SCOTT®
Serving collectors since 1863

1988 Standard Postage Stamp Catalogue

ONE HUNDRED AND FORTY-FOURTH EDITION IN FOUR VOLUMES

VOLUME II

EUROPEAN COUNTRIES and COLONIES INDEPENDENT NATIONS of AFRICA, ASIA, LATIN AMERICA A—F

Scott Publishing Co.

911 Vandemark Road, Sidney, Ohio 45365

A division of AMOS PRESS INC., publishers of *Linn's Stamp News, Coin World, Cars & Parts* magazine and *The Sidney Daily News.*

TABLE OF CONTENTS

See Volumes 3 and 4 for nations of Africa, Asia, Europe, Latin America and their affiliated territories, G-Z.

See Volume 1 for United States and Affiliated Territories, United Nations, and British Commonwealth of Nations.

ISBN 0-89487-091-2

Library of Congress Card No. 2-3301

SPECIAL NOTICES

This Catalogue lists adhesive postage stamps of the various countries, except for the United States where additional listings cover revenue stamps and postal stationery.

To facilitate identification, the following style of listing is used:

Canada

41	A24	3c	bright vermilion	17.50	30
		a.	3c rose carmine	300.00	6.00

The number (41) in the first column is the index or identifcation number; the letter and number combination (A24) indicates the design and refers to the illustration having this (A24) designation; next comes the denomination (3c) followed by the color (bright vermilion) or a description of the stamp; the prices are in two columns at the right, the first (17.50) being that of an unused stamp and the last (30) of a canceled one. This is known as a major listing or variety.

Variations from so-called "normal" stamps are listed in small type and designated by lowercase letters of the alphabet. These are called minor varieties. When they immediately follow the major listing in the catalogue the original index and design numbers are understood to be the same. In the preceding example, the minor variety, No. 41a, differs from the major variety, No. 41, only in shade; its design, perforation, etc., remain unchanged.

When year, perforation, watermark or printing method is mentioned, the description applies to all succeeding listings until a change is noted. The heading note "Without Gum" applies only to the set it precedes.

When a stamp is printed in black on colord paper, the color of the paper alone is given in italics.

With stamps printed in two or more colors, the color given first is that of the frame or outer parts of the design starting at the upper left corner. The colors that follow are those of the vignette or inner parts of the design.

For some sets which include both vertical and horizontal format stamps, a single illustration is used, with the various designs and formats described beneath the illustration.

Abbreviations

The most frequently used abbreviations are:

Imperf. = Imperforate. Perf. = Perforated. Wmk. = Watermark. Unwmkd. = Unwatermarked. Litho. = Lithographed. Photo. = Photogravure. Engr. = Engraved. Typo. = Typographed.

When no color is given for an overprint or surcharge, it is understood to be in black. Abbreviations are sometimes used, as (B) or (Bk) Black, (Bl) Blue, (R) Red, (G) Green, etc.

New Issue Listings

Scott's Catalogue Update appears regularly in the Scott Stamp Monthly and reports new listings.

Condition

A stamp's condition is a crucial factor of its price. Prices quoted in this catalogue are for stamps with no flaws; all perforations intact; unfaded color; reasonable centering, i.e., no worse than the design not quite touching the perforations on some issues and much closer to perfect centering on more recent issues; and for unused stamps with the major part of original gum intact (unless, of course, the stamp was issued without gum). Exceptional copies often bring higher prices. For some countries, or for specific issues within countries, a note with the listing indicates that prices are for specimens without gum.

Slightly defective stamps which are off-center, heavily canceled, faded, or stained are usually sold at large discounts. Damaged stamps which are torn or mutilated or have serious defects seldom bring more than a small fraction of the price of a fine specimen.

Standards of condition may vary greatly in the stamps of different countries. By way of example, early stamps of the United States, Great Britain, Victoria, and Japan were perforated in such a manner as to make most examples appear severely off center. They also normally were heavily canceled. It therefore is difficult to obtain early stamps from these countries, and others, in as fine a condition as stamps from countries where more care was taken during the perforating process and where lighter cancellations were applied.

Pricing Limitations

Each price appearing in this catalogue represents an estimate by Scott Publishing Co. of the current value basis for a specimen of that single stamp (or, where noted, set of stamps) of the condition noted in the first section of this explanation, offered by a retail stamp dealer to a collector. Because this catalogue is issued only once each year, it is impossible for it to reflect the price fluctuations that may occur over the short term. What should remain constant, however, is the relative price (value) of items over the long term.

These prices are not intended to reflect "wholesale" transactions, i.e., between dealers or a collector selling to a dealer. Many factors may affect the differential between an individual price shown in these pages and the actual price of a transaction: individual bargaining, the effect of dealer mark-up and profit margins, condition of the item in question, changes in popularity of the item, temporary change in supply of the item, local custom, unusual postal markings on a used example of the item, unexpected political situations within the country of issue, newly discovered philatelic or other information, or changes in the relative value of that nation's currency against the U.S. dollar.

As a point of philatelic economic fact, the lower the pricc shown for an item in this catalogue, the greater the percentage of that price which is attributed to dealer mark-up and profit margin. Thus, packets of 1,000 different stamps — all of which have a catalogue price of at least 5 cents — normally sell for considerably less than $50!

Scott Publishing Co. endeavors to obtain more than one judgment of the prices and to incorporate in its pricing the various price factors listed above. There can be no assurnce, however, that all of the prices listed are accurate estimates of prices which would be paid in actual transactions. Some of the items listed have not been publicly traded recently. The pricing, therefore, is based on the editors' estimates of the probable prices which the stamp would command if it were offered individually for sale to a collector.

Users of this Catalogue should not enter into any transaction solely in reliance on the prices, valuations, or stamp availability information set forth in the Catalogue. Persons wishing to further establish the value of a particular stamp or other material may wish to consult with recognized stamp experts (collector or dealer) and review current information or recent developments which could affect stamp prices.

Scott Publishing Co. assumes no obligation to revise the prices during the distribution period of this Catalogue or to advise users of other factors, such as stamp availability, political and economic conditions, or collecting preferences, all of which may have an immediate positive or negative impact on prices. The publisher endeavors to balance these factors with its general understanding of stamp pricing considerations to avoid unnecessary fluctuations in the prices included in this Catalogue:

It should be noted that persons relied upon for pricing information also may deal in stamps and/or may maintain substantial personal stamp collections. They may buy, sell, and deal in stamps for their own account and for the account of others and therefore may have both a direct and indirect interest in the price of the stamps. In some cases, the references to prices may reflect valuations of their personal holdings or stamps in which they deal for themselves and others.

Understanding Pricing Notations

The absence of a price does not necessarily indicate that the stamp is scarce or rare. In the United States listings, a dash in the price column means that the stamp is known in a stated form or variety, but that information is lacking or insufficient for pricing.

The minimum price of a stamp is fixed at 5 cents to cover a dealer's labor and service cost of purchasing that stamp at wholesale and preparing it for resale. As noted above, the sum of these list prices does not properly represent the "value" of a packet of unsorted or unmounted stamps sold in bulk which generally consists of only the lesser valued stamps.

Prices in the "unused" column are for stamps that have been hinged for items through 1960. Prices for unused stamps after those dates are for unhinged examples. Where prices for a used example of a stamp is considerably higher than for the unused stamp, the price applies to a stamp showing a distinct contemporary postmark of origin.

Beginning with issues of about 1900, and sometimes for earlier issues, prices for sets are provided for most issues of five or more stamps. Unless otherwise noted, the set price excludes minor varieties. The parenthetical number in the set-price line notes the number of stamps in the priced total. Set prices are the sum of the individual prices.

Many countries sell canceled-to-order stamps at a marked reduction of face value. Exceptions which sell or have sold canceled-to-order stamps at full face value include Australia, Netherlands, France, and Switzerland. It is almost impossible to identify such stamps, if the gum has been removed, as the official government canceling devices are used. Postally used copies on cover are worth more than the canceled-to-order stamps with original gum.

How To Order From Your Dealer

It is not necessary to write the full description of a stamp as listed in this Catalogue. All that is needed is the name of the country, the index number and whether unused or used. For example. "Japan Scott No. 422 unused" is sufficient to identify the stamp of Japan listed as: "422 A206 5y brown."

Addenda And Number Changes

Stamps received too late to be included in the body of the Catalogue are listed in the Addenda at the back of this volume.

A list of stamps whose catalogue numbers have been changed from those of the preceding edition appears at the back of this volume.

Examination

Scott Publishing Co. cannot undertake to pass upon genuineness or condition of stamps, due to the time and responsibility involved, but refers collectors to the several expertizing/verification groups which undertake this work. Neither can Scott Publishing Co. undertake to appraise or identify. The Company cannot take responsibility for unsolicited stamps or covers.

INFORMATION FOR COLLECTORS

The anatomy of a stamp can be divided into the following parts: paper, watermark, separation, impression, design and gum.

Paper

Paper is a material composed of a compacted web of cellulose fibers formed into sheets. The fibers most often used for the paper on which stamps are printed are mulberry bark, wood, straw and certain grasses, with linen or cotton rags added for greater strength. These fibers are ground, bleached and boiled until they are reduced to a slushy pulp known as "stuff." Sizing, or weak glue, and coloring matter may be added to the pulp. Thin coatings of pulp are poured on sieve-like frames which allow the water to run off while retaining the matted pulp. When it is almost dry, the appearance of the pulp is converted by mechanical processes. It may be passed through smooth or engraved rollers (dandy rolls) or placed between cloth in a press that flattens and dries the product under pressure, thus forming a sheet of paper.

Stamp paper falls broadly into two types — "wove" and "laid." The differences in appearance are caused by the surface of the frame onto which the pulp is first fed. If the surface is smooth and even, the paper will be of uniform texture throughout, showing no light and dark areas when held up to a light. This is called *Wove Paper.* Early paper making machines poured the pulp on to continuously circulating webs of felt, but modern machines feed the pulp on to a cloth-like screen made of closely interwoven fine wires. This paper, when held up to a light, will show little dots or points, very close together. Technically, it is called "wire wove," but because it is the most common form, it is generally known as "wove paper." Any United States or British stamp printed after 1880 will furnish an example of wire wove paper.

The frames utilized for *Laid Paper* are made of closely spaced parallel wires, with cross wires at wider intervals. Obviously a greater thickness of the pulp will settle between the wires, and the paper, when held up to a light, will show alternate light and dark lines. The spacing and the thickness of the lines may vary, but on any one sheet of paper, they are all alike. (Russia Nos. 31-38.)

If the lines are spaced quite far apart, like the ruling on a writing tablet, the paper is called *Batonne* from the French word meaning a staff. Batonne paper may be either wove or laid. If it is laid, fine laid lines can be seen between the batons. The laid lines, which are actually a form of watermark, may be geometrical figures such as squares, diamonds, rectangles, or wavy lines.

When the lines form little squares, the paper is called *Quadrille.* When they form rectangles instead of squares, the paper is called *Oblong Quadrille.* (Mexico-Guadalajara Nos. 35-37.)

Paper is also classified as thick or thin, hard or soft, and by color if dye was added during production, such as yellowish, greenish, bluish and reddish.

Pelure Paper—An extremely thin, hard and often brittle paper. It is sometimes bluish or grayish. (Serbia No. 170.)

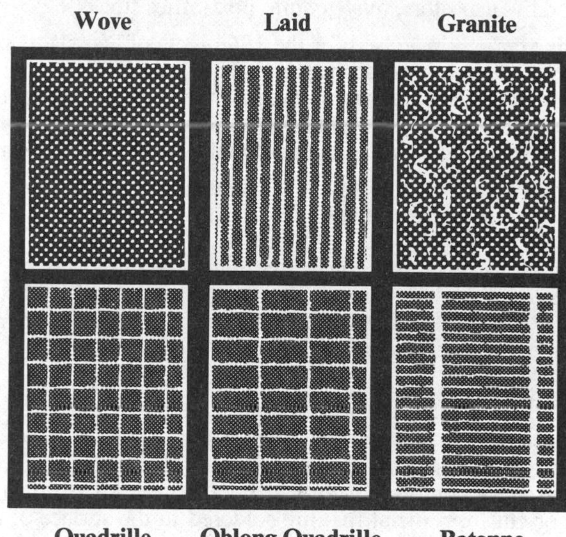

Native Paper—A term applied to the handmade papers on which some of the early stamps of the Indian States were printed. Japanese paper, originally made of mulberry fibers and rice flour, is part of this group. (Japan Nos. 1-18.)

Manila Paper—Often used to make stamped envelopes and wrappers, it is a coarse textured stock, usually smooth on one side and rough on the other. It is made in a variety of colors.

Silk Paper—Introduced by the British in 1847 as a safeguard against counterfeiting, there are scattered bits of colored silk thread in it. Silk-thread paper has continuous threads of colored silk arranged so that one or more threads run through the stamp or postal stationery. (Great Britain Nos. 5-8.)

Granite Paper—Not to be confused with either of the silk papers, it is filled with minute fibers of various colors and lengths in the paper substance. (Austria Nos. 172-175.)

Chalky Paper—Coated with a chalk-like substance to discourage the cleaning and reuse of canceled stamps. As the design is imprinted on the water-soluble coating of the stamp, any attempts to remove a cancellation will destroy the stamp. **Collectors are warned not to soak these stamps in any fluid.** If one is to be removed from envelope paper, a good way is to wet the paper from underneath until the gum dissolves enough to slip the stamp off it. (St. Kitts-Nevis Nos. 89-90.)

India Paper—Originally introduced from China about 1750, it is sometimes referred to as China Paper. It is a thin, opaque paper often used for plate and die proofs by many countries.

Double Paper—In philately this has two distinct meanings. The first, used experimentally as a means to discourage reuse, is two-ply paper, usually of a thick and thin sheet, joined together during the process of manufacture. Any attempt to remove a cancellation would destroy the design which is printed on the thin paper. The second occurs on the rotary press when the printer glues the end of one paper roll onto the next roll to save time in feeding the paper through the press. Stamp designs are printed over the joined paper and if overlooked by inspectors, may get into post-office stocks.

Goldbeater's Skin—Used for the 1866 issue of Prussia, it was made of a tough translucent paper. The design was printed in reverse on the back of the stamp, and the gum applied on top of the printing. It is impossible to remove them from the paper to which they are affixed without destroying the design.

Ribbed Paper—An uneven, corrugated surface made by passing it through ridged rollers. (Exists on some copies of U.S. No. 163.)

Various other substances that have been used for stamp manufacture include aluminum, copper, silver and gold foil, plastic, silk and cotton fabrics. Most of these are considered novelties designed for sale to novice collectors.

Watermarks

Watermarks are an integral part of the paper as they are formed in the process of manufacture. They consist of small designs such as crowns, stars, anchors, letters, etc. formed of wire or cut from metal that are soldered to the surface of the dandy roll or mold. These pieces of metal (referred to as "bits") impress a design into the paper which may be seen by holding the stamp up to the light. They are more easily seen in a watermark detector, a small black tray. The stamp is placed face down in the tray and dampened with a watermark detection fluid which brings up the watermark in dark lines against a lighter background.

Multiple Watermarks of Crown Agents and Burma

Watermarks of Uruguay, Vatican and Jamaica

WARNING
Some inks used in the photogravure process dissolve in watermark fluids. (See SOLUBLE PRINTING INKS.) There are also electric watermark detectors that come with plastic discs of various colors. When the light is turned on the watermark can be seen through the disc that neutralizes the color of the stamp.

Watermarks may be found reversed, inverted, sideways or diagonal, as seen from the back of the stamp, depending on the position of the printing plates or the manner in which paper was fed through the press. On machine-made paper they normally read from right to left. In a "multiple watermark" the design is repeated closely throughout the sheet. In a "sheet watermark" the design appears only once on the sheet, but extends over many stamps. Individual stamps may carry only a small fraction or none of the watermark.

"Marginal watermarks" occur in the margins of sheets or panes of stamps. Outside the border of some papers a large row of letters may spell the name of the country or of the manufacturer of the paper. Careless press feeding may cause parts of these letters to show on stamps of the outer rows. **For easier reference watermarks are numbered in the Scott Catalogue. See numerical index of Watermarks at back of this volume.**

Separation

Separation is the general term used to describe methods of separating stamps. The earliest issues, such as the 1840 Penny Blacks, did not have any means provided for separating and were intended to be cut apart with scissors. These are called imperforate stamps. As many stamps that were first issued imperforate were later issued perforated, care must be observed in buying imperforate stamps to be sure they are really imperforate and not perforated copies that have been trimmed. Although sometimes priced as singles, it is recommended that imperforate varieties of normally perforated stamps be collected in pairs or larger pieces as indisputable evidence of their imperforate character.

Separation is effected by two general methods, rouletting and perforating. In rouletting the paper is cut partly or wholly through, but no paper is removed. In perforating a part of the paper is removed. Rouletting derives its name from the French roulette, a spur-like wheel. As the wheel is rolled over the paper, each point makes a small cut. The number of cuts

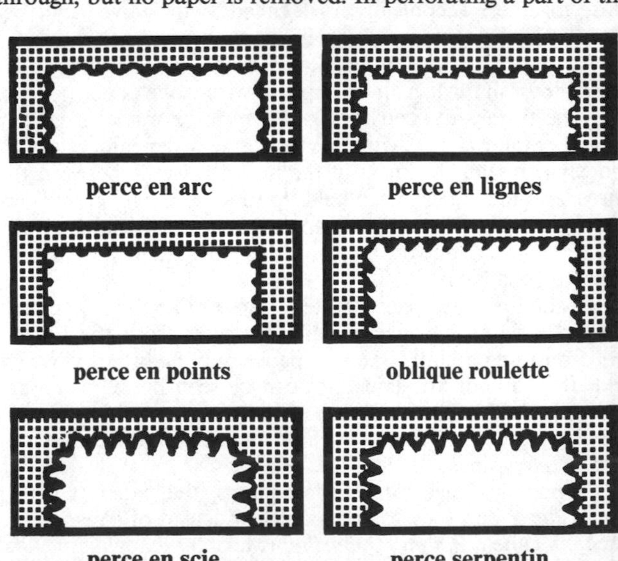

made in two centimeters determines the gauge of the roulette. This is fully explained under "Perforation."

ROULETTING

The shape and arrangement of the teeth on the wheels varies. French names are usually used to describe the various roulettes:

Perce en lignes: rouletted in lines. The paper receives short, straight cuts in lines. (Mexico No. 500.)

Perce en points: pin-perforated. Round, equidistant holes are pricked through the paper, but no paper is removed. which distinguishes it from a small perforation. (Mexico Nos. 242-256.)

Perce en arc and perce en scie: pierced in an arc or saw-toothed rouletted, forming half circles or small triangles. (Hanover Nos. 25-29.)

Perce en serpentin: serpentine roulette. The cuts form a serpentine or wavy line. (Brunswick Nos. 13-18.)

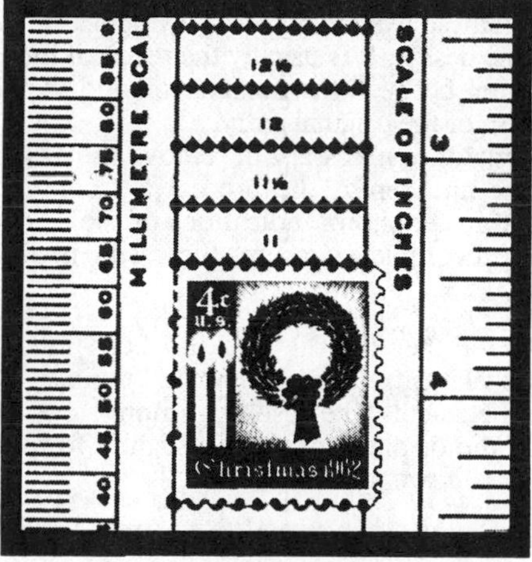

Perforation gauge

PERFORATION

The second chief style of separation of stamps, and the one which is in universal use today, is called perforating. By this process the paper between the stamps is cut away in a line of holes, usually round, leaving little bridges of paper between the stamps to hold them together. These little bridges, which project from the stamp when it is torn from the sheet are called the teeth of the perforation. As the size of the perforation is sometimes the only way to differentiate between two otherwise identical stamps, it is necessary to be able to measure and describe them. This is done with a perforation gauge, a ruler-like device that has dots to show how many perforations can be counted in the space of 2 centimeters, the space universally adopted as the length in which perforations are measured. Run your stamp along the gauge until the dots on it fit exactly into the perforations. If the number alongside the dots into which it fits is 11, this means that 11 perforations fit between two centimeters and the stamp is described as "perf. 11." If the gauge of the perforations on the top and bottom of a stamp differs from that on the sides, it is called a "compound perforation." In measuring compound perforations the gauge at the top and bottom is always given first, then the sides. Thus a stamp that measures 10½ at top and bottom and 11 at the sides is described as "10½ x 11." (U.S. No. 1526.)

A perforation with small holes and teeth close together is called a "fine perforation." One with large holes and teeth far apart is a "coarse perforation." If the holes are jagged rather than clean cut, it is called "rough perforation." Blind perforations are the slight impressions left by the perforating pins if they fail to puncture the paper. Multiples showing blind perfs may command a slight premium over normally perforated stamps.

Printing Processes

ENGRAVING (Intaglio)

Master Die—The initial operation in the engraving process is the making of the master die. The die is a small flat block of soft steel on which the stamp design is recess engraved in reverse.

The original art is reduced photographically to the appropriate size, and serves as a tracing guide for the initial outline of the design. After the engraving is completed, the die is hardened to withstand the stress and pressures of subsequent transfer operations.

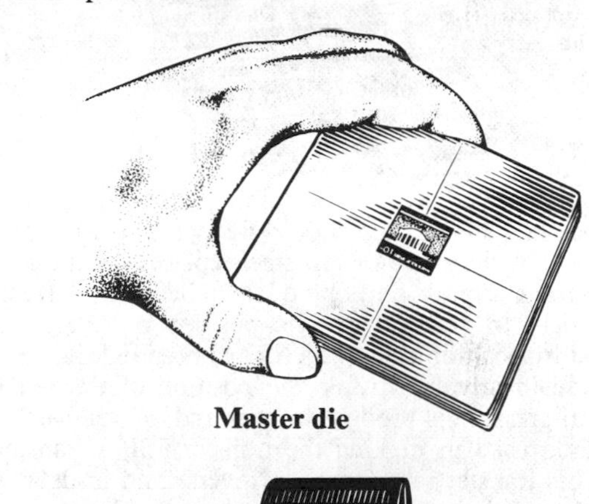

Master die

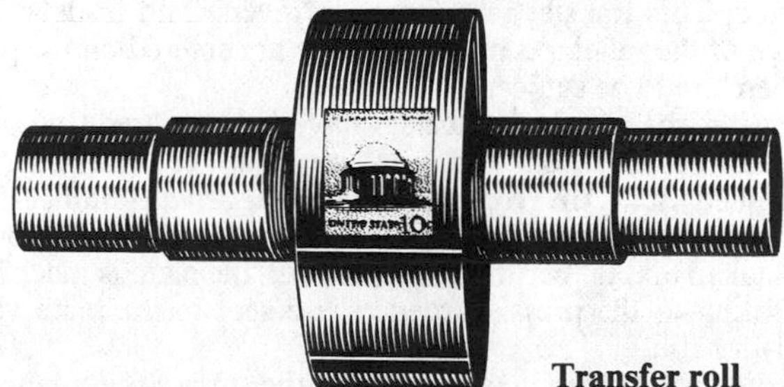

Transfer roll

Transfer Roll—The next operation is the making of the transfer roll which, as the name implies, is the medium used to transfer the subject from the die to the plate. A blank roll of soft steel, mounted on a mandrel, is placed under the bearers of a transfer press, so as to allow it to roll freely on its axis. The hardened die is placed on the bed of the press and the face of the transfer roll is brought to bear on the die under pressure. The bed is then rocked back and forth under increasing pressure until the soft steel of the roll is forced into every engraved line of the die. The resulting impression on the roll is known as a "relief" of a "relief transfer." When the required number of reliefs are "rocked in," the soft steel transfer roll is also hardened.

A "relief" is the normal reproduction of the design on the die in reverse. A "defective relief" may occur during the "rocking in" process due to a minute piece of foreign material lodging on the die, or other causes. Imperfections in the steel of the transfer roll may result in a breaking away of parts of the design. If the damaged relief is continued in use, it will transfer a repeating defect to the plate. Sometimes reliefs are deliberately altered. "Broken relief" and "altered relief" are terms used to designate these changed conditions.

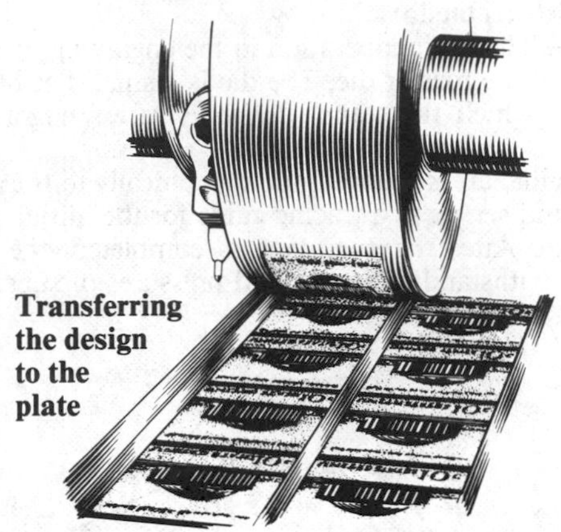

Transferring the design to the plate

Plate—The final step in the procedure is the making of the printing plate. A flat piece of soft steel replaces the die on the bed of the transfer press and one of the reliefs on the transfer roll is brought to bear on it. The position on the plate is determined by position dots, which have been lightly marked on the plate in advance. After the position of the relief is determined, pressure is brought to bear and, by following the same method used in making the transfer roll, a transfer is entered. This transfer reproduces in reverse and in detail the design of the relief. As many transfers are entered on the plate as there are to be subjects.

After the required transfers have been entered, the position dots, layout dots and lines, scratches, etc. are generally burnished out. Any required *guide lines, plate numbers* or other *marginal markings* are added. A proof impression is then taken and if "certified" (approved), the plate is machined for fitting to the press, hardened and sent to the plate vault ready for use.

On press, the plate is inked and the surface automatically wiped clean, leaving the ink only in the depressed lines. Damp paper under pressure is forced down into the engraved depressed lines, thereby receiving the ink. Consequently, the lines on engraved stamps are slightly raised; and, conversely, slight depressions occur on the back of the stamp.

The expressions *taille douce,* engraved, line engraved and steel plate all designate substantially the same processes for producing engraved stamps.

Rotary Press—Engraved stamps were printed only with flat plates until 1915, when rotary press printing was introduced. *Rotary press plates,* after being certified, require additional machining. They are curved to fit the press cylinder and "gripper slots" are cut into the back of each plate to receive the "grippers," which hold the plate securely on the press, after which the plate is hardened. Stamps printed from rotary press plates are usually longer or wider than the same stamps printed from flat press plates. The stretching of the plate during the curving process causes this enlargement.

Re-entry—In order to execute a re-entry the transfer roll is reapplied to the plate, usually at some time after it has been put to press. Thus worn-out designs can be resharpened by carefully re-entering the transfer roll. If the transfer roll is not precisely in line with the impression on the plate, the registration will not be true and a double transfer will result. After a plate has been curved for the rotary press, it is impossible to make a re-entry.

Double Transfer—A description of the condition of a transfer on a plate that shows evidence of a duplication of all, or a portion of the design. It is usually the result of the changing of the registration between the transfer roll and the plate during the rocking-in of the original entry.

It is sometimes necessary to remove the original transfer from a plate and repeat the process a second time. If the finished re-transfer shows indications of the original impression due to incomplete erasure, the result is also a double transfer.

Re-engraved—Either the die that has been used to make a plate or the plate itself may have its "temper" drawn (softened) and be re-cut. The resulting impressions from such a re-engraved die or plate may differ slightly from the original issue, and are known as "re-engraved."

Short Transfer—It sometimes happens that the transfer roll is not rocked its entire length in entering a transfer on a plate, with the result that the finished transfer fails to show the complete design. This is known as a "short transfer." (U.S. No. 8, type III of 1851-56 1c.)

TYPOGRAPHY (Letterpress, Surface Printing)

As related to the printing of postage stamps, typography is the reverse of engraving. It includes all printing wherein the design is raised above the surface area, whether it is wood, metal, or in some instances hard rubber.

The master die is made in much the same manner as the engraved die. However, in this instance the area not being utilized as a printing surface is cut away, leaving the surface area raised. The original die is then reproduced by stereotyping or electrotyping. The resulting electrotypes are assembled in the required number and format of the desired sheet of stamps. The plate used in printing the stamps is an electroplate of these assembled electrotypes.

Ink is applied to the raised surface and the pressure of the press transfers the ink impression to the paper. Again, as opposed to engraving, the fine lines of typography are impressed on the surface of the stamp. When viewed from the back (as on a typewritten page) the corresponding linework will be raised slightly above the surface.

PHOTOGRAVURE (Rotogravure, Heliogravure)
In this process the basic principles of photography are applied to a sensitized metal plate, as opposed to photographic paper. The design is photographically transferred to the plate through a halftone screen, breaking the reproduction into tiny dots. The plate is treated chemically and the dots form depressions of varying depths, depending on the degrees of shade in the design. The depressions in the plate hold the ink, which is lifted out when the paper is pressed against the plate, in a manner similar to that of engraved printing.

LITHOGRAPHY
This process is based on the principle that oil and water will not mix. The design is drawn by hand or transferred from an engraving to the surface of a lithographic stone or metal plate in a greasy (oily) ink. The stone (or plate) is wet with an acid fluid, causing it to repel the printing ink in all areas not covered by the greasy ink.

Transfers are made from the original stone or plate by means of transfer paper. A series of duplicate transfers are grouped and these in turn are transferred to the final printing plate.

Photolithography—The application of photographic processes to lithography. This process allows greater flexibility of design, relating to use of halftone screens combined with line-work.

Offset—A development of the lithographic process. A rubber-covered blanket cylinder takes up the impression from the inked lithographic plate. From the "blanket" the impression is *offset* or transferred to the paper. Because of its greater flexibility and speed, offset printing has largely displaced lithography. Since the processes and results are almost identical, stamps printed by either method are designated as lithographed.

Sometimes two or even three printing methods are combined in producing stamps.

EMBOSSED (RELIEF) PRINTING
A method in which the design is sunk into the metal of the die and the printing is done against a yielding platen, such as leather or linoleum, which is forced up into the depression of the die, thus forming the design on the paper in relief.

Embossing may be done without color (Sardinia Nos. 4-6); with color printed around the embossed area (Great Britain No. 5 and most U.S. envelopes); and with color in exact registration with the embossed subject (Canada Nos. 656-657).

INK COLORS
Pigments or dyes, usually of mineral origin, are used in the manufacture of inks or colored papers on which stamps are printed. The tone of any given color may be affected by numerous factors: heavier pressure will cause a more intense color; slight interruptions in the ink feed will cause a lighter tint.

Hand-mixed ink formulas produced under different conditions (humidity, temperature) at different times account for notable color variations in early printings, mostly 19th century, of the same stamp (U.S. Nos. 248-250, 279B, etc.).

Colors may vary in shade because papers of different quality and consistency were used for the same printing. Most pelure papers, for example, show a richer color when compared to wove or laid papers. (Russia No. 181a.)

The very nature of the printing processes can cause a variety of differences in shades or hues of the same stamp. Some of these shades are scarcer than others, and are of particular interest to the advanced collector.

Soluble Printing Inks

WARNING
Most stamp colors are permanent. That is, they are not seriously affected by light or water. Some colors may fade from excessive exposure to light. Other stamps are printed in inks which dissolve easily in water or fluids used to detect watermarks. These inks were often used intentionally to prevent the removal of cancellations. Water affects all aniline prints, those on safety paper, and some photogravure printings. All the above are called *fugitive colors.*

Tagged Stamps

(Luminiscence, Fluorescence, Phosphorescence)—Some tagged stamps have bars (Great Britain, Canada), frames (South Africa), or an overall coating of luminescent material applied after the stamps have been printed (United States). Another tagging method is to incorporate the luminescent material into some or all colors of the printing ink (Australia No. 366, Netherlands No. 478). A third is to mix the luminescent material with the pulp during the paper manufacturing process or apply it as a surface coating afterwards. These are called "fluorescent" papers. (Switzerland Nos. 510-514, Germany No. 848.)

The treated stamps show up in specific colors when exposed to ultraviolet light. The wave length of the luminescent material determines the colors and activates the triggering mechanism of the electronic machinery for sorting, facing or canceling letters.

Various fluorescent substances have been used as paper whiteners, but the resulting "hi-brite papers" show up differently under ultraviolet light and do not trigger the machines. They are not noted in the Catalogue.

Introduced in Great Britain in 1959 on an experimental basis, tagging in its various forms is now used by many countries to expedite the handling of mail. Following Great Britain were Germany ('61); Canada and Denmark ('62); United States, Australia, Netherlands and Switzerland ('63); Belgium and Japan ('66); Sweden and Norway ('67); Italy ('68); Russia ('69), and so forth.

Certain stamps were issued both with and without the luminescent factor. In these instances, the "tagged" variety is listed in the United States, Canada, Great Britain and Switzerland, and is noted in some of the other countries.

Gum

The gum on a stamp's back may be smooth, crinkly, dark, white, colored or tinted, and either obvious or virtually invisible as on Canada No. 453 or Rwanda Nos. 287-294. Most stamp gumming has been carried out with adhesives using gum arabic or dextrine as a base, but certain polymers such as polyvinyl alcohol (PVA) have been used extensively since World War II. The PVA gum which Harrison & Sons of Great Britain introduced in 1968 is dull, slightly yellowish and almost invisible.

Stamps having full *original gum* sell for more than those from which the gum has been removed. Reprints may have gum differing from the originals.

Reprints And Reissues

Reprints—These are impressions of stamps (usually obsolete) made from the original plates or stones. If valid for postage and from obsolete issues, they are called reissues. If they are from current issues, they are *second, third,* etc. *printings.* If designated for a particular purpose, they are called *special printings.*

When reprints are not valid for postage, but made from original dies and plates by authorized persons they are *official reprints*—to distinguish them from *private reprints* made from original plates and dies by private hands. *Official reproductions* or imitations are made from new dies and plates by government authorization.

For the 1876 Centennial, the U.S. government made official imitations of its first postage stamps, which are listed as Nos. 3-4; official reprints of the demonetized pre-1861 issues; re-issued the 1869 stamps and made special printings of the current 1875 denominations. An example of the private reprint is that of the New Haven postmaster's provisional.

Most reprints differ slightly from the original stamp in some characteristic such as gum, paper, perforation, color, watermark (or lack thereof). Sometimes the details have been followed so meticulously that only a student of that stamp can tell the reprint from the original.

Remainders And Canceled To Order

Some countries sell their stock of old stamps when a new issue replaces them. The *remainders* are usually canceled with a punch hole, a heavy line or bar, or a more or less regular cancellation to avoid postal use. The most famous merchant of remainders was Nicholas F. Seebeck, who arranged printing contracts between the Hamilton Bank Note Co., of which he was a director, and several Central and Latin American countries in the 1880's and 1890's. The contracts provided that the plates and all remainders of the yearly issues became the property of Hamilton, and Seebeck saw to it that ample stock remained. The "Seebecks," both remainders and reprints, were standard packet fillers for decades.

Some countries also issue stamps *canceled to order* (CTO), either in sheets with original gum or stuck onto pieces of paper or envelopes and canceled. Such CTO items generally are worth less than postally used stamps. Most can be detected by the presence of gum. However, as the CTO practice goes back at least to 1885, the gum inevitably has been washed off some stamps so they could pass for postally used. The normally applied postmarks usually differ slightly and specialists can tell the difference. When applied individually to envelopes by philatelically minded persons, CTO material is known as *favor canceled* and generally sells at large discounts.

Cinderellas And Facsimiles

Cinderella is a catchall term used by collectors of phantoms, fantasies, bogus items, municipal issues, exhibition seals, local revenues, transportation stamps, labels, poster stamps, etc. Cinderellas are not issued by any national government for postal purposes. Some cinderella collectors include local postage issues, telegraph stamps, essays and proofs, forgeries and counterfeits.

A fantasy is an adhesive created for a nonexisting stamp issuing authority. Fantasy items range from imaginary countries (Kingdom of Sedang or Principality of Trinidad) to nonexisting locals (Winans City Post), or nonexisting transportation lines (McRobish & Co.'s Acapulco-San Francisco Line). On the other hand, if the entity exists and might have issued stamps or did issue other stamps, the items are *bogus* stamps. These would include the Mormon postage stamps of Utah, S. Allan Taylor's Guatemala and Paraguay inventions, the propaganda issues for the South Moluccas and the adhesives of the Page & Keyes local post of Boston.

Both fantasies and bogus issues are sometimes called *phantoms.*

Facsimilies—These are copies or imitations made to represent original stamps, but which do not pretend to be originals. A catalogue illustration is such a facsimile. Illustrations from the Moens catalogue of the last century were occasionally colored and passed as stamps. Since the beginning of stamp collecting, facsimilies have been made for collectors as space fillers or for reference. They often carry the words "facsimile" "falsch" (German), "sanko" or "mozo" (Japanese), or "faux" (French) overprinted on the face or stamped on the back. Naturally, they have only curio value.

Counterfeits Or Forgeries

Postal counterfeits or *postal forgeries* are unauthorized imitations of stamps intended to deprive the post of revenue. They often command higher prices than the genuine stamps they imitate. Sales are illegal and governments can, and do, prosecute.

The first postal forgery was of Spain's 4-cuartos carmine of 1854, No. 25. The forgers lithographed it, though the original was typographed. Apparently they were not satisfied and soon made an engraved forgery which is fairly common, unlike the scarce lithographed counterfeit. Postal forgeries quickly followed in Spain, Austria, Naples, Sardinia and the Roman States.

An infamous counterfeit to defraud the government is the 1-shilling Great Britain "Stock Exchange" forgery of 1872 used on telegrams at the exchange that year. It escaped detection until a stamp dealer noticed it in 1898. Many postal counterfeits are known of U.S. stamps.

Because the governments concerned did not issue them, the *wartime propaganda* stamps of both World Wars may be classed as postal counterfeits. They were put out by other governments or resistance groups.

Philatelic forgeries or *counterfeits* are unauthorized imitations of stamps designed to deceive and defraud collectors. Such spurious items first appeared on the market around 1860 and most old-time collections contain one or more. Many are crude and easily spotted even by the non-specialist, but some can deceive the better-than-average collector.

An important supplier of these early philatelic forgeries was the Hamburg printer, Gebruder Spiro. Many others indulged in this craft including S. Allan Taylor, George Hussey, James Chute, Georges Foure, Benjamin & Sarpy, Julius Goldner, E. Oneglia and L. H. Mercier. Among the noted 20th century forgers are Francois Fournier, Jean Sperati and the prolific Raoul DeThuin.

Most classic rarities, many medium priced stamps and, in this century, cheap stamps on a wholesale basis destined for beginners' packets, have been fraudulently produced. However, few new philatelic forgeries have appeared in recent decades and virtually no new frauds of valuable classics. Successful imitation of engraved work is virtually impossible.

It has proven far easier to produce a fake by altering a genuine stamp than to duplicate a stamp completely.

Repairs And Fakes

Most collectors will not object to restoration of a stamp or cover, although they will not accept repairs on the same basis. *Restoration* in this sense includes cleaning with a soft eraser or soap and water. It may include the ironing out of a crease or removal of a cellophane tape stain. Removal of old hinges is acceptable. Some collectors believe that freshening of a stamp is valid restoration, whether done by the removal of oxides, "toning," or the effect of wax paper left on stamps shipped to the tropics between such sheets. Regumming may have been acceptable restoration half a century ago, but today it is considered faking. Restored stamps or covers do not normally sell at a discount, and may even change hands at a premium.

Repairs include filling in thin spots, mending tears by reweaving, adding a missing corner or perforation "tooth." Repaired stamps sell at substantial discounts.

Fakes—Genuine stamps altered in some way to make them more desirable and sold without revealing the alterations. According to one major student, 30,000 varieties of fakes were known in the 1950's. The number has grown. The widespread existence of fakes makes it important for collectors to study their philatelic holdings and relevant literature. For the same reason they should buy from reputable dealers who will guarantee their stamps and make full prompt refund should a purchase be declared not genuine by some mutually agreed-upon authority. Because fakes always have some genuine characteristics, it is not always possible to obtain unanimity among expert students regarding specific items. These students may change their opinions as philatelic knowledge increases. More than 80 per cent of all fakes on the market today are regummed, reperforated or altered in regard to overprints, surcharges or cancellations.

Stamps can be chemically treated to alter or eliminate colors. For example a pale rose can be recolored into a blue of a higher value, or a "missing color" variety created. Designs may be changed by "painting," or a stroke or dot added or bleached out to turn an ordinary variety into a scarce stamp. Part of a stamp can be bleached and reprinted in a different version, achieving an inverted center or frame. Margins can be added or repairs done so deceptively that the stamp moves from the repaired to the fake category.

The fakers have not left the backs of stamps untouched. They may create false watermarks or add fake grills (or press out genuine ones). A thin India paper proof may be glued onto a thicker backing to "create" an issued stamp, or a cardboard proof may be shaved down. Silk threads have been impressed in and stamps have been split so that a rare paper variety, from a cheap stamp, can be applied as a back to falsely identify the stamp. However, the most common back treatment is regumming.

Some operators openly advertise "foolproof" application of "original gum" to stamps that lack it. This is faking, not counterfeiting. As few early stamps have survived without being hinged, the large number of never-hinged examples now offered for sale suggests the extent of regumming that has been and is being done. Regumming may be used to hide repairs and thin spots, but dipping in watermark fluid will often reveal these flaws.

The fakers also tamper with separations. Ingenious ways to add margins are known, and perforated wide-margin stamps may be falsely represented as imperforate when trimmed. Reperforating is commonly done to create scarce coil or perforation varieties and to eliminate the straight-edge stamps found in sheet margin positions of many earlier issues. Custom has made straight edges less desirable and the fakers have obliged by reperforating them so extensively that many are now uncommon if not rare.

Another main field of the faker is that of the overprint, surcharge and cancellation. The forging of rare surcharges or overprints began in the 1880's or 1890's. These forgeries are sometimes difficult to detect, but the better experts have probably identified almost all of them. Only occasionally are the overprints or cancellations removed to create unoverprinted stamps or unused items. The SPECIMEN overprints are sometimes removed — scraping and repainting is one way — to create unoverprinted varieties. Cheap revenues or pen-canceled stamps are used to generate "unused" stamps for further faking by adding other markings. The quartz lamp and a high-powered magnifying glass help in detecting cancellation removals.

The big problem, however, is the addition of overprints, surcharges or cancellations — many quite dangerous. Plating of the stamps or the overprint can be an important detecting method.

Fake postmarks can range from numerous spurious fancy cancellations, to the host of markings applied to transatlantic covers to create rare uses. With the advance of cover collecting and the wide interest in postal history, a fertile new field for fakers arose. Some have tried to create entire covers. Others specialize in adding stamps, tied by fake cancellations, to genuine stampless covers, or replacing cheaper or damaged stamps with more valuable ones. Detailed study of rates and postmarks (including the analysis of "breaks" in each handstamp over a period), ink analysis, etc. will usually unmask the fraud.

Classifications Of Stamps

The various functions of stamps are classified by their names. Postage stamps; air post stamps; postage due stamps for unpaid postage, collected at time of delivery; late fee stamps, a special fee for forwarding a letter after regular mail delivery; registration stamps, fee for keeping special record of letter and ensuring its delivery; special delivery and express stamps, for delivery of letter in advance of regular delivery. With the exception of regular postage, all numbers in the Catalogue include a prefix letter denoting the class to which the stamp belongs. (B=Semi-Postal; C=Air Post; E=Special Delivery; J=Postage Due; O=Official; CO=Air Post Official; etc.).

Terminology

BOOKLETS

Many countries have issued stamps in small booklets for the convenience of users. They are usually sold by the post office at a small premium. Booklets have been issued in all sizes and forms, often with advertising on the covers, on the panes of stamps or on the interleaving. The panes may be printed from special plates or made from regular sheets. All panes from booklets issued by the United States and many from those of other countries are straight edged on the bottom and both sides, but perforated between the stamps. Any unit in the pane, either printed or blank, which is not a postage stamp, is called a *label* in the catalogue listings.

CANCELLATIONS

The marks or obliterations put on a stamp by the postal authorities to show that it has done service and is no longer valid for postage. If it is made with a pen, it is called a pen cancellation. When the location of the post office appears in the cancellation, it is called a town cancellation. When it calls attention to a cause or celebration, it is a slogan cancellation. Many other types and styles of cancellations exist, such as duplex, numerals, targets, etc.

COIL STAMPS

Stamps issued in rolls for use in affixing and vending machines. Those of the United States, Canada, etc., are perforated horizontally or vertically only, with the outer edges imperforate. Coil stamps of some countries (Great Britain) are perforated on all four sides.

COVERS

Envelopes, with or without adhesive postage stamps, which have passed through the mail and bear postal or other markings of philatelic interest. Before the introduction of envelopes (1840), people folded letters and wrote the address on the outside. Many people covered their letters with an extra sheet of paper on the outside for the address. Hence the word "cover." Used air letter sheets, stamped envelopes, and other items of postal stationery are also referred to as "covers."

ERRORS

Stamps having some unintentional deviation from the normal. Errors include, but are not limited to, mistakes in color, paper or watermark; inverted centers (or frames), surcharges or overprints, and double impressions. A factually wrong or misspelled inscription, if it appears on all examples of a stamp, is not classified as a philatelic error. (Panama No. J1.)

OVERPRINTED AND SURCHARGED STAMPS

Overprinting is a wording placed on stamps to alter the place of use ("Canal Zone" on U.S. issues); to adapt them for a special purpose ("Porto" on Denmark's 1913-20 regular issues for use as postage dues, Nos. J1-J7); or for a special occasion. (Guatemala Nos. 374-378.)

The term *surcharge* is used when the overprint changes or restates the value (1923 "Inflation Issues" of Germany; Australia No. 580).

Surcharges and overprints may be handstamped, typeset or, occasionally, lithographed or engraved.

PRECANCELS

Stamps canceled before they are placed on mail. Precanceling is done to expedite the handling of large mailings.

In the United States precancellations generally identify the point of origin. That is, the city and state names (or initials) appear, usually centered by an arrangement of parallel lines.

In France the abbreviation *Affranchts* in a semicircle together with the word *Postes* is the general form. Belgian precancellations are usually a square box in which the name of the city appears. Netherlands' precancellations have the name of the city enclosed between a large and small circle, sometimes called a "life-saver."

Precancellations of other countries usually follow these patterns, but may be any arrangement of bars, boxes and city names.

PROOFS AND ESSAYS

Proofs are impressions taken from an approved die, plate or stone in which the design and color are the same as the stamp issued to the public. Trial color proofs are impressions taken from approved dies, plates or stones in varying colors. An essay is the impression of a design that differs in some way from the stamp as issued.

PROVISIONALS

Stamps issued on short notice and intended for temporary use pending the arrival of regular (definitive) issues. They are usually issued to meet contingencies: changes in government or currency; shortage of necessary postage values, or military occupation.

In the 1840's, postmasters in certain American cities issued stamps that were valid only at specific post offices. Postmasters of the Confederate States also issued stamps with limited validity. These are known as Postmasters' Provisionals.

SE-TENANT

Joined together, referring to an unsevered pair, strip or block of stamps differing in design, denomination or overprint. (U.S. Nos. 1530-1537.)

TETE BECHE

A pair of stamps in which one is upside down in relation to the other. Some of these are the result of intentional sheet arrangement (Morocco Nos. B10-B11). Others occurred when one or more electrotypes were accidentally placed upside down on the plate. (Colombia No. 57a.) Separation of course destroys the tete beche variety.

SPECIMENS

One of the regulations of the Universal Postal Union requires member nations to send samples of all stamps they put into service to the International Bureau in Switzerland. These are then sent to all other member nations as samples of what stamps are valid for postage. Many are overprinted, handstamped or initial-perforated "Specimen," "Canceled" or "Muestra." Some are marked with bars across the denominations (China), punched holes (Czechoslovakia) or back inscriptions (Mongolia).

Stamps distributed to government officials or for publicity purposes, and stamps submitted by private security printers for official approval may also receive such defacements.

These markings prevent postal use, and all such items are generally known as "specimens."

Color Abbreviations

amb.	amber
anil	aniline
ap	apple
aqua	aquamarine
az.	azure
bis	bister
bl	blue
bld	blood
blk	black
bril	brilliant
brn	brown
brnsh.	brownish
brnz.	bronze
brt	bright
brnt	burnt
car	carmine
cer	cerise
chlky	chalky
cham	chamois
chnt	chestnut
choc.	chocolate
chr	chrome
cit	citron
cl	claret
cob	cobalt
cop	copper
crim.	crimson
cr	cream
dk	dark
dl	dull
dp	deep
db	drab
emer	emerald
gldn	golden
grysh	grayish
grn	green
grnsh	greenish
hel	heliotrope
hn	henna
ind	indigo
int	intense
lav	lavender
lem	lemon
lil	lilac
lt	light
mag	magenta
man	manila
mar	maroon
mv	mauve
multi	multicolored
mlky	milky
myr	myrtle
ol	olive
olvn	olivine
org	orange
pck	peacock
pnksh	pinkish
Prus	Prussian
pur	purple
redsh	reddish
res	reseda
ros	rosine
ryl	royal
sal	salmon
saph	sapphire
scar	scarlet
sep	sepia
sien	sienna
sil	silver
sl	slate
stl	steel
turq	turquoise
ultra	ultramarine
ven	venctian
ver	vermilion
vio	violet
yel	yellow
yelsh	yellowish

COLONIES, FORMER COLONIES, OFFICES, TERRITORIES CONTROLLED BY PARENT STATES

Belgium

Belgian Congo
Ruanda-Urundi

Denmark

Danish West Indies
Faroe Islands
Greenland
Iceland

France

COLONIES PAST AND PRESENT, CONTROLLED TERRITORIES

Afars & Issas, Territory of
Alaouites
Alexandretta
Algeria
Alsace & Lorraine
Ajouan
Annam & Tonkin
Benin
Cambodia (Khmer)
Cameroun
Castellorizo
Chad
Cilicia
Cochin China
Comoro Islands
Dahomey
Diego Suarez
Djibouti (Somali Coast)
Fezzan
French Congo
French Equatorial Africa
French Guiana
French Guinea
French India
French Morocco
French Polynesia (Oceania)
French Southern & Antarctic Territories
French Sudan
French West Africa
Gabon
Germany
Ghadames
Grand Comoro
Guadeloupe
Indo-China
Inini
Ivory Coast
Laos
Latakia
Lebanon
Madagascar
Martinique
Mauritania
Mayotte
Memel

France (cont.)

Middle Congo
Moheli
New Caledonia
New Hebrides
Niger Territory
Nossi-Be
Obock
Reunion
Rouad, Ile
Ste.-Marie de Madagascar
St. Pierre & Miquelon
Senegal
Senegambia & Niger
Somali Coast
Syria
Tahiti
Togo
Tunisia
Ubangi-Shari
Upper Senegal & Niger
Upper Volta
Viet Nam
Wallis & Futuna Islands

POST OFFICES IN FOREIGN COUNTRIES

China
Crete
Egypt
Turkish Empire
Zanzibar

Germany

EARLY STATES

Baden
Bavaria
Bergedorf
Bremen
Brunswick
Hamburg
Hanover
Lubeck
Mecklenburg-Schwerin
Mecklenburg-Strelitz
Oldenburg
Prussia
Saxony
Schleswig-Holstein
Wurttemberg

FORMER COLONIES

Cameroun (Kamerun)
Caroline Islands
German East Africa
German New Guinea
German South-West Africa
Kiauchau
Mariana Islands
Marshall Islands
Samoa
Togo

Italy

Early States

Modena
Parma
Romagna
Roman States
Sardinia
Tuscany
Two Sicilies
  Naples
  Neapolitan Provinces
  Sicily

FORMER COLONIES, CONTROLLED TERRITORIES, OCCUPATION AREAS

Aegean Islands
  Calimno (Calino)
  Caso
  Cos (Coo)
  Karki (Carchi)
  Leros (Lero)
  Lipso
  Nisiros (Nisiro)
  Patmos (Patmo)
  Piscopi
  Rodi (Rhodes)
  Scarpanto
  Simi
  Stampalia
Castellorizo
Corfu
Cyrenaica
Eritrea
Ethiopia (Abyssinia)
Fiume
Ionian Islands
  Cephalonia
  Ithaca
  Paxos
Italian East Africa
Libya
Oltre Giuba
Saseno
Somalia (Italian Somaliland)
Tripolitania

POST OFFICES IN FOREIGN COUNTRIES

"ESTERO"*
Austria
China
  Peking
  Tientsin
Crete
Tripoli
Turkish Empire
  Constantinople
  Durazzo
  Janina
Jerusalem

Italy (cont.)

Salonika
Scutari
Smyrna
Valona

*Stamps overprinted "ESTERO" were used in various parts of the world.

Netherlands

Netherlands Antilles (Curacao)
Netherlands Indies
Netherlands New Guinea
Surinam (Dutch Guiana)

Portugal

COLONIES PAST AND PRESENT, CONTROLLED TERRITORIES

Angola
Angra
Azores
Cape Verde
Funchal
Horta
Inhambane
Kionga
Lourenco Marques
Macao
Madeira
Mozambique
Mozambique Co.
Nyassa
Ponta Delgada
Portuguese Africa
Portuguese Congo
Portuguese Guinea
Portuguese India
Quelimane
St. Thomas & Prince Islands
Tete
Timor
Zambezia

Russia

ALLIED TERRITORIES AND REPUBLICS, OCCUPATION AREAS

Armenia
Aunus (Olonets)
Azerbaijan
Batum
Estonia
Far Eastern Republic
Georgia
Karelia
Latvia
Lithuania
North Ingermanland
Ostland
Russian Turkestan
Siberia

Russia (cont.)

South Russia
Tannu Tuva
Transcaucasian Fed. Republics
Ukraine
Wenden (Livonia)
Western Ukraine

Spain

COLONIES PAST AND PRESENT, CONTROLLED TERRITORIES

Aguera, La
Cape Juby
Cuba
Elobey, Annobon & Corisco

Spain (cont.)

Fernando Po
Ifni
Mariana Islands
Philippines
Puerto Rico
Rio de Oro
Rio Muni
Spanish Guinea
Spanish Morocco
Spanish Sahara
Spanish West Africa

POST OFFICES IN FOREIGN COUNTRIES

Morocco
Tangier
Tetuan

ACKNOWLEDGMENTS

The Editors thank all those many good friends of Scott who have helped this year or in previous years in the task of revising the *Scott Standard Postage Stamp Catalogue.* They have generously shared their stamp knowledge with others through this medium.

No lists of aides can be complete, and several helpers prefer anonymity. The following men are chiefly those who have undertaken to assist on one or more specific countries:

Bruce W. Ball
John K. Bash
Brian M. Bleckwenn
Hamish Bird
Wally A. Bizer
Herbert J. Bloch
John R. Boker, Jr.
Paul Brenner
George W. Brett
Alex A. Cohen
Herbert E. Conway
Ellery Denison
Pandelis J. Drossos
Daniel S. Franklin
Frank P. Geiger
Henry Gitner
Brian M. Green
David Gronbeck-Jones
Mihran B. Hagopian
Calvet M. Hahn
John Hain
Leo John Harris
Clifford O. Herrick
Juan J. Holler
Robert L. Huggins
Lewis S. Kaufman
Joseph E. Landry, Jr.
Andrew Levitt
David MacDonnell
Nick Macris
Robert L. Markovits
Robert P. Odenweller
Souren Panirian
Frank E. Patterson III
Gilbert N. Plass
Henrik Pollak
Alex Rendon
Stanley J. Richmond
Milo D. Rowell
Otto G. Schaffling
Jacques Schiff
Richard Schwartz
Alfredo M. Seiferheld
F. Burton Sellers
Michael Shamilzadeh
James W. Smith
Sherwood Springer
Willard F. Stanley
Carlos Vieiro
Richard A. Washburn
John M. Wilson
Edmund H. Wright

Among the organizations that have helped are:

American Air Mail Society
102 Arbor Road, Cinnaminson, NJ 08077

American Philatelic Society
P.O. Box 8000, State College, PA 16803

American Revenue Association
Bruce Miller, Sec'y, 701 S. First Ave., Suite 332, Arcadia, CA 91006

American Stamp Dealers' Association
5 Dakota Dr., Suite 102, Lake Success, NY 11042

Arabian Philatelic Association
Aramco Box 1929, Dhahran 31311, Saudi Arabia

Brazil Philatelic Association
Tony DeBellis, 30 W. 60th St., New York, NY 10023

Bureau Issues Association
4630 Greylock, St., Boulder, CO 80301

Canadian Society of Russian Philately
P.O. Box 5722, Station A, Toronto, Ontario, Canada M5W 1P2

Canadian Stamp Dealers' Association
P.O. Box 1123, Adelaide St., P.O., Toronto, Ontario, Canada M5C 2K5

Canal Zone Study Group
Alfred R. Bew, Sec'y., 29 S. South Carolina Ave., Atlantic City, NJ 08401

China Stamp Society
J. Lewis Blackburn, Pres., 21816 8th Place W., Bothell, WA 98011

Confederate Stamp Alliance
Brian M. Green, c/o Philatelic Foundation, 270 Madison Ave., New York, NY 10016

Costa Rica Collectors, Society of
T. C. Willoughby, 7600 Ridgemont Dr., Newburgh, IN 47630

Croatian Philatelic Society
1512 Lancelot Rd., Borger, TX 79007

Czechoslovak Philately, Society for
87 Carmita Ave., Rutherford, NJ 07070

Eire Philatelic Association
Robert C. Jones, Sec'y., 8 Beach St., Brockton, MA 02402

Estonian Philatelic Society
Rudolf Hamar, Pres., 243 E. 34th St., New York, NY 10016

France & Colonies Philatelic Society
Walter Parshall, Sec'y., 103 Spruce St., Bloomfield, NJ 07003

Germany Philatelic Society
P.O. Box 779, Arnold, MD 21012

Guatemala Collectors, International Society of
Henry B. Madden, Pres., 4003 N. St. Charles St., Baltimore, MD 21218

Hellenic Philatelic Society of America
Dr. Nicholas Asimakopulos, Sec'y., 541 Cedar Hill Ave., Wyckoff, NJ 07481

Japanese Philately, International Society for
Kenneth Kamholz, Sec'y., P.O. Box 1283, Haddonfield, NJ 08033

Korea Stamp Society, Inc.
Forrest W. Calkins, Sec'y., P.O. Box 1057, Grand Junction, CO 81502

Mexico-Elmhurst Philatelic Society International
Quintus Fernando, Sec'y., 2402 E. 8th St., Tucson, AZ 85719

Oceania Philatelic Society
William Hagan, Pres., 1523 East Meadowbrook Drive, Loveland, OH 45140

Philatelic Foundation
270 Madison Ave., New York, NY 10016

Polonus Philatelic Society
864 N. Ashland Ave., Chicago, IL 60622

Portuguese Philately, International Society for
Nancy M. Gaylord, 1116 Marineway West, North Palm Beach, FL 33408

Rossica, Society of Russian Philately
Norman Epstein, Treas., 33 Crooke Ave., Brooklyn, NY 11226

El Salvador, Associated Collectors of
Robert Fisher, Box 306, Oaks, PA 19456

Scandinavian Collectors Club
Robert B. Brandeberry, 58 W. Salisbury Dr., Wilmington, DE 19809

Turkey & Ottoman Philatelic Society
George Tarnowski, 2050 Spring Valley Rd., Lansdale, PA 19446

United Postal Stationery Society
P.O. Box 48, Redlands, CA 92373

COMMON DESIGN TYPES

Pictured in this section are issues where one illustration has been used for a number of countries in the Catalogue. Not included in this section are overprinted stamps or those issues which are illustrated in each country.

EUROPA

Europa Issue, 1956

The design symbolizing the cooperation among the six countries comprising the Coal and Steel Community is illustrated in each country.

Belgium	444–445
France	805–806
Germany	748–749
Italy	715–716
Luxembourg	318–320
Netherlands	368–369

Europa Issue, 1958

"E" and Dove
CD1

European Postal Union at the service of European integration.

1958, Sept. 13

Belgium	478–479
France	889–890
Germany	790–791
Italy	750–751
Luxembourg	341–343
Netherlands	375–376
Saar	317–318

Europa Issue, 1959

6-Link Endless Chain
CD2

1959, Sept. 19

Belgium	479–498
France	929–930
Germany	805–806
Italy	791–792
Luxembourg	354–355
Netherlands	379–380

Europa Issue, 1960

19-Spoke Wheel
CD3

First anniversary of the establishment of C.E.P.T. (Conférence Européenne des Administrations des Postes et des Télécommunications.)

The spokes symbolize the 19 founding members of the Conference.

1960, Sept.

Belgium	518–519
Denmark	379
Finland	376–377
France	970–971
Germany	818–820
Great Britain	377–378
Greece	688
Iceland	327–328
Ireland	175–176
Italy	809–810
Luxembourg	374–375
Netherlands	385–386
Norway	387
Portugal	866–867
Spain	941–942
Sweden	562–563
Switzerland	400–401
Turkey	1493–1494

Europa Issue, 1961

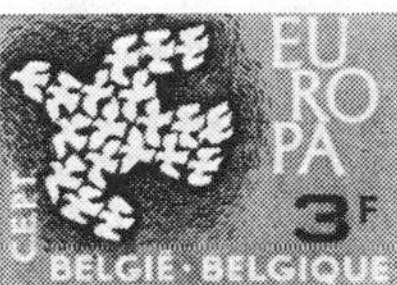

19 Doves Flying as One
CD4

The 19 doves represent the 19 members of the Conference of European Postal and Telecommunications Administrations, C.E.P.T.

1961–62

Belgium	536–537
Cyprus	201–203
France	1005–1006
Germany	844–845
Great Britain	383–384
Greece	718–719
Iceland	340–341
Italy	845–846
Luxembourg	382–383
Netherlands	387–388
Spain	1010–1011
Switzerland	410–411
Turkey	1518–1520

Europa Issue 1962

Young Tree with 19 Leaves
CD5

The 19 leaves represent the 19 original members of C.E.P.T.

1962–63

Belgium	546–547
Cyprus	219–221
France	1045–1046
Germany	852–853
Greece	739–740
Iceland	348–349
Ireland	184–185
Italy	860–861
Luxembourg	386–387
Netherlands	394–395
Norway	414–415
Switzerland	416–417
Turkey	1553–1555

Europa Issue, 1963

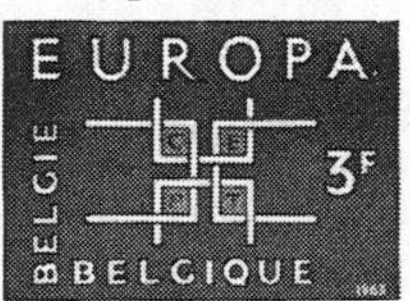

Stylized Links, Symbolizing Unity
CD6

1963, Sept.

Belgium	562–563
Cyprus	229–231
Finland	419
France	1074–1075
Germany	867–868
Greece	768–769
Iceland	357–358
Ireland	188–189
Italy	880–881
Luxembourg	403–404
Netherlands	416–417
Norway	441–442
Switzerland	429
Turkey	1602–1603

Europa Issue, 1964

Symbolic Daisy
CD7

5th anniversary of the establishment of C.E.P.T. The 22 petals of the flower symbolize the 22 members of the Conference.

1964, Sept.

Austria	738
Belgium	578–579
Cyprus	244–246
France	1109–1110
Germany	897–898
Greece	801–802
Iceland	367–368
Ireland	196–197
Italy	894–895
Luxembourg	411–412
Monaco	590–591
Netherlands	428–429
Norway	458
Portugal	931–933
Spain	1262–1263
Switzerland	438–439
Turkey	1628–1629

Europa Issue, 1965

Leaves and "Fruit"
CD8

1965

Belgium	600–601
Cyprus	262–264
Finland	437
France	1131–1132
Germany	934–935
Greece	833–834
Iceland	375–376
Ireland	204–205
Italy	915–916
Luxembourg	432–433
Monaco	616–617
Netherlands	438–439
Norway	475–476
Portugal	958–960
Switzerland	469
Turkey	1665–1666

Europa Issue, 1966

Symbolic Sailboat
CD9

1966, Sept.

Andorra, French	172
Belgium	622–628
Cyprus	275–277
France	1163–1164
Germany	963–964
Greece	862–863
Iceland	384–385
Ireland	216–217
Italy	942–943
Liechtenstein	415
Luxembourg	440–441
Monaco	639–640
Netherlands	441–442
Norway	496–497
Portugal	980–982
Switzerland	477–478
Turkey	1718–1719

Europa Issue, 1967

Cogwheels
CD10

1967

Andorra, French	174–175
Belgium	641–642
Cyprus	297–299
France	1178–1179
Greece	891–892
Germany	969–970
Iceland	389–390
Ireland	232–233
Italy	951–952
Liechtenstein	420
Luxembourg	449–450
Monaco	669–670
Netherlands	444–447
Norway	504–505
Portugal	994–996
Spain	1465–1466
Switzerland	482
Turkey	B120–B121

Europa Issue, 1968

Golden Key with C.E.P.T. Emblem
CD11

1968

Andorra, French	182–183
Belgium	664–665
Cyprus	314–316
France	1209–1210
Germany	983–984
Greece	916–917
Iceland	395–396
Ireland	242–243
Italy	979–980
Liechtenstein	442
Luxembourg	466–467
Monaco	689–691
Netherlands	452–453
Portugal	1019–1021
San Marino	687
Spain	1526
Turkey	1775–1776

Europa Issue, 1969

"EUROPA" and "CEPT"
CD12

Tenth anniversary of C.E.P.T.

1969

Andorra, French	188–189
Austria	837
Belgium	683–684
Cyprus	326–328
Denmark	458
Finland	483
France	1245–1246
Germany	996–997
Great Britain	585
Greece	947–948
Iceland	406–407
Ireland	270–271
Italy	1000–1001
Jugoslavia	1003–1004
Liechtenstein	453
Luxembourg	474–475
Monaco	722–724
Netherlands	475–476
Norway	533–534
Portugal	1038–1040
San Marino	701–702
Spain	1567
Sweden	814–816
Switzerland	500–501
Turkey	1799–1800
Vatican	470–472

Europa Issue, 1970

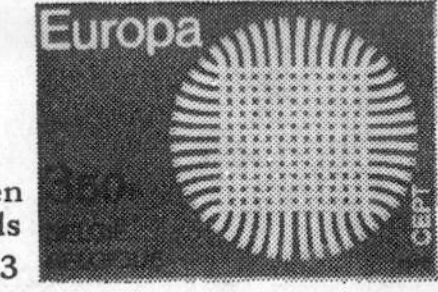

Interwoven Threads
CD13

1970

Andorra, French	196–197
Belgium	708–709
Cyprus	340–342
France	1271–1272
Germany	1018–1019
Greece	985, 987
Iceland	420–421
Ireland	279–281
Italy	1013–1014
Jugoslavia	1024–1025
Liechtenstein	470
Luxembourg	489–490
Monaco	768–770
Netherlands	483–484
Portugal	1060–1062
San Marino	729–730
Spain	1607
Switzerland	515–516
Turkey	1848–1849

Europa Issue, 1971

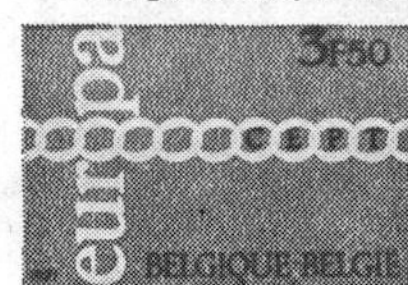

"Fraternity, Cooperation, Common Effort"—CD14

1971

Andorra, French	205–206
Belgium	742–743
Cyprus	365–367
Finland	504
France	1304
Germany	1064–1065
Greece	1029–1030
Iceland	429–430
Ireland	305–306
Italy	1038–1039
Jugoslavia	1052–1053
Liechtenstein	485
Luxembourg	500–501
Malta	425–427
Monaco	797–799
Netherlands	488–489
Portugal	1094–1096
San Marino	749–750
Spain	1675–1676
Switzerland	531–532
Turkey	1876–1877

Europa Issue, 1972

Sparkles, Symbolic of Communications
CD15

1972

Andorra, French	210–211
Andorra, Spanish	62
Belgium	768–769
Cyprus	380–382
Finland	512–513
France	1341
Germany	1089–1090
Greece	1049–1050
Iceland	439–440
Ireland	316–317
Italy	1065–1066
Jugoslavia	1100–1101
Liechtenstein	504
Luxembourg	512–513
Malta	450–453
Monaco	831–832
Netherlands	494–495
Portugal	1141–1143
San Marino	771–772
Spain	1718
Switzerland	544–545
Turkey	1907–1908

Europa Issue, 1973

Post Horn and Arrows
CD16

1973

Andorra, French	319–320
Andorra, Spanish	76
Belgium	782–783
Cyprus	396–398
Finland	526
France	1367
Germany	1114–1115
Greece	1090–1092
Iceland	447–448
Ireland	329–330
Italy	1108–1109
Jugoslavia	1138–1139
Liechtenstein	528–529
Luxembourg	523–524
Malta	469–471
Monaco	866–867
Netherlands	504–505
Norway	604–605
Portugal	1170–1172
San Marino	802–803
Spain	1753
Switzerland	580–581
Turkey	1935–1936

PORTUGAL & COLONIES

Vasco da Gama Issue

Fleet Departing—CD20

Fleet Arriving at Calicut
CD21

Embarking at Rastello—CD22

Muse of History
CD23

Flagship San Gabriel, da Gama and Camoens
CD24

Archangel Gabriel, the Patron Saint
CD25

Flagship San Gabriel
CD26

Vasco da Gama
CD27

Fourth centenary of Vasco da Gama's discovery of the route to India.

1898

Azores	93–100
Macao	67–74
Madeira	37–44
Portugal	147–154
Port. Africa	1–8
Port. India	189–196
Timor	45–52

Pombal Issue

POSTAL TAX

Marquis de Pombal
CD28

Planning Reconstruction of Lisbon, 1755
CD29

Pombal Monument, Lisbon
CD30

Sebastiao José de Carvalho e Mello, Marquis de Pombal (1699–1782), statesman, rebuilt Lisbon after earthquake of 1755. Tax was for the erection of Pombal monument. Obligatory on all mail on certain days throughout the year.

1925

Angola	RA1–RA3
Azores	RA9–RA11
Cape Verde	RA1–RA3
Macao	RA1–RA3
Madeira	RA1–RA3
Mozambique	RA1–RA3
Portugal	RA11–RA13
Port. Guinea	RA1–RA3
Port. India	RA1–RA3
St. Thomas & Prince Islands	RA1–RA3
Timor	RA1–RA3

Pombal Issue

POSTAL TAX DUES

Marquis de Pombal
CD31

Planning Reconstruction of Lisbon, 1755
CD32

Pombal Monument, Lisbon
CD33

1925	
Angola	RAJ1–RAJ3
Azores	RAJ2–RAJ4
Cape Verde	RAJ1–RAJ3
Macao	RAJ1–RAJ3
Madeira	RAJ1–RAJ3
Mozambique	RAJ1–RAJ3
Portugal	RAJ2–RAJ4
Port. Guinea	RAJ1–RAJ3
Port. India	RAJ1–RAJ3
St. Thomas & Prince Islands	RAJ1–RAJ3
Timor	RAJ1–RAJ3

Vasco da Gama
CD34

Mousinho de Albuquerque
CD35

Dam
CD36

Prince Henry the Navigator
CD37

Affonso de Albuquerque
CD38

1938–39	
Angola	274–291
Cape Verde	234–251
Macao	289–305
Mozambique	270–287
Port. Guinea	233–250
Port. India	439–453
St. Thomas & Prince Islands	302–319, 323–340
Timor	223–239

Plane over Globe
CD39

1938–39	
Angola	C1–C9
Cape Verde	C1–C9
Macao	C7–C15
Mozambique	C1–C9
Port. Guinea	C1–C9
Port. India	C1–C8
St. Thomas & Prince Islands	C1–C18
Timor	C1–C9

Lady of Fatima Issue

Our Lady of the Rosary, Fatima, Portugal
CD40

1948–49	
Angola	315–318
Cape Verde	266
Macao	336
Mozambique	325–328
Port. Guinea	271
Port. India	480
St. Thomas & Prince Islands	351
Timor	254

A souvenir sheet of 9 stamps was issued in 1951 to mark the extension of the 1950 Holy Year. The sheet contains: Angola No. 316, Cape Verde No. 266, Macao No. 336, Mozambique No. 325, Portuguese Guinea No. 271, Portuguese India Nos. 480, 485, St. Thomas & Prince Islands No. 351, Timor No. 254.

The sheet also contains a portrait of Pope Pius XII and is inscribed "Encerramento do Ano Santo, Fatima 1951." It was sold for 11 escudos.

Holy Year Issue

Church Bells and Dove — **CD41**

Angel Holding Candelabra — **CD42**

Holy Year, 1950.

1950–51	
Angola	331–332
Cape Verde	268–269
Macao	339–340
Mozambique	330–331
Port. Guinea	273–274
Port. India	490–491, 496–503
St. Thomas & Prince Islands	353–354
Timor	258–259

A souvenir sheet of 8 stamps was issued in 1951 to mark the extension of the Holy Year. The sheet contains: Angola No. 331, Cape Verde No. 269, Macao No. 340, Mozambique No. 331, Portuguese Guinea No. 275, Portuguese India No. 490, St. Thomas & Prince Islands No. 354, Timor No. 258, some with colors changed. The sheet contains doves and is inscribed "Encerramento do Ano Santo, Fatima 1951." It was sold for 17 escudos.

Holy Year Conclusion Issue

Our Lady of Fatima
CD43

Conclusion of Holy Year. Sheets contain alternate vertical rows of stamps and labels bearing quotation from Pope Pius XII, different for each colony.

1951	
Angola	357
Cape Verde	270
Macao	352
Mozambique	356
Port. Guinea	275
Port. India	506
St. Thomas & Prince Islands	355
Timor	270

Medical Congress Issue

Medical Examination
CD44

First National Congress of Tropical Medicine, Lisbon, 1952.

Each stamp has a different design.

1952	
Angola	358
Cape Verde	287
Macao	364
Mozambique	359
Port. Guinea	276
Port. India	516
St. Thomas & Prince Islands	356
Timor	271

POSTAGE DUE STAMPS

CD45

1952	
Angola	J37–J42
Cape Verde	J31–J36
Macao	J53–J58
Mozambique	J51–J56
Port. Guinea	J40–J45
Port. India	J47–J52
St. Thomas & Prince Islands	J52–J57
Timor	J31–J36

Sao Paulo Issue

Father Manuel da Nobrega and View of Sao Paulo
CD46

400th anniversary of the founding of Sao Paulo, Brazil.

1954	
Angola	385
Cape Verde	297
Macao	382
Mozambique	395
Port. Guinea	291
Port. India	530
St. Thomas & Prince Islands	369
Timor	279

Tropical Medicine Congress Issue

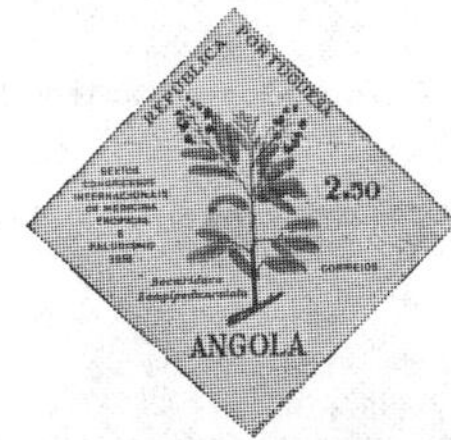

Securidaca Longipedunculata
CD47

Sixth International Congress for Tropical Medicine and Malaria, Lisbon, Sept. 1958.

Each stamp shows a different plant.

1958	
Angola	409
Cape Verde	303
Macao	392
Mozambique	404
Port. Guinea	295
Port. India	569
St. Thomas & Prince Islands	371
Timor	289

Sports Issue

Flying
CD48

Each stamp shows a different sport.

1962

Angola	433–438
Cape Verde	320–325
Macao	394–399
Mozambique	424–429
Port. Guinea	299–304
St. Thomas & Prince Islands	374–379
Timor	313–318

Anti-Malaria Issue

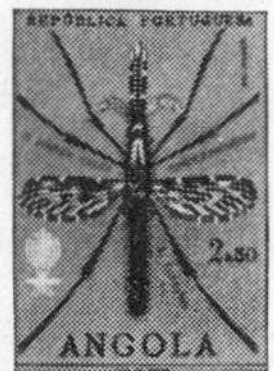

Anopheles Funestus and Malaria Eradication Symbol

CD49

World Health Organization drive to eradicate malaria.

1962

Angola	439
Cape Verde	326
Macao	400
Mozambique	430
Port. Guinea	305
St. Thomas & Prince Islands	380
Timor	319

Airline Anniversary Issue

Map of Africa, Super Constellation and Jet Liner

CD50

Tenth anniversary of Transportes Aéreos Portugueses (TAP).

1963

Angola	490
Cape Verde	327
Mozambique	434
Port. Guinea	318
St. Thomas & Prince Islands	381

National Overseas Bank Issue

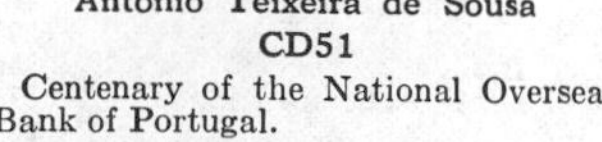

Antonio Teixeira de Sousa

CD51

Centenary of the National Overseas Bank of Portugal.

1964, May 16

Angola	509
Cape Verde	328
Port. Guinea	319
St. Thomas & Prince Islands	382
Timor	320

ITU Issue

ITU Emblem and St. Gabriel

CD52

Centenary of the International Communications Union.

1965, May 17

Angola	511
Cape Verde	329
Macao	402
Mozambique	464
Port. Guinea	320
St. Thomas & Prince Islands	383
Timor	321

National Revolution Issue

St. Pauls's Hospital, and Commercial and Industrial School

CD53

40th anniversary of the National Revolution.
Different buildings on each stamp.

1966, May 28

Angola	525
Cape Verde	338
Macao	403
Mozambique	465
Port. Guinea	329
St. Thomas & Prince Islands	392
Timor	322

Navy Club Issue

Mendes Barata and Cruiser Dom Carlos I

CD54

Centenary of Portugal's Navy Club.
Each stamp has a different design.

1967, Jan. 31

Angola	527–528
Cape Verde	339–340
Macao	412–413
Mozambique	478–479
Port. Guinea	330–331
St. Thomas & Prince Islands	393–394
Timor	323–324

Admiral Coutinho Issue

Admiral Gago Coutinho and his First Ship

CD55

Centenary of the birth of Admiral Carlos Viegas Gago Coutinho (1869–1959), explorer and aviation pioneer.
Each stamp has a different design.

1969, Feb. 17

Angola	547
Cape Verde	355
Macao	417
Mozambique	484
Port. Guinea	335
St. Thomas & Prince Islands	397
Timor	335

Administration Reform Issue

Luiz Augusto Rebello da Silva

CD56

Centenary of the administration reforms of the overseas territories.

1969, Sept. 25

Angola	549
Cape Verde	357
Macao	419
Mozambique	491
Port. Guinea	337
St. Thomas & Prince Islands	399
Timor	338

Marshal Carmona Issue

Marshal A. O. Carmona

CD57

Birth centenary of Marshal Antonio Oscar Carmona de Fragoso (1869–1951), President of Portugal.
Each stamp has a different design.

1970, Nov. 15

Angola	563
Cape Verde	359
Macao	422
Mozambique	493
Port. Guinea	340
St. Thomas & Prince Islands	403
Timor	341

Olympic Games Issue

Racing Yachts and Olympic Emblem

CD59

20th Olympic Games, Munich, Aug. 26–Sept. 11.
Each stamp shows a different sport.

1972, June 20

Angola	569
Cape Verde	361
Macao	426
Mozambique	504
Port. Guinea	342
St. Thomas & Prince Islands	408
Timor	343

Lisbon-Rio de Janeiro Flight Issue

"Santa Cruz" over Fernando de Noronha

CD60

50th anniversary of the Lisbon to Rio de Janeiro flight by Arturo de Sacadura and Coutinho, March 30–June 5, 1922.
Each stamp shows a different stage of the flight.

1972, Sept. 20

Angola	570
Cape Verde	362
Macao	427
Mozambique	505
Port. Guinea	343
St. Thomas & Prince Islands	409
Timor	344

WMO Centenary Issue

WMO Emblem

CD61

Centenary of international meteorological cooperation.

1973, Dec. 15

Angola	571
Cape Verde	363
Macao	429
Mozambique	509
Port. Guinea	344
St. Thomas & Prince Islands	410
Timor	345

FRENCH COMMUNITY

Colonial Exposition Issue

People of French Empire

CD70

Women's Heads

CD71

France Showing Way to Civilization

CD72

"Colonial Commerce"

CD73

International Colonial Exposition, Paris 1931.

1931

Cameroun	213–216
Chad	60–63
Dahomey	97–100
Fr. Guiana	152–155
Fr. Guinea	116–119
Fr. India	100–103
Fr. Polynesia	76–79
Fr. Sudan	102–105
Gabon	120–123
Guadeloupe	138–141
Indo-China	140–142
Ivory Coast	92–95
Madagascar	169–172
Martinique	129–132
Mauritania	65–68
Middle Congo	61–64
New Caledonia	176–179
Niger	73–76
Reunion	122–125
St. Pierre & Miquelon	132–135
Senegal	138–141
Somali Coast	135–138
Togo	254–257
Ubangi-Shari	82–85
Upper Volta	66–69
Wallis & Futuna Isls.	85–88

Paris International Exposition Issue

Colonial Arts Exposition Issue

"Colonial Resources"

CD74 CD77

Overseas Commerce

CD75

Exposition Buildings and Women

CD76

"France and the Empire"

CD78

Cultural Treasures of the Colonies

CD79

Souvenir sheets contain one imperf. stamp.

1937

Cameroun	217–222A
Dahomey	101–107
Fr. Equatorial Africa	27–32, 73
Fr. Guiana	162–168
Fr. Guinea	120–126
Fr. India	104–110
Fr. Polynesia	117–123
Fr. Sudan	106–112
Guadeloupe	148–154
Indo-China	193–199
Inini	41
Ivory Coast	152–158
Kwangchowan	132
Madagascar	191–197
Martinique	179–185
Mauritania	69–75
New Caledonia	208–214
Niger	72–83
Reunion	167–173
St. Pierre & Miquelon	165–171
Senegal	172–178
Somali Coast	139–145
Togo	258–264
Wallis & Futuna Isls.	89

Curie Issue

Pierre and Marie Curie

CD80

40th anniversary of the discovery of radium. The surtax was for the benefit of the International Union for the Control of Cancer.

1938

Cameroun	B1
Dahomey	B2
France	B76
Fr. Equatorial Africa	B1
Fr. Guiana	B3
Fr. Guinea	B2
Fr. India	B6
Fr. Polynesia	B5
Fr. Sudan	B1
Guadeloupe	B3
Indo-China	B14
Ivory Coast	B2
Madagascar	B2
Martinique	B2
Mauritania	B3
New Caledonia	B4
Niger	B1
Reunion	B4
St. Pierre & Miquelon	B3
Senegal	B3
Somali Coast	B2
Togo	B1

Caillié Issue

René Caillié and Map of Northwestern Africa

CD81

Death centenary of René Caillié (1799–1838), French explorer.

All three denominations exist with colony name omitted.

1939

Dahomey	108–110
Fr. Guinea	161–163
Fr. Sudan	113–115
Ivory Coast	160–162
Mauritania	109–111
Niger	84–86
Senegal	188–190
Togo	265–267

New York World's Fair Issue

Natives and New York Skyline

CD82

1939

Cameroun	223–224
Dahomey	111–112
Fr. Equatorial Africa	78–79
Fr. Guiana	169–170
Fr. Guinea	164–165
Fr. India	111–112
Fr. Polynesia	124–125
Fr. Sudan	116–117
Guadeloupe	155–156
Indo-China	203–204
Inini	42–43
Ivory Coast	163–164
Kwangchowan	121–122
Madagascar	209–210
Martinque	186–187
Mauritania	112–113
New Caledonia	215–216
Niger	87–88
Reunion	174–175
St. Pierre & Miquelon	205–206
Senegal	191–192
Somali Coast	179–180
Togo	268–269
Wallis & Futuna Isls.	90–91

French Revolution Issue

Storming of the Bastille

CD83

150th anniversary of the French Revolution. The surtax was for the defense of the colonies.

1939

Cameroun	B2–B6
Dahomey	B3–B7
Fr. Equatorial Africa	B4–B8, CB1
Fr. Guiana	B4–B8, CB1
Fr. Guinea	B3–B7
Fr. India	B7–B11
Fr. Polynesia	B6–B10, CB1
Fr. Sudan	B2–B6
Guadeloupe	B4–B8
Indo-China	B15–B19, CB1
Inini	B1–B5
Ivory Coast	B3–B7
Kwangchowan	B1–B5
Madagascar	B3–B7, CB1
Martinique	B3–B7
Mauritania	B4–B8
New Caledonia	B5–B9, CB1
Niger	B2–B6
Reunion	B5–B9, CB1
St. Pierre & Miquelon	B4–B8
Senegal	B4–B8, CB1
Somali Coast	B3–B7
Togo	B2–B6
Wallis & Futuna Isls.	B1–B5

Plane over Coastal Area

CD85

All five denominations exist with colony name omitted.

1940

Dahomey	C1–C5
Fr. Guinea	C1–C5
Fr. Sudan	C1–C5
Ivory Coast	C1–C5
Mauritania	C1–C5
Niger	C1–C5
Senegal	C12–C16
Togo	C1–C5

Colonial Infantryman

CD86

1941

Cameroun	B13B
Dahomey	B13
Fr. Equatorial Africa	B8B
Fr. Guiana	B10
Fr. Guinea	B13
Fr. India	B13
Fr. Polynesia	B12
Fr. Sudan	B12
Guadeloupe	B10
Indo-China	B19B
Inini	B7
Ivory Coast	B13
Kwangchowan	B7
Madagascar	B9
Martinique	B9
Mauritania	B14
New Caledonia	B11
Niger	B12
Reunion	B11
St. Pierre & Miquelon	B8B
Senegal	B14
Somali Coast	B9
Togo	B10B
Wallis & Futuna Isls.	B7

Cross of Lorraine and Four-motor Plane

CD87

1941–5

Cameroun	C1–C7
Fr. Equatorial Africa	C17–C23
Fr. Guiana	C9–C10
Fr. India	C1–C6
Fr. Polynesia	C3–C9
Fr. West Africa	C1–C3
Guadeloupe	C1–C2
Madagascar	C37–C43
Martinique	C1–C2
New Caledonia	C7–C13
Reunion	C18–C24
St. Pierre & Miquelon	C1–C7
Somali Coast	C1–C7

Transport Plane

CD88

Caravan and Plane—CD89

1942

Dahomey	C6–C13
Fr. Guinea	C6–C13
Fr. Sudan	C6–C13
Ivory Coast	C6–C13
Mauritania	C6–C13
Niger	C6–C13
Senegal	C17–C25
Togo	C6–C13

Red Cross Issue

Marianne
CD90

The surtax was for the French Red Cross and national relief.

1944

Cameroun	B28
Fr. Equatorial Africa	B38
Fr. Guiana	B12
Fr. India	B14
Fr. Polynesia	B13
Fr. West Africa	B1
Guadeloupe	B12
Madagascar	B15
Martinique	B11
New Caledonia	B13
Reunion	B15
St. Pierre & Miquelon	B13
Somali Coast	B13
Wallis & Futuna Isls.	B9

Eboué Issue

Félix Eboué
CD91

Félix Eboué, first French colonial administrator to proclaim resistance to Germany after French surrender in World War II.

1945

Cameroun	296–297
Fr. Equatorial Africa	156–157
Fr. Guiana	171–172
Fr. India	210–211
Fr. Polynesia	150–151
Fr. West Africa	15–16
Guadeloupe	187–188
Madagascar	259–260
Martinique	196–197
New Caledonia	274–275
Reunion	238–239
St. Pierre & Miquelon	322–323
Somali Coast	238–239

Victory Issue

Victory
CD92

European victory of the Allied Nations in World War II.

1946, May 8

Cameroun	C8
Fr. Equatorial Africa	C24
Fr. Guiana	C11
Fr. India	C7
Fr. Polynesia	C10
Fr. West Africa	C4
Guadeloupe	C3
Indo-China	C19
Madagascar	C44
Martinique	C3
New Caledonia	C14
Reunion	C25
St. Pierre & Miquelon	C8
Somali Coast	C8
Wallis & Futuna Isls.	C1

Chad to Rhine Issue

Leclerc's Departure from Chad
CD93

Battle at Cufra Oasis
CD94

Tanks in Action, Mareth
CD95

Normandy Invasion
CD96

Entering Paris
CD97

Liberation of Strasbourg
CD98

"Chad to the Rhine" march, 1942–44, by Gen. Jacques Leclerc's column, later French 2nd Armored Division.

1946, June 6

Cameroun	C9–C14
Fr. Equatorial Africa	C25–C30
Fr. Guiana	C12–C17
Fr. India	C8–C13
Fr. Polynesia	C11–C16
Fr. West Africa	C5–C10
Guadeloupe	C4–C9
Indo-China	C20–C25
Madagascar	C45–C50
Martinique	C4–C9
New Caledonia	C15–C20
Reunion	C26–C31
St. Pierre & Miquelon	C9–C14
Somali Coast	C9–C14
Wallis & Futuna Isls.	C2–C7

UPU Issue

French Colonials, Globe and Plane
CD99

75th anniversary of the Universal Postal Union.

1949, July 4

Cameroun	C29
Fr. Equatorial Africa	C34
Fr. India	C17
Fr. Polynesia	C20
Fr. West Africa	C15
Indo-China	C26
Madagascar	C55
New Caledonia	C24
St. Pierre & Miquelon	C18
Somali Coast	C18
Togo	C18
Wallis & Futuna Isls.	C10

Tropical Medicine Issue

Doctor Treating Infant
CD100

The surtax was for charitable work.

1950

Cameroun	B29
Fr. Equatorial Africa	B39
Fr. India	B15
Fr. Polynesia	B14
Fr. West Africa	B3
Madagascar	B17
New Caledonia	B14
St. Pierre & Miquelon	B14
Somali Coast	B14
Togo	B11

Military Medal Issue

Medal, Early Marine and Colonial Soldier
CD101

Centenary of the creation of the French Military Medal.

1952

Cameroun	332
Comoro Isls.	39
Fr. Equatorial Africa	186
Fr. India	233
Fr. Polynesia	179
Fr. West Africa	57
Madagascar	286
New Caledonia	295
St. Pierre & Miquelon	345
Somali Coast	267
Togo	327
Wallis & Futuna Isls.	149

Liberation Issue

Allied Landing, Victory Sign and Cross of Lorraine
CD102

10th anniversary of the liberation of France.

1954, June 6

Cameroun	C32
Comoro Isls.	C4
Fr. Equatorial Africa	C38
Fr. India	C18
Fr. Polynesia	C23
Fr. West Africa	C17
Madagascar	C57
New Caledonia	C25
St. Pierre & Miquelon	C19
Somali Coast	C19
Togo	C19
Wallis & Futuna Isls.	C11

FIDES Issue

Plowmen
CD103

Efforts of FIDES, the Economic and Social Development Fund for Overseas Possessions (Fonds d' Investissement pour le Developpement Economique et Social.)

Each stamp has a different design.

1956

Cameroun	326–329
Comoro Isls.	43
Fr. Polynesia	181
Madagascar	292–295
New Caledonia	303
Somali Coast	268
Togo	331

Flower Issue

Euadania
CD104

Each stamp shows a different flower.

1958–9

Cameroun	333
Comoro Isls.	45
Fr. Equatorial Africa	200–201
Fr. Polynesia	192
Fr. So. & Antarctic Terr.	11
Fr. West Africa	79–83
Madagascar	301–302
New Caledonia	304–305
St. Pierre & Miquelon	357

Somali Coast 270
Togo 348–349
Wallis & Futuna Isls. 152

Human Rights Issue

Sun, Dove and U. N. Emblem

CD105

10th anniversary of the signing of the Universal Declaration of Human Rights.

1958

Comoro Isls. 44
Fr. Equatorial Africa 202
Fr. Polynesia 191
Fr. West Africa 85
Madagascar 300
New Caledonia 306
St. Pierre & Miquelon 356
Somali Coast 274
Wallis & Futuna Isls. 153

C.C.T.A. Issue

Map of Africa and Cogwheels

CD106

10th anniversary of the Commission for Technical Cooperation in Africa south of the Sahara.

1960

Air Afrique Issue, 1961

Modern and Ancient Africa, Map and Planes

CD107

Founding of Air Afrique (African Airlines).

1961–62

Cameroun C37
Cent. African Rep. C5
Chad C7
Congo, P.R. C5
Dahomey C17
Gabon C5
Ivory Coast C18
Mauritania C17
Niger C22
Senegal C31
Upper Volta C4

Anti-Malaria Issue

Malaria Eradication Emblem

CD108

World Health Organization drive to eradicate malaria.

1962, Apr. 7

Cameroun B36
Cent. African Rep. B1
Chad B1
Comoro Isls. B1
Congo, P.R. B3
Dahomey B15
Gabon B4
Ivory Coast B15
Madagascar B19
Mali B1
Mauritania B16
Niger B14
Senegal B16
Somali Coast B15
Upper Volta B1

Abidjan Games Issue

Relay Race

CD109

Abidjan Games, Ivory Coast, Dec. 24–31, 1961.

Each stamp shows a different sport.

1962

Chad 83–84
Cent. African Rep. 19–20
Congo, P.R. 103–104
Gabon 163–164
Niger 109–111
Upper Volta 103–105

African and Malagasy Union Issue

Flag of African and Malagasy Union

CD110

First anniversary of the Union.

1962, Sept. 8

Cameroun 373
Cent. African Rep. 21
Chad 85
Congo, P.R. 105
Dahomey 155
Gabon 165
Ivory Coast 198
Madagascar 332
Mauritania 170
Niger 112
Senegal 211
Upper Volta 106

Telstar Issue

Telstar and Globe Showing Andover and Pleumeur-Bodou

CD111

First television connection of the United States and Europe through the Telstar satellite, July 11–12, 1962.

1962–63

Andorra, French 154
Comoro Isls. C7
Fr. Polynesia C29
Fr. So. & Antarctic Terr. C5
New Caledonia C33
Somali Coast C31
St. Pierre & Miquelon C26
Wallis & Futuna Isls. C17

Freedom From Hunger Issue

World Map and Wheat Emblem

CD112

United Nations Food and Agriculture Organization's "Freedom from Hunger" campaign.

1963, Mar. 21

Cameroun B37–B38
Cent. African Rep. B2
Chad B2
Congo, P.R. B4
Dahomey B16
Gabon B5
Ivory Coast B16
Madagascar B21
Mauritania B17
Niger B15
Senegal B17
Upper Volta B2

Red Cross Centenary Issue

Centenary Emblem

CD113

Centenary of the International Red Cross.

1963, Sept. 2

Comoro Isls. 55
Fr. Polynesia 205
New Caledonia 328
St. Pierre & Miquelon 367
Somali Coast 297
Wallis & Futuna Isls. 165

African Postal Union Issue

UAMPT Emblem, Radio Masts, Plane and Mail

CD114

Establishment of the African and Malagasy Posts and Telecommunications Union, UAMPT.

1963, Sept. 8

Cameroun C47
Cent. African Rep. C10
Chad C9
Congo, P.R. C13
Dahomey C19
Gabon C13
Ivory Coast C25
Madagascar C75
Mauritania C22
Niger C27
Rwanda 36
Senegal C32
Upper Volta C9

Air Afrique Issue, 1963

Symbols of Flight

CD115

First anniversary of Air Afrique and inauguration of DC-8 service.

1963, Nov. 19

Cameroun C48
Chad C10
Congo, P.R. C14
Gabon C18
Ivory Coast C26
Mauritania C26
Niger C35
Senegal C33

Europafrica Issue

Europe and Africa Linked Together

CD116

Signing of an economic agreement between the European Economic Community and the African and Malagasy Union, Yaoundé, Cameroun, July 20, 1963.

1963–64

Cameroun 402
Chad C11
Cent. African Rep. C12
Congo, P.R. C16

Gabon	C19
Ivory Coast	217
Niger	C43
Upper Volta	C11

Human Rights Issue

Scales of Justice and Globe

CD117

15th anniversary of the Universal Declaration of Human Rights.

1963, Dec. 10

Comoro Isls.	58
Fr. Polynesia	206
New Caledonia	329
St. Pierre & Miquelon	368
Somali Coast	300
Wallis & Futuna Isls.	166

PHILATEC Issue

Stamp Album, Champs Elysées Palace and Horses of Marly

CD118

"PHILATEC," International Philatelic and Postal Techniques Exhibition, Paris, June 5-21, 1964.

1963-64

Comoro Isls.	60
France	1078
Fr. Polynesia	207
New Caledonia	341
St. Pierre & Miquelon	369
Somali Coast	301
Wallis & Futuna Isls.	167

Cooperation Issue

Maps of France and Africa and Clasped Hands

CD119

Cooperation between France and the French-speaking countries of Africa and Madagascar.

1964

Cameroun	409-410
Cent. African Rep.	39
Chad	103
Congo, P.R.	121
Dahomey	193
France	1111
Gabon	175
Ivory Coast	221
Madagascar	360
Mauritania	181
Niger	143
Senegal	236
Togo	495

ITU Issue

Telegraph, Syncom Satellite and ITU Emblem

CD120

Centenary of the International Telecommunication Union.

1965, May 17

Comoro Isls.	C14
Fr. Polynesia	C33
Fr. So. & Antarctic Terr.	C8
New Caledonia	C40
New Hebrides	124-125
St. Pierre & Miquelon	C29
Somali Coast	C36
Wallis & Futuna Isls.	C20

French Satellite A-1 Issue

Diamant Rocket and Launching Installations

CD121

Launching of France's first satellite, Nov. 26, 1965.

1965-66

Comoro Isls.	C15-C16
France	1137-1138
Fr. Polynesia	C40-C41
Fr. So. & Antarctic Terr.	C9-C10
New Caledonia	C44-C45
St. Pierre & Miquelon	C30-C31
Somali Coast	C39-C40
Wallis & Futuna Isls.	C22-C23

French Satellite D-1 Issue

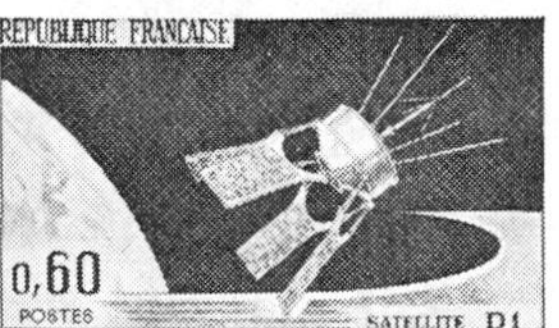

D-1 Satellite in Orbit

CD122

Launching of the D-1 satellite at Hammaguir, Algeria, Feb. 17, 1966.

1966

Comoro Isls.	C17
France	1148
Fr. Polynesia	C42
Fr. So. & Antarctic Terr.	C11
New Caledonia	C46
St. Pierre & Miquelon	C32
Somali Coast	C49
Wallis & Futuna Isls.	C24

Air Afrique Issue, 1966

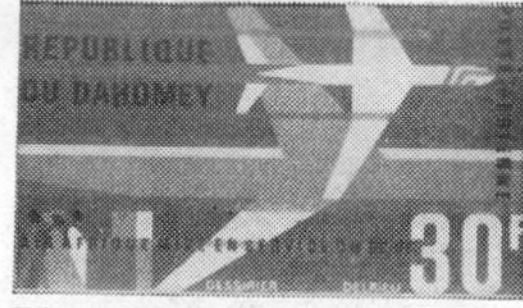

Planes and Air Afrique Emblem

CD123

Introduction of DC-8F planes by Air Afrique.

1966

Cameroun	C79
Cent. African Rep.	C35
Chad	C26
Congo, P.R.	C42
Dahomey	C42
Gabon	C47
Ivory Coast	C32
Mauritania	C57
Niger	C63
Senegal	C47
Togo	C54
Upper Volta	C31

African Postal Union Issue, 1967

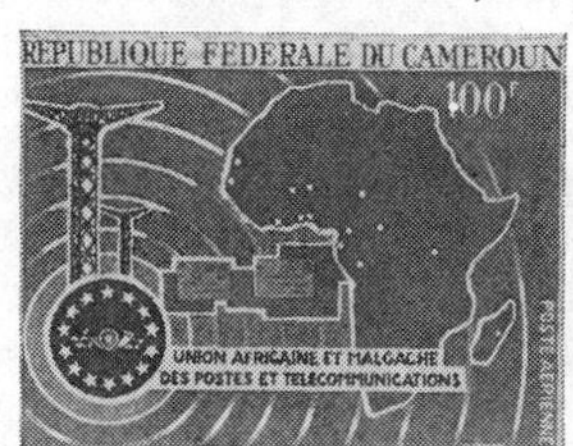

Telecommunications Symbols and Map of Africa

CD124

Fifth anniversary of the establishment of the African and Malagasy Union of Posts and Telecommunications, UAMPT.

1967

Cameroun	C90
Cent. African Rep.	C46
Chad	C37
Congo, P.R.	C57
Dahomey	C61
Gabon	C58
Ivory Coast	C34
Madagascar	C85
Mauritania	C65
Niger	C75
Rwanda	C1-C3
Senegal	C60
Togo	C81
Upper Volta	C50

Monetary Union Issue

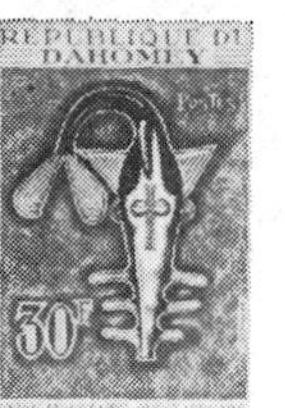

Gold Token of the Ashantis, 17-18th Centuries

CD125

Fifth anniversary of the West African Monetary Union.

1967, Nov. 4

Dahomey	244
Ivory Coast	259
Mauritania	238
Niger	204
Senegal	294
Togo	623
Upper Volta	181

WHO Anniversary Issue

Sun, Flowers and WHO Emblem

CD126

20th anniversary of the World Health Organization.

1968, May 4

Afars & Issas	317
Comoro Isls.	73
Fr. Polynesia	241-242
Fr. So. & Antarctic Terr.	31
New Caledonia	367
St. Pierre & Miquelon	377
Wallis & Futuna Isls.	169

Human Rights Year Issue

Human Rights Flame

CD127

International Human Rights Year.

1968, Aug. 10

Afars & Issas	322-323
Comoro Isls.	76
Fr. Polynesia	243-244
Fr. So. & Antarctic Terr.	32
New Caledonia	369
St. Pierre & Miquelon	382
Wallis & Futuna Isls.	170

2nd PHILEXAFRIQUE Issue

Gabon No. 131 and Industrial Plant

CD128

Opening of PHILEXAFRIQUE, Abidjan, Feb. 14.

Each stamp shows a local scene and stamp.

1969, Feb. 14

Cameroun	C118
Cent. African Rep.	C65
Chad	C48
Congo, P.R.	C77
Dahomey	C94
Gabon	C82
Ivory Coast	C38-C40
Madagascar	C92
Mali	C65
Mauritania	C80
Niger	C104
Senegal	C68
Togo	C104
Upper Volta	C62

Concorde Issue

Concorde in Flight
CD129

First flight of the prototype Concorde super-sonic plane at Toulouse, Mar. 1, 1969.

1969

Afars & Issas	C56
Comoro Isls.	C29
France	C42
Fr. Polynesia	C50
Fr. So. & Antarctic Terr.	C18
New Caledonia	C63
St. Pierre & Miquelon	C40
Wallis & Futuna Isls.	C30

Development Bank Issue

Bank Emblem—CD130

Fifth anniversary of the African Development Bank.

1969

Cameroun	499
Chad	217
Congo, P.R.	181–182
Ivory Coast	281
Mali	127–128
Mauritania	267
Niger	220
Senegal	317–318
Upper Volta	201

ILO Issue

ILO Headquarters, Geneva, and Emblem
CD131

50th anniversary of the International Labor Organization.

1969–70

Afars & Issas	337
Comoro Isls.	83
Fr. Polynesia	251–252
Fr. So. & Antarctic Terr.	35
New Caledonia	379
St. Pierre & Miquelon	396
Wallis & Futuna Isls.	172

ASECNA Issue

Map of Africa, Plane and Airport
CD132

10th anniversary of the Agency for the Security of Aerial Navigation in Africa and Madagascar (ASECNA, Agence pour la Sécurité de la Navigation Aérienne en Afrique et à Madagascar).

1969–70

Cameroun	500
Cent. African Rep.	119
Chad	222
Congo, P.R.	197
Dahomey	269
Gabon	260
Ivory Coast	287
Mali	130
Niger	221
Senegal	321
Upper Volta	204

U.P.U. Headquarters Issue

U.P.U. Headquarters and Emblem
CD133

New Universal Postal Union headquarters, Bern, Switzerland.

1970

Afars & Issas	342
Algeria	443
Cameroun	503–504
Cent. African Rep.	125
Chad	225
Comoro Isls.	84
Congo, P.R.	216
Fr. Polynesia	261–262
Fr. So. & Antarctic Terr.	36
Gabon	258
Ivory Coast	295
Madagascar	444
Mali	134–135
Mauritania	283
New Caledonia	382
Niger	231–232
St. Pierre & Miquelon	397–398
Senegal	328–329
Tunisia	535
Wallis & Futuna Isls.	173

De Gaulle Issue

General de Gaulle, 1940
CD134

First anniversary of the death of Charles de Gaulle, (1890-1970), President of France.

1971–72

Afars & Issas	356–357
Comoro Isls.	104–105
France	1322–1325
Fr. Polynesia	270–271
Fr. So. & Antarctic Terr.	52–53
New Caledonia	393–394
Reunion	377, 380
St. Pierre & Miquelon	417–418
Wallis & Futuna Isls.	177–178

African Postal Union Issue, 1971

Carved Stool, UAMPT Building, Brazzaville, Congo
CD135

10th anniversary of the establishment of the African and Malagasy Posts and Telecommunications Union, UAMPT.

Each stamp has a different native design.

1971, Nov. 13

Cameroun	C177
Cent. African Rep.	C89
Chad	C94
Congo, P.R.	C136
Dahomey	C146
Gabon	C120
Ivory Coast	C47
Mauritania	C113
Niger	C164
Rwanda	C8
Senegal	C105
Togo	C166
Upper Volta	C97

West African Monetary Union Issue

African Couple, City, Village and Commemorative Coin
CD136

10th anniversary of the West African Monetary Union.

1972, Nov. 2

Dahomey	300
Ivory Coast	331
Mauritania	299
Niger	258
Senegal	374
Togo	825
Upper Volta	280

African Postal Union Issue, 1973

Telecommunications Symbols and Map of Africa
CD137

11th anniversary of the African and Malagasy Posts and Telecommunications Union (UAMPT).

1973, Sept. 12

Cameroun	574
Cent. African Rep.	194
Chad	272
Congo, P.R.	289
Dahomey	311
Gabon	320
Ivory Coast	361
Madagascar	500
Mauritania	304
Niger	287
Rwanda	540
Senegal	393
Togo	849
Upper Volta	285

Philexafrique II—Essen Issue

Buffalo and Dahomey No. C33
CD138

Wild Ducks and Baden No. 1
CD139

Designs: Indigenous fauna, local and German stamps.

Types CD138–CD139 printed horizontally and vertically se-tenant in sheets of 10 (2x5). Label between horizontal pairs alternately commemorates Philexafrique II, Libreville, Gabon, June 1978, and 2nd International Stamp Fair, Essen, Germany, Nov. 1–5.

1978-1979

Benin	C285-C286
Central Africa	C200-C201
Chad	C238-C239
Congo Republic	C245-C246
Djibouti	C121-C122
Gabon	C215-C216
Ivory Coast	C64-C65
Mali	C356-C357
Mauritania	C185-C186
Niger	C291-C292
Rwanda	C12-C13
Senegal	C146-C147
Togo	C363-C364
Upper Volta	C253-C254

HISTORICAL FOOTNOTES

Scouting Year: 75th anniversary of scouting and 125th birth anniversary of its founder, Lord Baden-Powell (1857-1941).

Robert Koch: Centenary of tuberculosis bacillus discovery by Robert Koch (1843-1910), German physician. Awarded 1905 Nobel Prize for physiology and medicine; also discovered cholera bacillus, 1883.

George Washington: 250th birth anniversary of George Washington (1732-1799), first U.S. president.

Charles Darwin: Death centenary of Charles Darwin (1809-1882), British naturalist. Traveled through South America and Australasia, 1831-1836, aboard the Beagle developing his theory of evolution. Published findings in *On the Origin of Species,* 1859.

Norman Rockwell (1894-1978): American illustrator who is best known for his paintings of people in everyday situations. Many of his works have been on the covers of *The Saturday Evening Post, Boy's Life, American Boy* and *St. Nicholas.*

Lewis B. Carroll (1832-1898): English author of the childhood classics *Alice in Wonderland* and *Through the Looking Glass.* He also wrote many works on mathematics under his real name, Charles Lutwidge Dodgson.

World Cup Soccer: The 12th World Cup Soccer Championship was held in Spain from June 13th to July 11th. The series, held every 4 years, opened in Barcelona with Belgium over Argentina before a crowd of 95,000. The 52 games were held in 17 stadiums in 14 cities with 24 participating teams. The final game was played in Madrid with Italy defeating Germany by a score of 3 to 1.

The 14th Winter Olympic Games were held in Sarajevo, Jugoslavia, Feb. 7-18, 1984. Russia captured 25 medals, though East Germany won the most gold, with 9. The United States received 4 gold and 4 silver medals, primarily on the surprisingly strong showing of the ski team.

The 23rd Olympic Games were held in Los Angeles, July 28-August 12, 1984, marred by a boycott by Russia and other eastern bloc nations. The boycott was viewed as a retaliatory action against the U.S. led boycott of the 1980 Moscow Olympics. The U.S. gathered 174 medals, 83 of them gold, to lead all participants.

The 19th Universal Postal Union Congress was held in Hamburg, Germany, June 18-July 27, 1984. It was attended by approximately 750 delegates from 166 member countries.

AUSIPEX '84 International Stamp Exhibition, Melbourne, Australia, Sept. 21-30, 1984.

PHILATELIA '84 International Stamp Exhibition, Stuttgart, Germany, Oct. 5-7, 1984.

FILACENTO '84 International Stamp Exhibition, The Hague, Netherlands, Sept. 6-9, 1984.

ITALIA '85 International Stamp Exhibition, Rome, Italy, Oct. 25-Nov. 3, 1985.

SCOTT'S STANDARD POSTAGE STAMP CATALOGUE

ABYSSINIA

(See Ethiopia.)

AFARS AND ISSAS, French Territory of the

(ä-färz′ and ĭ-säz′)

LOCATION—East Africa.
GOVT.—French Overseas Territory.
AREA—8,880 sq. mi.
POP.—150,000 (est. 1974).
CAPITAL—Djibouti (Jibuti).

The French overseas territory of Somali Coast was renamed the French Territory of the Afars and Issas in 1967. It became the Djibouti Republic (which see) on June 27, 1977.

100 Centimes = 1 Franc

Imperforates

Most stamps of Afars and Issas exist imperforate in issued and trial colors, and also in small presentation sheets in issued colors.

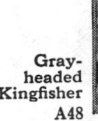

Gray-headed Kingfisher
A48

Designs: 15fr, Oystercatcher. 50fr, Greenshanks. 55fr, Abyssinian roller. 60fr, Ground squirrel (vert.).

Unwmkd.

1967 Engraved Perf. 13

310	A48	10fr brt bl, gray grn & blk	1.75	1.75
311	A48	15fr dk brn, bl, ol & ocher	2.50	2.50
312	A48	50fr blk, sl grn & brn	9.50	6.00
313	A48	55fr vio, brt bl & gray grn	12.00	7.75
314	A48	60fr ocher, brt grn & sl grn	17.50	12.00
		Nos. 310-314 (5)	43.25	30.00

Dates of Issue: 10fr, 55fr, Aug. 21; 15fr, 50fr, 60fr, Sept. 25. See No. C50.

Soccer
A49

Design: 30fr, Basketball.

1967, Dec. 18 Engraved Perf. 13

315	A49	25fr bl, brn & emer	2.50	1.75
316	A49	30fr red lil, Prus bl & brn	3.50	3.00

WHO Anniversary Issue

Common Design Type

1968, May 4 Engraved Perf. 13

317	CD126	15fr multi	1.90	1.40

Issued to commemorate the 20th anniversary of the World Health Organization.

Common Design Types

pictured in section at front of book.

Damerdjog Fortress
A50

Administration Buildings: 25fr, Ali Addé. 30fr, Dorra. 40fr, Assamo.

1968, May 17 Engraved Perf. 13

318	A50	20fr sl, brn & emer	1.25	90
319	A50	25fr brt grn, bl & brn	1.40	90
320	A50	30fr brn ol, brn org & sl	1.75	1.25
321	A50	40fr brn ol, sl & brt grn	3.50	2.50

Human Rights Year Issue

Common Design Type

1968, Aug. 10 Engraved Perf. 13

322	CD127	10fr pur, ver & org	1.25	1.00
323	CD127	70fr grn, pur & org	2.50	2.00

International Human Rights Year.

Radio-television Station, Djibouti
A52

High Commission Palace, Djibouti
A53

Designs: 2fr, Justice Building. 5fr, Chamber of Deputies. 8fr, Great Mosque. 15fr, Monument of Free French Forces (vert.). 40fr, Djibouti Post Office. 70fr, Residence of Gov. Léonce Lagarde at Obock. No. 332, Djibouti Harbormaster's Building. No. 333, Control tower, Djibouti Airport.

1968–70 Engraved Perf. 13

324	A52	1fr dk red, sky bl & ind ('69)	26	18
325	A52	2fr grn, bl & ind ('69)	30	18
326	A52	5fr brn, sky bl & grn ('69)	42	26
327	A52	8fr choc, emer & gray ('69)	48	26
328	A52	15fr grn, sky bl & yel brn ('69)	3.50	2.50
329	A52	40fr grn, brn & sl ('70)	2.25	1.25
330	A53	60fr multi	2.50	2.00
331	A53	70fr dl grn, gray & ol bis ('69)	3.50	2.50
332	A53	85fr multi ('69)	4.75	3.00
333	A52	85fr dk grn, bl & gray ('70)	5.25	3.50
		Nos. 324-333 (10)	23.21	15.63

Locust
A54

Designs: 50fr, Pest control by helicopter. 55fr, Pest control by plane.

1969, Oct. 6 Engraved Perf. 13

334	A54	15fr brn, grn & sl	1.75	1.00
335	A54	50fr dk grn, bl & ol brn	2.50	1.50
336	A54	55fr red brn, bl & brn	3.50	2.50

Campaign against locusts.

ILO Issue

Common Design Type

1969, Nov. 24 Engraved Perf. 13

337	CD131	30fr org, gray & lil	2.00	1.25

Afar Dagger in Ornamental Scabbard
A56

1970, Apr. 3 Engraved Perf. 13

338	A56	10fr yel grn, dk grn & org brn	70	42
339	A56	15fr yel grn, bl & org brn	90	42
340	A56	20fr yel grn, red & org brn	1.00	60
341	A56	25fr yel grn, plum & org brn	1.75	60

See No. 364.

U.P.U. Headquarters Issue

Common Design Type

1970, May 20 Engr. Perf. 13

342	CD133	25fr brn, brt grn & choc	1.50	90

Trap-shooting
A57

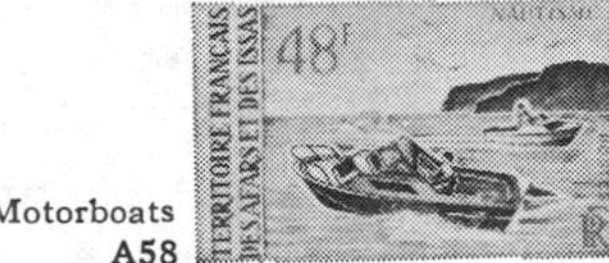

Motorboats
A58

Designs: 50fr, Steeplechase. 55fr, Sailboat (vert.). 60fr, Equestrians.

1970 Engraved Perf. 13

343	A57	30fr dp brn, yel grn & brt bl	2.00	1.40
344	A58	48fr bl & multi	2.25	1.25
345	A58	50fr cop red, bl & pur	2.50	1.75
346	A58	55fr red brn, bl & ol	2.25	1.40
347	A58	60fr ol, blk & red brn	3.50	2.50
		Nos. 343-347 (5)	12.50	8.30

Issue dates: 30fr, June 5; 48fr, Oct. 9; 50fr, 60fr, Nov. 6.

Automatic Ferry, Tadjourah
A59

1970, Nov. 25

348	A59	48fr bl, brn & grn	2.25	1.25

Volcanic Geode
A60

Diabase and Chrysolite
A61

Designs: 10fr, Doleritic basalt. 15fr, Olivine basalt.

1971 Photogravure Perf. 13

349	A61	10fr blk & multi	60	52
350	A61	15fr blk & multi	70	52
351	A60	25fr blk, crim & brn	1.75	1.25
352	A61	40fr blk & multi	3.00	2.00

Issue dates: 10fr, Nov. 22; 15fr, Oct. 8; 25fr, Apr. 26; 40fr, Jan. 25.

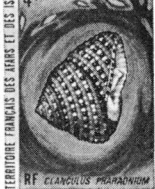

Manta Ray
A62

Strawberry Top
A63

Fishes: 5fr, Dolphinfish. 9fr, Smalltooth sawfish.

1971, July 1 Photo. Perf. 12x12½

353	A62	4fr grn & multi	85	52
354	A62	5fr bl & multi	85	52
355	A62	9fr red & multi	1.40	1.10

See No. C60.

De Gaulle Issue

Common Design Type

Designs: 60fr, Gen. Charles de Gaulle, 1940. 85fr, Pres. de Gaulle, 1970.

1971, Nov. 9 Engraved Perf. 13

356	CD134	60fr dk vio bl & blk	3.00	2.50
357	CD134	85fr dk vio bl & blk	4.75	2.50

1972, Mar. 8 Photo. Perf. 12½x13

Shells: 9fr, Cypraea pantherina. 20fr, Bull-mouth helmet. 50fr, Ethiopian volute.

358	A63	4fr ol & multi	48	35
359	A63	9fr dk bl & multi	65	52
360	A63	20fr dp grn & multi	1.50	80
361	A63	50fr dp cl & multi	3.00	1.40

Shepherd—A64

Design: 10fr, Dromedary breeding.

1973, Apr. 11 Photo. *Perf. 13*

362	A64	9fr bl & multi	60	42
363	A64	10fr bl & multi	60	42

Afar Dagger A65

1974, Jan. 29 Engraved *Perf. 13*

364	A65	30fr sl grn & dk brn	1.75	1.00

Flamingos, Lake Abbé—A66

Designs: Flamingos and different views of Lake Abbé.

1974, Feb. 22 Photogravure *Perf. 13*

370	A60	5fr multi	42	26
371	A60	15fr multi	70	35
372	A60	50fr multi	2.25	1.10

Soccer Ball—A67

1974, May 24 Engr. *Perf. 13*

373	A67	25fr blk & emer	1.90	1.25

World Cup Soccer Championship, Munich, June 13–July 7.

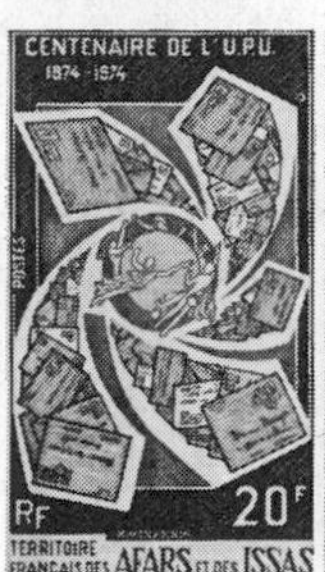

Letters Around UPU Emblem A68

Oleo Chrysophylla A69

1974, Oct. 9 Engraved *Perf. 13*

374	A68	20fr multi	1.75	90
375	A68	100fr multi	4.25	3.50

Centenary of Universal Postal Union.

1974, Nov. 22 Photogravure

Multicolored

376	A69	10fr *shown*	70	52

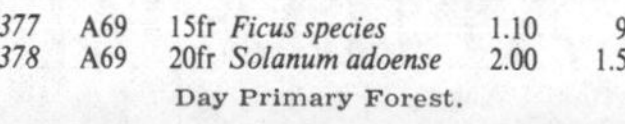

377	A69	15fr *Ficus species*	1.10	95
378	A69	20fr *Solanum adoense*	2.00	1.50

Day Primary Forest.

No. 364 Surcharged with New Value and Two Bars in Red

1975, Jan. 1 Engr. *Perf. 13*

379	A65	40fr on 30fr multi	2.00	1.40

Treasury—A70

Design: 25fr, Government buildings.

1975, Jan. 7 Engr. *Perf. 13*

380	A70	8fr bl, gray & red	60	42
381	A70	25fr red, bl & ind	1.10	90

Ranella Spinosa—A71

Sea Shells: No. 382, Darioconus textile. No. 383, Murex palmarosa. 10fr, Conus sumatrensis. 15fr, Cypraea pulchra. No. 386, 45fr, Murex scolopax. No. 387, Cypraea exhusta. 55fr, Cypraea erythraensis. 60fr, Conus taeniatus.

1975–76 Engraved *Perf. 13*

382	A71	5fr bl grn & brn	52	30
383	A71	5fr bl & multi ('76)	40	18
384	A71	10fr lil, blk & brn	60	40
385	A71	15fr bl, ind & brn	90	48
386	A71	20fr pur & lt brn	1.50	90
387	A71	20fr brt grn & multi ('76)	55	35
388	A71	40fr grn & brn	2.25	1.25
389	A71	45fr grn, bl & bis	2.00	1.25
390	A71	55fr turq & multi ('76)	1.50	1.00
391	A71	60fr buff & sep ('76)	2.25	1.40
		Nos. 382-391 (10)	12.47	7.51

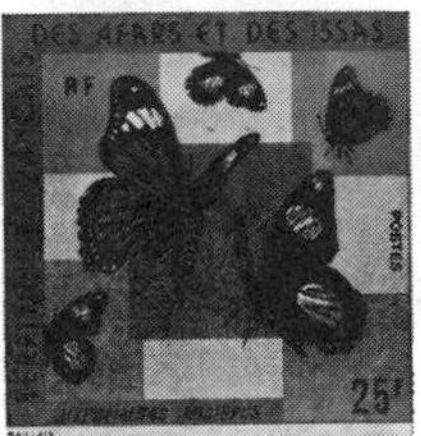

Hypolimnas Misippus A72

Butterflies: 40fr, Papilio nireus. 50fr, Acraea anemosa. 65fr, Holocerina smilax menieri. 70fr, Papilio demodocus. No. 397, Papilio dardanus. No. 398, Balachowsky gonimbrasca. 150fr, Vanessa cardui.

1975–76 Photogravure *Perf. 13*

392	A72	25fr emer & multi	1.25	90
393	A72	40fr yel & multi	1.50	1.00
394	A72	50fr ultra & multi ('76)	1.75	1.25
395	A72	65fr ol & multi ('76)	2.25	1.25
396	A72	70fr vio & multi	3.25	2.50
397	A72	100fr bl & multi	4.00	2.50
398	A72	100fr Prus bl & multi ('76)	3.00	2.25
399	A72	150fr grn & multi ('76)	4.00	2.50
		Nos. 392-399 (8)	21.00	14.15

Mongoose—A73

Animals: 10fr, Hyena. No. 401, Catarrhine monkeys (vert.). No. 402, Wild ass (vert.). 30fr, Antelope. 60fr, Porcupines (vert.). 70fr, Skunks. 200fr, Aardvarks.

Perf. 13x12½, 12½x13

1975–76 Photogravure

400	A73	10fr lt vio & multi ('76)	42	26
401	A73	15fr yel grn & multi	90	52
402	A73	15fr grn & multi ('76)	60	42
403	A73	30fr bl & multi ('76)	1.00	70
404	A73	50fr dp org & multi	2.50	1.50
405	A73	60fr yel brn & multi	2.75	1.90
406	A73	70fr blk & brn	4.25	2.50
407	A73	200fr bl gray & multi	6.00	4.25
		Nos. 400-407 (8)	18.42	12.05

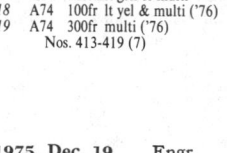

Pin-tailed Whydah A74

Palms A75

Birds: 25fr, Rose-ringed parakeet. 50fr, Variable sunbird. 60fr, Purple heron. No. 417, Hammerhead. No. 418, Turtle dove. 300fr, African spoonbill.

1975–76 Photo. *Perf. 12½x13*

413	A74	20fr lil, blk & org	90	60
414	A74	25fr car rose & multi ('76)	90	35
415	A74	50fr bl & multi	1.75	1.10
416	A74	60fr multi	2.50	1.65
417	A74	100fr lt grn & multi	3.50	2.25
418	A74	100fr lt yel & multi ('76)	2.50	1.75
419	A74	300fr multi ('76)	7.00	5.00
		Nos. 413-419 (7)	19.05	12.70

1975, Dec. 19 Engr. *Perf. 13*

421	A75	20fr brt bl & multi	70	42

Satellite and Alexander Graham Bell A76

1976, Mar. 10 Engr. *Perf. 13*

422	A76	200fr dp bl, org & sl grn	4.75	3.50

Centenary of the first telephone call by Alexander Graham Bell, Mar. 10, 1876.

Basket-ball A77

Designs: 15fr, Bicycling. 40fr, Soccer. 60fr, Running.

1976, July 7 Litho. *Perf. 12½*

423	A77	10fr lt bl & multi	42	22
424	A77	15fr yel & multi	60	30
425	A77	40fr org red & multi	1.10	70
426	A77	60fr lt grn & multi	1.75	1.10

21st Olympic Games, Montreal, Canada, July 17–Aug. 1.

Turkeyfish—A78

1976, Aug. 10 Photo. *Perf. 13x13½*

428	A78	45fr bl & multi	1.75	1.50

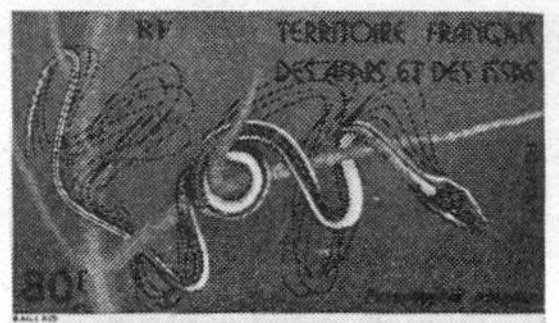

Psammophis Elegans—A79

Design: 70fr, Naja nigricollis (vert.).

Perf. 13x13½, 13½x13

1976, Sept. 27 Photogravure

430	A79	70fr ocher & multi	2.50	2.25
431	A79	80fr emer & multi	3.00	2.50

Motorcyclist A80

1977, Jan. 27 Litho. *Perf. 12x12½*

432	A80	200fr multi	5.75	4.00

Moto-Cross motorcycle race.

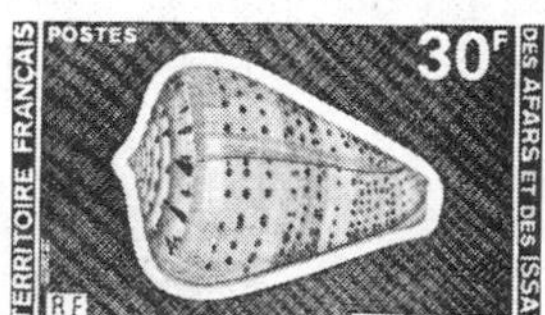

Conus Betulinus—A81

Sea Shells: 5fr, Cyprea tigris. 70fr, Conus striatus. 85fr, Cyprea mauritiana.

1977 Engr. *Perf. 13*

433	A81	5fr multi	60	42
434	A81	30fr multi	80	52

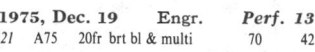

435 A81 70fr multi 2.75 1.75
436 A81 85fr multi 4.50 3.00

Gaterin Gaterinus
A82

Design: 65fr, Barracudas.

1977, Apr. 15 Photo. *Perf. 13x12½*

437 A82 15fr multi 80 42
438 A82 65fr multi 2.25 1.25

Stamps of the French Territory of the Afars and Issas were replaced in 1977 by those of the Republic of Djibouti.

AIR POST STAMPS

Tawny Eagles AP16 **Unwmkd.** Parachutists AP17

1967, Aug. 21 Engraved *Perf. 13*

C50 AP16 200fr multi 17.50 9.50

1968 Engraved *Perf. 13*

Design: 85fr, Water skier and skin diver.

C51 AP17 48fr brn ol, Prus bl & brn 4.00 2.50
C52 AP17 85fr dk brn, ol & Prus bl 5.75 4.00

Issue dates: 48fr. Jan. 5; 85fr, Mar. 15.

Aerial Map of the Territory
AP18

1968, Nov. 15 Engraved *Perf. 13*

C53 AP18 500fr bl, dk brn & ocher 42.50 12.00

Buildings Type of Regular Issue

Designs: 100fr, Cathedral (vert.). 200fr, Sayed Hassan Mosque (vert.).

1969 Engraved *Perf. 13*

C54 A53 100fr grn, sky bl & bis brn 4.00 2.25
C55 A53 200fr lil, bl, brn & blk 8.25 4.75

Issue dates: 100fr, Apr. 4; 200fr, May 8.

Concorde Issue

Common Design Type

1969, Apr. 17

C56 CD129 100fr org red & ol 24.00 17.50

Arta Ionospheric Station—AP19

Japanese Sword Guard, Fish Design—AP20

1970, May 8 Engraved *Perf. 13*

C57 AP19 70fr multi 4.00 3.00

Gold Embossed

1970, Sept. 29 *Perf. 12½*

Design: 200fr, Japanese sword guard, horse design.

C58 AP20 100fr gold, yel grn, ultra & brn 10.50 7.00
C59 AP20 200fr gold, car, yel grn & brn 14.00 8.75

EXPO '70 International Exposition, Osaka, Japan, Mar. 15–Sept. 13.

Parrot-fish
AP21

1971, July 1 Photo. *Perf. 12½*

C60 AP21 30fr blk & multi 3.50 2.50

Djibouti Harbor—AP22

1971, Nov. 26

C61 AP22 100fr bl & multi 5.25 3.50

New Djibouti harbor.

Lichtenstein's Sandgrouse
AP23

Running, Olympic Rings
AP24

Birds: 49fr, Hoopoe. 66fr, Great snipe. 500fr, Tawny-breasted francolin.

1972 Photogravure *Perf. 12½x13*

C62 AP23 30fr multi 2.25 1.75
C63 AP23 49fr multi 3.50 2.50
C64 AP23 66fr bl & multi 4.75 3.50
C65 AP23 500fr multi 21.00 10.50

Issue dates: No. C65, Nov. 3, others Apr. 21.

1972, June 8 Engr. *Perf. 13*

Designs (Olympic Rings and): 10fr, Basketball. 55fr, Swimming (horiz.). 60fr, Olympic torch and Greek frieze (horiz.).

C66 AP24 5fr pur, bl grn & dk brn 52 35
C67 AP24 10fr dk red, sl grn & dk brn 60 42
C68 AP24 55fr grn, brn & bl 2.25 1.40
C69 AP24 60fr bl grn, dk red & pur 3.00 1.75

20th Olympic Games, Munich, Aug. 26–Sept. 11.

Louis Pasteur—AP25

Design: 100fr, Albert Calmette and C. Guérin.

1972, Oct. 5 Engraved *Perf. 13*

C70 AP25 20fr rose car, ol bis & brt grn 1.25 70
C71 AP25 100fr dk brn, brt grn & dl red 4.25 3.25

Pasteur, Calmette, Guérin, chemists and bacteriologists, benefactors of mankind.

Map and Views of Territory—AP26

Design: 200fr, Woman and Mosque of Djibouti (vert.).

1973, Jan. 15 Photo. *Perf. 13*

C72 AP26 30fr brn & multi 5.25 4.25
C73 AP26 200fr multi 12.00 9.50

Visit of Pres. Georges Pompidou of France, Jan. 15–17.

Oryx—AP27

Animals: 50fr, Dik-dik. 66fr, Caracal.

1973, Feb. 26 Photo. *Perf. 13x12½*

C74 AP27 30fr grn & multi 1.75 1.10
C75 AP27 50fr rose & multi 3.00 1.50
C76 AP27 66fr lil & multi 4.00 3.00

See also Nos. C94–C96.

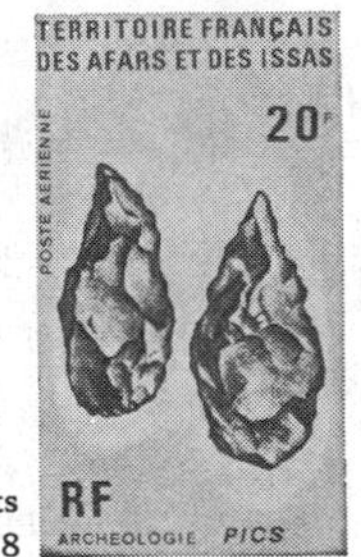

Celts
AP28

Designs: Various pre-historic flint tools. 40fr, 60fr, horizontal.

1973 Photographed *Perf. 13*

C77 AP28 20fr yel grn, blk & brn 1.75 1.25
C78 AP28 40fr yel & multi 1.75 1.25
C79 AP28 49fr lil & multi 3.00 2.25
C80 AP28 60fr bl & multi 3.00 2.25

Issue dates: 20fr, 49fr, Mar. 16; 40fr, 60fr, Sept. 7.

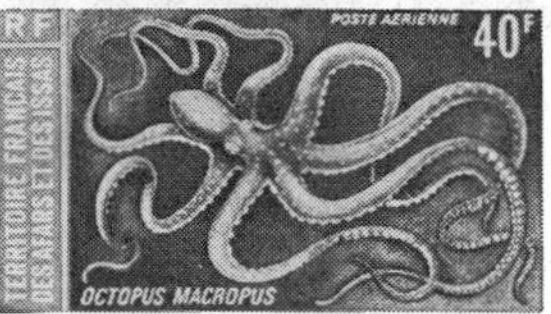

Octopus—AP29

Design: 60fr, Dugong.

1973, Mar. 16

C81 AP29 40fr multi 2.25 1.25
C82 AP29 60fr brn & multi 4.00 2.50

Copernicus
AP30

Baboons
AP31

Designs: 8fr, Nicolaus Copernicus (1473–1534), Polish astronomer. 9fr, William C. Roentgen (1845–1923), physicist, X-ray discoverer. C85, Edward Jenner (1749–1823), physician, discoverer of vaccination. No. C86, Marie Curie (1867–1934), discoverer of radium and polonium. 49fr, Robert Koch (1843–1910), physician and bacteriologist. 50fr, Clément Ader (1841–1925), French aviation pioneer. 55fr, Guglielmo Marconi (1874–1937), Italian electrical engineer, inventor. 85fr, Molière (1622–1673), French playwright. 100fr, Henri Farman (1874–1937), French aviation pioneer. 150fr, André-Marie Ampère (1775–1836), French physicist. 250fr, Michelangelo Buonarroti (1475–1564), Italian sculptor, painter and architect.

1973–75 Engraved *Perf. 13*

C83	AP30	8fr	blk, dk bis & mar	70	42
C84	AP30	9fr	brn, ocher & vio brn	60	42
C85	AP30	10fr	car, brn & vio brn	60	42
C86	AP30	10fr	red lil, dp cl & bl	70	42
C87	AP30	49fr	sl grn, yel grn & vio brn	3.25	2.25
C88	AP30	50fr	ol brn, sl grn & bl	2.50	1.75
C89	AP30	55fr	multi ('74)	2.25	1.75
C90	AP30	85fr	bl, vio & ind	4.50	3.00
C91	AP30	100fr	yel grn, vio brn & bl ('74)	4.25	3.50
C92	AP30	150fr	multi	4.25	3.50
C93	AP30	250fr	blk, grn & brn	7.00	5.25
			Nos. C83-C93 (11)	30.60	22.68

Issue dates: 8fr, 85fr, May 9, 1973. 9fr, C85, 49fr, Oct. 12, 1973. 100fr, Jan. 29, 1974. 55fr, Mar. 22, 1974. C86, Aug. 23, 1974. 150fr, July 24, 1975. 250fr, June 26, 1975. 50fr, Sept. 25, 1975.

Perf. 12½x13, 13x12½

1973, Dec. 12 Photogravure

Designs: 50fr, Genets (horiz.). 66fr, Hares.

C94	AP31	20fr	org & multi	1.25	90
C95	AP31	50fr	multi	2.50	1.25
C96	AP31	66fr	bl & multi	4.00	2.50

Spearfishing—AP32

1974, Apr. 14 Engr. *Perf. 13*

C97	AP32	200fr	multi	7.75	6.50

No. C97 was prepared for release in Nov. 1972, to commemorate the 3rd Underwater Spearfishing Contest in the Red Sea. Dates have been obliterated with a rectangle and the stamp was not issued without this obliteration.

Rock Carvings, Balho—AP33

1974, Apr. 26

C98	AP33	200fr	car & sl	8.75	7.00

Lake Assal—AP34

Designs (Lake Assal): 50fr, Rock formations on shore. 85fr, Crystallized wood.

1974, Oct. 25 Photogravure *Perf. 13*

C99	AP34	49fr	multi	1.50	1.25
C100	AP34	50fr	multi	1.90	1.40
C101	AP34	85fr	multi	3.50	3.00

Guinea Dove
AP35

1975, May 23 Photo. *Perf. 13*

C102	AP35	500fr	multi	16.00	8.75

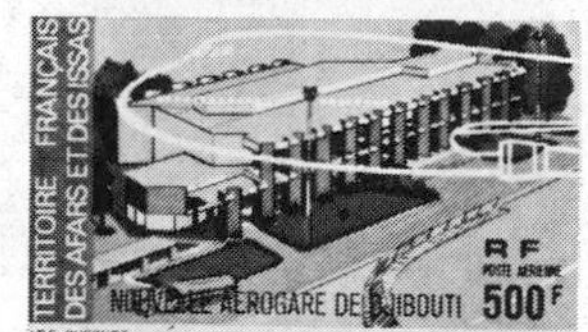

Djibouti Airport—AP36

1977, Mar. 1 Litho. *Perf. 12*

C103	AP36	500fr	multi	13.00	10.50

Opening of new Djibouti Airport.

Thomas A. Edison and Phonograph—AP37

Design: 75fr, Alexander Volta, electric train, lines and light bulb.

1977, May 5 Engr. *Perf. 13*

C104	AP37	55fr	multi	3.00	2.00
C105	AP37	75fr	multi	4.75	3.50

Famous inventors: Thomas Alva Edison (1847–1931) and Alexander Volta (1745–1827).

POSTAGE DUE STAMPS

Nomad's Milk Jug
D3

Unwmkd.

1969, Dec. 15 Engr. *Perf. 14x13*

J49	D3	1fr	red brn, red lil & sl	10	10
J50	D3	2fr	red brn, emer & sl	18	18
J51	D3	5fr	red brn, bl & sl	40	40
J52	D3	10fr	red brn, brn & sl	90	90

AFGHANISTAN

(ăf·găn'ĭ·stăn ; ăf·găn'ĭs·tän')

LOCATION — Central Asia, bounded by Iran, Russian Turkestan, Pakistan, Baluchistan and China.
GOVT.—Republic.
AREA—251,773 sq. mi.
POP.—17,150,000 (1984 est.).
CAPITAL—Kabul.

Afghanistan changed from a constitutional monarchy to a republic in July 1973.

12 Shahi = 6 Sanar = 3 Abasi =
2 Krans = 1 Rupee Kabuli
60 Paisas = 1 Rupee (1921)
100 Pouls = 1 Rupee Afghani (1927)

CHARACTERS OF VALUE.

Shahi.

1871-78 A7 A8

Sanar. Abasi. 6 Shahi.

1871-78 1871 1872

1 Rupee. ½ Rupee.

1874 1876(A8) 1876 (A7)

1 Rupee. Rupee.

1872 1874 1876 (A8) 1877-78

From 1871 to 1892 and 1898 the Moslem year date appears on the stamp. Numerals as follows:

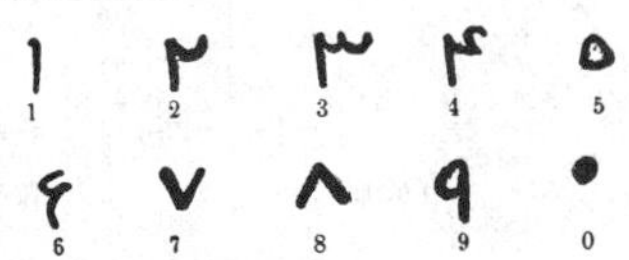

Until 1891 cancellation consisted of cutting or tearing a piece from the stamps. Such copies should not be considered as damaged.

Prices are for cut square examples of good color. Cut to shape or faded copies sell for much less, particularly Nos. 2-10.

Nos. 2-108 are on laid paper of varying thickness except where wove is noted.

Until 1907 all stamps were issued ungummed.

The tiger's head on types A2 to A11 symbolizes the name of the contemporary amir, Sher (Tiger) Ali.

Kingdom of Kabul

Tiger's Head—A2
(Both circles dotted.)

Dated "1288".
Lithographed

1871 *Imperf.* **Unwmkd.**

No.	Type	Description	Unused	Used
2	A2	1sh black	175.00	35.00
3	A2	1sa black	110.00	30.00
4	A2	1ab black	55.00	30.00

Thirty varieties of the shahi, 10 of the sanar and 5 of the abasi.

Similar designs without the tiger's head in the center are revenues.

A3
(Outer circle dotted.)

Dated "1288".

No.	Type	Description	Unused	Used
5	A3	1sh black	250.00	50.00
6	A3	1sa black	110.00	32.50
7	A3	1ab black	55.00	35.00

Five varieties of each.

A4
Dated "1289".
Toned Wove Paper

1872

No.	Type	Description	Unused	Used
8	A4	6sh violet	*850.00*	*550.00*
9	A4	1rup violet	*1,100.*	*650.00*

Two varieties of each. Date varies in location. Printed in sheets of 4 (2x2) containing two of each denomination.

Most used copies are smeared with a greasy ink cancel.

A4a
Dated "1290"

1873 White Laid Paper

No.	Type	Description	Unused	Used
10	A4a	1sh black	13.00	6.75
a.		Corner ornament missing	*600.00*	*500.00*
b.		Corner ornament retouched	*90.00*	*37.50*

15 varieties. Nos. 10a, 10b are the sixth stamp on the sheet.

A5

1873

No.	Type	Description	Unused	Used
11	A5	1sh black	3.25	2.75
11A	A5	1sh violet	*725.00*	

Sixty varieties of each.

1874 Dated "1291".

No.	Type	Description	Unused	Used
12	A5	1ab black	55.00	37.50
13	A5	½rup black	30.00	27.50
14	A5	1rup black	35.00	30.00

Five varieties of each.

Nos. 12-14 were printed on the same sheet. Se-tenant varieties exist.

A6 A7

1875 Dated "1292".

No.	Type	Description	Unused	Used
15	A6	1sa black	*250.00*	*175.00*
a.		Wide outer circle	*900.00*	
16	A6	1ab black	350.00	250.00
17	A6	1sa brn vio	35.00	35.00
a.		Wide outer circle	175.00	
18	A6	1ab brn vio	60.00	37.50

Ten varieties of the sanar, five of the abasi.

Nos. 15-16 and 17-18 were printed in the same sheets. Se-tenant pairs exist.

1876 Dated "1293"

No.	Type	Description	Unused	Used
19	A7	1sh black	425.00	225.00
20	A7	1sa black	550.00	300.00
21	A7	1ab black	750.00	300.00
22	A7	½rup black	550.00	300.00
23	A7	1rup black	750.00	300.00
24	A7	1sh violet	550.00	300.00
25	A7	1sa violet	525.00	300.00
26	A7	1ab violet	650.00	300.00
27	A7	½rup violet	135.00	80.00
28	A7	1rup violet	135.00	110.00

12 varieties of the shahi and 3 each of the other values.

A8

1876 Dated "1293".

No.	Type	Description	Unused	Used
29	A8	1sh gray	7.50	6.00
30	A8	1sa gray	11.00	6.00
31	A8	1ab gray	22.50	11.00
32	A8	½rup gray	25.00	15.00
33	A8	1rup gray	32.50	15.00
34	A8	1sh ol blk	190.00	
35	A8	1sa ol blk	250.00	
36	A8	1ab ol blk	525.00	
37	A8	½rup ol blk	350.00	
38	A8	1rup ol blk	425.00	
39	A8	1sh green	32.50	5.50
40	A8	1sa green	50.00	23.50
41	A8	1ab green	75.00	52.50
42	A8	½rup green	150.00	60.00
43	A8	1rup green	150.00	120.00
44	A8	1sh ocher	32.50	11.00
45	A8	1sa ocher	50.00	22.50
46	A8	1ab ocher	85.00	40.00
47	A8	½rup ocher	110.00	90.00
48	A8	1rup ocher	190.00	160.00
49	A8	1sh violet	32.50	8.00
50	A8	1sa violet	32.50	11.00
51	A8	1ab violet	50.00	15.00
52	A8	½rup violet	85.00	32.50
53	A8	1rup violet	110.00	50.00

24 varieties of the shahi, 4 of which show denomination written

12 varieties of the sanar, 6 of the abasi and 3 each of the ½ rupee and rupee.

A9

1877 Dated "1294".

No.	Type	Description	Unused	Used
54	A9	1sh gray	5.25	3.25
55	A9	1sa gray	8.50	4.25
56	A9	1ab gray	14.00	8.50
57	A9	½rup gray	18.00	18.00
58	A9	1rup gray	18.00	18.00
59	A9	1sh black	14.00	
60	A9	1sa black	27.50	
61	A9	1ab black	62.50	
62	A9	½rup black	67.50	
63	A9	1rup black	67.50	
64	A9	1sh green	6.75	5.00
a.		Wove paper	18.00	
65	A9	1sa green	11.00	5.00
a.		Wove paper	25.00	18.00
66	A9	1ab green	14.00	14.00
a.		Wove paper	40.00	
67	A9	½rup green	20.00	20.00
a.		Wove paper	45.00	45.00
68	A9	1rup green	21.00	21.00
a.		Wove paper	45.00	45.00
69	A9	1sh ocher	5.00	3.00
70	A9	1sa ocher	14.00	5.00
71	A9	1ab ocher	27.50	24.00
72	A9	½rup ocher	45.00	45.00
73	A9	1rup ocher	45.00	45.00
74	A9	1sh violet	5.50	3.00
75	A9	1sa violet	11.00	4.00
76	A9	1ab violet	16.50	11.00
77	A9	½rup violet	27.50	21.00
78	A9	1rup violet	27.50	21.00

25 varieties of the shahi, 8 of the sanar, 3 of the abasi and 2 each of the ½ rupee and rupee.

A10

A11

1878 Dated "1295"

No.	Type	Description	Unused	Used
79	A10	1sh gray	2.25	2.25
80	A10	1sa gray	2.75	2.75
81	A10	1ab gray	5.50	5.50
82	A10	½rup gray	14.00	11.00
83	A10	1rup gray	14.00	11.00
84	A10	1sh black	4.50	
85	A10	1sa black	4.50	
86	A10	1ab black	15.00	
87	A10	½rup black	30.00	
88	A10	1rup black	30.00	
89	A10	1sh green	32.50	30.00
90	A10	1sa green	4.50	4.50
91	A10	1ab green	16.00	14.00
92	A10	½rup green	32.50	27.50
93	A10	1rup green	32.50	27.50
94	A10	1sh ocher	14.00	4.50
95	A10	1sa ocher	4.50	3.50
96	A10	1ab ocher	16.00	14.00
97	A10	½rup ocher	32.50	32.50
98	A10	1rup ocher	25.00	25.00
99	A10	1sh violet	2.50	2.50
100	A10	1sa violet	2.50	2.50
101	A10	1ab violet	8.00	8.00
102	A10	½rup violet	32.50	27.50
103	A10	1rup violet	32.50	27.50
104	A11	1sh gray	3.00	2.75
105	A11	1sh black	*135.00*	
106	A11	1sh green	2.50	2.50
107	A11	1sh ocher	2.00	2.00
108	A11	1sh violet	3.00	2.75

40 varieties of the shahi, 30 of the sanar, 6 of the abasi and 2 each of the ½ rupee and 1 rupee.

The 1876, 1877 and 1878 issues were printed in separate colors for each main post office on the Peshawar-Kabul-Khulm (Tashkurghan) postal route. Some specialists consider the black printings to be proofs or trial colors.

There are many shades of these colors.

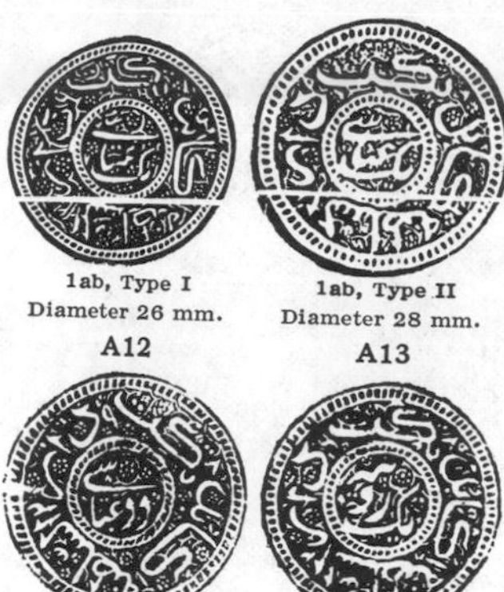

1ab, Type I Diameter 26 mm. — 1ab, Type II Diameter 28 mm.

A12 A13

A14 A15

1881–90

Handstamped, in watercolor.
Dated "1298", numerals scattered through design.

Thin White Laid Batonné Paper

109	A12	1ab violet	2.50	1.75
109A	A13	1ab violet	5.00	3.75
110	A12	1ab blk brn	5.00	2.75
111	A12	1ab rose	3.00	3.00
b.		Se-tenant with 111A	25.00	
111A	A13	1ab rose	3.75	3.00
112	A14	2ab violet	2.75	2.25
113	A14	2ab blk brn	7.50	6.00
114	A14	2ab rose	4.50	4.50
115	A15	1rup violet	3.75	2.25
116	A15	1rup blk brn	10.00	10.00
117	A15	1rup rose	4.50	4.50

Thin White Wove Batonné Paper

118	A12	1ab violet	10.00	6.00
119	A12	1ab vermilion	6.25	
120	A12	1ab rose		
121	A14	2ab violet		
122	A14	2ab vermilion	7.50	
122A	A14	2ab blk brn		
123	A15	1rup violet	12.50	
124	A15	1rup vermilion	10.00	
125	A15	1rup blk brn	12.50	

Thin White Laid Batonné Paper

126	A12	1ab brn org	3.75	3.75
126A	A13	1ab brn org (II)	5.00	5.00
127	A12	1ab car lake	3.75	3.75
a.		Laid paper		
128	A14	2ab brn org	3.75	3.75
129	A14	2ab car lake	4.50	4.50
130	A15	1rup brn org	15.00	15.00
131	A15	1rup car lake	6.25	6.25

Yellowish Laid Batonné Paper

132	A12	1ab purple		5.00
133	A12	1ab red	10.00	5.00

1884

Colored Wove Paper

133A	A13	1ab pur, *yel*(II)	27.50	27.50
134	A12	1ab pur, *grn*	30.00	
135	A12	1ab pur, *bl*	47.50	32.50
136	A12	1ab red, *grn*	55.00	
137	A12	1ab red, *yel*	2.50	
139	A12	1ab red, *rose*	8.75	
140	A14	2ab red, *yel*	8.75	
142	A14	2ab red, *rose*	8.00	
143	A15	1rup red, *yel*	10.00	10.00
145	A15	1rup red, *rose*	11.00	11.00

Thin Colored Ribbed Paper

146	A14	2ab red, *yel*	4.50	
147	A15	1rup red, *yel*	12.50	
148	A12	1ab lake, *lil*	6.00	
149	A14	2ab lake, *lil*	7.25	
150	A15	1rup lake, *lil*	6.00	
151	A12	1ab lake, *grn*	3.00	
152	A14	2ab lake, *grn*	6.00	
153	A15	1rup lake, *grn*	6.00	

1886–88

Colored Wove Paper.

155	A12	1ab *magenta*	42.50	
156	A12	1ab cl brn, *org*	30.00	
156A	A12	1ab red, *org*	3.00	
156B	A14	2ab red, *org*	7.00	
156C	A15	1rup red, *org*	5.00	

Laid Batonné Paper.

157	A12	1ab *lavender*	4.00	
158	A12	1ab cl brn, *grn*	10.00	
159	A12	1ab *pink*	27.50	
160	A14	2ab *pink*	50.00	
161	A15	1rup *pink*	30.00	

Laid Paper.

162	A12	1ab *pink*	10.00	
163	A14	2ab *pink*	10.00	
164	A15	1rup *pink*	10.00	
165	A12	1ab brn, *yel*	10.00	
166	A14	2ab brn, *yel*	10.00	
167	A15	1rup brn, *yel*	10.00	
168	A12	1ab bl, *grn*	10.00	
169	A14	2ab bl, *grn*	10.00	
170	A15	1rup bl, *grn*	10.00	

1891

Colored Wove Paper.

175	A12	1ab grn, *rose*	35.00	
176	A15	1rup pur, *grn batonné*	35.00	

Nos. 109–176 fall into three categories:
1. Those regularly issued and in normal postal use from 1881 on, handstamped on thin white laid or wove paper in strip sheets containing 12 or more impressions of the same denomination arranged in two irregular rows, with the impressions often touching or overlappng.
2. The 1884 postal issues provisionally printed on smooth or ribbed colored wove paper as needed to supplement low stocks of the normal white paper stamps.
3. The "special" printings made in a range of colors on several types of laid or wove colored papers, most of which were never used for normal printings. These were produced periodically from 1886 to 1891 to meet philatelic demands. Although nominally valid for postage, most of the special printings were exported directly to fill dealers' orders, and few were ever postally used. Many of the sheets contained all three denominations with impressions separated by ruled lines. Sometimes different colors were used, so se-tenant multiples of denomination or color exist. Many combinations of stamp and paper colors exist besides those listed.

Various shades of each color exist.

Type A12 is known dated "1297".

Counterfeits, lithographed or typographed, are plentiful.

Kingdom of Afghanistan

A16

A17 A18

Dated "1309".

1891 Pelure Paper Lithographed

177	A16	1ab sl bl	1.25	1.25
a.		Tête bêche pair	20.00	
178	A17	2ab sl bl	8.75	7.50
179	A18	1rup sl bl	18.50	15.00

Revenue stamps of similar design exist in various colors.

Nos. 177–179 were printed in panes on the same sheet, so se-tenant gutter pairs exist. Examples in black or red are proofs.

A Mosque Gate and Crossed Cannons (National Seal)
A19

Dated "1310" in Upper Right Corner.

1892 Flimsy Wove Paper

180	A19	1ab *green*	3.00	2.50
181	A19	1ab *orange*	3.75	3.75
182	A19	1ab *yellow*	3.00	2.50
183	A19	1ab *pink*	3.75	2.50
184	A19	1ab *lil rose*	3.75	3.75
185	A19	1ab *blue*	6.25	5.00
186	A19	1ab *salmon*	3.75	3.00
187	A19	1ab *magenta*	3.75	3.75
188	A19	1ab *violet*	3.75	3.75
188A	A19	1ab *scarlet*	3.75	2.50

Many shades exist.

A20

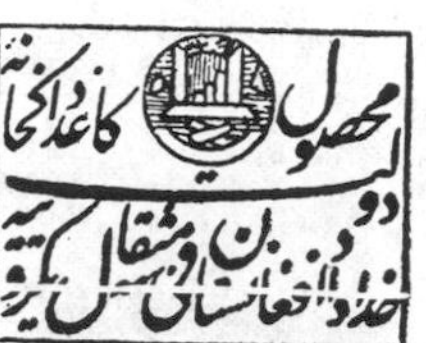

A21

Undated

1894 Flimsy Wove Paper

189	A20	2ab *green*	10.00	10.00
190	A21	1rup *green*	15.00	15.00

24 varieties of the 2 abasi and 12 varieties of the rupee.

Nos. 189–190 and F3 were printed se-tenant in the same sheet. Pairs exist.

A21a

Dated "1316"

1898 Flimsy Wove Paper

191	A21a	2ab *pink*	3.75	
192	A21a	2ab *magenta*	3.75	
193	A21a	2ab *yellow*	1.75	
193A	A21a	2ab *salmon*	4.50	
194	A21a	2ab *green*	2.00	
195	A21a	2ab *purple*	2.50	
195A	A21a	2ab *blue*	35.00	

Nos. 191–195A were not regularly issued. Genuinely used copies are scarce. No. 195A was found in remainder stocks and probably was never released.

National Coat of Arms
A22 A23

A24

1907 Engraved *Imperf.*

Medium Wove Paper

196	A22	1ab bl grn	3.75	2.50
a.		emerald	8.50	5.00
197	A22	1ab brt bl	7.50	6.25
198	A23	2ab dp bl	1.85	1.25
199	A24	1rup green	3.00	2.50
a.		bl grn	6.00	6.00

Zigzag Roulette 10

200	A22	1ab green	35.00	25.00
201	A23	2ab blue	50.00	45.00
201A	A24	1rup bl grn	*70.00*	*60.00*

1908 *Perf. 12*

202	A22	1ab green	6.25	6.25
203	A23	2ab dp bl	1.25	1.25
204	A24	1rup bl grn	3.00	3.00

Twelve varieties of the 1 abasi, 6 of the 2 abasi, 4 of the 1 rupee.

Nos. 196–204 were issued in small sheets containing 3 or 4 panes. Gutter pairs, normal and tête bêche, exist.

A25 A26

A27

1909–19 Typo. *Perf. 12*

205	A25	1ab ultra	50	35
a.		Imperf., pair	3.00	
206	A25	1ab red ('16)	35	25
a.		Imperf.		
207	A25	1ab rose ('18)	35	25
208	A26	2ab green	75	75
a.		Imperf., pair	7.00	
b.		Horizontal pair, imperf. between		
208C	A26	2ab yel ('16)	1.25	1.25
209	A26	2ab bis ('18-'19)	90	90
210	A27	1rup lil brn	1.50	1.50
a.		red brn	1.50	1.50
211	A27	1rup ol bis ('16)	1.50	1.50
		Nos. 205-211 (8)	7.10	6.75

A28

1913

212	A28	2pa db brn	1.25	1.25
a.		red brn	1.25	1.25

No. 212 is inscribed "Tiket waraq dak" (Postal card stamps). It was usable only on postcards and not accepted for postage on letters.

Nos. 196–212 sometimes show letters of a papermaker's watermark, "Howard & Jones, London."

Royal Star
A29

1920, Aug. 24 *Perf. 12*

Size: 39x47mm.

214 A29 10pa rose 18.50 16.00
215 A29 20pa red brn 42.50 25.00
216 A29 30pa green 87.50 87.50

Issued in sheets of two.

1921, Mar.

Size: 22½x28¼mm.

217 A29 10pa rose 50 25
a. Perf. 11 ('27) 1.00 1.50
218 A29 20pa red brn 1.50 75
219 A29 30pa yel grn 1.50 75
a. Tête bêche pair 7.50 7.50
b. 30pa grn 1.50 75
c. As "b," Tête bêche pair 7.50 7.50

Two types of the 10pa, three of the 20pa.

Crest of King Amanullah
A30

1924, Feb. 26 *Perf. 12*

220 A30 10pa chocolate 16.00 10.00
a. Tête bêche pair 35.00 30.00

Issued to commemorate the 6th Independence Day.

Printed in sheets of four consisting of two tête bêche pairs, and in sheets of two. Two types exist.

Some authorities believe that Nos. Q15–Q16 were issued as regular postage stamps.

Crest of King Amanullah
A32

1925, Feb. 26 *Perf. 12*

Size: 29x37mm.

222 A32 10pa lt brn 15.00 8.75

Issued to commemorate the 7th Independence Day.

Printed in sheets of 8 (two panes of 4).

1926, Feb. 28 Wove Paper

Size: 26x33mm.

224 A32 10pa dk bl 2.00 2.00
a. Imperf., pair 12.50 12.50
b. Horizontal pair, imperf. between 15.00
c. Vertical pair, imperf. between 12.50
d. Laid paper 10.00 7.50

Issued for the 7th anniversary of Independence. Printed in sheets of 4, and in sheets of 8 (two panes of 4). Tête bêche gutter pairs exist.

Tughra and Crest of Amanullah—A33

1927, Feb.

225 A33 10pa magenta 6.00 4.25
a. Vertical pair, imperf. between 20.00

Dotted Background.

226 A33 10pa magenta 5.50 4.25
a. Horizontal pair, imperf. between 15.00

The surface of No. 226 is covered by a net of fine dots.

Nos. 225 and 226 were issued to commemorate the eighth anniversary of Independence. Printed in sheets of 8 (two panes of 4). Tête bêche gutter pairs exist.

National Seal
A34

A35

A35a

A36

1927, Oct. *Imperf.*

227 A34 15p pink 35 35
228 A35 30p Prus grn 80 40
229 A36 60p lt bl 1.50 1.50
a. Tête bêche pair 4.50 5.00

1927–30 *Perf. 11, 12*

230 A34 15p pink 35 25
231 A34 15p ultra ('29) 1.00 75
232 A35 30p Prus grn 50 50
233 A35a 30p dp grn ('30) 1.25 1.25
234 A36 60p brt bl 2.50 2.50
a. Tête bêche pair 6.00 6.00
235 A36 60p blk ('29) 2.00 1.00
Nos. 230-235 (6) 7.60 6.25

Nos. 230, 232 and 234 are usually imperforate on one or two sides.

No. 233 has been redrawn. A narrow border of pearls has been added and "30", in European and Arabic numerals, inserted in the upper spandrels.

Tughra and Crest of Amanullah
A37

1928, Feb. 27

236 A37 15p pink 3.75 3.75
a. Tête bêche pair 10.00 10.00
b. Imperf. vertically, pair 12.50
c. Same as "a", imperf. vertically, block of 4

Issued to commemorate the ninth anniversary of Independence. This stamp is always imperforate on one or two sides.

A 15p blue of somewhat similar design was prepared for the 10th anniversary, but was not issued due to Amanullah's dethronement. Price, $5.

National Seal—A38

A39

A40

A41

A42

1928–30 *Perf. 11, 12*

237 A38 2p dl bl 3.75 2.50
a. Vertical pair, imperf. between
238 A38 2p lt rose ('30) 25 25
239 A39 10p gray grn 25 15
a. Tête bêche pair 7.50 7.50
b. Imperf. horizontally, pair 1.00
c. Vertical pair, imperf. between 75
240 10p choc ('30) 1.00 1.00
a. 10p brn pur ('29) 4.50 2.50
241 A40 25p car rose 35 25
242 A40 25p Prus grn ('29) 75 60
243 A41 40p ultra 40 35
a. Tête bêche pair 7.50 7.50
244 A41 40p rose ('29) 1.50 1.25
a. Tête bêche pair 10.00 10.00
b. Imperf. horizontally, pair 5.00
245 A42 50p red 40 40
246 A42 50p dk bl ('29) 2.50 2.00
Nos. 237-246 (10) 11.15 8.75

The sheets of these stamps are often imperforate at the outer margins.

Nos. 237–238 are newspaper stamps.

Revolutionary Gov't. Issue

Stamps of 1927–28 Handstamped

On Stamps of 1927.

1929 *Imperf.*

252 A34 15p pink 5.75
253 A35 30p Prus grn 6.25
253A A36 60p lt bl 11.00

Perf. 11

254 A34 15p pink 5.75
255 A35 30p Prus grn 6.25
256 A36 60p brt bl 11.00

On Stamps of 1928.

257 A38 2p dl bl 4.50
258 A39 10p gray grn 4.50
a. Vertical pair, imperf. between
259 A40 25p car rose 6.25
260 A41 40p ultra 8.00
a. Tête bêche pair 75.00
261 A42 50p red 12.50
Nos. 257-261 (5) 35.75

Impressions of the overprint vary greatly. It reads: "Khadim Din Mohammed Rasul Ullah Amir Habib Ullah, 1347." (The Servant of the Faith of Mohammed, Prophet of God. Amir Habibullah). Genuinely used copies are not known. Counterfeit overprints and bogus cancellations are plentiful.

Independence Monument
A46

Lithographed.

Wmkd. Large Seal in the Sheet.

1931, Aug. Laid Paper *Perf. 12*

262 A46 20p red 1.25 75

Issued to commemorate the 13th Independence Day. Issued without gum.

National Assembly Chamber
A47

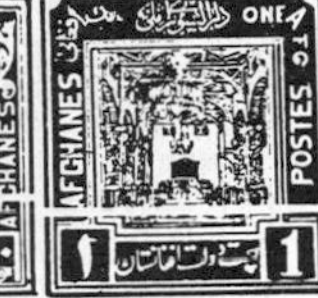

National Assembly Chamber
A48 A50

National Assembly Building
A49

National Assembly Chamber
A51

National Assembly Building
A52

Typographed

Wove Paper

1932 *Perf. 12* **Unwmkd.**

263 A47 40p olive 60 40
264 A48 60p violet 1.00 75
265 A49 80p dk red 1.50 1.25
266 A50 1af black 15.00 6.25
267 A51 2af ultra 5.00 4.00
268 A52 3af gray grn 6.50 5.00
Nos. 263-268 (6) 29.60 17.65

Issued to commemorate the formation of the National Council. Imperforate or perforated examples of Nos. 263–268 on ungummed chalky paper are proofs.

See also Nos. 304–305.

Mosque at Balkh
A53

Kabul Fortress
A54

Parliament House, Darul Funun
A55

Parliament House, Darul Funun
A56

Arch of Qalai Bist
A57

Memorial Pillar of Knowledge and Ignorance
A58

Independence Monument
A59

Minaret at Herat
A60

Arch of Paghman
A61

Ruins at Balkh
A62

Minarets of Herat
A63

Great Buddha at Bamian
A64

1932 Typographed *Perf. 12*

269	A53	10p brown	18	15
270	A54	15p dk brn	30	15
271	A55	20p red	40	25
272	A56	25p dk grn	40	20
273	A57	30p red	60	40
274	A58	40p orange	1.00	50
275	A59	50p blue	1.25	50
a.		Tête bêche pair	8.00	
276	A60	60p blue	1.50	75
277	A61	80p violet	2.50	1.50
278	A62	1af dk bl	4.00	85
279	A63	2af dk red vio	4.50	3.00
280	A64	3af claret	6.50	3.75
		Nos. 269-280 (12)	23.13	12.00

Counterfeits of types A53—A65 exist.
See also Nos. 290–295, 298–299, 302–303.

Entwined 2's
A65

Two types:
Type I. Numerals shaded. Size about 21x29mm.
Type II. Numerals unshaded. Size about 21¾x30mm.

1931–38 *Perf. 12, 11x12*

281	A65	2p red brn (I)	8	8
282	A65	2p ol blk (I) ('34)	10	8
283	A65	2p grnsh gray (I) ('34)	25	8
283A	A65	2p blk (II) ('36)	15	8
284	A65	2p sal (II) ('38)	25	8
284A	A65	2p rose (I) ('38)	10	10
b.		Imperf., pair	75	

Imperf.

285	A65	2p blk (II) ('37)	25	10
286	A65	2p sal (II) ('38)	10	10
		Nos. 281-286 (8)	1.28	70

The newspaper rate was 2 pouls.

Independence Monument
A66

1932, Aug. *Perf. 12*

287	A66	1af dp rose	2.75	2.25

Issued to commemorate the 14th Independence Day.

1929 Liberation Monument, Kabul
A67

1932, Oct. Typographed

288	A67	80p red brn	1.25	75

Arch of Paghman
A68

1933, Aug.

289	A68	50p lt ultra	1.50	1.50

Issued to commemorate the 15th Independence Day.

Types of 1932 and

Royal Palace, Kabul
A69

Darrah-Shikari Pass, Hindu Kush
A70

1934–38 Typographed *Perf. 12*

290	A53	10p dp vio	25	12
291	A54	15p turq grn	30	15
292	A55	20p magenta	35	15
293	A56	25p dp rose	40	25
294	A57	30p orange	60	30
295	A58	40p bl blk	90	40
296	A69	45p dk bl	1.75	1.50
297	A69	45p red ('38)	30	25
298	A59	50p orange	40	25
299	A60	60p purple	60	25
300	A70	75p red	90	50
301	A70	75p dk bl ('38)	90	60
302	A61	80p brn vio	1.50	75
303	A62	1af red vio	2.00	1.50
304	A51	2af gray blk	4.50	3.00
305	A52	3af ultra	6.00	4.50
		Nos. 290-305 (16)	21.65	14.47

Nos. 290, 292, 300, 304, 305 exist imperf.

Independence Monument
A71

1934, Aug. Litho. Without Gum

306	A71	50p pale grn	1.50	1.50
a.		Tête bêche pair	4.50	4.50

Issued to commemorate the 16th year of Independence. Each sheet of 40 (4x10) included 4 tête bêche pairs as lower half of sheet was inverted.

Independence Monument
A74

Fireworks Display
A75

1935, Aug. 15 Laid Paper

309	A74	50p dk bl	1.50	1.50

Issued in commemoration of the 17th year of Independence.

Wove Paper

1936, Aug. 15 *Perf. 12*

310	A75	50p red vio	1.75	1.50

Issued in commemoration of the 18th year of Independence.

Independence Monument and Nadir Shah—A76

1937

311	A76	50p vio & bis brn	1.25	75
a.		Imperf., pair	2.75	

Issued in commemoration of the 19th year of Independence.

Mohammed Nadir Shah
A77 A78

1938 *Perf. 11x12*

315	A77	50p brt bl & sep	1.00	1.00
a.		Imperf. pair	6.25	3.75

Issued in commemoration of the 20th year of Independence. Issued without gum.

1939 *Perf. 11, 12x11*

317	A78	50p dp sal	1.50	1.00

Issued in commemoration of the 21st year of Independence.

National Arms
A79

Parliament House, Darul Funun
A80

Royal Palace, Kabul
A81

Independence Monument
A82

Independence Monument and Nadir Shah
A83

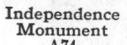

Mohammed Zahir Shah
A84

Mohammed Zahir Shah
A85

Perf. 11, 11x12, 12x11, 12

1939–61 Typographed

318	A79	2p int blk	10	10
318A	A79	2p brt pink ('61)	25	15
319	A80	10p brt pur	10	10
320	A80	15p brt grn	12	10
321	A80	20p red lil	15	10
322	A81	25p rose red	50	25
322A	A81	25p grn ('41)	25	8
323	A81	30p orange	20	15
324	A81	40p dk gray	20	15
325	A82	45p brt car	20	15
326	A82	50p dp org	30	20
327	A82	60p violet	30	20
328	A83	75p ultra	3.00	75
328A	A83	75p red vio ('41)	75	30
328C	A83	75p brt red ('44)	1.75	1.35
328D	A83	75p chnt brn ('49)	2.00	1.65
329	A83	80p chocolate	50	50
a.		80p dl red vio (error)		
330	A84	1af brt red vio	1.50	75
330A	A85	1af brt red vio ('44)	2.50	1.50
331	A85	2af dp rose red	2.50	1.35
a.		2af cop red	1.75	50
332	A84	3af dp bl	3.75	1.60
		Nos. 318-332 (21)	20.92	11.48

On No. 332 the King faces slightly left.
No. 318A issued with and without gum.
See Nos. 795A-795B.

Mohammed Nadir Shah
A86

1940, Aug. 23 ***Perf. 11***

333	A86	50p gray grn	1.00	85

Issued in commemoration of the 22nd year of Independence.

Independence Monument
A87

Arch of Paghman
A88

1941, Aug. 23 ***Perf. 12***

334	A87	15p gray grn	6.50	2.75
335	A88	50p red brn	1.25	85

Issued in commemoration of the 23rd year of Independence.

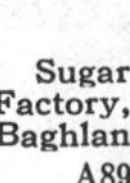

Sugar Factory, Baghlan
A89

1942, April ***Perf. 12***

336	A89	1.25af ultra	2.50	1.75
a.		1.25af bl (shades)	1.50	50

In 1949, a 1.50af brown, type A89, was sold for 3af by the Philatelic Office, Kabul. It was not valid for postage. Price $3.50.

Independence Monument
A90

Mohammed Nadir Shah and Arch of Paghman
A91

1942, Aug. 23 ***Perf. 12***

337	A90	35p brt grn	4.00	3.00
338	A91	125p chlky bl	2.00	1.75

Issued in commemoration of the 24th year of Independence.

Independence Monument and Nadir Shah
A92

Mohammed Nadir Shah
A93

Perf. 11x12, 12x11

1943, Aug. 25 **Typo.** **Unwmkd.**

339	A92	35p carmine	15.00	9.00
340	A93	1.25af dk bl	5.00	1.75

25th year of Independence.

Tomb of Gohar Shad, Herat
A94

Ruins of Qalai Bist
A95

1944, May 1 ***Perf. 12, 11x12***

341	A94	35p orange	60	40
342	A95	70p violet	1.20	75
a.		70p rose lil	4.75	1.00

Arch of Paghman
A96

Independence Monument and Mohammed Nadir Shah
A97

1944, Aug. ***Perf. 12***

343	A96	35p crimson	1.00	75
344	A97	1.25af ultra	1.75	1.50

Issued to commemorate the 26th year of Independence.

Independence Monument
A98

Mohammed Nadir Shah and Arch of Paghman
A99

1945, July

345	A98	35p dp red lil	1.00	90
346	A99	1.25af blue	2.50	2.00

Issued to commemorate the 27th year of Independence.

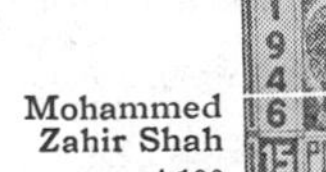

Mohammed Zahir Shah
A100

Independence Monument
A101

Mohammed Nadir Shah
A102

1946, July

347	A100	15p emerald	60	45
348	A101	20p dp red lil	90	70
349	A102	125p blue	2.25	2.25

Issued to commemorate the 28th year of Independence.

Zahir Shah and Ruins of Qalai Bist—A103

Arch of Paghman
A104

Nadir Shah and Independence Monument
A105

1947, Aug.

350	A103	15p yel grn	40	20
351	A104	35p plum	50	30
352	A105	125p dp bl	1.85	1.85

Issued to commemorate the 29th year of Independence.

Begging Child
A106

A107

Typographed.

1948, May ***Perf. 12*** **Unwmkd.**

353	A106	35p yel grn	4.00	2.75
354	A107	125p gray bl	4.00	3.25

Issued to commemorate Children's Day, May 29, 1948, and valid only on that day. Proceeds were used for Child Welfare.

Arch of Paghman
A108

Independence Monument
A109

Mohammed Nadir Shah
A110

1948, Aug.

355	A108	15p green	30	20
356	A109	20p magenta	50	25
357	A110	125p dk bl	1.10	90

Issued to commemorate the 30th year of Independence.

United Nations Emblem
A111

1948, Oct. 24

358	A111	125p dk vio bl	10.00	8.50

Issued to commemorate the third anniversary of the formation of the United Nations. Valid one day only. Sheets of 9.

Maiwand Victory Column, Kandahar
A112

Zahir Shah and Ruins of Qalai Bist
A113

Independence Monument and Nadir Shah
A114

1949, Aug. Typo. ***Perf. 12***

359	A112	25p green	35	25
360	A113	35p magenta	50	35
361	A114	1.25af blue	1.25	1.00

Issued to commemorate the 31st year of Independence.

Nadir Shah
A117

1950, Aug.

364	A117	35p red brn	40	40
365	A117	125p blue	1.00	75

Issued to commemorate the 32nd year of Independence.

Medical School and Nadir Shah
A119

1950, Dec. 22 Typo. ***Perf. 12***

Size: 38x25mm.

367	A119	35p emerald	75	75

Size: 46x30mm.

368	A119	1.25af dp bl	2.50	2.00
a.		1.25af blk (error)	6.00	

Issued to commemorate the 19th anniversary of the founding of Afghanistan's Faculty of Medicine. On sale and valid for use on Dec. 22–23, 1950.

Minaret, Herat
A120

Zahir Shah
A121

Mosque of Khodja Abu Parsar, Balkh
A122

Zahir Shah
A123 A124

Designs: 20p, Buddha at Bamian. 40p, Ruined arch. 45p, Maiwand Victory Monument. 50p, View of Kandahar. 60p, Ancient tower. 70p, Afghanistan flag. 80p, 1af, Profile of Zahir Shah in uniform.

Photogravure, Engraved, Engraved and Lithographed.

Perf. 12, 12½, 13x12½, 13½.

1951, Mar. 21 **Unwmkd.**

Imprint:
"Waterlow & Sons Limited, London."

369	A120	10p yel & brn	10	8
370	A120	15p bl & brn	15	8
371	A120	20p black	7.00	3.50
372	A121	25p green	18	10
373	A122	30p cerise	25	12
374	A121	35p violet	25	12
375	A122	40p chnt brn	30	12
376	A120	45p dp bl	25	15
377	A122	50p ol blk	60	18
378	A120	60p black	60	20
379	A122	70p dk grn, blk, red & grn	35	20
380	A123	75p cerise	80	25
381	A123	80p car & blk	85	50
382	A123	1af dp grn & vio	60	50
383	A124	1.25af rose lil & blk	*4.00*	50
384	A124	2af ultra	1.40	50
385	A124	3af ultra & blk	3.25	1.25
		Nos. 369-385 (17)	*20.93*	8.35

Nos. 372, 374 and 381 to 385 are engraved, No. 379 is engraved and lithographed.

See also Nos. 445–451, 453, 552A–552D.

Arch of Paghman
A125

Nadir Shah and Independence Monument
A126

Overprint in Violet سال ۳۳ استقلال

Perf. 13½x13, 13

1951, Aug. 25 **Engraved**

386	A125	35p dk grn & blk	85	50
387	A126	1.25af dp bl	2.10	1.25

Overprint reads "Sol 33 Istiqlal" or "33rd Year of Independence." Overprint measures about 11 mm. wide.

See also Nos. 398–399B, 441–442.

Proposed Flag of Pashtunistan
A127

Design: 1.25af, Flag and Pashtunistan warrior.

1951, Sept. 2 Litho. ***Perf. 11½***

388	A127	35p dl choc	1.25	1.00
389	A127	125p blue	3.00	2.75

Issued to publicize "Free Pashtunistan" Day.

Imperforates

From 1951 to 1958, quantities of nearly all locally-printed stamps were left imperforate and sold by the government at double face. From 1959 until March, 1964, many of the imperforates were sold for more than face value.

Avicenna—A128

1951, Nov. 4 Typo. ***Perf. 11½***

390	A128	35p dp cl	75	50
391	A128	125p blue	2.10	1.65

Issued to commemorate the 20th anniversary of the founding of the national Graduate School of Medicine.

A129

Dove and U. N. Symbols
A130

1951, Oct. 24

392	A129	35p magenta	2.00	1.50
393	A130	125p blue	5.00	4.00

Issued to commemorate the 7th anniversary of the formation of the United Nations.

Amir Sher Ali Khan and Tiger Head Stamp
A131

Design: Nos. 395 and 397, Zahir Shah and stamp.

1951, Dec. 23 **Lithographed**

394	A131	35p chocolate	50	50
395	A131	35p rose lil	50	50
396	A131	125p ultra	1.00	90
a.		Cliche of 35p in plate of 125p	125.00	125.00
397	A131	125p aqua	1.00	90

Issued to commemorate the 76th anniversary of the formation of the Universal Postal Union.

Types of 1951
Without Overprint.

Perf. 13½x13, 13

1952, Aug. 24 **Engraved**

398	A125	35p dk grn & blk	2.50	2.50
399	A126	1.25af dp bl	2.50	2.50

Same Overprinted in Violet

۳۴ استقلال

399A	A125	35p dk grn & blk	90	60
399B	A126	1.25af dp bl	2.50	1.50

Nos. 398–399B were issued to commemorate the 34th Independence Day.

Globe—A132

Lithographed

1952, Oct. 25 ***Perf. 11½*** **Unwmkd.**

400	A132	35p rose	80	70
401	A132	125p aqua	1.75	1.50

Issued to honor the United Nations.

Symbol of Medicine
A134

Tribal Warrior and National Flag
A135

1952, Nov. ***Perf. 11½***

403	A134	35p chocolate	60	50
404	A134	125p vio bl	1.75	1.75

Issued to commemorate the 21st anniversary of the national Graduate School of Medicine.

No. 404 is inscribed in French with white letters on a colored background.

1952, Sept. 1 ***Perf. 11***

405	A135	35p red	40	40
406	A135	125p dk bl	85	85

No. 406 is inscribed in French "Pashtunistan Day, 1952."

Flags of Afghanistan and Pashtunistan
A139

Badge of Pashtunistan
A140

Perf. 10½x11, 11

1953, Sept. 1 **Unwmkd.**

411	A139	35p vermilion	30	25
412	A140	125p blue	85	65

Issued to publicize "Free Pashtunistan" Day.

Nadir Shah and Flag Bearer
A141

Nadir Shah and Independence Monument
A142

1953, Aug. 24 ***Perf. 11***

413 A141 35p green 25 20
414 A142 125p violet 1.00 75

Issued to commemorate the 35th anniversary of Independence.

United Nations Emblem
A143

1953, Oct. 24

415 A143 35p lilac 75 75
416 A143 125p vio bl 1.85 1.50

Issued to publicize United Nations Day, 1953.

Nadir Shah
A144 A145

1953, Nov. 29

417 A144 35p orange 1.00 1.00
418 A145 125p chlky bl 2.25 2.25

Issued to commemorate the 22nd anniversary of the founding of the national Graduate School of Medicine.

Redrawn.

35p. Original - Right character in second line of Persian inscription: ٣

Redrawn - Persian character: ٢

125p. Original - Inscribed "XXIII," "MADECINE" and "ANNIVERAIRE"
Redrawn - Inscribed "XXII," "MEDECINE" and "ANNIVERSAIRE"

1953

419 A144 35p dp org 5.00
420 A145 125p chlky bl 6.50

Nadir Shah and Symbols of Independence
A146

1954, Aug. **Typo.** ***Perf. 11***

421 A146 35p car rose 50 40
422 A146 125p vio bl 1.50 1.25

Issued to commemorate the 36th year of Independence.

Raising Flag of Pashtunistan
A147

1954, Sept. ***Perf. 11½***

423 A147 35p chocolate 50 40
424 A147 125p blue 1.50 1.25

Issued to publicize "Free Pashtunistan" Day.

U.N. Flag and Map
A148

1954, Oct. 24 ***Perf. 11***

425 A148 35p car rose 1.00 1.00
426 A148 125p dk vio bl 3.00 3.00

Issued to commemorate the 9th anniversary of the United Nations.

U. N. Symbols
A149

Design: 125p, U. N. emblem & flags.

1955, June 26 **Litho.** ***Perf. 11***

Size: 26½x36mm.

427 A149 35p dk grn 60 50

Size: 28½x36mm.

428 A149 125p aqua 1.50 1.25

Issued to commemorate the 10th anniversary of the signing of the United Nations charter.

Nadir Shah (center) and Brothers
A150

1929 Civil War Scene and Zahir Shah
A151

Tribal Elders' Council and Pashtun Flag
A152

1955, Aug. ***Perf. 11*** **Unwmkd.**

429 A150 35p brt pink 40 40
430 A150 35p vio bl 40 40
431 A151 125p rose lil 1.25 1.00
432 A151 125p lt vio 1.25 1.00

Issued to commemorate the 37th anniversary of Independence.

1955, Sept. 5

433 A152 35p org brn 35 35
434 A152 125p yel grn 1.25 1.00

Issued for "Free Pashtunistan" Day.

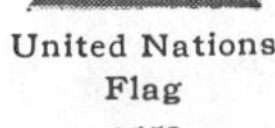

United Nations Flag
A153

Nadir Shah and Independence Monument
A154

1955, Oct. 24 ***Perf. 11*** **Unwmkd.**

435 A153 35p org brn 90 75
436 A153 125p brt ultra 1.85 1.50

Issued to commemorate the tenth anniversary of the United Nations, Oct. 24, 1955.

1956, Aug. **Lithographed**

437 A154 35p lt grn 35 30
438 A154 140p lt vio bl 1.35 1.10

Issued to commemorate the 38th year of Independence.

Jesh'n Exhibition Hall
A155

1956, Aug. 25

439 A155 50p chocolate 45 30
440 A155 50p lt vio bl 45 30

International Exposition at Kabul.
Of the 50p face value, only 35p paid postage. The remaining 15p went to the Exposition.

Nos. 398-399 Handstamped in Violet

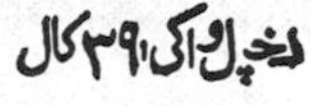

a

39 em Anv

b

Perf. 13½x13, 13

1957, Aug. **Engraved**

441 A125 (a) 35p dk grn & blk 60 30
442 A126 (b) 1.25af dp bl 90 75

Arabic overprint on No. 441 measures 19mm. No. 442 overprinted: "39 em Anv". Issued to commemorate the 39th year of independence.

Pashtunistan Flag
A156

1957, Sept. 1 **Litho.** ***Perf. 11***

443 A156 50p pale lil rose 75 50
444 A156 155p lt vio 1.25 1.00

Issued for "Free Pashtunistan" Day. French inscription on No. 444.

Types of 1951 and

Game of Buzkashi—A157

Photogravure, Engraved, Engraved and Lithographed.

Perf. 12, 12½, 12½x13, 13, 13x12, 13x12½, 13½x14

1957, Nov. 23 **Unwmkd.**

Imprint: " Waterlow & Sons Limited, London."

445 A122 30p brown 22 6
446 A122 40p rose red 32 6
447 A122 50p yellow 48 8
448 A120 60p ultra 55 10
449 A123 75p brt vio 70 10
450 A123 80p vio & brn 75 10
451 A123 1af car & ultra 1.50 20
452 A157 140p ol & dp cl 3.00 75
453 A124 3af org & blk 3.75 75
Nos. 445-453 (9) 11.27 2.20

No. 452 lacks imprint.

Nadir Shah and Flag-bearer
A158

1958, Aug. 25 ***Perf. 13½x14***

454 A158 35p dp yel grn 25 20
455 A158 140p brown 60 50

Issued to commemorate the 40th year of Independence.

Exposition Buildings
A159

1958, Aug. 23 **Litho.** ***Perf. 11***

456 A159 35p brt bl grn 25 20
457 A159 140p vermilion 70 60

Issued for the International Exposition at Kabul.

Pres. Celal Bayar of Turkey
A160

Flags of U.N. and Afghanistan
A161

1958, Sept. 13 **Unwmkd.**

458 A160 50p lt bl 30 20
459 A160 100p brown 50 40

Issued to commemorate the visit of President Celal Bayar of Turkey.

Perf. 14x13½

1958, Oct. 24 **Photogravure**

Flags in Original Colors.

460 A161 50p dk gray 75 75
461 A161 100p green 1.50 1.25

Issued for United Nations Day, Oct. 24.

Atomic Energy Encircling the Hemispheres—A162

1958, Oct. 20 ***Perf. 13½x14***

462 A162 50p blue 50 50
463 A162 100p dp red lil 85 85

Issued to promote Atoms for Peace.

UNESCO Building, Paris
A163

1958, Nov. 3

464 A163 50p dp yel grn 75 60
465 A163 100p brn ol 1.10 90

Issued to commemorate the opening of UNESCO (U.N. Educational, Scientific and Cultural Organization) Headquarters in Paris, Nov. 3.

Globe and Torch
A164

Perf. 13½x14

1958, Dec. 10 Unwmkd.

466	A164	50p lil rose	50	50
467	A164	100p maroon	1.00	1.00

Issued to commemorate the tenth anniversary of the signing of the Universal Declaration of Human Rights.

Nadir Shah and Flags
A165

1959, Aug. Litho. *Perf. 11 Rough*

468	A165	35p lt ver	30	30
469	A165	165p lt vio	1.00	60

Issued to commemorate the 41st year of Independence.

Uprooted Oak Emblem
A166

1960, Apr. 7 *Perf. 11*

470	A166	50p dp org	20	15
471	A166	165p blue	50	40

Issued to publicize World Refugee Year, July 1, 1959–June 30, 1960.

Two imperf. souvenir sheets exist. Both contain a 50p and a 165p, type A166, with marginal inscriptions and WRY emblem in maroon. On one sheet the stamps are in the colors of Nos. 470–471 (size 108x81 mm.). On the other, the 50p is blue and the 165p is deep orange (size 107x80 mm.). Price $6 each.

Buzkashi—A167

1960, May 4 *Perf. 11, Imperf.*

472	A167	25p rose red	35	20
473	A167	50p bluish grn	75	50
a.		Cliché of 25p in plate of 50p	20.00	20.00

See also Nos. 549–550A.

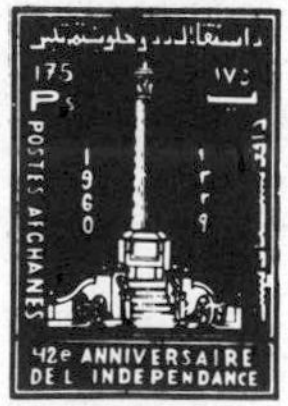

Independence Monument
A168

1960, Aug.

474	A168	50p lt bl	15	15
475	A168	175p brt pink	50	50

Issued to commemorate the 42nd Independence Day.

Globe and Flags
A169

1960, Oct. 24 Litho. *Perf. 11*

476	A169	50p rose lil	30	25
477	A169	175p ultra	1.00	85

Issued to commemorate United Nations Day.

An imperf. souvenir sheet contains one each of Nos. 476–477 with marginal inscriptions ("La Journée des Nations Unies 1960" in French and Persian) and UN emblem in light blue. Size: 127x85½mm. Price $5.

This sheet was surcharged "+20ps" in 1962. Price $8.50.

Teacher Pointing to Globe
A170

1960, Oct. 23 *Perf. 11*

478	A170	50p brt pink	25	18
479	A170	100p brt grn	90	60

Issued to publicize Teacher's Day.

Mohammed Zahir Shah
A171

1960, Oct. 15

480	A171	50p red brn	40	20
481	A171	150p dk car rose	1.25	40

Issued to honor the King on his 46th birthday.

Buzkashi
A172

1960, Nov. 9 *Perf. 11*

482	A172	175p lt red brn	1.50	60

See also Nos. 551–552.

No. 482 Overprinted "1960" and Olympic Rings in Bright Green.

1960, Dec. 24

483	A172	175p red brn	3.25	3.00
a.		Souvenir sheet	12.00	

Issued to commemorate the 17th Olympic Games, Rome, Aug. 25–Sept. 11.

No. 483a contains one of No. 483, imperf. Bright green marginal inscription. Size: 86x61mm.

Mir Wais
A173

1961, Jan. 5 *Perf. 10½* Unwmkd.

484	A173	50p brt rose lil	30	20
485	A173	175p ultra	75	50
a.		Souv. sheet of 2	2.25	2.25

Issued to honor Mir Wais (1665–1708), national leader.

No. 485a contains one each of Nos. 484–485, imperf. Emerald marginal inscription. Size: 108x78mm.

No Postal Need

existed for the 1p to 15p denominations released with commemorative or semipostal sets of 1961–63 (between Nos. 486 and 649, B37 and B65). The lowest denomination actually used for non-philatelic postage in that period was 25p (except for the 2p newspaper rate for which separate stamps were provided).

Horse, Sheep and Camel
A174

Designs: No. 487, 175p, Rock partridge. 10p, 100p, Afghan hound. 15p, 150p, Grain and grasshopper (vert.).

1961, Mar. 29 Photo. *Perf. 13½x14*

486	A174	2p mar & buff		
487	A174	2p ultra & org		
488	A174	5p brn & yel		
489	A174	10p blk & sal		
490	A174	15p bl grn & yel		
491	A174	25p blk & pink		
492	A174	50p blk & cit		
493	A174	100p blk & pink		
494	A174	150p grn & yel		
495	A174	175p ultra & pink		
		Nos. 486-495 (10)	3.00	

Two souvenir sheets, perf. and imperf., contain two stamps, one each of Nos. 492–493. Black marginal inscriptions, "Journee d'Agriculture 1961" in Persian and French. Size: 111x64mm. Price $2 each.

Afghan Fencing
A175

Designs: No. 497, 5p, 25p, 50p, Wrestlers. 10p, 100p, Man with Indian clubs. 15p, 150p, Afghan fencing. 175p, Children skating.

1961, July 6 *Perf. 13½x14*

496	A175	2p grn & rose lil		
497	A175	2p brn & cit		
498	A175	5p gray & rose		
499	A175	10p bl & bis		
500	A175	15p sl bl & dl lil		
501	A175	25p blk & dl bl		
502	A175	50p sl grn & bis brn		
503	A175	100p brn & bl grn		
504	A175	150p brn & org yel		
505	A175	175p blk & bl		
		Nos. 496-505 (10)	1.75	

Issued for Children's Day.

A souvenir sheet exists, perf. and imperf., containing one each of Nos. 502-503. Size: 111x65mm. Price $3.50 each.

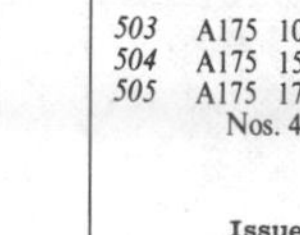

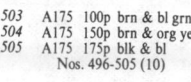

Bandé Amir Lakes
A176

1961, Aug. 7 Photo. *Perf. 13½x14*

506	A176	3af brt bl	50	40
507	A176	10af rose cl	1.75	1.50

Nadir Shah
A177

Girl Scout
A178

1961, Aug. 23 *Perf. 14x13½*

508	A177	50p rose red & blk	50	40
509	A177	175p brt grn & org brn	1.00	80

Issued to commemorate the 43rd Independence Day.

Two souvenir sheets, perf. and imperf., contain one each of Nos. 508–509. Black marginal inscription and control number, flag in black, red & green. Size: 104x 74mm. Price, each $2.50.

Perf. 14x13½

1961, July 23 Unwmkd.

510	A178	50p dp car & dk gray	40	20
511	A178	175p dp grn & rose brn	90	60

Issued for Women's Day.

Two souvenir sheets exist, perf. and imperf., containing one each of Nos. 510–511. Black marginal inscription. Size: 105x75mm. Price $4 each.

Exhibition Hall, Kabul
A179

1961, Aug. 23 *Perf. 13½x14*

512	A179	50p yel brn & yel grn	25	20
513	A179	175p bl & brn	60	40

International Exhibition at Kabul.

Pathan with Pashtunistan Flag
A180

Photogravure

1961, Aug. 31 ***Perf. 14x13½***

514	A180	50p blk, lil & red	20	18
515	A180	175p brn, grnsh bl & red	50	40

Issued for "Free Pashtunistan Day."
Souvenir sheets exist perf. and imperf. containing one each of Nos. 514–515 with black marginal inscription and flag in red and black. Size: 104x75mm. Price $2 each.

Assembly Building—A181

1961, Sept. 10 ***Perf. 12***

516	A181	50p dk gray & brt grn	25	18
517	A181	175p ultra & brn	65	45

Issued to commemorate the anniversary of the founding of the National Assembly.
Souvenir sheets exist, perf. and imperf., containing one each of Nos. 516–517 with black marginal inscription and flower in ultramarine and green. Size: 106x70mm. Price $1 each.

Exterminating Anopheles Mosquito
A182

1961, Oct. 5 ***Perf. 13½x14***

518	A182	50p blk & brn lil	70	40
519	A182	175p mar & brt grn	1.50	75

Issued to publicize the Anti-Malaria campaign. Souvenir sheets exist, perf. and imperf., containing one each of Nos. 518–519 with black marginal inscription and mosquito. Size: 110x65mm. Price $5 each.

Zahir Shah
A183

1961, Oct. 15 ***Perf. 13½***

520	A183	50p lil & bl	25	20
521	A183	175p emer & red brn	60	50

Issued to honor King Mohammed Zahir Shah on his 47th birthday.
See also Nos. 609–612.

Pomegranates—A184

Fruit: No. 523, 5p, 25p, 50p, Grapes. 10p, 150p, Apples. 15p, 175p, Pomegranates. 100p, Melons.

1961, Oct. 16 ***Perf. 13½x14***

Fruit in Natural Colors.

522	A184	2p black		
523	A184	2p green		
524	A184	5p lil rose		
525	A184	10p lilac		
526	A184	15p dk bl		
527	A184	25p dl red		
528	A184	50p purple		
529	A184	100p brt bl		
530	A184	150p brown		
531	A184	175p ol gray		
		Nos. 522-531 (10)	2.00	

For Afghan Red Crescent Society.
Souvenir sheets exist, perf. and imperf., containing one each of Nos. 528–529 with black marginal inscription and red crescent. Size: 110x65mm. Price $1.75 each.

U.N. Headquarters, N.Y.—A185

1961, Oct. 24 ***Perf. 13½x14***

Vertical Borders in Emerald, Red and Black.

532	A185	1p rose lil		
533	A185	2p slate		
534	A185	3p brown		
535	A185	4p ultra		
536	A185	50p rose red		
537	A185	75p gray		
538	A185	175p brt grn		
		Nos. 532-538 (7)	1.25	

Issued to commemorate the 16th anniversary of the United Nations. Souvenir sheets exist, perf. and imperf., containing one each of Nos. 536–538. Black marginal inscription with U.N. emblem and control number. Size: 114x95mm. Price $2.25 each.

Children Giving Flowers to Teacher
A186

People Raising UNESCO Symbol
A187

Designs: No. 540, 5p, 25p, 50p, Tulips. 10p, 100p, Narcissus. 15p, 150p, Children giving flowers to teacher. 175p, Teacher with children in front of school.

1961, Oct. 26 **Photo.** ***Perf. 12***

539	A186	2p multi		
540	A186	2p multi		
541	A186	5p multi		
542	A186	10p multi		
543	A186	15p multi		
544	A186	25p multi		
545	A186	50p multi		
546	A186	100p multi		
547	A186	150p multi		
548	A186	175p multi		
		Nos. 539-548 (10)	2.00	

Issued for Teacher's Day.
Souvenir sheets exist, perf. and imperf. containing one each of Nos. 545–546. Gray marginal inscription and black control number. Size: 104x78mm. Price, 2 sheets, $3.

Buzkashi Types of 1960.

1961-72 **Litho.** ***Perf. 10½, 11***

549	A167	25p violet	10	5
b.		25p brt vio, typo. ('72)	5	5
549A	A167	25p cit ('63)	15	5
550	A167	50p blue	30	5
550A	A167	50p yel org ('69)	10	5
551	A172	100p citron	40	10
551A	A172	150p org ('64)	30	15
552	A172	2af lt grn	1.00	60
		Nos. 549-552 (7)	2.35	1.05

Zahir Shah Types of 1951
Imprint: "Thomas De La Rue & Co. Ltd."
Photo., Engr., Engr. & Litho.

1962 ***Perf. 13x12, 13***

552A	A123	75p brt pur	1.50	35
552B	A123	1af car & ultra	1.85	42
552C	A124	2af blue	2.25	95
552D	A124	3af org & blk	5.25	1.40

1962, July 2 **Photo.** ***Perf. 14x13½***

553	A187	2p rose lil & brn		
554	A187	2p ol bis & brn		
555	A187	5p dp org & dk grn		
556	A187	10p gray & mag		
557	A187	15p bl & brn		
558	A187	25p org yel & pur		
559	A187	50p lt grn & pur		
560	A187	75p brt cit & brn		
561	A187	100p dp org & brn		
		Nos. 553-561 (9)	1.40	

Issued to commemorate the 15th anniversary of UNESCO (U.N. Educational, Scientific and Cultural Organization). Souvenir sheets exist, perf. and imperf. One contains Nos. 558–559 with purple marginal inscription; the other contains one each of Nos. 560–561 with brown marginal inscription and black control numbers. Size: 99x80mm. Price, $4 each.

Ahmad Shah
A188

Afghan Hound
A189

1962, Feb. 24 **Photo.** ***Perf. 13½***

562	A188	50p red brn & gray	15	10
563	A188	75p grn & sal	25	20
564	A188	100p cl & bis	40	30

Issued to honor Ahmad Shah (1724–1773), who founded the Afghan kingdom in 1747 and ruled until 1773.

1962, Apr. 21 ***Perf. 14x13½***

Designs: 5p, 75p, Afghan cock. 10p, 100p, Kondjid plant. 15p, 125p, Astrakhan skins.

565	A189	2p rose & brn		
566	A189	2p lt grn & brn		
567	A189	5p dp rose & cl		
568	A189	10p lt grn & sl grn		
569	A189	15p bl grn & blk		
570	A189	25p bl & brn		
571	A189	50p gray & brn		
572	A189	75p rose lil & lil		
573	A189	100p gray & dl grn		
574	A189	125p rose brn & blk		
		Nos. 565-574 (10)	2.00	

Issued for Agriculture Day. Perf. and imperf. souvenir sheets exist. Set of 4 sheets, price $4.

Athletes with Flag and Nadir Shah
A190

Woman in National Costume
A191

1962, Aug. 23 ***Perf. 12***

575	A190	25p multi	12	5
576	A190	50p multi	18	6
577	A190	150p multi	25	8

44th Independence Day.

1962, Aug. 30 ***Perf. 11½x12***

578	A191	25p lil & brn	12	6
579	A191	50p grn & brn	25	15

Issued for Women's Day. For souvenir sheet see note after No. C16.

Man and Woman with Flag
A192

Malaria Eradication Emblem and Swamp
A193

1962, Aug. 31 **Photogravure**

580	A192	25p blk, pale bl & red	12	6
581	A192	50p blk, grn & red	25	12
582	A192	150p blk, pink & red	60	20

Issued for "Free Pashtunistan Day."

1962, Sept. 5 ***Perf. 14x13½***

583	A193	2p dk grn & ol gray		
584	A193	2p dk grn & sal		
585	A193	5p red brn & ol		
586	A193	10p red brn & brt grn		
587	A193	15p red brn & gray		
588	A193	25p brt bl & bluish grn		
589	A193	50p brt bl & rose lil		
590	A193	75p blk & bl		
591	A193	100p blk & brt pink		
592	A193	150p blk & bis brn		
593	A193	175p blk & org		
		Nos. 583-593 (11)	2.25	

Issued for the World Health Organization drive to eradicate malaria. Perf. and imperf. souvenir sheets exist. Set of 4 sheets, price $6.50.

National Assembly Building
A194

Lithographed

1962, Sept. 10 ***Perf. 10½*** **Unwmkd.**

594	A194	25p lt grn	8	6
595	A194	50p blue	12	8
596	A194	75p rose	15	12
597	A194	100p violet	25	20
598	A194	125p ultra	28	25
		Nos. 594-598 (5)	88	71

Establishment of the National Assembly.

Stamps not listed in this Catalogue or mentioned in "For the Record" (unless recent issues) usually are revenues, locals or labels.

Horse Racing
A195

Designs: 3p, Wrestling. 4p, Weight lifting. 5p, Soccer.

1962, Sept. 22 Photo. *Perf. 12*

Black Inscriptions

599 A195 1p lt ol & red brn
600 A195 2p lt grn & red brn
601 A195 3p yel & dk pur
602 A195 4p pale bl & grn
603 A195 5p bluish grn & dk brn
Nos. 599-603,C17-C22 (11) 2.50

Issued to commemorate the 4th Asian Games, Djakarta, Indonesia. Two souvenir sheets exist. A perforated one contains a 125p blue, dark blue and brown stamp in horse racing design. An imperf. one contains a 2af buff, purple and black stamp in soccer design. Both sheets have black control number. Size: 64x90mm. Price, $4.50 each.

Runners
A196

Designs: 1p, 2p, Diver (vert.). 4p, Peaches. 5p, Iris (vert.).

Perf. 11½x12, 12x11½

1962, Oct. 2 Unwmkd.

604 A196 1p rose lil & brn
605 A196 2p bl & brn
606 A196 3p brt bl & lil
607 A196 4p ol gray & multi
608 A196 5p gray & multi
Nos. 604-608, C23-C25 (8) 2.00

Issued for Children's Day.

King Type of 1961, Dated "1962"

Various Frames

1962, Oct. 15 *Perf. 13½*

609 A183 25p lil rose & brn 8 8
610 A183 50p org brn & grn 15 15
611 A183 75p bl & lake 22 22
612 A183 100p grn & red brn 30 30

Issued to honor King Mohammed Zahir Shah on his 48th birthday.

Grapes
A197

Designs: 3p, Pears. 4p, Wistaria. 5p, Blossoms.

1962, Oct. 16 *Perf. 12*

Fruit and Flowers in Natural Colors; Carmine Crescent

613 A197 1p dp rose
614 A197 2p blue
615 A197 3p lilac
616 A197 4p gray brn
617 A197 5p gray
Nos. 613-617, C26-C28 (8) 1.20

For the Afghan Red Crescent Society.

U.N. Headquarters, N.Y. and Flags of U.N. and Afghanistan
A198

1962, Oct. 24 Unwmkd.

Flags in Original Colors, Black Inscriptions

618 A198 1p ol bis
619 A198 2p lil rose
620 A198 3p dl vio
621 A198 4p green
622 A198 5p redsh brn
Nos. 618-622, C29-C31 (8) 1.50

Issued for United Nations Day. Souvenir sheets exist. One contains a single 4af ultramarine stamp, perforated; the other, a 4af ocher stamp, imperf. Both sheets have a black marginal inscription and control number. Size: 89x65mm. Price, 2 sheets, $6.50.

Boy Scout Pole Vault
A199 A200

1962, Oct. 18 Photo. *Perf. 12*

623 A199 1p yel, dk grn & sal
624 A199 2p dl yel, sl & sal
625 A199 3p rose, blk & sal
626 A199 4p multi
Nos. 623-626, C32-C35 (8) 1.75

Issued to honor the Boy Scouts.

1962, Oct. 25 *Perf. 12* Unwmkd.

Designs: 3p, High jump. 4p, 5p, Different blossoms.

627 A200 1p lil & dk grn
628 A200 2p yel grn & brn
629 A200 3p bis & vio
630 A200 4p sal pink, grn & ultra
631 A200 5p yel, grn & bl
Nos. 627-631, C36-C37 (7) 1.40

Issued for Teacher's Day.

Rockets—A201

1962, Nov. 29

632 A201 50p pale lil & dk bl 60
633 A201 100p lt bl & red brn 1.25

Issued to commemorate the United Nations World Meteorological Day. A souvenir sheet contains one 5af pink and green stamp, green marginal inscription and black control number. Size: 89x65mm. Price $8.

Ansari Mausoleum, Herat
A202

Photogravure

1963, Jan. 3 *Perf. 13½* Unwmkd.

634 A202 50p pur & grn 12 12
635 A202 75p gray & mag 18 18
636 A202 100p org brn & brn 30 30

Issued to honor Khwaja Abdullah Ansari, Sufi, religious leader and poet, on the 900th anniversary of his death.

Sheep—A203

Silkworm, Cocoons, Moth and Mulberry Branch
A204

1963, March 1 *Perf. 12*

637 A203 1p grnsh bl & blk
638 A203 2p yel grn & blk
639 A203 3p lil rose & blk
640 A204 4p gray, grn & brn
641 A204 5p red lil, grn & brn
Nos. 637-641, C42-C44 (8) 1.75

Issued for the Day of Agriculture.

Rice—A205

Designs: 3p, Corn. 300p, Wheat emblem.

1963, March 27 *Perf. 14* Unwmkd.

642 A205 2p gray, cl & grn 8 8
643 A205 3p grn, yel & ocher 12 12
644 A205 300p dk bl & yel 45 45

Issued for the "Freedom from Hunger" campaign of the U.N. Food and Agriculture Organization.

Meteorological Measuring Instrument
A206

Designs: 3p, 10p, Weather station. 4p, 5p, Rockets in space.

1963, May 23 Photo. *Perf. 13½x14*

645 A206 1p dp mag & brn
646 A206 2p brt bl & brn
647 A206 3p red & brn
648 A206 4p org & lil
649 A206 5p grn & dl vio

Imperf.

650 A206 10p red brn & grn
Nos. 645-650, C46-C50 (11) 9.50

Issued to commemorate the United Nations Third World Meteorological Day, Mar. 23.

Independence Monument
A207

1963, Aug. 23 Litho. *Perf. 10½*

651 A207 25p lt grn 10 6
652 A207 50p orange 20 15
653 A207 150p rose car 50 35

Issued to commemorate the 45th Independence Day.

Pathans in Forest
A208

1963, Aug. 31 *Perf. 10½* Unwmkd.

654 A208 25p pale vio 10 6
655 A208 50p sky bl 20 18
656 A208 150p dl red brn 60 50

Issued for "Free Pashtunistan Day."

National Assembly Building
A209

1963, Sept. 10 *Perf. 11*

657 A209 25p gray 6 6
658 A209 50p dl red 12 8
659 A209 75p brown 20 15
660 A209 100p olive 30 15
661 A209 125p lilac 40 20
Nos. 657-661 (5) 1.08 64

Issued to honor the National Assembly.

Balkh Gate
A210

1963, Oct. 8

662 A210 3af choc (screened margins) 60 40
a. white margins 1.50 50

In the original printing (No. 662), a halftone screen extended across the plate, covering the space between the stamps. A retouch removed the screen between the stamps (No. 662a).

Zahir Shah A211 — Kemal Ataturk A212

1963, Oct. 15 *Perf. 10½*

663	A211	25p green	10	5
664	A211	50p gray	20	8
665	A211	75p car rose	30	15
666	A211	100p dl redsh brn	40	18

Issued to honor King Mohammed Zahir Shah on his 49th birthday.

1963, Oct. 10 *Perf. 10½*

667	A212	1af blue	15	12
668	A212	3af rose lil	60	50

Issued to commemorate the 25th anniversary of the death of Kemal Ataturk, president of Turkey.

"Tiger's Head" of 1878—A214

1964, March 22 Photo. *Perf. 12*

675	A214	1.25af gold, grn & blk	20	10
676	A214	5af gold, rose car & blk	50	35

Issued to honor philately.

Unisphere and Flags—A215

1964, May 3 *Perf. 13½x14*

677	A215	6af crim, gray & grn	40	30

New York World's Fair, 1964–65.

Hand Holding Torch
A216

Photogravure

1964, May 12 *Perf. 14x13½*

678	A216	3.75af brt bl, org, yel & blk	25	25

Issued to commemorate the first United Nations Seminar on Human Rights in Kabul, May 1964. The denomination in Persian at right erroneously reads "3.25" but the stamp was sold and used as 3.75af.

Kandahar Airport
A217

1964, Apr. **Litho.** *Perf. 10½, 11*

679	A217	7.75af dk red brn	60	30
680	A217	9.25af lt grn	75	35
681	A217	10.50af lt grn	75	40
682	A217	13.75af car rose	90	50

Inauguration of Kandahar Airport.

Snow Leopard
A218

Designs: 50p, Ibex (vert.). 75p, Head of argali. 5af, Yak.

1964, June 25 Photogravure *Perf. 12*

683	A218	25p yel & bl	8	8
684	A218	50p dl red & grn	8	8
685	A218	75p Prus bl & lil	8	8
686	A218	5af brt grn & dk brn	30	30

View of Herat
A219

Flag and Map of Afghanistan
A220

Design: 75p, Tomb of Queen Gowhar Shad (vert.).

Perf. 13½x14, 14x13½

1964, July 12

687	A219	25p sep & bl	5	5
688	A219	75p dp bl & buff	5	5
689	A220	3af red, blk & grn	30	10

Issued for tourist publicity.

Wrestling
A221

Designs: 25p, Hurdling (vert.). 1af, Diving (vert.). 5af, Soccer.

1964, July 26 *Perf. 12*

690	A221	25p ol bis, blk & car	5	5
691	A221	1af bl grn, blk & car	8	8
692	A221	3.75af yel grn, blk & car	35	35
693	A221	5af brn, blk & car	45	45
a.		Souv. sheet of 4	1.10	1.10

Issued to commemorate the 18th Olympic Games, Tokyo, Oct. 10–25, 1964. No. 693a contains 4 imperf. stamps similar to Nos. 690–693, black inscription. Size: 95x95mm. Sold for 15af. The additional 5af went to the Afghanistan Olympic Committee.

Flag and Outline of Nadir Shah's Tomb
A222

1964, Aug. 24 Photogravure

695	A222	25p gold, bl, blk, red & grn	7	7
696	A222	75p gold, bl, blk, red & grn	10	10

Issued to commemorate Independence Day. The stamps were printed with an erroneous inscription in upper left corner: "33rd year of independence." This was locally obliterated with a typographed gold bar.

Pashtunistan Flag A223 — Zahir Shah A225

1964, Sept. 1 **Unwmkd.**

697	A223	100p gold, blk, red, bl & grn	7	7

Issued for "Free Pashtunistan Day."

1964, Oct. 17 *Perf. 14x13½*

699	A225	1.25af gold & yel grn	10	5
700	A225	3.75af gold & rose	20	15
701	A225	50af gold & gray	3.00	2.50

Issued to honor King Mohammed Zahir Shah on his 50th birthday.

Coat of Arms of Afghanistan and U.N. Emblem
A226

1964, Oct. 24 *Perf. 13½x14*

702	A226	5af gold, blk & dl bl	30	20

Issued for United Nations Day.

Emblem of Afghanistan Women's Association
A227

1964, Nov. 9 Photo. **Unwmkd.**

703	A227	25p pink, dk bl & emer	5	5
704	A227	75p aqua, dk bl & emer	5	5
705	A227	1af sil, dk bl & emer	10	5

Issued for Women's Day.

Abdul Rahman Jami
A228

Lithographed

1964, Nov. 23 *Perf. 11 Rough*

706	A228	1.50af blk, emer & yel	1.25	

Issued to commemorate the 550th anniversary of the birth of the poet Mowlana Nooruddin Abdul Rahman Jami (1414–1492).

Woodpecker
A229

Birds: 3.75af, Black-throated jay (vert.). 5af, Impeyan pheasant (vert.).

Perf. 13½x14, 14x13½

1965, Apr. 20 Photo. **Unwmkd.**

707	A229	1.25af multi	12	6
708	A229	3.75af multi	30	20
709	A229	5af multi	40	20

ITU Emblem, Old and New Communication Equipment
A230

1965, May 17 *Perf. 13½x14*

710	A230	5af lt bl, blk & red	35	35

Issued to commemorate the centenary of the International Telecommunication Union.

"Red City," Bamian
A231

Designs: 3.75af, Ruins of ancient Bamian city. 5af, Bandé Amir, mountain lakes.

1965, May 30 *Perf. 13x13½*

711	A231	1.25af pink & multi	10	10
712	A231	3.75af lt bl & multi	25	25
713	A231	5af yel & multi	40	40

Issued for tourist publicity.

ICY Emblem
A232

1965, June 25 *Perf. 13½x13*

714	A232	5af grn, yel, blk, red & vio bl	25	25

International Cooperation Year, 1965.

ARIANA Air Lines Emblem and DC-3
A233

Designs: 5af, DC-6 at right. 10af, DC-3 on top.

Perf. 13½x14

1965, July 15 Photo. **Unwmkd.**

715	A233	1.25af brt bl, gray & blk	10	10
716	A233	5af red lil, blk & bl	30	30
717	A233	10af bis, blk, bl gray & grn	75	75
a.		Souv. sheet of 3	1.25	1.25

Issued to commemorate the 10th anniversary of Afghan Air Lines, ARIANA. No. 717a contains 3 imperf. stamps similar to Nos. 715-717; blue marginal inscription, black control number. Size: 90x90mm.

Nadir Shah
A234

1965, Aug. 23 *Perf. 14x13½*

718	A234	1af dl grn, blk & red brn	12	12

For the 47th Independence Day.

Flag of Pashtunistan
A235

Perf. 13½x14

1965, Aug. 31 Photo. **Unwmkd.**

719	A235	1af ultra, blk, gold, car & grn	10	10

Issued for "Free Pashtunistan Day."

Zahir Shah Signing Constitution
A236

1965, Sept. 11 *Perf. 13x13½*

720	A236	1.50af brt grn & blk	25	25

Promulgation of the new Constitution.

Zahir Shah and Oak Leaves
A237

1965, Oct. 14 *Perf. 14x13½*

721	A237	1.25af blk, ultra & sal	20	15
722	A237	6af blk, lt bl & rose lil	60	50

Issued to honor King Mohammed Zahir Shah on his 51st birthday.

Flags of UN and Afghanistan
A238

1965, Oct. 24 *Perf. 13½x14*

723	A238	5af multi	30	30

Issued for United Nations Day.

Dappled Ground Gecko
A239

Designs: 4af, Caucasian agamid (lizard). 8af, Horsfield's tortoise.

Perf. 13½x14

1966, May 10 Photo. **Unwmkd.**

724	A239	3af tan & multi	30	30
725	A239	4af brt grn & multi	30	30
726	A239	8af vio & multi	50	50

Soccer Player and Globe
A240

1966, July 31 Litho. *Perf. 14x13½*

727	A240	2af rose red & blk	75	25
728	A240	6af vio bl & blk	1.50	35
729	A240	12af bis brn & blk	3.00	75

Issued to commemorate the World Cup Soccer Championship, Wembley, England, July 11-30.

Cotton Flower and Boll
A241

Designs: 5af, Silkworm. 7af, Farmer plowing with oxen.

1966, July 31 *Perf. 13½x14*

730	A241	1af multi	15	10
731	A241	5af multi	40	30
732	A241	7af multi	60	40

Issued for the Day of Agriculture.

Independence Monument
A242

1966, Aug. 23 Photo. *Perf. 13½x14*

733	A242	1af multi	10	10
734	A242	3af multi	35	25

Issued to commemorate Independence Day.

Flag of Pashtunistan
A243

1966, Aug. 31 Litho. *Perf. 11 rough*

735	A243	1af brt bl	25	10

Issued for "Free Pashtunistan Day."

Bagh-i-Bala Park Casino
A244

Designs: 2af, Map of Afghanistan. 8af, Tomb of Abd-er-Rahman. The casino on 4af is tne former summer palace of Abd-er-Rahman near Kabul.

1966, Oct. 3 Photo. *Perf. 13½x14*

736	A244	2af red & multi	18	15
737	A244	4af multi	40	30
738	A244	8af multi	65	60
a.		Souvenir sheet of 3	1.50	1.50

Issued for tourist publicity. No. 738a contains 3 imperf. stamps similar to Nos. 736-738: light yellow margin with black inscription and control number. Size: 110x80mm.

Zahir Shah
A245

UNESCO Emblem
A246

1966, Oct. 14 *Perf. 14x13½*

739	A245	1af dk sl grn	20	10
740	A245	5af red brn	50	25

Issued to honor King Mohammed Zahir Shah on his 52nd birthday. See Nos. 760-761.

1967, Mar. 6 **Litho.** *Perf. 12*

741	A246	2af multi	75	20
742	A246	6af multi	1.00	20
743	A246	12af multi	2.00	40

Issued to commemorate the 20th anniversary of UNESCO (United Nations Educational, Scientific and Cultural Organization).

Zahir Shah and U.N. Emblem
A247

1967 **Photogravure**

744	A247	5af multi	50	20
745	A247	10af multi	1.00	40

Issued to commemorate the 20th anniversary of the U.N. International Organization for Refugees.

New Power Station
A248

Designs: 5af, Carpet (vert.). 8af, Cement factory.

1967, Jan. 7 Photo. *Perf. 13½x14*

746	A248	2af red lil & ol grn	12	8
747	A248	5af multi	30	25
748	A248	8af blk, dk bl & tan	50	35

Issued to publicize industrial development.

International Tourist Year Emblem
A249

Designs: 6af, International Tourist Year emblem and map of Afghanistan.

1967, May 11 **Photo.** *Perf. 12*

749	A249	2af yel, blk & lt bl	15	10
750	A249	6af bis brn, blk & lt bl	50	30
a.		Souv. sheet of 3	1.00	1.00

Issued for International Tourist Year, 1967. No. 750a contains 2 imperf. stamps similar to Nos. 749-750 with black marginal inscription. Size: 110x70mm. Sold for 10af.

Power Dam, Dorunta
A250

Macaque
A251

Designs: 6af, Sirobi Dam (vert.). 8af, Reservoir at Jalalabad.

1967, July 2 **Photo.** *Perf. 12*

751	A250	1af dk grn & lil	6	6
752	A250	6af red brn & grnsh bl	35	35
753	A250	8af plum & dk bl	50	50

Issued to publicize progress in agriculture through electricity.

1967, July 28 **Photo.** *Perf. 12*

Designs: 6af, Striped hyena (horiz.). 12af, Persian gazelles (horiz.).

754	A251	2af dl yel & ind	12	12
755	A251	6af lt grn & sep	35	35
756	A251	12af lt bl & red brn	75	75

Pashtun Dancers
A252

1967, Sept. 1 **Photo.** *Perf. 12*

757	A252	2af mag & vio	12	12

Issued for "Free Pashtunistan Day."

Retreat of British at Maiwand
A253

Fireworks and U.N. Emblem
A254

1967, Aug. 24

758	A253	1af dk brn & org ver	7	7
759	A253	2af dk brn & brt pink	12	12

Issued to commemorate Independence Day.

King Type of 1966.

1967, Oct. 15 Photo. *Perf. 14x13½*

760 A245 2af brn red 12 10
761 A245 8af dk bl 50 25

Issued to honor King Mohammed Zahir Shah on his 53rd birthday.

1967, Oct. 24 Litho. *Perf. 12*

762 A254 10af vio bl & multi 65 35

Issued for United Nations Day.

Greco-Roman Wrestlers A255

Said Jamalluddin Afghan A256

Design: 6af, Wrestlers (free style).

1967, Nov. 20 Photogravure

763 A255 4af ol grn & rose lil 25 12
764 A255 6af dp car & brn 40 20
a. Souv. sheet of 2 1.10 1.10

Issued to publicize the 1968 Olympic Games. No. 764a contains 2 imperf. stamps similar to Nos. 763–764. Rose lilac marginal inscription and black control number. Size: 100x65mm.

1967, Nov. 27

765 A256 1af magenta 7 7
766 A256 5af brown 35 20

Issued to honor Said Jamalluddin Afghan, politician (1839–1897).

Bronze Vase, 11th–12th Centuries A257

WHO Emblem A258

Design: 7af, Bronze vase, Ghasnavide era, 11th–12th centuries.

1967, Dec. 23 Photo. *Perf. 12*

767 A257 3af lt grn & brn 18 15
768 A257 7af yel & sl grn 42 30
a. Souv. sheet of 2 1.25 1.25

No. 768a contains 2 imperf. stamps similar to Nos. 767–768. Slate green marginal inscription and black control number. Size: 65x100mm.

1968, Apr. 7 Photo. *Perf. 12*

769 A258 2af cit & brt bl 8 8
770 A258 7af rose & brt bl 28 22

Issued to commemorate the 20th anniversary of the World Health Organization.

Karakul A259

1968, May 20 Photo. *Perf. 12*

771 A259 1af yel & blk 6 5
772 A259 6af lt bl & blk 35 20
773 A259 12af lt ultra & dk brn 70 40

Issued for the Day of Agriculture.

Map of Afghanistan A260

Victory Tower, Ghazni A261

Cinereous Vulture A262

Design: 16af, Mausoleum, Ghazni.

1968, June 3 *Perf. 13½x14, 12*

774 A260 2af red, blk, lt bl & grn 12 8
775 A261 3af yel, dk brn & lt bl 18 10
776 A261 16af pink & multi 95 50

Issued for tourist publicity.

1968, July 3 *Perf. 12*

Birds: 6af, Eagle owl. 7af, Greater flamingoes.

777 A262 1af sky bl & multi 7 5
778 A262 6af yel & multi 45 20
779 A262 7af multi 50 30

Game of "Peg-sticking" A263

Designs: 2af, Olympic flame and rings (vert.). 12af, Buzkashi.

1968, July 20 Photo. *Perf. 12*

780 A263 2af multi 12 7
781 A263 8af org & multi 50 30
782 A263 12af multi 75 45

19th Olympic Games, Mexico City, Oct. 12–27.

Flower-decked Armored Car A264

1968, Aug. 23

783 A264 6af multi 40 20

Issued to commemorate Independence Day.

Flag of Pashtunistan A265

1968, Aug. 31 Photo. *Perf. 12*

784 A265 3af multi 25 10

Issued for "Free Pashtunistan Day."

Zahir Shah A266

Human Rights Flame A267

1968, Oct. 14 Photo. *Perf. 12*

785 A266 2af ultra 12 6
786 A266 8af brown 45 28

Issued to honor King Mohammed Zahir Shah on his 54th birthday.

1968, Oct. 24

787 A267 1af multi 10 5
788 A267 2af vio, bis & blk 25 6
789 A267 6af vio blk, bis & vio 50 20

Souvenir Sheet

Imperf.

790 A267 10af plum, bis & red org 1.00 1.00

Issued for International Human Rights Year. No. 790 contains one stamp. Bister margin with plum inscription and black control number. Size: 100x65mm.

Maolana Djalalodine Balkhi A268

Kushan Mural A269

1968, Nov. 26 Photo. *Perf. 12*

791 A268 4af dk grn & mag 27 12

Maolana Djalalodine Balkhi (1207–1273), historian.

1969, Jan. 2 *Perf. 12*

Design: 3af, Jug shaped like female torso.

792 A269 1af dk grn, mar & yel 10 5
793 A269 3af vio, gray & mar 25 10
a. Souv. sheet of 2 40 40

Issued to publicize the archaeological finds at Bagram, 1st century B.C. to 2nd century A.D.

No. 793a contains 2 imperf. stamps similar to Nos. 792–793. Maroon marginal inscription and black control number. Size: 100x65mm.

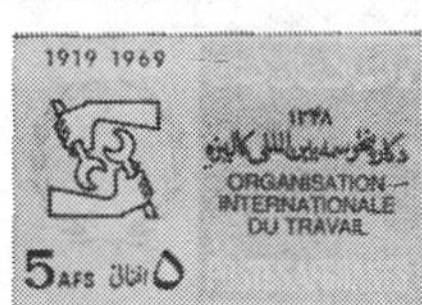

ILO Emblem A270

1969, Mar. 23 Photo. *Perf. 12*

794 A270 5af lt yel, lem & blk 30 18
795 A270 8af lt bl, grnsh bl & blk 50 30

Issued for the 50th anniversary of the International Labor Organization.

Arms Type of 1939

1969, May (?) Typographed

795A A79 100p dk grn 8 5
795B A79 150p dp brn 10 6

Nos. 795A–795B were normally used as newspaper stamps.

Badakhshan Scene A271

Designs: 2af, Map of Afghanistan. 7af, Three men on mules ascending the Pamir Mountains.

1969, July 6 Photo. *Perf. 13½x14*

796 A271 2af ocher & multi 15 6
797 A271 4af multi 25 12
798 A271 7af multi 55 22
a. Souv. sheet of 3 1.10 1.10

Issued for tourist publicity. No. 798a contains 3 imperf. stamps similar to Nos. 796–798. Black marginal inscription and control number. Size: 136x90½mm. Sold for 15af.

Bust, from Hadda Treasure, 3rd–5th Centuries A272

Zahir Shah and Queen Humeira A273

Designs: 5af, Vase and jug. 10af, Statue of crowned woman. 5af and 10af from Bagram treasure, 1st–2nd centuries.

1969, Aug. 3 Photo. *Perf. 14x13½*

799 A272 1af ol grn & gold 5 5
800 A272 5af pur & gold 20 16
801 A272 10af dp bl & gold 40 32

1969, Aug. 23 *Perf. 12*

802 A273 5af gold, dk bl & red brn 35 20
803 A273 10af gold, dp lil & bl grn 65 35

Issued to commemorate Independence Day.

Map of Pashtunistan and Rising Sun A274

1969, Aug. 31 Typo. *Perf. 10½*

804 A274 2af lt bl & red 12 6

Issued for "Free Pashtunistan Day."

Zahir Shah A275

1969, Oct. 14 Photo. *Perf. 12*

Portrait in Natural Colors

805 A275 2af dk brn & gold 15 6
806 A275 6af brn & gold 45 20

Issued to honor King Mohammed Zahir Shah on his 55th birthday.

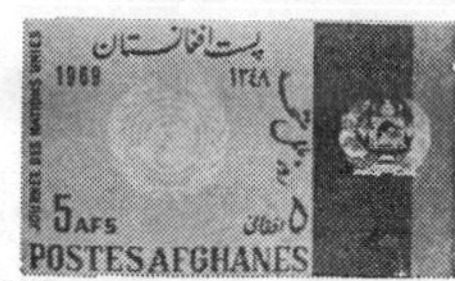

U.N. Emblem and Flag of Afghanistan—A276

1969, Oct. 24 Litho. ***Perf. 13½***

807 A276 5af bl & multi 27 16

Issued for United Nations Day.

ITU Emblem A277 — Wild Boar A278

1969, Nov. 12

808 A277 6af ultra & multi 30 20
809 A277 12af rose & multi 60 35

Issued for World Telecommunications Day.

1969, Dec. 7 Photo. ***Perf. 12***

Designs: 1af, Long-tailed porcupine. 8af, Red deer.

810 A278 1af yel & multi 6 5
811 A278 3af bl & multi 18 10
812 A278 8af pink & multi 50 25

Man's First Footprints on Moon, and Earth A279

1969, Dec. 28 ***Perf. 13½x14***

813 A279 1af yel grn & multi 6 5
814 A279 3af yel & multi 17 10
815 A279 6af bl & multi 30 20
816 A279 10af rose & multi 50 32

Moon landing. See note after Algeria No. 427.

Anti-cancer Symbol A280 — Mirza Abdul Quader Bedel A281

1970, Apr. 7 Photogravure ***Perf. 14***

817 A280 2af dk grn & rose car 15 6
818 A280 6af dk bl & rose cl 40 20

Issued to publicize the fight against cancer.

1970, May 6 ***Perf. 14x13½***

819 A281 5af multi 27 15

Issued for the 250th anniversary of the death of Mirza Abdul Quader Bedel (1643–1720), poet.

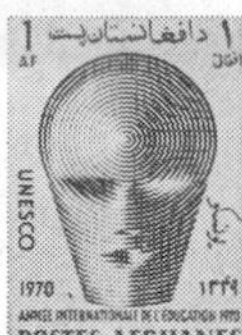

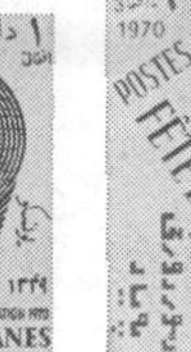

Education Year Emblem A282 — Mother and Child A283

1970, June 7 Photo. ***Perf. 12***

820 A282 1af black 6 5
821 A282 6af dp rose 35 20
822 A282 12af green 75 35

International Education Year 1970.

1970, June 15 ***Perf. 13½***

823 A283 6af yel & multi 27 20

Issued for Mother's Day.

U.N. Emblem, Scales of Justice, Spacecraft A284

1970, June 26

824 A284 4af yel, dk bl & dp bl 20 12
825 A284 6af sal pink, dk bl & brt bl 35 20

25th anniversary of United Nations.

Mosque of the Amir of the two Swords, Kabul—A285

Designs: 2af, Map of Afghanistan. 7af, Arch of Paghman.

1970, July 6 ***Perf. 12***

Size: 30½x30½mm.

826 A285 2af lt bl, blk & cit 12 6

Size: 36x26mm.

827 A285 3af pink & multi 18 10
828 A285 7af yel & multi 42 22

Issued for tourist publicity.

Zahir Shah Reviewing Troops A286

1970, Aug. 23 Photo. ***Perf. 13½***

829 A286 8af multi 60 25

Issued to commemorate Independence Day.

Pathans A287

1970, Aug. 31 Typo. ***Perf. 10½***

830 A287 2af ultra & red 12 6

Issued for "Free Pashtunistan Day."

Quail A288

Dsigns: 4af, Golden eagle. 6af, Ring-necked pheasant.

1970, Sept. Photo. ***Perf. 12***

831 A288 2af multi 8 6
832 A288 4af multi 16 12
833 A288 6af multi 24 20

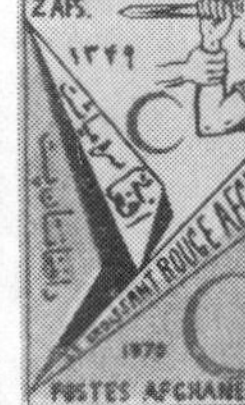

Zahir Shah A289 — Red Crescents A290

1970, Oct. 14 Photo. ***Perf. 14x13½***

834 A289 3af grn & vio 20 10
835 A289 7af dk bl & vio brn 60 22

Issued to honor King Mohammed Zahir Shah on his 56th birthday.

1970, Oct. 16 Typo. ***Perf. 10½***

836 A290 2af blk, gold & red 12 6

Issued for the Red Crescent Society.

U. N. Emblem and Charter A291

1970, Oct. 24 Photo. ***Perf. 14***

837 A291 1af gold & multi 10 5
838 A291 5af gold & multi 20 16

United Nations Day.

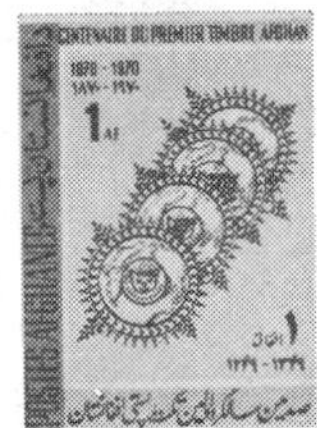

Tiger Heads of 1871 A292

1970, Nov. 10 ***Perf. 12***

839 A292 1af sal, lt grnsh bl & blk 5 5
840 A292 4af lt ultra, yel & blk 16 12
841 A292 12af lil, lt bl & blk 48 35

Issued to commemorate the centenary of the first Afghan postage stamps. The postal service was established in 1870, but the first stamps were issued in May, 1871.

Globe and Waves A293

1971, May 17 Photo. ***Perf. 13½***

842 A293 12af grn, blk & bl 60 35

3rd World Telecommunications Day.

Callimorpha Principalis A294

Designs: 3af, Epizygaenella species. 5af, Parnassius autocrator.

1971, May 30 ***Perf. 13½x14***

843 A294 1af ver & multi 5 5
844 A294 3af yel & multi 12 10
845 A294 5af ultra & multi 20 15

"UNESCO" and Half of Ancient Kushan Statue A295

1971, June 26 Photo. ***Perf. 13½***

846 A295 6af ocher & vio 40 20
847 A295 10af lt bl & mar 65 30

UNESCO-sponsored International Kushani Seminar.

Tughra and Independence Monument A296

1971, Aug. 23

848 A296 7af rose red & multi 40 22
849 A296 9af red org & multi 65 28

Independence Day.

Pashtunistan Square, Kabul A297

1971, Aug. 31 Typo. ***Perf. 10½***

850 A297 5af dp rose lil 27 15

"Free Pashtunistan Day."

Zahir Shah
A298

1971, Oct. 14 Photo. *Perf. 12½x12*

851 A298 9af lt grn & multi 40 28
852 A298 17af yel & multi 75 55

57th birthday of King Mohammed Zahir Shah.

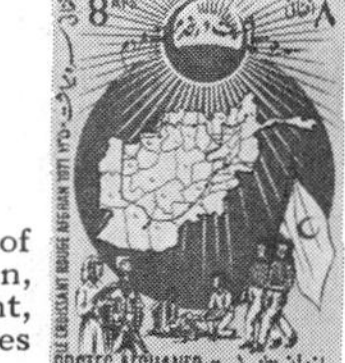

Map of Afghanistan, Red Crescent, Various Activities
A299

1971, Oct. 16 *Perf. 14x13½*

853 A299 8af lt bl, red, grn & blk 45 25

For Afghan Red Crescent Society.

Equality Year Emblem
A300

1971, Oct. 24 *Perf. 12*

854 A300 24af brt bl 1.25 70

International Year Against Racial Discrimination and United Nations Day.

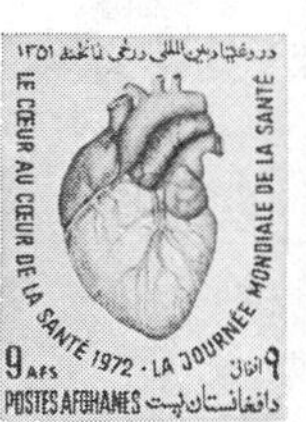

"Your Heart is your Health"
A301

Tulip
A302

1972, Apr. 7 Photo. *Perf. 14*

855 A301 9af pale yel & multi 36 28
856 A301 12af gray & multi 48 35

World Health Day.

1972, June 5 Photo. *Perf. 14*

Designs: 10af, Rock partridge (horiz.). 12af, Lynx (horiz.). 18af, Allium stipitatum (flower).

857 A302 7af grn & multi 28 22
858 A302 10af bl & multi 40 32
859 A302 12af lt grn & multi 48 35
860 A302 18af bl grn & multi 72 60

Buddhist Shrine, Hadda
A302a

Designs: 7af, Greco-Bactrian animal seal, 250 B.C. 9af, Greco-Oriental temple, Ai-Khanoum, 3rd–2nd centuries B.C.

1972, July 16 Photo. *Perf. 12*

861 A302a 3af brn & dl bl 12 9
862 A302a 7af rose cl & dl grn 28 22
863 A302a 9af grn & lil 36 30

Tourist publicity.

King and Queen Reviewing Parade
A303

1972, Aug. 23 Photo. *Perf. 13½*

864 A303 25af gold & multi 4.00 1.00

Independence Day.

Used later with king and queen part removed.

Wrestling
A304

Designs: 8af, Like 4af. 10af, 19af, 21af, Wrestling, different hold.

1972, Aug. 26

865 A304 4af ol bis & multi 20 12
866 A304 8af lt bl & multi 40 25
867 A304 10af yel grn & multi 50 32
868 A304 19af multi 90 40
869 A304 21af lil & multi 1.00 45
a. Souv. sheet of 5 3.25 3.25
Nos. 865-869 (5) 3.00 1.54

20th Olympic Games, Munich, Aug. 26–Sept. 11. No. 869a contains 5 imperf. stamps similar to Nos. 865–869. Olive bister marginal inscription and ornament, black control number. Size: 159x110mm. Sold for 60af.

Pathan and View of Tribal Territory
A305

Zahir Shah
A306

1972, Aug. 31 *Perf. 12½x12*

870 A305 5af ultra & multi 27 15

Pashtunistan day.

1972, Oct. 14 Photo. *Perf. 14x13½*

871 A306 7af gold, blk & Prus bl 1.50 30
872 A306 14af gold, blk & lt brn 3.00 50

58th birthday of King Mohammed Zahir Shah.

City Destroyed by Earthquake, Refugees—A307

1972, Oct. 16 *Perf. 13½*

873 A307 7af lt bl, red & blk 40 22

For Afghan Red Crescent Society.

U.N. Emblem
A308

1972, Oct. 24

874 A308 12af lt ultra & blk 65 35

United Nations Economic Commission for Asia and the Far East (ECAFE), 25th anniversary.

Ceramics
A309

Designs: 9af, Leather coat (vert.). 12af, Metal ware (vert.). 16af, Inlaid artifacts.

1972, Dec. 10 Photo. *Perf. 12*

875 A309 7af gold & multi 42 22
876 A309 9af gold & multi 55 28
877 A309 12af gold & multi 70 35
878 A309 16af gold & multi 1.00 50
a. Souvenir sheet of 4 2.75 2.75

Handicraft industries. No. 878a contains 4 imperf. stamps similar to Nos. 875–878. Gold marginal inscription and black control number. Size: 109x109mm. Sold for 45af.

WMO and National Emblems—A310

1973, Apr. 3 Photo. *Perf. 14*

879 A310 7af lt lil & dk grn 42 22
880 A310 14af lt bl & dp cl 85 45

Centenary of international meteorological cooperation.

Abu Rayhan al-Biruni
A311

Family
A312

1973, June 16 Photo. *Perf. 13½*

881 A311 10af multi 55 32

Millennium of birth (973-1048), philosopher and mathematician.

1973, June 30 Photo. *Perf. 13½*

882 A312 9af org & red lil 50 30

International Family Planning Federation, 21st anniversary.

Republic

Impeyan Pheasant
A313

Birds: 9af, Great crested grebe. 12af, Himalayan snow cock.

1973, July 29 Photo. *Perf. 12x12½*

883 A313 8af yel & multi 65 25
884 A313 9af bl & multi 90 30
885 A313 12af multi 1.25 35

Stylized Buzkashi Horseman
A314

1973, Aug. *Perf. 13½*

886 A314 8af black 32 25

Tourist publicity.

Fireworks
A315

1973, Aug. 23 Photo. *Perf. 12*

887 A315 12af multi 48 35

55th Independence Day.

Lake Abassine, Pashtunistan Flag
A316

1973, Aug. 31 *Perf. 14x13½*

888 A316 9af multi 50 30

Pashtunistan Day.

Red Crescent
A317

1973, Oct. 16 *Perf. 13½*

889 A317 10af red, blk & gold 60 32

Red Crescent Society.

Kemal Ataturk
A318

1973, Oct. 28 Litho. *Perf. 10½*

890	A318	1af blue	6	5
891	A318	7af redsh brn	42	22

50th anniversary of the Turkish Republic.

Human Rights Flame, Arms of Afghanistan
A319

1973, Dec. 10 Photo. *Perf. 12*

892	A319	12af sil, blk & lt bl	45	35

25th anniversary of the Universal Declaration of Human Rights.

Asiatic Black Bears
A320

1974, Mar. 26 Lithographed *Perf. 12*
Multicolored

893	A320	5af *shown*	15	12
894	A320	7af *Afghan hound*	22	20
895	A320	10af *Persian goat*	30	25
896	A320	12af *Leopard*	40	30
a.		Souvenir sheet of 4	1.25	1.25

No. 896a contains 4 imperf. stamps similar to Nos. 893–896. Magenta border and black marginal inscription. Size: 120x100mm.

Worker and Farmer
A321

1974, May 1 Photo. *Perf. 13½x12½*

897	A321	9af rose red & multi	40	25

International Labor Day, May 1.

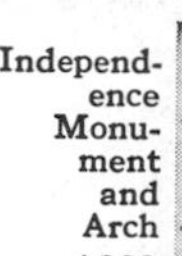

Independence Monument and Arch
A322

1974, May 27 Photo. *Perf. 12*

898	A322	4af bl & multi	12	10
899	A322	11af gold & multi	35	30

56th Independence Day.

Arms of Afghanistan and Symbol of Cooperation—A323

Pres. Mohammad Daoud Khan
A324

Designs: 5af, Flag of Republic of Afghanistan. 15af, Soldiers and coat of arms of the Republic.

1974, July 25 *Perf. 13½x12½, 14*
Sizes: 4af, 15af, 36x22mm.; 5af, 7af, 36x26, 26x36mm.

900	A323	4af multi	18	10
901	A323	5af multi	22	12
902	A324	7af grn, brn & blk	32	18
a.		Souvenir sheet of 2	70	70
903	A323	15af multi	65	40
a.		Souvenir sheet of 2	1.00	1.00

First anniversary of the Republic of Afghanistan. No. 902a contains 2 imperf. stamps similar to Nos. 901–902, No. 903a contains 2 imperf. stamps similar to Nos. 900 and 903. Both sheets have yellow margins, black inscriptions and control numbers. Sizes: No. 902a, 99x99mm., No. 903a, 120x80mm.

Lesser Spotted Eagle
A325

Birds: 6af, White-fronted goose, ruddy shelduck and gray-lag goose. 11af, European coots and European crane.

1974, Aug. 6 Photo. *Perf. 13½x13*

904	A325	1af car rose & multi	6	5
905	A325	6af bl & multi	35	15
906	A325	11af yel & multi	70	30

Nos. 904–906 printed se-tenant.

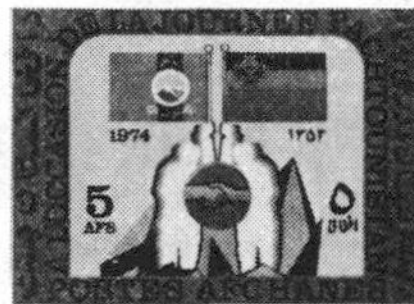

Flags of Pashtunistan and Afghanistan—A326

1974, Aug. 31 Photo. *Perf. 14*

907	A326	5af multi	27	12

Pashtunistan Day.

Coat of Arms
A327

1974, Oct. 9

908	A327	7af gold, grn & blk	22	18

Centenary of Universal Postal Union.

"UN" and UN Emblem
A328

1974, Oct. 24 Photo. *Perf. 14*

909	A328	5af lt ultra & dk bl	27	12

United Nations Day.

Minaret of Jam A329 · Buddha, Hadda A330

Design: 14af, Lady riding griffin, 2nd century, Bagram.

1975, May 5 Photo. *Perf. 13½*

910	A329	7af multi	22	15
911	A330	14af multi	44	30
912	A330	15af multi	48	30
a.		Souvenir sheet of 3	1.50	1.50

South Asia Tourism Year 1975.

No. 912a contains 3 imperf. stamps similar to Nos. 910–912. Tourism Year emblem in margin and black control number. Size: 130x90mm.

New Flag of Afghanistan
A331

1975, May 27 Photo. *Perf. 12*

913	A331	16af multi	75	35

57th Independence Day.

Celebrating Crowd
A332

1975, July 17 Photo. *Perf. 13½*

914	A332	9af bl & multi	42	20
915	A332	12af car & multi	55	28

Second anniversary of the Republic.

Women's Year Emblems
A333

1975, Aug. 24 Photo. *Perf. 12*

916	A333	9af car, lt bl & blk	28	22

International Women's Year 1975.

Pashtunistan Flag, Sun Rising Over Mountains
A334

Mohammed Akbar Khan
A335

1975, Aug. 31 *Perf. 13½*

917	A334	10af multi	30	25

Pashtunistan Day.

1976, Feb. 4 Photo. *Perf. 14*

918	A335	15af lt brn & multi	45	35

Mohammed Akbar Khan (1816–1846), warrior son of Amir Dost Mohammed Khan.

Pres. Mohammad Daoud Khan
A336 A337

1974-78 Photo. *Perf. 14*

919	A336	10af multi	60	25
920	A336	16af multi ('78)	2.50	*1.00*
921	A336	19af multi	1.00	48
922	A336	21af multi	1.25	50
923	A336	22af multi ('78)	3.50	*2.00*
924	A336	30af multi ('78)	4.50	*2.75*
925	A337	50af multi('75)	2.75	1.25
926	A337	100af multi('75)	5.25	2.50
		Nos. 919-926 (8)	21.35	*10.73*

Arms of Republic, Independence Monument
A338

1976, June 1 Photo. *Perf. 14*

927	A338	22af bl & multi	65	45

58th Independence Day.

Flag Raising
A339

1976, July 17 Photo. *Perf. 14*

928	A339	30af multi	90	75

Republic Day.

Mountain Peaks and Flag of Pashtunistan
A340

1976, Aug. 31 Photo. *Perf. 14*

929	A340	16af multi	48	38

Pashtunistan Day.

Coat of Arms—A340a

1976, Sept. Litho. *Rough Perf. 11*

929A A340a 25p salmon 25 15
930 A340a 50p lt grn 25 15
931 A340a 1af ultra 25 15

Flag and Views on Open Book A341

1977, May 27 Photo. *Perf. 14*

937 A341 20af grn & multi 60 50

59th Independence Day.

Pres. Daoud and National Assembly A342

President Taking Oath of Office A343

Designs: 10af, Inaugural address. 18af, Promulgation of Constitution.

1977, June 22

938 A342 7af multi 65 45
939 A343 8af multi 70 60
940 A343 10af multi 90 75
941 A342 18af multi 1.65 1.25
a. Souvenir sheet of 4 3.00 3.00

Election of first President and promulgation of Constitution. No. 941a contains 4 imperf. stamps similar to Nos. 938–941. Black marginal inscription and control number. Size: 135x105mm.

Jamalluddin Medal A344

1977, July 6 Photo. *Perf. 14*

942 A344 12af bl, blk & gold 35 30

Sajo Jamalluddin Afghani, reformer, 80th death anniversary.

Afghanistan Flag over Crowd A345

1977, July 17

943 A345 22af multi 65 55

Dancers, Fountain, Pashtunistan Flag A346

1977, Aug. 31

944 A346 30af multi 90 75

Pashtunistan Day.

Arms and Carrier Pigeon—A346a

1977, Oct. 30 Litho. *Perf. 11*

944A A346a 1af blk & bl 5 5

Members of Parliament Congratulating Pres. Daoud—A347

1978, Feb. 5 Litho. *Perf. 14*

945 A347 20af multi 1.75

Election of first president, first anniversary.

Map of Afghanistan, UPU Emblem A348

1978, Apr. 1 Photo. *Perf. 14*

946 A348 10af grn, blk & gold 30 25

50th anniversary of Afghanistan's membership in Universal Postal Union.

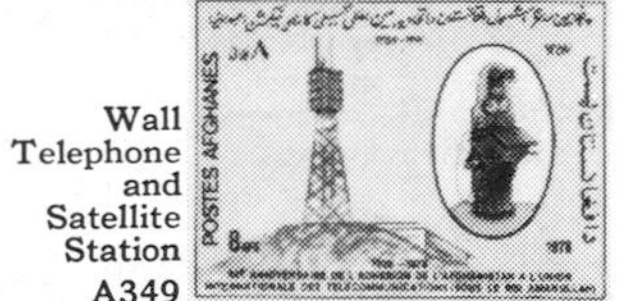

Wall Telephone and Satellite Station A349

1978, Apr. 12

947 A349 8af multi 24 20

50th anniversary of Afghanistan's membership in International Telecommunications Union.

Arrows Pointing to Crescent, Cross and Lion A350

1978, July 6 Litho. *Perf. 11 Rough*

948 A350 3af black 10 6

50th anniversary of Afghani Red Crescent Society.

Khala Party Emblem—A350a

1978, Aug. Litho. *Perf. 11*

948A A350a 1af rose red & gold 5 5
948B A350a 4af rose red & gold 12 8

Arch A351

1978, Aug. 19 *Perf. 14*

949 A351 16af Bamian Buddha 45 40
949A A351 22af shown 65 55
949B A351 30af Hazara Women 1.20 90

Democratic Republic of Afghanistan.

Men with Pashtunistan Flag A352

Coat of Arms and Emblems A353

1978, Aug. 31 *Perf. 11 Rough*

950 A352 7af ultra & red 22 16

Pashtunistan Day.

1978, Sept. 8 *Perf. 11*

951 A353 20af rose red 60 50

World Literacy Day.

A354

1978, Oct. 25 Litho. *Perf. 11½ Rough*

952 A354 18af lt grn 55 45

Hero of Afghanistan.

Khala Party Flag A355

1978, Oct. 19 Photo. *Perf. 11½*

953 A355 8af blk, red & gold 24 20
954 A355 9af blk, red & gold 30 22

"The mail serving the people."

Nour Mohammad Taraki A356

1979, Jan. 1 Litho. *Perf. 12*

955 A356 12af multi 35 10

Nour Mohammad Taraki, founder of People's Democratic Party of Afghanistan, installation as president.

Woman Breaking Chain A357

1979, Mar. 8 Litho. *Perf. 11*

956 A357 14af red & ultra 1.50 50

Women's Day. Inscribed "POSSTES."

Map of Afghanistan, Census Emblem A358

1979, Mar. 25 Litho. *Perf. 12*

957 A358 3af multi 15 10

First comprehensive population census.

Farmers A359

1979, Mar. 21

958 A359 1af multi 15 10

Agricultural advances.

Pres. Taraki Reading First Issue of Khalq—A360

1979, Apr. 11 *Perf. 12½x12*

959 A360 2af multi 10 8

Khalq, newspaper of People's Democratic Republic of Afghanistan.

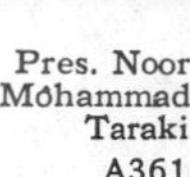

Pres. Noor Mohammad Taraki
A361

Plaza with Tank Monument and Fountain—A362

House where Revolution Started
A363

Design: 12af, House where 1st Khalq Party Congress was held.

Perf. 12, 12½x12 (A362)

1979, Apr. 27 **Lithographed**

959A A353 50p Taraki, tank 5 5
960 A361 4af multi 12 10
961 A362 5af multi 15 12
962 A363 6af multi 18 15
963 A363 12af multi 35 30
Nos. 959A-963 (5) 85 72

1st anniversary of revolution.

Carpenter and Blacksmith
A364

1979, May 1 ***Perf. 12***
964 A364 10af multi 30 25

Int'l Labor Day.

Children, Flag and Map of Afghanistan—A366

1979, June 1 **Litho.** ***Perf. 12½x12***
966 A366 16af multi 48 40

International Year of the Child.

Doves Circling Asia in Globe—A366a

1979 **Litho.** ***Perf. 11x10½***
966A A366a 2af red & bl 6 5

Armed Afghans, Kabul Memorial and Arch
A367

Pashtunistan Citizens, Flag
A368

1979, Aug. 19 **Litho.** ***Perf. 12***
967 A367 30af multi 90 75

60th anniv. of independence.

1979, Aug. 31
968 A368 9 af multi 28 22

Pashtunistan Day.

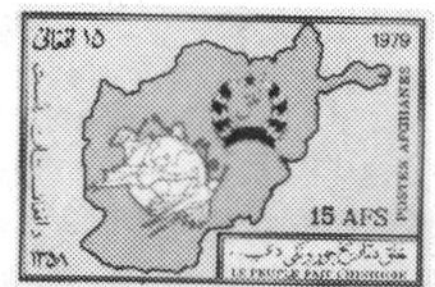

UPU Day—A369

1979, Oct. **Litho.** ***Perf. 12***
969 A369 15af multi 45 38

Tombstone—A369a

1979, Oct. 25 **Litho.** ***Perf. 12½x12***
969A A369a 22af multi 65 45

International Women's Day—A370

1980, Mar. 8 **Litho.** ***Perf. 12***
970 A370 8af multi 1.00

Farmers' Day—A371

1980, Mar. 21 **Litho.** ***Perf. 11½x12***
971 A371 2af multi 10 8

Non-smoker and Smoker—A372

1980, Apr. 7 ***Perf. 11½***
972 A372 5af multi 15 12

Anti-smoking campaign; World Health Day.

Lenin, 110th Birth Anniversary—A373

1980, Apr. 22 ***Perf. 12x12½***
973 A373 12af multi 35 30

People and Fist on Map of Afghanistan—A374

1980, Apr. 27 **Litho.** ***Perf. 12½x12***
974 A374 1af multi 5 5

Saur Revolution, 2nd anniversary.

International Workers' Solidarity Day—A375

1980, May 1
975 A375 9af multi 28 22

Wrestling, Moscow '80 Emblem—A376

1980, July 19 ***Perf. 12x12½, 12½x12***
976 A376 3af *Soccer*, vert. 20 8
977 A376 6af *shown* 35 15
978 A376 9af *Buzkashi* 55 22
979 A376 10af *Pigsticking* 60 25

22nd Summer Olympic Games, Moscow, July 19-Aug. 3.

61st Anniversary of Independence—A377

1980, Aug. 19 **Litho.** ***Perf. 12½x12***
980 A377 3af multi 10 8

Pashtunistan Day—A378

1980, Aug. 30
981 A378 25af multi 80 65

International U.P.U. Day—A379

1980, Oct. 9 **Litho.** ***Perf. 12½x12***
982 A379 20af multi 60 50

International Women's Day—A381

1981, Mar. 9 **Litho.** ***Perf. 12½x12***
984 A381 15af multi 45 38

Farmers' Day—A382

1981, Mar. 20 **Litho.** ***Perf. 12½x12***
985 A382 1af multi 5 5

Bighorn Mountain Sheep (Protected Species)—A383

1981, Apr. 4 ***Perf. 12x12½***
986 A383 12af multi 36 30

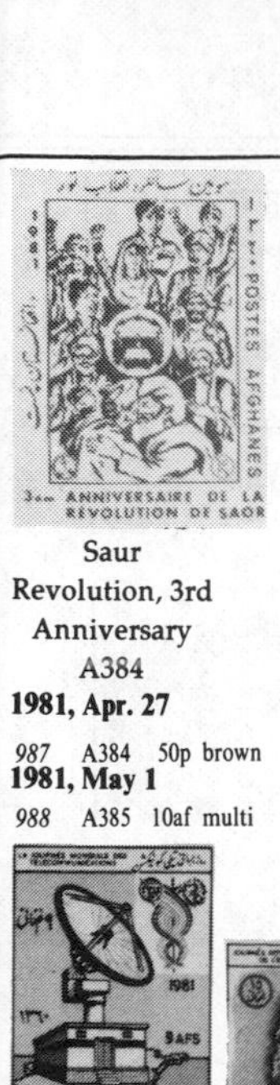

Saur Revolution, 3rd Anniversary
A384

International Workers' Solidarity Day
A385

1981, Apr. 27 ***Perf. 11***

987 A384 50p brown 5 5

1981, May 1 ***Perf. 12½x12***

988 A385 10af multi 30 25

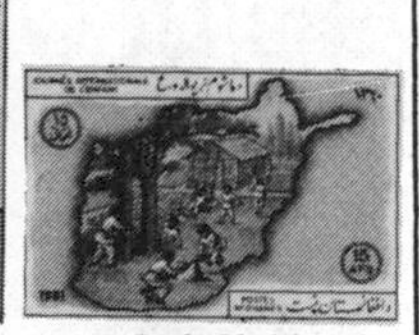

13th World Telecommunications Day
A387

Intl. Children's Day
A388

1981, May 17 **Litho.** ***Perf. 12½x12***

990 A387 9af multi 28 22

1981, June 1 ***Perf. 12x12½***

991 A388 15af multi 45 38

People's Independence Monument
62nd Anniv. of Independence—A389

1981, Aug. 19

992 A389 4af multi 12 10

Pashtunistan Day—A389a

1981, Aug. 31 **Litho.** ***Perf. 12***

992A A389a 2af multi 6 5

Intl. Tourism Day
A390

1981, Sept. 27 ***Perf. 12½x12***

993 A390 5af multi 15 12

World Food Day—A392

1981, Oct. 16

995 A392 7af multi 22 15

Asia—Africa Solidarity Meeting—A393

1981, Nov. 18 **Litho.** ***Perf. 11***

996 A393 8af blue 24 20

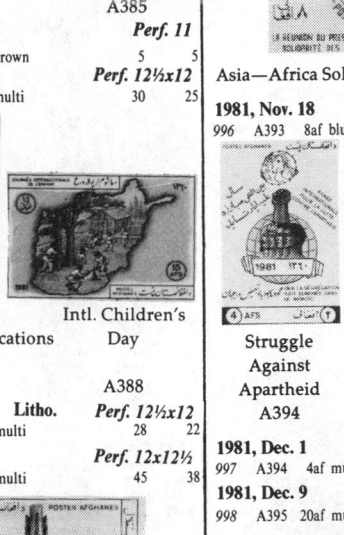

Struggle Against Apartheid
A394

1300th Anniv. of Bulgaria
A395

1981, Dec. 1 ***Perf. 12½x12***

997 A394 4af multi 12 10

1981, Dec. 9 ***Perf. 12x12½***

998 A395 20af multi 60 50

Buzkashi Game—A395a

1980 **Photo.** ***Perf. 14***

998A	A395a	50af multi	1.50	1.00
998B	A395a	100af multi	3.00	2.00

Intl. Women's Day—A396

1982, Mar. 8 **Litho.** ***Perf. 12***

999 A396 6af multi 18 15

Farmers' Day
A397

1982, Mar. 21

1000 A397 4af multi 12 10

Rhubarb Plant
A398

Saur Revolution, 4th Anniv.
A399

Designs: Various local plants.

1982, Apr. 9 **Litho.** ***Perf. 12***

1001	A398	3af Judas trees	10	8
1002	A398	4af Rose of Sharan	12	10
1003	A398	16af shown	50	40

1982, Apr. 27

1004 A399 1af multi 5 5

George Dimitrov (1882-1947), First Prime Minister of Bulgaria
A400

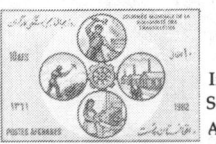

Intl. Workers' Solidarity Day
A401

1982, Apr. 30

1005 A400 30af multi 90 75

1982, May 1

1006 A401 10af multi 30 25

Storks—A402

1982, May 31

1007	A402	6af shown	20	15
1008	A402	11af Nightingales	35	28

Hedgehogs—A403

1982, July 6 **Litho.** ***Perf. 12***

1009	A403	3af shown	10	8
1010	A403	14af Cobra	45	35

See Nos. 1020-1022.

63rd Anniv. of Independence—A404

1982, Aug. 19

1011 A404 20af multi 60 50

Pashtunistan Day—A405

1982, Aug. 31

1012 A405 32af multi 1.00 80

World Tourism Day—A406

1982, Sept. 27 **Litho.** ***Perf. 12***

1013 A406 9af multi 30 22

UPU Day—A407

1982, Oct. 9

1014 A407 4af multi 12 10

World Food Day—A408

1982, Oct. 16

1015 A408 9af multi 30 22

37th Anniv. of UN—A409

1982, Oct. 24

1016 A409 15af multi 45 38

ITU Plenipotentiaries Conference, Nairobi, Sept.—A410

1982, Oct. 26

1017	A410	8af multi	25	20

TB Bacillus Centenary

A411

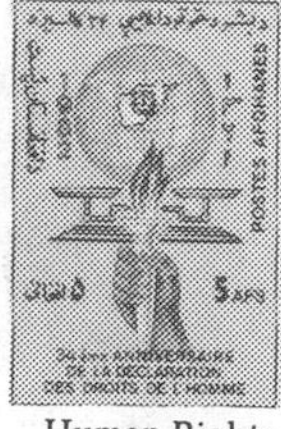

Human Rights Declaration, 34th Anniv.

A412

1982, Nov. 24 Litho. *Perf. 12*

1018	A411	7af multi	22	18

1982, Dec. 10

1019	A412	5af multi	15	12

Animal Type of 1982

1982, Dec. 16

1020	A403	2af Lions	6	5
1021	A403	7af Donkeys	22	18
1022	A403	12af Marmots, vert.	36	28

Intl. Women's Day

A413

Mir Alicher Nawai Research Decade

A414

1983, Mar. 8

1023	A413	3af multi	10	8

1983, Mar. 19

1024	A414	22af multi	70	50

Farmers' Day—A415

1983, Mar. 21 Litho. *Perf. 12*

1025	A415	10af multi	30	25

5th Anniv. of Saur Revolution—A416

1983, Apr. 27 Litho. *Perf. 12*

1026	A416	15af multi	45	38

Intl. Workers' Solidarity Day—A417

1983, May 1

1027	A417	20af multi	60	50

World Communications Year—A418

1983, May 17

1028	A418	4af Modes of communication	12	10
1029	A418	11af Building	34	28

Intl. Children's Day—A419

1983, June 1 Litho. *Perf. 12*

1030	A419	25af multi		

2nd Anniv. of National Front—A420

1983, June 15

1031	A420	1af multi		

Local Butterflies—A421

Various butterflies. 9af, 13af vert.

1983, July 6

1032	A421	9af multi		
1033	A421	13af multi		
1034	A421	21af multi		

Struggle Against Apartheid—A422

1983, Aug. 1 Litho. *Perf. 12*

1035	A422	10 af multi		

64th Anniv. of Independence—A423

1983, Aug. 19

1036	A423	6 af multi		

Parliament House—A423a

1983, Sept. Litho. *Perf. 12*

1036A	A423a	50af shown		
1036B	A423a	100af Afghan Woman, Camel		

A424

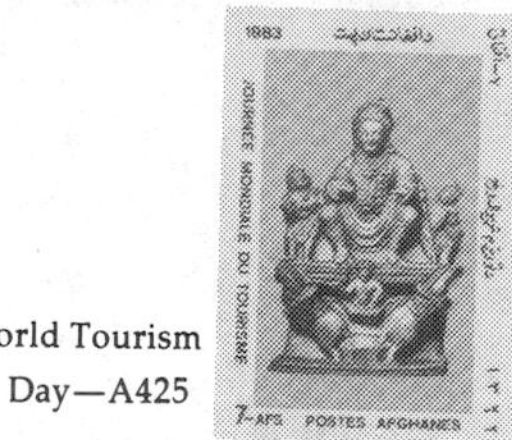

World Tourism Day—A425

1983, Sept. 27 Litho. *Perf. 12*

1037	A424	5af shown		
1038	A425	7af shown		
1039	A424	12af Golden statues		
1040	A425	16af Stone carving		

World Communications Year—A426

1983, Oct. 9 Litho. *Perf. 12*

1041	A426	14af Dish antenna, dove		
1042	A426	15af shown		

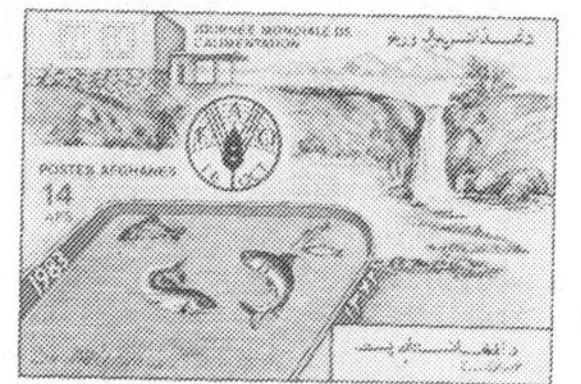

World Food Day—A427

1983, Oct. 16 Litho. *Perf. 12*

1043	A427	14af multi		

Boxing—A428

1983, Nov. 1 Litho. *Perf. 12*

1044	A428	1af Running		
1045	A428	18af shown		
1046	A428	21af Wrestling		

Pashtunistan Day—A428a

1983, Litho. *Perf. 12*

1046A	A428a	3af Afghans Waving Flag		

Handicrafts—A429

1983, Nov. 22

1047	A429	2af Jewelry		
1048	A429	8af Stone ashtrays, dishes		
1049	A429	19af Furniture		
1050	A429	30af Leather goods		

U.N. Declaration of Human Rights, 35th Anniv.—A430

1983, Dec. 10 Litho. *Perf. 12*

1051	A430	20af multi		

Kabul Polytechnical Institute, 20th Anniv.—A431

1983, Dec. 28 *Perf. 12½x12*

1052	A431	30af multi		

1984 Winter Olympics—A432

1984, Jan. *Perf. 12*

1053	A432	5af Figure skating	
1054	A432	9af Skiing	
1055	A432	11af Speed skating	
1056	A432	15af Hockey	
1057	A432	18af Biathlon	
1058	A432	20af Ski jumping	
1059	A432	22af Bobsledding	

Intl. Women's Day—A433

1984, Mar. 8

1060	A433	4af multi	

Farmers' Day—A434

Various agricultural scenes.

1984, Mar. 21 **Litho.** *Perf. 12*

1061	A434	2af multi	5
1062	A434	4af multi	16
1063	A434	7af multi	28
1064	A434	9af multi	36
1065	A434	15af multi	60
1066	A434	18af multi	72
1067	A434	20af multi	80
		Nos. 1061-1067 (7)	2.97

World Aviation Day—A435

1984, Apr. 12

1068	A435	5af Luna 1	20
1069	A435	8af Luna 2	32
1070	A435	11af Luna 3	45
1071	A435	17af Apollo 11	68
1072	A435	22af Soyuz 6	90
1073	A435	28af Soyuz 7	1.15
1074	A435	34af Soyuz 6,7,8	1.35
		Nos. 1068-1074 (7)	5.05

Souvenir Sheet
Perf. 12x12½

1075	A435	25af S. Koroliov	1.00

No. 1075 contains one stamp (30x41mm.); multicolored margin continues design. Size: 66x88mm.

Saur Revolution, 6th Anniv.—A436

1984, Apr. 27 *Perf. 12*

1076	A436	3af multi	12

65th Anniv. of Independence—A437

1984, Aug. 19 **Litho.** *Perf. 12*

1077	A437	6af multi	24

Pashto's and Balutchi's Day—A438

1984, Aug. 31

1078	A438	3af Symbolic sun, tribal terr.	12

Wildlife—A439

1984, May 5 **Litho.** *Perf. 12½x12, 12x12½*

1079	A439	1af Cape hunting dog, vert.	5
1080	A439	2af Argali sheep, vert.	8
1081	A439	6af Przewalski's horse	22
1082	A439	8af Wild boar, vert.	30
1083	A439	17af Snow leopard	65
1084	A439	19af Tiger	68
1085	A439	22af Indian elephant, vert.	85
		Nos. 1079-1085 (7)	2.83

19th UPU Congress, Hamburg—A440

1984, June 18 *Perf. 12x12½*

1086	A440	25af German postman, 17th cent.	1.00
1087	A440	35af Postrider, 16th cent.	1.40
1088	A440	40af Carrier pigeon, letter	1.50

Souvenir Sheet

1089	A440	50af Hamburg No. 3 in black	2.00

No. 1089 contains one stamp (size: 30x40mm); multicolored decorative margin pictures aerial view of Hamburg, Germany, and UPU emblem. Size: 97x67mm.

Natl. Aviation, 40th Anniv.—A441

Soviet civil aircraft.

1984, June 29

1090	A441	1af Antonov AN-2	5
1091	A441	4af Ilyushin IL-12	15
1092	A441	9af Tupolev TU-104	35
1093	A441	10af Ilyushin IL-18	40
1094	A441	13af Tupolev TU-134	50
1095	A441	17af Ilyushin IL-62	65
1096	A441	21af Ilyushin IL-28	85
		Nos. 1090-1096 (7)	2.95

Ettore Bugatti (1881-1947), Type 43, Italy—A442

Classic automobiles and their designers: 5af, Henry Ford (1863-1947), 1903 Model A, USA. 8af, Rene Panhard (1841-1908), 1899 Landau, France. 11af, Gottlieb Daimler (1834-1900), 1935 Daimler-Benz, Germany. 12af, Carl Benz (1844-1929), 1893 Victoris, Germany. 15af, Armand Peugeot (1848-1915), 1892 Vis-a-Vis, France. 22af, Louis Chevrolet (1879-1941), 1925 Sedan, USA.

1984, June 30

1097	A442	2af multi	8
1098	A442	5af multi	20
1099	A442	8af multi	30
1100	A442	11af multi	42
1101	A442	12af multi	48
1102	A442	15af multi	60
1103	A442	22af multi	85
		Nos. 1097-1103 (7)	2.93

Ornamental Arch—A443

World Tourism Day: 2af, Ornamental buckled harness. 5af, Victory Monument and Memorial Arch, Kabul. 9af, Standing sculpture of Afghani ruler and attendants. 10af, Buffalo riders in snow. 19af, Camel driver, tent, camel in caparison. 21af, Horsemen playing buzkashi.

1984, Sept. 27

1104	A443	1af multi	5
1105	A443	2af multi	8
1106	A443	5af multi	20
1107	A443	9af multi	35
1108	A443	10af multi	40
1109	A443	19af multi	75
1110	A443	21af multi	85
		Nos. 1104-1110 (7)	2.68

UN World Food Day—A444

Fruit-bearing trees.

1984, Oct. 16

1111	A444	2af multi	8
1112	A444	4af multi	16
1113	A444	6af multi	24
1114	A444	9af multi	35
1115	A444	13af multi	50
1116	A444	15af multi	60
1117	A444	26af multi	1.00
		Nos. 1111-1117 (7)	2.93

People's Democratic Party, 20th Anniv.—A445

1985, Jan. 1

1118	A445	25af multi	1.00

Farmer's Day—A446

1985

1119	A446	1af Oxen	5
1120	A446	3af Mare, foal	12
1121	A446	7af Brown horse	28
1122	A446	8af White horse, vert.	30
1123	A446	15af Sheep, sheepskins	60
1124	A446	16af Shepherd, cattle, sheep	62
1125	A446	25af Family, camels	1.00
		Nos. 1119-1125 (7)	2.97

Geologist's Day—A447

1985

1126	A447	4af multi	15

Lenin Leading Red Army, 1917—A448

Lenin and: 10af, Soviet Workers' Party deputies, Smolny. 15af, Revolutionaries, 1917, Leningrad. 50af, Portrait.

1985 *Perf. 12x12½*

1127	A448	10af multi	40
1128	A448	15af multi	60
1129	A448	25af multi	1.00

Souvenir Sheet

1130	A448	50af multi	2.00

No. 1130 has red and black margin picturing a scene from the 1917 Revolution, Russia. Size: 90x122mm.

Saor Revolution, 7th Anniv.—A449

1985

1131 A449 21af multi 85

Berlin-Treptow Soviet War Memorial, Red Army at Siege of Berlin, 1945—A450

Designs: 9af, Victorious Motherland monument, fireworks over Kremlin. 10af, Caecilienhof, site of Potsdam Treaty signing, flags of Great Britain, USSR and US.

1985 ***Perf. 12½x12***

1132 A450 6af multi 22
1133 A450 9af multi 35
1134 A450 10af multi 38

End of World War II, defeat of Nazi Germany, 40th anniv.

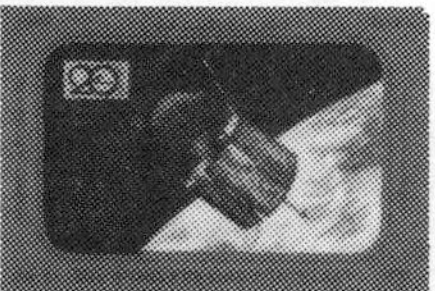

INTELSAT, 20th Anniv.—A451

Designs: 6af, INTELSAT satellite orbiting Earth. 9af, INTELSAT III. 10af, Rocket launch, Baikanur Space Center, vert.

1985, Apr. 6 Litho. ***Perf. 12x12½, 12½x12***

1135 A451 6af multi 22
1136 A451 9af multi 35
1137 A451 10af multi 40

12th World Youth Festival, Moscow—A452

1985, May 5

1138 A452 7af Olympic stadium, Moscow 28
1139 A452 12af Festival emblem 48
1140 A452 13af Kremlin 50
1141 A452 18af Folk doll, emblem 65

Intl. Child Survival Campaign—A453

1985, June 1

1142 A453 1af Weighing child 5
1143 A453 2af Immunization 8
1144 A453 4af Breastfeeding 15
1145 A453 5af Mother, child 20

Flowers—A454

1985, July 5

1146 A454 2af Oenothera affinis 8
1147 A454 4af Erythrina crista-galli 15
1148 A454 8af Tillandsia aeranthos 30
1149 A454 13af Vinca major 50
1150 A454 18af Mirabilis jalapa 65
1151 A454 25af Cypella herbertii 1.00
1152 A454 30af Clytostoma callistegioides 1.15
Nos. 1146-1152 (7) 3.83

Souvenir Sheet

Perf. 12½x11½

1153 A454 75af Sesbania punicea, horiz. 3.00

ARGENTINA '85. No. 1153 has multicolored decorative margin continuing the illustration. Size: 79x100mm.

Independence, 66th Anniv.—A455

1985, Aug. 19 ***Perf. 12x12½***

1154 A455 33af Mosque 1.25

Pashto's and Baluchi's Day—A456

1985, Aug. 30

1155 A456 25af multi 1.00

UN Decade for Women—A457

1985, Sept. 22

1156 A457 10af Emblems 40

UN 40th Anniv. A458

Birds A459

1985, Oct. 24 ***Perf. 12½x12***

1157 A458 22af multi 85

1985, Oct. 25 ***Perf. 12½x12, 12x12½***

1158 A459 2af Jay 8
1159 A459 4af Plover, hummingbird 15
1160 A459 8af Pheasant 30
1161 A459 13af Hoopoe 50
1162 A459 18af Falcon 65
1163 A459 25af Partridge 1.00
1164 A459 30af Pelicans, horiz. 1.15
Nos. 1158-1164 (7) 3.83

Souvenir Sheet

Perf. 12x12½

1165 A459 75af Parakeets 3.00

No. 1165 has multicolored decorative margin continuing the design. Size: 88x119mm.

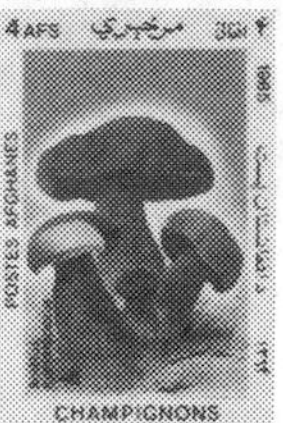

Mushrooms—A460

1985, June 10 Litho. ***Perf. 12½x12***

1166 A460 4af Boletus miniatoporus 16
1167 A460 7af Amanita rubescens 28
1168 A460 11af Boletus scaber 45
1169 A460 12af Coprinus atramentarius 48
1170 A460 18af Hypholoma 72
1171 A460 20af Boletus aurantiacus 80
Nos. 1166-1171 (6) 2.89

World Wildlife Fund—A461

1985, Nov. 25

1172 A461 2af Leopard, cubs 8
1173 A461 9af Adult's head 38
1174 A461 11af Adult 45
1175 A461 15af Cub 60

Motorcycle, Cent.—A462

Designs: Different makes and landmarks.

1985, Dec. 16

1176 A462 2af multi 8
1177 A462 4af multi 16
1178 A462 8af multi 32
1179 A462 13af multi 52
1180 A462 18af multi 72
1181 A462 25af multi 1.00
1182 A462 30af multi 1.20
Nos. 1176-1182 (7) 4.00

Souvenir Sheet

Perf. 11½x12½

1183 A462 75af multi 3.00

No. 1183 has multicolored margin continuing the design. Size: 100x80mm.

People's Democratic Party, 21st Anniv.—A463

1986, Jan. 1 ***Perf. 12½x12***

1184 A463 2af multi 8

27th Soviet Communist Party Congress—A464

1986, Mar. 31

1185 A464 25af Lenin 1.00

First Man in Space, 25th Anniv.—A465

Designs: 3af, Spacecraft, 7af, Soviet space achievement medal, vert. 9af, Rocket lift-off, vert. 11af, Yuri Gagarin, military decorations, vert. 13af, Gagarin, cosmonaut. 15af, Gagarin, politician. 17af, Gagarin wearing flight suit, vert.

1986, Apr. 12 Litho. ***Perf. 12½x12, 12x12½***

1186 A465 3af multi 12
1187 A465 7af multi 28
1188 A465 9af multi 38
1189 A465 11af multi 45
1190 A465 13af multi 52
1191 A465 15af multi 60
1192 A465 17af multi 68
Nos. 1186-1192 (7) 3.03

Intl. Children's Day—A466

1986, June 1 *Perf. 12*

1193 A466 1af Mother, children, vert. 4
1194 A466 3af Mother, child, vert. 12
1195 A466 9af Children, map 38

Pashtos' and Baluchis' Day—A467

1986, Aug. 31 *Perf. 12x12½*

1196 A467 4af multi 16

Intl. Peace Year—A468

1986, Sept. 30 **Photo.** *Perf. 12½x12*

1197 A468 12af blk & Prus bl 48

A469

1986 World Cup Soccer Championships, Mexico—A470

Various soccer plays.

1986, Apr. 15 **Litho.** *Perf. 12*

1198 A469 3af multi, vert. 12
1199 A469 4af multi 16
1200 A469 7af multi 28
1201 A469 11af multi, vert. 45
1202 A469 12af multi 48
1203 A469 18af multi, vert. 72
1204 A469 20af multi, vert. 80
Nos. 1198-1204 (7) 3.01

Souvenir Sheet
Perf. 12½x12

1205 A470 75af multi 3.00

No. 1205 has multicolored inscribed margin continuing the design. Size: 120x89mm.

Lenin—A471

1986, Apr. 21 *Perf. 12½x12*

1206 A471 16af multi 65

Natl. Independence, 67th Anniv.—A473

1986, Aug. 19 **Litho.** *Perf. 12½x12*

1208 A473 10af multi 40

Literacy Day—A474

1986, Sept. 18 *Perf. 12x12½*

1209 A474 2af multi 8

SEMI-POSTAL STAMPS.

No. 373 Surcharged in Violet

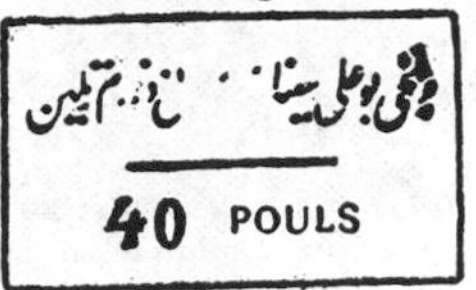

a

MILLIEME ANNIVERSAIRE
DE BOALI SINAI BALKI
125 POULS

b

1952, July 12 ***Perf. 12½*** **Unwmkd.**

B1 A122(a) 40p +30p cer 1.85 1.85
B2 A122(b) 125p +30p cer 3.00 2.50

Issued to commemorate the 1000th anniversary of the birth of Avicenna.

Children at Play
SP1

1955, July 3 **Typo.** ***Perf. 11***

B3 SP1 35p +15p dk grn 60 40
B4 SP1 125p +25p pur 1.25 1.00

The surtax was for child welfare.

Amir Sher Ali Khan, Tiger Head Stamp and Zahir Shah
SP2

Children at Play
SP3

1955, July 2 **Lithographed**

B5 SP2 35p +15p car 60 40
B6 SP2 125p +25p pale vio bl 1.25 80

Issued to commemorate the 85th anniversary of the Afghan post.

1956, June 20 **Typographed**

B7 SP3 35p +15p brt vio bl 40 40
B8 SP3 140p +15p dk org brn 1.00 1.00

Issued for Children's Day. The surtax was for child welfare. No. B8 inscribed in French.

Pashtunistan Monument, Kabul
SP4

1956, Sept. 1 **Lithographed**

B9 SP4 35p +15p dp vio 25 25
B10 SP4 140p +15p dk brn 75 75

Issued for "Free Pashtunistan" Day. The surtax aided the "Free Pashtunistan" movement.

No. B9 measures 30½x19½mm.; No. B10, 29x19mm. On sale and valid for use only on Sept. 1–2.

Globe and Sun SP5 — Children on Seesaw SP6

1956, Oct. 24 ***Perf. 11***

B11	SP5	35p +15p ultra	1.00	85
B12	SP5	140p +15p red brn	1.85	1.50

Issued for the tenth anniversary of Afghanistan's admission to the United Nations.

1957, June 20 **Unwmkd.**

B13	SP6	35p +15p brt rose	50	30
B14	SP6	140p +15p ultra	1.25	90

Issued for Children's Day. The surtax was for child welfare.

U. N. Headquarters and Emblems
SP7

1957, Oct. 24 ***Perf. 11 Rough***

B15	SP7	35p +15p red brn	50	30
B16	SP7	140p +15p lt ultra	1.00	90

Issued for United Nations Day.

Swimming Pool and Children
SP8

1958, June 22 ***Perf. 11***

B17	SP8	35p +15p rose	40	30
B18	SP8	140p +15p dl red brn	1.00	75

Issued for Children's Day. The surtax was for child welfare.

Pashtunistan Flag
SP9

1958, Aug. 31

B19	SP9	35p +15p lt bl	25	25
B20	SP9	140p +15p red brn	75	75

Issued for "Free Pashtunistan Day."

Children Playing Tug of War
SP10

1959, June 23 **Litho.** ***Perf. 11***

B21	SP10	35p +15p brn vio	35	25
B22	SP10	165p +15p brt pink	1.10	75

Issued for Children's Day. The surtax was for child welfare.

Pathans in Tribal Dance—SP11

Perf. 11 Rough

1959, Sept. **Unwmkd.**

B23	SP11	35p +15p grn	20	20
B24	SP11	165p +15p org	75	75

Issued for "Free Pashtunistan Day."

Afghan Cavalryman with U.N. Flag
SP12

1959, Oct. 24 ***Perf. 11 Rough***

B25	SP12	35p +15p org	30	25
B26	SP12	165p +15p lt bl grn	65	60

Issued for United Nations Day.

Children
SP13

1960, Oct. 23 **Lithographed**

B27	SP13	75p +25p lt ultra	35	30
B28	SP13	175p +25p lt grn	60	45

Issued for Children's Day. The surtax was for child welfare.

Man with Spray Gun—SP14

1960, Sept. 6 ***Perf. 11 Rough***

B29	SP14	50p +50p org	1.25	1.00
B30	SP14	175p +50p red brn	3.00	2.00

11th anniversary of the WHO malaria control program in Afghanistan.

SP15

1960, Sept. 1 **Unwmkd.**

B31	SP15	50p +50p rose	35	30
B32	SP15	175p +50p dk bl	85	60

Issued for "Free Pashtunistan Day."

Ambulance—SP16

Crescent in Red

1960, Oct. 16 ***Perf. 11***

B33	SP16	50p +50p vio	50	25
B34	SP16	175p +50p bl	1.10	90

Issued for the Red Crescent Society.

Nos. 470–471 Surcharged in Blue or Orange.

1960, Dec. 31 **Litho.** ***Perf. 11***

B35	A166	50p +25p dp org (Bl)	3.00	3.00
B36	A166	165p +25p bl (O)	3.00	3.00

The souvenir sheets described after No. 471 were surcharged in carmine "+25 Ps" on each stamp. Price $5 each.

See general note after No. 485.

Nos. 496–500 Surcharged UNICEF يونيسف +25PS

Photogravure

1961 ***Perf. 13½x14*** **Unwmkd.**

B37	A175	2p +25p grn & rose lil		
B38	A175	2p +25p brn & cit		
B39	A175	5p +25p gray & rose		
B40	A175	10p +25p bl & bis		
B41	A175	15p +25p sl bl & dl lil		
		Nos. B37-B41 (5)	2.25	

Issued for the United Nations Children's Fund, UNICEF. The same surcharge was applied to an imperf. souvenir sheet like that noted after No. 505. Price $4.50.

Nos. 522–526 Surcharged "+25PS" and Crescent in Red.

1961, Oct. 16 ***Perf. 13½x14***

B42	A184	2p +25p blk		
B43	A184	2p +25p grn		
B44	A184	5p +25p lil rose		
B45	A184	10p +25p lil		
B46	A184	15p +25p dk bl		
		Nos. B42-B46 (5)	2.50	

Issued for the Red Crescent Society.

Nos. 539–543 Surcharged in Red: "UNESCO + 25PS"

1962 ***Perf. 12***

B47	A186	2p +25p multi		
B48	A186	2p +25p multi		
B49	A186	5p +25p multi		
B50	A186	10p +25p multi		
B51	A186	15p +25p multi		
		Nos. B47-B51 (5)	1.50	

Issued for the United Nations Educational, Scientific and Cultural Organization. The same surcharge was also applied to the souvenir sheets mentioned after No. 548. Price, 2 sheets, $3.50.

Nos. 553–561 Surcharged: "Dag Hammarskjöld +20PS"

1962, Sept. 17 ***Perf. 14x13½***

B52	A187	2p +20p rose lil & brn		
B53	A187	2p +20p ol bis & brn		
B54	A187	5p +20p dp org & dk grn		
B55	A187	10p +20p gray & mag		
B56	A187	15p +20p bl & brn		
B57	A187	25p +20p org yel & pur		
B58	A187	50p +20p lt grn & pur		
B59	A187	75p +20p brt cit & brn		
B60	A187	100p +20p dp org & brn		
		Nos. B52-B60 (9)	2.25	

Issued in memory of Dag Hammarskjold, Secretary General of the United Nations, 1953–61. Perf. and imperf. souvenir sheets exist. Price, 2 sheets, $3.

Nos. 583–593 Surcharged "+15PS"

1963, Mar. 15 ***Perf. 14x13½***

B61	A193	2p +15p dk grn & ol gray		
B62	A193	2p +15p dk grn & sal		
B63	A193	5p +15p red brn & ol		
B64	A193	10p +15p red brn & brt grn		
B65	A193	15p +15p red brn & gray		
B66	A193	25p +15p brt bl & bluish grn		
B67	A193	50p +15p brt bl & rose lil		
B68	A193	75p +15p blk & bl		
B69	A193	100p +15p blk & brt pink		
B70	A193	150p +15p blk & bis brn		
B71	A193	175p +15p blk & org		
		Nos. B61-B71 (11)	10.00	

Issued for the World Health Organization drive to eradicate malaria.

Postally used copies of Nos. B35–B71 are uncommon and command a considerable premium over the prices for unused copies.

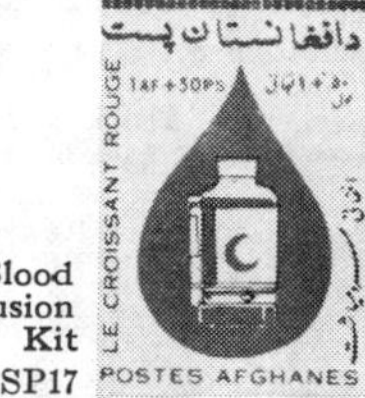

Blood Transfusion Kit
SP17

1964, Oct. 18 **Litho.** ***Perf. 10½***

B72	SP17	1af +50p blk & rose	15	10

Issued for the Red Crescent Society and Red Crescent Week, Oct. 18–24.

First Aid Station
SP18

1965, Oct. **Photo.** ***Perf. 13½x14***

B73	SP18	1.50af +50p grn, choc & red	25	10

Issued for the Red Crescent Society.

Children Playing
SP19

1966, Nov. 28 **Photo.** ***Perf. 13½x14***

B74	SP19	1af +1af yel grn & cl	18	12
B75	SP19	3af +2af yel & brn	40	30
B76	SP19	7af +3af rose lil & grn	85	60

Children's Day.

Nadir Shah Presenting Society Charter—SP20

1967 Photogravure *Perf. 13x14*

B77	SP20	2af + 1af red & dk grn	25	15
B78	SP20	5af + 1af lil rose & brn	50	25

Issued for the Red Crescent Society.

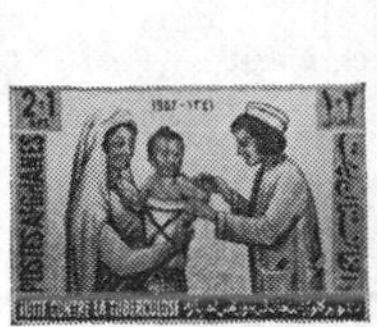

Vaccination SP21

Red Crescent SP22

1967, June 6 Photo. *Perf. 12*

B79	SP21	2af + 1af yel & blk	25	10
B80	SP21	5af + 2af pink & brn	50	25

The surtax was for anti-tuberculosis work.

1967, Oct. 18 Photo. *Perf. 12*

Crescent in Red

B81	SP22	3af + 1af gray ol & blk	25	15
B82	SP22	5af + 1af dl bl & blk	35	20

Issued for the Red Crescent Society.

Queen Humeira SP23

Red Crescent SP24

1968, June 14 Photo. *Perf. 12*

B83	SP23	2af + 2af red brn	25	20
B84	SP23	7af + 2af dl grn	75	50

Issued for Mother's Day.

1968, Oct. 16 Photo. *Perf. 12*

B85	SP24	4af + 1af yel, blk & red	45	27

Issued for the Red Crescent Society.

Red Cross, Crescent, Lion and Sun Emblems SP25

Mother and Child SP26

1969, May 5 Litho. *Perf. 14x13½*

B86	SP25	3af + 1af multi	30	18
B87	SP25	5af + 1af multi	50	30

Issued to commemorate the 50th anniversary of the League of Red Cross Societies.

1969, June 14 Photo. *Perf. 12*

B88	SP26	1af + 1af yel org & brn	18	12
B89	SP26	4af + 1af rose lil & pur	40	27
a.		Souv. sheet of 2	1.10	1.10

Issued for Mother's Day. No. B89a contains 2 imperf. stamps similar to Nos. B88–B89. Brown marginal inscription and black control number. Size: 120x80mm. Sold for 10af.

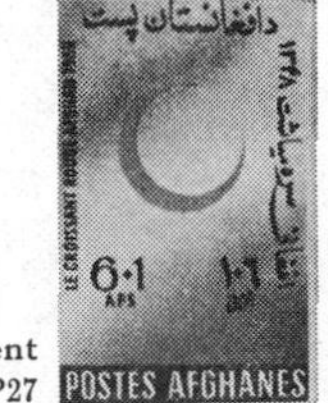

Red Crescent SP27

1969, Oct. 16 Photo. *Perf. 12*

B90	SP27	6af + 1af multi	55	30

Issued for the Red Crescent Society.

UN and FAO Emblems, Farmer SP28

1973, May 24 Photo. *Perf. 13½*

B91	SP28	14af + 7af grnsh bl & lil	1.10	75

World Food Program, 10th anniversary.

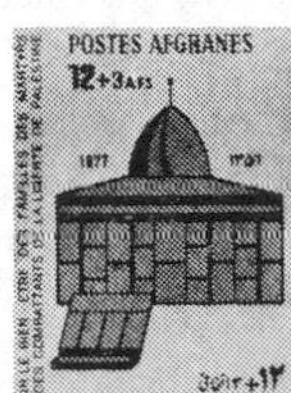

Dome of the Rock, Jerusalem SP29

1977, Sept. 11 Photo. *Perf. 14*

B92	SP29	12af + 3af multi	45	36

The surtax was for Palestinian families and soldiers.

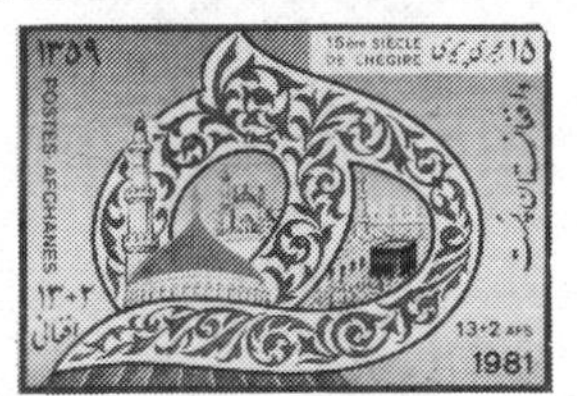

15 cent. (lunar) of Islamic pilgrimage (Hegira)—SP30

1981, Jan. 17 Litho. *Perf. 12½x12*

B93	SP30	13 + 2af multi	45	38

Red Crescent Aid Programs—SP31

1981, May 8 *Perf. 12x12½*

B94	SP31	1 + 4af multi	15	12

Intl. Year of the Disabled A391

1981, Oct. 12 *Perf. 12x12½*

B95	SP32	6 + 1af multi	22	15

AIR POST STAMPS

Plane over Kabul—AP1

Perf. 12, 12x11, 11

1939, Oct. 1 Typographed. Unwmkd.

C1	AP1	5af orange	3.00	3.00
a.		Imperf. pair ('47)	35.00	35.00
b.		Imperf. vertically, pair	30.00	
C2	AP1	10af blue	3.00	2.50
a.		lt bl	4.00	4.00
b.		Imperf. pair ('47)	35.00	
c.		Imperf. vertically, pair	30.00	
C3	AP1	20af emerald	7.00	7.00
a.		Imperf. pair ('47)	35.00	
b.		Imperf. vertically, pair	30.00	
c.		Imperf. horiz., pair	35.00	

These stamps come with clean-cut or rough perforations. Counterfeits exist.

1948, June 14 *Perf. 12x11½.*

C4	AP1	5af emerald	27.50	27.50
C5	AP1	10af red org	27.50	27.50
C6	AP1	20af blue	27.50	27.50

Imperforates exist.

Plane over Palace Grounds, Kabul—AP2

Imprint: "Waterlow & Sons, Limited, London"

1951-54 Engraved. *Perf. 13½.*

C7	AP2	5af hn brn	2.00	80
C8	AP2	5af dp grn ('54)	1.50	70
C9	AP2	10af gray	6.00	2.00
C10	AP2	20af dk bl	10.00	3.50

1957

C11	AP2	5af ultra	1.25	75
C12	AP2	10af dk vio	2.50	1.50

See also No. C38.

Ariana DC-3 Plane over Hindu Kush AP3

Perf. 11, Imperf.

1960–63 Lithographed Unwmkd.

C13	AP3	75p lt vio	30	30
C14	AP3	125p blue	40	45

Perf. 10½, 11

C14A	AP3	5af cit ('63)	1.10	1.10

Girl Scout AP4

1962, Aug. 30 Photo. *Perf. 11½x12*

C15	AP4	100p ocher & brn	60	60
C16	AP4	175p brt yel grn & brn	85	85

Issued for Women's Day. A souvenir sheet exists containing one each of Nos. 578–579 and C15–C16. Brown inscription. Size: 109x105mm. Price $3.

Sports Type of Regular Issue, 1962

Designs: 25p, 50p, Horse racing. 75p, 100p, Wrestling. 150p, Weight lifting. 175p, Soccer.

1962, Sept. 25 *Perf. 12* Unwmkd.

Black Inscriptions.

C17	A195	25p rose & red brn		
C18	A195	50p gray & red brn		
C19	A195	75p pale vio & dk grn		
C20	A195	100p gray ol & dk pur		
C21	A195	150p rose lil & grn		
C22	A195	175p sal & brn		
		Nos. C17-C22 (6)		2.25

4th Asian Games, Djakarta, Indonesia.

Children's Day Type of Regular Issue

Designs: 75p, Runners. 150p, Peaches. 200p, Iris (vert.).

Perf. 11½x12, 12x11½

1962, Oct. 14 Unwmkd.

C23	A196	75p lt grn & lil
C24	A196	150p bl & multi
C25	A196	200p ol & multi

Issued for Children's Day. A souvenir sheet contains one each of Nos. C23–C25. Lilac marginal inscription and black control number. Size: 119x90mm. Price $2.50.

Red Crescent Type of Regular Issue

Designs: 25p, Grapes. 50p, Pears. 100p, Wistaria.

1962, Oct. 16 *Perf. 12*

Fruit and Flowers in Natural Colors; Carmine Crescent

C26	A197	25p brown
C27	A197	50p dl grn
C28	A197	100p dk bl gray

Issued for the Afghan Red Crescent Society. Two souvenir sheets exist. One contains a 150p gray brown stamp in blossom design, the other a 200p gray stamp in wistaria design, imperf. Each sheet has marginal inscriptions in color of stamp, and black control number. Size: 89x65mm. Price, each $5.

U.N. Type of Regular Issue

1962, Oct. 24 Photogravure

Flags in Original Colors, Black Inscriptions

C29	A198	75p blue
C30	A198	100p lt brn

C31 A198 125p brt grn

Issued for United Nations Day.

Boy Scout Type of Regular Issue

1962, Oct. 25 *Perf. 12* Unwmkd.

C32 A199 25p gray, blk, dl grn & sal
C33 A199 50p grn, brn & sal
C34 A199 75p bl grn, red brn & sal
C35 A199 100p bl, sl & sal

Issued to honor the Boy Scouts.

Teacher's Day Type of Regular Issue

Designs: 100p, Pole vault. 150p, High jump.

1962, Oct. 25

C36 A200 100p yel & blk
C37 A200 150p bluish grn & brn

Issued for Teacher's Day. A souvenir sheet contains one 250p pink and slate green stamp in design of 150p. Slate green marginal inscription and black control number. Size: 65x89mm. Price $2.50.

Type of 1951-54

1962 Engraved *Perf. 13½*

Imprint: "Thomas De La Rue & Co. Ltd."

C38 AP2 5af ultra 9.00 1.00

Agriculture Types of Regular Issue

Photogravure

1963, March 1 *Perf. 12* Unwmkd.

C42 A204 100p dk car, grn & brn
C43 A203 150p ocher & blk
C44 A204 200p ultra, grn & brn

Issued for the Day of Agriculture.

Hands Holding Wheat Emblem
AP5

1963, Mar. 27 Photo. *Perf. 14*

C45 AP5 500p lil, lt brn & brn 85 85

Issued for the "Freedom from Hunger" campaign of the U.N. Food and Agriculture Organization.

Two souvenir sheets exist. One contains a 1000p blue green, light brown and brown, type AP5, imperf. Claret marginal inscription. Size: 76x100mm. The other contains a 200p brown and green and 300p ultramarine, yellow and ocher in rice and corn designs, type A205. Green marginal inscription. Size: 100x75mm. Both sheets have black control number. Prices $6 and $2.50.

Meteorological Day Type of Regular Issue

Designs: 100p, 500p, Meteorological measuring instrument. 200p, 400p, Weather station. 300p, Rockets in space.

1963, May 23 *Imperf.*

C46 A206 100p brn & bl

Perf. 13½x14

C47 A206 200p brt grn & lil
C48 A206 300p dk bl & rose
C49 A206 400p bl & dl red brn
C50 A206 500p car rose & gray grn

Issued to commemorate the United Nations Third World Meteorological Day, March 23. Nos. C47 and C50 printed se-tenant.

Two souvenir sheets exist. One contains a 125p red and brown stamp in rocket design. Red marginal inscription. The other contains a 100p blue and dull red brown in "rockets in space" design. Blue marginal inscription. Both sheets have black control number, and measure 100x 75mm. Prices $5 and $7.50.

Kabul International Airport
AP8

Photogravure

1964, Apr. *Perf. 12x11* Unwmkd.

C57 AP8 10af red lil & grn 80 35
C58 AP8 20af dk grn & red lil 1.20 60
C59 AP8 50af dk bl & grnsh bl 3.25 1.50

Inauguration of Kabul Airport Terminal.

Nos. C58-C59 are 36mm. wide. They were reissued in 1968, 35½mm. wide.

Zahir Shah and Ariana Plane—AP9

Design: 50af, Zahir Shah and Kabul Airport.

1971 Photo. *Perf. 12½x13½*

C60 AP9 50af multi 15.00 12.00
C61 AP9 100af blk, red & grn 8.00 5.00

No C60 was used, starting in 1978, with king's portrait removed.

REGISTRATION STAMPS.

R1

Lithographed

Dated "1309"

1891 *Imperf.* Unwmkd.

Pelure Paper.

F1 R1 1r sl bl 2.00
a. Tête bêche pair 15.00

R2

Thin Wove Paper.

1893 Dated "1311".

F2 R2 1r *grn* 1.60

Genuinely used copies of Nos. F1-F2 are rare. Counterfeit cancellations exist.

R3

1894 Undated.

F3 R3 2ab *green* 11.00 14.00

12 varieties. See note below Nos. 189-190.

R4

1898-1900 Undated

F4 R4 2ab *dp rose* 6.25 7.50
F5 R4 2ab *lil rose* 6.25 7.50
F6 R4 2ab *magenta* 6.25 7.50
F7 R4 2ab *salmon* 6.25 7.50
F8 R4 2ab *orange* 6.25 7.50
F9 R4 2ab *yellow* 6.25 7.50
F10 R4 2ab *green* 6.25 7.50
Nos. F4-F10 (7) 43.75 52.50

Many shades of paper.

Nos. F4-F10 come in two sizes, measured between outer frame lines: 52x36 mm., first printing; 46x33mm., second printing. The outer frame line (not pictured) is 3-6mm. from inner frame line.

Used on P.O. receipts.

OFFICIAL STAMPS.
(Used only on interior mail.)

Coat of Arms
O1

Typographed

1909 *Perf. 12* Unwmkd.

Wove Paper.

O1 O1 red 1.00 1.00
a. car ('19?) 1.25 1.25

Later printings of No. O1 in scarlet, vermilion, claret, etc., on various types of paper, were issued until 1927.

Official Stamp of 1909 Handstamped like Regular Issues of 1929.

1929

O2 O1 red 12.50

See note after No. 261.

Coat of Arms
O2

1939-68? Typo. *Perf. 11, 12*

O3 O2 15p emerald 50 25
O4 O2 30p ocher ('40) 75 75
O5 O2 45p dk car 60 50
O6 O2 50p brt car ('68?) 40 40
a. car rose ('55) 75 60
O7 O2 1af brt red vio 1.25 75
Nos. O3-O7 (5) 3.50 2.65

Size of 50p, 24x31mm. Others 22½x 28mm.

1964-65 Lithographed *Perf. 11*

O8 O2 50p rose 75 75
a. sal ('65) 1.50 1.50

Stamps of this type are revenues.

PARCEL POST STAMPS.

Coat of Arms
PP1

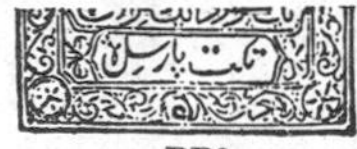

PP2

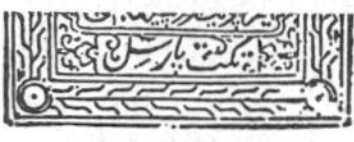

PP3

PP4

Typographed.

1909 *Perf. 12.* Unwmkd.

Q1 PP1 3sh bister 50 60
a. Imperf., pair 1.25
Q2 PP2 1kr ol gray 75 1.00
a. Imperf., pair 2.00
Q3 PP3 1r orange 3.00 2.25
Q4 PP3 1r ol grn 1.25 2.75
Q5 PP4 2r red 3.75 2.50
Nos. Q1-Q5 (5) 9.25 9.10

1916-18

Q6 PP1 3sh green 1.00 75
Q7 PP2 1kr pale red 1.50 1.25
a. rose red ('18) 2.00 2.00
Q8 PP3 1r brn org 1.50 1.25
a. dp brn ('18) 2.50 2.50
Q9 PP4 2r blue 3.00 3.00

Nos. Q1-Q9 sometimes show letters of the papermaker's watermark "HOWARD & JONES LONDON."

Ungummed copies are remainders. They sell for one-third the price of mint examples.

The indexes in each volume of the Scott Catalogue contain many listings which help to identify stamps.

Old Habibia College, near Kabul

PP5

1921 **Wove Paper.**

Q10	PP5	10pa chocolate	1.75	1.75
a.		Tête bêche pair	6.25	
Q11	PP5	15pa lt brn	2.50	2.50
a.		Tête bêche pair	6.25	
Q12	PP5	30pa red vio	3.50	2.75
a.		Tête bêche pair	8.75	
b.		Laid paper	15.00	7.50
Q13	PP5	1r brt bl	5.50	5.50
a.		Tête bêche pair	12.00	

Stamps of this issue are usually perforated on one or two sides only.

The laid paper of No. Q12b has a papermaker's watermark in the sheet.

PP6

1924-26 **Wove Paper**

Q15	PP6	5kr ultra ('26)	25.00	15.00
Q16	PP6	5r lilac	8.75	8.75

A 15r rose exists, but is not known to have been placed in use.

PP7

PP8

1928-29 ***Perf. 11, 11xImperf.***

Q17	PP7	2r yel org	5.00	4.00
Q18	PP7	2r grn ('29)	4.00	3.50
Q19	PP8	3r dp grn	6.50	6.00
Q20	PP8	3r brn ('29)	6.50	6.00

Nos. Q17 and Q19 Handstamped

1929

Q21	PP7	2r yel org	*15.00*
Q22	PP8	3r dp grn	18.50

See note after No. 261.

POSTAL TAX STAMPS.

Aliabad Hospital near Kabul

PT1

Pierre and Marie Curie

PT2

Perf. 12x11½, 12

1938, Dec. 22 **Typo.** **Unwmkd.**

RA1	PT1	10p pck grn	2.75	2.75
RA2	PT2	15p dl bl	2.75	2.75

Obligatory on all mail Dec. 22-28, 1938. The money was used for the Allabad Hospital. See note with CD80.

Begging Child

PT3 PT4

1949, May 28 **Typo.** ***Perf. 12***

RA3	PT3	35p red org	2.00	2.00
RA4	PT4	125p ultra	3.00	2.00

United Nations Children's Day, May 28. Obligatory on all foreign mail on that date. Proceeds were used for child welfare.

Paghman Arch and U. N. Emblem

PT5

1949, Oct. 24

RA5	PT5	125p dk bl grn	12.50	11.00

Issued to commemorate the fourth anniversary of the formation of the United Nations. Valid one day only. Issued in sheets of 9 (3x3).

Zahir Shah and Map of Afghanistan

PT6

1950, Mar. 30 **Typographed**

RA6	PT6	125p bl grn	2.50	1.25

Issued to celebrate the return of Zahir Shah from a trip to Europe for his health. Valid for two weeks. The tax was used for public health purposes.

Hazara Youth

PT7

1950, May 28 **Typo.** ***Perf. 11½***

RA7	PT7	125p dk bl grn	3.00	2.00

The tax was for Child Welfare. Obligatory and valid only on May 28, 1950, on foreign mail.

Ruins of Qalai Bist and Globe

PT8

1950, Oct. 24

RA8	PT8	1.25af ultra	6.50	5.00

Issued to commemorate the 5th anniversary of the formation of the United Nations. Proceeds went to Afghanistan's U.N. Projects Committee.

Zahir Shah and Medical Center

PT9

Typographed.

1950, Dec. 22 ***Perf. 11½***

Size: 38x25mm.

RA9	PT9	35p carmine	50	50
RA10	PT9	1.25af black	6.00	3.00

The tax was for the national Graduate School of Medicine.

Koochi Girl with Lamb

PT10

Kohistani Boy and Sheep

PT11

1951, May 28

RA11	PT10	35p emerald	1.25	1.00
RA12	PT11	1.25af ultra	1.25	1.00

The tax was for Child Welfare.

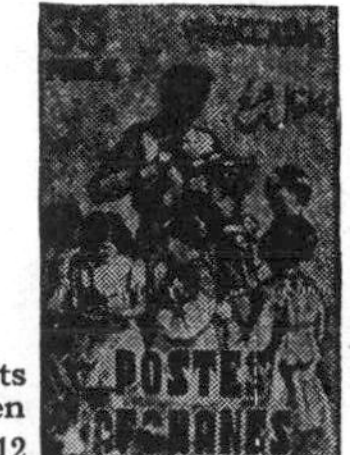

Distributing Gifts to Children

PT12

Qandahari Boys Dancing the 'Attan'

PT13

1952, May 28 **Lithographed**

RA13	PT12	35p chocolate	40	40
RA14	PT13	125p violet	1.10	1.10

The tax was for Child Welfare.

Soldier Receiving First Aid

PT14

1952, Oct.

RA15	PT14	10p lt grn	50	45

Stretcher-bearers and Wounded
PT15

Soldier Assisting Wounded
PT16

1953, Oct.

RA16	PT15	10p yel grn & org red	60	50
RA17	PT16	10p vio brn & org red	60	50

Prince Mohammed Nadir
PT17

Map and Young Musicians
PT18

1953, May 28

RA18	PT17	35p org yel	25	20
RA19	PT17	125p chlky bl	75	75

No. RA19 is inscribed in French "Children's Day." The tax was for child welfare.

1954, May 28 *Perf. 11* **Unwmkd.**

RA20	PT18	35p purple	40	20
RA21	PT18	125p ultra	1.50	1.50

No. RA21 is inscribed in French. The tax was for child welfare.

Red Crescent
PT19 PT20

1954, Oct. 17 *Perf. 11½*

RA22	PT19	20p bl & red	35	30

1955, Oct. 18 *Perf. 11*

RA23	PT20	20p dl grn & car	30	25

Zahir Shah and Red Crescent
PT21

1956, Oct. 18

RA24	PT21	20p lt grn & rose car	35	25

Red Crescent Headquarters, Kabul
PT22

1957, Oct. 17

RA25	PT22	20p lt ultra & car	35	25

Map and Crescent
PT23

1958, Oct. *Perf. 11* **Unwmkd.**

RA26	PT23	25p yel grn & red	25	20

PT24

1959, Oct. 17 Lithographed *Perf. 11*

RA27	PT24	25p lt vio & red	25	15

The tax on Nos. RA15–RA17, RA22–RA27 was for the Red Crescent Society. Use of these stamps was required for one week.

AGUERA, LA

(ä·gwā'rä)

LOCATION—An administrative district in southern Rio de Oro on the northwest coast of Africa.

GOVT.—Spanish possession.

AREA—Because of indefinite political boundaries, figures for area and population are not available.

See Spanish Sahara.

100 Centimos = 1 Peseta

Type of 1920 Issue of Rio de Oro Overprinted **LA AGÜERA**

1920 *Perf. 13* **Unwmkd.**

1	A8	1c bl grn	2.00	2.00
2	A8	2c ol brn	2.00	2.00
3	A8	5c dp grn	2.00	2.00
4	A8	10c lt red	2.00	2.00
5	A8	15c yellow	2.00	2.00
6	A8	20c lilac	2.00	2.00
7	A8	25c dp bl	2.00	2.00
8	A8	30c dk brn	2.00	2.00
9	A8	40c pink	2.00	2.00
10	A8	50c brt bl	5.25	4.75
11	A8	1p red brn	9.00	7.75
12	A8	4p dk vio	30.00	25.00
13	A8	10p orange	60.00	55.00
		Nos. 1-13 (13)	122.25	110.50

King Alfonso XIII
A2

1922 **Typographed**

14	A2	1c turq bl	1.00	1.00
15	A2	2c dk grn	1.00	1.00
16	A2	5c bl grn	1.00	1.00
17	A2	10c red	1.00	1.00
18	A2	15c red brn	1.00	1.00
19	A2	20c yellow	1.00	1.00
20	A2	25c dp bl	1.00	1.00
21	A2	30c dk brn	1.00	1.00
22	A2	40c rose red	1.25	1.25
23	A2	50c red vio	4.00	3.50
24	A2	1p rose	7.75	7.25
25	A2	4p violet	17.50	15.00
26	A2	10p orange	27.50	25.00
		Nos.14-26 (13)	66.00	60.00

For later issues see Spanish Sahara in Vol. IV.

ALAOUITES

(å·lå'wēt')

LOCATION—A division of Syria, in Western Asia.

GOVT.—Under French Mandate.

AREA—2,500 sq. mi.

POP.—278,000 (approx. 1930).

CAPITAL—Latakia.

This territory became an independent state in 1924, although still administered under the French Mandate. In 1930 it was renamed Latakia and Syrian stamps overprinted "Lattaquie" superseded the stamps of Alaouites. For these and subsequent issues see Latakia and Syria.

100 Centimes = 1 Piastre

Issued under French Mandate.

Stamps of France Surcharged:

ALAOUITES
0 P. 25
العلويين
١/٤ الغرش
a

ALAOUITES
2 PIASTRES
العلويين
غروش ٢
b

1925 *Perf. 14x13½* **Unwmkd.**

1	A16 (a)	10c on 2c vio brn	1.50	1.50
2	A22 (a)	25c on 5c org	1.00	1.00
3	A20 (a)	75c on 15c gray grn	1.90	1.90
4	A22 (a)	1p on 20c red brn	1.25	1.25
5	A22 (a)	1.25p on 25c bl	1.75	1.75
6	A22 (a)	1.50p on 30c red	5.25	5.25
7	A22 (b)	2p on 35c vio	1.25	1.25
8	A18 (b)	2p on 40c red & pale bl	2.50	2.50
9	A18 (b)	2p on 45c grn & bl	5.25	5.25
10	A18 (b)	3p on 60c vio & ultra	3.00	3.00
11	A20 (b)	3p on 60c lt vio	5.25	5.25
12	A20 (b)	4p on 85c ver	90	90
13	A18 (b)	5p on 1fr cl & ol grn	3.75	3.75
14	A18 (b)	10p on 2fr org & pale bl	4.75	4.75
15	A18 (b)	25p on 5fr Bl & buff	6.50	6.50
		Nos. 1-15 (15)	45.80	45.80

Same Surcharges on Stamps of France, 1923-24 (Pasteur)

16	A23 (a)	50c on 10c grn	95	95
17	A23 (a)	75c on 15c grn	95	95
18	A23 (a)	1.50p on 30c red	1.25	1.25
19	A23 (b)	2p on 45c red	1.40	1.40
20	A23 (b)	2.50p on 50c bl	1.75	1.75
21	A23 (b)	4p on 75c bl	2.50	2.50
		Nos. 16-21 (6)	8.80	8.80

Stamps of Syria, 1925, Overprinted in Red, Black or Blue:

ALAOUITES
العلويين
c

ALAOUITES
العلويين
d

1925, Mar. 1 *Perf. 12½, 13½*

25	A3 (c)	10c dk vio (R)	42	42
a.		Dbl. ovpt.	17.50	17.50
26	A4 (d)	25c ol blk (R)	80	80
a.		Inverted overprint	10.00	10.00
b.		Blue ovpt.	17.50	17.50
27	A4 (d)	50c yel grn	60	60
a.		Inverted overprint	8.75	8.75
b.		Blue ovpt.	17.50	17.50
c.		Red ovpt.	17.50	17.50
28	A4 (d)	75c brn org	70	70
a.		Inverted overprint	10.00	10.00
29	A5 (c)	1p magenta	1.10	1.10
30	A4 (d)	1.25p dp grn	80	80
a.		Red ovpt.	15.00	15.00
31	A4 (d)	1.50p rose red (Bl)	70	70
a.		Inverted overprint	10.00	10.00
b.		Black ovpt.	17.50	17.50
32	A4 (d)	2p dk brn (R)	80	80
a.		Blue ovpt.	10.00	10.00
33	A4 (d)	2.50p pck bl (R)	1.00	1.00
a.		Black ovpt.	10.00	10.00
34	A4 (d)	3p org brn	80	80
a.		Inverted overprint	10.00	10.00
b.		Blue ovpt.	21.00	21.00
35	A4 (d)	5p violet	90	90
a.		Red ovpt.	21.00	21.00
36	A4 (d)	10p vio brn	1.40	1.40
37	A4 (d)	25p ultra (R)	3.00	3.00
		Nos. 25-37 (13)	13.02	13.02

Stamps of Syria, 1925, Surcharged in Black or Red:

=4P. غ٤=
ALAOUITES
العلويين
e

=4P.50 غ٤ ١/٢=
Alaouites
العلويين
f

1926

38	A4 (e)	3.50p on 75c brn org	95	80
a.		Surcharged on face and back	7.00	7.00
39	A4 (e)	4p on 25c ol blk (R)	1.00	80
40	A4 (e)	6p on 2.50p pck bl (R)	90	80
41	A4 (e)	12p on 1.25p dp grn	90	80
a.		Inverted surch.	9.50	9.50
42	A4 (e)	20p on 1.25p dp grn	1.50	1.25
43	A4 (f)	4.50p on 75c brn org	3.00	1.75
a.		Invtd. surch.	10.00	
44	A4 (f)	7.50p on 2.50p pck bl	2.25	1.25
45	A4 (f)	15p on 25p ultra	4.25	3.00
		Nos. 38-45 (8)	14.75	10.45

Syria No. 199 Overprinted Type "c" in Red.

1928

46	A3 (c)	5c on 10c dk vio	42	42
a.		Double surcharge	13.00	

Syria Nos. 178 and 174 Surcharged in Red.

47	A4 (f)	2p on 1.25p dp grn	7.75	4.75
48	A4 (f)	4p on 25c ol blk	4.75	3.50

= 4P ٤٤ =
ALAOUITES
العلويين
g

49	A4 (g)	4p on 25c ol blk	37.50	35.00
a.		Double impression		

AIR POST STAMPS.

Nos. 8, 10, 13 & 14 with Additional Overprint in Black

Perf. 14 x 13½.

1925, Jan. 1 **Unwmkd.**

C1	A18	2p red & pale bl	5.75	5.75
a.		Overprint reversed	65.00	
C2	A18	3p on 60c vio & ultra	8.75	8.75
a.		Overprint reversed	65.00	65.00
C3	A18	5p on 1fr cl & ol grn	5.75	5.75
C4	A18	10p on 2fr org & pale bl	5.75	5.75

Nos. 32, 34, 35 & 36 With Additional Overprint in Green

1925, Mar. 1 ***Perf. 13½***

C5	A4	2p dk brn	1.50	1.50
C6	A4	3p org brn	1.50	1.50
C7	A4	5p violet	1.50	1.50
C8	A4	10p vio brn	1.50	1.50

Nos. 32, 34, 35 & 36 With Additional Overprint in Red

k

1926, May 1

C9	A4	2p dk brn	2.25	2.25
C10	A4	3p org brn	2.25	2.25
C11	A4	5p violet	2.25	2.25
C12	A4	10p vio brn	2.25	2.25

No. C9 has the type "d" overprint in black.

Double or inverted overprints, types "d" or "k," are known on most of Nos. C9–C12. Price, $8–$10.

The red plane overprint, "k," was also applied to Nos. C5–C8. These are believed to have been essays, and were not regularly issued.

Nos. 27, 29, and 37 With Additional Overprint of Airplane (k) in Red or Black.

1929, June-July

C17	A4	50c yel grn (R)	1.25	1.25
a.		Red overprint (k) double	13.00	
b.		Red overprint (k) on face and back	13.00	
c.		Pair with overprint (k) tête bêche	40.00	
C18	A5	1p mag (Bk)	4.00	4.00
C19	A4	25p ultra (R)	21.00	21.00
a.		Overprint (k) inverted	65.00	65.00

Nos. 47 and 45 With Additional Overprint of Airplane (k) in Red.

1929-30

C20	A4	2p on 1.25p dp grn ('30)	1.75	1.75
a.		Surcharge inverted	6.00	
b.		Double surch.	5.00	
C21	A4	15p on 25p ultra (Bk + R)	32.50	21.00
a.		Overprint (k) inverted	50.00	50.00

POSTAGE DUE STAMPS.

Postage Due Stamps of France, 1893-1920, Surcharged in Black.

1925 ***Perf. 14 x 13½.*** **Unwmkd.**

J1	D2 (a)	50c on 10c choc	2.25	2.25
J2	D2 (a)	1p on 20c ol grn	2.25	2.25
J3	D2 (b)	2p on 30c red	2.25	2.25
J4	D2 (b)	3p on 50c vio brn	2.25	2.25
J5	D2 (b)	5p on 1 fr red brn, *straw*	2.25	2.25
		Nos. J1-J5 (5)	11.25	11.25

Postage Due Stamps of Syria, 1925, Overprinted in Black, Blue or Red.

1925 ***Perf. 13½***

J6	D5 (d)	50c brn, *yel*	90	90
J7	D6 (c)	1p vio *rose* (Bl)	90	90
a.		Blk. overprint	13.00	13.00
b.		Double overprint (Bk + Bl)	21.00	21.00
J8	D5 (d)	2p *blue*	1.40	1.40
J9	D5 (d)	3p *red org*	2.00	2.00
J10	D5 (d)	5p *bl grn*	3.00	3.00
		Nos. J6-J10 (5)	8.20	8.20

The stamps of Alaouites were superseded in 1930 by those of Latakia.

ALBANIA

(ăl·bā'nĭ·ȧ)

LOCATION — Southeastern Europe.
GOVT.—Republic.
AREA—11,101 sq. mi.
POP.—2,750,000 (1982 est.).
CAPITAL—Tirana.

After the outbreak of World War I, the country fell into a state of anarchy when the Prince and all members of the International Commission left Albania. Subsequently General Ferrero in command of Italian troops declared Albania an independent country. A constitution was adopted and a republican form of government was instituted which continued until 1928 when, by constitutional amendment, Albania was declared to be a monarchy. The President of the republic, Ahmed Zogu, became king of the new state. Many unlisted varieties of surcharges and lithographed labels are said to have done postal duty in Albania and Epirus during this unsettled period.

In March 1939, Italy invaded Albania. King Zog fled but did not abdicate. The King of Italy acquired the crown.

Germany occupied Albania from September, 1943, until late 1944 when it became an independent state. The People's Republic began in January, 1946.

40 Paras = 1 Piastre = 1 Grossion
100 Centimes = 1 Franc (1917)
100 Qintar = 1 Franc
100 Qintar (Qindarka) = 1 Lek (1947)

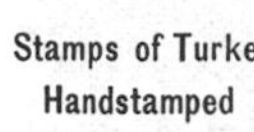

1913, June **Unwmkd.**
Perf. 12, 13½ and Compound.

Handstamped on Issue of 1908.

1	A19	2½pi vio brn	300.00	250.00

With Additional Overprint in Carmine ب

2	A19	10pa bl grn	250.00	225.00

The eagle handstamp was applied to other Turkish stamps of 1908: 25pi green and 50 pi red brown. The 5pa ocher, Albania #4, was surcharged "2 paras" These three stamps were retained by officials.

Prices, $3,000, $7,500, $500.

Handstamped on Issue of 1909.

4	A21	5pa ocher	125.00	100.00
5	A21	10pa bl grn	100.00	90.00
6	A21	20pa car rose	75.00	60.00
7	A21	1pi ultra	85.00	75.00
8	A21	2pi bl blk	130.00	110.00
10	A21	5pi dk vio	450.00	325.00
11	A21	10pi dl red	1,400.	1,200.

With Additional Overprint in Blue or Carmine ب

14	A21	20pa car rose (Bl)	225.00	175.00
15	A21	1pi brt bl (C)	575.00	525.00

Handstamped on Newspaper Stamp of 1911

17	A21	2pa ol grn	130.00	120.00

Handstamped on Postage Due Stamp of 1908.

18	A19	1pi *dp rose*	800.00	600.00

No. 18 was used for regular postage.

No. 6 Surcharged With New Value.

19	A21	10pa on 20pa car rose	300.00	275.00

The overprint on Nos. 1 to 19 was handstamped and, as usual, is found inverted, double, etc.

Nos. 6, 7 and 8 exist with the handstamp in red, blue or violet, but these varieties are not known to have been regularly issued.

Excellent counterfeits exist of Nos. 1 to 19.

A1

1913, July ***Imperf.***

Handstamped on White Laid Paper Without Eagle and Value.

20	A1	(1pi) black	135.00	120.00
		Cut to shape	60.00	60.00
a.		Sewing machine perf.	200.00	175.00

1913, Aug. **With Eagle.**

Value Typewritten in Violet

21	A1	10pa violet	5.50	3.50
22	A1	20pa red & blk	5.50	3.75
23	A1	1gr black	5.50	3.50
24	A1	2gr bl & vio	6.50	5.00
25	A1	5gr vio & bl	8.75	7.00
26	A1	10gr blue	9.00	7.00
		Nos. 21-26 (6)	40.75	29.75

Nos. 21-26 exist with the eagle inverted or omitted and with numerous errors in the figures of value and the spelling of the word "grosh".

A2

SHQIPENIA E LIRË
GJERGJI KASTRIOTI
2 QINT. 2

Skanderbeg (George Castriota)
A3

1913, Nov. ***Perf. 11½***

Handstamped on White Laid Paper Eagle and Value in Black.

27	A2	10pa green	2.00	1.00
b.		Eagle and value in grn	20.00	
c.		10pa red (error)	15.00	15.00
d.		10pa vio (error)	15.00	15.00
29	A2	20pa red	2.00	1.00
b.		20pa grn (error)	15.00	15.00
30	A2	30pa violet	2.25	1.25
a.		30pa ultra (error)	15.00	15.00
b.		30pa red (error)	15.00	15.00
31	A2	1gr ultra	3.00	1.75
a.		1gr grn (error)	15.00	15.00
b.		1gr blk (error)	15.00	15.00
c.		1gr vio (error)	15.00	15.00
33	A2	2gr black	5.00	3.50
a.		2gr vio (error)	15.00	15.00
b.		2gr bl (error)	15.00	15.00
		Nos. 27-33 (5)	14.25	8.50

The stamps of this issue are known with eagle or value inverted or omitted.

The stamps were issued in commemoration of the first anniversary of Albanian independence.

1913, Dec. **Typographed** ***Perf. 14***

35	A3	2q org brn & buff	65	50
36	A3	5q grn & bl grn	65	50
37	A3	10q rose red	60	40
38	A3	25q dk bl	80	60
39	A3	50q vio & red	1.25	1.00
40	A3	1fr dp brn	6.00	6.00
		Nos. 35-40 (6)	9.95	9.00

Nos. 35–40 Handstamped in Black or Violet

7.Mars
1407. RROFTË MBRETI. 1914

1914, Mar. 7

41	A3	2q org brn & buff	12.50	10.00
42	A3	5q grn & bl grn (V)	12.50	10.00
43	A3	10q rose red	12.50	10.00
44	A3	25q dk bl (V)	12.50	10.00
45	A3	50q vio & red	12.50	10.00
46	A3	1fr dp brn	12.50	10.00
		Nos. 41-46 (6)	75.00	60.00

Issued to celebrate the arrival of Prince Wilhelm zu Wied on Mar. 7, 1914.

Nos. 35–40 Surcharged in Black:

5 • PARA •
a

1 GROSH
b

1914, Apr. 2

47	A3 (a)	5pa on 2q org brn & buff	60	60
a.		Inverted surcharge	5.00	5.00
48	A3 (a)	10pa on 5q grn & bl grn	60	60
a.		Inverted surcharge	5.00	5.00
49	A3 (a)	20pa on 10q rose red	90	70
a.		Inverted surcharge	5.00	5.00
50	A3 (b)	1gr on 25q bl	90	90
a.		Inverted surcharge	6.00	6.00
51	A3 (b)	2gr on 50q vio & red	1.25	1.10
a.		Inverted surcharge	7.50	7.50
52	A3 (b)	5gr on 1fr dp brn	7.50	7.50
b.		Invtd. surch.	10.00	10.00
		Nos. 47-52 (6)	11.75	11.40

Korce (Korytsa) Issues

A4

1914 Handstamped *Imperf.*

52A	A4	10pa vio & red	60.00	50.00
c.		10pa blk & red	85.00	70.00
53	A4	25pa vio & red	60.00	50.00
a.		25pa blk & red	110.00	100.00

Nos. 52A–53a originally were handstamped directly on the cover, so the paper varies. Later they were also produced in sheets; these are rarely found. Nos. 52A–53a were issued by Albanian military authorities.

A5 A6

1917 Typo. & Litho. *Perf. 11½*

54	A5	1c dk brn & grn	12.50	10.00
55	A5	2c red & grn	12.50	10.00
56	A5	3c gray grn & grn	12.50	10.00
57	A5	5c grn & blk	9.00	5.00
58	A5	10c rose red & blk	9.00	5.00
59	A5	25c bl & blk	9.00	5.00
60	A5	50c vio & blk	9.00	5.00
61	A5	1fr brn & blk	12.50	10.00
		Nos. 54-61 (8)	86.00	60.00

1917-18

62	A6	1c dk brn & grn	4.00	3.25
63	A6	2c red brn & grn	4.00	3.25
a.		"CTM" for "CTS"	17.50	17.50
64	A6	3c blk & grn	4.00	3.25
a.		"CTM" for "CTS"	17.50	17.50
65	A6	5c grn & blk	4.50	4.50
66	A6	10c dl red & blk	4.50	4.50
67	A6	50c vio & blk	8.50	8.50
68	A6	1fr red brn & blk	15.00	10.00
		Nos. 62-68 (7)	44.50	37.25

Counterfeits abound of Nos. 54-68, 80-81.

No. 65 Surcharged in Red

QARKU
I
KORÇËS
25 CTS

1918

80	A6	25c on 5c grn & blk	60.00	50.00

A7

1918

81	A7	25c bl & blk	37.50	30.00

General Issue

A8 A9

Handstamped in Rose or Blue

XV I MCMXIX

1919 *Perf. 12½*

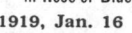

84	A8	(2)q on 2h brn	5.00	4.50
85	A8	5q on 16h grn	5.00	4.50
86	A8	10q on 8h rose (Bl)	5.00	4.50
87	A8	25q on 64h bl	5.00	4.50
88	A9	25q on 64h bl	200.00	175.00
89	A8	50q on 32h vio	5.00	4.50
90	A8	1fr on 1.28k org, *bl*	5.00	4.50
		Nos. 84-90 (7)	230.00	202.00

Handstamped in Rose or Blue

1919, Jan. 16

91	A8	(2)q on 2h brn	6.50	6.50
92	A8	5q on 16h grn	6.50	6.50
93	A8	10q on 8h rose (Bl)	6.50	6.50
94	A8	25q on 64h bl	35.00	35.00
95	A9	25q on 64h bl	30.00	30.00
96	A8	50q on 32h vio	6.50	6.50
97	A8	1fr on 1.28k org, *bl*	6.50	6.50
		Nos. 91-97 (7)	97.50	97.50

Handstamped in Violet

1919

98	A8	(2)q on 2h brn	7.00	7.00
99	A8	5q on 16h grn	7.00	7.00
100	A8	10q on 8h rose	7.00	7.00
101	A8	25q on 64h bl	7.00	7.00
102	A9	25q on 64h bl	30.00	30.00
103	A8	50q on 32h vio	7.00	7.00
104	A8	1fr on 1.28k org, *bl*	7.00	7.00
		Nos. 98-104 (7)	72.00	72.00

No. 50 Overprinted in Violet

1919 *Perf. 14*

105	A3	1gr on 25q bl	3.00	4.00

A10 A11

1919, June 5 *Perf. 11½, 12½*

106	A10	10q on 2h brn	4.00	4.00
107	A11	15q on 8h rose	4.00	4.00
108	A11	20q on 16h grn	4.00	4.00
109	A10	25q on 64h bl	4.00	4.00
110	A11	50q on 32h vio	4.00	4.00
111	A11	1fr on 96h org	4.00	4.00
112	A10	2fr on 1.60k vio, *buff*	8.00	8.00
		Nos. 106-112 (7)	32.00	32.00

Nos. 106–108, 110 exist with inverted surcharge.

A12 A13

Black or Violet Surcharge

1919

113	A12	10q on 8h car	4.00	4.00
114	A12	15q on 8h car (V)	4.00	4.00
115	A13	20q on 16h grn	4.00	4.00
116	A13	25q on 32h vio	4.00	4.00
117	A13	50q on 64h bl	8.50	8.50
118	A13	1fr on 96h org	5.00	5.00
119	A12	2fr on 1.60k vio, *buff*	5.00	5.00
		Nos. 113-119 (7)	34.50	34.50

A14 A15

Overprinted in Blue or Black. Without New Value.

1920 *Perf. 12½.*

120	A14	1q gray (Bl)	30.00	35.00
121	A14	10q rose (Bk)	2.50	4.00
a.		Double overprint	35.00	40.00
122	A14	20q brn (Bl)	15.00	17.50
123	A14	25q bl (Bk)	160.00	175.00
124	A14	50q brn vio (Bk)	20.00	25.00
		Nos. 120-124 (5)	227.50	256.50

Counterfeit overprints exist of Nos. 120-128.

Surcharged with New Value.

125	A14	2q on 10q rose (R)	4.00	6.00
126	A14	5q on 10q rose (G)	4.00	6.00
127	A14	25q on 10q rose (Bl)	4.00	6.00
128	A14	50q on 10q rose (Br)	4.00	6.00

Stamps of type A14 (Portrait of the Prince zu Wied) were not placed in use without overprint or surcharge.

Post Horn Overprinted in Black.

1920 *Perf. 14x13*

129	A15	2q orange	2.00	2.00
130	A15	5q dp grn	2.75	2.25
131	A15	10q red	7.00	5.50
132	A15	25q lt bl	12.50	7.00
133	A15	50q gray grn	2.00	2.00
134	A15	1fr claret	2.00	2.00
		Nos. 129-134 (6)	28.25	20.75

Type A15 was never placed in use without post horn or "Besa" overprint.

Stamps of Type A15 (No Post Horn) Overprinted

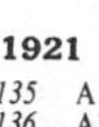

1921

135	A15	2q orange	1.50	1.50
136	A15	5q dp grn	2.00	2.00
137	A15	10q red	3.50	3.50
138	A15	25q lt bl	7.50	6.00
139	A15	50q gray grn	2.50	2.50
140	A15	1fr claret	2.00	2.00
		No. 135-140 (6)	19.00	17.50

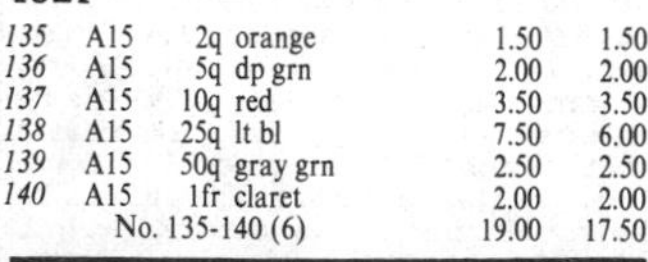

Stamps of these types, and with "TAKSE" overprint, were unauthorized and never placed in use.

Gjinokaster
A18

Korcha
A19

Designs: 5q, Kanina. 10q, Berati. 25q, Bridge at Vezirit. 50q, Rozafat. 2fr, Dursit.

1923 Typo. *Perf. 12½, 11½*

147	A18	2q orange	70	95
148	A18	5q yel grn	55	30
149	A18	10q carmine	55	30
150	A18	25q dk bl	55	30
151	A18	50q dk grn	55	30
152	A19	1fr dk vio	80	1.10
153	A19	2fr ol grn	2.25	3.00
		Nos. 147-153 (7)	5.95	6.25

No. 135 Surcharged

Q 1

1922 *Perf. 14x13*

154	A15	1q on 2q org	2.00	2.00

Stamps of Type A15 (No Post Horn) Overprinted

BESA

1922

156	A15	5q dp grn	2.75	2.75
157	A15	10q red	2.75	2.75

Nos. 147–151 Overprinted (top line in Black; diamond in Violet)

Mbledhje Kushtetuese
TIRANE
KALLNUER
1924

1924, Jan *Perf. 12½*

158	A18	2q red org	3.00	4.00
159	A18	5q yel grn	3.00	4.00
160	A18	10q carmine	3.00	4.00
161	A18	25q dk bl	3.00	4.00
162	A18	50q dk grn	3.00	4.00
		Nos. 158-162 (5)	15.00	20.00

The words "Mbledhje Kushtetuese" are in taller letters on the 25q than on the other values. This issue was to commemorate the opening of the Constituent Assembly.

No. 147 Surcharged

= 1 =

1924

163	A18	1q on 2q red org	75	75

Nos. 163, 147–152 Overprinted

Triumf' i legalitetit
24 Dhetuer 1924

1924

164	A18	1q on 2q org	1.75	1.75
165	A18	2q orange	1.75	1.75
166	A18	5q yel grn	1.75	1.75
167	A18	10q carmine	1.75	1.75
168	A18	25q dk bl	1.75	1.75
169	A18	50q dk grn	1.75	1.75
170	A19	1fr dk vio	1.75	1.75
		Nos. 164-170 (7)	12.25	12.25

Issued to celebrate the return of the Government to the Capital after a revolution.

Nos. 163, 147–152 Overprinted

Republika Shqiptare

21 Kallnduer 1925

1925

171	A18	1q on 2q org	1.50	1.50
172	A18	2q orange	1.50	1.50
173	A18	5q yel grn	1.50	1.50
174	A18	10q carmine	1.50	1.50
175	A18	25q dk bl	1.50	1.50
176	A18	50q dk grn	1.50	1.50
177	A19	1fr dk vio	1.50	1.50
		Nos. 171-177 (7)	10.50	10.50

Issued in honor of the proclamation of the Republic, Jan. 21, 1925. The date "1921" instead of "1925" occurs once in each sheet of 50.

Nos. 163, 147–153 Overprinted

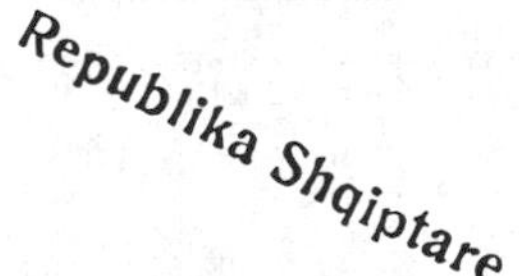

1925

178	A18	1q on 2q org	65	65
a.		Inverted overprint	8.25	8.25
179	A18	2q orange	65	65
180	A18	5q yel grn	65	65
a.		Inverted overprint	8.25	8.25
181	A18	10q carmine	65	65
182	A18	25q dk bl	65	65
183	A18	50q dk grn	65	65
184	A19	1fr dk vio	80	80
185	A19	2fr ol grn	80	80
		Nos. 178-185 (8)	5.50	5.50

President Ahmed Zogu
A25 A26

1925 ***Perf. 13½, 13½x13***

186	A25	1q orange	15	15
187	A25	2q red brn	15	15
188	A25	5q green	15	15
189	A25	10q rose red	15	15
190	A25	15q gray brn	1.75	1.75
191	A25	25q dk bl	15	15
192	A25	50q bl grn	60	60
193	A26	1fr red & ultra	1.10	1.10
194	A26	2fr grn & org	1.10	1.10
195	A26	3fr brn & vio	1.75	1.75
196	A26	5fr vio & blk	4.25	4.25
		Nos. 186-196 (11)	11.30	11.30

No. 193 in ultramarine and brown, and No. 194 in gray and brown were not regularly issued.

Price, both $15.

Nos. 186–196 Overprinted in Various Colors

1927

197	A25	1q org (V)	50	50
198	A25	2q red brn (G)	20	20
199	A25	5q grn (R)	1.00	20
200	A25	10q rose red (Bl)	20	10
201	A25	15q gray brn (G)	10.00	10.00
202	A25	25q dk bl (R)	20	10
203	A25	50q bl grn (Bl)	20	10
204	A26	1fr red & ultra (Bk)	20	20
205	A26	2fr grn & org (Bk)	20	20
206	A26	3fr brn & vio (Bk)	75	75
207	A26	5fr vio & blk (Bk)	1.25	1.25
		Nos. 197-207 (11)	14.70	13.60

No. 200 exists perf. 11.

Nos. 200, 202 Surcharged ═ 5 ═ in Black or Red.

1928

208	A25	1q on 10q rose red	40	30
a.		Inverted surcharge	5.00	5.00
209	A25	5q on 25q dk bl (R)	40	30
a.		Inverted surcharge	5.00	5.00

King Zog I
A27 A28

Black Overprint.

1928 ***Perf. 14x13½.***

210	A27	1q org brn	2.50	2.50
211	A27	2q slate	2.50	2.50
212	A27	5q bl grn	2.50	2.50
213	A27	10q rose red	2.50	2.50
214	A27	15q bister	13.50	13.50
215	A27	25q dp bl	2.00	2.00
216	A27	50q lil rose	2.50	2.50

Red Overprint.

Perf. 13½x14.

217	A28	1fr bl & sl	2.75	2.75
		Nos. 210-217 (8)	30.75	30.75

A29 A30

Black or Red Overprint.

1928 ***Perf. 14x13½.***

218	A29	1q org brn	8.50	8.50
219	A29	2q sl (R)	8.50	8.50
220	A29	5q bl grn	7.00	7.00
221	A29	10q rose red	4.50	4.50
222	A29	15q bister	5.00	5.00
223	A29	25q dp bl (R)	5.00	5.00
224	A29	50q lil rose	5.50	5.50

Perf. 13½x14.

225	A30	1fr bl & sl (R)	8.00	8.00
226	A30	2fr grn & sl (R)	9.50	9.50
		Nos. 218-226 (9)	61.50	61.50

Issued in commemoration of the proclamation of Ahmed Zogu as King of Albania.

A31 A32

Black Overprint.

1928 ***Perf. 14x13½.***

227	A31	1q org brn	40	40
228	A31	2q slate	20	20
229	A31	5q bl grn	1.50	20
230	A31	10q rose red	20	15
231	A31	15q bister	11.00	8.00
232	A31	25q dp bl	25	15
233	A31	50q lil rose	25	15

Perf. 13½x14.

234	A32	1fr bl & sl	50	75
235	A32	2fr grn & sl	60	75
236	A32	3fr dk red & ol bis	1.00	1.25
237	A32	5fr dl vio & gray	2.00	2.25
		Nos. 227-237 (11)	17.90	14.25

The overprint reads "Kingdom of Albania".

Mbr. Shqiptare

Nos. 203, 202, 200 Surcharged in Black

■ 5 ■

1929 ***Perf. 13½x13, 11½***

238	A25	1q on 50q bl grn	40	40
239	A25	5q on 25q dk bl	40	40
240	A25	15q on 10q rose red	65	60

RROFT-MBRETI

Nos. 186–189, 191–194 Overprinted in Black or Red

8X1929.

1929 ***Perf. 11½, 13½.***

241	A25	1q orange	4.00	4.00
242	A25	2q red brn	4.00	4.00
243	A25	5q green	4.00	4.00
244	A25	10q rose red	4.00	4.00
245	A25	25q dk bl	4.00	4.00
246	A25	50q bl grn (R)	4.50	4.50
247	A26	1fr red & ultra	7.00	7.00
248	A26	2fr grn & org	8.50	8.50
		Nos. 241-248 (8)	40.00	40.00

Issued to commemorate the 34th birthday of King Zog. The overprint reads "Long live the King."

Lake Butrinto King Zog I
A33 A34

Zog Bridge Ruin at Zog Manor
A35 A36

Wmk. 220

Wmkd.

Double Headed Eagle. (220)

1930, Sept. 1 Photo. *Perf. 14, 14½*

250	A33	1q slate	15	10
251	A33	2q org red	15	10
252	A34	5q yel grn	15	10
253	A34	10q carmine	15	10
254	A34	15q dk brn	20	20
255	A34	25q dk ultra	25	20
256	A33	50q sl grn	35	30
257	A35	1fr violet	90	90
258	A35	2fr indigo	1.00	1.00
259	A36	3fr gray grn	2.25	2.25
260	A36	5fr org brn	3.50	3.50
		Nos. 250-260 (11)	9.05	8.75

2nd anniversary of accession of King Zog I.

Nos. 250–259 Overprinted in Black

1 1
9 9
2 3
4=24Dhetuer=4

1934, Dec. 24

261	A33	1q slate	2.00	2.00
262	A33	2q org red	2.00	2.00
263	A34	5q yel grn	2.00	2.00
264	A34	10q carmine	2.00	2.00
265	A34	15q dk brn	2.00	2.00
266	A34	25q dk ultra	2.00	2.00
267	A33	50q sl grn	2.00	2.00
268	A35	1fr violet	4.50	4.50
269	A35	2fr indigo	9.00	9.00
270	A36	3fr gray grn	12.50	12.50
		Nos. 261-270 (10)	40.00	40.00

Tenth anniversary of the Constitution.

Allegory of Death of Skanderbeg Albanian Eagle in Turkish Shackles
A37 A38

Designs: 5q, 25q, 40q, 2fr, Eagle with wings spread.

1937 ***Perf. 14*** **Unwmkd.**

271	A37	1q brn vio	20	20
272	A38	2q brown	20	20
273	A38	5q lt grn	30	30
274	A37	10q ol brn	40	40
275	A38	15q rose red	50	50
276	A38	25q blue	90	90
277	A37	50q dp grn	1.25	1.25
278	A38	1fr violet	2.25	2.25
279	A38	2fr org brn	5.50	5.50
		Nos. 271-279 (9)	11.50	11.50

Souvenir Sheet.

280		Sheet of three	12.50	15.00
a.		A37 20q red vio	2.50	3.00
b.		A38 30q ol brn	2.50	3.00
c.		A38 40q red	2.50	3.00

Nos. 271–280 commemorate the 25th anniversary of independence from Turkey, proclaimed Nov. 26, 1912. No. 280 measures 138x140mm.

Queen Geraldine and King Zog
A40

1938 ***Perf. 14***

281	A40	1q sl vio	15	15
282	A40	2q red brn	15	15
283	A40	5q green	15	15
284	A40	10q ol brn	25	30
285	A40	15q rose red	35	50
286	A40	25q blue	60	75
287	A40	50q Prus grn	1.75	2.00
288	A40	1fr purple	3.75	4.00
		Nos. 281-288 (8)	7.15	8.00

Souvenir Sheet.

289	A40	Sheet of four	17.50	20.00
a.		20q dk red vio	1.75	1.75
b.		30q brn ol	1.75	1.75

Nos. 281–289 were issued to commemorate the wedding of King Zog and Countess Geraldine Apponyi, April 27, 1938. Souvenir sheet measures 110½x139mm.

Queen Geraldine
A42

National Emblems
A43

King Zog I
A44

1938

290	A42	1q dp red vio	15	20
291	A43	2q red org	15	20
292	A42	5q dp grn	15	20
293	A44	10q red brn	15	20
294	A42	15q dp rose	45	45
295	A44	25q dp bl	60	75
296	A43	50q gray blk	1.50	1.75
297	A44	1fr sl grn	5.00	5.50
		Nos. 290-297 (8)	8.15	9.25

Souvenir Sheet.

298		Sheet of three	17.50	20.00
b.		A43 20q Prus grn	2.25	2.25
c.		A44 30q dp vio	2.25	2.25

Nos. 290–298 were issued to commemorate the 10th anniversary of royal rule. They were on sale for three days (Aug. 30–31, Sept. 1) only, during which their use was required on all mail.

No. 298 has marginal inscriptions in Prussian green. Size: 110x65mm. The 15q deep rose (type A42) is identical with No. 294.

Issued under Italian Dominion.

Nos. 250–260 Overprinted in Black

Mbledhja Kushtetuëse 12-IV-1939 XVII

1939 ***Perf. 14*** **Wmk 220**

299	A33	1q slate	10	10
300	A33	2q org red	15	15
301	A34	5q yel grn	15	15
302	A34	10q carmine	20	20
303	A34	15q dk brn	20	20
304	A34	25q dk ultra	30	30
305	A33	50q sl grn	40	40
306	A35	1fr violet	75	75
307	A35	2fr indigo	1.00	1.00
308	A36	3fr gray grn	2.25	2.25
309	A36	5fr org brn	3.00	3.00
		Nos. 299-309 (11)	8.50	8.50

Issued in commemoration of the resolution adopted by the National Assembly, April 12, 1939, offering the Albanian Crown to Italy.

Native Costumes
A46 A47 A48

King Victor Emmanuel III
A49 A50

Native Costume
A51

Monastery
A52

Designs: 2fr, Bridge at Vezirit. 3fr, Ancient Columns. 5fr, Amphitheater.

Photogravure

1939 ***Perf. 14*** **Unwmkd.**

310	A46	1q bl gray	12	12
311	A47	2q ol grn	10	10
312	A48	3q gldn brn	10	10
313	A49	5q green	10	10
314	A50	10q brown	15	10
315	A50	15q crimson	20	15
316	A50	25q sapphire	30	20
317	A50	30q brt vio	40	25
318	A51	50q dl pur	50	25
319	A49	65q red brn	75	75
320	A52	1fr myr grn	1.00	1.00
321	A52	2fr brn lake	2.25	2.25
322	A52	3fr brn blk	4.50	4.50
323	A52	5fr gray vio	8.75	8.75
		Nos. 310-323 (14)	19.22	18.62

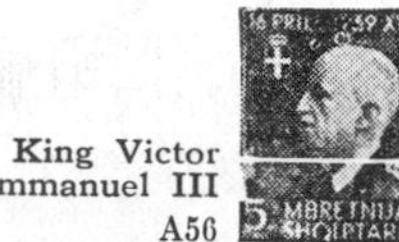
King Victor Emmanuel III
A56

1942 **Photogravure**

324	A56	5q green	12	12
325	A56	10q brown	12	12
326	A56	15q rose red	12	12
327	A56	25q blue	20	20
328	A56	65q red brn	30	30
329	A56	1fr myr grn	60	60
330	A56	2fr gray vio	1.25	1.25
		Nos. 324-330 (7)	2.71	2.71

Issued to commemorate the third anniversary of the conquest of Albania by Italy.

No. 311 Surcharged in Black **1 QIND**

331	A47	1q on 2q ol grn	40	40

Issued under German Administration

Stamps of 1939 Overprinted in Carmine or Brown

14 Shtator 1943

1943

332	A47	2q ol grn	1.25	2.00
333	A48	3q gldn brn	1.25	2.00
334	A49	5q green	1.25	2.00
335	A50	10q brown	1.25	2.00
336	A50	15q crim (Br)	1.25	2.00
337	A50	25q sapphire	1.25	2.00
338	A50	30q brt vio	1.25	2.00
339	A49	65q red brn	1.50	3.50
340	A52	1fr myr grn	9.00	15.00
341	A52	2fr brn lake	12.00	*30.00*
342	A52	3fr brn blk	52.50	*80.00*

Surcharged with New Values.

343	A48	1q on 3q gldn brn	1.25	2.00
344	A49	50q on 65q red brn	1.50	3.50
		Nos. 332-344 (13)	86.50	*148.00*

Proclamation of Albanian independence.
The overprint "14 Shtator 1943" on Nos. 324 to 328 is private and fraudulent.

Independent State

Nos. 312 to 317 and 319 to 321 Surcharged with New Value and Bars in Black or Carmine, and

QEVERIJA DEMOKRAT. E SHQIPERISE 22-X-1944

1945

345	A48	30q on 3q gldn brn	2.50	2.50
346	A49	40q on 5q grn	2.50	2.50
347	A50	50q on 10q brn	2.50	2.50
348	A50	60q on 15q crim	2.50	2.50
349	A50	80q on 25q saph (C)	2.50	2.50
350	A50	1fr on 30q brt vio	2.50	2.50
351	A49	2fr on 65q red brn	2.50	2.50
352	A52	3fr on 1fr myr grn	2.50	2.50
353	A52	5fr on 2fr brn lake	2.50	2.50
		Nos. 345-353 (9)	22.50	22.50

"DEMOKRATIKE" is not abbreviated on Nos. 352 and 353.

Nos. 250, 251, 256 and 258 Surcharged in Black or Carmine, and

1943 U.N.ÇL.SHQ. 1945 10 KORRIK FR.SHQ. 5

1945 **Wmk. 220**

354	A33	30q on 1q sl	50	50
355	A33	60q on 1q sl	60	60
356	A33	80q on 1q sl	70	70
357	A33	1fr on 1q sl	1.00	1.00
358	A33	2fr on 2q org red	1.50	1.50
359	A33	3fr on 50q sl grn	3.75	3.75
360	A35	5fr on 2fr ind	5.00	5.50
		Nos. 354-360 (7)	13.05	13.55

Albanian National Army of Liberation, second anniversary.
The surcharge on No. 360 is condensed to fit the size of the stamp.

Country House, Labinot
A57

Designs: 40q, 60q, Bridge at Berat. 1fr, 3fr, Permet.

Typographed.

1945, Nov. 28 ***Perf. 11*** **Unwmkd.**

361	A57	20q bluish grn	25	25
362	A57	30q dp org	50	50
363	A57	40q brown	50	50
364	A57	60q red vio	75	75
365	A57	1fr rose red	1.50	1.50
366	A57	3fr dk bl	7.50	7.50
		Nos. 361-366 (6)	11.00	11.00

Counterfeits exist. See note after No. B33.

Nos. 361 to 366 Overprinted in Black

ASAMBLEJA KUSHTETUESE

10 KALLHUER 1946

1946

367	A57	20q bluish grn	75	75
368	A57	30q dp org	75	75
369	A57	40q brown	1.25	1.25
370	A57	60q red vio	2.25	2.25
371	A57	1fr rose red	6.00	6.00
372	A57	3fr dk bl	9.50	9.50
		Nos. 367-372 (6)	20.50	20.50

Issued to commemorate the convocation of the Constitutional Assembly, January 10, 1946.

People's Republic

Nos. 361 to 366 Overprinted in Black

REPUBLIKA POPULLORE E SHQIPERISE

1946

373	A57	20q bluish grn	75	75
374	A57	30q dp org	1.25	1.25
375	A57	40q brown	1.75	1.75
376	A57	60q red vio	2.75	2.75
377	A57	1fr rose red	5.00	5.00
378	A57	3fr dk bl	8.50	8.50
		Nos. 373-378 (6)	20.00	20.00

Issued to commemorate the proclamation of the Albanian People's Republic.

Globe, Dove and Olive Branch
A60

Typographed

1946, Mar. 8 ***Perf. 11½, Imperf.***

Denomination in Black.

379	A60	20q lil & dl red	15	15
380	A60	40q dp lil & dl red	25	25
381	A60	50q vio & dl red	40	40
382	A60	1fr lt bl & red	60	60
383	A60	2fr dk bl & red	1.25	1.25
		Nos. 379-383 (5)	2.65	2.65

International Women's Congress.

Athletes with Shot and Indian Club
A61

Perf. 11½

1946, Oct. 6 **Litho.** **Unwmkd.**

384	A61	1q grnsh blk	8.00	8.00
385	A61	2q green	8.00	8.00
386	A61	5q brown	8.00	8.00
387	A61	10q crimson	8.00	8.00
388	A61	20q ultra	8.00	8.00
389	A61	40q rose vio	8.00	8.00
390	A61	1fr dp org	12.50	12.50
		Nos. 384-390 (7)	60.50	60.50

Balkan Games, Tirana, Oct. 6–13.

Qemal Stafa
A62

1947, May 5 ***Perf. 12½x11½***

391	A62	20q brn & yel brn	1.75	1.75
392	A62	28q dk bl & bl	1.75	1.75
393	A62	40q brn blk & gray brn	3.00	3.00
a.		Souvenir sheet	6.50	6.50

Nos. 391 to 393a commemorate the 5th anniversary of the death of Qemal Stafa, May 5, 1942. No. 393a contains one each of Nos. 391-393 imperf. with illustrations above and below the stamps.

Young Railway Laborers
A64

1947, May 16 ***Perf. 11½***

395	A64	1q brn blk & gray brn	1.00	50
396	A64	4q dk grn & grn	1.00	50
397	A64	10q blk brn & bis brn	1.00	50
398	A64	15q dk red & red	1.25	50

399	A64	20q	ind & bl gray	1.75	75
400	A64	28q	dk bl & bl	2.50	75
401	A64	40q	brn vio & rose vio	6.50	3.50
402	A64	68q	dk brn & org brn	10.00	6.50
			Nos. 395-402 (8)	25.00	13.50

Issued to publicize the construction of the Durrës Elbasan Railway by Albanian youths.

Citizens Led by Hasim Zeneli
A65

Enver Hoxha and Vasil Shanto
A66

Vojo Kushi
A68

Inauguration of Vithkuq Brigade
A67

947, July 10 Lithographed

403	A65	16q	brn org & red brn	2.00	2.00
404	A66	20q	org brn & dk brn	2.00	2.00
405	A67	28q	bl & dk bl	2.25	2.25
406	A68	40q	lil & dk brn	3.25	3.25

Issued to commemorate the 4th anniver-ary of the formation of Albania's army, uly 10, 1943.

Conference Building Ruins, Peza
A69

Disabled Soldiers
A70

.947, Sept. 16

407	A69	2 l	red vio	2.50	2.00
408	A69	2.50 l	dp bl	2.50	2.00

Issued to commemorate the 5th anniver-sary of the Peza Conference, September 16, 1942.

947, Nov. 17 *Perf. 12½x11½*

408A	A70	1 l	red	3.50	3.50

Issued to publicize the Disabled War Veterans Congress, November 14-20, 1947.

A71

A73

Designs: 2 l, Banquet. 2.50 l, Peasants rejoicing.

Perf. 11½x12½, 12½x11½

1947, Nov. 17 Unwmkd.

409	A71	1.50 l	dl vio	2.75	2.75
410	A71	2 l	brown	2.75	2.75
411	A71	2.50 l	blue	2.75	2.75
412	A73	3 l	rose red	2.75	2.75

Issued to commemorate the 1st anniversary of the agrarian reform law of November 17, 1946.

Burning Farm Buildings
A74

Designs: 2.50 l, Trench scene. 5 l, Firing line. 8 l, Winter advance. 12 l, Infantry column.

1947, Nov. 29 *Perf. 11½x12½*

Inscribed: "29-XI-1944-1947 Pervjetori I IIIte Iclirimit."

413	A74	1.50 l	red	2.00	2.00
414	A74	2.50 l	rose brn	2.50	2.50
415	A74	5 l	blue	3.00	3.00
416	A74	8 l	purple	5.00	5.00
417	A74	12 l	brown	7.50	7.50
			Nos. 413-417 (5)	20.00	20.00

Issued to commemorate the third anniversary of Albania's liberation.

Nos. 373 to 378 Surcharged with New Value and Bars in Black.

1948, Feb. 22 *Perf. 11*

418	A57	50q	on 30q dp org	30	30
419	A57	1 l	on 20q bluish grn	60	60
420	A57	2.50 l	on 60q red vio	1.25	1.25
421	A57	3 l	on 1fr rose red	1.75	1.75
422	A57	5 l	on 3fr dk bl	2.75	2.75
423	A57	12 l	on 40q brn	6.00	6.00
			Nos. 418-423 (6)	12.65	12.65

The two bars consist of four type squares each set close together.

Map, Train and Construction Workers
A75

1948, June 1 Litho. *Perf. 11½*

424	A75	50q	dk car rose	1.00	60
425	A75	1 l	lt grn & blk	1.25	60
426	A75	1.50 l	dp rose	1.25	60
427	A75	2.50 l	org brn & dk brn	1.25	60
428	A75	5 l	dl bl	2.00	1.25
429	A75	8 l	sal & dk brn	4.50	2.50
430	A75	12 l	red vio & dk vio	6.50	2.75
431	A75	20 l	ol gray	12.50	6.00
			Nos. 424-431 (8)	30.25	14.90

Issued to publicize the construction of the Durrës-Tirana Railway.

Marching Soldiers
A76

Design: 8 l, Battle scene.

1948, July 10

432	A76	2.50 l	yel brn	75	75
433	A76	5 l	dk bl	1.00	1.00
434	A76	8 l	vio gray	2.00	2.00

Issued to commemorate the 5th anniversary of the formation of Albania's army.

Bricklayer, Flag, Globe and "Industry"
A77

Map and Soldier
A78

1949, May 1 Photo. *Perf. 12½x12*

435	A77	2.50 l	ol brn	25	25
436	A77	5 l	blue	65	65
437	A77	8 l	vio brn	1.00	1.00

Issued to publicize Labor Day, May 1, 1949.

1949, July 10 Unwmkd.

438	A78	2.50 l	brown	35	35
439	A78	5 l	lt ultra	50	50
440	A78	8 l	brn org	1.25	1.25

Issued to commemorate the 6th anniversary of the formation of Albania's army.

Enver Hoxha
A79

Albanian Citizen and Spasski Tower, Kremlin
A80

1949, Oct. 16 Engr. *Perf. 12½*

441	A79	50q	purple	7	5
442	A79	1 l	dl grn	7	5
443	A79	1.50 l	car lake	15	5
444	A79	2.50 l	brown	30	5
445	A79	5 l	vio bl	60	15
446	A79	8 l	sepia	1.00	75
447	A79	12 l	rose lil	2.25	1.25
448	A79	20 l	gray bl	4.50	2.00
			Nos. 441-448 (8)	8.94	4.35

Photogravure.

1949, Sept. 10 *Perf. 12½x12*

449	A80	2.50 l	org brn	45	45
450	A80	5 l	dp ultra	90	90

Albanian-Soviet friendship.

Albanian Soldier and Flag
A81

Battle Scene
A82

1949, Nov. 29 *Perf. 12* Unwmkd.

451	A81	2.50 l	brown	20	20
452	A82	3 l	dk red	30	40
453	A81	5 l	violet	45	55
454	A82	8 l	black	1.50	1.50

Fifth anniversary of Albania's liberation.

Joseph V Stalin
A83

Symbols of UPU and Postal Transport
A84

1949, Dec. 21

455	A83	2.50 l	dk brn	25	30
456	A83	5 l	vio bl	65	75
457	A83	8 l	rose brn	1.10	1.25

Issued to commemorate the 70th anniversary of the birth of Joseph V. Stalin.

Canceled to Order

Beginning in 1950, Albania sold some issues in sheets canceled to order. Prices in second column when much less than unused are for "CTO" copies. Postally used stamps are valued at slightly less than, or the same as, unused.

1950, July 1 Photo. *Perf. 12x12½*

458	A84	5 l	blue	1.00	1.00
459	A84	8 l	rose brn	1.50	1.50
460	A84	12 l	sepia	2.00	2.00

Issued to commemorate the 75th anniversary (in 1949) of the formation of the Universal Postal Union.

Sami Frasheri
A85

Arms and Albanian Flags
A86

Authors: 2.50 l, Andon Zako. 3 l, Naim Frasheri. 5 l, Kostandin Kristoforidhi.

1950, Nov. 5 *Perf. 14*

461	A85	2 l	dk grn	25	15
462	A85	2.50 l	red brn	35	20
463	A85	3 l	brn car	50	25
464	A85	5 l	dp bl	75	60

Issued to commemorate the "Jubilee of the Writers of the Renaissance."

1951, Jan. 11 Engr. *Perf. 14x13½*

465	A86	2.50 l	brn car	50	25
466	A86	5 l	dp bl	1.00	50
467	A86	8 l	sepia	1.50	1.00

Issued to commemorate the 5th anniversary of the formation of the Albanian People's Republic.

Skanderbeg
A87

Enver Hoxha and Congress of Permet
A88

1951, Mar. 1

468	A87	2.50 l brown	40	25
469	A87	5 l violet	85	50
470	A87	8 l ol bis	1.50	1.00

Issued to commemorate the 483rd anniversary of the death of George Castriota (Skanderbeg).

1951, May 24 Photo. *Perf. 12*

471	A88	2.50 l dk brn	30	20
472	A88	3 l rose brn	45	30
473	A88	5 l vio bl	75	50
474	A88	8 l rose lil	1.25	80

Congress of Permet, 7th anniversary.

Child and Globe
A89

Weighing Baby
A90

1951, July 16

475	A89	2 l green	45	30
476	A90	2.50 l brown	60	40
477	A90	3 l red	85	50
478	A89	5 l blue	1.25	80

Issued to publicize International Children's Day, June 1, 1951.

Enver Hoxha and Birthplace of Albanian Communist Party
A91

1951, Nov. 8 Photo. *Perf. 14*

479	A91	2.50 l ol brn	25	25
480	A91	3 l rose brn	35	35
481	A91	5 l dk sl bl	60	60
482	A91	8 l black	85	85

Issued to commemorate the 10th anniversary of the founding of Albania's Communist Party.

Battle Scene
A92

Designs: 5 l, Schoolgirl, "Agriculture and Industry." 8 l, Four portraits.

1951, Nov. 28 *Perf. 12x12½*

483	A92	2.50 l brown	30	15
484	A92	5 l blue	50	40
485	A92	8 l brn car	1.00	75

Issued to commemorate the 10th anniversary of the formation of the Albanian Communist Youth Organization.

Albanian Heroes (Haxhija, Lezhe, Giyebegej, Mezi and Dedej)
A93

1950, Dec. 25 *Perf. 14* **Unwmkd.**

Various Portraits

486	A93	2 l dk grn	30	20
487	A93	2.50 l purple	35	25
488	A93	3 l scarlet	45	35
489	A93	5 l brt bl	75	50
490	A93	8 l ol brn	2.00	1.50
		Nos. 486-490 (5)	3.85	2.80

Isssued to commemorate the 6th anniversary of Albania's liberation. Nos. 486–489 each show five "Heroes of the People"; No. 490 shows two (Stafa and Shanto).

Tobacco Factory, Shkoder
A94

Composite, Lenin Hydroelectric Plant
A95

Designs: 1 l, Canal. 2.50 l, Textile factory. 3 l, "8 November" Cannery. 5 l, Motion Picture Studio, Tirana. 8 l, Stalin Textile Mill, Tirana. 20 l, Central Hydroelectric Dam.

Perf. 12x12½, 12½x12

1953, Aug. 1

491	A94	50q red brn	5	5
492	A94	1 l dl grn	10	5
493	A94	2.50 l brown	30	5
494	A94	3 l rose brn	45	10
495	A94	5 l blue	65	12
496	A94	8 l brn ol	1.00	25
497	A95	12 l dp plum	1.75	50
498	A94	20 l sl bl	3.00	75
		Nos. 491-498 (8)	7.30	1.87

Liberation Scene
A96

1954, Nov. 29 *Perf. 12x12½*

499	A96	50q brn vio	9	5
500	A96	1 l ol grn	20	5
501	A96	2.50 l yel brn	45	10
502	A96	3 l car rose	60	25
503	A96	5 l gray bl	75	25
504	A96	8 l rose brn	1.50	85
		Nos. 499-504 (6)	3.59	1.55

10th anniversary of Albania's liberation.

School
A97

Pandeli Sotiri, Petro Nini Luarasi, Nuci Naci
A98

1956, Feb. 23 **Unwmkd.**

505	A97	2 l rose vio	20	6
506	A98	2.50 l lt grn	30	12
507	A98	5 l ultra	60	30
508	A97	10 l brt grnsh bl	1.35	50

Issued to commemorate the 70th anniversary of the opening of the first Albanian school.

Flags
A99

Designs: 5 l, Labor Party headquarters, Tirana. 8 l, Marx and Lenin.

1957, June 1 Engr. *Perf. 11½x11*

509	A99	2.50 l brown	25	10
510	A99	5 l lt vio bl	50	20
511	A99	8 l rose lil	1.10	30

Issued to commemorate the 15th anniversary of the founding of Albania's Labor Party.

Congress Emblem
A100

1957, Oct. 4 *Perf. 11½* **Unwmkd.**

512	A100	2.50 l gray brn	25	8
513	A100	3 l rose red	35	10
514	A100	5 l dk bl	45	15
515	A100	8 l green	90	30

Issued to publicize the fourth International Trade Union Congress, Leipzig, Oct. 4-15.

Lenin and Cruiser "Aurora"
A101

1957, Nov. 7 Litho. *Perf. 10½*

516	A101	2.50 l vio brn	20	12
517	A101	5 l vio bl	45	22
518	A101	8 l gray	60	40

Issued to commemorate the 40th anniversary of the Russian Revolution.

Albanian Fighter Holding Flag
A102

Naum Veqilharxhj
A103

1957, Nov. 28 *Perf. 10½*

519	A102	1.50 l magenta	20	6
520	A102	2.50 l brown	35	10
521	A102	5 l blue	65	25
522	A102	8 l green	1.10	40

Issued to commemorate the 45th anniversary of the proclamation of independence.

1958, Feb. 1 **Unwmkd.**

523	A103	2.50 l dk brn	25	12
524	A103	5 l vio bl	50	20
525	A103	8 l rose lil	90	40

Issued to commemorate the 160th anniversary of the birth of Naum Veqilharxhj, patriot and writer.

Luigi Gurakuqi
A104

Soldiers
A105

1958, Apr. 15 Photo. *Perf. 10½*

526	A104	1.50 l dk grn	15	5
527	A104	2.50 l brown	25	10
528	A104	5 l blue	45	20
529	A104	8 l sepia	90	30

Issued to commemorate the transfer of the ashes of Luigi Gurakuqi.

1958, July 10 **Lithographed**

Design: 2.50 l, 11 l, Airman, sailor, soldier and tank.

530	A105	1.50 l bl grn	12	5
531	A105	2.50 l dk red brn	20	6
532	A105	8 l rose red	60	20
533	A105	11 l brt bl	90	30

15th anniversary of Albanian army.

Cerciz Topulli and Mihal Grameno
A106

Buildings and Tree
A107

1958, July 1

534	A106	2.50 l dk ol bis	20	8
535	A107	3 l green	25	10
536	A106	5 l blue	45	18
537	A107	8 l red brn	70	30

50th anniversary, Battle of Mashkullore.

Ancient Amphitheater and Goddess of Butrinto
A108

1959, Jan. 25 Litho. *Perf. 10½*

538	A108	2.50 l redsh brn	30	6
539	A108	6.50 l lt bl grn	75	25
540	A108	11 l dk bl	1.25	50

Cultural Monuments Week.

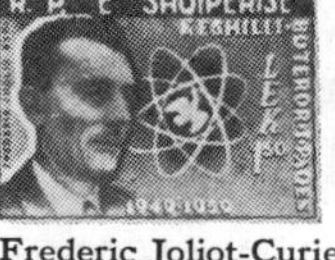

Frederic Joliot-Curie and World Peace Congress Emblem
A109

Basketball
A110

1959, July 1 **Unwmkd.**

541	A109	1.50 l car rose	75	20
542	A109	2.50 l rose vio	1.35	30
543	A109	11 l blue	3.75	1.50

Issued to commemorate the 10th anniversary of the World Peace Movement.

1959, Nov. 20 *Perf. 10½*

Sports: 2.50 l, Soccer. 5 l, Runner. 11 l, Man and woman runners with torch and flags.

544	A110	1.50 l brt vio	20	8

545 A110 2.50 l emerald 25 15
546 A110 5 l car rose 60 25
547 A110 11 l ultra 1.75 75

Issued to publicize the first Albanian Spartacist Games.

Fighter and Flags
A111

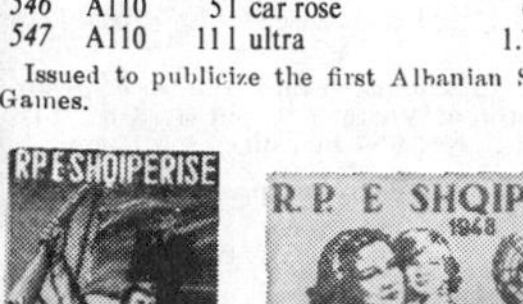

Mother and Child, U.N. Emblem
A112

1959, Nov. 29

Designs: 2.50 l, Miner with drill standing guard. 3 l, Farm woman with sheaf of grain. 6.50 l, Man and woman in laboratory.

548 A111 1.50 l brt car 25 5
549 A111 2.50 l red brn 35 5
550 A111 3 l brt bl grn 45 10
551 A111 6.50 l brt red 90 30
a. Souvenir sheet 5.50 5.50

15th anniversary of Albania's liberation.
No. 551a contains one each of Nos. 548–551, imperf. and all in bright carmine. Inscribed ribbon frame of sheet and frame lines for each stamp are blue green. Size: 144x97mm.

1959, Dec. 5 **Unwmkd.**

552 A112 5 l lt grnsh bl 1.65 60
a. Miniature sheet 4.00 4.00

Issued to commemorate the 10th anniversary (in 1958) of the signing of the Universal Declaration of Human Rights.
No. 552a contains one imperf. stamp similar to No. 552; ornamental border. Size: 74½x66mm.

Woman with Olive Branch
A113

Alexander Moissi
A114

1960, Mar. 8 **Litho.** ***Perf. 10½***

553 A113 2.50 l chocolate 30 12
554 A113 11 l rose car 1.25 40

Issued to commemorate the 50th anniversary of International Women's Day, March 8.

1960, Apr. 20

555 A114 3 l dp brn 20 8
556 A114 11 l Prus grn 75 25

80th anniversary of the birth of Alexander Moissi (Moisiu) (1880–1935), German actor.

Lenin
A115

School Building
A116

1960, Apr. 22

557 A115 4 l Prus bl 60 8
558 A115 11 l lake 1.35 20

90th anniversary of birth of Lenin.

1960, May 30 **Litho.** ***Perf. 10½***

559 A116 5 l green 75 30
560 A116 6.50 l plum 75 30

Issued to commemorate the 50th anniversary of the first Albanian secondary school.

Soldier on Guard Duty
A117

Liberation Monument, Tirana, Family and Policeman
A118

1960, May 12 ***Perf. 10½*** **Unwmkd.**

561 A117 1.50 l car rose 20 8
562 A117 11 l Prus bl 1.25 30

15th anniversary of the Frontier Guards.

1960, May 14

563 A118 1.50 l green 20 5
564 A118 8.50 l brown 1.25 30

15th anniversary of the People's Police.

Congress Site
A119

Pashko Vasa
A120

1960, Mar. 25

565 A119 2.50 l sepia 15 10
566 A119 7.50 l dl bl 60 25

40th anniversary, Congress of Louchnia.

1960, May 5

Designs: 1.50 l, Jani Vreto. 6.50 l, Sami Frasheri. 11 l, Page of statutes of association.

567 A120 1 l gray ol 12 5
568 A120 1.50 l brown 20 5
569 A120 6.50 l blue 45 12
570 A120 11 l rose red 90 25

Issued to commemorate the 80th anniversary (in 1959) of the Association of Albanian Authors.

Albanian Fighter and Cannon
A121

TU-104 Plane, Clock Tower, Tirana, and Kremlin, Moscow
A122

1960, Aug. 2 **Litho.** ***Perf. 10½***

571 A121 1.50 l ol brn 20 5
572 A121 2.50 l maroon 25 10
573 A121 5 l dk bl 60 20

Issued to commemorate the 40th anniversary of the Battle of Viona (against Italian troops.)

1960, Aug. 18

574 A122 1 l redsh brn 35 12
575 A122 7.50 l brt grnsh bl 1.25 50
576 A122 11.50 l gray 2.25 90

Issued to commemorate the 2nd anniversary of TU-104 flights, Moscow-Tirana.

Rising Sun and Federation Emblem
A123

Ali Kelmendi
A124

1960, Nov. 10 ***Perf. 10½*** **Unwmkd.**

577 A123 1.50 l ultra 15 6
578 A123 8.50 l red 60 20

Issued to commemorate the 15th anniversary of the International Youth Federation.

1960, Dec. 5 **Litho.** ***Perf. 10½***

579 A124 1.50 l pale gray grn 20 6
580 A124 11 l dl rose lake 55 20

Issued to honor Ali Kelmendi, communist leader, on his 60th birthday.

Flags of Russia and Albania and Clasped Hands
A125

Marx and Lenin
A126

1961, Jan. 10 ***Perf. 10½*** **Unwmkd.**

581 A125 2 l violet 20 6
582 A125 8 l dl red brn 55 20

Issued to commemorate the 15th anniversary of the Albanian-Soviet Friendship Society.

1961, Feb. 13 **Lithographed**

583 A126 2 l rose red 20 6
584 A126 8 l vio bl 70 20

Fourth Communist Party Congress.

Man from Shkoder
A127

Otter
A128

1961, Apr. 28 ***Perf. 10½***

Costumes: 1.50 l, Woman from Shkoder. 6.50 l, Man from Lume. 11 l, Woman from Mirdite.

585 A127 1 l slate 20 5
586 A127 1.50 l dl cl 30 6
587 A127 6.50 l ultra 1.10 25
588 A127 11 l red 1.75 50

1961, June 25 ***Perf. 10½*** **Unwmkd.**

Designs: 6.50 l, Badger. 11 l, Brown bear.

589 A128 2.50 l grysh bl 90 25
590 A128 6.50 l bl grn 2.00 60
591 A128 11 l dk red brn 3.50 1.00

Dalmatian Pelicans
A129

Cyclamen
A130

Birds: 7.50 l, Gray herons. 11 l, Little egret.

1961, Sept. 30 ***Perf. 14***

592 A129 1.50 l rose car, *pnksh* 60 20
593 A129 7.50 l vio, *bluish* 1.25 40
594 A129 11 l red brn, *pnksh* 1.75 60

1961, Oct. 27 **Lithographed**

Designs: 8 l, Forsythia. 11 l, Lily.

595 A130 1.50 l brt bl & lil rose 60 15
596 A130 8 l red lil & org 1.10 35
597 A130 11 l brt grn & car rose 1.50 60

Milosh G. Nikolla
A131

Flag with Marx and Lenin
A132

1961, Oct. 30 ***Perf. 14***

598 A131 50q vio brn 15 6
599 A131 8.50 l Prus grn 60 25

Issued to commemorate the 50th anniversary of the birth of Milosh Gjergi Nikolla, poet.

1961, Nov. 8

600 A132 2.50 l vermilion 30 10
601 A132 7.50 l dl red brn 60 30

Issued to commemorate the 20th anniversary of the founding of Albania's Communist Party.

Worker, Farm Woman and Emblem
A133

Yuri Gagarin and Vostok 1
A134

1961, Nov. 23 ***Perf. 14*** **Unwmkd.**

602 A133 2.50 l vio bl 30 12
603 A133 7.50 l rose cl 60 35

Issued to commemorate the 20th anniversary of the Albanian Workers' Party.

1962, Feb. 15 ***Perf. 14*** **Unwmkd.**

604 A134 50q blue 35 7
605 A134 4 l red lil 1.50 20
606 A134 11 l dk sl grn 3.00 90

Issued to commemorate the first manned space flight, made by Yuri A. Gagarin, Soviet astronaut, Apr. 12, 1961.
Nos. 604–606 were overprinted with an over-all yellow tint and with "POSTA AJRORE" (Air Mail) in maroon in 1962.

Price, set $50.

Petro Nini Luarasi

A135

Malaria Eradication Emblem

A136

1962, Feb. 28 **Lithographed**

607 A135 50q Prus bl 20 5
608 A135 8.50 l ol gray 1.20 25

Issued to commemorate the 50th anniversary (in 1961) of the death of Petro Nini Luarasi, Albanian patriot.

1962, Apr. 30 ***Perf. 14*** **Unwmkd.**

609 A136 1.50 l brt grn 10 6
610 A136 2.50 l brn red 10 8
611 A136 10 l red lil 40 25
612 A136 11 l blue 65 35

Issued for the World Health Organization drive to eradicate malaria.

A souvenir sheet, issued both perf. and imperf., contains one each of Nos. 609-612, with blue marginal inscription and U.N. emblem. Size: 88x106½mm.

Price $10 each.
Nos. 609-612 imperf., price, set $10.

Camomile

A137

Woman Diver

A138

1962, May 10

Medicinal Plants: 8 l, Linden. 11.50 l, Garden sage.

613 A137 50q gray vio, yel & grn 10 7
614 A137 8 l gray, yel & grn 60 25
615 A137 11.50 l bis, grn & pur 1.50 50

Price, imperf. set $10.

1962, May 31 ***Perf. 14***

Designs: 2.50 l, Pole vault. 3 l, Mt. Fuji and torch (horiz.). 9 l, Woman javelin thrower. 10 l, Shot putting.

616 A138 50q brt grnsh bl & blk 10 5
617 A138 2.50 l gldn brn & sep 15 7
618 A138 3 l bl & gray 30 8
619 A138 9 l rose car & dk brn 90 25
620 A138 10 l ol & blk 1.05 30
Nos. 616-620 (5) 2.50 75

1964 Olympic Games, Tokyo.

Price, imperf. set $10.
A 15 l (like 3 l) exists in souv. sheet, perf. and imperf.

Globe and Orbits

A139

Dog Laika and Sputnik 2

A140

Designs: 1.50 l, Rocket to the sun. 20 l, Lunik 3 photographing far side of the moon.

1962, June ***Perf. 14*** **Unwmkd.**

621 A139 50q vio & org 20 5
622 A140 1 l bl grn & brn 35 10
623 A140 1.50 l yel & ver 50 15
624 A139 20 l mag & bl 3.50 1.00

Russian space explorations.
Nos. 621-624 exist imperforate in changed colors.
Two miniature sheets exist (101x77mm.), each containing one 14-lek picturing Sputnik 1. The perforated 14-lek is yellow and brown; the imperf. red and brown. Marginal design in blue and black.

Soccer Game, Map of South America

A141

Design: 2.50 l, 15 l, Soccer game and globe as ball.

1962, July **Lithographed**

625 A141 1 l org & dk pur 10 5
626 A141 2.50 l emer & bluish grn 20 5
627 A141 6.50 l lt brn & pink 60 10
628 A141 15 l bluish grn & mar 1.05 40

Issued to commemorate the World Soccer Championships, Chile, May 30–June 17.
Nos. 625–628 exist imperforate in changed colors.
Two miniature sheets exist (67x49mm.), each containing a single 20-lek in design similar to A141. The perforated sheet is brown and green; the imperforate sheet, brown and orange.

Map of Europe and Albania

A142

Woman of Dardhë

A143

Designs: 1 l, 2.50 l, Map of Adriatic Sea and Albania and Roman statue.

1962, Aug.

630 A142 50q multi 25 25
631 A142 1 l ultra & red 50 50
632 A142 2.50 l bl & red 1.75 1.75
633 A142 11 l multi 3.75 3.75

Issued for tourist propaganda. Imperforates in changed colors exist.
Miniature sheets containing a 7 l and 8 l stamp, perf. and imperf., exist.

1962, Sept.

Regional Costumes: 1 l, Man from Devoll. 2.50 l, Woman from Lunxheri. 14 l, Man from Gjirokastër.

635 A143 50q car, bl & pur 7 5
636 A143 1 l red brn & ocher 10 5
637 A143 2.50 l vio, yel grn & blk 35 15
638 A143 14 l red brn & pale grn 1.25 50

Price, imperf. set $10.

Chamois

A144

Ismail Qemali

A145

Animals: 1 l, Lynx (horiz.). 1.50 l, Wild boar (horiz.). 15 l, 20 l, Roe deer.

1962, Oct. 24 ***Perf. 14*** **Unwmkd.**

639 A144 50q sl grn & dk pur 20 5
640 A144 1 l org & blk 35 10
641 A144 1.50 l red brn & blk 50 12
642 A144 15 l yel ol & red brn 2.50 1.00

Miniature Sheet

643 A144 20 l yel ol & red brn 12.50 12.50

No. 643 measures 71½x89mm.

Imperfs. in changed colors, price #639-642 $10, #643 $15.

1962, Dec. 28 **Lithographed**

Designs: 1 l, Albanian eagle. 16 l, Eagle over fortress formed by "RPSH."

644 A145 1 l red & red brn 15 5
645 A145 3 l org brn & blk 30 10
646 A145 16 l dk car rose & blk 1.85 70

50th anniv. of independence

Imperfs. in changed colors, price, set $10.

Monument of October Revolution

A146

Henri Dunant, Cross, Globe and Nurse

A147

Design: 10 l, Lenin statue.

1963, Jan. 5 ***Perf. 14*** **Unwmkd.**

647 A146 5 l yel & dl vio 25 10
648 A146 10 l red org & blk 65 25

Issued to commemorate the 45th anniversary of the October Revolution (Russia, 1917).

1963, Jan 25 ***Perf. 14*** **Unwmkd.**

649 A147 1.50 l rose lake, red & blk 20 5
650 A147 2.50 l lt bl, red & blk 30 15
651 A147 6 l emer, red & blk 70 30
652 A147 10 l dl yel, red & blk 1.25 50

Issued to commemorate the centenary of the Geneva Conference, which led to the establishment of the International Red Cross in 1864.

Imperfs. in changed colors, price, set $10.

Stalin and Battle of Stalingrad

A148

Andrian G. Nikolayev

A149

1963, Feb. 2

653 A148 8 l dk grn & sl 1.00 25

Issued to commemorate the 20th anniversary of the Battle of Stalingrad. See No. C67.

1963, Feb. 28 **Lithographed**

Designs: 7.50 l, Vostoks 3 and 4 and globe (horiz.). 20 l, Pavel R. Popovich. 25 l, Nikolayev, Popovich and globe with trajectories.

654 A149 2.50 l vio bl & sep 35 5
655 A149 7.50 l lt bl & blk 70 15
656 A149 20 l vio & sep 2.10 75

Miniature Sheet

657 A149 25 l vio bl & sep 12.00 12.00

Issued to commemorate the first group space flight of Vostoks 3 and 4, Aug. 11–15, 1962. No. 657 measures 88x73mm.

Imperfs. in changed colors, price #654-656 $10, #657 $12.

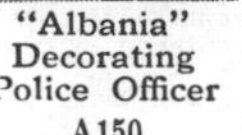

"Albania" Decorating Police Officer

A150

Polyphylla Fullo

A151

1963, Mar. 20 ***Perf. 14*** **Unwmkd.**

658 A150 2.50 l crim, mag & blk 35 10
659 A150 7.50 l org ver, dk red & blk 1.25 25

20th anniversary of the security police.

1963, Mar. 20

Beetles: 1.50 l, Lucanus cervus. 8 l, Procerus gigas. 10 l, Cicindela Albanica.

660 A151 50q ol grn & brn 15 5
661 A151 1.50 l bl & brn 35 10
662 A151 8 l dl rose & blk vio 1.60 70
663 A151 10 l brt cit & blk 1.90 85

1913 Stamp and Postmark

A152

Design: 10 l, Stamps of 1913, 1937 and 1962.

1963, May 5

664 A152 5 l yel, buff, bl & blk 70 20
665 A152 10 l car rose, grn & blk 1.35 40

50th anniversary of Albanian stamps.

Boxer

A153

Crested Grebe

A154

Designs: 3 l, Basketball baskets. 5, l, Volleyball. 6 l, Bicyclists. 9 l, Gymnast. 15 l, Hands holding torch, and map of Japan.

1963, May 25 ***Perf. 13½***

666 A153 2 l yel, blk & red brn 20 5
667 A153 3 l ocher, brn & bl 30 10
668 A153 5 l gray bl, red brn & brn 50 15
669 A153 6 l gray, dk gray & grn 70 25
670 A153 9 l rose, red brn & bl 1.40 30
Nos. 666-670 (5) 3.10 85

Miniature Sheet

671 A153 15 l lt bl, car, blk & brn 6.00 6.00

Issued to publicize the 1964 Olympic Games in Tokyo. No. 671 contains one stamp (31x49mm.) with ocher border. Size: 60x80mm.

Price, imperfs. #666-670 $5, #671 $6.

1963, Apr. 20 Litho. *Perf. 14*

Birds: 3 l, Golden eagle. 6.50 l, Gray partridges. 11 l, Capercaillie.

672 A154 50q multi 15 7
673 A154 3 l multi 60 20
674 A154 6.50 l multi 1.40 45
675 A154 11 l multi 2.25 70

Soldier and Building
A155

Designs: 2.50 l, Soldier with pack, ship and plane. 5 l, Soldier in battle. 6 l, Soldier and bulldozer.

1963, July 10 *Perf. 12* Unwmkd.

676 A155 1.50 l brick red, yel & blk 15 5
677 A155 2.50 l bl, ocher & brn 20 6
678 A155 5 l bluish grn, gray & blk 45 20
679 A155 6 l red brn, buff & bl 60 35

Albanian army, 20th anniversary.

Maj. Yuri A. Gagarin
A156

Designs: 5 l, Maj. Gherman Titov. 7 l, Maj. Andrian G. Nikolayev. 11 l, Lt. Col. Pavel R. Popovich. 14 l, Lt. Col. Valeri Bykovski. 20 l, Lt. Valentina Tereshkova.

1963, July 30

Portraits in Yellow and Black

680 A156 3 l brt pur 35 10
681 A156 5 l dl bl 50 15
682 A156 7 l gray 70 15
683 A156 11 l dp cl 1.20 35
684 A156 14 l bl grn 1.75 55
685 A156 20 l ultra 2.50 1.00
Nos. 680-685 (6) 7.00 2.30

Man's conquest of space.
Price, imperf. set $12.50.

Volleyball
A157

Sports: 3 l, Weight lifting. 5 l, Soccer. 7 l, Boxing. 8 l, Rowing.

1963, Aug. 31 *Perf. 12x12½*

686 A157 2 l cit, red & blk 15 5
687 A157 3 l dk red, bis & blk 25 8
688 A157 5 l emer, org & blk 45 15
689 A157 7 l dp pink, emer & blk 55 25
690 A157 8 l dp bl, dp pink & blk 1.05 30
Nos. 686-690 (5) 2.45 83

European championships.

Imperfs. in changed colors, price set $10.

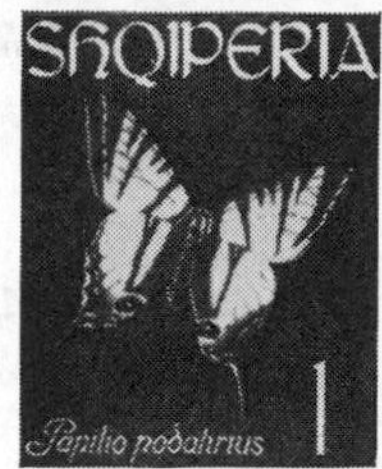

Papilio Podalirius
A158

Various Butterflies and Moths in Natural Colors

1963, Sept. 29 Lithographed

691 A158 1 l red 15 5
692 A158 2 l blue 30 10
693 A158 4 l dl lil 50 25
694 A158 5 l pale grn 90 40
695 A158 8 l bister 1.10 55
696 A158 10 l lt bl 1.65 70
Nos. 691-696 (6) 4.60 2.05

Oil Refinery, Cerrik
A159

Flag and Shield
A160

Designs: 2.50 l, Food processing plant, Tirana (horiz.). 30 l, Fruit canning plant. 50 l, Tannery (horiz.).

1963, Nov. 15 *Perf. 14* Unwmkd.

697 A159 2.50 l rose red, *pnksh* 20 8
698 A159 20 l sl grn, *grnsh* 75 20
699 A159 30 l dl pur, *grysh* 1.75 50
700 A159 50 l ocher, *yel* 2.00 75

Industrial development in Albania.

1963, Nov. 24 *Perf. 12½x12*

701 A160 2 l grnsh bl, blk, ocher & red 35 6
702 A160 8 l bl, blk, ocher & red 1.00 65

1st Congress of Army Aid Assn.

Chinese, Caucasian and Negro Men
A161

1963, Dec. 10 *Perf. 12x11½*

703 A161 3 l bis & blk 35 15
704 A161 5 l bis & ultra 60 25
705 A161 7 l bis & vio 1.00 40

Issued to commemorate the 15th anniversary of the Universal Declaration of Human Rights.

Slalom Ascent
A162

Lenin
A163

Designs: 50q, Bobsled (horiz.). 6.50 l, Ice hockey (horiz.). 12.50 l, Women's figure skating. No. 709A, Ski jumper.

1963, Dec. 25 *Perf. 14*

706 A162 50q grnsh bl & blk 10 5
707 A162 2.50 l red, gray & blk 20 6
708 A162 6.50 l yel, blk & gray 50 20
709 A162 12.50 l red, blk & yel grn 1.05 50

Miniature Sheet

709A A162 12.50 l multi 4.50 4.50

Issued to publicize the 9th Winter Olympic Games, Innsbruck, Jan. 29–Feb. 9, 1964. Size of No. 709A: 56x75mm.

Imperfs. in changed colors, price #706-709 $12.50, #709A $15.

1964, Jan. 21 *Perf. 12½x12*

710 A163 5 l gray & bis 30 12
711 A163 10 l gray & ocher 60 30

40th anniversary, death of Lenin.

Hurdling
A164

Sturgeon
A165

Designs: 3 l, Track (horiz.). 6.50 l, Rifle shooting (horiz.). 8 l, Basketball.

Perf. 12½x12, 12x12½

1964, Jan. 30 Lithographed

712 A164 2.50 l pale vio & ultra 20 10
713 A164 3 l lt grn & red brn 30 15
714 A164 6.50 l bl & cl 60 25
715 A164 8 l lt bl & ocher 85 30

Issued to commemorate the 1st Games of the New Emerging Forces, GANEFO, Jakarta, Indonesia, Nov. 10–22, 1963.

1964, Feb. 26 *Perf. 14* Unwmkd.

Designs: Various fish.

Multicolored

716 A165 50q *shown* 10 5
717 A165 1 l *Gilthead* 10 5
718 A165 1.50 l *Striped mullet* 20 10
719 A165 2.50 l *Carp* 35 15
720 A165 6.50 l *Mackerel* 1.00 40
721 A165 10 l *Lake Ohrid trout* 1.75 50
Nos. 716-721 (6) 3.50 1.25

Red Squirrel
A166

Designs: Wild animals.

1964, March 28 *Perf. 12½x12*

Multicolored

722 A166 1 l *shown* 10 5
723 A166 1.50 l *Beech marten* 15 5
724 A166 2 l *Red fox* 30 5
725 A166 2.50 l *Hedgehog* 35 10
726 A166 3 l *Hare* 40 15
727 A166 5 l *Jackal* 70 25
728 A166 7 l *Wildcat* 1.00 35
729 A166 8 l *Wolf* 1.25 50
Nos. 722-729 (8) 4.25 1.50

Scott's editorial staff cannot undertake to identify, authenticate or appraise stamps and postal markings.

Lighting Olympic Torch
A167

Designs: 5 l, Torch and globes. 7 l, 15 l, Olympic flag and Mt. Fuji. 10 l, National Stadium, Tokyo.

1964, May 18 *Perf. 12x12½*

730 A167 3 l lt yel grn, yel & buff 20 6
731 A167 5 l red & vio bl 35 10
732 A167 7 l lt bl, ultra & yel 50 20
733 A167 10 l org, bl & vio 70 30

Miniature Sheet

734 A167 15 l lt bl, ultra & org 6.50 6.50

Issued to publicize the 18th Olympic Games, Tokyo, October 10–25, 1964. No. 734 contains one stamp (49x62mm.) with orange border. Size: 80x90mm.

Imperfs. in changed colors, price #730-733 $6.50, #734 $9.

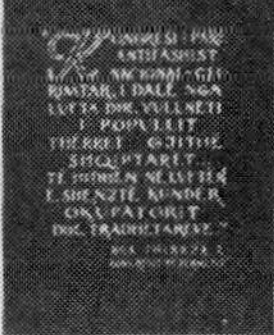

Partisans—A168

Designs: 5 l, Arms of Albania. 8 l, Enver Hoxha.

Perf. 12½x12

1964, May 24 Litho. Unwmkd.

735 A168 2 l org, red & blk 15 6
736 A168 5 l multi 35 10
737 A168 8 l red brn, blk & red 70 20

Issued to commemorate the 20th anniversary of the National Anti-Fascist Congress of Liberation, Permet, May 24, 1944. The label attached to each stamp, without perforations between, carries a quotation from the 1944 Congress.

Albanian Flag and Revolutionists
A169

Full Moon
A170

Perf. 12½x12

1964, June 10 Litho. Unwmkd.

738 A169 2.50 l red & gray 10 10
739 A169 7.50 l lil rose & gray 35 20

Issued to commemorate the 40th anniversary of the Albanian revolution of 1924.

1964, June 27 *Perf. 12x12½*

Designs: 5 l, New moon. 8 l, Half moon. 11 l, Waning moon. 15 l, Far side of moon.

740 A170 1 l pur & yel 15 5
741 A170 5 l vio & yel 40 15
742 A170 8 l bl & yel 70 30
743 A170 11 l grn & yel 1.05 45

Miniature Sheet
Perf. 12 on 2 sides

744	A170	15 l ultra & yel	7.00	7.00

No. 744 contains one stamp (35x36mm.) with bister border, perforated at top and bottom. Size: 66½x79mm.

Imperfs. in changed colors, price #740-743 $7, #744 $9.

No. 733 with Added Inscription: "Rimini 25-VI-64"

1964 ***Perf. 12x12½***

745	A167	10 l org, bl & vio	2.10	2.10

Issued to commemorate the "Toward Tokyo 1964" Philatelic Exhibition at Rimini, Italy, June 25–July 6.

Wren
A171

Birds: 1 l, Penduline titmouse. 2.50 l, Green woodpecker. 3 l, Tree creeper. 4 l, Nuthatch. 5 l, Great titmouse. 6 l, Goldfinch. 18 l, Oriole.

1964, July 31 ***Perf. 12x12½***

746	A171	50q multi	10	5
747	A171	1 l org & multi	10	5
748	A171	2.50 l multi	20	5
749	A171	3 l bl & multi	30	7
750	A171	4 l yel & multi	40	10
751	A171	5 l bl & multi	50	15
752	A171	6 l lt vio & multi	70	30
753	A171	18 l pink & multi	2.10	85
		Nos. 746-753 (8)	4.40	1.62

Running and Gymnastics
A172

Sport: 2 l, Weight lifting, judo. 3 l, Equestrian, bicycling. 4 l, Soccer, water polo. 5 l, Wrestling, boxing. 6 l, Pentathlon, hockey. 7 l, Swimming, sailing. 8 l, Basketball, volleyball. 9 l, Rowing, canoeing. 10 l, Fencing, pistol shooting. 20 l, Three winners.

Perf. 12x12½

1964, Sept. 25 Litho. Unwmkd.

754	A172	1 l lt bl, rose & emer	10	5
755	A172	2 l bis brn, bluish grn & vio	10	5
756	A172	3 l vio, red org & ol bis	25	5
757	A172	4 l grnsh bl, ol & ultra	25	10
758	A172	5 l grnsh bl, car & pale lil	40	15
759	A172	6 l dk bl, org & lt bl	45	20
760	A172	7 l dk bl, lt ol & org	50	20
761	A172	8 l emer, gray & yel	70	30
762	A172	9 l bl, yel & lil rose	85	40
763	A172	10 l brt grn, org brn & yel grn	2.10	65
		Nos. 754-763 (10)	5.70	2.15

Miniature Sheet
Perf. 12

764	A172	20 l vio & lem	8.00	8.00

Issued to commemorate the 18th Olympic Games, Tokyo, Oct. 10–25. No. 764 contains one stamp (41x68mm.) with violet border. Size: 55x82mm.

Imperfs. in changed colors, price #754-763 $8, #764 $8.

Arms of People's Republic of China
A173

Mao Tse-tung and Flag
A174

Perf. 11½x12, 12x11½

1964, Oct. 1

765	A173	7 l blk, red & yel	55	30
766	A174	8 l blk, red & yel	85	40

Issued to commemorate the 15th anniversary of the People's Republic of China.

Karl Marx
A175

Jeronim de Rada
A176

Designs: 5 l, St. Martin's Hall, London. 8 l, Friedrich Engels.

1964, Nov. 5 ***Perf. 12x11½***

767	A175	2 l red, lt vio & blk	30	10
768	A175	5 l gray bl	70	20
769	A175	8 l ocher, blk & red	1.35	35

Centenary of First Socialist International.

1964, Nov. 15 ***Perf. 12½x11½***

770	A176	7 l sl grn	55	30
771	A176	8 l dl vio	70	35

Issued to commemorate the 150th anniversary of the birth of Jeronim de Rada, poet.

Arms of Albania
A177

Factories
A178

Designs: 3 l, Combine harvester. 4 l, Woman chemist. 10 l, Hands holding Constitution, hammer and sickle.

Perf. 11½x12, 12x11½

1964, Nov. 29

772	A177	1 l multi	10	5
773	A178	2 l red, yel & vio bl	15	6
774	A178	3 l red, yel & brn	35	8
775	A178	4 l red, yel & gray grn	45	15
776	A177	10 l red, bl & blk	70	45
		Nos. 772-776 (5)	1.75	79

20th anniversary of liberation.

Planet Mercury
A179

Planets: 2 l, Venus and rocket. 3 l, Earth, moon and rocket. 4 l, Mars and rocket. 5 l, Jupiter. 6 l, Saturn. 7 l, Uranus. 8 l, Neptune. 9 l, Pluto. 15 l, Solar system and rocket.

1964, Dec. 15 ***Perf. 12x12½***

777	A179	1 l yel & pur	10	5
778	A179	2 l multi	15	5
779	A179	3 l multi	25	5
780	A179	4 l multi	30	15
781	A179	5 l yel, dk pur & brn	45	15
782	A179	6 l lt grn, vio brn & yel	70	20
783	A179	7 l yel & grn	80	25
784	A179	8 l yel & vio	1.00	30
785	A179	9 l lt grn, yel & blk	1.35	50
		Nos. 777-785 (9)	5.10	1.70

Miniature Sheet
Perf. 12 on 2 sides

786	A179	15 l car, bl, yel & grn	10.00	10.00

No. 786 contains one stamp (62x51mm.) with yellow marginal inscription, perforated at top and bottom. Size: 87x72mm.

Imperfs. in changed colors, price #777-785 $10, #786 $10.

European Chestnut
A180

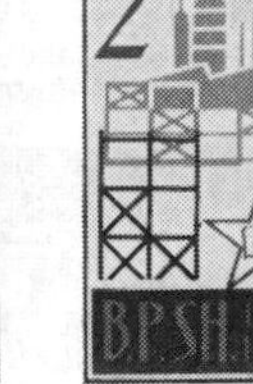

Symbols of Industry
A181

1965, Jan. 25 ***Perf. 11½x12***

Multicolored

787	A180	1 l *shown*	10	5
788	A180	2 l *Medlars*	15	5
789	A180	3 l *Persimmon*	30	10
790	A180	4 l *Pomegranate*	35	15
791	A180	5 l *Quince*	50	20
792	A180	10 l *Orange*	1.00	35
		Nos. 787-792 (6)	2.40	90

1965, Feb. 20

Designs: 5 l, Books, triangle and compass. 8 l, Beach, trees and hotel.

793	A181	2 l blk, car rose & pink	40	40
794	A181	5 l yel, gray & blk	85	85
795	A181	8 l blk, vio bl & lt bl	1.60	1.60

Issued to commemorate the 20th anniversary of professional trade associations.

Water Buffalo
A182

Various designs: Water buffalo.

1965, Mar. ***Perf. 12x11½***

796	A182	1 l lt yel grn, yel & brn blk	15	5
797	A182	2 l lt bl, dk gray & blk	35	10
798	A182	3 l yel, brn & grn	50	15
799	A182	7 l brt grn, yel & brn blk	1.25	35
800	A182	12 l pale lil, dk brn & ind	2.10	65
		Nos. 796-800 (5)	4.35	1.30

Mountain View, Valbona
A183

Views: 1.50 l, Seashore. 3 l, Glacier and peak (vert.). 4 l, Gorge (vert.). 5 l, Mountain peaks. 9 l, Lake and hills.

1965, Mar. Lithographed ***Perf. 12***

801	A183	1.50 l multi	50	20
802	A183	2.50 l multi	70	30
803	A183	3 l multi	85	35
804	A183	4 l multi	1.20	50
805	A183	5 l multi	1.60	70
806	A183	9 l multi	2.75	1.00
		Nos. 801-806 (6)	7.60	3.05

Frontier Guard
A184

Small-bore Rifle Shooting, Prone
A185

1965, Apr. 25 Unwmkd.

807	A184	2.50 l lt bl & multi	50	15
808	A184	12.50 l ultra & multi	2.10	90

20th anniversary of the Frontier Guards.

1965, May 10

Designs: 2 l, Rifle shooting, standing. 3 l, Target over map of Europe, showing Bucharest. 4 l, Pistol shooting. 15 l, Rifle shooting, kneeling.

809	A185	1 l lil, car rose, blk & brn	10	5
810	A185	2 l bl, blk, brn & vio bl	25	5
811	A185	3 l pink & car rose	30	15
812	A185	4 l bis, blk & vio brn	40	15
813	A185	15 l brt grn, brn & vio brn	1.40	50
		Nos. 809-813 (5)	2.45	90

Issued to commemorate the European Shooting Championships, Bucharest.

ITU Emblem, Old and New Communications Equipment
A186

Col. Pavel Belyayev
A187

1965, May 17 *Perf. 12½x12*

814 A186 2.50 l brt grn, blk & lil rose 50 10
815 A186 12.50 l vio, blk & brt bl 3.00 45

Issued to commemorate the centenary of the International Telecommunication Union.

1965, June 15 *Perf. 12*

Designs: 2 l, Voskhod II. 6.50 l, Lt. Col. Alexei Leonov. 20 l, Leonov floating in space.

816 A187 1.50 l lt bl & brn 10 5
817 A187 2 l dk bl, lt vio & lt ultra 15 5
818 A187 6.50 l lil & brn 60 20
819 A187 20 l chlky bl, yel & blk 1.75 45

Miniature Sheet
Perf. 12 on 2 sides

820 A187 20 l brt bl, org & blk 7.00 7.00

Issued to commemorate the space flight of Voskhod II and the first man walking in space, Lt. Col. Alexei Leonov. No. 820 contains one stamp (size: 51x59½mm.), orange border, perforated at top and bottom; size: 72x85mm.

Imperf., brt grn background, price $7.

Marx and Lenin
A188

1965, June 21 *Perf. 12*

821 A188 2.50 l dk brn, red & yel 50 15
822 A188 7.50 l sl grn, org ver & buff 1.25 35

Issued to commemorate the 6th Conference of Postal Ministers of Communist Countries, Peking, June 21–July 15.

Mother and Child
A189

Designs: 2 l, Pioneers. 3 l, Boy and girl at play (horiz.). 4 l, Child on beach. 15 l, Girl with book.

Perf. 12½x12, 12x12½

1965, June 29 Litho. Unwmkd.

823 A189 1 l brt bl, rose lil & blk 10 5
824 A189 2 l sal, vio & blk 20 10
825 A189 3 l grn, org & vio 30 10
826 A189 4 l multi 40 15
827 A189 15 l lil rose, brn & ocher 1.25 50
Nos. 823-827 (5) 2.25 90

Issued for International Children's Day.

Statue of Magistrate
A190

Fuchsia
A191

1965, July 20 *Perf. 12*

Designs: 1 l, Amphora. 2 l, Illyrian armor. 3 l, Mosaic (horiz.). 15 l, Torso, Apollo statue.

828 A190 1 l lt ol, org & brn 10 5
829 A190 2 l gray grn, grn & brn 20 5
830 A190 3 l tan, brn, car & lil 35 10
831 A190 4 l grn, bis & brn 50 20
832 A190 15 l gray & pale cl 1.25 65
Nos. 828-832 (5) 2.40 1.05

1965, Aug. 11 *Perf. 12½x12*

Flowers: 2 l, Cyclamen. 3 l, Tiger lily. 3.50 l, Iris. 4 l, Dahlia. 4.50 l, Hydrangea. 5 l, Rose. 7 l, Tulips.

833 A191 1 l multi 10 5
834 A191 2 l multi 15 5
835 A191 3 l multi 25 10
836 A191 3.50 l multi 30 15
837 A191 4 l multi 35 15
838 A191 4.50 l multi 40 15
839 A191 5 l multi 50 20
840 A191 7 l multi 90 30
Nos. 833-840 (8) 2.95 1.15

Nos. 698–700 Surcharged New Value and Two Bars

1965, Aug. 16 *Perf. 14*

841 A159 5q on 30 l dl pur, *grysh* 12 10
842 A159 15q on 30 l dl pur, *grysh* 30 12
843 A159 25q on 50 l ocher, *yel* 45 12
844 A159 80q on 50 l ocher, *yel* 90 30
845 A159 1.10 l on 20 l sl grn, *grnsh* 1.35 45
846 A159 2 l on 20 l sl grn, *grnsh* 2.75 90
Nos. 841-846 (6) 5.87 1.99

White Stork
A192

"Homecoming," by Bukurosh Sejdini
A193

Migratory Birds: 20q, Cuckoo. 30q, Hoopoe. 40q, European bee-eater. 50q, European nightjar. 1.50 l, Quail.

1965, Aug. 31 *Perf. 12*

847 A192 10q yel, blk & gray 10 5
848 A192 20q brt pink, blk & dk bl 20 10
849 A192 30q vio, blk & bis 30 15
850 A192 40q emer, blk yel & org 65 20
851 A192 50q ultra, brn & red brn 75 30
852 A192 1.50 l bis, red brn & dp org 2.10 1.00
Nos. 847-852 (6) 4.10 1.80

1965, Sept. 26 Litho. *Perf. 12x12½*

853 A193 25q ol blk 90 20
854 A193 65q bl blk 2.10 40
855 A193 1.10 l black 3.00 75

Second war veterans' meeting.

Hunter and Capercaillie
A194

Oleander
A195

Hunting: 20q, Deer. 30q, Pheasant. 40q, Mallards. 50q, Boar. 1 l, Rabbit.

1965, Oct. 6 Litho. Unwmkd.

856 A194 10q gray & multi 12 5
857 A194 20q lt grn, red brn & dk brn 20 10
858 A194 30q bl & multi 40 18
859 A194 40q rose lil & grn 60 20
860 A194 50q lt vio bl, blk & brn 70 25
861 A194 1 l cit, ol & brn 2.10 55
Nos. 856-861 (6) 4.12 1.33

1965, Oct. 26 *Perf. 12½x12*

Flowers: 20q, Forget-me-nots. 30q, Pink. 40q, White water lily. 50q, Bird's foot. 1 l, Corn poppy.

862 A195 10q brt bl, grn & car rose 18 5
863 A195 20q org red, bl, brn & grn 20 10
864 A195 30q vio, car rose & grn 40 12
865 A195 40q emer, yel & blk 60 18
866 A195 50q org brn, yel & grn 70 20
867 A195 1 l yel grn, blk & rose red 1.50 70
Nos. 862-867 (6) 3.58 1.35

Hotel Turizmi, Fier
A196

Freighter "Teuta"
A197

Buildings: 10q, Hotel, Peshkopi. 15q, Sanatorium, Tirana. 25q, Rest home, Pogradec. 65q, Partisan Sports Arena, Tirana. 80q, Rest home, Mali Dajt. 1.10 l, Culture House, Tirana. 1.60 l, Hotel Adriatik, Durrës. 2 l, Migjeni Theater, Shkoder. 3 l, Alexander Moissi House of Culture, Durrës.

1965, Oct. *Perf. 12x12½*

868 A196 5q bl & blk 5 5
869 A196 10q ocher & blk 6 5
870 A196 15q dl grn & blk 10 5
871 A196 25q vio & blk 18 10
872 A196 65q lt brn & blk 65 12
873 A196 80q yel grn & blk 80 20
874 A196 1.10 l lil & blk 1.25 30
875 A196 1.60 l lt vio bl & blk 1.60 50
876 A196 2 l dl rose & blk 2.25 70
877 A196 3 l gray & blk 3.75 1.00
Nos. 868-877 (10) 10.69 3.07

1965, Nov. 16

Ships: 20q, Raft. 30q, Sailing ship, 19th century. 40q, Sailing ship, 18th century. 50q, Freighter "Vlora." 1 l, Illyric galleys.

878 A197 10q brt grn & dk grn 10 5
879 A197 20q ol bis & dk grn 20 10
880 A197 30q lt & dp ultra 35 12
881 A197 40q vio & dp vio 60 18
882 A197 50q pink & dk red 75 20
883 A197 1 l bis & brn 1.50 45
Nos. 878-883 (6) 3.50 1.10

Brown Bear
A198

Basketball and Players
A199

Designs: Various Albanian bears. 50q, 55q, 60q, horizontal.

1965, Dec. 7 *Perf. 11½x12*

884 A198 10q bis & dk brn 18 5
885 A198 20q pale brn & dk brn 25 10
886 A198 30q bis, dk brn & car 40 12
887 A198 35q pale brn & dk brn 50 15
888 A198 40q bis & dk brn 70 18
889 A198 50q bis & dk brn 90 20
890 A198 55q bis & dk brn 90 30
891 A198 60q pale brn, dk brn & car 1.00 45
Nos. 884-891 (8) 4.83 1.55

1965, Dec. 15 Litho. *Perf. 12½x12*

Designs: 10q, Games' emblem (map of Albania and basket). 30q, 50q, Players with ball (diff. designs). 1.40 l, Basketball medal on ribbon.

892 A199 10q bl, yel & car 18 5
893 A199 20q rose lil, lt brn & blk 30 6
894 A199 30q bis, lt brn, red & blk 40 12
895 A199 50q lt grn, lt brn & blk 90 20
896 A199 1.40 l rose, blk, brn & yel 1.75 70
Nos. 892-896 (5) 3.53 1.13

Issued to commemorate the Seventh Balkan Basketball Championships, Tirana, Dec. 15–19.

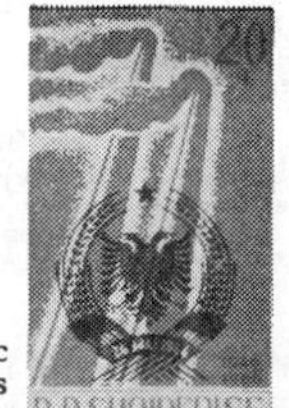

Arms of Republic and Smokestacks
A200

Designs (Arms and): 10q, Book. 30q, Wheat. 60q, Book, hammer and sickle. 80q, Factories.

1966, Jan. 11 Litho. *Perf. 11½x12*
Coat of Arms in Gold

897 A200 10q crim & brn 10 5
898 A200 20q bl & vio bl 12 5
899 A200 30q org yel & brn 25 7
900 A200 60q yel grn & brt grn 40 20
901 A200 80q crim & brn 90 25
Nos. 897-901 (5) 1.77 62

Issued to commemorate the 20th anniversary of the Albanian People's Republic.

Cow
A201

Perf. 12½x12, 12x12½

1966, Feb. 25

Multicolored

902	A201	10q *shown*	12	6
903	A201	20q *Pig*	20	10
904	A201	30q *Ewe & lamb*	30	12
905	A201	35q *Ram*	40	18
906	A201	40q *Dog*	60	20
907	A201	50q *Cat,* vert.	70	20
908	A201	55q *Horse,* vert.	80	30
909	A201	60q *Ass,* vert.	1.00	35
		Nos. 902-909 (8)	4.12	1.51

Soccer Player and Map of Uruguay
A202

Andon Zako Cajupi
A203

Designs: 5q, Globe in form of soccer ball. 15q, Player and map of Italy. 20q, Goalkeeper and map of France. 25q, Player and map of Brazil. 30q, Player and map of Switzerland. 35q, Player and map of Sweden. 40q, Player and map of Chile. 50q, Player and map of Great Britain. 70q, World Championship cup and ball.

1966, March 20 Litho. *Perf. 12*

910	A202	5q gray & dp org	10	5
911	A202	10q lt brn, bl & vio	12	5
912	A202	15q cit, dk bl & brt bl	20	5
913	A202	20q org, vio bl & brt bl	30	10
914	A202	25q sal & sep	35	10
915	A202	30q lt yel grn & brn	40	18
916	A202	35q lt ultra & emer	45	20
917	A202	40q pink & brn	70	20
918	A202	50q pale grn, mag & rose red	70	25
919	A202	70q gray, brn, yel & blk	90	40
		Nos. 910-919 (10)	4.22	1.58

Issued to publicize the World Cup Soccer Championship, Wembley, England, July 11–30.

1966, March 27 Unwmkd.

920	A203	40q bluish blk	30	12
921	A203	1.10 l dk grn	90	25

Issued to commemorate the centenary of the birth of the poet Andon Zako Cajupi.

Painted Lady
A204

WHO Headquarters, Geneva, and Emblem
A205

Designs: 20q, Blue dragonfly. 30q, Cloudless sulphur butterfly. 35q, 40q, Splendid dragonfly. 50q, Machaon swallowtail. 55q, Sulphur butterfly. 60q, White-marbled butterfly.

1966, Apr. 21 Litho. *Perf. 11½x12*

922	A204	10q multi	10	6
923	A204	20q yel & multi	18	6
924	A204	30q yel & multi	30	10
925	A204	35q sky bl & multi	35	12
926	A204	40q multi	40	15
927	A204	50q rose & multi	55	20
928	A204	55q multi	60	20
929	A204	60q multi	1.00	25
		Nos. 922-929 (8)	3.48	1.14

Perf. 12x12½, 12½x12

1966, May 3 Lithographed

Designs (WHO Emblem and): 35q, Ambulance and stretcher bearers (vert.). 60q, Albanian mother and nurse weighing infant (vert.). 80q, X-ray machine and hospital.

930	A205	25q lt bl & blk	30	5
931	A205	35q sal & ultra	60	10
932	A205	60q lt grn, bl & red	90	18
933	A205	80q yel, bl, grn & lt brn	1.35	35

Issued to commemorate the inauguration of the World Health Organization Headquarters, Geneva.

Bird's Foot Starfish
A206

Designs: 25q, Starfish. 35q, Brittle star. 45q, But-thorn starfish. 50q, Starfish. 60q, Sea cucumber. 70q, Sea urchin.

1966, May 10 *Perf. 12x12½*

934	A206	15q multi	15	5
935	A206	25q multi	25	8
936	A206	35q multi	35	10
937	A206	45q multi	50	15
938	A206	50q multi	60	18
939	A206	60q multi	70	20
940	A206	70q multi	1.00	35
		Nos. 934-940 (7)	3.55	1.11

Luna 10
A207

Designs: 30q, 80q, Trajectory of Luna 10, earth and moon.

1966, June 10 *Perf. 12x12½*

941	A207	20q bl, yel & blk	30	10
942	A207	30q yel grn, blk & bl	45	15
943	A207	70q vio, yel & blk	90	25
944	A207	80q yel, vio, grn & blk	1.25	25

Issued to commemorate the launching of the first artificial moon satellite, Luna 10, April 3, 1966.

Jules Rimet Cup and Soccer
A208

Designs: Various scenes of soccer play.

1966, July 12 Litho. *Perf. 12x12½*

Black Inscriptions

945	A208	10q ocher & lil	10	5
946	A208	20q lt bl & cit	15	6
947	A208	30q brick red & Prus bl	25	10
948	A208	35q lt ultra & rose	35	15
949	A208	40q yel grn & lt red brn	40	15
950	A208	50q lt red brn & yel grn	65	18
951	A208	55q rose lil & yel grn	70	20
952	A208	60q dp rose & ocher	1.35	35
		Nos. 945-952 (8)	3.95	1.24

Issued to commemorate the World Cup Soccer Championship, Wembley, England, July 11–30.

Water Level Map of Albania
A209

Designs: 30q, Water measure and fields. 70q, Turbine and pylon. 80q, Hydrological decade emblem.

1966, July *Perf. 12½x12*

953	A209	20q brick red, blk & org	18	10
954	A209	30q emer, blk & lt brn	25	12
955	A209	70q brt vio & blk	65	30
956	A209	80q brt bl, org, yel & blk	70	35

Issued to publicize the Hydrological Decade (UNESCO), 1965–74.

Greek Turtle—A210

Designs: 15q, Grass snake. 25q, European pond turtle. 30q, Wall lizard. 35q, Wall gecko. 45q, Emerald lizard. 50q, Slowworm. 90q, Horned viper (or sand viper).

1966, Aug. 10 Litho. *Perf. 12½x12*

957	A210	10q gray & multi	10	5
958	A210	15q yel & multi	20	10
959	A210	25q ultra & multi	30	15
960	A210	30q multi	40	18
961	A210	35q multi	55	20
962	A210	45q multi	65	25
963	A210	50q org & multi	75	30
964	A210	90q lil & multi	1.65	55
		Nos. 957-964 (8)	4.60	1.78

Persian Cat
A211

Cats: 10q, Siamese (vert.). 15q, European tabby (vert.). 25q, Black kitten. 60q, 65q, 80q, Various Persians.

Perf. 12x12½, 12½x12

1966, Sept. 20 Lithographed

965	A211	10q multi	10	5
966	A211	15q blk, sep & car	18	6
967	A211	25q blk, dk & lt brn	25	12
968	A211	45q blk, org & yel	50	20
969	A211	60q blk, brn & yel	65	25
970	A211	65q multi	70	25
971	A211	80q blk, gray & yel	1.25	35
		Nos. 965-971 (7)	3.63	1.28

Pjeter Budi
A212

1966, Oct. 5 *Perf. 12x12½*

972	A212	25q buff & sl grn	20	10
973	A212	1.75 l gray & dl cl	1.35	65

Issued to honor Pjeter Budi, writer.

UNESCO Emblem
A213

Designs (UNESCO Emblem and): 15q, Open book, rose and school. 25q, Male folk dancers. 1.55 l, Jug, column and old building.

1966, Oct. 20 Litho. *Perf. 12*

974	A213	5q lt gray & multi	12	5
975	A213	15q dp bl & multi	25	10
976	A213	25q gray & multi	50	18
977	A213	1.55 l multi	2.25	60

Issued to commemorate the 20th anniversary of UNESCO (United Nations Educational, Scientific and Cultural Organization).

Hand Holding Book with Pictures of Marx, Engels, Lenin and Stalin
A214

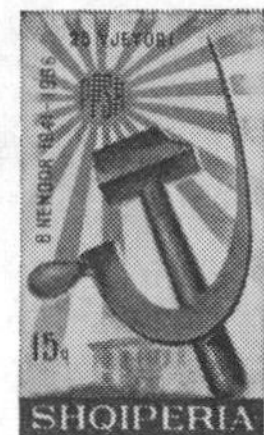

Hammer and Sickle, Party Emblem in Sunburst
A215

Designs: 25q, Map of Albania, hammer and sickle, symbols of agriculture and industry. 65q, Symbolic grain and factories. 95q, Fists holding rifle, spade, axe, sickle and book.

1966, Nov. 1 Litho. *Perf. 11½x12*

978	A214	15q ver & gold	18	5
979	A214	25q multi	25	8
980	A214	65q brn, brn org & gold	65	20
981	A214	95q yel & multi	90	45

Issued to commemorate the 5th Congress of the Albanian Communist Party.

1966, Nov. 8

Designs: 25q, Partisan and sunburst. 65q, Steel worker and blast furnace. 95q, Combine harvester, factories, and pylon.

982	A215	15q org & multi	18	5
983	A215	25q red & multi	25	8
984	A215	65q multi	65	20
985	A215	95q bl & multi	90	45

Issued to commemorate the 25th anniversary of the founding of the Albanian Workers Party.

Russian Wolfhound—A216

Dogs: 15q, Sheep dog. 25q, English setter. 45q, English springer spaniel. 60q, Bulldog. 65q, Saint Bernard. 80q, Dachshund.

1966 Litho. *Perf. 12½x12*

986	A216	10q grn & multi	18	6
987	A216	15q multi	25	10
988	A216	25q lil & multi	35	15
989	A216	45q rose & multi	75	45
990	A216	60q brn & multi	90	50
991	A216	65q ultra & multi	1.00	55
992	A216	80q bl grn & multi	1.50	65
		Nos. 986-992 (7)	4.93	2.46

Ndre Mjeda A217

Proclamation A218

1966 *Perf. 12½x12*

993	A217	25q brt bl & dk brn	45	10
994	A217	1.75 l brt grn & dk brn	1.75	65

Birth Centenary of the priest Ndre Mjeda.

1966 *Perf. 11½x12, 12x11½*

Designs: 10q, Banner, man and woman holding gun and axe (horiz.). 1.85 l, man with axe and banner and partisan with gun.

995	A218	5q lt brn, red & blk	5	5
996	A218	10q red, blk, gray & bl	18	5
997	A218	1.85 l red, blk & sal	1.35	45

Issued to commemorate the 25th anniversary of the Albanian Communist Party.

Golden Eagle A219

Birds of Prey: 15q, European sea eagle. 25q, Griffon vulture. 40q, Common sparrowhawk. 50q, Osprey. 70q, Egyptian vulture. 90q, Kestrel.

1966, Dec. 20 Litho. *Perf. 11½x12*

998	A219	10q gray & multi	12	5
999	A219	15q multi	18	10
1000	A219	25q cit & multi	35	18
1001	A219	40q multi	55	25
1002	A219	50q multi	65	30
1003	A219	70q yel & multi	90	45
1004	A219	90q multi	1.25	65
		Nos. 998-1004 (7)	4.00	1.98

Hake A220

Fish: 15q, Red mullet. 25q, Opah. 40q, Atlantic wolf fish. 65q, Lumpfish. 80q, Swordfish. 1.15 l, Shorthorn sculpin.

1967, Jan. Photo. *Perf. 12x11½*

Fish in Natural Colors

1005	A220	10q blue	12	5
1006	A220	15q lt yel grn	20	5
1007	A220	25q Prus bl	25	10
1008	A220	40q emerald	60	18
1009	A220	65q brt bl grn	70	25
1010	A220	80q blue	1.00	35
1011	A220	1.15 l brt grn	1.35	60
		Nos. 1005-1011 (7)	4.22	1.58

White Pelican A221

Designs: Various groups of pelicans.

1967, Feb. 22 Litho. *Perf. 12*

1012	A221	10q pink & multi	10	5
1013	A221	15q pink & multi	15	6
1014	A221	25q pink & multi	40	10
1015	A221	50q pink & multi	70	20
1016	A221	2 l pink & multi	2.75	1.00
		Nos. 1012-1016 (5)	4.10	1.41

Camellia A222

Flowers: 10q, Chrysanthemum. 15q, Hollyhock. 25q, Flowering Maple. 35q, Peony. 65q, Gladiolus. 80q, Freesia. 1.15 l, Carnation.

Lithographed

1967, Apr. 12 *Perf. 12* Unwmkd.

Flowers in Natural Colors

1017	A222	5q pale brn	10	5
1018	A222	10q lt lil	10	5
1019	A222	15q gray	15	6
1020	A222	25q ultra	25	10
1021	A222	35q lt bl	45	10
1022	A222	65q lt bl grn	70	20
1023	A222	80q lt bluish gray	1.00	35
1024	A222	1.15 l dl yel	1.35	65
		Nos. 1017-1024 (8)	4.10	1.56

Congress Emblem and Power Station A223

1967, Apr. 24 Litho. *Perf. 12*

1025	A223	25q gray lil, sep & brt rose	25	10
1026	A223	1.75 l gray, blk & brt rose	2.00	55

Issued to commemorate the Congress of the Union of Professional Workers, Tirana, Apr. 24.

Rose A224

Various Roses in Natural Colors

1967, May 15 *Perf. 12x12½*

1027	A224	5q bl gray	5	5
1028	A224	10q brt bl	7	5
1029	A224	15q rose vio	10	5
1030	A224	25q lemon	30	5
1031	A224	35q brt grnsh bl	40	10
1032	A224	65q gray	70	20
1033	A224	80q brown	90	30
1034	A224	1.65 l gray grn	2.00	55
		Nos. 1027-1034 (8)	4.52	1.35

Seashore, Bregdet Borsh A225

Views: 15q, Buthrotum (vert.). 25q, Shore, Fshati Piqeras. 45q, Shore, Bregdet. 50q, Shore, Bregdet Himare. 65q, Ship, Sarande (Santi Quaranta). 80q, Shore, Dhermi. 1 l, Sunset, Bregdet (vert.).

Perf. 12x12½, 12½x12

1967, June 10

1035	A225	15q multi	10	5
1036	A225	20q multi	15	6
1037	A225	25q multi	18	10
1038	A225	45q multi	45	15
1039	A225	50q multi	50	20
1040	A225	65q multi	70	25
1041	A225	80q multi	75	30
1042	A225	1 l multi	1.00	45
		Nos. 1035-1042 (8)	3.83	1.56

Fawn A226

Roe Deer: 20q, Stag (vert.). 25q, Doe (vert.). 30q, Young stag and doe. 35q, Doe and fawn. 40q, Young stag (vert.). 65q, Stag and doe (vert.). 70q, Running stag and does.

Perf. 12½x12, 12x12½

1967, July 20 Lithographed

1043	A226	15q yel grn, gldn brn & blk	20	5
1044	A226	20q lt bl, org brn & blk	20	6
1045	A226	25q yel, org brn & blk	30	8
1046	A226	30q vio bl, ol bis & blk	35	10
1047	A226	35q pink, dk red brn & blk	45	10
1048	A226	40q lt vio, bis brn & blk	55	10
1049	A226	65q yel, org brn & blk	90	30
1050	A226	70q grnsh bl, org brn & blk	90	35
		Nos. 1043-1050 (8)	3.85	1.14

Man and Woman from Madhe A227

Fighters and Newspaper A228

Regional Costumes: 20q, Woman from Zadrimës. 25q, Dancer and drummer, Kukesit. 45q, Woman spinner, Dardhës. 50q, Farm couple, Myseqesë. 65q, Dancer with tambourine, Tirana. 80q, Man and woman, Dropullit. 1 l, Piper, Labërisë.

1967, Aug. 25 *Perf. 12*

1051	A227	15q tan & multi	10	6
1052	A227	20q lt yel grn	20	10
1053	A227	25q multi	20	10
1054	A227	45q sky bl & multi	40	25
1055	A227	50q lem & multi	60	30
1056	A227	65q pink & multi	70	45
1057	A227	80q multi	90	50
1058	A227	1 l gray & multi	1.25	65
		Nos. 1051-1058 (8)	4.35	2.41

1967, Aug. 25 *Perf. 12½x12*

Designs: 75q, Printing plant, newspapers and microphone. 2 l, People holding newspaper.

1059	A228	25q multi	30	8
1060	A228	75q pink & multi	70	18
1061	A228	2 l multi	1.75	50

Issued for the Day of the Press.

Street Scene, by Kolé Idromeno A229

Hakmarrja Battalion, by Sali Shijaku A230

Designs: 20q, David, fresco by Onufri, 16th century (vert.). 45q, Woman's head, ancient mosaic (vert.). 50q, Men on horseback from 16th century icon (vert.). 65q, Farm Women, by Zef Shoshi. 80q, Street Scene, by Vangjush Mio. 1 l, Bride, by Kolé Idromeno (vert.).

Perf. 12, 12x12½, (A230)

1967, Oct. 25 Lithographed

1062	A229	15q multi	25	5
1063	A229	20q multi	30	5
1064	A230	25q multi	35	6
1065	A229	45q multi	75	8
1066	A229	50q multi	85	10
1067	A230	65q multi	1.00	14
1068	A230	80q multi	1.25	25
1069	A230	1 l multi	1.75	30
		Nos. 1062-1069 (8)	6.50	1.03

Lenin at Storming of Winter Palace
A231

Rabbit
A232

Designs: 15q, Lenin and Stalin (horiz.). 50q, Lenin and Stalin addressing meeting. 1.10 l, Storming of the Winter Palace (horiz.).

1967, Nov. 7 ***Perf. 12***

1070	A231	15q red & multi	15	5
1071	A231	25q sl grn & blk	25	10
1072	A231	50q brn, blk & brn vio	40	15
1073	A231	1.10 l lil, gray & blk	1.25	30

Issued to commemorate the 50th anniversary of the Russian October Revolution.

1967, Nov. 25

Designs: Various hares and rabbits. The 15q, 25q, 35q, 40q and 1 l are horizontal.

1074	A232	15q org & multi	10	5
1075	A232	20q brt yel & multi	10	5
1076	A232	25q lt brn & multi	12	5
1077	A232	35q multi	18	8
1078	A232	40q yel & multi	30	8
1079	A232	50q pink & multi	35	15
1080	A232	65q multi	65	30
1081	A232	1 l lil & multi	95	45
		Nos. 1074-1081 (8)	2.75	1.21

University, Torch and Book
A233

1967 **Lithographed** ***Perf. 12***

1082	A233	25q multi	25	5
1083	A233	1.75 l multi	1.60	40

Issued to commemorate the 10th anniversary of the founding of the State University, Tirana.

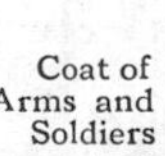

Coat of Arms and Soldiers
A234

Designs: 65q, Arms, Factory, grain, flag, gun and radio tower. 1.20 l, Arms and hand holding torch.

1967 ***Perf. 12x11½***

1084	A234	15q multi	15	5
1085	A234	65q multi	65	15
1086	A234	1.20 l multi	1.10	20

25th anniversary of the Democratic Front.

Turkey
A235

Designs: 20q, Duck. 25q, Hen. 45q, Rooster. 50q, Guinea fowl. 65q, Goose (horiz.). 80q, Mallard (horiz.). 1 l, Chicks (horiz.).

Perf. 12x12½, 12½x12

1967, Nov. 25 **Photogravure**

1087	A235	15q gold & multi	10	5
1088	A235	20q gold & multi	10	5
1089	A235	25q gold & multi	12	6
1090	A235	45q gold & multi	20	10
1091	A235	50q gold & multi	30	10
1092	A235	65q gold & multi	40	20
1093	A235	80q gold & multi	70	30
1094	A235	1 l gold & multi	90	40
		Nos. 1087-1094 (8)	2.82	1.26

Skanderbeg
A236

Designs: 10q, Arms of Skanderbeg. 25q, Helmet and sword. 30q, Kruje Castle. 35q, Petreles Castle. 65q, Berati Castle. 80q, Skanderbeg addressing national chiefs. 90q, Battle of Albulenes.

1967, Dec. 10 Litho. ***Perf. 12x12½***

Medallion in Bister and Dark Brown

1095	A236	10q gold & vio	6	5
1096	A236	15q gold & rose car	8	5
1097	A236	25q gold & vio bl	13	6
1098	A236	30q gold & dk bl	15	9
1099	A236	35q gold & mar	20	12
1100	A236	65q gold & grn	35	18
1101	A236	80q gold & gray brn	60	20
1102	A236	90q gold & ultra	1.00	25
		Nos. 1095-1102 (8)	2.57	1.00

Issued to commemorate the 500th anniversary of the death of Skanderbeg (George Castriota), national hero.

Ice Hockey
A237

Designs: 15q, 2 l, Winter Olympics emblem. 30q, Women's figure skating. 50q, Slalom. 80q, Downhill skiing. 1 l, Ski jump.

1967-68

1103	A237	15q multi	6	5
1104	A237	25q multi	10	5
1105	A237	30q multi	15	6
1106	A237	50q multi	30	12
1107	A237	80q multi	60	20
1108	A237	1 l multi	85	30
		Nos. 1103-1108 (6)	2.06	78

Miniature Sheet

Imperf.

1109	A237	2 l red, gray & brt bl ('68)	5.50	5.50

Issued to publicize the 10th Winter Olympic Games, Grenoble, France, Feb. 6–18. Size of No. 1109: 55x66mm.
Nos. 1103–1108 issued Dec. 29, 1967.

Skanderbeg Monument, Kruje
A238

Designs: 10q, Skanderbeg monument, Tirana. 15q, Skanderbeg portrait, Uffizi Galleries, Florence. 25q, Engraved portrait of Gen. Tanush Topia. 35q, Portrait of Gen. Gjergj Arianti (horiz.). 65q, Portrait bust of Skanderbeg by O. Paskali. 80q, Title page of "The Life of Skanderbeg." 90q, Skanderbeg battling the Turks, painting by S. Rrota (horiz.).

Perf. 12x12½, 12½x12

1968, Jan 17 **Lithographed**

1110	A238	10q multi	15	5
1111	A238	15q multi	25	5
1112	A238	25q blk, yel & lt bl	35	5
1113	A238	30q multi	40	5
1114	A238	35q lt vio, pink & blk	60	10
1115	A238	65q multi	1.00	15
1116	A238	80q pink, blk & yel	1.25	20
1117	A238	90q beige & multi	1.75	25
		Nos. 1110-1117 (8)	5.75	90

Issued to commemorate the 500th anniversary of the death of Skanderbeg (George Castriota), national hero.

Carnation
A239

1968, Feb. 15 ***Perf. 12***

Various Carnations in Natural Colors

1118	A239	15q green	8	5
1119	A239	20q dk brn	10	5
1120	A239	25q brt bl	12	5
1121	A239	50q gray ol	20	10
1122	A239	80q bluish gray	55	20
1123	A239	1.10 l vio gray	75	30
		Nos. 1118-1123 (6)	1.80	75

"Electrification"
A240

Designs: 65q, Farm tractor (horiz.). 1.10 l, Cow and herd.

1968, Mar. 5 **Litho.** ***Perf. 12***

1124	A240	25q multi	20	5
1125	A240	65q multi	60	10
1126	A240	1.10 l multi	85	25

Fifth Farm Cooperatives Congress.

Goat
A241

Designs: Various goats. 15q, 20q and 25q are vertical.

Perf. 12x12½, 12½x12

1968, Mar. 25

1127	A241	15q multi	10	5
1128	A241	20q multi	10	5
1129	A241	25q multi	15	5
1130	A241	30q multi	18	5
1131	A241	40q multi	25	8
1132	A241	50q multi	30	10
1133	A241	80q multi	50	20
1134	A241	1.40 l multi	1.25	40
		Nos. 1127-1134 (8)	2.83	98

Zee N. Jubani
A242

Physician and Hospital
A243

1968, Mar. 30 ***Perf. 12***

1135	A242	25q yel & choc	20	10
1136	A242	1.75 l lt vio & blk	85	35

Issued to commemorate the sesquicentennial of the birth of Zee N. Jubani, writer and scholar.

Perf. 12½x12, 12x12½

1968, Apr. 7 **Lithographed**

Designs (World Health Organization Emblem and): 65q, Hospital and microscope (horiz.). 1.10 l, Mother feeding child.

1137	A243	25q grn & cl	20	6
1138	A243	65q blk, yel & bl	60	15
1139	A243	1.10 l blk & dp org	90	25

Issued to commemorate the 20th anniversary of the World Health Organization.

Scientist
A244

Women: 15q, Militia member. 60q, Farm worker. 1 l, Factory worker.

1968, Apr. 14 ***Perf. 12***

1140	A244	15q ver & dk red	15	5
1141	A244	25q bl grn & grn	20	10
1142	A244	60q dl yel & brn	35	18
1143	A244	1 l lt vio & vio	85	35

Issued to commemorate the 25th anniversary of the Albanian Women's Organization.

Karl Marx
A245

Designs: 25q, Marx lecturing to students. 65q, "Das Kapital," "Communist Manifesto" and marching crowd. 95q, Full-face portrait.

1968, May 5 Litho. *Perf. 12*

1144 A245 15q gray, dk bl & bis 15 6
1145 A245 25q brn vio, dk brn & dl yel 30 10
1146 A245 65q gray, blk, brn & car 80 25
1147 A245 95q gray, ocher & blk 1.25 50

Karl Marx, 150th birth anniversary.

Heliopsis
A246

Flowers: 20q, Red flax. 25q, Orchid. 30q, Gloxinia. 40q, Turk's-cap lily. 80q, Amaryllis. 1.40 l, Red magnolia.

1968, May 10 *Perf. 12x12½*

1148 A246 15q gold & multi 6 5
1149 A246 20q gold & multi 8 5
1150 A246 25q gold & multi 10 5
1151 A246 30q gold & multi 15 5
1152 A246 40q gold & multi 40 10
1153 A246 80q gold & multi 50 10
1154 A246 1.40 l gold & multi 75 30
Nos. 1148-1154 (7) 2.04 70

Proclamation of Prizren
A247

Designs: 25q, Abdyl Frasheri. 40q, House in Prizren.

1968, June 10 Litho. *Perf. 12*

1155 A247 25q emer & blk 20 5
1156 A247 40q multi 45 10
1157 A247 85q yel & multi 85 25

Issued to commemorate the 90th anniversary of the League of Prizren against the Turks.

Shepherd, by A. Kushi
A248

Paintings from Tirana Art Gallery: 20q, View of Tirana, by V. Mio (horiz.). 25q, Mountaineer, by G. Madhi. 40q, Refugees, by A. Buza. 80q, Guerrillas of Shahin Matrakut, by S. Xega. 1.50 l, Portrait of an Old Man, by S. Papadhimitri. 1.70 l, View of Scutari, by S. Rrota. 2.50 l, Woman in Scutari Costume, by Z. Colombi.

1968, June 20 *Perf. 12x12½*

1158 A248 15q gold & multi 10 5
1159 A248 20q gold & multi 12 5
1160 A248 25q gold & multi 15 6
1161 A248 40q gold & multi 30 10
1162 A248 80q gold & multi 50 10
1163 A248 1.50 l gold & multi 90 25
1164 A248 1.70 l gold & multi 1.00 50
Nos. 1158-1164 (7) 3.07 1.11

Miniature Sheet
Perf. 12½xImperf.

1165 A248 2.50 l multi 2.50 1.00

No. 1165 contains one stamp with picture frame in margin. Size of stamp: 50x71mm.; size of sheet: 89x113mm.

Soldier and Guns—A249

Designs: 25q, Sailor and warships. 65q, Aviator and planes (vert.). 95q, Militiamen and woman.

1968, July 10 Litho. *Perf. 12*

1166 A249 15q multi 15 5
1167 A249 25q multi 25 10
1168 A249 65q multi 65 15
1169 A249 95q multi 1.20 25

25th anniversary of the People's Army.

Squid
A250

Designs: 20q, Crayfish. 25q, Whelk. 50q, Crab. 70q, Spiny lobster. 80q, Shore crab. 90q, Norway lobster.

1968, Aug. 20

1170 A250 15q multi 10 5
1171 A250 20q multi 10 5
1172 A250 25q multi 15 5
1173 A250 50q multi 25 10
1174 A250 70q multi 40 25
1175 A250 80q multi 50 30
1176 A250 90q multi 75 35
Nos. 1170-1176 (7) 2.25 1.15

Women's Relay Race
A251

Sport: 20q, Running. 25q, Women's discus. 30q, Equestrian. 40q, High jump. 50q, Women's hurdling. 80q, Soccer. 1.40 l, Woman diver. 2 l, Olympic stadium.

1968, Sept. 23 Photo. *Perf. 12*

1177 A251 15q multi 8 5
1178 A251 20q multi 12 5
1179 A251 25q multi 15 5
1180 A251 30q multi 25 5
1181 A251 40q multi 30 10
1182 A251 50q multi 45 10
1183 A251 80q multi 70 20
1184 A251 1.40 l multi 1.25 45
Nos. 1177-1184 (8) 3.30 1.05

Souvenir Sheet
Perf. 12½ Horizontally

1185 A251 2 l multi 3.00 1.00

Issued to publicize the 19th Olympic Games, Mexico City, Oct. 12–27. No. 1185 contains one rectangular stamp, size: 64x54mm. Sheet has ocher marginal inscription. Size: 90x82mm.

Price of imperfs., #1177-1184 $6, #1185 $5.

Enver Hoxha
A252

1968, Oct. 16 Litho. *Perf. 12*

1186 A252 25q bl gray 25 12
1187 A252 35q rose brn 40 18
1188 A252 80q violet 70 35
1189 A252 1.10 l brown 90 50

Souvenir Sheet
Imperf.

1190 A252 1.50 l rose red, bl vio & gold 55.00 55.00

Issued for the 60th birthday of Enver Hoxha, First Secretary of the Central Committee of the Communist Party of Albania. No. 1190 contains portrait (size: 45x55mm.) with name of country, denomination and commemorative inscription in margin. Size: 79x90mm.

Book and Pupils
A253

1968, Nov. 14 Photogravure

1191 A253 15q mar & sl grn 20 10
1192 A253 85q gray ol & sep 1.30 25

Issued to commemorate the 60th anniversary of the Congress of Monastir, Nov. 14–22, 1908, which adopted a unified Albanian alphabet.

Waxwing
A254

Birds: 20q, Rose-colored starling. 25q, Kingfishers. 50q, Long-tailed tits. 80q, Wallcreeper. 1.10 l, Bearded tit.

1968, Nov. 15 Lithographed
Birds in Natural Colors

1193 A254 15q lt bl & blk 10 5
1194 A254 20q bis & blk 15 5
1195 A254 25q pink & blk 25 10
1196 A254 50q lt yel grn & blk 30 15
1197 A254 80q bis brn & blk 65 25
1198 A254 1.10 l pale grn & blk 85 30
Nos. 1193-1198 (6) 2.30 90

Mao Tse-tung—A255

1968, Dec. 26 Litho. *Perf. 12½x12*

1199 A255 25q gold, red & blk 25 15
1200 A255 1.75 l gold, red & blk 1.25 30

Issued to commemorate the 75th birthday of Mao Tse-tung, Chairman of the Communist Party of the People's Republic of China.

Adem Reka and Crane
A256

Portraits: 10q, Pjeter Lleshi and power lines. 15q, Mohammed Shehu and Myrteza Kepi. 25q, Shkurte Vata and women railroad workers. 65q, Agron Elezi, frontier guard. 80q, Ismet Bruçaj and mountain road. 1.30 l, Fuat Cela, blind revolutionary.

1969, Feb. 10 Litho. *Perf. 12x12½*

1201 A256 5q multi 5 5
1202 A256 10q multi 6 5
1203 A256 15q multi 10 5
1204 A256 25q multi 12 6
1205 A256 65q multi 35 10
1206 A256 80q multi 60 15
1207 A256 1.30 l multi 1.00 30
Nos. 1201-1207 (7) 2.28 76

Issued to honor a contemporary heroine and heroes.

Meteorological Instruments
A257

Designs: 25q, Water gauge. 1.60 l, Radar, balloon and isobars.

1969, Feb. 25 *Perf. 12*

1208 A257 15q multi 15 5
1209 A257 25q ultra, org & blk 25 10
1210 A257 1.60 l rose vio, yel & blk 1.35 35

Issued to commemorate the 20th anniversary of Albanian hydrometeorology.

Partisans, 1944, by F. Haxmiu
A258

Paintings: 5q, Student Revolutionists, by P. Mele (vert.). 65q, Steel Mill, by C. Ceka. 80q, Reconstruction, by V. Kilica. 1.10 l, Harvest, by N. Jonuzi. 1.15 l, Terraced Landscape, by S. Kaceli. 2 l, Partisans' Meeting.

Perf. 12x12½, 12½x12

1969, Apr. 25 Lithographed

Size: 31½x41½mm.

1211 A258 5q buff & multi 5 5

Size: 51½x30½mm.

1212 A258 25q buff & multi 10 6

Size: 40½x32mm.

1213 A258 65q buff & multi 25 10

Size: 51½x30½mm.

1214	A258	80q	buff & multi	35	15
1215	A258	1.10 l	buff & multi	55	20
1216	A258	1.15 l	buff & multi	70	25
			Nos. 1211-1216 (6)	2.00	81

Miniature Sheet

Imperf.

Size: 111x90mm.

1217	A258	2 l	ocher & multi	1.50	90

Leonardo da Vinci, Self-portrait
A259

Designs (after Leonardo da Vinci): 35q, Lilies. 40q, Design for a flying machine (horiz.). 1 l, Portrait of Beatrice. No. 1222, Portrait of a Noblewoman. No. 1223, Mona Lisa.

Perf. 12x12½, 12½x12

1969, May 2 **Lithographed**

1218	A259	25q	gold & sep	15	5
1219	A259	35q	gold & sep	25	10
1220	A259	40q	gold & sep	30	10
1221	A259	1 l	gold & multi	80	20
1222	A259	2 l	gold & sep	1.50	55
			Nos. 1218-1222 (5)	3.00	1.00

Miniature Sheet

Imperf.

1223	A259	2 l	gold & multi	3.00	2.25

Issued to commemorate the 450th anniversary of the death of Leonardo da Vinci (1452–1519), painter, sculptor, architect and engineer. Size of No. 1223: 64x95 mm.

First Congress Meeting Place
A260

Designs: 1 l, Albanian coat of arms. 2.25 l, Two partisans with guns and flag.

1969, May 24 ***Perf. 12***

1224	A260	25q	lt grn, blk & red	25	15
1225	A260	2.25 l	multi	1.75	1.10

Souvenir Sheet

1226	A260	1 l	gold, bl, blk & red	*22.50*	*15.00*

25th anniversary of the First Anti-Fascist Congress of Permet, May 24, 1944.

No. 1226 contains one stamp; blue, black and red decorative margin. Size: 94½x100mm.

Albanian Violet
A261

Designs: Violets and Pansies.

1969, June 30 Litho. ***Perf. 12x12½***

1227	A261	5q	gold & multi	5	5
1228	A261	10q	gold & multi	10	5
1229	A261	15q	gold & multi	10	5
1230	A261	20q	gold & multi	15	10
1231	A261	25q	gold & multi	25	10
1232	A261	80q	gold & multi	40	30
1233	A261	1.95 l	gold & multi	1.00	65
			Nos. 1227-1233 (7)	2.05	1.30

Plum, Fruit and Blossoms
A262

Designs: Blossoms and Fruits.

1969, Aug. 10 **Litho.** ***Perf. 12***

Multicolored

1234	A262	10q	*shown*	5	5
1235	A262	15q	*Lemon*	10	5
1236	A262	25q	Pomegranate	15	5
1237	A262	50q	*Cherry*	30	10
1238	A262	80q	*Peach*	50	20
1239	A262	1.20 l	*Apple*	90	35
			Nos. 1234-1239 (6)	2.00	80

Basketball
A263

Designs: 10q, 80q, 2.20 l, Various views of basketball game. 25q, Hand aiming ball at basket and map of Europe (horiz.).

1969, Sept. 15 **Litho.** ***Perf. 12***

1240	A263	10q	multi	7	5
1241	A263	15q	buff & multi	10	5
1242	A263	25q	bl & multi	25	7
1243	A263	80q	multi	60	15
1244	A263	2.20 l	multi	1.50	45
			Nos. 1240-1244 (5)	2.52	77

Issued to publicize the 16th European Basketball Championships, Naples, Italy, Sept. 27–Oct. 5.

Runner
A264

Designs: 5q, Games' emblem. 10q, Woman gymnast. 20q, Pistol shooting. 25q, Swimmer at start. 80q, Bicyclist. 95q, Soccer.

1969, Sept. 30

1245	A264	5q	multi	5	5
1246	A264	10q	multi	8	5
1247	A264	15q	multi	10	5
1248	A264	20q	multi	18	6
1249	A264	25q	multi	25	8
1250	A264	80q	multi	55	18
1251	A264	95q	multi	85	25
			Nos. 1245-1251 (7)	2.06	72

Second National Spartakiad.

Electronic Technicians, Steel Ladle
A265

Designs: 25q, Mao Tse-tung with microphones (vert.). 1.40 l, Children holding Mao's red book (vert.).

1969, Oct. 1 **Litho.** ***Perf. 12***

1252	A265	25q	multi	20	5
1253	A265	85q	multi	50	15
1254	A265	1.40 l	multi	80	30

Issued to commemorate the 20th anniversary of the People's Republic of China.

Enver Hoxha
A266

Designs: 80q, Pages from Berat resolution. 1.45 l, Partisans with flag.

1969, Oct. 20 **Litho.** ***Perf. 12***

1255	A266	25q	multi	20	5
1256	A266	80q	gray & multi	50	15
1257	A266	1.45 l	ocher & multi	80	30

Issued to commemorate the 25th anniversary of the second reunion of the National Antifascist Liberation Council, Berat.

Soldiers—A267

Designs: 30q, Oil refinery. 35q, Combine harvester. 45q, Hydroelectric station and dam. 55q, Militia woman, man and soldier. 1.10 l, Dancers and musicians.

1969, Nov. 29

1258	A267	25q	multi	10	5
1259	A267	30q	multi	10	5
1260	A267	35q	multi	10	5
1261	A267	45q	multi	15	10
1262	A267	55q	multi	35	10
1263	A267	1.10 l	multi	75	15
			Nos. 1258-1263 (6)	1.55	50

Issued to commemorate the 25th anniversary of the socialist republic.

Joseph V. Stalin
A268

1969, Dec. 21 **Litho.** ***Perf. 12***

1264	A268	15q	lilac	6	5
1265	A268	25q	sl bl	10	5
1266	A268	1 l	brown	40	15
1267	A268	1.10 l	vio bl	70	20

Issued to commemorate the 90th anniversary of the birth of Joseph V. Stalin (1879–1953), Russian political leader.

Head of Woman
A269

1969, Dec. 25 ***Perf. 12½x12***

Greco-Roman Mosaics: 25q, Geometrical floor design (horiz.). 80q, Bird and tree (horiz.). 1.10 l, Floor with birds and grapes (horiz.). 1.20 l, Fragment with corn within oval design.

1268	A269	15q	gold & multi	10	5
1269	A269	25q	gold & multi	15	5
1270	A269	80q	gold & multi	40	10
1271	A269	1.10 l	gold & multi	60	20
1272	A269	1.20 l	gold & multi	80	35
			Nos. 1268-1272 (5)	2.05	75

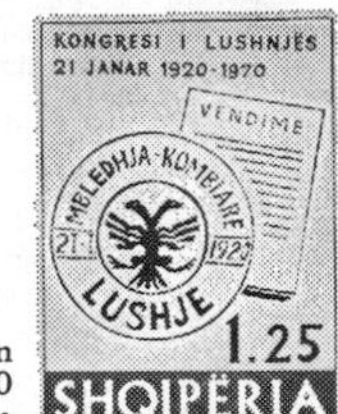

Cancellation of 1920
A270

Design: 25q, Proclamation and congress site.

1970, Jan. 21 **Litho.** ***Perf. 12***

1273	A270	25q	red, gray & blk	15	6
1274	A270	1.25 l	dk grn, yel & blk	85	15

Congress of Louchnia, 50th anniversary.

Worker, Student and Flag
A271

1970, Feb. 11 ***Perf. 12½x12***

1275	A271	25q	red & multi	15	5
1276	A271	1.75 l	red & multi	85	30

Issued to commemorate the 25th anniversary of vocational organizations in Albania.

Turk's-cap Lily
A272

Lilies: 5q, Cernum (vert.). 15q, Madonna (vert.). 25q, Royal (vert.). 1.10 l, Tiger. 1.15 l, Albanian.

Perf. 11½x12, 12x11½

1970, Mar. 10 **Lithographed**

1277	A272	5q	multi	5	5

1278 A272 15q multi 8 5
1279 A272 25q multi 15 5
1280 A272 80q multi 40 12
1281 A272 1.10 l multi 60 20
1282 A272 1.15 l multi 75 30
Nos. 1277-1282 (6) 2.03 77

Lenin
A273

Designs (Lenin): 5q, Portrait (vert.). 25q, As volunteer construction worker. 95q, Addressing crowd. 1.10 l, Saluting (vert.).

1970, Apr. 22 Litho. *Perf. 12*

Red, Black & Silver

1283 A273 5q 5 5
1284 A273 15q 7 5
1285 A273 25q 14 5
1286 A273 95q 40 10
1287 A273 1.10 l 65 20
Nos. 1283-1287 (5) 1.31 45

Centenary of birth of Lenin (1870–1924).

Frontier Guard
A274

1970, Apr. 25

1288 A274 25q multi 15 5
1289 A274 1.25 l multi 85 25

25th anniversary of Frontier Guards.

Soccer Players
A275

Designs: 5q, Jules Rimet Cup and globes. 10q, Aztec Stadium, Mexico City. 25q, Defending goal. 65q, 80q, No. 1296, Two soccer players in various plays. No. 1297, Mexican horseman and volcano Popocatepetl.

1970, May 15 Litho. *Perf. 12½x12*

1290 A275 5q multi 5 5
1291 A275 10q multi 5 5
1292 A275 15q multi 10 5
1293 A275 25q lt grn & multi 15 6
1294 A275 65q pink & multi 32 10
1295 A275 80q lt bl & multi 50 18
1296 A275 2 l yel & multi 1.35 30
Nos. 1290-1296 (7) 2.52 79

Souvenir Sheet

Perf. 12x Imperf.

1297 A275 2 l multi 2.00 1.00

Issued to publicize the World Soccer Championships for the Jules Rimet Cup, Mexico City, May 31–June 21, 1970. No. 1297 contains one large horizontal stamp, decorative border and inscription. Size: 81x74mm. Nos. 1290-1297 exist imperf.

U.P.U. Headquarters and Monument, Bern
A276

1970, May 30 Litho. *Perf. 12½x12*

1298 A276 25q ultra, gray & blk 15 5
1299 A276 1.10 l org, buff & blk 60 25
1300 A276 1.15 l grn, gray & blk 80 30

Issued to commemorate the inauguration of the new Universal Postal Union Headquarters in Bern.

Bird and Grapes Mosaic
A277

Mosaics, 5th–6th centuries, excavated near Pogradec: 10q, Waterfowl and grapes. 20q, Bird and tree stump. 25q, Bird and leaves. 65q, Fish. 2.25 l, Peacock (vert.).

Perf. 12½x12, 12x12½

1970, July 10

1301 A277 5q multi 5 5
1302 A277 10q multi 10 5
1303 A277 20q multi 15 5
1304 A277 25q multi 20 8
1305 A277 65q multi 35 15
1306 A277 2.25 l multi 1.25 40
Nos. 1301-1306 (6) 2.10 78

Fruit Harvest and Dancers
A278

Designs: 25q, Contour-plowed fields and conference table. 80q, Cattle and newspapers. 1.30 l, Wheat harvest.

1970, Aug. 28 Litho. *Perf. 12x11½*

1307 A278 15q brt vio & blk 10 5
1308 A278 25q dp bl & blk 15 5
1309 A278 80q dp brn & blk 40 10
1310 A278 1.30 l org brn & blk 60 20

Issued to commemorate the 25th anniversary of the agrarian reform law.

Attacking Partisans
A279

Designs: 25q, Partisans with horses and flag. 1.60 l, Partisans.

1970, Sept. 3 *Perf. 12*

1311 A279 15q org brn & blk 5 5
1312 A279 25q brn, yel & blk 10 6
1313 A279 1.60 l dp grn & blk 85 35

50th anniversary of liberation of Vlona.

Miners, by Nexhmedin Zajmi
A280

Paintings from the National Gallery, Tirana: 5q, Bringing in the Harvest, by Isuf Sulovari (vert.). 15q, The Activists, by Dhimitraq Trebicka (vert.). 65q, Instruction of Partisans, by Hasan Nallbani. 95q, Architectural Planning, by Vilson Kilica. No. 1319, Woman Machinist, by Zef Shoshi (vert.). No. 1320, Partisan Destroying Tank, by Sali Shijaku (vert.).

Perf. 12½x12, 12x12½

1970, Sept. 25 Lithographed

1314 A280 5q multi 5 5
1315 A280 15q multi 6 5
1316 A280 25q multi 15 5
1317 A280 65q multi 20 8
1318 A280 95q multi 35 15
1319 A280 2 l multi 1.20 40
Nos. 1314-1319 (6) 2.01 78

Miniature Sheet

Imperf.

1320 A280 2 l multi 1.50 1.25

Size of No. 1320: 66x93½mm.

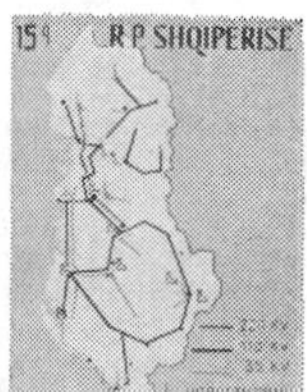

Electrification Map of Albania
A281

Designs: 25q, Light bulb, hammer and sickle emblem, map of Albania and power graph. 80q, Linemen at work. 1.10 l, Use of electricity on the farm, in home and business.

1970, Oct. 25 Litho. *Perf. 12*

1321 A281 15q multi 10 5
1322 A281 25q multi 10 5
1323 A281 80q multi 50 10
1324 A281 1.10 l multi 70 15

Issued to publicize the completion of Albanian village electrification.

Friedrich Engels
A282

Designs: 1.10 l, Engels as young man. 1.15 l, Engels addressing crowd.

1970, Nov. 28 Litho. *Perf. 12x12½*

1325 A282 25q bis & dk bl 15 5
1326 A282 1.10 l bis & dp cl 55 20
1327 A282 1.15 l bis & dk ol grn 65 25

Issued to commemorate the 150th anniversary of the birth of Friedrich Engels (1820–1895), German socialist, collaborator with Karl Marx.

Ludwig van Beethoven
A283

Designs: 5q, Birthplace, Bonn. 25q, 65q, 1.10 l, various portraits. 1.80 l, Scene from Fidelio (horiz.).

1970, Dec. 16 Litho. *Perf. 12*

1328 A283 5q dp plum & gold 5 5
1329 A283 15q brt rose lil & sil 5 5
1330 A283 25q grn & gold 10 5
1331 A283 65q mag & sil 30 10
1332 A283 1.10 l dk bl & gold 60 22
1333 A283 1.80 l blk & sil 1.25 45
Nos. 1328-1333 (6) 2.35 92

Bicentenary of the birth of Ludwig van Beethoven (1770–1827), composer.

Coat of Arms
A284

Designs: 25q, Proclamation. 80q, Enver Hoxha reading proclamation. 1.30 l, Young people and proclamation.

1971, Jan. 11 Litho. *Perf. 12*

1334 A284 15q lt bl, gold, blk & red 10 5
1335 A284 25q rose lil, blk, gold & gray 10 5
1336 A284 80q emer, blk & gold 40 12
1337 A284 1.30 l yel org, blk & gold 65 30

Declaration of the Republic, 25th anniversary.

"Liberty" A285 — Black Men A286

Designs: 50q, Women's brigade. 65q, Street battle (horiz.). 1.10 l, Execution (horiz.).

Perf. 12x11½, 11½x12

1971, March 18 Lithographed

1338 A285 25q dk bl & bl 13 5
1339 A285 50q sl grn 25 7
1340 A285 65q dk brn & chnt 35 15
1341 A285 1.10 l purple 55 20

Centenary of the Paris Commune.

1971, March 21 *Perf. 12x12½*

Designs: 1.10 l, Men of 3 races. 1.15 l, Black protest.

1342 A286 25q blk & bis brn 12 5
1343 A286 1.10 l blk & rose car 45 15
1344 A286 1.15 l blk & ver 55 20

International year against racial discrimination.

Tulip A287 — Horseman, by Dürer A288

Designs: Various tulips.

1971, March 25

1345	A287	5q multi	5	5
1346	A287	10q yel & multi	5	5
1347	A287	15q pink & multi	6	5
1348	A287	20q lt bl & multi	8	5
1349	A287	25q multi	18	6
1350	A287	80q multi	35	10
1351	A287	1 l multi	50	18
1352	A287	1.45 l cit & multi	75	25
		Nos. 1345-1352 (8)	2.02	79

Perf. 11½x12, 12x11½

1971, May 15 **Lithographed**

Art Works by Dürer: 15q, Three peasants. 25q, Dancing peasant couple. 45q, The bagpiper. 65q, View of Kalkreut (horiz.). 2.40 l, View of Trent (horiz.). 2.50 l, Self-portrait.

1353	A288	10q blk & pale grn	5	5
1354	A288	15q blk & pale lil	10	5
1355	A288	25q blk & pale bl	15	5
1356	A288	45q blk & pale rose	20	7
1357	A288	65q blk & multi	30	18
1358	A288	2.40 l blk & multi	1.25	40
		Nos. 1353-1358 (6)	2.05	80

Miniature Sheet

Imperf.

1359	A288	2.50 l multi	1.50	1.00

500th anniversary of the birth of Albrecht Dürer (1471–1528), German painter and engraver. Size of No. 1359: 93x90 mm.

Satellite Orbiting Globe—289

Designs: 1.20 l, Government Building, Tirana, and Red Star emblem. 2.20 l, like 60q, 2.50 l, Flag of People's Republic of China forming trajectory around globe.

1971, June 10 Litho. *Perf. 12x12½*

1360	A289	60q pur & multi	40	15
1361	A289	1.20 l ver & multi	1.00	25
1362	A289	2.20 l grn & multi	1.60	45

Imperf.

1363	A289	2.50 l vio blk & multi	2.50	90

Space developments of People's Republic of China. Size of No. 1363: 64x112mm.

Mao Tse-tung A290

Designs: 1.05 l, House where Communist Party was founded (horiz.). 1.20 l, Peking crowd with placards (horiz.).

Perf. 12x12½, 12½x12

1971, July 1

1364	A290	25q sil & multi	18	5
1365	A290	1.05 l sil & multi	55	15
1366	A290	1.20 l sil & multi	70	25

50th anniversary of Chinese Communist Party.

Crested Titmouse—A291

1971, Aug. 15 Litho. *Perf. 12½x12*

Multicolored

1367	A291	5q *shown*	5	5
1368	A291	10q *European serin*	6	5
1369	A291	15q *Linnet*	8	5
1370	A291	25q *Firecrest*	10	6
1371	A291	45q *Rock thrush*	30	12
1372	A291	60q *Blue tit*	45	25
1373	A291	2.40 l *Chaffinch*	1.50	60
		Nos. 1367-1373 (7)	2.54	1.18

Printed se-tenant in blocks of 8 (2x4) including a label showing bird's nest. The label is se-tenant horizontally with the 5q, and vertically with the 10q.

Olympic Rings and Running—A292

Designs (Olympic Rings and): 10q, Hurdles. 15q, Canoeing. 25q, Gymnastics. 80q, Fencing. 1.05 l, Soccer. 2 l, Runner at finish line. 3.60 l, Diving, women's.

1971, Sept. 15

1374	A292	5q grn & multi	5	5
1375	A292	10q multi	6	5
1376	A292	15q bl & multi	8	5
1377	A292	25q vio & multi	10	10
1378	A292	80q lil & multi	30	15
1379	A292	1.05 l multi	40	20
1380	A292	3.60 l multi	2.00	65
		Nos. 1374-1380 (7)	2.99	1.25

Souvenir Sheet

Imperf.

1381	A292	2 l brt bl & multi	1.50	1.00

20th Olympic Games, Munich, Aug. 26–Sept. 10, 1972. No. 1381 contains one stamp, gray margin with brown inscription. Olympic rings and deep orange and silver flame emblem. Size: 68x82mm.

Workers with Flags A293

Designs: 1.05 l, Party Headquarters, Tirana, and Red Star. 1.20 l, Rifle, star, flag and "VI" (vert.).

1971, Nov. 1 ***Perf. 12***

1382	A293	25q gold, sil, red & bl	15	5
1383	A293	1.05 l gold, sil, red & bl	50	14
1384	A293	1.20 l gold, sil, red & blk	60	25

6th Congress of Workers' Party.

Factories and Workers A294

Designs: 80q, "XXX" and flag (vert.). 1.55 l, Enver Hoxha and flags.

1971, Nov. 8

1385	A294	15q gold, sil, lil & yel	10	5
1386	A294	80q gold, sil & red	40	12
1387	A294	1.55 l gold, sil, red & brn	75	30

30th anniversary of Workers' Party.

Construction Work, by M. Fushekati A295

Albanian Paintings: 5q, Young Man, by R. Kuci (vert.). 25q, Partisan, by D. Jukniu (vert.). 80q, Fliers, by S. Kristo. 1.20 l, Girl in Forest, by A. Sadikaj. 1.55 l, Warriors with Spears and Shields, by S. Kamberi. 2 l, Freedom Fighter, by I. Lulani.

Perf. 12x12½, 12½x12

1971, Nov. 20

1388	A295	5q gold & multi	5	5
1389	A295	15q gold & multi	7	5
1390	A295	25q gold & multi	11	5
1391	A295	80q gold & multi	30	10
1392	A295	1.20 l gold & multi	65	22
1393	A295	1.55 l gold & multi	85	30
		Nos. 1388-1393 (6)	2.03	77

Miniature Sheet

Imperf.

1394	A295	2 l gold & multi	1.50	90

Contemporary Albanian paintings. Size of No. 1394: 87x67½mm.

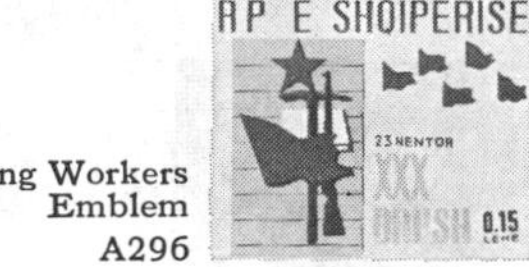

Young Workers Emblem A296

1971, Nov. 23 ***Perf. 12x12½***

1395	A296	15q lt bl & multi	10	5
1396	A296	1.35 l grnsh gray & multi	70	25

30th anniversary of the Albanian Young Workers' Union.

"Halili and Hajria" Ballet—A297

Scenes from "Halili and Hajria" Ballet: 10q, Brother and sister. 15q, Hajria before Sultan Suleiman. 50q, Hajria and husband. 80q, Execution of Halili. 1.40 l, Hajria killing her husband.

1971, Dec. 27 ***Perf. 12½x12***

1397	A297	5q sil & multi	5	5
1398	A297	10q sil & multi	8	5
1399	A297	15q sil & multi	7	5
1400	A297	50q sil & multi	35	10
1401	A297	80q sil & multi	55	15
1402	A297	1.40 l sil & multi	90	40
		Nos. 1397-1402 (6)	2.00	80

Albanian ballet Halili and Hajria after drama by Kol Jakova.

Biathlon and Olympic Rings—A298

Designs (Olympic Rings and): 10q, Sledding. 15q, Ice hockey. 20q, Bobsledding. 50q, Speed skating. 1 l, Slalom. 2 l, Ski jump. 2.50 l, Figure skating, pairs.

1972, Feb. 10

1403	A298	5q lt ol & multi	5	5
1404	A298	10q lt vio & multi	6	5
1405	A298	15q multi	7	5
1406	A298	20q pink & multi	10	5
1407	A298	50q lt bl & multi	25	10
1408	A298	1 l ocher & multi	60	25
1409	A298	2 l lil & multi	1.25	45
		Nos. 1403-1409 (7)	2.38	1.00

Souvenir Sheet

Imperf.

1410	A298	2.50 l bl & multi	1.75	75

11th Winter Olympic Games, Sapporo, Japan, Feb. 3–13. No. 1410 contains one stamp. Blue, ultramarine and silver margin with inscription. Size: 71x90mm.

Wild Strawberries A299

Wild Fruits and Nuts: 10q, Blackberries. 15q, Hazelnuts. 20q, Walnuts. 25q, Strawberry-tree fruit. 30q, Dogwood berries. 2.40 l, Rowan berries.

1972, Mar. 20 **Litho.** ***Perf. 12***

1411	A299	5q lt grn & multi	5	5
1412	A299	10q yel & multi	6	5
1413	A299	15q lt vio & multi	10	5
1414	A299	20q pink & multi	15	5
1415	A299	25q multi	20	15
1416	A299	30q multi	30	15
1417	A299	2.40 l multi	1.50	55
		Nos. 1411-1417 (7)	2.36	1.05

"Your Heart is your Health" A300

Worker and Student A301

Design: 1.20 l, Cardiac patient and electrocardiogram.

1972, Apr. 7 ***Perf. 12x12½***

1418	A300	1.10 l multi	60	20
1419	A300	1.20 l rose & multi	75	30

World Health Day 1972.

1972, Apr. 24 Litho. *Perf. 11½x12½*

Design: 2.05 l, Assembly Hall, dancers and emblem.

1420	A301	25q multi	15	5
1421	A301	2.05 l bl & multi	1.00	45

7th Trade Union Congress, May 8.

Qemal Stafa
A302

Designs: 15q, Memorial flame. 25q, Monument "Spirit of Defiance" (vert.).

Perf. 12½x12, 12x12½

1972, May 5

1422	A302	15q gray & multi	7	5
1423	A302	25q sal rose, blk & gray	15	8
1424	A302	1.90 l dl yel & blk	1.10	30

30th anniversary of the murder of Qemal Stafa and of Martyrs' Day.

Camellia
A303

Designs: Various camellias.

1972, May 10 *Perf. 12x12½*

Flowers in Natural Colors

1425	A303	5q lt bl & blk	5	5
1426	A303	10q cit & blk	6	5
1427	A303	15q grnsh gray & blk	7	5
1428	A303	25q pale sal & blk	10	5
1429	A303	45q gray & blk	20	10
1430	A303	50q sal pink & blk	35	15
1431	A303	2.50 l bluish gray & blk	1.50	85
		Nos. 1425-1431 (7)	2.33	1.30

High Jump—A304

Designs (Olympic and Motion Emblems and): 10q, Running. 15q, Shot put. 20q, Bicycling. 25q, Pole vault. 50q, Hurdles, women's. 75q, Hockey. 2 l, Swimming. 2.50 l, Diving, women's.

1972, June 30 Litho. *Perf. 12½x12*

1432	A304	5q multi	5	5
1433	A304	10q lt brn & multi	5	5
1434	A304	15q lt lil & multi	7	5
1435	A304	20q multi	8	5
1436	A304	25q lt vio & multi	10	6
1437	A304	50q lt grn & multi	25	10
1438	A304	75q multi	50	15
1439	A304	2 l multi	95	30
		Nos. 1432-1439 (8)	2.05	81

Miniature Sheet

Imperf.

1440	A304	2.50 l multi	2.00	1.10

20th Olympic Games, Munich, Aug. 26–Sept. 11. Nos. 1432–1439 each issued in sheets of 8 stamps and one label (3x3) showing Olympic rings in gold. Size of No. 1440: 70x87mm.

Autobus
A305

Designs: 25q, Electric train. 80q, Ocean liner Tirana. 1.05 l, Automobile. 1.20 l, Trailer truck.

1972, July 25 Litho. *Perf. 12*

1441	A305	15q org brn & multi	10	5
1442	A305	25q gray & multi	8	5
1443	A305	80q dp grn & multi	40	8
1444	A305	1.05 l multi	55	15
1445	A305	1.20 l multi	70	18
		Nos. 1441-1445 (5)	1.83	51

Arm Wrestling
A306

Folk Games: 10q, Piggyback ball game. 15q, Women's jumping. 25q, Rope game (srum). 90q, Leapfrog. 2 l, Women throwing pitchers.

1972, Aug. 18

1446	A306	5q multi	5	5
1447	A306	10q lt bl & multi	5	5
1448	A306	15q rose & multi	10	5
1449	A306	25q lt bl & multi	15	5
1450	A306	90q ocher & multi	50	15
1451	A306	2 l lt grn & multi	95	30
		Nos. 1446-1451 (6)	1.80	65

1st National Festival of People's Games.

Mastheads—A307

Designs: 25q, Printing press. 1.90 l, Workers reading paper.

1972, Aug. 25

1452	A307	15q lt bl & blk	10	5
1453	A307	25q red, grn & blk	15	5
1454	A307	1.90 l lt vio & blk	1.00	35

30th Press Day.

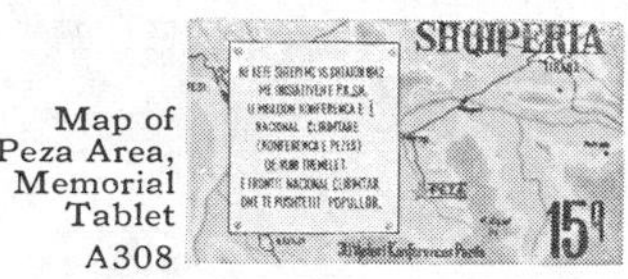

Map of Peza Area, Memorial Tablet
A308

1972, Sept. 16 Multicolored

1455	A308	15q *shown*	10	5
1456	A308	25q *Guerrillas with flag*	15	5
1457	A308	1.90 l *Peza Conference memorial*	1.00	35

30th anniversary, Conference of Peza.

Partisans, by Sotir Capo—A309

Paintings: 10q, Woman, by Ismail Lulani (vert.). 15q, "Communists," by Lec Shkreli (vert.). 20q, View of Nendorit, 1941, by Sali Shijaku (vert.). 50q, Woman with Sheaf, by Zef Shoshi (vert.). 1 l, Landscape with Children, by Dhimitraq Trebicka. 2 l, Women on Bicycles, by Vilson Kilica. 2.30 l, Folk Dance, by Abdurrahim Buza.

Perf. 12½x12, 12x12½

1972, Sept. 25 Lithographed

1458	A309	5q gold & multi	5	5
1459	A309	10q gold & multi	5	5
1460	A309	15q gold & multi	7	5
1461	A309	20q gold & multi	10	5
1462	A309	50q gold & multi	25	10
1463	A309	1 l gold & multi	50	20
1464	A309	2 l gold & multi	1.10	50
		Nos. 1458-1464 (7)	2.12	1.00

Miniature Sheet

Imperf.

1465	A309	2.30 l gold & multi	1.50	1.00

No. 1465 contains one stamp (41x68 mm.); silver margin. Size: 55x82mm.

Congress Emblem
A310

Design: 2.05 l, Young worker with banner.

1972, Oct. 23 Litho. *Perf. 12*

1466	A310	25q sil, red & gold	10	5
1467	A310	2.05 l sil & multi	1.00	45

Union of Working Youth, 6th Congress.

Hammer and Sickle
A311

Ismail Qemali
A312

Design: 1.20 l, Lenin as orator.

1972, Nov. 7 Litho. *Perf. 11½x12*

1468	A311	1.10 l multi	60	25
1469	A311	1.20 l multi	65	30

55th anniversary of the Russian October Revolution.

Perf. 12x11½, 11½x12

1972, Nov. 29

Designs: 15q, Albanian fighters (horiz.). 65q, Rally (horiz.). 1.25 l, Coat of arms.

1470	A312	15q red, brt bl & blk	10	5
1471	A312	25q yel, blk & red	15	5
1472	A312	65q red, sal & blk	35	10
1473	A312	1.25 l dl red & blk	70	25

60th anniv. of independence.

Cock, Mosaic
A313

Mosaics, 2nd–5th centuries, excavated near Buthrotium and Apollonia: 10q, Bird (vert.). 15q, Partridges (vert.). 25q, Warrior's legs. 45q, Nymph riding dolphin (vert.). 50q, Fish (vert.). 2.50 l, Warrior with helmet.

1972, Dec. 10 *Perf. 12½x12, 12x12½*

1474	A313	5q sil & multi	5	5
1475	A313	10q sil & multi	5	5
1476	A313	15q sil & multi	10	6
1477	A313	25q sil & multi	14	8
1478	A313	45q sil & multi	25	9
1479	A313	50q sil & multi	30	10
1480	A313	2.50 l sil & multi	1.40	50
		Nos. 1474-1480 (7)	2.29	93

Nicolaus Copernicus
A314

Designs: 10q, 25q, 80q, 1.20 l, Various portraits of Copernicus. 1.60 l, Heliocentric solar system.

1973, Feb. 19 Litho. *Perf. 12x12½*

1481	A314	5q lil rose & multi	5	5
1482	A314	10q dl ol & multi	5	5
1483	A314	25q multi	15	7
1484	A314	80q lt vio & multi	50	15
1485	A314	1.20 l bl & multi	75	30
1486	A314	1.60 l gray & multi	1.00	40
		Nos. 1481-1486 (6)	2.50	1.02

500th anniversary of the birth of Nicolaus Copernicus (1473–1543), Polish astronomer.

Flowering Cactus—A315

Designs: Various flowering cacti.

1973, Mar. 25 Litho. *Perf. 12*

1487	A315	10q multi	5	5
1488	A315	15q multi	7	5
1489	A315	20q beige & multi	7	5
1490	A315	25q gray & multi	10	5
1491	A315	30q beige & multi	15	6
1492	A315	65q gray & multi	40	10
1493	A315	80q multi	50	15
1494	A315	2 l multi	1.25	35
		Nos. 1487-1494 (8)	2.59	86

Nos. 1487–1494 printed se-tenant.

Guard and Factories
A316

Design: 1.80 l, Guard and guards with prisoner.

1973, Mar. 20 Litho. *Perf. 12½x12*

1495	A316	25q	ultra & blk	18	10
1496	A316	1.80 l	dk red & multi	85	60

30th anniversary of the State Security Branch.

Common Tern A317

Sea Birds: 15q, White-winged black terns (vert.). 25q, Black-headed gull (vert.). 45q, Great black-headed gull. 80q, Slender-billed gull (vert.). 2.40 l, Sandwich terns.

Perf. 12½x12, 12x12½

1973, Apr. 30

1497	A317	5q	gold & multi	5	5
1498	A317	15q	gold & multi	8	5
1499	A317	25q	gold & multi	15	5
1500	A317	45q	gold & multi	20	10
1501	A317	80q	gold & multi	45	25
1502	A317	2.40 l	gold & multi	1.35	55
			Nos. 1497-1502 (6)	2.28	1.05

Letters, 1913 Cancellation and Post Horn A318

Design: 1.80 l, Mailman and 1913 cancelation.

1973, May. 5 Litho. *Perf. 12x11½*

1503	A318	25q	red & multi	20	10
1504	A318	1.80 l	red & multi	1.25	75

60th anniversary of Albanian stamps.

Farmer, Worker, Soldier A319

Design: 25q, Woman and factory (vert.).

1973, June 4 *Perf.12*

1505	A319	25q	car rose	20	10
1506	A319	1.80 l	yel, dp org & blk	1.00	50

7th Congress of Albanian Women's Union.

Creation of General Staff, by G. Madhi—A320

Designs: 40q, "August 1949," sculpture by Sh. Haderi (vert.). 60q, "Generation after Generation," sculpture by H. Dule (vert.). 80q, "Defend Revolutionary Victories," by M. Fushekati.

1973, July 10 Litho. *Perf. 12½x12*

1507	A320	25q	gold & multi	25	10
1508	A320	40q	gold & multi	40	15
1509	A320	60q	gold & multi	60	25
1510	A320	80q	gold & multi	75	30

30th anniversary of the People's Army.

"Electrification," by S. Hysa—A321

Albanian Paintings: 10q, Woman Textile Worker, by N. Nallbani. 15q, Gymnasts, by M. Fushekati. 50q, Aviator, by F. Stamo. 80q, Fascist Prisoner, by A. Lakuriqi. 1.20 l, Workers with Banner, by P. Mele. 1.30 l, Farm Woman, by Zef Shoshi. 2.05 l, Battle of Tenda, by F. Haxhiu. 10q, 50q, 80q, 1.20 l, 1.30 l, vertical.

Perf. 12½x12, 12x12½

1973, Aug. 10

1511	A321	5q	gold & multi	5	5
1512	A321	10q	gold & multi	7	5
1513	A321	15q	gold & multi	10	5
1514	A321	50q	gold & multi	30	10
1515	A321	80q	gold & multi	60	12
1516	A321	1.20 l	gold & multi	90	15
1517	A321	1.30 l	gold & multi	1.00	25
			Nos. 1511-1517 (7)	3.02	77

Souvenir Sheet

Imperf.

1518	A321	2.05 l	multi	1.50	75

No. 1518 contains one stamp; light yellow margin. Size: 98x62mm.

Mary Magdalene, by Caravaggio A322

Paintings by Michelangelo da Caravaggio: 10q, The Lute Player (horiz.). 15q, Self-portrait. 50q, Boy Carrying Fruit and Flowers. 80q, Still Life (horiz.). 1.20 l, Narcissus. 1.30 l, Boy Peeling Apple. 2.05 l, Man with Feathered Hat.

Perf. 12x12½, 12½x12

1973, Sept. 28

1519	A322	5q	gold & multi	5	5
1520	A322	10q	gold & multi	5	5
1521	A322	15q	gold, blk & gray	7	5
1522	A322	50q	gold & multi	18	5
1523	A322	80q	gold & multi	40	10
1524	A322	1.20 l	gold & multi	60	30
1525	A322	1.30 l	gold & multi	70	30
			Nos. 1519-1525 (7)	2.05	90

Souvenir Sheet

Imperf.

1526	A322	2.05 l	multi	2.00	75

400th anniversary of the birth of Michelangelo da Caravaggio (Merisi; 1573?–1609), Italian painter. No. 1526 contains one stamp (63x73mm.); gray marginal inscription. Size: 81x99mm.

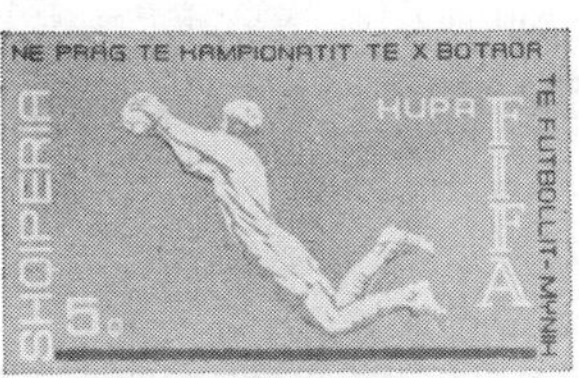

Soccer—A323

Designs: 5q–1.25 l, Various soccer scenes. 2.05 l, Ball in goal and list of cities where championships were held.

1973, Oct. 30 Litho. *Perf. 12½x12*

1527	A323	5q	multi	5	5
1528	A323	10q	multi	5	5
1529	A323	15q	multi	7	5
1530	A323	20q	multi	10	5
1531	A323	25q	multi	15	5
1532	A323	90q	multi	60	10
1533	A323	1.20 l	multi	80	20
1534	A323	1.25 l	multi	1.00	25
			Nos. 1527-1534 (8)	2.82	80

Minature Sheet

Imperf.

1535	A323	2.05 l	multi	2.00	75

World Soccer Cup, Munich 1974. Size of No. 1535: 82x54mm.

Weight Lifter A324

Designs: Various stages of weight lifting. 1.20 l, 1.60 l, horizontal.

1973, Oct. 30 Litho. *Perf. 12*

1536	A324	5q	multi	5	5
1537	A324	10q	multi	5	5
1538	A324	25q	multi	11	5
1539	A324	90q	multi	40	18
1540	A324	1.20 l	multi	30	10
1541	A324	1.60 l	multi	65	15
			Nos. 1536-1541 (6)	1.56	58

Weight Lifting Championships, Havana, Cuba.

Ballet A325 Harvester Combine A326

Perf. 12½x12, 12x12½

1973–74 Lithographed

Designs: 5q, Cement factory, Kavaje. 10q, Ali Kelmendi truck factory and tank cars (horiz.). 25q, "Communication." 35q, Skiers and hotel (horiz.). 60q, Resort (horiz.). 80q, Mountain lake. 1 l, Mao Tse-tung textile mill. 1.20 l, Steel workers. 2.40 l, Welder and pipe. 3 l, Skanderbeg Monument, Tirana. 5 l, Roman arches, Durrës.

1543	A325	5q	gold & multi	5	5
1544	A325	10q	gold & multi	5	5
1545	A325	15q	gold & multi	7	5
1545A	A326	20q	gold & multi	10	5
1546	A326	25q	gold & multi	15	5
1547	A326	35q	gold & multi	16	7
1548	A326	60q	gold & multi	25	10
1549	A326	80q	gold & multi	36	17
1549A	A326	1 l	gold & multi	30	10
1549B	A326	1.20 l	gold & multi	50	15
1549C	A326	2.40 l	gold & multi	1.10	40
1550	A326	3 l	gold & multi	1.25	40
1551	A326	5 l	gold & multi	2.00	75
			Nos. 1543-1551 (13)	6.34	2.39

Issue dates: Nos. 1545–1546, 1549–1550, Dec. 5, 1973; others in 1974.

Mao Tse-tung A327

Design: 1.20 l, Mao Tse-tung addressing crowd.

1973, Dec. 26 *Perf. 12*

1552	A327	85q	gold, red & sep	30	10
1553	A327	1.20 l	gold, red & sep	50	15

80th birthday of Mao Tse-tung.

Old Man and Dog, by Gericault A328

Paintings by Jean Louis André Theodore Gericault: 10q, Horse's Head. 15q, Male Model. 25q, Head of Black Man. 1.20 l, Self-portrait. 2.05 l, Raft of the Medusa (horiz.). 2.20 l, Battle of the Giants.

Perf. 12x12½, 12½x12

1974, Jan. 18 Lithographed

1554	A328	10q	gold & multi	5	5
1555	A328	15q	gold & multi	7	5
1556	A328	20q	gold & multi	10	5
1557	A328	25q	gold & blk	15	5
1558	A328	1.20 l	gold & multi	55	15
1559	A328	2.20 l	gold & multi	1.10	40
			Nos. 1554-1559 (6)	2.02	75

Souvenir Sheet

Imperf.

1560	A328	2.05 l	gold & multi	1.35	55

No. 1560 contains one stamp (87x78 mm.). Sheet has gold margin and inscription. Size: 100x78mm.

Lenin, by Pandi Mele A329

Designs: 25q, Lenin with Sailors on Cruiser Aurora, by Dhimitraq Trebicka (horiz.). 1.20 l, Lenin, by Vilson Kilica.

Perf. 12½x12, 12x12½

1974, Jan. 21

1561	A329	25q	gold & multi	15	5
1562	A329	60q	gold & multi	35	10
1563	A329	1.20 l	gold & multi	75	25

50th anniversary of the death of Lenin (1870–1924).

Swimming Duck, Mosaic—A330

Designs: Mosaics from the 5th–6th Centuries A.D., excavated near Buthrotium, Pogradec and Apollonia.

1974, Feb. 20 Litho. *Perf. 12½x12*

Multicolored

1564	A330	5q	*shown*	5	5
1565	A330	10q	*Bird and flower*	5	5
1566	A330	15q	*Vase and grapes*	7	5
1567	A330	25q	*Duck*	15	5
1568	A330	40q	*Donkey and bird*	25	6
1569	A330	2.50 l	*Sea horse*	1.25	35
			Nos. 1564-1569 (6)	1.82	61

Soccer—A331

Designs: Various scenes from soccer. 2.05 l, World Soccer Cup and names of participating countries.

1974, Apr. 25 Litho. *Perf. 12½x12*

1570	A331	10q	gold & multi	5	5
1571	A331	15q	gold & multi	7	5
1572	A331	20q	gold & multi	8	5
1573	A331	25q	gold & multi	15	5
1574	A331	40q	gold & multi	25	6
1575	A331	80q	gold & multi	50	15
1576	A331	1 l	gold & multi	75	25
1577	A331	1.20 l	gold & multi	1.00	35
			Nos. 1570-1577 (8)	2.85	1.01

Souvenir Sheet

Imperf.

1578	A331	2.05 l	gold & multi	2.25	90

World Cup Soccer Championship, Munich, June 13–July 7. No. 1578 contains one stamp (60x60mm.) with simulated perforations. Size: 72x75mm.

Nos. 1570-1577 exist imperf, No. 1578 with simulated perfs omitted.

Arms of Albania, Soldier A332

Design: 1.80 l, Soldier and front page of 1944 Congress Book.

1974, May 24 Litho. *Perf. 12*

1579	A332	25q	multi	11	5
1580	A332	1.80 l	multi	75	25

30th anniversary of the First Anti-Fascist Liberation Congress of Permet.

Bittersweet A333

Designs: Medicinal Plants. 40q, 80q, 2.20 l, horizontal.

1974, May 5 *Perf. 12x12½*

Multicolored

1581	A333	10q	*shown*	5	5
1582	A333	15q	*Arbutus*	7	5
1583	A333	20q	*Lilies of the valley*	8	5
1584	A333	25q	*Autumn crocus*	11	5
1585	A333	40q	*Borage*	15	6
1586	A333	80q	*Soapwort*	45	15
1587	A333	2.20 l	*Gentian*	1.00	40
			Nos. 1581-1587 (7)	1.91	81

Revolutionaries with Albanian Flag A334

Design: 1.80 l, Portraits of 5 revolutionaries (vert.).

Perf. 12½x12, 12x12½

1974, June 10

1588	A334	25q	red, blk & lil	11	5
1589	A334	1.80 l	yel, red & blk	70	25

50th anniversary Albanian Bourgeois Democratic Revolution.

European Redwing—A335

Designs: Songbirds; Nos. 1597–1600 vertical.

Perf. 12½x12, 12x12½

1974, July 15 Lithographed

Multicolored

1594	A335	10q	*shown*	5	5
1595	A335	15q	*European robin*	7	5
1596	A335	20q	*Greenfinch*	5	5
1597	A335	25q	*Bullfinch*	8	5
1598	A335	40q	*Hawfinch*	20	6
1599	A335	80q	*Blackcap*	50	20
1600	A335	2.20 l	*Nightingale*	1.10	45
			Nos. 1594-1600 (7)	2.05	91

Globe A336

Designs: 1.20 l, UPU emblem. 2.05 l, Jet over globe.

1974, Aug. 25 Litho. *Perf. 12x12½*

1601	A336	85q	grn & multi	45	15
1602	A336	1.20 l	vio & ol grn	65	20

Miniature Sheet

Imperf.

1603	A336	2.05 l	bl & multi	12.00	12.00

Centenary of Universal Postal Union. No. 1603 contains one stamp, gold margin. Size: 77x78mm.

Widows, by Sali Shijaku—A337

Albanian Paintings: 15q, Drillers, by Danish Jukniu (vert.). 20q, Workers with Blueprints, by Clirim Ceka. 25q, Call to Action, by Spiro Kristo (vert.). 40q, Winter Battle, by Sabaudin Xhaferi. 80q, Comrades, by Clirim Ceka (vert.). 1 l, Aiding the Partisans, by Guri Madhi. 1.20 l, Teacher with Pupils, by Kleo Nini Brezat. 2.05 l, Comrades in Arms, by Guri Madhi.

Perf. 12½x12, 12x12½

1974, Sept. 25

1604	A337	10q	sil & multi	5	5
1605	A337	15q	sil & multi	7	5
1606	A337	20q	sil & multi	8	5
1607	A337	25q	sil & multi	11	5
1608	A337	40q	sil & multi	20	6
1609	A337	80q	sil & multi	35	12
1610	A337	1 l	sil & multi	45	15
1611	A337	1.20 l	sil & multi	50	25
			Nos. 1604-1611 (8)	1.81	78

Miniature Sheet

Imperf.

1612	A337	2.05 l	sil & multi	1.25	50

No. 1612 contains one stamp. Size: 86x 77mm.

Crowd on Tien An Men Square A338

Design: 1.20 l, Mao Tse-tung (vert.).

1974, Oct. 1 *Perf. 12*

1613	A338	85q	gold & multi	42	12
1614	A338	1.20 l	gold & multi	60	20

25th anniversary of the proclamation of the People's Republic of China.

Women's Volleyball A339

Designs (Spartakiad Medal and): 15q, Women hurdlers. 20q, Women gymnasts. 25q, Mass exercises in Stadium. 40q, Weight lifter. 80q, Wrestlers. 1 l, Military rifle drill. 1.20 l, Soccer.

1974, Oct. 9 *Perf. 12x12½*

1615	A339	10q	multi	5	5
1616	A339	15q	multi	7	5
1617	A339	20q	multi	8	5
1618	A339	25q	gray & multi	11	5
1619	A339	40q	multi	15	6
1620	A339	80q	multi	40	12
1621	A339	1 l	multi	45	15
1622	A339	1.20 l	tan & multi	50	20
			Nos. 1615-1622 (8)	1.81	73

National Spartakiad, Oct. 9–17.

View of Berat A340

Designs: 80q, Enver Hoxha addressing Congress, bas-relief (horiz.). 1 l, Hoxha and leaders leaving Congress Hall.

Perf. 12x12½, 12½x12

1974, Oct. 20 Lithographed

1623	A340	25q	rose car & blk	15	5
1624	A340	80q	yel, brn & blk	30	12
1625	A340	1 l	dp lil & blk	45	15

30th anniversary of 2nd Congress of Berat.

Anniversary Emblem, Factory Guards A341

Designs (Anniversary Emblem and): 35q, Chemical industry. 50q, Agriculture. 80q, Arts. 1 l, Atomic diagram and computer. 1.20 l, Youth education. 2.05 l, Anniversary emblem: Crowd and History Book.

1974, Nov. 29 Litho. *Perf. 12½x12*

1626	A341	25q	grn & multi	5	5
1627	A341	35q	ultra & multi	12	7
1628	A341	50q	brn & multi	22	10
1629	A341	80q	multi	40	12
1630	A341	1 l	vio & multi	45	15
1631	A341	1.20 l	multi	50	20
			Nos. 1626-1631 (6)	1.74	69

Miniature Sheet

Imperf.

1632	A341	2.05 l	gold & multi	1.50	60

30th anniversary of liberation from Fascism. No. 1632 contains one stamp. Size: 80x69mm.

Artemis, from Apolloni A342

1974, Dec. 25 Photo. *Perf. 12x12½*

Silver & Multicolored

1633	A342	10q	*shown*	5	5
1634	A342	15q	*Zeus statue*	8	5
1635	A342	20q	*Poseidon statue*	8	5
1636	A342	25q	*Illyrian helmet*	8	5
1637	A342	40q	*Amphora*	15	6
1638	A342	80q	*Agrippa*	40	10
1639	A342	1 l	*Demosthenes*	45	12
1640	A342	1.20 l	*Head of Bilia*	55	20
			Nos. 1633-1640 (8)	1.84	68

Miniature Sheet

Imperf.

1641	A342	2.05 l	*Artemis & amphora*	1.50	60

Archaeological discoveries in Albania. No. 1641 contains one stamp. Size: 95x95 mm.

Workers and Factories A343

Design: 25q, Handshake, tools and book (vert.).

1975, Feb. 11 Litho. *Perf. 12*

1642	A343	25q	brn & multi	8	5
1643	A343	1.80 l	yel & multi	75	30

Albanian Trade Unions, 30th anniversary.

Chicory
A344

1975, Feb. 15

Gray and Multicolored

1644	A344	5q	*shown*	5	5
1645	A344	10q	*Houseleek*	5	5
1646	A344	15q	*Columbine*	7	5
1647	A344	20q	*Anemone*	8	5
1648	A344	25q	*Hibiscus*	10	5
1649	A344	30q	*Gentian*	10	6
1650	A344	35q	*Hollyhock*	12	6
1651	A344	2.70 l	*Iris*	1.20	40
			Nos. 1644-1651 (8)	1.77	77

Protected flowers.

Jesus, from Doni Madonna
A345

Works by Michelangelo: 10q, Slave, sculpture. 15q, Head of Dawn, sculpture. 20q, Awakening Giant, sculpture. 25q, Cumaenian Sybil, Sistine Chapel. 30q, Lorenzo di Medici, sculpture. 1.20 l, David, sculpture. 2.05 l, Self-portrait. 3.90 l, Delphic Sybil, Sistine Chapel.

1975, Mar. 20 Litho. *Perf. 12x12½*

1652	A345	5q	gold & multi	5	5
1653	A345	10q	gold & multi	5	5
1654	A345	15q	gold & multi	7	5
1655	A345	20q	gold & multi	8	5
1656	A345	25q	gold & multi	8	5
1657	A345	30q	gold & multi	10	6
1658	A345	1.20 l	gold & multi	40	20
1659	A345	3.90 l	gold & multi	1.75	60
			Nos. 1652-1659 (8)	2.58	1.11

Miniature Sheet

Imperf.

1660	A345	2.05 l	gold & multi	1.25	60

500th birth anniversary of Michelangelo Buonarroti (1475–1564), Italian sculptor, painter and architect. Size of No. 1660: 76x85mm.

Two-wheeled Cart—A346

Albanian Transportation of the Past: 5q, Horseback rider. 15q, Lake ferry. 20q, Coastal three-master. 25q, Phaeton. 3.35 l, Early automobile on bridge.

1975, Apr. 15 Litho. *Perf. 12½x12*

1661	A346	5q	bl grn & multi	5	5
1662	A346	10q	ol & multi	5	5
1663	A346	15q	lil & multi	7	5
1664	A346	20q	multi	8	5
1665	A346	25q	multi	15	6
1666	A346	3.35 l	ocher & multi	1.40	50
			Nos. 1661-1666 (6)	1.80	76

Guard at Frontier Stone
A347

Guardsman and Militia
A348

1975, Apr. 25 ***Perf. 12***

1667	A347	25q	multi	11	5
1668	A348	1.80 l	multi	75	25

30th anniversary of Frontier Guards.

Posting Illegal Poster—A349

Designs: 60q, Partisans in battle. 1.20 l, Partisan killing German soldier, and Albanian coat of arms.

1975, May 9 ***Perf. 12½x12***

1669	A349	25q	multi	11	5
1670	A349	60q	multi	20	10
1671	A349	1.20 l	red & multi	50	25

30th anniversary of victory over Fascism.

European Widgeons
A350

Waterfowl: 10q, Red-crested pochards. 15q, White-fronted goose. 20q, Northern pintails. 25q, Red-breasted merganser. 30q, Eider ducks. 35q, Whooper swan. 2.70 l, Shovelers.

1975, June 15 Litho. *Perf. 12*

1672	A350	5q	brt bl & multi	5	5
1673	A350	10q	yel grn & multi	5	5
1674	A350	15q	brt rose lil & multi	7	5
1675	A350	20q	bl grn & multi	8	5
1676	A350	25q	multi	10	5
1677	A350	30q	multi	10	6
1678	A350	35q	org & multi	12	6
1679	A350	2.70 l	multi	1.35	40
			Nos. 1672-1679 (8)	1.92	77

Shyqyri Kanapari, by Musa Qarri
A351

Albanian Paintings: 10q, Woman Saving Children in Sea, by Agim Faja. 15q, "November 28, 1912" (revolution), by Petrit Ceno (horiz.). 20q, "Workers Unite," by Sali Shijaku. 25q, The Partisan Shota Galica, by Ismail Lulani. 30q, Victorious Resistance Fighters, 1943, by Nestor Jonuzi. 80q, Partisan Couple in Front of Red Flag, by Vilson Halimi. 2.05 l, Dancing Procession, by Abdurahim Buza. 2.25 l, Republic Day Celebration, by Fatmir Haxhiu (horiz.).

Perf. 12x12½, 12½x12

1975, July 15 **Lithographed**

1680	A351	5q	gold & multi	5	5
1681	A351	10q	gold & multi	5	5
1682	A351	15q	gold & multi	7	5
1683	A351	20q	gold & multi	10	5
1684	A351	25q	gold & multi	10	5
1685	A351	30q	gold & multi	17	6
1686	A351	80q	gold & multi	30	10
1687	A351	2.25 l	gold & multi	1.00	35
			Nos. 1680-1687 (8)	1.84	76

Miniature Sheet

Imperf.

1688	A351	2.05 l	gold & multi	1.10	60

No. 1688 contains one stamp. Size: 67x98mm. Nos. 1680–1687 issued in sheets of 8 stamps and gold center label showing palette and easel.

Farmer Holding Reform Law
A352

Design: 2 l, Produce and farm machinery.

1975, Aug. 28 ***Perf. 12***

1689	A352	15q	multi	7	5
1690	A352	2 l	multi	75	35

Agrarian reform, 30th anniversary.

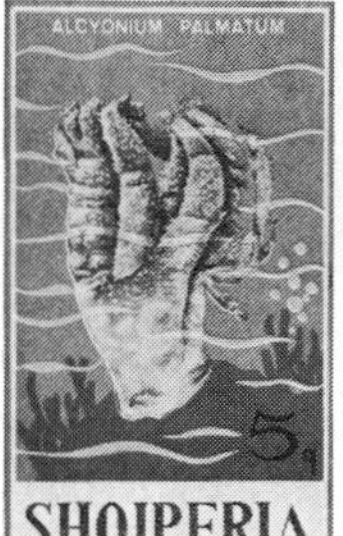

Alcynonium Palmatum
A353

Corals: 10q, Paramuricea chamaeleon. 20q, Coralium rubrum. 25q, Eunicella covalini. 3.70 l, Cladocora cespitosa.

1975, Sept. 25 Litho. *Perf. 12*

1691	A353	5q	bl, ol & blk	5	5
1692	A353	10q	bl & multi	5	5
1693	A353	20q	bl & multi	10	5
1694	A353	25q	bl & blk	18	6
1695	A353	3.70 l	bl & blk	1.50	60
			Nos. 1691-1695 (5)	1.88	81

Bicycling
A354

Designs (Montreal Olympic Games Emblem and): 10q, Canoeing. 15q, Fieldball. 20q, Basketball. 25q, Water polo. 30q, Hockey. 1.20 l, Pole vault. 2.05 l, Fencing. 2.15 l, Montreal Olympic Games emblem and various sports.

1975, Oct. 20 Litho. *Perf. 12½*

1696	A354	5q	multi	5	5
1697	A354	10q	multi	5	5
1698	A354	15q	multi	7	5
1699	A354	20q	multi	8	5
1700	A354	25q	multi	12	6
1701	A354	30q	multi	12	8
1702	A354	1.20 l	multi	45	20
1703	A354	2.05 l	multi	95	30
			Nos. 1696-1703 (8)	1.89	84

Miniature Sheet

Imperf.

1704	A354	2.15 l	org & multi	3.00	2.50

21st Olympic Games, Montreal, July 18–Aug. 8, 1976. Size of No. 1704: 72x76mm.

No. 1696-1703 exist imperf.

Power Lines Leading to Village
A355

Designs: 25q, Transformers and insulators. 80q, Dam and power station. 85q, Television set, power lines, grain and cogwheel.

1975, Oct. 25 ***Perf. 12x12½***

1705	A355	15q	ultra & yel	7	5
1706	A355	25q	brt vio & pink	11	5
1707	A355	80q	lt grn & gray	35	10
1708	A355	85q	ocher & brn	35	15

General electrification, 5th anniversary.

Child, Rabbit and Teddy Bear Planting Tree—A356

Fairy Tales: 10q, Mother fox. 15q, Ducks in school. 20q, Little pigs building house. 25q, Animals watching television. 30q, Rabbit and bear at work. 35q, Working and playing ants. 2.70 l, Wolf in sheep's clothes.

1975, Dec. 25 Litho. *Perf. 12½x12*

1709	A356	5q	blk & multi	5	5
1710	A356	10q	blk & multi	5	5
1711	A356	15q	blk & multi	7	5
1712	A356	20q	blk & multi	8	5
1713	A356	25q	blk & multi	10	5
1714	A356	30q	blk & multi	10	6
1715	A356	35q	blk & multi	20	6
1716	A356	2.70 l	blk & multi	1.25	35
			Nos. 1709-1716 (8)	1.90	72

Arms, People, Factories
A357

Design: 1.90 l, Arms, government building, celebrating crowd.

1976, Jan. 11 Litho. *Perf. 12*

1717 A357 25q gold & multi 10 5
1718 A357 1.90 l gold & multi 70 30

30th anniversary of proclamation of Albanian People's Republic.

Ice Hockey, Olympic Games' Emblem
A358

Designs: 10q, Speed skating. 15q, Biathlon. 50q, Ski jump. 1.20 l, Slalom. 2.15 l, Figure skating, pairs. 2.30 l, One-man bobsled.

1976, Feb. 4

1719 A358 5q sil & multi 5 5
1720 A358 10q sil & multi 5 5
1721 A358 15q sil & multi 7 5
1722 A358 50q sil & multi 20 10
1723 A358 1.20 l sil & multi 45 15
1724 A358 2.30 l sil & multi 1.10 40
Nos. 1719-1724 (6) 1.92 80

Miniature Sheet

Perf. 12 on 2 sides x imperf.

1725 A358 2.15 l sil & multi 1.25 1.00

12th Winter Olympic Games, Innsbruck, Austria, Feb. 4–15. Size of No. 1725 66x79mm.

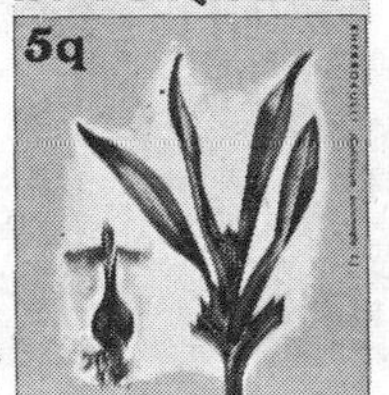

Meadow Saffron
A359

Medicinal Plants: 10q, Deadly nightshade. 15q, Yellow gentian. 20q, Horse chestnut. 70q, Shield fern. 80q, Marsh mallow. 2.30 l, Thorn apple.

1976, Apr. 10 Litho. *Perf. 12x12½*

1726 A359 5q blk & multi 5 5
1727 A359 10q blk & multi 5 5
1728 A359 15q blk & multi 7 5
1729 A359 20q blk & multi 8 5
1730 A359 70q blk & multi 20 10
1731 A359 80q blk & multi 40 12
1732 A359 2.30 l blk & multi 1.10 35
Nos. 1726-1732 (7) 1.95 77

Bowl and Spoon—A360

Designs: 15q, Flask (vert.). 20q, Carved handles (vert.). 25q, Pistol and dagger. 80q, Wall hanging (vert.). 1.20 l, Earrings and belt buckle. 1.40 l, Jugs (vert.).

1976 Litho. *Perf. 12½x12, 12x12½*

1733 A360 10q lil & multi 5 5
1734 A360 15q gray & multi 7 5
1735 A360 20q multi 8 5
1736 A360 25q car & multi 12 5
1737 A360 80q yel & multi 35 12
1738 A360 1.20 l multi 50 15
1739 A360 1.40 l tan & multi 65 25
Nos. 1733-1739 (7) 1.82 72

National Ethnographic Conference, Tirana, June 28.

Founding of Cooperatives, by Zef Shoshi
A361

Paintings: 10q, Going to Work, by Agim Zajmi (vert.). 25q, Crowd Listening to Loudspeaker, by Vilson Kilica. 40q, Woman Welder, by Sabaudin Xhaferi (vert.). 50q, Factory, by Isuf Sulovari (vert.). 1.20 l, 1942 Revolt, by Lec Shkreli (vert.). 1.60 l, Coming Home from Work, by Agron Dine. 2.05 l, Honoring a Young Pioneer, by Andon Lakuriqi.

Perf. 12½x12, 12x12½

1976, Aug. 8 Lithographed

1740 A361 5q gold & multi 5 5
1741 A361 10q gold & multi 5 5
1742 A361 25q gold & multi 11 5
1743 A361 40q gold & multi 15 8
1744 A361 50q gold & multi 15 10
1745 A361 1.20 l gold & multi 54 15
1746 A361 1.60 l gold & multi 75 30
Nos. 1740-1746 (7) 1.80 78

Miniature Sheet

Perf. 12 on 2 sides x imperf.

1747 A361 2.05 l gold & multi 1.00 50

Size of No. 1747: 92x79mm.

Red Flag, Agricultural Symbols
A362

Enver Hoxha, Partisans and Albanian Flag
A363

Design: 1.20 l, Red flag and raised pickax.

1976, Nov. 1

1748 A362 25q multi 12 5
1749 A362 1.20 l multi 50 20

7th Workers Party Congress.

1976, Oct. 28 *Perf. 12x12½*

Design: 1.90 l, Demonstrators with Albanian flag.

1750 A363 25q multi 12 5
1751 A363 1.90 l multi 80 30

35th anniversary of anti-Fascist demonstrations.

Attacking Partisans, Meeting House
A364

Designs (Red Flag and): 25q, Partisans, pickax and gun. 80q, Workers, soldiers, pickax and gun. 1.20 l, Agriculture and industry. 1.70 l, Dancers, symbols of science and art.

1976, Nov. 8 Litho. *Perf. 12x12½*

1752 A364 15q gold & multi 5 5
1753 A364 25q gold & multi 10 5
1754 A364 80q gold & multi 20 10
1755 A364 1.20 l gold & multi 40 15
1756 A364 1.70 l gold & multi 80 20
Nos. 1752-1756 (5) 1.55 55

35th anniversary of 1st Workers Party Congress.

Young Workers and Track
A365

Design: 1.25 l, Young soldiers and Albanian flag.

1976, Nov. 23 *Perf. 12*

1757 A365 80q yel & multi 35 12
1758 A365 1.25 l car & multi 50 25

Union of Young Communists, 35th anniversary.

"Cuca e Maleve" Ballet
A366

Designs: Scenes from ballet "Mountain Girl."

1976, Dec. 14 *Perf. 12*

1759 A366 10q gold & multi 5 5
1760 A366 15q gold & multi 8 5
1761 A366 20q gold & multi 10 5
1762 A366 25q gold & multi 12 5
1763 A366 80q gold & multi 40 12
1764 A366 1.20 l gold & multi 50 20
1765 A366 1.40 l gold & multi 70 25
Nos. 1759-1765 (7) 1.95 77

Miniature Sheet

Perf. 12 on 2 sides x imperf.

1766 A366 2.05 l gold & multi 1.00 50

Size of No. 1766: 77x68mm.

Bashtoves Castle
A367

Albanian Castles: 15q, Gjirokastres. 20q, Ali Pash Tepelenes. 25q, Petreles. 80q, Beratit. 1.20 l, Durresit. 1.40 l, Krujes.

1976, Dec. 30 Litho. *Perf. 12*

1767 A367 10q blk & dl bl 5 5
1768 A367 15q blk & grn 8 5
1769 A367 20q blk & gray 10 5
1770 A367 25q blk & brn 12 5
1771 A367 80q blk & rose 30 12
1772 A367 1.20 l blk & vio 35 20
1773 A367 1.40 l blk & brn red 70 20
Nos. 1767-1773 (7) 1.70 72

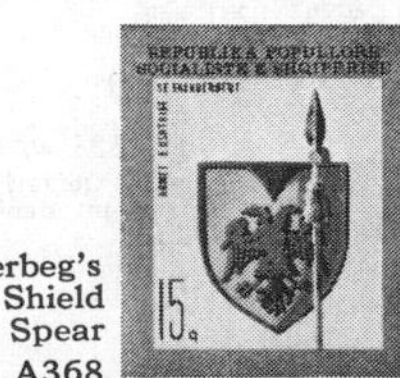

Skanderbeg's Shield and Spear
A368

Skanderbeg's Weapons: 80q, Helmet, sword and scabbard. 1 l, Halberd, quiver with arrows, crossbow and spear.

1977, Jan. 28 Litho. *Perf. 12*

1774 A368 15q sil & multi 35 8
1775 A368 80q sil & multi 1.40 40
1776 A368 1 l sil & multi 2.00 50

Skanderbeg (1403–1468), national hero.

Ilia Oiqi, Messenger in Storm
A369

Polyvinylchloride Plant, Vlore
A370

Modern Heroes: 10q, Ilia Dashi, sailor in battle. 25q, Fran Ndue Ivanaj, fisherman in storm. 80q, Zeliha Allmetaj, woman rescuing child. 1 l, Ylli Zaimi, rescuing goats from flood. 1.90 l, Isuf Plloci, fighting forest fire.

1977, Feb. 28 Litho. *Perf. 12x12½*

1777 A369 5q brn & multi 5 5
1778 A369 10q ultra & multi 5 5
1779 A369 25q bl & multi 10 5
1780 A369 80q ocher & multi 40 10
1781 A369 1 l brn & multi 60 15
1782 A369 1.90 l brn & multi 1.10 25
Nos. 1777-1782 (6) 2.30 65

1977, Mar. 29 Litho. *Perf. 12½x12*

Designs: 25q, Naphtha fractioning plant, Ballsh. 65q, Hydroelectric station and dam, Fjerzes. 1 l, Metallurgical plant and blast furance, Elbasan.

1783 A370 15q sil & multi 5 5
1784 A370 25q sil & multi 15 5
1785 A370 65q sil & multi 35 12
1786 A370 1 l sil & multi 55 20

6th Five-year plan.

Qerime Halil Galica
A371

Victory Monument, Tirana
A372

Design: 1.25 l, Qerime Halil Galica "Shota" and father Azem Galica.

1977, Apr. 20 Litho. *Perf. 12*

1787 A371 80q dk red 30 12
1788 A371 1.25 l gray bl 50 20

"Shota" Galica, communist fighter.

1977, May 5 Litho. *Perf. 12*

Designs (Red Star and): 80q, Clenched fist, Albanian flag. 1.20 l, Bust of Qemal Stafa and poppies.

1789 A372 25q multi 12 5
1790 A372 80q multi 35 12
1791 A372 1.20 l multi 55 20

35th anniversary of Martyrs' Day.

Physician Visiting Farm, Mobile Clinic
A373

Designs: 10q, Cowherd and cattle ranch. 20q, Militia woman helping with harvest, rifle and combine. 80q, Modern village, highway and power lines. 2.95 l, Tractor and greenhouses.

1977, June 18

1792	A373	5q multi	5	5
1793	A373	10q multi	5	5
1794	A373	20q multi	10	5
1795	A373	80q multi	30	12
1796	A373	2.95 l multi	1.80	50
		Nos. 1792-1796 (5)	2.30	77

"Socialist transformation of the villages."

Armed Workers, Flag and Factory
A374

Design: 1.80 l, Workers with proclamation and flags.

1977, June 20

1797	A374	25q multi	12	5
1798	A374	1.80 l multi	75	25

9th Labor Unions Congress.

Kerchief Dance
A375

Designs: Various folk dances.

1977, Aug. 20 Litho. *Perf. 12*

1799	A375	5q multi	5	5
1800	A375	10q multi	5	5
1801	A375	15q multi	8	5
1802	A375	25q multi	8	5
1803	A375	80q multi	30	12
1804	A375	1.20 l multi	60	20
1805	A375	1.55 l multi	75	25
		Nos. 1799-1805 (7)	1.91	77

Miniature Sheet

Perf. 12 on 2 sides x imperf.

1806	A375	2.05 l multi	1.00	50

Size of No. 1806: 56x74mm.
See Nos. 1836-1840, 1884-1888.

Attack
A376

Designs: 25q, Enver Hoxha addressing Army. 80q, Volunteers and riflemen. 1 l, Volunteers, hydrofoil patrolboat and MiG planes. 1.90 l, Volunteers and Albanian flag.

1977, July 10 Litho. *Perf. 12*

1807	A376	15q gold & multi	5	5
1808	A376	25q gold & multi	8	5
1809	A376	80q gold & multi	30	12
1810	A376	1 l gold & multi	45	12
1811	A376	1.90 l gold & multi	90	25
		Nos. 1807-1811 (5)	1.78	59

"One People—One Army."

Armed Workers, Article 3 of Constitution
A377

Design: 1.20 l, Symbols of farming and fertilizer industry, Article 25 of Constitution.

1977, Oct.

1812	A377	25q red, gold & blk	15	5
1813	A377	1.20 l red, gold & blk	55	20

New Constitution.

Picnic
A378

Film Frames: 15q, Telephone lineman in winter. 25q, Two men and a woman. 80q, Workers. 1.20 l, Boys playing in street. 1.60 l, Harvest.

1977, Oct. 25 Litho. *Perf. 12½x12*

1814	A378	10q bl grn	5	5
1815	A378	15q multi	5	5
1816	A378	25q black	8	5
1817	A378	80q multi	35	12
1818	A378	1.20 l dp cl	60	15
1819	A378	1.60 l multi	75	25
		Nos. 1814-1819 (6)	1.88	67

Albanian films.

Farm Workers in Field, by V. Mio
A379

Paintings by V. Mio: 10q, Landscape in Snow. 15q, Grazing Sheep under Walnut Tree in Spring. 25q, Street in Korce. 80q, Horseback Riders on Mountain Pass. 1 l, Boats on Shore. 1.75 l, Tractors Plowing Fields. 2.05 l, Self-portrait.

1977, Dec. 25 Litho. *Perf. 12½x12*

1820	A379	5q gold & multi	5	5
1821	A379	10q gold & multi	5	5
1822	A379	15q gold & multi	8	5
1823	A379	25q gold & multi	8	5
1824	A379	80q gold & multi	35	12
1825	A379	1 l gold & multi	40	15
1826	A379	1.75 l gold & multi	70	20
		Nos. 1820-1826 (7)	1.71	67

Miniature Sheet

Imperf.; Perf. 12 Horiz. between Vignette and Value Panel.

1827	A379	2.05 l gold & multi	90	40

Size of No. 1827: 66x101mm.

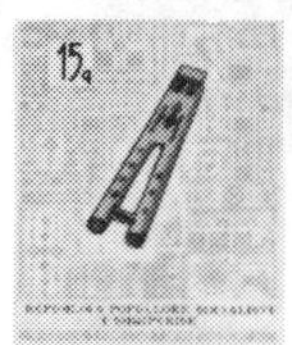

Pan Flute
A380

Albanian Flag, Monument and People
A381

Folk Musical Instruments: 25q, Single-string goat's-head fiddle. 80q, Woodwind. 1.20 l, Drum. 1.70 l, Bagpipe. Background shows various woven folk patterns.

1978, Jan. 20 *Perf. 12x12½*

1828	A380	15q multi	8	5
1829	A380	25q multi	12	5
1830	A380	80q multi	35	12
1831	A380	1.20 l multi	55	15
1832	A380	1.70 l multi	75	20
		Nos. 1828-1832 (5)	1.85	57

1978 *Perf. 12½x12, 12x12½*

Designs: 25q, Ismail Qemali and fighters (horiz.). 1.65 l, People dancing around Albanian flag (horiz.).

1833	A381	15q multi	8	5
1834	A381	25q multi	12	5
1835	A381	1.65 l multi	75	25

65th anniversary of independence.

Folk Dancing Type of 1977

Designs: Various dances.

1978, Feb. 15 Litho. *Perf. 12*

1836	A375	5q multi	5	5
1837	A375	25q multi	8	5
1838	A375	80q multi	30	12
1839	A375	1 l multi	45	15
1840	A375	2.30 l multi	90	30
		Nos. 1836-1840 (5)	1.78	67

Nos. 1836–1840 have white background around dancers, Nos. 1799–1805 have pinkish shadows.

Tractor Drivers, by Dhimitraq Trebicka
A382

Working Class Paintings: 80q, Steeplejack, by Spiro Kristo. 85q, "A Point in the Discussion," by Skender Milori. 90q, Oil rig crew, by Anesti Cini (vert.). 1.60 l, Metal workers, by Ramadan Karanxha. 2.20 l, Political discussion, by Sotiraq Sholla.

1978, Mar. 25 Litho. *Perf. 12*

1841	A382	25q multi	8	5
1842	A382	80q multi	30	12
1843	A382	85q multi	30	12
1844	A382	90q multi	35	16
1845	A382	1.60 l multi	75	25
		Nos. 1841-1845 (5)	1.78	70

Miniature Sheet

Perf. 12 on 2 sides x imperf.

1846	A382	2.20 l multi	1.00	40

Size of No. 1846: 72x98mm.

Woman with Rifle and Pickax—A383

Design: 1.95 l, Farm and Militia women, industrial plant.

1978, June 1 Litho. *Perf. 12*

1847	A383	25q gold & red	12	5
1848	A383	1.95 l gold & red	75	25

8th Congress of Women's Union.

Children and Flowers
A384

Designs: 10q, Children with rifle, ax, book and flags. 25q, Dancing children in folk costume. 1.80 l, Children in school.

1978, June 1 Lithographed

1849	A384	5q multi	5	5
1850	A384	10q multi	5	5
1851	A384	25q multi	12	5
1852	A384	1.80 l multi	75	25

International Children's Day.

Spirit of Skanderbeg as Conqueror
A385

Designs: 10q, Battle at Mostar Bridge. 80q, Marchers and Albanian flag. 1.20 l, Riflemen in winter battle. 1.65 l, Abdyl Frasheri (1839–1892). 2.20 l, Rifles, scroll and pen, League building. 2.60 l, League headquarters, Prizren.

1978, June 10 Litho. *Perf. 12*

1853	A385	10q multi	5	5
1854	A385	25q multi	8	5
1855	A385	80q multi	25	12
1856	A385	1.20 l multi	50	15
1857	A385	1.65 l multi	75	20
1858	A385	2.60 l multi	90	35
		Nos. 1853-1858 (6)	2.53	92

Miniature Sheet

Perf. 12 on 2 sides x imperf.

1859	A385	2.20 l multi	1.00	40

Centenary of League of Prizren. Size of No. 1859: 74x69mm.

Guerrillas and Flag, 1943
A386

Designs: 25q, Soldier, sailor, airman, militiaman (horiz.). 1.90 l, Members of armed forces, civil guards, and Young Pioneers.

1978, July 10 *Perf. 11½x12½*

1860	A386	5q multi	5	5
1861	A386	25q multi	12	5
1862	A386	1.90 l multi	1.00	25

35th anniversary of People's Army.

Woman with Machine Carbine
A387

Kerchief Dance
A388

Designs: 25q, Man with target rifle (horiz.). 95q, Man shooting with telescopic sights (horiz.). 2.40 l, Woman target shooting with pistol.

Perf. 12½x12, 12x12½

1978, Sept. 20 Lithographed

1863	A387	25q blk & yel	12	5
1864	A387	80q org & blk	30	12
1865	A387	95q red & blk	42	14
1866	A387	2.40 l car & blk	1.00	30

32nd National Rifle-shooting Championships, Sept. 20.

1978, Oct. 6 *Perf. 12*

Designs: 15q, Musicians. 25q, Fiddler with single-stringed instrument. 80q, Dancers, men. 1.20 l, Saber dance. 1.90 l, Singers, women.

1867	A388	10q multi	5	5
1868	A388	15q multi	8	5
1869	A388	25q multi	12	5
1870	A388	80q multi	25	12
1871	A388	1.20 l multi	50	15
1872	A388	1.90 l multi	80	25
		Nos. 1867-1872 (6)	1.80	67

National Folklore Festival.

No. 1736 Surcharged with New Value, 2 Bars and "RICCIONE 78"

1978 Litho. *Perf. 12½x12*

1873	A360	3.30 l on 25q multi	4.00	1.50

Riccione 78 Philatelic Exhibition.

Enver Hoxha
A389

1978, Oct. 16 Litho. *Perf. 12x12½*

1874	A389	80q	red & multi	30	12
1875	A389	1.20 l	red & multi	45	15
1876	A389	3.40 l	red & multi	90	25

Miniature Sheet

Perf. 12½ on 2 sides x imperf.

1877	A389	2.20 l	red & multi	85	40

70th birthday of Enver Hoxha, First Secretary of Central Committee of the Communist Party of Albania. Size of No. 1877: 67x88½mm.

Woman and Wheat
A390

Designs: 25q, Woman with egg crates. 80q, Shepherd and sheep. 2.60 l, Milkmaid and cows.

1978, Dec. 15 *Perf. 12x12½*

1878	A390	15q	multi	10	5
1879	A390	25q	multi	15	5
1880	A390	80q	multi	40	12
1881	A390	2.60 l	multi	1.10	50

Dora d'Istria
A391

Tower House
A392

Design: 1.10 l, Full portrait of Dora d'Istria, author; birth sesquicentennial.

1979, Jan. 22 Litho. *Perf. 12*

1882	A391	80q	lt grn & blk	45	12
1883	A391	1.10 l	vio brn & blk	55	18

Costume Type of 1977

Designs: Various folk dances.

1979, Feb. 25

1884	A375	15q	multi	8	5
1885	A375	25q	multi	12	5
1886	A375	80q	multi	45	12
1887	A375	1.20 l	multi	60	18
1888	A375	1.40 l	multi	85	30
			Nos. 1884-1888 (5)	2.10	70

Nos. 1884–1888 have white background. Denomination in upper left on No. 1885, in upper right on No. 1802; lower left on No. 1886, upper left on No. 1803.

1979, Mar. 20

Traditional Houses: 15q, Stone gallery house (horiz.). 80q, House with wooden galleries (horiz.). 1.20 l, Galleried tower house. 1.40 l, 1.90 l, Tower houses (diff.).

1889	A392	15q	multi	8	5
1890	A392	25q	multi	12	5
1891	A392	80q	multi	45	12
1892	A392	1.20 l	multi	60	18
1893	A392	1.40 l	multi	85	30
			Nos. 1889-1893 (5)	2.10	70

Miniature Sheet

Perf. 12 on 2 sides x imperf.

1894	A392	1.90 l	multi	1.00	50

Size of No. 1894: 62x75mm.

Soldier, Factories, Wheat
A393

Design: 1.65 l, Soldiers, workers and coat of arms.

1979, May 14 Litho. *Perf. 12*

1895	A393	25q	multi	18	5
1896	A393	1.65 l	multi	80	25

Congress of Permet, 35th anniversary.

Albanian Flag
A394

1979, June 4

1897	A394	25q	multi	18	5
1898	A394	1.65 l	multi	80	25

5th Congress of Albanian Democratic Front.

Vasil Shanto
A395

Alexander Moissi
A396

1979

1899	A395	15q	multi	8	5
1900	A395	25q	multi	12	8
1901	A395	60q	multi	35	10
1902	A396	80q	multi	45	12
1903	A395	90q	multi	45	15
1904	A396	1.10 l	multi	60	18
			Nos. 1899-1904 (6)	2.05	68

Vasil Shanto (1913–1944) and Qemal Stafa (1921–1942), Anti-Fascist fighters; Alexander Moissi (1880–1935), actor.

Winter Campaign, by Arben Basha
A397

Paintings of Military Scenes by: 25q, Ismail Lulani. 80q, Myrteza Fushekati. 1.20 l, Muhamet Deliu. 1.40 l, Jorgji Gjikopulli. 1.90 l, Fatmir Haxhiu.

1979, Oct. Litho. *Perf. 12½×12*

1905	A397	15q	multi	8	5
1906	A397	25q	multi	12	8
1907	A397	80q	multi	35	12
1908	A397	1.20 l	multi	60	18
1909	A397	1.40 l	multi	65	30
			Nos. 1905-1909 (5)	1.80	73

Miniature Sheet

Perf. 12 on 2 sides x imperf.

1910	A397	1.90 l	multi	1.00	50

Size of No. 1910: 78×103mm.

Athletes Surrounding Flag-A398

Literary Society Headquarters-A399

1979, Oct. 1 Litho. *Perf. 12*

1911	A398	15q	*shown*	8	5
1912	A398	25q	*Shooting*	12	5
1913	A398	80q	*Dancing*	35	12
1914	A398	1.20 l	*Soccer*	65	18
1915	A398	1.40 l	*High jump*	85	30
			Nos. 1911-1915 (5)	2.05	70

Liberation Spartakiad, 35th anniversary.

1979, Oct. 12

Albanian Literary Society Centenary: 25q, Seal and charter. 80q, Founder. 1.55 l, 1879 Headquarters. 1.90 l, Founders.

1916	A399	25q	multi	15	5
1917	A399	80q	multi	40	12
1918	A399	1.20 l	multi	55	18
1919	A399	1.55 l	multi	75	25

Miniature Sheet

Perf. 12½ on 2 sides × imperf.

1920	A399	1.90 l	multi	1.00	50

Size of No. 1920: 78½×66mm.

Congress Statute, Coat of Arms—A400

1979, Oct. 20 Photo. *Perf. 12×12½*

1921	A400	25q	multi	18	5
1922	A400	1.65 l	multi	80	30

2nd Congress of Berat, 35th anniversary.

Children Entering School, Books—A401

1979 Litho. *Perf. 12½x12*

1923	A401	5q	shown	5	5
1924	A401	10q	Communications	5	5
1925	A401	15q	Steel workers	12	5
1926	A401	20q	Dancers, instruments	12	5
1927	A401	25q	Newspapers, radio, television	18	5
1928	A401	60q	Textile worker	35	15
1929	A401	80q	Armed forces	50	20
1930	A401	1.20 l	Industry	70	30
1931	A401	1.60 l	transportation	90	45
1932	A401	2.40 l	Agriculture	1.30	60
1932A	A401	3 l	Medicine	1.70	85
			Nos. 1923-1932A (11)	5.97	2.80

Workers and Factory—A402

Worker, Red Flag and: 80q, Hand holding sickle and rifle. 1.20l, Red star and open book. 1.55l, Open book and cogwheel.

1979, Nov. 29

1933	A402	25q	multi	12	5
1934	A402	80q	multi	35	10
1935	A402	1.20 l	multi	55	18
1936	A402	1.55 l	multi	65	20

35th anniversary of independence.

Joseph Stalin—A403

Design: 1.10l, Stalin on dais (horiz.).

1979, Dec. 21 Litho. *Perf. 12*

1937	A403	80q	red & dk bl	40	12
1938	A403	1.10 l	red & dk bl	55	20

Joseph Stalin (1879-1953), birth centenary.

Fireplace and Pottery, Korcar—A404

Home Furnishings: 80q, Cupboard bed, dagger, pistol, ammunition pouch, Shkodar. 1.20 l, Stool, pot, chair, Mirdit. 1.35 l, Chimney, dagger, jacket, Gjirokastro.

1980, Feb. 27 Litho. *Perf. 12*

1939	A404	25q	multi	10	5
1940	A404	80q	multi	35	12
1941	A404	1.20 l	multi	55	20
1942	A404	1.35 l	multi	60	30

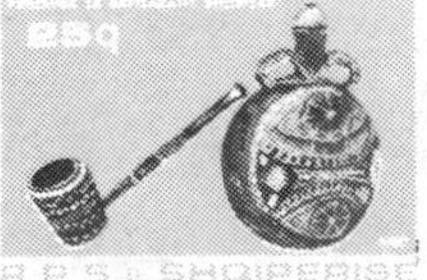

Pipe, Painted Flask—A405

1980, Mar. 4

1943	A405	25q	*shown*	10	5
1944	A405	80q	*Leather handbags*	35	12
1945	A405	1.20 l	*Carved eagle, embroidered rug*	55	20
1946	A405	1.35 l	*Lace*	60	30

Prof. Aleksander Xhuvanit Birth Centenary—A406

1980, Mar. 14

1947	A406	80q	multi	35	12
1948	A406	1 l	multi	45	18

Revolutionaries on Horseback—A407

Insurrection at Kosove, 70th Anniversary: 1 l, Battle scene.

1980, Apr. 4

1949	A407	80q	red & blk	35	12
1950	A407	1 l	red & blk	45	18

Soldiers and Workers Laboring to Aid the Stricken Populations, by D. Jukinui and I. Lulani—A408

1980, Apr. 15 **Litho.** ***Perf. 12½***

1951	A408	80q	lt bl & multi	35	12
1952	A408	1 l	lt bl grn & multi	45	18

Lenin, 110th Birth Anniversary—A409

1980, Apr. 22

1953	A409	80q	multi	35	12
1954	A409	1 l	multi	45	18

Misto Mame and Ali Demi, War Martyrs—A410

War Martyrs: 80q, Sadik Staveleci, Vojo Kusji, Hoxhi Martini. 1.20 l, Bule Naipi, Persefoni Kokedhima. 1.35 l, Ndoc Deda, Hydajet Lezha, Naim Gjylbegu, Ndoc Mazi, Ahmed Haxha.

1980, May 5

1955	A410	25q	multi	12	5
1956	A410	80q	multi	35	12
1957	A410	1.20 l	multi	50	20
1958	A410	1.35 l	multi	60	30

See Nos. 2025-2028, 2064-2067, 2122-2125, 2171-2174, 2207-2209.

Scene from "Mirela"—A411

1980, June 7

1959	A411	15q	*shown*	8	5
1960	A411	25q	*The Scribbler*	10	5
1961	A411	80q	*Circus Bears*	35	12
1962	A411	2.40 l	*Waterdrops*	1.00	45

Carrying Iron Castings in the Enver Hoxha Tractor Combine, by S. Shijaku and M. Fushekati—A412

Paintings (Gallery of Figurative Paintings, Tirana): 80q, The Welder, by Harilla Dhima. 1.20 l, Steel Erectors, by Petro Kokushta. 1.35 l, Pandeli Lena, 1.80 l Communists, by Vilson Kilica.

1980, July 22

1963	A412	25q	multi	12	5
1964	A412	80q	multi	35	12
1965	A412	1.20 l	multi	50	20
1966	A412	1.35 l	multi	65	30

Souvenir Sheet

1967	A412	1.80 l	multi	85	60

Gate, Parchment Miniature, 11th Cent.—A413

Bas reliefs of the Middle Ages: 80q, Eagle, 13th cent. 1.20 l, Heraldic lion, 14th cent. 1.35 l, Pheasant, 14th cent.

1980, Sept. 27 **Litho.** ***Perf. 12***

1968	A413	25q	gold & blk	12	5
1969	A413	80q	gold & blk	35	15
1970	A413	1.20 l	gold & blk	55	20
1971	A413	1.35 l	gold & blk	70	30

Divjaka National Park—A414

1980, Nov. 6 **Photo.**

1972	A414	80q	shown	35	15
1973	A414	1.20 l	Lura	55	30
1974	A414	1.60 l	Thethi	75	35

Park Type of 1980
Souvenir Sheet

1980, Nov. 6 **Photo.** ***Perf. 12½***

1975	A414	1.80 l	Llogara Park	90	90

No. 1975 has multicolored decorative margin. Size: 90x90mm.

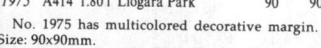

Citizens, Flag and Arms of Albania—A415

1981, Jan. 11 **Litho.** ***Perf. 12***

1976	A415	80q	shown	35	15
1977	A415	1 l	People's Party Headquarters, Tirana	50	25

35th anniversary of the Republic.

Child's Bed—A416

1981, Mar. 20 **Litho.** ***Perf. 12***

1978	A416	25q	shown	12	5
1979	A416	80q	Wooden bucket, brass bottle	40	25
1980	A416	1.20 l	Shoes	60	30
1981	A416	1.35 l	Jugs	65	35

Soldiers Fighting with Rifles—A417

1981, Apr. 20

1982	A417	80q	shown	40	25
1983	A417	1 l	Sword combat	55	30

Souvenir Sheet
Perf. 12½ Vert.

1984	A417	1.80 l	Soldier with pistol	90	90

Battle of Shtimje centenary. No. 1984 contains one stamp; purple margin shows battle scene. Size: 85x68mm.

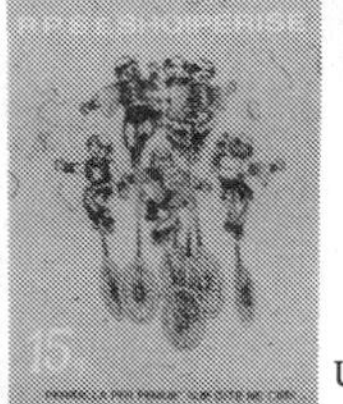

House Interior, Labara—A418

1981, Feb. 25 **Litho.** ***Perf. 12***

1985	A418	25q	shown	12	5
1986	A418	80q	Labara, diff.	40	25
1987	A418	1.20 l	Mat	60	30
1988	A418	1.35 l	Dibres	65	35

Boys Riding Unicycles—A419

Designs: Children's circus.

1981, June ***Perf. 12***

1989	A419	15q	multi	8	5
1990	A419	25q	multi	12	5
1991	A419	80q	multi	40	25
1992	A419	2.40 l	multi	1.20	70

Soccer Players A420

1982 World Cup Soccer Elimination Games: Various soccer players.

1981, Mar. 31 **Litho.** ***Perf. 12***

1993	A420	25q	multi	50	25
1994	A420	80q	multi	1.30	60
1995	A420	1.20 l	multi	2.00	95
1996	A420	1.35 l	multi	2.25	1.20

Allies, by S. Hysa—A421

Paintings: 80q, Warriors, by A. Buza. 1.20 l, Rallying to the Flag, Dec. 1911, by A. Zajmi (vert.). 1.35 l, My Flag is My Heart, by L. Cefa (vert.). 1.80 l, Circling the Flag in a Common Cause, by N. Vasia.

1981, July 10 ***Perf. 12½x12***

1997	A421	25q	multi	15	5
1998	A421	80q	multi	50	25
1999	A421	1.20 l	multi	70	35
2000	A421	1.35 l	multi	75	40

Souvenir Sheet

2001	A421	1.80 l	multi	1.20	1.10

No. 2001 contains one stamp (55x55mm.); multicolored margin. Size: 82x109mm.

Rifleman—A422

1981, Aug. 30 ***Perf. 12***

2002	A422	25q	shown	15	5
2003	A422	80q	Weight lifting	50	25
2004	A422	1.20 l	Volleyball	70	35
2005	A422	1.35 l	Soccer	80	40

Albanian Workers' Party, 8th Congress—A423

1981, Nov. 1

2006	A423	80q	Flag, star	40	25
2007	A423	1 l	Flag, hammer and sickle	55	30

Albanian Workers' Party, 40th Anniv. A424

Communist Youth Org., 40th Anniv. A425

1981, Nov. 8

2008	A424	80q	Symbols of industrialization	40	25
2009	A424	2.80 l	Fist, emblem	1.50	80

Souvenir Sheet

2010	A424	1.80 l	Enver Hoxha, Memoirs	1.00	1.00

Size of No. 2010: 79x99mm.

1981, Nov. 23

2011	A425	80q	Star, ax, map	40	25
2012	A425	1 l	Flags, star	55	30

Fan S. Noli, Writer, Birth Centenary A426

Traditional House, Bulqize A427

1982, Jan. 6 **Litho.** ***Perf. 12***

2013	A426	80q	lt ol grn & gold	40	25
2014	A426	1.10 l	lt red brn & gold	55	30

1982, Feb. ***Perf. 12½x12***

2015	A427	25q	shown	40	25
2016	A427	80q	Lebush	40	25
2017	A427	1.20 l	Bicaj	65	35
2018	A427	1.55 l	Klos	90	55

TB Bacillus Centenary—A428

1982, Mar. 24 ***Perf. 12***

2019	A428	80q	Globe	50	25
2020	A428	1.10 l	Koch	70	35

Albanian League House, Prizren, by K. Buza—A429

Kosova Landscapes: 25q, Castle at Prizrenit, by G. Madhi. 1.20 l, Mountain Gorge at Rogove, by K. Buza. 1.55 l, Street of the Hadhji at Zekes, by G. Madhi. 25q, 1.20 l, 1.55 l vert.

Perf. 12x12½, 12½x 12

1982, Apr. 15 **Litho.**

2021	A429	25q	multi	15	5
2022	A429	80q	multi	40	18
2023	A429	1.20 l	multi	60	25
2024	A429	1.55 l	multi	80	35

War Martyr Type of 1980

Designs: 25q, Hibe Palikuqi, Liri Gero. 80q, Mihal Duri, Kajo Karafili. 1.20 l, Fato Dudumi, Margarita Tutulani, Shejnaze Juka. 1.55 l, Memo Meto, Gjok Doci.

1982, May ***Perf. 12***

2025	A410	25q	multi	15	5
2026	A410	80q	multi	40	25
2027	A410	1.20 l	multi	65	35
2028	A410	1.55 l	multi	90	55

Loading Freighter—A430

Children's Paintings.

1982, June 15 ***Perf. 12½x12***

2029	A430	15q	shown	10	5
2030	A430	80q	Forest	40	25
2031	A430	1.20 l	City	65	35
2032	A430	1.65 l	Park	95	55

9th Congress of Trade Unions—A431

1982, June 6 **Litho.** ***Perf. 12***

2033	A431	80q	Workers, factories	40	18
2034	A431	1.10 l	Emblem, flag	55	22

Alpine Village Festival, by Danish Jukniu—A432

Industrial Development Paintings: 80q, Hydroelectric Station Builders, by Ali Miruku. 1.20 l, Steel Workers, by Clirim Ceka. 1.55 l, Oil drillers, by Pandeli Lena. 1.90 l, Trapping the Furnace, by Jorgji Gjikopulli.

1982, July ***Perf. 12½***

2035	A432	25q	multi	12	5
2036	A432	80q	multi	40	18
2037	A432	1.20 l	multi	60	25
2038	A432	1.55 l	multi	80	35

Souvenir Sheet

2039	A432	1.90 l	multi	1.25	50

No. 2039 contains one stamp (54x48mm., perf. 12); silver and black margin. Size: 76x91mm.

40th Anniv. of Democratic Front—A433

1982, Sept. 16 ***Perf. 12***

2040	A433	80q	Glory to the Heroes of Peza Monument	40	18
2041	A433	1.10 l	Marchers	55	22

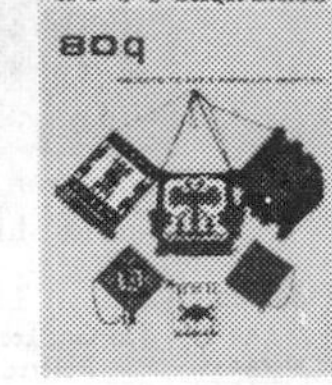

8th Youth Congress A434

Handmade Shoulder Bags A435

1982, Oct. 4

2042	A434	80q	multi	40	18
2043	A434	1.10 l	multi	55	22

1982, Nov.

2044	A435	25q	Rug, horiz.	12	5
2045	A435	80q	shown	40	18
2046	A435	1.20 l	Wooden pots, bowls, horiz.	60	25
2047	A435	1.55 l	Jug	80	35

70th Anniv. of Independence—A436

1982, Nov. 28

2048	A436	20q	Ishamil Qemali	10	5
2049	A436	1.20 l	Partisans	60	25
2050	A436	2.40 l	Partisans, diff.	1.20	50

Souvenir Sheet

2051	A436	1.90 l	Independence Monument, Tirana	1.25	50

Size of No. 2051: 91x88mm.

Dhermi Beach—A437

1982, Dec. 20

2052	A437	25q	shown	12	5
2053	A437	80q	Sarande	40	18
2054	A437	1.20 l	Ksamil	60	25
2055	A437	1.55 l	Lukove	80	35

Handkerchief Dancers—A438

Folkdancers.

1983, Feb. 20 **Litho.** ***Perf. 12***

2056	A438	25q	shown	12	5
2057	A438	80q	With kerchief, drum	40	18
2058	A438	1.20 l	With guitar, flute, tambourine	60	25
2059	A438	1.55 l	Women	80	35

Karl Marx (1818-1883)—A439

1983, Mar. 14 **Litho.** ***Perf. 12***

2060	A439	80q	multi	40	18
2061	A439	1.10 l	multi	55	22

Energy Development—A440

1983, Apr. 20

2062	A440	80q	Electricity generation	40	18
2063	A440	1.10 l	Gas & oil production	55	22

War Martyr Type of 1980

Designs: 25q, Asim Zeneli (1916-1943), Nazmi Rushiti (1919-1942). 80q, Shyqyri Ishmi (1922-1942), Shyqyri Alimerko (1923-1943), Myzafer Asqeriu (1918-1942). 1.20 l, Qybra Sokoli (1924-1944), Qeriba Derri (1905-1944), Ylbere Bilibashi (1928-1944). 1.55 l, Themo Vasi (1915-1943), Abaz Shehu (1905-1942).

1983, May 5 **Litho.** ***Perf. 12***

2064	A410	25q	multi	12	5
2065	A410	80q	multi	40	18
2066	A410	1.20 l	multi	60	25
2067	A410	1.55 l	multi	80	35

Women's Union, 9th Congress—A441

1983, June 1 **Litho.** ***Perf. 12x12½***

2068	A441	80q	red & gold	40	18
2069	A441	1.10 l	bl & gold	55	22

Bicycling—A442

1983, June 20 ***Perf. 12***

2070	A442	25q	shown	12	5
2071	A442	80q	Chess	40	18
2072	A442	1.20 l	Gymnastics	60	25
2073	A442	1.55 l	Wrestling	80	35

40th Anniv. of People's Army—A443

1983, July 10

2074	A443	20q	Armed services	10	5
2075	A443	1.20 l	Soldier, gun barrels	60	25
2076	A443	2.40 l	Factory guard, crowd	1.20	50

Sunny Day, by Myrteza Fushekati—A444

Paintings: 80q, Messenger of the Grasp, by Niko Progi. 1.20l, 29 November 1944, by Harilla Dhimo. 1.55l, Fireworks, by Pandi Mele. 1.90l, Partisan Assault,, by Sali Shijaku and M. Fushekati.

1983, Aug. 28 Litho. *Perf. 12½x12*

2077	A444	25q	multi	12	5
2078	A444	80q	multi	40	18
2079	A444	1.20 l	multi	60	25
2080	A444	1.55 l	multi	80	35

Souvenir Sheet
Perf. 12

2081	A444	1.90 l	multi	1.00	50

Size of No. 2081: 112x76mm.

Gjirokaster Folklore Festival—A445

Folkdances.

1983, Oct. 6 Litho. *Perf. 12*

2082	A445	25q	Sword dance	12	5
2083	A445	80q	Kerchief dance	40	18
2084	A445	1.20 l	Shepherd flautists	60	25
2085	A445	1.55 l	Garland dance	80	35

World Communications Year—A446

1983, Nov. 10

2086	A446	60q	multi	30	12
2087	A446	1.20 l	multi	60	25

75th Birthday of Enver Hoxha—A447

1983, Oct. 16 Litho. *Perf. 12½*

2088	A447	80q	multi	40	18
2089	A447	1.20 l	multi	60	25
2090	A447	1.80 l	multi	90	38

Souvenir Sheet
Perf. 12

2091	A447	1.90 l	multi	1.00	50

Size of No. 2091: 77x100mm.

The Right to a Joint Triumph, by J. Keraj—A448

Era of Skanderbeg in Figurative Art: 80q, The Heroic Center of the Battle of Krujes, by N. Bakalli. 1.20 l, The Rights of the Enemy after our Triumph, by N. Progri. 1.55 l, The Discussion at Lezhes, by B. Ahmeti. 1.90 l, Victory over the Turks, by G. Madhi.

1983, Dec. 10 *Perf. 12½x12*

2092	A448	25q	multi	12	5
2093	A448	80q	multi	40	18
2094	A448	1.20 l	multi	60	25
2095	A448	1.55 l	multi	80	35

Souvenir Sheet
Perf. 12

2096	A448	1.90 l	multi	1.00	50

Size of No. 2096: 79x92mm.

Greco-Roman Ruins of Illyris—A449

1983, Dec. 28 *Perf. 12*

2097	A449	80q	Amphitheater, Buthroxtum	40	18
2098	A449	1.20 l	Colonnade, Apollonium	60	25
2099	A449	1.80 l	Vaulted gallery, amphitheater at Epidamnus	90	38

Archeological Discoveries—A450

Designs: Apollo, 3rd cent. 25q, Tombstone, Korce, 3rd cent. 80q, Apollo, diff. 1st cent. 1.10 £, Earthenware pot (child's head), Tren, 1st cent. 1.20 £, Man's head, Dyrrah, 2.20 £, Eros with Dolphin, statue Bronze Dyrrah, 3rd cent.

1984, Feb. 25 *Perf. 12x12½*

2100	A450	15q	multi	8	5
2101	A450	25q	multi	12	5
2102	A450	80q	multi	40	18
2103	A450	1.10 l	multi	55	22
2104	A450	1.20 l	multi	60	25
2105	A450	2.20 l	multi	1.10	50
			Nos. 2100-2105 (6)	2.85	1.25

Clock Towers—A451

1984, Mar. 30 Litho. *Perf. 12*

2106	A451	15q	Gjirokaster	8	5
2107	A451	25q	Kavaje	12	5
2108	A451	80q	Elbasan	40	18
2109	A451	1.10 l	Tirana	55	22
2110	A451	1.20 l	Peqin	60	25
2111	A451	2.20 l	Kruje	1.10	50
			Nos. 2106-2111 (6)	2.85	1.25

40th Anniv. of Liberation—A452

1984, Apr. 20 Litho. *Perf. 12*

2112	A452	15q	Student & microscope	8	5
2113	A452	25q	Guerrilla with flag	12	5
2114	A452	80q	Children with flag	40	18
2115	A452	1.10 l	Soldier	55	22
2116	A452	1.20 l	Workers with flag	60	25
2117	A452	2.20 l	Militia at dam	1.10	50
			Nos. 2112-2117 (6)	2.85	1.25

Children—A453

1984, May Litho. *Perf. 12*

2118	A453	15q	Children reading	8	5
2119	A453	25q	Young pioneers	12	5
2120	A453	60q	Gardening	30	14
2121	A453	2.80 l	Kite flying	1.40	60

War Martyr Type of 1980

Designs: 15q, Manush Almani, Mustafa Matohiti, Kastriot Muco. 25q, Zaho Koka, Reshit Collaku, Maliq Muco. 1.20 l, Lefter Talo, Tom Kola, Fuat Babani. 2.20 l, Myslysm Shyri, Dervish Hexali, Skender Caci.

1984, May 5 Litho. *Perf. 12*

2122	A410	15q	multi	8	5
2123	A410	25q	multi	12	5
2124	A410	1.20 l	multi	65	30
2125	A410	2.20 l	multi	1.25	60

40th Anniv. of Permet Congress—A454

1984, May 24 Litho. *Perf. 12*

2126	A454	80q	Enver Hoxha	45	20
2127	A454	1.10 l	Resistance fighter	65	30

European Soccer Championships—A455

1984, June 12 Litho. *Perf. 12*

2128	A455	15q	Goalkeeper	12	6
2129	A455	25q	Referee	20	10
2130	A455	1.20 l	Map of Europe	90	45
2131	A455	2.20 l	Field diagram	1.75	90

Freedom Came, by Myrteza Fushekati—A456

Paintings, Tirana Gallery of Figurative Art: 25q, Morning, by Zamir Mati, vert. 80q, My Darling, by Agim Zajmi, vert. 2.60 l, For the Partisans, by Arben Basha. 1.90 l, Eagle, by Zamir Mati, vert.

1984, July 12 *Perf. 12½*

2132	A456	15q	multi	12	6
2133	A456	25q	multi	20	10
2134	A456	80q	multi	60	30
2135	A456	2.60 l	multi	2.00	1.00

Souvenir Sheet
Perf. 12 Horiz.

2136	A456	1.90 l	multi	1.50	75

Size: 80x96mm.

AUSIPEX '84, Melbourne, Sept. 21-30—A458

Perf. 12 Horiz.

1984, Sept. 21 Litho.

2141	A458	1.90 l	Sword dancers, emblem	1.50	75

No. 2141 has gray inscribed margin. Size: 72x101mm.

Forestry, Logging, UNFAO Emblem—A459

1984, Sept. 25 *Perf. 12*

2142	A459	15q	Beech trees, transport	12	6
2143	A459	25q	Pine forest, logging cable	20	10
2144	A459	1.20 l	Firs, sawmill	90	45
2145	A459	2.20 l	Forester clearing woods	1.75	90

EURPHILA '84, Rome—A460

1984, Oct. 13 *Perf. 12½*

2146	A460	1.20 l	View of Gjirokaster	90	45

5th National Spartakiad—A461

1984, Oct. 19 *Perf. 12*

2147	A461	15q	Soccer	12	6
2148	A461	25q	Women's track & field	20	10
2149	A461	80q	Weight lifting	60	30
2150	A461	2.20 l	Pistol shooting	1.75	90

Souvenir Sheet
Perf. 12 Horiz.

2151	A461	1.90 l	Opening ceremony, red flags	1.50	75

No. 2151 has orange inscribed margin. Size: 70x90mm.

November 29 Revolution, 40th Anniv.—A462

1984, Nov. 29 *Perf. 12*

2152	A462	80q	Industrial reconstruction	60	30
2153	A462	1.10 l	Natl. flag, partisans	80	40

Souvenir Sheet
Perf. 12 Horiz.

2154	A462	1.90 l	Gen. Enver Hoxha reading 1944 declaration	1.50	75

No. 2154 has grayish margin. Size: 69x90mm.

Archaeological Discoveries from Illyria—A463

1985, Feb. 25 *Perf. 12x12½*

2155	A463	15q	Iron Age water container	16	8
2156	A463	80q	Terra-cotta woman's head, 6th-7th century B.C.	78	40
2157	A463	1.20 l	Aphrodite, bust, 3rd century B.C.	1.15	55
2158	A463	1.70 l	Nike, A.D. 1st-2nd century bronze statue	1.75	85

Hysni Kapo (1915-1980), Natl. Labor Party Leader—A464

1985, Mar. 4 *Perf. 12*

2159	A464	90q	red & blk	85	42
2160	A464	1.10 l	chlky bl & blk	1.10	55

OLYMPHILEX '85, Lausanne—A465

1985, Mar. 18

2161	A465	25q	Women's track & field	25	12
2162	A465	60q	Weight lifting	58	30
2163	A465	1.20 l	Soccer	1.15	55
2164	A465	1.50 l	Women's pistol shooting	1.25	65

Johann Sebastian Bach—A466

1985, Mar. 31

2165	A466	80q	Portrait, manuscript	78	40
2166	A466	1.20 l	Eisenach, birthplace	1.15	55

Gen. Enver Hoxha (1908-1985)—A467

1985, Apr. *Perf. 12½*

2167	A467	80q	multi	78	40

Souvenir Sheet
Imperf.

2168	A467	1.90 l	multi	2.00	1.00

No. 2168 has gold and black inscribed margin. Size: 67x91mm.

Natl. Frontier Guards, 40th Anniv.—A468

1985, Apr. 25 *Perf. 12*

2169	A468	25q	Guardsman, family	25	12
2170	A468	80q	At frontier post	78	40

War Martyrs Type of 1980

Cameo portraits: 25q, Mitro Xhani (1916-1944), Nimete Progonati (1929-1944), Kozma Nushi (1909-1944). 40q, Ajet Xhindoli (1922-1943), Mustafa Kacaci (1903-1944), Estref Caka Osaja (1919-1944). 60q, Celo Sinani (1929-1944), Lt. Ambro Andoni (1920-1944), Meleq Gosnishti (1913-1944). 1.20 l, Thodhori Mastora (1920-1944), Fejzi Micoli (1919-1945), Hysen Cino (1920-1944).

1985, May 5

2171	A410	25q	multi	25	12
2172	A410	40q	multi	40	20
2173	A410	60q	multi	58	30
2174	A410	1.20 l	multi	1.15	55

Victory over Fascism—A469

Designs: 25q, Rifle, red flag, inscribed May 9. 80q, Hand holding rifle, globe, broken swastika.

1985, May 9

2175	A469	25q	multi	25	12
2176	A469	80q	multi	78	40

End of World War II, 40th anniv.

Primary School, by Thoma Malo—A470

Paintings, Tirana Gallery of Figurative Art: 80q, The Heroes, by Hysen Devolli, vert. 90q, In Our Days, by Angjelin Dodmasej, vert. 1.20 l, Going Off to Sow, by Ksenofon Dilo. 1.90 l, Foundry Workers, by Mikel Gurashi.

1985, June 25 *Perf. 12½*

2177	A470	25q	multi	25	12
2178	A470	80q	multi	78	40
2179	A470	90q	multi	85	42
2180	A470	1.20 l	multi	1.15	55

Souvenir Sheet
Perf. 12 Horiz.

2181	A470	1.90 l	multi	2.00	1.00

No. 2181 has gray inscribed margin. Size: 75x90mm.

Basketball Championships, Spain
A471

Fruits
A472

Various plays.

1985, July 20 **Litho.** *Perf. 12*

2182	A471	25q	dl bl & blk	22	10
2183	A471	80q	dl grn & blk	78	40
2184	A471	1.20 l	dl vio & blk	1.15	58
2185	A471	1.60 l	dl rose & blk	1.50	75

1985, Aug. 20

2186	A472	25q	Oranges	22	10
2187	A472	80q	Plums	78	40
2188	A472	1.20 l	Apples	1.15	58
2189	A472	1.60 l	Cherries	1.50	75

Architecture—A473

1985, Sept. 20

2190	A473	25q	Kruja	22	10
2191	A473	80q	Gjirokastra	78	40
2192	A473	1.20 l	Berati	1.15	58
2193	A473	1.60 l	Shkodera	1.50	75

Natl. Folk Theater Festival—A474

Various scenes from folk plays.

1985, Oct. 6

2194	A474	25q	multi	22	10
2195	A474	80q	multi	78	40
2196	A474	1.20 l	multi	1.15	58
2197	A474	1.60 l	multi	1.50	75

Size: 56x82mm.
Imperf.

2198	A474	1.90 l	multi	1.75	88
	Nos. 2194-2198 (5)			5.40	2.71

Socialist People's Republic, 40th Anniv.—A475

1986, Jan. 11 **Litho.** ***Perf. 12½***

2199	A475	25q	Natl. crest, vert.	25	12
2200	A475	80q	Proclamation, 1946	78	40

Enver Hoxha Hydro-electric Power Station, Koman—A476

Designs: 25q, Dam, River Drin, Melgun. 80q, Bust of Enver Hoxha, dam power house.

1986, Feb. 20 ***Perf. 12***

2201	A476	25q	multi	25	12
2202	A476	80q	multi	78	40

Flowers—A477

1986, Mar. 20 **Litho.** ***Perf. 12***

2203	A477	25q	Gymnospermium shqipetarum	22	10
2204	A477	1.20 l	Leucojum valentinum	1.15	58

Nos. 2203-2204 printed se-tenant. Sold only in booklets of 2; exists imperf.

A478

Famous Men—A479

Designs: 25q, Maxim Gorky (1868-1936), Russian author. 80q, Andre Marie Ampere (1775-1836), French physicist. 1.20 l, James Watt (1736-1819), English inventor of modern steam engine. 2.40 l, Franz Liszt (1811-1886), Hungarian composer.

1986, Apr. 20

2205	Strip of 4	4.40	2.20
a.	A478 25q dl red brn	25	12
b.	A478 80q dl vio	78	40
c.	A478 1.20 l ol grn	1.15	58
d.	A478 2.40 l dl lil rose	2.20	1.10

Size: 88x72mm.
Imperf.

2206	A479	1.90 l	multi	1.75	88

No. 2206 has central area picturing Gorky, Ampere, Watt and Liszt, perf. 12½.

War Martyrs Type of 1980

Portraits: 25q, Ramiz Aranitasi (1923-1943), Inajete Dumi (1924-1944) and Laze Nuro Ferraj (1897-1944). 80q, Dine Kalenja (1919-1944), Kozma Naska (1921-1944), Met Hasa (1929-1944) and Fahri Ramadani (1920-1944). 1.20 l, Hiqmet Buzi (1927-1944), Bajram Tusha (1922-1942), Mumin Selami (1923-1942) and Hajrfdin Bylyshi (1923-1942).

1986, May 5 ***Perf. 12***

2207	A410	25q	multi	25	12
2208	A410	80q	multi	78	40
2209	A410	1.20 l	multi	1.15	55

A480

1986 World Cup Soccer Championships, Mexico—A481

1986, May 31 **Litho.** ***Perf. 12***

2210	A480	25q	Globe, world cup	22	10
2211	A480	1.20 l	Player, soccer ball	1.15	58

Size: 97x64mm.
Imperf.

2212	A481	1.90 l	multi	1.75	88

No. 2212 has central label, perf. 12½.

Transportation Workers' Day, 40th Anniv.—A482

1986, Aug. 10 **Litho.** ***Perf. 12***

2213	A482	1.20 l	multi	1.15	58

SEMI-POSTAL STAMPS.

Nos. 148–151 Surcharged in Red and Black

+ 5 qind.

1924

B1	A18	5q +5q yel grn	4.00	5.00
B2	A18	10q +5q car	4.00	5.00
B3	A18	25q +5q dk bl	4.00	5.00
B4	A18	50q +5q dk grn	4.00	5.00

Nos. B1 to B4 with Additional Surcharge in Red and Black

+ 5 qind.

1924

B5	A18	5q +5q+5q yel grn	4.00	5.00
B6	A18	10q +5q+5q car	4.00	5.00
B7	A18	25q +5q+5q dk bl	4.00	5.00
B8	A18	50q +5q+5q dk grn	4.00	5.00

Issued under Italian Dominion.

Nurse and Child
SP1

Photogravure

1943 ***Perf. 14*** **Unwmkd.**

B9	SP1	5q +5q dk grn	10	15
B10	SP1	10q +10q ol brn	10	15
B11	SP1	15q +10q rose red	15	20
B12	SP1	25q +15q saph	20	25
B13	SP1	30q +20q vio	25	30
B14	SP1	50q +25q dk org	30	35
B15	SP1	65q +30q grnsh blk	45	50
B16	SP1	1fr +40q chnt	1.00	1.10
		Nos. B9-B16 (8)	2.55	3.00

The surtax was for the control of tuberculosis.

Issued under German Administration.

War Victims
SP2

1944

B17	SP2	5q +5(q) dp grn	3.00	4.00
B18	SP2	10q +5(q) dp brn	3.00	4.00
B19	SP2	15q +5(q) car lake	3.00	4.00
B20	SP2	25q +10(q) dp bl	3.00	4.00
B21	SP2	1fr +50q dk ol	3.00	4.00
B22	SP2	2fr +1(fr) pur	3.00	4.00
B23	SP2	3fr +1.50(fr) dk org	3.00	4.00
		Nos. B17-B23 (7)	21.00	28.00

The surtax was for victims of World War II.

Independent State

Nos. B9 to B12 Surcharged in Carmine

1945 ***Perf. 14.*** **Unwmkd.**

B24	SP1	30q +15q on 5q+5q	1.75	1.75
B25	SP1	50q +25q on 10q+10q	1.75	1.75
B26	SP1	1fr +50q on 15q+10q	5.25	5.25
B27	SP1	2fr +1fr on 25q+15q	9.00	9.00

The surtax was for the Albanian Red Cross.

People's Republic

Nos. 361 to 366 Overprinted in Red (cross) and Surcharged in Black

KONGRESI
K.K.SH.
24-25-11-46
+0.10

1946 ***Perf. 11***

B28	A57	20q +10q bluish grn	7.00	7.00
B29	A57	30q +15q dp org	7.00	7.00
B30	A57	40q +20q brn	7.00	7.00
B31	A57	60q +30q red vio	7.00	7.00
B32	A57	1fr +50q rose red	7.00	7.00
B33	A57	3fr +1.50fr dk bl	7.00	7.00
		Nos. B28-B33 (6)	42.00	42.00

To honor and benefit the Congress of the Albanian Red Cross.

Counterfeits: lithographed, dull gum. Genuine: typographed, shiny gum.

First Aid and Red Cross
SP3

Designs: 25q+5q, Nurse carrying child on stretcher. 65q+25q, Symbolic blood transfusion. 80q+40q, Mother and child.

1967, Dec. 1 Litho. ***Perf. 11½x12***

B34	SP3	15q +5q blk, red & brn	90	70
B35	SP3	25q +5q multi	1.00	90
B36	SP3	65q +25q multi	3.00	1.00
B37	SP3	80q +40q multi	5.00	2.25

6th congress of the Albanian Red Cross.

AIR POST STAMPS.

Airplane Crossing Mountains
AP1

Wmk. 125

Wmkd. Lozenges. (125)

1925, May 30 Typo. ***Perf. 14***

C1	AP1	5q green	60	60
C2	AP1	10q rose red	60	60
C3	AP1	25q dp bl	65	65
C4	AP1	50q dk grn	1.25	1.25
C5	AP1	1fr dk vio & blk	2.25	2.25
C6	AP1	2fr ol grn & vio	3.50	3.50
C7	AP1	3fr brn org & dk grn	6.25	6.25
		Nos. C1-C7 (7)	15.10	15.10

Nos. C1-C7 exist imperforate but are not known to have been regularly issued in that condition.

Nos. C1-C7 Overprinted

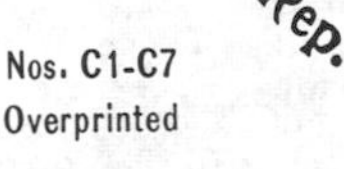

1927, Jan. 18

C8	AP1	5q green	4.50	4.50
a.		Double overprint, one inverted	40.00	
C9	AP1	10q rose red	4.50	4.50
a.		Inverted overprint	40.00	
b.		Double overprint, one inverted	40.00	
C10	AP1	25q dp bl	2.25	2.25
C11	AP1	50q dk grn	2.25	2.25
a.		Inverted overprint	40.00	
C12	AP1	1fr dk vio & blk	2.25	2.25
a.		Inverted overprint	40.00	
b.		Double overprint	40.00	
C13	AP1	2fr ol grn & vio	2.25	2.25
C14	AP1	3fr brn org & dk grn	4.00	4.00
		Nos. C8-C14 (7)	22.00	22.00

Nos. C1-C7 Overprinted

REP. SHQYPTARE
Fluturim' i I-ar
Vlonë--Brindisi
21. IV. 1928

1928, Apr. 21

C15	AP1	5q green	1.50	1.50
a.		Inverted overprint	30.00	
C16	AP1	10q rose red	1.50	1.50
C17	AP1	25q dp bl	1.50	1.50
C18	AP1	50q dk grn	1.50	1.50
C19	AP1	1fr dk vio & blk	22.50	22.50
C20	AP1	2fr ol grn & vio	22.50	22.50
C21	AP1	3fr brn org & dk grn	22.50	22.50
		Nos. C15-C21 (7)	73.50	73.50

First flight across the Adriatic, Valona to Brindisi, Apr. 21, 1928.

The variety "SHQYRTARE" occurs once in the sheet for each value. Price 3 times normal.

Nos. C1-C7 Overprinted in Red Brown

Mbr. Shqiptare

1929, Dec. 1

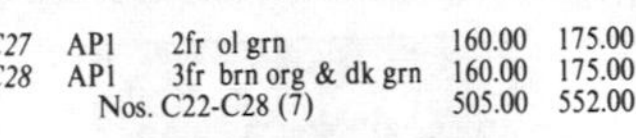

C22	AP1	5q green	4.00	4.00
C23	AP1	10q rose red	4.00	4.00
C24	AP1	25q dp bl	4.00	4.00
C25	AP1	50q dk grn	13.00	15.00
C26	AP1	1fr dk vio & blk	160.00	175.00
C27	AP1	2fr ol grn	160.00	175.00
C28	AP1	3fr brn org & dk grn	160.00	175.00
		Nos. C22-C28 (7)	505.00	552.00

Excellent counterfeits exist of Nos. C22 to C28.

King Zog and Airplane over Tirana
AP2

AP3

1930, Oct. 8 Photo. Unwmkd.

C29	AP2	5q yel grn	30	30
C30	AP2	15q rose red	40	40
C31	AP2	20q sl bl	60	60
C32	AP2	50q ol grn	75	75
C33	AP3	1fr dk bl	1.75	1.75
C34	AP3	2fr ol brn	6.00	6.00
C35	AP3	3fr purple	7.50	7.50
		Nos. C29-C35 (7)	17.30	17.30

Nos. C29-C35 Overprinted

TIRANE-ROME
6 KORRIK 1931

1931, July 6

C36	AP2	5q yel grn	2.00	2.00
a.		Double overprint	100.00	
C37	AP2	15q rose red	2.00	2.00
C38	AP2	20q sl bl	2.00	2.00
C39	AP2	50q ol grn	2.00	2.00
C40	AP3	1fr dk bl	15.00	15.00
C41	AP3	2fr ol brn	15.00	15.00
C42	AP3	3fr purple	15.00	15.00
a.		Inverted overprint	250.00	
		Nos. C36-C42 (7)	53.00	53.00

Issued in connection with the first air post flight from Tirana to Rome.

Only a very small part of this issue was sold to the public. Most of the stamps were given to the Aviation Company to help provide funds for conducting the service.

Issued under Italian Dominion.

Nos. C29–C30 Overprinted in Black

Mbledhja
Kushtetuëse
12-IV-1939
XVII

1939, Apr. 19 ***Perf. 14.*** **Unwmkd.**

C43	AP2	5q yel grn	75	75
C44	AP2	15q rose red	75	75

No. C32 With Additional Surcharge of New Value

C45	AP2	20q on 50q ol grn	1.50	1.50
a.		Inverted ovpt.		

See note after No. 309.

King Victor Emmanuel III and Plane over Mountains
AP4

1939, Aug. 4 **Photogravure.**

C46	AP4	20q brown	7.00	3.50

Shepherds
AP5

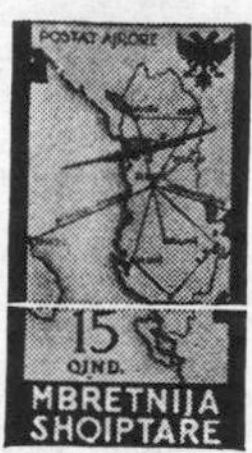

Map of Albania Showing Air Routes
AP6

Designs: 20q, Victor Emmanuel III and harbor view. 50q, Woman and river valley. 1fr, Bridge at Vezirit. 2fr, Ruins. 3fr, Women waving to plane.

1940, Mar. Unwmkd.

C47	AP5	5q green	20	20
C48	AP6	15q rose red	20	20
C49	AP5	20q dp bl	20	20
C50	AP6	50q brown	50	50
C51	AP5	1fr myr grn	1.00	1.10
C52	AP6	2fr brn blk	3.00	3.50
C53	AP6	3fr rose vio	9.00	10.00
		Nos.C47-C53 (7)	14.10	15.70

People's Republic

Vuno-Himare
AP12

Designs (Albanian towns): 1 l and 10 l, Rozafat-Shkoder. 2 l and 20 l, Keshtjelle-Butrinto.

1950, Dec. 15 Engr. *Perf. 12½x12*

C54	AP12	50q gray blk	10	5
C55	AP12	1 l red brn	15	7
C56	AP12	2 l ultra	35	12
C57	AP12	5 l dp grn	80	25
C58	AP12	10 l dp bl	1.75	1.00
C59	AP12	20 l purple	5.00	2.25
		Nos. C54-C59 (6)	8.15	3.74

Nos. C56-C58 Surcharged with New Value and Bars in Red or Black

1952–53

C60	AP12	50q on 2 l (R)	50.00	50.00
C61	AP12	50q on 5 l ('53)	7.00	4.00
C62	AP12	2.50 l on 5 l (R)	100.00	100.00
C63	AP12	2.50 l on 10 l ('53)	8.00	4.00

Banner with Lenin, Map of Stalingrad and Tanks
AP13

1963, Feb. 2 Litho. *Perf. 14*

C67	AP13	7 l grn & dp car	2.00	60

20th anniversary, Battle of Stalingrad.

Sputnik and Sun
AP14

Designs: 3 l, Lunik 4. 5 l, Lunik 3 photographing far side of the Moon. 8 l, Venus space probe. 12 l, Mars 1.

1963, Oct. 31 *Perf. 12* Unwmkd.

C68	AP14	2 l org, yel & blk	25	10
C69	AP14	3 l multi	30	10
C70	AP14	5 l rose lil, yel & blk	70	40
C71	AP14	8 l dl vio, yel & dp car	1.10	55
C72	AP14	12 l bl & org	2.50	1.25
		Nos. C68-72 (5)	4.85	2.40

Russian interplanetary explorations.

Nos. C68 and C71 Overprinted: "Riccione 23-8-1964"

1964, Aug. 23

C73	AP14	2 l org, yel & blk	4.50	4.50
C74	AP14	8 l dl vio, yel & dp car	7.00	7.00

Issued to commemorate the International Space Exhibition in Riccione, Italy.

Plane over Berat
AP15

Designs (Plane over): 40q, Gjirokaster. 60q, Sarande. 90q, Dürres. 1.20 l, Kruje. 2.40 l, Boga. 4.05 l, Tirana.

1975, Nov. 25 Litho. *Perf. 12*

C75	AP15	20q multi	10	5
C76	AP15	40q multi	10	8
C77	AP15	60q multi	15	8
C78	AP15	90q multi	30	15
C79	AP15	1.20 l multi	50	15
C80	AP15	2.40 l multi	1.15	40
C81	AP15	4.05 l multi	1.75	90
		Nos. C75-C81 (7)	4.05	1.81

SPECIAL DELIVERY STAMPS.

Issued under Italian Dominion.

King Victor Emmanuel III
SD1

Photogravure.

1940 *Perf. 14.* Unwmkd.

E1	SD1	25q brt vio	40	40
E2	SD1	50q red org	1.35	1.60

Issued under German Administration.

No. E1 Overprinted in Carmine

14
Shtator
1943

1943

E3	SD1	25q brt vio	15.00	17.50

Proclamation of Albanian independence.

POSTAGE DUE STAMPS.

Nos. 35–39 Handstamped in Various Colors

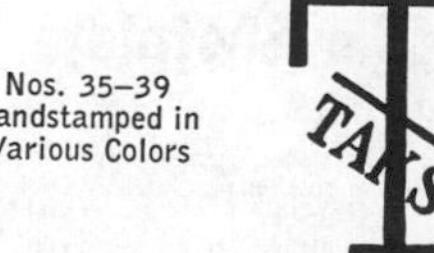

1914 *Perf. 14.* Unwmkd.

J1	A3	2q org brn & buff	2.00	1.20
J2	A3	5q green	2.00	1.50
J3	A3	10q rose red	2.75	1.50
J4	A3	25q dk bl	3.25	2.00
J5	A3	50q vio & red	4.00	2.75
		Nos. J1-J5 (5)	14.00	8.95

The two parts of the overprint are handstamped separately. Stamps exist with one or both handstamps inverted, double, omitted or in wrong color.

Nos. 48–51 Overprinted in Black TAKSË

1914

J6	A3 (a)	10pa on 5q grn	2.50	2.50
J7	A3 (a)	20pa on 10q rose red	2.50	2.50
J8	A3 (b)	1gr on 25q bl	2.50	2.50
J9	A3 (b)	2gr on 50q vio & red	2.50	2.50

Same Design as Regular Issue of 1919, Overprinted TAXE

1919 *Perf. 11½, 12½*

J10	A8	(4)q on 4h rose	6.00	6.00
J11	A8	(10)q on 10k red, *grn*	6.00	6.00
J12	A8	20q on 2k org, *gray*	6.00	6.00
J13	A8	50q on 5k brn, *yel*	6.00	6.00

Fortress at Scutari
D3

D5

Post Horn Overprinted in Black.

1920 *Perf. 14x13.*

J14	D3	4q ol grn	40	50
J15	D3	10q rose red	40	50
J16	D3	20q bis brn	40	50
J17	D3	50q black	70	80

1922 *Perf. 12½, 11½*

Background of Red Wavy Lines.

J23	D5	4q *red*	85	1.10
J24	D5	10q *red*	85	1.10
J25	D5	20q *red*	85	1.10
J26	D5	50q *red*	85	1.10

Same Overprinted in White

Republika Shqiptare

1925

J27	D5	4q *red*	85	1.10
J28	D5	10q *red*	85	1.10
J29	D5	20q *red*	85	1.10
J30	D5	50q *red*	85	1.10

The 10q with overprint in gold was a trial printing. It was not put in use.

D7

Coat of Arms
D8

Overprinted "QINDAR" in Red.

1926 *Perf. 13½x13*

J31	D7	10q dk bl	15	25
J32	D7	20q green	30	50
J33	D7	30q red brn	50	75
J34	D7	50q dk brn	75	1.25

Wmkd. Double Headed Eagle. (220)

1930 Photogravure *Perf. 14, 14½*

J35	D8	10q dk bl	5.00	5.00
J36	D8	20q rose red	1.25	1.25
J37	D8	30q violet	1.25	1.25
J38	D8	50q dk grn	1.50	1.50

Nos. J36–J38 exist with overprint "14 Shtator 1943" (see Nos. 332–344) which is private and fraudulent on these stamps.

No. 253 Overprinted **Taksë**

1936 *Perf. 14*

J39	A34	10q carmine	6.00	8.00

Issued under Italian Dominion.

Coat of Arms
D9

Photogravure.

1940 *Perf. 14.* Unwmkd.

J40	D9	4q red org	8.00	8.00
J41	D9	10q brt vio	2.50	2.50
J42	D9	20q brown	2.50	2.50
J43	D9	30q dk bl	3.00	3.00
J44	D9	50q car rose	6.00	6.00
		Nos. J40-J44 (5)	22.00	22.00

ALEXANDRETTA

(ăl'ĕg·zăn·drĕt'ȧ)

LOCATION—A political territory in northern Syria, bordering on Turkey.

GOVT.—A former French mandate.

AREA—10,000 sq. mi. (approx.).

POP.—270,000 (approx.).

Included in the Syrian territory mandated to France under the Versailles Treaty, the name was changed to Hatay in 1938. The following year France returned the territory to Turkey in exchange for certain concessions. See Hatay.

100 Centimes = 1 Piastre

Stamps of Syria, 1930–36, Overprinted or Surcharged in Black or Red:

Sandjak d'Alexandrette
a

SANDJAK D'ALEXANDRETTE
b

Sandjak d'Alexandrette
c

Sandjak d'Alexandrette 2P50
d

POSTES
Sandjak d'Alexandrette

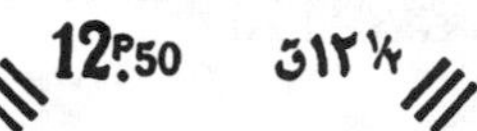

e

1938	Perf. 12x12½, 13½.		Unwmkd.	
1	A6 (a)	10c vio brn	52	52
2	A6 (a)	20c brn org	52	52
3	A9 (b)	50c vio (R)	52	52
4	A10 (b)	1p bis brn	70	70
5	A9 (b)	2p dk vio (R)	95	95
6	A13 (b)	3p yel grn (R)	2.00	2.00
7	A10 (b)	4p yel org	2.25	2.25
8	A16 (b)	6p grnsh blk (R)	2.50	2.50
9	A18 (b)	25p vio brn	7.75	7.75
		Perf. 13½		
10	A15 (c)	75c org red	70	70
11	A10 (d)	2.50p on 4p yel org	1.40	1.40
12	AP2 (e)	12.50p on 15p org red	4.25	4.25
		Nos. 1-12 (12)	24.06	24.06

Nos. 4, 7, 10–12 Overprinted in Black

1938, Dec.				
13	A15	75c org red	42.50	42.50
14	A10	1p bis brn	26.00	25.00
15	A10	2.50p on 4p yel org	17.50	15.00
16	A10	4p yel org	21.00	19.00
17	AP2	12.50p on 15p org red	42.50	42.50
		Nos. 13-17 (5)	149.50	144.00

Death of Kemal Atatürk, president of Turkey.

AIR POST STAMPS.

Air Post Stamps of Syria, 1937, Overprinted Type "b" in Red or Black

1938	Perf. 13.		Unwmkd.	
C1	AP14	½p dk vio (R)	85	85
C2	AP15	1p blk (R)	85	85
C3	AP14	2p bl grn (R)	2.25	2.25
C4	AP15	3p dp ultra	2.75	2.75
C5	AP14	5p rose lake	6.75	6.75
C6	AP15	10p red brn	7.25	7.25
C7	AP14	15p lake brn	8.75	8.75
C8	AP15	25p dk bl (R)	11.00	11.00
		Nos. C1-C8 (8)	40.45	40.45

POSTAGE DUE STAMPS.

Postage Due Stamps of Syria, 1925–31, Overprinted Type "b" in Black or Red

1938	Perf. 13½.		Unwmkd.	
J1	D5	50c brn, *yel*	1.25	1.25
J2	D6	1p vio, *rose*	1.75	1.75
J3	D5	2p *bl* (R)	2.50	2.50
J4	D5	3p *red org*	4.75	4.75
J5	D5	5p *bl grn* (R)	7.75	7.75
J6	D7	8p *gray bl* (R)	7.75	7.75
		Nos. J1-J6 (6)	25.75	25.75

On No. J2, the overprint is vertical, reading up. On the other denominations, it is horizontal.

Stamps of Alexandretta were discontinued in 1938 and replaced by those of Hatay.

ALGERIA

(ăl·jēr'ĭ·ȧ)

LOCATION — North Africa.

GOVT.—Republic.

AREA—919,595 sq. mi.

POP.—21,463,000 (1984 est.).

CAPITAL—Algiers.

The former French colony of Algeria became an integral part of France on Sept. 1, 1958, when French stamps replaced Algerian stamps. Algeria became an independent country July 3, 1962.

100 Centimes = 1 Franc

100 Centimes = 1 Dinar (1964)

Stamps of France Overprinted in Red, Blue or Black:

ALGÉRIE
a

ALGÉRIE
b

ALGÉRIE
c

ALGÉRIE
d

1924-26	Perf. 14x13½		Unwmkd.	
1	A16 (a)	1c dk gray (R)	5	5
2	A16 (a)	2c vio brn	5	5
3	A16 (a)	3c orange	5	5
4	A16 (a)	4c yel brn (Bl)	10	10
5	A22 (a)	5c org (Bl)	14	14
6	A16 (a)	5c grn ('25)	26	26
7	A23 (a)	10c green	8	6
b.		Booklet pane of 10	3.00	
8	A22 (a)	10c grn ('25)	25	15
9	A20 (a)	15c sl grn	8	6
10	A23 (a)	15c grn ('25)	18	18
11	A22 (a)	15c red brn (Bl) ('26)	10	10
12	A22 (a)	20c red brn (Bl)	6	5
13	A22 (a)	25c bl (R)	6	5
a.		Booklet pane of 10	5.75	
14	A23 (a)	30c red (Bl)	26	26
15	A22 (a)	30c cer ('25)	52	26
16	A22 (a)	30c lt bl (R) ('25)	6	5
a.		Booklet pane of 10	4.00	
17	A22 (a)	35c violet	26	8
18	A18 (b)	40c red & pale bl	30	18
19	A22 (a)	40c ol brn (R) ('25)	60	42
20	A18 (b)	45c grn & bl (R)	40	30
21	A23 (a)	45c red (Bl) ('25)	30	18
22	A23 (a)	50c bl (R)	18	6
23	A20 (a)	60c lt vio	30	10
a.		Inverted overprint	475.00	
24	A20 (a)	65c rose (Bl)	30	10
25	A23 (a)	75c bl (R)	42	26
a.		Double overprint	125.00	
26	A20 (a)	80c ver ('26)	80	35
27	A20 (a)	85c ver (Bl)	52	26
28	A18 (b)	1fr cl & ol grn	1.10	30
29	A22 (a)	1.05fr ver ('26)	1.10	52
30	A18 (c)	2fr org & pale bl	90	60
31	A18 (b)	3fr vio & bl ('26)	4.50	1.10
32	A18 (d)	5fr bl & buff (R)	10.00	6.50
		Nos. 1-32 (32)	24.28	13.18

No. 15 was issued precanceled only. Prices for precanceled stamps in first column are for those which have not been through the post and have original gum. Prices in second column are for postally used, gumless stamps.

Street in Kasbah, Algiers
A1

Mosque of Sidi Abd-er-Rahman
A2

La Pêcherie Mosque
A3

Marabout of Sidi Yacoub
A4

1926-39	Typo.		Perf. 14x13½	
33	A1	1c olive	18	18
34	A1	2c red brn	6	5
35	A1	3c orange	18	18
36	A1	5c bl grn	5	5
37	A1	10c brt vio	5	5
a.		Booklet pane of 10	4.75	
38	A2	15c org brn	8	6
39	A2	20c green	5	5
40	A2	20c dp rose	18	5
41	A2	25c bl grn	25	25
42	A2	25c bl ('27)	35	6
43	A2	25c vio bl ('39)	5	5
44	A2	30c blue	35	22
45	A2	30c bl grn ('27)	90	52
46	A2	35c dp vio	1.25	1.00
47	A2	40c ol grn	5	5
a.		Booklet pane of 10	4.00	
48	A3	45c vio brn	35	30
49	A3	50c blue	35	22
a.		Booklet pane of 10	5.25	
50	A3	50c dk red ('30)	5	5
a.		Booklet pane of 10	7.00	
51	A3	60c yel grn	18	5
52	A3	65c blk brn ('27)	1.75	1.50
53	A1	65c ultra ('38)	22	5
a.		Booklet pane of 10	2.75	
54	A3	75c carmine	42	35
55	A3	75c bl ('29)	3.00	26
56	A3	80c org red	42	38
57	A3	90c red ('27)	6.00	2.75
58	A4	1fr gray grn & red brn	80	26
59	A3	1.05fr lt brn	50	40
60	A3	1.10fr mag ('27)	6.00	2.75
61	A4	1.25fr dk bl & ultra	90	90
62	A4	1.50fr dk bl & ultra ('27)	2.50	22
63	A4	2fr Prus bl & blk brn	2.75	26
64	A4	3fr vio & org	4.50	1.10
65	A4	5fr red & vio	8.75	3.50
66	A4	10fr ol brn & rose ('27)	45.00	30.00
67	A4	20fr vio & grn ('27)	7.00	4.50
		Nos. 33-67 (35)	95.47	52.62

Type A4, 50c blue and rose red, inscribed "CENTENAIRE-ALGERIE" is France No. 255.

Stamps of 1926 Surcharged with New Values.

1927				
68	A2	10c on 35c dp vio	10	10
69	A2	25c on 30c bl	6	6
70	A2	30c on 25c bl grn	16	8
71	A3	65c on 60c yel grn	90	70
72	A3	90c on 80c org red	48	40
73	A3	1.10fr on 1.05fr lt brn	48	32
74	A4	1.50fr on 1.25fr dk bl & ultra	1.75	90
		Nos. 68-74 (7)	3.93	2.56

Bars cancel the old value on Nos. 68, 69, 73 and 74.

No. 4 Surcharged 5c

1927				
75	A16	5c on 4c yel brn	14	8

Bay of Algiers
A5

1930, May 4	Engr.	Perf. 11, 12½		
78	A5	10fr red brn	13.00	13.00
a.		Imperf. (pair)	47.50	

Centenary of Algeria and for International Philatelic Exhibition of North Africa, May, 1930.

One copy of No. 78 was sold with each 10fr admission.

Travel across the Sahara
A6

Arch of Triumph, Lambese
A7

Admiralty Building, Algiers
A8

Kings' Tombs near Touggourt
A9

El-Kebir Mosque, Algiers
A10

Oued River at Colomb-Béchar
A11

Sidi Bon Medine Cemetery at Tlemcen
A13

View of Ghardaia
A12

1936–41 Engraved *Perf. 13*

79	A6	1c ultra	5	5
80	A11	2c dk vio	5	5
81	A7	3c dk bl grn	15	15
82	A12	5c red vio	6	6
83	A8	10c emerald	6	5
84	A9	15c red	6	5
85	A13	20c dk bl grn	6	5
86	A10	25c rose vio	60	6
87	A12	30c yel grn	52	8
88	A9	40c brn vio	6	6
89	A13	45c dp ultra	1.25	90
90	A8	50c red	70	5
91	A6	65c red brn	3.75	3.00
92	A6	65c rose car ('37)	42	5
93	A6	70c red brn ('39)	8	8
94	A11	75c sl bl	35	10
95	A7	90c hn brn	1.25	1.00
96	A10	1fr brown	35	5
97	A8	1.25fr lt vio	60	35
98	A8	1.25fr car rose ('39)	26	18
99	A11	1.50fr turq bl	1.75	35
99A	A11	1.50fr rose ('40)	35	22
100	A12	1.75fr hn brn	14	6
101	A7	2fr dk brn	14	8
102	A6	2.25fr yel grn	12.50	10.00
103	A12	2.50fr dk ultra ('41)	52	40
104	A13	3fr magenta	26	14
105	A10	3.50fr pck bl	3.50	3.00
106	A8	5fr sl bl	35	18
107	A11	10fr hn brn	42	35
108	A9	20fr turq bl	95	60
		Nos. 79-108 (31)	31.56	21.80

See also Nos. 124–125, 162.

Nos. 82 and 100 with surcharge "E. F. M. 30frs" (Emergency Field Message) were used in 1943 to pay cable tolls for U. S. and Canadian servicemen.

Algerian Pavilion
A14

1937 *Perf. 13*

109	A14	40c brt grn	65	52
110	A14	50c rose car	40	14
111	A14	1.50fr blue	90	40
112	A14	1.75fr brn blk	1.00	90

Paris International Exposition.

Constantine in 1837
A15

1937

113	A15	65c dp rose	48	22
114	A15	1fr brown	5.25	80
115	A15	1.75fr bl grn	40	30
116	A15	2.15fr red vio	26	22

Issued in commemoration of the centenary of the taking of Constantine by the French.

Ruins of a Roman Villa
A16

1938

117	A16	30c green	70	48
118	A16	65c ultra	5	5
119	A16	75c rose vio	80	55
120	A16	3fr car rose	2.25	2.25
121	A16	5fr yel brn	3.50	3.50
		Nos. 117-121 (5)	7.30	6.83

Centenary of Philippeville.

No. 90 Surcharged in Black

0,25

1938

122	A8	25c on 50c red	6	6
a.		Dbl. surch.	40.00	35.00
b.		Invtd. surch.	26.00	22.50

1939 Types of 1936.

Numerals of Value on Colorless Background.

124	A7	90c hn brn	8	5
125	A10	2.25fr bl grn	26	30

American Export Liner Unloading Cargo
A17

1939

126	A17	20c green	1.00	70
127	A17	40c red vio	1.00	70
128	A17	90c brn blk	52	35
129	A17	1.25fr rose	4.00	1.25
130	A17	2.25fr ultra	1.00	90
		Nos. 126-130 (5)	7.52	3.90

New York World's Fair.

Type of 1926, Surcharged in Black

1F

Two types of surcharge:
I. Bars 6mm.
II. Bars 7mm.

1939–40 *Perf. 14x13½*

131	A1	1fr on 90c crim (I)	12	5
a.		Booklet pane of 10		
b.		Dbl. surcharge (I)	52.50	
c.		Invtd. surcharge (I)	35.00	
d.		Pair, one without surch. (I)	1,200.	
e.		Type II ('40)	2.25	22
f.		Invtd. surcharge (II)	40.00	
g.		Pair, one without surch. (II)	1,200.	

View of Algiers
A18

1941 Typographed

132	A18	30c ultra	14	5
133	A18	70c sepia	14	5
134	A18	1fr car rose	14	5

See also No. 163.

Marshal Pétain
A19 A20

1941 Engraved *Perf. 13*

135	A19	1fr dk bl	18	8

No. 53 Surcharged in Black with New Value and Bars.

1941 *Perf. 14x13½*

136	A1	50c on 65c ultra	40	6
a.		Booklet pane of 10		
b.		Inverted surch.	32.50	
c.		Pair, one without surch.	77.50	

1942 *Perf. 14x13*

137	A20	1.50fr org red	15	8

Four other denominations of type A20 exist (4fr, 5fr, 10fr, 20fr), but were not placed in use.

Arms of
Constantine A21 · Oran A22 · Algiers A23

Engraver's Name at Lower Left.

1942-43 Photogravure. *Perf. 12.*

138	A21	40c dk vio ('43)	15	15
139	A22	60c rose ('43)	8	8
140	A21	1.20fr yel grn ('43)	12	10
141	A23	1.50fr car rose	8	8
142	A22	2fr sapphire	28	8
143	A21	2.40fr rose ('43)	10	8
144	A23	3fr sapphire	28	8
145	A21	4fr bl ('43)	15	15
146	A22	5fr yel grn ('43)	10	10
		Nos. 138-146 (9)	1.34	90

Imperforates

Nearly all of Algeria Nos. 138–285, B39–B96, C1–C12 and CB1–CB3 exist imperforate. See note after France No. 395.

Without Engraver's Name.

1942–45 Typo. *Perf. 14x13½*

147	A23	10c dl brn vio ('45)	6	6
148	A22	30c dp bl grn ('45)	8	8
149	A21	40c dl brn vio ('45)	6	6
150	A22	60c rose ('45)	8	8
151	A21	70c dp bl ('45)	8	6
152	A23	80c dk bl grn ('43)	35	35
153	A21	1.20fr dp bl grn ('45)	8	8
154	A23	1.50fr brt rose ('43)	6	6
155	A22	2fr dp bl ('45)	8	6
156	A21	2.40fr rose ('45)	35	35
157	A23	3fr dp bl ('45)	10	8
158	A22	4.50fr brn vio	18	18
		Nos. 147-158 (12)	1.56	1.50

La Pêcherie Mosque
A24

1942 Typographed

159	A24	50c dl red	14	5
a.		Booklet pane of 10	4.00	

1942 Photogravure *Perf. 12*

160	A24	40c gray grn	14	8
161	A24	50c red	14	8

Types of 1936–41, Without "RF"

1942 Engraved *Perf. 13*

162	A11	1.50fr rose	14	5

Typographed.
Perf. 14x13½.

163	A18	30c ultra	14	6

"One Aim Alone—Victory"
A25 A26

1943 Lithographed *Perf. 12*

164	A25	1.50fr dp rose	14	5
165	A26	1.50fr dk bl	14	5

Type of 1942–3 Surcharged with New Value in Black.

1943 Photogravure

166	A22	2fr on 5fr red org	14	8
a.		Surcharge omitted	190.00	

Summer Palace, Algiers
A27

1944, Dec. 1 **Lithographed**

167	A27	15fr slate	1.25	1.25
168	A27	20fr lt bl grn	90	52
169	A27	50fr dk car	70	60
170	A27	100fr dp bl	1.90	1.50
171	A27	200fr dl bis brn	3.00	1.75
		Nos. 167-171 (5)	7.75	5.62

Marianne A28 **Gallic Cock** A29

1944-45

172	A28	10c gray	5	5
173	A28	30c red vio	5	5
174	A29	40c rose car ('45)	14	14
175	A28	50c red	6	5
176	A28	80c emerald	6	6
177	A29	1fr grn ('45)	6	5
178	A28	1.20fr rose lil	8	6
179	A28	1.50fr dk bl	5	5
a.		Dbl impression	30.00	
180	A29	2fr red	6	5
a.		Double impression	35.00	
181	A29	2fr dk brn ('45)	6	5
182	A28	2.40fr rose red	8	6
183	A28	3fr purple	8	5
184	A29	4fr ultra ('45)	8	6
185	A28	4.50fr ol blk	35	35
186	A29	10fr grnsh blk ('45)	55	40
		Nos. 172-186 (15)	1.81	1.53

No. 38 Surcharged in Black **0f.30**

1944 ***Perf. 14x13½.***

187	A2	30c on 15c org brn	18	6
a.		Inverted surch.	14.00	6.00

This stamp exists precanceled only. See note below No. 32.

No. 154 Surcharged "RF" and New Value.

1945

190	A23	50c on 1.50fr brt rose	14	5
a.		Inverted surch.	22.50	

Stamps of France, 1944, Overprinted in Black **ALGÉRIE** *a*

1945-46

191	A99	80c yel grn	5	5
192	A99	1fr grnsh bl	8	6
193	A99	1.20fr violet	14	14
194	A99	2fr vio brn	35	14
195	A99	2.40fr car rose	35	14
196	A99	3fr orange	35	14
		Nos. 191-196 (6)	1.32	67

Same Overprint on Stamps of France, 1945-47, in Black, Red or Carmine.

1945-47

197	A145	40c lil rose	6	6
198	A145	50c vio bl (R)	6	6
199	A146	60c brt ultra (R)	35	14
200	A146	1fr rose red ('47)	6	5
201	A146	1.50fr rose lil ('47)	6	5
202	A147	2fr myr grn (R) ('46)	6	5
203	A147	3fr dp rose	5	5
204	A147	4.50fr ultra (C) ('47)	80	14
205	A147	5fr lt grn ('46)	6	5
206	A147	10fr ultra	42	40
		Nos. 197-206 (10)	1.98	1.05

Same Overprint on France No. 383 and New Value Surcharged in Black

1946

207	A99	2fr on 1.50fr hn brn	6	5
a.		Without "2F"	160.00	

Same Overprint on France Nos. 562 and 564, in Carmine or Blue.

1947

208	A153	10c dp ultra & blk (C)	5	5
209	A155	50c brn, yel & red (Bl)	35	35

Constantine A30 **Arms of: Algiers** A31 **Oran** A32

Typographed

1947-49 ***Perf. 14x13½*** **Unwmkd.**

210	A30	10c dk grn & brt red	5	5
211	A31	50c blk & org	6	5
212	A32	1fr ultra & yel	5	5
213	A30	1.30fr blk & grnsh bl	80	52
214	A31	1.50fr pur & org yel	5	5
215	A32	2fr blk & brt grn	6	5
216	A30	2.50fr blk & brt red	52	42
217	A31	3fr vio brn & grn	14	5
218	A32	3.50fr lt grn & rose lil	14	8
219	A30	4fr dk brn & brt grn	14	14
220	A31	4.50fr ultra & scar	6	5
221	A31	5fr blk & grnsh bl	5	5
222	A32	6fr brn & scar	35	12
223	A32	8fr choc & ultra ('48)	26	6
224	A30	10fr car & choc ('48)	48	5
225	A31	15fr blk & red ('49)	52	5
		Nos. 210-225 (16)	3.73	1.84

See also Nos. 274-280, 285.

Peoples of the World
A33

1949, Oct. 24 **Engr.** ***Perf. 13***

226	A33	5fr green	1.75	1.40
227	A33	15fr scarlet	1.75	1.40
228	A33	25fr ultra	4.25	4.25

Issued to commemorate the 75th anniversary of the formation of the Universal Postal Union.

Grapes A34 **Apollo of Cherchell** A35

Designs: 25fr, Dates. 40fr, Oranges and lemons.

1950, Feb. 25

229	A34	20fr vio brn, grn & cl	1.25	35
230	A34	25fr dk brn, dk grn & brn org	1.40	70
231	A34	40fr brn, grn, red org & org	3.50	1.00

1952 ***Perf. 13*** **Unwmkd.**

Designs: 12fr, 18fr, Isis statue, Cherchell. 15fr, 20fr, Child with eagle.

240	A35	10fr gray blk	35	5
241	A35	12fr org brn	52	8
242	A35	15fr dp bl	35	6
243	A35	18fr rose red	52	35
244	A35	20fr dp grn	52	18
245	A35	30fr dp bl	95	52
		Nos. 240-245 (6)	3.21	1.24

War Memorial, Algiers A38 **Fossilized Nautilus** A39

Phonolite Dike
A40

1952, Apr. 11

246	A38	12fr dk grn	70	52

Issued to honor the French Africa Army.

1952, Aug. 11

247	A39	15fr brt crim	1.25	90
248	A40	30fr dp ultra	1.40	1.00

Issued to publicize the 19th International Geological Congress, Algiers, Sept. 8-15, 1952.

French and Algerian Soldiers and Camel
A41

1952, Nov. 30

249	A41	12fr chnt brn	1.25	90

Issued to commemorate the 50th anniversary of the establishment of the Sahara Companies.

Eugène Millon
A42

François C. Maillot A43 **Oranges** A44

Portrait: 50fr, Alphonse Laveran.

Engraved.

1954, Jan. 4 ***Perf. 13*** **Unwmkd.**

250	A42	25fr dk grn & choc	1.75	26
251	A43	40fr org brn & brn car	2.25	90
252	A42	50fr ultra & ind	2.25	35

Military Health Service.

1954, May 8

253	A44	15fr ind & bl	90	70

Issued to publicize the third International Congress on Agronomy, Algiers, 1954.

Type of France, 1954
Overprinted type "a" in Black.
Engraved.

1954, June 6 ***Perf. 13*** **Unwmkd.**

254	A240	15fr rose car	70	70

Liberation of France, 10th anniversary.

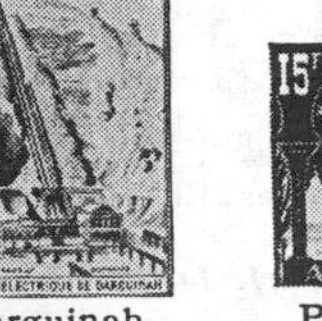

Darguinah Hydroelectric Works A45 **Patio of Bardo Museum** A46

1954, June 19

255	A45	15fr lil rose	90	70

Issued to commemorate the opening of Darguinah hydroelectric works.

1954 **Typographed** ***Perf. 14x13½***

257	A46	12fr red brn & brn org	30	14
258	A46	15fr dk bl & bl	35	5

See also Nos. 267-271.

Type of France, 1954,
Overprinted type "a" in Carmine.

1954 **Engraved** ***Perf. 13***

260	A247	12fr dk grn	80	70

Issued to commemorate the 150th anniversary of the first Legion of Honor awards at Camp de Boulogne.

St. Augustine—A47

1954, Nov. 11

261	A47	15fr chocolate	70	70

Issued to commemorate the 1600th anniversary of the birth of St. Augustine.

Aesculapius Statue and El Kattar Hospital, Algiers
A48

1955, Apr. 3 ***Perf. 13*** **Unwmkd.**

262	A48	15fr red	60	52

Issued to publicize the 30th French Congress of Medicine, Algiers, April 3-6, 1955.

Chenua Mountain and View of Tipasa
A49

1955, May 31

263	A49	50fr brn car	95	26

Issued to commemorate the 2000th anniversary of the founding of Tipasa.

Type of France, 1955
Overprinted type "a" in Red

1955, June 13

264	A251	30fr dp ultra	1.00	70

Issued to commemorate the 50th anniversary of the founding of Rotary International.

Marianne A50 Great Kabylia Mountains A51

Perf. 14x13½

1955, Oct. 3 **Typo.** **Unwmkd.**

265	A50	15fr carmine	35	5

See also No. 284.

1955, Dec. 17 **Engraved** ***Perf. 13***

266	A51	100fr ind & ultra	3.00	35

Bardo Type of 1954, "Postes" and "Algerie" in White. Typographed.

1955-57 ***Perf. 14x13½*** **Unwmkd.**

267	A46	10fr dk brn & lt brn	22	5
268	A46	12fr red brn & brn org ('56)	18	5
269	A46	18fr crim & ver ('57)	70	26
270	A46	20fr grn & yel grn ('57)	52	42
271	A46	25fr pur & brt pur	60	8
		Nos. 267-271 (5)	2.22	86

Marshal Franchet d'Esperey
A52

1956, May 25 **Engraved** ***Perf. 13***

272	A52	15fr saph & ind	90	90

Birth centenary of Marshal Franchet d'Esperey.

Marshal Jacques Leclerc
A53

1956, Nov. 29

273	A53	15fr red brn & sep	70	70

Issued to commemorate the death of Marshal Leclerc.

Type of 1947-49 and

Arms of Bône
A54

Designs: 2fr, Arms of Tizi-Ouzou. 3fr, Arms of Mostaganem. 5fr, Arms of Tlemcen. 10fr, Arms of Setif. 12fr, Arms of Orleansville.

1956-58 **Typographed.** ***Perf. 14x13½***

274	A54	1fr grn & ver	5	5
275	A54	2fr ver & ultra ('58)	52	40
276	A54	3fr ultra & emer ('58)	60	22
277	A54	5fr ultra & yel	26	18
278	A31	6fr red & grn ('57)	70	52
279	A54	10fr dp cl & emer ('58)	70	52
280	A54	12fr ultra & red ('58)	70	52
		Nos. 274-280 (7)	3.53	2.41

Nos. 275 and 279 are inscribed "Republique Francaise." See also No. 285.

View of Oran
A55

1956-58 **Engraved.** ***Perf. 13.***

281	A55	30fr dl pur	70	26
282	A55	35fr car rose ('58)	1.00	70

Electric Train Crossing Bridge
A56

1957, Mar. 25

283	A56	40fr dk bl grn & emer	90	26

Marianne Type of 1955 Inscribed "Algerie" Vertically.

Perf. 14x13½

1957, Dec. 2 **Typo.** **Unwmkd.**

284	A50	20fr ultra	60	8

Arms Type of 1947-49 Inscribed "Republique Francaise"

1958, July

285	A31	6fr red & grn	15.00	15.00

Independent State

France Nos. 939, 968, 945-946 and 1013 Overprinted "EA" and Bars, Handstamped or Typographed, in Black or Red

1962, July 2

286	A336	10c brt grn	35	26
a.		Typographed ovpt.	60	42
287	A349	25c lake & gray	42	26
a.		Handstamped ovpt.	52	26
288	A339	45c brt vio & ol gray	5.25	4.00
a.		Handstamped ovpt.	22.50	16.00
289	A339	50c sl grn & lt cl	6.00	4.00
a.		Handstamped ovpt.	25.00	17.00
290	A372	1fr dk bl, sl & bis	2.50	1.50
a.		Handstamped ovpt.	3.50	2.00
		Nos. 286-290 (5)	14.52	10.02

Post offices were authorized to overprint their stock of these 5 French stamps. The size of the letters was specified as 3x6mm. each, but various sizes were used. The post offices had permission to make their own rubber stamps. Typography, pen or pencil were also used. Many types exist. Colors of handstamped overprints include black, red, blue, violet. "EA" stands for Etat Algérien.

Mosque, Tlemcen
A57

Roman Gates of Lodi, Médéa
A58

Designs: 5c, Kerrata Gorge. 10c, Dam at Foum el Gherza. 95c, Oil field, Hassi Messaoud.

1962, Nov. 1 **Engr.** ***Perf. 13***

291	A57	5c Prus grn, grn & choc	18	8
292	A58	10c ol blk & dk bl	22	8
293	A57	25c sl grn, brn & ver	60	8
294	A57	95c dk bl, blk & bis	2.50	80
295	A58	1fr grn & blk	2.50	1.75
		Nos. 291-295 (5)	6.00	2.79

The designs of Nos. 291-295 are similar to French issues of 1959-61 with "Republique Algeriénne" replacing "Republique Francaise."

Flag, Rifle, Olive Branch
A59

Design: Nos. 300-303, Broken chain and rifle added to design A59.

1963, Jan. 6 **Litho.** ***Perf. 12½***

Flag in Green and Red

296	A59	5c bis brn	18	14
297	A59	10c blue	26	14
298	A59	25c vermilion	1.90	5
299	A59	95c violet	1.75	90
300	A59	1fr green	1.50	26
301	A59	2fr brown	4.00	90
302	A59	5fr lilac	6.00	2.50
303	A59	10fr gray	22.50	14.00
		Nos. 296-303 (8)	38.09	18.89

Nos. 296-299 commemorate the successful revolution and Nos. 300-303 commemorate the return of peace.

Men of Various Races, Wheat Emblem and Globe
A60

1963, Mar. 21 **Engraved** ***Perf. 13***

304	A60	25c mar, dl grn & yel	42	35

Issued for the "Freedom from Hunger" campaign of the U.N. Food and Agriculture Organization.

Map of Algeria and Emblems A61 Physicians from 13th Century Manuscript A62

1963, July 5 ***Perf. 13*** **Unwmkd.**

305	A61	25c bl, dk brn, grn & red	60	35

Issued to commemorate the first anniversary of Algeria's independence.

1963, July 29 **Engraved**

306	A62	25c brn red, grn & bis	1.40	52

Issued to commemorate the Second Congress of the Union of Arab physicians.

Orange and Blossom A63 Scales and Scroll A64

1963 ***Perf. 14x13***

307	A63	8c gray grn & org	50	15
308	A63	20c sl & org red	65	25
309	A63	40c grnsh bl & org	90	38
310	A63	55c ol grn & org red	1.50	65

Nos. 307-310 issued precanceled only. See note below No. 32.

1963, Oct. 13 ***Perf. 13*** **Unwmkd.**

311	A64	25c blk, grn & rose red	65	40

Issued to honor the new constitution.

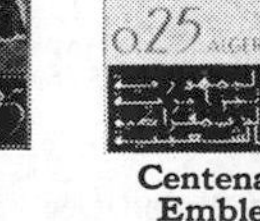

Guerrilla Fighters A65 Centenary Emblem A66

1963, Nov. 1

312	A65	25c dk brn, yel grn & car	65	38

9th anniversary of Algerian revolution.

1963, Dec. 8 Photo. *Perf. 12*

313	A66	25c lt vio bl, yel & dk red	80	42

Centenary of International Red Cross.

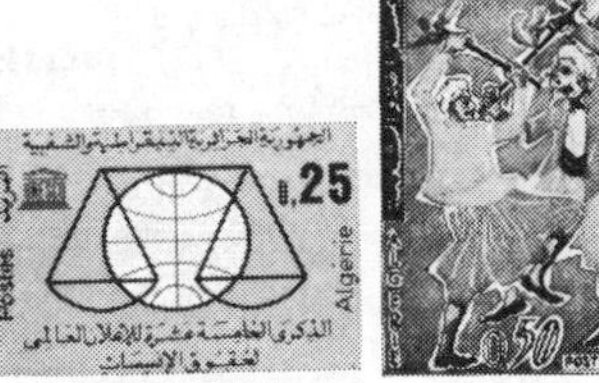

UNESCO Emblem, Scales and Globe A67 — Workers A68

1963, Dec. 16 *Perf. 12* Unwmkd.

314	A67	25c lt bl & blk	70	30

Issued to commemorate the 15th anniversary of the Universal Declaration of Human Rights.

1964, May 1 Engraved *Perf. 13*

315	A68	50c dl red, red org & bl	1.25	48

Issued for the Labor Festival.

Map of Africa and Flags
A69

1964, May 25 *Perf. 13* Unwmkd.

316	A69	45c bl, org & car	90	40

Issued for Africa Day on the first anniversary of the Addis Ababa charter on African unity.

Ramses II Battling the Hittites (from Abu Simbel)—A70

Design: 30c, Two statues of Ramses II.

1964, June 28 Engraved *Perf. 13*

317	A70	20c choc, red & vio bl	80	48
318	A70	30c brn, red & grnsh bl	95	55

Issued to publicize the UNESCO world campaign to save historic monuments in Nubia.

Tractors A71 — Communications Tower A72

Designs: 5c, 25c, 85c, Tractors. 10c, 30c, 65c, Men working with lathe. 12c, 15c, 45c, Electronics center and atom symbol. 20c, 50c, 95c, Draftsman and bricklayer.

1964–65 Typographed *Perf. 14x13½*

319	A71	5c red lil	6	6
320	A71	10c brown	10	6
321	A71	12c emer ('65)	38	10
322	A71	15c dk bl ('65)	22	12
323	A71	20c yellow	28	15
324	A71	25c red	48	6
325	A71	30c pur ('65)	40	6
326	A71	45c rose car	48	22
327	A71	50c ultra	60	10
328	A71	65c orange	85	22
329	A71	85c green	1.40	28
330	A71	95c car rose	1.65	35
		Nos. 319-330 (12)	6.90	1.78

1964, Aug. 30 Engraved *Perf. 13*

331	A72	85c bl, blk & red brn	1.90	75

Inauguration of tne Hertzian cable telephone line Algiers-Annaba.

Industrial and Agricultural Symbols A73 — Gas Flames and Pipes A74

1964, Sept. 26 Typo. *Perf. 13½x14*

332	A73	25c lt ultra, yel & red	40	22

Issued to publicize the first International Fair at Algiers, Sept. 26—Oct. 11.

1964, Sept. 27

333	A74	30c vio, bl & yel	55	40

Issued to commemorate the opening of the Arzew natural gas liquification plant.

Planting Trees A75 — Children and UNICEF Emblem A76

1964, Nov. 29 Unwmkd.

334	A75	25c sl grn, yel & car	42	30

National reforestation campaign.

1964, Dec. 13 *Perf. 13½x14*

335	A76	15c pink, vio bl & lt grn	40	30

Issued for Children's Day.

Decorated Camel Saddle A77

1965, May 29 Typo. *Perf. 13½x14*

336	A77	20c blk, red, emer & brn	35	22

Handicrafts of Sahara.

ICY Emblem A78

1965, Aug. 29 Engraved *Perf. 13*

337	A78	30c blk, mar & bl grn	90	48
338	A78	60c blk, brt bl & bl grn	1.25	55

International Cooperation Year, 1965.

ITU Emblem A79

1965, Sept. 19

339	A79	60c pur, emer & buff	90	55
340	A79	95c dk brn, mar & buff	1.25	65

Issued to commemorate the centenary of the International Telecommunication Union.

Musicians A80

Miniatures by Mohammed Racim: 60c, Two female musicians. 5d, Algerian princess and antelope.

1965, Dec. 27 Photo. *Perf. 11½*

341	A80	30c multi	1.00	70
342	A80	60c multi	1.50	1.00
343	A80	5d multi	11.00	7.00

Bulls, Painted in 6000 B.C. A81

Wall Paintings from Tassili-N-Ajjer, c. 6000 B.C.: No. 345, Shepherd (vert.). 2d, Fleeing ostriches. 3d, Two girls (vert.).

1966, Jan. 29 Photo. *Perf. 11½*

344	A81	1d brn, bis & red brn	3.50	2.50
345	A81	1d gray, blk, ocher & dk brn	3.50	2.50
346	A81	2d brn, ocher & red brn	8.25	4.25
347	A81	3d buff, blk, ocher & brn red	10.00	6.00

See also Nos. 365–368.

Pottery A82

Handicrafts from Great Kabylia: 50c, Weaving, woman at loom (horiz.). 70c, Jewelry.

1966, Feb. 26 Engraved *Perf. 13*

348	A82	40c Prus bl, brn red & blk	42	35
349	A82	50c dk red, ol & ocher	55	42
350	A82	70c vio bl, blk & red	1.00	60

Weather Balloon, Compass Rose and Anemometer
A83

1966, Mar. 23 Engr. Unwmkd.

351	A83	1d cl, brt bl & grn	1.25	55

World Meteorological Day.

Book, Grain, Cogwheel and UNESCO Emblem
A84

Design: 60c, Grain, cogwheel, book and UNESCO emblem.

1966, May 2 Typo. *Perf. 13x14*

352	A84	30c yel bis & blk	35	30
353	A84	60c dk red, gray & blk	60	35

Literacy as basis for development.

WHO Headquarters, Geneva
A85

1966, May 30 Engraved *Perf. 13*

354	A85	30c multi	48	35
355	A85	60c multi	85	42

Issued to commemorate the inauguration of the World Health Organization Headquarters, Geneva.

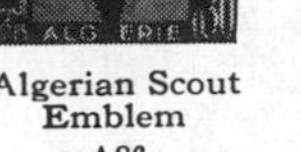

Algerian Scout Emblem A86 — Arab Jamboree Emblem A87

1966, July 23 Photo. *Perf. 12x12½*

356	A86	30c multi	50	35
357	A87	1d multi	1.50	70

No. 356 commemorates the 30th anniversary of the Algerian Mohammedan Boy Scouts. No. 357, the 7th Arab Boy Scout Jamboree, held at Good Daim, Libya, Aug. 12.

Map of Palestine and Victims
A88

Abd-el-Kader
A89

1966, Sept. 26 Typo. *Perf. 10½*

358	A88	30c red & blk	35	22

Deir Yassin Massacre, Apr. 9, 1948.

1966, Nov. 2 Photo. *Perf. 11½*

359	A89	30c multi	30	14
360	A89	95c multi	1.00	40

Issued to commemorate the transfer from Damascus to Algiers of the ashes of Abd-el-Kader (1807?–1883), Emir of Mascara. See also Nos. 382–387.

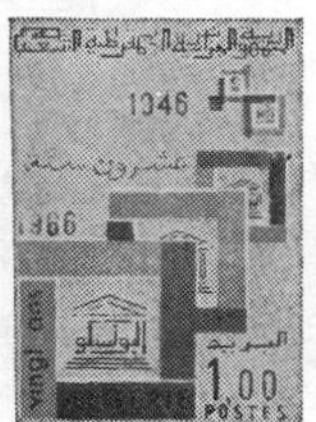

UNESCO Emblem
A90

1966, Nov. 19 Typo. *Perf. 10½*

361	A90	1d multi	1.25	52

Issued to commemorate the 20th anniversary of UNESCO (United Nations Educational, Scientific and Cultural Organization).

Horseman
A91

Miniatures by Mohammed Racim: 1.50d, Woman at her toilette. 2d, The pirate Barbarossa in front of the Admiralty.

1966, Dec. 17 Photo. *Perf. 11½*

Granite Paper

362	A91	1d multi	3.50	1.75
363	A91	1.50d multi	5.25	2.50
364	A91	2d multi	8.75	4.25

Wall Paintings Type of 1966

Wall Paintings from Tassili-N-Ajjer, c.6000 B.C.: 1d, Cow. No. 366, Antelope. No. 367, Archers. 3d, Warrior (vert.).

1967, Jan. 28 Photo. *Perf. 11½*

365	A81	1d brn, bis & dl vio	3.50	2.25
366	A81	2d brn, ocher & red brn	5.75	4.00
367	A81	2d brn, yel & red brn	5.75	4.00
368	A81	3d blk, gray, yel & red brn	9.50	5.75

Bardo Museum
A92

La Kalaa Minaret
A93

Design: 1.30d, Ruins at Sedrata.

1967, Feb. 27 Photo. *Perf. 13*

369	A92	35c multi	35	26
370	A93	95c multi	90	55
371	A92	1.30d multi	1.50	80

Moretti and International Tourist Year Emblem
A94

Design: 70c, Tuareg riding camel, Tassili, and Tourist Year Emblem (vert.).

1967, Apr. 29 Litho. *Perf. 14*

372	A94	40c multi	52	35
373	A94	70c multi	1.00	52

International Tourist Year, 1967.

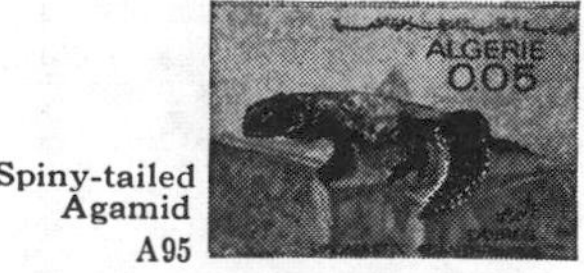

Spiny-tailed Agamid
A95

Designs: 20c, Ostrich (vert.). 40c, Slender-horned gazelle (vert.). 70c, Fennec.

1967, June 24 Photo. *Perf. 11½*

374	A95	5c bis & blk	45	36
375	A95	20c ocher, blk & pink	90	60
376	A95	40c ol bis, blk & red brn	1.50	80
377	A95	70c gray, blk & dp org	2.75	1.40

Dancers
A96

Typographed and Engraved

1967, July 4 *Perf. 10½*

378	A96	50c gray vio, yel & blk	75	48

National Youth Festival.

Map of the Mediterranean and Sport Scenes—A97

1967, Sept. 2 Typo. *Perf. 10½*

379	A97	30c blk, red & bl	42	30

Issued to publicize the 5th Mediterranean Games, Tunis, Sept. 8–17.

Skiers
A98

Olympic Emblem and Sports
A99

1967, Oct. 21 Engraved *Perf. 13*

380	A98	30c brt bl & ultra	60	40
381	A99	95c brn org, pur & brt grn	1.50	1.00

Issued to publicize the 10th Winter Olympic Games, Grenoble, Feb. 6–18, 1968.

Abd-el-Kader Type of 1966

Lithographed, Photogravure

1967–71 *Perf. 13½, 11½*

382	A89	5c dl pur ('68)	5	5
383	A89	10c green	75	30
383A	A89	10c sl grn (litho.,'69)	14	5
383B	A89	25c org ('71)	26	8
384	A89	30c blk ('68)	30	6
385	A89	30c lt vio ('68)	35	25
386	A89	50c rose cl	75	26
387	A89	70c vio bl	90	35
		Nos. 382-387 (8)	3.50	1.40

The 10c (No. 383), 50c and 70c are on granite paper, photogravure, and were issued Nov. 13, 1967. The 5c, 10c (No. 383A), 25c and both 30c are lithographed and perf. 13½; others, perf. 11½.

The three 1967 stamps (No. 383, 50c, 70c) have numerals thin, narrow and close together; the Arabic inscription at lower right is 2mm. high. The five lithographed stamps are redrawn, with numerals thicker and spaced more widely; Arabic at lower right 3mm. high.

Boy Scouts Holding Jamboree Emblem
A100

1967, Dec. 23 Engraved *Perf. 13*

388	A100	1d multi	1.50	85

Issued to commemorate the 12th Boy Scout World Jamboree, Farragut State Park, Idaho, Aug. 1–9.

No. 324 Surcharged

1967 Typographed *Perf. 14x13½*

389	A71	30c on 25c red	50	30

Mandolin
A101

Musical Instruments: 40c, Lute. 1.30d, Rebec.

1968, Feb. 17 Photo. *Perf. 12½x13*

390	A101	30c dk brn, ocher & lt bl	52	35
391	A101	40c multi	60	40
392	A101	1.30d multi	2.00	1.00

Nememcha Rug
A102

Algerian Rugs: 70c, Guergour. 95c, Djebel-Amour. 1.30d, Kalaa.

1968, Apr. 13 Photo. *Perf. 11½*

393	A102	30c multi	70	42
394	A102	70c multi	1.40	80
395	A102	95c multi	2.25	1.25
396	A102	1.30d multi	2.50	1.50

Human Rights Flame
A103

1968, May 18 Typo. *Perf. 10½*

397	A103	40c bl, red & yel	60	42

International Human Rights Year, 1968.

WHO Emblem
A104

1968, May 18

398	A104	70c blk, lt bl & yel	80	42

Issued for the 20th anniversary of the World Health Organization.

Welder A105 — Athletes, Olympic Flame and Rings A106

1968, June 15 Engr. *Perf. 13*

399 A105 30c gray, brn & ultra 40 26

Algerian emigration to Europe.

Perf. 12½x13, 13x12½

1968, July 4 Photogravure

Designs: 50c, Soccer player. 1d, Mexican pyramid, emblem, Olympic flame, rings and athletes (horiz.).

400 A106 30c grn, red & yel 52 42
401 A106 50c rose car & multi 90 48
402 A106 1d dk grn, org, brn & red 1.65 1.00

Issued to publicize the 19th Olympic Games, Mexico City, Oct. 12–27.

Scouts and Emblem A107 — Barbary Sheep A108

1968, July 4 *Perf. 13*

403 A107 30c multi 42 26

Issued to publicize the 8th Arab Boy Scout Jamboree, Algiers, 1968.

1968, Oct. 19 Photo. *Perf. 11½*

Design: 1d, Red deer.

404 A108 40c red brn, bis & blk 70 38
405 A108 1d lt & dk ol grn & brn 1.90 85

Hunting Scenes, Djemila A109 — "Industry" A110

Design: 95c, Neptune's chariot, Timgad (horiz.). Both designs are from Roman mosaics.

Perf. 12½x13, 13x12½

1968, Nov. 23 Photogravure

406 A109 40c gray & multi 52 35
407 A109 95c gray & multi 1.25 70

1968, Dec. 14 *Perf. 11½*

Designs: No. 409, Miner with drill. 95c, "Energy" (circle and rays).

408 A110 30c dp org & sil 42 26
409 A110 30c brn & multi 42 26
410 A110 95c sil, red & blk 1.25 52

Issued to publicize industrial development.

Opuntia Ficus Indica A111

Flowers: 40c, Carnations. 70c, Roses. 95c, Bird-of-paradise flower.

1969, Jan. Photo. *Perf. 11½*

Flowers in Natural Colors

411 A111 25c pink & blk 42 30
412 A111 40c yel & blk 60 40
413 A111 70c gray & blk 1.10 52
414 A111 95c brt bl & blk 1.75 90

See also Nos. 496–499.

Irrigation Dam at Djorf Torba-Oued Guir A112

Design: 1.50d, Truck on Highway No. 51 and camel caravan.

1969, Feb. 22 Photo. *Perf. 11½*

415 A112 30c multi 42 26
416 A112 1.50d multi 2.25 1.00

Public works in the Sahara.

Mail Coach A113

1969, Mar. 22 Photo. *Perf. 11½*

417 A113 1d multi 1.75 90

Issued for Stamp Day, 1969.

Capitol, Timgad A114

Design: 1d, Septimius Temple, Djemila (horiz.).

1969, Apr. 5 Photo. *Perf. 13x12½*

418 A114 30c gray & multi 52 26
419 A114 1d gray & multi 1.25 52

Second Timgad Festival, Apr. 4–8.

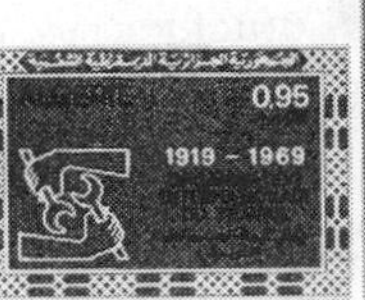

ILO Emblem A115 — Arabian Saddle A116

1969, May 24 Photo. *Perf. 11½*

420 A115 95c dp car, yel & blk 1.40 55

50th anniversary of the International Labor Organization.

1969, June 28 Photo. *Perf. 12x12½*

Algerian Handicrafts: 30c, Bookcase. 60c, Decorated copper plate.

Granite Paper

421 A116 30c multi 42 30
422 A116 60c multi 80 38
423 A116 1d multi 1.40 70

No. 321 Surcharged **0,20**

1969 Typographed *Perf. 14x13½*

424 A71 20c on 12c emer 35 18

Pan-African Culture Festival Emblem A117 — African Development Bank Emblem A118

1969, July 19 Photo. *Perf. 12½*

425 A117 30c multi 38 26

Issued to commemorate the First Pan-African Culture Festival, Algiers, July 21–Aug. 1.

1969, Aug. 23 Typo. *Perf. 10½*

426 A118 30c dl bl, yel & blk 38 30

Issued to commemorate the 5th anniversary of the African Development Bank.

Astronauts and Landing Module on Moon A119

Photogravure

1969, Aug. 23 *Perf. 12½x11½*

427 A119 50c gold & multi 90 52

Issued to commemorate man's first landing on the moon, July 20, 1969. U.S. astronauts Neil A. Armstrong and Col. Edwin E. Aldrin, Jr., with Lieut. Col. Michael Collins piloting Apollo 11.

Algerian Women, by Dinet A120

Design: 1.50d, The Watchmen, by Etienne Dinet.

1969, Nov. 29 Photo. *Perf. 14½*

428 A120 1d multi 1.90 1.10
429 A120 1.50d multi 2.75 1.75

Mother and Child A121

1969, Dec. 27 Photo. *Perf. 11½*

430 A121 30c multi 60 42

Issued to promote mother and child protection.

Agricultural Growth Chart, Tractor and Dam A122

Designs: 30c, Transportation and development. 50c, Abstract symbols of industrialization.

1970, Jan. 31 Photo. *Perf. 12½*

Size: 37x23mm.

431 A122 25c dk brn, yel & org 26 22

Lithographed *Perf. 14*

Size: 49x23mm.

432 A122 30c bl & multi 42 26

Photogravure *Perf. 12½*

Size: 37x23mm.

433 A122 50c rose lil & blk 52 30

Issued to publicize the Four-Year Development Plan.

Old and New Mail Delivery A123 — Spiny Lobster A124

1970, Feb. 28 Photo. *Perf. 11½*

Granite Paper

434 A123 30c multi 42 26

Issued for Stamp Day.

1970, Mar. 28

Designs: 40c, Mollusks. 75c, Retepora cellulosa. 1d, Red coral.

435 A124 30c ocher & multi 42 26
436 A124 40c multi 52 35
437 A124 75c ultra & multi 1.00 52
438 A124 1d lt bl & multi 1.50 70

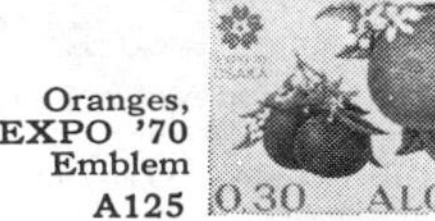

Oranges, EXPO '70 Emblem A125

Designs (EXPO '70 Emblem and): 60c, Algerian pavilion. 70c, Grapes.

1970, Apr. 25 Photo. *Perf. 12½x12*

439 A125 30c lt bl, grn & org 42 22
440 A125 60c multi 52 26

441 A125 70c multi 80 48

EXPO '70 International Exhibition, Osaka, Japan, Mar. 15–Sept. 13, 1970.

Olives, Oil Bottle A126 — Saber A127

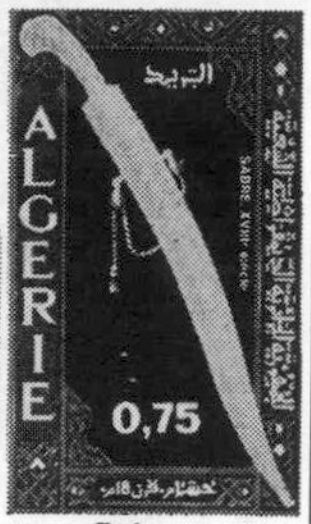

1970, May 16 Photo. *Perf. 12½x12*

442 A126 1d yel & multi 1.25 70

Olive Year, 1969–1970.

U.P.U. Headquarters Issue

Common Design Type

1970, May 30 *Perf. 13*

Size: 36x26mm.

443 CD133 75c multi 80 42

1970, June 27 Photo. *Perf. 12½*

Designs: 40c, Guns, 18th century (horiz.). 1d, Pistol, 18th century (horiz.).

444 A127 40c yel & multi 70 42
445 A127 75c red & multi 1.00 80
446 A127 1d multi 1.75 1.00

Map of Arab Countries and Arab League Flag A128

Typographed and Engraved

1970, July 25 *Perf. 10½*

447 A128 30c grn, ocher & lt bl 35 22

25th anniversary of the Arab League.

Lenin A129

1970, Aug. 29 Litho. *Perf. 11½x12*

448 A129 30c brn & buff 30 22

Issued to commemorate the centenary of the birth of Lenin (1870–1924), Russian communist leader.

Exhibition Hall and Algiers Fair Emblem—A130

1970, Sept. 11 Engr. *Perf. 14x13½*

449 A130 60c lt ol grn 52 30

New Exhibition Hall for Algiers International Fair.

Common Design Types

pictured in section at front of book.

Education Year Emblem, Blackboard, Atom Symbol—A131

Koran Page A132

1970, Oct. 24 Photo. *Perf. 14*

450 A131 30c pink, blk, gold & lt bl 35 26
451 A132 3d multi 3.00 2.25

Issued for International Education Year.

Great Mosque, Tlemcen A133

Design: 40c, Ketchaoua Mosque, Algiers (vert.). 1d, Mosque, Sidi-Okba (vert.).

1970–71 Lithographed *Perf. 14*

456 A133 30c multi 35 22
457 A133 40c sep & lem ('71) 38 18
458 A133 1d multi 1.00 42

Symbols of the Arts A134

1970, Dec. 26 Photo. *Perf. 13x12½*

459 A134 1d grn, lt grn & org 1.00 52

Main Post Office, Algiers A135

1971, Jan. 23 *Perf. 11½*

460 A135 30c multi 48 30

Stamp Day, 1971.

Hurdling A136

Designs: 40c, Vaulting (vert.). 75c, Basketball (vert.).

1971, Mar. 7 Photo. *Perf. 11½*

461 A136 20c lt bl & sl 38 22
462 A136 40c lt ol grn & sl 55 40
463 A136 75c sal pink & sl 95 60

Mediterranean Games, Izmir, Turkey, Oct. 1971.

Symbolic Head A137

1971, March 27 *Perf. 12½*

464 A137 60c car rose, blk & sil 55 30

International year against racial discrimination.

Emblem and Technicians A138

1971, Apr. 24 Photo. *Perf. 12½x12*

465 A138 70c cl, org & bluish blk 65 35

Founding of the Institute of Technology.

Woman from Aurès A139

Regional Costumes: 70c, Man from Oran. 80c, Man from Algiers. 90c, Woman from Amour Mountains.

1971, Oct. 16 *Perf. 11½*

466 A139 50c gold & multi 90 52
467 A139 70c gold & multi 95 70
468 A139 80c gold & multi 1.40 90
469 A139 90c gold & multi 1.50 1.00

See Nos. 485–488, 534–537.

UNICEF Emblem, Birds and Plants A140

1971, Dec. 6 *Perf. 11½*

470 A140 60c multi 70 48

25th anniversary of United Nations International Children's Fund (UNICEF).

Lion of St. Mark—A141

Design: 1.15d, Bridge of Sighs, Venice (vert.).

1972, Jan. 24 Litho. *Perf. 12*

471 A141 80c multi 90 60
472 A141 1.15d multi 1.50 95

UNESCO campaign to save Venice.

Javelin A142 — Book and Book Year Emblem A143

Designs: 25c, Bicycling (horiz.). 60c, Wrestling. 1d, Gymnast on rings.

1972, Mar. 25 Photo. *Perf. 11½*

473 A142 25c mar & multi 38 22
474 A142 40c ocher & multi 48 30
475 A142 60c ultra & multi 70 42
476 A142 1d rose & multi 1.25 60

20th Olympic Games, Munich, Aug. 26–Sept. 11.

1972, Apr. 15

477 A143 1.15d bis, brn & red 90 60

International Book Year 1972.

Mailmen A144 — Jasmine A145

1972, Apr. 22

478 A144 40c gray & multi 38 22

Stamp Day 1972.

1972, May 27

Flowers: 60c, Violets. 1.15d, Tuberose.

Flowers in Natural Colors

479 A145 50c brn & pale sal 60 42
480 A145 60c vio & gray 70 52
481 A145 1.15d lt bl & Prus bl 1.50 80

Olympic Stadium, Chéraga A146

1972, June 10

482 A146 50c gray, choc & grn 52 35

New Day, Algerian Flag A147

1972, July 5

483 A147 1d grn & multi 1.00 65

10th anniversary of independence.

Festival Emblem A148 — Mailing a Letter A149

1972, July 5 Litho. *Perf. 10½*

484 A148 40c grn, dk brn & org 35 18

First Arab Youth Festival, Algiers, July 5–11.

Costume Type of 1971

Regional Costumes: 50c, Woman from Hoggar. 60c, Kabyle woman. 70c, Man from Mzab. 90c, Woman from Tlemcen.

1972, Nov. 18 Photo. *Perf. 11½*

485 A139 50c gold & multi 1.00 70
486 A139 60c gold & multi 1.00 70
487 A139 70c gold & multi 1.25 90
488 A139 90c gold & multi 1.50 1.25

1973, Jan. 20 Photo. *Perf. 11*

489 A149 40c org & multi 40 22

Stamp Day.

Ho Chi Minh, Map of Viet Nam A150

1973, Feb. 17 Photo. *Perf. 11½*

490 A150 40c multi 40 22

To honor the people of Viet Nam.

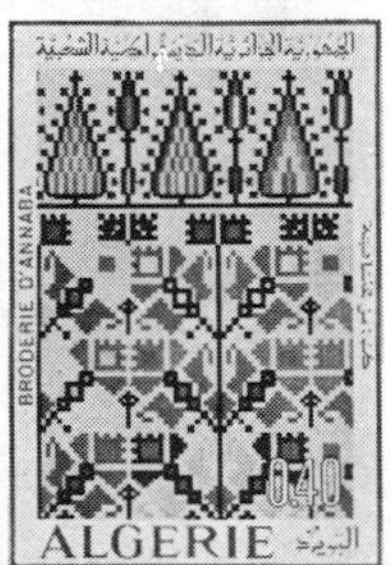

Embroidery from Annaba A151

Designs: 60c, Tree of Life pattern from Algiers. 80c, Constantine embroidery.

1973, Feb. 24

491 A151 40c gray & multi 60 40
492 A151 60c bl and multi 90 55
493 A151 80c dk red, gold & blk 1.10 80

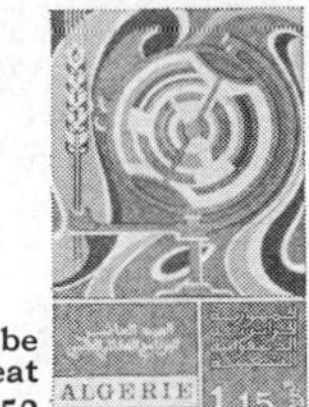

Stylized Globe and Wheat A152

1973, Mar. 26 Photo. *Perf. 11½*

494 A152 1.15d brt rose lil, org & grn 80 42

World Food Program, 10th anniversary.

Soldier and Flag—A153

1973, Apr. 23 Photo. *Perf. 14x13½*

495 A153 40c multi 35 22

Honoring the National Service.

Flower Type of 1969

Flowers: 30c, Opuntia ficus indica. 40c, Roses. 1d, Carnations. 1.15d, Bird-of-paradise flower.

1973, May 21 Photo. *Perf. 11½*

Flowers in Natural Colors

496 A111 30c pink & blk 35 26
497 A111 40c gray & blk 42 30
498 A111 1d yel & multi 1.10 60
499 A111 1.15d multi 1.50 75

OAU Emblem A154

1973, May 28 Photo. *Perf. 12½x13*

500 A154 40c multi 40 26

Organization for African Unity, 10th anniversary.

Desert and Fruitful Land, Farmer and Family—A155

1973, June 18 *Perf. 11½*

501 A155 40c gold & multi 52 35

Agricultural revolution.

Map of Africa, Scout Emblem A156

1973, July 16 Litho. *Perf. 10½*

502 A156 80c purple 70 42

24th Boy Scout World Conference (1st in Africa), Nairobi, Kenya, July 16–21.

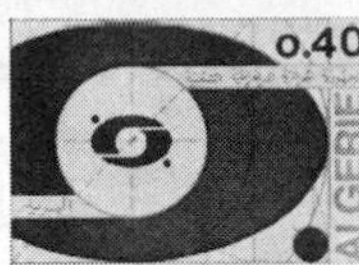

Algerian PTT Emblem A157

1973, Aug. 6 *Perf. 14*

503 A157 40c bl & org 35 22

Adoption of new emblem for Post, Telegraph and Telephone System.

Conference Emblem A158

1973, Sept. 5 Photo. *Perf. 13½x12½*

504 A158 40c dp rose & multi 35 26
505 A158 80c bl grn & multi 70 35

4th Summit Conference of Non-aligned Nations, Algiers, Sept. 5–9.

Port of Skikda A159

1973, Sept. 29 Photo. *Perf. 11½*

506 A159 80c ocher, blk & ultra 70 40

New port of Skikda.

Young Workers A160

1973, Oct. 22 Photo. *Perf. 13*

507 A160 40c multi 35 22

Voluntary work service.

Arms of Algiers A161

1973, Dec. 22 Photo. *Perf. 13*

508 A161 2d gold & multi 2.50 1.75

Millennium of Algiers.

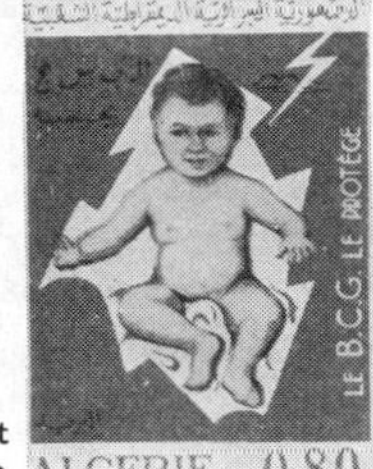

Infant A162

1974, Jan. 7 Litho. *Perf. 10½x11*

509 A162 80c org & multi 90 52

Fight against tuberculosis.

Man and Woman, Industry and Transportation A163

1974, Feb. 18 Photo. *Perf. 11½*

510 A163 80c multi 70 30

Four-year plan.

A164

1974, Feb. 25 Photo. *Perf. 11½*

511 A164 1.50d multi 1.75 1.00

Millennium of the birth of abu-al-Rayhan al-Biruni (973–1048), philosopher and mathematician.

Map and Colors of Algeria, Tunisia, Morocco A165

1974, Mar. 4 Photo. *Perf. 13*

512 A165 40c gold & multi 40 30

Maghreb Committee for Coordination of Posts and Telecommunications.

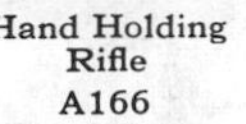

Hand Holding Rifle A166 — Mother and Children A167

1974, Mar. 25 *Perf. 11½*

513 A166 80c red & blk 52 30

Solidarity with the struggle of the people of South Africa.

1974, Apr. 8 *Perf. 13½*

514 A167 85c multi 65 35

Honoring Algerian mothers.

Village—A168

Designs: 80c, Harvest. 90c, Tractor and sun. Designs after children's drawings.

1974, June 15 **Size: 45x26mm.**

515 A168 70c multi 60 26

Size: 48x33mm.

516 A168 80c multi 70 42
517 A168 90c multi 90 65

Nos. 498–499 Overprinted "FLORALIES/1974"

1974, June 22 Photo. *Perf. 11½*

518 A111 1d multi 95 52
519 A111 1.15d multi 1.10 60

1974 Flower Show.

Stamp Vending Machine A169

1974, Oct. 7 Photogravure *Perf. 13*

520 A169 80c multi 65 30

Stamp Day 1974.

UPU Emblem and Globe A170

1974, Oct. 14 *Perf. 14*

521 A170 80c multi 75 42

Centenary of Universal Postal Union.

"Revolution" A171

Soldiers and Mountains A172

Raising New Flag A173

Design: 1d, Algerian struggle for independence (people, sun and fields).

1974, Nov. 4 Photogravure *Perf. 14*

522 A171 40c multi 40 26
523 A172 70c multi 55 35
524 A173 95c multi 70 35
525 A171 1d multi 90 42

20th anniversary of the start of the revolution.

"Horizon 1980" A174

Ewer and Basin A175

1974, Nov. 23 Photo. *Perf. 13*

526 A174 95c ocher, dk red & blk 80 40

10-year development plan, 1971–1980.

1974, Dec. 21 *Perf. 11½*

Designs: 60c, Coffee pot. 95c, Sugar bowl. 1d, Bath tub.

527 A175 50c pink & multi 42 30
528 A175 60c pale yel & multi 52 40
529 A175 95c cit & multi 90 52
530 A175 1d ultra & multi 1.00 70

17th century Algerian copperware.

No. 497 Surcharged with New Value and Heavy Bar

1975, Jan. 4

531 A111 50c on 40c multi 52 30

Mediterranean Games' Emblem—A176

1975, Jan. 27 *Perf. 13½*

532 A176 50c pur, yel & grn 42 26
533 A176 1d org, bl & mar 90 35

Mediterranean Games, Algiers, 1975.

Costume Type of 1971

Regional Costumes: No. 534, Woman from Hoggar. No. 535, Woman from Algiers. No. 536, Woman from Oran. No. 537, Man from Tlemcen.

1975, Feb. 22 Photo. *Perf. 11½*

534 A139 1d gold & multi 1.25 90
535 A139 1d gold & multi 1.25 90
536 A139 1d gold & multi 1.25 90
537 A139 1d gold & multi 1.25 90

Map of Arab Countries, ALO Emblem A177

1975, Mar. 10 Litho. *Perf. 10½x11*

538 A177 50c red brn 40 18

Arab Labor Organization, 10th anniversary.

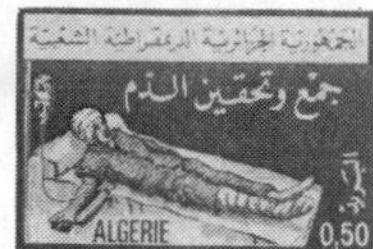

Blood Transfusion A178

1975, Mar. 15 *Perf. 14*

539 A178 50c car rose & multi 48 26

Blood donations and transfusions.

Post Office, Al-Kantara A179

Policeman and Map of Algeria A180

1975, May 10 Photo. *Perf. 11½*
Granite Paper

540 A179 50c multi 40 18

Stamp Day 1975.

1975, June 1 Photo. *Perf. 13*

541 A180 50c multi 50 25

National Security and 10th National Police Day.

Ground Receiving Station A181

Designs: 1d, Map of Algeria with locations of radar sites, transmission mast and satellite. 1.20d, Main and subsidiary stations.

1975, June 28 Photo. *Perf. 13*

542 A181 50c bl & multi 42 22
543 A181 1d bl & multi 80 30
544 A181 1.20d bl & multi 95 35

National satellite telecommunications network.

Revolutionary with Flag A182

1975, Aug. 20 Photo. *Perf. 11½*

545 A182 1d multi 75 40

August 20th Revolutionary Movement (Skikda), 20th anniversary.

Swimming and Games' Emblem A183

Perf. 13x13½, 13½x13

1975, Aug. 23 Photogravure
Multicolored

546 A183 25c *shown* 22 18
547 A183 50c *Wrestling and map* 40 26
548 A183 70c *Soccer* (vert.) 70 35
549 A183 1d *Running* (vert.) 80 40
550 A183 1.20d *Handball* (vert.) 1.10 55
a. Souvenir sheet of 5 6.75 6.75
Nos. 546-550 (5) 3.22 1.74

7th Mediterranean Games, Algiers, Aug. 23–Sept. 6.

No. 550a contains one each of Nos. 546–550, perf. 13, buff margin with marginal inscription and ornament in blue and maroon. Size: 135x135mm. Sold for 4.50d. Exists imperf.; same price.

Setif, Guelma, Kherrata A184

1975 Litho. *Perf. 13½x14*

551 A184 5c org & blk 10 5
552 A184 10c emer & brn 14 5
553 A184 25c dl bl & blk 18 6
554 A184 30c lem & blk 22 8
555 A184 50c brt grn & blk 35 8
556 A184 70c fawn & blk 52 18
557 A184 1d ver & blk 75 40
Nos. 551-557 (7) 2.26 90

30th anniversary of victory in World War II.

Issue dates: 50c, 1d, Nov. 3; others, Dec. 17.

Map of Maghreb and APU Emblem A185

1975 Nov. 20 Photo. *Perf. 11½*

558 A185 1d multi 80 42

10th Congress of Arab Postal Union, Algiers.

Mosaic, Bey Constantine's Palace A186

Dey-Alger Palace—A187

Design: 2d, Prayer niche, Medersa Sidi—Boumediene, Tlemcen.

1975, Dec. 22

559 A186 1d lt bl & multi 90 35
560 A186 2d buff & multi 1.75 90
561 A187 2.50d buff & blk 2.50 1.25

Famous buildings.

Al-Azhar University
A188

Lithographed

1975, Dec. 29 ***Perf. 11½x12½***

562 A188 2d multi 1.75 90

Millennium of Al-Azhar University.

Red-billed Firefinch
A189

Birds: 1.40d, Black-headed bush shrike (horiz.). 2d, Blue tit. 2.50d, Black-bellied sandgrouse (horiz.).

1976, Jan. 24 Photo. ***Perf. 11½***

563 A189 50c multi 52 26
564 A189 1.40d multi 1.25 80
565 A189 2d multi 1.75 1.00
566 A189 2.50d multi 2.25 1.40

See Nos. 595–598.

Telephones 1876 and 1976
A190

Map of Africa with Angola and its Flag
A191

1976, Feb. 23 Photo. ***Perf. 13½x13***

567 A190 1.40d rose, dk & lt bl 95 55

Centenary of first telephone call by Alexander Graham Bell, Mar. 10, 1876.

1976, Feb. 23 ***Perf. 11½***

568 A191 50c brn & multi 40 22

Algeria's solidarity with the People's Republic of Angola.

Sahraoui Flag and Child, Map of former Spanish Sahara
A192

1976, Mar. 15 Photo. ***Perf. 11½***

569 A192 50c multi 40 22

Algeria's solidarity with Sahraoui Arab Democratic Republic, former Spanish Sahara.

Mailman
A193

1976, Mar. 22

570 A193 1.40d multi 95 48

Stamp Day 1976.

Microscope, Slide with TB Bacilli, Patients
A194

1976, Apr. 26 ***Perf. 13x13½***

571 A194 50c multi 42 22

Fight against tuberculosis.

"Setif, Guelma, Kherrata"
A195

1976, May 24 Photo. ***Perf. 13½x13***

572 A195 50c bl & yel 50 8
a. Booklet pane of 6 3.25
b. Booklet pane of 10 5.00

No. 572 was issued in booklets only.

Ram's Head over Landscape
A196

1976, June 17 Photo. ***Perf. 11½***

573 A196 50c multi 42 26

Livestock breeding.

People Holding Torch, Map of Algeria
A197

Palestine Map and Flag
A198

1976, June 29 Photo. ***Perf. 14x13½***

574 A197 50c multi 42 18

National Charter.

1976, July 12 ***Perf. 11½***

Granite Paper

575 A198 50c multi 1.00 25

Solidarity with the Palestinians.

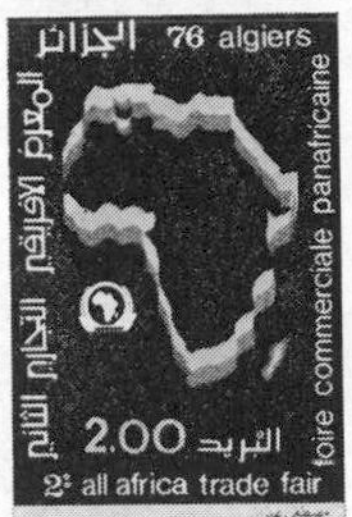

Map of Africa
A199

1976, Oct. 3 Litho. ***Perf. 10½x11***

576 A199 2d dk bl & multi 1.50 75

2nd Pan-African Commercial Fair, Algiers.

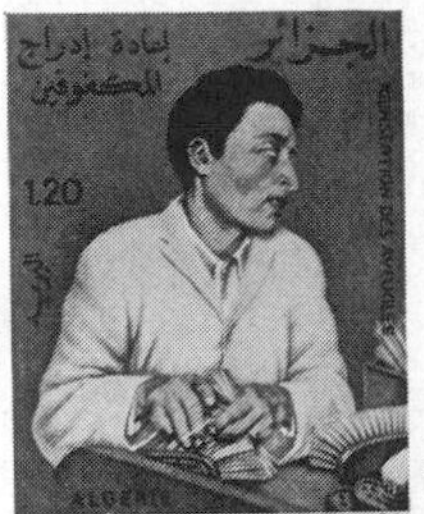

Blind Brushmaker
A200

The Blind, by Dinet
A201

1976, Oct. 23 Photo. ***Perf. 14½***

577 A200 1.20d bl & multi 1.00 52
578 A201 1.40d gold & multi 1.40 70

Rehabilitation of the blind.

"Constitution 1976"—A202

1976, Nov. 19 Photo. ***Perf. 11½***

579 A202 2d multi 1.50 80

New Constitution.

Soldiers Planting Seedlings
A203

1976, Nov. 25 Litho. ***Perf. 12***

580 A203 1.40d multi 1.10 52

Green barrier against the Sahara.

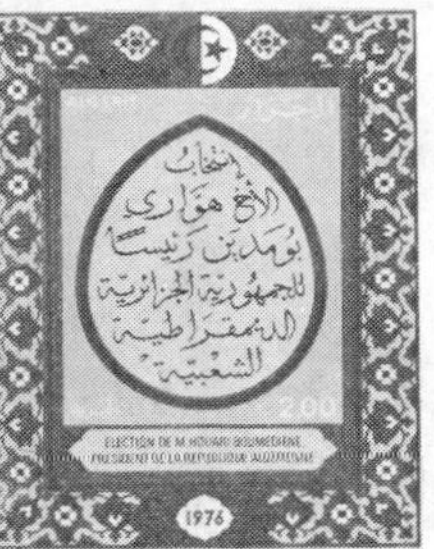

Ornamental Border and Inscription
A204

1976, Dec. 18 Photo. ***Perf. 11½***

Granite Paper

581 A204 2d multi 1.50 80

Re-election of Pres. Houari Boumediene.

Map with Charge Zones and Dials
A205

People and Buildings
A206

1977, Jan. 22 ***Perf. 13***

582 A205 40c sil & multi 40 22

Inauguration of automatic national and international telephone service.

1977, Jan. 29 Photo. ***Perf. 11½***

583 A206 60c on 50c multi 52 26

2nd General Population and Buildings Census. No. 583 was not issued without the typographed red brown surcharge, date, and bars.

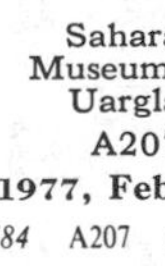

Sahara Museum, Uargla
A207

1977, Feb. 12 Litho. ***Perf. 14***

584 A207 60c multi 52 30

El-Kantara Gorge
A208

1977, Feb. 19 Photo. ***Perf. 12½x13½***

585 A208 20c grn & yel 8 6
a. Booklet pane of 7 (3 #585, 4 #586 + label) 2.00
b. Booklet pane of 7 (5 #585, 2 #587 + label) 2.25
586 A208 60c brt lil & yel 26 14
587 A208 1d brn & yel 60 22

National Assembly—A209

1977, Feb. 27 ***Perf. 11½***

588	A209	2d multi	1.40	70

People and Flag A210

Soldier and Flag A211

Perf. 13½, 11½ (3d)

1977, Mar. 12 **Photogravure**

589	A210	2d multi	1.40	65
590	A211	3d multi	2.00	1.00

Solidarity with the peoples of Zimbabwe (Rhodesia), 2d; Namibia, 3d.

Winter, Roman Mosaic A212

The Seasons from Roman Villa, 2nd century A.D.: 1.40d, Fall. 2d, Summer. 3d, Spring.

1977, Apr. 21 **Photo.** ***Perf. 11½***

Granite Paper

591	A212	1.20d multi	1.00	52
592	A212	1.40d multi	1.25	52
593	A212	2d multi	1.75	1.00
594	A212	3d multi	2.50	1.75
a.		Souv. sheet of 4, perf. imperf.	10.00	10.00

No. 594a contains one each of Nos. 591-594; gray marginal inscription. Size: 101x145mm. Sold for 8d.

Bird Type of 1976

Birds: 60c, Tristram's warbler. 1.40d, Moussier's redstart (horiz.). 2d, Temminck's horned lark (horiz.). 3d, Eurasian hoopoe.

1977, May 21 **Photo.** ***Perf. 11½***

595	A189	60c multi	52	35
596	A189	1.40d multi	1.00	60
597	A189	2d multi	1.75	1.00
598	A189	3d multi	2.75	1.75

Horseman A213

Design: 5d, Attacking horsemen (horiz.).

1977, June 25 **Photo.** ***Perf. 11½***

599	A213	2d multi	1.90	1.00
600	A213	5d multi	4.25	2.50

Helpful notes abound in the "Information for Collectors" section at the front of this volume.

Flag Colors, Games Emblem A214

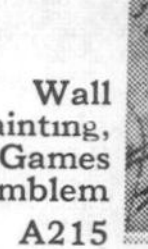

Wall Painting, Games Emblem A215

1977, Sept. 24 **Photo.** ***Perf. 11½***

601	A214	60c multi	52	35
602	A215	1.40d multi	1.25	70

3rd African Games, Algiers 1978.

Village and Tractor A216

1977, Nov. 12 ***Perf. 14x13***

603	A216	1.40d multi	1.00	52

Socialist agricultural village.

Almohades Dirham, 12th Century—A217

Ancient Coins: 1.40d, Almohades coin, 12th century. 2d, Almoravides dinar, 11th century.

1977, Dec. 17 **Photo.** ***Perf. 11½***

604	A217	60c ultra, sil & blk	52	35
605	A217	1.40d grn, gold & brn	1.25	52
606	A217	2d red brn, gold & brn	1.75	1.00

Cherry Blossoms A218

Flowering Trees: 1.20d, Peach. 1.30d, Almond. 1.40d, Apple.

1978, Feb. 11 **Photo.** ***Perf. 11½***

607	A218	60c multi	42	26
608	A218	1.20d multi	90	52
609	A218	1.30d multi	90	52
610	A218	1.40d multi	95	60

No. 555 Surcharged with New Value and Bar

1978, Feb. 11 **Litho.** ***Perf. 13½x14***

611	A184	60c on 50c	42	6

Children with Traffic Signs and Car A219

1978, Apr. 29 **Photo.** ***Perf. 11½***

612	A219	60c multi	42	22

Road safety and protection of children.

Sports and Games Emblems A220

Designs (Games Emblem and): 60c, Rower (vert.). 1.20d, Flag colors. 1.30d, Fireworks (vert.). 1.40d, Map of Africa and dancers (vert.).

1978, July 13 **Photo.** ***Perf. 11½***

613	A220	40c multi	26	18
614	A220	60c multi	42	26
615	A220	1.20d multi	90	42
616	A220	1.30d multi	90	52
617	A220	1.40d multi	1.00	52
		Nos. 613-617 (5)	3.48	1.90

3rd African Games, Algiers, July 13–28.

TB Patient Returning to Family A221

1978, Oct. 5 **Photo.** ***Perf. 13½x14***

618	A221	60c multi	50	25

Anti-tuberculosis campaign.

Holy Kaaba A222

1978, Oct. 28 **Photo.** ***Perf. 11½***

619	A222	60c multi	42	18

Pilgrimage to Mecca.

National Servicemen Building Road A223

1978, Nov. 4

620	A223	60c multi	42	22

African Unity Road from El Goleah to In Salah, inauguration.

Fibula A224

Jewelry: 1.35d, Pendant. 1.40d, Ankle ring.

1978, Dec. 21 **Photo.** ***Perf. 12x11½***

621	A224	1.20d multi	90	42
622	A224	1.35d multi	1.00	42
623	A224	1.40d multi	1.10	70

Pres. Boumediène—A225

1979, Jan. 7 **Photo.** ***Perf. 12x11½***

624	A225	60c grn, red & brn	42	14

Houari Boumediène, president of Algeria 1965–1978.

Torch and Books A226

1979, Jan. 27 **Photo.** ***Perf. 11½***

625	A226	60c multi	42	26

National Front of Liberation Party Congress.

Pres. Boumediène—A227

1979, Feb. 4 **Photo.** ***Perf. 11½***

626	A227	1.40d multi	1.00	42

40 days after death of Pres. Houari Boumediène.

Proclamation of New President A228

1979, Feb. 10

627	A228	2d multi	1.40	52

Election of Pres. Chadli Bendjedid.

Sheik Abdul-Hamid Ben Badis (1889–1940) A229

1979, Apr. 18 Photo. *Perf. 11½*

628	A229	60c multi	42	22

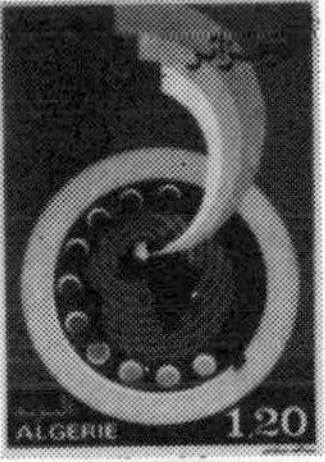

Telephone Dial, Map of Africa A230

1979, May 19 Photo. *Perf. 13½x14*

Design: 1.40d, Symbolic Morse key and waves.

629	A230	1.20d multi	80	35
630	A230	1.40d multi	95	35

Telecom '79 Exhibition, Geneva, Sept. 20–26.

Harvest, IYC Emblem A231

Design: 1.40d, Dancers and IYC emblem (vert.).

Perf. 11½x11, 11x11½

1979, June 21

631	A231	60c multi	42	18
632	A231	1.40d multi	95	52

International Year of the Child.

Nuthatch—A232

1979, Oct. 20 Photo. *Perf. 11½*

633	A232	1.40d multi	1.00	42

Flag, Soldiers and Workers—A233

Design: 3rd, Revolutionaries and emblem.

1979, Nov. 1 Photo. *Perf. 12½*

634	A233	1.40d multi	90	35

Size: 37×48mm. *Perf. 11½*

635	A233	3d multi	2.00	1.00

November 1 revolution, 25th anniversary.

Hegira, 1500 Anniv.—A234

1979, Dec. 2 Photo. *Perf. 11½*

636	A234	3d multi	1.90	95

Camels, Lion, Men and Slave—A235

Dionysian Procession (Setif Mosaic): 1.35d, Elephants, tigers and women. Men in tiger-drawn cart. Nos. 637-639 se-tenant in continuous design.

1980, Feb. 16 Photo. *Perf. 11½*

Granite Paper

637	A235	1.20d multi	80	35
638	A235	1.35d multi	90	52
639	A235	1.40d multi	95	70

Science Day—A236

1980, Apr. 19 Photo. *Perf. 12*

640	A236	60c multi	42	18

Dam and Workers—A237

1980, June 17 Photo. *Perf. 11½*

641	A237	60c multi	42	22

Extraordinary Congress of the National Liberation Front Party.

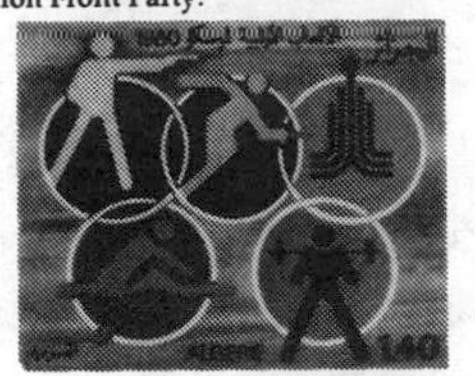

Olympic Sports, Moscow '80 Emblem—A238

1980, June 28

642	A238	50c Flame, rings, vert.	35	18
643	A238	1.40d *shown*	95	52

22nd Summer Olympic Games, Moscow, July 19-Aug. 3.

20th Anniversary of OPEC—A239

Engr.

1980, Sept. 15 *Perf. 11x10½, 10½x11*

644	A239	60c *Men holding OPEC emblem*, vert.	42	18
645	A239	1.40d *shown*	95	52

Aures Valley—A240

1980, Sept. 25 Litho. *Perf. 13½x14*

646	A240	50c *shown*	35	18
647	A240	1d *El Oued Oasis*	60	26
648	A240	1.40d *Tassili Rocks*	90	35
649	A240	2d *View of Algiers*	1.40	60

World Tourism Conference, Manila, Sept. 27.

Avicenna (980-1037), Philosopher and Physician—A241

1980, Oct. 25 Photo. *Perf. 12*

650	A241	2d multi	1.75	70

Ruins of El Asnam—A242

1980, Nov. 13 Photo. *Perf. 12*

651	A242	3d multi	1.90	70

Earthquake relief.

Crown—A243

1980, Dec. 20 Photo. *Perf. 12*

Granite Paper

652	A243	60c *Necklace*, vert.	42	26
653	A243	1.40d *Earrings, bracelet*, vert.	90	42
654	A243	2d *shown*	1.25	70

See Nos. 705-707.

1980-1984 Five-Year Plan—A244

1981, Jan. 29 Litho. *Perf. 14*

655	A244	60c multi	40	8

Basket Weaving—A245

1981, Feb. 19 Photo. *Perf. 12½*

Granite Paper

656	A245	40c shown	30	18
657	A245	60c Rug weaving	40	22
658	A245	1d Coppersmith	60	26
659	A245	1.40d Jeweler	90	48

Cedar Tree—A246

Arbor Day: 1.40d, Cypress tree (vert.).

1981, Mar. 19 Photo. *Perf. 12*
Granite Paper

660 A246 60c multi 45 14
661 A246 1.40d multi 85 48

Mohamed Bachir el Ibrahimi (1869-1965) A247

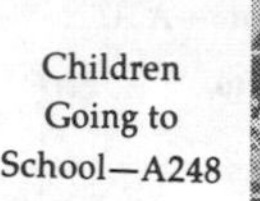

Children Going to School—A248

1981, Apr. 16 Granite Paper

662 A247 60c multi 40 18
663 A248 60c multi 40 8

Science Day.

12th International Hydatidological Congress, Algiers—A249

1981, Apr. 23 *Perf. 14x13½*

664 A249 2d multi 1.25 48

13th World Telecommunications Day—A250

1981, May 14 Photo. *Perf. 14x13½*

665 A250 1.40d multi 90 30

Disabled People and Hand Offering Flower—A251

1981, June 20 Litho. *Perf. 12½x13, 13x12½*

666 A251 1.20d Symbolic globe, vert. 80 26
667 A251 1.40d shown 90 26

Intl. Year of the Disabled.

Papilio Machaon—A252

1981, Aug. 20 Photo. *Perf. 11½*
Granite Paper

668 A252 60c shown 40 18
669 A252 1.20d Rhodocera rhamni 80 30
670 A252 1.40d Charaxes jasius 90 40
671 A252 2d Papilio podalirius 1.25 52

Monk Seal—A253

1981, Sept. 17 *Perf. 14x13½*

672 A253 60c shown 40 18
673 A253 1.40d Macaque 90 52

World Food Day A254

Cave Drawings of Tassili A255

1981, Oct. 16 Photo. *Perf. 14x14½*

674 A254 2d multi 1.25 52

1981, Nov. 21 *Perf. 11½*

Designs: Various cave drawings. 1.60d, 2d horiz.

675 A255 60c multi 40 22
676 A255 1d multi 60 26
677 A255 1.60d multi 1.00 48
678 A255 2d multi 1.25 60

Galley, 17-18th Cent.—A256

1981, Dec. 17 Photo. *Perf. 11½*

679 A256 60c shown 40 26
680 A256 1.60d Ship, diff. 1.00 52

1982 World Cup Soccer—A257

Designs: Various soccer players.

Litho.
1982, Feb. 25 *Perf. 13x12½x 12½x13*

681 A257 80c multi, vert. 52 22
682 A257 2.80d multi 1.75 75

TB Bacillus Centenary—A258

1982, Mar. 20 Photo. *Perf. 14½x14*

683 A258 80c multi 52 22

Painted Stand—A259

1982, Apr. 24 Photo. *Perf. 11½*
Granite Paper

684 A259 80c Mirror, vert. 52 26
685 A259 2d shown 1.25 60

Size: 48x33mm.

686 A259 2.40d Chest 1.50 80

Djamaael Djadid Mosque, Algiers—A260

1982, May 15 Litho. *Perf. 14*

687 A260 80c shown 52 22
688 A260 2.40d Sidi Boumediene Mosque, Tlemcen 1.40 70
689 A260 3d Garden of Dey, Algiers 1.90 85

Callitris Articulata A261

Independence, 20th Anniv. A262

Designs: Medicinal plants.

1982, May 27 Photo. *Perf. 11½*
Granite Paper

690 A261 50c shown 30 18
691 A261 80c Artemisia herba-alba 40 22
692 A261 1d Ricinus communis 70 30
693 A261 2.40d Thymus fontanesii 1.40 70

1982, July 5 Granite Paper

694 A262 50c Riflemen 30 18
695 A262 80c Soldiers, horiz. 48 26
696 A262 2d Symbols, citizens, horiz. 1.25 70

Souvenir Sheet

697 A262 5d Emblem 3.00 3.00

No. 697 contains one stamp (32x39mm.); green and red decorative margin. Size: 75x83mm.

Soummam Congress—A263

1982, Aug. 20 Litho.

698 A263 80c Congress building 52 18

Scouting Year—A264

1982, Oct. 21 Photo.
Granite Paper

699 A264 2.80d multi 1.75 70

Palestinian Child A265

Chlamydotis Undulata A266

1982, Nov. 25 Litho. *Perf. 10½*

700 A265 1.60d multi 1.50 50

1982, Dec. 23 Photo. Perf 15x14, 14x15

Protected birds. 50c, 2d horiz.

701 A266 50c Geronticus eremita 35 18
702 A266 80c shown 60 26
703 A266 2d Aguila rapax 1.25 60
704 A266 2.40d Gypaetus barbatus 1.50 70

Jewelry Type of 1980

1983, Feb. 10 *Perf. 11½*
Granite Paper

705 A243 50c Picture frame 30 18
706 A243 1d Flasks 60 42
707 A243 2d Brooch, horiz. 1.25 70

Intl. Arbor Day—A267

1983, Mar. 17 Photo.
Granite Paper

708 A267 80c Abies numidica, vert. 48 22
709 A267 2.80d Acacia raddiana 1.75 90

Minerals—A268

Various minerals. 70c, 80c vert.

1983, Apr. 21 Photo. ***Perf. 12x12½, 12½x12***
Granite Paper

710	A268 70c multi		42	18
711	A268 80c multi		48	26
712	A268 1.20d multi		75	52
713	A268 2.40d multi		1.40	90

30th Anniv. of Intl. Customs Cooperation Council—A269

1983, May 14 Photo. ***Perf. 11½***
Granite Paper

714	A269 80c multi	52	26

Emir Abdelkader Death Centenary—A270

1983, May 22 Photo. ***Perf. 12***
Granite Paper

715	A270 4d multi	2.50	1.10

Local Mushrooms—A271

1983, July 21 ***Perf. 14x15***

716	A271 50c Amanita muscaria	30	18
717	A271 80c Amanita phalloides	48	26
718	A271 1.40d Pleurotus eryngii	80	52
719	A271 2.80d Terfezia leonis	1.50	90

ibn-Khaldun, Historian, Philosopher—A272

1983, Sept. 1 Photo. ***Perf. 11½***

720	A272 80c multi	52	22

World Communications Year—A273

1983, Sept. 22 Litho. ***Perf. 11½x12½***

721	A273 80c Post Office, Algiers	52	22
722	A273 2.40d Telephone, circuit box	1.40	55

Goat and Tassili Mountains—A274

1983, Oct. 20 Litho. ***Perf. 12½x13***

723	A274 50c shown	30	18
724	A274 80c Tuaregs in native costume	48	26
725	A274 2.40d Animals, rock painting	1.40	60
726	A274 2.80d Rock formation	1.50	90

Sloughi Dog—A275

1983, Nov. 24 Photo. ***Perf. 14x14½, 14½x14***

727	A275 80c Sloughi, vert.	48	26
728	A275 2.40d shown	1.40	90

Natl. Liberation Party, 5th Congress—A276

1983, Dec. 19 Photo. ***Perf. 11½***

729	A276 80c Symbols of development	52	35

Souvenir Sheet

730	A276 5d Emblem	3.00	3.00

No. 730 contains one stamp (32x38mm.); multicolored decorative margin. Size: 75x83mm.

View of Oran, 1830—A277

1984, Jan. 26 Litho. ***Perf. 14***

731	A277 10c shown	5	5
732	A277 1d Sidi Abderahman and Taalibi Mosques	60	26
733	A277 2d Bejaia, 1830	1.25	52
734	A277 4d Constantine, 1830	2.50	90

See Nos. 745-747.

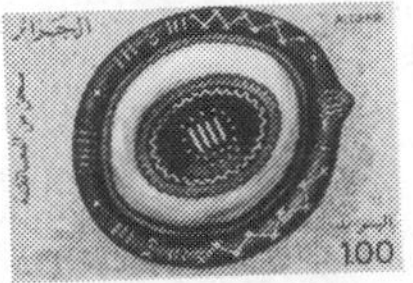

Pottery—A278

1984, Feb. 23 Photo. ***Perf. 11½x12, 12x11½***
Granite Paper

735	A278 80c Jug, vert.	52	35
736	A278 1d Platter	60	35
737	A278 2d Oil lamp, vert.	1.25	70
738	A278 2.40d Pitcher	1.50	90

Fountains of Old Algiers—A279

Various fountains.

1984, Mar. 22 Photo. ***Perf. 11½***
Granite Paper

739	A279 50c multi	30	22
740	A279 80c multi	55	30
741	A279 2.40d multi	1.50	90

1984 Summer Olympics—A280

1984, May 19 Photo. ***Perf. 11½***
Granite Paper

742	A280 1d multi	70	42

Brown Stallion—A281

1984, June 14 Photo. ***Perf. 11½***
Granite Paper

743	A281 80c shown	52	26
744	A281 2.40d White mare	1.50	90

View Type of 1984

1984 Litho. ***Perf. 14***

745	A277 5c Mustapha Pacha	5	5
746	A277 20c Bab Azzoun	14	5
746A	A277 30c Algiers	14	6
746B	A277 40c Kolea	18	8
746C	A277 50c Algiers	22	10
747	A277 70c Mostaganem	48	22
	Nos. 745-747 (6)	1.21	56

Issue dates: Nos. 745, 746, 747, July 19. Nos. 746A-746C, Oct. 20.

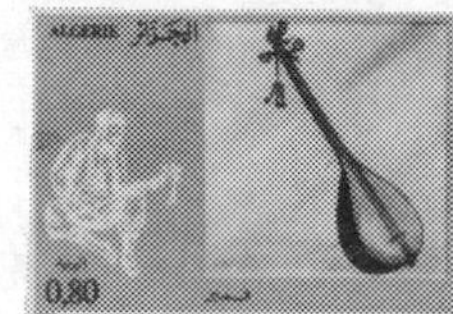

Lute—A282

Native musical instruments.

1984, Sept. 22 Litho. ***Perf. 15x14***

748	A282 80c shown	32	16
749	A282 1d Drum	40	20
750	A282 2.40d Fiddle	1.00	50
751	A282 2.80d Bagpipe	1.15	55

30th Anniv. of Algerian Revolution—A284

1984, Nov. 3 Photo. ***Perf. 11½x12***

757	A284 80c Partisans	32	16

Souvenir Sheet

758	A284 5d Algerian flags, vert.	2.00	1.00

Size: 75x82mm.

M'Zab Valley—A285

1984, Dec. 15 Photo. ***Perf. 15x14, 14x15***

759	A285 80c Map of valley	32	16
760	A285 2.40d Town of M'Zab, vert.	96	48

18th and 19th Century Metalware—A286

1985, Jan. 26 Photo. ***Perf. 11½***

761	A286 80c Coffee pot	32	16
762	A286 2d Bowl, horiz.	78	40
763	A286 2.40d Covered bowl	96	48

Fish—A287

1985, Feb. 23 **Photo.** ***Perf. 15x14***

764	A287	50c	Thunnus thynnus	20	10
765	A287	80c	Sparus aurata	30	15
766	A287	2.40d	Epinephelus guaza	90	45
767	A287	2.80d	Mustelus mustelus	1.00	50

National Games—A288

Granite Paper

1985, Mar. 28 ***Perf. 11½x12***

768	A288	80c	Doves, emblem	30	15

Environmental Conservation—A289

1985, Apr. 25 ***Perf. 13½***

769	A289	80c	Stylized trees	30	15
770	A289	1.40d	Stylized waves	55	28

The Casbah—A290

Perf. 13½x12½ on 3 or 4 Sides

1985, June 1

773	A290	20c	dk bl & buff	8	5
777	A290	80c	sage grn & buff	30	15
779	A290	2.40d	chnt & buff	90	45
a.			Bklt. pane of 5 (20c, 3 80c, 2.40d) + label	2.00	65
			Nos. 771-783 (13)	1.28	65

Issued only in booklet panes.

UN, 40th Anniv.—A291

1985, June 26 **Photo.** ***Perf. 14***

784	A291	1d	Dove, emblem, 40	40	20

Natl. Youth Festival—A292

1985, July 5 **Litho.** ***Perf. 13½***

785	A292	80c	multi	30	15

Intl. Youth Year—A293

1985, July 5

786	A293	80c	Silhouette, globe, emblem, vert.	30	15
787	A293	1.40d	Doves, globe	55	28

World Map, OPEC—A294

1985, Sept. 14 **Photo.** ***Perf. 12½x13***

788	A294	80c	multi	30	15

Organization of Petroleum Exporting Countries, 25th anniv.

Family Planning A295

El-Meniaa Township A296

1985, Oct. 3 **Litho.** ***Perf. 14***

789	A295	80c	Mother and sons	30	15
790	A295	1.40d	Weighing infant	55	28
791	A295	1.70d	Breast-feeding	68	35

1985, Oct. 24 **Engr.** ***Perf. 13***

792	A296	80c	Chetaibi Bay, horiz.	30	15
793	A296	2d	shown	78	40
794	A296	2.40d	Bou Noura Town, horiz.	95	48

The Palm Grove, by N. Dinet—A297

1985, Nov. 21 **Photo.** ***Perf. 11½x12***

Granite Paper

795	A297	2d	multi	78	40
796	A297	3d	multi, diff.	1.15	58

Tapestries—A298

Various designs.

1985, Dec. 19 **Granite Paper**

797	A298	80c	multi	30	15
798	A298	1.40d	multi	55	28
799	A298	2.40d	multi	95	48
800	A298	2.80d	multi	1.10	55

Wildcats—A299

1986, Jan. 23 ***Perf. 12x11½, 11½x12***

Granite Paper

801	A299	80c	Felis margarita	30	15
802	A299	1d	Felis caracal	40	20
803	A299	2d	Felis sylvestris	78	40
804	A299	2.40d	Felis serval, vert.	95	48

UN Child Survival Campaign

A300

Algerian General Worker's Union, 30th Anniv. A301

1986, Feb. 13 **Litho.** ***Perf. 13½***

805	A300	80c	Oral vaccine	30	15
806	A300	1.40d	Mother, child, sun	55	28
807	A300	1.70d	Three children	68	35

1986, Feb. 24 **Granite Paper** ***Perf. 12½***

808	A301	2d	multi	78	40

National Charter A302

Natl. Day of the Disabled A303

1986, Mar. 6 **Photo.** ***Perf. 11½***

Granite Paper

809	A302	4d	multi	1.60	80

1986, Mar. 15 ***Perf. 12½x13***

810	A303	80c	multi	30	15

Anti-Tuberculosis Campaign-A304

1986 World Cup Soccer Championships, Mexico-A305

1986, Apr. 17 **Litho.** ***Perf. 14x15***

811	A304	80c	multi	30	15

1986, Apr. 24 ***Perf. 14***

812	A305	2d	Soccer ball, sombrero	78	40

Inner Courtyards—A306

1986, May 15 **Photo.** ***Perf. 11½***

Granite Paper

814	A306	80c	multi	30	15
815	A306	2.40d	multi, diff.	95	48
816	A306	3d	multi, diff.	1.20	60

Blood Donation Campaign—A307

1986, June 26 Litho. *Perf. 13½*

817	A307	80c multi	32	16

Southern District Radio Communication Inauguration—A308

1986, July *Perf. 13*

818	A308	60c multi	24	12

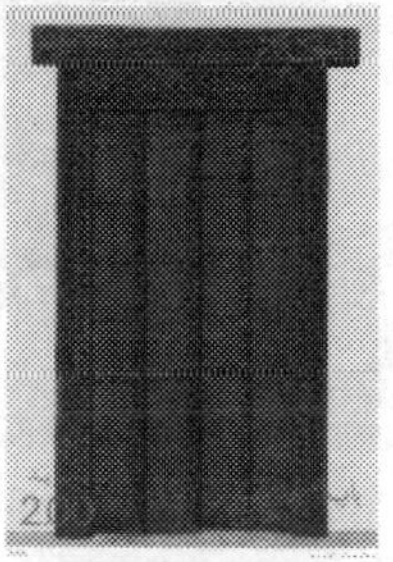

Mosque Gateways—A309

1986, Sept. 27 Photo. *Perf. 12x11½*
Granite Paper

819	A309	2d Door	78	40
820	A309	2.40d Ornamental arch	95	48

Intl. Peace Year—A310

1986, Oct. 16 Photo. *Perf. 13½x14½*

821	A310	2.40d multi	95	48

Folk Dancing—A311

1986, Nov. 22 Litho. *Perf. 14x13½*

822	A311	80c Woman, scarf	32	16
823	A311	2.40d Woman, diff.	95	48
824	A311	2.80d Man, sword	1.10	55

Flowers—A312

1986, Dec. 18 Photo. *Perf. 14*

825	A312	80c Narcissus tazetta	32	16
826	A312	1.40d Iris unguicularis	55	28
827	A312	2.40d Capparis spinosa	95	48
828	A312	2.80d Gladiolus segetum	1.10	55

Abstract Paintings by Mohammed Issia Khem—A313

1987, Jan. 29 Litho. *Perf. 11½x12, 12x11½*

829	A313	2d Man and woman, vert.	1.00	50
830	A313	5d Man and books	2.50	1.25

SEMI-POSTAL STAMPS.

Regular Issue of 1926 Surcharged in Black or Red

1927 *Perf. 14x13½.* **Unwmkd.**

B1	A1	5c +5c bl grn	50	50
B2	A1	10c +10c lil	50	50
B3	A2	15c +15c org brn	50	50
B4	A2	20c +20c car rose	50	50
B5	A2	25c +25c bl grn	50	50
B6	A2	30c +30c lt bl	50	50
B7	A2	35c +35c dp vio	50	50
B8	A2	40c +40c ol grn	50	50
B9	A3	50c +50c dp bl (R)	50	50
a.		Dbl. surch.	165.00	165.00
B10	A3	80c +80c red org	50	50
B11	A4	1fr +1fr gray grn & red brn	50	50
B12	A4	2fr +2fr Prus bl & blk brn	17.00	17.00
B13	A4	5fr +5fr red & vio	25.00	25.00
		Nos. B1-B13 (13)	47.50	47.50

The surtax was for the benefit of wounded soldiers. Government officials speculated in this issue.

Railroad Terminal, Oran
SP1

Ruins at Djemila
SP2

Mosque of Sidi Abd-er-Rahman
SP3

Designs: 10c+10c, Rummel Gorge, Constantine. 15c+15c, Admiralty Buildings, Algiers. 25c+25c, View of Algiers. 30c+30c, Trajan's Arch, Timgad. 40c+40c, Temple of the North, Djemila. 75c+75c Mansourah Minaret, Tlemcen. 1f+1f, View of Ghardaia. 1.50f+1.50f, View of Tolga. 2f+2f, Tuareg warriors. 3f+3f, Kasbah, Algiers.

1930 **Engraved.** *Perf. 12½.*

B14	SP1	5c +5c org	7.00	7.00
B15	SP1	10c +10c ol grn	7.00	7.00
B16	SP1	15c +15c dk brn	7.00	7.00
B17	SP1	25c +25c blk	7.00	7.00
B18	SP1	30c +30c dk red	7.00	7.00
B19	SP1	40c +40c ap grn	7.00	7.00
B20	SP2	50c +50c ultra	7.00	7.00
B21	SP2	75c +75c red pur	7.00	7.00
B22	SP2	1fr +1fr org red	7.00	7.00
B23	SP2	1.50fr +1.50fr dp ultra	7.00	7.00
B24	SP2	2fr +2fr dk car	7.00	7.00
B25	SP2	3fr +3fr dk grn	7.00	7.00
B26	SP3	5fr +5fr grn & car	15.00	15.00
a.		Center inverted	475.00	
		Nos. B14-B26 (13)	99.00	99.00

Issued in connection with the celebration of the centenary of the French occupation of Algeria. The surtax on the stamps was given to the funds for the celebration.

Nos. B14–B26 exist imperf. Price, set in pairs, $350.

No. 102 Surcharged in Red

1918-11 Nov.-1938
0.65 + 0.35
= =

1938 *Perf. 13.*

B27	A6	65c +35c on 2.25fr yel grn	60	60

20th anniversary of Armistice.

René Caillié, Charles Lavigerie and Henri Duveyrier—SP14

1939 **Engraved.**

B28	SP14	30c +20c dk bl grn	90	90
B29	SP14	90c +60c car rose	90	90
B30	SP14	2.25fr +75c ultra	9.00	9.00
B31	SP14	5fr +5fr brn blk	21.00	21.00

Pioneers of the Sahara.

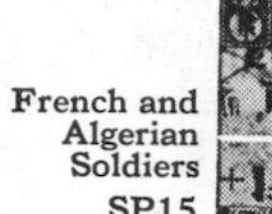

French and Algerian Soldiers
SP15

1940 **Photogravure** *Perf. 12*

B32	SP15	1fr +1fr bl & car	60	60
B33	SP15	1fr +2fr brn rose & blk	60	60
B34	SP15	1fr +4fr dp grn & red	90	90
B35	SP15	1fr +9fr brn & car	1.40	1.40

The surtax was used to assist the families of mobilized men.

Type of Regular Issue, 1941 Surcharged in Carmine **+ 4f**

1941 **Engraved.** *Perf. 13.*

B36	A19	1fr +4fr blk	26	26

No. 135 Surcharged in Carmine

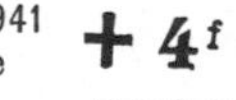

B37	A19	1fr +4fr dk bl	26	26

The surtax was for National Relief.

No. 124 Surcharged in Black "+60c"

1942

B38	A7	90c +60c hn brn	10	6
a.		Double surch.	80.00	

The surtax was used for National Relief. The stamp could also be used as 1.50 francs for postage.

Mother and Child
SP16

1943, Dec. 1 **Litho.** *Perf. 12*

B39	SP16	50c +4.50fr brt pink	48	48
B40	SP16	1.50fr +8.50fr lt grn	48	48
B41	SP16	3fr +12fr dp bl	48	48
B42	SP16	5fr +15fr vio brn	48	48

The surtax was for the benefit of soldiers and prisoners of war.

Planes over Fields
SP17

Engraved.

1945, July 2 *Perf. 13* **Unwmkd.**

B43	SP17	1.50fr +3.50fr lt ultra, red org & blk	35	35

The surtax was for the benefit of Algerian airmen and their families.

France No. B192 Overprinted in Black

ALGÉRIE
a

1945

B44	SP146	4fr +6fr dk vio brn	30	30

The surtax was for war victims of the P. T. T.

Overprinted in Blue on Type of France, 1945.

1945, Oct. 15

B45	SP150	2fr +3fr dk brn	52	52

For Stamp Day.

Overprinted in Blue on Type of France, 1946.

1946, June 29

B46	SP160	3fr +2fr red	70	70

For Stamp Day.

Children Playing by Stream
SP18

Girl
SP19

Athlete
SP20

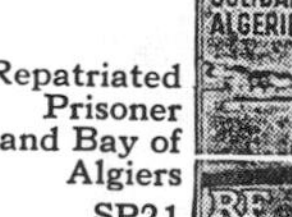

Repatriated Prisoner and Bay of Algiers
SP21

1946, Oct. 2 **Engraved** *Perf. 13*

B47	SP18	3fr +17fr dk grn	1.00	1.00
B48	SP19	4fr +21fr red	1.00	1.00
B49	SP20	8fr +27fr rose lil	4.50	4.50
B50	SP21	10fr +35fr dk bl	1.10	1.10

Type of France, 1947, Overprinted type "a" in Carmine.

1947, Mar. 15

B51	SP172	4.50fr +5.50fr dp ultra	55	55

For Stamp Day.

Same on Type of France, 1947, Surcharged Like No. B36 in Carmine.

1947, Nov. 13

B52	A173	5fr +10fr dk Prus grn	52	52

Type of France, 1948, Overprinted in Dark Green

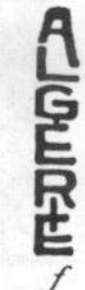

1948, Mar. 6

B53	SP176	6fr +4fr dk grn	70	70

For Stamp Day.

Type of France, 1948, Overprinted type "a" in Blue and New Value.

1948, May

B54	A176	6fr +4fr red	52	52

Battleship Richelieu and the Admiralty, Algiers
SP22

Aircraft Carrier Arromanches
SP23

Engraved.

1949, Jan. 15 *Perf. 13* **Unwmkd.**

B55	SP22	10fr +15fr dp bl	5.75	5.75
B56	SP23	18fr +22fr red	5.75	5.75

The surtax was for naval charities.

Type of France, 1949, Overprinted in Blue

ALGÉRIE
g

1949, Mar. 26

B57	SP180	15fr +5fr lil rose	1.40	1.40

For Stamp Day, Mar. 26–27.

Type of France, 1950, Overprinted type "f" in Green.

1950, Mar. 11

B58	SP183	12fr +3fr blk brn	1.40	1.40

For Stamp Day, Mar. 11–12.

Foreign Legionary
SP24

1950, Apr. 30

B59	SP24	15fr +5fr dk grn	1.75	1.75

Charles de Foucauld and Gen. J. F. H. Laperrine
SP25

1950, Aug. 21 *Perf. 13* **Unwmkd.**

B60	SP25	25fr +5fr brn ol & brn blk	4.25	4.25

50th anniversary of the presence of the French in the Sahara.

Emir Abd-el-Kader and Marshal T. R. Bugeaud
SP26

1950, Aug. 21

B61	SP26	40fr +10fr dk brn & blk brn	4.25	4.25

Unveiling of a monument to Emir Abd-el-Kader at Cacheron.

Col. Colonna d'Ornano and Fine Arts Museum, Algiers
SP27

1951, Jan. 11

B62	SP27	15fr +5fr blk brn, vio brn & red brn	90	90

Issued to commemorate the tenth anniversary of the death of Col. Colonna d'Ornano.

Type of France, 1951, Overprinted type "a" in Black.

1951, Mar. 10

B63	SP186	12fr +3fr brn	1.25	1.25

For Stamp Day.

Type of France, 1952, Overprinted type "g" in Dark Blue.

1952, Mar. 8 ***Perf. 13*** **Unwmkd.**

B64	SP190	12fr +3fr dk bl	2.00	2.00

For Stamp Day.

French Military Medal
SP28

Engraved.

1952, July 5 ***Perf. 13*** **Unwmkd.**

B65	SP28	15fr +5fr grn, yel & brn	2.00	2.00

Issued to commemorate the centenary of the creation of the French Military Medal.

Type of France 1952, Surcharged type "g" and Surtax in Black

1952, Sept. 15

B66	A222	30fr +5fr dp ultra	1.75	1.75

Issued to commemorate the 10th anniversary of the defense of Bir-Hakeim.

View of El Oued
SP29

Design: 12fr+3fr, View of Bou-Noura.

1952, Nov. 15 **Engraved**

B67	SP29	8fr +2fr ultra & red	1.75	1.75
B68	SP29	12fr +3fr red	2.50	2.50

The surtax was for the Red Cross.

Type of France, 1953, Overprinted type "a" in Black.

1953, Mar. 14 **Engraved**

B69	SP193	12fr +3fr pur	1.50	1.40

For Stamp Day. Surtax for Red Cross.

Victory of Cythera
SP30

Engraved.

1953, Dec. 18 ***Perf. 13*** **Unwmkd.**

B70	SP30	15fr +5fr blk brn & brn	90	90

The surtax was for army welfare work.

Type of France, 1954, Overprinted type "a" in Black.

1954, Mar. 20 ***Perf. 13*** **Unwmkd.**

B71	SP196	12fr +3fr scar	1.00	1.00

For Stamp Day.

Soldiers and Flags **SP31** — **Foreign Legionary** **SP32**

1954, Mar. 27

B72	SP31	15fr +5fr dk brn	52	52

The surtax was for old soldiers.

1954, Apr. 30

B73	SP32	15fr +5fr dk grn	1.40	1.40

The surtax was for the welfare fund of the Foreign Legion.

Nurses and Verdun Hospital, Algiers—SP33

Design: 15fr+5fr, J. H. Dunant & ruins at Djemila.

1954, Oct. 30

B74	SP33	12fr +3fr ind & red	3.00	3.00
B75	SP33	15fr +5fr pur & red	3.50	3.50

The surtax was for the Red Cross.

Earthquake Victims and Ruins **SP34** — **First Aid** **SP35**

Designs: 15fr+5fr, As No. B76, 20fr+7fr, As No. B78. 25fr+8fr & 30fr+10fr, Removing wounded.

1954, Dec. 5

B76	SP34	12fr +4fr dk vio brn	1.90	1.90
B77	SP34	15fr +5fr dp bl	1.90	1.90
B78	SP35	18fr +6fr lil rose	2.25	2.25
B79	SP35	20fr +7fr vio	2.25	2.25
B80	SP35	25fr +8fr rose brn	2.50	2.50
B81	SP35	30fr +10fr brt bl grn	2.50	2.50
		Nos. B76-B81 (6)	13.30	13.30

The surtax was for victims of the Orleansville earthquake disaster of September 1954.

Type of France, 1955, Overprinted type "a" in Black.

1955, Mar. 19

B82	SP199	12fr +3fr dp ultra	1.25	1.25

For Stamp Day, Mar. 19—20.

Women and Children **SP36** — **Cancer Victim** **SP37**

1955, Nov. 5

B83	SP36	15fr +5fr bl & ind	70	70

The tax was for war victims.

1956, Mar. 3 ***Perf. 13*** **Unwmkd.**

B84	SP37	15fr +5fr dk brn	70	70

The surtax was for the Algerian Cancer Society. The male figure in the design is Rodin's "Age of Bronze."

Type of France, 1956, Overprinted type "a" in Black.

1956, Mar.

B85	SP202	12fr +3fr red	70	70

For Stamp Day, Mar. 17—18.

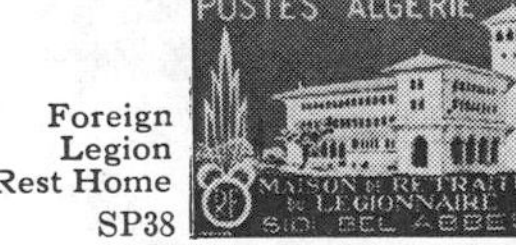

Foreign Legion Rest Home
SP38

1956, Apr. 29

B86	SP38	15fr +5fr dk bl grn	1.50	1.50

Issued in honor of the French Foreign Legion.

Type of France, 1957, Overprinted type "f" in Black

1957, Mar. 16 **Engraved** ***Perf. 13***

B87	SP204	12fr +3fr dl pur	1.00	1.00

For Stamp Day and to honor the Maritime Postal Service.

Fennec
SP39

Design: 15fr+5fr, Stork flying over roofs.

1957, Apr. 6

B88	SP39	12fr +3fr red brn & red	5.75	5.75
B89	SP39	15fr +5fr sep & red	5.75	5.75

The surtax was for the Red Cross.

Type of Regular Issue, 1956 Surcharged in Dark Blue

18 JUIN 1940
+ 5F

1957, June 18

B90	A53	15fr +5fr scar & rose red	90	90

Issued to commemorate the 17th anniversary of General de Gaulle's appeal for a Free France.

The Giaour, by Delacroix
SP40

On the Banks of the Oued, by Fromentin
SP41

Design: 35fr+10fr, Dancer, by Chasseriau.

Engraved.

1957, Nov. 30 ***Perf. 13*** **Unwmkd.**

B91	SP40	15fr +5fr dk car	5.25	5.25
B92	SP41	20fr +5fr grn	5.25	5.25
B93	SP40	35fr +10fr dk bl	5.25	5.25

The surtax was for army welfare organizations.

Type of France Overprinted type "f" in Blue.

1958, Mar. 15 ***Perf. 13*** **Unwmkd.**

B94	SP206	15fr +5fr org brn	1.00	1.00

For Stamp Day.

Bird-of-Paradise Flower **SP42** — **Arms and Marshal's Baton** **SP43**

1958, June 14 **Engr.** ***Perf. 13***

B95	SP42	20fr +5fr grn, org & vio	2.50	2.50

The surtax was for Child Welfare.

1958, July 20

B96	SP43	20fr +5fr ultra, car & grn	1.50	1.50

Issued for the Marshal de Lattre Foundation.

Independent State

Clasped Hands, Wheat and Olive Branch
SP44

Burning Books
SP45

1963, May 27 *Perf. 13* Unwmkd.

B97	SP44	50c +20c sl grn, brt grn & car	1.25	90

The surtax was for the National Solidarity Fund.

1965, June 7 Engraved *Perf. 13*

B98	SP45	20c +5c ol grn, red & blk	52	38

Issued to commemorate the burning of the Library of Algiers, June 7, 1962.

Soldiers and Woman Comforting Wounded Soldier
SP46

1966, Aug. 20 Photo. *Perf. 11½*

B99	SP46	30c +10c multi	1.00	90
B100	SP46	95c +10c multi	2.00	1.50

Issued for the Day of the Moudjahid (Moslem volunteers).

Red Crescent, Boy and Girl
SP47

1967, May 27 Litho. *Perf. 14*

B101	SP47	30c +10c brt grn, brn & car	70	52

Algerian Red Crescent Society.

Flood Victims
SP48

Design: 95c+25c, Rescuing flood victims.

1969, Nov. 15 Typo. *Perf. 10½*

B102	SP48	30c +10c dl bl, sal & blk	70	52

Lithographed

B103	SP48	95c +25c multi	1.50	1.00

Red Crescent Flag
SP49

1971, May 17 Engraved *Perf. 10½*

B104	SP49	30c +10c sl grn & car	52	42

Algerian Red Crescent Society.

AIR POST STAMPS.

Plane over Algiers Harbor
AP1

Two types of 20fr:

Type I. Monogram "F" without serifs. "POSTE" indented 3mm.

Type II. Monogram "F" with serifs. "POSTE" indented 4½mm.

Engraved.

1946, June 20 *Perf. 13.* Unwmkd.

C1	AP1	5fr red	6	5
C2	AP1	10fr dp bl	6	5
C3	AP1	15fr dp grn	52	5
C4	AP1	20fr brn (II)	26	5
C4A	AP1	20fr brn (I)	110.00	77.50
C5	AP1	25fr violet	60	14
C6	AP1	40fr gray blk	70	14
		Nos. C1-C4, C5-C6 (6)	2.20	48

No. C1 Surcharged in Black **—10 %**

1947, Jan. 18

C7		AP1(4.50fr) on 5fr red	5	5

Storks over Mosque
AP2

Plane over Village
AP3

1949–53

C8	AP2	50fr green	3.25	42
C9	AP3	100fr brown	2.50	42
C10	AP2	200fr brt red	6.50	4.25
C11	AP3	500fr ultra ('53)	21.00	15.00

Beni Bahdel Dam
AP4

1957, July 1 *Perf. 13* Unwmkd.

C12	AP4	200fr dk red	5.25	1.25

Caravelle over Ghardaia
AP5

Designs: 2d, Caravelle over El Oued. 5d, Caravelle over Tipasa.

1967–68 Engraved *Perf. 13*

C13	AP5	1d lil, org brn & emer	1.25	60
C14	AP5	2d brt bl, org brn & emer	3.00	1.50
C15	AP5	5d brt bl, grn & org brn ('68)	7.75	3.50

Plane over Casbah, Algiers
AP6

Designs: 3d, Plane over Oran. 4d, Plane over Rhumel Gorge.

1971–72 Photogravure *Perf. 12½*

C16	AP6	2d grysh blk & multi	1.90	1.00
C17	AP6	3d vio & blk ('72)	3.00	1.75
C18	AP6	4d blk & multi ('72)	4.00	2.25

Issue dates: 2d, June 12, 1971; 3d, 4d, Feb. 28, 1972.

AIR POST SEMI-POSTAL STAMPS.

No. C2 Surcharged in Carmine

‡
18 Juin 1940
+10Fr.

1947, June 18 *Perf. 13.*

CB1	AP1	10fr +10fr dp bl	70	70

Issued to commemorate the 7th anniversary of Gen. Charles de Gaulle's speech in London, June 18, 1940.

No. C1 Surcharged in Blue

‡
18 JUIN 1940
+10 Fr.

1948, June 18

CB2	AP1	5fr +10fr red	70	70

Issued to commemorate the 8th anniversary of Gen. Charles de Gaulle's speech in London, June 18, 1940.

Monument, Clock Tower and Plane
SPAP1

1949, Nov. 10 Engraved Unwmkd.

CB3	SPAP1	15fr +20fr dk brn	4.25	4.25

Issued to commemorate the 25th anniversary of Algeria's first postage stamps.

POSTAGE DUE STAMPS.

D1

D2

Perf. 14x13½.

1926-27 Typographed. Unwmkd

J1	D1	5c lt bl	5	
J2	D1	10c dk brn	5	
J3	D1	20c ol grn	26	2
J4	D1	25c car rose	52	5
J5	D1	30c rose red	26	2
J6	D1	45c bl grn	60	5
J7	D1	50c brn vio	5	
J8	D1	60c grn ('27)	1.90	5
J9	D1	1fr red brn, *straw*	18	1
J10	D1	2fr lil rose ('27)	26	2
J11	D1	3fr dp bl ('27)	26	2
		Nos. J1-J11 (11)	4.39	2.8

1926-27

J12	D2	1c ol grn	5	
J13	D2	10c violet	60	2
J14	D2	30c bister	52	3
J15	D2	60c dl red	35	3
J16	D2	1fr brt vio ('27)	14.00	2.5
J17	D2	2fr lt bl ('27)	10.00	1.0
		Nos. J12-J17 (6)	25.52	4.4

See note below France No. J51.

Stamps of 1926
1927 Surcharged with New Values.

J18	D1	60c on 20c ol grn	1.25	42
J19	D1	2fr on 45c bl grn	1.50	1.00
J20	D1	3fr on 25c car rose	70	42

Recouvrement Stamps of 1926 Surcharged **= 10c**

1927-32

J21	D2	10c on 30c bis ('32)	2.50	2.25
J22	D2	1fr on 1c ol grn	1.00	90
J23	D2	1fr on 60c dl red ('32)	16.00	35
J24	D2	2fr on 10c vio	9.50	9.50

Type of 1926, Without "R F".

1942 Typographed *Perf. 14x13½*

J25	D1	30c dk red	6	6
J26	D1	2fr magenta	26	26

Type of 1926 Surcharged in Red **T 0.50**

1944 *Perf. 14x13½.*

J27	A2	50c on 20c yel grn	18	14
a.		Inverted surch.	5.25	
b.		Double surch.	14.00	

No. J27 was issued precanceled only. See note after No. 32.

Type of 1926.

1944 Lithographed. *Perf. 12.*

J28	D1	1.50fr brt rose lil	42	35
J29	D1	2fr grnsh bl	42	35
J30	D1	5fr rose car	42	30

Type of 1926.

1947 Typographed *Perf. 14x13½*

J32	D1	5fr green	90	70

France Nos. J80–J81 Overprinted in Carmine or Black **ALGÉRIE**

1947

J33	D5	10c sep (C)	18	14
J34	D5	30c brt red vio	18	14

D3

Engraved.

1947-55 *Perf. 14x13* Unwmkd.

J35	D3	20c red	18	18
J36	D3	60c ultra	35	30
J37	D3	1fr dk org brn	5	5
J38	D3	1.50fr dl grn	60	55
J39	D3	2fr red	5	5

J40	D3	3fr	violet	10	10
J41	D3	5fr	ultra ('49)	18	14
J42	D3	6fr	black	30	26
J43	D3	10fr	lil rose	30	18
J44	D3	15fr	ol grn ('55)	70	70
J45	D3	20fr	brt grn	35	18
J46	D3	30fr	red org ('55)	60	55
J47	D3	50fr	ind ('51)	1.40	1.40
J48	D3	100fr	brt bl ('53)	6.00	5.00
			Nos. J35-J48 (14)	11.16	9.64

Independent State

France Nos. J93-J97 Overprinted "EA" in Black like Nos. 286-290

Perf. 14x13½

1962, July 2 Typo. Unwmkd.

Handstamped Overprint

J49	D6	5c	brt pink	3.50	2.50
J50	D6	10c	red org	3.50	1.90
J51	D6	20c	ol bis	3.50	1.90
J52	D6	50c	dk grn	5.50	4.25
J53	D6	1fr	dp grn	8.00	7.50
			Nos. J49-J53 (5)	24.00	18.05

Typographed Overprint

J49a	D6	5c	brt pink	9.00	9.00
J50a	D6	10c	red org	9.00	9.00
J51a	D6	20c	ol bis	8.00	8.00
J52a	D6	50c	dk grn	21.00	21.00
J53a	D6	1fr	dp grn	37.50	37.50
			Nos. J49a-J53a (5)	84.50	84.50

See note after No. 290.

Scales—D4

Grain—D5

1963, June 25 *Perf. 14x13½*

J54	D4	5c	car rose & blk	8	5
J55	D4	10c	ol & car	18	8
J56	D4	20c	ultra & blk	26	14
J57	D4	50c	bis brn & grn	70	52
J58	D4	1fr	lil & org	1.40	1.00
			Nos. J54-J58 (5)	2.62	1.79

No. J58 Surcharged with New Value and 3 Bars

1968, Mar. 28 Typo. *Perf. 14x13½*

J59	D4	60c	on 1fr lil & org	60	42

1972, Oct. 21 Litho. *Perf. 13½x14*

J60	D5	10c	bister	6	6
J61	D5	20c	dp brn	10	6
J62	D5	40c	orange	30	12
J63	D5	50c	dk vio bl	32	14
J64	D5	80c	dk ol gray	55	20
J65	D5	1d	green	65	38
J66	D5	2d	blue	1.40	65
			Nos. J60-J66 (7)	3.38	1.61

NEWSPAPER STAMPS.

No. 1 Surcharged in Red

1/2 centime

1924 *Perf. 14x13½* **Unwmkd.**

P1	A16	½c	on 1c dk gray	5	5
a.			Triple surcharge	87.50	

1926

Same Surcharge in Red on No. 33

P2	A1	½c	on 1c ol	14	14

ALLENSTEIN

(äl'ĕn·shtīn)

LOCATION—In East Prussia.

AREA—4,457 sq. mi.

POP.—540,000 (estimated 1920).

CAPITAL—Allenstein.

Allenstein, a district of East Prussia, held a plebiscite in 1920 under the Versailles Treaty, voting to join Germany rather than Poland. Later that year, Allenstein became part of the German Republic.

100 Pfennig = 1 Mark

Stamps of Germany, 1906-20, Overprinted

PLÉBISCITE
OLSZTYN
ALLENSTEIN

Perf. 14, 14½, 14x14½, 14½x14

1920 Wmkd. Lozenges. (125)

1	A16	5pf	green	25	25
2	A16	10pf	carmine	25	25
3	A22	15pf	dk vio	25	25
4	A22	15pf	vio brn	8.00	8.00
5	A16	20pf	bl vio	25	25
6	A16	30pf	org & blk, *buff*	38	38
7	A16	40pf	lake & blk	28	28
8	A16	50pf	pur & blk, *buff*	30	30
9	A16	75pf	grn & blk	30	28
10	A17	1m	car rose	1.00	1.00
a.			Double ovpt.	500.00	825.00
11	A17	1.25m	green	85	85
a.			Double ovpt.	650.00	1,400.
12	A17	1.50m	yel brn	85	85
13	A21	2.50m	lil rose	1.00	2.50
14	A19	3m	blk vio	2.00	2.00
a.			Double ovpt.	450.00	1,250.
b.			Inverted overprint	500.00	825.00
			Nos. 1-14 (14)	15.96	17.44

Overprinted

15	A16	5pf	green	25	38
16	A16	10pf	carmine	25	38
17	A22	15pf	dk vio	25	25
18	A22	15pf	vio brn	35.00	40.00
19	A16	20pf	bl vio	25	25
20	A16	30pf	org & blk, *buff*	38	38
21	A16	40pf	lake & blk	38	38
22	A16	50pf	pur & blk, *buff*	25	25
23	A16	75pf	grn & blk	25	25
24	A17	1m	car rose	85	85
a.			Inverted overprint	750.00	1,000.
25	A17	1.25m	green	85	85
26	A17	1.50m	yel brn	85	85
27	A21	2.50m	lil rose	1.25	2.50
28	A19	3m	blk vio	1.50	1.50
a.			Inverted overprint	400.00	750.00
b.			Double ovpt.	375.00	600.00
			Nos 15-28 (14)	42.56	49.07

The 40pf carmine rose (Germany No. 124) exists with this oval overprint, but it is doubtful whether it was regularly issued. Price $400.

ANATOLIA

(ăn'ȧ·tō'lĭ·ȧ)

See Turkey in Asia, Vol. IV.

ANDORRA

(ăn·dŏr'ȧ)

LOCATION—On the southern slope of the Pyrenees Mountains between France and Spain.

GOVT.—Co-principality.

AREA—179 sq. mi.

POP.—26,500 (1976).

CAPITAL—Andorre-la-Vieille.

Andorra is subject to the joint control of France and the Spanish Bishop of Urgel and pays annual tribute to both. The country has no monetary unit of its own, the peseta and franc both being in general use.

100 Centimos = 1 Peseta
100 Centimes = 1 Franc

Spanish Administration.

Stamps of Spain, 1922-26, Overprinted in Red or Black

:-: CORREOS :-:
ANDORRA

Perf. 14, 13½x12½, 12½x11½.

1928 Unwmkd.

1	A49	2c	ol grn	30	20

Control Numbers on Back

2	A49	5c	car rose (Bk)	40	30
3	A49	10c	green	40	30
4	A49	15c	sl bl	2.00	2.00
5	A49	20c	violet	2.00	2.00
6	A49	25c	rose red (Bk)	2.00	2.00
7	A49	30c	blk brn	11.50	7.00
8	A49	40c	dp bl	11.50	5.00
9	A49	50c	org (Bk)	11.50	7.25
10	A49a	1p	bl blk	14.00	10.00
11	A49a	4p	lake (Bk)	100.00	85.00
12	A49a	10p	brn (Bk)	165.00	120.00
			Nos. 1-12 (12)	320.60	241.05

Counterfeit overprints exist.

La Vall
A1

St. Juan de Caselles
A2

St. Julia de Loria
A3

St. Coloma
A4

General Council
A5

1929 Engraved *Perf. 14, 11½*

13	A1	2c	ol grn	1.00	30
a.			Perf. 11½	7.50	60

Control Numbers on Back

14	A2	5c	car lake	2.25	40
a.			Perf. 11½	7.50	1.75
15	A3	10c	yel grn	2.25	1.50
a.			Perf. 11½	12.00	2.25
16	A4	15c	sl grn	2.25	1.50
a.			Perf. 11½	40.00	27.50
17	A3	20c	violet	2.25	1.50
a.			Perf. 11½	12.00	6.75
18	A4	25c	car rose	5.50	2.25
a.			Perf. 11½	12.00	6.75
19	A1	30c	ol brn	100.00	65.00
a.			Perf. 11½	120.00	75.00
20	A2	40c	dk bl	4.50	1.00
a.			Perf. 11½	20.00	15.00
21	A3	50c	dp org	4.50	1.50
22	A5	1p	slate	9.50	5.00
a.			Perf. 11½	50.00	27.50
b.			Perf. 11½, control # omitted	2,750.	
23	A5	4p	dp rose	72.50	35.00
24	A5	10p	bis brn	80.00	50.00
			Nos. 13-24 (12)	286.50	164.95

Nos. 13-24, 26, 28, 32 exist imperforate.

Without Control Numbers.

1936-43 *Perf. 11½x11*

25	A1	2c	red brn ('37)	1.65	70
26	A2	5c	dk brn	1.65	70
27	A3	10c	bl grn	8.25	1.50
a.			10c yel grn	100.00	24.00
28	A4	15c	grn ('37)	5.00	1.50
29	A3	20c	violet	5.00	1.50
30	A4	25c	dp rose ('37)	1.90	1.50
31	A1	30c	carmine	3.50	1.50
31A	A2	40c	dk bl	*650.00*	30.00
32	A1	45c	rose red ('37)	1.50	70
33	A3	50c	dp org	7.00	2.75
34	A1	60c	dp bl ('37)	5.00	1.50
35	A5	4p	dp rose ('43)	26.00	24.00
36	A5	10p	bis brn ('43)	37.50	24.00
			Nos. 25-36 (13)	*753.95*	91.85

Edelweiss
A6

Provost
A7

Coat of Arms
A8

Plaza of Ordino
A9

Chapel of Meritxell
A10

Map
A11

Photogravure.

1948-53 *Perf. 12½* **Unwmkd.**

37	A6	2c	dk ol grn ('51)	50	30
38	A6	5c	dp org ('53)	50	30
39	A6	10c	dp bl ('53)	50	30

Engraved

Perf. 9½x10

40	A7	20c	brn vio	15.00	1.25
41	A7	25c	org, perf. 12½ ('53)	9.25	65
42	A8	30c	dk sl grn	15.00	1.70
43	A9	50c	dp grn	18.00	2.25
44	A10	75c	dk bl	24.00	2.25
45	A9	90c	dp car rose	12.00	2.25
46	A10	1p	brt org ver	18.00	2.25
47	A8	1.35p	dk bl vio	12.00	3.25

Perf. 10.

48	A11	4p	ultra ('53)	18.00	6.00
49	A11	10p	dk vio brn ('51)	37.50	14.00
			Nos. 37-49 (13)	180.25	36.75

Bridge of St. Anthony
A12

Madonna of Meritxell, 8th Century
A13

Designs: 70c, Aynos pasture. 1p, View of Canillo. 2p, St. Coloma. 2.50p, Arms of Andorra. 3p, Old Andorra (horiz.). 5p, View of Ordino (horiz.).

Engraved

1963-64 ***Perf. 13*** **Unwmkd.**

50	A12	25c dk gray & sep	25	6
51	A12	70c dk sl grn & brn blk	25	6
52	A12	1p sl & dl pur	40	6
53	A12	2p vio & dl pur	40	6
54	A12	2.50p rose cl ('64)	1.00	60
55	A12	3p blk & grnsh gray ('64)	1.75	60
56	A12	5p dk brn & choc ('64)	2.75	1.10
57	A13	6p sep & car ('64)	4.25	1.10
		Nos. 50-57 (8)	11.05	3.64

Narcissus
A14

Encamp Valley
A15

Flowers: 1p, Pinks. 5p, Jonquils. 10p, Hellebore.

1966, June 10 **Engraved** ***Perf. 13***

58	A14	50c sl bl & vio bl	10	10
59	A14	1p brn & cl	25	10
60	A14	5p brt grn & sl bl	1.50	60
61	A14	10p dk vio & blk	3.25	75

Europa Issue 1972

Common Design Type

1972, May 2 **Photo.** ***Perf. 13***

Size: 25½x38mm.

62	CD15	8p dk grn & multi	200.00	135.00

1972, July 4 **Photo.** ***Perf. 13***

Designs: 1.50p, Massana (village). 2p, Skiing on De La Casa Pass. 5p, Pessons Lake (horiz.).

63	A15	1p multi	25	10
64	A15	1.50p multi	80	45
65	A15	2p multi	1.90	45
66	A15	5p multi	2.50	80

Tourist publicity.

Butterfly Stroke
A16

Design: 2p, Volleyball (vert.).

1972, Oct. **Photo.** ***Perf. 13***

67	A16	2p lt bl & multi	60	30
68	A16	5p multi	70	40

20th Olympic Games, Munich, Aug. 26–Sept. 11.

Common Design Types pictured in section at front of book.

St. Anthony Singers
A17

1972, Dec. 5 **Photo.** ***Perf. 13***

Multicolored

69	A17	1p *shown*	20	6
70	A17	1.50p *Les Caramelles (boys' choir)*	20	6
71	A17	2p *Nativity scene*	15	10
72	A17	5p *Man holding giant cigar* (vert.)	90	15
73	A17	8p *Hermit of Meritxell* (vert.)	1.10	45
74	A17	15p *Marratxa dancers*	2.75	65
		Nos. 69-74 (6)	5.30	1.47

Andorran customs. No. 71 is for Christmas 1972.

Europa Issue 1973

Common Design Type and

Symbol of Unity
A18

1973, Apr. 30 **Photo.** ***Perf. 13***

75	A18	2p ultra, red & blk	40	20

Size: 37x25mm.

76	CD16	8p tan, red & blk	1.65	55

Nativity
A19

Virgin of Ordino
A20

Design: 5p, Adoration of the Kings. Designs are from altar panels of Meritxell Parish Church.

1973, Dec. 14 **Photo.** ***Perf. 13***

77	A19	2p multi	25	20
78	A19	5p multi	1.00	40

Christmas 1973.

Europa Issue 1974

1974, Apr. 29 **Photo.** ***Perf. 13***

Design: 8p, Les Banyes Cross.

79	A20	2p multi	1.25	30
80	A20	8p sl & brt bl	3.75	1.00

Cupboard
A21

Crowns of Virgin and Child of Roser
A22

1974, July 30 **Photo.** ***Perf. 13***

81	A21	10p multi	1.65	60
82	A22	25p dk red & multi	4.00	1.50

UPU Monument, Bern
A23

1974, Oct. **Photogravure** ***Perf. 13***

83	A23	15p multi	2.00	75

Centenary of Universal Postal Union.

Nativity
A24

Design: 5p, Adoration of the Kings.

1974, Dec. 4 **Photo.** ***Perf. 13***

84	A24	2p multi	60	20
85	A24	5p multi	2.25	45

Christmas 1974.

Mail Delivery, Andorra, 19th Century
A25

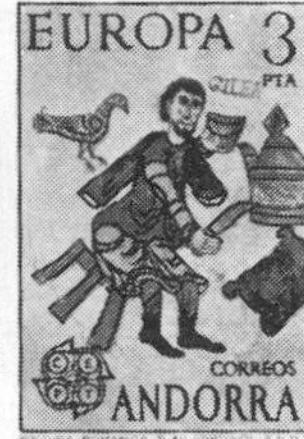

12th Century Painting, Ordino Church
A26

1975, Apr. 4 **Photo.** ***Perf. 13***

86	A25	3p multi	45	18

España 75 International Philatelic Exhibition, Madrid, Apr. 4–13.

1975, Apr. 28 **Photo.** ***Perf. 13***

Design: 12p, Christ in Glory, 12th century Romanesque painting, Ordino church.

87	A26	3p multi	1.75	40
88	A26	12p multi	3.25	65

Urgel Cathedral and Document
A27

1975, Oct. 4 **Photo.** ***Perf. 13***

89	A27	7p multi	2.25	1.10

Millennium of consecration of Urgel Cathedral, and Literary Festival 1975.

Nativity, Ordino
A28

Design: 7p, Adoration of the Kings, Ordino.

1975, Dec. 3 **Photo.** ***Perf. 13***

90	A28	3p multi	45	20
91	A28	7p multi	65	35

Christmas 1975.

Caldron and CEPT Emblem
A29

Slalom and Montreal Olympic Emblem
A30

Europa Issue 1976

Design: 12p, Chest and CEPT emblem (horiz.).

1976, May 3 **Photo.** ***Perf. 13***

92	A29	3p bis & multi	50	15
93	A29	12p yel & multi	1.50	40

1976, July 9 **Photo.** ***Perf. 13***

Design: 15p, One-man canoe and Montreal Olympic emblem (horiz.).

94	A30	7p multi	35	15
95	A30	15p multi	85	40

21st Olympic Games, Montreal, Canada, July 17–Aug. 1.

Nativity
A31

Design: 25p, Adoration of the Kings. Wall paintings in La Massana Church.

1976, Dec. 7 **Photo.** ***Perf. 13***

96	A31	3p multi	25	10
97	A31	25p multi	1.00	45

Christmas 1976.

Europa Issue 1977

View of Ansalonge
A32

Design: 12p, Xuclar, valley and mountains.

1977, May 2 **Litho.** ***Perf. 13***

98	A32	3p multi	25	15
99	A32	12p multi	80	35

Cross of Terme
A33

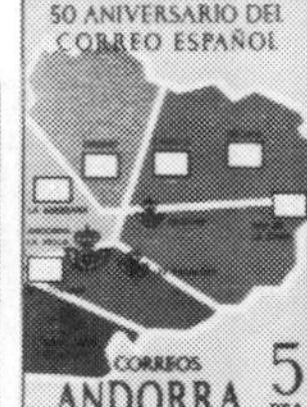

Map of Post Offices
A34

Design: 12p, Church of St. Miguel d'Engolasters.

1977, Dec. 2 **Photo.** ***Perf. 13x12½***

100	A33	5p multi	45	30
101	A33	12p multi	1.10	65

Christmas 1977.

Souvenir Sheet

Designs: 10p, Mail delivery. 20p, Post Office, 1928. 25p, Andorran coat of arms.

1978, Mar. 31 Photo. *Perf. 13x13½*

102	Sheet of 4	1.00	1.00
a.	A34 5p multi	10	6
b.	A34 10p multi	20	15
c.	A34 20p multi	30	30
d.	A34 25p multi	35	35

Spanish postal service in Andorra, 50th anniversary. No. 102 has black marginal inscription. Size: 105x149mm.

Europa Issue 1978

La Vall A35

Design: 12p, St. Juan de Caselles.

1978, May 2 *Perf. 13*

103	A35	5p multi	25	10
104	A35	12p multi	60	30

Crown, Bishop's Mitre and Staff A36

1978, Sept. 24 Photo. *Perf. 13*

105	A36	5p brn, car & yel	65	20

700th anniversary of the signing of treaty establishing Co-Principality of Andorra.

Holy Family A37

Design: 25p, Adoration of the Kings. Both designs after frescoes in the Church of St. Mary d'Encamp.

1978, Dec. 5 Photo. *Perf. 13*

106	A37	5p multi	15	10
107	A37	25p multi	65	40

Christmas 1978.

Young Woman A38

Designs: 5p, Young man. 12p, Bride-groom and bride riding mule.

1978, Feb. 14 Photo. *Perf. 13*

108	A38	3p multi	10	6
109	A38	5p multi	15	6
110	A38	12p multi	35	20

Europa Issue 1979

Old Mail Truck A39

Design: 12p, Stampless covers of 1846 and 1854.

1979, Apr. 30 Engr. *Perf. 13*

111	A39	5p yel grn & dk bl	30	10
112	A39	12p dk red & vio	70	30

Children Holding Hands—A40

1979, Oct. 18 Photo. *Perf. 13*

113	A40	19p multi	70	35

International Year of the Child.

St. Coloma's Church—A41

Design: 25p, Agnus Dei roundel, St. Coloma's Church.

1979, Nov. 28 Photo. *Perf. 13½*

114	A41	8p multi	25	8
115	A41	25p multi	55	35

Christmas 1979.

Bishop Pere d'Arg—A42

Bishops of Urgel: 5p, Josep Caixal. 13p, Joan Benlloch.

1979, Dec. 27 Engraved

116	A42	1p dk bl & brn	5	5
117	A42	5p rose lake & pur	10	6
118	A42	13p brn & dk grn	25	15

Europa Issue 1980

Antoni Fiter I. Rosell, Magistrate—A43

Design: 19p, Francesc Cairat I. Freixes, magistrate.

1980, Apr Photo. *Perf. 13x13½*

119	A43	8p bis, blk & brn	12	10
120	A43	19p lt grn & blk	35	18

Boxing, Moscow '80 Emblem—A44

1980 Photo. *Perf. 13½x13*

121	A44	5p *Downhill skiing*	10	6
122	A44	8p *shown*	12	10
123	A44	50p *Target shooting*	70	40

12th Winter Olympic Games, Lake Placid, N.Y., Feb. 12-24 (5p); 22nd Summer Olympic Games, Moscow, July 19-Aug. 3.

Nativity—A45

1980 Litho. *Perf. 13*

124	A45	10p *Nativity*, vert.	15	10
125	A45	22p *shown*	40	20

Christmas 1980.

Europa Issue 1981

Children Dancing at Santa Anna Feast—A46

Design: 30p, Going to church on Aplec de la Verge de Canolich Day.

1981, May 7 Photo. *Perf. 13*

126	A46	12p multi	20	10
127	A46	30p multi	45	25

50th Anniv. of Police Force—A47

1981, July 2 Photo. *Perf. 13½x13*

128	A47	30p multi	45	20

Intl. Year of the Disabled—A48

1981, Oct. 8 Photo. *Perf. 13½*

129	A48	50p multi	75	30

Christmas 1981—A49

Designs: Encamp Church retable.

1981, Dec. 3 Photo. *Perf. 13½*

130	A49	12p Nativity	18	10
131	A49	30p Adoration	45	20

Bishops of Urgel—A50

1981, Dec. 12 Engr. *Perf. 13½*

132	A50	7p Salvador Casanas	10	6
133	A50	20p Josep de Boltas	30	12

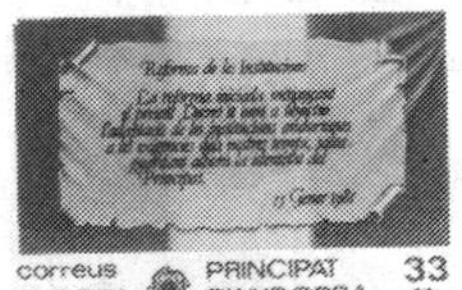

Natl. Arms—A51

1982, Feb. 17 Photo. *Perf. 13x13½*

134	A51	1p brt pink	5	5
135	A51	3p bis brn	10	6
136	A51	7p red org	10	10
137	A51	12p lake	18	10
138	A51	15p ultra	25	10
139	A51	20p bl grn	30	10
140	A51	30p crim rose	45	15

1982, July Engr. *Perf. 13x12½*

Size: 25½x30½mm

141	A51	50p dk grn	75	25
142	A51	100p dk bl	1.50	50
		Nos. 134-142 (9)	3.68	1.41

Europa 1982—A52

1982, May 12 Photo. *Perf. 13*

143	A52	14p New Reforms, 1866, vert.	20	10
144	A52	33p Reform of Institutions, 1981	50	25

1982 World Cup—A53

Designs: Various soccer players.

1982, June 13 Photo. *Perf. 13x13½*

145	A53	14p multi	75	75
146	A53	33p multi	1.50	1.50

Centenary of Permanent Spanish and French Delegations—A54

Anniversaries: 14p, 50th anniv. of Andorran stamps. 23p, St. Francis of Assisi (1182-1226). 33p, Anyos Pro-Vicarial District membership centenary (Relacio sobre la Vall de Andorra titlepage).

1982, Sept. 7 **Engr.** ***Perf. 13***

147 A54 9p dk bl & brn 15 10
148 A54 14p blk & grn 55 25
149 A54 23p dk bl & brn 35 15
150 A54 33p blk & ol grn 1.00 50

Christmas 1982—A55

Designs: 14p, Madonna and Child, Andorra la Vella Church (vert.). 33p, El Tio de Nadal (children in traditional costumes striking hollow tree).

1982, Dec. 9 **Photo.** ***Perf. 13x13½, 13½x13***

151 A55 14p multi 20 10
152 A55 33p multi 50 25

Europa 1983—A56

1983, June 7 **Photo.** ***Perf. 13***

153 A56 16p La Cortinada Church, architect, 12th cent. 25 8
154 A56 38p Water mill, 16th cent. 60 30

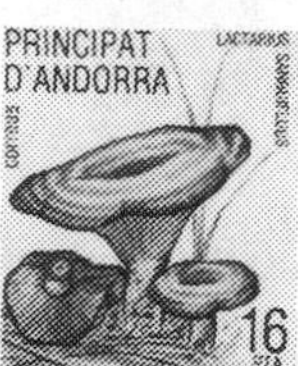

Local Mushrooms—A57

1983, July 20 **Photo.** ***Perf. 13x12½***

155 A57 16p Lactarius sanguifluus 25 8

See Nos. 169, 172.

Universal Suffrage, 50th Anniv. A58

1983, Sept. 6 **Photo. & Engr.** ***Perf. 13***

156 A58 10p multi 15 8

Visit of Monsignor Jacinto Verdaguer, Bishop and Co-Prince—A59

1983, Sept. 6 **Photo. & Engr.** ***Perf. 13***

157 A59 50p multi 75 35

Christmas 1983—A60

Unidentified saint, Romanesque fresco, Church of San Cerni de Nagol.

1983, Nov. 24 **Photo.** ***Perf. 13½***

158 A60 16p multi 25 8

Joan J. Laguarda Fenollera, Bishop of Urgel, 1902-06—A61

1983, Dec. 7 **Engr.** ***Perf. 13***

159 A61 26p red & brn 40 15

1984 Winter Olympics—A62

1984, Feb. 17 **Litho.** ***Perf. 13½x14***

160 A62 16p Ski jumping 25 8

ESPANA '84—A63

1984, Apr. 27 **Photo.** ***Perf. 13***

161 A63 26p Emblems 40 15

Europa (1959-84)—A64

1984, May 5 **Engr.**

162 A64 16p brown 25 8
163 A64 38p blue 60 30

1984 Summer Olympics—A65

1984, Aug. 9 **Litho.** ***Perf. 13½x14***

164 A65 40p Running 60 30

Mushroom Type of 1983

1984, Sept. 27 **Photo.** ***Perf. 13x12½***

165 A57 11p Morchella esculenta 1.00 15

Christmas 1984—A66

1984, Dec. 6 **Photo.** ***Perf. 13½***

166 A66 17p Nativity carving 25 10

Europa 1985—A67

Designs: 18p, Mossen Enric Arfany, composer, natl. hymn score. 45p, Musician Playing Viol, Romanesque fresco detail, La Cortinada Church, vert.

1985, May 3 **Engr.** ***Perf. 13½***

167 A67 18p dk vio, grn & choc 30 10
168 A67 45p grn & choc 70 20

Mushroom Type of 1983

1985, Sept. 19 **Photo.** ***Perf. 13½x12½***

169 A57 30p Gyromitra esculenta 45 15

Pal Village—A68

1985, Nov. 7 **Engr.** ***Perf. 13½***

170 A68 17p brt ultra & dk bl 25 10

Christmas 1985—A69

Fresco: Angels Playing Trumpet and Psaltery St. Bartholomew Chapel.

1985, Dec. 11 **Photo.** ***Perf. 13½x1***

171 A69 17p multi 25 1

Mushroom Type of 1983

1986, Apr. 10 **Photo.** ***Perf. 13½x12½***

172 A57 30p Marasmius oreades 45 1

Europa 1986—A70

1986, May 5 **Engr.** ***Perf. 13***

173 A70 17p Water 25 1
174 A70 45p Soil and air 70 2

Santa Roma de Les Bons Church Bell—A72

1986, Dec. 11 **Litho.** ***Perf. 14***

176 A72 19p multi 30 15

Christmas.

AIR POST STAMPS

AP1

Engraved.

1951, June 27 ***Perf. 11.*** **Unwmkd.**

C1	AP1	1p dk vio brn	32.50	3.50

Jaime Sansa Nequi, Episcopal Church Official—AP2

1983, Oct. 20 **Litho. & Engr.** ***Perf. 13***

C2	AP2	20p brn & bis brn	30	20

Pyrenees Art Center—AP3

1984, Oct. 25 **Photo.** ***Perf. 13***

C3	AP3	20p multi	30	20

Ramon Iglesias, Bishop of Urgel—AP4

1985, June 13 **Engr.** ***Perf. 13½***

C4	AP4	20p org brn & yel brn	30	15

No.	Type	Denomination	Unused	Used
21	A18	10fr grn & red	325.00	325.00
22	A18	20fr mag & grn	400.00	400.00
		Nos. 1-22 (22)	1,193.80	1,193.80

See No. P1 for ½c on 1c gray.

Nos. 9, 15 and 17 were not issued in France without overprint.

Chapel of Meritxell
A50

Bridge of St. Anthony
A51

St. Miguel d'Engolasters
A52

Gorge of St. Julia
A53

Old Andorra
A54

1932–43 Engraved Perf. 13

No.	Type	Denomination	Unused	Used
23	A50	1c gray blk	45	38
24	A50	2c violet	65	65
25	A50	3c brown	45	35
26	A50	5c bl grn	65	50
27	A51	10c dl lil	1.00	85
28	A50	15c dp red	1.40	1.40
29	A51	20c lt rose	11.50	9.00
30	A52	25c brown	4.50	4.50
31	A51	25c brn car ('37)	8.50	12.50
32	A51	30c emerald	2.75	2.50
33	A51	40c ultra	9.50	8.25
34	A51	40c brn blk ('39)	1.00	90
35	A51	45c lt red	11.00	9.00
36	A51	45c bl grn ('39)	5.25	4.50
37	A52	50c lil rose	11.50	9.00
38	A51	50c lt vio ('39)	5.25	4.50
38A	A51	50c grn ('40)	2.00	2.00
39	A51	55c lt vio ('38)	18.00	13.00
40	A51	60c yel brn ('38)	90	75
41	A52	65c bl grn	50.00	47.50
42	A51	65c bl ('38)	12.50	10.00
43	A51	70c red ('39)	2.00	1.50
44	A52	75c violet	6.00	5.25
45	A51	75c ultra ('39)	4.25	3.50
46	A51	80c grn ('38)	24.00	18.00
46A	A51	80c bl grn ('40)	40	45
47	A53	90c dp rose	6.00	3.75
48	A53	90c dk grn ('39)	3.50	3.50
49	A53	1fr bl grn	18.00	11.00
50	A53	1fr scar ('38)	24.00	18.00
51	A53	1fr dp ultra ('39)	38	38
51A	A53	1.20fr brt vio ('42)	38	35
52	A50	1.25fr rose car ('33)	42.50	26.00
52A	A50	1.25fr rose ('38)	5.25	2.00
52B	A53	1.30fr sep ('40)	38	35
53	A54	1.50fr ultra	16.00	15.00
53A	A53	1.50fr crim ('40)	38	35
54	A53	1.75fr vio ('33)	115.00	110.00
55	A53	1.75fr dk bl ('38)	45.00	35.00
56	A53	2fr red vio	6.75	6.00
56A	A50	2fr rose red ('40)	1.40	1.00
56B	A50	2fr dk bl grn ('42)	40	30
57	A50	2.15fr dk vio ('38)	52.50	42.50
58	A50	2.25fr ultra ('39)	7.50	5.75
58A	A50	2.40fr red ('42)	38	30
59	A50	2.50fr gray blk ('39)	7.50	6.00
59A	A50	2.50fr dp ultra ('40)	2.00	1.90
60	A53	3fr org brn	6.75	6.00
60A	A50	3fr red brn ('40)	45	38
60B	A50	4fr sl bl ('42)	45	38
60C	A50	4.50fr dp vio ('42)	1.25	1.25
61	A54	5fr brown	60	45
62	A54	10fr violet	70	60
62B	A54	15fr dp ultra ('42)	75	55
63	A54	20fr rose lake	75	60
63A	A51	50fr turq bl ('43)	1.50	75
		Nos. 23-63A (56)	563.80	471.12

A 20c ultra exists. Price $12,500.

No. 37 Surcharged with Bars and New Value in Black.

1935

No.	Type	Denomination	Unused	Used
64	A52	20c on 50c lil rose	16.00	13.00
a.		Double surcharge	950.00	

Coat of Arms
A55 A56

1936–42 Perf. 14x13

No.	Type	Denomination	Unused	Used
65	A55	1c blk ('37)	12	12
66	A55	2c blue	12	12
67	A55	3c brown	12	12
68	A55	5c rose lil	12	12
69	A55	10c ultra ('37)	12	12
70	A55	15c red vio	80	80
71	A55	20c emer ('37)	12	12
72	A55	30c cop red ('38)	38	38
72A	A55	30c blk brn ('42)	22	22
73	A55	35c Prus grn ('38)	50.00	50.00
74	A55	40c cop red ('42)	22	22
75	A55	50c Prus grn ('42)	22	22
76	A55	60c turq bl ('42)	22	22
77	A55	70c vio ('42)	22	22
		Nos. 65-77 (14)	53.00	53.00

1944

No.	Type	Denomination	Unused	Used
78	A56	10c violet	5	5
79	A56	30c dp mag	5	5
80	A56	40c dl bl	15	15
81	A56	50c org red	6	6
82	A56	60c black	6	6
83	A56	70c brt red vio	6	6
84	A56	80c bl grn	15	15
		Nos. 78-84 (7)	58	58

See also No. 114.

St. Jean de Caselles
A57

La Maison des Vallees
A58

Old Andorra
A59

Provost
A60

1944–47 Perf. 13

No.	Type	Denomination	Unused	Used
85	A57	1fr brn vio	18	15
86	A57	1.20fr blue	15	15
87	A57	1.50fr red	18	15
88	A57	2fr dk bl grn	15	15
89	A58	2.40fr rose red	22	18
90	A58	2.50fr rose red ('46)	1.25	50
91	A58	3fr sepia	15	15
92	A58	4fr ultra	18	15
93	A59	4.50fr brn blk	18	15
94	A58	4.50fr dk bl grn ('47)	4.00	3.50
95	A59	5fr ultra	22	18
96	A59	5fr Prus grn ('46)	40	30
97	A59	6fr rose car ('45)	30	15
98	A59	10fr Prus grn	15	12
99	A59	10fr ultra ('46)	18	12
100	A60	15fr rose lil	38	25
101	A60	20fr dp bl	55	45
102	A60	25fr lt rose red ('46)	1.40	1.10
103	A60	40fr dk grn ('46)	1.40	1.10
104	A60	50fr sepia	1.40	1.10
		Nos. 85-104 (20)	13.02	10.10

1948-49

No.	Type	Denomination	Unused	Used
105	A58	4fr lt bl grn	70	70
106	A59	6fr vio brn	35	35
107	A59	8fr indigo	1.00	1.00
108	A59	12fr brt red	75	75
109	A59	12fr bl grn ('49)	90	75
110	A59	15fr crim ('49)	45	45
111	A60	18fr dp bl	2.50	1.50
112	A60	20fr dk vio	2.00	1.65
113	A60	25fr ultra ('49)	1.40	1.10
		Nos. 105-113 (9)	10.05	8.25

1949–51 Perf. 14x13, 13

No.	Type	Denomination	Unused	Used
114	A56	1fr dp bl	60	55
115	A57	3fr red ('51)	4.50	3.25
116	A57	4fr sepia	2.00	2.00
117	A58	5fr emerald	2.25	1.65
118	A58	5fr pur ('51)	2.25	1.40
119	A58	6fr bl grn ('51)	2.00	1.65
120	A58	8fr brown	60	60
121	A59	15fr blk brn ('51)	2.00	1.65
122	A59	18fr rose red ('51)	10.00	7.25
123	A60	30fr ultra ('51)	16.00	7.50
		Nos. 114-123 (10)	42.20	27.50

Les Escaldres Spa
A61

St. Coloma Belfry
A62

SPECIAL DELIVERY STAMPS.

Special Delivery Stamp of Spain, 1905 Overprinted

CORREOS

ANDORRA

1928 Perf. 14. Unwmkd.

Without Control Number on Back.

No.	Type	Denomination	Unused	Used
E1	SD1	20c red	62.50	42.50

With Control Number on Back.

No.	Type	Denomination	Unused	Used
E2	SD1	20c pale red	32.50	17.50

Eagle over Mountain Pass
SD2

Arms and Squirrel
SD3

1929 Perf. 14

With Control Number on Back.

No.	Type	Denomination	Unused	Used
E3	SD2	20c scarlet	19.00	8.00
a.		Perf. 11½	450.00	

Without Control Number on Back.

1937 Perf. 11½x11.

No.	Type	Denomination	Unused	Used
E4	SD2	20c red	6.75	4.00

Engraved.

1949 Perf. 10x9½. Unwmkd.

No.	Type	Denomination	Unused	Used
E5	SD3	25c red	8.00	4.00

French Administration.

Stamps and Types of France, 1900-1929, Overprinted ANDORRE

1931 Perf. 14x13½ Unwmkd.

No.	Type	Denomination	Unused	Used
1	A16	1c gray	80	80
a.		Double ovpt.	1,000.	1,000.
2	A16	2c red brn	1.00	1.00
3	A16	3c orange	1.00	1.00
4	A16	5c green	1.50	1.50
5	A16	10c lilac	2.25	2.25
6	A22	15c red brn	4.50	4.50
7	A22	20c red vio	6.75	6.75
8	A22	25c yel brn	6.75	6.75
9	A22	30c green	6.75	6.75
10	A22	40c ultra	11.00	11.00
11	A20	45c lt vio	12.00	12.00
12	A20	50c vermilion	10.00	10.00
13	A20	65c gray grn	16.00	16.00
14	A20	75c rose lil	21.00	21.00
15	A22	90c red	27.50	27.50
16	A20	1fr dl bl	30.00	30.00
17	A22	1.50fr lt bl	37.50	37.50

Overprinted ANDORRE

No.	Type	Denomination	Unused	Used
18	A18	2fr org & pale bl	27.50	27.50
19	A18	3fr brt vio & rose	95.00	95.00
20	A18	5fr dk bl & buff	150.00	150.00

Designs: 15fr, 18fr, 20fr, 25fr, Gothic cross. 30fr, 35fr, 40fr 50fr, 65fr, 70fr, 75fr, Village of Les Bons.

Engraved.

1955-58 ***Perf. 13*** **Unwmkd.**

124	A61	1fr dk gray bl	18	15
125	A61	2fr dp grn	18	15
126	A61	3fr red	18	15
127	A61	5fr chocolate	18	15
128	A62	6fr dk bl grn	45	38
129	A62	8fr rose brn	45	45
130	A62	10fr brt vio	70	55
131	A62	12fr indigo	75	60
132	A61	15fr red	1.00	85
133	A61	18fr bl grn	1.00	85
134	A61	20fr dp pur	1.65	1.50
135	A61	25fr sepia	2.00	1.50
136	A62	30fr dp bl	26.00	15.00
137	A62	35fr Prus bl ('57)	10.00	7.50
138	A62	40fr dk grn	27.50	20.00
139	A62	50fr cerise	3.00	2.25
140	A62	65fr pur ('58)	8.50	5.75
141	A62	70fr chnt ('57)	6.00	5.75
142	A62	75fr vio bl	45.00	37.50
		Nos. 124-142 (19)	134.72	101.03

Coat of Arms A63 — **Gothic Cross, Meritxell** A64

Designs: 65c, 85c, 1fr, Pond of Engolasters. 30c, 45c, 50c, as 25c.

1961, June 19 **Typo.** ***Perf. 14x13***

143	A63	5c brt grn & blk	5	5
144	A63	10c red, pink & blk	5	5
145	A63	15c bl & blk	6	6
146	A63	20c yel & brn	10	10

Engraved ***Perf. 13***

147	A64	25c vio, bl & grn	22	22
148	A64	30c mar, ol grn & brn	38	38
149	A64	45c ind, bl & grn	13.00	8.00
150	A64	50c pur, lt brn & ol grn	1.40	1.40
151	A64	65c bl, ol & brn	16.00	12.00
152	A64	85c rose lil, vio bl & brn	16.00	12.00
153	A64	1fr grnsh bl, ind & brn	1.25	90
		Nos. 143-153 (11)	48.51	35.16

See also Nos. 161–166A.

Imperforates

Most stamps of Andorra, French Administration, from 1961 onward exist imperforate in issued and trial colors, and also in small presentation sheets in issued colors.

Telstar and Globe Showing Andover and Pleumeur-Bodou
A65

1962, Sept. 29 **Engraved**

154	A65	50c ultra & pur	1.90	1.90

Issued to commemorate the first television connection of the United States and Europe through the Telstar satellite, July 11–12.

"La Sardane"
A66

Charlemagne Crossing Andorra
A67

Design: 1fr, Louis le Debonnaire giving founding charter.

1963, June 22 ***Perf. 13*** **Unwmkd.**

155	A66	20c lil rose, cl & ol grn	4.50	4.50
156	A67	50c sl grn & dk car rose	7.50	7.50
157	A67	1fr red brn, ultra & dk grn	12.00	12.00

Old Andorra Church and Champs-Elysées Palace
A68

1964, Jan. 20 **Engraved**

158	A68	25c blk, grn & vio brn	1.40	90

Issued to publicize "PHILATEC," International Philatelic and Postal Techniques Exhibition, Paris, June 5–21, 1964.

Bishop of Urgel and Seigneur of Caboët Confirming Co-Principality, 1288
A69

Design: 60c, Napoleon re-establishing Co-principality, 1806.

1964, Apr. 25 **Engraved** ***Perf. 13***

159	A69	60c dk brn, red brn & sl grn	16.00	16.00
160	A69	1fr brt bl, org brn & blk	16.00	16.00

Arms Type of 1961

1964, May 16 **Typo.** ***Perf. 14x13***

161	A63	1c dk bl & gray	10	10
162	A63	2c blk & org	5	5
163	A63	12c pur, emer & yel	30	30
164	A63	18c blk, lil & pink	30	30

Scenic Type of 1961

Designs: 40c, 45c, Gothic Cross, Meritxell. 60c, 90c, Pond of Engolasters.

1965–71 **Engraved** ***Perf. 13***

165	A64	40c dk brn, org brn & sl grn	50	50
165A	A64	45c vio bl, ol bis & sl ('70)	1.00	75
166	A64	60c org brn & dk brn	60	60
166A	A64	90c ultra, bl grn & bis ('71)	50	50

Syncom Satellite over Pleumeur-Bodou Station
A70

Andorra House, Paris
A71

1965, May 17 **Unwmkd.**

167	A70	60c dp car, lil & bl	5.25	4.50

Issued to commemorate the centenary of the International Telecommunication Union.

1965, June 5

168	A71	25c dk bl, org brn & ol gray	1.00	85

Ski Lift
A72

Design: 25c, Chair lift (vert.).

1966, Apr. 2 **Engraved** ***Perf. 13***

169	A72	25c brt bl, grn & dk brn	1.25	1.00
170	A72	40c mag, brt ultra & sep	1.75	1.50

Winter sports in Andorra.

FR-1 Satellite
A73

1966, May 7 ***Perf. 13***

171	A73	60c brt bl, grn & dk grn	1.90	1.90

Issued to commemorate the launching of the scientific satellite FR-1, Dec. 6, 1965.

Europa Issue, 1966

Common Design Type

1966, Sept. 24 **Engraved** ***Perf. 13***

Size: 21½x35½mm.

172	CD9	60c brown	3.75	3.25

Folk Dancers, Sculpture by Josep Viladomat
A74

Telephone Encircling the Globe
A75

1967, Apr. 29 **Engraved** ***Perf. 13***

173	A74	30c ol grn, dp grn & sl	60	45

Issued to commemorate the centenary (in 1966) of the New Reform, which reaffirmed and strengthened political freedom in Andorra.

Europa Issue, 1967

Common Design Type

1967, Apr. 29

Size: 22x36mm.

174	CD10	30c bluish blk & lt bl	2.25	1.90
175	CD10	60c dk red & brt pink	3.75	2.75

1967, Apr. 29

176	A75	60c dk car, vio & blk	1.40	1.10

Automatic telephone service.

Injured Father at Home
A76

1967, Sept. 23 **Engraved** ***Perf. 13***

177	A76	2.30fr ocher, dk red brn & brn red	8.00	5.75

Introduction of Social Security System.

Jesus in Garden of Gethsemane
A77

Designs (from 16th century frescoes in La Maison des Vallees): 30c, The Kiss of Judas. 60c, The Descent from the Cross (Picta).

1967, Sept. 23

178	A77	25c blk & red brn	70	55
179	A77	30c pur & red lil	1.00	75
180	A77	60c ind & Prus bl	1.75	1.10

See also Nos. 185–187.

Downhill Skier
A78

1968, Jan. 27 **Engraved** ***Perf. 13***

181	A78	40c org, ver & red lil	90	75

Issued to publicize the 10th Winter Olympic Games, Grenoble, France, Feb. 6–18.

Europa Issue, 1968

Common Design Type

1968, Apr. 27 **Engraved** ***Perf. 13***

Size: 36x22mm.

182	CD11	30c gray & brt bl	4.25	3.50
183	CD11	60c brn & lil	5.75	4.25

High Jump
A79

1968, Oct. 12 Engraved *Perf. 13*

184	A79	40c brt bl & brn	1.40	1.25

Issued to commemorate the 19th Olympic Games, Mexico City, Oct. 12–27.

Fresco Type of 1967

Designs (from 16th century frescoes in La Maison des Vallees): 25c, The Scourging of Christ. 30c, Christ Carrying the Cross. 60c, The Crucifixion. (All horizontal.)

1968, Oct. 12

185	A77	25c dk grn & gray grn	75	75
186	A77	30c dk brn & lil	1.25	1.25
187	A77	60c dk car & vio brn	1.75	1.75

Europa Issue, 1969
Common Design Type

1969, Apr. 26 Engraved *Perf. 13*

188	CD12	40c rose car, gray & dl bl	3.75	3.00
189	CD12	70c ind, dl red & ol	6.00	4.25

Issued to commemorate the 10th anniversary of the Conference of European Postal and Telecommunications Administrations.

Kayak on Isère River
A80

Drops of Water and Diamond
A80a

1969, Aug. 2 Engraved *Perf. 13*

190	A80	70c dk sl grn, ultra & ind	1.75	1.75

Issued to commemorate the International Canoe and Kayak Championships, Bourg-Saint-Maurice, Savoy, July 31–Aug. 6.

1969, Sept. 27 Engraved *Perf. 13*

191	A80a	70c blk, dp ultra & grnsh bl	3.00	3.00

European Water Charter.

St. John, the Woman and the Dragon
A81

The Revelation (From the Altar of St. John, Caselles): 40c, St. John Hearing Voice from Heaven on Patmos. 70c, St. John and the Seven Candlesticks.

1969, Oct. 18

192	A81	30c brn, dp pur & brn red	80	80
193	A81	40c gray, dk brn & brn ol	1.25	1.25
194	A81	70c dk red, mar & brt rose lil	2.25	2.25

See also Nos. 199–201, 207–209, 214–216.

Field Ball
A82

Shot Put
A83

1970, Feb. 21 Engraved *Perf. 13*

195	A82	80c multi	2.25	1.75

Issued to publicize the 7th International Field Ball Games, France, Feb. 26–Mar. 8.

Europa Issue, 1970
Common Design Type

1970, May 2 Engraved *Perf. 13*
Size: 36x22mm.

196	CD13	40c orange	2.25	1.90
197	CD13	80c vio bl	3.25	2.75

1970, Sept. 11 Engraved *Perf. 13*

198	A83	80c bl & dk brn	1.50	1.25

Issued to publicize the First European Junior Athletic Championships, Colombes, France, Sept. 11–13.

Altar Type of 1969

The Revelation (from the Altar of St. John, Caselles): 30c, St. John recording angel's message. 40c, Angel erecting column symbolizing faithful in heaven. 80c, St. John's trial in kettle of boiling oil.

1970, Oct. 24

199	A81	30c dp car, dk brn & brt pur	1.00	1.00
200	A81	40c vio & sl grn	1.25	1.25
201	A81	80c ol, dk bl & car rose	2.25	2.25

Ice Skating
A84

1971, Feb. 20 Engraved *Perf. 13*

202	A84	80c dk red, red lil & pur	2.75	2.25

World Figure Skating Championships, Lyons, France, Feb. 23–28.

Capercaillie
A85

Design: No. 204, Brown bear.

1971, Apr. 24 Photo. *Perf. 13*

203	A85	80c multi	2.50	1.75

Engraved

204	A85	80c bl, grn & brn	2.50	1.75

Nature Protection.

Europa Issue, 1971
Common Design Type

1971, May 8 Engraved *Perf. 13*
Size: 35½x22mm.

205	CD14	50c rose red	2.75	2.25
206	CD14	80c lt bl grn	4.00	3.00

Altar Type of 1969

The Revelation (from the Altar of St. John, Caselles): 30c, St. John preaching, Rev. 1:3. 50c, "The Sign of the Beast . . ." Rev. 16:1–2. 90c, The Woman, Rev. 17:1.

1971, Sept. 18

207	A81	30c dl grn, ol & brt grn	1.00	1.00
208	A81	50c rose car, org & ol brn	1.25	1.25
209	A81	90c blk, dk pur & bl	2.25	2.25

Europa Issue 1972
Common Design Type

1972, Apr. 29 Photo. *Perf. 13*
Size: 21½x37mm.

210	CD15	50c brt mag & multi	3.00	2.75
211	CD15	90c multi	3.75	3.25

Golden Eagle
A86

1972, May 27 Engraved

212	A86	60c dk grn, ol & plum	2.00	1.65

Nature protection.

Shooting
A87

1972, July 8

213	A87	1fr dk pur	2.00	1.65

20th Olympic Games, Munich, Aug. 26–Sept. 11.

Altar Type of 1969

The Revelation (from the Altar of St. John, Caselles): 30c, St. John, bishop and servant. 50c, Resurrection of Lazarus. 90c, Angel with lance and nails.

1972, Sept. 16 Engraved *Perf. 13*

214	A81	30c dk ol, gray & red lil	90	90
215	A81	50c vio bl & sl	1.40	1.40
216	A81	90c dk Prus bl & sl grn	2.25	2.25

De Gaulle as Co-prince of Andorra
A88

Design: 90c, De Gaulle in front of Maison des Vallées.

1972, Oct. 23 Engr. *Perf. 13*

217	A88	50c vio bl	1.50	1.50
218	A88	90c dk car	2.25	2.25

5th anniversary of the visit of Charles de Gaulle to Andorra. Nos. 217–218 printed se-tenant in sheets of 10 stamps and 5 labels showing Andorran coat of arms and commemorative inscription.

Europa Issue 1973
Common Design Type

1973, Apr. 28 Photo. *Perf. 13*
Size: 36x22mm.

219	CD16	50c vio & multi	3.00	2.75
220	CD16	90c dk red & multi	4.00	3.00

Virgin of Canòlich
A89

1973, June 16 Engraved *Perf. 13*

221	A89	1fr ol, Prus bl & vio	2.00	2.00

Lily
A90

Designs: 45c, Iris. 50c, Columbine. 65c, Tobacco. No. 226, Pinks. No. 227, Narcissuses.

1973–74 Photo. *Perf. 13*

222	A90	30c car rose & multi	45	45
223	A90	45c yel grn & multi	25	25
224	A90	50c buff & multi	1.50	1.50
225	A90	65c gray & multi	40	40
226	A90	90c ultra & multi	1.00	1.00
227	A90	90c grnsh bl & multi	80	80
		Nos. 222-227 (6)	4.40	4.40

See Nos. 238–240.

Blue Titmouse
A91

Designs: 60c, Citril finch and mistletoe. 80c, Eurasian bullfinch. 1fr, Lesser spotted woodpecker.

1973–74 Photo. *Perf. 13*

228	A91	60c buff & multi	1.65	1.40
229	A91	80c gray & multi	1.65	1.40
230	A91	90c gray & multi	1.40	1.10
231	A91	1fr yel grn & multi	2.00	1.50

Nature protection.

Europa Issue 1974

Virgin of Pal
A92

Design: 90c, Virgin of Santa Coloma. Statues are polychrome 12th century carvings by rural artists.

1974, Apr. 27 Engr. *Perf. 13*

232	A92	50c multi	3.75	2.75
233	A92	90c multi	5.25	3.75

Arms of Andorra and Cahors Bridge
A93

Mail Box, Chutes and Globe
A94

1974, Aug. 24 Engr. *Perf. 13*
234 A93 1fr bl, vio & org 1.25 90

First anniversary of meeting of the co-princes of Andorra: Pres. Georges Pompidou of France and Msgr. Juan Marti Alanis, Bishop of Urgel.

1974, Oct. 5 Engraved *Perf. 13*
235 A94 1.20fr multi 1.65 1.40

Centenary of Universal Postal Union.

Europa Issue 1975

Coronation of St. Marti, 16th Century—A95

Design: 80c, Crucifixion, 16th century (vert.).

Perf. 11½x13, 13x11½

1975, Apr. 26 Photogravure
236 A95 80c gold & multi 4.50 4.00
237 A95 1.20fr gold & multi 5.25 4.00

Flower Type of 1973

Designs: 60c, Gentian. 80c, Anemone. 1.20fr, Autumn crocus.

1975, May 10 Photo. *Perf. 13*
238 A90 60c ol & multi 35 35
239 A90 80c brt rose & multi 80 80
240 A90 1.20fr grn & multi 85 85

Abstract Design—A96

1975, June 7 Engr. *Perf. 13*
241 A96 2fr bl, mag & emer 2.25 2.25

ARPHILA 75 International Philatelic Exhibition, Paris, June 6–16.

Pres. Georges Pompidou
A97

1975, Aug. 23 Engr. *Perf. 13*
242 A97 80c vio bl & blk 90 90

Georges Pompidou (1911–1974), president of France and co-prince of Andorra (1969–1974).

Costume and IWY Emblem
A98

1975, Nov. 8 Engr. *Perf. 13*
243 A98 1.20fr multi 1.40 1.25

International Women's Year.

Skier and Snowflake
A99

1976, Jan. 31 Engr. *Perf. 13*
244 A99 1.20fr multi 1.40 1.25

12th Winter Olympic Games, Innsbruck, Austria, Feb. 4–15.

Telephone and Satellite
A100

1976, Mar. 20 Engr. *Perf. 13*
245 A100 1fr multi 1.00 1.00

Centenary of first telephone call by Alexander Graham Bell, Mar. 10, 1976.

Europa Issue 1976

Catalan Forge
A101

Design: 1.20fr, Lacemaker.

1976, May 8 Engr. *Perf. 13*
246 A101 80c multi 1.10 90
247 A101 1.20fr multi 1.50 1.40

Thomas Jefferson
A102

Trapshooting
A103

1976, July 3 Engr. *Perf. 13*
248 A102 1.20fr multi 1.40 1.25

American Bicentennial.

1976, July 17 Engr. *Perf. 13*
249 A103 2fr multi 1.65 1.50

21st Olympic Games, Montreal, Canada, July 17–Aug. 1.

Meritxell Sanctuary and Old Chapel—A104

1976, Sept. 4 Engr. *Perf. 13*
250 A104 1fr multi 1.25 1.00

Dedication of rebuilt Meritxell Church, Sept. 8, 1976.

Apollo
A105

Ermine
A106

Design: 1.40fr, Morio butterfly.

1976, Oct. 16 Photo. *Perf. 13*
251 A105 80c blk & multi 1.00 90
252 A105 1.40fr sal & multi 1.50 1.25

Nature protection.

1977, Apr. 2 Photo. *Perf. 13*
253 A106 1fr vio bl, gray & blk 1.40 1.10

Nature protection.

St. Jean de Caselles
A107

Manual Digest, 1748, Arms of Andorra
A108

Europa Issue 1977

Design: 1.40fr, Sant Vicens Castle.

1977, Apr. 30 Engr. *Perf. 13*
254 A107 1fr multi 1.10 90
255 A107 1.40fr multi 1.65 1.40

1977, June 11 Engr. *Perf. 13*
256 A108 80c grn, bl & brn 80 70

Establishment of Institute of Andorran Studies.

St. Romanus of Caesarea
A109

1977, July 23 Engr. *Perf. 12½x13*
257 A109 2fr multi 1.50 1.25

Design from altarpiece in Church of St. Roma de les Bons.

General Council Chamber
A110

Guillem d'Arény Plandolit
A111

1977, Sept. 24 Engr. *Perf. 13*
258 A110 1.10fr multi 1.25 1.10
259 A111 2fr car & dk brn 1.40 1.10

Andorran heritage. Guillem d'Arény Plandolit started Andorran reform movement in 1866.

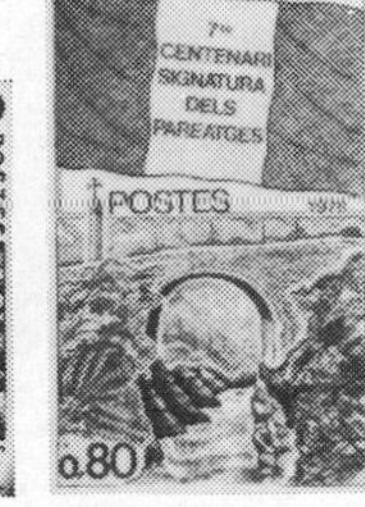

Squirrel
A112

Flag and Valira River Bridge
A113

1978, Mar. 18 Engr. *Perf. 13*
260 A112 1fr multi 75 60

1978, Apr. 8
261 A113 80c multi 60 55

700th anniversary of the signing of the treaty establishing the Co-Principality of Andorra.

Europa Issue 1978

Pal Church
A114

Design: 1.40fr, Charlemagne's Castle, Charlemagne on horseback (vert.).

1978, Apr. 29 Engr. *Perf. 13*
262 A114 1fr multi 1.10 90
263 A114 1.40fr multi 1.65 1.40

Virgin of Sispony
A115

1978, May 20 Engr. *Perf. 12x13*
264 A115 2fr multi 1.50 1.25

Visura Tribunal A116

1978, June 24 Engr. *Perf. 13*

265	A116 1.20fr multi		90	75

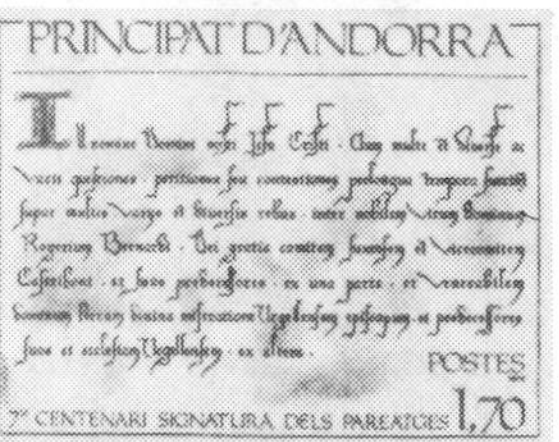

Preamble of 1278 Treaty—A117

1978, Sept. 2 Engr. *Perf. 13x12½*

266	A117 1.70fr multi		90	75

700th anniversary of the signing of treaty establishing Co-Principality of Andorra.

Pyrenean Chamois A118

White Partridges A119

1979, Mar. 26 Engr. *Perf. 13*

267	A118 1fr multi		45	38

1979, Apr. 9 Photo. *Perf. 13*

268	A119 1.20fr multi		80	60

Nature protection. See Nos. 288-289.

Europa Issue 1979

French Mailman, 1900 A120

Design: 1.70fr, First French post office in Andorra.

1979, Apr. 28 Engr. *Perf. 13*

269	A120 1.20fr multi		1.40	1.10
270	A120 1.70fr multi		2.00	1.50

Falcon, Pre-Roman Painting A121

1979, June 2 Engr. *Perf. 12½x13*

271	A121 2fr multi		1.25	90

Child with Lambs, Church, IYC Emblem A122

1979, July 7 Photo. *Perf. 13*

272	A122 1.70fr multi		90	75

International Year of the Child.

Bas-relief, Trobada Monument A123

1979, Sept. 29 Engraved *Perf. 13*

273	A123 2fr multi		1.10	90

700th anniversary of Co-Principality of Andorra.

Judo Hold—A124

1979, Nov. 24 Engr. *Perf. 13*

274	A124 1.30fr multi		75	60

World Judo Championships, Paris, Dec. 1979.

Farm House, Cortinada—A125

1980, Jan. 26 Engraved *Perf. 13*

275	A125 1.10fr multi		60	55

Cross-Country Skiing—A126

1980, Feb. 9

276	A126 1.80fr ultra & lil rose		1.90	1.25

13th Winter Olympic Games, Lake Placid, N.Y., Feb. 12-24.

World Bicycling Championships—A128

1980, Aug. 30 Engr. *Perf. 13*

278	A128 1.20fr multi		45	38

Europa Issue 1980

Charlemagne (742-814) —A129

Design: 1.80fr, Napoleon I (1769-1821).

1980, Apr. 26 Engraved *Perf. 13*

279	A129 1.30fr multi		60	45
280	A129 1.80fr gray grn & brn		90	70

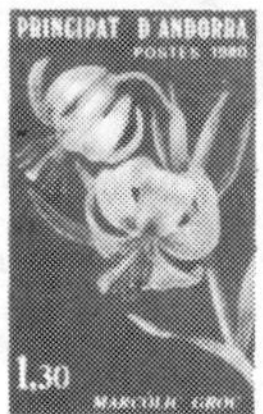

Pyrenees Lily—A130

1980 Photo.

281	A130 1.10fr *Dog-toothed violet*		50	38
282	A130 1.30fr *shown*		55	45

Nature protection. Issue dates: 1.10fr, June 21, 1.30fr, May 17.

De La Vall House, 400th Anniversary of Restoration—A131

1980, Sept. 6 Engraved

283	A131 1.40fr multi		40	38

Angel, Church of St. Cerni de Nagol, Pre-Romanesque Fresco—A132

1980, Oct. 27 *Perf. 13x12½*

284	A132 2fr multi		1.25	90

Bordes de Mereig Mountain Village—A133

1981, Mar. 21 Engr. *Perf. 13*

285	A133 1.40fr bl gray & dk brn		50	40

Europa Issue 1981

Ball de l'Ossa, Winter Game—A134

1981, May 16 Engr.

286	A134 1.40fr shown		65	45
287	A134 2fr El Contrapas dance		80	60

Bird Type of 1979

1981, June 20 Photo.

288	A119 1.20fr Phylloscopus bonelli		38	30
289	A119 1.40fr Tichodroma muraria		50	38

World Fencing Championship, Clermont-Ferrand, July 2-13—A135

1981, July 4 Engr.

290	A135 2fr bl & blk		75	50

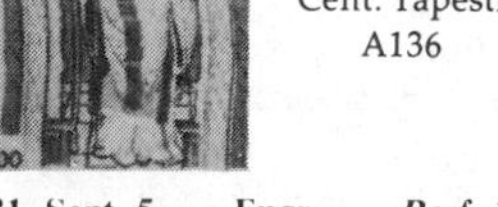

St. Martin, 12th Cent. Tapestry A136

1981, Sept. 5 Engr. *Perf. 12x13*

291	A136 3fr multi		1.25	90

ntl. Drinking Vater Decade A137

Intl. Year of the Disabled A138

81, Oct. 17 *Perf. 13*

2 A137 1.60fr multi 55 40

81, Nov. 7

3 A138 2.30fr multi 70 60

Europa 1982—A139

82, May 8 **Engr.** *Perf. 13*

94 A139 1.60fr Creation of Andorran govt., 1982 55 40
95 A139 2.30fr Land Council, 1419 80 55

1982 World Cup—A140

Designs: Various soccer players. Nos. 296-297 -tenant with label showing natl. arms.

982, June 12 **Engr.** *Perf. 13*

96 A140 1.60fr red & dk brn 60 45
97 A140 2.60fr red & dk brn 90 65

Souvenir Sheet

No. 52—A141

982, Aug. 21 **Engr.**

98 A141 5fr blk & rose car 1.75 1.7

First Andorran Stamp Exhibition, Aug. 21-Sept. 9. Black marginal inscription. Size: 143x93mm.

Horse, Roman Wall Painting—A142

982, Sept. 4 **Photo.** *Perf. 13x12½*

99 A142 3fr multi 1.10 90

Wild Cat—A143

1982, Oct. 9 **Engr.** *Perf. 13*

300 A143 1.80fr shown 65 50
301 A143 2.60fr Pine trees 1.00 65

TB Bacillus Centenary A144

St. Thomas Aquinas (1225-1274) A145

1982, Nov. 13

302 A144 2.10fr Koch, lungs 60 50

1982, Dec. 4

303 A145 2fr multi 75 60

Manned Flight Bicentenary—A146

1983, Feb. 26 **Engr.**

304 A146 2fr multi 75 60

Nature Protection—A147

1983, Apr. 16 **Engr.** *Perf. 13*

305 A147 1fr Birch trees 35 22
306 A147 1.50fr Trout 50 38

Europa 1983—A148

Catalane Gold Works.

1983, May 7 **Engr.** *Perf. 13*

307 A148 1.80fr Exterior 60 45
308 A148 2.60fr Interior 80 60

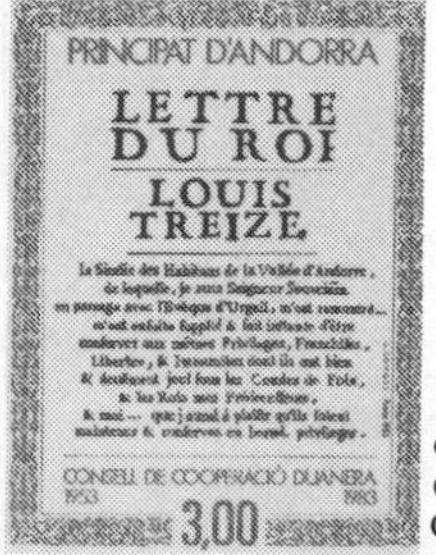

30th Anniv. of Customs Cooperation Council—A149

1983, May 14

309 A149 3fr Letter to King Louis XIII 1.10 80

First Arms of Valleys of Andorra—A150

1983, Sept. 3 **Engr.** *Perf. 13*

310 A150 5c ol grn & red 5 5
311 A150 10c grn & ol grn 5 5
312 A150 20c brt pur & red 5 5
313 A150 30c brn vio & red 6 5
314 A150 40c dk bl & ultra 10 6
315 A150 50c gray & red 12 6
316 A150 1fr dp mag 25 18
317 A150 2fr org red & red brn 50 35
318 A150 5fr dk brn & red 1.25 85
Nos. 310-318 (9) 6.68 4.95

See Nos. 332-335.

Painting, Cortinada Church—A151

1983, Sept. 24 *Perf. 12x13*

319 A151 4fr multi 1.40 1.00

Plandolit House—A152

1983, Oct. 15 **Photo.** *Perf. 13*

320 A152 1.60fr dp ultra & brn 50 38

1984 Winter Olympics—A153

1984, Feb. 18 **Engr.**

321 A153 2.80fr multi 80 70

Pyrennes Region Work Community (Labor Org.)—A154

1984, Apr. 28 **Engr.** *Perf. 13*

322 A154 3fr brt bl & sep 80 65

Europa (1959-84)—A155

1984, May 5 **Engr.**

323 A155 2fr brt grn 60 38
324 A155 2.80fr rose car 90 60

Nature Protection Type of 1983

1984, July 7 **Engr.** *Perf. 13*

325 A147 1.70fr Chestnut Tree 50 30
326 A147 2.10fr Walnut Tree 60 38

Pyranees Art Center—A155a

1984, Sept. 7 **Engr.**

327 A155a 3fr multi 90 60

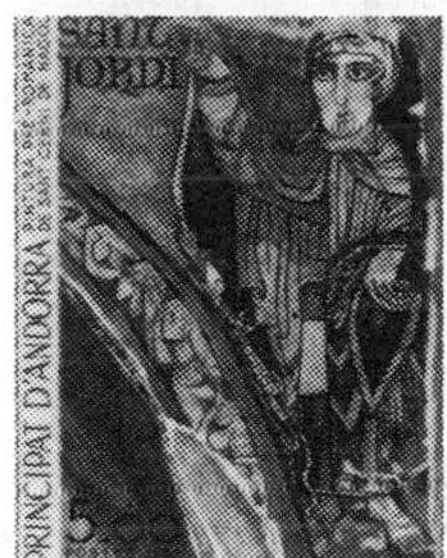

Romanesque Fresco, Church of St. Cerni de Nagol—A156

1984, Nov. 17 *Perf. 12x13*

328 A156 5fr multi 1.65 1.10

Arms Type of 1983

1984-86 *Perf. 13*

332 A150 3fr bl grn & red brn 75 45
333 A150 4fr brt org & brn ('86) 1.15 85
334 A150 10fr brn org & blk ('85) 2.50 1.50
334A A150 15fr grn & dk grn ('86) 4.25 3.25
335 A150 20fr brt bl & red brn 5.25 3.00

Saint Julia Valley—A157

1985, Apr. 13 **Engr.**

336 A157 2fr multi 55 45

Europa 1985—A158

1985, May 4 **Engr.**

337	A158	2.10fr	Le Val D'Andorre	60	45
338	A158	3fr	Instruments	80	65

Intl. Youth Year—A159

1985, June 8 **Engr.**

339	A159	3fr	multi	80	60

Wildlife Conservation—A160

1985, Aug. 3 **Photo.**

340	A160	1.80fr	Anas platyrhynchos	50	38
341	A160	2.20fr	Carduelis carduelis	60	45

Two Saints, Medieval Fresco in St. Cerni de Nagol Church—A161

1985, Sept. 14 **Engr.** ***Perf. 12½x13***

342	A161	5fr	multi	1.40	1.10

Postal Museum Inauguration—A162

1986, Mar. 22 **Engr.** ***Perf. 13***

343	A162	2.20fr	like No. 269	62	12

Europa 1986—A163

1986, May 3 **Engr.** ***Perf. 13***

344	A163	2.20fr	Ansalonga	62	12
345	A163	3.20fr	Isard	80	16

1986 World Cup Soccer Championships, Mexico—A164

1986, June 14

346	A164	3fr	multi	75	15

Angonella Lake—A165

1986, June 28

347	A165	2.20fr	multi	62	12

Manual Digest Frontispiece, 1748—A166

1986, Sept. 6 **Engr.**

348	A166	5fr	chnt brn, gray ol & blk	1.55	30

Intl. Peace Year—A167

1986, Sept. 29

349	A167	1.90fr	bl gray & grnsh bl	58	12

St. Vicenc D'Enclar—A168

1986, Oct. 18 **Engr.** ***Perf. 13½x13***

350	A168	1.90fr	dl gray vio, gray grn & ol brn	60	12

SEMI-POSTAL STAMP

Virgin of St. Coloma
SP1

Engraved

1964, July 25 *Perf. 13* Unwmkd.

B1	SP1	25c +10c multi	30.00	30.00

The surtax was for the Red Cross.

AIR POST STAMPS.

Chamois—AP1

Engraved.

1950, Feb. 20 *Perf. 13* Unwmkd.

C1	AP1	100fr indigo	70.00	45.00

East Branch of Valira River
AP2

1955–57

C2	AP2	100fr dk grn	9.00	7.50
C3	AP2	200fr cerise	18.00	15.00
C4	AP2	500fr dp bl ('57)	100.00	70.00

D'Inclès Valley
AP3

1961, June 19 *Perf. 13* Unwmkd.

C5	AP3	2fr red, ol gray & cl	90	75
C6	AP3	3fr bl, mar & sl grn	1.40	1.40
C7	AP3	5fr rose lil & red org	2.25	2.00

1964, Apr. 25

C8	AP3	10fr bl grn & sl grn	4.50	4.25

POSTAGE DUE STAMPS.

Postage Due Stamps of France, 1893-1931, Overprinted **ANDORRE**

On Stamps of 1893-1926.

1931–33 *Perf. 14x13½* Unwmkd.

J1	D2	5c blue	1.50	1.50
J2	D2	10c brown	1.50	1.50
J3	D2	30c rose red	45	45
J4	D2	50c vio brn	1.50	1.50
J5	D2	60c green	15.00	15.00
J6	D2	1fr red brn, *straw*	75	75
J7	D2	2fr brt vio	9.00	9.00
J8	D2	3fr magenta	1.75	1.75
		Nos. J1-J8 (8)	31.45	31.45

On Stamps of 1927-31.

J9	D4	1c ol grn	1.65	1.65
J10	D4	10c rose	3.50	3.50
J11	D4	60c red	22.50	22.50
J12	D4	1fr Prus grn ('32)	90.00	90.00
J13	D4	1.20fr on 2fr bl	70.00	70.00
J14	D4	2fr ol brn ('33)	150.00	150.00
J15	D4	5fr on 1fr vio	82.50	82.50
		Nos. J9-J15 (7)	420.15	420.15

D5 D6

1935-41 Typographed.

J16	D5	1c gray grn	2.25	1.65
J17	D6	5c lt bl ('37)	6.75	6.00
J18	D6	10c brn ('41)	5.25	6.00
J19	D6	2fr vio ('41)	7.50	4.50
J20	D6	5fr red org ('41)	9.50	4.50
		Nos. J16-J20 (5)	31.25	22.65

Wheat Sheaves
D7

1943–46 *Perf. 14x13½*

J21	D7	10c sepia	60	60
J22	D7	30c brt red vio	90	90
J23	D7	50c bl grn	1.10	1.10
J24	D7	1fr brt ultra	50	50
J25	D7	1.50fr rose red	4.00	4.00
J26	D7	2fr turq bl	90	90
J27	D7	3fr brn org	1.75	1.75
J28	D7	4fr dp vio ('45)	3.00	3.00
J29	D7	5fr brt pink	3.00	3.00
J30	D7	10fr red org ('45)	4.00	4.00
J31	D7	20fr ol brn ('46)	4.25	4.25
		Nos. J21-J31 (11)	24.00	24.00

Inscribed: "Timbre Taxe."

1946-53

J32	D7	10c sep ('46)	90	90
J33	D7	1fr ultra	60	60
J34	D7	2fr turq bl	75	75
J35	D7	3fr org brn	2.00	2.00
J36	D7	4fr violet	2.75	2.75
J37	D7	5fr brt pink	1.65	1.65
J38	D7	10fr red org	2.75	2.75
J39	D7	20fr ol brn	6.00	6.00
J40	D7	50fr dk grn ('50)	16.00	16.00
J41	D7	100fr dp grn ('53)	82.50	82.50
		Nos. J32-J41 (10)	115.90	115.90

Inscribed: "Timbre Taxe."

1961, June 19 *Perf. 14x13½*

J42	D7	5c rose pink	3.00	3.00
J43	D7	10c red org	6.00	6.00
J44	D7	20c olive	9.00	9.00
J45	D7	50c dk sl grn	15.00	15.00

Flower Type of France, 1964.

Designs: 5c, Centaury. 10c, Gentian. 15c, Corn poppy. 20c, Violets. 30c, Forget-me-not. 40c, Columbine. 50c, Clover.

1964–71 Typo. *Perf. 14x13½*

J46	D7	5c car rose, red & grn ('65)	5	5
J47	D7	10c car rose, brt bl & grn ('65)	6	6
J48	D7	15c brn, grn & red	6	6
J49	D7	20c dk grn, grn & vio ('71)	8	8
J50	D7	30c brn, ultra & grn	12	12
J51	D7	40c dk grn, scar & yel ('71)	15	15
J52	D7	50c vio bl, car & grn ('65)	22	22
		Nos. J46-J52 (7)	74	74

Wildflowers & Berries—D9

1985, Oct. 21 Engr. *Perf. 13*

J53	D9	10c Holly	5	5
J54	D9	20c Blueberries	5	5
J55	D9	30c Raspberries	8	8
J56	D9	40c Bilberries	12	12
J57	D9	50c Blackberries	15	15
J58	D9	1fr Broom	30	30
J59	D9	2fr Rosehips	60	38
J60	D9	3fr Nightshade	90	58
J61	D9	4fr Nabiu	1.25	75
J62	D9	5fr Strawberries	1.50	95
		Nos. J53-J62 (10)	5.00	3.41

NEWSPAPER STAMP.

France No. P7 Overprinted **ANDORRE**

1931 *Perf. 14x13½.* Unwmkd.

P1	A16	½c on 1c gray	80	80

ANGOLA

(ăng·gō'lȧ)

LOCATION — Southwestern Africa between Congo and South-West Africa.
GOVT.—Republic.
AREA—481,351 sq. mi.
POP.—7,108,000 (1983 est.).
CAPITAL—Luanda.

Angola was a Portuguese overseas territory until it became independent November 11, 1975, as the People's Republic of Angola.

1000 Reis = 1 Milreis
100 Centavos = 1 Escudo (1913, 1954)
100 Centavos = 1 Angolar (1932)
10 Lweys = 1 Kwanza (1977)

Portuguese Crown
A1

Perf. 12½, 13½.

1870–77 Typographed Unwmkd.

1 A1 5r black 2.00 1.75
a. Perf. 13½ 10.00 5.00
2 A1 10r yellow 20.00 10.00
3 A1 20r bister 3.00 1.90
a. Perf. 13½ 100.00 75.00
4 A1 25r red 12.00 5.00
a. 25r rose 12.00 5.00
b. Laid paper
c. 25r rose, perf. 14 165.00 100.00
d. Perf. 13½ 24.00 12.00
5 A1 40r bl ('77) 150.00 90.00
6 A1 50r green 50.00 14.00
a. Perf. 13½ 275.00 100.00
7 A1 100r lilac 2.50 2.25
a. Perf. 12½ 10.00 6.00
8 A1 200r org ('77) 4.00 2.00
a. Perf. 12½ 5.00 2.50
9 A1 300r choc ('77) 4.00 3.50
a. Perf. 12½ 12.00 5.50

1881-85

10 A1 10r grn ('83) 5.00 2.50
a. Perf. 12½ 17.50 3.50
11 A1 20r car rose ('85) 11.00 8.50
a. Cliche of 40r in plate of 20r 750.00
12 A1 25r vio ('85) 9.00 3.00
a. Perf. 13½ 9.00 4.00
13 A1 40r buff ('82) 5.50 3.25
a. Perf. 12½ 6.00 3.25
15 A1 50r blue 25.00 2.75
a. Perf. 13½ 30.00 2.75

Two types of numerals are found on No. 2 and Nos. 11 to 15.

The error, No. 11a, was discovered before the stamps were issued. All copies were cancelled by a blue pencil mark.

In perf. 12½, Nos. 1–4, 4a and 6, as well as 7a, were printed in 1870 on thicker paper and 1875 on normal paper. Stamps of the earlier printing sell for 2 to 15 times more than those of the 1875 printing.

Some reprints of the 1870–85 issues are on a smooth white chalky paper, ungummed and perf. 13½. Price each, $1.50.

Other reprints of these issues are on thin white paper with shiny white gum and clear-cut perf. 13½. Price each, $2.50.

King Luiz
A2

King Carlos
A3

1886 Embossed *Perf. 12½*

16 A2 5r black 10.00 6.00
a. Perf. 13½ 17.50 13.00
17 A2 10r green 10.00 5.50
a. Perf. 13½ 20.00 11.00
18 A2 20r rose 15.00 12.50
a. Perf. 13½ 19.00 10.00
19 A2 25r red vio 11.00 2.50
20 A2 40r chocolate 12.00 6.00
21 A2 50r blue 16.00 4.00
22 A2 100r yel brn 22.50 9.00
23 A2 200r gray vio 27.50 12.50
24 A2 300r orange 30.00 14.00

Reprints of 5, 20 & 100r have cleancut perf. 13½. Price, each $3.

Typographed.

1893-94 *Perf. 11½, 12½, 13½.*

25 A3 5r yellow 1.50 1.25
26 A3 10r redsh vio 3.25 1.40
27 A3 15r chocolate 4.25 2.10
28 A3 20r lavender 4.50 2.25
29 A3 25r green 2.00 1.25
a. Perf. 12½ 4.50 1.75
30 A3 50r lt bl 3.75 1.75
a. Perf. 13½ 7.50 4.50
31 A3 75r carmine 7.50 4.50
a. Perf. 11½ 9.50 7.50
32 A3 80r lt grn 10.00 5.50
33 A3 100r brn, *buff* 10.50 5.50
a. Perf. 11½ 75.00 50.00
34 A3 150r car, *rose* 18.00 12.00
35 A3 200r dk bl, *lt bl* 22.50 15.00
36 A3 300r dk bl, *sal* 22.50 15.00

No. P1 Surcharged in Blue

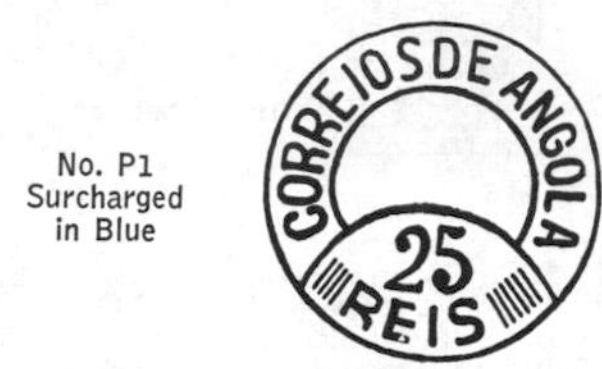

1894, Aug.

37 N1 25r on 2½r brn 90.00 60.00

King Carlos
A5

1898–1903 *Perf. 11½*

Name and Value in Black except 500r

38 A5 2½r gray 30 20
39 A5 5r orange 30 20
40 A5 10r yel grn 30 20
41 A5 15r vio brn 2.25 1.25
42 A5 15r gray grn ('03) 1.00 75
43 A5 20r gray vio 40 30
44 A5 25r sea grn 1.50 60
45 A5 25r car ('03) 50 20
46 A5 50r blue 2.25 70
47 A5 50r brn ('03) 6.00 3.00
48 A5 65r dl bl ('03) 8.00 6.50
49 A5 75r rose 8.00 2.50
50 A5 75r red vio ('03) 2.00 1.50
51 A5 80r violet 8.00 2.75
52 A5 100r dk bl, *bl* 1.50 1.00
53 A5 115r org brn, *pink* ('03) 8.00 5.00
54 A5 130r brn, *straw* ('03) 8.00 5.00
55 A5 150r brn, *straw* 8.00 4.25
56 A5 200r red vio, *pink* 3.50 1.50
57 A5 300r dk bl, *rose* 4.25 4.00
58 A5 400r dl bl, *straw* ('03) 3.75 2.50
59 A5 500r blk & red, *bl* ('01) 5.00 4.00
60 A5 700r vio, *yelsh* ('01) 27.50 15.00
Nos. 38-60 (23) 110.30 62.90

Stamps of 1886–94 Surcharged in Black or Red

65 RÉIS

Two types of surcharge:
I. 3mm. between numeral and REIS.
II. 4½mm. spacing.

1902 *Perf. 12½*

61 A2 65r on 40r choc 8.00 4.00
62 A2 65r on 300r org, I 8.00 4.00
a. Type II 50.00 27.50
63 A2 115r on 10r grn 6.50 4.00
a. Inverted surcharge
b. Perf. 13½ 27.50 25.00
64 A2 115r on 200r gray vio 6.00 3.50
65 A2 130r on 50r bl 8.75 6.50
66 A2 130r on 100r brn 5.50 3.25
67 A2 400r on 20r rose 50.00 32.50
a. Perf. 13½ 60.00 42.50
68 A2 400r on 25r vio 12.50 7.50
69 A2 400r on 5r blk (R) 12.00 9.00
a. Double surcharge
Nos. 61-69 (9) 117.25 74.25

Perf. 11½, 12½, 13½.

70 A3 65r on 5r yel, I 6.00 4.00
a. Type II 15.00 15.00
71 A3 65r on 10r red vio, I 5.00 3.50
a. Type II 20.00 8.00
b. Perf. 11½, type I 13.50 8.00
c. Perf. 11½, type II 5.25 3.75
72 A3 65r on 20r lav 6.00 4.00
a. Type II 10.00 9.00
73 65r on 25r grn 4.50 3.50
a. Perf. 11½ 14.00 11.00
74 A3 115r on 80r lt grn 8.50 6.25
75 A3 115r on 100r brn, *buff* 8.50 5.00
a. Perf. 13½ 14.00 10.00
76 A3 115r on 150r car, *rose* 12.00 8.00
a. Perf. 13½ 15.00 9.00
77 A3 130r on 15r choc 4.25 3.00
78 A3 130r on 75r car 5.50 3.50
a. Perf. 13½ 22.50 17.50
79 A3 130r on 300r dk bl, *sal* 16.00 9.00
80 A3 400r on 50r lt bl 5.25 4.00
81 A3 400r on 200r bl, *bl* 6.00 4.50
a. Perf. 13½ 32.50 13.50
82 N1 400r on 2½r brn 1.25 1.25
a. Type II 3.75 3.50
Nos. 70-82 (13) 88.75 59.50

Reprints of Nos. 65, 67, 68 and 69 have clean-cut perforation 13½. Price $2.50 each.

Stamps of 1898 Overprinted

PROVISORIO
a

1902 *Perf. 11½*

83 A5 15r brown 1.50 90
84 A5 25r sea grn 1.25 60
85 A5 50r blue 2.25 1.40
86 A5 75r rose 4.25 3.00

No. 48 Surcharged in Black

50 RÉIS

1905

87 A5 50r on 65r dl bl 3.50 2.25

Stamps of 1898-1903 Overprinted in Carmine or Green

REPUBLICA
b

1911

88 A5 2½r gray 30 20
89 A5 5r org yel 30 20
90 A5 10r lt grn 35 30
a. Inverted overprint 5.75 5.75
91 A5 15r gray grn 50 30
92 A5 20r gray vio 50 30
93 A5 25r car (G) 50 25
a. Inverted overprint 5.00 4.00
94 A5 50r brown 2.25 1.50
95 A5 75r lilac 4.00 4.00
96 A5 100r dk bl, *bl* 4.00 4.00
97 A5 115r org brn, *pink* 1.50 90
98 A5 130r brn, *straw* 1.50 90
99 A5 200r red lil, *pnksh* 1.50 90
100 A5 400r dl bl, *straw* 2.00 1.00
101 A5 500r blk & red, *bl* 2.00 1.00
102 A5 700r vio, *yelsh* 2.25 1.10
Nos. 88-102 (15) 23.45 16.85

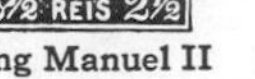

King Manuel II
A6

Ceres
A7

1912 *Perf. 11½x12.*

Overprinted in Carmine or Green.

103 A6 2½r violet 35 50
104 A6 5r black 45 60
105 A6 10r gray grn 55 45
106 A6 20r car (G) 55 45
107 A6 25r vio brn 55 45
108 A6 50r dk bl 90 75
109 A6 75r bis brn 1.00 1.50
110 A6 100r brn, *lt grn* 2.50 1.25
111 A6 200r dk grn, *sal* 2.00 1.25
112 A6 300r *azure* 2.00 1.25
Nos. 103-112 (10) 10.85 8.45

No. 91 Surcharged with New Values as 5

1912, June *Perf. 11½*

113 A5 2½r on 15r gray grn 4.00 4.00
114 A5 5r on 15r gray grn 3.00 2.25
115 A5 10r on 15r gray grn 3.00 2.25

Inverted and double surcharges of Nos. 113-115 were made intentionally.

Nos. 86 and 50 Surcharged "25" in Black and Overprinted in Violet

c

1912

116 A5 25r on 75r rose 65.00 40.00
117 A5 25r on 75r red vio 4.00 2.50
a. "REUPBLICA" 40.00 37.50
b. "25" omitted 40.00 37.50
c. "REPUBLICA" omitted 40.00 37.50

Typographed.

Name and Value in Black.

1914-26 *Perf. 12x11½, 15x14.*

118 A7 ¼c ol brn 12 25
a. Inscriptions inverted 3.00
119 A7 ½c black 12 25
120 A7 1c bl grn 12 25
121 A7 1c yel grn ('22) 12 12
122 A7 1½c lil brn 12 12
123 A7 2c carmine 12 12
124 A7 2c gray ('25) 40 1.00
125 A7 2½c lt vio 12 12
126 A7 3c org ('22) 12 1.00
127 A7 4c dl rose ('22) 12 12
128 A7 4½c gray ('22) 12 1.00
130 A7 5c blue 12 12
131 A7 6c lil ('22) 12 12
132 A7 7c ultra ('22) 12 12
133 A7 7½c yel brn 12 12
134 A7 8c slate 12 12
135 A7 10c org brn 40 12
136 A7 12c ol brn ('22) 65 35
137 A7 12c dp grn ('25) 35 15
138 A7 15c plum 40 30
139 A7 15c brn rose ('22) 17 15
140 A7 20c yel grn 35 15
141 A7 24c ultra ('25) 1.75 65
142 A7 25c choc ('25) 1.75 65
143 A7 30c brn, *grn* 2.00 2.00
144 A7 30c gray grn ('22) 1.00 10

145 A7 40c brn, *pink* 3.50 2.00
146 A7 40c turq bl ('22) 90 12
147 A7 50c org, *sal* 9.00 5.00
148 A7 50c lt vio ('25) 1.50 15
149 A7 60c dk bl ('22) 80 15
150 A7 60c dp rose ('26) 75.00 60.00
151 A7 80c pink ('22) 2.00 15
152 A7 1e grn, *bl* 4.50 3.50
153 A7 1e rose ('22) 2.25 15
154 A7 1e dp bl ('25) 2.00 1.50
155 A7 2e dk vio ('22) 2.25 80
156 A7 5e buff ('25) 7.50 3.50
157 A7 10e pink ('25) 17.50 11.00
158 A7 20e pale turq ('25) 75.00 40.00
Nos. 118-158 (40) 214.72 *137.59*

Two kinds of chalky-surfaced paper, ordinary and coated, were used for Nos. 118–120, 122–123, 130, 133–135, 138 and 140. Those on coated paper sell unused for 10 to 40 times the prices listed; used for about 5 to 20 times.

Stamps of 1898–1903 Overprinted type "c" in Red or Green

On Stamps of 1898-1903.

1914 ***Perf. 11½, 12.***

159 A5 10r yel grn (R) 4.25 3.25
160 A5 15r gray grn (R) 4.25 3.25
161 A5 20r gray vio (G) 1.00 75
163 A5 75r red vio (G) 90 60
164 A5 100r bl, *bl* (R) 2.00 2.00
165 A5 115r org brn, *pink* (R) *30.00*
167 A5 200r red vio, *pnksh* (G) 1.50 75
169 A5 400r dl bl, *straw* (R) 25.00 17.00
170 A5 500r blk & red, *bl* (R) 3.75 3.25
171 A5 700r vio, *yelsh* (G) 13.00 12.00

Inverted and double surcharges were made intentionally. No. 165 was not regularly issued.

On Provisional Stamps of 1902.

Perf. 11½, 12½, 13½.

172 A2 115r on 10r grn (R) 11.00 8.25
a. Perf. 13½ 12.50 12.50
173 A2 115r on 200r gray vio (R) 11.00 10.00
174 A2 130r on 50r bl (R) 14.00 12.00
175 A3 115r on 80r lt grn (R) 150.00 125.00
176 A3 115r on 100r brn, *buff* (R) 200.00 175.00
177 A3 115r on 150r car, *rose* (G) 175.00 150.00
178 A3 130r on 75r car (G) 3.00 2.75
179 A3 130r on 300r dk bl, *sal* (R) 5.50 3.50
a. Perf. 12½ 10.00 6.50
180 N1 400r on 2½r brn (R) 50 50
a. Perf. 11½ 2.50 2.00
Nos. 172-180 (9) 570.00 487.00

On Stamps of 1902.

Overprinted PROVISORIO

Perf. 11½, 12.

181 A5 50r bl (R) 1.35 90
a. "Republica" double
182 A5 75r rose (G) 3.50 2.75
a. "Republica" inverted

On Stamp of 1905.

183 A5 50r on 65r dl bl (R) 3.50 2.75
a. "Republica" inverted
b. "Republica" double

Vasco da Gama Issue of Various Portuguese Colonies

Common Design Types CD20–CD27 Surcharged

REPUBLICA
ANGOLA
¼ C.

On Stamps of Macao.

1913 ***Perf. 12½ to 16.***

184 ¼c on ½a bl grn 2.00 2.00
185 ½c on 1a red 1.65 1.65
186 1c on 2a red vio 1.65 1.65
187 2½c on 4a yel grn 1.40 1.40
188 5c on 8a dk bl 1.40 1.40
189 7½c on 12a vio brn 3.50 3.50
190 10c on 16a bis brn 1.90 1.90
191 15c on 24a bis 1.90 1.90
Nos. 184-191 (8) 15.40 15.40

On Stamps of Portuguese Africa.

Perf. 14 to 15.

192 ¼c on 2½r bl grn 1.00 1.00
193 ½c on 5r red 1.00 1.00
194 1c on 10r red vio 1.00 1.00
195 2½c on 25r yel grn 1.00 1.00
196 5c on 50r dk bl 1.00 1.00
197 7½c on 75r vio brn 4.00 4.00
198 10c on 100r bis brn 1.40 1.40
199 15c on 150r bis 2.25 2.25
Nos. 192-199 (8) 12.65 12.65

On Stamps of Timor

200 ¼c on ½a bl grn 2.00 2.00
201 ½c on 1a red 2.00 2.00
202 1c on 2a red vio 2.00 2.00
203 2½c on 4a yel grn 1.90 1.90
204 5c on 8a dk bl 1.90 1.90
205 7½c on 12a vio brn 3.25 3.25
206 10c on 16a bis brn 2.25 2.25
207 15c on 24a bis 2.25 2.25
Nos. 200-207 (8) 17.55 17.55

Provisional Issue of 1902 Overprinted in Carmine

REPUBLICA

1915 ***Perf. 11½, 12½, 13½.***

208 A2 115r on 10r grn 1.65 *2.00*
209 A2 115r on 200r gray vio 1.40 *1.75*
210 A2 130r on 100r brn 1.20 *1.75*
211 A3 115r on 80r lt grn 1.65 *2.00*
212 A3 115r on 100r brn, *buff* 1.40 *1.75*
a. Perf. 11½ 22.50 *22.50*
213 A3 115r on 150r car, *rose* 2.25 *3.00*
214 A3 130r on 15r choc 1.10 *1.75*
a. Perf. 12½ 6.00 4.50
215 A3 130r on 75r car 2.25 *2.75*
216 A3 130r on 300r dk bl, *sal* 1.75 *2.75*
Nos. 208-216 (9) 14.65 *19.50*

Stamps of 1911-14 Surcharged in Black:

½ C.

½ C. ═ ═ ═
d e

On Stamps of 1911.

1919 ***Perf. 11½***

217 A5 (d) ½c on 75r red lil 2.25 *2.50*
218 A5 (d) 2½c on 100r bl, *grysh* 2.50 *2.75*

On Stamps of 1912.

Perf. 11½x12.

219 A6 (e) ½c on 5r bis brn 1.00 *1.00*
220 A6 (e) 2½c on 100r brn, *lt grn* 1.25 75

On Stamps of 1914.

221 A5 (d) ½c on 75r red lil 1.10 75
222 A5 (d) 2½c on 100r bl, *grysh* 1.25 90

Inverted and double surcharges were made for sale to collectors.

Nos. 163, 98 and Type of 1914 Surcharged with New Values and Bars in Black.

1921

223 A5 (c) 00.5c on 75c red vio *120.00* *120.00*
224 A5 (b) 4c on 130r brn, *straw* (#98) 1.25 *1.25*
225 A5 (c) 4c on 130r brn, *straw* 4.00 3.00
a. Surch. omitted 150.00

Nos. 109 and 108 Surcharged with New Values and Bars in Black.

226 A6 00.5c on 75c bis brn 1.25 90
227 A6 1c on 50r dk bl 1.25 80

Nos. 133 and 138 Surcharged with New Values and Bars in Black.

228 A7 00.5c on 7½c yel brn 1.25 90
229 A7 04c on 15c plum 1.25 90

Nos. 81–82 Surcharged

República
40 C.

1925 ***Perf. 12½***

234 A3 40c on 400r on 200r bl, *bl* 85 55
a. Perf. 13½ 5.00 3.50
235 N1 40c on 400c on 2½r brn 55 45
a. Perf. 13½ 55 45

Nos. 150–151, 154–155 Surcharged

70 C.

1931 ***Perf. 11½.***

236 A7 50c on 60c dp rose 1.40 1.20
237 A7 70c on 80c pink 2.75 1.50
238 A7 70c on 1e dp bl 2.25 1.75
239 A7 1.40e on 2e dk vio 1.65 1.25

Ceres
A14

Wmk. 232

Wmkd. Maltese Cross. (232)

1932–46 **Typo.** ***Perf. 12x11½***

243 A14 1c bis brn 12 12
244 A14 5c dk brn 12 12
245 A14 10c dp vio 12 12
246 A14 15c black 12 12
247 A14 20c gray 12 12
248 A14 30c myr grn 12 12
249 A14 35c yel grn ('46) 4.50 1.50
250 A14 40c dp org 12 12
251 A14 45c lt bl 1.00 60
252 A14 50c lt brn 12 12
253 A14 60c ol grn 45 20
254 A14 70c org brn 45 25
255 A14 80c emerald 40 15
256 A14 85c rose 3.00 3.00
257 A14 1a claret 80 18
258 A14 1.40a dk bl 6.75 1.75
258A A14 1.75a dk bl ('46) 9.00 2.00
259 A14 2a dl vio 2.50 30
260 A14 5a pale yel grn 4.50 75
261 A14 10a ol bis 12.00 1.50
262 A14 20a orange 30.00 3.00
Nos. 243-262 (21) 76.31 16.14

Stamps of 1932

Surcharged with New Value and Bars.

5½mm. between bars and new value.

1934

263 A14 10c on 45c lt bl 2.00 1.25
264 A14 20c on 85c rose 1.75 1.25
265 A14 30c on 1.40a dk bl 1.75 1.25
266 A14 70c on 2a dl vio 2.25 1.75
267 A14 80c on 5a pale yel grn 3.50 1.60

See also Nos. 294A–300.

Nos. J26, J30 Surcharged in Black

CORREIOS
═ 5
CENTAVOS

1935 ***Perf. 11½*** **Unwmkd.**

268 D2 5c on 6c lt brn 1.50 1.00
269 D2 30c on 50c gray 1.50 1.00
270 D2 40c on 50c gray 1.50 1.00

No. 255 Surcharged in Black

0,15 Cent.

1938 ***Perf. 12x11½*** **Wmk. 232**

271 A14 5c on 80c emer 60 *1.00*
272 A14 10c on 80c emer 80 *2.00*
273 A14 15c on 80c emer 1.25 *3.50*

Vasco da Gama Issue
Common Design Types
Engraved; Name and Value Typographed in Black.
Perf. 13½x13

1938, July 26 **Unwmkd.**

274 CD34 1c gray grn 12 12
275 CD34 5c org brn 12 12
276 CD34 10c dk car 12 12
277 CD34 15c dk vio brn 25 12
278 CD34 20c slate 28 12
279 CD35 30c rose vio 40 12
280 CD35 35c brt grn 55 30
281 CD35 40c brown 40 25
282 CD35 50c brt red vio 40 25
283 CD36 60c gray blk 50 25
284 CD36 70c brn vio 45 25
285 CD36 80c orange 45 25
286 CD36 1a red 45 25
287 CD37 1.75a blue 1.25 60
288 CD37 2a brn car 2.25 60
289 CD37 5a ol grn 6.75 60
290 CD38 10a bl vio 15.00 1.00
291 CD38 20a red brn 30.00 1.75
Nos. 274-291 (18) 59.74 7.07

Common Design Types
pictured in section at front of book.

Marble Column and Portuguese Arms with Cross
A20

1938, July 29 *Perf. 12½*

No.	Type	Description	Unused	Used
292	A20	80c bl grn	2.25	1.90
293	A20	1.75a dp bl	17.50	3.75
294	A20	20a dk red brn	42.50	22.50

Issued to commemorate the visit of the President of Portugal to this colony in 1938.

Stamps of 1932 Surcharged with New Value and Bars.

8mm. between bars and new value.

1941-45 *Perf. 12x11½.* **Wmk. 232**

No.	Type	Description	Unused	Used
294A	A14	5c on 80c emer ('45)	45	35
295	A14	10c on 45c lt bl	1.00	75
296	A14	15c on 45c lt bl	1.50	75
297	A14	20c on 85c rose	1.00	75
298	A14	35c on 85c rose	1.00	75
299	A14	50c on 1.40a dk bl	1.00	75
300	A14	60c on 1a cl	5.50	4.00
		Nos. 294A-300 (7)	11.45	8.10

Nos. 285 to 287 Surcharged with New Values and Bars in Black or Red.

1945 *Perf. 13½x13.* **Unwmkd.**

No.	Type	Description	Unused	Used
301	CD36	5c on 80c org	45	35
302	CD36	50c on 1a red	60	35
303	CD37	50c on 1.75a bl (R)	45	35
304	CD37	50c on 1.75a bl	60	35

São Miguel Fort, Luanda
A21

Chiumbe River
A24

John IV
A22

Designs: 10c, Our Lady of Nazareth Church, Luanda. 50c, Salvador Correia de Sa e Benevides. 1a, Surrender of Luanda. 1.75a, Diogo Cao. 2a, Manuel Cerveira Pereira. 5a, Stone Cliffs, Yelala. 10a, Paulo Dias de Novais. 20a, Massangano Fort.

Lithographed.

1948, May *Perf. 14½* **Unwmkd.**

No.	Type	Description	Unused	Used
305	A21	5c dk vio	12	12
306	A21	10c dk brn	50	30
307	A22	30c bl grn	20	20
308	A22	50c vio brn	20	10
309	A21	1a carmine	50	20
310	A22	1.75a sl bl	1.00	30
311	A22	2a green	1.00	30
312	A21	5a gray blk	3.00	60
313	A22	10a rose lil	6.00	65
314	A21	20a gray bl	12.00	1.75
a.		Sheet of ten	60.00	60.00
		Nos. 305-314 (10)	24.52	4.52

Issued to commemorate the 300th anniversary of the restoration of Angola to Portugal.

No. 314a measures 225x162mm. and contains one each of Nos. 305-314 with marginal inscriptions in gray. The sheet sold for 42.50 angolars.

Lady of Fatima Issue
Common Design Type

1948, Dec.

No.	Type	Description	Unused	Used
315	CD40	50c carmine	1.25	1.00
316	CD40	3a ultra	4.50	2.75
317	CD40	6a red org	22.50	6.50
318	CD40	9a dp cl	45.00	9.00

Issued to honor Our Lady of the Rosary at Fatima, Portugal.

Black Rocks
A25

Designs: 50c, View of Luanda. 2.50a, Sa da Bandeira. 3.50a, Mocamedes. 15a, Cubal River. 50a, Duke of Bragança Falls.

1949 *Perf. 13½* **Unwmkd.**

No.	Type	Description	Unused	Used
319	A24	20c dk sl bl	30	20
320	A25	40c blk brn	30	15
321	A24	50c rose brn	30	15
322	A24	2.50a bl vio	1.80	45
323	A24	3.50a sl gray	1.80	45
323A	A24	15a dk grn	20.00	2.00
324	A24	50a dp grn	135.00	7.00
		Nos. 319-324 (7)	159.50	10.40

Sailing Vessel
A26

U.P.U. Symbols
A27

1949, Aug. *Perf. 14*

No.	Type	Description	Unused	Used
325	A26	1a chocolate	6.00	50
326	A26	4a dk Prus grn	20.00	1.25

Centenary of founding of Mocamedes.

1949, Oct.

No.	Type	Description	Unused	Used
327	A27	4a dk grn & lt grn	7.50	2.25

Issued to commemorate the 75th anniversary of the formation of the Universal Postal Union.

Stamp of 1870
A28

1950, Apr. 2 *Perf. 11½x12*

No.	Type	Description	Unused	Used
328	A28	50c yel grn	1.25	35
329	A28	1a fawn	1.25	40
330	A28	4a black	5.00	1.25

Angola's first philatelic exhibition, marking the 80th anniversary of Angola's first stamps.

A sheet of three, perf. 11½, contains one each of Nos. 328, 329 (inverted) and 330, and sold for 6.50 angolars. Size: 119x80 mm. All copies carry an oval exhibition cancellation.

Holy Year Issue
Common Design Types

1950, May *Perf. 13x13½*

No.	Type	Description	Unused	Used
331	CD41	1a dl rose vio	1.00	20
332	CD42	4a black	5.00	60

Issued to commemorate the Holy Year, 1950.

Dark Chanting Goshawk
A31

European Bee Eater
A32

Designs: 10c, Racquet-tailed roller. 15c, Bataleur eagle. 50c, Giant kingfisher. 1a, Yellow-fronted barbet. 1.50a, Openbill (stork). 2a, Southern ground hornbill. 2.50a, African skimmer. 3a, Shikra. 3.50a, Denham's bustard. 4a, African golden oriole. 4.50a, Long-tailed shrike. 5a, Red-shouldered glossy starling. 6a, Sharp-tailed glossy starling. 7a, Red-shouldered widow bird. 10a, Half-colored kingfisher. 12.50a, White-crowned shrike. 15a, White-winged babbling starling. 20a, Yellow-billed hornbill. 25a, Amethyst starling. 30a, Orange-breasted shrike. 40a, Secretary bird. 50a, Rosy-faced lovebird.

Photogravure and Lithographed.

1951 *Perf. 11½* **Unwmkd.**

Birds in Natural Colors.

No.	Type	Description	Unused	Used
333	A31	5c lt bl	20	*1.00*
334	A32	10c aqua	20	20
335	A32	15c sal pink	40	*2.00*
336	A32	20c pale yel	55	45
337	A31	50c gray bl	40	20
338	A31	1a lilac	40	20
339	A31	1.50a gray buff	60	20
340	A31	2a cream	60	20
341	A32	2.50a gray	60	30
342	A32	3a lem yel	50	35
343	A31	3.50a lt gray	50	35
344	A31	4a rose buff	80	35
345	A32	4.50a rose lil	80	50
346	A31	5a green	4.50	50
347	A31	6a blue	4.50	1.20
348	A31	7a orange	4.50	1.50
349	A31	10a lil rose	37.50	2.25
350	A32	12.50a sl gray	5.00	3.50
351	A31	15a pale ol	5.00	3.50
352	A31	20a pale bis brn	60.00	10.00
353	A31	25a lil rose	20.00	5.50
354	A32	30a pale sal	20.00	7.00
355	A31	40a yellow	30.00	8.50
356	A31	50a turquoise	90.00	27.50
		Nos. 333-356 (24)	287.55	*77.25*

Holy Year Extension Issue.
Common Design Type

1951, Oct. **Litho.** *Perf. 14*

No.	Type	Description	Unused	Used
357	CD43	4a orange	2.25	90

Issued to publicize the extension of the Holy Year into 1951.

Sheets contain alternate vertical rows of stamps and labels bearing quotations from Pope Pius XII or the Patriarch Cardinal of Lisbon.

Medical Congress Issue.
Common Design Type
Design: Medical examination

1952, June *Perf. 13½*

No.	Type	Description	Unused	Used
358	CD44	1a vio bl & brn blk	60	30

Issued to publicize the first National Congress of Tropical Medicine, Lisbon, 1952.

Head of Christ
A35

1952, Oct. *Perf. 13* **Unwmkd.**

No.	Type	Description	Unused	Used
359	A35	10c dk bl & buff	10	5
360	A35	50c dk ol grn & ol gray	50	15
361	A35	2a rose vio & cr	2.75	35

Issued to commemorate the Exhibition of Sacred Missionary Art held at Lisbon in 1951.

Leopard
A36

Sable Antelope
A37

Animals: 20c, Elephant. 30c, Eland. 40c, African crocodile. 50c, Impala. 1a, Mountain zebra. 1.50a, Sitatunga. 2a, Black rhinoceros. 2.30a, Gemsbok. 2.50a, Lion. 3a, Buffalo. 3.50a, Springbok. 4a, Brindled gnu. 5a, Hartebeest. 7a, Wart hog. 10a, Defassa waterbuck. 12.50a, Hippopotamus. 15a, Greater kudu. 20a, Giraffe.

1953, Aug. 15 *Perf. 12½*

No.	Type	Description	Unused	Used
362	A36	5c multi	10	10
363	A37	10c multi	10	10
364	A37	20c multi	10	10
365	A37	30c multi	10	10
366	A36	40c multi	10	10
367	A37	50c multi	10	10
368	A37	1a multi	35	10
369	A37	1.50a multi	25	10
370	A36	2a multi	30	15
371	A37	2.30a multi	40	15
372	A37	2.50a multi	50	10
373	A36	3a multi	50	15
374	A37	3.50a multi	30	12
375	A37	4a multi	13.00	50
376	A37	5a multi	55	20
377	A37	7a multi	1.25	40
378	A37	10a multi	2.00	35
379	A37	12.50a multi	4.50	1.50
380	A37	15a multi	4.50	2.00
381	A37	20a multi	6.00	75
		Nos. 362-381 (20)	35.00	7.17

Stamp of Portugal and Arms of Colonies
A38

1953, Nov. **Photo.** *Perf. 13*

Stamp and Arms Multicolored.

No.	Type	Description	Unused	Used
382	A38	50c gray & dk gray	85	55

Issued to commemorate the centenary of Portugal's first postage stamps.

Map and Plane
A39

Typographed and Lithographed.

1954, May 27 *Perf. 13½*

No.	Type	Description	Unused	Used
383	A39	35c dk grn, ol, bl grn & red	15	15
384	A39	4.50e blk, dl vio, aqua & red	1.10	45

Issued to publicize the visit of Pres. Francisco H C. Lopes.

Sao Paulo Issue
Common Design Type

1954 **Lithographed**

No.	Type	Description	Unused	Used
385	CD46	1e bis & gray	50	30

Issued to commemorate the 400th anniversary of the founding of Sao Paulo.

Map of Angola A41 — Artur de Paiva A42

1955, Aug. Perf. 13½ Unwmkd.

Blue Outline, Red Highways, Black Inscriptions

386	A41	5c gray & pale grn	6	6
387	A41	20c gray, lt bl & sal	7	6
388	A41	50c brn buff, pale grn & lt bl	15	6
389	A41	1e gray, lt bl grn, & org yel	20	6
390	A41	2.30e brn buff, aqua & yel	55	30
391	A41	4e bis, pale grn & lt bl	1.75	20
392	A41	10e lil, aqua & cit	1.65	20
393	A41	20e ol grn & pale grn	3.00	40
		Nos. 386-393 (8)	7.43	1.34

1956, Oct. 9 Perf. 13½x12½

394	A42	1e blk, dk bl & ocher	30	20

Issued to commemorate the centenary of the birth of Col. Artur de Paiva.

Man of Malange A43 — José M. Antunes A44

Various Costumes in Multicolor; Inscriptions in Black Brown.

1957, Jan. 1 Photo. Perf. 11½

Granite Paper.

395	A43	5c gray	5	5
396	A43	10c org yel	7	6
397	A43	15c lt bl grn	12	8
398	A43	20c pale rose vio	12	8
399	A43	30c brt rose	12	8
400	A43	40c bl gray	12	8
401	A43	50c pale ol	12	8
402	A43	80c lt vio	20	20
403	A43	1.50e buff	1.75	20
404	A43	2.50e lt yel grn	2.00	18
405	A43	4e salmon	50	18
406	A43	10e sal pink	1.25	40
		Nos. 395-406 (12)	6.42	1.67

1957, April Perf. 13½

407	A44	1e aqua & brn	80	40

Issued to commemorate the centenary of the birth of Father José Maria Antunes.

Fair Emblem, Globe and Arms A45

1958, July Litho. Perf. 12x11½

408	A45	1.50e multi	60	35

World's Fair, Brussels, Apr. 17–Oct. 19.

Tropical Medicine Congress Issue

Common Design Type

Design: Securidaca longipedunculata.

1958, Dec. 15 Perf. 13½

409	CD47	2.50e multi	1.90	1.10

Issued to publicize the 6th International Congress for Tropical Medicine and Malaria, Lisbon, Sept. 1958.

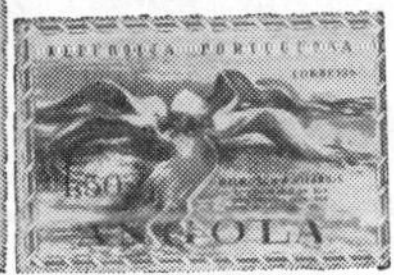

Medicine Man A47 — Welwitschia Mirabilis A48

Designs: 1.50e, Early government doctor. 2.50e, Modern medical team.

1958, Dec. 18 Perf. 11½x12

410	A47	1e bl blk & brn	30	15
411	A47	1.50e gray, blk & brn	80	35
412	A47	2.50e multi	1.50	60

Issued to commemorate the 75th anniversary of the Maria Pia Hospital, Luanda.

1959, Oct. 1 Litho. Perf. 14½

Various Views of Plant and Various Frames.

413	A48	1.50e lt brn, grn & blk	80	70
414	A48	2.50e multi	1.20	55
415	A48	5e multi	1.60	90
416	A48	10e multi	4.50	1.50

Centenary of discovery of Welwitschia mirabilis, desert plant.

Map of West Africa, c. 1540, by Jorge Reinel—A49

1960, June 25 Perf. 13½

417	A49	2.50e multi	30	20

Issued to commemorate the 500th anniversary of the death of Prince Henry the Navigator.

Distributing Medicines A50 — Girl of Angola A51

1960, Oct. Litho. Perf. 14½

418	A50	2.50e multi	45	25

Issued to commemorate the 10th anniversary of the Commission for Technical Co-operation in Africa South of the Sahara (C.C.T.A.).

1961, Nov. 30 Perf. 13 Unwmkd.

Portraits of Angolese Women in Natural Colors

419	A51	10c blk, yel grn & grn	8	5
420	A51	15c blk, gray bl & lil	8	8
421	A51	30c blk, yel & dk bl	10	10
422	A51	40c blk, gray & dk red	5	5
423	A51	60c blk, sal & ol	8	8
424	A51	1.50e blk, bl & red	20	5
425	A51	2e blk, lil & bis	90	15
426	A51	2.50e blk, yel & brn	1.25	15
427	A51	3e blk, pink & ol	3.00	30
428	A51	4e blk, gray grn & brn	1.40	30
429	A51	5e blk, lt bl & car	1.10	30
430	A51	7.50e blk, dl yel & brn	1.40	70
431	A51	10e blk, ocher & grn	1.10	40
432	A51	15e blk, beige & grn	1.00	60
432A	A51	25e blk, rose & red brn	2.50	1.00
432B	A51	50e blk, gray & vio bl	4.00	1.50
		Nos. 419-432B (16)	18.24	5.81

Sports Issue

Common Design Type

Sports: 50c, Flying. 1e, Rowing. 1.50e, Water polo. 2.50e, Hammer throwing. 4.50e, High jump. 15e, Weight lifting.

1962, Jan. 18 Perf. 13½

Multicolored Design

433	CD48	50c lt bl	15	10
434	CD48	1e ol bis	95	20
435	CD48	1.50e salmon	50	15
436	CD48	2.50e lt brn	60	15
437	CD48	4.50e pale bl	50	40
438	CD48	15e yellow	2.00	1.00
		Nos. 433-438 (6)	4.70	2.00

Anti-Malaria Issue

Common Design Type

Design: Anopheles funestus.

1962, April Litho. Perf. 13½

439	CD49	2.50e multi	1.00	50

Issued for the World Health Organization drive to eradicate malaria.

Gen. Norton de Matos A54

1962, Aug. 8 Perf. 14½ Unwmkd.

440	A54	2.50e multi	45	20

Issued to commemorate the 50th anniversary of the founding of Nova Lisboa.

Locusts A56

1963, June 2 Litho. Perf. 14

447	A56	2.50e multi	60	30

Issued to commemorate the 15th anniversary of the International Anti-Locust Organization.

Arms of Luanda A57

Vila de Santo Antonio do Zaire A58

Coats of Arms (Provinces and Cities): 10c, Massangano. 15c, Sanza-Pombo. 25c, Ambriz. 30c, Muxima. 40c, Ambrizete. 50c, Carmona. 60c, Catete. 70c, Quibaxe. No. 458, Maquelo do Zombo. 1e, Salazar. 1.20e, Bembe. No. 461, Caxito. 1.50e, Malanje. 1.80e, Dondo. No. 465, Damba. 2e, Henrique de Carvalho. 2.50e, Moçâmedes. 3e, Novo Redondo. 3.50e, S. Salvador do Congo. 4e, Cuimba. 5e, Luso. 6.50e, Negage. 7e, Quitexe. 7.50e, S. Filipe de Benguela. 8e, Mucaba. 9e, 31 de Janeiro. 10e, Lobito. 11e, Nova Caipemba. 12.50e, Gabela. 14e, Songo. 15e Sa' da Bandeira. 17e, Quimbele. 17.50e, Silva Porto. 20e, Nova Lisboa. 22.50e, Cabinda. 25e, Noqui. 30e, Serpa Pinto. 35e, Santa Cruz. 50e, General Freire.

1963 Perf. 13½

Arms in Original Colors; Red and Violet Blue Inscriptions.

448	A57	5c tan	10	10
449	A57	10c lt bl	10	10
450	A58	15c salmon	10	10
451	A58	20c olive	10	10
452	A58	25c lt bl	12	10
453	A57	30c buff	10	10
454	A58	40c gray	12	10
455	A57	50c lt grn	10	10
456	A58	60c brt yel	18	12
457	A58	70c dl rose	18	12
458	A57	1e pale lil	45	10
459	A58	1e dl yel	30	10
460	A58	1.20e rose	15	10
461	A57	1.50e pale sal	90	10
462	A58	1.50e lt grn	60	12
463	A58	1.80e yel ol	35	20
464	A57	2e lt yel grn	45	10
465	A57	2.50e lt gray	2.25	15
466	A58	2.50e dl bl	2.00	18
467	A57	3e yel ol	65	12
468	A57	3.50e gray	75	15
469	A58	4e citron	55	20
470	A57	5e citron	60	35
471	A58	6.50e tan	60	40
472	A58	7e rose lil	65	40
473	A57	7.50e pale lil	85	60
474	A58	8e lt aqua	70	55
475	A58	9e yellow	90	60
476	A57	10e dp sal	1.10	55
477	A58	11e dl yel grn	1.10	85
478	A57	12.50e pale bl	1.40	90
479	A58	14e lt gray	1.40	90
480	A57	15e lt bl	1.50	90
481	A58	17e pale bl	1.65	1.25
482	A57	17.50e dl yel	2.25	1.50
483	A57	20e lt aqua	2.25	1.20
484	A57	22.50e gray	2.25	1.50
485	A58	25e citron	2.25	1.25
486	A57	30e yellow	3.00	2.00
487	A58	35e grysh bl	3.00	2.25
488	A58	50e dp yel	4.50	2.00
		Nos. 448-488 (41)	42.55	22.61

Pres. Américo Rodrigues Thomaz A59

1963, Sept. 16 Lithographed

489	A59	2.50e multi	50	20

Visit of the President of Portugal.

Airline Anniversary Issue

Common Design Type

1963, Oct. 5 Perf. 14½ Unwmkd.

490	CD50	1e lt bl & multi	40	20

Issued to commemorate the 10th anniversary of Transportes Aéreos Portugueses.

Cathedral of Sá da Bandeira — A61

Malange Cathedral — A62

Churches: 20c, Landana. 30c, Luanda Cathedral. 40c, Gabela. 50c, St. Martin's Chapel, Baia dos Tigres. 1.50e, St. Peter, Chibia. 2e, Church of Our Lady, Benguela. 2.50e, Church of Jesus, Luanda. 3e, Camabatela. 3.50e, Mission, Cabinda. 4e, Vila Folgares. 4.50e, Church of Our Lady, Lobito. 5e, Church of Cabinda. 7.50e, Cacuso Church, Malange. 10e, Lubango Mission. 12.50e, Huila Mission. 15e, Church of Our Lady, Luanda Island.

1963, Nov. 1 **Lithographed**
Multicolored Design and Inscription

491	A61	10c gray bl	10	10
492	A61	20c pink	10	10
493	A61	30c lt bl	10	10
494	A61	40c tan	10	10
495	A61	50c lt grn	10	10
496	A62	1e buff	12	10
497	A61	1.50e lt vio bl	15	10
498	A62	2e pale rose	18	10
499	A61	2.50e gray	25	10
500	A62	3e buff	28	10
501	A61	3.50e olive	33	12
502	A62	4e buff	35	30
503	A62	4.50e pale bl	42	35
504	A61	5e tan	45	35
505	A62	7.50e gray	70	60
506	A61	10e dl yel	90	75
507	A62	12.50e bister	1.20	90
508	A62	15e pale gray vio	2.00	1.10
		Nos. 491-508 (18)	7.83	5.47

National Overseas Bank Issue
Common Design Type

Design: Antonio Teixeira de Sousa.

1964, May 16 ***Perf. 13½***

509	CD51	2.50e multi	60	35

Issued to commemorate the centenary of the National Overseas Bank of Portugal.

Commerce Building and Arms of Chamber of Commerce—A64

1964, Nov. **Litho.** ***Perf. 12***

510	A64	1e multi	20	10

Luanda Chamber of Commerce centenary.

ITU Issue
Common Design Type

1965, May 17 ***Perf. 14½*** **Unwmkd.**

511	CD52	2.50e gray & multi	1.00	40

Issued to commemorate the centenary of the International Telecommunication Union.

Plane over Luanda Airport — A65

Harquebusier, 1539 — A66

1965, Dec. 3 **Litho.** ***Perf. 13***

512	A65	2.50e multi	35	20

Issued to commemorate the 25th anniversary of DTA, Direccão dos Transportes Aéreos.

1966, Feb. 25 **Litho.** ***Perf. 14½***

Designs: 50c, Harquebusier, 1539. 1e, Harquebusier, 1640. 1.50e, Infantry officer, 1777. 2e, Standard bearer, infantry, 1777. 2.50e, Infantry soldier, 1777. 3e, Cavalry officer, 1783. 4e, Cavalry soldier, 1783. 4.50e, Infantry officer, 1807. 5e, Infantry soldier, 1807. 6e, Cavalry officer, 1807. 8e, Cavalry soldier, 1807. 9e, Infantry soldier, 1873.

513	A66	50c multi	15	15
514	A66	1e multi	18	18
515	A66	1.50e multi	15	15
516	A66	2e multi	18	18
517	A66	2.50e multi	30	15
518	A66	3e multi	30	15
519	A66	4e multi	40	30
520	A66	4.50e multi	40	30
521	A66	5e multi	60	20
522	A66	6e multi	70	40
523	A66	8e multi	1.00	55
524	A66	9e multi	1.25	55
		Nos. 513-524 (12)	5.61	3.26

National Revolution Issue
Common Design Type

Design: St. Paul's Hospital and Commercial and Industrial School.

1966, May 28 **Litho.** ***Perf. 12***

525	CD53	1e multi	30	15

40th anniversary, National Revolution.

Emblem of Holy Ghost Society — A68

1966 **Lithographed** ***Perf. 13***

526	A68	1e bl & multi	20	10

Centenary of the Holy Ghost Society.

Navy Club Issue
Common Design Type

Designs: 1e, Mendes Barata and cruiser Dom Carlos I. 2.50e, Capt. Augusto de Castilho and corvette Mindelo.

1967, Jan. 31 **Litho.** ***Perf. 13***

527	CD54	1e multi	50	20
528	CD54	2.50e multi	90	30

Centenary of Portugal's Navy Club.

Fatima Basilica — A70

Angola Map, Manuel Cerveira Pereira — A71

1967, May 13 **Litho.** ***Perf. 12½x13***

529	A70	50c multi	15	15

Issued to commemorate the 50th anniversary of the apparition of the Virgin Mary to three shepherd children at Fatima.

1967, Aug. 15 **Litho.** ***Perf. 12½x13***

530	A71	50c multi	18	15

Issued to commemorate the 350th anniversary of the founding of Benguela.

Administration Building, Carmona—A72

1967 **Lithographed** ***Perf. 12***

531	A72	1e multi	15	15

Issued to commemorate the 50th anniversary of the founding of Carmona.

Military Order of Valor — A73

Our Lady of Hope — A74

Designs: 50c, Ribbon of the Three Orders. 1.50e, Military Order of Avis. 2e, Military Order of Christ. 2.50e, Military Order of St. John of Espada. 3e, Order of the Empire. 4e, Order of Prince Henry. 5e, Order of Benemerencia. 10e, Order of Public Instruction. 20e, Order for Industrial and Agricultural Merit.

1967, Oct. 31 ***Perf. 14***

532	A73	50c lt gray & multi	10	6
533	A73	1e lt grn & multi	10	6
534	A73	1.50e yel & multi	12	6
535	A73	2e multi	18	6
536	A73	2.50e multi	20	10
537	A73	3e lt ol & multi	28	10
538	A73	4e gray & multi	30	10
539	A73	5e multi	40	10
540	A73	10e lil & multi	60	40
541	A73	20e lt bl & multi	1.50	80
		Nos. 532-541 (10)	3.78	1.84

Cabral Issue

Designs: 1e, Belmonte Castle (horiz.). 1.50e, St. Jerome's Convent. 2.50e, Cabral's Armada.

1968, Apr. 22 **Litho.** ***Perf. 14***

542	A74	50c yel & multi	10	10
543	A74	1e gray & multi	40	10
544	A74	1.50e lt bl & multi	60	10
545	A74	2.50e buff & multi	90	20

Issued to commemorate the 500th anniversary of the birth of Pedro Alvares Cabral, navigator who took possession of Brazil for Portugal.

Francisco Inocencio de Souza Coutinho — A75

1969, Jan. 7 **Litho.** ***Perf. 14***

546	A75	2e multi	40	30

Issued to commemorate the 200th anniversary of the founding of Novo Redondo.

Admiral Coutinho Issue
Common Design Type

Design: Adm. Gago Coutinho and his first ship.

1969, Feb. 17 **Litho.** ***Perf. 14***

547	CD55	2.50e multi	45	20

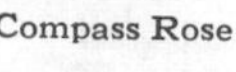

Compass Rose — A77

Portal of St. Jeronimo's Monastery — A79

1969, Aug. 29 **Litho.** ***Perf. 14***

548	A77	1e multi	20	20

Issued to commemorate the 500th anniversary of the birth of Vasco da Gama (1469–1524), navigator.

Administration Reform Issue
Common Design Type

1969, Sept. 25 **Litho.** ***Perf. 14***

549	CD56	1.50e multi	20	20

Issued to commemorate the centenary of the administration reforms of the overseas territories.

1969, Dec. 1 **Litho.** ***Perf. 14***

550	A79	3e multi	30	20

Issued to commemorate the 500th anniversary of the birth of King Manuel I.

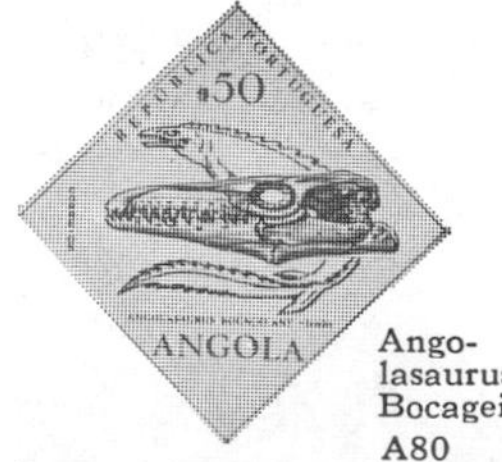

Angolasaurus Bocagei — A80

Fossils and Minerals: 1e, Ferrometeorite. 1.50e, Dioptase crystals. 2e, Gondwanidium. 2.50e, Diamonds. 3e, Estromatolite. 3.50e, Procarcharodon megalodon. 4e, Microceratodus angolensis. 4.50e, Moscovite. 5e, Barite. 6e, Nostoceras. 10e, Rotula orbiculus angolensis.

1970, Oct. 31 **Litho.** ***Perf. 13***

551	A80	50c tan & multi	15	10
552	A80	1e multi	20	10
553	A80	1.50e multi	25	10
554	A80	2e multi	30	10
555	A80	2.50e lt gray & multi	30	10
556	A80	3e multi	30	10
557	A80	3.50e bl & multi	40	20
558	A80	4e lt gray & multi	40	20
559	A80	4.50e gray & multi	40	20
560	A80	5e gray & multi	40	20
561	A80	6e pink & multi	60	30
562	A80	10e lt bl & multi	80	50
		Nos. 551-562 (12)	4.50	2.20

Marshal Carmona Issue
Common Design Type

1970, Nov. 15 ***Perf. 14***

563	CD57	2.50e multi	30	15

Birth centenary of Marshal Antonio Oscar Carmona de Fragoso (1869–1951), President of Portugal.

Arms of Malanje, Cotton Boll and Field — A82

1970, Nov. 20 ***Perf. 13***

564	A82	2.50e multi	35	20

Centenary of the municipality of Malanje.

Mail Ships and Angola No. 1 — A83

Designs: 4.50e, Steam locomotive and Angola No. 4.

1970, Dec. 1 ***Perf. 13½***

565	A83	1.50e multi	30	20
566	A83	4.50e multi	75	35

Centenary of stamps of Angola. See No. C36.

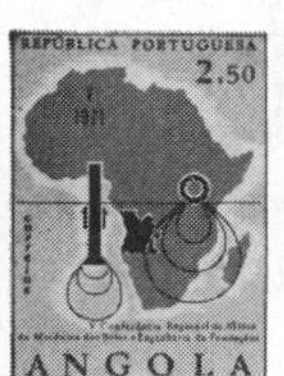

Map of Africa, Diagram of Seismic Tests
A84

Galleon on Congo River
A85

1971, Aug. 22 Litho. *Perf. 13*

567 A84 2.50e multi 20 10

5th Regional Conference of Soil and Foundation Engineers, Luanda, Aug. 22–Sept. 5.

1972, May 25 Litho. *Perf. 13*

568 A85 1e emer & multi 20 15

4th centenary of the publication of The Lusiads by Luiz Camoëns.

Olympic Games Issue
Common Design Type

1972, June 20 *Perf. 14x13½*

569 CD59 50c multi 20 15

20th Olympic Games, Munich, Aug. 26–Sept. 11.

Lisbon-Rio de Janeiro Flight Issue
Common Design Type

1972, Sept. 20 Litho. *Perf. 13½*

570 CD60 1e multi 20 15

WMO Centenary Issue
Common Design Type

1973, Dec. 15 Litho. *Perf. 13*

571 CD61 1e dk gray & multi 20 15

Centenary of international meteorological cooperation.

Radar Station
A89

1974, June 25 Litho. *Perf. 13*

572 A89 2e multi 30 20

Establishment of satellite communications network via Intelsat among Portugal, Angola and Mozambique.

Harpa Doris
A90

Designs: Sea shells.

1974, Oct. 25 Litho. *Perf. 12x12½*
Multicolored

573 A90 25c *shown* 12 12
574 A90 30c *Murex melanamathos* 12 12
575 A90 50c *Venus foliaceo lamellosa* 12 12
576 A90 70c *Lathyrus filosus* 12 12
577 A90 1e *Cymbium cisium* 12 12
578 A90 1.50e *Cassis tesselata* 20 15
579 A90 2e *Cypraea stercoraria* 20 12
580 A90 2.50e *Conus prometheus* 20 20
581 A90 3e *Strombus latus* 20 20
582 A90 3.50e *Tympanotonus fuscatus* 20 20
583 A90 4e *Cardium costatum* 30 20
584 A90 5e *Natica fulminea* 30 20
585 A90 6e *Lyropecten nodosus* 40 20
586 A90 7e *Tonna galea* 50 20
587 A90 10e *Donax rugosus* 60 30
588 A90 25e *Cymatium trigonum* 1.50 50
589 A90 30e *Olivancilaria acuminata* 2.00 60
590 A90 35e *Semifusus morio* 2.25 80
591 A90 40e *Clavatula lineata* 2.50 1.50
592 A90 50e *Solarium granulatum* 3.00 1.75
Nos. 573-592 (20) 14.95 7.72

No. 386 Overprinted in Blue:
"1974 / FILATELIA / JUVENIL"

1974, Dec. 21 Litho. *Perf. 13½*

593 A41 5c multi 20 20

Youth philately.

Republic

Star and Hand Holding Rifle
A91

1975, Nov. 11 Litho. *Perf. 13x13½*

594 A91 1.50e red & multi 20 20

Independence in 1975.

Diquiche Mask
A92

Design: 3e, Bui ou Congolo mask.

1976, Feb. 6 *Perf. 13½*

595 A92 50c lt bl & multi 10 10
596 A92 3e multi 30 10

Workers
A93

President Agostinho Neto
A94

1976, May 1 Litho. *Perf. 12*

597 A93 1e red & multi 20 20

International Workers' Day.

No. 392 Overprinted Bar and:
"DIA DO SELO / 15 Junho 1976 / REP. POPULAR / DE"

1976, June 15 Litho. *Perf. 13½*

598 A41 10e multi 60 40

Stamp Day.

1976, Nov. 11 Litho. *Perf. 13*

599 A94 50c yel & dk brn 10 10
600 A94 2e lt gray & plum 20 10
601 A94 3e gray & ind 20 10
602 A94 5e buff & brn 30 10
603 A94 10e tan & sep 60 20
a. Souvenir sheet 3.00 2.00
Nos. 599-603 (5) 1.40 60

First anniversary of independence. No. 603a contains one imperf. stamp. Gold margin with brown inscription. Size: 60x75mm.

Nos. 393, 588–589, 592 Overprinted with Bar over Republica Portuguesa and:
"REPUBLICA POPULAR DE"

1977, Feb. 9 *Perf. 13½, 12x12½*

604 A41 20e multi 1.25 40
605 A90 25e multi 1.50 50
606 A90 30e multi 2.00 60
607 A90 50e multi 3.00 1.00

Overprint in 3 lines on No. 604, in 2 lines on others.

No. 438 Overprinted with Bar over Republica Portuguesa and: "S. Silvestre / 1976 / Rep. Popular / de"

1976, Dec. 31 *Perf. 13½*

608 CD48 15e multi 90 40

Child and WHO Emblem
A95

Map of Africa, Flag of Angola
A96

1977 Litho. *Perf. 10½*

609 A95 2.50k blk & lt bl 20 10

Campaign for vaccination against poliomyelitis.

1977 Photogravure

610 A96 6k blk, red & bl 30 20

First congress of Popular Movement for the Liberation of Angola.

Anti-Apartheid Emblem
A97

1979, July Litho. *Perf. 13½*

611 A97 1k multi 15 15

Anti-Apartheid Year.

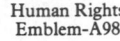

Human Rights Emblem-A98

Child Flowers, Globe, IYC Emblem—A99

1979 Litho. *Perf. 13½*

612 A98 2.50k multi 20 10

Declaration of Human Rights, 30th anniversary, in 1975.

1980, Aug. Litho. *Perf. 14x14½*

613 A99 3.50k multi 20 10

International Year of the Child (1979).

Running, Moscow '80 Emblem
A100

5th Anniv. of Independence
A101

1980 Litho. *Perf. 13½*

614 A100 9k shown 50 30
615 A100 12k Swimming, horiz. 60 30

22nd Summer Olympic Games, Moscow, July 19-Aug. 3.

1980

616 A101 5.50k multi 20 20

Nos. 572, 566 Overprinted with Bar and:
"REPUBLICA POPULAR / DE"

1980 Litho. *Perf. 13½x13*

616A A89 2e multi (bar only) 20
616B A83 4.50e multi 45

See No. C37.

Nos. 577-580, 582-591 Overprinted with Black Bar over "Republica Portuguesa"

1981, Sept. Litho. *Perf. 12x12½*

617 A90 1e multi
618 A90 1.50e multi
619 A90 2e multi
620 A90 2.50e multi
621 A90 3.50e multi
622 A90 4e multi
623 A90 5e multi
624 A90 6e multi
625 A90 7e multi
626 A90 10e multi
627 A90 25e multi
628 A90 30e multi
629 A90 35e multi
630 A90 40e multi
Nos. 617-630 (14) 10.00 5.50

Man Walking with Canes, Tchibinda Ilunga Statue—A102

1981, Sept. Litho. *Perf. 13½*

631 A102 9k multi 50 30

Turipex '81 tourism exhibition.

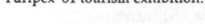

M.P.L.A. Workers' Party Congress—A103

1981 Litho. *Perf. 14*

632 A103 50l Millet 10 10
633 A103 5k Coffee 30 20
634 A103 7.50k Sunflowers 40 20
635 A103 13.50k Cotton 60 30
636 A103 14k Oil 70 40
637 A103 16k Diamonds 70 40
Nos. 632-637 (6) 2.80 1.60

People's Power
A104

Natl. Heros' Day
A105

1981

638 A104 40k lt bl & blk 2.00 60

1981 ***Perf. 14x13½***

639 A105 4.50k Former Pres. Neto 20 10
640 A105 50k Neto, diff. 2.25 1.00

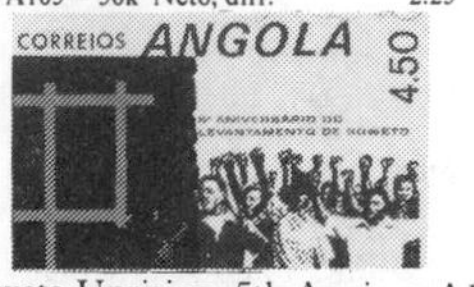

Soweto Uprising, 5th Anniv.—A106

1981

641 A106 4.50k multi 30 10

2nd Central African Games—A107

1981 **Litho.** ***Perf. 13½***

642 A107 50 l Bicycling, tennis 20 10
643 A107 5k Judo, boxing 30 20
644 A107 6k Basketball, volleyball 35 22
645 A107 10k Handball, soccer 60 40

Souvenir Sheet
Imperf.

646 A107 15k multi 1.00

Size of No. 646: 112x130mm.

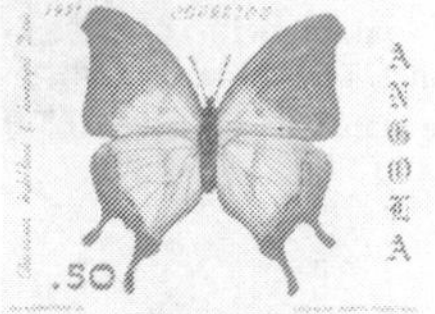

Charaxes Kahldeni—A108

1982, Feb. 26 **Litho.** ***Perf. 13½***

647 A108 50 l shown 10 10
648 A108 1k Abantis zambesiaca 10 10
649 A108 5k Catacroptera cloanthe 30 20
650 A108 9k Myrina ficedula, vert. 60 20
651 A108 10k Colotis danae 60 20
652 A108 15k Acraea acrita 80 40
653 A108 100k Precis hierta 4.00 2.00
a. 30k Souvenir sheet 3.00 1.50
Nos. 647-653 (7) 6.50 3.20

No. 653a contains Nos. 647-653 (imperf.); blue and black margin. Size: 155x105mm.

5th Anniv. of UN Membership—A109

Designs: 5.50k, The Silence of the Night, by Musseque Catambor. 7.50k, Cotton picking, Catete.

1982, Sept. 22 **Litho.**

654 A109 5.50k multi 30 20
655 A109 7.50k multi 40 20

20th Anniv. of Engineering Laboratory—A110

1982, Dec. 21 **Litho.** ***Perf. 14***

656 A110 9k Lab 40 20
657 A110 13k Worker, vert. 60 30
658 A110 100k Equipment, vert. 5.00 2.00

Local Flowers—A111

1983, Feb. 18 ***Perf. 13½***

659 A111 5k Dichrostachys glomerata 20 20
660 A111 12k Amblygonocarpus obtusangulus 60 20
661 A111 50k Albizzia versicolor 3.00 1.00

Women's Org., First Congress
A112

Africa Day
A113

1983 **Litho.** ***Perf. 13½***

662 A112 20k multi 1.20

1983, June 30 ***Perf. 13***

663 A113 6.5k multi 40

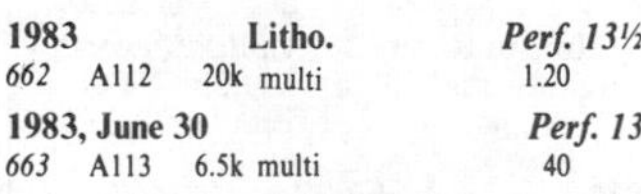

BRASILIANA '83 Stamp Exhibition, Rio de Janeiro, July 29—Aug. 7—A115

Crop-eating insects.

1983, July 29 **Litho.** ***Perf. 13***

666 A115 4.5k Antestiopsis lineaticollis 28
667 A115 6.5k Stephanoderes hampei ferr. 40
668 A115 10k Zonocerus variegatus 62

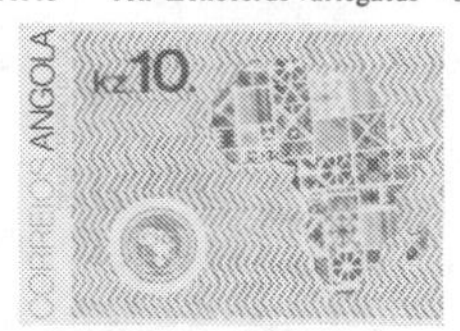

25th Anniv. of Economic Commission for Africa—A116

1983, Aug. 2

669 A116 10k Map, emblem 62

185th Anniv. of Post Office—A117

1983, Dec. 7 **Litho.** ***Perf. 13½***

670 A117 50 l Mail collection, vert. 5
671 A117 3.5k Unloading mail plane 22
672 A117 5k Sorting mail 32
673 A117 15k Mailing letter, vert. 92
674 A117 30k Post office box delivery 1.85
a. Miniature sheet of 3 6.25
Nos. 670-674 (5) 3.36

No. 674a contains Nos. 671-672, 674. Size: 142x78mm. Sold for 100k.

Local Butterflies—A118

1984, Jan. 20 **Litho.** ***Perf. 13½***

675 A118 50 l Parasa karschi 5
676 A118 1k Diaphone angolensis 6
677 A118 3.5k Choeropais jucunda 22
678 A118 6.5k Hespagarista rendalli 40
679 A118 15k Euchromia guineensis 92
680 A118 17.5k Mazuca roseistriga 1.10
681 A118 20k Utetheisa callima 1.25
Nos. 675-681 (7) 4.00

First Natl. Worker's Union Congress, Apr. 11-16—A119

1984, Apr. 11 **Litho.** ***Perf.13½***

682 A119 30k multi 1.85

Local Birds—A120

1984, Oct. 24 **Litho.** ***Perf. 13½***

683 A120 10.50k Bucorvos leadbeateri 70
684 A120 14k Gypohicax angolensis 85
685 A120 16k Ardea goliath 95
686 A120 19.50k Pelicanus onocrotalus 1.20
687 A120 22k Platelea alba 1.30
688 A120 26k Balearica pavonnia 1.55
Nos. 683-688 (6) 6.55

Local Animals—A121

1984, Nov. 12

689 A121 1k Tragelephus strepsicerus 6
690 A121 4k Antidorcos marsupialis angolerusis 24
691 A121 5k Pan troglodytes 30
692 A121 10k Sycerus caffer 60
693 A121 15k Hippotragus niger variani 90
694 A121 20k Orycteropus afer 1.20
695 A121 25k Crocuta crocuta 1.50
Nos. 689-695 (7) 4.80

Angolan Monuments—A122

1985, Feb. 21 **Litho.** ***Perf. 13½***

696 A122 5k San Pedro da Barra 35
697 A122 12.5k Nova Oeiras 85
698 A122 18k M'Banza Kongo 1.20
699 A122 26k Massangano 1.75
700 A122 39k Escravatura Museum 2.60
Nos. 696-700 (5) 6.75

United Workers' Party, 25th Anniv.—A123

1985, May **Litho.** ***Perf. 12***

701 A123 77k XXV, red flags 2.25

Printed in sheets of 5.

Southern African Development Council, 5th Anniv.—A124

1985, May

702	A124	1k	Flags	5
703	A124	11k	Oil drilling platform, Cabindha	35
704	A124	57k	Conference	1.65
a.			Strip of 3, #702-704	2.05

Medicinal Plants—A125

1985, July 5 Litho. & Typo. *Perf. 11*

705	A125	1k	Lonchocarpus sericeus	5
706	A125	4k	Gossypium	12
707	A125	11k	Cassia occidentalis	35
708	A125	25.50k	Gloriosa superba	75
709	A125	55k	Cochlospermum angolensis	1.60
			Nos. 705-709 (5)	2.87

ARGENTINA '85 exhibition.

5th Natl. Heroes Day—A126

Natl. flag and: 10.50k, Portrait of Agostinho Neto, party leader. 36.50k, Neto working.

1985 Litho. *Perf. 13½*

710	A126	10.50k	multi	30
711	A126	36.50k	multi	1.05

Ministerial Conference of Non—Aligned Countries, Luanda—A127

1985, Sept. 4 Photo. *Perf. 11*

712	A127	35k	multi	2.25

UN, 40th Anniv.—A128

1985, Oct. 29 Litho. *Perf. 11*

713	A128	12.50k	multi	85

Industry and Natural Resources—A129

1985, Nov. 11

714	A129	50 l	Cement Factory	5
715	A129	5k	Logging	32
716	A129	7k	Quartz	45
717	A129	10k	Iron mine	65
a.			Souvenir sheet of 4, #714-717, imperf.	1.50

Natl. independence, 10th anniv.

No. 717a has multicolored margin picturing natl. crest, family, industry, aircraft and historical data. Size: 210x124mm.

2nd Natl. Workers' Party Congress (MPLA)—A130

1985, Nov. 28 *Perf. 13½*

718	A130	20k	multi	1.25

Demostenes de Almeida Clington Races, 30th Anniv.—A131

Various runners.

1985, Dec. 13

719	A131	50 l	multi	5
720	A131	5k	multi	32
721	A131	6.50k	multi	42
722	A131	10k	multi	65

1986 World Cup Soccer Championships, Mexico—A132

Map, soccer field and various plays.

1986, May 6 Litho. *Perf. 11½x11*

723	A132	50 l	multi	5
724	A132	3.50k	multi	22
725	A132	5k	multi	32
726	A132	7k	multi	45
727	A132	10k	multi	65
728	A132	18k	multi	1.29
			Nos. 723-728 (6)	2.98

Struggle against Portugal, 25th Anniv.—A133

1986, May 6 *Perf. 11x11½*

729	A133	15k	multi	1.00

First Man in Space, 25th Anniv.—A134

1986, Aug. 21 Litho. *Perf. 11x11½*

730	A134	50 l	Skylab, US	5
731	A134	1k	Spacecraft	6
732	A134	5k	A. Leonov space-walking	32
733	A134	10k	Lunokhod on Moon	65
734	A134	13k	Apollo-Soyuz link-up	88
			Nos. 730-734 (5)	1.96

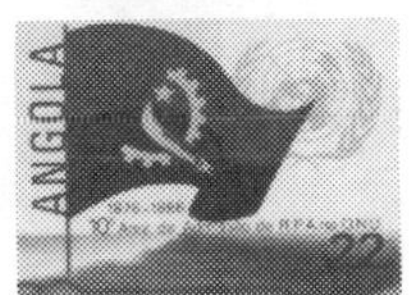

Admission of Angola to UN, 10thAnniv.—A135

1986, Dec. 1 Litho. *Perf. 11x11½*

735	A135	22k	multi	1.40

Liberation Movement, 30th Anniv.—A136

Angolans at work, fighting and: No. 736a, "1956." No. 736b, Congress emblem, "1980." No. 736c, Labor Party emblem, "1985."

1986, Dec. 3 *Perf. 11½x11*

736		Strip of 3	1.00
a.-c.	A136	5k, any single	30

Agostinho Neto University, 10th Anniv.—A137

1986, Dec. 30 Litho. *Perf. 11x11½*

737	A137	50 l	Mathematics	5
738	A137	1k	Law	8
739	A137	10k	Medicine	70

AIR POST STAMPS.

Common Design Type

Perf. 13½x13.

1938, July 26 Engraved Unwmkd.

Name and Value in Black.

C1	CD39	10c scarlet		30	30
C2	CD39	20c purple		40	30
C3	CD39	50c orange		30	30
C4	CD39	1a ultra		40	30
C5	CD39	2a lil brn		1.00	30
C6	CD39	3a dk grn		2.50	45
C7	CD39	5a red brn		4.00	55
C8	CD39	9a rose car		5.50	1.60
C9	CD39	10a magenta		7.50	1.75
		Nos. C1-C9 (9)		21.90	5.85

No. C7 exists with overprint "Exposicao Internacional de Nova York, 1939-1940" and Trylon and Perisphere.

AP2

1947, Aug. Litho. *Perf. 10½*

C10	AP2	1a red brn	7.50	2.50
C11	AP2	2a yel grn	7.50	2.50
C12	AP2	3a orange	9.00	2.50
C13	AP2	3.50a orange	15.00	6.00
C14	AP2	5a ol grn	110.00	7.50
C15	AP2	6a rose	110.00	10.00
C16	AP2	9a red	275.00	150.00
C17	AP2	10a green	225.00	50.00
C18	AP2	20a blue	225.00	50.00
C19	AP2	50a black	350.00	175.00
C20	AP2	100a yellow	600.00	500.00
		Nos. C10-C20 (11)	1,934.	956.00

Planes Circling Globe
AP3

1949, May 1 Photo. *Perf. 11½*

C21	AP3	1a hn brn	30	10
C22	AP3	2a red brn	60	12
C23	AP3	3a plum	1.00	30
C24	AP3	6a dl grn	3.00	60
C25	AP3	9a vio brn	4.50	1.50
		Nos. C21-C25 (5)	9.40	2.62

Cambambe Dam
AP4

Designs: 1.50e, Oil refinery (vert.). 3e, Salazar Dam. 4e, Capt. Teófilo Duarte Dam. 4.50e, Craveiro Lopes Dam. 5e, Cuango Dam. 6e, Quanza River Bridge. 7e, Capt. Teófilo Duarte Bridge. 8.50e, Oliveira Salazar Bridge. 12.50e, Capt. Silva Carvalho Bridge.

Perf. 11½x12, 12x11½

1965, July 12 Litho. Unwmkd.

C26	AP4	1.50e multi	1.50	10
C27	AP4	2.50e multi	90	10
C28	AP4	3e multi	1.30	20
C29	AP4	4e multi	60	20
C30	AP4	4.50e multi	60	30
C31	AP4	5e multi	1.00	30
C32	AP4	6e multi	1.00	30
C33	AP4	7e multi	1.25	30
C34	AP4	8.50e multi	1.75	85
C35	AP4	12.50e multi	2.00	1.00
		Nos. C26-C35 (10)	11.90	3.65

Stamp Centenary Type of Regular Issue

Design: 2.50e, Boeing 707 jet and Angola No. 2.

1970, Dec. 1 Litho. *Perf. 13½*

C36	A83	2.50e multi	40	20
a.		Souvenir sheet of 3	3.00	3.00

Centenary of stamps of Angola.

No. C36a contains one each of No. 565-566, C36. Margin shows Duke of Bragança Waterfall, with commemorative inscription. Size: 150x105mm. Sold for 15e.

No. C36 Overprinted with Bar and: "REPUBLICA POPULAR / DE"

1980 Litho. *Perf. 13½*

C37	A83	2.50e multi	25

POSTAGE DUE STAMPS.

D1

D2

Typographed.

1904 *Perf. 11½x12.* Unwmkd.

J1	D1	5r yel grn	40	30
J2	D1	10r slate	40	30
J3	D1	20r yel brn	50	45
J4	D1	30r orange	60	50
J5	D1	50r gray brn	60	50
J6	D1	60r red brn	6.00	2.75
J7	D1	100r lilac	2.75	2.00
J8	D1	130r dl bl	2.75	2.00
J9	D1	200r carmine	6.00	3.00
J10	D1	500r gray vio	6.00	3.00
		Nos. J1-J10 (10)	26.00	14.80

Postage Due Stamps of 1904 Overprinted in Carmine or Green

REPUBLICA

1911

J11	D1	5r yel grn	30	30
J12	D1	10r slate	30	30
J13	D1	20r yel brn	30	30
J14	D1	30r orange	45	45
J15	D1	50r gray brn	45	45
J16	D1	60r red brn	1.00	1.00
J17	D1	100r lilac	1.00	1.00
J18	D1	130r dl bl	1.00	1.00
J19	D1	200r car (G)	1.00	1.00
J20	D1	500r gray vio	1.25	1.25
		Nos. J11-J20 (10)	7.05	7.05

1921 *Perf. 11½.*

J21	D2	½c yel grn	12	12
J22	D2	1c slate	12	12
J23	D2	2c org brn	12	12
J24	D2	3c orange	12	12
J25	D2	5c gray brn	12	12
J26	D2	6c lt brn	12	12
J27	D2	10c red vio	12	12
J28	D2	13c dl bl	35	35
J29	D2	20c carmine	35	35
J30	D2	50c gray	35	35
		Nos. J21-J30 (10)	1.89	1.89

Stamps of 1932 Surcharged in Black

PORTEADO
10
Centavos

1948 *Perf. 12x11½.* Wmk. 232

J31	A14	10c on 20c gray	20	20
J32	A14	20c on 30c myr grn	20	20
J33	A14	30c on 50c lt brn	40	30
J34	A14	40c on 1a cl	45	45
J35	A14	50c on 2a dl vio	80	45
J36	A14	1a on 5a pale yel grn	1.10	90
		Nos. J31-J36 (6)	3.15	2.50

Common Design Type

Photogravure and Typographed.

1952 *Perf. 14.* Unwmkd.

Numeral in Red, Frame Multicolored.

J37	CD45	10c red brn	15	15
J38	CD45	30c ol grn	15	15
J39	CD45	50c chocolate	15	15
J40	CD45	1a dk vio bl	15	15
J41	CD45	2a red brn	30	30
J42	CD45	5a blk brn	50	50
		Nos. J37-J42 (6)	1.40	1.40

NEWSPAPER STAMP.

N1

Perf. 11½, 12½, 13½.

1893 Typographed Unwmkd.

P1	N1	2½r brown	1.75	1.10

No. P1 was also used for ordinary postage.

POSTAL TAX STAMPS.

Pombal Issue.

Common Design Types

1925 *Perf. 12½.* Unwmkd.

RA1	CD28	15c lil & blk	50	40
RA2	CD29	15c lil & blk	50	40
RA3	CD30	15c lil & blk	50	40

"Charity" PT1 Coat of Arms PT2

Without Gum

1929 Lithographed. *Perf. 11.*

RA4	PT1	50c dk bl	4.00	1.25

1939 Without Gum. *Perf. 10½.*

RA5	PT2	50c turq grn	3.00	20
RA6	PT2	1a red	4.00	2.00

A 1.50a, type PT2, was issued for fiscal use.

Old Man PT3 Mother and Child PT4

Designs: 1e, Boy. 1.50e, Girl.

Imprint: "Foto-Lito—E.G.A.—Luanda"

1955 *Perf. 13* Unwmkd.

Heads in dark brown.

RA7	PT3	50c dk ocher	20	15
RA8	PT3	1e org ver	90	30
RA9	PT3	1.50e brt yel grn	55	25

A 2.50e, type PT3 showing an old woman, was issued for revenue use.

See also Nos. RA16, RA19–RA21, RA25–RA27.

No. RA7 Surcharged with New Values and two Bars in Red or Black.

1957-58 Head in dark brown.

RA11	PT3	10c on 50c dk ocher (R)	40	25
RA12	PT3	10c on 50c dk ocher ('58)	30	20
RA13	PT3	30c on 50c dk ocher	35	25

1959 Lithographed. *Perf. 13*

Design: 30c, Boy and girl.

RA14	PT4	10c org & blk	15	15
RA15	PT4	30c sl & blk	15	15

Type of 1955 Redrawn

Design: 1e, Boy.

1961, Nov. *Perf. 13*

RA16	PT3	1e sal pink & dk brn	30	30

Denomination in italics.

Yellow, White and Black Men PT5

1962 Typographed *Perf. 10½*

Without Gum

RA17	PT5	50c multi	50	50
RA18	PT5	1e multi	60	60

Issued for the Provincial Settlement Committee (Junta Provincial do Povoamento). The tax was used to promote Portuguese settlement in Angola, and to raise educational and living standards of recent immigrants.

See also No. RAJ4. Denominations higher than 2e were used for revenue purposes.

Head Type of 1955

Without Imprint

Designs: 50c, Old man. 1e, Boy. 1.50e, Girl.

1964-65 Litho. *Perf. 11½*

Heads in dark bown

RA19	PT3	50c orange	22	15
RA20	PT3	1e dl red org ('65)	30	15
RA21	PT3	1.50e yel grn ('65)	40	25

No. RA20 is second redrawing of 1e, with bolder lettering and denomination in gothic. Space between "Assistencia" and denomination on RA19–RA21 is ½mm.; on 1955 issue space is 2mm.

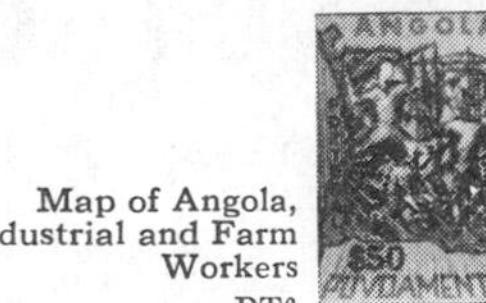

Map of Angola, Industrial and Farm Workers PT6

1965 Lithographed *Perf. 13*

RA22	PT6	50c multi	30	30
RA23	PT6	1e multi	45	45

See also No. RAJ5.

Head Type of 1955

1966

Imprint: "I.N.A." or "INA" (1e)

Heads in dark brown

RA25	PT3	50c dl org	15	15
RA26	PT3	1e dl brick red	25	15
RA27	PT3	1.50e lt yel grn	25	20

Woman Planting Tree PT7

Designs: 1e, Workers. 2e, Produce.

1972 Lithographed *Perf. 13*

RA28	PT7	50c gray & pink	10	10
RA29	PT7	1e grn & blk	20	20
RA30	PT7	2e brn & blk	30	30

POSTAL TAX DUE STAMPS.

Pombal Issue.

Common Design Types

1925 *Perf. 12½.* Unwmkd.

RAJ1	CD31	30c lil & blk	75	*1.25*
RAJ2	CD32	30c lil & blk	75	*1.25*
RAJ3	CD33	30c lil & blk	75	*1.25*

See note after Portugal No. RAJ4.

Three-Men Type of Postal Tax Stamps, 1962.

1962 Typographed *Perf. 10½*

Without Gum

RAJ4	PT5	2e multi	80	*1.00*

See note after Nos. RA17–RA18.

Type of Postal Tax Stamps, 1965

1965 Lithographed *Perf. 13*

RAJ5	PT6	2e multi	35	*1.00*

ANGRA

(äng'grȧ)

LOCATION — An administrative district of the Azores, consisting of the islands of Terceira, São Jorge and Graciosa.

GOVT.—A district of Portugal.

AREA—275 sq. mi.

POP.—70,000 (approx.).

CAPITAL—Angra do Heroismo.

1000 Reis = 1 Milreis

King Carlos

A1 A2

Perf. 11½, 12½, 13½.

1892-93 Typographed. Unwmkd.

No.	Type	Description	Unused	Used
1	A1	5r yellow	2.00	1.25
a.		Perf. 11½	6.00	3.00
2	A1	10r redsh vio	2.75	1.75
3	A1	15r chocolate	3.25	2.25
4	A1	20r lavender	3.50	2.25
a.		Perf. 13½	7.50	2.50
5	A1	25r green	2.50	35
a.		Perf. 12½	6.50	75
7	A1	50r blue	5.25	2.25
a.		Perf. 13½	8.50	5.00
8	A1	75r carmine	9.00	4.25
9	A1	80r yel grn	10.00	6.50
10	A1	100r brn, *yel*, perf. 13½ ('93)	35.00	17.50
a.		Perf. 12½	125.00	100.00
11	A1	150r car, *rose* ('93)	40.00	30.00
12	A1	200r dk bl, *bl* ('93)	40.00	30.00
13	A1	300r dk bl, *sal* ('93)	40.00	30.00

Reprints of 50r, 150r, 200r and 300r, made in 1900, are perf. 11½ and ungummed. Price, each $7.50. Reprints of all values, made in 1905, have shiny white gum and clean-cut perf. 13½. Price, each $1.

1897–1905 ***Perf. 11½***

Name and Value in Black except Nos. 26 and 35.

No.	Type	Description	Unused	Used
14	A2	2½r gray	35	25
15	A2	5r orange	35	25
a.		Diagonal half used as 2½r on cover		12.50
16	A2	10r yel grn	35	25
17	A2	15r brown	6.50	2.75
18	A2	15r gray grn ('99)	1.25	70
19	A2	20r gray vio	1.25	45
20	A2	25r sea grn	1.50	50
a.		Imperf., pair	12.50	
21	A2	25r car rose ('99)	90	25
22	A2	50r dk bl	2.50	90
23	A2	50r ultra ('05)	9.00	7.50
24	A2	65r sl bl ('98)	45	30
25	A2	75r rose	1.50	75
26	A2	75r gray brn & car, *straw* ('05)	9.50	8.00
27	A2	80r violet	55	45
28	A2	100r dk bl, *bl*	1.50	60
29	A2	115r org brn, *pink* ('98)	1.10	90
30	A2	130r gray brn, *straw* ('98)	1.10	90
31	A2	150r lt brn, *straw*	1.00	75
32	A2	180r sl, *pnksh* ('98)	1.60	1.25
33	A2	200r red vio, *pnksh*	3.00	2.25
34	A2	300r bl, *rose*	5.50	4.00
35	A2	500r blk & red, *bl*	11.00	8.00
a.		Perf. 12½	22.50	14.00
		Nos. 14-35 (22)	61.75	41.95

Azores stamps were used in Angra from 1906 to 1931, when they were superseded by those of Portugal.

ANJOUAN

(än'jōō·än')

LOCATION—One of the Comoro Islands in the Mozambique Channel between Madagascar and Mozambique.

GOVT.—Former French colony.

AREA—89 sq. mi.

POP.—20,000 (approx. 1912).

CAPITAL—Mossamondu.

See Comoro Islands.

100 Centimes = 1 Franc

Navigation and Commerce

A1

Perf. 14x13½.

1892–1907 Typographed Unwmkd.

Name of Colony in Blue or Carmine.

No.	Type	Description	Unused	Used
1	A1	1c *blue*	1.00	1.00
2	A1	2c brn, *buff*	1.50	1.40
3	A1	4c cl, *lav*	2.25	2.00
4	A1	5c grn, *grnsh*	4.75	3.50
5	A1	10c *lavender*	4.75	3.75
6	A1	10c red ('00)	14.00	11.00
7	A1	15c bl, quadrille paper	5.75	4.75
8	A1	15c gray, *lt gray* ('00)	9.50	7.75
9	A1	20c red, *grn*	6.00	4.75
10	A1	25c *rose*	7.25	6.00
11	A1	25c bl ('00)	10.50	10.50
12	A1	30c brn, *bis*	15.00	12.00
13	A1	35c *yel* ('06)	7.75	6.00
14	A1	40c red, *straw*	24.00	20.00
15	A1	45c *gray grn* ('07)	110.00	100.00
16	A1	50c car, *rose*	27.50	20.00
17	A1	50c brn, *az* ('00)	19.00	13.00
18	A1	75c vio, *org*	25.00	20.00
19	A1	1fr brnz grn, *straw*	57.50	57.50
		Nos. 1-19 (19)	353.00	304.90

Issues of 1892-1907 Surcharged in Black or Carmine

05 10

1912

No.	Type	Description	Unused	Used
20	A1	5c on 2c brn, *buff*	60	60
21	A1	5c on 4c cl, *lav* (C)	60	60
22	A1	5c on 15c bl (C)	60	60
23	A1	5c on 20c red, *grn*	60	60
24	A1	5c on 25c *rose* (C)	60	60
25	A1	5c on 30c brn, *bis* (C)	60	60
26	A1	10c on 40c red, *straw*	90	90
27	A1	10c on 45c *gray grn* (C)	1.25	1.25
28	A1	10c on 50c car, *rose*	2.25	2.25
29	A1	10c on 75c vio, *org*	1.50	1.50
30	A1	10c on 1fr brnz grn, *straw*	1.75	1.75
		Nos. 20-30 (11)	11.25	11.25

Nos. 21-23, 30 exist in pairs, one without surcharge. Price, $225 each.

Two spacings between the surcharged numerals are found on Nos. 20 to 30.

Nos. 20 to 30 were available for use in Madagascar and the entire Comoro archipelago.

The stamps of Anjouan were superseded by those of Madagascar, and in 1950 by those of Comoro Islands.

ANNAM AND TONKIN

(ă·năm' & tŏn'kĭn')

LOCATION — In French Indo-China bordering on the China Sea on the east and Siam on the west.

GOVT.—French Protectorate.

AREA—97,503 sq. mi.

POP.—14,124,000 (approx. 1890).

CAPITALS—Annam: Hué. Tonkin: Hanoi.

For administrative purposes, the Protectorates of Annam, Tonkin, Cambodia, Laos and the Colony of Cochin-China were grouped together and were known as French Indo-China.

100 Centimes = 1 Franc

Stamps of French Colonies, 1881-86 Surcharged in Black:

A&T 1 or **A&T 5**

1888 ***Perf. 14x13½.*** **Unwmkd.**

No.	Type	Description	Unused	Used
1	A9	1c on 2c brn, *buff*	24.00	21.00
a.		Inverted surch.	82.50	82.50
2	A9	1c on 4c cl, *lav*	17.50	16.00
a.		Inverted surch.	82.50	82.50
3	A9	5c on 10c *lav*	19.00	17.50
a.		Inverted surch.	82.50	82.50

A 5c on 2c was prepared but not issued.

Hyphen between "A" and "T"

No.	Type	Description	Unused	Used
7	A9	1c on 2c brn, *buff*	225.00	225.00
8	A9	1c on 4c cl, *lav*	350.00	325.00
9	A9	5c on 10c *lav*	175.00	175.00

In these surcharges there are different types of numerals and letters.

These stamps were superseded in 1892 by those of Indo-China.

ARABIA

See Saudi Arabia, Vol. IV.

ARGENTINA

(är'jĕn·tē'nȧ)

LOCATION — In South America.

GOVT. — Republic.

AREA — 1,084,120 sq. mi.

POP. — 27,949,480 (1980).

CAPITAL — Buenos Aires.

100 Centavos = 1 Peso

Argentine Confederation.

Symbolical of the Argentine Confederation

A1 A2

Lithographed

1858, May 1 ***Imperf.*** **Unwmkd.**

No.	Type	Description	Unused	Used
1	A1	5c red	2.25	12.50
a.		Colon after '5'	1.75	15.00
b.		Colon after 'V'	1.75	15.00
2	A1	10c green	3.25	75.00
a.		Half used as 5c on cover		275.00
3	A1	15c blue	22.50	200.00
a.		One-third used as 5c on cover		5,000.

1860, Jan.

No.	Type	Description	Unused	Used
4	A2	5c red	3.25	100.00
4A	A2	10c green	8.00	
4B	A2	15c blue	37.50	

Nos. 4A and 4B were never placed in use. There are nine varieties of Nos. 1, 2 and 3, sixteen of No. 4 and eight of Nos. 4A and 4B. Forged cancellations are plentiful.

Prices for Unused

Unused prices for Nos. 5-15, 17-67 are for copies without gum. Copies with original gum command higher prices. From No. 68 onward, unused prices are for stamps with original gum.

Argentine Republic.

Seal of the Republic

A3

Broad "C" in "CENTAVOS", Accent on "U" of "REPUBLICA".

1862, Jan. 11

No.	Type	Description	Unused	Used
5	A3	5c rose	65.00	60.00
a.		rose lil	125.00	50.00
6	A3	10c green	250.00	110.00
b.		Diagonal half used as 5c on cover		6,000.
7	A3	15c blue	500.00	400.00
a.		Without accent on 'U'	8,000.	4,000.
b.		Tête bêche pair	50,000.	30,000.
i.		15c ultra	600.00	450.00

Broad "C" in "CENTAVOS", No Accent on "U"

1863

No.	Type	Description	Unused	Used
7C	A3	5c rose	30.00	35.00
d.		5c rose lil	150.00	165.00
e.		Worn plate	300.00	75.00
7F	A3	10c yel grn	500.00	250.00
g.		10c ol grn	900.00	350.00

Narrow "C" in "CENTAVOS", No Accent on "U"

1864

No.	Type	Description	Unused	Used
7H	A3	5c rose red	300.00	50.00

The so-called reprints of 10c and 15c are counterfeits. They have narrow "C" and straight lines in shield. Nos. 7C and 7H have been extensively counterfeited.

Rivadavia Issue.

Bernardino Rivadavia

A4 A5

Rivadavia

A6

Wmk. 84

Wmkd. RA in Italics (84)

1864-67 Engraved *Imperf.*

Clear Impressions.

8	A4	5c brn rose	1,800.	250.00
a.		5c org red ('67)	2,500.	200.00
9	A5	10c green	3,000.	2,250.
10	A6	15c blue	10,000.	6,000.

Perf. 11½.

Dull to Worn Impressions.

11	A4	5c brn rose ('65)	45.00	20.00
11B	A4	5c lake	125.00	30.00
12	A5	10c green	100.00	40.00
a.		Diagonal half used as 5c on cover		1,000.
13	A6	15c blue	250.00	150.00

1867-72 *Imperf.* Unwmkd.

14	A4	5c car ('72)	300.00	100.00
15	A4	5c rose	300.00	125.00
15A	A5	10c green	6,000.	6,000.
16	A6	15c blue	3,000.	3,000.

Nos. 15A-16 issued without gum.

1867 *Perf. 11½.*

17	A4	5c carmine	500.00	225.00

Nos. 14, 15 and 17 exist with part of papermaker's wmk. "LACROIX FRERES"

Rivadavia
A7

Manuel Belgrano
A8

José de San Martín
A9

Groundwork of Horizontal Lines.

1867-68 *Perf. 12.*

18	A7	5c vermilion	300.00	15.00
18A	A8	10c green	45.00	7.50
b.		Diagonal half used as 5c on cover		750.00
19	A9	15c blue	75.00	22.50

Groundwork of Crossed Lines.

20	A7	5c vermilion	15.00	1.00
21	A9	15c blue	150.00	17.50

See also Nos. 27, 33-34, 39 and types A19, A33, A34, A37.

Gen. Antonio G. Balcarce
A10

Mariano Moreno
A11

Carlos Maria de Alvear
A12

Gervasio Antonio Posadas
A13

Cornelio Saavedra
A14

1873

22	A10	1c purple	5.50	3.50
a.		1c gray vio	9.00	3.50
23	A11	4c brown	8.50	55
a.		4c red brn	25.00	3.00
24	A12	30c orange	150.00	25.00
25	A13	60c black	150.00	8.00
26	A14	90c blue	35.00	4.00

1873 Laid Paper.

27	A8	10c green	225.00	25.00

A15 A16

Surcharged in Black.

1877, Feb. Wove Paper

30	A15	1c on 5c ver	75.00	25.00
a.		Inverted surcharge	500.00	300.00
31	A15	2c on 5c ver	150.00	100.00
a.		Inverted surcharge	1,000.	750.00
32	A16	8c on 10c grn	175.00	50.00
b.		Inverted surcharge	750.00	600.00

Forgeries of these surcharges include the inverted and double varieties.

1876-77 *Rouletted*

33	A7	5c vermilion	225.00	100.00
34	A7	8c lake ('77)	35.00	50

Belgrano
A17

Dalmacio Vélez Sarsfield
A18

San Martín
A19

1878 *Rouletted*

35	A17	16c green	12.50	2.00
36	A18	20c blue	15.00	5.00
37	A19	24c blue	27.50	4.50

See also No. 56.

Vicente López
A20

Alvear
A21

1877-80 *Perf. 12.*

38	A20	2c yel grn	6.50	1.50
39	A7	8c lake ('80)	6.50	50
a.		8c brn lake	40.00	50
40	A21	25c lake ('78)	35.00	10.00

A22 A23

1882 Surcharged in Black.

41	A22	½c on 5c ver	1.50	1.50
a.		Double surcharge	35.00	20.00
b.		Inverted surcharge	25.00	20.00
c.		"PROVISORIO" omitted	50.00	50.00
d.		Fraction omitted	35.00	
e.		"PROVISOBIO"	12.50	12.50
f.		Pair, one without surcharge	125.00	

Perforated across Middle of Stamp.

42	A22	½c on 5c ver	2.50	2.50
a.		"PROVISORIQ"	15.00	12.50

The "½ (PROVISORIO)" surcharge on Nos. 41-42 is found in two types: I. Small "P" and narrow "V." II. Large "P" and wider "V."

1882 Typographed *Perf. 12*

43	A23	½c brown	2.25	1.25
a.		Imperf., pair	35.00	35.00
44	A23	1c red, perf. 14	4.50	1.35
a.		Perf. 12	12.50	6.00
45	A23	12c ultra	90.00	15.00
a.		Perf. 14	65.00	15.00

Perf. 14

46	A23	12c grnsh bl	160.00	20.00

No. 21 Surcharged in Red:

1884 ½ *a*

1 C 1884 *b*

1884 Engr. *Perf. 12*

47	A9 (a)	½c on 15c bl	3.00	2.00
a.		Groundwork of horizontal lines	90.00	70.00
b.		Inverted surcharge	20.00	15.00
48	A9 (b)	1c on 15c bl	15.00	12.00
a.		Groundwork of horizontal lines	9.00	7.00
b.		Inverted surcharge	60.00	50.00
c.		Double surcharge	22.50	20.00
d.		Triple surch.	450.00	

Nos. 20-21 Surcharged in Black

CUATRO Centavos 1884 *c*

49	A7 (a)	½c on 5c ver	3.25	2.50
a.		Inverted surcharge	125.00	100.00
b.		Date omitted	45.00	
c.		Pair, one without surcharge	160.00	
50	A9 (a)	½c on 15c bl	10.00	8.00
a.		Groundwork of horizontal lines	35.00	25.00
b.		Inverted surcharge	35.00	30.00
51	A7 (c)	4c on 5c ver	12.50	8.00
a.		Inverted surcharge	20.00	15.00
b.		Double surcharge	350.00	225.00
c.		Pair, one without surcharge but with "4" in manuscript	275.00	150.00

A29

1884-85 Engraved *Perf. 12*

52	A29	½c red brn	1.50	60
a.		Imperf., pair	65.00	
53	A29	1c rose red	7.50	60
a.		Imperf., pair	65.00	
54	A29	12c grnsh bl ('85)	35.00	2.00
a.		12c dp bl	35.00	2.00
b.		Imperf., pair	65.00	

San Martin Type of 1878

1887 Engraved

56	A19	24c blue	25.00	2.00

Justo José de Urquiza
A30

López
A31

Miguel Juárez Celman
A32

Rivadavia (Large head)
A33

Rivadavia (Small head)
A34

Domingo F. Sarmiento
A35

Nicolás Avellaneda
A36

San Martin
A37

Julio A. Roca
A37a

Belgrano
A37b

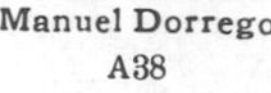

Manuel Dorrego
A38

Moreno
A39

Bartolomé Mitre
A40

CINCO CENTAVOS.

Type I. A33. Shows collar on left side only.

Type II. A34. Shows collar on both sides. Lozenges in background larger and clearer than in type I.

1888–90 Lithographed *Perf. 11½*

No.	Type			
57	A30	½c blue	85	75
a.		Imperf. pair	50.00	35.00
58	A31	2c yel grn	15.00	10.00
a.		Imperf., pair	40.00	
59	A32	3c bl grn	2.25	1.00
a.		Imperf., pair	25.00	17.50
b.		Imperf. vert., pair	35.00	
c.		Horizontal pair, imperf. between	40.00	
d.		Vertical pair, imperf. between	15.00	
60	A33	5c car, type I	17.50	3.00
61	A34	5c car, type II	12.50	1.00
a.		Imperf., pair		75.00
b.		Vertical pair, imperf. between	50.00	
62	A35	6c red	35.00	25.00
a.		Imperf., pair	40.00	
b.		Vertical pair, imperf. between	50.00	
c.		Perf. 12	75.00	60.00
63	A36	10c brown	25.00	1.75
a.		Imperf. pair	40.00	
64	A37	15c orange	25.00	2.75
c.		Imperf., pair		150.00
64A	A37a	20c green	20.00	2.00
64B	A37b	25c purple	25.00	2.75
65	A38	30c chocolate	35.00	4.00
a.		Imperf., pair	200.00	150.00
66	A39	40c sl, perf.12	35.00	5.00
a.		Perf. 11½	85.00	22.50
67	A40	50c blue	130.00	13.50
		Nos. 57-67 (13)	378.10	72.50

In this issue there are several varieties of each value, the difference between them being in the relative position of the head to the frame.

Urquiza
A41

Vélez Sarsfield
A42

Miguel Juárez Celman
A43

Rivadavia
(Large head)
A44

Sarmiento
A45

Juan Bautista Alberdi
A46

1888–89 Engr. *Perf. 11½, 11½x12*

No.	Type			
68	A41	½c ultra	50	15
a.		Imperf. horiz., pair	25.00	15.00
b.		Imperf., pair	25.00	15.00
69	A42	1c brown	1.50	30
a.		Imperf. horiz., pair	25.00	
b.		Vertical pair, imperf. between	25.00	
c.		Imperf. pair	25.00	
70	A43	3c bl grn	3.75	75
71	A44	5c rose	5.00	20
a.		Imperf., pair	35.00	25.00
72	A45	6c bl blk	2.50	1.00
b.		Perf. 11½x12	15.00	4.00
73	A46	12c blue	7.50	2.00
a.		Imperf., pair	20.00	
b.		bluish paper	5.00	1.25
c.		Perf. 11½	12.50	5.00
		Nos. 68-73 (6)	20.75	4.40

Nos. 69-70 exist with papermakers' watermarks.

See also Nos. 77 and 89.

José Maria Paz
A48

Santiago Derqui
A49

Rivadavia
(Small head)
A50

Avellaneda
A51

Moreno
A53

Mitre
A54

Posadas—A55

A56

1890 Engraved *Perf. 11½*

No.	Type			
75	A48	¼c green	20	10
76	A49	2c violet	1.50	30
a.		2c pur	1.50	30
b.		2c sl	2.25	50
c.		Horizontal pair, imperf. between	22.50	
d.		Imperf., pair	27.50	
e.		Perf. 11½x12	6.00	50
77	A50	5c carmine	3.25	12
a.		Imperf., pair	60.00	30.00
b.		Perf. 11½x12	3.25	60
78	A51	10c brown	3.00	40
b.		Imperf., pair		150.00
80	A53	40c ol grn	7.00	1.25
a.		Imperf., pair	30.00	
81	A54	50c orange	7.00	1.25
a.		Imperf., pair	45.00	
b.		Perf. 11½x12	7.50	1.75
82	A55	60c black	22.50	4.00
a.		Imperf., pair	50.00	50.00
		Nos. 75-82 (7)	44.45	7.42

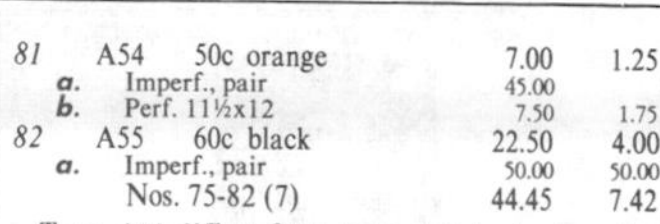

Type A50 differs from type A44 in having the head smaller, the letters of "Cinco Centavos" not as tall, and the curved ornaments at sides close to the first and last letters of "Republica Argentina".

1890 *Perf. 11½x12*

Black or Red Lithographed Surcharge.

No.	Type			
83	A56	¼c on 12c bl (Blk)	60	50
a.		Perf. 11½	50.00	30.00
84	A56	¼c on 12c bl (R)	60	50
a.		Double surcharge	75.00	75.00
b.		Perf. 11½	10.00	3.00

Rivadavia
A57

José de San Martin
A58

Gregorio Araoz de Lamadrid
A59

Admiral Guillermo Brown
A60

1891 Engraved. *Perf. 11½*

No.	Type			
85	A57	8c car rose	2.25	35
a.		Imperf., pair	85.00	
86	A58	1p dp bl	65.00	10.00
87	A59	5p ultra	325.00	35.00
88	A60	20p green	450.00	100.00

A 10p brown and a 50p red were prepared but not issued.

Prices $1,500 and $1,000.

Vélez Sarsfield
A61

1890 *Perf. 11½*

No.	Type			
89	A61	1c brown	1.50	40

Type A61 is a re-engraving of A42. The figure "1" in each upper corner has a short horizontal serif instead of a long one pointing downward. In type A61 the first and last letters of "Correos y Telegrafos" are closer to the curved ornaments below than in type A42. Background is of horizontal lines (crosshatching on No. 69).

"Santa Maria," "Niña" and "Pinta"—A62

Wmk. 85

Wmk. 86

The Small Sun (85) is 4½mm. in diameter and the Large Sun (86) 6mm.

Wmkd. Small Sun. (85)

1892, Oct. 12 *Perf. 11½*

No.	Type			
90	A62	2c lt bl	10.00	5.0
a.		Dbl. impression	275.00	
91	A62	5c dk bl	14.00	7.0

Discovery of America, 400th anniv. Counterfeits of Nos. 90-91 are litho.

Rivadavia
A63

Belgrano
A64

San Martín
A65

Perf. 11½, 12 and Compound.

1892–95 Wmk. 85

No.	Type			
92	A63	½c dl bl	30	10
a.		½c brt ultra	35.00	10.00
b.		Imperf., pair	40.00	
93	A63	1c brown	60	8
a.		Imperf., pair	40.00	
94	A63	2c green	60	8
a.		Imperf., pair	17.50	
95	A63	3c org ('95)	1.50	10
96	A63	5c carmine	2.00	5
a.		Imperf., pair	17.50	17.50
b.		5c grn (error)	500.00	375.00
98	A64	10c car rose	9.00	12
a.		Imperf., pair	45.00	
99	A64	12c dp bl ('93)	9.00	40
a.		Imperf., pair	45.00	
100	A64	16c gray	16.50	1.00
a.		Imperf., pair	45.00	
101	A64	24c gray brn	16.50	1.00
a.		Imperf., pair	45.00	
b.		Perf. 12	35.00	10.00
102	A64	50c bl grn	24.00	1.00
a.		Imperf., pair	35.00	
b.		Perf. 12	35.00	4.00
103	A65	1p lake ('93)	15.00	1.35
a.		1p red brn	25.00	7.00
b.		Imperf., pair	50.00	
104	A65	2p dk grn	35.00	3.50
a.		Perf. 12	110.00	40.00
105	A65	5p dk bl	60.00	4.00
a.		Imperf., pair	100.00	
		Nos. 92-105 (13)	190.00	12.78

Part-perforate varieties of Nos. 92–98 include vert. or horiz. pairs imperf. between and pairs imperf. vert. or horiz. Price $6–$35.

The high values of this and succeeding issues are frequently punched with the word "INUTILIZADO," parts of the letters showing on each stamp. These punched stamps sell for only a small fraction of the catalogue prices.

Reprints of No. 96b have white gum. The original stamp has yellowish gum. *Price $125.*

1896–97 Wmkd. Large Sun. (86)

No.	Type			
106	A63	½c slate	50	10
a.		½c gray bl	50	10
b.		½c ind	50	10
107	A63	1c brown	60	5
108	A63	2c yel grn	1.00	5
109	A63	3c orange	1.00	10
110	A63	5c carmine	1.00	5
a.		Imperf., pair	30.00	
111	A64	10c car rose	10.00	5
112	A64	12c dp bl	5.00	5
a.		Imperf., pair	45.00	
113	A64	16c gray	15.00	85
114	A64	24c gray brn	17.50	2.25
a.		Imperf., pair	25.00	
115	A64	30c org ('97)	16.00	85
116	A64	50c bl grn	16.00	85
117	A64	80c dl vio	22.50	1.10
118	A65	1p lake	35.00	1.10
119	A65	1p20c blk ('97)	17.50	4.00
120	A65	2p dk grn	25.00	10.00
121	A65	5p dk bl	125.00	10.00
a.		Perf. 12	275.00	70.00
		Nos. 106-121 (16)	308.60	31.45

Allegory, Liberty Seated
A66 A67

Perf. 11½, 12 and Compound

1899-1903

122	A66	½c yel brn	12	5
a.		Imperf., pair	25.00	
123	A66	1c green	30	5
a.		Imperf., pair	35.00	
124	A66	2c slate	30	5
a.		Imperf., pair	9.00	5.00
125	A66	3c org ('01)	1.00	30
a.		Imperf., pair	140.00	85.00
126	A66	4c yel ('03)	2.00	35
127	A66	5c car rose	30	5
a.		Imperf., pair	7.50	6.00
128	A66	6c blk ('03)	1.10	40
a.		Imperf., pair	45.00	
129	A66	10c dk grn	2.00	5
a.		Imperf., pair	45.00	
130	A66	12c dl bl	1.50	60
131	A66	12c ol grn ('01)	1.50	50
132	A66	15c sea grn ('01)	4.00	25
a.		Imperf., pair	45.00	
132B	A66	15c dl bl ('01)	3.00	30
133	A66	16c orange	11.00	8.00
134	A66	20c claret	3.00	15
135	A66	24c violet	5.00	1.50
136	A66	30c rose	11.00	85
137	A66	30c ver ('01)	5.50	30
a.		30c scar	75.00	4.00
138	A66	50c brt bl	7.00	35
139	A67	1p bl & blk, perf. 11½	20.00	1.50
a.		Center inverted	2,250.	800.00
b.		Perf. 12	275.00	80.00
140	A67	5p org & blk	85.00	20.00
		Punch cancellation		1.25
a.		Center inverted	2,250.	
141	A67	10p grn & blk	100.00	20.00
		Punch cancellation		1.25
a.		Center invtd.	5,000.	
		Punch cancellation		1,100.
142	A67	20p red & blk	300.00	60.00
		Punch cancellation		60
a.		Center inverted (punch canc.)		2,500.
		Nos. 122-142 (22)	564.62	115.60

Part-perforate varieties of Nos. 122–129 include vert. or horiz. pairs imperf. between and pairs imperf. vert. or horiz. Price 50 cents to $10.

River Port of Rosario
A68

1902, Oct. 26 Perf. 11½, 11½x12

143	A68	5c dp bl	7.00	3.00
a.		Imperf., pair	120.00	

Completion of port facilities at Rosario.

San Martín
A69 A70

Perf. 13½, 13½x12½.

1908-09 Typographed.

144	A69	½c violet	20	10
145	A69	1c brnsh buff	30	10
146	A69	2c chocolate	90	10
147	A69	3c green	1.10	50
148	A69	4c redsh vio	2.25	50
149	A69	5c carmine	50	10
150	A69	6c ol bis	1.25	40
151	A69	10c gray grn	2.50	15
152	A69	12c yel buff	65	60
153	A69	12c dk bl ('09)	2.00	20
154	A69	15c ap grn	2.75	1.35
155	A69	20c ultra	2.00	15
156	A69	24c red brn	5.00	1.00
157	A69	30c dl rose	8.00	1.00
158	A69	50c black	7.50	70
159	A70	1p sl bl & pink	17.50	2.75
		Nos. 144-159 (16)	54.40	9.70

The 1c in blue was not issued. Price $250.

Wmk. 86 appears on ½, 1, 6, 20, 24 and 50c. Other values have similar wmk. with wavy rays.

Stamps lacking wmk. are from outer rows printed on sheet margin.

Centenary of the Republic Issue.

Pyramid of May
A71

Nicolás Rodríguez Peña and Hipólito Vieytes
A72

Meeting at Peña's Home
A73

Designs: 3c, Miguel de Azcuénaga (1754–1833) and Father Manuel M. Alberti (1763–1811). 4c, Viceroy's house and Fort Buenos Aires. 5c, Cornelio Saavedra (1759–1829). 10c, Antonio Luis Beruti (1772–1842) and French distributing badges. 12c, Congress building. 20c, Juan José Castelli (1764–1812) and Domingo Matheu (1765–1831). 24c, First council. 30c, Manuel Belgrano (1770–1820) and Juan Larrea (1782–1847). 50c, First meeting of republican government, May 25, 1810. 1p, Mariano Moreno (1778–1811) and Juan José Paso (1758–1833). 5p, Oath of the Junta. 10p, Centenary Monument. 20p, José Francisco de San Martin (1778–1850).

Inscribed "1810 1910"
Various Frames

1910, May 1 Engraved Perf. 11½

160	A71	½c bl & gray bl	60	20
a.		Center inverted	800.00	
161	A72	1c bl grn & blk	60	15
a.		Center inverted	800.00	
b.		Horiz. pair, imperf. between	80.00	
162	A73	2c ol & gray	45	10
a.		Center inverted	950.00	
163	A72	3c green	1.25	25
164	A73	4c dk bl & grn	1.25	40
a.		Center inverted	450.00	
165	A71	5c carmine	1.00	5
166	A73	10c yel brn & blk	3.00	35
167	A73	12c brt bl	2.50	40
a.		Center inverted	800.00	
168	A72	20c gray brn & blk	4.00	60
169	A73	24c org brn & bl	3.00	1.50
170	A72	30c lil & blk	3.00	1.10
171	A71	50c car & blk	8.00	1.50
a.		Center inverted	800.00	
172	A72	1p brt bl	17.50	6.00
173	A73	5p org & vio	135.00	50.00
		Punch cancel		4.00
a.		Center inverted	800.00	
174	A71	10p org & blk	225.00	110.00
		Punch cancel		5.00
175	A71	20p dp bl & ind	350.00	150.00
		Punch cancel		7.50
		Nos. 160-175 (16)	756.15	322.60

Domingo F. Sarmiento — Agriculture
A87 A88

1911, May 15 Typo. Perf. 13½

176	A87	5c gray brn & blk	1.25	60

Issued to commemorate the centenary of the birth of Domingo Faustino Sarmiento (1811-88), president of Argentina, 1868-74.

Wmk. 86, without Face

1911 Engraved. Perf. 12.

Size: 19x25mm.

177	A88	5c vermilion	60	10
178	A88	12c dp bl	7.50	30

Wmk. 86, with Face

1911 Typographed Perf. 13½x12½

Size: 18x23mm.

179	A88	½c violet	15	8
180	A88	1c brn ocher	20	8
181	A88	2c chocolate	30	6
a.		Perf. 13½	7.50	3.00
b.		Imperf., pair	45.00	
182	A88	3c green	75	15
183	A88	4c brn vio	60	35
184	A88	10c gray grn	90	10
185	A88	20c ultra	7.50	1.50
186	A88	24c red brn	9.00	5.00
187	A88	30c claret	3.00	85
188	A88	50c black	15.00	1.50
		Nos. 179-188 (10)	37.40	9.67

The 5c dull red is a proof. In this issue Wmk. 86 comes: straight rays (4c,20c,24c) and wavy rays (2c). All other values exist with both forms.

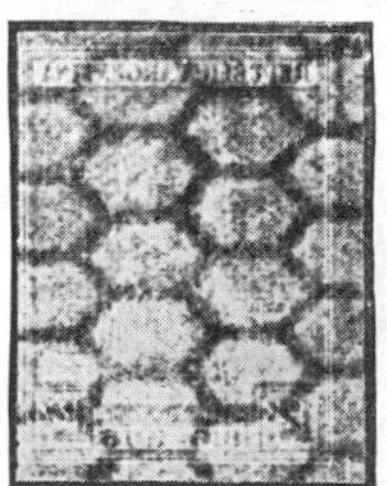

Wmk. 87

Wmkd. Honeycomb. (87) (Horizontal or Vertical)

1912-14 Perf. 13½x12½

189	A88	½c violet	30	10
a.		Perf. 13½	1.50	50
190	A88	1c ocher	30	10
a.		Perf. 13½	1.50	50
191	A88	2c chocolate	60	6
a.		Perf. 13½	1.50	30
192	A88	3c green	1.10	30
a.		Perf. 13½	65.00	30.00
193	A88	4c brn vio	1.10	30
a.		Perf. 13½	3.00	1.25
194	A88	5c red	30	5
a.		Perf. 13½	60	10
195	A88	10c dp grn	2.50	15
196	A88	12c dp bl	2.50	5
a.		Perf. 13½	6.00	1.50
197	A88	20c ultra	15.00	1.25
a.		Perf. 13½	9.00	1.25
198	A88	24c red brn	6.00	3.00
199	A88	30c claret	15.00	1.10
200	A88	50c black	9.00	1.10
		Nos. 189-200 (12)	53.70	7.56

See also Nos. 208–212.

A89

1912-13 Perf. 13½.

201	A89	1p dl bl & rose	11.00	1.75
		Punch cancel		25
202	A89	5p sl & ol grn	35.00	10.00
		Punch cancel		50
203	A89	10p vio & bl	135.00	16.50
		Punch cancel		1.25
204	A89	20p bl & cl	325.00	100.00
		Punch cancel		1.75

1915 Perf. 13½x12½. Unwmkd.

208	A88	1c ocher	75	12
209	A88	2c chocolate	75	8
212	A88	5c red	60	7

Only these denominations were printed on paper without watermark.

Other stamps of the series are known unwatermarked but they are from the outer rows of sheets the other parts of which are watermarked.

Francisco Narciso de Laprida — Declaration of Independence
A90 A91

José de San Martín
A92 A92a

Perf. 13½, 13½x12½.

1916, July 9 Lithographed Wmk. 87

215	A90	½c violet	30	6
216	A90	1c buff	40	8

Perf. 13½x12½

217	A90	2c chocolate	30	10
218	A90	3c green	75	15
219	A90	4c red vio	1.10	15

Perf. 13½

220	A91	5c red	50	5
a.		Imperf., pair	65.00	
221	A91	10c gray grn	2.00	15
222	A92	12c blue	1.10	20
223	A92	20c ultra	1.10	25
224	A92	24c red brn	3.00	1.25
225	A92	30c claret	3.00	60
226	A92	50c gray blk	6.00	75
227	A92a	1p sl bl & red	15.00	6.00
		Punch cancel		60
a.		Imperf., pair	400.00	
228	A92a	5p blk & gray grn	175.00	75.00
		Punch cancel		6.00
229	A92a	10p vio & bl	300.00	135.00
		Punch cancel		4.00
230	A92a	20p dl bl & cl	275.00	120.00
		Punch cancel		1.50
a.		Imperf., pair	800.00	
		Nos. 215-230 (16)	784.55	339.79

Issued to commemorate the centenary of Argentina's declaration of independence of Spain, July 9, 1816.

The watermark is either vertical or horizontal on Nos. 215-220, 222; only vertical on No. 221, and only horizontal on Nos. 223-230.

A93

A94

A94a

1917 ***Perf. 13½, 13½x12½***

No.	Type	Description	Unused	Used
231	A93	½c violet	30	6
232	A93	1c buff	30	6
233	A93	2c brown	30	5
234	A93	3c lt grn	1.00	10
235	A93	4c red vio	1.00	50
236	A93	5c red	30	5
a.		Imperf., pair	20.00	
237	A93	10c gray grn	2.00	10

Perf. 13½

No.	Type	Description	Unused	Used
238	A94	12c blue	1.25	10
239	A94	20c ultra	2.00	30
240	A94	24c red brn	6.50	3.00
241	A94	30c claret	6.50	85
242	A94	50c gray blk	6.00	90
243	A94a	1p sl bl & red	6.00	60
244	A94a	5p blk & gray grn	25.00	4.00
		Punch cancel		1.00
245	A94a	10p vio & bl	60.00	16.00
		Punch cancel		60
246	A94a	20p dl bl & cl	135.00	25.00
		Punch cancel		60
a.		Center inverted	1,500.	1,100.
		Nos. 231-246 (16)	253.45	51.67

The watermark is either vertical or horizontal on Nos. 231–236, 238; only vertical on No. 237, and only horizontal on Nos. 239–246.

Juan Gregorio Pujol
A95

1918, June 15 **Litho.** ***Perf. 13½***

No.	Type	Description	Unused	Used
247	A95	5c bis & gray	1.25	30

Issued to commemorate the centenary of the birth of Juan G. Pujol (1817–61), lawyer and legislator.

Perf. 13½, 13½x12½

1918–19 **Unwmkd.**

No.	Type	Description	Unused	Used
248	A93	½c violet	20	10
249	A93	1c buff	20	6
a.		Imperf., pair	25.00	
250	A93	2c brown	25	5
251	A93	3c lt grn	45	10
252	A93	4c red vio	45	15
253	A93	5c red	25	5
254	A93	10c gray grn	2.00	5

Perf. 13½

No.	Type	Description	Unused	Used
255	A94	12c blue	2.00	8
256	A94	20c ultra	3.00	8
257	A94	24c red brn	3.50	85
258	A94	30c claret	4.25	50
259	A94	50c gray blk	10.00	45
		Nos. 248-259 (12)	26.55	2.52

The stamps of this issue sometimes show letters of papermakers' watermarks.

There were two printings, in 1918 and 1923, using different ink and paper.

Wmk. 88

Wmkd. Multiple Suns. (88)

1920 ***Perf. 13½, 13½x12½***

No.	Type	Description	Unused	Used
264	A93	½c violet	30	10
265	A93	1c buff	40	6
266	A93	2c brown	40	8
267	A93	3c green	2.25	60
268	A93	4c red vio	3.00	1.50
269	A93	5c red	60	5
270	A93	10c gray grn	5.00	12

Perf. 13½

No.	Type	Description	Unused	Used
271	A94	12c blue	2.75	15
272	A94	20c ultra	4.00	15
274	A94	30c claret	12.50	1.25
275	A94	50c gray blk	7.50	1.75
		Nos. 264-275 (11)	38.70	5.81

See also Nos. 292–300, 304–307A, 310–314, 318, 322.

Belgrano's Mausoleum
A96

Gen. Manuel Belgrano
A98

Creation of Argentine Flag
A97

1920, June 18 ***Perf. 13½***

No.	Type	Description	Unused	Used
280	A96	2c red	75	25
a.		Perf. 13½x12½	75	25
281	A97	5c rose & bl	75	10
282	A98	12c grn & bl	1.50	1.10

Issued to commemorate the centenary of the death of Manuel Belgrano (1770–1820), Argentine general, patriot and diplomat.

Gen. Justo José de Urquiza
A99

Bartolomé Mitre
A100

1920, Nov. 11

No.	Type	Description	Unused	Used
283	A99	5c gray bl	45	20

Issued to honor Gen. Justo José de Urquiza (1801–1870), president of Argentina, 1854–1860. See also No. 303.

1921, June 26 **Unwmkd.**

No.	Type	Description	Unused	Used
284	A100	2c vio brn	50	25
285	A100	5c lt bl	50	20

Issued to commemorate the centenary of the birth of Bartolomé Mitre (1821–1906), president of Argentina, 1862–65.

Allegory, Pan-America
A101

1921, Aug. 25 ***Perf. 13½***

No.	Type	Description	Unused	Used
286	A101	3c violet	1.10	40
287	A101	5c blue	1.50	20
288	A101	10c vio brn	2.75	50
289	A101	12c rose	4.00	1.00

Inscribed "Buenos Aires—Agosto de 1921"
A102

Inscribed "Republica Argentina"
A103

1921, Oct. ***Perf. 13½x12½***

No.	Type	Description	Unused	Used
290	A102	5c rose	50	8
a.		Perf. 13½	2.25	8
291	A103	5c rose	2.75	6
a.		Perf. 13½	4.00	6

Issued to commemorate the first Pan-American Postal Congress, held at Buenos Aires, August, 1921.

See also Nos. 308–309, 319.

Wmk. 89

In this watermark the face of the sun is 7 mm. in diameter, the rays are heavier than in the large sun watermark of 1896-1911 and the watermarks are placed close together, so that parts of several frequently appear on one stamp. This paper was intended to be used for fiscal stamps and is usually referred to as "fiscal sun paper".

Wmkd. Large Sun. (89)

1920 ***Perf. 13½, 13½x12½***

No.	Type	Description	Unused	Used
292	A93	½c violet	2.50	1.00
293	A93	1c buff	7.00	1.00
294	A93	2c brown	4.00	1.00
297	A93	5c red	5.50	60
298	A93	10c gray grn	5.50	60

Perf. 13½

No.	Type	Description	Unused	Used
299	A94	12c blue	3,500.	150.00
300	A94	20c ultra	20.00	1.50
		Nos. 292-298, 300 (6)	44.50	5.70

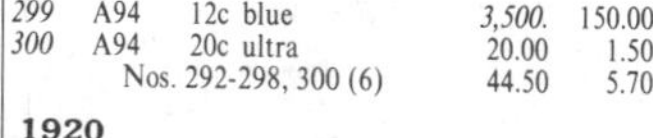

1920

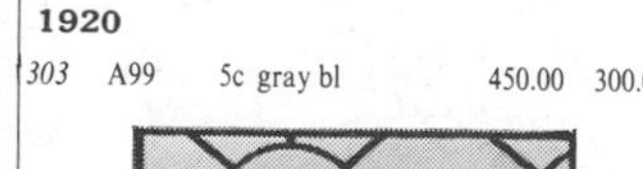

No.	Type	Description	Unused	Used
303	A99	5c gray bl	450.00	300.00

Wmk. 90

In 1928 the watermark R. A. in Sun (90) was slightly modified, making the diameter of the Sun 9 mm. instead of 10 mm. Several types of this watermark exist.

Wmkd. RA in Sun. (90)

1922–23 ***Perf. 13½, 13½x12½***

No.	Type	Description	Unused	Used
304	A93	½c violet	25	10
305	A93	1c buff	25	5
306	A93	2c brown	25	5
307	A93	3c green	75	50
307A	A93	4c red vio	6.00	1.50
308	A102	5c rose	3.75	20
309	A103	5c red	2.50	10
310	A93	10c gray grn	7.50	50

Perf. 13½

No.	Type	Description	Unused	Used
311	A94	12c blue	1.10	20
312	A94	20c ultra	2.00	10
313	A94	24c red brn	15.00	7.00
314	A94	30c claret	9.00	75
		Nos. 304-314 (12)	48.35	11.05

Paper with Gray Overprint RA in Sun.

Perf. 13½, 13½x12½

1922-23 **Unwmkd.**

No.	Type	Description	Unused	Used
318	A93	2c brown	4.00	1.25
319	A103	5c red	2.50	35

Perf. 13½

No.	Type	Description	Unused	Used
322	A94	20c ultra	25.00	1.75

San Martín
A104 A105

With Period after Value.

1923, May **Litho.** **Wmk. 90**

No.	Type	Description	Unused	Used
323	A104	½c red vio	40	30
324	A104	1c buff	60	15
325	A104	2c dk brn	60	6
326	A104	3c lt grn	60	35
327	A104	4c red brn	60	30
328	A104	5c red	60	5
329	A104	10c dl grn	5.00	15
330	A104	12c dp bl	75	15
331	A104	20c ultra	2.00	8
332	A104	24c lt brn	5.00	2.75
333	A104	30c claret	15.00	85
334	A104	50c black	7.50	60

Without Period after Value.

Wmkd. Honeycomb. (87) ***Perf. 13½***

No.	Type	Description	Unused	Used
335	A105	1p bl & red	7.50	20
336	A105	5p gray lil & grn	30.00	3.00
		Punch cancel		75
337	A105	10p cl & bl	100.00	17.50
		Punch cancel		1.25
338	A105	20p sl & brn lake	150.00	45.00
		Punch cancel		70
a.		Center inverted		
		Nos. 323-338 (16)	326.15	71.49

Nos. 335 to 338 and 353 to 356 cancelled with round or oval killers in purple (revenue cancellations) sell for one-fifth to one-half the price of postally used copies.

Design of 1923.

Without Period after Value.

Wmkd. RA in Sun. (90)

1923–31 ***Perf. 13½, 13½x12½***

No.	Type	Description	Unused	Used
340	A104	½c red vio	12	5
341	A104	1c buff	12	5
342	A104	2c dk brn	12	5
343	A104	3c green	20	5
a.		Imperf., pair	15.00	
b.		Typographed	2.00	40
344	A104	4c red brn	75	5
345	A104	5c red	12	5
a.		Typographed	3.75	75
346	A104	10c dl grn	50	5
a.		Typographed	6.00	30
347	A104	12c dp bl	90	10
a.		Typographed	12.50	2.25
348	A104	20c ultra	1.25	5
a.		Typographed	50.00	2.50
349	A104	24c lt brn	3.00	1.50
350	A104	25c purple	1.50	5
a.		Typographed	30.00	1.10
351	A104	30c claret	3.00	10
a.		Typographed	22.50	60
352	A104	50c black	3.00	10
353	A105	1p bl & red	3.75	10

354 A105 5p dk vio & grn 27.50 1.00
a. Punch cancel 30
355 A105 10p cl & bl 60.00 5.00
Punch cancel 35
356 A105 20p sl & lake 90.00 15.00
Punch cancel 35
Nos. 340-356 (17) 195.83 23.35

There were two printings of many of the stamps of type A104: lithographed (1923-24), clear impression, and typographed (1931-33), rough impression with heavy shading about the eyes and nose. The typographed stamps were issued only in coils. Nos. 343 and 346 are known without watermark.

Nos. 341-345, 347-349, 351 (litho.) may be found in pairs, one with period.

See note after No. 338. See also Nos. 362-368.

Rivadavia
A106

1926, Feb. 8 ***Perf. 13½***

357 A106 5c rose 75 20

Issued in commemoration of the centenary of the Presidency of Bernardino Rivadavia.

Rivadavia
A108

San Martín
A109

General Post Office, 1926
A110

General Post Office, 1826
A111

1926, July 1 ***Perf. 13½x12½***

358 A108 3c gray grn 25 10
359 A109 5c red 25 8

Perf. 13½

360 A110 12c dp bl 1.50 30
361 A111 25c chocolate 2.75 15
a. "1326" for "1826" 9.00 1.25

Centenary of the Post Office.

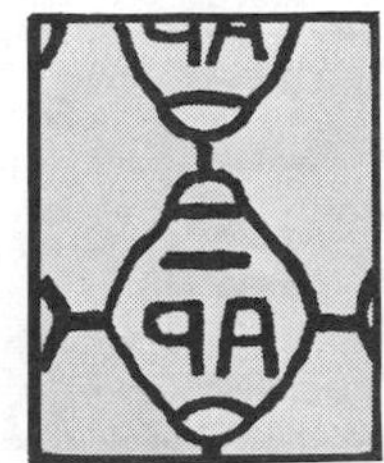

Wmk. 205

The letters "A. P." in the watermark are the initials of "AHORRO POSTAL". This paper was formerly used exclusively for Postal Savings stamps.

Type of 1923-31 Issue.
Without Period after Value.
Wmkd. AP in Oval. (205)

1927 ***Perf. 13½x12½***

362 A104 ½c red vio 40 30
a. Pelure paper 3.00 2.50
363 A104 1c buff 40 30
364 A104 2c dk brn 40 15
a. Pelure paper 60 30
365 A104 5c red 50 15
a. Period after value 6.00 3.00
b. Pelure paper 75 35
366 A104 10c dl grn 7.50 3.00
367 A104 20c ultra 30.00 3.00

Perf. 13½

368 A105 1p bl & red 60.00 9.00
Nos. 362-368 (7) 99.20 15.90

Arms of Argentina and Brazil
A112

Wmkd. RA in Sun. (90)

1928, Aug. 27 ***Perf. 12½x13***

369 A112 5c rose red 1.50 50
370 A112 12c dp bl 3.00 1.00

Commemorative of the centenary of peace between the Empire of Brazil and the United Provinces of the Rio de la Plata.

Allegory, Discovery of the New World
A113

"Spain" and "Argentina"
A114

"America" Offering Laurels to Columbus
A115

1929, Oct. 12 **Litho.** ***Perf. 13½***

371 A113 2c lil brn 1.50 30
372 A114 5c lt red 1.50 12
373 A115 12c dl bl 3.50 1.10

Issued to commemorate the 437th anniversary of the discovery of America by Columbus.

Spirit of Victory Attending Insurgents
A116

March of the Victorious Insurgents
A117

Perf. 13½x12½ (A116),
12½x13 (A117)

1930

374 A116 ½c vio gray 30 20
375 A116 1c myr grn 40 20
376 A117 2c dl vio 50 10
377 A116 3c green 75 35
378 A116 4c violet 60 35
379 A116 5c rose red 30 10
380 A116 10c gray blk 1.75 50
381 A117 12c dl bl 1.25 35
382 A117 20c ocher 1.25 30
383 A117 24c red brn 5.00 2.25
384 A117 25c green 6.00 2.25
385 A117 30c dp vio 10.00 3.00
386 A117 50c black 15.00 4.00
387 A117 1p sl bl & red 25.00 15.00
388 A117 2p blk & org 50.00 15.00
389 A117 5p dl grn & blk 150.00 60.00
390 A117 10p dp red brn & dl bl 200.00 75.00
391 A117 20p yel grn & dl bl 575.00 175.00
392 A117 50p dk grn & vio 1,350. 1,000.
Nos. 374-392 (19) 2,393.10 1,353.95

Issued to commemorate the Revolution of 1930.

Nos. 387-392 with oval (parcel post) cancellation sell for less.

1931 ***Perf. 12½x13***

393 A117 ½c red vio 20 15
394 A117 1c gray blk 1.50 60
395 A117 3c green 75 35
396 A117 4c red brn 60 30
397 A117 5c red 20 5
a. Plane omitted, top left corner 5.00 2.50
398 A117 10c dl grn 1.50 40
Nos. 393-398 (6) 4.75 1.85

Issued to commemorate the Revolution of 1930.

Stamps of 1924-25 Overprinted in Red or Green **-6- Septiembre 1930 - 1931**

Perf. 13½, 13½x12½

1931, Sept. 6

399 A104 3c grn (R) 35 35
400 A104 10c dl grn (R) 1.00 1.00
401 A104 30c cl (G) 5.50 3.50
402 A104 50c blk (R) 5.50 3.50

Overprinted in Blue **1930 Septiembre 6 1931**

403 A105 1p bl & red 6.50 3.50
404 A105 5p dk vio & grn 120.00 32.50

No. 388 Overprinted in Blue
6 Septiembre 1931

Perf. 12½x13

405 A117 2p blk & org 22.50 12.50
Nos. 399-405 (7) 161.35 56.85

Issued in commemoration of the first anniversary of the Revolution of 1930.

Refrigeration Compressor
A118

Lithographed.

1932, Aug. 29 ***Perf. 13½x12½***

406 A118 3c green 75 40
407 A118 10c scarlet 2.50 25
408 A118 12c gray bl 6.00 1.50

Issued to commemorate the sixth International Refrigeration Congress.

Port of La Plata
A119

President Julio A. Roca
A120

Municipal Palace
A121

Cathedral of La Plata
A122

Dardo Rocha
A123

Perf. 13½x13, 13x13½ (10c)

1933, Jan.

409 A119 3c grn & dk brn 60 40
410 A120 10c org & dk vio 90 30
411 A121 15c dk bl & dp bl 6.00 3.00
412 A122 20c vio & yel brn 3.00 1.50
413 A123 30c dk grn & vio brn 25.00 8.50
Nos.409-413 (5) 35.50 13.70

Issued in commemoration of the 50th anniversary of the founding of the city of La Plata, November 19th, 1882.

Christ of the Andes
A124

Buenos Aires Cathedral
A125

Perf. 13x13½, 13½x13

1934, Oct. 1

414 A124 10c rose & brn 1.25 35
415 A125 15c dk bl 2.50 85

Issued to commemorate the 32nd International Eucharistic Congress, Oct. 10–14, 1934.

"Liberty" with Arms of Brazil and Argentina
A126

Symbolical of "Peace" and "Friendship"
A127

1935, May 15 ***Perf. 13x13½***

416	A126	10c red	1.50	40
417	A127	15c blue	3.00	80

Visit of Pres. Getulio Vargas of Brazil.

Belgrano
A128

Sarmiento
A129

Urquiza
A130

Louis Braille
A131

San Martín
A132

Brown
A133

Moreno
A134

Alberdi
A135

Nicolás Avellaneda
A136

Rivadavia
A137

Mitre
A138

Bull (Cattle Breeding)
A139

Martín Güemes
A140

Agriculture
A141

Oil Well (Petroleum)
A144

Merino Sheep (Wool)
A142

Sugar Cane
A143

Map of South America
A145 A146

Fruit
A147

Iguacu Falls (Scenic Wonders)
A148

Grapes (Vineyards)
A149

Cotton
A150

Two types of A140:
Type I—Inscribed Juan Martín Guemes.
Type II—Inscribed Martín Güemes.

Lithographed

Wmkd. RA in Sun. (90)

1935-51 ***Perf. 13, 13½x13, 13x13½***

418	A128	½c red vio	12	5
419	A129	1c buff	12	5
a.		Typographed	12	5
420	A130	2c dk brn	20	5
421	A131	2½c blk ('39)	12	6
422	A132	3c green	20	5
423	A132	3c lt gray ('39)	12	5
424	A134	3c lt gray ('46)	20	6
425	A133	4c lt gray	20	5
426	A133	4c sage grn ('39)	20	5
427	A134	5c yel brn	2.50	5
a.		Tête bêche pair, typo.	8.00	4.00
b.		Booklet pane of 8, typo.		
c.		Booklet pane of 4, typo.		
d.		Typographed	20	5
428	A135	6c ol grn	40	5
429	A136	8c org ('39)	20	8
430	A137	10c car, typo.	50	5
431	A137	10c brn ('42)	20	5
a.		Typographed	75	5
432	A138	12c brown	35	10
433	A138	12c red ('39)	15	5
434	A139	15c sl bl ('36)	1.50	5
435	A139	15c pale ultra ('39)	90	5
436	A140	15c lt gray bl (II) ('42)	65.00	2.50
437	A140	20c lt ultra (I)	1.00	6
438	A140	20c lt ultra (II) ('36)	60	5
439	A140	20c bl gray (II) ('39)	60	5
439A	A139	20c dk bl & pale bl, 22x33mm ('42)	1.50	5
440	A139	20c bl ('51)	20	5
a.		Typographed	20	5
441	A141	25c car ('36)	40	5
442	A142	30c org brn ('36)	90	5
443	A143	40c dk vio ('36)	75	5
444	A144	50c red & org ('36)	60	5
445	A145	1p brn blk & lt bl ('36)	32.50	1.25
446	A146	1p brn blk & lt bl ('37)	12.50	30
a.		Chalky paper	75.00	1.50
447	A147	2p brn lake & dk ultra ('36)	1.50	20
448	A148	5p ind & ol grn ('36)	11.00	50
449	A149	10p brn lake & blk	60.00	3.50
450	A150	20p bl grn & brn ('36)	85.00	12.00
		Nos. 418-450 (34)	282.23	21.71

See Nos. 485-500, 523-540, 659, 668.

No. 439A exists with attached label showing medallion.
Price $75 unused, $40 used.

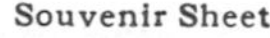

Souvenir Sheet.

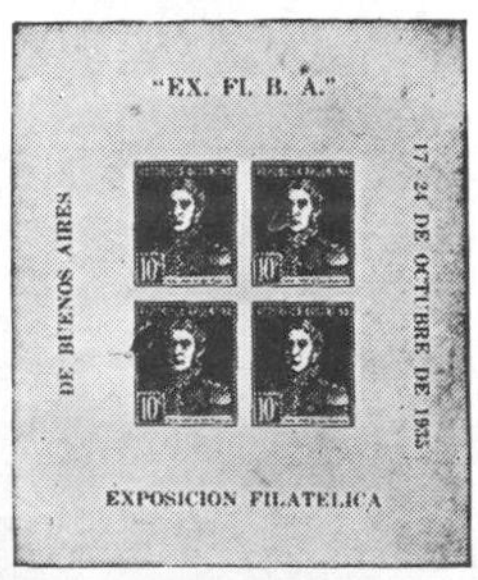

A151

Without Period after Value.

1935, Oct. 17 **Litho.** ***Imperf.***

452	A151	10c dl grn, sheet of four	90.00	50.00
a.		Single stamp	12.00	7.00

Issued in commemoration of the Philatelic Exhibition at Buenos Aires, October 17–24, 1935. The stamps were on sale during the eight days of the exhibition only. Sheets measure 83x101mm.

Plaque
A152

1936, Dec. 1 ***Perf. 13x13½***

453	A152	10c rose	90	30

Issued in commemoration of the Inter-American Conference for Peace.

Domingo Faustino Sarmiento
A153

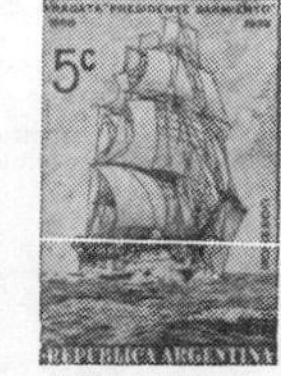

"Presidente Sarmiento"
A154

1938, Sept. 5

454	A153	3c sage grn	30	10
455	A153	5c red	30	5
456	A153	15c dp bl	1.00	25
457	A153	50c orange	3.00	1.10

Issued in commemoration of the 50th anniversary of the death of Domingo Faustino Sarmiento, president, educator and author.

1939, Mar. 16

458	A154	5c grnsh bl	60	25

Issued in commemoration of the final voyage of the training ship "Presidente Sarmiento."

Allegory of the Universal Postal Union
A155

Coat of Arms
A157

Post Office, Buenos Aires
A156

Iguacu Falls—A158

Bonete Hill, Nahuel Huapi Park
A159

Allegory of Modern Communications
A160

Argentina, Land of Promise
A161

Lake Frias, Nahuel Huapi Park
A162

Perf. 13x13½, 13½x13

1939, Apr. 1 Photogravure

459	A155	5c rose car	30	10
460	A156	15c grnsh blk	75	50
461	A157	20c brt bl	75	25
462	A158	25c dp bl grn	1.50	75
463	A159	50c brown	3.00	1.25
464	A160	1p brn vio	3.50	1.50
465	A161	2p magenta	16.00	10.00
466	A162	5p purple	65.00	30.00
		Nos. 459-466 (8)	90.80	44.35

Universal Postal Union, 11th Congress.

Souvenir Sheets.

A163

A164

1939, May 12 *Imperf.* Wmk. 90

467	A163	Sheet of four	10.00	7.00
a.		5c rose car (A155)	1.75	1.25
b.		20c brt bl (A157)	1.75	1.25
c.		25c dp bl grn (A158)	1.75	1.25
d.		50c brn (A159)	1.75	1.25
468	A164	Sheet of four	10.00	7.00

Issued in four forms:

a.	Unsevered horizontal pair of sheets Type A163 at left Type A164 at right	25.00	25.00
b.	Unsevered vertical pair of sheets Type A163 at top Type A164 at bottom	25.00	25.00
c.	Unsevered block of four sheets Type A163 at left Type A164 at right	90.00	90.00
d.	Unsevered block of four sheets Type A163 at top Type A164 at bottom	90.00	90.00

Issued in commemoration of the 11th Congress of the Universal Postal Union and the Argentina International Philatelic Exposition (C.Y.T.R.A.).

No. 468 contains one each of Nos. 467a-467d.

Size: No. 468a, 190x95mm. No. 468b, 95x190mm.

Family and New House
A165

Perf. 13½x13

1939, Oct. 2 Litho. Wmk. 90

469	A165	5c bluish grn	45	10

Issued to commemorate the first Pan-American Housing Congress.

Bird Carrying Record
A166

Head of Liberty and Arms of Argentina
A167

Record and Winged Letter
A168

1939, Dec. 11 Photo. *Perf. 13*

470	A166	1.18p indigo	27.50	15.00
471	A167	1.32p brt bl	27.50	15.00
472	A168	1.50p dk brn	95.00	60.00

These stamps were issued for the recording and mailing of flexible phonograph records.

Map of the Americas
A169

1940, Apr. 14 *Perf. 13x13½*

473	A169	15c ultra	75	20

Issued to commemorate the 50th anniversary of the Pan American Union.

Souvenir Sheet.

Reproductions of Early Argentine Stamps
A170

Wmkd. RA in Sun. (90)

1940, May 25 Litho. *Imperf.*

474	A170	Sheet of five	17.50	10.00
a.		5c dk bl (*Corrientes*)	2.00	1.25
b.		5c red (*Argentine Republic*)	2.00	1.25
c.		5c dk bl (*Cordoba*)	2.00	1.25
d.		5c red (*Argentine Republic*)	2.00	1.25
e.		10c dk bl (*Buenos Aires*)	2.00	1.25

Issued in sheets measuring 111x116mm., in commemoration of the 100th anniversary of the first postage stamp.

General Domingo French and Colonel Antonio Beruti
A171

1941, Feb. 20 *Perf. 13½x13*

475	A171	5c dk gray bl & lt bl	60	10

Issued in honor of General French and Colonel Beruti, patriots.

Marco M. de Avellaneda
A172

Statue of Gen. Julio Roca
A173

1941, Oct. 3 *Perf. 13x13½*

476	A172	5c dl sl bl	60	10

Issued in commemoration of the centenary of the death of Marco M. de Avellaneda, (1814-41), Army leader and martyr.

1941, Oct. 19 Photo. Wmk. 90

477	A173	5c dk ol grn	60	10

Issued to commemorate the dedication of a monument to Lt. Gen. Julio Argentino Roca (1843-1914).

Carlos Pellegrini and Bank of the Nation
A174

1941, Oct. 26 *Perf. 13½x13*

478	A174	5c brn car	60	10

Issued to commemorate the 50th anniversary of the founding of the Bank of the Nation.

Gen. Juan Lavalle
A175

1941, Dec. 5 *Perf. 13x13½*

479	A175	5c brt bl	60	10

Issued to commemorate the centenary of the death of Gen. Juan Galo de Lavalle (1797-1841).

National Postal Savings Bank
A176

1942, Apr. 5 Litho. *Perf. 13½x13*

480	A176	1c pale ol	25	10

José Manuel Estrada
A177

1942, July 13 *Perf. 13x13½*

481	A177	5c brn vio	60	10

Issued to commemorate the centenary of the birth of José Estrada (1842-1894), writer and diplomat.

No. 481 exists with label, showing medallion, attached. The pair sells for 15 times the price of the single stamp.

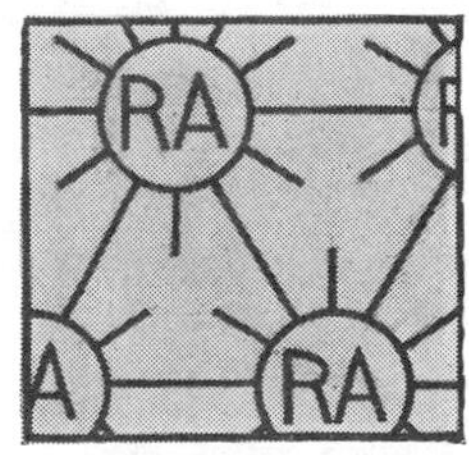

Wmk. 288

Types of 1935-51.

Wmkd. RA in Sun with Straight Rays. (288)

Perf. 13, 13x13½, 13½x13.

1942-50 Lithographed.

485	A128	½c brn vio	7.50	1.25
486	A129	1c buff ('50)	12	5
487	A130	2c dk brn ('50)	12	5
488	A132	3c lt gray	25.00	1.50
489	A134	3c lt gray ('49)	25	5
490	A137	10c red brn ('49)	30	5
491	A138	12c red	30	10
492	A140	15c lt gray bl (II)	45	5
493	A139	20c dk sl bl & pale bl	2.00	5
494	A141	25c dl rose ('49)	90	10
495	A142	30c org brn ('49)	2.00	6
496	A143	40c vio ('49)	12.50	20
497	A144	50c red & org ('49)	12.50	30
498	A146	1p brn blk & lt bl	10.00	30
499	A147	2p brn lake & bl ('49)	20.00	1.00
500	A148	5p ind & ol grn ('49)	80.00	6.00
		Nos. 485-500 (16)	173.94	11.11

No. 493 measures 22x33 mm.

Post Office, Buenos Aires
A178

Proposed Columbus Lighthouse
A179

Inscribed: "Correos y Telegrafos".

1942, Oct. 5 Litho. *Perf. 13*

503 A178 35c lt ultra 5.00 6

See also Nos. 541-543.

1942, Oct. 12 Wmk. 288

504 A179 15c dl bl 4.00 10

Wmk. 90

505 A179 15c dl bl 100.00 7.00

Nos. 504–505 were issued to commemorate the 450th anniversary of the discovery of America by Columbus.

José C. Paz
A180

Books and Argentine Flag
A181

1942, Dec. 15 Wmk. 288

506 A180 5c dk gray 60 5

Issued in commemoration of the centenary of the birth of José C. Paz, statesman and founder of the newspaper La Prensa.

1943, Apr. 1 Litho. *Perf. 13*

507 A181 5c dl bl 25 5

Issued to commemorate the first Book Fair of Argentina.

Arms of Argentina Inscribed "Honesty, Justice, Duty"
A182

1943–50 *Perf. 13* Wmk. 288

Size: 20x26mm.

508 A182 5c red ('50) 3.50 5

Wmk. 90

509 A182 5c red 30 5
a. 5c dl red, unsurfaced paper 5.00 8
510 A182 15c green 1.00 15

Perf. 13x13½

Size: 22x33mm.

511 A182 20c dk bl 1.50 15

Issued to commemorate the change of political organization on June 4, 1943.

Independence House, Tucuman
A183

Liberty Head and Savings Bank
A184

1943–51 *Perf. 13* Wmk. 90

512 A183 5c bl grn 1.20 8

Wmk. 288

513 A183 5c bl grn ('51) 50 8

Issued to commemorate the restoration of Independence House.

1943, Oct. 25 Wmk. 90

514 A184 5c vio brn 25 5

Wmk. 288

515 A184 5c vio brn 55.00 3.00

Issued to commemorate the first conference of National Postal Savings.

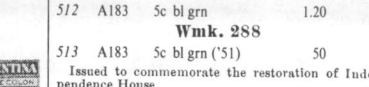

Port of Buenos Aires in 1800
A185

1943, Dec. 11 Wmk. 90

516 A185 5c gray blk 25 5

Day of Exports.

Warship, Merchant Ship and Sailboat
A186

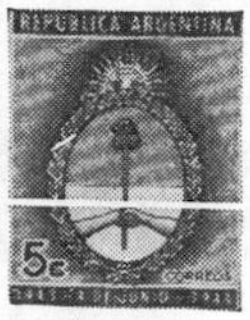

Arms of Argentine Republic
A187

1944, Jan. 31 *Perf. 13*

517 A186 5c blue 25 6

Issued to commemorate Sea Week.

1944, June 4

518 A187 5c dl bl 15 6

Issued to commemorate the first anniversary of the change of political organization in Argentina.

St. Gabriel
A188

Cross at Palermo
A189

1944, Oct. 11

519 A188 3c yel grn 25 8
520 A189 5c dp rose 25 8

Fourth national Eucharistic Congress.

Allegory of Savings
A190

Reservists
A191

1944, Oct. 24

521 A190 5c gray 15 5

Issued to commemorate the 20th anniversary of the National Savings Bank.

1944, Dec. 1

522 A191 5c blue 15 5

Day of the Reservists.

Types of 1935-51.

Perf. 13x13½, 13½x13.

1945-47 Lithographed. Unwmkd.

523 A128 ½c brn vio ('46) 12 5
524 A129 1c yel brn 12 5
525 A130 2c sepia 15 5
526 A132 3c lt gray (*San Martin*) 70 5
527 A134 3c lt gray (*Moreno*) ('46) 25 5
528 A135 6c ol grn ('47) 30 15
529 A137 10c brn ('46) 2.50 5
530 A140 15c lt gray bl (II) 1.25 5
531 A139 20c dk sl bl & pale bl 2.50 5
532 A141 25c dl rose 75 5
533 A142 30c org brn 60 5
534 A143 40c violet 2.50 12
535 A144 50c red & org 2.50 5
536 A146 1p brn blk & lt bl 3.75 10
537 A147 2p brn lake & bl 20.00 35
538 A148 5p ind & ol grn ('46) 100.00 4.00
539 A149 10p dp cl & int blk 12.00 1.50
540 A150 20p bl grn & brn ('46) 12.50 1.50
Nos. 523-540 (18) 162.49 8.27

No. 531 measures 22x33mm.

Post Office Type

Inscribed: "Correos y Telecommunicaciones".

1945 *Perf. 13x13½* Unwmkd.

541 A178 35c lt ultra 2.00 5

Wmk. 90

542 A178 35c lt ultra 2.00 5

Wmk. 288

543 A178 35c lt ultra 60 5

Bernardino Rivadavia
A192 A193

Mausoleum of Rivadavia
A194

Perf. 13½x13.

1945, Sept. 1 Litho. Unwmkd.

544 A192 3c bl grn 20 6
545 A193 5c rose 20 5
546 A194 20c blue 50 6

Issued to commemorate the centenary of the death of Bernardino Rivadavia, Argentina's first president.

No. 546 exists with mute label attached. The pair sells for four times the price of the single stamp.

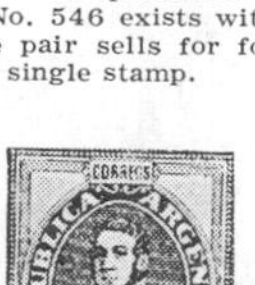

General José de San Martín
A195

Monument to Army of the Andes, Mendoza
A196

Lithographed or Typographed.

1945-46 Wmk. 90

547 A195 5c car, typo. 15 6
a. Lithographed ('46) 20 6

Wmk. 288

548 A195 5c car, litho. 175.00 30.00

Unwmkd.

549 A195 5c car, typo. ('46) 75 5
a. Lithographed ('46) 30 5

1946, Jan. 14 Litho. *Perf. 13½x13*

550 A196 5c vio brn 15 5

Issued to honor the Unknown Soldier of the War for Independence.

Franklin D. Roosevelt
A197

Liberty Administering Presidential Oath—A198

1946, Apr. 12

551 A197 5c sl blk 20 8

Issued in memory of Franklin D. Roosevelt.

1946, June 4 *Perf. 13x13½*

552 A198 5c blue 15 5

Issued to commemorate the inauguration of President Juan D. Perón, June 4, 1946.

Argentina Receiving Popular Acclaim
A199

1946, Oct. 17 *Perf. 13½x13*

553 A199 5c rose vio 30 10
554 A199 10c bl grn 45 15
555 A199 15c dk bl 90 20
556 A199 50c red brn 1.25 40
557 A199 1p car rose 2.50 1.10
Nos. 553-557 (5) 5.40 1.95

First anniversary of the political organization change of Oct. 17, 1945.

Coin Bank and World Map
A200

1946, Oct. 31 Unwmkd.

558 A200 30c dk rose car & pink 1.00 15

Issued to commemorate the Universal Day of Savings, October 31, 1946.

Argentine Industry
A201

International Bridge Connecting Argentina and Brazil
A202

1946, Dec. 6 ***Perf. 13x13½***

559 A201 5c vio brn 15 5

Day of Argentine Industry, Dec. 6.

1947, May 21 Litho. ***Perf. 13½x13***

560 A202 5c green 15 5

Issued to commemorate the opening of the Argentina-Brazil International Bridge, May 21, 1947.

Map of Argentine Antarctic Claims A203

Justice A204

1947–49 ***Perf. 13x13½*** **Unwmkd.**

561 A203 5c vio & lil 60 6
562 A203 20c dk car rose & rose 1.25 10

Wmk. 90

563 A203 20c dk car rose & rose 3.00 20

Wmk. 288

564 A203 20c dk car rose & rose ('49) 3.50 20

Issued to note the 43rd anniversary of the first Argentine Antarctic mail.

1947, June 4 **Unwmkd.**

565 A204 5c brn vio & pale yel 15 5

Issued to commemorate the 1st anniversary of the Perón government.

Icarus Falling A205

1947, Sept. 25 ***Perf. 13½x13***

566 A205 15c red vio 25 8

Aviation Week.

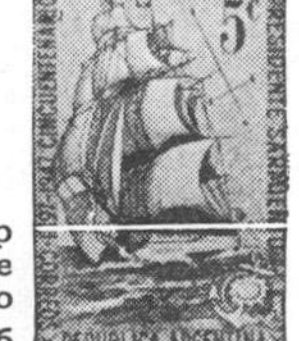

Training Ship Presidente Sarmiento A206

1947, Oct. 5 ***Perf. 13x13½***

567 A206 5c blue 30 15

Issued to commemorate the 50th anniversary of the launching of the Argentine training frigate "Presidente Sarmiento".

Cervantes and Characters from Don Quixote—A207

Perf. 13½x13

1947, Oct. 12 Photo. Wmk. 90

568 A207 5c ol grn 20 5

Issued to commemorate the 400th anniversary of the birth of Miguel de Cervantes Saavedra, playwright and poet.

Gen. José de San Martin A208

Lithographed.

1947–49 ***Perf. 13½x13*** **Unwmkd.**

569 A208 5c dl grn 15 6

Wmk. 288

570 A208 5c dl grn ('49) 25 5

Issued to commemorate the transfer of the remains of Gen. José de San Martin's parents.

School Children A209

Statue of Araucanian Indian A210

1947–49 ***Perf. 13x13½*** **Unwmkd.**

571 A209 5c green 15 5

Wmk. 90

574 A209 20c brown 50 10

Wmk. 288

575 A209 5c green 50 5

Argentine School Crusade for World Peace.

1948, May 21 **Wmk. 90**

576 A210 25c yel brn 50 10

American Indian Day, Apr. 19.

Cap of Liberty A211

Manual Stop Signal A212

1948, July 16

577 A211 5c ultra 15 5

Issued to commemorate the 5th anniversary of the Revolution of June 4, 1943.

1948, July 22

578 A212 5c choc & yel 15 5

Traffic Safety Day, June 10.

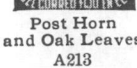

Post Horn and Oak Leaves A213

Argentine Farmers A214

1948, July 22 **Unwmkd.**

579 A213 5c lil rose 15 5

Issued to commemorate the 200th anniversary of the establishment of regular postal service on the Plata River.

Perf. 13x13½

1948, Sept. 20 **Wmk. 288**

580 A214 10c red brn 25 6

Agriculture Day, Sept. 8, 1948.

Liberty and Symbols of Progress A215

Wmk. 287

Wmkd. Double Circle and Letters in Sheet. (287)

1948, Nov. 23 Photo. ***Perf. 13x13½***

581 A215 25c red brn 30 6

Issued to commemorate the third anniversary of President Juan D. Peron's return to power, October 17, 1945.

Souvenir Sheets.

A216

Designs: 15c, Mail coach. 45c, Buenos Aires in 18th century. 55c, First train, 1857. 85c, Sailing ship, 1767.

1948, Dec. 21 ***Imperf.*** **Unwmkd.**

582 A216 Sheet of four 4.00 3.00
a. 15c dk grn 60 60
b. 45c org brn 60 60
c. 55c lil brn 60 60
d. 85c ultra 60 60

A217

Designs: 85c, Domingo de Basavilibaso (1709–75). 1.05p, Postrider. 1.20p, Sailing ship, 1798. 1.90p, Courier in the Andes, 1772.

583 A217 Sheet of four 18.00 14.00
a. 85c brn 4.00 3.00
b. 1.05p dk grn 4.00 3.00
c. 1.20p dk bl 4.00 3.00
d. 1.90p red brn 4.00 3.00

Issued in sheets measuring 143x101mm. (No. 582) and 101x143mm. (No. 583) to commemorate the 200th anniversary of the establishment of regular postal service on the Plata River.

Winged Wheel A218

Perf. 13½x13

1949, Mar. 1 **Wmk. 288**

584 A218 10c blue 40 5

Nationalization of the railroads, first anniversary.

Liberty A219

1949, June 20 Engraved Wmk. 90

585 A219 1p red & red vio 75 15

Ratification of the Constitution of 1949.

Allegory of the U.P.U. A220

1949, Nov. 19

586 A220 25c dk grn & yel grn 40 10

Issued to commemorate the 75th anniversary of the formation of the Universal Postal Union.

Gen. José de San Martín A221

Mausoleum of San Martín A223

San Martín at Boulogne sur Mer
A222

Designs: 20c, 50c, 75c, Different Portraits of San Martin. 1p, House where San Martin died.

Inscribed:
"Centenario de la Muerte del General Don José de San Martin 1850-1950."

Engraved, Photogravure (25c, 1p, 2p)

1950, Aug. 17 *Perf. 13½* Wmk. 90

587	A221	10c ind & dk pur	20	5
588	A221	20c red brn & dk brn	20	6
589	A222	25c brown	25	8
590	A221	50c dk grn & ind	75	12
591	A221	75c choc & dk grn	75	18
a.		Souv. sheet of 4	2.00	1.25
592	A222	1p dk grn	1.50	30
593	A223	2p dp red lil	1.25	50
		Nos. 587-593 (7)	4.90	1.29

Issued to commemorate the centenary of the death of General José de San Martin. No. 591a measures 120x150mm. and contains one each of Nos. 587, 588, 590 and 591, imperf., with marginal inscriptions and ornamental border in brown.

Map Showing Antarctic Claims
A224

1951, May 21 Litho. *Perf. 13x13½*

594	A224	1p choc & lt bl	1.25	10

Pegasus and Train
A225

Communications Symbols
A226

Design: 25c, Ship and dolphin.

1951, Oct. 17 Photo. *Perf. 13½*

595	A225	5c dk brn	20	5
596	A225	25c Prus grn	40	12
597	A226	40c rose brn	45	15

Close of Argentine Five Year Plan.

Woman Voter and "Argentina"
A227

1951, Dec. 14 *Perf. 13½x13*

598	A227	10c brn vio	15	6

Granting of women's suffrage.

Eva Perón
A228 A229

Lithographed
or Engraved (#605).

1952, Aug. 26 *Perf. 13* Wmk. 90

599	A228	1c org brn	12	5
600	A228	5c gray	12	5
601	A228	10c rose lil	12	5
602	A228	20c rose pink	12	5
603	A228	25c dl grn	12	8
604	A228	40c dl vio	20	5
605	A228	45c dp bl	25	10
606	A228	50c dl brn	25	10

Photogravure

607	A229	1p dk brn	45	10
608	A229	1.50p dp grn	2.50	15
609	A229	2p brt car	75	15
610	A229	3p indigo	1.25	20
		Nos. 599-610 (12)	6.25	1.13

Inscribed: "Eva Perón."

1952–53 *Perf. 13x13½*

611	A229	1p dk brn	90	5
612	A229	1.50p dp grn	90	5
613	A229	2p brt car ('53)	2.00	15
614	A229	3p indigo	2.75	20

Engraved

Size: 30x40mm.

Perf. 13½x13.

615	A229	5p red brn	2.75	60
616	A228	10p red	7.50	2.50
617	A229	20p green	20.00	7.00
618	A228	50p ultra	30.00	17.50
		Nos. 611-618(8)	66.80	28.05

Indian Funeral Urn
A230

1953, Aug. 28 Photo. *Perf. 13x13½*

619	A230	50c bl grn	25	10

Issued to commemorate the 400th anniversary of the founding of Santiago del Estero.

Rescue Ship "Uruguay"
A231

1953, Oct. 8 *Perf. 13½*

620	A231	50c ultra	1.50	12

Issued to commemorate the 50th anniversary of the rescue of the Antarctic expedition of Otto C. Nordenskjold.

Planting Argentine Flag in the Antarctic
A232

Engraved

1954, Jan. 20 *Perf. 13½x13*

621	A232	1.45p blue	2.25	15

Issued to commemorate the 50th anniversary of Argentina's first antarctic post office and the establishing of the La Hoy radio post office in the South Orkneys.

Wired Communications
A233

Television
A234

Design: 3p, Radio.

Perf. 13x13½, 13½x13.

1954, Apr. Photo. Wmk. 90

622	A233	1.50p vio brn	60	25
623	A233	3p vio bl	2.00	50
624	A234	5p carmine	2.50	1.00

Issued to publicize the International Plenipotentiary Conference of Telecommunications, Buenos Aires, 1952.

Pediment, Buenos Aires Stock Exchange
A235

1954, July 13 *Perf. 13½x13*

625	A235	1p dk grn	50	10

Issued to commemorate the centenary of the establishment of the Buenos Aires Stock Exchange.

Eva Perón
A236

1954 Wmk. 90

626	A236	3p dp car rose	2.00	30

Wmk. 288

627	A236	3p dp car rose	250.00	50.00

Issued to commemorate the second anniversary of the death of Eva Perón.

José de San Martin
A237

Eva Perón Foundation Building
A239

Wheat
A238

Industry
A238a

Cliffs of Humahuaca
A240

Gen. José de San Martin
A241

Designs: 50c, Buenos Aires harbor. 1p, Cattle ranch (Ganaderia). 3p, Nihuil Dam. 5p, Iguassu Falls (vert.). 20p, Mt. Fitz Roy (vert.).

1954-59 **Wmk. 90**
Engr. (#632, 638-642), Photo. (#634-637)
Perf. 13½, 13x13½ (80c), 13½x13 (#639, 641-642)

628 A237 20c brt red, typo. 12 5
629 A237 20c red, litho. ('55) 90 5
630 A237 40c red, litho. ('56) 25 5
631 A237 40c brt red, typo. ('55) 40 5
632 A239 50c bl ('56) 15 5
633 A239 50c bl, litho. ('59) 25 5
634 A238 80c brown 35 5
635 A239 1p brn ('58) 40 5
636 A238a 1.50p ultra ('58) 30 7
637 A239 2p dk rose lake 50 6
638 A239 3p vio brn ('56) 50 6
639 A240 5p gray grn ('55) 8.00 6
a. Perf. 13½ 10.00 6
640 A240 10p yel grn ('55) 6.00 8
641 A240 20p dl vio ('55) 12.00 15
a. Perf. 13½ 15.00 15
642 A241 50p ultra & ind ('55) 12.00 15
a. Perf. 13½ 12.00 15
Nos. 628-642 (15) 42.12 1.03

See Nos. 699–700. For similar designs inscribed "Republica Argentina" see Nos. 823–827, 890, 935, 937, 940, 990, 995, 1039, 1044, 1048.

Allegory
A242

1954, Aug. 26 **Typo.** ***Perf. 13½***
643 A242 1.50p sl blk 1.00 10
Issued to commemorate the centenary of the establishment of the Buenos Aires Grain Exchange.

Clasped Hands and Congress Medal
A243

1955, Mar. 21 **Photo.** ***Perf. 13½x13***
644 A243 3p red brn 1.25 15
Issued to publicize the National Productivity and Social Welfare Congress.

Allegory of Aviation
A244

Argentina Breaking Chains
A245

Perf. 13½.
1955, June 18 **Wmk. 90**
645 A244 1.50p ol gray 1.00 8
Issued to commemorate the 25th anniversary of commercial aviation in Argentina.

1955, Oct. 16 **Lithographed**
647 A245 1.50p ol grn 50 6
Liberation Revolution of Sept. 16, 1955.

Army Navy and Air Force Emblems—A246

Perf. 13½x13
1955, Dec. 31 **Photo.** **Wmk. 90**
648 A246 3p blue 75 10
"Brotherhood of the Armed Forces."

Justo José de Urquiza
A247

1956, Feb. 3 ***Perf. 13½***
649 A247 1.50p green 50 6
Battle of Caseros, 104th anniversary.

Coin and Die
A248

Engraved.
1956, July 28 ***Perf. 13½x13***
650 A248 2p gray brn & redsh brn 50 10

75th anniversary of the Argentine Mint.

1856 Stamp of Corrientes
A249

Juan G. Pujol
A250

Design: 2.40p, Stamp of 1860–78.

1956, Aug. 21
651 A249 40c dk grn & bl 25 10
652 A249 2.40p brn & lil rose 50 12

Photogravure.
653 A250 4.40p brt bl 1.10 30
a. Souvenir sheet 2.50 2.25
Centenary of Argentine postage stamps.
No. 653a commemorates both the Argentine stamp centenary and the Philatelic Exhibition for the Centenary of Corrientes Stamps, Oct. 12–21. It is imperf. and contains one each of Nos. 651–653, with the 4.40p in photogravure and the other two stamps and border lithographed. Colors of 40c and 2.40p differ slightly from engraved stamps. Marginal inscriptions, coats of arms and scroll work in dull purple. Size: 146x170mm.

Felling Trees, La Pampa
A251

Maté Herb and Gourd, Misiones
A252

Design: 1p, Cotton plant and harvest, Chaco.

1956, Sept. 1 ***Perf. 13½***
654 A251 50c ultra 12 5
655 A251 1p magenta 30 6
656 A252 1.50p green 40 8
Issued to commemorate the elevation of the territories of La Pampa, Chaco and Misiones to provinces.

"Liberty"
A253

Florentino Ameghino
A254

Photogravure.
1956, Sept. 15 ***Perf. 13½*** **Wmk. 90**
657 A253 2.40p lil rose 50 10
Issued to commemorate the first anniversary of the Revolution of Liberation.

1956, Nov. 30
658 A254 2.40p brown 40 5
Issued to honor Florentino Ameghino (1854–1911), anthropologist.

Adm. Brown Type of 1935–51.

1956 **Lithographed** ***Perf. 13***
Two types:
I. Bust touches upper frame line of name panel at bottom.
II. White line separates bust from frame line.

Size: 19½–20½x26–27mm.
659 A133 20c dl pur (I) 30 5
a. Type II 30 5
b. Size 19½x25¼ mm (I) 25 5

Benjamin Franklin
A255

1956, Dec. 22 **Photo.** ***Perf. 13½***
660 A255 40c int bl 50 8
Issued to commemorate the 250th anniversary of the birth of Benjamin Franklin.

Frigate "Hercules"
A256

Guillermo Brown
A257

1957, Mar. 2
661 A256 40c brt bl 15 6
662 A257 2.40p gray blk 60 15
Issued to commemorate the centenary of the death of Admiral Guillermo (William) Brown (1777–1857), founder of the Argentine navy.

Roque Saenz Peña
A258

Church of Santo Domingo, 1807
A259

1957, Apr. 1
663 A258 4.40p grnsh gray 60 12
Issued to honor Roque Saenz Peña (1851–1914), president in 1910–1914.

1957, July 6 **Wmk. 90**
664 A259 40c brt bl grn 15 7
Issued to commemorate the 150th anniversary of the defense of Buenos Aires.

"La Portena"
A260

1957, Aug. 31 ***Perf. 13½*** **Wmk. 90**
665 A260 40c pale brn 30 15
Centenary of Argentine railroads.

Esteban Echeverria
A261

"Liberty"
A262

1957, Sept. 2 ***Perf. 13x13½***
666 A261 2p claret 30 5
Esteban Echeverria (1805–1851), poet.

1957, Sept. 28 ***Perf. 13½***

667	A262	40c car rose	12	6

Constitutional reform convention.

Portrait Type of 1935-51.

Portrait: 5c, Jose Hernandez.

1957, Oct. 28 **Litho.** ***Perf. 13½***

Size: 16½x22mm.

668	A128	5c buff	15	6

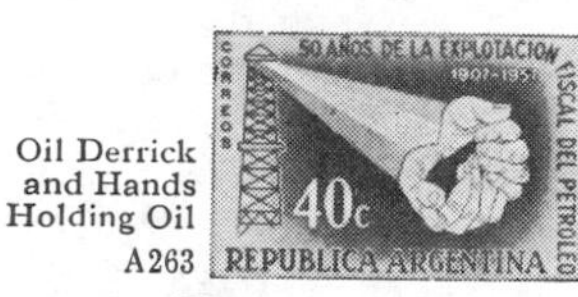

Oil Derrick and Hands Holding Oil
A263

Photogravure.

1957, Dec. 21 ***Perf. 13½*** **Wmk. 90**

669	A263	40c brt bl	30	15

Issued to commemorate the 50th anniversary of the national oil industry.

Museum, La Plata
A264

1958, Jan. 11

670	A264	40c dk gray	20	10

City of La Plata, 75th anniversary.

Locomotive and Arms of Argentina and Bolivia
A265

Map of Argentine-Bolivian Boundary and Plane
A266

1958, Apr. 19 ***Perf. 13½*** **Wmk. 90**

671	A265	40c sl & dp car	40	15
672	A266	1p dk brn	40	15

Issued to celebrate Argentine-Bolivian friendship. No. 671 commemorates the opening of the Jacuiba-Santa Cruz railroad; No. 672, the exchange of presidential visits.

Symbols of the Republic
A267

Flag Monument
A268

Engraved and Photogravure

1958, Apr. 30 **Wmk. 90**

673	A267	40c multi	15	5
674	A267	1p multi	25	6
675	A267	2p multi	40	12

Transmission of Presidential power.

1958, June 21 **Litho.** **Wmk. 90**

676	A268	40c bl & vio bl	15	6

Issued to commemorate the first anniversary of the Flag Monument of Rosario.

Map of Antarctica
A269

Stamp of Cordoba and Mail Coach
A270

1958, July 12 ***Perf. 13½***

677	A269	40c car rose & blk	80	30

International Geophysical Year, 1957-58.

1958, Oct. 18

678	A270	40c pale bl & sl	20	10

Centenary of Cordoba postage stamps.
See also Nos. C72-C73.

"Slave" by Michelangelo and U. N. Emblem
A271

Engraved and Lithographed

1959, Mar. 14 ***Perf. 13½*** **Wmk. 90**

679	A271	40c vio brn & gray	20	10

Issued to commemorate the tenth anniversary (in 1958) of the signing of the Universal Declaration of Human Rights.

Orchids and Globe
A272

1959, May 23 **Photo.** ***Perf. 13½***

680	A272	1p dl cl	30	15

1st International Horticulture Exposition.

Pope Pius XII
A273

William Harvey
A274

1959, June 20 **Engraved** ***Perf. 13½***

681	A273	1p yel & blk	30	15

Issued in memory of Pope Pius XII, 1876-1958.

1959, Aug. 8 **Litho.** **Wmk. 90**

Portraits: 1p, Claude Bernard. 1.50p, Ivan P. Pavlov.

682	A274	50c green	15	8
683	A274	1p dk red	20	12
684	A274	1.50p brown	40	10

Issued to publicize the 21st International Congress of Physiological Sciences, Buenos Aires.

Type of 1958 and

Domestic Horse
A275

José de San Martin
A276

Tierra del Fuego
A277

Inca Bridge, Mendoza
A278

Ski Jumper
A279

Mar del Plata
A280

Designs: 10c, Cayman. 20c, Llama. 50c, Puma. No. 690, Sunflower. 3p, Zapata Slope, Catamarca. 12p, 23p, 25p, Red quebracho tree. 20p, Nahuel Huapi Lake. 22p, "Industry" (cogwheel and factory).

Two overall paper sizes for 1p, 5p:
I. 27x37½mm. or 37½x27mm.
II. 27x39mm. or 39x27mm.

Perf. 13x13½

1959-70 **Lithographed** **Wmk. 90**

685	A275	10c sl grn	10	5
686	A275	20c dl red brn ('61)	10	5
687	A275	50c bis, litho. ('60)	10	5
688	A275	50c bis, typo. ('60)	30	5
689	A275	1p rose red	10	5

Perf. 13½

690	A278	1p brn, photogravure, paper I ('61)	10	5
a.		Paper II ('69)	30	5
690B	A278	1p brn, litho., paper I	1.00	5
691	A276	2p rose red, litho. ('61)	40	6
692	A276	2p red, typo. (19½x26mm) ('61)	50	5
a.		Redrawn (19½x25mm)	7.50	5
693	A277	3p dk bl, photo. ('60)	25	5
694	A276	4p red, typo ('62)	30	5
694A	A276	4p red, litho. ('62)	60	5
695	A277	5p gray brn, photo., paper I	60	5
e.		5p dk brn, paper II ('70)	10.00	5
695A	A276	8p ver, litho. ('65)	2.00	6
695B	A276	8p red, typo. ('65)	50	5
695C	A276	10p ver, litho. ('66)	1.00	8
695D	A276	10p red, typo. ('66?)	75	6

Photogravure

696	A278	10p lt red brn ('60)	75	9
697	A278	12p dk brn vio ('62)	1.25	5
697A	A278	12p dk brn, litho. ('64)	12.50	10
698	A278	20p Prus grn ('60)	4.50	8
698A	A276	20p red, typo. ('67)	40	5
699	A238a	22p ultra ('62)	2.50	8
700	A238a	22p ultra, litho. ('62)	37.50	10
701	A278	23p grn ('65)	7.50	6
702	A278	25p dp vio ('66)	2.00	6
703	A278	25p pur, litho. ('66?)	10.00	6
704	A279	100p bl ('61)	8.00	15
705	A280	300p dp vio ('62)	4.50	20
		Nos. 685-705 (29)	100.10	1.99

See Nos. 882-887, 889, 892, 923-925, 928-930, 938, 987-989, 991.

The 300p remained on sale as a 3p stamp after the 1970 currency exchange.

Symbolic Sailboat
A281

Child Playing with Doll
A282

1959, Oct. 3 **Litho.** ***Perf. 13½***

706	A281	1p blk, red & bl	20	10

Red Cross sanitary education campaign.

1959, Oct. 17

707	A282	1p red & blk	20	10

Issued for Mother's Day, 1959.

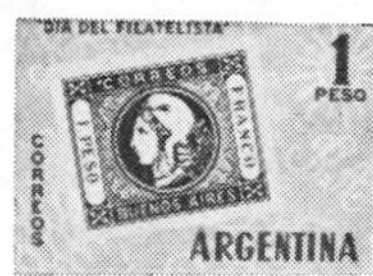

Buenos Aires 1p Stamp of 1859
A283

1959, Nov. 21 ***Perf. 13½*** **Wmk. 90**

708	A283	1p gray & dk bl	20	10

Issued for the Day of Philately.

Bartolomé Mitre and Justo José de Urquiza
A284

1959, Dec. 12 **Photo.** ***Perf. 13½***

709	A284	1p purple	20	10

Treaty of San Jose de Flores, centenary.

WRY Emblem A285 Abraham Lincoln A286

1960, Apr. 7 Litho. Wmk. 90

710 A285 1p bis & car 15 10
711 A285 4.20p ap grn & dp cl 45 30

World Refugee Year, July 1, 1959–June 30, 1960. See also No. B25.

1960, Apr. 14 Photo. *Perf. 13½*

712 A286 5p ultra 60 25

Issued to commemorate the sesquicentennial (in 1959) of the birth of Abraham Lincoln.

Cornelio Saavedra and Cabildo, Buenos Aires—A287

"Cabildo" and: 2p, Juan José Paso. 4.20p, Manuel Alberti and Miguel Azcuénaga. 10.70p, Juan Larrea and Domingo Matheu.

Photogravure

1960, May 28 *Perf. 13½* Wmk. 90

713 A287 1p rose lil 15 5
714 A287 2p bluish grn 15 6
715 A287 4.20p gray & grn 35 15
716 A287 10.70p gray & ultra 65 30
Nos. 713-716, C75-C76 (6) 1.80 76

150th anniversary of the May Revolution. Souvenir sheets are Nos. C75a and C76a.

Luis Maria Drago A288 Juan Bautista Alberdi A289

1960, July 8

717 A288 4.20p brown 30 10

Issued to commemorate the centenary of the birth of Dr. Luis Maria Drago, statesman and jurist.

1960, Sept. 10 *Perf. 13½* Wmk. 90

718 A289 1p green 20 10

Issued to commemorate the 150th anniversary of the birth of Juan Bautista Alberdi, statesman and philosopher.

Map of Argentina and Antarctic Sector A290 Caravel and Emblem A291

1960, Sept. 24 Litho. *Perf. 13½*

719 A290 5p violet 1.25 30

National census of 1960.

1960, Oct. 1 Photogravure

720 A291 1p dk ol grn 20 6
721 A291 5p brown 70 18

Issued to commemorate the 8th Congress of the Postal Union of the Americas and Spain. See also Nos. C78–C79.

Virgin of Luján, Patroness of Argentina—A292 Argentine Boy Scout Emblem—A293

1960, Nov. 12 *Perf. 13½* Wmk. 90

722 A292 1p dk bl 15 8

First Inter-American Marian Congress.

1961, Jan. 17 Lithographed

723 A293 1p car rose & blk 40 20

International Patrol Encampment of the Boy Scouts, Buenos Aires.

"Shipment of Cereals," by Quinquela Martin—A294

Photogravure

1961, Feb. 11 *Perf. 13½* Wmk. 90

724 A294 1p red brn 40 15

Export drive: "To export is to advance."

Naval Battle of San Nicolás A295 Mariano Moreno by Juan de Dios Rivera A296

1961, Mar. 2 *Perf. 13½*

725 A295 2p gray 40 15

Issued to commemorate the 150th anniversary of the naval battle of San Nicolás.

1961, Mar. 25 *Perf. 13½* Wmk. 90

726 A296 2p blue 20 6

Issued to commemorate the 150th anniversary of the death of Mariano Moreno (1778–1811), writer, politician, member of the 1810 Junta.

Emperor Trajan Statue A297

1961, Apr. 11

727 A297 2p sl grn 20 8

Issued to commemorate the visit of Pres. Giovanni Gronchi of Italy to Argentina, April 1961.

Rabindranath Tagore A298

1961, May 13 Photo. *Perf. 13½*

728 A298 2p pur, *grysh* 20 6

Issued to commemorate the centenary of the birth of Rabindranath Tagore, Indian poet.

San Martin Statue, Madrid—A299

1961, May 24 Wmk. 90

729 A299 1p ol gray 20 6

Issued to commemorate the unveiling of a statue of General José de San Martin in Madrid.

Manuel Belgrano A300

1961, June 17 *Perf. 13½*

730 A300 2p vio bl 20 6

Issued to commemorate the erection of a monument by Hector Rocha, to General Manuel Belgrano in Buenos Aires.

Explorers, Sledge and Dog Team A301

1961, Aug. 19 Photo. Wmk. 90

731 A301 2p black 1.00 30

Issued to commemorate the 10th anniversary of the General San Martin Base, Argentine Antarctic.

Spanish Conquistador and Sword A302 Sarmiento Statue by Rodin, Buenos Aires A303

1961, Aug. 19 Lithographed

732 A302 2p red & blk 20 8

First city of Jujuy, 400th anniversary.

1961, Sept. 9 Photogravure

733 A303 2p violet 20 8

Issued to commemorate the 150th anniversary of the birth of Domingo Faustino Sarmiento (1811–1888), political leader and writer.

Symbol of World Town Planning A304

Lithographed

1961, Nov. 25 *Perf. 13½* Wmk. 90

734 A304 2p ultra & yel 20 8

World Town Planning Day, Nov. 8.

Manuel Belgrano Statue, Buenos Aires A305 Grenadier, Flag and Regimental Emblem A306

1962, Feb. 24 Photogravure

735 A305 2p Prus bl 20 10

150th anniversary of the Argentine flag.

Perf. 13½

1962, March 31 Wmk. 90

736 A306 2p car rose 20 10

Issued to commemorate the 150th anniversary of the San Martin Grenadier Guards regiment.

Mosquito and Malaria Eradication Emblem A307

1962, Apr. 7 Lithographed

737 A307 2p ver & blk 20 10

Issued for the World Health Organization drive to eradicate malaria.

Church of the Virgin of Lujàn A308 Bust of Juan Jufrè A309

1962, May 12 *Perf. 13½* Wmk. 90

738 A308 2p org brn & blk 20 8

Issued to commemorate the 75th anniversary of the pontifical coronation of the Virgin of Lujan.

1962, June 23 Photogravure

739 A309 2p Prus bl 20 8

Issued to commemorate the fourth centenary of the founding of San Juan.

"Soaring into Space"
A310

Juan Vucetich
A311

1962, Aug. 18 Litho. *Perf. 13½*

740 A310 2p mar, blk & bl 20 8

Argentine Air Force, 50th anniversary.

1962, Oct. 6 Photo. Wmk. 90

741 A311 2p green 20 8

Issued to honor Juan Vucetich (1864–1925), inventor of the Argentine system of fingerprinting.

Domingo F. Sarmiento
A312

February 20th Monument, Salta
A313

Design: 4p, José Hernandez.

1962–66 Photogravure *Perf. 13½*

742 A312 2p dp grn 90 5

Lithographed

742A A312 2p lt grn ('64) 75 5

Photogravure

742B A312 4p dl red ('65) 60 5

Lithographed

742C A312 4p rose red ('66) 60 5

See also No. 817–819.

1963, Feb. 23 Photo. Wmk. 90

743 A313 2p dk grn 20 8

Issued to commemorate the 150th anniversary of the Battle of Salta, War of Independence.

Gear Wheels
A314

1963, Mar. 16 Litho. *Perf. 13½*

744 A314 4p gray, blk & brt rose 20 8

Issued to commemorate the 75th anniversary of the Argentine Industrial Union.

National College, Buenos Aires
A315

Child Draining Cup
A316

1963, Mar. 16 Wmk. 90

745 A315 4p dl org & blk 25 8

Issued to commemorate the centenary of the National College of Buenos Aires.

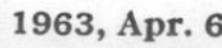

1963, Apr. 6

746 A316 4p multi 20 8

Issued for the "Freedom from Hunger" campaign of the U.N. Food and Agriculture Organization.

Frigate "La Argentina," 1817, by Emilio Biggeri
A317

1963, May 18 Photogravure

747 A317 4p bluish grn 40 20

Issued for Navy Day, May 17.

Seat of 1813 Assembly and Official Seal
A318

Lithographed

1963, July 13 *Perf. 13½* Wmk. 90

748 A318 4p lt bl & blk 20 8

150th anniversary of the 1813 Assembly.

Battle of San Lorenzo, 1813
A319

1963, Aug. 24

749 A319 4p grn & blk, *grnsh* 25 8

Issued to commemorate the sesquicentennial of the Battle of San Lorenzo.

Queen Nefertari Offering Papyrus Flowers, Abu Simbel
A320

1963, Sept. 14 *Perf. 13½* Wmk. 90

750 A320 4p ocher, blk & bl grn 40 20

Campaign to save the historic monuments in Nubia.

Government House, Buenos Aires
A321

1963, Oct. 12 *Perf. 13½* Wmk. 90

751 A321 5p rose & brn 20 8

Inauguration of President Arturo Illia.

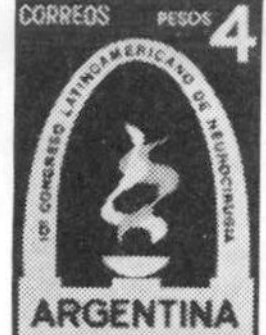

"Science"
A322

Francisco de las Carreras, Supreme Court Justice—A323

1963, Oct. 16 Lithographed

752 A322 4p org brn, bl & blk 20 8

Issued to publicize the 10th Latin-American Neurosurgery Congress.

Photogravure

1963, Nov. 23 *Perf. 13½* Wmk. 90

753 A323 5p bluish grn 20 8

Centenary of judicial power.

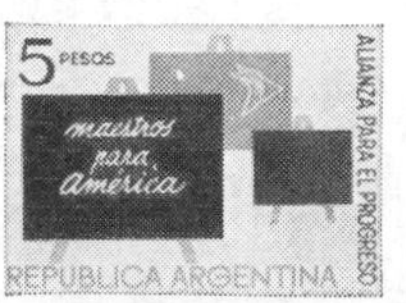

Blackboards
A324

1963, Nov. 23 Lithographed

754 A324 5p red, blk & bl 20 8

Issued to publicize "Teachers for America" through the Alliance for Progress program.

Kemal Atatürk
A325

"Payador" by Juan Carlos Castagnino
A326

1963, Dec. 28 Photo. *Perf. 13½*

755 A325 12p dk gray 40 15

Issued to commemorate the 25th anniversary of the death of Kemal Atatürk, president of Turkey.

1964, Jan. 25 Lithographed

756 A326 4p ultra, blk & lt bl 40 20

Fourth National Folklore Festival.

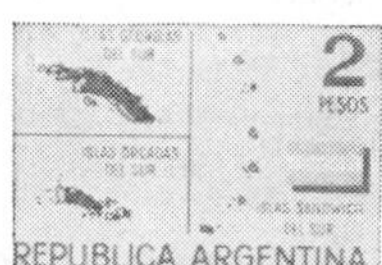

Maps of South Georgia, South Orkney and South Sandwich Islands
A327

Design: 4p, Map of Argentina and Antarctic claims (vert.).

1964, Feb. 22 *Perf. 13½* Wmk. 90

Size: 33x22mm.

757 A327 2p lt & dk bl & bis 2.00 40

Size: 30x40mm.

758 A327 4p lt & dk bl & ol grn 3.00 50

Issued to commemorate the 60th anniversary of Argentina's claim to Antarctic territories. See also No. C92.

Jorge Newbery in Cockpit
A328

1964, Feb. 23 Photogravure

759 A328 4p dp grn 20 8

Issued to commemorate the 50th anniversary of the death of Jorge Newbery, aviator.

John F. Kennedy
A329

José Brochero by José Cuello
A330

1964, Apr. 14 Engraved Wmk. 90

760 A329 4p cl & dk bl 50 10

Issued in memory of President John F. Kennedy (1917–63).

1964, May 9 Photo. *Perf. 13½*

761 A330 4p lt sep 20 8

Issued to commemorate the 50th anniversary of the death of Father José Gabriel Brochero.

Soldier of Patricios Regiment
A331

Pope John XXIII
A332

1964, May 29 Litho. Wmk. 90

762 A331 4p blk, ultra & red 60 30

Issued for Army Day. Later Army Day stamps, inscribed "Republica Argentina," are of type A340a.

1964, June 27 Engraved

763 A332 4p org & blk 30 20

Issued in memory of Pope John XXIII.

University of Cordoba Arms
A333

Pigeons and U.N. Building, N.Y.
A334

1964, Aug. 22 Litho. Wmk. 90

764 A333 4p blk, ultra & yel 20 10

Issued to commemorate the 350th anniversary of the University of Cordoba.

1964, Oct. 24 ***Perf. 13½***

765 A334 4p dk bl & lt bl 20 10

Issued for United Nations Day.

Joaquin V. Gonzalez
A335

Julio Argentino Roca
A336

1964, Nov. 14 **Photogravure**

766 A335 4p dk rose car 20 10

Issued to commemorate the centenary (in 1963) of the birth of Joaquin V. Gonzalez, writer.

1964, Dec. 12 ***Perf. 13½*** **Wmk. 90**

767 A336 4p vio bl 20 10

Issued to commemorate the 50th anniversary of the death of General Julio A. Roca, (1843–1914), president of Argentina, (1880–86, 1898–1904).

Market at Montserrat Square, by Carlos Morel
A337

1964, Dec. 19 **Photogravure**

768 A337 4p sepia 50 30

Issued to honor the 19th century Argentine painter Carlos Morel.

Icebreaker General San Martin
A338

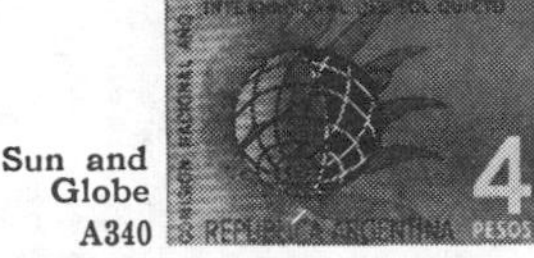

Girl with Piggy Bank
A339

Design: 2p, General Belgrano Base, Antarctica.

1965 ***Perf. 13½*** **Wmk. 90**

769 A338 2p dl pur 70 20
770 A338 4p ultra 80 20

Issued to publicize the national territory of Tierra del Fuego, Antarctic and South Atlantic Isles.

Issue dates: 4p, Feb. 27; 2p, June 5.

1965, Apr. 3 **Lithographed**

771 A339 4p red org & blk 15 10

Issued to commemorate the 50th anniversary of the National Postal Savings Bank.

Sun and Globe
A340

1965, May 29

772 A340 4p blk, org & dl bl 40 20

Issued for the International Quiet Sun Year, 1964–65. See also Nos. C98–C99.

Hussar of Pueyrredon Regiment
A340a

Ricardo Rojas (1882–1957)
A341

1965, June 5 ***Perf. 13½*** **Wmk. 90**

773 A340a 8p dp ultra, blk & red 80 30

Issued for Army Day. See also Nos. 796, 838, 857, 893, 944, 958, 974, 1145.

1965, June 26 **Photogravure**

Portraits: No. 775, Ricardo Guiraldes (1886–1927). No. 776, Enrique Larreta (1873–1961). No. 777, Leopoldo Lugones (1874–1938). No. 778, Roberto J. Payro (1867–1928).

774 A341 8p brown 50 20
775 A341 8p brown 50 20
776 A341 8p brown 50 20
777 A341 8p brown 50 20
778 A341 8p brown 50 20
Nos. 774-778 (5) 2.50 1.00

Issued to honor Argentine writers. Printed se-tenant in sheets of 100 (10x10); 2 horizontal rows of each design with Guiraldes in top rows and Rojas in bottom rows.

Hipolito Yrigoyen
A342

1965, July 3 **Lithographed**

779 A342 8p pink & blk 30 20

Issued in memory of Hipolito Yrigoyen (1852–1933), president of Argentina 1916–22 and 1928–30.

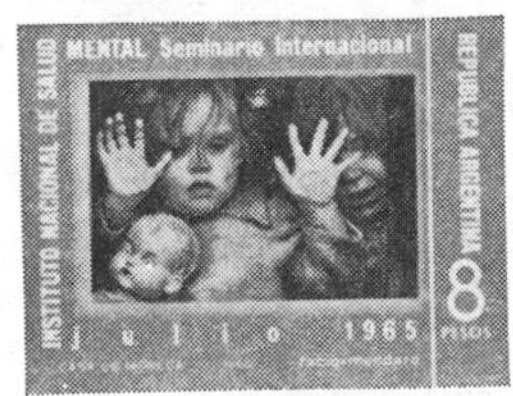

Children Looking Through Window
A343

1965, July 24 **Photogravure**

780 A343 8p sal & blk 30 10

International Seminar on Mental Health.

Child's Funerary Urn and 16th Century Map
A344

1965, Aug. 7 **Lithographed**

781 A344 8p lt grn, dk red, brn & ocher 40 20

City of San Miguel de Tucuman, 400th anniversary.

Cardinal Cagliero
A345

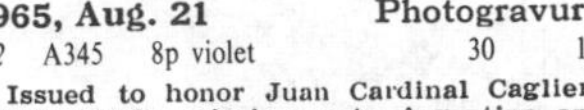

Dante Alighieri
A346

1965, Aug. 21 **Photogravure**

782 A345 8p violet 30 10

Issued to honor Juan Cardinal Cagliero (1839–1926), missionary to Argentina and Bishop of Magida.

1965, Sept. 16 ***Perf. 13½*** **Wmk. 90**

783 A346 8p lt ultra 40 20

Issued to commemorate the 700th anniversary of the birth of Dante Alighieri (1265–1321), Italian poet.

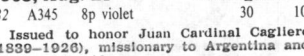

Clipper "Mimosa" and Map of Patagonia—A347

1965, Sept. 25 **Lithographed**

784 A347 8p red & blk 40 20

Issued to commemorate the centenary of Welsh colonization of Chubut, and the founding of the city of Rawson.

Map of Buenos Aires, Cock and Compass Emblem of Federal Police
A348

1965, Oct. 30 **Photo.** ***Perf. 13½***

785 A348 8p car rose 40 20

Issued for Federal Police Day.

Child's Drawing of Children
A349

1965, Nov. 6 **Litho.** **Wmk. 90**

786 A349 8p lt yel grn & blk 40 20

Public education law, 81st anniversary.

Church of St. Francis, Catamarca
A350

Ruben Dario
A351

1965, Dec. 8

787 A350 8p org yel & red brn 30 10

Issued to honor Brother Mamerto de la Asuncion Esquiu, preacher, teacher and official of 1885 Provincial Constitutional Convention.

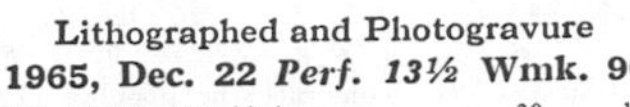

Lithographed and Photogravure

1965, Dec. 22 ***Perf. 13½*** **Wmk. 90**

788 A351 15p bl vio, *gray* 30 15

Issued to honor Ruben Dario (pen name of Felix Ruben Garcia Sarmiento, 1867–1916), Nicaraguan poet, newspaper correspondent and diplomat.

"The Orange Seller"
A352

Pueyrredon Paintings: No. 790, "Stop at the Grocery Store." No. 791, "Landscape at San Fernando" (sailboats). No. 792, "Bathing Horses at River Plata."

1966, Jan. 29 **Photo.** ***Perf. 13½***

789 A352 8p bluish grn 1.00 45
790 A352 8p bluish grn 1.00 45
791 A352 8p bluish grn 1.00 45
792 A352 8p bluish grn 1.00 45

Issued to honor Prilidiano Pueyrredon (1823–1870), painter. Nos. 789–792 are printed in one sheet of 40 stamps and 20 labels.

Sun Yat-sen, Flags of Argentina and China
A353

1966, March 12 ***Perf. 13½*** **Wmk. 90**

793 A353 8p dk red brn 1.00 30

Issued to commemorate the centenary of the birth of Dr. Sun Yat-sen (1866–1925), founder of the Republic of China.

Souvenir Sheet

Rivadavia Issue of 1864
A354

Lithographed

1966, Apr. 20 ***Imperf.*** **Wmk. 90**

794 A354 Sheet of three 1.00 1.00
a. 4p gray & red brn 15 15
b. 5p gray & grn 20 20
c. 8p gray & dk bl 25 25

Issued to commemorate the Second Rio de la Plata Stamp Show, Buenos Aires, March 16–24. No. 794 shows flags of Argentina and Uruguay in margin. Marginal inscriptions in gray and red brown, flags in blue and border in green. Size of stamps: 33x43mm. Size of sheet: 140x99mm.

People of Various Races and WHO Emblem
A355

1966, Apr. 23 ***Perf. 13½***

795 A355 8p brn & blk 40 20

Issued to commemorate the opening of the World Health Organization Headquarters, Geneva.

Soldier Type of 1965

Design: 8p, Cavalryman, Guëmes Infernal Regiment.

1966, May 28 **Lithographed**

796 A340a 8p multi 80 30

Issued for Army Day.

Coat of Arms
A356

Designs (all 10p): Arms of Buenos Aires, Federal Capital, Catamarca, Cordoba, Corrientes, Chaco, Chubut, Entre Rios, Formosa, Jujuy, La Pampa, La Rioja, Mendoza, Misiones, Neuquen, Salta, San Juan, San Luis, Santa Cruz, Santa Fe, Santiago del Estero, Tucuman; maps of Rio Negro, and of Tierra del Fuego, Antarctica and South Atlantic Islands.

1966, July 30 ***Perf. 13½*** **Wmk. 90**

797 A356 10p blk & multi 1.50 1.00
a. Sheet of 25 40.00

Issued to commemorate the 150th anniversary of Argentina's Declaration of Independence.

Sheets of 25 (5x5) contain 25 different designs with commemorative inscription and border in sheet margin.

Three Crosses, Caritas Emblem
A357

1966, Sept. 10 **Litho.** ***Perf. 13½***

798 A357 10p ol grn, blk & lt bl 30 8

Caritas, charity organization.

Hilario Ascasubi (1807–75)
A358

Portraits: No. 800, Estanislao del Campo (1834–80). No. 801, Miguel Cane (1851–1905). No. 802, Lucio V. Lopez (1848–94). No. 803, Rafael Obligado (1851–1920). No. 804, Luis Agote (1868–1954), M.D. No. 805, Juan B. Ambrosetti (1865–1917), naturalist and archaeologist. No. 806, Miguel Lillo (1862–1931), botanist and chemist. No. 807, Francisco P. Moreno (1852–1919), naturalist and paleontologist. No. 808, Francisco J. Muñiz (1795–1871), physician.

1966 **Photogravure** **Wmk. 90**

799 A358 10p dk bl grn *(Ascasubi)* 60 30
800 A358 10p dk bl grn *(del Campo)* 60 30
801 A358 10p dk bl grn *(Cane)* 60 30
802 A358 10p dk bl grn *(Lopez)* 60 30
803 A358 10p dk bl grn *(Obligado)* 60 30
804 A358 10p dp vio *(Agote)* 60 30
805 A358 10p dp vio *(Ambrosetti)* 60 30
806 A358 10p dp vio *(Lillo)* 60 30
807 A358 10p dp vio *(Moreno)* 60 30
808 A358 10p dp vio *(Muniz)* 60 30
Nos. 799-808 (10) 6.00 3.00

Nos. 799–803 issued Sept. 17 to honor Argentine writers. Printed se-tenant in sheets of 100 (10x10); 2 horizontal rows of each portrait with Ascasubi in top two rows and Obligado in bottom rows. Nos. 804–808 issued Oct. 22 to honor Argentine scientists; 2 horizontal rows of each portrait with Agote in top two rows and Muñiz in bottom rows. Scientists set has value at upper left, frame line with rounded corners.

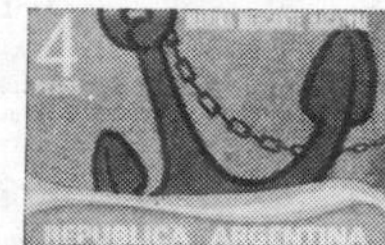

Anchor
A359

1966, Oct. 8 **Lithographed**

809 A359 4p multi 30 20

Argentine merchant marine.

Flags and Map of the Americas
A360

Argentine National Bank
A361

1966, Oct. 29 ***Perf. 13½*** **Wmk. 90**

810 A360 10p gray & multi 30 20

7th Conference of American Armies.

1966, Nov. 5 **Photogravure**

811 A361 10p brt bl grn 25 8

Issued to commemorate the 75th anniversary of the Argentine National Bank.

La Salle Monument and College, Buenos Aires
A362

1966, Nov. 26 **Litho.** ***Perf. 13½***

812 A362 10p brn org & blk 25 8

Issued to commemorate the 75th anniversary of the Colegio de la Salle, Buenos Aires, and to honor Saint Jean Baptiste de la Salle (1651–1719), educator.

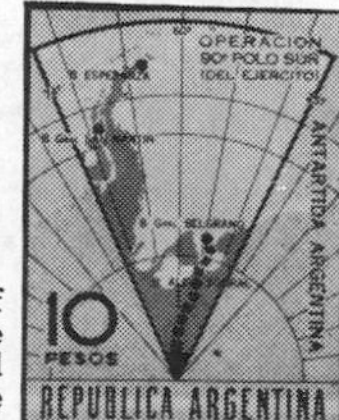

Map of Argentine Antarctica and Expedition Route
A363

1966, Dec. 10 **Wmk. 90**

813 A363 10p multi 1.00 40

Issued to commemorate the 1965 Argentine Antarctic expedition, which planted the Argentine flag on the South Pole. See also No. 851.

Juan Martin de Pueyrredon
A364

Gen. Juan de Las Heras
A365

1966, Dec. 17 **Photo.** ***Perf. 13½***

814 A364 10p dl red brn 25 10

Issued to honor Juan Martin de Pueyrredon (1777–1850), Governor of Cordoba and of the United Provinces of the River Plata.

1966, Dec. 17 **Engraved**

815 A365 10p black 25 10

Issued to honor Gen. Juan Gregorio de Las Heras (1780–1866), Peruvian field marshal and aide-de-camp to San Martin.

Inscribed "Republica Argentina" Types of 1955–61 and

Guillermo Brown
A366

Trout Leaping in National Park
A366a

Designs: 6p, José Hernandez. 50p, Gen. José de San Martin. 500p, Red deer in forest.

Two overall paper sizes for 6p, 50p (No. 827) and 90p:
I. 27x37½mm.
II. 27x39mm.

Photogravure

1965–68 ***Perf. 13½*** **Wmk. 90**

817 A366 6p rose red, litho, paper I ('67) 1.75 8
818 A366 6p rose red, photo. ('67) 3.25 8
819 A366 6p brn, 15x22mm ('68) 10 6
823 A238a 43p dk car rose 9.00 10
824 A238a 45p brn, photo ('66) 6.00 10
825 A238a 45p brn, litho ('67) 10.00 20
826 A241 50p dk bl, 29x40mm 10.00 18
827 A241 50p dk bl, 22x31½ mm, paper I ('67) 6.75 8
a. Paper II 3.75 8
828 A366 90p ol bis, paper I ('67) 4.50 15
a. Paper II 18.00 15

Engraved

829 A495 500p yel grn ('66) 2.00 40
829A A366a 1,000p vio bl ('68) 8.00 1.50
Nos. 817-829A (11) 61.35 2.93

The 500p and 1,000p remained on sale as 5p and 10p stamps after the 1970 currency exchange.

See also Nos. 888, 891, 939, 941, 992, 1031, 1040, 1045–1047.

Pre-Columbian Pottery
A367

1967, Feb. 18 **Litho.** ***Perf. 13½***

830 A367 10p multi 40 20

Issued to commemorate the 20th anniversary of UNESCO (United Nations Educational, Scientific and Cultural Organization).

"The Meal" by Fernando Fader
A368

1967, Feb. 25 **Photo.** **Wmk. 90**

831 A368 10p red brn 40 20

Issued in memory of the Argentine painter Fernando Fader (1882–1935).

Col. Juana Azurduy de Padilla (1781–1862), Soldier
A369

Schooner "Invencible," 1811
A370

Famous Women: No. 833, Juana Manuela Gorriti, writer. No. 834, Cecilia Grierson (1858–1934), physician. No. 835, Juana Paula Manso (1819–75), writer and educator. No. 836, Alfonsina Storni (1892–1938), writer and educator.

1967, May 13 **Photo.** ***Perf. 13½***

832 A369 6p dk brn 40 20
833 A369 6p dk brn 40 20
834 A369 6p dk brn 40 20
835 A369 6p dk brn 40 20
836 A369 6p dk brn 40 20
Nos. 832-836 (5) 2.00 1.00

Issued to honor famous Argentine women. Printed se-tenant in sheets of 100 (10x10); 2 horizontal rows of each portrait with Azurduy in two top rows and Storni in bottom rows.

1967, May 20 **Lithographed**

837 A370 20p multi 1.25 40

Issued for Navy Day.

Soldier Type of 1965

Design: 20p, Highlander (Arribeños Corps).

1967, May 27

838 A340a 20p multi 1.00 40

Issued for Army Day.

Souvenir Sheet

Manuel Belgrano and José Artigas
A371

1967, June 22 ***Imperf.***

839 A371 Souv. sheet of 2 60 60
a. 6p gray & brn 15 15
b. 22p brn & gray 35 35

Third Rio de la Plata Stamp Show, Montevideo, Uruguay, June 18–25. Gray marginal inscription. Size: 56x42mm.

Peace Dove and Valise
A372

PADELAI Emblem
A373

1967, Aug. 5 **Litho.** ***Perf. 13½***

840 A372 20p multi 30 10

Issued for International Tourist Year 1967.

1967, Aug. 12 **Lithographed**

841 A373 20p multi 30 10

Issued to commemorate the 75th anniversary of the Children's Welfare Association (Patronato de la Infancia—PADELAI).

Stagecoach and Modern City
A374

1967, Sept. 23 ***Perf. 13½*** **Wmk. 90**

842 A374 20p rose, yel & blk 35 10

Centenary of Villa Maria, Córdoba.

San Martin by Ibarra
A375

"Battle of Chacabuco" by P. Subercaseaux
A376

1967, Sept. 30 **Lithographed**

843 A375 20p blk brn & pale yel 80 10

Engraved

844 A376 40p bl blk 1.25 24

Battle of Chacabuco, 150th anniversary.

Exhibition Rooms
A377

1967, Oct. 11 **Photogravure**

845 A377 20p bl gray 30 10

Issued to commemorate the 10th anniversary of the Government House Museum.

Pedro L. Zanni, Fokker and 1924 Flight Route
A378

1967, Oct. 21 **Litho.** ***Perf. 13½***

846 A378 20p multi 40 20

Issued for Aviation Week and to commemorate the 1924 flight of the Fokker seaplane "Province of Buenos Aires" from Amsterdam, Netherlands, to Osaka, Japan.

Training Ship General Brown, by Emilio Biggeri
A379

1967, Oct. 28 **Wmk. 90**

847 A379 20p multi 1.25 40

Issued to honor the Military Naval School.

Ovidio Lagos and Front Page
A380

St. Barbara
A381

1967, Nov. 11 **Photogravure**

848 A380 20p sepia 20 10

Centenary of La Capital, Rosario newspaper.

1967, Dec. 2 ***Perf. 13½*** **Wmk. 90**

849 A381 20p rose red 40 20

Issued to honor St. Barbara, patron saint of artillerymen.

Portrait of his Wife, by Eduardo Sivori
A382

1968, Jan. 27 **Photo.** ***Perf. 13½***

850 A382 20p bl grn 40 20

Issued to commemorate the 50th anniversary of the death of Eduardo Sivori (1847–1918), painter.

Antarctic Type of 1966 and

Admiral Brown Scientific Station
A383

Planes over Map of Antarctica
A384

Design: 6p, Map showing radio-postal stations 1966–67.

1968, Feb. 17 **Litho.** **Wmk. 90**

851 A363 6p multi 75 30
852 A383 20p multi 1.00 40
853 A384 40p multi 1.75 50

Issued to publicize Argentine research projects in Argentine Antarctica.

The Annunciation, by Leonardo da Vinci
A385

Man in Wheelchair and Factory
A386

1968, Mar. 23 **Photo.** ***Perf. 13½***

854 A385 20p lil rose 30 10

Issued for the Day of the Army Communications System and its patron saint, Gabriel.

1968, Mar. 23 **Lithographed**

855 A386 20p grn & blk 30 10

Day of Rehabilitation of the Handicapped.

Children and WHO Emblem
A387

1968, May 11 ***Perf. 13½*** **Wmk. 90**

856 A387 20p dk vio bl & ver 30 10

Issued for the 20th anniversary of the World Health Organization.

Soldier Type of 1965

Design: 20p, Uniform of First Artillery Regiment "General Iriarte."

1968, June 8 **Lithographed**

857 A340a 20p multi 1.25 40

Issued for Army Day.

Frigate "Libertad," Painting by Emilio Biggeri
A388

1968, June 15 **Wmk. 90**

858 A388 20p multi 1.25 40

Issued for Navy Day.

Guillermo Rawson and Old Hospital
A389

1968, July 20 **Photo.** ***Perf. 13½***

859 A389 6p ol bis 20 10

Issued to commemorate the centenary of Rawson Hospital, Buenos Aires.

Student Directing Traffic for Schoolmates
A390

1968, Aug. 10 **Litho.** ***Perf. 13½***

860 A390 20p lt bl, blk, buff & car 20 10

Traffic safety and education.

O'Higgins Joining San Martin at Battle of Maipu, by P. Subercaseaux
A391

1968, Aug. 15 **Engraved**

861 A391 40p bluish blk 90 40

Sesquicentennial of the Battle of Maipu.

Osvaldo Magnasco
A392

1968, Sept. 7 Photo. ***Perf. 13½***

862 A392 20p brown 30 10

Issued to honor Osvaldo Magnasco (1864–1920), lawyer, Professor of Law and Minister of Justice.

Grandmother's Birthday, by Patricia Lynch
A393

The Sea, by Edgardo Gomez
A394

1968, Sept. 21 Lithographed

863 A393 20p multi 30 10
864 A394 20p multi 30 10

The designs were chosen in a competition among kindergarten and elementary school children.

Mar del Plata at Night
A395

1968, Oct. 19 Litho. ***Perf. 13½***

865 A395 20p blk, ocher & bl 35 10

Issued to publicize the 4th Plenary Assembly of the International Telegraph and Telephone Consultative Committee, Mar del Plata, Sept. 23–Oct. 25. See Nos. C113–C114.

Frontier Gendarme
A396

Patrol Boat
A397

1968, Oct. 26

866 A396 20p multi 40 20
867 A397 20p bl, vio bl & blk 40 20

No. 866 honors the Gendarmery; No. 867 the Coast Guard.

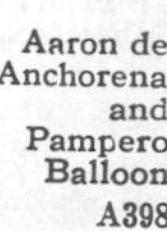

Aaron de Anchorena and Pampero Balloon
A398

1968, Nov. 2 Photogravure

868 A398 20p bl & multi 40 20

22nd Aeronautics and Space Week.

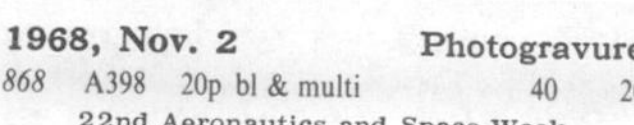

St. Martin of Tours, by Alfredo Guido
A399

1968, Nov. 9 Lithographed

869 A399 20p lil & dk brn 30 10

Issued to honor St. Martin of Tours, patron saint of Buenos Aires.

Municipal Bank Emblem
A400

1968, Nov. 16

870 A400 20p multi 30 10

Issued to commemorate the 90th anniversary of the Buenos Aires Municipal Bank.

Anniversary Emblem
A401

1968, Dec. 14 ***Perf. 13½*** **Wmk. 90**

871 A401 20p car rose & dk grn 30 10

Issued to commemorate the 25th anniversary of ALPI (Fight Against Polio Association).

Shovel and State Coal Fields Emblem
A402

Pouring Ladle and Army Manufacturing Emblem
A403

1968, Dec. 21 Lithographed

872 A402 20p org, bl & blk 30 10
873 A403 20p dl vio, dl yel & blk 30 10

Issued to publicize the National Coal and Steel industry at the Rio Turbio coal fields and the Zapla blast furnaces.

Woman Potter, by Ramon Gomez Cornet
A404

1968, Dec. 21 Photo. ***Perf. 13½***

874 A404 20p car rose 60 40

Centenary of the Witcomb Gallery.

View of Buenos Aires and Rio de la Plata by Ulrico Schmidl—A405

1969, Feb. 8 Litho. **Wmk. 90**

875 A405 20p yel, blk & ver 60 40

Issued to honor Ulrico Schmidl (c. 1462–1554) who wrote "Journey to the Rio de la Plata and Paraguay."

Types of 1955–67

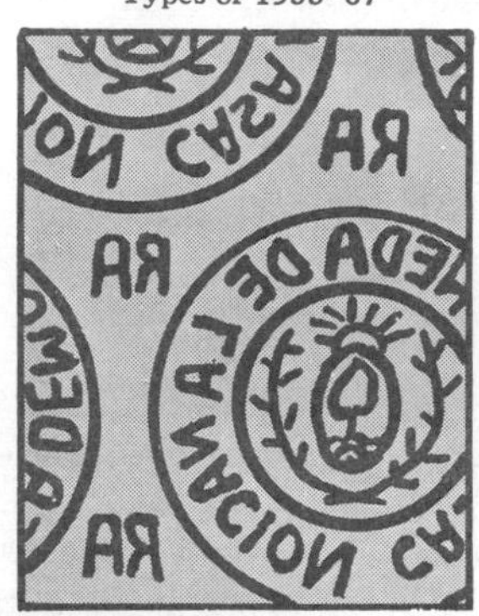

Wmk. 365

Designs: 50c, Puma. 1p, Sunflower. 3p, Zapata Slope, Catamarca. 5p, Tierra del Fuego. 6p, José Hernandez. 10p, Inca Bridge, Mendoza. 50p, José de San Martin. 90p, Guillermo Brown. 100p, Ski jumper.

Wmkd. Argentine Arms, 'Casa de Moneda de la Nacion' & 'RA' Mult. (365)

Photo.; Litho. (50c, 3p, 10p)

1969–70 ***Perf. 13½***

882 A275 50c bis ('70) 1.00 8
883 A277 5p brown 1.50 12
884 A279 100p blue 37.50 1.00

Unwmkd.

885 A278 1p brn ('70) 90 8
886 A277 3p dk bl ('70) 90 8
a. Wmk. 90 7.50 50
887 A277 5p brn ('70) 1.10 8
888 A366 6p red brn, 15x22mm ('70) 1.50 12
889 A278 10p dl red ('70) 75 18
a. Wmk. 90 500.00 40.00
890 A241 50p dk bl, 22x31½mm ('70) 2.50 15
891 A366 90p ol brn, 22x32mm ('70) 4.00 25
892 A279 100p bl ('70) 13.00 30
Nos. 882-892 (11) 64.65 2.44

Soldier Type of 1965

Design: 20p, Sapper (gastador) of Buenos Aires Province, 1856.

Lithographed

1969, May 31 ***Perf. 13½*** **Wmk. 365**

893 A340a 20p multi 1.25 40

Issued for Army Day.

Frigate Hercules, by Emilio Biggeri
A406

1969, May 31

894 A406 20p multi 1.25 40

Issued for Navy Day.

"All Men are Equal"
A407

ILO Emblem
A408

1969, June 28 **Wmk. 90**

895 A407 20p blk & ocher 30 10

International Human Rights Year.

1969, June 28 Litho. **Wmk. 365**

896 A408 20p lt grn & multi 30 10

Issued to commemorate the 50th anniversary of the International Labor Organization.

Pedro N. Arata (1849–1922), Chemist
A409

Radar Antenna, Balcarce Station and Satellite
A410

Portraits: No. 898, Miguel Fernandez (1883–1950), zoologist. No. 899, Angel P. Gallardo (1867–1934), biologist. No. 900, Cristobal M. Hicken (1875–1933), botanist. No. 901, Eduardo Ladislao Holmberg, M.D. (1852–1937), natural scientist.

1969, Aug. 9 ***Perf. 13½*** **Wmk. 365**

Red Brown Design on Orange Yellow Background

897 A409 6p (*Arata*) 60 10
898 A409 6p (*Fernandez*) 60 10
899 A409 6p (*Gallardo*) 60 10
900 A409 6p (*Hicken*) 60 10
901 A409 6p (*Holmberg*) 60 10
Nos. 897-901 (5) 3.00 50

Argentine scientists. See #778 note.

1969, Aug. 23 **Wmk. 90**

902 A410 20p yel & blk 40 20

Issued to publicize communications by satellite through International Telecommunications Satellite Consortium (INTELSAT). See No. C115.

Nieuport 28, Flight Route and Map of Buenos Aires Province
A411

1969, Sept. 13 Litho. Wmk. 90

903 A411 20p multi 40 20

Issued to commemorate the 50th anniversary of the first Argentine airmail service from El Palomar to Mar del Plata, flown Feb. 23–24, 1919, by Capt. Pedro L. Zanni.

Military College Gate and Emblem
A412

1969, Oct. 4 *Perf. 13½* Wmk. 365

904 A412 20p multi 40 20

Issued to commemorate the centenary of the National Military College, El Palomar (Greater Buenos Aires).

Gen. Angel Pacheco
A413

La Farola, Logotype of La Prensa
A414

1969, Nov. 8 Photo. Wmk. 365

905 A413 20p dp grn 30 10

Issued to commemorate the centenary of the death of Gen. Angel Pacheco (1795–1869).

1969, Nov. 8 Litho. *Perf. 13½*

Design: No. 907, Bartolomé Mitre and La Nacion logotype.

906 A414 20p org, yel & blk 1.00 30
907 A414 20p brt grn & blk 1.00 30

Centenary of newspapers La Prensa and La Nacion.

Julian Aguirre
A415

Musicians: No. 909, Felipe Boero. No. 910, Constantino Gaito. No. 911, Carlos Lopez Buchardo. No. 912, Alberto Williams.

Photogravure

1969, Dec. 6 *Perf. 13½* Wmk. 365

Dark Green Design on Light Blue Background

908 A415 6p *(Aguirre)* 80 30
909 A415 6p *(Boero)* 80 30
910 A415 6p *(Gaito)* 80 30
911 A415 6p *(Buchardo)* 80 30
912 A415 6p *(Williams)* 80 30
Nos. 908-912 (5) 4.00 1.50

Argentine musicians. See #778 note.

Lt. Benjamin Matienzo and Nieuport Plane
A416

1969, Dec. 13 Lithographed

913 A416 20p multi 90 40

23rd Aeronautics and Space Week.

High Power Lines and Map
A417

Design: 20p, Map of Santa Fe Province and schematic view of tunnel.

1969, Dec. 13

914 A417 6p multi 70 10
915 A417 20p multi 1.50 20

Issued to publicize the completion of development projects. The 6p commemorates the hydroelectric dams on the Limay and Neuquen Rivers, the 20p the tunnel under the Rio Grande from Sante Fe to Parana.

Lions Emblem
A418

1969, Dec. 20 *Perf. 13½* Wmk. 365

916 A418 20p blk, emer & org 1.00 40

Issued to commemorate the 50th anniversary of the Argentine Lions International Club.

Madonna and Child, by Raul Soldi
A419

1969, Dec. 27 Lithographed

917 A419 20p multi 1.00 40

Christmas 1969.

Manuel Belgrano, by Jean Gericault
A420

The Creation of the Flag, Bas-relief by José Fioravanti
A421

Photogravure

1970, July 4 *Perf. 13½* Unwmkd.

918 A420 20c dp brn 50 20

Lithographed

Perf. 12½

919 A421 50c bis, blk & bl 1.25 50

Issued to commemorate the sesquicentennial of the death of Gen. Manuel Belgrano (1770–1820), Argentine patriot.

San José Palace
A422

1970, Aug. 9 Litho. *Perf. 13½*

920 A422 20c yel grn & multi 30 10

Issued to commemorate the centenary of the death of Gen. Justo José de Urquiza (1801–1870), president of Argentina, 1854–60.

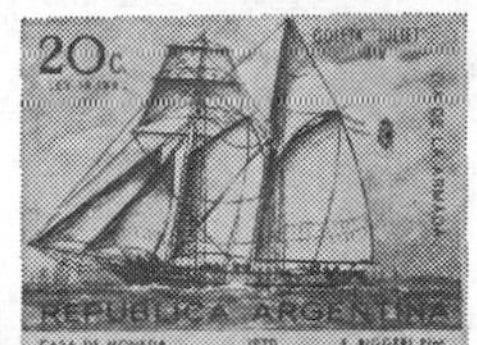

Schooner "Juliet"
A423

1970, Aug. 8 Unwmkd.

921 A423 20c multi 1.25 40

Issued for Navy Day.

Receiver of 1920 and Waves—A424

1970, Aug. 29

922 A424 20c lt bl & multi 40 20

Issued to commemorate the 50th anniversary of Argentine broadcasting.

Types of 1955–67 Inscribed "Republica Argentina" and Types A425, A426

Manuel Belgrano
A425

Lujan Basilica
A426

Designs: 1c, Sunflower. 3c, Zapata Slope, Catamarca. 5c, Tierra del Fuego. 8c, No. 931, Belgrano. 10c, Inca Bridge, Mendoza. 25c, 50c, 70c, Jose de San Martin. 65c, 90c, 1.20p, San Martin. 1p, Ski jumper. 1.15p, 1.80p, Adm. Brown.

Unwmkd.

1970–73 Photogravure *Perf. 13½*

923 A278 1c dk grn ('71) 20 5
924 A277 3c car rose ('71) 20 5
925 A277 5c bl ('71) 20 5
926 A425 6c dp bl 20 5
927 A425 8c grn ('72) 20 5
928 A278 10c dl red ('71) 60 6
929 A278 10c brn, litho. ('71) 80 6
930 A278 10c org brn ('72) 70 5
931 A425 10c brn ('73) 30 5
932 A426 18c yel & dk brn, litho ('73) 30 5
933 A425 25c brn ('71) 50 5
934 A425 50c scar ('72) 2.00 5
935 A241 65c brn, 22x31½mm, paper II ('71) 1.00 5
936 A425 70c dk bl ('73) 50 5
937 A241 90c emer, 22x31½mm('72) 5.00 5
938 A279 1p brn, 22½x29½ mm ('71) 3.00 5
939 A366 1.15p dk bl, 22½x32mm('71) 1.75 5
940 A241 1.20p org, 22x31½mm('73) 1.75 5
941 A366 1.80p brn ('73) 1.75 5
Nos. 923-941 (19) 20.95 97

The imprint "Casa de Moneda de la Nacion" (in capitals) appears on 3c, 5c, Nos. 928–929; 65c, 90c, 1p, 1.20p.

On type A425 only the 6c is inscribed "Ley 18.188" below denomination.

Fluorescent paper was used in printing the 25c, 50c, and 70c. The 3c, 8c, No. 931 and 65c were issued on both ordinary and fluorescent paper.

See also Nos. 987-996, 1032-1038, 1042-1043, 1089-1107.

Soldier Type of 1965

Design: 20c, Galloping messenger of Field Army, 1879.

1970, Oct. 17 Litho. *Perf. 13½*

944 A340a 20c multi 1.25 40

Dome of Cathedral of Cordoba
A430

1970, Nov. 7 Unwmkd.

945 A430 50c gray & blk 1.25 20

Bishopric of Tucuman, 400th anniversary. See No. C131.

People Around U.N. Emblem
A431

1970, Nov. 7

946 A431 20c tan & multi 30 10

25th anniversary of the United Nations.

State Mint and Medal
A432

1970, Nov. 28 *Perf. 13½* Unwmkd.

947 A432 20c gold, grn & blk 30 10

Inauguration of the State Mint Building, 25th anniversary.

St. John Bosco and Dean Funes College
A433

1970, Dec. 19 Lithographed

948 A433 20c ol & blk 30 10

Honoring the work of the Salesian Order in Patagonia.

Nativity, by Horacio Gramajo Gutierrez—A434

1970, Dec. 19

949 A434 20c multi 80 40

Christmas 1970.

Argentine Flag, Map of Argentine Antarctica
A435

1971, Feb. 20 Litho. *Perf. 13½*

950 A435 20c multi 2.00 60

Fifth anniversary of Argentine South Pole Expedition.

Phosphorescent Sorting Code and Albert Einstein
A436

1971, Apr. 30 *Perf. 13½* Unwmkd.

951 A436 25c multi 80 40

Electronics in postal development.

Symbolic Road Crossing
A437

1971, May 29 Lithographed

952 A437 25c bl & blk 40 20

Inter-American Regional Meeting of the International Federation of Roads, Buenos Aires, March 28–31.

Elias Alippi
A438

Actors: No. 954, Juan Aurelio Casacuberta. No. 955, Angelina Pagano. No. 956, Roberto Casaux. No. 957, Florencio Parravicini. See #778 note.

1971, May 29 Lithographed

Black Design on Pale Rose Background

953 A438 15c (*Alippi*) 50 10
954 A438 15c (*Casacuberta*) 50 10
955 A438 15c (*Pagano*) 50 10
956 A438 15c (*Casaux*) 50 10
957 A438 15c (*Parravicini*) 50 10
Nos. 953-957 (5) 2.50 50

Soldier Type of 1965

Design: 25c, Artilleryman, 1826.

1971, July 3 *Perf. 13½* Unwmkd.

958 A340a 25c multi 2.00 60

Army Day, May 29.

Bilander "Carmen," by Emilio Biggeri
A439

1971, July 3

959 A439 25c multi 1.75 20

Navy Day

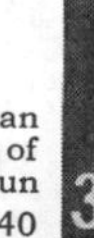

Peruvian Order of the Sun
A440

1971, Aug. 28

960 A440 31c multi 50 10

Sesquicentennial of Peru's independence.

Güemes in Battle, by Lorenzo Gigli
A441

Design: No. 962, Death of Güemes, by Antonio Alice.

1971, Aug. 28 Size: 39x29mm.

961 A441 25c multi 75 40

Size: 84x29mm.

962 A441 25c multi 75 40

Sesquicentennial of the death of Martin Miguel de Güemes, leader in Gaucho War, Governor and Captain General of Salta Province.

Stylized Tulip
A442

1971, Sept. 18

963 A442 25c tan & multi 35 10

3rd International and 8th National Horticultural Exhibition.

Father Antonio Saenz, by Juan Gut
A443

1971, Sept. 18

964 A443 25c gray & multi 35 10

Sesquicentennial of University of Buenos Aires, and to honor Father Antonio Saenz, first Chancellor and Rector.

Fabricaciones Militares Emblem
A444

1971, Oct. 16 *Perf. 13½* Unwmkd.

965 A444 25c brn, gold, bl & blk 35 10

30th anniversary of military armament works.

Cars and Trucks
A445

Design: 65c, Tree converted into paper.

1971, Oct. 16

966 A445 25c dl bl & multi 85 20
967 A445 65c grn & multi 2.00 60

Nationalized industries. See No. C134.

Luis C. Candelaria and his Plane, 1918
A446

1971, Nov. 27

968 A446 25c multi 40 20

25th Aeronautics and Space Week.

Observatory and Nebula of Magellan
A447

1971, Nov. 27

969 A447 25c multi 40 20

Centenary of Cordoba Astronomical Observatory.

Christ in Majesty
A448

1971, Dec. 18 Lithographed

970 A448 25c blk & multi 40 20

Christmas 1971. Design is from a tapestry by Horacio Butler in Basilica of St. Francis, Buenos Aires.

Mother and Child, by J. C. Castagnino
A449

1972, May 6 *Perf. 13½* Unwmkd.

971 A449 25c fawn & blk 40 20

25th anniversary (in 1971) of the International United Nations Children's Fund (UNICEF).

Mailman's Bag
A450

1972, Sept. 2 Litho. *Perf. 13½*

972 A450 25c lem & multi 20 8

Bicentenary of appointment of first Argentine mailman.

Adm. Brown Station, Map of Antarctica
A451

1972, Sept. 2

973 A451 25c bl & multi 1.00 40

10th anniversary (in 1971) of Antarctic Treaty.

Soldier Type of 1965

Design: 25c, Sergeant, Negro and Mulatto Corps, 1806–1807.

1972, Sept. 23

974 A340a 25c multi 1.25 40

Army Day, May 29.

Brigantine "Santisima Trinidad"
A452

1972, Sept. 23

975 A452 25c multi 1.25 40

Navy Day. See also No. 1006.

Oil Pump
A453

1972, Sept. 30 Litho. ***Perf. 13½***

976 A453 45c blk & multi 1.50 15

50th anniversary of the organization of the state oil fields (Yacimientos Petroliferos Fiscales).

Sounding Balloon
A454

1972, Sept. 30

977 A454 25c blk, bl & ocher 40 20

Centenary of National Meteorological Service.

Trees and Globe—A455

1972, Oct. 14 ***Perf. 13x13½***

978 A455 25c bl, blk & lt bl 1.10 15

7th World Forestry Congress, Buenos Aires, Oct. 4–18.

Arms of Naval School, Frigate "Presidente Sarmiento"—A456

1972, Oct. 14

979 A456 25c gold & multi 1.00 40

Centenary of Military Naval School.

Early Balloon and Plane, Antonio de Marchi—A457

Bartolomé Mitre
A458

1972, Nov. 4 ***Perf. 13½***

980 A457 25c multi 40 20

Aeronautics and Space Week, and in honor of Baron Antonio de Marchi (1875–1934), aviation pioneer.

1972, Nov. 4 **Engraved**

981 A458 25c dk bl 20 8

Pres. Bartolomé Mitre (1821–1906), writer, historian, soldier.

Flower and Heart
A459

1972, Dec. 2 Litho. ***Perf. 13½***

982 A459 90c lt bl, ultra & blk 80 40

"Your heart is your health," World Health Day.

"Martin Fierro," by Juan C. Castignano
A460

"Spirit of the Gaucho," by Vicente Forte
A461

1972, Dec. 2 Litho. ***Perf. 13½***

983 A460 50c multi 50 25
984 A461 90c multi 1.00 40

International Book Year 1972, and to commemorate the centenary of publication of the poem, Martin Fierro, by José Hernandez (1834–1886).

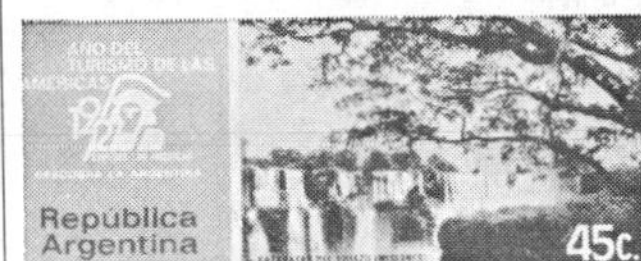

Iguassu Falls and Tourist Year Emblem—A462

1972, Dec. 16 ***Perf. 13x13½***

985 A462 45c multi 45 12

Tourism Year of the Americas.

King, Wood Carving, 18th Century
A463

1972, Dec. 16 ***Perf. 13½***

986 A463 50c multi 80 40

Christmas 1972.

Types of 1955–73 Inscribed "Republica Argentina" and

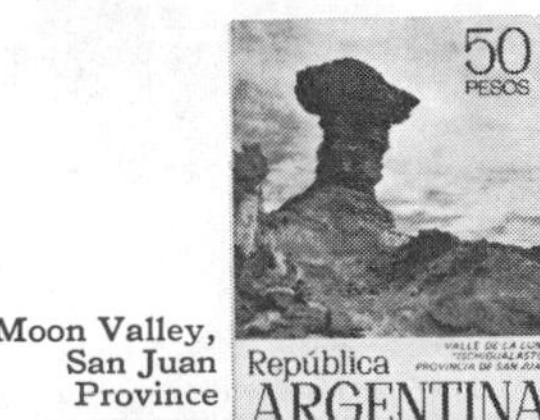

Moon Valley, San Juan Province
A463a

Designs: 1c, Sunflower. 5c, Tierra del Fuego. 10c, Inca Bridge, Mendoza. 50c, Lujan Basilica. 65c, 22.50p, San Martin. 1p, Ski jumper. 1.15p, 4.50p, Guillermo Brown. 1.80p, Manuel Belgrano.

Perf. 13½, 12½ (1.80p)

Litho.; Photo. (1c, 65c, 1p)

1972–75 **Wmk. 365**

987	A278	1c	dk grn	25	5
988	A277	5c	dk bl	25	5
989	A278	10c	bis brn	25	5
989A	A426	50c	dl pur ('75)	25	5
990	A241	65c	gray brn	5.00	10
991	A279	1p	brown	2.00	6
992	A366	1.15p	dk gray bl	2.00	6
993	A425	1.80p	bl ('75)	25	5
994	A366	4.50p	grn ('75)	1.00	6
995	A241	22.50p	vio bl ('75)	2.00	10
996	A463a	50p	multi ('75)	4.00	50
			Nos. 987-996 (11)	17.25	1.13

Paper size of 1c is 27½x39mm.; others of 1972, 37x27, 27x37mm.

Size of 22.50p, 50p: 26½x38½mm.

See No. 1050.

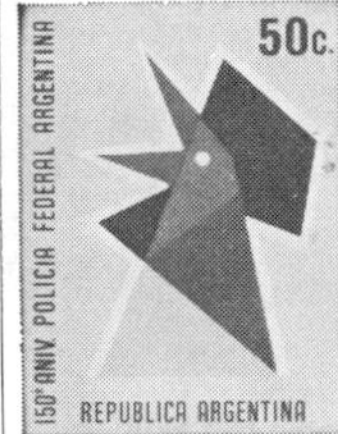

Cock (Symbolic of Police)
A464

First Coin of Bank of Buenos Aires
A465

1973, Feb. 3 Litho. **Unwmkd.**

997 A464 50c lt grn & multi 40 20

Sesquicentennial of Federal Police of Argentina.

1973, Feb. 3 ***Perf. 13½***

998 A465 50c pur, yel & brn 20 10

Sesquicentennial of the Bank of Buenos Aires Province.

DC-3 Planes Over Antarctica
A466

1973, Apr. 28 Litho. ***Perf. 13½***

999 A466 50c lt bl & multi 2.00 60

10th anniversary of Argentina's first flight to the South Pole.

Rivadavia's Chair, Argentine Arms and Colors
A467

1973, May 19 Litho. ***Perf. 13½***

1000 A467 50c multi 35 12

Inauguration of Pres. Hector J. Cámpora, May 25, 1973.

San Martin, by Gil de Castro
A468

San Martin and Bolívar
A469

1973, July 7 Litho. ***Perf 13½***

1001 A468 50c lt grn & multi 45 10
1002 A469 50c yel & multi 45 10

Gen. San Martin's farewell to the people of Peru and his meeting with Simon Bolívar at Guayaquil July 26–27, 1822.

Eva Perón
A470

1973, July 26 Litho. ***Perf. 13½***

1003 A470 70c blk, org & bl 30 10

Maria Eva Duarte de Perón (1919–1952), political leader.

House of Viceroy Sobremonte, by Hortensia de Virgilion—A471

1973, July 28 ***Perf. 13x13½***

1004 A471 50c bl & multi 30 10

400th anniversary of the city of Córdoba.

Woman, by Lino Spilimbergo
A472

New and Old Telephones
A473

1973, Aug. 28 Litho. ***Perf. 13½***

1005 A472 70c multi 1.10 10

Philatelists' Day. See Nos. B60–B61.

Ship Type of 1972

Design: 70c, Frigate "La Argentina."

1973, Oct. 27 Litho. ***Perf. 13½***

1006 A452 70c multi 90 40

Navy Day.

1973, Oct. 27

1007 A473 70c brt bl & multi 60 30

25th anniversary of national telecommunications system.

Plume Made of Flags of Participants
A474

1973, Nov. 3 ***Perf. 13½***

1008 A474 70c yel bis & multi 35 10

12th Congress of Latin Notaries, Buenos Aires.

No. 940 Overprinted

TRANSMISION DEL MANDO PRESIDENCIAL
12 OCTUBRE 1973

1973, Nov. 30 Photogravure

1010 A241 1.20p orange 1.10 20

Assumption of presidency by Juan Peron, Oct. 12.

Virgin and Child, Window, La Plata Cathedral
A476

Design: 1.20p, Nativity, by Bruno Venier, b. 1914.

1973, Dec. 15 Litho. ***Perf. 13½***

1011 A476 70c gray & multi 50 25
1012 A476 1.20p blk & multi 1.00 50

Christmas 1973.

The Lama, by Juan Batlle Planas
A477

Paintings: 50c, Houses in Boca District, by Eugenio Daneri (horiz.). 90c, The Blue Grotto, by Emilio Pettoruti (horiz.).

1974, Feb. 9 Litho. ***Perf. 13½***

1013 A477 50c multi 40 20
1014 A477 70c multi 50 30
1015 A477 90c multi 90 40

Argentine painters. See No. B64.

Mar del Plata
A478

1974, Feb. 9

1016 A478 70c multi 40 20

Centenary of Mar del Plata.

Weather Symbols
A479

Justo Santa Maria de Oro
A480

1974, Mar. 23 Litho. ***Perf. 13½***

1017 A479 1.20p multi 50 20

Centenary of international meteorological cooperation.

1974, Mar. 23

1018 A480 70c multi 30 10

Bicentenary of the birth of Brother Justo Santa Maria de Oro (1772–1836), theologian, patriot, first Argentine bishop.

Belisario Roldan
A481

1974, June 29 Photo. **Unwmkd.**

1019 A481 70c bl & brn 30 20

Birth centenary of Belisario Roldan (1873–1922), writer.

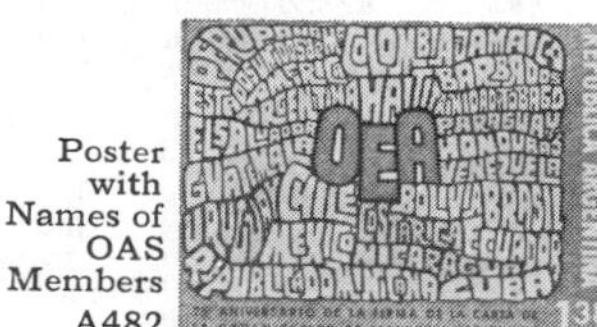

Poster with Names of OAS Members
A482

1974, June 29 Lithographed

1020 A482 1.38p multi 25 15

25th anniversary of the Organization of American States.

ENCOTEL Emblem—A483

1974, Aug. 10 Litho. ***Perf. 13***

1021 A483 1.20p bl, gold & blk 60 15

ENCOTEL, National Post and Telegraph Press.

Flags of Argentina, Bolivia, Brazil, Paraguay, Uruguay
A484

1974, Aug. 16 ***Perf. 13½***

1022 A484 1.38p multi 30 20

6th Meeting of Foreign Ministers of Rio de la Plata Basin Countries.

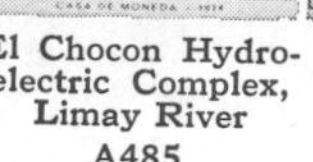

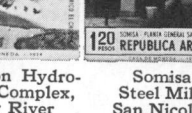

El Chocon Hydroelectric Complex, Limay River
A485

Somisa Steel Mill, San Nicolas
A486

Gen. Belgrano Bridge, Chaco-Corrientes—A487

Perf. 13½, 13x13½ (4.50p)

1974, Sept. 14

1023 A485 70c multi 50 25
1024 A486 1.20p multi 75 50
1025 A487 4.50p multi 3.00 75

Development projects.

Brigantine Belgrano, by Emilio Biggeri
A488

1974, Oct. 26 Litho. ***Perf. 13½***

1026 A488 1.20p multi 1.00 40

Departure into exile in Chile of General San Martin, Sept. 22, 1822.

Alberto R. Mascias and Bleriot Plane
A489

1974, Oct. 26 **Unwmk.**

1027 A489 1.20p multi 80 40

Air Force Day, Aug. 10, and to honor Alberto Roque Garcias (1878–1951), aviation pioneer.

Exists with wmk. 365.

Hussar, 1812, by Eleodoro Marenco
A490

1974, Oct. 26

1028 A490 1.20p multi 80 40

Army Day.

Post Horn and Flags
A491

1974, Nov. 23 ***Perf. 13½*** **Unwmkd.**

1029 A491 2.65p multi 1.25 15

Centenary of Universal Postal Union. Exists with wmk. 365.

Franciscan Monastery
A492

1974, Nov. 23 Lithographed

1030 A492 1.20p multi 60 15

400th anniversary, city of Santa Fe.

Trout Type of 1968.

1974 **Engraved** **Unwmkd.**

1031 A366a 1000p vio bl 5.00 1.00

Due to a shortage of 10p stamps a quantity of this 1,000p was released for use as 10p.

Types of 1954–73
Inscribed "Republica Argentina" and

Red Deer in Forest
A495

Congress Building
A497

Designs: 30c, 60c, 1.80p, Manuel Belgrano. 50c, Lujan Basilica. No. 1036, 2p, 6p, San Martin (16x22½mm.). 2.70p, 7.50p, 22.50p, San Martin (22x31½mm.). 4.50p, 13.50p, Guillermo Brown. 10p, Leaping trout.

Photogravure

1974–75 ***Perf. 13½*** **Unwmkd.**

1032 A425 30c brn vio 15 5
1033 A426 50c blk & brn red ('75) 15 5
1034 A426 50c bis & bl ('75) 15 5
1035 A425 60c ocher ('75) 15 5
1036 A425 1.20p red 45 5
1037 A425 1.80p dp bl ('75) 20 5
1038 A425 2p dk pur ('75) 30 5
1039 A241 2.70p dk bl 22x31½mm 35 5
1040 A366 4.50p green 1.30 5
1041 A495 5p yel grn 60 5
1042 A425 6p red org ('75) 30 5
1043 A425 6p emer ('75) 30 5
1044 A241 7.50p grn, 22x31½mm('75) 1.25 6
1045 A366a 10p vio bl 1.50 6
1046 A366 13.50p scar, 16x22½mm ('75) 1.25 6
1047 A366 13.50p scar, 22x31½mm('75) 1.25 8

1048	A241	22.50p dp bl, 22x31½mm('75)	1.10	10
1049	A497	30p yel & dk red brn	1.75	12
1050	A463a	50p multi ('76)	2.25	15
		Nos. 1032-1050 (19)	14.75	1.23

Fluorescent paper was used in printing No. 1036, 2p, Nos. 1044 and 1047. The 30p was issued on both ordinary and fluorescent paper.

See also No. 829.

Miniature Sheet

A498

1974, Dec. 7 Litho. *Perf. 13½*

1052	A498	Sheet of 6, multi	5.00	4.00
a.		1p *Mariano Necochea*	35	
b.		1.20p *Jose de San Martin*	35	
c.		1.70p *Manuel Isidoro Suarez*	50	
d.		1.90p *Juan Pascual Pringles*	60	
e.		2.70p *Latin American flags*	90	
f.		4.50p *Jose Felix Bogado*	1.50	

Sesquicentennial of Battles of Junin and Ayacucho. No. 1052 has black control number. Size: 140x132mm.

Dove, by Vito Campanella
A499

St. Anne, by Raul Soldi
A500

1974, Dec. 21 Litho. *Perf. 13½*

1053	A499	1.20p multi	80	30
1054	A500	2.65p multi	1.25	50

Christmas 1974.

Boy Looking at Stamp
A501

1974, Dec. 21

1055	A501	1.70p blk & yel	50	18

World Youth Philately Year.

Space Monsters, by Raquel Forner
A502

Design: 4.50p, Dream, by Emilio Centurion.

1975, Feb. 22 Litho. *Perf. 13½*

1056	A502	2.70p multi	1.40	40
1057	A502	4.50p multi	2.75	60

Argentine modern art.

Indian Woman and Cathedral, Catamarca—A503

Designs: No. 1059, Carved chancel and street scene. No. 1060, Grazing cattle and monastery yard. No. 1061, Painted pottery and power station. No. 1062, Farm cart and colonial mansion. No. 1063, Perito Moreno glacier and spinning mill. No. 1064, Lake Lapataia and scientific surveyor. No. 1065, Los Alerces National Park and oil derrick.

1975 Lithographed *Perf. 13½*
Unwmkd.; Wmk. 365 (6p)

1058	A503	1.20p *shown*	35	25
1059	A503	1.20p *Jujuy*	35	25
1060	A503	1.20p *Salta*	35	25
1061	A503	1.20p *Santiago del Estero*	35	25
1062	A503	1.20p *Tucuman*	35	25
1063	A503	6p *Santa Cruz*	75	25
1064	A503	6p *Tierra del Fuego*	75	25
1065	A503	6p *Chubut*	75	25
		Nos. 1058-1065 (8)	4.00	2.00

Tourist publicity.
Issue dates: 1.20p, Mar. 8; 6p, Dec. 20.

"We Have Been Inoculated"
A504

1975, Apr. 26 Unwmkd. *Perf. 13½*

1066	A504	2p multi	60	30

Children's inoculation campaign (child's painting).

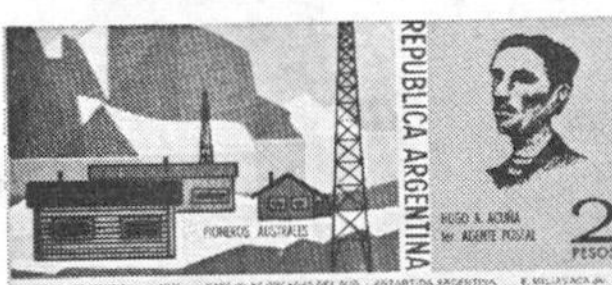

Hugo A. Acuña and South Orkney Station—A505

Designs: No. 1068, Francisco P. Moreno and Lake Nahuel Huapi. No. 1069, Lt. Col. Luis Piedra Buena and cutter, Luisito. No. 1070, Ensign José M. Sobral and Snow Hill House. No. 1071, Capt. Carlos M. Moyano and Cerro del Toro (mountain).

1975, June 28 Litho. *Perf. 13*

1067	A505	2p grnsh bl & multi	40	20
1068	A505	2p yel grn & multi	40	20
1069	A505	2p lt vio & multi	40	20
1070	A505	2p gray bl & multi	40	20
1071	A505	2p pale grn & multi	40	20
		Nos. 1067-1071 (5)	2.00	1.00

Pioneers of Antarctica.

Frigate "25 de Mayo"
A506

1975, Sept. 27 *Perf. 13½* Unwmkd.

1072	A506	6p multi	60	30

Navy Day 1975.

Eduardo Bradley and Balloon
A507

1975, Sept. 27 Wmk. 365

1073	A507	6p multi	60	30

Air Force Day.

Declaration of Independence, by Juan M. Blanes
A508

1975, Oct. 25

1074	A508	6p multi	45	12

Sesquicentennial of Uruguay's declaration of independence.

Flame
A509

1975, Oct. 17 Unwmkd.

1075	A509	6p gray & multi	45	12

Loyalty Day, 30th anniversary of Pres. Peron's accession to power.

Nos. 886, 891 and 932 Surcharged

REVALORIZADO
6 c.
a

REVALORIZADO
30 c
b

REVALORIZADO
5 pesos
c

1975 Litho., Photo.

1076	A277	6c on 3p	20	10
1077	A366	30c on 90p	20	10
1078	A426	5p on 18c	60	30

Issue dates: 6c, Oct. 30; 30c, Nov. 20; 5p, Oct. 24. The 6c also exists on No. 886a.

International Bridge, Flags of Argentina and Uruguay
A510

1975, Oct. 25 Litho. Wmk. 365

1081	A510	6p multi	60	30

Opening of bridge connecting Colon, Argentina, and Paysandu, Uruguay.

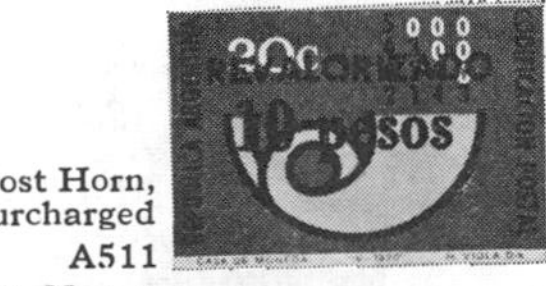

Post Horn, Surcharged
A511

1975, Nov. 8

1082	A511	10p on 20c multi	75	20

Introduction of postal code. Not issued without surcharge.

CENTENARIO DEL HOSPITAL DE NIÑOS
REPUBLICA ARGENTINA

Nurse Holding Infant
A512

1975, Dec. 13 Litho. *Perf. 13½*

1083	A512	6p multi	75	20

Children's Hospital, centenary.

Nativity, Nueva Pompeya Church
A513

1975, Dec. 13 Litho. Unwmkd.

1084	A513	6p multi	50	30

Christmas 1975.

Types of 1970–75 and

Church of St. Francis, Salta
A515

Designs: 3p, No. 1099, 60p, 90p, Manuel Belgrano. 12p, 15p, 20p, 30p, No. 1100, 100p, 110p, 120p, 130p, San Martin. 15p, 70p, Guillermo Brown. 300p, Moon Valley (lower inscriptions italic). 500p, Adm. Brown Station, Antarctica.

Photo.; *Perf. 13½*; Unwmkd.
Litho.; *Perf. 12½x13*; Wmk. 365

1976–78

1089	A425	3p slate	20	10
1090	A425	12p rose red	30	10

1091	A425	12p rose red, litho.	30	10
1092	A425	12p emer, litho.	30	10
1093	A425	12p emer ('77)	30	10
1094	A425	15p rose red	30	10
1095	A425	15p vio bl ('77)	30	10
1097	A425	20p rose red ('77)	50	10
1098	A425	30p rose red ('77)	50	14
1099	A425	40p dp grn	75	20
1100	A425	40p rose red ('77)	50	15
1101	A425	60p dk bl ('77)	1.00	28
1102	A425	70p dk bl ('77)	1.25	30
1103	A425	90p emer ('77)	1.50	40
1104	A425	100p red	1.10	35
1105	A425	110p rose red ('78)	75	25
1106	A425	120p rose red ('78)	85	30
1107	A425	130p rose red ('78)	1.00	35

Litho.; *Perf. 13½;* Unwmkd.

1108	A463a	300p multi	5.00	2.25
1109	A515	500p multi ('77)	12.00	2.00
1110	A515	1000p multi ('77)	15.00	3.00
		Nos. 1089-1110 (21)	43.70	10.77

Fluorescent paper was used in printing both 12p rose red, 15p rose red, 20p, 30p, 40p rose red, 100p, 110p, 120p, 130p. No. 1099 and the 300p were issued on both ordinary and fluorescent paper.

300p and 500p exist with wmk. 365.

Numeral
A516

Photo.; *Perf. 13½;* Unwmkd.
Litho.; *Perf. 13x12½;* Wmk. 365
1976

1112	A516	12c gray & blk	5	5
1113	A516	50c gray & grn	10	5
1114	A516	1p red & blk	10	5
1115	A516	4p bl & blk	20	5
1116	A516	5p org & blk	20	5
1117	A516	5p org & blk, litho.	20	5
1118	A516	6p dp brn & blk	20	5
1119	A516	10p gray & vio bl	30	5
1120	A516	27p lt grn & blk	75	8
1121	A516	27p lt grn & blk, litho.	75	8
1122	A516	30p lt bl & blk	1.25	10
1123	A516	45p yel & blk	1.25	15
1124	A516	45p yel & blk, litho.	1.25	15
1125	A516	50p dl grn & blk	1.75	18
1126	A516	100p brt grn & red	2.25	35
		Nos. 1112-1126 (15)	10.60	1.49

The 1p, 6p, 10p, 50p and No. 1116 were issued on both ordinary and fluorescent paper.

Jet and Airlines Emblem—A517
Unwmkd.

1976, Apr. 24 Litho. *Perf. 13x13½*

1130 A517 30p bl, lt bl & dk bl 1.50 20

Argentine Airlines, 25th anniversary.

Frigate Heroina and Map of Falkland Islands—A518

1976, Apr. 26

1131 A518 6p multi 1.50 60

Argentina's claim to Falkland Islands.

Louis Braille—A519
Wmk. 365

1976, May 22 Engr. *Perf. 13½*

1132 A519 19.70 dp bl 45 15

Sesquicentennial of the invention of the Braille system of writing for the blind by Louis Braille (1809–1852).

Private, 7th Infantry Regiment
A520

1976, May 29 Litho. *Unwmkd.*

1133 A520 12p multi 60 30

Army Day.

Schooner Rio de la Plata, by Emilio Biggeri
A521

1976, June 19

1134 A521 12p multi 60 30

Navy Day.

Dr. Bernardo Houssay
A522

Nobel Prize Winners: 15p, Luis F. Leloir, chemistry, 1970. 20p, Carlos Saavedra Lamas, peace, 1936. Bernardo Houssay, medicine and physiology, 1947.

1976, Aug. 14 Litho. *Perf. 13½*

1135	A522	10p org & blk	35	20
1136	A522	15p yel & blk	50	25
1137	A522	20p ocher & blk	75	35

Argentine Nobel Prize winners.

Rio de la Plata International Bridge—A523

1976, Sept. 18 Litho. *Perf. 13½*

1138 A523 12p multi 40 20

Inauguration of International Bridge connecting Puerte Unzue, Argentina, and Fray Bentos, Uruguay.

Pipelines and Cooling Tower, Gen. Mosconi Plant—A524

1976, Nov. 20 Litho. *Perf. 13½*

1139 A524 28p multi 60 30

Pablo Teodoro Fels and Bleriot Monoplane, 1910—A525

1976, Nov. 20

1140 A525 15p multi 40 20

Air Force Day.

Nativity
A526

1976, Dec. 18 Litho. *Perf. 13½*

1141 A526 20p multi 80 40

Christmas 1976. Painting by Edith Chiapetto.

Water Conference Emblem
A527

1977, Mar. 19 Litho. *Perf. 13½*

1142 A527 70p multi 1.00 35

U.N. Water Conference, Mar del Plata, Mar. 14–25.

Dalmacio Vélez Sarsfield
A528

1977, Mar. 19 Engraved

1143 A528 50p blk & red brn 1.00 40

Dalmacio Vélez Sarsfield (1800–1875), author of Argentine civil code.

Red Deer Type of 1974 Surcharged

1977, July 30 Photo. *Perf. 13½*

1144 A495 100p on 5p brn 2.00 60

Sesquicentennial of Uruguayan postal service. Not issued without surcharge.

Soldier, 16th Lancers
A529

1977, July 30

1145 A529 30p multi 60 30

Army Day.

Schooner Sarandi, by Emilio Biggeri
A530

1977, July 30

1146 A530 30p multi 60 30

Navy Day.

Soccer Games' Emblem
A531

Design: 70p, Argentina '78 emblem, flags and soccer field.

1977, May 14

1147	A531	30p multi	65	30
1148	A531	70p multi	1.40	70

11th World Cup Soccer Championship, Argentina, June 1–25, 1978.

The Visit, by Horacio Butler
A532

Consecration, by Miguel P. Caride
A533

1977, Mar. 26 **Lithographed**

1149	A532	50p multi	85	40
1150	A533	70p multi	1.10	60

Argentine artists.

Sierra de la Ventana—A534

Views: No. 1152, Civic Center, Santa Rosa. No. 1153, Skiers, San Martin de los Andes. No. 1154, Boat on Lake Fonck, Rio Negro.

1977, Oct. 8 **Litho.** ***Perf. 13x13½***

1151	A534	30p multi	50	25
1152	A534	30p multi	50	25
1153	A534	30p multi	50	25
1154	A534	30p multi	50	25

Guillermo Brown, by R. del Villar
A535

1977, Oct. 8 ***Perf. 13½***

1155	A535	30p multi	50	30

Adm. Guillermo Brown (1777–1857), leader in fight for independence, bicentenary of birth.

Jet
A536

Double-decker, 1926
A537

1977 **Litho.** ***Perf. 13½***

1156	A536	30p multi	35	15
1157	A537	40p multi	45	20

50th anniversary of military plane production (30p); Air Force Day (40p).
Issue dates: 30p, Dec. 3; 40p, Nov. 26.

Adoration of the Kings
A538

1977, Dec. 17

1158	A538	100p multi	1.50	40

Christmas 1977.

Historic City Hall, Buenos Aires
A539

Chapel of Rio Grande Museum, Tierra del Fuego
A540

Designs: 5p, 20p, La Plata Museum. 10p, Independence Hall, Tucuman. 40p, City Hall, Salta (vert.). No. 1165, City Hall, Buenos Aires. 100p, Columbus Theater, Buenos Aires. 200p, flag Monument, Rosario. 280p, 300p, Chapel of Rio Grande Museum, Tierra del Fuego. 480p, 520p, 800p, Ruins of Jesuit Mission Church of San ignacio, Misiones. 500p, Candonga Chapel, Cordoba. 1000p, G.P.O., Buenos Aires. 2000p, Civic Center, Bariloche, Rio Negro.

Three types of 10p: I. Nine vertical window bars; small imprint "E. MILIAVACA Dib." II. Nine bars; large imprint "E. MILIAVACA DIB." III. Redrawn; 5 bars; large imprint.

Unwmkd.

1977– **Photogravure** ***Perf. 13½***

Size: 32x21mm., 21x32mm.

1159	A540	5p gray & blk ('78)	5	5
1160	A540	10p lt ultra & blk, I ('78)	5	5
a.		Type II ('78)	5	5
1161	A540	10p lt bl & blk, III ('79)	5	5
1162	A540	20p cit & blk, litho. ('78)	5	5
1163	A540	40p gray bl & blk ('78)	30	5
1164	A539	50p yel & blk	35	15
1165	A540	50p cit & blk ('79)	20	5
1166	A540	100p org & blk, litho. ('78)	45	10
a.		Wmk. 365	120.00	30.00
1167	A540	100p red org & blk, photo. ('79)	5	5
1168	A540	100p turq & blk ('81)	5	5
1169	A539	200p lt bl & blk ('79)	60	30
1170	A540	280p rose & blk	17.50	20
1171	A540	300p lem & blk ('78)	1.25	15
1172	A540	480p org & blk ('78)	2.25	30
1173	A540	500p yel grn & blk ('78)	2.25	25
1174	A540	520p org & blk ('78)	2.25	30
1175	A540	800p rose lil & blk ('79)	2.75	40
1176	A540	1000p lem bis & blk ('79)	3.00	50
1177	A540	1000p gold & blk, 40x29mm ('78)	5.00	50
1178	A540	2000p multi ('80)	2.80	50
		Nos. 1159-1178 (20)	41.25	4.05

Soccer Games' Emblem
A544

1978, Feb. 10 **Photo.** ***Perf. 13½***

1179	A544	200p yel grn & bl	1.25	40

11th World Cup Soccer Championship, Argentina, June 1-25. Exists with wmk. 365.

View of El Rio, Rosario—A545

Designs (Argentina '78 Emblem and): 100p, Rio Tercero Dam, Cordoba. 150p, Cordillera Mountains, Mendoza. 200p, City Center, Mar del Plata. 300p, View of Buenos Aires.

1978, May 6 **Litho.** ***Perf. 13***

1180	A545	50p multi	25	20
1181	A545	100p multi	50	20
1182	A545	150p multi	75	25
1183	A545	200p multi	75	35
1184	A545	300p multi	1.75	50
		Nos. 1180-1184 (5)	4.00	1.50

Sites of 11th World Cup Soccer Championship, June 1–25.

Children—A546

1978, May 20

1185	A546	100p multi	50	20

50th anniversary of Children's Institute.

Labor Day, by B. Quinquela Martin
A547

Design: No. 1187, Woman's torso, sculpture by Orlando Pierri.

1978, May 20 ***Perf. 13½***

1186	A547	100p multi	50	20
1187	A547	100p multi	50	20

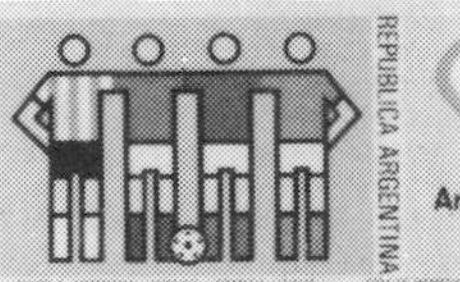

Argentina, Hungary, France, Italy and Emblem—A548

Stadium
A549

Teams and Argentina '78 Emblem: 200p, Poland, Fed. Rep. of Germany, Tunisia, Mexico. 300p, Austria, Spain, Sweden, Brazil. 400p, Netherlands, Iran, Peru, Scotland.

1978 **Litho.** ***Perf. 13***

1188	A548	100p multi	45	10
1189	A548	200p multi	90	10
1190	A548	300p multi	1.35	15
1191	A548	400p multi	1.75	25

Souvenir Sheet

Litho. and Engr. ***Perf. 13½***

1192	A549	700p buff & blk	3.50	2.00

11th World Cup Soccer Championship, Argentina, June 1–25. No. 1192 contains one stamp; blue and black margin shows sports and communications emblems. Size: 89x60mm. Issue dates, Nos. 1188–1191, June 6, No. 1192, June 3.

Stadium Type of 1978 Inscribed in Red:
"ARGENTINA / CAMPEON"

Lithographed and Engraved

1978, Sept. 2 ***Perf. 13½***

1193	A549	1000p buff, blk & red	5.00	2.00

Argentina's victory in 1978 Soccer Championship. No. 1193 has margin similar to No. 1192 with Rimet Cup emblem added in red. Size: 89x60mm.

Young Tree Nourished by Old Trunk, U.N. Emblem—A550

1978, Sept. 2 **Lithographed**

1194	A550	100p multi	50	30

Technical Cooperation among Developing Countries Conference, Buenos Aires, Sept. 1978.

Emblems of Buenos Aires and Bank
A551

1978, Sept. 16

1195	A551	100p multi	50	30

Bank of City of Buenos Aires, centenary.

General Savio and Steel Production
A552

1978, Sept. 16

1196	A552	100p multi	50	30

Gen. Manuel N. Savio (1892–1948), general manager of military heavy industry, 30th death anniversary.

San Martin
A553

1978, Oct. **Engraved**

1197	A553	2000p grnsh blk	9.00	1.50
1198	A553	2000p grnsh blk, wmk. 365 ('79)	6.00	50

Gen Jose de San Martin (1778-1850), soldier and statesman. See No. 1292.

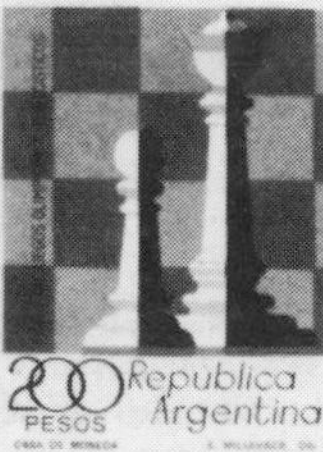

Globe and Argentine Flag A554 — Chessboard, Queen and Pawn A555

1978, Oct. 7 Litho. *Perf. 13½*

1199 A554 200p multi 1.00 40

12th International Cancer Congress, Buenos Aires, Oct. 5-11.

1978, Oct. 7

1200 A555 200p multi 3.00 1.00

23rd National Chess Olympics, Buenos Aires, Oct. 25-Nov. 12.

Correct Positioning of Stamps A557

Design: 50p, Use correct postal code number.

1978 Photogravure *Perf. 13½*

1201 A557 20p ultra 20 10
1203 A557 50p carmine 30 10

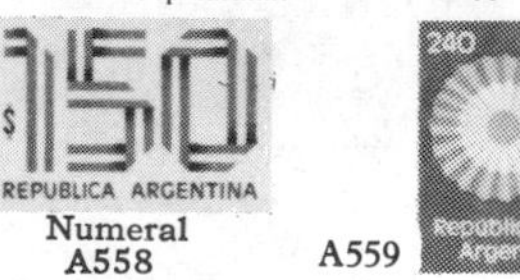

Numeral A558 — A559

1978 Photogravure *Perf. 13½*

No.	Type	Description	Unused	Used
1204	A558	150p bl & ultra	45	10
1205	A558	180p bl & ultra	55	15
1206	A558	200p bl & ultra	40	12
1207	A559	240p ol bis & bl ('79)	48	16
1208	A559	260p blk & lt bl ('79)	52	18
1209	A559	290p blk & lt bl ('79)	58	18
1210	A559	310p mag & bl ('79)	62	22
1211	A559	350p ver & bl ('79)	70	25
1212	A559	450p ultra & bl	65	22
1213	A559	600p grn & bl ('80)	85	30
1214	A559	700p blk & bl ('80)	85	30
1215	A559	800p red & bl ('81)	80	10
1216	A559	1100p gray & bl ('81)	1.10	10
1217	A559	1500p blk & bl ('81)	45	10
1218	A559	1700p grn & bl ('82)	55	10
		Nos. 1204-1218 (15)	9.55	2.58

No. 1206 issued on fluorescent and ordinary paper.

Balsa "24" A561

Ships: 200p, Tug Legador. 300p, River Parana tug No. 34. 400p, Passenger ship Ciudad de Parana.

1978, Nov. 4 Litho. *Perf. 13½*

1220 A561 100p multi 30 5
1221 A561 200p multi 60 5
1222 A561 300p multi 90 10
1223 A561 400p multi 1.20 15

20th anniversary of national river fleet. Nos. 1220 and 1223, 1221-1222 printed se-tenant in sheets of 50. Issued on fluorescent paper.

View and Arms of Bahia Blanca A562

1978, Nov. 25 Litho. *Perf. 13½*

1224 A562 20p multi 60 10

Sesquicentennial of Bahia Blanca.

"Spain," (Queen Isabella and Columbus) by Arturo Dresco—A563

1978, Nov. 25

1225 A563 300p multi 4.00 25

Visit of King Juan Carlos and Queen Sofia of Spain to Argentina, Nov. 26.

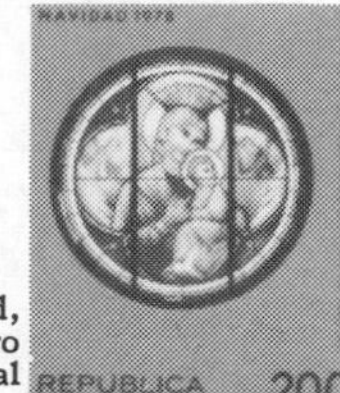

Virgin and Child, San Isidro Cathedral A564

1978, Dec. 16

1226 A564 200p gold & multi 80 40

Christmas 1978.

Slope at Chacabuco, by Pedro Subercaseaux—A565

Painting: 1000p, The Embrace of Maipu (San Martin and O'Higgins), by Pedro Subercaseaux (vert.).

1978, Dec. 16 Litho. *Perf. 13½*

1227 A565 500p multi 1.50 40
1228 A565 1000p multi 3.00 60

José de San Martin, 200th birth anniversary.

Adolfo Alsina A566

Design: No. 1230, Mariano Moreno.

1979, Jan. 20

1229 A566 200p lt bl & blk 75 20
1230 A566 200p yel red & blk 75 20

Adolfo Alsina (1828-1877), political leader, vice-president; Mariano Moreno (1778-1811), lawyer, educator, political leader.

Argentina No. 37 and UPU Emblem—A567

1979, Jan. 20

1231 A567 200p multi 40 14

Centenary of Argentina's UPU membership.

Still-life, by Cárcova A568

Painting: 300p, The Laundresses, by Faustino Brughetti.

1979, Mar. 3

1232 A568 200p multi 75 15
1233 A568 300p multi 1.00 25

Ernesto de la Cárcova (1866-1927) and Faustino Brughetti (1877-1956), Argentine painters.

Balcarce Earth Station A569

1979, Mar. 3

1234 A569 200p multi 1.00 30

Third Inter-American Telecommunications Conference, Buenos Aires, March 5-9.

Stamp Collecting A570

1979

1235 A570 30p brt grn 20 10

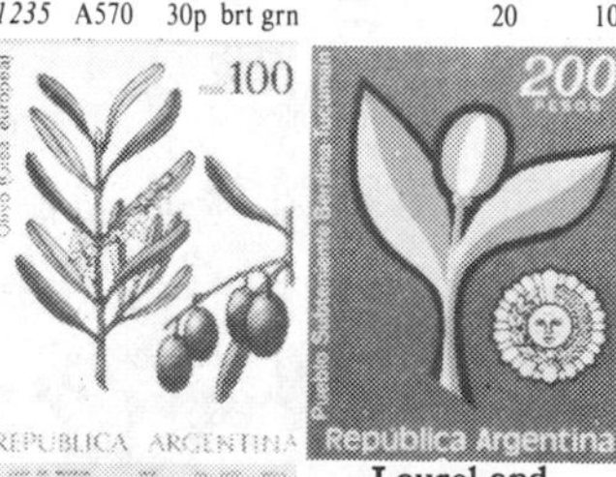

European Olive A571 — Laurel and Regimental Emblem A572

Designs: 200p, Tea. 300p, Sorghum. 400p, Common flax.

1979, June 2 Litho. *Perf. 13½*

1236 A571 100p multi 40 20
1237 A571 200p multi 80 40
1238 A571 300p multi 1.25 60
1239 A571 400p multi 1.65 80

1979, June 9

1240 A572 200p gold & multi 60 30

Founding of Subteniente Berdina Village in memory of Sub-lieutenant Rodolfo Hernan Berdina, killed by terrorists in 1975.

"75" and Automobile Club Emblem A573

1979, June 9

1241 A573 200p gold & multi 60 30

Argentine Automobile Club, 75th anniversary.

Exchange Building and Emblem A574

1979, June 9

1242 A574 200p bl, blk & gold 60 30

Grain Exchange, 125th anniversary.

Cavalry Officer, 1817 A575

1979, July 7 Litho. *Perf. 13½*

1243 A575 200p multi 1.25 30

Army Day.

Corvette Uruguay and Navy Emblem A576

Design: No. 1245, Hydrographic service ship and emblem.

1979 *Perf. 13*

1244 A576 250p multi 1.25 40
1245 A576 250p multi 1.25 40

Navy Day (No. 1244); Centenary of Naval Hydrographic Service (No. 1245). Issue dates: No. 1244, July 28; No. 1245, July 7.

See "Special Notices" at the front of this volume for data on the listing methods of this Catalogue, abbreviations, condition, prices and examination.

Tree and Man
A577

1979, July 28 ***Perf. 13½***

1246 A577 250p multi 80 30

Protection of the Environment Day, June 5.

"Spad" Flying over Andes, and Vicente Almandos Almonacid—A578

1979, Aug. 4

1247 A578 250p multi 1.00 30

Air Force Day.

Gen. Julio A. Roca Occupying Rio Negro, by Juan M. Blanes—A579

1979, Aug. 4

1248 A579 250p multi 1.00 30

Conquest of Rio Negro Desert, centenary.

Rowland Hill—A580

1979, Sept. 29 **Litho.** ***Perf. 13½***

1249 A580 300p gray, red & blk 80 30

Sir Rowland Hill (1795-1879), originator of penny postage.

Viedma y Navarez Monument—A581

1979, Sept. 29

1250 A581 300p multi 80 30

Viedma and Carmen de Patagones towns, bicentenary.

Pope Paul VI—A582

Design: No. 1252, Pope John Paul I.

1979, Oct. 27 **Engr.** ***Perf. 13½***

1251 A582 500p black 1.50 40
1252 A582 500p sepia 1.50 40

No. 1169 Overprinted in Red: "75 ANNIV. / SOCIEDAD/ FILATELICA / DE ROSARIO"

1979, Nov. 10 **Photo.** ***Perf. 13½***

1253 A539 200p lt bl & blk 1.00 30

Rosario Philatelic Society, 75th anniversary.

Frontier Resettlement—A583

1979, Nov. 10 **Litho.**

1254 A583 300p multi 1.00 40

Military Geographic Institute Centenary
A584

1979, Dec. 1 **Litho.** ***Perf. 13½***

1255 A584 300p multi 1.00 40

Christmas 1979—A585

1979, Dec. 1

1256 A585 300p multi 80 30

General Mosconi Birth Centenary
A586

1979, Dec. 15 **Engr.** ***Perf. 13½***

1257 A586 1000p blk & bl 2.50 40

Rotary Emblem and Globe—A587

1979, Dec. 29 **Litho.**

1258 A587 300p multi 3.00 60

Rotary International, 75th anniversary.

Child and IYC Emblem—A588

Family, by Pablo Menicucci—A589

1979, Dec. 29

1259 A588 500p lt bl & sep 1.00 20
1260 A589 1000p multi 2.00 30

International Year of the Child.

Microphone, Waves, ITU Emblem—A590

1980, Mar. 22 **Litho.** ***Perf. 13x13½***

1261 A590 500p multi 1.50 40

Regional Administrative Conference on Broadcasting by Hectometric Waves for Area 2, Buenos Aires, Mar. 10-29.

Guillermo Brown—A591

1980 **Engraved** ***Perf. 13½***

1262 A591 5000p black 7.00 15

See No. 1372.

Argentine Red Cross Centenary—A592

1980, Apr. 19 **Litho.** ***Perf. 13½***

1263 A592 500p multi 80 30

OAS Emblem—A593

1980, Apr. 19

1264 A593 500p multi 80 30

Day of the Americas, Apr. 14.

Dish Antennae, Balcarce—A594

1980, Apr. 26 **Litho. & Engr.**

1265 A594 300p *shown* 60 30
1266 A594 300p *Hydroelectric Station, Salto Grande* 60 30
1267 A594 300p *Bridge, Zarate-Brazo Largo* 60 30

Capt. Hipolito Bouchard, Frigate "Argentina"—A595

1980, May 31 **Litho.** ***Perf. 13x13½***

1268 A595 500p multi 1.00 40

Navy Day.

"Villarino," San Martin, by Theodore Gericault—A596

1980, May 31

1269 A596 500p multi 1.00 40

Return of the remains of Gen. José de San Martin to Argentina, centenary.

Buenos Aires Gazette, 1810, Signature—A597

1980, June 7 *Perf. 13½*

1270 A597 500p multi 80 30

Journalism Day.

Coaches in Victoria Square—A598

1980, June 14

1271 Block of 14 multi 10.00 3.50
a. A598 500p, any single 70 25

Buenos Aires, 400th anniversary. No. 1271 shows ceramic mural of Victoria Square by Rodolfo Franco in continuous design.

See No. 1285.

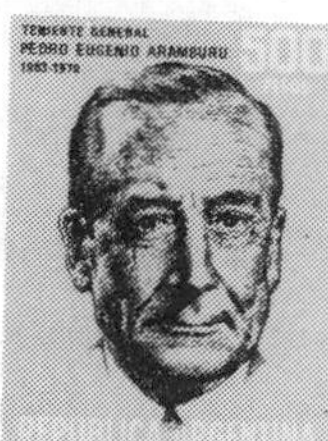

Gen. Pedro Aramburu—A599

1980, July 12 **Litho.** *Perf. 13½*

1272 A599 500p yel & blk 80 30

Gen. Pedro Eugenio Aramburu (1903-1970), provisional president, 1955.

Army Day—A600

1980, July 12

1273 A600 500p multi 1.25 40

Gen. Juan Gregorio de Las Heras (1780-1866), Hero of 1817 War of Independence—A601

Grandees of Argentina Bicentenary: No. 1275, Bernardino Rivadavia (1780-1845), stateman and president. No. 1276, Brig. Gen José Matias Zapiola (1780-1874), naval commander and statesman.

1980, Aug. 2 **Litho.** *Perf. 13½*

1274 A601 500p tan & blk 80 30
1275 A601 500p multi 80 30
1276 A601 500p lt lil & blk 80 30

Avro "Gosport" Biplane, Maj. Francisco de Artega—A602

1980, Aug. 16 *Perf. 13*

1277 A602 500p multi 1.00 30

Air Force Day. Artega (1882-1930) was first director of Military Aircraft Factory where Avro "Gosport" was built (1927).

University of La Plata, 75th Anniversary—A603

1980, Aug. 16 *Perf. 13½*

1278 A603 500p multi 80 30

Souvenir Sheets

Emperor Penguin—A604

South Orkneys Argentine Base A605 A606

1980 Sept. 27 **Litho.** *Perf. 13½*

1279 Sheet of 12 15.00 10.00
a. A604 500p *shown* 1.00 75
b. A604 500p *Bearded penguin* 1.00 75
c. A604 500p *Adeli penguins* 1.00 75
d. A604 500p *Papua penguins* 1.00 75
e. A604 500p *Sea elephants* 1.00 75
f. A605 500p *shown* 1.00 75
g. A606 500p *shown* 1.00 75
h. A604 500p *Fur seals* 1.00 75
i. A604 500p *Giant petrels* 1.00 75
j. A604 500p *Blue-eyed cormorants* 1.00 75
k. A604 500p *Stormy petrel* 1.00 75
m. A604 500p *Antarctic doves* 1.00 75
1280 Sheet of 12 15.00 10.00
a. A605 500p *Puerto Soledad* 70 30
b. A606 500p *Different view* 70 30

75th anniversary of Argentina's presence in the South Orkneys and 150th anniversary of political and military command in the Falkland Islands. Nos. 1279-1280 each contain 12 stamps (4x3) with landscape designs in center of sheets. Silhouettes of Argentine exploration ships in margins. Size: 150x173mm. No. 1280 contains Nos. 1279a-1279e, 1279h-1279m, 1280a-1280b.

Anti-smoking Campaign—A608

1980, Oct. 11

1282 A608 700p multi 1.25 30

National Census—A609

1980, Sept.

1283 A609 500p blk & bl 1.25 30

Madonna and Child (Congress Emblem)—A610

1980, Oct. 1 **Litho.**

1284 A610 700p multi 1.00 15

National Marian Congress, Mendoza, Oct. 8-12

Mural Type of 1980

1980, Oct. 25

1285 Block of 14, multi 10.00 3.50
a. A598 500p, any single 70 25

Buenos Aires, 400th anniversary/Buenos Aires '80 Stamp Exhibition, Oct. 24-Nov. 2. No. 1285 shows ceramic mural Arte bajo la Cuidad by Alfredo Guido in continuous design.

Technical Military Academy, 50th Anniversary A611

Amateur Radio Operation A612

1980, Nov. 1

1286 A611 700p multi 1.00 15

1980, Nov. 1

1287 A612 700p multi 1.00 15

Medal A613

Lujan Cathedral Floor Plan A614

1980, Nov. 29 **Litho.** *Perf. 13½*

1288 A613 700p multi 1.00 15
1289 A614 700p ol & brn 1.00 15

Christmas 1980. 150th anniversary of apparition of Holy Virgin to St. Catherine Laboure, Paris (No. 1288), 350th anniversary of apparition at Lujan.

150th Death Anniversary of Simon Bolivar—A615

1980, Dec. 13

1290 A615 700p multi 1.00 15

Soccer Gold Cup Championship, Montevideo, 1980—A616

1981, Jan. 3 **Litho.**

1291 A616 1000p multi 1.40 15

San Martin Type of 1978

1981, Jan. 20 **Engraved** *Perf. 13½*

1292 A553 10,000p dk bl 10.00 20

Landscape in Lujan, by Marcos Tiglio—A617

Paintings: No. 1304, Expansion of Light along a Straight Line, by Miguel Angel Vidal (vert.).

1981, Apr. 11 **Litho.**

1303 A617 1000p multi 1.25 30
1304 A617 1000p multi 1.25 30

Intl. Sports Medicine Congress, June 7-12—A618

1981, June 6 **Litho.** ***Perf. 13½***

1305 A618 1000p bl & dk brn 1.00 15

Esperanza Base, Antarctica—A619

Cargo Plane, Map of Vice-Commodore Marambio Island—A620

Perf. 13½,13x13½(No. 1308)

1981, June 13

1306 A619 1000p shown 2.00 75
1307 A619 2000p Almirante Irizar 3.50 1.00
1308 A620 2000p shown 3.50 1.50

Antarctic Treaty 20th anniv.

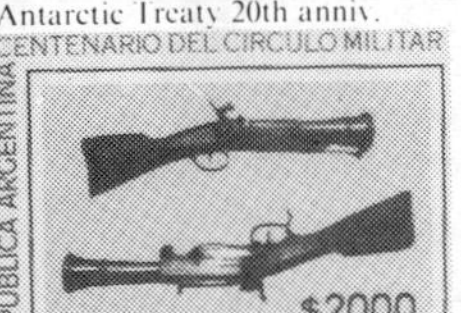

Antique Pistols (Military Club Centenary) A621

1981, June 27 ***Perf. 13½***

1309 A621 1000p Club building 1.00 15
1310 A621 2000p shown 2.00 15

Gen. Juan A. Alvarez de Arenales (1770-1831)—A622

Famous Men: No. 1312, Felix G. Frias (1816-1881), writer. No. 1313, José E. Uriburu (1831-1914), statesman.

1981, Aug. 8 **Litho.** ***Perf. 13½***

1311 A622 1000p multi 1.00 15
1312 A622 1000p multi 1.00 15
1313 A622 1000p multi 1.00 15

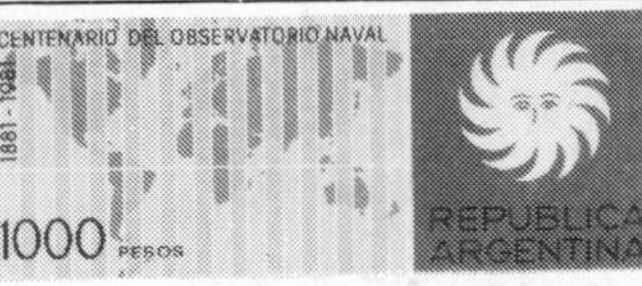

Naval Observatory Centenary—A623

1981, Aug. 15 **Litho.** ***Perf. 13x13½***

1314 A623 1000p multi 1.25 40

No. 1176 Overprinted in Red: "50° ANNIV. DE LA ASOCIACION / FILATELICA Y NUMISMATICA / DE BAHIA BLANCA"

1981, Aug. 15 **Photo.** ***Perf. 13½***

1315 A540 1000p lem & blk 3.00 40

50th anniv. of Bahia Blanca Philatelic and Numismatic Society.

St. Cayetano, Stained-glass Window, Buenos Aires—A624

1981, Sept. 5 **Litho.** ***Perf. 13½***

1316 A624 1000p multi 1.00 15

St. Cayetano, founder of Teatino Order, 500th birth anniv.

Pablo Castaibert (1883-1909) and his Monoplane (Air Force Day)—A625

1981, Sept. 5 ***Perf. 13x13½***

1317 A625 1000p multi 1.00 15

Intl. Year of the Disabled A626

1981, Sept. 10 ***Perf. 13½***

1318 A626 1000p multi 1.00 15

22nd Latin—American Steelmakers' Congress, Buenos Aires, Sept. 21-23—A627

1981, Sept. 19

1319 A627 1000p multi 1.00 15

Army Regiment No. 1 (Patricios), 175th Anniv.—A628

1981, Oct. 10 **Litho.** ***Perf. 13½***

1320 A628 1500p Natl. arms 70 15
1321 A628 1500p shown 70 15

Nos. 1320-1321 se-tenant.

Jose San Martin as Artillery Captain in Battle of Bailen, 1808—A629

1981, Oct. 5

1322 Sheet of 8 4.00 1.50
a.-d. A629 1000p multi 30 15
e.-h. A629 1500p multi 45 15

Espamer '81 Intl. Stamp Exhibition (Americas, Spain, Portugal), Buenos Aires, Nov. 13-22. No. 1322 has multicolored margin. Size 136x212mm.

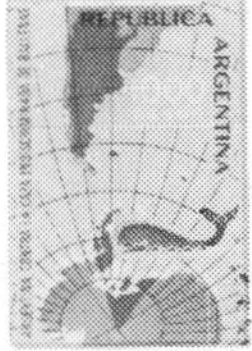

Anti-indiscriminate Whaling A630

Espamer '81 Emblem and Ship A631

1981, Oct. 5

1323 A630 1000p multi 1.00 60

1981

1324 A631 1300p multi 1.00 30

No. 1324 Overprinted in Blue: "CURSO SUPERIOR DE ORGANIZACION DE SERVICIOS FILATELICOS-UPAE-BUENOS AIRES-1981"

1981, Nov. 7 **Photo.** ***Perf. 13½***

1325 A631 1300p multi 1.00 30

Postal Administration philatelic training course.

Soccer Players—A632

Designs: Soccer players.

1981, Nov. 13 **Litho.**

1326 Sheet of 4 + 2 labels 10.00 6.00
a. A632 1000p multi 30 20
b. A632 3000p multi 90 30
c. A632 5000p multi 1.50 50
d. A632 15000p multi 4.50 1.50

Espamer '81. No. 1326 has black marginal inscription and control number. Size: 137x130mm.

"Peso" Coin Centenary—A633

1981, Nov. 21

1327 A633 2000p Patacon, 1881 60 15
1328 A633 3000p Argentine Oro, 1881 90 15

Christmas 1981 A634

1981, Dec. 12

1329 A634 1500p multi 1.00 40

Traffic Safety—A635

1981, Dec. 19 **Litho.**

1330 A635 1000p Observe traffic lights, vert. 1.00 50
1331 A635 2000p Drive carefully, vert. 1.00 50
1332 A635 3000p Cross at white lines 1.50 50
1333 A635 4000p Don't shine headlights 2.00 50

Francisco Luis Bernardez, Ciuda Laura—A636

Designs: Writers and title pages from their works.

1982, Mar. 20 **Litho.**

1334 A636 1000p shown 90 30
1335 A636 2000p Lucio V. Mansilla, Excursion a los indios ranqueles 1.25 30
1336 A636 3000p Conrado Nale Roxlo, El Grillo 1.75 40
1337 A636 4000p Victoria Ocampo, Sur 2.50 40

No. 1219A Overprinted:
"LAS / MALVINAS / SON/ ARGENTINAS"

1982, Apr. 17 Photo. Perf. 13½

1338 A559 1700p grn & bl 75 30

Argentina's claim on Falkland Islds.

Robert Koch A637

American Airforces Commanders' 22nd Conference A638

1982, Apr. 17 Litho.

1339 A637 2000p multi 80 40

TB bacillus centenary and 25th Intl. Tuberculosis Conference.

1982, Apr. 17

1340 A638 2000p multi 1.00 40

Stone Carving, City Founder's Signature (Don Hernando de Lerma)—A639

1982, Apr. 17

1341 A639 2000p multi 1.00 40

Souvenir Sheet

1342 A639 5000p multi 3.00 3.00

City of Salta, 400th anniv. No. 1342 contains one stamp (43x30mm.); multicolored margin shows map. Size: 89x60mm.

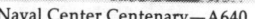

Naval Center Centenary—A640

1982, Apr. 24 Perf. 13x13½

1343 A640 2000p multi 1.00 40

Chorisia Speciosa—A641

1982 Photo. Perf. 13½

1344 A641 200p Zinnia peruviana 5 5
1345 A641 300p Ipomola purpurea 5 5
1346 A641 400p Tillandsia aeranthos 5 5
1347 A641 500p shown 8 5
1348 A641 800p Oncidium bifolium 12 5
1349 A641 1000p Erythrina crista-galli 15 8
1350 A641 2000p Jacaranda mimosifolia 30 8
1351 A641 3000p Bauhinia candicans 45 15
1352 A641 5000p Tecoma stans 75 20
1353 " 10,000p Tabebuia ipe 1.50 30
1354 " 20,000p Passiflora coerulea 3.00 50
1355 " 30,000p Aristolochia littoralis 4.50 75
1356 " 50,000p Oxalis enneaphylla 7.50 1.00
Nos. 1344-1356 (13) 18.50 3.31

See Nos. 1429-1442, 1515-1530.

10th Death Anniv. of Gen. Juan C. Sanchez—A641a

1982, May 29 Litho.

1364 A641a 5000 grn & blk 1.25 40

153rd Anniv. of Malvinas Political and Military Command District—A641b

1982, June 12

1365 A641b 5000 Luis Venet, 1st commander 1.50 60

Size: 83x28mm.

1366 A641b 5000 Map 1.50 60

Visit of Pope John Paul II—A641c

1982, June 12

1367 A641c 5000 multi 2.50 80

Organ Grinder, by Aldo Severi (b. 1928)—A641d

1982, July 3

1368 A641d 2000 shown 40 30
1369 A641d 3000 Still Life, by Santiago Cogorno (b. 1915) 60 30

Guillermo Brown Type of 1980 and:

Jose de San Martin—A641e

1982 Litho. & Engr. Perf. 13½

1372 A591 30000 blk & bl 5.00 75
1376 A641e 50000 sep & car 9.00 1.00

Issue dates: 30,000, June; 50,000, July.

Scouting Year—A641f

1982, Aug. 7 Litho. Perf. 13½

1380 A641f 5000 multi 2.50 30

Alconafta Fuel Campaign—A641g

1982, Aug. 7

1381 A641g 2000 multi 45 10

No. 1351 Overprinted:
"50 ANIVERSARIO SOCIEDAD FILATELICA DE TUCUMAN"

1982, Aug. 7 Photo.

1382 A641 5000p multi 2.00 1.50

Rio III Central Nuclear Power Plant, Cordoba—A642

1982, Sept. 4 Litho. Perf. 13½

1383 A642 2000p shown 50 10
1384 A642 2000p Control room 50 10

Namibia Day—A643

1982, Sept. 4

1385 A643 5000p Map 1.25 15

Formosa Cathedral—A644

Churches and Cathedrals of the Northeast: 2000p, Our Lady of Itati, Corrientes (vert.). 3000p, Resistencia Cathedral, Chaco (vert.). 10,000p, St. Ignatius Church ruins, Misiones.

1982, Sept. 18 Wmk. 365 Engr.

1386 A644 2000p dk grn & blk 30 20
1387 A644 3000p dk brn & brn 45 20
1388 A644 5000p dk bl & brn 75 30
1389 " 10,000p dp org & blk 1.50 50

Tension Sideral, by Mario Alberto Agatiello—A645

Sculpture (Espamer '81 and Juvenex '82 Exhibitions): 3000p, Sugerencia II, by Eduardo Mac Entyre. 5000p, Storm, by Carlos Silva.

1982, Oct. 2 Litho. Perf. 13½

1390 A645 2000p multi 40 15
1391 A645 3000p multi 75 20
1392 A645 5000p multi 1.00 30

Sante Fe Bridge—A646

1982, Oct. 16 Litho. & Engr.

1393 A646 2000p bl & blk 75 10

2nd Southern Cross Games, Santa Fe and Rosario, Nov. 26-Dec. 5.

10th World Men's Volleyball Championship—A647

1982, Oct. 16 **Litho.**

1394 A647 2000p multi 40 20
1395 A647 5000p multi 80 30

Los Andes Newspaper Centenary—A648

Design: Army of the Andes Monument, Hill of Glory, Mendoza.

1982, Oct. 30

1396 A648 5000p multi 80 30

50th Anniv. of Natl. Roads, Administration—A649

1982, Oct. 30

1397 A649 5000p Signs 80 30

La Plata City Centenary—A650

1982, Nov. 20 **Litho.**

1398 A650 5000p Cathedral 90 15
1399 A650 5000p City Hall 90 15
1400 Sheet of 6 2.75 1.25
a. A650 2500p Cathedral, diff. 35 10
b. A650 2500p Head, top 35 10
c. A650 2500p Observatory 35 10
d. A650 2500p City Hall, diff. 35 10
e. A650 2500p Head, bottom 35 10
f. A650 2500p University 35 10

No. 1400 has black control number. Size: 120x115mm.

75th Anniv. of Oil Discovery, Comodoro Rivadavia—A651

1982, Nov. 20

1401 A651 5000p Well, Natl. Hydrocarbon Congress emblem 1.00 40

Jockey Club of Buenos Aires Centenary
A652

Christmas 1982
A653

1982, Dec. 4 **Litho.**

1402 A652 5000p Emblem 75 15
1403 A652 5000p Carlos Pellegrini, 1st pres. 75 15

1982, Dec. 18 ***Perf. 13½***

1404 A653 3000p St. Vincent de Paul 2.50 10

Size: 29x38mm.

1405 A653 5000p St. Francis Assisi 2.00 15

Pedro B. Palacios (1854-1917), Writer—A654

Writers: 2000p, Leopoldo Marechal (1900-1970). 3000p, Delfina Bunge de Galvez (1881-1952). 4000p, Manuel Galvez (1882-1962). 5000p, Evaristo Carriego (1883-1912). Se-tenant.

1983, Mar. 26 **Litho.** ***Perf. 13½***

1406 A654 1000p multi 15 10
1407 A654 2000p multi 30 10
1408 A654 3000p multi 45 15
1409 A654 4000p multi 60 20
1410 A654 5000p multi 75 25
Nos. 1406-1410 (5) 2.25 80

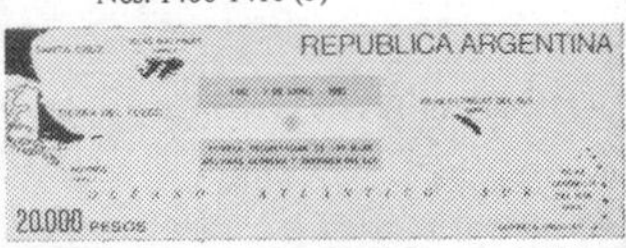

Recovery of the Malvinas—A655

1983, Apr. 9 **Litho.** ***Perf. 13½***

1411 A655 20,000p Map, flag 1.00 50

Telecommunications Systems—A656

1983, Apr. 16 **Wmk. 365**

1412 A656 5000p SITRAM 1.50 10
1413 A656 5000p red ARPAC 1.50 10

Naval League Emblem
A657

Natl. Arts Fund, 25th Anniv.
A658

1983, May 14 **Litho.** ***Perf. 13½***

1414 A657 5000p multi 60 10

Navy Day and 50th anniv. of Naval League.

1983, May 14

1415 A658 5000p Allegory, by Victor Rebuffo 60 10

75th Anniv. of Colon Opera House, Buenos Aires—A659

1983, May 28 **Wmk.**

1416 A659 5000p Main hall 1.00 10
1417 A659 10000p Stage 1.50 15

Protected Species—A660

1983, July 2 **Litho.** ***Perf. 13½***

1418 A660 1p Chrysocyon brachtyurus 50 10
1419 A660 1.50p Ozotocerus bezoarticus 75 15
1420 A660 2p Myrmecophaga tridactyla 90 20
1421 A660 2.50p Leo onca 1.00 25

City of Catamarca, 300th Anniv.
A661

Mamerto Esquiu (1826-1883)
A662

Foundation of the City of Catamarca, by Luis Varela Lezana (1900-1982).

1983, July 16 **Litho.** ***Perf. 13½***

1422 A661 1p multi 45 10

1983, July 16

1423 A662 1p multi 45 10

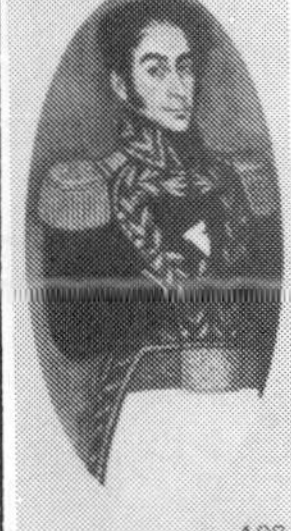

Bolivar, by Herrera Toro
A663

Bolivar, Engraving by Kepper
A664

Perf. 13 (A663), 13½ (A664)

1983 **Wmk. 365**

1424 A663 1p multi 45 10
1425 A664 2p black 90 15
1426 A664 10p San Martin 4.50 2.25

Issue dates: 1p, 2p, July 23. 10p, Aug. 20.

See No. 1457.

Gen. Toribio de Luzuriaga (1782-1842)—A665

1983, Aug. 20 **Litho.** ***Perf. 13½***

1427 A665 1p multi 45 10

50th Anniv. of San Martin National Institute—A666

1983, Aug. 20 **Engr.**

1428 A666 2p sepia 90 25

Flower Type of 1982 in New Currency

1983-85		**Photo.**	**Perf. 13½**	
1429	A641	5c like #1347	5	5
1430	A641	10c like #1349	5	5
1431	A641	20c like #1350	5	5
1432	A641	30c like #1351	5	5
1433	A641	40c Eichhornia crassipes	6	5
1434	A641	50c like #1352	8	5
1435	A641	1p like #1353	14	5
1435A	A641	1.80p Mutisia retusa	15	6
1436	A641	2p like #1354	28	10
1437	A641	3p like #1355	42	15
1438	A641	5p like #1356	70	25
1439	A641	10p Alstroemeria aurantiaca	1.40	1.00
1440	A641	20p like #1345 ('84)	70	20
1441	A641	30p Embothrium coccineum	4.25	3.00
1442	A641	50p like #1346 ('84)	1.40	50
1443	A641	100p Oncidium bifolium ('84)	2.00	60
1443A	A641	300p Cassia carnaval ('85)	1.00	30
		Nos. 1429-1443A (17)	12.78	6.51

Issue Dates: 20p, Aug. 27. 50p, Oct. 19. 100p, Dec. 300p, June 15.

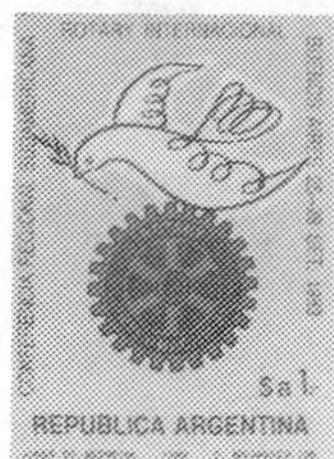

Intl. Rotary South American Regional Conference, Buenos Aires, Sept. 25-28—A667

1983, Sept. 24		**Litho.**		
1444	A667	1p multi	90	40

9th Pan American Games, Caracas, Aug. 13-28—A668

1983, Sept. 24				
1445	A668	1p Track	45	20
1446	A668	2p Emblem	90	40

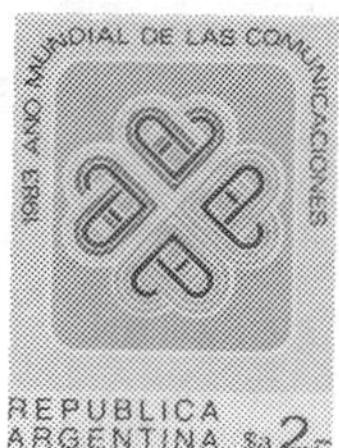

World Communications Year—A669

1983, Oct. 8			**Perf. 13½**	
1447	A669	2p multi	75	30

Squash Peddler by Antonio Berni (1905-1981)—A670

Designs: 2p, Figure in Yellow by Luis Seoane (1910-1979).

1983, Oct. 15			**Perf. 13½**	
1448	A670	1p multi	45	15
1449	A670	2p multi	75	30

World Communications Year—A671

1983, Nov. 19		**Litho.**	**Perf. 13½**	
1450	A671	1p Wagon, 18th cen.	20	10
1451	A671	2p Post-chaise, 19th cen.	35	20
1452	A671	4p Steam locomotive, 1857	75	30
1453	A671	5p Tramway, 1910	95	40

World Communications Year—A672

Return to Elected Government—A673

1983, Nov. 26		**Litho.**	**Perf. 12½x12**	
1454	A672	2p General Post Office	60	25

1983, Dec. 10		**Photo.**	**Perf. 13½**	
1455	A673	2p Coin, 1813	45	25

Eudyptes crestatus—A674

Designs: b, Diomedea exulans. c, Diomedea melanophris. d, Eudyptes chrysolophus. e, Luis Piedra Buena. f, Carlos Maria Moyano. g, Luis Py. h, Augusto Lasserre. i, Phoebetria palpebrata. j, Hydrurga leptonyx. k, Lobodon carcinophagus. l, Leptonychotes weddelli.

1983, Dec. 10		**Litho.**		
1456		Sheet of 12	6.00	3.00
a.-l.		A674 2p any single	45	20

Southern pioneers and fauna. Margin depicts various airplanes and emblems.

Bolivar Type of 1983

Famous men: 10p, Angel J. Carranza (1834-1899), historian. 20p, Estanislao del Campo (1834-1880), poet. 30p, Jose Hernandez (1834-1886), author. 40p, Vicente Lopez y Planes (1784-1856), poet and patriot. 50p, Gen. Jose de San Martin (1778-1850), statesman. 200p, Gen. Manuel Belgrano (1770-1820), patriot. 500p Adm. Guillermo Brown.

1983-85		**Litho. & Engr.**	**Perf. 13½**	
1457	A664	10p pale bl & dk bl ('85)	6	5
1458	A664	20p Guillermo Brown	3.50	1.75
1459	A664	20p dl brn ol & ol blk ('85)	12	5
1460	A664	30p pale bl & bluish blk ('85)	18	8
1461	A664	40p lt bl grn & blk ('85)	24	10
1462	A664	50p Prus & choc ('85)	1.50	30
1462A	A664	200p int bl & blk ('85)	4.00	1.25
1462B	A664	500p brn & int bl ('85)	2.00	40
		Nos. 1457-1462B (8)	11.60	3.98

Issue dates: 10p, 20p, 30p, 40p, Mar. 23. 50p, Apr. 23. 200p, Nov. 2.

Christmas 1983—A675

Nativity Scenes: 2p,Tapestry, by Silke. 3p, Stained-glass window, San Carlos de Bariloche's Wayn Church (vert.).

1983, Dec. 17		**Litho.**	**Perf. 13½**	
1463	A675	2p multi	45	22
1464	A675	3p multi	80	40

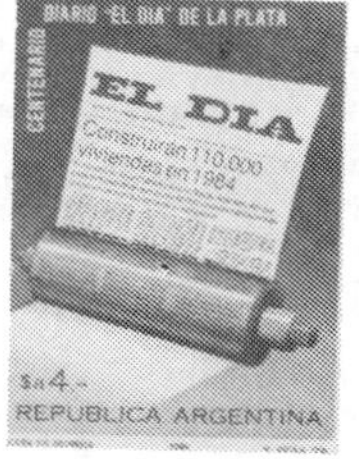

Centenary of El Dia Newspaper—A676

1984, Mar. 24		**Litho.**		
1465	A676	4p Masthead, printing roll	55	28

Alejandro Carbo Teachers' College Centenary—A677

1984, June 2		**Litho.**	**Perf. 13½**	
1466	A677	10p Building	60	30

1984 Olympics—A678

1984, July 28		**Litho.**	**Perf. 13½**	
1467	A678	5p Rowing, basketball	30	15
1468	A678	5p Weightlifting, discus, shot put	30	15
1469	A678	10p Javelin, fencing	60	30
1470	A678	10p Bicycling, swimming	60	30

Rosario Stock Exchange Centenary—A679

1984, Aug. 11				
1471	A679	10p multi	60	30

Wheat—A680

1984, Aug. 11				
1472	A680	10p shown	60	30
1473	A680	10p Corn	60	30
1474	A680	10p Sunflower	60	30

18th FAO Regional Conference for Latin America and Caribbean (No. 1472); 3rd Natl. Corn Congress (No. 1473); World Food Day (No. 1474).

Wildlife Protection—A681

1984, Sept. 22		**Litho.**	**Perf. 13½**	
1475	A681	20p Hippocamelus bisulcus	50	12
1476	A681	20p Vicugna vicugna	50	12
1477	A681	20p Aburria jacutinga	50	12
1478	A681	20p Mergus octosetaceus	50	12
1479	A681	20p Podiceps gallardoi	50	12
		Nos. 1475-1479 (5)	2.50	60

First Latin American Theater Festival, Cordoba, Oct.—A682

1984, Oct. 13 Litho. *Perf. 13½*

1480	A682	20p Mask	24	12

Intl. Eucharistic Congress, 50th Anniv.—A683

1984, Oct. 13

1481	A683	20p Apostles' Communion, by Fra Angelico	30	12

Glaciares Natl. Park (UNESCO World Heritage List)—A684

1984, Nov. 17 Litho.

1482	A684	20p Sea	30	12
1483	A684	30p Glacier	50	18

City of Puerto Deseado Centenary—A685

1984, Nov. 17 *Perf. 13½*

1484	A685	20p shown	50	12
1485	A685	20p Ushuaia centenary	50	12

Childrens' Paintings, Christmas 1984—A686

1984, Dec. 1 Litho. *Perf. 13½*

1486	A686	20p Diego Aguero	50
1487	A686	30p Leandro Ruiz	60
1488	A686	50p Maria Castillo, vert.	90

No. 1439 Overprinted with the Philatelic Center emblem and: "1934 - 50th Anniversary - 1984"

1984, Dec. 1 Photo. *Perf. 13½*

1489	A641	10p multi	26

50th anniversary of the Buenos Aires Philatelic Center.

Vista Del Jardin Zoologico, by Fermin Eguia—A687

Paintings: No. 1491, El Congreso Iluminado, by Francisco Travieso. No. 1492, Galpones (La Boca), by Marcos Borio.

1984, Dec. 15 *Perf. 13½*

1490	A687	20p multi	40
1491	A687	20p multi, vert.	40
1492	A687	20p multi, vert.	40

Gen. Martin Miguel de Guemes (1785-1821)—A688

1985, Mar. 23 Litho. *Perf. 13½*

1493	A688	30p multi	40

ARGENTINA '85 Exhibition—A689

Premier airmail service from: 20p, Buenos Aires to Montevideo, 1917. 40p, Cordoba to Villa Dolores, 1925. 60p, Bahia Blanca to Comodoro Rivadavia, 1929. 80p, Argentina to Germany, 1934. 100p, naval service to the Antarctic, 1952.

1985, Apr. 27

1494	A689	20p Bleriot Gnome	25
1495	A689	40p Junker F-13L	50
1496	A689	60p Latte 25	75
1497	A689	80p L.Z. 127 Graf Zeppelin	1.00
1498	A689	100p Consolidated PBY Catalina	1.25
		Nos. 1494-1498 (5)	3.75

Central Bank, 50th Anniv.—A690

1985, June 1

1499	A690	80p Bank Bldg., Buenos Aires	90

Jose A. Ferreyra (1889-1943), Director of Munequitas Portenas—A691

Famous directors and their films: No. 1501, Leopoldo Torre Nilsson (1924-1978), scene from Martin Fierro.

1985, June 1

1500	A691	100p dk bl & multi	1.00
1501	A691	100p pale grn, Prus & multi	1.00

Carlos Gardel (1890-1935), Entertainer—A692

Paintings: No. 1502, Gardel playing the guitar on stage, by Carlos Alonso (b. 1929). No. 1503, Gardel in a wide-brimmed hat, by Hermegildo Sabat (b. 1933). No. 1504, Portrait of Gardel in an ornamental frame, by Aldo Severi (b. 1928) and Martiniano Arce (b. 1939).

1985, June 15

1502	A692	200p multi	1.25
1503	A692	200p multi	1.25
1504	A692	200p multi	1.25

The Arrival, by Pedro Figari—A693

Oil paintings (details): 30c, The Wagon Square, by C. B. de Quiros. No. 1507, A Halt on the Plains, by Prilidiano Pueyrredon.

1985, July 6 Litho. *Perf. 13½*

1505	A693	20c multi	1.25
1506	A693	30c multi	1.50

Souvenir Sheet *Perf. 12*

1507	Sheet of 2	3.00
a.	A693 20c Pilgrims, vert.	32
b.	A693 30c Wagon	48

ARGENTINA '85. No. 1507 contains 2 stamps (size: 30x40mm); multicolored margin continue the painting and is inscribed in silver with the exhibition and Inter-American Philatelic Federation emblems. Size: 146x74mm.

Buenos Aires to Montevideo, 1917 Teodoro Fels Flight—A694

Historic flight covers: No. 1508, Shown. No. 1509, Villa Dolores to Cordoba, 1925. No. 1510, Buenos Aires to France, 1929 St. Exupery flight. No. 1511, Buenos Aires to Bremerhaven, 1934 Graf Zeppelin flight. No. 1512, First Antarctic flight, 1952.

1985, July 13 *Perf. 12x12½*

1508	A694	10c emer & multi	50
1509	A694	10c ultra & multi	50
1510	A694	10c lt choc & multi	50
1511	A694	10c chnt & multi	50
1512	A694	10c ap grn & multi	50
		Nos. 1508-1512 (5)	2.50

ARGENTINA '85.

Illuminated Fruit, by Fortunato Lacamera (1887-1951)—A695

Paintings: 20c, Woman with Bird, by Juan del Prete (1897-?), vert.

1985, Sept. 7 *Perf. 13½*

1513	A695	20c multi	1.25
1514	A695	30c multi	1.50

Flower Types of 1982-85

1985, Sept. 7 Photo.

1515	A641	3c like #1441	15
1516	A641	5c like #1346	25
1517	A641	10c like #1348	40
1520	A641	50c like #1344	2.00
1522	A641	1a Begonia micranthera var. hieronymi	4.00
		Nos. 1515-1522 (15)	6.80

Folk Musical Instruments—A699

1985, Sept. 14 **Litho.** ***Perf. 13½***

1531	A699	20c Frame drum	75
1532	A699	20c Long flute	75
1533	A699	20c Jew's harp	75
1534	A699	20c Pan flutes	75
1535	A699	20c Musical bow	75
		Nos. 1531-1535 (5)	3.75

Juan Bautista Alberdi (1810-1884), Historian, Politician—A700

Famous men: Nicolas Avellaneda (1836-1885), President in 1874. 30c, Fr. Luis Beltran (1784-1827), military and naval engineer. 40c, Ricardo Levene (1885-1959), historian, author.

1985, Oct. 5

1536	A700	10c multi	30
1537	A700	20c multi	60
1538	A700	30c multi	90
1539	A700	40c multi	1.50

Skaters—A701

Deception, by J. H. Rivoira—A702

1985, Oct. 19 **Litho.** ***Perf. 13½***

1540	A701	20c multi	32
1541	A702	30c multi	48

Size: 147x75mm.

Imperf.

1542	A693	1a multi	1.75

IYY. No. 1542 is inscribed in silver with the UN 40th anniversary and IYY emblems.

Provincial Views—A703

Designs: No. 1543, Rock Window, Buenos Aires. No. 1544, Forclaz Windmill, Entre Rios. No. 1545, Lake Potrero de los Funes, San Luis. No. 1546, Mission church, north-east province. No. 1547, Penguin colony, Punta Tombo, Chubut. No. 1548, Water Mirrors, Cordoba.

1985, Nov. 23 ***Perf. 13½***

1543	A703	10c multi	16
1544	A703	10c multi	16
1545	A703	10c multi	16
1546	A703	10c multi	16
1547	A703	10c multi	16
1548	A703	10c multi	16
		Nos. 1543-1548 (6)	96

Christmas 1985—A704

Designs: 10c, Birth of Our Lord, by Carlos Cortes. 20c, Christmas, by Hector Viola.

1985, Dec. 7

1549	A704	10c multi	16
1550	A704	20c multi	32

Natl. Campaign for the Prevention of Blindness—A705

1985, Dec. 7

1551	A705	10c multi	16

Rio Gallegos City, Cent.—A716

1985, Dec. 21 **Litho.** ***Perf. 13½***

1552	A716	10c Church	20

Natl. Grape Harvest Festival, 50th Anniv.—A717

1986, Mar. 15

1553	A717	10c multi	20

Historical Architecture in Buenos Aires—A718

Designs: No. 1554, Valentin Alsina House, Italian Period, 1860-1870. No. 1555, House on Cerrito Street, French influence, 1880-1900. No. 1556, House on the Avenida de Mayo y Santiago del Estero, Art Nouveau, 1900-1910. No. 1557, Customs Building, academic architecture, 1900-1915. No. 1558, Isaac Fernandez Blanco Museum, house of architect Martin Noel, national restoration, 1910-1930. Nos. 1554-1556 vert.

1986, Apr. 19

1554	A718	20c multi	40
1555	A718	20c multi	40
1556	A718	20c multi	40
1557	A718	20c multi	40
1558	A718	20c multi	40
		Nos. 1554-1558 (5)	2.00

Antarctic Bases, Pioneers and Fauna—A719

Designs: No. 1559a, Base, Jubany. No. 1559b, Arctocephalus gazella. No. 1559c, Otaria byronia. No. 1559d, Gen. Belgrano Base. No. 1559e, Daption capensis. No. 1559f, Diomedia melanophris. No. 1559g, Apterodytes patagonica. No. 1559h, Macronectes giganteus. No. 1559i, Hugo Alberto Acuna (1885-1953). No. 1559j, Spheniscus magellanicus. No. 1559k, Gallinago gallinago. No. 1559 l, Capt. Agustin del Castillo (1855-1889).

1986, May 31

1559		Sheet of 12	2.50
a.-l.		A719 10c, any single	20

No. 1559 has margin picturing Antarctic postmarks. Size: 150x180mm.

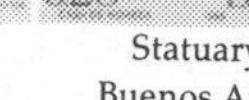

Famous People A720

Statuary, Buenos Aires A721

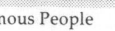

Designs: No. 1560, Dr. Alicia Moreau de Justo, human rights activist. No. 1561, Dr. Emilio Ravignani (1886-1954), historian. No. 1562, Indira Gandhi (1917-1984), prime minister of India.

1986, July 5 **Litho.** ***Perf. 13½***

1560	A720	10c multi	18
1561	A720	10c multi	18
1562	A720	30c multi	55

1986, July 5

Designs: 20c, Fountain of the Nereids, by Dolores Lola Mora (1866-1936). 30c, Lamenting at Work, by Rogelio Yrurtia (1879-1950), horiz.

1563	A721	20c multi	35
1564	A721	30c multi	55

Famous Men—A722

Designs: No. 1565, Francisco N. Laprida (1786-1829), politician. No. 1566, Estanislao Lopez (1786-1838), brigadier general. No. 1567, Francisco Ramirez (1786-1821), general.

1986, Aug. 9 **Litho.** ***Perf. 13***

1565	A722	20c dl yel, brn & blk	35
1566	A722	20c dl yel, brn & blk	35
1567	A722	20c dl yel, brn & blk	35

Fr. Ceferino Namuncura (1886-1905)—A723

1986, Aug. 30 ***Perf. 13½***

1568	A723	20c multi	35

Miniature Sheets

Natl. Team Victory, 1986 World Cup Soccer Championships, Mexico—A724

Designs: No. 1569a-1569d, Team. Nos. 1569e-1569h, Shot on goal. Nos. 1570a-1570d, Action close-up. Nos. 1570e-1570h, Diego Maradona holding soccer cup.

1986, Nov. 8 **Litho.** ***Perf. 13½***

1569	Sheet of 8	9.20
a.-h.	A724 75c, any single	1.15
1570	Sheet of 8	9.20
a.-h.	A724 75c, any single	1.15

Nos. 1569-1570 have bright blue and black margins inscribed with final scores. Sizes: 120x171mm.

San Francisco (Cordoba), Cent.—A725

1986, Nov. 8

1571	A725	20c Municipal Building	32

Trelew City (Chubut), Cent.—A726

1986, Nov. 22 **Litho.** ***Perf. 13½***

1572	A726	20c Old railroad station, 1865	30

Mutualism Day—A727

1986, Nov. 22

1573	A727	20c multi	30

Christmas—A728

Designs: 20c, Naif retable, by Aniko Szabo (b. 1945). 30c, Everyone's Tree, by Franca Delacqua (b. 1947).

1986, Dec. 13 **Litho.** ***Perf. 13½***

1574	A728	20c multi	30
1575	A728	30c multi	45

Santa Rosa de Lima, 400th Birth Anniv. A729

Rio Cuarto Municipal Building A730

1986, Dec. 13

1576	A729	50c multi	75

1986, Dec. 20

1577	A730	20c shown	30
1578	A730	20c Court Building, Cordoba	30

Rio Cuarto City, bicent. Court Building, Cordoba, 50th anniv.

Antarctic Treaty, 25th Anniv.—A731

1987, Mar. 7 **Litho.** ***Perf. 13½***

1579	A731	20c Marine biologist	30
1580	A731	30c Ornithologist	45

Souvenir Sheet

Perf. 12

1581	Sheet of 2	75
a.	A731 20c like No. 1579	30
b.	A731 30c like No. 1580	45

No. 1581 contains 2 stamps (size: 40x50mm); multicolored margin pictures penguin and offspring. Size: 160x90mm.

Natl. Mortgage Bank, Cent.—A732

1987, Mar. 21 ***Perf. 13½***

1582	A732	20c multi	30

Natl. Cooperative Associations Movement—A733

1987, Mar. 21

1583	A733	20c multi	30

SEMI-POSTAL STAMPS.

Samuel F. B. Morse SP1

Globe SP2

Landing of Columbus SP5

Designs: 10c+5c, Alexander Graham Bell. 25c+15c, Rowland Hill.

Wmkd. RA in Sun. (90)

1944, Jan. 5 Lithographed *Perf. 13*

B1	SP1	3c	+2c lt vio & sl bl	60	35
B2	SP2	5c	+5c dl red & sl bl	1.25	30
B3	SP1	10c	+5c org & sl bl	2.50	90
B4	SP1	25c	+15c red brn & sl bl	3.25	1.50
B5	SP5	1p	+50c lt grn & sl bl	16.00	12.00
	Nos. B1-B5 (5)			23.60	15.05

The surtax was for the Postal Employees Benefit Association.

Map of Argentina SP6

1944, Feb. 17 *Perf. 13* Wmk. 90

B6	SP6	5c	+10c ol yel & sl	1.50	75
B7	SP6	5c	+50c vio brn & sl	6.00	3.00
B8	SP6	5c	+1p dl org & sl	17.50	12.50
B9	SP6	5c	+20p dp bl & sl	45.00	25.00

The surtax was for the victims of the San Juan earthquake.

Souvenir Sheets

National Anthem and Flag SP7

1944, July 17 ***Imperf.***

B10	SP7	5c	+1p vio brn & lt bl	3.00	3.00
B11	SP7	5c	+50p bl blk & lt bl	450.00	400.00

The sheets measure 75x110mm. The surtax was for the needy in the provinces of La Rioja and Catamarca.

Stamp Designing
SP8

1950, Aug. 26 Photo. *Perf. 13½*

B12	SP8	10c +10c vio	40	40

Issued to publicize the Argentine International Philatelic Exhibition, 1950.
See also Nos. CB1-CB5 and note after No. CB5.

Poliomyelitis Victim
SP9

1956, Apr. 14 *Perf. 13½x13*

B13	SP9	20c +30c sl	40	15

The surtax was for the poliomyelitis fund. Head in design is from Correggio's "Antiope," Louvre.

Stamp of 1858 and Mail Coach on Raft
SP10

Designs: 2.40p+1.20p, Album, magnifying glass and stamp of 1858. 4.40p+2.20p, Government seat of Confederation, Parana.

Lithographed

1958, Mar. 29 *Perf. 13½* Wmk. 90

B14	SP10	40c +20c brt grn & dl pur	50	35
B15	SP10	2.40p +1.20p ol gray & bl	60	40
B16	SP10	4.40p +2.20p lt bl & dp cl	90	60
		Nos. B14-B16, CB8-CB12 (8)	8.80	7.05

The surtax was for the International Centennial Philatelic Exhibition, Paraná, Entre Rios, April 19-27.

View of Flooded Land
SP11

1958, Oct. 4 Photo. *Perf. 13½*

B17	SP11	40c +20c brn	15	10

The surtax was for flood victims in the Buenos Aires district. See Nos. CB13-CB14.

Child Receiving Blood
SP12

Runner
SP13

1958, Dec. 20 Litho. Wmk. 90

B18	SP12	1p +50c blk & rose red	20	15

The surtax went to the Anti-Leukemia Foundation.

1959, Sept. 5 *Perf. 13½*

Designs: 50c+20c, Basketball players (vert.). 1p+50c, Boxers (vert.).

B19	SP13	20c +10c emer & blk	30	25
B20	SP13	50c +20c yel & blk	20	20
B21	SP13	1p +50c mar & blk	25	25
		Nos. B19-B21, CB15-CB16 (5)	2.25	1.85

Issued to commemorate the third Pan American Games, Chicago, Aug. 27-Sept. 7, 1959.

Condor
SP14

Birds: 50c+20c, Fork-tailed flycatchers. 1p+50c, Magellanic woodpecker.

1960, Feb. 6

B22	SP14	20c +10c dk bl	12	10
B23	SP14	50c +20c dp vio bl	20	12
B24	SP14	1p +50c brn & buff	30	15
		Nos. B22-B24, CB17-CB18(5)	1.62	1.12

The surtax was for child welfare work. See also No. B30, CB29.

Souvenir Sheet

Uprooted Oak Emblem—SP15

1960, Apr. 7 *Imperf.* Wmk. 90

B25	SP15	Sheet of two	1.75	1.75
a.		1p+50c bis & car	75	75
b.		4.20p+2.10p ap grn & dp cl	75	75

Issued to publicize World Refugee Year, July 1, 1959—June 30, 1960. No. B25 measures 112x84mm. with deep claret marginal inscription.
The surtax was for aid to refugees.

Jacaranda
SP16

Flowers: 1p+1p, Passionflower. 3p+3p, Orchid. 5p+5p, Tabebuia.

1960, Dec. 3 Photo. *Perf. 13½*

B26	SP16	50c +50c dp bl	12	8
B27	SP16	1p +1p bluish grn	20	12
B28	SP16	3p +3p hn brn	45	30
B29	SP16	5p +5p dk brn	75	50

Issued to publicize "TEMEX 61" (International Thematic Exposition).

Type of 1960

Bird: 4.20p+2.10p, Blue-eyed shag.

1961, Feb. 25 *Perf. 13½* Wmk. 90

B30	SP14	4.20p +2.10p chnt brn	75	50

The surtax was for child welfare work. See also No. CB29.

Nos. B26-B29 Overprinted in Black, Brown, Blue or Red:
"14 DE ABRIL DIA DE LAS AMERICAS"

1961, Apr. 15

B31	SP16	50c +50c dp bl	12	12
B32	SP16	1p +1p bluish grn (Brn)	20	15
B33	SP16	3p +3p hn brn (Bl)	45	35
B34	SP16	5p +5p dk brn (R)	75	60

Day of the Americas, Apr. 14.

Cathedral, Cordoba
SP17

Stamp of 1862
SP18

Flight into Egypt, by Ana Maria Moncalvo
SP19

Design: 10p+10p, Cathedral, Buenos Aires.

Photogravure

1961, Oct. 21 *Perf. 13½* Wmk. 90

B35	SP17	2p +2p rose cl	30	20
B36	SP18	3p +3p grn	45	25
B37	SP17	10p +10p brt bl	1.25	75
a.		Souvenir sheet of 3	2.25	1.50

Issued to publicize the 1962 International Stamp Exhibition.
No. B37a contains three imperf. stamps similar to Nos. B35-B37 in dark blue. Violet brown marginal inscription. Size: 85x86mm.

1961, Dec. 16 Lithographed

B38	SP19	2p +1p lil & blk brn	20	12
B39	SP19	10p +5p lt cl & dp cl	75	20

The surtax was for child welfare.

Chalk-browed Mockingbird
SP20

Soccer
SP21

Design: 12p+6p, Rufous-collared sparrow.

1962, Dec. 29 *Perf. 13½* Wmk. 90

B40	SP20	4p +2p bis, brn & bl grn	1.25	1.00
B41	SP20	12p +6p gray, yel, grn & brn	2.25	1.75

The surtax was for child welfare. See also Nos. B44, B47, B48-B50, CB32, CB35-CB36.

1963, May 18 *Perf. 13½* Wmk. 90

Design: 12p+6p, Horsemanship.

B42	SP21	4p +2p brt pink, grn & blk	30	15
B43	SP21	12p +6p sal, dk car & blk	65	50
a.		Dark car (jacket) omitted		

Issued to commemorate the 4th Pan American Games, Sao Paulo. See also No. CB31.

Bird Type of 1962.

Design: Vermilion flycatcher.

1963, Dec. 21 Lithographed

B44	SP20	4p +2p blk, red, org & grn	75	50

The surtax was for child welfare. See also No. CB32.

Fencers
SP22

Design: 4p+2p, National Stadium, Tokyo (horiz.).

1964, July 18 *Perf. 13½* Wmk. 90

B45	SP22	4p +2p red, ocher & brn	25	20
B46	SP22	12p +6p bl grn & blk	60	50

Issued to publicize the 18th Olympic Games, Tokyo, Oct. 10-25, 1964. See also No. CB33.

Bird Type of 1962

Design: Red-crested cardinal.

1964, Dec. 23 Lithographed

B47	SP20	4p +2p dk bl, red & grn	1.00	50

The surtax was for child welfare. See also No. CB35.

Bird Type of 1962
Inscribed "R. ARGENTINA"

Designs: 8p+4p, Lapwing. 10p+5p, Scarlet-headed marshbird (horiz.). 20p+10p, Amazon kingfisher.

1966-67 *Perf. 13½* Wmk. 90

B48	SP20	8p +4p blk, ol, brt grn & red	1.00	50
B49	SP20	10p +5p blk, bl, org & grn ('67)	1.00	75
B50	SP20	20p +10p blk, yel, bl & pink ('67)	60	50

The surtax was for child welfare.
Issue dates: 8p+4p, Mar. 26, 1966. 10p+5p, Jan. 14, 1967. 20p+10p, Dec. 23, 1967.
See also Nos. CB36, CB38-CB39.

Grandmother's Birthday, by Patricia Lynch; Lions Emblem—SP23

Perf. 12½x13½

1968, Dec. 14 Litho. Wmk. 90

B51	SP23	40p +20p multi	60	50

Issued to publicize the First Lions International Benevolent Philatelic Exhibition. The surtax was for the Children's Hospital Benevolent Fund.

White-faced Tree Duck SP24

1969, Sept. 20 *Perf. 13½* Wmk. 365

B52	SP24	20p +10p multi	60	50

The surtax was for child welfare. See No. CB40.

Slender-tailed Woodstar (Hummingbird) SP25

1970, May 9 *Perf. 13½* Wmk. 365

B53	SP25	20c +10c multi	70	60

The surtax was for child welfare. See Nos. CB41, B56–B59, B62–B63.

Dolphinfish—SP26

1971, Feb. 20 *Perf. 12½* Unwmkd.

Size: 75x15mm.

B54	SP26	20c +10c multi	70	60

The surtax was for child welfare. See No. CB42.

Children with Stamps, by Mariette Lydis SP27

1971, Dec. 18 Litho. *Perf. 13½*

B55	SP27	1p +50p multi	75	50

2nd Lions International Solidarity Stamp Exhibition.

Bird Type of 1970

Birds: 25c+10c, Saffron finch. 65c+30c, Rufous-bellied thrush (horiz.).

1972, May 6 *Perf. 13½* Unwmkd.

B56	SP25	25c +10c multi	50	30
B57	SP25	65c +30c multi	70	50

Surtax was for child welfare.

Bird Type of 1970

Birds: 50c+25c, Southern screamer (chaja). 90c+45c, Saffron-cowled blackbird (horiz.).

1973, Apr. 28

B58	SP25	50c +25c multi	60	50
B59	SP25	90c +45c multi	90	75

Surtax was for child welfare.

Painting Type of Regular Issue

Designs: 15c+15c, Still Life, by Alfredo Guttero (horiz.). 90c+90c, Nude, by Miguel C. Victorica (horiz.).

1973, Aug. 28 Litho. *Perf. 13½*

B60	A472	15c +15c multi	40	25
B61	A472	90c +90c multi	1.40	1.00

Philatelists' Day.

Bird Type of 1970

Birds: 70c+30c, Blue seed-eater. 1.20p +60c, Hooded siskin.

1974, May 11 Litho. *Perf. 13½*

B62	SP25	70c +30c multi	70	50
B63	SP25	1.20p +60c multi	1.10	60

Surtax was for child welfare.

Painting Type of 1974

Design: 70c+30c, The Lama, by Juan Batlle Planas.

1974, May 11 Litho. *Perf. 13½*

B64	A477	70c +30c multi	40	30

PRENFIL-74 UPU, International Exhibition of Philatelic Periodicals, Buenos Aires, Oct. 1–12.

Plush-crested Jay SP28

Designs: 13p+6.50p, Golden-collared macaw. 20p+10p, Begonia. 40p+20p, Teasel.

1976, June 12 Litho. *Perf. 13½*

B65	SP28	7p +3.50p multi	30	20
B66	SP28	13p +6.50p multi	50	30
B67	SP28	20p +10p multi	75	50
B68	SP28	40p +20p multi	1.50	75

Argentine philately.

Telegraph, Communications Satellite SP29

Designs: 20p+10p, Old and new mail trucks. 60p+30p, Old, new packet boats. 70p+35p, Biplane and jet.

1977, July 16 Litho. *Perf. 13½*

B69	SP29	10p +5p multi	35	25
B70	SP29	20p +10p multi	60	75
B71	SP29	60p +30p multi	1.25	1.00
B72	SP29	70p +35p multi	1.50	1.00

Surtax was for Argentine philately.
No. B70 exists with wmk. 365.

Church of St. Francis Type, 1977, Inscribed: "EXPOSICION ARGENTINA '77"

1977, Aug. 27

B73	A515	160p +80p multi	3.50	3.00

Surtax was for Argentina '77 Philatelic Exhibition. Issued in sheets of 4.

No. B73 Overprinted with Soccer Cup Emblem

1978, Feb. 4 Litho. *Perf. 13½*

B74	A515	160p +80p multi	7.50	7.00
a.		Souvenir sheet of 4	25.00	20.00

11th World Cup Soccer Championship, Argentina, June 1–25.

No. B74a contains 4 No. B74, light blue margin with black inscription. Size: 103x133mm.

Spinus Magellanicus SP30

Birds: 100p+100p, Variable seedeater. 150p+150p, Yellow thrush. 200p+200p, Pyrocephalus rubineus. 500p+500p, Great kiskadee.

1978, Aug. 5 Litho. *Perf. 13½*

B75	SP30	50p +50p multi	1.50	1.00
B76	SP30	100p +100p multi	1.75	1.50
B77	SP30	150p +150p multi	2.25	2.00
B78	SP30	200p +200p multi	3.00	3.00
B79	SP30	500p +500p multi	14.00	12.00
		Nos. B75-B79 (5)	22.50	19.50

ARGENTINA '78, Inter-American Philatelic Exhibition, Buenos Aires, Oct. 27–Nov. 5. Nos. B75–B79 issued in sheets of 4 with marginal inscriptions commemorating Exhibition and 1978 Soccer Championship.

Caravel "Magdalena," 16th Century SP31

Sailing Ships: 500+500p, Three master "Rio de la Plata," 17th century. 600+600p, Corvette "Descubierta," 18th century. 1500+1500p, Naval Academy yacht "A.R.A. Fortuna," 1979.

1979, Sept. 8 Litho. *Perf. 13½*

B80	SP31	400p +400p multi	6.00	4.00
B81	SP31	500p +500p multi	7.50	5.00
B82	SP31	600p +600p multi	9.00	6.00
B83	SP31	1500p +1500p multi	22.50	15.00

Buenos Aires '80, International Philatelic Exhibition, Buenos Aires, Oct. 24-Nov. 2, 1980. Issued in sheets of 4.

Purmamarca Church—SP32

Churches: 200p + 100p, Molinos. 300p + 150p, Animana. 400p + 200p, San Jose de Lules.

1979, Nov. 3 Litho. *Perf. 13½*

B84	SP32	100p +50p multi	22	15
B85	SP32	200p +100p multi	42	20
B86	SP32	300p +150p multi	65	30
B87	SP32	400p +200p multi	85	40

Buenos Aires No. 3, Exhibition and Society Emblems—SP33

Argentine Stamps: 750p+750p, type A588. 1000p+1000p, No. 91. 2000p+2000p, type A588.

1979, Dec. 15 Litho. *Perf. 13½*

B88	SP33	250p +250p multi	1.25	1.00
B89	SP33	750p +750p multi	3.25	2.50
B90	SP33	1000p +1000p multi	4.25	3.50
B91	SP33	2000p +2000p multi	8.50	7.00

PRENFIL '80, International Philatelic Literature and Publications Exhibition, Buenos Aires, Nov. 7-16, 1980. Multicolored margins show Exhibition and Society emblems. Size: 89×60mm.

Minuet, by Carlos E. Pellegrini—SP34

Paintings: 700p+350p, Media Cana, by Carlos Morel. 800p+400p, Cielito, by Pellegrini. 1000p+500p, El Gato, by Juan Leon Palliere.

1981, July 11 Litho. *Perf. 13½*

B92	SP34	500 + 250p multi	1.00	50
B93	SP34	700 + 350p multi	1.50	1.00
B94	SP34	800 + 400p multi	1.50	1.25
B95	SP34	1000 + 500p multi	2.00	1.75

Espamer '81 Intl. Stamp Exhibition (Americas, Spain, Portugal), Buenos Aires, Nov. 13-22.

Canal, by Beatriz Bongliani (b. 1933)—SP35

Tapestries: 1000p+500p, Shadows, by Silvia Sieburger (vert.). 2000p+1000p, Interpretation of a Rectangle, by Silke R. de Haupt (vert.). 4000p+2000p, Tilcara, by Tana Sachs.

1982, July 31 Litho. *Perf. 13½*

B96	SP35	1000 +500p multi	25	25
B97	SP35	2000 +1000p multi	50	50
B98	SP35	3000 +1500p multi	75	75
B99	SP35	4000 +2000p multi	1.00	1.00

Boy Playing Marbles—SP36

1983, July 2 **Litho.** ***Perf. 13½***

B100	SP36	20c +10c shown	10	10
B101	SP36	30c +15c Jumping rope	50	25
B102	SP36	50c +25c Hopscotch	50	30
B103	SP36	1p +50c Flying kites	90	75
B104	SP36	2p +1p Spinning top	1.00	1.00
		Nos. B100-B104 (5)	3.00	2.40

Surtax was for youth programs.

See Nos. B106-B110.

Compass, 15th Cent.—SP37

ARGENTINA '85 Intl. Stamp Show: b. Arms of Spain, Argentina. c. Columbus' arms. d.-f. Columbus' arrival at San Salvador Island. Nos. B105d-B105f in continuous design; ships shown on singles range in size, left to right, from small to large. Surtax was for exhibition.

1984, Apr. 28 **Litho.** ***Perf. 13½***

B105	Block of 6	4.00	2.00
a-f.	SP37 5p+2.50p, any single	65	32

Children's Game Type of 1983

1984, July 7 **Litho.** ***Perf. 13½***

B106	SP36	2p +1p Blind Man's Bluff	25	20
B107	SP36	3p +1.50p The Loop	50	40
B108	SP36	4p +2p Leap Frog	60	50
B109	SP36	5p +2.50p Rolling the loop	75	60
B110	SP36	6p +3p Ball Mold	90	75
		Nos. B106-B110 (5)	3.00	2.45

Butterflies—SP38

1985, Nov. 9 **Litho.** ***Perf. 13½***

B111	SP38	5c + 2c Rothschildia jacobaeae	10
B112	SP38	10C + 5c Heliconius erato phyllis	24
B113	SP38	20c + 10c Precis evarete hilaris	48
B114	SP38	25c +13c Cyanopepla pretiosa	60
B115	SP38	40c +20c Papilio androgeus	95
		Nos. B111-B115 (5)	2.37

Children's Drawings—SP39

1986, Aug. 30 **Litho.**

B116	SP39	5c +2c N. Pastor	10
B117	SP39	10c +5c T. Valleistein	24
B118	SP39	20c +10c J.M. Flores	48
B119	SP39	25c +13c M.E. Pezzuto	60
B120	SP39	40c +20c E. Diehl	95
		Nos. B116-B120 (5)	2.37

Surtax for natl. philatelic associations.

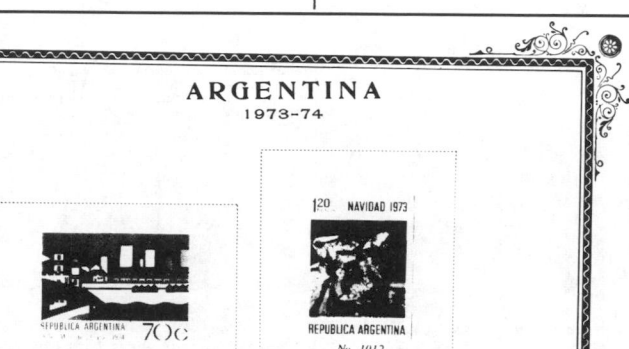

AIR POST STAMPS.

Airplane Circles the Globe
AP1

Eagle
AP2

Wings Cross the Sea
AP3

Condor on Mountain Crag
AP4

Perforations of Nos. C1-C37 vary from clean-cut to rough and uneven, with many skipped perfs.

Lithographed

Wmkd. RA in Sun. (90)

1928, Mar. 1 ***Perf. 13x13½, 13½x13***

C1	AP1	5c lt red	1.75	75
C2	AP1	10c Prus bl	3.50	1.25
C3	AP2	15c lt brn	3.50	1.25
C4	AP1	18c lil gray	5.00	4.00
a.		18c brn lil	5.50	4.00
b.		Double impression	*500.00*	
C5	AP2	20c ultra	3.50	1.25
C6	AP2	24c dp bl	6.00	4.00
C7	AP3	25c brt vio	6.00	2.00
C8	AP3	30c rose red	8.50	1.50
C9	AP4	35c rose	6.00	1.50
C10	AP1	36c bis brn	4.00	2.00
C11	AP4	50c gray blk	6.00	75
C12	AP2	54c chocolate	6.00	3.00
C13	AP2	72c yel grn	7.00	3.00
a.		Double impression	*400.00*	
C14	AP3	90c dk brn	14.00	2.75
C15	AP3	1p sl bl & red	17.50	1.00
C16	AP3	1.08p rose & dk bl	25.00	7.00
C17	AP4	1.26p dl vio & grn	32.50	12.00
C18	AP4	1.80p bl & lil rose	32.50	12.00
C19	AP4	3.60p gray & bl	65.00	30.00
		Nos. C1-C19 (19)	253.25	91.00

The watermark on No. C4a is larger than on the other stamps of this set, measuring 10 mm. across Sun.

Zeppelin First Flight.

Air Post Stamps of 1928 Overprinted in Blue

1930, May

C20	AP2	20c ultra	16.00	10.00
C21	AP4	50c gray blk	32.50	20.00
a.		Invtd. ovpt.	*750.00*	
C22	AP3	1p sl bl & red	35.00	20.00
a.		Invtd. ovpt.	*1,100.*	
C23	AP4	1.80p bl & lil rose	90.00	50.00
C24	AP4	3.60p gray & bl	250.00	150.00
		Nos. C20-C24 (5)	423.50	250.00

Overprinted in Green.

C25	AP2	20c ultra	15.00	10.00
C26	AP4	50c gray blk	20.00	12.50

C27 AP3 90c dk brn 15.00 10.00
C28 AP3 1p sl bl & red 35.00 20.00
C29 AP4 1.80p bl & lil rose 1,100. 750.00
a. Thick paper 1,200.
Nos. C25-C29 (5) 1,185. 802.50

Air Post Stamps of 1928 Overprinted in Red — **1930 6 Septiembre -1931-**

1931

C30 AP1 18c lil gray 3.50 1.50
C31 AP2 72c yel grn 25.00 16.00

Overprinted in Red or Blue — **6 de Septiembre 1930 — 1931**

C32 AP3 90c dk brn 25.00 16.00
C33 AP4 1.80p bl & lil rose (Bl) 50.00 30.00
C34 AP4 3.60p gray & bl 100.00 60.00
Nos. C30-C34 (5) 203.50 123.50

Issued in commemoration of the first anniversary of the Revolution of 1930.

Zeppelin Issue.

Air Post Stamps of 1928 Overprinted in Blue or Red — **GRAF ZEPPELIN 1932**

1932, Aug. 4

C35 AP1 5c lt red (Bl) 4.00 2.50
C36 AP1 18c lil gray (R) 18.00 11.00
a. 18c brn lil (R) 110.00 65.00

Overprinted **GRAF ZEPPELIN 1932**

C37 AP3 90c dk brn (R) 30.00 25.00

Plane and Letter
AP5

Mercury
AP6

Plane in Flight
AP7

Photogravure
Wmkd. RA in Sun. (90)

1940, Oct. 23 *Perf. 13½x13, 13x13½*

C38 AP5 30c dp org 10.00 15
C39 AP6 50c dk brn 15.00 25
C40 AP5 1p carmine 3.00 10
C41 AP7 1.25p dp grn 75 15
C42 AP5 2.50p brt bl 2.50 25
Nos. C38-C42 (5) 31.25 90

Plane and Letter
AP8

Mercury and Plane
AP9

Perf. 13½x13, 13x13½

1942, Oct. 6 Lithographed Wmk. 90

C43 AP8 30c orange 25 5
C44 AP9 50c dl brn & buff 60 5

See also Nos. C49–C52, C57, C61.

Plane over Iguaçu Falls
AP10

Plane over the Andes
AP11

Perf. 13½x13

1946, June 10 Unwmkd.

C45 AP10 15c dl red brn 40 8
C46 AP11 25c gray grn 25 8

See also Nos. C53–C54.

Allegory of Flight
AP12

Astrolabe
AP13

Surface-Tinted Paper.

Perf. 13½x13, 13x13½.

1946, Sept. 25 Litho. Unwmkd.

C47 AP12 15c sl grn, *pale grn* 90 25
C48 AP13 60c vio brn, *ocher* 90 40

Types of 1942.

1946–48 *Perf. 13½x13* Unwmkd.

C49 AP8 30c orange 2.25 10
C50 AP9 50c dl brn & buff 4.00 25
C51 AP8 1p car ('47) 2.00 20
C52 AP8 2.50p brt bl ('48) 9.00 1.25

Types of 1946.

1948 Wmk. 90

C53 AP10 15c dl red brn 20 10
C54 AP11 25c gray grn 40 10

Atlas (National Museum, Naples)
AP14

Map of Argentine Republic, Globe and Caliper—AP15

Perf. 13½x13, 13x13½.

1948-49 Photogravure. Wmk. 288

C55 AP14 45c dk brn ('49) 50 25
C56 AP15 70c dk grn 75 35

Issued to commemorate the 4th Pan-American Reunion of Cartographers, Buenos Aires, October–November, 1948.

Mercury Type of 1942.

Lithographed

1949 *Perf. 13x13½* Wmk. 288

C57 AP9 50c dl brn & buff 60 18

Marksmanship Trophy
AP16

1949, Nov. 4 Photogravure.

C58 AP16 75c brown 1.10 30

World Rifle Championship, 1949.

Douglas DC-3 and Condor
AP17

Perf. 13x13½.

1951, June 20 Wmk. 90

C59 AP17 20c dk ol grn 20 8

10th anniversary of the State air lines.

Douglas DC-6 and Condor
AP18

1951, Oct. 17 *Perf. 13½.*

C60 AP18 20c blue 20 9

End of Argentine 5-year Plan.

Plane-Letter Type of 1942.

Lithographed

1951 *Perf. 13½x13* Wmk. 90

C61 AP8 1p carmine 50 18

Jesus by Leonardo da Vinci (detail, "Virgin of the Rocks")
AP19

Perf. 13½x13

1956, Sept. 29 Photo. Wmk. 90

C62 AP19 1p dl pur 50 20

Issued to express the gratitude of the children of Argentina to the people of the world for their help against poliomyelitis.

Battle of Montevideo
AP20

Leonardo Rosales and Tomas Espora
AP21

Guillermo Brown
AP22

Map of Americas and Arms of Buenos Aires
AP23

1957, March 2 *Perf. 13½*

C63 AP20 60c bl gray 20 10
C64 AP21 1p brt pink 20 10
C65 AP22 2p brown 35 15

Issued to commemorate the centenary of the death of Admiral Guillermo Brown, founder of the Argentine navy.

1957, Aug. 16

C66 AP23 2p rose vio 60 25

Issued to publicize the Inter-American Economic Conference in Buenos Aires.

Modern Locomotive
AP24

1957, Aug. 31 *Perf. 13½* Wmk. 90

C67 AP24 60c gray 15 8

Centenary of Argentine railroads.

Globe, Flag and Compass Rose
AP25

Design: 2p, Key.

1957, Sept. 14

C68	AP25	1p redsh brn	25	10
C69	AP25	2p Prus bl	40	12

Issued to publicize the 1957 International Congress for Tourism.

Birds Carrying Letters
AP26

1957, Nov. 6

C70	AP26	1p brt bl	20	8

Issued for Letter Writing Week, Oct. 6–12.

Early Plane
AP27

1958, May 31 *Perf. 13½* Wmk. 90

C71	AP27	2p maroon	25	18

Issued to commemorate the 50th anniversary of the Argentine Aviation Club.

Stamp of 1858 and "The Post of Santa Fe"
AP28

Design: 80c, Stamp of Buenos Aires and view of the Plaza de la Aduana.

1958 Lithographed *Perf. 13½*

C72	AP28	80c pale bis & sl bl	25	10
C73	AP28	1p red org & dk bl	30	18

Issued to commemorate the centenary of the first postage stamps of Buenos Aires and the Argentine Confederation.
Issue dates: 80c, Oct. 18; 1p, Aug. 23.

Comet Jet over World Map
AP29

1959, May 16 *Perf. 13½* Wmk. 90

C74	AP29	5p blk & ol	40	10

Issued to commemorate the inauguration of jet flights by Argentine Airlines.

Type of Regular Issue, 1960.

"Cabildo" and: 1.80p, Mariano Moreno. 5p, Manuel Belgrano and Juan José Castelli.

Photogravure

1960, May 28 *Perf. 13½* Wmk. 90

C75	A287	1.80p red brn	20	10
a.		Souvenir sheet of 3	90	60
C76	A287	5p buff & pur	45	15
a.		Souvenir sheet of 3	2.00	1.25

Issued to commemorate the 150th anniversary of the May Revolution.

Souvenir sheets are imperf. No. C75a contains one No. C75 and 1p and 2p resembling Nos. 713–714; stamps in reddish brown, marginal inscriptions in green. No. C76a contains one No. C76 and 4.20p and 10.70p resembling Nos. 715–716; stamps are in green, marginal inscriptions in reddish brown. Sheet size: 152x106mm.

Symbolic of New Provinces
AP30

1960, July 8 Lithographed

C77	AP30	1.80p dp car & bl	20	10

Issued to commemorate the elevation of the territories of Chubut, Formosa, Neuquen, Rio Negro and Santa Cruz to provinces.

Type of Regular Issue, 1960
Photogravure

1960, Oct. 1 *Perf. 13½* Wmk. 90

C78	A291	1.80p rose lil	25	10
C79	A291	10.70p brt grnsh bl	60	25

Issued to commemorate the 8th Congress of the Postal Union of the Americas and Spain.

UNESCO Emblem
AP31

1962, July 14 Lithographed

C80	AP31	13p ocher & brn	60	40

Issued to commemorate the 15th anniversary of UNESCO (U.N. Educational, Scientific and Cultural Organization).

Mail Coach
AP32

1962, Oct. 6 *Perf. 13½* Wmk. 90

C81	AP32	5.60p gray brn & blk	30	15

Mailman's Day, Sept. 14, 1962.

No. 695 and Type of 1959 Surcharged in Green

AEREO
5 60 PESOS

1962, Oct. 31 Photogravure

C82	A277	5.60p on 5p brn	40	20
C83	A277	18p on 5p brn, *grnsh*	1.50	30

UPAE Emblem
AP33

Skylark
AP34

Photogravure

1962, Nov. 24 *Perf. 13½* Wmk. 90

C84	AP33	5.60p dk bl	25	15

Issued to commemorate the 50th anniversary of the founding of the Postal Union of the Americas and Spain, UPAE.

1963, Feb. 9 Lithographed

Design: 11p, Super Albatros.

C85	AP34	5.60p bl & blk	25	15
C86	AP34	11p bl, blk & red	45	20

9th World Gliding Championships.

Symbolic Plane
AP35

1963–65 *Perf. 13½* Wmk. 90

C87	AP35	5.60p dk pur, car & brt grn	50	20
C88	AP35	7p blk & bis ('64)	75	15
C88A	AP35	7p blk & bis ('65)	6.00	75
C89	AP35	11p blk, dk pur & grn	75	35
C90	AP35	18p dk pur, red & vio bl	1.50	50
C91	AP35	21p brn, red & gray	2.00	75
		Nos. C87-C91 (6)	11.50	2.70

"Argentina" reads down on No. C88, up on No. C88A. See also Nos. C101–C104, C108–C111, C123–C126, C135–C141.

Type of Regular Issue, 1964

Design: 18p, Map of Falkland Islands (Islas Malvinas).

1964, Feb. 22 *Perf. 13½* Wmk. 90
Size: 33x22mm.

C92	A327	18p lt & dk bl & ol grn	2.50	1.00

Issued to commemorate the 60th anniversary of Argentina's claim to Antarctic territories.

U.P.U. Monument, Bern, and U.N. Emblem
AP36

Engraved

1964, May 23 *Perf. 13½* Wmk. 90

C93	AP36	18p red & dk brn	75	30

Issued to commemorate the 15th Universal Postal Union Congress, Vienna, Austria, May–June 1964.

Discovery of America, Florentine Woodcut
AP37

1964, Oct. 10 Lithographed

C94	AP37	13p tan & blk	45	25

Issued for the Day of the Race, Columbus Day.

Lt. Matienzo Base, Antarctica
AP38

1965, Feb. 27 Photo. *Perf. 13½*

C95	AP38	11p sal pink	75	2

Issued to publicize the national territory of Tierra del Fuego, Antarctic and South Atlantic Isles.

No. C88A Overprinted in Silver: "PRIMERAS / JORNADAS FILATELICAS / RIOPLATENSES"

1965, Mar. 17 Lithographed

C96	AP35	7p blk & bis	30	2

Issued to commemorate the First Rio de la Plata Stamp Show, sponsored jointly by the Argentine and Uruguayan Philatelic Associations, Montevideo, March 19–28.

ITU Emblem
AP39

Ascending Rocket
AP40

1965, May 11 *Perf. 13½* Wmk. 90

C97	AP39	18p sl, blk & red	60	30

Issued to commemorate the centenary of the International Telecommunication Union.

1965, May 29 Photo. *Perf. 13½*

Design: 50p, Earth with trajectories and magnetic field (horiz.).

C98	AP40	18p vermilion	60	30
C99	AP40	50p dp vio bl	1.50	65

Issued to commemorate the 6th Symposium on Space Research, held in Buenos Aires, and to honor the National Commission of Space Research.

Type of 1963–65 Inscribed "Republica Argentina" Reading Down

1965, Oct. 13 Litho. Wmk. 90

C101	AP35	12p dk car rose & brn	2.00	30
C102	AP35	15p vio bl & dk red	1.25	40
C103	AP35	27.50p dk bl grn & gray	2.00	60
C104	AP35	30.50p dk brn & dk bl	3.00	75

Argentine Antarctica Map and Centaur Rocket
AP41

1966, Feb. 19 *Perf. 13½* Wmk. 90

C105	AP41	27.50p bl, blk & dp org	1.50	1.00

Issued to commemorate the launchings of sounding balloons and of a Gamma Centaur rocket in Antarctica during February, 1965.

Sea Gull and Southern Cross
AP42

1966, May 14 ***Perf. 13½*** **Wmk. 90**

C106 AP42 12p Prus bl, blk & red 40 20

Issued to commemorate the 50th anniversary of the Naval Aviation School.

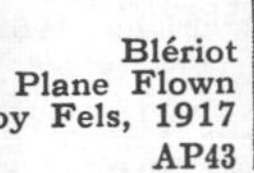

Blériot Plane Flown by Fels, 1917
AP43

1967, Sept. 2 **Litho.** ***Perf. 13½***

C107 AP43 26p ol, bl & blk 40 15

Issued to commemorate the flight by Theodore Fels from Buenos Aires to Montevideo, Sept. 2, 1917, allegedly the first International airmail flight.

Type of 1963–65 Inscribed "Republica Argentina" Reading Down

1967, Dec. 20 ***Perf. 13½*** **Wmk. 90**

C108 AP35 26p brown 1.00 35
C109 AP35 40p violet 7.00 50
C110 AP35 68p bl grn 5.00 75
C111 AP35 78p ultra 2.00 1.00

Vito Dumas and Ketch "Legh II"
AP44

1968, July 27 **Litho.** **Wmk. 90**

C112 AP44 68p bl, blk, red & vio bl 1.00 50

Issued to commemorate Vito Dumas's one-man voyage around the world in 1943.

Type of Regular Issue and

Assembly Emblem
AP45

Design: 40p, Globe and map of South America.

1968, Oct. 19 **Litho.** ***Perf. 13½***

C113 A395 40p brt pink, lt bl & blk 60 25
C114 AP45 68p bl, lt bl, gold & blk 1.00 40

Issued to publicize the 4th Plenary Assembly of the International Telegraph and Telephone Consultative Committee, Mar del Plata, Sept. 23–Oct. 25.

Radar Antenna, Balcarce Station
AP46

Photogravure

1969, Aug. 23 ***Perf. 13½*** **Wmk. 90**

C115 AP46 40p bl gray 1.00 30

Issued to publicize communications by satellite through International Telecommunications Consortium (INTELSAT).

Atucha Nuclear Center
AP47

1969, Dec. 13 **Litho.** **Wmk. 365**

C116 AP47 26p bl & multi 2.00 1.00

Completion of Atucha Nuclear Center.

Type of 1963–65 Inscribed "Republica Argentina" Reading Down

1969–71 ***Perf. 13½*** **Wmk. 365**

C123 AP35 40p violet 7.50 50
C124 AP35 68p dk bl grn ('70) 2.50 75

Unwmkd.

C125 AP35 26p yel brn ('71) 50 25
C126 AP35 40p vio ('71) 4.00 50

Old Fire Engine and Fire Brigade Emblem
AP48

1970, Aug. 8 **Litho.** **Unwmkd.**

C128 AP48 40c grn & multi 80 40

Centenary of the Fire Brigade.

Education Year Emblem
AP49

1970, Aug. 29 ***Perf. 13½***

C129 AP49 68c bl & blk 60 25

Issued for International Education Year.

Fleet Leaving Valparaiso, by Antonio Abel
AP50

1970, Oct. 17 **Litho.** ***Perf. 13½***

C130 AP50 26c multi 1.25 30

Issued to commemorate the 150th anniversary of the departure for Peru of the liberation fleet from Valparaiso, Chile.

Sumampa Chapel
AP51

1970, Nov. 7 **Photogravure**

C131 AP51 40c multi 1.50 40

Bishopric of Tucuman, 400th anniversary.

Buenos Aires Planetarium
AP52

1970, Nov. 28 **Litho.** ***Perf. 13½***

C132 AP52 40c multi 90 40

Jorge Newbery and Morane Saulnier Plane
AP53

1970, Dec. 19

C133 AP53 26c bl, blk, yel & grn 60 35

24th Aeronautics and Space Week.

Industries Type of Regular Issue

Design: 31c, Refinery.

1971, Oct. 16 **Litho.** ***Perf. 13½***

C134 A445 31c red, blk & yel 1.00 40

Nationalized industries.

Type of 1963–65 Inscribed "Republica Argentina" Reading Down

1971–74 **Unwmkd.**

C135 AP35 45c brown 5.00 10
C136 AP35 68c red 75 10
C137 AP35 70c vio bl ('73) 1.25 10
C138 AP35 90c emer ('73) 3.00 15
C139 AP35 1.70p bl ('74) 75 35
C140 AP35 1.95p emer ('74) 75 40
C141 AP35 2.65p dp cl ('74) 75 50
Nos. 135-C141 (7) 12.25 1.70

Fluorescent paper was used for Nos. C135–C136, C138–C141. The 70c was issued on both ordinary and fluorescent paper.

Don Quixote, Drawing by Ignacio Zuloaga
AP54

1975, Apr. 26 **Photo.** ***Perf. 13½***

C145 AP54 2.75p yel, blk & red 80 40

Day of the Race and for España 75 International Philatelic Exhibition, Madrid, Apr. 4–13.

No. C87 Surcharged

100 ● PESOS

1975, Sept. 15 **Litho.** **Wmk. 90**

C146 AP35 9.20p on 5.60p 1.25 25
C147 AP35 19.70p on 5.60p 1.75 50
C148 AP35 100p on 5.60p 8.00 3.00

No. C87 Surcharged

REVALORIZADO
9 20 PESOS

1975, Oct. 15

C149 AP35 9.20p on 5.60p 1.00 30
C150 AP35 19.70p on 5.60p 1.75 70

AIR POST SEMI-POSTAL STAMPS.

Stamp Engraving
SPAP1

Designs: 70c+70c, Proofing stamp die. 1p+1p, Sheet of stamps. 2.50p+2.50p, The letter. 5p+5p, Gen. San Martín.

Photogravure.

1950, Aug. 26 *Perf. 13½.* Wmk. 90

CB1	SPAP1	45c +45c vio bl	60	40
CB2	SPAP1	70c +70c dk brn	90	60
a.		Souvenir sheet of 3	5.00	5.00
CB3	SPAP1	1p +1p cer	2.50	2.50
CB4	SPAP1	2.50p +2.50p ol gray	14.00	10.00
CB5	SPAP1	5p +5p dl grn	15.00	12.00
		Nos. CB1-CB5 (5)	33.00	25.50

Issued to publicize the Argentine International Philatelic Exhibition, 1950.

No. CB2a measures 120x150mm., and contains one each of Nos. B12, CB1 and CB2, imperf., with marginal inscriptions and ornamental border in olive green.

Pieta by Michelangelo
SPAP2

1951, Dec. 22 *Perf. 13½x13.*

CB6	SPAP2	2.45p +7.55p grnsh blk	35.00	22.50

The surtax was for the Eva Perón Foundation.

Flower and Child's Head
SPAP3

Stamp of 1858
SPAP4

1958, Mar. 15 *Perf. 13½*

CB7	SPAP3	1p +50c dp cl	35	35

Surtax for National Council for Children.

1958, Mar. 29 Litho. Wmk. 90

CB8	SPAP4	1p +50c gray ol & bl	60	50
CB9	SPAP4	2p +1p rose lil & vio	80	65
CB10	SPAP4	3p +1.50p grn & brn	90	80
CB11	SPAP4	5p +2.50p gray ol & car rose	1.50	1.25
CB12	SPAP4	10p +5p gray ol & brn	3.00	2.50
		Nos. CB8-CB12 (5)	6.80	5.70

The surtax was for the International Centennial Philatelic Exhibition, Buenos Aires, April 19–27.

Type of Semi-Postal Issue, 1958.

Designs: 1p+50c, Flooded area. 5p+2.50p, House and truck under water.

Photogravure.

1958, Oct. 4 *Perf. 13½* Wmk. 90

CB13	SP11	1p +50c dl pur	30	25
CB14	SP11	5p +2.50p grnsh bl	1.00	90

The surtax was for victims of a flood in the Buenos Aires district.

Type of Semi-Postal Issue, 1959.

Designs: 2p+1p, Rowing. 3p+1.50p, Woman diver.

1959, Sept. 5 Litho. *Perf. 13½*

CB15	SP13	2p +1p brt bl & blk	60	40
CB16	SP13	3p +1.50p ol & blk	90	75

Issued to commemorate the third Pan American Games, Chicago, Aug. 27–Sept. 7, 1959.

Type of Semi-Postal Issue, 1960.

Birds: 2p+1p, Rufous tinamou. 3p+1.50p, Rhea.

1960, Feb. 6 *Perf. 13½*

CB17	SP14	2p +1p rose car & sal	40	25
CB18	SP14	3p +1.50p sl grn	60	50

The surtax was for child welfare work. See also No. CB29.

Buenos Aires Market Place, 1810
SPAP5

Seibo, National Flower
SPAP6

Designs: 6p+3p, Oxcart water carrier. 10.70p+5.30p, Settlers landing. 20p+10p, The Fort.

1960, Aug. 20 Photo. Wmk. 90

CB19	SPAP5	2 +1p rose brn	25	12
CB20	SPAP5	6 +3p gray	50	35
CB21	SPAP5	10.70 +5.30p bl	90	50
CB22	SPAP5	20 +10p bluish grn	1.50	1.25

Issued to publicize the Inter-American Philatelic Exhibition EFIMAYO 1960, Buenos Aires, Oct. 12–24, held to commemorate the sesquicentennial of the May Revolution of 1910.

1960, Sept. 10 *Perf. 13½*

Design: 10.70p+5.30p, Copihue, Chile's national flower.

CB23	SPAP6	6 +3p lil rose	50	40
CB24	SPAP6	10.70 +5.30p ver	75	60

The surtax was for earthquake victims in Chile.

Nos. CB19–CB22 Overprinted:
"DIA DE LAS NACIONES UNIDAS
24 DE OCTUBRE"

1960, Oct. 8

CB25	SPAP5	2 +1p rose brn	35	25
CB26	SPAP5	6 +3p gray	60	50
CB27	SPAP5	10.70 +5.30p bl	80	75
CB28	SPAP5	20 +10p bluish grn	1.50	1.35

United Nations Day, Oct. 24, 1960.

Type of Semi-Postal Issue, 1960

Design: Emperor penguins.

1961, Feb. 25 Photo. Wmk. 90

CB29	SP14	1.80p +90c gray	40	30

The surtax was for child welfare work.

Stamp of 1862
SPAP7

Crutch, Olympic Torch and Rings
SPAP8

1962, May 19 Lithographed

CB30	SPAP7	6.50p +6.50p Prus bl & grnsh bl	90	80

Issued to publicize the opening of the "Argentina 62" Philatelic Exhibition, Buenos Aires, May 19–29.

Type of Semi-Postal Issue, 1963

Design: 11p+5p, Bicycling.

1963, May 18 *Perf. 13½* Wmk. 90

CB31	SP21	11p +5p grn, red & blk	70	60

Issued to commemorate the 4th Pan American Games, Sao Paulo, Brazil.

Type of Semi-Postal Issue, 1962.

Design: 11p+5p, Great kiskadee.

1963, Dec. 21 *Perf. 13½* Wmk. 90

CB32	SP20	11p +5p dk brn, brn, yel & grn	1.25	1.00

The surtax was for child welfare.

Type of Semi-Postal Issue, 1964.

Design: 11p+5p, Sailboat.

1964, July 18 Lithographed

CB33	SP22	11p +5p brt bl & blk	75	75

Issued to publicize the 18th Olympic Games, Tokyo, Oct. 10–25, 1964.

1964, Sept. 19 Litho. *Perf. 13½*

CB34	SPAP8	18p +9p bluish grn, blk, red & yel	80	80

Issued to publicize the 13th "Olympic" games for the handicapped, Tokyo, 1964.

Bird Type of Semi-Postal Issue, 1962

Design: Chilean swallow.

1964, Dec. 23 Litho. Wmk. 90

CB35	SP20	18p +9p brn, dk bl & grn	1.50	1.25

The surtax was for child welfare.

Bird Type of Semi-Postal Issue, 1962, Inscribed "R. ARGENTINA"

Design: Rufous ovenbird.

1966, Mar. 26 *Perf. 13½* Wmk. 90

CB36	SP20	27.50p +12.50p bl, ocher, yel & grn	1.50	1.25

The surtax was for child welfare.

Coat of Arms—SPAP9

1966, June 25 Litho. *Perf. 13½*

CB37	SPAP9	10p +10p yel & multi	2.50	2.00

Issued to publicize the ARGENTINA '66 Philatelic Exhibition held in connection with the sesquicentennial celebration of the Declaration of Independence, Buenos Aires, July 16–23. The surtax was for the Exhibition. Issued in sheets of 4.

Bird Type of Semi-Postal Issue, 1962, Inscribed "R. ARGENTINA"

Designs: 15p+7p, Blue and yellow tanager. 26p+13p, Toco toucan.

1967 Lithographed Wmk. 90

CB38	SP20	15p +7p blk, bl, grn & yel	1.50	1.25
CB39	SP20	26p +13p blk, org, yel & bl	90	70

The surtax was for child welfare.

Issue dates: 15p+7p, Jan. 14. 26p+13p, Dec. 23.

Bird Type of Semi-Postal Issue, 1969

Design: 26p+13p, Lineated woodpecker.

1969, Sept. 20 *Perf. 13½* Wmk. 365

CB40	SP24	26p +13p multi	60	50

The surtax was for child welfare.

Bird Type of Semi-Postal Issue, 1970

Design: 40c+20c, Chilean flamingo.

1970, May 9 Litho. Wmk. 365

CB41	SP25	40c +20c multi	70	60

The surtax was for child welfare.

Fish Type of Semi-Postal Issue, 1971

Design: Pejerrey (atherinidae family).

1971, Feb. 20 *Perf. 12½* Unwmkd.

Size: 75x15mm.

CB42	SP26	40c +20c lt bl & multi	50	40

The surtax was for child welfare.

OFFICIAL STAMPS.

Regular Issues Overprinted in Black

1884–87 *Perf. 12, 14.* Unwmkd.

O1	A29	½c brown	9.00	6.00
a.		Inverted overprint	9.00	6.00
O2	A23	1c red	5.50	4.00
a.		Invtd. ovpt., perf.14	50.00	37.50
b.		Perf. 12	55.00	40.00
c.		As "a," perf. 12	35.00	35.00
O3	A29	1c red	60	40
a.		Inverted overprint	1.25	85
b.		Double overprint	30.00	30.00
O4	A20	2c green	60	40
a.		Inverted overprint	55.00	27.50
b.		Double overprint	30.00	30.00
O5	A11	4c brown	60	40
a.		Inverted overprint	40.00	27.50
O6	A7	8c lake	60	40
a.		Inverted overprint	55.00	55.00
O7	A8	10c green	55.00	27.50
O8	A23	12c ultra (#45)	4.00	3.00
a.		Perf. 14	55.00	55.00
O9	A29	12c grnsh bl	90	75
a.		Inverted overprint	110.00	80.00
O10	A19	24c blue	1.25	90
a.		Inverted overprint	4.00	2.50
O11	A21	25c lake	11.00	7.00
O12	A12	30c orange	22.50	15.00
O13	A13	60c black	15.00	9.00
a.		Inverted overprint	55.00	35.00
O14	A14	90c blue	11.00	6.50
a.		Inverted overprint	45.00	35.00
b.		Double overprint	45.00	
		Nos. O1-O14 (14)	137.55	81.25

1884 *Rouletted.*

O15	A17	16c green	2.00	1.00
a.		Double overprint	15.00	15.00
b.		Inverted overprint	110.00	
O16	A18	20c blue	9.00	6.50
a.		Inverted overprint	55.00	37.50
O17	A19	24c blue	1.25	1.10
a.		Inverted overprint	4.00	3.50
b.		Double ovpt., one inverted	27.50	

Overprinted Diagonally in Red.

1885 *Perf. 12.*

O18 A20 2c green 2.00 1.00
a. Inverted overprint 45.00 27.50
O19 A11 4c brown 2.00 1.25
a. Inverted overprint 45.00 27.50
b. Double overprint 45.00 45.00
O20 A13 60c black 25.00 15.00
O21 A14 90c blue 275.00 200.00

1885 *Rouletted*

O22 A19 24c blue 20.00 11.00

On all of these stamps, the overprint is found reading both upwards and downwards.

Counterfeits exist of No. O21 overprint and others.

Regular Issues Handstamped Horizontally in Black **OFICIAL**

1884 *Perf. 12, 14.*

O23 A23 1c red 70.00 25.00
a. Perf. 12 225.00 125.00
O24 A20 2c green 225.00 175.00
a. Diagonal ovpt. 35.00 20.00
O25 A11 4c brown 15.00 11.00
O26 A7 8c lake 15.00 11.00
O27 A23 12c ultra 40.00 25.00

Overprinted Diagonally.

O28 A19 24c bl, rouletted 30.00 20.00
O29 A13 60c black 20.00 10.00

Counterfeit overprints exist.

Liberty Head O1

1901, Dec. 1 Engraved *Perf. 11½*

O31 O1 1c gray 30 20
O32 O1 2c org brn 45 25
O33 O1 5c red 60 25
O34 O1 10c dk grn 70 30
O35 O1 30c dk bl 4.50 1.10
O36 O1 50c orange 2.50 75
Nos. O31-O36 (6) 9.05 2.85

Regular Stamps of 1935-51 Overprinted in Black **SERVICIO OFICIAL** *c*

Wmkd. RA in Sun. (90)

Perf. 13x13½, 13½x13, 13.

1938-54

O37 A129 1c buff ('40) 10 5
O38 A130 2c dk brn ('40) 10 5
O39 A132 3c grn ('39) 12 5
O40 A132 3c lt gray ('39) 10 5
O41 A134 5c yel brn 10 5
O42 A195 5c car ('53) 12 5
O43 A137 10c carmine 10 5
O44 A137 10c brn ('39) 10 5
O45 A140 15c lt gray bl, type II ('47) 12 5
O46 A139 15c sl bl 35 5
O47 A139 15c pale ultra ('39) 12 5
O48 A139 20c bl ('53) 30 5
O49 A141 25c carmine 12 5
a. Overprint 11mm 20 5
O49B A143 40c dk vio 75 8
O50 A144 50c red & org 10 5
a. Overprint 11mm 25 5
O51 A146 1p brn blk & lt bl ('40) 20 5
a. Overprint 11mm
O52 A224 1p choc & lt bl ('51) 20 8
a. Overprint 11mm 20 8
O53 A147 2p brn lake & dk ultra (ovpt. 11mm) ('54) 75 8
Nos. O37-O53 (18) 3.85 99

Overprinted in Black on Stamps and Types of 1945-47

Perf. 13x13½, 13½x13.

1945-46 **Unwmkd.**

O54 A130 2c sepia 1.25 30
O55 A134 3c lt gray 1.25 20
O56 A134 5c yel brn 30 5
O57 A195 5c dp car 8 5
O58 A137 10c brown 8 5
a. Double overprint
O59 A140 15c lt gray bl, type II 12 5
O61 A141 25c dl rose 12 5
O62 A144 50c red & org 30 5
O63 A146 1p brn blk & lt bl 12 5
O64 A147 2p brn lake & bl 12 5
O65 A148 5p ind & ol grn 12 6
O66 A149 10p dp cl & int blk 25 8
O67 A150 20p bl grn & brn 50 20
Nos. O54-O67 (13) 4.61 1.24

Overprinted in Black on Stamps and Types of 1942-50

Perf. 13, 13x13½.

1944-51 **Wmk. 288**

O73 A134 3c lt gray 1.50 40
O74 A134 5c yel brn 25 6
O75 A137 10c red brn 10 5
O76 A140 15c lt gray bl, type II 25 5
O77 A144 50c red & org (overprint 11 mm) 2.25 40
O78 A146 1p brn blk & lt bl (overprint 11mm) 2.25 30
Nos. O73-O78 (6) 6.60 1.26

Regular Issue of 1952 Overprinted in Black SERVICIO OFICIAL *d*

1953 *Perf. 13.* **Wmk. 90**

O79 A228 5c gray 8 5
O80 A228 10c rose lil 8 5
O81 A228 20c rose pink 8 5
O82 A228 25c dl grn 12 5
O83 A228 40c dl vio 8 5
O84 A228 45c dp bl 20 5
O85 A228 50c dl brn 12 5

Nos. 611-617 Overprinted Type "e" in Blue

SERVICIO OFICIAL *e* **SERVICIO OFICIAL** *f*

Perf. 13x13½, 13½x13

O86 A229 1p dk brn 15 6
O87 A229 1.50p dp grn 30 8
O88 A229 2p brt car 20 10
O89 A229 3p indigo 60 20

Size: 30x40mm.

O90 A229 5p red brn 60 35
O91 A228 10p red 3.00 1.50
O92 A229 20p green 32.50 15.00
Nos. O79-O92 (14) 38.11 17.64

No. 612 Overprinted Type "f" in Blue.

O93 A229 1.50p dp grn 1.00 15

Regular Issue of 1954-59 Variously Overprinted in Black or Blue

S. OFICIAL *g* SERVICIO OFICIAL *h*

Perf. 13½, 13x13½, 13½x13

1955-61 **Lithographed** **Wmk. 90**

O94 A237 (c) 20c red (#629) 12 5
O95 A237 (d) 20c red (#629) 10 5
O96 A237 (d) 40c red, ovpt. 15mm (#630) 12 5

Engraved

O97 A239 (g) 50c bl (#632) ('58) 10 5

Photogravure

O98 A239 (h) 1p brn (#635) ('59) 10 5
O99 A239 (e) 1p brn (Bl,#635) ('59) 10 5
O100 A239 (e) 1p brn (Bk,#635) ('60) 10 5

Engraved

O101 A239 (h) 3p vio brn (#638) ('58) 12 5
O102 A240 (h) 5p gray grn (#639) ('57) 30 8
O103 A240 (e) 10p yel grn (#640) ('58) 50 15
O104 A240 (f) 20p dl vio (#641) ('59) 90 30
O105 A240 (h) 20p dl vio (#641) ('58) 90 25
O106 A241 (e) 50p ultra & ind (#642) ('61) 1.25 15
Nos. O94-O106 (13) 4.71 1.33

The overprints on Nos. O99-O100 and O103-O104 are horizontal; that on No. O109 is vertical. On No. O106 overprint measures 23mm.

No. 659 Overprinted Type "d".

Lithographed.

1957 *Perf. 13* **Wmk. 90**

O108 A133 20c dl pur (ovpt. 15mm) 10 5

Nos. 666, 658 and 663 Variously Overprinted

1957 **Photo.** *Perf. 13x13½, 13½*

O109 A261 (g) 2p claret 20 5
O110 A254(e) 2.40p brown 20 5
O111 A258(c) 4.40p grnsh gray 25 8

Nos. 668, 685-687, 690-691, 693-705, 742, 742C and Types of 1959-65 Overprinted in Black, Blue or Red Types "e," "g" or

S. OFICIAL *i* **S. OFICIAL** *j*

S. OFICIAL *k* **S. OFICIAL** *m* **S. OFICIAL** *n*

Lithographed; Photogravure

1960-68 *Perf. 13x13½, 13½*

O112 A128 (g) 5c buff (vert. ovpt.) ('62) 10 5
O113 A275 (j) 10c sl grn ('62) 8 5
O114 A275 (j) 20c dl red brn ('62) 8 5
O115 A275 (i) 50c bister 8 5
O116 A278 (k) 1p brn ('62) 12 5
O117 A278 (j) 1p brn, photo. (vert. ovpt.) ('65) 20 5
O117A A278 (j) 1p brn, litho., (vert. ovpt., down, '68) 20 7
O118 A276 (j) 2p rose red ('62) 12 5
O119 A312 (m) 2p dp grn (vert. ovpt., down) ('64) 25 8
O120 A312 (j) 2p brt grn (vert. ovpt., up) ('66) 12 5
O121 A312 (j) 2p grn litho. (vert. ovpt., down) ('67) 25 8
O122 A277 (e) 3p dk bl (horiz.) ('61) 20 7
O123 A277 (j) 3p dk bl ('67) 20 7
O124 A276 (j) 4p red, litho. ('63?) 20 5
O125 A312 (j) 4p rose red, litho. (vert. ovpt., down) ('65) 20 5
O126 A277 (e) 5p brn (Bl) (horiz.) 25 8
O127 A277 (e) 5p brn (Bk) (horiz.) ('61) 25 8
O128 A277 (j) 5p sep ('66) 15 5
O129 A277 (e) 5p sep (horiz. ovpt.) ('67) 15 5
O130 A276 (j) 8p red ('65) 20 8
O131 A278 (i) 10p lt red brn 50 10
O132 A276 (j) 10p ver ('66) 20 5
O133 A278 (j) 10p brn car (vert. ovpt., up) ('66) 20 5
O134 A278 (m) 12p dk brn vio ('64) 40 5
O135 A278 (k) 20p Prus grn ('61) 60 10
O136 A278 (j) 20p Prus grn (vert. ovpt., up) ('66) 45 6
O137 A276 (j) 20p red, litho. ('67) 40 6
O138 A276 (m) 20p red, litho. ('67) 25 5
O139 A278 (j) 23p grn (vert. ovpt.) ('65) 60 10
O140 A278 (j) 25p dp vio, photo. (R) (vert. ovpt., up) ('66) 60 6
O141 A278 (j) 25p pur, litho. (R) (vert. ovpt., down) ('67) 60 10
O142 A241 (n) 50p dk bl ('66) 1.25 10
O143 A279(m) 100p bl (horiz. ovpt.) ('64) 1.25 25
O144 A279(m) 100p bl (vert. ovpt., up) ('65) 1.25 25
O145 A280(m) 300p dp vio ('66) 2.50 50

The "m" overprint measures 15½mm. on 2p; 14½mm. on 12p, 100p and 300p; 13mm. on 20p.

Nos. 699, 818, 823-825, 827-829, and Type of 1962 Overprinted in Black or Red Types "j," "m" or "o"

SERVICIO OFICIAL *o*

Inscribed: "Republica Argentina"

Litho., Photo., Engraved

1964-67 *Perf. 13½* **Wmk. 90**

O149 A312 (j) 6p rose red (vert. ovpt., down) ('67) 30 5
O153 A238a(m) 22p ultra ('64) 60 6
O154 A238a (j) 43p dk car rose (vert. ovpt., down) 85 6
O155 A238a (j) 45p brn, photo. (vert. ovpt., up) ('66) 85 6
O156 A238a (j) 45p brn, litho. (vert. ovpt., up) ('67) 1.25 15
O157 A241 (j) 50p dk bl (vert. ovpt., up) (R) ('67) 2.50 15
O158 A366 (j) 90p ol bis (vert. ovpt., up) ('67) 3.00 15
O162 A279 (o) 500p yel grn ('67) 4.00 75

Type of 1959-67 Overprinted Type "j"

Perf. 13½

1969 **Lithographed** **Wmk. 365**

O163 A276 20p vermilion 25 10

OFFICIAL DEPARTMENT STAMPS

Regular issues of 1911-37 Overprinted in Black

Ministry of Agriculture

M. A. (Type I) | **M. A.** (Type II)

1913-37 **On Stamp of 1911**

OD1 A88 2c #181 10 5

On Stamps of 1912-14

OD2 A88 1c #190 10 5
OD3 A88 2c #191 15 6
OD4 A88 5c #194 30 5
OD5 A88 12c #196 10 5

On Stamps of 1915-16

OD6 A88 1c #208 15 12
OD7 A88 2c #209 10 6
OD8 A88 5c #212 10 6
OD9 A91 5c #220 10 5

On Stamp of 1917

OD10 A94 12c #238 30 5

On Stamps of 1918-19

OD11	A93	1c #249	10	5
OD12	A93	2c #250	10	5
OD13	A93	5c #253	10	5
OD14	A94	12c #255	10	5
OD15	A94	20c #256	15	10

On Stamps of 1920

OD16	A93	1c #265	30	20
OD17	A93	2c #266	50	20
OD18	A93	5c #269	20	5

On Stamps of 1922-23

OD19	A94	12c #311	75	25
OD20	A94	20c #312	20.00	

On Stamps of 1923

OD21	A104	1c #324	5	5
OD22	A104	2c #325	25	10
OD23	A104	5c #328	5	5
OD24	A104	12c #330	5	5
OD25	A104	20c #331	5	5

On Stamps of 1923-31

OD26	A104	1c #341	5	5
OD27	A104	2c #342, I	5	5
a.	Type II		1.20	60
OD28	A104	3c #343	10	5
OD29	A104	5c #345, II	5	5
a.	Type I		10	5
OD30	A104	10c #346, II	5	5
a.	Type I		10	5
OD31	A104	12c #347	10	5
OD32	A104	20c #348, I	15	5
a.	Type II		15	5
OD33	A104	30c #351	15	5

On Stamp of 1926

OD34	A110	12c #360	5	5

Type II

On Stamps of 1935-37

OD35	A129	1c #419	5	5
OD36	A130	2c #420	5	5
OD37	A132	3c #422	5	5
OD38	A134	5c #427	5	5
OD39	A137	10c #430	5	5
OD40	A139	15c #434	30	5
OD41	A140	20c #437	20	6
OD42	A140	20c #438	10	5
OD43	A141	25c #441	20	5
OD44	A142	30c #442	15	5
OD45	A145	1p #445	2.00	1.00
OD46	A146	1p #446	25	10

Ministry of War

M. G. (Type I) | **M. G.** (Type II)

On Stamp of 1911

OD47	A88	2c #181	10	5

On Stamps of 1912-14

OD48	A88	1c #190	10	5
OD49	A88	2c #191	75	5
OD50	A88	5c #194	10	5
OD51	A88	12c #196	10	5

On Stamps of 1915-16

OD52	A88	1c #208	6.00	60
OD53	A88	2c #209	50	10
OD54	A88	5c #212	60	5
OD55	A91	5c #220	75	15
OD56	A92	12c #222	75	25

On Stamps of 1917

OD57	A93	1c #232	20	5
OD58	A93	2c #233	30	5
OD59	A93	5c #236	30	5
OD60	A94	12c #238	45	5

On Stamps of 1918-19

OD61	A93	1c #249	15	5
OD62	A93	2c #250	10	5
OD63	A93	5c #253	10	5
OD64	A94	12c #255	30	5
OD65	A94	20c #256	90	5

On Stamps of 1920

OD66	A93	2c #266	30	5
OD67	A93	5c #269	30	5
OD68	A94	12c #271	25	5

On Stamp of 1920

OD69	A94	12c #299	1.50	15

On Stamps of 1922-23

OD70	A93	1c #305	60	10
OD71	A93	2c #306	1.25	30
OD72	A103	5c #309	60	5
OD73	A94	20c #312	20	5

On Stamp of 1922-23

OD74	A93	2c #318	3.50	50

On Stamps of 1923

OD75	A104	1c #324	10	5
OD76	A104	2c #325	10	5
OD77	A104	5c #328	10	5
OD78	A104	12c #330	10	5
OD79	A104	20c #331	75	5

On Stamps of 1923-31

OD80	A104	1c #341	1.00	30
OD81	A104	2c #342	15	5
OD82	A104	3c #343, I	5	5
a.	Type II		30	5
OD83	A104	5c #345, I	5	5
a.	Type II		15	5
OD84	A104	10c #346, II	5	5
a.	Type I		45	5
OD85	A104	20c #348, I	10	5
a.	Type II		30	5
OD86	A104	30c #351, II	15	5
a.	Type I		90	10
OD87	A105	1p #353	1.25	20

On Stamp of 1926

OD88	A109	5c #359	45	5

Type II

On Stamps of 1935-37

OD89	A129	1c #419	5	5
OD90	A130	2c #420	5	5
OD91	A132	3c #422	5	5
OD92	A134	5c #427	6	5
OD93	A137	10c #430	10	5
OD94	A139	15c #434	15	5
OD95	A140	20c #437	75	5
OD96	A140	20c #438	15	5
OD97	A141	25c #441	10	5
OD98	A142	30c #442	10	5
OD99	A144	50c #444	15	5
OD100	A145	1p #445	80	20
OD101	A146	1p #446	25	10

Ministry of Finance

M. H. (Type I) | **M. H.** (Type II)

Type I

On Stamp of 1911

OD102	A88	2c #181	10	5

On Stamps of 1912-14

OD103	A88	1c #190	10	5
OD104	A88	2c #191	10	5
OD105	A88	5c #194	10	5
OD106	A88	12c #196	10	5

On Stamps of 1915-16

OD107	A88	2c #209	10	6
OD108	A88	5c #212	10	5
OD109	A91	5c #220	10	5

On Stamps of 1917

OD110	A93	2c #233	10	5
OD111	A93	5c #236	90	5
OD112	A94	12c #238	10	5

On Stamps of 1918-19

OD113	A93	2c #250		20.00
OD114	A93	5c #253	10	5
OD115	A94	12c #255	30	5
OD116	A94	20c #256	30	5

On Stamps of 1920

OD117	A93	1c #265	60	30
OD118	A93	2c #266	90	30
OD119	A93	5c #269	20	5
OD120	A94	12c #271	45	10

On Stamp of 1922-23

OD121	A94	20c #312	10.00	2.00

On Stamps of 1923

OD122	A104	1c #324	60	30
OD123	A104	2c #325	5	5
OD124	A104	5c #328	5	5
OD125	A104	12c #330	5	5
OD126	A104	20c #331	5	5

On Stamps of 1923-31

OD127	A104	3c #343	6.00	1.00
OD128	A104	5c #345	5	5
OD129	A104	10c #346	5	5
OD130	A104	12c #347	6.00	3.00
OD131	A104	20c #348, I	10	5
a.	Type II		25	5
OD132	A104	30c #351	15	5
OD133	A105	1p #353	30	15

On Stamp of 1926

OD134	A110	12c #360	10.00	10.00

Type II

On Stamps of 1935-37

OD135	A129	1c #419	5	5
OD136	A130	2c #420	5	5
OD137	A132	3c #422	5	5
OD138	A134	5c #427	5	5
OD139	A137	10c #430	10	5
OD140	A139	15c #434	30	5
OD141	A140	20c #437	15	5
OD142	A140	20c #438	10	5
OD143	A142	30c #442	10	5
OD144	A145	1p #445	1.20	40
OD145	A146	1p #446	25	5

Ministry of the Interior

M. I. (Type I) | **M. I.** (Type II)

Type I

On Stamp of 1911

OD146	A88	2c #181	25	5

On Stamps of 1912-14

OD147	A88	1c #190	10	5
OD148	A88	2c #191	10	5
OD149	A88	5c #194	10	5
OD150	A88	12c #196	10	5

On Stamps of 1915-17

OD151	A88	2c #209	75	30
OD152	A88	5c #212	60	10
OD153	A91	5c #220	45	10
OD154	A93	5c #236	1.20	10

On Stamps of 1918-19

OD155	A93	2c #250	10	5
OD156	A93	5c #253	10	5

On Stamps of 1920

OD157	A93	1c #265	3.00	75
OD158	A93	5c #269	60	25

On Stamps of 1922-23

OD159	A93	2c #306	10.00	10.00
OD160	A103	5c #309	2.50	75
OD161	A94	12c #311	75	25
OD162	A94	20c #312	75	25

On Stamps of 1923

OD163	A104	1c #324	5	5
OD164	A104	2c #325	5	5
OD165	A104	5c #328	5	5
OD166	A104	12c #330	1.50	1.50
OD167	A104	20c #331	50	5

On Stamps of 1923-31

OD168	A104	1c #341	5	5
OD169	A104	2c #342	5	5
OD170	A104	3c #343, II	5	5
a.	Type I		90	20
OD171	A104	5c #345, I	5	5
a.	Type II		5	5
OD172	A104	10c #346	5	5
OD173	A104	12c #347	30	5
OD174	A104	20c #348, II	5	5
a.	Type I		60	5
OD175	A104	30c #351	5	15

Type II

On Stamps of 1935-37

OD176	A129	1c #419	5	[illegible]
OD177	A130	2c #420	5	[illegible]
OD178	A132	3c #422	5	[illegible]
OD178A	A134	5c #427	5	[illegible]
OD179	A137	10c #430	5	[illegible]
OD180	A139	15c #434	20	[illegible]
OD181	A140	20c #437	60	[illegible]
OD182	A140	20c #438	10	[illegible]
OD182A	A142	30c #442	10	[illegible]
OD182B	A145	1p #445	1.20	[illegible]
OD182C	A146	1p #446	25	[illegible]

Ministry of Justice and Instruction

M. J. I. (Type I) | **M. J. I.** (Type II)

Type I

On Stamp of 1911

OD183	A88	2c #181	90	5

On Stamps of 1912-14

OD184	A88	1c #190	1.20	5
OD185	A88	2c #191	75	15
OD186	A88	5c #194	30	5
OD187	A88	12c #196	30	5

On Stamps of 1915-17

OD188	A88	1c #208	20	5
OD189	A88	2c #209	20	5
OD190	A88	5c #212	75	10
OD191	A91	5c #220	15	5
OD192	A92	12c #222	50	5

On Stamps of 1917

OD193	A93	1c #232	20	5
OD194	A93	2c #233	60	5
OD195	A93	5c #236	20	5
OD196	A94	12c #238	17.50	5.00

On Stamps of 1918-19

OD197	A93	1c #249	10	5
OD198	A93	2c #250	10	5
OD199	A93	5c #253	10	5
OD200	A94	12c #255	20	5
OD201	A94	20c #256	40	5

On Stamps of 1920

OD202	A93	1c #265	15	5
OD203	A93	2c #266	10	5
OD204	A93	5c #269	10	5
OD205	A94	12c #271	25	5

On Stamps of 1922-23

OD206	A93	1c #305	15	5
OD207	A93	2c #306	1.20	30
OD208	A103	5c #309	15	5
OD209	A94	12c #311	7.50	1.20
OD210	A94	20c #312	1.20	20

On Stamp of 1922-23

OD211	A93	2c #318	2.00	2.00

On Stamps of 1923

OD212	A104	1c #324	10	5
OD213	A104	2c #325	5	5
OD214	A104	5c #328	10	5
OD215	A104	12c #330	10	5
OD216	A104	20c #331	30	5

On Stamps of 1923-31

OD217	A104	½c #340	1.50	50
OD218	A104	1c #341, I	5	5
a.	Type II		5	5
OD219	A104	2c #342	5	5
OD220	A104	3c #343, I	5	5
a.	Type II		5	5
OD221	A104	5c #345, I	5	5
a.	Type II		5	5
OD222	A104	10c #346, II	5	5
a.	Type I		20	5
OD223	A104	12c #347, I	5	5
a.	Type II		30	15
OD224	A104	20c #348, I	5	5
a.	Type II		5	5
OD225	A104	30c #351	5	5
OD226	A105	1p #353	30	50

On Stamps of 1926

OD227	A109	5c #359	10	5
OD228	A110	12c #360	15	5

Type II

On Stamps of 1935-37

OD229	A129	1c #419	5	5
OD230	A130	2c #420	5	5
OD231	A132	3c #422	5	5
OD232	A134	5c #427	6	5
OD233	A137	10c #430	5	5
OD234	A139	15c #434	30	5
OD234A	A140	20c #437	10	5
OD234B	A140	20c #438	15	5
OD234C	A141	25c #441	10	5
OD234D	A142	30c #442	10	5
OD234E	A145	1p #445	60	30
OD234F	A146	1p #446	15	10

Ministry of Marine

M. M. (Type I) | **M. M.** (Type II)

Type I

On Stamp of 1911

OD235	A88	2c #181	20	5

On Stamps of 1912-14

OD236	A88	1c #190	10	5
OD237	A88	2c #191	10	5
OD238	A88	5c #194	2.00	10
OD239	A88	12c #196	15	5

On Stamps of 1915-16

OD240	A88	2c #209	50	5
OD241	A88	5c #212	30	5

On Stamps of 1917

OD242	A93	1c #232	10	5
OD243	A93	2c #233	10	5
OD244	A93	5c #236	10	5

On Stamps of 1918-19

OD245	A93	1c #249	10	5
OD246	A93	2c #250	10	5
OD247	A93	5c #253	20	5
OD248	A94	12c #255	20	10
OD249	A94	20c #256	2.50	25

On Stamps of 1920

OD250	A93	1c #265	10	5
OD251	A93	2c #266	15	5
OD252	A93	5c #269	20	5

On Stamps of 1922-23

OD253	A103	5c #309	60	10
OD254	A94	12c #311	7.50	7.50
OD255	A94	20c #312	6.00	1.00

On Stamps of 1923

OD256	A104	1c #324	5	5
OD257	A104	2c #325	10	5
OD258	A104	5c #328	25	5
OD259	A104	12c #330	50	15
OD260	A104	20c #331	50	5

On Stamps of 1923-31

OD261	A104	1c #341	60	15
OD262	A104	2c #342	15	5
OD263	A104	3c #343	45	15
OD264	A104	5c #345, I	10	5
a.		Type II	45	5
OD265	A104	10c #346	45	5
OD266	A104	20c #348, II	45	5
a.		Type I	60	5
OD267	A104	30c #351	90	5
OD268	A105	1p #353	9.00	2.00

On Stamp of 1926

OD269	A109	5c #359	50	5

Type II

On Stamps of 1935-37

OD270	A129	1c #419	5	5
OD271	A130	2c #420	5	5
OD272	A132	3c #422	5	5
OD273	A134	5c #427	5	5
OD274	A137	10c #430	20	5
OD275	A139	15c #434	20	5
OD276	A140	20c #437	30	5
OD277	A140	20c #438	20	5
OD278	A142	30c #442	20	5
OD279	A145	1p #445	2.50	60
OD280	A146	1p #446	60	15

Ministry of Public Works

M. O. P. (Type I) | **M. O. P.** (Type II)

Type I

On Stamp of 1911

OD281	A88	2c #181	30	5

On Stamps of 1912-14

OD282	A88	1c #190	30	5
OD283	A88	5c #194	15	5
OD284	A88	12c #196	1.50	25

On Stamps of 1916-19

OD285	A91	5c #220	12.00	75
OD286	A94	12c #238	20.00	
OD287	A94	20c #256	20.00	

On Stamps of 1920

OD288	A93	2c #266	5.00	2.00
OD289	A93	5c #269	1.50	10
OD290	A94	12c #271	18.00	5.00

On Stamps of 1923

OD291	A104	1c #324	30	10
OD292	A104	2c #325	30	5
OD293	A104	5c #328	30	5
OD294	A104	12c #330	50	10
OD295	A104	20c #331	75	10

On Stamps of 1923-31

OD296	A104	1c #341	5	5
OD297	A104	2c #342	5	5
OD298	A104	3c #343	5	5
OD299	A104	5c #345, I	5	5
a.		Type II	5	5
OD300	A104	10c #346	5	5
OD301	A104	12c #347	7.50	90
OD302	A104	20c #348, I	5	5
a.		Type II	1.80	50
OD303	A104	30c #351	30	5
OD304	A105	1p #353	18.00	5.00

On Stamp of 1926

OD305	A109	5c #359	50	5

Type II

On Stamps of 1935-37

OD306	A129	1c #419	5	5
OD307	A130	2c #420	5	5
OD308	A132	3c #422	5	5
OD309	A134	5c #427	5	5
OD310	A137	10c #430	30	5
OD311	A139	15c #434	45	5
OD312	A140	20c #437	60	6
OD313	A140	20c #438	10	5
OD314	A142	30c #442	10	5
OD315	A144	50c #444	10	5
OD316	A145	1p #445	1.20	40
OD317	A146	1p #446	25	10

Ministry of Foreign Affairs and Religion

M. R. C. (Type I) | **M. R. C.** (Type II)

Type I

On Stamp of 1911

OD318	A88	2c #181	7.50	1.25

On Stamps of 1912-14

OD319	A88	1c #190	10	5
OD320	A88	2c #191	10	5
OD321	A88	5c #194	30	5
OD322	A88	12c #196	1.50	25

On Stamps of 1915-19

OD323	A88	5c #212	30	5
OD324	A91	5c #220	15	5
OD325	A94	20c #256	1.50	50

On Stamps of 1920

OD326	A93	1c #265	30	10
OD327	A93	5c #269	10	5

On Stamps of 1922-23

OD328	A93	2c #306	10.00	4.00
OD329	A103	5c #309	25.00	
OD330	A93	10c #311	20.00	

On Stamps of 1923

OD331	A104	1c #324	5	5
OD332	A104	2c #325	5	5
OD333	A104	5c #328	5	5
OD334	A104	12c #330	10	5
OD335	A104	20c #331	15	5

On Stamps of 1923-31

OD336	A104	½c #340	75	30
OD337	A104	1c #341	6	5
OD338	A104	2c #342	6	5
OD339	A104	3c #343	5	5
OD340	A104	5c #345	5	5
OD341	A104	10c #346, II	5	5
a.		Type I	1.20	5
OD342	A104	12c #347	5	5
OD343	A104	20c #348, I	5	5
a.		Type II	15	5
OD344	A104	30c #351, I	15	5
a.		Type II	15	5
OD345	A105	1p #353	30	10

On Stamp of 1926

OD346	A110	12c #360	10	5

Type II

On Stamps of 1935-37

OD347	A129	1c #419	5	5
OD348	A130	2c #420	5	5
OD349	A132	3c #422	5	5
OD350	A134	5c #427	5	5
OD351	A137	10c #430	10	5
OD352	A139	15c #434	10	5
OD353	A140	20c #437	10	5
OD354	A140	20c #438	10	5
OD355	A142	30c #442	10	5
OD356	A145	1p #445	1.50	60
OD357	A146	1p #446	75	35

Buenos Aires

(bwā'nos ī'rās)

The central point of the Argentine struggle for independence. At intervals Buenos Aires maintained an independent government but after 1862 became a province of the Argentine Republic.

8 REALES=1 PESO

> Prices of Buenos Aires Nos. 1–8 vary according to condition. Quotations are for fine copies. Very fine to superb specimens sell at much higher prices, and inferior or poor copies sell at reduced prices, depending on the condition of the individual specimen.

Steamship

A1

Typographed.

1858 ***Imperf.*** **Unwmkd.**

1	A1	1 (in) pesos lt brn	*500.00*	*350.00*
2	A1	2 (dos) pesos bl	250.00	190.00
3	A1	3 (tres) pesos grn	1,600.	*1,000.*
a.		3p dk grn	2,000.	*1,250.*
4	A1	4 (cuato) pesos ver	5,500.	*3,500.*
5	A1	5 (cinco) pesos org	5,000.	*3,000.*
a.		5p ocher	5,000.	*3,000.*
b.		5p ol yel	5,000.	*3,000.*

Issue dates: Nos. 2–5, Apr. 29, 1858. No. 1, Oct. 26, 1858.

1858, Oct. 26

6	A1	4 (cuato) reales brn	350.00	300.00
a.		4r gray brn	350.00	300.00
b.		4r yel brn	350.00	300.00

1859, Jan. 1

7	A1	1 (in) pesos bl	225.00	150.00
a.		1p ind	300.00	175.00
b.		Impression on reverse of stamp in bl	*2,500.*	
c.		Double impression	300.00	225.00
d.		Tête bêche pair		*50,000.*
8	A1	1 (to) pesos bl	500.00	400.00

Nos. 1, 2, 3 and 7 have been reprinted on very thick, hand-made paper. The same four stamps and No. 8 have been reprinted on thin, hard, white wove paper.

Counterfeits of Nos. 1–8 are plentiful.

Liberty Head

A2

1859, Sept. 3

9	A2	4r grn, *bluish*	350.00	200.00
10	A2	1p blue	50.00	27.50
11	A2	2p vermilion	500.00	300.00
a.		2p red	500.00	300.00

Both clear and rough impressions of these stamps may be found. They have generally been called Paris and Local prints, respectively, but the opinion now obtains that the differences are due to the impression and that they do not represent separate issues.

Many shades exist of Nos. 1–11.

1862, Oct. 4

12	A2	1p rose	175.00	75.00
13	A2	2p blue	500.00	125.00

All three values have been reprinted in black, brownish black, blue and red brown on thin hard white paper. The 4r has also been reprinted in green on bluish paper.

Cordoba

(kôr'dô·bä)

A province in the central part of the Argentine Republic.

100 CENTAVOS=1 PESO

Arms of Cordoba

A1

Lithographed

Laid Paper.

1858, Oct. 28 ***Imperf.*** **Unwmkd.**

1	A1	5c blue	125.00	
2	A1	10c black	*2,500.*	

Cordoba stamps were printed on laid paper, but stamps from edges of the sheets sometimes do not show any laid lines and appear to be on wove paper. Counterfeits are plentiful.

Corrientes

(kŏr'rě·ěn'těs)

The northeast province of the Argentine Republic.

1 REAL M(ONEDA) C(ORRIENTE)=12½ CENTAVOS M. C.=50 CENTAVOS

100 CENTAVOS FUERTES=1 PESO FUERTE

Ceres

A1 A2

1856, Aug. 21 *Imperf.* **Unwmkd.**

1 A1 1r *blue* 125.00 400.00

1860, Feb. 8

Pen Stroke Through "Un Real"

2 A1 (3c) *blue* 500.00 750.00

1860-78

3 A2 (3c) *blue* 12.50 40.00
4 A2 (2c) *yel grn* ('64) 50.00 60.00
a. (2c) *bl grn* 125.00 150.00
5 A2 (2c) *yel* ('67) 10.00 25.00
6 A2 (3c) *dk bl* ('71) 4.00 25.00
7 A2 (3c) *lil rose* ('75) 250.00 100.00
a. (3c) *rose red* ('76) 150.00 75.00
8 A2 (3c) *red vio* ('78) 60.00 50.00

Pen cancels sell for much less.

Printed from settings of eight varieties, three or four impressions constituting a sheet. Some impressions were printed inverted and tête bêche pairs may be cut from adjacent impressions.

From Jan. 1st to Feb. 24th, 1864, No. 4 was used as a 5 centavos stamp but copies so used can only be distinguished when they bear dated cancellations.

The reprints show numerous spots and small defects which are not found on the originals. They are printed on gray blue, dull blue, gray green, dull orange and light magenta papers

ARMENIA

(är·mē'ni·ȧ)

LOCATION—In southern Russia bounded by Georgia, Azerbaijan, Persia and Turkey.
GOVT.—A Soviet Socialist Republic.
AREA—11,945 sq. mi.
POP.—1,214,391 (1923).
CAPITAL—Erevan.

With Azerbaijan and Georgia, Armenia made up the Transcaucasian Federation of Soviet Republics. Stamps of Armenia were replaced in 1923 by those of Transcaucasian Federated Republics.

100 Kopecks = 1 Ruble

Counterfeits abound of all overprinted and surcharged stamps.

National Republic.

Russian Stamps of 1902-19

Handstamped

Thirteen types exist of both framed and unframed overprints. The device is the Armenian "H," initial of Hayasdan (Armenia). Inverted and double overprints are found.

Surcharged K 60 K

Type I. Without periods.
Type II. Periods after first "K" and "60".

Black Surcharge.

1919 *Perf. 14, 14½x15.* **Unwmkd.**

1 A14 60k on 1k org (II) 35 40
a. Imperf. (I) 25 30
b. Imperf. (II) 25 30

Violet Surcharge.

2 A14 60k on 1k org (II) 45 50

Handstamped in Violet

a

Perf. 14, 14½x15, 13½.

6 A15 4k carmine 75 75
7 A14 5k claret 3.50 4.00
a. Imperf. 2.25 2.50
9 A14 10k on 7k lt bl 1.75 2.00
10 A11 15k red brn & bl 40 40
11 A8 20k bl & car 1.25 1.50
13 A11 35k red brn & grn 75 75
14 A8 50k vio & grn 60 60
15 A14 60k on 1k org (II) 3.00 3.50
a. Imperf. (I) 2.50 2.75
b. Imperf. (II) 14.00 15.00

18 A13 5r dk bl, grn & pale bl 6.00 7.00
a. Imperf. 1.50 1.50
19 A12 7r dk grn & pink 2.00 2.25
20 A13 10r scar, yel & gray 2.00 2.25

Handstamped in Black.

Perf. 14, 14½x15, 13½.

31 A14 2k green 6.50 7.00
a. Imperf. 25 25
32 A14 3k red 4.00 4.00
a. Imperf. 25 25
33 A15 4k carmine 15 20
34 A14 5k claret 25 30
a. Imperf. 2.00 2.00
36 A15 10k dk bl 1.50 1.00
37 A14 10k on 7k lt bl 10 15
38 A11 15k red brn & bl 10 15
a. Imperf. 2.00 2.00
39 A8 20k bl & car 15 20
40 A11 25k grn & gray vio 15 20
41 A11 35k red brn & grn 10 15
42 A8 50k vio & grn 10 15
43 A14 60k on 1k org (II) 4.00 4.00
43A A11 70k brn & org 30 35
b. Imperf. 25 30
44 A9 1r pale brn, dk brn & org 70 75
a. Imperf. 40 50
45 A12 3½r mar & lt grn 1.50 1.25
a. Imperf. 75 85
46 A13 5r dk bl, grn & pale bl 75 85
a. Imperf. 1.25 1.25
47 A12 7r dk grn & pink 1.75 1.75
48 A13 10r scar, yel & gray 1.50 1.50

Vertically Laid Paper.

Wmkd. Wavy Lines. (168)

1920 *Imperf.*

60 A13 5r dk bl, grn & pale bl 30.00

Handstamped in Violet

c

Unwmkd.

Perf. 14, 14½x15, 13½.

Wove Paper.

62 A14 2k green 8.00 8.00
a. Imperf. 50 50
63 A14 3k red 5.00 4.50
a. Imperf. 25 25
64 A15 4k carmine 60 60
65 A14 5k claret 60 60
a. Imperf. 1.00 1.00
67 A15 10k dk bl 1.50 1.25
68 A14 10k on 7k lt bl 1.50 1.00
69 A11 15k red brn & bl 50 50
70 A8 20k bl & car 60 60
71 A11 25k grn & gray vio 50 50
72 A11 35k red brn & grn 40 40
73 A8 50k vio & grn 30 30
74 A14 60k on 1k org (II) 4.00 3.00
a. Imperf. (I) 2.50 2.50
b. Imperf. (II) 3.00 3.00
75 A9 1r pale brn, dk brn & org 1.00 1.00
a. Imperf. 75 75
76 A12 3½r mar & lt grn 1.50 1.50
a. Imperf. 1.00 1.00
77 A13 5r dk bl, grn & pale bl 3.00 3.00
a. Imperf. 1.50 1.50
78 A12 7r dk grn & pink 3.00 2.50
79 A13 10r scar, yel & gray 3.00 2.50

Imperf.

85 A11 70k brn & org 3.00 3.00

Handstamped in Black.

Perf. 14, 14½x15, 13½.

90 A14 1k orange 7.50 6.50
a. Imperf. 9.00 9.00
91 A14 2k green 6.00 5.00
a. Imperf. 10 10
92 A14 3k red 6.00 5.00
a. Imperf. 25 25
93 A15 4k carmine 20 20
94 A14 5k claret 10 10
a. Imperf. 1.00 1.00
95 A14 7k lt bl 7.00 6.00
96 A15 10k dk bl 1.50 1.25
97 A14 10k on 7k lt bl 20 10
98 A11 15k red brn & bl 20 12
99 A8 20k bl & car 20 12
100 A11 25k grn & gray vio 40 25
101 A11 35k red brn & grn 20 15
102 A8 50k vio & grn 20 12
102A A14 60k on 1k org (II) 4.00 2.00
b. Imperf. (I) 40 40
c. Imperf. (II) 60 60
103 A9 1r pale brn, dk brn & org 50 50
a. Imperf. 35 35
104 A12 3½r mar & lt grn 75 75
a. Imperf. 50 50
105 A13 5r dk bl, grn & pale bl 1.00 1.00
a. Imperf. 1.25 1.25
106 A12 7r dk grn & pink 1.00 1.00
107 A13 10r scar, yel & gray 1.00 1.00

Imperf.

113 A11 70k brn & org 40 40

Handstamped in Violet or Black:

5r f 10r g

Violet Surcharge.

1920 *Perf. 14, 14½x15*

120 A14 (f) 3r on 3k red 4.00 4.00
a. Imperf. 1.25 1.25
121 A14 (f) 5r on 3k red 6.00 5.00
122 A15 (f) 5r on 4k car 4.00 3.50
123 A14 (f) 5r on 5k cl 4.00 3.00
a. Imperf. 2.50 2.50
124 A15 (f) 5r on 10k dk bl 4.00 3.50
125 A14 (f) 5r on 10k on 7k lt bl 4.00 3.00
126 A8 (f) 5r on 20k bl & car

Imperf.

127 A14 (f) 5r on 2k grn 12.50 12.50
128 A11 (f) 5r on 35k red brn & grn 12.50 12.50

Black Surcharge.

Perf. 14 to 15 and Compound, 13½

130 A14 (g) 1r on 1k org 15 15
a. Imperf. 25 25
131 A14 (f) 3r on 3k red 15 8
a. Imperf. 8 8
132 A15 (f) 3r on 4k car 5.00 5.00
133 A14 (f) 5r on 2k grn 1.00 1.00
a. Imperf. 15 12
134 A14 (f) 5r on 3k red 2.50 2.50
a. Imperf. 2.50 2.50
135 A15 (f) 5r on 4k car 60 60
a. Imperf. 7.50 7.50
136 A14 (f) 5r on 5k cl 12 12
a. Imperf. 25 25
137 A14 (f) 5r on 7k lt bl 1.00 1.00
138 A15 (f) 5r on 10k dk bl 12 12
139 A14 (f) 5r on 10k on 7k lt bl 12 12
140 A11 (f) 5r on 14k bl & rose 3.50 3.50
141 A11 (f) 5r on 15k red brn & bl 20 20
a. Imperf. 4.00 4.00
142 A8 (f) 5r on 20k bl & car 20 20
a. Imperf. 4.00 4.00
143 A11 (f) 5r on 20k on 14k bl & rose 5.00 5.00
144 A11 (f) 5r on 25k grn & gray vio 5.00 5.00
145 A14 (g) 10r on 1k org *175.00* *175.00*
a. Imperf. 1.25 1.25
146 A14 (g) 10r on 3k red *90.00* *90.00*
147 A14 (g) 10r on 5k cl 6.00 6.00
a. Imperf. 8.00
148 A8 (g) 10r on 20k bl & car 6.00 6.00
148A A11 (f) 10r on 25k grn & gray vio 2.50 2.50
149 A11 (g) 10r on 25k grn & gray vio 2.00 2.00
a. Imperf. 12.00 12.00
150 A11 (g) 10r on 35k red brn & grn 25 25
151 A8 (f) 10r on 50k brn vio & grn 2.50 2.50
152 A8 (g) 10r on 50k brn vio & grn 65 65
152A A11 (g) 10r on 70k brn & org *100.00* *100.00*
b. Imperf. 4.50 4.50
152C A8 (g) 25r on 20k bl & car 1.50 1.50
153 A11 (g) 25r on 25k grn & gray vio 1.25 1.25
154 A11 (g) 25r on 35k red brn & grn 1.25 1.25
a. Imperf. 6.00 6.00
155 A8 (g) 25r on 50k vio & grn 1.75 1.75
a. Imperf. 3.00 3.00
156 A11 (g) 25r on 70k brn & org 3.00 3.00
a. Imperf. 3.00 3.00
157 A9 (g) 50r on 1r pale brn, dk brn & org 2.00 2.00
a. Imperf. 50 50
158 A13 (g) 50r on 5r dk bl, grn & lt bl 4.00 4.00
a. Imperf. 4.00 4.00
159 A12 (g) 100r on 3½r mar & lt grn 3.50 3.50
a. Imperf. 3.50 3.50
160 A13 (g) 100r on 5r dk bl, grn & pale bl 3.50 3.50
a. Imperf. 3.50 3.50
161 A12 (g) 100r on 7r dk grn & pink 4.00 4.00
a. Imperf. 16.00 16.00
162 A13 (g) 100r on 10r scar, yel & gray 3.50 3.50

Wmkd. Wavy Lines. (168)

Perf. 11½.

Vertically Laid Paper.

163 A12 (g) 100r on 3½r blk & gray 15.00 15.00
164 A12 (g) 100r on 7r blk & yel 12.50 12.50

1920 ***Imperf.*** **Unwmkd.**

Wove Paper.

166	A14 (g)	1r on 60k on 1k org (I)	4.00	4.00
168	A14 (f)	5r on 1k org	12.50	12.50
173	A11 (f)	5r on 35k red brn & grn	4.00	4.00
177	A11 (g)	50r on 70k brn & org	4.00	4.00
179	A12 (g)	50r on 3½r mar & lt grn	3.00	3.00
181	A9 (g)	100r on 1r pale brn, dk brn & org	6.00	6.00

Romanov Issues Surcharged Types "f" or "g".

On Stamps of 1913.

1920 ***Perf. 13½***

184	A16 (g)	1r on 1k brn org	4.00	4.00
185	A18 (f)	3r on 3k rose red	3.50	3.50
186	A19 (f)	5r on 4k dl red	3.50	3.50
187	A22 (f)	5r on 14k bl grn	20.00	20.00
187A	A19 (g)	10r on 4k dl red	22.50	
187B	A26 (g)	10r on 35k gray vio & dk grn		
187C	A19 (g)	25r on 4k dl red	4.50	4.50
188	A26 (g)	25r on 35k gray vio & dk grn	4.50	4.50
189	A28 (g)	25r on 70k yel grn & brn	4.50	4.50
190	A31 (f)	50r on 3r dk vio	3.50	3.50
190A	A16 (g)	100r on 1k brn org	75.00	75.00
190B	A17 (g)	100r on 2k grn	75.00	75.00
191	A30 (g)	100r on 2r brn	17.50	17.50
192	A31 (g)	100r on 3r dk vio	17.50	17.50

On Stamps of 1915.

Thin Cardboard.

Inscriptions on Back.

Perf. 12.

193	A21 (g)	100r on 10k bl	5.00
194	A23 (g)	100r on 15k brn	5.00
195	A24 (g)	100r on 20k ol grn	5.00

On Stamps of 1916.

Perf. 13½.

196	A20 (f)	5r on 10k on 7k brn	3.50	3.50
197	A22 (f)	5r on 20k on 14k bl grn	5.50	5.50

Surcharged

Type "f" or "g" over type "c",

Type "c" in Violet.

Perf. 14, 14½x15, 13½.

200	A15 (f)	5r on 4k car	1.75	1.75
201	A15 (f)	5r on 10k dk bl	1.75	1.75
202	A11 (f)	5r on 15k red brn & bl	3.50	3.50
203	A8 (f)	5r on 20k bl & car	3.00	3.00
204	A11 (g)	10r on 25k grn & gray vio	3.00	3.00
205	A11 (g)	10r on 35k red brn & grn	5.00	5.00
205A	A8 (g)	10r on 50k brn vio & grn	6.00	6.00
206	A8 (f)	25r on 50k brn vio & grn	*75.00*	*75.00*
207	A9 (g)	50r on 1r pale brn, dk brn & org	50.00	50.00
a.		Imperf.	6.00	6.00
207B	A12 (g)	100r on 3½r mar & lt grn	15.00	
207C	A12 (g)	100r on 7r dk grn & pink	15.00	

Imperf.

208	A14 (f)	5r on 2k grn	9.00	9.00
209	A14 (f)	5r on 5k cl	2.50	2.50
210	A11 (g)	25r on 70k brn & org	9.00	9.00
211	A13 (g)	100r on 5r dk bl, grn & pale bl	1.25	1.25

Type "c" in Black.

Perf. 14, 14½x15, 13½.

212	A14 (f)	5r on 7k lt bl	*100.00*	*100.00*
213	A14 (f)	5r on 10k on 7k lt bl	1.75	1.75
214	A11 (g)	5r on 15k red brn & bl	70	70
215	A8 (f)	5r on 20k bl & car	50	50
215A	A11 (g)	10r on 5r on 25k grn & gray vio	7.50	7.50
216	A11 (g)	10r on 35k red brn & grn	75	75
217	A8 (g)	10r on 50k brn vio & grn	1.25	1.25
217A	A9 (g)	50r on 1r pale brn, dk brn & org	1.50	1.50
a.		Imperf.	1.75	1.75
217C	A12 (g)	100r on 3½r mar & lt grn	2.50	2.50
218	A13 (g)	100r on 5r dk bl, grn & pale bl	3.50	3.50
a.		Imperf.	3.00	3.00
219	A12 (f)	100r on 7r dk grn & pink	5.00	5.00
219A	A13 (f)	100r on 10r scar, yel & gray	5.00	5.00

Imperf.

220	A14 (g)	1r on 60k on 1k org (I)	8.00	8.00
221	A14 (f)	5r on 2k grn	1.00	1.00
222	A14 (f)	5r on 5k cl	5.00	5.00
223	A11 (g)	10r on 70k brn & org	3.50	3.50
224	A11 (g)	25r on 70k brn & org	3.00	3.00

Surcharged

Type "f" or "g" over type "a".

Type "a" in Violet.

Imperf.

231	A9 (g)	50r on 1r pale brn, dk brn & org	*60.00*	*60.00*
232	A13 (g)	100r on 5r dk bl, grn & pale bl	17.50	

Type "a" in Black.

Perf. 14, 14½x15, 13½.

233	A8 (f)	5r on 20k bl & car	1.00	1.00
233A	A11 (g)	10r on 25k grn & gray vio	*75.00*	*75.00*
234	A11 (g)	10r on 35k red brn & grn	1.25	1.25
235	A12 (g)	100r on 3½r mar & lt grn	2.00	2.00
a.		Imperf.	2.50	2.50

Imperf.

237	A14 (g)	5r on 2k grn	50.00	50.00
237A	A11 (g)	10r on 70k brn & org		

Surcharged Type "a" and New Value.

Type "a" in Violet.

Perf. 14, 14½x15.

238	A11	10r on 15k red brn & bl	1.00	1.00

Type "a" in Black.

239	A8	5r on 20k bl & car	1.75	1.75
239A	A8	10r on 20k bl & car	5.00	5.00
239B	A8	10r on 50k brn red & grn	10.00	

Imperf.

240	A12	100r on 3½r mar & lt grn	3.00	3.00

Surcharged Type "c" and New Value.

Type "c" in Black.

1920 ***Perf. 14, 14½x15, 13½***

241	A15	5r on 4k red	3.00	3.00
242	A11	5r on 15k red brn & bl	1.75	1.75
243	A8	10r on 20k bl & car	3.00	3.00
243A	A11	10r on 25k grn & gray vio	1.25	1.25
244	A11	10r on 35k red brn & grn	1.00	1.00
a.		With additional surcharge "5r"	2.00	2.00
245	A12	100r on 3½r mar & lt grn	2.00	2.00

Imperf.

247	A14	3r on 3k red	8.00	8.00
248	A14	5r on 2k grn	50	50
249	A9	50r on 1r pale brn, dk brn & org	1.50	1.50

Type "c" in Violet.

249A	A14	5r on 2k grn	10.00

Postal Savings Stamps Surcharged.

A1 A2

A3 Wmk. 171

Wmkd. Diamonds. (171)

Perf. 14½x15.

250	A1	60k on 1k red & buff	17.50	17.50
251	A2	1r on 1k red & buff	8.50	8.50
252	A3	5r on 5k grn & buff	12.00	12.00
253	A3	5r on 10k brn & buff	12.00	12.00

Russian Semi-Postal Stamps of 1914-18 Surcharged with Armenian Monogram and New Values like Regular Issues.

Unwmkd.

Perf. 11½, 12½, 13½.

On Stamps of 1914.

255	SP5	25r on 1k red brn & dk grn *straw*	70.00	75.00
256	SP6	25r on 3k mar & gray grn, *pink*	50.00	60.00
257	SP7	50r on 7 dk brn & dk grn, *buff*	14.00	15.00
258	SP5	100r on 1k red brn & dk grn, *straw*	5.50	6.00
259	SP6	100r on 3k mar & gray grn, *pink*	5.50	6.00
260	SP7	100r on 7k dk brn & dk grn, *buff*	5.50	6.00

On Stamps of 1915-19.

261	SP5	25r on 1k org brn & gray	60.00	80.00
262	SP6	25r on 3k car & gray	50.00	50.00
263	SP8	50r on 10k dk bl & brn	17.50	20.00
264	SP5	100r on 1k org brn & gray	5.50	6.00
265	SP8	100r on 10k dk bl & brn	5.50	6.00

These surcharged semi-postal stamps were used for ordinary postage.

A set of 10 stamps in the above designs, and in a third design showing a woman quilling, was prepared in 1920, but not issued. Price of set, $2. Exist with "SPECIMEN" overprint and imperf. Counterfeits exist.

Soviet Socialist Republic.

Hammer and Sickle
A7

Mythological Monster
A8

Symbols of Soviet Republics on Designs from old Armenian Manuscripts
A9

Ruined City of Ani
A10

Mythological Monster
A11

Armenian Soldier
A12

Fisherman on River Aras
A16

Mythological Monster
A13

Soviet Symbols, Armenian Designs
A14

Mt. Alagöz and Plain of Shirak
A15

Post Office in Erevan and Mt. Ararat
A17

Ruin in City of Ani
A18

Street in Erevan
A19

Lake Gökcha and Sevan Monastery
A20

Mythological Subject from old Armenian Monument
A21

Mt. Ararat
A22

Perf. 11½, Imperf.

1921			**Unwmkd.**	
278	A7	1r gray grn	20	
279	A8	2r sl gray	20	
280	A9	3r carmine	20	
281	A10	5r dk brn	20	
282	A11	25r gray	20	15
283	A12	50r red	10	
284	A13	100r orange	10	
285	A14	250r dk bl	10	
286	A15	500r brn vio	10	
287	A16	1000r sea grn	20	
288	A17	2000r bister	25	
289	A18	5000r dk brn	25	
290	A19	10,000r dl red	25	
291	A20	15,000r sl bl	25	
292	A21	20,000r lake	25	
293	A22	25,000r gray bl	50	
294	A22	25,000r brn ol	4.00	
		Nos. 278-294 (17)	7.35	

Except the 25r, Nos. 278–294 were not regulary issued and used. Counterfeits exist.

Russian Stamps of 1909-17 Surcharged

Wove Paper
Lozenges of Varnish on Face

1921, August			***Perf. 13½***
295	A9	5000r on 1r pale brn, dk brn & org	3.50
296	A12	5000r on 3½r mar & lt grn	3.50
297	A13	5000r on 5r dk bl, grn & pale bl	3.50
298	A12	5000r on 7r dk grn & pink	3.50
299	A13	5000r on 10r scar, yel & gray	3.50
		Nos. 295-299 (5)	17.50

Nos. 295–299 were not officially issued. Counterfeits abound.

Mt. Ararat and Soviet Star
A23 A24

Soviet Symbols
A25

Crane
A26

Peasant
A27

Harpy
A28

Peasant Sowing
A29

Soviet Symbols
A30

Forging
A31

Plowing
A32

1922			***Perf. 11½.***
300	A23	50r grn & red	20
301	A24	300r sl bl & buff	25
302	A25	400r bl & pink	25
303	A26	500r vio & pale lil	25
304	A27	1000r dl bl & pale bl	25
305	A28	2000r blk & gray	40
306	A29	3000r blk & grn	40
307	A30	4000r blk & lt brn	40
308	A31	5000r blk & dl red	30
309	A32	10,000r blk & pale rose	30
a.		Tête bêche pair	15.00
		Nos. 300-309 (10)	3.00

Nos. 300 to 309 were not placed in use without surcharge.

Stamps of types A23 to A32, printed in other colors than Nos. 300 to 309, are essays.

1922-23

Stamps of Preceding Issue with Handstamped Surcharge of New Values in Rose, Violet or Black

310	A23	10,000 on 50r grn & red (R)	8.00	8.00
311	A23	10,000 on 50r grn & red (V)	2.50	2.50
312	A23	10,000 on 50r grn & red (Bk)	75	75
313	A24	15,000 on 300r sl bl & buff (R)	12.00	12.00
314	A24	15,000 on 300r sl bl & buff (V)	2.50	2.50
315	A24	15,000 on 300r sl bl & buff (Bk)	1.25	1.25
316	A25	25,000 on 400r bl & pink (V)	2.50	2.50
317	A25	25,000 on 400r bl & pink (Bk)	50	50
318	A26	30,000 on 500r vio & pale lil (R)	15.00	15.00
319	A26	30,000 on 500r vio & pale lil (V)	1.25	1.25
320	A26	30,000 on 500r vio & pale lil (Bk)	75	75
321	A27	50,000 on 1000r dl bl & pale bl (R)	12.00	12.00
322	A27	50,000 on 1000r dl bl & pale bl (V)	5.00	5.00
323	A27	50,000 on 1000r dl bl & pale bl (Bk)	1.25	1.25
324	A29	75,000 on 3000r blk & grn (Bk)	1.50	1.50
325	A28	100,000 on 2000r blk & gray (R)	16.00	16.00
326	A28	100,000 on 2000r blk & gray (V)	5.00	5.00
327	A28	100,000 on 2000r blk & gray (Bk)	1.25	1.25
328	A30	200,000 on 4000r blk & lt brn (V)	1.25	1.25
329	A30	200,000 on 4000r blk & lt brn (Bk)	1.25	1.25
330	A31	300,000 on 5000r blk & dl red (V)	8.50	8.50
331	A31	300,000 on 5000r blk & dl red (Bk)	1.00	1.00
332	A32	500,000 on 10,000r blk & pale rose (V)	5.00	5.00
333	A32	500,000 on 10,000r blk & pale rose (Bk)	1.00	1.00
		Nos. 310-333 (24)	107.00	107.00

Goose
A33

Armenian Woman at Well
A35

Armenian Village Scene
A34

Mt. Ararat
A36

Mt. Ararat
A37

New Values in Gold Kopecks, Handstamped Surcharge in Black.

922				*Imperf.*
34	A33	1(k) on 250r rose	3.00	3.00
35	A33	1(k) on 250r gray	6.00	6.00
36	A34	2(k) on 500r rose	2.50	2.50
37	A34	3(k) on 500r gray	2.00	2.00
38	A35	4(k) on 1000r rose	2.00	2.00
39	A35	4(k) on 1000r gray	3.50	3.50
40	A36	5(k) on 2000r gray	2.00	2.00
41	A36	10(k) on 2000r rose	2.00	2.00
42	A37	15(k) on 5000r rose	12.00	12.00
43	A37	20(k) on 5000r gray	2.00	2.00
		Nos. 334-343 (10)	37.00	37.00

Nos. 334–343 were issued for postal tax purposes.

Nos. 334 to 343 exist without surcharge but are not known to have been issued in that condition. Counterfeits exist of both sets.

Regular Issue of 1921 Handstamped with New Values in Black or Red.
Short, Thick Numerals.

1922-23				*Imperf.*
47	A8	2(k) on 2r sl gray (R)	17.50	17.50
50	A11	4(k) on 25r gray (R)	6.00	6.00
53	A13	10(k) on 100r org (R)	12.50	12.50
54	A14	15(k) on 250r dk bl	1.00	1.00
55	A15	20(k) on 500r brn vio	1.50	1.50
a.		With "k" written in red	2.00	2.00
57	A22	50(k) on 25,000r bl (R)	20.00	20.00
58	A22	50(k) on 25,000r brn ol (R)	15.00	15.00
59	A22	50(k) on 25,000r brn ol		
		Nos. 347-358 (7)	73.50	73.50

Perf. 11½.

360	A7	1(k) on 1r gray grn	10.00	10.00
a.		Imperf.	3.00	3.00
361	A7	1(k) on 1r gray grn (R)	6.00	6.00
a.		Imperf.	10.00	10.00
362	A8	2(k) on 2r sl gray	15.00	15.00
a.		Imperf.	6.00	6.00
363	A15	2(k) on 500r brn vio	3.50	3.50
a.		Imperf.	3.00	3.00
364	A15	2(k) on 500r brn vio (R)	15.00	15.00
365	A11	4(k) on 25r gray	12.00	12.00
a.		Imperf.	6.00	6.00
366	A12	5(k) on 50r red	4.00	4.00
a.		Imperf.	3.00	3.00
367	A13	10(k) on 100r org	3.50	3.50
a.		Imperf.	3.50	3.50
368	A21	35(k) on 20,000r cl	15.00	15.00
a.		With "k" written in vio	15.00	15.00
b.		Imperf.	6.00	6.00
c.		As "a," imperf.	6.00	6.00
d.		With "kop" written in vio, imperf.		
		Nos. 360-368 (9)	84.00	84.00

Manuscript Surcharge in Red.
Perf. 11½.

371	A14	1k on 250r dk bl	4.00	4.00

Handstamped in Black or Red.
Tall, Thin Numerals.
Imperf.

377	A11	4(k) on 25r gray (R)	7.00	7.00
379	A13	10(k) on 100r org	4.00	4.00
380	A15	20(k) on 500r brn vio	10.00	10.00
381	A22	50k on 25,000r bl	1.50	1.50
a.		Surcharged "50" only	25.00	25.00
382	A22	50k on 25,000r bl (R)	20.00	20.00
382A	A22	50k on 25,000r brn ol	40.00	40.00
		Nos. 377-382A (6)	82.50	82.50

On Nos. 381, 382 and 382A the letter "k" forms part of the surcharge.

Perf. 11½.

383	A7	1(k) on 1r gray grn (R)	5.00	5.00
a.		Imperf.		
384	A14	1(k) on 250r dk bl	3.00	3.00
385	A15	2(k) on 500r brn vio	3.75	3.75
a.		Imperf.	4.00	4.00
386	A15	2(k) on 500r brn vio (R)	8.00	8.00
387	A9	3(k) on 3r rose	10.00	10.00
a.		Imperf.	10.00	10.00
388	A21	3(k) on 20,000r cl	30.00	30.00
a.		Imperf.	5.00	5.00
389	A11	4(k) on 25r gray	4.00	4.00
a.		Imperf.	7.00	7.00
390	A12	5(k) on 50r red	3.00	3.00
a.		Imperf.	2.00	2.00
		Nos. 383-390 (8)	66.75	66.75

Foreign postal stationery (stamped envelopes, postal cards and air letter sheets) lies beyond the scope of this Catalogue which is limited to adhesive postage stamps.

ARUBA

Traditional House—A1

1986		Litho.		*Perf. 14x13*
1	A1	5c shown	5	5
3	A1	15c King William III Tower	12	12
5	A1	30c Snake	22	22
6	A1	35c Owl	26	26
9	A1	60c Water skier	45	45
10	A1	65c Net fishing	48	48
15	A1	150c Watapana tree	1.15	1.15
16	A1	250c Aloe plant	1.85	1.85
		Nos. 1-16 (8)	4.58	4.58

Issue dates: 5c, 30c, 60c, 150c, Jan. 1. Others, Feb. 5.

Independence—A2

1986, Jan. 1				*Perf. 14x13, 13x14*
18	A2	25c Map	20	20
19	A2	45c Coat of arms, vert.	35	35
20	A2	55c Natl. anthem, vert.	42	42
21	A2	100c Flag	75	75

Intl. Peace Year—A3

1986, Aug. 29				*Perf. 14x13*
22	A3	60c shown	45	45
23	A3	100c Barbed wire	75	75

SEMI-POSTAL STAMPS

Solidarity—SP1

1986, May 7		Litho.		*Perf. 14x13*
B1	SP1	30c + 10c shown	30	30
B2	SP1	35c + 15c Three ropes	38	38
B3	SP1	60c + 25c One rope	65	65

Child Welfare—SP2

1986, Oct. 29		Litho.		*Perf. 14x13*
B4	SP2	45c + 20c Boy, caterpillar	55	55
B5	SP2	70c + 25c Boy, cocoon	80	80
B6	SP2	100c + 40c Girl, butterfly	1.20	1.20

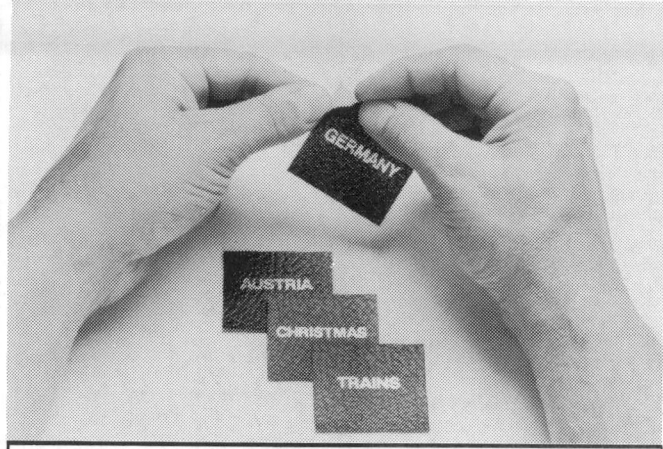

AUSTRIA

(ôs'trĭ·ȧ)

LOCATION — Central Europe.
GOVT.—Republic.
AREA—32,376 sq. mi.
POP.—7,555,338 (1981).
CAPITAL—Vienna.

Before 1867 Austria was an absolute monarchy, which included Hungary and Lombardy-Venetia. In 1867 the Astro-Hungarian Monarchy was established, with Austria and Hungary as equal partners. After World War I, in 1918, the different nationalities established their own states and only the German-speaking parts remained, forming a republic under the name "Deutschosterreich" (German Austria), which name was shortly again changed to "Austria." In 1938 German forces occupied Austria, which became part of the German Reich. After the liberation by Allied troops in 1945, an independent republic was re-established.

60 Kreuzer = 1 Gulden
100 Neu-Kreuzer = 1 Gulden (1858)
100 Heller = 1 Krone (1899)
100 Groschen = 1 Schilling (1925)

Prices of early Austrian stamps vary according to condition. Quotations for Nos. 1–5, P1–P7 and PR1–PR4 are for fine copies. Very fine to superb specimens sell at much higher prices, and inferior or poor copies sell at reduced prices, depending on the condition of the individual specimen.

Prices for unused stamps of 1850–80 issues are for copies in fine condition with original gum. Specimens without gum sell for about one-third of the figures quoted.

Issues of the Austrian Monarchy (including Hungary).

Coat of Arms
A1

Wmkd. K. K. H. M. in Sheet or Unwmkd.

1850 Typographed *Imperf.*

Thin to Thick Paper.

The stamps of this issue were at first printed on a rough hand-made paper, varying in thickness and having a watermark in script letters K. K. H. M., the initials of Kaiserlich Königliches Handels-Ministerium (Imperial and Royal Ministry of Commerce), vertically in the gutter between the panes. Parts of these letters show on margin stamps in the sheet. From 1854 a thick, smooth machine-made paper without watermark was used.

NINE KREUZER.

Type I. The top of "9" is about on a level with "Kreuzer" and not near the top of the label.

Type IA. Similar to type I but with 1¼mm. instead of ½mm. space between "9" and "Kreuzer."

Type II. The top of "9" is much higher than the top of the word "Kreuzer" and nearly touches the top of the label.

No.	Type	Description	Unused	Used
1	A1	1kr yellow	850.00	70.00
a.		Printed on both sides	*1,750.*	160.00
b.		1kr org	1,400.	100.00
c.		1kr brn org	2,500.	400.00
2	A1	2kr black	950.00	65.00
a.		Ribbed paper		*1,750.*
b.		2kr gray blk	1,300.	80.00
3	A1	3kr red	400.00	3.00
a.		Ribbed paper	*2,000.*	75.00
b.		Laid paper		*10,000.*
c.		Printed on both sides		*10,000.*
4	A1	6kr brown	450.00	4.00
a.		Ribbed paper		*1,500.*

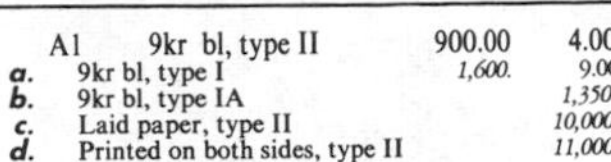

No.	Type	Description	Unused	Used
5	A1	9kr bl, type II	900.00	4.00
a.		9kr bl, type I	*1,600.*	9.00
b.		9kr bl, type IA		*1,350.*
c.		Laid paper, type II		*10,000.*
d.		Printed on both sides, type II		*11,000.*

In 1852–54, Nos. 1 to 5, rouletted 14, were used in Tokay. A 12kr blue exists, but was not issued.

The reprints are printed in brighter colors, some on paper watermarked "Briefmarken" in the sheet.

Emperor Franz Josef
A2 A3 A4

A5 A6

1858-59 Embossed. ***Perf. 14½.***

Two Types of Each Value.

Type I. Loops of the bow at the back of the head broken, except the 2kr. In the 2kr, the "2" has a flat foot, thinning to the right.

Type II. Loops complete. Wreath projects further at top of head. In the 2kr, the "2" has a more curved foot of uniform thickness, with a shading line in the upper and lower curves.

No.	Type	Description	Unused	Used
6	A2	2kr yel, type II	550.00	25.00
a.		2kr yel, type I	1,250.	225.00
b.		2kr org, type II	1,250.	225.00
7	A3	3kr blk, type II	1,750.	150.00
a.		3kr blk, type I	750.00	175.00
8	A3	3kr grn, type II ('59)	500.00	87.50
9	A4	5kr red, type II	175.00	90
a.		5kr red, type I	250.00	7.50
10	A5	10kr brn, type II	450.00	2.25
a.		10kr brn, type I	450.00	19.00
11	A6	15kr bl, type II	350.00	1.50
a.		Type I	800.00	12.00

The reprints are of type II and are perforated 10½, 11, 12, 12½ and 13. There are also imperforate reprints of Nos. 6 to 8.

Emperor Franz Josef
A7

Coat of Arms
A8

1860–61 Embossed ***Perf. 14***

No.	Type	Description	Unused	Used
12	A7	2kr yellow	325.00	17.50
13	A7	3kr green	300.00	12.50
14	A7	5kr red	175.00	90
15	A7	10kr brown	250.00	2.00
16	A7	15kr blue	200.00	1.00

The reprints are perforated 9, 9½, 10, 10½, 11, 11½, 12, 12½, 13 and 13½. There are also imperforate reprints of the 2 and 3kr.

1863

No.	Type	Description	Unused	Used
17	A8	2kr yellow	450.00	75.00
18	A8	3kr green	350.00	65.00
19	A8	5kr rose	200.00	5.00
20	A8	10kr blue	700.00	6.00
21	A8	15kr yel brn	800.00	8.50

Wmk. 91

Unwmkd. or, after June 1864, Wmkd. "BRIEF-MARKEN" in Double-lined Capitals Across the Middle of the Sheet (91).

1863-64 ***Perf. 9½.***

22	A8	2kr	yel ('64)	125.00	7.50
23	A8	3kr	grn ('64)	125.00	6.50
24	A8	5kr	rose	45.00	25
25	A8	10kr	blue	100.00	1.75
26	A8	15kr	yel brn	110.00	1.25

The reprints are perforated 10½, 11½, 13 and 13½. There are also imperforate reprints of the 2 and 3kr.

Issues of Austro-Hungarian Monarchy

From 1867 to 1871 the independent postal administrations of Austria and Hungary used the same stamps.

Emperor Franz Josef

A9 A10

5 kr:

Type I. In arabesques in lower left corner, the small ornament at left of the curve nearest the figure "5" is short and has three points at bottom.

Type II. The ornament is prolonged within the curve and has two points at bottom. The corresponding ornament at top of the lower left corner does not touch the curve (1872).

Type III. Similar to type II but the top ornament is joined to the curve (1881).

Two different printing methods were used for the 1867-74 issues. The first produced stamps on which the hair and whiskers were coarse and thick, from the second they were fine and clear.

Typographed

1867-72 ***Perf. 9½*** **Wmk. 91**

Coarse Print.

27	A9	2kr	yellow	110.00	2.00
28	A9	3kr	green	110.00	2.25
29	A9	5kr	rose, type I	70.00	10
a.			5kr rose, type II	65.00	13
b.			Perf. 10½, type II	125.00	
c.			Cliché of 3kr in plate of 5kr		*30,000.*
30	A9	10kr	blue	135.00	2.00
31	A9	15kr	brown	150.00	4.50
32	A9	25kr	lilac	20.00	15.00
a.			25kr gray lil	20.00	15.00
b.			25kr brn vio	110.00	32.50

Perf. 12.

33	A10	50kr	lt brn	30.00	*62.50*
a.			50kr pale red brn	120.00	75.00
b.			50kr brnsh rose	400.00	150.00
c.			Pair, imperf. btwn., vert. or horizontal	500.00	*1,000.*

Issues for Austria only.

1874-80 ***Perf. 9½***

Fine Print.

34	A9	2kr	yel ('76)	11.00	90
a.			Perf. 9	175.00	22.50
b.			Perf. 10½	45.00	4.25
c.			Perf. 12	250.00	85.00
d.			Perf. 13	190.00	150.00
35	A9	3kr	grn ('76)	32.50	1.10
a.			Perf. 9	160.00	20.00
b.			Perf. 10½	45.00	2.50
c.			Perf. 12	190.00	9.00
d.			Perf. 13	150.00	22.50
36	A9	5kr	rose, type III	3.00	6
a.			Perf. 9	75.00	3.50
b.			Perf. 10½	11.00	75
c.			Perf. 12	60.00	2.50
d.			Perf. 13	90.00	10.00
37	A9	10kr	bl ('75)	75.00	25
a.			Perf. 9	300.00	22.50
b.			Perf. 10½	80.00	2.50
c.			Perf. 12	375.00	100.00
d.			Perf. 13	190.00	80.00
38	A9	15kr	brn ('77)	7.00	4.00
a.			Perf. 9	375.00	70.00
b.			Perf. 10½	190.00	20.00
c.			Perf. 12	600.00	110.00
d.			Perf. 13	350.00	200.00
39	A9	25kr	gray lil ('78)	2.00	*80.00*
40	A10	50kr	brn, perf. 12 ('80)	12.50	*65.00*
a.			Perf. 13	15.00	*75.00*
b.			Perf. 10½x12	300.00	

Various compound perforations exist.

A11

Inscriptions in Black

Perf. 9, 9½, 10, 10½, 11½, 12, 12½

1883

41	A11	2kr	brown	6.00	50
42	A11	3kr	green	6.00	35
43	A11	5kr	rose	10.00	5
a.			Vertical pair, imperf. between	300.00	400.00
44	A11	10kr	blue	6.00	40
45	A11	20kr	gray	60.00	6.00
46	A11	50kr	red lil	350.00	62.50

The last printings of Nos. 41 to 46 are watermarked "ZEITUNGS-MARKEN" instead of "BRIEF-MARKEN."

The 5kr has been reprinted in a dull red rose, perforated 10½.

Emperor Franz Josef

A12 A13

Granite Paper.

Perf. 9 to 13½, also Compound.

1890-96 **Unwmkd.**

Numerals in black, Nos. 51 to 61.

51	A12	1kr	dk gray	2.25	10
a.			Pair, imperf. between	300.00	500.00
52	A12	2kr	lt brn	40	5
53	A12	3kr	gray grn	50	5
a.			Pair, imperf. between	325.00	500.00
54	A12	5kr	rose	40	5
a.			Pair, imperf. between	300.00	400.00
55	A12	10kr	ultra	70	6
a.			Pair, imperf. between	375.00	550.00
56	A12	12kr	claret	2.75	25
57	A12	15kr	lilac	1.75	25
a.			Pair, imperf. between	375.00	550.00
58	A12	20kr	ol grn	35.00	2.50
59	A12	24kr	gray bl	3.50	85
a.			Pair, imperf. between	400.00	550.00
60	A12	30kr	dk brn	3.00	40
61	A12	50kr	violet	12.50	7.50

Engraved

62	A13	1gld	dk bl	2.25	2.75
63	A13	1gld	pale lil ('96)	55.00	3.75
64	A13	2gld	carmine	5.00	10.00
65	A13	2gld	gray grn ('96)	30.00	30.00

Nearly all values of the 1890-1907 issues are found with numerals missing in one or more corners, some with nnmerals printed on the back.

A14

1891 **Typographed.**

Numerals in black.

Perf. 9 to 13½, also Compound.

66	A14	20kr	ol grn	1.50	12
67	A14	24kr	gray bl	3.00	60
68	A14	30kr	brown	1.50	12
a.			Pair, imperf. between	425.00	600.00
b.			Perf. 9	175.00	35.00
69	A14	50kr	violet	2.00	35

A15

A16

A17 A18

Perf. 10½ to 13½ and Compound.

Numerals in black, Nos. 70 to 82.

1899 **Without Varnish Bars.**

70	A15	1h	lilac	1.10	7
b.			Imperf.	100.00	125.00
c.			Perf. 10½	20.00	5.50
d.			Numerals inverted	550.00	750.00
71	A15	2h	dk gray	3.75	25
72	A15	3h	bis brn	5.00	6
b.			"3" in lower right corner sideways		*1,100.*
73	A15	5h	bl grn	12.50	5
c.			Perf. 10½	17.50	5.00
74	A15	6h	orange	60	5
75	A16	10h	rose	8.00	5
b.			Perf. 10½	400.00	100.00
76	A16	20h	brown	1.00	10
77	A16	25h	ultra	75.00	20
78	A16	30h	red vio	27.50	2.75
b.			Horizontal pair, imperf. between	375.00	
80	A17	40h	green	45.00	3.25
81	A17	50h	gray bl	32.50	4.25
b.			All four "50's" parallel		*1,500.*
82	A17	60h	brown	55.00	1.25
b.			Horizontal pair, imperf. between	375.00	
c.			Perf. 10½	65.00	1.50

Engraved

83	A18	1k	car rose	3.00	12
a.			1k car	7.50	12
b.			Vertical pair, imperf. between	375.00	400.00
84	A18	2k	gray lil	70.00	50
a.			Vertical pair, imperf. between	500.00	550.00
85	A18	4k	gray grn	7.50	7.00

1901 **With Varnish Bars.**

70a	A15	1h	lilac	1.75	3
71a	A15	2h	dk gray	1.75	2
72a	A15	3h	bis brn	60	
73a	A15	5h	bl grn	30	
74a	A15	6h	orange	30	
75a	A16	10h	rose	40	
76a	A16	20h	brown	1.25	
77a	A16	25h	ultra	1.50	1
78a	A16	30h	red vio	1.50	1.0
79	A17	35h	green	1.50	2
80a	A17	40h	green	2.75	5.0
81a	A17	50h	gray bl	7.00	7.5
82a	A17	60h	brown	3.50	6
			Nos. 70a-78a, 79, 80a-82a (13)	24.10	15.2

The diagonal yellow bars of varnish were printed across the face to prevent cleaning.

A19

A20

A21

Perf. 12½ to 13½ and Compound.

Colored Numerals.

1905-07 **Typographed**

Without Varnish Bars.

86	A19	1h	lilac	18	20
87	A19	2h	dk gray	25	10
88	A19	3h	bis brn	28	8
89	A19	5h	dk bl grn	12.50	8
90	A19	5h	yel grn ('06)	50	5
91	A19	6h	dp org	50	8
92	A20	10h	car ('06)	75	5
93	A20	12h	vio ('07)	1.50	50
94	A20	20h	brn ('06)	2.75	10
95	A20	25h	ultra ('06)	4.00	30
96	A20	30h	red vio ('06)	7.50	25

Black Numerals.

97	A20	10h	carmine	9.00	8
98	A20	20h	brown	50.00	1.25
99	A20	25h	ultra	50.00	3.00
100	A20	30h	red vio	50.00	3.00

White Numerals.

101	A21	35h	green	3.00	30
102	A21	40h	dp vio	3.00	1.00
103	A21	50h	dl bl	3.75	4.50
104	A21	60h	yel brn	3.75	50
105	A21	72h	rose	3.75	1.75
			Nos. 86-105 (20)	206.96	17.17

1904 **With Varnish Bars**

86a	A19	1h	lilac	75	55
87a	A19	2h	dk gray	2.75	55
88a	A19	3h	bis brn	2.75	8
89a	A19	5h	dk bl grn	6.50	12
91a	A19	6h	dp org	10.00	40
97a	A20	10h	carmine	3.75	5
98a	A20	20h	brown	52.50	75
99a	A20	25h	ultra	60.00	75
100a	A20	30h	red vio	65.00	1.40
101a	A21	35h	green	55.00	60
102a	A21	40h	dp vio	52.50	5.00
103a	A21	50h	dl bl	50.00	7.50
104a	A21	60h	yel brn	50.00	1.25
105a	A21	72h	rose	1.50	90
			Nos. 86a-105a (14)	413.00	19.90

Stamps of the 1901, 1904 and 1905 issues perf. 9 or 10½, also compound with 12½, were not sold at any post office, but were supplied only to some high-ranking officials. This applies also to the contemporary issues of Austrian Offices Abroad.

Emperor Karl VI

A22

Emperor Franz Josef

A23

Schönbrunn Castle
A24

Emperor Franz Josef
A25

Designs: 2h, Empress Maria Theresa. 3h, Emperor Joseph II. 5h, 10h, 25h, Emperor Franz Josef. h, Emperor Leopold II. 12h, Emperor Franz I. 0h, Emperor Ferdinand I. 30h, Franz Josef as outh. 35h, Franz Josef in middle age. 60h, Franz osef on horseback. 1k, Franz Josef in royal robes. k, Hofburg, Vienna.

1908-13		Typographed.	*Perf. 12½.*	
10	A22	1h gray blk	50	10
11	A22	2h bl vio ('13)	35	10
a.		2h vio	50	8
12	A22	3h magenta	22	10
13	A22	5h yel grn	22	5
a.		Booklet pane of 6	30.00	
14	A22	6h buff	90	65
a.		6h ocher ('13)	1.75	1.60
b.		6h org brn ('13)	1.75	1.60
15	A22	10h rose	22	5
a.		Booklet pane of 6	110.00	
16	A22	12h scarlet	1.75	45
17	A22	20h chocolate	2.75	22
18	A22	25h ultra ('13)	1.60	15
a.		25h dp bl	2.75	28
19	A22	30h ol grn	5.50	28
20	A22	35h slate	4.00	28
		Engraved.		
21	A23	50h dk grn	90	28
a.		Pair, imperf. btwn., vert. or horizontal	300.00	325.00
22	A23	60h dp car	50	12
a.		Pair, imperf. btwn., vert. or horizontal	400.00	450.00
23	A23	72h dk brn ('13)	2.25	28
24	A23	1k purple	16.00	28
a.		Pair, imperf. btwn., vert. or horizontal	300.00	325.00
25	A24	2k lake & ol grn	22.50	55
26	A24	5k bis & dk vio	40.00	5.50
27	A25	10k bl, bis & dp brn	225.00	72.50
		Nos. 110-127 (18)	325.16	81.94

Issued in commemoration of the 60th year of e reign of Emperor Franz Josef for permanent se.

The 1 to 35h inclusive exist on both ordinary and alk-surfaced paper.

All values exist imperforate. They were not sold any post office, but presented to a number of high overnment officials. This applies also to all imperorate stamps of later issues, including semi-postals, c., and those of the Austrian Offices Abroad.

Forgeries of No. 127 exist.

Birthday Jubilee Issue.

Similar to 1908 Issue, but designs nlarged by labels at top and bottom bearing dates "1830" and "1910".

910		Typographed.		
8	A22	1h gray blk	5.00	4.50
9	A22	2h violet	6.25	6.75
0	A22	3h magenta	6.25	6.75
1	A22	5h yel grn	22	22
2	A22	6h buff	2.75	2.25
3	A22	10h rose	22	22
4	A22	12h scarlet	3.50	3.50
5	A22	20h chocolate	5.00	5.75
6	A22	25h dp bl	90	90
7	A22	30h ol grn	5.00	5.25
8	A22	35h slate	5.00	5.25
		Engraved		
9	A23	50h dk grn	5.25	6.75
0	A23	60h dp car	5.25	6.75
1	A23	1k purple	5.75	9.00
2	A24	2k lake & ol grn	140.00	210.00
3	A24	5k bis & dk vio	125.00	175.00

144	A25	10k bl, bis & dp brn	225.00	325.00
		Nos. 128-144 (17)	546.34	773.84

Issued in celebration of the eightieth birthday of Emperor Franz Josef.

All values exist imperforate.

Forgeries of Nos. 142 to 144 exist.

Austrian Crown
A37

Emperor Franz Josef
A38

Coat of Arms
A39 A40

1916-18		Typographed.		
145	A37	3h brt vio	5	5
146	A37	5h lt grn	5	5
a.		Bklt. pane of 6	20.00	
b.		Booklet pane of 4 + 2 labels	35.00	
147	A37	6h dp org	28	65
148	A37	10h magenta	5	5
a.		Bklt. pane of 6	35.00	
149	A37	12h lt bl	45	1.40
150	A38	15h rose red	60	5
a.		Booklet pane of 6	20.00	
151	A38	20h chocolate	5.25	12
152	A38	25h blue	8.00	65
153	A38	30h slate	7.25	90
154	A39	40h ol grn	18	5
155	A39	50h bl grn	28	5
156	A39	60h dp bl	22	5
157	A39	80h org brn	18	5
158	A39	90h red vio	18	6
159	A39	1k car, *yel* ('18)	45	8
		Engraved.		
160	A40	2k dk bl	65	22
161	A40	3k claret	7.50	1.10
162	A40	4k dp grn	1.40	2.25
163	A40	10k dp vio	27.50	42.50
		Nos. 145-163 (19)	60.52	50.33

Stamps of type A38 have two varieties of the frame. Stamps of type A40 have various decorations about the shield.

Nos. 145–163 exist imperf. Price, set $425.

1917		Ordinary Paper		
164	A40	2k lt bl	90	45
165	A40	3k car rose	11.00	90
166	A40	4k yel grn	1.40	1.40
167	A40	10k violet	125.00	65.00

Nos. 164–167 exist imperf. Price, set $325.

See Nos. 172–175 (granite paper).

Emperor Karl I
A42

1917-18		Typographed		
168	A42	15h dl red	5	5
a.		Booklet pane of 6	20.00	
169	A42	20h dk grn ('18)	8	5
a.		20h grn ('17)	75	8
170	A42	25h blue	20	5
171	A42	30h dl vio	15	5

Nos. 168–171 exist imperf. Price, set $50.

Engraved.

1918-19		Granite Paper.		
172	A40	2k lt bl	12	65
a.		Perf. 11½	550.00	450.00
173	A40	3k car rose	30	1.50
174	A40	4k yel grn ('19)	5.25	13.00
175	A40	10k dp vio ('19)	6.25	11.00

Issues of the Republic.

Austrian Stamps of 1916-18 Overprinted

1918-19		*Perf. 12½.*	Unwmkd.	
181	A37	3h brt vio	5	5
182	A37	5h lt grn	5	5
183	A37	6h dp org	8	32
184	A37	10h magenta	5	5
185	A37	12h lt bl	15	55
186	A42	15h dl red	8	55
187	A42	20h dp grn	6	5
188	A42	25h blue	15	8
189	A42	30h dl vio	10	8
190	A39	40h ol grn	10	12
191	A39	50h dp grn	45	55
192	A39	60h dp bl	35	55
193	A39	80h org brn	8	15
a.		Inverted overprint	275.00	275.00
194	A39	90h red vio	12	15
195	A39	1k car, *yel*	15	15
		Granite Paper.		
196	A40	2k lt bl	8	8
a.		Pair, imperf. between	275.00	275.00
b.		Perf. 11½	11.00	6.75
197	A40	3k car rose	18	50
198	A40	4k yel grn	1.40	1.75
a.		Perf. 11½	15.00	13.00
199	A40	10k dp vio	10.50	13.00
		Nos. 181-199 (19)	14.18	18.78

Nos. 181, 182, 184, 187 to 191, 194, 197 and 199 exist imperforate.

Post Horn
A43

Coat of Arms
A44

Allegory of New Republic
A45

Ordinary Paper.

1919-20		Typographed.	*Perf. 12½.*	
200	A43	3h gray	5	12
201	A44	5h yel grn	5	5
202	A44	5h gray ('20)	5	5
203	A43	6h orange	10	32
204	A44	10h dp rose	5	5
205	A44	10h red ('20)	5	5
a.		Thick grysh paper ('20)	5	5
206	A43	12h grnsh bl	6	40
207	A43	15h bis ('20)	22	65
a.		Thick grysh paper ('20)	5	5
208	A45	20h dk grn	5	5
a.		20h yel grn	5	5
b.		As "a," thick grysh paper ('20)	45	1.25
209	A44	25h blue	5	5
210	A43	25h vio ('20)	5	5
211	A45	30h dk brn	5	5
212	A45	40h violet	5	12
213	A45	40h lake ('20)	5	5
214	A44	45h ol grn	18	45
215	A45	50h dk bl	6	5
a.		Thick grysh paper ('20)	8	15
216	A43	60h ol grn ('20)	5	8
217	A44	1k car, *yel*	5	8
218	A44	1k lt bl ('20)	5	6
		Nos. 200-218 (19)	1.32	2.78

All values exist imperf. (For regularly issued imperfs, see Nos. 227–235).

Parliament Building
A46

Granite Paper.

1919-20		Engraved	*Perf. 12½, 11½*	
219	A46	2k ver & blk	25	45
a.		Center inverted	3,250.	
220	A46	2½k ol bis ('20)	6	20
221	A46	3k bl & blk brn	6	12
222	A46	4k car & blk	6	12
a.		Center invert.	1,850.	1,600.
223	A46	5k blk ('20)	8	12
a.		Perf. 11½x12½	37.50	52.50
224	A46	7½k plum	8	32
a.		Perf. 11½	100.00	135.00
b.		Perf. 11½x12½	87.50	135.00
225	A46	10k ol grn & blk brn	20	45
a.		Perf. 11½x12½	75.00	100.00
b.		Perf. 11½	16.00	27.50
226	A46	20k lil & red ('20)	8	55
a.		Center invert.	8,500.	7,000.
b.		Perf. 11½	45.00	75.00
		Nos. 219-226 (8)	87	2.33

A number of values exist imperforate between. Prices, $300 to $400 a pair.

See No. 248.

Ordinary Paper.

1920		Typographed.	*Imperf.*	
227	A44	5h yel grn	8	30
228	A44	5h gray	5	5
229	A44	10h dp rose	5	5
230	A44	10h red	5	5
231	A43	15h bister	5	10
232	A43	25h violet	5	5
233	A45	30h dk brn	5	10
234	A45	40h violet	5	7
235	A43	60h ol grn	5	12
		Nos. 227-235 (9)	48	89

Arms
A47 A48

Ordinary Paper.

1920-21		Typo.	*Perf. 12½*	
238	A47	80h rose	5	5
239	A47	1k blk brn	5	5
241	A47	1½k grn ('21)	6	10
242	A47	2k blue	5	5
243	A48	3k yel grn & dk grn ('21)	5	5
244	A48	4k red & cl ('21)	6	5
245	A48	5k vio & cl ('21)	6	6
246	A48	7½k yel & brn ('21)	6	6
247	A48	10k ultra & bl ('21)	5	8
		Nos. 238-247 (9)	49	55

Nos. 238–245, 247 exist on white paper of good quality and on thick grayish paper of inferior quality; No. 246 only on white paper.

1921		Engraved		
248	A46	50k dk vio, *yel*	30	90
a.		Perf. 11½	40.00	67.50

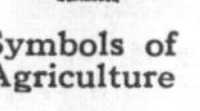

Symbols of Agriculture
A49

Symbols of Labor and Industry
A50

1922–24 Typographed *Perf. 12½*

No.	Type	Description	Unused	Used
250	A49	½k ol bis	5	65
251	A50	1k brown	5	5
252	A50	2k cob bl	5	18
253	A49	2½k org brn	5	8
254	A50	4k dl vio	5	80
255	A50	5k gray grn	5	8
256	A49	7½k gray vio	5	8
257	A50	10k claret	5	8
258	A49	12½k gray grn	5	8
259	A49	15k bluish grn	5	15
260	A49	20k dk bl	5	8
261	A49	25k claret	5	8
262	A50	30k pale gray	5	15
263	A50	45k pale red	5	15
264	A50	50k org brn	5	8
265	A50	60k yel grn	5	8
266	A50	75k ultra	5	8
267	A50	80k yellow	5	8
268	A49	100k gray	5	8
269	A49	120k brown	5	8
270	A49	150k orange	5	8
271	A49	160k lt grn	5	8
272	A49	180k red	5	8
273	A49	200k pink	5	8
274	A49	240k dk vio	5	8
275	A49	300k lt bl	6	8
276	A49	400k dp grn	1.00	12
a.		400k gray grn	1.00	28
277	A49	500k yellow	5	8
278	A49	600k slate	5	8
279	A49	700k brn ('24)	50	8
280	A49	800k vio ('24)	1.00	3.25
281	A50	1000k vio ('23)	50	22
282	A50	1200k car rose ('23)	25	55
283	A50	1500k org ('24)	1.50	12
284	A50	1600k sl ('23)	2.25	3.00
285	A50	2000k dp bl ('23)	4.50	55
286	A50	3000k lt bl ('23)	14.00	1.10
287	A50	4000k dk bl, *bl* ('24)	5.75	2.75
		Nos. 250-287 (38)	32.66	15.55

Nos. 250–287 exist imperf. Price, set $700.

Symbols of Art and Science
A51

1922–24 Engraved *Perf. 12½*

No.	Type	Description	Unused	Used
288	A51	20k dk brn	8	8
a.		Perf. 11½	1.25	1.40
289	A51	25k blue	8	6
a.		Perf. 11½	1.25	1.40
290	A51	50k brn red	6	8
a.		Perf. 11½	3.75	4.50
291	A51	100k dp grn	8	8
a.		Perf. 11½	7.50	8.00
292	A51	200k dk vio	5	8
a.		Perf. 11½	10.00	15.00
293	A51	500k dp org	12	90
294	A51	1000k blk vio, *yel*	5	6
a.		Perf. 11½	120.00	200.00
295	A51	2000k ol grn *yel*	12	8
296	A51	3000k cl brn ('23)	9.50	65
297	A51	5000k gray blk ('23)	2.50	1.75

Granite Paper.

No.	Type	Description	Unused	Used
298	A51	10,000k red brn ('24)	3.50	4.50
		Nos. 288-298 (11)	16.14	8.32

On Nos. 281 to 287 and Nos. 291 to 298 "kronen" is abbreviated to "k" and transposed with the numerals.

Nos. 288–298 exist imperf. Price, set $425.

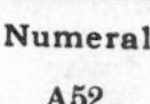

Numeral
A52

Fields Crossed by Telegraph Wires
A53

White-Shouldered Eagle
A54

Church of Minorite Friars
A55

1925–27 Typographed *Perf. 12*

No.	Type	Description	Unused	Used
303	A52	1g dk gray	20	5
304	A52	2g claret	30	5
305	A52	3g scarlet	35	5
306	A52	4g grnsh bl ('27)	90	5
307	A52	5g brn org	1.90	5
308	A52	6g ultra	1.10	5
309	A52	7g chocolate	2.00	5
310	A52	8g yel grn	8.00	5
311	A53	10g orange	28	5
313	A53	15g red lil	28	5
314	A53	16g dk bl	28	5
315	A53	18g ol grn	65	32
316	A54	20g dk vio	38	5
317	A54	24g carmine	50	32
318	A54	30g dk brn	45	5
319	A54	40g ultra	65	8
320	A54	45g yel brn	90	8
321	A54	50g gray	1.10	15
322	A54	80g turq bl	4.00	3.75

Engraved.
Perf. 12½

No.	Type	Description	Unused	Used
323	A55	1s dp grn	17.50	32
a.		1s lt grn	75.00	1.40
324	A55	2s brn rose	8.00	9.00
		Nos. 303-324 (21)	49.72	14.67

Nos. 303–305 and 307–324 exist imperf. Price, set $400.

Güssing
A56

National Library, Vienna
A57

Designs: 15g, Hochosterwitz. 16g, 20g, Durnstein. 18g, Traunsee. 24g, Salzburg. 30g, Seewiesen. 40g, Innsbruck. 50g, Worthersee. 60g, Hohenems. 2s, St. Stephen's Cathedral, Vienna.

1929–30 Typo. *Perf. 12½*

Size: 25½x21½mm

No.	Type	Description	Unused	Used
326	A56	10g brn org	1.10	5
327	A56	10g bis ('30)	1.10	5
328	A56	15g vio brn	75	1.50
329	A56	16g dk gray	25	10
330	A56	18g bl grn	55	55
331	A56	20g dk gray ('30)	55	5
332	A56	24g maroon	5.25	7.50
333	A56	24g lake ('30)	9.50	55
334	A56	30g dk vio	5.50	12
335	A56	40g dk bl	10.50	20
336	A56	50g gray vio ('30)	40.00	22
337	A56	60g ol grn	30.00	32

Engraved.

Size: 21x26mm.

No.	Type	Description	Unused	Used
338	A57	1s blk brn	6.75	28
339	A57	2s dk grn	12.00	8.00
		Nos. 326-339 (14)	123.80	19.49

Type of 1929–30 Issue.

Designs: 12g, Traunsee. 64g, Hohenems.

1932 *Perf. 12*

Size: 21 x 16½ mm.

No.	Type	Description	Unused	Used
340	A56	10g ol brn	1.10	5
341	A56	12g bl grn	1.75	5
342	A56	18g bl grn	85	2.75
343	A56	20g dk gray	1.40	5
344	A56	24g car rose	6.75	5
345	A56	24g dl vio	5.50	5
346	A56	30g dk vio	21.00	6
347	A56	30g car rose	5.00	10
348	A56	40g dk bl	25.00	90
349	A56	40g dk vio	7.25	35
350	A56	50g gray vio	30.00	35
351	A56	50g dl bl	8.25	35
352	A56	60g gray grn	65.00	2.25
353	A56	64g gray grn	10.00	22
		Nos. 340-353 (14)	188.85	7.58

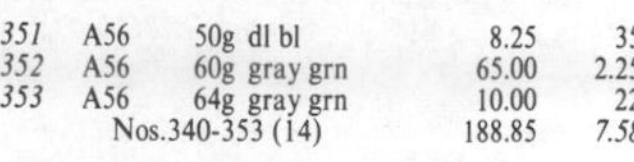

Burgenland
A67

Tyrol
A68

Designs (costumes of various districts): 3g, Burgenland. 4g, 5g, Carinthia. 6g, 8g, Lower Austria. 12g, 20g, Upper Austria. 24g, 25g, Salzburg. 30g, 35g, Styria. 45g, Tyrol. 60g, Vorarlberg bridal couple. 64g, Vorarlberg. 1s, Viennese family. 2s, Military.

1934–35 Typographed *Perf. 12*

No.	Type	Description	Unused	Used
354	A67	1g dk vio	5	5
355	A67	3g scarlet	5	5
356	A67	4g ol grn	8	6
357	A67	5g red vio	8	5
358	A67	6g ultra	28	25
359	A67	8g green	15	5
360	A67	12g dk brn	15	5
361	A67	20g yel brn	18	5
362	A67	24g grnsh bl	18	5
363	A67	25g violet	28	15
364	A67	30g maroon	25	5
365	A67	35g rose car	42	40

Perf. 12½

No.	Type	Description	Unused	Used
366	A68	40g sl gray	50	12
367	A68	45g brn red	42	12
368	A68	60g ultra	75	22
369	A68	64g brown	95	8
370	A68	1s dp vio	80	45
371	A68	2s dl grn	40.00	62.50

Designs Redrawn
Perf. 12 (6g), 12½ (2s)

No.	Type	Description	Unused	Used
372	A67	6g ultra ('35)	20	12
373	A68	2s emer ('35)	3.25	6.00
		Nos. 354-373 (20)	49.02	70.87

The design of No. 358 looks as though the man's ears were on backwards, while No. 372 appears correctly.

On No. 373 there are seven feathers on each side of the eagle instead of five.

Nos. 354–373 exist imperf. Price, set $500.

Dollfuss Mourning Issue.

Engelbert Dollfuss
A85

1934 Engraved *Perf. 12½*

No.	Type	Description	Unused	Used
374	A85	24g grnsh blk	65	35

1935

No.	Type	Description	Unused	Used
375	A85	24g indigo	1.25	1.00

"Mother and Child" by Joseph Danhauser
A86

"Madonna and Child", after Painting by Albrecht Dürer
A87

1935, May 1

No.	Type	Description	Unused	Used
376	A86	24g dk bl	65	2

Issued for Mother's Day.

Nos. 376–377 exist imperf. Price, each $225.

1936, May 5 Photogravure

No.	Type	Description	Unused	Used
377	A87	24g vio bl	28	3

Issued for Mother's Day.

Farm Workers
A88

Design: 5s, Factory workers.

1936, June Engraved *Perf. 12½*

No.	Type	Description	Unused	Used
378	A88	3s red org	15.00	20.0
379	A88	5s brn blk	30.00	55.0

Nos. 378–379 exist imperf. Price, set $225.

Engelbert Dollfuss
A90

Mother and Child
A91

1936, July 25

No.	Type	Description	Unused	Used
380	A90	10s dk bl	800.00	1,100.

Second anniversary of death of Engelbert Dollfuss, chancellor. Exists imperf. Price, $2,250.

1937, May 5 Photo. *Perf. 12*

No.	Type	Description	Unused	Used
381	A91	24g hn brn	32	28

Issued for Mother's Day. Exists imperf. Price, $160.

S. S. Maria Anna
A92

Steamships: 24g, Uranus, 64g, Oesterreich.

1937, June 9

No.	Type	Description	Unused	Used
382	A92	12g red brn	80	30
383	A92	24g dp bl	80	30
384	A92	64g dk grn	80	1.00

Centenary of steamship service on Danube River.

Exist imperf. Price, set $160.

First Locomotive, "Austria"
A95

Designs: 25g, Modern steam locomotive. 35g, Modern electric train.

1937, Nov. 22

No.	Type	Description	Unused	Used
385	A95	12g blk brn	10	8
386	A95	25g dk vio	50	90
387	A95	35g brn red	1.25	1.40

Centenary of Austrian railways. Exist imperf. Price, set $135

Rose and Zodiac Signs
A98

1937 Engraved. ***Perf. 13x12½.***

No.	Type	Description	Unused	Used
388	A98	12g dk grn	12	15
389	A98	24g dk car	12	15

For Use in Vienna, Lower Austria and Burgenland.

Germany Nos. 509-511 and 511B Overprinted in Black

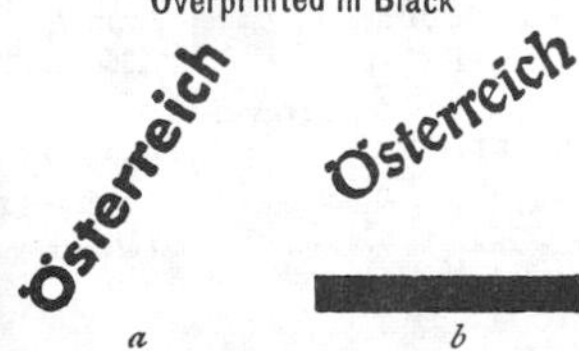

a b

1945 ***Perf. 14.*** **Unwmkd.**

No.	Type	Description	Unused	Used
390	A115 (a)	5(pf) dp yel grn	5	6
391	A115 (b)	6(pf) purple	6	15
392	A115 (a)	8(pf) red	5	6
393	A115 (b)	12(pf) carmine	6	15

Nos. 390–393 exist with overprint inverted or double.

Germany No. 507, the 3pf, with overprint "a" was prepared, not issued, but sold to collectors after the definitive Republic issue had been placed in use. Price $75.

German Semi-Postal Stamps, Nos. B207, B209, B210 and B283 Surcharged in Black

ÖSTERREICH
5 Pf.
c

ÖSTERREICH
8 Pf.

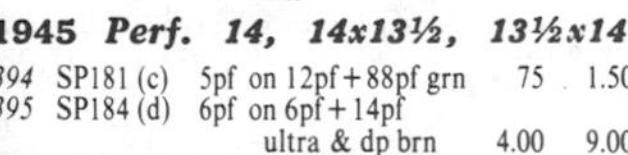

d

1945 ***Perf. 14, 14x13½, 13½x14***

No.	Type	Description	Unused	Used
394	SP181 (c)	5pf on 12pf+88pf grn	75	1.50
395	SP184 (d)	6pf on 6pf+14pf ultra & dp brn	4.00	9.00
396	SP242 (d)	8pf on 42pf+108pf brn	75	1.50
397	SP183 (d)	12pf on 3pf+7pf dl bl	75	1.50

The surcharges are spaced to fit the stamps.

Stamps not listed in this Catalogue or mentioned in "For the Record" (unless recent issues) usually are revenues, locals or labels.

Stamps of Germany, Nos. 509 to 511, 511B, 519 and 529 Overprinted

e f

1945 **Typo.** ***Perf. 14***

Size: 18½x22½mm.

No.	Type	Description	Unused	Used
398	A115 (e)	5(pf) dp yel grn	40	70
399	A115 (f)	5(pf) dp yel grn	7.50	13.00
400	A115 (e)	6(pf) purple	22	45
401	A115 (e)	8(pf) red	22	45
402	A115 (e)	12(pf) carmine	35	60

Engraved.

Size: 21½x26mm.

No.	Type	Description	Unused	Used
403	A115 (e)	30(pf) ol grn	6.00	11.00
a.		Thin bar at bottom	20.00	25.00
404	A118 (e)	42(pf) brt grn	12.00	40.00
a.		Thin bar at bottom	22.50	27.50
		Nos. 398-404 (7)	26.69	66.20

On Nos. 403a and 404a, the bottom bar of the overprint is 2½mm. wide, and, as the overprint was applied in two operations, "Osterreich" is usually not exactly centered in its diagonal slot. On Nos. 403 and 404, the bottom bar is 3mm. wide, and "Osterreich" is always well centered.

Germany Nos. 524–527 (the 1m, 2m, 3m and 5m), overprinted with vertical bars and "Osterreich" similar to "e" and "f", were prepared, not issued, but sold to collectors after the definitive Republic issue had been placed in use. Price for set $175.

For Use in Styria.

Stamps of Germany Nos. 506 to 511, 511A, 511B, 514 to 523 and 529 Overprinted in Black

Österreich

Typographed

1945 ***Perf. 14*** **Unwmkd.**

Size: 18½x22½mm.

No.	Type	Description	Unused	Used
405	A115	1(pf) gray blk	1.90	4.50
406	A115	3(pf) lt brn	1.50	4.50
407	A115	4(pf) slate	7.00	15.00
408	A115	5(pf) dp yel grn	1.40	3.00
409	A115	6(pf) purple	22	45
410	A115	8(pf) red	1.00	2.50
411	A115	10(pf) dk brn	2.00	5.00
412	A115	12(pf) carmine	22	45

Engraved.

No.	Type	Description	Unused	Used
413	A115	15(pf) brn lake	1.00	2.75
414	A115	16(pf) pck grn	12.00	27.50
415	A115	20(pf) blue	3.25	8.00
416	A115	24(pf) org brn	12.00	27.50

Size: 22½x26mm.

No.	Type	Description	Unused	Used
417	A115	25(pf) brt ultra	1.40	4.00
418	A115	30(pf) ol grn	1.40	3.00
419	A115	40(pf) brt red vio	1.50	3.50
420	A118	42(pf) brt grn	2.00	5.25
421	A115	50(pf) myr grn	2.00	5.25
422	A115	60(pf) dk red brn	3.25	7.25
423	A115	80(pf) indigo	2.50	5.75
		Nos. 405-423 (19)	57.54	135.15

Overprinted on Nos. 524 to 527.

Perf. 12½, 14.

No.	Type	Description	Unused	Used
424	A116	1m dk sl grn	10.00	30.00
a.		Perf. 12½	160.00	
425	A116	2m violet	8.75	30.00
a.		Perf. 14	18.00	67.50
426	A116	3m cop red	20.00	72.50
a.		Perf. 14	185.00	
427	A116	5m dk bl	225.00	750.00
a.		Perf. 14	850.00	

On the preceding four stamps the innermost vertical lines are 10½ mm. apart; on the pfennig values 6½ mm. apart.

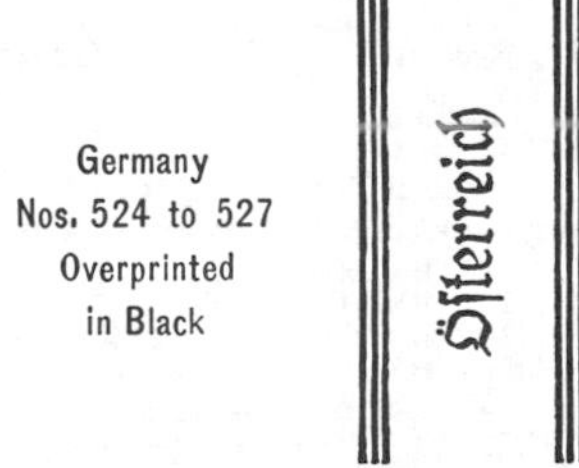

Germany Nos. 524 to 527 Overprinted in Black

Perf. 14

No.	Type	Description	Unused	Used
428	A116	1m dk sl grn	11.00	27.50
429	A116	2m violet	11.00	30.00

Perf. 12½

No.	Type	Description	Unused	Used
430	A116	3m cop red	22.50	57.50
431	A116	5m dk bl	160.00	400.00
a.		Perf. 14	900.00	

On the preceding four stamps, "Osterreich" is thinner, measuring 16 mm. On the previous set of 23 values it measures 18 mm.

Counterfeits exist of Nos. 424–431 overprints.

For Use in Vienna, Lower Austria and Burgenland.

Coat of Arms
A99 A100

Typographed or Lithographed.

Perf. 14x13½

1945, July 3 **Unwmkd.**

Size: 21x25mm.

No.	Type	Description	Unused	Used
432	A99	3(pf) brown	5	5
433	A99	4(pf) slate	5	12
434	A99	5(pf) dk grn	5	5
435	A99	6(pf) dp vio	5	5
436	A99	8(pf) org brn	5	5
437	A99	10(pf) dp brn	5	8
438	A99	12(pf) rose car	5	5
439	A99	15(pf) org red	5	12
440	A99	16(pf) dl bl grn	5	32

Perf. 14.

Size: 24x28½mm.

No.	Type	Description	Unused	Used
441	A99	20(pf) lt bl	5	8
442	A99	24(pf) orange	5	18
443	A99	25(pf) dk bl	5	8
444	A99	30(pf) dp gray grn	5	5
445	A99	38(pf) ultra	5	5
446	A99	40(pf) brt red vio	5	8
447	A99	42(pf) sage grn	5	5
448	A99	50(pf) bl grn	5	45
449	A99	60(pf) maroon	5	15
450	A99	80(pf) dl lil	6	15

Engraved

Perf. 14x13½

No.	Type	Description	Unused	Used
451	A100	1(m) dk grn	6	45
452	A100	2(m) dk pur	8	45
453	A100	3(m) dk vio	12	45
454	A100	5(m) brn red	15	45
		Nos. 432-454 (23)	1.37	4.01

Nos. 432, 433, 437, 439, 440, 443, 446, 448 and 449 are typographed. Nos. 434, 435, 441 and 442 are lithographed; the other values exist both ways.

For General Use.

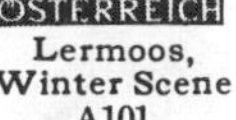

Lermoos, Winter Scene
A101

The Prater Woods, Vienna
A105

Hochosterwitz, Carinthia
A106

Lake Constance
A110

Dürnstein, Lower Austria
A124

Designs: 4g, Eisenerz surface mine. 5g, Leopoldsberg, near Vienna. 6g, Hohensalzburg, Salzburg Province. 12g, Wolfgang See, near Salzburg. 15g, Forchtenstein Castle, Burgenland. 16g, Gesäuse Valley. 24g, Höldrichs Mill, Lower Austria. 25g, Oetz Valley Outlet, Tyrol. 30g, Neusiedler Lake, Burgenland. 35g, Belvedere Palace, Vienna. 38g, Langbath Lake. 40g, Mariazell, Styria. 42g, Traunkirchen. 45g, Hartenstein Castle. 50g, Silvretta Mountains, Vorarlberg. 60g, Railroad viaducts near Semmering. 70g, Waterfall of Bad-Gastein, Salzburg. 80g, Kaiser Mountains, Tyrol. 90g, Wayside Shrine, Tragöss, Styria. 2s, St. Christof am Arlberg, Tyrol. 3s, Heiligenblut, Carinthia. 5s, Schönbrunn, Vienna.

Perf. 14x13½

1945–46 **Photogravure** **Unwmkd.**

No.	Type	Description	Unused	Used
455	A101	3g sapphire	5	5
456	A101	4g dp org ('46)	5	5
457	A101	5g dk car rose	5	5
458	A101	6g dk sl grn	5	5
459	A105	8g gldn brn	5	5
460	A106	10g dk grn	5	5
461	A106	12g dk brn	5	5
462	A106	15g dk sl bl ('46)	5	8
463	A106	16g chnt brn ('46)	5	5

Perf. 13½x14

No.	Type	Description	Unused	Used
464	A110	20g dp ultra ('46)	5	5
465	A110	24g dp yel grn ('46)	5	5
466	A110	25g gray blk ('46)	5	8
467	A110	30g dk red	5	8
468	A110	35g brn red ('46)	5	5
469	A110	38g brn ol ('46)	5	5
470	A110	40g gray	5	5
471	A110	42g brn org ('46)	5	5
472	A110	45g dk bl ('46)	20	40
473	A110	50g dk bl	5	12
474	A110	60g dk vio	5	12
a.		Imperf. (pair)	60.00	80.00
475	A110	70g Prus bl ('46)	15	40
476	A110	80g brown	18	60
477	A110	90g Prus grn	75	1.25
478	A124	1s dk red brn ('46)	50	80
479	A124	2s bl gray ('46)	1.75	3.00
480	A124	3s dk sl grn ('46)	60	1.00
481	A124	5s dk red ('46)	1.00	2.00
		Nos. 455-481 (27)	6.08	10.63

See also Nos. 486–488, 496–515.

No. 461 Overprinted in Carmine

1946, Sept. 26

482	A106	12g dk brn	10	20

Issued to commemorate the meeting of the Society for Cultural and Economic Relations with the Soviet Union, Vienna, September 26 to 29, 1946.

City Hall Park, Vienna
A128

Hochosterwitz, Carinthia
A129

Perf. 14x13½

1946-47 Photogravure. Unwmkd.

483	A128	8g dp plum	5	5
484	A128	8g ol brn	5	5
a.		8g dk ol grn	5	5
485	A129	10g dk brn vio ('47)	5	5

Perf. 13½x14

486	A110	30g bl gray ('47)	5	20
487	A110	50g brn vio ('47)	22	40
488	A110	60g vio bl ('47)	1.50	1.75
		Nos. 483-488 (6)	1.92	2.50

See also No. 502.

Franz Grillparzer
A130

Franz Schubert
A131

1947 Engraved. *Perf. 14x13½.*

489	A130	18g chocolate	5	8

Photogravure.

490	A130	18g dk vio brn	8	10

Issued to commemorate the 75th anniversary of the death of Franz Grillparzer, dramatic poet.

A second printing of No. 490 on thicker paper has a darker frame and clearer delineation of the portrait.

1947, Mar. 31 Engraved

491	A131	12g dk grn	6	10

Issued to commemorate the 150th anniversary of the birth of Franz Schubert, musician and composer.

Nos. 469 and 463 Surcharged in Brown

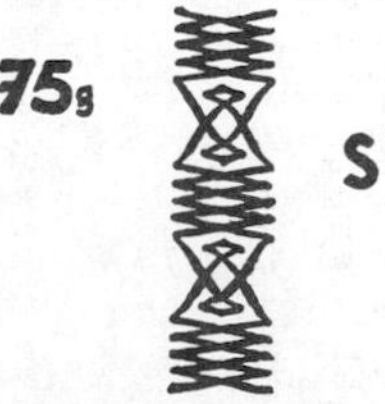

1947, Sept. 1 Photo. *Perf. 14*

492	A110	75g on 38g brn ol	20	80
493	A106	1.40s on 16g chnt brn	5	12

The surcharge on No. 493 varies from brown to black brown.

Symbols of Global Telegraphic Communication
A132

Engraved

1947, Nov. 5 *Perf. 14x13½*

495	A132	40g dk vio	5	15

Centenary of the telegraph in Austria.

Scenic Type of 1946.

1946, Aug. Photo. *Perf. 13½x14*

496	A124	1s dk brn	1.00	60
497	A124	2s dk bl	5.00	3.75
498	A124	3s dk sl grn	1.50	1.10
499	A124	5s dk red	25.00	12.00

On Nos. 478 to 481 the upper and lower panels show a screen effect. On Nos. 496 to 499 the panels appear to be solid color.

Scenic Types of 1945–46.

1947–48 Photo. *Perf. 14x13½*

500	A101	3g brt red	5	5
501	A101	5g brt red	5	5
502	A129	10g brt red	8	5
503	A106	15g brt red ('48)	80	80

Perf. 13½x14

504	A110	20g brt red	25	5
505	A110	30g brt red	40	20
506	A110	40g brt red	40	5
507	A110	50g brt red	55	5
508	A110	60g brt red ('48)	4.00	1.65
509	A110	70g brt red ('48)	2.25	8
510	A110	80g brt red ('48)	2.25	12
511	A110	90g brt red ('48)	2.50	40
512	A124	1s dk vio	40	5
513	A124	2s dk vio	55	20
514	A124	3s dk vio ('48)	5.75	1.25
515	A124	5s dk vio ('48)	6.75	1.60
		Nos. 500-515 (16)	27.03	6.65

Carl Michael Ziehrer
A133

Designs: No. 517, Adalbert Stifter. No. 518, Anton Bruckner. 60g, Friedrich von Amerling.

1948–49 Engraved

516	A133	20g dl grn	25	15
517	A133	40g chocolate	5.00	4.50
518	A133	40g dk grn ('49)	4.50	7.50
519	A133	60g rose brn	50	35

Issued to commemorate anniversaries of the death of Carl Michael Ziehrer (1843–1922), composer; Adalbert Stifter (1805–1868), novelist; Friedrich von Amerling (1803–1887), painter, and the birth of Anton Bruckner (1824–1896), composer.

Vorarlberg, Montafon Valley
A134

Costume of Vienna, 1850
A135

Designs (Austrian Costumes): 3g, Tyrol, Inn Valley. 5g, Salzburg, Pinzgau. 10g, Styria, Salzkammergut. 15g, Burgenland, Lutzmannsburg. 25g, Vienna, 1850. 30g, Salzburg, Pongau. 40g, Vienna, 1840. 45g, Carinthia, Lesach Valley. 50g, Vorarlberg, Bregenzer Forest. 60g, Carinthia, Lavant Valley. 70g, Lower Austria, Wachau. 75g, Styria, Salzkammergut. 80g, Styria, Enns Valley. 90g, Central Styria. 1s, Tyrol, Puster Valley. 1.20s, Lower Austria, Vienna Woods. 1.40s, Upper Austria, Inn District. 1.45s, Wilten. 1.50s, Vienna, 1853. 1.60s, Vienna, 1830. 1.70s, East Tyrol, Kals. 2s, Upper Austria. 2.20s, Ischl, 1820. 2.40s, Kitzbuhel. 2.50s, Upper Steiermark, 1850. 2.70s, Little Walser Valley. 3s, Burgenland. 3.50s, Lower Austria, 1850. 4.50s, Gail Valley. 5s, Ziller Valley. 7s, Steiermark, Sulm Valley.

Photogravure

1948–52 *Perf. 14x13½* Unwmkd.

520	A134	3g gray ('50)	38	60
521	A134	5g dk grn ('49)	5	5
522	A134	10g dp bl	5	5
523	A134	15g brown	38	5
524	A134	20g yel grn	8	5
525	A134	25g brn ('49)	8	5
526	A134	30g dk car rose	1.65	5
527	A134	30g dk vio ('50)	38	5
528	A134	40g violet	1.65	5
529	A134	40g grn ('49)	12	5
530	A134	45g vio bl	1.50	40
531	A134	50g org brn ('49)	38	5
532	A134	60g scarlet	12	5
533	A134	70g brt bl grn ('49)	12	5
534	A134	75g blue	2.50	40
535	A134	80g car rose ('49)	25	5
536	A134	90g brn vio ('49)	15.00	32
537	A134	1s ultra	2.75	5
538	A134	1s rose red ('50)	42.50	12
539	A134	1s dk grn ('51)	12	5
540	A134	1.20s vio ('49)	25	6
541	A134	1.40s brown	1.65	20
542	A134	1.45s dk car ('51)	75	10
543	A134	1.50s ultra ('51)	38	5
544	A134	1.60s org red ('49)	12	5
545	A134	1.70s vio bl ('50)	1.65	80
546	A134	2s bl grn	25	5
547	A134	2.20s sl ('52)	3.25	5
548	A134	2.40s bl ('51)	65	12
549	A134	2.50s brn ('52)	3.00	25
550	A134	2.70s dk brn ('51)	30	50
551	A134	3s brn car ('49)	1.25	5
552	A134	3.50s dl grn ('51)	6.50	5
553	A134	4.50s brn vio ('51)	38	50
554	A134	5s dk red vio	65	8
555	A134	7s ol ('52)	1.00	6

Engraved

556	A135	10s gray ('50)	17.50	4.00
		Nos. 520-556 (37)	109.59	9.56

In 1958–59, 21 denominations of this set were printed on white paper, differing from the previous grayish paper with yellowish gum.

Pres. Karl Renner
A136

1948, Nov. 12 *Perf. 14x13½*

557	A136	1sh dp bl	1.90	1.75

Issued to commemorate the 30th anniversary of the founding of the Austrian Republic. See also Nos. 573, 636.

Franz Gruber and Josef Mohr
A137

1948, Dec. 18 *Perf. 13½x14*

558	A137	60g red brn	3.75	6.25

Issued to commemorate the 130th anniversary of the hymn "Silent Night, Holy Night."

Symbolical of Child Welfare
A138

Johann Strauss, the Younger
A139

Photogravure

1949, May 14 *Perf. 14x13½*

559	A138	1s brt bl	11.00	1.90

Issued to commemorate the first year of activity of the United Nations International Children's Emergency Fund in Austria.

1949 Engraved

Designs: 30g, Johann Strauss, the elder. No. 561, Johann Strauss, the younger. No. 562, Karl Millöcker.

560	A139	30g vio brn	1.90	2.75
561	A139	1s dk bl	2.50	1.65
562	A139	1s dk bl	10.00	11.00

Issued to commemorate the centenary of the death of Johann Strauss, the elder (1804–1849), and the 50th anniversary of the deaths of Johann Strauss, the younger (1825–1899), and Karl Millöcker (1842–1899), composers. See also No. 574.

Esperanto Star, Olive Branches
A140

St. Gebhard
A141

1949, June 25 Photogravure

563	A140	20g bl grn	90	80

Austrian Esperanto Congress at Graz.

1949, Aug. 6 Engraved

564	A141	30g dk vio	1.50	2.00

Issued to commemorate the millenary of the birth of St. Gebhard (949–995), Bishop of Vorarlberg.

Letter, Roses and Post Horn
A142

Designs: 60g, Plaque. 1s, "Austria," wings and monogram.

1949, Oct. 8 *Perf. 13½x14*

565	A142	40g dk grn	2.75	2.75
566	A142	60g dk car	2.75	2.75
567	A142	1s dk vio bl	4.75	8.00

Issued to commemorate the 75th anniversary of the formation of the Universal Postal Union.

Moritz Michael Daffinger
A143

Andreas Hofer
A144

Designs: 30g, Alexander Girardi. No. 569, Daffinger. No. 570, Hofer. No. 571, Josef Madersperger.

1950 ***Perf. 14x13½*** **Unwmkd.**

568	A144	30g dk bl	1.25	1.25
569	A143	60g red brn	6.00	6.00
570	A144	60g dk vio	9.50	11.00
571	A144	60g purple	4.50	3.75

Issued to commemorate the centenary of the birth of Alexander Girardi (1850–1918), actor; the death centenary of Moritz Michael Daffinger (1790–1849), painter; the 140th anniversary of the death of Andreas Hofer (1767–1810), patriot, and the death centenary of Josef Madersperger (1768–1850), inventor.

Austrian Stamp of 1850
A146

1950, May 20 ***Perf. 14½***

572 A146 1s *straw* 1.50 1.40

Centenary of Austrian postage stamps.

Renner Type of 1948, Frame and Inscriptions Altered.

1951, Mar. 3

573 A136 1s *straw* 1.40 18

Issued in memory of Pres. Karl Renner, 1870–1950.

Strauss Type of 1949.

Portrait: 60g, Joseph Lanner.

1951, Apr. 12

574 A139 60g dk bl grn 3.25 1.75

Issued to commemorate the 150th anniversary of the birth of Joseph Lanner, composer.

Martin Johann Schmidt
A147

Boy Scout Emblem
A148

Engraved.

1951, June 28 ***Perf. 14x13½***

575 A147 1sh brn red 4.50 3.25

Issued to commemorate the 150th anniversary of the death of Martin Johann Schmidt, painter.

1951, Aug. 3 **Engr. & Litho.**

576 A148 1sh dk grn, ocher & pink 3.25 4.50

Issued in connection with the 7th World Scout Jamboree, Bad Ischl-St. Wolfgang, Aug. 3–13, 1951.

Wilhelm Kienzl
A149

Josef Schrammel
A150

Design: 1s, Karl von Ghega.

1951–52 **Engraved** **Unwmkd.**

577	A149	1s dp grn ('52)	5.25	1.65
578	A149	1.50s indigo	2.50	1.40
579	A150	1.50s vio bl ('52)	5.25	1.65

Issued to commemorate the 150th anniversary of the birth of Karl von Ghega (1802–1860), civil engineer; the 10th anniversary of the death of Wilhelm Kienzl (1857–1941), composer, and the birth centenary of Josef Schrammel (1852–1895), composer. See also No. 582.

Breakfast Pavilion, Schönbrunn
A151

1952, May 24 ***Perf. 13½x14***

580 A151 1.50s dk grn 4.75 1.75

Issued to commemorate the 200th anniversary of the founding of the Vienna Zoological Gardens.

Globe as Dot Over "i"
A152

School Girl
A153

1952, July 1 ***Perf. 14x13½***

581 A152 1.50s dk bl 5.25 1.00

Issued to publicize the formation of the International Union of Socialist Youth Camp, Vienna, July 1-10, 1952.

Type Similar to A150.

Portrait: 1s, Nikolaus Lenau.

1952, Aug. 13

582 A150 1s dp grn 5.50 1.65

Issued to commemorate the 150th anniversary of the birth of Nikolaus Lenau, pseudonym of Nikolaus Franz Niembsch von Strehlenau (1802–1850), poet.

1952, Sept. 6

583 A153 2.40s dp vio bl 9.25 2.75

Issued to stimulate letter-writing between Austrian and foreign school children.

Hugo Wolf
A154

Pres. Theodor Körner
A155

Engraved.

1953, Feb. 21 ***Perf. 14x13½***

587 A154 1.50s dk bl 6.00 1.10

Issued to commemorate the 50th anniversary of the death of Hugo Wolf, composer.

1953, Apr. 24

588 A155 1.50s dk vio bl 5.75 1.10

Issued to commemorate the 80th birthday of Pres. Theodor Körner. See also Nos. 591, 614.

State Theater, Linz, and Masks
A156

1953, Oct. 17 ***Perf. 13½x14***

589 A156 1.50s dk gray 12.50 2.25

Issued to commemorate the 150th anniversary of the founding of the State Theater at Linz.

Child and Christmas Tree
A157

Karl von Rokitansky
A158

1953, Nov. 30 ***Perf. 14x13½***

590 A157 1s dk grn 1.25 22

See also No. 597.

Type Similar to A155.

Portrait: 1.50s, Moritz von Schwind.

1954, Jan. 21 ***Perf. 14x13½***

591 A155 1.50s purple 9.75 1.75

Issued to commemorate the 150th anniversary of the birth of Moritz von Schwind, painter.

1954, Feb. 19

592 A158 1.50s purple 14.00 2.25

Issued to commemorate the 150th anniversary of the birth of Karl von Rokitansky, physician. See also No. 595.

Esperanto Star and Wreath
A159

Engraved and Photogravure

1954, June 5 ***Perf. 13½ 14***

593 A159 1s dk brn & emer 4.25 22

Issued to commemorate the 50th anniversary of the Esperanto movement in Austria.

Johann Michael Rottmayr
A160

Engraved

1954, Aug. 4 ***Perf. 14x13½***

594 A160 1s dk bl grn 9.75 3.25

300th birth anniversary of Johann Michael Rottmayr von Rosenbrunn, painter.

Type Similar to A158

Portrait: 1.50s, Carl Auer von Welsbach.

595 A158 1.50s vio bl 30.00 2.25

25th death anniversary of Carl Auer von Welsbach (1858–1929), chemist.

Organ, St. Florian Monastery and Cherub
A161

1954, Oct. 2 **Unwmkd.**

596 A161 1s brown 2.25 28

Issued to publicize the second International Congress for Catholic Church Music, Vienna, October 4-10, 1954.

Christmas Type of 1953

1954, Nov. 30

597 A157 1s dk bl 2.75 40

Arms of Austria and Official Publication
A162

1954, Dec. 18 **Engraved**

598 A162 1s sal & blk 2.25 22

Issued to commemorate the 150th anniversary of the founding of Austria's State Printing Plant and the 250th year of publication of the government newspaper, Wiener Zeitung.

Parliament Building
A163

Designs: 1s, Western railroad station, Vienna. 1.45s, Letters forming flag. 1.50s, Public housing, Vienna. 2.40s, Limberg dam.

1955, Apr. 27 ***Perf. 13½x14***

599	A163	70g rose vio	1.25	22
600	A163	1s dp ultra	4.75	22
601	A163	1.45s scarlet	7.50	3.25
602	A163	1.50s brown	16.00	22
603	A163	2.40s dk bl grn	7.50	6.75
		Nos. 599-603 (5)	37.00	10.66

Issued to commemorate the 10th anniversary of Austria's liberation.

Type of 1945 Overprinted in Blue **STAATSVERTRAG 1955**

1955, May 15 ***Perf. 14x13½***

604 A100 2(s) bl gray 1.90 35

Issued to commemorate the signing of the state treaty with the United States, France, Great Britain and Russia, May 15, 1955.

Workers of Three Races Climbing Globe
A164

1955, May 20 ***Perf. 13½x14***

605 A164 1s indigo 1.90 2.75

Issued to publicize the 4th congress of the International Confederation of Free Trade Unions, Vienna, May 1955.

Burgtheater, Vienna
A165

Design: 2.40s, Opera House, Vienna.

1955, July 25

606 A165 1.50s lt sep 2.75 22
607 A165 2.40s dk bl 3.50 2.25

Issued to celebrate the re-opening of the Burgtheater and Opera House in Vienna.

Symbolic of Austria's Desire to Join the U. N.
A166

1955, Oct. 24 **Unwmkd.**

608 A166 2.40s green 12.50 3.00

Tenth anniversary of United Nations.

Wolfgang Amadeus Mozart
A167

Symbolic of Austria's Joining the U. N.
A168

1956, Jan. 21 ***Perf. 14x13½***

609 A167 2.40s sl bl 2.75 85

Issued to commemorate the 200th anniversary of the birth of Wolfgang Amadeus Mozart, composer.

1956, Feb. 20

610 A168 2.40s chocolate 11.00 1.75

Issued to commemorate Austria's admission to the United Nations Organization.

Globe Showing Energy of the Earth
A169

1956, May 8 ***Perf. 13½14***

611 A169 2.40s dp bl 10.50 2.50

Issued to publicize the Fifth International Power Conference, Vienna, June 17-23, 1956.

Map of Europe and City Maps
A170

J. B. Fischer von Erlach
A171

Photogravure and Typographed

1956, June 8 ***Perf. 14x13½***

612 A170 1.45s lt grn blk & red 2.50 85

Issued to publicize the 23rd International Housing and Town Planning Congress, Vienna, July 22–28.

1956, July 20 **Engraved**

613 A171 1.50s brown 1.25 1.75

Issued to commemorate the 300th anniversary of the birth of Johann Bernhard Fischer von Erlach, architect.

Körner Type of 1953.

1957, Jan. 11

614 A155 1.50s gray blk 1.25 1.90

Issued to commemorate the death of Pres. Theodor Körner.

Dr. Julius Wagner-Jauregg
A172

Anton Wildgans
A173

1957, Mar. 7 ***Perf. 14x13½***

615 A172 2.40s brn vio 3.25 2.25

Issued to commemorate the centenary of the birth of Dr. Julius Wagner-Jauregg, psychiatrist.

1957, May 3 **Unwmkd.**

616 A173 1s vio bl 35 25

Issued to commemorate the 25th anniversary of the death of Anton Wildgans, poet.

Old and New Postal Motor Coach
A174

1957, June 14 ***Perf. 13½x14***

617 A174 1s *yellow* 35 25

Issued to commemorate the 50th anniversary of Austrian Postal Motor Coach Service.

Gasherbrum II and Glacier
A175

1957, July 27

618 A175 1.50s gray bl 35 20

Issued in honor of the Austrian Karakorum Expedition, which climbed Mount Gasherbrum II on July 7, 1956.

Mariazell
A176

Heidenreichstein Castle
A177

Designs: 20g, Farmhouse at Mörbisch. 50g, Heiligenstadt, Vienna. 1.40s, County seat, Klagenfurt. 1.50s, Rabenhof Building, Erdberg, Vienna. 1.80s, The Mint, Hall, Tyrol. 2s, Christkindl Church. 3.40s, Steiner Gate, Krems. 4s, Vienna Gate, Hainburg. 4.50s, Schwechat Airport, Vienna. 5.50s, Chur Gate, Feldkirch. 6s, County seat, Graz. 6.40s, "Golden Roof," Innsbruck.

1957–61 ***Perf. 14x13½***

Lithographed.

Size: 20x25mm.

618A A176 20g vio blk ('61) 5 5
619 A176 50g bluish blk ('59) 5 5

Engraved.

620 A176 1s chocolate 1.00 12

Typographed.

621 A176 1s chocolate 1.40 8

Lithographed.

622 A176 1s choc ('59) 70 5
622A A176 1.40s brt grnsh bl ('60) 25 5
623 A176 1.50s rose lake ('58) 40 5
624 A176 1.80s brt ultra ('60) 25 5
625 A176 2s dl bl ('58) 4.75 5
626 A176 3.40s yel grn ('60) 70 80
627 A176 4s brt red lil ('60) 60 5
627A A176 4.50s dl grn ('60) 80 50
628 A176 5.50s grnsh gray ('60) 45 20
629 A176 6s brt vio ('60) 80 5
629A A176 6.40s brt bl ('60) 75 90

Engraved.

Size: 22x28mm.

630 A177 10s dk bl grn 2.50 45
Nos. 618A-630 (16) 15.45 3.50

Of the three 1s stamps above, Nos. 620 and 621 have two names in imprint (designer H. Strohofer, engraver G. Wimmer). No. 622 has only Strohofer's name.

Prices for Nos. 618A–624, 626–630 are for stamps on white paper. Most denominations also come on grayish paper with yellowish gum.

See also Nos. 688–702.

1960–65 Photogravure ***Perf. 14½x14***

Size: 17x21mm.

630A A176 50g sl ('64) 6 5

Size: 18x21½ mm.

630B A176 1s chocolate 12 8

Size: 17x21mm.

630C A176 1.50s dk car ('65) 18 12

Nos. 630A–630C issued in sheets and coils.

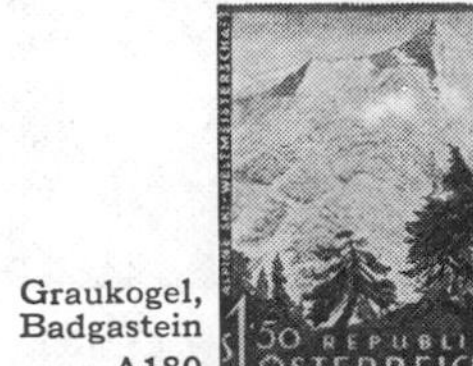

Graukogel, Badgastein
A180

1958, Feb. 1 **Engr.** ***Perf. 14x13½***

631 A180 1.50s dk bl 22 10

Alpine championships of the International Ski Federation, Badgastein, Feb. 2–7.

Plane over Map of Austria
A181

1958, Mar. 27 ***Perf. 13½x14***

632 A181 4s red 45 25

Re-opening of Austrian Airlines.

Mother and Daughter
A182

Walther von der Vogelweide
A183

Perf. 14x13½

1958, May 8 **Unwmkd.**

633 A182 1.50s dk bl 25 12

Issued for Mother's Day, 1958.

1958, July 17 **Litho. & Engr.**

634 A183 1.50s multi 25 12

Issued to commemorate the 3rd Austrian Song Festival, Vienna, July 17-20.

Oswald Redlich
A184

Giant "E" on Map
A185

1958, Sept. 17 **Engraved**

635 A184 2.40s ultra 50 28

Issued to commemorate the centenary of the birth of Prof. Oswald Redlich (1858–1944), historian.

Renner Type of 1948.

1958, Nov. 12

636 A136 1.50s dp grn 35 35

Issued to commemorate the 40th anniversary of the founding of the Austrian Republic.

1959, Mar. 9

637 A185 2.40s emerald 25 32

Issued to promote the idea of a United Europe.

Cigarette Machine and Trademark of Tobacco Monopoly
A186

Archduke Johann
A187

1959, May 8 *Perf. 13½* **Unwmkd.**

638 A186 2.40s dk ol bis 25 25

Issued to commemorate the 175th anniversary of the establishment of the Austrian tobacco monopoly.

1959, May 11 *Perf. 14x13½*

639 A187 1.50s dp grn 25 18

Issued to commemorate the centenary of the death of Archduke Johann of Austria, military leader and humanitarian.

Capercaillie A188 — Joseph Haydn A189

Animals: 1.50s, Roe buck. 2.40s, Wild boar. 3.50s, Red deer, doe and fawn.

1959, May 20 **Engraved**

640 A188 1s rose vio 25 20
641 A188 1.50s bl vio 60 12
642 A188 2.40s dk bl grn 45 65
643 A188 3.50s dk brn 30 28

Issued to publicize the Congress of the International Hunting Council, Vienna, May 20-24.

1959, May 30 **Unwmkd.**

644 A189 1.50s vio brn 45 18

Issued to commemorate the sesquicentennial of the death of Joseph Haydn, composer.

Coat of Arms, Tyrol A190 — Antenna, Zugspitze A191

1959, June 13 *Perf. 14x13½*

645 A190 1.50s rose red 25 12

Issued to commemorate the 150th anniversary of the fight for the liberation of Tyrol.

1959, June 19 *Perf. 13½*

646 A191 2.40s dk bl grn 25 20

Inauguration of Austria's relay system.

Field Ball Player A192 — Orchestral Instruments A193

Designs: 1s, Runner. 1.80s, Gymnast on vaulting horse. 2s, Woman hurdler. 2.20s, Hammer thrower.

1959–70 **Engr.** *Perf. 14x13½*

647 A192 1s lilac 18 20
648 A192 1.50s bl grn 50 25
648A A192 1.80s car ('62) 45 40
648B A192 2s rose lake ('70) 25 18
648C A192 2.20s bluish blk ('67) 25 18
Nos. 647-648C (5) 1.63 1.21

Lithographed and Engraved

1959, Aug. 19 *Perf. 14x13½*

649 A193 2.40s dl bl & blk 30 28

Issued to publicize the 1959 world tour of the Vienna Philharmonic Orchestra.

Family Fleeing over Mountains
A194

Engraved

1960, Apr. 7 *Perf. 13½x14*

650 A194 3s Prus grn 90 45

Issued to publicize World Refugee Year, July 1, 1959–June 30, 1960.

President Adolf Schärf
A195

1960, Apr. 20 *Perf. 14x13½*

651 A195 1.50s gray ol 90 28

Issued to honor President Adolf Schärf on his 70th birthday.

Young Hikers and Hostel
A196

1960, May 20 *Perf. 13½x14*

652 A196 1s car rose 30 25

Issued to publicize youth hiking and the youth hostel movement.

Anton Eiselsberg A197 — Gustav Mahler A198

Lithographed and Engraved

1960, June 20 *Perf. 14x13½*

653 A197 1.50s buff & dk brn 95 28

Issued to commemorate the centenary of the birth of Dr. Anton Eiselsberg, surgeon.

1960, July 7 **Engraved**

654 A198 1.50s chocolate 95 28

Issued to commemorate the centenary of the birth of Gustav Mahler, composer.

Jakob Prandtauer, Melk Abbey A199 — Gross Glockner Mountain Road A200

1960, July 16 **Unwmkd.**

655 A199 1.50s red brn 95 28

Issued to commemorate the 300th anniversary of the birth of Jakob Prandtauer, architect.

1960, Aug. 3

656 A200 1.80s dk bl 85 80

Issued to commemorate the 25th anniversary of the opening of the Gross Glockner Mountain Road.

Europa Issue, 1960

Ionic Capital
A201

1960, Aug. 29 *Perf. 14x13½*

657 A201 3s black 1.90 1.25

Issued to promote the idea of a united Europe.

Griffen, Carinthia
A202

Engraved

1960, Oct. 10 *Perf. 13½x14*

658 A202 1.50s sl grn 45 20

Issued to commemorate the 40th anniversary of the plebiscite which kept Carinthia with Austria.

Flame and Broken Chain
A203

Perf. 14x13½

1961, May 8 **Unwmkd.**

659 A203 1.50s scarlet 45 18

Issued to honor the victims in Austria's fight for freedom.

First Austrian Mail Plane, 1918
A204

1961, May 15 *Perf. 13½x14*

660 A204 5s vio bl 95 50

Issued to publicize the Airmail Philatelic Exhibition, LUPOSTA 1961, Vienna, May, 1961.

Transportation by Road, Rail and Waterway A205 — Mountain Mower, by Albin Egger-Lienz A206

Engraved and Typographed

1961, May 29 *Perf. 13½*

661 A205 3s rose red & ol 60 50

Issued to commemorate the 13th European Conference of Transportation ministers, Vienna, May 29–31.

Engraved

1961, June 12 *Perf. 13½x14*

Designs: 1.50s, The Kiss, by August von Pettenkofen. 3s, Girl, by Anton Romako. 5s, Ariadne's Triumph, by Hans Makart.

Inscriptions in Red Brown

662 A206 1s rose lake 20 20
663 A206 1.50s dl vio 32 32
664 A206 3s ol grn 1.10 1.10
665 A206 5s bl vio 60 60

Issued to commemorate the centenary of the Society of Creative Artists, Künstlerhaus, Vienna.

Sonnblick Mountain and Observatory A207 — Mercury and Globe A208

1961, Sept. 1 *Perf. 14x13½*

666 A207 1.80s vio bl 55 45

Issued to commemorate the 75th anniversary of the establishment of the Sonnblick meteorological observatory.

1961, Sept. 18

667 A208 3s black 1.00 70

Issued to publicize the International Banking Congress, Vienna, Sept. 1961. English inscription listing United Nations financial groups.

Coal Mine Shaft
A209

Designs: 1.50s, Generator. 1.80s, Iron blast furnace. 3s, Pouring steel. 5s, Oil refinery.

Engraved

1961, Sept. 15 ***Perf. 14x13½***

668	A209	1s black	20	18
669	A209	1.50s green	32	28
670	A209	1.80s dk car rose	65	60
671	A209	3s brt lil	90	80
672	A209	5s blue	1.10	1.10
		Nos. 668-672 (5)	3.17	2.96

15th anniversary of nationalized industry.

Arms of Burgenland — A210; Franz Liszt — A211

Engraved and Lithographed

1961, Oct. 9

673	A210	1.50s blk, yel & dk red	50	25

Issued to commemorate the 40th anniversary of Burgenland's joining the Austrian Republic.

1961, Oct. 20 **Engraved**

674	A211	3s dk brn	80	65

Issued to commemorate the 150th anniversary of the birth of Franz Liszt, composer.

Parliament
A212

1961, Dec. 18 ***Perf. 13½x14***

675	A212	1s brown	28	18

Issued to commemorate the 200th anniversary of the Austrian Bureau of Budget.

Kaprun-Mooserboden Reservoir
A213

Hydroelectric Power Plants: 1.50s, Ybbs-Persenbeug dam and locks. 1.80s, Lünersee dam and reservoir. 3s, Grossraming dam. 4s, Bisamberg transformer plant. 6.40s, St. Andrä power plant.

1962, March 26 **Unwmkd.**

676	A213	1s vio bl	20	20
677	A213	1.50s red lil	32	32
678	A213	1.80s green	50	50
679	A213	3s brown	50	50
680	A213	4s rose red	50	50
681	A213	6.40s gray	1.60	1.60
		Nos. 676-681 (6)	3.62	3.62

Issued to commemorate the 15th anniversary of the nationalization of the electric power industry.

Johann Nestroy — A214; Friedrich Gauermann — A215

1962, May 25 ***Perf. 14x13½***

682	A214	1s violet	28	20

Issued to commemorate the centenary of the death of Johann Nepomuk Nestroy, Viennese playwright, author and actor.

1962, July 6 **Engraved**

683	A214	1.50s int bl	28	18

Issued to commemorate the centenary of the death of Friedrich Gauermann (1807–1862), landscape painter.

Scout Emblem and Handshake
A216

1962, Oct. 5

684	A216	1.50s dk grn	50	28

Issued to commemorate the 50th anniversary of Austria's Boy Scouts.

Lowlands Forest
A217

Designs: 1.50s, Deciduous forest. 3s, Fir and larch forest.

1962, Oct. 12 ***Perf. 13½x14***

685	A217	1s grnsh gray	20	20
686	A217	1.50s redsh brn	32	32
687	A217	3s dk sl grn	1.10	1.10

Buildings Types of 1957–61

Designs: 30g, City Hall, Vienna. 40g, Porcia Castle, Spittal on the Drau. 60g, Tanners' Tower, Wels. 70g, Residenz Fountain, Salzburg. 80g, Old farmhouse, Pinzgau. 1s, Romanesque columns, Millstatt Abbey. 1.20s, Kornmesser House, Bruck on the Mur. 1.30s, Schatten Castle, Feldkirch, Vorarlberg. 2s, Dragon Fountain, Klagenfurt. 2.20s, Beethoven House, Vienna. 2.50s, Danube Bridge, Linz. 3s, Swiss Gate, Vienna. 3.50s, Esterhazy Palace, Eisenstadt. 8s, City Hall, Steyr. 20s, Melk Abbey

1962–70 **Litho.** ***Perf. 14x13½***

Size: 20x25mm.

688	A176	30g grnsh gray	50	5
689	A176	40g rose red	12	5
690	A176	60g vio brn	32	5
691	A176	70g dk bl	25	5
692	A176	80g yel brn	32	5
693	A176	1s brn ('70)	20	5
694	A176	1.20s red lil	40	5
695	A176	1.30s grn ('67)	15	5
696	A176	2s dk bl ('68)	25	5
697	A176	2.20s green	1.40	5
698	A176	2.50s violet	80	12
699	A176	3s brt bl	70	5
700	A176	3.50s rose car	80	6
701	A176	8s cl ('65)	1.00	20

Engraved

Perf. 13½

Size: 28x36½mm.

702	A177	20s rose cl ('63)	2.40	50
		Nos. 688-702 (15)	9.61	1.43

Prices for Nos. 688–702 are for stamps on white paper. Some denominations also come on grayish paper with yellowish gum.

Electric Locomotive and Train of 1837
A218

Lithographed and Engraved

1962, Nov. 9 ***Perf. 13½x14***

703	A218	3s buff & blk	1.00	70

125th anniversary of Austrian railroads.

Postilions and Postal Clerk, 1863 — A219; Hermann Bahr — A220

1963, May 7 **Photo.** ***Perf. 14x13½***

704	A219	3s dk brn & cit	90	70

Issued to commemorate the centenary of the first International Postal Conference, Paris, 1863.

Lithographed and Engraved

1963, July 19 ***Perf. 14x13½***

705	A220	1.50s bl & blk	32	12

Centenary of birth of Hermann Bahr, poet.

St. Florian Statue, Kefermarkt, Contemporary and Old Fire Engines
A221

1963, Aug. 30 **Unwmkd.**

706	A221	1.50s brt rose & blk	32	12

Issued to commemorate the centenary of the Austrian volunteer fire brigades.

Factory, Flag and "ÖGB" on Map of Austria
A222

Lithographed

1963, Sept. 23 ***Perf. 13½x14***

707	A222	1.50s gray, red & dk brn	32	12

Issued to commemorate the 5th Congress of the Austrian Trade Union Federation (ÖGB), Sept. 23–28.

Arms of Austria and Tyrol
A223

1963, Sept. 27 **Unwmkd.**

708	A223	1.50s tan, blk, red & yel	32	12

Issued to commemorate the 600th anniversary of Tyrol's union with Austria.

Prince Eugene of Savoy — A224; Centenary Emblem — A225

Engraved

1963, Oct. 18 ***Perf. 14x13½***

709	A224	1.50s violet	32	12

Issued to commemorate the 300th anniversary of the birth of Prince Eugene of Savoy (1663–1736), Austrian general.

Engraved and Photogravure

1963, Oct. 25 **Unwmkd.**

710	A225	3s blk, sil & red	60	35

Issued to commemorate the centenary of the founding of the International Red Cross.

Slalom
A226

Sports: 1.20s, Biathlon (skier with rifle). 1.50s, Ski jump. 1.80s, Women's figure skating. 2.20s, Ice hockey. 3s, Tobogganing. 4s, Bobsledding.

Photogravure and Engraved

1963, Nov. 11 ***Perf. 13½x14***

Inscriptions in Gold; Athletes in Black

711	A226	1s lt gray	12	12
712	A226	1.20s lt bl	16	16
713	A226	1.50s gray	20	20
714	A226	1.80s pale lil	25	25
715	A226	2.20s lt grn	40	40
716	A226	3s gray	32	32

17 A226 4s grysh bl 60 60
Nos. 711-717 (7) 2.05 2.05

Issued to publicize the 9th Winter Olympic Games, Innsbruck, Jan. 29–Feb. 9, 1964.

Baroque Crèche by Josef Thaddäus Stammel
A227

Engraved

1963, Nov. 29 ***Perf. 14x13½***

718 A227 2s dk Prus grn 30 15

Nasturtium
A228

Flowers: 1.50s, Peony. 1.80s, Clematis. 2.20s, Dahlia. 3s, Morning glory. 4s, Hollyhock.

Lithographed

1964, Apr. 17 ***Perf. 14*** **Unwmkd.**

Gray Background

719 A228 1s yel, grn & dk red 12 12
720 A228 1.50s pink, grn & yel 20 20
721 A228 1.80s lil, grn & yel 25 25
722 A228 2.20s car, grn & yel 32 32
723 A228 3s bl, grn & yel 38 38
724 A228 4s grn, yel & pink 50 50
Nos. 719-724 (6) 1.77 1.77

Issued to publicize the Vienna International Garden Show, Apr. 16–Oct. 11.

St. Mary Magdalene and Apostle
A229

Pallas Athena and National Council Chamber
A230

1964, May 21 Engraved ***Perf. 13½***

725 A229 1.50s bluish blk 28 20

Issued to publicize Romanesque art in Austria. The 12th century stained-glass window is from the Weitensfeld Church, the bust of the Apostle from the portal of St. Stephen's Cathedral, Vienna.

Engraved and Lithographed

1964, May 25 ***Perf. 14x13½***

726 A230 1.80s blk & emer 35 25

Issued to commemorate the second Parliamentary and Scientific Conference, Vienna.

The Kiss, by Gustav Klimt
A231

1964, June 5 Litho. ***Perf. 13½***

727 A231 3s multi 60 40

Issued to commemorate the re-opening of the Vienna Secession, a museum devoted to early 20th century art (art nouveau).

Brother of Mercy and Patient
A232

Perf. 14x13½

1964, June 11 Engr. Unwmkd.

728 A232 1.50s dk bl 28 18

Issued to commemorate the 350th anniversary of the Brothers of Mercy in Austria.

"Bringing the News of Victory at Kunersdorf" by Bernardo Bellotto
A233

"The Post in Art": 1.20s, Changing Horses at Relay Station, by Julius Hörmann. 1.50s, The Honeymoon Trip, by Moritz von Schwind. 1.80s, After the Rain, by Ignaz Raffalt. 2.20s, Mailcoach in the Mountains, by Adam Klein. 3s, Changing Horses at Bavarian Border, by Friedrich Gauermann. 4s, Postal Sleigh (Truck) in the Mountains, by Adalbert Pilch. 6.40s, Saalbach Post Office, by Adalbert Pilch.

1964, June 15 ***Perf. 13½x14***

729 A233 1s rose cl 8 8
730 A233 1.20s sepia 20 20
731 A233 1.50s vio bl 18 18
732 A233 1.80s brt vio 20 20
733 A233 2.20s black 25 25
734 A233 3s dl car rose 40 40
735 A233 4s sl grn 50 50
736 A233 6.40s dl cl 1.10 1.10
Nos. 729-736 (8) 2.91 2.91

Issued to commemorate the 15th Universal Postal Union Congress, Vienna, May–June 1964.

Workers
A234

1964, Sept. 4 ***Perf. 14x13½***

737 A234 1s black 20 12

Centenary of Austrian Labor Movement.

Europa Issue, 1964

Common Design Type

Lithographed

1964, Sept. 14 ***Perf. 12*** **Unwmkd.**

Size: 21x36mm.

738 CD7 3s dk bl 35 28

Emblem of Radio Austria and Transistor Radio Panel
A235

1964, Oct. 1 Photogravure ***Perf. 13½***

739 A235 1s blk brn & red 20 12

Forty years of Radio Austria.

Old Printing Press
A236

Lithographed and Engraved

1964, Oct. 12 ***Perf. 14x13½***

740 A236 1.50s tan & blk 20 12

Issued to publicize the 6th Congress of the International Graphic Federation, Vienna, Oct. 12–17.

Pres. Adolf Schärf and Schärf Student Center
A237

Ruins and New Buildings
A238

Typographed and Engraved

1965, Apr. 20 ***Perf. 12***

741 A237 1.50s bluish blk 32 20

Issued in memory of Dr. Adolf Schärf (1890–1965), President of Austria (1957–65).

Engraved

1965, Apr. 27 ***Perf. 14x13½***

742 A238 1.80s car lake 25 15

Twenty years of reconstruction.

Oldest Seal of Vienna University
A239

St. George, 16th Century Wood Sculpture
A240

Photogravure and Engraved

1965, May 10 ***Perf. 14x13½***

743 A239 3s gold & red 40 28

Issued to commemorate the 600th anniversary of the founding of the University of Vienna.

1965, May 17 **Engraved**

744 A240 1.80s bluish blk 28 25

Issued to publicize the art of the Danube Art School, 1490–1540, in connection with an art exhibition, May–Oct. 1965. The stamp background shows an engraving by Albrecht Altdorfer.

ITU Emblem, Telegraph Key and TV Antenna
A241

Ferdinand Raimund
A242

1965, May 17 **Unwmkd.**

745 A241 3s vio bl 35 28

Issued to commemorate the centenary of the International Telecommunication Union.

1965 Engraved ***Perf. 14x13½***

Portraits: No. 746, Ignaz Philipp Semmelweis. No. 747, Bertha von Suttner. No. 749, Ferdinand Georg Waldmüller.

746 A242 1.50s violet 20 12
747 A242 1.50s bluish blk 20 15
748 A242 3s dk brn 38 25
749 A242 3s grnsh blk 38 30

No. 746 commemorates the centenary of the death of Dr. Ignaz Philipp Semmelweis (1818–65), who discovered the cause of puerperal fever and introduced antisepsis into obstetrics. No. 747, the 60th anniversary of the awarding of the Nobel Prize for Peace to Bertha von Suttner (1843–1914), pacifist and author. No. 748, the 175th anniversary of the birth of Ferdinand Raimund (1790–1836), actor and playwright. No. 749, the centenary of the death of Ferdinand Georg Waldmüller (1793–1865), painter.

Issue dates: No. 746, Aug. 13; No. 747, Dec. 1; No. 748, June 1; No. 749, Aug. 23.

Dancers with Tambourines
A243

Red Cross and Strip of Gauze
A244

Design: 1.50s, Male gymnasts with practice bars.

1965, July 20 Photo. and Engraved

750 A243 1.50s gray & blk 20 15
751 A243 3s bis & blk 40 32

Issued to commemorate the Fourth Gymnaestrada, international athletic meet, Vienna, July 20–24.

1965, Oct. 1 Litho. ***Perf. 14x13½***

752 A244 3s blk & red 35 25

Issued to publicize the 20th International Red Cross Conference, Vienna.

Austrian Flag and Eagle with Mural Crown
A245

Austrian Flag, U.N. Headquarters and Emblem
A246

1965, Oct. 7 Photo. and Engraved

753 A245 1.50s gold, red & blk 20 18

Issued to commemorate the 50th anniversary of the Union of Austrian Towns.

Lithographed and Engraved

1965, Oct. 25 *Perf. 12* Unwmkd.

754 A246 3s blk, brt bl & red 50 30

Issued to commemorate the 10th anniversary of Austria's admission to the United Nations.

University of Technology, Vienna
A247

1965, Nov. 8 Engraved *Perf. 13½x14*

755 A247 1.50s violet 20 15

Issued to commemorate the 150th anniversary of the founding of the Vienna University of Technology.

Map of Austria with Postal Zone Numbers—A248

1966, Jan. 14 Photo. *Perf. 12*

756 A248 1.50s yel, red & blk 20 8

Issued to publicize the introduction of postal zone numbers, Jan. 1, 1966.

PTT Building, Emblem and Churches of Sts. Maria Rotunda and Barbara
A249

Maria von Ebner Eschenbach
A250

Lithographed and Engraved

1966, March 4 *Perf. 14x13½*

757 A249 1.50s *dl yel* 20 10

Issued to commemorate the centenary of the headquarters of the Post and Telegraph Administration.

1966, March 11 Engraved

758 A250 3s plum 35 20

Issued to commemorate the 50th anniversary of the death of Maria von Ebner Eschenbach (1830–1916), novelist and poet.

Ferris Wheel, Prater
A251

1966, Apr. 19 Engr. *Perf. 14x13½*

759 A251 1.50s sl grn 20 15

Issued to commemorate the 200th anniversary of the opening of the Prater (park), Vienna, to the public by Emperor Joseph II.

Josef Hoffmann
A252

Unwmkd.

1966, May 6 Engraved *Perf. 12*

760 A252 3s dk brn 35 20

Issued to commemorate the tenth anniversary of the death of Josef Hoffmann (1870–1956), architect.

Arms of Wiener Neustadt
A253

Photogravure and Engraved

1966, May 27 *Perf. 14*

761 A253 1.50s gray & multi 20 15

Issued to publicize the Wiener Neustadt Art Exhibition, centered around the time and person of Emperor Frederick III (1440–1493).

Austrian Eagle and Emblem of National Bank
A254

1966, May 27 *Perf. 14*

762 A254 3s gray grn, dk brn & dk grn 35 20

Issued to commemorate the 150th anniversary of the Austrian National Bank.

Puppy
A255

Lithographed and Engraved

1966, June 16 *Perf. 12*

763 A255 1.80s yel & blk 20 12

Issued to commemorate the 120th anniversary of the Vienna Humane Society.

Columbine
A256

Alpine Flowers: 1.80s, Turk's cap. 2.20s, Wulfenia carinthiaca. 3s, Globeflowers. 4s, Fire lily. 5s, Pasqueflower.

Lithographed

1966, Aug. 17 *Perf. 13½* Unwmkd.

Flowers in Natural Colors

764	A256	1.50s dk bl	15	15
765	A256	1.80s dk bl	20	20
766	A256	2.20s dk bl	32	32
767	A256	3s dk bl	50	50
768	A256	4s dk bl	55	55
769	A256	5s dk bl	55	55
		Nos. 764-769 (6)	2.27	2.27

Fair Building
A257

1966, Aug. 26 Engr. *Perf. 13½x13*

770 A257 3s vio bl 35 20

First International Fair at Wels.

Peter Anich, Map, Globe and Books
A258

Sick Worker and Health Emblem
A259

1966, Sept. 1 *Perf. 14x13½*

771 A258 1.80s black 20 12

Issued to commemorate the 200th anniversary of the death of Peter Anich (1723–1766), Tirolean cartographer and farmer.

1966, Sept. 19 Engr. and Litho.

772 A259 3s blk & ver 35 20

Issued to publicize the 15th Occupational Medicine Congress, Vienna, Sept. 19–24.

Theater Collection: "Eunuchus" by Terence from a 1496 Edition
A260

Designs: 1.80s, Map Collection: Title page of Geographia Blavania (Cronus, Hercules and celestial sphere). 2.20s, Picture Archive and Portrait Collection: View of Old Vienna after a watercolor by Anton Stutzinger. 3s, Manuscript Collection: Illustration from the 15th century "Livre du Cuer d'Amours Espris" of the Duke René d'Anjou.

Photogravure and Engraved

1966, Sept. 28 *Perf. 13½x14*

773	A260	1.50s multi	12	12
774	A260	1.80s multi	20	20
775	A260	2.20s multi	25	25
776	A260	3s multi	28	28

Austrian National Library.

Young Girl
A261

Lithographed and Engraved

1966, Oct. 3 *Perf. 14x13½*

777 A261 3s lt bl & blk 35 20

Issued to commemorate the 10th anniversary of the "Save the Child" society.

Strawberries
A262

Coat of Arms of University of Linz
A263

Fruit: 1s, Grapes. 1.50s, Apple. 1.80s, Blackberries. 2.20s, Apricots. 3s, Cherries.

1966, Nov. 25 Photo. *Perf. 13½x13*

778	A262	50g multi	18	18
779	A262	1s multi	15	15
780	A262	1.50s multi	15	15
781	A262	1.80s multi	25	25
782	A262	2.20s multi	25	25
783	A262	3s multi	30	30
		Nos. 778-783 (6)	1.28	1.28

Photogravure and Engraved

1966, Dec. 9 *Perf. 14x13½*

784 A263 3s gray, blk, red, sil & gold 35 20

Issued to commemorate the inauguration of the Universary of Linz, Oct. 8, 1966.

Ice Skater, 1866
A264

Ballet Dancer
A265

Photogravure and Engraved

1967, Feb. 3 *Perf. 14x13½*

785 A264 3s pale bl & dk bl 35 20

Centenary of Vienna Ice Skating Club.

1967, Feb. 15 Engr. *Perf. 11½x12*

786 A265 3s dp cl 35 20

a. Perf. 12 1.20 1.20

Issued to commemorate the centenary of the "Blue Danube" waltz by Johann Strauss.

Karl Schönherr
A266

1967, Feb. 24 Engr. *Perf. 14x13½*

787 A266 3s gray brn 35 20

Issued to commemorate the centenary of the birth of Dr. Karl Schönherr (1867–1943), poet, playwright and physician.

Ice Hockey Goalkeeper
A267

Photogravure and Engraved

1967, March 17 ***Perf. 13½x14***

788 A267 3s pale grn & dk bl 35 20

Issued to publicize the Ice Hockey Championships, Vienna, March 18–29.

Violin, Organ and Laurel
A268

1967, Mar. 28 **Engr.** ***Perf. 13½***

789 A268 3.50s indigo 45 20

Issued to commemorate the 125th anniversary of the Vienna Philharmonic Orchestra.

Motherhood, Water-color by Peter Fendi
A269

Lithographed

1967, Apr. 28 ***Perf. 14*** **Unwmkd.**

790 A269 2s multi 25 15

Issued for Mother's Day, 1967.

Gothic Mantle Madonna
A270

1967, May 19 **Engr.** ***Perf. 13½x14***

791 A270 3s slate 35 20

Issued to publicize the art exhibition "Austrian Gothic," Krems, 1967. The Gothic wood carving is from Frauenstein in Upper Austria.

Medieval Gold Cross
A271

Swan, Tapestry by Oscar Kokoschka
A272

Lithographed and Engraved

1967, June 9 ***Perf. 13½***

792 A271 3.50s Prus grn & multi 40 25

Issued to publicize the Salzburg Treasure Chamber in connection with an exhibition at Salzburg Cathedral, June 12–Sept. 15.

1967, June 9 **Photogravure**

793 A272 2s multi 25 15

Issued to publicize the Nibelungen District Art Exhibition, Pöchlarn, celebrating the 700th anniversary of Pöchlarn as a city. The design is from the border of the Amor and Psyche tapestry at the Salzburg Festival Theater.

View and Arms of Vienna
A273

Engraved and Photogravure

1967, June 12 ***Perf. 13x13½***

794 A273 3s blk & red 35 20

Issued to publicize the 10th Europa Talks, "Science and Society in Europe," Vienna, June 13–17.

Prize Bull "Mucki"
A274

1967, Aug. 28 **Engr.** ***Perf. 13½***

795 A274 2s dp cl 25 15

Issued to commemorate the centenary of the Ried Festival and the Agricultural Fair.

Potato Beetle
A275

Engraved and Photogravure

1967, Aug. 29 ***Perf. 13½x14***

796 A275 3s blk & multi 35 20

Issued to publicize the 6th International Congress for Plant Protection, Vienna.

First Locomotive Used on Brenner Pass—A276

1967, Sept. 23 **Photo.** ***Perf. 12***

797 A276 3.50s tan & sl grn 45 25

Centenary of railroad over Brenner Pass.

Christ in Glory
A277

1967, Oct. 9 ***Perf. 13½***

798 A277 2s multi 25 15

Issued to commemorate the restoration of the Romanesque (11th century) frescoes in the Lambach monastery church.

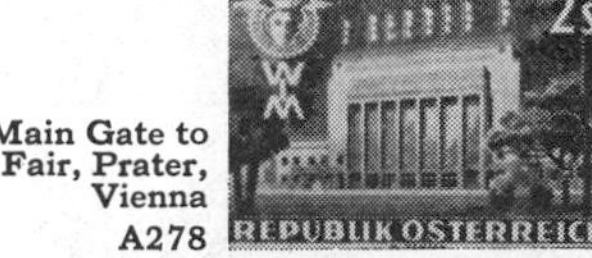

Main Gate to Fair, Prater, Vienna
A278

1967, Oct. 24 **Photo.** ***Perf. 13½x14***

799 A278 2s choc & buff 25 15

Issued to publicize the Congress of International Trade Fairs, Vienna, Oct., 1967.

Medal Showing Minerva and Art Symbols
A279

Frankfurt Medal for Reformation, 1717
A280

Lithographed and Engraved

1967, Oct. 25 ***Perf. 13½***

800 A279 2s dk brn, dk bl & yel 25 15

Issued to commemorate the 275th anniversary of the Vienna Academy of Fine Arts. The medal was designed by Georg Raphael Donner (1693–1741) and is awarded as an artist's prize.

1967, Oct. 31 **Engr.** ***Perf. 14x13½***

801 A280 3.50s bl blk 40 25

450th anniversary of the Reformation.

Mountain Range and Stone Pines
A281

1967, Nov. 7 ***Perf. 13½***

802 A281 3.50s green 40 25

Centenary of academic study of forestry.

Land Survey Monument, 1770
A282

St. Leopold, Window, Heiligenkreuz Abbey
A283

1967, Nov. 7 **Photogravure**

803 A282 2s ol blk 25 15

150th anniversary of official land records.

1967, Nov. 15 **Engr. & Photo.**

804 A283 1.80s multi 25 15

Issued in memory of Margrave Leopold III (1075–1136), patron saint of Austria.

Tragic Mask and Violin
A284

Nativity from 15th Century Altar
A285

1967, Nov. 17 ***Perf. 13½***

805 A284 3.50s bluish lil & blk 40 25

Issued to commemorate the 150th anniversary of the Academy of Music and Dramatic Art.

1967, Nov. 27 **Engr.** ***Perf. 14x13½***

806 A285 2s green 25 15

Christmas 1967.

The design shows the late Gothic carved center panel of the altar in St. John's Chapel in Nonnberg Convent, Salzburg.

Innsbruck Stadium, Alps and FISU Emblem
A286

Camillo Sitte
A287

1968, Jan. 22 **Engraved** ***Perf. 13½***

807 A286 2s dk bl 25 15

Issued to publicize the Winter University Games under the auspices of FISU (Fédération Internationale du Sport Universitaire), Innsbruck, Jan. 21–28.

1968, Apr. 17 ***Perf. 13½***

808 A287 2s blk brn 25 15

Issued to commemorate the 125th anniversary of the birth of Camillo Sitte (1843–1903), architect and city planner.

Mother and Child
A288

Cup and Serpent Emblem
A289

1968, May 7

809 A288 2s sl grn 25 15

Issued for Mother's Day, 1968.

1968, May 7 **Photogravure**

810 A289 3.50s dp plum, gray & gold 40 25

Bicentenary of the Veterinary College.

Bride with Lace Veil
A290

1968, May 24 Engraved *Perf. 12*

811	A290	3.50s bl blk	40	25

Issued to commemorate the centenary of the embroidery industry of Vorarlberg.

Horse Race
A291

1968, June 4 *Perf. 13½*

812	A291	3.50s sepia	40	28

Issued to commemorate the centenary of horse racing at Freudenau, Vienna.

Dr. Karl Landsteiner
A292

Peter Rosegger
A293

1968, June 14 *Perf. 14x13½*

813	A292	3.50s dk bl	40	28

Issued to commemorate the centenary of the birth of Dr. Karl Landsteiner (1868–1943), pathologist, discoverer of the four main human blood types.

1968, June 26

814	A293	2s sl grn	25	15

Issued to commemorate the 50th anniversary of the death of Peter Rosegger (1843–1918), poet and writer.

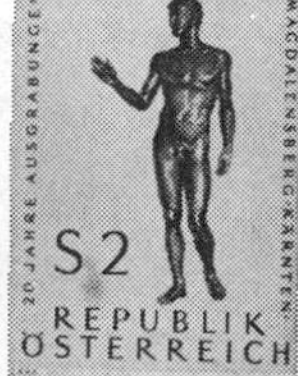

Angelica Kauffmann, Self-portrait
A294

Bronze Statue of Young Man, 1st Century B.C.
A295

1968, July 15 Engr. *Perf. 14x13½*

815	A294	2s int blk	25	15

Issued to publicize the art exhibitions "Angelica Kauffmann and her Contemporaries," Bregenz, July 28–Oct. 13, 1968, and Vienna, Oct. 22, 1968–January 6, 1969.

1968, July 15 Litho. and Engr.

816	A295	2s grnsh gray & blk	25	15

Issued to publicize 20 years of excavations on Magdalene Mountain, Carinthia.

Bishop, Romanesque Bas-relief
A296

1968, Sept. 20 Engr. *Perf. 14x13½*

817	A296	2s bl gray	25	15

Issued to commemorate the 750th anniversary of the Graz-Seckau Bishopric.

Koloman Moser
A297

Human Rights Flame—A298

Engraved and Photogravure

1968, Oct. 18 *Perf. 12*

818	A297	2s blk brn & ver	25	15

Issued to commemorate the 50th anniversary of the death of Koloman Moser (1868–1918), stamp designer and painter.

1968, Oct. 18 Photo. *Perf. 14x13½*

819	A298	1.50s gray, dp car & dk grn	40	15

International Human Rights Year.

Pres. Karl Renner and States' Arms
A299

Designs: No. 821, Coats of arms of Austria and Austrian states. No. 822, Article I of Austrian Constitution and States' coats of arms.

Engraved and Photogravure

1968 Nov. 11 *Perf. 13½*

820	A299	2s blk & multi	40	40
821	A299	2s blk & multi	40	40
822	A299	2s blk & multi	40	40

50th anniversary of Republic of Austria.

Crèche, Memorial Chapel, Oberndorf-Salzburg
A300

Perf. 14x13½

1968, Nov. 29 Engraved

823	A300	2s sl grn	25	15

Christmas 1968. 150th anniversary of "Silent Night, Holy Night."

Angels, from Last Judgment by Troger (Röhrenbach-Greillenstein Chapel)—A301

Baroque Frescoes: No. 825, Vanquished Demons, by Paul Troger, Altenburg Abbey. No. 826, Sts. Peter and Paul, by Troger, Melk Abbey. No. 827, The Glorification of Mary, by Franz Anton Maulpertsch, Maria Treu Church, Vienna. No. 828, St. Leopold Carried into Heaven, by Maulpertsch, Ebenfurth Castle Chapel. No. 829, Symbolic figures from The Triumph of Apollo, by Maulpertsch, Halbthurn Castle.

Engraved and Photogravure

1968, Dec. 11 *Perf. 13½x14*

824	A301	2s multi	32	32
825	A301	2s multi	32	32
826	A301	2s multi	32	32
827	A301	2s multi	32	32
828	A301	2s multi	32	32
829	A301	2s multi	32	32
		Nos. 824-829 (6)	1.92	1.92

St. Stephen
A302

Statues in St. Stephen's Cathedral, Vienna: No. 831, St. Paul. No. 832, Mantle Madonna. No. 833, St. Christopher. No. 834, St. George and the Dragon. No. 835, St. Sebastian.

1969, Jan. 28 Engraved *Perf. 13½*

830	A302	2s black	32	32
831	A302	2s rose cl	32	32
832	A302	2s gray vio	32	32
833	A302	2s sl bl	32	32
834	A302	2s sl grn	32	32
835	A302	2s dk red brn	32	32
		Nos. 830-835 (6)	1.92	1.92

500th anniversary of Diocese of Vienna.

Parliament and Pallas Athena Fountain, Vienna
A303

1969, Apr. 8 Engraved *Perf. 13½*

836	A303	2s grnsh blk	25	15

Issued to publicize the Interparliamentary Union Conference, Vienna, Apr. 7–13.

Europa Issue, 1969

Common Design Type

1969, Apr. 28 Photo. *Perf. 12*

837	CD12	2s gray grn, brick red & bl	25	15

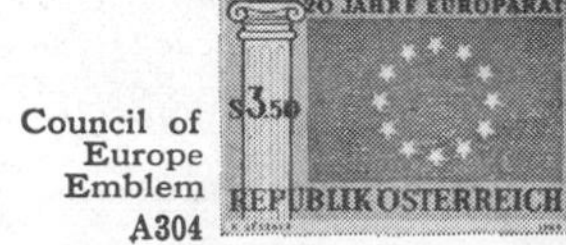

Council of Europe Emblem
A304

1969, May 5

838	A304	3.50s gray, ultra, blk & yel	50	32

20th anniversary of Council of Europe.

Frontier Guards
A305

Engraved and Photogravure

1969, May 14 *Perf. 12*

839	A305	2s sep & red	25	15

Honor to Austrian Federal Army.

Don Giovanni, by Mozart
A306

Gothic Armor of Maximilian I
A307

1969, May 23 *Perf. 13½*

840	A306	Sheet of 8, gold, red & brn blk	5.00	5.00
a.		2s *Don Giovanni, Mozart*	40	40
b.		2s *Magic Flute, Mozart*	40	40
c.		2s *Fidelio, Beethoven*	40	40
d.		2s *Lohengrin, Wagner*	40	40
e.		2s *Don Carlos, Verdi*	40	40
f.		2s *Carmen, Bizet*	40	40
g.		2s *Rosencavalier, Richard Strauss*	40	40
h.		2s *Swan Lake, Ballet by Tchaikovsky*	40	40

Centenary of Vienna Opera House.

No. 840 contains 8 stamps arranged around gold and red center label showing Opera House. Printed in sheets containing 4 Nos. 840 with wide gutters between.

1969, June 4 Engraved

841	A307	2s bluish blk	25	15

Issued to publicize the Emperor Maximilian I Exhibition, Innsbruck, May 30–Oct. 5.

Oldest Municipal Seal of Vienna
A308

Girl's Head and Village House
A309

1969, June 16 Photo. *Perf. 13½*

842	A308	2s tan, red & blk	25	15

Issued to publicize the 19th Congress of the International Organization of Municipalities, Vienna, June 1969.

Engraved and Photogravure

1969, June 16 *Perf. 13½x14*

843	A309	2s yel grn & sep	25	15

Issued to publicize the 20th anniversary of the Children's Village Movement in Austria (SOS Villages).

Hands Holding Wrench, and U.N. Emblem
A310

Austria's Flag and Shield Circling the World
A311

1969, Aug. 22 Photo. ***Perf. 13x13½***

844	A310	2s dp grn	25	15

Issued to commemorate the 50th anniversary of the International Labor Organization.

Engraved and Lithographed

1969, Aug. 22 ***Perf. 14x13½***

845	A311	3.50s sl & red	40	25

Issued to publicize 1969 as the Year of Austrians Living Abroad.

Young Hare, by Dürer
A312

Etchings: No. 847, El Cid Killing a Bull, by Francisco de Goya. No. 848, Madonna with the Pomegranate, by Raphael. No. 849, The Painter, by Peter Brueghel. No. 850, Rubens' Son Nicolas, by Rubens. No. 851, Self-portrait, by Rembrandt. No. 852, Lady Reading, by Francois Guerin. No. 853, Wife of the Artist, by Egon Schiele.

Engraved and Photogravure

1969, Sept. 26 ***Perf. 13½***

Gray Frame, Buff Background

846	A312	2s blk & brn	32	32
847	A312	2s black	32	32
848	A312	2s black	32	32
849	A312	2s black	32	32
850	A312	2s blk & sal	32	32
851	A312	2s black	32	32
852	A312	2s blk & sal	32	32
853	A312	2s black	32	32
		Nos. 846-853 (8)	2.56	2.56

Bicentenary of the etching collection in the Albertina, Vienna.

President Franz Jonas
A313

1969, Oct. 3

854	A313	2s gray & vio bl	25	15

Issued to commemorate the 70th birthday of Franz Jonas, president of Austria.

Post Horn, Globe and Lightning
A314

1969, Oct. 17 ***Perf. 13½x14***

855	A314	2s multi	25	15

Issued to commemorate the 50th anniversary of the Union of Postal and Telegraph employees.

Savings Box, about 1450
A315

Madonna, by Albin Egger-Lienz
A316

1969, Oct. 31 Photo. ***Perf. 13x13½***

856	A315	2s sil & sl grn	25	15

Issued to publicize the importance of savings.

Engraved and Photogravure

1969, Nov. 24 ***Perf. 12***

857	A316	2s dp cl & pale yel	25	15

Christmas 1969.

Josef Schöffel
A317

St. Klemens M. Hofbauer
A318

1970, Feb. 6 Engr. ***Perf. 14x13½***

858	A317	2s dl pur	25	15

Issued to commemorate the 60th anniversary of the death of Josef Schöffel, (1832–1910), who saved the Vienna Woods.

Engraved and Photogravure

1970, Mar. 13 ***Perf. 14x13½***

859	A318	2s dk brn & lt tan	25	15

Issued to commemorate the 150th anniversary of the death of St. Klemens Maria Hofbauer (1751–1820); Redemptorist preacher in Poland and Austria, canonized in 1909.

Chancellor Leopold Figl
A319

Belvedere Palace, Vienna
A320

1970, Apr. 27 Engraved ***Perf. 13½***

860	A319	2s dk ol gray	25	15
861	A320	2s dk rose brn	25	15

25th anniversary of Second Republic.

Krimml Waterfalls
A321

1970, May 19 Engraved ***Perf. 13½***

862	A321	2s sl grn	25	15

Issued for the European Nature Conservation Year, 1970.

St. Leopold on Oldest Seal of Innsbruck University
A322

Lithographed and Engraved

1970, June 5 ***Perf. 13½***

863	A322	2s red & blk	25	15

Issued to commemorate the 300th anniversary of the founding of the Leopold Franzens University in Innsbruck.

Organ, Great Hall, Music Academy
A323

Photogravure and Engraved

1970, June 5 ***Perf. 14***

864	A323	2s gold & dp cl	25	15

Issued to commemorate the centenary of the Vienna Music Academy Building.

Tower Clock, 1450–1550
A324

The Beggar Student, by Carl Millöcker
A325

Old Clocks from Vienna Horological Museum: No. 866, Lyre clock, 1790–1815. No. 867, Pendant clock 1600–1650. No. 868, Pendant watch, 1800–1830. No. 869, Bracket clock, 1720–1760. No. 870, French column clock, 1820–1850.

1970

865	A324	1.50s buff & sep	25	25
866	A324	1.50s grnsh & grn	25	25
867	A324	2s pale & dk bl	32	32
868	A324	2s pale rose & lake	32	32
869	A324	3.50s buff & brn	60	60
870	A324	3.50s pale lil & brn vio	60	60
		Nos. 865-870 (6)	2.34	2.34

Issue dates: Nos. 865, 867, 869, June 22. Others, Oct. 23.

1970 Photo. and Engr. ***Perf. 13½***

Operettas: No. 872, Fledermaus, by Johann Strauss. No. 873, The Dream Waltz, by Oscar Strauss. No. 874, The Bird Seller, by Carl Zeller. No. 875, The Merry Widow, by Franz Lehar. No. 876, Two Hearts in Three-quarter Time, by Robert Stolz.

871	A325	1.50s pale grn & grn	25	25
872	A325	1.50s yel & vio bl	25	25
873	A325	2s pale rose & vio brn	32	32
874	A325	2s pale grn & sep	32	32
875	A325	3.50s pale bl & ind	60	60
876	A325	3.50s beige & sl	60	60
		Nos. 871-876 (6)	2.34	2.34

Issue dates: Nos. 871, 873, 875, July 3. Others Sept. 11.

Bregenz Festival Stage
A326

1970, July 23 **Photogravure**

877	A326	3.50s dk bl & buff	40	32

25th anniversary of Bregenz Festival.

Salzburg Festival Emblem
A327

1970, July 27 ***Perf. 14***

878	A327	3.50s blk, red, gold & gray	40	32

50th anniversary of Salzburg Festival.

St. John, by Thomas Schwanthaler
A328

1970, Aug. 31 **Engraved**

879	A328	3.50s dk gray	40	32

Issued to publicize the 13th General Assembly of the World Veterans Federation, Aug. 28–Sept. 4. The head of St. John is from a sculpture showing the Agony in the Garden in the chapel of the Parish Church in Ried. It is attributed to Thomas Schwanthaler (1634–1702).

Thomas Koschat
A329

1970, Sept. 16 ***Perf. 14x13½***

880	A329	2s chocolate	25	15

Issued to commemorate the 125th anniversary of the birth of Thomas Koschat (1845–1914), Carinthian composer of songs.

Mountain Scene
A330

1970, Sept. 16 Photo. ***Perf. 14x13½***

881	A330	2s vio bl & pink	25	15

Issued to publicize hiking and mountaineering in Austria.

Alfred Cossmann
A331

Arms of Carinthia
A332

1970, Oct. 2 Engraved ***Perf. 14x13½***

882	A331	2s dk brn	25	15

Issued to commemorate the centenary of the birth of Alfred Cossmann (1870–1951), engraver.

Photogravure and Engraved

1970, Oct. 2 ***Perf. 14***

883	A332	2s ol, red, gold, blk & sil	25	15

Carinthian plebiscite, 50th anniversary.

U.N. Emblem
A333

1970, Oct. 23 Litho. ***Perf. 14x13½***

884	A333	3.50s lt bl & blk	50	32

25th anniversary of the United Nations.

Adoration of the Shepherds, Carving from Garsten Vicarage
A334

1970, Nov. 27 Engr. ***Perf. 13½x14***

885	A334	2s dk vio bl	25	15

Christmas 1970.

Karl Renner
A335

Beethoven, by Georg Waldmüller
A336

1970, Dec. 14 Engr. ***Perf. 14x13½***

886	A335	2s dp cl	25	15

Centenary of the birth of Karl Renner (1870–1950), President of Austria.

Photogravure and Engraved

1970, Dec. 16 ***Perf. 13½***

887	A336	3.50s blk & buff	40	32

Bicentenary of the birth of Ludwig van Beethoven (1770–1827), composer.

Enrica Handel-Mazzetti
A337

1971, Jan. 11 Engr. ***Perf. 14x13½***

888	A337	2s sepia	25	15

Centenary of the birth of Enrica von Handel-Mazzetti (1871–1955), novelist and poet.

"Watch Out for Children!"
A338

1971, Feb. 18 Photo. ***Perf. 13½***

889	A338	2s blk, red brn & brt grn	32	15

Traffic safety.

Saltcellar, by Benvenuto Cellini
A339

Art Treasures: 1.50s, Covered vessel, made of prase, gold and precious stones, Florentine, 1580. 2s, Emperor Joseph I, ivory statue by Matthias Steinle, 1693.

Photogravure and Engraved

1971, March 22 ***Perf. 14***

890	A339	1.50s gray & sl grn	25	25
891	A339	2s gray & dp plum	32	32
892	A339	3.50s gray, blk & bis	60	60

Emblem of Austrian Wholesalers' Organization
A340

1971, Apr. 16 Photo. ***Perf. 13½***

893	A340	3.50s multi	40	32

International Chamber of Commerce, 23rd Congress, Vienna, Apr. 17–23.

Jacopo de Strada, by Titian
A341

Seal of Paulus of Franchenfordia, 1380—A342

Paintings in Vienna Museum: 2s, Village Feast, by Peter Brueghel, the Elder. 3.50s, Young Venetian Woman, by Albrecht Dürer.

1971, May 6 Engraved ***Perf. 13½***

894	A341	1.50s rose lake	25	25
895	A341	2s grnsh blk	32	32
896	A341	3.50s dp brn	60	60

Photogravure and Engraved

1971, May 6 ***Perf. 13½x14***

897	A342	3.50s dk brn & bis	40	32

Congress commemorating the centenary of the Austrian Notaries' Statute, May 5–8.

St. Matthew
A343

August Neilreich
A344

1971, May 27 ***Perf. 12½x13½***

898	A343	2s brt rose lil & brn	25	15

Exhibition of "1000 Years of Art in Krems." The statue of St. Matthew is from the Lentl Altar, created about 1520 by the Master of the Pulkau Altar.

1971, June 1 Engr. ***Perf. 14x13½***

899	A344	2s brown	25	15

Centenary of the death of August Neilreich (1803–1871), botanist.

Singer with Lyre
A345

Photogravure and Engraved

1971, July 1 ***Perf. 13½x14***

900	A345	4s lt bl, vio bl & gold	55	40

International Choir Festival, Vienna, July 1–4.

Coat of Arms of Kitzbuhel
A346

1971, Aug. 23 ***Perf. 14***

901	A346	2.50s gold & multi	28	20

700th anniversary of the town of Kitzbuhel.

Vienna Stock Exchange—A347

1971, Sept. 1 Engr. ***Perf. 13½x14***

902	A347	4s redsh brn	45	28

Bicentenary of the Vienna Stock Exchange.

First and Latest Exhibition Halls
A348

1971, Sept. 6 Photo. ***Perf. 13½x13***

903	A348	2.50s dp rose lil	32	20

50th anniversary of Vienna International Fair.

Trade Union Emblem
A349

Arms of Burgenland
A350

1971, Sept. 20 ***Perf. 14x13½***

904	A349	2s gray, buff & red	25	15

25th anniversary of Austrian Trade Union Association.

1971, Oct. 1

905	A350	2s dk bl, gold, red & blk	25	15

50th anniversary of Burgenland's joining Austria.

Marcus Car
A351

Photogravure and Engraved

1971, Oct. 1 ***Perf. 14***

906	A351	4s pale grn & blk	45	32

75th anniversary of the Austrian Automobile, Motorcycle and Touring Club.

Europa Bridge
A352

1971, Oct. 8 Engr. *Perf. 14x13½*

907 A352 4s vio bl 45 32

Opening of highway over Brenner Pass.

Styria's Iron Mountain
A353

Designs: 2s, Austrian Nitrogen Products, Ltd., Linz. 4s, United Austrian Iron and Steel Works, Ltd. (VÖEST), Linz Harbor.

1971, Oct. 15 *Perf. 13½*

908 A353 1.50s redsh brn 25 25
909 A353 2s bluish blk 35 32
910 A353 4s dk sl grn 55 50

25 years of nationalized industry.

High-speed Train on Semmering Pass—A354

Trout Fisherman
A355

1971, Oct. 21 *Perf. 14*

911 A354 2s claret 25 15

Inter-city rapid train service.

1971, Nov. 15 *Perf. 13½*

912 A355 2s dk red brn 25 15

Erich Tschermak-Seysenegg
A356

Infant Jesus as Savior, by Dürer
A357

Photogravure and Engraved

1971, Nov. 15 *Perf. 14x13½*

913 A356 2s pale ol & dk pur 25 15

Centenary of the birth of Dr. Erich Tschermak-Seysenegg (1871–1962), botanist.

1971, Nov. 26 *Perf. 13½*

914 A357 2s gold & multi 25 15

Christmas 1971.

Franz Grillparzer, by Moritz Daffinger
A358

Fountain, Main Square, Friesach
A359

Lithographed and Engraved

1972, Jan. 21 *Perf. 14x13½*

915 A358 2s buff, gold & blk 25 15

Death centenary of Franz Grillparzer (1791–1872), dramatic poet.

1972, Feb. 23 Engr. *Perf. 14x13½*

Designs: 2s, Fountain, Heiligenkreuz Abbey. 2.50s, Leopold Fountain, Innsbruck.

916 A359 1.50s rose lil 25 20
917 A359 2s brown 32 28
918 A359 2.50s olive 40 40

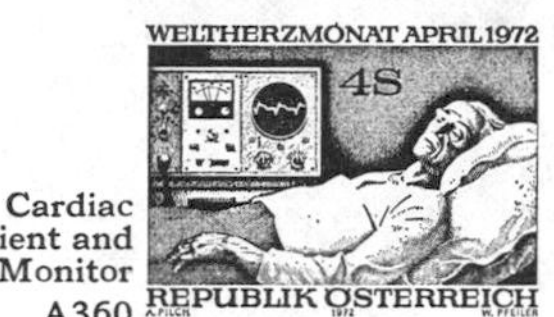

Cardiac Patient and Monitor
A360

1972, Apr. 11 *Perf. 13½x14*

919 A360 4s vio brn 45 38

World Health Day 1972.

St. Michael's Gate, Royal Palace, Vienna
A361

1972, Apr. 11 *Perf. 14x13½*

920 A361 4s vio bl 45 38

Conference of European Post and Telecommunications Ministers, Vienna, Apr. 11–14.

Sculpture, Gurk Cathedral
A362

Photogravure and Engraved

1972, May 5 *Perf. 14*

921 A362 2s gold & dk brn vio 25 15

900th anniversary of Gurk (Carinthia) Diocese. The design is after the central column supporting the sarcophagus of St. Hemma in Gurk Cathedral.

City Hall, Congress Emblem
A363

1972, May 23 Litho. and Engr.

922 A363 4s red, blk & yel 45 32

9th International Congress of Public and Cooperative Economy, Vienna, May 23–25.

Power Line in Carnic Alps
A364

Designs: 2.50s, Power Station, Simmering. 4s, Zemm Power Station (lake in Zillertaler Alps).

1972, June 28 *Perf. 13½x14*

923 A364 70g gray & vio 8 8
924 A364 2.50s gray & red brn 32 32
925 A364 4s gray & sl 45 45

25 years of nationalization of the power industry.

Runner with Olympic Torch
A365

St. Hermes, by Conrad Laib
A366

Engraved and Photogravure

1972, Aug. 21 *Perf. 14x13½*

926 A365 2s sep & red 25 15

Olympic torch relay from Olympia, Greece, to Munich, Germany, passing through Austria.

1972, Aug. 21 Engraved

927 A366 2s vio brn 25 15

Exhibition of Late Gothic Art, Salzburg.

Pears
A367

1972, Sept. *Perf. 14*

928 A367 2.50s dk bl & multi 28 20

World Congress of small plot Gardeners, Vienna, Sept. 7–10.

Souvenir Sheet

Spanish Walk
A368

1972, Sept. 12 *Perf. 13½*

929 A368 Sheet of 6, gold, car & dk brn 3.00 3.00
a. 2s *Spanish walk* 32 32
b. 2s *Piaffe* 32 32
c. 2.50s *Levade* 40 40
d. 2.50s *On long rein* 40 40
e. 4s *Capriole* 65 65
f. 4s *Courbette* 65 65

400th anniversary of the Spanish Riding School in Vienna. Gold and carmine margin. Size: 135x180mm.

Arms of University of Agriculture
A369

Church and Old University
A370

Photogravure and Engraved

1972, Oct. 17 *Perf. 14x13½*

930 A369 2s blk & multi 25 15

Centenary of the University of Agriculture, Vienna.

1972, Nov. 7 Engraved

931 A370 4s red brn 45 32

350th anniversary of the Paris Lodron University, Salzburg.

Carl Michael Ziehrer
A371

1972, Nov. 14

932 A371 2s rose cl 25 15

50th anniversary of the death of Carl Michael Ziehrer (1843–1922), composer.

Virgin and Child, Wood, 1420–30
A372

Photogravure and Engraved

1972, Dec. 1 *Perf. 13½*

933 A372 2s ol & choc 25 15

Christmas 1972.

Racing Sleigh, 1750
A373

Designs: 2s, Coronation landau, 1824. 2.50s, Imperial state coach, 1763.

1972, Dec. 12

934 A373 1.50s pale gray & brn 25 25
935 A373 2s pale gray & sl grn 32 32
936 A373 2.50s pale gray & plum 40 40

Collection of historic state coaches and carriages in Schönbrunn Palace.

Map of Austrian Telephone System
A374

1972, Dec. 14 Photo. *Perf. 14*

937 A374 2s yel & blk 25 15

Completion of automation of Austrian telephone system.

"Drugs are Death"
A375

1973, Jan. 26 Photo. *Perf. 13½x14*

938 A375 2s scar & multi 1.65 50

Fight against drug abuse.

Alfons Petzold A376 — Theodor Körner A377

1973, Jan. 26 Engr. *Perf. 14x13½*

939 A376 2s redsh brn 25 15

50th anniversary of the death of Alfons Petzold (1882–1923), poet.

Photogravure and Engraved

1973, Apr. 24 *Perf. 14x13½*

940 A377 2s gray & dp cl 25 15

Centenary of the birth of Theodor Körner (1873–1957), President of Austria.

Douglas DC-9
A378

1973, May 14 *Perf. 13½x14*

941 A378 2s vio bl & rose red 25 15

Austrian aviation anniversaries: First international airmail service Vienna to Kiev, Mar. 31, 1918, 55th anniversary; Austrian Aviation Corporation, 50th anniversary; Austrian Airlines, 15th anniversary.

Otto Loewi A379 — "Support" A380

1973, June 4 Engr. *Perf. 14x13½*

942 A379 4s dp vio 50 32

Centenary of the birth of Otto Loewi (1873–1961), pharmacologist, winner of 1936 Nobel prize.

1973, June 25

943 A380 2s dk bl 25 15

Federation of Austrian Social Insurance Institutes, 25th anniversary.

Europa Issue 1973

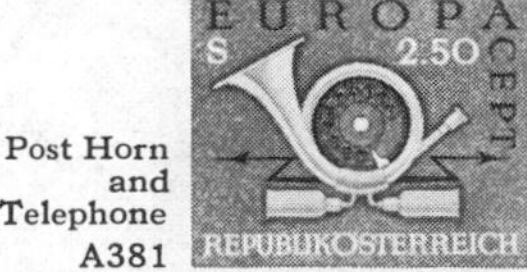

Post Horn and Telephone
A381

1973, July 9 Photo. *Perf. 14*

944 A381 2.50s ocher, blk & yel 28 20

Dornbirn Fair Emblem
A382

1973, July 27 *Perf. 13½x14*

945 A382 2s multi 25 15

Dornbirn Trade Fair, 25th anniversary.

Hurdles A383 — Leo Slezak A384

1973, Aug. 13 Engr. *Perf. 14x13½*

946 A383 4s gray ol 50 32

23rd International Military Pentathlon Championships, Wiener Neustadt, Aug. 13–18.

1973, Aug. 17 *Perf. 14*

947 A384 4s dk brn 50 32

Centenary of the birth of Leo Slezak (1873–1946), operatic tenor.

Gate, Vienna Hofburg, and ISI Emblem
A385

Photogravure and Engraved

1973, Aug. 20 *Perf. 14x13½*

948 A385 2s gray, dk brn & ver 25 15

39th Congress of International Statistical Institute, Vienna, Aug. 20–30.

Tegetthoff off Franz Josef Land, by Julius Prayer
A386

1973, Aug. 30 Engr. *Perf. 13½x14*

949 A386 2.50s Prus grn 28 20

Centenary of the discovery of Franz Josef Land by an Austrian North Pole expedition.

Academy of Science, by Canaletto
A387

1973, Sept. 4

950 A387 2.50s violet 28 20

Centenary of international meteorological cooperation.

Arms of Viennese Tanners A388 — Max Reinhardt A389

Photogravure and Engraved

1973, Sept. 4 *Perf. 14*

951 A388 4s red & multi 50 32

13th Congress of the International Union of Leather Chemists' Societies, Vienna, Sept. 1—7.

1973, Sept. 7 Engr. *Perf. 13x13½*

952 A389 2s rose mag 25 15

Centenary of the birth of Max Reinhardt (1873–1943), theatrical director and stage manager.

Trotter
A390

1973, Sept. 28 *Perf. 13½*

953 A390 2s green 25 15

Centenary of Vienna Trotting Association.

Ferdinand Hanusch
A391

1973, Sept. 28 *Perf. 14x13½*

954 A391 2s rose brn 25 15

50th anniversary of the death of Ferdinand Hanusch (1866–1923), secretary of state.

Police Radio Operator
A392

1973, Oct. 2 *Perf. 13½x14*

955 A392 4s vio bl 50 32

50th anniversary of International Criminal Police Organization (INTERPOL).

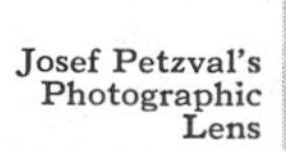

Josef Petzval's Photographic Lens
A393

Lithographed and Engraved

1973, Oct. 8 *Perf. 14*

956 A393 2.50s bl & multi 28 20

EUROPHOT Photographic Congress, Vienna.

Emperor's Spring, Hell Valley
A394

Photogravure and Engraved

1973, Oct. 23 *Perf. 13½x14*

957 A394 2s sep, bl & red 25 15

Centenary of Vienna's first mountain spring water supply system.

Almsee, Upper Austria A395 — Hofburg and Prince Eugene Statue, Vienna A395a

Designs: 50g, Farmhouses, Zillertal, Tirol. 1s, Kahlenbergerdorf. 1.50s, Bludenz, Vorarlberg. 2s, Inn Bridge, Alt Finstermunz. 2.50s, Murau, Styria. 3s, Bischofsmütze, Salzburg. 3.50s, Easter Church, Oberwart. 4.50s, Windmill, Retz. 5s, Aggstein Castle, Lower Austria. 6s, Lindauer Hut, Vorarlberg. 6.50s, Holy Cross Church, Villach, Carinthia. 7s, Falkenstein Castle, Carinthia. 7.50s, Hohensalzburg. 8s, Votive column, Reiteregg, Styria. 10s, Lake Neusiedl, Burgenland. 11s, Old Town, Enns. 16s, Open-air Museum, Bad Tatzmannsdorf. 20s, Myra waterfalls.

Photogravure and Engraved

1973–78 *Perf. 13½x14*

Size: 23x29mm.

No.	Type	Value	Color	Unused	Used
958	A395	50g	gray & sl grn ('75)	6	5
959	A395	1s	brn & dk brn ('75)	10	5
960	A395	1.50s	rose & brn ('74)	15	5
961	A395	2s	gray bl & dk bl ('74)	20	5
962	A395	2.50s	vio & dp vio ('74)	25	5
963	A395	3s	lt ultra & vio bl ('74)	30	5
963A	A395	3.50s	dl org & brn ('78)	35	8
964	A395	4s	brt lil & pur	40	5
965	A395	4.50s	brt grn & bl grn ('76)	45	8
966	A395	5s	lil & vio	50	5
967	A395	6s	dp rose & dk vio ('75)	60	8
968	A395	6.50s	bl grn & ind ('77)	65	12
969	A395	7s	sage grn & sl grn	70	8
970	A395	7.50s	lil rose & cl ('77)	75	20
971	A395	8s	dl red & dp brn ('76)	80	15
972	A395	10s	gray grn & dk grn	1.00	15
973	A395	11s	ver & dk car ('76)	1.10	12
974	A395	16s	ocher & blk ('77)	1.60	50
975	A395	20s	ol bis & ol grn ('77)	2.00	1.00
976	A395a	50s	gray vio & vio bl ('75)	5.00	2.00
			Nos. 958-976 (20)	16.96	4.96

See Nos. 1100-1109.

Nativity A396 — Fritz Pregl A397

1973, Nov. 30 *Perf. 14*

977 A396 2s multi 25 15

Christmas 1973. Design from 14th century stained-glass window.

1973, Dec. 12 Engr. *Perf. 14x13½*

978 A397 4s dp bl 50 32

50th anniversary of the awarding of the Nobel prize for chemistry to Fritz Pregl (1869–1930).

Telex Machine

A398

Hugo Hofmannsthal

A399

1974, Jan. 14 Photo. *Perf. 14x13½*

979 A398 2.50s ultra 28 20

50th anniversary of Radio Austria.

1974, Feb. 1 Engraved *Perf. 14*

980 A399 4s vio bl 50 32

Centenary of the birth of Hugo Hofmannsthal (1874–1929), poet and playwright.

Anton Bruckner and Bruckner House—A400

1974, Mar. 22 Engraved *Perf. 14*

981 A400 4s brown 50 32

Founding of Anton Bruckner House (concert hall), Linz, and sesquicentennial of the birth of Anton Bruckner (1824–1896), composer.

Vegetables A401

Photogravure and Engraved

1974, Apr. 18 *Perf. 14*

Multicolored

982 A401 2s *shown* 28 20
983 A401 2.50s *Fruits* 35 30
984 A401 4s *Flowers* 50 50

International Garden Show, Vienna, Apr. 18–Oct. 14.

Seal of Judenburg

A402

Karl Kraus

A403

1974, Apr. 24 Photo. *Perf. 14x13½*

985 A402 2s plum & multi 25 15

750th anniversary of Judenburg.

1974, Apr. 6 Engraved

986 A403 4s dk red 50 32

Centenary of the birth of Karl Kraus (1874–1936), poet and satirist.

St. Michael, by Thomas Schwanthaler

A404

King Arthur, from Tomb of Maximilian I

A405

1974, May 3

987 A404 2.50s sl grn 28 20

Exhibition of the works by the Schwanthaler Family of sculptors, (1633–1848), Reichersberg am Inn, May 3–Oct. 13.

Europa Issue 1974

1974, May 8 *Perf. 13½*

988 A405 2.50s ocher & sl bl 28 20

De-Dion-Bouton Motor Tricycle

A406

Photogravure and Engraved

1974, May 17 *Perf. 14x13½*

989 A406 2s gray & vio brn 25 15

75th anniversary of the Austrian Automobile Association.

Satyr's Head, Terracotta

A407

1974, May 22 *Perf. 13½x14*

990 A407 2s org brn, gold & blk 25 15

Exhibition, "Renaissance in Austria," Schallaburg Castle, May 22–Nov. 14.

Road Transport Union Emblem

A408

F. A. Maulbertsch, Self-portrait

A409

1974, May 24 Photo. *Perf. 14x13½*

991 A408 4s dp org & blk 50 32

14th Congress of the International Road Transport Union, Innsbruck.

1974, June 7 Engr. *Perf. 14x13½*

992 A409 2s vio brn 25 15

250th anniversary of the birth of Franz Anton Maulbertsch (1724–1796), painter.

Gendarmes, 1824 and 1974

A410

1974, June 7 Photo. *Perf. 13½x14*

993 A410 2s red & multi 25 15

125th anniversary of Austrian gendarmery.

Fencing A411

Photogravure and Engraved

1974, June 14 *Perf. 13½*

994 A411 2.50s red org & blk 28 20

Transportation Symbols

A412

St. Virgil, Sculpture from Nonntal Church

A413

1974, June 18 Photo. *Perf. 14x13½*

995 A412 4s lt ultra & multi 50 32

European Conference of Transportation Ministers, Vienna, June 18–21.

1974, June 28 Engr. *Perf. 13½x14*

996 A413 2s vio bl 25 15

1200th anniversary of the consecration of the Cathedral of Salzburg by Scotch-Irish Bishop Feirgil (St. Virgil). Salzburg was a center of Christianization in the 8th century.

Franz Jonas and Austrian Eagle

A414

1974, June 28

997 A414 2s black 25 15

Franz Jonas (1899–1974), President of Austria 1965–1974.

Franz Stelzhamer

A415

Diver

A416

1974, July 12 Engr. *Perf. 14x13½*

998 A415 2s indigo 25 15

Death centenary of Franz Stelzhamer (1802–1874), poet who wrote in Upper Austrian vernacular.

Perf. 13x13½

1974, Aug. 16 Photo. and Engr.

999 A416 4s bl & sep 50 32

13th European Swimming, Diving and Water Polo Championships, Vienna, Aug. 18–25.

Ferdinand Ritter von Hebra

A417

1974, Sept. 10 Engr. *Perf. 14x13½*

1000 A417 4s brown 50 32

30th Meeting of the Association of German-speaking Dermatologists, Graz, Sept. 10–14. Dr. von Hebra (1816–1880) was a founder of modern dermatology.

Arnold Schönberg

A418

1974, Sept. 13 *Perf. 13½x14*

1001 A418 2.50s purple 28 20

Centenary of the birth of Arnold Schönberg (1874–1951), composer.

Radio Station, Salzburg

A419

1974, Oct. 1 Photo. *Perf. 13½x14*

1002 A419 2s multi 25 15

50th anniversary of Austrian broadcasting.

Edmund Eysler

A420

1974, Oct. 4 Engr. *Perf. 14x13½*

1003 A420 2s dk ol 25 15

25th death anniversary of Edmund Eysler (1874–1949), composer.

Mailman, Mail Coach and Train, UPU Emblem—A421

Design: 4s, Mailman, jet, truck, 1974, and UPU emblem.

1974, Oct. 9 Photo. *Perf. 13½*

1004 A421 2s dp cl & lil 25 15
1005 A421 4s dk bl & gray 50 32

Centenary of Universal Postal Union.

Gauntlet Protecting Rose

A422

1974, Oct. 23 Photo. ***Perf. 13½x14***

1006 A422 2s multi 25 15

Environment protection.

Austrian Sports Pool Emblem
A423

1974, Oct. 23 Photo. ***Perf. 13½x14***

1007 A423 70g multi 8 6

Austrian Sports Pool (lottery), 25th anniversary.

Carl Ditters von Dittersdorf
A424

Virgin and Child, Wood, c. 1600
A425

1974, Oct. 24 Engr. ***Perf. 14x13½***

1008 A424 2s Prus grn 25 15

175th death anniversary of Carl Ditters von Dittersdorf (1739–1799), composer.

1974, Nov. 29 Photo. & Engr.

1009 A425 2s brn & gold 25 15

Christmas 1974.

Franz Schmidt
A426

St. Christopher
A427

1974, Dec. 18

1010 A426 4s gray & blk 50 32

Birth centenary of Franz Schmidt (1874–1939), composer.

Photogravure and Engraved

1975, Jan. 24 ***Perf. 13½***

1011 A427 2.50s gray & brn 28 20

European Architectural Heritage Year. The design shows part of a wooden figure from central panel of the retable in the Kefermarkt Church, 1490–1497.

Safety Belt and Skeleton Arms
A428

Stained Glass Window, Vienna City Hall
A429

1975, Apr. 1 Photo. ***Perf. 14x13½***

1012 A428 70g vio & multi 8 6

Introduction of obligatory use of automobile safety belts.

1975, Apr. 2 ***Perf. 14***

1013 A429 2.50s multi 28 20

11th meeting of the Council of European Municipalities, Vienna, Apr. 2–5.

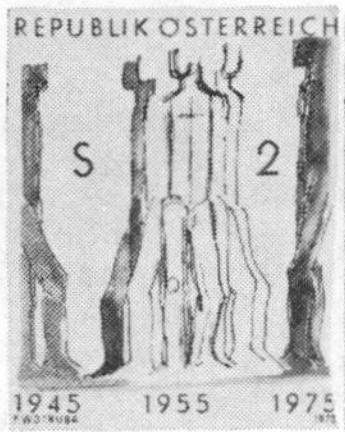

Austria as Mediator
A430

Forest
A431

1975, May 2 Litho. ***Perf. 14***

1014 A430 2s blk & bis 25 15

30th anniversary of the Second Republic of Austria.

1975, May 6 Engraved

1015 A431 2s green 25 15

National forests, 50th anniversary.

High Priest, by Michael Pacher
A432

Gosaukamm Funicular
A433

Europa Issue 1975

Photogravure and Engraved

1975, May 27 ***Perf. 14x13½***

1016 A432 2.50s blk & multi 28 20

Design is detail from painting "The Marriage of Joseph and Mary," by Michael Pacher (c. 1450–1500).

1975, June 23 ***Perf. 14x13½***

1017 A433 2s sl & red 25 15

4th International Funicular Congress, Vienna, June 23–27.

Josef Misson and Mühlbach am Manhartsberg
A434

1975, June 27 ***Perf. 13½x14***

1018 A434 2s choc & redsh brn 25 15

Death centenary of Josef Misson (1803–1875), poet who wrote in Lower Austrian vernacular.

Setting Sun and "P"
A435

1975, Aug. 27 Litho. ***Perf. 14x13½***

1019 A435 1.50s org, blk & bl 20 12

Austrian Association of Pensioners 25th anniversary meeting, Vienna, Aug. 1975.

Ferdinand Porsche
A436

Photogravure and Engraved

1975, Sept. 3 ***Perf. 13½x14***

1020 A436 1.50s gray & pur 20 12

Ferdinand Porsche (1875–1951), engineer, developer of Porsche and Volkswagen cars, birth centenary.

Leo Fall
A437

1975, Sept. 16 Engr. ***Perf. 14x13½***

1021 A437 2s violet 25 15

Leo Fall (1873–1925), composer, 50th death anniversary.

Judo Throw
A438

Heinrich Angeli
A439

1975, Oct. 20 Photo. ***Perf. 14x13½***

1022 A438 2.50s gold & multi 28 20

10th World Judo Championships, Vienna, Oct. 20–26.

1975, Oct. 21 Engr. ***Perf. 14x13½***

1023 A439 2s rose lake 25 15

Heinrich Angeli (1840–1925), painter, 50th death anniversary.

Johann Strauss and Dancers
A440

Photogravure and Engraved

1975, Oct. 24 ***Perf. 13½x14***

1024 A440 4s ocher & sep 50 32

Johann Strauss (1825–1899), composer, 150th birth anniversary.

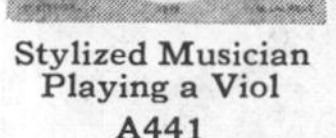

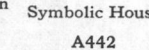

Stylized Musician Playing a Viol
A441

Symbolic House
A442

1975, Oct. 30 ***Perf. 14x13½***

1025 A441 2.50s sil & vio bl 28 20

Vienna Symphony Orchestra, 75th anniversary.

1975, Oct. 31 Photogravure

1026 A442 2s multi 25 15

Austrian building savings societies, 50th anniversary.

Fan with "Hanswurst" Scene, 18th Century
A443

1975, Nov. 14 Photo. ***Perf. 13½x14***

1027 A443 1.50s grn & multi 20 12

Salzburg Theater bicentenary.

Virgin and Child, from 15th Century Altar
A444

"The Spiral Tree," by Hundertwasser
A445

Photogravure and Engraved

1975, Nov. 28 ***Perf. 13x13½***

1028 A444 2s gold & dl pur 25 15

Christmas 1975.

Photo., Engr. and Typo.

1975, Dec. 11 ***Perf. 13½x14***

1029 A445 4s multi 50 40

Austrian modern art. Friedensreich Hundertwasser is the pseudonym of Friedrich Stowasser (b. 1928).

Old Burgtheater—A446

Design: No. 1030b, Grand staircase, new Burgtheater.

Perf. 14 (pane), 13½x14 (stamps)

1976, Apr. 8 Engraved

1030 Pane of 2 + label 1.20 1.20

a. A446 3s vio bl 40 40

b. A446 3s dp brn 40 40

Bicentenary of Vienna Burgtheater. Printed in sheets of 5 panes. Label (head of Pan) and commemorative inscription in vermilion. Size: 130x60mm.

Dr. Robert Barany
A447

Photogravure and Engraved

1976, Apr. 22 ***Perf. 14x13½***

1031 A447 3s bl & brn 35 25

Robert Barany (1876–1936), winner of Nobel Prize for Medicine, 1914, birth centenary.

Ammonite A448

1976, Apr. 30 Photo. ***Perf. 13½x14***

1032 A448 3s red & multi 35 25

Vienna Museum of Natural History, Centenary Exhibition.

Carinthian Dukes' Coronation Chair A449

Siege of Linz, 17th Century Etching A450

Photogravure and Engraved

1976, May 6 ***Perf. 14½x13½***

1033 A449 3s grnsh blk & org 35 25

Millennium of Carinthia.

1976, May 14

1034 A450 4s blk & gray grn 50 32

Upper Austrian Peasants' War, 350th anniversary.

Skittles A451

1976, May 14 ***Perf. 13½x14***

1035 A451 4s blk & org 50 32

11th World Skittles Championships, Vienna.

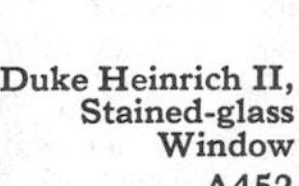

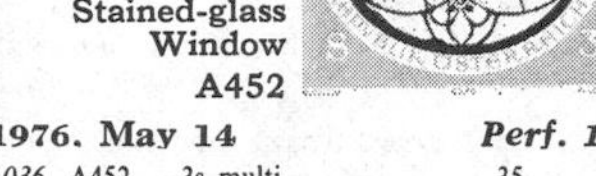

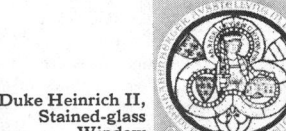

Duke Heinrich II, Stained-glass Window A452

1976. May 14 ***Perf. 14***

1036 A452 3s multi 35 25

Babenberg Exhibition, Lilienfeld.

St. Wolfgang, from Pacher Altar A453

1976, May 26 **Engr.** ***Perf. 13½***

1037 A453 6s brt vio 70 50

International Art Exhibition at St. Wolfgang.

Europa Issue 1976

Tassilo Cup, Kremsmunster, 777 A454

Photogravure & Engraved

1976, Aug. 13 ***Perf. 14x13½***

1038 A454 4s ultra & multi 50 32

Timber Fair Emblem A455

Constantin Economo, M.D. A456

1976, Aug. 13 **Photogravure**

1039 A455 3s grn & multi 35 25

25 years of Austrian Timber Fair, Klagenfurt.

1976, Aug. 23 **Engraved**

1040 A456 3s dk red brn 35 25

Dr. Constantin Economo (1876–1931); neurologist.

Administrative Court, by Salomon Klein A457

1976, Oct. 25 Engr. ***Perf. 13½x14***

1041 A457 6s dp brn 70 50

Austrian Central Administrative Court, centenary.

Souvenir Sheet

Arms of Lower Austria A458

Designs: Coats of Arms of Austrian Provinces.

Photogravure and Engraved

1976, Oct. 25 ***Perf. 14***

1042	A458	Sheet of 9, multi	2.50	2.50
a.		*2s shown*	25	25
b.		*2s Upper Austria*	25	25
c.		*2s Styria*	25	25
d.		*2s Carinthia*	25	25
e.		*2s Tyrol*	25	25
f.		*2s Vorarlberg*	25	25
g.		*2s Salzburg*	25	25
h.		*2s Burgenland*	25	25
i.		*2s Vienna*	25	25

Millennium of Austria. Austrian coat of arms, red border and black inscription in margin. Size: 135x180mm.

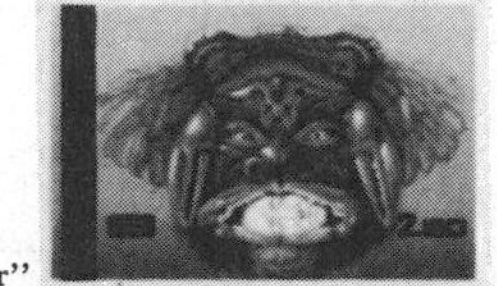

"Cancer" A459

1976, Nov. 17 Photo. ***Perf. 14x13½***

1043 A459 2.50s multi 28 20

Fight against cancer.

UN Emblem and Bridge A460

1976, Nov. 17

1044 A460 3s bl & gold 40 25

UN Industrial Development Organization (UNIDO), 10th anniversary.

Punched Tape, Map of Europe A461

1976, Nov. 17 ***Perf. 14***

1045 A461 1.50s multi 15 12

Austrian Press Agency (APA), 30th anniversary.

Viktor Kaplan, Kaplan Turbine A462

Photogravure and Engraved

1976, Nov. 26 ***Perf. 13½x14***

1046 A462 2.50s multi 28 20

Viktor Kaplan (1876–1934), inventor of Kaplan turbine, birth centenary.

Nativity, by Konrad von Friesach c. 1450 A463

1976, Nov. 26 ***Perf. 13½***

1047 A463 3s multi 32 25

Christmas 1976.

Augustin, the Piper A464

Photogravure and Engraved

1976. Dec. 29 ***Perf. 13½***

1048 A464 6s multi 65 40

Modern Austrian art.

Rainer Maria Rilke A465

Vienna City Synagogue A466

1976, Dec. 29 Engr. ***Perf. 14x13½***

1049 A465 3s dp vio 30 20

Rainer Maria Rilke (1875–1926), poet.

1976, Dec. 29 **Photo.** ***Perf. 13½***

1050 A466 1.50s multi 15 10

Sesquicentennial of Vienna City Synagogue.

Nikolaus Joseph Jacquin A467

1977. Feb. 16 Engr. ***Perf. 14x13½***

1051 A467 4s chocolate 40 32

Nikolaus Joseph von Jacquin (1727–1817), botanist.

Oswald von Wolkenstein A468

Photogravure and Engraved

1977, Feb. 16 ***Perf. 14***

1052 A468 3s multi 30 20

Oswald von Wolkenstein (1377–1445), poet, 600th birth anniversary.

Handball A469

1977, Feb. 25 Photo. ***Perf. 13½x14***

1053 A469 1.50s multi 15 10

World Indoor Handball Championships, Austria, Feb. 5–Mar. 6.

Alfred Kubin A470

1977, Apr. 12 Engr. *Perf. 14x13½*

1054 A470 6s dk vio bl 70 40

Alfred Kubin (1877–1959), illustrator and writer, birth centenary.

Great Spire, St. Stephen's Cathedral
A471

Designs: 3s, Heathen Tower and Frederick's Gable. 4s, Interior view with Albertinian Choir.

1977, Apr. 22 Engr. *Perf. 13½*

1055 A471 2.50s dk brn 32 15
1056 A471 3s dk bl 35 35
1057 A471 4s rose lake 50 40

Restoration and re-opening of St. Stephen's Cathedral, Vienna, 25th anniversary.

Fritz Hermanovsky-Orlando
A472

Photogravure and Engraved

1977, Apr. 29 *Perf. 13½x14*

1058 A472 6s Prus grn & gold 70 40

Fritz Hermanovsky-Orlando (1877–1954), poet and artist, birth centenary.

IAEA Emblem
A473

Arms of Schwanenstadt
A474

1977, May 2 Photo. *Perf. 14*

1059 A473 3s brt bl, lt bl & gold 35 20

International Atomic Energy Agency (IAEA), 20th anniversary.

1977, June 10 Photo. *Perf. 14x13½*

1060 A474 3s dk brn & multi 35 20

350th anniversary of the town Schwanenstadt.

Europa Issue 1977

Attersee, Upper Austria—A475

1977, June 10 Engr. *Perf. 14*

1061 A475 6s ol grn 65 50

Globe, by Vincenzo Coronelli, 1688
A476

Photogravure and Engraved

1977, June 29 *Perf. 14*

1062 A476 3s blk & buff 30 25

5th International Symposium of the Coronelli World Federation of Friends of the Globe, Austria, June 29–July 3.

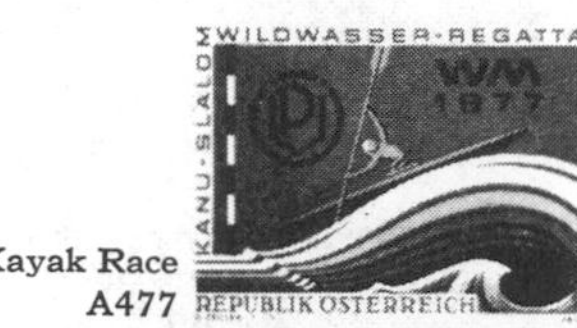

Kayak Race
A477

1977, July 15 Photo. *Perf. 13½x14*

1063 A477 4s multi 40 28

3rd Kayak Slalom White Water Race on Lieser River, Spittal.

The Good Samaritan, by Francesco Bassano
A478

Photogravure and Engraved

1977, Sept. 16

1064 A478 1.50s brn & red 20 12

Workers' Good Samaritan Organization, 50th anniversary.

Papermakers' Coat of Arms
A479

Man with Austrian Flag Lifting Barbed Wire
A480

1977, Oct. 10 *Perf. 14x13½*

1065 A479 3s multi 30 20

17th Conference of the European Committee of Pulp and Paper Technology (EUCEPA), Vienna.

1977, Nov. 3 *Perf. 14*

1066 A480 2.50s sl & red 30 20

Honoring the martyrs for Austria's freedom.

"Austria," First Steam Locomotive in Austria—A481

Designs: 2.50s, Steam locomotive 214. 3s, Electric locomotive 1044.

Photogravure and Engraved

1977, Nov. 17 *Perf. 13½*

1067 A481 1.50s multi 15 12
1068 A481 2.50s multi 28 15
1069 A481 3s multi 35 32

140th anniversary of Austrian railroads.

Virgin and Child, Wood Statue, Mariastein, Tyrol
A482

1977, Nov. 25 *Perf. 14x13½*

1070 A482 3s multi 32 15

Christmas 1977.

The Danube Maiden, by Wolfgang Hutter
A483

1977, Dec. 2 *Perf. 13½x14*

1071 A483 6s multi 65 28

Modern Austrian art.

Egon Friedell
A484

Photogravure and Engraved

1978, Jan. 23

1072 A484 3s lt bl & blk 35 25

Egon Friedell (1878–1938), writer and historian.

Subway Train
A485

1978, Feb. 24 Photo. *Perf. 13½x14*

1073 A485 3s multi 35 25

New Vienna subway system.

Biathlon Competition
A486

1978, Feb. 28 Photo. & Engr.

1074 A486 4s multi 45 32

Biathlon World Championships, Hochfilzen, Tyrol, Feb. 28–Mar. 5.

Leopold Kunschak
A487

1978, Mar. 13 Engr. *Perf. 14x13½*

1075 A487 3s vio bl 32 22

Leopold Kunschak (1871–1953), political leader, 25th death anniversary.

Coyote, Aztec Feather Shield
A488

1978, Mar. 13 Photo. *Perf. 13½x14*

1076 A488 3s multi 32 22

Ethnographical Museum, 50th anniversary exhibition.

Alpine Farm, Woodcut by Suitbert Lobisser
A489

1978, Mar. 23 Engr. *Perf. 13½*

1077 A489 3s dk brn, *buff* 32 22

Suitbert Lobisser (1878–1943), graphic artist, birth centenary.

Capercaillie, Hunting Bag, 1730, and Rifle, 1655
A490

Photogravure and Engraved

1978, Apr. 28 *Perf. 13½*

1078 A490 6s multi 70 50

International Hunting Exhibition, Marchegg.

Europa Issue 1978

Riegersburg, Styria—A491

1978, May 3 Engraved

1079 A491 6s dp rose lil 70 50

Parliament, Vienna, and Map of Europe
A492

Admont Pietà, c. 1410
A493

1978, May 3 Photo. *Perf. 14x13½*

1080 A492 4s multi 45 30

3rd Interparliamentary Conference for European Cooperation and Security, Vienna.

Photogravure and Engraved

1978, May 26

1081 A493 2.50s ocher & blk 25 15

Gothic Art in Styria Exhibition, St. Lambrecht, 1978.

Ort Castle, Gmunden
A494

1978, June 9

1082 A494 3s multi 32 25

700th anniversary of Gmunden City.

Child with Flowers and Fruit
A495

Lehar and his Home, Bad Ischl
A496

Photogravure and Engraved

1978, June 30 *Perf. 14x13½*

1083 A495 6s gold & multi 70 50

25 years of Social Tourism.

1978, July 14 Engr. *Perf. 14x13½*

1084 A496 6s slate 65 45

International Lehar Congress, Bad Ischl. Franz Lehar (1870–1948), operetta composer.

Congress Emblem
A497

1978, Aug. 21 Photo. *Perf. 13½x14*

1085 A497 1.50s blk, red & yel 20 12

Congress of International Federation of Building Construction and Wood Workers, Vienna, Aug. 20–24.

Ottokar of Bohemia and Rudolf of Hapsburg—A498

Photogravure and Engraved

1978, Aug. 25

1086 A498 3s multi 35 25

Battle of Durnkrut and Jedenspeigen (Marchfeld), which established Hapsburg rule in Austria, 700th anniversary.

First Documentary Reference to Villach, "ad pontem uillah"
A499

1978, Sept. 8 Litho. *Perf. 13½x14*

1087 A499 3s multi 35 25

1100th anniversary of Villach, Carinthia.

Seal of Graz, 1440
A500

Emperor Maximilian Fishing
A501

Photogravure and Engraved

1978, Sept. 13 *Perf. 14x13½*

1088 A500 4s multi 50 35

850th anniversary of Graz.

1978, Sept. 15 *Perf. 14x13½*

1089 A501 4s multi 50 32

World Fishing Championships, Vienna, Sept. 1978.

"Aid to the Handicapped"
A502

1978, Oct. 2 Photo. *Perf. 13½x14*

1090 A502 6s org brn & blk 65 45

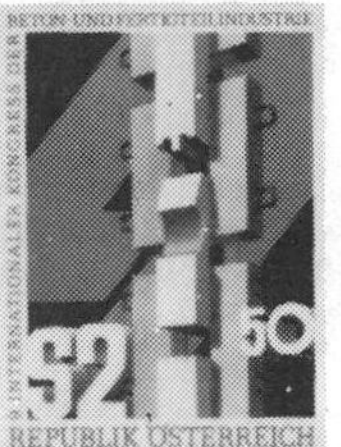

Symbolic Column
A503

1978, Oct. 9 Photo. *Perf. 13½*

1091 A503 2.50s org, blk & gray 30 22

9th International Congress of Concrete and Prefabrication Industries, Vienna, Oct. 8–13.

Grace, by Albin Egger-Lienz
A504

1978, Oct. 27 *Perf. 13½x14*

1092 A504 6s multi 65 45

European Family Congress, Vienna, Oct. 26–29.

Lise Meitner and Atom Symbol
A505

1978, Nov. 7 Engr. *Perf. 14x13½*

1093 A505 6s dk vio 65 45

Lise Meitner (1878–1968), physicist.

Viktor Adler, by Anton Hanak
A506

Photogravure and Engraved

1978, Nov. 10 *Perf. 13½x14*

1094 A506 3s ver & blk 35 25

Viktor Adler (1852–1918), leader of Social Democratic Party, 60th death anniversary.

Franz Schubert, by Josef Kriehuber
A507

Virgin and Child, Wilhering Church
A508

1978, Nov. 17 Engr. *Perf. 14*

1095 A507 6s redsh brn 70 50

Franz Schubert (1797–1828), composer.

Photogravure and Engraved

1978, Dec. 1 *Perf. 12½x13½*

1096 A508 3s multi 35 25

Christmas 1978.

Archduke Johann Shelter, Grossglockner—A509

1978, Dec. 6 *Perf. 13½x14*

1097 A509 1.50s gold & dk vio bl 20 12

Austrian Alpine Club, centenary.

Adam, by Rudolf Hausner
A510

Bound Hands
A511

1978, Dec. 6 Photo. *Perf. 13½x14*

1098 A510 6s multi 70 50

Modern Austrian art.

1978, Dec. 6 *Perf. 14x13½*

1099 A511 6s dp cl 65 45

30th anniversary of Universal Declaration of Human Rights.

Type of 1973

Designs: 20g, Freistadt, Upper Austria. 3s, Bishofsmutze, Salzburg. 4.20s, Hirschegg, Kleinwalsertal. 5.50s, Peace Chapel, Stoderzinken. 5.60s, Riezlern, Kleinwalsertal. 9s, Asten Carinthia. 12s, Kufstein Fortress. 14s, Weiszsee, Salzburg.

Sizes: 20g, 27x33mm. 3s, 17x21mm. 4.20s, 5.50s, 5.60s, 9s, 12s, 14s, 23x29mm.

Photo. and Engraved

1978-84 *Perf. 13½x14*

1100 A395 20g vio bl & dk bl ('80) 5 5
1102 A395 3s lt ultra & vio bl 35 20
1104 A395 4.20s blk & grysh bl ('79) 45 20
1105 A395 5.50s lil & pur ('82) 60 28
1106 A395 5.60s yel grn & ol grn ('82) 60 30
1107 A395 9s red 1.00 70
1108 A395 12s ocher & vio brn ('80) 1.35 25
1109 A395 14s lt grn & grn ('82) 1.65 32
Nos. 1100-1109 (8) 6.05 2.30

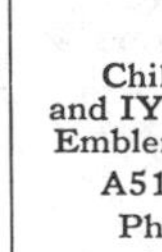

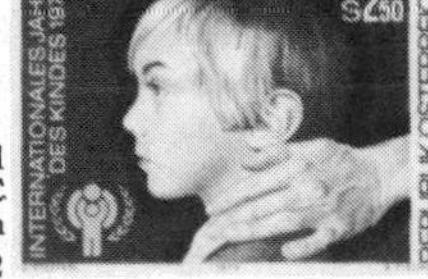

Child and IYC Emblem
A512

Photogravure and Engraved

1979, Jan. 16 *Perf. 14*

1110 A512 2.50s dk bl, blk & brn 25 20

International Year of the Child.

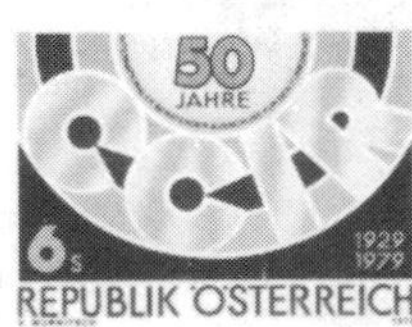

CCIR Emblem
A513

1979, Jan. 16 Photo. *Perf. 13½x14*

1111 A513 6s multi 65 45

International Radio Consultative Committee (CCIR) of the International Telecommunications Union, 50th anniversary.

Air Rifle, Air Pistol and Club Emblem—A514

Photogravure and Engraved

1979, Mar. 7 *Perf. 13½*

1112 A514 6s multi 65 45

Centenary of Austrian Shooting Club, and European Air Rifle and Air Pistol Championships, Graz.

Figure Skater
A515

1979, Mar. 7 Photo. ***Perf. 14x13½***

1113 A515 4s multi 45 35

World Ice Skating Championships, Vienna.

Steamer Franz I
A516

Designs: 2.50s, Tugboat Linz. 3s, Passenger ship Theodor Körner.

1979, Mar. 13 Engr. ***Perf. 13½***

1114 A516 1.50s vio bl 20 15
1115 A516 2.50s sepia 28 20
1116 A516 3s magenta 32 28

First Danube Steamship Company, 150th anniversary.

Fashion Design, by Theo Zasche, 1900
A517

Photogravure and Engraved

1979, Mar. 26 ***Perf. 13x13½***

1117 A517 2.50s multi 30 20

50th International Fashion Week, Vienna.

Wiener Neustadt Cathedral
A518

1979, Mar. 27 Engr. ***Perf. 13½***

1118 A518 4s vio bl 50 35

Cathedral of Wiener Neustadt, 700th anniversary.

Teacher and Pupils, by Franz A. Zauner
A519

Population Chart and Barock Angel
A520

Photogravure and Engraved

1979, Mar. 30 ***Perf. 14x13½***

1119 A519 2.50s multi 30 20

Education of the deaf in Austria, 200th anniversary.

1979, Apr. 6

1120 A520 2.50s multi 30 20

Austrian Central Statistical Bureau, 150th anniversary.

Laurenz Koschier
A521

Diesel Motor
A522

Europa Issue, 1979

1979, May 4

1121 A521 6s ocher & pur 65 45

1979, May 4 Photogravure

1122 A522 4s multi 45 32

13th CIMAC Congress (International Organization for Internal Combustion Machines).

Arms of Ried, Schärding and Braunau
A523

Photogravure and Engraved

1979, June 1 ***Perf. 14x13½***

1123 A523 3s multi 32 20

200th anniversary of Innviertel District.

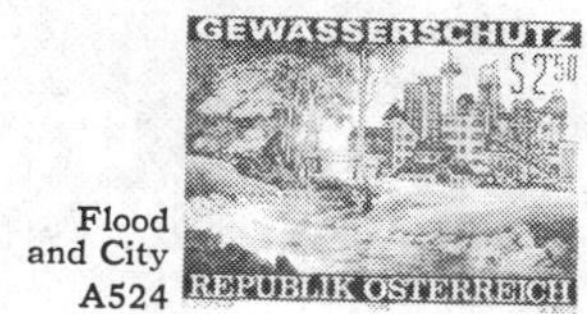

Flood and City
A524

1979, June 1 ***Perf. 13½x14***

1124 A524 2.50s multi 30 20

Control and eliminate water polution.

Arms of Rottenmann
A525

Jodok Fink
A526

Photogravure and Engraved

1979, June 22 ***Perf. 14x13½***

1125 A525 3s multi 32 22

700th anniversary of Rottenmann.

1979, June 29 Engr. ***Perf. 14***

1126 A526 3s brn car 32 22

Jodok Fink (1853–1929), governor of Vorarlberg.

Arms of Wels, Returnees' Emblem, "Europa Sail"
A527

1979, July 6 Photo. ***Perf. 14x13½***

1127 A527 4s yel grn & blk 45 32

5th European Meeting of the International Confederation of Former Prisoners of War, Wels, July 6–8.

Symbolic Flower, Conference Emblem
A528

1979, Aug. 20 Litho. ***Perf. 14x13½***

1128 A528 4s turq bl 45 32

U.N. Conference for Science and Technology, Vienna, Aug. 20-31.

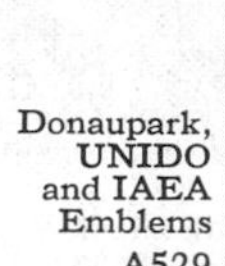

Donaupark, UNIDO and IAEA Emblems
A529

1979, Aug. 24 Engr. ***Perf. 13½x14***

1129 A529 6s grysh bl 65 45

Opening of the Donaupark International Center in Vienna, seat of the United Nations Industrial Development Organization (UNIDO) and the International Atomic Energy Agency (IAEA).

Diseased Eye and Blood Vessels
A530

1979, Sept. 10 Photo. ***Perf. 14***

1130 A530 2.50s multi 35 25

10th World Congress of International Diabetes Federation, Vienna, Sept. 9-14.

View of Stanz Valley through East Portal of Arlberg Tunnel—A531

1979, Sept. 14 Photo. & Engr.

1131 A531 4s multi 45 30

16th World Road Congress, Vienna, Sept. 16-21.

COLORS

Please refer to page v for a complete list of color abbreviations used in this book.

Steam Printing Press
A532

Photogravure and Engraved

1979, Sept. 18 ***Perf. 13½x14***

1132 A532 3s multi 32 20

175th anniversary of Austrian Government Printing Office.

Richard Zsigmondy
A533

1979, Sept. 21 Engr. ***Perf. 14x13½***

1133 A533 6s multi 65 50

Richard Zsigmondy (1865–1929), chemist.

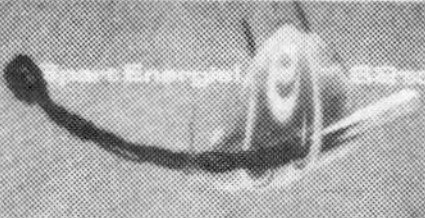

"Save Energy"
A534

1979, Oct. 1 Photo. ***Perf. 14x13½***

1134 A534 2.50s multi 28 20

Festival and Convention Center, Bregenz (Model)—A535

1979, Oct. 1 Engr. ***Perf. 14***

1135 A535 2.50s purple 28 20

Lions International Emblem
A536

1979, Oct. 11 Photo. & Engr.

1136 A536 4s multi 45 30

25th Lions Europa Forum, Vienna, Oct. 11-13.

Wilhelm Exner
A537

Photogravure and Engraved

1979, Oct. 19 ***Perf. 13½x14***

1137 A537 2.50s vio brn & blk 28 20

Centenary of Technological Handicraft Museum, founded by Wilhelm Exner.

The Compassionate Christ, by Hans Fronius A538

1979, Oct. 23 Litho. *Perf. 13½x14*

1138	A538	4s ol & ol blk	45	32

Modern Austrian art.

Locomotive and Arms A539

1979, Oct. 24 Photo. *Perf. 13½x14*

1139 A539	2.50s multi	30	25

Centenary of Raab-Odenburg-Ebenfurt railroad.

August Musger A540

Photo. & Engr.

1979, Oct. 30 *Perf. 14x13½*

1140	A540	2.50s bl gray & blk	30	20

August Musger (1868–1929), developer of slow-motion film technic.

Nativity, St. Barbara's Church—A541

Photogravure and Engraved

1979, Nov. 30 *Perf. 13½×14*

1141	A541	4s multi	45	32

Christmas 1979.

Arms of Baden—A542

Photogravure and Engraved

1980, Jan. 25 *Perf. 14*

1142	A542	4s multi	45	32

Baden, 500th anniversary.

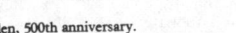

Fight Rheumatism—A543

1980, Feb. 21 *Perf. 13½*

1143	A543	2.50s red & aqua	30	20

Austrian Exports A544

Rudolph Kirchschlager A546

Austrian Red Cross Centenary A545

1980, Feb. 21 Photo. *Perf. 14×13½*

1144	A544	4s dk bl & red	45	32

1980, Mar. 14 Photo. *Perf. 13½×14*

1145	A545	2.50s multi	30	20

Photo. & Engr.

1980, Mar. 20 *Perf. 14×13½*

1146	A546	4s sep & red	45	32

Robert Hamerling—A547

1980, Mar. 24 Engr. *Perf. 13½×14*

1147	A547	2.50s ol grn	28	20

Robert Hamerling (1830-1889), poet.

Seal of Hallein A548

Maria Theresa, by Andreas Moller A549

1980, Apr. 30 Photo. & Engr. *Perf. 14x13½*

1148	A548	4s red & blk	45	32

Hallein, 750th anniversary.

1980, May 13 Engraved *Perf. 13½*

Empress Maria Theresa (1717-1780) Paintings by: 4s, Martin van Meytens. 6s, Josef Ducreux.

1149	A549	2.50s vio brn	28	28
1150	A549	4s dk bl	45	45
1151	A549	6s rose lake	65	65

Flags of Austria and Four Powers A550

1980, May 14 Photo. *Perf. 13½x14*

1152	A550	4s multi	45	32

State Treaty, 25th anniversary.

St. Benedict, by Meinrad Guggenbichler A551

Hygeia by Gustav Klimt A552

1980, May 16 Engraved *Perf. 14½*

1153	A551	2.50s ol grn	28	20

Congress of Benedictine Order of Austria.

1980, May 20 Photo. *Perf. 14*

1154	A552	4s multi	45	32

175th anniversary of academic teaching of hygiene.

Aflenz Ground Satellite Receiving Station Inauguration—A553

1980, May 30 Photo. *Perf. 14*

1155	A553	6s multi	65	45

Steyr, Etching, 1693—A554

1980, June 4 Photo. & Engr. *Perf. 13½*

1156	A554	4s multi	45	32

Millennium of Steyr.

Worker, Oil Drill Head—A555

1980, June 12

1157	A555	2.50s multi	28	20

Austrian oil production, 25th anniversary.

Seal of Innsbruck, 1267—A556

1980, June 23 *Perf. 13½x14½*

1158	A556	2.50s multi	28	20

Innsbruck, 800th anniversary.

Duke's Hat A557

Bible Illustration, Book of Genesis A559

Leo Ascher (1880-1942), composer—A558

1980, June 23 Photo. *Perf. 14½x13½*

1159	A557	4s multi	45	32

800tn anniversary of Styria as a Duchy.

1980, Aug. 18 Engraved *Perf. 14*

1160	A558	3s dk pur	32	28

1980, Aug. 25 *Perf. 13½*

1161	A559	4s multi	45	35

10th International Congress of the Organization for Old Testament Studies.

Europa Issue 1980

Robert Stolz—A560

1980, Aug. 25 **Engraved** ***Perf. 14x13½***
1162 A560 6s red brn 65 45

Robert Stolz (1880-1975), composer.

Old and Modern Bridges—A561

1980, Sept. 1 **Photo.** ***Perf. 13½***
1163 A561 4s multi 45 35

11th Congress of the International Association for Bridge and Structural Engineering, Vienna.

Moon Figure, by Karl Brandstätter A562

Customs Service, Sesquicentennial A563

Photogravure and Engraved

1980, Oct. 10 ***Perf. 14x13½***
1164 A562 4s multi 45 35

1980, Oct. 13 **Photogravure**
1165 A563 2.50s multi 28 20

Gazette Masthead, 1810—A564

1980, Oct. 23 **Photo.** ***Perf. 13½***
1166 A564 2.50s multi 28 20

Official Gazette of Linz, 350th anniversary.

Waidhofen Town Book Title Page, 14th Century—A565

1980, Oct. 24 **Photo. & Engr.** ***Perf. 14***
1167 A565 2.50s multi 28 20

Waidhofen on Thaya, 750th anniversary.

Federal Austrian Army, 25th Anniversary—A566

1980, Oct. 24 **Photo.** ***Perf. 13½x14***
1168 A566 2.50s grnsh blk & red 28 20

Alfred Wegener—A567

1980, Oct. 31 **Engraved**
1169 A567 4s vio bl 45 35

Alfred Wegener (1880-1930), scientist, discovered theory of continental drift.

Robert Musil (1880-1942), Poet—A568

1980, Nov. 6 ***Perf. 14x13½***
1170 A568 4s dk red brn 45 35

Nativity, Stained Glass Window, Klagenfurt—A569

1980, Nov. 28 **Photo. & Engr.** ***Perf. 13½***
1171 A569 4s multi 45 35

Christmas 1980.

25th Anniversary of Social Security—A570

1981, Jan. 19 **Litho.** ***Perf. 13½x14***
1172 A570 2.50s multi 28 20

Niebelungen Saga, 1926, by Wilhelm Dachauer A571

Machinist in Wheelchair A572

1981, Apr. 6 **Engr.** ***Perf. 14x13½***
1173 A571 3s sepia 35 25

Wilhelm Dachauer (1881-1951), artist and engraver.

1981,Apr. 6 **Photo & Engr.**
1174 A572 6s multi 65 50

Rehabilitation International, 3rd European Regional Conference.

Sigmund Freud A573

UNICHAL Congress, Vienna A574

1981, May 6 **Engr.**
1175 A573 3s rose vio 35 25

Sigmund Freud (1856-1939), psychoanalyst.

1981, May 11 **Photo.**
1176 A574 4s multi 45 35

Azzo (Founder of House of Kuenringer) and his Followers, Bear-skin Manuscript—A575

1981, May 15 **Photo. & Engr.**
1177 A575 3s multi 35 25

Kuenringer Exhibition, Zwettl Monastery.

Europa Issue 1981

Maypole—A576

1981, May 22 **Photo.**
1178 A576 6s multi 65 50

Telephone Service Centenary—A577

1981, May 29 **Photo. & Engr.**
Perf. 13½x14
1179 A577 4s multi 45 35

Seibersdorf Research Center, 25th Anniv. A578

1981, June 29 **Photo.** ***Perf. 13½***
1180 A578 4s multi 45 35

The Frog King (Child's Drawing) A579

1981, June 29 ***Perf. 13½x14***
1181 A579 3s multi 35 25

Town Hall and Town Seal of 1250—A580

1981, July 17 **Photo. & Engr.** ***Perf. 13½x14***
1182 A580 4s multi 45 35

St. Veit and der Glan, 800th anniv.

Johann Florian Heller (1813-1871), Pioneer of Urinalysis A581

1981, Aug. 31 ***Perf. 14x13½***
1183 A581 6s red brn 65 50

11th Intl. Clinical Chemistry Congress.

Ludwig Boltzmann (1844-1906), Physicist A582

Scale A583

1981, Sept. 4 **Engr.** ***Perf. 14x13½***
1184 A582 3s dk grn 35 25

1981, Sept. 7 **Photo. & Engr.** ***Perf. 14***
1185 A583 6s multi 65 50

Intl. Pharmaceutical Federation World Congress, Vienna, Sept. 6-11.

Otto Bauer, Politician, Birth Centenary A584

Escher's Impossible Cube A585

1981, Sept. 7 **Photo.** ***Perf. 14x13½***
1186 A584 4s multi 45 35

1981, Sept. 14
1187 A585 4s dk bl & brt bl 45 35

10th Intl. Mathematicians' Congress, Innsbruck.

Kneeling Virgin, Detail of Coronation of Mary Altarpiece, St. Wolfgang, 500th Anniv.—A586

1981, Sept. 25 **Engr.** ***Perf. 14x13½***
1188 A586 3s dk bl 35 25

South-East Fair, Graz, 75th Anniv.—A587

1981, Sept. 25 **Photo.** ***Perf. 13½x14***
1189 A587 4s multi 45 35

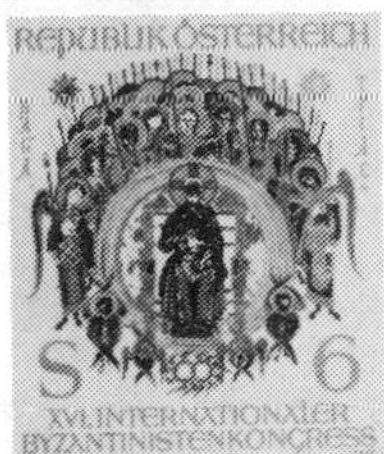

Holy Trinity, 12th Cent. Byzantine Miniature—A588

1981, Oct. 5
1190 A588 6s multi 65 50

16th Intl. Byzantine Congress.

Hans Kelsen (1881-1973), Co-author of Federal Constitution—A589

1981, Oct. 9 **Engr.**
1191 A589 3s dk car 35 25

Emperor Joseph II (Edict of Tolerance Bicentenary)—A590

1981, Oct. 9 **Photo. & Engr.** ***Perf. 14***
1192 A590 4s multi 45 35

World Food Day—A591

1981, Oct. 16 **Photo.** ***Perf. 13½***
1193 A591 6s multi 65 50

Between the Times, by Oscar Asboth—A592

1981, Oct. 22 **Litho.** ***Perf. 13½x14***
1194 A592 4s multi 45 35

Intl. Catholic Workers' Day—A593

1981, Oct. 23 **Photo. & Engr.** ***Perf. 14x13½***
1195 A593 3s multi 35 25

Baron Josef Hammer-Purgstall, Founder of Oriental Studies, 125th Death Anniv.—A594

1981, Nov. 23 **Photo. & Engr.** ***Perf. 14***
1196 A594 3s multi 35 25

Julius Raab (1891-1964), Politician—A595

1981, Nov. 27 **Engr.** ***Perf. 13½***
1197 A595 6s rose lake 65 50

Nativity, Corn Straw Figures—A596

1981, Nov. 27 **Photo. & Engr.**
1198 A596 4s multi 45 32

Christmas 1981.

Stefan Zweig (1881-1942), Poet—A597

1981, Nov. 27 **Engr.** ***Perf. 14x13½***
1199 A597 4s dl vio 45 32

800th Anniv. of St. Nikola on the Danube—A598

1981, Dec. 4
1200 A598 4s multi 45 32

Vienna Emergency Medical Service Centenary—A599

1981, Dec. 9 **Photo.** ***Perf. 13½x14***
1201 A599 3s multi 35 25

Schladming-Haus Alpine World Skiing Championship—A600

1982, Jan. 27 ***Perf. 14***
1202 A600 4s multi 45 32

Dorotheum (State Auction Gallery), 275th Anniv.
A601

Water Rescue Service, 25th Anniv.
A602

1982, Mar. 12 **Photo. & Engr.** ***Perf. 14***
1203 A601 4s multi 45 32

1982, Mar. 19 **Photo.** ***Perf. 14x13½***
1204 A602 5s multi 60 40

St. Severin
A603

Intl. Kneipp Hydropathy Congress, Vienna
A604

1982, Apr. 23 **Photo. & Engr.** ***Perf. 14x13½***
1205 A603 3s multi 35 25

St. Severin and the End of the Roman Era exhibition.

1982, May 4 ***Perf. 14***
1206 A604 4s multi 45 32

Arms of Printers' Guild
A605

Urine Analysis, Canone di Avicenna Manuscript
A606

1982, May 7
1207 A605 4s multi 50 32

Printing in Austria, 500th anniv.

1982, May 12 **Photo.**
1208 A606 6s multi 65 50

5th European Urology Society Congress, Vienna.

800th Birth Anniv. of St. Francis of Assisi
A607

Haydn and His Time Exhibition, Rohrau
A608

1982, May 14 **Photo. & Engr.**
1209 A607 3s multi 35 25

1982, May 19 **Engr.** ***Perf. 13½***
1210 A608 3s ol grn 35 25

25th World Milk Day
A609

800th Anniv of Gfohl (Market Town)
A610

1982, May 25 **Photo.** ***Perf. 14x13½***
1211 A609 7s multi 75 55

1982, May 28 **Photo. & Engr.** ***Perf. 14***
1212 A610 4s multi 45 32

Tennis Player and Austrian Tennis Federation Emblem—A611

1982, June 11
1213 A611 3s multi 35 25

900th Anniv. of City of Langenlois—A612

1982, June 11 **Photo. & Engr.** ***Perf. 13½x14***
1214 A612 4s multi 45 32

800th Anniv. of City of Weiz—A613

1982, June 18 **Photo.** ***Perf. 14x13½***
1215 A613 4s Arms 45 32

Ignaz Seipel (1876-1932), Statesman—A614

1982, July 30 **Engr.** ***Perf. 14x13½***
1216 A614 3s brn vio 35 25

Europa Issue 1982

Sesquicentennial of Linz-Freistadt-Budweis Horse-drawn Railroad—A615

1982, July 30 ***Perf. 13½***
1217 A615 6s brown 65 50

Mail Bus Service, 75th Anniv.
A616

Rocket Lift-off
A617

1982, Aug. 6 **Photo.** ***Perf. 14x13½***
1218 A616 4s multi 45 32

1982, Aug. 9 ***Perf. 14***
1219 A617 4s multi 45 32

2nd UN Conference on Peaceful Uses of Outer Space, Vienna, Aug. 9-21.

Geodesists' Day—A618

1982, Sept. 1 **Photo. & Engr.** ***Perf. 13½x14***
1220 A618 3s Tower, Office of Standards 35 25

Protection of Endangered Species—A619

1982, Sept. 9 ***Perf. 14***
1221 A619 3s Bustard 35 25
1222 A619 4s Beaver 45 32
1223 A619 6s Capercaillie 65 50

10th Anniv. of Intl. Institute for Applied Systems Analysis, Vienna—A620

1982, Oct. 4 **Photo.**
1224 A620 3s Laxenburg Castle 35 25

St. Apollonia (Patron Saint of Dentists)—A621

1982, Oct. 11 **Photo. & Engr.**
1225 A621 4s multi 45 32

70th Annual World Congress of Dentists.

Emmerich Kalman (1882-1953), Composer—A622

1982, Oct. 22 **Engr.** ***Perf. 13½***
1226 A622 3s dk bl 35 25

Max Mell (1882-19), Poet
A623

Christmas 1982
A624

1982, Nov. 10 **Photo.** ***Perf. 14x13½***
1227 A623 3s multi 35 25

1982, Nov. 25 **Photo. & Engr.** ***Perf. 13½***

Design: Christmas crib, Damuls Church, Vorarlberg, 1630.

1228 A624 4s multi 45 32

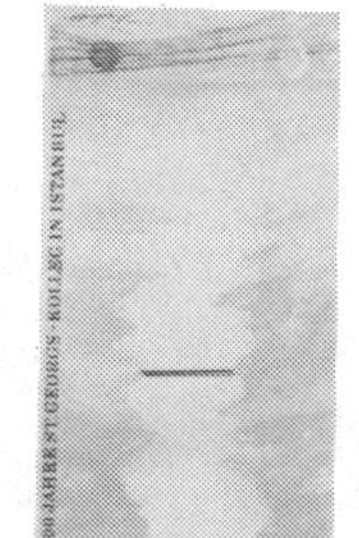

Centenary of St. George's College, Istanbul—A625

1982, Nov. 26 **Litho.** ***Perf. 14***
1229 A625 4s Bosphorus 45 32

Portrait of a Girl, by Ernst Fuchs—A626

1982, Dec. 10 **Photo & Engr.**
1230 A626 4s multi 45 32

Postal Savings Bank Centenary—A627

1983, Jan. 12 **Photo. & Engr.** ***Perf. 14***
1231 A627 4s Bank 45 32

Hildegard Burjan (1883-1933), Founder of Caritas Socialis—A628

1983, Jan. 28 **Engr.**
1232 A628 4s rose lake 45 32

World Communications Year
A629

75th Anniv. Children's Friends Org.
A630

1983, Feb. 18 **Photo.** ***Perf. 13½x14***
1233 A629 7s multi 75 55

1983, Feb. 23 **Photo. & Engr.** ***Perf. 14x13½***
1234 A630 4s multi 45 32

Josef Matthias Hauer (1883-1959), Composer—A631

1983, Mar. 18 **Engr.** ***Perf. 14***
1235 A631 3s dp lil rose 35 25

25th Anniv. of Austrian Airlines—A632

1983, Mar. 31 Photo. *Perf. 13½x14*
1236 A632 6s multi 65 50

Work Inspection Centenary—A633

1983, Apr. 8 Photo. *Perf. 13½*
1237 A633 4s multi 45 32

Upper Austria Millennium Provincial Exhibition—A634

1983, Apr. 28 Photo. *Perf. 13½*
1238 A634 3s Wels Castle, by Matthaus Merian 35 25

Gottweig Monastery, 900th Anniv. A635

7th World Pacemakers' Symposium A636

1983, Apr. 29 Photo. & Engr. *Perf. 13½*
1239 A635 3s multi 35 25

1983, Apr. 29 Photo. *Perf. 14x13½*
1240 A636 4s multi 45 32

Catholic Students' Org.—A637

1983, May 20 Photo. *Perf. 14*
1241 A637 4s multi 45 32

800th Anniv. of City of Weitra—A638

1983, May 20 Photo. & Engr. *Perf. 13½*
1242 A638 4s multi 45 32

Granting of Town Rights to Hohenems, 650th Anniv.—A639

1983, May 27 Photo. *Perf. 14*
1243 A639 4s multi 45 32

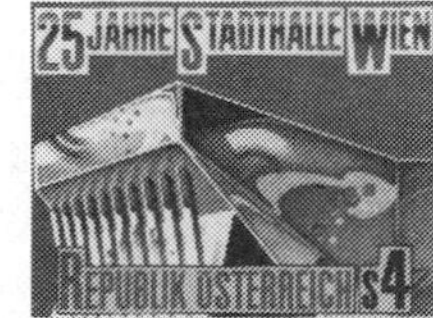

25th Anniv. of Stadthall, Vienna—A640

1983, June 24 Photo. *Perf. 14*
1244 A640 4s multi 45 32

Europa 1983—A641

Design: Viktor Franz Hess (1883-1964), 1936 Nobel Prize winner in physics.

1983, June 24 Engr. *Perf. 14x13½*
1245 A641 6s dk grn 65 50

Kiwanis Intl. Convention, Vienna, July 3-6—A642

1983, July 1 Photo. *Perf. 13½*
1246 A642 5s multi 55 40

7th World Congress of Psychiatry, Vienna—A643

1983, July 11 Photo. *Perf. 14*
1247 A643 4s Emblem, St. Stephen's Cathedral 45 32

Baron Carl von Hasenauer (1833-1894), Architect—A644

1983, July 20 Engr. *Perf. 13½x14*
1248 A644 3s Natural History Museum, Vienna 35 25

27th Intl. Chamber of Commerce Professional Competition, Linz—A645

1983, Aug. 16 Photo.
1249 A645 4s Chamber building 45 32

13th Intl. Chemotherapy Congress, Vienna, Aug. 28-Sept. 2—A646

1983, Aug. 26
1250 A646 5s Penicillin test on cancer 55 40

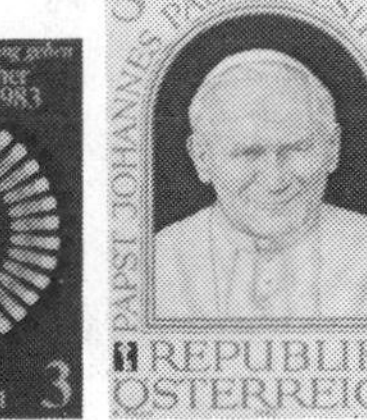

Catholics' Day A647

Visit of Pope John Paul II A648

1983, Sept. 9 Photo. *Perf. 14x13½*
1251 A647 3s multi 32 25

1983, Sept. 9 Photo. & Engr. *Perf. 13½*
1252 A648 6s multi 65 50

Souvenir Sheet

Battle of 1683 to Relieve Vienna, by Frans Geffel—A649

1983, Sept. 9 *Perf. 14*
1253 A649 6s multi 65 65

300th anniv. of Vienna's rescue from Turkey. Size:

Vienna Rathaus Centenary—A650

1983, Sept. 23 *Perf. 13½x14*
1254 A650 4s multi 45 32

Karl von Terzaghi (1883-1963), Founder of Scientific Subterranean Engineering—A651

1983, Oct. 3 Engr.
1255 A651 3s dk bl 35 25

10th Trade Unions Federal Congress, Oct. 3-8—A652

1983, Oct. 3 Photo. *Perf. 13½*
1256 A652 3s blk & red 35 25

Evening Sun in Burgenland, by Gottfried Kumpf—A653

1983, Oct. 7 Photo. & Engr. *Perf. 13½x14*
1257 A653 4s multi 45 32

Modling-Hinterbruhl Electric Railroad Centenary—A654

1983, Oct. 21 Photo.
1258 A654 3s multi 35 25

Provincial Museum of Upper Austria Sesquicentennial—A655

1983, Nov. 4 **Photo. & Engr.**

1259 A655 4s Francisco-Carolinum Museum 45 32

Creche, St. Andreas Parish Church, Kitzbuhel—A656

1983, Nov. 25 **Photo. & Engr.** ***Perf. 14***

1260 A656 4s multi 45 32

Christmas 1983.

Parliament Bldg. Vienna, 100th Anniv.—A657

1983, Dec. 2 **Engr.**

1261 A657 4s sl bl 45 32

Altar Picture, St. Nikola/Pram Church—A658

1983, Dec. 6 **Photo.** ***Perf. 14x13½***

1262 A658 3s multi 35 25

Wolfgang Pauli (1900-58), Physicist, Nobel Prize Winner—A659

1983, Dec. 15 **Engr.** ***Perf. 14½x13½***

1263 A659 6s dk red brn 65 50

Gregor Mendel (1822-1884), Genetics Founder—A660

1984, Jan. 5 **Photo. & Engr.** ***Perf. 13½***

1264 A660 4s multi 45 32

Anton Hanak (1875-1934), Sculptor—A661

1984, Jan. 5

1265 A661 3s red brn & blk 35 25

50th Anniv. of 1934 Uprising—A662

1984, Feb. 10 **Photo.** ***Perf. 14***

1266 A662 4.50s Memorial, Woellersdorf 50 38

900th Anniv. of Reichersberg Monastery—A663

Perf. 14x13½

1984, Apr. 25 **Photo. & Engr.**

1267 A663 3.50s Wernher von Reichersberg family, bas-relief, 15th cent. 40 28

Tobacco Monopoly Bicentenary—A665

1984, May 4 **Photo. & Engr.** ***Perf. 13½***

1269 A665 4.50s Cigar wrapper, tobacco plant 50 38

1200th Anniv. of Kostendorf Municipality—A666

1984, May 4

1270 A666 4.50s View, arms 50 38

Automobile Engineers World Congress—A667

1984, May 4 **Photo.** ***Perf. 13½x14***

1271 A667 5s Wheel bearing cross-section 60 40

Europa (1959-84)—A668

1984, May 4 ***Perf. 13½***

1272 A668 6s multi 65 50

Archduke Johann (1782-1859) by S. von Carolsfeld A669

Aragonite A670

1984, May 11 **Photo. & Engr.** ***Perf. 14***

1273 A669 4.50s multi 50 38

1984, May 11 ***Perf. 13½***

1274 A670 3.50s multi 40 28

Ore and Iron Provincial Exhibition.

Era of Emperor Francis Joseph Exhibition—A671

Design: Cover of Viribus Unitis, publ. by Max Herzig, 1898.

1984, May 18

1275 A671 3.50s red & gold 40 28

City of Vocklabruck, 850th Anniv. A672

Dionysius, Virinum Mosaic A673

Photo. & Engr.

1984, May 30 ***Perf. 14x13½***

1276 A672 4.50s Tower, arms 50 38

1984, June 1 ***Perf. 13½***

1277 A673 3.50s multi 40 28

Museum of Carinthia centenary.

Erosion Prevention Systems Centenary—A674

1984, June 5 **Engr.** ***Perf. 14***

1278 A674 4.50s Stone reinforcement wall 50 38

Tyrol Provincial Celebration, 1809-1984—A675

Art Exhibition: Meeting of Imperial Troops with South Tyrolean Reserves under Andreas Hofer near Sterzing in April 1809, by Ludwig Schnorr von Carolsfeld, 1830.

1984, June 5 **Photo. & Engr.** ***Perf. 14x13½***

1279 A675 3.50s multi 40 38

Ralph Benatzky (1884-1957), Composer—A676

1984, June 5 **Engr.**

1280 A676 4s vio brn 45 32

Christian von Ehrenfels (1859-1932), Philosopher—A677

1984, June 22 **Photo.** ***Perf. 14***

1281 A677 3.50s multi 40 28

25th Anniv. of Minimundus (Model City)—A678

1984, June 22 ***Perf. 13½x14***

1282 A678 4s Eiffel Tower, Tower of Pisa, ferris wheel 45 32

Blockheide Eibenstein Nature Park—A679

1984 **Photo. & Engr.**

1283 A679 4s shown 45 32
1284 A679 4s Lake Neusiedl 45 32

Issue dates: No. 1283, June 29; No. 1284, Aug. 13. See No. 1349.

Monasteries and Abbeys—A679a

Designs: 3.50s, Geras Monastery, Lower Austria. 4s, Stams. 4.50s, Schagl. 5s, Benedictine Abbey of St. Paul Levanttal. 6s, Rein-Hohenfurth.

1984-85 **Photo & Engr.** ***Perf. 14***

1285 A679a 3.50s multi 40 28
1286 A679a 4s multi 40 30
1287 A679a 4.50s multi 50 38

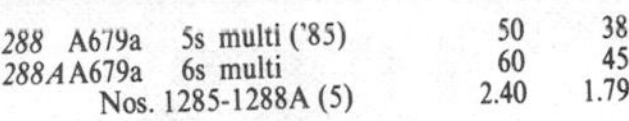
1288 A679a 5s multi ('85) 50 38
1288A A679a 6s multi 60 45
Nos. 1285-1288A (5) 2.40 1.79

Issue dates: 3.50s. Apr. 27; 4s, Sept. 28; 4.50s, May 18; 5s, Sept. 27; 6s, Oct. 4. See Nos. 1361-1364.

Schanatobel Railroad Bridge—A680

Railroad Anniversaries: 3.50s, Arlberg centenary. 4.50s, Tauern, 75th.

1984, July 6 ***Perf. 14***

1289 A680 3.50s shown 40 28
1290 A680 4.50s Falkenstein Bridge 50 38

Balloon Flight in Austria Bicentenary—A681

1984, July 6 **Photo.**

1291 A681 6s Johan Stuwer's balloon 65 50

Intl. Lawyers' Congress, Vienna—A682

1984, Aug. 31 **Photo. & Engr.**

1292 A682 7s Vienna Palace of Justice, emblem 80 60

7th European Anatomy Congress, Innsbruck, Sept. 3-7—A683

1984, Sept. 3 **Photo.**

1293 A683 6s Josef Hyrtl, anatomist 65 50

Window, by Karl Korab—A684

1984, Oct. 12

1294 A684 4s multi 45 32

Johannes of Gmunden, Mathematician, 600th Birth Anniv.—A685

1984, Oct. 18

1295 A685 3.50s Clock (Immset Uhr), 1555 40 28

Concordia Press Club, 125th Anniv.—A686

1984, Nov. 9 **Photo.** ***Perf. 13½***

1296 A686 4.50s Quill 50 38

Fanny Eissler, Dancer, Birth Centenary—A687

1984, Nov. 23

1297 A687 4s multi 45 38

Christmas 1984—A688

Design: Christ is Born, Aggsbacher Altar, Herzogenburg Monastery.

1984, Nov. 30 **Photo. & Engr.** ***Perf. 14***

1298 A688 4.50s multi 45 30

Karl Franzens University, Graz, 400th Anniv.—A689

1985, Jan. 4 **Photo. & Engr.** ***Perf. 14x13½***

1299 A689 3.50s Seal 32 22

Dr. Lorenz Bohler, Surgeon, Birth Cent.—A690

1985, Jan. 15 **Engr.**

1300 A690 4.50s dk rose lake 40 28

Nordic Events, Ski Championships, Seefeld—A691

1985, Jan. 17 **Photo.** ***Perf. 13½***

1301 A691 4s Ski jumper, cross country racer 35 25

Linz Diocese Bicentenary—A692

1985, Jan. 25
1302 A692 4.50s Linz Cathedral interior 40 28

Alban Berg (1885-1935), Composer—A693

1985, Feb. 8 **Engr.**
1303 A693 6s bluish blk 52 35

Vocational Training Inst., 25th Anniv.—A694

1985, Feb. 15 **Photo.** ***Perf. 13½x14***
1304 A694 4.50s multi 40 28

City of Bregenz, Bimillennium—A695

1985, Feb. 22 ***Perf. 14x13½***
1305 A695 4s multi 35 25

Austrian Registration Labels Cent.—A696

1985, Mar. 15 ***Perf. 13½x14***
1306 A696 4.50s Label, 1885 40 28

Josef Stefan (1835-1893), Physicist—A697

Photo. & Engr.

1985, Mar. 22 ***Perf. 14x13½***
1307 A697 6s buff, dl red brn & dk brn 52 36

St. Leopold Exhibition, Klosterneuberg—A698

Design: St. Leopold, 16th-17th century embroidery.

1985, Mar. 29
1308 A698 3.50s multi 32 22

Liberation from German Occupation Forces, 40th Anniv.—A699

1985, Apr. 26 **Photo.**
1309 A699 4.50s multi 42 28

Painter Franz von Defregger (1835-1921)—A700

1985, Apr. 26
1310 A700 3.50s Fairy tale teller 32 22

Europa 1985—A701

Design: Composer Johann Joseph Fux (1660-1741), violin and trombone.

1985, May 3 **Photo. & Engr.** ***Perf. 13½***
1311 A701 6s lil gray & dk brn 52 35

Boheimkirchen (Market Town) Millennium—A702

1985, May 10 ***Perf. 14***
1312 A702 4.50s View, coat of arms 40 28

European Free Trade Assoc., 25th Anniv.—A703

Design: Mercury staff, flags of member and affiliate nations.

1985, May 10 **Photo.** ***Perf. 13½***
1313 A703 4s multi 35 25

St. Polten Diocese Bicentenary—A704

Design: Episcopal residence gate, Polten diocese arms.

1985, May 15 **Photo. & Engr.**
1314 A704 4.50s multi 40 28

The Gumpp Family of Builders, Innsbruck—A705

1985, May 17 **Photo.** ***Perf. 14½x13½***
1315 A705 3.50s multi 35 25

Garsten Market Town Millennium—A706

Design: 17th century engraving by George Matthaus Fischer (1628-1696).

1985, June 7 **Photo. & Engr.** ***Perf. 13½x14***
1316 A706 4.50s multi 45 32

UN 40th Anniv.—A707

1985, June 26 **Photo.** ***Perf. 13½x14½***
1317 A707 4s multi 40 30

Austrian membership, 30th anniv.

Intl. Assoc. for the Prevention of Suicide, 13th Congress—A708

1985, June 28 **Photo. & Engr.** ***Perf. 14***
1318 A708 5s brn, lt ap grn & yel 50 38

Souvenir Sheet

Year of the Forest—A709

1985, June 28 ***Perf. 13½***
1319 A709 6s Healthy and damaged woodland 60 45

No. 1319 has multicolored margin continuing the design. Size: 90x71mm.

Bad Ischl Festival, 25th Anniv.—A710

Design: Kurhaus, Bad Ischl operetta activities emblem.

1985, July 5 *Perf. 14*
1320 A710 3.50s multi 35 25

Intl. Competition of Fire Brigades, Vocklabruck—A711

1985, July 18 **Photo.** *Perf. 14x13½*
1321 A711 4.50s Fireman, emblem 45 32

Grossglockner Alpine Motorway, 50th Anniv.—A712

1985, Aug. 2 **Photo. & Engr.** *Perf. 13½*
1322 A712 4s View of Fuschertorl 40 30

World Chess Federation Congress, Graz—A713

1985, Aug. 28 **Photo.** *Perf. 13½*
1323 A713 4s Checkered globe, emblem 40 30

The Legendary Founding of Konigstetten, by Charlemagne, by Auguste Stephan, c. 1870—A714

1985, Aug. 30 **Photo. & Engr.** *Perf. 14*
1324 A714 4.50s multi 45 32

Konigstetten millennium.

Hofkirchen-Taufkirchen-Weibern Municipalities, 1200th Anniv.—A715

1985, Aug. 30 Photo. & Engr. *Perf. 13½x14*
1325 A715 4.50s View of Weiburn, municipal arms 45 32

Dr. Adam Politzer (1835-1923), Physician—A716

1985, Sept. 12 **Engr.** *Perf. 14*
1326 A716 3.50s bl vio 35 25

Politzer pioneered aural therapy for auditory disorders.

Intl. Assoc. of Forwarding Agents, World Congress, Vienna—A717

1985, Oct. 7 **Photo.** *Perf. 13½*
1327 A717 6s multi 60 45

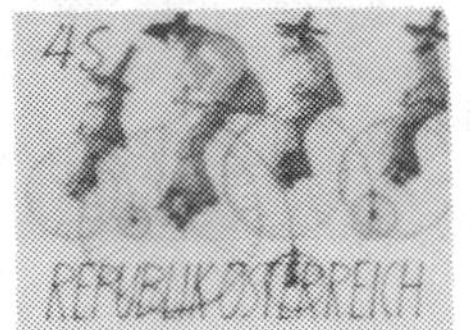

Carnival Figures Riding High Bicycles, By Paul Flora—A718

1985, Oct. 25 **Photo. & Engr.** *Perf. 14*
1328 A718 4s multi 45 32

St. Martin on Horseback—A719

1985, Nov. 8 **Photo.**
1329 A719 4.50s multi 50 38

Eisenstadt Diocese, 25th anniv.

Creche, Marble Bas-relief, Salzburg—A720

1985, Nov. 29 **Photo. & Engr.** *Perf. 13½*
1330 A720 4.50s gold, dl vio & buff 50 38

Christmas 1985.

Hanns Horbiger (1860-1931), Inventor—A721

1985, Nov. 29 *Perf. 14*
1331 A721 3.50s gold & sep 40 30

Aqueduct, Hundsau Brook, Near Gostling—A722

1985, Nov. 29 *Perf. 13½x14½*
1332 A722 3.50s red, bluish blk & brt ultra 40 30

Vienna Aqueduct, 75th anniv.

Chateau de la Muette, Paris Headquarters—A723

1985, Dec. 13
1333 A723 4s sep, rose lil & gold 48 35

Org. for Economic Cooperation and Development, 25th anniv.

Johann Bohm (1886-1959), Pres. Austrian Trade Fed.—A724

1986, Jan. 24 **Photo.** *Perf. 14*
1334 A724 4.50s blk, ver & GRYH blk 52 38

Intl. Peace Year—A725

1986, Jan. 24 **Photo.** *Perf. 13½x14½*
1335 A725 6s multi 70 52

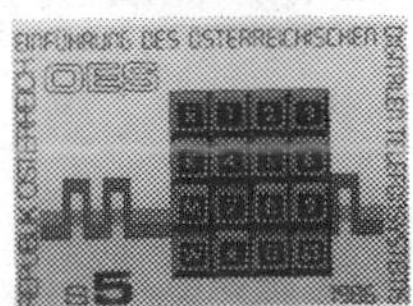

Digital Telephone Service Introduction—A726

1986, Jan. 29 **Photo.**
1336 A726 5s Push-button keyboard 60 45

Johann Georg Albrechtsberger (b. 1736), Composer—A727

Photo & Engr.

1986, Jan. 31 *Perf. 13½x14½*
1337 A727 3.50s Klosterneuberg organ 42 32

Korneuberg, 850th Anniv.—A728

1986, Feb. 7 **Photo.** *Perf. 14*
1338 A728 5s multi 60 45

Self-portrait, by Oskar Kokoschka (b.1886)—A729

1986, Feb. 28 **Photo.** *Perf. 14½x13½*
1339 A729 4s multi 50 38

Admission to Council of Europe, 30th Anniv.—A730

1986, Feb. 28 **Photo.** ***Perf. 13x13½***
1340 A730 6s multi 75 58

Clemens Holzmeister (b. 1886), Architect, Salzburg Festival Theater, 1926—A731

1986, Mar. 27 **Photo. & Engr.** ***Perf. 13½***
1341 A731 4s sep & redsh brn 52 40

3rd Intl. Geotextile Congress, Vienna—A732

1986, Apr. 7 **Photo.** ***Perf. 13½x14½***
1342 A732 5s multi 62 48

Prince Eugen and Schlosshof Castle—A733

1986, Apr. 21 **Photo. & Engr.** ***Perf. 14***
1343 A733 4s multi 52 40

Prince Eugen Exhibition, Schlosshof and Niederweiden.

St. Florian Monastery, Upper Austria—A734

1986, Apr. 24
1344 A734 4s multi 52 40

The World of Baroque provincial exhibition, St. Florian.

Herberstein Castle, Arms of Styria—A735

1986, May 2 ***Perf. 13½x14½***
1345 A735 4s multi 52 40

Europa 1986—A736

1986, May 2 ***Perf. 13½***
1346 A736 6s Pasque flower 80 60

Wagner, Scene from Opera Lohengrin—A737

1986, May 21
1347 A737 4s multi 52 40

Intl. Richard Wagner Congress, Vienna.

Antimonite—A738

1986, May 23 ***Perf. 13½x14½***
1348 A738 4s multi 52 40

Burgenland Provincial Minerals Exhibition.

Scenery Type of 1984

1986 **Photo. & Engr.** ***Perf. 14***
1349 A679 5s Martinswall, Tyrol 65 50
1350 A679 5s Tschauko Falls, Carinthia 65 50

Waidhofen on Ybbs Township, 800th Anniv.—A739

1986, June 20 **Photo.** ***Perf. 13½***
1355 A739 4s multi 52 40

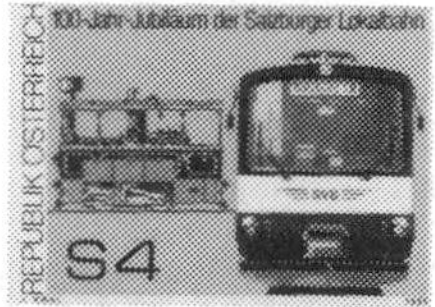

Salzburg Local Railway, Cent.—A740

1986, Aug. 8 **Photo.** ***Perf. 14***
1356 A740 4s multi 55 42

Georgenberg Treaty, 800th Anniv.—A741

Design: Seals, Dukes Leopold of Austria, Otakar of Styria, and Georgenberg Church.

1986, Aug. 14 **Photo. & Engr.**
1357 A741 5s multi 68 52

Julius Tandler (1869-1936), Social Reformer—A742

1986, Aug. 22
1358 A742 4s multi 55 42

Sonnblick Observatory, Cent.—A743

Perf. 13½x14½
1986, Aug. 27 **Photo. & Engr.**
1359 A743 4s Observatory, 1886 55 42

European Assoc. for Anesthesiology, 7th Congress—A744

Design: Discovery of mandrake root.

1986, Aug. 27 ***Perf. 14½x13½***
1360 A744 5s multi 68 52

Monasteries and Abbeys Type of 1986

Designs: 5.50s, St. Gerold's Provostry, Vorarlberg. 7.50s, Dominican Convent, Vienna.

1986 **Photo. & Engr.** ***Perf. 14***
1361 A679a 5.50s brt vio, vio & buff 78 60
1364 A679a 7.50s gold brn, redsh brn & buff 1.10 85

Issue dates: 5.50s, Sept. 12. 7.50s, Oct. 3.

Otto Stoessl (d. 1936), Writer—A745

1986, Sept. 3 **Photo. & Engr.** ***Perf. 14***
1366 A745 4s multi 55 42

Vienna Fire Brigade, 300th Anniv.—A746

1986, Sept. 3 **Photo.**
1367 A746 4s Fireman, 1686 55 42

Intl. Conference on Oriental Carpets, Vienna, Budapest—A747

Design: Silk Viennese hunting tapestry.

1986, Sept. 3 **Photo. & Engr.** ***Perf. 14***
1368 A747 5s multi 68 52

Minister at Pulpit—A748

1986, Oct. 10 **Photo. & Engr.** *Perf. 14*
1369 A748 5s vio, blk & gray 72 55

Protestant Act, 25th anniv., and Protestant Patent of Franz Josef I ensuring religious equality, 125th anniv.

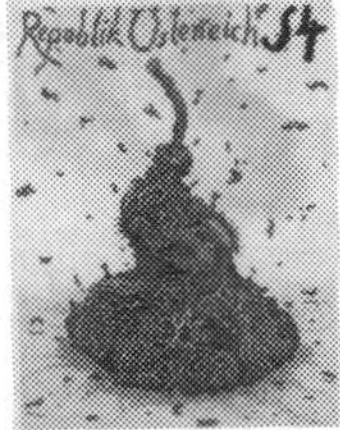

Disintegration, by Walter Schmogner—A749

1986, Oct. 17 *Perf. 13½x14*
1370 A749 4s multi 58 45

Franz Liszt, Composer, and Birthplace, Burgenland—A750

1986, Oct. 17 *Perf. 13½*
1371 A750 5s grn & sep 72 55

Souvenir Sheet

European Security Conference, Vienna—A751

1986, Nov. 4 *Perf. 13½x14*
1372 A751 6s Vienna 88 65

No. 1372 has multicolored margin continuing the design.

Strettweg Cart, 7th Cent. B.C.—A752

1986, Nov. 26 **Photo. & Engr.** *Perf. 14*
1373 A752 4s multi 58 45

Joanneum Styrian Land Museum, 175th anniv.

Christmas—A753

Design: The Little Crib, bas-relief by Schwanthaler (1740-1810), Schlierbach Monastery.

1986, Nov. 28
1374 A753 5s gold & rose lake 72 55

Federal Chamber of Commerce, 40th Anniv.—A754

1986, Dec. 2 **Photo.**
1375 A754 5s multi 72 55

Industry—A755

1986, Dec. 4
1376 A755 4s Steel workers 58 45

The Educated Eye, by Arnulf Rainer—A756

1987, Jan. 13 **Photo.** *Perf. 13½x14*
1386 A756 5s multi 72 55

Adult education in Vienna, cent.

The Large Blue Madonna, by Anton Faistauer (1887-1970)—A757

Paintings: 6s, Self-portrait, 1922, by A. Paris Gutersloh (1887-1973).

1987, Jan. 29 *Perf. 14*
1387 A757 4s multi 58 45
1388 A757 6s multi 88 65

SEMI-POSTAL STAMPS.
Issues of the Monarchy.

Emperor Franz Josef
SP1

Perf. 12½

1914, Oct. 4 Typo. Unwmkd.

B1	SP1	5h green	10	8
B2	SP1	10h rose	15	15

Nos. B1–B2 were sold at an advance of 2h each over face value. Exist imperf.; price, set $80.

The Firing Step
SP2

Designs: 5h+2h, Cavalry. 10h+2h, Siege gun. 20h+3h, Battleship. 35h+3h, Airplane.

1915, May 1

B3	SP2	3h +1h vio brn	15	45
B4	SP2	5h +2h grn	5	5
B5	SP2	10h +2h dp rose	5	5
B6	SP2	20h +3h Prus bl	32	1.40
B7	SP2	35h +3h ultra	3.50	2.25
		Nos. B3-B7 (5)	4.07	4.20

Exist imperf. Price, set $135.

Issues of the Republic.

Types of Austria, 1919-20, Overprinted in Black

Kärnten

Abstimmung

1920, Sept. 16 *Perf. 12½*

B11	A44	5h gray, *yel*	35	60
B12	A44	10h red, *pink*	65	1.10
B13	A43	15h bis, *yel*	35	60
B14	A45	20h dk grn, *bl*	35	60
B15	A43	25h vio, *pink*	35	60
B16	A45	30h brn, *buff*	1.10	1.90
B17	A45	40h car, *yel*	55	90
B18	A45	50h dk bl, *bl*	55	90
B19	A43	60h ol grn, *az*	1.25	2.25
B20	A47	80h red	35	60
B21	A47	1k org brn	40	70
B22	A47	2k pale bl	35	60

Granite Paper.
Imperf.

B23	A46	2½k brn red	45	80
B24	A46	3k dk bl & grn	45	80
B25	A46	4k car & vio	70	1.25
B26	A46	5k blue	90	1.50
B27	A46	7½k yel grn	90	1.50
B28	A46	10k gray grn & red	90	1.50
B29	A46	20k lil & org	90	1.50
		Nos. B11-B29 (19)	11.80	20.20

Carinthia Plebiscite. Sold at three times face value for the benefit of the Plebiscite Propaganda Fund.

Nos. B11-B19 exist imperf. Price, set $175.

Types of Regular Issues of 1919-21 Overprinted

Hochwasser

1920

1921, Mar. 1 *Perf. 12½*

B30	A44	5h gray, *yel*	28	45
B31	A44	10h org brn	28	45
B32	A43	15h gray	28	45
B33	A45	20h grn, *yel*	28	45
B34	A43	25h bl, *yel*	28	45
B35	A45	30h vio, *bl*	28	45
B36	A45	40h org brn, *pink*	35	70
B37	A45	50h grn, *bl*	1.10	2.75
B38	A43	60h lil, *yel*	28	45
B39	A47	80h pale bl	28	45
B40	A47	1k red org, *bl*	70	1.65
B41	A47	1½k grn, *yel*	32	45
B42	A47	2k lil brn	32	45

Overprinted

Hochwasser

1920

B43	A46	2½k lt bl	32	45
B44	A46	3k ol grn & brn red	32	45
B45	A46	4k lil & org	90	2.00
B46	A46	5k ol grn	50	90
B47	A46	7½k brn red	50	90
B48	A46	10k bl & ol grn	65	1.40
B49	A46	20k car rose & vio	80	1.65
		Nos. B30-B49 (20)	9.02	17.35

Exists imperf. Price, set $250.

Nos. B30–B49 were sold at three times face value, the excess going to help flood victims.

Franz Joseph Haydn
SP9

View of Bregenz
SP16

Musicians: 5k, Mozart. 7½k, Beethoven. 10k, Schubert. 25k, Anton Bruckner. 50k, Johann Strauss (son). 100k, Hugo Wolf.

Engraved

1922, Apr. 24 *Perf. 11½, 12½*

B50	SP9	2½k brown	7.00	6.00
B51	SP9	5k dk bl	1.50	1.75
B52	SP9	7½k black	1.75	2.75
	a.	Perf. 11½	87.50	125.00
B53	SP9	10k dk vio	2.75	3.00
B54	SP9	25k dk grn	3.25	4.00
B55	SP9	50k claret	2.25	3.75
B56	SP9	100k brn ol	8.00	8.00
		Nos. B50-B56 (7)	26.50	29.25

These stamps were sold at 10 times face value, the excess being given to needy musicians.

All values exist imperf. on both regular and handmade papers. Price, set $350.

A 1969 souvenir sheet without postal validity contains reprints of the 5k in black, 7½k in claret and 50k in dark blue, each overprinted "NEUDRUCK" in black at top. It was issued for the Vienna State Opera Centenary Exhibition.

1923, May 22 *Perf. 12½*

Designs: 120k, Mirabelle Gardens, Salzburg. 160k, Church at Eisenstadt. 180k, Assembly House, Klagenfurt. 200k, "Golden Roof," Innsbruck. 240k, Main Square, Linz. 400k, Castle Hill, Graz. 600k, Abbey at Melk. 1000k, Upper Belvedere, Vienna.

Various Frames.

B57	SP16	100k dk grn	3.75	3.75
B58	SP16	120k dp bl	3.75	3.75
B59	SP16	160k dk vio	3.75	3.75
B60	SP16	180k red vio	3.75	3.75
B61	SP16	200k lake	3.75	3.75
B62	SP16	240k red brn	3.75	3.75
B63	SP16	400k dk brn	3.75	3.75
B64	SP16	600k ol brn	3.75	3.75
B65	SP16	1000k black	3.75	3.75
		Nos. B57-B65 (9)	33.75	33.75

Nos. B57–B65 were sold at five times face value, the excess going to needy artists.

All values exist imperf. on both regular and handmade papers. Price, set $375.

Feebleness
SP25

Siegfried Slays the Dragon
SP30

Designs: 300k+900k, Aid to industry. 500k+1500k, Orphans and widow. 600k+1800k, Indigent old man. 1000k+3000k, Alleviation of hunger.

1924, Sept. 6 Photogravure

B66	SP25	100k +300k yel grn	4.00	3.00
B67	SP25	300k +900k red brn	5.50	6.75
B68	SP25	500k +1500k brn vio	5.50	6.75
B69	SP25	600k +1800k pck bl	5.50	6.75
B70	SP25	1000k +3000k brn org	9.50	10.50
		Nos. B66-B70 (5)	30.00	33.75

The surtax was for child welfare and anti-tuberculosis work. Set exists imperf.

Price, $350.

1926, Mar. 8 Engraved

Designs: 8g+2g, Gunther's voyage to Iceland. 15g+5g, Brunhild accusing Kriemhild. 20g+5g, Nymphs telling Hagen the future. 24g+6g, Rudiger von Bechelaren welcomes the Nibelungen. 40g+10g, Dietrich von Bern vanquishes Hagen.

B71	SP30	3g +2g ol blk	1.25	45
B72	SP30	8g +2g ind	28	45
B73	SP30	15g +5g dk cl	28	45
B74	SP30	20g +5g ol grn	50	90
B75	SP30	24g +6g dk vio	50	90
B76	SP30	40g +10g red brn	3.75	5.00
		Nos. B71-B76 (6)	6.56	8.15

Nibelungen issue.

The surtax was for child welfare. Set exists imperf. Price, $350.

President Michael Hainisch
SP36

President Wilhelm Miklas
SP37

1928, Nov. 5

B77	SP36	10g dk brn	5.50	8.50
B78	SP36	15g red brn	5.50	8.50
B79	SP36	30g black	5.50	8.50
B80	SP36	40g indigo	5.50	8.50

Tenth anniversary of Austrian Republic. Sold at double face value, the premium aiding war orphans and children of war invalids.

Set exists imperf. Price $300.

1930, Oct. 4

B81	SP37	10(g) lt brn	8.50	11.00
B82	SP37	20(g) red	8.50	11.00
B83	SP37	30(g) brn vio	8.50	11.00
B84	SP37	40(g) indigo	8.50	11.00
B85	SP37	50(g) dk grn	8.50	11.00
B86	SP37	1s blk brn	8.50	11.00
		Nos. B81-B86 (6)	51.00	66.00

Nos. B81–B86 were sold at double face value. The excess aided the anti-tuberculosis campaign and the building of sanatoria in Carinthia.

Set exists imperf. Price, $425.

Regular Issue of 1929-30 Overprinted in Various Colors

CONVENTION
WIEN 1931

1931, June 20

B87	A56	10g bis (Bl)	40.00	45.00
B88	A56	20g dk gray (R)	40.00	45.00
B89	A56	30g dk vio (Gl)	40.00	45.00
B90	A56	40g dk bl (Gl)	40.00	45.00
B91	A56	50g gray vio (O)	40.00	45.00
B92	A57	1s blk brn (Bk)	40.00	45.00
		Nos. B87-B92 (6)	240.00	270.00

Rotary convention, Vienna.

Nos. B87 to B92 were sold at double their face values. The excess was added to the beneficent funds of Rotary International.

Exists imperf. Price, set $900.

Ferdinand Raimund
SP38

Poets: 20g, Franz Grillparzer. 30g, Johann Nestroy. 40g, Adalbert Stifter. 50g, Ludwig Anzengruber. 1s, Peter Rosegger.

1931, Sept. 12

B93	SP38	10(g) dk vio	14.00	19.00
B94	SP38	20(g) gray blk	14.00	19.00
B95	SP38	30(g) org red	14.00	19.00
B96	SP38	40(g) dl bl	14.00	19.00
B97	SP38	50(g) gray grn	14.00	19.00
B98	SP38	1s yel brn	14.00	19.00
		Nos. B93-B98 (6)	84.00	114.00

Nos. B93–B98 were sold at double face value. The surtax aided unemployed young people.

Set exists imperf. Price, $625.

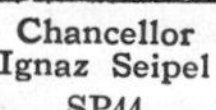

Chancellor Ignaz Seipel
SP44

Ferdinand Georg Waldmüller
SP45

1932, Oct. 12 *Perf. 13*

B99	SP44	50g ultra	10.00	18.00

Msgr. Ignaz Seipel, Chancellor of Austria, 1922–29. Sold at double face value, the excess aiding wounded veterans of World War I.

Exists imperf. Price, $225.

1932, Nov. 21

Artists: 24g, Moritz von Schwind. 30g, Rudolf von Alt. 40g, Hans Makart. 64g, Gustav Klimt. 1s, Albin Egger-Lienz.

B100	SP45	12(g) sl grn	20.00	30.00
B101	SP45	24(g) dp vio	20.00	30.00
B102	SP45	30(g) dk red	20.00	30.00
B103	SP45	40(g) dk gray	20.00	30.00
B104	SP45	64(g) dk brn	20.00	30.00
B105	SP45	1s claret	20.00	30.00
		Nos. B100-B105 (6)	120.00	180.00

Nos. B100 to B105 were sold at double their face values. The surtax was for the assistance of charitable institutions.

Set exists imperf. Price, $725.

Mountain Climbing
SP51

Designs: 24g, Ski gliding. 30g, Walking on skis. 50g, Ski jumping.

1933, Jan. 9 Photo. *Perf. 12½*

B106	SP51	12(g) dk grn	10.00	13.00
B107	SP51	24(g) dk vio	85.00	120.00

B108	SP51	30(g) brn red	20.00	22.50
B109	SP51	50(g) dk bl	85.00	120.00

Issued in connection with a meeting of the International Ski Federation at Innsbruck, Feb. 8–13, 1933.

These stamps were sold at double their face value. The surtax was for the benefit of "Youth in Distress."

Nos. B106–B109 exist imperf. Price $1,500.

Vienna Philatelic Exhibition Issue.

Stagecoach, after Painting by Moritz von Schwind
SP55

Ordinary Paper.

1933, June 23 Engraved *Perf. 12½*

B110	SP55	50g dp ultra	140.00	225.00
a.		Granite paper	300.00	500.00

Sheets of 25.

Nos. B110 and B110a exist imperf. Prices four times those of perf. stamps.

Souvenir Sheet

SP55a

Perf. 12.

Granite Paper.

B111	SP55a	50g dp ultra, sheet of 4	2,000.	3,250.
a.		Single stamp	325.00	525.00

Issued in connection with the International Philatelic Exhibition at Vienna in 1933. In addition to the postal value of 50g the stamp was sold at a premium of 50g for charity and of 1s60g for the admission fee to the exhibition.

Size of No. B111: 126x103mm.

The 50g dark red in souvenir sheet, with dark blue overprint ("NEUDRUCK WIPA 1965"), had no postal validity.

St. Stephen's Cathedral in 1683
SP56

Marco d'Aviano, Papal Legate
SP57

Designs: 30g, Count Ernst Rudiger von Starhemberg. 40g, John III Sobieski, King of Poland. 50g, Karl V, Duke of Lorraine. 64g, Burgomaster Johann Andreas von Liebenberg.

1933, Sept. 6 Photo. *Perf. 12½*

B112	SP56	12(g) dk grn	27.50	35.00
B113	SP57	24(g) dk vio	25.00	30.00
B114	SP57	30(g) brn red	25.00	30.00
B115	SP57	40(g) bl blk	35.00	47.50
B116	SP57	50(g) dk bl	25.00	30.00
B117	SP57	64(g) ol brn	35.00	45.00
		Nos. B112-B117 (6)	172.50	217.50

Issued in commemoration of the 250th anniversary of the deliverance of Vienna from the Turks and in connection with the Pan-German Catholic Congress on September 6th, 1933.

The stamps were sold at double their face value, the excess being for the aid of Catholic works of charity.

Set exists imperf. Price, $900.

Types of Regular Issue of 1925-30 Surcharged:

+2g Winterhilfe
a

WINTERHILFE +6g
b

+50g WINTERHILFE
c

1933, Dec. 15

B118	A52 (a)	5g +2g ol grn	28	60
B119	A56 (b)	12g +3g lt bl	28	60
B120	A56 (b)	24g +6g brn org	28	60
B121	A57 (c)	1s +50g org red	35.00	45.00

Winterhelp. Exists imperf. Price, set $175.

Anton Pilgram
SP62

Architects: 24g, J. B. Fischer von Erlach. 30g, Jakob Prandtauer. 40g, A. von Siccardsburg & E. van der Null. 60g, Heinrich von Ferstel. 64g, Otto Wagner.

Thick Yellowish Paper.

1934, Dec. 2 Engr. *Perf. 12½*

B122	SP62	12gr (+12gr) blk	10.00	14.00
B123	SP62	24gr (+24gr) dl vio	10.00	14.00
B124	SP62	30gr (+30gr) car	10.00	14.00
B125	SP62	40gr (+40gr) brn	10.00	14.00
B126	SP62	60gr (+60gr) bl	10.00	14.00
B127	SP62	64gr (+64gr) dl grn	10.00	14.00
		Nos. B122-B127 (6)	60.00	84.00

Exist imperf. Price, set $550.

Nos. B124-B126 exist in horiz. pairs imperf. between. Price, each $275.

The surtax on this and the following issues was devoted to general charity.

Types of Regular Issue of 1934 Surcharged in Black:

+50g

Winterhilfe +2g
a

WINTERHILFE
b

1935, Nov. 11 *Perf. 12, 12½*

B128	A67 (a)	5g +2g emer	50	90
B129	A67 (a)	12g +3g bl	50	90
B130	A67 (a)	24g +6g lt brn	50	90
B131	A68 (b)	1s +50g ver	27.50	42.50

Winterhelp. Set exists imperf. Price, $150.

Prince Eugene of Savoy
SP68

Slalom Turn
SP74

Military Leaders: 24g, Field Marshal Laudon. 30g, Archduke Karl. 40g, Field Marshal Josef Radetzky. 60g, Admiral Wilhelm Tegetthoff. 64g, Field Marshal Franz Conrad Hotzendorff.

1935, Dec. 1 *Perf. 12½*

B132	SP68	12g (+12g) brn	10.00	14.00
B133	SP68	24g (+24g) dk grn	10.00	14.00
B134	SP68	30g (+30g) cl	10.00	14.00
B135	SP68	40g (+40g) sl	10.00	14.00
B136	SP68	60g (+60g) dp ultra	10.00	14.00
B137	SP68	64g (+64g) dk vio	10.00	14.00
		Nos. B132-B137 (6)	60.00	84.00

Set exists imperf. Price, $475.

1936, Feb. 20 Photogravure

Designs: 24g, Jumper taking off. 35g, Slalom turn. 60g, Innsbruck view.

B138	SP74	12g (+12g) Prus grn	3.25	3.50
B139	SP74	24g (+24g) dp vio	5.50	5.50
B140	SP74	35g (+35g) rose car	27.50	37.50
B141	SP74	60g (+60g) saph	27.50	42.50

Ski concourse issue. Set exists imperf. Price, $525.

St. Martin of Tours
SP78

Designs: 12g+3g, Medical clinic. 24g+6g, St. Elizabeth of Hungary. 1s+1s, "Flame of Charity."

1936, Nov. 2

B142	SP78	5g +2g dp grn	35	45
B143	SP78	12g +3g dp vio	35	45
B144	SP78	24g +6g dp bl	35	45
B145	SP78	1s +1s dk car	6.50	12.00

Winterhelp. Set exists imperf. Price, $175.

Josef Ressel
SP82

Nurse and Infant
SP88

Inventors: 24g, Karl von Ghega. 30g, Josef Werndl. 40g, Carl Auer von Welsbach. 60g, Robert von Lieben. 64g, Viktor Kaplan.

1936, Dec. 6 Engraved

B146	SP82	12g (+12g) dk brn	2.50	4.00
B147	SP82	24g (+24g) dk vio	2.50	4.00
B148	SP82	30g (+30g) dp cl	2.50	4.00
B149	SP82	40g (+40g) gray vio	2.50	4.00
B150	SP82	60g (+60g) vio bl	2.50	4.00
B151	SP82	64g (+64g) dk sl grn	2.50	4.00
		Nos. B146-B151 (6)	15.00	24.00

Exists imperf. Price, set $375.

1937, Oct. 18 Photogravure

Designs: 12g+3g, Mother and child. 24g+6g, Nursing the aged. 1s+1s, Sister of Mercy with patient.

B152	SP88	5g +2g dk grn	15	28
B153	SP88	12g +3g dk brn	15	28
B154	SP88	24g +6g dk bl	15	28
B155	SP88	1s +1s dk car	3.75	6.00

Winterhelp. Set exists imperf. Price, $135.

Gerhard van Swieten
SP92

The Dawn of Peace
SP101

Physicians: 8g, Leopold Auenbrugger von Auenbrugg. 12g, Karl von Rokitansky. 20g, Joseph Skoda. 24g, Ferdinand von Hebra. 30g, Ferdinand von Arlt. 40g, Joseph Hyrtl. 60g, Theodor Billroth. 64g, Theodor Meynert.

1937, Dec. 5 Engr. *Perf. 12½*

B156	SP92	5g +(5g) choc	2.00	3.75
B157	SP92	8g +(8g) dk red	2.00	3.75
B158	SP92	12g +(12g) brn blk	2.00	3.75
B159	SP92	20g +(20g) dk grn	2.00	3.75
B160	SP92	24g +(24g) dk vio	2.00	3.75
B161	SP92	30g +(30g) brn car	2.00	3.75
B162	SP92	40g +(40g) dp ol grn	2.00	3.75
B163	SP92	60g +(60g) ind	2.00	3.75
B164	SP92	64g +(64g) brn vio	2.00	3.75
		Nos. B156-B164 (9)	18.00	33.75

Set exists imperf. Price, $450.

Photogravure.

1945, Sept. 10 *Perf. 14* Unwmkd.

B165	SP101	1s +10s dk grn	60	1.40

No. 467 Surcharged in Black

1946, June 25

B166	A110	30g +20g dk red	2.25	4.50

First anniversary of United Nations.

Pres. Karl Renner
SP102

1946 Engraved. *Perf. 13½x14.*

B167	SP102	1s +1s dk sl grn	1.90	4.00

B168	SP102	2s +2s dk bl vio	1.90	4.00
B169	SP102	3s +3s dk pur	1.90	4.00
B170	SP102	5s +5s dk vio brn	1.90	4.00

See also Nos. B185-B188.

Nazi Sword Piercing Austria
SP103

Sweeping Away Fascist Symbols
SP104

Designs: 8g + 6g, St. Stephen's Cathedral in Flames. 12g+12g, Pleading hand in concentration camp. 30g + 30g, Hand choking Nazi serpent. 42g + 42g, Hammer breaking Nazi pillar. 1s + 1s, Oath of allegiance. 2s + 2s, Austrian eagle and burning swastika.

Photogravure

1946, Sept. 16 ***Perf. 14*** **Unwmkd.**

B171	SP103	5(g) +3(g) dk brn	32	60
B172	SP104	6(g) +4(g) dk sl grn	25	50
B173	SP104	8(g) +6(g) org red	25	50
B174	SP104	12(g) +12(g) sl blk	25	50
B175	SP104	30(g) +30(g) vio	25	50
B176	SP104	42(g) +42(g) dl brn	25	50
B177	SP104	1s +1s dk red	32	60
B178	SP104	2s +2s dk car rose	45	60
		Nos. B171-B178 (8)	2.34	4.30

Issued as anti-fascist propaganda.

Race Horse with Foal—SP111

Engraved.

1946, Oct. 20 ***Perf. 13½x14***

Various Race Horses.

B179	SP111	16g +16g rose brn	1.50	3.25
B180	SP111	24g +24g dk pur	1.50	3.25
B181	SP111	60g +60g dk grn	1.50	3.25
B182	SP111	1s +1s dk bl gray	1.50	3.25
B183	SP111	2s +2s yel brn	1.50	3.25
		Nos. B179-B183 (5)	7.50	16.25

Austria Prize race, Vienna.

St. Ruprecht's Church, Vienna
SP116

1946, Oct. 30 ***Perf. 14x13½***

B184	SP116	30g +70g dk red	32	60

Issued to commemorate the 950th anniversary of the founding of Austria. The surtax aided the Stamp Day celebration.

Souvenir Sheets.

President Karl Renner
SP117

1946, Sept. 5 ***Imperf.***

B185	SP117	1s +1s dk sl grn	525.00	1,000.
a.		Single stamp	55.00	110.00
B186	SP117	2s +2s dk bl vio	525.00	1,000.
a.		Single stamp	55.00	110.00
B187	SP117	3s +3s dk pur	525.00	1,000.
a.		Single stamp	55.00	110.00
B188	SP117	5s +5s dk vio brn	525.00	1,000.
a.		Single stamp	55.00	110.00

First anniversary of Austria's liberation. Sheets of 8. Size: 180x153mm.

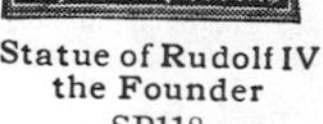

Statue of Rudolf IV the Founder
SP118

Reaping Wheat
SP128

Designs: 5g+20g, Tomb of Frederick III. 6g+24g, Main pulpit. 8g+32g, Statue of St. Stephen. 10g+40g, Madonna of the Domestics statue. 12g+48g, High altar. 30g+1.20s, Organ, destroyed in 1945. 50g+1.80s, Anton Pilgram statue. 1s+5s, Cathedral from northeast. 2s+10s, Southwest corner of cathedral.

Engraved.

1946, Dec. 12 ***Perf. 14x13½***

B189	SP118	3g +12g brn	15	38
B190	SP118	5g +20g dk vio brn	15	38
B191	SP118	6g +24g dk bl	15	38
B192	SP118	8g +32g dk grn	15	38
B193	SP118	10g +40g dp bl	25	42
B194	SP118	12g +48g dk vio	30	55
B195	SP118	30g +1.20s car	75	1.25
B196	SP118	50g +1.80s dk bl	1.10	2.00
B197	SP118	1s +5s brn vio	1.50	2.75
B198	SP118	2s +10s vio brn	3.00	5.25
		Nos. B189-B198 (10)	7.50	13.74

The surtax aided reconstruction of St. Stephen's Cathedral, Vienna.

1947, Mar. 23 ***Perf. 14x13½***

Designs: 8g+2g, Log raft. 10g+5g, Cement factory. 12g+8g, Coal mine. 18g+12g, Oil derricks. 30g+10g, Textile machinery. 35g+15g, Iron furnace. 60g+20g, Electric power lines.

B199	SP128	3g +2g yel brn	25	38
B200	SP128	8g +2g dk bl grn	25	38
B201	SP128	10g +5g sl blk	25	38
B202	SP128	12g +8g dk pur	25	38
B203	SP128	18g +12g ol grn	25	38
B204	SP128	30g +10g dp cl	25	38
B205	SP128	35g +15g crim	25	38
B206	SP128	60g +20g dk bl	25	38
		Nos. B199-B206 (8)	2.00	3.04

Vienna International Sample Fair, 1947.

Race Horse and Jockey
SP136

1947, June 29 ***Perf. 13½x14***

B207	SP136	60g +20g dp bl, *pale pink*	10	20

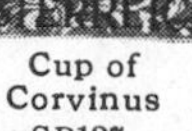

Cup of Corvinus
SP137

Prisoner of War
SP147

Designs: 8g+2g, Statue of Providence, Vienna. 10g+5g, Abbey at Melk. 12g+8g, Picture of a Woman, by Kriehuber. 18g+12g, Children at the Window, by Waldmuller. 20g + 10g, Entrance, Upper Belvedere Palace. 30g+10g, Nymph Egeria, Schönbrunn Castle. 35g+15g, National Library, Vienna. 48g + 12g, "Workshop of a Printer of Engravings," by Schmutzer. 60g+20g, Girl with Straw Hat, by Amerling.

1947, June 20 ***Perf. 14x13½***

B208	SP137	3g +2g brn	20	35
B209	SP137	8g +2g dk bl grn	20	35
B210	SP137	10g +5g dp cl	20	35
B211	SP137	12g +8g dk pur	20	35
B212	SP137	18g +12g gldn brn	20	35
B213	SP137	20g +10g sep	20	35
B214	SP137	30g +10g dk yel grn	20	35
B215	SP137	35g +15g dp car	20	35
B216	SP137	48g +12g dk brn vio	20	35
B217	SP137	60g +20g dp bl	20	35
		Nos. B208-B217 (10)	2.00	3.50

1947, Aug. 30

Designs: 12g+8g, Prisoners' Mail, 18g+12g, Prison camp visitor. 35g + 15g, Family reunion. 60g+20g, "Industry" beckoning. 1s+40g, Sower.

B218	SP147	8g +2(g) dk grn	12	20
B219	SP147	12g +8(g) dk vio brn	12	20
B220	SP147	18g +12(g) blk brn	12	20
B221	SP147	35g +15(g) rose brn	12	20
B222	SP147	60g +20(g) dp bl	12	20
B223	SP147	1s +40(g) redsh brn	12	20
		Nos. B218-B223 (6)	72	1.20

Olympic Flame and Emblem
SP153

Laabenbach Bridge Neulengbach
SP154

1948, Jan. 16 **Engraved.**

B224	SP153	1s +50g dk bl	28	35

The surtax was used to help defray expenses of Austria's 1948 Olympics team.

1948, Feb. 18 ***Perf. 14x13½***

Designs: 20g+10g, Dam, Vermunt Lake. 30g+10g, Danube Port, Vienna. 40g+20g, Mining, Erzberg. 45g+20g, Tracks, Southern Railway Station, Vienna. 60g + 30g, Communal housing project, Vienna. 75g+35g, Gas Works, Vienna. 80g+40g, Oil refinery. 1s+50g, Gesäuse Highway, Styria. 1.40s+70g, Parliament Building, Vienna.

B225	SP154	10g +5g sl blk	12	20
B226	SP154	20g +10g lil	12	20
B227	SP154	30g +10g dl grn	38	45
B228	SP154	40g +20g ol brn	10	15
B229	SP154	45g +20g dk bl	5	8
B230	SP154	60g +30g dk red	5	8
B231	SP154	75g +35g dk vio brn	5	8
B232	SP154	80g +40g vio brn	5	8
B233	SP154	1s +50g dp bl	8	12
B234	SP154	1.40s +70g dp car	28	42
		Nos. B225-B234 (10)	1.28	1.86

The surtax was for the Reconstruction Fund.

Violet
SP155

Designs: 20g+10g, Anemone. 30g+10g, Crocus. 40g+20g, Yellow primrose. 45g+20g, Pasqueflower. 60g + 30g, Rhododendron. 75g + 35g, Dogrose. 80g + 40g, Cyclamen. 1s + 50g, Alpine Gentian. 1.40s + 70g, Edelweiss.

Engraved and Typographed.

1948, May 14 **Unwmkd.**

B235	SP155	10g +5g multi	22	18
B236	SP155	20g +10g multi	10	8
B237	SP155	30g +10g multi	2.25	3.25
B238	SP155	40g +20g multi	35	32
B239	SP155	45g +20g multi	10	8
B240	SP155	60g +30g multi	10	12
B241	SP155	75g +35g multi	10	12
B242	SP155	80g +40g multi	20	25
B243	SP155	1s +50g multi	25	40
B244	SP155	1.40s +70g multi	60	80
		Nos. B235-B244 (10)	4.27	5.60

Hans Makart
SP156

St. Rupert
SP157

Designs: 20g+10g, Künstlerhaus, Vienna. 40g+20g, Carl Kundmann. 50g+25g, A. S. von Siccardsburg. 60g+30g, Hans Cannon. 1s+50g, William Unger. 1.40s+70g, Friedrich von Schmidt.

1948, June 15 **Engraved**

B245	SP156	20g +10g dp yel grn	4.75	8.00
B246	SP156	30g +15g dk brn	2.25	3.00
B247	SP156	40g +20g ind	2.25	3.00
B248	SP156	50g +25g dk vio	2.75	4.50
B249	SP156	60g +30g dk red	2.75	4.50
B250	SP156	1s +50g dk bl	4.75	8.00
B251	SP156	1.40s +70g red brn	6.50	11.00
		Nos. B245-B251 (7)	26.00	42.00

Issued to commemorate the 80th anniversary of the Kunstlerhaus, home of the leading Austrian Artists Association.

1948, Aug. 6 ***Perf. 14x13½***

Designs: 30g + 15g, Cathedral and Fountain. 40g+20g, Facade of Cathedral. 50g+25g, Cathedral from South. 60g+30g, Abbey of St. Peter. 80g + 40g, Inside Cathedral. 1s + 50g, Salzburg Cathedral and Castle. 1.40s + 70g, Madonna by Michael Pacher.

B252	SP157	20g +10g dp grn	5.25	7.25
B253	SP157	30g +15g red brn	2.25	3.50

B254 SP157 40g +20g sl blk 1.75 2.75
B255 SP157 50g +25g choc 38 60
B256 SP157 60g +30g dk red 38 60
B257 SP157 80g +40g dk brn vio 38 60
B258 SP157 1s +50g dp bl 65 75
B259 SP157 1.40s +70g dk grn 1.15 1.50
Nos. B252-B259 (8) 12.19 17.55

The surtax was to aid in the reconstruction of Salzburg Cathedral.

Easter SP158   Arms of Austria, 1230 SP159

Designs: 60g + 20g, St. Nicholas Day. 1s+25g, Birthday. 1.40s+35g, Christmas.

1949, Apr. 13 **Unwmkd.**

Inscribed: "Glückliche Kindheit".

B260 SP158 40g +10g brn vio 12.50 19.00
B261 SP158 60g +20g brn red 12.50 19.00
B262 SP158 1s +25g dp ultra 12.50 19.00
B263 SP158 1.40s +35g dk grn 12.50 19.00

The surtax was for Child Welfare.

1949, Aug. 17

Designs: 60g+15g, Arms, 1450. 1s+25g, Arms, 1600. 1.60s+40g, Arms, 1945.

Engraved and Photogravure.

B264 SP159 40g +10g yel brn & yel 5.25 8.00

Engraved and Typographed.

B265 SP159 60g +15g brn car & sal 5.25 8.00
B266 SP159 1s +25g dp bl & ver 5.25 8.00
B267 SP159 1.60s +40g dp grn & sal 5.25 8.00

The surtax was for returned prisoners of war.

Laurel Branch, Stamps and Magnifier
SP160

1949, Dec. 3 **Engraved**

B268 SP160 60g +15g dk red 2.00 2.25

Stamp Day, Dec. 3-4.

Arms of Austria and Carinthia SP161   Carinthian with Austrian Flag SP162

Design: 1.70s+40g, Casting ballot.

Photogravure.

1950, Oct. 10 ***Perf. 14x13½***

B269 SP161 60g +15g bl grn & choc 20.00 24.00
B270 SP162 1s +25g red org & red 27.50 30.00
B271 SP162 1.70s +40g dp bl & grnsh bl 30.00 35.00

Issued to mark the 30th anniversary of the plebiscite in Carinthia.

Collector Examining Cover SP163   Miner and Mine SP164

1950, Dec. 2 **Engraved**

B272 SP163 60g +15g bl grn 7.00 7.25

Stamp Day.

1951, Mar. 10 **Unwmkd.**

Designs: 60g + 15g, Mason holding brick and trowel. 1s + 25g, Bridge builder with hook and chain. 1.70s+40g, Electrician, pole and insulators.

B273 SP164 40g +10g dk brn 10.50 16.00
B274 SP164 60g +15g dk grn 10.50 16.00
B275 SP164 1s +25g red brn 10.50 16.00
B276 SP164 1.70s +40g vio bl 10.50 16.00

Issued to publicize Austrian reconstruction.

Laurel Branch and Olympic Circles
SP165

1952, Jan. 26 ***Perf. 13½x14***

B277 SP165 2.40s +60g grnsh blk 13.00 20.00

The surtax was used to help defray expenses of Austria's athletes in the 1952 Olympic Games.

Cupid as Postman
SP166

1952, Mar. 10 ***Perf. 14x13½***

B278 SP166 1.50s +35g dk brn car 15.00 21.00

Stamp Day.

Sculpture, "Christ, The Almighty"
SP167

1952, Sept. 6 ***Perf. 13½x14***

B279 SP167 1s +25g grnsh gray 9.00 14.00

Issued to publicize the Austrian Catholic Convention, Vienna, Sept. 11-14, 1952.

Type of 1945-46 Overprinted in Gold

1s+25g

1953, Aug. 29 **Unwmkd.**

B280 A124 1s +25g on 5s dl bl 2.50 3.50

Issued to commemorate the 60th anniversary of labor unions in Austria.

Bummerlhaus Steyr SP168   Globe and Philatelic Accessories SP169

Designs: 1s+25g, Johannes Kepler. 1.50s+40g, Lutheran Bible, 1st edition. 2.40s+60g, Theophil von Hansen. 3s+75g, Reconstructed Lutheran School, Vienna.

1953, Nov. 5 **Engr.** ***Perf. 14x13½***

B281 SP168 70g +15g vio brn 20 32
B282 SP168 1s +25g dk gray bl 20 32
B283 SP168 1.50s +40g choc 60 90
B284 SP168 2.40s +60g dk grn 2.25 3.50
B285 SP168 3s +75g dk pur 5.25 8.50
Nos. B281-B285 (5) 8.50 13.54

The surtax was used toward reconstruction of the Lutheran School, Vienna.

1953, Dec. 5

B286 SP169 1s +25g choc 5.50 6.00

Stamp Day.

Type of 1945-46 with Denomination Replaced by Asterisks

Surcharged in Brown

LAWINENOPFER
1954
1s + 20g

1954, Feb. 19 ***Perf. 13½x14***

B287 A124 1s +20g bl gray 15 8

The surtax was used for aid to avalanche victims.

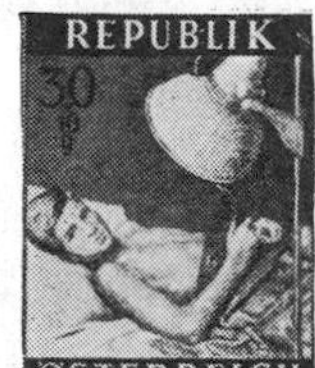

Patient Under Sun Lamp
SP170

Designs: 70g+15g, Physician using microscope. 1s+25g, Mother and children. 1.45s+35g, Operating room. 1.50s+35g, Baby on scale. 2.40s+60g, Nurse.

1954 **Engraved.** ***Perf. 14x13½.***

B288 SP170 30g +10g pur 1.10 1.50
B289 SP170 70g +15g dk brn 15 18
B290 SP170 1s +25g dk bl 20 25
B291 SP170 1.45s +35g dk bl grn 28 35
B292 SP170 1.50s +35g dk red 4.50 6.00
B293 SP170 2.40s +60g dk red brn 5.25 8.00
Nos. B288-B293 (6) 11.48 16.28

The surtax was for social welfare.

Early Vienna-Ulm Ferryboat
SP171

1954, Dec. 4 ***Perf. 13½x14***

B294 SP171 1s +25g dk gray grn 4.50 7.00

Stamp Day.

"Industry" Welcoming Returned Prisoner of War
SP172

1955, June 29

B295 SP172 1s +25g red brn 2.00 2.75

The surtax was for returned prisoners of war and relatives of prisoners not yet released.

Collector Looking at Album SP173   Ornamental Shield and Letter SP174

1955, Dec. 3 ***Perf. 14x13½***

B296 SP173 1s +25g vio brn 3.00 4.75

Issued for the Day of the Stamp. The surtax was for the promotion of Austrian philately.

1956, Dec. 1 **Engraved**

B297 SP174 1s +25g scar 2.50 4.00

Stamp Day. See note after No. B296.

Arms of Austria, 1945
SP175

Engraved and Typographed

1956, Dec. 21 ***Perf. 14x13½***

B298 SP175 1.50s +50g on 1.60s +40g gray & red 28 40

The surtax was for Hungarian refugees.

New Post Office, Linz 2
SP176

1957, Nov. 30 Engr. *Perf. 13½x14*

B299 SP176 1s +25g dk sl grn 2.25 3.75

Stamp Day. See note after No. B296.

1958, Dec. 6

Design: 2.40s+60g, Post office, Kitzbuhel.

B300 SP176 2.40s +60g bl 75 1.10

Stamp Day. See note after B296. See also No. B303.

Roman Carriage from Tomb at Maria Saal SP177

Lithographed and Engraved

1959, Dec. 5 *Perf. 13½x14*

B301 SP177 2.40s +60g pale lil & blk 60 90

Stamp Day.

Progressive Die Proof under Magnifying Glass SP178

1960, Dec. 2 Engr. *Perf. 13½x14*

B302 SP178 3s +70g vio brn 1.10 1.10

Stamp Day.

P. O. Type of 1957

Design: 3s+70g, Post Office, Rust.

1961, Dec. 1 *Perf. 13½*

B303 SP176 3s +70g dk bl grn 1.10 1.10

Stamp Day. See note after No. B296.

Hands of Stamp Engraver at Work—SP179

1962, Nov. 30 *Perf. 13½x14*

B304 SP179 3s +70g dl pur 1.10 1.10

Stamp Day.

Railroad Exit, Post Office Vienna 101—SP180

Lithographed and Engraved

1963, Nov. 29 Unwmkd.

B305 SP180 3s +70g tan & blk 75 75

Stamp Day.

View of Vienna, North SP181

Designs: Various views of Vienna with compass indicating direction.

1964, July 20 Litho. *Perf. 13½x14*

Multicolored

B306	SP181	1.50s +30g ("N")	18	18
B307	SP181	1.50s +30g ("NO")	18	18
B308	SP181	1.50s +30g ("O")	18	18
B309	SP181	1.50s +30g ("SO")	18	18
B310	SP181	1.50s +30g ("S")	18	18
B311	SP181	1.50s +30g ("SW")	18	18
B312	SP181	1.50s +30g ("W")	18	18
B313	SP181	1.50s +30g ("NW")	18	18
		Nos. B306-B313 (8)	1.44	1.44

Issued to publicize the Vienna International Philatelic Exhibition (WIPA 1965).

Post Bus Terminal, St. Gilgen, Wolfgangsee—SP182

1964, Dec. 4 *Perf. 13½* Unwmkd.

B314 SP182 3s +70g multi 45 45

Stamp Day.

Wall Painting, Tomb at Thebes SP183

Development of Writing: 1.80s+50g, Cuneiform writing on stone tablet and man's head from Assyrian palace. 2.20s+60g, Wax tablet with Latin writing, Corinthian column. 3s+80g, Gothic writing on sealed letter, Gothic window from Munster Cathedral. 4s+1s, Letter with seal and postmark and upright desk. 5s+1.20s, Typewriter.

Lithographed and Engraved

1965, June 4 *Perf. 14x13½*

B315	SP183	1.50s +40g dp rose & blk	12	12
B316	SP183	1.80s +50g yel & blk	20	20
B317	SP183	2.20s +60g pale vio & blk	40	40
B318	SP183	3s +80g ap grn & blk	25	25
B319	SP183	4s +1s lt bl & blk	55	55
B320	SP183	5s +1.20s brt grn & blk	75	75
		Nos. B315-B320 (6)	2.27	2.27

Issued to commemorate the Vienna International Philatelic Exhibition, WIPA, June 4–13.

Mailman Distributing Mail SP184

Perf. 13½x14

1965, Dec. 3 Engraved Unwmkd.

B321 SP184 3s +70g bl grn 45 45

Stamp Day.

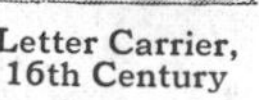

Letter Carrier, 16th Century SP185

Letter Carrier, 16th Century Playing Card SP186

Lithographed and Engraved

1966, Dec. 2 *Perf. 13½* Unwmkd.

B322 SP185 3s +70g multi 45 40

Stamp Day. Design is from Ambras Heroes' Book, Austrian National Library.

Engraved and Photogravure

1967, Dec. 1 *Perf. 13x13½*

B323 SP186 3.50s +80g multi 50 50

Stamp Day.

Mercury, Bas-relief from Purkersdorf SP187

Unken Post Station Sign, 1710 SP188

1968, Nov. 29 Engr. *Perf. 13½*

B324 SP187 3.50s +80g sl grn 45 45

Stamp Day.

Engraved and Photogravure

1969, Dec. 5 *Perf. 12*

B325 SP188 3.50s +80g tan, red & blk 40 40

Stamp Day. Design is from a watercolor by Friedrich Zeller.

Saddle, Bag, Harness and Post Horn SP189

Engraved and Lithographed

1970, Dec. 4 *Perf. 13½x14*

B326 SP189 3.50s +80g gray blk & yel 50 40

Stamp Day.

"50 Years" SP190

Engraved and Photogravure

1971, Dec. 3 *Perf. 13½*

B327 SP190 4s +1.50s gold & red brn 65 6

50th anniversary of the Federation of Austrian Philatelic Societies.

Local Post Carrier SP191

Gabriel, by Lorenz Luchsperger, 15th Century SP192

1972, Dec. 1 Engraved *Perf. 14x13½*

B328 SP191 4s +1s ol grn 65 65

Stamp Day.

1973, Nov. 30

B329 SP192 4s +1s mar 60 60

Stamp Day.

Mail Coach Leaving Old PTT Building SP193

1974, Nov. 29 Engr. *Perf. 14x13½*

B330 SP193 4s +2s vio bl 70 70

Stamp Day.

Alpine Skiing, Women's SP194

Designs (Innsbruck Winter Olympic Games Emblem and): 1.50s+70g, Ice hockey. 2s+90g, Ski jump. 4s+1.90s, Bobsledding.

1975, Mar. 14 Photo. *Perf. 13½x14*

B331	SP194	1s +50g multi	25	25
B332	SP194	1.50s +70g multi	32	32
B333	SP194	2s +90g multi	40	40
B334	SP194	4s +1.90s multi	80	80

1975, Nov. 14

Designs (Innsbruck Winter Olympic Games Emblem and): 70g+30g, Figure skating, pair. 2s+1s, Cross-country skiing. 2.50s+1s, Luge. 4s+2s, Biathlon.

B335	SP194	70g +30g multi	18	18
B336	SP194	2s +1s multi	35	35
B337	SP194	2.50s +1s multi	40	40
B338	SP194	4s +2s multi	75	75

12th Winter Olympic Games, Innsbruck, Feb. 4–15, 1976.

Austria Nos. 5, 250, 455 SP195

Photogravure and Engraved

1975, Nov. 28 *Perf. 14*

B339 SP195 4s +2s multi 75 75

Stamp Day and 125th anniversary of Austrian stamps.

Postilion's Gala Hat and Horn
SP196

1976, Dec. 3 ***Perf. 13½x14***

B340 SP196 6s +2s blk & lt vio 90 90

Stamp Day 1976.

Emanuel Herrmann
SP197

1977, Dec. 2 ***Perf. 14x13½***

B341 SP197 6s +2s multi 90 90

Stamp Day 1977. Emanuel Herrmann (1839–1902), economist, invented postal card. Austria issued first postal card in 1869.

Post Bus, 1913
SP198

1978, Dec. 1 **Photo.** ***Perf. 13½x14***

B342 SP198 10s +5s multi 1.75 1.75

Stamp Day 1978.

Heroes' Square, Vienna—SP199

Photo. & Engr.

1979, Nov. 30 ***Perf. 13½***

B343 SP199 16s +8s multi 2.75 2.75

No. B343 Inscribed "2. Phase"

1980, Nov. 21 **Photo. & Engr.** ***Perf. 13½***

B344 SP199 16s +8s multi 2.75 2.75

WIPA 1981 Philatelic Exhibition, Vienna, May 22-31, 1981.

Souvenir Sheet

1981, Feb. 20 **Photo. & Engr.** ***Perf. 13½***

B345 SP199 16s +8s multi 3.25 3.25

WIPA 1981 Philatelic Exhibition, Vienna, May 22-31. No. B345 contains one stamp (without inscription); black and red margin. Size: 90x72mm.

Stamp Day 1982—SP200

1982, Nov. 26 **Photo. & Engr.**

B346 SP200 6s +3s Mainz-Weber mailbox, 1870 1.00 1.00

Stamp Day 1983—SP201

1983, Oct. 21 **Photo. & Engr.** ***Perf. 14***

B347 SP201 6s +3s Boy examining cover 1.00 1.00

World Winter Games for the Handicapped—SP202

1984, Jan. 5 **Photo.** ***Perf. 13½x13***

B348 SP202 4s +2s Downhill skier 65 65

Stamp Day 1984—SP203

Design: 6s+3s, Seschemnofer III burial chamber detail, pyramid of Cheops, Gizeh.

1984, Nov. 30 **Photo. & Engr.** ***Perf. 13½***

B349 SP203 6s +3s multi 1.10 1.10

Stamp Day 1985—SP204

1985, Nov. 28 **Photo. & Engr.** ***Perf. 14***

B350 SP204 6s + 3s Roman messenger on horseback 1.00 75

Nuremberg Messenger, 16th Cent.—SP205

1986, Nov. 28 **Photo.** ***Perf. 14***

B351 SP205 6s +3s multi 1.30 1.00

Stamp Day 1986.

AIR POST STAMPS.
Issues of the Monarchy.

FLUGPOST

Types of Regular Issue of 1916 Surcharged

2·50 K 2·50

Perf. 12½.

1918, Mar. 30 Unwmkd.

C1	A40	1.50k on 2k lil	2.50	3.00
C2	A40	2.50k on 3k ocher	11.00	20.00
a.		Inverted surch.	1,500.	
b.		Perf. 11½	325.00	225.00
c.		Perf. 12½x11½	27.50	37.50

Overprinted **FLUGPOST**

C3	A40	4k gray	6.75	10.00

Set exists imperf. Price, $500.

Nos. C1-C3 also exist without surcharge or overprint. Price, set perf., $900; imperf., $750.

Nos. C1-C3 were printed on grayish and on white paper.

A 7k on 10k red brown was prepared but not regularly issued. Price, perf. or imperf., $600.

Issues of the Republic.

Hawk AP1 — Wilhelm Kress AP2

1922-24 Typographed *Perf. 12½*

C4	AP1	300k claret	35	1.25
C5	AP1	400k grn ('24)	5.50	10.00
C6	AP1	600k bister	10	60
C7	AP1	900k brn org	10	60

Engraved

C8	AP2	1200k brn vio	10	60
C9	AP2	2400k slate	10	60
C10	AP2	3000k dp brn ('23)	2.00	2.75
C11	AP2	4800k dk bl ('23)	2.50	3.25
		Nos. C4-C11 (8)	10.75	19.65

Set exists imperf. Price, $900.

Plane and Pilot's Head AP3 — Airplane Passing Crane AP4

1925-30 Typographed *Perf. 12½*

C12	AP3	2g gray brn	55	1.00
C13	AP3	5g red	30	25
a.		Horizontal pair, imperf. between	275.00	
C14	AP3	6g dk bl	1.25	1.75
C15	AP3	8g yel grn	1.40	2.00
C16	AP3	10g dp org ('26)	1.40	2.00
a.		Horiz. pair, imperf. between	300.00	
C17	AP3	15g red vio ('26)	60	90
a.		Horiz. pair, imperf. between	375.00	
C18	AP3	20g org brn ('30)	14.00	4.75
C19	AP3	25g blk vio ('30)	3.50	7.00
C20	AP3	30g bis ('26)	9.00	7.00
C21	AP3	50g bl gray ('26)	16.00	12.00
C22	AP3	80g dk grn ('30)	1.75	4.75

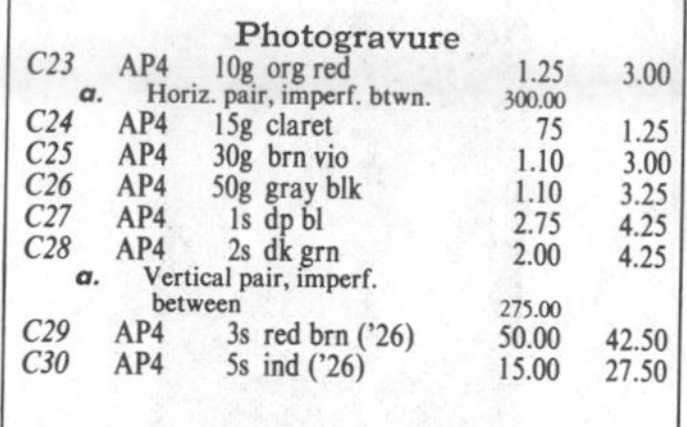

Photogravure

C23	AP4	10g org red	1.25	3.00
a.		Horiz. pair, imperf. btwn.	300.00	
C24	AP4	15g claret	75	1.25
C25	AP4	30g brn vio	1.10	3.00
C26	AP4	50g gray blk	1.10	3.25
C27	AP4	1s dp bl	2.75	4.25
C28	AP4	2s dk grn	2.00	4.25
a.		Vertical pair, imperf. between	275.00	
C29	AP4	3s red brn ('26)	50.00	42.50
C30	AP4	5s ind ('26)	15.00	27.50

Size: 25½x32mm.

C31	AP4	10s blk brn, *gray* ('26)	12.50	20.00
		Nos. C12-C31 (20)	136.20	152.40

Exists imperf. Price, set $1,100.

Airplane over Güssing Castle AP5

Airplane over the Danube AP6

Designs (each includes plane): 10g, Maria-Worth. 15g, Durnstein. 20g, Hallstatt. 25g, Salzburg. 30g, Upper Dachstein and Schladminger Glacier. 40g, Lake Wetter. 50g, Arlberg. 60g, St. Stephen's Cathedral. 80g, Church of the Minorites. 2s, Railroad viaduct, Carinthia. 3s, Gross Glockner mountain. 5s, Aerial railway. 10s, Seaplane and yachts.

1935, Aug. 16 Engraved. *Perf. 12½.*

C32	AP5	5g rose vio	12	18
C33	AP5	10g red org	12	18
C34	AP5	15g yel grn	70	55
C35	AP5	20g gray bl	15	32
C36	AP5	25g vio brn	15	32
C37	AP5	30g brn org	18	38
C38	AP5	40g gray grn	18	38
C39	AP5	50g lt sl bl	18	38
C40	AP5	60g blk brn	40	65
C41	AP5	80g lt brn	40	65
C42	AP6	1s rose red	40	90
C43	AP6	2s ol grn	2.25	4.50
C44	AP6	3s yel brn	9.00	13.00
C45	AP6	5s dk grn	5.50	13.00
C46	AP6	10s sl bl	40.00	72.50
		Nos. C32-C46 (15)	59.73	107.89

Set exists imperf. Price, $425.

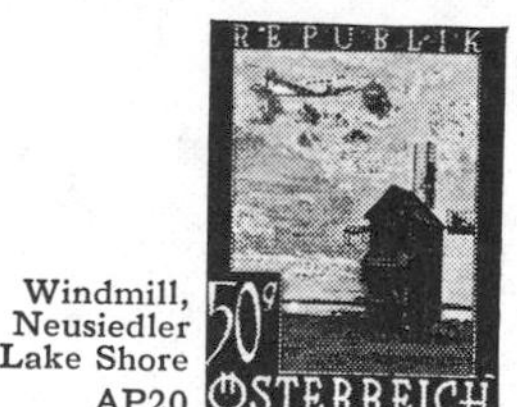

Windmill, Neusiedler Lake Shore AP20

Designs: 1s, Roman arch, Carnuntum. 2s, Town Hall, Gmund. 3s, Schieder Lake, Hinterstoder. 4s, Praegraten, Eastern Tyrol. 5s, Torsäule, Salzburg. 10s, St. Charles Church, Vienna.

1947 *Perf. 14x13½* Unwmkd.

C47	AP20	50g blk brn	12	28
C48	AP20	1s dk brn vio	25	35
C49	AP20	2s dk grn	28	45
C50	AP20	3s chocolate	1.65	3.00
C51	AP20	4s dk grn	1.10	2.00
C52	AP20	5s dk bl	1.10	2.00
C53	AP20	10s dk bl	55	1.25
		Nos. C47-C53 (7)	5.05	9.33

Rooks AP27

Birds: 1s, Barn swallows. 2s, Black-headed gulls. 3s, Great cormorants. 5s, Buzzard. 10s, Gray heron. 20s, Golden eagle.

1950-53 *Perf. 13½x14*

C54	AP27	60g dk bl vio	2.25	2.00
C55	AP27	1s dk vio bl ('53)	14.00	22.50
C56	AP27	2s dk bl	9.50	6.75
C57	AP27	3s dk sl grn ('53)	80.00	90.00
C58	AP27	5s red brn ('53)	80.00	90.00
C59	AP27	10s gray vio ('53)	35.00	35.00
C60	AP27	20s brn blk ('52)	6.50	5.75
		Nos C54-C60 (7)	227.25	252.00

Value at lower left on Nos. C59 and C60. No. C60 exists imperf.

Etrich "Dove" AP28

Designs: 3.50s, Twin-engine jet airliner. 5s, Four-engine jet airliner.

1968, May 31 Engr. *Perf. 13½x14*

C61	AP28	2s ol bis	32	32
C62	AP28	3.50s sl grn	55	55
C63	AP28	5s dk bl	80	80

Issued to publicize IFA WIEN 1968 (International Air Post Exhibition), Vienna, May 30-June 4.

POSTAGE DUE STAMPS.
Issues of the Monarchy.

D1 — D2

Wmkd.

ZEITUNGS-MARKEN. (91)

1894-95 Typo. *Perf. 10 to 13½*

J1	D1	1kr brown	2.50	1.25
a.		Perf. 13½	22.50	6.50
J2	D1	2kr brn ('95)	4.50	1.25
a.		Pair, imperf. btwn.	200.00	225.00
J3	D1	3kr brown	4.00	30
J4	D1	5kr brown	3.50	40
a.		Perf. 13½	15.00	6.50
b.		Pair, imperf. btwn.	175.00	200.00
J5	D1	6kr brn ('95)	3.50	3.50
J6	D1	7kr brn ('95)	1.00	1.75
a.		Pair, imperf. btwn.	225.00	250.00
J7	D1	10kr brown	6.00	38
J8	D1	20kr brown	90	2.25
J9	D1	50kr brown	45.00	35.00
		Nos. J1-J9 (9)	70.90	46.08

See also Nos. J204-J231.

1899-1900 *Imperf.*

J10	D2	1h brown	25	40
J11	D2	2h brown	25	40
J12	D2	3h brn ('00)	25	30
J13	D2	4h brown	4.00	1.10
J14	D2	5h brn ('00)	3.50	30
J15	D2	6h brown	35	1.40
J16	D2	10h brown	25	30
J17	D2	12h brown	50	2.75
J18	D2	15h brown	50	1.40
J19	D2	20h brown	22.50	75
J20	D2	40h brown	1.00	2.75
J21	D2	100h brown	5.00	2.25
		Nos. J10-J21 (12)	38.35	14.10

Perf. 10½, 12½, 13½ and Compound.

J22	D2	1h brown	70	25
J23	D2	2h brown	55	20
J24	D2	3h brn ('00)	50	12
J25	D2	4h brown	50	12
J26	D2	5h brn ('00)	35	12
J27	D2	6h brown	35	12
J28	D2	10h brown	50	10
J29	D2	12h brown	55	40
J30	D2	15h brown	90	40
J31	D2	20h brown	60	3
J32	D2	40h brown	1.00	9
J33	D2	100h brown	25.00	1.4
		Nos. J22-J33 (12)	31.50	4.4

Nos. J10 to J33 exist on unwatermarked paper.

D3

1908-13 *Perf. 12½* Unwmkd.

J34	D3	1h carmine	1.25	1.25
J35	D3	2h carmine	50	50
J36	D3	4h carmine	50	25
J37	D3	6h carmine	50	25
J38	D3	10h carmine	50	25
J39	D3	14h car ('13)	3.75	1.50
J40	D3	20h carmine	4.50	25
J41	D3	25h car ('10)	9.00	2.50
J42	D3	30h carmine	5.50	25
J43	D3	50h carmine	6.50	35
J44	D3	100h carmine	14.00	40
		Nos. J34-J44 (11)	46.50	7.75

All values exist on ordinary paper, Nos. J34 to J38, J40 and J42 to J44 on chalky paper and Nos. J34 to J38, J40 and J44 on thin ordinary paper. All values exist imperforate.

1911

J45	D3	5k violet	50.00	10.00
J46	D3	10k violet	275.00	5.00

Regular Issue of 1908 Overprinted or Surcharged in Carmine or Black:

a — b

1916

J47	A22	1h gray (C)	8	8
a.		Pair, one without overprint	150.00	
J48	A22	15h on 2h vio (Bk)	25	35

D4 — D5

1916

J49	D4	5h rose red	12	8
J50	D4	10h rose red	12	8
J51	D4	15h rose red	12	8
J52	D4	20h rose red	12	8
J53	D4	25h rose red	50	40
J54	D4	30h rose red	20	12
J55	D4	40h rose red	25	12
J56	D4	50h rose red	1.25	1.25
J57	D5	1k ultra	40	12
a.		Horizontal pair, imperf. btwn.	450.00	450.00
J58	D5	5k ultra	1.65	1.75
J59	D5	10k ultra	1.65	1.25
		Nos. J49-J59 (11)	6.38	5.33

Exists imperf. Price, set $115.

Type of Regular Issue of 1916 Surcharged

15 ✻ 15

1917

J60	A38	10h on 24h bl	2.00	35
J61	A38	15h on 36h vio	30	20

J62	A38	20h on 54h org	30	35
J63	A38	50h on 42h choc	30	20

All values of this issue are known imperforate, also without surcharge, perforated and imperforate.

Issues of the Republic.

Postage Due Stamps of 1916 Overprinted

1919

J64	D4	5h rose red	20	25
a.		Inverted ovpt.	275.00	275.00
J65	D4	10h rose red	20	25
J66	D4	15h rose red	25	50
J67	D4	20h rose red	45	38
J68	D4	25h rose red	8.50	20.00
J69	D4	30h rose red	25	25
J70	D4	40h rose red	25	38
J71	D4	50h rose red	50	1.25
J72	D5	1k ultra	7.50	7.00
J73	D5	5k ultra	10.00	7.00
J74	D5	10k ultra	11.00	5.00
		Nos. J64-J74 (11)	39.10	42.26

Nos. J64, J65, J67 and J70 exist imperforate.

D6

D7

1920-21 *Perf. 12½.*

J75	D6	5h brt red	8	22
J76	D6	10h brt red	5	6
J77	D6	15h brt red	5	45
J78	D6	20h brt red	5	8
J79	D6	25h brt red	10	45
J80	D6	30h brt red	5	12
J81	D6	40h brt red	5	8
J82	D6	50h brt red	5	12
J83	D6	80h brt red	5	12
J84	D7	1k ultra	5	12
J85	D7	1½k ultra ('21)	5	12
J86	D7	2k ultra ('21)	5	10
J87	D7	3k ultra ('21)	5	20
J88	D7	4k ultra ('21)	5	20
J89	D7	5k ultra	5	12
J90	D7	8k ultra ('21)	5	20
J91	D7	10k ultra	5	12
J92	D7	20k ultra ('21)	15	60
		Nos. J75-J92 (18)	1.08	3.48

Nos. J84 to J92 exist on white paper and on grayish white paper. They also exist imperf.; price, set $120

Imperf.

J93	D6	5h brt red	10	30
J94	D6	10h brt red	5	8
J95	D6	15h brt red	5	38
J96	D6	20h brt red	5	8
J97	D6	25h brt red	5	45
J98	D6	30h brt red	5	18
J99	D6	40h brt red	5	12
J100	D6	50h brt red	5	32
J101	D6	80h brt red	5	18
		Nos. J93-J101 (9)	50	2.09

No. 207a Surcharged in Dark Blue

Nachmarke

7½K

1921 *Perf. 12½*

J102	A43	7½k on 15h bis	5	18
a.		Inverted surch.	250.00	250.00

D8

1922

J103	D8	1k redsh buff	5	*18*
J104	D8	2k redsh buff	5	*18*
J105	D8	4k redsh buff	5	*25*
J106	D8	5k redsh buff	5	*18*
J107	D8	7½k redsh buff	5	*20*
J108	D8	10k bl grn	5	*18*
J109	D8	15k bl grn	6	*25*
J110	D8	20k bl grn	6	*20*
J111	D8	25k bl grn	6	*23*
J112	D8	40k bl grn	6	*18*
J113	D8	50k bl grn	6	*40*
		Nos. J103-J113 (11)	60	*2.45*

D9

D10

1922-24

J114	D9	10k cob bl	5	*18*
J115	D9	15k cob bl	6	*20*
J116	D9	20k cob bl	5	*18*
J117	D9	50k cob bl	6	*28*
J118	D10	100k plum	5	5
J119	D10	150k plum	5	*12*
J120	D10	200k plum	5	5
J121	D10	400k plum	6	6
J122	D10	600k plum ('23)	6	*18*
J123	D10	800k plum	6	5
J124	D10	1,000k plum ('23)	5	6
J125	D10	1,200k plum ('23)	45	*1.40*
J126	D10	1,500k plum ('24)	10	15
J127	D10	1,800k plum ('24)	1.50	*4.50*
J128	D10	2,000k plum ('23)	20	40
J129	D10	3,000k plum ('24)	5.75	8.00
J130	D10	4,000k plum ('24)	4.00	*10.00*
J131	D10	6,000k plum ('24)	4.00	*16.00*
		Nos. J114-J131 (18)	16.60	*41.86*

Price, #J103-J131 imperf, $350.

D11

D12

1925-34 *Perf. 12½*

J132	D11	1g red	6	6
J133	D11	2g red	6	6
J134	D11	3g red	6	12
J135	D11	4g red	6	10
J136	D11	5g red ('27)	6	6
J137	D11	6g red	25	50
J138	D11	8g red	25	25
J139	D11	10g dk bl	15	6
J140	D11	12g dk bl	15	12
J141	D11	14g dk bl ('27)	25	12
J142	D11	15g dk bl	15	12
J143	D11	16g dk bl ('29)	40	20
J144	D11	18g dk bl ('34)	1.40	4.50
J145	D11	20g dk bl	15	12
J146	D11	23g dk bl	75	20
J147	D11	24g dk bl ('32)	1.25	12
J148	D11	28g dk bl ('27)	55	30
J149	D11	30g dk bl	25	18
J150	D11	31g dk bl ('29)	1.00	25
J151	D11	35g dk bl ('30)	65	20
J152	D11	39g dk bl ('32)	1.10	12
J153	D11	40g dk bl	1.10	2.25
J154	D11	60g dk bl	75	1.25
J155	D12	1s dk grn	4.25	1.25
J156	D12	2s dk grn	32.50	4.50
J157	D12	5s dk grn	100.00	37.50
J158	D12	10s dk grn	50.00	5.25
		Nos. J132-J158 (27)	197.60	59.76

Issues of 1925-27 (21 values) imperf, price, set $650.

D13

D14

Coat of Arms

1935

J159	D13	1g red	12	18
J160	D13	2g red	12	18
J161	D13	3g red	12	18
J162	D13	5g red	18	12
J163	D13	10g blue	18	5
J164	D13	12g blue	18	5
J165	D13	15g blue	25	60
J166	D13	20g blue	18	12
J167	D13	24g blue	20	5
J168	D13	30g blue	25	12
J169	D13	39g blue	32	6
J170	D13	60g blue	60	1.65
J171	D14	1s green	1.00	60
J172	D14	2s green	1.50	80
J173	D14	5s green	4.00	1.65
J174	D14	10s green	6.00	90
		Nos. J159-J174 (16)	15.20	7.31

On Nos. J163–J170, background lines are horizontal.

Nos. J159–J174 exist imperf. Price, set $125.

D15

D16

Coat of Arms

Typographed.

1945 *Perf. 10½* Unwmkd.

J175	D15	1g vermilion	5	*10*
J176	D15	2g vermilion	5	*10*
J177	D15	3g vermilion	5	*10*
J178	D15	5g vermilion	5	5
J179	D15	10g vermilion	5	5
J180	D15	12g vermilion	5	10
J181	D15	20g vermilion	5	*12*
J182	D15	24g vermilion	5	5
J183	D15	30g vermilion	5	*12*
J184	D15	60g vermilion	5	*18*
J185	D15	1s violet	5	*35*
J186	D15	2s violet	6	*45*
J187	D15	5s violet	6	*20*
J188	D15	10s violet	6	*20*
		Nos. J175-J188 (14)	73	*2.17*

Occupation Stamps of the Allied Military Government Overprinted in Black

PORTO

1946 *Perf. 11.*

J189	OS1	3g dp org	5	12
J190	OS1	5g brt grn	5	5
J191	OS1	6g red vio	5	10
J192	OS1	8g rose pink	5	5
J193	OS1	10g lt gray	5	20
J194	OS1	12g pale buff brn	5	5
J195	OS1	15g rose red	5	20
J196	OS1	20g cop brn	5	8
J197	OS1	25g dp bl	5	10
J198	OS1	30g brt vio	5	5
J199	OS1	40g lt ultra	5	6
J200	OS1	60g lt ol grn	5	8
J201	OS1	1s dk vio	8	18
J202	OS1	2s yellow	18	28
J203	OS1	5s dp ultra	18	28
		Nos. J189-J203 (15)	1.04	1.88

Nos. J189–J203 were issued by the Renner Government. Inverted overprints exist on about half of the denominations.

Type of 1894-95.

Inscribed "Republik Osterreich".

1947 Typographed *Perf. 14*

J204	D1	1g chocolate	5	5
J205	D1	2g chocolate	5	5
J206	D1	3g chocolate	5	5
J207	D1	5g chocolate	5	5
J208	D1	8g chocolate	5	5
J209	D1	10g chocolate	5	5
J210	D1	12g chocolate	5	5
J211	D1	15g chocolate	5	5
J212	D1	16g chocolate	15	40
J213	D1	17g chocolate	15	40
J214	D1	18g chocolate	15	40
J215	D1	20g chocolate	32	6
J216	D1	24g chocolate	20	30
J217	D1	30g chocolate	12	25
J218	D1	36g chocolate	32	60
J219	D1	40g chocolate	6	8
J220	D1	42g chocolate	30	60
J221	D1	48g chocolate	35	60
J222	D1	50g chocolate	40	12
J223	D1	60g chocolate	12	15
J224	D1	70g chocolate	6	15
J225	D1	80g chocolate	2.50	1.65
J226	D1	1s blue	12	12
J227	D1	1.15s blue	1.65	28
J228	D1	1.20s blue	2.00	1.00
J229	D1	2s blue	25	40
J230	D1	5s blue	25	40
J231	D1	10s blue	30	40
		Nos. J204-J231 (28)	10.17	8.76

1949-57

J232	D16	1g carmine	12	6
J233	D16	2g carmine	12	6
J234	D16	4g car ('51)	50	12
J235	D16	5g carmine	1.25	25
J236	D16	8g car ('51)	1.50	1.20
J237	D16	10g carmine	10	5
J238	D16	20g carmine	10	5
J239	D16	30g carmine	10	5
J240	D16	40g carmine	8	5
J241	D16	50g carmine	10	5
J242	D16	60g car ('50)	4.25	12
J243	D16	63g car ('57)	2.50	3.25
J244	D16	70g carmine	10	5
J245	D16	80g carmine	8	8
J246	D16	90g car ('50)	12	12
J247	D16	1s purple	12	5
J248	D16	1.20s purple	18	8
J249	D16	1.35s purple	15	8
J250	D16	1.40s pur ('51)	25	20
J251	D16	1.50s pur ('53)	12	5
J252	D16	1.65s pur ('50)	20	12
J253	D16	1.70s purple	20	12
J254	D16	2s purple	18	5
J255	D16	2.50s pur ('51)	25	6
J256	D16	3s pur ('51)	50	6
J257	D16	4s pur ('51)	50	40
J258	D16	5s purple	90	20
J259	D16	10s purple	1.50	20
		Nos. J232-J259 (28)	16.07	7.23

MILITARY STAMPS.

Issues of the Austro-Hungarian Military Authorities for the Occupied Territories in World War I.

Stamps of Bosnia of 1912-14 Overprinted

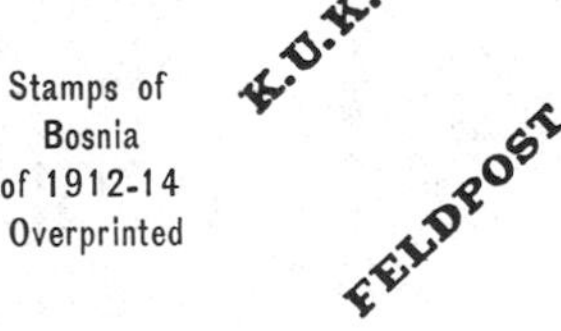

1915 *Perf. 12½* Unwmkd.

M1	A23	1h ol grn	18	25
M2	A23	2h brt bl	18	25
M3	A23	3h claret	18	25
M4	A23	5h green	10	12
M5	A23	6h dk gray	18	25
M6	A23	10h rose car	10	12
M7	A23	12h dp ol grn	28	40
M8	A23	20h org brn	40	48
M9	A23	25h ultra	40	40
M10	A23	30h org red	3.50	*6.00*
M11	A24	35h myr grn	3.00	*4.75*
M12	A24	40h dk vio	3.00	*4.75*
M13	A24	45h ol brn	3.25	*5.25*
M14	A24	50h sl bl	3.00	*4.75*
M15	A24	60h brn vio	45	60
M16	A24	72h dk bl	3.00	*4.75*
M17	A25	1k brn vio, *straw*	3.50	*6.00*
M18	A25	2k dk gray, *bl*	3.50	*4.75*
M19	A26	3k car, *grn*	*22.50*	*32.50*
M20	A26	5k dk vio, *gray*	*22.50*	*32.50*

M21	A25	10k dk ultra, *gray*	150.00	180.00
		Nos. M1-M21 (21)	*223.20*	*289.12*

Exists imperf. Price, set $400.

Nos. M1–M21 also exist with overprint double, inverted and in red. These varieties were made by order of an official but were not regularly issued.

Emperor Franz Josef

M1 M2

1915-17 Engraved.

Perf. 11½, 12½ and Compound.

M22	M1	1h ol grn	10	10
M23	M1	2h dl bl	12	10
M24	M1	3h claret	10	10
M25	M1	5h green	10	10
a.		Perf. 11½	40.00	*45.00*
b.		Perf. 11½x12½	50.00	*75.00*
c.		Perf. 12½x11½	80.00	*100.00*
M26	M1	6h dk gray	10	10
M27	M1	10h rose car	12	10
M28	M1	10h gray bl ('17)	12	10
M29	M1	12h dp ol grn	12	15
M30	M1	15h car rose ('17)	6	6
a.		Perf. 11½	8.00	7.25
M31	M1	20h org brn	35	15
M32	M1	20h ol grn ('17)	35	15
M33	M1	25h ultra	18	12
M34	M1	30h vermilion	18	15
M35	M1	35h dk grn	32	40
M36	M1	40h dk vio	32	40
M37	M1	45h ol brn	30	40
M38	M1	50h myr grn	30	25
M39	M1	60h brn vio	30	40
M40	M1	72h dk bl	30	40
M41	M1	80h org brn ('17)	18	20
M42	M1	90h mag ('17)	90	90
M43	M2	1k brn vio, *straw*	1.65	2.00
M44	M2	2k dk gray, *bl*	1.40	80
M45	M2	3k car, *grn*	1.00	1.10
M46	M2	4k dk vio, *gray* ('17)	1.00	1.10
M47	M2	5k dk vio, *gray*	21.00	24.00
M48	M2	10k dk ultra, *gray*	3.00	6.00
		Nos. M22-M48 (27)	33.97	39.83

Nos. M22–M48 exist imperf. Price, set $90.

Emperor Karl I

M3 M4

1917–18 ***Perf. 12½***

M49	M3	1h grnsh bl ('18)	6	5
a.		Perf. 11½	3.50	4.00
M50	M3	2h red org ('18)	6	5
M51	M3	3h ol gray	6	5
a.		Perf. 11½, 11½x12½	12.50	15.00
M52	M3	5h ol grn	6	5
M53	M3	6h violet	8	5
M54	M3	10h org brn	6	5
M55	M3	12h blue	6	6
a.		Perf. 11½	2.75	3.00
M56	M3	15h brt rose	6	5
M57	M3	20h red brn	8	5
M58	M3	25h ultra	40	40
M59	M3	30h slate	10	5
M60	M3	40h ol bis	10	8
a.		Perf. 11½	1.40	1.50
M61	M3	50h dp grn	10	5
a.		Perf. 11½	4.50	6.00
M62	M3	60h car rose	10	10
M63	M3	80h dl bl	8	5
M64	M3	90h dk vio	45	55
M65	M4	2k rose, *straw*	10	5
a.		Perf. 11½	2.25	3.00
M66	M4	3k grn, *bl*	1.10	1.10
M67	M4	4k rose, *grn*	18.00	14.00
a.		Perf. 11½	27.50	35.00
M68	M4	10k dl vio, *gray*	2.75	4.00
a.		Perf. 11½	11.00	16.00
		Nos. M49-M68 (20)	26.61	23.89

Nos. M49–M68 exist imperf. Price, set $45.

Emperor Karl I

M5

1918 Typographed ***Perf. 12½***

M69	M5	1h grnsh bl	26.00
M70	M5	2h orange	13.00
M71	M5	3h ol gray	10.50
M72	M5	5h yel grn	28
M73	M5	10h dk brn	28
M74	M5	20h red	1.00
M75	M5	25h blue	1.00
M76	M5	30h bister	100.00
M77	M5	45h dk sl	100.00
M78	M5	50h dp grn	65.00
M79	M5	60h violet	125.00
M80	M5	80h rose	65.00
M81	M5	90h brn vio	2.50

Engraved.

M82	M4	1k ol bis, *bl*	28
		Nos. M69-M82 (14)	509.84

Nos. M69–M82 were on sale at the Vienna post office for a few days before the Armistice signing. They were never issued at the Army Post Offices. They exist imperf.; price, set $700.

MILITARY SEMI-POSTAL STAMPS.

Emperor Karl I Empress Zita

MSP7 MSP8

Typographed

1918 ***Perf. 12½x13*** **Unwmkd.**

MB1	MSP7	10h gray grn	22	28
MB2	MSP8	20h magenta	22	28
MB3	MSP7	45h blue	22	28

These stamps were sold at a premium of 10h each over face value. The surtax was for "Karl's Fund."

Nos. MB1–MB3 exist imperf. Price, set $10.

MILITARY NEWSPAPER STAMPS.

Mercury MN1

Typographed

1916 ***Perf. 12½*** **Unwmkd.**

MP1	MN1	2h blue	5	5
a.		Perf. 11½	1.75	1.00
b.		Perf. 12½x11½	125.00	*125.00*
MP2	MN1	6h orange	70	60
MP3	MN1	10h carmine	90	60
MP4	MN1	20h brown	50	55
a.		Perf. 11½	2.00	1.25

Exists imperf. Price, set $47.50.

NEWSPAPER STAMPS.

From 1851 to 1866, the Austrian Newspaper Stamps were also used in Lombardy-Venetia.

> Prices for unused stamps 1851–67 are for fine copies with original gum. Specimens without gum sell for about a third of the figures quoted.

Issues of the Monarchy.

Mercury

N1

Typographed.

Machine-made Paper.

Two Types.

Type I. The "G" of "Zeitungs" has no crossbar.
Type II. The "G" of "Zeitungs" has a crossbar.

1851–56 ***Imperf.*** **Unwmkd.**

P1	N1	(0.6kr) bl, type II	160.00	80.00
a.		bl, type I	185.00	125.00
b.		Ribbed paper	400.00	160.00
P2	N1	(6kr) yel, type I	*12,500.*	*7,500.*
P3	N1	(30kr) rose, type I	*17,500.*	*9,000.*
P4	N1	(6kr) scar, type II ('56)		
			37,500.	*40,000.*

From 1852 No. P3 and from 1856 No. P2 were used as 0.6 kreuzer values.

Pale shades of Nos. P2 and P3 sell at considerably lower prices.

Originals of Nos. P2 and P3 are usually in pale colors and poorly printed. Prices are for stamps clearly printed and in bright colors. Numerous reprints of Nos. P1 to P4 were made between 1866 and 1904. Those of Nos. P2 and P3 are always well printed and in much deeper colors. All reprints are in type I, but occasionally show faint traces of a crossbar on "G" of "ZEITUNGS."

N2 N3

Two Types of the 1858–59 Issue

Type I. Loops of the bow at the back of the head broken.

Type II. Loops complete. Wreath projects further at top of head.

1858–59 Embossed

P5	N2	(1kr) bl, type I	450.00	600.00
P6	N2	(1kr) lil, type II ('59)	625.00	250.00

1861

P7	N3	(1kr) gray	150.00	100.00
a.		(1kr) gray lil	350.00	135.00
b.		(1kr) dp lil	1,600.	450.00

The embossing on the reprints of the 1858–59 and 1861 issues is not as sharp as on the originals.

N4

1863

Unwmkd., or, after June 1864, Wmkd. "ZEITUNGS-MARKEN" in Double-lined Capitals across the Sheet. (91)

P8	N4	(1.05kr) gray	30.00	10.00
a.		Tête bêche pair	*20,000.*	
b.		(1.05kr) gray lil	60.00	17.50

The embossing of the reprints is not as sharp as on the originals.

Mercury

N5 N6

Typographed.

Wmkd. "ZEITUNGS-MARKEN" in Double-lined Capitals across the Sheet. (91)

Three Types.

Type I. Helmet not defined at back, more or less blurred. Two thick short lines in front of wing of helmet. Shadow on front of face not separated from hair.

Type II. Helmet distinctly defined. Four thin short lines in front of wing. Shadow on front of face clearly defined from hair.

Type III. Outer white circle around head is open at top (closed on types I and II). Greek border at top and bottom is wider than on types I and II.

1867-73 Coarse Print.

P9	N5	(1kr) vio, type I	55.00	1.75
a.		(1kr) vio, type II ('73)	210.00	15.00

1874-76 Fine Print.

P9B	N5	(1kr) vio, type III ('76)	40	22
c.		(1kr) gray lil, type I ('76)	160.00	22.50
d.		(1kr) vio, type II	40.00	4.00
e.		Double impression, type III		225.00

Stamps of this issue, except No. P9Bc, exist in many shades, from gray to lilac brown and deep violet. Stamps in type III exist also privately perforated or rouletted.

1880

P10	N6	½kr green	8.00	90

Nos. P9B and P10 also exist on thicker paper without sheet watermark and No. P10 exists with unofficial perforation.

N7

1899 ***Imperf.*** **Unwmkd.**

Without Varnish Bars.

P11	N7	2h dk bl	25	5
P12	N7	6h orange	3.25	1.40
P13	N7	10h brown	1.50	1.40
P14	N7	20h rose	2.00	2.00

1901 With Varnish Bars

P11a	N7	2h dk bl	1.00	30
P12a	N7	6h orange	14.00	15.00
P13a	N7	10h brown	12.50	12.50
P14a	N7	20h rose	25.00	30.00

Nos. P11 to P14 were re-issued in 1905.

Mercury

N8 N9

1908 ***Imperf.***

P15	N8	2h dk bl	1.75	8
a.		Tête bêche pair	375.00	375.00
P16	N8	6h orange	2.50	40
P17	N8	10h carmine	2.50	40
P18	N8	20h brown	2.50	30

All values are found on chalky, regular and thin ordinary paper. They exist privately perforated.

1916 ***Imperf.***

P19	N9	2h brown	5	5
P20	N9	4h green	20	50
P21	N9	6h dk bl	25	1.00
P22	N9	10h orange	25	50
P23	N9	30h claret	30	50
		Nos. P19-P23 (5)	1.05	2.55

Issues of the Republic.

Newspaper Stamps of 1916 Overprinted

1919

No.	Design	Description	Unused	Used
P24	N9	2h brown	5	5
P25	N9	4h green	8	*90*
P26	N9	6h dk bl	8	*1.40*
P27	N9	10h orange	25	*90*
P28	N9	30h claret	12	*1.40*
		Nos. P24-P28 (5)	58	*4.65*

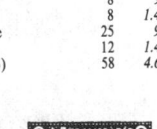

Mercury

N10 N11

1920–21 ***Imperf.***

No.	Design	Description	Unused	Used
P29	N10	2h violet	5	5
P30	N10	4h brown	5	6
P31	N10	5h slate	5	6
P32	N10	6h turq bl	5	6
P33	N10	8h green	5	6
P34	N10	9h yel ('21)	5	6
P35	N10	10h red	5	6
P36	N10	12h blue	5	12
P37	N10	15h lil ('21)	5	8
P38	N10	18h bl grn ('21)	5	8
P39	N10	20h orange	5	12
P40	N10	30h yel brn ('21)	5	5
P41	N10	45h grn ('21)	5	18
P42	N10	60h claret	5	28
P43	N10	72h choc ('21)	5	45
P44	N10	90h vio ('21)	10	45
P45	N10	1.20k red ('21)	8	45
P46	N10	2.40k yel grn ('21)	8	45
P47	N10	3k gray ('21)	10	45
		Nos. P29-P47 (19)	1.11	3.57

Nos. P37–P40, P42, P44 and P47 exist also on thick gray paper.

1921–22

No.	Design	Description	Unused	Used
P48	N11	45h gray	6	10
P49	N11	75h brn org ('22)	6	15
P50	N11	1.50k ol bis ('22)	6	22
P51	N11	1.80k gray bl ('22)	6	22
P52	N11	2.25k lt brn	6	22
P53	N11	3k dl grn ('22)	6	45
P54	N11	6k cl ('22)	6	45
P55	N11	7.50k bister	18	45
		Nos. P48-P55 (8)	60	2.26

Nos. P24-P55 exist privately perforated.

NEWSPAPER TAX STAMPS.

Prices for unused stamps 1853–59 are for copies in fine condition with gum. Specimens without gum sell for about one-third of the figures quoted.

Issues of the Monarchy.

NT1 NT2

Typographed

1853 ***Imperf.*** **Unwmkd.**

No.	Design	Description	Unused	Used
PR1	NT1	2kr green	2,100.	80.00

The reprints are in finer print than the more coarsely printed originals, and on a smooth toned paper.

Unwmkd. or, after June 1864, Wmkd. ZEITUNGS-MARKEN. (91)

1858-59 **Two Types.**

Type I. The banderol on the Crown of the left eagle touches the beak of the eagle.

Type II. The banderol does not touch the beak.

No.	Design	Description	Unused	Used
PR2	NT2	1kr bl, type II ('59)	50.00	9.00
a.		1kr bl, type I	700.00	150.00
b.		Printed on both sides, type II		
PR3	NT2	2kr brn, type II ('59)	25.00	7.50
a.		2kr red brn, type II	400.00	150.00
PR4	NT2	4kr brn, type I	475.00	*1,200.*

Nos. PR2a, PR3a, and PR4 were printed only on unwatermarked paper. Nos. PR2 and PR3 exist on unwatermarked and watermarked paper.

Nos. PR2 and PR3 exist in coarse and (after 1874) in fine print, like the contemporary postage stamps.

The reprints of the 4kr brown are of type II and on a smooth toned paper.

NT3 NT4

1877 **Redrawn.**

No.	Design	Description	Unused	Used
PR5	NT3	1kr blue	15.00	1.25
a.		1kr pale ultra		*1,200.*
PR6	NT3	2kr brown	15.00	1.50

In the redrawn stamps the shield is larger and the vertical bar has eight lines above the white square and nine below, instead of five.

Nos. PR5 and PR6 exist also watermarked "WECHSEL" instead of "ZEITUNGS-MARKEN".

1890

No.	Design	Description	Unused	Used
PR7	NT4	1kr brown	12.50	80
PR8	NT4	2kr green	14.00	1.50

Nos. PR5 to PR8 exist with private perforation.

NT5

Wmkd. "STEMPEL-MARKEN" in Double-lined Capitals, across the Sheet. (91)

Perf. 13, 12½

No.	Design	Description	Unused	Used
PR9	NT5	25kr carmine	125.00	160.00

Nos. PR1 to PR9 did not pay postage, but were a fiscal tax, collected by the postal authorities on newspapers.

SPECIAL HANDLING STAMPS (For Printed Matter Only.)

Issues of the Monarchy.

Mercury

SH1

1916 ***Perf. 12½*** **Unwmkd.**

No.	Design	Description	Unused	Used
QE1	SH1	2h cl, *yel*	45	60
QE2	SH1	5h dp grn, *yel*	45	60

SH2

1917 ***Perf. 12½***

No.	Design	Description	Unused	Used
QE3	SH2	2h cl, *yel*	18	20
a.		Pair, imperf. between	300.00	300.00
b.		Perf. 11½x12½	62.50	87.50
c.		Perf. 12½x11½	87.50	125.00
d.		Perf. 11½	1.75	2.50
QE4	SH2	5h dp grn, *yel*	18	20
a.		Pair, imperf. between	275.00	275.00
b.		Perf. 11½x12½	62.50	87.50
c.		Perf. 12½x11½	87.50	125.00
d.		Perf. 11½	1.75	2.50

Nos. QE1–QE4 exist imperforate.

Issues of the Republic.

Nos. QE3 and QE4 Overprinted

Deutschösterreich

1919

No.	Design	Description	Unused	Used
QE5	SH2	2h cl, *yel*	5	25
a.		Inverted overprint	325.00	
b.		Perf. 11½x12½	6.00	10.00
c.		Perf. 12½x11½	80.00	110.00
QE6	SH2	5h dp grn, *yel*	5	35
a.		Perf. 11½x12½	2.50	4.50
b.		Perf. 12½x11½	30.00	45.00

Nos. QE5 and QE6 exist imperforate.

SH3

1921 **Dark Blue Surcharge.**

No.	Design	Description	Unused	Used
QE7	SH3	50h on 2h cl, *yel*	6	8

SH4

1922 ***Perf. 12½***

No.	Design	Description	Unused	Used
QE8	SH4	50h lil, *yel*	6	18

Nos. QE5 to QE8 exist in vertical pairs, imperforate between. No. QE8 exists imperforate.

OCCUPATION STAMPS.

Issued under Italian Occupation.

Issued in Trieste.

Austrian Stamps of 1916-18 Overprinted

Regno d'Italia
Venezia Giulia
3. XI. 18.

1918 ***Perf. 12½.*** **Unwmkd.**

No.	Design	Description	Unused	Used
N1	A37	3h brt vio	30	38
a.		Double overprint	13.00	16.00
b.		Inverted ovpt.	13.00	16.00
N2	A37	5h lt grn	20	38
a.		Inverted ovpt.	13.00	16.00
b.		"3.XI." omitted	13.00	13.00
c.		Double overprint		16.00
N3	A37	6h dp org	38	48
N4	A37	10h magenta	30	38
a.		Inverted overprint	9.00	11.00
N5	A37	12h lt bl	95	1.25
a.		Double overprint	13.00	16.00
N6	A42	15h dl red	30	38
a.		Inverted ovpt.	11.00	15.00
b.		Double overprint	13.00	16.00
c.		"3.XI." omitted	13.00	13.00
N7	A42	20h dk grn	30	38
a.		Inverted ovpt.	9.00	11.00
b.		"3.XI." omitted	13.00	15.00
c.		Double overprint	26.00	
N8	A42	25h dp bl	2.50	3.25
a.		Inverted ovpt.	37.50	45.00
b.		"3.XI." omitted	75.00	75.00
N9	A42	30h dl vio	75	1.00
N10	A39	40h ol grn	26.00	32.50
N11	A39	50h dk grn	1.10	1.50
N12	A39	60h dp bl	1.90	2.50
N13	A39	80h org brn	1.10	1.50
a.		Inverted overprint		
N14	A39	1k car, *yel*	1.10	1.50
a.		Double ovpt.	26.00	26.00
N15	A40	2k lt bl	45.00	55.00
N16	A40	4k yel grn	100.00	130.00

Handstamped.

No.	Design	Description	Unused	Used
N17	A40	10k dp vio	*10,000.*	*12,000.*

Granite Paper.

No.	Design	Description	Unused	Used
N18	A40	2k lt bl		
N19	A40	3k car rose	75.00	92.50

Some authorities question the authenticity of No. N18. Counterfeits of Nos. N10, N15–N19 are plentiful.

Italian Stamps of 1901-18 Overprinted

Venezia
Giulia

Wmkd. Crown. (140) ***Perf. 14.***

No.	Design	Description	Unused	Used
N20	A42	1c brown	30	75
a.		Inverted overprint	6.00	9.00
N21	A43	2c org brn	30	75
a.		Inverted overprint	4.50	*6.75*
N22	A48	5c green	15	55
a.		Inverted overprint	9.00	*13.00*
b.		Double overprint	26.00	
N23	A48	10c claret	15	55
a.		Inverted overprint	13.00	*18.00*
b.		Double overprint	26.00	
N24	A50	20c brn org	18	55
a.		Inverted overprint	18.00	*27.50*
b.		Double overprint	26.00	*37.50*
N25	A49	25c blue	22	55
a.		Double overprint	*75.00*	
b.		Invtd. overprint	26.00	*37.50*
N26	A49	40c brown	1.50	*3.75*
a.		Inverted overprint	*65.00*	
N27	A45	45c ol grn	38	90
a.		Inverted overprint	26.00	*37.50*
N28	A49	50c violet	55	*1.40*
N29	A49	60c brn car	6.00	*15.00*
N30	A46	1l brn & grn	2.50	*6.25*
		Nos. N20-N30 (11)	12.23	*31.00*

Italian Stamps of 1901-18 Surcharged

Venezia
Giulia
5 Heller

No.	Design	Description	Unused	Used
N31	A48	5h on 5c grn	22	48
a.		"5" omitted	18.00	*27.50*
b.		Inverted surch.	22.50	*32.50*
N32	A50	20h on 20c brn org	22	45
a.		Double surcharge	22.50	*32.50*

Issued in the Trentino.

Austrian Stamps of 1916-18 Overprinted

Regno d Italia
Trentino
3 nov 1918

1918 ***Perf. 12½*** **Unwmkd.**

No.	Design	Description	Unused	Used
N33	A37	3h brt vio	90	1.25
a.		Double ovpt.	26.00	*37.50*
b.		Inverted ovpt.	22.50	*30.00*
N34	A37	5h lt grn	55	80
a.		"8 nov. 1918"	*1,000.*	
b.		Inverted ovpt.	22.50	*30.00*
N35	A37	6h dp org	24.00	32.50
N36	A37	10h magenta	75	1.10
a.		"8 nov. 1918"	30.00	40.00
N37	A37	12h lt bl	75.00	110.00
N38	A42	15h dl red	2.00	3.00
N39	A42	20h dk grn	30	45
a.		"8 nov. 1918"	45.00	*60.00*
b.		Double ovpt.	26.00	37.50
c.		Inverted ovpt.	9.00	11.00
N40	A42	25h dp bl	16.00	24.00
N41	A42	30h dl vio	3.75	5.50
N42	A39	40h ol grn	24.00	32.50
N43	A39	50h dk grn	9.00	13.00
a.		Inverted ovpt.	37.50	47.50
N44	A39	60h dp bl	16.00	24.00
a.		Double ovpt.	45.00	*60.00*
N45	A39	80h org brn	26.00	37.50
N46	A39	90h red vio	375.00	550.00
N47	A39	1k car, *yel*	26.00	37.50
N48	A40	2k lt bl	115.00	170.00
N49	A40	4k yel grn	*600.00*	*925.00*
N50	A40	10k dp vio	*33,000.*	

Granite Paper.

N51	A40	2k lt bl	*185.00*	

Counterfeits of Nos. N33–N51 are plentiful.

Italian Stamps of 1901-18 Overprinted **Venezia Tridentina**

Wmkd. Crown. (140) *Perf. 14.*

N52	A42	1c brown	38	90
a.		Inverted overprint	11.00	16.00
N53	A43	2c org brn	38	90
a.		Inverted overprint	11.00	16.00
N54	A48	5c green	38	90
a.		Inverted overprint	11.00	16.00
b.		Double overprint	15.00	22.50
N55	A48	10c claret	38	90
a.		Inverted overprint	15.00	22.50
b.		Double overprint	15.00	22.50
N56	A50	20c brn org	38	90
a.		Inverted overprint	15.00	22.50
N57	A49	40c brown	7.50	19.00
N58	A45	45c ol grn	4.50	11.00
a.		Double overprint	47.50	*75.00*
N59	A49	50c violet	4.50	11.00
N60	A46	1 l brn & grn	4.50	11.00
a.		Double overprint	47.50	*75.00*
		Nos. N52-N60 (9)	22.90	56.50

Italian Stamps of 1906-18 Surcharged **Venezia Tridentina 5 Heller**

N61	A48	5h on 5c grn	18	50
N62	A48	10h on 10c cl	18	50
a.		Inverted overprint	19.00	*26.00*
N63	A50	20h on 20c brn org	18	50
a.		Double surcharge	19.00	*26.00*

General Issue.

Italian Stamps of 1901-18 Surcharged **5 centesimi di corona**

1919

N64	A42	1c on 1c brn	15	38
a.		Inverted surcharge	3.75	5.50
N65	A43	2c on 2c org brn	15	38
a.		Double surcharge	67.50	
b.		Inverted surcharge	1.90	3.00
N66	A48	5c on 5c grn	15	38
a.		Inverted surcharge	9.00	13.00
b.		Double surcharge	18.00	18.00
N67	A48	10c on 10c cl	15	38
a.		Inverted surcharge	9.00	13.00
b.		Double surcharge	18.00	*27.50*
N68	A50	20c on 20c brn org	15	38
a.		Double surcharge	26.00	*37.50*
N69	A49	25c on 25c bl	15	38
a.		Double surcharge	26.00	26.00
N70	A49	40c on 40c brn	15	38
a.		"ccrona"	30.00	*45.00*
N71	A45	45c on 45c ol grn	15	38
a.		Inverted surcharge	26.00	37.50
N72	A49	50c on 50c vio	15	38
N73	A49	60c on 60c brn car	15	38
a.		"00" for "60"	30.00	*45.00*

Surcharged: **1 corona**

N74	A46	1 cor on 1 l brn & grn	15	38
		Nos. N64-N74 (11)	1.65	4.18

Surcharges similar to these but differing in style or arrangement of type were used in Dalmatia.

SPECIAL DELIVERY STAMPS.

Issued in Trieste.

Special Delivery Stamp of Italy of 1903 Overprinted

Venezia Giulia

Wmkd. Crown. (140)

1918 *Perf. 14.*

NE1	SD1	25c rose red	4.50	11.00
a.		Invtd. ovpt.	30.00	45.00

General Issue.

1919

Special Delivery Stamps of Italy of 1903-09 Surcharged **25 centesimi di corona**

NE2	SD1	25c on 25c rose	18	38
a.		Double surcharge	15.00	*22.50*
NE3	SD2	30c on 30c bl & rose	26	75

POSTAGE DUE STAMPS.

Issued in Trieste.

Postage Due Stamps of Italy, 1870-94, Overprinted **Venezia Giulia**

Wmkd. Crown. (140)

1918 *Perf. 14.*

NJ1	D3	5c buff & mag	15	55
a.		Inverted overprint	3.75	5.50
b.		Double overprint	45.00	
NJ2	D3	10c buff & mag	15	55
a.		Inverted overprint	13.00	*19.00*
NJ3	D3	20c buff & mag	22	55
a.		Double overprint	45.00	
b.		Inverted overprint	13.00	*19.00*
NJ4	D3	30c buff & mag	38	90
NJ5	D3	40c buff & mag	3.75	9.25
a.		Inverted overprint	67.50	*100.00*
NJ6	D3	50c buff & mag	9.00	22.50
a.		Inverted overprint	67.50	*100.00*
NJ7	D3	1 l bl & mag	24.00	60.00
		Nos. NJ1-NJ7 (7)	37.65	94.30

General Issue.

Postage Due Stamps of Italy, 1870–1903 Surcharged **5 centesimi di corona**

1919

NJ8	D3	5c on 5c buff & mag	18	55
a.		Inverted overprint	3.75	5.50
NJ9	D3	10c on 10c buff & mag	18	55
a.		Center and surcharge invtd.	18.00	*27.00*
NJ10	D3	20c on 20c buff & mag	22	55
a.		Double overprint	37.50	*55.00*
NJ11	D3	30c on 30c buff & mag	22	55
NJ12	D3	40c on 40c buff & mag	22	55
NJ13	D3	50c on 50c buff & mag	22	55

Surcharged **una corona**

NJ14	D3	1 cor on 1 l bl & mag	22	55
NJ15	D3	2 cor on 2 l bl & mag	8.25	20.00
NJ16	D3	5 cor on 5 l bl & mag	8.25	20.00
		Nos. NJ8-NJ16 (9)	17.96	43.85

A. M. G. Issue for Austria.

Issued jointly by the Allied Military Government of the United States and Great Britain, for civilian use in areas under American, British and French occupation. (Upper Austria, Salzburg, Tyrol, Vorarlberg, Styria and Carinthia).

OS1

Lithographed.

1945 *Perf. 11.* **Unwmkd.**

4N1	OS1	1g aqua	6	12
4N2	OS1	3g dp org	5	5
4N3	OS1	4g buff	5	5
4N4	OS1	5g brt grn	5	5
4N5	OS1	6g red vio	5	5
4N6	OS1	8g rose pink	5	5
4N7	OS1	10g lt gray	5	8
4N8	OS1	12g pale buff brn	5	5
4N9	OS1	15g rose red	5	5
4N10	OS1	20g cop brn	5	5
4N11	OS1	25g dp bl	5	6
4N12	OS1	30g brt vio	5	5
4N13	OS1	40g lt ultra	5	8
4N14	OS1	60g lt ol grn	5	18
4N15	OS1	1s dk vio	5	28
4N16	OS1	2s yellow	12	30
4N17	OS1	5s dp ultra	25	45
		Nos. 4N1-4N17 (17)	1.13	2.00

AUSTRIAN OFFICES ABROAD

Offices in Crete.

100 CENTIMES=1 FRANC

These stamps were on sale and usable at all Austrian post-offices in Crete and in the Turkish Empire.

> Used prices are italicized for stamps often found with false cancellations.

Stamps of Austria of 1899–1901 Issue, Surcharged in Black:

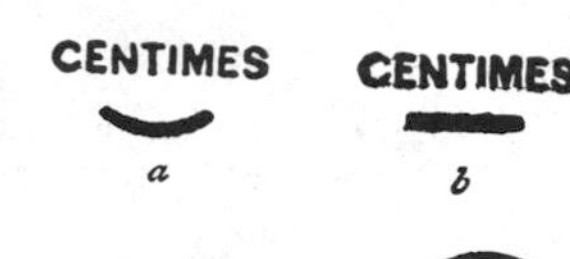

a *b*

FRANC

c *d*

Granite Paper.

1903–04 *Perf. 12½, 13½* **Unwmkd.**

With Varnish Bars

(On Nos. 73a, 75a, 77a, 81a)

1	A15 (a)	5c on 5h bl grn	1.90	2.75
2	A16 (b)	10c on 10h rose	90	*3.00*
3	A16 (b)	25c on 25h ultra	32.50	22.50
4	A17 (c)	50c on 50h gray bl	5.75	*45.00*

Without Varnish Bars

(On Nos. 83, 83a, 84, 85)

5	A18 (d)	1fr on 1k car rose	2.75	*47.50*
a.		1fr on 1k car	5.00	
b.		Horiz. or vert. pair, imperf. between	225.00	
6	A18 (d)	2fr on 2k gray lil ('04)	10.00	*165.00*
7	A18 (d)	4fr on 4k gray grn ('04)	11.00	*250.00*

Surcharged on Austrian Stamps of 1904–05.

1905 **Without Varnish Bars**

(On Nos. 89, 97)

8	A19 (a)	5c on 5h bl grn	40.00	20.00
9	A20 (b)	10c on 10h car	1.10	*5.75*

With Varnish Bars.

(On Nos. 89a, 97a, 99a, 103a)

8a	A19 (a)	5c on 5h bl grn	4.50	4.
9a	A20 (b)	10c on 10h car	22.50	14.
10	A20 (b)	25c on 25h ultra	90	*45.*
11	A21 (b)	50c on 50h dl bl	1.25	*185.*

Surcharged on Austrian Stamps and Type of 1906-07.

1907 *Perf. 12½, 13½.*

Without Varnish Bars

12	A19 (a)	5c on 5h yel grn (#90)	1.10	*3.*
13	A20 (b)	10c on 10h car (#92)	1.40	*11.*
14	A20 (b)	15c on 15h vio	1.75	*16.*

A5

A6

1908 **Typographed** *Perf. 12½*

15	A5	5c grn, *yel*	38	2
16	A5	10c scar, *rose*	45	4
17	A5	15c brn, *buff*	50	*3.0*
18	A5	25c dp bl, *bl*	13.00	3.0

Engraved.

19	A6	50c lake, *yel*	2.75	*20.0*
20	A6	1fr brn, *gray*	3.75	*30.0*
a.		Vert pair, imperf. btwn.	225.00	
		Nos. 15-20 (6)	20.83	

Nos. 15 to 18 are on paper colored on the surface only. All values exist imperforate.

Issued to commemorate the sixtieth year of the reign of Emperor Franz Josef, for permanent use.

Paper Colored Through.

1914 **Typographed.**

21	A5	10c rose, *rose*	1.75	*650.00*
22	A5	25c ultra, *bl*	75	*72.50*

Nos. 21 and 22 exist imperforate.

Offices in the Turkish Empire.

From 1863 to 1867 the stamps of Lombardy-Venetia (Nos. 15 to 24) were used at the Austrian Offices in the Turkish Empire.

> Prices for unused stamps are for copies with gum. Specimens without gum sell for about one-third the figures quoted.
>
> Used prices are italicized for stamps often found with false cancellations.

100 SOLDI=1 FLORIN
40 PARAS=1 PIASTRE

A1

A2

Typographed

Wmkd.

"BRIEF-MARKEN" in Double-lined Capitals, across the Sheet. (91)

Two different printing methods were used, as in the 1867-74 issues of Austria. They may be distinguished by the coarse or fine lines of the hair and whiskers.

1867 **Coarse Print.** *Perf. 9½.*

1	A1	2sld orange	1.10	*14.00*
a.		2sld yel	50.00	25.00
2	A1	3sld green	72.50	22.50
a.		3sld dk grn	85.00	28.50

3 A1 5sld red 72.50 10.00
a. 5sld car 80.00 14.00
4 A1 10sld blue 72.50 1.25
a. 10sld lt bl 80.00 2.25
b. 10sld dk bl 80.00 2.50
5 A1 15sld brown 11.00 4.50
a. 15sld dk brn 37.50 13.00
b. 15sld redsh brn 13.00 9.50
6 A1 25sld gray lil 9.00 *22.50*
a. 25sld brn vio 11.00 *25.00*
7 A2 50sld brn, perf. 10½ 1.10 *37.50*
a. Perf. 12 80.00 52.50
b. Perf. 13 265.00
k. Perf. 9 or 10½x9 22.50 *45.00*
l. 50sld pale red brn, perf. 12 45.00 47.50
m. Vertical pair, imperf. between 350.00 *800.00*
n. Horiz. pair, imperf. btwn. 400.00 *900.00*

Fine Print.

Perf. 9, 9½, 10½ and Compound.

1876-83

7C A1 2sld yel ('83) 18 *1,200.*
7D A1 3sld grn ('78) 1.10 *16.00*
7E A1 5sld red ('78) 38 *15.00*
7F A1 10sld blue 60.00 75
7I A1 15sld org brn ('81) 5.25 *90.00*
7J A1 25sld gray lil ('83) 55 *180.00*

The 10 soldi has been reprinted in deep dull blue, perforated 10½.

A3

1883 ***Perf. 9½, 10, 10½.***

8 A3 2sld brown 18 *72.50*
9 A3 3sld green 90 *9.50*
10 A3 5sld rose 18 *5.50*
11 A3 10sld blue 75 38
12 A3 20sld gray 2.00 *3.75*
13 A3 50sld red lil 2.00 *9.00*

A4 A5

10 PARAS ON 3 SOLDI:

Type I. Surcharge 16½mm. across. "PARA" about ½mm. above bottom of "10". 2mm. space between "10" and "P"; 1½mm. between "A" and "10". Perf. 9½ only.

Type II. Surcharge 15½ to 16mm. across. "PARA" on same line with figures or slightly higher or lower. 1½mm. space between "10" and "P"; 1mm. between "A" and "10". Perf. 9½ and 10.

1886 ***Perf. 9½ and 10***

14 A4 10pa on 3sld grn, type II 28 *3.75*
a. 10pa on 3sld grn, type I 250.00 300.00
b. Inverted surcharge, type I *2,250.*

1888

15 A5 10pa on 3kr grn 3.75 4.50
a. "01 PARA 10" *500.00*
16 A5 20pa on 5kr rose 75 *5.00*
17 A5 1pi on 10kr bl 47.50 1.10
a. Perf. 13½ 160.00
b. Double surcharge 160.00
18 A5 2pi on 20kr gray 1.75 2.75
19 A5 5pi on 50kr vio 2.75 *13.00*

A6

Granite Paper.

1890-92 ***Perf. 9 to 13½*** **Unwmkd.**

20 A6 8pa on 2kr brn ('92) 18 20
a. Perf. 9½ 3.75 2.25
21 A6 10pa on 3kr grn 75 18
a. Pair, imperf. between 90.00
22 A6 20pa on 5kr rose 18 18
23 A6 1pi on 10kr ultra 38 8
24 A6 2pi on 20kr ol grn 11.00 *18.50*
25 A6 5pi on 50kr vio 14.00 *45.00*

See note after Austria No. 65 on missing numerals, etc.

A7 A8

1891 ***Perf. 9 to 13½***

26 A7 2pi on 20kr ol grn 5.25 32
a. Perf. 9½ 90.00 14.00
27 A7 5pi on 50kr vio 3.75 2.00

There are two types of the surcharge on No. 26.

1892 ***Perf. 10½, 11½***

28 A8 10pi on 1gld bl 14.00 18.00
29 A8 20pi on 2gld car 14.00 22.50
a. Double surcharge

1896 ***Perf. 10½, 11½, 12½***

30 A8 10pi on 1gld pale lil 14.00 18.00
31 A8 20pi on 2gld gray grn 45.00 45.00

A9 A10

A11 A12

Perf. 10½, 12½, 13½ and Compound.

1900 **Without Varnish Bars**

32 A9 10pa on 5h bl grn 4.50 1.00
33 A10 20pa on 10h rose 4.50 1.00
b. Perf. 12½x10½ 265.00 32.50
34 A10 1pi on 25h ultra 4.50 18
35 A11 2pi on 50h gray bl 9.50 1.40
36 A12 5pi on 1k car rose 1.40 18
a. 5pi on 1k car 1.75 70
b. Horiz. or vert. pair, imperf. between 135.00
37 A12 10pi on 2k gray lil 3.75 2.25
a. Horizontal pair, imperf. between
38 A12 20pi on 4k gray grn 2.85 *5.00*
Nos. 32-38 (7) 31.00 *11.01*

In the surcharge on Nos. 37 and 38 "piaster" is printed "PIAST."

1901 **With Varnish Bars.**

32a A9 10pa on 5h bl grn 2.85 1.50
33a A10 20pa on 10h rose 2.85 *72.50*
34a A10 1pi on 25h ultra 2.25 32
35a A11 2pi on 50h gray bl 4.50 1.40

A13 A14

A15

1906 ***Perf. 12½ to 13½***

Without Varnish Bars.

39 A13 10pa dk grn 15.00 1.10
40 A14 20pa rose 95 38
41 A14 1pi ultra 38 18
42 A15 2pi gray bl 1.10 50

1903 **With Varnish Bars.**

39a A13 10pa dk grn 6.00 90
40a A14 20pa rose 2.75 38
41a A14 1pi ultra 2.25 18
42a A15 2pi gray bl 130.00 1.10

1907 **Without Varnish Bars.**

43 A13 10pa yel grn 38 *1.50*
45 A14 30pa violet 65 *2.50*

A16 A17

1908 **Typographed.** ***Perf. 12½.***

46 A16 10pa grn, *yel* 18 10
47 A16 20pa scar, *rose* 28 15
48 A16 30pa brn, *buff* 40 55
49 A16 1pi dp bl, *bl* 16.00 6
50 A16 60pa vio, *bluish* 75 3.00

Engraved

51 A17 2pi lake, *yel* 45 10
52 A17 5pi brn, *gray* 65 55
53 A17 10pi grn, *yel* 1.10 1.40
54 A17 20pi bl, *gray* 2.00 3.00
Nos. 46-54 (9) 21.81 8.91

Nos. 46 to 50 are on paper colored on the surface only. Issued in commemoration of the sixtieth year of the reign of Emperor Franz Josef I for permanent use. All values exist imperforate.

1913-14 **Typographed**

Paper Colored Through.

57 A16 20pa rose, *rose* ('14) 1.10 *225.00*
58 A16 1pi ultra, *bl* 45 40

Nos. 57 and 58 exist imperforate.

POSTAGE DUE STAMPS.

D1 D2

Black Surcharge.

1902 ***Perf. 12½, 13½*** **Unwmkd.**

J1 D1 10pa on 5h grn 1.65 2.75
J2 D1 20pa on 10h grn 1.65 2.50
J3 D1 1pi on 20h grn 2.75 3.75
J4 D1 2pi on 40h grn 2.75 2.75
J5 D1 5pi on 100h grn 4.00 1.65
Nos. J1-J5 (5) 12.80 13.40

Shades of Nos. J1 to J5 exist, varying from yellowish green to dark green.

1908 **Typographed.** ***Perf. 12½.***

J6 D2 ¼pi green 3.75 6.50
J7 D2 ½pi green 1.75 *4.50*
J8 D2 1pi green 2.50 *6.50*
J9 D2 1½pi green 75 *8.00*
J10 D2 2pi green 2.75 *10.00*
J11 D2 5pi green 2.75 *6.50*
J12 D2 10pi green 22.50 *100.00*
J13 D2 20pi green 18.50 *125.00*
J14 D2 30pi green 14.00 9.00
Nos. J6-J14 (9) 69.25 *276.00*

Nos. J6 to J14 exist in distinct shades of green and on thick chalky, regular and thin ordinary paper. All values exist imperforate.

LOMBARDY-VENETIA

(lŏm'bĕr·dĭ; lŭm'-·; vĕ·nē'shĭ·ȧ;- shȧ)

Formerly a kingdom in the north of Italy forming part of the Austrian Empire. Milan and Venice were the two principal cities. Lombardy was annexed to Sardinia in 1859, and Venetia to the kingdom of Italy in 1866.

100 CENTESIMI = 1 LIRA
100 SOLDI = 1 FLORIN (1858)

Prices of the earliest Lombardy-Venetia stamps vary according to condition. Quotations for Nos. 1-6, PR1-PR3 are for fine copies. Very fine to superb specimens sell at much higher prices, and inferior or poor copies sell at reduced prices, depending on the condition of the individual specimen.

Prices for unused stamps are for fine copies with gum. Specimens without gum sell for about one-quarter of the prices quoted.

Coat of Arms
A1

15 CENTESIMI:

Type I. "5" of "15" is on a level with the "1."

Type II. "5" is a trifle sideways and is higher than the "1."

45 CENTESIMI:

Type I. Lower part of "45" is lower than "Centes."

Type II. Lower part of "45" is on a level with lower part of "Centes."

Wmkd. K. K. H. M. in Sheet or Unwmkd.

1850 **Typographed** ***Imperf.***

Thick to Thin Paper.

1 A1 5c buff 900.00 75.00
a. Printed on both sides *6,000.* 150.00
b. 5c yel *4,500.* 400.00
c. 5c org 900.00 90.00
d. 5c lem yel *800.00*
3 A1 10c black 1,300. 65.00
a. 10c gray blk 1,400. 75.00
4 A1 15c pale red, type II 275.00 2.25
b. 15c red, type I *1,400.* 12.50
c. Ribbed paper, type II *12,500.* 200.00
d. Ribbed paper, type I *7,500.* 65.00
e. Laid paper, type II *4,000.*
5 A1 30c brown 1,100. 4.25
a. Ribbed paper 3,000. 32.50
6 A1 45c bl, type II *3,250.* 10.00
a. 45c bl, type I *5,500.* 17.50
b. Ribbed paper, type I *12,500.* 135.00

The note about the paper of the 1850 issue of Austria will also apply here. No. 1 and its minor varieties exist only on hand-made paper.

The reprints are in brighter colors.

A2 A3 A4

A5 A6

Two Types of Each Value.

Type I. Loops of the bow at the back of the head broken.

Type II. Loops complete. Wreath projects further at top of head.

1858-62 Embossed. *Perf. 14½.*

7	A2	2s yel, type II	325.00	55.00
a.		2s yel, type I	900.00	300.00
8	A3	3s blk, type II	1,300.	85.00
a.		3s blk, type I	675.00	175.00
b.		Perf. 16, type I		400.00
c.		Perf. 15x16 or 16x15, type I	*1,200.*	350.00
9	A3	3s grn, type II ('62)	250.00	50.00
10	A4	5s red, type II	135.00	3.00
a.		5s red, type I	225.00	8.50
b.		Printed on both sides, type II		*2,250.*
11	A5	10s brn, type II	625.00	9.00
a.		10s brn, type I	180.00	30.00
12	A6	15s bl, type II	650.00	11.00
a.		15s bl, type I	900.00	50.00

The reprints are of type II and are perforated 10½, 11, 11½, 12, 12½ and 13. There are also imperforate reprints of Nos. 7, 8 and 9.

A7

A8

1861-62 *Perf. 14.*

13	A7	5s red	725.00	2.25
14	A7	10s brn ('62)	675.00	15.00

The reprints are perforated 9, 9½, 10½, 11, 12, 12½ and 13. There are also imperforate reprints of the 2 and 3s.

The 2, 3 and 15s of this type exist only as reprints.

1863

15	A8	2s yellow	75.00	95.00
16	A8	3s green	550.00	60.00
17	A8	5s rose	550.00	9.00
18	A8	10s blue	1,350.	50.00
19	A8	15s yel brn	1,000.	85.00

Wmkd. "BRIEF-MARKEN" in Double-lined Capitals across the Sheet. (91)

1864-65 *Perf. 9½.*

20	A8	2s yel ('65)	75.00	*225.00*
21	A8	3s green	12.50	10.00
22	A8	5s rose	1.50	1.25
23	A8	10s blue	12.50	4.25
24	A8	15s yel brn	17.50	17.50

The reprints are perforated 10½ and 13. There are also imperforate reprints of the 2s and 3s.

NEWSPAPER TAX STAMPS.

From 1853 to 1858 the Austrian Newspaper Tax Stamp 2kr green (No. PR1) was also used in Lombardy-Venetia, at the value of 10 centesimi.

NT1

Type I. The banderol of the left eagle touches the beak of the eagle.

Type II. The banderol does not touch the beak.

Typographed

1858-59 *Imperf.* Unwmkd.

PR1	NT1	1kr blk, type I ('59)	1,150.	*3,250.*
PR2	NT1	2kr red, type II ('59)	180.00	55.00
PR3	NT1	4kr red, type I	*40,000.*	*3,000.*

No. PR2 exists also with watermark "ZEITUNGS-MARKEN" (91).

The reprints are on a smooth toned paper and are all of type II.

AZERBAIJAN

(ă'zĕr·bī'jan'; ăz'ĕr-)

(Azerbaidjan)

LOCATION—Southernmost part of Russia in Eastern Europe. Bounded by Georgia, Dagestan, Caspian Sea, Persia and Armenia.

GOVT.—A Soviet Socialist Republic.

AREA—32,686 sq. mi.

POP.—2,096,973 (1923).

CAPITAL—Baku.

100 Kopecks = 1 Ruble

National Republic.

Standard Bearer
A1

Farmer at Sunset
A2

Baku
A3

Temple of Eternal Fires
A4

Lithographed

1919 *Imperf.* Unwmkd.

1	A1	10k multi	15	20
2	A1	20k multi	15	20
3	A2	40k grn, yel & blk	15	20
4	A2	60k red, yel & blk	15	20
5	A2	1r bl, yel & blk	25	35
6	A3	2r red, bis & blk	25	35
7	A3	5r bl, bis & blk	35	60
8	A3	10r ol grn, bis & blk	50	70
9	A4	25r bl, red & blk	90	1.10
10	A4	50r ol grn, red & blk	1.00	1.25
		Nos. 1-10 (10)	3.85	5.15

The two printings of Nos. 1-10 are distinguished by the grayish or thin white paper. Both have yellowish gum.

Soviet Socialist Republic.

Symbols of Labor
A5

Oil Well
A6

Bibi Eibatt Oil Field
A7

Khan's Palace, Baku
A8

Globe and Workers
A9

Maiden's Tower, Baku
A10

Blacksmiths
A12

Goukasoff House
A11

Hall of Judgment, Baku
A13

1922

15	A5	1r gray grn	20	35
16	A6	2r ol blk	20	35
17	A7	5r gray brn	20	35
18	A8	10r gray	50	65
19	A9	25r org brn	20	40
20	A10	50r violet	20	40
21	A11	100r dl red	35	50
22	A12	150r blue	35	50
23	A9	250r vio & buff	35	50
24	A13	400r dk bl	35	50
25	A12	500r gray vio & blk	35	50
26	A13	1000r dk bl & rose	35	50
27	A8	2000r bl & blk	35	50
28	A7	3000r brn & bl	35	50
a.		Tête bêche pair	14.00	15.00
29	A11	5000r *ol grn*	60	75
		Nos. 15-29 (15)	4.90	7.25

Counterfeits exist of Nos. 1-29.

Stamps of 1922 Handstamped from Metal Dies in a Numbering Machine

15000

1922

32	A5	10.000r on 1r gray grn	7.00	7.50
33	A7	15.000r on 5r gray brn	9.50	10.00
34	A9	33.000r on 250r vio & buff	3.50	3.5
35	A7	50.000r on 3.000r brn & bl	5.00	5.0
36	A8	66.000r on 2.000r bl & blk	10.00	9.0
		Nos. 32-36 (5)	35.00	35.0

Same Surcharges on Regular Issue and Semi-Postal Stamps of 1922.

1922-23

36A	A7	500r on 5r gray brn	80.00	90.0
37	A6	1.000r on 2r ol blk	12.50	12.5
38	A8	2.000r on 10r gray	4.00	4.0
39	A8	5.000r on 2.000r bl & blk	2.25	2.2
40	A11	15.000r on 5.000r *ol grn*	9.00	9.0
41	A5	20.000r on 1r gray grn	10.00	10.0
42	SP1	25.000r on 500r bl & pale bl	32.50	
43	A7	50.000r on 5r gray brn	15.00	15.0
44	SP2	50.000r on 1.000r brn & bis	32.50	
45	A11	50.000r on 5.000r *ol grn*	4.50	3.5
45A	A8	60.000r on 2.000r bl & blk	15.00	18.0
46	A11	70.000r on 5.000r *ol grn*	24.00	24.0
47	A6	100.000r on 2r ol blk	12.00	12.0
48	A8	200.000r on 10r gray	5.00	5.0
49	A9	200.000r on 25r org brn	19.00	19.0
50	A7	300.000r on 3.000r brn & bl	5.00	5.00
51	A8	500.000r on 2.000r bl & blk	11.00	10.00

Revalued.

52	A7	500r on 15.000r on 5r gray brn	37.50	*70.00*
53	A11	15.000r on 70.000r on 5.000r *ol grn*	37.50	*70.00*
54	A7	300.000r on 50.000r on 3.000r brn & bl	60.00	*70.00*
55	A8	500.000r on 66.000r on 2.000r bl & blk	67.50	*100.00*

The surcharged semi-postal stamps were used for regular postage.

Same Surcharges on Stamps of 1919.

57	A1	25.000r on 10k grn, bl, red & blk	60	90
58	A1	50.000r on 20k bl, red, grn & blk	60	90
59	A2	75.000r on 40k grn, yel & blk	1.65	2.25
60	A2	100.000r on 60k red, yel & blk	60	85
61	A2	200.000r on 1r bl, yel & blk	60	85
62	A3	300.000r on 2r red, bis & blk	75	1.00
63	A3	500.000r on 5r bl, bis & blk	90	1.00
64	A2	750.000r on 40k grn, yel & blk	3.00	2.50
		Nos. 57-64 (8)	8.70	10.25

Handstamped from Settings of Rubber Type in Black or Violet

100000 *b* **200.000** *c*

On Stamps of 1922.

65	A6	(b) 100.000r on 2r ol blk	12.00	12.00
66	A8	(b) 200.000r on 10r gray	20.00	17.00
67	A8	(b) 200.000r on 10r gray (V)	14.00	15.00

No.	Type	Description	Unused	Used
68	A9 (b)	200,000r on 25r org brn (V)	12.00	11.00
a.		blk surch.	30.00	32.50
69	A7 (c)	300.000r on 3.000r brn & bl (V)	27.50	27.50
70	A8 (c)	500.000r on 2.000r bl & blk (V)	22.50	22.50
a.		Black surch.	30.00	32.50
71	A11 (b)	1.500.000r on 5.000r *ol grn*	17.50	15.00
72	A11 (b)	1.500.000r on 5.000r *ol grn* (V)	17.50	15.00

On Stamps of 1919.

No.	Type	Description	Unused	Used
75	A1 (b)	50.000r on 20k bl, red, grn & blk	75	
76	A2 (b)	75.000r on 40k grn, yel & blk	50	
77	A2 (b)	100.000r on 60k red, yel & blk	1.00	
78	A2 (b)	200.000r on 1r bl, yel & blk	25	25
79	A3 (b)	300.000r on 2r red, bis & blk	75	
80	A3 (b)	500,000r on 5r bl, bis & blk	1.00	

Inverted and double surcharges of Nos. 32–80 sell for twice the normal price.
Counterfeits exist of Nos. 32–80.

Baku Province.

Regular and Semi-Postal Stamps of 1922 Handstamped in Violet or Black

БАКИНСКОИ П. К.

The overprint reads "Bakinskoi P(ochtovoy) K(ontory)," meaning Baku Post Office.

1922		*Imperf.*	Unwmkd.	
300	A5	1r gray grn	20.00	
301	A7	5r gray brn	20.00	
302	A12	150r blue	6.00	
303	A9	250r vio & buff	9.00	
304	A13	400r dk bl	8.00	
305	SP1	500r bl & pale bl	9.00	
306	SP2	1000r brn & bis	12.00	
307	A8	2000r bl & blk	12.00	
308	A7	3000r brn & bl	20.00	
309	A11	5000r *ol grn*	20.00	
		Nos. 300-309 (10)	136.00	

Stamps of 1922 Handstamped in Violet

БАКИНСКАГО Г.-П.-Т.О. №1

Overprint reads: Baku Post, Telegraph Office No. 1.

1924

Overprint 24x2mm.

No.	Type	Description	Unused	Used
312	A12	150r blue	9.00	
313	A9	250r vio & buff	9.00	
314	A13	400r dk bl	9.00	
317	A8	2000r bl & blk	10.00	
318	A7	3000r brn & bl	10.00	
319	A11	5000r *ol grn*	10.00	

Overprint 30x3½mm.

No.	Type	Description	Unused	Used
323	A12	150r blue	9.00	
324	A9	250r vio & buff	9.00	
325	A13	400r dk bl	9.00	
328	A8	2000r bl & blk	9.00	
329	A7	3000r brn & bl	10.00	
330	A11	5000r *ol grn*	9.00	

Overprinted on Nos. 32–33, 35.

No.	Type	Description	Unused	Used
331	A5	10,000r on 1r gray grn	32.50	
332	A7	15,000r on 5r gray brn	32.50	
333	A7	50,000r on 3000r brn & bl	37.50	
		Nos. 312-333 (15)	214.50	

The overprinted semipostal stamps were used for regular postage.

This handstamp on Nos. 17, B1–B2 in size 24x2mm., and on Nos. 15, 17, B1–B2 in size 30x3½mm., was of private origin and not officially issued.

SEMI-POSTAL STAMPS.

Carrying Food to Sufferers
SP1

1922		*Imperf.*	Unwmkd.	
B1	SP1	500r bl & pale bl	50	75

Widow and Orphans
SP2

No.	Type	Description	Unused	Used
B2	SP2	1000r brn & bis	1.00	1.50

Counterfeits exist.

OCCUPATION AZIRBAYEDJAN

Russian stamps of 1909–18 were privately overprinted as above in red, blue or black by a group of Entente officers working with Russian soldiers returning from Persia. Azerbaijan was not occupied by the Allies. There is evidence that existing covers (some seemingly postmarked at Baku, dated Oct. 19, 1917, and at Tabriz, Russian Consulate, Apr. 25, 1917) are fakes.

AZORES

(ȧ-zōrz')

LOCATION—A group of islands in the North Atlantic Ocean, due west of Portugal.

GOVT.—Integral part of Portugal, former colony.

AREA—922 sq. mi.

POP.—253,935 (1930).

CAPITAL—Ponta Delgada.

Azores stamps were supplanted by those of Portugal in 1931.

1000 Reis = 1 Milreis
100 Centavos = 1 Escudo (1912)

> Prices of early Azores stamps vary according to condition. Quotations for Nos. 1–37 are for fine copies. Very fine to superb specimens sell at much higher prices, and inferior or poor copies sell at reduced prices, depending on the condition of the individual specimen.

Stamps of Portugal Overprinted in Black or Carmine

AÇORES
a

A second type of this overprint has a broad "O" and open "S".

1868		*Imperf.*	Unwmkd.	
1	A14	5r black	1,750.	1,200.
2	A14	10r yellow	4,000.	3,000.
3	A14	20r bister	170.00	120.00
4	A14	50r green	175.00	125.00
5	A14	80r orange	175.00	135.00
6	A14	100r lilac	175.00	135.00

The reprints are on thick chalky white wove paper, ungummed, and on thin white paper with shiny white gum. Price $7.50 each.

1868-70 *Perf. 12½.*

5 REIS:

Type I. The "5" at the right is 1mm. from end of label.

Type II. The "5" is 1½mm. from end of label.

No.	Type	Description	Unused	Used
7	A14	5r blk (C)	45.00	30.00
8	A14	10r yellow	60.00	50.00
a.		Inverted overprint	100.00	100.00
9	A14	20r bister	50.00	37.50
10	A14	25r rose	45.00	6.00
a.		Inverted overprint	75.00	75.00
11	A14	50r green	150.00	120.00
12	A14	80r orange	150.00	120.00
13	A14	100r lilac	150.00	120.00
14	A14	120r blue	90.00	60.00
15	A14	240r violet	375.00	275.00

The reprints are on thick chalky white paper ungummed and perforated 13, and on thin white paper with shiny white gum and perforated 13½. Price $6 each.

1871-75 *Perf. 12½, 13½*

No.	Type	Description	Unused	Used
21	A15	5r blk (C)	8.50	6.00
a.		Inverted overprint	50.00	50.00
23	A15	10r yellow	14.00	10.00
a.		Inverted overprint	50.00	50.00
24	A15	20r bister	15.00	12.00
25	A15	25r rose	10.00	2.25
a.		Inverted overprint	50.00	50.00
b.		Double overprint	50.00	
c.		Perf. 14	140.00	40.00
d.		Double impression of stamp		
26	A15	50r green	45.00	15.00
27	A15	80r orange	60.00	37.50
28	A15	100r lilac	45.00	22.50
a.		Perf. 14	150.00	90.00
29	A15	120r blue	95.00	60.00
a.		Inverted overprint	150.00	125.00
30	A15	240r violet	675.00	500.00

The reprints are of the second type. They are on thick chalky white paper ungummed and perforated 13, also on thin white paper with shiny white gum and perforated 13½. Price $4 each.

Overprinted in Black

AÇORES
b

1875-80

15 REIS:

Type I. The figures of value, 1 and 5, at the right in upper label are close together.

Type II. The figures of value at the right in upper label are spaced.

No.	Type	Description	Unused	Used
31	A15	10r bl grn	90.00	75.00
32	A15	10r yel grn	52.50	37.50
33	A15	15r lil brn	10.00	7.50
a.		Inverted overprint	50.00	50.00
34	A15	50r blue	80.00	37.50
35	A15	150r blue	100.00	80.00
36	A15	150r yellow	120.00	100.00
37	A15	300r violet	37.50	30.00

The reprints have the same papers, gum and perforations as those of the preceding issue. Price $4 each.

1880 Black Overprint.

Perf. 11½, 12½ and 13½.

No.	Type	Description	Unused	Used
38	A17	25r gray	60.00	12.50
39	A18	25r red lil	15.00	5.00
a.		25r gray	15.00	5.00
b.		Dbl. ovpt.		

Overprinted in Carmine or Black

1881-82

No.	Type	Description	Unused	Used
40	A16	5r blk (C)	10.00	4.50
41	A23	25r brn ('82)	13.50	2.75
a.		Double overprint		
42	A19	50r blue	75.00	20.00

Reprints of Nos. 38, 39, 39a, 40 and 42 have the same papers, gum and perforations as those of preceding issues. Price $1.50 each.

Overprinted in Red or Black

AÇORES
c

1882-85

15, 20 REIS

Type I. The figures of value are some distance apart and close to the end of the label.

Type II. The figures are closer together and farther from the end of the label. On the 15 reis this is particularly apparent in the upper right figures.

No.	Type	Description	Unused	Used
43	A16	5r blk (R)	9.50	5.50
44	A21	5r slate	6.00	1.75
a.		Dbl. ovpt.		
c.		Inverted overprint		
45	A15	10r green	37.50	30.00
a.		Inverted overprint		
46	A22	10r green	12.00	5.25
a.		Dbl. ovpt.		
47	A15	15r lil brn	22.50	13.50
a.		15r red brn	22.50	13.50
b.		Inverted overprint		
48	A15	20r bister	40.00	30.00
a.		Inverted overprint		
49	A15	20r carmine	60.00	45.00
a.		Double overprint		
50	A23	25r brown	10.00	2.25
51	A15	50r blue	375.00	300.00
52	A24	50r blue	12.00	2.25
a.		Double overprint		
53	A15	80r orange	37.50	30.00
a.		80r yel	30.00	18.00
b.		Double overprint		
54	A15	100r lilac	22.50	15.00
55	A15	150r blue	375.00	300.00
56	A15	150r yellow	25.00	15.00
57	A15	300r violet	37.50	30.00

Reprints of the 1882-85 issues have the same papers, gum and perforations as those of preceding issues. Price $3 each.

Red Overprint.

No.	Type	Description	Unused	Used
58	A21	5r slate	7.50	2.25
59	A24a	500r black	100.00	90.00
60	A15	1000r black	45.00	40.00

1887 Black Overprint.

No.	Type	Description	Unused	Used
61	A25	20r pink	15.00	7.50
a.		Inverted overprint		
b.		Dbl. ovpt.		
62	A26	25r lil rose	15.00	1.25
a.		Inverted overprint		
b.		Double overprint, one inverted		
63	A26	25r red vio	15.00	1.25
a.		Dbl. ovpt.		
64	A24a	500r red vio	75.00	45.00
a.		Perf. 13½	125.00	90.00

Nos. 58 to 64 inclusive have been reprinted on thin white paper with shiny white gum and perforated 13½. Price $2 each.

Prince Henry the Navigator Issue.

Portugal Nos. 97–109 Overprinted

AÇORES

1894 *Perf. 14.*

No.	Type	Description	Unused	Used
65	A46	5r org yel	2.25	1.50
a.		Inverted overprint	13.50	11.00
66	A46	10r vio rose	2.25	1.50
a.		Dbl. ovpt.	18.50	
b.		Inverted overprint	15.00	11.00
67	A46	15r brown	3.00	1.50
68	A46	20r violet	3.00	1.50
a.		Double overprint		16.50
69	A47	25r green	3.00	1.50
a.		Double overprint	13.50	13.50
b.		Inverted overprint	13.50	13.50
70	A47	50r blue	6.00	3.00
71	A47	75r dp car	10.00	6.00
72	A47	80r yel grn	12.00	6.00
73	A47	100r lt brn, *pale buff*	10.00	4.50
a.		Dbl. ovpt.	22.50	
74	A48	150r lt car, *pale rose*	15.00	11.00
75	A48	300r dk bl, *sal buff*	22.50	13.50
76	A48	500r brn vio, *pale lil*	37.50	20.00

77	A48	1000r gray blk, *yelsh*	75.00	37.50
a.		Double overprint		
		Nos. 65-77 (13)	212.00	118.50

St. Anthony of Padua Issue.

Portugal Nos. 132–146 Overprinted in Red or Black — AÇORES

1895 ***Perf. 12***

78	A50	2½r blk (R)	2.25	2.00
79	A51	5r brn yel	4.50	2.00
80	A51	10r red lil	4.50	3.00
81	A51	15r red brn	5.25	3.00
82	A51	20r gray lil	5.25	3.00
83	A51	25r grn & vio	4.50	3.25
84	A52	50r bl & brn	15.00	7.50
85	A52	75r rose & brn	22.50	20.00
86	A52	80r lt grn & brn	37.50	22.50
87	A52	100r choc & blk	25.00	20.00
88	A53	150r vio rose & bis	60.00	55.00
89	A53	200r bl & bis	70.00	50.00
90	A53	300r sl & bis	90.00	60.00
91	A53	500r vio brn & grn	125.00	90.00
92	A53	1000r vio & grn	250.00	175.00
		Nos. 78-92 (15)	721.25	516.25

Issued in commemoration of the seventh centenary of the birth of Saint Anthony of Padua.

Vasco da Gama Issue.

Common Design Types

1898 ***Perf. 14, 15.***

93	CD20	2½r bl grn	1.25	75
94	CD21	5r red	1.50	90
a.		Horizontal pair, imperf. between		
95	CD22	10r gray lil	2.50	1.50
96	CD23	25r yel grn	2.25	90
97	CD24	50r dk bl	4.50	3.50
98	CD25	75r vio brn	10.00	6.00
99	CD26	100r bis brn	10.00	5.50
100	CD27	150r bister	15.00	7.50
		Nos. 93-100 (8)	47.00	26.55

King Carlos

A28

King Manuel II

A29

1906 **Typographed** ***Perf. 11½x12***

101	A28	2½r gray	20	15
a.		Inverted overprint	13.50	13.50
102	A28	5r org yel	20	15
a.		Inverted overprint	13.50	13.50
103	A28	10r yel grn	20	15
104	A28	20r gray vio	50	25
105	A28	25r carmine	25	15
106	A28	50r ultra	3.00	2.50
107	A28	75r brn, *straw*	70	*1.00*
108	A28	100r dk bl, *bl*	70	*1.25*
109	A28	200r red lil, *pnksh*	1.00	*1.50*
110	A28	300r dk bl, *rose*	1.75	*1.75*
111	A28	500r blk, *bl*	2.25	1.50
		Nos. 101-111 (11)	10.75	*10.35*

"Acores" and letters and figures in the corners are in red on the 2½, 10, 20, 75 and 500r and in black on the other values.

1910 ***Perf. 14x15***

112	A29	2½r violet	25	20
113	A29	5r black	35	30
114	A29	10r dk grn	40	35
115	A29	15r lil brn	65	60
116	A29	20r carmine	65	60
117	A29	25r vio brn	35	20
a.		Perf. 11½	1.50	1.00
118	A29	50r blue	1.25	75
a.		Booklet pane of 6		
119	A29	75r bis brn	2.50	1.75
120	A29	80r slate	2.50	1.75
121	A29	100r brn, *lt grn*	3.00	2.50
122	A29	200r grn, *sal*	3.00	2.50
123	A29	300r *blue*	4.50	3.00
124	A29	500r ol & brn	6.50	5.00
125	A29	1000r bl & blk	11.00	8.00
		Nos. 112-125 (14)	36.90	27.50

The errors of color 10r black, 15r dark green, 25r black and 50r carmine were not regularly issued.

Stamps of 1910 Overprinted in Carmine or Green — REPUBLICA

1910

126	A29	2½r violet	15	10
a.		Inverted overprint	2.00	2.00
127	A29	5r black	25	15
a.		Inverted overprint	2.00	2.00
128	A29	10r dk grn	25	20
a.		Inverted overprint	2.00	2.00
129	A29	15r lil brn	1.00	80
a.		Inverted overprint	2.00	2.00
130	A29	20r car (G)	1.25	1.00
a.		Inverted overprint	3.00	3.00
b.		Double overprint	3.00	3.00
131	A29	25r vio brn	20	15
a.		Perf. 11½	30.00	25.00
132	A29	50r blue	90	70
133	A29	75r bis brn	50	25
a.		Double overprint	2.00	2.00
134	A29	80r slate	65	35
135	A29	100r brn, *grn*	50	30
136	A29	200r grn, *sal*	50	*1.00*
137	A29	300r *blue*	1.50	1.50
138	A29	500r ol & brn	1.75	*2.50*
139	A29	1000r bl & blk	3.25	*4.00*
		Nos. 126-139 (14)	12.65	*13.00*

Vasco da Gama Issue Overprinted or Surcharged in Black:

REPUBLICA
d

REPUBLICA **REPUBLICA**

REIS 15 REIS
e

1$000
f

1911 ***Perf. 14, 15***

141	CD20 (d)	2½r bl grn	40	35
142	CD21 (e)	15r on 5r red	35	35
143	CD23 (d)	25r yel grn	50	30
144	CD24 (d)	50r dk bl	1.25	85
145	CD25 (d)	75r vio brn	90	90
146	CD27 (e)	80r on 150r bis	90	90
147	CD26 (d)	100r yel brn	90	90
a.		Dbl. surch.	10.00	10.00
148	CD22 (f)	1000r on 10r lil	8.00	6.00
		Nos. 141-148 (8)	13.20	10.55

Postage Due Stamps of Portugal Overprinted or Surcharged in Black "ACORES" and

REPUBLICA

REPUBLICA
g

Rs 300 Rs
h

1911 ***Perf. 12***

149	D1 (g)	5r black	60	50
a.		Half used as 2½r on cover		
150	D1 (g)	10r magenta	1.50	80
a.		"Acores" double	7.50	7.50
151	D1 (g)	20r orange	2.25	2.00
152	D1 (g)	200r brn, *buff*	8.00	5.50
a.		"Acores" inverted		
153	D1 (h)	300r on 50r sl	8.00	5.50
154	D1 (h)	500r on 100r car, *pink*	8.00	5.50
		Nos. 149-154 (6)	28.35	19.80

Ceres
A30

Ceres Issue of Portugal Overprinted "ACORES" in Black or Carmine

With Imprint.

1912–31 ***Perf. 12x11½, 15x14***

155	A30	¼c ol brn	10	10
a.		Inverted overprint	2.00	
156	A30	½c blk (C)	10	10
157	A30	1c dp grn	70	40
a.		Inverted overprint	4.50	
158	A30	1c dp brn ('18)	12	5
a.		Inverted overprint		
159	A30	1½c choc ('13)	75	60
a.		Inverted overprint	3.00	
160	A30	1½c dp grn ('18)	25	15
a.		Inverted overprint		
161	A30	2c carmine	35	25
a.		Inverted overprint	4.50	
162	A30	2c org ('18)	20	10
a.		Inverted overprint	11.00	
163	A30	2½c violet	30	15
164	A30	3c rose ('18)	20	10
165	A30	3c dl ultra ('25)	20	15
166	A30	3½c lt grn ('18)	25	10
167	A30	4c lt grn ('19)	15	6
168	A30	4c org ('30)	40	30
169	A30	5c dp bl	40	12
170	A30	5c yel brn ('18)	35	25
171	A30	5c ol brn ('23)	15	8
172	A30	5c blk brn ('30)	3.50	3.00
173	A30	6c dl rose ('20)	25	15
174	A30	6c choc ('25)	25	15
175	A30	6c red brn ('31)	25	*1.00*
176	A30	7½c yel brn	4.00	1.50
177	A30	7½c dp bl ('18)	85	60
178	A30	8c sl ('13)	35	25
179	A30	8c bl grn ('22)	30	20
180	A30	8c org ('25)	65	35
181	A30	10c org brn	35	10
182	A30	12c bl gray ('20)	1.25	90
183	A30	12c dp grn ('22)	65	50
184	A30	13½c chlky bl ('20)	1.25	*3.00*
185	A30	14c dk bl, *yel*('20)	4.00	*5.00*
186	A30	15c plum ('13)	75	25
187	A30	15c blk (R) ('23)	50	50
188	A30	16c brt ultra ('24)	1.00	30
189	A30	16c dp bl ('30)	1.50	*2.00*
190	A30	20c vio brn, *grn* ('13)	10.00	5.00
191	A30	20c choc ('20)	75	25
192	A30	20c dp grn ('23)	1.00	1.00
a.		Double overprint		
193	A30	20c gray ('24)	75	25
194	A30	24c grnsh bl ('21)	75	25
195	A30	25c sal ('23)	35	20
196	A30	30c brn, *pink* ('13)	45.00	30.00
197	A30	30c brn, *yel* ('19)	2.75	2.75
198	A30	30c gray brn ('21)	1.00	80
199	A30	32c dp grn ('25)	1.75	1.25
200	A30	36c red ('21)	50	25
201	A30	40c dp bl ('23)	50	50
202	A30	40c blk brn ('24)	25	10
203	A30	40c brt grn ('30)	1.75	50
204	A30	48c brt rose ('24)	1.75	1.25
205	A30	48c dl pink ('31)	2.00	1.50
206	A30	50c org, *sal* ('13)	5.00	1.25
207	A30	50c yel ('23)	1.50	1.25
208	A30	50c bis ('30)	3.00	2.25
209	A30	50c red brn ('31)	2.50	1.75
210	A30	60c bl ('21)	1.10	90
211	A30	64c pale ultra ('24)	1.75	1.25
212	A30	64c brn rose ('31)	15.00	10.00
213	A30	75c dl rose ('23)	5.00	5.00
214	A30	75c car rose ('30)	2.00	1.50
215	A30	80c dl rose ('21)	1.50	85
216	A30	80c vio ('24)	1.50	1.00
217	A30	80c dk grn ('31)	2.00	1.50
218	A30	90c chlky bl ('21)	1.50	85
219	A30	96c dp rose ('26)	8.50	4.00
220	A30	1e dp grn, *bl*	6.00	2.50
221	A30	1e vio ('21)	1.50	85
222	A30	1e gray vio ('24)	2.00	1.25
223	A30	1e brn lake ('30)	22.50	16.00
224	A30	1.10e yel brn ('21)	1.50	1.50
225	A30	1.20e yel grn ('21)	1.75	1.2
226	A30	1.20e buff ('24)	4.50	2.2
227	A30	1.25e dk bl ('30)	1.75	8
228	A30	1.50e blk vio ('23)	3.25	2.2
229	A30	1.50e lil ('25)	3.50	2.2
230	A30	1.60e dp bl ('25)	3.50	2.2
231	A30	2e sl grn ('21)	5.00	2.5
232	A30	2.40e ap grn ('26)	40.00	20.0
233	A30	3e lil pink ('26)	40.00	20.0
234	A30	3.20e gray grn ('25)	10.00	5.0
235	A30	5e emer ('24)	14.00	7.0
236	A30	10e pink ('24)	27.50	11.0
237	A30	20e pale turq ('25)	90.00	57.5
		Nos. 155-237 (83)	427.57	*258.2*

Castello-Branco Issue.

Stamps of Portugal, 1925, Overprinted in Black or Red — AÇORES

1925 ***Perf. 12½***

238	A73	2c orange	20	20
239	A73	3c green	20	20
240	A73	4c ultra (R)	20	20
241	A73	5c scarlet	20	20
242	A74	10c pale bl	20	20
243	A74	16c red org	30	30
244	A75	25c car rose	30	30
245	A74	32c green	50	50
246	A75	40c grn & blk (R)	30	30
247	A74	48c red brn	1.00	1.00
248	A76	50c bl grn	1.00	1.00
249	A76	64c org brn	1.00	1.00
250	A76	75c gray blk (R)	1.25	1.25
251	A75	80c brown	1.25	1.25
252	A76	96c car rose	1.50	1.50
253	A77	1.50e dk bl, *bl* (R)	1.50	1.10
254	A75	1.60e ind (R)	1.50	1.10
255	A77	2e dk grn, *grn* (R)	2.00	2.00
256	A77	2.40e red, *org*	2.50	2.25
257	A77	3.20e *grn* (R)	3.75	3.00
		Nos. 238-257 (20)	20.65	18.85

First Independence Issue.

Stamps of Portugal, 1926, Overprinted in Red — AÇÔRES

1926 ***Perf. 14, 14½***

Center in Black.

258	A79	2c orange	30	30
259	A80	3c ultra	30	30
260	A79	4c yel grn	30	30
261	A80	5c blk brn	30	30
262	A79	6c ocher	30	30
263	A80	15c dk grn	60	60
264	A81	20c dl vio	60	60
265	A82	25c scarlet	60	60
266	A81	32c dp grn	60	60
267	A82	40c yel brn	60	60
268	A82	50c ol bis	1.25	1.25
269	A82	75c red brn	1.25	1.25
270	A83	1e blk vio	2.00	2.00
271	A84	4.50e ol grn	4.50	4.50
		Nos. 258-271 (14)	13.50	13.50

The use of these stamps instead of those of the regular issue was obligatory on Aug. 13th and 14th Nov. 30th and Dec. 1st, 1926.

Second Independence Issue.

Stamps of Portugal, 1927, Overprinted in Red — AÇÔRES

1927 **Center in Black.**

272	A86	2c lt brn	30	30
273	A87	3c ultra	30	30
274	A86	4c orange	30	30
275	A88	5c dk brn	30	30
276	A89	6c org brn	30	30
277	A87	15c blk brn	30	30
278	A86	25c gray	1.25	1.25
279	A89	32c bl grn	1.25	1.25
280	A90	40c yel grn	1.25	1.25
281	A90	96c red	3.00	3.00
282	A88	1.60e myr grn	3.00	3.00
283	A91	4.50e bister	6.00	6.00
		Nos. 272-283 (12)	17.55	17.55

Third Independence Issue.

Stamps of Portugal, 1928, Overprinted in Red **AÇÔRES**

1928 **Center in Black.**

284	A93	2c lt bl	30	30
285	A94	3c lt grn	30	30
286	A95	4c lake	30	30
287	A96	5c ol grn	30	30
288	A97	6c org brn	30	30
289	A94	15c slate	50	50
290	A95	16c dk vio	85	85
291	A93	25c ultra	85	85
292	A97	32c dk grn	85	85
293	A96	40c ol brn	85	85
294	A95	50c red org	1.75	1.75
295	A94	80c lt gray	1.75	1.75
296	A97	96c carmine	2.25	2.25
297	A96	1e claret	2.25	2.25
298	A93	1.60e dk bl	2.25	2.25
299	A98	4.50e yellow	5.50	5.50
		Nos. 284-299 (16)	21.15	21.15

A31

A32

1929-30 ***Perf. 12x11½, 15x14***

300	A31	4c on 25c pink ('30)	50	50
301	A31	4c on 60c dp bl	50	50
302	A31	10c on 25c pink	60	50
303	A31	12c on 25c pink	60	50
304	A31	15c on 25c pink	75	60
305	A31	20c on 25c pink	1.00	85
306	A31	40c on 1.10e yel brn	3.25	2.75
		Nos. 300-306 (7)	7.20	6.20

Black or Red Overprint.

1930 ***Perf. 14.***

Without Imprint at Foot.

307	A32	4c orange	60	50
308	A32	5c dp brn	2.25	1.50
309	A32	10c vermilion	1.00	70
310	A32	15c blk (R)	1.00	70
311	A32	40c brt grn	1.00	70
312	A32	80c violet	14.00	11.00
313	A32	1.60e dk bl	2.25	1.25
		Nos. 307-313 (7)	22.10	16.35

POSTAGE DUE STAMPS.

D2

D3

Portugal Nos. J7-J13 Overprinted in Black

1904 ***Perf. 12*** **Unwmkd.**

J1	D2	5r brown	60	60
J2	D2	10r orange	60	60
J3	D2	20r lilac	1.00	1.00
J4	D2	30r gray grn	1.00	1.00
a.		Double overprint		
J5	D2	40r gray vio	1.75	1.75
J6	D2	50r carmine	2.00	2.00
J7	D2	100r dl bl	3.50	3.50
		Nos J1-J7 (7)	10.45	10.45

Same Overprinted in Carmine or Green (Portugal Nos. J14-J20) **REPUBLICA**

1911

J8	D2	5r brown	30	30
J9	D2	10r orange	30	30
J10	D2	20r lilac	30	30
J11	D2	30r gray grn	30	30
J12	D2	40r gray vio	50	50
J13	D2	50r car (G)	2.50	2.50
J14	D2	100r dl bl	1.50	1.50
		Nos. J8-J14 (7)	5.70	5.70

Portugal Nos. J21-J27 Overprinted in Black

1918

J15	D3	½c brown	15	15
a.		Inverted overprint	50	50
b.		Double overprint	50	50
J16	D3	1c orange	15	15
a.		Inverted overprint	50	50
b.		Double overprint	50	50
J17	D3	2c red lil	15	15
a.		Inverted overprint	1.00	1.00
b.		Double overprint	1.00	1.00
J18	D3	3c green	15	15
a.		Inverted overprint	1.00	1.00
b.		Double overprint	1.00	1.00
J19	D3	4c gray	15	15
a.		Inverted overprint	1.00	1.00
b.		Double overprint	1.00	1.00
J20	D3	5c rose	15	15
b.		Double overprint	1.00	1.00
J21	D3	10c dk bl	25	25
		Nos. J15-J21 (7)	1.15	1.15

Stamps and Type of Portugal Postage Dues, 1921-27, Overprinted in Black

1922-24 ***Perf. 11½x12.***

J30	D3	½c gray grn ('23)	15	15
J31	D3	1c gray grn ('23)	15	15
J32	D3	2c gray grn ('23)	15	15
J33	D3	3c gray grn ('24)	50	50
J34	D3	8c gray grn ('24)	30	30
J35	D3	10c gray grn ('24)	30	30
J36	D3	12c gray grn ('24)	30	30
J37	D3	16c gray grn ('24)	30	30
J38	D3	20c gray grn	60	60
J39	D3	24c gray grn	30	30
J40	D3	32c gray grn ('24)	30	30
J41	D3	36c gray grn	30	30
J42	D3	40c gray grn ('24)	60	60
J43	D3	48c gray grn ('24)	35	35
J44	D3	50c gray grn	60	60
J45	D3	60c gray grn	40	40
J46	D3	72c gray grn	40	40
J47	D3	80c gray grn ('24)	1.75	1.75
J48	D3	1.20e gray grn	1.75	1.75
		Nos. J30-J48 (19)	9.50	9.50

NEWSPAPER STAMPS.

N1

N2

N3

Newspaper Stamps of Portugal Overprinted in Black or Red

Perf. 11½, 12½ and 13½.

1876-88 **Unwmkd.**

P1	N1	2½r olive	6.00	2.25
a.		Inverted overprint		
P2	N2	2½r ol ('82)	4.25	1.25
a.		Inverted overprint		
b.		Double overprint		
P3	N3	2r blk ('85)	2.25	1.25
a.		Inverted overprint		
b.		Double overprint, one inverted		
P4	N2	2½r bis ('82)	4.25	1.00
a.		Double overprint		
P5	N3	2r blk (R) ('88)	7.00	4.50

Reprints of the newspaper stamps have the same papers, gum and perforations as reprints of the regular issues. Price $2 each.

PARCEL POST STAMPS.

Mercury and Commerce
PP1

Portugal Nos. Q1-Q17 Overprinted in Black or Red.

1921-22 ***Perf. 12.*** **Unwmkd.**

Q1	PP1	1c lil brn	20	18
a.		Inverted overprint	50	50
Q2	PP1	2c orange	20	18
a.		Inverted overprint	50	50
Q3	PP1	5c lt brn	20	18
a.		Inverted overprint	1.00	1.00
b.		Double overprint	1.00	1.00
Q4	PP1	10c red brn	40	30
a.		Inverted overprint	1.00	1.00
b.		Double overprint	1.00	1.00
Q5	PP1	20c gray bl	40	30
a.		Inverted overprint	1.00	1.00
b.		Double overprint	1.00	1.00
Q6	PP1	40c carmine	40	40
a.		Double overprint	1.50	1.50
Q7	PP1	50c blk (R)	70	70
Q8	PP1	60c dk bl (R)	70	70
Q9	PP1	70c gray brn	1.75	1.50
a.		Double overprint		
Q10	PP1	80c ultra	1.75	1.50
Q11	PP1	90c lt vio	1.75	1.50
Q12	PP1	1e lt grn	1.75	1.50
Q13	PP1	2e pale lil	2.50	2.50
Q14	PP1	3e olive	3.00	3.00
Q15	PP1	4c ultra	5.00	5.00
Q16	PP1	5e gray	5.00	5.00
Q17	PP1	10e chocolate	15.00	15.00
		Nos. Q1-Q17 (17)	40.70	39.44

POSTAL TAX STAMPS.

These stamps represent a special fee for the delivery of postal matter on certain days in the year. The money derived from their sale is applied to works of public charity.

Nos. 114 and 157 Overprinted in Carmine **ASSISTENCIA**

1911-13 ***Perf. 14x15*** **Unwmkd.**

RA1	A29	10r dk grn	75	60

The 20r of this type was for use on telegrams.

Perf. 15x14

RA2	A30	1c dp grn	1.50	1.50

The 2c of this type was for use on telegrams.

Charity Sheltering Poor
PT1

Postal Tax Stamp of Portugal Overprinted in Black.

1915 ***Perf. 12.***

RA3	PT1	1c carmine	15	12

The 2c of this type was for use on telegrams.

Postal Tax Stamp of 1915 Surcharged **15 ctvs.**

1924

RA4	PT1	15c on 1c rose	50	*1.00*

Comrades of the Great War Issue.

Postal Tax Stamps of Portugal, 1925, Overprinted AÇORES

1925 ***Perf. 11.***

RA5	PT3	10c brown	40	40
RA6	PT3	10c green	40	40
RA7	PT3	10c rose	40	40
RA8	PT3	10c ultra	40	40

The use of Nos. RA5-RA11 in addition to the regular postage was compulsory on certain days. If the tax represented by these stamps was not prepaid, it was collected by means of Postal Tax Due Stamps.

Pombal Issue.

Common Design Types

1925 ***Perf. 12½.***

RA9	CD28	20c dp grn & blk	45	35
RA10	CD29	20c dp grn & blk	45	35
RA11	CD30	20c dp grn & blk	45	35

POSTAL TAX DUE STAMPS.

Postal Tax Due Stamp of Portugal Overprinted **AÇORES**

1925 ***Perf. 11x11½.*** **Unwmkd.**

RAJ1	PTD1	20c brn org	50	50

See note after No. RA8.

Pombal Issue.

Common Design Types

1925 ***Perf. 12½.***

RAJ2	CD31	40c dp grn & blk	75	*1.25*
RAJ3	CD32	40c dp grn & blk	75	*1.25*
RAJ4	CD33	40c dp grn & blk	75	*1.25*

See note after No. RA8.

See Portugal for later issues.

BADEN

See Vol. III, Early German States group preceding Germany.

BATUM

See Vol. I, British section.

BAVARIA

See Vol. III, Early German States group preceding Germany.

BELGIAN CONGO

LOCATION—Central Africa.
GOVT.—Belgian colony.
AREA—902,082 sq. mi. (estimated).
POP.—12,660,000 (1956).
CAPITAL—Léopoldville.

Congo was an independent state, founded by Leopold II of Belgium, until 1908 when it was annexed to Belgium as a colony. In 1960 it became the independent Republic of the Congo. See Congo Democratic Republic and Zaire.

100 Centimes = 1 Franc

Independent State

King Leopold II
A1 A2 A3

Typographed.

1886 *Perf. 15.* **Unwmkd.**

1	A1	5c green	12.50	20.00
2	A1	10c rose	4.50	5.00
3	A2	25c blue	55.00	42.50
4	A3	50c ol grn	7.50	6.25
5	A1	5fr lilac	375.00	250.00
a.		Perf. 14	750.00	

King Leopold II
A4

1887-94

6	A4	5c grn ('89)	75	75
7	A4	10c rose ('89)	1.25	1.10
8	A4	25c bl ('89)	1.00	90
9	A4	50c brown	62.50	18.00
10	A4	50c gray ('94)	2.50	*15.00*
11	A4	5fr violet	875.00	375.00
12	A4	5fr gray ('92)	125.00	100.00
13	A4	10fr buff ('91)	350.00	225.00

The 25fr and 50fr in gray were not issued. Prices $22.50, $21.

Port Matadi
A5

River Scene on the Congo, Stanley Falls
A6

Inkissi Falls
A7

Railroad Bridge on M'pozo River
A8

Hunting Elephants
A9

Bangala Chief and Wife
A10

Engraved.

1894–1901 *Perf. 12½ to 15*

14	A5	5c pale bl & blk	15.00	14.00
15	A5	5c red brn & blk ('95)	3.50	1.50
16	A5	5c grn & blk ('00)	2.25	50
17	A6	10c red brn & blk	15.00	14.00
18	A6	10c grnsh bl & blk ('95)	1.25	1.25
a.		Center invtd.	*1,500.*	*1,900.*
19	A6	10c car & blk ('00)	3.00	50
20	A7	25c yel org & blk	3.75	2.25
21	A7	25c lt bl & blk ('00)	3.25	1.25
22	A8	50c grn & blk	1.40	1.25
23	A8	50c ol & blk ('00)	3.25	65
24	A9	1fr lil & blk	24.00	11.00
a.		1fr rose lil & blk	150.00	17.50
25	A9	1fr car & blk ('01)	175.00	2.00
26	A10	5fr lake & blk	37.50	14.00
		Nos. 14-26 (13)	288.15	64.15

Climbing Oil Palms
A11

Congo Canoe
A12

1896

27	A11	15c ocher & blk	3.75	50
28	A12	40c bluish grn & blk	4.00	2.75

Congo Village—A13

River Steamer on the Congo
A14

1898

29	A13	3.50fr red & blk	125.00	62.50
30	A14	10fr yel grn & blk	87.50	17.50
a.		Center invtd.	*5,750.*	
b.		Perf. 12	450.00	17.50
c.		Perf. 12x14	325.00	125.00

Belgian Congo

Overprinted CONGO BELGE

1908

31	A5	5c grn & blk	7.50	7.50
a.		Handstamped	2.50	1.75
32	A6	10c car & blk	12.50	12.50
a.		Handstamped	2.50	1.75
33	A11	15c ocher & blk	6.50	3.50
a.		Handstamped	5.00	2.75
34	A7	25c lt bl & blk	5.00	3.50
a.		Handstamped	7.50	3.25
35	A12	40c bluish grn & blk	2.25	2.25
a.		Handstamped	7.50	5.25
36	A8	50c ol & blk	4.25	2.50
a.		Handstamped	4.00	2.50
37	A9	1fr car & blk	21.00	2.50
a.		Handstamped	25.00	2.00
38	A13	3.50fr red & blk	20.00	12.50
a.		Handstamped	150.00	75.00
39	A10	5fr car & blk	37.50	20.00
a.		Handstamped	57.50	25.00
40	A14	10fr yel grn & blk	87.50	17.50
a.		Perf. 14	250.00	150.00
b.		Handstamped	110.00	27.50
c.		Handstamped, perf. 14	300.00	175.00
		Nos. 31-40 (10)	204.00	84.25

Most of the above handstamps are also found inverted and double.

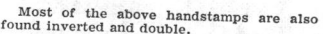

Port Matadi—A15

River Scene on the Congo, Stanley Falls
A16

Climbing Oil Palms
A17

Railroad Bridge on M'pozo River
A18

1909 *Perf. 14*

41	A15	5c grn & blk	75	75
42	A16	10c car & blk	65	50
43	A17	15c ocher & blk	21.00	12.00
44	A18	50c ol & blk	3.25	2.50

Port Matadi
A19

River Scene on the Congo, Stanley Falls
A20

Climbing Oil Palms
A21

Bangala Chief and Wife
A27

Inkissi Falls
A22

Congo Canoe
A23

Railroad Bridge on M'pozo River
A24

Hunting Elephants
A25

Congo Village
A26

River Steamer on the Congo
A28

1910-15 Engraved. *Perf. 14, 15.*

No.	Type	Description	Unused	Used
45	A19	5c grn & blk	1.25	28
46	A20	10c car & blk	70	25
47	A21	15c ocher & blk	70	25
48	A21	15c grn & blk ('15)	38	25
a.		Bklt pane of 10	12.50	
49	A22	25c bl & blk	1.75	38
50	A23	40c bluish grn & blk	2.25	2.25
51	A23	40c brn red & blk ('15)	4.50	2.25
52	A24	50c ol & blk	3.75	2.00
53	A24	50c brn lake & blk ('15)	7.00	2.25
54	A25	1fr car & blk	3.50	2.75
55	A25	1fr ol bis & blk ('15)	2.25	90
56	A26	3fr red & blk	17.50	13.00
57	A27	5fr car & blk	20.00	17.50
58	A27	5fr ocher & blk ('15)	1.90	90
59	A28	10fr grn & blk	19.00	16.00
		Nos. 45-59 (15)	86.43	61.21

Nos. 48, 51, 53, 55 and 58 exist imperforate.

Port Matadi
A29

Stanley Falls, Congo River
A30

Inkissi Falls—A31

TEN CENTIMES.

Type I. Large white space at top of picture and two small white spots at lower edge. Vignette does not fill frame.

Type II. Vignette completely fills frame.

1915

No.	Type	Description	Unused	Used
60	A29	5c grn & blk	25	20
a.		Booklet pane of 10	8.75	
61	A30	10c car & blk (II)	30	20
a.		10c car & blk (I)	30	20
d.		Booklet pane of 10 (II)	12.50	
62	A31	25c bl & blk	1.40	38
a.		Booklet pane of 10	62.50	

Nos. 60 to 62 exist imperforate.

Stamps of 1910 Issue Surcharged in Red or Black

10c 10c

1921

No.	Type	Description	Unused	Used
64	A23	5c on 40c bluish grn & blk (R)	30	30
65	A19	10c on 5c grn & blk (R)	30	30
66	A24	15c on 50c ol & blk (R)	30	30
67	A21	25c on 15c ocher & blk (R)	1.90	1.40
68	A20	30c on 10c car & blk	30	30
69	A22	50c on 25c bl & blk (R)	1.75	1.25
		Nos. 64-69 (6)	4.85	3.85

The position of the new value and the bars varies on Nos. 64 to 69.

Overprinted **1921**

1921

No.	Type	Description	Unused	Used
70	A25	1fr car & blk	1.10	1.10
a.		Double overprint	17.50	
71	A26	3fr red & blk	3.25	3.25
72	A27	5fr car & blk	6.25	6.25
73	A28	10fr grn & blk (R)	5.00	3.75

Belgian Surcharges.

Stamps of 1915 Surcharged in Black or Red **·10c**

1922

No.	Type	Description	Unused	Used
74	A24	5c on 50c brn lake & blk	50	45
75	A29	10c on 5c grn & blk (R)	50	38
76	A23	25c on 40c brn red & blk (R)	2.50	45
77	A30	30c on 10c car & blk (II)	28	25
a.		30c on 10c car & blk (I)	28	25
b.		Double surcharge	6.00	6.00
78	A31	50c on 25c bl & blk (R)	60	38
		Nos. 74-78 (5)	4.38	1.91

No. 74 has the surcharge at each side.

Nos. 74-78 were issued only in sheets of 50. Blocks of 10 (5x2), so-called "booklet panes," are believed to be from the sheets of 50.

Congo Surcharges.

Nos. 60, 51 Surcharged in Red or Black:

10 c.

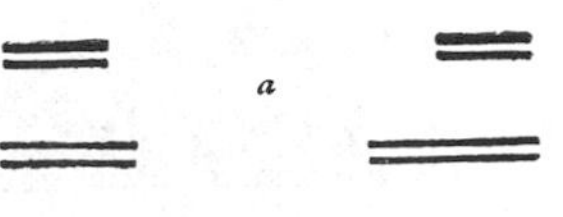
a

25 c.
b

1922

No.	Type	Description	Unused	Used
80	A29 (a)	10c on 5c grn & blk (R)	75	75
a.		Invtd. surch	20.00	20.00
b.		Double surcharge	6.00	
c.		Double surcharge, one inverted	40.00	
d.		Pair, one without surcharge	45.00	
e.		On No.45	150.00	150.00
81	A23 (b)	25c on 40c brn red & blk	1.00	50
a.		Inverted surcharge	20.00	20.00
b.		Double surcharge	7.00	
c.		"25c" double		
d.		25c on 5c, No. 60	110.00	110.00

Nos. 55, 58 Surcharged **10 c.**

and vertical bars over original values.

1922

No.	Type	Description	Unused	Used
84	A25	10c on 1fr ol bis & blk (R)	75	75
a.		Double surcharge	15.00	
b.		Inverted surcharge	20.00	20.00
85	A27	25c on 5fr ocher & blk	2.00	2.00

Nos. 68, 77 Handstamped **0,25**

No.	Type	Description	Unused	Used
86	A20	25c on 30c on 10c car & blk	10.00	10.00
87	A30	25c on 30c on 10c car & blk (II)	10.00	10.00

Nos. 86-87 exist with handstamp surcharge inverted.

Ubangi Woman
A32

Watusi Cattle
A44

Designs: 10c, Baluba woman. 15c, Babuende woman. No. 90, 40c, 1.25fr, 1.50fr, 1.75fr. Ubangi man. 25c, Basketmaking. 30c, 35c, Nos. 101, 102, Carving wood. 50c, Archer. Nos. 92, 100, Weaving. 1fr, Making pottery. 3fr, Working rubber. 5fr. Making palm oil. 10fr, African elephant.

1923-27 Engraved *Perf. 12*

No.	Type	Description	Unused	Used
88	A32	5c yellow	20	12
89	A32	10c green	20	12
90	A32	15c ol brn	20	12
91	A32	20c ol grn ('24)	18	12
92	A44	20c grn ('26)	20	15
93	A44	25c red brn	30	12
94	A44	30c rose red ('24)	75	90
95	A44	30c ol grn ('25)	20	15
96	A44	35c grn ('27)	50	50
97	A32	40c vio ('25)	20	15
98	A44	50c gray bl	30	22
99	A44	50c buff ('25)	35	12
100	A44	75c red org	42	42
101	A44	75c gray bl ('25)	45	28
102	A44	75c sal red ('26)	25	15
103	A44	1fr bis brn	55	22
104	A44	1fr dl bl ('25)	45	12
105	A44	1fr rose red ('27)	75	15
106	A32	1.25fr dl bl ('26)	38	28
107	A32	1.50fr dl bl ('26)	38	22
108	A32	1.75fr dl bl ('27)	3.75	2.85
109	A44	3fr gray brn ('24)	4.50	1.40
110	A44	5fr gray ('24)	9.25	4.00
111	A44	10fr gray blk ('24)	21.00	6.25

1925-26 *Perf. 12*

No.	Type	Description	Unused	Used
112	A44	45c dk vio ('26)	45	38
113	A44	60c car rose	45	22
		Nos. 88-113 (26)	46.61	19.73

No. 107 Surcharged **1.75**

1927, June 14

No.	Type	Description	Unused	Used
114	A32	1.75fr on 1.50fr dl bl	50	38

Sir Henry Morton Stanley
A45

1928, June 30 *Perf. 14*

No.	Type	Description	Unused	Used
115	A45	5c gray blk	8	8
116	A45	10c dp vio	12	12
117	A45	20c org red	22	22
118	A45	35c green	80	65
119	A45	40c red brn	32	20
120	A45	60c blk brn	32	20
121	A45	1fr carmine	32	12
122	A45	1.60fr dk gray	3.50	3.00
123	A45	1.75fr dp bl	1.40	90
124	A45	2fr dk brn	1.00	38
125	A45	2.75fr red vio	4.00	45
126	A45	3.50fr rose lake	1.25	75
127	A45	5fr sl grn	1.00	30
128	A45	10fr vio bl	1.40	75
129	A45	20fr claret	5.00	2.75
		Nos. 115-129 (15)	20.73	10.87

Issued in memory of Sir Henry M. Stanley (1841-1904), explorer.

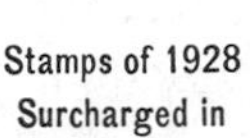

Stamps of 1928 Surcharged in Red, Blue or Black **1F25**

1931, Jan. 15

No.	Type	Description	Unused	Used
130	A45	40c on 35c grn (R)	70	55
131	A45	1.25fr on 1fr car (Bl)	55	15
132	A45	2fr on 1.60fr dk gray (R)	1.10	38
133	A45	2fr on 1.75fr dp bl (R)	1.00	35
134	A45	3.25fr on 2.75fr red vio (Bk)	3.00	2.25
135	A45	3.25fr on 3.50fr rose lake (Bk)	3.75	2.50

Stamps of 1923-27 Surcharged in Red **50c**

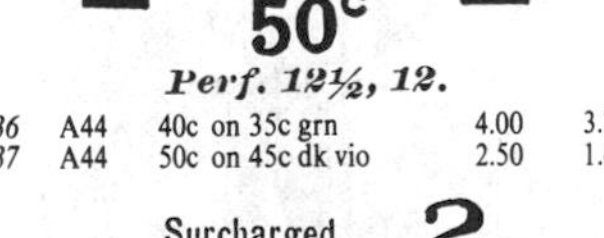

Perf. 12½, 12.

No.	Type	Description	Unused	Used
136	A44	40c on 35c grn	4.00	3.75
137	A44	50c on 45c dk vio	2.50	1.40

Surcharged **2**

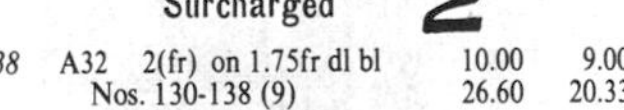

No.	Type	Description	Unused	Used
138	A32	2(fr) on 1.75fr dl bl	10.00	9.00
		Nos. 130-138 (9)	26.60	20.33

View of Sankuru River
A46

Flute Players
A50

Designs: 15c, Kivu Kraal. 20c, Sankuru River rapids. 25c, Uele hut. 50c, Musicians of Lake Leopold II. 60c, Batetelas drummers. 75c, Mangbetu woman. 1fr, Domesticated elephant of Api. 1.25fr, Mangbetu chief. 1.50fr, 2fr, Village of Mondimbi. 2.50fr, 3.25fr, Okapi. 4fr, Canoes at Stanleyville. 5fr, Woman preparing cassava. 10fr, Baluba chief. 20fr, Young woman of Irumu.

1931-37 Engraved. *Perf. 11½.*

139	A46	10c gray brn ('32)	8	8
140	A46	15c gray ('32)	8	8
141	A46	20c brn lil ('32)	8	8
142	A46	25c dp bl ('32)	8	8
143	A50	40c dp grn ('32)	25	25
144	A46	50c vio ('32)	8	8
b.		Booklet pane of 8	7.50	
145	A50	60c vio brn ('32)	15	12
146	A50	75c rose ('32)	12	12
b.		Booklet pane of 8	1.65	
147	A50	1fr rose red ('32)	20	12
148	A50	1.25fr red brn	18	12
b.		Booklet pane of 8	1.65	
149	A46	1.50fr dk ol gray ('37)	20	15
b.		Booklet pane of 8	7.50	
150	A46	2fr ultra ('32)	25	15
151	A46	2.50fr dp bl ('37)	45	18
b.		Bklt pane of 8	11.00	
152	A46	3.25fr gray blk ('32)	70	40
153	A46	4fr dl vio ('32)	30	20
154	A50	5fr dp vio ('32)	70	30
155	A50	10fr red ('32)	75	50
156	A50	20fr blk brn ('32)	1.90	1.50
		Nos.139-156 (18)	6.55	4.51

No. 109 Surcharged in Red

3F25

══ ══

1932, Mar. 15 ***Perf. 12***

157	A44	3.25fr on 3fr gray brn	3.50	2.50

King Albert Memorial Issue.

King Albert
A62

1934, May 7 **Photo.** ***Perf. 11½***

158	A62	1.50fr black	1.00	25

Leopold I, Leopold II, Albert I, Leopold III
A63

1935, Aug. 15 Engr. *Perf. 12½x12*

159	A63	50c green	90	65
160	A63	1.25fr dk car	90	22
161	A63	1.50fr brn vio	90	15
162	A63	2.40fr brn org	3.00	2.50
163	A63	2.50fr lt bl	2.50	1.00
164	A63	4fr brt vio	3.00	1.50
165	A63	5fr blk brn	3.00	1.75
		Nos. 159-165 (7)	14.20	7.77

Issued to commemorate the 50th anniversary of the founding of Congo Free State.

Molindi River
A64

Bamboos
A65

Suza River
A66

Rutshuru River
A67

Karisimbi
A68

Mitumba Forest
A69

1937-38 Photo. *Perf. 11½*

166	A64	5c pur & blk	8	8
167	A65	90c car & brn	70	55
168	A66	1.50fr dp red brn & blk	18	12
169	A67	2.40fr ol blk & brn	30	20
170	A68	2.50fr dp ultra & blk	45	22
171	A69	4.50fr dk grn & brn	45	20
172	A69	4.50fr car & sep	35	35
		Nos. 166-172 (7)	2.51	1.72

National Parks.

No. 172 was issued in sheets of four measuring 140x111mm. It was sold by subscription, the subscription closing Oct. 20, 1937. Price, $1.60.

Nos. 166–171 were issued Mar. 1, 1938.

King Albert Memorial, Leopoldville
A70

1941, Feb. 7 Litho. *Perf. 11*

173	A70	10c lt gray	30	28
174	A70	15c brn vio	30	28
175	A70	25c lt bl	38	30
176	A70	50c lt vio	30	28
177	A70	75c rose pink	1.25	50
178	A70	1.25fr gray	30	30
179	A70	1.75fr orange	1.00	80
180	A70	2.50fr carmine	60	20
181	A70	2.75fr vio bl	1.25	1.00
182	A70	5fr lt ol grn	2.50	2.50
183	A70	10fr rose red	3.75	3.75
		Nos.173-183 (11)	11.93	10.19

Exist imperforate.

Stamps of 1938-41 Surcharged in Blue or Black

5 c.

75 c.

a b

1941-42 *Perf. 11½, 11.*

184	A66 (a)	5c on 1.50fr dp red brn & blk (Bl)	12	12
a.		Inverted surcharge	15.00	15.00
185	A70 (b)	75c on 1.75fr org (Bk) ('42)	50	50
a.		Inverted surcharge	15.00	15.00
186	A67 (a)	2.50(fr) on 2.40fr ol blk & brn (Bk) ('42)	1.25	1.00
a.		Double surcharge	30.00	30.00
b.		Inverted surcharge	15.00	15.00

Oil Palms
A71 A72

Congo Woman
A73

Askari
A75

Leopard
A74

Okapi
A76

1942, May 23 Engr. *Perf. 12½*

Inscribed "Congo Belge Belgisch Congo".

187	A71	5c red	6	6
188	A72	10c ol grn	8	6
189	A72	15c brn car	8	6
190	A72	20c dp ultra	8	6
191	A72	25c brn vio	8	6
192	A72	30c blue	8	8
193	A72	50c dp grn	8	8
194	A72	60c chestnut	10	10
195	A73	75c dl lil & blk	12	10
196	A73	1fr dk brn & blk	15	10
197	A73	1.25fr rose red & blk	15	12
198	A74	1.75fr dk gray brn	75	55
199	A74	2fr ocher	75	18
200	A74	2.50fr carmine	75	10
201	A75	3.50fr dk ol grn	30	12
202	A75	5fr orange	55	20
203	A75	6fr brt ultra	50	12
204	A75	7fr black	50	12
205	A75	10fr dp brn	65	12
206	A76	20fr plum & blk	4.00	95
		Nos. 187-206 (20)	9.81	3.34

Same

Inscribed "Belgisch Congo Congo Belge".

207	A72	10c ol grn	8	6
208	A72	15c brn car	8	6
209	A72	20c dp ultra	8	6
210	A72	25c brn vio	8	6
211	A72	30c blue	8	8
212	A72	50c dp grn	8	8
213	A72	60c chestnut	10	10
214	A73	75c dl lil & blk	12	10
215	A73	1fr dk brn & blk	15	10
216	A73	1.25fr rose red & blk	15	12
217	A74	1.75fr dk gray brn	75	55
218	A74	2fr ocher	75	18
219	A74	2.50fr carmine	75	10
220	A75	3.50fr dk ol grn	30	12
221	A75	5fr orange	55	20
222	A75	6fr brt ultra	50	12
223	A75	7fr black	50	12
224	A75	10fr dp brn	65	12
225	A76	20fr plum & blk	4.00	95
		Nos. 207-225 (19)	9.75	3.28

Miniature sheets of Nos. 193, 194, 197, 200, 211, 214, 217 and 219 were printed in 1944 by the Belgian Government in London and given to the Belgian political review, Message, which distributed them to its subscribers, one a month. Price per sheet, about $12.50.

Remainders of these eight miniature sheets received marginal overprints in various colors in 1950, specifying a surtax of 100fr per sheet and paying tribute to the Universal Postal Union. These sheets, together with four of Ruanda-Urundi, were sold by the Committee of Cultural Works (and not at post offices) in sets of 12 for 1,217.15 francs. Set price, about $150.

Nos. 187 to 227 exist imperforate but had no franking value.

Congo Woman
A77

Askari
A78

1943, Jan. 1

226	A77	50fr ultra & blk	5.00	65
227	A78	100fr car & blk	6.50	1.00

Slaves and Arab Guards
A79

Auguste Lambermont
A80

Design: 10fr, Leopold II.

Perf. 13x11½, 12½x12.

1947 Engraved. Unwmkd.

228	A79	1.25fr blk brn	25	10
229	A80	3.50fr dk bl	38	12
230	A80	10fr red org	75	22

Issued to commemorate the 50th anniversary of the abolition of slavery in Belgian Congo. See also Nos. 261-262.

Baluba Carving of Former King
A82

Carved Figures and Masks of Baluba Tribe: 10c, 50c, 2fr, "Ndoha," figure of tribal king. 15c, 70c, 1.20fr, 2.50fr, "Tshimanyi," an idol. 20c, 75c, 1.60fr, 3.50fr, "Buangakokoma," statue of kneeling beggar. 25c, 1fr, 2.40fr, 5fr, "Mbuta," sacred double cup, carved with two faces, Man and Woman. 40c, 1.25fr, 6fr, 8fr, "Ngadimuashi," female mask. 1.50fr, 3fr, 10fr, 50fr, "Buadi-Muadi," mask with squared features. 6.50fr, 20fr, 100fr, "Mbowa," executioner's mask with buffalo horns.

1947-50 ***Perf. 12½.***

231	A82	10c dp org ('48)	12	8
232	A82	15c ultra ('48)	12	8
233	A82	20c brt bl ('48)	12	10
234	A82	25c rose car ('48)	25	12
235	A82	40c vio ('48)	15	8
236	A82	50c ol brn	15	8
237	A82	70c yel grn ('48)	12	10
238	A82	75c mag ('48)	15	10
239	A82	1fr yel org & dk vio	1.25	8
240	A82	1.20fr gray & brn ('50)	15	12
241	A82	1.25fr lt bl grn & mag ('48)	25	18
242	A82	1.50fr ol & mag ('50)	8.00	2.25
243	A82	1.60fr bl gray & brt bl ('50)	20	18
244	A82	2fr org & mag ('48)	18	8
245	A82	2.40fr bl grn & dk grn ('50)	25	18
246	A82	2.50fr brn red & bl grn	15	8
247	A82	3fr lt ultra & ind ('49)	3.75	8
248	A82	3.50fr lt bl & blk ('48)	2.75	25
249	A82	5fr bis & mag ('48)	50	10
250	A82	6fr brn org & ind ('48)	65	10
251	A82	6.50fr red org & red brn ('49)	1.25	10
252	A82	8fr gray bl & dk grn ('50)	65	25
253	A82	10fr pale vio & red brn ('48)	2.00	12
254	A82	20fr red org & vio brn ('48)	1.00	10
255	A82	50fr dp org & blk ('48)	2.50	30
256	A82	100fr crim & blk brn ('48)	3.75	60
		Nos. 231-256 (26)	30.41	5.89

Railroad Train and Map
A83

1948, July 1 ***Perf. 13½*** **Unwmkd.**

257	A83	2.50fr dp bl & grn	85	25

50th anniversary of railway service in the Congo.

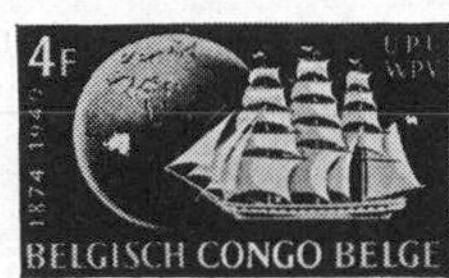

Globe and Ship—A84

1949, Nov. 21 ***Perf. 11½***

Granite Paper

258	A84	4fr vio bl	75	25

Issued to commemorate the 75th anniversary of the formation of the Universal Postal Union.

Allegorical Figure and Map
A85

1950, Aug. 12 ***Perf. 12x12½***

259	A85	3fr bl & ind	1.50	25
260	A85	6.50fr car rose & blk brn	1.75	38

Issued to commemorate the 50th anniversary of the establishment of Katanga Province.

Portrait Type of 1947.

Designs: 1.50fr, Cardinal Lavigerie. 3fr, Baron Dhanis.

Perf. 12½x12

1951, June 25 Unwmkd.

261	A80	1.50fr purple	2.00	38
262	A80	3fr blk brn	2.00	10

Littonia
A86

Flowers: 10c, Dissotis. 15c, Protea. 20c, Vellozia. 40c, Ipomoea. 50c, Angraecum. 60c, Euphorbia. 75c, Ochna. 1fr, Hibiscus. 1.25fr, Protea. 1.50fr, Schizoglossum. 2fr, Ansellia. 3fr, Costus. 4fr, Nymphaea. 5fr, Thunbergia. 6.50fr, Thonningia. 7fr, Gerbera. 8fr, Gloriosa. 10fr, Silene. 20fr, Aristolochia. 50fr, Eulophia. 100fr, Cryptosepalum.

Granite Paper.

1952-53 Photogravure. ***Perf. 11½.***

Flowers in Natural Colors.

Size: 21x25½mm.

263	A86	10c dp plum & ocher	5	5
264	A86	15c red & yel grn	5	5
265	A86	20c grn & gray	5	5
266	A86	25c dk grn & dl org	5	5
267	A86	40c grn & sal	18	15
268	A86	50c dk car & aqua	8	5
269	A86	60c bl grn & pink	8	5
270	A86	75c dp plum & gray	8	5
271	A86	1fr car & yel	8	5
272	A86	1.25fr dk grn & bl ('53)	65	50
273	A86	1.50fr vio & ap grn	15	5
274	A86	2fr ol grn & buff	25	5
275	A86	3fr ol grn & pink	25	5
276	A86	4fr choc & lil	30	5
277	A86	5fr dp plum & lt bl grn	45	5
278	A86	6.50fr dk car & lil	55	5
279	A86	7fr dk grn & fawn	55	5
280	A86	8fr grn & lt yel ('53)	90	15
281	A86	10fr dp plum & pale ol ('53)	1.65	5
282	A86	20fr vio bl & dl sal	1.40	5

Size: 22x32mm.

283	A86	50fr dp plum & gray bl ('53)	7.00	50
284	A86	100fr grn & buff ('53)	11.00	1.10
		Nos. 263-284 (22)	25.80	3.25

No. 264 surcharged "10c" is Congo Democratic Republic No. 324a.

St. Francis Xavier
A86a

1953, Jan. 5 Engr. ***Perf. 12½x13***

285	A86a	1.50fr ultra & gray blk	75	60

Issued to commemorate the 400th anniversary of the death of St. Francis Xavier.

Canoe on Lake Kivu
A87

1953, Jan. 5 ***Perf. 14***

286	A87	3fr car & blk	1.50	30
287	A87	7fr dp bl & brn org	1.65	45

Issued to publicize the Kivu Festival, 1953.

Royal Colonial Institute Jubilee Medal
A88

Design: 6.50fr, Same with altered background and transposed inscriptions.

1954, Dec. 27 Photo. ***Perf. 13½***

288	A88	4.50fr ind & gray	1.40	45
289	A88	6.50fr dk grn & brn	1.10	18

Issued to commemorate the 25th anniversary of the founding of the Belgian Royal Colonial Institute.

King Baudouin and Tropical Scene
A89

Designs: King and various views.

Engraved; Portrait Photogravure.

1955, Feb. 15 ***Perf. 11½*** **Unwmkd.**

Portrait in Black.

Inscribed "Congo Belge - Belgisch Congo."

290	A89	1.50fr rose car	90	38
291	A89	3fr green	32	12
292	A89	4.50fr ultra	42	15
293	A89	6.50fr dp cl	65	12

Inscribed "Belgisch Congo - Congo Belge."

294	A89	1.50fr rose car	42	28
295	A89	3fr green	32	8
296	A89	4.50fr ultra	42	15
297	A89	6.50fr dp cl	65	12
		Nos. 290-297 (8)	4.10	1.40

Map of Africa and Emblem of Royal Touring Club
A90

1955, July 26 Engr. ***Perf. 11½***

Inscription in French.

298	A90	6.50fr vio bl	3.25	50

Inscription in Flemish.

299	A90	6.50fr vio bl	3.25	50

5th International Congress of African Tourism, Elisabethville, July 26-Aug. 4. Nos. 298-299 printed in alternate rows.

Kings of Belgium—A91

1958, July 1 ***Perf. 12½*** **Unwmkd.**

300	A91	1fr rose vio	25	8
301	A91	1.50fr ultra	25	8
302	A91	3fr rose car	25	8
303	A91	5fr green	80	55
304	A91	6.50fr brn red	50	10
305	A91	10fr dl vio	70	15
		Nos. 300-305 (6)	2.75	1.04

Issued to commemorate the 50th anniversary of Belgium's annexation of Congo.

Roan Antelope
A92

Black Buffaloes
A93

Animals: 20c, White rhinoceros. 40c, Giraffe. 50c, Thick-tailed bushbaby. 1fr, Gorilla. 2fr, Black-and-white colobus (monkey). 3fr, Elephants. 5fr, Okapis. 6.50fr, Impala. 8fr, Giant pangolin. 10fr, Eland and zebras.

1959 Photogravure. ***Perf. 11½***

Granite Paper.

306	A92	10c bl & brn	5	5
307	A93	20c red org & sl	5	5
308	A92	40c brn & bl	8	8
309	A93	50c brt ultra, red & sep	8	8
310	A92	1fr brn, grn & blk	10	8
311	A93	1.50fr blk & org yel	12	8

312	A92	2fr crim, blk & brn	15	8
313	A93	3fr blk, gray & lil rose	25	10
314	A92	5fr brn, dk brn & brt grn	40	18
315	A93	6.50fr bl, brn & org yel	45	10
316	A92	8fr org brn, ol bis & lil	50	30
317	A93	10fr multi	60	15
		Nos. 306-317 (12)	2.83	1.33

Madonna and Child
A94

1959, Dec. 1 *Perf. 11½* Unwmkd.

318	A94	50c gldn brn, ocher & red brn	10	6
319	A94	1fr dk bl, pur & red brn	10	8
320	A94	2fr gray, brt bl & red brn	18	12

Map of Africa and Symbolic Honeycomb
A95

1960, Feb. 19 *Perf. 11½* Unwmkd.

Inscription in French.

321	A95	3fr gray & red	25	15

Inscription in Flemish.

322	A95	3fr gray & red	25	15

Issued to commemorate the 10th anniversary of the Commission for Technical Co-operation in Africa South of the Sahara. (C. C. T. A.)

Succeeding issues are listed under Congo Democratic Republic.

SEMI-POSTAL STAMPS.

Types of 1910-15 Issues

Surcharged in Red **+ 10c**

Perf. 14, 15

1918, May 15 Unwmkd.

B1	A29	5c +10c grn & bl	30	38
B2	A30	10c +15c car & bl (I)	30	38
B3	A21	15c +20c bl grn & bl	30	38
B4	A31	25c +25c dp bl & pale bl	38	38
B5	A23	40c +40c brn red & bl	50	65
B6	A24	50c +50c brn lake & bl	50	65
B7	A25	1fr +1fr ol bis & bl	1.90	2.25
B8	A27	5fr +5fr ocher & bl	11.50	12.00
B9	A28	10fr +10fr grn & bl	90.00	90.00
		Nos. B1-B9 (9)	105.68	107.07

The position of the cross and the added value varies on the different stamps.

Nos. B1 to B9 exist imperforate.

SP1

Design: No. B11 inscribed "Belgisch Congo."

1925 ***Perf. 12½.***

B10	SP1	25c +25c car & blk	25	25
B11	SP1	25c +25c car & blk	25	25

Colonial campaigns in 1914–1918.

The stamps with French and Flemish inscriptions alternate in the sheet.

The surtax helped erect at Kinshasa a monument to those who died in World War I.

Nurse Weighing Child
SP3

First Aid Station
SP5

Designs: 20c+10c, Missionary and Child. 60c+30c, Congo hospital. 1fr+50c, Dispensary service. 1.75fr+75c, Convalescent area. 3.50fr+1.50fr, Instruction on bathing infant. 5fr+2.50fr, Operating room. 10fr+5fr, Students.

1930, Jan. 16 Engr. *Perf. 11½*

B12	SP3	10c +5c ver	55	55
B13	SP3	20c +10c dp brn	70	70
B14	SP5	35c +15c dp grn	1.25	1.25
B15	SP5	60c +30c dl vio	1.50	1.50
B16	SP3	1fr +50c dk car	2.25	2.25
B17	SP5	1.75fr +75c dp bl	3.25	3.25
B18	SP5	3.50fr +1.50fr rose lake	6.25	6.25
B19	SP5	5fr +2.50fr red brn	6.00	6.00
B20	SP5	10fr +5fr gray blk	6.25	6.25
		Nos. B12-B20 (9)	28.00	28.00

The surtax on these stamps was intended to aid welfare work among the natives, especially the children.

Nos. 161, 163
Surcharged "+50c" in Blue or Red.

1936, May 15 ***Perf. 12½x12***

B21	A63	1.50fr +50c brn vio (Bl)	2.50	2.50
B22	A63	2.50fr +50c lt bl (R)	2.50	2.50

The surtax was for the benefit of the King Albert Memorial Fund.

Queen Astrid with Congolese Children
SP12

1936, Aug. 29 Photo. *Perf. 12½*

B23	SP12	1.25fr +5c dk brn	75	65
B24	SP12	1.50fr +10c dl rose	75	65
B25	SP12	2.50fr +25c dk bl	90	90

Issued in memory of Queen Astrid. The surtax was for the aid of the National League for Protection of Native Children.

Souvenir Sheet.

SP13

1938, Oct. 3 ***Perf. 11½***

B26	SP13	Sheet of six	10.50	10.50
a.		A64 5c ultra & lt brn	1.75	1.75
b.		A65 90c ultra & lt brn	1.75	1.75
c.		A66 1.50fr ultra & lt brn	1.75	1.75
d.		A67 2.40fr ultra & lt brn	1.75	1.75
e.		A68 2.50fr ultra & lt brn	1.75	1.75
f.		A69 4.50fr ultra & lt brn	1.75	1.75

Issued in sheets measuring 139x122mm. The star is printed in yellow. Issued in commemoration of the International Tourist Congress. A surtax of 3.15fr was for the benefit of the Congo Tourist Service.

Marabou Storks and Vultures
SP14

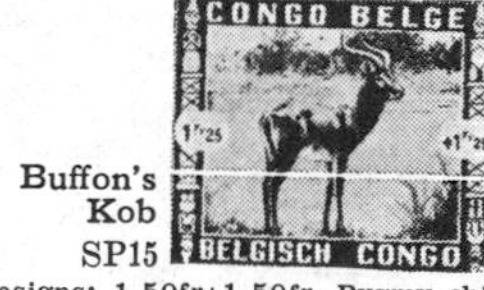

Buffon's Kob
SP15

Designs: 1.50fr+1.50fr, Pygmy chimpanzees. 4.50fr+4.50fr, Dwarf crocodiles. 5fr+5fr, Lioness.

1939 Photogravure *Perf. 14*

B27	SP14	1fr +1fr dp cl	5.00	5.00
B28	SP15	1.25fr +1.25fr car	5.00	5.00
B29	SP15	1.50fr +1.50fr brt pur	7.50	7.50
B30	SP14	4.50fr +4.50fr sl grn	5.00	5.00
B31	SP15	5fr +5fr brn	5.50	5.50
		Nos. B27-B31 (5)	28.00	28.00

The surtax was for the Leopoldville Zoological Gardens.

Nos. B27–B31 were sold in full sets by subscription.

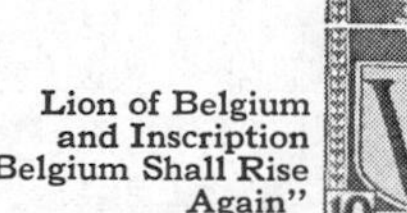

Lion of Belgium and Inscription "Belgium Shall Rise Again"
SP19

1942, Feb. 17 Engr. *Perf. 12½*

B32	SP19	10fr +40fr brt grn	1.40	1.40
B33	SP19	10fr +40fr vio bl	1.40	1.40

Nos. 193, 216, 198 and 220
Surcharged in Red

Au profit
de la
Croix Rouge
+ 50 Fr.
Ten voordeele
van het
Roode Kruis
a

Ten voordeele
van het
Roode Kruis
+ 100 Fr.
Au profit
de la
Croix Rouge
b

Au profit de la
Croix Rouge
+ 100 Fr.
Ten voordeele van het
Roode Kruis
c

1945

B34	A72 (a)	50c +50fr dp grn	2.50	2.50
B35	A73 (b)	1.25fr +100fr rose red & blk	2.50	2.50
B36	A74 (c)	1.75fr +100fr dk gray brn	2.50	2.75
B37	A75 (b)	3.50fr +100fr dk ol grn	2.50	2.75

The surtax was for the Red Cross.

Nos. B34–B37 were sold in full sets by subscription.

Mozart at Age 7
SP20

Queen Elisabeth and Sonata by Mozart
SP21

Engraved.

1956, Oct. 10 *Perf. 11½* Unwmkd.

B38	SP20	4.50fr +1.50fr brt lil	1.50	1.50
B39	SP21	6.50fr +2.50fr ultra	2.50	2.50

Issued to commemorate the 200th anniversary of the birth of Wolfgang Amadeus Mozart.

The surtax was for the Pro-Mozart Committee.

Nurse and Children
SP22

Designs: 4.50fr+50c, Patient receiving injection. 6.50fr+40c, Patient being bandaged.

1957, Dec. 10 Photo. *Perf. 13x10½*

Cross in Carmine.

B40	SP22	3fr +50c dk bl	1.10	1.10
B41	SP22	4.50fr +50c dk grn	1.00	1.00
B42	SP22	6.50fr +50c red brn	1.25	1.25

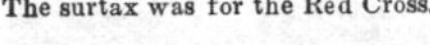

The surtax was for the Red Cross.

High Jumper
SP23

Sports: 1.50fr+50c, Hurdlers. 2fr+1fr, Soccer. 3fr+1.25fr, Javelin thrower. 6.50fr+3.50fr, Discus thrower.

1960, May 2 *Perf. 13½* Unwmkd.

B43	SP23	50c +25c ultra & red	12	12
B44	SP23	1.50fr +50c car & grn	22	22
B45	SP23	2fr +1fr grn & ver	22	22
B46	SP23	3fr +1.25fr rose cl & bl	95	95
B47	SP23	6.50fr +3.50fr red brn & car	1.25	1.25
		Nos. B43-B47 (5)	2.76	2.76

Issued to commemorate the 17th Olympic Games, Rome, Aug. 25–Sept. 11. The surtax was for the youth of Congo.

AIR POST STAMPS.

Wharf on Congo River
AP1

Congo "Country Store"
AP2

View of Congo River
AP3

Stronghold in the Interior
AP4

Engraved.

1920, July 1 *Perf. 12* Unwmkd.

C1	AP1	50c org & blk	25	15
C2	AP2	1fr dl vio & blk	25	12
C3	AP3	2fr bl & blk	80	30
C4	AP4	5fr grn & blk	1.50	70

Kraal
AP5

Porters on Safari
AP6

1930, Apr. 2

C5	AP5	15fr dk brn & blk	3.50	1.25
C6	AP6	30fr brn vio & blk	4.00	1.25

Fokker F VII over Congo
AP7

1934, Jan. 22 *Perf. 13½x14*

C7	AP7	50c gray blk	20	20
C8	AP7	1fr dk car	30	20
a.		Bklt pane of 8	7.00	
C9	AP7	1.50fr green	20	15
C10	AP7	3fr brown	30	15
C11	AP7	4.50fr brt ultra	45	15
a.		Bklt pane of 8	15.00	
C12	AP7	5fr red brn	35	15
C13	AP7	15fr brn vio	70	45
C14	AP7	30fr red org	1.25	1.10
C15	AP7	50fr violet	3.75	1.75
		Nos. C7-C15 (9)	7.50	4.30

The 1fr, 3fr, 4.50fr, 5fr and 15fr exist imperf.

No. C10 Surcharged in Blue with New Value and Bars.

1936, Mar. 25

C16	AP7	3.50fr on 3fr brn	25	15

No. C9 Surcharged in Black

50 c.

1942, Apr. 27

C17	AP7	50c on 1.50fr grn	30	30
a.		Inverted surcharge	7.50	7.50

POSTAGE DUE STAMPS.

In 1908–23 regular postage stamps handstamped "TAXES" or "TAXE," usually boxed, were used in lieu of postage due stamps.

D1

D2

Perf. 14, 14½.

1923-29 Typographed. Unwmkd.

J1	D1	5c blk brn	18	18
J2	D1	10c rose red	20	18
J3	D1	15c violet	25	20
J4	D1	30c green	40	38
J5	D1	50c ultra	55	50
J6	D1	50c bl ('29)	55	50
J7	D1	1fr gray	65	45
		Nos. J1-J7 (7)	2.78	2.39

1943 *Perf. 14x14½*

J8	D2	10c ol grn	6	6
J9	D2	20c dk ultra	6	6
J10	D2	50c green	15	15
J11	D2	1fr dk brn	18	18
J12	D2	2fr yel org	22	22
		Nos. J8-J12 (5)	67	67

1943 *Perf. 12½*

J8a	D2	10c ol grn	25	25
J9a	D2	20c dk ultra	25	25
J10a	D2	50c green	25	25
J11a	D2	1fr dk brn	38	38
J12a	D2	2fr yel org	38	38
		Nos. J8a-J12a (5)	1.51	1.51

D3

1957 Engraved. *Perf. 11½*

J13	D3	10c ol brn	6	6
J14	D3	20c claret	10	10
J15	D3	50c green	15	15
J16	D3	1fr lt bl	30	30
J17	D3	2fr vermilion	45	40
J18	D3	4fr purple	60	55
J19	D3	6fr vio bl	85	70
		Nos. J13-J19 (7)	2.51	2.26

PARCEL POST STAMPS.

PP1

PP2 PP3

Handstamped Surcharges on Nos. 5, 11–12

1887–1893 *Perf. 15* Unwmkd.

Blue-Black Surcharge

Q1	PP1	3.50fr on 5fr lil	750.00	500.00

Black Surcharge

Q3	PP2	3.50fr on 5fr vio	700.00	375.00
Q4	PP3	3.50fr on 5fr vio ('88)	500.00	300.00
a.		bl surcharge	500.00	300.00
Q6	PP3	3.50fr on 5fr gray ('93)	95.00	62.50

Nos. Q1, Q3–Q4, Q4a and Q6 are known with inverted surcharge, No. Q1 with double surcharge and No. Q6 in pair with unsurcharged stamp. Most of these handstamp varieties sell for more than the normal surcharges.

BELGIAN EAST AFRICA

(See Ruanda-Urundi in Vol. IV.)

BELGIUM

(bĕl'jĭ·ŭm)

LOCATION — Western Europe, bordering the North Sea.
GOVT.—Constitutional Monarchy.
AREA—11,778 sq. mi.
POP.—9,853,000 (est. 1983).
CAPITAL—Brussels.

100 Centimes = 1 Franc

Prices of early Belgian stamps vary according to condition. Quotations for Nos. 1–12 are for fine copies. Very fine to superb specimens sell at much higher prices, and inferior or poor copies sell at reduced prices, depending on the condition of the individual specimen.

Prices for unused stamps of 1849–1863 issues are for copies with original gum. Copies without gum sell for one third of the figures quoted, or less.

King Leopold I
A1 A2

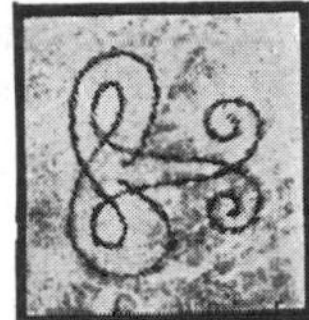

Wmk. 96

Wmkd. Two "L"s Framed. (96)

1849 Engraved. *Imperf.*

1	A1	10c brown	*2,250.*	100.00
a.		10c red brn	*3,500.*	300.00
2	A1	20c blue	*3,250.*	90.00
a.		20c mlky bl	*3,750.*	225.00

The reprints are on thick and thin wove and thick laid paper unwatermarked.

A souvenir sheet containing reproductions of the 10c, 20c and 40c of 1849–51 with black burelage on back was issued Oct. 17, 1949, for the centenary of the first Belgian stamps. It was sold at BEPITEC 1949, an international stamp exhibition at Brussels, and was not valid. Size: 139x90mm.

1849-50

3	A2	10c brn ('50)	*2,000.*	100.00
4	A2	20c bl ('50)	*2,250.*	77.50
5	A2	40c car rose	*2,000.*	325.00

Nos. 3–5 on thin paper are as priced. Copies on thick paper sell for 5 to 12 percent more.

Wmkd. Two "L"s Without Frame. (96)

1851–54

6	A2	10c brown	1,100.	13.00
a.		Ribbed paper ('54)	1,300.	57.50
7	A2	20c blue	1,100.	13.00
a.		Ribbed paper ('54)	1,300.	57.50
8	A2	40c car rose	*2,200.*	90.00
a.		Ribbed paper ('54)	*2,600.*	250.00

Nos. 6–8 were printed on thin and thick paper. Nos. 6–7 on thick paper, unused, sell for 7 to 10 percent more.

1858–61 Unwmkd.

9	A2	1c grn ('61)	*250.00*	200.00
a.		Laid paper		
10	A2	10c brown	500.00	13.00
11	A2	20c blue	500.00	13.00

12	A2	40c car rose	2,500.	90.00

Nos. 9 and 13 were valid for postage on newspapers and printed matter only.

Reprints of Nos. 9 to 12 are on thin wove paper. The colors are brighter than those of the originals. They were made from the dies and show lines outside the stamps.

1863

Perf. 12½, 12½x13, 12½x13½, 14½

13	A2	1c green	52.50	45.00
14	A2	10c brown	75.00	2.25
15	A2	20c blue	80.00	2.25
16	A2	40c car rose	525.00	22.50

King Leopold I

A3 A3a

A4 A4a

A5

London Print.

1865 **Typographed** ***Perf. 14***

17	A5	1fr pale vio	900.00	135.00

Brussels Print.

Thick or Thin Paper.

1865–66 ***Perf. 15, 14½x14***

18	A3	10c sl ('66)	110.00	1.25
a.		Pair, imperf. between		175.00
19	A3a	20c bl ('66)	135.00	1.25
a.		20c lil bl	135.00	1.40
20	A4	30c brown	275.00	9.00
a.		Pair, imperf. between	900.00	
21	A4a	40c rose ('66)	400.00	18.00
22	A5	1fr violet	1,000.	135.00

Nos. 18 to 22 on thin paper are perf. 14½x14; on thick paper, perf. 15.

The reprints are on thin paper, imperforate and ungummed.

Coat of Arms

A6

1866–67 ***Imperf.***

23	A6	1c gray	250.00	200.00

Perf. 15, 14½x14

24	A6	1c gray	37.50	16.00
25	A6	2c bl ('67)	135.00	90.00
a.		2c ultra	150.00	110.00
26	A6	5c brown	135.00	90.00

Nos. 23-26 were valid for postage on newspapers and printed matter only.

Nos. 24 to 26 on thin paper are perf. 14½ x 14; on thick paper, perf. 15.

Reprints of Nos. 24 to 26 are on thin paper, imperforate and ungummed.

King Leopold II

A7 A8

A9 A10

A11 A12

1869–70 ***Perf. 15***

28	A7	1c green	12.00	45
29	A7	2c ultra ('70)	16.00	45
30	A7	5c buff ('70)	57.50	65
31	A7	8c lil ('70)	90.00	62.50
32	A8	10c green	30.00	45
33	A9	20c lt ultra ('70)	125.00	90
34	A10	30c buff ('70)	100.00	5.50
35	A11	40c brt rose ('70)	125.00	5.75
36	A12	1fr dl lil ('70)	300.00	20.00
a.		1fr rose lil	325.00	22.50

The frames and inscriptions of Nos. 30, 31 and 42 differ slightly from the illustration.

Minor "broken letter" varieties exist on several values.

Imperf. varieties of 1869–1912 (between Nos. 28–105) are without gum.

See also Nos. 40–43, 49–51, 55.

A13 A14 A15

1875–78

37	A13	25c ol bis	80.00	1.40
a.		25c ocher	80.00	1.40
38	A14	50c gray	300.00	8.00
a.		50c gray blk	500.00	67.50
39	A15	5fr pale brn ('78)	3,750.	1,000.
		Roller cancel		450.00
a.		5fr dp red brn	2,100.	1,000.

Printed in Aniline Colors.

1881 ***Perf. 14, 15***

40	A7	1c gray grn	11.00	45
41	A7	2c lt ultra	17.50	85
42	A7	5c org buff	57.50	65
a.		5c red org	57.50	65
43	A8	10c gray grn	45.00	45
44	A13	25c ol bis	80.00	1.40
		Nos. 40-44 (5)	211.00	3.80

King Leopold II

A16 A17

A18 A19

1883

45	A16	10c carmine	40.00	1.75
46	A17	20c gray	175.00	4.50
47	A18	25c blue	350.00	32.50
		Roller cancel		12.50
48	A19	50c violet	300.00	35.00
		Roller cancel		12.50

A20 A21

A22

1884–85 ***Perf. 14***

49	A7	1c ol grn	13.00	65
50	A7	1c gray	5.25	8
51	A7	5c green	27.50	15
52	A20	10c rose, *bluish*	9.00	10
a.		grysh paper	10.00	35
c.		yelsh paper	100.00	20.00
53	A21	25c bl, *pink* ('85)	16.00	55
54	A22	1fr brn, *grnsh*	1,000.	13.00

The frame and inscription of No. 51 differ slightly from the illustration. See note after No. 36.

A23 A24

A25 A26

1886–91

55	A7	2c pur brn ('88)	13.00	55
56	A23	20c ol, *grnsh*	160.00	70
57	A24	35c vio brn, *brnsh* ('91)	30.00	3.00
58	A25	50c bis, *yelsh*	16.00	2.25
59	A26	2fr vio, *pale lil*	150.00	30.00
		Roller cancel		6.00

Coat of Arms King Leopold

A27 A28

1893-1900

60	A27	1c gray	1.40	10
61	A27	2c yellow	1.75	1.40
a.		Wmkd. coat of arms in sheet ('95)		
62	A27	2c vio brn ('94)	2.25	25
63	A27	2c red brn ('98)	4.25	25
64	A27	5c yel grn	6.75	15
65	A28	10c org brn	6.75	15
66	A28	10c brt rose ('00)	4.50	15
67	A28	20c ol grn	30.00	50
68	A28	25c ultra	27.50	50
a.		No ball to "5" in upper left corner	45.00	16.00
69	A28	35c vio brn	50.00	1.25
a.		35c brn	57.50	1.65
70	A28	50c bister	85.00	11.00
71	A28	50c gray ('97)	75.00	2.50
72	A28	1fr car, *lt grn*	100.00	15.00
73	A28	1fr org ('00)	140.00	6.75
74	A28	2fr lil, *rose*	150.00	110.00
75	A28	2fr lil ('00)	200.00	18.00

Prices quoted for Nos. 60–107, B1–B24 are for stamps with label attached. Stamps without label sell for about half.

Antwerp Exhibition Issue.

Arms of Antwerp

A29

1894

76	A29	5c grn, *rose*	6.75	3.75
77	A29	10c car, *bluish*	6.25	1.65
78	A29	25c bl, *rose*	90	90

Brussels Exhibition Issue.

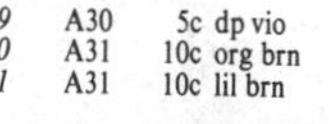

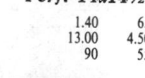

St. Michael and Satan

A30 A31

1896–97 ***Perf. 14x14½.***

79	A30	5c dp vio	1.40	65
80	A31	10c org brn	13.00	4.50
81	A31	10c lil brn	90	55

Coat of Arms King Leopold II

A32 A33

King Leopold II

A34 A35

A36

A37

A38

A39

Two types of 1c:
I. Periods after "Dimanche" and "Zondag" in label.
II. No period after "Dimanche". Period often missing after "Zondag".

1905-07 ***Perf. 14.***

82	A32	1c gray (I) ('07)	1.40	22
a.		Type II ('08)	1.40	25
83	A32	2c red brn ('07)	9.00	2.25
84	A32	5c grn ('07)	9.00	22
85	A33	10c dl rose	3.50	20
86	A34	20c ol grn	25.00	90
87	A35	25c ultra	20.00	75
a.		25c dl bl	20.00	75
88	A36	35c pur brn	37.50	1.90
89	A37	50c bluish gray	100.00	2.50
90	A38	1fr yellow	125.00	8.00
91	A39	2fr violet	125.00	22.50
		Bar cancellation		4.00
		Nos. 82-91 (10)	455.40	39.44

Numeral

A40

Coat of Arms

A41

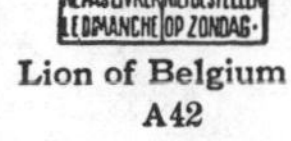

Lion of Belgium

A42

King Albert I

A43

A44

1912

92	A40	1c orange	22	10
93	A41	2c org brn	45	45
94	A42	5c green	35	10
95	A43	10c red	1.65	35
96	A43	20c ol grn	13.00	1.40
97	A43	35c bis brn	2.00	65
98	A43	40c green	20.00	11.00
99	A43	50c gray	2.00	90
100	A43	1fr orange	9.00	6.75
101	A43	2fr violet	22.50	20.00
102	A44	5fr plum	135.00	30.00
		Nos. 92-102 (11)	206.17	71.70

A45

1912-13 **Larger Head**

103	A45	10c red	55	22
a.		Without engraver's name	25	15
104	A45	20c ol grn ('13)	75	50
a.		Without engraver's name	1.10	1.10
105	A45	25c ultra	4.25	1.90
a.		Without engraver's name	35	45
107	A45	40c grn ('13)	90	75

King Albert I

A46

Cloth Hall of Ypres

A47

Bridge of Dinant

A48

Library of Louvain

A49

Scheldt River at Antwerp

A50

Anti-slavery Campaign in the Congo

A51

King Albert I at Furnes

A52

Kings of Belgium
Leopold I, Albert I, Leopold II

A53

1915-20 **Typographed.** ***Perf. 14, 14½***

108	A46	1c orange	18	5
109	A46	2c chocolate	18	5
110	A46	3c gray blk ('20)	25	6
111	A46	5c green	45	5
112	A46	10c carmine	90	5
113	A46	15c purple	1.10	6
114	A46	20c red vio	1.10	5
115	A46	25c blue	1.25	22
		Engraved.		
116	A47	35c brn org & blk	90	22
117	A48	40c grn & blk	1.40	22
a.		Vertical pair, imperf. between		
118	A49	50c car rose & blk	4.50	22
119	A50	1fr violet	27.50	40
120	A51	2fr slate	32.50	1.75
121	A52	5fr dp bl	300.00	125.00
		Telegraph or railroad cancel		100.00
122	A53	10fr brown	32.50	30.00
		Nos. 108-122 (15)	404.71	158.40

Two types each of the 1c, 10c and 20c; three of the 2c and 15c; four of the 5c, differing in the top left corner.

Nos. 108 to 120 and 122 exist imperforate. See also No. 138.

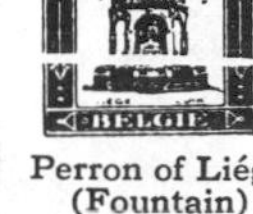

Perron of Liége (Fountain)

A54

King Albert in Trench Helmet

A55

1919 ***Perf. 11½***

123	A54	25c dp bl	3.25	20
a.		Sheet of ten	11,000.	11,000.

1919 ***Perf. 11, 11½, 11½x11, 11x11½.***

Size: 18½x22mm.

124	A55	1c lil brn	8	8
125	A55	2c olive	8	8
		Size: 23x26mm.		
126	A55	5c green	28	22
127	A55	10c carmine	15	8
128	A55	15c gray vio	22	15
129	A55	20c ol blk	1.10	1.25
130	A55	25c dp bl	1.25	1.40
131	A55	35c bis brn	1.90	1.75
132	A55	40c red	3.00	3.00
133	A55	50c red brn	7.50	7.75
134	A55	1fr lt org	45.00	45.00
135	A55	2fr violet	475.00	450.00
		Size: 28x33½mm.		
136	A55	5fr car lake	150.00	150.00
137	A55	10fr claret	175.00	175.00
		Nos. 124-137 (14)	860.56	835.76

Type of 1915 Inscribed: "FRANK" instead of "FRANKEN"

1919, Dec. ***Perf. 14, 15***

138	A52	5fr dp bl	2.25	1.25

Town Hall at Termonde

A56 A57

1920 ***Perf. 11½***

139	A56	65c cl & blk	1.75	30
a.		Center inverted	30,000.	

Semi-Postal Stamps of 1920 Surcharged in Red or Black

20c X 20c X

1921 ***Perf. 12***

140	SP6	20c on 5c dp grn (R)	1.40	38
a.		Invtd. surcharge	250.00	250.00
141	SP7	20c on 10c car	1.00	38
b.		Invtd. surcharge	250.00	250.00
142	SP8	20c on 15c dk brn (R)	1.10	38
a.		Invtd. surcharge	250.00	250.00

Red Surcharge.

143	A57	55c on 65c cl & blk	1.75	60
a.		Pair, one without surcharge	3.00	1.25

A58

A59

1922-27 **Typographed** ***Perf. 14***

144	A58	1c orange	8	5
145	A58	2c ol ('26)	10	10
146	A58	3c fawn	8	5
147	A58	5c gray	8	5
148	A58	10c bl grn	12	5
149	A58	15c plum ('23)	12	8
150	A58	20c blk brn	30	6
151	A58	25c dl vio	22	8
152	A58	30c vermilion	70	10
153	A58	30c rose ('25)	55	8
154	A58	35c red brn	45	12
155	A58	35c bl grn ('27)	1.10	30

No.	Type	Description	Unused	Used
156	A58	40c rose	70	12
157	A58	50c bis ('25)	70	8
158	A58	60c ol brn ('27)	4.50	5
159	A58	1.25fr dp bl ('26)	1.25	90
160	A58	1.50fr brt bl ('26)	3.50	22
161	A58	1.75fr ultra ('27)	2.25	12
a.		Tête bêche pair	18.00	9.00
c.		Bklt. pane of 4 + 2 labels	57.50	
		Nos. 144-161 (18)	16.80	2.61

See also Nos. 185–190.

Perf. 11½, 11½x11, 11½x12, 11½x12½.

1921-25 **Engraved**

No.	Type	Description	Unused	Used
162	A59	50c dl bl	45	5
163	A59	75c scar ('22)	22	15
164	A59	75c ultra ('24)	55	12
165	A59	1fr blk brn ('22)	1.10	12
166	A59	1fr dk bl ('25)	75	12
167	A59	2fr dk grn ('22)	90	30
168	A59	5fr brn vio ('23)	22.50	27.50
169	A59	10fr mag ('22)	14.00	3.50
		Nos. 162-169 (8)	40.47	31.86

No. 162 measures 18x20¾mm. and was printed in sheets of 100.

Philatelic Exhibition Issue.

1921, May 26 ***Perf. 11½***

No.	Type	Description	Unused	Used
170	A59	50c dk bl	6.75	6.75
a.		Sheet of 25	375.00	300.00

No. 170 measures 17½x21¼mm., was printed in sheets of 25 and sold at the Philatelic Exhibition at Brussels.

Philatelic Exhibition Issue.
Souvenir Sheet.

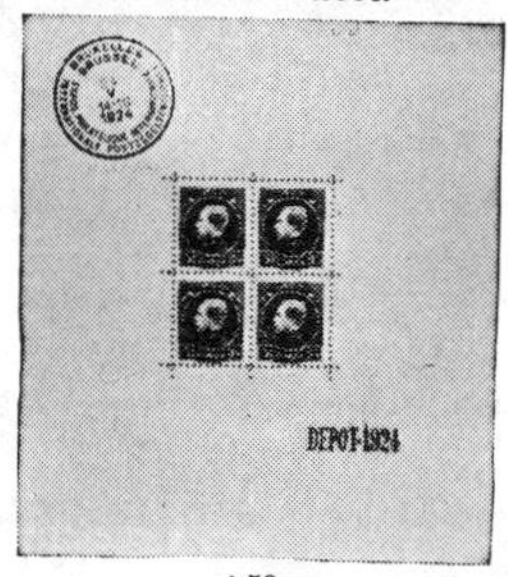

A59a

1924, May 24 ***Perf. 11½***

No.	Type	Description	Unused	Used
171	A59a	5fr red brn, sheet of 4	150.00	160.00
a.		Single stamp (A59)	20.00	20.00

Sold only at the International Philatelic Exhibition, Brussels. Sheet size: 130x145 mm.

Kings Leopold I and Albert I
A60

1925 ***Perf. 14***

No.	Type	Description	Unused	Used
172	A60	10c dp grn	12.50	10.00
173	A60	15c dl vio	7.50	7.50
174	A60	20c red brn	7.50	7.50
175	A60	25c grnsh blk	7.50	7.50
176	A60	30c vermilion	7.50	7.50
177	A60	35c lt bl	7.50	7.50
178	A60	40c brnsh blk	7.50	7.50
179	A60	50c yel brn	7.50	7.50
180	A60	75c dk bl	7.50	7.50
181	A60	1fr dk vio	12.50	11.00
182	A60	2fr ultra	7.50	7.50
183	A60	5fr bl blk	7.50	7.50
184	A60	10fr dp rose	12.50	13.00
		Nos. 172-184 (13)	112.50	109.00

75th anniversary of Belgian postage stamps.

Nos. 172–184 were sold only in sets and only by The Administration of Posts, not at post offices.

A61

1926-27 **Typographed.**

No.	Type	Description	Unused	Used
185	A61	75c dk vio	90	65
186	A61	1fr pale yel	80	22
187	A61	1fr rose red ('27)	1.10	12
a.		Tête bêche pair	10.00	6.00
c.		Bklt pane 4 + 2 labels	30.00	
188	A61	2fr Prus bl	3.00	12
189	A61	5fr emer ('27)	22.50	90
190	A61	10fr dk brn ('27)	50.00	2.50
		Nos. 185-190 (6)	78.30	4.51

Stamps of 1921-27 Surcharged in Carmine, Red or Blue

≡ 1F75 ≡

1927

No.	Type	Description	Unused	Used
191	A58	3c on 2c ol (C)	6	12
192	A58	10c on 15c plum (R)	12	10
193	A58	35c on 40c rose (Bl)	50	12
194	A58	1.75fr on 1.50fr brt bl (C)	2.50	80

Nos. 153, 185 and 159 Surcharged in Black

BRUXELLES
1929
BRUSSEL
=5c=

1929, Jan. 1

No.	Type	Description	Unused	Used
195	A58	5c on 30c rose	12	10
196	A61	5c on 75c dk vio	30	30
197	A58	5c on 1.25fr dp bl	12	12

The surcharge on Nos. 195 to 197 is a precancelation which alters the value of the stamp to which it is applied.

Prices for precanceled stamps in first column are for those which have not been through the post and have original gum. Prices in second column are for postally used, gumless stamps.

A63

A64

1929-32 **Typographed** ***Perf. 14***

No.	Type	Description	Unused	Used
198	A63	1c orange	8	10
199	A63	2c emer ('31)	35	35
200	A63	3c red brn	8	5
201	A63	5c slate	12	5
a.		Tête bêche pair	1.65	1.35
c.		Bklt pane of 4 + 2 labels	11.00	
202	A63	10c ol grn	12	5
a.		Tête bêche pair	90	80
c.		Bklt pane of 4 + 2 labels	6.00	
203	A63	20c brt vio	1.50	10
204	A63	25c rose red	70	5
a.		Tête bêche pair	4.00	3.25
c.		Bklt pane of 4 + 2 labels	11.00	
205	A63	35c green	1.00	12
a.		Tête bêche pair	6.00	5.00
c.		Bklt pane of 4 + 2 labels	13.00	
206	A63	40c red vio ('30)	45	5
a.		Tête bêche pair	5.75	4.25
c.		Bklt pane of 4 + 2 labels	13.00	
207	A63	50c dp bl	80	5
a.		Tête bêche pair	4.75	3.50
c.		Bklt pane of 4 + 2 labels	11.00	
208	A63	60c rose ('30)	1.75	20
a.		Tête bêche pair	16.00	13.00
c.		Bklt pane of 4 + 2 labels	40.00	
209	A63	70c org brn ('30)	1.10	5
a.		Tête bêche pair	11.00	9.00
c.		Bklt pane of 4 + 2 labels	30.00	
210	A63	75c dk bl ('30)	2.75	10
a.		Tête bêche pair	16.50	15.00
211	A63	75c dp brn ('32)	13.00	5
a.		Tête bêche pair	57.50	40.00
b.		Bklt pane of 4 + 2 labels	135.00	
		Nos. 198-211 (14)	23.80	1.37

Nos. 198 and 199 exist se-tenant in booklets.

1929, Jan. 25 Engr. ***Perf. 14½, 14***

No.	Type	Description	Unused	Used
212	A64	10fr dk brn	22.50	6.75
213	A64	20fr dk grn	135.00	9.00
214	A64	50fr red vio	13.00	9.00
a.		Perf. 14½	30.00	30.00
215	A64	100fr rose lake	17.50	17.50
a.		Perf. 14½	40.00	40.00

Peter Paul Rubens
A65

Zenobe Gramme
A66

1930, Apr. 26 Photo. ***Perf. 12½x12***

No.	Type	Description	Unused	Used
216	A65	35c bl grn	65	25
217	A66	35c bl grn	65	25

No. 216 issued for the Antwerp Exhibition, No. 217 the Liege Exhibition.

King Leopold I, by Jacques de Winne
A67

King Leopold II, by Joseph Lempoels
A68

Design: 1.75fr, King Albert I.

1930, July 1 Engraved ***Perf. 11½***

No.	Type	Description	Unused	Used
218	A67	60c brn vio	30	12
219	A68	1fr carmine	2.25	2.25
220	A68	1.75fr dk bl	5.50	1.65

Centenary of Belgian independence.

Antwerp Exhibition Issue.
Souvenir Sheet.

Arms of Antwerp
A70

1930, Aug. 9 ***Perf. 11½***

No.	Type	Description	Unused	Used
221	A70	Sheet of one	150.00	200.00
a.		4fr dk grn & gray grn	60.00	90.00

Issued in sheets of one stamp measuring 142x141 mm. Inscription in lower margin "ATELIER DU TIMBRE—1930—ZEGELFABRIEK." Each purchaser of a ticket to the Antwerp Philatelic Exhibition, August 9th to 15th 1930, was allowed to purchase one of the exhibition stamps. The ticket cost 6 francs.

Nos. 218–220 Overprinted in Blue or Red

B.I.T.
OCT. 1930

1930, Oct.

No.	Type	Description	Unused	Used
222	A67	60c brn vio (Bl)	2.75	2.25
223	A68	1fr car (Bl)	12.50	11.50
224	A68	1.75fr dk bl (R)	21.00	21.00

Issued to commemorate the 50th meeting of the administrative council of the International Labor Bureau at Brussels.

The names of the painters and the initials of the engraver have been added at the foot of these stamps.

Stamps of 1929-30 Surcharged in Blue or Black:

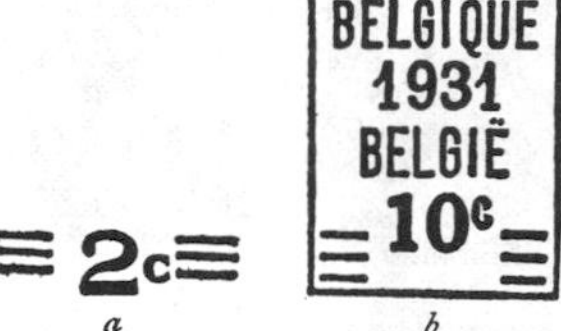

a b

1931, Feb. 20 ***Perf. 14***

No.	Type	Description	Unused	Used
225	A63 (a)	2c on 3c red brn (Bl)	12	10
226	A63 (b)	10c on 60c rose (Bk)	90	22

The surcharge on No. 226 is a precancelation which alters the denomination. See note after No. 197.

King Albert
A71 A71a

1931, June 15 **Photogravure**

No.	Type	Description	Unused	Used
227	A71	1fr brn car	85	12

1932, June 1

No.	Type	Description	Unused	Used
228	A71a	75c bis brn	60	5
a.		Tête bêche pair	21.00	21.00
c.		Bklt pane 4 + 2 labels	27.50	

See also No. 257.

A72

1931-32 **Engraved**

No.	Type	Description	Unused	Used
229	A72	1.25fr gray blk	1.25	35
230	A72	1.50fr brn vio	1.65	30
231	A72	1.75fr dp bl	1.25	12
232	A72	2fr red brn	1.65	12
233	A72	2.45fr dp vio	2.25	30
234	A72	2.50fr blk brn ('32)	17.50	35
235	A72	5fr dp grn	19.00	90
236	A72	10fr claret	45.00	11.00
		Nos. 229-236 (8)	89.55	13.44

Nos. 206 and 209 Surcharged as No. 226, but dated "1932."

1932, Jan. 1

240	A63	10c on 40c red vio	5.25	50
241	A63	10c on 70c org brn	4.00	25

The surcharge on Nos. 240 and 241 is a precancelation which alters the value of the stamps. See note after No. 197.

Gleaner A73

Mercury A74

1932, June 1 Typo. Perf. 13½x14

245	A73	2c pale grn	20	45
246	A74	5c dp org	20	10
247	A73	10c ol grn	38	5
a.		Tête bêche pair	8.50	6.75
c.		Bklt pane 4 + 2 labels	15.00	
248	A74	20c brt vio	80	12
249	A73	25c dp red	80	5
a.		Tête bêche pair	6.75	6.00
c.		Bklt pane 4 + 2 labels	15.00	
250	A74	35c dp grn	4.50	10
		Nos. 245-250 (6)	6.88	87

Auguste Piccard's Balloon A75

1932, Nov. 26 Engraved Perf. 11½

251	A75	75c red brn	5.25	30
252	A75	1.75fr dk bl	12.00	1.75
253	A75	2.50fr dk vio	16.00	13.00

Issued in commemoration of Prof. Auguste Piccard's two ascents to the stratosphere.

Nos. 206 and 209 Surcharged as No. 226, but dated "1933."

1933, Nov. Perf. 14

254	A63	10c on 40c red vio	22.50	7.00
255	A63	10c on 70c org brn	18.00	2.50

No. 206 Surcharged as No. 226, but dated "1934."

1934, Feb.

256	A63	10c on 40c red vio	13.00	2.50

The surcharge on Nos. 254 to 256 is a precancelation which alters the value of the stamps. See note after No. 197.

Regummed copies of Nos. 254-256 abound.

King Albert Memorial Issue.

Type of 1932 with Black Margins.

1934, Mar. 10 Photogravure

257	A71a	75c black	45	8

Brussels International Exhibition of 1935.

Congo Pavilion A76

Designs: 1fr, Brussels pavilion. 1.50fr, "Old Brussels." 1.75fr, Belgian pavilion.

1934, July 1 Perf. 14x13½

258	A76	35c green	1.00	10
259	A76	1fr dk car	1.40	25
260	A76	1.50fr brown	3.50	1.10
261	A76	1.75fr blue	8.00	20

King Leopold III A80 A81

1934-35 Perf. 13½x14.

262	A80	70c ol blk ('35)	45	5
a.		Tête bêche pair	2.25	1.25
c.		Bklt pane 4 + 2 labels	7.50	
263	A80	75c brown	1.40	15

Perf. 14x13½

264	A81	1fr rose car ('35)	6.75	45

Coat of Arms A82

1935-48 Typographed. Perf. 14.

265	A82	2c grn ('37)	10	5
266	A82	5c orange	10	5
267	A82	10c ol bis	10	5
a.		Tête bêche pair	35	30
b.		Bklt pane 4 + 2 labels	6.00	
268	A82	15c dk vio	10	5
269	A82	20c lilac	10	5
270	A82	25c car rose	10	5
a.		Tête bêche pair	80	60
c.		Bklt pane 4 + 2 labels	6.00	
271	A82	25c yel org ('46)	25	5
272	A82	30c brown	28	5
273	A82	35c green	12	5
a.		Tête bêche pair	35	30
c.		Bklt pane 4 + 2 labels	4.00	
274	A82	40c red vio ('38)	60	5
275	A82	50c blue	28	5
276	A82	60c sl ('41)	18	5
277	A82	65c red lil ('46)	75	5
278	A82	70c lt bl grn ('45)	38	5
279	A82	75c lil rose ('45)	80	5
280	A82	80c grn ('48)	9.00	45
281	A82	90c dl vio ('46)	80	5
282	A82	1fr red brn ('45)	80	5
		Nos. 265-282 (18)	14.84	1.30

Several stamps of type A82 exist in various shades.

Nos. 265, 361 were privately overprinted and surcharged "+10FR." by the Association Belgo-Americaine for the dedication of the Bastogne Memorial, July 16, 1950. The overprint is in four types.

King Leopold III A83 A83a

1936-51 Photo. Perf. 14, 14x13½

Size: 17½x21¾ mm.

283	A83	70c brown	55	5
a.		Tête bêche pair	2.75	2.00
c.		Bklt pane 4 + 2 labels	10.00	

Size: 20¾x24 mm.

284	A83a	1fr rose car	60	8
285	A83a	1.20fr dk brn ('51)	2.00	5
286	A83a	1.50fr brt red vio ('43)	45	12
287	A83a	1.75fr dp ultra ('43)	20	18
288	A83a	1.75fr dk car ('50)	75	5
289	A83a	2fr dk pur ('43)	90	85
290	A83a	2.25fr grnsh blk ('43)	45	8
291	A83a	2.50fr org red ('51)	6.00	10
292	A83a	3.25fr chnt ('43)	22	5
293	A83a	5fr dp grn ('43)	2.50	40
		Nos. 283-293 (11)	14.62	2.01

Nos. 287-288, 290-291, 293 inscribed "Belgie-Belgique."

King Leopold III A84 A85

1936-51 Engraved Perf. 14x13½

294	A84	1.50fr rose lil	90	10
295	A84	1.75fr dl bl	45	5
296	A84	2fr dl vio	90	10
297	A84	2.25fr gray vio ('41)	45	12
298	A84	2.45fr black	45.00	45
299	A84	2.50fr ol blk ('40)	4.50	25
300	A84	3.25fr org brn ('41)	45	12
301	A84	5fr dl grn	3.25	35
302	A84	10fr dk vio brn	1.40	5
303	A84	20fr vermilion	2.75	15

Perf. 11½

304	A84	3fr yel brn ('51)	2.00	5
305	A84	4fr bl, *bluish* ('50)	8.75	10
a.		White paper	19.00	5
306	A84	6fr brt rose car ('51)	8.75	8
307	A84	10fr brn vio ('51)	90	5
308	A84	20fr red ('51)	2.25	6
		Nos. 294-308 (15)	82.70	2.08

See No. 1159.

No. 206 Surcharged as No. 226, but dated "1937."

1937 Perf. 14. Unwmkd.

309	A63	10c on 40c red vio	45	35

The surcharge is a precancelation which alters the value of the stamp. See note after No. 197.

1938-41 Photo. Perf. 13½x14

310	A85	75c ol gray	80	5
a.		Tête bêche pair	3.00	1.65
c.		Bklt pane 4 + 2 labels	9.00	
311	A85	1fr rose pink ('41)	15	5
a.		Tête bêche pair	45	30
b.		Booklet pane of 6	3.00	
c.		Bklt pane 4 + 2 labels	3.00	

Nos. 272, 274, 283, 310, 299, 298 Surcharged in Blue, Black, Carmine or Red

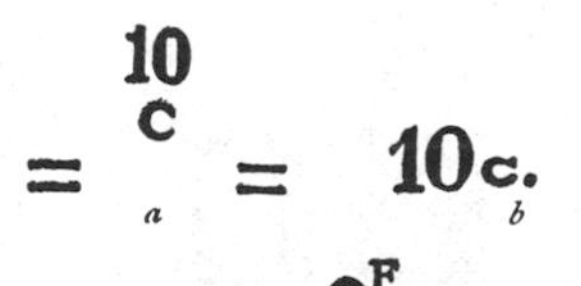

a b c

1938-42 Perf. 14, 14x13½

312	A82 (a)	10c on 30c brn (Bl)	18	12
313	A82 (a)	10c on 40c red vio (Bl)	18	12
314	A83 (b)	10c on 70c brn (Bk)	22	15
315	A85 (b)	50c on 75c ol gray (C)	45	20
316	A84 (c)	2.25fr on 2.50fr ol blk (C)	1.10	90
317	A84 (c)	2.50fr on 2.45fr blk (R)	22.50	35
		Nos. 312-317 (6)	24.63	1.84

Issue date: No. 317, Oct. 31, 1938.

Basilica and Bell Tower A86

Water Exhibition Buildings A87

Designs: 1.50fr, Albert Canal and Park. 1.75fr, Eygenbilsen Cut in Albert Canal.

Perf. 14x13½, 13½x14

1938, Oct. 31

318	A86	35c dk bl grn	15	15
319	A87	1fr rose red	90	18
320	A87	1.50fr vio brn	2.25	70
321	A87	1.75fr ultra	2.50	22

Publicity for the International Water Exhibition, Liège, 1939.

Lion Rampant A90

King Leopold III with Crown and V A91

Photogravure.

1944 Perf. 12½. Unwmkd.

Inscribed: "Belgique-Belgie".

322	A90	5c chocolate	8	5
323	A90	10c green	8	5
324	A90	25c lt bl	8	5
325	A90	35c brown	8	5
326	A90	50c lt bl grn	12	5
327	A90	75c purple	12	12
328	A90	1fr vermilion	8	5
329	A90	1.25fr chestnut	15	22
330	A90	1.50fr orange	40	50
331	A90	1.75fr brt ultra	12	5
332	A90	2fr aqua	3.25	2.50
333	A90	2.75fr dp mag	18	12
334	A90	3fr claret	65	85
335	A90	3.50fr sl blk	65	85
336	A90	5fr dk ol	5.75	6.25
337	A90	10fr black	1.10	1.40
		Nos. 322-337 (16)	12.89	13.16

Inscribed: "Belgie-Belgique".

338	A90	5c chocolate	8	5
339	A90	10c green	8	5
340	A90	25c lt bl	8	5
341	A90	35c brown	8	5
342	A90	50c lt bl grn	12	5
343	A90	75c purple	12	12
344	A90	1fr vermilion	8	5
345	A90	1.25fr chestnut	16	22
346	A90	1.50fr orange	35	50
347	A90	1.75fr brt ultra	15	5
348	A90	2fr aqua	2.25	2.25
349	A90	2.75fr dp mag	20	12
350	A90	3fr claret	75	85
351	A90	3.50fr sl blk	75	85
352	A90	5fr dk ol	6.25	5.50
353	A90	10fr black	1.10	1.40
		Nos. 338-353 (16)	12.60	12.16

1944-57 Perf. 14x13½

354	A91	1fr brt rose red	35	6
355	A91	1.50fr magenta	50	6
356	A91	1.75fr dp ultra	50	55
357	A91	2fr dp vio	1.50	8
358	A91	2.25fr grnsh blk	55	65
359	A91	3.25fr chnt brn	75	5
360	A91	5fr dk bl grn	3.00	5
a.		Perf. 11½ ('57)	82.50	10
		Nos. 354-360 (7)	7.15	1.50

Nos. 355, 357, 359 inscribed "Belgique-Belgie."

Stamps of 1935-41 Overprinted in Red **V**

1944 *Perf. 14.*

361	A82	2c pale grn	6	5
362	A82	15c indigo	6	6
363	A82	20c brt vio	10	6
364	A82	60c slate	20	15

See note following No. 282.

Nos. 355, 357, and 360 Surcharged Typographically in Black or Carmine **−10%**

1946 *Perf. 14x13½.*

365	A91	On 1.50fr mag	75	10
366	A91	On 2fr dp vio (C)	2.75	65
367	A91	On 5fr dk bl grn (C)	3.75	40

To provide denominations created by a reduction in postal rates, the Government produced Nos. 365-367 by surcharging typographically. Also, each post office was authorized on May 20, 1946, to surcharge its stock of 1.50fr, 2fr and 5fr stamps "—10 percent." Hundreds of types and sizes of this surcharge exist, both hand-stamped and typographed. These include the "1,35", "1,80" and "4,50" applied at Ghislenghien.

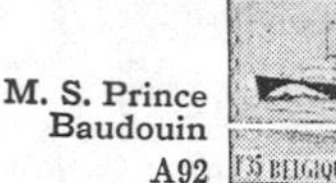

M. S. Prince Baudouin
A92

Designs: 2.25fr, S. S. Marie Henriette. 3.15fr, S. S. Diamant.

Perf. 14x13½, 13½x14.

1946, June 15 Photo. Unwmkd.

368	A92	1.35fr brt bluish grn	18	6
369	A92	2.25fr sl grn	45	18
370	A92	3.15fr sl blk	45	25

Centenary of the steamship line between Ostend and Dover.

No. 368 exists in two sizes: 21¼x18¼mm and 21x17mm. Nos. 369-370 are 24½x20mm

Capt. Adrien de Gerlache
A95

Belgica and Explorers
A96

1947, June *Perf. 14x13½, 11½*

371	A95	1.35fr crim rose	25	6
372	A96	2.25fr gray blk	1.50	1.40

Issued to commemorate the 50th anniversary of Capt. Adrien de Gerlache's Antarctic Expedition.

Joseph A. F. Plateau
A97

1947, June *Perf. 14x13½*

373	A97	3.15fr dp bl	60	15

Issued to mark the World Film and Fine Arts Festival, Brussels, June, 1947.

Chemical Industry
A98

Industrial Arts
A99

Agriculture
A100

Communications Center
A101

Textile Industry
A102

Iron Manufacture
A103

Photogravure (#357-359, 361), Typographed (#360, 363), Engraved.

1948 *Perf. 11½* **Unwmkd.**

374	A98	60c bl grn	50	15
375	A98	1.20fr brown	2.00	10
376	A99	1.35fr red brn	50	5
377	A100	1.75fr brt red	1.25	6
378	A99	1.75fr dk gray grn	1.00	5
379	A101	2.25fr gray bl	1.75	1.10
380	A100	2.50fr dk car rose	6.25	12
381	A101	3fr brt red vio	8.25	18
382	A102	3.15fr dp bl	1.65	15
383	A102	4fr brt ultra	7.25	12
384	A103	6fr bl grn	12.00	12
385	A103	6.30fr brt red vio	3.50	3.75
		Nos. 374-385 (12)	45.90	5.95

King Leopold I
A104

Engraved

1949, July 1 *Perf. 14x13½*

386	A104	90c dk grn	75	60
387	A104	1.75fr brown	60	15
388	A104	3fr red	3.50	4.50
389	A104	4fr dp bl	5.00	1.25

Issued to commemorate the centenary of Belgium's first postage stamps.

See note on souvenir sheet below No. 2.

Stamps of 1935-45 Precanceled and Surcharged in Black

1949 *Perf. 14*

390	A82	5c on 15c dk vio	8	10
391	A82	5c on 30c brn	8	10
392	A82	5c on 40c red vio	8	10
393	A82	20c on 70c lt bl grn	20	25
394	A82	20c on 75c lil rose	12	10

Similar Surcharge and Precancelation in Black on Nos. B455-B458.

Perf. 14x13½.

395	SP251	10c on 65+35 rose red	3.25	5.75
396	SP251	40c on 90c+60c gray	90	1.65
397	SP251	80c on 1.35fr+1.15fr hn brn	60	90
398	SP251	1.20fr on 3.15+1.85 brt bl	2.00	2.75
		Nos. 390-398 (9)	7.31	11.70

The surcharges on Nos. 390-398 are combined with the precancellations. See note after No. 197.

St. Mary Magdalene, from Painting by Gerard David
A105

1949, July 15 Photo. *Perf. 11*

399	A105	1.75fr dk brn	75	35

Issued to publicize the Gerard David Exhibition at Bruges, 1949.

Allegory of U.P.U.—A106

1949, Oct. 1 Engr. *Perf. 11½*

400	A106	4fr dp bl	3.75	3.25

Issued to commemorate the 75th anniversary of the formation of the Universal Postal Union.

Symbolical of Pension Fund
A107

Lion Rampant
A108

Photogravure.

1950, May 1 *Perf. 11½* **Unwmkd.**

401	A107	1.75fr dk brn	50	25

Issued to commemorate the centenary of the foundation of the General Pension Fund.

1951, Feb. 15 Engr. *Perf. 11½*

402	A108	20c blue	25	8

1951-75 Typographed *Perf. 13½x14*

Size: 17½x21mm

403	A108	2c org brn ('60)	10	5
404	A108	3c brt lil ('60)	10	5
405	A108	5c pale vio	12	5
406	A108	5c brt pink ('74)	15	5
407	A108	10c red org	8	5
408	A108	15c brt pink ('59)	10	5
409	A108	20c claret	5	5
410	A108	25c green	1.50	22
411	A108	25c lt bl grn ('66)	15	5
412	A108	30c gray grn ('57)	12	5
413	A108	40c brn ol	12	5
414	A108	50c ultra	5	5
a.		50c lt bl	12	5
415	A108	60c lil rose	5	5
416	A108	65c vio brn	15.00	55
417	A108	75c bluish lil	30	5
418	A108	80c emerald	1.00	5
419	A108	90c dp bl	1.25	12
420	A108	1fr rose	12	5
421	A108	2fr emer ('73)	30	5
422	A108	2.50fr brn ('70)	30	8
423	A108	3fr brt pink ('70)	30	5
424	A108	4fr brt rose lil ('74)	30	5
425	A108	4.50fr bl ('74)	45	5
426	A108	5fr brt lil ('75)	30	5

Size: 17x20½mm

427	A108	1.50fr dk sl grn ('69)	15	10

Perf. 13½x13

428	A108	2fr emer ('68)	25	5

Photo. *Perf. 11½*

Size: 20½x24mm

429	A108	50c lt bl ('61)	1.00	15
430	A108	60c lil rose ('66)	2.25	2.00
431	A108	1fr car rose ('59)	15	5

Perf. 13½x12½

Size: 17½x22mm

432	A108	50c lt bl ('75)	15	5
a.		Booklet pane of 4 (#432, 784 and 2 #785) + labels	1.00	
b.		Booklet pane of 4 (#432 and 3 #787) + labels	1.35	
433	A108	1fr rose ('69)	9.00	1.50
434	A108	2fr emer ('72)	60	30
e.		Booklet pane of 6 (4 #434 + 2 #475)	5.50	
f.		Booklet pane of 5 (#434, 4 #476 + label)	8.00	
		Nos. 403-434 (32)	35.86	6.17

Counterfeits exist of No. 416. Nos. 429, 431 also issued in coils with black control number on back of every fifth stamp. Nos. 432-434 issued in booklet panes only. No. 432 has one straight-edge, and stamps in the pane are tete-beche. Each pane has 2 labels showing Belgian postal emblem and a large selvage with postal code instructions.

Nos. 433-434 have 1 or 2 straight-edges. Panes have a large selvage with inscription or map of Belgium showing postal zones.

Francois de Tassis (Franz von Taxis)
A109

Portraits: 1.75fr, Jean-Baptiste of Thurn & Taxis. 2fr, Baron Leonard I. 2.50fr, Count Lamoral I. 3fr, Count Leonard II. 4fr, Count Lamoral II. 5fr, Prince Eugene Alexander. 5.75fr, Prince Anselme Francois. 8fr, Prince Alexander Ferdinand. 10fr, Prince Charles Anselme. 20fr, Prince Charles Alexander.

Laid Paper.

Inscribed: "Congres 1952 U.P.U." etc.

1952, May 14 Engraved *Perf. 11½*

435	A109	80c ol grn	75	90
436	A109	1.75fr red org	75	30
437	A109	2fr vio brn	1.75	50
438	A109	2.50fr carmine	2.50	1.50
439	A109	3fr ol bis	2.25	90
440	A109	4fr ultra	3.25	75
441	A109	5fr red brn	4.25	1.65
442	A109	5.75fr bl vio	7.50	2.00
443	A109	8fr gray	11.50	2.50

44	A109	10fr rose vio	20.00	4.00
45	A109	20fr brown	50.00	25.00
		Nos. 435-445 (11)	104.50	40.00

Issued on the occasion of the 13th Universal Postal Union Congress, Brussels, 1952. See No. B514.

King Baudouin
A110 A111

1952-58 Engraved *Perf. 11½*

Size: 21x24mm

446	A110	1.50fr gray	55	8
447	A110	2fr crimson	42	5
448	A110	4fr ultra	3.50	30

Size: 24½x35mm

449	A110	50fr gray brn	1.75	30
a.		50fr vio brn	27.50	90
450	A110	100fr rose red ('58)	5.00	35

1953-72 Photo. *Perf. 11½*

451	A111	1.50fr gray	25	5
452	A111	2fr rose car	6.75	5
453	A111	2fr green	25	5
454	A111	2.50fr red brn ('57)	60	5
a.		2.50fr org brn ('70)	45	5
455	A111	3fr rose lil ('58)	38	5
456	A111	3.50fr brt yel grn ('58)	75	5
457	A111	4fr brt ultra	50	5
458	A111	4.50fr dk red brn ('62)	3.00	5
459	A111	5fr vio ('57)	1.25	5
460	A111	6fr dp pink ('58)	75	5
461	A111	6.50fr gray ('60)	80.00	17.00
462	A111	7fr bl ('60)	90	5
463	A111	7.50fr grysh brn ('58)	52.50	20.00
464	A111	8fr bluish gray ('58)	1.25	8
465	A111	8.50fr cl ('58)	20.00	45
466	A111	9fr gray ('58)	55.00	1.10
467	A111	12fr lt bl grn ('66)	90	15
468	A111	30fr red org ('58)	5.50	15

Redrawn

469	A111	2.50fr org brn ('71)	35	7
470	A111	4.50fr brn ('72)	2.25	90
471	A111	7fr bl ('71)	60	12

Perf. 13½x12½

Size: 17½x22mm.

472	A111	1.50fr gray ('70)	60	45
b.		Bklt pane of 10	8.50	
c.		Bklt. pane of 6 (3 #472 + 3 #475)	20.00	
473	A111	2.50fr org brn ('70)	9.00	9.00
h.		Bklt. pane of 6 (#473 + 5 #475)	22.50	
474	A111	3fr lil rose ('69)	60	15
a.		Bklt pane of 5 + label	35.00	
b.		Bklt pane of 8 (2 #433 + 6 #474)	25.00	
475	A111	3.50fr brt yel grn ('70)	60	35
476	A111	4.50fr dl red brn ('72)	75	60
		Nos. 446-476 (31)	256.50	52.20

Nos. 451, 453, 454a, 455, 456, 458 also issued in coils with black control number on back of every fifth stamp. These coils, except for No. 451, are on luminescent paper.

On Nos. 469-471, the 2, 4 and 7 are 3mm high. The background around the head is white. On Nos. 454, 458, 462 the 2, 4 and 7 are 2½mm high and the background is tinted.

Nos. 472-476 issued in booklets only and have 1 or 2 straight-edges. All panes have a large selvage with inscription or map.

Luminescent Paper

Stamps issued on both ordinary and luminescent paper include: Nos. 307-308, 430-431, 449-451, 453-460, 462, 464, 467-468, 472, 643-644, 650-651, 837, Q385, Q410.

Stamps issued only on luminescent paper include: Nos. 433, 454a, 472b, 473-474, 649, 652-658, 664-670, 679-682, 688-690, 694-696, 698-703, 705-711, 713-726, 729-747, 751-754, 756-757, 759, 761-762, 764, 766, 769, 772, 774, 778, 789, 791-793, 795, 797-799, 801-807, 809-811, 814-818, 820-834, 836, 838-848.

See note after No. 857.

Nos. 396 and 398 Surcharged and Precanceled in Black

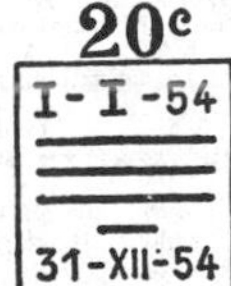

Perf. 13½x14

1954, Jan. 1 **Unwmkd.**

477	A108	20c on 65c vio brn	1.75	65
478	A108	20c on 90c dp bl	1.75	45

The surcharge is combined with the precancellation. See note after No. 197.

Map and Rotary Emblem
A112

Designs: 80c, Mermaid and Mercury holding emblem. 4fr, Rotary emblem and two globes.

1954, Sept. 10 **Engr.** ***Perf. 11½***

479	A112	20c red	25	25
480	A112	80c dk grn	65	50
481	A112	4fr ultra	1.40	75

5th regional conf. of Rotary International at Ostend. No. 481 for Rotary 50th Anniv. (in 1955).

A souv. sheet containing one each, imperf., was sold for 500 francs. It was not valid for postage.

The Rabot and Begonia
A113

Designs: 2.50fr, The Oudeburg and azalea. 4fr, "Three Towers" and orchid.

1955, Feb. 15 **Photogravure**

482	A113	80c brt car	75	55
483	A113	2.50fr blk brn	4.50	5.50
484	A113	4fr dk rose brn	4.00	1.75

Issued to publicize the Ghent International Flower Exhibition, 1955.

Homage to Charles V as a Child, by Albrecht de Vriendt
A114

Charles V, by Titian
A115

Design: 4fr, Abdication of Charles V, by Louis Gallait.

1955, Mar. 25 ***Perf. 11½*** **Unwmkd.**

485	A114	20c rose red	18	25
486	A115	2fr dk gray grn	1.65	10
487	A114	4fr blue	4.50	1.65

Issued to publicize the Charles V Exhibition, Ghent, 1955.

Emile Verhaeren, by Montald Constant
A116

1955, May 11 **Engraved**

488	A116	20c dk gray	18	8

Issued to commemorate the centenary of the birth of Emile Verhaeren, poet.

Allegory of Textile Manufacture
A117

1955, May 11

489	A117	2fr vio brn	1.25	18

Issued to publicize the second International Textile Exhibition, Brussels, June 1955.

"The Foolish Virgin" by Rik Wouters
A118

"Departure of Volunteers from Liege, 1830" by Charles Soubre
A119

1955, June 10

490	A118	1.20fr ol grn	1.00	1.10
491	A118	2fr violet	1.50	15

Issued to publicize the third biennial exhibition of sculpture, Antwerp, June 11–Sept. 10, 1955.

1955, Sept. 10 **Photogravure**

492	A119	20c grnsh sl	18	25
493	A119	2fr chocolate	90	22

Issued to publicize the exhibition "The Romantic Movement in Liege Province," Sept. 10 - Oct. 31, 1955; and to mark the 125th anniversary of Belgium's independence from the Netherlands.

Pelican Giving Blood to Young
A120

Buildings of Tournai, Ghent and Antwerp
A121

1956, Jan. 14 **Engraved**

494	A120	2fr brt car	55	18

Issued in honor of the blood donor service of the Belgian Red Cross.

1956, July 14 **Photogravure**

495	A121	2fr brt ultra	38	18

Issued to publicize the Scheldt exhibition (Scaldis) at Tournai, Ghent and Antwerp, July–Sept. 1956.

Europa Issue.

"Rebuilding Europe"
A122

1956, Sept. 15 **Engraved**

496	A122	2fr lt grn	1.75	15
497	A122	4fr purple	8.00	1.00

Issued to symbolize the cooperation among the six countries comprising the Coal and Steel Community.

Train on Map of Belgium and Luxembourg—A123

1956, Sept. 29

498	A123	2fr dk bl	60	18

Issued to mark the electrification of the Brussels-Luxembourg railroad.

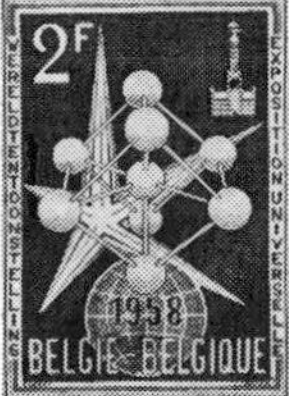

Edouard Anseele
A124

"The Atom" and Exposition Emblem
A125

1956, Oct. 27

499	A124	20c vio brn	12	6

Issued to commemorate the centenary of the birth of Edouard Anseele, statesman, and in connection with an exhibition held in his honor at Ghent.

1957-58 **Unwmkd.**

500	A125	2fr car rose	45	12
501	A125	2.50fr grn ('58)	60	18
502	A125	4fr brt vio bl	1.50	38
503	A125	5fr cl ('58)	1.25	1.00

Issued to publicize the 1958 World's Fair at Brussels.

Emperor Maximilian I Receiving Letter
A126

1957, May 19

504 A126 2fr claret 55 15

Issued for the Day of the Stamp, May 19, 1957.

Sikorsky S-58 Helicopter
A127

1957, June 15

505 A127 4fr gray grn & brt bl 90 80

Issued to publicize the 100,000th passenger carried by Sabena helicopter service, June 15, 1957.

Zeebrugge Harbor
A128

1957, July 6

506 A128 2fr dk bl 55 15

Issued to commemorate the 50th anniversary of the completion of the port of Zeebrugge-Bruges.

Leopold I Entering Brussels, 1831
A129

Leopold I Arriving at Belgian Border
A130

1957, July 17 Photogravure

507 A129 20c dk gray grn 8 12
508 A130 2fr lilac 75 30

Issued to commemorate the 126th anniversary of the arrival in Belgium of King Leopold I.

Boy Scout and Girl Scout Emblems
A131

Design: 4fr, Robert Lord Baden-Powell, painted by David Jaggers (vert.).

Engraved.

1957, July 29 ***Perf. 11½*** **Unwmkd.**

509 A131 80c gray 38 25
510 A131 4fr lt grn 1.50 75

Issued to commemorate the centenary of the birth of Lord Baden-Powell, founder of the Boy Scout movement.

"Kneeling Woman" by Lehmbruck
A132

"United Europe"
A133

1957, Aug. 20 Photogravure

511 A132 2.50fr dk bl grn 1.50 2.00

Issued to commemorate the fourth Biennial Exposition of Sculpture, Antwerp, May 25–Sept. 15.

Europa Issue, 1957.

1957, Sept. 16 Engr. ***Perf. 11½***

512 A133 2fr dk vio brn 1.25 25
513 A133 4fr dk bl 2.50 75

Issued to publicize a united Europe for peace and prosperity.

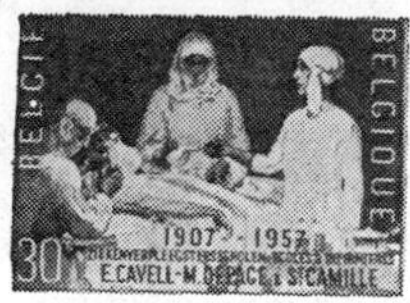

Queen Elisabeth Assisting at Operation, by Allard L'Olivier
A134

Engraved.

1957, Nov. 23 ***Perf. 11½*** **Unwmkd.**

514 A134 30c rose lil 15 10

Issued to commemorate the 50th anniversary of the founding of the Edith Cavell-Marie Depage and St. Camille schools of nursing.

Post Horn and Historic Postal Insignia
A135

1958, Mar. 16 Photo. ***Perf. 11½***

515 A135 2.50fr gray 30 15

Postal Museum Day.

United Nations Issue

International Labor Organization
A136

Allegory of U. N.
A137

Designs: 1fr, Food and Agriculture Organization. 2fr, World Bank. 2.50fr, UNESCO. 3fr, U. N. Pavilion. 5fr, International Telecommunication Union. 8fr, International Monetary Fund. 11fr, World Health Organization. 20fr, U. P. U.

Engraved.

1958, Apr. 17 ***Perf. 11½*** **Unwmkd.**

516 A136 50c gray 80 1.40
517 A136 1fr claret 25 45
518 A137 1.50fr dp ultra 25 45
519 A137 2fr gray brn 75 1.25
520 A136 2.50fr ol grn 25 45
521 A136 3fr grnsh bl 75 1.25
522 A137 5fr rose lil 50 90
523 A136 8fr red brn 90 1.65
524 A136 11fr dl lil 1.10 2.00
525 A136 20fr car rose 1.50 2.50
Nos. 516-525 (10) 7.05 12.30

World's Fair, Brussels, Apr. 17–Oct. 19. See Nos. C15–C20.

Postally valid only from the UN pavilion at the Brussels Fair. Proceeds went toward financing the UN exhibits.

Eugène Ysaye
A138

1958, Sept. 1

526 A138 30c dk bl & plum 12 8

Issued to commemorate the centenary of the birth of Eugène Ysaye (1858–1931), violinist and composer.

Europa Issue, 1958
Common Design Type

1958, Sept. 13 Photogravure

Size: 24½x35mm.

527 CD1 2.50fr brt red & bl 22 6
528 CD1 5fr brt bl & red 38 45

Issued to show the European Postal Union at the service of European integration.

Infant and U. N. Emblem
A140

Charles V and Jean-Baptiste of Thurn and Taxis
A141

1958, Dec. 10 Engraved

529 A140 2.50fr bl gray 38 10

Issued to commemorate the tenth anniversary of the signing of the Universal Declaration of Human Rights.

1959, Mar. 15 **Unwmkd.**

530 A141 2.50fr green 60 15

Issued for the Day of the Stamp. Design from painting by J.-E. van den Bussche.

NATO Emblem
A142

City Hall, Audenarde
A143

1959, Apr. 3 Photo. ***Perf. 11½***

531 A142 2.50fr dp red & dk bl 60 15
532 A142 5fr emer & dk bl 1.65 1.90

Issued to commemorate the 10th anniversary of the North Atlantic Treaty Organization.

See No. 720

1959, Aug. 17 Engraved

533 A143 2.50fr dp cl 45 6

Pope Adrian VI, by Jan van Scorel
A144

1959, Aug. 31 ***Perf. 11½***

534 A144 2.50fr dk red 30 10
535 A144 5fr Prus bl 85 85

Issued to commemorate the 500th anniversary of the birth of Pope Adrian VI.

Europa Issue, 1959
Common Design Type

1959, Sept. 19 Photogravure

Size: 24 x 35½mm.

536 CD2 2.50fr dk red 20 12
537 CD2 5fr brt grnsh bl 45 55

No. 536 inscribed Belgie-Belgique.

Boeing 707
A146

Engraved and Photogravure

1959, Dec. 1 ***Perf. 11½***

538 A146 6fr dk bl gray & car 1.90 1.25

Issued to commemorate the inauguration of jet flights by Sabena Airlines.

Countess of Taxis
A147

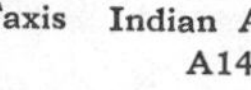

Indian Azalea
A148

Engraved

960, Mar. 21 ***Perf. 11½***

39 A147 3fr dk bl 1.50 15

Issued to honor Alexandrine de Rye, ountess of Taxis, Grand Mistress of the etherlands Posts, 1628–1645, and to publicize the day of the stamp, March 21, 960. The painting of the Countess is by icholas van der Eggermans.

960, Mar. 28 **Unwmkd.**

Flowers: 3fr, Begonia. 6fr, Anthurium nd bromelia.

40 A148 40c dl vio & dp car 32 15
41 A148 3fr emer, red & org yel 1.50 15
42 A148 6fr dk bl, grn & brt red 1.75 1.50

Issued to publicize the 24th Ghent International Flower Exhibition, Apr. 23–ay 2, 1960.

Steel Workers, by Constantin Meunier
A149

Design: 3fr, The sower, field and dock workers, from "Monument to Labor," Brussels, by Constantin Meunier (horiz.).

Engraved and Photogravure

1960, Apr. 30 ***Perf. 11½***

43 A149 40c cl & brt red 28 15
44 A149 3fr brn & brt red 1.65 55

Issued to commemorate the 75th anniversary of the Socialist Party of Belgium.

Congo River Boat Pilot
A150

Designs: 40c, Medical team. 1fr, Planting tree. 2fr, Sculptors. 2.50fr, Shot put. 3fr, Congolese officials. 6fr, Congolese and Belgian girls playing with doll. 8fr, Boy pointing on globe to independent Congo.

1960, June 30 **Photo.** ***Perf. 11½***

Size: 35x24mm.

545 A150 10c brt red 45 15
546 A150 40c rose cl 65 20
547 A150 1fr brt lil 1.75 90
548 A150 2fr gray grn 1.90 1.10
549 A150 2.50fr blue 1.75 90
550 A150 3fr dk bl gray 2.00 60

Size: 51x35mm.

551 A150 6fr vio bl 6.00 3.00
552 A150 8fr dk brn 10.00 6.75
Nos. 545-552 (8) 24.50 13.60

Independence of Congo.

Europa Issue, 1960

Common Design Type

1960, Sept. 17

Size: 35x24½mm.

553 CD3 3fr claret 1.00 15
554 CD3 6fr gray 2.00 65

Common Design Types pictured in section at front of book.

Children Examining Stamp and Globe
A152

H. J. W. Frère-Orban
A153

1960, Oct. 1 **Photo.** ***Perf. 11½***

555 A152 40c bis & blk +label 18 15

Issued to promote stamp collecting among children. Issued in sheets of 30 with alternating label. Label shows post horn and inscription in Flemish and French.

Photogravure and Engraved

1960, Oct. 17 **Unwmkd.**

Portrait in Brown

556 A153 10c org yel 15 15
557 A153 40c bl grn 15 15
558 A153 1.50fr brt vio 1.50 1.50
559 A153 3fr red 2.25 15

Centenary of Communal Credit Society.

King Baudouin and Queen Fabiola—A154

1960, Dec. 13 **Photo.** ***Perf. 11½***

Portraits in Dark Brown

560 A154 40c green 15 15
561 A154 3fr red lil 45 15
562 A154 6fr dl bl 2.25 1.00

Issued to commemorate the wedding of King Baudouin and Dona Fabiola de Mora y Aragon, Dec. 15, 1960.

Nos. 412, 414 Surcharged

1961 **Typographed** ***Perf. 13½x14***

563 A108 15c on 30c gray grn 35 8
564 A108 15c on 50c bl ('68) 15 5
565 A108 20c on 30c gray grn 35 15

No. 412 Surcharged and Precanceled

1961

566 A108 15c on 30c gray grn 1.50 12
567 A108 20c on 30c gray grn 3.25 2.25

The surcharges are combined with the precancellations. See note after No. 197.

Nicolaus Rockox, by Anthony Van Dyck
A155

Seal of Jan Bode, Alderman of Antwerp, 1264
A156

Engraved and Photogravure

1961, Mar. 18 ***Perf. 11½***

568 A155 3fr bis, blk & brn 45 15

Issued to commemorate the 400th anniversary of the birth of Nicolaus Rockox, mayor of Antwerp.

1961, Apr. 16 **Photogravure**

569 A156 3fr buff & brn 45 15

Issued for Stamp Day, April 16.

Senate Building, Brussels, Laurel and Sword
A157

Engraved and Photogravure

1961, Sept. 14 ***Perf. 11½*** **Unwmkd.**

570 A157 3fr brn & Prus grn 30 12
571 A157 6fr dk brn & dk car 1.75 1.75

Issued to commemorate the 50th Conference of the Interparliamentary Union, Brussels, Sept. 14–22.

Europa Issue, 1961

Common Design Type

1961, Sept. 16 **Photogravure**

Size: 35x25½mm.

572 CD4 3fr yel grn & dk grn 30 10
573 CD4 6fr org brn & blk 45 40

Atomic Reactor Plant, BR2, Mol
A159

Designs: 3fr, Atomic Reactor BR3 (vert.). 6fr, Atomic Reactor plant BR3.

1961, Nov. 8 ***Perf. 11½*** **Unwmkd.**

574 A159 40c dk bl grn 15 10
575 A159 3fr red lil 30 6
576 A159 6fr brt bl 60 45

Issued to publicize the atomic nuclear research center at Mol.

Horta Museum
A160

1962, Feb. 15 **Engraved**

577 A160 3fr red brn 30 10

Issued to honor Baron Victor Horta (1861–1947), architect.

Postrider, 16th Century
A161

Engraved and Photogravure

1962, March 25 ***Perf. 11½***

Chalky Paper

578 A161 3fr brn & sl grn 30 15

Stamp Day. See No. 677.

Gerard Mercator
A162

Bro. Alexis-Marie Gochet
A163

Engraved and Photogravure

1962, Apr. 14 **Unwmkd.**

579 A162 3fr sep & gray 30 15

Issued to commemorate the 450th anniversary of the birth of Mercator (Gerhard Kremer, 1512–1594), geographer and map maker.

1962, May 19 **Engr.** ***Perf. 11½***

Portrait: 3fr, Canon Pierre-Joseph Triest.

580 A163 2fr dk bl 30 18
581 A163 3fr gldn brn 30 10

Issued to honor Brother Alexis-Marie Gochet (1835–1910), geographer and educator, and Canon Pierre-Joseph Triest (1760–1836), educator and founder of hospitals and orphanages.

Europa Issue, 1962

Common Design Type

1962, Sept. 15 **Photogravure**

Size: 35x24mm.

582 CD5 3fr dp car, cit & blk 30 10
583 CD5 6fr ol, cit & blk 45 45

Hand with Barbed Wire and Freed Hand
A165

Engraved and Photogravure

1962, Sept. 16

584 A165 40c lt bl & blk 15 6

Issued in memory of concentration camp victims.

Adam, by Michelangelo, Broken Chain and U.N. Emblem
A166

1962, Nov. 24 *Perf. 11½*

585 A166 3fr gray & blk 30 15
586 A166 6fr lt redsh brn & dk brn 60 45

Issued to publicize the U.N. Declaration of Human Rights.

Henri Pirenne
A167

1963, Jan. 15 Engraved

587 A167 3fr ultra 30 15

Issued to commemorate the centenary of the birth of Henri Pirenne (1862–1935), historian.

Swordsmen and Ghent Belfry
A168

Designs: 3fr, Modern fencers. 6fr, Arms of the Royal and Knightly Guild of St. Michael (vert.).

Engraved and Photogravure

1963, Mar. 23 *Perf. 11½* Unwmkd.

588 A168 1fr brn red & pale bl 15 15
589 A168 3fr dk vio & yel grn 25 10
590 A168 6fr gray, blk, red, bl & gold 45 45

Issued to commemorate the 350th anniversary of the granting of a charter to the Ghent guild of fencers.

Stagecoach
A169

1963, Apr. 7

591 A169 3fr gray & ocher 45 10

Stamp Day. See No. 678.

Hotel des Postes, Paris, Stagecoach and Stamp, 1863
A170

Engraved

1963, May 7 *Perf. 11½* Unwmkd.

592 A170 6fr dk brn, gray & yel grn 60 60

Issued to commemorate the centenary of the first International Postal Conference, Paris, 1863.

"Peace," Child in Rye Field
A171

Engraved and Photogravure

1963, May 8

593 A171 3fr grn, blk, yel & brn 30 12
594 A171 6fr buff, blk, brn & org 60 45

Issued to publicize the May 8th Movement for Peace. (On May 8, 1945, World War II ended in Europe).

Allegory and Shields of 17 Member Nations
A172

1963, June 13 *Perf. 11½* Unwmkd.

595 A172 6fr bl & blk 60 45

10th anniversary of the Conference of European Transport Ministers.

Seal of Union of Belgian Towns
A173

1963, June 17

596 A173 6fr grn, red, blk & gold 45 45

50th anniversary of the International Union of Municipalities.

Caravelle over Brussels National Airport
A174

Photogravure and Engraved

1963, Sept. 1 *Perf. 11½* Unwmkd.

597 A174 3fr grn & gray 30 15

40th anniversary of SABENA airline.

Europa Issue, 1963
Common Design Type

1963, Sept. 14 Photogravure

Size: 35x24mm.

598 CD6 3fr blk, dl red & lt brn 90 12
599 CD6 6fr blk, lt bl & lt brn 2.50 50

Jules Destrée
A176

Design: No. 565, Henry Van de Velde.

Engraved

1963, Nov. 16 *Perf. 11½* Unwmkd.

600 A176 1fr rose lil 15 12
601 A176 1fr green 15 12

Issued to commemorate the centenary of the birth of Jules Destrée (1863–1936), statesman and founder of the Royal Academy of French Language and Literature (No. 600), and of Henry Van de Velde (1863-1957), architect (No. 601).

No. 600 incorrectly inscribed "1864."

Development of the Mail, Bas-relief
A177

Engraved and Photogravure

1963, Nov. 23

602 A177 50c dl red, sl & blk 15 7

50th anniversary of the establishment of postal checking service.

Dr. Armauer G. Hansen
A178

Designs: 2fr, Leprosarium. 5fr, Father Joseph Damien.

1964, Jan. 25 *Perf. 11½* Unwmkd.

603 A178 1fr brn org & blk 15 15
604 A178 2fr brn org & blk 30 15
605 A178 5fr brn org & blk 45 35
a. Souvenir sheet of 3 1.90 1.90

Fight against leprosy. No. 605a contains one each of Nos. 603-605. Size: 137x97mm. Sold for 12fr.

Andreas Vesalius
A179

Jules Boulvin
A180

Design: 2fr, Henri Jaspar.

Engraved and Photogravure

1964, March 2 *Perf. 11½* Unwmkd.

606 A179 50c pale grn & blk 15
607 A180 1fr pale grn & blk 15
608 A180 2fr pale grn & blk 25

Issued to commemorate 400th anniversary of the death of Andreas Vesalius (1514–64), anatomist (50c); honor Jules Boulvin (1855–1920), mechanical engineer (1fr) and to commemorate the 25th anniversary of the death of Henri Jaspar (1870–1939), satesman and lawyer (2fr).

Postilion of Liège, 1830–40
A181

1964, Apr. 5 Engraved *Perf. 11½*

609 A181 3fr black 30 6

Issued for Stamp Day 1964.

Arms of Ostend
A182

1964, May 16 Photogravure

610 A182 3fr ultra, ver, gold & blk 30 6

Millennium of Ostend.

Flame, Hammer and Globe
A183

Designs: 1fr, "SI" and globe. 2fr, Flame over wavy lines.

1964, July 18 *Perf. 11½* Unwmkd.

611 A183 50c dk bl & red 15 10
612 A183 1fr dk bl & red 15 12
613 A183 2fr dk bl & red 15 15

Issued to commemorate the centenary of the First Socialist International, founded in London, Sept. 28, 1864.

Europa Issue, 1964
Common Design Type

1964, Sept. 12 Photo. *Perf. 11½*

Size: 24x35½mm.

614 CD7 3fr yel grn, dk car & gray 30 15
615 CD7 6fr car rose, yel grn & bl 45 45

Benelux Issue

King Baudouin, Queen Juliana and Grand Duchess Charlotte
A185

964, Oct. 12

6	A185	3fr ol, lt grn & mar	30	10

Issued to commemorate the 20th anniersary of the customs union of Belgium, etherlands and Luxembourg.

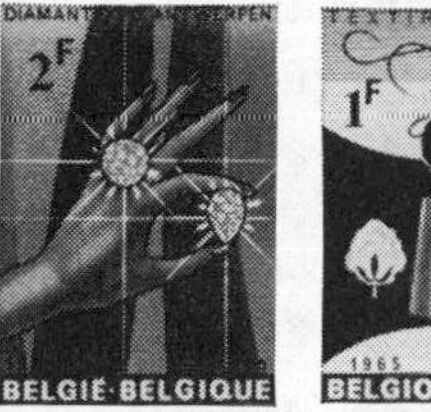

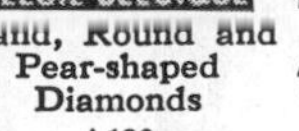

Hand, Round and Pear-shaped Diamonds
A186

Symbols of Textile Industry
A187

965, Jan. 23 *Perf. 11½* Unwmkd.

17	A186	2fr ultra, dp car & blk	15	15

Issued to publicize the Diamond Exhibiton "Diamantexpo," Antwerp, July 10–28, 965.

965, Jan. 25 Photogravure

18	A187	1fr bl, red & blk	18	18

Issued to publicize the eighth textile inustry exhibition "Textirama," Ghent, Jan. 9–Feb. 2, 1965.

Vriesia
A188

Paul Hymans
A189

Designs: 2fr, Echinocactus. 3fr, Stapelia.

Engraved and Photogravure

1965, Feb. 13

19	A188	1fr multi	15	15
20	A188	2fr multi	15	15
21	A188	3fr multi	15	15
a.		Souv. sheet of 3	1.75	1.75

Issued to publicize the 25th Ghent International Flower Exhibition, Apr. 24–May 3, 1965.

No. 621a contains one each of Nos. 619-621, and was issued Apr. 26. It carries the UNRWA and Belgian Postal emblems in the margin. Sold for 20fr.

1965, Feb. 24 Engraved *Perf. 11½*

22	A189	1fr dl pur	15	7

Issued to commemorate the centenary of the birth of Paul Hymans (1865–1941), Belgian Foreign Minister and first president of the League of Nations.

Peter Paul Rubens
A190

Sir Rowland Hill as Philatelist
A191

Portraits: 2fr, Frans Snyders. 3fr, Adam van Noort. 6fr, Anthony Van Dyck. 8fr, Jacob Jordaens.

Photogravure and Engraved

1965, Mar. 15

Portraits in Sepia

623	A190	1fr car rose	15	15
624	A190	2fr bl grn	15	15
625	A190	3fr plum	15	15
626	A190	6fr dp car	30	15
627	A190	8fr dk bl	45	45
		Nos. 623-627 (5)	1.20	1.05

Issued to commemorate the founding of the General Savings and Pensions Bank.

1965, Mar. 27 Engraved *Perf. 11½*

628	A191	50c bl grn	15	7

Issued to publicize youth philately. The design is from a mural by J. E. Van den Bussche in the General Post Office, Brussels.

Postmaster, c. 1833
A192

Staircase, Affligem Abbey
A194

Telephone, Globe and Teletype Paper
A193

1965, Apr. 26 *Perf. 11½* Unwmkd.

629	A192	3fr emerald	30	7

Issued for Stamp Day.

1965, May 8 Photogravure

630	A193	2fr dl pur & blk	15	15

Issued to commemorate the centenary of the International Telecommunication Union.

1965, May 27 Engraved

631	A194	1fr gray bl	15	10

St. Jean Berchmans and his Birthplace
A195

Engraved and Photogravure

1965, May 27

632	A195	2fr dk brn & red brn	15	12

Issued to honor St. Jean Berchmans (1599–1621), Jesuit "Saint of the Daily Life."

TOC H Lamp and Arms of Poperinge
A196

Farmer with Tractor
A197

1965, June 19 Photo. *Perf. 11½*

633	A196	3fr ol bis, blk & car	30	7

Issued to commemorate the 50th anniversary of the founding of Talbot House in Poperinge, which served British soldiers in World War I, and where the TOC H Movement began (Christian Social Service; TOC H is army code for Poperinge Center).

Engraved and Photogravure

1965, July 17 *Perf. 11½* Unwmkd.

Design: 3fr, Farmer with horse-drawn roller.

634	A197	50c bl, ol, bis brn & blk	15	10
635	A197	3fr bl, ol grn, ol & blk	22	10

Issued to commemorate the 75th anniversary of the Belgian Farmers' Association (Boerenbond).

Europa Issue, 1965

Common Design Type

1965, Sept. 25 *Perf. 11½*

Size: 35½x24mm.

636	CD8	1fr dl rose & blk	15	12
637	CD8	3fr grnsh gray & blk	18	12

King Leopold I
A199

Joseph Lebeau
A200

1965, Nov. 13 Engraved

638	A199	3fr sepia	30	10
639	A199	6fr brt vio	45	45

Issued to commemorate the centenary of the death of King Leopold I (1790–1865). The designs of the vignettes are similar to the 30c and 1fr of 1865.

1965, Nov. 13 Photogravure

640	A200	1fr multi	15	12

Issued to commemorate the centenary of the death of Joseph Lebeau (1794–1865), Foreign Minister.

Tourist Issue

Grapes and Houses, Hoeilaart
A201

Bridge and Castle, Huy
A202

Designs: No. 643, British War Memorial, Ypres. No. 644, Castle Spontin. No. 645, City Hall, Louvain. No. 646, Ourthe Valley. No. 647, Romanesque Cathedral, gothic fountain, Nivalles. No. 648, Water mill, Kasterlee. No. 649, City Hall, Cloth Guild and Statue of Margarethe of Austria, Malines. No. 650, Town Hall, Lier. No. 651, Castle Bouillon. No. 652, Fountain and Kursaal Spa. No. 653, Windmill, Bokrijk. No. 654, Mountain road, Vielsalm. No. 655, View of Furnes. No. 656, City Hall and Belfry, Mons. No. 657, St. Martin's Church, Aalst. No. 658, Abbey and fountain, St. Hubert.

1965-71 Engraved *Perf. 11½*

641	A201	50c vio bl, lt bl & yel grn	15	7
642	A202	50c sl grn, lt bl & red brn	15	7
643	A202	1fr grn, lt bl, sal & brn	15	5
644	A202	1fr ind, lt bl & ol	15	5
645	A201	1fr brt rose lil, lt bl & blk	15	7
646	A202	1fr blk, grnsh bl & ol	15	8
647	A201	1.50fr sl, sky bl & bis	15	10
648	A202	1.50fr blk, bl & ol	15	10
649	A202	1.50fr dk bl & buff	18	8
650	A201	2fr brn, lt bl & ind	18	8
651	A202	2fr dk brn, grn & ocher	18	8
652	A202	2fr bl, brt grn & blk	15	10
653	A202	2fr blk, lt bl & yel	15	10
654	A202	2fr blk, lt bl & yel grn	15	12
655	A202	2fr car, lt bl & dk brn	15	12
656	A201	2.50fr vio, buff & blk	18	8
657	A201	2.50fr vio, lt bl, blk & ol	25	8
658	A201	2.50fr vio bl & yel	25	8
		Nos. 641-658 (18)	3.02	1.51

Issue dates: Nos. 641-642, Nov. 13, 1965; Nos. 643-644, July 15, 1967; Nos. 645-646, Dec. 16, 1968; Nos. 647-648, July 6, 1970; Nos. 649, 656, Dec. 11, 1971; Nos. 650-651, Nov. 11, 1966; Nos. 652-653, June 24, 1968, Nos. 654-655, Sept. 6, 1969; Nos. 657-658, Sept. 11, 1971.

Queen Elisabeth Type of Semi-Postal Issue, 1956

1965, Dec. 23 Photo. *Perf. 11½*

659	SP305	3fr dk gray	30	12

Issued in memory of Queen Elisabeth (1876–1965).

A dark frame has been added in design of No. 659; 1956 date has been changed to 1965; inscription in bottom panel is Koningin Elisabeth Reine Elisabeth 3F.

"Peace on Earth"
A203

Arms of Pope Paul VI
A204

Rural Mailman, 19th Century
A205

Design: 1fr, "Looking toward a Better Future" (family, new buildings, sun and landscape).

1966, Feb. 12 Photo. *Perf. 11½*

660	A203	50c multi	15	10
661	A203	1fr ocher, blk & bl	15	12
662	A204	3fr gray, gold, car & blk	18	15

Issued to commemorate the 75th anniversary of the encyclical by Pope Leo XIII "Rerum Novarum," which proclaimed the general principles for the organization of modern industrial society.

1966, Apr. 17 Photo. Unwmkd.

663 A205 3fr blk, dl yel & pale lil 18 7

Issued for Stamp Day 1966.

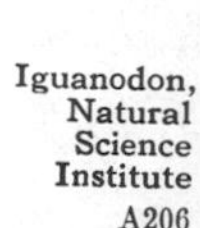

Iguanodon, Natural Science Institute
A206

Arend-Roland Comet, Observatory
A207

Designs: No. 617, Ancestral head and spiral pattern, Kasai; Central Africa Museum. No. 618, Snowflakes, Meteorological Institute. No. 619, Seal of Charles V, Royal Archives. No. 620, Medieval scholar, Royal Library. 8fr, Satellite and rocket, Space Aeronautics Institute.

1966, May 28 Engr. and Photo.

664 A206 1fr grn & blk 15 10
665 A206 2fr gray, blk & brn org 18 12
666 A206 2fr bl, blk & yel 18 12
667 A207 3fr dp rose, blk & gold 18 10
668 A207 3fr multi 18 10
669 A207 6fr ultra, yel & blk 45 18
670 A207 8fr multi 60 60
Nos. 664-670 (7) 1.92 1.32

Issued to publicize the national scientific heritage.

Atom Symbol and Retort
A208

August Kekulé, Benzene Ring
A209

Engraved and Photogravure
1966, July 9 *Perf. 11½* Unwmkd.

671 A208 6fr gray, blk & red 45 35

Issued to publicize the European chemical plant, EUROCHEMIC, at Mol.

1966, July 9

672 A209 3fr brt bl & blk 18 12

Issued to honor August Friedrich Kekulé (1829–96), chemistry professor at University of Ghent (1858–67).

No. *663* Overprinted with Red and Blue Emblem

1966, July 11 Photogravure

673 A205 3fr multi 18 12

Issued to commemorate the 19th International P.T.T. Congress (Postal, Telegraph and Telephone Administrations), Brussels, July 11–15.

Rik Wouters, Self-portrait
A210

1966, Sept. 6 Photo. *Perf. 11½*

674 A210 60c multi 18 12

Issued to commemorate the 50th anniversary of the death of Rik Wouters (1882–1916), painter.

Europa Issue, 1966
Common Design Type
1966, Sept. 24 Engraved *Perf. 11½*
Size: 24x34mm.

675 CD9 3fr brt grn 25 15
676 CD9 6fr brt rose lil 60 50

Types of 1962–1963 Overprinted in Black and Red

1966, Nov. 11 Engraved and Photo.

677 A161 60c sep & grnsh gray 15 10
678 A169 3fr sep & pale bis 18 10

75th anniversary, Royal Federation of Philatelic Circles of Belgium. Overprint shows emblem of International Philatelic Federation (F.I.P.).

Lions Emblem
A214

Engraved and Photogravure
1967, Jan. 14 *Perf. 11½*

679 A214 3fr gray, blk & bl 18 12
680 A214 6fr lt grn, blk & vio 45 25

Issued to commemorate the 50th anniversary of the founding of the International Association of Lions Clubs.

Pistol by Leonhard Cleuter
A215

1967, Feb. 11 Photogravure

681 A215 2fr dp car, blk & cr 15 10

Fire Arms Museum in Liège.

International Tourist Year Emblem
A216

1967, Feb. 11

682 A216 6fr ver, ultra & blk 35 18

International Tourist Year, 1967.

Birches and Trientalis
A217

Design: No. *684*, Dunes, beach grass, privet and blue thistles.

1967, Mar. 11 Photo. *Perf. 11½*

683 A217 1fr multi 15 8
684 A217 1fr multi 15 8

Issued to publicize the nature preserves at Hautes Fagnes and Westhoek.

Paul E. Janson
A218

1967, Apr. 15 Engraved *Perf. 11½*

685 A218 10fr blue 60 30

Issued in memory of Paul Emile Janson (1872–1944), lawyer and statesman.

Postilion
A219

1967, Apr. 16 Photo. and Engr.

686 A219 3fr rose red & cl 18 10

Issued for Stamp Day, 1967.

Inscribed: "FITCE"
Engraved and Photogravure
1967, June 24 *Perf. 11½*

687 A219 10fr ultra, sep & emer 60 45

Issued to commemorate the meeting of the Federation of Common Market Telecommunications Engineers, Brussels, July 3–8.

Europa Issue, 1967
Common Design Type
1967, May 2 Photogravure
Size: 24x35mm.

688 CD10 3fr blk, lt bl & red 30 12
689 CD10 6fr blk, grnsh gray & yel 55 45

Flax, Shuttle and Mills
A221

1967, June 3 Photo. *Perf. 11½*

690 A221 6fr tan & multi 35 25

Belgian linen industry.

Old Kursaal, Ostend
A222

1967, June 3 Engraved and Photo

691 A222 2fr dk brn, lt bl & yel 15 1

700th anniversary of Ostend as a city.

Caesar Crossing Rubicon, 15th Century Tapestry
A223

Design : No. 693, Emperor Maximilian Killing a Boar, 16th cent. tapestry.

1967, Sept. 2 Photo. *Perf. 11½*

692 A223 1fr multi 15 1
693 A223 1fr multi 15 1

Issued for the Charles Plisnier and Lodewijk de Raet Foundations.

Arms of University of Ghent
A224

Princess Margaret of York
A225

Design: No. 651, Arms of University of Liège.

Engraved and Photogravure
1967, Sept. 30 *Perf. 11½*

694 A224 3fr gray & multi 18 10
695 A224 3fr gray & multi 18 10

Issued to commemorate the 150th anniversaries of the Universities of Ghent and Liège.

1967, Sept. 30 Photogravure

696 A225 6fr multi 35 30

British Week, Sept. 28–Oct. 2.

"Virga Jesse," Hasselt
A226

1967, Nov. 11 Engraved *Perf. 11½*

697 A226 1fr sl bl 15 12

Christmas, 1967.

Hand Guarding Worker
A227

Military Mailman, 1916, by James Thiriar
A228

.968, Feb. 3 Photo. ***Perf. 11½***

98 A227 3fr multi 18 7

Issued to publicize industrial safety.

Engraved and Photogravure

.968, Mar. 17 ***Perf. 11½***

99 A228 3fr sep, lt bl & brn 18 7

Issued for Stamp Day, 1968.

View of Grammont and Seal of Baudouin VI
A229

Stamp of 1866, No. 23
A230

Historic Sites: 3fr, Theux-Franchimont fortress, sword and seal. 6fr, Neolithic cave and artifacts, Spiennes. 10fr, Roman oil lamp and St. Medard's Church, Wervik.

1968, Apr. 13 Photo. ***Perf. 11½***

700 A229 2fr bl, blk, lil & rose 20 20
701 A229 3fr org, blk & car 20 12
702 A229 6fr ultra, ind & bis 45 25
703 A229 10fr tan, blk, yel & gray 75 50

1968, Apr. 13 Engr. ***Perf. 13***

'04 A230 1fr black 15 10

Centenary of the Malines Stamp Printery.

Europa Issue, 1968
Common Design Type

1968, Apr. 27 Photo. ***Perf. 11½***
Size: 35x24mm.

'05 CD11 3fr dl grn, gold & blk 18 12
'06 CD11 6fr car, sil & blk 60 42

St. Laurent Abbey, Liège
A232

Designs: 3fr, Gothic Church, Lisseweghe. No. 709. Barges in Zandvliet locks. No.710, Ship in Neuzen lock, Ghent Canal. 10fr, Ronquieres canal ship lift.

Engraved and Photogravure

1968, Sept. 7 ***Perf. 11½***

707 A232 2fr ultra, gray ol & sep 20 20
708 A232 3fr ol bis, gray & sep 20 10
709 A232 6fr ind, brt bl & sep 45 25
710 A232 6fr blk, grnsh bl & ol 35 25
711 A232 10fr bis, brt bl & sep 75 50
Nos. 707-711 (5) 1.95 1.30

No. 710 issued Dec. 14 for opening of lock at Neuzen, Netherlands.

Christmas Candle
A233

Engraved and Photogravure

1968, Dec. 7 ***Perf. 11½***

712 A233 1fr multi 15 7

Christmas, 1968.

St. Albertus Magnus—A234

1969, Feb. 15 Engraved *Perf. 11½*

713 A234 2fr sepia 15 12

The Church of St. Paul in Antwerp (16th century) was destroyed by fire in Apr. 1968.

Ruins of Aulne Abbey, Gozee
A235

1969, Feb. 15 **Engr. and Photo.**

714 A235 3fr brt pink & blk 18 10

Aulne Abbey was destroyed in 1794 during the French Revolution.

The Travelers, Roman Sculpture
A236

Broodjes Chapel, Antwerp
A237

1969, Mar. 15 Engraved *Perf. 11½*

715 A236 2fr vio brn 15 10

2,000th anniversary of city of Arlon.

1969, Mar. 15 **Engraved & Photo.**

716 A237 3fr gray & blk 18 10

Issued to commemorate the 150th anniversary of public education in Antwerp.

Post Office Train
A238

1969, Apr. 13 Photo. ***Perf. 11½***

717 A238 3fr multi 18 7

Issued for Stamp Day.

Europa Issue, 1969
Common Design Type

1969, Apr. 26
Size: 35x24mm.

718 CD12 3fr lt grn, brn & blk 30 12
719 CD12 6fr sal, rose car & blk 45 45

NATO Type of 1959 Redrawn and Dated "1949–1969"

1969, May 31 Photo. ***Perf. 11½***

720 A142 6fr org brn & ultra 45 45

20th anniv. of NATO. No. 720 inscribed Belgique-Belgie and OTAN-NAVO.

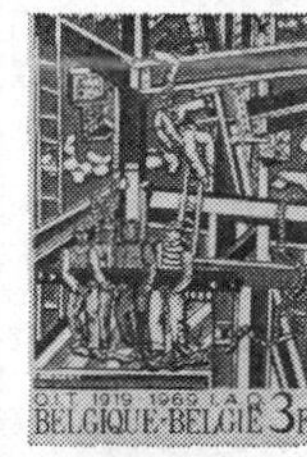

Construction Workers, by F. Leger
A240

Bicyclist
A241

1969, May 31

721 A240 3fr multi 18 7

Issued to commemorate the 50th anniversary of the International Labor Organization.

1969, July 5 Photo. ***Perf. 11½***

722 A241 6fr rose & multi 35 30

Issued to publicize the World Bicycling Road Championships, Terlaemen to Zolder, Aug. 10.

Ribbon in Benelux Colors
A242

1969, Sept. 6 Photo. ***Perf. 11½***

723 A242 3fr blk, red, ultra & yel 25 10

Issued to commemorate the 25th anniversary of the signing of the customs union of Belgium, Netherlands and Luxembourg.

Annevoie Garden and Pascali Rose
A243

Design: No. 690, Lochristi Garden and begonia.

1969, Sept. 6

724 A243 2fr multi 15 12
725 A243 2fr multi 15 12

Armstrong, Collins, Aldrin and Map Showing Tranquillity Base
A245

1969, Sept. 20 **Photogravure**

726 A245 6fr black 35 30

See note after Algeria No. 427. See also No. B846.

Wounded Veteran
A246

Mailman
A247

1969, Oct. 11 **Engr.** ***Perf. 11½***

727 A246 1fr bl gray 15 7

Issued to publicize the national war veterans' aid organization (O.N.I.G.). The design is similar to type SP10.

1969, Oct. 18 **Photogravure**

728 A247 1fr dp rose & multi 15 7

Issued to publicize youth philately. Design by Danielle Saintenoy, 14.

Kennedy Tunnel Under the Schelde, Antwerp
A248

Design: 6fr, Three highways crossing near Loncin.

1969, Nov. 8 Engraved *Perf. 11½*

729 A248 3fr multi 30 12
730 A248 6fr multi 45 45

Issued to publicize the John F. Kennedy Tunnel under the Schelde and the Walloon auto route and interchange near Loncin.

Henry Carton de Wiart, by Gaston Geleyn
A249

1969, Nov. 8

731 A249 6fr sepia 35 25

Issued to commemorate the centenary of the birth of Count Henry Carton de Wiart (1869–1951), statesman.

The Census at Bethlehem (detail), by Peter Brueghel
A250

1969, Dec. 13 **Photogravure**

732	A250	1.50fr multi	15	7

Christmas, 1969.

Symbols of Bank's Activity, 100fr Coin
A251

Engraved and Photogravure

1969, Dec. 13

733	A251	3.50fr lt ultra, blk & sil	20	7

Issued to commemorate the 50th anniversary of the Industrial Credit Bank (Société nationale de crédit à l'industrie).

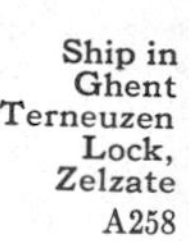

Camellia A252 — Beeches in Botanical Garden A253

Flowers: 2.50fr, Water lily. 3.50fr, Azalea.

1970, Jan. 31 **Photo.** ***Perf. 11½***

734	A252	1.50fr multi	15	10
735	A252	2.50fr multi	30	30
736	A252	3.50fr multi	30	12
a.		Souvenir sheet of 3	2.75	2.75

Ghent Int'l Flower Exhibition.

No. 736a contains one each of Nos. 734-736, and was issued Apr. 25. It carries gray UN and UN Refugees emblems in margin. Size: 121x90mm. Sold for 25fr.

Engraved and Photogravure

1970, Mar. 7 ***Perf. 11½***

Design: 7fr, Birches.

737	A253	3.50fr yel & multi	30	10
738	A253	7fr grn & multi	45	45

European Nature Conservation Year.

Mailman
A254

1970, Apr. 4 **Photogravure**

739	A254	1.50fr multi	15	7

Issued for Youth Stamp Day.

New UPU Headquarters and Monument, Bern
A255

1970, Apr. 12 **Engr. and Photo.**

740	A255	3.50fr grn & lt grn	30	8

Issued to commemorate the opening of the new Universal Postal Union Headquarters, Bern.

Europa Issue, 1970

Common Design Type

1970, May 1 **Photo.** ***Perf. 11½***

Size: 35x24mm.

741	CD13	3.50fr rose cl, yel & blk	30	15
742	CD13	7fr ultra, pink & blk	60	45

Cooperative Alliance Emblem
A257

1970, June 27 **Photo.** ***Perf. 11½***

743	A257	7fr blk & org	45	18

Issued to commemorate the 75th anniversary of the International Cooperative Alliance.

Ship in Ghent Terneuzen Lock, Zelzate
A258

Design: No. 745, Clock Tower, Virton (vert.).

1970, June 27 **Engr. & Photo.**

744	A258	2.50fr ind & lt bl	18	15
745	A258	2.50fr dk pur & ocher	18	15

King Baudouin
A259

1970-80 **Engraved** ***Perf. 11½***

746	A259	1.75fr grn ('71)	30	15
747	A259	2.25fr gray grn ('72)	45	15
748	A259	2.50fr gray grn ('74)	20	5
749	A259	3fr emer ('73)	3.75	3.00
750	A259	3.25fr vio brn ('75)	25	5
751	A259	3.50fr org brn	30	5
752	A259	3.50fr brn ('71)	30	5
753	A259	4fr bl ('72)	45	5
754	A259	4.50fr brn ('72)	30	5
755	A259	4.50fr grnsh bl ('74)	30	5
756	A259	5fr lil ('72)	30	6
757	A259	6fr rose car ('72)	35	12
758	A259	6.50fr vio blk '74)	45	6
759	A259	7fr ver ('71)	45	8
760	A259	7.50fr brt pink ('75)	45	5
761	A259	8fr blk ('72)	45	6
762	A259	9fr ol bis ('71)	75	8
763	A259	9fr red brn ('80)	55	6
764	A259	10fr rose car ('71)	60	8
765	A259	11fr gray ('76)	65	15
766	A259	12fr Prus bl ('72)	75	10
767	A259	13fr sl ('75)	90	6
768	A259	14fr gray grn ('76)	85	15
769	A259	15fr lt vio ('71)	90	10
770	A259	16fr grn ('77)	90	8
771	A259	17fr dl mag ('75)	1.00	15
772	A259	18fr stl bl ('71)	1.25	20
773	A259	18fr grnsh bl ('80)	1.10	12
774	A259	20fr vio bl ('71)	1.25	10
775	A259	22fr blk ('74)	1.75	1.75
776	A259	22fr lt grn ('79)	1.40	15
777	A259	25fr lil ('75)	1.50	15
778	A259	30fr ocher ('72)	2.00	15
779	A259	35fr emer ('80)	2.00	30
780	A259	40fr dk bl ('77)	2.50	15
781	A259	45fr brn ('80)	2.75	30

Photo. ***Perf. 12½x13½***

Size: 22x17mm

782	A259	3fr emer ('73)	3.75	3.50
a.		Booklet pane of 4 (#782 and 3 #783) + labels	10.00	
783	A259	4fr bl ('73)	90	90
784	A259	4.50fr grnsh bl ('75)	50	45
785	A259	5fr lil ('73)	30	15
a.		Booklet pane of 4 + labels	2.75	
786	A259	6fr car ('78)	35	25
787	A259	6.50fr dl pur ('75)	55	30
788	A259	8fr gray ('78)	45	18
		Nos. 746-788 (43)	41.20	14.19

No. 751 issued Sept. 7, 1970, King Baudouin's 40th birthday, and is inscribed "1930-1970." Dates are omitted on other stamps of type A259.

Nos. 754, 756 also issued in coils in 1973 and Nos. 757, 761 in 1978, with black control number on back of every fifth stamp.

Nos. 782-788 issued in booklets only. Nos. 782, 784 have one straight-edge, Nos. 786, 788 have two. The rest have one or two. Stamps in the panes are tete-beche. Each pane has two labels showing Belgian Postal emblem with a large selvage with postal code instructions. Nos. 786, 788 not luminescent.

See Nos. 432a, 432b, 977a, 977b.

U.N. Headquarters, N.Y. A260 — Fair Emblem A261

1970, Sept. 12 **Engr. and Photo.**

789	A260	7fr dk brn & Prus bl	45	25

25th anniversary of the United Nations.

1970, Sept. 19

790	A261	1.50fr bis, org & brn	15	7

Issued to publicize the 25th International Fair at Ghent, Sept. 12–27.

Queen Fabiola A262 — The Mason, by Georges Minne A263

1970, Sept. 19

791	A262	3.50fr lt bl & blk	20	7

Issued to publicize the Queen Fabiola Foundation for Mental Health.

1970, Oct. 17 ***Perf. 11½***

Engraved and Photogravure

792	A263	3.50fr dl yel & sep	20	7

Issued to commemorate the 50th anniversary of the National Housing Society.

Man, Woman and City—A264

1970, Oct. 17 **Photogravure**

793	A264	2.50fr blk & multi	15	15

Issued to commemorate the 25th anniversary of the Social Security System.

Madonna with the Grapes, by Jean Gossaert
A265

1970, Nov. 14 **Engraved** ***Perf. 11½***

794	A265	1.50fr dk brn	15	7

Christmas 1970.

Arms of Eupen, Malmédy and Saint-Vith
A266

Engraved and Photogravure

1970, Dec. 12 ***Perf. 11½***

795	A266	7fr sep & dk brn	45	18

The 50th anniversary of the return of the districts of Eupen, Malmédy and Saint-Vith.

Automatic Telephone A267

Touring Club Emblem A269

"Auto" A268

1971, Jan. 16 Photo. ***Perf. 11½***

96	A267	1.50fr multi	15	7

Automatization of Belgian telephone system.

1971, Jan. 16

97	A268	2.50fr car & blk	15	15

Fiftieth Automobile Show, Brussels, Jan. 19–31.

1971, Feb. 13

98	A269	3.50fr ultra & multi	25	7

Belgian Touring Club, 75th anniversary.

Tournai Cathedral A270

1971, Feb. 13 Engraved

99	A270	7fr brt bl	45	30

Cathedral of Tournai, 8th centenary.

"The Letter Box," by T. Lobrichon A271

1971, March 13 Engr. ***Perf. 11½***

00	A271	1.50fr dk brn	15	8

Youth philately.

Albert I, Jules Destrée and Academy—A272

Engraved and Photogravure

1971, Apr. 17 ***Perf. 11½***

801	A272	7fr gray & blk	45	30

50th anniversary of the founding of the Royal Academy of Language and French Literature.

Mailman A273

1971, Apr. 25

802	A273	3.50fr multi	25	7

Stamp Day.

Europa Issue, 1971

Common Design Type

1971, May 1 Photogravure

Size: 35x24mm.

803	CD14	3.50fr ol & blk	30	10
804	CD14	7fr dk ol grn & blk	45	15

Radar Ground Station A275

1971, May 15 Photo. ***Perf. 11½***

805	A275	7fr multi	45	25

3rd World Telecommunications Day.

Antarctic Explorer, Ship and Penguins—A276

1971, June 19 Photo. ***Perf. 11½***

806	A276	10fr multi	75	75

Tenth anniversary of the Antarctic Treaty pledging peaceful uses of and scientific cooperation in Antarctica.

Orval Abbey A277

1971, June 26 Engraved ***Perf. 11½***

807	A277	2.50fr chocolate	15	12

9th centenary of the Abbey of Notre Dame, Orval.

Georges Hubin A278

1971, June 26 Engr. and Photo.

808	A278	1.50fr vio bl & blk	15	12

Georges Hubin (1863–1947), socialist leader and Minister of State.

Mr. and Mrs. Goliath, the Giants of Ath A279

View of Ghent—A280

1971, Aug. 7 Photogravure

809	A279	2.50fr multi	15	12

Engraved

810	A280	2.50fr gray brn	15	15

Test Tubes and Insulin Molecular Diagram—A281

1971, Aug. 7 Photogravure

811	A281	10fr lt gray & multi	60	45

50th anniversary of the discovery of insulin.

Family and "50"—A283

1971, Sept. 11 Photogravure

812	A283	1.50fr grn & multi	15	12

50th anniversary of the Belgian Large Families League.

Achaemenidaen Tomb, Buzpar, and Persian Coat of Arms—A284

Engraved and Photogravure

1971, Oct. 2 ***Perf. 11½***

813	A284	7fr multi	45	25

2500th anniversary of the founding of the Persian empire by Cyrus the Great.

Dr. Jules Bordet A285

Flight into Egypt, Anonymous A286

Portrait: No. 758, Stijn Streuvels.

1971, Oct. 2 Engraved

814	A285	3.50fr sl grn	25	8
815	A285	3.50fr dk brn	25	8

No. 757 honors Dr. Jules Bordet (1870–1945), serologist and immunologist; No. 758, Stijn Streuvels (1871–1945), novelist whose pen name was Frank Lateur.

1971, Nov. 13 Photogravure

816	A286	1.50fr multi	15	12

Christmas 1971.

Federation Emblem A287

Book Year Emblem A288

1971, Nov. 13

817	A287	3.50fr blk, ultra & gold	25	10

25th anniversary of the Federation of Belgian Industries (FIB).

1972, Feb. 19

818	A288	7fr bis, blk & bl	45	30

International Book Year 1972.

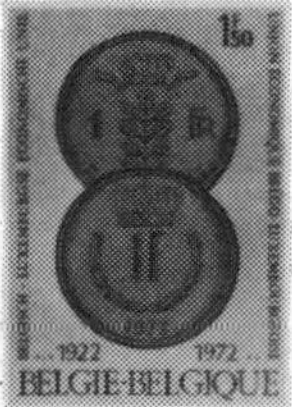

Coins of Belgium and Luxembourg A289

1972, Feb. 19 **Engr. & Photo.**

819 A289 1.50fr org blk & sil 15 12

Economic Union of Belgium and Luxembourg, 50th anniversary.

Traffic Signal and Road Signs
A290

1972, Feb. 19 **Photogravure**

820 A290 3.50fr bl & multi 25 10

Via Secura (road safety), 25th anniversary.

Belgica '72 Emblem
A291

1972, Mar. 27

821 A291 3.50fr choc, bl & lil 25 7

International Philatelic Exhibition, Brussels, June 24–July 9.

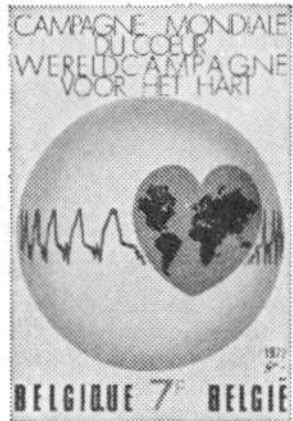

"Your Heart is your Health"
A292

Auguste Vermeylen
A293

1972, Mar. 27

822 A292 7fr blk, gray, red & bl 45 30

World Health Day.

1972, Mar. 27

823 A293 2.50fr multi 15 12

Centenary of the birth of Auguste Vermeylen (1872–1945), Flemish writer and educator. Portrait by Isidore Opsomer.

Astronaut on Moon
A294

1972, Apr. 23

824 A294 3.50fr multi 25 12

Stamp Day 1972.

Europa Issue 1972

Common Design Type

1972, Apr. 29

Size: 24x35mm.

825 CD16 3.50fr lt bl & multi 30 10
826 CD16 7fr rose & multi 60 45

"Freedom of the Press"
A296

1972, May 13 **Photo.** ***Perf. 11½***

827 A296 2.50fr org brn, buff & blk 15 12

50th anniversary of the BELGA news information agency and 25th Congress of the International Federation of Newspaper Editors (F.I.E.J.), Brussels, May 15–19.

Freight Cars with Automatic Coupling
A297

1972, June 3

828 A297 7fr bl & multi 45 30

International Railroad Union, 50th anniversary.

View of Couvin
A298

Design: No. 830, Aldeneik Church, Maaseik (vert.).

1972, June 24 Engr. ***Perf. 13½x14***

829 A298 2.50fr bl, vio brn & sl grn 30 30
830 A298 2.50fr dk brn & bl 30 30

Beatrice, by Gustave de Smet
A299

Radar Station, Intelsat 4
A300

1972, Sept. 9 **Photo.** ***Perf. 11½***

831 A299 3fr multi 18 12

Youth philately.

1972, Sept. 16

832 A300 3.50fr lt bl, sil & blk 25 10

Opening of the Lessive satellite earth station.

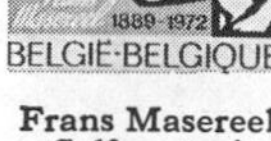

Frans Masereel, Self-portrait
A301

Adoration of the Kings, by Felix Timmermans
A302

1972, Oct. 21

833 A301 4.50fr lt ol & blk 30 6

Frans Masereel (1889–1972), wood engraver.

1972, Nov. 11 **Photo.** ***Perf. 11½***

834 A302 3.50fr blk & multi 25 12

Christmas 1972.

Maria Theresa, Anonymous
A303

1972, Dec. 16 **Photo.** ***Perf. 11½***

835 A303 2fr multi 15 15

200th anniversary of the Belgian Academy of Science, Literature and Art, founded by Empress Maria Theresa.

WMO Emblem, Meterological Institute, Ukkel
A304

1973, Mar. 24 **Photo.** ***Perf. 11½***

836 A304 9fr bl & multi 60 30

Centenary of international meteorological cooperation.

"Fire"
A305

Man and WHO Emblem
A306

1973, Mar. 24

837 A305 2fr multi 25 15

National industrial fire prevention campaign.

1973, Apr. 7

838 A306 8fr dk red, ocher & blk 45 35

25th anniversary of World Health Organization.

Europa Issue 1973

Common Design Type

1973, Apr. 28

Size: 35x24mm.

839 CD16 4.50fr org brn, vio bl & yel 30 10
840 CD16 8fr ol, dk bl & yel 75 45

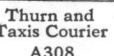

Thurn and Taxis Courier
A308

Arrows Circling Globe
A309

1973, Apr. 28 ***Perf. 11½***

Engraved and Photogravure

841 A308 4.50fr blk & red brn 30

Stamp Day.

1973, May 12 **Photogravure**

842 A309 3.50fr dp ocher & multi 25

5th International Telecommunications Day.

Workers' Sports Exhibition Poster, Ghent, 1913
A310

1973, May 12

843 A310 4.50fr multi 30 12

60th anniversary of the International Workers' Sports Movement.

Fair Emblem
A311

1973, May 12 **Photo.** ***Perf. 11½***

844 A311 4.50fr multi 30 10

25th International Fair, Liège, May 12–27.

DC-10 and 1923 Biplane over Brussels Airport—A312

Design: 10fr, Tips biplane, 1908.

1973, May 19 **Engr. & Photo.**

845 A312 8fr gray bl, blk & ultra 45 35
846 A312 10fr grn, lt bl & blk 75 60

50th anniversary of SABENA, Belgian airline (No. 788) and 25th anniversary of the "Vieilles Tiges" Belgian flying pioneers' society (No. 789).

Adolphe Sax and Tenor Saxophone
A313

Fresco from Bathhouse, Ostend
A314

1973, Sept. 15 Photogravure

47 A313 9fr grn, blk & bl 60 30

Adolphe Sax (1814–1894), inventor of axophone.

1973, Sept. 15

48 A314 4.50fr multi 30 10

Year of the Spa.

St. Nicholas Church, Eupen
A315

Charley, by Henri Evenepoel
A316

Designs: No. 850, Town Hall, Leau. No. 851, Aarshot Church. No. 852, Chiman Castle. No. 853, Gemmenich Border: Belgium, Germany, Netherlands. No. 854, St. Monan and church, Nassogne. No. 855, Church tower, Dottignes. No. 856, Grand-Place, Sint-Truiden.

973-75 **Engraved** *Perf. 13*

49 A315 2fr plum, sep & lt vio 18 12
50 A315 3fr blk, lt bl & mar 45 12
51 A315 3fr brn blk & yel 28 12
52 A315 4fr grnsh blk & grnsh bl 30 12
53 A315 4fr grnsh blk & bl 35 15
54 A315 4fr grnsh blk & bl 35 15
55 A315 4.50fr multi 45 18
56 A315 5fr multi 45 15
Nos. 849-856 (8) 2.81 1.11

Nos. 851, 855 not luminescent. Nos. 850, 852-354, 856 horiz.

973, Oct. 13 Photo. *Perf. 11½*

57 A316 3fr multi 18 15

Youth philately.

Luminescent Paper

Starting with No. 858, all stamps are on luminescent paper unless otherwise noted.

Jean-Baptiste Moens
A317

973, Oct. 13 Photo. & Engr.

58 A317 10fr gray & multi 60 30

50th anniversary of the Belgian Stamp Dealers' Association. Printed in sheets of 2 stamps and 12 labels showing association emblem.

Adoration of the Shepherds, by Hugo van der Goes
A318

Louis Pierard, by M. I. Ianchelevici
A319

1973, Nov. 17 Engr. *Perf. 11½*

859 A318 4fr blue 25 12

Christmas 1973.

1973, Nov. 17 Photo. & Engr.

860 A319 4fr ver & buff 25 12

Louis Pierard (1886–1952), journalist, member of Parliament.

Highway, Automobile Club Emblem
A320

1973, Nov. 17 Photogravure

861 A320 5fr yel & multi 30 12

50th anniversary of the Vlaamse Automobile Club.

Early Microphone, Emblem of Radio Belgium
A321

1973, Nov. 24 Photo. & Engr.

862 A321 4fr bl & blk 25 12

50th anniversary of Radio Belgium.

Felicien Rops, Self-portrait
A323

Photogravure and Engraved

1973, Dec. 8 *Perf. 11½*

863 A323 7fr tan & blk 45 25

Felicien Rops (1833–1898), painter and engraver.

King Albert
A324

Sun, Bird, Flowers and Girl
A325

1974, Feb. 16 Photo. *Perf. 11½*

864 A324 4fr Prus grn & blk 30 12

King Albert, 1875–1934.

1974, Mar. 25 Photo. *Perf. 11½*

865 A325 3fr vio & multi 30 12

Protection of the environment.

NATO Emblem
A326

1974, Apr. 20 Photo. *Perf. 11½*

866 A326 10fr dp to lt bl 60 35

25th anniversary of the signing of the North Atlantic Treaty.

Hubert Krains
A327

"Destroyed City," by Ossip Zadkine
A328

Engraved and Photogravure

1974, Apr. 27 *Perf. 11½*

867 A327 5fr blk & gray 30 8

Stamp Day.

Europa Issue 1974

1974, May 4

Design: 10fr, Solidarity, by Georges Minne.

868 A328 5fr blk & red 35 10
869 A328 10fr blk & ultra 90 45

Children
A329

1974, May 18 Photo. *Perf. 11½*

870 A329 4fr lt bl & multi 28 15

10th Lay Youth Festival.

Planetarium, Brussels
A330

Soleilmont Abbey Ruins—A331

Engraved and Photogravure

1974, June 22 *Perf. 11½*

Designs: 4fr, Pillory, Braine-le-Chateau. 7fr, Fountain, Ghent (procession symbolic of Chamber of Rhetoric). 10fr, Belfry, Bruges (vert.).

871 A330 3fr sky bl & blk 20 10
872 A330 4fr lil rose & blk 30 10
873 A331 5fr lt grn & blk 45 12
874 A331 7fr dl yel & blk 60 35
875 A330 10fr blk, bl & brn 75 25
Nos. 871-875 (5) 2.30 92

Historic buildings and monuments.

"BENELUX"
A332

1974, Sept. 7 Photo. *Perf. 11½*

876 A332 5fr bl grn, dk grn & lt bl 30 8

30th anniversary of the signing of the customs union of Belgium, Netherlands and Luxembourg.

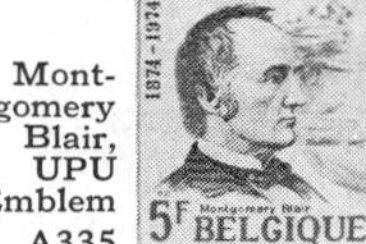

Jan Vekemans, by Cornelis de Vos
A333

1974, Sept. 14

877 A333 3fr multi 18 12

Youth philately.

Leon Tresignies, Willebroek Canal Bridge
A334

1974, Sept. 28 Engr. & Photo.

878 A334 4fr brn & ol grn 25 12

60th death anniversary of Corporal Leon Tresignies (1886–1914), hero of World War I.

Montgomery Blair, UPU Emblem
A335

Design: 10fr, Heinrich von Stephan and UPU emblem.

Engraved and Photogravure

1974, Oct. 5 *Perf. 11½*

879 A335 5fr grn & blk 35 12
880 A335 10fr brick red & blk 75 50

Centenary of Universal Postal Union.

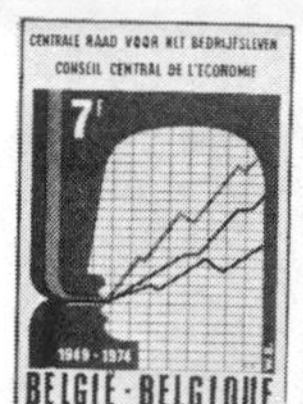

Symbolic Chart
A336

1974, Oct. 12 Photo. ***Perf. 11½***

881 A336 7fr multi 45 30

Central Economic Council, 25th anniversary.

Rotary Emblem
A337

1974, Oct. 19

882 A337 10fr multi 60 30

Rotary International of Belgium.

Wild Boar (Regiment's Emblem)
A338

1974, Oct. 26

883 A338 3fr multi 25 15

Granting of the colors to the Ardennes Chasseurs Regiment, 40th anniversary.

Angel, by Van Eyck Brothers
A341

1974, Nov. 16 ***Perf. 11½***

884 A341 4fr rose lil 28 15

Christmas 1974. The Angel shown is from the triptyque "The Mystical Lamb" in the Saint-Bavon Cathedral, Ghent.

Adolphe Quetelet, by J. Odevaere
A342

1974, Dec. 14 Engr. & Photo.

885 A342 10fr blk & buff 60 30

Death centenary of Adolphe Quetelet (1796–1874), statistician, astronomer and Secretary of Royal Academy of Brussels.

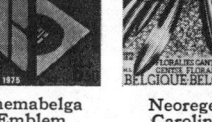

Themabelga Emblem
A343

Neoregelia Carolinae
A344

1975, Feb. 15 Photo. ***Perf. 11½***

912 A343 6.50fr grn, blk & org 35 10

Themabelga, International Thematic Stamp Exhibition, Brussels, Dec. 13–21, 1975.

1975, Feb. 22

Flowers: 5fr, Coltsfoot. 6.50fr, Azalea.

913 A344 4.50fr multi 30 15

Photogravure and Engraved

914 A344 5fr multi 35 20
915 A344 6.50fr multi 45 15

Ghent International Flower Exhibition, Apr. 26–May 5.

School Emblem, Man Leading Boy
A345

Engraved and Photogravure

1975, Mar. 15 ***Perf. 11½***

916 A345 4.50fr blk & multi 30 8

Centenary of the founding of the Charles Buls Normal School for Boys, Brussels.

Davids Foundation Emblem
A346

1975, Mar. 22 Photogravure

917 A346 5fr yel & multi 30 6

Centenary of the Davids Foundation, a Catholic organization for the promotion of Flemish through education and books.

King Albert
A347

Mailman, 1840, by James Thiriar
A348

1975, Apr. 5 Engr. & Photo.

918 A347 10fr blk & mar 60 35

King Albert (1875–1934), birth centenary.

1975, Apr. 19 Engr. ***Perf. 11½***

919 A348 6.50fr dl mag 45 8

Stamp Day 1975.

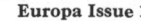

St. John, from Last Supper, by Bouts
A349

Concentration Camp Symbols
A350

Europa Issue 1975

Design: 10fr, Woman's Head, detail from "Trial by Fire," by Dirk Bouts.

1975, Apr. 26 Engr. & Photo.

920 A349 6.50fr blk, grn & bl 45 18
921 A349 10fr blk, ocher & red 75 42

1975, May 3 Photogravure

Design: "B" denoted political prisoners, "KG" prisoners of war.

922 A350 4.50fr multi 30 12

Liberation of concentration camps, 30th anniversary.

Hospice of St. John, Bruges
A351

Church of St. Loup, Namur
A352

Design: 10fr, Martyrs' Square, Brussels.

1975, May 12 Engr. ***Perf. 11½***

926 A351 4.50fr dp rose lil 30 28
927 A352 5fr sl grn 30 18
928 A351 10fr brt bl 60 30

European Architectural Heritage Year.

Library, Louvain University, Ryckmans and Cerfaux
A355

1975, June 7 Photo. ***Perf. 11½***

931 A355 10fr dl bl & sep 60 30

25th anniversary of Louvain Bible Colloquium, founded by Professors Gonzague Ryckmans (1887–1969) and Lucien Cerfaux (1883–1968).

"Metamorphose" by Pol Mara
A356

Marie Popelin, Palace of Justice, Brussels
A357

1975, June 14

932 A356 7fr multi 45 30

Queen Fabiola Mental Health Foundation.

1975, June 21 Engr. & Photo.

933 A357 6.50fr grn & cl 45 10

International Women's Year 1975. Marie Popelin (1846–1913), first Belgian woman doctor of law.

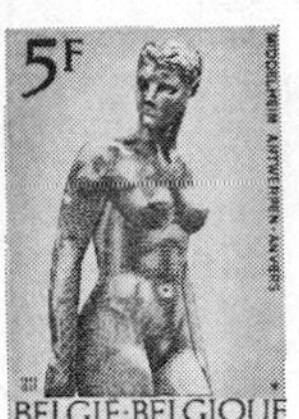

Assia, by Charles Despiau
A358

Cornelia Vekemans, by Cornelis de Vos
A359

Engraved & Photogravure

1975, Sept. 6 *Perf. 11½*

934 A358 5fr yel grn & blk 30 12

Middelheim Outdoor Museum, 25th anniversary.

1975, Sept. 20 Photogravure

935 A359 4.50fr multi 30 12

Youth philately.

Map of Schelde-Rhine Canal
A360

1975, Sept. 20

936 A360 10fr multi 60 30

Opening of connection between the Schelde and Rhine, Sept. 23, 1975.

National Bank, W. F. Orban, Founder
A361

Photogravure and Engraved

1975, Oct. 11 *Perf. 12½x13*

937 A361 25fr multi 1.50 45

National Bank of Belgium, 125th anniversary.

Edmond Thieffry and Plane, 1925
A362

1975, Oct. 18 *Perf. 11½*

938 A362 7fr blk & lil 45 30

First flight Brussels to Kinshasa, Congo, 50th anniversary.

"Seat of Wisdom" St. Peter's, Louvain
A363

Photogravure and Engraved

1975, Nov. 8 *Perf. 11½*

939 A363 6.50fr bl, blk & grn 45 8

University of Louvain, 550th anniversary.

Angels, by Rogier van der Weyden
A364

1975, Nov. 15

940 A364 5fr multi 30 12

Christmas 1975.

Willemsfonds Emblem
A365

American Bicentennial Emblem
A366

1976, Feb. 21 Photo. *Perf. 11½*

941 A365 5fr multi 30 10

125th anniversary of the Willems Foundation, which supports Flemish language and literature.

1976, Mar. 13 Photo. *Perf. 11½*

942 A366 14fr gold, red, bl & blk 90 45

American Bicentennial.

No. 942 printed checkerwise in sheets of 30 stamps and 30 gold and black labels which show medal with 1626 seal of New York. Black engraved inscription on labels commemorates arrival of first Walloon settlers in Nieu Nederland.

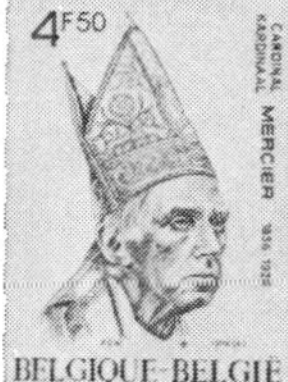

Cardinal Mercier
A367

Symbolic of V.E.V.
A368

1976, Mar. 20 Engraved

943 A367 4.50fr brt rose lil 30 12

Désiré Joseph Cardinal Mercier (1851–1926), professor at Louvain University, spiritual and patriotic leader during World War I, 50th death anniversary.

1976, Apr. 3 Photo. *Perf. 11½*

944 A368 6.50fr multi 45 6

Flemish Economic Organization (Vlaams Ekonomisch Verbond), 50th anniversary.

General Post Office, Brussels
A369

1976, Apr. 24 Engr. *Perf. 11½*

945 A369 6.50fr sepia 45 6

Stamp Day.

Europa Issue 1976

Potter's Hands
A370

Design: 6.50fr, Basket maker (vert.).

1976, May 8 Photogravure

946 A370 6.50fr multi 60 12
947 A370 14fr multi 90 50

Truck on Road
A371

1976, May 8

948 A371 14fr blk, yel & red 90 45

15th International Road Union Congress, Brussels, May 9–13.

Queen Elisabeth
A372

1976, May 24 *Perf. 11½*

949 A372 14fr green 90 45

Queen Elisabeth (1876–1965), birth centenary.

Ardennes Draft Horses
A373

1976, June 19

950 A373 5fr multi 35 12

Ardennes Draft Horses Association, 50th anniversary.

Souvenir Sheets

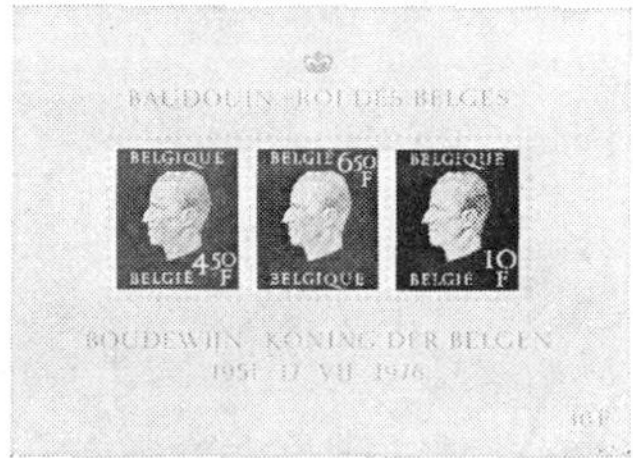

King Baudouin—A374

1976, June 26

951	A374	Sheet of 3	5.50	5.50
a.		4.50fr gray	1.75	1.75
b.		6.50fr ocher	1.75	1.75
c.		10fr brick red	1.75	1.75
952	A374	Sheet of 2	7.50	7.50
a.		20fr yel grn	2.25	2.25
b.		30fr Prus bl	2.25	2.25

25th anniversary of the reign of King Baudouin. Nos. 951–952 have silver marginal inscriptions. Size: 110x82mm. No. 951 sold for 30fr, No. 952 for 70fr. The surtax went to a new foundation for the improvement of living conditions in honor of the King.

Electric Train and Society Emblem
A375

1976, Sept. 11 Photo. *Perf. 11½*

953 A375 6.50fr multi 45 8

National Belgian Railroad Society, 50th anniversary.

William of Nassau, Prince of Orange
A376

1976, Sept. 11 Engraved

954 A376 10fr sl grn 60 30

400th anniversary of the pacification of Ghent.

New Subway Train
A377

1976, Sept. 18 Photogravure

955 A377 6.50fr multi 45 8

Opening of first line of Brussels subway.

Young Musician, by W. C. Duyster
A378

1976, Oct. 2 Photo. ***Perf. 11½***

956	A378	4.50fr	multi	30	15

Young musicians and youth philately.

Charles Bernard
A379

St. Jerome in the Mountains, by Le Patinier
A380

Blind Leading the Blind, by Breughel the Elder
A381

Design: No. 958, Fernand Victor Toussaint van Boelaere.

1976, Oct. 16 Engraved

957	A379	5fr	violet	30	30
958	A379	5fr	red brn & sep	30	30
959	A380	6.50fr	dk brn	45	8
960	A381	6.50fr	sl grn	45	8

Charles Bernard (1875-1961), Frenchspeaking journalist; Toussaint van Boelaere (1875-1947), Flemish journalist; No. 959, Charles Plisnier Belgian-French Cultural Society. No. 960, Assoc. for Language Promotion.

Remouchamps Caves
A382

Hunnegem Priory, Gramont, and Madonna
A383

Designs: No. 963, River Lys and St. Martin's Church. No. 964, Ham-sur-Heure Castle.

1976, Oct. 23 Engr. ***Perf. 13***

961	A382	4.50fr	multi	30	25
962	A383	4.50fr	multi	30	25
963	A383	5fr	multi	45	25
964	A383	5fr	multi	45	25

Tourism. Nos. 961–962 are not luminescent.

Nativity, by Master of Flemalle
A384

1976, Nov. 20 ***Perf. 11½***

965	A384	5fr	violet	30	25

Christmas 1976.

Rubens' Monogram—A385

Photogravure and Engraved

1977, Feb. 12 ***Perf. 11½***

966	A385	6.50fr	lil & blk	45	6

Peter Paul Rubens (1577–1640), painter, 400th birth anniversary.

Heraldic Lion
A386

1977-84 Typo. ***Perf. 13½x14***

Size: 17x20mm.

967	A386	50c	brn ('80)	15	5
a.			org brn ('85)	5	5
968	A386	1fr	brt lil	15	5
a.			brt rose lil ('84)	6	5
969	A386	1.50fr	gray ('78)	15	5
970	A386	2fr	yel ('78)	15	5
970A	A386	2.50fr	yel grn ('81)	15	5
971	A386	2.75fr	Prus bl ('80)	30	10
972	A386	3fr	vio ('78)	30	5
a.			dl vio ('84)	18	5
973	A386	4fr	red brn ('80)	25	6
974	A386	4.50fr	lt ultra	30	5
975	A386	5fr	grn ('80)	30	8
a.			dp grn ('84)	20	8
976	A386	6fr	dl red brn	35	5
			Nos. 967-976 (11)	2.55	64

Perf. 13½x12½, 12½x13½

1978, Aug. Photogravure

Size: 17x22mm, 22x17mm.

977	A386	1fr	brt lil	15	5
a.			Booklet pane of 4 (#977-978 and 2 #786)	1.50	
b.			Booklet pane of 4 (#977, 979 and 2 #788)	2.00	
978	A386	2fr	yellow	30	30
979	A386	3fr	violet	45	45

See Nos. 1085-1088.

Nos. 977-979 issued in booklets only and have one straight-edge. Each pane has 2 labels showing Belgian Postal emblem, also a large selvage with zip code instructions. No. 977-979 not luminescent.

Anniversary Emblem
A387

1977, Mar. 14 Photo. ***Perf. 11½***

982	A387	6.50fr	sil & multi	45	6

Royal Belgian Association of Civil and Agricultural Engineers, 50th anniversary.

Birds and Lions Emblem
A388

1977, Mar. 28

983	A388	14fr	multi	90	45

Belgian District No. 112 of Lions International, 25th anniversary.

Pillar Box, 1852
A389

1977, Apr. 23 Engraved

984	A389	6.50fr	sl grn	45	6

Stamp Day 1977.

Europa Issue 1977

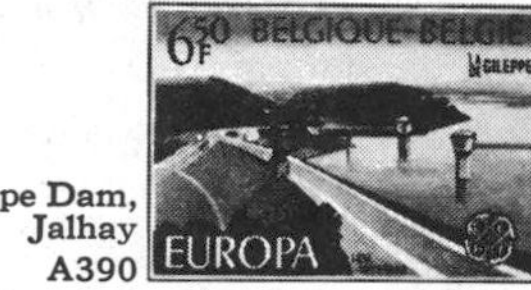

Gileppe Dam, Jalhay
A390

Design: 14fr, War Memorial, Yser at Nieuport.

1977, May 7 Photo. ***Perf. 11½***

985	A390	6.50fr	multi	60	10
986	A390	14fr	multi	1.25	15

Mars and Mercury Association Emblem
A391

1977, May 14

987	A391	5fr	multi	30	18

Mars and Mercury Association of Reserve and Retired Officers, 50th anniversary.

Prince de Hornes Coat of Arms
A392

Conversion of St. Hubertus
A394

Battle of the Golden Spur, from Oxford Chest—A393

Design: 6.50fr, Froissart writing book.

1977, June 11 Engr. ***Perf. 11½***

988	A392	4.50fr	violet	35	12
989	A393	5fr	red	42	20
990	A394	6.50fr	dk brn	45	6
991	A394	14fr	sl grn	85	45

300th anniversary of the Principality of Overijse (4.50fr); 675th anniversary of the Battle of the Golden Spur (5fr); 600th anniversary of publication of first volume of the Chronicles of Jehan Froissart (6.50fr); 1250th anniversary of the death of St. Hubertus (14fr).

Rubens, Self-portrait
A395

1977, June 25 Photogravure

992	A395	5fr	multi	30	18
a.			Souvenir sheet of 3	1.25	1.25

Peter Paul Rubens (1577–1640), painter, 400th birth anniversary. No. 992a contains 3 No. 992; decorative margin. Size: 100x152mm. Sold for 20fr.

Open Book, from The Lamb of God, by Van Eyck Brothers—A396

1977, Sept. 3 Photo. ***Perf. 11½***

993	A396	10fr	multi	60	30

International Federation of Library Associations (IFLA), 50th Anniversary Congress, Brussels, Sept. 5–10.

Gymnast and Soccer Player
A397

Designs: 6.50fr, Fencers in wheelchairs (horiz.). 10fr, Basketball players. 14fr, Hockey players.

1977, Sept. 10

994	A397	4.50fr	multi	30	12
995	A397	6.50fr	multi	45	6
996	A397	10fr	multi	60	30
997	A397	14fr	multi	90	45

Workers' Gymnastics and Sports Center, 50th anniversary (4.50fr); sport for the Handicapped (6.50fr); 20th European Basketball Championships (10fr); First World Hockey Cup (14fr).

Europalia 77 Emblem—A398

1977, Sept. 17

998	A398	5fr	gray & multi	30	18

5th Europalia Arts Festival, featuring German Federal Republic, Belgium, Oct.–Nov. 1977.

The Egg Farmer, by Gustave De Smet
A399

977, Oct. 8 Engr. & Photo.

99	A399	4.50fr bis & blk	30	12

Publicity for Belgian eggs.

Mother and Daughter with Album, by Constant Cap
A400

977, Oct. 15 Engraved

000	A400	4.50fr dk brn	30	12

Youth Philately.

Bailiff's House, Gembloux
A401

Market Square, t. Nicholas
A402

Designs: No. 1002, St. Aldegonde Church nd Cultural Center. No. 1004, Statue and ridge, Liège.

977, Oct. 22

001	A401	4.50fr multi	30	15
002	A401	4.50fr multi	30	15
003	A402	5fr multi	30	25
004	A402	5fr multi	30	25

Tourism. Nos. 1001-1004 are not luminescent. See Nos. 1017-1018, 1039-1040.

Nativity, by Rogier van der Weyden
A403

1977, Nov. 11 Engraved

005	A403	5fr rose red	30	15

Christmas 1977.

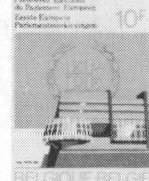

Symbols of Transportation and Map
A404

Parliament of Europe, Strasbourg, and Emblem
A405

Campidoglio Palace, Rome, and Map
A406

Design: No. 1009, Paul-Henri Spaak and map of 19 European member countries.

1978, Mar. 18 Photo. *Perf. 11½*

1006	A404	10fr bl & multi	75	30
1007	A405	10fr bl & multi	1.50	30
1008	A406	14fr bl & multi	90	90
1009	A406	14fr bl & multi	90	90

European Action: 25th anniversary of the European Transport Ministers' Conference; 1st general elections for European Parliament; 20th anniversary of the signing of the Treaty of Rome; Paul-Henri Spaak (1899–1972), Belgian statesman who worked for the establishment of European Community.

Grimbergen Abbey—A407

1978, Apr. 1 Engraved

1010	A407	4.50fr red brn	30	12

850th anniversary of the Premonstratensian Abbey at Grimbergen.

Emblem
A408

No. 39 with First Day Cancel
A409

1978, Apr. 8 Photogravure

1011	A408	8fr multi	45	6

Ostend Chamber of Commerce and Industry, 175th anniversary.

1978, Apr. 15

1012	A409	8fr multi	45	6

Stamp Day.

Europa Issue

Pont des Trous, Tournai
A410

Design: 8fr, Antwerp Cathedral, by Vaclav Hollar (vert.).

Photogravure and Engraved

1978, May 6 *Perf. 11½*

1013	A410	8fr multi	60	8
1014	A410	14fr multi	90	35

Virgin of Ghent, Porcelain Plaque
A411

Paul Pastur Workers' University, Charleroi
A412

1978, Sept. 16 Photo. *Perf. 11½*

1015	A411	6fr multi	42	15
1016	A412	8fr multi	55	6

Municipal education in Ghent, 150th anniversary; Paul Pastur Workers' University, Charleroi, 75th anniversary. Nos. 1015–1016 are not luminescent.

Types of 1977 and

Tourist Guide, Brussels
A413

Designs: No. 1017, Jonathas House, Enghien. No. 1018, View of Wetteren and couple in local costume. No. 1020, Prince Carnival, Eupen-St. Vith.

1978, Sept. 25 Photo. & Engr.

1017	A401	4.50fr multi	30	15
1018	A402	4.50fr multi	30	15
1019	A413	6fr multi	45	15
1020	A413	6fr multi	45	15

Tourism. Nos. 1017–1020 are not luminescent.

Emblem
A414

1978, Oct. 7 Photogravure

1021	A414	8fr red & blk	45	8

Royal Flemish Engineer's Organization, 50th anniversary.

Young Philatelist
A415

1978, Oct. 14 Engr. *Perf. 11½*

1022	A415	4.50fr dk vio	30	8

Youth philately.

Nativity, Notre Dame, Huy
A416

1978, Nov. 18 Engr. *Perf. 11½*

1023	A416	6fr black	35	15

Christmas 1978.

Tyll Eulenspiegel Lay Action Emblem
A417

European Parliament Emblem
A418

1979, Mar. 3 Photo. *Perf. 11½*

1024	A417	4.50fr multi	30	6

10th anniversary of Lay Action Centers.

1979, Mar. 3

1025	A418	8fr multi	60	12

European Parliament, first direct elections, June 7–10.

St. Michael Banishing Lucifer
A419

1979, Mar. 17 Photo. & Engr.

1026	A419	4.50fr rose red & blk	30	12
1027	A419	8fr brt grn & blk	45	15

Millennium of Brussels.

NATO Emblem and Monument
A420

1979, Mar. 31 Photogravure

1028	A420	30fr multi	90	45

North Atlantic Treaty Organization, 30th anniversary.

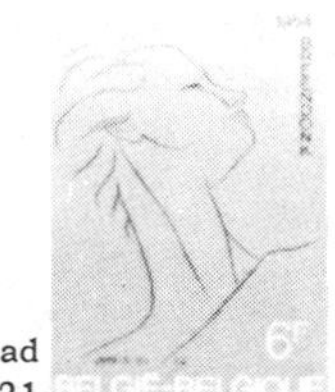

Prisoner's Head
A421

1979, Apr. 7 Photo. & Engr.

1029	A421	6fr org & blk	35	12

25th anniversary of the National Political Prisoners' Monument at Breendonk.

Belgium No. Q2
A422

1979, Apr. 21 Photo. *Perf. 11½*

1030	A422	8fr multi	45	12

Stamp Day 1979.

Europa Issue 1979

Mail Coach and Truck—A423

Design: 14fr, Chappe's heliograph, Intelsat satellite and dish antenna.

Photo. & Engr.

1979, Apr. 28 ***Perf. 11½***

1031 A423 8fr multi 45 15
1032 A423 14fr multi 90 40

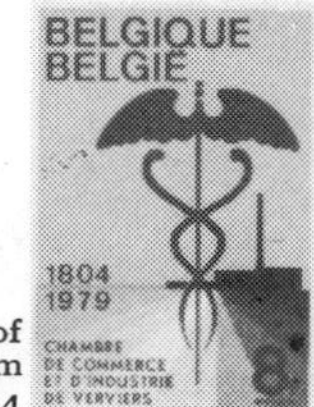

Chamber of Commerce Emblem A424

1979, May 19 **Photo.** ***Perf. 11½***

1033 A424 8fr multi 45 12

Verviers Chamber of Commerce and Industry, 175th anniversary.

"50" Emblem A425

1979, June 9 **Photo.** ***Perf. 11½***

1034 A425 4.50fr gold & ultra 28 6

National Fund for Professional Credit, 50th anniversary.

Merchants, Roman Bas-relief—A426

1979, June 9

1035 A426 10fr multi 60 25

Belgian Chamber of Trade and Commerce, 50th anniversary.

"Tintin" as Philatelist A427

1979, Sept. 29 **Photo.** ***Perf. 11½***

1036 A427 8fr multi 60 20

Youth philately.

Tourism Types of 1977

Designs: No. 1037, Belfry, Thuin. No. 1038, Royal Museum of Central Africa, Tervuren. No. 1039, St. Nicholas Church and cattle, Ciney. No. 1040, St. John's Church and statue of Our Lady, Poperinge.

Perf. 11½ (#1037, 1039), 13 (#1038, 1040)

1979, Oct. 22 **Photo & Engr.**

1037 A401 5fr multi 30 8
1038 A402 5fr multi 30 8
1039 A401 6fr multi 45 18
1040 A402 6fr multi 45 18

Francois Auguste Gevaert A429

Piano, String Instruments A430

Design: 6fr, Emmanuel Durlet.

Photo. & Engr.

1979, Nov. 3 ***Perf. 11½***

1041 A429 5fr brown 35 8
1042 A429 6fr brown 42 10
1043 A430 14fr brown 90 35

Francois Auguste Gevaert (1828-1908), musicologist and composer; Emmanuel Durlet (1893-1977), pianist; Queen Elisabeth Musical Chapel Foundation, 40th anniversary.

Virgin and Child, Notre Dame, Foy A431

1979, Nov. 24 **Photo. & Engr.**

1044 A431 6fr lt grnsh bl 35 10

Christmas 1979.

Independence, 150th Anniversary A432

1980, Jan. 26 **Photo** ***Perf. 11½***

1045 A432 9fr purple 60 15

Frans van Cauwelaert A433

Spring Flowers A434

1980, Feb. 25 **Engraved**

1046 A433 5fr gray 30 8

Frans van Cauwelaert (1880-1961), Minister of State.

1980, Mar. 10 **Photo.**

Multicolored

1047 A434 5fr *shown* 30 8
1048 A434 6.50fr *Summer flowers* 40 10
1049 A434 9fr *Autumn flowers* 55 15

Ghent Flower Show, Apr. 19-27.

Telephone and Telegraph Administration, 50th Anniversary—A435

1980, Apr. 14 **Photo.** ***Perf. 11½***

1050 A435 10fr multi 60 30

Belgium No. C4—A436

1980, Apr. 21

1051 A436 9fr multi 55 15

Stamp Day.

Europa Issue 1980

St. Benedict, by Hans Memling—A437

Design: 14fr, Margaret of Austria (1480-1530).

1980, Apr. 28

1052 A437 9fr multi 55 15
1053 A437 14fr multi 85 30

Palais des Nations, Brussels—A438

1980, May 10 **Photo.** ***Perf. 11½***

1054 A438 5fr multi 30 10

4th Interparliamentary Conference for European Cooperation and Security, Brussels, May 12-18.

Golden Carriage, 1780, Mons—A439

Design: No. 1056, Canal landscape, Damme.

1980, May 17

1055 A439 6.50fr multi 40 25
1056 A439 6.50fr multi 40 25

Tourism.

Souvenir Sheet

Royal Mint Theater, Brussels—A440

1980, May 31 **Photo. & Engr.** ***Perf. 11½***

1057 A440 50fr black 4.50 4.5

150th anniversary of independence. Multicolored decorative margin; sold for 75fr. Size. 100½x151mm.

King Baudouin, 50th Birthday—A441

1980, Sept. 6 **Photo.** ***Perf. 11½***

1058 A441 9fr rose cl 55 1

View of Chiny—A442

Portal and Court, Diest—A443

1980 **Engr.** ***Perf. 13***

1059 A442 5fr multi 30 1
1060 A443 5fr multi 30 1

Tourism. Nos. 1059-1060 are not luminescent. Issue dates: No. 1059, Sept. 27; No. 1060, Dec. 13. See Nos. 1072-1075.

Emblem of Belgian Heart League—A444

1980, Oct. 4 **Photo.** ***Perf. 11½***

1061 A444 14fr bl & mag 85 4

Heart Week, Oct. 20-25.

Rodenbach Statue, Roulers—A445

1980, Oct. 11

1062 A445 9fr multi 60 1

Albrecht Rodenbach (1856-1880), poet.

Youth Philately—A446

980, Oct. 27 Photo. *Perf. 11½*

63	A446	5fr multi	30	10

National Broadcasting Service, 50th Anniversary—A447

980, Nov. 10

064	A447	10fr gray & blk	60	30

Garland and Nativity, by Daniel Seghers, 17th Century—A448

980, Nov. 17

065	A448	6.50fr multi	40	12

Christmas 1980.

Baron de ›rlache, by F.J. Navez A449

Leopold I, By Geefs A450

Design: 9fr, Baron de Stassart, by F.J. Navez.

81, Mar. 16 Photo. *Perf. 11½*

6	A449	6fr multi	35	18
7	A449	9fr multi	55	12

Photogravure & Engraved

8	A450	50fr multi	3.00	75

›esquicentennial of Chamber of Deputies, ›ate and Dynasty.

Europa Issue 1981

Tchantchès and Op-Signoorke, Puppets—A451

1981, May 4 Photo. & Engr. *Perf. 11½*

1069	A451	9fr shown	55	12
1070	A451	14fr d'Artagnan and Woltje	90	45

Impression of M.A. de Cock (Founder of Post Museum)—A452

1981, May 18 Photo.

1071	A452	9fr multi	55	12

Stamp Day.

Tourism Types of 1980

Designs: No. 1072, Virgin and Child statue, Our Lady's Church, Tongre-Notre Dame. No. 1073, Egmont Castle, Zottegem. No. 1074, Eau d'Heure River. No. 1075, Tongerlo Abbey, Antwerp.

1981, June 15 Engr. *Perf. 11½*

1072	A442	6fr multi	45	18
1073	A442	6fr multi	45	25
1074	A443	6.50fr multi	45	25
1075	A443	6.50fr multi	45	25

Soccer Player A453

E. Remouchamps, Founder—A454

1981, Sept. 5 Photo. *Perf. 11½*

1076	A453	6fr multi	35	18

Soccer in Belgium centenary; Royal Antwerp Soccer Club.

1981, Sept. 5 Photo. & Engr.

1077	A454	6.50fr multi	40	18

Walloon Language and Literature Club 125th anniv.

Audit Office Sesquicentennial—A455

1981, Sept. 12 Engr.

1078	A455	10fr tan & dk brn	60	30

French Horn—A456

1981, Sept. 12 Photo.

1079	A456	6.50fr multi	40	18

Vredekring (Peace Circle) Band of Antwerp centenary.

Souvenir Sheet

Pieta, by Ben Genaux—A457

1981, Sept. 19 Photo. *Perf. 11½*

1080	A457	20fr multi	1.75	1.75

Mining disaster at Marcinelle, 25th anniv. Red brown and black margin shows mine fire. Size: 150x100mm. Sold for 30fr.

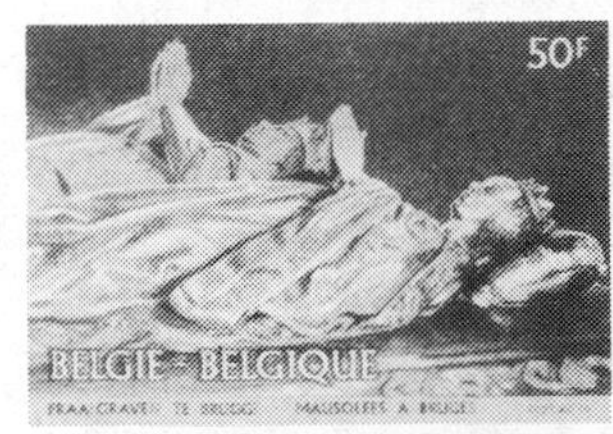

Mausoleum of Marie of Burgundy and Charles the Bold, Bruges—A458

1981, Oct. 10 Photo. & Engr.

1081	A458	50fr multi	3.00	75

Youth Philately—A459

1981, Oct. 24 Photo.

1082	A459	6fr multi	35	18

Type of 1977

A459a A460

King Baudouin—A460a

Photo. & Engr.; Photo.

1981-85 *Perf. 13½x14, 11½*

1083	A386	65c brt rose ('85)	5	5
1085	A386	1fr on 5fr grn ('82)	5	5
1086	A386	7fr brt rose ('82)	42	5
1087	A386	8fr grnsh bl ('83)	45	6
1088	A386	9fr dl org ('85)	38	8
1089	A459a	10fr bl ('82)	60	10
1090	A459a	11fr dl red ('83)	65	8
1091	A459a	12fr grn ('84)	70	6
1092	A459a	13fr scar ('86)	60	6
1093	A459a	15fr red org ('84)	90	20
1094	A459a	20fr dk bl ('84)	1.25	28
1095	A459a	22fr lil ('84)	1.40	30
1096	A459a	23fr gray grn ('85)	75	55
1097	A459a	30fr brn ('84)	1.75	40
1098	A459a	40fr red org ('84)	2.50	55
1099	A460	50fr lt grnsh bl & bl	3.00	30
1100	A460a	50fr tan & dk brn ('84)	3.00	60
1101	A460	65fr pale lil & blk	4.00	90
1102	A460	100fr lt bis brn & dk bl	6.00	1.25
1103	A460a	100fr lt bl & dk bl ('84)	6.00	1.25

See No. 1231.

Max Waller, Movement Founder A461

The Spirit Drinkers, by Gustave van de Woestyne A462

Fernand Severin, Poet, 50th Death Anniv. A463

Jan van Ruusbroec, Flemish Mystic, 500th Birth Anniv. A464

Thought and Man TV Series, 25th Anniv. A465

Nativity, 16th Cent. Engraving A466

1981, Nov. 7

1104	A461	6fr multi	35	18
1105	A462	6.50fr multi	40	25
1106	A463	9fr multi	55	15
1107	A464	10fr multi	90	30
1108	A465	14fr multi	85	45
		Nos. 1104-1108 (5)	3.05	1.33

La Jeune Belgique cultural movement centenary (6fr).

1981, Nov. 21

1109	A466	6.50fr multi	40	18

Christmas 1981.

Royal Conservatory of Music Sesquicentennial—A467

Design: 9fr, Judiciary sesquicentennial.

1982, Jan. 25 Photo. *Perf. 11½*

1110 A467 6.50fr multi 40 18
1111 A467 9fr multi 55 8

Galaxy and Microscope A468

1982, Mar. 1

1112 A468 6fr Cyclatron 35 18
1113 A468 14fr shown 85 45
1114 A468 50fr Koch 3.00 90

Radio-isotope production, Natl. Radio-elements Institute, Fleurus (6fr); Royal Belgian Observatory (14fr); centenary of TB bacillus discovery (50fr).

Joseph Lemaire (1882-1966), Minister of State—A469

1982, Apr. 17 Photo. *Perf. 11½*

1115 A469 6.50fr multi 40 18

Europa 1982—A470

1982, May 1

1116 A470 10fr Universal suffrage 60 8
1117 A470 17fr Edict of Tolerance, 1781 1.00 45

Stamp Day—A471

1982, May 22 Photo. & Engr. *Perf. 11½*

1118 A471 10fr multi 60 8

67th World Esperanto Congress, Anvers—A472

1982, June 7 Photo. *Perf. 11½*

1119 A472 12fr Tower of Babel 75 35

Tourism Type of 1980

Designs: No. 1120, Tower of Gosselies. No. 1121, Zwijveke Abbey, Dendermonde. No. 1122, Stavelot Abbey. No. 1123, Villers-la-Ville Abbey ruins. No. 1124, Geraardsbergen Abbey entrance. No. 1125, Beveren Pillory.

1982, June 21 Photo. & Engr.

1120 A443 7fr lt bl & blk 42 6
1121 A443 7fr lt grn & blk 42 6
1122 A442 7.50fr tan & dk brn 45 30
1123 A442 7.50fr lt vio & pur 45 30
1124 A443 7.50fr sl & blk 45 30
1125 A443 7.50fr beige & blk 45 30
Nos. 1120-1125 (6) 2.64 1.32

Self Portrait, by L.P. Boon (b. 1912)

Abraham Hans, Writer (1882-1932)—A474

Designs: 10fr, Adoration of the Shepherds, by Hugo van der Goes (1440-1482). 12fr, The King on His Throne, carving by M. de Ghelderode (1898-1962). 17fr, Madonna and Child, by Pieter Paulus (1881-1959).

1982, Sept. 13 Photo. *Perf. 11½*

1126 A473 7fr multi 45 6
1127 A473 10fr multi 60 6
1128 A473 12fr multi 75 45
1129 A473 17fr multi 1.00 45

1982, Sept. 27

1130 A474 17fr multi 1.00 45

Youth Philately and Scouting Year—A475

1982, Oct. 2 Photo. *Perf. 11½*

1131 A475 7fr multi 45 6

Grand Orient Lodge of Belgium Sesquicentennial—A476

1982, Oct. 16 Photo. & Engr.

1132 A476 10fr Man taking oath 60 6

Cardinal Joseph Cardijn (1882-1967)—A477

1982, Nov. 13 Photo.

1133 A477 10fr multi 60 6

St. Francis of Assisi (1182-1226)—A478

1982, Nov. 27

1134 A478 20fr multi 1.25 45

Horse-drawn Trolley—A479

1983, Feb. 12 Photo. *Perf. 11½*

1135 A479 7.50fr shown 45 25
1136 A479 10fr Electric trolley 60 15
1137 A479 50fr Trolley, diff. 3.00 60

Intl. Fed. for Periodical Press, 24th World Congress, Brussels, May 11-13—A480

1983, Mar. 19 Photo. *Perf. 11½*

1138 A480 20fr multi 1.25 30

Homage to Women—A481

1983, Apr. 16

1139 A481 8fr Operator 60 5
1140 A481 11fr Homemaker 75 8
1141 A481 20fr Executive 1.25 25

Stamp Day—A482

1983, Apr. 23

1142 A482 11fr multi 65

Procession of the Precious Blood, Bruges—A483

1983, Apr. 30 Photo. *Perf. 11*

1143 A483 8fr multi 50

Europa 1983—A484

Paintings by P. Delvaux. 11fr vert.

1983, May 14

1144 A484 11fr Common Man 65
1145 A484 20fr Night Train 1.25 4

Manned Flight Bicentenary—A485

1983, June 11 Photo. *Perf. 11*

1146 A485 11fr Balloon over city 65
1147 A485 22fr Country 1.40 4

Our Lady's Church, Hastiere—A486

1983, June 25

1148 A486 8fr shown 45
1149 A486 8fr Landen 45 1
1150 A486 8fr Park, Mouscron 45 1
1151 A486 8fr Wijnendale Castle, Torhout 45 1

Tineke Festival, Heule—A487

1983, Sept. 10 Photo.

1152 A487 8fr multi 45

Enterprise Year Emblem—A488

983, Sept. 24
153 A488 11fr multi 65 12

European year for small and medium-sized terprises and craft industry.

Youth Philately—A489

983, Oct. 10 **Photo.** ***Perf. 11½***
154 A489 8fr multi 45 8

Belgian Exports—A490

983, Oct. 24 ***Perf. 11½***
155 A490 10fr Diamond industry 60 10
156 A490 10fr Metallurgy 60 10
157 A490 10fr Textile industry 60 10

See Nos. 1161-1164

Hendrik Conscience, Novelist (1812-1883)—A491

983, Nov. 7
158 A491 20fr multi 1.25 25

Leopold III Type of 1936

983, Dec. 12 **Engr.** ***Perf. 12x11½***
159 A84 11fr black 65 12

Leopold III memorial (1901-1983), King 934-1951.

Free University of Brussels Sesquicentennial—A492

984, Jan. 14 **Photo. & Engr.** ***Perf. 11½***
160 A492 11fr multi 65 12

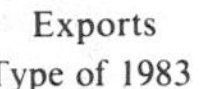

Exports
Type of 1983

1984, Jan. 28 **Photo.**
1161 A490 11fr Chemicals 65 12
1162 A490 11fr Food 65 12
1163 A490 11fr Transportation equipment 65 12
1164 A490 11fr Technology 65 12

50th Death Anniv. of King Albert I—A494

1984, Feb. 11 **Photo. & Engr.**
1165 A494 8fr tan & dk brn 45 10

Souvenir Sheet

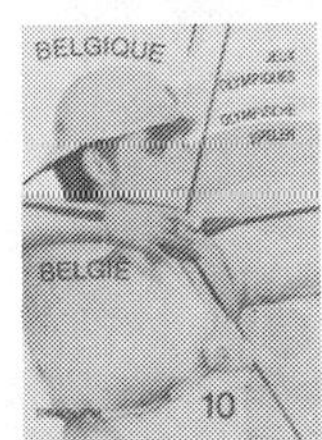

Archery—A495

1984, Mar. 3 **Photo.**
1166 Sheet of 2 2.25 2.25
a. A495 10fr shown 60 60
b. A495 24fr Dressage 1.75 1.75

1984 Olympics. See Nos. B1029-B1030. Size: 125x90mm.

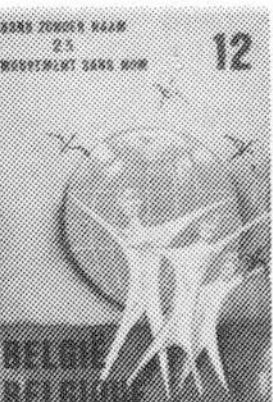

Family, Globe, Birds
A496

St. John Roscho Canonization
A497

1984, Mar. 24 **Photo.** ***Perf. 11½***
1167 A496 12fr multi 70 14

"Movement without a Name" peace org.

1984, Apr. 7
1168 A497 8fr multi 45 10

Europa (1959-84)—A498

1984, May 5 **Photo.** ***Perf. 11½***
1169 A498 12fr blk & red 75 14
1170 A498 22fr blk & ultra 1.40 30

Stamp Day—A499

1984, May 19
1171 A499 12fr No. 52 70 14

2nd European Parliament Elections—A500

1984, May 26
1172 A500 12fr multi 70 14

Royal Military School, 150th Anniv.—A501

1984, June 9 **Photo.** ***Perf. 11½***
1173 A501 22fr Hat 1.40 30

Notre-Dame de la Chappelle, Brussels—A502

Churches: No. 1175, St. Martin's, Montigny-le-Tilleul. No. 1176, Tielt (vert.).

Photo. & Engr.
1984, June 23 ***Perf. 11½x12, 12x11½***
1174 A502 10fr multi 60 14
1175 A502 10fr multi 60 14
1176 A502 10fr multi 60 14

50th Anniv. of Chirojeugd (Christian Youth Movement)—A503

1984, Sept. 15 **Photo.** ***Perf. 11½***
1177 A503 10fr Emblem 60 14

Affligem Abbey—A504

1984, Oct. 6 **Photo. & Engr.**
1178 A504 8fr Averbode, vert. 48 30
1179 A504 22fr Chimay, vert. 1.40 30
1180 A504 24fr Rochefort, vert. 1.50 45
1181 A504 50fr shown 3.00 60

Youth Philately—A505

1984, Oct. 20 **Photo.**
1182 A505 8fr Postman smurf 45 12

Arthur Meulemans (1884-1966), Composer—A506

1984, Nov. 17 **Photo. & Engr.**
1183 A506 12fr multi 75 14

St. Norbert, 850th Death Anniv.—A507

1985, Jan. 14 **Photo. & Engr.**
1184 A507 22fr sep & beige 90 30

Europalia '85—A508

1985, Jan. 21 **Photo.**
1185 A508 12fr Virgin with Lion 40 14

Belgian Assoc. of Professional Journalists, Cent.—A509

1985, Feb. 11 **Photo.**
1186 A509 9fr multi 30 10

Ghent Flower Festival, Orchids—A510

1985, Mar. 18 Photo. & Engr. *Perf. 11½*

1187	A510	12fr	Vanda coerules	40	14
1188	A510	12fr	Phalaenopsis	40	14
1189	A510	12fr	Suphrolaelio cattlea riffe	40	14

Visit of Pope John-Paul II—A511

1985, Apr. 1 Photo.

1190	A511	12fr	multi	40	14

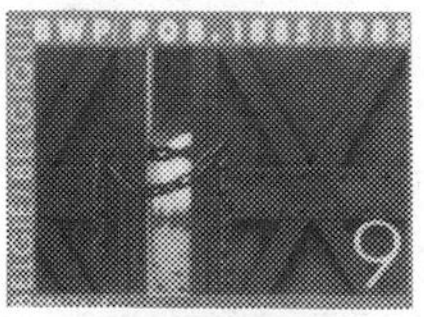

Belgian Worker's Party Cent.—A512

1985, Apr. 15 Photo.

1191	A512	9fr	Chained factory gate	30	10
1192	A512	12fr	Broken wall, red flag	40	14

Jean de Bast (1883-1975), Engraver—A513

Stamp Day.

1985, Apr. 22 Engr.

1193	A513	12fr	bl blk	40	14

Public Transportation Year—A514

Design: 9fr, Steam tram locomotive Type 18, 1896. 12fr, Locomotive Elephant and tender, 1835. 23fr, Type 23 tank engine, 1904. 24fr, Type I Pacific locomotive, 1935. 50fr, Type 27 electric locomotive, 1975.

1985, May 6 Photo.

1194	A514	9fr	multi	30	10
1195	A514	12fr	multi	40	14
1196	A514	23fr	multi	75	25
1197	A514	24fr	multi	80	28

Souvenir Sheet

1198	A514	50fr	multi	1.75	1.00

No. 1198 has multicolored margin continuing design. Size 150x100mm.

Europa 1985—A515

1985, May 13 Photo.

1199	A515	12fr	Cesar Franck at organ, 1887	40	14
1200	A515	23fr	Folk figures	75	25

26th Navigation Congress, Brussels—A516

1985, June 10 Photo. *Perf. 11½*

1201	A516	23fr	Zeebruge Harbor	78	25
1202	A516	23fr	Projected lock at Strepy-Thieu	78	25

St. Martin's Church, Marcinelle—A517

Tourism: No. 1203, Church of the Assumption of Our Lady, Avernas-le-Baudouin (vert.). No. 1204, Church of the Old Beguinage, Tongres (vert.). No. 1206, Private residence, Puyenbroeck.

1985, June 24 *Perf. 11½*

1203	A517	12fr	multi	40	12
1204	A517	12fr	multi	40	12
1205	A517	12fr	multi	40	12
1206	A517	12fr	multi	40	12

Queen Astrid (1905-1935)

A518

Baking Pies for the Mattetart of Geraardsbergen

A519

1985, Sept. 2 *Perf. 11½*

1207	A518	12fr	brown	42	14

1985, Sept. 16

Folk events: 24fr, Children dancing, centenary of the St. Lambert de Hermalle-Argenteau Le Rouges youth organization.

1208	A519	12fr	multi	42	14
1209	A519	24fr	multi	85	28

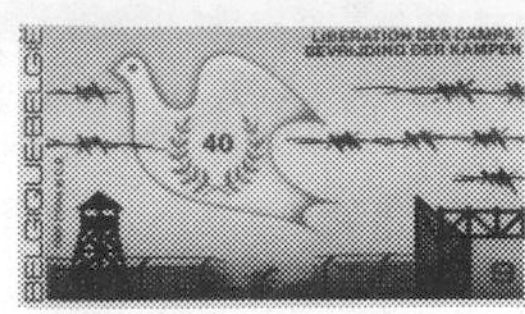

Liberation from German Occupation, 40th Anniv.—A520

Allegories: 9fr, Dove, liberation of concentration camps. 23fr, Battle of Ardennes. 24fr, Destroyer, liberation of the River Scheldt estuary.

1985, Sept. 30 Photo. *Perf. 11½*

1210	A520	9fr	multi	35	25
1211	A520	23fr	multi	85	65
1212	A520	24fr	multi	90	68

Ernest Claes (1885-1968), Author—A521

1985, Oct. 7

1213	A521	9fr	Portrait, book character	35	25

Intl. Youth Year—A522

1985, Oct. 21

1214	A522	9fr	Nude in repose, angel	35	25

King Baudouin & Queen Fabiola, 25th Wedding Anniv.—A523

1985, Dec. 9

1215	A523	12fr	multi	48	38

Birds—A524

1985, Sept. 30 Typo. *Perf. 11½*

1218	A524	3fr	Hawkfinch	10	5
1219	A524	3.50fr	Robin	18	14
1220	A524	8fr	Kingfisher	40	30
1221	A524	9fr	Goldfinch	30	10

King Type of 1981

1986 Photo. *Perf. 11½*

1231	A459a	24fr	dk grysh grn ('86)	1.10	8.
1234	A460a	200fr	sage grn & dl gray grn	9.50	7.0

Congo Stamp Cent.—A525

1986, Jan. 27 Photo. *Perf. 11½*

1236	A525	10fr	Belgian Congo No. 3	42	14

See Zaire No. 1230.

Carnival Cities of Aalst and Binche—A526

Folklore: masks, giants.

1986, Feb. 3

1237	A526	9fr	Aalst Belfry	38	12
1238	A526	12fr	Binche Gilles	50	18

Intl. Peace Year—A527

1986, Mar. 10

1239	A527	23fr	Emblem, dove	1.00	35

Stamp Day—A528

1986, Apr. 21 Photo. *Perf. 11½*

1240	A528	13fr	Artifacts	55	42

Europa 1986—A529

1986, May 5

1241	A529	13fr	Fish	55	42
1242	A529	24fr	Flora	1.10	85

Dogs
A530

St. Ludger's Church, Zele
A531

1986, May 26 **Photo.** ***Perf. 11½***

1243	A530	9fr	Malines sheepdog	40	30
1244	A530	13fr	Tervueren sheepdog	58	45
1245	A530	24fr	Groenendael sheepdog	1.10	82
1246	A530	26fr	Flemish cattle dog	1.15	85

1986, June 30 **Photo. & Engr.**

1247	A531	9fr	shown	40	30
1248	A531	9fr	Waver Town Hall	40	30
1249	A531	13fr	Nederzwalm Canal, horiz.	58	45
1250	A531	13fr	Chapel of Our Lady of the Dunes, Bredene	58	45
1251	A531	13fr	Licot Castle, Viroinval, horiz.	58	45
1252	A531	13fr	Eynenbourg Castle, La Calamine, horiz.	58	45
			Nos. 1247-1252 (7)	3.12	2.40

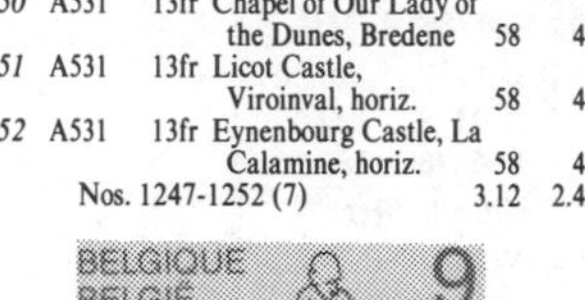

Youth Philately—A532

1986, Sept. 1 **Photo.** ***Perf. 11½***

1253	A532	9fr	dl ol grn, blk & dk red	42	32

Cartoon Exhibition, Knokke.

Famous Men—A533

Designs: 9fr, Constant Permeke, painter, sculptor. 13fr, Baron Michel-Edmond de Selys Longchamps, scientist. 24fr, Felix Timmermans, writer. 26fr, Maurice Careme, poet.

1986, Sept. 29

1254	A533	9fr	multi	42	32
1255	A533	13fr	multi	60	45
1256	A533	24fr	multi	1.10	82
1257	A533	26fr	multi	1.20	90

Royal Academy for Dutch Language and Literature, Cent.—A534

1986, Oct. 6 **Engr.**

1258	A534	9fr	42	32

Natl. Beer Industry—A535

1986, Oct. 13 **Photo. *Perf. 12½x11½***

1259	A535	13fr	Glass, barley, hops	65	50

Provincial Law and Councils, 150th Anniv.—A536

1986, Oct. 27 ***Perf. 11½***

1260	A536	13fr	Stylized map	65	50

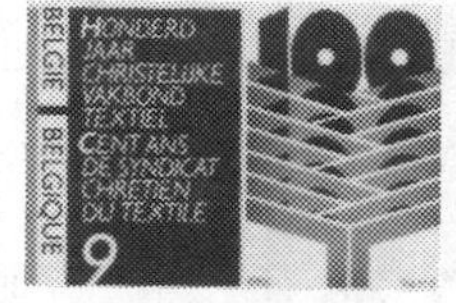

Christian Trade Union, Cent.—A537

1986, Dec. 13 **Photo.** ***Perf. 11½***

1261	A537	9fr	shown	45	35
1262	A537	13fr	design reversed	65	50

Flanders Technology Intl.—A538

1987, Mar. 2 **Photo.**

1263	A538	13fr	multi	65	50

NUMBER CHANGES

No. in 1987 Cat.	No. in 1988 Cat.
BELGIUM	
28a, 29a, 30a, 32a, 34a, 35a, 36b	deleted
37b	deleted
41a, 42b, 43a, 44a	deleted
45a, 46a, 47a, 48a	deleted
50a, 51a, 52b, 53a, 54a	deleted
56a, 57a	deleted
65a, 67a, 73a	deleted
85a, 86a, 87b, 88a, 90a	deleted
92a	deleted
103b	deleted
138a, 141a	deleted
270B	271
271-274	272-275
274A	276
274B-274C	278-279
274D	282
275-276	283-284
277-278	286-287
279-280	289-290
281-292	292-303
293-295	309-311
296-300	317-321
301-305	312-316
306-340	322-360
345-351	361-370
352	277
352A-353	280-281
354-383	371-400
385	401
388	402
389	405
390	407
391-392	409-410
393-396	413-416
397-399	418-420
400	285
401	288
402	291
403-406A	304-308
407-421	435-449
422-423	451-452
424	457
425-461	477-513
462	412
463	454
464	459
465-479	514-528
480	453
481-482	455-456
482A	458
483-487	460-466
488	468
489	450
490-499	529-538
500-501	403-404
502	408
502A	429
503	431
504-528	539-563
529-606	565-642
607-611	659-663
612	411
613	430
614	417
614A-614B	427-428
615	467
616-628	664-676
629-630	650-651
631-640	677-686
641-644	688-691
645	687
646-647	643-644
648-653	692-697

No. in 1987 Cat.	No. in 1988 Cat.
655-656	698-699
657	564
659-665	700-706
666-667	645-646
668-669	652-653
670-672	707-709
673-674	711-712
675	710
676-679	713-716
680	433
680A	472
680D	434
680G-681	473-474
681C-681D	475-476
682-690	717-725
691-692	654-655
693-710	726-743
711-712	647-648
713-714	744-745
714A-716	421-423
717-717A	746-747
717B	749
718-720A	751-754
720B-720C	756-757
721	759
722-723	761-762
724	764
724A	766
725	769
726	772
727	774
727A	778
728-738	789-799
738A-738C	469-471
739-750	800-811
751	649
752-754	656-658
755-792	812-849
793-798	857-862
799	850
800	852
801	863
802-803	782-783
804	785
805-816	864-875
865-872	876-883
873	851
874-875	853-854
876-877	884-885
878	406
882-884	424-426
890	748
891	750
893	755
894	758
895	760
896	763
897	765
898-899	767-768
900-901	770-771
902	773
903-905	775-777
906	779
910-911	780-781
923	432
924	784
925	787
929-930	855-856
980	786
981	788
B12a, B15a	deleted
B13a	B9a
P7a, P12a, P26a	deleted

Binder Labels for Specialty and National Albums

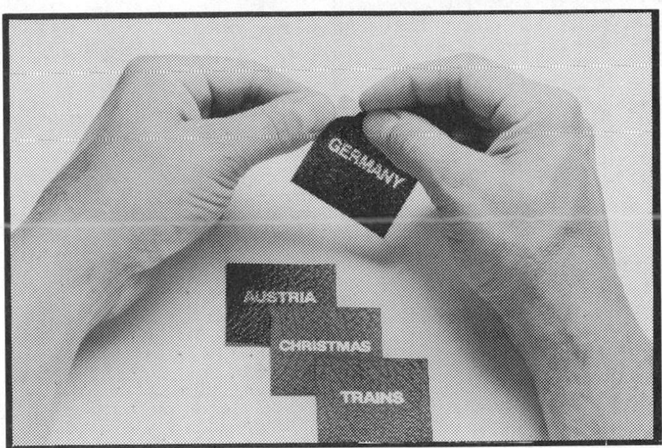

Argentina
Australia
Australia & Dependencies
Austria
Belgium & Colonies
Brazil
British Africa
British America
British Asia
British Europe
British Oceania
Canada
Central America
Czechoslovakia
East & South Europe
Ecuador
Finland
France
French Andorra
French Colonies
Germany
Germany I
Germany II
Germany III
Germany IV
Great Britain/British
Europe/Ireland
Greece

Guernsey/Isle of Man/Jersey
Hungary
Independent Asia
Independent Country/Africa
Ireland
Israel
Israel Tabs
Italy

Japan
Korea
Latin/West Indies
Liechtenstein
Luxembourg
Mexico
Monaco
Netherlands

New Zealand
Philippines
Poland
Portugal
Portugal/Colonies
Ryukyu Islands
San Marino
Scandinavia
Scandinavia/Finland
South America
Soviet Republics
Spain
Switzerland
National Postage
Stamp Album
Turkey
U.S. Trust Territories
United Nations
U.S. 20th Century Comm.
U.S. Administration
U.S. Postal Cards
U.S. Revenue Stamps
Vatican City
Audubon
Christmas
Europa
Queen Mother
Space
Trains

SEMI-POSTAL STAMPS.

St. Martin of Tours Dividing His Cloak with a Beggar
SP1 SP2

Perf. 14

1910, June 1 Typo. Unwmkd.

B1	SP1	1c gray	1.75	1.75
B2	SP1	2c pur brn	12.50	12.50
B3	SP1	5c pck bl	3.50	3.50
B4	SP1	10c brn red	3.50	3.50
B5	SP2	1c gray grn	3.50	3.50
B6	SP2	2c vio brn	9.50	9.50
B7	SP2	5c pck bl	3.50	3.50
B8	SP2	10c carmine	3.25	3.25
		Nos. B1-B8 (8)	41.00	41.00

Overprinted "1911" in Black.

1911, Apr. 1

B9	SP1	1c gray	25.00	16.00
a.		Inverted overprint		
B10	SP1	2c pur brn	57.50	52.50
B11	SP1	5c pck bl	6.00	4.75
B12	SP1	10c brn red	6.00	4.75
B13	SP2	1c gray grn	45.00	40.00
B14	SP2	2c vio brn	40.00	32.50
B15	SP2	5c pck bl	6.00	4.75
B16	SP2	10c carmine	6.00	4.75
		Nos. B9-B16 (8)	191.50	160.00

Overprinted "CHARLEROI—1911".

1911, June

B17	SP1	1c gray	6.00	6.00
B18	SP1	2c pur brn	22.50	21.00
B19	SP1	5c pck bl	10.00	9.00
B20	SP1	10c brn red	9.00	8.00
B21	SP2	1c gray grn	6.00	6.00
B22	SP2	2c vio brn	20.00	18.00
B23	SP2	5c pck bl	8.00	7.25
B24	SP2	10c carmine	6.00	6.00
		Nos. B17-B24 (8)	87.50	81.25

Nos. B1–B24 were sold at double face value, except the 10c denominations which were sold for 15c. The surtax benefited the national anti-tuberculosis organization.

SP3

Mérode Monument SP4 — King Albert I SP5

1914, Oct. 3 Lithographed

B25	SP3	5c grn & red	2.25	2.75
B26	SP3	10c red	45	45
B27	SP3	20c vio & red	16.00	19.00

1914, Oct. 3

B28	SP4	5c grn & red	6.75	6.75
B29	SP4	10c red	6.75	6.75
B30	SP4	20c vio & red	62.50	62.50

Counterfeits of Nos. B25–B30 abound.

1915, Jan. 1 *Perf. 12, 14*

B31	SP5	5c grn & red	6.75	3.50
a.		Perf. 12x14	22.50	13.00
B32	SP5	10c rose & red	13.00	6.75
B33	SP5	20c vio & red	37.50	19.00
a.		Perf. 14x12	400.00	325.00
b.		Perf. 12	75.00	35.00

Nos. B25–B33 were sold at double face value. The surtax benefited the Red Cross.

Types of Regular Issue of 1915 Surcharged in Red:

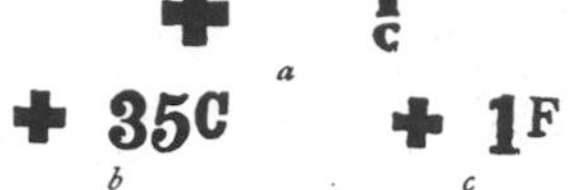

1918, Jan. 15 Typographed *Perf. 14*

B34	A46 (a)	1c +1c dp org	40	40
B35	A46 (a)	2c +2c brn	50	50
B36	A46 (a)	5c +5c bl grn	1.65	1.65
B37	A46 (a)	10c +10c red	3.00	3.00
B38	A46 (a)	15c +15c brt vio	4.50	4.50
B39	A46 (a)	20c +20c plum	9.50	9.50
B40	A46 (a)	25c +25c ultra	10.00	10.00

Engraved.

B41	A47 (b)	35c +35c lt vio & blk	14.00	14.00
B42	A48 (b)	40c +40c dl red & blk	14.00	14.00
B43	A49 (b)	50c +50c turq bl & blk	17.50	17.50
B44	A50 (c)	1f +1f bluish sl	50.00	50.00
B45	A51 (c)	2f +2f dp gray grn	130.00	130.00
B46	A52 (c)	5f +5f brn	350.00	350.00
B47	A53 (c)	10f +10f dp bl	675.00	625.00
		Nos. B34-B47 (14)	1,280.05	1,230.05

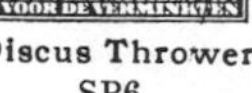

Discus Thrower SP6 — Runner SP8

Racing Chariot SP7

1920, May 20 Engraved *Perf. 12*

B48	SP6	5c +5c dp grn	3.00	3.50
B49	SP7	10c +5c car	3.00	3.50
B50	SP8	15c +15c dk brn	6.00	1.75

Issued to commemorate the 7th International Olympic Games of 1920. The surtax was to benefit wounded soldiers. Imperforates exist.

Allegory: Asking Alms from the Crown SP9 — Wounded Veteran SP10

1922, May 20

B51	SP9	20c +20c brn	2.50	2.25

1923, July 5

B52	SP10	20c +20c sl gray	3.50	3.50

The surtax on Nos. B51–B52 was to aid wounded veterans.

SP11 SP12

St. Martin, by Van Dyck
SP13 SP14

1925, Dec. 15 Typo. *Perf. 14*

B53	SP11	15c +15c dl vio & red	45	22
B54	SP11	30c +5c gray & red	28	12
B55	SP11	1fr +10c chlky bl & red	1.65	1.90

The surtax on Nos. B53–B55 benefited the National Anti-Tuberculosis League.

1926, Feb. 10

B56	SP12	30c +30c bluish grn (red surch.)	75	85
B57	SP13	1fr +1fr lt bl	11.00	11.00
B58	SP14	1fr +1fr lt bl	1.75	2.00

The surtax on Nos. B56–B58 aided victims of the Meuse flood.

Lion and Cross of Lorraine SP15

Queen Elisabeth and King Albert SP16

1926, Dec. 6 Typographed *Perf. 14*

B59	SP15	5c +5c dk brn	28	22
B60	SP15	20c +5c red brn	75	70
B61	SP15	50c +5c dl vio	32	22

Engraved *Perf. 11½.*

B62	SP16	1.50fr +25c dk bl	1.25	1.25
B63	SP16	5fr +1fr rose red	11.00	11.00
		Nos. B59-B63 (5)	13.60	13.39

The surtax on Nos. B59–B63 was used to benefit tubercular war veterans.

Boat Adrift SP17

1927, Dec. 15 Engr. *Perf. 11½, 14*

B64	SP17	25c +10c dk brn	1.25	1.25
B65	SP17	35c +10c yel grn	1.25	1.25
B66	SP17	60c +10c dp vio	1.00	65
B67	SP17	1.75fr +25c dk bl	2.75	3.75
B68	SP17	5fr +1fr plum	8.00	8.50
		Nos. B64-B68 (5)	14.25	15.40

The surtax on these stamps was divided among several charitable associations.

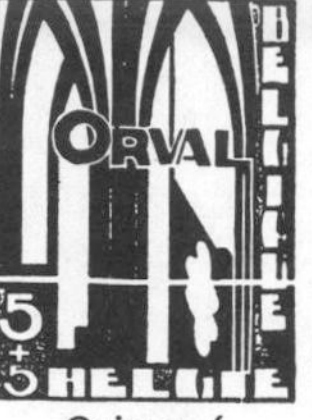

Ogives of Orval Abbey SP18 — Monk Carving Capital of Column SP19

Ruins of Orval Abbey SP20

Design: 60c+15c, 1.75fr+25c, 3fr+1fr, Countess Matilda recovering her ring.

1928, Sept. 15 Photo. *Perf. 11½*

B69	SP18	5c +5c red & gold	28	50
B70	SP18	25c +5c dk vio & gold	55	1.10

Engraved.

B71	SP19	35c +10c dp grn	2.00	2.75
B72	SP19	60c +15c red brn	2.75	80
B73	SP19	1.75fr +25c dk bl	6.50	6.50
B74	SP19	2fr +40c dp vio	24.00	18.00
B75	SP19	3fr +1fr red	26.00	22.50

Perf. 14.

B76	SP20	5fr +5fr rose lake	26.00	27.50
B77	SP20	10fr +10fr ol brn	26.00	30.00
		Nos. B69-B77 (9)	114.08	109.65

The surtax on these stamps was to be used toward the restoration of the ruined Abbey of Orval.

St. Waudru, Mons SP22

St. Rombaut, Malines SP23

Designs: 25c + 15c, Cathedral of Tournai. 60c + 15c, St. Bavon, Ghent. 1.75fr + 25c, St. Gudule, Brussels. 5fr + 5fr, Louvain Library.

1928, Dec. 1 Photo. *Perf. 14, 11½*

B78	SP22	5c +5c car	20	22
B79	SP22	25c +15c ol brn	38	45

Engraved.

B80	SP23	35c +10c dp grn	1.25	1.40
B81	SP23	60c +15c red brn	50	30
B82	SP23	1.75fr +25c vio bl	13.00	12.50
B83	SP23	5fr +5fr red vio	25.00	27.50
		Nos. B78-B83 (6)	40.33	42.37

The surtax was for anti-tuberculosis work.

Orval Abbey Stamps of 1928 Overprinted in Blue or Red

1929, Aug. 19

B84	SP18	5c +5c red & gold	125.00	125.00

85	SP18	25c	+5c dk vio & gold (R)	125.00	125.00
86	SP19	35c	+10c dp grn (R)	125.00	125.00
87	SP19	60c	+15c red brn	125.00	125.00
88	SP19	1.75fr	+25c dk bl (R)	125.00	125.00
89	SP19	2fr	+40c dp vio (R)	125.00	125.00
90	SP19	3fr	+1fr red	125.00	125.00
91	SP20	5fr	+5fr rose lake	125.00	125.00
92	SP20	10fr	+10fr dk brn (R)	125.00	125.00
			Nos. B84-B92 (9)	1,125.	1,125.

Issued in commemoration of the laying of the first stone toward the restoration of the ruined Abbey of Orval. Forgeries of the overprint exist.

Waterfall at Coo
SP28

Bayard Rock, Dinant
SP29

Designs: 35c+10c, Menin Gate, Ypres. 60c+15c, Promenade d'Orleans, Spa. 1.75fr+25c, Antwerp Harbor. 5fr+5fr, Quai Vert, Bruges.

1929, Dec. 2 Engr. *Perf. 11½, 14*

B93	SP28	5c	+5c red brn	20	22
B94	SP29	25c	+15c gray blk	1.00	90
B95	SP28	35c	+10c grn	1.10	1.40
B96	SP28	60c	+15c rose lake	50	45
B97	SP28	1.75fr	+25c dp bl	6.00	6.25
B98	SP29	5fr	+5fr dl vio	37.50	37.50
			Nos. B93-B98 (6)	46.30	46.72

Bornhem
SP34

Beloeil
SP35

Gaesbeek
SP36

Designs: 25c + 15c, Wynendaele. 70c + 15c, Oydonck. 1fr+25c, Ghent. 1.75fr+25c, Bouillon.

1930, Dec. 1 Photo. *Perf. 14*

B99	SP34	10c	+5c vio	35	45
B100	SP34	25c	+15c ol brn	90	90

Engraved.

B101	SP35	40c	+10c brn vio	1.10	1.40
B102	SP35	70c	+15c gray blk	65	65
B103	SP35	1fr	+25c rose lake	4.50	4.50
B104	SP35	1.75fr	+25c dp bl	5.25	3.50
B105	SP36	5fr	+5fr gray grn	32.50	40.00
			Nos. B99-B105 (7)	45.25	51.40

Prince Leopold
SP41

Queen Elisabeth
SP42

Philatelic Exhibition Issue.
Souvenir Sheet.

1931, July 18 Photo. *Perf. 14*

B106	SP41	2.45fr	+55c car brn	160.00	160.00

Issued in sheets measuring 122x159mm. Sold exclusively at the Brussels Philatelic Exhibition, July 18th to 21st, 1931. The surtax was for the Veterans' Relief Fund.

1931, Dec. 1 Engraved

B107	SP42	10c	+5c red brn	28	50
B108	SP42	25c	+15c dk vio	1.50	1.75
B109	SP42	50c	+10c dk grn	1.40	1.25
B110	SP42	75c	+15c blk brn	80	60
B111	SP42	1fr	+25c rose lake	9.50	8.00
B112	SP42	1.75fr	+25c ultra	7.00	5.25
B113	SP42	5fr	+5fr brn vio	75.00	75.00
			Nos. B107-B113 (7)	95.48	92.35

The surtax was for the National Anti-Tuberculosis League.

Désiré Cardinal Mercier
SP43

Mercier Protecting Children and Aged at Malines
SP44

Mercier as Professor at Louvain University
SP45

Mercier in Full Canonicals, Giving His Blessing
SP46

1932, June 10 Photo. *Perf. 14½x14*

B114	SP43	10c	+10c dk vio	65	65
B115	SP43	50c	+30c brt vio	3.25	3.50
B116	SP43	75c	+25c ol brn	3.25	2.75
B117	SP43	1fr	+2fr brn red	9.50	9.00

Engraved.
Perf. 11½.

B118	SP44	1.75fr	+75c dp bl	95.00	110.00
B119	SP45	2.50fr	+2.50fr dk brn	95.00	100.00
B120	SP44	3fr	+4.50fr dl grn	95.00	100.00
B121	SP45	5fr	+20fr vio brn	110.00	110.00
B122	SP46	10fr	+40fr brn lake	275.00	300.00
			Nos. B114-B122 (9)	686.65	735.90

Issued in commemoration of Cardinal Mercier and to obtain funds to erect a monument to his memory.

Belgian Infantryman
SP47

Sanatorium at Waterloo
SP48

1932, Aug. 4 *Perf. 14½x14*

B123	SP47	75c	+3.25fr red brn	72.50	72.50
B124	SP47	1.75fr	+4.25fr dk bl	72.50	72.50

Issued in commemoration of the Belgian soldiers who fought in World War I and to obtain funds to erect a national monument to their glory.

1932, Dec. 1 Photo. *Perf. 13½x14*

B125	SP48	10c	+5c dk vio	25	90
B126	SP48	25c	+15c red vio	1.25	1.75
B127	SP48	50c	+10c red brn	1.25	1.75
B128	SP48	75c	+15c ol brn	1.25	1.10
B129	SP48	1fr	+25c dp red	16.50	15.00
B130	SP48	1.75fr	+25c dp bl	13.00	13.00
B131	SP48	5fr	+5fr gray grn	110.00	120.00
			Nos. B125-B131 (7)	143.50	153.50

The surtax was for the assistance of the National Anti-Tuberculosis Society at Waterloo.

View of Old Abbey—SP49

Ruins of Old Abbey
SP50

Count de Chiny Presenting First Abbey to Countess Matilda
SP56

Restoration of Abbey in XVI and XVII Centuries
SP57

Abbey in XVIII Century, Maria Theresa and Charles V
SP58

Madonna and Arms of Seven Abbeys
SP60

Designs: 25c + 15c, Guests, courtyard. 50c + 25c, Transept. 75c + 50c, Bell Tower. 1fr + 1.25fr, Fountain. 1.25fr + 1.75fr, Cloisters. 5fr + 20fr, Duke of Brabant placing first stone of new abbey.

1933, Oct. 15 *Perf. 14*

B132	SP49	5c	+5c dl grn	65.00	72.50
B133	SP50	10c	+15c ol grn	57.50	65.00
B134	SP49	25c	+15c dk brn	57.50	65.00
B135	SP50	50c	+25c red brn	57.50	65.00
B136	SP50	75c	+50c dp grn	57.50	65.00
B137	SP50	1fr	+1.25fr cop red	57.50	65.00
B138	SP49	1.25fr	+1.75fr gray blk	57.50	65.00
B139	SP56	1.75fr	+2.75fr bl	72.50	72.50
B140	SP57	2fr	+3fr mag	72.50	70.00
B141	SP58	2.50fr	+5fr dl brn	72.50	70.00
B142	SP56	5fr	+20fr vio	72.50	72.50

Perf. 11½.

B143	SP60	10fr	+40fr bl	450.00	375.00
			Nos. B132-B143 (12)	1,150.	1,122.50

The surtax was for a fund to aid in the restoration of Orval Abbey. Counterfeits exist.

"Tuberculosis Society"
SP61

Peter Benoit
SP62

1933, Dec. 1 Engr. *Perf. 14x13½*

B144	SP61	10c	+5c blk	1.00	1.50
B145	SP61	25c	+15c vio	3.75	4.25

B146	SP61	50c +10c red brn	3.50	3.75
B147	SP61	75c +15c blk brn	13.00	1.10
B148	SP61	1fr +25c cl	15.00	17.50
B149	SP61	1.75fr +25c vio bl	17.50	16.00
B150	SP61	5fr +5fr lil	175.00	200.00
		Nos. B144-B150 (7)	228.75	244.10

The surtax was for anti-tuberculosis work.

1934, June 1 **Photogravure**

B151	SP62	75c +25c ol brn	11.00	11.00

The surtax was to raise funds for the Peter Benoit Memorial.

King Leopold III

SP63 SP64

1934, Sept. 15

B152	SP63	75c +25c ol blk	32.50	30.00
a.		Sheet of 20	1,300.	1,300.
B153	SP64	1fr +25c red vio	30.00	27.50
a.		Sheet of 20	1,300.	1,300.

The surtax aided the National War Veterans' Fund. Sold for 4.50fr a set at the Exhibition of War Postmarks 1914–18, held at Brussels by the Royal Philatelic Club of Veterans. The price included an exhibition ticket. Sold at Brussels post office Sept. 18–22. No. B152 printed in sheets of 20 (4x5) and 100 (10x10). No. B153 printed in sheets of 20 (4x5) and 150 (10x15).

1934, Sept. 24

B154	SP63	75c +25c vio	2.25	2.25
B155	SP64	1fr +25c red brn	12.50	13.00

The surtax aided the National War Veterans' Fund. No. B154 printed in sheets of 100 (10x10); No. B155 in sheets of 150 (10x15). These stamps remained in use one year.

Crusader

SP65

1934, Nov. 17 **Engr.** ***Perf. 13½x14***

B156	SP65	10c +5c blk & red	1.00	45
B157	SP65	25c +15c brn & red	1.65	1.50
B158	SP65	50c +10c dl grn & red	1.65	1.50
B159	SP65	75c +15c vio brn & red	80	45
B160	SP65	1fr +25c rose & red	13.00	14.00
B161	SP65	1.75fr +25c ultra & red	11.00	11.50
B162	SP65	5fr +5fr brn vio & red	150.00	150.00
		Nos. B156-B162 (7)	179.10	179.40

The surtax was for anti-tuberculosis work.

Prince Baudouin, Princess Josephine and Prince Albert

SP66

1935, Apr. 10 **Photogravure**

B163	SP66	35c +15c dk grn	1.25	1.40
B164	SP66	70c +30c red brn	1.25	1.10
B165	SP66	1.75fr +50c dk bl	4.75	6.00

Surtax was for Child Welfare Society.

Brussels Exhibition Issue.

Stagecoach—SP67

1935, Apr. 27

B166	SP67	10c +10c ol blk	1.00	1.40
B167	SP67	25c +25c bis brn	3.50	3.50
B168	SP67	35c +25c dk grn	4.50	4.50

Nos. B166–B168 were printed in sheets of 10. Price, set of 3, $175.

Franz von Taxis SP68 Queen Astrid SP69

Souvenir Sheet.

1935, May 25 **Engr.** ***Perf. 14***

B169	SP68	5fr +5fr grnsh blk	175.00	175.00

Issued in sheets measuring 91½x117 mm., containing one stamp.

Nos. B166–B169 were issued for the Brussels Philatelic Exhibition (SITEB).

Queen Astrid Memorial Issue.

1935, Dec. 1 **Photo.** ***Perf. 11½***

Borders in Black.

B170	SP69	10c +5c ol blk	12	18
B171	SP69	25c +15c brn	15	35
B172	SP69	35c +5c dk grn	22	30
B173	SP69	50c +10c rose lil	80	65
B174	SP69	70c +5c gray blk	12	18
B175	SP69	1fr +25c red	1.65	1.40
B176	SP69	1.75fr +25c bl	3.75	3.25
B177	SP69	2.45fr +55c dk vio	4.50	5.25
		Nos. B170-B177 (8)	11.31	11.56

The surtax was divided among several charitable organizations.

Borgerhout Philatelic Exhibition Issue.

Souvenir Sheet.

Town Hall, Borgerhout

SP70

1936, Oct. 3

B178	SP70	70c +30c pur brn	55.00	55.00

Issued in sheets, measuring 115x126 mm., containing one stamp.

Town Hall and Belfry of Charleroi SP71 Prince Baudouin SP72

Charleroi Youth Exhibition.

Souvenir Sheet.

1936, Oct. 18 **Engraved**

B179	SP71	2.45fr +55c gray bl	55.00	50.00

Issued in sheets, measuring 95x120 mm., containing one stamp.

1936, Dec. 1 **Photo.** ***Perf. 14x13½***

B180	SP72	10c +5c dk brn	12	22
B181	SP72	25c +5c vio	28	35
B182	SP72	35c +5c dk grn	28	35
B183	SP72	50c +5c vio brn	40	45
B184	SP72	70c +5c ol grn	28	22
B185	SP72	1fr +25c cer	1.40	90
B186	SP72	1.75fr +25c ultra	2.25	1.40
B187	SP72	2.45fr +2.55fr vio rose	6.50	8.00
		Nos. B180-B187 (8)	11.51	11.89

The surtax was for the assistance of the National Anti-Tuberculosis Society.

1937, Jan. 10

B188	SP72	2.45fr +2.55fr sl	2.00	2.25

Issued in commemoration of International Stamp Day. The surtax was for the benefit of the Brussels Postal Museum, the Royal Belgian Philatelic Federation and the Anti-Tuberculosis Society.

Queen Astrid and Prince Baudouin SP73 Queen Mother Elisabeth SP74

1937, Apr. 15 ***Perf. 11½***

B189	SP73	10c +5c mag	12	20
B190	SP73	25c +5c ol blk	28	35
B191	SP73	35c +5c dk grn	28	35
B192	SP73	50c +5c vio	70	75
B193	SP73	70c +5c sl	28	40
B194	SP73	1fr +25c dk car	1.40	1.40
B195	SP73	1.75fr +25c dp ultra	2.25	2.25
B196	SP73	2.45fr +1.55fr dk brn	5.75	5.00
		Nos. B189-B196 (8)	11.06	10.70

The surtax was to raise funds for Public Utility Works.

SP74a

1937, Sept. 15 ***Perf. 14x13½***

B197	SP74	70c +5c int blk	45	45
B198	SP74	1.75fr +25c brt ultra	1.10	1.10

Souvenir Sheet.

Perf. 11½.

B199	SP74a	Sheet of four	35.00	27.50
a.		1.50fr +2.50fr red brn	8.00	6.75
b.		2.45fr +3.55fr red vio	6.50	4.50

Nos. B197–B199 were issued for the benefit of the Queen Elisabeth Music Foundation in connection with the Eugene Ysaye international competition.

No. B199 contains two se-tenant pairs of Nos. B199a and B199b. Size: 111x145mm. On sale one day, Sept. 15, at Brussels.

Princess Josephine-Charlotte

SP75

1937, Dec. 1 ***Perf. 14x13½***

B200	SP75	10c +5c sl grn	12	2
B201	SP75	25c +5c lt brn	25	2
B202	SP75	35c +5c yel grn	25	2
B203	SP75	50c +5c ol gray	50	4
B204	SP75	70c +5c brn red	18	2
B205	SP75	1fr +25c red	1.40	1.1
B206	SP75	1.75fr +25c vio bl	1.50	1.4
B207	SP75	2.45fr +2.55fr mag	6.00	6.2
		Nos. B200-B207 (8)	10.20	10.0

King Albert Memorial Issue

Souvenir Sheet

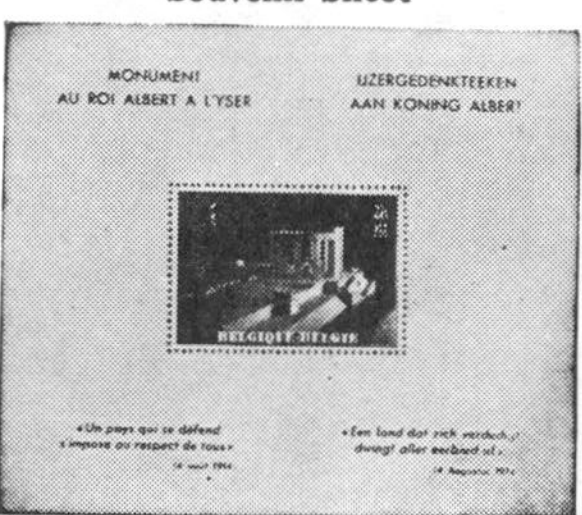

King Albert Memorial—SP76

1938, Feb. 17 ***Perf. 11½***

B208	SP76	2.45fr +7.55fr brn vio	16.00	16.00

Issued in connection with the dedication of the monument to King Albert. Sheet size: 143x115mm.

King Leopold III in Military Plane

SP77

1938, Mar. 15

B209	SP77	10c +5c car brn	22	40
B210	SP77	35c +5c dp grn	42	1.75
B211	SP77	70c +5c gray blk	1.25	90
B212	SP77	1.75fr +25c ultra	3.00	2.75
B213	SP77	2.45fr +2.55fr pur	6.50	5.75
		Nos. B209-B213 (5)	11.39	11.55

The surtax was for the benefit of the National Fund for Aeronautical Propaganda.

Basilica of Koekelberg

SP78

Interior View of the Basilica of Koekelberg

SP79

1938, June 1 Photogravure

B214 SP78	10c	+5c lt brn	12	22
B215 SP78	35c	+5c grn	22	22
B216 SP78	70c	+5c gray grn	22	22
B217 SP78	1fr	+25c car	1.25	1.10
B218 SP78	1.75fr	+25c ultra	1.25	1.25
B219 SP78	2.45fr	+2.55fr brn vio	5.25	6.75

Engraved.

B220 SP79	5fr	+5fr dl grn	21.00	20.00
Nos. B214-B220 (7)			29.31	29.76

The surtax was for a fund to aid in completing the National Basilica of the Sacred Heart at Koekelberg.

Nos. B214, B216 and B218 are different views of the exterior of the Basilica.

Souvenir Sheet

Interior of Koekelberg Basilica
SP80

1938, July 21 **Engr.** ***Perf. 14***

B221 SP80	5fr	+5fr lt vio	16.00	15.00

Sheet size 94x120mm.

Stamps of 1938 Surcharged in Black:

40c (a) 2.50 Fr (b)

1938, Nov. 10 ***Perf. 11½***

B222 SP78 (a)	40c on 35c+5c grn		38	45
B223 SP78 (a)	75c on 70c+5c gray grn		50	65
B224 SP78 (b)	2.50fr	+2.50fr on 2.45fr+2.55fr	8.00	9.00

Prince Albert of Liège
SP81

1938, Dec. 10 **Photo.** ***Perf. 14x13½***

B225 SP81	10c	+5c brn	12	22
B226 SP81	30c	+5c mag	25	35
B227 SP81	40c	+5c ol gray	25	35
B228 SP81	75c	+5c sl grn	20	22
B229 SP81	1fr	+25c dk car	1.00	1.40
B230 SP81	1.75fr	+25c ultra	1.00	1.40
B231 SP81	2.50fr	+2.50fr dp grn	6.00	10.00
B232 SP81	5fr	+5fr brn lake	20.00	15.00
Nos. B225-B232 (8)			28.82	28.94

Henri Dunant
SP82

Florence Nightingale
SP83

King Leopold and Royal Children
SP85

Queen Mother Elisabeth and Royal Children
SP84

Queen Astrid
SP86

Queen Mother Elisabeth and Wounded Soldier
SP87

1939, Apr. 1 **Photo.** ***Perf. 11½***

The Cross is Printed in Carmine.

B233 SP82	10c	+5c brn	12	22
B234 SP83	30c	+5c brn car	35	35
B235 SP84	40c	+5c ol gray	25	35
B236 SP85	75c	+5c sl blk	75	22
B237 SP84	1fr	+25c brt rose	3.50	2.00
B238 SP85	1.75fr	+25c brt ultra	1.10	1.50
B239 SP86	2.50fr	+2.50fr dl vio	2.25	3.00
B240 SP87	5fr	+5fr gray grn	7.50	10.00
Nos. B233-B240 (8)			15.82	17.64

75th anniversary of the founding of the International Red Cross Society.

Rubens' House, Antwerp
SP88

"Albert and Nicolas Rubens"
SP89

Arcade, Rubens' House
SP90

"Helena Fourment and Her Children"
SP91

Rubens and Isabelle Brandt
SP92

Peter Paul Rubens
SP93

"The Velvet Hat"
SP94

"Descent from the Cross"
SP95

1939, July 1

B241 SP88	10c	+5c brn	10	22
B242 SP89	40c	+5c brn car	35	35
B243 SP90	75c	+5c ol blk	1.10	90
B244 SP91	1fr	+25c rose	3.00	2.75
B245 SP92	1.50fr	+25c sep	3.00	2.75
B246 SP93	1.75fr	+25c dp ultra	4.00	3.00
B247 SP94	2.50fr	+2.50fr brt red vio	18.00	19.00
B248 SP95	5fr	+5fr sl gray	25.00	25.00
Nos. B241-B248 (8)			54.55	53.97

Issued to honor Peter Paul Rubens. The surtax was used to restore Rubens' home in Antwerp.

"Martin van Nieuwenhove" by Hans Memling
SP96

1939, July 1

B249 SP96	75c	+75c ol blk	4.00	4.00

Issued in honor of Hans Memling, (1430?-1495), Flemish painter.

Twelfth Century Monks at Work
SP97

Reconstructed Tower Seen through Cloister
SP98

Monks Laboring in the Fields
SP99

Orval Abbey, Aerial View
SP100

Bishop Heylen of Namur, Madonna and Abbot General Smets of the Trappists
SP101

King Albert I and King Leopold III and Shrine—SP102

1939, July 20

B250	SP97	75c	+75c ol blk	4.00	4.50
B251	SP98	1fr	+1fr rose red	2.75	2.75
B252	SP99	1.50fr	+1.50fr dl brn	2.75	2.75
B253	SP100	1.75fr	+1.75fr saph	2.75	2.75
B254	SP101	2.50fr	+2.50fr brt red vio	12.00	11.00
B255	SP102	5fr	+5fr brn car	12.00	12.00
			Nos. B250-B255 (6)	36.25	35.75

The surtax was used for the restoration of the Abbey of Orval.

Belfry at Bruges SP103 — Belfry at Furnes SP104

Designs (Belfries): 30c + 5c, Thuin. 40c + 5c, Lierre. 75c + 5c, Mons. 1.75fr+25c, Namur. 2.50fr + 2.50fr, Alost. 5fr + 5fr, Tournai.

1939, Dec. 1 Photo. *Perf. 14x13½*

B256	SP103	10c	+5c ol gray	12	22
B257	SP103	30c	+5c brn org	25	35
B258	SP103	40c	+5c brt red vio	40	45
B259	SP103	75c	+5c ol blk	20	22

Engraved

B260	SP104	1fr	+25c rose car	1.50	1.75
B261	SP104	1.75fr	+25c dk bl	1.50	1.75
B262	SP104	2.50fr	+2.50fr dp red brn	11.50	11.50
B263	SP104	5fr	+5fr pur	15.00	16.00
			Nos. B256-B263 (8)	30.47	32.24

Arms of Mons SP111 — Arms of Ghent SP112

Designs (Coats of Arms): 40c + 10c, Arel. 50c + 10c, Bruges. 75c + 15c, Namur. 1fr + 25c, Hasselt. 1.75fr. + 50c, Brussels. 2.50fr + 2.50fr, Antwerp. 5fr + 5fr, Liege.

1940-41 Typographed *Perf. 14x13½*

B264	SP111	10c	+5c multi ('41)	18	22
B265	SP112	30c	+5c multi	28	22
B266	SP111	40c	+10c multi	28	22
B267	SP112	50c	+10c multi	28	22
B268	SP111	75c	+15c multi	18	22
B269	SP112	1fr	+25c multi ('41)	60	65
B270	SP111	1.75fr	+50c multi ('41)	90	80
B271	SP112	2.50fr	+2.50fr multi ('41)	2.75	2.75
B272	SP111	5fr	+5fr multi ('41)	3.50	3.50
			Nos. B264-B272 (9)	8.95	8.80

The surtax was used for winter relief.

Queen Elisabeth Music Chapel SP120

Bust of Prince Albert of Liège SP121

1940, Nov. Photo. *Perf. 11½*

B273	SP120	75c	+75c sl	2.75	2.75
B274	SP120	1fr	+1fr rose red	1.65	1.50
B275	SP121	1.50fr	+1.50fr Prus grn	1.90	2.50
B276	SP121	1.75fr	+1.75fr ultra	1.90	2.50
B277	SP120	2.50fr	+2.50fr brn org	3.75	2.75
B278	SP121	5fr	+5fr red vio	4.75	4.75
			Nos. B273-B278 (6)	16.70	16.75

The surtax was for the Queen Elisabeth Music Foundation. Nos. B273-B278 were not authorized for postal use, but were sold to advance subscribers either mint or cancelled to order. See also Nos. B317-B318.

Souvenir Sheets.

Arms of Various Cities SP122

Typographed.

1941, May *Perf. 14x13½, Imperf.*

Cross and City Name in Carmine.

B279	SP122	Sheet of nine	15.00	17.50
a.		10c+5c sl	1.25	1.35
b.		30c+5c emer	1.25	1.35
c.		40c+10c choc	1.25	1.35
d.		50c+10c lt vio	1.25	1.35
e.		75c+15c dl pur	1.25	1.35
f.		1fr+25c car	1.25	1.35
g.		1.75fr+50c dl bl	1.25	1.35
h.		2.50fr+2.50fr ol gray	1.25	1.35
i.		5fr+5fr dl vio	4.50	5.00

The sheets measure 106x148 mm. The surtax was used for relief work.

Painting SP123 — Sculpture SP124

Monks Studying Plans of Orval Abbey SP128

Designs: 40c+60c, 2fr+3.50fr, Monk carrying candle. 50c+65c, 1.75fr+2.50fr, Monk praying. 75c+1fr, 3fr+5fr, Two monks singing.

1941, June Photo. *Perf. 11½*

B281	SP123	10c	+15c brn org	65	75
B282	SP124	30c	+30c ol gray	65	75
B283	SP124	40c	+60c dp brn	65	75
B284	SP124	50c	+65c vio	65	75
B285	SP124	75c	+1fr brt red vio	65	75
B286	SP124	1fr	+1.50fr rose red	65	75
B287	SP123	1.25fr	+1.75fr dp yel grn	65	75
B288	SP123	1.75fr	+2.50fr dp ultra	65	75
B289	SP123	2fr	+3.50fr red vio	65	75
B290	SP124	2.50fr	+4.50fr dl red brn	65	75
B291	SP124	3fr	+5fr dk ol grn	65	75
B292	SP128	5fr	+10fr grnsh blk	2.25	2.25
			Nos. B281-B292 (12)	9.40	10.50

The surtax was used for the restoration of the Abbey of Orval.

Maria Theresa SP129 — Charles the Bold SP130

Portraits (in various frames): 35c+5c, Charles of Lorraine. 50c+10c, Margaret of Parma. 60c+10c, Charles V. 1fr+15c, Johanna of Castile. 1.50fr+1fr, Philip the Good. 1.75fr+1.75fr, Margaret of Austria. 3.25fr+3.25fr, Archduke Albert. 5fr+5fr, Archduchess Isabella.

1941-42 Photogravure.

B293	SP129	10c	+5c ol blk	18	22
B294	SP129	35c	+5c dl grn	18	22
B295	SP129	50c	+10c brn	18	22
B296	SP129	60c	+10c pur	18	22
B297	SP129	1fr	+15c brt car rose	18	22
B298	SP129	1.50fr	+1fr red vio	55	45
B299	SP129	1.75fr	+1.75fr ryl bl	55	45
B300	SP130	2.25fr	+2.25fr dl red brn	70	65
B301	SP129	3.25fr	+3.25fr lt brn	90	90
B302	SP129	5fr	+5fr sl grn	1.00	1.10
			Nos. B293-B302 (10)	4.60	4.65

Souvenir Sheet.

Archduke Albert and Archduchess Isabella SP139

B302A	SP139	Sheet of two ('42)	5.25	5.25
b.		3.25fr+6.75fr turq bl	2.25	2.50
c.		5fr+10fr dk car	2.25	2.50

The sheets measure 77x59mm.

The surtax was for the benefit of National Social Service Work among soldiers' families.

Souvenir Sheets.

Monks Studying Plans of Orval Abbey SP140

1941, Oct. Photo. *Perf. 11½*

Inscribed "Belgie-Belgique".

B303	SP140	5fr	+15fr ultra	9.50	13.00

Imperf.

Inscribed "Belgique-Belgie".

B304	SP140	5fr	+15fr ultra	9.50	13.00

The sheets measure 185x165 mm. and are inscribed in black, gold and ultramarine.

The surtax was for the restoration of Orval Abbey.

No. B304 exists perforated.

In 1942 these sheets were privately trimmed and overprinted "1142 1942" and ornament.

St. Martin Statue, Church of Dinant SP141 — Lennik, Saint-Quentin SP142

St. Martin's Church, Saint-Trond SP146

Designs (Statues of St. Martin): 50c+10c, 3.25fr +3.25fr, Beck, Limburg. 60c+10c, 2.25fr+2.25fr, Dave on the Meuse. 1.75fr+50c, Hal, Brabant.

1941-42 Photogravure *Perf. 11½*

B305	SP141	10c	+5c chnt	15	22
B306	SP142	35c	+5c dk bl grn	15	22
B307	SP142	50c	+10c vio	15	22
B308	SP142	60c	+10c dp brn	15	22
B309	SP142	1fr	+15c car	15	22
B310	SP141	1.50fr	+25c sl grn	45	55
B311	SP142	1.75fr	+50c dk ultra	55	65
B312	SP142	2.25fr	+2.25fr red vio	55	65
B313	SP142	3.25fr	+3.25fr brn vio	55	65
B314	SP146	5fr	+5fr dk ol grn	80	90
			Nos. B305-B314 (10)	3.65	4.50

Souvenir Sheets.
Inscribed "Belgie-Belgique".

B315	SP146	5fr	+20fr vio brn ('42)	16.00	16.00

Imperf.
Inscribed "Belgique-Belgie"

B316	SP146	5fr	+20fr vio brn ('42)	13.00	13.00

Nos. B315–B316 contain one stamp each. Size: 105x139mm.

In 1956, the Bureau Européen de la Jeunesse et de l'Enfance privately overprinted Nos. B315–B316: "Congrés Européen de l'education 7–12 Mai 1956," in dark red and dark green respectively. A black bar obliterates "Winterhulp-Secours d'Hiver."

Queen Elisabeth Music Chapel
SP147

1941, Dec. 1 Photo. *Perf. 11½*
Inscribed "Belgique-Belgie".

B317	SP147	10fr	+15fr ol blk	2.75	4.50

Imperf.
Inscribed "Belgie-Belgique".

B318	SP147	10fr	+15fr ol blk	2.75	4.50

Issued in sheets measuring 105x139mm.

The surtax was for the Queen Elisabeth Music Foundation. These sheets were perforated with the monogram of Queen Elisabeth in 1942.

In 1954 Nos. B317–B318 were overprinted to commemorate the birth centenary of Edgar Tinel, composer. Inscriptions in French, border in brown on No. B317; inscriptions in Flemish, border in green on No. B318. These overprinted sheets were not postally valid.

Jean Bollandus
SP148

Christophe Plantin
SP156

Designs: 35c+5c, Andreas Vesalius. 50c+10c, Simon Stevinus. 60c+10c, Jean Van Helmont. 1fr+15c, Rembert Dodoens. 1.75fr+50c, Gerardus Mercator. 3.25fr+3.25fr, Abraham Ortelius. 5fr+5fr, Justus Lipsius.

Photogravure.

1942, May 15 *Perf. 14x13½*

B319	SP148	10c	+5c dl brn	12	18
B320	SP148	35c	+5c gray grn	20	22
B321	SP148	50c	+10c fawn	20	22
B322	SP148	60c	+10c grnsh blk	20	22

Engraved.

B323	SP148	1fr	+15c brt rose	25	32
B324	SP148	1.75fr	+50c dl bl	38	32
B325	SP148	3.25fr	+3.25fr lil rose	38	32
B326	SP148	5fr	+5fr vio	42	45

Perf. 13½x14.

B327	SP156	10fr	+30fr red org	2.50	2.75
			Nos. B319-B327 (9)	4.65	5.00

The surtax was used to help fight tuberculosis.

No. B327 was sold by subscription at the Brussels Post Office, July 1–10, 1942.

Belgian Prisoner
SP158

1942, Oct. 1 *Perf. 11½*

B331	SP158	5fr	+45fr ol gray, with Label	9.00	9.00

The surtax was for prisoners of war. A brown label, inscribed "1942 POUR NOS PRISONNIERS/ VOOR ONZE GEVANGENEN," alternates with the stamps in the sheet.

SP159

SP164

SP162

SP168

Various Statues of St. Martin

1942–43

B332	SP159	10c	+5c org	20	8
B333	SP159	35c	+5c dk bl grn	22	22
B334	SP159	50c	+10c dp brn	28	28
B335	SP162	60c	+10c blk	30	30
B336	SP159	1fr	+15c brt rose	38	35
B337	SP164	1.50fr	+25c grnsh blk	45	45
B338	SP164	1.75fr	+50c dk bl	55	55
B339	SP162	2.25fr	+2.25fr brn	75	65
B340	SP162	3.25fr	+3.25fr brt red vio	85	80
B341	SP168	5fr	+10fr hn brn	1.25	1.10
B342	SP168	10fr	+20fr rose brn & vio brn ('43)	1.75	1.75

Inscribed "Belgique-Belgie".

B343	SP168	10fr	+20fr gldn brn & vio brn ('43)	1.75	1.75
			Nos. B332-B343 (12)	8.73	8.28

The surtax was for winter relief.

Issue dates: Nos. B332–B341, Nov. 12, 1942. Nos. B342–B343, Apr. 3, 1943.

Prisoners of War—SP170

Design: No. B345, Two prisoners with package from home.

1943, May Photo. *Perf. 11½*

B344	SP170	1fr	+30fr ver	4.00	4.50
B345	SP170	1fr	+30fr brn rose	4.00	4.50

The surtax was used for prisoners of war.

Roof Tiler
SP172

Coppersmith
SP173

Designs: (Statues in Petit Sablon Park, Brussels). 35c+5c, Blacksmith. 60c+10c, Gunsmith. 1fr+15c, Armsmith. 1.75fr+75c, Goldsmith. 3.25fr+3.25fr, Fishdealer. 5fr+25fr, Watchmaker.

1943, June 1

B346	SP172	10c	+5c chnt brn	18	18
B347	SP172	35c	+5c grn	20	22
B348	SP173	50c	+10c dk brn	22	28
B349	SP173	60c	+10c sl	25	32
B350	SP173	1fr	+15c dl rose brn	32	45
B351	SP173	1.75fr	+75c ultra	50	60
B352	SP173	3.25fr	+3.25fr brt red vio	80	1.00
B353	SP173	5fr	+25fr dk pur	1.25	1.40
			Nos. B346-B353 (8)	3.72	4.45

The surtax was for the control of tuberculosis.

"O"
SP180

"ORVAL"
SP185

Designs: 60c+1.90fr, "R." 1fr+3fr, "V." 1.75fr+5.25fr, "A." 3.25fr+16.75fr, "L."

1943, Oct. 9

B354	SP180	50c	+1fr ol blk	95	1.10
B355	SP180	60c	+1.90fr dl vio	50	45
B356	SP180	1fr	+3fr rose brn	50	45
B357	SP180	1.75fr	+5.25fr dk bl	50	45
B358	SP180	3.25fr	+16.75fr dk bl grn	80	90
B359	SP185	5fr	+30fr dp brn	1.40	1.50
			Nos. B354-B359 (6)	4.65	4.85

The surtax aided restoration of Orval Abbey.

St. Léonard Church, Léau
SP186

St. Martin Church, Courtrai
SP190

Basilica of St. Martin, Angre
SP191

Notre Dame, Hal
SP193

St. Martin—SP194

Designs: 35c+5c, St. Martin Church, Dion-le-Val. 50c+15c, St. Martin Church, Alost. 60c+20c, St. Martin Church, Liege. 3.25fr+11.75fr, St. Martin Church, Loppem. No. B369, St. Martin, beggar and Meuse landscape.

1943-44

B360	SP186	10c	+5c dp brn	18	22
B361	SP186	35c	+5c dk bl grn	38	45
B362	SP186	50c	+15c ol blk	45	55
B363	SP186	60c	+20c brt red vio	55	65
B364	SP190	1fr	+1fr rose brn	65	65
B365	SP191	1.75fr	+4.25fr dp ultra	2.25	1.50
B366	SP186	3.25fr	+11.75fr red lil	2.25	1.75
B367	SP193	5fr	+25fr dk bl	3.00	3.00
B368	SP194	10fr	+30fr gray grn ('44)	2.25	2.25
B369	SP194	10fr	+30fr blk brn ('44)	2.25	2.25
			Nos. B360-B369 (10)	14.21	13.27

Surtax for winter relief.

"Daedalus and Icarus"
SP196

Sir Anthony Van Dyck, Self-portrait
SP200

Paintings by Van Dyck: 50c+2.50fr. "The Good Samaritan." 60c+3.40fr, Detail of "Christ Healing the Paralytic." 1fr+5fr, "Madonna and Child." 5fr+30fr, "St. Sebastian."

1944, Apr. 16 Photo. *Perf. 11½*
Crosses in Carmine.

B370	SP196	35c	+1.65fr dk sl grn	45	45
B371	SP196	50c	+2.50fr grnsh blk	45	45
B372	SP196	60c	+3.40fr blk brn	45	45
B373	SP196	1fr	+5fr dk car	65	65
B374	SP200	1.75fr	+8.25fr int bl	80	90
B375	SP196	5fr	+30fr cop brn	80	90
			Nos. B370-B375 (6)	3.60	3.80

The surtax was for the Belgian Red Cross.

Jan van Eyck
SP202

Godfrey of Bouillon
SP203

Designs: 50c+25c, Jacob van Maerlant. 60c+40c, Jean Joses de Dinant. 1fr+50c, Jacob van Artevelde. 1.75fr+4.25fr, Charles Joseph de Ligne. 2.25fr+8.25fr, Andre Gretry. 3.25fr+11.25fr, Jan Moretus-Plantin. 5fr+35fr, Jan van Ruysbroeck.

1944, May 31

B376	SP202	10c	+15c dk pur	42	45
B377	SP203	35c	+15c grn	42	45
B378	SP203	50c	+25c chnt brn	42	45
B379	SP203	60c	+40c ol blk	42	45
B380	SP203	1fr	+50c rose brn	42	45
B381	SP203	1.75fr	+4.25fr ultra	42	45
B382	SP203	2.25fr	+8.25fr grnsh blk	1.10	1.10
B383	SP203	3.25fr	+11.25fr dk brn	42	45
B384	SP203	5fr	+35fr sl bl	85	1.40
			Nos. B376-B384 (9)	4.89	5.65

The surtax was for prisoners of war.

Sons of Aymon Astride Bayard
SP211

Brabo Slaying the Giant Antigoon
SP212

Till Eulenspiegel Singing to Nele
SP214

Designs: 50c+10c, St. Hubert converted by stag with crucifix. 1fr+15fr, St. George slaying the dragon. 1.75fr+5.25fr, Genevieve of Brabant with son and roe-deer. 3.25fr+11.75fr, Tchantches wrestling with the Saracen. 5fr+25fr, St. Gertrude rescuing the knight with the cards.

1944, June 25

B385	SP211	10c	+5c choc	12	22
B386	SP212	35c	+5c dk bl grn	12	22
B387	SP211	50c	+10c dl vio	12	22
B388	SP214	60c	+10c blk brn	12	22
B389	SP214	1fr	+15c rose brn	12	22
B390	SP214	1.75fr	+5.25fr ultra	25	45
B391	SP211	3.25fr	+11.75fr grnsh blk	38	65
B392	SP211	5fr	+25fr dk bl	50	90
			Nos. B385-B392 (8)	1.73	3.10

The surtax was for the control of tuberculosis.

Nos. B385–B389 were overprinted "Breendonk+10fr." in 1946 by the Union Royale Philatelique for an exhibition at Brussels. They had no postal validity.

Union of the Flemish and Walloon Peoples in their Sorrow
SP219

Union in Reconstruction
SP220

Photogravure

1945, May 1 *Perf. 11½* Unwmkd.

B395	SP219	1fr	+30fr car	1.10	1.90
B396	SP220	1¾fr	+30fr brt ultra	1.10	1.90

1945, July 21

Size: 34½x23½mm.

B397	SP219	1fr	+9fr scar	25	45
B398	SP220	1fr	+9fr car rose	25	45

The surtax was for the postal employees' relief fund.

Prisoner of War
SP221

Reunion
SP222

Awaiting Execution
SP223

Symbolical Figures "Recovery of Freedom"
SP225

Design: 70c+30c, 3.50fr+3.50fr, Member of Resistance Movement.

1945, Sept. 10

B399	SP221	10c	+15c org	8	12
B400	SP222	20c	+20c dp pur	8	12
B401	SP223	60c	+25c sep	8	12
B402	SP221	70c	+30c dp yel grn	10	12
B403	SP221	75c	+50c org brn	10	18
B404	SP222	1fr	+75c brt bl grn	18	22
B405	SP223	1.50fr	+1fr brt red	18	22
B406	SP221	3.50fr	+3.50fr brt bl	1.25	1.75
B407	SP225	5fr	+40fr brn	1.10	1.50
			Nos. B399-B407 (9)	3.15	4.35

The inscriptions are transposed on Nos. B403–B406.

The surtax was for the benefit of prisoners of war, displaced persons, families of executed victims and members of the Resistance Movement.

Arms of West Flanders
SP226

Arms of Provinces: 20c+20c, Luxembourg. 60c+25c, East Flanders. 70c+30c, Namur. 75c+50c, Limburg. 1fr+75c, Hainaut. 1.50fr+1fr, Antwerp. 3.50fr+1.50fr, Liege. 5fr+45fr, Brabant.

1945, Dec. 1

B408	SP226	10c	+15c sl blk & sl gray	8	12
B409	SP226	20c	+20c rose car & rose	10	18
B410	SP226	60c	+25c dk brn & pale brn	10	[illegible]
B411	SP226	70c	+30c dk grn & lt grn	10	[illegible]
B412	SP226	75c	+50c org brn & pale org brn	18	[illegible]
B413	SP226	1fr	+75c pur & lt pur	10	[illegible]
B414	SP226	1.50fr	+1fr car & rose	10	[illegible]
B415	SP226	3.50fr	+1.50fr dp bl & gray bl	20	[illegible]
B416	SP226	5fr	+45fr dp mag & cer	2.25	[illegible]
			Nos. B408-B416 (9)	3.21	[illegible]

The surtax was for tuberculosis prevention.

Father Joseph Damien
SP227

Father Damien Comforting Leper
SP229

Leper Colony, Molokai Island, Hawaii
SP228

Photogravure.

1946, July 15 *Perf. 11½* Unwmkd.

B417	SP227	65c	+75c dk bl	90	1.40
B418	SP228	1.35fr	+2fr brn	90	1.40
B419	SP229	1.75fr	+18fr rose brn	1.40	2.25

The surtax was for the erection of a museum in Louvain.

Symbols of Wisdom and Patriotism
SP230

"In Memoriam"
SP232

François Bovesse
SP231

1946, July 15

B420	SP320	65c	+75c vio	90	1.40
B421	SP231	1.35fr	+2fr dk org brn	1.10	1.75
B422	SP232	1.75fr	+18fr car rose	1.65	2.50

The surtax was for the erection of a "House of the Fine Arts" at Namur.

Emile Vandervelde
SP233

Sower
SP235

Vandervelde, Laborer and Family
SP234

1946, July 15

B423	SP233	65c	+75c dk sl grn	1.00	1.40
B424	SP234	1.35fr	+2fr dk vio bl	1.10	1.75
B425	SP235	1.75fr	+18fr dp car	1.65	2.25
			Nos. B417-B425 (9)	10.60	16.10

The surtax was for the Emile Vandervelde Institute, to promote social, economic and cultural activities.

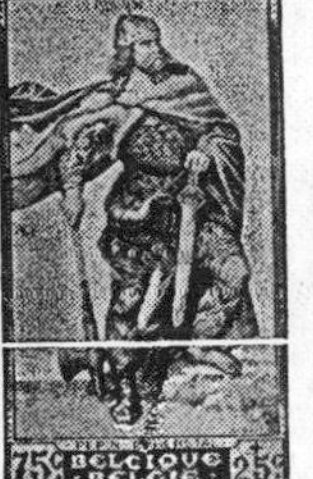
Pepin of Herstal
SP236

Arms of Malines
SP241

Designs: 1fr+50c, Charlemagne. 1.50fr +1fr, Godfrey of Bouillon. 3.50fr+1.50fr, Robert of Jerusalem. Nos. B430–B431, Baldwin of Constantinople.

1946, Sept. 15 Engr. *Perf. 11½x11*

B426	SP236	75c	+25c grn	65	75
B427	SP236	1fr	+50c vio	90	1.10
B428	SP236	1.50fr	+1fr plum	1.10	1.40
B429	SP236	3.50fr	+1.50fr brt bl	1.25	1.75
B430	SP236	5fr	+45fr red vio	11.00	15.00
B431	SP236	5fr	+45fr red org	14.00	18.00
			Nos. B426-B431 (6)	28.90	38.00

The surtax on Nos. B426–B429 was for the benefit of former prisoners of war, displaced persons, the families of executed patriots, and former members of the Resistance Movement.

The surtax on Nos. B430–B431 was divided among several welfare, national celebration and educational organizations.

Issue dates: Nos. B426–B429, Apr. 15; No. B430, Sept. 15; No. B431, Nov. 15.

See also Nos. B437–B441, B465–B466, B472–B476.

1946, Dec. 2 *Perf. 11½*

Designs (Coats of Arms): 90c+60c, Dinant. 1.35fr+1.15fr, Ostend. 3.15fr+1.85fr, Verviers. 4.50fr+45.50fr, Louvain.

B432	SP241	65c	+35c rose car	38	45
B433	SP241	90c	+60c lem	38	45
B434	SP241	1.35fr	+1.15fr dp grn	38	45
B435	SP241	3.15fr	+1.85fr bl	1.50	1.10
B436	SP241	4.50fr	+45.50fr dk vio brn	14.00	17.50
			Nos. B432-B436 (5)	16.64	19.95

The surtax was for anti-tuberculosis work
See also Nos. B442-B446.

Type of 1946.

Designs: 65c+35c, John II, Duke of Brabant. 90c+60c, Count Philip of Alsace. 1.35fr+1.15fr, William the Good. 3.15fr+1.85fr, Bishop Notger of Liege. 20fr+20fr, Philip the Noble.

1947, Sept. 25 Engr. *Perf. 11½x11*

B437	SP236	65c	+35c Prus grn	50	1.25
B438	SP236	90c	+60c yel grn	75	1.75
B439	SP236	1.35fr	+1.15fr car	1.10	2.25
B440	SP236	3.15fr	+1.85fr ultra	1.50	4.50
B441	SP236	20fr	+20fr red vio	42.50	55.00
			Nos. B437-B441 (5)	46.35	64.75

The surtax was for victims of World War II.

Arms Type of 1946 Dated "1947"

Coats of Arms: 65c+35c, Nivelles. 90c+60c, St. Trond. 1.35fr+1.15fr, Charleroi. 3.15fr+1.85fr, St. Nicolas. 20fr+20fr, Bouillon.

1947, Dec. 15 *Perf. 11½*

B442	SP241	65c	+35c org	85	90
B443	SP241	90c	+60c dp cl	65	1.00
B444	SP241	1.35fr	+1.15fr dk brn	95	1.10
B445	SP241	3.15fr	+1.85fr dp bl	2.25	2.75
B446	SP241	20fr	+20fr dk grn	19.00	20.00
			Nos. B442-B446 (5)	23.70	25.75

The surtax was for anti-tuberculosis work.

St. Benedict and King Totila
SP247

Achel Abbey
SP248

Designs: 3.15fr+2.85fr, St. Benedict, legislator and builder. 10fr+10fr, Death of St. Benedict.

1948, Apr. 5 Photogravure

B447	SP247	65c	+65c red brn	1.25	1.10
B448	SP248	1.35fr	+1.35fr gray	1.75	1.10
B449	SP247	3.15fr	+2.85fr dp ultra	2.50	3.50
B450	SP247	10fr	+10fr brt red vio	12.50	19.00

The surtax was to aid the Abbey of the Trappist Fathers at Achel.

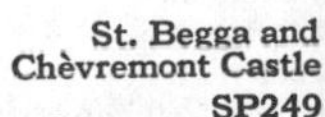
St. Begga and Chèvremont Castle
SP249

Chèvremont Basilica and Convent
SP250

Designs: 3.15fr+2.85fr, Madonna of Chevremont and Chapel. 10fr+10fr, Madonna of Mt. Carmel.

1948, Apr. 5 Unwmkd.

B451	SP249	65c	+65c bl grn	1.25	1.10
B452	SP250	1.35fr	+1.35fr dk car rose	1.75	1.10
B453	SP249	3.15fr	+2.85fr dp bl	2.50	3.25
B454	SP249	10fr	+10fr dp brn	12.50	19.00

The surtax was to aid the Basilica of the Carmelite Fathers of Chèvremont.

Anseele Monument Showing French Inscription
SP251

Designs: 90c + 60c, View of Ghent. 1.35fr+1.15fr, Van Artevelde monument, Ghent. 3.15fr+1.85fr. Anseele Monument, Flemish inscription.

1948, June 21 *Perf. 14x13½*

B455	SP251	65c	+35c rose red	2.00	2.25
B456	SP251	90c	+60c gray	3.00	3.50
B457	SP251	1.35fr	+1.15fr hn brn	1.50	3.00
B458	SP251	3.15fr	+1.85fr brt bl	6.25	6.75
a.			Souvenir sheet of 4	50.00	67.50

Issued to honor Edouard Anseele, statesman, founder of the Belgian Socialist Party.

No. B458a contains one each of Nos. B455–B458. Size: 144x81mm. Sold for 50fr.

Statue "The Unloader"
SP252

Underground Fighter
SP253

1948, Sept. 4 *Perf. 11½x11*

B460	SP252	10fr	+10fr gray grn	27.50	32.50
B461	SP253	10fr	+10fr red brn	17.50	20.00

The surtax was used toward erection of monuments at Antwerp and Liège.

Portrait Type of 1946 and SP254

Double Barred Cross
SP254

Designs: 4fr+3.25fr, Isabella of Austria. 20fr+20fr, Archduke Albert of Austria.

1948, Dec. 15 Photo. *Perf. 13½x14*

B462	SP254	20c	+5c dk sl grn	25	22
B463	SP254	1.20fr	+30c mag	1.00	1.50
B464	SP254	1.75fr	+25c red	1.25	1.40

Engraved
Perf. 11½x11

B465	SP236	4fr	+3.25fr ultra	7.50	9.00
B466	SP236	20fr	+20fr Prus grn	35.00	40.00
			Nos. B462-B466 (5)	45.00	52.12

The surtax was divided among several charities.

Souvenir Sheets

Rogier van der Weyden Paintings—SP255

Paintings by van der Weyden (No. B466A): 90c, Virgin and Child. 1.75fr, Christ on the Cross. 4fr, Mary Magdalene.

Paintings by Jordaens (No. B466B): 90c, Woman Reading. 1.75fr, The Flutist. 4fr, Old Woman Reading Letter.

1949, Apr. 1 Photo. *Perf. 11½*

B466A SP255		Sheet of 3	95.00	150.00
c.		90c dp brn	30.00	45.00
d.		1.75fr dp rose lil	30.00	45.00
e.		4fr dk vio bl	30.00	45.00
B466B SP255		Sheet of 3	95.00	150.00
f.		90c dk vio	30.00	45.00
g.		1.75fr red	30.00	45.00
h.		4fr bl	30.00	45.00

The surtax went to various cultural and philanthropic organizations. Nos. B466A and B466B have dark brown and orange decorative border. Size: 140x90½mm. Sheets sold for 50fr each.

Guido Gezelle
SP256

1949, Nov. 15 Photo. *Perf. 14x13½*

B467	SP256	1.75fr	+75c dk Prus grn	2.50	3.25

Issued to commemorate the 50th anniversary of the death of Guido Gezelle, poet. The surtax was for the Guido Gezelle Museum, Bruges.

Portrait Type of 1946 and

Arnica
SP257

Designs: 65c+10c, Sand grass. 90c+10c, Wood myrtle. 1.20fr+30c, Field poppy. 1.75fr+25c, Philip the Good. 3fr+1.50fr, Charles V. 4fr+2fr, Maria-Christina. 6fr+3fr, Charles of Lorraine. 8fr+4fr, Maria-Theresa.

1949, Dec. 20 Typo. *Perf. 13½x14*

B468	SP257	20c	+5c multi	25	65
B469	SP257	65c	+10c multi	1.00	2.00
B470	SP257	90c	+10c multi	1.50	2.50
B471	SP257	1.20fr	+30c multi	2.00	3.00

Engraved

Perf. 11½x11

B472	SP236	1.75fr	+25c red org	75	1.40
B473	SP236	3fr	+1.50fr dp cl	6.25	11.50
B474	SP236	4fr	+2fr ultra	7.50	13.00
B475	SP236	6fr	+3fr choc	12.50	19.00
B476	SP236	8fr	+4fr dl grn	12.50	15.00
			Nos. B468-B476 (9)	44.25	68.05

The surtax was apportioned among several welfare organizations.

Arms of Belgium and Great Britain
SP258

British Memorial
SP260

Design: 2.50fr+50c, British tanks at Hertain.

Engraved.

1950, Mar. 15 *Perf. 13½x14, 11½*

B477	SP258	80c	+20c grn	1.25	1.40
B478	SP258	2.50fr	+50c red	5.00	5.50
B479	SP260	4fr	+2fr dp bl	9.00	9.00

Issued to commemorate the 6th anniversary of the liberation of Belgian territory by the British army.

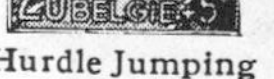

Hurdle Jumping
SP261

Relay Race
SP262

Designs: 90c+10c, Javelin throwing. 4fr+2fr, Pole vault. 8fr+4fr, Foot race.

Inscribed: "Heysel 1950."

Perf. 14x13½, 13½x14.

1950, July 1 Engr. Unwmkd.

B480	SP261	20c	+5c brt grn	50	90
B481	SP261	90c	+10c vio brn	3.00	3.50
B482	SP262	1.75fr	+25c car	3.75	3.50
	a.		Souvenir sheet	35.00	45.00
B483	SP261	4fr	+2fr lt bl	30.00	35.00

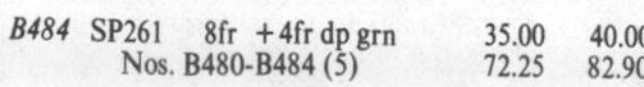

B484	SP261	8fr	+4fr dp grn	35.00	40.00
			Nos. B480-B484 (5)	72.25	82.90

Issued to publicize the European Athletic Games, Brussels, August 1950.

No. B482a measures 89 x 68½ mm., and contains a single copy of No. B482 with inscriptions typographed in black in upper and lower margins.

The margins of No. B482a were trimmed in April, 1951, and an overprint ("25 Francs pour le Fonds Sportif—25e Fofre Internationale Bruxelles") was added in red in French and in black in Flemish by a private committee. These pairs of altered sheets were sold at the Brussels Fair.

Gentian
SP263

Tombeek Sanatorium
SP265

Sijsele Sanatorium
SP264

Designs: 65c+10c, Cotton Grass. 90c+10c, Foxglove. 1.20fr+30c, Limonia. 4fr+2fr, Jauche Sanatorium.

Typographed.

1950, Dec. 20 *Perf. 14x13½*

Cross in Red.

B485	SP263	20c	+5c mar, bl & emer	50	45
B486	SP263	65c	+10c brn, buff & emer	1.50	1.25
B487	SP263	90c	+10c bluish grn, dp mag & yel grn	1.75	1.75
B488	SP263	1.20fr	+30c vio bl, bl & grn	2.25	2.75

Engraved.

Perf. 11½.

B489	SP264	1.75fr	+25c car	1.75	1.75
B490	SP264	4fr	+2fr bl	11.50	9.00
B491	SP265	8fr	+4fr bl grn	19.00	22.50
			Nos. B485-B491 (7)	38.25	39.45

The surtax was for tuberculosis prevention and other charitable purposes.

Chemist
SP266

Allegory of Peace
SP268

Colonial Instructor and Class
SP267

1951, Mar. 27 Unwmkd.

B492	SP266	80c	+20c grn	1.25	2.25
B493	SP267	2.50fr	+50c vio brn	9.00	11.00
B494	SP268	4fr	+2fr dp bl	10.00	13.50

The surtax was for the reconstruction fund of the United Nations Educational, Scientific and Cultural Organization.

Monument to Political Prisoners
SP269

Fort of Breendonk
SP270

Design: 8fr+4fr, Monument: profile of figure on pedestal.

1951, Aug. 20 Photo. *Perf. 11½*

B495	SP269	1.75fr	+25c blk brn	1.75	2.25
B496	SP270	4fr	+2fr bl & sl gray	16.00	20.00
B497	SP269	8fr	+4fr dk bl grn	20.00	25.00

The surtax was for the erection of a national monument.

Queen Elisabeth
SP271

1951, Sept. 22

B498	SP271	90c	+10c grnsh gray	1.25	1.40
B499	SP271	1.75fr	+25c plum	1.75	2.25
B500	SP271	3fr	+1fr grn	14.00	15.00
B501	SP271	4fr	+2fr gray bl	17.50	20.00
B502	SP271	8fr	+4fr sep	21.00	22.50
			Nos. B498-B502 (5)	55.50	61.15

The surtax was for the Queen Elisabeth Medical Foundation.

Cross, Sun Rays and Dragon
SP272

Beersel Castle
SP273

Horst Castle
SP274

Castles: 4fr+2fr, Lavaux St. Anne. 8fr+4fr, Veves.

1951, Dec. 17 Engr. Unwmkd.

B503	SP272	20c	+5c red	12	2
B504	SP272	65c	+10c dp ultra	65	9
B505	SP272	90c	+10c sep	75	1.2
B506	SP272	1.20fr	+30c rose vio	1.00	1.4
B507	SP273	1.75fr	+75c red brn	1.25	1.7
B508	SP274	3fr	+1fr yel grn	9.00	9.0
B509	SP273	4fr	+2fr bl	11.50	11.0
B510	SP274	8fr	+4fr gray	16.00	15.0
			Nos. B503-B510 (8)	40.27	40.5

The surtax was for anti-tuberculosis work. See also Nos. B523-B526, B547-B550.

Main Altar
SP275

Basilica of the Sacred Heart Koekelberg
SP276

Procession Bearing Relics of St. Albert of Louvain
SP277

1952, Mar. 1 Photo. *Perf. 11½*

B511	SP275	1.75fr	+25c blk brn	1.25	1.75
B512	SP276	4fr	+2fr ind	10.00	12.00

Engraved.

B513	SP277	8fr	+4fr vio brn	12.50	16.00
	a.		Souv. sheet	125.00	135.00

No. B513a measures 122x72mm., and contains one each of Nos. B511-B513, with inscriptions in indigo and black brown. Sold for 30 fr.

Issued to commemorate the 25th anniversary of the Cardinalate of J. E. Van Roey, Primate of Belgium. The surtax was for the Basilica.

Beaulieu Castle, Malines
SP278

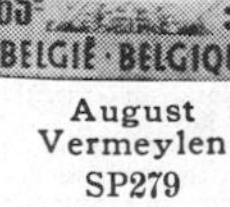

August Vermeylen
SP279

1952, May 14 Engraved

Laid Paper.

B514	SP278	40fr	+10fr lt grnsh bl	175.00	210.00

Issued on the occasion of the 13th Universal Postal Union Congress, Brussels, 1952.

1952, Oct. 24 *Perf. 11½* Unwmkd.

Portraits: 80c+40c, Karel Van de Woestijne. 90c+45c, Charles de Coster. 1.75fr+75c, M. Maeterlinck. 4fr+2fr, Emile Verhaeren. 8fr+4fr, Hendrik Conscience.

Photogravure.

B515	SP279	65c	+30c pur	1.25	1.50

B516	SP279	80c	+40c dk grn	2.50	2.00
B517	SP279	90c	+45c sep	2.00	2.50
B518	SP279	1.75fr	+75c cer	2.50	2.75
B519	SP279	4fr	+2fr bl vio	21.00	27.50
B520	SP279	8fr	+4fr dk brn	21.00	35.00
			Nos. B515-B520 (6)	50.25	71.25

1952, Nov. 15

Portraits: 4fr, Emile Verhaeren. 8fr, Hendrik Conscience.

B521	SP279	4fr	(+9fr) bl	90.00	130.00
B522	SP279	8fr	(+9fr) dk car rose	90.00	130.00

On Nos. B521–B522, the denomination is repeated at either side of the stamp. The surtax is expressed on se-tenant labels bearing quotations of Verhaeren (in French) and Conscience (in Flemish).

A 9-line black overprint was privately applied to these labels: "Conference Internationale de la Musique Bruxelles UNESCO International Music Conference Brussels 1953*"

Price is for stamp with label.

Type of 1951 Dated "1952," and

Arms of Malmédy
SP281

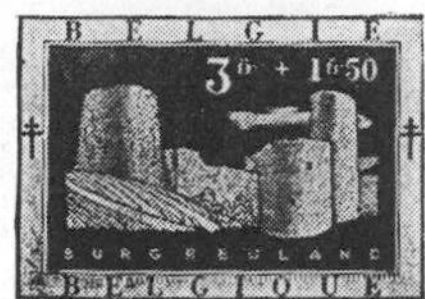

Castle Ruins, Burgreuland
SP282

Designs: 4fr+2fr, Vesdre Dam, Eupen. 8fr+4fr, St. Vitus, patron saint of Saint-Vith.

1952, Dec. 15 **Engraved**

B523	SP272	20c	+5c red brn	25	45
B524	SP272	80c	+20c grn	75	1.10
B525	SP272	1.20fr	+30c lil rose	1.50	1.75
B526	SP272	1.50fr	+50c ol brn	1.50	1.75
B527	SP281	2fr	+75c car	2.50	3.75
B528	SP282	3fr	+1.50fr choc	11.50	15.00
B529	SP281	4fr	+2fr bl	10.00	13.50
B530	SP281	8fr	+4fr vio brn	17.50	21.00
			Nos. B523-B530 (8)	45.50	58.30

The surtax on Nos. B523–B530 was for anti-tuberculosis and other charitable works.

Walthère Dewé
SP283

Princess Josephine-Charlotte
SP284

1953, Feb. 16 **Photogravure**

B531	SP283	2fr	+1fr brn car	2.75	3.00

The surtax was for the construction of a memorial to Walthère Dewé, Underground leader in World War II.

1953, Mar. 14 **Cross in Red**

B532	SP284	80c	+20c ol grn	1.00	1.40
B533	SP284	1.20fr	+30c brn	1.25	1.75
B534	SP284	2fr	+50c rose lake	1.00	2.25
a.			Bklt pane of 8	90.00	90.00
B535	SP284	2.50fr	+50c crim	11.50	12.00
B536	SP284	4fr	+1fr brt bl	7.50	10.00
B537	SP284	5fr	+2fr sl grn	9.00	12.00
			Nos. B532-B537 (6)	31.25	39.40

The surtax was for the Belgian Red Cross.

The selvage of No. B534a is inscribed in French or Dutch. The price is for the French.

Boats at Dock
SP285

Bridge and Citadel, Namur
SP286

Allegory
SP287

Designs: 1.20fr+30c, Bridge at Bouillon. 2fr+50c, Antwerp waterfront. 4fr+2fr, Wharf at Ghent. 8fr+4fr, Meuse River at Freyr.

1953, June 22 ***Perf. 11½*** **Unwmkd.**

B538	SP285	80c	+20c grn	75	1.40
B539	SP285	1.20fr	+30c redsh brn	1.50	2.25
B540	SP285	2fr	+50c sep	2.00	3.00
B541	SP286	2.50fr	+50c dp mag	9.00	13.00
B542	SP286	4fr	+2fr vio bl	14.00	13.00
B543	SP286	8fr	+4fr gray blk	16.50	13.00
			Nos. B538-B543 (6)	43.75	45.65

The surtax was used to promote tourism in the Ardenne-Meuse region and for various cultural works.

1953, Oct. 26 **Engraved**

B544	SP287	80c	+20c grn	3.75	4.50
B545	SP287	2.50fr	+1fr rose car	35.00	47.50
B546	SP287	4fr	+1.50fr bl	40.00	57.50

The surtax was for the European Bureau of Childhood and Youth.

Type of 1951 Dated "1953," and

Ernest Malvoz
SP288

Robert Koch
SP289

Portraits: 3fr+1.50fr, Carlo Forlanini. 4fr+2fr, Leon Charles Albert Calmette.

1953, Dec. 15

B547	SP272	20c	+5c bl	25	45
B548	SP272	80c	+20c rose vio	1.00	90
B549	SP272	1.20fr	+30c choc	1.25	1.40
B550	SP272	1.50fr	+50c dk gray	1.50	1.75
B551	SP288	2fr	+75c dk grn	2.75	2.75
B552	SP288	3fr	+1.50fr dk red	11.50	13.00
B553	SP288	4fr	+2fr ultra	10.00	11.00
B554	SP289	8fr	+4fr choc	15.00	16.00
			Nos. B547-B554 (8)	43.25	47.25

The surtax was for anti-tuberculosis and other charitable works.

King Albert I Statue
SP290

Albert I Monument, Namur
SP291

Design: 9fr+4.50fr, Cliffs of Marche-les-Dames.

1954, Feb. 17 **Photogravure**

B555	SP290	2fr	+50c chnt brn	2.00	2.75
B556	SP291	4fr	+2fr bl	11.50	15.00
B557	SP290	9fr	+4.50fr ol blk	15.00	17.50

Issued to commemorate the 20th anniversary of the death of King Albert I. The surtax aided in the erection of the monument pictured on B556.

Political Prisoners' Monument
SP292

Camp and Fort, Breendonk
SP293

Design: 9fr+4.50fr, Political prisoners' monument (profile).

1954, Apr. 1 ***Perf. 11½*** **Unwmkd.**

B558	SP292	2fr	+1fr red	10.00	11.00
B559	SP293	4fr	+2fr dk brn	22.50	27.50
B560	SP292	9fr	+4.50fr ol grn	25.00	27.50

The surtax was used toward the creation of a monument to political prisoners.

Gatehouse and Gateway
SP294

Nuns in Courtyard
SP295

Our Lady of the Vine
SP296

Designs: 2fr+1fr, Swans in stream. 7fr+3.50fr Nuns at well. 8fr+4fr, Statue above door.

1954, May 15

B561	SP294	80c	+20c dk bl grn	1.25	1.75
B562	SP294	2fr	+1fr crim	10.00	2.25
B563	SP295	4fr	+2fr vio	14.00	16.00
B564	SP295	7fr	+3.50fr lil rose	30.00	37.50
B565	SP295	8fr	+4fr brn	27.50	35.00
B566	SP296	9fr	+4.50fr gray bl	45.00	45.00
			Nos. B561-B566 (6)	127.75	137.50

The surtax was for the Friends of the Beguinage of Bruges.

Child's Head
SP297

"The Blind Man and the Paralytic," by Antoine Carte
SP298

1954, Dec. 1 **Engraved**

B567	SP297	20c	+5c dk grn	38	55
B568	SP297	80c	+20c dk gray	1.00	1.40
B569	SP297	1.20fr	+30c org brn	1.50	1.75
B570	SP297	1.50fr	+50c pur	2.00	2.75
B571	SP298	2fr	+75c rose car	7.50	5.75
B572	SP298	4fr	+1fr brt bl	16.50	16.00
			Nos. B567-B572 (6)	28.88	28.20

The surtax was for anti-tuberculosis work.

Ernest Solvay
SP299

Jean-Jacques Dony
SP300

Portraits: 1.20fr+30c, Egide Walschaerts. 25fr+50c, Leo H. Baekeland. 3fr+1fr, Jean-Etienne Lenoir. 4fr+2fr, Emile Fourcault and Emile Gobbe.

Photogravure.

1955, Oct. 22 *Perf. 11½* Unwmkd.

B573	SP299	20c	+5c brn & dk brn	25	45
B574	SP300	80c	+20c vio	1.00	90
B575	SP299	1.20fr	+30c ind	1.25	1.40
B576	SP300	2fr	+50c dp car	3.75	4.50
B577	SP300	3fr	+1fr dk grn	11.50	11.00
B578	SP299	4fr	+2fr brn	11.50	11.00
			Nos. B573-B578 (6)	29.25	29.25

Issued in honor of Belgian scientists.
The surtax was for the benefit of various cultural organizations.

"The Joys of Spring" by E. Canneel
SP301

Einar Holböll
SP302

Portraits: 4fr+2fr, John D. Rockefeller. 8fr+4fr, Sir Robert W. Philip.

1955, Dec. 5 *Perf. 11½* Unwmkd.

B579	SP301	20c	+5c red lil	50	45
B580	SP301	80c	+20c grn	75	90
B581	SP301	1.20fr	+30c redsh brn	1.00	1.40
B582	SP301	1.50fr	+50c vio bl	1.25	1.75
B583	SP302	2fr	+50c car	7.00	6.75
B584	SP302	4fr	+2fr ultra	14.00	17.50
B585	SP302	8fr	+4fr ol gray	17.50	20.00
			Nos. B579-B585 (7)	42.00	48.75

The surtax was for anti-tuberculosis work.

Palace of Charles of Lorraine
SP303

Queen Elisabeth and Sonata by Mozart
SP304

Design: 2fr+1 fr, Mozart at age 7.

1956, Mar. 5 Engraved

B586	SP303	80c	+20c stl bl	60	1.40
B587	SP303	2fr	+1fr rose lake	3.75	6.25
B588	SP304	4fr	+2fr dl pur	6.00	8.00

Issued to commemorate the 200th anniversary of the birth of Wolfgang Amadeus Mozart, composer.
The surtax was for the benefit of the Pro-Mozart Committee in Belgium.

Queen Elisabeth
SP305

1956, Aug. 16 Photogravure

B589	SP305	80c	+20c sl grn	70	1.40
B590	SP305	2fr	+1fr dp plum	3.25	3.50
B591	SP305	4fr	+2fr brn	4.25	5.50

Issued in honor of the 80th birthday of Queen Elisabeth. The surtax went to the Queen Elisabeth Foundation.
See also No. 607.

Ship with Cross
SP306

Rehabilitation
SP308

Infant on Scales
SP307

Design: 4fr+2fr, X-Ray examination.

1956, Dec. 17 Engraved

B592	SP306	20c	+5c redsh brn	25	35
B593	SP306	80c	+20c grn	75	1.10
B594	SP306	1.20fr	+30c dl lil	90	1.00
B595	SP306	1.5fr	+50c lt sl bl	1.00	1.50
B596	SP307	2fr	+50c ol grn	2.50	2.75
B597	SP307	4fr	+2fr dl pur	11.50	11.00
B598	SP308	8fr	+4fr dp car	11.50	12.50
			Nos. B592-B598 (7)	28.40	30.20

The surtax was for anti-tuberculosis work.

Charles Plisnier and Albrecht Rodenbach
SP309

Portraits: 80c+20c, Emiel Vliebergh and Maurice Wilmotte. 1.20fr+30c, Paul Pastur and Julius Hoste. 2fr+50c, Lodewijk de Raet and Jules Destree. 3fr+1fr, Constantin Meunier and Constant Permeke. 4fr+2fr, Lieven Gevaert and Edouard Empain.

Photogravure.

1957, June 8 *Perf. 11½* Unwmkd.

B599	SP309	20c	+5c brt vio	25	45
B600	SP309	80c	+20c lt red brn	50	65
B601	SP309	1.20f	+30c blk brn	65	90
B602	SP309	2fr	+50c cl	1.65	1.75
B603	SP309	3fr	+1fr dk ol grn	2.50	3.50
B604	SP309	4fr	+2fr vio bl	3.50	5.00
			Nos. B599-B604 (6)	9.05	12.25

The surtax was for the benefit of various cultural organizations.

Dogs and Antarctic Camp
SP310

1957, Oct. 18 Engr. *Perf. 11½*

B605	SP310	5fr	+2.50fr gray, org & vio brn	2.50	4.25
a.			Sheet of four	110.00	175.00
b.			bl, sl and red brn	22.50	40.00

Surtax for Belgian Antarctic Expedition, 1957–58.
No. B605a contains 4 No. B605b. Inscribed "Expedition Antarctique Belge 1957–1958" in French and Flemish. Size: 115x83mm.

Gen. Patton's Grave and Flag
SP311

Gen. George S. Patton, Jr.
SP312

Designs: 2.50fr+50c, Memorial, Bastogne. 3fr+1fr, Gen. Patton decorating Brig. Gen. Anthony C. McAuliffe. 6fr+3fr, Tanks of 1918 and 1944.

1957, Oct. 28 Photogravure

Size: 36x25mm., 25x36mm.

B606	SP311	1fr	+50c dk gray	1.25	1.75
B607	SP311	2.50fr	+50c ol grn	1.75	2.75
B608	SP311	3fr	+1fr red brn	2.50	3.50
B609	SP312	5fr	+2.50fr grysh bl	6.25	9.00

Size: 53x35mm.

B610	SP311	6fr	+3fr pale brn car	9.00	12.0
			Nos. B606-B610 (5)	20.75	29.0

The surtax was for the General Patton Memorial Committee and Patriotic Societies.

Adolphe Max
SP313

1957, Nov. 10 Engraved

B611	SP313	2.50fr	+1fr ultra	1.65	3.2

18th anniversary of the death of Adolphe Max, mayor of Brussels. The surtax was for the national "Adolphe Max" fund.

"Chinels," Fosses
SP314

"Op Signoorken," Malines
SP315

Infanta Isabella Shooting Crossbow
SP316

Legends: 1.50fr+50c, St. Remacle and the wolf. 2fr+1fr, Longman and the pea soup. 5fr+2fr, The Virgin with Inkwell (vert.). 6fr+2.50fr, "Gilles" (clowns), Binche.

Engraved and Photogravure.

1957, Dec. 14

B612	SP314	30c	+20c pur & org yel	22	45
B613	SP315	1fr	+50c brn & lt bl	60	65
B614	SP314	1.50fr	+50c gray & red	1.25	1.10
B615	SP315	2fr	+1fr gray & brt grn	1.50	2.25
B616	SP316	2.50fr	+1fr bl grn & lil	1.75	2.00
B617	SP316	5fr	+2fr bl & dk gray	4.50	4.75
B618	SP316	6fr	+2.50fr vio brn & red org	6.00	6.75
			Nos. B612-B618 (7)	15.82	17.95

The surtax was for anti-tuberculosis work.
See also Nos. B631–B637.

Benelux Gate—SP317

Designs: 1fr+50c, Civil Engineering Pavilion. 1.50fr+50c, Ruanda-Urundi Pavilion. 2.50fr+1fr, Belgium 1900. 3fr+1.50fr, Atomium. 5fr+3fr, Telexpo Pavilion.

Engraved.

1958, Apr. 15 *Perf. 11½* Unwmkd.

Size: 35½x24½mm.

No.	Type	Denom.	Description	Unused	Used
B619	SP317	30c	+20c brn red, vio bl & sep	12	12
B620	SP317	1fr	+50c gray bl, dk brn & emer	12	18
B621	SP317	1.50fr	+50c grnsh bl, pur & cit	25	35
B622	SP317	2.50fr	+1fr ultra, red & brn red	38	65
B623	SP317	3fr	+1.50fr gray, car & lt ultra	1.25	1.10

Size: 49x33mm.

No.	Type	Denom.	Description	Unused	Used
B624	SP317	5fr	+3fr gray, ultra & red lil	1.50	1.10
			Nos. B619-B624 (6)	3.62	3.50

World's Fair, Brussels, Apr. 17–Oct. 19.

Marguerite van Eyck
by Jan van Eyck
SP318

Christ Carrying Cross,
by Hieronymus Bosch
SP319

Paintings: 1.50fr+50c, St. Donatien, Jan Gossart. 2.50fr+1fr, Self-portrait, Lambert Lombard. 3fr+150fr, The Rower, James Ensor. 5fr+3fr, Henriette, Henri Evenepoel.

1958, Oct. 30 Photo. *Perf. 11½*

Various Frames in Ochre and Brown.

No.	Type	Denom.	Description	Unused	Used
B625	SP318	30c	+20c dk ol grn	22	45
B626	SP319	1fr	+50c mar	90	1.50
B627	SP318	1.50fr	+50c vio bl	1.25	1.75
B628	SP318	2.50fr	+1fr dk brn	2.50	3.00
B629	SP319	3fr	+1.50fr dl red	3.00	4.50
B630	SP318	5fr	+3fr brt bl	6.00	11.00
			Nos. B625-B630 (6)	13.87	22.20

The surtax was for the benefit of various cultural organizations.

Type of 1957.

Legends: 40c+10c, Elizabeth, Countess of Hoogstraten. 1fr+50c, Jean de Nivelles. 1.50fr+50c, St. Evermare play, Russon. 2fr+1fr, The Penitents of Furnes. 2.50fr+1fr, Manger and "Pax." 5fr+2fr, Sambre-Meuse procession. 6fr+2.50fr, Our Lady of Peace and "Pax" (vert.).

Engraved and Photogravure

1958, Dec. 6 *Perf. 11½* Unwmkd.

No.	Type	Denom.	Description	Unused	Used
B631	SP314	40c	+10 ultra & brt grn	38	45
B632	SP315	1fr	+50 gray brn & org	55	60
B633	SP315	1.50fr	+50c cl & brt grn	75	80
B634	SP314	2fr	+1fr brn & red	1.00	1.10
B635	SP316	2.50fr	+1fr vio brn & bl grn	3.25	4.25

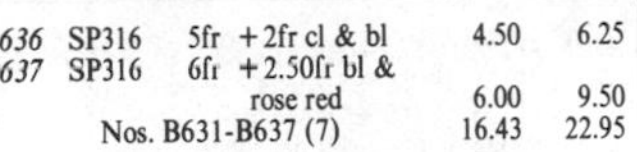

No.	Type	Denom.	Description	Unused	Used
B636	SP316	5fr	+2fr cl & bl	4.50	6.25
B637	SP316	6fr	+2.50fr bl & rose red	6.00	9.50
			Nos. B631-B637 (7)	16.43	22.95

The surtax was for anti-tuberculosis work.

"Europe of the Heart"
SP320

1959, Feb. 25 Photo. Unwmkd.

No.	Type	Denom.	Description	Unused	Used
B638	SP320	1fr	+50c red lil	75	65
B639	SP320	2.50fr	+1fr dk grn	2.00	2.75
B640	SP320	5fr	+2.50fr dp brn	2.75	3.50

The surtax was for aid for displaced persons.

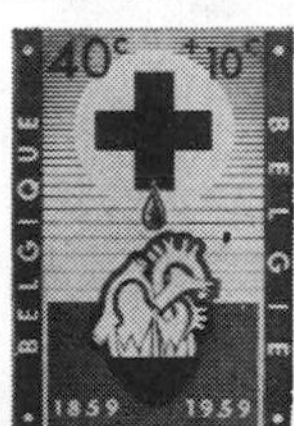

Allegory of Blood Transfusion
SP321

Henri Dunant and Battlefield
at Solferino—SP322

Design: 2.50fr+1fr, 3fr+1.50fr, Red Cross, broken sword and drop of blood (horiz.).

1959, June 10 Photo. *Perf. 11½*

No.	Type	Denom.	Description	Unused	Used
B641	SP321	40c	+10c bl gray & car	50	65
B642	SP321	1fr	+50c brn & car	90	1.00
B643	SP321	1.50fr	+50c dl vio & car	1.10	1.40
B644	SP321	2.50fr	+1fr sl grn & car	1.50	2.50
B645	SP321	3fr	+1.50fr vio bl & car	3.75	5.50
B646	SP322	5fr	+3fr dk brn & car	6.25	7.25
			Nos. B641-B646 (6)	14.00	18.30

Issued to commemorate the centenary of the International Red Cross idea. The surtax was for the Red Cross and patriotic organizations.

Philip the Good
SP323

Arms of Philip the Good
SP324

Designs: 1fr+50c, Charles the Bold. 1.50fr+50c, Emperor Maximilian of Austria. 2.50fr+1fr, Philip the Fair. 3fr+1.50fr, Charles V. Portraits from miniatures by Simon Bening (c. 1483–1561).

1959, July 4 Engraved

No.	Type	Denom.	Description	Unused	Used
B647	SP323	40c	+10c multi	50	65
B648	SP323	1fr	+50c multi	90	1.00
B649	SP323	1.50fr	+50c multi	1.10	1.40
B650	SP323	2.50fr	+1fr multi	1.50	2.50
B651	SP323	3fr	+1.50fr multi	3.75	5.50
B652	SP324	5fr	+3fr multi	6.25	7.00
			Nos. B647-B652 (6)	14.00	18.05

The surtax was for the Royal Library, Brussels.

Portraits show Grand Masters of the Order of the Golden Fleece.

Whale, Antwerp
SP325

Carnival, Stavelot
SP326

Designs: 1fr+50c, Dragon, Mons. 2fr+50c, Prince Carnival, Eupen. 3fr+1fr, Jester and cats, Ypres. 6fr+2fr, Holy Family (horiz.). 7fr+3fr, Madonna, Liége (horiz.).

Engraved and Photogravure

1959, Dec. 5 *Perf. 11½*

No.	Type	Denom.	Description	Unused	Used
B653	SP325	40c	+10c cit, Prus bl & red	38	65
B654	SP325	1fr	+50c ol & grn	90	1.00
B655	SP325	2fr	+50c lt brn, org & cl	65	65
B656	SP326	2.50fr	+1fr gray, pur & ultra	1.00	1.00
B657	SP326	3fr	+1fr gray, mar & yel	2.25	1.75
B658	SP326	6fr	+2fr ol, brt bl & hn brn	4.00	4.50
B659	SP326	7fr	+3fr chlky bl & org yel	6.00	6.25
			Nos. B653-B659 (7)	15.18	15.80

The surtax was for anti-tuberculosis work.

Child Refugee
SP327

Designs: 3fr+1.50fr, Man. 6fr+3fr, Woman.

1960, Apr. 7 Engraved

No.	Type	Denom.	Description	Unused	Used
B660	SP327	40c	+10c rose cl	15	15
B661	SP327	3fr	+1.50fr gray brn	75	75
B662	SP327	6fr	+3fr dk bl	2.00	1.75
a.			Souv. sheet of 3	45.00	45.00

Issued to publicize World Refugee Year, July 1, 1959–June 30, 1960.

No. B662a contains one each of Nos. B660–B662 with colors changed: 40c+10c, dull purple; 3fr+1.50fr, red brown; 6fr+3fr, henna brown. Black marginal inscription and uprooted oak emblem. Size: 121x92mm.

Parachutists and Plane
SP328

Designs: 2fr+50c, 2.50fr+1fr, Parachutists coming in for landing (vert.) 3fr+1fr, 6fr+2fr, Parachutist walking with parachute.

Photogravure and Engraved

1960, June 13 *Perf. 11½*

No.	Type	Denom.	Description	Unused	Used
B663	SP328	40c	+10c lt ultra & blk	15	15
B664	SP328	1fr	+50c bl & blk	90	90
B665	SP328	2fr	+50c bl, blk & ol	2.25	1.65
B666	SP328	2.50fr	+1fr grnsh bl, blk & gray ol	3.00	3.00
B667	SP328	3fr	+1fr bl, blk & sl grn	3.00	3.00
B668	SP328	6fr	+2fr lt vio bl, blk & ol	5.50	5.25
			Nos. B663-B668 (6)	14.80	13.95

The surtax was for various patriotic and cultural organizations.

Mother and Child,
Planes and Rainbow
SP329

Designs: 40c+10c, Brussels Airport, planes and rainbow. 6fr+3fr, Rainbow connecting Congo and Belgium, and planes (vert.)

Photogravure

1960, Aug. 3 *Perf. 11½* Unwmkd.

Size: 35x24mm.

No.	Type	Denom.	Description	Unused	Used
B669	SP329	40c	+10c grnsh bl	15	15
B670	SP329	3fr	+1.50fr brt red	4.50	4.00

Size: 35x52mm.

No.	Type	Denom.	Description	Unused	Used
B671	SP329	6fr	+3fr vio	6.50	5.00

The surtax was for refugees from Congo.

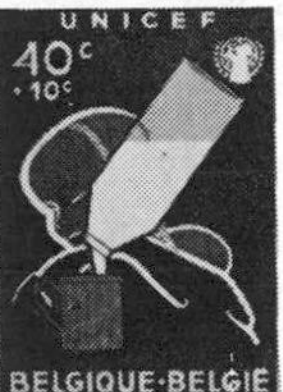

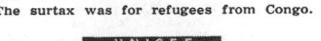

Infant, Milk Bottle and Mug
SP330

Designs: 1fr+50c, Nurse and children of 3 races. 2fr+50c, Refugee woman carrying gift clothes. 2.50fr+1fr, Negro nurse weighing infant. 3fr+1fr, Children of various races dancing. 6fr+2fr, Refugee boys.

Photogravure and Engraved

1960, Oct. 8 ***Perf. 11½***

B672	SP330	40c	+10c gldn brn, yel & bl grn	15	15
B673	SP330	1fr	+50c ol gray, mar & sl	1.50	1.00
B674	SP330	2fr	+50c vio, pale brn & brt grn	1.80	1.40
B675	SP330	2.50fr	+1fr dk red, sep & lt bl	2.25	1.75
B676	SP330	3fr	+1fr bl grn, red org & dl vio	1.20	1.20
B677	SP330	6fr	+2fr ultra, emer & brn	4.25	4.00
			Nos. B672-B677 (6)	11.15	9.50

Issued for the United Nations Children's Fund, UNICEF.

Tapestry
SP331

Belgian handicrafts: 1fr+50c, Cut crystal vases (vert.). 2fr+50c, Lace (vert.). 2.50fr+1fr, Metal plate & jug. 3fr+1fr, Diamonds. 6fr+2fr, Ceramics.

Photogravure and Engraved

1960, Dec. 5 ***Perf. 11½***

B678	SP331	40c	+10c bl, bis & brn	15	15
B679	SP331	1fr	+50c ind & org brn	1.20	1.20
B680	SP331	2fr	+50c dk red brn, blk & cit	2.25	2.00
B681	SP331	2.50fr	+1fr choc & yel	3.00	3.00
B682	SP331	3fr	+1fr org brn, blk & ultra	1.50	1.50
B683	SP331	6fr	+2fr dp blk & yel	6.00	4.75
			Nos. B678-B683 (6)	14.10	12.60

The surtax was for anti-tuberculosis work.

Jacob Kats and Abbe Nicolas Pietkin
SP332

Portraits: 1fr+50c, Albert Mockel and J. F. Willems. 2fr+50c, Jan van Rijswijck and Xavier M. Neujean. 2.50fr+1fr, Joseph Demarteau and A. Van de Perre. 3fr+1fr, Canon Jan-Baptist David and Albert du Bois. 6fr+2fr, Henri Vieuxtemps and Willem de Mol.

Photogravure and Engraved

1961, Apr. 22 ***Perf. 11½*** **Unwmkd.**

Portraits in Gray Brown

B684	SP332	40c	+10c ver & mar	15	15
B685	SP332	1fr	+50c bis brn & mar	1.50	1.40
B686	SP332	2fr	+50c yel & crim	2.25	2.00
B687	SP332	2.50fr	+1fr pale cit & dk grn	3.00	2.25
B688	SP332	3fr	+1fr lt & dk bl	3.00	3.00
B689	SP332	6fr	+2fr lil & ultra	5.50	5.50
			Nos. B684-B689 (6)	15.40	14.30

The surtax was for the benefit of various cultural organizations.

White Rhinoceros
SP333

Antonius Cardinal Perrenot de Granvelle
SP334

Animals: 1fr+50c, Przewalski horses. 2fr+50c, Okapi. 2.50fr+1fr, Giraffe (horiz.). 3fr+1fr, Lesser panda (horiz.). 6fr+2fr, European elk (horiz.).

Photogravure

1961, June 5 ***Perf. 11½*** **Unwmkd.**

B690	SP333	40c	+10c bis brn & dk brn	15	15
B691	SP333	1fr	+50c gray & brn	1.50	1.50
B692	SP333	2fr	+50c dp rose & blk	2.10	2.00
B693	SP333	2.50fr	+1fr red org & brn	1.75	1.40
B694	SP333	3fr	+1fr org & brn	1.50	1.50
B695	SP333	6fr	+2fr bl & bis brn	3.75	2.25
			Nos. B690-B695 (6)	10.75	8.80

The surtax was for various philanthropic organizations.

1961, July 29 **Engraved**

Designs: 3fr+1.50fr, Arms of Cardinal de Granvelle. 6fr+3fr, Tower and crosier, symbolic of collaboration between Malines and the Archbishopric.

B696	SP334	40c	+10c mag, car & brn	15	15
B697	SP334	3fr	+1.50fr multi	1.20	90
B698	SP334	6fr	+3fr mag pur & bis	2.50	2.25

Issued to commemorate the 400th anniversary of Malines as an Archbishopric.

Mother and Child by Pierre Paulus
SP335

Castle of the Counts of Male
SP336

Paintings: 1fr+50c, Mother Love, Francois-Joseph Navez. 2fr+50c, Motherhood, Constant Permeke. 2.50fr+1fr, Madonna and Child, Rogier van der Weyden. 3fr+1fr, Madonna with Apple, Hans Memling. 6fr+2fr, Madonna of the Forget-me-not, Peter Paul Rubens.

1961, Dec. 2 Photo. ***Perf. 11½***

Gold Frame

B699	SP335	40c	+10c dp brn	15	15
B700	SP335	1fr	+50c brt bl	75	60
B701	SP335	2fr	+50c rose red	1.10	90
B702	SP335	2.50fr	+1fr mag	1.65	1.40
B703	SP335	3fr	+1fr vio bl	2.00	1.50
B704	SP335	6fr	+2fr dk sl grn	3.25	2.75
			Nos. B699-B704 (6)	8.90	7.30

The surtax was for anti-tuberculosis work.

1962, Mar. 12 **Engr.** ***Perf. 11½***

Designs: 90c+10c, Royal library (horiz.). 1fr+50c, Church of Our Lady, Tongres. 2fr+50c, Collegiate Church, Soignies (horiz.). 2.50fr+1fr, Church of Our Lady, Malines. 3fr+1fr, St. Denis Abbey, Broqueroi. 6fr+2fr, Cloth Hall, Ypres (horiz.).

B705	SP336	40c	+10c brt grn	15	15
B706	SP336	90c	+10c lil rose	30	30
B707	SP336	1fr	+50c dl vio	75	70
B708	SP336	2fr	+50c vio	1.00	1.00
B709	SP336	2.50fr	+1fr red brn	1.75	1.50
B710	SP336	3fr	+1fr bl grn	1.75	1.50
B711	SP336	6fr	+2fr car rose	2.50	2.25
			Nos. B705-B711 (7)	8.20	7.40

The surtax was for various cultural and philanthropic organizations.

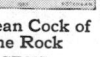

Andean Cock of the Rock
SP337

Handicapped Child
SP338

Birds: 1fr+50c, Red lory. 2fr+50c, Guinea touraco. 2.50fr+1fr, Keel-billed toucan. 3fr+1fr, Great bird of paradise. 6fr+2fr, Congolese peacock.

Engraved and Photogravure

1962, June 23 ***Perf. 11½*** **Unwmkd.**

Birds in Natural Colors

B712	SP337	40c	+10c bl	15	15
B713	SP337	1fr	+50c ultra & car	60	50
B714	SP337	2fr	+50c blk & car rose	70	60
B715	SP337	2.50fr	+1fr grnsh bl & ver	80	70
B716	SP337	3fr	+1fr red brn & grn	1.75	1.40
B717	SP337	6fr	+2fr red & ultra	3.00	2.75
			Nos. B712-B717 (6)	7.00	6.10

The surtax was for various philanthropic organizations.

Photogravure

1962, Sept. 22 ***Perf. 11½*** **Unwmkd.**

Handicapped Children: 40c+10c, Reading Braille. 2fr+50c, Deaf-mute girl with earphones and electronic equipment (horiz.). 2.50fr+1fr, Child with ball (cerebral palsy). 3fr+1fr, Girl with crutches (polio). 6fr+2fr, Sitting boys playing ball (horiz.).

B718	SP338	40c	+10c choc	15	15
B719	SP338	1fr	+50c rose red	50	45
B720	SP338	2fr	+50c brt lil	1.10	1.00
B721	SP338	2.50fr	+1fr dl grn	1.25	1.10
B722	SP338	3fr	+1fr dk bl	1.65	1.50
B723	SP338	6fr	+2fr dk brn	3.00	2.50
			Nos. B718-B723 (6)	7.65	6.70

The surtax was for various institutions for handicapped children.

Queen Louise-Marie
SP339

Belgian Queens: No. B725, like No. B724 with "ML" initials. 1fr+50c, Marie-Henriette. 2fr+1fr, Elisabeth. 3fr+1.50fr, Astrid. 8fr+2.50fr, Fabiola.

Photogravure and Engraved

1962, Dec. 8 ***Perf. 11½***

B724	SP339	40c	+10c gray, blk & gold ("L")	15	15
B725	SP339	40c	+10c gray, blk & gold ("ML")	15	15
B726	SP339	1fr	+50c gray, blk & gold	90	90
B727	SP339	2fr	+1fr gray, blk & gold	1.50	1.40
B728	SP339	3fr	+1.50fr gray, blk & gold	1.75	1.40
B729	SP339	8fr	+2.50fr gray, blk & gold	2.75	2.00
			Nos. B724-B729 (6)	7.20	6.00

The surtax was for anti-tuberculosis work.

British War Memorial (Porte de Menin), Ypres
SP340

1962, Dec. 26 **Engr.** ***Perf. 11½***

B730	SP340	1fr	+50c blk, grn, bl & red brn	90	90

Millennium of the city of Ypres. Issued in sheets of eight.

Peace Bell Ringing over Globe
SP341

The Sower by Brueghel
SP342

Engraved and Photogravure

1963, Feb. 18 ***Perf. 11½*** **Unwmkd.**

B731	SP341	3fr	+1.50fr blk, bl, org & grn	2.25	2.25
	a.		Sheet of 4	11.50	11.50
B732	SP341	6fr	+3fr blk, brn & org	1.40	1.40

The surtax was for the installation of the Peace Bell (Bourdon de la Paix) at Koekelberg Basilica and for the benefit of various cultural organizations.

No. B731 was issued in sheets of 4. The sheet is inscribed "Bourdon de la Paix," repeated in Flemish, and measures 85x115 mm. No. B732 was issued in sheets of 30.

1963, Mar. 21 ***Perf. 11½***

Designs: 3fr+1fr, The Harvest, by Brueghel (horiz.). 6fr+2fr, "Bread," by Anton Carte (horiz.).

B733	SP342	2fr	+1fr grn, ocher & blk	30	30

B734	SP342	3fr +1fr red lil, ocher & blk	75	60
B735	SP342	6fr +2fr red brn, cit & blk	1.10	90

Issued for the "Freedom from Hunger" campaign of the U.N. Food and Agriculture Organization.

Speed Racing
SP343

Designs: 2fr+1fr, Bicyclists at check point (horiz.). 3fr+1.50fr, Team racing (horiz.). 6fr+3fr, Pace setters.

Engraved

1963, July 13 *Perf. 11½* Unwmkd.

B736	SP343	1fr +50c multi	15	15
B737	SP343	2fr +1fr bl, car, blk & ol gray	30	30
B738	SP343	3fr +1.50fr multi	60	60
B739	SP343	6fr +3fr multi	90	90

Issued to commemorate the 80th anniversary of the founding of the Belgian Bicycle League. The surtax was for athletes at the 1964 Olympic Games.

Princess Paola with Princess Astrid
SP344

Prince Albert and Family
SP345

Designs: 40c+10c, Prince Philippe. 2fr+50c, Princess Astrid. 2.50fr+1fr, Princess Paola. 6fr+2fr, Prince Albert.

1963, Sept. 28 Photogravure

Cross in Red

B740	SP344	40c +10c dk car rose & buff	15	15
B741	SP344	1fr +50c sl & buff	45	45
B742	SP344	2fr +50c dk car rose & buff	60	60
B743	SP344	2.50fr +1fr brt bl & buff	75	75
B744	SP345	3fr +1fr gray brn & buff	75	75
B745	SP345	3fr +1fr sl grn & buff	2.25	2.25
a.		Bklt pane of 8	55.00	55.00
B746	SP344	6fr +2fr sl & buff	1.25	1.25
		Nos. B740-B746 (7)	6.20	6.20

Issued to commemorate the centenary of the International Red Cross. No. B745 issued only in booklet panes of 8, which are in two forms: French and Flemish inscriptions in top and bottom margins transposed.

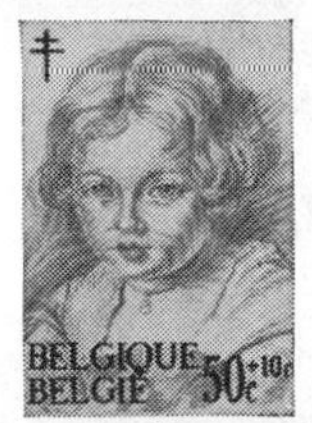

Daughter of Balthazar Gerbier, Painted by Rubens
SP346

Jesus, St. John and Cherubs by Rubens
SP347

Portraits (Rubens' sons): 1fr+40c, Nicolas, 2 yrs. old. 2fr+50c, Franz. 2.50fr+1fr, Nicolas, 6 yrs. old. 3fr+1fr, Albert.

Photogravure and Engraved

1963, Dec. 7 *Perf. 11½* Unwmkd.

B747	SP346	50c +10c buff, gray & dk brn	15	15
B748	SP346	1fr +40c buff, red brn & dk brn	15	15
B749	SP346	2fr +50c buff, vio brn & dk brn	30	30
B750	SP346	2.50fr +1fr buff, grn & dk brn	75	75
B751	SP346	3fr +1fr buff, red brn & dk brn	60	60
B752	SP347	6fr +2fr buff & gray	90	90
		Nos. B747-B752 (6)	2.85	2.85

The surtax was for anti-tuberculosis work.
See also No. B771.

John Quincy Adams and Lord Gambier Signing Treaty of Ghent, by Amédée Forestier—SP348

1964, May 16 Photo. *Perf. 11½*

B753	SP348	6fr +3fr dk bl	75	75

Issued to commemorate the 150th anniversary of the signing of the Treaty of Ghent between the United States and Great Britain, Dec. 24, 1814.

Philip van Marnix
SP349

Portraits: 3fr+1.50fr, Ida de Bure Calvin. 6fr+3fr, Jacob Jordaens.

1964, May 30 Engraved

B754	SP349	1fr +50c bl gray	15	15
B755	SP349	3fr +1.50fr rose pink	30	30
B756	SP349	6fr +3fr redsh brn	60	60

Issued to honor Protestantism in Belgium. The surtax was for the erection of a Protestant church.

Foot Soldier, 1918
SP350

Battle of Bastogne
SP351

Designs: 2fr+1fr, Flag bearer, Guides Regiment, 1914. 3fr+1.50fr, Trumpeter of the Grenadiers and drummers, 1914.

1964, Aug. 1 Photo. *Perf. 11½*

B757	SP350	1fr +50c multi	15	15
B758	SP350	2fr +1fr multi	30	30
B759	SP350	3fr +1.50fr multi	30	30

Issued to commemorate the 50th anniversary of the German aggression against Belgium in 1914. The surtax aided patriotic undertakings.

1964, Aug. 1 Unwmkd.

Design: 6fr+3fr, Liberation of the estuary of the Escaut.

B760	SP351	3fr +1fr multi	30	30
B761	SP351	6fr +3fr multi	45	45

Issued to commemorate Belgium's Resistance and liberation of World War II. The surtax was to help found an International Student Center at Antwerp and to aid cultural undertakings.

Souvenir Sheets

Rogier van der Weyden Paintings
SP352

Descent From the Cross
SP353

Designs: 1fr, Philip the Good. 2fr, Portrait of a Lady. 3fr, Man with Arrow.

1964, Sept. 19 Photo. *Perf. 11½*

B762	SP352	Sheet of 3	4.50	4.50
a.		1fr multi	1.10	1.10
b.		2fr multi	1.10	1.10
c.		3fr multi	1.10	1.10

Engraved

B763	SP353	8fr red brn, sheet of 1	4.50	4.50

Issued to commemorate the 5th centenary of the death of the painter Rogier van der Weyden (Roger de La Pasture, 1400-1464). The surtax went to various cultural organizations. Sheets have gray brown frames and marginal inscriptions. Size of sheets: 153x114mm. Size of stamps: 24x36mm. (Nos. B762a,b,c); 54x35mm. (No. B763). No. B762 sold for 14fr, No. B763 for 16fr.

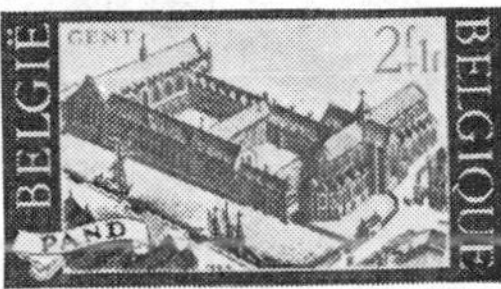

Ancient View of the Pand
SP354

Design: 3fr+1fr, Present view of the Pand from Lys River.

1964, Oct. 10 Photogravure

B764	SP354	2fr +1fr blk, grnsh bl & ultra	30	30
B765	SP354	3fr +1fr lil rose, bl & dk brn	30	30

The surtax was for the restoration of the Pand Dominican Abbey in Ghent.

Type of 1963 and

Child of Charles I, Painted by Van Dyck
SP355

Designs: 1fr+40c, William of Orange with his bride, by Van Dyck. 2fr+1fr, Portrait of a small boy with dogs by Erasmus Quellin and Jan Fyt. 3fr+1fr, Alexander Farnese by Antonio Moro. 4fr+2fr, William II, Prince of Orange by Van Dyck. 6fr+3fr, Artist's children by Cornelis De Vos.

1964, Dec. 5 Engraved *Perf. 11½*

B766	SP355	50c +10c rose cl	15	15
B767	SP355	1fr +40c car rose	15	15
B768	SP355	2fr +1fr vio brn	30	30
B769	SP355	3fr +1fr gray	30	30
B770	SP355	4fr +2fr vio bl	45	45
B771	SP347	6fr +3fr brt pur	45	45
		Nos. B766-B771 (6)	1.80	1.80

The surtax was for anti-tuberculosis work.

Liberator, Shaking Prisoner's Hand, Concentration Camp
SP356

Designs: 1fr+50c, Prisoner's hand reaching for the sun. 3fr+1.50fr, Searchlights and tank breaking down barbed wire (horiz.). 8fr+5fr, Rose growing amid the ruins (horiz.).

Engraved and Photogravure

1965, May 8 *Perf. 11½* Unwmkd.

B772	SP356	50c +50c tan, blk & buff	15	15
B773	SP356	1fr +50c multi	15	15

B774	SP356	3fr +1.50fr dl lil & blk	30	30
B775	SP356	8fr +5fr multi	60	60

Issued to commemorate the 20th anniversary of the liberation of the concentration camps for political prisoners and prisoners of war.

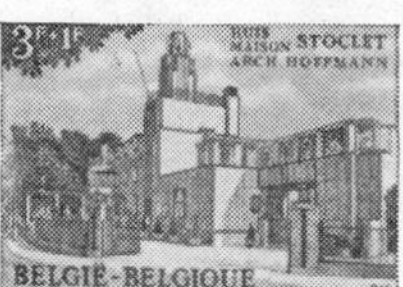

Stoclet House, Brussels
SP357

Stoclet House: 6fr+3fr, Hall with marble foundation (vert.). 8fr+4fr, View of house from garden.

1965, June 21

B776	SP357	3fr +1fr sl & tan	30	30
B777	SP357	6fr +3fr sep	45	45
B778	SP357	8fr +4fr vio brn & tan	60	60

Issued to commemorate the 95th anniversary of the birth of the Austrian architect Josef Hoffmann (1870–1956), builder of the art nouveau residence of Adolphe Stoclet, engineer and financier.

Jackson's Chameleon
SP358

Animals from Antwerp Zoo: 2fr+1fr, Common iguanas. 3fr+1.50fr, African monitor. 6fr+3fr, Komodo monitor. 8fr+4fr, Nile softshell turtle.

1965, Oct. 16 Photo. *Perf. 11½*

B779	SP358	1fr +50c multi	15	15
B780	SP358	2fr +1fr multi	20	20
B781	SP358	3fr +1.50fr multi	28	28
B782	SP358	6fr +3fr multi	55	55

Miniature Sheet

B783	SP358	8fr +4fr multi	2.25	2.25

The surtax was for various cultural and philanthropic organizations. No. B783 contains one stamp (52x35mm.) and has gray animal border. Size: 117x95mm.

Boatmen's and Archers' Guild Halls
SP359

Buildings on Grand-Place, Brussels: 1fr+40c, Brewers' Hall. 2fr+1fr, "King of Spain." 3fr+1.50fr, "Dukes of Brabant." 10fr+4.50fr, Tower of City Hall and St. Michael.

1965, Dec. 4 Engraved *Perf. 11½*

Size: 35x24mm.

B784	SP359	50c +10c ultra	15	15
B785	SP359	1fr +40c bl grn	18	18
B786	SP359	2fr +1fr rose cl	25	25
B787	SP359	3fr +1.50fr vio	30	30

Size: 24x44mm.

B788	SP359	10fr +4.50fr sep & gray	45	45
		Nos. B784-B788 (5)	1.33	1.33

The surtax was for anti-tuberculosis work.

Souvenir Sheets

Queen Elisabeth
SP360

Design: No. B790, Types of 1931 and 1956.

1966, Apr. 16 Photo. *Perf. 11½*

B789	SP360	Sheet of 2	2.50	2.50
a.		SP74 3fr dk brn & gray grn	1.00	1.00
b.		SP87 3fr dk brn, yel grn & gold	1.00	1.00
B790	SP360	Sheet of 2	2.50	2.50
a.		SP42 3fr dk brn & dl bl	1.00	1.00
b.		SP304 3fr dk brn & gray	1.00	1.00

The surtax went to various cultural organizations.

Each sheet contains two stamps plus label with the Queen's initial; sold for 20fr. Dark brown marginal inscription. Size: 81½x115mm.

Luminescent Paper

was used in printing Nos. B789–B790, B801–B806, B808–B809, B811–B823, B825–B831, B833–B835, B837–B840, B842–B846, B848–B850, B852–B854, B856–B863, and from B865 onward unless otherwise noted.

Diver
SP361

Design: 10fr+4fr, Swimmer at start.

1966, May 9 Engraved

B791	SP361	60c +40c Prus grn, ol & org brn	15	15
B792	SP361	10fr +4fr ol grn, org brn & mag	55	55

Issued to publicize the importance of swimming instruction.

Minorites' Convent, Liège
SP362

Designs: 1fr+50c, Val-Dieu Abbey, Aubel. 2fr+1fr, View and seal of Huy. 10fr+4.50fr, Statue of Ambiorix by Jules Bertin, and tower, Tongeren.

1966, Aug. 27 Engr. *Perf. 11½*

B793	SP362	60c +40c bl, vio brn & org brn	10	10
B794	SP362	1fr +50c vio brn, bl & grnsh bl	15	15
B795	SP362	2fr +1fr car rose, vio brn & org brn	18	18
B796	SP362	10fr +4.50fr brt grn, vio brn & sl bl	70	70

The surtax was for various patriotic and cultural organizations.

Surveyor and Dog Team
SP363

Designs: 3fr+1.50fr, Adrien de Gerlache and "Belgica." 6fr+3fr, Surveyor, weather balloon and ship. 10fr+5fr, Penguins and "Magga Dan" (ship used for 1964, 1965 and 1966 expeditions).

1966, Oct. 8 Engraved *Perf. 11½*

B797	SP363	1fr +50c bl grn	15	15
B798	SP363	3fr +1.50fr pale vio	25	25
B799	SP363	6fr +3fr dk car	45	45

Souvenir Sheet

Engraved and Photogravure

B800	SP363	10fr +5fr dk gray, sky bl & dk red	90	90

Issued to publicize Belgian Antarctic expeditions. No. B800 contains one stamp (52x35mm.); inscriptions, map of Antarctica and observation post in margin. Size: 130x95mm.

Boy with Ball and Dog
SP364

Designs: 2fr+1fr, Girl skipping rope. 3fr+1.50fr, Girl and boy blowing soap bubbles. 6fr+3fr, Girl and boy rolling hoops (horiz.). 8fr+3.50fr, Four children at play and cat (horiz.).

Engraved and Photogravure

1966, Dec. 3 *Perf. 11½*

B801	SP364	1fr +1fr pink & blk	15	15
B802	SP364	2fr +1fr lt bluish grn & blk	18	18
B803	SP364	3fr +1.50fr lt vio & blk	25	25
B804	SP364	6fr +3fr pale sal & dk brn	40	40
B805	SP364	8fr +3.50fr lt yel grn & dk brn	50	50
		Nos. B801-B805 (5)	1.48	1.48

The surtax was for anti-tuberculosis work.

Souvenir Sheet

Refugees
SP365

Designs: 1fr, Boy receiving clothes. 2fr, Tibetan children. 3fr, African mother and children.

1967, Mar. 11 Photo. *Perf. 11½*

B806	SP365	Sheet of 3	1.75	1.75
a.		1fr blk & yel	40	40
b.		2fr blk & bl	40	40
c.		3fr blk & org	60	60

Issued to help refugees around the world. Sheet has black border with Belgian P.T.T. and U.N. Refugee emblems. Size: 110x76 mm. Sold for 20fr.

Robert Schuman
SP366

Colonial Brotherhood Emblem
SP368

Kongolo Memorial, Gentinnes
SP367

1967, June 24 Engraved *Perf. 11½*

B807	SP366	2fr +1fr gray bl	40	40

Engraved and Photogravure

B808	SP367	5fr +2fr brn & ol	45	45
B809	SP368	10fr +5fr multi	70	60

Issued to commemorate respectively: Robert Schuman (1886–1963), French statesman, one of the founders of European Steel and Coal Community, first president of European Parliament (2fr+1fr); Kongolo Memorial, erected in memory of missionary and civilian victims in the Congo (5fr+2fr); a memorial for African Troops, Brussels (10fr+5fr).

Preaching Fool from "Praise of Folly" by Erasmus
SP369

Erasmus, by Quentin Massys
SP370

Designs: 2fr+1fr, Exhorting Fool from Praise of Folly. 5fr+2fr, Thomas More's Family, by Hans Holbein (horiz.). 6fr+3fr, Pierre Gilles (Aegidius), by Quentin Massys.

Photogravure and Engraved (SP369); Photogravure (SP370)

1967, Sept. 2 *Perf. 11* Unwmkd.

B810	SP369	1fr +50c tan, blk, bl & car	15	15
B811	SP369	2fr +1fr tan, blk & car	18	18
B812	SP370	3fr +1.50fr multi	25	25
B813	SP369	5fr +2fr tan, blk & car	35	35
B814	SP370	6fr +3fr multi	45	45
		Nos. B810-B814 (5)	1.38	1.38

Issued to commemorate Erasmus (1466(?)–1536), Dutch scholar and his era.

Souvenir Sheet

Pro-Post Association Emblem
SP371

Engraved and Photogravure

1967, Oct. 21 *Perf. 11½*

B815	SP371	10fr +5fr multi	1.25	1.25

Issued to publicize the POSTPHILA Philatelic Exhibition, Brussels, Oct. 21-29. No. B815 has black marginal inscription and ornaments. Size: 112x77mm.

Detail from Brueghel's "Children's Games"
SP372

Designs: Various Children's Games. Singles of Nos. B816-B821 arranged in 2 rows of 3 show complete painting by Pieter Brueghel.

1967, Dec. 9 Photo. *Perf. 11½*

B816	SP372	1fr +50c multi	15	15
B817	SP372	2fr +50c multi	25	25
B818	SP372	3fr +1fr multi	25	25
B819	SP372	6fr +3fr multi	40	40
B820	SP372	10fr +4fr multi	55	55
B821	SP372	13fr +6fr multi	80	80
		Nos. B816-B821 (6)	2.40	2.40

Queen Fabiola Holding Refugee Child from Congo
SP373

Design: 6fr+3fr, Queen Elisabeth and Dr. Depage.

1968, Apr. 27 Photo. *Perf. 11½*

Cross in Red

B822	SP373	6fr +3fr sep & gray	40	40
B823	SP373	10fr +5fr sep & gray	75	75

The surtax was for the Red Cross.

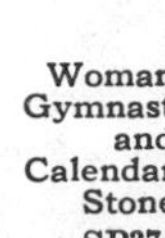

Woman Gymnast and Calendar Stone
SP374

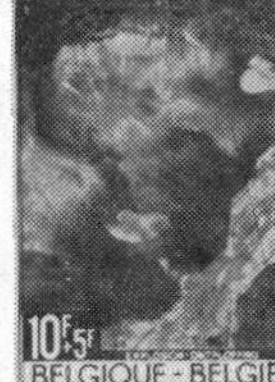

Yachting and "The Swimmer" by Andrien
SP375

"Explosion"
SP376

Designs: 2fr+1fr, Weight lifter and Mayan motif. 3fr+1.50fr, Hurdler, colossus of Tula and animal head from Kukulkan. 6fr+2fr, Bicyclists and Chichen Itza Temple.

Engraved and Photogravure

1968, May 27 *Perf. 11½*

B824	SP374	1fr +50c multi	15	15
B825	SP374	2fr +1fr multi	18	18
B826	SP374	3fr +1.50fr multi	25	25
B827	SP374	6fr +2fr multi	40	40

Photogravure

B828	SP375	13fr +5fr multi	95	95
		Nos. B824-B828 (5)	1.93	1.93

Issued to publicize the 19th Olympic Games, Mexico City, Oct. 12-27.

1968, June 22 Photogravure

Designs (Paintings by Pol Mara): 12fr+5fr, "Fire." 13fr+5fr, "Tornado."

B829	SP376	10fr +5fr multi	60	60
B830	SP376	12fr +5fr multi	1.00	1.00
B831	SP376	13fr +5fr multi	1.10	1.10

The surtax was for disaster victims.

Undulate Triggerfish
SP377

Tropical Fish: 3fr+1.50fr, Angelfish. 6fr+3fr, Turkeyfish (Pterois volitans). 10fr+5fr, Orange butterflyfish.

Engraved and Photogravure

1968, Oct. 19 *Perf. 11½*

B832	SP377	1fr +50c multi	18	18
B833	SP377	3fr +1.50fr multi	30	30
B834	SP377	6fr +3fr multi	55	55
B835	SP377	10fr +5fr multi	80	80

King Albert and Queen Elisabeth Entering Brussels—SP378

Tomb of the Unknown Soldier and Eternal Flame, Brussels
SP379

Designs: 1fr+50c, King Albert, Queen Elisabeth and Crown Prince Leopold on balcony, Bruges (vert.). 6fr+3fr, King and Queen entering Liège.

1968, Nov. 9 Photo. *Perf. 11½*

B836	SP378	1fr +50c multi	15	15
B837	SP378	3fr +1.50fr multi	30	30
B838	SP378	6fr +3fr multi	55	55

Engraved and Photogravure

B839	SP379	10fr +5fr multi	75	75

Issued to commemorate the 50th anniversary of the victory in World War I.

Souvenir Sheet

The Painter and the Amateur, by Peter Brueghel
SP380

1969, May 10 Engraved *Perf. 11½*

B840	SP380	10fr +5fr sep	1.75	1.75

Issued to publicize the POSTPHILA 1969 Philatelic Exhibition, Brussels, May 10-18. Size of stamp: 40x47mm.; size of sheet: 90x123mm.

Huts, by Ivanka D. Pancheva, Bulgaria
SP381

Msgr. Victor Scheppers
SP382

Children's Drawings and UNICEF Emblem: 3fr+1.50fr, "My Art" (Santa Claus), by Claes Patric, Belgium. 6fr+3fr, "In the Sun" (young boy), by Helena Rejchlova, Czechoslovakia. 10fr+5fr, "Out for a Walk" by Phillis Sporn, USA (horiz.).

1969, May 31 Photo. *Perf. 11½*

B841	SP381	1fr +50c multi	15	15
B842	SP381	3fr +1.50fr multi	25	25
B843	SP381	6fr +3fr multi	55	55
B844	SP381	10fr +5fr multi	80	80

The surtax was for philanthropic purposes.

1969, July 5 Engraved

B845	SP382	6fr +3fr rose cl	60	60

Issued to commemorate Msgr. Victor Scheppers (1802-77), prison reformer and founder of the Brothers of Mechlin (Scheppers).

Souvenir Sheet

Moon Landing Type of 1969

Design: 20fr+10fr, Armstrong, Collins and Aldrin and moon with Tranquillity Base (vert.).

1969, Sept. 20 Photo. *Perf. 11½*

B846	A245	20fr +10fr ind	6.00	6.00

See note after No. 693. No. B846 contains one stamp. Margin has commemorative inscription and picture of Armstrong stepping on moon. Size: 94x129mm.

Heads from Alexander the Great Tapestry, 15th Century
SP383

Designs from Tapestries: 3fr+1.50fr, Fiddler from "The Feast," c. 1700. 10fr+4fr, Head of beggar from "The Healing of the Paralytic," 16th century.

1969, Sept. 20

B847	SP383	1fr +50c multi	15	15
B848	SP383	3fr +1.50fr multi	30	30
B849	SP383	10fr +4fr multi	75	75

The surtax was for philanthropic purposes.

Bearded Antwerp Bantam
SP384

Engraved and Photogravure

1969, Nov. 8 *Perf. 11½*

B850	SP384	10fr +5fr multi	90	90

Angel Playing Lute
SP385

Designs from Stained Glass Windows: 1.50fr+50c, Angel with trumpet, St. Waudru's, Mons. 7fr+3fr, Angel with viol, St. Jacques', Liege. 9fr+4fr, King with bagpipes, Royal Art Museum, Brussels.

1969, Dec. 13 Photogravure

Size: 24x35mm.

B851	SP385	1.50fr +50c multi	18	18
B852	SP385	3.50fr +1.50fr multi	30	30
B853	SP385	7fr +3fr multi	55	55

Size: 35x52mm.

B854	SP386	9fr +4fr multi	90	90

The surtax was for philanthropic purposes.

Farm and Windmill, Open-air Museum, Bokrijk
SP386

Belgian Museums: 3.50fr+1.50fr, Stage Coach Inn, Courcelles. 7fr+3fr, "The Thresher of Trevires," Gallo-Roman sculpture, Gaumais Museum, Virton. 9fr+4fr, "The Sovereigns," by Henry Moore, Middelheim Museum, Antwerp.

Engraved and Photogravure

1970, May 30 ***Perf. 11½***

B855	SP386	1.50fr +50c multi	30	30
B856	SP386	3.50fr +1.50fr multi	45	45
B857	SP386	7fr +3fr multi	60	60
B858	SP386	9fr +4fr multi	75	75

The surtax went to various culture organizations.

"Resistance"
SP387

Design: 7fr+3fr, "Liberation of Camps." The designs were originally used as book covers.

1970, July 4 **Photo.** ***Perf. 11½***

B859	SP387	3.50fr +1.50fr blk, gray grn & dp car	30	30
B860	SP387	7fr +3fr blk, lil & dp car	60	60

Issued to honor the Resistance Movement and to commemorate the 25th anniversary of the liberation of concentration camps.

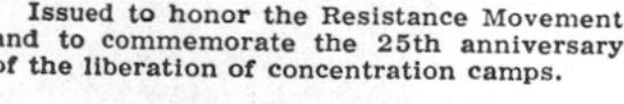

Fishing Rod and Reel
SP388

Design: 9fr+4fr, Hockey stick and puck (vert.).

Engraved and Photogravure

1970, Sept. 19 ***Perf. 11½***

B861	SP388	3.50fr +1.50fr multi	45	45
B862	SP388	9fr +4fr brt grn & multi	75	75

Souvenir Sheet

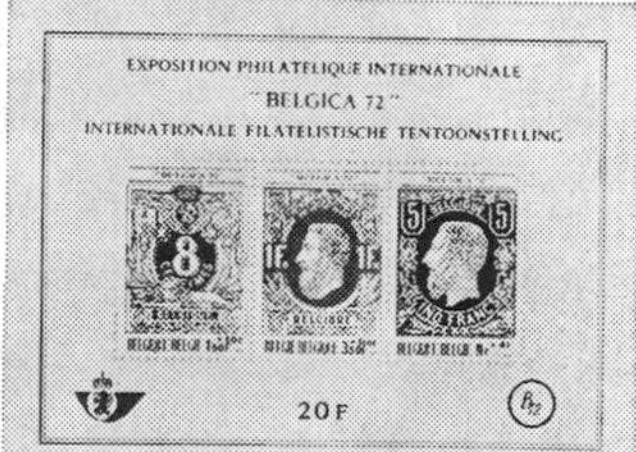

Belgium Nos. 31, 36 and 39
SP389

Engraved and Photogravure

1970, Oct. 10 ***Perf. 11½***

B863	SP389	20fr sheet of 3	5.50	5.50
a.		1.50fr+50c blk & dl lil	1.65	1.65
b.		3.50fr+1.50fr blk & lil	1.65	1.65
c.		9fr+4fr blk & red brn	1.65	1.65

Issued to publicize BELGICA 72 International Philatelic Exhibition, Brussels, June 24–July 9. No. B863 has black marginal inscription and lilac frame. Size: 130x97mm.

Camille Huysmans (1871–1968)
SP390

"Anxious City" (Detail) by Paul Delvaux
SP391

Portraits: 3.50fr+1.50fr, Joseph Cardinal Cardijn (1882–1967). 7fr+3fr, Maria Baers (1883–1959). 9fr+4fr, Paul Pastur (1866–1938).

Engraved and Photogravure

1970, Nov. 14 ***Perf. 11½***

Portraits in Sepia

B864	SP390	1.50fr +50c car rose	20	20
B865	SP390	3.50fr +1.50fr lil	30	30
B866	SP390	7fr +3fr grn	60	60
B867	SP390	9fr +4fr bl	75	75

1970, Dec. 12 **Photogravure**

Design: 7fr+3fr, "The Memory," by René Magritte.

B868	SP391	3.50fr +1.50fr multi	30	30
B869	SP391	7fr +3fr multi	60	60

Notre Dame du Vivier, Marche-les-Dames
SP392

Design: 7fr+3fr, Turnhout Beguinage and Beguine.

1971, March 13 ***Perf. 11½***

B870	SP392	3.50fr +1.50 multi	30	60
B871	SP392	7fr +3fr multi	60	60

The surtax was for philanthropic purposes.

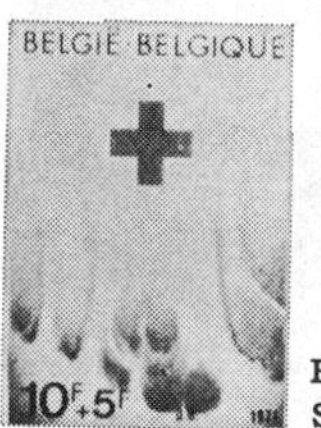

Red Cross
SP393

1971, May 22 **Photo.** ***Perf. 11½***

B872	SP393	10fr +5fr crim & blk	90	90

Belgian Red Cross.

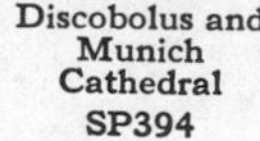

Discobolus and Munich Cathedral
SP394

Festival of Flanders
SP395

Engraved and Photogravure

1971, June 19 ***Perf. 11½***

B873	SP394	7fr +3fr bl & blk	75	75

Publicity for the 20th Summer Olympic Games, Munich 1972.

1971, Sept. 11 **Photo.** ***Perf. 11½***

Design: 7fr+3fr, Wallonia Festival.

B874	SP395	3.50fr +1.50fr multi	30	30
B875	SP395	7fr +3fr multi	60	60

Attre Palace—SP396

Steen Palace, Elewijt
SP397

Design: 10fr+5fr, Royal Palace, Brussels.

1971, Oct. 23 **Engraved**

B876	SP396	3.50fr +1.50fr sl grn	45	45
B877	SP397	7fr +3fr red brn	75	75
B878	SP396	10fr +5fr vio bl	1.10	1.10

Surtax was for BELGICA 72, International Philatelic Exposition.

Ox Fly
SP398

Insects: 1.50fr+50c, Luna moth (vert.). 7fr+3fr, Wasp, polistes gallicus. 9fr+4fr, Tiger beetle (vert.).

1971, Dec. 11 **Photo.** ***Perf. 11½***

B879	SP398	1.50fr +50c multi	30	30
B880	SP398	3.50fr +1.50fr multi	30	30
B881	SP398	7fr +3fr multi	60	60
B882	SP398	9fr +4fr multi	90	90

Surtax was for philanthropic purposes.

Leopold I on No. 1
SP399

Epilepsy Emblem
SP400

Designs: 2fr+1fr, Leopold I on No. 5. 2.50fr+1fr, Leopold II on No. 45. 3.50fr+1.50fr, Leopold II on No. 48. 6fr+3fr, Albert I on No. 135. 7fr+3fr, Albert I on No. 214. 10fr+5fr, Albert I on No. 231. 15fr+7.50fr, Leopold III on No. 290. 20fr+10fr, King Baudouin on No. 718.

Engraved and Photogravure

1972, June 24 ***Perf. 11½***

"B" in Gold

B883	SP399	1.50fr +50c brn & blk	30	3
B884	SP399	2fr +1fr brick red & brn	30	3
B885	SP399	2.50 +1fr car & blk	45	4
B886	SP399	3.50fr +1.50fr vio & blk	75	7
B887	SP399	6fr +3fr rose lil & blk	1.10	1.1
B888	SP399	7fr +3fr rose car & blk	1.50	1.5
B889	SP399	10fr +5fr sl bl & blk	1.75	1.7
B890	SP399	15fr +7fr gray grn & bl grn	2.50	2.5
B891	SP399	20fr +10fr red brn & brn	3.75	3.7
		Nos. B883-B891 (9)	12.40	12.4

Belgica 72, International Philatelic Exhibition, Brussels, June 24–July 9. Nos. B883–B891 issued in sheets of 10 and of 20 (2 tête bêche sheets with gutter between). Belgica 72 emblem in stamp color and gray blue border and inscription in margin. Sold in complete sets.

1972, Sept. 9 **Photo.** ***Perf. 11½***

B892	SP400	10fr +5fr multi	90	90

The surtax was for the William Lennox Center for epilepsy research and treatment.

Gray Lag Goose
SP401

Designs: 4.50fr+2fr, Lapwing. 8fr+4fr, Stork. 9fr+4.50fr, Kestrel (horiz.).

1972, Dec. 16 **Photo.** ***Perf. 11½***

B893	SP401	2fr +1fr multi	30	30
B894	SP401	4.50fr +2fr multi	45	45
B895	SP401	8fr +4fr multi	90	90
B896	SP401	9fr +4.50fr multi	90	90

Bijloke Abbey, Ghent—SP402

Designs: 4.50fr+2fr, St. Ursmer Collegiate Church, Lobbes. 8fr+4fr, Park Abbey, Heverle. 9fr+4.50fr, Abbey, Floreffe.

1973, Mar. 24 **Engr.** ***Perf. 11½***

B897	SP402	2fr +1fr sl grn	30	30
B898	SP402	4.50fr +2fr brn	45	45
B899	SP402	8fr +4fr rose lil	90	90
B900	SP402	9fr +4.50fr brt bl	1.10	1.10

Basketball
SP403

1973, Apr. 7 **Photo. & Engr.**

B901	SP403	10fr +5fr multi	90	90

First World Basketball Championships of the Handicapped, Bruges, Apr. 16–21.

Dirk Martens' Printing Press
SP404

Lady Talbot, by Petrus Christus
SP405

Hadrian and Marcus Aurelius Coins
SP406

Council of Malines, by Coussaert—SP407

Designs: 3.50fr+1.50fr, Head of Amon and Tutankhamen's cartouche. 10fr+5fr, Three-master of Ostend Merchant Company.

Photo. & Engr.; Photo. (B906)

1973, June 23 ***Perf. 11½***

B902	SP404	2fr	+1fr multi	30	30
B903	SP404	3.50fr	+1.50fr multi	30	30
B904	SP405	4.50fr	+2fr multi	45	45
B905	SP406	8fr	+4fr multi	1.25	1.25
B906	SP407	9fr	+4.50fr multi	1.75	1.75
B907	SP407	10fr	+5fr multi	3.00	3.00
			Nos. B902-B907 (6)	7.05	7.05

Historical Anniversaries: 500th anniversary of first book printed in Belgium (B902); 50th anniversary of Queen Elisabeth Egyptological Foundation (B903); 500th anniversary of death of painter Petrus Christus (B904); Discovery of Roman treasure at Luttre-Liberchies (B905); 500th anniversary of Great Council of Malines (B906); 250th anniversary of the Ostend Merchant Company (B907).

No. B902 is not luminescent.

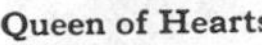

Queen of Hearts
SP408

Symbol of Blood Donations
SP409

Old Playing Cards: No. B909, King of Clubs. No. B910, Jack of Diamonds. No. B911, King of Spades.

1973, Dec. 8 **Photo.** ***Perf. 11½***

B908	SP408	5	+2.50fr multi	75	75
B909	SP408	5	+2.50fr multi	75	75
B910	SP408	5	+2.50fr multi	75	75
B911	SP408	5	+2.50fr multi	75	75

Surtax was for philanthropic purposes. Nos. B908–B911 printed se-tenant in sheets of 24 (4x6).

1974, Feb. 23 **Photo.** ***Perf. 11½***

Design: 10fr+5fr, Traffic lights, Red Cross (symbolic of road accidents).

B912	SP409	4fr	+2fr multi	45	45
B913	SP409	10fr	+5fr multi	1.00	1.00

The Red Cross as blood collector and aid to accident victims.

Armand Jamar, Self-portrait
SP410

Van Gogh, Self-portrait and House at Cuesmes
SP411

Designs: 5fr+2.50fr, Anton Bergmann and view of Lierre. 7fr+3.50fr, Henri Vieuxtemps and view of Verviers. 10fr+5fr, James Ensor, self-portrait, and masks.

1974, Apr. 6 **Photo.** ***Perf. 11½***

Size: 24x35mm.

B914	SP410	4fr	+2fr multi	45	45
B915	SP410	5fr	+2.50fr multi	60	60
B916	SP410	7fr	+3.50fr multi	75	75

Size: 35x52mm.

B917	SP410	10fr	+5fr multi	1.25	1.25

1974, Sept. 21 **Photo.** ***Perf. 11½***

B918	SP411	10fr	+5fr multi	90	90

Opening of Vincent van Gogh House at Cuesmes, where he worked as teacher.

Gentian
SP412

Spotted Cat's Ear
SP414

Badger
SP413

Design: 7fr+3.50fr, Beetle.

1974, Dec. 8 **Photo.** ***Perf. 11½***

B919	SP412	4fr	+2fr multi	40	40
B920	SP413	5fr	+2.50fr multi	45	45
B921	SP413	7fr	+3.50fr multi	60	60
B922	SP414	10fr	+5fr multi	90	90

Pesaro Palace, Venice
SP415

St. Bavon Abbey, Ghent
SP416

Virgin and Child, by Michelangelo
SP417

1975, Apr. 12 **Engr.** ***Perf. 11½***

B923	SP415	6.50fr	+2.50fr brn	60	60
B924	SP416	10fr	+4.50 vio brn	1.10	1.10
B925	SP417	15fr	+6.50fr brt bl	1.40	1.40

Surtax was for various cultural organizations.

Frans Hemerijckx and Leprosarium, Kasai
SP418

1975, Sept. 13 **Photo.** ***Perf. 11½***

B926	SP418	20fr	+10fr multi	1.75	1.75

Dr. Frans Hemerijckx (1902–1969), tropical medicine and leprosy expert.

Emile Moyson
SP419

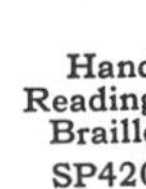

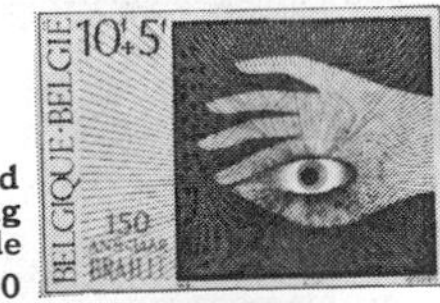

Hand Reading Braille
SP420

Beheading of St. Dympna
SP420a

Design: 6.50fr+3fr, Dr. Ferdinand Augustin Snellaert.

1975, Nov. 22 **Engr.** ***Perf. 11½***

B927	SP419	4.50fr	+2fr lil	45	45
B928	SP419	6.50fr	+3fr grn	60	60

Engraved and Photogravure

B929	SP420	10fr	+5fr multi	90	90

Photogravure

B930	SP420a	13fr	+6fr multi	1.25	1.25

Emile Moyson (1838–1868), freedom fighter for the rights of Flemings and Walloons; Dr. Snellaert (1809–1872), physician and Flemish patriot; Louis Braille (1809–1852), sesquicentennial of invention of Braille system of writing for the blind; St. Dympna, patron saint of Geel, famous for treatment of mentally ill.

The Cheese Vendor
SP421

Designs (THEMABELGA Emblem and): No. B932, Potato vendor. No. B933, Basket carrier. No. B934, Shrimp fisherman with horse (horiz.). No. B935, Knife grinder (horiz.). No. B936, Milk vendor with dog cart (horiz.).

Engraved and Photogravure

1975, Dec. 13 ***Perf. 11½***

B931	SP421	4.50fr	+1.50fr multi	30	30
B932	SP421	6.50fr	+3fr multi	60	60
B933	SP421	6.50fr	+3fr multi	60	60
B934	SP421	10fr	+5fr multi	90	90
B935	SP421	10fr	+5fr multi	90	90
B936	SP421	30fr	+15fr multi	2.75	2.75
			Nos. B931-B936 (6)	6.05	6.05

THEMABELGA International Topical Philatelic Exhibition, Brussels, Dec. 13–21. Issued in sheets of 10 (5x2).

Blackface Fund Collector
SP422

1976, Feb. 14 **Photo.** ***Perf. 11½***

B937	SP422	10fr	+5fr multi	90	90

Centenary of the "Conservatoire Africain" philanthropic society, and to publicize the Princess Paola crèches.

Swimming and Olympic Emblem
SP423

Designs (Montreal Olympic Games Emblem and): 5fr+2fr, Running (vert.). 6.50fr+2.50fr, Equestrian.

1976, Apr. 10 **Photo.** ***Perf. 11½***

B938	SP423	4.50fr	+1.50fr multi	30	30
B939	SP423	5fr	+2fr multi	45	45
B940	SP423	6.50fr	+2.50fr multi	75	75

21st Olympic Games, Montreal, Canada, July 17–Aug. 1.

Queen Elisabeth Playing Violin
SP424

Engraved and Photogravure

1976, May 1 ***Perf. 11½***

B941	SP424	14fr	+6fr blk & cl	1.25	1.25

Queen Elisabeth International Music Competition, 25th anniversary.

Souvenir Sheet

Jan Olieslagers, Bleriot Monoplane, Aero Club Emblem—SP425

Engraved and Photogravure

1976, June 12 *Perf. 11½*

B942	SP425	25fr +10fr multi	3.25	3.25

Royal Belgian Aero Club, 75th anniversary, and Jan Olieslagers (1883–1942), aviation pioneer. No. B942 has blue marginal decorations and black inscription. Size: 83x116mm.

Adoration of the Shepherds (detail), by Rubens
SP426

Dwarf, by Velazquez
SP427

Rubens Paintings (Details): 4.50fr, Descent from the Cross. No. B945, The Virgin with the Parrot. No. B946, Adoration of the Kings. No. B947, Last Communion of St. Francis. 30fr+15fr, Virgin and Child.

1976, Sept. 4 Photo. *Perf. 11½*

Size: 30x52mm.

B943	SP426	4.50fr +1.50fr multi	45	45

Size: 24x35mm.

B944	SP426	6.50fr +3fr multi	75	75
B945	SP426	6.50fr +3fr multi	75	75
B946	SP426	10fr +5fr multi	1.10	1.10
B947	SP426	10fr +5fr multi	1.10	1.10

Size: 30x52mm.

B948	SP426	30fr +15fr multi	2.25	2.25
		Nos. B943-B948 (6)	6.40	6.40

Peter Paul Rubens (1577–1640), Flemish painter, 400th birth anniversary.

1976, Nov. 6 Photo. *Perf. 11½*

B949	SP427	14fr +6fr multi	1.25	1.25

Surtax was for the National Association for the Mentally Handicapped.

Dr. Albert Hustin
SP428

Red Cross and Rheumatism Year Emblem
SP429

1977, Feb. 19 Photo. *Perf. 11½*

B950	SP428	6.50fr +2.50 multi	60	60
B951	SP429	14fr +7fr multi	1.10	1.10

Belgian Red Cross.

Bordet Atheneum, Empress Maria Theresa
SP430

Conductor and Orchestra, by E. Tytgat
SP431

Lucien Van Obbergh, Stage
SP432

Humanistic Society Emblem
SP433

Camille Lemonnier
SP434

Design: No. B953, Marie-Therese College, Herve, and coat of arms.

1977, Mar. 21 Photo. *Perf. 11½*

B952	SP430	4.50fr +1fr multi	40	40
B953	SP430	4.50fr +1fr multi	40	40
B954	SP431	5fr +2fr multi	45	45
B955	SP432	6.50fr +2fr multi	60	60
B956	SP433	6.50fr +2fr blk & red	60	60

Engraved

B957	SP434	10fr +5fr sl bl	90	90
		Nos. B952-B957 (6)	3.35	3.35

Bicentenaries of the Jules Bordet Atheneum, Brussels, and the Marie-Therese College, Herve (Nos. B952–B953); 50th anniversaries of the Brussels Philharmonic Society, and Artists' Union (Nos. B954–B955): 25th anniversary of the Flemish Humanistic Organization (No. B956); 75th anniversary of the French-speaking Belgian writers' organization (No. B957).

Young Soccer Players
SP435

1977, Apr. 18 Photogravure

B958	SP435	10fr +5fr multi	90	90

30th International Junior Soccer Tournament.

Albert-Edouard Janssen, Financier
SP436

Famous Men: No. B960, Joseph Wauters (1875–1929), editor of Le Peuple, and newspaper. No. B961, Jean Capart (1877–1947), Egyptologist, and hieroglyph. No. B962, August de Boeck (1865–1937), composer, and score.

1977, Dec. 3 Engr. *Perf. 11½*

B959	SP436	5fr +2.50fr brn	45	45
B960	SP436	5fr +2.50fr red	45	45
B961	SP436	10fr +5fr mag	90	90
B962	SP436	10fr +5fr bl gray	90	90

Abandoned Child
SP437

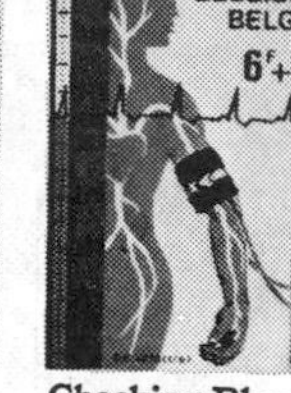

Checking Blood Pressure
SP438

De Mick Sanatorium, Brasschaat—SP439

1978, Feb. 18 Photo. *Perf. 11½*

B963	SP437	4.50fr +1.50fr multi	30	30
B964	SP438	6fr +3fr multi	60	60
B965	SP439	10fr +5fr multi	90	90

Help for abandoned children (No. B963); fight against hypertension (No. B964); fight against tuberculosis (No. B965).

Actors and Theater
SP440

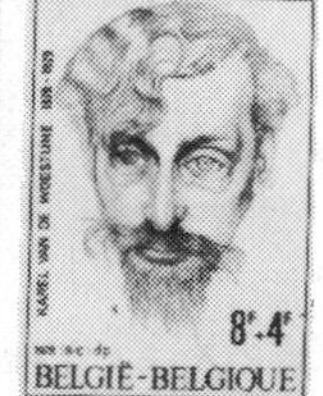

Karel van de Woestijne
SP441

Designs: No. B967, Harquebusier, Harquebusier Palace and coat of arms. 10fr+5fr, John of Austria and his signature.

Engraved and Photogravure

1978, June 17 *Perf. 11½*

B966	SP440	6fr +3fr multi	60	60
B967	SP440	6fr +3fr multi	60	60

Engraved

B968	SP441	8fr +4fr blk	70	70
B969	SP441	10fr +5fr blk	90	90

Centenary of Royal Flemish Theater, Brussels (No. B966); 400th anniversary of Harquebusiers' Guild of Visé, Liège (No. B967); Karel van de Woestijne (1878–1929), poet (No. B968); 400th anniversary of signing of Perpetual Edict by John of Austria (No. B969).

Lake Placid '80 and Belgian Olympic Emblems
SP442

Designs (Moscow '80 Emblem and): 8fr+3.50fr, Kremlin Towers and Belgian Olympic Committee emblem. 7fr+3fr, Runners from Greek vase, Lake Placid '80 emblem and Olympic rings. 14fr+6fr, Olympic flame, Lake Placid '80 and Belgian emblems, Olympic rings.

1978, Nov. 4 Photo. *Perf. 11½*

B970	SP442	6fr +2.50fr multi	60	60
B971	SP442	8fr +3.50fr multi	90	90

Souvenir Sheet

B972		Sheet of 2	2.00	2.00
a.		SP442 7fr + 3fr multi	80	80
b.		SP442 14fr + 6fr multi	1.25	1.25

Surtax was for 1980 Olympic Games. No. B972 has marginal inscription, Olympic Flame and Rings in blue and brown. Size: 150x100mm.

Great Synagogue, Brussels
SP443

Dancers
SP444

Father Pire, African Village
SP445

1978, Dec. 2 Engr. *Perf. 11½*

B973	SP443	6fr +2fr sep	75	75

Photogravure

B974	SP444	8fr +3fr multi	60	60
B975	SP445	14fr +7fr multi	1.10	1.10

Centenary of Great Synagogue of Brussels; Flemish Catholic Youth Action Organization, 50th anniversary; Nobel Peace Prize awarded to Father Dominique Pire for his "Heart Open to the World" movement, 20th anniversary.

Young People Giving First Aid
SP446

Skull with Bottle, Cigarette, Syringe
SP447

1979, Feb. 10 Photo. *Perf. 11½*

B976	SP446	8fr +3fr multi	60	60
B977	SP447	16fr +8fr multi	1.40	1.40

Belgian Red Cross.

Beatrice Soetkens with Statue of Virgin Mary
SP448

Details from Tapestries, 1516–1518, Showing Legend of Our Lady of Sand: 8fr+3fr, Francois de Tassis accepting letter from Emperor Frederick III (beginning of postal service). 14fr+7fr, Arrival of statue, Francois de Tassis and Philip the Fair. No. B981, Statue carried in procession by future Emperor Charles V and his brother Ferdinand. No. B982, Ship carrying Beatrice Soetkens with statue to Brussels (horiz.).

1979, May 5 Photo. *Perf. 11½*

B978	SP448	6fr +2fr multi	40	40
B979	SP448	8fr +3fr multi	60	60
B980	SP448	14fr +7fr multi	1.00	1.00
B981	SP448	20fr +10fr multi	1.65	1.65

Souvenir Sheet

B982	SP448	20fr +10fr multi	1.40	1.40

The surtax was for festivities in connection with the millennium of Brussels. No. B982 has multicolored margin showing entire tapestry with burghers receiving letter from kneeling messenger. Size: 100x 150mm.

Notre Dame Abbey, Brussels—SP449

Designs: 8fr+3fr, Beauvoorde Castle. 14fr+7fr, First issue of "Courrier de L'Escaut" and Barthelemy Dumortier, founder. 20fr+10fr, Shrine of St. Hermes, Renaix.

Engraved and Photogravure

1979, Sept. 15 *Perf. 11½*

B983	SP449	6fr +2fr multi	50	50
B984	SP449	8fr +3fr multi	60	60
B985	SP449	14fr +7fr multi	90	90
B986	SP449	20fr +10fr multi	1.65	1.65

50th anniversary of restoration of Notre Dame de la Cambre Abbey; historic Beauvoorde Castle, 15th century; sesquicentennial of the regional newspaper "Le Courrier de L'Escaut;" 850th anniversary of the consecration of the Collegiate Church of St. Hermes, Renaix.

Grand-Hornu Coal Mine—SP450

1979, Oct. 22 Engraved *Perf. 11½*

B987	SP450	10fr +5fr blk	70	70

Henry Heyman
SP451

Veterans Organization Medal
SP452

Boy and IYC Emblem—SP453

1979, Dec. 8 Photo. *Perf. 11½*

B988	SP451	8fr +3fr multi	60	60
B989	SP452	10fr +5fr multi	80	80
B990	SP453	16fr +8fr multi	1.10	1.10

Henri Heyman (1879-1958), Minister of State; Disabled Veterans' Organization, 50th anniversary; International Year of the Child.

Ivo Van Damme, Olympic Rings—SP454

1980, May 3 Photo. *Perf. 11½*

B991	SP454	20fr +10fr multi	1.40	1.40

Ivo Van Damme (1954-1976), silver medalist, 800-meter race, Montreal Olympics, 1976. Surtax was for Van Damme Memorial Foundation.

Queen Louis, King Leopold I—SP455

150th Anniversary of Independence (Queens and Kings): 9fr+3fr, Marie Henriette. Leopold II. 14fr+6fr, Elisabeth, Albert I. 17fr+8fr, Astrid, Leopold III. 25fr+10fr, Fabiola, Baudouin.

1980, May 31 Photo. & Engr. *Perf. 11½*

B992	SP455	6.50 +1.50fr multi	40	40
B993	SP455	9 +3fr multi	60	60
B994	SP455	14 +6fr multi	1.00	1.00
B995	SP455	17 +8fr multi	1.40	1.40
B996	SP455	25 +10fr multi	1.75	1.75
		Nos. B992-B996 (5)	5.15	5.15

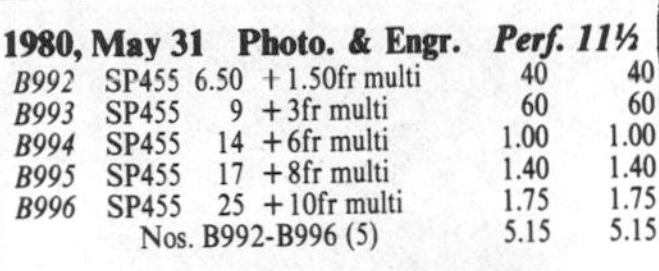

Miner, by Constantine Meunier—SP456

Seal of Bishop Notger, First Prince-Bishop—SP457

Designs: 9fr+3fr, Brewer, 16th century, from St. Lambert's reliquary (vert.). 25fr+10fr, Virgin and Child, 13th century, St. John's Collegiate Church, Liége.

1980, Sept. 13 Photo. *Perf. 11½*

B997	SP456	9 +3fr multi	55	55
B998	SP456	17 +6fr multi	1.10	1.10
B999	SP456	25 +10fr multi	1.75	1.75

Souvenir Sheet

B1000	SP457	20 +10fr multi	2.00	2.00

Millennium of the Principality of Liége. No. B1000 has gray and brown margin showing baptism of Centurion Cornelius from baptismal font in St. Bartholomew's Church, Liége. Size: 150x100mm.

Visual and Oral Handicaps—SP458

International Year of the Disabled: 10fr+5fr, Cerebral handicap (vert.).

1981, Feb. 9 Photo. *Perf. 11½*

B1001	SP458	10 +5fr multi	70	70
B1002	SP458	25 +10fr multi	1.65	1.65

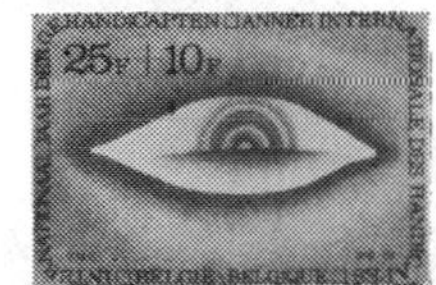

Dove with Red Cross Carrying Globe—SP459

Design: 10fr+5fr, Atomic model (vert.).

1981, Apr. 6 Photo. *Perf. 11½*

B1003	SP459	10 +5fr multi	70	70
B1004	SP459	25 +10fr multi	1.65	1.65

Red Cross and: 15th International Radiology Congress, Brussels, June 24-July 1 (No. B1003); international disaster relief (No. B1004).

Ovide Decroly—SP460

1981, June 1 Photo. *Perf. 11½*

B1005	SP460	35 +15fr multi	2.25	2.25

Ovide Decroly (1871-1932), developer of educational psychology.

Mounted Police Officer—SP461

Anniversaries: 9fr+4fr, Gendarmerie (State Police Force), 150th. 20fr+7fr, Carabineers Regiment, 150th. 40fr+20fr, Guides Regiment.

1981, Dec. 7 Photo *Perf. 11½*

B1006	SP461	9 +4fr multi	60	60
B1007	SP461	20 +7fr multi	1.25	1.25
B1008	SP461	40 +20fr multi	2.75	2.75

Billiards—SP462

1982, Mar. 29 Photo. *Perf. 11½*

B1009	SP462	6 +2fr shown	35	35
B1010	SP462	9 +4fr Cycling	55	55
B1011	SP462	10 +5fr Soccer	65	65
B1012	SP462	50 +14fr Yachting	2.65	2.65

Souvenir Sheet

B1013		Sheet of 4	4.25	4.25
a.		SP462 25fr like #B1009	1.20	1.20
b.		SP462 25fr like #B1010	1.20	1.20
c.		SP462 25fr like #B1011	1.20	1.20
d.		SP462 25fr like #B1012	1.20	1.20

No. B1013 shows designs in changed colors. Size: 105x100mm.

Christmas 1982—SP463

1982, Nov. 6

B1014	SP463	10 +1fr multi	60	45

Surtax was for tuberculosis research.

Belgica '82 Intl. Stamp Exhibition, Brussels, Dec. 11-19—SP464

Messengers (Prints). Nos. B1016-B1018 vert.

1982, Dec. 11 Photo. & Engr. *Perf. 11½*

B1015	SP464	7 +2fr multi	35	35
B1016	SP464	7.50 +2.50fr multi	40	40
B1017	SP464	10 +3fr multi	50	50
B1018	SP464	17 +7fr multi	95	95
B1019	SP464	20 +9fr multi	1.10	1.10
B1020	SP464	25 +10fr multi	1.40	1.40
		Nos. B1015-B1020 (6)	4.70	4.70

Souvenir Sheet

B1021	SP464	50 +25fr multi	3.00	3.00

No. B1021 contains one stamp (48x37mm.); multicolored margin continues design. Size: 125x90mm.

50th Anniv. of Catholic Charities—SP465

1983, Jan. 22 **Photo.** ***Perf. 11½***

B1022	SP465	10 +2fr multi	50	50

Mountain Climbing—SP466

1983, Mar. 7 **Photo.**

B1023	SP466	12 +3fr shown	60	60
B1024	SP466	20 +5fr Hiking	1.00	1.00

Surtax was for Red Cross.

Madonna by Jef Wauters—SP467

1983, Nov. 21 **Photo.** ***Perf. 11½***

B1025	SP467	11 +1fr multi	45	45

Rifles Uniform—SP468

1983, Dec. 5 **Photo.** ***Perf. 11½***

B1026	SP468	8 +2fr shown	38	38
B1027	SP468	11 +2fr Lancers uniform	50	50
B1028	SP468	50 +12fr Grenadiers uniform	2.25	2.25

Type of 1984

1984, Mar. 3 **Photo.** ***Perf. 11½***

B1029	A495	8 +2fr Judo, horiz.	40	40
B1030	A495	12 +3fr Wind surfing	60	60

50th Anniv. of Natl. Lottery—SP469

1984, Mar. 31 **Photo.** ***Perf. 11½***

B1031	SP469	12 +3fr multi	60	60

Brussels Modern Art Museum Opening—SP470

Paintings: 8fr+2fr, Les Masques Singuliers, by James Ensor. 12fr+3fr, Empire des Lumieres, by Rene Magritte. 22fr+5fr, The End, by Jan Cox. 50fr+13fr, Rhythm No. 6, by Jo Delahaut.

1984, Sept. 1 **Photo.**

B1032	SP470	8 +2fr multi	40	40
B1033	SP470	12 +3fr multi	60	60
B1034	SP470	22 +5fr multi	1.10	1.10
B1035	SP470	50 +13fr multi	2.50	2.50

Child with Parents—SP471

1984, Nov. 3 **Photo.**

B1036	SP471	10 +2fr shown	48	48
B1037	SP471	12 +3fr Siblings	60	60
B1038	SP471	15 +3fr Merry-go-round	72	72

Surtax was for children's programs.

Christmas 1984—SP472

1984, Dec. 1

B1039	SP472	12 +1fr Three Kings	52	52

Belgian Red Cross Blood Transfusion Service, 50th Anniv.—SP473

1985, Mar. 4 **Photo.** ***Perf. 11½***

B1040	SP473	9 +2fr Tree	38	38
B1041	SP473	23 +5fr Hearts	90	90

Surtax was for the Belgian Red Cross.

Solidarity—SP474

Castles.

1985, Nov. 4 **Photo. & Engr.**

B1042	SP474	9 + 2fr Trazegnies	42	42
B1043	SP474	12 + 3fr Laarne	58	58
B1044	SP474	23 + 5fr Turnhout	1.00	1.00
B1045	SP474	50 + 12fr Colonster	2.50	2.50

Christmas 1985, New Year 1986—SP475

Painting: Miniature from the Book of Hours, by Jean duc de Berry.

1985, Nov. 25 **Photo.**

B1046	SP475	12 + 1fr multi	50	50

King Baudouin Foundation—SP476

1986, Mar. 24 **Photo.**

B1047	SP476	12 + 3fr Emblem	65	65

Surtax for the foundation.

Madonna—SP477

Paintings by Hubert van Eyck (c. 1370-1426).

1986, Apr. 7 **Photo.** ***Perf. 11½***

B1048	SP477	9 + 2fr shown	48	48
B1049	SP477	13 + 3fr Christ in Majesty	68	68
B1050	SP477	24 + 6fr St. John the Baptist	1.25	1.25

Souvenir Sheet

Adoration of the Mystic Lamb, St. Bavon Cathedral Altarpiece, Ghent—SP478

B1051	SP478	50 + 12fr shown	2.75	2.75

Surtax for cultural organizations. No. B1051 has multicolored margin continuing design. Size: 93x150mm.

Antique Automobiles—SP479

1986, Nov. 3 **Photo.**

B1052	SP479	9 + 2fr Lenoir, 1863	55	55
B1053	SP479	13 + 3fr Pipe de Tourisme, 1911	80	80
B1054	SP479	24 + 6fr Minerva 22 HP, 1930	1.50	1.50
B1055	SP479	26 + 6fr FN 8 Cylinder, 1931	1.60	1.60

Christmas 1986, New Year 1987—SP480

1986, Nov. 24 **Photo.**

B1056	SP480	13 + 1fr Village in winter	68	68

Natl. Red Cross

SP482

European Conservation Year

SP483

Nobel Prize winners for physiology (1938) and medicine (1974): No. B1058, Corneille Heymans (1892-1968). No. B1059, A. Claude (1899-1983).

1987, Feb. 16 **Photo. & Engr.** ***Perf. 11½***

B1058	SP482	13 + 3fr	88	65
B1059	SP482	24 + 6fr	1.65	1.25

1987, Mar. 16 **Photo.**

B1060	SP483	9 + 2fr Bee orchid	60	45
B1061	SP483	24 + 6fr Horseshoe bat	1.65	1.25
B1062	SP483	26 + 6fr Peregrine falcon	1.75	1.30

AIR POST STAMPS.

Fokker FVII/3m over Ostend
AP1

Designs: 1.50fr, Plane over St. Hubert. 2fr, over Namur. 5fr, over Brussels.

Photogravure.

1930, Apr. 30 Perf. 11½ Unwmkd.

No.	Type	Description	Unused	Used
C1	AP1	50c blue	50	45
C2	AP1	1.50fr blk brn	4.00	4.75
C3	AP1	2fr dp grn	3.75	65
C4	AP1	5fr brn lake	3.50	1.10

1930, Dec. 5

No.	Type	Description	Unused	Used
C5	AP1	5fr dk vio	45.00	45.00

Issued for use on a mail carrying flight from Brussels to Leopoldville, Belgian Congo, starting Dec. 7.
Nos. C1-C5 exist imperforate.

Nos. C2 and C4 Surcharged in Carmine or Blue

1Fr 1Fr

1935, May 23

No.	Type	Description	Unused	Used
C6	AP1	1fr on 1.50fr blk brn (C)	90	90
C7	AP1	4fr on 5fr brn lake (Bl)	13.00	8.00

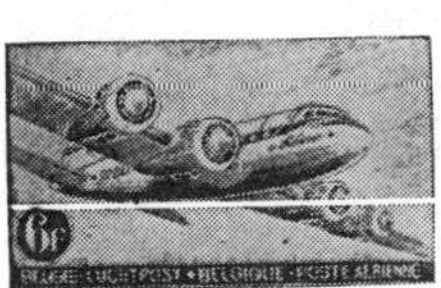

DC-4 Skymaster, Sabena Airline
AP5

1946-54 Engraved Perf. 11½

No.	Type	Description	Unused	Used
C8	AP5	6fr blue	75	32
C9	AP5	8.50fr vio brn	1.00	65
C10	AP5	50fr yel grn	5.00	75
a.		Perf. 12x11½ ('54)	160.00	1.10
C11	AP5	100fr gray	8.00	1.00
a.		Perf. 12x11½ ('54)	90.00	1.50

The French and Flemish inscriptions are transposed on Nos. C9 and C11.

Evolution of Postal Transportation
AP6

1949, July 1

No.	Type	Description	Unused	Used
C12	AP6	50fr dk brn	17.50	20.00

Centenary of Belgian postage stamps.

Glider—AP7

Design: 7fr, "Tipsy" plane.

1951, June 18 Photo. Perf. 13½

No.	Type	Description	Unused	Used
C12A	AP7	Strip of 2 + label	55.00	60.00
b.		6fr dk bl	20.00	25.00
c.		7fr car rose	20.00	25.00

For the 50th anniversary of the Aero Club of Belgium. The label is inscribed "1901 — 1951 + 37FR. BELGIE BELGIQUE" and carries the club emblem. The strip sold for 50fr.

1951, July 25 Perf. 13½

No.	Type	Description	Unused	Used
C13	AP7	6fr sepia	3.75	15
C14	AP7	7fr Prus grn	3.00	95

United Nations Issue

Types of Regular Issue, 1958

Designs: 5fr, International Civil Aviation Organization. 6fr, World Meteorological Organization. 7.50fr, Protection of Refugees. 8fr, General Agreement on Tariffs and Trade. 9fr, UNICEF. 10fr, Atomic Energy Agency.

Engraved.

1958, Apr. 17 Perf. 11½ Unwmkd.

No.	Type	Description	Unused	Used
C15	A137	5fr dl bl	32	55
C16	A136	6fr yel grn	55	1.00
C17	A137	7.50fr lilac	32	55
C18	A136	8fr sepia	32	55
C19	A137	9fr carmine	75	1.40
C20	A136	10fr redsh brn	1.00	1.65
		Nos. C15-C20 (6)	3.26	5.70

World's Fair, Brussels, Apr. 17-Oct. 19. See note after No. 476.

AIR POST SEMI-POSTAL STAMPS.

American Soldier in Combat
SPAP1

Engraved.

Perf. 11x11½

1946, June 15 Unwmkd.

No.	Type	Description	Unused	Used
CB1	SPAP1	17.50fr +62.50fr dl brn	1.10	1.75
CB2	SPAP1	17.50fr +62.50fr dl gray grn	1.10	1.75

The French and Flemish inscriptions are transposed on No. CB2. The surtax was to erect an American memorial at Bastogne.

An overprint, "Hommage a Roosevelt", was privately applied to Nos. CB1 and CB2 in 1947 by the Association Belgo-Americaine.

In 1950 another private overprint was applied, in red, to Nos. CB1-2. It consists of "16-12-1944, 25-1-1945, Dedication July 16, 1950" and outlines of the American eagle emblem and the Bastogne Memorial. Similar overprints were applied to Nos. 265 and 345.

Flight Allegory
SPAP2

1946, Sept. 7 Perf. 11½

No.	Type	Description	Unused	Used
CB3	SPAP2	2fr +8fr brt vio	60	1.00

The surtax was for the benefit of aviation.

A particular stamp may be scarce, but if few want it, its market potential may remain relatively low.

Nos. B417-B425 Surcharged in Various Arrangements in Red or Dark Blue

POSTE AERIENNE
LUCHTPOST
1F 2F

LUCHTPOST
POSTE AERIENNE
1F +2F

Type I. Top line "POSTE AERIENNE."
Type II. Top line "LUCHTPOST."

1947, May 18 Photo. Perf. 11½

No.	Type	Description	Unused	Used
CB4	SP227	1fr +2fr on 65c+75c dk bl (R)	1.00	1.40
a.		Type II	1.00	1.40
CB5	SP228	1.50fr +2.50 on 1.35+2 brn (Bl)	1.00	1.40
a.		Type II	1.00	1.40
CB6	SP229	2fr +45fr on 1.75fr+18fr rose brn (Bl)	1.00	1.40
a.		Type II	1.00	1.40
CB7	SP230	1fr +2fr on 65c+75c vio (R)	1.00	1.40
a.		Type II	1.00	1.40
CB8	SP231	1.50fr +2.50fr on 1.35fr+2fr dk org brn (Bl)	1.00	1.40
a.		Type II	1.00	1.40
CB9	SP232	2fr +45fr on 1.75fr+18fr car rose (Bl)	1.00	1.40
a.		Type II	1.00	1.40
CB10	SP233	1fr +2fr on 65c+75c dk sl grn (R)	1.00	1.40
a.		Type II	1.00	1.40
CB11	SP234	1.50fr +2.50fr on 1.35fr+2fr dk vio bl (R)	1.00	1.40
a.		Type II	1.00	1.40
CB12	SP235	2fr +45fr on 1.75fr+18fr dp car (Bl)	1.00	1.40
a.		Type II	1.00	1.40
		Nos. CB4-CB12, CB4a-CB12a (18)	18.00	25.20

In 1948 Nos. CB4-CB12 and CB4a-CB12a were punched with the letters "IMABA," and the inscription "Imaba du 21 au 29 aout 1948" was applied to the backs. Price $20.

Helicopter Leaving Airport
SPAP3

1950, Aug. 7

No.	Type	Description	Unused	Used
CB13	SPAP3	7fr +3fr bl	6.75	9.50

The surtax was for the National Aeronautical Committee.

SPECIAL DELIVERY STAMPS

From 1874 to 1903 certain hexagonal telegraph stamps were used as special delivery stamps.

Town Hall, Brussels SD1 — **Eupen** SD2

Designs: 2.35fr, Street in Ghent. 3.50fr, Bishop's Palace, Liege. 5.25fr, Notre Dame Cathedral, Antwerp.

Photogravure.

1929 Perf. 11½. Unwmkd.

No.	Type	Description	Unused	Used
E1	SD1	1.75fr dk bl	80	32
E2	SD1	2.35fr carmine	2.25	45
E3	SD1	3.50fr dk vio	6.25	10.00
E4	SD1	5.25fr ol grn	6.25	7.25

1931

No.	Type	Description	Unused	Used
E5	SD2	2.45fr dk grn	17.50	2.75
		Nos. E1-E5 (5)	33.05	20.77

No. E5 Surcharged in Red 2Fr 50

1932

No.	Type	Description	Unused	Used
E6	SD2	2.50fr on 2.45fr dk grn	13.00	1.65

POSTAGE DUE STAMPS.

D1 D2

Typographed.

1870 Perf. 15. Unwmkd.

No.	Type	Description	Unused	Used
J1	D1	10c green	5.50	2.25
a.		Half used as 5c on piece		6.75
J2	D1	20c ultra	25.00	3.50

1895-09 Perf. 14.

No.	Type	Description	Unused	Used
J3	D2	5c yel grn	22	22
J4	D2	10c org brn	6.75	1.75
J5	D2	10c car ('00)	22	22
J6	D2	20c ol grn	22	22
J7	D2	30c pale bl ('09)	45	35
J8	D2	50c yel brn	15.00	5.50
J9	D2	50c gray ('00)	90	65
J10	D2	1fr carmine	32.50	17.50
J11	D2	1fr ocher ('00)	11.00	7.25
		Nos. J3-J11 (9)	67.26	33.66

1916 Redrawn

No.	Type	Description	Unused	Used
J12	D2	5c bl grn	9.00	4.50
J13	D2	10c carmine	9.00	3.50
J14	D2	20c dp gray grn	22.50	11.50
J15	D2	30c brt bl	3.50	2.75
J16	D2	50c gray	45.00	37.50
		Nos. J12-J16 (5)	89.00	59.75

In the redrawn stamps the lions have a heavy, colored outline. There is a thick vertical line at the outer edge of the design on each side.

D3 D4

1919 Perf. 14

No.	Type	Description	Unused	Used
J17	D3	5c green	55	40
J18	D3	10c carmine	1.25	35
J19	D3	20c gray grn	10.00	1.00
J20	D3	30c brt bl	2.00	30
J21	D3	50c gray	4.00	40
		Nos. J17-J21 (5)	17.80	2.45

1922-32

No.	Type	Description	Unused	Used
J22	D4	5c dk gray	12	12
J23	D4	10c green	15	12
J24	D4	20c dp brn	18	15
J25	D4	30c ver ('24)	32	15
a.		30c rose red	1.10	65
J26	D4	40c red brn ('25)	32	18
J27	D4	50c ultra	2.75	18
J28	D4	70c red brn ('29)	40	18
J29	D4	1fr vio ('25)	65	18
J30	D4	1fr rose lil ('32)	55	18
J31	D4	1.20fr ol grn ('29)	95	65
J32	D4	1.50fr ol grn ('32)	95	65
J33	D4	2fr vio ('29)	1.10	28
J34	D4	3.50fr dp bl ('29)	1.40	32
		Nos. J22-J34 (13)	9.84	3.34

1934-46 *Perf. 14x13½.*

J35 D4 35c grn ('35) 55 65
J36 D4 50c slate 32 18
J37 D4 60c car ('38) 55 40
J38 D4 80c sl ('38) 45 28
J39 D4 1.40fr gray ('35) 95 60
J39A D4 3fr org brn ('46) 1.65 90
J39B D4 7fr brt red vio ('46) 3.25 4.50
Nos. J35-J39B (7) 7.72 7.51

See also Nos. J54-J61.

D5 D6

1945 Typographed *Perf. 12½*

Inscribed "TE BETALEN" at Top.

J40 D5 10c gray ol 10 15
J41 D5 20c ultra 10 15
J42 D5 30c carmine 8 10
J43 D5 40c blk vio 8 10
J44 D5 50c dl bl grn 10 10
J45 D5 1fr sepia 15 10
J46 D5 2fr red org 18 15

Inscribed "A PAYER" at Top.

J47 D5 10c gray ol 10 15
J48 D5 20c ultra 10 15
J49 D5 30c carmine 8 10
J50 D5 40c blk vio 8 10
J51 D5 50c dl bl grn 10 10
J52 D5 1fr sepia 15 10
J53 D5 2fr red org 18 15
Nos. J40-J53 (14) 1.58 1.70

Type of 1922-32.

1949 Typographed. *Perf. 14x13½.*

J54 D4 65c emerald 6.25 8.00
J55 D4 1.80fr red 11.00 11.00
J56 D4 5fr red brn 3.00 65
J57 D4 8fr lil rose 7.50 10.00
J58 D4 10fr dk vio 6.25 8.00
Nos. J54-J58 (5) 34.00 37.65

1953

J59 D4 1.60fr lil rose 7.50 11.00
J60 D4 2.40fr gray lil 6.50 3.00
J61 D4 4fr dp bl 7.50 1.75

1966-70 Photogravure

J62 D6 1fr brt pink 8 5
J63 D6 2fr bl grn 10 10
J64 D6 3fr blue 15 13
J65 D6 5fr purple 28 25
J66 D6 6fr bis brn 32 32
J67 D6 7fr red org ('70) 45 38
J68 D6 20fr sl grn 1.75 1.40
Nos. J62-J68 (7) 3.13 2.63

MILITARY STAMPS

King Baudouin

M1 M2

Photogravure

1967, July 17 *Perf. 11* Unwmkd.

M1 M1 1.50fr grnsh gray 75 45

1971-75 Engraved *Perf. 11½*

M2 M2 1.75fr green 2.25 1.10
M3 M2 2.25fr gray grn ('72) 2.00 75
M4 M2 2.50fr gray grn ('74) 75 65
M5 M2 3.25fr vio brn ('75) 60 32

Nos. M1-M3 are luminescent, Nos. M4-M5 are not.

MILITARY PARCEL POST STAMP.

Type of Parcel Post Stamp of 1938 Surcharged with New Value and "M" in Blue.

1939 *Perf. 13½* Unwmkd.

MQ1 PP19 3fr on 5.50fr cop red 45 20

OFFICIAL STAMPS.

For franking the official correspondence of the Administration of the Belgian National Railways.

Regular Issue of 1921-27 Overprinted in Black

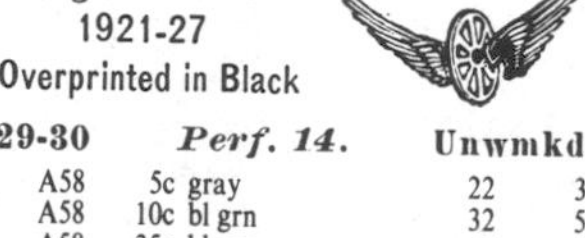

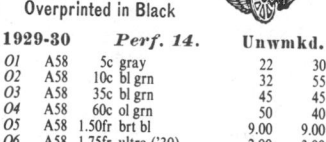

1929-30 *Perf. 14.* Unwmkd.

O1 A58 5c gray 22 30
O2 A58 10c bl grn 32 55
O3 A58 35c bl grn 45 45
O4 A58 60c ol grn 50 40
O5 A58 1.50fr brt bl 9.00 9.00
O6 A58 1.75fr ultra ('30) 2.00 3.00
Nos. O1-O6 (6) 12.49 13.70

Same Overprint, in Red or Black, on Regular Issues of 1929-30.

1929-31

O7 A63 5c sl (R) 22 40
O8 A63 10c ol grn (R) 45 50
O9 A63 25c rose red (Bk) 1.25 1.10
O10 A63 35c dp grn (R) 1.65 65
O11 A63 40c red vio (Bk) 1.10 55
O12 A63 50c dp bl (R) ('31) 70 40
O13 A63 60c rose (Bk) 6.00 7.50
O14 A63 70c org brn (Bk) 4.00 1.40
O15 A63 75c blk vio (R) ('31) 3.50 1.10
Nos. O7-O15 (9) 18.87 13.60

Overprinted on Regular Issue of 1932.

1932

O16 A73 10c ol grn (R) 75 90
O17 A74 35c dp grn 13.00 1.10
O18 A71a 75c bis brn (R) 2.25 40

Overprinted on No. 262 in Red.

1935 *Perf. 13½x14*

O19 A80 70c ol blk 2.75 40

Regular Stamps of 1935-36 Overprinted in Red.

1936-38 *Perf. 13½, 13½x14, 14.*

O20 A82 10c ol bis 18 35
O21 A82 35c green 28 40
O22 A82 50c dk bl 55 35
O23 A83 70c brown 1.75 75

Overprinted in Black or Red on Regular Issue of 1938.

Perf. 13½x14.

O24 A82 40c red vio (Bk) 35 35
O25 A85 75c ol gray (R) 80 30
Nos. O20-O25 (6) 3.91 2.50

Regular Issues of 1935-41 Overprinted in Red or Dark Blue

1941-44 *Perf. 14, 14x13½, 13½x14.*

O26 A82 10c ol bis 12 15
a. Inverted overprint 40.00
O27 A82 40c red vio 55 75
O28 A82 50c dk bl 12 15
a. Inverted overprint
O29 A83a 1fr rose car (Bl) 45 35
O30 A85 1fr rose pink (Bl) 10 12
O31 A83a 2.25fr grnsh blk ('44) 28 50
O32 A84 2.25fr gray vio 45 70
Nos. O26-O32 (7) 2.07 2.72

Nos. O21, O23 and O25 Surcharged with New Values in Black or Red.

1942

O33 A82 10c on 35c grn 18 32
O34 A83 50c on 70c brn 15 18
O35 A85 50c on 75c ol gray (R) 15 18

O1 O2

1946-48 *Perf. 14.* Unwmkd.

O36 O1 10c ol bis 20 20
O37 O1 20c brt vio 1.75 75
O38 O1 50c dk bl 25 22
O39 O1 65c red lil ('48) 2.75 1.10
O40 O1 75c lil rose 20 30
O41 O1 90c brn vio 3.50 50
Nos. O36-O41 (6) 8.65 3.07

Types A99, A101 and A102 with "B" Emblem Added to Design.

1948 *Perf. 11½.*

O42 A99 1.35fr red brn 2.50 1.10
O43 A99 1.75fr dk gray grn 3.00 38
O44 A101 3fr brt red vio 16.00 5.25
O45 A102 3.15fr dp bl 6.75 11.00
O46 A102 4fr brt ultra 12.50 21.00
Nos. O42-O46 (5) 40.75 38.73

1953-66 Typo. *Perf. 13½x14*

O47 O2 10c orange 65 85
O48 O2 20c red lil 75 60
O49 O2 30c gray grn ('58) 75 1.00
O50 O2 40c ol gray 50 40
O51 O2 50c lt bl 70 50
O51A O2 60c lil rose ('66) 1.10 90
O52 O2 65c red lil 27.50 42.50
O53 O2 80c emerald 1.50 85
O54 O2 90c dp bl 3.00 1.25
O55 O2 1fr rose 38 40
Nos. O47-O55 (10) 36.83 49.25

King Baudouin

O3 O4

1954-70 Photogravure *Perf. 11½*

O56 O3 1.50fr gray 1.00 38
O57 O3 2fr rose red 37.50 75
O58 O3 2fr bl grn ('59) 75 30
O59 O3 2.50fr red brn ('58) 24.00 75
O60 O3 3fr red lil ('58) 2.00 60
O61 O3 3.50fr yel grn ('70) 1.10 60
O62 O3 4fr brt bl 2.25 1.00
O63 O3 6fr car rose ('58) 5.00 1.65
Nos. O56-O63 (8) 73.60 6.03

Type of 1953-66 Redrawn

1970-75 Typo. *Perf. 13½x14*

O66 O2 1.50fr grnsh gray ('75) 18 10
O68 O2 2.50fr brown 18 10

1971-73 Engraved *Perf. 11½*

O71 O4 3.50fr org brn ('73) 1.75 1.25
O72 O4 4.50fr brn ('73) 1.10 90
O73 O4 7fr red 45 40
O74 O4 15fr violet 90 90

Nos. O71-O74 are on luminescent paper.

1974-80

O75 O4 3fr yel grn 5.75 1.75
O76 O4 4fr blue 2.25 1.10
O77 O4 4.50fr grnsh bl ('75) 65 38
O78 O4 5fr lilac 30 30
O79 O4 6fr car ('78) 40 40
O80 O4 6.50fr blk ('76) 65 60
O81 O4 8fr bluish blk ('78) 50 45
O82 O4 9fr lt red brn ('80) 50 45
O83 O4 10fr rose car 55 50
O84 O4 25fr lil ('76) 1.40 1.40
O85 O4 30fr org brn ('78) 1.90 1.75
Nos. O75-O85 (11) 14.85 9.08

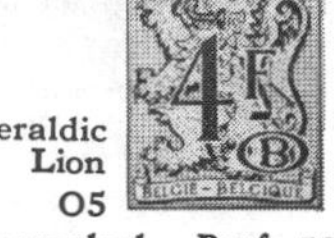

Heraldic Lion
O5

1977-82 Typographed *Perf. 13½x14*

O87 O5 50c brn ('82) 5 5
O92 O5 1fr lil ('82) 8 8
O94 O5 2fr org ('82) 12 8
O95 O5 4fr red brn 30 25
O96 O5 5fr grn ('80) 35 28
Nos. O87-O96 (5) 90 74

NEWSPAPER STAMPS.

Parcel Post Stamps of 1923-27 Overprinted

JOURNAUX DAGBLADEN 1928

Perf. 14½x14, 14x14½.

1928 Unwmkd.

P1 PP12 10c vermilion 18 30
P2 PP12 20c turq bl 22 30
P3 PP12 40c ol grn 22 30
P4 PP12 60c orange 45 60
P5 PP12 70c dk brn 28 30
P6 PP12 80c violet 35 50
P7 PP12 90c slate 1.50 1.40
P8 PP13 1fr brt bl 55 40
a. 1fr ultra 8.00 3.75
P10 PP13 2fr ol grn 1.00 42
P11 PP13 3fr org red 1.10 60
P12 PP13 4fr rose 1.40 80
P13 PP13 5fr violet 1.40 75
P14 PP13 6fr bis brn 2.75 1.25
P15 PP13 7fr orange 3.25 1.65
P16 PP13 8fr dk brn 3.75 2.00
P17 PP13 9fr red vio 6.75 2.25
P18 PP13 10fr bl grn 5.75 2.00
P19 PP13 20fr magenta 10.00 5.00
Nos. P1-P8, P10-P19 (18) 40.90 20.82

Parcel Post Stamps of 1923-28 Overprinted

JOURNAUX DAGBLADEN

1929-31

P20 PP12 10c vermilion 28 25
P21 PP12 20c turq bl 28 25
P22 PP12 40c ol grn 35 30
a. Inverted overprint
P23 PP12 60c orange 45 50
P24 PP12 70c dk brn 55 30
P25 PP12 80c violet 65 35
P26 PP12 90c gray 1.75 1.40
P27 PP13 1fr ultra 60 38
a. 1fr brt bl 3.00 70
P28 PP13 1.10fr org brn ('31) 9.00 2.00
P29 PP13 1.50fr gray vio ('31) 9.00 2.75
P30 PP13 2fr ol grn 1.75 38
P31 PP13 2.10fr sl gray ('31) 32.50 13.00
P32 PP13 3fr org red 2.00 60
P33 PP13 4fr rose 2.00 1.00
P34 PP13 5fr violet 3.00 80
P35 PP13 6fr bis brn 3.50 1.40
P36 PP13 7fr orange 3.75 1.40
P37 PP13 8fr dk brn 3.75 1.50
P38 PP13 9fr red vio 5.00 2.25
P39 PP13 10fr bl grn 3.75 1.50
P40 PP13 20fr magenta 12.50 6.50
Nos. P20-P40 (21) 96.41 38.81

PARCEL POST AND RAILWAY STAMPS.

Prices for used stamps are for copies with railway cancellations. Stamps with postal cancellations sell for twice as much.

Coat of Arms
PP1

Typographed.

1879–82 *Perf. 14* **Unwmkd.**

Q1	PP1	10c vio brn	42.50	2.75
Q2	PP1	20c blue	140.00	12.50
Q3	PP1	25c grn ('81)	175.00	7.00
Q4	PP1	50c carmine	1,200.	5.25
Q5	PP1	80c yellow	1,250.	37.50
Q6	PP1	1fr gray ('82)	125.00	9.50

Used copies of Nos. Q1–Q6 with pinholes, a normal state, sell for half price.

PP2

Most of the stamps of 1882-1902 (Nos. Q7 to Q28) are without watermark. Twice in each sheet of 100 stamps they have one of three watermarks: (1) A winged wheel and "Chemins de Fer de l'Etat Belge", (2) Coat of Arms of Belgium and "Royaume de Belgique", (3) Larger Coat of Arms, without inscription.

1882-94 *Perf. 15x14½.*

Q7	PP2	10c brn ('86)	14.00	90
Q8	PP2	15c gray ('94)	12.00	9.00
Q9	PP2	20c bl ('86)	60.00	3.00
a.		20c ultra ('90)	55.00	3.00
Q10	PP2	25c yel grn ('91)	52.50	3.50
a.		25c bl grn ('87)	62.50	3.50
Q11	PP2	50c carmine	60.00	45
Q12	PP2	80c brnsh buff	52.50	65
Q13	PP2	80c lemon	65.00	2.75
Q14	PP2	1fr lavender	325.00	2.75
Q15	PP2	2fr yel buff ('94)	215.00	47.50

Counterfeits exist.

PP3

Name of engraver below frame.

1895–97

Numerals in Black, except 1fr, 2fr.

Q16	PP3	10c red brn ('96)	10.00	40
Q17	PP3	15c gray	9.50	7.25
Q18	PP3	20c blue	20.00	90
Q19	PP3	25c green	20.00	1.25
Q20	PP3	50c carmine	22.50	40
Q21	PP3	60c vio ('96)	37.50	55
Q22	PP3	80c ol yel ('96)	32.50	55
Q23	PP3	1fr lil brn	140.00	90
Q24	PP3	2fr yel buff ('97)	150.00	4.50

Counterfeits exist.

1902 **Numerals in Black.**

Q25	PP3	30c orange	22.50	1.40
Q26	PP3	40c green	25.00	1.40
Q27	PP3	70c blue	40.00	70
a.		Numerals omitted	*1,000.*	
Q28	PP3	90c red	47.50	90

Winged Wheel
PP4

Without engraver's name.

1902–14 *Perf. 15*

Q29	PP3	10c yel brn & sl	18	12
Q30	PP3	15c sl & vio	28	15
Q31	PP3	20c ultra & yel brn	18	12
Q32	PP3	25c yel grn & red	28	15
Q33	PP3	30c org & bl grn	28	15
Q34	PP3	35c bis & bl grn ('12)	50	30
Q35	PP3	40c bl grn & vio	28	15
Q36	PP3	50c pale rose & vio	18	12
Q37	PP3	55c lil brn & ultra ('14)	50	30
Q38	PP3	60c vio & red	28	15
Q39	PP3	70c bl & red	22	12
Q40	PP3	80c lem & vio brn	18	12
Q41	PP3	90c red & yel grn	28	15
Q42	PP4	1fr vio brn & org	28	15
Q43	PP4	1.10fr rose & blk ('06)	30	20
Q44	PP4	2fr ocher & bl grn	30	20
Q45	PP4	3fr blk & ultra	50	30
Q46	PP4	4fr yel grn & red ('13)	1.90	1.10
Q47	PP4	5fr org & bl grn ('13)	80	80
Q48	PP4	10fr ol yel & brn vio ('13)	1.40	85
		Nos. Q29-Q48 (20)	9.10	5.70

Exist imperforate.

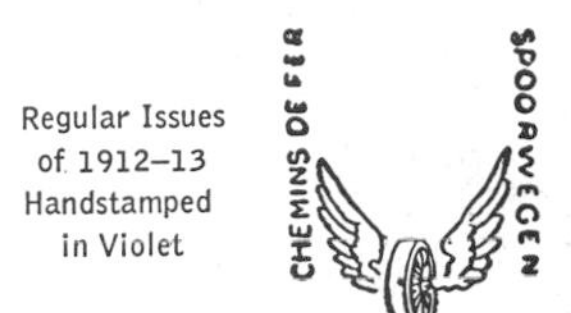

Regular Issues of 1912–13 Handstamped in Violet

1915 *Perf. 14*

Q49	A42	5c green	120.00	120.00
Q50	A43	10c red	700.00	700.00
Q51	A45	10c red	120.00	120.00
a.		With engraver's name	450.00	450.00
Q52	A43	20c ol grn	*1,100.*	*1,100.*
Q53	A45	20c ol grn	140.00	140.00
a.		With engraver's name	450.00	450.00
Q54	A45	25c ultra	140.00	140.00
a.		With engraver's name	450.00	450.00
Q55	A43	35c bis brn	200.00	200.00
Q55A	A43	40c green	*1,600.*	*1,600.*
Q56	A45	40c green	140.00	140.00
Q57	A43	50c gray	165.00	165.00
Q58	A43	1fr orange	210.00	210.00
Q59	A43	2fr violet	*1,200.*	*1,200.*
Q60	A44	5fr plum	*2,350.*	*2,350.*

Excellent forgeries of this overprint exist.

Locomotive
PP5 PP6

1916 **Lithographed** *Perf. 13½*

Q61	PP5	10c pale bl	90	28
Q62	PP5	15c ol grn	1.10	55
Q63	PP5	20c red	1.65	55
Q64	PP5	25c lt brn	1.65	55
Q65	PP5	30c lilac	1.10	45
Q66	PP5	35c gray	1.10	45
Q67	PP5	40c org yel	2.25	1.40
Q68	PP5	50c bister	2.00	45
Q69	PP5	55c brown	2.25	2.00
Q70	PP5	60c gray vio	1.65	45
Q71	PP5	70c green	1.65	45
Q72	PP5	80c red brn	1.65	45
Q73	PP5	90c blue	1.65	45
Q74	PP6	1fr gray	1.65	45
Q75	PP6	1.10fr ultra (*Franken*)	25.00	25.00
Q76	PP6	2fr red	18.00	45
Q77	PP6	3fr violet	18.50	45
Q78	PP6	4fr emerald	30.00	90
Q79	PP6	5fr brown	30.00	1.40
Q80	PP6	10fr orange	30.00	90
		Nos. Q61-Q80 (20)	173.75	38.03

Type of 1916 Inscribed "FRANK" instead of "FRANKEN."

1920

Q81	PP6	1.10fr ultra	2.00	45

PP7 PP8

1920 *Perf. 14.*

Q82	PP7	10c bl grn	1.25	40
Q83	PP7	15c ol grn	1.50	1.25
Q84	PP7	20c red	1.50	40
Q85	PP7	25c gray brn	2.00	1.00
Q86	PP7	30c red vio	12.50	10.00
Q87	PP7	40c pale org	8.50	80
Q88	PP7	50c bister	6.00	60
Q89	PP7	55c pale brn	4.75	2.00
Q90	PP7	60c dk vio	7.50	1.00
Q91	PP7	70c green	11.00	1.65
Q92	PP7	80c red brn	32.50	1.40
Q93	PP7	90c dl bl	6.00	60
Q94	PP8	1fr gray	57.50	1.00
Q95	PP8	1.10fr ultra	16.00	3.25
Q96	PP8	1.20fr dk grn	12.50	50
Q97	PP8	1.40fr blk brn	7.25	50
Q98	PP8	2fr vermilion	62.50	80
Q99	PP8	3fr red vio	75.00	1.25
Q100	PP8	4fr yel grn	75.00	75
Q101	PP8	5fr bis brn	75.00	75
Q102	PP8	10fr brn org	75.00	75
		Nos. Q82-Q102 (21)	550.75	30.65

PP9

PP10

Types PP7 and PP9 differ in the position of the wheel and the tablet above it.

Types PP8 and PP10 differ in the bars below "FR".

There are many other variations in the designs.

1920-21 **Typographed.**

Q103	PP9	10c carmine	45	25
Q104	PP9	15c yel grn	42	25
Q105	PP9	20c bl grn	1.10	35
Q106	PP9	25c ultra	1.00	35
Q107	PP9	30c chocolate	1.25	35
Q108	PP9	35c org brn	1.40	45
Q109	PP9	40c orange	1.65	25
Q110	PP9	50c rose	1.65	25
Q111	PP9	55c yel ('21)	3.50	1.75
Q112	PP9	60c dl rose	1.65	25
Q113	PP9	70c emerald	3.25	30
Q114	PP9	80c violet	3.00	20
Q115	PP9	90c lemon	14.00	15.00
Q116	PP9	90c claret	6.75	60
Q117	PP10	1fr buff	7.00	50
Q118	PP10	1fr red brn	6.00	40
Q119	PP10	1.10fr ultra	2.25	75
Q120	PP10	1.20fr orange	3.00	20
Q121	PP10	1.40fr yellow	12.50	1.50
Q122	PP10	1.60fr turq bl	21.00	50
Q123	PP10	1.60fr emerald	50.00	50
Q124	PP10	2fr pale rose	24.00	30
Q125	PP10	3fr dp rose	21.00	30
Q126	PP10	4fr emerald	21.00	40
Q127	PP10	5fr lt vio	18.00	35
Q128	PP10	10fr lemon	115.00	3.75
Q129	PP10	10fr dk brn	19.00	28
Q130	PP10	15fr dp rose ('21)	19.00	35
Q131	PP10	20fr dk bl ('21)	275.00	2.50
		Nos. Q103-Q131 (29)	654.82	33.18

PP11

1922 **Engraved.** *Perf. 11½.*

Q132	PP11	2fr black	4.00	15
Q133	PP11	3fr brown	40.00	28
Q134	PP11	4fr green	10.00	18
Q135	PP11	5r claret	10.00	18
Q136	PP11	10fr yel brn	11.50	25
Q137	PP11	15fr rose red	11.50	35
Q138	PP11	20fr blue	70.00	38
		Nos. Q132-Q138 (7)	157.00	1.77

PP12

PP13

Perf. 14x13½, 13½x14.

1923–40 **Typographed**

Q139	PP12	5c red brn	28	35
Q140	PP12	10c vermilion	15	12
Q141	PP12	15c ultra	32	45
Q142	PP12	20c turq bl	15	10
Q143	PP12	30c brn vio ('27)	32	15
Q144	PP12	40c ol grn	28	10
Q145	PP12	50c mag ('27)	28	5
Q146	PP12	60c orange	32	15
Q147	PP12	70c dk brn ('24)	20	5
Q148	PP12	80c violet	28	10
Q149	PP12	90c sl ('27)	1.50	18
Q150	PP13	1fr ultra	42	5
Q151	PP13	1fr brt bl ('28)	85	10
Q152	PP13	1.10fr orange	4.25	18
Q153	PP13	1.50fr turq bl	4.75	35
Q154	PP13	1.70fr dp brn ('31)	1.10	25
Q155	PP13	1.80fr claret	8.00	25
Q156	PP13	2fr ol grn ('24)	40	25
Q157	PP13	2.10fr gray grn	8.50	38
Q158	PP13	2.40fr dp vio	8.50	55
Q159	PP13	2.70fr gray ('24)	17.00	25
Q160	PP13	3fr org red	65	12
Q161	PP13	3.30fr brn ('24)	18.00	38
Q162	PP13	4fr rose ('24)	85	15
Q163	PP13	5fr vio ('24)	1.25	15
Q163A	PP13	5fr brn vio ('40)	65	55
Q164	PP13	6fr bis brn ('27)	75	10
Q165	PP13	7fr org ('27)	1.25	10
Q166	PP13	8fr dp brn ('27)	1.10	12
Q167	PP13	9fr red vio ('27)	3.00	15
Q168	PP13	10fr bl grn ('27)	1.25	12
Q168A	PP13	10fr blk ('40)	3.50	4.00

Q169	PP13	20fr mag ('27)	2.75	12
Q170	PP13	30fr turq grn ('31)	8.75	25
Q171	PP13	40fr gray ('31)	60.00	45
Q172	PP13	50fr bis ('27)	13.00	30
		Nos. Q139-Q172 (36)	174.60	11.47

See Nos. Q239-Q262.

Stamps overprinted "Bagages Reisgoed" are revenues.

PP14

1924 Green Surcharge.

Q173	PP14	2.30fr on 2.40fr vio	4.50	25
a.		Inverted surcharge	57.50	

Type of Regular Issue of 1926-27 Overprinted

1928 *Perf. 14.*

Q174	A61	4fr buff	6.50	90
Q175	A61	5fr bister	6.50	1.10

Central P.O., Brussels
PP15

1929-30 Engraved *Perf. 11½*

Q176	PP15	3fr blk brn	1.75	22
Q177	PP15	4fr gray	1.75	15
Q178	PP15	5fr carmine	1.75	15
Q179	PP15	6fr vio brn ('30)	27.50	30.00

No. Q179 Surcharged in Blue

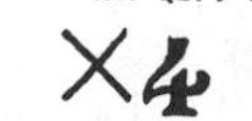

4X

1933

Q180	PP15	4(fr) on 6fr vio brn	27.50	28

Modern Locomotive
PP16

1934 Photogravure *Perf. 13½x14*

Q181	PP16	3fr dk grn	4.50	2.25
Q182	PP16	4fr red vio	1.40	12
Q183	PP16	5fr dp rose	5.00	12

Modern Railroad Train
PP17

Old Railroad Train
PP18

Perf. 14x13½, 13½x14.

1935 Engraved.

Q184	PP17	10c rose car	30	18
Q185	PP17	20c violet	38	15
Q186	PP17	30c blk brn	50	50
Q187	PP17	40c dk bl	60	20
Q188	PP17	50c org red	65	15
Q189	PP17	60c green	75	25
Q190	PP17	70c ultra	85	20
Q191	PP17	80c ol blk	75	25
Q192	PP17	90c rose lake	1.00	70
Q193	PP18	1fr brn vio	1.00	15
Q194	PP18	2fr gray blk	2.00	20
Q195	PP18	3fr red org	2.25	25
Q196	PP18	4fr vio brn	2.75	25
Q197	PP18	5fr plum	3.00	20
Q198	PP18	6fr dp grn	3.50	25
Q199	PP18	7fr dp vio	4.00	20
Q200	PP18	8fr ol blk	5.25	30
Q201	PP18	9fr dk bl	6.00	25
Q202	PP18	10fr car lake	6.00	20
Q203	PP18	20fr green	27.50	30
Q204	PP18	30fr violet	87.50	1.50
Q205	PP18	40fr blk brn	87.50	2.25
Q206	PP18	50fr rose car	100.00	1.75
Q207	PP18	100fr ultra	225.00	30.00
		Nos. Q184-Q207 (24)	569.03	40.63

Centenary of Belgian State Railway.

Winged Wheel
PP19

Surcharge in Red or Blue.

1938 Photogravure *Perf. 13½*

Q208	PP19	5fr on 3.50fr dk grn (R)	10.00	65
Q209	PP19	5fr on 4.50fr rose vio (Bl)	22	10
Q210	PP19	6fr on 5.50fr cop red (Bl)	50	15
a.		Half used as 3fr on piece		2.25

See also Nos. MQ1, Q297-Q299.

Symbolizing Unity Achieved Through Railroads
PP20

1939 Engraved *Perf. 13½x14*

Q211	PP20	20c redsh brn	4.50	5.00
Q212	PP20	50c vio bl	4.50	5.00
Q213	PP20	2fr rose red	4.50	5.00
Q214	PP20	9fr sl grn	4.50	5.00
Q215	PP20	10fr dk vio	4.50	5.00
		Nos. Q211-Q215 (5)	22.50	25.00

Issued in commemoration of the Railroad Exposition and Congress held at Brussels.

Parcel Post Stamps of 1925-27 Overprinted in Blue or Carmine

Perf. 14½x14, 14x14½.

1940 Unwmkd.

Q216	PP12	10c vermilion	12	10
Q217	PP12	20c turq bl (C)	12	10
Q218	PP12	30c brn vio	15	10
Q219	PP12	40c ol grn (C)	12	12
Q220	PP12	50c magenta	12	10
Q221	PP12	60c orange	25	30
Q222	PP12	70c dk brn	18	20
Q223	PP12	80c vio (C)	20	25
Q224	PP12	90c sl (C)	28	30
Q225	PP13	1fr ultra (C)	28	25
Q226	PP13	2fr ol grn (C)	28	25
Q227	PP13	3fr org red	28	25
Q228	PP13	4fr rose	28	25
Q229	PP13	5fr vio (C)	28	25
Q230	PP13	6fr bis brn	40	32
Q231	PP13	7fr orange	40	25
Q232	PP13	8fr dp brn	40	25
Q233	PP13	9fr red vio	40	25
Q234	PP13	10fr bl grn (C)	40	30
Q235	PP13	20fr magenta	1.10	30
Q236	PP13	30fr turq grn (C)	1.90	1.50
Q237	PP13	40fr gray (C)	2.75	3.75
Q238	PP13	50fr bister	3.25	2.00
		Nos. Q216-Q238 (23)	13.94	11.74

1941 Types of 1923-40.

Q239	PP12	10c dl ol	12	10
Q240	PP12	20c lt vio	12	10
Q241	PP12	30c fawn	12	10
Q242	PP12	40c dl bl	12	15
Q243	PP12	50c lt grn	12	5
Q244	PP12	60c gray	14	15
Q245	PP12	70c chlky grn	14	15
Q246	PP12	80c orange	18	25
Q247	PP12	90c rose lil	18	25
Q248	PP13	1fr lt yel grn	18	20
Q249	PP13	2fr vio brn	30	20
Q250	PP13	3fr slate	35	20
Q251	PP13	4fr dl ol	42	20
Q252	PP13	5fr rose lil	55	20
Q253	PP13	5fr black	80	35
Q254	PP13	6fr org ver	75	30
Q255	PP13	7fr lilac	75	15
Q256	PP13	8fr chlky grn	75	20
Q257	PP13	9fr blue	90	15
Q258	PP13	10fr rose lil	90	15
Q259	PP13	20fr mlky bl	2.00	15
Q260	PP13	30fr orange	4.75	35
Q261	PP13	40fr rose	5.50	40
Q262	PP13	50fr brt red vio	7.00	25
		Nos. Q239-Q262 (24)	27.14	4.75

Adjusting Tie Plates
PP21

Engineer at Throttle
PP22

Freight Station Interior
PP23

Signal and Electric Train
PP24

1942 Engraved *Perf. 14x13½*

Q263	PP21	9.20fr red org	60	80
Q264	PP22	12.30fr dp grn	60	85
Q265	PP23	14.30fr dk car	85	1.25

Perf. 11½.

Q266	PP24	100fr ultra	16.00	24.00

Engineer at Throttle
PP25

Adjusting Tie Plates
PP26

Freight Station Interior
PP27

1945-46 Photogravure Unwmkd.

Nos. Q268, Q270, Q272, Q274, Q287 and Q289 are inscribed "Belgique-Belgie", Nos. Q277, Q279, Q281 and Q283 are inscribed "Belgie-Belgique".

Q267	PP25	10c ol blk ('46)	20	5
Q268	PP25	20c dp vio	20	5
Q269	PP25	30c chnt brn ('46)	20	12
Q270	PP25	40c dp bl ('46)	20	10
Q271	PP25	50c pck grn	20	6
Q272	PP25	60c blk ('46)	22	15
Q273	PP25	70c emer ('46)	30	25
Q274	PP25	80c orange	50	20
Q275	PP25	90c brn vio ('46)	30	25
Q276	PP26	1fr bl grn ('46)	20	12
Q277	PP26	2fr blk brn	22	10
Q278	PP26	3fr grnsh blk ('46)	1.25	20
Q279	PP26	4fr dk bl	30	20
Q280	PP26	5fr sepia	30	5
Q281	PP26	6fr dk ol grn ('46)	1.50	15
Q282	PP26	7fr dk vio ('46)	50	18
Q283	PP26	8fr red org	50	10
Q284	PP26	9fr dp bl ('46)	65	7
Q285	PP27	10fr dk red ('46)	2.25	15
Q286	PP27	10fr sep ('46)	1.10	25
Q287	PP27	20fr dk yel grn ('46)	50	5
Q288	PP27	30fr dp vio	75	5
Q289	PP27	40fr rose pink	65	5
Q290	PP27	50fr brt bl ('46)	8.00	12
		Nos. Q267-Q290 (24)	20.99	3.07

Mercury
PP28

1945-46 *Perf. 13½x13*

Q291	PP28	3fr emer ('46)	45	25
Q292	PP28	5fr ultra	12	18
Q293	PP28	6fr red	18	12

Inscribed "Belgique-Belgie".

Q294	PP28	3fr emer ('46)	45	25
Q295	PP28	5fr ultra	12	18
Q296	PP28	6fr red	18	12
		Nos. Q291-Q296 (6)	1.50	1.10

Winged Wheel Type of 1938.
Carmine Surcharge.

1946 *Perf. 13½x14*

Q297	PP19	8fr on 5.50fr brn	65	15
Q298	PP19	10fr on 5.50fr dk bl	75	25
Q299	PP19	12fr on 5.50fr vio	1.10	25

Railway Crossing
PP29

1947 **Engraved** *Perf. 12½*

Q300	PP29	100fr dk grn	8.50	25

Crossbowman with Train
PP30

1947 **Photogravure** *Perf. 11½*

Q301	PP30	8fr dk ol brn	75	25
Q302	PP30	10fr gray & bl	90	30
Q303	PP30	12fr dk vio	1.40	50

Surcharged with
New Value and Bars in Carmine.

1948

Q304	PP30	9fr on 8fr dk ol brn	75	25
Q305	PP30	11fr on 10fr gray & bl	90	40
Q306	PP30	13.50fr on 12fr dk vio	1.40	40

Delivery of Parcel
PP31

1948

Q307	PP31	9fr chocolate	4.25	12
Q308	PP31	11fr brn car	4.50	12
Q309	PP31	13.50fr gray	6.50	35

Locomotive of 1835
PP32

Various Locomotives.
Lathe Work in Frame Differs.

1949 **Engraved** *Perf. 12½*

Q310	PP32	½fr dk brn	32	12
Q311	PP32	1fr car rose	45	12
Q312	PP32	2fr dp ultra	50	15
Q313	PP32	3fr dp mag	1.00	12
Q314	PP32	4fr bl grn	1.25	15
Q315	PP32	5fr org red	1.25	15
Q316	PP32	6fr brn vio	1.50	18
Q317	PP32	7fr yel grn	2.00	12
Q318	PP32	8fr grnsh bl	2.25	15
Q319	PP32	9fr yel brn	3.00	18
Q320	PP32	10fr citron	3.75	12
Q321	PP32	20fr orange	6.50	12
Q322	PP32	30fr blue	9.00	12
Q323	PP32	40fr lil rose	11.50	18
Q324	PP32	50fr violet	12.00	25
Q325	PP32	100fr red	35.00	18
		Nos. Q310-Q325 (16)	91.27	2.41

See also No. Q337.

Engraved; Center Typographed.

Q326	PP32	10fr car rose & blk	4.50	70

1949 **Engraved**
Design: Electric locomotive.

Q327	PP32	60fr blk brn	15.00	25

Opening of Charleroi-Brussels electric railway line, Oct. 15, 1949.

Mailing Parcel Post
PP33

Sorting
PP34

Loading
PP35

1950–52 *Perf. 12, 12½*

Q328	PP33	11fr red org	4.00	40
Q329	PP33	12fr red vio ('51)	10.00	1.10
Q330	PP34	13fr dk bl grn	3.50	20
Q331	PP34	15fr ultra ('51)	9.50	30
Q332	PP35	16fr gray	3.75	20
Q333	PP33	17fr brn ('52)	5.00	40
Q334	PP35	18fr brt car ('51)	8.50	40
Q335	PP35	20fr brn org ('52)	5.00	45
		Nos. Q328-Q335 (8)	49.25	3.45

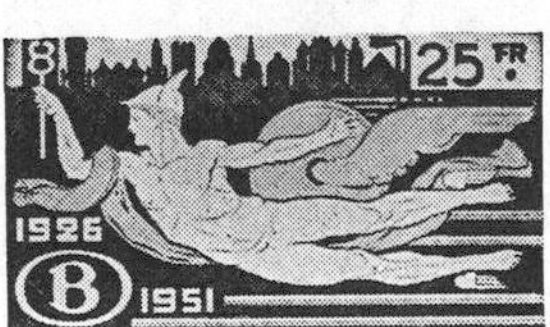

Mercury and Winged Wheel
PP36

1951

Q336	PP36	25fr dk bl	9.00	8.00

Issued to commemorate the 25th anniversary of the founding of the National Society of Belgian Railroads.

Type of 1949.

1952 *Perf. 11½* **Unwmkd.**
Design: Electric locomotive.

Q337	PP32	300fr red vio	75.00	65

Nos. Q331, Q328 and Q334 Surcharged with New Value and "X" in Red, Blue or Green.

1953 *Perf. 12.*

Q338	PP34	13fr on 15fr ultra (R)	32.50	1.40
Q339	PP33	17fr on 11fr red org (Bl)	20.00	1.10
Q340	PP35	20fr on 18fr brt car (G)	16.50	1.50

Electric Train, 1952
PP37

1953 **Engraved**

Q341	PP37	200fr dk yel grn & vio brn	140.00	3.25
Q342	PP37	200fr dk grn	120.00	80

No. Q341 was issued to commemorate the opening of the railway link connecting Brussels North and South Stations, Oct. 4, 1952.

New North Station, Brussels
PP38

Chapelle Station, Brussels—PP39

Designs: No. Q348, 15fr, Congress Station. 10fr, 20fr, 30fr, 40fr, 50fr, South Station. 100fr, 200fr, 300fr, Central Station.

1953-57 *Perf. 11½* **Unwmkd.**

Q343	PP38	1fr bister	38	5
Q344	PP38	2fr slate	50	8
Q345	PP38	3fr bl grn	65	5
Q346	PP38	4fr orange	1.00	5
Q347	PP38	5fr red brn	1.00	5
Q348	PP38	5fr dk red brn	7.00	25
Q349	PP38	6fr rose vio	1.20	5
Q350	PP38	7fr brt grn	1.20	5
Q351	PP38	8fr rose red	1.50	5
Q352	PP38	9fr brt grnsh bl	2.00	5
Q353	PP38	10fr lt grn	2.00	5
Q354	PP38	15fr dl red	8.75	10
Q355	PP38	20fr blue	3.25	5
Q356	PP38	30fr purple	5.00	5
Q357	PP38	40fr brt pur	6.25	5
Q358	PP38	50fr lil rose	7.50	5
Q359	PP39	60fr brt pur	15.00	12
Q360	PP39	80fr brn vio	18.00	15
Q361	PP39	100fr emerald	17.50	10
Q361A	PP39	200fr brt vio bl	40.00	1.25
Q361B	PP39	300fr lil rose	62.50	1.65
		Nos. Q343-Q361B (21)	202.18	4.35

Issue dates: No. Q347, 20fr and 30fr, 1953; 80fr, 1955; 200fr, 1956; 300fr, 1957. Rest of set, 1954.
See Nos. Q407, Q431–Q432.

Electric Train
PP40

Mercury and Winged Wheel
PP41

1954

Q362	PP40	13fr chocolate	7.00	15
Q363	PP40	18fr dk bl	8.00	12
Q364	PP40	21fr lil rose	9.00	50

Nos. Q362-Q364 Surcharged with New Value and "X" in Blue, Red or Green.

1956

Q365	PP40	14fr on 13fr choc (B)	7.00	15
Q366	PP40	19fr on 18fr dk bl (R)	7.50	25
Q367	PP40	22fr on 21fr lil rose (G)	8.00	45

1957 **Engraved.** *Perf. 11½*

Q368	PP41	14fr brt grn	6.75	25
Q369	PP41	19fr ol gray	7.75	35
Q370	PP41	22fr car rose	8.00	60

Nos. Q369-Q370 Surcharged with New Value and "X" in Pink or Green.

1959

Q371	PP41	20fr on 19fr ol gray (P)	19.00	38
Q372	PP41	20fr on 22fr car rose (G)	21.00	60

Old North Station, Brussels
PP42

1959 **Engraved** *Perf. 11½*

Q373	PP42	20fr ol grn	12.50	38

See also No. Q381.

Diesel and Electric Locomotives and Association Emblem
PP43

1960 *Perf. 11½* **Unwmkd.**

Q374	PP43	20fr red	62.50	47.50
Q375	PP43	50fr dk bl	62.50	40.00
Q376	PP43	60fr red lil	62.50	40.00
Q377	PP43	70fr emerald	62.50	40.00

Issued to commemorate the 75th anniversary of the International Association of Railway Congresses.

No. Q373 Surcharged with New Value and "X" in Red.

1961

Q378	PP42	24fr on 20fr ol grn	80.00	38

South Station, Brussels
PP44

1962 *Perf. 11½* **Unwmkd.**

Q379	PP44	24fr dl red	9.00	38

No. Q379 Surcharged with New Value and "X" in Light Green

1963

Q380	PP44	26fr on 24fr dl red	9.00	38

Type of 1959

Design: 26fr, Central Station, Antwerp.

1963 Engraved *Perf. 11½*

Q381	PP42	26fr blue	9.00	75

No. Q381 Surcharged in Red

1964, Apr. 20

Q382	PP42	28fr on 26fr bl	9.00	50

Type of 1959.

Design: 28fr, St. Peter's Station, Ghent.

1965 Engraved *Perf. 11½*

Q383	PP42	28fr red lil	9.00	1.25

Nos. Q383 Surcharged with New Value and "X" in Green

1966

Q384	PP42	35fr on 28fr red lil	9.00	1.00

Arlon Railroad Station PP45

Engraved

1967, Aug. *Perf. 11½* Unwmkd.

Q385	PP45	25fr bister	13.50	30
Q386	PP45	30fr bl grn	6.75	38
Q387	PP45	35fr dp bl	9.00	65

Electric Train PP46

Designs: 2fr, 3fr, 4fr, 5fr, 6fr, 7fr, 8fr, 9fr, like 1fr. 10fr, 20fr, 30fr, 40fr, Train going right. 50fr, 60fr, 70fr, 80fr, 90fr, Train going left. 100fr, 200fr, 300fr, Diesel train.

1968–73 Engraved *Perf. 11½*

Q388	PP46	1fr ol bis	6	5
Q389	PP46	2fr slate	12	5
Q390	PP46	3fr bl grn	18	5
Q391	PP46	4fr orange	25	6
Q392	PP46	5fr brown	30	8
Q393	PP46	6fr plum	40	5
Q394	PP46	7fr brt grn	45	8
Q395	PP46	8fr carmine	50	8
Q396	PP46	9fr blue	55	8
Q397	PP46	10fr green	60	5
Q398	PP46	20fr dk bl	1.10	5
Q399	PP46	30fr dk pur	1.65	5
Q400	PP46	40fr brt lil	2.00	5
Q401	PP46	50fr brt pink	2.50	5
Q402	PP46	60fr brt vio	3.00	8
Q402A	PP46	70fr dp bis ('73)	4.00	1.00
Q403	PP46	80fr dk brn	4.00	25
Q403A	PP46	90fr yel grn ('73)	5.50	1.25
Q404	PP46	100fr emerald	5.75	45
Q405	PP46	200fr vio bl	12.50	80
Q406	PP46	300fr lil rose	27.50	1.25
		Nos. Q388-Q406 (21)	72.91	5.91

Types of 1953–68

Designs: 10fr, Congress Station, Brussels. 40fr, Arlon Station. 500fr, Electric train going left.

1968, June Engraved *Perf. 11½*

Q407	PP38	10fr gray	75	10
Q408	PP45	40fr vermilion	27.50	40
Q409	PP46	500fr yellow	30.00	2.25

Nos. Q385, Q387 and Q408 Surcharged with New Value and "X"

1970, Dec.

Q410	PP45	37fr on 25fr bis	55.00	3.50
Q411	PP45	48fr on 35fr dp bl	16.00	5.50
Q412	PP45	53fr on 40fr ver	18.00	6.75

Ostend Station PP47

1971, March Engraved *Perf. 11½*

Q413	PP47	32fr bis & blk	2.25	90
Q414	PP47	37fr gray & blk	2.75	1.25
Q415	PP47	42fr bl & blk	3.00	1.40
Q416	PP47	44fr brt rose & blk	3.50	1.50
Q417	PP47	46fr vio & blk	3.50	1.50
Q418	PP47	50fr brick red & blk	4.00	1.65
Q419	PP47	52fr sep & blk	4.00	1.65
Q420	PP47	54fr yel grn & blk	4.50	1.75
Q421	PP47	61fr grnsh bl & blk	4.50	2.00
		Nos. Q413-Q421 (9)	32.00	13.60

Nos. Q413–Q416, Q419-Q421 Surcharged wth New Value and "X"

1971, Dec. 15

Denomination in Black

Q422	PP47	34fr on 32fr bis	2.25	80
Q423	PP47	40fr on 37fr gray	2.75	1.00
Q424	PP47	47fr on 44fr brt rose	3.00	1.10
Q425	PP47	53fr on 42fr bl	3.50	1.25
Q426	PP47	56fr on 52fr sep	4.00	1.40
Q427	PP47	59fr on 54fr yel grn	4.50	1.40
Q428	PP47	66fr on 61fr grnsh bl	5.50	1.65
		Nos. Q422-Q428 (7)	25.50	8.60

Track, Underpinning of Railroad Car and Emblems—PP48

1972, Mar. Photogravure

Q429	PP48	100fr emer, red & blk	20.00	2.75

Centenary of International Railroad Union.

Congress Emblem PP49

1974, Apr. Photo. *Perf. 11½*

Q430	PP49	100fr yel, blk & red	18.00	2.00

4th International Symposium on Railroad Cybernetics, Washington, D.C., Apr. 1974.

Type of 1953–1957

1975, June 1 Engr. *Perf. 11½*

Q431	PP38	20fr emerald	1.40	80
Q432	PP38	50fr blue	3.50	2.00

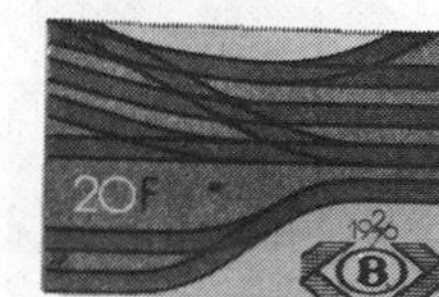

Railroad Tracks PP50

1976, June 10 Photo. *Perf. 11½*

Q433	PP50	20fr ultra & multi	5.00	1.00
Q434	PP50	50fr brt grn & multi	3.00	2.25
Q435	PP50	100fr dp org & multi	6.75	4.75
Q436	PP50	150fr brt lil & multi	10.00	8.00

Railroad Station PP51

1977 Photo. *Perf. 11½*

Q437	PP51	1000fr multi	55.00	*45.00*

Freight Car—PP52

Designs: 2fr, 3fr, 4fr, 5fr, 6fr, 7fr, 8fr, 9fr, Freight car. 10fr, 20fr, 30fr, 40fr, Hopper car. 50fr, 60fr, 70fr, 80fr, 90fr, Maintenance car. 100fr, 200fr, 300fr, 500fr, Liquid fuel car.

1980, Dec. 16 Engraved *Perf. 11½*

Q438	PP52	1fr bis brn & blk	6	5
Q439	PP52	2fr cl & blk	12	5
Q440	PP52	3fr brt bl & blk	15	5
Q441	PP52	4fr grnsh blk & blk	22	6
Q442	PP52	5fr sep & blk	28	10
Q443	PP52	6fr dp org & blk	30	12
Q444	PP52	7fr pur & blk	38	14
Q445	PP52	8fr black	42	14
Q446	PP52	9fr grn & blk	45	15
Q447	PP52	10fr yel bis & blk	50	20
Q448	PP52	20fr grnsh bl & blk	1.10	40
Q449	PP52	30fr bis & blk	1.65	60
Q450	PP52	40fr lt lil & blk	2.00	80
Q451	PP52	50fr dk brn & blk	2.65	1.00
Q452	PP52	60fr ol & blk	3.00	1.20
Q453	PP52	70fr vio bl & blk	3.75	1.40
Q454	PP52	80fr vio brn & blk	4.25	1.60
Q455	PP52	90fr lil rose & blk	4.75	1.80
Q456	PP52	100fr crim rose & blk	5.25	2.00
Q457	PP52	200fr brn & blk	10.00	4.00
Q458	PP52	300fr ol gray & blk	15.00	6.00
Q459	PP52	500fr dl pur & blk	26.00	10.00
		Nos. Q438-Q459 (22)	82.28	31.86

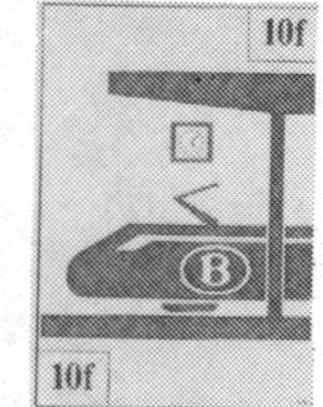

Train in Station—PP53

1982 Engr. *Perf. 11½*

Q460	PP53	10fr red & blk	45	20
Q461	PP53	20fr grn & blk	90	40
Q462	PP53	50fr sep & blk	2.50	1.00
Q463	PP53	100fr bl & blk	5.00	2.00

BB-150 Electric Locomotive—PP54

1985, May 3 Photo. *Perf. 11½*

Q464	PP54	250fr shown	8.00	6.00
Q465	PP54	500fr BB-120 electric locomotive	16.00	12.00

OCCUPATION STAMPS.

Issued under German Occupation.

German Stamps of 1906-11 Surcharged

Belgien
3 Centimes
a

✱ 1Fr.25C. ✱

Belgien
b

Wmkd. Lozenges. (125)

1914-15 *Perf. 14, 14½.*

N1	A16 (a)	3c on 3pf brn	40	28
N2	A16 (a)	5c on 5pf grn	32	22
N3	A16 (a)	10c on 10pf car	50	22
N4	A16 (a)	25c on 20pf ultra	55	40
N5	A16 (a)	50c on 40pf lake & blk	2.75	1.75
N6	A16 (a)	75c on 60pf mag	1.10	1.40
N7	A16 (a)	1fr on 80pf lake & blk, *rose*	2.75	2.25
N8	A17 (b)	1fr 25c on 1m car	27.50	17.50
N9	A21 (b)	2fr 50c on 2m gray bl	20.00	22.50
		Nos. N1-N9 (9)	55.87	46.52

German Stamps of 1906-18 Surcharged

Belgien
3 Cent.
c

Belgien
1 F.
d

✱ 1F.25Cent. ✱

Belgien
e

1916–18

N10	A22 (c)	2c on 2pf db	22	22
N11	A16 (c)	3c on 3pf brn	28	18
N12	A16 (c)	5c on 5pf grn	28	22
N13	A22 (c)	8c on 7½pf org	45	45
N14	A16 (c)	10c on 10pf car	22	18
N15	A22 (c)	15c on 15pf yel brn	50	25
N16	A22 (c)	15c on 15pf dk vio	50	45
N17	A16 (c)	20c on 25pf org & blk, *yel*	28	28
N18	A16 (c)	25c on 20pf ultra	28	18
a.		25c on 20pf bl	35	22
N19	A16 (c)	40c on 30pf org & blk, *buff*	30	28
N20	A16 (c)	50c on 40pf lake & blk	28	28
N21	A16 (c)	75c on 60pf mag	50	*18.00*
N22	A16 (d)	1f on 80pf lake & blk, *rose*	1.65	*4.00*
N23	A17 (e)	1f 25c on 1m car	2.75	2.75
N24	A21 (e)	2f 50c on 2m gray bl	30.00	30.00
a.		2f50c on 1m car (error)		*4,500.*
N25	A20 (e)	6f 25c on 5m sl & car	32.50	45.00
		Nos. N10-N25 (16)	70.99	*102.72*

A similar series of stamps without "Belgien" was used in parts of Belgium and France while occupied by German forces. See France Nos. N15–N26.

BENADIR

(See Vol. IV, Somalia.)

BENIN

(bĕ·nēn')

French Colony

LOCATION — West Coast of Africa.
GOVT.—Republic.
AREA—43,483 sq. mi.
POP.—3,832,000 (est. 1984).
CAPITAL—Porto Novo.

In 1895 the French possessions known as Benin were incorporated into the colony of Dahomey and postage stamps of Dahomey superseded those of Benin. Dahomey took the name Benin when it became a republic in 1975.

100 Centimes = 1 Franc

Handstamped on Stamps of French Colonies **BÉNIN**

Black Overprint.

1892 ***Perf. 14x13½.*** **Unwmkd.**

1	A9	1c *bluish*	140.00	110.00
2	A9	2c brn, *buff*	110.00	95.00
3	A9	4c cl, *lav*	40.00	35.00
4	A9	5c grn, *grnsh*	12.00	10.50
5	A9	10c *lavender*	67.50	52.50
6	A9	15c blue	26.00	10.50
7	A9	20c red, *grn*	210.00	160.00
8	A9	25c *rose*	77.50	47.50
9	A9	30c brn, *yelsh*	165.00	125.00
10	A9	35c *orange*	165.00	125.00
11	A9	40c red, *straw*	125.00	110.00
12	A9	75c car, *rose*	325.00	260.00
13	A9	1fr brnz grn, *straw*	350.00	275.00

Red Overprint.

14	A9	15c blue	77.50	57.50

Blue Overprint.

15	A9	5c grn, *grnsh*	2,100.	600.00
15A	A9	15c blue	2,100.	600.00

Nos. 1-13 all exist with overprint inverted, and several with it double. These sell for slightly more than normal stamps. The overprints of Nos. 1-15A are of four types, three without accent mark on "E." They exist diagonal.

Counterfeits exist of Nos. 1-19.

Additional Surcharge Red or Black **40**

1892

16	A9	01c on 5c grn, *grnsh*	250.00	190.00
17	A9	40c on 15c bl	175.00	65.00
18	A9	75c on 15c bl	775.00	525.00
19	A9	75c on 15c bl (Bk)	3,000.	2,400.

Navigation and Commerce
A3 A4

1893 **Typographed.**

Name of Colony in Blue or Carmine.

20	A3	1c *bluish*	2.25	2.00
21	A3	2c brn, *buff*	3.00	2.50
22	A3	4c cl, *lav*	3.25	2.50
23	A3	5c grn, *grnsh*	4.25	3.25
24	A3	10c *lavender*	4.25	3.50
25	A3	15c bl, quadrille paper	21.00	17.00
26	A3	20c red, *grn*	12.00	7.75
27	A3	25c *rose*	32.50	17.50
28	A3	30c brn, *bis*	14.00	12.00
29	A3	40c red, *straw*	3.75	2.50
30	A3	50c car, *rose*	3.50	2.50
31	A3	75c vio, *org*	7.00	5.50
32	A3	1fr brnz grn, *straw*	45.00	40.00
		Nos. 20-32 (13)	155.75	118.50

1894

33	A4	1c *bluish*	2.00	1.50
34	A4	2c brn, *buff*	2.00	1.50
35	A4	4c cl, *lav*	2.00	1.50
36	A4	5c grn, *grnsh*	2.25	1.50
37	A4	10c *lavender*	4.00	2.75
38	A4	15c bl, quadrille paper	5.50	2.75
39	A4	20c red, *grn*	5.75	4.00
40	A4	25c *rose*	7.00	3.25
41	A4	30c brn, *bis*	4.25	3.25
42	A4	40c red, *straw*	12.00	7.75
43	A4	50c car, *rose*	16.00	8.25
44	A4	75c vio, *org*	10.50	7.75
45	A4	1fr brnz grn, *straw*	2.50	2.50
		Nos. 33-45 (13)	75.75	48.25

People's Republic

LOCATION—West Coast of Africa.
GOVT.—Republic.
AREA—43,483 sq. mi.
POP.—3,290,000 (est. 1977).
CAPITAL—Porto-Novo.

The Republic of Dahomey proclaimed itself the People's Republic of Benin on Nov. 30, 1975. See Dahomey for stamps issued before then.

Allamanda Cathartica — **A83**

Flag Bearers, Arms of Benin — **A84**

Photogravure

1975, Dec. 8 ***Perf. 13*** **Unwmkd.**

Flowers: 35fr, Ixora coccinea. 45fr, Hibiscus. 60fr, Phaemeria magnifica.

342	A83	10fr lil & multi	15	10
343	A83	35fr gray & multi	35	20
344	A83	45fr multi	50	35
345	A83	60fr bl & multi	60	45

1976, Apr. 30 **Litho.** ***Perf. 12***

Designs: 60fr, Speaker, wall with "PRPB," flag and arms of Benin. 100fr, Flag and arms of Benin.

346	A84	50fr ocher & multi	40	30
347	A84	60fr ocher & multi	45	30
348	A84	100fr multi	80	60

Proclamation of the People's Republic of Benin, Nov. 30, 1975.

A. G. Bell, Satellite and 1876 Telephone—A85

1976, July 9 **Litho.** ***Perf. 13***

349	A85	200fr lil, red & brn	1.65	70

Centenary of first telephone call by Alexander Graham Bell, Mar. 10, 1876.

Dahomey
Nos. 277-278 Surcharged

1976, July 19 **Photo.** ***Perf. 12½x13***

350	A57	50fr on 1fr multi	40	18
351	A57	60fr on 2fr multi	50	20

Scouts Cooking—A86

Design: 70fr, Three Scouts.

1976, Aug. 16 **Litho.** ***Perf. 12½x13***

352	A86	50fr blk, lil & brn	40	30
353	A86	70fr blk, ol & red brn	55	40

African Jamboree, Nigeria 1976.

Blood Bank, Cotonou—A87

Designs: 50fr, Accident and first aid station. 60fr, Blood donation.

1976, Sept. 24 **Litho.** ***Perf. 13***

354	A87	5fr multi	5	5
355	A87	50fr multi	40	30
356	A87	60fr multi	50	35

National Blood Donors Day.

Manioc A88

Designs: 50fr, Corn. 60fr, Cacao. 150fr, Cotton.

1976, Oct. 4 **Litho.** ***Perf. 13x12½***

357	A88	20fr multi	15	10
358	A88	50fr multi	40	30
359	A88	60fr multi	45	30
360	A88	150fr multi	1.25	90

National Agricultural production campaign.

Classroom A89

1976, Oct. 25

361	A89	50fr multi	40	30

Third anniversary of KPARO newspaper, used in local language studies.

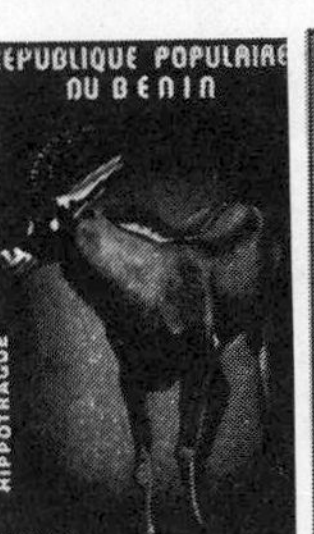

Roan Antelope — **A90**

Flags, Wall, Broken Chains — **A91**

Designs: 30fr, Buffalo. 50fr, Hippopotamus (horiz.). 70fr, Lion.

1976, Nov. 8 **Photogravure**

362	A90	10fr multi	10	6
363	A90	30fr multi	25	18
364	A90	50fr multi	40	30
365	A90	70fr multi	55	35

Penjari National Park.

1976, Nov. 30 **Litho.** ***Perf. 12½***

Design: 150fr, Corn, raised hands with weapons.

366	A91	40fr multi	30	20
367	A91	150fr multi	1.20	90

First anniversary of proclamation of the People's Republic of Benin.

Table Tennis, Map of Africa (Games' Emblem)—A92

Design: 50fr, Stadium, Cotonou.

1976, Dec. 26 **Litho.** ***Perf. 13***

368	A92	10fr multi	10	6
369	A92	50fr multi	40	30

West African University Games, Cotonou, Dec. 26-31.

Europafrica Issue

Planes over Africa and Europe A93

1977, May 13 **Litho.** ***Perf. 13***

370	A93	200fr multi	1.60	1.20

Snake A94

Designs: 3fr, Tortoise. 5fr, Zebus. 10fr, Cats.

1977, June 13 **Litho.** ***Perf. 13x13½***

371	A94	2fr multi	5	5
372	A94	3fr multi	5	5
373	A94	5fr multi	5	5
374	A94	10fr multi	10	6

Patients at Clinic
A95

1977, Aug. 2 Litho. *Perf. 12½*

375	A95	100fr multi	85	60

World Rheumatism Year.

Karate, Map of Africa
A96

Designs: 100fr, Javelin, map of Africa, Benin flag (horiz.). 150fr, Hurdles.

1977, Aug. 30 Litho. *Perf. 12½*

376	A96	90fr multi	70	55
377	A96	100fr multi	85	60
378	A96	150fr multi	1.25	90
a.		Souvenir sheet of 3	2.75	2.75

2nd West African Games, Lagos, Nigeria. No. 378a contains one each of Nos. 376-378; black marginal inscription. Size: 143x92mm.

Chairman Mao
A97

Lister and Vaporizer
A98

1977, Sept. 9 Litho. *Perf. 13x12½*

379	A97	100fr multi	85	60

Chairman Mao Tse-tung (1893-1976), Chinese communist leader, first death anniversary.

1977, Sept. 20 Engr. *Perf. 13*

Design: 150fr, Scalpels and flames, symbols of antisepsis, and Red Cross.

380	A98	150fr multi	1.20	90
381	A98	210fr multi	1.75	1.25

Joseph Lister (1827-1912), surgeon, founder of antiseptic surgery, birth sesquicentennial.

Guelede Mask, Ethnographic Museum, Porto Novo—A99

Designs: 50fr, Jar, symbol of unity, emblem of King Ghezo, Historical Museum, Abomey (vert.). 210fr, Abomey Museum.

1977, Oct. 17 *Perf. 13*

382	A99	50fr red & multi	40	30
383	A99	60fr blk, bl & bis	50	35
384	A99	210fr multi	1.75	1.25

Atacora Falls
A100

Mother and Child, Owl of Wisdom
A101

Designs: 60fr, Pile houses, Ganvie (horiz.). 150fr, Round huts, Savalou.

1977, Oct. 24 Litho. *Perf. 12½*

385	A100	50fr multi	40	30
386	A100	60fr multi	50	35
387	A100	150fr multi	1.25	90
a.		Souvenir sheet of 3	2.80	2.80

Tourist publicity. No. 387a contains one each of Nos. 385-387; black marginal inscription. Size: 143x91mm.

Perf. 12½x13, 13x12½

1977, Dec. 3 Photogravure

Design: 150fr, Chopping down magical tree (horiz.).

388	A101	60fr multi	50	35
389	A101	150fr multi	1.25	90

Campaign against witchcraft.

Battle Scene—A102

1978, Jan. 16 Litho *Perf. 12½*

390	A102	50fr multi	50	28

Victory of people of Benin over imperialist forces.

Map, People and Houses of Benin
A103

1978, Feb. 1

391	A103	50fr multi	50	28

General population and dwellings census.

Alexander Fleming, Microscope and Penicillin—A104

1978, Mar. 12 Litho. *Perf. 13*

392	A104	300fr multi	3.00	1.65

Alexander Fleming (1881-1955), 50th anniversary of discovery of penicillin.

Abdoulaye Issa, Weapons and Fighters
A105

1978, Apr. 1 *Perf. 12½x13*

393	A105	100fr red, blk & gold	1.00	55

First anniversary of death of Abdoulaye Issa and National Day of Benin's Youth.

El Hadj Omar and Horseback Rider
A106

Design: 90fr, L'Almamy Samory Toure (1830-1900) and horseback riders.

1978, Apr. 10 *Perf. 13x12½*

394	A106	90fr red & multi	90	50
395	A106	100fr multi	1.00	55

African heroes of resistance against colonialism.

ITU Emblem, Satellite, Landscape
A107

1978, May 17 Litho. *Perf. 13*

396	A107	100fr multi	1.00	55

10th World Telecommunications Day.

Soccer Player, Stadium, Argentina '78 Emblem—A108

Designs (Argentina '78 Emblem and): 300fr, Soccer players and ball (vert.). 500fr, Soccer player, globe with ball on map.

1978, June 1 Litho. *Perf. 12½*

397	A108	200fr multi	2.00	1.10
398	A108	300fr multi	3.00	1.65
399	A108	500fr multi	5.00	2.75
a.		Souvenir sheet of 3	11.00	11.00

11th World Cup Soccer Championship, Argentina, June 1-25. No. 399a contains 3 stamps similar to Nos. 397-399 in changed colors; red marginal inscription and blue border. Size: 190x120mm.

Nos. 397-399a Overprinted in Red Brown:
a. FINALE / ARGENTINE: 3 / HOLLANDE: 1
b. CHAMPION / 1978 / ARGENTINE
c. 3e BRESIL / 4e ITALIE

1978, June 25 Litho. *Perf. 12½*

400	A108 (a)	200fr multi	2.00	1.10
401	A108 (b)	300fr multi	3.00	1.65
402	A108 (c)	500fr multi	5.00	2.75
a.		Souvenir sheet of 3	11.00	11.00

Argentina's victory in 1978 Soccer Championship.

Games' Flag over Africa, Basketball Players—A109

Designs (Games' Emblem and): 60fr, Map of Africa and volleyball players. 80fr, Map of Benin and bicyclists.

1978, July 13 *Perf. 13x12½*

403	A109	50fr lt bl & multi	50	28
404	A109	60fr ultra & multi	60	35
405	A109	80fr multi	80	50
a.		Souvenir sheet of 3	2.00	2.00

3rd African Games, Algiers, July 13-28. No. 405a contains 3 stamps in changed colors similar to Nos. 403-405; rose lilac and black margin. Size: 208-80mm.

Martin Luther King, Jr.
A110

1978, July 30 *Perf. 12½*

406	A110	300fr multi	3.00	1.65

Martin Luther King, Jr. (1929-1968), American civil rights leader.

Kanna Taxi, Oueme
A111

Designs: 60fr, Leatherworker and goods. 70fr, Drummer and tom-toms. 100fr, Metalworker and calabashes.

1978, Aug. 26

407	A111	50fr multi	50	28
408	A111	60fr multi	60	35
409	A111	70fr multi	70	42
410	A111	100fr multi	1.00	55

Getting to know Benin through its provinces.

Map of Italy and Exhibition Poster—A112

1978, Aug. 26 Litho. ***Perf. 13***

411	A112	200fr multi	2.00	1.10

Riccione 1978 Philatelic Exhibition.

Turkeys A113

Poultry: 20fr, Ducks. 50fr, Chicken. 60fr, Guinea fowl.

1978, Oct. 5 Photo. ***Perf. 12½x13***

412	A113	10fr multi	10	10
413	A113	20fr multi	20	20
414	A113	50fr multi	50	50
415	A113	60fr multi	60	60

Poultry breeding.

Royal Messenger, UPU Emblem A114

Designs (UPU Emblem and): 60fr, Boatsman, ship and car (vert.). 90fr, Special messenger and plane (vert.).

Perf. 13x12½, 12½x13

1978, Oct. 16

416	A114	50fr multi	50	50
417	A114	60fr multi	60	60
418	A114	90fr multi	90	90

Centenary of change of "General Postal Union" to "Universal Postal Union."

Raoul Follereau A115

1978, Dec. 17 Litho. ***Perf. 12½***

419	A115	200fr multi	2.00	2.00

Raoul Follereau (1903–1977), apostle to the lepers and educator of the blind.

See "Special Notices" at the front of this volume for data on the listing methods of this Catalogue, abbreviations, condition, prices and examination.

IYC Emblem A116

Designs: 20fr, Globe as balloon carrying children. 50fr, Children of various races surrounding globe.

1979, Feb. 20 Litho. ***Perf. 12x13***

420	A116	10fr multi	10	10
421	A116	20fr multi	20	20
422	A116	50fr multi	50	50

International Year of the Child.

Hydrangea A117

Flowers: 25fr, Assangokan. 30fr, Geranium. 40fr, Water lilies (horiz.).

Perf. 13x12½, 12½x13

1979, Feb. 28 Lithographed

423	A117	20fr multi	20	20
424	A117	25fr multi	25	25
425	A117	30fr multi	30	30
426	A117	40fr multi	40	40

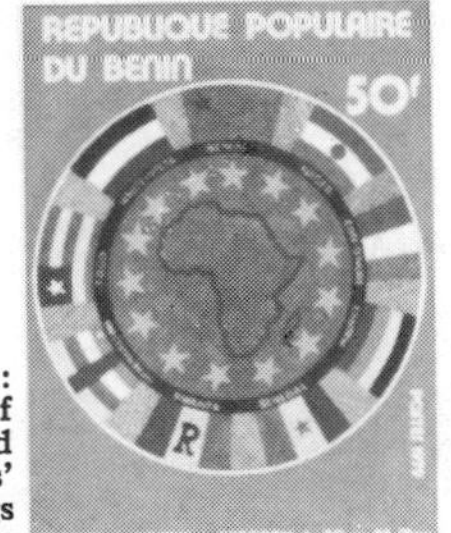

Emblem: Map of Africa and Members' Flags A118

Designs: 60fr, Map of Benin and flags. 80fr, OCAM flag and map of Africa showing member states.

1979, Mar. 20 Litho. ***Perf. 12x13***

427	A118	50fr multi	50	50
428	A118	60fr multi	60	60
429	A118	80fr multi	80	80

OCAM Summit Conference, Cotonou, Mar. 20–28.

Tower, Waves, Satellite, ITU Emblem A119

1979, May 17 Litho. ***Perf. 12½***

430	A119	50fr multi	50	50

World Telecommunications Day.

Bank Building and Sculpture A120

1979, May 26 Litho.

431	A120	50fr multi	50	50

Opening of Headquarters of West African Savings Bank in Dakar.

Guelede Mask, Abomey Tapestry, Malaconotus Bird—A121

Design: 50fr, Jet, canoe, satellite, UPU and exhibition emblems.

1979, June 8 Litho. ***Perf. 13***

432	A121	15fr multi	15	15

Engraved

433	A121	50fr multi	50	50

Philexafrique II, Libreville, Gabon, June 8–17. Nos. 432, 433 each printed in sheets of 10 with 5 labels showing exhibition emblem.

Nos. 427-429 Overprinted: "26 au 28 juin 1979" and Dots

1979, June 26

434	A118	50fr multi	50	50
435	A118	60fr multi	60	60
436	A118	80fr multi	80	80

2nd OCAM Summit Conference, June 26-28.

Olympic Flame and Emblems—A122

Pre-Olympic Year: 50fr, High jump.

1979, July 1 Litho.

437	A122	10fr multi	10	10
438	A122	50fr multi	50	50

Antelope—A123

Animals: 10fr, Giraffes, map of Benin (vert.) 20fr, Chimpanzee 50fr, Elephants, map of Benin (vert).

1979, Oct.1 Litho. ***Perf. 13***

439	A123	5fr multi	5	5
440	A123	10fr multi	10	10
441	A123	20fr multi	20	20
442	A123	50fr multi	50	50

Map of Africa, Emblem and Jet—A124

1979, Dec. 12 Litho. ***Perf. 12½***

443	A124	50fr multi	50	50
444	A124	60fr multi	60	60

ASECNA (Air Safety Board), 20th anniversary.

Mail Services—A125

Design: 50fr, Post Office and headquarters (vert.).

1979, Dec. 19 Litho. ***Perf. 13***

445	A125	50fr multi	50	50
446	A125	60fr multi	60	60

Office of Posts and Telecommunications, 20th anniversary.

Lenin and Globe—A126

1980, Apr. 22 Litho. ***Perf. 12½***

447	A126	50fr *shown*	50	50
448	A126	150fr *Lenin in library*	1.50	1.50

Lenin, 110th birth anniversary.

Cotonou Club Emblem A127

Galileo, Astrolabe A128

1980, Feb. 23 **Litho.** ***Perf. 12½***

449	A127	90fr	*shown*	90	90
450	A127	200fr	*Rotary emblem on globe*, horiz.	2.00	2.00

Rotary International, 75th anniversary.

1980, Apr. 2

451	A128	70fr	*shown*	70	70
452	A128	100fr	*Copernicus, solar system*	1.00	1.00

Discovery of Pluto, 50th anniversary.

Abu Simbel, UNESCO Emblem—A129

1980, Apr. 15 ***Perf. 13***

453	A129	50fr	*Column*, vert.	50	50
454	A129	60fr	*Ramses II*, vert.	60	60
455	A129	150fr	*shown*	1.50	1.50

UNESCO campaign to save Nubian monuments, 20th anniversary.

Monument, Martyrs' Square, Cotonou—A130

Designs: Various monuments in Martyrs' Square. Cotonou. 60fr, 70fr, 100fr, horiz.

1980, May 2 ***Perf. 12½x13, 13x12½***

456	A130	50fr	multi	50	50
457	A130	60fr	multi	60	60
458	A130	70fr	multi	70	70
459	A130	100fr	multi	1.00	1.00

Tinbo—A131

Musical Instruments: 5fr, Assan (vert.). 15fr, Tam-tam sato (vert.). 20fr, Kora. 30fr, Gangan. 50fr, Sinhoun.

1980, May 20 ***Perf. 12½***

460	A131	5fr	multi	5	5
461	A131	10fr	multi	10	10
462	A131	15fr	multi	15	15
463	A131	20fr	multi	20	20
464	A131	30fr	multi	30	30
465	A131	50fr	multi	50	50
			Nos. 460-465 (6)	1.30	1.30

First Non-stop Flight, Paris-New York—A132

1980, June 2 **Litho.** ***Perf. 12½***

466	A132	90fr	*shown*	90	90
467	A132	100fr	*Dieudonne Coste, Maurice Bellonte*	1.00	1.00

Lunokhod I on the Moon—A133

1980, June 15 **Engraved** ***Perf. 13***

468	A133	90fr	multi	90	90

Lunokhod I Soviet unmanned moon mision, 10th anniversary. See No. C290.

Olympic Flame and Mischa, Moscow '80 Emblem—A134

1980, July 16 **Litho.** ***Perf. 12½***

469	A134	50fr	*shown*	50	50
470	A134	60fr	*Equestrian*, vert.	60	60
471	A134	70fr	*Judo*	70	70
472	A134	200fr	*Flag, sports, globe*, vert.	2.00	2.00
473	A134	300fr	*Weight lifting*, vert.	3.00	3.00
			Nos. 469-473 (5)	6.80	6.80

22nd Summer Olympic Games, Moscow, July 19-Aug. 3.

Telephone and Rising Sun—A135

World Telecommunications Day: 50fr, Farmer on telephone (vert.).

1980, May 17 **Litho.** ***Perf. 12½***

474	A135	50fr	multi	50	50
475	A135	60fr	multi	60	60

Cotonou West African Community Village—A136

Designs: Views of Cotonou.

1980, July 26 ***Perf. 13x13½***

476	A136	50fr	multi	50	50
477	A136	60fr	multi	60	60
478	A136	70fr	multi	70	70

Agbadja Dancers—A137

Designs: Dancers and musicians.

1980, Aug. 1 ***Perf. 12½***

479	A137	30fr	multi	30	30
480	A137	50fr	multi	50	50
481	A137	60fr	multi	60	60

Fisherman

A138

Philippines under Magnifier

A139

Designs: 5fr, Throwing net. 15fr, Canoe and shore fishing. 20fr, Basket traps. 50fr, Hauling net. 60fr, River fishing. All horiz.

1980, Sept. 1

482	A138	5fr	multi	5	5
483	A138	10fr	multi	10	10
484	A138	15fr	multi	15	15
485	A138	20fr	multi	20	20
486	A138	50fr	multi	50	50
487	A138	60fr	multi	60	60
			Nos. 482-487 (6)	1.60	1.60

1980, Sept. 27 ***Perf. 13x13½, 13½x13***

World Tourism Conference, Manila, Sept. 27: 60fr, Emblem on flag, hand pointing to Manila on globe (horiz.).

488	A139	50fr	multi	50	50
489	A139	60fr	multi	60	60

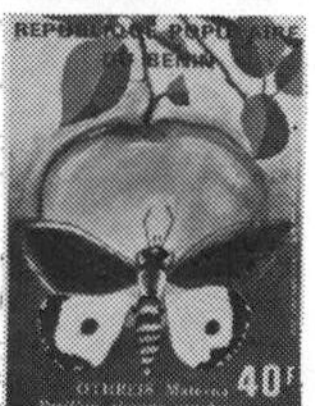

Othreis Materna—A140

1980, Oct. 1 ***Perf. 12½***

490	A140	40fr	shown	40	40
491	A140	50fr	Othreis fullonia	50	50
492	A140	200fr	Oryctes sp.	2.00	2.00

African Postal Union, 5th Anniversary

A141

Clasped Hands Breaking Chain, UN Emblem

A142

1980, Oct. 24 **Photo.** ***Perf. 13½***

493	A141	75fr	multi	75	75

1980, Nov. 4 ***Perf. 12½x13***

494	A142	30fr	shown	30	30
495	A142	50fr	Freed prisoner	50	50
496	A142	60fr	Man holding torch	60	60

Declaration of human rights, 30th anniversary.

Self-portrait, by Vincent van Gogh, 1888—A143

1980, Dec. 1 **Litho.** ***Perf. 13***

497	A143	100fr	shown	1.00	1.00
498	A143	300fr	Facteur Roulin	3.00	3.00

Vincent Van Gogh (1853-1890), artist.

Offenbach and Scene from Orpheus in the Underworld—A144

1980, Dec. 15 **Engr.**

499	A144	50fr	shown	50	50
500	A144	60fr	Paris Life	60	60

Jacques Offenbach (1819-1880), composer.

Kepler and Satellites—A145

1980, Dec. 20

501	A145	50fr	Kepler, diagram, vert.	50	50
502	A145	60fr	shown	60	60

Johannes Kepler (1571-1630), astronomer, 350th death anniversary.

Intl. Year of the Disabled—A146

1981, Apr. 10 **Litho.** ***Perf. 12½***

503	A146	115fr	multi	1.15	1.15

20th Anniv. of Manned Space Flight—A147

1981, May 30 ***Perf. 13***

504	A147	500fr	multi	5.00	5.00

13th World Telecommunications Day—A148

1981, May 30 **Litho.** ***Perf. 12½***
505 A148 115fr multi 1.15 1.15

Amaryllis A149

1981, June 20 ***Perf. 12½***
506 A149 10fr shown 10 10
507 A149 20fr Eischornia crassipes, vert. 20 20
508 A149 80fr Parkia biglobosa, vert. 80 80

Benin Sheraton Hotel—A150

1981, July 1
509 A150 100fr multi 1.00 1.00

Guinea Pig A151

1981, July 31 ***Perf. 13x13½***
510 A151 5fr shown 5 5
511 A151 60fr Cat 60 60
512 A151 80fr Dogs 80 80

World UPU Day—A152

1981, Oct. 9 **Engr.** ***Perf. 13***
513 A152 100fr red brn & blk 1.00 1.00

25th Intl. Letter Writing Week, Oct. 6-12—A153

1981, Oct. 15
514 A153 100fr dk bl & pur 1.00 1.00

West African Economic Community A154

1981, Nov. 20 **Litho.** ***Perf. 12½***
515 A154 60fr multi 60 60

West African Rice Development Assoc. 10th Anniv.—A155

1981, Dec. 10 ***Perf. 13x13½***
516 A155 60fr multi 60 60

TB Bacillus Centenary—A156

1982, Mar. 1 **Litho.** ***Perf. 13***
517 A156 115fr multi 1.15 1.15

West African Economic Community, 5th Summit Conference—A157

1982, May 27 ***Perf. 12½***
518 A157 60fr multi 60 60

1982 World Cup—A158

1982, June 1 ***Perf. 13***
519 A158 90fr Players 90 90
520 A158 300fr Flags on leg 3.00 3.00

France No. B349 Magnified, Map of France—A159

1982, June 11
521 A159 90fr multi 90 90

PHILEXFRANCE '82 Stamp Exhibition, Paris, June 11-21.

George Washington—A160

1982, Mar. 10 **Litho.** ***Perf. 14***
522 A160 200fr Washington, flag, map 2.00 2.00

Nos. 519-520 Overprinted with Finalists Names.

1982, Aug. 16 ***Perf. 12½***
523 A158 90fr multi 90 90
524 A158 300fr multi 3.00 3.00

Italy's victory in 1982 World Cup.

Bluethroat—A161

1982, Sept. 1 ***Perf. 14x14½, 14½x14***
525 A161 5fr Daoelo gigas, vert. 5 5
526 A161 10fr shown 10 10
527 A161 15fr Swallow, vert. 15 15
528 A161 20fr Kingfisher, weaver bird, vert. 20 20
529 A161 30fr Great sedge warbler 30 30
530 A161 60fr Common warbler 60 60
531 A161 80fr Owl, vert. 80 80
532 A161 100fr Cockatoo, vert. 1.00 1.00
Nos. 525-532 (8) 3.20 3.20

ITU Plenipotentiaries Conference, Nairobi, Sept.—A162

1982, Sept. 26 ***Perf. 13***
533 A162 200fr Map 2.00 2.00

13th World UPU Day—A163

1982, Oct. 9 **Engr.** ***Perf. 13***
534 A163 100fr Monument 1.00 1.00

Nos. 411, 482, 510 Overprinted in Red or Blue:
#537 "RICCIONE 1982"
#536 "UAPT 1982"
#535 "Croix Rouge / 8 Mai 1982"

1982, Nov. **Litho.** ***Perf. 13, 12½, 13x13½***
535 A138 60fr on 5fr multi 60 60
536 A151 60fr on 5fr multi 60 60
537 A112 200fr multi (Bl) 2.00 2.00

Visit of French Pres. Francois Mitterand—A164

1983, Jan. 15 **Litho.** ***Perf. 12½x13***
538 A164 90fr multi 90 90

Nos. 458, 476, 508-509, 512 Surcharged.

1983 **Litho.** ***Perf. 13x12½, 13x13½, 12½***
539 A130 60fr on 70fr multi 60 60
540 A136 60fr on 50fr multi 60 60
541 A150 60fr on 100fr multi 60 60
542 A149 75fr on 80fr multi 75 75
543 A151 75fr on 80fr multi 75 75
Nos. 539-543 (5) 3.30 3.30

Seme Oil Rig—A165

1983, Apr. 28 **Litho.** ***Perf. 13x12½***
544 A165 125fr multi 1.25 1.25

World Communications Year—A166

1983, May 17 **Litho.** ***Perf. 13***
545 A166 185fr multi 1.85 1.85

Riccione '83, Stamp Show—A167

1983, Aug. 27 **Litho.** ***Perf. 13***
546 A167 500fr multi 5.00 5.00

Benin Red Cross, 20th Anniv.—A168

1983, Sept. 5 **Photo.** ***Perf. 13***
547 A168 105fr multi 1.05 1.05

Handicrafts—A169

Designs: 75fr, Handcarved lion chairs and table. 90fr, Natural tree table and stools. 200fr, Monkeys holding jar.

1983, Sept. 18 **Litho.** ***Perf. 13***

548	A169	75fr multi	75	75
549	A169	90fr multi	90	90
550	A169	200fr multi	2.00	2.00

14th UPU Day—A170

1983, Oct. 9 **Engr.** ***Perf. 13***

551	A170	125fr multi	1.25	1.25

Religious Movements A171

Plaited Hair Styles A172

1983, Oct. 31 **Litho.** ***Perf. 14x15***

552	A171	75fr	Zangbeto	50	50
553	A171	75fr	Egoun	50	50

1983, Nov. 14

554	A172	30fr	Rockcoco	20	20
555	A172	75fr	Serpent	50	50
556	A172	90fr	Songas	60	60

Types of 1976-81 Surcharged.

1983, Nov.

557	A139	5fr on 50fr #486	5	5
558	A153	10fr on 100fr #514	8	8
559	A134	15fr on 200fr #472	10	10
560	A98	15fr on 210fr #381	10	10
561	A134	25fr on 70fr #471	18	18
562	A99	25fr on 210fr #384	18	18
563	A151	75fr on 5fr #510	50	50
564	A132	75fr on 100fr #467	50	50
565	A88	75fr on 150fr #360	50	50
566	A98	75fr on 150fr #380	50	50
		Nos. 557-566 (10)	2.69	2.69

Alfred Nobel (1833-96)—A173

1983, Dec. 19 **Litho.** ***Perf. 15x14***

567	A173	300fr multi	2.00	2.00

Council of Unity—A174

1984, May 29 **Litho.** ***Perf. 12***

568	A174	75fr multi	50	50
569	A174	90fr multi	60	60

1984 UPU Congress—A175

1984, June 18 **Litho.** ***Perf. 13***

570	A175	90fr multi	60	60

Abomey Calavi Earth Station—A176

1984, June 29 **Litho.** ***Perf. 12½x13***

571	A176	75fr Satellite dish	38	38

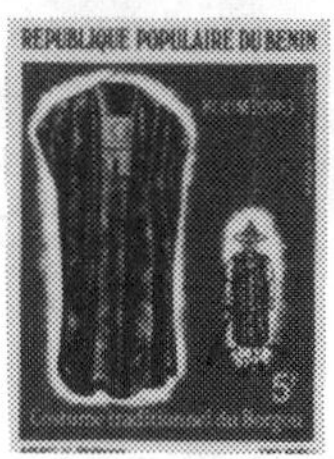

Traditional costumes—A177

1984, July 2 **Litho.** ***Perf. 13½x13***

572	A177	5fr	Koumboro	5	5
573	A177	10fr	Taka	5	5
574	A177	20fr	Toko	10	10

Nos. 389, 498, 503-505, 517, 522, 533, 547, 550 and 551 Surcharged.

1984, Sept.

575	A170	5fr on 125fr multi	5	5
576	A101	5fr on 150fr multi	5	5
577	A160	10fr on 200fr multi	5	5
578	A169	10fr on 200fr multi	5	5
579	A143	15fr on 300fr multi	8	8
580	A147	40fr on 500fr multi	20	20
581	A168	75fr on 105fr multi	38	38
582	A146	75fr on 115fr multi	38	38
583	A148	75fr on 115fr multi	38	38
584	A156	75fr on 115fr multi	38	38
585	A162	75fr on 200fr multi	38	38
		Nos. 575-585 (11)	2.38	2.38

World Food Day A178

Dinosaurs A179

1984, Oct. 16 **Litho.** ***Perf. 12½***

586	A178	100fr Malnourished child	45	45

1984, Dec. 14 **Litho.** ***Perf. 13½***

587	A179	75fr	Anatosaurus	35	35
588	A179	90fr	Brontosaurus	40	40

Cultural & Technical Cooperation Agency, 15th Anniv.—A180

1985, Mar. 20 **Litho.** ***Perf. 13***

589	A180	300fr Emblem, globe, hands, book	1.30	1.30

Stamps of 1977-82 Surcharged.

1985, Mar.

590	A93	75fr on 200fr No. 370	30	30
591	A108	75fr on 200fr No. 397	30	30
592	A110	75fr on 300fr No. 406	30	30
593	A108	75fr on 300fr No. 398	30	30
594	A158	90fr on 300fr No. 520	38	38
595	A108	90fr on 500fr No. 399	38	38
596	A108	90fr on 500fr No. 402	38	38
		Nos. 590-596 (7)	2.34	2.34

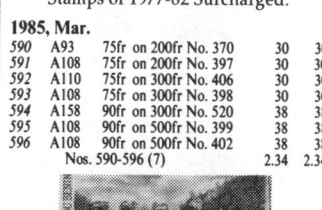

Traditional Dances—A181

1985, June **Litho.** ***Perf. 15x14½***

597	A181	75fr	Teke, Borgou Tribe	30	30
598	A181	100fr	Tipen'ti, L'Atacora Tribe	42	42

Intl. Youth Year—A182

1985, July 16 ***Perf. 13½***

599	A182	150fr multi	62	62

1986 World Cup Soccer Championships, Mexico—A183

1985, July 22 ***Perf. 13x12½***

600	A183	200fr multi	85	85

Dahomey No. 336 Ovptd. "REPUBLIQUE POPULAIRE DU BENIN" and Surcharged with Black Bars and New Value.

1985, Aug. ***Perf. 12½***

601	A78	15fr on 40fr multi	8	8

ASECNA Airlines, 25th Anniv.—A184

1985, Sept. 16 ***Perf. 13***

602	A184	150fr multi	62	62

UN 40th Anniv.—A185

1985, Oct. 24 ***Perf. 12½***

603	A185	250fr multi	1.00	1.00

Benin UN membership, 25th anniv.

ITALIA '85, Rome—A186

1985, Oct. 25 ***Perf. 13½***

604	A186	200fr multi	85	85

PHILEXAFRICA '85, Lome—A187

1985, Nov. 16 *Perf. 13*

605	A187	250fr	No. 569, labor emblem	1.00	1.00
606	A187	250fr	No. C252, Gabon No. 365, magnified stamp	1.00	1.00

Nos. 605-606 printed se-tenant with center label picturing map of Africa or UAPT emblem.

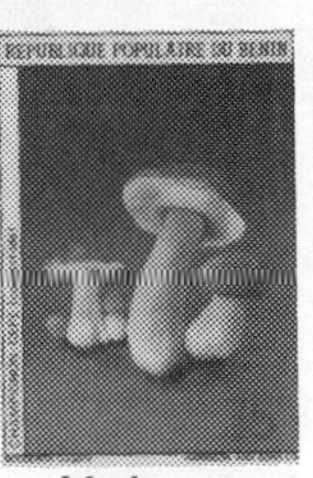

Audubon Birth Bicent. A188

Mushrooms and Toadstools A189

1985, Oct. 17 **Litho.** *Perf. 14x15*

607	A188	150fr	Skua gull	82	82
608	A188	300fr	Oyster catcher	1.65	1.65

1985, Oct. 17

609	A189	35fr	Boletus edible	20	20
610	A189	40fr	Amanite phalloide	22	22
611	A189	100fr	Brown chanterelle	55	55

Stamps Inscribed Dahomey Surcharged and Ovptd. with 2 Black Bars and "Populaire Republique du Benin" in 3 lines.

1986, Mar. **Photo.** **Perfs. as before**

612	A83	75fr	on 35fr #343	40	40
613	A57	90fr	on 70fr #282	50	50
614	A60	90fr	on 140fr #292	50	50

African Parliamentary Union, 10th Anniv.—A190

1986, May 8 **Litho.** *Perf. 13x12½*

615	A190	100fr	multi	55	55

9th Conference, Cotonou, May 8-10.

Halley's Comet—A191

1986, May 30 *Perf. 12½x12*

616	A191	205fr	multi	1.10	1.10

Stamps Inscribed Dahomey Surcharged with Bar, "Republique/Populaire/du Benin" and New Value.

1986, June **Engr., Photo.** *Perf. 13*

617	A58	100fr	on 40fr #283	55	55
618	A83	150fr	on 45fr #344	82	82

1986 World Cup Soccer Championships, Mexico—A192

1986, June 29 **Litho.**

619	A192	500fr	multi	2.75	2.75

Fight against Desert Encroachment—A193

1986, July 16 *Perf. 13½*

620	A193	150fr	multi	82	82

Amazon A194

Flowers A195

1986, Aug. 1 **Engr.** *Perf. 13*

622	A194	100fr	brt bl	28	28
624	A194	150fr	violet	82	82

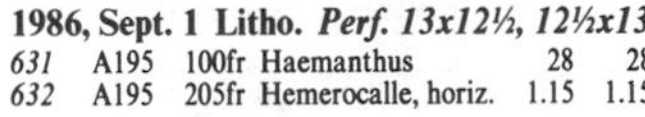

1986, Sept. 1 **Litho.** *Perf. 13x12½, 12½x13*

631	A195	100fr	Haemanthus	28	28
632	A195	205fr	Hemerocalle, horiz.	1.15	1.15

Butterflies—A196

Designs: No. 633, Day peacock, little tortoise-shell, morio. No. 634, Aurora, machaon and fair lady.

1986, Sept. 15

633	A196	150fr	multi	82	82
634	A196	150fr	multi	82	82

Statue of Liberty, Cent. A197

King Behanzin A198

1986, Oct. 28 **Litho.** *Perf. 12½*

635	A197	250fr	multi	1.40	1.40

1986, Oct. 30 *Perf. 13½*

636	A198	440fr	multi	2.50	2.50

Behanzin, leader of resistance movement against French occupation (1886-1894).

Brazilian Cultural Week, Cotonou—A200

1987, Jan. 17 *Perf. 12½*

638	A200	150fr	multi	88	88

AIR POST STAMPS

People's Republic

Nativity, by Aert van Leyden
AP84

Paintings: 85fr, Adoration of the Kings, by Rubens (vert.). 140fr, Adoration of the Shepherds, by Charles Lebrun. 300fr, The Virgin with the Blue Diadem, by Raphael (vert.).

1975, Dec. 19 Litho. *Perf. 13*

C240	AP84	40fr gold & multi	40	15
C241	AP84	85fr gold & multi	85	30
C242	AP84	140fr gold & multi	1.20	50
C243	AP84	300fr gold & multi	2.75	1.25

Christmas 1975.

Slalom, Innsbruck Olympic Emblem—AP85

Designs (Innsbruck Olympic Games Emblem and): 150fr, Bobsledding (vert.). 300fr, Figure skating, pairs.

1976, June 28 Litho. *Perf. 12½*

C244	AP85	60fr multi	50	20
C245	AP85	150fr multi	1.25	50
C246	AP85	300fr multi	2.50	1.10

12th Winter Olympic Games, Innsbruck, Austria, Feb. 4–15.

Dahomey Nos. C235–C237 Overprinted: "POPULAIRE / DU BENIN" and Bars, with Surcharge Added on Nos. C236—C237

1976, July 4 Engr. *Perf. 13*

C247	AP82	135fr multi	1.10	50
C248	AP82	210fr on 300fr multi	1.75	70
C249	AP82	380fr on 500fr multi	3.00	1.30

The overprint includes a bar covering "DU DAHOMEY" in shades of brown; "POPULAIRE DU BENIN" is blue on Nos. C247–C248, red on No. C249. The surcharge and bars over old value are blue on No. C248, red, brown on No. C249.

Long Jump—AP86

Designs (Olympic Rings and): 150fr, Basketball (vert.). 200fr, Hurdles.

1976, July 16 Photo. *Perf. 13*

C250	AP86	60fr multi	50	20
C251	AP86	150fr multi	1.25	50
C252	AP86	200fr multi	1.65	70
a.		Souvenir sheet of 3	3.50	3.50

21st Olympic Games, Montreal, Canada, July 17–Aug 1. No. C252a contains one each of Nos. C250–C252; brown marginal inscription. Size:150x120mm.

Konrad Adenauer and Cologne Cathedral—AP87

Design: 90fr, Konrad Adenauer (vert.).

1976, Aug. 27 Engr. *Perf. 13*

C253	AP87	90fr multi	70	30
C254	AP87	250fr multi	2.00	80

Konrad Adenauer (1876–1967), German Chancellor, birth centenary.

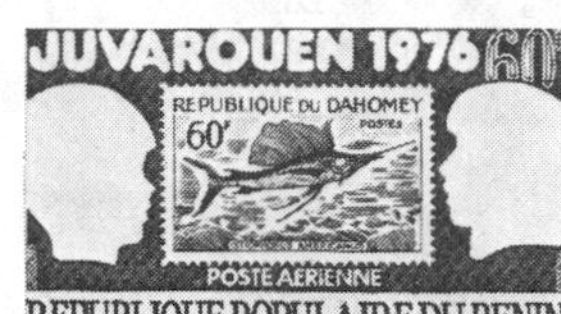

Children's Heads and Flying Fish (Dahomey Type A32)—AP88

Design: 210fr, Lion cub's head and Benin type A3 (vert.).

1976, Sept. 13

C255	AP88	60fr Prus bl & vio bl	50	20
C256	AP88	210fr multi	1.65	70

JUVAROUEN 76, International Youth Philatelic Exhibition, Rouen, France, Apr. 25–May 2.

Apollo 14 Emblem and Blast-off AP89

Design: 270fr, Landing craft and man on moon.

1976, Oct. 18 Engr. *Perf. 13*

C257	AP89	130fr multi	1.00	45
C258	AP89	270fr multi	2.25	95

Apollo 14 Moon Mission, 5th anniversary.

Annunciation, by Master of Jativa AP90

Paintings: 60fr, Nativity, by Gerard David. 270fr, Adoration of the Kings, Dutch School. 300fr, Flight into Egypt, by Gentile Fabriano (horiz.).

1976, Dec. 20 Litho. *Perf. 12½*

C259	AP90	50fr gold & multi	40	25

C260	AP90	60fr gold & multi	50	35
C261	AP90	270fr gold & multi	2.25	95
C262	AP90	300fr gold & multi	2.50	1.50

Christmas 1976.

Gamblers and Lottery Emblem AP91

1977, Mar. 13 Litho. *Perf. 13*

C263	AP91	50fr multi	40	30

National lottery, 10th anniversary.

Sassenage Castle, Grenoble—AP92

1977, May 16 *Perf. 12½*

C264	AP92	200fr multi	1.65	1.20

10th anniversary of International French Language Council.

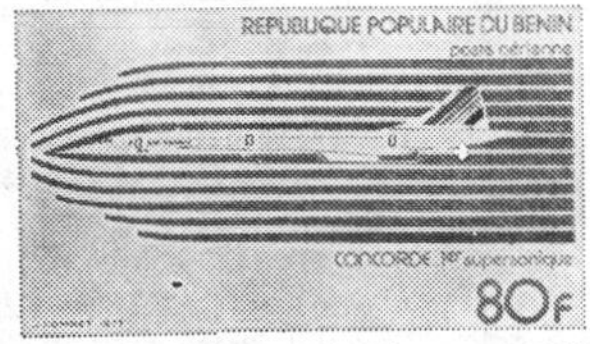

Concorde, Supersonic Plane—AP93

Designs: 150fr, Zeppelin. 300fr, Charles A. Lindbergh and Spirit of St. Louis. 500fr, Charles Nungesser and François Coli, French aviators lost over Atlantic, 1927.

1977, July 25 Engr. *Perf. 13*

C265	AP93	80fr ultra & red	65	50
C266	AP93	150fr multi	1.25	90
C267	AP93	300fr multi	2.50	1.80
C268	AP93	500fr multi	4.00	3.00

Aviation history.

Soccer Player AP94

Design: 200fr, Soccer players and Games' emblem.

1977, July 28 Litho. *Perf. 12½x12*

C269	AP94	60fr multi	50	30
C270	AP94	200fr multi	1.65	1.20

World Soccer Cup elimination games.

Miss Haverfield, by Gainsborough AP95

Designs: 150fr, Self-portrait, by Rubens. 200fr, Anguish, man's head by Da Vinci.

1977, Oct. 3 Engr. *Perf. 13*

C271	AP95	100fr sl grn & mar	80	60
C272	AP95	150fr red brn & dk brn	1.25	90
C273	AP95	200fr brn & red	1.65	1.20

Birth anniversaries: Thomas Gainsborough (1727–1788); Peter Paul Rubens (1577–1640); Leonardo da Vinci (1452–1519).

No. C265 Overprinted:
"1er VOL COMMERCIAL / 22.11.77 PARIS NEW–YORK"

1977, Nov. 22 Engr. *Perf. 13*

C274	AP93	80fr ultra & red	65	50

Concorde, first commercial flight, Paris to New York.

Viking on Mars—AP96

Designs: 150fr, Isaac Newton, apple globe, stars. 200fr, Vladimir M. Komarov, spacecraft and earth. 500fr, Dog Laika, rocket and space.

1977, Nov. 28 Engr. *Perf. 13*

C275	AP96	100fr multi	80	60
C276	AP96	150fr multi	1.25	90
C277	AP96	200fr multi	1.65	1.20
C278	AP96	500fr multi	4.00	3.00

Operation Viking on Mars; 250th death anniversary of Isaac Newton (1642–1727); 10th death anniversary of Russian cosmonaut Vladimir M. Komarov; 20th anniversary of first living creature in space.

Monument, Red Star Place, Cotonou—AP97

Litho.; Gold Embossed

1977 Nov. 30 *Perf. 12½*

C279	AP97	500fr multi	4.00	2.50

Common Design Types
pictured in section at front of book.

Suzanne Fourment, by Rubens AP98

Design: 380fr, Nicholas Rubens, By Rubens.

1977, Dec. 12 Engr. *Perf. 13*

C280	AP98	200fr multi	1.65	1.20
C281	AP98	380fr cl & ocher	3.00	2.10

Peter Paul Rubens (1577–1640), 400th birth anniversary.

Parthenon and UNESCO Emblem AP99

Designs: 70fr, Acropolis and frieze showing Pan-Athenaic procession (vert.). 250fr, Parthenon and frieze showing horsemen (vert.).

1978, Sept. 22 Litho. *Perf. 12½x12*

C282	AP99	70fr multi	70	40
C283	AP99	250fr multi	2.50	1.50
C284	AP99	500fr multi	5.00	3.00

Save the Parthenon in Athens campaign.

Philexafrique II—Essen Issue
Common Design Types

Designs: No. C285, Buffalo and Dahomey No. C33. No. C286, Wild ducks and Baden No. 1.

1978, Nov. 1 Litho. *Perf. 12½*

C285	CD138	100fr multi	1.00	60
C286	CD139	100fr multi	1.00	60

Nos. C285–C286 printed se-tenant.

Wilbur and Orville Wright and Flyer—AP100

1978, Dec. 28 Engr. *Perf. 13*

C287	AP100	500fr multi	5.00	3.00

75th anniversary of 1st powered flight.

Cook's Ships, Hawaii, World Map AP101

Design: 50fr, Battle at Kowrowa.

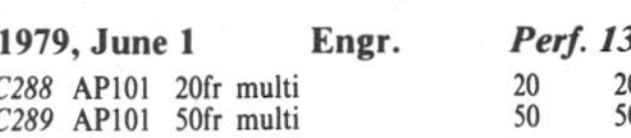

1979, June 1 Engr. *Perf. 13*

C288	AP101	20fr multi	20	20
C289	AP101	50fr multi	50	50

Capt. James Cook (1728-1779), explorer, death bicentenary.

Lunokhod Type of 1980

1980, June 15 Engraved *Perf. 13*
Size: 27x48mm.

C290	A133	210fr multi	2.10	2.10

Soccer Players AP102

1981, Mar. 31 Litho. *Perf. 13*

C291	AP102	200fr Ball, globe	2.00	2.00
C292	AP102	500fr shown	5.00	5.00

ESPANA '82 World Soccer Cup eliminations.

Prince Charles and Lady Diana, London Bridge—AP103

1981, July 29 Litho. *Perf. 12½*

C293	AP103	500fr multi	5.00	5.00

Royal wedding.

Three Musicians, by Pablo Picasso (1881-1973)—AP104

1981, Nov. 2 Litho. *Perf. 12½x13, 13x12½*

C294	AP104	300fr Dance, vert.	3.00	3.00
C295	AP104	500fr shown	5.00	5.00

1300th Anniv. of Bulgaria—AP105

1981, Dec. 2 Litho. *Perf. 13*

C296	AP105	100fr multi	1.00	1.00

Visit of Pope John Paul II—AP106

1982, Feb. 17 **Litho.** *Perf. 13*
C297 AP106 80fr multi 80 80

20th Anniv. of John Glenn's Flight—AP107

1982, Feb. 21 **Litho.** *Perf. 13*
C298 AP107 500fr multi 5.00 5.00

Scouting Year—AP108

1982, June 1 *Perf. 12½*
C299 AP108 105fr multi 1.05 1.05

Nos. C256, C275 Surcharged.

1982, Nov. **Engr.** *Perf. 13*
C300 AP88 50fr on 210fr multi 50 50
C301 AP96 50fr on 100fr multi 50 50

Monet in Boat, by Claude Monet (1832-1883)—AP109

1982, Dec. 6 **Litho.** *Perf. 13x12½*
C302 AP109 300fr multi 3.00 3.00

Christmas 1982—AP110

Virgin and Child Paintings.

1982, Dec. 20 *Perf. 12½x13*
C303 AP110 200fr Matthias Grunewald 2.00 2.00
C304 AP110 300fr Correggio 3.00 3.00

No. C290 Surcharged.

1983 **Engr.** *Perf. 13*
C305 A133 75fr on 210fr multi 75 75

Bangkok '83 Stamp Exhibition—AP111

1983, Aug. 4 **Photo.** *Perf. 13*
C306 AP111 300fr multi 3.00 3.00

Christmas 1983—AP112

1983, Dec. 26 **Litho.** *Perf. 12½x13*
C307 AP112 200fr Loretto Madonna, by Raphael 1.00 1.00

Types of 1976-82 Surcharged.

1983, Nov.
C308 AP94 10fr on 200fr #C270 8 8
C309 AP95 15fr on 200fr #C273 10 10
C310 AP90 15fr on 270fr #C261 10 10
C311 AP98 20fr on 200fr #C280 15 15
C312 AP89 25fr on 270fr #C258 18 18
C313 AP98 25fr on 380fr #C281 18 18
C314 AP96 30fr on 200fr #C277 20 20
C315 AP107 40fr on 500fr #C298 30 30
C316 AP93 75fr on 150fr #C266 55 55
C317 AP95 75fr on 150fr #C272 55 55
Nos. C308-C317 (10) 2.39 2.39

Summer Olympics—AP113

1984, July 16 **Litho.** *Perf. 13x13½*
C318 AP113 300fr Sam the Eagle, mascot 1.50 1.50

Nos. C262, C293-C294, C299, C302-C303, C306-C307 Surcharged

1984, Sept.
C319 AP112 15fr on 200fr multi 8 8
C320 AP104 15fr on 300fr multi 8 8
C321 AP90 25fr on 300fr multi 14 14
C322 AP111 25fr on 300fr multi 14 14
C323 AP103 40fr on 500fr multi 20 20
C324 AP108 75fr on 105fr multi 38 38
C325 AP110 90fr on 200fr multi 45 45
C326 AP109 90fr on 300fr multi 45 45
Nos. C319-C326 (8) 1.92 1.92

Christmas 1984—AP114

1984, Dec. 17 **Litho.** *Perf. 12½x13*
C327 AP114 500fr Virgin and Child, by Murillo 2.25 2.25

Ships—AP115

1984, Dec. 28 **Litho.** *Perf. 13*
C328 AP115 90fr Sidon merchant ship 40 40
C329 AP115 125fr Wavertree, vert. 55 55

Benin - S.O.M. Postal Convention—AP116

1985, Apr. 15 **Litho.** *Perf. 13½*
C330 AP116 75fr Benin arms 32 32
C331 AP116 75fr Sovereign Order of Malta 32 32

Se-tenant.

PHILEXAFRICA III, Lome—AP117

1985, June 24 *Perf. 13*
C332 AP117 200fr Oil platform 85 85
C333 AP117 200fr Soccer players 85 85

Nos. C332-C333 printed se-tenant with center labels picturing the conference emblem or a map of Africa showing Lome.

Stamps of 1977-82 Surcharged.

1985, Mar.
C334 AP92 75fr on 200fr No. C264 30 30
C335 AP102 75fr on 200fr No. C291 30 30
C336 AP93 75fr on 300fr No. C267 30 30
C337 AP110 75fr on 300fr No. C304 30 30
C338 AP99 90fr on 500fr No. C284 38 38
C339 AP100 90fr on 500fr No. C287 38 38
C340 AP104 90fr on 500fr No. C295 38 38
Nos. C334-C340 (7) 2.34 2.34

Dahomey Stamps of 1971-75 Ovptd. "REPUBLIQUE POPULAIRE DU BENIN" or "POPULAIRE DU BENIN" and Surcharged with Black Bar and New Value.

1985, Aug.
C341 AP83 25fr on 40fr No. C238 12 12
C342 AP49 40fr No. C142 18 18
C343 AP56 75fr on 85fr No. C164 30 30
C344 AP60 75fr on 100fr No. C173 30 30
C345 AP64 75fr on 125fr No. C186 30 30
C346 AP56 90fr on 20fr No. C163 38 38
C347 A61 90fr on 150fr No. C153 38 38
C348 AP49 90fr on 200fr No. C143 38 38
C349 AP76 90fr on 200fr No. C221 38 38
C350 AP76 150fr No. C220 62 62
Nos. C341-C350 (10) 3.34 3.34

Christmas—AP118

1985, Dec. 20 **Litho.** *Perf. 13x12½*
C351 AP118 500fr multi 2.75 2.75

Stamps of Dahomey Surcharged and Ovptd. with 2 Black Bars and "Republique Populaire du Benin" in 3 lines.

1986, Mar. **Photo.** **Perfs. as before**
C352 AP33 75fr on 70fr #C84 40 40
C353 AP14 75fr on 100fr #C34 40 40
C354 AP15 75fr on 200fr #C35 40 40
C355 AP15 90fr on 250fr #C36 50 50

Stamps of Dahomey Ovptd. or Surcharged with One or Two Bars, "Republique/Populaire/du Benin."

1986, June **Photo.** *Perf. 12½*
C356 AP45 100fr #C131 55 55
C357 AP14 150fr on 500fr #C37 82 82

Christmas—AP119

1986, Dec. 24 **Litho.** *Perf. 13x12½*
C358 AP119 300fr multi 1.75 1.75

Air Africa, 25th Anniv.—AP120

1986, Dec. 30 *Perf. 12½*
C359 AP120 100fr multi 58 58

POSTAGE DUE STAMPS.

French Colony

Handstamped in Black on Postage Due Stamps of French Colonies **BENIN**

1894		*Imperf.*	Unwmkd.	
J1	D1	5c black	125.00	55.00
J2	D1	10c black	125.00	55.00
J3	D1	20c black	125.00	55.00
J4	D1	30c black	125.00	55.00

Nos. J1–J4 exist with overprint in various positions.

People's Republic

Pineapples D6

Mail Delivery D7

Designs: 20fr, Cashew (vert.). 40fr, Oranges. 50fr, Akee. 80fr, Mail delivery by boat.

1978, Sept. 5		Photo.	*Perf. 13*	
J44	D6	10fr multi	12	10
J45	D6	20fr multi	18	15
J46	D6	40fr multi	38	25
J47	D6	50fr multi	55	38
		Engraved		
J48	D7	60fr multi	42	35
J49	D7	80fr multi	55	42
		Nos. J44-J49 (6)	2.20	1.65

PARCEL POST STAMPS

Nos. 448, 459, 473 Overprinted "Colis Postaux"

1982, Nov.		Litho.	*Perf. 12½, 13x12½*	
Q8	A126	100fr on 150fr multi	60	30
Q9	A130	100fr multi	60	30
Q10	A134	300fr multi	1.75	90

BERGEDORF

See Early German States group preceding Germany.

BHUTAN

(bōōt·än′; bōō·tăn′)

LOCATION — Eastern Himalayas.
GOVT.—Kingdom.
AREA—18,000 sq. mi.
POP.—1,250,000 (est. 1983).
CAPITAL—Thimphu.

100 Chetrum = 1 Ngultrum or Rupee.

Postal Runner
A1

Designs: 3ch, 70ch, Archer. 5ch, 1.30nu, Yak. 15ch, Map of Bhutan, portrait of Druk Gyalpo (Dragon King) Ugyen Wangchuk (1867–1902) and Paro Dzong (fortress-monastery). 33ch, Postal runner. All horiz. except 2ch and 33ch.

Perf. 14x14½, 14½x14

1962 Litho. Unwmkd.

No.	Type	Description	Unused	Used
1	A1	2ch red & gray	5	5
2	A1	3ch red & ultra	15	15
3	A1	5ch grn & brn	60	60
4	A1	15ch red, blk & org yel	8	8
5	A1	33ch bl grn & lil	15	15
6	A1	70ch dp ultra & lt bl	45	45
7	A1	1.30nu bl & blk	1.25	1.25
		Nos. 1-7 (7)	2.73	2.73

Nos. 1–7 were issued for inland use in April, 1962, and became valid for international mail on Oct. 10, 1962.

Refugee Year Emblem and Arms of Bhutan
A2

1962, Oct. 10 ***Perf. 14½x14***

No.	Type	Description	Unused	Used
8	A2	1nu dk bl & dk car rose	60	60
9	A2	2nu yel grn & red lil	1.50	1.50

World Refugee Year.

Equipment of Ancient Warrior
A3

Boy Filling Grain Box and Wheat Emblem
A4

1963 ***Perf. 14x14½*** **Unwmkd.**

No.	Type	Description	Unused	Used
10	A3	33ch multi	20	20
11	A3	70ch multi	40	40
12	A3	1.30nu multi	90	90

Bhutan's membership in Colombo Plan.

1963, Sept. 17 ***Perf. 13½x14***

No.	Type	Description	Unused	Used
13	A4	20ch lt bl, yel & red brn	25	25
14	A4	1.50nu rose lil, bl & red brn	1.00	1.00

Issued for the "Freedom from Hunger" Campaign of the U.N. Food and Agriculture Organization.

Masked Dancer—A5

Various Bhutanese Dancers (Five Designs; 2ch, 5ch, 20ch, 1nu, 1.30nu vertical)

1964, Mar. ***Perf. 14½x14, 14x14½***

Dancers Multicolored

No.	Type	Description	Unused	Used
15	A5	2ch bl grn & brn	5	5
16	A5	3ch lt vio & blk	7	7
17	A5	5ch lt ultra & dk bl	7	7
18	A5	20ch yel & red	8	8
19	A5	33ch gray & blk	15	15
20	A5	70ch emer & blk	35	35
21	A5	1nu cit & red	60	60
22	A5	1.30nu bis & dk bl	70	70
23	A5	2nu org & blk	1.10	1.10
		Nos. 15-23 (9)	3.17	3.17

Stone Throwing
A6

Sport: 5ch, 33ch, Boxing. 1nu, 3nu, Archery. 2nu, Soccer.

1964, Oct. 10 Litho. ***Perf. 14½***

No.	Type	Description	Unused	Used
24	A6	2ch emer & multi	5	5
25	A6	5ch org & multi	7	7
26	A6	15ch brt cit & multi	8	8
27	A6	33ch rose lil & multi	20	20
28	A6	1nu multi	70	70
29	A6	2nu rose lil & multi	1.10	1.10
30	A6	3nu lt bl & multi	1.65	1.65
		Nos. 24-30 (7)	3.77	3.77

Issued to commemorate the 18th Olympic Games, Tokyo, Oct. 10–25. See No. B4.
Nos. 24–30 exist imperf. Price $4.

Flags of the World at Half-mast
A7

1964, Nov. 22 ***Perf. 14½*** **Unwmkd.**

Flags in Original Colors

No.	Type	Description	Unused	Used
31	A7	33ch stl gray	20	20
32	A7	1nu silver	75	75
33	A7	3nu gold	1.75	1.75
a.		Souv. sheets perf. 13½, imperf.	4.25	4.25

Issued in memory of those who died in the service of their country. Nos. 31–33 exist imperf.
No. 33a contains 2 stamps similar to Nos. 32–33 with flag of Bhutan and gold inscription in margin. Size: 83x118mm.

Primrose
A8

Flowers: 5ch, 33ch, Gentian. 50ch, 1nu, Rhododendron. 75ch, 2nu, Peony.

1964, Dec. Lithographed ***Perf. 13***

No.	Type	Description	Unused	Used
34	A8	2ch lt bl, vio bl & grn	5	5
35	A8	5ch vio, grn & yel	6	6
36	A8	15ch yel, vio & grn	10	10
37	A8	33ch gray, vio bl & grn	15	15
38	A8	50ch lt gray, grn & car	25	25
39	A8	75ch lt grn, yel & brn	40	40
40	A8	1nu pink, grn & dk gray	45	45
41	A8	2nu sep, yel & grn	95	95
		Nos. 34-41 (8)	1.96	1.96

Nos. 5, 40, 32, 41 and 33 Overprinted: "WINSTON CHURCHILL 1874–1965"

1965, Feb. 27

No.	Type	Description	Unused	Used
42	A1	33ch bl grn & lil	25	25
43	A8	1nu pink, grn & dk gray	65	65
44	A7	1nu sil & multi	65	65
45	A8	2nu sep, yel & grn	1.10	1.10
46	A7	3nu gold & multi	1.50	1.50
		Nos. 42-46 (5)	4.15	4.15

Issued in memory of Sir Winston Churchill (1874–1965), British statesman. The overprint is in three lines on Nos. 42–43 and 45; in two lines on Nos. 43 and 46.
Nos. 44 and 46 exist imperf. Price, both, $4.50.

Skyscraper, Pagoda and World's Fair Emblem—A9

Designs: 10ch, 2nu, Pieta by Michelangelo and statue of Khmer Buddha. 20ch, Skyline of New York and Bhutanese village. 33ch, George Washington Bridge, N. Y., and foot bridge, Bhutan.

1965, Apr. 21 Litho. ***Perf. 14½***

No.	Type	Description	Unused	Used
47	A9	1ch bl & multi	5	5
48	A9	10ch grn & multi	8	8
49	A9	20ch rose lil & multi	12	12
50	A9	33ch bis & multi	18	18
51	A9	1.50nu bis & multi	75	75
52	A9	2nu multi	1.00	1.00
a.		Souv. sheets perf. 13½, imperf.	3.00	3.00
		Nos.47-52 (6)	2.18	2.18

Nos. 47–52 exist imperf.; price $3.50.
No. 52a contains two stamps similar to Nos. 51–52. World's Fair emblems in margin in bister and inscription in black. Size: 118½x86½mm.

Telstar, Short-wave Radio and ITU Emblem—A10

Designs (ITU Emblem and): 2nu, Telstar and Morse key. 3nu, Syncom and ear phones.

1966, March 2 Litho. ***Perf. 14½***

No.	Type	Description	Unused	Used
53	A10	35ch multi	15	15
54	A10	2nu multi	70	70
55	A10	3nu multi	1.00	1.00

Issued to commemorate the centenary (in 1965) of the International Telecommunication Union. Souvenir sheets exist containing two stamps similar to Nos. 54–55, perf. 13½ and imperf. Dark blue margin with white inscription and pictures of satellites in space. Size: 119x78mm. Price, 2 sheets, $5.

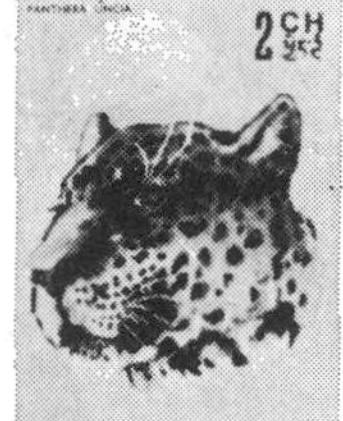

Leopard
A11

Animals: 1ch, 4nu, Asiatic black bear. 4ch, 2nu, Pigmy hog. 8ch, 75ch, Tiger. 10ch, 1.50nu, Dhole (Asiatic hunting dog). 1nu, 5nu, Takin (goat).

1966 Lithographed ***Perf. 13***

Animals in Natural Colors

No.	Type	Description	Unused	Used
56	A11	1ch yel & blk	10	10
57	A11	2ch pale grn & blk	10	10
58	A11	4ch lt cit & blk	10	10
59	A11	8ch lt bl & blk	10	10
60	A11	10ch lt lil & blk	10	10
61	A11	75ch lt yel grn & blk	30	30
62	A11	1nu lt grn & blk	75	75
63	A11	1.50nu lt bl grn & blk	60	60
64	A11	2nu dl org & blk	75	75
65	A11	3nu bluish lil & blk	1.10	1.10
66	A11	4nu lt grn & blk	1.50	1.50
67	A11	5nu pink & blk	2.00	2.00
		Nos. 56-67 (12)	7.50	7.50

Issue dates: Nos. 56–60, 62, March 28; Nos. 61, 63–67, Apr. 26.

Nos. 6–9, 20–23 Surcharged

10 CH

1965(?) ***Perf. 14½x14, 14x14½***

No.	Type	Description	Unused	Used
68	A2	5ch on 1nu dk bl & dk car rose		
69	A2	5ch on 2nu yel grn & red lil		
70	A5	10ch on 70ch multi		
71	A5	10ch on 2nu multi		
72	A1	15ch on 70ch dp ultra & lt bl		
73	A1	15ch on 1.30nu bl & blk		
74	A5	20ch on 1nu multi		
75	A5	20ch on 1.30nu multi		
		Nos. 68-75 (8)	*110.00*	

The surcharges on Nos. 68–69 contain two bars at left and right obliterating the denomination on both sides of the design. Four bars on Nos. 72–73.

Simtokha Dzong
A12

Tashichho Dzong—A13

Daga Dzong A14

Designs: 5ch, Rinpung Dzong. 50ch, Tongsa Dzong. 1nu, Lhuntsi Dzong.

Perf. 14½x14 (A12), 13½ (A13, A14)

1966–70 **Photogravure**

No.	Type	Description	Unused	Used
76	A12	5ch org brn ('67)	12	8
77	A13	10ch dk grn & rose vio ('68)	12	8
78	A12	15ch brown	12	8
79	A12	20ch green	20	20
80	A13	50ch bl grn ('68)	30	20
81	A14	75ch dk bl & ol gray ('70)	30	30
82	A14	1nu dk vio & vio bl ('70)	40	40
		Nos. 76-82 (7)	1.56	1.34

Sizes: 5ch, 15ch, 20ch, 37x20½mm. 10ch, 53½x28½mm. 50ch, 35½x25½ mm.

Certain unlisted issues of Bhutan, starting in 1966, are mentioned and briefly described in "For the Record" at the back of this volume.

Mahatma Gandhi—A14a

1969, Oct. 2 **Litho.** ***Perf. 13x13½***

No.	Type	Description	Unused	Used
83	A14a	20ch lt bl & brn	60	60
84	A14a	2nu lem & brn ol	1.50	1.50

Mohandas K. Gandhi (1869–1948), leader in India's struggle for independence, birth centenary.

Various Forms of Mail Transport, UPU Headquarters, Bern—A14b

1970, Feb. 25 **Photo.** ***Perf. 13½***

No.	Type	Description	Unused	Used
85	A14b	3ch ol grn & gold	15	15
86	A14b	10ch red brn & gold	15	15
87	A14b	20ch Prus bl & gold	20	20
88	A14b	2.50nu dp mag & gold	1.00	1.00

New Headquarters of Universal Postal Union, Bern, Switzerland.
Exist imperf. Price $4.

Wangdiphodrang Dzong and Bridge A15

1971–73 **Photogravure** ***Perf. 13½***

No.	Type	Description	Unused	Used
89	A15	2ch gray ('73)	5	5
90	A15	3ch dp red lil ('73)	5	5
91	A15	4ch vio ('73)	5	5
92	A15	5ch dk grn	15	15
93	A15	10ch org brn	15	15
94	A15	15ch dp bl	15	15
95	A15	20ch dp plum	15	15
		Nos. 89-95 (7)	75	75

U.N. Emblem and Bhutan Flag A16

Designs (Bhutan Flag and): 10ch, UN Headquarters, New York. 20ch, Security Council Chamber and mural by Per Krohg. 3nu, General Assembly Hall.

1971, Sept. 21 **Photo.** ***Perf. 13½***

No.	Type	Description	Unused	Used
96	A16	5ch gold, bl & multi	5	5
97	A16	10ch gold & multi	5	5
98	A16	20ch gold & multi	6	6
99	A16	3nu gold & multi	85	85
		Nos. 96-99, C1-C3 (7)	5.26	5.26

Bhutan's admission to the United Nations. Exist imperf.

Boy Scout Crossing Stream in Rope Sling—A17

Designs (Emblem and Boy Scouts): 20ch, 2nu, mountaineering. 50ch, 6nu, reading map. 75ch, as 10ch.

1971, Nov. 30 **Litho.** ***Perf. 13½***

No.	Type	Description	Unused	Used
143	A17	10ch gold & multi	5	5
144	A17	20ch gold & multi	7	7
145	A17	50ch gold & multi	17	17
146	A17	75ch sil & multi	25	25
147	A17	2nu sil & multi	65	65
148	A17	6nu sil & multi	2.00	2.00
a.		Souvenir sheet of 2	2.75	2.75
		Nos. 143-148 (6)	3.19	3.19

60th anniversary of the Boy Scouts. No. 148a contains one each of Nos. 147–148 and 2 labels. Silver fleur-de-lis pattern on labels and margin. Size: 92½x92½mm. Exist imperf.

Nos. 87–90 Overprinted in Gold

UNHCR
UNRWA
1971

1971, Dec. 23

No.	Type	Description	Unused	Used
149	A16	5ch gold & multi	5	5
150	A16	10ch gold & multi	5	5
151	A16	20ch gold & multi	7	7
152	A16	3nu gold & multi	1.00	1.00
		Nos. 149-152, C4-C6 (7)	5.57	5.57

World Refugee Year. Exist imperf.

Book Year Emblem A17a

1972, May 15 **Photo.** ***Perf. 13½x13***

No.	Type	Description	Unused	Used
153	A17a	2ch multi	8	8
154	A17a	3ch multi	8	8
155	A17a	5ch multi	12	8
156	A17a	20ch multi	25	10

International Book Year.

King Jigme Singye Wangchuk and Royal Crest—A18

Designs (King and): 25ch, 90ch, Flag of Bhutan. 1.25nu, Wheel with 8 good luck signs. 2nu, 4nu, Punakha Dzong, former winter capital. 3nu, 5nu, Crown. 5ch, same as 10ch.

1974, June 2 **Litho.** ***Perf. 13½***

No.	Type	Description	Unused	Used
157	A18	10ch mar & multi	5	5
158	A18	25ch gold & multi	10	10
159	A18	1.25nu multi	45	45
160	A18	2nu gold & multi	70	70
161	A18	3nu multi	1.00	1.00
		Nos. 157-161 (5)	2.30	2.30

Souvenir Sheets

Perf. 13½, Imperf.

No.	Type	Description	Unused	Used
162	A18	Sheet of 2	2.00	2.00
a.		5ch mar & multi	5	
b.		5nu red org & multi	1.70	
163	A18	Sheet of 2	2.00	2.00
a.		90ch gold & multi	45	
b.		4nu gold & multi	1.40	

Coronation of King Jigme Singye Wangchuk, June 2, 1974. Nos. 162–163 have maroon and multicolored borders with picture of the king wearing peacock crown. Size: 177x127mm.

Mailman on Horseback A19

Old and New Locomotives A20

Designs (UPU Emblem, Carrier Pigeon and): 3ch, Sailing and steam ships. 4ch, Old biplane and jet. 25ch, Mail runner and jeep.

1974, Oct. 9 **Litho.** ***Perf. 14½***

No.	Type	Description	Unused	Used
164	A19	1ch grn & multi	5	5
165	A20	2ch lil & multi	5	5
166	A20	3ch ocher & multi	5	5
167	A20	4ch yel grn & multi	5	5
168	A20	25ch sal & multi	10	10
		Nos. 164-168, C7-C9 (8)	1.90	1.90

Centenary of Universal Postal Union. Issued in sheets of 50 and sheets of 5 plus label with multicolored margin. Exist imperf.

Family and WPY Emblem—A21

1974, Dec. 17 ***Perf. 13½***

No.	Type	Description	Unused	Used
169	A21	25ch bl & multi	6	6
170	A21	50ch org & multi	12	12
171	A21	90ch ver & multi	22	22
172	A21	2.50nu brn & multi	60	60
a.		Souv. sheet, 10nu	3.50	3.50

Sephisa Chandra A22

Designs: Indigenous butterflies.

1975, Sept. **Lithographed** ***Perf. 14½***

Multicolored

No.	Type	Description	Unused	Used
173	A22	1ch *shown*	5	5
174	A22	2ch *Lethe kansa*	5	5
175	A22	3ch *Neope bhadra*	5	5
176	A22	4ch *Euthalia duda*	5	5
177	A22	5ch *Vindula erota*	5	5
178	A22	10ch *Bhutanitis Lidderdale*	5	5
179	A22	3nu *Limenitis zayla*	90	90
180	A22	5nu *Delis thysbe*	2.00	2.00
		Nos. 173-180 (8)	3.20	3.20

Souvenir Sheet

Perf. 13

No.	Type	Description	Unused	Used
181	A22	10nu *Dabasa gyas*	3.75	3.75

No. 181 contains one stamp; Bhutanese landscape in multicolored margin. Size: 115x90mm.

Apollo and Apollo-Soyuz Emblem—A23

Design: No. 183, Soyuz and emblem.

1975, Oct. **Litho.** ***Perf. 14x13½***

No.	Type	Description	Unused	Used
182	A23	10nu multi	3.00	3.00
183	A23	10nu multi	3.00	3.00
a.		Souvenir sheet of 2, 15nu	10.00	10.00

Apollo Soyuz link-up in space, July 17. Nos. 182–183 printed se-tenant in sheets of 10. No. 183a contains two 15nu stamps similar to Nos 182–183; light green margin with U.S. and U.S.S.R. flags and Apollo-Soyuz emblem. Size: 130x90 mm. Exist imperf.

Jewelry A24

Designs: 2ch, Coffee pot, bell and sugar cup. 3ch, Container and drinking horn. 4ch, Pendants and box cover. 5ch, Painter. 15ch, Silversmith. 20ch, Wood carver with tools. 1.50nu, Mat maker. 5nu, 10nu, Printer.

1975, Nov. ***Perf. 14½***

No.	Type	Description	Unused	Used
184	A24	1ch multi	5	5
185	A24	2ch multi	5	5
186	A24	3ch multi	5	5
187	A24	4ch multi	5	5
188	A24	5ch multi	5	5
189	A24	15ch multi	5	5
190	A24	20ch multi	6	6
191	A24	1.50nu multi	45	45
192	A24	10nu multi	3.00	3.00
		Nos. 184-192 (9)	3.81	3.81

Souvenir Sheet

Perf. 13

No.	Type	Description	Unused	Used
193	A24	5nu multi	1.50	1.50

Handicrafts and craftsmen. No. 193 contains one stamp; multicolored margin with black inscription. Size: 105x80mm.

King Jigme Singye Wangchuk
A25

Designs: 25ch, 90ch, 1nu, 2nu, 4nu, like 15ch. 1.30nu, 3nu, 5nu, Coat of arms. Sizes (Diameter): 15ch, 1nu, 1.30nu, 38mm. 25ch, 2nu, 3nu, 49mm. 90ch, 4nu, 5nu, 63mm.

Lithographed, Embossed on Gold Foil

1975, Nov. 11 ***Imperf.***

194	A25	15ch emerald	5	5
195	A25	25ch emerald	8	8
196	A25	90ch emerald	28	28
197	A25	1nu brt car	30	30
198	A25	1.30nu brt car	35	35
199	A25	2nu brt car	50	50
200	A25	3nu brt car	80	80
201	A25	4nu brt car	1.20	1.20
202	A25	5nu brt car	1.50	1.50
		Nos. 194-202 (9)	5.06	5.06

King Jigme Singye Wangchuk's 20th birthday.

Rhododendron Cinnabarinum
A28

Designs (Rhododendron): 2ch, Campanulatum. 3ch, Fortunei. 4ch, Red arboreum. 5ch, Pink arboreum. 1nu, Falconeri. 3nu, Hodgsonii. 5nu, Keysii. 10nu, Cinnabarinum.

1976, Feb. 15 Litho. *Perf. 15*

203	A28	1ch rose & multi	5	5
204	A28	2ch lt grn & multi	5	5
205	A28	3ch gray & multi	5	5
206	A28	4ch lil & multi	5	5
207	A28	5ch ol gray & multi	5	5
208	A28	1nu brn org & multi	30	24
209	A28	3nu ultra & multi	90	72
210	A28	5nu gray & multi	1.50	1.20
		Nos. 203-210 (8)	2.95	2.41

Souvenir Sheet

Perf. 13½

211	A28	10nu multi	3.50	3.50

No. 211 contains one stamp; multicolored margin showing rhododendrons around pool. Size: 105x80mm.

Slalom and Olympic Games Emblem
A29

Designs (Olympic Games Emblem and): 2ch, 4-men bobsled. 3ch, Ice hockey. 4ch, Cross-country skiing. 5ch, Figure skating, women's. 2nu, Downhill skiing. 4nu, Speed skating. 6nu, Ski jump. 10nu, Figure skating, pairs.

1976, Mar. 29 Litho. *Perf. 13½*

212	A29	1ch multi	5	5
213	A29	2ch multi	5	5
214	A29	3ch multi	5	5
215	A29	4ch multi	5	5
216	A29	5ch multi	5	5
217	A29	2nu multi	50	45
218	A29	4nu multi	1.20	90
219	A29	10nu multi	3.00	2.25
		Nos. 212-219 (8)	4.95	3.85

Souvenir Sheet

220	A29	6nu multi	2.00	2.00

12th Winter Olympic Games, Innsbruck, Austria, Feb. 4-15. No. 220 has orange and brown margin showing ski jump. Size: 78x104mm.

Orchid
A30

Designs: Various orchids.

1976, June Litho. *Perf. 14½*

221	A30	1ch multi	5	5
222	A30	2ch multi	5	5
223	A30	3ch multi	5	5
224	A30	4ch multi	5	5
225	A30	5ch multi	5	5
226	A30	2nu multi	60	45
227	A30	4nu multi	1.20	90
228	A30	6nu multi	1.80	1.50
		Nos. 221-228 (8)	3.85	3.10

Souvenir Sheet

Perf. 13½

229	A30	10nu multi	3.25	3.00

No. 229 contains one stamp; multicolored margin with orchid design. Size: 106x 80mm.

Double Carp Design—A31

Designs: Various symbolic designs and Colombo Plan emblem.

1976, July 1 Litho. *Perf. 14½*

230	A31	3ch red & multi	5	5
231	A31	4ch ver & multi	5	5
232	A31	5ch multi	5	5
233	A31	25ch bl & multi	20	15
234	A31	1.25nu multi	38	30
235	A31	2nu yel & multi	60	48
236	A31	2.50nu vio & multi	75	60
237	A31	3nu multi	90	72
		Nos. 230-237 (8)	2.98	2.40

Colombo Plan, 25th anniversary.

Bandaranaike Conference Hall—A32

1976, Aug. 16 Litho. *Perf. 13½*

238	A32	1.25nu multi	45	30
239	A32	2.50nu multi	85	60

5th Summit Conference of Non-aligned Countries, Colombo, Sri Lanka, Aug. 9-19.

Queen Elizabeth II
A33

Liberty Bell
A34

Spirit of St. Louis
A35

Bhutanese Archer, Olympic Rings
A36

Designs: No. 242, Alexander Graham Bell. No. 245, LZ 3 Zeppelin docking, 1907. No. 246, Alfred B. Nobel.

1978, Nov. 15 Litho. *Perf. 14½*

240	A33	20nu multi	5.00	5.00
241	A34	20nu multi	5.00	5.00
242	A33	20nu multi	5.00	5.00
243	A35	20nu multi	5.00	5.00
244	A36	20nu multi	5.00	5.00
245	A35	20nu multi	5.00	5.00
246	A33	20nu multi	5.00	5.00
		Nos. 240-246 (7)	35.00	35.00

Commemoration: 25th anniversary of coronation of Queen Elizabeth II; American Bicentennial; centenary of first telephone call by Alexander Graham Bell; Charles A. Lindbergh crossing the Atlantic, 50th anniversary; Olympic Games; 75th anniversary of the Zeppelin; 75th anniversary of Nobel Prize. Seven souvenir sheets exist, each 25nu, commemorating same events with different designs. Size: 103x80mm.

Issues of 1967-1976 Surcharged with New Value and Bars

Perforations and Printing as Before

1978 Multicolored

252	A16	25ch on 3nu (#99)		
253	A17	25ch on 6nu (#148)		
254	A21	25ch on 2.50nu (#172)		
255	A22	25ch on 3nu (#179)		
256	A22	25ch on 5nu (#180)		
257	A23	25ch on 10nu (#182)		
258	A23	25ch on 10nu (#183)		
259	A24	25ch on 10nu (#192)		
260	A28	25ch on 5nu (#210)		
261	A29	25ch on 4nu (#218)		
262	A29	25ch on 10nu (#219)		
263	A30	25ch on 4nu (#227)		
264	A30	25ch on 6nu (#228)		
265	A31	25ch on 2.50nu (#236)		
266		25ch on 5nu *Girl Scout*		
267		25ch on 3nu *INDIPEX*		
268		25ch on 4nu *Dog*		
269		25ch on 8nu *Dogs*		
		Nos. 252-269, C11-C18 (26)	*50.00*	*50.00*

Nos. 266-269 on unlisted issues (see For the Record).

Mother and Child, IYC Emblem
A37

IYC Emblem and: 5nu, Mother and two children. 10nu, Boys with blackboards and stylus.

1979, June Litho. *Perf. 14x13½*

289	A37	2nu multi	65	50
290	A37	5nu multi	1.60	1.25
291	A37	10nu multi	3.00	2.50
a.		Souvenir sheet of 3	5.50	4.50

International Year of the Child. No. 291a contains Nos. 289-291, perf. 15x 13½, and label; olive green decorative margin. Size: 130x103mm.

Conference Emblem and Dove—A38

Design: 10nu, Emblem and Bhutanese symbols.

1979, Sept. 3 Litho. *Perf. 14x13½*

292	A38	25ch multi	8	6
293	A38	10nu multi	3.25	2.50

6th Non-Aligned Summit Conference, Havana, August 1979.

Silver Rattle, Dorji—A39

Antiques: 10ch, Silver handbell, Dilbu (vert.). 15ch, Cylindrical jar, Jadum (vert.). 25ch, Ornamental teapot, Jamjee. 1nu, Leather container, Kem (vert.). 1.25nu, Brass teapot, Jamjee. 1.70nu, Vessel with elephant-head legs, Sangphor (vert.). 2nu, Teapot with ornamental spout, Jamjee (vert.). 3nu, Metal pot on claw-shaped feet, Yangtho (vert.). 4nu, Dish inlaid with precious stones, Battha. 5nu, Metal circular flask, Chhap (vert.).

1979, Dec. 17 Photo. *Perf. 14*

294	A39	5ch multi	5	5
295	A39	10ch multi	5	5
296	A39	15ch multi	5	5
297	A39	25ch multi	8	6
298	A39	1nu multi	30	25
299	A39	1.25nu multi	35	32
300	A39	1.70nu multi	45	45
301	A39	2nu multi	60	50
302	A39	3nu multi	80	75
303	A39	4nu multi	1.10	1.00
304	A39	5nu multi	1.50	1.25
		Nos. 294-304 (11)	5.33	4.73

Hill, Rinpiang Dzong
A40

Hill Statue, Stamps of Bhutan and : 2nu, Dzong. 5nu, Ounsti Dzong. 10nu, Lingzi Dzong, Gt. Britain Type 81. 20nu, Rope bridge, Penny Black.

1980, May 6 Litho. *Perf. 14x13½*

305	A40	1nu multi	30	25
306	A40	2nu multi	60	50
307	A40	5nu multi	1.60	1.25
308	A40	10nu multi	3.00	2.50

Souvenir Sheet

309	A40	20nu multi	6.50	5.00

Sir Rowland Hill (1795-1879), originator of penny postage. No. 309 has multicolored margin showing postal runner and Hill. Size: 102x103mm.

Kichu Lhakhang Monastery, Phari—A41

Guru Padma Sambhava's Birthday: Monasteries.

1981, July 11 Litho. *Perf. 14*

310	A41	1nu Dungtse, Phari (vert.)	32	25
311	A41	2nu shown	65	50
312	A41	2.25nu Kurjey	75	55
313	A41	3nu Tangu, Thimphu	1.00	75
314	A41	4nu Cheri, Thimphu	1.30	1.00
315	A41	5nu Chorten, Kora	1.65	1.25
316	A41	7nu Tak-Tsang, Phari (vert.)	2.30	1.75
		Nos. 310-316 (7)	7.97	6.05

Prince Charles and Lady Diana
A42

1981, Sept. 10 Litho. *Perf. 14½*

317	A42	1nu St. Paul's Cathedral	32	25
318	A42	5nu like #317	1.65	1.25
319	A42	20nu shown	6.50	5.00
320	A42	25nu like #319	8.25	6.00

Souvenir Sheet

321	A42	20nu Wedding procession	6.50	5.00

Royal wedding. Nos. 318-319 issued in sheets of 5 plus label. No. 321 has multicolored decorative margin. Size: 69x91mm.

Orange-bellied Chloropsis—A43

1982, Apr. 19 Litho. *Perf. 14*

322	A43	2nu shown	65	50
323	A43	3nu Monal pheasant	1.00	75
324	A43	5nu Ward's trogon	1.65	1.25
325	A43	10nu Mrs. Gould's sunbird	3.25	2.50

Souvenir Sheet

326	A43	25nu Maroon oriole	8.25	6.25

No. 326 has multicolored margin showing birds, map. Size: 95x101mm.

1982 World Cup—A44

Designs: Various soccer players.

1982, June 25 Litho. *Perf. 14½x14*

327	A44	1nu multi	30	25
328	A44	2nu multi	65	50
329	A44	3nu multi	1.00	75
330	A44	20nu multi	6.50	5.00

Souvenir Sheets

331	A44	25nu multi	8.50	6.25

Nos. 331 have multicolored margins continuing design and listing finalists (Algeria, etc. or Hungary, etc.). Sizes: 80x118mm.

21st Birthday of Princess Diana—A45

1982, Aug.

332	A45	1nu St. James' Palace	32	30
332A	A45	10nu Diana, Charles	3.25	2.50
332B	A45	15nu Windsor Castle	5.00	5.50
333	A45	25nu Wedding	8.50	6.25

Souvenir Sheet

334	A45	20nu Diana	6.50	5.00

No. 334 has multicolored margin showing family tree, Franklin Roosevelt. Size: 104x75mm.

10nu, 15 nu issued only in sheets of 5 plus label.

Scouting Year—A46

1982, Aug. 23 Litho. *Perf. 14*

335	A46	3nu Baden-Powell, vert.	1.00	75
336	A46	5nu Eating around fire	1.65	1.25
337	A46	15nu Reading map	5.00	3.75
338	A46	20nu Pitching tents	6.75	5.00

Souvenir Sheet

339	A46	25nu Mountain climbing	8.25	6.25

No. 339 has multicolored margin continuing design. Size: 91x70mm.

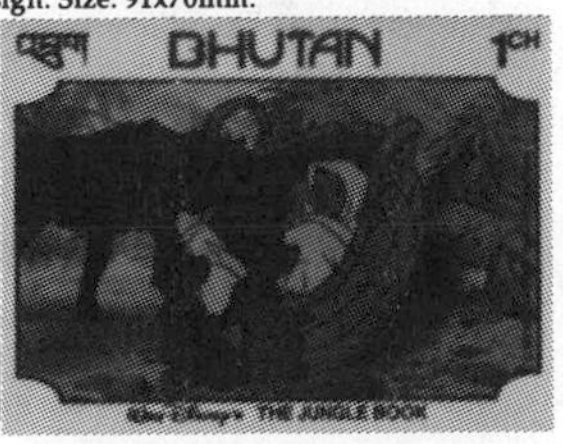

Rama and Cubs with Mowgli—A47

Designs: Scenes from Walt Disney's The Jungle Book.

1982, Sept. 1 *Perf. 11*

340	A47	1ch multi	5	5
341	A47	2ch multi	5	5
342	A47	3ch multi	5	5
343	A47	4ch multi	5	5
344	A47	5ch multi	5	5
345	A47	10ch multi	5	5
346	A47	30ch multi	10	8
347	A47	2nu multi	65	50
348	A47	20nu multi	6.50	5.00
		Nos. 340-348 (9)	7.55	5.88

Souvenir Sheets
Perf. 13½

349	A47	20nu Baloo and Mowgli in forest	6.50	5.00
350	A47	20nu Baloo and Mowgli floating	6.50	5.00

Nos. 349-350 have multicolored margins. Size: 127x102mm.

George Washington Surveying—A48

1982, Nov. 15 Litho. *Perf. 15*

351	A48	50ch shown	16	12
352	A48	1nu FDR, Harvard	32	25
353	A48	2nu Washington at Valley Forge	65	50
354	A48	3nu FDR, family	1.00	75
355	A48	4nu Washington, Battle of Monmouth	1.30	1.00
356	A48	5nu FDR, White House	1.65	1.25
357	A48	15nu Washington, Mt. Vernon	5.00	3.75
358	A48	20nu FDR, Churchill, Stalin	6.50	5.00
		Nos. 351-358 (8)	16.58	12.62

Souvenir Sheets

359	A48	25nu Washington, vert.	8.25	6.25
360	A48	25nu FDR, vert.	8.25	6.25

George Washington (1732-1799) and Franklin D. Roosevelt (1882-1945). Size of Nos. 359-360: 103x73mm.

Nos. 332, 333-334 Overprinted: "ROYAL BABY / 21.6.82"

1982, Nov. 19 *Perf. 14½x14*

361	A45	1nu multi	32	32
362	A45	25nu multi	8.50	6.25

Souvenir Sheet

363	A45	20nu multi	6.50	5.00

Birth of Prince William of Wales, June 21.

500th Birth Anniv. of Raphael—A51

Portraits.

1983, Mar. 23 *Perf. 13½*

375	A51	1nu Angelo Doni	32	25
376	A51	4nu Maddalena Doni	1.30	1.00
377	A51	5nu Baldassare Castiglione	1.65	1.25
378	A51	20nu La Donna Velata	6.50	5.00

Souvenir Sheets

379	A51	25nu Expulsion of Heliodorus	8.25	6.25
380	A51	25nu Mass of Bolsena	8.25	6.25

Nos. 148, 184 and Issues of 1972-73 Overprinted: "Druk Air"

Litho. (30ch), Photo.
1983, Feb. 11 *Perf. 14½ (30ch), 13½*

381	A24	30ch on 1ch multi	10	8
382		5nu multi INDIPEX	1.65	1.25
383	A17	6nu multi	2.00	1.50
384		7nu multi, olympics	2.30	1.75
385		8nu multi, dogs	2.60	2.00
		Nos. 381-385 (5)	8.65	6.58

Druk Air Service inauguration. Overprint of 8nu all caps. Nos. 382, 384 air mail.

Manned Flight Bicentenary—A52

1983, Aug. 15 Litho. *Perf. 15*

386	A52	50ch Dornier Wal	16	12
387	A52	3nu Savoia-Marchetti S-66	1.00	75
388	A52	10nu Hawker Osprey	3.25	2.50
389	A52	20nu Ville de Paris	6.50	5.00

Souvenir Sheet

390	A52	25nu Balloon Captif	8.25	6.00

Buddhist Symbols—A53

1983, Aug. 11 Litho. *Perf. 13½*
391 A53 25ch Sacred vase 8 6
392 A53 50ch Five Sensory Symbols 16 12
393 A53 2nu Seven Treasures 65 50
394 A53 3nu Five Sensory Organs 1.00 75
395 A53 8nu Five Fleshes 2.60 2.00
396 A53 9nu Sacrificial cake 3.00 2.25
a. Souvenir sheet of 6 7.50 5.75
Nos. 391-396 (6) 7.49 5.68

Size of Nos. 393, 396: 45x40mm. No. 396a contains Nos. 391-396. Size: 180x135mm.

World Communications Year (1983)—A54

Various Disney characters and history of communications.

1984, Apr. 10 Litho. *Perf. 14½x14*
397 A54 4ch multi 5 5
398 A54 5ch multi 5 5
399 A54 10ch multi 5 5
400 A54 20ch multi 6 5
401 A54 25ch multi 8 6
402 A54 50ch multi 16 12
403 A54 1nu multi 32 25
404 A54 5nu multi 1.65 1.25
405 A54 20nu multi 6.50 5.00
Nos. 397-405 (9) 8.92 6.88

Souvenir Sheets
Perf. 14x14½
406 A54 20nu Donald Duck on phone, horiz. 6.50 5.00
407 A54 20nu Mickey Mouse on TV 6.50 5.00

Nos. 406-407 have multicolored margin continuing design. Size: 128x103mm.

1984 Winter Olympics—A55

1984, Apr. *Perf. 14*
408 A55 50ch Skiing 16 12
409 A55 1nu Cross-country skiing 32 25
410 A55 3nu Speed skating 1.00 75
411 A55 20nu Bobsledding 6.40 5.00

Souvenir Sheet
412 A55 25nu Hockey 8.25 6.25

Golden Langur A56

Locomotives A57

1984, June 1 Litho. *Perf. 14½*
413 A56 50ch shown 10 8
414 A56 1nu Group in tree, horiz. 20 15
415 A56 2nu Family, horiz. 40 30
416 A56 4nu Group walking 80 60

Souvenir Sheets
417 A56 20nu Snow leopard 4.50 3.00
418 A56 25nu Yak 4.50 3.00
419 A56 25nu Blue sheep, horiz. 4.50 3.00

Size: 122x88mm, 88x122mm.

1984, July 16
420 A57 50ch Sans Pareil, 1829 10 8
421 A57 1nu Planet, 1830 20 15
422 A57 3nu Experiment, 1832 60 45
423 A57 4nu Black Hawk, 1835 80 60
424 A57 5.50nu Jenny Lind, 1847 1.10 85
425 A57 8nu Semmering-Bavaria, 1851 1.60 1.25
426 A57 10nu Great Northern #1, 1870 2.00 1.50
427 A57 25nu German Natl. Tinder, 1880 5.00 3.75
Nos. 420-427 (8) 11.40 8.63

Souvenir Sheets
428 A57 20nu Darjeeling Himalayan Railway, 1984 4.00 3.00
429 A57 20nu Sondermann Freight, 1896 4.00 3.00
430 A57 20nu Crampton's locomotive, 1846 4.00 3.00
431 A57 20nu Erzsebet, 1870 4.00 3.00

Nos. 424-427 horiz. Sizes (Nos. 428-431): 93x65mm.

Classic Cars—A58

1984, Aug. 29 Litho. *Perf. 14*
432 A58 50ch Riley Sprite, 1936 10 8
433 A58 1nu Lanchester, 1919 20 15
434 A58 3nu Itala, 1907 60 45
435 A58 4nu Morris Oxford Bullnose, 1913 80 60
436 A58 5.50nu Lagonda LG6, 1939 1.10 85
437 A58 6nu Wolseley, 1903 1.20 90
438 A58 8nu Buick Super, 1952 1.60 1.20
439 A58 20nu Maybach Zeppelin, 1933 4.00 3.00
Nos. 432-439 (8) 9.60 7.23

Souvenir Sheet
440 A58 25nu Simplex, 1912 4.50 3.00
441 A58 25nu Renault, 1901 4.50 3.00

Nos. 440-441 have multicolored margins showing flowers. Size: 126x99mm.

Summer Olympic Games—A59

1984, Oct. 27 Litho.
442 A59 15ch Women's archery 5 5
443 A59 25ch Men's archery 5 5
444 A59 2nu Table tennis 40 30
445 A59 2.25nu Basketball 45 35
446 A59 5.50nu Boxing 1.10 85
447 A59 6nu Running 1.20 90
448 A59 8nu Tennis 1.60 1.20
Nos. 442-448 (7) 4.85 3.70

Souvenir Sheet
449 A59 25nu Archery 4.50 3.25

No. 449 shows Himalayas in margin. Size: 116x83mm.

Nos. 335-339 Surcharged with New Values and Bars in Black or Silver.

1984, Oct. Litho. *Perf. 14*
450 A46 10 nu on 3 nu multi 1.75 1.35
451 A46 10 nu on 5 nu multi 1.75 1.35
452 A46 10 nu on 15 nu multi 1.75 1.35
453 A46 10 nu on 20 nu multi 1.75 1.35

Souvenir Sheet
454 A46 20 nu on 25 nu multi 3.50 2.75

Nos. 332, 332A, 332B, 333-334 Surcharged with New Values and Bars.

1984, Oct.
455 A45 5 nu on 1 nu multi 90 68
456 A45 5 nu on 10 nu multi 90 68
457 A45 5 nu on 15 nu multi 90 68
458 A45 40 nu on 25 nu multi 7.25 5.25

Souvenir Sheet
459 A45 25 nu on 20 nu multi 4.50 3.50

50th Anniv. of Donald Duck—A60

1984, Dec. 10 Litho. *Perf. 13½x14*
460 A60 4ch Magician Mickey 5 5
461 A60 5ch Slide, Donald, Slide 5 5
462 A60 10ch Donald's Golf Game 5 5
463 A60 20ch Mr. Duck Steps Out 5 5
464 A60 25ch Lion Around 5 5
465 A60 50ch Alpine Climbers 10 8
466 A60 1nu Flying Jalopy 20 15
467 A60 5nu Frank Duck 1.00 75
468 A60 20nu Good Scouts 4.00 3.00
Nos. 460-468 (9) 5.55 4.23

Souvenir Sheets
469 A60 20nu Three Caballeros 4.00 3.00
470 A60 20nu Sea Scouts 4.00 3.00

Size: 128x102mm.

Nos. 317-321 Surcharged with New Values and Bars.

1984, Oct. Litho. *Perf. 14½*
471 A42 10 nu on 1 nu multi 1.75 1.35
472 A42 10 nu on 5 nu multi 1.75 1.35
473 A42 10 nu on 20 nu multi 1.75 1.35
474 A42 10 nu on 25 nu multi 1.75 1.35

Souvenir Sheet
475 A42 25 nu on 20 nu multi 4.50 3.50

Nos. 361, 361A, 361B, 362-363 Surcharged with New Values and Bars.

1984, Oct. *Perf. 14½x14*
476 A45 5 nu on 1 nu multi
477 A45 5 nu on 10 nu multi
478 A45 5 nu on 15 nu multi
479 A45 40 nu on 25 nu multi

Souvenir Sheet
480 A45 25 nu on 20 nu multi

Nos. 327-331 Surcharged with New Values and Bars in Black or Silver.

1984, Dec.
481 A44 5 nu on 1 nu multi 90 68
482 A44 5 nu on 2 nu multi 90 68
483 A44 5 nu on 3 nu multi 90 68
484 A44 5 nu on 20 nu multi 90 68

Souvenir Sheets
485 A44 20 nu on 25 nu multi 3.50 2.75

Mask Dance of the Judgement of Death—A61

1984, Dec. *Perf. 13½*
486 A61 5 ch Shinje Choegyel 5 5
487 A61 35 ch Raksh Lango 6 5
488 A61 50 ch Druelgo 10 8
489 A61 2.50 nu Pago 45 35
490 A61 3 nu Telgo 55 42
491 A61 4 nu Due Nakcung 75 58
492 A61 5 nu Lha Karpo 90 68
a. Souvenir sheet of 4, #486-487, 491-492 1.75 1.40
493 A61 5.50 nu Nyalbum 1.00 75
494 A61 6 nu Khimda Pelkyi 1.10 85
Nos. 486-494 (9) 4.96 3.81

No. 492a has multicolored margin containing inscriptions. Size: 91x136mm.

Monasteries—A62

1984, Dec. 1 Litho. *Perf. 12*
495 A62 10ch Domkhar 5 5
496 A62 25ch Shemgang 5 5
497 A62 50ch Chapcha 8 8
498 A62 1nu Tashigang 14 14
499 A62 2nu Pungthang Chhug 28 28
500 A62 5nu Dechhenphoda 70 70
Nos. 495-500 (6) 1.30 1.30

Veteran's War Memorial Building, San Francisco—A63

1985, Oct. 24 Litho. *Perf. 14*
502 A63 50ch Flags of Bhutan, U.N., vert. 9 6
503 A63 15nu Headquarters, New York, vert. 2.50 1.75
504 A63 20nu shown 3.50 2.50

Souvenir Sheet
505 A63 25nu UN Human Rights Declaration 4.25 3.00

UN, 40th anniv. No. 505 has bright blue and black margin picturing the emblems of the UN agencies. Size: 65x80mm.

Audubon Birth Bicentenary—A64

Illustrations of North American bird species by Audubon.

1985

506	A64	50ch Anas breweri	9	6
507	A64	1nu Lagopus lagopus	18	14
508	A64	2nu Charadrius montanus	35	25
509	A64	3nu Cavia stellata	52	40
510	A64	4nu Canachites canadensis	70	52
511	A64	5nu Mergus cucullatus	85	62
512	A64	15nu Olor buccinator	2.50	1.75
513	A64	20nu Bucephala clangula	3.50	2.50
		Nos. 506-513 (8)	8.69	6.24

Souvenir Sheets

514	A64	25nu Accipiter striatus	4.25	3.00
515	A64	25nu Parus bicolor	4.25	3.00

Nos. 507, 510-511, 514 Nov. 15. Nos. 506, 508-509, 513, 515 Dec. 6. Nos. 514-515 have multicolored margins continuing the illustrations. Sizes: 75x105mm.

A Tramp Abroad, by Mark Twain (1835-1910)—A65

Walt Disney animated characters.

1985, Nov. 15

516	A65	50ch multi	9	6
517	A65	2nu multi	35	25
518	A65	5nu multi	85	62
519	A65	9nu multi	1.50	1.15
520	A65	20nu multi	3.50	2.50
		Nos. 516-520 (5)	6.29	4.58

Souvenir Sheet

521	A65	25nu Goofy, Mickey Mouse	4.25	3.00

Intl. Youth Year. No. 521 has multicolored decorative margin continuing design and picturing Donald Duck and Hirschhorn Castle. Size: 126x101mm.

Rapunzel, by Jacob and Wilhelm Grimm—A66

Walt Disney animated characters.

1985, Nov. 15

522	A66	1nu multi	18	14
523	A66	4nu multi	70	52
524	A66	7nu multi	1.25	95
525	A66	8nu multi	1.40	1.05
526	A66	15nu multi	2.50	1.75
		Nos. 522-526 (5)	6.03	4.41

No. 525 printed in sheets of 8.

Souvenir Sheet

527	A66	25nu multi	4.25	3.00

No. 527 has multicolored margin continuing the design. Size: 127x101mm.

First South Asian Regional Cooperation Summit, Dec. 7-8, Dacca, Bangladesh—A67

1985, Dec. 8 *Perf. 14*

528	A67	50ch multi	9	6
529	A67	5nu multi	85	62

Seven Precious Attributes of the Universal King—A68

1986, Feb. 12 **Litho.** *Perf. 13x12½*

530	A68	30ch Wheel	5	5
531	A68	50ch Gem	8	8
532	A68	1.25nu Queen	18	18
533	A68	2nu Minister	28	28
534	A68	4nu Elephant	55	55
535	A68	6nu Horse	85	85
536	A68	8nu General	1.15	1.15
		Nos. 530-536 (7)	3.14	3.14

Nos. 442-443, 445-449 Ovptd. with Medal, Winners' Names and Countries. No. 449 Ovptd. for Men's and Women's Events.

1986, May 5 **Litho.** *Perf. 14*

537	A59	15ch Hyang Soon Seo, So. Korea	5	5
538	A59	25ch Darrell Pace, US	5	5
539	A59	2.25nu US	32	32
540	A59	5.50nu Mark Breland, US	78	78
541	A59	6nu Daley Thompson, Britain	85	85
542	A59	8nu Stefan Edberg, Sweden	1.15	1.15
		Nos. 537-542 (6)	3.20	3.20

Souvenir Sheets

543	A59	25nu Hyang Soon Seo	3.50	3.50
544	A59	25nu Darrel Pace	3.50	3.50

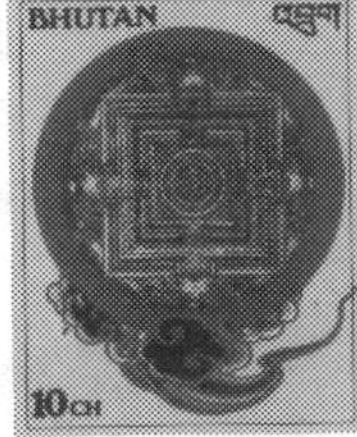

Kilkhor Mandalas, Deities—A69

Religious art: 10ch, 1nu, Phurpa, ritual dagger. 25ch, 3nu, Amitayus in wrath. 50ch, 5nu, Overpowering Deities. 75ch, 7nu, Great Wrathful One, Guru Rinpoche.

1986, June 17 *Perf. 13½*

545	A69	10ch multi	5	5
546	A69	25ch multi	5	5
547	A69	50ch multi	8	8
548	A69	75ch multi	12	12
549	A69	1nu multi	14	14
550	A69	3nu multi	42	42
551	A69	5nu multi	70	70
552	A69	7nu multi	1.00	1.00
		Nos. 545-552 (8)	2.56	2.56

Nos. 525, 519, 526, 520, 521 and 527 Ovptd. with AMERIPEX '86 Emblem.

1986, June 16 **Litho.** *Perf. 14*

553	A66	8nu multi	1.40	1.05
554	A65	9nu multi	1.50	1.15
555	A66	15nu multi	2.50	1.75
556	A65	20nu multi	3.50	2.50

Souvenir Sheets

557	A65	25nu #521	4.25	3.00
558	A66	25nu #527	4.25	3.00

A70

A71

Halley's Comet—A72

Designs: 50ch, Babylonian tablet fragments, 2349 B.C. sighting. 1nu, 17th cent. print, A.D. 66 sighting. 2nu, French silhouette art, 1835 sighting. 3nu, Bayeux Tapestry, 1066 sighting. 4nu, Woodblock, 684 sighting. 5nu, Illustration from Bybel Printen, 1650. 15nu, 1456 Sighting, Cancer constellation. 20nu, Delft plate, 1910 sighting. No. 572, Comet over Himalayas. No. 573, Comet over domed temple Dug-gye Jong.

1986, Nov. 4 **Litho.** *Perf. 15*

564	A70	50ch multi	10	8
565	A70	1nu multi	18	14
566	A71	2nu multi	35	28
567	A70	3nu multi	50	35
568	A70	4nu multi	68	52
569	A71	5nu multi	85	65
570	A70	15nu multi	2.50	2.00
571	A70	20nu multi	3.50	2.50
		Nos. 564-571 (8)	8.66	6.52

Souvenir Sheets

572	A72	25nu multi	4.25	3.00
573	A72	25nu multi	4.25	3.00

Nos. 572-573 have multicolored margins continuing the designs. Sizes: 110x80mm.

SEMI-POSTAL STAMPS

Nos. 10–12 Surcharged

+ 50 ch

Perf. 14x14½

1964, March **Litho.** **Unwmkd.**

B1	A3	33ch +50ch multi	3.75	3.75
B2	A3	70ch +50ch multi	3.75	3.75
B3	A3	1.30nu +50ch multi	3.75	3.75

Issued to commemorate the 9th Winter Olympic Games, Innsbruck, Jan. 29–Feb. 9, 1964.

Olympic Games Type of Regular Issue, 1964

Souvenir Sheet

Designs: 1nu+50ch, Archery. 2nu+50ch, Soccer.

1964, Oct. 10 ***Perf. 13½, Imperf.***

B4	A6	Sheet of 2	6.00	6.00
a.		1nu+50ch multi	75	75
b.		2nu+50ch multi	1.75	1.75

18th Olympic Games, Tokyo, Oct. 10–25. No. B4 has multicolored border. Size: 86x117½mm.

AIR POST STAMPS

U.N. Type of Regular Issue

Designs (Bhutan Flag and): 2.50nu, U.N. Headquarters, New York. 5nu, Security Council Chamber and mural by Per Krohg. 6nu, General Assembly Hall.

1971, Sept. 21 **Photo.** ***Perf. 13½***

C1	A16	2.50nu sil & multi	75	75
C2	A16	5nu sil & multi	1.50	1.50
C3	A16	6nu sil & multi	2.00	2.00

Bhutan's admission to the United Nations. Exist imperf.

Nos. C1–C3 Overprinted in Gold: "UNHCR / UNRWA / 1971" Like Nos. 153–156

1971, Dec. 23 **Litho.** ***Perf. 13½***

C4	A16	2.50nu sil & multi	80	80
C5	A16	5nu sil & multi	1.60	1.60
C6	A16	6nu sil & multi	2.00	2.00

World Refugee Year. Exist imperf.

UPU Types of 1974

Designs (UPU Emblem, Carrier Pigeon and): 1nu, Mail runner and jeep. 1.40nu, 10nu, Old and new locomotives. 2nu, Old biplane and jet.

1974, Oct. 9 **Litho.** ***Perf. 14½***

C7	A19	1nu sal & multi	35	35
C8	A20	1.40nu lil & multi	55	55
C9	A20	2nu multi	70	70

Souvenir Sheet

Perf. 13

C10	A20	10nu lil & multi	3.75	3.75

Centenary of Universal Postal Union. No. C10 contains one stamp; yellow and multicolored margin with UPU emblem and black inscription. Size: 91x78mm. Nos. C7–C9 were issued in sheets of 50 and sheets of 5 plus label with multicolored margin. Exist imperf.

Issues of 1968–1974 Surcharged 25ch and Bars

Perforations and Printing as Before

1978 **Multicolored**

C11	A16	25ch on 5nu (#C2)
C12	A16	25ch on 6nu (#C3)
C13	A20	25ch on 1.40nu (#C8)
C14	A20	25ch on 2nu (#C9)
C15		25ch on 4nu *Mythological creature*
C16		25ch on 10nu *Mythological creature*
C17		25ch on 5nu *INDIPEX*
C18		25ch on 6nu *INDIPEX*

Nos. C15–C18 on unlisted issues (see For the Record).

BOHEMIA AND MORAVIA

Listed under Czechoslovakia.

BOLIVIA

(bô·liv'i·á)

LOCATION — Central South America, separated from the Pacific Ocean by Chile and Peru.
GOVT.—Republic.
AREA—424,165 sq. mi.
POP.—6,252,250 (est. 1984).
CAPITAL—Sucre (La Paz is the actual seat of government).

100 Centavos = 1 Boliviano
100 Centavos = 1 Peso Boliviano (1963)

On February 21st, 1863, the Bolivian Government decreed contracts for carrying the mails should be let to the highest bidder, the service to commence on the day the bid was accepted, and stamps used for the payment of postage. On March 18th, 1863, the contract was awarded to Sr. Justiniano Garcia and was in effect until April 29th, 1863, when it was rescinded by the government. Stamps in the form illustrated above were prepared in denominations of ½, 1, 2 and 4 reales. All values exist in black and in blue. It is said that used copies exist on covers, but the authenticity of these covers remains to be established.

Condor
A1

A2

A3

72 varieties of each of the 5c, 78 varieties of the 10c, 30 varieties of each of the 50c and 100c.

The plate of the 5c stamps was entirely re-engraved four times and retouched at least six times. Various states of the plate have distinguishing characteristics, each of which is typical of most, though not all the stamps in a sheet. These characteristics (usually termed types) are found in the shading lines at the right side of the globe. (a.): vertical and diagonal lines; (b.): diagonal lines only; (c.): diagonal and horizontal with traces of vertical lines; (d): diagonal and horizontal lines; (e.): horizontal lines only; (f.): no lines except the curved ones forming the outlines of the globe.

Engraved.

1867–68 *Imperf.* Unwmkd.

1 A1 5c bl grn (b) 7.00 *20.00*
a. 5c bl grn (a) 7.00 *20.00*
b. 5c dp grn (a) 7.00 *20.00*
c. 5c ol grn, thick paper (a) 50.00 40.00
d. 5c yel grn, thick paper (a) 125.00 125.00
e. 5c yel grn, thick paper (b) 125.00 125.00
f. 5c yel grn, thin paper (a,b) 5.00 7.00
2 A1 5c grn (d) 6.00 11.00
a. 5c grn (c) 7.00 11.00
b. 5c grn (e) 6.00 11.00
c. 5c grn (f) 6.00 11.00
3 A1 5c vio ('68) 400.00 275.00
a. 5c rose lil ('68) 400.00 275.00
4 A3 10c brown 450.00 275.00
5 A2 50c orange 27.50
6 A2 50c bl ('68) *475.00*
a. 50c dk bl ('68) *475.00*
7 A3 100c blue 85.00
8 A3 100c grn ('68) 200.00
a. 100c pale bl grn ('68) 200.00

Used prices are for postally canceled copies. Pen cancellations usually indicate that the stamps have been used fiscally and such stamps sell for about one-fifth as much as those with postal cancellations.

Nos. 2-8 have been reprinted.

(9 stars)

(11 stars)

Coat of Arms
A4 A5

1868–69 *Perf. 12*

Nine Stars

10 A4 5c green 25.00 12.50
11 A4 10c vermilion 35.00 12.50
12 A4 50c blue 60.00 35.00
13 A4 100c orange 60.00 40.00
14 A4 500c black 750.00 650.00

Eleven Stars

15 A5 5c green 12.50 7.50
16 A5 10c vermilion 17.50 12.50
a. Half used as 5c as cover 600.00
17 A5 50c blue 45.00 20.00
18 A5 100c dp org 40.00 20.00
19 A5 500c black *2,000.* *2,000.*

Arms and "The Law"
A6

1878 Various Frames. *Perf. 12*

20 A6 5c ultra 12.50 5.00
21 A6 10c orange 10.00 4.00
a. Half used as 5c on cover 75.00
22 A6 20c green 30.00 5.00
a. Half used as 10c on cover 250.00
23 A6 50c dl car 150.00 15.00

(11 stars)

(9 stars)

Numerals Upright
A7 A8

1887 *Rouletted*

24 A7 1c rose 3.00 1.25
25 A7 2c violet 3.00 1.25
26 A5 5c blue 10.00 2.00
27 A5 10c orange 10.00 2.00

1890 *Perf. 12*

28 A8 1c rose 2.75 1.50
29 A8 2c violet 6.00 2.00
30 A4 5c blue 3.50 1.50
31 A4 10c orange 7.50 1.75
32 A4 20c dk grn 17.50 2.50
33 A4 50c red 7.50 2.50
34 A4 100c yellow 17.50 6.00
Nos. 28-34 (7) 62.25 17.75

1893 Lithographed. *Perf. 11.*

35 A8 1c rose 5.00 2.00
a. Imperf. pair 50.00
b. Imperf. vert., pair 30.00
c. Horizontal pair, imprf. between 50.00
36 A8 2c violet 5.00 2.00
a. Block of 4 imperf. vert. and horiz. through center 75.00
b. Horizontal pair, imperf. between 40.00
37 A7 5c blue 7.00 2.00
a. Imperf. horiz., pair 40.00
b. Horizontal pair imperf. between 50.00
38 A8 10c orange 20.00 3.00
a. Horizontal pair, imperf. between 75.00
39 A8 20c dk grn 65.00 20.00
a. Imperf. pair, vert. or horiz. 200.00
b. Pair, imperf. btwn., vert. or horiz. 200.00
Nos. 35-39 (5) 102.00 29.00

Coat of Arms
A9

Engraved.

Thin Paper.

1894 *Perf. 14, 14½.* Unwmkd.

40 A9 1c bister 2.00 1.00
41 A9 2c red org 2.00 1.00
42 A9 5c green 2.00 1.00
43 A9 10c yel brn 2.00 1.00
44 A9 20c dk bl 6.00 2.50
45 A9 50c claret 15.00 3.50
46 A9 100c brn rose 35.00 12.50
Nos. 40-46 (7) 64.00 22.50

Stamps of type A9 on thick paper were surreptitiously printed in Paris on the order of an official and without government authorization. Some of these stamps were substituted for part of a shipment of stamps on thin paper, which had been printed in London on government order. When the thick paper stamps reached Bolivia they were at first repudiated but afterwards were allowed to do postal duty. A large quantity of the thick paper stamps were fraudulently cancelled in Paris with a cancellation of heavy bars forming an oval.

To be legitimate, copies of the thick paper stamps must have been bought at post offices in Bolivia, or must have genuine cancellations of Bolivia.

The 10c blue on thick paper is not known to have been issued.

President Tomás Frías
A10

President José M. Linares
A11

Pedro Domingo Murillo
A12

Bernardo Monteagudo
A13

Gen. José Ballivián
A14

Gen. Antonio José de Sucre
A15

Simón Bolívar
A16

Coat of Arms
A17

1897 Lithographed. *Perf. 12.*

47 A10 1c pale yel grn 2.00 1.25
a. Imperf. horiz. pair 75.00
b. Vertical pair, imperf. between 75.00
48 A11 2c red 3.50 2.50
49 A12 5c dk grn 3.50 1.25
a. Horizontal pair, imperf. between 75.00
50 A13 10c brn vio 3.50 1.25
a. Vertical pair, imperf. between 75.00
51 A14 20c lake & blk 8.00 1.50
a. Imperf., pair 225.00
52 A15 50c orange 8.00 3.00
53 A16 1b Prus bl 8.00 7.50
54 A17 2b red, yel, grn & blk 45.00 60.00
Nos. 47-54 (8) 81.50 78.25

Excellent forgeries of No. 54 exist.

Nos. 40-44 Handstamped in Violet or Blue

E.F.
1899

1899 *Perf. 14½.*

55 A9 1c yel bis 25.00 25.00
56 A9 2c red org 30.00 30.00
57 A9 5c green 20.00 20.00
58 A9 10c yel brn 25.00 20.00
59 A9 20c dk bl 40.00 40.00
Nos. 55-59 (5) 140.00 135.00

The handstamp is found inverted, double, etc. Forgeries of this handstamp are plentiful. "E.F." stands for Estado Federal.

The 50c and 100c (Nos. 45-46) with similar handstamp are considered bogus.

Antonio José de Sucre
A18

Thin Paper.

1899 Engraved *Perf. 11½, 12*

62 A18 1c gray bl 2.25 1.00
63 A18 2c brnsh red 1.50 1.00
64 A18 5c dk grn 6.00 2.00
65 A18 10c yel org 2.25 1.50
66 A18 20c rose pink 3.00 1.00
67 A18 50c bis brn 6.00 2.50
68 A18 1b gray vio 2.50 2.00
Nos. 62-68 (7) 23.50 11.00

1901

69 A18 5c dk red 2.50 1.00

Col. Adolfo Ballivián
A19

Eliodoro Camacho
A20

President Narciso Campero
A21

José Ballivián
A22

Gen. Andrés Santa Cruz
A23

Coat of Arms
A24

1901-02 Engraved.

No.	Type	Denomination	Unused	Used
70	A19	1c claret	50	25
71	A20	2c green	60	35
73	A21	5c scarlet	60	40
74	A22	10c blue	1.50	25
75	A23	20c vio & blk	80	25
76	A24	2b brown	4.50	4.00
		Nos. 70-71, 73-76 (6)	8.50	5.50

1904 Lithographed

No.	Type	Denomination	Unused	Used
77	A19	1c claret	3.00	1.00

In No. 70 the panel above "CENTAVO" is shaded with continuous lines. In No. 77 the shading is of dots.

See also Nos. 103-105, 107, 110.

Coat of Arms of Dept. of La Paz
A25

Murillo
A26

José Miguel Lanza
A27

Ismael Montes
A28

1909 Lithographed *Perf. 11*

No.	Type	Denomination	Unused	Used
78	A25	5c bl & blk	14.00	6.50
79	A26	10c grn & blk	14.00	6.50
80	A27	20c org & blk	14.00	6.50
81	A28	2b red & blk	14.00	6.50

Centenary of Revolution of July, 1809.

Nos. 78-81 exist imperf. and tête bêche. Nos. 79-81 exist with center inverted.

Miguel Betanzos
A29

Col. Ignacio Warnes
A30

Murillo
A31

Monteagudo
A32

Esteban Arce
A33

Antonio José de Sucre
A34

Simón Bolívar
A35

Manuel Belgrano
A36

Dated 1809-1825.

1909 *Perf. 11½.*

No.	Type	Denomination	Unused	Used
82	A29	1c lt brn & blk	75	60
83	A30	2c grn & blk	90	75
84	A31	5c red & blk	90	50
85	A32	10c dl bl & blk	90	50
86	A33	20c vio & blk	1.00	75
87	A34	50c ol bis & blk	1.50	1.00
88	A35	1b gray brn & blk	1.50	1.50
89	A36	2b choc & blk	2.00	1.50
		Nos. 82-89 (8)	9.45	7.10

Issued in commemoration of the War of Independence, 1809-1825.

Warnes
A37

Betanzos—A38

Arce—A39

Dated 1910-1825.

1910 *Perf. 13x13½.*

No.	Type	Denomination	Unused	Used
92	A37	5c grn & blk	40	20
a.		Imperf., pair	5.00	
93	A38	10c cl & ind	40	20
a.		Imperf., pair	7.50	
94	A39	20c dl bl & ind	85	50
a.		Imperf., pair	5.00	

Issued in commemoration of the War of Independence.

Nos. 92-94 may be found with parts of a papermaker's watermark: "A I & Co/ EXTRA STRONG/9303."

Nos. 71 and 75 Surcharged in Black

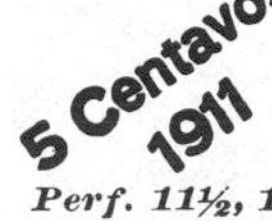

1911 *Perf. 11½, 12.*

No.	Type	Denomination	Unused	Used
95	A20	5c on 2c grn	60	30
a.		Inverted surcharge	7.00	7.00
b.		Double surcharge		
c.		Period after "1911"	5.00	1.25
d.		Blue surcharge	100.00	75.00
96	A23	5c on 20c vio & blk	22.50	22.50
a.		Inverted surch.	45.00	45.00

No. 83 Handstamp Surcharged in Green

No.	Type	Denomination	Unused	Used
97	A30	20c on 2c grn & blk		1,300.

This provisional was issued by local authorities at Villa Bella, a town on the Brazilian border. The 20c surcharge was applied after the stamp had been affixed to the cover. Excellent forgeries of No. 96-97 exist.

"Justice"
A40 A41

1912

Black or Dark Blue Overprint.

No.	Type	Denomination	Unused	Used
98	A40	2c grn (Bk)	60	40
a.		Inverted overprint	7.50	
99	A41	10c ver (Bl)	1.25	70
a.		Inverted overprint	7.50	

A42

A43

Red or Black Overprint.

Engraved.

No.	Type	Denomination	Unused	Used
100	A42	5c org (R)	50	50
a.		Inverted overprint	6.00	
b.		Pair, one without overprint	15.00	
c.		Black overprint	75.00	

Red or Black Surcharge.

No.	Type	Denomination	Unused	Used
101	A43	10c on 1c bl (R)	50	25
a.		Inverted surch.	7.50	
b.		Double surch.	7.50	
c.		Double surcharge, one inverted	8.50	
d.		Black surcharge	200.00	200.00

Revenue Stamp Surcharged "CORREOS / 10 Cts. / — 1917 —" in Red

1917 Lithographed

No.	Type	Denomination	Unused	Used
102		10c on 1c bl	2,000.	1,750.

Design similar to type A43.

Frias
A45

Sucre
A46

Bolívar
A47

1913 Engraved. *Perf. 12.*

No.	Type	Denomination	Unused	Used
103	A19	1c car rose	50	40
104	A20	2c vermilion	50	30
105	A21	5c green	60	20
106	A45	8c yellow	1.00	90
107	A22	10c gray	1.00	40
108	A46	50c dl vio	2.00	1.00
109	A47	1b sl bl	3.50	2.00
110	A24	2b black	7.00	4.00
		Nos. 103-110 (8)	16.10	9.20

Monolith of Tiahuanacu
A48

Mt. Potosí
A49

Lake Titicaca
A50

Mt. Illimani
A51

Legislature Building
A53

FIVE CENTAVOS.

Type I. Numerals have background of vertical lines. Clouds formed of dots.

Type II. Numerals on white background. Clouds near the mountain formed of wavy lines.

1916-17 Lithographed. *Perf. 11½.*

No.	Type	Denomination	Unused	Used
111	A48	½c brown	30	30
a.		Imperf. vert., pair	7.50	
112	A49	1c gray grn	35	20
a.		Imperf., pair	2.50	
113	A50	2c car & blk	35	20
a.		Imperf., pair	2.50	
b.		Imperf. horiz.		
c.		Center inverted	25.00	22.50
d.		Imperf., center inverted	27.50	
114	A51	5c dk bl (I)	75	35
a.		Imperf., pair	2.50	
b.		Imperf. horiz., pair	5.00	
c.		Imperf. vert., pair	5.00	
115	A51	5c dk bl (II)	75	15
a.		Imperf., pair	3.50	
116	A53	10c org & bl	1.25	15
a.		Imperf., pair	5.00	
b.		No period after "Legislativo"	1.25	25
c.		Center inverted	75.00	75.00
d.		Vertical pair, imperf. between	7.50	
		Nos. 111-116 (6)	3.75	1.35

Coat of Arms
A54 A55

Printed by the American Bank Note Co.

1919-20 Engraved. *Perf. 12.*

No.	Type	Denomination	Unused	Used
118	A54	1c carmine	35	35
119	A54	2c dk vio	6.00	4.00
120	A54	5c dk grn	50	15
121	A54	10c vermilion	50	15
122	A54	20c dk bl	2.00	50
123	A54	22c lt bl	1.25	1.25
124	A54	24c purple	1.25	75
125	A54	50c orange	6.00	1.00
126	A55	1b red brn	7.50	2.00
127	A55	2b blk brn	12.50	7.50
		Nos. 118-127 (10)	37.85	17.65

Printed by Perkins, Bacon & Co., Ltd.

Types of 1919-20 Issue.

Re-engraved.

1923-27 *Perf. 13½.*

No.	Type	Denomination	Unused	Used
128	A54	1c car ('27)	25	15
129	A54	2c dk vio	35	20

130	A54	5c dp grn	1.00	15
131	A54	10c vermilion	22.50	20.00
132	A54	20c sl bl	2.00	35
135	A54	50c orange	4.00	1.00
136	A55	1b red brn	1.00	50
137	A55	2b blk brn	75	50
		Nos. 128-137 (8)	31.85	22.85

The stamps of 1919–20 are perf. 12, those of 1923 are perf. 13½. The two issues may thus be readily distinguished. There are many differences in the designs of the two issues but they are too minute to be illustrated or described.

See also Nos. 144–146.

Stamps of 1919–20 Surcharged in Blue, Black or Red

Habilitada 15 cts.

1924 *Perf. 12.*

138	A54	5c on 1c car (Bl)	50	35
a.		Inverted surcharge	7.50	7.50
b.		Double surcharge	7.50	7.50
139	A54	15c on 10c ver (Bk)	1.00	60
a.		Inverted surcharge	10.00	10.00
140	A54	15c on 22c lt bl (Bk)	1.00	50
a.		Inverted surcharge	9.00	9.00
b.		Double surcharge, one inverted		
c.		Red surcharge	35.00	

Same Surcharge on No. 131.

Perf. 13½

142	A54	15c on 10c ver (Bk)	50	40
a.		Inverted surch.	10.00	10.00

No. 121 Surcharged

Habilitada 15 cts.

Perf. 12.

143	A54	15c on 10c ver (Bk)	60	50
a.		Inverted surch.	10.00	10.00
b.		Double surcharge	8.50	8.50
		Nos. 138-143 (5)	3.60	2.35

Printed by Waterlow & Sons.

Type of 1919-20 Issue.

Second Re-engraving.

1925 *Perf. 12½* **Unwmkd.**

144	A54	5c dp grn	75	35
145	A54	15c ultra	75	20
146	A54	20c dk bl	50	20

These stamps may be identified by the perforation.

Miner
A56

Condor Looking Toward the Sea
A57

Designs: 2c, Sower. 5c, Torch of Eternal Freedom. 10c, National flower (kantuta). 15c, Pres. Bautista Saavedra. 50c, Liberty head. 1b, Archer on horse. 2b, Mercury. 5b, Gen. A. J. de Sucre.

1925 **Engraved.** *Perf. 14.*

150	A56	1c dk grn	1.50	1.00
151	A56	2c rose	1.50	1.00
152	A56	5c red, *grn*	1.50	50
153	A56	10c car, *yel*	1.75	1.00
154	A56	15c red brn	1.00	50
155	A57	25c ultra	1.25	75
156	A56	50c dp vio	1.25	75
157	A56	1b red	2.25	2.00
158	A57	2b orange	3.50	3.00
159	A56	5b blk brn	4.00	3.00
		Nos. 150-159 (10)	19.50	13.50

Issued to commemorate the centenary of the Republic.

Stamps of 1919-27 Surcharged in Blue, Black or Red

1927 5 CENTAVOS

1927

160	A54	5c on 1c car (Bl)	1.50	1.25
a.		Inverted surcharge	6.00	6.00
b.		Black surcharge	30.00	30.00

Perf. 12.

162	A54	10c on 24c pur (Bk)	1.50	1.25
a.		Inverted surcharge	40.00	40.00
b.		Red surcharge	30.00	30.00

Coat of Arms
A66

Printed by Waterlow & Sons.

1927 **Lithographed.** *Perf. 13½.*

165	A66	2c yellow	50	35
166	A66	3c pink	60	50
167	A66	4c red brn	60	50
168	A66	20c lt ol grn	90	35
169	A66	25c dp bl	90	50
170	A66	30c violet	90	75
171	A66	40c orange	2.00	75
172	A66	50c dp brn	2.00	75
173	A55	1b red	2.25	75
174	A55	2b plum	3.50	1.00
175	A55	3b ol grn	3.50	2.50
176	A55	4b claret	5.00	3.00
177	A55	5b bis brn	6.00	2.00
		Nos. 165-177 (13)	28.65	13.70

Type of 1927 Issue Overprinted

Octubre 1927

1927

178	A66	5c dk grn	35	25
179	A66	10c slate	50	25
180	A66	15c carmine	75	50

Stamps of 1919-27 Surcharged

15 cts. 1928

Perf. 12, 12½, 13½

1928 Red Surcharge.

181	A54	15c on 20c dk bl (No. 122)	10.00	10.00
182	A54	15c on 20c sl bl (No. 132)	10.00	10.00
a.		Black surcharge	35.00	
183	A54	15c on 20c dk bl (No. 146)	250.00	250.00

Black Surcharge.

184	A54	15c on 24c pur (No. 124)	2.00	1.50
a.		Inverted surcharge	5.00	5.00
b.		Blue surcharge	55.00	
185	A54	15c on 50c org (No. 125)	65.00	65.00
186	A54	15c on 50c org (No. 135)	1.50	1.00
		Nos. 181-186 (6)	338.50	337.50

Condor
A67

Hernando Siles
A68

Map of Bolivia
A69

Printed by Perkins, Bacon & Co., Ltd.

1928 **Engraved.** *Perf. 13½.*

189	A67	5c green	50	10
190	A68	10c slate	50	10
191	A69	15c car lake	1.00	15

Stamps of 1913-17 Surcharged in Various Colors

0.03 Centavos R. S. 21-4 1930

1930 *Perf. 12, 11½.*

193	A20	1c on 2c ver (Bl)	1.00	1.00
a.		"0.10" for "0.01"	15.00	15.00
194	A50	3c on 2c car & blk (Br)	1.25	1.00
195	A48	25c on ½c brn (Bk)	1.00	75
196	A50	25c on 2c car & blk (V)	1.00	75

The lines of the surcharges were spaced to fit the various shapes of the stamps. The surcharges exist inverted, double, etc.

Trial printings were made of the surcharges on Nos. 193 and 194 in black and on No. 196 in brown.

Mt. Potosí
A70

Mt. Illimani
A71

Eduardo Abaroa
A72

Map of Bolivia
A73

Sucre
A74

Bolívar
A75

1931 **Engraved.** *Perf. 14.*

197	A70	2c green	60	50
198	A71	5c lt bl	50	25
199	A72	10c red org	60	25
200	A73	15c violet	1.00	25
201	A73	35c carmine	2.00	1.00
202	A73	45c orange	2.00	1.00
203	A74	50c gray	1.00	75
204	A75	1b brown	2.00	2.00
		Nos. 197-204 (8)	9.70	6.00

See also Nos. 207, 241.

Symbols of 1930 Revolution—A76

1931 **Lithographed.** *Perf. 11.*

205	A76	15c scarlet	3.00	50
a.		Pair, imperf. between		
206	A76	50c brt vio	1.00	75
a.		Pair, imperf. between	10.00	

Revolution of June 25, 1930.

Map Type of 1931.
Without Imprint.

1932 **Lithographed.**

207	A73	15c violet	1.50	40

Stamps of 1927-31 Surcharged

Habilitada A 15 Cts. D. S. 13-7.1933

1933 *Perf. 13½, 14.*

208	A66	5c on 1b red	60	30
a.		Without period after "Cts"	1.25	1.25
209	A73	15c on 35c car	30	30
210	A73	15c on 45c org	30	30
a.		Inverted surcharge	3.00	3.00
211	A66	15c on 50c dp brn	60	25
212	A66	25c on 40c org	60	20
		Nos. 208-212 (5)	2.40	1.35

The hyphens in "13-7-33" occur in three positions.

Coat of Arms
A77

1933 **Engraved** *Perf. 12*

213	A77	2c bl grn	35	20
214	A77	5c blue	25	15
215	A77	10c red	60	40
216	A77	15c dp vio	35	20
217	A77	25c dk bl	90	60
		Nos. 213-217 (5)	2.45	1.55

Mariano Baptista
A78

Map of Bolivia
A79

1935

218	A78	15c dl vio	75	30

1935

219	A79	2c dk bl	35	25
220	A79	3c yellow	35	25
221	A79	5c vermilion	35	20
222	A79	5c bl grn	35	20
223	A79	10c blk brn	35	20
224	A79	15c dp rose	40	20
225	A79	15c ultra	40	20
226	A79	20c yel grn	50	25

227	A79	25c lt bl	50	20
228	A79	30c dp rose	90	35
229	A79	40c orange	90	30
230	A79	50c gray vio	90	20
231	A79	1b yellow	90	60
232	A79	2b ol brn	2.00	1.25
		Nos. 219-232 (14)	9.15	4.65

Regular Stamps of 1925-33 Surcharged in Black

Comuni-
caciones
D. S.
25-2-37
0.05

1937 *Perf. 11, 12, 13½.*

233	A77	5c on 2c bl grn	30	30
234	A77	15c on 25c dk bl	40	40
235	A77	30c on 25c dk bl	60	60
236	A55	45c on 1b red brn	75	75
237	A55	1b on 2b plum	90	90
a.		"1" missing	5.00	5.00
238	A77	2b on 25c dk bl	90	90

"Comunicaciones" on one line.

239	A76	3b on 50c brt vio	1.25	1.25
a.		"3" of value missing	6.00	6.00
240	A76	5b on 50c brt vio	2.00	2.00
		Nos. 233-240 (8)	7.10	7.10

President Siles—A80

1937 *Perf. 14* **Unwmkd.**

241	A80	1c yel brn	40	35

Native School
A81

Oil Wells
A82

Modern Factories
A83

Torch of Knowledge
A84

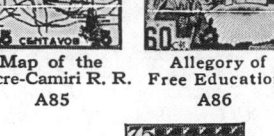

Map of the Sucre-Camiri R. R.
A85

Allegory of Free Education
A86

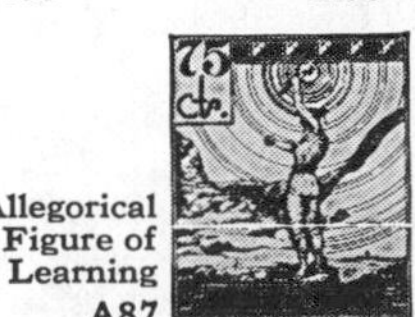

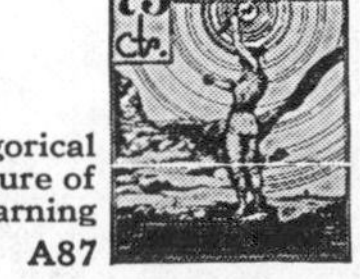

Allegorical Figure of Learning
A87

Symbols of Industry
A88

Modern Agriculture
A89

1938 Lithographed. *Perf. 10½, 11.*

242	A81	2c dl red	50	35
243	A82	10c pink	60	35
244	A83	15c yel grn	75	40
245	A84	30c yellow	1.00	50
246	A85	45c rose red	1.25	1.00
247	A86	60c dk vio	1.25	50
248	A87	75c dl bl	1.50	50
249	A88	1b lt brn	2.00	50
250	A89	2b bister	2.50	1.00
		Nos. 242-250 (9)	11.35	5.10

Llamas
A90

Vicuna
A91

Coat of Arms
A92

Cocoi Herons
A93

Chinchilla
A94

Toco Toucan
A95

Condor
A96

Jaguar
A97

Perf. 10½, 11½x10½

1939, Jan. 21

251	A90	2c green	75	50
252	A90	4c fawn	75	50
253	A90	5c red vio	75	40
254	A91	10c black	75	50
255	A91	15c emerald	75	60
256	A91	20c dk sl grn	75	40
257	A92	25c lemon	75	40
258	A92	30c dk bl	75	50
259	A93	40c vermilion	1.50	50
260	A93	45c gray	1.50	50
261	A94	60c rose red	1.75	1.00
262	A94	75c sl bl	1.75	1.00
263	A95	90c orange	2.50	1.00
264	A95	1b blue	3.00	1.00
265	A96	2b rose lake	4.00	1.00
266	A96	3b dk vio	5.00	1.50
267	A97	4b brn org	6.00	2.00
268	A97	5b gray brn	7.50	2.50
		Nos. 251-268 (18)	40.50	15.80

Imperforate counterfeits of some values exist.

Flags of 21 American Republics
A98

1940, Apr. **Litho.** *Perf. 10½*

269	A98	9b multi	3.00	2.50

Pan American Union, 150th anniversary.

Statue of Murillo
A99

Pedro Domingo Murillo
A102

Urns of Murillo and Sagarnaga
A100

Dream of Murillo
A101

1941, Apr. 15

270	A99	10c dl vio brn	15	10
271	A100	15c lt grn	25	15
a.		Imperf. (pair)	5.00	
272	A101	45c car rose	25	20
a.		Double impression		
273	A102	1.05b dk ultra	50	25

Issued to commemorate the 130th anniversary of the death (by execution) of Pedro Domingo Murillo (1759–1810), patriot.

First Stamp of Bolivia and 1941 Airmail Stamp—A103

1942. Oct. **Litho.** *Perf. 13½*

274	A103	5c pink	1.00	75
275	A103	10c orange	1.00	75
276	A103	20c yel grn	2.00	1.00
277	A103	40c car rose	2.50	1.25
278	A103	90c ultra	5.00	1.50
279	A103	1b violet	6.00	3.00
280	A103	10b ol bis	20.00	12.50
		Nos. 274-280 (7)	37.50	20.75

Issued in commemoration of the first School Philatelic Exposition held in La Paz, October, 1941.

Gen. Ballivian Leading Cavalry Charge, Battle of Ingavi
A104

1943 **Photogravure** *Perf. 12½*

281	A104	2c lt bl grn	15	10
282	A104	3c orange	15	10
283	A104	25c dp plum	25	15
284	A104	45c ultra	35	20
285	A104	3b scarlet	75	50
286	A104	4b brt rose lil	1.00	60
287	A104	5b blk brn	1.50	90
		Nos. 281-287 (7)	4.15	2.55

Souvenir Sheets.

Perf. 13, Imperf.

288	A104	Sheet of 4	3.00	2.50
289	A104	Sheet of 3	9.00	7.50

Centenary of the Battle of Ingavi, 1841. No. 288 contains 4 stamps similar to Nos. 281–284, No. 289 three stamps similar to Nos. 285–287: black marginal inscriptions. Size: 139x100mm.

Potosi
A107

Quechisla
A108

Miner
A109

Dam
A110

Mine Interior
A111

Chaquiri Dam
A112

Entrance to Pulacayo Mine
A113

1943 Engraved. *Perf. 12½.*

290	A107	15c red brn	35	25
291	A108	45c vio bl	35	25
292	A109	1.25b brt rose vio	50	40
293	A110	1.50b emerald	50	40
294	A111	2b brn blk	60	50
295	A112	2.10b lt bl	75	60
296	A113	3b red org	1.00	90
		Nos. 290-296 (7)	4.05	3.30

General José Ballivián and Cathedral at Trinidad

A114

1943, Nov. 18

297	A114	5c dk grn & brn	15	15
298	A114	10c dl pur & brn	20	20
299	A114	30c rose red & brn	25	25
300	A114	45c brt ultra & brn	35	35
301	A114	2.10b dp org & brn	50	50
		Nos. 297-301, C91-C95 (10)	3.25	2.80

Department of Beni centenary.

"Honor—Work —Law"

A115

"United for the Country"

A116

1944 Lithographed *Perf. 13½*

302	A115	20c orange	10	10
303	A115	90c ultra	15	10
304	A116	1b brt red vio	20	15
305	A116	2.40b dl brn	30	20

1945

306	A115	20c green	5	5
307	A115	90c dp rose	15	10
		Nos. 302-307, C96-C99 (10)	2.05	1.25

Nos. 302–307 were issued to commemorate the Revolution of Dec. 20, 1943.

Leopold Benedetto Vincenti, Joseph Ignacio de Sanjines and Bars of Anthem

A117

1946, Aug. 21 Litho. *Perf. 10½*

308	A117	5c rose vio & blk	20	15
309	A117	10c ultra & blk	20	15
310	A117	15c bl grn & blk	20	15
311	A117	30c ver & brn	25	20
a.		Souvenir sheet	1.25	1.25
312	A117	90c dk bl & brn	25	20
313	A117	2b blk & brn	60	25
a.		Souvenir sheet	2.50	2.50
		Nos. 308-313 (6)	1.70	1.10

Issued to commemorate the centenary of the adoption of Bolivia's national anthem.

Nos. 311a and 313a measure 86x136½ mm., contain respectively one each of Nos. 311 and 313, and are imperforate. The price of each sheet included a surtax of 4 bolivianos.

Nos. 248 and 262 Surcharged in Carmine, Black or Orange

1947, Mar. 12 *Perf. 10½, 11*

314	A87	1.40b on 75c dl bl (C)	20	8
315	A94	1.40b on 75c sl bl (Bk)	20	8
316	A94	1.40b on 75c sl bl (C)	20	8
317	A94	1.40b on 75c sl bl (O)	20	8
		Nos. 314-317, C112 (5)	1.10	62

People Attacking Presidential Palace

A118

Arms of Bolivia and Argentina

A119

1947, Sept. Litho. *Perf. 13½*

318	A118	20c bl grn	5	5
a.		Imperf. (pair)		
319	A118	50c lil rose	10	6
320	A118	1.40b grnsh bl	15	8
a.		Imperf. (pair)		
321	A118	3.70b dl org	25	12
322	A118	4b violet	35	20
323	A118	10b olive	75	45
		Nos. 318-323, C113-C117 (11)	2.90	1.92

Issued to commemorate the first anniversary of the Revolution of July 21, 1946.

1947, Oct. 23

324	A119	1.40b dp org	12	8

Issued to commemorate the meeting of Presidents Enrique Hertzog of Bolivia and Juan D. Peron of Argentina at Yacuiba on October 23, 1947. See also No. C118.

Statue of Christ above La Paz

A120

Designs: 2b, Child kneeling before cross of Golgotha. 3b, St. John Bosco. No. 328, Virgin of Copacabana. No. 329, Pope Pius XII blessing University of La Paz.

1948, Sept. 26 *Perf. 11½* Unwmkd.

325	A120	1.40b bl & yel	50	18
326	A120	2b yel grn & sal	75	22
327	A120	3b grn & gray	1.25	25
328	A120	5b vio & sal	1.50	30
329	A120	5b red brn & lt grn	2.00	30
		Nos. 325-329, C119-C123 (10)	11.05	3.00

Issued to publicize the 3rd Inter-American Congress of Catholic Education.

Map and Emblem of Bolivia Auto Club

A125

Pres. Gregorio Pacheco, Map and Post Horn

A126

1948, Oct. 20

330	A125	5b ind & sal	3.50	25

Issued to publicize the International Automobile Races of South America, September–October 1948. See also No. C124.

1950, Jan. 2 Litho. *Perf. 11½*

331	A126	1.40b vio bl	15	10
332	A126	4.20b red	15	10
		Nos. 331-332, C125-C127 (5)	70	60

Issued to commemorate the 75th anniversary of the formation of the Universal Postal Union.

No. 273 Surcharged in Black

Bs.2.-
Habilitada
D.S.6·VII·50

1950 *Perf. 10½*

333	A102	2b on 1.05b dk ultra	25	10

Crucifix and View of Potosí

A127

Symbols of United Nations

A128

Perf. 11½

1950, Sept. 14 Litho. Unwmkd.

334	A127	20c violet	10	6
335	A127	30c dp org	10	6
336	A127	50c lil rose	10	6
337	A127	1b carmine	15	6
338	A127	2b blue	20	6
339	A127	6b chocolate	35	15
		Nos. 334-339 (6)	1.00	45

Issued to commemorate the 400th anniversary of the appearance of a crucifix at Potosí.

1950, Oct. 24

340	A128	60c ultra	1.50	20
341	A128	2b green	2.00	35

Issued to commemorate the 5th anniversary of the formation of the United Nations, October 24, 1945. See also Nos. C138–C139.

Gate of the Sun and Llama

A129

Church of San Francisco

A130

Designs: 40c, Avenue Camacho. 50c, Consistorial Palace. 1b, Legislative Palace. 1.40b, Communications Bldg. 2b, Arms. 3b, La Gasca ordering Mendoza to found La Paz. 5b, Capt. Alonso de Mendoza founding La Paz. 10b, Arms; portrait of Mendoza.

1951, Mar. Engraved *Perf. 12½*

Center in Black.

342	A129	20c green	10	10
343	A130	30c dp org	10	10
344	A129	40c bis brn	10	10
345	A129	50c dk red	10	10
346	A129	1b dp pur	15	15
347	A129	1.40b dk vio bl	20	20
348	A129	2b dp pur	20	20
349	A129	3b red lil	30	20
a.		Sheet, Nos. 345, 346, 348, 349	1.75	1.75
b.		Sheet, imperf.	1.75	1.75
350	A129	5b dk red	35	25
a.		Sheet, Nos. 344, 347, 350	1.75	1.75
b.		Sheet, imperf.	1.75	1.75
351	A129	10b sepia	75	35
a.		Sheet, Nos. 342, 343, 351	1.75	1.75
b.		Sheet, imperf.	1.75	1.75
		Nos. 342-351, C140-C149 (20)	6.70	6.10

Issued to commemorate the 400th anniversary of the founding of La Paz.

The souvenir sheets measure 150x100 mm., and contain marginal inscriptions in black.

Boxing

A131

Designs: 50c, Tennis. 1b, Diving. 1.40b, Soccer. 2b, Skiing. 3b, Handball. 4b, Cycling.

Engraved

1951, July 1 *Perf. 12½* Unwmkd.

Center in Black.

352	A131	20c dp bl	25	10
353	A131	50c red	25	15
354	A131	1b claret	30	15
355	A131	1.40b yellow	30	20
356	A131	2b brt car	75	35
357	A131	3b yel brn	1.25	75
a.		Sheet, Nos. 352, 353, 356, 357	3.50	3.50
b.		Sheet, imperf.	3.50	3.50
358	A131	4b vio bl	1.50	75
a.		Sheet, Nos. 354, 355, 358	3.00	3.00
b.		Sheet, imperf.	3.00	3.00
		Nos. 352-358, C150-C156 (14)	12.45	5.85

The stamps were intended to commemorate the 5th athletic championship matches held at La Paz, October 1948.

The sheets measure 150x100 mm., and contain marginal inscriptions in black.

Eagle and Flag of Bolivia

A132

1951, Nov. 5 Litho. *Perf. 11½*

Flag in Red, Yellow and Green.

359	A132	2b aqua	15	15
360	A132	3.50b ultra	15	15
361	A132	5b purple	25	20
362	A132	7.50b gray	40	20
363	A132	15b dp car	50	40
364	A132	30b sepia	1.00	75
		Nos. 359-364 (6)	2.45	1.85

Issued to commemorate the centenary of the adoption of Bolivia's national flag.

Eduardo Abaroa

A133

Queen Isabella I

A134

1952, Mar. *Perf. 11*

365	A133	80c dk car	15	5
366	A133	1b red org	15	15
367	A133	2b emerald	25	15
368	A133	5b ultra	30	20
369	A133	10b lil rose	50	25
370	A133	20b dk brn	1.00	60
		Nos. 365-370, C157-C162 (12)	6.40	4.05

Issued to commemorate the 73rd anniversary of the death of Eduardo Abaroa.

1952, July 16 ***Perf. 13½*** **Unwmkd.**

371	A134	2b vio bl	15	10
372	A134	6.30b carmine	35	25

Issued to commemorate the 500th anniversary of the birth of Queen Isabella I of Spain. See also Nos. C163–C164.

Columbus Lighthouse
A135

1952, July 16 **Lithographed**

373	A135	2b vio bl, *bl*	25	20
374	A135	5b car, *sal*	50	30
375	A135	9b emer, *grn*	75	50
		Nos. 373-375, C165-C168 (7)	2.55	1.58

Miner
A136

1953, Apr. 9

376	A136	2.50b vermilion	10	8
377	A136	8b violet	15	12

Issued to publicize the nationalization of the mines.

Gualberto Villarroel, Victor Paz Estenssoro and Hernan Siles Zuazo
A137

1953, Apr. 9 ***Perf. 11½***

378	A137	50c rose lil	5	5
379	A137	1b brt rose	10	10
380	A137	2b vio bl	10	10
381	A137	3b lt grn	15	15
382	A137	4b yel org	15	15
383	A137	5b dl vio	25	15
		Nos. 378-383, C169-C175 (13)	2.80	2.20

Issued to commemorate the first anniversary of the Revolution of Apr. 9, 1952.

Map of Bolivia and Cow's Head
A138

Designs: 17b, Same as 5b. 25b, 85b, Map and ear of wheat.

1954, Aug. 2 ***Perf. 12x11½***

384	A138	5b car rose	5	5
385	A138	17b aqua	15	7
386	A138	25b chlky bl	25	8
387	A138	85b blk brn	50	25
		Nos. 384-387, C176-C181 (10)	4.65	1.45

Nos. 384–385 were issued to commemorate the agrarian reform laws of 1953–54. Nos. 386–387 commemorate the 1st National Congress of Agronomy.

Oil Refinery
A139

Perf. 12x11½

1955, Oct. 9 **Unwmkd.**

388	A139	10b ultra & lt ultra	10	10
389	A139	35b rose car & rose	15	10
390	A139	40b dk & lt yel grn	15	10
391	A139	50b red vio & lil rose	20	10
392	A139	80b brn & bis brn	35	15
		Nos. 388-392, C182-C186 (10)	4.95	3.00

Nos. 342-351, Surcharged with New Values and Bars in Ultramarine.

1957, Feb. 14 **Engr.** ***Perf. 12½***

Center in Black.

393	A129	50b on 3b red lil	15	5
394	A129	100b on 2b dp pur	15	5
395	A129	200b on 1b dp pur	20	10
396	A129	300b on 1.40b dk vio bl	25	10
397	A129	350b on 20c grn	35	10
398	A129	400b on 40c bis brn	35	10
399	A130	600b on 30c dp org	50	15
400	A129	800b on 50c dk red	60	15
401	A129	1000b on 10b sep	60	25
402	A129	2000b on 5b dk red	1.00	40
		Nos. 393-402 (10)	4.15	1.45

See also Nos. C187–C196.

CEPAL Building, Santiago de Chile, and Meeting Hall in La Paz
A140

1957, May 15 **Litho.** ***Perf. 13***

403	A140	150b gray & ultra	15	5
404	A140	350b bis brn & gray	30	10
405	A140	550b chlky bl & brn	35	15
406	A140	750b dp rose & grn	50	20
407	A140	900b grn & brn blk	75	25
		Nos. 403-407, C197-C201 (10)	8.90	4.75

Issued to commemorate the seventh session of the C. E. P. A. L. (Comision Economica para la America Latina de las Naciones Unidas), La Paz.

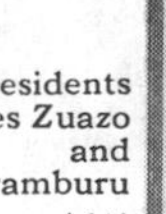

Presidents Siles Zuazo and Aramburu
A141

1957, Dec. 15 ***Perf. 11½*** **Unwmkd.**

408	A141	50b red org	15	5
409	A141	350b blue	40	10
410	A141	1000b redsh brn	75	15
		Nos. 408-410, C202-C204 (6)	2.90	70

Issued to commemorate the opening of the Santa Cruz-Yacuiba Railroad and the meeting of the Presidents of Bolivia and Argentina.

Flags of Bolivia and Mexico and Presidents Hernan Siles Zuazo and Adolfo Lopez Mateos
A142

1960, Jan. 30 **Litho.** ***Perf. 11½***

411	A142	350b olive	25	8
412	A142	600b red brn	35	15
413	A142	1500b blk brn	75	25
		Nos. 411-413, C205-C207 (6)	4.60	1.53

Issued for an expected visit of Mexico's President Adolfo Lopez Mateos. On sale Jan. 30–Feb. 1, 1960.

Indians and Mt. Illimani
A143

Refugee Children
A144

1960, Mar. 26 **Unwmkd.**

414	A143	500b ol bis	35	10
415	A143	1000b blue	60	20
416	A143	2000b brown	1.25	50
417	A143	4000b green	2.50	75
		Nos. 414-417, C208-C211 (8)	24.70	10.30

1960, Apr. 7 ***Perf. 11½***

418	A144	50b brown	15	5
419	A144	350b claret	20	6
420	A144	400b stl bl	25	8
421	A144	1000b gray brn	75	25
422	A144	3000b sl grn	1.50	70
		Nos. 418-422, C212-C216 (10)	6.20	4.34

Issued to publicize World Refugee Year, July 1, 1959–June 30, 1960.

Jaime Laredo
A145

Rotary Emblem and Nurse with Children
A146

1960, Aug. 15 **Litho.** ***Perf. 11½***

423	A145	100b olive	40	10
424	A145	350b dp rose	60	10
425	A145	500b Prus grn	75	15
426	A145	1,000b brown	1.00	25
427	A145	1,500b vio bl	1.75	35
428	A145	5,000b gray	6.00	1.25
		Nos. 423-428, C217-C222 (12)	25.25	8.10

Issued to honor violinist Jaime Laredo.

1960, Nov. 19 ***Perf. 11½***

429	A146	350b grn, yel & dp bl	25	10
430	A146	500b brn, yel & dp bl	35	10
431	A146	600b vio, yel & dp bl	50	15
432	A146	1,000b gray, yel & dp bl	60	25
		Nos. 429-432, C223-C226 (8)	8.45	3.65

Issued for the Children's Hospital, sponsored by the Rotary Club of La Paz.

Designs from Gate of the Sun
A147 A148

Designs: Various prehistoric gods and ornaments from Tiahuanacu excavations.

Lithographed

1960, Dec. 16 ***Perf. 13x12, 12x13***

Gold Background.

Surcharge in Black or Dark Red (#436)

Size: 21x23, 23x21mm.

433	A147	50b on ½c red	75	50
434	A147	100b on 1c red	50	25
435	A147	200b on 2c blk	1.50	15
436	A147	300b on 5c grn	35	20
437	A147	350b on 10c grn	35	1.25
438	A148	400b on 15c ind	50	25
439	A148	500b on 20c red	50	25
440	A148	500b on 50c red	60	25
441	A148	600b on 22½c grn	75	40
442	A148	600b on 60c vio	90	50
443	A148	700b on 25c vio	1.25	30
444	A148	700b on 1b grn	1.75	1.00
445	A148	800b on 30c red	85	30
446	A148	900b on 40c grn	75	40
447	A148	1000b on 2b bl	90	50
448	A148	1800b on 3b gray	9.00	6.00

Perf. 11

Size: 49½x23mm.

449	A148	4000b on 4b gray	65.00	55.00

Perf. 11x13½

Size: 49x53mm.

450	A147	5000b on 5b gray	17.50	12.50
		Nos. 433-450 (18)	103.70	80.00

Nos. 433–450 were not regularly issued without surcharge. Price (set), $20.

The decree for Nos. 433–450 stipulated that seven were for air mail (500b on 50c, 600b on 60c, 700b on 1b, 1,000b, 1,800b, 4,000b and 5,000b), but the overprinting failed to include "Aereo."

The 800b surcharge also exists on the 1c red and gold. This was not listed in the decree.

Miguel de Cervantes
A149

Nuflo de Chaves
A150

1961, Nov. **Photo.** ***Perf. 13x12½***

451	A149	600b ocher & dl vio	50	12

Issued to commemorate Cervantes' appointment as Chief Magistrate of La Paz. See also No. C230.

1961, Nov. **Unwmkd.**

452	A150	1500b dk bl, *buff*	75	30

Issued to commemorate the 400th anniversary of the founding of Santa Cruz de la Sierra. See also Nos. 468, C246.

People below Eucharist Symbol
A151

Hibiscus
A152

1962, Mar. 19 **Litho.** ***Perf. 10½***

453	A151	1000b gray grn, red & yel	1.00	50

Issued to commemorate the Fourth National Eucharistic Congress, Santa Cruz, 1961. See also No. C231.

Nos. 418–422 Surcharged Horizontally with New Value and Bars or Greek Key Border Segment

1962, June ***Perf. 11½***

454	A144	600b on 50b brn	30	20
455	A144	900b on 350b cl	40	20
456	A144	1,000b on 400b stl bl	60	25
457	A144	2,000b on 1,000b gray brn	75	40

458 A144 3,500b on 3,000b sl grn 1.25 75
Nos.454-458, C232-C236 (10) 9.20 4.80

Old value obliterated with two short bars on No. 454; four short bars on Nos. 455–456 and Greek key border on Nos. 457–458. The Greek key obliteration comes in two positions: two full "keys" on top, and one full and two half keys on top.

1962, June 28 Litho. *Perf. 10½*

Flowers in Natural Colors

Flowers: 400b, Bicolored vanda. 600b, Lily. 1000b, Orchid.

459 A152 200b sl bl 30 10
460 A152 400b brown 30 15
461 A152 600b dk bl 60 20
462 A152 1000b violet 1.00 35
Nos. 459-462, C237-C240 (8) 9.80 4.65

Infantry

A153

Anti-Malaria Emblem

A154

Designs: 500b, Cavalry. 600b, Artillery. 2000b, Engineers.

1962, Sept. 5 *Perf. 11½*

Insigne in Red, Yellow & Green

463 A153 400b blk, mar & buff 15 10
464 A153 500b blk, lt & dk grn 20 15
465 A153 600b blk & pale bis 25 20
466 A153 2000b blk & brn 75 50
Nos. 463-466, C241-C244 (8) 4.30 2.95

Issued in honor of Bolivia's Armed Forces.

1962, Oct. 4

467 A154 600b dk & lt vio & yel 40 20

Issued for the World Health Organization drive to eradicate malaria. See No. C245.

Portrait Type of 1961.

Design: 600b, Alonso de Mendoza.

1962 Photogravure *Perf. 13x12½*

468 A150 600b rose vio, *bluish* 40 20

Soccer and Flags

A155

Design: 1p, Goalkeeper catching ball (vert.).

1963, Mar. 21 Litho. *Perf. 11½*

Flags in National Colors

469 A155 60c gray 60 15
470 A155 1p gray 90 25

Issued to publicize the 21st South American Soccer Championships. See also Nos. C247–C248.

Globe and Wheat Emblem

A156

1963, Aug. 1 *Perf. 11½* Unwmkd.

471 A156 60c dk bl, bl & yel 35 15

Issued for the "Freedom from Hunger" campaign of the U.N. Food and Agriculture Organization. See also No. C249.

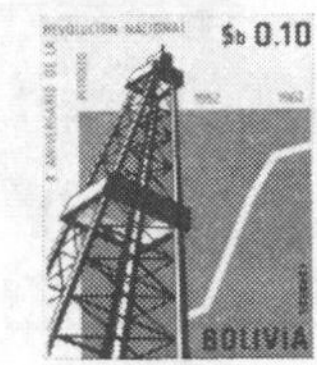

Oil Derrick and Chart

A157

Designs: 60c, Map of Bolivia. 1p, Students.

1963, Dec. 21 Litho. *Perf. 11½*

472 A157 10c grn & dk brn 15 10
473 A157 60c ocher & dk brn 40 15
474 A157 1p dk bl, grn & yel 50 25
Nos. 472-474, C251-C253 (6) 3.90 1.95

Issued to commemorate the 10th anniversary of the Revolution of Apr. 9, 1952.

Flags of Bolivia and Peru

A158

1966, Aug. 10 *Perf. 13½* Wmk. 90

Flags in National Colors

475 A158 10c blk & tan 15 10
476 A158 60c blk & lt grn 30 15
477 A158 1p blk & gray 50 20
478 A158 2p blk & rose 75 30
Nos. 475-478, C254-C257 (8) 3.65 1.85

Issued to commemorate the centenary (in 1965) of the death of Marshal Andrés Santa Cruz (1792–1865), president of Bolivia and of Peru-Bolivian Confederation.

Children

A159

Lithographed

1966, Dec. 16 *Perf. 13½* Unwmkd.

479 A159 30c ocher & sep 25 10

Issued to help poor children. See No. C258.

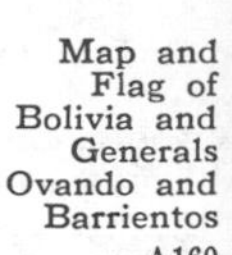

Map and Flag of Bolivia and Generals Ovando and Barrientos

A160

1966, Dec. 16 Litho. *Perf. 13½*

Flag in Red, Yellow and Green

480 A160 60c vio brn & tan 30 10
481 A160 1p dl grn & tan 45 15

Issued to honor Generals Rene Barrientos Ortuno and Alfredo Ovando C., co-Presidents, 1965–66. See also Nos. C259–C260.

A161

Various Issues 1957–60 and Type A161 Surcharged with New Values and Bars

1966, Dec. 21

On No. 403:
"Centenario de la / Cruz Roja / Internacional"

482 A140 20c on 150b gray & ultra 15 5

On Nos. 405–406:
"Homenaje a la / Generala / J. Azurduy de / Padilla"

483 A140 30c on 550b chlky bl & brn 15 5
484 A140 2.80p on 750b dp rose & grn 90 50

On No. 424:
"CL Aniversario / Heroinas Coronilla"

485 A145 60c on 350b dp rose 25 10

Nos. 429–430 Surcharged

486 A146 1.60p on 350b multi 60 25
487 A146 2.40p on 500b multi 90 40

Revenue Stamps of 1946 surcharged with New Value, "X" and:
"XXV Aniversario / Gobierno Busch"

488 A161 20c on 5b red 15 5

Overprinted:
"XX Aniversario / Gob. Villaroel"

489 A161 60c on 2b grn 25 10

Overprinted:
"Centenario do / Rurrenabaque"

490 A161 1p on 10b brn 40 15

Overprinted:
"XXV Aniversario / Dpto. Pando"

491 A161 1.60p on 50c vio 60 25
Nos. 482-491, C261-C272 (22) 14.20 10.20

Sower

A162

"Macheteros"

A163

1967, Sept. 20 Litho. *Perf. 13½x13*

492 A162 70c multi 50 15

Issued to commemorate the 50th anniversary of Lions International. See Nos. C273–C273a.

1968, June 24 *Perf. 13½x13*

Designs (Folklore characters): 60c, Chunchos. 1p, Wiphala. 2p, Diablada.

493 A163 30c gray & multi 15 8
494 A163 60c sky bl & multi 25 15
495 A163 1b gray & multi 40 20
496 A163 2b gray ol & multi 75 30
Nos. 493-496, C274-C277 (8) 4.45 2.43

Issued to publicize the 9th Congress of the Postal Union of the Americas and Spain.

A souvenir sheet exists containing 4 imperf. stamps similar to Nos. 493–496. Bister and gray marginal inscription. Size: 131x81½mm.

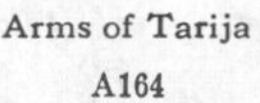

Arms of Tarija

A164

Pres. Gualberto Villaroël

A165

1968, Oct. 29 Litho. *Perf. 13½x13*

497 A164 20c pale sal & multi 15 6
498 A164 30c gray & multi 15 8
499 A164 40c dl yel & multi 20 10
500 A164 60c lt yel grn & multi 30 12
Nos. 497-500, C278-C281 (8) 4.40 2.11

Battle of Tablada sesquicentennial.

1968, Nov. 6 Unwmkd.

501 A165 20c sep & org 20 6
502 A165 30c sep & dl bl grn 20 6
503 A165 40c sep & dl rose 20 8
504 A165 50c sep & yel grn 25 10
505 A165 1b sep & ol bis 50 15
Nos. 501-505 (5) 1.35 45

Issued to commemorate the 4th centenary of the founding of Cochabamba. See Nos. C282–C286.

ITU Emblem

A166

1968, Dec. 3 Litho. *Perf. 13x13½*

506 A166 10c gray, blk & yel 25 6
507 A166 60c org, blk & ol 50 10

Issued to commemorate the centenary (in 1965) of the International Telecommunication Union. See Nos. C287–C288.

Polychrome Painted Clay Cup, Inca Period

A167

1968, Nov. 14 *Perf. 13½x13*

508 A167 20c dk bl grn & multi 25 6
509 A167 60c vio bl & multi 50 10

Issued to commemorate the 20th anniversary (in 1966) of UNESCO (United Nations Educational, Scientific and Cultural Organization). See Nos. C289–C290.

John F. Kennedy

A168

Tennis Player

A169

1968, Nov. 22 *Perf. 13x13½*

510 A168 10c yel grn & blk 20 10
511 A168 4b vio & blk 2.00 60

Issued in memory of Pres. John F. Kennedy (1917–1963).

A souvenir sheet contains one imperf. stamp similar to No. 511. Green marginal inscription. Size: 131x81½mm.

See Nos. C291–C292.

1968, Dec. 10 *Perf. 13x13½*

512 A169 10c gray, blk & lt brn 20 10
513 A169 20c yel, blk & lt brn 20 10
514 A169 30c ultra, blk & lt brn 20 10

Issued to commemorate the 32nd South American Tennis Championships, La Paz, 1965. See Nos. C293–C294.

A souvenir sheet exists containing 3 imperf. stamps similar to Nos. 512–514. Light brown marginal inscription. Size: 131x81½mm.

Issue of 1863
A170

1968, Dec. 23 Litho. *Perf. 13x13½*

515 A170 10c yel grn, brn & blk 20 10
516 A170 30c lt bl, brn & blk 20 10
517 A170 2b gray, brn & blk 35 20
Nos. 515-517, C295-C297 (6) 3.90 2.25

Issued to commemorate the centenary of Bolivian postage stamps. See Nos. C295-C297.

A souvenir sheet exists containing 3 imperf. stamps similar to Nos. 515-517. Yellow green marginal inscription. Size: 131x81½mm.

Rifle Shooting
A171

Sports: 50c, Equestrian. 60c, Canoeing.

1969, Oct. 29 Litho. *Perf. 13x13½*

518 A171 40c red brn, org & blk 20 10
519 A171 50c emer, red & blk 20 10
520 A171 60c bl, emer & blk 35 15
Nos. 518-520, C299-C301 (6) 4.60 2.10

Issued to commemorate the 19th Olympic Games, Mexico City, Oct. 12-27, 1968.

A souvenir sheet exists containing 3 imperf. stamps similar to Nos. 518-520. Marginal inscription in red brown, emerald and blue. Size: 130½x81mm.

Temenis Laothoe Violetta
A172

Butterflies: 10c, Papilio crassus. 20c, Catagramma cynosura. 30c, Eunica eurota flora. 80c, Ituna phenarete.

1970, Apr. 24 Litho. *Perf. 13x13½*

521 A172 5c pale lil & multi 15 5
522 A172 10c pink & multi 15 5
523 A172 20c gray & multi 15 5
524 A172 30c yel & multi 15 5
525 A172 80c multi 35 20
Nos. 521-525, C302-C306 (10) 7.70 3.35

A souvenir sheet exists containing 3 imperf. stamps similar to Nos. 521-523. Black marginal inscription. Size: 129½x80mm.

Boy Scout
A173

Design: 10c, Girl Scout planting rose bush.

1970, June 17 *Perf. 13½x13*

526 A173 5c multi 20 5
527 A173 10c multi 20 5

Issued to honor the Bolivian Scout movement. See Nos. C307-C308.

No. 437 Surcharged "EXFILCA 70 / $b. 0.30" and Two Bars in Red

1970, Dec. 6 Litho. *Perf. 13x12*

528 A147 30c on 350b on 10c gold & grn 20 10

EXFILCA 70, 2nd Interamerican Philatelic Exhibition, Caracas, Venezuela, Nov. 27-Dec. 6.

Nos. 455 and 452 Surcharged in Black or Red

1970, Dec. Photo. *Perf. 11½*

529 A144 60c on 900b on 350b cl 35 12
533 A150 1.20b on 1500b dk bl, *buff* (R) 65 20

Amaryllis Yungacensis
A174

Sica Sica Church, EXFILIMA Emblem
A175

Bolivian Flowers: 30c, Amaryllis escobar uriae (horiz.). 40c, Amaryllis evansae (horiz.). 2b, Gymnocalycium chiquitanum.

Perf. 13x13½, 13½x13

1971, Aug. 9 Litho. Unwmkd.

534 A174 30c gray & multi 15 10
535 A174 40c multi 15 10
536 A174 50c multi 25 20
537 A174 2b multi 75 50
Nos. 534-537, C310-C313 (8) 5.90 2.50

1971, Nov. 6 *Perf. 14x13½*

538 A175 20c red & multi 25 10

EXFILIMA '71, 3rd Inter-American Philatelic Exhibition, Lima, Peru, Nov. 6-14.

Pres. Hugo Banzer Suarez
A176

1972, Jan. 24 Litho. *Perf. 13½*

539 A176 1.20b blk & multi 75 20

Bolivia's development, Aug. 19, 1971, to Jan. 24, 1972.

Chiriwano de Achocalla Dance
A177

Folk Dances: 40c, Rueda Chapaca. 60c, Kena-kena. 1b, Waca Thokori.

1972, Mar. 23 Litho. *Perf. 13½x13*

540 A177 20c red & multi 10 10
541 A177 40c rose lil & multi 25 20
542 A177 60c cr & multi 35 25
543 A177 1b cit & multi 50 35
Nos. 540-543, C314-C315 (6) 2.95 1.40

Madonna and Child by B. Bitti
A178

Tarija Cathedral, EXFILBRA Emblem
A179

Paintings: 10c, Nativity, by Melchor Perez de Holguín. 50c, Coronation of the Virgin, by G. M. Berrio. 70c, Harquebusier, anonymous. 80c, St. Peter of Alcantara, by Holguín.

1972 Lithographed *Perf. 14x13½*

544 A178 10c gray & multi 15 10
545 A178 50c sal & multi 30 10
546 A178 70c lt grn & multi 35 15
547 A178 80c buff & multi 40 20
548 A178 1b multi 50 25
Nos. 544-548, C316-C319 (9) 4.50 1.95

Bolivian paintings. Issue dates: 1b, Aug. 17; others, Dec. 4.

1972, Aug. 26

549 A179 30c multi 25 10

4th Inter-American Philatelic Exhibition, EXFILBRA, Rio de Janeiro, Brazil, Aug. 26-Sept. 2.

Echinocactus Notocactus
A180

Designs: Various cacti.

1973, Aug. 6 Litho. *Perf. 13½*

550 A180 20c crim & multi 15 5
551 A180 40c multi 20 8
552 A180 50c multi 25 10
553 A180 70c multi 35 12
Nos. 550-553, C321-C323 (7) 3.20 1.25

Power Station, Santa Isabel
A181

Designs: 20c, Tin industry. 90c, Bismuth industry. 1b, Natural gas plant.

1973, Nov. 26 Litho. *Perf. 13½*

554 A181 10c gray & multi 10 5
555 A181 20c tan & multi 10 5
556 A181 90c lt grn & multi 40 12
557 A181 1b yel & multi 40 15
Nos. 554-557, C324-C325 (6) 2.25 87

Bolivia's development.

Cattleya Nobilior
A182

Orchids: 50c, Zygopetalum bolivianum. 1b, Huntleya melagris.

1974, May 15 *Perf. 13½*

558 A182 20c gray & multi 15 5
559 A182 50c lt bl & multi 25 10
560 A182 1b cit & multi 40 15
Nos. 558-560, C327-C330 (7) 7.80 2.45

UPU and Philatelic Exposition Emblems—A183

1974, Oct. 9

561 A183 3.50b grn, blk & bl 1.50 60

Centenary of Universal Postal Union; PRENFIL-UPU Philatelic Exhibition, Buenos Aires, Oct. 1-12; EXPO-UPU Philatelic Exhibition, Montevideo, Oct. 20-27.

Gen. Sucre, by I. Wallpher
A184

1974, Dec. 9 Litho. *Perf. 13½*

562 A184 5b multi 1.75 75

Sesquicentennial of the Battle of Ayacucho.

Lions Emblem and Steles
A185

1975, Mar. Litho. *Perf. 13½*

563 A185 30c red & multi 50 10

Lions International in Bolivia, 25th anniversary.

España 75 Emblem
A186

1975, Mar.

564 A186 4.50b yel, red & blk 1.25 50

España 75 International Philatelic Exhibition, Madrid, Apr. 4-13.

Emblem
A187

1975 Lithographed *Perf. 13½*

565 A187 2.50b lil, blk & sil 1.00 40

First meeting of Postal Ministers, Quito, Ecuador, March 1974, and for the Cartagena Agreement.

Pando Coat of Arms
A188

Designs: Departmental coats of arms.

1975, July 16 Litho. *Perf. 13½*

Gold & Multicolored

566	A188	20c *shown*	10	10
567	A188	2b *Chuquisaca*	75	50
568	A188	3b *Cochabamba*	1.00	75
		Nos. 566-568, C336-C341 (9)	4.35	3.50

Sesquicentennial of Republic of Bolivia.

Simón Bolívar
A189

Presidents and Statesmen of Bolivia: 30c, Victor Paz Estenssoro. 60c, Tomas Frias. 1b, Ismael Montes. 2.50b, Aniceto Arce. 7b, Bautista Saavedra. 10b, José Manuel Pando. 15b, José Maria Linares. 50b, Simón Bolívar.

1975 Litho. *Perf. 13½*

Size: 24x32mm.

569	A189	30c multi	15	5
569A	A189	60c multi	20	10
570	A189	1b multi	30	15
571	A189	2.50b multi	75	35
572	A189	7b multi	2.00	1.00
573	A189	10b multi	3.00	1.50
574	A189	15b multi	4.00	2.00

Size: 28x39mm.

575	A189	50b multi	15.00	
		Nos. 569-575, C346-C353 (16)	53.90	

Sesquicentennial of Republic of Bolivia.

"EXFIVIA 75"
A190

1975, Dec. 1 Litho. *Perf. 13½*

576	A190	3b multi	1.00	50
a.		Souvenir sheet	2.25	1.75

EXFIVIA 75, first Bolivian Philatelic Exposition. No. 576a contains one stamp similar to No. 576 with simulated perforations. Multicolored margin shows emblems of various international philatelic exhibitions. Size: 130x80mm. Sold for 5b.

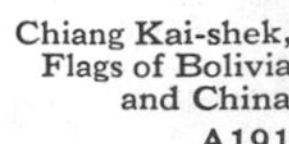

Chiang Kai-shek, Flags of Bolivia and China
A191

1976, Apr. 4 Litho. *Perf. 13½*

577	A191	2.50b multi, red circle	90	40
578	A191	2.50b multi, bl circle	90	40

Pres. Chiang Kai-shek of China (1887–1975), first death anniversary.

Erroneous red of sun's circle on Chinese flag of No. 577 was corrected on No. 578 with a dark blue overlay.

Naval Insignia
A192

1976, Apr. Litho. *Perf. 13½*

579	A192	50c bl & multi	35	10

Navy anniversary.

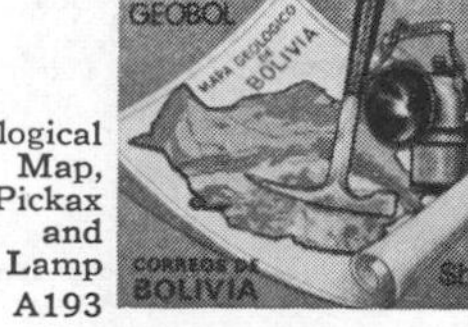

Geological Map, Pickax and Lamp
A193

1976, May

580	A193	4b multi	1.25	75

Bolivian Geological Institute.

Lufthansa Jet, Bolivian and German Colors—A194

1976, May

581	A194	3b multi	1.25	50

Lufthansa, 50th anniversary.

Boy Scout and Scout Emblem
A195

1976, May Litho. *Perf. 13½*

582	A195	1b multi	50	30

Bolivian Boy Scouts, 60th anniversary.

Battle Scene, U.S. Bicentennial Emblem
A196

1976, May 25

583	A196	4.50b bis & multi	2.00	1.00

American Bicentennial.

A souvenir sheet contains one stamp similar to No. 583 with simulated perforations. Multicolored, inscribed margin shows U.S. flags of 1776 and 1976. Size: 130x80mm.

Family, Map of Bolivia
A197

Brother Vicente Bernedo
A198

1976 *Perf. 13½*

584	A197	2.50b multi	75	50

National Census 1976.

1976, Oct.

585	A198	1.50b multi	50	25

Brother Vicente Bernedo de Potosi (1544–1619), missionary to the Indians.

Policeman with Dog, Rainbow over La Paz
A199

1976, Oct.

586	A199	2.50b multi	75	40

Bolivian Police, 150 years of service.

Emblem, Bolivar and Sucre
A200

1976, Nov. 18 Litho. *Perf. 13½*

587	A200	1.50b multi	75	40

International Congress of Bolivarian Societies.

Pedro Poveda, View of La Paz
A201

1976, Dec.

588	A201	1.50b multi	50	25

Pedro Poveda (1874–1936), educator.

A202

1976, Dec. 17 *Perf. 10½*

594	A202	20c brown	10	5
595	A202	1b ultra	30	10
596	A202	1.50b green	50	10

Boy and Girl
A203

1977, Feb. 4 Litho. *Perf. 13½*

599	A203	50c multi	20	5

Christmas 1976, and for 50th anniversary of the Inter-American Children's Institute.

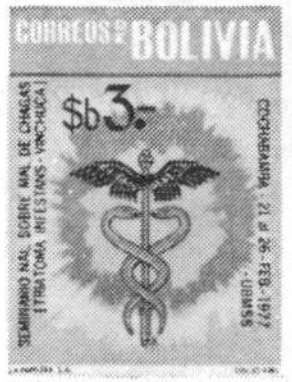

Staff of Aesculapius
A204

Supreme Court, La Paz
A205

1977, Mar. 18 Litho. *Perf. 13½x13*

600	A204	3b multi	90	15

National Seminar on Chagas' disease, Cochabamba, Feb. 21–26.

1977, May 3

Designs: 4b, Manuel Maria Urcullu, first President of Supreme Court. 4.50b, Pantaleon Dalence, President 1883–1889.

601	A205	2.50b multi	45	12
602	A205	4b multi	65	18
603	A205	4.50b multi	75	20

Sesquicentennial of Bolivian Supreme Court.

Newspaper Mastheads
A206

Map of Bolivia, Tower and Flag
A207

Designs: 2.50b, Alfredo Alexander and Hoy (horiz.). 3b, José Carrasco and El Diario (horiz.). 4b, Demetrio Canelas and Los Tiempos. 5.50b, Frontpage of Presencia.

1977, June Lithographed *Perf. 13½*

604	A206	1.50b multi	35	10
605	A206	2.50b multi	50	15
606	A206	3b multi	65	20
607	A206	4b multi	75	25
608	A206	5.50b multi	1.00	30
		Nos. 604-608 (5)	3.25	1.00

Bolivian newspapers and their founders.

1977, June

609	A207	3b multi	75	25

90th anniversary of Oruro Club.

Games' Poster
A208

Tin Miner and Emblem
A209

1977, Oct. 20 Litho. *Perf. 13½*

610	A208	5b bl & multi	1.00	30

8th Bolivian Games, La Paz, Oct. 1977.

1977, Oct. 31 Litho. *Perf. 13*

611	A209	3b multi	75	25

Bolivian Mining Corporation, 25th anniversary.

Miners, Globe, Tin Symbol
A210

Map of Bolivia, Radio Masts
A211

1977, Nov. 3

612 A210 6b sil & multi 1.25 40

International Tin Symposium, La Paz, Nov. 14–21.

1977, Nov. 11

613 A211 2.50b bl & multi 50 12

Radio Bolivia, ASBORA, 50th anniversary.

No. 450 Surcharged with New Value, 3 Bars and "EXFIVIA–77"

1977, Nov. 25 Litho. *Perf. 11x13½*

614 A147 5b on 5000b on 5b gold & gray 1.10 25

EXFIVIA '77 Philatelic Exhibition, Cochabamba.

Eye, Compass, Book of Law
A212

1978, May 3 Litho. *Perf. 13½x13*

615 A212 5b multi 1.00 25

Audit Department, 50th anniversary.

Mt. Illimani
A213

Pre-Columbian Monolith
A214

Design: 1.50b, Mt. Cerro de Potosi.

Perf. 11x10½, 10½x11

1978, June 1 Litho.

616 A213 50c bl & Prus bl 15 5
617 A214 1b brn & lem 25 5
618 A213 1.50b red & bl gray 40 6

Andean Countries, Staff of Aesculapius
A215

Map of Americas with Bolivia
A216

1978, June 1 *Perf. 10½x11*

626 A215 2b org & blk 50 15

Health Ministers of Andean Countries, 5th meeting.

1978, June 1

627 A216 2.50b dp ultra & red 50 20

World Rheumatism Year.

Central Bank Building
A217

1978, July 26 Litho. *Perf. 13½*

628 A217 7b multi 1.50 40

50th anniversary of Bank of Bolivia.

Jesus and Children
A218

1979, Feb. 20 Litho. *Perf. 13½*

629 A218 8b multi 1.40 25

International Year of the Child.

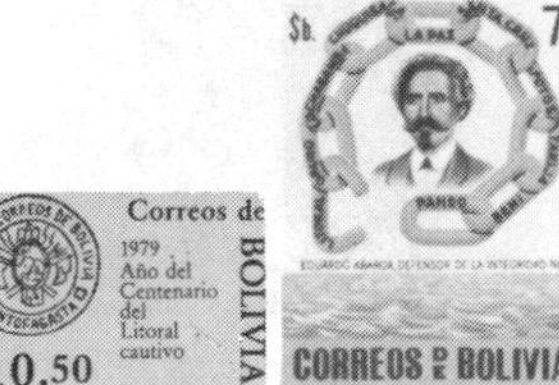

Antofagasta Cancel
A219

Eduardo Abaroa, and Chain
A220

Designs: 1b, La Chimba cancel. 1.50b, Mejillones cancel. 5.50b, View of Antofagasta (horiz.). 6.50b, Woman in chains, symbolizing captive province. 8b, Map of Antofagasta Province, 1876. 10b, Arms of province.

1979, Mar. 23 Litho. *Perf. 10½*

630 A219 50c buff & blk 10 5
631 A219 1b pink & blk 18 5
632 A219 1.50b pale grn & blk 28 6

Perf. 13½

633 A220 5.50b multi 95 25
634 A220 6.50b multi 1.20 28
635 A220 7b multi 1.25 28
636 A220 8b multi 1.40 35
637 A220 10b multi 1.75 48
Nos. 630-637 (8) 7.11 1.80

Centenary of loss of Antofagasta coastal area to Chile.

Emblem and Map of Bolivia
A221

Gymnast
A222

1979, Mar. 26 *Perf. 13½x13*

638 A221 3b multi 55 12

Radio Club of Bolivia.

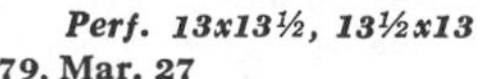

Perf. 13x13½, 13½x13

1979, Mar. 27

Design: 6.50b, Runner and Games emblem (horiz.).

639 A222 6.50b multi 1.20 28
640 A222 10b multi 1.75 48

Southern Cross Sports Games, Bolivia, Nov. 3–12, 1978.

A souvenir sheet contains 1 stamp similar to No. 640 with simulated perforations. Multicolored margin shows various exhibition and sports emblems. Sold for 20b. Size: 80x130mm.

Bulgaria No. 1
A223

EXFILMAR Emblem
A224

1979, Mar. 30 *Perf. 10½*

641 A223 2.50b multi 45 12

PHILASERDICA '79 International Philatelic Exhibition, Sofia, Bulgaria, May 18–27.

1979, Apr. 2

642 A224 6b multi 1.10 30

Bolivian Maritime Philatelic Exhibition, La Paz, Nov. 18–28.

OAS Emblem, Map of Bolivia—A226

1979, Oct. 22 Litho. *Perf. 14×13½*

644 A226 6b multi 1.10 30

Organization of American States, 9th Congress, La Paz, Oct.-Nov.

Franz Tamayo
A227

Bolivian and Japanese Flags, Hospital
A228

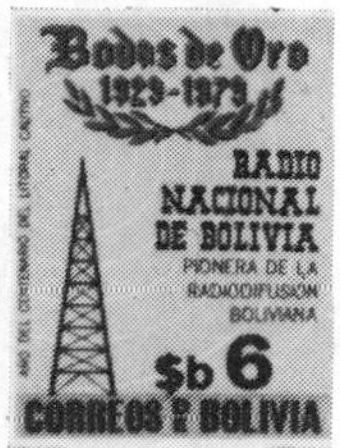

U.N. Emblem and Meeting
A229

Radio Tower and Waves
A230

1979, Dec.

645 A227 2.80b blk & gray 50 15
646 A228 5b multi 90 25
648 A229 5b multi 90 25
649 A230 6b multi 1.10 30

Franz Tamayo, lawyer, birth centenary; Japanese-Bolivian health care cooperation; CEPAL, 18th Congress, La Paz, Sept. 18-26; Bolivian National Radio, 50th anniversary.

Puerto Suarez Iron Ore Deposits—A231

1979 Litho. *Perf. 13½x14*

650 A231 9.50b multi 1.70 45

Bolivia No. 19, EXFILMAR Emblem, Bolivian Flag—A232

1980 Litho. *Perf. 13½*

651 A232 4b multi 72 16

EXFILMAR, Bolivian Maritime Philatelic Exhibition, La Paz, Nov. 18-28, 1979.

Juana Azurduy on Horseback—A233

1980 Litho. *Perf. 14x13½*

652 A233 4b multi 72 16

Juana Azurduy de Padilla, independence fighter, birth bicentenary.

La Salle and World Map—A234

1980 *Perf. 13½x14*
653 A234 9b multi 1.60 40

St. Jean Baptiste de la Salle (1651-1719), educator.

"Victory" in Chariot, Madrid, Exhibition Emblem, Flags of Bolivia and Spain—A235

1980, Oct. **Litho.** *Perf. 13½x14*
654 A235 14b multi 2.50 65

ESPAMER '80 Stamp Exhibition, Madrid.

Map of South America, Flags of Argentina, Bolivia and Peru—A236

1980, Oct. *Perf. 14x13½*
655 A236 2b multi 36 8

Ministers of Public Works and Transport of Argentina, Bolivia and Peru meeting.

Santa Cruz-Trinidad Railroad, Inauguration of Third Section—A237

1980, Oct.
656 A237 3b multi 52 12

Flag on Provincial Map
A238

Ara Macao
A239

1981, May 11 Litho. *Perf. 14x13½, 13½x14*

657	A238	1b Soldier, flag, map	18	5
658	A238	3b Flag, map	52	12
659	A238	40b shown	7.25	1.60
660	A238	50b Soldier, civilians, horiz.	9.00	2.00

July 17 Revolution memorial.

1981, May 11 *Perf. 14x13½*

Designs: Parrots.

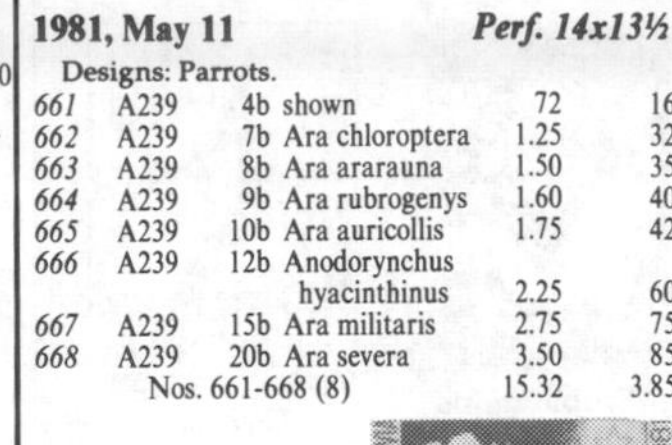

661	A239	4b shown	72	16
662	A239	7b Ara chloroptera	1.25	32
663	A239	8b Ara ararauna	1.50	35
664	A239	9b Ara rubrogenys	1.60	40
665	A239	10b Ara auricollis	1.75	42
666	A239	12b Anodorynchus hyacinthinus	2.25	60
667	A239	15b Ara militaris	2.75	75
668	A239	20b Ara severa	3.50	85
		Nos. 661-668 (8)	15.32	3.85

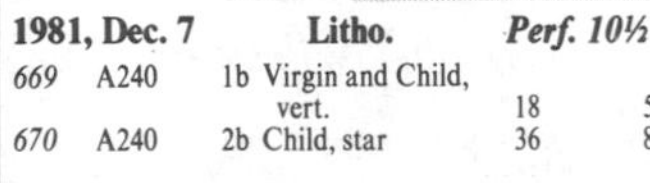

Christmas 1981
A240

1981, Dec. 7 **Litho.** *Perf. 10½*
669 A240 1b Virgin and Child, vert. 18 5
670 A240 2b Child, star 36 8

American Airforces Commanders' 22nd Conference, Buenos Aires—A241

1982, Apr. 12 **Litho.** *Perf. 13½*
671 A241 14b multi 2.50 70

75th Anniv. of Cobija
A242

Simon Bolivar Birth Bicentenary (1983)
A243

1982, July 8 **Litho.** *Perf. 13½*
672 A242 28b multi 62 24

1982, July 12
673 A243 18b multi 40 16

1983 World Telecommunications Day
A244

1982 World Cup
A245

1982, July 15
674 A244 26b Receiving station 58 20

1982, July 21 *Perf. 11*
675 A245 4b shown 10 5
676 A245 100b Final Act, by Picasso 2.25 90

Girl Playing Piano—A246

1982, July 25 *Perf. 13½*
677 A246 16b Boy playing soccer 35 14
678 A246 20b shown 45 18

Bolivian-Chinese Agricultural Cooperation, 1972-1982—A247

1982, Aug. 12
679 A247 30b multi 65 26

First Bolivian-Japanese Gastroenterology Conference, La Paz, Jan—A248

1982, Aug. 26
680 A248 22b multi 50 20

10th Anniv. of Bolivian Philatelic Federation—A249

1982, Aug. 31 **Litho.** *Perf. 14x13½*
681 A249 19b Stamps 40 15

Pres. Hernando Siles Birth Centenary—A250

1982, Sept. 1
682 A250 20b tan & dk brn 45 18

Scouting Year
A251

Cochabamba Philatelic Center, 25th Anniv.
A252

1982, Sept. 3 *Perf. 11*
683 A251 5b Baden-Powell 12 5

1982, Sept. 14
684 A252 3b multi 6 5

Cochabamba Superior Court of Justice Sesquicentennial—A253

1982 **Litho.** *Perf. 13½*
685 A253 10b multi 25 10

Entronement of Virgin of Copacabana, 400th Anniv.
A254

Navy Day
A255

1982, Nov. 15 **Litho.** *Perf. 13½*
686 A254 13b multi 34 15

1982, Nov. 17
687 A255 14b Port Busch Naval Base 35 15

Christmas 1982—A256

1982, Nov. 19 *Perf. 11*
688 A256 10b grn & gray 25 10

10th Youth Soccer Championship, Jan. 22-Feb. 13—A257

1983, Feb. 13 **Litho.** *Perf. 13½*
689 A257 50b multi 1.25 50

EXFIVIA '83 Philatelic Exhibition—A258

1983, Nov. 5 **Litho.** ***Perf. 13½***

690	A258	150b brn car	1.50	60

Visit of Brazilian Pres. Joao Figueiredo, Feb.—A259

1984, Feb. 7 **Litho.** ***Perf. 13½x14***

691	A259	150b multi	60	25

Simon Bolivar Entering La Paz, by Carmen Baptista—A260

Paintings of Bolivar: 50b, Riding Horse, by Mulato Gil de Quesada (vert.).

1984, Mar. 30 ***Perf. 14x13½, 13½x14***

692	A260	50b multi	20	8
693	A260	200b multi	80	32

Types of 1957-79 Surcharged.

1984, Mar.

694	A223	40b on 2.50b #641	16	5
695	A227	40b on 2.80b #645	16	5
696	A219	60b on 1.50b #632	24	10
697	A216	60b on 2.50b #627	24	10
698	A226	100b on 2b #642	40	16
699	A141	200b on 350b #409	80	32
		Nos. 694-699 (6)	2.00	78

Nos. 675, 683-684, 688 C328 Surcharged.

1984, June 27 **Litho.** ***Perf. 11***

700	A252	500b on 3b #684		
701	A245	1000b on 4b #675		
702	A256	2000b on 10b #688		
703	A251	5000b on 5b #683		

Perf. 13½

704	A182	10,000b on 3.80b #C328		

Road Safety Education

A261

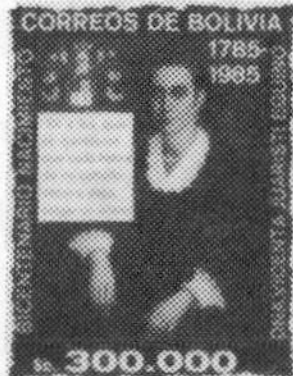

Jose Eustaquio Mendez, 200th Birth Anniv.

A262

Cartoons.

1984, Sept. 7 **Litho.** ***Perf. 11***

705	A261	80b Jaywalker	5	5
706	A261	120b Motorcycle policeman, ambulance	8	5

1984, Sept. 19 ***Perf. 14x13½, 13½x14***

Paintings: 300b, Birthplace, by Jorge Campos. 500b, Mendez Leading the Battle of La Tablada, by M. Villegas, horiz.

707	A262	300b multi	18	8
708	A262	500b multi	22	10

1986 World Cup Soccer Championships, Mexico

A263

Chasqui, Postal Runner

A264

Sponsoring shoe-manufacturers' trademarks and: 100b, 200b, Outline map of Bolivia, national colors. 600b, World map and soccer ball, horiz.

1984, Oct. 26 ***Perf. 11***

709	A263	100b multi	5	5
710	A263	200b multi	8	5
711	A263	600b multi	20	8

1985

712	A264	11000b vio bl	40	16

Intl. Year of Professional Education

A265

Intl. Anti-Polio Campaign

A266

1985, Apr. 25

713	A265	2000b Natl. Manual Crafts emblem	5	5

1985, May 22

714	A266	20000b lt bl & vio	36	15

Endangered Wildlife—A267

1985, May 22

715	A267	23000b Altiplano boliviano	30	12
716	A267	25000b Sarcorhamphus gryphus	35	14
717	A267	30000b Blastocaros dichotomus	45	18

Nos. 716-717 vert.

Dona Vicenta Juaristi Eguino (b. 1785), Independence Heroine

A268

UN, 40th Anniv.

A269

1985, Oct. **Litho.** ***Perf. 13½***

718	A268	300000b multi	30	12

1985, Oct. 24 ***Perf. 11***

719	A269	1000000b bl & gold	1.00	40

Natl. Soccer Team, 75th Anniv.—A270

1985, Nov.

720	A270	200000b multi	20	8

No. 713 Surcharged.

1986 **Litho.** ***Perf. 11***

721	A265	200000b on 2000b multi	22	10
722	A265	5000000b on 2000b multi	5.25	2.10

1986 World Cup Soccer Championships—A271

Intl. Youth Year

A272 A273

1986

723	A271	300000 Emblems, vert.	32	12
724	A271	550000 Pique trademark, vert.	58	24
725	A271	1000000 Azteca Stadium	1.05	42
726	A271	2500000 World cup, vert.	2.65	1.05

1986

727	A272	150000 brt car rose	16	6
728	A272	500000 bl grn	55	35
729	A273	3000000 multi	3.15	1.25

Inscribed 1985.

Alfonso Sobieta Viaduct, Carretera Quillacollo, Confital—A274

1986 ***Perf. 13½***

730	A274	400000 int bl & gray	42	16

Inter-American Development Bank, 25th anniv.

Admission of Bolivia to the UPU, Cent.—A275

1986 ***Perf. 11***

731	A275	800000 multi	85	35

Postal Workers Society, 50th Anniv.—A276

1986

732	A276	2000000 brn & pale brn	2.10	85

Founding of Trinidad, 300th Anniv.—A277

1986 ***Perf. 13½x14***

733	A277	1400000 Bull and Rider, by Vaca	1.50	60

Bolivian Philatelic Federation, 15th Anniv.—A278

1986

734	A278	600000b No. 19	62	25

Death of a Priest, by Jose Antonio Zampa

A279

Intl. Peace Year

A280

1986 ***Perf. 14x13½***

735	A279	400000 multi	42	16

1986 ***Perf. 11***

736	A280	200000 yel grn & pale grn	22	10

AIR POST STAMPS.

Aviation School
AP1 AP2

Engraved.

1924, Dec. *Perf. 14* **Unwmkd.**

C1	AP1	10c ver & blk	35	35
a.		Inverted center	1,250.	
C2	AP1	15c car & blk	1.50	1.00
C3	AP1	25c dk bl & blk	75	50
C4	AP1	50c org & blk	1.25	1.00
C5	AP2	1b red brn & blk	1.25	1.25
C6	AP2	2b blk brn & blk	2.75	2.75
C7	AP2	5b dk vio & blk	4.50	4.50
		Nos. C1-C7 (7)	12.35	11.35

Issued to commemorate the establishing of the National Aviation School.

These stamps were available for ordinary postage. Nos. C1, C3, C5 and C6 exist imperforate. Proofs of the 2b with inverted center exist imperforate and privately perforated.

Emblem of
Lloyd Aéreo Boliviano
AP3

1928 **Lithographed.** *Perf. 11.*

C8	AP3	15c green	1.25	75
a.		Imperf. (pair)	35.00	
C9	AP3	20c dk bl	25	15
C10	AP3	35c red brn	75	40

Graf Zeppelin Issues.

Nos. C1–C5 Surcharged or Overprinted in Various Colors:

CORREO AEREO
R. S. 6-V-1930
5 Cts.
a

CORREO AEREO
R. S.
6-V- 1930
b

1930, May 6 *Perf. 14.*

C11	AP1 (a)	5c on 10c ver & blk (G)	15.00	15.00
C12	AP1 (b)	10c ver & blk (Bl)	15.00	15.00
C13	AP1 (b)	10c ver & blk (Br)	750.00	1,000.
C14	AP1 (b)	15c car & blk (V)	15.00	15.00
C15	AP1 (b)	25c dk bl & blk (R)	15.00	15.00
C16	AP1 (b)	50c org & blk (Br)	15.00	15.00
C17	AP1 (b)	50c org & blk (R)	750.00	1,000.
C18	AP2 (b)	1b red brn & blk (gold)	175.00	150.00

Experts consider the 50c with silver overprint to be a trial color proof.

Surcharged or Overprinted
in Bronze Inks of Various Colors.

C19	AP1 (a)	5c on 10c ver & blk (G)	85.00	85.00
C20	AP1 (b)	10c ver & blk (Bl)	70.00	70.00
C21	AP1 (b)	15c car & blk (V)	85.00	85.00
C22	AP1 (b)	25c dk bl & blk (cop)	85.00	85.00
C23	AP2 (b)	1b red brn & blk (gold)	175.00	175.00

Issued in commemoration of the flight of the airship Graf Zeppelin from Europe to Brazil and return via Lakehurst, N.J.

Nos. C11 to C18 exist with the surcharges inverted, double, or double with one inverted, but the regularity of these varieties is questioned.

Nos. C19 to C23 were intended for use on postal matter forwarded by the Graf Zeppelin.

No. C18 was overprinted with light gold or gilt bronze ink. No. C23 was overprinted with deep gold bronze ink. Nos. C13 and C17 were overprinted with trial colors but were sold with the regular printings. The 5c on 10c is known surcharged in black and in blue.

Air Post Stamps of 1928 Issue, Surcharged

Z 1930
Bs. 3.—

1930, May 6 *Perf. 11.*

C24	AP3	1.50b on 15c grn	40.00	40.00
a.		Inverted surcharge	80.00	80.00
b.		Comma instead of period after "1"	50.00	50.00
C25	AP3	3b on 20c dk bl	40.00	40.00
a.		Inverted surcharge	80.00	80.00
b.		Comma instead of period after "3"	55.00	55.00
C26	AP3	6b on 35c red brn	60.00	65.00
a.		Inverted surcharge	135.00	135.00
b.		Comma instead of period after "6"	75.00	75.00

Airplane and Bullock Cart
AP6

Airplane and River Boat
AP7

1930, July 24 **Litho.** *Perf. 14*

C27	AP6	5c dp vio	60	40
C28	AP7	15c red	60	40
C29	AP7	20c yellow	60	40
C30	AP6	35c yel grn	60	25
C31	AP7	50c dp bl	60	25
C32	AP6	1b lt brn	60	25
C33	AP7	2b dp rose	60	35
C34	AP6	3b slate	3.00	2.00
		Nos. C27-C34 (8)	7.20	4.30

Nos. C27 to C34 exist imperforate.

Air Service Emblem
AP8

1932, Sept. 16 *Perf. 11.*

C35	AP8	5c ultra	1.00	60
C36	AP8	10c gray	60	30
C37	AP8	15c dk rose	1.00	75
C38	AP8	25c orange	1.00	75
C39	AP8	30c green	80	40
C40	AP8	50c violet	80	40
C41	AP8	1b dk brn	80	40
		Nos. C35-C41 (7)	6.00	3.60

Map of Bolivia
AP9

1935, Feb. 1 **Engraved.** *Perf. 12.*

C42	AP9	5c brn red	25	20
C43	AP9	10c dk grn	25	20
C44	AP9	20c dk vio	25	20
C45	AP9	30c ultra	25	20
C46	AP9	50c orange	35	20
C47	AP9	1b bis brn	35	30
C48	AP9	1½b yellow	80	20
C49	AP9	2b carmine	80	40
C50	AP9	5b green	1.50	50
C51	AP9	10b dk brn	2.50	1.00
		Nos. C42-C51 (10)	7.30	3.40

Air Post Stamps of 1924–30 Surcharged in Red or Green

Correo Aéreo
D. S. 25-2-37
0.05
c

1937, Oct. 6 *Perf. 11, 14.*

C52	AP6	5c on 35c yel grn (R)	50	40
a.		"Carreo"	15.00	
C53	AP3	20c on 35c red brn (R)	60	40
C54	AP3	50c on 35c red brn (R)	75	60
a.		Inverted surcharge	25.00	
C55	AP3	1b on 35c red brn (R)	1.25	75
C56	AP1	2b on 50c org & blk (R)	1.75	1.00
C57	AP1	12b on 10c ver & blk (G)	7.00	5.00
a.		Inverted surcharge	30.00	
C58	AP1	15b on 10c ver & blk (G)	7.00	3.00

Regular Postage Stamps of 1925 Surcharged in Green or Red

Correo
Aéreo
D. S.
25-2-37
Bs. 4.—
d

Perf. 14.

C59	A56 (d)	3b on 50c dp vio (G)	1.75	1.50
C60	A56 (d)	4b on 1b red (G)	2.25	2.00
C61	A57 (c)	5b on 2b org (G)	2.75	2.50
C62	A56 (d)	10b on 5b blk brn (R)	7.00	5.00
a.		Double surcharge	50.00	
		Nos. C52-C62 (11)	32.60	22.15

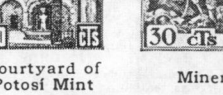

Courtyard of Potosí Mint
AP10

BOLIVIA CORREO AEREO
30 cts 30

Miner
AP11

Emancipated Woman
AP12

Pincers, Torch and Good Will Principles
AP15

Airplane over Field
AP13

Airplanes and Liberty Monument
AP14

Airplane over River
AP16

Emblem of New Government
AP17

Transport Planes over Map of Bolivia
AP18

1938, May **Lithographed.** *Perf. 10½.*

C63	AP10	20c dp rose	35	30
C64	AP11	30c gray	35	30
C65	AP12	40c yellow	35	30
C66	AP13	50c yel grn	50	30
C67	AP14	60c dl bl	50	30
C68	AP15	1b dl red	75	30
C69	AP16	2b bister	1.50	30
C70	AP17	3b lt brn	1.50	30
C71	AP18	5b dk vio	2.00	30
		Nos. C63-C71 (9)	7.80	2.70

Chalice
AP19

Virgin of Copacabana
AP20

Jesus Christ
AP21

Church of San Francisco, La Paz
AP22

St. Anthony of Padua
AP23

Lithographed.

1939, July 19 ***Perf. 13½, 10½.***

C72	AP19	5c dl vio	75	50
a.		Pair, imperf. between	60.00	
C73	AP20	30c lt bl grn	60	30
C74	AP21	45c vio bl	75	30
a.		Vertical pair, imperf. between	85.00	
C75	AP22	60c carmine	75	50
C76	AP23	75c vermilion	1.25	1.00
C77	AP23	90c dp bl	85	40
C78	AP22	2b dl brn	1.50	40
C79	AP21	4b dp plum	2.00	60
C80	AP20	5b lt bl	4.00	40
C81	AP19	10b yellow	10.00	40
		Nos. C72-C81 (10)	22.45	4.80

Issued to commemorate the second National Eucharistic Congress.

Plane over Lake Titicaca
AP24

Mt. Illimani and Condor
AP25

1941, Aug. 21 ***Perf. 13½.***

C82	AP24	10b dl grn	6.00	75
C83	AP24	20b lt ultra	7.00	1.25
C84	AP25	50b rose lil	12.50	1.75
C85	AP25	100b ol bis	30.00	6.00

Counterfeits exist.

Liberty and Clasped Hands
AP26

1942, Nov. 12

C86	AP26	40c rose lake	50	35
C87	AP26	50c ultra	50	35
C88	AP26	1b org brn	60	50
C89	AP26	5b magenta	1.50	35
a.		Double impression		
C90	AP26	10b dl brn vio	5.00	2.50
		Nos. C86-C90 (5)	8.10	4.05

Issued to commemorate the Conference of Chancellors held January 15, 1942.

General José Ballivián; Old and Modern Transportation
AP27

1943, Nov. 18 **Engr.** ***Perf. 12½***

C91	AP27	10c rose vio & brn	15	15
C92	AP27	20c emer & brn	20	15
C93	AP27	30c rose car & brn	30	25
C94	AP27	3b bl & brn	40	30
C95	AP27	5b blk & brn	75	50
		Nos. C91-C95 (5)	1.80	1.35

Department of Beni centenary.

Condor and Sun Rising
AP28

Plane
AP29

Lithographed.

1944, Sept. 19 ***Perf. 13½.***

C96	AP28	40c red vio	15	10
C97	AP28	1b lt vio	20	10
C98	AP29	1.50b yel grn	25	10
C99	AP29	2.50b dk gray bl	50	25

Revolution of Dec. 20, 1943.

Map of National Airways
AP30

Map of Bolivian Air Lines
AP31

1945, May 31 ***Perf. 11***

C100	AP30	10c red	15	10
a.		Imperf. (pair)	12.50	
C101	AP30	50c yellow	20	10
a.		Imperf. (pair)	20.00	
C102	AP30	90c lt grn	30	10
C103	AP30	5b lt ultra	50	20
C104	AP30	20b dp brn	1.50	60
		Nos. C100-C104 (5)	2.65	1.10

10th anniversary of first flight, La Paz to Tacna, Peru, by Panagra Airways.

Centers in Red and Blue.

1945, Sept. 15 ***Perf. 13½.***

C105	AP31	20c violet	12	10
C106	AP31	30c org brn	12	10
C107	AP31	50c brt bl grn	12	10
C108	AP31	90c brt vio	12	10
C109	AP31	2b blue	20	15
C110	AP31	3b magenta	30	20
C111	AP31	4b ol bis	50	25
		Nos. C105-C111 (7)	1.48	1.00

Issued to commemorate the 20th anniversary of the founding of Lloyd Aéreo Boliviano.

No. C76 Surcharged in Blue

1947, Mar. 23

C112	AP23	1.40b on 75c ver	30	30

Mt. Illimani
AP32

Arms of Bolivia and Argentina
AP33

1947, Sept. 15 **Litho.** ***Perf. 11½***

C113	AP32	1b rose car	10	10
C114	AP32	1.40b emerald	15	10
C115	AP32	2.50b blue	25	20
C116	AP32	3b dp org	35	30
C117	AP32	4b rose lil	40	25
		Nos. C113-C117 (5)	1.25	95

Issued to commemorate the first anniversary of the Revolution of July 21, 1946.

1947, Oct. 23 ***Perf. 13½***

C118	AP33	2.90b ultra	40	40
a.		Imperf. (pair)	30.00	
b.		Perf. 10½	7.50	6.00

Issued to commemorate the meeting of Presidents Enrique Hertzog of Bolivia and Juan D. Perón of Argentina at Yacuiba, Oct. 23, 1947.

Types of Regular Issue of 1948.

Designs: 2.50b, Statue of Christ above La Paz. 3.70b, Child kneeling before cross. No. C121, St. John Bosco. No. C122, Virgin of Copacabana. 13.60b, Pope Pius XII blessing University of La Paz.

1948, Sept. 26 ***Perf. 11½.***

C119	A120	2.50b ver & yel	85	50
C120	A120	3.70b rose & cr	1.00	50
C121	A120	4b rose lil & gray	1.00	40
C122	A120	4b lt ultra & sal	1.00	25
C123	A120	13.60b ultra & lt grn	1.25	40
		Nos. C119-C123 (5)	5.10	2.05

Issued to publicize the 3rd Inter-American Congress of Catholic Education.

Type of Regular Issue of 1948

1948, Oct.

C124	A125	10b emer & sal	2.50	30

Issued to publicize the International Automobile Races of South America, September–October 1948.

Pres. Gregorio Pacheco, Map and Post Horn
AP34

L. A. B. Plane
AP35

1950, Jan. 2 **Unwmkd.**

C125	AP34	1.40b org brn	15	15
C126	AP34	2.50b orange	10	10
C127	AP34	3.30b rose vio	15	15

Issued to commemorate the 75th anniversary of the formation of the Universal Postal Union.

Nos. C100 and C104 Surcharged in Black

XV ANIVERSARIO
PANAGRA
Bs
4.-
1935-1950

1950, May 31 ***Perf. 11.***

C128	AP30	4b on 10c red	15	15
C129	AP30	10b on 20b dp brn	40	30
a.		Inverted surcharge	25.00	25.00

Issued to commemorate the 15th anniversary of Panagra air services in Bolivia.

1950, Sept. 15 **Litho.** ***Perf. 13½***

C130	AP35	20c red org	15	15
C131	AP35	30c purple	15	15
C132	AP35	50c green	15	15
C133	AP35	1b orange	15	15
C134	AP35	3b ultra	15	15
C135	AP35	15b carmine	50	20
C136	AP35	50b chocolate	1.50	50
		Nos. C130-C136 (7)	2.75	1.45

Issued to commemorate the 25th anniversary of the founding of Lloyd Aéreo Boliviano. No. C132 exists imperforate.

No. C116 Surcharged in Black

Triunfo de la
Democracia
24 de Sept. 49
Bs. 1,40

1950, Sept. 24 ***Perf. 11½***

C137	AP32	1.40b on 3b dp org	25	25

Issued to commemorate the 1st anniversary of the ending of the Civil War of Aug. 24–Sept. 24, 1949.

Symbols of United Nations
AP36

1950, Oct. 24 **Unwmkd.**

C138	AP36	3.60b crim rose	75	25
C139	AP36	4.70b blk brn	1.00	25

Issued to commemorate the 5th anniversary of the formation of the United Nations, October 24, 1945.

Gate of the Sun and Llama
AP37

Church of San Francisco
AP38

Designs: 40c, Avenue Camacho. 50c, Consistorial Palace. 1b, Legislative Palace. 2b, Communications Bldg. 3b, Arms. 4b, La Gasca ordering Mendoza to found La Paz. 5b, Capt. Alonso de Mendoza founding La Paz. 10b, Arms; portrait of Mendoza.

1951, Mar. 1 **Engr.** ***Perf. 12½.***

Center in Black.

C140	AP37	20c carmine	20	20
C141	AP38	30c dk vio bl	20	20
C142	AP37	40c dk bl	20	20
C143	AP37	50c bl grn	25	25
C144	AP37	1b red	30	30
C145	AP37	2b red org	50	50

C146	AP37	3b dp bl	50	50
C147	AP37	4b vermilion	60	60
a.		Souv. sheet of 4	1.50	1.50
C148	AP37	5b dk grn	60	60
a.		Souv. sheet of 3	1.50	1.50
C149	AP37	10b red brn	1.00	1.00
a.		Souv. sheet of 3	1.50	1.50
		Nos. C140-C149 (10)	4.35	4.35

400th anniversary of the founding of La Paz.

No. C147a contains C143–C145, C147; No. C148a contains C142, C146, C148; No. C149a contains 140, C141, C149. Black marginal inscriptions. Perf. and imperf., size: 150x100mm.

Horsemanship
AP39

Designs: 30c, Basketball. 50c, Fencing. 1b, Hurdling. 2.50b, Javelin throwing. 3b, Relay race. 5b, La Paz stadium.

1951, Aug. 23 **Unwmkd.**

Center in Black.

C150	AP39	20c purple	35	10
C151	AP39	30c rose vio	50	15
C152	AP39	50c dp red org	75	15
C153	AP39	1b chocolate	75	15
C154	AP39	2.50b orange	1.00	60
C155	AP39	3b blk brn	1.50	75
a.		Souv. sheet of 3	6.00	5.00
C156	AP39	5b red	3.00	1.50
a.		Souv. sheet of 4	7.00	6.50
		Nos. C150-C156 (7)	7.85	3.40

The stamps were intended to commemorate the 5th South American Games and the 2nd National Sports Congress held at La Paz, October 1948.

No. C155a contains C153–C155; No. C156a contains C150–C152, C156. Black marginal inscriptions. Perf. and imperf., size: 150x100mm.

Eduardo Abaroa
AP40

Queen Isabella I
AP41

1952, Mar. 24 Litho. ***Perf. 11***

C157	AP40	70c rose red	15	15
C158	AP40	2b org yel	20	25
C159	AP40	3b yel grn	20	25
C160	AP40	5b blue	25	25
C161	AP40	50b rose lil	1.50	75
C162	AP40	100b gray blk	1.75	1.00
		Nos. C157-C162 (6)	4.05	2.65

Issued to commemorate the 73rd anniversary of the death of Eduardo Abaroa.

1952, July 16 ***Perf. 13½***

C163	AP41	50b emerald	50	40
C164	AP41	100b brown	1.00	50

Issued to commemorate the 500th anniversary of the birth of Queen Isabella I of Spain. Exist imperforate.

Columbus Lighthouse
AP42

1952, July 16

C165	AP42	2b rose lil, *sal*	15	15
C166	AP42	3.70b bl grn, *bl*	15	15
C167	AP42	4.40b org, *sal*	25	10
C168	AP42	20b dk brn, *cr*	50	18

No. C168 exists imperforate.

Soldiers
AP43

Gualberto Villarroel, Victor Paz Estenssoro and Hernan Siles Zuazo
AP44

Perf. 13½ (AP43), 11½ (AP44)

1953, Apr. 9 Lithographed

C169	AP44	3.70b chocolate	20	20
C170	AP43	6b red vio	20	20
C171	AP44	9b brn rose	20	20
C172	AP44	10b aqua	20	20
C173	AP44	16b vermilion	20	20
C174	AP43	22.50b dk brn	40	30
C175	AP44	40b gray	60	20
		Nos. C169-C175 (7)	2.00	1.50

Issued to commemorate the first anniversary of the Revolution of Apr. 9, 1952. Nos. C170 and C174 exist imperf.

Pres. Victor Paz Estenssoro Embracing Indian
AP45

Map and Peasant
AP46

1954, Aug. 2 ***Perf. 12x11½.***

C176	AP45	20b org brn	15	10
C177	AP46	27b brt pink	15	20
C178	AP46	30b red org	25	15
C179	AP46	45b vio brn	40	10
C180	AP45	100b bl grn	75	10
C181	AP46	300b yel grn	2.00	35
		Nos. C176-C181 (6)	3.70	1.00

Nos. C176 and C180 were issued to commemorate the 3rd Inter-American Indian Congress. Nos. C177–C179 and C181 commemorate the agrarian reform laws of 1953–1954.

Oil Derricks
AP47

Map of South America and La Paz Arms
AP48

1955, Oct. 9 ***Perf. 10½***

C182	AP47	55b dk & lt grnsh bl	15	10
C183	AP47	70b dk gray & gray	25	10
C184	AP47	90b dk & lt grn	30	15

Perf. 13.

C185	AP47	500b red lil	1.25	60
C186	AP47	1000b blk brn & fawn	2.00	1.50
		Nos. C182-C186 (5)	3.95	2.45

Nos. C140–C149 Surcharged with New Values and Bars in Black or Carmine.

1957 **Engraved.** ***Perf. 12½***

Center in Black

C187	AP37	100b on 3b dp bl (C)	15	10
C188	AP37	200b on 2b red org	15	10
C189	AP37	500b on 4b ver	25	15
C190	AP37	600b on 1b red	25	15
C191	AP37	700b on 20c car	40	20
C192	AP37	800b on 40c dk bl (C)	50	30
C193	AP38	900b on 30c dk vio bl (C)	60	15
C194	AP37	1800b on 50c bl grn (C)	1.00	50
C195	AP37	3000b on 5b dk grn (C)	1.50	90
C196	AP37	5000b on 10b red brn (C)	2.50	1.75
		Nos. C187-C196 (10)	7.30	4.30

Lithographed.

1957, May 25 ***Perf. 12*** **Unwmkd.**

C197	AP48	700b lil & vio	60	40
C198	AP48	1200b pale brn	75	60
C199	AP48	1350b rose car	1.00	75
C200	AP48	2700b bl grn	2.00	1.00
C201	AP48	4000b vio bl	2.50	1.25
		Nos. C197-C201 (5)	6.85	4.00

Issued to commemorate the seventh session of the C. E. P. A. L. (Comision Economica para la America Latina de las Naciones Unidas), La Paz.

Type of Regular Issue, 1957

1957, Dec. 19 ***Perf. 11½***

C202	A141	600b magenta	35	10
C203	A141	700b vio bl	50	18
C204	A141	900b pale grn	75	12

Issued to commemorate the opening of the Santa Cruz-Yacuiba Railroad and the meeting of the Presidents of Bolivia and Argentina.

Type of Regular Issue, 1960.

1960, Jan. 30

C205	A142	400b rose cl	75	15
C206	A142	800b sl bl	1.00	30
C207	A142	2000b slate	1.50	60

Issued for an expected visit of Mexico's Pres. Adolfo Lopez Mateos. On sale Jan. 30-Feb. 1, 1960.

Gate of the Sun, Tiahuanacu
AP49

Uprooted Oak Emblem
AP50

1960, Mar. 26 **Litho.** ***Perf. 11½***

C208	AP49	3,000b gray	2.00	75
C209	AP49	5,000b orange	3.00	1.50
C210	AP49	10,000b rose cl	6.00	2.50
C211	AP49	15,000b bl vio	9.00	4.00

1960, Apr. 7 ***Perf. 11½***

C212	AP50	600b ultra	50	50
C213	AP50	700b lt red brn	50	50
C214	AP50	900b dk bl grn	50	50
C215	AP50	1,800b violet	85	85
C216	AP50	2,000b gray	1.00	85
		Nos. C212-C216 (5)	3.35	3.20

Issued to publicize World Refugee Year, July 1, 1959–June 30, 1960.

No. C215 exists with "1961" overprint in dark carmine, but was not regularly issued in this form.

Jaime Laredo
AP51

Lithographed

1960, Aug. 15 ***Perf. 11½*** **Unwmkd.**

C217	AP51	600b rose vio	1.25	40
C218	AP51	700b ol gray	1.50	50
C219	AP51	800b vio brn	1.50	50
C220	AP51	900b dk bl	2.00	50
C221	AP51	1,800b green	2.50	1.50
C222	AP51	4,000b dk gray	6.00	2.50
		Nos. C217-C222 (6)	14.75	5.90

Issued to honor the violinist Jaime Laredo.

Type of Regular Issue, 1960.
(Children's Hospital)

1960, Nov. 21 ***Perf. 11½***

C223	A146	600b red brn, yel & dp bl	60	35
C224	A146	1,000b ol grn, yel & dp bl	90	35
C225	A146	1,800b plum, yel & dp bl	1.25	60
C226	A146	5,000b blk, yel & dp bl	4.00	1.75

Issued for the Children's Hospital, sponsored by the Rotary Club of La Paz.

Pres. Paz Estenssoro and Pres. Getulio Vargas of Brazil
AP52

1960, Dec. 14 **Litho.** ***Perf. 11½***

C227	AP52	1,200b on 10b org & blk	1.25	1.00

Exists with surcharge inverted.

No. C227 without surcharge was not regularly issued, although a decree authorizing its circulation was published. Counterfeits of surcharge exist.

Pres. Paz Estenssoro and Pres. Frondizi of Argentina
AP53

Design: 4,000b, Flags of Bolivia and Argentina.

1961, May 23 ***Perf. 10½***

C228	AP53	4,000b brn, red, yel, grn & bl	1.00	90
C229	AP53	6,000b dk grn & blk	1.50	1.25

Issued to commemorate the visit of the President of Argentina, Dr. Arturo Frondizi, to Bolivia.

See "Special Notices" at the front of this volume for data on the listing methods of this Catalogue, abbreviations, condition, prices and examination.

Miguel de Cervantes
AP54

1961, Oct. Photogravure *Perf. 13*
C230 AP54 1400b pale grn & dk ol grn 75 35

Issued to commemorate Cervantes' appointment as Chief Magistrate of La Paz.

Virgin of Cotoca and Symbol of Eucharist
AP55

Planes and Parachutes
AP56

1962, Mar. 19 Litho. *Perf. 10½*
C231 AP55 1400b brn, pink & yel 1.00 50

Issued to commemorate the 4th National Eucharistic Congress, Santa Cruz, 1961.

Nos. C212–C216 Surcharged Vertically with New Value and Greek Key Border.

1962, June *Perf. 11½* **Unwmkd.**
C232 AP50 1,200b on 600b ultra 1.00 50
C233 AP50 1,300b on 700b lt red brn 90 50
C234 AP50 1,400b on 900b dk bl grn 1.00 50
C235 AP50 2,800b on 1,800b vio 1.50 75
C236 AP50 3,000b on 2,000b gray 1.50 75
Nos. C232-C236 (5) 5.90 3.00

The overprinted segment of Greek key border on Nos. C232–C236 comes in two positions: two full "keys" on top, and one full and two half keys on top.

Flower Type of 1962

Flowers: 100b, 1,800b, Cantua buxifolia. 800b, 10,000b, Cantua bicolor.

1962, June 28 Litho. *Perf. 10½*

Flowers in Natural Colors

C237 A152 100b dk bl 10 10
C238 A152 800b green 50 25
C239 A152 1,800b violet 1.00 50
a. Souv. sheet of 3 5.00 5.00
C240 A152 10,000b dk bl 6.00 3.00

No. C239a contains 3 imperf. stamps similar to Nos. C237–C239, but with the 1,800b background color changed to dark violet blue. Green marginal inscriptions. Size: 130x80mm.

1962, Sept. 5 Litho. *Perf. 11½*

Designs: 1,200b, 5,000b, Plane and ox-cart. 2,000b, Aerial photography (plane over South America).

Emblem in Red, Yellow & Green

C241 AP56 600b blk & bl 35 20
C242 AP56 1200b multi 50 30
C243 AP56 2000b multi 60 50
C244 AP56 5000b multi 1.50 1.00

Armed Forces of Bolivia.

Malaria Type of 1962

Design: Inscription around mosquito, laurel around globe.

1962, Oct. 4
C245 A154 2000b ind, grn & yel 1.25 75

Issued for the World Health Organization drive to eradicate malaria.

Type of Regular Issue, 1961

Design: 1,200b Pedro de la Gasca (1485–1567).

Photogravure

1962 *Perf. 13x12½* **Unwmkd.**
C246 A150 1,200b brn, *yel* 50 30

Condor, Soccer Ball and Flags
AP57

Alliance for Progress Emblem
AP58

Design: 1.80p, Map of Bolivia, soccer ball, goal and flags.

1963, Mar. 21 Litho. *Perf. 11½*

Flags in National Colors

C247 AP57 1.40p blk, ocher & red 1.50 1.00
C248 AP57 1.80p blk, red & ocher 1.50 1.00

Issued to publicize the 21st South American Soccer Championships.

Freedom from Hunger Issue

Type of Regular Issue

Design: 1.20p, Wheat, globe and wheat emblem.

1963, Aug. 1 *Perf. 11½* **Unwmkd.**
C249 A156 1.20p dk grn, bl & yel 1.00 75

Issued for the "Freedom from Hunger" campaign of the U.N. Food and Agriculture Organization.

1963, Nov. 15 *Perf. 11½*
C250 AP58 1.20p dl yel, ultra & grn 1.25 50

Issued to commemorate the second anniversary of the Alliance for Progress, which aims to stimulate economic growth and raise living standards in Latin America.

Type of Regular Issue, 1963

Designs: 1.20p, Ballot box and voters. 1.40p, Map and farmer breaking chain. 2.80p, Miners.

1963, Dec. 21 *Perf. 11½*
C251 A157 1.20p gray, dk brn & rose 60 30
C252 A157 1.40p bis & grn 75 40
C253 A157 2.80p sl & buff 1.50 75

Issued to commemorate the 10th anniversary of the Revolution of Apr. 9, 1952.

Andrés Santa Cruz
AP59

Lithographed

1966, Aug. 10 *Perf. 13½* **Wmk. 90**
C254 AP59 20c dp bl 15 10
C255 AP59 60c dp grn 30 15
C256 AP59 1.20p red brn 75 25
C257 AP59 2.80p black 1.25 60

Issued to commemorate the centenary (in 1965) of the death of Marshal Andrés Santa Cruz (1792–1865), president of Bolivia and of Peru-Bolivia Confederation.

Children Type of 1966

Design: 1.40p, Mother and children.

1966, Dec. 16 *Perf. 13½* **Unwmkd.**
C258 A159 1.40p gray bl & blk 1.50 65

Issued to help poor children.

Co-Presidents Type of Regular Issue

1966, Dec. 16 Litho. *Perf. 12½*

Flag in Red, Yellow and Green

C259 A160 2.80p gray & tan 2.00 1.50
C260 A160 10p sep & tan 2.50 1.75
a. Souv. sheet of 4 10.00 10.00

Issued to honor Generals Rene Barrientos Ortuno and Alfredo Ovando C., Co-Presidents, 1965–66.

No. C260a contains 4 imperf. stamps similar to Nos. 480–481 and C259–C260. Dark green marginal inscription. Size: 135x82mm.

Various Issues 1954–62 Surcharged with New Values and Bars

1966, Dec. 21

On No. C177:
"XII Aniversario / Reforma / Agraria"
C261 AP46 10c on 27b brt pink 20 20

On No. C182:
"XXV / Aniversario Paz / del Chaco"
C262 AP47 10c on 55b dk & lt grnsh bl 20 20

On No. C199:
"Centenario de / Tupiza"
C263 AP48 60c on 1350b rose car 30 30

On No. C200:
"XXV / Aniversario / Automovil Club / Boliviano"
C264 AP48 2.80p on 2700b bl grn 3.00 2.50

On No. C201:
"Centenario de la / Cruz Roja / Internacional"
C265 AP48 4p on 4000b vio bl 2.00 1.50

On No. C219:
"CL Aniversario / Heroinas Coronilla"
C266 AP51 1.20p on 800b vio brn 60 50

On No. C222:
"Centenario Himno / Paceño"
C267 AP51 1.40p on 4,000b dk gray 60 50

Nos. C224–C225 Surcharged
C268 A146 1.40p on 1,000b multi 60 60
C269 A146 1.40p on 1,800b multi 60 60

On Nos. C238–C239:
"Aniversario / Centro Filatelico / Cochabamba"
C270 A152 1.20p on 800b multi 50 40
C271 A152 1.20p on 1,800b multi 50 40

Revenue Stamp of 1946 Surcharged with New Value "X" and:
"XXV Aniversario / Dpto. Pando / Aéreo"
C272 A161 1.20p on 1b dk bl 75 60
Nos. C261-C272 (12) 9.85 8.30

Lions Emblem and Pre-historic Sculptures
AP60

1967, Sept. 20 Litho. *Perf. 13x13½*
C273 AP60 2p red & multi 1.25 1.00
a. Souv. sheet of 2 5.00 5.00

Issued to commemorate the 50th anniversary of Lions International. No. C273a contains 2 imperf. stamps similar to Nos. 492 and C273. Black marginal inscription. Size: 129x80mm.

Folklore Type of Regular Issue

Designs (Folklore characters): 1.20p, Pujllay. 1.40p, Ujusiris. 2p, Morenada. 3p, Auki-aukis.

1968, June 24 *Perf. 13½x13*
C274 A163 1.20b lt yel grn & multi 40 25
C275 A163 1.40b gray & multi 50 30
C276 A163 2b dk ol bis & multi 75 40
C277 A163 3b sky bl & multi 1.25 75

Issued to publicize the 9th Congress of the Postal Union of the Americas and Spain.

A souvenir sheet exists containing 4 imperf. stamps similar to Nos. C274–C277. Bister and gray marginal inscription. Size: 131x81½mm.

Moto Mendez
AP61

1968, Oct. 29 Litho. *Perf. 13½x13*
C278 AP61 1b dp org & multi 50 25
C279 AP61 1.20b lt ultra & multi 60 25
C280 AP61 2b bis brn & multi 1.00 50
C281 AP61 4b bluish lil & multi 1.50 75

Battle of Tablada sesquicentennial.

Pres. Guálberto Villaroël
AP62

1968, Nov. 6 *Perf. 13x13½*
C282 AP62 1.40b org & blk 50 40
C283 AP62 3b lt bl & blk 1.00 60
C284 AP62 4b rose & blk 1.25 75
C285 AP62 5b gray grn & blk 1.50 1.00
C286 AP62 10b pale pur & blk 3.00 2.00
Nos. C282-C286 (5) 7.25 4.75

4th centenary of Cochabamba.

ITU Type of Regular Issue

1968, Dec. 3 Litho. *Perf. 13x13½*
C287 A166 1.20b gray, blk & yel 40 20
C288 A166 1.40b bl, blk & gray ol 50 30

Issued to commemorate the centenary (in 1965) of the International Telecommunication Union.

UNESCO Emblem
AP63

1968, Nov. 14 *Perf. 13½x13*

C289 AP63 1.20b pale vio & blk 50 25
C290 AP63 2.80b yel grn & blk 1.00 50

Issued to commemorate the 20th anniversary (in 1966) of UNESCO (United Nations Educational, Scientific and Cultural Organization).

Kennedy Type of Regular Issue

1968, Nov. 22 **Unwmkd.**

C291 A168 1b grn & blk 40 30
C292 A168 10b scar & blk 3.00 2.00

Issued in memory of Pres. John F. Kennedy, 1917–1963.

A souvenir sheet contains one imperf. stamp similar to No. C291. Dark violet marginal inscription. Size: 131x81½mm.

Tennis Type of Regular Issue

1968, Dec. 10 *Perf. 13x13½*

C293 A169 1.40b org, blk & lt brn 50 35
C294 A169 2.80b sky bl, blk & lt brn 1.00 75

Issued to commemorate the 32nd South American Tennis Championships, La Paz, 1965.

A souvenir sheet exists containing one imperf. stamp similar to No. C293. Light brown marginal inscription. Size: 131x 81½mm.

Stamp Centenary Type of Regular Issue

Design: 1.40b, 2.80b, 3b, Bolivia No. 1.

1968, Dec. 23 Litho. *Perf. 13x13½*

C295 A170 1.40b org, grn & blk 75 35
C296 A170 2.80b pale rose, grn & blk 1.50 75
C297 A170 3b lt vio, grn & blk 1.50 75

Issued to commemorate the centenary of Bolivian postage stamps.

A souvenir sheet exists containing 3 imperf. stamps similar to Nos. C295–C297. Dark brown marginal inscription. Size: 131x81½mm.

Franklin D. Roosevelt
AP64

1969, Oct. 29 Litho. *Perf. 13½x13*

C298 AP64 5b brn, blk & buff 2.00 1.50

Issued to honor Franklin D. Roosevelt (1882–1945), 32nd President of the United States.

Olympic Type of Regular Issue

Sports: 1.20b, Woman runner (vert.). 2.80b, Discus thrower (vert.). 5b, Hurdler.

Perf. 13½x13, 13x13½

1969, Oct. 29 Lithographed

C299 A171 1.20b yel grn, bis & blk 60 25
C300 A171 2.80b red, org & blk 1.25 50
C301 A171 5b bl, lt bl, red & blk 2.00 1.00

Issued to commemorate the 19th Olympic Games, Mexico City, Oct. 12–27, 1968.

A souvenir sheet exists containing 3 imperf. stamps similar to Nos. C299–C301. Marginal inscription in blue, yellow green and red brown. Size: 130½x81mm.

Butterfly Type of Regular Issue

Butterflies: 1b, Metamorpha dido wernichei. 1.80b, Heliconius felix. 2.80b, Morpho casica. 3b, Papilio yuracares. 4b, Heliconius melitus.

1970, Apr. 24 Litho. *Perf. 13x13½*

C302 A172 1b sal & multi 50 20
C303 A172 1.80b lt bl & multi 75 40
C304 A172 2.80b multi 1.50 75
C305 A172 3b multi 1.50 75
C306 A172 4b multi 2.00 85
Nos. C302-C306 (5) 6.25 2.95

A souvenir sheet exists containing 3 imperf. stamps similar to Nos. C302–C304. Black marginal inscription. Size: 129½x 80mm.

Scout Type of Regular Issue

Designs: 50c, Boy Scout building brick wall. 1.20b, Bolivian Boy Scout emblem.

1970, June 17 Litho. *Perf. 13½x13*

C307 A173 50c yel & multi 20 10
C308 A173 1.20b multi 40 20

Issued to honor the Bolivian Boy Scout movement.

No. C228 Surcharged

1970, Dec. **Litho.** *Perf. 10½*

C309 AP53 1.20b on 4,000b multi 40 20

Flower Type of Regular Issue

Bolivian Flowers: 1.20b, Amaryllis pseudopardina (horiz.). 1.40b, Rebutia kruegeri. 2.80b, Lobivia pentlandii (horiz.). 4b, Rebutia tunariensis.

Perf. 13x13½, 13½x13

1971, Aug. 9 **Litho.** **Unwmkd.**

C310 A174 1.20b multi 60 20
C311 A174 1.40b multi 75 25
C312 A174 2.80b multi 1.25 40
C313 A174 4b multi 2.00 75

Two souvenir sheets of 4 exist. One contains imperf. stamps similar to Nos. 534–535 and C310, C312. The other contains imperf. stamps similar to Nos. 536–537, C311, C313. Black marginal inscriptions. Size: 130x80mm.

Dance Type of Regular Issue

Folk Dances: 1.20b, Kusillo. 1.40b, Taquirari.

1972, Mar. 23 Litho. *Perf. 13½x13*

C314 A177 1.20b yel & multi 75 25
C315 A177 1.40b org & multi 1.00 25

Two souvenir sheets of 3 exist. One contains imperf. stamps similar to Nos. 542–543, C314. The other contains imperf. stamps similar to Nos. 540–541, C315. Sheets have Sapporo '72 Olympic Games emblem in multicolor and marginal inscriptions in yellow, green and orange. Size: 80x129mm.

Painting Type of Regular Issue

Bolivian Paintings: 1.40b, Portrait of Chola Paceña, by Cecilio Guzmán de Rojas. 1.50b, Adoration of the Kings, by G. Gamarra. 1.60b, Adoration of Pachamama (mountain), by A. Borda. 2b, The Kiss of the Idol, by Guzman de Rojas.

1972 **Lithographed** *Perf. 13½*

C316 A178 1.40b multi 60 25
C317 A178 1.50b multi 60 25
C318 A178 1.60b multi 60 25
C319 A178 2b multi 1.00 40

Two souvenir sheets of 2 exist. One contains imperf. stamps similar to Nos. 548 and C318. The other contains imperf. stamps similar to Nos. C317 and C319. Sheets have "Munich 1972," Olympic and Munich emblems in margins. Size: 129x80mm.

Issue dates: 1.40b, Dec. 4. Others, Aug. 17.

Bolivian Coat of Arms
AP65

1972, Dec. 4 *Perf. 13½x14*

C320 AP65 4b lt bl & multi 2.00 1.50

Cactus Type of Regular Issue

Designs: Various cacti.

1973, Aug. 6 **Litho.** *Perf. 13½*

C321 A180 1.20b tan & multi 50 20
C322 A180 1.90b org & multi 75 30
C323 A180 2b multi 1.00 40

Development Type of Regular Issue

Designs: 1.40b, Highway 1Y4. 2b, Bus crossing bridge.

1973, Nov. 26 **Litho.** *Perf. 13½*

C324 A181 1.40b sal & multi 50 20
C325 A181 2b multi 75 30

Bolivia's development.

Santos-Dumont and 14-Bis Plane
AP66

1973, July 20

C326 AP66 1.40b yel & blk 1.00 50

Centenary of the birth of Alberto Santos-Dumont (1873–1932), Brazilian aviation pioneer.

Orchid Type of 1974

Orchids: 2.50b, Cattleya luteola (horiz.). 3.80b, Stanhopaea. 4b, Catasetum (horiz.). 5b, Maxillaria.

1974 **Lithographed** *Perf. 13½*

C327 A182 2.50b multi 1.00 35
C328 A182 3.80b rose & multi 1.50 50
C329 A182 4b multi 2.00 60
C330 A182 5b sal & multi 2.50 70

Air Force Emblem, Plane over Map of Bolivia
AP67

Designs: 3.80b, Plane over Andes. 4.50b, Triple decker and jet. 8b, Rafael Pabon and double decker. 15b, Jet and "50."

1974 **Lithographed** *Perf. 13x13½*

C331 AP67 3b multi 1.00 75
C332 AP67 3.80b multi 1.50 1.00
C333 AP67 4.50b multi 1.50 1.00
C334 AP67 8b multi 2.50 2.00
C335 AP67 15b multi 5.00 3.00
Nos. C331-C335 (5) 11.50 7.75

Bolivian Air Force, 50th anniversary.

Coat of Arms Type of 1975

Designs: Departmental coats of arms.

1975, July 16 **Litho.** *Perf. 13½*

Gold & Multicolored

C336 A188 20c *Beni* 10 10
C337 A188 30c *Tarija* 15 10
C338 A188 50c *Potosi* 15 15
C339 A188 1b *Oruro* 35 30
C340 A188 2.50b *Santa Cruz* 75 75
C341 A188 3b *La Paz* 1.00 75
Nos. C336-C341 (6) 2.50 2.15

Sesquicentennial of Republic of Bolivia.

LAB Emblem
AP68

Bolivia on Map of Americas
AP69

Map of Bolivia, Plane and Kyllmann
AP70

1975 **Lithographed** *Perf. 13½*

C342 AP68 1b gold, bl & blk 25 1
C343 AP69 1.50b multi 35 2
C344 AP70 2b multi 50 3

Lloyd Aereo Boliviano, 50th anniversary, founded by Guillermo Kyllmann.

Bolivar, Presidents Perez and Banzer, and Flags
AP71

1975, Aug. 4 **Litho.** *Perf. 13½*

C345 AP71 3b gold & multi 1.00 75

Visit of Pres. Carlos A. Perez of Venezuela.

Bolivar Type of 1975.

Presidents and Statesmen of Bolivia: 50c, Rene Barrientes O. 2b, Francisco B. O'Connor. 3.80b, Gualberto Villarroel. 4.20b, German Busch. 4.50b, Hugo Banzer Suarez. 20b, José Ballivian. 30b, Andres de Santa Cruz. 40b, Antonio Jose de Sucre.

1975 **Litho.** *Perf. 13½*

Size: 24x33mm.

C346 A189 50c multi 25 15
C347 A189 2b multi 75 40
C348 A189 3.80b multi 1.00 75
C349 A189 4.20b multi 1.50 1.00

Size: 28x39mm.

C350 A189 4.50b multi 1.50 1.00

Size: 24x33mm.

C351 A189 20b multi 6.00 4.00
C352 A189 30b multi 7.50 5.00
C353 A189 40b multi 10.00 7.00
Nos. C346-C353 (8) 28.50 19.30

UPU Emblem
AP72

1975, Dec. 7 **Litho.** *Perf. 13½*

C358 AP72 25b bl & multi 6.00 3.50

Centenary of Universal Postal Union (in 1974).

POSTAGE DUE STAMPS.

D1

Engraved.

1931 *Perf. 14, 14½.* **Unwmkd.**

No.	Type	Description	Unused	Used
J1	D1	5c ultra	2.25	1.50
J2	D1	10c red	2.25	1.50
J3	D1	15c yellow	2.25	1.50
J4	D1	30c dp grn	2.25	1.50
J5	D1	40c dp vio	2.25	1.50
J6	D1	50c blk brn	2.25	1.50
		Nos. J1-J6 (6)	13.50	9.00

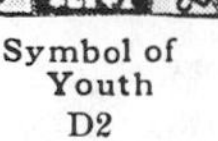

Symbol of Youth
D2

Torch of Knowledge
D3

Symbol of the Revolution of May 17, 1936
D4

1938 **Lithographed.** *Perf. 11.*

No.	Type	Description	Unused	Used
J7	D2	5c dp rose	1.00	75
a.		Pair, imperf. between		
J8	D3	10c green	1.00	75
J9	D4	30c gray bl	1.00	75

POSTAL TAX STAMPS.

Worker
PT1

Symbols of Communications
PT2

Imprint: "LITO. UNIDAS LA PAZ."

Perf. 13½x10½, 10½, 13½.

1939 **Lithographed.** **Unwmkd.**

No.	Type	Description	Unused	Used
RA1	PT1	5c dl vio	60	15
a.		Double impression		

Redrawn

Imprint: "TALL. OFFSET LA PAZ."

1940 *Perf. 12x11, 11.*

No.	Type	Description	Unused	Used
RA2	PT1	5c violet	50	15
a.		Horizontal pair, imperf. between	2.50	
b.		Imperf. horiz., pair		

Tax of Nos. RA1–RA2 was for the Workers' Home Building Fund.

1944–45 **Lithographed** *Perf. 10½*

No.	Type	Description	Unused	Used
RA3	PT2	10c salmon	45	15
RA4	PT2	10c bl ('45)	45	15

A 30c orange inscribed "Centenario de la Creacion del Departmento del Beni" was issued in 1946 and required to be affixed to all air and surface mail to and from the Department of Beni in addition to regular postage. Five higher denominations in the same scenic design were used for local revenue purposes.

Type of 1944 Redrawn.

1947-48 *Perf. 10½.* **Unwmkd.**

No.	Type	Description	Unused	Used
RA5	PT2	10c carmine	30	5
RA6	PT2	10c org yel ('48)	25	5
RA7	PT2	10c yel brn ('48)	25	5
RA8	PT2	10c emer ('48)	25	5

Post horn and envelope reduced in size.

Condor, Envelope and Post Horn
PT3

Communication Symbols
PT4

1951-52

No.	Type	Description	Unused	Used
RA9	PT3	20c dp org	40	20
a.		Imperf., pair		
RA10	PT3	20c grn ('52)	40	20
RA11	PT3	20c bl ('52)	40	20

1952–54 *Perf. 13½, 10½, 10½x12*

No.	Type	Description	Unused	Used
RA12	PT4	50c green	50	20
RA13	PT4	50c carmine	50	20
RA14	PT4	3b green	50	20
RA15	PT4	3b ol bis	75	60
RA16	PT4	5b vio ('54)	75	20
		Nos. RA12-RA16 (5)	3.00	1.40

No. RA10 and Type of 1951-52, Surcharged with New Value in Black.

1953 *Perf. 10½.*

No.	Type	Description	Unused	Used
RA17	PT3	50c on 20c grn	40	20
RA18	PT3	50c on 20c red vio	40	20

Postman Blowing Horn
PT5

1954-55 *Perf. 10½.* **Unwmkd.**

No.	Type	Description	Unused	Used
RA19	PT5	1b brown	30	15
RA20	PT5	1b car rose ('55)	30	15

Nos. RA15 and RA14 Surcharged in Black "Bs. 5.—/D. S./21-IV-55"

1955 *Perf. 10½, 10½x12*

No.	Type	Description	Unused	Used
RA21	PT4	5b on 3b ol bis	30	10
RA22	PT4	5b on 3b grn	30	10

Tax of Nos. RA3–RA22 was for the Communications Employees Fund.

No. RA21 is known with surcharge in thin type of different font and with comma added after "55".

Plane over Airport
PT6

Planes
PT7

Lithographed.

1955 *Perf. 10½, 12, 13½,* **Unwmkd.**

No.	Type	Description	Unused	Used
RA23	PT6	5b dp ultra	40	10
a.		Vertical pair imperf. between		

Perf. 11½

No.	Type	Description	Unused	Used
RA24	PT7	10b lt grn	30	10

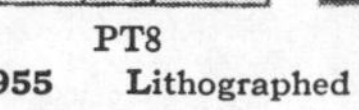

PT8 PT9

1955 **Lithographed** *Perf. 10½*

No.	Type	Description	Unused	Used
RA25	PT8	5b red	40	10

Perf. 12

No.	Type	Description	Unused	Used
RA26	PT9	20b dk brn	40	20

Tax of Nos. RA23–RA26 was for the building of new airports.

General Alfredo Ovando and Three Men
PT10

1970, Sept. 26 Litho. *Perf. 13x13½*

No.	Type	Description	Unused	Used
RA27	PT10	20c blk & red	25	15

See No. RAC1.

Pres. German Busch
PT11

1971, May 13 Litho. *Perf. 13x13½*

No.	Type	Description	Unused	Used
RA28	PT11	20c lil & blk	35	10

AIR POST POSTAL TAX STAMPS

Type of Postal Tax Issue

1970, Sept. 26 Litho. *Perf. 13x13½*

Design: 30c, General Ovando and oil well.

No.	Type	Description	Unused	Used
RAC1	PT10	30c blk & grn	30	15

Pres. Gualberto Villarroel, Refinery
PTAP1

1971, May 25 Litho. *Perf. 13x13½*

No.	Type	Description	Unused	Used
RAC2	PTAP1	30c lt bl & blk	30	15

Type of 1971 Inscribed: "XXV ANIVERSARIO DE SU GOBIERNO"

1975 **Litho.** *Perf. 13x13½*

No.	Type	Description	Unused	Used
RAC3	PTAP1	30c lt bl & blk	30	15

BOSNIA AND HERZEGOVINA

(bŏz'ni·ȧ & hĕr'tsĕ·gō·vē'nä)

LOCATION—In what is now Jugoslavia, between Dalmatia and Serbia.

GOVT.—Provinces of Turkey under Austro-Hungarian occupation, 1879-1908; provinces of Austria-Hungary 1908-1918.

AREA—19,768 sq. mi.

POP.—2,000,000 (approx. 1918).

CAPITAL—Sarajevo.

Following World War I Bosnia and Herzegovina united with the kingdoms of Montenegro and Serbia, and Croatia, Dalmatia and Slovenia, to form the Kingdom of Jugoslavia (See Jugoslavia.)

100 Novcica (Neukreuzer) = 1 Florin (Gulden)

100 Heller = 1 Krone (1900)

Coat of Arms
A1

Type I. The heraldic eaglets on the right side of the escutcheon are entirely blank. The eye of the lion is indicated by a very small dot, which sometimes fails to print. All values except the ½n exist in this type.

Type II. There is a colored line across the lowest eaglet. A similar line sometimes appears on the middle eaglet. The eye of the lion is formed by a large dot which touches the outline of the head above it. All values are found in this type.

Type III. The eaglets and eye of the lion are similar to type I. Each tail feather of the large eagle has two lines of shading and the lowest feather does not touch the curved line below it. In types I and II there are several shading lines in these feathers, and the lowest feather touches the curved line. Only the 5n is found in type III.

Varieties of the Numerals.

2 NOVCICA:

A. The "2" has curved tail. All are type I.

B. The "2" has straight tail. All are type II.

15 NOVCICA:

C. The serif of the "1" is short and forms a wide angle with the vertical stroke.

D. The serif of the "1" forms an acute angle with the vertical stroke.

The numerals of the 5n were retouched several times and show minor differences, especially in the flag.

Other Varieties.

½ NOVCICA:

All printings of the ½n are type II.

There is a black dot between the curved ends of the ornaments near the lower spandrels.

G. This dot touches the curve at its right. Stamps of this (first) printing are lithographed.

H. This dot stands clear of the curved lines. Stamps of this (second) printing are typographed.

10 NOVCICA:

Ten stamps in each sheet of type II show a small cross in the upper section of the right side of the escutcheon.

Wmk. 91

Lithographed.

Wmkd. BRIEF-MARKEN or (from 1890) ZEITUNGS-MARKEN in Double-lined Capitals, Across the Sheet (91)

Perf. 9 to 13½ and Compound

1879–94 **Type 1.**

No.	Type	Description	Unused	Used
1	A1	½n blk (type II) ('94)	10.00	*25.00*
2	A1	1n gray	6.00	2.50
c.		1n gray lil		3.00
4	A1	2n yellow	7.50	1.50
5	A1	3n green	10.00	3.00
6	A1	5n rose red	15.00	60
7	A1	10n blue	50.00	1.25
8	A1	15n brown	55.00	7.50
9	A1	20n gray grn ('93)	225.00	10.00
10	A1	25n violet	45.00	10.00

No. 2c was never issued. It is usually cancelled by blue pencil marks and "mint" copies generally have been cleaned.

Typographed.

Perf. 10½ to 13 and Compound.

1894-98 **Type II.**

No.	Type	Description	Unused	Used
1a	A1	½n black	14.00	*20.00*
2a	A1	1n gray	5.50	1.50
4a	A1	2n yellow	4.00	75
5a	A1	3n green	5.50	1.75
6a	A1	5n rose red	75.00	50
7a	A1	10n blue	7.50	1.00
8a	A1	15n brown	6.50	4.50
9a	A1	20n gray grn	9.00	5.00
10a	A1	25n violet	10.00	8.00

Type III.

No.	Type	Description	Unused	Used
6b	A1	5n rose red ('98)	2.00	50

All the preceding stamps exist in various shades.

Nos. 1a to 10a were reprinted in 1911 in lighter colors, on very white paper and perf. 12½. Price, set $25.

A2

A3

Perf. 10½, 12½ and Compound

1900 Typographed.

11	A2	1h gray blk	38	8
12	A2	2h gray	38	8
13	A2	3h yellow	40	12
14	A2	5h green	38	5
15	A2	6h brown	75	12
16	A2	10h red	35	5
17	A2	20h rose	125.00	5.00
18	A2	25h blue	1.10	25
19	A2	30h bis brn	140.00	6.00
20	A2	40h orange	200.00	10.00
21	A2	50h red lil	1.25	45
22	A3	1k dk rose	1.50	65
23	A3	2k ultra	2.00	1.75
24	A3	5k dl bl grn	4.50	4.50
		Nos. 11-24 (14)	477.99	29.10

All values of this issue except the 3h exist on ribbed paper.

Nos. 17, 19 and 20 were reprinted in 1911. The reprints are in lighter colors and on whiter paper than the originals. Reprints of Nos. 17 and 19 are perf. 10½ and those of No. 20 are perf. 12½. Price each $3.

Numerals in Black.

1901-04 ***Perf. 12½.***

25	A2	20h pink ('02)	75	50
26	A2	30h bis brn ('03)	75	50
27	A2	35h blue	1.00	50
a.		35h ultra	*100.00*	*6.00*
28	A2	40h org ('03)	1.25	1.00
29	A2	45h grnsh bl ('04)	85	55
		Nos. 25-29 (5)	4.60	3.05

Nos. 11-16, 18, 21-29 exist imperf. Most of Nos. 11-29 exist perf. 6½; compound with 12½; part perf.; in pairs imperf. between. These were supplied only to some high-ranking officials and never sold at any P.O.

View of Deboj
A4

The Carsija at Sarajevo
A17

Designs: 2h, View of Mostar. 3h, Pliva Gate, Jajce. 5h, Narenta Pass and Prenj River. 6h, Rama Valley. 10h, Vrbas Valley. 20h, Old Bridge, Mostar. 25h, Bey's Mosque, Sarajevo. 30h, Donkey post. 35h, Jezero and tourists' pavilion. 40h, Mail wagon. 45h, Bazaar at Sarajevo. 50h, Postal car. 2k, St. Luke's Campanile, Jajce. 5k, Emperor Franz Josef.

Perf. 6½, 9½, 10½ and 12½, also Compounds.

1906 Engraved. **Unwmkd.**

30	A4	1h black	10	12
31	A4	2h violet	10	12
32	A4	3h olive	10	12
33	A4	5h dk grn	10	12
34	A4	6h brown	20	25
a.		Perf. 13½	*20.00*	*25.00*
35	A4	10h carmine	10	12
36	A4	20h dk brn	50	30
a.		Perf. 13½	*50.00*	*50.00*
37	A4	25h dp bl	1.50	1.25
38	A4	30h green	1.65	50
39	A4	35h myr grn	1.75	50
40	A4	40h org red	1.75	50
41	A4	45h brn red	1.75	1.50
42	A4	50h dl vio	2.00	1.00
43	A17	1k maroon	4.50	2.00
44	A17	2k gray grn	6.00	10.00
45	A17	5k dl bl	5.00	7.50
		Nos. 30-45 (16)	27.10	25.90

Nos. 30-45 exist imperf. Price, set $60 unused, $45 canceled.

Birthday Jubilee Issue.

Designs of 1906 Issue, with "1830-1910" in label at bottom.

1910 ***Perf. 12½.***

46	A4	1h black	50	22
47	A4	2h violet	60	22
48	A4	3h olive	60	30
49	A4	5h dk grn	70	12
50	A4	6h org brn	75	30
51	A4	10h carmine	70	12
52	A4	20h dk brn	1.50	1.75
53	A4	25h dp bl	3.50	3.75
54	A4	30h green	2.50	3.25
55	A4	35h myr grn	3.50	3.25
56	A4	40h org red	3.50	4.00
57	A4	45h brn red	6.00	7.25
58	A4	50h dl vio	6.00	7.50
59	A17	1k maroon	6.00	7.50
60	A17	2k gray grn	22.50	22.50
61	A17	5k dl bl	4.00	5.00
		Nos. 46-61 (16)	62.85	67.03

80th birthday of Emperor Franz Josef.

Scenic Type of 1906.

Designs (Views): 12h, Jaice. 60h, Konjica. 72h, Vishegrad.

1912

62	A4	12h ultra	5.00	6.00
63	A4	60h dl bl	3.00	5.50
64	A4	72h carmine	15.00	20.00

Price, imperf. set, $75.

Emperor Franz Josef
A23 A24

A25 A26

1912-14 **Various Frames.**

65	A23	1h ol grn	50	5
66	A23	2h brt bl	50	5
67	A23	3h claret	50	5
68	A23	5h green	50	5
69	A23	6h dk gray	50	5
70	A23	10h rose car	50	5
71	A23	12h dp ol grn	1.50	30
72	A23	20h org brn	6.00	6
73	A23	25h ultra	3.00	8
74	A23	30h org red	3.00	8
75	A24	35h myr grn	3.00	8
76	A24	40h dk vio	9.00	8
77	A24	45h ol brn	4.00	25
78	A24	50h sl bl	4.00	8
79	A24	60h brn vio	3.75	8
80	A24	72h dk bl	4.50	4.00
81	A25	1k brn vio, *straw*	17.50	50
82	A25	2k dk gray, *bl*	10.00	35
83	A26	3k car, *grn*	15.00	12.50
84	A26	5k dk vio, *gray*	30.00	30.00
85	A25	10k dk ultra, *gray* ('14)	100.00	110.00
		Nos. 65-85 (21)	217.25	158.74

Price, imperf. set, $450.

A27

A28

1916-17 ***Perf. 12½***

86	A27	3h dk gray	25	28
87	A27	5h ol grn	38	50
88	A27	6h violet	42	50
89	A27	10h bister	1.90	2.50
90	A27	12h bl gray	50	70
91	A27	15h car rose	8	8
92	A27	20h brown	45	60
93	A27	25h blue	35	50
94	A27	30h dk grn	35	50
95	A27	40h vermilion	35	50
96	A27	50h green	35	50
97	A27	60h lake	38	55
98	A27	80h org brn	1.50	50
a.		Perf. 11½	*5.00*	*4.50*
99	A27	90h dk vio	90	75
a.		Perf. 11½	*600.00*	*900.00*
101	A28	2k cl, *straw*	60	75
102	A28	3k grn, *bl*	1.75	3.25
103	A28	4k car, *grn*	8.00	11.00
104	A28	10k dp vio, *gray*	20.00	30.00
		Nos. 86-104 (18)	38.51	53.96

Price, imperf. set, $175.

Emperor Karl I
A29 A30

1917 ***Perf. 12½***

105	A29	3h ol gray	20	28
a.		Perf. 11½	*100.00*	*110.00*
b.		Perf. 12½x11½	*20.00*	*32.50*
106	A29	5h ol grn	12	20
107	A29	6h violet	50	75
108	A29	10h org brn	25	6
a.		Perf. 11½x12½	*85.00*	*120.00*
b.		Perf. 11½		
109	A29	12h blue	75	1.00
110	A29	15h brt rose	12	8
111	A29	20h red brn	12	12
112	A29	25h ultra	1.25	65
113	A29	30h gray grn	35	25
114	A29	40h ol bis	38	20
115	A29	50h dp grn	1.25	65
116	A29	60h car rose	1.25	55
a.		Perf. 11½	*22.50*	*25.00*
117	A29	80h stl bl	35	28
118	A29	90h dl vio	1.50	2.00
119	A30	2k car, *straw*	80	50
120	A30	3k grn, *bl*	20.00	25.00
121	A30	4k car, *grn*	8.00	10.00
122	A30	10k dp vio, *gray*	5.00	8.00
		Nos. 105-122 (18)	42.19	50.57

Price, imperf. set, $85.

Nos. 47 and 66 Overprinted in Red **1918**

1918

126	A4	2h violet	65	65
b.		Inverted overprint	*25.00*	
d.		Double overprint	*20.00*	
f.		Double overprint, one inverted		
127	A23	2h brt bl	75	75
a.		Pair, one without overprint		
b.		Inverted overprint	*25.00*	
c.		Double overprint	*20.00*	
d.		Double overprint, one inverted		

Emperor Karl I
A31

1918 **Typo.** ***Perf. 12½, Imperf.***

128	A31	2h orange	11.50	
129	A31	3h dk grn	11.50	
130	A31	5h lt grn	11.50	
131	A31	6h bl grn	11.50	
132	A31	10h brown	11.50	
133	A31	20h brick red	11.50	
134	A31	25h ultra	11.50	
135	A31	45h dk sl	11.50	
136	A31	50h lt bluish grn	11.50	
137	A31	60h bl vio	11.50	
138	A31	70h ocher	11.50	
139	A31	80h rose	11.50	
140	A31	90h vio brn	11.50	

Engraved

141	A30	1k ol grn, *grnsh*	*2,250.*	
		Nos. 128-140 (13)	149.50	

Nos. 128–141 were prepared for use in Bosnia and Herzegovina, but were not issued there. They were sold after the Armistice at the Vienna post office for a few days.

SEMI-POSTAL STAMPS.

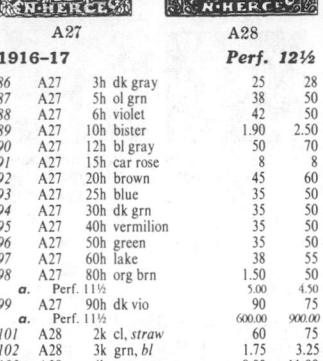

Nos. 33 and 35 Surcharged in Red **1914. 7 Heller**

1914 ***Perf. 12½.*** **Unwmkd.**

B1	A4	7h on 5h dk grn	50	50
B2	A4	12h on 10h car	50	50

Various minor varieties of the surcharge include "4" with open top, narrow "4" and wide "4".

Nos. B1–B2 exist with double and inverted surcharges. Price about $20 each.

Nos. 33 and 35 Surcharged in Red or Blue **1915. 7 Heller**

1915 ***Perf. 12½***

B3	A4	7h on 5h dk grn (R)	12.50	12.50
a.		Perf. 9½	*200.00*	*200.00*
B4	A4	12h on 10h car (Bl)	40	40

Nos. B3–B4 exist with double and inverted surcharges. Price about $18.50 each.

Nos. 68 and 70 Surcharged in Red or Blue **1915 7 Heller.**

1915

B5	A23	7h on 5h grn (R)	1.00	1.00
a.		"1915" at top and bottom	*45.00*	*55.00*
B6	A23	12h on 10h rose car (Bl)	1.75	2.00
a.		Surcharged "7 Heller."	*45.00*	*55.00*

Nos. B5–B6 are found in three types differing in length of surcharge lines: I, date 18mm., denomination 14mm. II, date 16mm., denomination 14mm. III, date 18mm., denomination 16mm.

Nos. B5–B6 exist with double and inverted surcharges. Price $15 each.

Nos. B5a and B6a exist double and inverted.

❖ 1916. ❖

Nos. 68 and 70 Surcharged in Red or Blue

7 Heller.

1916				
B7	A23	7h on 5h grn (R)	75	1.00
B8	A23	12h on 10h rose car (Bl)	75	1.00

Nos. B7–B8 exist with double and inverted surcharges. Price $12.50 each.

Wounded Soldier SP1

Blind Soldier SP2

1916		Engraved.		
B9	SP1	5h (+2h) grn	1.00	1.00
B10	SP2	10h (+2h) mag	1.50	1.50

Nos. B9–B10 exist imperf. Price, set $27.50.

Nos. 89, 91 Overprinted

WITWEN- UND WAISENWOCHE 1917

1917				
B11	A27	10h bister	10	15
B12	A27	15h car rose	10	15

Nos. B11-B12 exist imperf. Price set, $16.

Nos. B11-B12 exist with double and inverted overprint. Price $9 each.

Design for Memorial Church at Sarajevo—SP3

Archduke Francis Ferdinand SP4

Duchess Sophia and Archduke Francis Ferdinand SP5

1917		Typo.	*Perf. 11½, 12½*	
B13	SP3	10h vio blk	15	38
B14	SP4	15h claret	15	38
B15	SP5	40h dp bl	15	38

Assassination of Archduke Ferdinand and Archduchess Sophia. Sold at a premium of 2h each which helped build a memorial church at Sarajevo.

Exist imperf. Price, set $3.

Blind Soldier SP6

Emperor Karl I SP8

Design: 15h, Wounded soldier.

1918		Engraved	*Perf. 12½*	
B16	SP6	10h (+10h) grnsh bl	75	75
B17	SP6	15h (+10h) red brn	75	75

Nos. B16–B17 exist imperf. Price, set $18.50.

1918 Typographed. ***Perf. 12½x13.***

Design: 15h, Empress Zita.

B18	SP8	10h gray grn	50	75
B19	SP8	15h brn red	50	75
B20	SP8	40h violet	50	75

Sold at a premium of 10h each which went to the "Karl's Fund."

Nos. B18–B20 exist imperf. Price, set $22.50.

POSTAGE DUE STAMPS.

D1

D2

Perf. 9½, 10½, 12½ and Compound.

1904			Unwmkd.	
J1	D1	1h blk, red & yel	50	8
J2	D1	2h blk, red & yel	50	25
J3	D1	3h blk, red & yel	50	8
J4	D1	4h blk, red & yel	50	8
J5	D1	5h blk, red & yel	50	8
J6	D1	6h blk, red & yel	25	8
J7	D1	7h blk, red & yel	3.00	3.25
J8	D1	8h blk, red & yel	3.00	70
J9	D1	10h blk, red & yel	75	12
J10	D1	15h blk, red & yel	60	22
J11	D1	20h blk, red & yel	3.50	25
J12	D1	50h blk, red & yel	2.50	20
J13	D1	200h blk, red & grn	10.00	1.00
		Nos. J1-J13 (13)	26.10	6.39

Price, imperf. set, $150.

1916–18			*Perf. 12½*	
J14	D2	2h red ('18)	50	50
J15	D2	4h red ('18)	38	38
J16	D2	5h red	50	50
J17	D2	6h red ('18)	38	38
J18	D2	10h red	45	45
J19	D2	15h red	4.00	4.00
J20	D2	20h red	45	45
J21	D2	25h red	1.40	1.40
J22	D2	30h red	1.25	1.25
J23	D2	40h red	10.00	10.00
J24	D2	50h red	32.50	32.50
J25	D2	1k dk bl	4.00	4.00
J26	D2	3k dk bl	17.00	17.00
		Nos. J14-J26 (13)	72.81	72.81

Nos. J25 and J26 have colored numerals on a white tablet.

Price, imperf. set, $110.

NEWSPAPER STAMPS.

Bosnian Girl N1

1913		*Imperf.*	Unwmkd.	
P1	N1	2h ultra	50	50
P2	N1	6h violet	2.00	2.00
P3	N1	10h rose	2.00	2.00
P4	N1	20h green	2.50	2.50

After Bosnia and Herzegovina became part of Jugoslavia stamps of type N1 perforated, also imperforate copies surcharged with new values, were used as regular postage stamps.

SPECIAL HANDLING STAMPS.

"Lightning" SH1

Engraved.

1916		*Perf. 12½.*	Unwmkd.	
QE1	SH1	2h vermilion	30	30
a.		Perf. 11½x12½	225.00	225.00
QE2	SH1	5h dp grn	50	50
a.		Perf. 11½	17.50	17.50

BRAZIL

(brȧ-zĭl')

Brasil (after 1918)

LOCATION — On the north and east coasts of South America, bordering on the Atlantic Ocean.
GOVT.—Republic.
AREA—3,286,000 sq. mi.
POP.—132,580,000 (est. 1984).
CAPITAL—Brasilia.

Brazil was an independent empire from 1822 to 1889, when a constitution was adopted and the country became officially known as The United States of Brazil.

1000 Reis = 1 Milreis
100 Centavos = 1 Cruzeiro (1942)

Prices of Brazil Nos. 1–13 vary according to condition. Quotations are for fine copies. Very fine to superb specimens sell at much higher prices, and inferior or poor copies sell at reduced prices, depending on the condition of the individual specimen.

Issues of the Empire.

A1

Engraved

Grayish or Yellowish Paper.

1843, Aug. 1		*Imperf.*	Unwmkd.	
1	A1	30r black	2,200.	525.00
a.		In pair with No. 2		*90,000.*
2	A1	60r black	750.00	250.00
3	A1	90r black	3,500.	1,450.

Early impressions of Nos. 1 to 3 bring higher prices than quoted which are for copies from worn plates.

A2

A3

Grayish or Yellowish Paper.

1844-46				
7	A2	10r black	90.00	30.00
8	A2	30r black	110.00	45.00
9	A2	60r black	90.00	30.00
10	A2	90r black	600.00	175.00
11	A2	180r black	4,500.	1,750.
12	A2	300r black	7,000.	2,400.
13	A2	600r black	6,500.	2,750.

Nos. 8, 9 and 10 exist on thick paper and are considerably scarcer.

Grayish or Yellowish Paper.

1850, Jan. 1				
21	A3	10r black	35.00	20.00
22	A3	20r black	90.00	125.00
23	A3	30r black	12.00	4.00
24	A3	60r black	12.00	3.00
25	A3	90r black	110.00	15.00
26	A3	180r black	110.00	70.00
27	A3	300r black	325.00	100.00
28	A3	600r black	450.00	125.00

All values except the 90r were reprinted in 1910 on very thick paper.

1854				
37	A3	10r blue	17.50	15.00
38	A3	30r blue	45.00	80.00

A4

1861				
39	A4	280r red	200.00	150.00
40	A4	430r yellow	300.00	200.00

Nos. 39 and 40 have been reprinted on thick white paper with white gum. They are printed in aniline inks and the colors are brighter than those of the originals.

1866			*Perf. 13½.*	
41	A3	10r black	*25.00*	*20.00*
42	A3	10r blue	80.00	*125.00*
43	A3	20r black	500.00	350.00
44	A3	30r black	225.00	125.00
45	A3	30r blue	*600.00*	*750.00*
46	A3	60r black	80.00	17.50
47	A3	90r black	400.00	225.00
48	A3	180r black	400.00	225.00
49	A4	280r red	450.00	650.00
50	A3	300r black	750.00	350.00
51	A4	430r yellow	450.00	425.00
52	A3	600r black	450.00	225.00

Fraudulent perforations abound.

Emperor Dom Pedro A5

A6

A7

A8

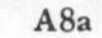
A8a

A9

A9a

Thick or Thin White Wove Paper.

1866, July 1 *Perf. 12*

53	A5	10r vermilion	10.00	5.00
a.		Bluish paper	550.00	650.00
54	A6	20r red lil	12.00	3.00
a.		20r dl vio	80.00	40.00
b.		Bluish paper	175.00	35.00
56	A7	50r blue	25.00	2.00
a.		Bluish paper	175.00	17.50
57	A8	80r sl vio	60.00	6.00
a.		Bluish paper	225.00	35.00
58	A8a	100r bl grn	22.50	50
a.		100r yel grn	90.00	5.00
b.		Bluish paper	1,000.	150.00
59	A9	200r black	90.00	6.00
60	A9a	500r orange	200.00	30.00
		Nos. 53-60 (7)	419.50	52.50

The 10r and 20r exist imperf. on both white and bluish paper. Some authorities consider them proofs.

Nos. 58 and 65 are found in two types.

1876-77 *Rouletted.*

61	A5	10r ver ('77)	45.00	40.00
62	A6	20r red lil ('77)	60.00	30.00
63	A7	50r bl ('77)	60.00	7.00
64	A8	80r vio ('77)	135.00	17.50
65	A8a	100r green	20.00	1.00
66	A9	200r blk ('77)	50.00	6.00
a.		Diagonal half used as 100r on cover		
67	A9a	500r orange	175.00	35.00
		Nos. 61-67 (7)	545.00	136.50

A10

A11

A12

A13

A14

A15

A16

A17

A18

A19

A20

1878-79 *Rouletted.*

68	A10	10r vermilion	8.00	3.00
69	A11	20r violet	12.00	2.50
70	A12	50r blue	17.50	1.50
71	A13	80r lake	20.00	9.00
72	A14	100r green	20.00	50
73	A15	200r black	125.00	15.00
a.		Diagonal half used as 100r on cover		
74	A16	260r dk brn	70.00	24.00
75	A18	300r bister	70.00	6.00
76	A19	700r red brn	160.00	110.00
77	A20	1000r gray lil	200.00	42.50
		Nos. 68-77 (10)	702.50	214.00

1878, Aug. 21 *Perf. 12*

78	A17	300r org & grn	75.00	20.00

Nos. 68-78 exist imperforate.

A21

A22

A23

Small Heads

1881, July 15 Laid Paper

Perf. 13, 13½ and Compound

79	A21	50r blue	125.00	20.00
80	A22	100r ol grn	400.00	40.00
81	A23	200r pale red brn	600.00	125.00

On Nos. 79 and 80 the hair above the ear curves forward. On Nos. 83 and 88 it is drawn backward. On the stamps of the 1881 issue the beard is smaller than in the 1882-85 issues and fills less of the space between the neck and the frame at the left.

See also No. 88.

A24

A25

A26

A27

Two types each of the 100 and 200 reis.

100 REIS:

Type I. Groundwork formed of diagonal crossed lines and horizontal lines.

Type II. Groundwork formed of diagonal crossed lines and vertical lines.

200 REIS:

Type I. Groundwork formed of diagonal and horizontal lines.

Type II. Groundwork formed of diagonal crossed lines.

Larger Heads.

Perf. 12½ to 14 and Compound.

1882-84 Laid Paper

82	A24	10r black	7.00	17.50
83	A25	100r ol grn, type I	30.00	3.50
a.		100r dk grn, type I	30.00	3.50
b.		100r dk grn, type II	175.00	15.00
84	A26	200r pale red brn, type I	80.00	27.50
85	A27	200r pale rose, type II	40.00	5.00
a.		Diagonal half used as 100r on cover		20.00

See also No. 86.

A28

A29

A30

Three types of A29.

Type I. Groundwork formed of horizontal lines.

Type II. Groundwork formed of diagonal crossed lines.

Type III. Groundwork solid.

Perf. 13, 13½, 14 and Compound

1884-85

86	A24	10r orange	1.75	1.75
87	A28	20r sl grn	8.00	3.00
a.		20r ol grn	8.00	2.00
88	A21	50r bl, head larger	20.00	3.50
89	A29	100r lil, type II,III	300.00	60.00
90	A29	100r lil, type I	75.00	2.50
91	A30	100r lilac	160.00	4.00

A31

Perf. 13, 13½, 14 and Compound.

1885

92	A31	100r lilac	40.00	1.50

A32

Southern Cross
A33

Crown
A34

1887

93	A32	50r chlky bl	20.00	4.00
94	A33	300r gray bl	125.00	20.00
95	A34	500r olive	80.00	15.00

A35

A36

Entrance to Bay of Rio de Janeiro
A37

1888

96	A35	100r lilac	30.00	1.00
a.		Imperf., pair	90.00	*125.00*
97	A36	700r violet	60.00	*90.00*
98	A37	1000r dl bl	200.00	90.00

Issues of the Republic.

Southern Cross
A38

Wove Paper, Thin to Thick.

Perf. 12½ to 14, 11 to 11½, and 12½ to 14 x 11 to 11½, Rough or Clean-Cut.

1890-91 Engr.; Typo. (#102)

99	A38	20r gray grn	1.75	1.25
a.		20r bl grn	1.75	1.25
b.		20r emer	13.00	6.00
100	A38	50r gray grn	2.50	1.00
a.		50r ol grn	10.00	1.00
b.		50r yel grn	10.00	5.00
c.		50r dk sl grn	10.00	5.00
d.		Horizontal pair, imperf. between		
101	A38	100r lil rose	300.00	5.00
102	A38	100r red lil, redrawn	25.00	50
a.		Tête bêche pair	*12,000.*	*18,000.*
103	A38	200r purple	8.00	1.25
a.		200r vio	15.00	2.25
b.		200r vio bl	30.00	3.00
104	A38	300r sl vio	50.00	2.50
a.		300r gray	50.00	7.50
b.		300r gray bl	70.00	10.00
c.		300r dk vio	35.00	6.00
105	A38	500r ol bis	16.00	10.00
a.		500r ol gray	16.00	10.00
106	A38	500r slate	16.00	8.00
107	A38	700r chocolate	20.00	20.00
a.		700r fawn	22.50	22.50
108	A38	1000r bister	12.00	2.50
a.		1000r yel buff	25.00	5.00
		Nos. 99-108 (10)	451.25	52.00

The redrawn 100r may be distinguished by the absence of the curved lines of shading in the left side of the central oval. The pearls in the oval are not well aligned and there is less shading at right and left of "CORREIO" and "100 REIS."

A 100 reis stamp of type A38 but inscribed "BRAZIL" instead of "E. U. DO BRAZIL" was not placed in issue but postmarked copies are known. A reprint on thick paper was made in 1910.

No. 101 exists imperf., not regularly issued.

Liberty Head
A39

Liberty Head
A40

Perf. 12½ to 14, 11 to 11½ and 12½ to 14 x 11 to 11½

1891, May 1 Typographed

109	A39	100r bl & red	20.00	50
a.		Head inverted	100.00	75.00
b.		Tête bêche pair	500.00	500.00
c.		100r ultra & red	22.50	60

Perf. 11, 11½, 13, 13½, 14 and Compound.

1893, Jan. 18 **Lithographed**

111	A40	100r rose	35.00	50

Sugarloaf Mountain

A41 A41a

A42

Liberty Head Hermes

A42a A43

Perf. 11 to 11½, 12½ to 14 and 12½ to 14x11 to 11½.

1894–97 **Unwmkd.**

112	A41	10r rose & bl	2.00	50
113	A41a	10r rose & bl	1.50	35
114	A41a	20r org & bl	1.75	40
115	A41a	50r dk bl & bl	5.00	1.50
116	A42	100r car & blk	2.50	25
a.		Vertical pair, imperf. between	100.00	
118	A42a	200r org & blk	1.50	25
a.		Imperf. horiz., pair	75.00	
b.		Vertical pair, imperf. between	75.00	
119	A42a	300r grn & blk	15.00	50
120	A42a	500r bl & blk	25.00	1.00
121	A42a	700r lil & blk	17.50	1.50
122	A43	1000r grn & vio	60.00	1.50
124	A43	2000r blk & gray lil	80.00	20.00
		Nos. 112-124 (11)	211.75	27.75

The head of No. 116 exists in five types. See also Nos. 140-150A, 159-161, 166-171d.

Newspaper Stamps Surcharged:

100 1898 100 — *a*

200 1898 200 — *b*

100 1898 100 — *c*

Surcharged on 1889 Issue of type N1.

1898 ***Rouletted***

Green Surcharge.

125	(b)	700r on 500r yel	7.00	10.00
126	(c)	1000r on 700r yel	30.00	30.00
a.		Surcharged "700r"	450.00	500.00
127	(c)	2000r on 1000r yel	20.00	12.50
128	(c)	2000r on 1000r brn	17.50	6.00

Violet Surcharge.

129	(a)	100r on 50r brn yel	2.00	*15.00*
130	(c)	100r on 50r brn yel	45.00	50.00
131	(c)	300r on 200r blk	3.50	1.25
a.		Double surcharge	150.00	90.00

The surcharge on No. 130 is handstamped. The impression is blurred and lighter in color than on No. 129. The two surcharges differ most in the shapes and serifs of the figures "1."

Counterfeits exist of No. 126a.

Black Surcharge.

132	(b)	200r on 100r vio	3.00	1.25
a.		Double surcharge	[illegible]	[illegible]
b.		Inverted surcharge	85.00	*135.00*
132C	(b)	500r on 300r car	4.50	2.50
133	(b)	700r on 500r grn	7.00	2.25

Blue Surcharge.

134	(b)	500r on 300r car	6.00	4.50

Red Surcharge.

135	(c)	1000r on 700r ultra	20.00	12.50
a.		Inverted surcharge	175.00	175.00

Surcharged on 1890-94 Issues:

200 1898 — *d*

1898 50 RÉIS 50 — *e*

Perf. 11 to 14 and Compound.

Black Surcharge.

136	N3 (e)	20r on 10r bl	1.25	2.50
137	N2 (d)	200r on 100r red lil	9.00	6.50
a.		Double surcharge	110.00	110.00

Surcharge on No. 137 comes blue to deep black.

Blue Surcharge.

138	N3 (e)	50r on 20r grn	2.50	4.00

Red Surcharge.

139	N3 (e)	100r on 50r grn	8.00	10.00
a.		Blue surch.	17.50	

The surcharge on Nos. 139 and 139a exists double, inverted, one missing, etc.

Types of 1894–97

Perf. 5½ to 7 and 11 to 11½x5½ to 7

140	A41a	10r rose & bl	4.00	8.00
141	A41a	20r org & bl	8.00	8.00
142	A41a	50r dk bl & lt bl	9.00	18.00
143	A42	100r car & blk	15.00	4.00
144	A42a	200r org & blk	9.00	4.00
145	A42a	300r grn & blk	55.00	9.00

Perf. 8½ to 9½ and 8½ to 9½x11 to 11½

146	A41a	10r rose & bl	5.00	2.50
147	A41a	20r org & bl	15.00	2.50
147A	A41a	50r dk bl & bl	125.00	35.00
148	A42	100r car & blk	25.00	1.50
149	A42a	200r org & blk	10.00	1.25
150	A42a	300r grn & blk	50.00	6.00
150A	A43	1000r grn & vio	120.00	12.00

Issue of 1890-93 Surcharged in Violet or Magenta

1899 50 RÉIS

Perf. 11 to 11½, 12½ to 14 and Compound

1899, June 25

151	A38	50r on 20r gray grn	1.00	1.50
a.		Double surcharge		
152	A38	100r on 50r gray grn	1.50	1.50
b.		Double surch.	60.00	60.00
153	A38	300r on 200r pur	6.00	*8.00*
a.		Double surcharge	60.00	60.00
154	A38	500r on 300r sl vio	18.00	9.00
a.		500r on 300r gray lil	16.00	6.00
b.		Pair, one without surcharge	300.00	
155	A38	700r on 500r ol bis	20.00	5.00
a.		Pair, one without surcharge	350.00	
156	A38	1000r on 700r choc	11.00	5.00
157	A38	1000r on 700r fawn	15.00	5.00
a.		Pair, one without surcharge	350.00	
158	A38	2000r on 1000r yel buff	45.00	3.50
a.		2000r on 1000r bis	17.50	3.50
b.		Pair, one without surcharge	350.00	
		Nos. 151-158 (8)	117.50	*38.50*

Types of 1894–97

Perf. 11, 11½, 13 and Compound.

1900

159	A41a	50r green	8.50	50
160	A42	100r rose	17.50	40
a.		Frame around inner oval	100.00	5.00
161	A42a	200r blue	12.00	40

Three types exist of No. 161, all of which have the frame around inner oval.

Cabral Arrives at Brazil

A44

Independence Proclaimed

A45

"Emancipation of Slaves" Allegory, Republic of Brazil

A46 A47

1900, Jan. 1 **Litho.** ***Perf. 12½***

162	A44	100r red	6.00	5.50
a.		Imperf. (pair)	350.00	350.00
163	A45	200r grn & yel	6.00	5.50
164	A46	500r blue	6.00	5.50
165	A47	700r emerald	6.00	5.50

Discovery of Brazil, 400th anniversary.

Wmk. 97 Wmk. 98

Types of 1894–97.

Wmkd. (97? or 98?)

1905 ***Perf. 11, 11½***

166	A41a	10r rose & bl	4.00	2.00
167	A41a	20r org & bl	7.00	60
168	A41a	50r green	12.50	50
169	A42	100r rose	17.50	25
170	A42a	200r dk bl	17.50	25
171	A42a	300r grn & blk	35.00	1.50
		Nos. 166-171 (6)	93.50	5.10

Positive identification of Wmk. 97 or 98 places stamp in specific watermark groups below.

Wmkd. "CORREIO FEDERAL REPUBLICA DOS ESTADOS UNIDOS DO BRAZIL" in Sheet. (97)

166b	A41a	10r rose & bl	30.00	13.00
167b	A41a	20r org & bl	30.00	7.50
168b	A41a	50r green	45.00	7.50
169b	A42	100r rose	225.00	25.00
170b	A42a	200r dk bl	90.00	2.00
171b	A42a	300r grn & blk	275.00	17.50
171A	A43	1000r grn & vio	225.00	22.50
		Nos. 166b-171A (7)	920.00	95.00

Wmkd. "IMPOSTO DE CONSUMO REPUBLICA DOS ESTADOS UNIDOS DO BRAZIL" in Sheet. (98)

166c	A41a	10r rose & bl	30.00	25.00
167c	A41a	20r org & bl	60.00	12.50
168c	A41a	50r green	110.00	22.50
169c	A42	100r rose	70.00	2.50
170c	A42a	200r dk bl	90.00	1.00
171d	A42a	300r grn & blk	200.00	22.50
		Nos. 166c-171d (6)	560.00	86.00

Allegory, Pan-American Congress

A48

1906, July 23 **Litho.** **Unwmkd.**

172	A48	100r car rose	30.00	30.00
173	A48	200r blue	60.00	7.50

Third Pan-American Congress.

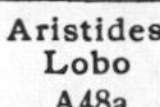

Aristides Lobo Benjamin Constant

A48a A49

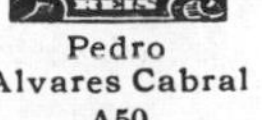

Pedro Alvares Cabral Eduardo Wandenkolk

A50 A51

Manuel Deodoro da Fonseca
A52

Floriano Peixoto
A53

Prudente de Moraes
A54

Manuel Ferraz de Campos Salles
A55

Francisco de Paula Rodrigues Alves
A56

Liberty Head
A57

A58

A59

1906–16 Engraved *Perf. 12*

174	A48a	10r bluish sl	40	6
175	A49	20r anil vio	25	6
176	A50	50r green	50	8
a.		Booklet pane of 6 ('08)	30.00	60.00
177	A51	100r anil rose	1.10	5
a.		Imperf. vert., coil ('16)	4.00	50
b.		Booklet pane of 6 ('08)	45.00	60.00
178	A52	200r blue	1.10	8
a.		Booklet pane of 6 ('08)	35.00	60.00
179	A52	200r ultra ('15)	1.50	8
a.		Imperf. vert., coil ('16)	2.00	50
180	A53	300r gray blk	3.50	15
181	A54	400r ol grn	22.50	1.50
182	A55	500r dk vio	4.50	20
183	A54	600r ol grn ('10)	1.50	50
184	A56	700r red brn	4.50	2.00
185	A57	1000r vermilion	35.00	60
186	A58	2000r yel grn	15.00	40
187	A58	2000r Prus bl ('15)	9.00	50
188	A59	5000r car rose	6.00	1.25
		Nos. 174-188 (15)	106.35	7.51

Allegorical Emblems: Liberty, Peace, Industry, etc.
A60

1908, July 14

189	A60	100r carmine	20.00	1.00

National Exhibition, Rio de Janeiro.

Emblems of Peace Between Brazil and Portugal
A61

1908, July 14

190	A61	100r red	7.50	75

Issued to commemorate the centenary of the opening of Brazilian ports to foreign commerce. Medallions picture King Carlos I of Portugal and Pres. Affonso Penna of Brazil.

Bonifacio, Bolívar, Hidalgo, O'Higgins, San Martin, Washington
A62

1909

191	A62	200r dp bl	3.50	50

Nilo Peçanha
A63

Baron of Rio Branco
A64

1910, Nov. 15

192	A63	10,000r brown	6.00	1.00

1913–16

193	A64	1000r dp grn	1.50	30
194	A64	1000r sl ('16)	15.00	30

Cabo Frio
A65

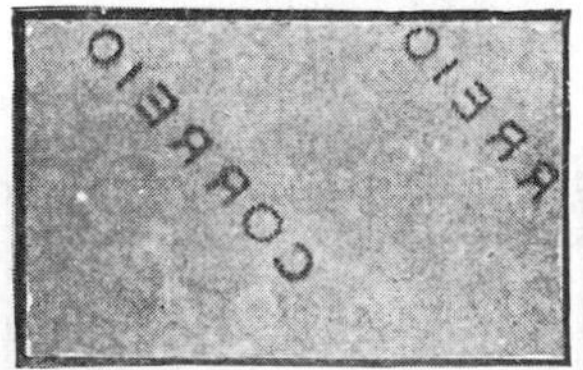

Wmk. 99

Wmkd. "CORREIO." (99)

1915, Nov. 13 Litho. *Perf. 11½*

195	A65	100r dk grn, *yelsh*	4.00	3.00

Founding of the town of Cabo Frio, 300th anniversary.

Bay of Guajara
A66

1916, Jan. 5

196	A66	100r carmine	8.00	4.50

City of Belem, 300th anniversary.

Revolutionary Flag
A67

1917, Mar. 6

197	A67	100r dp bl	20.00	7.50

Centenary of Revolution of Pernambuco, Mar. 6, 1817.

Rodrígues Alves
A68

Engraved.

1917, Aug. 31 *Perf. 12* Unwmkd.

198	A68	5000r red brn	55.00	9.00

Liberty Head
A69 A70

Perf. 12½, 13, 13x13½.

1918-20 Typographed. Unwmkd.

200	A69	10r org brn	25	15
201	A69	20r slate	25	15
202	A69	25r ol gray ('20)	25	15
203	A69	50r green	30.00	1.75
204	A70	100r rose	85	15
a.		Imperf. (pair)		
205	A70	300r red org	15.00	1.75
206	A70	500r dl vio	15.00	75
		Nos. 200-206 (7)	61.60	4.85

Wmk. 100

Because of the spacing of this watermark, a few stamps in each sheet may show no watermark.

Wmkd. CASA DA MOEDA in Sheet. (100)

207	A69	10r red brn	4.00	1.25
a.		Imperf. (pair)		
207B	A69	20r slate	1.00	80
c.		Imperf. (pair)		
208	A69	25r ol gray ('20)	50	30
209	A69	50r green	50	10
210	A70	100r rose	37.50	10
a.		Imperf. (pair)		
211	A70	200r dl bl	5.50	30
212	A70	300r orange	37.50	3.00
213	A70	500r dl vio	37.50	7.00
214	A70	600r orange	1.50	*7.00*
		Nos. 207-214 (9)	125.50	*19.85*

"Education"
A72

1918 Engraved. *Perf. 11½.*

215	A72	1000r blue	3.00	20
216	A72	2000r red brn	20.00	5.00
217	A72	5000r dk vio	6.00	6.00

Watermark note below No. 257 also applies to Nos. 215–217.

See also Nos. 233–234, 283–285, 404, 406, 458, 460.

Railroad
A73

"Industry"
A74

"Aviation"
A75

Mercury
A76

"Navigation"
A77

Perf. 13½x13, 13x13½

1920-22 Typographed. Unwmkd.

218	A73	10r red vio	40	10
219	A73	20r ol grn	40	10
220	A74	25r brn vio	30	10
221	A74	50r bl grn	50	10
222	A74	50r org brn ('22)	80	20
223	A75	100r rose red	1.50	10
224	A75	100r org ('22)	3.00	20
225	A75	150r vio ('21)	80	20
226	A75	200r blue	1.50	15
227	A75	200r rose red ('22)	5.00	15
228	A76	300r ol gray	5.00	25
229	A76	400r dl bl ('22)	15.00	1.75
230	A76	500r red brn	10.00	40
		Nos. 218-230 (13)	44.20	3.80

See also Nos. 236–257, 265–266, 268–271, 273–274, 276–281, 302–311, 316–322, 326–340, 357–358, 431–434, 436–441, 461–463B, 467–470, 472–474, 488–490, 492–494.

***Perf. 11, 11½* Engr. Wmk. 100**

231	A77	600r red org	1.25	20
232	A77	1000r claret	3.00	15
a.		Perf. 8½	22.50	4.00
233	A72	2000r dl vio	12.00	40
234	A72	5000r brown	10.00	5.00

Nos. 233 and 234 are inscribed "BRASIL CORREIO". Watermark note below No. 257 also applies to Nos. 231–234.

See also No. 282.

King Albert of Belgium and President Epitacio Pessoa
A78

1920, Sept. 19 Engr. *Perf. 11½x11*

235	A78	100r dl red	1.00	75

This stamp was issued to commemorate the visit of the King and Queen of Belgium to Brazil.

Types of 1920–22 Issue.

Perf. 13x13½, 13x12½.

1922–29 Typographed Wmk. 100

236	A73	10r red vio	20	10
237	A73	20r ol grn	20	10
238	A75	20r gray vio ('29)	20	10

239 A74 25r brn vio 25 10
240 A74 50r bl grn *2.50* *30.00*
241 A74 50r org brn ('23) 35 25
a. Booklet pane of 6
242 A75 100r rose red 18.00 30
243 A75 100r org ('26) 40 10
a. Booklet pane of 6
244 A75 100r turq grn ('28) 25 15
245 A75 150r violet 2.00 15
246 A75 200r blue 300.00 10.00
247 A75 200r rose red 30 15
a. Booklet pane of 6
248 A75 200r ol grn ('28) 2.00 2.50
249 A76 300r ol gray 1.50 20
a. Booklet pane of 6
250 A76 300r rose red ('29) 25 20
251 A76 400r blue 1.50 15
252 A76 400r org ('29) 75 50
253 A76 500r red brn 6.00 40
a. Booklet pane of 6
254 A76 500r ultra ('29) 7.00 15
255 A76 600r brn org ('29) 6.00 2.50
256 A76 700r dl vio ('29) 5.50 1.75
257 A76 1000r turq bl ('29) 8.00 60
Nos. 236-257 (22) *363.15* *50.45*

Because of the spacing of the watermark, a few stamps in each sheet show no watermark.

"Agriculture"
A79

1922 ***Perf. 13x13½.*** **Unwmkd.**

258 A79 40r org brn 50 10
259 A79 80r grnsh bl 40 *3.00*

See also Nos. 263, 267, 275.

Declaration of Ypiranga
A80

Dom Pedro I and José Bonifacio
A81

National Exposition and President Pessoa
A82

Engraved.

1922, Sept. 7 ***Perf. 14*** **Unwmkd.**

260 A80 100r ultra 6.00 40
261 A81 200r red 2.50 30
262 A82 300r green 4.50 30

Issued in commemoration of the centenary of independence and the National Exposition of 1922.

Agriculture Type of 1922
Typographed

1923 ***Perf. 13½x12*** **Wmk. 100**

263 A79 40r org brn 35 *1.00*

Brazilian Army Entering Bahia
A83

Perf. 13

1923, July 12 **Litho.** **Unwmkd.**

264 A83 200r rose 9.00 4.50

Centenary of the taking of Bahia from the Portuguese.

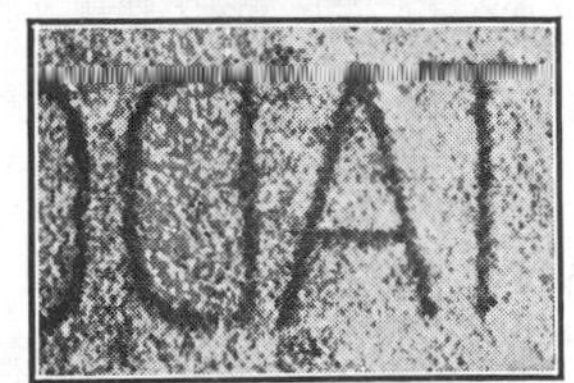
Wmk. 193

Types of 1920–22 Issues
Typographed
Wmkd.
ESTADOS UNIDOS DO BRASIL. (193)

1924 ***Perf. 13x13½***

265 A73 10r red vio 4.50 3.00
266 A73 20r ol grn 5.00 3.00
267 A79 40r org brn 3.50 50
268 A74 50r org brn 3.00 *10.00*
269 A75 100r orange 3.50 25
270 A75 200r rose 5.00 20
271 A76 400r blue 3.00 3.00
Nos. 265-271 (7) 27.50 *19.95*

Arms of Equatorial Confederation, 1824
A84

Perf. 11

1924, July 2 **Litho.** **Unwmkd.**

272 A84 200r bl, blk, yel, & red 3.50 2.25
a. Red omitted 450.00 450.00

Centenary of the Equatorial Confederation.

Wmk. 101

Types of 1920–22 Issues.
Wmkd. Stars and CASA DA MOEDA. (101)
Perf. 9½ to 13½ and Compound.

1924–28 **Typographed**

273 A73 10r red vio 15 8
274 A73 20r ol gray 15 8
275 A79 40r org brn 30 12
276 A74 50r org brn 30 10
277 A75 100r red org 60 10
278 A75 200r rose 40 10
279 A76 300r ol gray ('25) 7.00 80
280 A76 400r blue 2.00 25
281 A76 500r red brn 9.00 35

Engraved.

282 A77 600r red org ('26) 75 15
283 A72 2000r dl vio ('26) 2.00 15
284 A72 5000r brn ('26) 10.00 60
285 A72 10,000r rose ('28) 12.00 75
Nos. 273-285 (13) 44.65 3.63

Nos. 283 to 285 are inscribed "BRASIL CORREIO".

Ruy Barbosa
A85

1925 ***Perf. 11½*** **Wmk. 100**

286 A85 1000r claret 4.00 2.00

1926 **Wmk. 101**

287 A85 1000r claret 1.75 25

"Justice"
A86

Scales of Justice and Map of Brazil
A87

Wmk. 206

Wmkd.
Star-framed CM, Multiple (206)

1927, Aug. 11 Typo. ***Perf. 13½x13***

288 A86 100r dp bl 1.00 50
289 A87 200r rose 1.00 50

Issued in commemoration of the centenary of the founding of the law courses.

Liberty Holding Coffee Leaves
A88

1928, Mar. 5

290 A88 100r bl grn 1.50 60
291 A88 200r carmine 1.00 50
292 A88 300r ol blk 8.50 40

Issued to commemorate the bicentenary of the introduction of the coffee tree in Brazil.

Official Stamps of 1919 Surcharged in Red or Black **700 Réis**

Engraved.

1928 ***Perf. 11, 11½*** **Wmk. 100**

293 O3 700r on 500r org (R) 3.25 2.25
a. Inverted surcharge 250.00 250.00
294 O3 1000r on 100r rose red (Bk) 2.25 40
295 O3 2000r on 200r dl bl (R) 3.00 60
296 O3 5000r on 50r grn (R) 3.00 75
a. Inverted surcharge
297 O3 10,000r on 10r ol grn (R) 16.00 1.25
Nos. 293-297 (5) 27.50 5.25

Nos. 293 to 297 were used for ordinary postage.

Stamps in the outer rows of the sheets are often without watermark.

Ruy Barbosa
A89

Perf. 9, 9½x11, 11, and Compound.

1929 **Wmk. 101**

300 A89 5000r bl vio 12.00 75

For other stamps of type A89, see Nos. 323, 405 and 459.

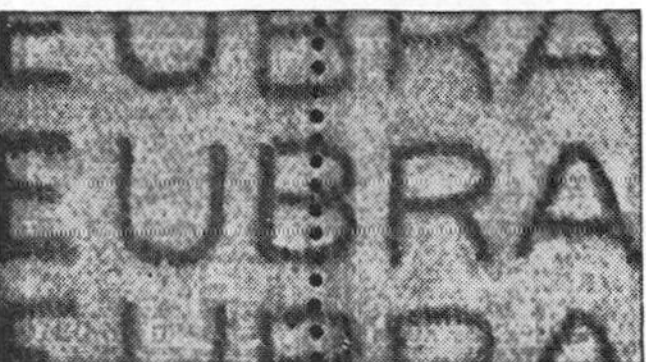
Wmk. 218

Types of 1920-21 Issue.
Typographed.
Wmkd. E U BRASIL Multiple. (218) (Letters 8 mm. high.)

Wmk. 218 exists both in vertical alignment and in echelon.

1929 ***Perf. 13½x12½.***

302 A75 20r gray vio 15 8
a. Wmk. in echelon 20 35
303 A75 50r red brn 15 8
a. Wmk. in echelon 80.00 30.00
304 A75 100r turq grn 25 8
305 A75 200r ol grn 13.00 2.50
306 A76 300r rose red 60 8
a. Wmk. in echelon 75 30
307 A76 400r orange 75 25
308 A76 500r ultra 7.50 50
a. Wmk. in echelon 125.00 17.50
309 A76 600r brn org 9.00 60
310 A76 700r dp vio 2.50 10
311 A76 1000r turq bl 4.00 10
a. Wmk. in echelon 7.50 7.50
Nos. 302-311 (10) 37.90 4.37

Architectural Fantasies
A90 A91

Architectural Fantasy
A92

Perf. 13x13½

1930, June 20 Wmk. 206

312	A90	100r turq bl	1.75	1.00
313	A91	200r ol gray	3.00	75
314	A92	300r rose red	5.00	1.25

Issued in connection with the Fourth Pan-American Congress of Architects and Exposition of Architecture.

Wmk. 221

Types of 1920-21 Issues.
Wmkd. ESTADOS UNIDOS DO BRASIL, Multiple. (221)
(Letters 6 mm. high.)

1930 *Perf. 13x12½.*

316	A75	20r gray vio	10	10
317	A75	50r red brn	15	10
318	A75	100r turq bl	20	10
319	A75	200r ol grn	2.50	20
320	A76	300r rose red	50	20
321	A76	500r ultra	1.25	20
322	A76	1000r turq bl	17.50	60
		Nos.316-322 (7)	22.20	1.50

Imperforates

Since 1930, imperforate or partly perforated sheets of nearly all commemorative and some definitive issues have become obtainable.

Wmk. 222

Types of 1920-29 Issue.
Wmkd. CORREIO BRASIL and 5 Stars in Squared Circle. (222)
Perf. 11, 13½x13, 13x12½.

1931-34 Typographed

326	A75	10r dp brn	10	5
327	A75	20r gray vio	10	5
328	A74	25r brn vio ('34)	10	50
330	A75	50r bl grn	15	10
331	A75	50r red brn	10	8
332	A75	100r orange	25	8
334	A75	200r dp car	35	8
335	A76	300r ol grn	50	8
336	A76	400r ultra	70	8
337	A76	500r red brn	3.00	10
338	A76	600r brn org	3.00	10
339	A76	700r dp vio	3.00	10
340	A76	1000r turq bl	10.00	10
		Nos. 326-340 (13)	21.35	1.50

Getulio Vargas and João Pessoa
A93

Vargas and Pessoa—A94

Oswaldo Aranha
A95 A96

Antonio Carlos
A97

Pessoa A98 Vargas A99

Lithographed.

1931, Apr. 29 *Perf. 14* Unwmkd.

342	A93	10r +10r lt bl	20	*8.00*
343	A93	20r +20r yel brn	20	*6.00*
344	A95	50r +50r dl grn, red & yel	20	20
a.		Red missing at left	1.25	1.25
345	A93	100r +50r org	40	40
346	A93	200r +100r grn	40	40
347	A94	300r +150r multi	40	40
348	A93	400r +200r dp rose	1.50	90
349	A93	500r +250r dk bl	1.00	80
350	A93	600r +300r brn vio	70	*10.00*
351	A94	700r +350r multi	1.25	75
352	A96	1000r +500r brt grn, red & yel	3.00	30
353	A97	2000r +1000r gray blk & red	6.00	75
354	A98	5000r +2500r blk & red	25.00	7.00
355	A99	10000r +5000r brt grn & yel	60.00	15.00
		Nos.342-355 (14)	100.25	*50.90*

Issued to commemorate the Revolution of Oct. 3, 1930. Prepared as semipostal stamps, Nos. 342–355 were sold as ordinary postage stamps with stated surtax ignored.

Nos. 306, 320 and 250 Surcharged **1931 200 Réis**

Wmkd. E U BRASIL Multiple. (218)

1931, July 20 *Perf. 13½x12½*

356	A76	200r on 300r rose red	1.00	75
a.		Wmk. in echelon	15.00	15.00
b.		Inverted surcharge	35.00	

Perf. 13x12½ **Wmk. 221**

357	A76	200r on 300r rose red	30	15
a.		Inverted surcharge	37.50	37.50

Perf. 13½x12½ **Wmk. 100**

358	A76	200r on 300r rose red	50.00	50.00

Map of South America Showing Meridian of Tordesillas
A100

João Ramalho and Tibiriçá
A101

Martim Affonso de Souza
A102

King John III of Portugal
A103

Disembarkation of M. A. de Souza at São Vicente
A104

Typographed.

1932, June 3 *Perf. 13* Wmk. 222

359	A100	20r dk vio	20	20
360	A101	100r black	50	40
361	A102	200r purple	1.25	20
362	A103	600r red brn	2.50	1.00

Perf. 9½, 11, 9½x11.

Engraved Wmk. 101

363	A104	700r ultra	3.00	1.50
		Nos.359-363 (5)	7.45	3.30

Nos. 359 to 363 commemorate the fourth centenary of the first colonization of Brazil at Sao Vicente, in 1532, under the hereditary captaincy of Martim Affonso de Souza.

Revolutionary Issue.

Map of Brazil
A105

Soldier and Flag
A106

Allegory: Freedom, Justice, Equality
A107

Soldier's Head
A108

"LEX" and Sword
A109

Symbolical of Law and Order
A110

Symbolical of Justice
A111

Perf. 11½

1932, Sept. 13 Litho. Unwmkd.

364	A105	100r brn org	60	3.00
365	A106	200r dk car	50	1.00
366	A107	300r gray grn	3.00	5.00
367	A108	400r dk bl	10.00	10.00
368	A105	500r blk brn	10.00	10.00
369	A107	600r red	10.00	10.00
370	A106	700r violet	4.50	10.00
371	A108	1000r orange	2.50	10.00
372	A109	2000r dk brn	20.00	27.50
373	A110	5000r yel grn	25.00	47.50
374	A111	10000r plum	27.50	55.00
		Nos. 364-374 (11)	113.60	189.00

Issued by the revolutionary forces in the state of Sao Paulo during the revolt of September, 1932. Subsequently the stamps were recognized by the Federal Government and placed in general use.

Excellent counterfeits of Nos. 373 and 374 exist.

Counterfeit cancellations abound.

City of Vassouras and Illuminated Memorial
A112

Typographed.

1933, Jan. 15 *Perf. 12* Wmk. 222

375	A112	200r rose red	1.50	75

Commemorative of the centenary of the founding of the city of Vassouras.

No. 306 Surcharged **200 RÉIS**

Perf. 13½x12½

1933, July 28 Wmk. 218

376	A76	200r on 300r rose red	85	75
a.		Wmk.218 in echelon (No. 306a)	15.00	15.00
b.		Wmk. 100 (No. 250)	90.00	90.00

Same Surcharge on No. 320.

Perf. 13x12½. **Wmk. 221**

377	A76	200r on 300r rose red	50	40
a.		Inverted surcharge	35.00	
b.		Double surcharge	35.00	

Religious Symbols and Inscriptions
A113

Typographed

1933, Sept. 3 *Perf. 13* Wmk. 222

378 A113 200r dk red 1.00 60

Issued in commemoration of the First National Eucharistic Congress in Brazil.

"Flag of the Race"
A114

1933, Aug. 18

379 A114 200r dp red 1.00 60

Commemorating the raising of the "Flag of the Race" and the 441st anniversary of the sailing of Columbus from Palos, Spain, August 3, 1492.

Republic Figure, Flags of Brazil and Argentina
A115

Wmk. 236

Engraved.

1933, Oct. 7 *Perf. 11½* Wmk. 101

380 A115 200r blue 60 35

Wmkd.

Coat of Arms in Sheet (236)

Watermark (reduced illustration) covers 22 stamps in sheet.

Thick Laid Paper.

Perf. 11, 11½.

381 A115 400r green 90 70
382 A115 600r brt rose 3.50 3.50
383 A115 1000r lt vio 5.00 3.00

Issued in commemoration of the visit of President Justo of the Argentine Republic to Brazil, October 2nd to 7th, 1933.

Allegory: "Faith and Energy"
A116

Allegory of Flight
A117

1933 Typographed. Wmk. 222

384 A116 200r dk red 30 15
385 A116 200r dk vio 35 10

See also Nos. 435, 471 and 491.

Wmk. 236

1934, Apr. 15 Engraved *Perf. 12*

386 A117 200r blue 75 1.00

Issued in commemoration of the first National Aviation Congress at Sao Paulo.

A118

Perf. 11

1934, May 12 Typo. Wmk. 222

387 A118 200r dk ol 50 50
388 A118 400r carmine 2.50 2.50
389 A118 700r ultra 2.50 1.50
390 A118 1000r orange 6.00 1.00

Issued in commemoration of the Seventh International Fair at Rio de Janeiro.

Christ of Corcovado
A119

1934, Oct. 20

392 A119 300r dk red 3.00 3.00
a. Tête bêche pair 9.00 9.00
393 A119 700r ultra 12.00 7.50
a. Tête bêche pair 35.00 35.00

Visit of Eugenio Cardinal Pacelli, later Pope Pius XII, to Brazil.

The three printings of Nos. 392-393, distinguishable by shades, sell for different prices.

José de Anchieta
A120

Thick Laid Paper.

1934, Nov. 8 *Perf. 11, 12* Wmk. 236

394 A120 200r yel brn 90 25
395 A120 300r violet 75 40
396 A120 700r blue 3.00 2.50
397 A120 1000r lt grn 6.00 1.50

Issued in commemoration of the 400th anniversary of the birth of Jose de Anchieta, S.J. (1534-1597), Portuguese missionary and "father of Brazilian literature."

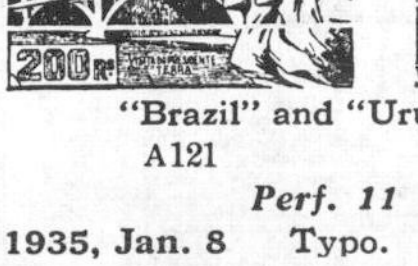

"Brazil" and "Uruguay"
A121 A122

Perf. 11

1935, Jan. 8 Typo. Wmk. 222

398 A121 200r orange 90 50
399 A122 300r yellow 1.25 75
400 A122 700r ultra 5.00 5.00
401 A121 1000r dk vio 12.00 6.00

Visit of President Terra of Uruguay.

View of Town of Igarassu
A123

1935, July 1

402 A123 200r mar & brn 1.50 75
403 A123 300r vio & ol brn 1.50 60

Issued in commemoration of the 400th anniversary of the founding of the captaincy of Pernambuco.

Types of 1918-29.

Thick Laid Paper.

Perf. 9½, 11, 12, 12x11.

1934-36 Engraved Wmk. 236

404 A72 2000r violet 4.50 50
405 A89 5000r bl vio ('36) 12.50 50
406 A72 10000r cl ('36) 10.00 1.00

No. 404 is inscribed "BRASIL CORREIO".

Revolutionist
A124

Bento Gonçalves da Silva
A125

Duke of Caxias
A126

1935, Sept. 20 *Perf. 11, 12*

407 A124 200r black 1.00 75
408 A124 300r rose lake 1.00 60
409 A125 700r dl bl 4.00 4.00
410 A126 1000r lt vio 4.50 2.50

Centenary of the "Ragged" Revolution.

Federal District Coat of Arms
A127

Perf. 11

1935, Oct. 19 Typo. Wmk. 222

411 A127 200r blue 4.00 3.00

Issued in commemoration of the Eighth International Sample Fair held at Rio de Janeiro.

Coutinho's Ship
A128

Arms of Fernandes Coutinho
A129

1935, Oct. 25

412 A128 300r maroon 3.50 1.00
413 A129 700r turq bl 4.50 2.50

Issued in commemoration of the 400th anniversary of the establishment of the first Portuguese colony at Espirito Santo by Vasco Fernandes Coutinho.

Gavea, Rock near Rio de Janeiro
A130

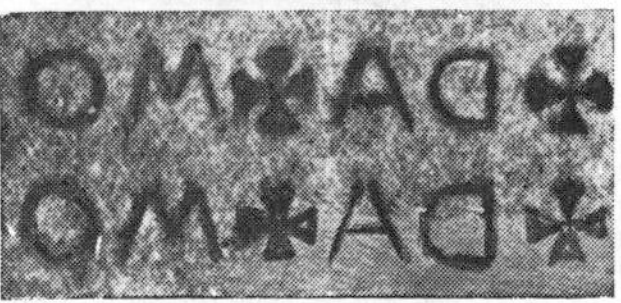

Wmk. 245

Wmkd. Multiple "CASA DA MOEDA DO BRASIL" and Small Formée Cross. (245)

1935, Oct. 12 *Perf. 11*

414 A130 300r brn & vio 2.00 1.50
415 A130 300r blk & turq bl 2.00 1.50
416 A130 300r Prus bl & ultra 2.00 1.50
417 A130 300r crim & blk 2.00 1.50

"Child's Day," Oct. 12.

Viscount of Cairú
A131

Perf. 11, 12x11

1936, Jan. 20 Engraved Wmk. 236

418 A131 1200r violet 10.00 5.00

Issued in commemoration of the centenary of the death of José da Silva Lisboa, Viscount of Cairu (1756-1835).

View of Cametá
A132

1936, Feb. 26 *Perf. 11, 12*

419	A132	200r brn org	1.75	1.25
420	A132	300r green	1.75	75

Issued in commemoration of the 300th anniversary of the founding of the city of Cameta, Dec. 24, 1635.

Coining Press
A133

Thick Laid Paper.

1936, Mar. 24 *Perf. 11*

421	A133	300r pur brn, *cr*	1.25	75

Issued in commemoration of the first Numismatic Congress at Sao Paulo, March, 1936.

Carlos Gomes—A134

"Il Guarany"
A135

1936, July 11 *Perf. 11, 11x12*

Thick Laid Paper.

422	A134	300r dl rose	90	60
423	A134	300r blk brn	90	60
424	A135	700r ocher	4.50	1.50
425	A135	700r blue	5.00	2.50

Issued in commemoration of the 100th anniversary of the birth of Antonio Carlos Gomes, who composed the opera "Il Guarany."

Scales of Justice
A136

Perf. 11

1936, July 4 Typo. **Wmk. 222**

426	A136	300r rose	3.00	1.00

First National Judicial Congress.

Federal District Coat of Arms
A137

Wmk. 249

Wmkd. "CORREIO BRASIL" Multiple. (249)

1936, Nov. 13 Typographed

427	A137	200r rose red	1.25	1.00

Issued in commemoration of the Ninth International Sample Fair held at Rio de Janeiro.

Eucharistic Congress Seal
A138

1936, Dec. 17 *Perf. 11½* **Wmk. 245**

428	A138	300r grn, yel, bl & blk	1.25	75

Issued in commemoration of the Second National Eucharistic Congress in Brazil.

Botafogo Bay
A139

Thick Laid Paper.

Engraved.

1937, Jan. 2 *Perf. 11* **Wmk. 236**

429	A139	700r blue	1.50	75
430	A139	700r black	1.50	75

Issued to commemorate the birth centenary of Francisco Pereira Passos, engineer who planned the modern city of Rio de Janeiro.

Types of 1920-21, 1933.

Perf. 11, 11½ and Compound.

1936-37 Typographed. **Wmk. 249**

431	A75	10r dp brn	15	10
432	A75	20r dl vio	15	10
433	A75	50r bl grn	15	10
434	A75	100r orange	25	10
435	A116	200r dk vio	50	10
436	A76	300r ol grn	25	10
437	A76	400r ultra	50	10
438	A76	500r lt brn	75	10
439	A76	600r brn org ('37)	1.75	10
440	A76	700r dp vio	3.50	10
441	A76	1000r turq bl	3.50	10
		Nos. 431-441 (11)	11.45	1.10

Massed Flags and Star of Esperanto
A140

1937, Jan. 19

442	A140	300r green	1.75	75

Ninth Brazilian Esperanto Congress.

Bay of Rio de Janeiro
A141

Perf. 12½

1937, June 9 **Unwmkd.**

443	A141	300r org red & blk	75	75
444	A141	700r bl & dk brn	2.00	75

Issued in commemoration of the Second South American Radio Communication Conference held in Rio de Janeiro, June 7 to 19, 1937.

Globe
A142

1937, Sept. 4 *Perf. 11, 12* **Wmk. 249**

445	A142	300r green	1.50	75

50th anniversary of Esperanto.

Monroe Palace, Rio de Janeiro
A143

Botanical Garden, Rio de Janeiro
A144

1937, Sept. 30 *Perf. 12½* **Unwmkd.**

446	A143	200r lt brn & bl	75	50
447	A144	300r org & ol grn	75	50
448	A143	2000r grn & cer	6.50	9.00
449	A144	10000r lake & ind	55.00	45.00

Brig. Gen. José da Silva Paes
A145

Eagle and Shield
A146

1937, Oct. 11 *Perf. 11½* **Wmk. 249**

450	A145	300r blue	1.00	40

Bicentenary of Rio Grande do Sul.

1937, Dec. 2 Typo. *Perf. 11*

451	A146	400r dk bl	1.25	50

Issued in commemoration of the 150th anniversary of the Constitution of the United States of America.

Bags of Brazilian Coffee
A147

Frame Engr., Center Typo.

Center Typographed.

1938, Jan. 17 *Perf. 12½* **Unwmkd.**

452	A147	1200r multi	6.00	1.00

Arms of Olinda
A148

Perf. 11, 11x11½.

1938, Jan. 24 Engraved Wmk. 249

453	A148	400r violet	75	40

Issued in commemoration of the fourth centenary of the founding of the city of Olinda.

Independence Memorial, Ypiranga
A149

1938, Jan. 24 Typo. *Perf. 11*

454	A149	400r brn ol	1.00	40

Issued to commemorate the proclamation of Brazil's independence by Dom Pedro, Sept. 7, 1822.

Iguaçu Falls
A150

Engraved.

1938, Jan. 10 *Perf. 12½* **Unwmkd.**

455	A150	1000r sep & yel brn	2.50	1.25
456	A150	5000r ol blk & grn	27.50	12.50

Couto de Magalhaes
A151

Perf. 11, 11x11½

1938, Mar. 17 **Wmk. 249**

457	A151	400r dl grn	75	35

Issued to commemorate the centenary of the birth of General Couto de Magalhaes (1837–1898), statesman, soldier, explorer, writer, developer.

Types of 1918–38

Perf. 11, 12x11, 12x11½, 12.

1938 Engraved **Wmk. 249**

458	A72	2000r bl vio	8.00	15
459	A89	5000r vio bl	30.00	60
a.		5000r dp bl	25.00	60
460	A72	10000r rose lake	35.00	1.20

No. 458 is inscribed "BRASIL CORREIO".

Types of 1920-22.

Typographed.

1938 *Perf. 11.* **Wmk. 245**

461	A75	50r bl grn	60	1.25
462	A75	100r orange	60	1.25
463	A76	300r ol grn	60	25

463A	A76	400r ultra	120.00	60.00
463B	A76	500r red brn	60	*12.00*
		Nos. 461-463B (5)	122.40	*74.75*

National Archives Building
A152

1938, May 20 **Wmk. 249**

464	A152	400r brown	75	35

Centenary of National Archives.

Souvenir Sheets.

Sir Rowland Hill
A153

1938, Oct. 22 ***Imperf.***

465	A153	Sheet of 10	20.00	20.00
a.		400r dl grn, Single stamp	1.25	1.25

Issued in commemoration of the Brazilian International Philatelic Exposition (Brapex).

Issued in sheets measuring 106x118 mm. A few perforated sheets exist.

President Vargas
A154

1938, Nov. 10 ***Perf. 11***

Without Gum

466	A154	Sheet of 10	9.00	15.00
a.		400r sl bl, Single stamp	65	65

Issued in commemoration of the Constitution of Brazil, set up by President Vargas, Nov. 10, 1937. Size: 113x135½mm.

Wmk. 256

Types of 1920-33.

Wmkd.

"CASA+DA+MOEDA+DO+BRAZIL" in 8mm. Letters (256)

1939 **Typographed.** ***Perf. 11.***

467	A75	10r red brn	40	30
468	A75	20r dl vio	40	15
469	A75	50r bl grn	40	10
470	A75	100r yel org	60	10
471	A116	200r dk vio	70	10
472	A76	400r ultra	1.25	10
473	A76	600r dl org	1.25	10
474	A76	1000r turq bl	9.00	10
		Nos. 467-474 (8)	14.00	1.05

View of Rio de Janeiro
A155

View of Santos
A156

1939, June 14 Engraved Wmk. 249

475	A155	1200r dl vio	2.50	25

1939, Aug. 23

476	A156	400r dl bl	60	30

Centenary of founding of Santos.

Chalice Vine and Blossoms
A157

Eucharistic Congress Seal
A158

1939, Aug. 23

477	A157	400r green	2.00	50

Issued in commemoration of the first South American Botanical Congress held in January, 1938.

1939, Sept. 3

478	A158	400r rose red	60	30

Third National Eucharistic Congress.

Duke of Caxias, Army Patron
A159

1939, Sept. 12 **Photo.** ***Rouletted***

479	A159	400r dp ultra	60	40

Issued for Soldiers' Day.

George Washington
A159a

Grover Cleveland
A159c

Emperor Pedro II
A159b

Statue of Friendship, Given by U. S. A.
A159d

Engraved.

1939, Oct. 7 ***Perf. 12*** **Unwmkd.**

480	A159a	400r yel org	75	40
481	A159b	800r dk grn	45	25
482	A159c	1200r rose car	1.00	25
483	A159d	1600r dk bl	1.00	40

New York World's Fair.

Benjamin Constant
A160

Fonseca on Horseback
A161

Manuel Deodoro da Fonseca and President Vargas
A162

Rouletted

1939, Nov. 15 **Photo.** **Wmk. 249**

484	A160	400r dp grn	60	30
485	A162	1200r chocolate	1.50	40

Engraved ***Perf. 11***

486	A161	800r gray blk	90	45

Issued in commemoration of the 50th anniversary of the Proclamation of the Republic.

President Roosevelt, President Vargas and Map of the Americas
A163

1940, Apr. 14

487	A163	400r sl bl	1.25	60

Pan American Union, 50th anniversary.

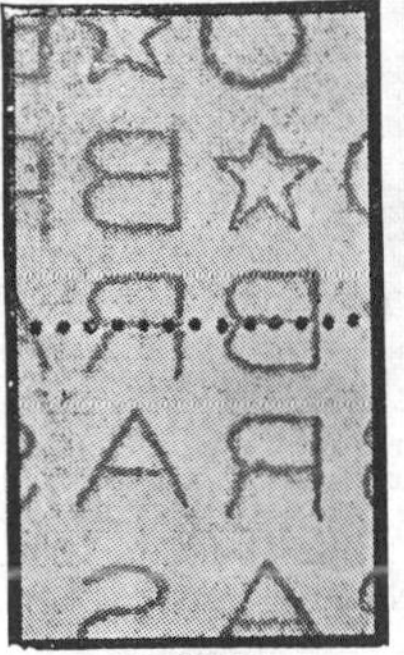

Wmk. 264

Types of 1920-33.

Wmkd.

"☆ CORREIO ☆ BRASIL ☆"

Multiple. Letters 7mm. high. (264)

1940-41 **Typographed.** ***Perf. 11.***

488	A75	10r red brn	10	25
489	A75	20r dl vio	25	25
489A	A75	50r bl grn ('41)	75	*1.50*
490	A75	100r yel org	1.00	8
491	A116	200r violet	75	8
492	A76	400r ultra	5.00	8
493	A76	600r dl org	5.00	8
494	A76	1000r turq bl	12.50	8
		Nos. 488-494 (8)	25.35	*2.40*

Map of Brazil
A164

1940, Sept. 7 **Engraved**

495	A164	400r carmine	65	35
a.		Unwmkd.	75.00	50.00

Issued in commemoration of the 9th Brazilian Congress of Geography held at Florianopolis.

Victoria Regia Water Lily
A165

President Vargas
A166

Relief Map of Brazil
A167

1940, Oct. 30 ***Perf. 11*** **Wmk. 249**

Without Gum

496	A165	1000r dl vio	1.50	1.50
a.		Sheet of ten	15.00	45.00
497	A166	5000r red	12.00	9.00
a.		Sheet of ten	130.00	200.00
498	A167	10,000r sl bl	13.50	4.50
a.		Sheet of ten	175.00	200.00

New York World's Fair.

All three sheets exist unwatermarked and also with papermaker's watermark of large globe and "AMERICA BANK" in sheet. A few imperforate sheets also exist.

Joaquim Machado de Assis
A168

Pioneers and Buildings of Porto Alegre
A169

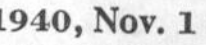

1940, Nov. 1

499	A168	400r black	75	40

Birth centenary of Joaquim Maria Machado de Assis, poet and novelist.

1940, Nov. 2 **Wmk. 264**

500	A169	400r green	60	35

Issued to commemorate the bicentenary of the colonization of Porto Alegre.

Proclamation of King John IV of Portugal
A173

1940, Dec. 1 **Wmk. 249**

501	A173	1200r bl blk	2.00	50

Issued in commemoration of the 800th anniversary of Portuguese independence and the 300th anniversary of the restoration of the monarchy.

No. 501 was also printed on paper with papermaker's watermark of large globe and "AMERICA BANK." Unwatermarked copies are from these sheets.

Brazilian Flags and Head of Liberty
A175

Calendar Sheet and Inscription "Day of the Fifth General Census of Brazil"
A176

Engraved.

1940, Dec. 18 ***Perf. 11*** **Wmk. 256**

502	A175	400r dl vio	75	40
b.	Unwmkd.		60.00	60.00

Wmk. 245

502A	A175	400r dl vio	50.00	50.00

Issued in commemoration of the 10th anniversary of the inauguration of President Vargas.

Typographed.

1941, Jan. 14 ***Perf. 11*** **Wmk. 256**

503	A176	400r bl & red	45	20

Wmk. 245

504	A176	400r bl & red	3.50	1.00

Fifth general census of Brazil.

The only foreign revenue stamps listed in this Catalogue are those authorized for prepayment of postage.

King Alfonso Henriques
A177

Father Antonio Vieira
A178

Salvador Corrêia de Sa e Benevides
A179

President Carmona of Portugal and President Vargas
A180

Photogravure.

1940-41 ***Rouletted*** **Wmk. 264**

504A	A177	200r pink	20	15
505	A178	400r ultra	30	20
506	A179	800r brt vio	35	20
506A	A180	5400r sl grn	2.25	80

Wmk. 249

507	A177	200r pink	7.50	4.50
507A	A178	400r ultra	35.00	12.00
508	A180	5400r sl grn	3.50	1.75
		Nos. 504A-508 (7)	49.10	19.60

Issued in commemoration of the 800th anniversary of Portuguese Independence.

José de Anchieta
A181

Amador Bueno
A182

Engraved

1941, Aug. 1 ***Perf. 11*** **Wmk. 264**

509	A181	1000r gray vio	1.75	1.00

Society of Jesus, 400th anniversary.

1941, Oct. 20 ***Perf. 11½***

510	A182	400r black	80	50

Issued in commemoration of the 300th anniversary of the acclamation of Amador Bueno (1572-1648) as king of Sao Paulo.

Air Force Emblem
A183

1941, Oct. 20 ***Perf. 11***

511	A183	5400r sl grn	6.00	3.50

Issued in connection with Aviation Week, as propaganda for the Brazilian Air Force.

Petroleum
A184

Agriculture
A185

Steel Industry
A186

Commerce
A187

Marshal Peixoto
A188

Count of Porto Alegre
A189

Admiral J. A. C. Maurity
A190

"Armed Forces"
A191

Vargas
A192

Typographed

1941-42 ***Perf. 11*** **Wmk. 264**

512	A184	10r yel brn	20	20
513	A184	20r ol grn	10	5
514	A184	50r ol bis	10	5
515	A184	100r bl grn	20	5
516	A185	200r brn org	50	5
517	A185	300r lil rose	25	15
518	A185	400r grnsh bl	75	10
519	A185	500r salmon	35	10
520	A186	600r violet	75	10
521	A186	700r brt rose	35	15
522	A186	1000r gray	2.00	10
523	A186	1200r dl bl	4.00	10
524	A187	2000r gray vio	3.00	10

Engraved

525	A188	5000r blue	6.00	15
526	A189	10,000r rose red	7.50	20
527	A190	20,000r dp brn	7.50	40
528	A191	50,000r red ('42)	30.00	25.00
529	A192	100,000r bl ('42)	60	*10.00*
		Nos. 512-529 (18)	64.15	*37.05*

Nos. 512 to 527 and later issues come on thick or thin paper. The stamps on both papers also exist with three vertical green lines printed on the back, a control mark.

See also Nos. 541-587, 592-593, 656-670.

Bernardino de Campos
A193

Prudente de Morais
A194

1942, Jan. 25

533	A193	1000r red	2.50	75
534	A194	1200r blue	6.00	50

Issued in commemoration of the 100th anniversary of the birth of Bernardino de Campos and Prudente de Morais, lawyers and statesmen of Brazil.

Head of Indo-Brazilian Bull
A195

1942, May 1 ***Perf. 11½*** **Wmk. 264**

535	A195	200r blue	75	40
536	A195	400r org brn	75	40
a.	Wmk. 267		75.00	75.00

Issued in commemoration of the second Agriculture and Livestock Show of Central Brazil held at Uberaba. Wmk. 267 is illustrated with Nos. 573-587.

Outline of Brazil and Torch of Knowledge
A196

Map of Brazil Showing Goiania
A197

Perf. 11

1942, July 5 **Typo.** **Wmk. 264**

537	A196	400r org brn	70	35

8th Brazilian Congress of Education.

1942, July 5

538	A197	400r lt vio	70	40

Founding of Goiania city.

Seal of Congress
A198

1942, Sept. 20 **Wmk. 264**

539	A198	400r ol bis	50	25
a.	Wmk. 267		30.00	15.00

Issued to commemorate the 4th National Eucharistic Congress at Sao Paulo. Wmk. 267 is illustrated with Nos. 573-587.

Types of 1941-42.

1942-47 ***Perf. 11.*** **Wmk. 245**

541	A184	20r ol grn	10	40
542	A184	50r ol bis	10	10
543	A184	100r bl grn	40	40
544	A185	200r brn org	65	50
545	A185	400r grnsh bl	40	10
546	A186	600r lt vio	3.00	10
547	A186	700r brt rose	35	80
548	A186	1200r dl bl	1.25	15
549	A187	2000r gray vio ('47)	10.00	10.00

Engraved

550	A188	5000r blue	10.00	40
551	A189	10,000r rose red	6.00	1.50
552	A190	20,000r dp brn ('47)	4.50	45
553	A192	100,000r blue	3.50	8.00
		Nos. 541-553 (13)	40.25	22.90

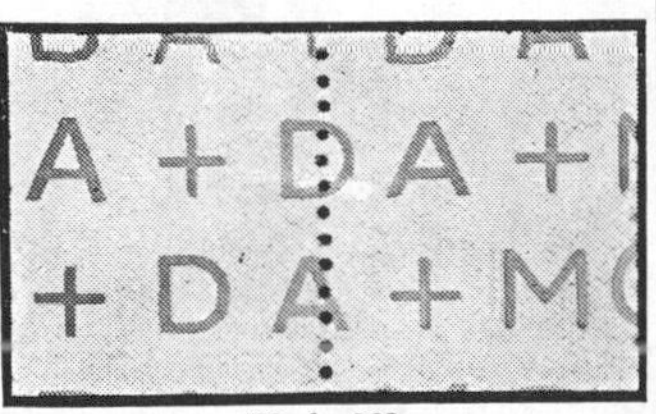

Wmk. 268

Types of 1941-42.

Wmkd. "CASA+DA+MOEDA+DO+BRASIL" in 6mm. Letters. (268)

1941-47 Typographed. *Perf. 11.*

554	A184	20r ol grn	20	15
555	A184	50r ol bis ('47)	60	60
556	A184	100r bl grn ('43)	20	15
557	A185	200r brn org ('43)	20	10
558	A185	300r lil rose ('43)	15	10
559	A185	400r grnsh bl ('42)	35	15
560	A185	500r sal ('43)	20	10
561	A186	600r violet	70	8
562	A186	700r brt rose ('45)	40	*1.00*
563	A186	1000r gray	75	8
564	A186	1200r dp bl ('44)	1.00	15
565	A187	2000r gray vio ('43)	3.50	10

Engraved

566	A188	5000r bl ('43)	5.00	15
567	A189	10,000r rose red ('43)	10.00	45
568	A190	20,000r dp brn ('42)	22.50	50
569	A191	50,000r red ('42)	25.00	3.50
a.		50,000r dk brn red ('47)	17.50	9.00
570	A192	100,000r blue	65	65
		Nos. 554-570 (17)	71.40	*8.01*

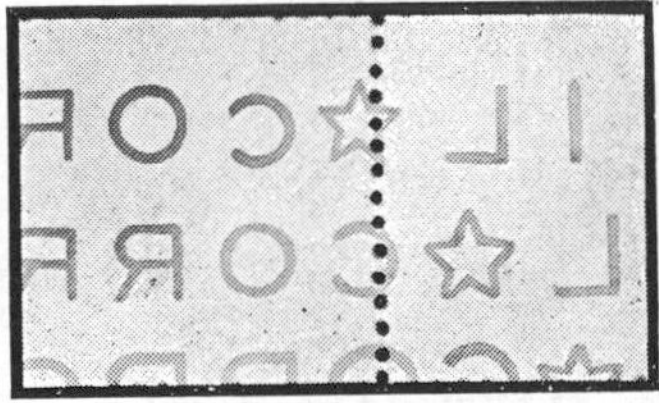

Wmk. 267

Wmkd. "☆ CORREIO ☆ BRASIL ☆" Multiple in Small Letters (5 mm. high). (267)

Types of 1941-42.

1942-47 Typographed Wmk. 267

573	A184	20r ol grn ('43)	20	10
574	A184	50r ol bis ('43)	10	10
575	A184	100r bl grn ('43)	25	10
576	A185	200r brn org ('43)	30	35
577	A185	400r grnsh bl	30	10
578	A185	500r sal ('43)	95.00	15.00
579	A186	600r vio ('43)	60	40
580	A186	700r brt rose ('47)	50	*5.00*
581	A186	1000r gray ('44)	2.50	15
582	A186	1200r dl bl	3.00	10
583	A187	2000r gray vio	3.50	10

Engraved

584	A188	5000r blue	6.00	20
585	A189	10,000r rose red ('44)	10.00	1.50
586	A190	20,000r dp brn ('45)	12.00	60
587	A191	50,000r red ('43)	35.00	7.50
		Nos. 573-587 (15)	169.25	*31.30*

1942 Typographed Wmk. 249

592	A184	100r bl grn	5.00	3.50
593	A186	600r violet	5.00	1.00

Map Showing Amazon River

A199

1943, Mar. 19 *Perf. 11* Wmk. 267

607	A199	40c org brn	50	50

Issued in commemoration of the 400th anniversary of the discovery of the Amazon River.

Reproduction of Brazil Stamp of 1866

A200

Adaptation of 1843 "Bull's-eye"

A201

1943, Mar. 28 Wmk. 267

608	A200	40c violet	75	40
a.		Wmk. 268	*1,000.*	

Centenary of city of Petropolis.

1943, Aug. 1 Engraved *Imperf.*

609	A201	30c black	1.00	50
610	A201	60c black	1.25	50
611	A201	90c black	1.00	50

Centenary of the first postage stamp of Brazil. The 30c and 90c exist unwatermarked; prices $25 and $65.

Souvenir Sheet.

A202

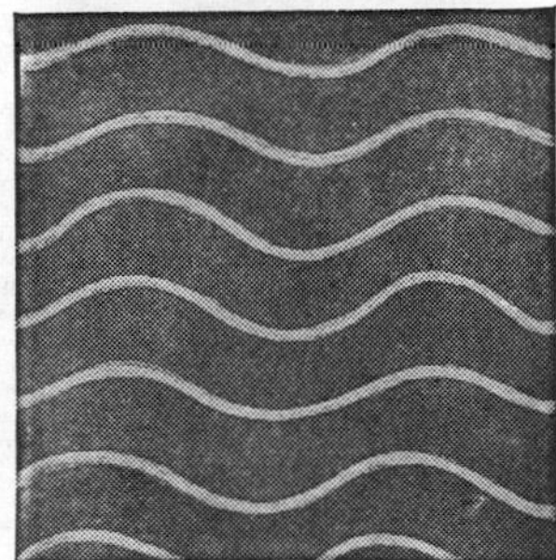

Wmk. 281

Wmkd. Wavy Lines. (281) Horizontally or Vertically. Without Gum.

1943 Engraved *Imperf.*

612	A202	Sheet of three	10.00	9.00
a.		30c blk	2.50	2.50
b.		60c blk	2.50	2.50
c.		90c blk	2.50	2.50

Sheet measures 125½x94½mm.

Ubaldino do Amaral

A203

"Justice"

A204

Perf. 11, 12

1943, Aug. 27 Typo. Wmk. 264

613	A203	40c dl sl grn	50	25
a.		Wmk. 267	30.00	25.00

Birth centenary of Ubaldino do Amaral, banker and statesman.

1943, Aug. 30 Wmk. 267

614	A204	2cr brt rose	1.00	75

Centenary of Institute of Brazilian Lawyers.

Indo-Brazilian Bull

A205

1943, Aug. 30 Engraved

615	A205	40c dk red brn	1.25	75

9th Livestock Show at Bahia.

José Barbosa Rodrigues

A206

1943, Nov. 13 Typographed

616	A206	40c bluish grn	60	25

Birth centenary of José Barbosa Rodrigues, botanist.

Charity Hospital, Santos

A207

1943, Nov. 7 Engraved

617	A207	1cr blue	75	40

400th anniversary of Charity Hospital, Santos.

Pedro Americo

A208

Perf. 11

1943, Dec. 16 Typo. Wmk. 267

618	A208	40c brn org	50	30

Issued to commemorate the birth centenary of Pedro Americo de Figueirido e Melo (1843-1905), artist-hero and statesman.

Gen. A. E. Gomes Carneiro

A209

1944, Feb. 9 Engraved

619	A209	1.20cr rose	1.00	50

50th anniversary of the Lapa siege.

Statue of Baron of Rio Branco

A210

1944, May 13 Typographed

620	A210	1cr blue	75	40

Issued to commemorate the unveiling of a statue of the Baron of Rio Branco.

Duke of Caxias

A211

Granite Paper.

1944, May 13 *Perf. 12* Unwmkd.

621	A211	1.20cr bl grn & pale org	90	50

Centenary of pacification of Sao Paulo and Minas Gerais in an independence movement in 1842.

YMCA Seal

A212

1944, June 7 Litho. *Perf. 11*

Granite Paper.

622	A212	40c dp bl, car & yel	40	30

Centenary of Young Men's Christian Assn.

Chamber of Commerce Rio Grande

A213

Engraved.

1944, Sept. 25 *Perf. 12* **Wmk. 268**

623	A213	40c lt yel brn	40	35

Issued to commemorate the centenary of the Chamber of Commerce of Rio Grande.

Martim F. R. de Andrada
A214

1945, Jan. 30 ***Perf. 11***

624	A214	40c blue	40	35

Issued to commemorate the centenary of the death of Martim F. R. de Andrada, statesman.

Meeting of Duke of Caxias and David Canabarro
A215

1945, Mar. 19 **Photogravure**

625	A215	40c ultra	40	25

Centenary of the pacification of Rio Grande do Sul.

Globe and "Esperanto"
A216

1945, Apr. 16

626	A216	40c lt bl grn	60	30

10th Esperanto Congress, Rio de Janeiro, Apr. 14–22.

Baron of Rio Branco's Bookplate
A217

1945, Apr. 20 ***Perf. 11*** **Wmk. 268**

627	A217	40c violet	30	25

Issued to commemorate the centenary of the birth of José Maria da Silva Paranhos, Baron of Rio Branco.

Tranquility
A218

Glory
A219

Victory
A220

Peace
A221

Cooperation
A222

Rouletted 7

1945, May 8 **Engraved** **Wmk. 268**

628	A218	20c dk rose vio	25	25
629	A219	40c dk car	28	25
630	A220	1cr dl org	60	50
631	A221	2cr stl bl	1.50	75
632	A222	5cr green	3.00	1.00
		Nos. 628-632 (5)	5.63	2.75

Victory of the Allied Nations in Europe.
Nos. 628–632 exist on thin card, imperf. and unwatermarked.

Francisco Manoel da Silva
A223

Perf. 12

1945, May 30 **Typo.** **Wmk. 245**

633	A223	40c brt rose	75	40
a.		Wmk. 268	11.00	11.00

Issued to commemorate the 150th anniversary of the birth of Francisco Manoel da Silva (1795–1865), composer (in 1831) of the national anthem.

Bahia Institute of Geography and History
A224

1945, May 30 ***Perf. 11*** **Wmk. 268**

634	A224	40c lt ultra	35	25

Issued to commemorate the 50th anniversary of the founding of the Institute of Geography and History at Bahia.

Emblems of 5th Army and B. E. F.
A225 A226

U.S. Flag and Shoulder Patches
A227

Brazilian Flag and Shoulder Patches—A228

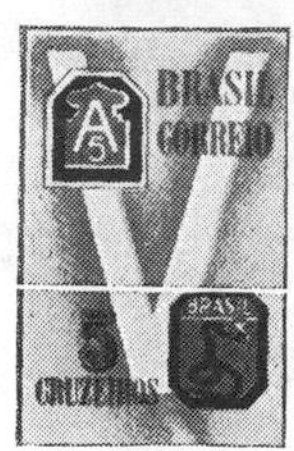

Victory Symbol and Shoulder Patches
A229

1945, July 18 **Lithographed**

635	A225	20c multi	25	25
636	A226	40c multi	25	25
637	A227	1cr multi	1.25	75
638	A228	2cr multi	1.75	1.00
639	A229	5cr multi	5.00	1.00
		Nos. 635-639 (5)	8.50	3.25

Issued in honor of the Brazilian Expeditionary Force and the United States Fifth Army Battle against the Axis in Italy.

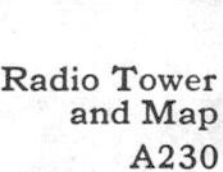

Radio Tower and Map
A230

1945, Sept. 3 **Engraved**

640	A230	1.20cr gray	60	25

Third Inter-American Conference on Radio Communications.

No. 640 was reproduced on a souvenir card with blue background and inscriptions. Size: 145x161mm.

A 40c lilac stamp, picturing the International Bridge between Argentina and Brazil and portraits of Presidents Justo and Vargas, was prepared late in 1945. It was not issued, but later was sold, without postal value, to collectors. Price, 15 cents.

Adm. Saldanha da Gama
A231

1946, Apr. 7

641	A231	40c gray blk	30	30

Issued to commemorate the centenary of the birth of Admiral Luiz Felipe Saldanha da Gama (1846–1895).

Princess Isabel d'Orleans-Braganca
A232

1946, July 29 **Unwmkd.**

642	A232	40c black	35	35

Issued to commemorate the centenary of the birth of Princess Isabel d'Orleans-Braganca.

Post Horn, V and Envelope
A233

Post Office, Rio de Janeiro
A234

Bay of Rio de Janeiro and Plane
A235

Perf. 11

1946, Sept. 2 **Litho.** **Wmk. 268**

643	A233	40c blk & pale org	30	25

Perf. 12½ **Engraved** **Unwmkd.**

Center in Ultramarine.

644	A234	2cr slate	75	25
645	A234	5cr org brn	4.50	1.50
646	A234	10cr dk vio	5.00	75

Center in Brown Orange.

647	A235	1.30cr dk grn	50	50
648	A235	1.70cr car rose	50	50
649	A235	2.20cr dp ultra	75	75
		Nos. 643-649 (7)	12.30	4.50

Nos. 643 to 649 were issued to commemorate the 5th Postal Union Congress of the Americas and Spain.

No. 643 was reproduced on a souvenir card with inscriptions and marginal illustrations of the Palacio da Fazenda, Rio de Janeiro. Size: 188x239mm. Sold for 10 cruzeiros.

Liberty
A236

Perf. 11x11½

1946, Sept. 18 — Wmk. 268

650	A236	40c blk & gray	20	15
a.		Unwmkd.	150.00	

Adoption of the Constitution of 1946

Columbus Lighthouse, Dominican Republic
A237

1946, Sept. 14 — Litho. — *Perf. 11*

651	A237	5cr Prus grn	6.50	2.50

Orchid
A238

Gen. A. E. Gomes Carneiro
A239

1946, Nov. 8 — Wmk. 268

652	A238	40c ultra, red & yel	55	30
a.		Unwmkd.	75.00	

Issued to publicize the 4th National Exhibition of Orchids, Rio de Janeiro, November, 1946.

Perf. 10½x12

1946, Dec. 6 — Engraved — Unwmkd.

653	A239	40c dp grn	20	20

Issued to commemorate the centenary of the birth of General Antonio Ernesto Gomes Carneiro.

Brazilian Academy of Letters
A240

1946, Dec. 14 — *Perf. 11*

654	A240	40c blue	25	20

Issued to commemorate the 50th anniversary of the foundation of the Brazilian Academy of Letters, Rio de Janeiro.

Antonio de Castro Alves—A241

1947, Mar. 14 — Litho. — Wmk. 267

655	A241	40c bluish grn	25	25

Issued to commemorate the birth centenary of Antonio de Castro Alves (1847–1871), poet.

Types of 1941–42, Values in Centavos or Cruzeiros.

Typographed

1947–54 — *Perf. 11* — Wmk. 267

656	A184	2c olive	12	8
657	A184	5c yel brn	12	8
658	A184	10c green	12	8
659	A185	20c brn org	15	8
660	A185	30c dk lil rose	50	8
661	A185	40c blue	25	8
b.		Wmk. 268	800.00	60.00
661A	A185	50c salmon	50	8
662	A186	60c lt vio	90	8
663	A186	70c brt rose ('54)	30	10
664	A186	1cr gray	90	10
665	A186	1.20cr dl bl	2.25	10
a.		Wmk. 268	10.00	9.00
666	A187	2cr gray vio	3.50	8
		Engraved		
667	A188	5cr blue	7.00	10
668	A189	10cr rose red	7.00	10
		Perf. 11, 13.		
669	A190	20cr dp brn	14.00	75
670	A191	50cr red	27.50	50
		Nos. 656-670 (16)	65.11	2.47

The 5cr, 20cr and 50cr also exist with perf. 12 to 13.

Pres. Gonzalez Videla of Chile
A242

1947, June 26 — *Perf. 12x11* — Unwmkd.

671	A242	40c dk brn org	25	20

Issued to commemorate the visit of President Gabriel Gonzalez Videla of Chile, June 1947.

A souvenir folder contains four impressions of No. 671, measures 6½x8¼ inches and has marginal inscriptions, including a coat of arms, in blue.

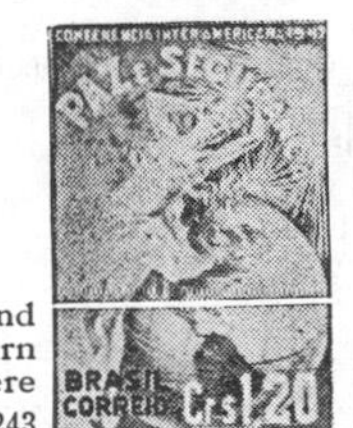

"Peace" and Western Hemisphere
A243

1947, Aug. 15 — *Perf. 11x12*

672	A243	1.20cr blue	35	25

Issued to commemorate the Inter-American Defense Conference at Rio de Janeiro, August–September, 1947.

Pres. Harry S Truman, Map and Statue of Liberty
A244

1947, Sept. 1 — Typo. — *Perf. 12x11*

673	A244	40c ultra	30	25

Visit of U.S. President Harry S Truman to Brazil, Sept. 1947.

Pres. Eurico Gaspar Dutra
A245

Mother and Child
A246

Engraved.

1947, Sept. 7 — *Perf. 11* — Wmk. 268

674	A245	20c green	20	20
675	A245	40c rose car	25	15
676	A245	1.20cr dp bl	50	22

The souvenir sheet containing Nos. 674–676 is listed as No. C73A. See also No. 679.

1947, Oct. 10 — Typo. — Unwmkd.

677	A246	40c brt ultra	25	20

Issued to mark Child Care Week, 1947.

Arms of Belo Horizonte
A247

Globe
A248

1947, Dec. 12 — Engraved — Wmk. 267

678	A247	1.20cr rose car	60	25

Issued to commemorate the 50th anniversary of the founding of the city of Belo Horizonte.

Dutra Type of 1947.

1948 — Engraved. — Wmk. 267

679	A245	20c green	3.00	3.00

1948, July 10 — Lithographed

680	A248	40c dl grn & pale lil	50	20

Issued to commemorate the International Exposition of Industry and Commerce, Petropolis, 1948.

Arms of Paranagua
A249

Child Reading Book
A250

1948, July 29

681	A249	5cr bis brn	3.00	1.00

Issued to commemorate the 300th anniversary of the founding of the city of Paranagua, July 29, 1648.

1948, Aug. 1

682	A250	40c green	30	30

National Education Campaign.

No. 682 was reproduced on a souvenir card with brown orange background and inscriptions. Size: 124x157mm.

Tiradentes
A251

Symbolical of Cancer Eradication
A252

1948, Nov. 12

683	A251	40c brn org	25	20

Issued to commemorate the 200th anniversary of the birth of Joaquim José da Silva Xavier (Tiradentes).

1948, Dec. 14

684	A252	40c claret	25	25

Anti-cancer publicity.

Adult Student
A253

1949, Jan. 3 — *Perf. 12x11* — Wmk. 267

685	A253	60c red vio & pink	25	15

Campaign for adult education.

"Battle of Guararapes," by Vitor Meireles—A254

1949, Feb. 15 — *Perf. 11½x12*

686	A254	60c lt bl	1.25	60

Issued to commemorate the 300th anniversary of the Second Battle of Guararapes.

Church of São Francisco de Paula
A255

Manuel de Nobrega
A256

Engraved.

1949, Mar. 8 — *Perf. 11x12* — Unwmkd.

687	A255	60c dk brn	30	25
a.		Souvenir sheet	40.00	40.00

Bicentenary of city of Ouro Fino, state of Minas Gerais.

No. 687a contains one imperf. stamp similar to No. 687, with dates in lower margin. Size: 70x89mm.

1949, Mar. 29 — *Imperf.*

688	A256	60c violet	25	25

Issued to commemorate the 400th anniversary of the founding of the City of Salvador.

Emblem of Brazilian Air Force and Plane—A257

1949, June 18

689 A257 60c bl vio 25 25

Issued to honor the Brazilian Air Force.

Star and Angel
A258

Lithographed.

1949 ***Perf. 11x12.*** **Wmk. 267**

690 A258 60c pink 25 25

Issued to publicize the first Ecclesiastical Congress, Salvador, Bahia.

"U. P. U." Encircling Globe
A259

1949, Oct. 22 Typo. ***Perf. 12x11***

691 A259 1.50cr blue 40 20

Issued to commemorate the 75th anniversary of the formation of the Universal Postal Union.

Ruy Barbosa
A260

Engraved.

1949, Dec. 14 ***Perf. 12*** **Unwmkd.**

692 A260 1.20cr rose car 75 40

Centenary of birth of Ruy Barbosa.

Joaquim Cardinal Arcoverde
A261

Perf. 11x12

1950, Feb. 27 Litho. Wmk. 267

693 A261 60c rose 30 25

Issued to commemorate the birth centenary of Joaquim Cardinal Arcoverde A. Cavalcanti.

Grapes and Factory
A262

1950, Mar. 15 ***Perf. 12x11***

694 A262 60c rose lake 20 20

Issued to commemorate the 75th anniversary of Italian immigration to the state of Rio Grande do Sul.

Virgin of the Globe
A263

Globe and Soccer Players
A264

1950, May 31 ***Perf. 11x12***

695 A263 60c blk & lt bl 30 20

Issued to commemorate the centenary of the establishment in Brazil of the Daughters of Charity of St. Vincent de Paul.

1950, June 24

696 A264 60c ultra, bl & gray 1.00 50

4th World Soccer Championship.

Symbolical of Brazilian Population Growth
A265

1950, July 10 Typo. ***Perf. 12x11***

697 A265 60c rose lake 30 20

Issued to publicize the 6th Brazilian census.

Dr. Oswaldo Cruz
A266

1950, Aug. 23 Litho. ***Perf. 11x12***

698 A266 60c org brn 30 25

Issued to publicize the 5th International Congress of Microbiology.

View of Blumenau and Itajai River
A267

1950, Sept. 9 ***Perf. 12x11*** **Wmk. 267**

699 A267 60c brt pink 25 20

Centenary of the founding of Blumenau.

Amazonas Theater, Manaus
A268

1950, Sept. 27

700 A268 60c lt brn red 20 20

Centenary of Amazonas Province.

Arms of Juiz de Fora
A269

1950, Oct. 24 ***Perf. 11x12***

701 A269 60c carmine 25 25

Centenary of the founding of Juiz de Fora.

Post Office at Recife
A270

1951, Jan. 10 Typo. ***Perf. 12x11***

702 A270 60c carmine 20 20
703 A270 1.20cr carmine 30 20

Issued to commemorate the opening of the new building of the Pernambuco Post Office.

Arms of Joinville
A271

Jean-Baptiste de La Salle
A272

1951, Mar. 9 ***Perf. 11x12***

704 A271 60c org brn 20 20

Centenary of the founding of Joinville.

1951, Apr. 30 **Lithographed**

705 A272 60c blue 30 25

Issued to commemorate the 300th anniversary of the birth of Jean-Baptiste de La Salle.

Heart and Flowers
A273

Sylvio Romero
A274

1951, May 13 **Engraved**

706 A273 60c dp plum 30 25

Issued to honor Mother's Day, May 14, 1951.

1951, Apr. 21 **Lithographed**

707 A274 60c dl vio brn 20 20

Issued to commemorate the centenary of the birth of Sylvio Romero (1851–1914), poet and author.

João Caetano, Stage and Masks
A275

1951, July 9 ***Perf. 12x11***

708 A275 60c lt gray bl 25 20

Issued to publicize the first Brazilian Theater Congress, Rio de Janeiro, July 9–13, 1951.

Orville A. Derby
A276

First Mass Celebrated in Brazil
A277

1951, July 23 ***Perf. 11x12***

709 A276 2cr slate 40 40

Issued to commemorate the centenary of the birth (in New York State) of Orville A. Derby, geologist.

1951, July 25

710 A277 60c dl brn & buff 30 25

Issued to publicize the 4th Inter-American Congress on Catholic Education, Rio de Janeiro, 1951.

Euclides Pinto Martins
A278

1951, Aug. 16 ***Perf. 12x11***

711 A278 3.80cr brn & cit 2.25 35

Issued to commemorate the 29th anniversary of the first flight from New York City to Rio de Janeiro.

Monastery of the Rock
A279

1951, Sept. 8

712 A279 60c dl brn & cr 25 25

Founding of Vitoria, 4th centenary.

Santos-Dumont and Model Plane Contest
A280

Dirigible and Eiffel Tower
A281

Lithographed.

1951, Oct. 19 *Perf. 11x12* **Wmk. 267**

713 A280 60c sal & dk brn 75 50

Engraved
Unwmkd.

714 A281 3.80cr dk pur 2.25 50

Issued to publicize the Week of the Wing and to commemorate the 50th anniversary of Santos-Dumont's flight around the Eiffel Tower.

In December 1951, Nos. 713 and 714 were privately overprinted: "Exposicao Filatelica Regional Distrito Federal 15-XII-1951 23-XII-1951." These were attached to souvenir sheets bearing engraved facsimiles of Nos. 38, 49 and 51, which were sold by Clube Filatelico do Brasil to mark its 20th anniversary. The overprinted stamps on the sheets were cancelled, but 530 "unused" sets were sold by the club.

Farmers and Ear of Wheat
A282

1951, Nov. 10 **Litho.** **Wmk. 267**

715 A282 60c dp grn & gray 40 30

Issued to publicize Festival of Grain at Bagé, 1951.

Map and Open Bible
A283

1951, Dec. 9 *Perf. 12x11*

716 A283 1.20cr brn org 75 40

Issued to publicize the Day of the Bible.

Queen Isabella A284 — Henrique Oswald A285

1952, Mar. 10 *Perf. 11x12*

717 A284 3.80cr lt bl 1.00 30

Issued to commemorate the 500th anniversary of the birth of Queen Isabella I of Spain.

1952, Apr. 22

718 A285 60c brown 30 25

Issued to commemorate the centenary of the birth of Henrique Oswald (1852–1931), composer.

Vicente Licinio Cardoso A286 — Map and Symbol of Labor A287

1952, May 2

719 A286 60c gray bl 30 25

4th Brazilian Homeopathic Congress.

1952, Apr. 30

720 A287 1.50cr brnsh pink 40 25

Issued to publicize the 5th International Labor Organization Conference for American Countries.

Gen. Polidoro da Fonseca A288 — Luiz de Albuquerque M. P. Caceres A289

Portraits: 5cr, Baron de Capanema. 10cr, Minister Eusebio de Queiros.

Engraved

1952, May 11 *Perf. 11* **Unwmkd.**

721	A288	2.40cr lt car	50	35
722	A288	5cr blue	3.50	45
723	A288	10cr dk bl grn	3.50	45

Centenary of telegraph in Brazil.

Perf. 11x12

1952, June 8 **Litho.** **Wmk. 267**

724 A289 1.20cr vio bl 30 20

Issued to commemorate the 200th anniversary of the founding of the city of Mato Grosso.

Symbolizing the Glory of Sports
A290

1952, July 21 *Perf. 12x11*

725 A290 1.20cr dp bl & bl 85 40

Fluminense Soccer Club, 50th anniversary.

José Antonio Saraiva A291 — Emperor Dom Pedro A292

1952, Aug. 16 *Perf. 11x12*

726 A291 60c lil rose 20 20

Issued to commemorate the centenary of the founding of Terezina, capital of Piaui State.

1952, Sept. 3 **Wmk. 267**

727 A292 60c lt bl & blk 25 20

Issued for Stamp Day and the 2nd Philatelic Exhibition of Sao Paulo.

Flag-encircled Globe
A293

1952, Oct. 24 *Perf. 13½*

728 A293 3.80cr blue 1.50 50

Issued to publicize United Nations Day.

View of Sao Paulo, Sun and Compasses
A294

1952, Nov. 8 **Litho.** *Perf. 12x11*

729 A294 60c dl bl, yel & gray grn 30 25

City Planning Day.

Father Diogo Antonio Feijo
A295

1952, Nov. 9 *Perf. 11x12*

730 A295 60c fawn 20 20

Rodolpho Bernardelli and His "Christ and the Adultress"
A297

1952, Dec. 18 *Perf. 12x11*

732 A297 60c gray bl 25 20

Issued to commemorate the centenary of the birth of Rodolpho Bernardelli, sculptor and painter.

Map of Western Hemisphere and View of Rio de Janeiro
A298

1952, Sept. 20

733 A298 3.80cr vio brn & lt grn 90 30

Issued to commemorate the 2nd Congress of American Industrial Medicine, Rio de Janeiro, 1952.

Arms and Head of Pioneer
A299

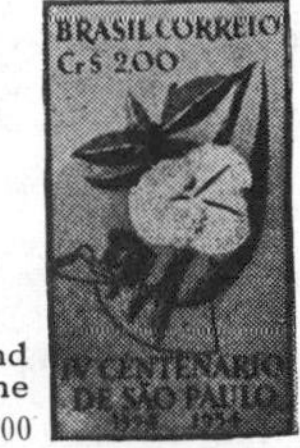

Coffee, Cotton and Sugar Cane
A300

Designs: 2.80cr, Jesuit monk planting tree. 3.80cr and 5.80cr, Spiral, symbolizing progress.

1953, Jan. 25 **Litho.** *Perf. 11*

734	A299	1.20cr ol brn & blk brn	75	50
735	A300	2cr ol grn & yel	2.50	50
736	A300	2.80cr red brn & dp org	1.75	30
737	A300	3.80cr dk brn & yel grn	1.50	30
738	A300	5.80cr int bl & yel grn	1.00	30
		Nos. 734-738 (5)	7.50	1.90

400th anniversary of Sao Paulo.

Ledger and Winged Cap
A301

1953, Feb. 22 *Perf. 12x11*

739 A301 1.20cr dl brn & fawn 40 20

6th Brazilian Accounting Congress.

Joao Ramalho
A302

Engraved

1953, Apr. 8 *Perf. 11½* **Wmk. 264**

740 A302 60c blue 25 20

Issued to commemorate the fourth centenary of the founding of the city of Santo Andre.

Aarao Reis and Plan of Belo Horizonte
A303

1953, May 6 **Photogravure**

741 A303 1.20cr red brn 35 25

Issued to commemorate the centenary of the birth of Aarao Leal de Carvalho Reis (1853–1936), civil engineer.

Training Ship Almirante Saldanha
A304

1953, May 16

742 A304 1.50cr vio bl 50 30

Issued to commemorate the fourth globe-circling voyage of the training ship Almirante Saldanha.

Joaquim Jose Rodrigues Torres, Viscount of Itaborai
A305

1953, July 5 Photogravure

743 A305 1.20cr violet 30 20

Centenary of the Bank of Brazil.

Lamp and Rio-Petropolis Highway
A306

1953, July 14

744 A306 1.20cr gray 30 20

Issued to publicize the tenth International Congress of Nursing, Petropolis, 1953.

Bay of Rio de Janeiro
A307

1953, July 15

745 A307 3.80cr dk bl grn 60 20

Issued to publicize the fourth World Congress of Baptist Youth, July 1953.

Arms of Jau and Map
A308

1953, Aug. 15 Engraved

746 A308 1.20cr purple 30 20

Centenary of the city of Jau.

Ministry of Health and Education Building, Rio
A309

Maria Quiteria de Jesus Medeiros
A310

1953, Aug. 1

747 A309 1.20cr dp grn 30 20

Issued to publicize the Day of the Stamp and the first Philatelic Exhibition of National Education.

1953, Aug. 21 Photogravure

748 A310 60c vio bl 25 20

Issued to commemorate the centenary of the death of Maria Quiteria de Jesus Medeiros (1792–1848), independence heroine.

Pres. Odria of Peru
A311

Duke of Caxias Leading his Troops
A312

1953, Aug. 25

749 A311 1.40cr rose brn 30 20

Issued to publicize the visit of Gen. Manuel A. Odria, President of Peru, Aug. 25, 1953.

Engraved (60c, 5.80cr); Photo.
Identical Frames.

1953, Aug. 25

Designs: 1.20cr, Caxias' tomb. 1.70cr, 5.80cr, Portrait of Caxias. 3.80cr, Arms of Caxias.

750	A312	60c dp grn	50	25
751	A312	1.20cr dp cl	75	25
752	A312	1.70cr sl grn	75	25
753	A312	3.80cr rose brn	1.25	25
754	A312	5.80cr gray vio	1.25	25
		Nos. 750-754 (5)	4.50	1.25

Issued to commemorate the 150th anniversary of the birth of Luis Alves de Lima e Silva, Duke of Caxias.

Quill Pen, Map and Tree
A313

Horacio Hora
A314

1953, Sept. 12 Photogravure

755 A313 60c ultra 25 20

5th National Congress of Journalism.

1953, Sept. 17 Litho. Wmk. 267

756 A314 60c org & dp plum 25 20

Issued to commemorate the centenary of the birth of Horacio Pinto de Hora (1853–1890), painter.

Pres. Somoza of Nicaragua
A315

Auguste de Saint-Hilaire
A316

1953, Sept. 24 Photo. Wmk. 264

757 A315 1.40cr dk vio brn 30 20

Issued to publicize the visit of Gen. Anastasio Somoza, president of Nicaragua.

1953, Sept. 30

758 A316 1.20cr dk brn car 40 25

Issued to commemorate the centenary of the death of Auguste de Saint-Hilaire, explorer and botanist.

José Carlos do Patrocinio
A317

Clock Tower, Crato
A318

1953, Oct. 9 Photogravure

759 A317 60c dk sl gray 25 20

Issued to commemorate the centenary of the birth of José Carlos do Patrocinio, (1853–1905), journalist and abolitionist.

1953, Oct. 17

760 A318 60c bl grn 25 20

Centenary of the city of Crato.

Joao Capistrano de Abreu
A319

Allegory: "Justice"
A320

1953, Oct. 23

761 A319 60c dl bl 30 30
762 A319 5cr purple 2.00 30

Issued to commemorate the centenary of the birth of Joao Capistrano de Abreu (1853–1927), historian.

1953, Nov. 17

763 A320 60c indigo 25 20
764 A320 1.20cr dp mag 25 20

Issued to commemorate the 50th anniversary of the Treaty of Petropolis.

Farm Worker in Wheat Field
A321

Teacher and Pupils
A322

1953, Nov. 29 Photo. ***Perf. 11½***

766 A321 60c dk grn 30 20

Issued to publicize the Third National Wheat Festival, Erechim, 1953.

1953, Dec. 14

767 A322 60c red 25 25

Issued to publicize the First National Conference of Primary School Teachers, Salvador, 1953.

Zacarias de Gois e Vasconsellos
A323

Alexandre de Gusmão
A324

Design: 5cr, Porters with Trays of Coffee Beans.

1953-54 Photogravure.

Inscribed: "Centenario do Parana."

768	A323	2cr org brn & blk ('54)	2.50	40
a.		Buff paper	90	40
769	A323	5cr dp org & blk	2.00	40

Centenary of the state of Paraná.

1954, Jan. 13

770 A324 1.20cr brn vio 30 20

Issued to commemorate the 200th anniversary of the death of Alexandre de Gusmao (1695–1753), statesman, diplomat and writer.

Symbolical of Sao Paulo's Growth
A325

Arms and View of Sao Paulo
A326

Designs: 2cr, Priest, settler and Indian. 2.80cr, José de Anchieta.

1954, Jan. 25 ***Perf. 11½x11***

771	A325	1.20cr dk vio brn	1.25	50
a.		Buff paper	1.75	1.00
772	A325	2cr lil rose	1.75	60
773	A325	2.80cr pur gray	1.75	1.00

Engraved.
Perf. 11x11½.

774	A326	3.80cr dl grn	2.00	50
a.		Buff paper	2.00	2.00
775	A326	5.80cr dl red	2.00	60
a.		Buff paper	5.00	75
		Nos. 771-775 (5)	8.75	3.20

400th anniversary of Sao Paulo.

J. Fernandes Vieira, A. Vidal de Negreiros, A. F. Camarao and H. Dias
A327

Perf. 11x11½

1954, Feb. 18 Photo. **Unwmkd.**

776 A327 1.20cr ultra 40 30

Issued to commemorate the 300th anniversary of the recovery of Pernambuco from the Dutch.

Sao Paulo and Minerva
A328

1954, Feb. 24

777 A328 1.50cr dp plum 30 25

Issued to publicize the 10th International Congress of Scientific Organizations, Sao Paulo, 1954.

Stylized Grapes, Jug and Map
A329

Monument of the Immigrants
A330

1954, Feb. 27 Photo. *Perf. 11½x11*

778 A329 40c dp cl 30 25

Grape Festival, Rio Grande do Sul.

1954, Feb. 28

779 A330 60c dp vio bl 30 25

Issued to commemorate the unveiling of the Monument to the Immigrants of Caxias do Sul.

First Brazilian Locomotive
A331

Perf. 11x11½

1954, Apr. 30 Unwmkd.

781 A331 40c carmine 50 25

Issued to commemorate the centenary of the first railroad engine built in Brazil.

Pres. Chamoun of Lebanon
A332

1954, May 12 Photo. *Perf. 11½x11*

782 A332 1.50cr maroon 35 30

Issued to commemorate the visit of Pres. Camille Chamonn of Lebanon, 1954.

Sao Jose College, Rio de Janeiro
A333

J. B. Champagnat Marcelin
A334

Apolonia Pinto
A335

1954, June 6 *Perf. 11x11½, 11½x11*

783 A333 60c purple 30 20
784 A334 1.20cr vio bl 35 25

Issued to commemorate the 50th anniversary of the founding of the Marist Brothers in Brazil.

1954, June 21 Photogravure

785 A335 1.20cr brt grn 15 12

Issued to commemorate the centenary of the birth of Apolonia Pinto (1854–1937), actress.

Adm. Margues Tamandare
A336

Portraits: 2c, 5c, 10c, Admiral Margues Tamandare. 20c, 30c, 40c, Oswaldo Cruz. 50c, 60c, 90c, Joaquim Murtinho. 1cr, 1.50cr, 2cr, Duke of Caxias. 5cr, 10cr, Ruy Barbosa. 20cr, 50cr, José Bonifacio.

1954–60 *Perf. 11x11½* Wmk. 267

786	A336	2c vio bl	15	12
787	A336	5c org red	10	5
788	A336	10c brt grn	15	5
789	A336	20c magenta	15	5
790	A336	30c dk gray grn	25	5
791	A336	40c rose red	50	5
792	A336	50c violet	30	5
793	A336	60c gray grn	15	5
794	A336	90c org ('55)	50	15
795	A336	1cr brown	15	5
796	A336	1.50cr blue	10	5
a.		Wmk. 264	20.00	10.00
797	A336	2cr dk bl grn ('56)	60	5
798	A336	5cr rose lil ('56)	50	10
799	A336	10cr lt grn ('60)	1.25	10
800	A336	20cr crim rose ('59)	1.25	10
801	A336	50cr ultra ('59)	7.50	20
		Nos. 786-801 (16)	13.60	1.27

See also Nos. 890, 930–933.

Boy Scout Waving Flag (Statue)
A337

Baltasar Fernandes, Explorer
A338

Perf. 11½x11

1954, Aug. 2 Unwmkd.

802 A337 1.20cr vio bl 60 30

Issued to publicize the International Boy Scout Encampment, Sao Paulo, 1954.

1954, Aug. 15

803 A338 60c dk red 30 25

300th anniversary of city of Sorocaba.

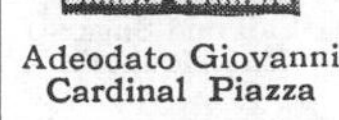

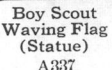

Adeodato Giovanni Cardinal Piazza
A339

Our Lady of Aparecida, Map of Brazil
A340

1954, Sept. 2

804 A339 4.20cr red org 75 35

Issued to commemorate the visit of Adeodato Cardinal Piazza, papal legate to Brazil.

1954

Design: 1.20cr, Virgin standing on globe.

805 A340 60c claret 75 35
806 A340 1.20cr vio bl 1.00 30

No. 805 was issued to commemorate the 1st Congress of Brazil's Patron Saint (Our Lady of Aparecida); No. 806, the centenary of the proclamation of the dogma of the Immaculate Conception. Both stamps also commemorate the Marian Year.

Issue dates: 60c, Sept. 6; 1.20cr, Sept. 8.

Benjamin Constant and Hand Reading Braille
A341

1954, Sept. 27 Photo. Unwmkd.

807 A341 60c dk grn 30 20

Issued to commemorate the centenary of the founding of the Benjamin Constant Institute.

River Battle of Riachuelo
A342

Admiral F. M. Barroso
A343

Dr. Christian F. S. Hahnemann
A344

1954, Oct. 6 *Perf. 11x11½, 11½x11*

808 A342 40c redsh brn 50 25
809 A343 60c purple 40 25

Issued to commemorate the 150th anniversary of the birth of Admiral Francisco Manoel Barroso da Silva (1804–82).

1954, Oct. 8 *Perf. 11½x11*

810 A344 2.70cr dk grn 40 25

Issued to publicize the first World Congress of Homeopathic Medicine.

Nizia Floresta
A345

Ears of Wheat
A346

1954, Oct. 12

811 A345 60c lil rose 30 25

Issued to commemorate the reburial of the remains of Nizia Floresta (Dio Nizia Pinto Lisboa), writer and educator.

1954, Oct. 22

812 A346 60c ol grn 40 25

4th National Wheat Festival, Carazinho.

Basketball Player and Ball-Globe
A347

Allegory of the Spring Games
A348

1954, Oct. 23 Photogravure

813 A347 1.40cr org red 50 30

Issued to publicize the second World Basketball Championship Matches, 1954.

Perf. 11½x11

1954, Nov. 6 Wmk. 267

814 A348 60c red brn 40 25

Issued to publicize the 6th Spring Games.

San Francisco Hydroelectric Plant
A349

1955, Jan. 15 *Perf. 11x11½*

815 A349 60c brn org 20 15

Issued to publicize the inauguration of the San Francisco Hydroelectric Plant.

Itutinga Hydroelectric Plant
A350

1955, Feb. 3

816 A350 40c blue 20 15

Issued to publicize the inauguration of the Itutinga Hydroelectric Plant at Lavras.

Rotary Emblem and Bay of Rio de Janeiro
A351

1955, Feb. 23 ***Perf. 12x11½***

817	A351	2.70cr sl gray & blk	75	25

Rotary International, 50th anniversary.

Fausto Cardoso Palace
A352

1955, Mar. 17 ***Perf. 11x11½***

818	A352	40c hn brn	25	25

Centenary of Aracaju.

Aviation Symbols
A353

1955, Mar. 13 Photo. ***Perf. 11½***

819	A353	60c dk gray grn	20	15

Issued to publicize the third National Aviation Congress at Sao Paulo, Mar. 6–13.

Arms of Botucatu
A354

1955, Apr. 14

820	A354	60c org brn	25	20
821	A354	1.20cr brt grn	35	20

Centenary of Botucatu.

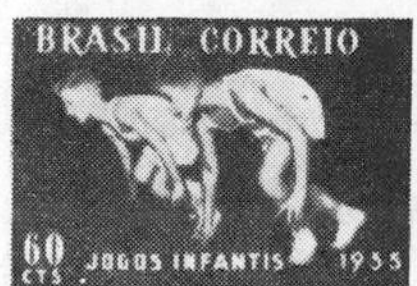

Young Racers at Starting Line
A355

Perf. 11½

1955, Apr. 30 Photo. Unwmkd.

823	A355	60c org brn	35	20

5th Children's Games.

Marshal Hermes da Fonseca
A356

Congress Altar, Sail and Sugar-loaf Mountain
A357

1955, May 12 **Wmk. 267**

824	A356	60c purple	25	20

Issued to commemorate the centenary of the birth of Marshal Hermes da Fonseca.

Engr.; Photo. (2.70cr)

1955, July 17 ***Perf. 11½*** **Unwmkd.**

Designs: 2.70cr, St. Pascoal. 4.20cr, Aloisi Benedetto Cardinal Masella.

825	A357	1.40cr green	25	25
826	A357	2.70cr dp cl	50	40
827	A357	4.20cr blue	60	25

Issued to commemorate the 36th World Eucharistic Congress in Rio de Janeiro.

Girl Gymnasts
A358

Granite Paper

1955, Nov. 12 **Engraved**

828	A358	60c rose lil	35	20

Issued to publicize the 7th Spring Games.

José B. Monteiro Lobato
A359

1955, Dec. 8 **Granite Paper**

829	A359	40c dk grn	20	15

Issued in honor of José B. Monteiro Lobato, author.

Adolfo Lutz
A360

Lt. Col. Vilagran Cabrita
A361

1955, Dec. 18 **Granite Paper**

830	A360	60c dk grn	20	15

Issued to commemorate the centenary of the birth of Adolfo Lutz, public health pioneer.

1955, Dec. 22 Photo. Wmk. 267

831	A361	60c vio bl	20	15

Issued to commemorate the centenary of the First Battalion of Engineers.

Salto Grande Hydroelectric Dam
A362

Granite Paper.

1956, Jan. 15 ***Perf. 11½*** **Unwmkd.**

832	A362	60c brick red	20	15

Arms of Mococa
A363

"G" and Globe
A364

Photogravure

1956, Apr. 17 ***Perf. 11½*** **Wmk. 256**

833	A363	60c brick red	20	15

Centenary of Mococa, Sao Paulo.

Granite Paper

1956, Apr. 14 **Unwmkd.**

834	A364	1.20cr vio bl	30	20

18th International Geographic Congress, Rio de Janeiro, August 1956.

Girls' Foot Race
A365

1956, Apr. 28 **Photogravure**

Granite Paper.

835	A365	2.50cr brt bl	50	20

6th Children's Games.

Plane over Map of Brazil
A366

1956, June 12 ***Perf. 11½*** **Wmk. 267**

836	A366	3.30cr brt vio bl	1.00	25

Issued to commemorate the 25th anniversary of the National Airmail Service.

Fireman Rescuing Child
A367

1956, July 2 **Wmk. 264**

837	A367	2.50cr crimson	60	25
a.		Buff paper	2.25	1.00

Centenary of the Fire Brigade.

Map of Brazil and Open Book
A368

1956, Sept. 8 **Wmk. 267**

838	A368	2.50cr brt vio bl	40	20

Issued to commemorate the 50th anniversary of the arrival of the Marist Brothers in Northern Brazil.

Church and Monument, Franca
A369

1956, Sept. 7 **Engraved**

839	A369	2.50cr dk bl	40	20

Centenary of city of Franca, Sao Paulo.

Woman Hurdler
A370

1956, Sept. 22 Photo. Unwmkd.

Granite Paper.

840	A370	2.50cr dk car	1.00	25

Issued to publicize the 8th Spring Games.

Forest and Map of Brazil
A371

1956, Sept. 30 ***Perf. 11½*** **Wmk. 267**

841	A371	2.50cr dk grn	35	20

Issued to publicize education in forestry.

Baron da Bocaina
A372

1956, Oct. 8 **Engraved** **Wmk. 268**

842	A372	2.50cr redsh brn	35	20

Issued to commemorate the centenary of the birth of Baron da Bocaina, who introduced the special delivery mail system to Brazil.

Marbleized Paper

Paper with a distinct wavy-line or marbleized watermark (which Brazilians call *marmorizado* paper) has been found on many stamps of Brazil, 1956–68, including Nos. 843–845, 847, 851–854, 858–858A, 864, 878, 880, 882, 884, 886–887, 896, 909, 918, 920–921, 925–928, 936–939, 949, 955–958, 960, 962–964, 978–979, 983, 985–987, 997–998, 1002–1003, 1005, 1009–1012, 1017, 1024, 1026, 1055, 1075, 1078, 1082, C82, C82a, C83–C87, C96, C99, C109.

Quantities are much less than those of stamps on regular paper.

Panama Stamp Showing Pres. Juscelino Kubitschek
A373

1956, Oct. 12 Photo. Wmk. 267

843 A373 3.30cr grn & blk 1.00 25

Issued on America Day, Oct. 12, to commemorate the meeting of the Presidents and the Pan-American Conference at Panama City, July 21-22.

Symbolical of Steel Production
A374

Photogravure.

1957, Jan. 31 *Perf. 11½* Wmk. 267

844 A374 2.50cr chocolate 40 15

Issued to commemorate the second expansion of the National Steel Company at Volta Redonda.

Joaquim E. Gomes da Silva
A375

Granite Paper.

1957, Mar. 1 Photo. Unwmkd.

845 A375 2.50cr dk bl grn 35 15

Issued to commemorate the centenary of the birth (in 1856) of Joaquim E. Gomes da Silva.

Allan Kardec
A376

Engraved.

1957, Apr. 18 *Perf. 11½* Wmk. 268

846 A376 2.50cr dk brn 35 15

Issued in honor of Allan Kardec, pen name of Leon Hippolyto Denizard Rivail, and for the centenary of the publication of his "Codification of Spiritism."

Boy Gymnast
A377

Granite Paper.

1957, Apr. 27 Photo. Unwmkd.

847 A377 2.50cr lake 75 25

7th Children's Games.

Pres. Craveiro Lopes
A378

Stamp of 1932
A379

1957, June 7 Engraved Wmk. 267

848 A378 6.50cr blue 75 25

Issued to commemorate the visit of Gen. Francisco Higino Craveiro Lopes, President of Portugal.

1957, July 9 Photogravure

849 A379 2.50cr rose 30 15

Issued to commemorate the 25th anniversary of the movement for a constitution.

St. Antonio Monastery, Pernambuco
A380

1957, Aug. 24 Engraved Wmk. 267

850 A380 2.50cr dp mag 30 15

Issued to commemorate the 300th anniversary of the emancipation of the Franciscan province of St. Antonio in Pernambuco State.

Volleyball
A381

Basketball
A382

1957, Sept. 28 Photo. *Perf. 11½*

851 A381 2.50cr dl org red 75 25

Issued for the 9th Spring Games.

1957, Oct. 12

852 A382 3.30cr org & brt grn 75 25

Issued to commemorate the second Women's International Basketball Championship, Rio de Janeiro.

Count of Pinhal and Sao Carlos
A383

1957, Nov. 4 *Perf. 11½* Wmk. 267

853 A383 2.50cr rose 60 25

Issued to commemorate the centenary of the city of Sao Carlos and to honor the Count of Pinhal, its founder.

Auguste Comte
A384

1957, Nov. 15

854 A384 2.50cr dk red brn 50 25

Issued to commemorate the centenary of the death of Auguste Comte, French mathematician and philosopher.

Radio Station
A385

1957, Dec. 10 Wmk. 268

855 A385 2.50cr dk grn 35 15

Opening of Sarapui Central Radio Station.

Admiral Tamandare and Warship
A386

Design: 3.30cr, Aircraft carrier.

1957–58 Photogravure

856 A386 2.50cr lt bl 45 20

Engraved

857 A386 3.30cr grn ('58) 50 20

Issued to commemorate the 150th anniversary of the birth of Admiral Joaquim Marques de Tamandare, founder of the Brazilian navy.

Coffee Plant and Symbolic "R"
A387

Photogravure.

1957–58 *Perf. 11½* Wmk. 267

858 A387 2.50cr magenta 85 35

Unwmkd.

Granite Paper.

858A A387 2.50cr mag ('58) 75 35

Issued to commemorate the centenary (in 1956) of the city of Ribeirao Preto in Sao Paulo state.

Dom John VI—A388

1958, Jan. 28 Engraved Wmk. 268

859 A388 2.50cr magenta 50 25

Issued to commemorate the 150th anniversary of the opening of the ports of Brazil to foreign trade.

Bugler
A389

1958, Mar. 18 Wmk. 267

860 A389 2.50cr red 60 25

Issued to commemorate the 150th anniversary of the Brazilian Marine Corps.

Station at Rio and Locomotive of 1858
A390

Court House
A391

Photogravure.

1958, Mar. 29 *Perf. 11½* Wmk. 267

861 A390 2.50cr red brn 50 25

Issued to commemorate the centenary of the Central Railroad of Brazil.

1958, Apr. 1 Engraved Wmk. 256

862 A391 2.50cr green 35 15

Issued to commemorate the 150th anniversary of the Military Superior Court.

Emblem and Brazilian Pavilion
A392

1958, Apr. 17 Wmk. 267

863 A392 2.50cr dk bl 30 25

World's Fair, Brussels, Apr. 17–Oct. 19.

High Jump
A393

1958, Apr. 20 Photo. Unwmkd.
Granite Paper

864 A393 2.50cr crim rose 45 15

8th Children's Games.

Marshal Mariano da Silva Rondon
A394

1958, Apr. 19 Engraved Wmk. 267

865 A394 2.50cr magenta 35 15

Issued to honor Marshal Mariano da Silva Rondon and the "Day of the Indian."

Hydroelectric Station
A395

1958, Apr. 28 *Perf. 11½* Wmk. 267

866 A395 2.50cr magenta 25 15

Opening of Sao Paulo State power plant.

National Printing Plant
A396

1958, May 22 Photogravure

867 A396 2.50cr redsh brn 25 15

Issued to commemorate the 150th anniversary of the founding of the National Printing Plant.

Marshal Osorio
A397

1958, May 24

868 A397 2.50cr brt vio 25 15

Issued to commemorate the 150th anniversary of the birth of Marshal Manoel Luiz Osorio.

Pres. Ramon Villeda Morales
A398

Fountain
A399

Engraved.
1958, June 7 *Perf. 11½* Wmk. 267

869 A398 6.50cr dk grn 2.00 75
a. Wmk. 268 6.00 2.00

Issued to commemorate the visit of Pres. Ramon Villeda Morales of Honduras.

1958, June 13

870 A399 2.50cr dk grn 35 15

Issued to commemorate the 150th anniversary of the Botanical Garden, Rio de Janeiro.

Symbols of Agriculture
A400

Prophet Joel
A401

1958, June 18 Photogravure

871 A400 2.50cr rose car 25 15

Issued to commemorate the 50th anniversary of Japanese immigration to Brazil.

1958, June 21 Engraved

872 A401 2.50cr dk bl 30 15

Issued to commemorate the bicentenary of the Cathedral of Bom Jesus at Matosinhos.

Stylized Globe
A402

1958, July 10 Photogravure

873 A402 2.50cr dk brn 25 15

Issued to publicize the International Investment Conference, Belo Horizonte.

Julio Bueno Brandao
A403

1958, Aug. 1 *Perf. 11½* Wmk. 268

874 A403 2.50cr red brn 25 15

Issued to commemorate the centenary of the birth of Julio Bueno Brandao, President of Minas Gerais.

Palacio Tiradentes
(House of Congress)
A404

1958, July 24 Engraved

875 A404 2.50cr sepia 25 15

Issued to honor the 47th Interparliamentary Conference, Rio de Janeiro, July 24–Aug. 1.

Presidential Palace, Brasilia
A405

1958, Aug. 8 Photo. Wmk. 267

876 A405 2.50cr ultra 35 15

Issued to publicize the construction of Brazil's new capital, Brasilia.

Freighters
A406

1958, Aug. 22

877 A406 2.50cr blue 45 15

Issued in honor of the Brazilian merchant marine.

Joaquim Caetano da Silva
A407

1958, Sept. 2 Unwmkd.
Granite Paper

878 A407 2.50cr redsh brn 35 15

Issued in honor of Joaquim Caetano da Silva, scientist and historian.

Giovanni Gronchi
A408

Archers
A409

1958, Sept. 4 Engraved Wmk. 268

879 A408 7cr dk bl 75 15

Issued to commemorate the visit of Italy's President Giovanni Gronchi to Brazil.

Perf. 11½
1958, Sept. 21 Photo. Unwmkd.
Granite Paper

880 A409 2.50cr red org 60 20

Issued to publicize the 10th Spring Games.

Elderly Couple
A410

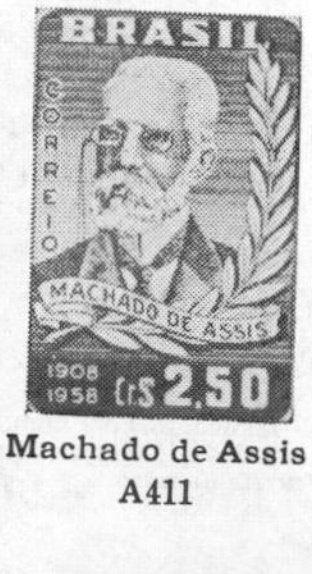

Machado de Assis
A411

1958, Sept. 27 Wmk. 267

881 A410 2.50cr magenta 40 15

Issued to publicize the Day of the Old People, Sept. 27.

1958, Sept. 28 Unwmkd.

882 A411 2.50cr red brn 35 15

Issued to commemorate the 50th anniversary of the death of Joaquim Maria Machado de Assis, writer.

Pres. Vargas and Oil Derrick
A412

1958, Oct. 6 Wmk. 268

883 A412 2.50cr blue 25 15

Issued to commemorate the 5th anniversary of Pres. Getulio D. Vargas' oil law.

Globe
A413

Gen. Lauro Sodré
A414

Perf. 11½
1958, Nov. 14 Photo. Wmk. 267

884 A413 2.50cr blue 50 15

Issued to commemorate the seventh Inter-American Congress of Municipalities.

1958, Nov. 15 Engraved

885 A414 3.30cr green 15 15

Issued to commemorate the centenary of the birth of Gen. Lauro Sodré.

U. N. Emblem
A415

Soccer Player
A416

1958, Dec. 26 Photo. *Perf. 11½*

886 A415 2.50cr brt bl 35 15

Issued to commemorate the tenth anniversary of the signing of the Universal Declaration of Human Rights.

1959, Jan. 20

887 A416 3.30cr emer & red brn 50 20

World Soccer Championships of 1958.

Railroad Track and Map
A417

Pres. Sukarno of Indonesia
A418

1959, Apr. *Perf. 11½* Wmk. 267

888 A417 2.50cr dp org 30 20

Issued to commemorate the centenary of the linking of Patos and Campina Grande by railroad.

1959, May 20

889 A418 2.50cr blue 25 15

Visit of President Sukarno of Indonesia.

Dom John VI
A419

Boy Polo Players
A420

Perf. 10½x11½

1959, June 12 Wmk. 267

890 A419 2.50cr crimson 30 10

1959, June 13 *Perf. 11½*

891 A420 2.50cr org brn 35 15

9th Children's Games.

Loading Freighter
A421

Organ and Emblem
A422

1959, July 10

892 A421 2.50cr dk grn 35 15

Issued to honor the merchant marine.

1959, July 16 Photogravure

893 A422 3.30cr magenta 20 15

Issued to commemorate the bicentenary of the Carmelite Order in Brazil.

Joachim Silverio de Souza
A423

Symbolic Road
A424

1959, July 20 *Perf. 11½*

894 A423 2.50cr red brn 20 15

Issued to commemorate the birth centenary of Joachim Silverio de Souza, first bishop of Diamantina, Minas Gerais.

1959, Sept. 27 Wmk. 267

895 A424 3.30cr bl grn & ultra 25 15

11th International Roadbuilding Congress.

Girl Athlete
A425

1959, Oct. 4

896 A425 2.50cr lil rose 40 20

11th Spring Games.

Map of Parana—A426

1959, Sept. 27

897 A426 2.50cr dk grn 25 15

Issued to commemorate the 25th anniversary of the founding of Londrina, Parana.

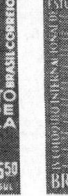

Globe and Snipes
A427

Lusignan Cross
A428

1959, Oct. 22 *Perf. 11½*

898 A427 6.50cr dl grn 15 15

Issued to commemorate the World Championship of Snipe Class Sailboats, Porto Alegre, won by Brazilian yachtsmen.

1959, Oct. 24 Engraved

899 A428 6.50cr dl bl 15 15

Issued to commemorate the 4th International Conference on Brazilian-Portuguese Studies, Univeristy of Bahia, Aug. 10–20.

Factory Entrance and Order of Southern Cross
A429

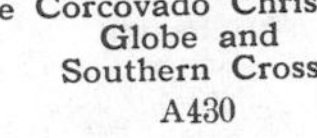

Corcovado Christ, Globe and Southern Cross
A430

1959, Nov. 19 Photogravure

900 A429 3.30cr org red 15 15

Issued to commemorate the 50th anniversary of the Pres. Vargas Gunpowder Factory.

1959, Nov. 26 *Perf. 11½*

901 A430 2.50cr blue 40 15

Universal Thanksgiving Day.

Burning Bush—A431

1959, Dec. 24 Wmk. 267

902 A431 3.30cr lt grn 15 15

Centenary of Presbyterian work in Brazil.

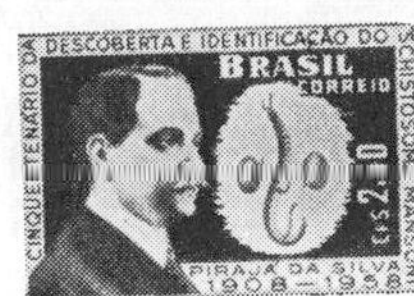

Piraja da Silva and Schistosoma Mansoni
A432

1959, Dec. 28

903 A432 2.50cr rose vio 35 15

Issued to commemorate the 25th anniversary of the discovery and identification of schistosoma mansoni, a parasite of the fluke family, by Dr. Piraja da Silva.

Luiz de Matos—A433

1960, Jan. 3 Photogravure

904 A433 3.30cr red brn 15 15

Birth centenary of Luiz de Matos.

L. L. Zamenhof
A434

Adél Pinto
A435

Perf. 11½

1960, Mar. 10 Wmk. 267

905 A434 6.50cr emerald 15 15

Issued to commemorate the birth centenary of Lazarus Ludwig Zamenhof (1859–1917), Polish oculist who invented Esperanto in 1887.

1960, Mar. 19 Engr. Wmk. 268

906 A435 11.50cr rose red 15 15

Issued to commemorate the centenary of the birth of Adél Pinto, civil engineer and railroad expert.

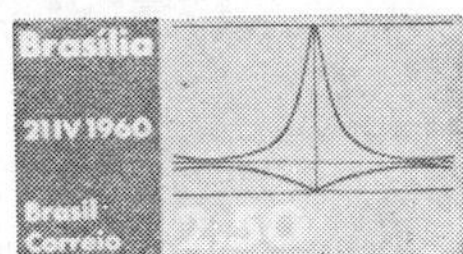

Presidential Palace, Colonnade
A436

Design: 27cr, Plan of Brasilia (like No. C98).

Perf. 11x11½

1960 Photogravure Wmk. 267

907 A436 2.50cr brt grn 40 15

908 A436 27cr salmon 1.00 1.00

Nos. 907-908, C95-C98 (6) 3.20 1.75

No. 907 issued Apr. 21 to commemorate the inauguration of Brazil's new capital, Brasilia, Apr. 21, 1960.

No. 908 issued Sept. 12 to commemorate the birthday of Pres. Juscelino Kubitschek. It measures 105x46½mm., carrying at center a 27cr in design of No. C98, flanked by the chief design features of Nos. 907, C95–C97, with Kubitschek signature below. Issued in sheets of 4 with wide horizontal gutter.

Grain, Coffee, Cotton and Cacao
A437

Paulo de Frontin
A438

Perf. 11½x11

1960, July 28 Wmk. 267

909 A437 2.50cr brown 30 15

Centenary of Ministry of Agriculture.

1960, Oct. 12 Wmk. 268

910 A438 2.50cr org red 20 15

Issued to commemorate the centenary of the birth of Paulo de Frontin, engineer.

Girl Athlete Holding Torch
A439

1960, Oct. 18 *Perf. 11½x11*

911 A439 2.50cr bl grn 30 15

12th Spring Games.

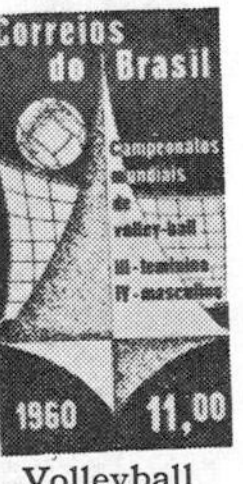

Volleyball and Net
A440

Locomotive Wheels
A441

Perf. 11½x11

1960, Nov. 12 Wmk. 268

912 A440 11cr blue 30 15

International Volleyball Championships.

1960, Oct. 15 *Perf. 11½x11*

913 A441 2.50cr ultra 20 10

10th Pan-American Railroad Congress.

Symbols of Flight
A442

1960, Dec. 16 Photo. *Perf. 11½*

914 A442 2.50cr brn & yel 20 15

Issued to commemorate the International Fair of Industry and Commerce, Rio de Janeiro.

Emperor Haile Selassie I
A443

1961, Jan. 31 *Perf. 11½x11*

915 A443 2.50cr dk brn 20 15

Issued to commemorate the visit of Emperor Haile Selassie I of Ethiopia to Brazil, Dec. 1960.

Map of Brazil, Open Book and Sacred Heart Emblem
A444

Perf. 11x11½

1961, Mar. 13 Wmk. 268

916 A444 2.50cr blue 30 15

The 50th anniversary of the operation in Brazil of the Order of the Blessed Heart of Mary.

Map of Guanabara
A445

1961, March 27 Wmk. 267

917 A445 7.50cr org brn 25 15

Issued to commemorate the promulgation of the constitution of the state of Guanabara.

Arms of Agulhas Negras
A446

Brazil and Senegal Linked on Map
A447

Design: 3.30cr, Dress helmet and sword.

Perf. 11½x11

1961, Apr. 23 Wmk. 267

918 A446 2.50cr green 35 15
919 A446 3.30cr rose car 15 15

Issued to commemorate the sesquicentennial of the Agulhas Negras Military Academy.

1961, Apr. 28 Photogravure

920 A447 27cr ultra 50 20

Issued to commemorate the visit of Afonso Arinos, Brazilian foreign minister, to Senegal to attend its independence ceremonies.

View of Ouro Preto, 1711
A448

1961, June 6 *Perf. 11x11½*

921 A448 1cr orange 20 20

250th anniversary of Ouro Preto.

War Arsenal
A449

1961, June 20 Wmk. 256

924 A449 5cr dk red brn 40 15

Issued to commemorate the 150th anniversary of the War Arsenal, Rio de Janeiro.

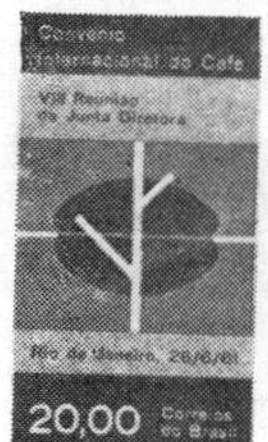

Coffee Bean and Branch
A450

Rabindranath Tagore
A451

Perf. 11½x11

1961, June 26 Wmk. 267

925 A450 20cr redsh brn 1.50 25

Issued to commemorate the 8th Directorial Committee meeting of the International Coffee Convention, Rio de Janeiro, June 26, 1961.

1961, July 28 Photo. Wmk. 267

926 A451 10cr rose car 30 15

Issued to commemorate the centenary of the birth of Rabindranath Tagore, Indian poet.

Stamp of 1861 and Map of English Channel
A452

Design: 20cr, 430r stamp of 1861 and map of Netherlands.

1961, Aug. 1 *Perf. 11x11½*

927 A452 10cr rose 75 20
928 A452 20cr sal pink 2.00 30

Centenary of 1861 stamp issue.

Portrait Type of 1954–60
Designs as Before.

1961 *Perf. 11x11½* Wmk. 268

930 A336 1cr brown 1.25 65
931 A336 2cr dk bl grn 1.75 65
932 A336 5cr red lil 4.50 40
933 A336 10cr emerald 9.00 40

The 1cr, 5cr and 10cr have patterned background.

Sun, Clouds, Rain and Weather Symbols
A453

Dedo de Deus Peak
A454

1962, March 23 *Perf. 11½x11*

936 A453 10cr red brn 1.25 30

World Meteorological Day, Mar. 23.

1962, Apr. 14 Photo. Wmk. 267

937 A454 8cr emerald 25 25

Issued to commemorate the 50th anniversary of the climbing of Dedo de Deus (Finger of God) peak.

Dr. Gaspar Vianna and Leishmania Protozoa
A455

1962, Apr. 24 *Perf. 11x11½*

938 A455 8cr blue 25 15

Issued to commemorate the 50th anniversary of the discovery by Gaspar Oliveiro Vianna (1885–1914) of a cure for leishmaniasis.

Henrique Dias—A456

1962, June 18 Wmk. 267

939 A456 10cr dk vio brn 50 15

Issued to commemorate the 300th anniversary of the death of Henrique Dias, Negro military leader who fought against the Dutch and Spaniards.

Millimeter Gauge
A457

Sailboats, Snipe Class
A458

1962, June 26 *Perf. 11½x11*

940 A457 100cr car rose 60 20

Issued to commemorate the centenary of the introduction of the metric system in Brazil.

1962, July 21 Photo. Wmk. 267

941 A458 8cr Prus grn 30 15

Issued to commemorate the 13th Brazilian championships for Snipe Class sailing.

Julio Mesquita—A459

1962, Aug. 18 *Perf. 11x11½*

942 A459 8cr dl brn 30 15

Issued to commemorate the centenary of the birth of Julio Mesquita, journalist and founder of Sao Paulo.

Empress Leopoldina
A460

1962, Sept. 7 *Perf. 11½x11*

943 A460 8cr rose cl 25 15

140th anniversary of independence.

Buildings, Brasilia—A461

Perf. 11x11½

1962, Oct. 24 Wmk. 267

944 A461 10cr orange 60 15

Issued to commemorate the 51st Interparliamentary Conference, Brasilia.

Pouring Ladle
A462

1962, Oct. 26 *Perf. 11½x11*

945 A462 8cr orange 25 15

Issued to mark the inauguration of the Usiminas State Iron and Steel Foundry at Belo Horizonte, Minas Gerais.

UPAE Emblem
A463

1962, Nov. 19 *Perf. 11x11½*

946 A463 8cr brt mag 20 15

Issued to commemorate the 50th anniversary of the founding of the Postal Union of the Americas and Spain, UPAE.

Chimney and Cogwheel Forming "10"
A464

1962, Nov. 26 ***Perf. 11½x11***

947 A464 10cr lt bl grn 40 15

Issued to commemorate the 10th anniversary of the National Economic and Development Bank.

Quintino Bocaiuva
A465

Soccer Player and Globe
A466

Perf. 11½x11

1962, Dec. 27 Photo. **Wmk. 267**

948 A465 8cr brn org 20 15

Issued to commemorate the 50th anniversary of the death of Quintino Bocaiuva, journalist.

1963, Jan. 14

949 A466 10cr bl grn 12 7

World Soccer Championship of 1962.

Carrier Pigeon
A467

Lithographed

1963, Jan. ***Perf. 14*** **Unwmkd.**

950 A467 8cr yel, dk bl, red & grn 25 15

Souvenir Sheet

Imperf.

951 A467 100cr yel, dk bl, red & grn 1.40 *2.50*

Issued to commemorate 300 years of Brazilian postal service. No. 951 contains one stamp. Black inscription and ultramarine border. Size: 145x57mm.

Issue dates: 8cr, Jan. 25; 100cr, Jan. 31.

Severino Neiva
A468

Perf. 10½x11½

1963, Jan. 31 Photo. **Wmk. 267**

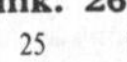

952 A468 8cr brt vio 25 10

Radar Tracking Station and Rockets
A469

"Cross of Unity"
A470

Perf. 11½x11

1963, Mar. 15 **Wmk. 268**

953 A469 21cr lt ultra 30 15

Issued to publicize the International Aeronautics and Space Exhibition, Sao Paulo.

1963 ***Perf. 11½x11*** **Wmk. 267**

954 A470 8cr red lil 20 15

Issued to commemorate Vatican II, the 21st Ecumenical Council of the Roman Catholic Church.

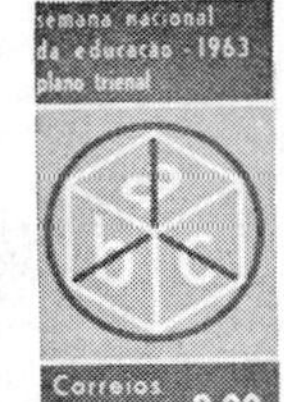

"ABC" in Geometric Form
A471

Basketball Player
A472

1963, Apr. 22 Photo. **Wmk. 267**

955 A471 8cr brt bl & lt bl 20 15

Issued for Education Week, Apr. 22–27, in connection with the 3-year alphabetization program.

1963, May 15

956 A472 8cr dp lil rose 35 15

Issued to commemorate the 4th International Basketball Championships, Rio de Janeiro, May 10–25, 1963.

Games Emblem
A473

"OEA" and Map of the Americas
A474

1963, May 22 ***Perf. 11½x11***

957 A473 10cr car rose 60 15

4th Pan American Games, Sao Paulo.

1963, June 6

958 A474 10cr org & dp org 60 15

Issued to commemorate the 15th anniversary of the charter of the Organization of American States.

José Bonifacio de Andrada
A475

1963, June 13

959 A475 8cr dk brn 20 15

Issued to commemorate the bicentenary of the birth of José Bonifacio de Andrada de Silva, statesman.

Wheat
A476

Perf. 11x11½

1963, June 19 Photo. **Wmk. 267**

960 A476 10cr blue 50 15

Issued for the "Freedom from Hunger" campaign of the U.N. Food and Agriculture Organization.

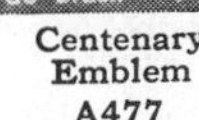

Centenary Emblem
A477

João Caetano
A478

1963, Aug. 19 ***Perf. 11½x11***

961 A477 8cr yel org & red 30 15

Centenary of International Red Cross.

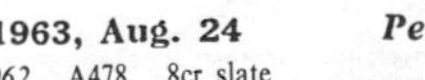

1963, Aug. 24 ***Perf. 11½x11***

962 A478 8cr slate 30 15

Death centenary of João Caetano, actor.

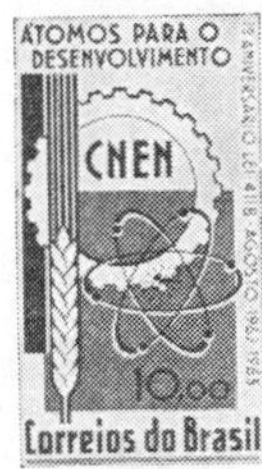
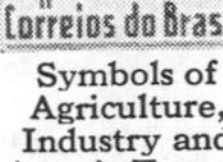

Symbols of Agriculture, Industry and Atomic Energy
A479

Hammer Thrower
A480

1963, Aug. 28

963 A479 10cr car rose 40 15

Issued to commemorate the first anniversary of the Atomic Development Law.

1963, Sept. 13

964 A480 10cr gray 75 10

International College Students' Games, Porto Alegre.

Marshal Tito
A481

Compass Rose, Map of Brazil and View of Rio de Janeiro
A482

1963, Sept. 19

965 A481 80cr sepia 60 30

Visit of Marshal Tito of Jugoslavia.

1963, Sept. 20

966 A482 8cr lt bl grn 20 15

8th International Leprology Congress.

Oil Derrick and Storage Tank
A483

1963, Oct. 3 ***Perf. 11x11½***

967 A483 8cr dk sl grn 20 15

Issued to commemorate the 10th anniversary of Petrobras, the national oil company.

"Spring Games"—A484

1963, Nov. 5 Photo. **Wmk. 267**

968 A484 8cr yel & org 25 20

1963 Spring Games.

Borges de Medeiros
A485

1963, Nov. 29 ***Perf. 11½x11***

969 A485 8cr red brn 20 15

Issued to commemorate the centenary of the birth of Dr. Borges de Medeiros (1863–1962), Governor of Rio Grande do Sul.

São João del Rei
A486

1963, Dec. 8 ***Perf. 11x11½***

970 A486 8cr vio bl 20 15

250th anniversary of São João del Rei.

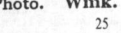

Dr. Alvaro Alvim
A487

1963, Dec. 19

971	A487	8cr dk gray	20	15

Issued to commemorate the centenary of the birth of Dr. Alvaro Alvim (1863–1928), X-ray specialist and martyr of science.

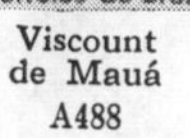

Viscount de Mauá
A488

Mandacaru Cactus and Emblem
A489

1963, Dec. 28 ***Perf. 11½x11***

972	A488	8cr rose car	20	15

Issued to commemorate the sesquicentennial of the birth of Viscount de Mauá, founder of first Brazilian railroad.

1964, Jan. 23 **Photo.** **Wmk. 267**

973	A489	8cr dl grn	25	15

Issued to commemorate the 10th anniversary of the Bank of Northeast Brazil.

Coelho Netto
A490

Lauro Müller
A491

1964, Feb. 21 ***Perf. 11½x11***

974	A490	8cr brt vio	20	15

Birth centenary of Coelho Netto, writer.

1964, March 8 **Wmk. 267**

975	A491	8cr dp org	20	15

Issued to commemorate the centenary of the birth of Lauro Siverino Müller, politician and member of the Brazilian Academy of Letters.

Child Holding Spoon
A492

1964, March 25 ***Perf. 11x11½***

976	A492	8cr yel brn & yel	25	15

Issued for "School Meals Week."

Chalice Rock
A493

Allan Kardec
A494

1964, Apr. 9 Engraved *Perf. 11½x11*

977	A493	80cr red org	40	20

Issued for tourist publicity.

1964, Apr. 18 **Photogravure**

978	A494	30cr sl grn	75	15

Issued to commemorate the centenary of "O Evangelho" (Gospel) of the codification of Spiritism.

Heinrich Lübke
A495

Pope John XXIII
A496

Perf. 11½x11

1964, May 8 **Photo.** **Wmk. 267**

979	A495	100cr red brn	75	18

Issued to commemorate the visit of President Heinrich Lübke of Germany.

1964, June 29 **Wmk. 267**

980	A496	20cr dk car rose	30	20
a.		Unwmkd.	30	20

Issued in memory of Pope John XXIII.

Pres. Senghor of Senegal
A497

1964, Sept. 19 **Wmk. 267**

981	A497	20cr dk brn	40	15

Issued to commemorate the visit of Léopold Sédar Senghor, President of Senegal.

Botafago Bay and Sugarloaf Mountain—A498

Designs: 100cr, Church of Our Lady of the Rock (vert.). 200cr, Copacabana beach.

Perf. 11x11½, 11½x11

1964–65 **Photogravure**

983	A498	15cr org & bl	40	25
984	A498	100cr brt grn & red brn, *yel*	50	18
985	A498	200cr blk & red	2.50	35
a.		Souv. sheet of 3 ('65)	6.00	5.00

Issued to commemorate the 4th centenary of Rio de Janeiro. See Nos. 993–995a.

No. 985a contains three imperf. stamps similar to Nos. 983–985, but printed in brown with marginal inscriptions and border in deep orange. Size: 129x79mm. Sold for 320cr. Issued Dec. 30, 1965.

A souvenir card containing one lithographed facsimile of No. 984, imperf., exists, but has no franking value. Marginal inscriptions in green. Size: 100x125mm. Sold by P.O. for 250cr.

Pres. Charles de Gaulle
A499

Pres. John F. Kennedy
A500

1964, Oct. 13 ***Perf. 11½x11***

986	A499	100cr org brn	30	15

Issued to commemorate the visit of Charles de Gaulle, President of France, Oct. 13–15.

1964, Oct. 24 **Photo.** **Wmk. 267**

987	A500	100cr slate	30	15

Issued in memory of President John F. Kennedy (1917–63).

"Prophet" by A. F. Lisbao
A501

1964, Nov. 18 ***Perf. 11½x11***

988	A501	10cr slate	10	6

Issued to commemorate the 150th anniversary of the death of the sculptor Antonio Francisco Lisbao, "O Aleijadinho" (The Cripple).

Antonio Goncalves Dias
A502

Designs: 30cr, Euclides da Cunha. 50cr, Prof. Angelo Moreira da Costa Lima. 200cr, Tiradentes. 500cr, Dom Pedro I. 1000cr, Dom Pedro II.

1965–66 ***Perf. 11x11½*** **Wmk. 267**

989	A502	30cr brt bluish grn ('66)	2.00	25
989A	A502	50cr dl brn ('66)	1.50	10
990	A502	100cr blue	60	10
991	A502	200cr brn org	2.00	10
992	A502	500cr red brn	6.00	50
992A	A502	1000cr sl bl ('66)	10.00	50
		Nos. 989-992A (6)	22.10	1.55

Statue of St. Sebastian, Guanatara Bay
A503

The Arches
A504

Design: 35cr, Estacio de Sá (1520–67), founder of Rio de Janeiro.

1965 **Photogravure** ***Perf. 11½***

Size: 24x37mm.

993	A503	30cr bl & rose red	60	15

Lithographed and Engraved

Perf. 11x11½

994	A504	30cr lt bl & blk	60	15

Photogravure

Perf. 11½

Size: 21x39mm.

995	A503	35cr blk & org	25	25
a.		Souv. sheet of 3	4.00	5.00

Issued to commemorate the 4th centenary of Rio de Janeiro. Issue dates: No. 993, Mar. 5. No. 994, Nov. 30. No. 995, July 28. No. 995a, Dec. 30.

No. 995a contains three imperf. stamps similar to Nos. 993–995, but printed in deep orange with marginal inscriptions and border in brown. Size: 130x79mm. Sold for 100cr.

Sword and Cross
A505

1965, Apr. 15 ***Perf. 11½*** **Wmk. 267**

996	A505	120cr gray	40	15

Issued to commemorate the first anniversary of the democratic revolution.

Vital Brazil
A506

Shah of Iran
A507

1965, Apr. 28 ***Perf. 11½*** **Wmk. 267**

997	A506	120cr dp org	50	15

Centenary of birth of Vital Brazil, M.D.

A souvenir card containing one impression similar to No. 997, imperf., exists, printed in dull plum. Sold by P.O. for 250cr. Size: 114x180mm.

1965, May 5 **Photogravure**

998	A507	120cr rose cl	40	15

Issued to commemorate the visit of Shah Mohammed Riza Pahlavi of Iran.

Marshal Mariano da Silva Rondon
A508

Lions' Emblem
A509

1965, May 7 Engraved

999 A508 30cr claret 50 15

Issued to commemorate the centenary of the birth of Marshal Mariano da Silva Rondon (1865–1958), explorer and expert on Indians.

1965, May 14 Photogravure

1000 A509 35cr pale vio & blk 30 15

Issued to commemorate the 12th convention of the Lions Clubs of Brazil, Rio de Janeiro, May 11–16.

ITU Emblem, Old and New Communication Equipment
A510

1965, May 21 ***Perf. 11½*** **Wmk. 267**

1001 A510 120cr yel & grn 50 20

Issued to commemorate the centenary of the International Telecommunication Union.

Epitácio Pessoa
A511

Statue of Admiral Barroso
A512

1965, May 23 Photogravure

1002 A511 35cr bl gray 20 15

Issued to commemorate the centenary of the birth of Epitácio da Silva Pessoa (1865–1942), jurist, president of Brazil, 1919–22.

1965, June 11

1003 A512 30cr blue 40 15

Centenary of the naval battle of Riachuelo.

A souvenir card containing one lithographed facsimile of No. 1003, imperf., exists. Size: 100x139½mm.

José de Alencar and Indian Princess
A513

1965, June 24 ***Perf. 11½x11***

1004 A513 30cr dp plum 50 15

Issued to commemorate the centenary of the publication of "Iracema" by José de Alencar.

A souvenir card containing one lithographed facsimile of No. 1004, printed in rose red and imperf., exists. Size: 100x141½mm.

Winston Churchill
A514

1965, June 25 ***Perf. 11x11½***

1005 A514 200cr slate 1.00 25

Issued in memory of Sir Winston Spencer Churchill (1874–1965), statesman and World War II leader.

Scout Jamboree Emblem
A515

1965, July 17 Photogravure

1006 A515 30cr dl bl grn 50 15

Issued to commemorate the First Pan-American Boy Scout Jamboree, Fundao Island, Rio de Janeiro, July 15–25.

ICY Emblem
A516

1965, Aug. 25 ***Perf. 11½*** **Wmk. 267**

1007 A516 120cr dl bl & blk 40 15

International Cooperation Year, 1965.

Leoncio Correias
A517

Emblem
A518

1965, Sept. 1 ***Perf. 11½x11***

1008 A517 35cr sl grn 20 15

Issued to commemorate the centenary of the birth of Leoncio Correias, poet.

1965, Sept. 4

1009 A518 30cr brt rose 30 15

Issued to publicize the Eighth Biennial Fine Arts Exhibition, Sao Paulo, Nov.–Dec., 1965.

Pres. Saragat of Italy
A519

1965, Sept. 11 **Photo.** **Wmk. 267**

1010 A519 100cr sl grn, *pink* 25 12

Visit of Pres. Giuseppe Saragat of Italy.

Grand Duke and Duchess of Luxembourg
A520

1965, Sept. 17 ***Perf. 11x11½***

1011 A520 100cr brn ol 25 12

Issued to commemorate the visit of Grand Duke Jean and Grand Duchess Josephine Charlotte of Luxembourg.

Biplane
A521

1965, Oct. 8 **Photo.** ***Perf. 11½x11***

1012 A521 35cr ultra 25 15

Issued to publicize the 3rd Aviation Week Philatelic Exhibition, Rio de Janeiro.

A souvenir card carries one impression of this 35cr, imperf. Size: 102x140mm. Sold for 100cr.

Flags of OAS Members
A522

1965, Nov. 17 ***Perf. 11x11½***

1013 A522 100cr brt bl & blk 40 20

Issued to commemorate the second meeting of Foreign Ministers of the Organization of American States, Rio de Janeiro.

King Baudouin and Queen Fabiola of Belgium—A523

1965, Nov. 18

1014 A523 100cr gray 40 20

Visit of King and Queen of Belgium.

"Coffee Beans"
A524

Perf. 11½x11

1965, Dec. 21 **Photo.** **Wmk. 267**

1015 A524 30cr brown 60 15

Brazilian coffee publicity.

Conveyor and Loading Crane
A525

1966, Apr. 1 ***Perf. 11x11½***

1016 A525 110cr tan & dk sl grn 40 25

Issued to commemorate the opening of the new terminal of the Rio Doce Iron Ore Company at Tubarao.

Pouring Ladle and Steel Beam
A526

Prof. de Rocha Dissecting Cadaver
A527

Perf. 11½x11

1966, Apr. 16 **Photo.** **Wmk. 267**

1017 A526 30cr *dp org* 35 15

Issued to commemorate the 25th anniversary of the National Steel Company (nationalization of the steel industry).

1966, Apr. 26

1018 A527 30cr brt bluish grn 60 15

Issued to commemorate the 50th anniversary of the discovery and description of Rickettsia prowazeki, the cause of typhus fever, by Prof. Henrique de Rocha Lima.

Battle of Tuiuti
A528

Perf. 11x11½

1966, May 24 **Photo.** **Wmk. 267**

1019 A528 30cr gray grn 60 15

Centenary of the Battle of Tuiuti.

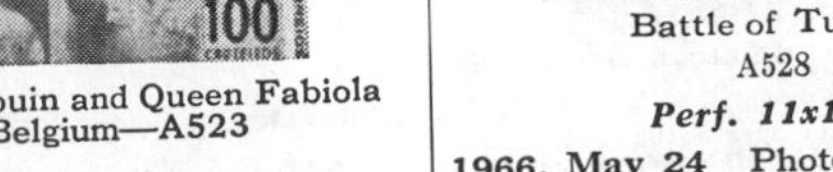

Symbolic Water Cycle
A529

Pres. Shazar of Israel
A530

1966, July 1 ***Perf. 11½x11***

1020 A529 100cr lt brn & bl 45 20

Hydrological Decade (UNESCO), 1965–74.

1966, July 18 Photo. Wmk. 267

1021 A530 100cr ultra 50 20

Visit of Pres. Zalman Shazar of Israel.

Imperial Academy of Fine Arts
A531

Perf. 11x11½

1966, Aug. 12 Engr. Wmk. 267

1022 A531 100cr red brn 90 20

150th anniversary of French art mission.

Military Service Emblem
A532

1966, Sept. 6 Photo. ***Perf. 11x11½***

1023 A532 30cr yel, ultra & grn 40 15
a. With commemorative border 3.00 3.00

Issued to publicize the new Military Service Law. No. 1023a, issued in sheets of four, measures 103½x47mm. It carries at left a single 30cr, type A532, in deeper tones of yellow and ultramarine, Wmk. 264. Top and bottom "frames" in ultramarine are inscribed "Departamento dos Correios e Telégrafos" and "100 Cruzeiros." Inscription at right: "Bloco Comemorativo da Nova Lei do Serviço Militar." Without gum. Sold for 100cr.

Rubén Dario
A533

Perf. 11½x11

1966, Sept. 20 Photo. Wmk. 267

1024 A533 100cr brt rose lil 40 15

Issued to commemorate the 50th anniversary of the death of Rubén Dario (pen name of Felix Rubén Garcia Sarmiento (1867–1916), Nicaraguan poet, newspaper correspondent and diplomat.

Ceramic Candlestick from Santarém
A534

1966, Oct. 6 ***Perf. 11x11½***

1025 A534 30cr dk brn, *sal* 40 15

Centenary of Goeldi Museum at Belém.

Arms of Santa Cruz
A535

Perf. 11½x11

1966, Oct. 15 Photo. Wmk. 267

1026 A535 30cr sl grn 45 15

Issued to publicize the First National Tobacco Exposition, Santa Cruz.

UNESCO Emblem
A536

1966, Oct. 24 Engraved ***Perf. 11½***

1027 A536 120cr black 90 25
a. With commemorative border 4.75 4.75

Issued to commemorate the 20th anniversary of UNESCO (United Nations Educational, Scientific and Cultural Organization). No. 1027a issued in sheets of 4 with red control number measures 102x48mm. It carries at right a design similar to No. 1027. Inscribed at left: "Bloco comemorativo do 20° aniversario da UNESCO," "Cr$150" and "Departamento dos Correios e Telegrafos". Unwatermarked granite paper, without gum. Sold for 150cr.

Captain Antonio Correia Pinto and Map of Lages
A537

Formée Cross and Southern Cross
A538

Perf. 11½x11

1966, Nov. 22 Photo. Wmk. 267

1028 A537 30cr sal pink 35 15

Issued to commemorate the bicentenary of the arrival of Capt. Antonio Correia Pinto.

1966, Dec. 4 ***Perf. 11½***

1029 A538 100cr bl grn 45 15

Issued to commemorate LUBRAPEX 1966 philatelic exhibition at the National Museum of Fine Arts, Rio de Janeiro.

Madonna and Child
A539

Madonna and Child
A540

Perf. 11½x11

1966, Dec. Photo. Wmk. 267

1030 A539 30cr bl grn 30 15

Perf. 11½

1031 A540 35cr sal & ultra 25 20
a. 150cr sal & ultra 2.50 3.00

Christmas 1966.

No. 1031a measures 46x103mm. and is printed in sheets of 4. It is inscribed "Pax Hominibus" (but not "Brasil Correio") and carries the Madonna shown on No. 1031. Issued without gum.

Issue dates: 30cr, Dec. 8; 35cr, Dec. 22; 150cr, Dec. 28.

Arms of Laguna
A541

1967, Jan. 4 Engr. ***Perf. 11x11½***

1032 A541 60cr sepia 25 15

Issued to commemorate the centenary of the Post and Telegraph Agency of Laguna, Santa Catarina.

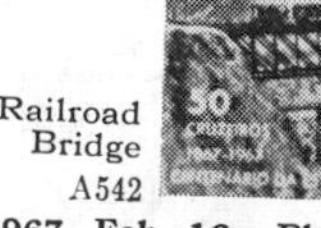

Railroad Bridge
A542

1967, Feb. 16 Photo. Wmk. 267

1033 A542 50cr dp org 60 20

Centenary of the Santos-Jundiai railroad.

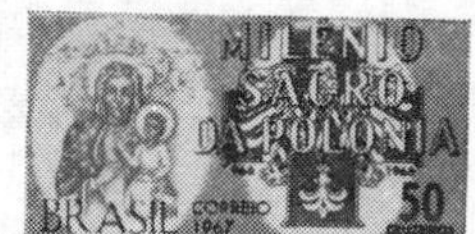

Black Madonna of Czestochowa, Polish Eagle and Cross
A543

1967, Mar. 12 ***Perf. 11x11½***

1034 A543 50cr yel, bl & rose red 60 20

Issued to commemorate the thousandth anniversary of the adoption of Christianity in Poland.

Research Rocket
A544

Anita Garibaldi
A545

1967, March 23 ***Perf. 11½x11***

1035 A544 50cr blk & brt bl 75 30

World Meteorological Day, March 23.

Perf. 11x11½

1967–69 Photo. Wmk. 267

Portraits: 1c, Mother Joana Angelica. 2c, Marilia de Dirceu. 3c, Dr. Rita Lobato. 6c, Ana Neri. 10c, Darcy Vargas.

1036 A545 1c dp ultra 15 5
1037 A545 2c red brn 15 5
1038 A545 3c brt grn 25 8
1039 A545 5c black 50 8
1040 A545 6c brown 50 8
1041 A545 10c dk sl grn ('69) 1.50 30
Nos. 1036-1041 (6) 3.05 64

Issue dates: 1c, May 3; 2c, Aug. 14; 3c, June 7; 5c, Apr. 14; 6c, May 14, 1967; 10c, June 18, 1969.

VARIG Airlines
A546

Madonna and Child, by Robert Feruzzi
A548

Lions Emblem and Globes
A547

1967, May 8 ***Perf. 11½x11***

1046 A546 6c brt bl & blk 30 25

40th anniversary of VARIG Airlines.

1967, May 9 Engr. ***Perf. 11x11½***

1047 A547 6c green 50 25
a. Souv. sheet 2.50 3.00

Issued to commemorate the 50th anniversary of Lions International. No. 1047a contains one imperf. stamp similar to No. 1047. Green inscription and Lions emblem in margin. Size: 131x80mm. Sold for 15c.

1967, May 14 Photo. ***Perf. 11½x11***

1048 A548 5c violet 30 25
a. 15c, souv. sheet 2.50 3.00

Issued for Mother's Day. No. 1048a contains one 15c imperf. stamp in design of No. 1048. Violet marginal inscription. Size: 129x77mm.

Prince Akihito and Princess Michiko
A549

1967, May 25 *Perf. 11x11½*

1049 A549 10c blk & pink 40 20

Issued to commemorate the visit to Brazil of Crown Prince Akihito and Princess Michiko of Japan.

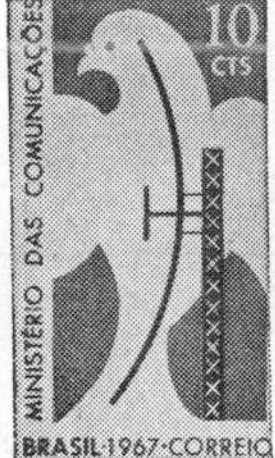

Carrier Pigeon and Radar Screen
A550

Brother Vicente do Salvador
A551

Perf. 11½x11

1967, June 20 Photo. Wmk. 267

1050 A550 10c sl & brt pink 40 20

Issued to commemorate the opening of the Communications Ministry in Brasilia.

1967, June 28 Engraved

1051 A551 5c brown 35 25

Issued to commemorate the 400th anniversary of the birth of Brother Vicente do Salvador (1564–1636), founder of Franciscan convent in Rio de Janeiro, and historian.

Boy, Girl and 4-S Emblem
A552

1967, July 12 Photo. *Perf. 11½*

1052 A552 5c grn & blk 30 20

National 4-S (4-H) Day.

Möbius Strip
A553

1967, July 21 *Perf. 11x11½*

1053 A553 5c brt bl & blk 30 25

Issued to commemorate the 6th Brazilian Mathematical Congress.

Fish
A554

1967, Aug. 1 *Perf. 11½*

1054 A554 5c slate 50 25

Bicentenary of city of Piracicaba.

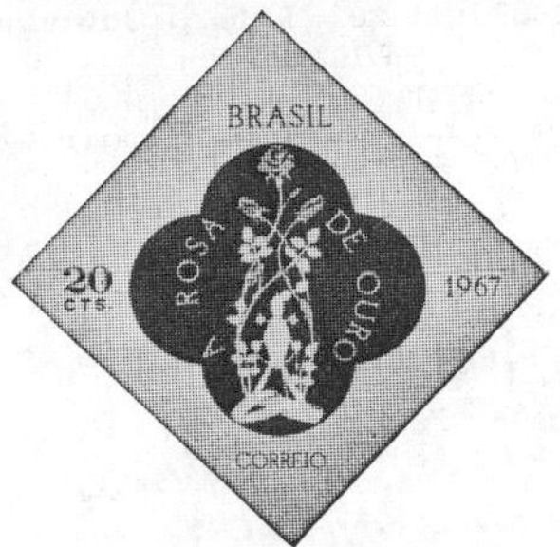

Golden Rose and Papal Arms
A555

1967, Aug. 15

1055 A555 20c mag & yel 1.25 50

Issued to commemorate the offering of a golden rose by Pope Paul VI to the Virgin Mary of Fatima (Our Lady of Peace), Patroness of Brazil.

General Sampaio
A556

King Olaf of Norway
A557

1967, Aug. 25 Engr. *Perf. 11½x11*

1056 A556 5c blue 30 25

Issued to honor General Antonio de Sampaio, hero of the Battle of Tutui.

1967, Sept. 8 Photogravure

1057 A557 10c brn org 30 25

Visit of King Olaf of Norway.

Sun over Sugar Loaf, Botafogo Bay
A558

Nilo Peçanha
A559

Photogravure and Embossed

1967, Sept. 25 *Perf. 11½* Wmk. 267

1058 A558 10c blk & dp org 30 20

Issued to commemorate the 22nd meeting of the International Monetary Fund, International Bank for Reconstruction and Development, International Financial Corporation and International Development Association.

Perf. 11½x11

1967, Oct. 1 Photo. Wmk. 267

1059 A559 5c brn vio 30 25

Issued to commemorate the centenary of the birth of Nilo Peçanha (1867–1924), President of Brazil 1909–1910.

Virgin of the Apparition and Basilica of Aparecida
A560

Cockerel, Festival Emblem
A561

1967, Oct. 11 *Perf. 11½*

1060 A560 5c ultra & dl yel 50 25
a. Souv. sheet of 2 3.50 4.50

Issued to commemorate the 250th anniversary of the discovery of the statue of Our Lady of the Apparition, now in the National Basilica of the Apparition at Aparecida do Norte.

No. 1060a contains imperf. 5c and 10c stamps similar to No. 1060. Blue marginal inscriptions with pink and blue design. Issued Dec. 27, 1967, for Christmas. Size: 77½x129mm.

Engraved and Photogravure

1967, Oct. 16 *Perf. 11½x11*

1061 A561 20c blk & multi 75 40

Second International Folksong Festival.

Balloon, Plane and Rocket
A562

Perf. 11x11½

1967, Oct. 18 Photo. Unwmkd.

1062 A562 10c blue 60 35
a. 15c, souv. sheet 3.00 3.50

Issued for the Week of the Wing, Oct. 18–23. No. 1062a contains one imperf. 15c stamp similar to No. 1062, blue marginal design and inscription; it was issued Oct. 23. Size: 130x75mm.

Pres. Arthur Bernardes
A563

Portraits of Brazilian Presidents: 20c, Campos Salles. 50c, Wenceslau Pereira Gomes Braz. 1cr, Washington Pereira de Souza Luiz. 2cr, Castello Branco.

Perf. 11x11½

1967–68 Photogravure Wmk. 267

1063 A563 10c blue 30 20
1064 A563 20c dk red brn 1.00 20

Engraved

1065 A563 50c blk ('68) 5.00 30
1066 A563 1cr lil rose ('68) 8.00 30
1067 A563 2cr emer ('68) 1.50 30
Nos. 1063-1067 (5) 15.80 1.30

Carnival of Rio
A564

Ships, Anchor and Sailor
A565

1967, Nov. 22 *Perf. 11½x11*

1070 A564 10c lem, ultra & pink 40 25
a. 15c, souv. sheet 3.50 4.50

Issued for International Tourist Year, 1967. No. 1070a contains a 15c imperf. stamp in design of No. 1070. Pink marginal design and inscription. Size: 76x130mm. Issued Nov. 24.

1967, Dec. 6

1071 A565 10c ultra 40 30

Issued for Navy Week.

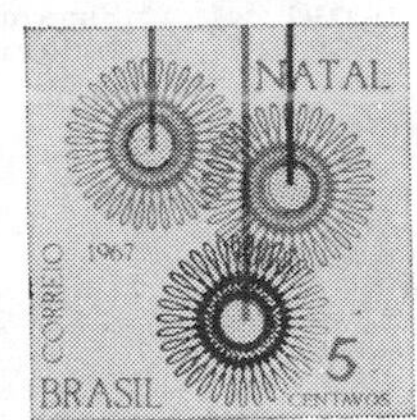

Christmas Decorations
A566

1967, Dec. 8 *Perf. 11½*

1072 A566 5c car, yel & bl 40 25

Christmas 1967.

Olavo Bilac, Planes, Tank and Aircraft Carrier—A567

Perf. 11x11½

1967, Dec. 16 Photo. Wmk. 267

1073 A567 5c brt bl & yel 40 25

Issued for Reservists' Day and to honor Olavo Bilac, sponsor of compulsory military service.

Rodrigues de Carvalho
A568

1967, Dec. 18 Engr. *Perf. 11½x11*

1074 A568 10c green 30 25

Issued to commemorate the centenary of the birth of Rodrigues de Carvalho, poet and lawyer.

Orlando Rangel
A569

Photogravure

1968, Feb. 29 *Perf. 11x11½*

1075 A569 5c lt grnsh bl & blk 60 35

Issued to commemorate the centenary of the birth of Orlando de Fonseca Rangel, pioneer of pharmaceutical industry in Brazil.

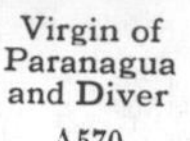
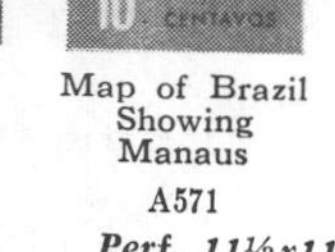

Virgin of Paranagua and Diver
A570

Map of Brazil Showing Manaus
A571

1968, Mar. 9 ***Perf. 11½x11***

1076 A570 10c dk sl grn & brt yel grn 50 30

Issued to commemorate the 250th anniversary of the first underwater explorations at Paranagua.

1968, Mar. 13 Photo. **Wmk. 267**

1077 A571 10c yel, grn & red 40 30

Issued to publicize the free port of Manaus on the Amazon River.

Human Rights Flame
A572

Paul Harris and Rotary Emblem
A573

1968, Mar. 21 ***Perf. 11½x11***

1078 A572 10c bl & sal 40 30

International Human Rights Year.

1968, Apr. 19 Litho. **Unwmkd.**
Without Gum

1079 A573 20c grn & org brn 1.50 70

Issued to commemorate the centenary of the birth of Paul Percy Harris (1868–1947), founder of Rotary International.

Pedro Alvares Cabral and his Fleet—A574

Design: 20c, First Mass celebrated in Brazil.

1968 Without Gum ***Perf. 11½***

1080 A574 10c multi 85 50
1081 A574 20c multi 1.15 60

Issued to commemorate the 500th anniversary of the birth of Pedro Alvares Cabral, navigator, who took possession of Brazil for Portugal.

Issue dates: 10c, Apr. 22; 20c, July 11.

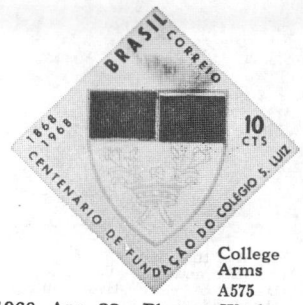

College Arms
A575

1968, Apr. 22 Photo. **Wmk. 267**

1082 A575 10c vio bl, red & gold 80 35

Centenary of St. Luiz College, São Paulo.

Motherhood, by Henrique Bernardeli
A576

1968, May 12 Litho. **Unwmkd.**
Without Gum

1083 A576 5c multi 50 30

Issued for Mother's Day.

Harpy Eagle
A577

Photogravure and Engraved

1968, May 28 **Wmk. 267**

1084 A577 20c brt bl & blk 1.75 60

Sesquicentennial of National Museum.

Brazilian and Japanese Women
A578

1968, June 28 Litho. **Unwmkd.**
Without Gum

1085 A578 10c yel & multi 80 50

Issued to commemorate the inauguration of Varig's direct Brazil-Japan airline.

Horse Race
A579

Perf. 11x11½

1968, July 16 Litho. **Unwmkd.**
Without Gum

1086 A579 10c multi 50 30

Centenary of the Jockey Club of Brazil.

Musician Wren—A580

Designs: 10c, Red-crested cardinal (vert.). 50c, Royal flycatcher (vert.).

Perf. 11½x11, 11x11½

1968–69 Engraved **Sheet Wmk.**
Without Gum

1087 A580 10c multi ('69) 75 30
1088 A580 20c multi 1.25 30
1089 A580 50c multi 1.75 60

Some stamps in each sheet of Nos. 1087–1089 show parts of a two-line papermaker's watermark: "WESTERPOST / INDUSTRIA BRASILEIRA" with diamond-shaped emblem between last two words. Entire watermark appears in one sheet margin.

Issue dates: 10c, Aug. 20, 1969. 20c, July 19, 1968. 50c, Aug. 2, 1968.

Mailbox and Envelope
A581

Photogravure and Engraved

1968, Aug. 1 ***Perf. 11*** **Wmk. 267**

1091 A581 5c cit, blk & grn 25 20

Issued for Stamp Day, 1968 and to commemorate the 125th anniversary of the first Brazilian postage stamps.

Emilio Luiz Mallet
A582

Map of South America
A583

Perf. 11½x11

1968, Aug. 25 Engraved **Wmk. 267**

1092 A582 10c pale pur 25 20

Issued to honor Marshal Emilio Luiz Mallet, Baron of Itapevi, patron of the marines.

1968, Sept. 5 **Photogravure**

1093 A583 10c dp org 20 20

Visit of President Eduardo Frei of Chile.

Seal of Portuguese Literary School
A584

Photogravure and Engraved

1968, Sept. 10 ***Perf. 11½***

1094 A584 5c pink & grn 25 20

Centenary of Portuguese Literary School.

Map of Brazil and Telex Tape
A585

1968, Sept. Photo. ***Perf. 11x11½***

1095 A585 20c cit & brt grn 60 25

Linking of 25 Brazilian cities by teletype.

Soldiers' Heads on Medal
A586

Perf. 11½x11

1968, Sept. 24 Litho. **Unwmkd.**
Without Gum

1096 A586 5c bl & gray 30 25

8th American Armed Forces Conference.

Clef, Notes and Sugarloaf Mountain
A587

1968, Sept. 30 ***Perf. 11½***
Without Gum

1097 A587 6c blk, yel & red 60 30

Third International Folksong Festival.

Catalytic Cracking Plant
A588

1968, Oct. 4 **Without Gum**

1098 A588 6c bl & multi 60 40

Issued to commemorate the 15th anniversary of Petrobras, the national oil company.

Child Protection
A589

Whimsical Girl
A590

Design: 5c, School boy walking toward the sun.

Perf. 11½x11, 11x11½

1968, Oct. 16 Litho. Unwmkd.

Without Gum

1099	A590	5c gray & lt bl	50	40
1100	A589	10c brt bl, dk red & blk	60	30
1101	A590	20c multi	75	30

Issued to commemorate the 22nd anniversary of the United Nations Children's Fund.

Children with Books
A591

1968, Oct. 23 ***Perf. 11x11½***

Without Gum

1102 A591 5c multi 35 25

Issued to publicize Book Week.

U.N. Emblem and Flags
A592

Perf. 11½x11

1968, Oct. 24 Without Gum

1103 A592 20c blk & multi 75 35

Issued to commemorate the 20th anniversary of the World Health Organization.

Jean Baptiste Debret, Self-portrait
A593

Perf. 11x11½

1968, Oct. 30 Litho. Unwmkd.

Without Gum

1104 A593 10c dk gray & pale yel 50 25

Issued to commemorate the bi-centenary of the birth of Jean Baptiste Debret, (1768–1848), French painter who worked in Brazil (1816–31). Design includes his "Burden Bearer."

Queen Elizabeth II
A594

1968, Nov. 4 ***Perf. 11½***

Without Gum

1105 A594 70c lt bl & multi 1.75 1.00

Issued to commemorate the visit of Queen Elizabeth II of Great Britain.

Francisco Braga
A595

Perf. 11½x11

1968, Nov. 19 Wmk. 267

1106 A595 5c dl red brn 40 25

Issued to commemorate the centenary of the birth of Antonio Francisco Braga, composer of the Hymn of the Flag.

Brazilian Flag
A596

1968, Nov. 19 ***Perf. 11½*** **Unwmkd.**

Without Gum

1107 A596 10c multi 50 30

Issued for Flag Day.

Clasped Hands and Globe
A597

Perf. 11x11½

1968, Nov. 25 Typo. Unwmkd.

Without Gum

1108 A597 5c multi 30 25

Issued for Voluntary Blood Donor's Day.

Old Locomotive—A598

1968, Nov. 28 Litho. ***Perf. 11½***

Without Gum

1109 A598 5c multi 1.00 50

Centenary of the São Paulo Railroad.

Bell
A599

Francisco Caldas, Jr.
A600

Design: 6c, Santa Claus and boy.

1968 Without Gum ***Perf. 11½x11***

1110	A599	5c multi	50	25
1111	A599	6c multi	50	25

Christmas 1968.
Issue dates: 5c, Dec. 12; 6c, Dec. 20.

1968, Dec. 13 Without Gum

1112 A600 10c crim & blk 35 20

Issued to commemorate the centenary of the birth of Francisco Caldas, Jr., journalist and founder of Correio de Povo, newspaper.

Map of Brazil, War Memorial and Reservists' Emblem
A601

Perf. 11x11½

1968, Dec. 16 Photo. Wmk. 267

1113 A601 5c bl grn & org brn 50 25

Issued for Reservists' Day.

Radar Antenna
A602

Viscount of Rio Branco
A603

Perf. 11½x11

1969, Feb. 28 Litho. Unwmkd.

Without Gum

1114 A602 30c ultra, lt bl & blk 1.25 60

Issued to publicize the inauguration of EMBRATEL, satellite communications ground station bringing U.S. television to Brazil via Telstar.

1969, Mar. 16 Without Gum

1115 A603 5c blk & buff 35 25

Issued to commemorate the 150th anniversary of the birth of José Maria da Silva Paranhos, Viscount of Rio Branco (1819–1880), statesman.

St. Gabriel
A604

1969, Mar. 24 Without Gum

1116 A604 5c multi 50 25

Issued to honor St. Gabriel as patron saint of telecommunications.

Shoemaker's Last and Globe
A605

Perf. 11x11½

1969, Mar. 29 Litho. Unwmkd.

Without Gum

1117 A605 5c multi 35 25

Issued to publicize the 4th International Shoe Fair, Novo Hamburgo.

Allan Kardec
A606

1969, Mar. 31 Photo. Wmk. 267

1118 A606 5c brt grn & org brn 40 25

Issued to commemorate the centenary of the death of Allan Kardec (pen name of Leon Hippolyto Denizard Rivail, 1803–1869), French physician and spiritist.

Men of 3 Races and Arms of Cuiabá
A607

1969, Apr. 8 Litho. Unwmkd.

Without Gum

1119 A607 5c blk & multi 30 25

Issued to commemorate the 250th anniversary of the founding of Cuiabá, capital of Matto Grosso.

State Mint—A608

1969, Apr. 11 ***Perf. 11½***

Without Gum

1120 A608 5c ol bis & org 60 40

Issued to commemorate the opening of the state money printing plant.

Brazilian Stamps and Emblem
A609

Perf. 11x11½

1969, Apr. 30 Litho. Unwmkd.

Without Gum

1121	A609	5c multi	40	25

Issued to commemorate the 50th anniversary of the São Paulo Philatelic Society.

St. Anne, Baroque Statue
A610

1969, May 8 ***Perf. 11½***

Without Gum

1122	A610	5c lem & multi	60	40

Issued for Mother's Day.

ILO Emblem
A611

Perf. 11x11½

1969, May 13 Photo. Wmk. 267

1123	A611	5c dp rose red & gold	40	20

Issued to commemorate the 50th anniversary of the International Labor Organization.

Diving Platform and Swimming Pool
A612

Mother and Child at Window
A613

Lithographed and Photogravure

Perf. 11½x11

1969, June 13 Unwmkd.

Without Gum

1124	A612	20c bis brn, blk & bl grn	1.00	60

40th anniversary of the Cearense Water Sports Club, Fortaleza.

1969 Lithographed ***Perf. 11½***

Designs: 20c, Modern sculpture by Felicia Leirner. 50c, "The Sun Sets in Brasilia," by Danilo di Prete. 1cr, Angelfish, painting by Aldemir Martins.

Size: 24x36mm.

1125	A613	10c org & multi	85	30

Size: 33x34mm.

1126	A613	20c red & multi	85	60

Size: 33x53mm.

1127	A613	50c yel & multi	3.00	1.50

Without Gum

1128	A613	1cr gray & multi	4.00	1.50

Issued to publicize the 10th Biennial Art Exhibition, São Paulo, Sept.-Dec. 1969.

Angelfish
A614

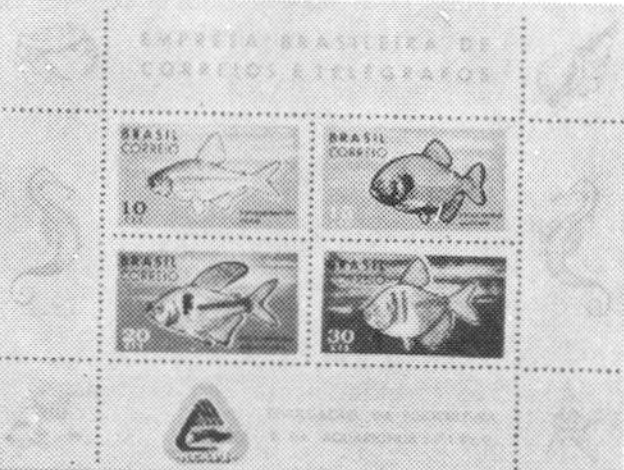

Fish
A615

Fish: 10c, Tetra. 15c, Piranha. No. 1130c, Megalamphodus megalopterus. 30c, Black tetra.

Perf. 11½

1969, July 21 Litho. Wmk. 267

1129	A614	20c multi	1.00	50

Souvenir Sheet

Imperf.

1969, July 24 Unwmkd.

1130	A615	Sheet of four	4.75	*6.00*
a.		10c yel & multi	85	85
b.		15c brt bl & multi	85	85
c.		20c grn & multi	85	85
d.		30c org & multi	85	85

Issued to publicize the work of ACAPI, an organization devoted to the preservation and development of fish in Brazil.

No. 1130 contains 4 stamps (size: 38½x21mm.). Greenish margin with commemorative inscription, marine life design and ACAPI emblem. Size: 132½x98½mm.

L. O. Teles de Menezes
A616

Mailman
A617

Perf. 11½x11

1969, July 26 Photo. Wmk. 267

1131	A616	50c dp org & bl grn	2.00	1.50

Centenary of Spiritism press in Brazil.

1969, Aug. 1

1132	A617	30c blue	2.00	1.00

Issued for Stamp Day.

Map of Brazil
A618

Gen. Tasso Fragoso
A620

Railroad Bridge
A619

Lithographed

1969, Aug. 25 ***Perf. 11½*** **Unwmkd.**

Without Gum

1133	A618	10c lt ultra, grn & yel	50	25

Perf. 11x11½

1134	A619	20c multi	1.00	40

Engraved ***Perf. 11½x11*** **Wmk. 267**

With Gum

1135	A620	20c green	1.00	50

No. 1133 honors the Army as guardian of security; No. 1134, as promoter of development. No. 1135 commemorates the birth centenary of Gen. Tasso Fragoso.

Jupia Dam, Parana River
A621

Perf. 11½

1969, Sept. 10 Litho. Unwmkd.

Without Gum

1136	A621	20c lt bl & multi	50	50

Issued to commemorate the inauguration of the Jupia Dam, part of the Urubupunga hydroelectric system serving Sao Paulo.

Gandhi and Spinning Wheel
A622

1969, Oct. 2 ***Perf. 11x11½***

1137	A622	20c yel & blk	50	30

Issued to commemorate the centenary of the birth of Mohandas K. Gandhi (1869-1948), leader in India's fight for independence.

Santos Dumont, Eiffel Tower and Module Landing on Moon
A623

1969, Oct. 17 ***Perf. 11½***

Without Gum

1138	A623	50c dk bl & multi	2.50	1.50

Man's first landing on the moon, July 20, 1969. See note after U.S. No. C76.

Smelting Plant
A624

1969, Oct. 26 ***Perf. 11½*** **Unwmkd.**

Without Gum

1139	A624	20c multi	50	40

Expansion of Brazil's steel industry.

Steel Furnace
A625

1969, Oct. 31 Litho. Without Gum

1140	A625	10c yel & multi	50	40

25th anniversary of Acesita Steel Works.

Water Vendor, by J. B. Debret
A626

Design: 30c, Street Scene, by Debret.

1969-70 Without Gum

1141	A626	20c multi	1.50	50
1141A	A626	30c multi	1.50	1.00

Issued to commemorate the 200th anniversary of the birth of Jean Baptiste Debret (1768-1848), painter.

Issue dates: 20c, Nov. 5, 1969; 30c, May 19, 1970.

Exhibition Emblem
A627

1969, Nov. 15 ***Perf. 11½x11***

Without Gum

1142 A627 10c multi 50 25

Issued to publicize the ABUEXPO 69 Philatelic Exposition, Sao Paulo, Nov. 15–23.

Plane—A628

1969, Nov. 23 Without Gum

1143 A628 50c multi 3.00 1.50

Issued to publicize the year of the expansion of the national aviation industry.

Pelé Scoring
A629

1969–70 Without Gum

1144 A629 10c multi 30 30

Souvenir Sheet

Imperf.

1145 A629 75c multi ('70) 3.00 3.00

Issued to commemorate the 1,000th goal scored by Pelé, Brazilian soccer player.

No. 1145 contains one imperf. stamp with simulated perforations, commemorative marginal inscription. Size: 80x119 mm.

Issued dates: 10c, Nov. 28, 1969. 75c, Jan. 23, 1970.

Madonna and Child from Villa Velha Monastery
A630

Lithographed

1969, Dec. ***Perf. 11½*** **Unwmkd.**

Without Gum

1146 A630 10c gold & multi 50 25

Souvenir Sheet

Imperf.

1147 A630 75c gold & multi 12.00 *15.00*

Christmas 1969.

No. 1147 has simulated perforations; commemorative inscription and Christmas decorations in margin. Size: 136x102mm.

Issue dates: 10c, Dec. 8; 75c, Dec. 18.

Destroyer and Submarine
A631

Perf. 11x11½

1969, Dec. 9 Engraved Wmk. 267

1148 A631 5c bluish gray 50 25

Issued for Navy Day.

Dr. Herman Blumenau
A632

1969, Dec. 26 ***Perf. 11½*** **Wmk. 267**

1149 A632 20c gray grn 1.25 40

Issued to commemorate the 150th anniversary of the birth of Dr. Herman Blumenau (1819–1899), founder of Blumenau, Santa Catarina State.

Carnival Scene—A633

Sugarloaf Mountain, Mask, Confetti and Streamers
A634

Designs: 5c, Jumping boy and 2 women (vert.). 20c, Clowns. 50c, Drummer.

1969–70 Litho. **Unwmkd.**

Without Gum

1150	A633	5c multi	60	30
1151	A633	10c multi	60	30
1152	A633	20c multi	75	40
1153	A634	30c multi ('70)	3.50	3.00
1154	A634	50c multi ('70)	3.00	2.50
		Nos. 1150-1154 (5)	8.45	6.50

Carico Carnival, Rio de Janeiro.

Issue dates: Nos. 1150–1152, Dec. 29, 1969. Nos. 1153–1154, Feb. 5, 1970.

Opening Bars of "Il Guarani" with Antonio Carlos Gomes Conducting
A635

1970, Mar. 19 Litho. ***Perf. 11½***

Without Gum

1155 A635 20c blk, yel, gray & brn 75 40

Issued to commemorate the centenary of the opera Il Guarani, by Antonio Carlos Gomes.

Church of Penha
A636

1970, Apr. 6 ***Perf. 11½*** **Unwmkd.**

Without Gum

1156 A636 20c blk & multi 40 20

Issued to commemorate the 400th anniversary of the Church of Penha, State of Esperito Santo.

Assembly Building
A637

Designs: 50c, Reflecting Pool. 1cr, Presidential Palace.

1970, Apr. 21 Without Gum

1157	A637	20c multi	1.50	75
1158	A637	50c multi	3.75	3.00
1159	A637	1cr multi	3.75	3.00

10th anniversary of Brasilia.

Symbolic Water Design
A638

1970, May 5 ***Perf. 11½*** **Unwmkd.**

Without Gum

1161 A638 50c multi 3.00 3.00

Issued to publicize the Rondon Project for the development of the Amazon River basin.

Marshal Manoel Luiz Osorio and Osorio Arms—A639

1970, May 8 Without Gum

1162 A639 20c multi 2.00 1.00

Issued to commemorate the inauguration of the Marshal Osorio Historical Park.

Madonna, from San Antonio Monastery, Rio de Janeiro
A640

Detail from Brasilia Cathedral
A641

1970, May 10 Without Gum

1163 A640 20c multi 60 50

Issued for Mother's Day.

1970, May 27 Engraved Wmk. 267

1164 A641 20c lt yel grn 40 30

8th National Eucharistic Congress, Brasilia.

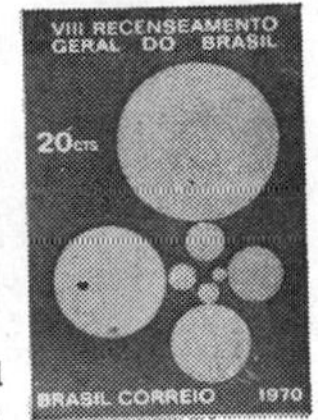

Census Symbol
A642

Lithographed

1970, June 22 ***Perf. 11½*** **Unwmkd.**

Without Gum

1165 A642 20c grn & yel 75 75

Issued to publicize the 8th general census.

Soccer Cup, Maps of Brazil and Mexico
A643

Swedish Flag and Player Holding Rimet Cup—A644

Designs: 2cr, Chilean flag and soccer. 3cr, Mexican flag and soccer.

1970 Without Gum

1166	A643	50c blk, lt bl & gold	1.00	1.00
1167	A644	1cr pink & multi	4.00	1.50
1168	A644	2cr gray & multi	6.00	2.00
1169	A644	3cr multi	5.00	1.00

Issued to commemorate the 9th World Soccer Championships for the Jules Rimet Cup, Mexico City, May 30–June 21. No. 1166 commemorates Brazil's victory.

Issue dates: No. 1166, June 24; Nos. 1167–1169, Aug. 4.

Corcovado Christ and Map of South America
A645

1970, July 18 **Without Gum**

1170	A645	50c brn, dk red & bl	3.00	3.00

Issued to publicize the 6th World Congress of Marist Brothers' Alumni.

Pandiá Calógeras
A646

Perf. 11½x11

1970, Aug. 25 **Photo.** **Unwmkd.**

1171	A646	20c bl grn	75	50

Issued to honor Pandiá Calógeras, Minister of War.

Brazilian Military Emblems and Map
A647

Perf. 11x11½

1970, Sept. 8 **Litho.** **Unwmkd.**

Without Gum

1172	A647	20c gray & multi	60	50

25th anniversary of victory in World War II.

Annunciation (Brazilian Primitive Painting)
A648

1970, Sept. 29 ***Perf. 11½***

Without Gum

1173	A648	20c multi	2.00	1.00

Issued for St. Gabriel's (patron saint of communications) Day.

Boy in Library
A649

U.N. Emblem
A650

1970, Oct. 23 **Without Gum**

1174	A649	20c multi	1.75	1.00

Issued to publicize Book Week.

1970, Oct. 24 **Without Gum**

1175	A650	50c dk bl, lt bl & sil	2.00	1.50

25th anniversary of the United Nations.

Rio de Janeiro, 1820—A651

Designs: 50c, LUBRAPEX 70 emblem. 1 cr, Rio de Janeiro with Sugar Loaf Mountain, 1970. No. 1179, like 20c.

1970, Oct. **Without Gum**

1176	A651	20c multi	2.00	1.00
1177	A651	50c yel brn & blk	3.75	2.00
1178	A651	1cr multi	3.75	3.75

Souvenir Sheet

Imperf.

1179	A651	1cr multi	12.00	*16.00*

Issued to commemorate LUBRAPEX 70, third Portuguese-Brazilian Philatelic Exhibition, Rio de Janeiro, Oct. 24–31. No. 1179 contains one stamp, black marginal inscription. Size: 60x80mm.

Issue dates: Nos. 1176–1178, Oct. 27. No. 1179, Oct. 31.

Holy Family by Candido Portinari
A652

1970, Dec. **Litho.** ***Perf. 11½***

Without Gum

1180	A652	50c multi	1.50	1.50

Souvenir Sheet

Imperf.

1181	A652	1cr multi	15.00	*22.50*

Christmas 1970. No. 1181 contains one stamp with simulated perforations. Light yellow green margin with red and black inscription. Size: 106x52mm. Issue dates: 50c, Dec. 1; 1cr, Dec. 8.

Battleship
A653

CIH Emblem
A654

1970, Dec. 11 **Litho.** ***Perf. 11½***

Without Gum

1182	A653	20c multi	1.75	75

Navy Day.

1971, Mar. 28 **Litho.** ***Perf. 11½***

Without Gum

1183	A654	50c blk & red	2.00	1.75

Third Inter-American Housing Congress, Mar. 27–Apr. 3.

Links Around Globe
A655

1971, Mar. 31 **Litho.** ***Perf. 12½x11***

Without Gum

1184	A655	20c grn, yel, blk & red	85	50

International year against racial discrimination.

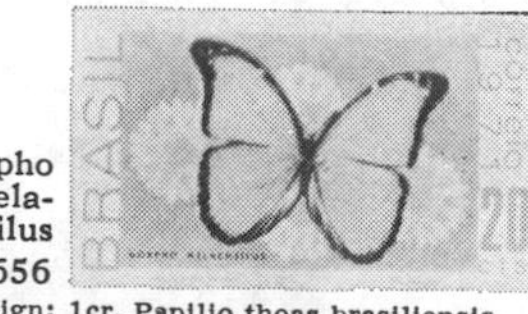

Morpho Melacheilus
A656

Design: 1cr, Papilio thoas brasiliensis.

Perf. 11x11½

1971, Apr. 28 **Litho.** **Unwmkd.**

Without Gum

1185	A656	20c multi	1.50	1.00
1186	A656	1cr multi	7.50	5.00

Madonna and Child
A657

1971, May 9 **Litho.** ***Perf. 11½***

Without Gum

1187	A657	20c multi	1.75	40

Mother's Day, 1971.

Basketball
A658

1971, May 19 **Without Gum**

1188	A658	70c multi	2.25	1.50

6th World Women's Basketball Championship.

Map of Trans-Amazon Highway
A660 A659

Lithographed

1971, July 1 ***Perf. 11½*** **Unwmkd.**

Without Gum

1189	A659	40c multi	7.50	3.00
1190	A660	1cr multi	7.00	6.00

Trans-Amazon Highway. Nos. 1189–1190 printed se-tenant in sheets of 28 (4x7). Horizontal rows contain 2 pairs of 1189–1190 with a label between. Each label carries different inscription.

Man's Head, by Victor Mairelles de Lima
A661

Design: 1cr, Arab Violinist, by Pedro Américo.

1971, Aug. 1 **Without Gum**

1191	A661	40c pink & multi	3.00	1.00
1192	A661	1cr gray & multi	4.00	2.00

Stamp Day.

Duke of Caxias and Map of Brazil
A662

1971, Aug. 23 **Photogravure**

1193	A662	20c yel grn & red brn	75	60

Army Day.

Anita Garibaldi
A663

1971, Aug. 30 **Litho.** **Without Gum**

1194	A663	20c multi	75	50

Anita Garibaldi (1821–1849), heroine in liberation of Brazil.

Xavante Jet and Santos Dumont's Plane, 1910—A664

1971, Sept. 6 **Without Gum**

1195	A664	40c yel & multi	2.00	90

First flight of Xavante jet plane.

Flags and Map of Central American Nations
A665

"71" in French Flag Colors
A666

1971, Sept. 15 **Without Gum**

1196 A665 40c ocher & multi 1.60 60

Sesquicentennial of the independence of Central American nations.

1971, Sept. 16 **Without Gum**

1197 A666 1.30cr ultra & multi 2.00 1.50

French Exhibition.

Black Mother, by Lucilio de Albuquerque
A667

Archangel Gabriel
A668

1971, Sept. 28 **Without Gum**

1198 A667 40c multi 1.00 60

Centenary of law guaranteeing personal freedom starting at birth.

Perf. 11½x11

1971, Sept. 29 **Without Gum**

1199 A668 40c multi 1.00 75

St. Gabriel's Day.

Bridge over River
A669

Children's Drawings: 35c, People crossing bridge. 60c, Woman with hat.

1971, Oct. 25 ***Perf. 11½***

Without Gum

1200 A669 35c pink, bl & blk 1.00 60
1201 A669 45c blk & multi 2.00 60
1202 A669 60c ol & multi 1.00 60

Children's Day.

Werkhäuserii Superba
A670

1971, Nov. 16 **Without Gum**

1203 A670 40c bl & multi 3.00 1.00

In memory of Carlos Werkhauser, botanist.

Greek Key Pattern "25"
A671

Design: 40c, like 20c but inscribed "sesc / servicio social / do comercio."

1971, Dec. 3

Without Gum

1204 A671 20c blk & bl 1.50 1.00
1205 A671 40c blk & org 1.50 1.00

25th anniversary of SENAC (national apprenticeship system) and SESC (commercial social service). Nos. 1204–1205 printed se-tenant.

Gunboat
A672

1971, Dec. 8 ***Perf. 11***

Without Gum

1206 A672 20c bl & multi 1.00 50

Navy Day.

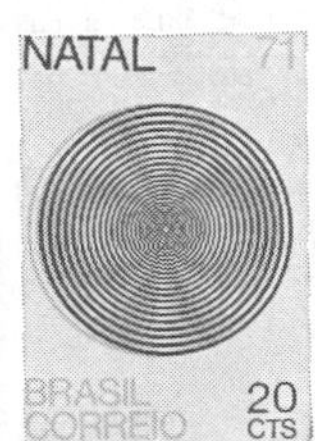

Cross and Circles
A673

Washing of Bonfim Church, Salvador, Bahia
A674

1971, Dec. 11

1207 A673 20c car & bl 50 40
1208 A673 75c sil & gray 1.00 *2.50*
1209 A673 1.30cr blk, yel, grn & bl 6.00 2.50

Christmas 1971.

1972, Feb. 18 Litho. ***Perf. 11½x11***

Designs: 40c, Grape Festival, Rio Grande do Sul. 75c, Festival of the Virgin of Nazareth, Belém. 1.30cr, Winter Arts Festival, Ouro Preto.

Without Gum

1210 A674 20c sil & multi 1.50 75
1211 A674 40c sil & multi 2.25 75
1212 A674 75c sil & multi 2.25 3.00
1213 A674 1.30cr sil & multi 5.00 3.00

Pres. Lanusse and Flag of Argentina
A675

1972, Mar. 13 ***Perf. 11x11½***

Without Gum

1214 A675 40c bl & multi 3.00 2.50

Visit of Lt. Gen. Alejandro Agustin Lanusse, president of Argentina.

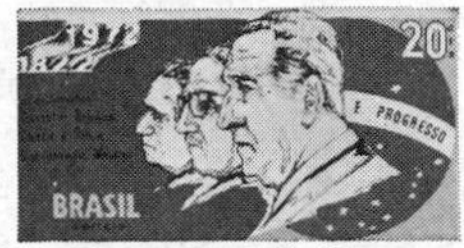

Presidents Castello Branco, Costa e Silva and Garrastazu Medici—A676

1972, Mar. 29 **Without Gum**

1215 A676 20c emer & multi 1.50 60

Anniversary of 1964 revolution.

Post Office Emblem
A677

Perf. 11½x11

1972, Apr. 10 **Photo.** **Unwmkd.**

1216 A677 20c red brn 2.00 20

No. 1216 is luminescent.

Pres. Thomas and Portuguese Flag
A678

1972, Apr. 22 **Litho.** ***Perf. 11***

Without Gum

1217 A678 75c ol brn & multi 2.50 2.00

Visit of Pres. Américo Thomas of Portugal to Brazil, Apr. 22–27.

Soil Research (CPRM)
A679

1972, May 3 ***Perf. 11½***

Without Gum; Multicolored

1218 A679 20c *shown* 1.50 50
1219 A679 40c *Offshore oil rig* 3.50 75
1220 A679 75c *Hydroelectric dam* 1.50 1.50
1221 A679 1.30cr *Iron ore production* 3.50 1.25

Industrial development. Stamps are inscribed with names of industrial firms.

Souvenir Sheet

Poster for Modern Art Week 1922
A680

1972, May 5

1222 A680 1cr blk & car 30.00 30.00

50th anniversary of Modern Art Week. No. 1222 contains one stamp. Silver margin with black inscription. Size: 78x110 mm.

Mailman, Map of Brazil and Letters
A681

Designs: 45c, "Telecommunications" (vert.). 60c, Tropospheric scatter system. 70c, Road map of Brazil and worker.

1972, May 26 **Without Gum**

1223 A681 35c bl & multi 1.50 50
1224 A681 45c sil & multi 1.75 1.75
1225 A681 60c blk & multi 1.75 1.50
1226 A681 70c multi 2.00 1.50

Unification of communications in Brazil.

Development Type and

Automobiles
A682

Designs: 45c, Ships. 70c, Ingots.

Perf. 11x11½, 11½x11

1972, June 21 **Photogravure**

1227 A682 35c blk, mag & org 1.25 50

Lithographed

1228 A679 45c lil & multi 1.25 60
1229 A679 70c vio & multi 1.25 40

Industrial development. The 35c is luminescent.

Soccer
A683

Designs: 75c, Folk music. 1.30cr, Plastic arts.

Perf. 11½x11

1972, July 7 **Photo.** **Unwmkd.**

1230 A683 20c blk & yel 1.00 50
1231 A683 75c blk & ver 2.00 3.00
1232 A683 1.30cr blk & ultra 3.50 3.00

150th anniversary of independence. No. 1230 publicizes the 1972 sports tournament, a part of independence celebrations. Nos. 1230–1232 are luminescent.

Souvenir Sheet

Shout of Independence, by Pedro Américo de Figueiredo e Melo
A684

1972, July 19 Litho. *Perf. 11½*
Without Gum

1233 A684 1cr multi 6.00 7.50

4th Interamerican Philatelic Exhibition, EXFILBRA, Rio de Janeiro, Aug 26–Sept. 2. No. 1233 contains one stamp (55x37mm.). Black and multicolored margin with white inscription. Size: 125x87mm.

Figurehead—A685

Designs: 60c, Gauchos dancing fandango. 75c, Acrobats (capoeira). 1.15cr, Karajá (ceramic) doll. 1.30cr, Mock bullfight (bumba meu boi).

1972, Aug. 6 Without Gum

1234	A685	45c multi	1.00	35
1235	A685	60c org & multi	2.00	1.50
1236	A685	75c gray & multi	35	35
1237	A685	1.15cr multi	65	65
1238	A685	1.30cr yel & multi	6.00	2.00
		Nos. 1234-1238 (5)	10.00	4.85

Brazilian folklore.

Map of Brazil, by Diego Homem, 1568
A686

Designs: 1cr, Map of Americas, by Nicholas Visscher, 1652. 2cr, Map of Americas, by Lopo Homem, 1519.

1972, Aug. 26 Litho. *Perf. 11½*
Without Gum

1239	A686	70c multi	50	50
1240	A686	1cr multi	9.00	1.00
1241	A686	2cr multi	4.50	1.50

4th Inter-American Philatelic Exhibition, EXFILBRA, Rio de Janeiro, Aug. 26–Sept. 2.

Dom Pedro Proclaimed Emperor, by Jean Baptiste Debret—A687

Designs: 30c, Founding of Brazil (people with imperial flag; vert.). 1cr, Coronation of Emperor Dom Pedro (vert.). 2cr, Dom Pedro commemorative medal. 3.50cr, Independence Monument, Ipiranga.

1972, Sept. 4 Litho. *Perf. 11½x11*

1242	A687	30c yel & grn	1.50	1.50
1243	A687	70c pink & rose lil	1.50	1.00
1244	A687	1cr buff & red brn	10.00	1.50
1245	A687	2cr pale yel & blk	6.00	1.50
1246	A687	3.50cr gray & blk	8.00	5.00
		Nos. 1242-1246 (5)	27.00	10.50

Sesquicentennial of independence.

Souvenir Sheet

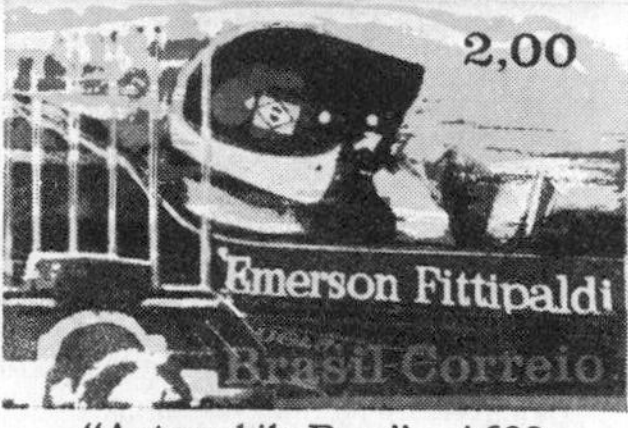

"Automobile Race"—A688

1972, Nov. 14 *Perf. 11½*

1247 A688 2cr multi 12.00 15.00

Emerson Fittipaldi, Brazilian world racing champion. No. 1247 contains one stamp. Multicolored margin with race car design and black inscription. Size: 120x86½mm.

Numeral and Post Office Emblem
A689

Möbius Strip
A689a

Photogravure

1972–75 *Perf. 11½x11* Unwmkd.

1248	A689	5c orange	30	5
a.		Wmk. 267	20	8
1249	A689	10c brn ('73)	20	5
a.		Wmk. 267	4.00	8
1250	A689	15c brt bl ('75)	10	5
1251	A689	20c ultra	30	5
1252	A689	25c sep ('75)	20	5
1253	A689	30c dp car	30	10
1254	A689	40c dk grn ('73)	15	10
1255	A689	50c olive	25	10
1256	A689	70c red lil ('75)	25	10

Engraved *Perf. 11½*

1257	A689a	1cr lil ('74)	40	10
1258	A689a	2cr grnsh bl ('74)	75	12
1259	A689a	4cr org & vio ('75)	1.25	20
1260	A689a	5cr brn, car & buff ('74)	2.00	20
1261	A689a	10cr grn, blk & buff ('74)	4.00	30
		Nos. 1248-1261 (14)	10.45	1.57

The 5cr and 10cr have beige lithographed multiple Post Office emblem underprint.

Nos. 1248–1261 are luminescent. Nos. 1248a and 1249a are not.

Hand Writing "Mobral"
A690

Designs: 20c, Multiracial group and population growth curve. 1cr, People and hands holding house. 2cr, People, industrial scene and upward arrow.

1972, Nov. 28 Litho. *Perf. 11½*
Without Gum

1262	A690	10c blk & multi	50	50
1263	A690	20c blk & multi	1.75	75
1264	A690	1cr blk & multi	11.00	30
1265	A690	2cr blk & multi	2.00	1.00

Publicity for: "Mobral" literacy campaign (10c); Centenary of census (20c); Housing and retirement fund (1cr); Growth of gross national product (2cr).

Congress Building, Brasilia, by Oscar Niemeyer, and "Os Guerreiros," by Bruno Giorgi—A691

1972, Dec. 4 Without Gum

1266 A691 1cr bl, blk & org 10.00 6.00

Meeting of National Congress, Brasilia, Dec. 4–8.

Holy Family (Clay Figurines)
A692

Retirement Plan
A693

1972, Dec. 13 Photo. *Perf. 11½x11*

1267 A692 20c ocher & blk 1.00 50

Christmas 1972. Luminescent.

Perf. 11½x11, 11x11½

1972, Dec. 20 Lithographed

Designs: No. 1269, School children and traffic lights (horiz.). 70c, Dr. Oswaldo Cruz with Red Cross, caricature. 2cr, Produce, fish and cattle (horiz.).

Without Gum

1268	A693	10c blk, bl & dl org	1.00	50
1269	A693	10c org & multi	1.50	1.00
1270	A693	70c blk, red & brn	9.00	3.75
1271	A693	2cr grn & multi	15.00	6.50

Publicity for: Agricultural workers' assistance program (No. 1268); highway and transportation development (No. 1269); centenary of the birth of Dr. Oswaldo Cruz (1872–1917), Director of Public Health Institute (70c); agricultural and cattle export (2cr). Nos. 1268–1271 are luminescent.

Sailing Ship, Navy
A694

Designs: 10c, Monument, Brazilian Expeditionary Force. No. 1274, Plumed helmet, Army. No. 1275, Rocket, Air Force.

Lithographed and Engraved

1972, Dec. 28 *Perf. 11x11½*
Without Gum

1272	A694	10c brn, dk brn & blk	2.00	1.50
1273	A694	30c lt ultra, grn & blk	2.00	1.50
1274	A694	30c yel grn, bl grn & blk	2.00	1.50
1275	A694	30c lil, mar & blk	2.00	1.50

Armed Forces Day. Nos. 1272–1275 are se-tenant in blocks of 4 with greenish blue label showing Navy, Army and Air Force insignia in black.

The first price column gives the catalogue value of an unused stamp, the second that of a used stamp.

Rotary Emblem and Cogwheels
A695

1973, Mar. 21 Litho. Unwmkd.
Perf. 11½

1276 A695 1cr ultra, grnsh bl & yel 2.50 1.50

Rotary International serving Brazil 50 years.

Swimming
A696

Designs: No. 1278, Gymnastics. No. 1279, Volleyball (vert.).

1973 Photo. *Perf. 11x11½, 11½x11*

1277	A696	40c brt bl & red brn	50	50
1278	A696	40c grn & org brn	3.75	1.00
1279	A696	40c vio & org brn	1.00	1.00

Issue dates: No. 1277, Apr. 19; No. 1278, May 22; No. 1279, Oct. 15.

Flag of Paraguay
A697

Perf. 11½

1973, Apr. 27 Litho. Unwmkd.

1280 A697 70c multi 3.00 1.25

Visit of Pres. Alfredo Stroessner of Paraguay, Apr. 25–27.

"Communications"
A698

Design: 1cr, Neptune, map of South America and Africa.

1973, May 5 *Perf. 11x11½*

1281	A698	70c multi	1.25	1.00
1282	A698	1cr multi	6.50	3.00

Inauguration of the Ministry of Communications Building, Brasilia (70c); and of the first underwater telephone cable between South America and Europe, Bracan 1 (1cr).

Congress Emblem
A699

1973, May 19 ***Perf. 11½x11***

1283 A699 1cr org & pur 4.50 3.00

24th Congress of the International Chamber of Commerce, Rio de Janeiro, May 19–26.

Swallow-tailed Manakin
A700

Birds: No. 1285, Orange-backed oriole. No. 1286, Brazilian ruby (hummingbird).

1973 Lithographed ***Perf. 11x11½***

1284 A700 20c multi 50 20
1285 A700 20c multi 50 20
1286 A700 20c multi 50 20

Issue dates: No. 1284, May 26; No. 1285, June 6; No. 1286, June 19.

Tourists
A701

1973, June 28 Litho. ***Perf. 11x11½***

1287 A701 70c multi 1.50 1.00

National Tourism Year.

Conference at Itu
A702

Satellite and Multi-spectral Image
A703

1973 ***Perf. 11½x11***

1288 A702 20c *shown* 75 50
1289 A702 20c *Decorated wagon* 75 50
1290 A702 20c *Indian* 75 50
1291 A702 20c *Graciosa Road* 75 50

Centenary of the Itu Convention (1288); sesquicentennial of the July 2 episode (1289); 400th anniversary of the founding of Niteroi (1290); centenary of Graciosa Road (1291).

Issue dates: No. 1291, July 29; others July 2.

1973, July 11 ***Perf. 11½***

Designs: 70c, Official opening of Engineering School, 1913. 1cr, Möbius strips and "IMPA."

1292 A703 20c blk & multi 30 50
1293 A703 70c dk bl & multi 2.50 1.25
1294 A703 1cr lil & multi 3.50 1.25

Institute for Space Research (20c); School of Engineering, Itajubá, 60th anniversary (70c); Institute for Pure and Applied Mathematics (1cr).

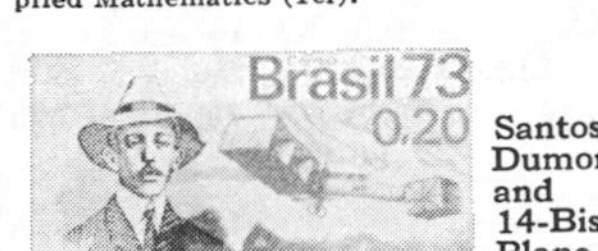

Santos-Dumont and 14-Bis Plane
A704

Designs (Santos-Dumont and): 70c, No. 6 Balloon and Eiffel Tower. 2cr Demoiselle plane.

Lithographed and Engraved

1973, July 20 ***Perf. 11x11½***

1295 A704 20c lt grn, brt grn & brn 1.25 30
1296 A704 70c yel, rose red & brn 3.00 1.50
1297 A704 2cr bl, vio bl & brn 3.00 1.50

Centenary of the birth of Alberto Santos-Dumont (1873–1932), aviation pioneer.

Mercator Map
A705

Design: No. 1299, Same, red border on top and at left.

Photogravure & Engraved

1973, Aug. 1 **Wmk. 267**

1298 A705 40c red & blk 3.75 1.50
1299 A705 40c red & blk 2.25 3.00
Block of 4 30.00 15.00

Stamp Day. Nos. 1298–1299 are printed se-tenant horizontally and tête bêche vertically in sheets of 55. Blocks of 4 have red border all around.

Gonçalves Dias
A706

Perf. 11½x11

1973, Aug. 10 **Wmk. 267**

1300 A706 40c vio & blk 1.00 50

Sesquicentenary of the birth of Antonio Gonçalves Dias (1823–1864), poet.

Souvenir Sheet

Copernicus and Sun—A707

Perf. 11x11½

1973, Aug. 15 Litho. Unwmkd.

1301 A707 1cr multi 4.50 5.00

500th anniversary of the birth of Nicolaus Copernicus (1473–1543), Polish astronomer. No. 1301 contains one stamp; multicolored margin. Size: 124x86mm.

Folklore Festival Banner
A708

1973, Aug. 22 ***Perf. 11½***

1302 A708 40c ultra & multi 1.25 60

Folklore Day, Aug. 22.

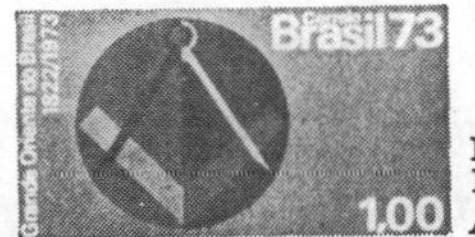

Masonic Emblem
A709

1973, Aug. 24 Photo. ***Perf. 11x11½***

1303 A709 1cr Prus bl 3.00 2.00

Free Masons of Brazil, 1822–1973.

Nature Protection
A710

Designs: No. 1305, Fire protection. No. 1306, Aviation safety. No. 1307, Safeguarding cultural heritage.

1973, Sept. 20 Litho. ***Perf. 11x11½***

1304 A710 40c brt grn & multi 75 40
1305 A710 40c dk bl & multi 75 40
1306 A710 40c lt bl & multi 75 40
1307 A710 40c pink & multi 75 40

Souvenir Sheet

St. Gabriel and Proclamation of Pope Paul VI—A711

Lithographed and Engraved

1973, Sept. 29 ***Perf. 11½*** **Unwmkd.**

1308 A711 1cr bis & blk 9.00 10.00

1st National Exhibition of Religious Philately, Rio de Janeiro, Sept. 29–Oct. 6. No. 1308 contains one stamp; bister margin and black inscription. Size: 123x87½mm.

St. Teresa
A712

Photogravure and Engraved

Perf. 11½x11

1973, Sept. 30 **Wmk. 267**

1309 A712 2cr dk org & brn 6.00 2.50

Centenary of the birth of St. Teresa of Lisieux, the Little Flower (1873–1897), Carmelite nun.

Monteiro Lobato and Emily
A713

Perf. 11½

1973, Oct. 12 Litho. Unwmkd.

Multicolored

1310 A713 40c *shown* 1.00 50
1311 A713 40c *Aunt Nastacia* 1.00 50
1312 A713 40c *Snubnose, Peter and Rhino* 1.00 50
1313 A713 40c *Viscount de Sabugosa* 1.00 50
1314 A713 40c *Dona Benta* 1.00 50
Block of 5 + label 5.00 5.00

Monteiro Lobato, author of children's books. Nos. 1310–1314 printed in sheets of 30 stamps and 6 labels.

Soapstone Sculpture of Isaiah (detail)
A714

Baroque Art in Brazil: No. 1316, Arabesque, gilded wood carving (horiz.). 70c, Father José Mauricio Nuñes Garcia and music score. 1cr, Church door, Salvador, Bahia. 2cr, Angels, church ceiling painting by Manoel da Costa Athayde (horiz.).

1973, Nov. 5

1315 A714 40c multi 30 30
1316 A714 40c multi 30 30
1317 A714 70c multi 1.50 1.40
1318 A714 1cr multi 9.00 3.00
1319 A714 2cr multi 3.00 3.00
Nos. 1315-1319 (5) 14.10 8.00

Old and New Telephones
A715

1973, Nov. 28 ***Perf. 11x11½***

1320 A715 40c multi 50 40

50th anniversary of Brazilian Telephone Company.

Symbolic Angel
A716

1973, Nov. 30 ***Perf. 11½***

1321 A716 40c ver & multi 50 40

Christmas 1973.

"Gaiola"
A717

Designs: River boats.

1973, Nov. 30 Litho. ***Perf. 11x11½***

Multicolored

1322 A717 40c *shown* 50 50
1323 A717 70c *"Regatao"* 1.50 1.50
1324 A717 1cr *"Jangada"* 6.50 3.00
1325 A717 2cr *"Saveiro"* 6.00 3.00

Nos. 1322–1325 are luminescent.

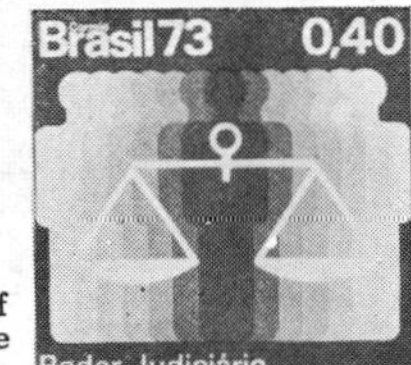

Scales of Justice
A718

1973, Dec. 5 ***Perf. 11½***

1326 A718 40c mag & vio 75 35

To honor the High Federal Court, created in 1891. Luminescent.

José Placido de Castro
A719

Scarlet Ibis and Victoria Regia
A720

Lithographed and Engraved

Perf. 11½x11

1973, Dec. 12 **Wmk. 267**

1327	A719	40c lil rose & blk	1.00	35

Centenary of the birth of José Placido de Castro, liberator of the State of Acre.

Perf. 11½x11

1973, Dec. 28 **Litho.** **Unwmkd.**

Designs: 70c, Jaguar and spathodea campanulata. 1cr, Scarlet macaw and carnauba palm. 2cr, Rhea and coral tree.

1328	A720	40c brn & multi	1.50	50
1329	A720	70c brn & multi	3.50	2.00
1330	A720	1cr bis & multi	6.50	50
1331	A720	2cr bis & multi	10.00	4.50

Nos. 1328–1331 are luminescent.

Saci Pereré, Mocking Goblin
A721

Characters from Brazilian Legends: 80c, Zumbi, last chief of rebellious slaves. 1cr, Chico Rei, African king. 1.30cr, Little Black Boy of the Pasture. 2.50cr, Iara, Queen of the Waters.

Perf. 11½x11

1974, Feb. 28 **Litho.** **Unwmkd.**

Size: 21x39mm.

1332	A721	40c multi	50	25
1333	A721	80c multi	1.00	75
1334	A721	1cr multi	2.00	50

Size: 32½x33mm.

Perf. 11½

1335	A721	1.30cr multi	3.50	1.00
1336	A721	2.50cr multi	13.50	3.00
		Nos. 1332-1336 (5)	20.50	5.50

Nos. 1332–1336 are luminescent.

Pres. Costa e Silva Bridge
A722

1974, Mar. 11

1337	A722	40c multi	75	35

Inauguration of the Pres. Costa e Silva Bridge, Rio Niteroi, connecting Rio de Janeiro and Guanabara State.

"The Press"
A723

1974, Mar. 25 ***Perf. 11½***

Multicolored

1338	A723	40c *shown*	60	40
1339	A723	40c *"Radio"*	30	30
1340	A723	40c *"Television"*	50	40

Communications Commemorations: No. 1338, bicentenary of first Brazilian newspaper, published in London by Hipolito da Costa; No. 1339, founding of the Radio Sociedade do Rio de Janeiro by Roquette Pinto; No. 1340, installation of first Brazilian television station by Assis Chateaubriand. Luminescent.

"Reconstruction"
A724

1974, Mar. 31

1341	A724	40c multi	1.00	50

10 years of progress. Luminescent.

Corcovado Christ, Marconi, Colors of Brazil and Italy
A725

1974, Apr. 25 **Litho.** ***Perf. 11½***

1342	A725	2.50cr multi	7.50	3.00

Centenary of the birth of Guglielmo Marconi (1874–1937), Italian physicist and inventor. Luminescent.

Stamp Printing Press, Stamp Designing
A726

1974, May 6

1343	A726	80c multi	1.00	50

Brazilian mint.

World Map, Indian, Caucasian and Black Men
A727

Designs (World Map and): No. 1345, Brazilians. No. 1346, Cabin and German horseback rider. No. 1347, Italian farm wagon. No. 1348, Japanese woman and torii.

1974, May 11 **Unwmkd.**

1344	A727	40c multi	50	35
1345	A727	40c multi	30	30
1346	A727	2.50cr multi	5.00	1.75
1347	A727	2.50cr multi	7.50	1.75
1348	A727	2.50cr multi	1.75	1.00
		Nos. 1344-1348 (5)	15.05	5.15

Ethnic and migration influences in Brazil.

Sandstone Cliffs, Sete Cidades National Park—A728

Design: 80c, Ruins of Cathedral of São Miguel das Missões.

Lithographed and Engraved

1974, June 8 ***Perf. 11x11½***

1349	A728	40c multi	1.00	50
1350	A728	80c multi	1.00	50

Tourist publicity.

Souvenir Sheet

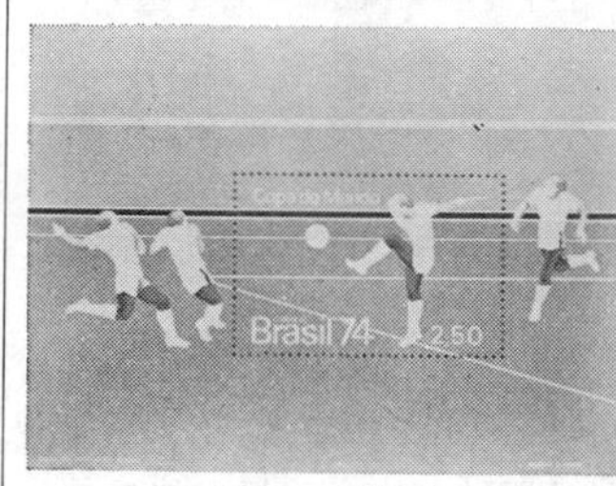

Soccer—A729

1974, June 20 **Litho.** ***Perf. 11½***

1351	A729	2.50cr multi	4.50	6.00

World Cup Soccer Championship, Munich, June 13–July 7. No. 1351 has multicolored margin. Size: 130x95mm.

Church and College, Caraça
A730

1974, July 6 **Litho.** ***Perf. 11x11½***

1352	A730	40c multi	75	35

Bicentenary of the College (Seminary) of Caraça.

Wave on Television Screen
A731

1974, July 15 ***Perf. 11½***

1353	A731	40c blk & bl	60	40

TELEBRAS, Third Brazilian Congress of Telecommunications, Brasilia, July 15–20.

Fernão Dias Paes
A732

1974, July 21 ***Perf. 11½***

1354	A732	20c grn & multi	50	30

3rd centenary of the expedition led by Fernão Dias Paes exploring Minas Gerais and the passage from South to North in Brazil.

Mexican Flag
A733

1974, July 24 **Litho.** ***Perf. 11½***

1355	A733	80c multi	3.50	1.25

Visit of Pres. Luis Echeverria Alvares of Mexico, July 24–29.

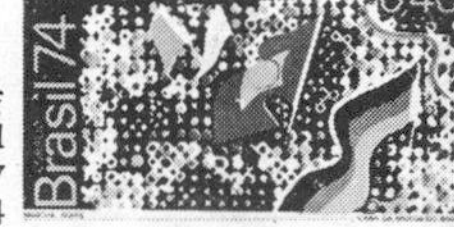

Flags of Brazil and Germany
A734

1974, Aug. 5 ***Perf. 11x11½***

1356	A734	40c multi	1.00	50

World Cup Soccer Championship, 1974, victory of German Federal Republic.

Souvenir Sheet

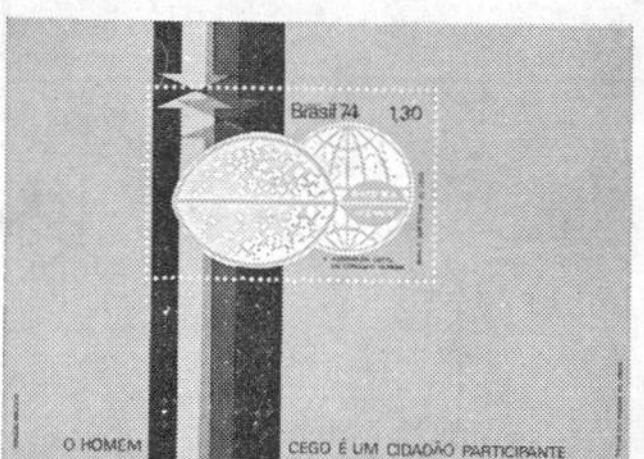

Congress Emblem—A735

1974, Aug. 7 ***Perf. 11½***

1357	A735	1.30cr multi	1.00	*2.00*

5th World Assembly of the World Council for the Welfare of the Blind, São Paulo, Aug. 7–16. No. 1357 has ocher margin with black inscription. Stamp and margin inscribed in Braille with name of Assembly. Size: 126x88½mm.

Raul Pederneiras, Caricature by J. Carlos
A736

Lithographed and Engraved

1974, Aug. 15 ***Perf. 11½x11***

1358	A736	40c buff, blk & ocher	50	40

Centenary of the birth of Raul Pederneiras (1874–1953), journalist, professor of law and fine arts.

Society Emblem and Landscape
A737

Perf. 11x11½

1974, Aug. 19 **Lithographed**

1359 A737 1.30cr multi 1.75 1.00

13th Congress of the International Union of Building and Savings Societies.

Souvenir Sheet

Five Women, by Di Cavalcanti—A738

1974, Aug. 26 **Litho.** ***Perf. 11½***

1360 A738 2cr multi 3.00 4.50

LUBRAPEX 74, 5th Portuguese-Brazilian Philatelic Exhibition, São Paulo, Nov. 26–Dec. 4. No. 1360 has gray marginal inscription. Size of stamp: 37x55mm., size of sheet: 87x125mm.

"UPU" and World Map
A739

1974, Oct. 9 **Litho.** ***Perf. 11½***

1361 A739 2.50cr blk & brt bl 6.50 2.25

Centenary of Universal Postal Union.

Hammock (Antillean Arawak Culture)
A740

Bilro Lace
A741

Singer of "Cord" Verses
A742

Ceramic Figure by Master Vitalino
A743

1974, Oct. 16 **Litho.** ***Perf. 11½***

1362 A740 50c dp rose lil 1.75 50
1363 A741 50c lt & dk bl 2.25 50
1364 A742 50c yel & red brn 50 50
1365 A743 50c brt yel & dk brn 65 50

Popular Brazilian crafts.

Branch of Coffee
A744

1974, Oct. 27 ***Perf. 11*** **Unwmkd.**

1366 A744 50c multi 1.00 75

Centenary of city of Campinas.

Hornless Tabapuã
A745

Animals of Brazil: 1.30cr, Creole horse. 2.50cr, Brazilian mastiff.

1974, Nov. 10 ***Perf. 11½***

1367 A745 80c multi 1.50 75
1368 A745 1.30cr multi 1.50 75
1369 A745 2.50cr multi 12.00 2.50

Angel
A746

1974, Nov. 18 ***Perf. 11½x11***

1370 A746 50c ultra & multi 85 40

Christmas 1974.

Solteira Island Hydroelectric Dam
A747

1974, Nov. 18 ***Perf. 11½***

1371 A747 50c blk & yel 1.25 50

Inauguration of the Solteira Island Hydroelectric Dam over Parana River.

The Girls, by Carlos Reis
A748

1974, Nov. 26

1372 A748 1.30cr multi 1.00 50

LUBRAPEX 74, 5th Portuguese-Brazilian Philatelic Exhibition, São Paulo, Nov. 26–Dec. 4.

Youths, Judge, Scales
A749

1974, Dec. 20 **Litho.** ***Perf. 11½***

1373 A749 90c yel, red & bl 50 35

Juvenile Court of Brazil, 50th anniversary.

Long Distance Runner
A750

1974, Dec. 23

1374 A750 3.30cr multi 1.25 75

São Silvestre long distance running, 50th anniversary.

News Vendor, 1875, Masthead, 1975
A751

1975, Jan. 4

1375 A751 50c multi 1.75 75

Centenary of the newspaper "O Estado de S. Paulo."

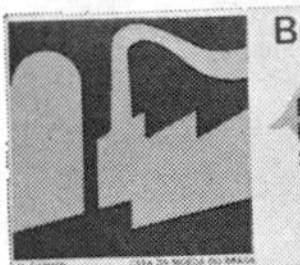

São Paulo Industrial Park
A752

Designs: 1.40cr, Natural rubber industry, Acre. 4.50cr, Manganese mining, Amapá.

1975, Jan. 24 **Litho.** ***Perf. 11x11½***

1376 A752 50c vio bl & yel 2.25 50
1377 A752 1.40cr yel & brn 1.00 75
1378 A752 4.50cr yel & blk 10.00 50

Economic development.

Fort of the Holy Cross
A753

Designs: No. 1380, Fort of the Three Kings. No. 1381, Fort of Montserrat. 90c, Fort of Our Lady of Help.

Lithographed, Engraved

1975, Mar. 14 ***Perf. 11½***

1379 A753 50c yel & red brn 25 25
1380 A753 50c yel & red brn 50 25
1381 A753 50c yel & red brn 1.00 25
1382 A753 90c yel & red brn 25 25

Colonial forts.

House on Stilts, Amazon Region
A754

Designs: 50c, Modern houses and plan of Brasilia. 1.40cr, Indian hut, Rondonia. 3.30cr, German-style cottage (Enxaimel), Santa Catarina.

1975, Apr. 18 **Litho.** ***Perf. 11½***

1383 A754 50c yel & multi 2.25 2.50
1384 A754 50c yel & multi 15.00 7.50
1385 A754 1cr yel & multi 1.50 25
1386 A754 1.40cr yel & multi 3.00 3.00
1387 A754 1.40cr yel & multi 1.00 1.00
1388 A754 3.30cr yel & multi 1.50 1.50
1389 A754 3.30cr yel & multi 6.00 4.50
Nos. 1383-1389 (7) 30.25 20.25

Brazilian architecture. Nos. 1383–1384, 1386–1387, 1388–1389 printed se-tenant in sheets of 50. Nos. 1383, 1386, 1388 have yellow strip at right side, others at left; No. 1385 has yellow strip on both sides.

Astronotus Ocellatus
A755

Designs: Brazilian fresh-water fish.

1975, May 2 **Litho.** ***Perf. 11½***

Pale Green and Multicolored

1390 A755 50c *shown* 2.25 40
1391 A755 50c *Colomesus psitacus* 25 25
1392 A755 50c *Phallocerus caudimaculatus* 40 40
1393 A755 50c *Symphysodon discus* 75 50

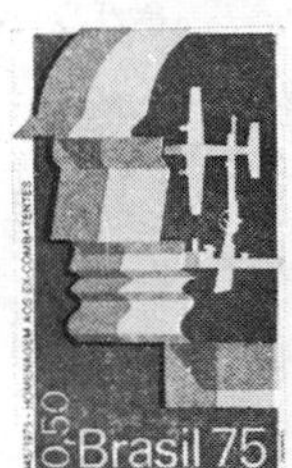
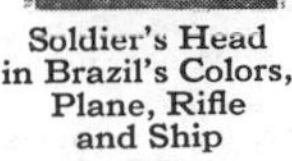
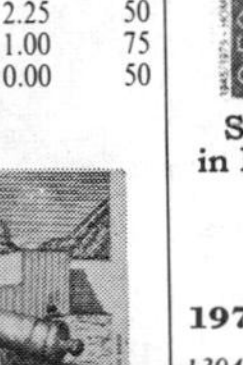

Soldier's Head in Brazil's Colors, Plane, Rifle and Ship
A756

Brazilian Otter
A757

1975, May 8 ***Perf. 11½x11***

1394 A756 50c vio bl & multi 50 35

In honor of the veterans of World War II, on the 30th anniversary of victory.

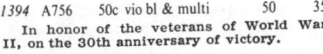

1975, June 17 **Litho.** ***Perf. 11½***

Designs: 70c, Brazilian pines (horiz.). 3.30cr, Marsh cayman (horiz.).

1395	A757	70c bl, grn & blk	1.50	50
1396	A757	1cr multi	1.50	1.00
1397	A757	3.30cr multi	1.25	75

Nature protection.

Petroglyphs, Stone of Ingá
A758

Marjoara Vase, Pará
A759

Vinctifer Comptoni, Petrified Fish
A760

1975, July 8 **Litho.** ***Perf. 11½***

1398	A758	70c multi	1.00	40
1399	A759	1cr multi	75	40
1400	A760	1cr multi	75	40

Archaeological discoveries.

Immaculate Conception, Franciscan Monastery, Vitoria
A761

Post and Telegraph Ministry
A762

1975, July 15

1401	A761	3.30cr bl & multi	1.50	1.25

Holy Year 1975 and 300th anniversary of establishment of the Franciscan Province in Southern Brazil.

1975, Aug. 8 **Engr.** ***Perf. 11½***

1402	A762	70c dk car	1.25	30

Stamp Day 1975.

Sword Dance, Minas Gerais
A763

Folk Dances: No. 1404, Umbrella Dance, Pernambuco. No. 1405, Warrior's Dance, Alagoas.

1975, Aug. 22 **Litho.** ***Perf. 11½***

1403	A763	70c gray & multi	50	50
1404	A763	70c pink & multi	50	50
1405	A763	70c yel & multi	50	50

Trees
A764

1975, Sept. 15 ***Perf. 11x11½***

1406	A764	70c multi	50	25

Annual Tree Festival.

Globe, Radar and Satellite
A765

1975, Sept. 16 ***Perf. 11½***

1407	A765	3.30cr multi	1.25	75

Inauguration of 2nd antenna of Tangua Earth Station, Rio de Janeiro State.

Woman Holding Flowers and Globe
A766

1975, Sept. 23

1408	A766	3.30cr multi	1.50	1.00

International Women's Year 1975.

Tile, Railing and Column, Alcantara
A767

Cross and Monastery, São Cristovão
A768

Design: No. 1411, Jug and Clock Tower, Goiás (vert.).

1975, Sept. 27 **Litho.** ***Perf. 11½***

1409	A767	70c multi	50	50
1410	A768	70c multi	90	50
1411	A768	70c multi	90	50

Historic cities.

"Books teach how to live"
A769

1975, Oct. 23 **Litho.** ***Perf. 11½***

1412	A769	70c multi	30	30

Day of the Book.

ASTA Congress Emblem
A770

1975, Oct. 27 ***Perf. 11x11½***

1413	A770	70c multi	30	30

American Society of Travel Agents, 45th World Congress, Rio de Janeiro, Oct. 27–Nov. 1.

Angels
A771

1975, Nov. 11

1414	A771	70c red & brn	35	20

Christmas 1975.

Map of Americas, Waves
A772

Dom Pedro II
A773

1975, Nov. 19 ***Perf. 11½x12***

1415	A772	5.20cr gray & multi	6.00	2.25

2nd Interamerican Conference of Telecommunications (CITEL), Rio de Janeiro, Nov. 19–27.

1975, Dec. 2 **Engr.** ***Perf. 12***

1416	A773	70c vio brn	1.25	50

Dom Pedro II (1825–1891), emperor of Brazil, birth sesquicentennial.

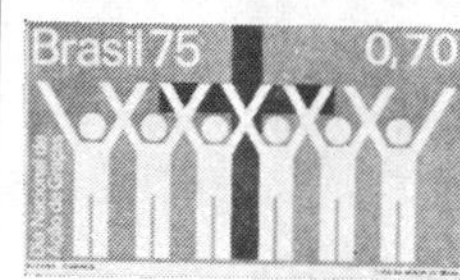

People and Cross
A774

1975, Dec. 4 **Litho.** ***Perf. 11x11½***

1417	A774	70c lt bl & dp bl	65	65

National Day of Thanksgiving.

Guarapari Beach, Espirito Santo
A775

Designs: No. 1419, Salt Stone beach, Piaui. No. 1420, Cliffs, Rio Grande Do Sul.

1975, Dec. 19 **Litho.** ***Perf. 11½***

1418	A775	70c multi	35	35
1419	A775	70c multi	35	35
1420	A775	70c multi	35	35

Tourist publicity.

Triple Jump, Games Emblem
A776

1975, Dec. 22 ***Perf. 11x11½***

1421	A776	1.60cr bl grn & blk	35	35

Triple jump world record by Joao Carlos de Oliveira in 7th Pan-American Games, Mexico City, Oct. 12–26.

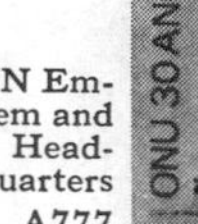

UN Emblem and Headquarters
A777

1975, Dec. 29 ***Perf. 11½***

1422	A777	1.30cr dp bl & vio bl	30	30

United Nations, 30th anniversary.

Light Bulbs, House and Sun
A778

Design: No. 1424, Gasoline drops, car and sun.

1976, Jan. 16

1423	A778	70c multi	50	20
1424	A778	70c multi	50	15

Energy conservation.

Concorde—A779

1976, Jan. 21 **Litho.** ***Perf. 11x11½***

1425	A779	5.20cr bluish blk	35	35

First commercial flight of supersonic jet Concorde from Paris to Rio de Janeiro, Jan. 21.

Souvenir Sheet

Nautical Map of South Atlantic, 1776—A780

1976, Feb. 2 ***Perf. 11½***

1426	A780	70c sal & multi	75	1.50

Centenary of the Naval Hydrographic and Navigation Institute. Size: 88x123mm.

Telephone Lines, 1876 Telephone
A781

1976, Mar. 10 Litho. *Perf. 11x11½*

1427	A781	5.20cr org & bl	75	75

Centenary of first telephone call by Alexander Graham Bell, March 10, 1876.

Eye and Exclamation Point
A782

Kaiapo Body Painting
A783

1976, Apr. 7 Litho. *Perf. 11½x11*

1428	A782	1cr vio red brn & brn	60	60

World Health Day: "Foresight prevents blindness."

1976, Apr. 19 Litho. *Perf. 11½*

Designs: No. 1430, Bakairi ceremonial mask. No. 1431, Karajá feather headdress.

1429	A783	1cr lt vio & multi	20	20
1430	A783	1cr lt vio & multi	20	20
1431	A783	1cr lt vio & multi	20	20

Preservation of indigenous culture.

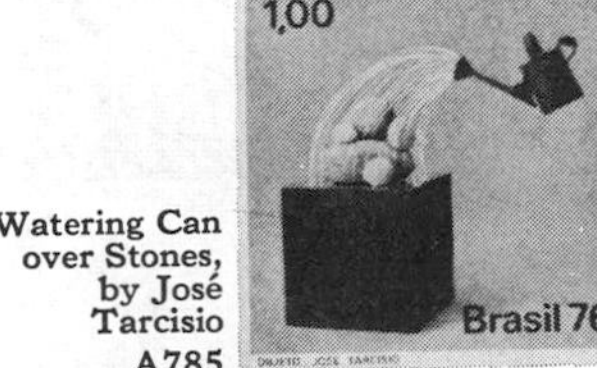

Itamaraty Palace, Brasilia
A784

1976, Apr. 20

1432	A784	1cr multi	75	75

Diplomats' Day. Itamaraty Palace, designed by Oscar Niemeyer, houses the Ministry of Foreign Affairs.

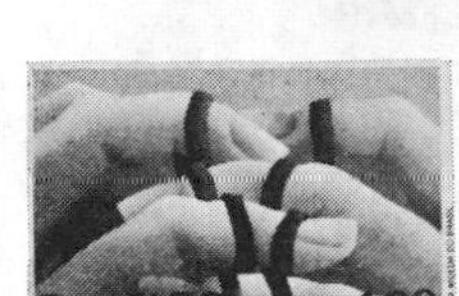

Fingers and Ribbons, by Pietrina Checcacci
A786

Watering Can over Stones, by José Tarcisio
A785

1976, May 14 Litho. *Perf. 11½*

1433	A785	1cr multi	40	35
1434	A786	1.60cr multi	50	35

Modern Brazilian art.

Basketball
A787

Orchid
A788

Designs (Olympic Rings and): 1.40cr, Yachting. 5.20cr, Judo.

1976, May 21 Litho. *Perf. 11½*

1435	A787	1cr emer & blk	20	15
1436	A787	1.40cr dk bl & blk	25	15
1437	A787	5.20cr org & blk	75	50

21st Olympic Games, Montreal, Canada, July 17–Aug. 1.

1976, June 4 *Perf. 11½x11*

Design: No. 1439, Golden-faced lion monkey.

1438	A788	1cr multi	35	30
1439	A788	1cr multi	35	30

Nature protection.

Film Camera, Brazilian Colors
A789

1976, June 19

1440	A789	1cr vio bl, brt grn & yel	35	25

Brazilian film industry.

Bahia Woman
A790

Designs: 10c, Oxcart driver (horiz.). 20c, Raft fishermen (horiz.). 30c, Rubber plantation worker. 40c, Cowboy (horiz.). 50c, Gaucho. 80c, Gold panner. 1cr, Banana plantation worker. 1.10cr, Grape harvester. 1.30cr, Coffee picker. 1.80cr, Farmer gathering wax palms. 2cr, Potter. 5cr, Sugar cane cutter. 7cr, Salt mine worker. 10cr, Fisherman. 15cr, Coconut seller. 20cr, Lacemaker.

Perf. 11½x11, 11x11½

1976–78 Photogravure

1441	A790	10c red brn ('77)	10	5
1442	A790	15c brown	50	50
1443	A790	20c vio bl	10	5
1444	A790	30c lil rose	10	5
1445	A790	40c org ('77)	15	5
1446	A790	50c citron	10	5
1447	A790	80c sl grn	60	5
1448	A790	1cr black	20	5
1449	A790	1.10cr mag ('77)	20	5
1450	A790	1.30cr red ('77)	20	5
1451	A790	1.80cr dk vio bl ('78)	30	5

Engraved

1452	A790	2cr brn ('77)	40	5
1453	A790	5cr dk pur ('77)	90	5
1454	A790	7cr violet	2.50	5
1455	A790	10cr yel grn ('77)	1.00	5
1456	A790	15cr gray grn ('78)	2.50	5
1457	A790	20cr blue	2.50	5
		Nos. 1441-1457 (17)	12.35	1.30

See Nos. 1653-1657

Hyphessobrycon Innesi
A791

Designs: Brazilian fresh-water fish.

1976, July 12 Litho. *Perf. 11x11½*
Multicolored

1460	A791	1cr *shown*	60	50
1461	A791	1cr *Copeina arnoldi*	60	50
1462	A791	1cr *Prochilodus insignis*	60	50
1463	A791	1cr *Crenicichla lepidota*	60	50
1464	A791	1cr *Ageneiosus*	60	50
1465	A791	1cr *Corydoras reticulatus*	60	50
		Nos. 1460-1465 (6)	3.60	3.00

Nos. 1460–1465 printed se-tenant in sheets of 36.

Santa Marta Lighthouse
A792

1976, July 29 Engr. *Perf. 12x11½*

1466	A792	1cr blue	50	30

300th anniversary of the city of Laguna.

Children on Magic Carpet
A793

1976, Aug. 1 Litho. *Perf. 11½x12*

1467	A793	1cr multi	25	20

Stamp Day.

Nurse's Lamp and Head
A794

1976, Aug. 12 Litho. *Perf. 11½*

1468	A794	1cr multi	35	20

Brazilian Nurses' Association, 50th anniversary.

Puppet, Soldier
A795

Winner's Medal
A796

Designs: 1.30cr, Girl's head. 1.60cr, Hand with puppet head on each finger (horiz.).

1976, Aug. 20

1469	A795	1cr multi	25	20
1470	A795	1.30cr multi	25	20
1471	A795	1.60cr multi	25	20

Mamulengo puppet show.

1976, Aug. 21

1472	A796	5.20cr multi	1.00	50

27th International Military Athletic Championships, Rio de Janeiro, Aug. 21–28.

Family Protection
A797

1976, Sept. 12

1473	A797	1cr lt & dk bl	25	20

National organizations SENAC and SESC helping commercial employees to improve their living standard, both commercially and socially.

Dying Tree
A798

1976, Sept. 20 Litho. *Perf. 11½*

1474	A798	1cr gray & multi	25	20

Protection of the environment.

Atom Symbol, Electron Orbits
A799

1976, Sept. 21

1475	A799	5.20cr multi	1.00	50

20th General Conference of the International Atomic Energy Agency, Rio de Janeiro, Sept. 21–29.

Train in Tunnel
A800

1976, Sept. 26

1476 A800 1.60cr multi 35 25

Inauguration of Sao Paulo subway, first in Brazil.

St. Francis and Birds
A801

1976, Oct. 4

1477 A801 5.20cr multi 1.00 50

St. Francis of Assisi, 750th death anniversary.

Ouro Preto School of Mining
A802

1976, Oct. 12 Engr. *Perf. 12x11½*

1478 A802 1cr dk vio 50 50

Ouro Preto School of Mining, centenary.

Three Kings
A803

Designs: Children's drawings.

1976, Nov. 4 Litho. *Perf. 11½*

Multicolored

1479	A803	80c *shown*	50	35
1480	A803	80c *Santa Claus on donkey*	50	35
1481	A803	80c *Virgin and Child and Angels*	30	35
1482	A803	80c *Angels with candle*	50	35
1483	A803	80c *Nativity*	50	35
		Nos. 1479-1483 (5)	2.30	1.75

Christmas 1976. Nos. 1479–1483 printed se-tenant in sheets of 35.

Souvenir Sheet

30,000 Reis Banknote—A804

1976, Nov. 5 Litho. *Perf. 11½*

1484 A804 80c multi 25 *1.50*

Opening of 1000th branch of Bank of Brazil, Barra do Bugres, Mato Grosso. No. 1484 contains one stamp. Size of stamp: 38x56½mm.; size of sheet: 125x87mm.

Virgin of Monte Serrat, by Friar Agostinho
A805

St. Joseph, 18th Century Wood Sculpture
A806

Designs: 5.60cr, The Dance, by Rodolfo Bernadelli, 19th century. 6.50cr, The Caravel, by Bruno Giorgi, 20th century abstract sculpture.

1976, Nov. 5

1485	A805	80c multi	20	10
1486	A806	5cr multi	75	40
1487	A805	5.60cr multi	90	40
1488	A806	6.50cr multi	90	40

Development of Brazilian sculpture.

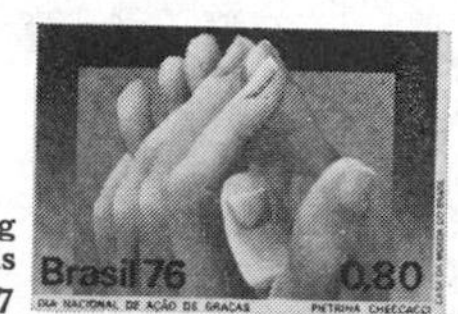

Praying Hands
A807

1976, Nov. 25

1489 A807 80c multi 25 25

National Day of Thanksgiving.

Sailor, 1840
A808

Design: 2cr, Marine's uniform, 1808.

1976, Dec. 13 Litho. *Perf. 11½x11*

1490	A808	80c multi	25	25
1491	A808	2cr multi	35	25

Brazilian Navy.

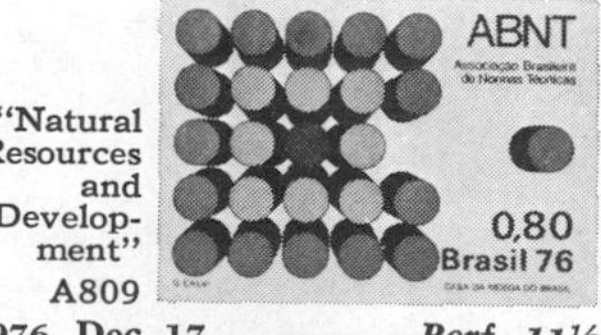

"Natural Resources and Development"
A809

1976, Dec. 17 *Perf. 11½*

1492 A809 80c multi 25 20

Brazilian Bureau of Standards, founded 1940.

Wheel of Life
A810

Designs: 5.60cr, Beggar, sculpture by Agnaldo dos Santos. 6.50cr, Benin mask.

1977, Jan. 14

1493	A810	5cr multi	1.00	40
1494	A810	5.60cr multi	1.00	40
1495	A810	6.50cr multi	1.75	40

FESTAC '77, 2nd World Black and African Festival, Lagos, Nigeria, Jan. 15–Feb. 12.

A811

1977, Jan. 20 Litho. *Perf. 11½*

1496 A811 6.50cr bl & yel grn 1.25 65

Rio de Janeiro International Airport.

Seminar Emblem with Map of Americas
A812

Salicylate, Microphoto
A813

1977, Feb. 6

1497 A812 1.10cr gray, vio bl & bl 50 20

6th Inter-American Budget Seminar.

1977, Apr. 10 Litho. *Perf. 11½*

1498 A813 1.10cr multi 25 10

International Rheumatism Year.

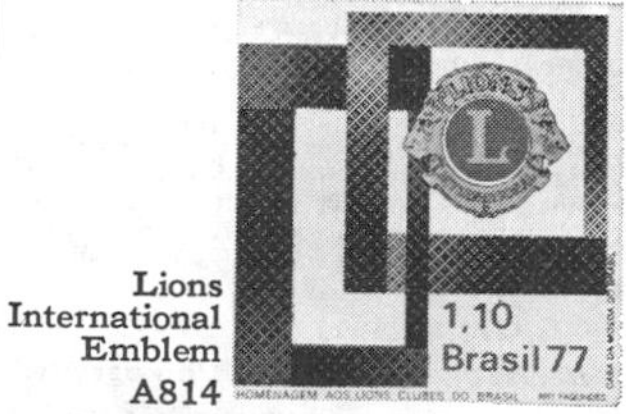

Lions International Emblem
A814

1977, Apr. 16

1499 A814 1.10cr multi 25 20

25th anniversary of Brazilian Lions International.

Heitor Villa Lobos
A815

1977, Apr. 26 *Perf. 11x11½*

Multicolored

1500	A815	1.10cr *shown*	25	20
1501	A815	1.10cr *Chiquinha Gonzaga*	25	20
1502	A815	1.10cr *Noel Rosa*	25	20

Brazilian composers.

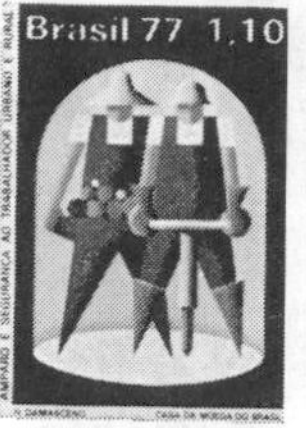

Farmer and Worker
A816

Medicine Bottles and Flask
A817

1977, May 8 Litho. *Perf. 11½*

1503	A816	1.10cr grn & multi	25	20
1504	A817	1.10cr lt & dk grn	25	20

Support and security for rural and urban workers (No. 1503) and establishment in 1971 of Medicine Distribution Center (CEME) for low-cost medicines (No. 1504).

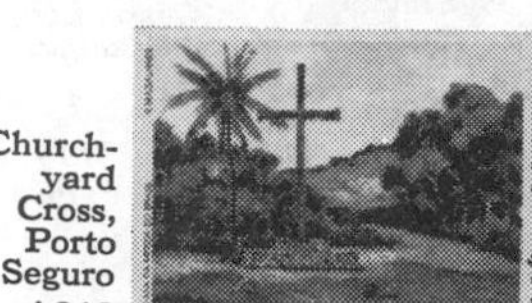

Churchyard Cross, Porto Seguro
A818

Views, Porto Seguro: 5cr, Beach and boats. 5.60cr, Our Lady of Pena Chapel. 6.50cr, Town Hall.

1977, May 25 Litho. *Perf. 11½*

1505	A818	1.10cr multi	25	15
1506	A818	5cr multi	2.25	40
1507	A818	5.60cr multi	1.00	50
1508	A818	6.50cr multi	1.75	60

Centenary of Brazil's membership in Universal Postal Union.

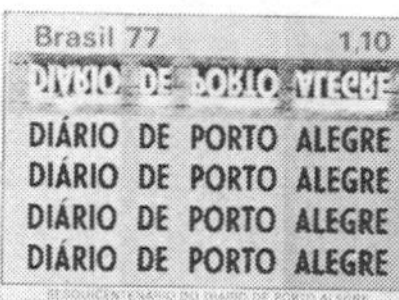

Diario de Porto Alegre
A819

1977, June 1

1509 A819 1.10cr multi 25 20

150th anniversary of Diario de Porto Alegre, newspaper.

Blue Whale
A820

1977, June 3

1510 A820 1.30cr multi 25 20

Protection of marine life.

"Life and Development"
A821

1977, June 20

1511 A821 1.30cr multi 25 20

National Development Bank, 25th anniversary.

Train Leaving Tunnel
A822

1977, July 8 **Engr.** ***Perf. 11½***

1512 A822 1.30cr black 25 20

Centenary of São Paulo-Rio de Janeiro railroad.

Vasum Cassiforme
A823

Caduceus, Formulas for Water and Fluoride
A824

Sea Shells: No. 1514, Strombus goliath. No. 1515, Murex tenuivaricosus.

1977, July 14 **Lithographed**

1513 A823 1.30cr bl & multi 25 20
1514 A823 1.30cr brn & multi 25 20
1515 A823 1.30cr grn & multi 25 20

1977, July 15 ***Perf. 11½x11***

1516 A824 1.30cr multi 25 20

3rd International Odontology Congress, Rio de Janeiro, July 15–21.

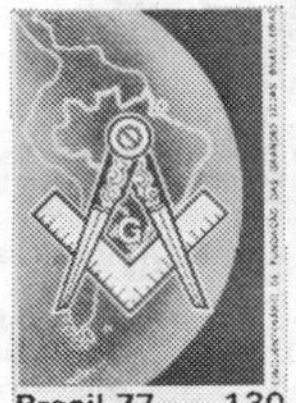

Masonic Emblem, Map of Brazil
A825

"Stamps Don't Sink or Lose their Way"
A826

1977, July 18 ***Perf. 11½***

1517 A825 1.30cr bl, lt bl & blk 25 20

50th anniversary of the founding of the Brazilian Grand Masonic Lodge.

1977, Aug. 1

1518 A826 1.30cr multi 25 20

Stamp Day 1977.

Dom Pedro's Proclamation
A827

Horses and Bulls
A828

1977, Aug. 11 **Litho.** ***Perf. 11½***

1519 A827 1.30cr multi 25 20

150th anniversary of Brazilian Law School.

Perf. 11½x11, 11x11½

1977, Aug. 20 **Lithographed**

Designs: No. 1521, King on horseback. No. 1522, Joust (horiz.).

1520 A828 1.30cr ocher & multi 25 20
1521 A828 1.30cr bl & multi 25 20
1522 A828 1.30cr yel & multi 25 20

Brazilian folklore.

2000-reis Doubloon
A829

Brazilian Colonial Coins: No. 1524, 640r pataca. No. 1525, 20r copper "vintem."

1977, Aug. 31 ***Perf. 11½***

1523 A829 1.30cr vio bl & multi 25 15
1524 A829 1.30cr dk red & multi 25 15
1525 A829 1.30cr yel & multi 25 15

Pinwheel
A830

Neoregelia Carolinae
A831

1977, Sept. 1

1526 A830 1.30cr multi 25 15

National Week.

1977, Sept. 21 **Litho.** ***Perf. 11½***

1527 A831 1.30cr multi 25 15

Nature preservation.

Pen, Pencil, Letters
A832

1977, Oct. 15 **Litho.** ***Perf. 11½***

1528 A832 1.30cr multi 25 15

Primary education, sesquicentennial.

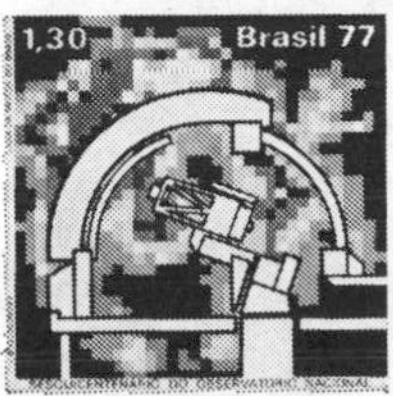

Dome and Telescope
A833

1977, Oct. 15

1529 A833 1.30cr multi 25 15

National Astrophysics Observatory, Brasópolis, sesquicentennial.

"Jahu" Hydroplane (Savoia Marchetti S-55)
A834

Design: No. 1531, PAX, dirigible.

1977, Oct. 17

1530 A834 1.30cr multi 50 25
1531 A834 1.30cr multi 50 25

50th anniversary of crossing of South Atlantic by Joao Ribeiro de Barros from Genoa to Sao Paulo (No. 1530) and 75th anniversary of the PAX airship (No. 1531).

O'Guarani
A835

1977, Oct. 24

1532 A835 1.30cr multi 25 15

Book Day and to honor José Martiniano de Alencar, writer, jurist.

Waves
A836

1977, Nov. 5 **Litho.** ***Perf. 11½***

1533 A836 1.30cr multi 25 15

Amateur Radio Operators' Day.

Nativity
A837

Designs (Folk Art): 2cr, Annunciation. 5cr, Nativity.

1977, Nov. 10

1534 A837 1.30cr bis & multi 35 15
1535 A837 2cr bis & multi 50 15
1536 A837 5cr bis & multi 1.00 25

Christmas 1977.

Emerald
A838

Designs: No. 1538, Topaz. No. 1539, Aquamarine.

1977, Nov. 19

1537 A838 1.30cr multi 25 20
1538 A838 1.30cr multi 25 20
1539 A838 1.30cr multi 25 20

PORTUCALE 77, 2nd International Topical Exhibition, Porto, Nov. 19–20.

Angel with Cornucopia
A839

1977, Nov. 24 **Litho.** ***Perf. 11½***

1540 A839 1.30cr multi 25 20

National Thanksgiving Day.

Army's Railroad Construction Battalion—A840

Designs: No. 1542, Navy's Amazon flotilla. No. 1543, Air Force's postal service (plane).

1977, Dec. 5

1541 A840 1.30cr multi 25 20
1542 A840 1.30cr multi 25 20
1543 A840 1.30cr multi 25 20

Civilian services of armed forces.

Varig Emblem, Jet
A841

1977, Dec. ***Perf. 11x11½***

1544 A841 1.30cr bl & blk 25 20

50th anniversary of Varig Airline.

Sts. Cosme and Damiao Church, Igaracu
A842

Woman Holding Sheaf
A843

Brazilian Architecture: 7.50cr, St. Bento Monastery Church, Rio de Janeiro. 8.50cr, Church of St. Francis of Assisi, Ouro Preto. 9.50cr, St. Anthony Convent Church, Joao Pessoa.

1977, Dec. 8

1545 A842 2.70cr multi 50 15
1546 A842 7.50cr multi 1.25 35
1547 A842 8.50cr multi 1.25 40
1548 A842 9.50cr multi 1.75 45

1977, Dec. 19 ***Perf. 11½***

1549 A843 1.30cr multi 25 20

Brazilian diplomacy.

Soccer Ball and Foot
A844

Designs: No. 1551, Soccer ball in net. No. 1552, Symbolic soccer player.

1978, Mar. 1 Litho. *Perf. 11½*

1550	A844	1.80cr multi	40	20
1551	A844	1.80cr multi	40	20
1552	A844	1.80cr multi	40	20

11th World Cup Soccer Championship, Argentina, June 1–25.

"La Fosca" on La Scala Stage and Carlos Gomes
A845

1978, Feb. 9

1553	A845	1.80cr multi	40	20

Bicentenary of La Scala in Milan, and to honor Carlos Gomes (1836–1893), Brazilian composer.

Symbols of Postal Mechanization
A846

1978, Mar. 15 Litho. *Perf. 11½*

1554	A846	1.80cr multi	25	20

Opening of Postal Staff College.

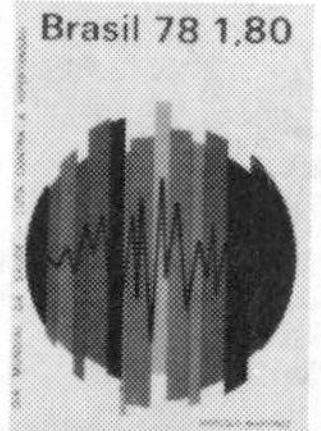

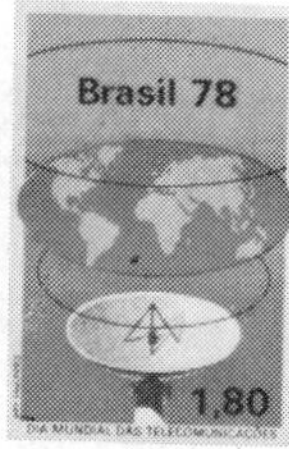

Hypertension Chart
A847

Waves from Antenna Uniting World
A848

1978, Apr. 4

1555	A847	1.80cr multi	25	20

World Health Day, fight against hypertension.

1978, May 17 Litho. *Perf. 12x11½*

1556	A848	1.80cr multi	25	20

10th World Telecommunications Day.

Brazilian Canary
A849

Birds: 8.50cr, Cotinga. 9.50cr, Tanager fastuosa.

1978, June 5 *Perf. 11½x12*

1557	A849	7.50cr multi	2.00	75
1558	A849	8.50cr multi	2.00	1.00
1559	A849	9.50cr multi	2.00	1.25

Inocencio Serzedelo Correa and Manuel Francisco Correa, 1893
A850

1978, June 20 Litho. *Perf. 11x11½*

1560	A850	1.80cr multi	25	20

85th anniversary of Union Court of Audit.

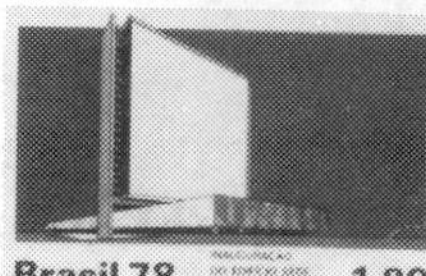

Post and Telegraph Building
A851

1978, June 22 *Perf. 11½*

1561	A851	1.80cr multi	25	25

Souvenir Sheet

Imperf.

1562	A851	7.50cr multi	80	1.50

Inauguration of Post and Telegraph Building (ECT), Brasilia, and for BRAPEX, 3rd Brazilian Philatelic Exhibition, Brasilia, June 23–28 (No. 1562). No. 1562 has buff margin with black inscription. Size: 70x 90mm.

Ernesto Geisel
A852

1978, June 22 Engr. *Perf. 11½*

1563	A852	1.80cr dl grn	25	15

Ernesto Geisel, President of Brazil.

Savoia-Marchetti S-64, Map of South Atlantic
A853

1978, July 3 Lithographed

1564	A853	1.80cr multi	25	20

50th anniversary of first crossing of South Atlantic by Carlos del Prete and Arturo Ferrarin.

Symbolic of Smallpox Eradication
A854

Brazil No. 68
A855

1978, July 25

1565	A854	1.80cr multi	25	20

Eradication of smallpox.

1978, Aug. 1

1566	A855	1.80cr multi	25	25

Stamp Day, centenary of the "Barba Branca" (white beard) issue.

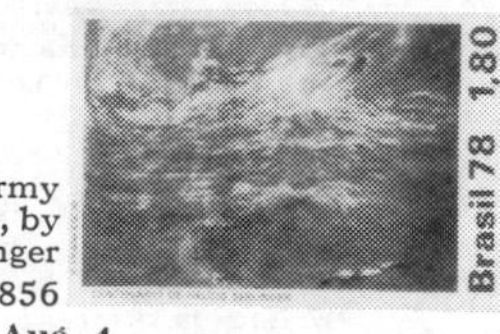

Stormy Sea, by Seelinger
A856

1978, Aug. 4

1567	A856	1.80cr multi	25	25

Helios Seelinger, painter, birth centenary.

Guitar Players
A857

Musicians and Instruments: No. 1569, Flutes. No. 1570, Percussion instruments.

1978, Aug. 22 Litho. *Perf. 11½*

1568	A857	1.80cr multi	25	15
1569	A857	1.80cr multi	25	15
1570	A857	1.80cr multi	25	20

Children at Play
A858

1978, Sept. 1 Litho. *Perf. 11½*

1571	A858	1.80cr multi	25	20

National Week.

Collegiate Church
A859

1978, Sept. 6 Engraved

1572	A859	1.80cr red brn	25	20

Restoration of patio of Collegiate Church, Sao Paulo.

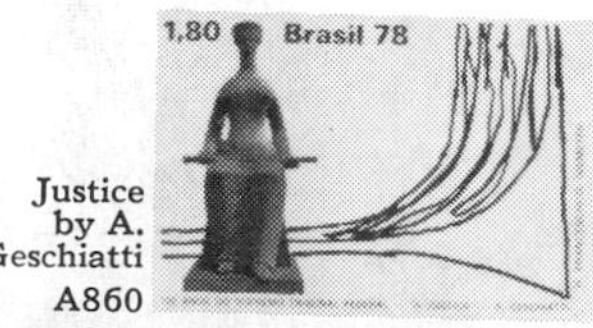

Justice by A. Geschiatti
A860

1978, Sept. 18 Lithographed

1573	A860	1.80cr blk & ol	25	20

Federal Supreme Court, sesquicentennial.

Iguacu Falls
A861

Design: No. 1575, Yellow ipecac.

1978, Sept. 21

1574	A861	1.80cr multi	25	20
1575	A861	1.80cr multi	25	20

Iguacu National Park.

Stages of Intelsat Satellite
A862

1978, Oct. 9 Litho. *Perf. 11½*

1576	A862	1.80cr multi	25	20

Flag of Order of Christ
A863

Brazilian Flags: No. 1578, Principality of Brazil. No. 1579, United Kingdom. No. 1580, Imperial Brazil. No. 1581, National flag (current).

1978, Oct. 13

1577	A863	1.80cr multi	1.25	65
1578	A863	1.80cr multi	1.25	65
1579	A863	1.80cr multi	1.25	65
1580	A863	8.50cr multi	1.25	65
1581	A863	8.50cr multi	1.25	65
	a.	Block of 5 + label	6.25	7.50

7th LUBRAPEX Philatelic Exhibition, Porto Alegre. Nos. 1577–1581 printed se-tenant in blocks of 5 plus label showing Acorianos monument.

Mail Street Car
A864

Mail Transportation: No. 1583, Overland mail truck. No. 1584, Mail delivery truck. 7.50cr. Railroad mail car. 8.50cr, Mail coach. 9.50cr, Post riders.

1978, Oct. 21 *Perf. 11x11½*

1582	A864	1.80cr multi	50	40
1583	A864	1.80cr multi	50	40
1584	A864	1.80cr multi	50	40
1585	A864	7.50cr multi	50	40
1586	A864	8.50cr multi	50	40
1587	A864	9.50cr multi	50	50
		Nos. 1582-1587 (6)	3.00	2.50

18th Universal Postal Union Congress, Rio de Janeiro, 1979. Nos. 1582–1587 printed se-tenant.

Brasil 78 1,80

Gaucho Herding Cattle, and Cactus
A865

1978, Oct. 23 *Perf. 11½x11*

1588	A865	1.80cr multi	25	20

Joao Guimaraes Rosa, poet and diplomat, 70th birthday.

A little time given to study of the arrangement of the Scott Catalogue can make it easier to use effectively.

St. Anthony's Hill, by Nicholas A. Taunay
A866

Landscape Paintings: No. 1590, Castle Hill, by Victor Meirelles. No. 1591, View of Sabara, by Alberto da Veiga Guignard. No. 1592, View of Pernambuco, by Frans Post.

1978, Nov. 6 **Litho.** ***Perf. 11½***

1589	A866	1.80cr	multi	25	20
1590	A866	1.80cr	multi	25	20
1591	A866	1.80cr	multi	25	20
1592	A866	1.80cr	multi	25	20

Angel with Harp
A867

Designs: No. 1594, Angel with lute. No. 1595, Angel with oboe.

1978, Nov. 10

1593	A867	1.80cr	multi	30	20
1594	A867	1.80cr	multi	30	20
1595	A867	1.80cr	multi	30	20

Christmas 1978.

Symbolic Candles
A868

1978, Nov. 23

1596	A868	1.80cr	blk, gold & car	25	20

National Thanksgiving Day.

Red Crosses and Activities—A869

1978, Dec. 5 **Litho.** ***Perf. 11x11½***

1597	A869	1.80cr	blk & red	25	20

70th anniversary of Brazilian Red Cross.

Paz Theater, Belem
A870

Designs: 12cr, José de Alencar Theater, Portaleza. 12.50cr, Municipal Theater, Rio de Janeiro.

1978, Dec. 6 ***Perf. 11½***

1598	A870	10.50cr	multi	1.00	25
1599	A870	12cr	multi	1.00	25
1600	A870	12.50cr	multi	1.00	25

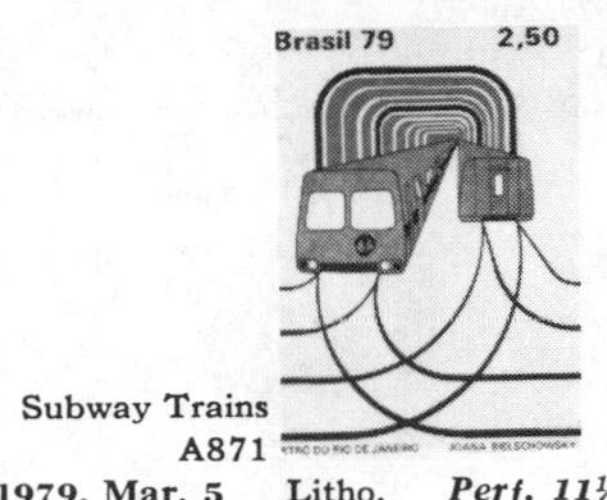

Subway Trains
A871

1979, Mar. 5 **Litho.** ***Perf. 11½***

1601	A871	2.50cr	multi	40	20

Inauguration of Rio de Janeiro's subway system.

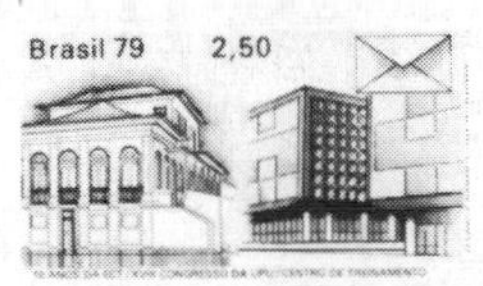

Old and New Post Offices—A872

Designs: No. 1603, Old and new mail boxes. No. 1604, Manual and automatic mail sorting. No. 1605, Old and new planes. No. 1606, Telegraph and telex machine. No. 1607, Mailmen's uniforms.

1979, Mar. 20 **Litho.** ***Perf. 11x11½***

1602	A872	2.50cr	multi	40	40
1603	A872	2.50cr	multi	40	40
1604	A872	2.50cr	multi	40	40
1605	A872	2.50cr	multi	40	40
1606	A872	2.50cr	multi	40	40
1607	A872	2.50cr	multi	40	40
		Nos. 1602-1607 (6)		2.40	2.40

10th anniversary of the new Post and Telegraph Department, and 18th Universal Postal Union Congress, Rio de Janeiro, Sept.–Oct., 1979.

O'Day 23 Class Yacht
A873

Yachts and Stamp Outlines: 10.50cr, Penguin Class. 12cr, Hobie Cat Class. 12.50cr, Snipe Class.

1979, Apr. 18 **Litho.** ***Perf. 11x11½***

1608	A873	2.50cr	multi	50	40
1609	A873	10.50cr	multi	1.00	70
1610	A873	12cr	multi	1.00	75
1611	A873	12.50cr	multi	1.25	75

Brasiliana '79, 3rd World Thematic Stamp Exhibition, São Conrado, Sept. 15–23.

Children, IYC Emblem
A874

1979, May 30 **Litho.** ***Perf. 11½***

1612	A874	2.50cr	multi	50	20

International Year of the Child and Children's Book Day.

Giant Water Lily
A875

Designs: 12cr, Amazon manatee. 12.50cr, Arrau (turtle).

1979, June 5 **Litho.** ***Perf. 11½***

1613	A875	10.50cr	multi	1.00	60
1614	A875	12cr	multi	1.25	60
1615	A875	12.50cr	multi	1.25	60

Amazon National Park, nature conservation.

Bank Emblem
A876

1979, June 7

1616	A876	2.50cr	multi	25	15

Northwest Bank of Brazil, 25th anniversary.

Physician Tending Patient 15th Cent. Woodcut—A877

1979, June 30

1617	A877	2.50cr	multi	25	15

National Academy of Medicine, 50th anniversary.

Flower made of Hearts
A878

1979, July 8 **Litho.** ***Perf. 11½***

1618	A878	2.50cr	multi	25	15

35th Brazilian Cardiology Congress.

Souvenir Sheet

Hotel Nacional, Rio de Janeiro
A879

1979, July 16

1619	A879	12.50cr	multi	70	1.50

Brasiliana '79 comprising 1st Inter-American Exhibition of Classical Philately and 3rd World Topical Exhibition, Rio de Janeiro, Sept. 15–23. No. 1619 has multicolored margin showing hang glider. Size: 87x125mm.

Cithaerias Aurora
A880

Moths: 10.50cr, Evenus regalis. 12cr, Caligo eurilochus. 12.50 cr, Diaethria clymena janeira.

1979, Aug. 1

1620	A880	2.50cr	multi	30	15
1621	A880	10.50cr	multi	1.00	60
1622	A880	12cr	multi	1.25	60
1623	A880	12.50cr	multi	1.25	60

Stamp Day 1979.

EMB-121 Xingo
A881

1979, Aug. 19 **Litho.** ***Perf. 11½***

1624	A881	2.50cr	vio bl	25	20

Embraer, Brazilian aircraft company, 10th anniversary.

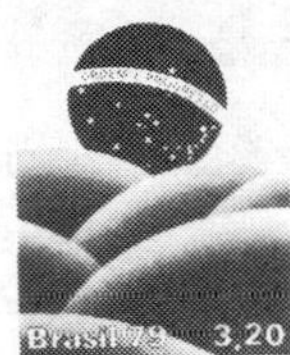

Symbolic Southern Sky over Landscape
A882

1979, Sept. 12

1625	A882	3.20cr	multi	25	20

National Week.

Our Lady of the Apparition
A883

1979, Sept. 8 **Litho.** ***Perf. 11½***

1626	A883	2.50cr	multi	25	20

Statue of Our Lady of the Apparition, 75th anniversary of coronation.

"UPU," Envelope and Mail Transport
A884

"UPU" and: No. 1628, Post Office emblems. 10.50cr, Globe. 12cr, Flags of Brazil and U.N. 12.50cr, UPU emblem.

1979, Sept. 12 *Perf. 11x11½*

1627	A884 2.50cr multi		30	20
1628	A884 2.50cr multi		30	20
1629	A88410.50cr multi		1.00	60
1630	A884 12cr multi		1.25	75
1631	A88412.50cr multi		1.25	75
	Nos. 1627-1631 (5)		4.10	2.50

18th Universal Postal Union Congress, Rio de Janeiro, Sept.–Oct. 1979.

Pyramid Fountain, Rio de Janeiro A885

Fountains: 10.50cr, Facade, Marilia, Ouro Preto (horiz.). 12cr, Boa Vista, Recife.

Perf. 12x11½, 11½x12

1979, Sept. 15

1632	A885 2.50cr multi	30	20
1633	A88510.50cr multi	1.00	60
1634	A885 12cr multi	1.25	75

Brasiliana '79, 1st Interamerican Exhibition of Classical Philately.

Church of the Glory A886

Landscapes by Leandro Joaquim: 12cr, Fishing on Guanabara Bay. 12.50cr, Boqueirao Lake and Carioca Arches.

1979, Sept. 15 *Perf. 11½*

1635	A886 2.50cr multi	30	20
1636	A886 12cr multi	1.25	75
1637	A88612.50cr multi	1.25	75

Brasiliana '79, 3rd World Topical Exhibition, São Conrado, Sept. 15–23.

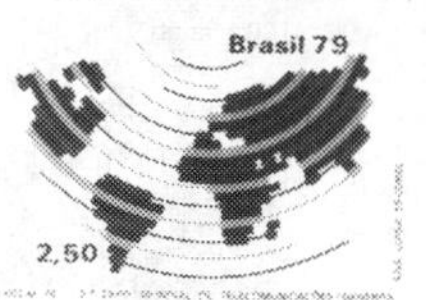

World Map A887

1979, Sept. 20

1638	A887 2.50cr multi	25	20

3rd World Telecommunications Exhibition, Geneva, Sept. 20–26.

"UPU" and UPU Emblem A888

1979, Oct. 9 **Litho.** ***Perf. 11½×11***

1639	A888 2.50cr multi	30	20
1640	A88810.50cr multi	1.00	60
1641	A888 12cr multi	1.25	75
1642	A88812.50cr multi	1.25	75

Universal Postal Union Day.

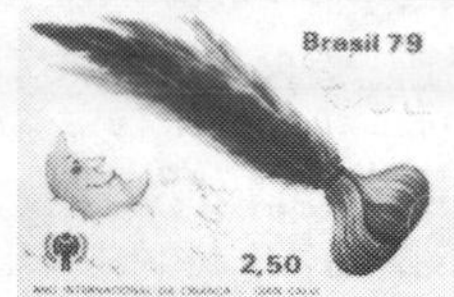

IYC Emblem, Feather Toy—A889

IYC Emblem and Toys: No. 1644, Bumble bee, ragdoll. No. 1645, Flower, top. No. 1646, Wooden acrobat.

1979, Oct. 12 ***Perf. 11½***

1643	A889 2.50cr multi	30	20
1644	A889 3.20cr multi	30	25
1645	A889 3.20cr multi	30	25
1646	A889 3.20cr multi	30	25

International Year of the Child.

Adoration of the Kings—A890

Christmas 1979: No. 1648, Nativity. No. 1649 Jesus and the Elders in the Temple.

1979, Nov. 12 **Litho.** ***Perf. 11½***

1647	A890 3.20cr multi	30	25
1648	A890 3.20cr multi	30	25
1649	A890 3.20cr multi	30	25

Souvenir Sheet

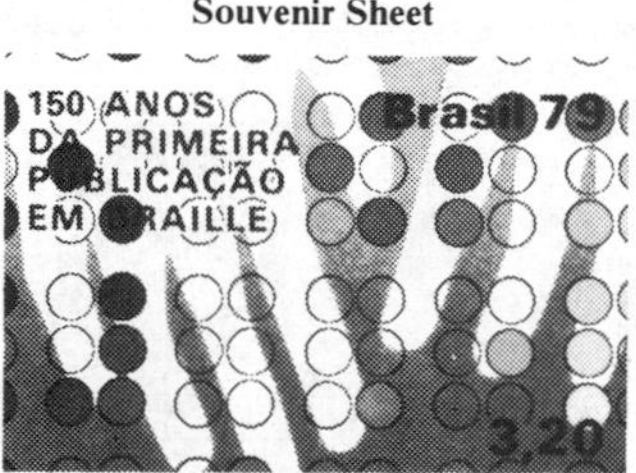

Hands Reading Braille—A891

Lithographed and Embossed

1979, Nov. 20. ***Perf. 11½***

1650	A891 3.20cr multi	75	1.25

Publication of Braille script, 150th anniversary. Multicolored margin shows extension of stamp design with Braille printed and embossed. Size: 127×87½mm.

Wheat Harvester A892

Steel Mill A893

1979, Nov. 22

1651	A892 3.20cr multi	25	25

Thanksgiving 1979.

1979, Nov. 23

1652	A893 3.20cr multi	30	25

COSIPA Steelworks, São Paulo, 25th anniversary.

Type of 1976 and

A894

Designs: 70c, Women grinding coconuts. 2cr, Coconuts. 2.50cr, Basket weaver. 3cr, Mangoes. 3.20cr, River boatman. 4cr, Corn. 5cr, Onions. 7cr, Oranges. 10cr, Maracuja. 12cr, Pineapple. 15cr, Bananas. 17cr, Guarana. 20cr, Sugar cane. 21cr, Harvesting ramie (China grass). 24cr, Beekeeping. 27cr, Man leading pack mule. 30cr, Silkworm. 34cr, Cacao. 38cr, Coffee. 42cr, Soybeans. 45cr, Mandioca. 50cr, Wheat. 57cr, Peanuts. 66cr, Grapes. 100cr, Cashews. 140cr, Tomatoes. 200cr, Mamona. 500cr, Cotton.

Perf. 11×11½, 11½×11

1979 **Photo., Engr. (21cr)**

1653	A790	70c gray grn		20	5
1654	A790	2.50cr sepia		15	5
1655	A790	3.20cr bl, horiz.		15	5
1656	A790	21cr purple		50	10
1657	A790	27cr sep, horiz.		60	15
		Nos. 1653-1657 (5)		1.60	40

1980-83 **Photo.** ***Perf. 11½x11***

1658	A894	2cr yel brn ('82)	5	5
1659	A894	3cr red ('82)	5	5
1660	A894	4cr orange	15	5
1661	A894	5cr dk pur ('82)	8	5
1662	A894	7cr org ('81)	20	5
1663	A894	10cr bl grn ('82)	15	5
1664	A894	12cr dk grn ('81)	18	5
1665	A894	15cr gldn brn ('83)	5	5
1666	A894	17cr brn org ('82)	20	5
1667	A894	20cr ol ('82)	20	10
1668	A894	24cr bis ('82)	20	5
1669	A894	30cr blk ('82)	20	10
1670	A894	34cr brown	45	10
1671	A894	38cr red ('83)	12	10
1672	A894	42cr green	7.50	50
1673	A894	45cr sep ('83)	75	10
1674	A894	50cr yel org ('82)	22	10
1675	A894	57cr brn ('83)	22	10
1676	A894	66cr pur ('81)	5.00	15
1677	A894	100cr dk red brn ('81)	75	5
1678	A894	140cr red ('82)	1.00	15

Engraved

1678A	A894	200cr grn ('82)	1.50	10
1679	A894	500cr brn ('82)	5.00	15
		Nos. 1658-1679 (23)	24.22	2.30

See Nos. 1928-1941.

Plant Inside Raindrop—A896

Light Bulb Containing: 17cr+7cr, Sun. 20cr+8cr, Windmill. 21cr+9cr, Dam.

1980, Jan. 2 **Litho.** ***Perf. 12***

1680	A896	3.20cr multi	25	15
1681	A896	24cr (17+7)	2.50	1.25
1682	A896	28cr (20+8)	3.00	1.50
1683	A896	30cr (21+9)	4.50	1.75

Anthracite Industry—A897

1980, Mar. 19 **Litho.** ***Perf. 11½***

1684	A897 4cr multi	30	15

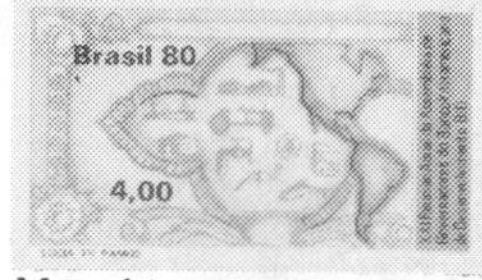

Map of Americas, Symbols of Development—A898

1980, Apr. 14 **Litho.** ***Perf. 11x11½***

1685	A898 4cr multi	30	15

21st Assembly of Inter-American Development Bank Governors, Rio de Janeiro, Apr. 14-16.

Tapirape Mask, Mato Grosso—A899

1980, Apr. 18 ***Perf. 11½***

1686	A899	4cr *shown*	30	15
1687	A899	4cr *Tukuna mask, Amazonas*, vert.	30	15
1688	A899	4cr *Kanela mask, Maranhao*, vert.	30	15

Brazilian Television, 30th Anniversary—A900

1980, May 5 **Litho.** ***Perf. 11½***

1689	A900 4cr multi	30	15

Duke of Caixas, by Miranda

A901

The Worker, by Candido Partinari

A902

1980, May 7

1690	A901 4cr multi	30	15

Duke of Caixas, death centenary.

980, May 18

'aintings: 28cr, Mademoiselle Pogany, by :onstantin Brancusi. 30cr, The Glass of Water, by rancisco Aurelio de Figueiredo.

1691	A902	24cr multi	2.00	1.00
1692	A902	28cr multi	2.00	1.00
1693	A902	30cr multi	3.00	1.00

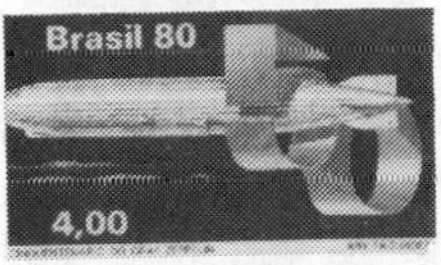

Graf Zeppelin, 50th Anniversary of Atlantic Crossing—A903

980, June **Litho.** ***Perf. 11x11½***

1694	A903	4cr multi	30	15

Pope John Paul II, St. Peter's, Rome, Congress Emblem—A904

Pope, Emblem and Brazilian Churches: No. 1696, Fortaleza (vert.) 24cr. Apericida 28cr. Rio de Janeiro, 30cr, Brasilia.

1980, June 24 ***Perf. 12***

1695	A904	4cr multi	30	15
1696	A904	4cr multi	30	15
1697	A904	24cr multi	1.50	40
1698	A904	28cr multi	1.50	40
1699	A904	30cr multi	3.00	40
		Nos. 1695-1699 (5)	6.60	1.50

Visit of Pope John Paul II to Brazil, June 30-July 12; 10th National Eucharistic Congress, Fortaleza, July 9-16.

First Transatlantic Flight, 50th Anniversary—A905

1980, June **Litho.** ***Perf. 11x11½***

1700	A905	4cr multi	30	15

Souvenir Sheet

Yacht Sail, Exhibition Emblem—A906

1980, June ***Perf. 11½***

1701	A906	30cr multi	90	2.00

Brapex IV Stamp Exhibition, Fortaleza, June 13-21. Multicolored margin shows sails on water. Size: 125x88mm.

Rowing, Moscow '80 Emblem—A907

1980, June 30

1702	A907	4cr *shown*	30	15
1703	A907	4cr *Target shooting*	30	15
1704	A907	4cr *Bicycling*	30	15

22nd Summer Olympic Games, Moscow, July 19-Aug. 3.

Rondon Community Works Project—A908

1980, July 11

1705	A908	4cr multi	30	15

Helen Keller and Anne Sullivan—A909

1980, July 28

1706	A909	4cr multi	30	15

Helen Keller (1880-1968), blind deaf writer and lecturer taught by Anne Sullivan (1867-1936).

Souvenir Sheet

São Francisco River Canoe—A910

1980, Aug. 1 **Litho.** ***Perf. 11½***

1707	A910	24cr multi	90	2.00

Stamp Day. Light blue and black margin shows river canoe, Postal and Telegraph Museum emblem. Size: 125½x86½mm.

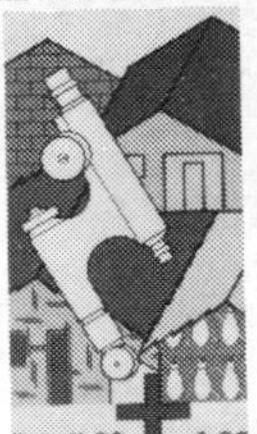

Microscope, Red Cross, Insects, Brick and Tile Houses—A911

1980, Aug. 5 ***Perf. 11½x11***

1708	A911	4cr multi	30	15

National Health Day.

Brazilian Postal Administration, 15th Anniversary—A912

1980, Sept. 16 **Litho.** ***Perf. 12***

1709	A912	5cr multi	40	20

Souvenir Sheet

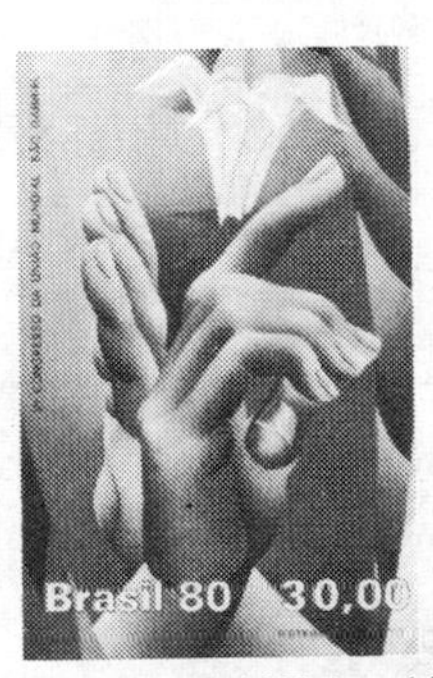

St. Gabriel World Union, 6th Congress—A913

1980, Sept. 29 ***Perf. 11½x12***

1710	A913	30cr multi	1.00	2.00

No. 1710 has red and orange margin. Size: 125x86mm.

Cattleya Amethystoglossa—A914

1980, Oct. 3 ***Perf. 11½***

1711	A914	5cr *shown*	35	20
1712	A914	5cr *Laelia cinnabarina*	35	20
1713	A914	24cr *Zygopetalum crinitum*	2.25	1.00
1714	A914	28cr *Laelia tenebrosa*	2.25	1.00

Espamer 80, American-European Philatelic Exhibition, Madrid, Oct. 3-12.

Red-tailed Amazon Parrot
A915

Capitao Rodrigo, Hero of Erico Verissimo's "O Continento"
A916

Parrots: No. 1716, Vinaceous Amazon. No. 1717, Brown-backed. No. 1718, Red-spectacled.

1980, Oct. 18 **Litho.** ***Perf. 12***

1715	A915	5cr multi	35	20
1716	A915	5cr multi	35	20
1717	A915	28cr multi	2.25	1.00
1718	A915	28cr multi	2.25	1.00

Lubrapex '80 Stamp Exhibition, Lisbon, Oct. 18-26.

1980, Oct. 23

1719	A916	5cr multi	35	20

Book Day.

Flight into Egypt—A917

1980, Nov. 5

1720	A917	5cr multi	35	20

Christmas 1980.

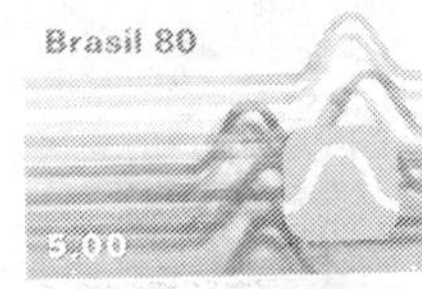

Sound Waves and Oscillator Screen—A918

1980, Nov. 7

1721	A918	5cr multi	35	20

Telebras Research Center inauguration.

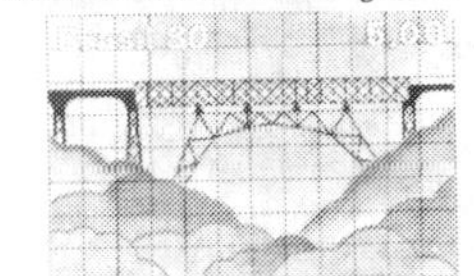

Carvalho Viaduct, Paranagua-Curitiba Railroad—A919

1980, Nov. 10

1722	A919	5cr multi	50	20

Engineering Club centenary.

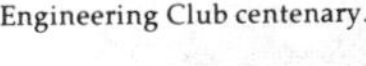

Portable Chess Board—A920

1980, Nov. 18 **Litho.** ***Perf. 11½***

1723	A920	5cr multi	50	50

Postal chess contest.

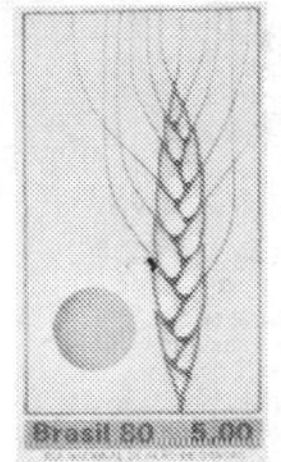

Sun and Wheat—A921

1980, Nov. 27 *Perf. 11½x11*

1724 A921 5cr multi 40 40

Thanksgiving 1980.

Father Anchieta Writing "Virgin Mary, Mother of God" on Sand of Iperoig Beach—A922

1980, Dec. 8 *Perf. 12*

1725 A922 5cr multi 35 20

Christ Carrying Cross, By O Aleijadinho—A923

Antonio Francisco Lisboa (O Aleijadinho), 250th Birth Anniversary: Paintings of the life of Christ: a. Mount of Olives. b. Arrest in the Garden. c. Flagellation. d. Crown of Thorns. f. Crucifixion.

1980, Dec. 29

1726 Block of 6 3.50 3.00
a.-f. A923 5cr any single 60 35

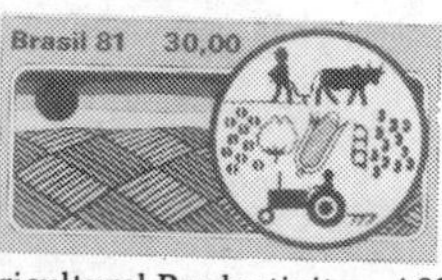

Agricultural Productivity—A924

1981, Jan. 2 **Litho.** *Perf. 11x11½*

1727 A924 30cr *shown* 1.00 35
1728 A924 35cr *Domestic markets* 90 35
1729 A924 40cr *Exports* 90 35

Boy Scout and Campfire—A925

1981, Jan. 22 **Litho.** *Perf. 11x11½*

1730 A925 5cr shown 35 20
1731 A925 5cr Scouts cooking 35 20
1732 A925 5cr Scout, tents 35 20

4th Pan-American Scout Jamboree.

Souvenir Sheet

Mailman, 1930—A926

1981, Mar. 11 **Litho.** *Perf. 11*

1733 Sheet of 3 4.50 6.00
a. A926 30cr shown 1.00 1.00
b. A926 35cr Mailman, 1981 1.00 1.00
c. A926 40cr Telegram messenger, 1930 1.00 1.00

Department of Posts and Telegraphs, 50th anniversary. No. 1733 has black marginal inscription. Size: 100x70mm.

Souvenir Sheet

The Hunter and the Jaguar, by Felix Taunay (1795-1881)—A927

1981, Apr. 10 **Litho.** *Perf. 11*

1734 A927 30cr multi 1.50 *2.50*

Size: 70x90mm.

Lima Barreto and Rio de Janeiro, 1900—A928

1981, May 13 **Litho.** *Perf. 11½*

1735 A928 7cr multi 35 30

Lima Barreto, writer, birth centenary.

Maraca Indian Funerary Urn A929

1981, May 18

1736 A929 7cr shown 35 30
1737 A929 7cr Marajoara triangular jug 35 30
1738 A929 7cr Tupi-Guarani bowl 35 30

Lophornis Magnifica—A930

Designs: Hummingbirds.

1981, May 22 *Perf. 11½*

1739 A930 7cr shown 60 30
1740 A930 7cr Phaethornis pretrei 60 30
1741 A930 7cr Chrysolampis mosquitus 60 30
1742 A930 7cr Heliactin cornuta 60 30

Rotary Emblem and Faces—A931

1981, May 31

1743 A931 7cr Emblem, hands 35 30
1744 A931 35cr shown 2.00 1.50

72nd Convention of Rotary Intl., Sao Paulo.

Environmental Protection—A932

1981, June 5 *Perf. 12*

1745 A932 7cr shown 35 30
1746 A932 7cr Forest 35 30
1747 A932 7cr Clouds (air) 35 30
1748 A932 7cr Village (soil) 35 30

Nos. 1745-1748 se-tenant.

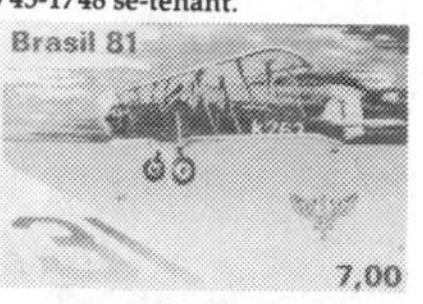

Biplane, 1931 (Airmail Service, 50th Anniv.)—A933

1981, June 10 *Perf. 11½*

1749 A933 7cr multi 35 30

Madeira-Mamore Railroad, 50th Anniv. of Nationalization—A934

1981, July 10 **Litho.** *Perf. 11x11½*

1750 A934 7cr multi 35 30

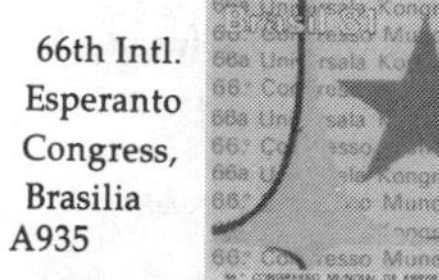

66th Intl. Esperanto Congress, Brasilia A935

1981, July 26 *Perf. 12*

1751 A935 7cr grn & blk 35 30

No. 79—A936

1981, Aug.1

1752 A936 50cr shown 2.50 50
1753 A936 55cr No. 80 2.50 50
1754 A936 60cr No. 81 2.50 50

Stamp Day; centenary of "small head" stamps.

Institute of Military Engineering, 50th Anniv.—A937

1981, Aug. 11 **Litho.** *Perf. 11½*

1755 A937 12cr multi 35 30

Reisado Dancers—A938

1981, Aug. 22

1756 A938 50cr Dancers, diff. 1.75 35
1757 A938 55cr Sailors 1.75 38
1758 A938 60cr shown 1.75 42

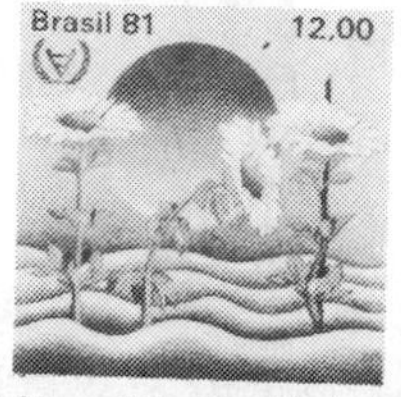

Intl. Year of the Disabled—A939

1981, Sept. 17 **Litho.** *Perf. 11½*

1759 A939 12cr multi 30 20

Flowers of the Central Plateau—A940

1981, Sept. 21 **Litho.** *Perf. 12*

1760 A940 12cr Palicourea rigida 35 20
1761 A940 12cr Dalechampia caperonioides 35 20
1762 A940 12cr Cassia clausseni, vert. 35 20
1763 A940 12cr Eremanthus sphaerocephalus, vert. 35 20

Virgin of Nazareth Statue A941

Christ the Redeemer Statue, Rio de Janeiro, 50th Anniv. A942

1981, Oct. 10 **Litho.** *Perf. 12*

1764 A941 12cr multi 35 20

Candle Festival of Nazareth, Belem.

1981, Oct. 12

1765 A942 12cr multi 35 20

World Food Day—A943

1981, Oct. 16

1766 A943 12cr multi 35 20

75th Anniv. of Santos-Dumont's First Flight—A944

1981, Oct. 23 **Litho.** ***Perf. 12***

1767	A944	60cr multi	1.75	50

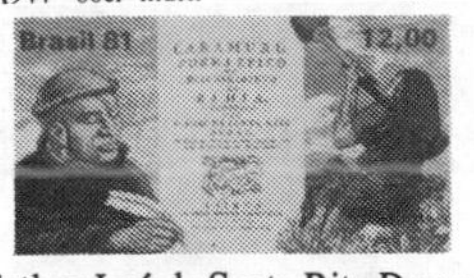

Father José de Santa Rita Durao, Titlepage of his Epic Poem Caramuru, Diego Alvares Correia (Character)—A945

1981, Oct. 29

1768	A945	12cr multi	35	20

Caramuru publication centenary; World Book Day.

Christmas 1981—A946

Designs: Creches and figurines. 55cr, 60cr vert.

1981, Nov. 10 **Litho.** ***Perf. 12***

1769	A946	12cr multi	18	10
1770	A946	50cr multi	1.75	35
1771	A946	55cr multi	1.75	38
1772	A946	60cr multi	1.75	50

State Flags A947

Designs: a. Alagoas. b. Bahia. c. Federal District. d. Pernambuco. e. Sergipe.

1981, Nov. 19

1773		Block of 5 plus label	1.50	1.50
a.-e.	A947	12cr, any single	30	30

Label shows arms of Brazil.

Thanksgiving 1981—A948

1981, Nov. 26 **Litho.** ***Perf. 11½***

1776	A948	12cr multi	30	15

Ministry of Labor, 50th Anniv.—A949

1981, Nov. 26

1777	A949	12cr multi	30	15

School of Engineering, Itajuba A950

1981, Nov. 30 ***Perf. 11x11½***

1778	A950	15cr lt grn & pur	45	15

Theodomiro C. Santiago, founder, birth centenary.

Sao Paulo State Police Sesquicentennial A951

1981, Dec. 15 **Litho.** ***Perf. 12***

1779	A951	12cr Policeman with saxophone	30	15
1780	A951	12cr Mounted policemen	30	15

Army Library Centenary A952

1981, Dec. 17

1781	A952	12cr multi	30	15

Souvenir Sheet

Philatelic Club of Brazil, 50th Anniv. A953

1981, Dec. 18 ***Perf. 11***

1782	A953	180cr multi	5.00	*6.00*

No. 1782 has multicolored margin showing "Bull's Eye" stamps designs, emblem. Size: 89x69mm.

Brigadier Eduardo Gomes—A954

1982, Jan. 20 **Litho.** ***Perf. 11x11½***

1783	A954	12cr bl & blk	45	15

Birth Centenary of Henrique Lage, Industrialist—A956

1982, Mar. 14 **Litho.** ***Perf. 11½***

1785	A956	17cr multi	70	16

1982 World Cup Soccer A957

TB Bacillus Centenary A958

Designs: Various soccer players.

1982, Mar. 19

1786	A957	75cr multi	1.50	70
1787	A957	80cr multi	1.50	75
1788	A957	85cr multi	1.50	76

Souvenir Sheet

Imperf.

1789		Sheet of 3	4.50	*9.00*
a.	A957	100cr like #1786	1.50	
b.	A957	100cr like #1787	1.50	
c.	A957	100cr like #1788	1.50	

No. 1789 has black marginal inscription. Size: 125x87mm.

1982, Mar. 24 ***Perf. 12***

1790	A958	90cr Microscope, lung	1.50	80
1791	A958	100cr Lung, pills	1.50	90

Nos. 1790-1791 se-tenant.

A959

1982, Apr. 17 **Litho.** ***Perf. 11***

1792		Sheet of 3	3.75	3.75
a.	A959	75cr Laelia Purpurata	1.15	70
b.	A959	80cr Oncidium flexuosum	1.20	75
c.	A959	85cr Cleistes revoluta	1.30	80

BRAPEX V Stamp Exhibition, Blumenau. No. 1792 has black marginal inscription. Size: 100x70mm.

Oil Drilling Centenary—A960

1982, Apr. 18 ***Perf. 11½***

1793	A960	17cr multi	30	15

400th Birth Anniv. of St. Vincent de Paul—A961

1982, Apr. 24 **Litho.** ***Perf. 11½***

1794	A961	17cr multi	30	15

Seven Steps of Guaira (Waterfalls)—A962

1982, Apr. 29

1795	A962	17cr Fifth Fall	30	15
1796	A962	21cr Seventh Fall	35	20

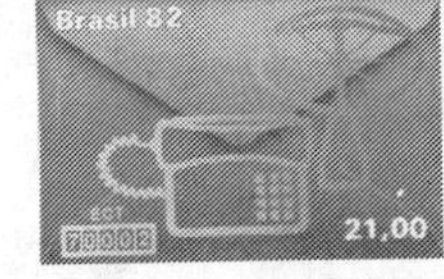

Ministry of Communications, 15th Anniv.—A963

1982, May 15

1797	A963	21cr multi	35	20

Museology Course, Natl. Historical Museum, 50th Anniv.—A964

1982, May 18

1798	A964	17cr blk & sal pink	30	15

Vale de Rio Doce Mining Co.—A965

1982, June 1

1799	A965	17cr Gears	30	15

Martin Afonso de Souza Reading Charter to Settlers—A966

1982, June 3 **Litho.** ***Perf. 11½***

1800 A966 17cr multi 30 15

Town of Sao Vincente, 450th anniv.

Armadillo—A967

1982, June 4

1801 A967 17cr shown 1.00 15
1802 A967 21cr Wolves 1.00 20
1803 A967 30cr Deer 3.00 25

Film Strip and Award—A968

1982, June 19

1804 A968 17cr multi 30 15

20th anniv. of Golden Palm award for The Promise Keeper, Cannes Film Festival.

Souvenir Sheet

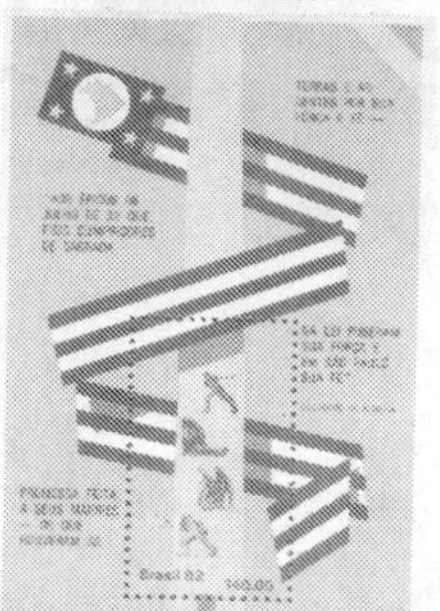

50th Anniv. of Constitutionalist Revolution—A969

1982, July 9 **Litho.** ***Perf. 11***

1805 A969 140cr multi 2.25 2.25

Multicolored margin continues design. Size: 70x100mm.

Church of Our Lady of O'Sabara A970

St. Francis of Assisi, 800th Birth Anniv. A971

Baroque Architecture, Minas Gerais State: No. 1807, Church of Our Lady of the Rosary, Diamantina (horiz.). No. 1808, Town Square, Mariana (horiz.).

1982, July 16 ***Perf. 11½***

1806 A970 17cr multi 30 15
1807 A970 17cr multi 30 15
1808 A970 17cr multi 30 15

1982, July 24

1809 A971 21cr multi 35 20

Stamp Day and Centenary of Pedro II "Large Head" Stamps—A972

1982, Aug. 1

1810 A972 21cr No. 82 35 20

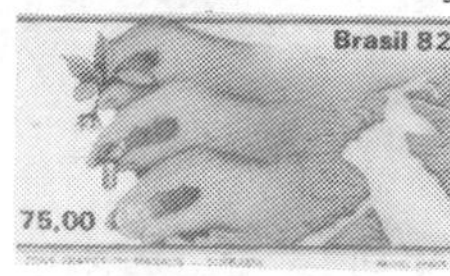

Port of Manaus Free Trade Zone—A973

1982, Aug. 15 ***Perf. 11x11½***

1811 A973 75cr multi 1.25 70

Scouting Year—A974

1982, Aug. 21 **Litho.** ***Perf. 11***

1812 Sheet of 2 4.75 6.50
a. A974 85cr Baden-Powell 1.75 2.00
b. A974 185cr Scout 2.80 4.50

Black marginal inscription, emblem. Size: 100x70mm.

Orixas Folk Costumes of African Origin—A975

1982, Aug. 21 ***Perf. 11½***

1813 A975 20cr Iemanja 30 16
1814 A975 20cr Xango 30 16
1815 A975 20cr Oxumare 30 16

10th Anniv. of Central Bank of Brazil Currency Museum—A976

1982, Aug. 31

1816 A976 25cr 12-florin coin, 1645, obverse and reverse 38 20
1817 A976 25cr Emperor Pedro's 6.40-reis coronation coin, 1822 38 20

National Week—A977

1982, Sept. 1

1818 A977 25cr Don Pedro proclaiming independence 38 20

St. Theresa of Avila (1515-1582)—A978

1982, Oct. 4

1819 A978 85cr Portrait 1.30 75

Instruments—A979

1982, Oct. 15 **Litho.** ***Perf. 11½x11***

1820 A979 75cr Instruments 1.15 70
1821 A979 80cr Dancers 1.20 72
1822 A979 85cr Musicians 1.30 75
a. Souvenir sheet of 3 3.75 4.50

Lubrapex '82, 4th Portuguese-Brazilian Stamp Exhibition. No. 1822a contains Nos. 1820-1822 (perf. 11), without "LUBRAPEX 82."

Aviation Industry Day—A980

1982, Oct. 17 ***Perf. 12***

1823 A980 24cr Embraer EMB-312 trainer plane 36 20

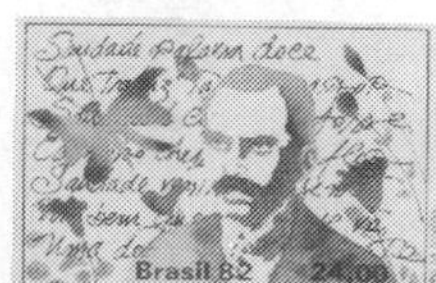

Bastos Tigre, Poet, Birth Centenary, and "Saudade" Text—A981

1982, Oct. 29

1824 A981 24cr multi 36 20

Book Day.

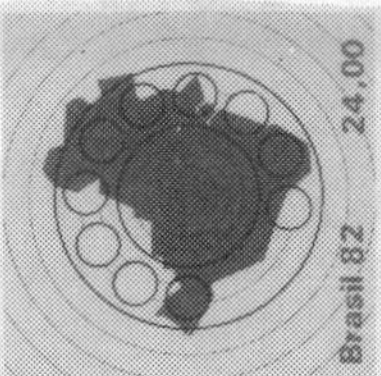

10th Anniv. of Brazilian Telecommunications Co.—A982

1982, Nov. 9 **Litho.** ***Perf. 11½***

1825 A982 24cr multi 36 20

Christmas 1982—A983

Children's Drawings.

1982, Nov. 10

1826 A983 24cr Nativity 36 20
1827 A983 24cr Angels 36 20
1828 A983 30cr Nativity, diff. 45 45
1829 A983 30cr Flight into Egypt 45 45

State Flags—A984

Designs: a. Ceara. b. Espirito Santo. c. Paraiba. d. Grande de Norte. e. Rondonia.

1982, Nov. 19

1830 Block of 5 plus label 6.00 6.00
a.-e. A984 24cr any single 1.00 20

Thanksgiving 1982—A985

1982, Nov. 25

1835 A985 24cr multi 36 20

Homage to the Deaf—A986

1982, Dec. 1

1836 A986 24cr multi 36 20

Naval Academy Bicentenary—A987

Training Ships.

1982, Dec. 14

1837	A987	24cr Brazil	36	20
1838	A987	24cr Benjamin Constant	36	20
1839	A987	24cr Almirante Saldanha	36	20

Souvenir Sheet

No. 12—A988

1982, Dec. 18 **Litho.** ***Perf. 11***

1840 A988 200cr multi 3.00 *4.50*

BRASILIANA '83 Intl. Stamp Exhibition, Rio de Janeiro, July 29-Aug. 7. Multicolored margin shows Regional Administration building. Size: 100x70mm.

Brasiliana '83 Carnival—A989

1983, Feb. 9 **Litho.** ***Perf. 11½***

1841	A989	24cr Samba drummers	18	10
1842	A989	130cr Street parade	1.25	50
1843	A989	140cr Dancer	1.25	52
1844	A989	150cr Male dancer	1.25	55

Antarctic Expedition—A990

1983, Feb. 20 **Litho.** ***Perf. 11½***

1845 A990 150cr Support ship Barano de Teffe 1.50 55

50th Anniv. of Women's Rights A991

1983, Mar. 8

1846 A991 130cr multi 1.25 50

Itaipu Hydroelectric Power Station Opening—A992

1983, Mar. **Litho.** ***Perf. 12***

1847 A992 140cr multi 1.25 45

Cancer Prevention A993

Martin Luther (1483-1546) A994

Designs: 30cr, Microscope. 38cr, Antonio Prudente, Paulista Cancer Assoc. founder, Camargo Hospital. Se-tenant.

1983, Apr. 18

1848	A993	30cr multi	20	10
1849	A993	38cr multi	25	12

1983, Apr. 18

1850 A994 150cr pale grn & blk 1.50 50

Agricultural Research—A994

1983, Apr. 26 **Litho.** ***Perf. 11½***

1851	A995	30cr Chestnut tree	12	6
1852	A995	30cr Genetic research	12	6
1853	A995	38cr Tropical soy beans	16	8

Father Rogerio Neuhaus (1863-1934), Centenary of Ordination—A996

1983, May 3 ***Perf. 11½x11***

1854 A996 30cr multi 12 6

Council—A997

30th Anniv. of Customs Cooperation Council—A997

1983, May 5 ***Perf. 11x11½***

1855 A997 30cr multi 12 6

World Communications Year—A998

1983, May 17 **Litho.** ***Perf. 11½***

1856 A998 250cr multi 1.00 50

Toucans—A999

1983, May 21

1857	A999	30cr Tucanucu	12	6
1858	A999	185cr White-breasted	1.50	38
1859	A999	205cr Green-beaked	1.50	40
1860	A999	215cr Black-beaked	1.50	45

Souvenir Sheet

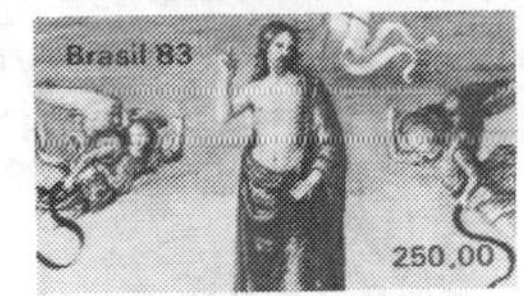

Resurrection, by Raphael (1483-1517)—A1000

1983, May 25 ***Perf. 11***

1861 A1000 250cr multi 1.50 *1.50*

Hohenzollern 980 Locomotive, 1875—A1001

Various locomotives.

1983, June 12 **Litho.** ***Perf. 11½***

1862	A1001	30cr shown	12	6
1863	A1001	30cr Baldwin No. 1, 1881	12	6
1864	A1001	38cr Fowler No. 1, 1872	15	8

9th Women's Basketball World Championship—A1002

1983, July 24 **Litho.** ***Perf. 11½x11***

1865	A1002	30cr Players, front view	12	6
1866	A1002	30cr Players, rear view	12	6

Simon Bolivar (1783-1830)—A1003

1983, July 24 ***Perf. 12***

1867 A1003 30cr multi 12 6

Children's Polio and Measles Vaccination Campaign—A1004

1983, July 25

1868	A1004	30cr Girl, measles	12	6
1869	A1004	30cr Boy, polio	12	6

20th Anniv. of Master's Program in Engineering—A1005

1983, July 28 ***Perf. 11½x11***

1870 A1005 30cr Minerva (goddess of wisdom), computer tape 12 6

No. 1, Guanabara Bay—A1006

1983, July 29 **Engr.**

1871	A1006	185cr shown	1.25	38
1872	A1006	205cr No. 2	1.25	40
1873	A1006	215cr No. 3	1.25	45

Souvenir Sheet

Perf. 11

1874		Sheet of 3	7.50	*9.00*
a.	A1006	185cr No. 1	2.00	*2.50*
b.	A1006	205cr No. 2	2.00	*2.50*
c.	A1006	215cr No. 3	2.00	*2.50*

BRASILIANA '83 Intl. Stamp Show, Rio de Janeiro, July 29-Aug. 7. No. 1874 View of Guanabara Bay in one continuous design. Size: 101x70mm.

Souvenir Sheet

The First Mass in Brazil, by Vitor Meireles (1833-1903)—A1007

1983, Aug. 18 ***Perf. 11***

1875 A1007 250cr multi 1.50 1.50

Size: 101x70mm.

EMB-120 Brasilia Passenger Plane—A1008

1983, Aug. 19 ***Perf. 12***

1876 A1008 30cr multi 12 6

Vision of Don Bosco Centenary—A1009

1983, Aug. 30

1877 A1009 130cr multi 75 25

Independence Week—A1010

1983, Sept. 1 **Litho.** ***Perf. 11½***

1878 A1010 50cr multi 25 12

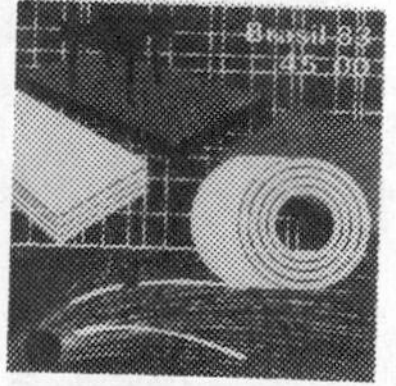

National Steel Corp., 10th Anniv. A1011

1983, Sept. 17 **Litho.** ***Perf. 11½***

1879 A1011 45cr multi 18 10

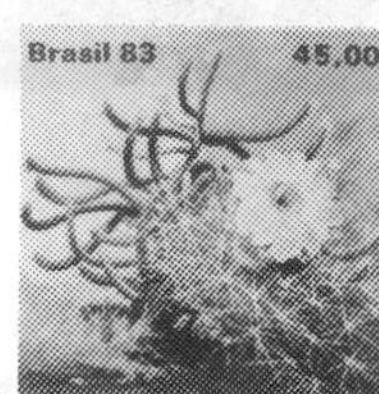

Cactus—A1012

1983, Sept. 12 **Litho.** ***Perf. 11½***

1880 A1012 45cr Pilosocereus gounellei 18 10
1881 A1012 45cr Melocactus bahiensis 18 10
1882 A1012 57cr Cereus jamacaru 24 12

1st National Eucharistic Congress—A1013

1983, Oct. 12 **Litho.** ***Perf. 11½***

1883 A1013 45cr multi 18 10

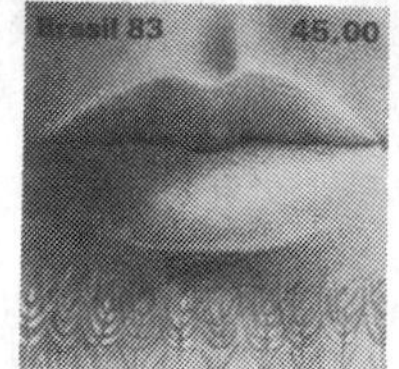

World Food Program—A1014

1983, Oct. 14 **Litho.** ***Perf. 11½***

1884 A1014 45cr Mouth, grain 18 10
1885 A1014 57cr Fish, sailboat 24 12

Souvenir Sheet

Louis Breguet, Death Centenary—A1015

1983, Oct. 27 **Litho.** ***Perf. 11***

1886 A1015 376cr Telegraph transmitter 1.50 1.50

Brown and multicolored margin shows portrait and telegraph lines. Size: 70x99mm.

Christmas 1983—A1016

17th-18th Cent. Statues: 45cr, Our Lady of the Angels. 315cr, Our Lady of the Parturition. 335cr, Our Lady of Joy. 345cr, Our Lady of the Presentation.

1983, Nov. 10 **Litho.** ***Perf. 11½***

1887 A1016 45cr multi 18 10
1888 A1016 315cr multi 1.50 60
1889 A1016 335cr multi 1.50 65
1890 A1016 345cr multi 1.50 70

Marshal Mascarenhas Birth Centenary—A1017

1983, Nov. 13 **Litho.** ***Perf. 11½***

1891 A1017 45cr Battle sites 18 10

Commander of Brazilian Expeditionary Force in Italy.

State Flags—A1018

Designs: a Amazonas. b. Goias. c. Rio de Janiero. d. Mato Grosso Do Sol. e. Parana.

1983, Nov. 17 **Litho.** ***Perf. 11½***

1892 Block of 5 plus label 3.00 3.00
a.-e.. A1018 45cr any single 50 20

Nos. 1892-1896 printed se-tenant with label showing arms of Republic.

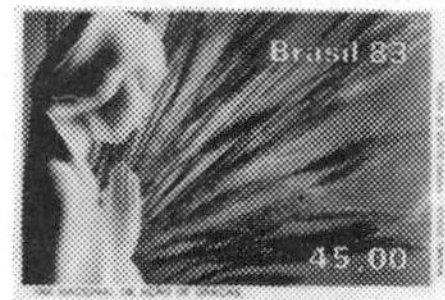

Thanksgiving 1983—A1018a

1983, Nov. 24 **Litho.** ***Perf. 12***

1896 A1018a 45cr Madonna, wheat 18 10

Manned Flight Bicentenary—A1019

1983, Dec. 15 **Litho.** ***Perf. 12***

1897 A1019 345cr Montgolfiere balloon, 1783 4.50 50

Ethnic Groups—A1020

1984, Jan. 20 **Litho.** ***Perf. 12***

1898 A1020 45cr multi 18 5

50th anniv. of publication of Masters and Slaves, sociological study by Gilberto Freyre.

Centenary of Crystal Palace, Petropolis—A1021

1984, Feb. 2

1899 A1021 45cr multi 18 5

Souvenir Sheet

Flags (Sculpture with 40 Figures), by Victor Brecheret (b. 1894)—A1022

1984, Feb. 22 **Litho.** ***Perf. 11***

1900 A1022 805cr multi 1.75 1.00

Size: 100x70mm.

Naval Museum Centenary—A1023

1984, Mar. 23 **Litho.** ***Perf. 11½***

1901 A1023 620cr Figurehead, frigate, 1847 1.30 80

Slavery Abolition Centenary—A1024

1984, Mar. 25

1902 A1024 585cr Broken chain, raft 1.15 65
1903 A1024 610cr Freed slave 1.25 70

Souvenir Sheet

Visit of King Carl XVI Gustaf of Sweden—A1025

1984, Apr. 2 *Perf. 11*
1904 A1025 2105cr multi 4.50 2.50

Multicolored margin shows palaces, arms. Size: 99x69mm.

1984 Summer Olympics—A1026

1984, Apr. 13 *Perf. 11½*
1905 A1026 65cr Long jump 14 8
1906 A1026 65cr 100 meter race 14 8
1907 A1026 65cr Relay race 14 8
1908 A1026 585cr Pole vault 1.15 65
1909 A1026 610cr High jump 1.25 70
1910 A1026 620cr Hurdles 1.30 80
Nos. 1905-1910 (6) 4.12 2.39

Nos. 1905-1910 se-tenant.

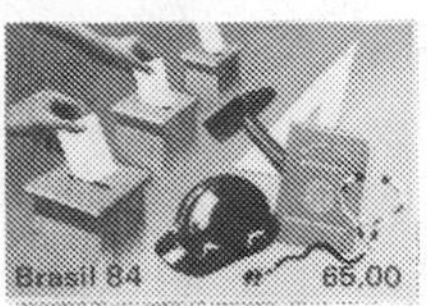

Voters Casting Ballots, Symbols of Labor—A1027

Pres. Getulio Vargas Birth Centenary: Symbols of Development.

1984, Apr. 19 **Litho.** *Perf. 11½*
1911 A1027 65cr shown 14 8
1912 A1027 65cr Oil rig, blast furnace 14 8
1913 A1027 65cr High-tension towers 14 8

Columbus, Espana '84 Emblem—A1028

1984, Apr. 27
1914 A1028 65cr Pedro Cabral 14 8
1915 A1028 610cr shown 1.25 70

Map of Americas, Heads
A1029

Lubrapex '84
A1030

1984, May 7 **Litho.** *Perf. 11½*
1916 A1029 65cr multi 14 8

Pan-American Association of Finance and Guarantees, 8th Assembly.

1984, May 8 *Perf. 11½x11*

18th Century Paintings, Mariana Cathedral.
1917 A1030 65cr Hunting scene 14 8
1918 A1030 585cr Pastoral scene 1.20 62
1919 A1030 610cr People under umbrellas 1.25 70
1920 A1030 620cr Elephants 1.30 72

Souvenir Sheet

Intl. Fedn. of Soccer Associations, 80th Anniv.—A1031

1984, May 21 *Perf. 11*
1921 A1031 2115cr Globe 4.50 2.50

Multicolored margin shows various World Cup games emblems. Size: 99x68mm.

Matto Grosso Lowland Fauna— A1032

1984, June 5 **Litho.** *Perf. 11½*
1922 Strip of 3 75 30
a. A1032 65cr Deer 25 8
b. A1032 65cr Jaguar 25 8
c. A1032 80cr Alligator 25 10

First Letter Mailed in Brazil, by Guido Mondin—A1033

1984, June 8 *Perf. 12x11½*
1923 A1033 65cr multi 14 8

Postal Union of Americas and Spain, first anniv. of new headquarters.

Brazil-Germany Air Service, 50th Anniv.
A1034 A1035

1984, June 19
1924 A1034 610cr Dornier-Wal seaplane 1.25 70
1925 A1035 620cr Steamer Westfalen 1.30 72

Woolly Spider Monkey, World Wildlife Fund Emblem—A1036

1984, July 6 *Perf. 11½*
1926 A1036 65cr Mother, baby 70 8
1927 A1036 80cr Monkey 50 10

Agriculture Type of 1980

Designs: 65cr, Rubber tree. 80cr, Brazil nuts. 120cr, Rice. 150cr, Eucalyptus. 300cr, Pinha da Parana. 800cr, Carnauba. 1000cr, Babacu. 2000cr, Sunflower.

Photo. (65, 80, 120, 150cr), Engr.

1984-85 *Perf. 11x11½*
1934 A894 65cr lilac 14 8
1935 A894 80cr brn red 18 10
1936 A894 120cr dk sl bl 26 8
1937 A894 150cr Eucalyptus 10 5
1938 A894 300cr rose mag 35 15
1939 A894 800cr grnsh bl 1.00 15
1940 A894 1000cr lemon 1.00 15
1941 A894 2000cr yel org ('85) 50 25
Nos. 1934-1941 (8) 3.53 1.01

Marajo Isld. Buffalo—A1037

1984, July 9 **Litho.** *Perf. 12*
1942 Strip of 3 75 25
a. A1037 65cr Approaching stream 20 8
b. A1037 65cr Standing on bank 20 8
c. A1037 65cr Drinking 20 8

Continuous design.

Banco Economico Sesquicentenary—A1038

1984, July 13 *Perf. 11½*
1943 A1038 65cr Bank, coins 20 8

Historic Railway Stations—A1039

1984, July 23 **Litho.** *Perf. 11½*
1944 A1039 65cr Japeri 14 8
1945 A1039 65cr Luz, vert. 14 8
1946 A1039 80cr Sao Joao del Rei 18 10

Souvenir Sheet

Girl Scouts in Brazil, 65th Anniv.—A1040

1984, Aug. 13 *Perf. 11*
1947 A1040 585cr Girl scout 1.50 1.00

Multicolored margin shows Juliet Lowe, scouts. Size: 100x70mm.

Housing Project Bank, 20th Anniv.—A1041

1984, Aug. 21 **Litho.** *Perf. 11½*
1948 A1041 65cr Couple sheltered from rain 14 8

Independence Week—A1042

Children's Drawings.

1984, Sept. 3
1949 A1042 100cr Explorer & ship 20 12
1950 A1042 100cr Sailing ships 20 12
1951 A1042 100cr "BRASIL" mural 20 12
1952 A1042 100cr Children under rainbow 20 12

Rio de Janeiro Chamber of Commerce Sesquicentenary—A1043

1984, Sept. 10
1953 A1043 100cr Monument, worker silhouette 20 12

Death Sesquicentenary of Don Pedro I (IV of Portugal)—A1044

1984, Sept. 23 *Perf. 12x11½*
1954 A1044 1000cr Portrait 2.00 1.25

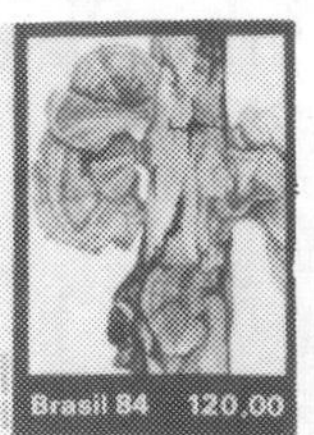

Local Mushrooms A1045

1984, Oct. 22 *Perf. 11½*
1955 A1045 120cr Pycnoporus sanguineus 24 15
1956 A1045 1050cr Calvatia sp 2.30 1.25
1957 A1045 1080cr Pleurotus sp, horiz. 2.40 1.30

Book Day—A1046

1984, Oct. 23 *Perf. 11½*
1958 A1046 120cr Girl in open book 24 15

New State Mint Opening—A1047

1984, Nov. 1
1959 A1047 120cr multi 24 15

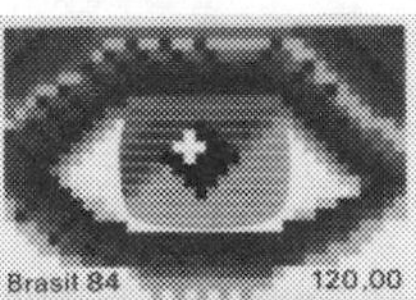

Informatics Fair & Congress—A1048

1984, Nov. 5 **Litho.** *Perf. 12*
1960 A1048 120cr Eye, computer terminal 8 5

Org. of American States, 14th Assembly—A1049

1984, Nov. 14
1961 A1049 120cr Emblem, flags 8 5

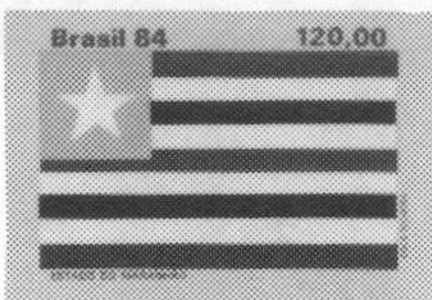

State Flags—A1050

Designs: a. Maranhaio. b. Mato Grosso. c. Minas Gerais. d. Piaui. e. Santa Catarina.

1984, Nov. 19 *Perf. 11½*
1962 Block of 5 plus label 1.50 1.50
a.-e. A1050 120cr, any single 30 10

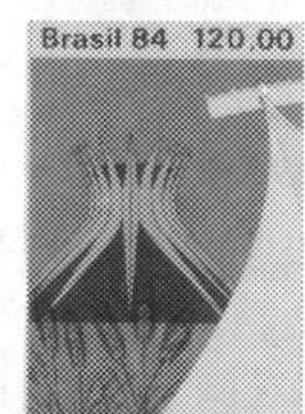

Thanksgiving 1984—A1051

1984, Nov. 22
1963 A1051 120cr Bell tower, Brasilia 10 6

Christmas 1984—A1052

Paintings: No. 1964, Nativity, by Djanira. No. 1965, Virgin and Child, by Glauco Rodrigues. No. 1966, Flight into Egypt, by Paul Garfunkel. No. 1967, Nativity, by Di Cavalcanti.

1984, Dec. 3 **Litho.** *Perf. 12*
1964 A1052 120cr multi 8 5
1965 A1052 120cr multi 8 5
1966 A1052 1050cr multi 64 40
1967 A1052 1080cr multi 65 40

40th Anniv., International Civil Aviation Organization—A1053

1984, Dec. 7 **Litho.** *Perf. 12*
1968 A1053 120cr Aircraft, Earth globe 8 5

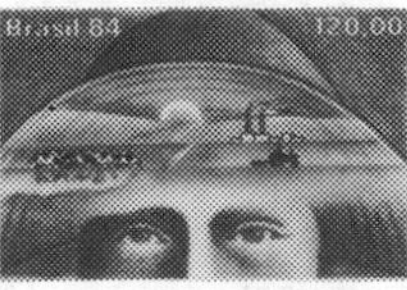

25th Anniv., North-Eastern Development—A1054

1984, Dec. 14 **Litho.** *Perf. 12*
1969 A1054 120cr Farmer, field 8 5

Emilio Rouede—A1055

Painting: Church of the Virgin of Safe Travels, by Rouede.

1985, Jan. 22 **Litho.** *Perf. 12*
1970 A1055 120cr multi 8 5

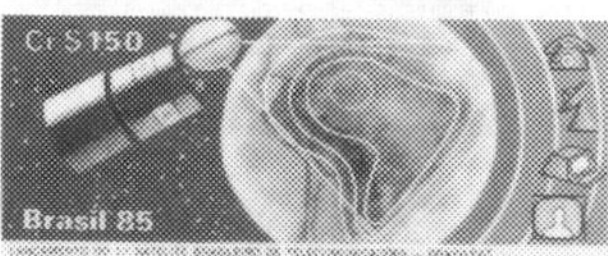

BRASILSAT—A1056

1985, Feb. 8 **Litho.** *Perf. 11½x12*
1971 A1056 150cr Satellite, Brazil 10 6

Metropolitan Railways—A1057

1985, Mar. 2 **Litho.** *Perf. 11x11½*
1972 A1057 200cr Passenger trains 14 8

Brasilia Botanical Gardens—A1058

1985, Mar. 8 **Litho.** *Perf. 11½x12*
1973 A1058 200cr Caryocar brasiliense 14 8

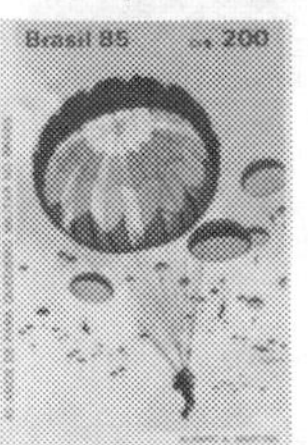

40th Anniv., Brazilian Paratroops—A1059

1985, Mar. 8 **Litho.** *Perf. 11½x12*
1974 A1059 200cr Parachute drop 14 8

Natl. Climate Awareness Program—A1060

1985, Mar. 18 **Litho.** *Perf. 11½x12*
1975 A1060 500cr multi 22 14

Thoroughbred Horses—A1061

1985, Mar. 19 **Litho.** *Perf. 12*
1976 A1061 1000cr Campolina 45 28
1977 A1061 1500cr Marajoara 68 42
1978 A1061 1500cr Mangalarga marchador 68 42

Ouro Preto—A1062

1985, Apr. 18 **Litho.** *Perf. 11½x12*
1979 A1062 220cr shown 10 6
1980 A1062 220cr St. Miguel des Missoes 10 6
1981 A1062 220cr Olinda 10 6

Polivolume, by Mary Vieira — A1063

Rio Branco Inst. 40th Anniv.

1985, Apr. 20 **Litho.**
1982 A1063 220cr multi 10 6

Natl. Capital, Brasilia, 25th Anniv.—A1064

1985, Apr. 22 **Litho.**
1983 A1064 220cr Natl. Theater, acoustic shell 10 6
1984 A1064 220cr Catetinho Palace, JK Memorial 10 6

Numerals—A1065

Dot Numeral—A1065a

1985-1986 **Photo.** *Perf. 11½*
1985 A1065 50cr lake 5 5
1986 A1065 100cr dp vio 6 5
1987 A1065 150cr violet 5 5
1988 A1065 200cr ultra 8 5
1989 A1065 220cr green 10 6
1990 A1065 300cr ryl bl 18 12

1991	A1065	500cr ol blk	30	22
1992	A1065a	1000cr brn ol ('86)	14	10
1993	A1065a	2000cr brt grn ('86)	28	22
1994	A1065a	3000 cr dl vio	42	32
1995	A1065a	5000 cr brn	58	42
		Nos. 1985-1995 (11)	2.24	1.66

Marshall Rondon, 120th Birth Anniv.—A1066

1985, May 5 *Perf. 11x11½*

1996 A1066 220cr multi 10 6

Educator, protector of the Indians, building superintendent of telegraph lines.

Candido Fontoura (1885-1974) A1067

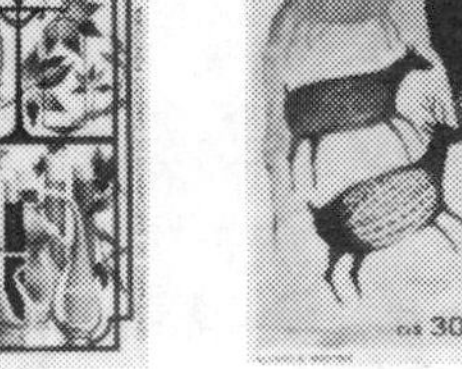

Brapex VI A1068

1985, May 14 *Perf. 12x11½*

1997 A1067 220cr multi 10 6

Pioneer of the Brazilian pharmaceutical industry.

1985, May 18 *Perf. 11½x11*

Cave paintings: No. 1998, Deer, Cerca Grande. No. 1999, Lizards, Lapa do Caboclo. No. 2000, Running deer, Grande Abrigo de Santana do Riacho.

1998	A1068	300cr multi	12	8
1999	A1068	300cr multi	12	8
2000	A1068	2000cr multi	75	50
a.		Souvenir sheet of 3, perf. 10½x11	1.10	75

No. 2000a contains Nos. 1998-2000; margin inscribed. Size: 100x70mm.

Wildlife Conservation—A1069

Birds in Marinho dos Abrolhos National Park.

1985, June 5 *Perf. 11½x12*

2001	A1069	220cr Fregata magnificens	8	5
2002	A1069	220cr Sula dactylatra	8	5
2003	A1069	220cr Anous stolidus	8	5
2004	A1069	2000cr Pluvialis squatarola	68	50

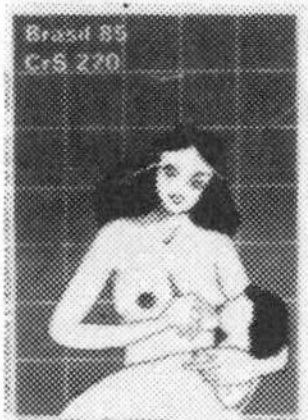

U.N. Infant Survival Campaign—A1070

1985, June 11 *Perf. 12x11½*

2005	A1070	220cr Mother breastfeeding infant	8	5
2006	A1070	220cr Hand, eyedropper, children	8	5
a.		Pair, #2005-2006	16	10

Helicopter Rescue, Search Ship, Diver—A1071

1985, June 22 **Litho.** *Perf. 11½x11*

2007 A1071 220cr multi 15 10

Sea Search & Rescue.

Souvenir Sheet

World Cup Soccer, Mexico, 1986—A1072

1985, June 23 *Perf. 11*

2008 A1072 2000cr Player dribbling, World Cup 1.25 85

No. 2008 has multicolored margin continuing the design. Size: 70x99mm.

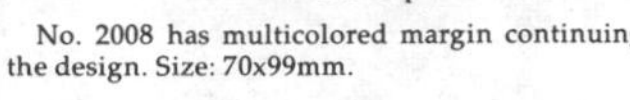

Intl. Youth Year A1073

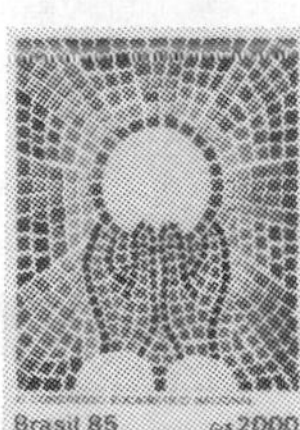

11th Natl. Eucharistic Congress A1074

1985, June 28 *Perf. 12*

2009 A1073 220cr Circle of children 15 10

1985, July 16 *Perf. 12x11½*

2010 A1074 2000cr Mosaic, Priest raising host 1.25 85

Director Humberto Mauro, Scene from Sangue Mineiro, 1929—A1075

1985, July 27

2011 A1075 300cr multi 18 12

Cataguases Studios, 60th anniv.

Escola e Sacro Museum, Convent St. Anthony, Joao Pessoa, Paraiba—A1076

1985, Aug. 5 *Perf. 11½x12*

2012 A1076 330cr multi 20 15

Paraiba State 400th anniv.

Inconfidencia Museum A1077

Cabanagem Insurrection, 150th Anniv. A1078

1985, Aug. 11 *Perf. 12x11½*

2013	A1077	300cr shown	18	12
2014	A1077	300cr Museum of History & Diplomacy	18	12

1985, Aug. 14

Design: Revolutionary, detail from an oil painting by Guido Mondin.

2015 A1078 330cr multi 20 15

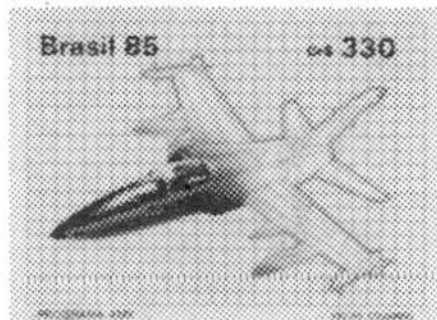

AMX Subsonic Air Force Fighter Plane—A1079

1985, Aug. 19 *Perf. 11½x12*

2016 A1079 330cr multi 20 15

AMX Project, joint program with Italy.

16th-17th Century Military Uniforms—A1080

1985, Aug. 26 *Perf. 12x11½*

2017	A1080	300cr Captain, crossbowman	18	12
2018	A1080	300cr Harquebusier, sergeant	18	12
2019	A1080	300cr Musketeer, pikeman	18	12
2020	A1080	300cr Fusilier, pikeman	18	12

Farrouphilha Insurrection, 150th Anniv.—A1081

Design: Bento Goncalves and insurrectionist cavalry on Southern battlefields, detail of an oil painting by Guido Mondin.

1985, Sept. 20 *Perf. 11½x12*

2021 A1081 330cr multi 20 15

Aparados da Serra National Park—A1082

1985, Sept. 23

2022 A1082 3100cr Ravine 80 52
2023 A1082 3320cr Mountains 85 55
2024 A1082 3480cr Forest, waterfall 90 60

President-elect Tancredo Neves—A1083

Design: Portrait, Natl. Congress, Alvorada Palace, Federal Supreme Court.

1985, Oct. 10 **Litho.** ***Perf. 11x11½***

2025 A1083 330cr multi 15 12

FEB, Postmark—A1084

1985, Oct. 10 ***Perf. 11½x12***

2026 A1084 500cr multi 20 15

Brazilian Expeditionary Force Postal Service, 41st anniv.

Rio de Janeiro-Niteroi Ferry Service, 150th Anniv.—A1085

1985, Oct. 14 ***Perf. 11½x12***

2027 A1085 500cr Segunda 20 15
2028 A1085 500cr Terceira 20 15
2029 A1085 500cr Especuladora 20 15
2030 A1085 500cr Urca 20 15

Muniz M-7 Inaugural Flight, 50th Anniv.—A1086

1985, Oct. 22

2031 A1086 500cr multi 20 15

UN 40th Anniv. A1087

Natl. Press System A1088

1985, Oct. 24 ***Perf. 11½x11***

2032 A1087 500cr multi 20 15

1985, Nov. 7

2033 A1088 500cr Newspaper masthead, reader 20 15

Diario de Pernambuco, newspaper, 160th anniv.

Christmas 1985—A1089

1985, Nov. 11 ***Perf. 11½x12***

2034 A1089 500cr Christ in Manger 20 15
2035 A1089 500cr Adoration of the Magi 20 15
2036 A1089 500cr Flight to Egypt 20 15

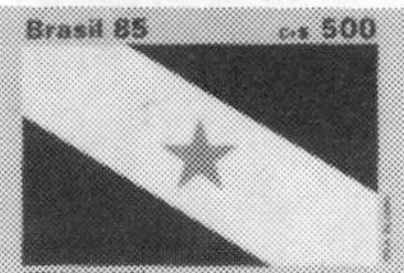

Para—A1090

State Flags: No. 2037b, Rio Grande do Sul. No. 2037c, Acre. No. 2037d, Sao Paulo.

1985, Nov. 19 ***Perf. 12***

2037 Block of 4 80 60
a.-d. A1090 500cr, any single 20 15

Thanksgiving Day—A1091

1985, Nov. 28 ***Perf. 12x11½***

2038 A1091 500cr Child gathering wheat 20 15

Economic Development of Serra dos Carajas Region—A1092

1985, Dec. 11 **Litho.** ***Perf. 11½x12***

2039 A1092 500cr multi 8 6

Fr. Bartholomeu Lourenco de Gusmao (1685-1724), Inventor, the Aerostat—A1093

1985, Dec. 19 **Litho.** ***Perf. 11x11½***

2040 A1093 500cr multi 8 6

The Trees, by Da Costa E Silva (b. 1885), Poet—A1094

1985, Dec. 20 **Litho.** ***Perf. 12x11½***

2041 A1094 500cr multi 8 6

Souvenir Sheet

1986 World Cup Soccer Championships, Mexico—A1095

1986, Mar. 3 **Litho.** ***Perf. 11***

2042 A109510000crmulti 1.25 95

LUBRAPEX '86, philatelic exhibition. No. 2042 has multicolored margin continuing the design and picturing FIFA emblem and flags. Size: 69x99mm.

1000 Cruzeiros = 1 Cruzado (1986)

Halley's Comet—A1096

1986, Apr. 11 **Litho.** ***Perf. 11½x12***

2043 A1096 .50cz multi 6 5

Commander Ferraz Antarctic Station, 2nd Anniv.—A1097

1986, Apr. 25

2044 A1097 .50cz multi 8 6

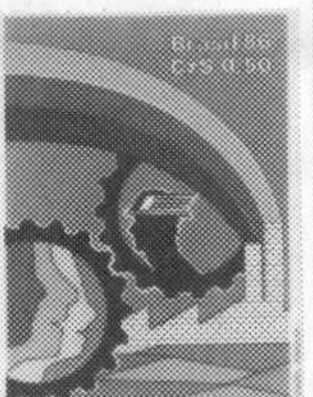

Labor Day A1098

Maternity, by Henrique Bernardelli (1858-1936) A1099

1986, May 1 **Litho.** ***Perf. 12x11½***

2045 A1098 .50cz multi 6 5

1986, May 8

2046 A1099 .50cz multi 6 5

Amnesty Intl., 25th Anniv.—A1100

1986, May 28 **Litho.** ***Perf. 11½x12***

2047 A1100 .50cz multi 6 5

Butterflies—A1101

1985, June 5 ***Perf. 12x11½***

2048 A1101 .50cz Pyrrhopyge ruficauda 6 5
2049 A1101 .50cz Prepona eugenes diluta 6 5
2050 A1101 .50cz Pierriballia mandela molione 6 5

Score from Opera "Il Guarani" and Antonio Carlos Gomes (1836-1896), Composer—A1102

1986, July 11 ***Perf. 11½x12***

2051 A1102 .50cz multi 6 5

Natl. Accident Prevention Campaign—A1103

1986, July 30 Litho. *Perf. 11½x11*

2052 A1103 .50cz Lineman 5 5

Souvenir Sheet

Stamp Day—A1104

1986, Aug. 1 *Perf. 11*

2053 A1104 5cz No. 53 45 35

Brazilian Philatelic Society, 75th anniv., and Dom Pedro II issue, Nos. 53-60, 120th anniv. No. 2053 has beige and vermilion inscribed margin picturing Emperor Dom Pedro II. Size: 70x99mm.

Architecture A1105

Famous Men A1106

Designs: No. 2055, House of Garcia D'Avila, Nazare de Mata, Bahia. No. 2059, Fort Reis Magos, Natal.

1986 Photo. *Perf. 11½x11*

2055 A1105 .10cz sage grn 5 5
2059 A1105 .50cz orange 5 5

Issue dates: No. 2055, Aug. 11. No. 2059, Aug. 19.

1986 *Perf. 12x11½, 11½x12*

Designs: No. 2074, Juscelino Kubitschek de Oliveira, president 1956-61, and Alvorado Palace, Brasilia. No. 2075, Octavio Mangabeira, statesman, and Itamaraty Palace, Rio de Janeiro, horiz.

2074 A1106 .50cz multi 5 5
2075 A1106 .50cz multi 5 5

Issue dates: No. 2074, Aug. 21. No. 2075, Aug. 27.

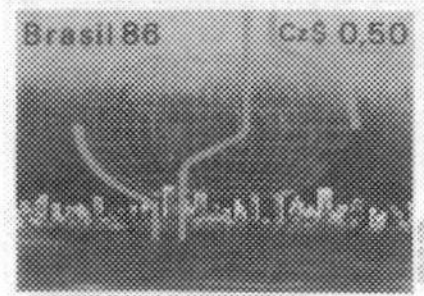

World Gastroenterology Congress, Sao Paulo—A1107

1986, Sept. 7 *Perf. 11½x12*

2076 A1107 .50cz multi 5 5

Federal Broadcasting System, 50th Anniv. A1108

Intl. Peace Year A1109

1986, Sept. 15 *Perf. 12x11½*

2077 A1108 .50cz multi 5 5

1986, Sept. 16

Painting (detail): War and Peace, by Candido Portinari.

2078 A1109 .50cz multi 5 5

Ernesto Simoes Filho (b. 1886), Publisher of La Tarde—A1110

1986, Oct. 4 Litho. *Perf. 11½x12*

2079 A1110 .50cz multi 8 6

Famous Men A1111

Federal Savings Bank, 125th Anniv. A1112

Designs: No. 2080, Title page from manuscript, c. 1683-94, by Gregorio Mattose e Guerra (b. 1636), author. No. 2081, Manuel Bandeira (1886-1968), poet, text from I'll Go Back to Pasargada.

1986, Oct. 29 *Perf. 11½x11*

2080 A1111 .50cz lake & beige 8 6
2081 A1111 .50cz lake & dl grn 8 6

1986, Nov. 4 *Perf. 12x11½*

2082 A1112 .50cz multi 8 6

Flowering Plants A1113

Glauber Rocha, Film Industry Pioneer A1114

1986, Nov. 10 *Perf. 12x11½, 11½x12*

2083 A1113 .50cz Urera mitis 8 6
2084 A1113 6.50cz Couroupita guyanensis 52 40
2085 A1113 6.90cz Bauhinia variegata, horiz. 55 42

1986, Nov. 20 *Perf. 12x11½*

2086 A1114 .50cz multi 8 6

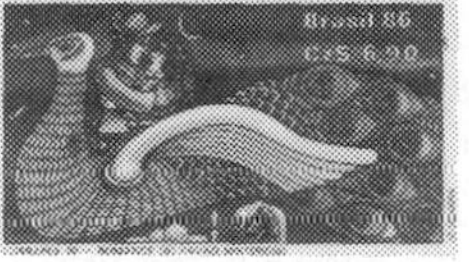

LUBRAPEX '86—A1115

Cordel Folk Tales: No. 2087, Romance of the Mysterious Peacock. No. 2088, History of the Empress Porcina.

1986, Nov. 21 *Perf. 11x12*

2087 A1115 6.90cz multi 55 42
2088 A1115 6.90cz multi 55 42
a Souv. sheet of 2, #2087-2088, perf. 11 1.10 85

No. 2088a has inscribed decorative margin picturing folk figures. Size: 70x100mm.

Christmas—A1116

Birds: .50cz, And Christ child. 6.50cz, And tree. 7.30cz, Eating fruit.

1986, Nov. 10 *Perf. 11½x12*

2089 A1116 .50cz multi 5 5
2090 A1116 6.50cz multi 65 48
2091 A1116 7.30cz multi 75 58

Military Uniforms, c. 1930 A1117

Bartolomeu de Gusmao Airport, 50th Anniv. A1118

Designs: No. 2092, Navy lieutenant commander, dreadnought Minas Gerais. No. 2093, Army flight lieutenant, WACO S.C.O. biplane, Fortaleza Airport.

1986, Dec. 15 *Perf. 12x11½*

2092 A1117 .50cz multi 5 5
2093 A1117 .50cz multi 5 5

Fortaleza Air Base, 50th anniv. (No. 2093).

1986, Dec. 26

2094 A1118 1cz multi 10 5

SEMI-POSTAL STAMPS

National Philatelic Exhibition Issue.

SP1

Wmkd. Coat of Arms in Sheet. (236)

1934, Sept. 16 Engraved *Imperf.*

Thick Paper

B1	SP1	200r +100r dp cl	75	1.50
B2	SP1	300r +100r ver	75	1.50
B3	SP1	700r +100r brt bl	8.00	15.00
B4	SP1	1000r +100r blk	8.00	15.00

The surtax was to help defray the expenses of the exhibition. Issued in sheets of 60, inscribed "EXPOSICAO FILATELICA NACIONAL".

Red Cross Nurse and Soldier
SP2

Perf. 11

1935, Sept. 19 Typo. Wmk. 222

B5	SP2	200r +100r pur & red	1.00	1.00
B6	SP2	300r +100r ol brn & red	1.00	75
B7	SP2	700r +100r turq bl & red	12.00	7.00

3rd Pan-American Red Cross Conference. Exist imperf.

Three Wise Men and Star of Bethlehem
SP3

Angel and Child
SP4

Southern Cross and Child
SP5

BRASIL CORREIO PRO JUVENTUDE 1200+400

Mother and Child
SP6

Perf. 10½

1939, Dec. 20 Litho. Wmk. 249

B8	SP3	100r +100r chlky bl & bl blk	50	50
a.		Horiz. or vert. pair, imperf. between	45.00	
B9	SP4	200r +100r brt grnsh bl	1.00	1.00
a.		Horizontal pair, imperf. between	45.00	
B10	SP5	400r +200r ol grn & ol	1.00	25
B11	SP6	1200r +400r crim & brn red	5.00	1.50
a.		Vertical pair, imperf. between	45.00	

The surtax was distributed to charitable institutions.

AIR POST STAMPS.

Official Stamps of 1913 Surcharged

SERVIÇO AEREO 200 Rs.

1927, Dec. 28 *Perf. 12* Unwmkd.

Center in Black.

C1	O2	50r on 10r gray	15	15
a.		Inverted surcharge	275.00	
b.		Top ornaments missing	50.00	
C2	O2	200r on 1000r blk brn	2.00	4.00
a.		Double surch.	275.00	
C3	O2	200r on 2000r red brn	2.00	7.00
a.		Double surch.	275.00	
C4	O2	200r on 5000r brn	1.50	1.50
a.		Double surch.	275.00	
b.		Double surcharge, one inverted	300.00	
c.		Triple surch.	400.00	
C5	O2	300r on 500r org	1.50	1.50
C6	O2	300r on 600r vio	60	50
b.		Pair, one without surch.		
C6A	O2	500r on 10r gray	375.00	475.00
C7	O2	500r on 50r gray	1.50	50
a.		Double surch.	275.00	275.00
C8	O2	1000r on 20r ol grn	90	25
a.		Double surch.	275.00	225.00
C9	O2	2000r on 100r ver	2.50	1.75
a.		Pair, one without surcharge	1,000.	
C10	O2	2000r on 200r bl	2.50	1.75
C11	O2	2000r on 10,000r blk	2.00	60
C12	O2	5000r on 20,000r bl	4.00	4.00
C13	O2	5000r on 50,000r grn	4.00	4.00
C14	O2	5000r on 100,000r org	20.00	25.00
C15	O2	10,000r on 500,000r brn	25.00	17.50
C16	O2	10,000r on 1,000,000r dk brn	20.00	20.00
		Nos. C1-C6, C7-C16 (16)	90.15	90.00

Nos. C1, C1b, C7, C8 and C9 have small diamonds printed over the numerals in the upper corners.

Monument to de Gusmão
AP1

Santos-Dumont's Airship
AP2

Augusto Severo's Airship "Pax"
AP3

Santos-Dumont's Biplane "14 Bis"
AP4

Ribeiro de Barros's Seaplane "Jahu"
AP5

Perf. 11, 12½x13, 13x13½.

1929 Typographed. Wmk. 206

C17	AP1	50r bl grn	25	20
C18	AP2	200r red	1.25	20
C19	AP3	300r brt bl	1.50	20
C20	AP4	500r red vio	2.00	20
C21	AP5	1000r org brn	5.00	40
		Nos. C17-C21 (5)	10.00	1.20

See also Nos. C32-C36.

Bartholomeu de Gusmão
AP6

Augusto Severo
AP7

BRASIL SERVIÇO POSTAL AEREO SANTOS DUMONT REIS 10.000 REIS

Alberto Santos-Dumont
AP8

Perf. 9, 11 and Compound.

1929-30 Engraved. Wmk. 101

C22	AP6	2000r lt grn ('30)	10.00	25
C23	AP7	5000r carmine	10.00	1.00
C24	AP8	10,000r ol grn	10.00	1.25

See also Nos. C37, C40.

Allegory: Airmail Service between Brazil and the United States
AP9

1929 Typographed Wmk. 206

C25	AP9	3000r violet	10.00	65

See also Nos. C38, C41. Nos. C23-C25 exist imperforate.

Air Post Stamps of 1929 Surcharged in Blue or Red

ZEPPELIN 2$500

1931, Aug. 16 *Perf. 12½x13½.*

C26	AP2	2500r on 200r red (Bl)	20.00	22.50
C27	AP3	5000r on 300r brt bl (R)	22.50	27.50

No. C25 Surcharged

2.500 REIS

1931, Sept. 2 *Perf. 11*

C28	AP9	2500r on 3000r vio	17.50	20.00
a.		Inverted surcharge	200.00	
b.		Surcharged on front and back	200.00	

Regular Issues of 1928-29 Surcharged

ZEPPELIN 3$500

Perf. 11, 11½.

1932, May Wmk. 101

C29	A89	3500r on 5000r gray lil	20.00	22.50
C30	A72	7000r on 10,000r rose	20.00	22.50
b.		Horiz. pair, imperf. between	750.00	

Imperforates

Since 1933, imperforate or partly perforated sheets of nearly all of the airmail issues have become available.

Flag and Airplane
AP10

Typographed

1933, June 7 *Perf. 11.* Wmk. 222

C31	AP10	3500r grn, yel & dk bl	4.00	85

See also Nos. C39, C42.

1934 Wmk. 222

C32	AP1	50r bl grn	1.00	1.00
C33	AP2	200r red	1.25	60
C34	AP3	300r brt bl	2.50	1.25
C35	AP4	500r red vio	1.25	50
C36	AP5	1000r org brn	3.00	40
		Nos. C32-C36 (5)	9.00	3.75

Engraved.

1934 *Perf. 12x11.* Wmk. 236

Thick Laid Paper.

C37	AP6	2000r lt grn	5.00	1.00

Types of 1929, 1933.

Perf. 11, 11½, 12.

1937-40 Typographed Wmk. 249

C38	AP9	3000r violet	20.00	1.50
C39	AP10	3500r grn, yel & dk bl	2.00	1.25

Engraved.

C40	AP7	5000r ver ('40)	4.50	60

Watermark note after No. 501 also applies to No. C40.

Types of 1929-33.

Perf. 11, 11½x12

1939-40 Typographed Wmk. 256

C41	AP9	3000r violet	90	50
C42	AP10	3500r bl, dl grn & yel ('40)	60	40

Map of the Western Hemisphere Showing Brazil
AP11

1941, Jan. 14 Engr. *Perf. 11*

C43	AP11	1200r dk brn	2.50	50

5th general census of Brazil.

No. 506A Overprinted in Carmine

AÉREO "10 Nov." 937-941

Rouletted.

1941, Nov. 10 Wmk. 264

C45	A180	5400r sl grn	2.00	1.00
a.		Overprint inverted	175.00	

Issued in commemoration of the fourth anniversary of President Vargas' new constitution.

Nos. 506A and 508 Surcharged in Black

AÉREO
"10 Nov."
937-942

Cr.$ 5,40

1942, Nov. 10 Wmk. 264

C47 A180 5.40cr on 5400r sl grn 2.00 1.00
a. Wmk. 249 50.00 50.00
b. Surcharge inverted 75.00 75.00

Issued in commemoration of the fifth anniversary of President Vargas' new constitution.

The status of No. C47a is questioned.

Southern Cross and Arms of Paraguay
AP12

Wmk. 270

Wmkd.
Wavy Lines and Seal. (270)

1943, May 11 Engr. *Perf. 12½*

C48 AP12 1.20cr lt gray bl 1.00 50

Issued in commemoration of the visit of President Higinio Morinigo of Paraguay.

Map of South America
AP13

Wmk. 271

Wmkd. Wavy Lines. (271)

1943, June 30 *Perf. 12½.*

C49 AP13 1.20cr multi 1.00 50

Visit of President Penaranda of Bolivia.

Numeral of Value
AP14

1943, Aug. 7

C50 AP14 1cr blk & dl yel 3.00 2.00
a. Double impression 50.00
C51 AP14 2cr blk & pale grn 4.00 2.00
a. Double impression 60.00
C52 AP14 5cr blk & pink 5.00 2.75

Centenary of Brazil's first postage stamps.

Souvenir Sheet.

AP15
Imperf.
Without Gum

C53 AP15 Sheet of three 37.50 35.00
a. 1cr blk & dl yel 10.00 10.00
b. 2cr blk & pale grn 10.00 10.00
c. 5cr blk & pink 10.00 10.00

Issued to commemorate the 100th anniversary of the first postage stamps of Brazil and the second Philatelic Exposition (Brapex). Printed in panes of 6 sheets, perforated 12½ between. Each sheet is perforated on two or three sides. Size approximately 155x155mm. Inscriptions are printed in light brown.

Law Book
AP16

1943, Aug. 13 *Perf. 12½*

C54 AP16 1.20cr rose & lil rose 60 25

Issued to commemorate the second Inter-American Conference of Lawyers.

Semi-Postal Stamps of 1939 Surcharged in Red, Carmine or Black

AÉREO
20
Cts.

1944, Jan. 3 *Perf. 10½* Wmk. 249

C55 SP5 20c on 400r+200r ol grn & ol (R) 50 50
C56 SP5 40c on 400r+200r ol grn & ol (Bk) 1.00 35
C57 SP5 60c on 400r+200r ol grn & ol (C) 1.00 25
C58 SP5 1cr on 400r+200r ol grn & ol (Bk) 1.25 30
C59 SP5 1.20cr on 400r+200r ol grn & ol (C) 1.50 30
Nos. C55-C59 (5) 5.25 1.70

No. C59 is known with surcharge in black but its status is questioned.

Bartholomeu de Gusmão and the "Aerostat"
AP17

Engraved

1944, Oct. 23 *Perf. 12* Wmk. 268

C60 AP17 1.20cr rose car 50 20

Week of the Wing.

L. L. Zamenhof
AP18

1945, Apr. 16 Litho. *Perf. 11*

C61 AP18 1.20cr dl brn 60 30

Issued to commemorate the Esperanto Congress held in Rio de Janeiro, April 14–22, 1945.

Map of South America
AP19

Baron of Rio Branco
AP20

1945, Apr. 20

C62 AP19 1.20cr gray brn 50 25
C63 AP20 5cr rose lil 1.50 40

Issued to commemorate the centenary of the birth of José Maria de Silva Paranhos, Baron of Rio Branco.

Dove and Flags of American Republics
AP21

Perf. 12x11

1947, Aug. 15 Engr. Unwmkd.

C64 AP21 2.20cr dk bl grn 50 25

Issued to commemorate the Inter-American Defense Conference at Rio de Janeiro August–September, 1947.

Santos-Dumont Monument, St. Cloud, France
AP22

Bay of Rio de Janeiro and Rotary Emblem
AP23

1947, Nov. 15 Typo. *Perf. 11x12*

C65 AP22 1.20cr org brn & ol 50 25

Issued to commemorate the Week of the Wing and to honor the Santos-Dumont monument which was destroyed in World War II.

1948, May 16 Engraved. *Perf. 11.*

C66 AP23 1.20cr dp cl 60 40
C67 AP23 3.80r dl vio 1.25 40

Issued in honor of the 39th convention of Rotary International, Rio de Janeiro, May 1948.

Hotel Quitandinha, Petropolis
AP24

1948, July 10 Litho. Wmk. 267

C68 AP24 1.20cr org brn 35 25
C69 AP24 3.80cr violet 65 30

Issued to commemorate the International Exposition of Industry and Commerce, Petropolis, 1948.

Musician and Singers
AP25

1948, Aug. 13 Engraved. Unwmkd.

C70 AP25 1.20cr blue 50 20

Issued to commemorate the centenary of the establishment of the National School of Music.

Luis Batlle Berres
AP26

1948, Sept. 2 Typographed.

C71 AP26 1.70cr blue 35 25

Issued to commemorate the visit of President Luis Batlle Berres of Uruguay, September, 1948.

Merino Ram
AP27

Perf. 12x11.

1948, Oct. 10 **Wmk. 267**

C72	AP27	1.20cr dp org	70	30

Issued to publicize the International Livestock Exposition at Bagé.

Eucharistic Congress Seal
AP28

Engraved.

1948, Oct. 23 ***Perf. 11*** **Unwmkd.**

C73	AP28	1.20cr dk car rose	40	30

Issued to commemorate the 5th National Eucharistic Congress, Porto Alegre, October 24 to 31.

Souvenir Sheet

AP28a

Without Gum

1948, Dec. 14 **Engraved** ***Imperf.***

C73A	AP28a	Sheet of three	50.00	60.00

No. C73A contains one each of Nos. 674-676. Issued in honor of President Eurico Gaspar Dutra and the armed forces. Exists both with and without number on back. Measures 130x75mm. Marginal inscriptions typographed in black.

Church of Prazeres, Guararapes
AP29

Perf. 11½x12.

1949, Feb. 15 **Litho.** **Wmk. 267**

C74	AP29	1.20cr pink	1.50	75

Issued to commemorate the 300th anniversary of the Second Battle of Guararapes.

Thomé de Souza Meeting Indians
AP30

Perf. 11x12.

1949, Mar. 29 **Engr.** **Unwmkd.**

C75	AP30	1.20cr blue	35	25

Issued to commemorate the 400th anniversary of the founding of the City of Salvador.

A souvenir folder, issued with No. C75, has an engraved 20cr red brown postage stamp portraying John III printed on it, and a copy of No. C75 affixed to it and postmarked. Paper is laid, inscriptions are in red brown and size of folder front is 100x150mm. Price, $5.

Franklin D. Roosevelt
AP31

1949, May 20 ***Imperf.*** **Unwmkd.**

C76	AP31	3.80cr dp bl	1.00	80
a.		Souvenir sheet	9.00	10.00

No. C76a measures 85x110mm., with deep blue inscriptions in upper and lower margins. It also exists with papermaker's watermark.

Joaquim Nabuco
AP32

1949, Aug. 30 ***Perf. 12***

C77	AP32	3.80cr rose lil	70	40
a.		Wmk. 256, imperf.	25.00	

Issued to commemorate the centenary of the birth of Joaquim Nabuco (1849–1910), lawyer and writer.

Maracanã Stadium
AP33

Soccer Player and Flag
AP34

Perf. 11x12, 12x11

1950, June 24 **Litho.** **Wmk. 267**

C78	AP33	1.20cr ultra & sal	1.25	40
C79	AP34	5.80cr bl, yel grn & yel	3.50	50

Issued to publicize the 4th World Soccer Championship at Rio de Janeiro.

Symbolical of Brazilian Population Growth
AP35

1950, July 10 ***Perf. 12x11***

C80	AP35	1.20cr red brn	40	15

Issued to publicize the 6th Brazilian census.

J. B. Marcelino Champagnat
AP36

Engraved.

1956, Sept. 8 ***Perf. 11½*** **Wmk. 267**

C81	AP36	3.30cr rose lil	35	15

Issued to commemorate the 50th anniversary of the arrival of the Marist Brothers in Northern Brazil.

Santos-Dumont's 1906 Plane
AP37

1956, Oct. 16 **Photogravure**

C82	AP37	3cr dk bl grn	1.25	30
a.		Souvenir sheet of four	1.75	1.75
b.		3cr dk car	35	25
C83	AP37	3.30cr brt ultra	30	10
C84	AP37	4cr dp cl	60	10
C85	AP37	6.50cr red brn	20	10
C86	AP37	11.50cr org red	1.25	35
		Nos. C82-C86 (5)	3.60	95

Issued to commemorate the 50th anniversary of the first flight by Santos-Dumont.

No. C82a measures 123½x156mm. and contains four copies of No. C82b. Inscribed in dark carmine in four languages: "50TH ANNIVERSARY OF THE FIRST FLIGHT OF THE HEAVIER THAN THE AIR." Issued Oct. 14, 1956.

Lord Baden-Powell
AP38

1957, Aug. 1 **Unwmkd.**

Granite Paper

C87	AP38	3.30cr dp red lil	40	15

Issued to commemorate the centenary of the birth of Lord Baden-Powell, founder of the Boy Scouts.

U.N. Emblem, Soldier and Map of Suez Canal Area
AP39

Engraved.

1957, Oct. 24 ***Perf. 11½*** **Wmk. 267**

C88	AP39	3.30cr dk bl	30	20

Issued to honor the Brazilian contingent of the United Nations Emergency Force.

Basketball Player
AP40

1959, May 30 **Photo.** ***Perf. 11½***

C89	AP40	3.30cr brt red brn & bl	40	15

Brazil's victory in the World Basketball Championships of 1959.

Symbol of Flight
AP41

1959, Oct. 21 **Wmk. 267**

C90	AP41	3.30cr dp ultra	20	10

Issued to publicize Week of the Wing.

Caravelle
AP42

1959, Dec. 18 ***Perf. 11½***

C91	AP42	6.50cr ultra	15	10

Inauguration of Brazilian jet flights.

Pres. Adolfo Lopez Mateos
AP43

Pres. Dwight D. Eisenhower
AP44

1960, Jan. 19 **Photo.** **Wmk. 267**

C92	AP43	6.50cr brown	15	10

Issued to commemorate the visit of President Adolfo Lopez Mateos of Mexico.

1960, Feb. 23 ***Perf. 11½***

C93	AP44	6.50cr dp org	20	12

Visit of Pres. Dwight D. Eisenhower.

World Refugee Year Emblem
AP45

Tower at Brasilia
AP46

1960, Apr. 7 Wmk. 268

C94	AP45	6.50cr blue	15	10

Issued to publicize World Refugee Year, July 1, 1959–June 30, 1960.

Type of Regular Issue and AP46.

Designs: 3.30cr, Square of the Three Entities. 4cr, Cathedral. 11.50cr, Plan of Brasilia.

Perf. 11x11½, 11½x11

1960, Apr. 21 Photo. Wmk. 267

C95	A436	3.30cr violet	20	15
C96	A436	4cr blue	1.25	15
C97	AP46	6.50cr rose car	15	15
C98	A436	11.50cr brown	20	15

Issued to commemorate the inauguration of Brazil's new capital, Brasilia, Apr. 21, 1960.

Chrismon and Oil Lamp
AP47

1960, May 16 ***Perf. 11x11½***

C99	AP47	3.30cr lil rose	15	15

Issued to publicize the Seventh National Eucharistic Congress at Curitiba.

Cross, Sugarloaf Mountain and Emblem—AP48

1960, July 1 Wmk. 267

C100	AP48	6.50cr brt bl	15	10

Issued to commemorate the 10th Congress of the World Baptist Alliance, Rio de Janeiro.

Boy Scout
AP49

Caravel
AP50

1960, July 23 ***Perf. 11½x11***

C101	AP49	3.30cr org ver	15	10

Boy Scouts of Brazil, 50th anniversary.

1960, Aug. 5 Engraved Wmk. 268

C102	AP50	6.50cr black	15	10

Issued to commemorate the 500th anniversary of the birth of Prince Henry the Navigator.

Maria E. Bueno
AP51

Photogravure

1960, Dec. 15 ***Perf. 11x11½***

C103	AP51	6cr pale brn	15	10

Issued to commemorate the victory at Wimbledon of Maria E. Bueno, women's singles tennis champion.

War Memorial, Sugarloaf Mountain and Allied Flags
AP52

1960, Dec. 22 Wmk. 268

C104	AP52	3.30cr lil rose	15	10

Issued to commemorate the reburial of Brazilian servicemen of World War II.

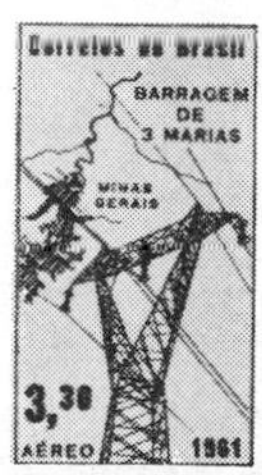

Power Line and Map
AP53

Malaria Eradication Emblem
AP54

1961, Jan. 20 ***Perf. 11½x11***

C105	AP53	3.30cr lil rose	10	10

Issued to commemorate the inauguration of Three Marias Dam and hydroelectric station in Minas Gerais.

Engraved

1962, May 24 Wmk. 267

C106	AP54	21cr blue	10	10

Issued for the World Health Organization drive to eradicate malaria.

F. A. de Varnhagen
AP55

1966, Feb. 17 Photo. Wmk. 267

C107	AP55	45cr red brn	30	15

Issued to commemorate the 150th anniversary of the birth of Francisco Adolfo de Varnhagen, Viscount of Porto Seguro (1816–1878), historian and diplomat.

Map of the Americas and Alliance for Progress Emblem
AP56

1966, March 14 ***Perf. 11x11½***

C108	AP56	120cr grnsh bl & vio bl	40	15

Issued to commemorate the fifth anniversary of the Alliance for Progress.

A souvenir card contains one impression of No. C108, imperf. Black inscriptions. Size: 113x160mm.

Nun and Globe
AP57

Face of Jesus from Shroud of Turin
AP58

1966, Mar. 25 Photo. ***Perf. 11½x11***

C109	AP57	35cr violet	20	10

Issued to commemorate the centenary of the arrival of the teaching Sisters of St. Dorothea.

1966, June 3 Photo. Wmk. 267

C110	AP58	45cr brn org	25	15

Issued to commemorate Vatican II, the 21st Ecumenical Council of the Roman Catholic Church, Oct. 11, 1962–Dec. 8, 1965.

A souvenir card contains one impression of No. C110, imperf. Brown orange inscription and head of Jesus in margin. Size: 100x39mm.

Admiral Mariz e Barros
AP59

"Youth" by Eliseu Visconti
AP60

1966, June 13 Photo. Wmk. 267

C111	AP59	35cr red brn	20	10

Death centenary of Admiral Antonio Carlos Mariz e Barros, who died in the Battle of Itaperu.

1966, July 31 ***Perf. 11½x11***

C112	AP60	120cr red brn	50	20

Birth centenary of Eliseu Visconti, painter.

SPECIAL DELIVERY STAMP.

No. 191 Surcharged

1000
REIS
EXPRESSO

1930 ***Perf. 12*** **Unwmkd.**

E1	A62	1000r on 200r dp bl	3.00	1.50
a.		Inverted surcharge	450.00	

POSTAGE DUE STAMPS.

D1 D2

Typographed.

1889 ***Rouletted.*** **Unwmkd.**

J1	D1	10r carmine	1.50	75
J2	D1	20r carmine	1.75	1.30
J3	D1	50r carmine	3.50	2.00
J4	D1	100r carmine	2.00	1.00
J5	D1	200r carmine	30.00	10.00
J6	D1	300r carmine	4.00	5.00
J7	D1	500r carmine	4.00	5.00
J8	D1	700r carmine	7.00	7.00
J9	D1	1000r carmine	7.00	7.00
		Nos. J1-J9 (9)	60.75	39.05

Counterfeits are common.

1890

J10	D1	10r orange	50	20
J11	D1	20r ultra	75	20
J12	D1	50r olive	1.00	20
J13	D1	200r magenta	3.00	30
J14	D1	300r bl grn	2.00	65
J15	D1	500r slate	2.50	2.25
J16	D1	700r purple	3.50	5.00
J17	D1	1000r dk vio	5.00	4.00
		Nos. J10-J17 (8)	18.25	12.80

Perf. 11 to 11½, 12½ to 14 and Compound.

1895-1901

J18	D2	10r dk bl ('01)	1.00	50
J19	D2	20r yel grn	10.00	3.00
J20	D2	50r yel grn ('01)	6.25	3.50
J21	D2	100r brick red	7.00	40
J22	D2	200r violet	4.50	25
a.		200r gray lil ('98)	12.00	1.50
J23	D2	300r dl bl	3.50	2.00
J24	D2	2000r brown	10.00	10.00
		Nos. J18-J24 (7)	42.25	19.65

1906 Wmk. 97

J25	D2	100r brick red	6.50	2.50

Wmkd. (97? or 98?)

J26	D2	200r violet	6.00	1.00
a.		Wmk. 97	225.00	75.00
b.		Wmk. 98	10.00	40.00

D3 D4

Engraved

1906–10 ***Perf. 12*** **Unwmkd.**

J28	D3	10r slate	15	10
J29	D3	20r brt vio	15	10
J30	D3	50r dk grn	20	10
J31	D3	100r carmine	1.50	50
J32	D3	200r dp bl	65	25
J33	D3	300r gray blk	25	50
J34	D3	400r ol grn	80	75
J35	D3	500r dk vio	30.00	30.00
J36	D3	600r vio ('10)	1.00	*2.00*
J37	D3	700r red brn	25.00	25.00
J38	D3	1000r red	1.25	*2.50*
J39	D3	2000r green	3.75	4.50
J40	D3	5000r choc ('10)	75	*10.00*
		Nos. J28-J40 (13)	65.45	*76.30*

Typographed.

1919-23 ***Perf. 12½, 11, 11x10½.***

J41	D4	5r red brn	15	30
J42	D4	10r violet	30	30
J43	D4	20r ol gray	25	20
J44	D4	50r grn ('23)	25	25
J45	D4	100r red	1.50	1.25
J46	D4	200r blue	7.00	2.00
J47	D4	400r brn ('23)	1.75	1.35
		Nos. J41-J47 (7)	11.20	5.65

Perf. 12½, 12½x13½.

1924–35 Wmk. 100

J48	D4	5r red brn	25	20
J49	D4	100r red	75	30
J50	D4	200r sl bl ('29)	75	50
J51	D4	400r dp brn ('29)	1.50	1.00
J52	D4	600r dk vio ('29)	1.75	1.10
J53	D4	600r org ('35)	75	50
		Nos. J48-J53 (6)	5.75	3.60

1924 ***Perf. 11x10½.*** **Wmk. 193**

J54	D4	100r red	40.00	40.00
J55	D4	200r sl bl	5.00	5.00

Perf. 11x10½, 13x13½.

1925-27 Wmk. 101

J56	D4	20r ol gray	25	20
J57	D4	100r red	1.00	40
J58	D4	200r sl bl	4.00	50

J59	D4	400r brown	2.50	1.75
J60	D4	600r dk vio	5.00	3.50
		Nos. J56-J60 (5)	12.75	6.35

Wmkd. E U BRASIL Multiple. (218)

1929-30 ***Perf. 12½x13½.***

J61	D4	100r lt red	25	20
J62	D4	200r bl blk	40	25
J63	D4	400r brown	40	25
J64	D4	1000r myr grn	75	50

Perf. 11, 12½x13, 13.

1931-36 **Wmk. 222**

J65	D4	10r lt vio ('35)	15	10
J66	D4	20r blk ('33)	20	15
J67	D4	50r bl grn ('35)	30	25
J68	D4	100r rose red ('35)	30	25
J69	D4	200r sl bl ('35)	40	35
J70	D4	400r blk brn ('35)	2.50	2.50
J71	D4	600r dk vio	30	25
J72	D4	1000r myr grn	50	40
J73	D4	2000r brn ('36)	1.00	1.00
J74	D4	5000r ind ('36)	1.25	1.25
		Nos. J65-J74 (10)	6.90	6.50

1938 ***Perf. 11.*** **Wmk. 249**

J75	D4	200r sl bl	2.00	75

1940 **Typographed.** **Wmk. 256**

J76	D4	10r lt vio	50	50
J77	D4	20r black	50	50
J79	D4	100r rose red	50	50
J80	D4	200r myr grn	50	50

1942 **Wmk. 264**

J81	D4	10r lt vio	15	10
J82	D4	20r ol blk	15	10
J83	D4	50r lt bl grn	15	10
J84	D4	100r vermilion	30	30
J85	D4	200r gray bl	30	30
J86	D4	400r claret	30	30
J87	D4	600r rose vio	20	20
J88	D4	1000r dk bl grn	20	20
J89	D4	2000r dp yel brn	50	50
J90	D4	5000r indigo	30	30
		Nos. J81-J90 (10)	2.55	2.40

1949 **Wmk. 268**

J91	D4	10c pale rose lil	5.00	4.00
J92	D4	20r black	30.00	30.00

No. J92 exists in shades of gray ranging to gray olive.

OFFICIAL STAMPS

Pres. Affonso Penna O1

Pres. Hermes da Fonseca O2

Engraved

1906, Nov. 15 ***Perf. 12*** **Unwmkd.**

O1	O1	10r org & grn	20	15
O2	O1	20r org & grn	35	15
O3	O1	50r org & grn	1.20	15
O4	O1	100r org & grn	35	15
O5	O1	200r org & grn	65	15
O6	O1	300r org & grn	1.75	30
O7	O1	400r org & grn	4.50	65
O8	O1	500r org & grn	2.00	50
O9	O1	700r org & grn	3.50	2.00
O10	O1	1000r org & grn	2.50	75
O11	O1	2000r org & grn	3.00	90
O12	O1	5000r org & grn	6.50	90
O13	O1	10,000r org & grn	8.00	50
		Nos. O1-O13 (13)	34.50	7.25

The portrait is the same but the frame differs for each denomination of this issue.

1913, Nov. 15 **Center in Black**

O14	O2	10r gray	30	20
O15	O2	20r ol grn	30	20
O16	O2	50r gray	35	15
O17	O2	100r vermilion	65	15
O18	O2	200r blue	75	25
O19	O2	500r orange	2.50	60
O20	O2	600r violet	4.00	90
O21	O2	1000r blk brn	5.00	75
O22	O2	2000r red brn	6.50	75
O23	O2	5000r brown	8.00	1.00
O24	O2	10,000r black	12.00	3.75
O25	O2	20,000r blue	30.00	30.00
O26	O2	50,000r green	45.00	35.00
O27	O2	100,000r org red	130.00	130.00
O28	O2	500,000r brown	200.00	220.00
O29	O2	1,000,000r dk brn	225.00	235.00
		Nos. O14-O29 (16)	670.35	658.70

The portrait is the same on all denominations of this series but there are eight types of the frame.

Pres. Wenceslau Braz

O3

Perf. 11, 11½

1919, Apr. 11 **Wmk. 100**

O30	O3	10r ol grn	40	1.00
O31	O3	50r green	50	50
O32	O3	100r rose red	75	40
O33	O3	200r dl bl	1.00	40
O34	O3	500r orange	6.50	7.50
		Nos. O30-O34 (5)	9.15	9.80

The official decree called for eleven stamps in this series but only five were issued.

See Nos. 293-297.

NEWSPAPER STAMPS.

N1

Lithographed.

1889, Feb. 1 ***Rouletted*** **Unwmkd.**

P1	N1	10r yellow	2.50	3.00
a.		Pair, imperf. between	125.00	175.00
P2	N1	20r yellow	6.00	7.00
P3	N1	50r yellow	10.00	6.00
P4	N1	100r yellow	4.00	3.00
P5	N1	200r yellow	2.50	1.50
P6	N1	300r yellow	3.00	1.50
P7	N1	500r yellow	17.50	8.00
P8	N1	700r yellow	3.00	10.00
P9	N1	1000r yellow	3.00	10.00
		Nos. P1-P9 (9)	51.50	50.00

1889, May 1

P10	N1	10r olive	50	20
P11	N1	20r green	50	25
P12	N1	50r brn yel	65	25
P13	N1	100r violet	1.35	1.00
P14	N1	200r black	1.25	1.00
P15	N1	300r carmine	8.00	8.00
P16	N1	500r green	40.00	40.00
P17	N1	700r ultra	20.00	25.00
P18	N1	1000r brown	8.00	15.00
		Nos. P10-P18 (9)	80.25	90.70

N2

N3

White Wove Paper Thin to Thick

Perf. 11 to 11½, 12½ to 14 and 12½ to 14x11 to 11½

1890 **Typographed**

P19	N2	10r blue	7.00	5.00
a.		10r ultra	7.00	5.00
P20	N2	20r emerald	20.00	7.50
P21	N2	100r violet	8.00	4.50

1890-93

P22	N3	10r blue	50	25
a.		10r ultra	1.25	50
P23	N3	10r ultra, *buff*	1.00	50
P24	N3	20r green	1.00	60
a.		20r emer	1.25	75
P25	N3	50r yel grn ('93)	6.00	4.00

POSTAL TAX STAMPS.

Icarus from the Santos-Dumont Monument at St. Cloud, France

PT1

Perf. 13½x12½, 11.

1933, Oct. 1 **Typo.** **Wmk. 222**

RA1	PT1	100r dp brn	50	10

No. RA1 was issued in commemoration of the Brazilian aviator, Santos-Dumont. It did not pay postage but its use was obligatory as a tax on all correspondence sent to countries in South America, the United States and Spain. Its use on correspondence to other countries was optional. The money obtained from its sale was added to funds for the construction of airports throughout Brazil.

Father Joseph Damien and Children

PT2

Father Bento Dias Pacheco

PT3

Perf. 12x11

1952, Nov. 24 **Litho.** **Wmk. 267**

RA2	PT2	10c yel brn	25	15

1953, Nov. 30

RA3	PT2	10c yel grn	25	15

1954, Nov. 22 **Photo.** ***Perf. 11½***

RA4	PT3	10c vio bl	20	15

1955-66, Nov. 24

RA5	PT3	10c dk car rose	20	15
RA6	PT3	10c org red ('57)	20	10
RA7	PT3	10c dp emer ('58)	15	10
RA8	PT3	10c red lil ('61)	15	10
RA9	PT3	10c choc ('62)	15	10
RA10	PT3	10c sl ('63)	15	10
RA11	PT3	2cr dp mag ('64)	15	10
RA12	PT3	2cr vio ('65)	15	10
RA13	PT3	2cr org ('66)	15	10

1968, Nov. 25

RA14	PT3	5c brt yel grn	1.25	75

1969, Nov. 28

RA15	PT3	5c dp plum	50	25

Eunice Weaver

PT4

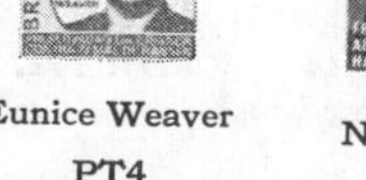

Father Nicodemos

PT5

1971, Nov. 24

RA16	PT4	10c sl grn	1.00	40

1973, Nov. 24

RA17	PT4	10c brt rose lil ('73)	20	10

1975, Nov. 24 **Litho.** **Unwmkd.**

RA18	PT5	10c sepia	20	10

Father Vicente Borgard (1888-1977)—PT6

Father Bento Dias Pacheco—PT7

1983, Nov. 24 **Photo.** ***Perf. 11½***

RA19	PT6	10cr brown	60	60

1984, Nov. 24 **Photo.** ***Perf. 11½***

RA20	PT7	30cr dp bl	5	5

1985, Nov. 24 **Litho.** ***Perf. 11½***

RA21	PT7	100cr lake	8	6

Use of Nos. RA2-RA21 was required for one week. The tax was for the care and treatment of lepers.

POSTAL TAX SEMI-POSTAL STAMP.

Icarus

PTSP1

Typographed.

1947, Nov. 15 ***Perf. 11*** **Wmk. 267**

RAB1	PTSP1	40c +10c brt red	35	20
a.		Pair, imperf. between	*350.00*	

Issued to commemorate Aviation Week, November 15-22, 1947, and compulsory on all domestic correspondence during that week.

BREMEN BRUNSWICK

See Early German States group preceding Germany.

BULGARIA

(bŭl·gâr'ĭ·*à*; bōōl·gâr'ĭ·*à*)

LOCATION — Southeastern Europe bordering on the Black Sea on the east and the Danube River on the north.

GOVT.—Republic.

AREA—42,823 sq. mi.

POP.—8,929,332 (1983).

CAPITAL—Sofia.

In 1885 Bulgaria, then a principality under the suzerainty of the Sultan of Turkey, was joined by Eastern Rumelia. Independence from Turkey was obtained in 1908.

100 Centimes = 1 Franc

100 Stotinki = 1 Lev (1881)

Lion of Bulgaria

A1 A2 A3

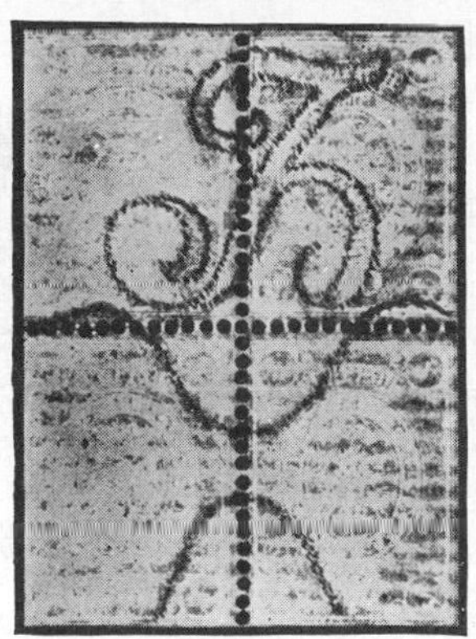

Wmk. 168

Typographed.

Laid Paper.

Wmkd. ЭЗГВ & Wavy Lines (168)

1879, June 1 ***Perf. 14½x15***

No.	Type	Description	Unused	Used
1	A1	5c blk & yel	60.00	20.00
2	A1	10c blk & grn	150.00	40.00
3	A1	25c blk & vio	150.00	15.00
a.		Imperf.		
4	A1	50c blk & bl	175.00	35.00
5	A2	1fr blk & red	60.00	20.00

1881, June 10

No.	Type	Description	Unused	Used
6	A3	3s red & sil	15.00	2.25
7	A3	5s blk & org	20.00	2.25
a.		Background inverted		2,500.
8	A3	10s blk & grn	72.50	6.00
9	A3	15s red & grn	100.00	6.00
10	A3	25s blk & vio	225.00	22.50
11	A3	30s bl & fawn	25.00	6.50

1882, Dec. 4

No.	Type	Description	Unused	Used
12	A3	3s org & yel	90	60
a.		Background inverted		2,500.
13	A3	5s grn & pale grn	7.00	60
a.		5s rose & pale rose (error)	2,250.	1,750.
14	A3	10s rose & pale rose	10.00	60
15	A3	15s red vio & pale lil	7.00	35
16	A3	25s bl & pale bl	7.00	60
17	A3	30s vio & grn	8.50	75
18	A3	50s bl & pink	8.50	90

See also Nos. 207–210, 286.

A4

A5

Surcharged in Black, Carmine or Vermilion

1884, May 1

Typographed Surcharge

No.	Type	Description	Unused	Used
19	A4	3s on 10s rose (Bk)	175.00	50.00
20	A4	5s on 30s bl & fawn (C)	75.00	32.50
20A	A4	5s on 30s bl & fawn (Bk)	2,500.	2,500.
21	A5	15s on 25s bl (C)	200.00	32.50

On some values the surcharge may be found inverted or double.

1885, June

Lithographed Surcharge

No.	Type	Description	Unused	Used
21B	A4	3s on 10s rose (Bk)	40.00	32.50
21C	A4	5s on 30s bl & fawn (V)	40.00	32.50
21D	A5	15s on 25s bl (V)	40.00	32.50
22	A5	50s on 1fr blk & red (Bk)	125.00	100.00

Forgeries of Nos. 19–22 are plentiful.

Word below left star in oval has 5 letters

A6

Third letter below left star is "A"

A7

1885, May 25

No.	Type	Description	Unused	Used
23	A6	1s gray vio & pale gray	11.00	4.00
24	A7	2s sl grn & pale gray	11.00	3.00

Word below left star has 4 letters

A8

Third letter below left star is "b" with cross-bar in upper half

A9

A10

1886–87

No.	Type	Description	Unused	Used
25	A8	1s gray vio & pale gray	85	20
26	A9	2s sl grn & pale gray	85	20
27	A10	1 l blk & red ('87)	25.00	4.00

A11

Perf. 10½, 11, 11½, 13, 13½.

1889 **Wove Paper.** **Unwmkd.**

No.	Type	Description	Unused	Used
28	A11	1s lilac	20	5
29	A11	2s gray	75	10
30	A11	3s bis brn	50	10
31	A11	5s yel grn	25	5
a.		Vertical pair, imperf. between		
32	A11	10s rose	1.50	12
33	A11	15s orange	80	10
34	A11	25s blue	1.25	12
35	A11	30s dk brn	10.50	8
36	A11	50s green	75	30
37	A11	1 l org red	65	35
		Nos. 28-37 (10)	17.15	1.37

The 10s orange is a proof.

Nos. 28–34 are known imperforate. Price, set $225. See Nos. 39, 41–42.

No. 35 Surcharged in Black **15**

1892, Jan. 26

No.	Type	Description	Unused	Used
38	A11	15s on 30s brn	9.00	1.00
a.		Inverted surcharge	100.00	75.00

1894 ***Perf. 10½, 11, 11½.***

Pelure Paper.

No.	Type	Description	Unused	Used
39	A11	10s red	11.00	60
a.		Imperf.	80.00	

No. 26 Surcharged in Red **01**

Wmkd. Wavy Lines. (168)

1895, Oct. 25 ***Perf. 14½x15***

Laid Paper.

No.	Type	Description	Unused	Used
40	A9	1s on 2s sl grn & pale gray	60	20
a.		Inverted surcharge	9.00	6.00
b.		Double surcharge	90.00	90.00
c.		Pair, one without surcharge	175.00	175.00

This surcharge on No. 24 is a proof.

Wmkd. Coat of Arms in the Sheet.

1896, Apr. 30 ***Perf. 11½, 13***

Wove Paper.

No.	Type	Description	Unused	Used
41	A11	2 l rose & pale rose	3.50	2.50
42	A11	3 l blk & buff	3.50	2.50

Coat of Arms

A14

Cherry Wood Cannon

A15

1896, Feb. 2 ***Perf. 13***

No.	Type	Description	Unused	Used
43	A14	1s bl grn	50	15
44	A14	5s dk bl	50	15
45	A14	15s purple	75	30
46	A14	25s red	7.00	1.50

Baptism of Prince Boris.

Examples of Nos. 41–46 from sheet edges show no watermark.

Nos. 43, 45–46 were also printed on rough unwatermarked paper.

1901, Apr. 20 **Litho.** **Unwmkd.**

No.	Type	Description	Unused	Used
53	A15	5s carmine	1.25	1.25
54	A15	15s yel grn	1.25	1.25

Insurrection of Independence in April, 1876, 25th anniversary.

Exist imperf. Forgeries exist.

Nos. 30 and 36 Surcharged in Black **5**

1901, Mar. 24 **Typographed**

No.	Type	Description	Unused	Used
55	A11	5s on 3s bis brn	2.00	1.00
a.		Inverted surcharge	60.00	60.00
b.		Pair, one without surcharge	100.00	100.00
56	A11	10s on 50s grn	2.50	1.00
a.		Inverted surcharge	70.00	70.00
b.		Pair, one without surcharge	100.00	100.00

Tsar Ferdinand

A17

Fighting at Shipka Pass

A18

ONE LEVA:

Type I. The numerals in the upper corners have, at the top, a sloping serif on the left side and a short straight serif on the right.

Type II. The numerals in the upper corners are of ordinary shape without the serif at the right.

1901–05 **Typo.** ***Perf. 12½***

No.	Type	Description	Unused	Used
57	A17	1s vio & gray blk	15	5
58	A17	2s brnz grn & ind	15	5
a.		Imperf.		
59	A17	3s org & ind	20	6
60	A17	5s emer & brn	3.50	5
61	A17	10s rose & blk	2.25	5
62	A17	15s cl & gray blk	1.00	5
63	A17	25s bl & blk	1.00	5
64	A17	30s bis & gray blk	22.50	12
65	A17	50s dk bl & brn	1.25	9
66	A17	1 l red org & brnz grn, type I	3.00	25
67	A17	1 l brn red & brnz grn, II('05)	60.00	2.00
68	A17	2 l car & blk	6.00	1.50
69	A17	3 l sl & red brn	7.50	3.50
		Nos. 57-69 (13)	108.50	7.82

1902, Aug. 29 **Litho.** ***Perf. 11½***

No.	Type	Description	Unused	Used
70	A18	5s lake	1.25	60
71	A18	10s bl grn	1.25	60
72	A18	15s blue	6.00	3.00

Battle of Shipka Pass, 1877.

Imperf. copies are proofs.

Excellent forgeries of Nos. 70 to 72 exist.

No. 62 Surcharged in Black **10**

1903, Oct. 1 ***Perf. 12½***

No.	Type	Description	Unused	Used
73	A17	10s on 15s cl & gray blk	8.50	40
a.		Invtd. surch.	80.00	70.00
b.		Double surcharge	80.00	70.00
c.		Pair, one without surcharge	150.00	150.00
d.		10s on 10s rose & blk	350.00	350.00

Ferdinand in 1887 and 1907

A19

1907, Aug. 12 **Litho.** ***Perf. 11½***

No.	Type	Description	Unused	Used
74	A19	5s dp grn	7.50	1.25
75	A19	10s red brn	13.00	1.25
76	A19	25s dp bl	20.00	2.50

Accession to the throne of Ferdinand I, 20th anniversary.

Nos. 74–76 imperf. are proofs. Nos. 74–76 exist in pairs imperforate between.

Stamps of 1889 Overprinted **1909**

1909

No.	Type	Description	Unused	Used
77	A11	1s lilac	1.50	50
a.		Inverted overprint	30.00	25.00
b.		Double overprint, one inverted	35.00	35.00
78	A11	5s yel grn	1.50	50
a.		Inverted ovpt.	35.00	35.00
b.		Double overprint	35.00	35.00

With Additional Surcharge **5** or **10**

No.	Type	Description	Unused	Used
79	A11	5s on 30s brn (Bk)	2.25	35
a.		"5" double		
b.		"1990" for "1909"	1,000.	800.00
80	A11	10s on 15s org (Bk)	2.25	75
a.		Inverted surcharge	25.00	25.00
b.		"1909" omitted	40.00	40.00
81	A11	10s on 50s dk grn (R)	2.25	75
a.		"1990" for "1909"	150.00	150.00
b.		Black surcharge	75.00	75.00

Stamps of 1901 Surcharged with Value Only.

No.	Type	Description	Unused	Used
83	A17	5s on 15s cl & gray blk (Bl)	2.25	75
a.		Inverted surcharge	30.00	30.00
84	A17	10s on 15s cl & gray blk (Bl)	6.00	50
a.		Inverted surcharge	30.00	30.00
85	A17	25s on 30s brn bis & gray blk (R)	7.50	1.00
a.		Double surcharge	100.00	100.00
b.		"2" of "25" omitted	125.00	125.00
c.		Blue surcharge	400.00	250.00

1910

Surcharged in Blue

5

1910, Oct.

No.	Type	Description	Unused	Used
87	A17	1s on 3s org & ind	5.00	1.00
a.		"1910" omitted	30.00	
88	A17	5s on 15s cl & gray blk	1.75	75

Tsar Assen's Tower
(Crown over lion)
A20

Tsar Ferdinand
A21

City of Trnovo
A22

Tsar Ferdinand
A23

Tsar Ferdinand
A24

Isker River
A25

Ferdinand
A26

Rila Monastery
(Crown at upper right)
A27

Tsar and Princes
A28

Ferdinand in Robes of Ancient Tsars
A29

Monastery of Holy Trinity
A30

View of Varna
A31

1911, Feb. 14 Engraved *Perf. 12*

89	A20	1s myr grn	15	5
90	A21	2s car & blk	15	5
91	A22	3s lake & blk	40	8
92	A23	5s grn & blk	1.00	5
93	A24	10s dp red & blk	1.25	5
94	A25	15s brn bis	3.00	10
95	A26	25s ultra & blk	50	6
96	A27	30s bl & blk	7.50	15
97	A28	50s ocher & blk	17.50	20
a.		Center inverted		*3,000.*
98	A29	1 l chocolate	6.50	25
99	A30	2 l dl pur & blk	1.50	90
100	A31	3 l bl vio & blk	7.00	3.00
		Nos. 89-100 (12)	46.45	4.94

See also Nos. 114–120, 161–162.

Tsar Ferdinand
A32

1912, Aug. 2 Typo. *Perf. 12½*

101	A32	5s ol grn	3.00	1.00
a.		5s pale grn	*350.00*	*150.00*
102	A32	10s claret	4.50	2.25
103	A32	25s slate	6.00	2.50

25th year of reign of Tsar Ferdinand.

ОСВОБ. ВОЙНА

1912-1913

Nos. 89-95 Overprinted in Various Colors

1913, Aug. 6 Engr.

104	A20	1s myr grn (C)	20	10
105	A21	2s car & blk (Bl)	20	10
107	A22	3s lake & blk (Bl Bk)	30	15
108	A23	5s grn & blk (R)	20	8
109	A24	10s dp red & blk (Bk)	45	7
110	A25	15s brn bis (G)	90	35
111	A26	25s ultra & blk (R)	4.00	50
		Nos. 104-111 (7)	6.25	1.35

Victory over the Turks in Balkan War of 1912–1913.

10 CT.

No. 95 Surcharged in Red

1915, July 6

112	A26	10s on 25s ultra & blk	50	10

No. 28 Surcharged in Green

3
СТОТИНКИ

113	A11	3s on 1s lil	4.50	4.50

Types of 1911 Re-engraved.

1915, Nov. 7 *Perf. 11½, 14*

114	A20	1s dk bl grn	5	5
115	A23	5s grn & brn vio	1.25	5
116	A24	10s red brn & brnsh blk	20	5
117	A25	15s ol grn	30	5
118	A26	25s ind & blk	20	5
119	A27	30s ol grn & red brn	20	5
120	A29	1 l dk brn	60	60
		Nos. 114-120 (7)	2.80	90

No. 114 is 19½mm. wide; No. 89, 18½mm. No. 118 is 19¼mm. wide; No. 95, 18¼mm. No. 120 is 20mm. wide; No. 98, 19mm. The re-engraved stamps also differ from the 1911 issue in many details of design. Nos. 114-120 exist imperforate.

The 5s and 10s exist perf. 14x11½.

For Nos. 114–116 and 118 overprinted with Cyrillic characters and "1916–1917," see Romania Nos. 2N1–2N4.

Coat of Arms
A33

Peasant and Bullock
A34

Soldier and Mt. Sonichka
A35

View of Nish
A36

Town and Lake Okhrida
A37

Demir-Kapiya (Iron Gate)
A37a

View of Gevgeli
A38

Perf. 11½, 12½x13, 13x12½.

1917–19 Typographed

122	A33	5s green	40	15
123	A34	15s slate	15	6
124	A35	25s blue	15	6
125	A36	30s orange	15	10
126	A37	50s violet	75	30
126A	A37a	2 l brn org ('19)	75	35
127	A38	3 l claret	1.00	75
		Nos. 122-127 (7)	3.35	1.77

Commemorative of the liberation of Macedonia. A 1 l dark green was prepared but not issued. Price $2.50.

View of Veles
A39

Monastery of St. Clement at Okhrida
A40

1918 *Perf. 13x14*

128	A39	1s gray	5	5
129	A40	5s green	5	5

Tsar Ferdinand
A41

Plowing with Oxen
A42

1918, July 1 *Perf. 12½x13*

130	A41	1s dk grn	5	5
131	A41	2s dk brn	5	5
132	A41	3s indigo	35	15
133	A41	10s brn red	35	15

30th anniversary of Tsar Ferdinand's accession to the throne.

1919 *Perf. 13½x13.*

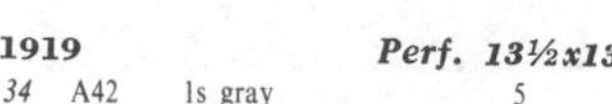

134	A42	1s gray	5	5

Sobranye Palace
A43

Tsar Boris III
A44

1919 *Perf. 11½x12, 12x11½*

135	A43	1s black	5	5
137	A43	2s ol grn	5	5

1919, Oct. 3

138	A44	3s org brn	5	5
139	A44	5s green	5	5
140	A44	10s rose red	5	5
141	A44	15s violet	5	5
142	A44	25s dp bl	5	5
143	A44	30s chocolate	15	5
144	A44	50s yel brn	15	5
		Nos. 138-144 (7)	55	35

First anniversary of enthronement of Tsar Boris III.

Nos. 135–144 exist imperforate.

Birthplace of Vazov at Sopot and Cherrywood Cannon
A47

"The Bear Fighter"—a Character from "Under the Yoke"
A48

Ivan Vazov in 1870 and 1920
A49

Vazov
A50

The Monk Paisii
A52

Homes of Vazov
at Plovdiv and Sofia
A51

1920, Oct. 20 Photo. *Perf. 11½*

147	A47	30s brn red	10	5
148	A48	50s dk grn	15	7
149	A49	1 l db	30	15
150	A50	2 l lt brn	85	35
151	A51	3 l blk vio	1.25	40
152	A52	5 l dp bl	1.50	50
		Nos. 147-152 (6)	4.15	1.52

Issued to commemorate the 70th birthday of Ivan Vazov (1850–1921), Bulgarian poet and novelist.

Several values of this series exist imperforate and in pairs imperforate between.

Tsar Ferdinand
A53 A54

Mt. Shar
A55

Bridge over Vardar River
A56

View of Ohrid
A57

Typographed.

1921, June 11 *Perf. 13x14, 14x13*

153	A53	10s claret	5	5
154	A54	10s claret	5	5
155	A55	10s claret	5	5
156	A56	10s rose lil	5	5
157	A57	20s blue	30	25
		Nos. 153-157 (5)	50	45

Nos. 153–157 were intended to be issued in 1915 to commemorate the liberation of Macedonia. They were not put in use until 1921. A 50s violet was prepared but never placed in use. Price $2.50.

View of Sofia
A58

"The Liberator,"
Monument to Alexander II
A59

Monastery at Shipka Pass
A62

Tsar Boris III
A63

Harvesting Grain
A64

Tsar Assen's Tower
(No crown over lion)
A65

Rila Monastery
(Rosette at upper right)
A66

1921–23 Engraved *Perf. 12*

158	A58	10s bl gray	8	5
159	A59	20s dp grn	8	5
160	A63	25s bl grn ('22)	8	5
161	A22	50s orange	8	5
162	A22	50s dk bl ('23)	3.00	3.00
163	A62	75s dl vio	20	5
164	A62	75s dp bl ('23)	35	12
165	A63	1 l carmine	35	15
166	A63	1 l dp bl ('22)	35	5
167	A64	2 l brown	40	6
168	A65	3 l brn vio	45	9
169	A66	5 l lt bl	3.00	30
170	A63	10 l vio brn	8.00	1.25
		Nos. 158-170 (13)	16.42	5.27

Bourchier in Bulgarian Costume
A67

James David Bourchier
A68

View of Rila Monastery
A69

1921, Dec. 31

171	A67	10s red org	5	5
172	A67	20s orange	5	5
173	A68	30s dp gray	7	5
174	A68	50s bluish gray	7	5
175	A68	1 l dl vio	25	7
176	A69	1½ l ol grn	25	15
177	A69	2 l dp grn	25	15
178	A69	3 l Prus bl	65	30
179	A69	5 l red brn	1.25	50
		Nos. 171-179 (9)	2.89	1.37

Issued to commemorate the death of James D. Bourchier, Balkan correspondent of the London Times.

Postage Due Stamps of 1919-22 Surcharged

10
СТОТИНКИ
a

1924

182	D6	10s on 20s yel	5	5
183	D6	20s on 5s gray grn	5	5
a.		20s on 5s emer	10.00	10.00
184	D6	20s on 10s vio	5	5
185	D6	20s on 30s org	5	5

Nos. 182 to 185 were used for ordinary postage.

Regular Issues of 1919-23 Surcharged in Blue or Red:

1 ЛЕВЪ
b

3 ЛЕВА
c

186	A43 (a)	10s on 1s blk (R)	5	5
187	A44 (b)	1 l on 5s emer (Bl)	15	5
188	A22 (c)	3 l on 50s dk bl (R)	30	15
189	A63 (b)	6 l on 1 l car (Bl)	90	30
		Nos. 182-189 (8)	1.60	75

The surcharge of No. 188 comes in three types: normal, thick and thin.

Nos. 182, 184–189 exist with inverted surcharge.

Lion of Bulgaria
A70 A71

Tsar Boris III
A72

New Sofia Cathedral
A73

Harvesting
A74

1925 Typo. *Perf. 13, 11½*

191	A70	10s red & bl, *pink*	7	5
192	A70	15s car & org, *bl*	7	5
193	A70	30s blk & buff	7	5
a.		Cliche of 15s in plate of 30s		
194	A71	50s choc, *grn*	10	5
195	A72	1 l dl grn	60	5
196	A73	2 l dk grn & buff	1.25	5
197	A74	4 l lake & yel	1.25	5
		Nos.191-197 (7)	3.41	35

Several values of this series exist imperforate and in pairs imperforate between. See also Nos. 199, 201.

Cathedral of Sveta Nedelya, Sofia, Ruined by Bomb—A75

1926 *Perf. 11½*

198	A75	50s gray blk	20	10

A76

A77

Type A72 Re-engraved.
(Shoulder at left does not touch frame.)

1926

199	A76	1 l gray	70	5
a.		1 l grn	70	5
201	A76	2 l ol brn	80	5

Center Embossed.

202	A77	6 l dp bl & pale lem	1.75	15
203	A77	10 l brn blk & brn org	6.00	1.00

Christo Botev
A78

Tsar Boris III
A79

1926, June 2

204	A78	1 l ol grn	45	15
205	A78	2 l sl vio	1.25	15
206	A78	4 l red brn	1.25	75

Issued to commemorate the 50th anniversary of the death of Christo Botev (1847-1876), Bulgarian revolutionary and poet.

Lion Type of 1881.

1927-29 *Perf. 13.*

207	A3	10s dk red & db	10	5
208	A3	15s blk & org ('29)	10	5
209	A3	30s dk bl & bis brn ('28)	10	5
a.		30s ind & buff	10	5
210	A3	50s blk & rose red ('28)	15	5

1928, Oct. 3 *Perf. 11½*

211	A79	1 l ol grn	1.25	5
212	A79	2 l dp brn	1.50	5

St. Clement
A80

Konstantin Miladinov
A81

George S. Rakovski
A82

Drenovo Monastery
A83

Paisii
A84

Tsar Simeon
A85

Lyuben Karavelov
A86

Vassil Levski
A87

Georgi Benkovski
A88

Tsar Alexander II
A89

1929, May 12

213	A80	10s dk vio	15	10
214	A81	15s vio brn	15	5
215	A82	30s red	15	5
216	A83	50s ol grn	30	5
217	A84	1 l org brn	75	10
218	A85	2 l dk bl	85	15
219	A86	3 l dl grn	2.00	50
220	A87	4 l ol brn	3.00	25
221	A88	5 l brown	2.00	40
222	A89	6 l Prus grn	2.75	1.00
		Nos. 213-222 (10)	12.10	2.65

Issued to commemorate the millenary of Tsar Simeon and the 50th anniversary of the liberation of Bulgaria from the Turks.

Royal Wedding Issue.

Tsar Boris and Fiancée, Princess Giovanna
A90

Queen Ioanna and Tsar Boris
A91

1930, Nov. 12 *Perf. 11½*

223	A90	1 l green	30	30
224	A91	2 l dl vio	40	40
225	A90	4 l rose red	40	40
226	A91	6 l dk bl	45	45

Fifty-five copies of a miniature sheet incorporating one each of Nos. 223-226 were printed and given to royal, governmental and diplomatic personages.

Tsar Boris III
A92 A93

Perf. 11½, 12x11½, 13.

1931-37 **Unwmkd.**

227	A92	1 l bl grn	30	5
228	A92	2 l carmine	50	5
229	A92	4 l red org ('34)	1.00	5
230	A92	4 l yel org ('37)	25	5
231	A92	6 l dp bl	90	5
232	A92	7 l dp bl ('37)	25	6
233	A92	10 l sl blk	11.00	60
234	A92	12 l lt brn	50	15
235	A92	14 l lt brn ('37)	35	20
236	A93	20 l cl & org brn	1.25	40
		Nos. 227-236 (10)	16.30	1.66

Nos. 230–233 and 235 have outer bars at top and bottom as shown on cut A92; Nos. 227–229 and 234 are without outer bars.

See also Nos. 251, 252, 279–280, 287.

Balkan Games Issues.

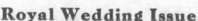

Gymnast
A95

Soccer
A96

Riding
A97

Swimmer
A100

"Victory"
A101

Designs: 6 l, Fencing. 10 l, Bicycle race.

1931, Sept. 18 *Perf. 11½*

237	A95	1 l lt grn	90	60
238	A96	2 l garnet	90	60
239	A97	4 l carmine	2.00	90
240	A95	6 l Prus bl	4.00	1.50
241	A95	10 l red org	10.00	4.50
242	A100	12 l dk bl	35.00	9.00
243	A101	50 l ol brn	32.50	27.50
		Nos. 237-243 (7)	85.30	44.60

1933, Jan. 5

244	A95	1 l bl grn	1.40	1.25
245	A96	2 l blue	2.50	1.25
246	A97	4 l brn vio	3.50	1.50
247	A95	6 l brt rose	6.50	2.25
248	A95	10 l ol brn	32.50	12.50
249	A100	12 l orange	65.00	25.00
250	A101	50 l red brn	120.00	110.00
		Nos. 244-250 (7)	231.40	153.75

Nos. 244–250 were sold only at the philatelic agency.

Boris Type of 1931.
Outer Bars at Top and Bottom Removed.

1933 *Perf. 13.*

251	A92	6 l dp bl	90	5

Type of 1931
Surcharged in Blue **2**

1934

252	A92	2(l) on 3 l ol brn	7.00	30

Soldier Defending Shipka Pass
A102

Shipka Battle Memorial
A103

Color-Bearer
A104

Widow and Orphans
A106

Veteran of the War of Liberation, 1878
A105

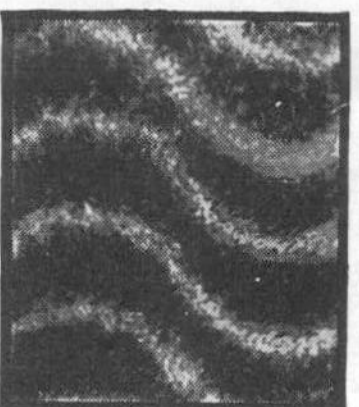
Wmk. 145

Wmkd. Wavy Lines. (145)

1934, Aug. 26 *Perf. 10½, 11½*

253	A102	1 l green	50	40
254	A103	2 l pale red	50	25
255	A104	3 l bis brn	1.50	1.25
256	A105	4 l dk car	1.25	60
257	A104	7 l dk bl	2.25	2.00
258	A106	14 l plum	6.00	6.00
		Nos. 253-258 (6)	12.00	10.50

Issued to commemorate the unveiling of the Shipka Pass Battle memorial.

An unwatermarked miniature sheet incorporating one each of Nos. 253-258 was put on sale in 1938 in five cities at a price of 8,000 leva. Printing: 100 sheets.

1934, Sept. 21

259	A102	1 l brt grn	50	40
260	A103	2 l dl org	50	25
261	A104	3 l yellow	1.50	1.25
262	A105	4 l rose	1.25	60
263	A104	7 l blue	2.25	2.00
264	A106	14 l ol bis	6.00	6.00
		Nos. 259-264 (6)	12.00	10.50

An unwatermarked miniature sheet incorporating one each of Nos. 259–263 was issued.

Velcho A. Djamjiyata
A108

Capt. G. S. Mamarchev
A109

1935, May 5 *Perf. 11½*

265	A108	1 l dp bl	1.00	35
266	A109	2 l maroon	1.00	40

Issued in commemoration of the centenary of a Bulgarian uprising against the Turks.

Soccer Game
A110

Cathedral of Alexander Nevski
A111

Symbolical of Victory
A113

Soccer Team
A112

Player and Trophy
A114

The Trophy
A115

1935, June 14

267	A110	1 l green	1.50	1.25
268	A111	2 l bl gray	3.50	1.90
269	A112	4 l crimson	5.50	3.00
270	A113	7 l brt bl	11.00	3.50
271	A114	14 l orange	11.00	4.75
272	A115	50 l lil brn	85.00	75.00
		Nos. 267-272 (6)	117.50	89.40

5th Balkan Soccer Tournament.

Gymnast on Parallel Bars
A116

Youth in "Yunak" Costume
A117

Girl in "Yunak" Costume
A118

Pole Vaulting
A119

Stadium, Sofia
A120

Yunak Emblem
A121

1935, July 10

273	A116	1 l green	2.00	1.40
274	A117	2 l lt bl	2.50	1.40
275	A118	4 l carmine	5.25	2.25
276	A119	7 l dk bl	5.25	3.50
277	A120	14 l dk brn	5.25	3.50
278	A121	50 l red	57.50	55.00
		Nos. 273-278 (6)	77.75	67.05

Issued to commemorate the 8th tournament of the Yunak Gymnastic Organization at Sofia, July 12-14.

Boris Type of 1931.
Wmkd. Wavy Lines. (145)

1935 *Perf. 12½, 13*

279	A92	1 l green	45	5
280	A92	2 l carmine	22.50	5

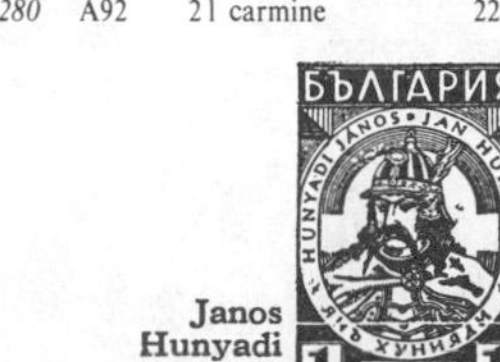

Janos Hunyadi
A122

King Ladislas Varnenchik
A123

Varna Memorial
A124

King Ladislas III
A125

Battle of Varna, 1444
A126

1935, Aug. 4 *Perf. 10½, 11½*

281	A122	1 l brn org	1.00	75
282	A123	2 l maroon	1.00	75
283	A124	4 l vermilion	5.00	3.50
284	A125	7 l dl bl	2.25	1.25
285	A126	14 l green	2.25	1.25
		Nos. 281-285 (5)	11.50	7.50

Issued to commemorate the Battle of Varna, and the death of the Polish King, Ladislas Varnenchik (1424-1444).

Lion Type of 1881.

1935 *Perf. 13.* **Wmk. 145**

286	A3	10s dk red & db	1.00	15

Boris Type of 1933.
Outer Bars at Top and Bottom Removed.

287	A92	6 l gray bl	60	10

Dimitr Monument
A127

Haji Dimitr
A128

Haji Dimitr and Stefan Karaja
A129

Taking the Oath
A130

Birthplace of Dimitr
A131

1935, Oct. 1 *Perf. 11½* **Unwmkd.**

288	A127	1 l green	1.50	50
289	A128	2 l brown	2.00	1.00
290	A129	4 l car rose	4.00	3.25
291	A130	7 l blue	5.25	5.00
292	A131	14 l orange	5.25	5.00
		Nos. 288-292 (5)	18.00	14.75

Issued to commemorate the 67th anniversary of the death of the Bulgarian patriots, Haji Dimitr and Stefan Karaja.

Numeral
A132

Lion
A133

1936-39 *Perf. 13x12½, 13*

293	A132	10s red org ('37)	5	5
294	A132	15s emerald	5	5
295	A133	30s maroon	8	5
296	A133	30s yel brn ('37)	8	5
297	A133	30s Prus bl ('37)	10	5
298	A133	50s ultra	12	5
299	A133	50s dk car ('37)	15	5
300	A133	50s sl grn ('39)	6	5
		Nos. 293-300 (8)	69	40

Meteorological Station, Mt. Moussalla
A134

Peasant Girl
A135

Town of Nessebr
A136

1936, Aug. 16 Photo. *Perf. 11½*

301	A134	1 l purple	1.40	1.00
302	A135	2 l ultra	1.40	90
303	A136	7 l dk bl	3.75	2.25

Issued to commemorate the fourth Geographical and Ethnographical Congress, Sofia, August, 1936.

Sts. Cyril and Methodius
A137

Displaying the Bible to the People
A138

1937, June 2

304	A137	1 l dk grn	25	20
305	A137	2 l dk plum	25	20
306	A138	4 l vermilion	45	30
307	A137	7 l dk bl	2.00	1.50
308	A138	14 l rose red	2.00	1.50
		Nos. 304-308 (5)	4.95	3.70

Millennium of Cyrillic alphabet.

Princess Marie Louise
A139

Tsar Boris III
A140

1937, Oct. 3

310	A139	1 l yel grn	30	8
311	A139	2 l brn red	30	12
312	A139	4 l scarlet	40	20

Issued in honor of Princess Marie Louise.

1937, Oct. 3

313	A140	2 l brn red	30	20

Issued to commemorate the 19th anniversary of the accession of Tsar Boris III to the throne. See No. B11.

National Products Issue.

Peasants Bundling Wheat
A141

Sunflower
A142

Wheat
A143

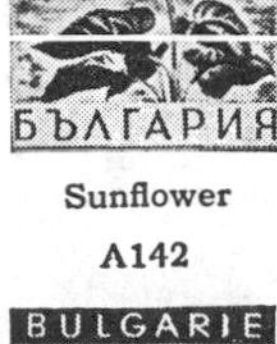

Chickens and Eggs
A144

Cluster of Grapes
A145

Rose and Perfume Flask
A146

Strawberries
A147

Girl Carrying Grape Clusters
A148

Rose
A149

Tobacco Leaves
A150

1938 ***Perf. 13.***

316	A141	10s orange	5	5
317	A141	10s red org	5	5
318	A142	15s brt rose	30	6
319	A142	15s dp plum	30	6
320	A143	30s gldn brn	10	6
321	A143	30s cop brn	10	6
322	A144	50s black	10	6
323	A144	50s indigo	10	9
324	A145	1 l yel grn	65	7
325	A145	1 l green	65	7
326	A146	2 l rose pink	50	8
327	A146	2 l rose brn	50	6
328	A147	3 l dp red lil	1.00	20
329	A147	3 l brn lake	1.00	20
330	A148	4 l plum	75	20
331	A148	4 l gldn brn	75	20
332	A149	7 l vio bl	1.35	75
333	A149	7 l dp bl	1.35	75
334	A150	14 l dk brn	2.00	1.25
335	A150	14 l red brn	2.00	1.25
		Nos. 316-335 (20)	13.60	5.57

Several values of this series exist imperforate.

Crown Prince Simeon
A151 A153

Designs: 2 l, Same portrait as 1 l, value at lower left. 14 l, Similar to 4 l, but no wreath.

1938, June 16

336	A151	1 l brt grn	10	6
337	A151	2 l rose pink	12	6
338	A153	4 l dp org	13	8
339	A151	7 l ultra	70	50
340	A151	14 l dp brn	70	50
		Nos. 336-340 (5)	1.75	1.20

First birthday of Prince Simeon.

Tsar Boris III
A155 A156

Various Portraits of Tsar.

1938, Oct. 3

341	A155	1 l lt grn	10	6
342	A156	2 l rose brn	60	8
343	A156	4 l gldn brn	15	6
344	A156	7 l brt ultra	30	30
345	A156	14 l dp red lil	35	35
		Nos. 341-345 (5)	1.50	85

20th anniversary, reign of Tsar Boris III.

Early Locomotive
A160

Designs: 2 l, Modern locomotive. 4 l, Train crossing bridge. 7 l, Tsar Boris in cab.

1939, Apr. 26

346	A160	1 l yel grn	15	8
347	A160	2 l cop brn	15	8
348	A160	4 l red org	1.00	30
349	A160	7 l dk bl	2.25	1.50

Issued in commemoration of the 50th anniversary of Bulgarian State Railways.

Post Horns and Arrows
A164

Central Post Office, Sofia
A165

1939, May 14 **Typographed**

350	A164	1 l yel grn	12	6
351	A165	2 l brt car	18	6

Issued in commemoration of the 60th anniversary of the establishment of the postal system.

Gymnast on Bar
A166

Yunak Emblem
A167

Discus Thrower
A168

Athletic Dancer
A169

Weight Lifter
A170

1939, July 7 **Photogravure**

352	A166	1 l yel grn & pale grn	20	15
353	A167	2 l brt rose	20	15
354	A168	4 l brn & gldn brn	30	30
355	A169	7 l dk bl & bl	90	90
356	A170	14 l plum & rose vio	3.75	3.75
		Nos. 352-356 (5)	5.35	5.25

Issued to commemorate the 9th tournament of the Yunak Gymnastic Organization at Sofia, July 4–8.

Tsar Boris III
A171

Bulgaria's First Stamp
A172

1940-41 **Typographed.**

356A	A171	1 l dl grn ('41)	75	5
357	A171	2 l brt crim	20	5

1940, May 19 **Photo.** ***Perf. 13***

Design: 20 l, Similar design, scroll dated "1840–1940."

358	A172	10 l ol blk	1.25	1.25
359	A172	20 l indigo	1.25	1.25

Centenary of first postage stamp. Exist imperf.

Peasant Couple and Tsar Boris
A174

Flags over Wheat Field and Tsar Boris
A175

Tsar Boris and Map of Dobrudja
A176

1940, Sept. 20

360	A174	1 l sl grn	5	5
361	A175	2 l rose red	10	7
362	A176	4 l dk brn	15	8
363	A176	7 l dk bl	60	40

Issued in commemoration of the return of Dobrudja from Romania.

Fruit
A177

Bees and Flowers
A178

Plowing
A179

Shepherd and Sheep
A180

Tsar Boris III
A181

Perf. 10, 10½x11½, 11½, 13.

1940–44 **Typographed.** **Unwmkd.**

364	A177	10s red org	5	5
365	A178	15s blue	5	5
366	A179	30s ol brn ('41)	5	5
367	A180	50s violet	15	5
368	A181	1 l brt grn	5	5
369	A181	2 l rose car	7	5
370	A181	4 l red org	15	5
371	A181	6 l red vio ('44)	35	5
372	A181	7 l blue	35	5
373	A181	10 l bl grn ('41)	40	15
		Nos. 364-373 (10)	1.67	60

See No. 440.

1940-41 ***Perf. 13.*** **Wmk. 145**

373A	A180	50s vio ('41)	10	5
374	A181	1 l brt grn	10	5
375	A181	2 l rose car	15	5
376	A181	7 l dl bl	40	8
377	A181	10 l bl grn	60	20
		Nos. 373A-377 (5)	1.35	43

Watermarked vertically or horizontally.

P. R. Slaveikov
A182

Sofronij, Bishop of Vratza
A183

Saint Ivan Rilski
A184

Martin S. Drinov
A185

Monk Khrabr
A186

Kolio Ficheto
A187

1940, Sept. 23 **Photo.** **Unwmkd.**

378	A182	1 l brt bl grn	7	5
379	A183	2 l brt car	8	5
380	A184	3 l dp red brn	15	8
381	A185	4 l red org	12	8
382	A186	7 l dp bl	1.00	75
383	A187	10 l dp red brn	1.50	1.10
		Nos. 378-383 (6)	2.92	2.11

Issued in commemoration of the liberation of Bulgaria from the Turks in 1878.

Johannes Gutenberg
A188

N. Karastoyanov, First Bulgarian Printer
A189

1940, Dec. 16

384	A188	1 l sl grn	10	8
385	A189	2 l org brn	10	8

Issued in commemoration of the 500th anniversary of the invention of the printing press and the 100th anniversary of the first Bulgarian printing press.

Christo Botev
A190

Monument to Botev
A192

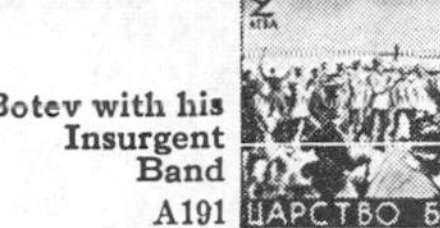

Botev with his Insurgent Band
A191

1941, May 3

386	A190	1 l dk bl grn	10	5
387	A191	2 l crim rose	15	5
388	A192	3 l dk brn	50	50

Issued in honor of Christo Botev, patriot and poet.

Palace of Justice, Sofia
A193

Designs: 20 l, Workers' hospital. 50 l, National Bank.

1941-43 Engraved *Perf. 11½*

389	A193	14 l lt gray brn ('43)	20	15
390	A193	20 l gray grn ('43)	40	25
391	A193	50 l lt bl gray	2.00	2.00

Macedonian Woman
A196

City of Okhrida
A200

Outline of Macedonia and Tsar Boris III
A197

View of Aegean Sea
A198

Poganovski Monastery
A199

1941, Oct. 3 Photo. *Perf. 13*

392	A196	1 l sl grn	5	5
393	A197	2 l crimson	6	5
394	A198	2 l red org	9	5
395	A199	4 l org brn	10	8
396	A200	7 l dp gray bl	40	40
		Nos. 392-396 (5)	70	63

Issued to commemorate the acquisition of Macedonian territory from neighboring countries.

Peasant Working in a Field
A201

Designs: 15s, Plowing. 30s, Apiary. 50s, Women harvesting fruit. 3 l, Shepherd and sheep. 5 l, Inspecting cattle.

1941-44

397	A201	10s dk vio	5	5
398	A201	10s dk bl	5	5
399	A201	15s Prus bl	5	5
400	A201	15s dk ol brn	5	5
401	A201	30s red org	5	5
402	A201	30s dk sl grn	5	5
403	A201	50s bl vio	6	5
404	A201	50s red lil	8	5
405	A201	3 l hn brn	60	40
406	A201	3 l dk brn ('44)	1.75	1.75
407	A201	5 l sepia	75	75
408	A201	5 l vio bl ('44)	1.75	1.75
		Nos. 397-408 (12)	5.29	5.05

Girls Singing
A207

Boys in Camp
A208

Raising Flag
A209

Folk Dancers
A211

Camp Scene
A210

1942, June 1 Photogravure

409	A207	1 l dk bl grn	8	5
410	A208	2 l scarlet	15	6
411	A209	4 l ol gray	15	6
412	A210	7 l dp bl	20	15
413	A211	14 l fawn	40	30
		Nos. 409-413 (5)	98	62

National "Work and Joy" movement.

Wounded Soldier
A212

Soldier's Farewell
A213

Designs: 4 l, Aiding wounded soldier. 7 l, Widow and orphans at grave. 14 l, Tomb of Unknown Soldier. 20 l, Queen Ioanna visiting wounded.

1942, Sept. 7

414	A212	1 l sl grn	8	6
415	A213	2 l brt rose	8	6
416	A213	4 l yel org	8	5
417	A213	7 l dk bl	9	5
418	A213	14 l brown	12	8
419	A213	20 l ol blk	20	10
		Nos. 414-419 (6)	65	40

Issued to aid war victims. No. 419 was printed in sheets of 50, alternating with 50 labels.

Legend of Kubrat
A218

Cavalry Charge
A219

Designs: 30s, Rider of Madara. 50s, Christening of Boris I. 1 l, School, St. Naum. 2 l, Crowning of Tsar Simeon by Boris I. 3 l, Golden era of Bulgarian literature. 4 l, Sentencing of the Bogomil Basil. 5 l, Proclamation of 2nd Bulgarian Empire. 7 l, Ivan Assen II at Trebizond. 10 l, Deporting the Patriarch Jeftimi. 14 l, Wandering minstrel. 20 l, Monk Paisii. 30 l, Monument, Shipka Pass.

1942, Oct. 12

420	A218	10s bluish blk	5	5
421	A219	15s Prus grn	5	5
422	A219	30s dk rose vio	5	5
423	A219	50s indigo	5	5
424	A219	1 l sl grn	5	5
425	A219	2 l crimson	5	5
426	A219	3 l brown	5	5
427	A219	4 l orange	6	6
428	A219	5 l grnsh blk	6	6
429	A219	7 l dk bl	7	7
430	A219	10 l brn blk	15	15
431	A219	14 l ol blk	15	15
432	A219	20 l hn brn	50	50
433	A219	30 l black	75	75
		Nos. 420-433 (14)	2.09	2.09

Tsar Boris III
A234

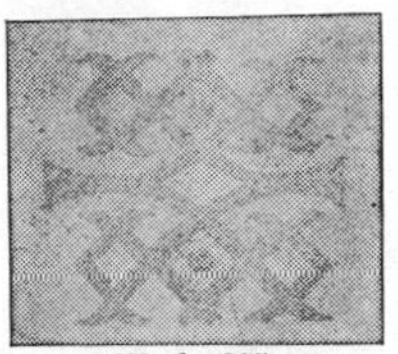
Wmk. 275

Designs: Various portraits of Tsar.

Wmkd. Entwined Curved Lines. (275)

Perf. 13, Imperf.

1944, Feb. 28 Photogravure

Frames in Black.

434	A234	1 l ol grn	5	5
435	A234	2 l red brn	12	12
436	A234	4 l brown	14	14
437	A234	5 l gray vio	25	25
438	A234	7 l sl bl	25	25
		Nos. 434-438 (5)	81	81

Issued in memory of Tsar Boris III (1894–1943).

Tsar Simeon II
A239

Perf. 11½, 13

1944, June 12 Typo. Unwmkd.

439	A239	3 l red org	20	5

Shepherd Type of 1940

1944

440	A180	50s yel grn	20	10

Parcel Post Stamps of 1944 Overprinted in Black or Orange

ВСИЧКО
ЗА
ФРОНТА

1945, Jan. 25 *Perf. 11½*

448	PP5	1 l dk car	5	5
449	PP5	7 l rose lil	5	5
450	PP5	20 l org brn	7	5
451	PP5	30 l dk brn car	15	5
452	PP5	50 l red org	30	15
453	PP5	100 l bl (O)	70	35

The overprint reads: "Everything for the Front".

No. 448 with Additional Surcharge of New Value in Black.

454	PP5	4 l on 1 l dk car	5	5
		Nos. 448-454 (7)	1.37	75

Nos. 368 to 370 Overprinted in Black

СЪБИРАЙТЕ
СТАРО
ЖЕЛЪЗО

1945, Mar. 15 *Perf. 11½, 13*

455	A181	1 l brt grn	5	5
456	A181	2 l rose car	8	5
457	A181	4 l red org	12	5

The overprint reads: "Collect old iron."

Overprinted in Black

СЪБИРАЙТЕ
ХАРТИЕНИ
ОТПАДЪЦИ

458	A181	1 l brt grn	5	5
459	A181	2 l rose car	8	5
460	A181	4 l red org	12	5

The overprint reads: "Collect discarded paper."

Overprinted in Black

СЪБИРАЙТЕ
ВСЪКАКВИ
ПАРЦАЛИ

461	A181	1 l brt grn	5	5
462	A181	2 l rose car	8	5

463 A181 4 l red org 12 5
Nos. 455-463 (9) 75 45

The overprint reads: "Collect all kinds of rags."

Oak Tree
A245

Imperf., Perf. 11½.

1945 Lithographed Unwmkd.

464 A245 4 l vermilion 8 6
465 A245 10 l blue 8 6

Imperf.

466 A245 50 l brn lake 25 20

Slav Congress, Sofia, March, 1945.

A246  A247

Lion Rampant
A248

Arms of Bulgaria
A249

A251

A252

Arms of Bulgaria
A253 A254

Two types of 2 l and 4 l: Type I: Large crown close to coat of arms. Type II: Smaller crown standing high.

1945-46 Photogravure *Perf. 13*

469 A246 30s yel grn 5 5
470 A247 50s pck grn 5 5
471 A248 1 l dk grn 5 5
472 A249 2 l choc (I) 5 5
a. Type II 5 5
473 A249 4 l dk bl (I) 8 5
a. Type II 5 5
475 A251 5 l red vio 5 5
476 A251 9 l sl gray 6 5
477 A252 10 l Prus bl 8 5
478 A253 15 l brown 10 5
479 A254 20 l carmine 20 6
480 A254 20 l gray blk 20 6
Nos. 469-480 (11) 97 57

Breaking Chain
A255

1 Lev Coin
A256

Water Wheel
A257

Coin and Symbols of Agriculture and Industry
A258

Lithographed.

1945, June 4 *Imperf.* Unwmkd.

Laid Paper.

481 A255 50 l brn red, *pink* 10 8
482 A255 50 l org, *pink* 10 8
483 A256 100 l gray bl, *pink* 15 12
484 A256 100 l brn, *pink* 15 12
485 A257 150 l dk ol gray, *pink* 35 25
486 A257 150 l dl car, *pink* 35 25
487 A258 200 l dp bl, *pink* 60 50
488 A258 200 l ol grn, *pink* 60 50
Nos. 481-488 (8) 2.40 1.90

Souvenir Sheets.

489 Sheet of four 2.50 2.50
a. 50 l vio bl 25 25
b. 100 l vio bl 25 25
c. 150 l vio bl 25 25
d. 200 l vio bl 25 25
490 Sheet of four 2.50 2.50
a. 50 l brn org 25 25
b. 100 l brn org 25 25
c. 150 l brn org 25 25
d. 200 l brn org 25 25

Nos. 481 to 490 were issued to publicize Bulgaria's Liberty Loan.

Nos. 489 and 490 measure 90x122mm. and contain one each of types A255—A258. Margin inscription: "March 9, 1935, Sofia" in Bulgarian characters.

Olive Branch
A260

1945, Sept. 1 Typo. *Perf. 13*

491 A260 10 l org brn & yel grn 7 5
492 A260 50 l dl red & dp grn 30 15

Victory of Allied Nations, World War II.

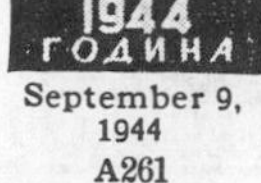

September 9, 1944
A261

Numeral and Broken Chain
A262

1945, Sept. 7

493 A261 1 l gray grn 5 5
494 A261 4 l dp bl 5 5
495 A261 5 l rose lil 5 5
496 A262 10 l lt bl 5 5
497 A262 20 l brt car 25 12
498 A261 50 l brt bl grn 60 30
499 A261 100 l org brn 65 50
Nos. 493-499 (7) 1.70 1.12

Issued to commemorate the 1st anniversary of Bulgaria's liberation.

Old Postal Savings Emblem— A263

First Bulgarian Postal Savings Stamp
A264

Child Putting Coin in Bank
A265

Postal Savings Building, Sofia
A266

1946, Apr. 12

500 A263 4 l brn org 6 5
501 A264 10 l dk ol 15 5
502 A265 20 l ultra 15 6
503 A266 50 l sl gray 75 75

Issued to commemorate the 50th anniversary of Bulgarian Postal Savings.

Refugee Children
A267

Nurse Assisting Wounded Soldier
A269

Wounded Soldier
A268

Design: 35 l, 100 l, Red Cross hospital train.

1946, Apr. 4

Cross in Carmine

504 A267 2 l dk ol 5 5
505 A268 4 l violet 10 5
506 A267 10 l plum 10 6
507 A268 20 l ultra 12 6
508 A269 30 l brn org 15 10
509 A268 35 l gray blk 20 20
510 A269 50 l vio brn 30 30
511 A268 100 l gray brn 1.00 1.00
Nos. 504-511 (8) 2.02 1.82

See also Nos. 553 to 560.

Advancing Troops
A271

Grenade Thrower
A272

Attacking Planes
A274

Designs: 5 l, Horse-drawn cannon. 9 l, Engineers building pontoon bridge. 10 l, 30 l, Cavalry charge. 40 l, Horse-drawn supply column. 50 l, Motor transport column. 60 l, Infantry, tanks and planes.

1946, Aug. 9 Typo. Unwmkd.

512 A271 2 l dk red vio 5 5
513 A272 4 l dk gray 5 5
514 A271 5 l dk org red 5 5
515 A274 6 l blk brn 5 5
516 A271 9 l rose lil 5 5
517 A271 10 l dp vio 5 5
518 A271 20 l dp bl 30 15
519 A271 30 l red org 30 15
520 A271 40 l dk ol bis 35 20
521 A271 50 l dk grn 35 20
522 A271 60 l red brn 50 35
Nos. 512-522 (11) 2.10 1.35

Bulgaria's participation in World War II.

Arms of Russia and Bulgaria
A279

Lion Rampant
A280

1946, May 23

523 A279 4 l red org 8 8
525 A279 20 l turq grn 20 15

Issued to commemorate the Congress of the Bulgarian-Soviet Association, May 1946.

The 4 l exists in dk car rose and 20 l in blue, price, set $10.

1946, May 25 *Imperf.*

526 A280 20 l blue 35 25

Issued to commemorate the Day of the Postage Stamp, May 26, 1946.

Alexander Stambolisky
A281

Flags of Albania, Romania, Bulgaria and Jugoslavia
A282

1946, June 13 ***Perf. 12***

527	A281	100 l red org	3.50	3.50

Issued to commemorate the 23rd anniversary of the death of Alexander Stambolisky, agrarian leader.

1946, July 6 ***Perf. 11½***

528	A282	100 l blk brn	90	90

Issued to publicize the 1946 Balkan Games.
Sheet of 100 arranged so that all stamps are tête bêche vertically and horizontally, except two center rows in left pane which provide 10 vertical pairs that are not tête bêche vertically.

St. Ivan Rilski
A283

Rila Monastery
A286

A284

A285

Views of Rila Monastery
A287

1946, Aug. 26

529	A283	1 l red brn	7	6
530	A284	4 l blk brn	8	6
531	A285	10 l dk grn	15	8
532	A286	20 l dp bl	20	10
533	A287	50 l dk red	90	75
		Nos. 529-533 (5)	1.40	1.05

Millenary of Rila Monastery.

People's Republic

A288

1946, Sept. 15 **Typographed**

534	A288	4 l brn lake	5	5
535	A288	20 l dl bl	5	5
536	A288	50 l dl bis	20	20

No. 535 is inscribed "BULGARIA" in Latin characters.
Issued to commemorate the referendum of September 8, 1946, resulting in the establishment of the Bulgarian People's Republic.

Partisan Army
A289

Snipers
A290

Soldiers: Past and Present
A291

Design: 30 l, Partisans advancing.

1946, Dec. 2

537	A289	1 l vio brn	5	5
538	A290	4 l dl grn	5	5
539	A291	5 l chocolate	5	5
540	A290	10 l crimson	5	5
541	A289	20 l ultra	30	15
542	A290	30 l ol bis	30	15
543	A291	50 l black	35	30
		Nos. 537-543 (7)	1.15	80

Relief Worker and Children
A294

Child with Gift Parcels
A295

Waiting for Food Distribution
A296

Mother and Child
A297

1946, Dec. 30

545	A294	1 l dk vio brn	5	5
546	A295	4 l brt red	5	5
547	A295	9 l ol bis	5	5
548	A294	10 l sl gray	10	5
549	A296	20 l ultra	15	6
550	A297	30 l dp brn org	15	10
551	A296	40 l maroon	30	20
552	A294	50 l pck grn	50	40
		Nos. 545-552 (8)	1.35	96

"Bulgaria" is in Latin characters on No. 548.

Red Cross Types of 1946

1947, Jan. 31

Cross in Carmine

553	A267	2 l ol bis	5	5
554	A268	4 l ol blk	5	5
555	A267	10 l bl grn	10	10
556	A268	20 l brt bl	25	25
557	A269	30 l yel grn	35	35
558	A268	35 l grnsh gray	40	40
559	A269	50 l hn brn	55	55
560	A268	100 l dk bl	85	85
		Nos. 553-560 (8)	2.60	2.60

Laurel Branch, Allied and Bulgarian Emblems
A298

Dove of Peace
A299

1947, Feb. 28

561	A298	4 l olive	5	5
562	A299	10 l brn red	6	6
563	A299	20 l dp bl	20	20

Issued to commemorate the return to peace at the close of World War II. "Bulgaria" in Latin characters on No. 563.

A302

Guerrilla Fighters
A303 A304

1947, Jan. 21 ***Perf. 11½***

567	A302	10 l choc & brn org	30	30
568	A303	20 l dk bl & bl	30	30
569	A304	70 l dp cl & rose	15.00	15.00

Issued to honor the anti-fascists.

Hydroelectric Station
A305

Miner
A306

Symbols of Industry
A307

Tractor
A308

1947, Aug. 6

570	A305	4 l ol grn	8	5
571	A306	9 l red brn	15	12
572	A307	20 l dp bl	25	25
573	A308	40 l ol brn	60	60

Exhibition Building
A309

Former Home of Alphonse de Lamartine
A310

Symbols of Agriculture and Horticulture
A311

Perf. 11x11½, 11½x11.

1947, Aug. 31 **Litho.** **Unwmkd.**

574	A309	4 l scarlet	7	5
575	A310	9 l brn lake	9	5
576	A311	20 l brt ultra	30	12

Issued to publicize the Plovdiv International Fair, 1947. See No. C54.

Basil Evstatiev Aprilov
A312

1947, Oct. 19 **Photo.** ***Perf. 11***

577	A312	40 l brt ultra	40	25

Issued to commemorate the centenary of the death of Basil Evstatiev Aprilov, educator and historian. See also No. 603.

Balkan Games Issue.

Bicycle Race
A313

Basketball
A314

Chess
A315

Designs: 20 l, Soccer players. 60 l, Four flags of participating nations.

1947, Sept. 29 **Typo.** ***Perf. 11½***

578	A313	2 l plum	30	20
579	A314	4 l dk ol grn	30	20
580	A315	9 l org brn	60	20
581	A315	20 l brt ultra	1.25	30
582	A315	60 l vio brn	2.50	1.50
		Nos. 578-582 (5)	4.95	2.40

People's Theater, Sofia
A316

National Assembly
A317

Central Post Office, Sofia
A318

Presidential Mansion
A319

1947–48 Typographed *Perf. 12½*

583	A316	50s yel grn	5	5
584	A317	50s yel grn	5	5
585	A318	1 l green	5	5
586	A319	1 l green	5	5
587	A316	2 l brn lake	5	5
588	A317	2 l lt brn	5	5
589	A316	4 l dp bl	6	5
590	A317	4 l dp bl	8	5
591	A316	9 l carmine	40	5
592	A317	20 l dp bl	85	30
		Nos. 583-592 (10)	1.69	75

On Nos. 583–592 inscription reads "Bulgarian Republic." No. 592 is inscribed in Latin characters.

Redrawn.

НАРОДНА

added to inscription.

593	A318	1 l green	6	5
594	A318	2 l brn lake	8	5
595	A318	4 l dp bl	10	5

Cyrillic inscription beneath design on Nos. 593–595 reads "Bulgarian People's Republic".

Geno Kirov
A320

Actors' Portraits: 1 l, Zlatina Nedeva. 2 l, Ivan Popov. 3 l, Athanas Kirchev. 4 l, Elena Snejina. 5 l, Stoyan Bachvarov.

Lithographed

1947, Dec. 8 *Perf. 10½* Unwmkd.

596	A320	50s bis brn	5	5
597	A320	1 l lt bl grn	5	5
598	A320	2 l sl grn	5	5
599	A320	3 l dp bl	6	6
600	A320	4 l scarlet	8	8
601	A320	5 l red brn	8	8
		Nos. 596-601, B22-B26 (11)	1.57	1.82

National Theater, 50th anniversary.

Merchant Ship "Fatherland"
A321

1947, Dec. 19

602	A321	50 l Prus bl, *cr*	50	25

B. E. Aprilov
A322

Bulgarian Worker
A323

1948, Feb. 19 *Perf. 11*

603	A322	4 l brn car, *cr*	10	10

Issued to commemorate the centenary of the death of Basil Evstatiev Aprilov, educator and historian.

1948, Feb. 29 Photo. *Perf. 11½x12*

604	A323	4 l dp bl, *cr*	20	10

2nd Bulgarian Workers' Congress.

Self-education
A324

Accordion Player
A325

Factory Recess
A326

Girl Throwing Basketball
A327

1948, Mar. 31 Photogravure

605	A324	4 l red	6	6
606	A325	20 l dp bl	20	15
607	A326	40 l dl grn	30	15
608	A327	60 l brown	80	50

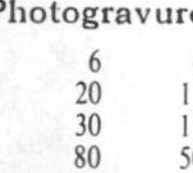

Nicholas Vaptzarov
A328

Portraits: 9 l, P. K. Iavorov. 15 l, Christo Smirnenski. 20 l, Ivan Vazov. 45 l, P. R. Slaveikov.

1948, May 18 Litho. *Perf. 11*

Cream Paper.

611	A328	4 l brt ver	7	5
612	A328	9 l lt brn	8	5
613	A328	15 l claret	10	6
614	A328	20 l dp bl	15	15
615	A328	45 l green	50	50
		Nos. 611-615 (5)	90	81

Soviet Soldier
A329

Civilians Offering Gifts to Soldiers
A330

Designs: 20 l, Soldiers, 1878 and 1944. 60 l, Stalin and Spasski Tower.

1948, July 5 Photogravure

Cream Paper.

616	A329	4 l brn org	6	5
617	A330	10 l ol grn	6	5
618	A330	20 l dp bl	15	12
619	A329	60 l ol brn	60	50

Issued to honor the Soviet Army.

Demeter Blagoev
A331

Monument to Bishop Andrey
A332

Designs: 9 l, Gabriel Genov. 60 l, Marching youths.

1948, Sept. 6 Lithographed

Cream Paper.

620	A331	4 l dk brn	5	5
621	A331	9 l brn org	5	5
622	A332	20 l dp bl	12	9
623	A332	60 l brown	80	65

No. 623 is inscribed in Cyrillic characters.

Issued to commemorate the 25th anniversary of the National Insurrection of 1923.

Christo Smirnenski
A333

Battle of Grivitza, 1877
A334

1948, Oct. 2 Photo. *Perf. 11½*

Cream Paper

624	A333	4 l blue	7	5
625	A333	16 l red brn	15	6

Issued to commemorate the 25th anniversary of the death of Christo Smirnenski, poet, 1898–1923.

1948, Nov. 1

626	A334	20 l blue	20	12

Issued to publicize Romanian-Bulgarian friendship. See Nos. C56–C57.

Bath, Gorna Banya
A335

Bath, Bankya
A336

Mineral Bath, Sofia
A337

Maliovitza
A338

1948-49 Typographed. *Perf. 12½.*

627	A335	2 l red brn	15	5
628	A336	3 l red org	15	5
629	A337	4 l dp bl	20	5
630	A338	5 l vio brn	18	5
631	A336	10 l red vio	25	5
632	A338	15 l ol grn ('49)	35	5
633	A335	20 l dp bl	1.25	20
		Nos. 627-633 (7)	2.53	50

Latin characters on No. 633. See also No. 653.

Emblem of the Republic
A339

1948–50

634	A339	50s red org	5	5
634A	A339	50s org brn ('50)	6	5
635	A339	1 l green	6	5
636	A339	9 l black	15	8

Botev's Birthplace, Kalofer
A340

Christo Botev
A341

Cyrillic Inscription:

"Chr. Botev 1848-1948."

Designs: 9 l, Steamer "Radetzky." 15 l, Kalofer village. 20 l, Botev in uniform. 40 l, Botev's mother. 50 l, Pen, pistol and wreath.

Photogravure.

1948, Dec. 21 *Perf. 11x11½, 11½*

Cream Paper.

638	A340	1 l dk grn	5	5
639	A341	4 l vio brn	5	5
640	A340	9 l violet	5	5
641	A340	15 l brown	8	6
642	A341	20 l blue	20	10
643	A340	40 l red brn	35	25
644	A341	50 l ol blk	45	35
		Nos. 638-644 (7)	1.23	91

Issued to commemorate the centenary of the birth of Christo Botev, Bulgarian national poet.

Lenin
A342

Lenin Speaking
A343

1949, Jan. 24 *Perf. 11½* Unwmkd.

Cream Paper.

645	A342	4 l brown	15	7
646	A343	20 l brn red	40	25

25th anniversary of the death of Lenin.

Road Construction
A344

Designs: 5 l, Tunnel construction. 9 l, Locomotive. 10 l, Textile worker. 20 l, Female tractor driver. 40 l, Workers in truck.

1949, Apr. 6 ***Perf. 10½***

Inscribed: "CHM".

Cream Paper.

647	A344	4 l dk red	10	5
648	A344	5 l dk brn	15	8
649	A344	9 l dk sl grn	30	15
650	A344	10 l violet	35	20
651	A344	20 l dl bl	70	55
652	A344	40 l brown	1.25	80
		Nos. 647-652 (6)	2.85	1.83

Issued to honor the Workers' Cultural Brigade.

Type of 1948.

Redrawn.

Country Name and "POSTA" in Latin Characters.

1949 **Typographed** ***Perf. 12½***

653	A337	20 l dp bl	80	15

Miner
A345

1949 ***Perf. 11x11½.***

654	A345	4 l dk bl	25	8

George Dimitrov
A347

A348

1949, July 10 **Photogravure**

656	A347	4 l red brn	15	5
657	A348	20 l dk bl	40	25

Issued in tribute to Prime Minister George Dimitrov, 1882–1949.

Power Station
A349

Grain Towers
A350

Farm Machinery
A351

Tractor Parade
A352

Agriculture and Industry
A353

Perf. 11½x11, 11x11½.

1949, Aug. 5

658	A349	4 l ol grn	12	5
659	A350	9 l dk red	20	10
660	A351	15 l purple	25	15
661	A352	20 l blue	80	55
662	A353	50 l org brn	2.50	1.25
		Nos. 658-662 (5)	3.87	2.10

Issued to publicize Bulgaria's Five Year Plan.

Grenade and Javelin Throwers
A354

Boy and Girl Athletes
A357

Hurdlers
A355

Motorcycle and Tractor
A356

1949, Sept. 5

663	A354	4 l brn org	35	20
664	A355	9 l ol grn	75	35
665	A356	20 l vio bl	1.50	1.00
666	A357	50 l red brn	3.50	2.00

Frontier Guards
A358 A359

1949, Oct. 31

667	A358	4 l chnt brn	15	5
668	A359	20 l gray bl	60	40

See also No. C60.

George Dimitrov
A360

Allegory of Labor
A361

Laborers of Both Sexes
A362

Workers and Flags of Bulgaria and Russia
A363

Perf. 11½

1949, Dec. 13 **Photo.** **Unwmkd.**

669	A360	4 l org brn	15	5
670	A361	9 l purple	25	8
671	A362	20 l dl bl	40	35
672	A363	50 l red	80	80

Joseph V. Stalin
A364

Stalin and Dove
A365

1949, Dec. 21

673	A364	4 l dp org	20	8
674	A365	40 l rose brn	70	50

Issued to commemorate the 70th anniversary of the birth of Joseph V. Stalin.

Kharalamby Stoyanov
A366

Communications Strikers
A368

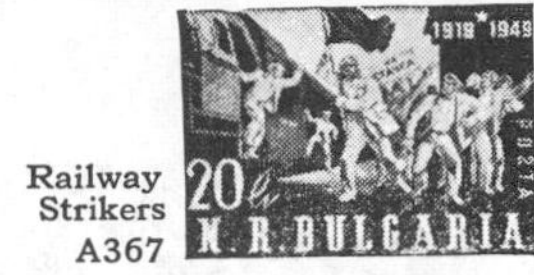

Railway Strikers
A367

1950, Feb. 15

675	A366	4 l yel brn	10	5
676	A367	20 l vio bl	20	10
677	A368	60 l brn ol	70	60

Issued to commemorate the 30th anniversary (in 1949) of the General Railway and Postal Employees' Strike of 1919.

Miner
A369

Shipbuilding
A371

Locomotive
A370

Tractor
A372

Farm Machinery
A373

Stalin Central Heating Plant
A374

Textile Worker
A375

1950-51 ***Perf. 11½, 13.***

678	A369	1 l ol	12	5
679	A370	2 l gray blk	20	5
680	A371	3 l gray bl	30	5
681	A372	4 l dk bl grn	2.50	75
682	A373	5 l hn brn	60	10
682A	A373	9 l gray blk ('51)	30	6
683	A374	10 l dp plum ('51)	40	10
684	A375	15 l dk car ('51)	60	6
685	A375	20 l dk bl ('51)	1.00	60
		Nos. 678-685 (9)	6.02	1.82

No. 685 is inscribed in Latin characters.

See Nos. 750–751A.

Vassil Kolarov
A377

1950, Mar. 6 ***Perf. 11½***

Size: 21½x31½ mm.

686	A377	4 l red brn	7	5

Size: 27x39½ mm.

687	A377	20 l vio bl	40	30

Issued in memory of Vassil Kolarov (1877–1950).

No. 687 has altered frame and is inscribed in Latin characters.

Stanislav Dospevski, Self-portrait
A378

King Kaloyan and Desislava
A379

Plowman Resting, by Christo Stanchev
A380

Statue of Dimtcho Debelianov, by Ivan Lazarov
A381

"Harvest," by V. Dimitrov
A382

Design: 9 l, Nikolai Pavlovich, self-portrait.

1950, Apr. 15 ***Perf. 11½***

688	A378	1 l dk ol grn	35	15
689	A379	4 l dk red	1.00	30
690	A378	9 l chocolate	1.00	30
691	A380	15 l brown	1.75	35
692	A380	20 l dp bl	2.25	1.10
693	A381	40 l red brn	3.25	1.75
694	A382	60 l dp org	4.50	2.25
		Nos. 688-694 (7)	14.10	6.20

Latin characters on No. 692.

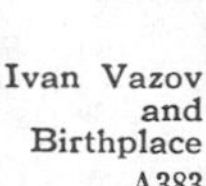

Ivan Vazov and Birthplace
A383

1950, June 26

695	A383	4 l ol grn	12	10

Issued to commemorate the centenary of the birth of Ivan Vazov (1850–1921), poet.

Road Building
A384

Men of Three Races and "Stalin" Flag
A385

Perf. 11½x11, 11x11½

1950, Sept. 19

696	A384	4 l brn red	5	5
697	A385	20 l vio bl	40	25

2nd National Peace Conference.

Molotov, Kolarov, Stalin and Dimitrov
A386

Spasski Tower and Flags
A387

Russian and Bulgarian Women
A388

Loading Russian Ship
A389

Photogravure.

1950, Oct. 10 ***Perf. 11½*** **Unwmkd.**

698	A386	4 l brown	10	5
699	A387	9 l rose car	15	6
700	A388	20 l gray bl	25	20
701	A389	50 l dk grnsh bl	1.25	65

Issued to commemorate the 2nd anniversary of the Soviet-Bulgarian treaty of mutual assistance.

St. Constantine Sanatorium
A390

Children at Seashore
A391

Design: 5 l, Rest home.

1950 **Typographed**

702	A390	1 l dk grn	6	5
703	A391	2 l carmine	20	5
704	A391	5 l dp org	30	15
705	A391	10 l dp bl	75	35

Originally prepared in 1945 as "Sunday Delivery Stamps," this issue was released for ordinary postage in 1950.

Runners
A393

Designs: 9 l, Cycling. 20 l, Putting the Shot. 40 l, Volleyball.

1950, Aug. 21 **Photo.** ***Perf. 11***

706	A393	4 l dk grn	30	20
707	A393	9 l red brn	50	40
708	A393	20 l gray bl	1.00	65
709	A393	40 l plum	2.25	1.50

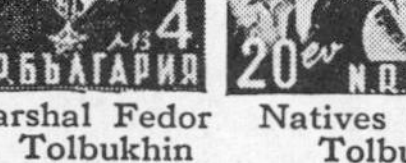

Marshal Fedor I. Tolbukhin
A394

Natives Greeting Tolbukhin
A395

Perf. 11½x11, 11x11½.

1950, Dec. 10 **Photo.** **Unwmkd.**

710	A394	4 l claret	15	10
711	A395	20 l dk bl	60	30

Issued to publicize the return of Dobrich and part of the province of Dobruja from Romania to Bulgaria.

Dimitrov's Birthplace
A396

George Dimitrov
A397 A398

Various Portraits, Inscribed:

Г.ДИМИТРОВ

1950, July 2 ***Perf. 10½***

712	A396	50s ol grn	15	5
713	A397	50s brown	15	5
714	A397	1 l redsh brn	25	5
715	A396	2 l gray (*Dimitrov Museum, Sofia*)	25	5
716	A397	4 l claret	45	15
717	A397	9 l red brn	60	35
718	A398	10 l brn red	65	50
719	A396	15 l ol gray	65	50
720	A396	20 l dk bl	1.75	75
		Nos. 712-720, C61 (10)	8.40	3.95

Issued to commemorate the first anniversary of the death of George Dimitrov, statesman. No. 720 is inscribed in Latin characters.

A. S. Popov
A400

1951, Feb. 10

722	A400	4 l red brn	25	15
723	A400	20 l dk bl	50	25

No. 723 is inscribed in Latin characters.

Arms of Bulgaria
A401 A402

Typographed

1950 ***Perf. 13*** **Unwmkd.**

724	A401	2 l dk brn	6	5
725	A401	3 l rose	7	5
726	A402	5 l carmine	10	5
727	A402	9 l aqua	25	5

Nos. 724–727 were prepared in 1947 for official use but were issued as regular postage stamps Oct. 1, 1950.

Heroes Chankova, Antonov-Malchik, Dimitrov and Dimitrova
A403

Stanke Dimitrov-Marek
A404

George Kirkov
A405

George Dimitrov at Leipzig
A406

Natcho Ivanov and Avr. Stoyanov
A407

Portraits: 9 l, Anton Ivanov. 15 l, Christo Michailov.

1951, Mar. 25 **Photo.** ***Perf. 11½***

728	A403	1 l red vio	15	6
729	A404	2 l dk red brn	15	8
730	A405	4 l car rose	15	10
731	A405	9 l org brn	50	15
732	A405	15 l ol brn	85	30
733	A406	20 l dk bl	1.25	75
734	A407	50 l ol gray	2.50	1.25
		Nos. 728-734 (7)	5.55	2.69

First Bulgarian Tractor
A408

First Steam Roller
A409

First Truck
A410

Bulgarian Embroidery
A411

Designs: 15 l, Carpet. 20 l, Tobacco and roses. 40 l, Fruits.

Perf. 11x10½

1951, Mar. 30 Photo. Unwmkd.

735	A408	1 l ol brn	10	5
736	A409	2 l violet	15	5
737	A410	4 l red brn	25	10
738	A411	9 l purple	40	20
739	A409	15 l dp plum	60	45
740	A411	20 l vio bl	80	50
741	A410	40 l dp grn	1.50	1.00

Perf. 13.

Size: 23x18½ mm.

742	A408	1 l purple	6	5
743	A409	2 l Prus grn	15	5
744	A410	4 l red brn	15	5
		Nos. 735-744 (10)	4.16	2.50

See also Nos. 894, 973.

Turkish Attack on Mt. Zlee Dol
A412

Designs: 4 l, Georgi Benkovski speaking to rebels. 9 l, Cherrywood cannon of 1876 and Russian cavalry, 1945. 20 l, Rebel, 1876 and partisan, 1944. 40 l, Benkovski and Dimitrov.

1951, May 3 ***Perf. 10½***

Cream Paper.

745	A412	1 l redsh brn	15	10
746	A412	4 l dk grn	15	10
747	A412	9 l vio brn	55	40
748	A412	20 l dp bl	70	70
749	A412	40 l dk red	1.00	1.00
		Nos. 745-749 (5)	2.55	2.30

Issued to commemorate the 75th anniversary of the "April" revolution.

Industrial Types of 1950.

1951 ***Perf. 13***

750	A369	1 l violet	15	5
751	A370	2 l dk brn	15	5
751A	A372	4 l dk yel grn	1.00	10

Demeter Blagoev Addressing 1891 Congress at Busludja
A413

1951 Photogravure ***Perf. 11***

752	A413	1 l purple	30	15
753	A413	4 l dk grn	40	15
754	A413	9 l dp cl	65	50

Issued to commemorate the 60th anniversary of the first Congress of the Bulgarian Social-Democratic Party.

See also Nos. 1174–1176.

Day Nursery
A414

Designs: 4 l, Model building construction. 9 l, Playground. 20 l, Children's town.

1951, Oct. 10 Unwmkd.

755	A414	1 l brown	15	6
756	A414	4 l dp plum	25	10
757	A414	9 l bl grn	75	30
758	A414	20 l dp bl	1.25	75

Issued to publicize Children's Day, Sept. 25, 1951.

Order of Labor
A415 A416

1952, Feb. 1 ***Perf. 13***

Reverse of Medal

759	A415	1 l red brn	5	5
760	A415	4 l bl grn	10	5
761	A415	9 l dk bl	35	10

Obverse of Medal

762	A416	1 l carmine	5	5
763	A416	4 l green	10	5
764	A416	9 l purple	35	10
		Nos. 759-764 (6)	1.00	40

No. 764 has numeral at lower left and different background.

Workers and Symbols of Industry
A417

Design: 4 l, Flags and Dimitrov, Chervenkov.

1951, Dec. 29 ***Perf. 11***

Inscribed: "16 XII 1951."

765	A417	1 l ol blk	7	5
766	A417	4 l chocolate	15	5

Issued to publicize the Third Congress of Bulgarian General Workers' Professional Union.

Dimitrov and Chemical Works
A418

George Dimitrov and V. Chervenkov
A419

Portrait: 80s, Dimitrov.

Photogravure.

1952, June 18 ***Perf. 11*** **Unwmkd.**

767	A418	16s brown	40	25
768	A419	44s brn car	55	30
769	A418	80s brt bl	1.25	60

Issued to commemorate the 70th anniversary of the birth of George Dimitrov.

Vassil Kolarov Dam
A420

Republika Power Station
A421

1952, May 16 ***Perf. 13***

770	A420	4s dk grn	6	5
771	A420	12s purple	9	5
772	A420	16s red brn	13	5
773	A420	44s rose brn	65	10
774	A420	80s brt bl	2.25	25
		Nos. 770-774 (5)	3.18	50

No. 774 is inscribed in Latin characters.

1952, June 30 ***Perf. 13, Pin Perf.***

775	A421	16s dk brn	30	5
776	A421	44s magenta	1.00	15

Nikolai I. Vapzarov
A422

Designs: Various portraits.

1952, July 23 ***Perf. 10½***

777	A422	16s rose brn	20	15
778	A422	44s dk red brn	65	25
779	A422	80s dk ol brn	1.50	80

Issued to commemorate the 10th anniversary of the death of Nikolai I. Vapzarov, poet and revolutionary.

Dimitrov and Youth Conference
A423

Designs: 16s, Resistance movement incident. 44s, Frontier guards and industrial scene. 80s, George Dimitrov and young workers.

1952, Sept. 1 ***Perf. 11x11½***

780	A423	2s brn car	15	5
781	A423	16s purple	20	15
782	A423	44s dk grn	55	40
783	A423	80s dk brn	1.25	85

Issued to commemorate the 40th anniversary of the founding conference of the Union of Social Democratic Youth.

Assault on the Winter Palace
A424

Designs: 8s, Volga-Don Canal. 16s, Symbols of world peace. 44s, Lenin and Stalin. 80s, Himlay hydroelectric station.

Photogravure.

1952, Nov. 6 ***Perf. 11½*** **Unwmkd.**

Dated: "1917-1952."

784	A424	4s red brn	6	5
785	A424	8s dk grn	9	5
786	A424	16s dk bl	13	5
787	A424	44s brown	35	20
788	A424	80s ol brn	80	40
		Nos. 784-788 (5)	1.43	75

Issued to commemorate the 35th anniversary of the Russian revolution.

Vassil Levski
A425

Design: 44s, Levski and comrades.

1953, Feb. 19 Cream Paper ***Perf. 11***

789	A425	16s brown	10	6
790	A425	44s brn blk	25	15

Issued to commemorate the 80th anniversary of the death of Vassil Levski, patriot.

Ferrying Artillery and Troops into Battle
A426

Soldier
A427

Mother and Children
A428

Designs: 44s, Victorious soldiers. 80s, Soldier welcomed. 1 l, Monuments.

1953, Mar. 3 ***Perf. 10½***

791	A426	8s Prus grn	15	5
792	A427	16s dp brn	20	6
793	A426	44s dk sl grn	40	20
794	A426	80s dl red brn	80	50
795	A426	1 l black	1.00	85
		Nos. 791-795 (5)	2.55	1.66

Issued to commemorate the 75th anniversary of Bulgaria's independence from Turkey.

1953, Mar. 9

796	A428	16s sl grn	10	5
797	A428	16s brt bl	10	5

Issued to commemorate Women's Day.

Certain countries cancel stamps in full sheets and sell them (usually with gum) for less than face value. Dealers generally sell "CTO" (canceled to order) stamps for much less than postally used copies.

Woodcarvings at Rila Monastery
A429 A430

Designs: 12s, 16s, 28s, Woodcarvings, Rila Monastery. 44s, Carved Ceilings, Trnovo. 80s, 1 l, 4 l, Carvings, Pasardjik.

Photogravure.

1953 *Perf. 13.* **Unwmkd.**

798	A429	2s gray brn	5	5
799	A430	8s dk sl grn	7	5
800	A430	12s brown	10	5
801	A430	16s rose lake	25	5
802	A429	28s dk ol grn	30	10
803	A430	44s dk brn	50	10
804	A430	80s ultra	85	20
805	A430	1 l vio bl	1.75	30
806	A430	4 l rose lake	3.50	1.25
		Nos. 798-806 (9)	7.37	2.15

Karl Marx A431 "Capital" A432

1953, Apr. 30 *Perf. 10½*

807	A431	16s brt bl	15	10
808	A432	44s dp brn	35	25

70th anniversary of the death of Karl Marx.

Labor Day Parade A433 Joseph V. Stalin A434

1953, Apr. 30 *Perf. 13*

809	A433	16s brn red	20	5

Issued to publicize Labor Day, May 1, 1953.

1953, May 23 *Perf. 13x13½*

810	A434	16s dk gray	20	5
811	A434	16s dk brn	20	5

Death of Joseph V. Stalin, Mar. 5, 1953.

Georgi Delchev A435 Battle Scene A436

Peasants Attacking Turkish Troops—A437

1953, Aug. 8 *Perf. 13*

812	A435	16s dk brn	8	5
813	A436	44s purple	35	20
814	A437	1 l dp cl	50	25

Issued to commemorate the 50th anniversary of the Ilinden Revolt (Nos. 812 and 814) and the Preobrazhene Revolt (No. 813).

Soldier and Rebels
A438

Design: 44s, Soldier guarding industrial construction.

1953, Sept. 18

815	A438	16s dp cl	10	5
816	A438	44s grnsh bl	25	15

Issued to publicize Army Day.

George Dimitrov and Vassil Kolarov A439 Demeter Blagoev A440

Designs: 16s, Citizens in revolt. 44s, Attack.

1953, Sept. 22

817	A439	8s ol gray	10	5
818	A439	16s dk red brn	15	5
819	A439	44s cerise	50	25

September Revolution, 30th anniversary.

1953, Sept. 21

Portraits: 44s, G. Dimitrov and D. Blagoev.

820	A440	16s brown	20	5
821	A440	44s red brn	30	20

Issued to commemorate the 50th anniversary of the formation of the Social Democratic Party.

Railway Viaduct A441 Pouring Molten Metal A442

Designs: 16s, Welder and storage tanks. 80s, Harvesting machine.

1953, Oct. 17

826	A441	8s brt bl	7	5
827	A441	16s grnsh blk	12	5
828	A442	44s brn red	30	18
829	A441	80s orange	50	40

Month of Bulgarian-Russian friendship.

Belladonna A443 Kolarov Library, Sofia A444

Medicinal Flowers: 4s, Jimson weed. 8s, Sage. 12s, Dog rose. 16s, Gentian. 20s, Poppy. 28s, Peppermint. 40s, Bear grass. 44s, Coltsfoot. 80s, Cowslip. 1 l, Dandelion. 2 l, Foxglove.

Photogravure.

1953 *Perf. 13.* **Unwmkd.**

White or Cream Paper

830	A443	2s dl bl	6	5
831	A443	4s brn org	6	5
832	A443	8s bl grn	10	6
833	A443	12s brn org	12	6
834	A443	12s bl grn	12	6
835	A443	16s vio bl	15	8
836	A443	16s dp red brn	15	8
837	A443	20s car rose	20	10
838	A443	28s dk gray grn	40	10
839	A443	40s dk bl	50	25
840	A443	44s brown	50	25
841	A443	80s yel brn	80	50
842	A443	1 l hn brn	3.00	65
843	A443	2 l purple	5.00	1.75
a.		Souvenir sheet	37.50	37.50
		Nos. 830-843 (14)	11.16	4.04

No. 843a contains 12 stamps, one of each denomination above, printed in dark green, with floral border and frame of inscriptions. Size: 161x172mm. Sold for 6 leva.

1953, Dec. 16

854	A444	44s brown	25	15

Issued to commemorate the 75th anniversary of the founding of the Kolarov Library, Sofia.

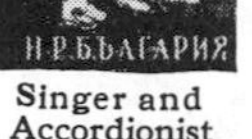

Singer and Accordionist A445 Lenin and Stalin A446

Design: 44s, Dancers.

1953, Dec. 26

855	A445	16s red brn	10	5
856	A445	44s dk grn	25	15

1954, Mar. 13

Designs: 44s, Lenin statue. 80s, Lenin mausoleum, Moscow. 1 l, Lenin.

Cream Paper.

857	A446	16s brown	15	5
858	A446	44s rose brn	25	5
859	A446	80s blue	40	20
860	A446	1 l dp ol grn	55	40

30th anniversary of the death of Lenin.

Demeter Blagoev and Followers
A447

Design: 44s, Blagoev at desk.

1954, Apr. 28 **Cream Paper**

861	A447	16s dp red brn	15	5
862	A447	44s blk brn	40	15

Issued to commemorate the 30th anniversary of the death of Demeter Blagoev.

George Dimitrov A448 Dimitrov and Refinery A449

1954, June 11 **Cream Paper**

863	A448	44s lake	20	8
864	A449	80s brown	45	12

Issued to commemorate the 5th anniversary of the death of George Dimitrov.

Train Leaving Tunnel
A450

1954, July 30 **Cream Paper**

865	A450	44s dk grn	50	15
866	A450	44s blk brn	50	15

Day of the Railroads, Aug. 1, 1954.

Miner at Work
A451

1954, Aug. 19 **Cream Paper**

867	A451	44s grnsh blk	25	10

Issued to publicize Miners' Day.

Academy of Science
A452

1954, Oct. 27 **Cream Paper**

868	A452	80s black	55	25

Issued to commemorate the 85th anniversary of the foundation of the Bulgarian Academy of Science.

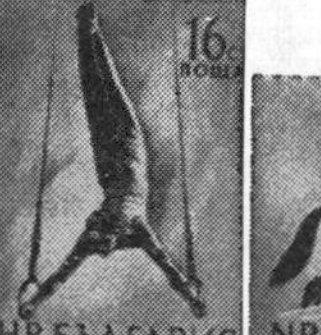

Gymnastics A453 Horsemanship A454

Designs: 44s, Wrestling. 2 l, Skiing.

1954, Dec. 21

869	A453	16s dk gray grn	70	25
870	A453	44s brn red	80	30
871	A454	80s cop brn	1.75	85
872	A453	2 l vio bl	4.00	2.50

Welcoming Liberators A455 Soldier's Return A456

Designs: 28s, Refinery. 44s, Dimitrov and workers. 80s, Girl and boy. 1 l, George Dimitrov.

1954, Oct. 4 **Cream Paper**

873	A455	12s brn car	5	5
874	A456	16s dp car	5	5
875	A455	28s indigo	15	5
876	A455	44s redsh brn	20	5
877	A456	80s dp bl	90	35
878	A456	1 l dk grn	90	35
		Nos. 873-878 (6)	2.25	90

10th anniversary of Bulgaria's liberation.

Recreation at Workers' Rest Home
A457

Metal Worker and Furnace
A458

Portraits: 80s, Dimitrov, Blagoev, and Kirkov.

Photogravure.

1954, Dec. 28 ***Perf. 13*** **Unwmkd.**

Cream Paper

879	A457	16s dk grn	20	5
880	A458	44s brn org	20	6
881	A457	80s dp vio bl	50	25

Issued to commemorate the 50th anniversary of Bulgaria's trade union movement.

Geese
A459

Designs: 4s, Chickens. 12s, Hogs. 16s, Sheep. 28s, Telephone building. 44s, Communist party headquarters. 80s, Apartment buildings. 1 l, St. Kiradgieff Mills.

1955–56

882	A459	2s dk bl grn	10	5
883	A459	4s ol grn	15	5
884	A459	12s dk red brn	25	5
885	A459	16s brn org	45	8
886	A459	28s vio bl	20	6
887	A459	44s lil red, *cr*	40	7
a.		44s brn red	2.50	20
888	A459	80s dk red brn	55	15
889	A459	1 l dk bl grn	1.00	25
		Nos. 882-889 (8)	3.10	76

Issue dates: No. 887, Apr. 20, 1956; others, Feb. 19, 1955.

Textile Worker
A460

Mother and Child
A461

Design: 16s, Woman feeding calf.

1955, Mar. 5

890	A460	12s dk brn	6	5
891	A460	16s dk grn	12	5
892	A461	44s dk car rose	50	10
893	A461	44s blue	50	10

Women's Day, Mar. 8, 1955.

No. 744 Surcharged in Blue.

1955, Mar. 8 ***Perf. 13***

894	A410	16s on 4 l red brn	50	5

May Day Demonstration of Workers
A462

Sts. Cyril and Methodius
A463

Design: 44s, Three workers and globe.

1955, Apr. 23 **Photogravure**

895	A462	16s car rose	9	5
896	A462	44s blue	25	10

Labor Day, May 1, 1955.

1955, May 21 **Cream Paper**

Designs: 8s, Paisii Hilendarski. 16s, Nicolas Karastoyanov's printing press. 28s, Christo Botev. 44s, Ivan Vazov. 80s, Demeter Blagoev and socialist papers. 2 l, Blagoev printing plant, Sofia.

897	A463	4s dp bl	5	5
898	A463	8s olive	5	5
899	A463	16s black	8	5
900	A463	28s hn brn	15	6
901	A463	44s brown	30	8
902	A463	80s rose red	50	25
903	A463	2 l black	1.50	65
		Nos. 897-903 (7)	2.63	1.19

Issued to commemorate the 1100th anniversary of the creation of the Cyrillic alphabet. Latin lettering at bottom on Nos. 901-903.

Sergei Rumyantzev
A464

Mother and Children
A465

Portraits: 16s, Christo Jassenov. 44s, Geo Milev.

Cream Paper

1955, June 30 ***Perf. 13*** **Unwmkd.**

904	A464	12s org brn	15	5
905	A464	16s lt brn	15	5
906	A464	44s grnsh blk	40	20

Issued to commemorate the 25th anniversary of the deaths of Sergei Rumyanchev, Christo Jassenov and Geo Milev. Latin lettering at bottom of No. 906.

1955, July 30 **Cream Paper**

907	A465	44s brn car	30	15

Issued to commemorate the World Congress of Mothers in Lausanne, 1955.

Young People of Three Races
A466

Friedrich Engels and Book
A467

1955, July 30 **Cream Paper**

908	A466	44s blue	30	8

Issued to commemorate the fifth World Festival of Youth in Warsaw, July 31–Aug. 14, 1955.

1955, July 30

909	A467	44s brown	35	15

Issued to commemorate the 60th anniversary of the death of Friedrich Engels.

Entrance to Fair, 1892
A468

Statuary Group at Fair, 1955
A469

Designs: 44s, "Fruit of our Land." 80s, Woman holding Fair emblem.

1955, Aug. 31 **Cream Paper**

910	A468	4s dp brn	5	5
911	A469	16s dk car rose	5	5
912	A468	44s ol blk	20	12
913	A469	80s dp bl	50	20

Issued to commemorate the 16th International Plovdiv Fair. Latin lettering on Nos. 912–913.

Friedrich von Schiller
A470

Portraits: 44s, Adam Mickiewicz. 60s, Hans Christian Andersen. 80s, Baron de Montesquieu. 1 l, Miguel de Cervantes. 2 l, Walt Whitman.

1955, Oct. 31 **Cream Paper**

914	A470	16s brown	10	5
915	A470	44s brn red	40	10
916	A470	60s Prus bl	60	10
917	A470	80s black	65	10
918	A470	1 l rose vio	1.50	45
919	A470	2 l ol grn	1.75	70
		Nos. 914-919 (6)	5.00	1.50

Issued in honor of various anniversaries of famous writers. Nos. 918 and 919 are issued in sheets alternating with labels without franking value. The labels show title pages for Leaves of Grass and Don Quixote in English and Spanish, respectively. Latin lettering on Nos. 915–919.

Karl Marx Industrial Plant
A471

Friendship Monument
A472

I. V. Michurin
A473

Designs: 4s, Alexander Stambolisky Dam. 16s, Bridge over Danube. 1 l, Vladimir V. Mayakovsky.

1955, Dec. 1 **Unwmkd.**

920	A471	2s sl blk	5	5
921	A471	4s dp bl	5	5
922	A471	16s dk bl grn	6	5
923	A472	44s red brn	25	8
924	A473	80s dk grn	40	15
925	A473	1 l gray blk	65	20
		Nos. 920-925 (6)	1.46	58

Issued to publicize Russian-Bulgarian friendship.

Library Seal
A474

Krusto Pishurka
A475

Portrait: 44s, Bacho Kiro.

1956, Feb. 10 ***Perf. 11x10½***

Cream Paper

926	A474	12s car lake	5	5
927	A475	16s dp brn	10	5
928	A475	44s sl blk	35	12

Issued to commemorate the 100th anniversary of the National Library. Latin lettering at bottom of No. 928.

Canceled to Order

Beginning about 1956, some issues were sold in sheets canceled to order. Prices in second column when much less than unused are for "CTO" copies. Postally used stamps are valued at slightly less than, or the same as, unused.

Quinces
A476

Cherrywood Cannon
A477

Designs: 8s, Pears. 16s, Apples. 44s, Grapes.

1956 **Photogravure** ***Perf. 13***

929	A476	4s carmine	1.00	8
930	A476	8s bl grn	45	10
931	A476	16s lil rose	1.10	5
932	A476	44s dp vio	1.10	25

Latin lettering on No. 932. See also Nos. 964–967.

1956, Apr. 28 ***Perf. 11x10½***

Design: 44s, Cavalry attack.

933	A477	16s dk cl	15	5
934	A477	44s dk sl grn	25	10

Issued to commemorate the 80th anniversary of the April (1876) Uprising against Turkish rule.

Demeter Blagoev and Birthplace
A478

Cherries
A479

1956, May 30 ***Perf. 11***

935	A478	44s Prus bl	30	10

Issued to commemorate the centenary of the birth of Demeter Blagoev (1856–1924), writer.

1956 ***Perf. 13*** **Unwmkd.**

Designs: 12s, Plums. 28s, Peaches. 80s, Strawberries.

936	A479	2s rose car	7	5
937	A479	12s blue	15	5
938	A479	28s org brn	30	5
939	A479	80s dp car	90	30

Latin lettering on No. 939.

Gymnastics
A480

Pole Vaulting
A481

Designs: 12s, Discus throw. 44s, Soccer. 80s, Basketball. 1 l, Boxing.

Perf. 11x10½, 10½x11

1956, Aug. 29

No.	Type	Description	Unused	Used
940	A480	4s brt ultra	15	5
941	A480	12s brick red	20	6
942	A481	16s yel brn	35	20
943	A481	44s dk grn	55	30
944	A480	80s dk red brn	1.10	70
945	A481	1 l dp mag	1.75	90
		Nos. 940-945 (6)	4.10	2.21

Latin lettering on Nos. 943–945.
Issued to publicize the forthcoming 16th Olympic Games at Melbourne, Nov. 22–Dec. 8, 1956.

Tobacco, Rose and Distillery
A482

People's Theater
A483

1956, Sept. 1 *Perf. 13*

No.	Type	Description	Unused	Used
946	A482	44s dp car	50	20
947	A482	44s ol grn	50	20

17th International Plovdiv Fair.

1956, Nov. 16 **Unwmkd.**

Design: 44s, Dobri Woinikoff and Sawa Dobroplodni, dramatists.

No.	Type	Description	Unused	Used
948	A483	16s dl red brn	15	6
949	A483	44s dk bl grn	25	10

Bulgarian Theater centenary.

Benjamin Franklin
A484

Cyclists, Palms and Pyramids
A485

Portraits: 20s, Rembrandt. 40s, Mozart. 44s, Heinrich Heine. 60s, G. B. Shaw. 80s, Dostoevski. 1 l, Henrik Ibsen. 2 l, Pierre Curie.

1956, Dec. 29

No.	Type	Description	Unused	Used
950	A484	16s dk ol grn	10	5
951	A484	20s brown	20	5
952	A484	40s dk car rose	20	6
953	A484	44s dk vio brn	25	8
954	A484	60s dk sl	35	15
955	A484	80s dk brn	50	15
956	A484	1 l bluish grn	85	45
957	A484	2 l Prus grn	1.75	80
		Nos. 950-957 (8)	4.20	1.79

Issued in honor of great personalities of the world.

1957, Mar. 6 Photo. *Perf. 10½*

No.	Type	Description	Unused	Used
958	A485	80s hn brn	75	30
959	A485	80s Prus grn	75	30

Fourth Egyptian bicycle race.

Woman Technician
A486

"New Times" Review
A487

Designs: 16s, Woman and children. 44s, Woman feeding chickens.

1957, Mar. 8

No.	Type	Description	Unused	Used
960	A486	12s dp bl	6	5
961	A486	16s hn brn	8	5
962	A486	44s sl grn	30	12

Women's Day, Mar. 8, 1957. Latin lettering on 44s.

1957, Mar. 8 **Unwmkd.**

No.	Type	Description	Unused	Used
963	A487	16s dp car	20	7

Issued to commemorate the 60th anniversary of the founding of the "New Times" review.

Fruit Type of 1956.

Designs: 4s, Quinces. 8s, Pears. 16s, Apples. 44s, Grapes.

1957 Photogravure. *Perf. 13*

No.	Type	Description	Unused	Used
964	A476	4s yel grn	5	5
965	A476	8s brn org	12	5
966	A476	16s rose red	15	5
967	A476	44s org yel	60	10

Latin lettering on No. 967.

Sts. Cyril and Methodius
A488

Basketball
A489

1957, May 22 *Perf. 11*

No.	Type	Description	Unused	Used
968	A488	44s ol grn & buff	50	15

Issued for the centenary of the first public veneration of Sts. Cyril and Methodius, inventors of the Cyrillic alphabet.

1957, June 20 Photo. *Perf. 10½x11*

No.	Type	Description	Unused	Used
969	A489	44s dk grn	1.25	30

Issued to commemorate the 10th European Basketball Championship at Sofia.

Dancer and Spasski Tower, Moscow
A490

1957, July 18 *Perf. 13*

No.	Type	Description	Unused	Used
970	A490	44s blue	35	15

Issued to publicize the Sixth World Youth Festival in Moscow.

George Dimitrov—A491

1957, July 18

No.	Type	Description	Unused	Used
971	A491	44s dp car	45	15

75th anniversary of the birth of George Dimitrov (1882–1949).

Vassil Levski
A492

1957, July 18 *Perf. 11*

No.	Type	Description	Unused	Used
972	A492	44s grnsh blk	45	15

Issued to commemorate the 120th anniversary of the birth of Vassil Levski, patriot and national hero.

No. 742 Surcharged in Carmine.

1957 *Perf. 13* **Unwmkd.**

No.	Type	Description	Unused	Used
973	A408	16s on 1 l pur	10	5

Trnovo and Lazarus L. Zamenhof
A493

1957, July 27

No.	Type	Description	Unused	Used
974	A493	44s sl grn	65	20

Issued to commemorate the 50th anniversary of the Bulgarian Esperanto Society and the 70th anniversary of Esperanto.

Bulgarian Veteran of 1877 War and Russian Soldier
A494

Design: 44s, Battle of Shipka Pass.

1957, Aug. 13

No.	Type	Description	Unused	Used
975	A494	16s dk bl grn	15	5
976	A494	44s brown	40	7

Issued to commemorate the 80th anniversary of Bulgaria's liberation from the Turks. Latin lettering on No. 976.

Woman Planting Tree
A495

Red Deer in Forest
A496

Designs: 16s, Dam, lake and forest. 44s, Plane over forest. 80s, Fields on edge of forest.

1957, Sept. 16 Photo. *Perf. 13*

No.	Type	Description	Unused	Used
977	A495	2s dp grn	5	5
978	A496	12s dk brn	7	5
979	A496	16s Prus bl	8	5
980	A496	44s Prus grn	20	8
981	A496	80s yel grn	40	20
		Nos. 977-981 (5)	80	43

Latin lettering on Nos. 980 and 981.

Lenin
A497

Designs: 16s, Cruiser "Aurora." 44s, Dove over map of communist area. 60s, Revolutionaries and banners. 80s, Oil refinery.

1957, Oct. 29 *Perf. 11*

No.	Type	Description	Unused	Used
982	A497	12s chocolate	15	5
983	A497	16s Prus grn	30	5
984	A497	44s dp bl	60	12
985	A497	60s dk car rose	70	25
986	A497	80s dk grn	1.25	35
		Nos. 982-986 (5)	3.00	82

Issued to commemorate the 40th anniversary of the Communist Revolution.
Latin lettering on Nos. 984–985.

Globes
A498

1957, Oct. 4 *Perf. 13*

No.	Type	Description	Unused	Used
987	A498	44s Prus bl	30	18

Issued to commemorate the fourth International Trade Union Congress, Leipzig, Oct. 4-15.

Vassil Kolarov Hotel
A499

Health Resorts: 4s, Skis and Pirin Mountains. 8s, Old house at Koprivspitsa. 12s, Rest home at Velingrad. 44s, Momin-Prochod Hotel. 60s, Nesebr Hotel, shoreline and peninsula. 80s, Varna beach scene. 1 l, Hotel at Varna.

1958 Photogravure *Perf. 13*

No.	Type	Description	Unused	Used
988	A499	4s blue	5	5
989	A499	8s org brn	6	5
990	A499	12s dk grn	6	5
991	A499	16s green	10	5
992	A499	44s dk bl grn	18	8
993	A499	60s dp bl	30	12
994	A499	80s fawn	45	20
995	A499	1 l dk red brn	55	30
		Nos. 988-995 (8)	1.75	90

Issued to publicize various Bulgarian health resorts. Latin lettering on 44s, 60s, 80s, and 1 l.
Issue dates: Nos. 991–994, Jan. 20. Others, July 5.

Mikhail I. Glinka
A500

Portraits: 16s, Jan A. Komensky (Comenius). 40s, Carl von Linné. 44s, William Blake. 60s, Carlo Goldoni. 80s, Auguste Comte.

1957, Dec. 30

No.	Type	Description	Unused	Used
996	A500	12s dk brn	20	5
997	A500	16s dk grn	20	5
998	A500	40s Prus bl	20	7
999	A500	44s maroon	20	10
1000	A500	60s org brn	70	20
1001	A500	80s dp plum	2.50	1.25
		Nos. 996-1001 (6)	4.00	1.72

Issued to honor famous men of other countries. Latin lettering on Nos. 999–1001.

Young Couple, Flag, Dimitrov
A501

People's Front Salute
A502

1957, Dec. 28 ***Perf. 11***

1002 A501 16s car rose 15 7

Issued to commemorate the 10th anniversary of Dimitrov's Union of the People's Youth.

1957, Dec. 28

1003 A502 16s dk vio brn 15 7

15th anniversary of the People's Front.

Hare
A503

Animals: 12s, Red deer (doe) (vert.). 16s, Red deer (stag). 44s, Chamois. 80s, Brown bear. 1 l, Wild boar.

Photogravure.

1958, Apr. 5 ***Perf. 10½*** **Unwmkd.**

1004 A503 2s lt & dk ol grn 6 5
1005 A503 12s sl grn & red brn 15 5
1006 A503 16s bluish grn & dk red brn 18 5
1007 A503 44s bl & brn 25 10
1008 A503 80s bis & dk brn 75 20
1009 A503 1 l stl bl & dk brn 1.10 35
Nos. 1004-1009 (6) 2.49 80

Price, imperf. set $4.

Marx and Lenin—A504

Designs: 16s, Marchers and flags. 44s, Lenin blast furnaces.

1958, July 2 ***Perf. 11***

1010 A504 12s dk brn 12 5
1011 A504 16s dk car 15 5
1012 A504 44s dk bl 60 15

Issued to commemorate the 7th Congress of the Bulgarian Communist Party.

Wrestlers
A505

1958, June 20 ***Perf. 10½***

1013 A505 60s dk car rose 85 50
1014 A505 80s dp brn 1.25 75

World Wrestling Championship, Sofia.

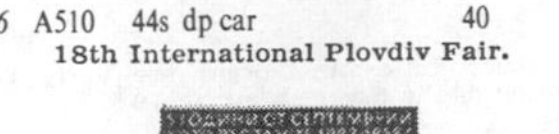

Chessmen and Globe
A506

Photogravure

1958, July 18 ***Perf. 10½*** **Unwmkd.**

1015 A506 80s grn & yel grn 1.75 1.25

5th World Students' Chess Games, Varna.

Conference Emblem
A507

1958, Sept. 24

1016 A507 44s blue 35 15

Issued to commemorate the World Trade Union Conference of Working Youth, Prague, July 14–20.

Swimmer
A508

Designs: 28s, Dancer (vertical). 44s, Volleyball (vertical).

1958, Sept. 19 ***Perf. 11x10½***

1017 A508 16s brt bl 15 7
1018 A508 28s brn org 30 15
1019 A508 44s brt grn 45 15

1958 Students' Games.

Onions
A509

Vegetables: 12s, Garlic. 16s, Peppers. 44s, Tomatoes. 80s, Cucumbers. 1 l, Eggplant.

1958, Sept. 20 ***Perf. 13***

1020 A509 2s org brn 5 5
1021 A509 12s Prus bl 5 5
1022 A509 16s dk grn 6 5
1023 A509 44s dp car 15 5
1024 A509 80s dp grn 40 12
1025 A509 1 l brt pur 65 15
Nos. 1020-1025 (6) 1.36 47

See No. 1072.

Price, imperf. set $3.50.

Plovdiv Fair Building
A510

1958, Sept. 14 ***Perf. 11*** **Unwmkd.**

1026 A510 44s dp car 40 12

18th International Plovdiv Fair.

Attack
A511

Design: 44s, Fighter dragging wounded man.

1958, Sept. 23 **Photo.** ***Perf. 11***

1027 A511 16s org ver 12 6
1028 A511 44s lake 35 10

Issued to commemorate the 35th anniversary of the September Revolution.

Emblem, Brussels Fair
A512

1958, Oct. 13 ***Perf. 11***

1029 A512 1 l blk & brt bl 2.50 2.50

Brussels World's Fair, Apr. 17-Oct. 19.

Price imperf. $10.

Runner at Finish Line
A513

Woman Throwing Javelin
A514

Sports: 60s, High jumper. 80s, Hurdler. 4 l, Shot putter.

1958, Nov. 30

1030 A513 16s red brn, *pnksh* 35 20
1031 A514 44s ol, *yelsh* 35 20
1032 A514 60s dk bl, *bluish* 65 30
1033 A514 80s dp grn, *grnsh* 80 30
1034 A513 4 l dp rose cl, *pnksh* 5.50 2.25
Nos. 1030-1034 (5) 7.65 3.25

1958 Balkan Games.
Latin lettering on Nos. 1032–1033.

Christo Smirnenski
A515

1958, Dec. 22

1035 A515 16s dk car 15 6

Issued to commemorate the 60th anniversary of the birth of Christo Smirnenski, poet, 1898–1923.

Girls Harvesting
A516

Girl Tending Calves
A517

Designs: 16s, Boy and girl laborers. 40s, Boy pushing wheelbarrow. 44s, Headquarters building.

1959, Nov. 29 **Photogravure**

1036 A516 8s dk ol grn 5 5
1037 A517 12s redsh brn 7 5
1038 A516 16s vio brn 8 5
1039 A517 40s Prus bl 15 5
1040 A516 44s dp car 75 20
Nos. 1036-1040 (5) 1.10 40

Issued to commemorate the 4th Congress of Dimitrov's Union of People's Youth.

UNESCO Building, Paris
A518

1959, Mar. 28 ***Perf. 11*** **Unwmkd.**

1041 A518 2 l dp red lil, *cr* 1.50 1.25

Opening of UNESCO Headquarters, Paris, Nov. 3, 1958.

Price imperf. $4.50.

Skier
A519

Soccer Players
A520

1959, Mar. 28 ***Perf. 11***

1042 A519 1 l bl, *cr* 1.50 60

Forty years of skiing in Bulgaria.

1959, Mar. 25

1043 A520 2 l chnt, *cr* 1.75 1.00

Issued to commemorate the 1959 European Youth Soccer Championship.

Russian Soldiers Installing Telegraph Wires
A251

First Bulgarian Postal Coach
A522

Designs: 60s, Stamp of 1879. 80s, First Bulgarian automobile. 1 l, Television tower. 2 l, Strike of railroad and postal workers, 1919.

1959, May 4

1044	A521	12s dk grn & cit	8	5
1045	A522	16s dp plum	12	5
1046	A521	60s dk brn & yel	30	10
1047	A522	80s hn brn & sal	40	20
1048	A521	1 l blue	60	25
1049	A522	2 l dk red brn	1.50	1.25
		Nos. 1044-1049 (6)	3.00	1.90

Issued to commemorate the 80th anniversary of the Bulgarian post. Latin lettering on Nos. 1046–1049.

Two imperf. souvenir sheets exist with olive borders and inscriptions. One contains one copy of No. 1046 in black & ochre, and measures 92x121mm. The other sheet contains one copy each of Nos. 1044–1045 and 1047–1048 in changed colors: 12s, olive green & ochre; 16s, deep claret & ochre; 80s, dark red & ochre; 1 l, olive & ochre. Each sheet sold for 5 leva.

Price, each $30.

Great Tits—A523

Birds: 8s, Hoopoe. 16s, Great spotted woodpecker (vert.). 45s, Gray partridge (vert.) 60s, Rock partridge. 80s, European cuckoo.

1959, June 30 **Photogravure**

1050	A523	2s ol & sl grn	5	5
1051	A523	8s dp org & blk	7	5
1052	A523	16s chnt & dk brn	15	10
1053	A523	45s brn & blk	20	15
1054	A523	60s dp bl & gray	45	20
1055	A523	80s dp bl grn & gray	80	30
		Nos. 1050-1055 (6)	1.72	85

Bagpiper
A524

Designs: 12s, Acrobats. 16s, Girls exercising with hoops. 20s, Male dancers. 80s, Ballet dancers. 1 l, Ceramic pitcher. 16s, 20s, 80s are horizontal.

1959, Aug. 29 ***Perf. 11*** **Unwmkd.**

Surface-colored Paper.

1056	A524	4s dk ol	5	5
1057	A524	12s scarlet	5	5
1058	A524	16s maroon	7	5
1059	A524	20s dk bl	25	10
1060	A524	80s brt grn	50	25
1061	A524	1 l brn org	85	40
		Nos. 1056-1061 (6)	1.77	90

Issued to publicize the 7th International Youth Festival, Vienna. Latin inscriptions on Nos. 1060–1061.

Partisans in Truck
A525

Designs: 16s, Partisans and soldiers shaking hands. 45s, Refinery. 60s, Tanks. 80s, Harvester. 1.25 l, Children with flag (vert.).

1959, Sept. 8

1062	A525	12s red & Prus grn	5	5
1063	A525	16s red & dk pur	6	5
1064	A525	45s red & int bl	10	5
1065	A525	60s red & ol grn	15	8
1066	A525	80s red & brn	40	15
1067	A525	1.25 l red & dp brn	1.10	45
		Nos. 1062-1067 (6)	1.86	83

15th anniversary of Bulgarian liberation.

Soccer—A526

1959, Oct. 10 ***Perf. 11.*** **Unwmkd.**

1068	A526	1.25 l dp grn, *yel*	5.00	3.50

50 years of Bulgarian soccer.

Price, set imperf. in changed colors, $10 unused, $6 canceled.

Batak Defenders
A527

1959, Aug. 8

1069	A527	16s dp cl	20	10

Issued to commemorate the 300th anniversary of the settlement of Batak.

Post Horn and Letter
A528

Bird-shaped Lyre
A529

Design: 1.25 l, Dove and letter.

1959, Nov. 23

1070	A528	45s emer & blk	35	10
1071	A528	1.25 l lt bl, red & blk	65	30

Issued for International Letter Writing Week Oct. 5-11.

Type of 1958 Surcharged "45 CT." in Dark Blue.

Design: Tomatoes.

1959 **Photogravure** ***Perf. 13***

1072	A509	45s on 44s scar	65	15

1960, Feb. 23 ***Perf. 10½*** **Unwmkd.**

Design: 1.25 l, Lyre.

1073	A529	80s emer & blk	45	15
1074	A529	1.25 l brt red & blk	75	30

Issued to commemorate the 50th anniversary of Bulgaria's State Opera.

N. I. Vapzarov
A530

Parachute and Radio Tower
A531

1959, Dec. 14 ***Perf. 11***

1075	A530	80s yel grn & red brn	40	12

Issued to commemorate the 50th anniversary of the birth of N. I. Vapzarov, poet and patriot.

1959, Dec. 3 **Photogravure**

1076	A531	1.25 l dp grnsh bl & yel	1.75	75

Issued to publicize the third Congress of Voluntary Participants in Defense.

Cotton Picker
A532

Harvester Combine
A533

Designs: 2s, Kindergarten. 4s, Woman doctor and child. 10s, Woman milking cow. 12s, Woman holding tobacco leaves. 15s, Woman working loom. 16s, Stalin textile mill, Dimitrovgrad. 25s, Rural electrification. 28s, Woman picking sunflowers. 40s, "Cold-well" hydroelectric dam. 45s, Miner. 60s, Foundry worker. 80s. Woman harvesting grapes. 1 l, Worker and peasant with cogwheel. 1.25 l, Industrial worker. 2 l, Party leader.

1959-61 **Photogravure** ***Perf. 13***

1077	A533	2s brn org ('60)	5	5
1077A	A532	4s gldn brn ('61)	5	5
1078	A532	5s dk grn	5	5
1079	A533	10s red brn ('61)	5	5
1080	A532	12s red brn	5	5
1081	A532	15s red lil ('60)	6	5
1082	A533	16s dp vio ('60)	6	5
1083	A533	20s orange	8	5
1084	A532	25s brt bl ('60)	8	5
1085	A532	28s brt grn	15	5
1086	A533	40s brt grnsh bl	25	5
1087	A532	45s choc ('60)	20	5
1088	A533	60s scarlet	35	10
1089	A532	80s ol ('60)	45	12
1090	A532	1 l maroon	45	12
1090A	A533	1.25 l dl bl ('61)	1.50	40
1091	A532	2 l dp car ('60)	1.00	30
		Nos. 1077-1091 (17)	4.88	1.64

Issued to commemorate the early completion of the 5-year plan (in 1959).

L. L. Zamenhof
A534

Path of Lunik 3
A535

1959, Dec. 5 ***Perf. 11*** **Unwmkd.**

1092	A534	1.25 l dk grn & yel grn	75	50

Lazarus Ludwig Zamenhof (1859-1917), inventor of Esperanto.

1960, Mar. 28 ***Perf. 11***

1093	A535	1.25 l Prus bl & brt yel	4.50	3.50

Flight of Lunik 3 around moon.
Price, imperf. $9.

Skier
A536

1960, Apr. 15 **Lithographed**

1094	A536	2 l ultra, blk & brn	1.50	50

8th Winter Olympics, Squaw Valley, CA, Feb. 18-29.

Price, imperf. $4 unused, $2 canceled.

Vela Blagoeva
A537

Portraits: 28s, Anna Maimunkova. 45s, Vela Piskova. 60s, Rosa Luxemburg. 80s, Klara Zetkin. 1.25 l, N. K. Krupskaya.

1960, Apr. 27 **Photo.** ***Perf. 11***

1095	A537	16s rose & red brn	5	5
1096	A537	28s cit & ol	8	5
1097	A537	45s ol grn & sl grn	20	5
1098	A537	60s lt bl & Prus bl	20	10
1099	A537	80s red org & dp brn	35	15
1100	A537	1.25 l dl yel & ol	60	25
		Nos. 1095-1100 (6)	1.48	65

International Women's Day, Mar. 8, 1960.

Lenin
A538

Design: 45s, Lenin sitting.

1960, May 12

1101	A538	16s red brn	35	20
1102	A538	45s sal pink & blk	75	30

90th anniversary of the birth of Lenin.

Women Playing Basketball
A539

1960, June 3 *Perf. 11*

1103	A539	1.25 l yel & sl grn	1.25	50

Issued to commemorate the seventh European Women's Basketball championships.

Parachutist
A541

Design: 1.25 l, Parachutes.

1960, June 29 **Lithographed**

1105	A541	16s lil & dk bl	60	30
1106	A541	1.25 l bl & cl	1.50	45

Issued to commemorate the 5th International Parachute Championships.

Yellow Gentian
A542

Flowers: 5s, Tulips. 25s, Turk's-cap lily. 45s, Rhododendron. 60s, Lady's-slipper. 80s, Violets.

1960, July 27 Photo. *Perf. 11*

1107	A542	2s beige, grn & yel	15	5
1108	A542	5s yel grn, grn & car rose	15	5
1109	A542	25s pink, grn & org	20	5
1110	A542	45s pale lil, grn & rose lil	35	15
1111	A542	60s yel, grn & org	75	15
1112	A542	80s gray, grn & vio bl	90	35
		Nos. 1107-1112 (6)	2.50	80

Soccer
A543

Sports: 12s, Wrestling. 16s, Weight lifting. 45s, Woman gymnast. 80s, Canoeing. 2 l, Runner.

1960, Aug. 29 *Perf. 11* **Unwmkd.**

Athletes' Figures in Pink

1113	A543	8s brown	5	5
1114	A543	12s violet	5	5
1115	A543	16s Prus bl	8	8
1116	A543	45s dp plum	20	10
1117	A543	80s blue	30	20
1118	A543	2 l dp grn	1.10	50
		Nos. 1113-1118 (6)	1.78	98

17th Olympic Games, Rome, Aug. 25-Sept. 11. Price, set imperf. in changed colors, $7.

Globes
A544

Photogravure

1960, Oct. 12 *Perf. 11* **Unwmkd.**

1125	A544	1.25 l bl & ultra	60	30

Issued to commemorate the 15th anniversary of the World Federation of Trade Unions.

Alexander Popov
A545

1960, Oct. 12

1126	A545	90s bl & blk	75	20

Issued to commemorate the centenary of the birth of Alexander Popov, radio pioneer.

Bicyclists
A546

1960, Sept. 22

1127	A546	1 l yel, red org & blk	1.25	75

The 10th Tour of Bulgaria Bicycle Race.

Jaroslav Vésin
A547

1960, Nov. 22 *Perf. 11* **Unwmkd.**

1128	A547	1 l brt cit & ol grn	2.25	1.00

Birth centenary of Jaroslav Vésin, painter.

U.N. Headquarters
A548

Costume of Kyustendil
A549

1961, Jan. 14 Photo. *Perf. 11*

1129	A548	1 l brn & yel	1.25	75
a.		Souvenir sheet	5.50	5.50

15th anniv. of the UN. No. 1129 sold for 2 l. Price, imperf. $4.50.

No. 1129a sold for 2.50 l and contains one copy of No. 1129, imperf. in dark olive and pink with orange marginal inscription. Size: 74x58mm.

1961, Jan. 28

Designs (Regional Costumes): 16s, Pleven. 28s, Sliven. 45s, Sofia. 60s, Rhodope. 80s, Karnobat.

1130	A549	12s sal, sl grn & yel	10	5
1131	A549	16s pale lil, brn vio & buff	10	5
1132	A549	28s pale grn, sl grn & rose	15	7
1133	A549	45s bl & red	30	8
1134	A549	60s grnsh bl, Prus bl & yel	50	15
1135	A549	80s yel, sl grn & pink	65	30
		Nos. 1130-1135 (6)	1.80	70

Theodor Tiro (Fresco)
A550

Designs: 60s, Boyana Church. 1.25 l, Duchess of Dessislava (fresco).

1961, Jan. 28 **Photogravure**

1136	A550	60s yel grn, blk & grn	50	15
1137	A550	80s yel, sl grn & org	50	15
1138	A550	1.25 l yel grn, hn brn & buff	1.00	35

700th anniversary of murals in Boyana Church.

Clock Tower, Vratsa
A551

Wooden Jug
A552

Designs: 12s, Clock tower, Bansko. 20s, Anguchev House, Mogilitsa. 28s, Oslekov House, Koprivspitsa (horiz.). 40s, Pasha's house, Melnik (horiz.). 45s, Lion sculpture. 60s, Man on horseback, Madara. 80s, Fresco, Bratchkovo monastery. 1 l, Tsar Assen coin.

1961, Feb. 25 *Perf. 11* **Unwmkd.**

Denomination and Stars in Vermilion.

1139	A551	8s ol grn	5	5
1140	A551	12s lt vio	5	5
1141	A552	16s dk red brn	5	5
1142	A551	20s brt bl	5	5
1143	A551	28s grnsh bl	8	5
1144	A551	40s red brn	12	7
1145	A552	45s ol gray	15	8
1146	A552	60s slate	30	10
1147	A552	80s dk ol gray	50	12
1148	A552	1 l green	65	25
		Nos. 1139-1148 (10)	2.00	87

Capercaillie
A553

Birds: 4s, Dalmatian pelican. 16s, Ring-necked pheasant. 80s, Great bustard. 1 l, Lammergeier. 2 l, Hazel hen.

1961, March 31

1149	A553	2s blk, sal & Prus grn	5	5
1150	A553	4s blk, yel grn & org	5	5
1151	A553	16s brn, lt grn & org	7	5
1152	A553	80s brn, bluish grn & yel	35	5
1153	A553	1 l blk, lt bl & yel	50	18
1154	A553	2 l brn, bl & yel	1.25	60
		Nos. 1149-1154 (6)	2.27	98

Radio Tower and Winged Anchor
A554

1961, Apr. 1 *Perf. 11* **Unwmkd.**

1155	A554	80s brt grn & blk	45	15

Issued to commemorate the 50th anniversary of the Transport Workers' Union.

T. G. Shevchenko
A555

Water Polo
A556

1961, Apr. 27

1156	A555	1 l ol & blk	2.00	1.00

Issued to commemorate the centenary of the death of Taras G. Shevchenko, Ukrainian poet.

1961, May 15

Designs: 5s, Tennis. 16s, Fencing. 45s, Throwing the discus. 1.25 l, Sports Palace. 2 l, Basketball. 5 l, Sports Palace, different view. 5s, 16s, 45s and 1.25 l, are horizontal.

Black Inscriptions

1157	A556	4s lt ultra	5	5
1158	A556	5s org ver	5	5
1159	A556	16s ol grn	15	5
1160	A556	45s dl bl	20	6
1161	A556	1.25 l yel brn	75	20
1162	A556	2 l lilac	95	45
		Nos. 1157-1162 (6)	2.15	86

Souvenir Sheet

Imperf.

1163	A556	5 l yel grn, dl bl & yel	10.00	10.00

Nos. 1157–1163 were issued to publicize the 1961 World University Games, Sofia, Aug. 26–Sept. 3.

No. 1163 measures 66x66mm.

Price, #1157-1162 in changed colors, imperf. $6.

Monk Seal—A557

Black Sea Fauna: 12s, Jellyfish. 16s, Dolphin. 45s, Black Sea sea horse (vert.). 1 l, Starred sturgeon. 1.25 l, Thornback ray.

1961, June 19 ***Perf. 11***

1164	A557	2s grn & blk	5	5
1165	A557	12s Prus grn & pink	5	5
1166	A557	16s ultra & vio bl	6	5
1167	A557	45s lt bl & brn	18	5
1168	A557	1 l yel grn & Prus grn	50	20
1169	A557	1.25 l lt vio bl & red brn	90	35
		Nos. 1164-1169 (6)	1.74	75

Hikers

A558

Designs: 4s, "Sredetz" hostel (horiz.). 16s, Tents. 1.25 l, Mountain climber.

1961, Aug. 25 **Litho.** ***Perf. 11***

1170	A558	4s yel grn, yel & blk	5	5
1171	A558	12s lt bl, cr & blk	5	5
1172	A558	16s grn, cr & blk	6	5
1173	A558	1.25 l bis, cr & blk	60	10

"Know Your Country" campaign.

Demeter Blagoev Addressing 1891 Congress at Busludja

A559

1961, Aug. 5 **Photogravure**

1174	A559	45s dk red & buff	20	15
1175	A559	80s bl & pink	35	20
1176	A559	2 l dk brn & pale cit	80	40

Issued to commemorate the 70th anniversary of the first Congress of the Bulgarian Social-Democratic Party.

The Golden Girl

A560

Fairy Tales: 8s, The Living Water. 12s, The Golden Apple. 16s, Krali-Marko, hero. 45s, Samovila-Vila, Witch. 80s, Tom Thumb.

1961, Oct. 10 ***Perf. 11*** **Unwmkd.**

1177	A560	2s bl, blk & org	15	5
1178	A560	8s rose lil, blk & gray	20	5
1179	A560	12s bl grn, blk & pink	20	5
1180	A560	16s red, blk, bl & gray	35	20
1181	A560	45s ol grn, blk & pink	65	30
1182	A560	80s ocher, blk & dk car	1.00	40
		Nos. 1177-1182 (6)	2.55	1.05

Caesar's Mushroom

A561

Miladinov Brothers and Title Page

A562

Designs: Various mushrooms.

1961, Dec. 20 **Photo.** ***Perf. 11***

Denominations in Black

1183	A561	2s lem & red	5	5
1184	A561	4s ol grn & red brn	5	5
1185	A561	12s bis & red brn	5	5
1186	A561	16s lil & red brn	5	5
1187	A561	45s car rose & yel	15	7
1188	A561	80s brn org & sep	30	15
1189	A561	1.25 l vio & dk brn	65	20
1190	A561	2 l org brn & brn	1.10	50
		Nos. 1183-1190 (8)	2.40	1.12

Price, denomination in dark grn, imperf. set $5 unused, $3 canceled.

1961, Dec. 21 ***Perf. 10½*** **Unwmkd.**

1191	A562	1.25 l ol & blk	50	15

Issued to commemorate the centenary of the publication of "Collected Folksongs" by the Brothers Miladinov, Dimitri and Konstantin.

Nos. 1079-1085, 1087, 992, 1023, 1090-1091 and 806 Surcharged with New Value in Black, Red or Violet.

1962, Jan. 1

1192	A533	1s on 10s red brn	5	5
1193	A532	1s on 12s red brn	5	5
1194	A532	2s on 15s red lil	7	5
1195	A533	2s on 16s dp vio (R)	7	5
1196	A533	2s on 20s org	7	5
a.		"2 CT." on 2 lines	7	5
1197	A532	3s on 25s brt bl (R)	10	5
a.		Black surch.	7.50	5.50
1198	A532	3s on 28s brt grn (R)	12	5
1199	A532	5s on 45s choc	15	5
1200	A499	5s on 44s dk bl grn (R)	15	10
1201	A509	5s on 44s dp car (V)	15	10
1202	A532	10s on 1 l mar	25	15
1203	A532	20s on 2 l dp car	65	25
1204	A430	40s on 4 l rose lake (V)	1.50	55
		Nos. 1192-1204 (13)	3.38	1.55

Freighter "Varna"

A563

Designs: 5s, Tanker "Komsomoletz." 20s, Liner "G. Dimitrov."

1962, Mar. 1 **Photo.** ***Perf. 10½***

1205	A563	1s lt grn & brt bl	5	5
1206	A563	5s lt bl & grn	20	6
1207	A563	20s gray bl & grnsh bl	75	20

Dimitrov working as Printer

A564

Roses

A565

Design: 13s, Griffin, emblem of state printing works.

1962, March 19 **Unwmkd.**

1208	A564	2s ver, blk & yel	5	5
1209	A564	13s red org, blk & yel	45	15

Issued to commemorate the 80th anniversary (in 1961) of the George Dimitrov state printing works.

1962, March 28

Various Roses in Natural Colors

1210	A565	1s dp vio	5	5
1211	A565	2s sal & dk car	5	5
1212	A565	3s gray & car	8	5
1213	A565	4s dk grn	15	5
1214	A565	5s ultra	20	10
1215	A565	6s bluish grn & dk car	45	20
1216	A565	8s cit & car	1.00	30
1217	A565	13s blue	2.00	1.00
		Nos. 1210-1217 (8)	3.98	1.80

Malaria Eradication Emblem and Mosquito—A566

Design: 20s, Malaria eradication emblem.

1962, Apr. 19

1218	A566	5s org brn, yel & blk	45	15
1219	A566	20s emer, yel & blk	90	40

WHO drive to eradicate malaria.
Price, imperf. $4.50 unused, $2.50 canceled.

Lenin and First Issue of Pravda

A567

1962, May 4 ***Perf. 10*** **Unwmkd.**

1220	A567	5s dp rose & sl	50	20

Issued to commemorate the 50th anniversary of Pravda, Russian newspaper founded by Lenin.

Blackboard and Book

A568

1962, May 21 **Photogravure**

1221	A568	5s Prus bl, blk & yel	20	6

The 1962 Teachers' Congress.

Soccer Player and Globe

A569

1962, May 26 ***Perf. 10½***

1222	A569	13s brt grn, blk & lt brn	1.00	35

World Soccer Championship, Chile, May 30-June 17.

Price, imperf. in changed colors, $5 unused, $3 canceled.

George Dimitrov

A570

1962, June 18 **Photogravure**

1223	A570	2s dk grn	15	5
1224	A570	5s turq bl	45	15

Issued to commemorate the 80th anniversary of the birth of George Dimitrov (1882–1949), communist leader and premier of the Bulgarian Peoples' Republic.

Bishop

A571

Chessmen: 2s, Rook. 3s, Queen. 13s, Knight. 20s, Pawn.

1962, July 7 ***Perf. 10½*** **Unwmkd.**

1225	A571	1s gray, emer & blk	5	5
1226	A571	2s gray, lem & blk	5	5
1227	A571	3s gray, lil & blk	10	5
1228	A571	13s gray, dk org & blk	55	20
1229	A571	20s gray, bl & blk	1.00	40
		Nos. 1225-1229 (5)	1.75	75

Issued to commemorate the 15th Chess Olympics, Varna. Nos. 1225–1229 were also issued imperf. in changed colors.

An imperf. souvenir sheet contains one 20s horizontal stamp showing five chessmen. Lilac and gray border of sea horses and waves. Size: 75x66mm.

Rila Mountain
A572

Designs: 2s, Pirin mountain. 6s, Nesebr, Black Sea. 8s, Danube. 13s, Vidin Castle. 1 l, Rhodope mountain.

1962-63 *Perf. 13*

1230	A572	1s dk bl grn	5	5
1231	A572	2s blue	6	5
1232	A572	6s grnsh bl	15	5
[illegible]	[illegible]	[illegible]	[illegible]	[illegible]
1234	A572	13s yel grn	50	15
1234A	A572	1 l dp grn ('63)	4.00	50
		Nos. 1230-1234A (6)	4.96	85

XXXV КОНГРЕС
1962

No. 974 Surcharged in Red

13 =

1962, July 14 *Perf. 13*

1235	A493	13s on 44s sl grn	2.25	1.25

Issued to commemorate the 25th Bulgarian Esperanto Congress, Burgas, July 14-16.

Girl and Festival Emblem
A573

Design: 5s, Festival emblem.

1962, Aug. 18 Photo. *Perf. 10½*

1236	A573	5s grn, lt bl & pink	20	6
1237	A573	13s lil, lt bl & gray	45	10

Issued to commemorate the 8th Youth Festival for Peace and Friendship, Helsinki, July 28-Aug. 6, 1962.

Parnassius Apollo—A574

1962, Sept. 13

Various Butterflies in Natural Colors

1238	A574	1s pale cit & dk grn	5	5
1239	A574	2s rose & brn	7	5
1240	A574	3s buff & red brn	10	5
1241	A574	4s gray & brn	12	5
1242	A574	5s lt gray & brn	15	5
1243	A574	6s gray & blk	20	5
1244	A574	10s pale grn & blk	95	30
1245	A574	13s buff & red brn	1.50	50
		Nos. 1238-1245 (8)	3.14	1.10

Planting Machine—A575

Designs: 2s, Electric locomotive. 3s, Blast furnace. 13s, Blagoev and Dimitrov and Communist flag.

1962, Nov. 1 *Perf. 11½*

1246	A575	1s bl grn & dk ol grn	5	5
1247	A575	2s bl & Prus bl	7	5
1248	A575	3s car & brn	15	5
1249	A575	13s plum, red & blk	45	20

Bulgarian Communist Party, 8th Congress.

Title Page of "Slav-Bulgarian History"
A576

Paisii Hilendarski Writing History
A577

1962, Dec. 8 *Perf. 10½* **Unwmkd.**

1250	A576	2s ol grn & blk	7	5
1251	A577	5s brn org & blk	25	5

Issued to commemorate the 200th anniversary of "Slav-Bulgarian History"

Aleco Konstantinov
A578

1963, Mar. 5 Photo. *Perf. 11½*

1252	A578	5s red, grn & blk	20	10

Issued to commemorate the centenary of the birth of Aleco Konstantinov (1863-1897), writer. Printed with alternating red brown and black label showing Bai Ganu, hero from Konstantinov's books.

Arms of Bulgaria
A579

Sofia University
A580

Designs: No. 1255, Levski Stadium, Sofia. No. 1256, Arch, Nissaria. No. 1257, Parachutist.

1963, Feb. 20 *Perf. 10* **Unwmkd.**

1253	A579	1s brn red	5	5
1254	A580	1s red brn	5	5
1255	A580	1s bl grn	5	5
1256	A580	1s dk grn	5	5
1257	A580	1s brt bl	5	5
		Nos. 1253-1257 (5)	25	25

Vassil Levski
A581

Boy, Girl and Dimitrov
A582

1963, Apr. 11 Photogravure

1258	A581	13s grnsh bl & buff	75	25

Issued to commemorate the 90th anniversary of the death of Vassil Levski, revolutionary leader in the fight for liberation from the Turks.

1963, Apr. 25 *Perf. 11½* **Unwmkd.**

Design: 13s, Girl with book and boy with hammer.

1259	A582	2s org, ver, red brn & blk	8	5
1260	A582	13s bluish grn, brn & blk	45	10

Issued to commemorate the 10th Congress of Dimitrov's Union of the People's Youth.

Red Squirrel
A583

Sun Coast Promenade
A584

Animals: 2s, Hedgehog. 3s, European polecat. 5s, Pine marten. 13s, Badger. 20s, Otter. (2s, 3s, 13s, horiz.)

1963, Apr. 30

Red Numerals

1261	A583	1s grn & brn, *grnsh*	5	5
1262	A583	2s grn & blk *yel*	5	5
1263	A583	3s grn & brn, *bis*	7	5
1264	A583	5s vio & red brn, *lil*	15	6
1265	A583	13s red brn & blk, *pink*	65	20
1266	A583	20s blk & brn, *bl*	1.00	25
		Nos. 1261-1266 (6)	1.97	66

1963, Mar. 12 *Perf. 13* **Unwmkd.**

Black Sea Resorts: 2s, 3s, 13s, Views of Gold Sand. 5s, 20s, Sun Coast.

1267	A584	1s blue	5	5
1268	A584	2s vermilion	35	5
1269	A584	2s car rose	50	5
1270	A584	3s ocher	25	5
1271	A584	5s lilac	25	5
1272	A584	13s bl grn	75	12
1273	A584	20s green	1.25	30
		Nos. 1267-1273 (7)	3.40	67

Freestyle Wrestling
A585

Design: 20s, Freestyle wrestling (horiz.).

1963, May 31 *Perf. 11½*

1274	A585	5s yel bis & blk	15	10
1275	A585	20s org brn & blk	75	30

Issued to commemorate the 15th International Freestyle Wrestling Competitions, Sofia.

"Women for Peace"
A586

1963, June 24 *Perf. 11½* **Unwmkd.**

1276	A586	20s bl & blk	60	20

Issued to commemorate the World Congress of Women, Moscow, June 24-29.

Esperanto Emblem and Arms of Sofia
A587

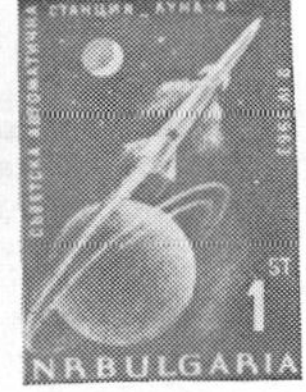

[illegible]
Lunik 4
A588

1963, June 29 Photogravure

1277	A587	13s multi	70	20

Issued to commemorate the 48th World Esperanto Congress, Sofia, Aug. 3-10.

1963, July 22

Designs: 2s, Radar equipment. 3s, Satellites and moon.

1278	A588	1s ultra	5	5
1279	A588	2s red lil	10	5
1280	A588	3s grnsh bl	15	5

Issued to commemorate Russia's rocket to the moon, Apr. 2, 1963.

Nos. 1211-1212 and 1215 Overprinted or Surcharged in Green, Ultramarine or Black

= MOSTRA EUROPEISTICA·1963
13
RICCIONE

1963, Aug. 31 *Perf. 10½*

Roses in Natural Colors

1281	A565	2s sal & dk car (G)	30	15
1282	A565	5s on 3s gray & dk car (U)	45	15
1283	A565	13s on 6s bluish grn & dk car	85	35

Issued to commemorate the International Stamp Fair, Riccione, Aug. 31.

Women's Relay Race
A589

Designs: 2s, Hammer thrower. 3s, Women's long jump. 5s, Men's high jump. 13s, Discus thrower.

Perf. 11½

1963, Sept. 13 Photo. **Unwmkd.**

Flags in National Colors

1284	A589	1s sl grn	10	5
1285	A589	2s purple	15	5
1286	A589	3s Prus bl	20	5
1287	A589	5s maroon	60	30
1288	A589	13s chnt brn	2.00	1.25
		Nos. 1284-1288 (5)	3.05	1.70

Issued to publicize the Balkan Games. A multicolored, 50s, imperf. souvenir sheet shows design of women's relay race. Size: 74x70mm.

"Slav-Bulgarian History"
A590

1963, Sept. 19 **Perf. 10½**

1289	A590	5s sal pink, sl & yel	20	5

5th International Slavic Congress.

Revolutionists A591   Christo Smirnenski A592

1963, Sept. 22 **Perf. 11½**

1290	A591	2s brt red & blk	15	5

Issued to commemorate the 40th anniversary of the September Revolution.

1963, Oct. 28 **Perf. 10½**

1291	A592	13s pale lil & ind	40	15

Issued to commemorate the 65th anniversary of the birth of Christo Smirnenski, poet.

Columbine A593   Horses A594

1963, Oct. 9 Photo. **Perf. 11½**

Multicolored

1292	A593	1s *shown*	5	5
1293	A593	2s *Edelweiss*	5	5
1294	A593	3s *Primrose*	10	5
1295	A593	5s *Water lily*	10	6
1296	A593	6s *Tulips*	15	8
1297	A593	8s *Larkspur*	30	12
1298	A593	10s *Alpine clematis*	65	20
1299	A593	13s *Anemone*	1.25	30
		Nos. 1292-1299 (8)	2.65	91

1963, Dec. 28 **Perf. 10½** **Unwmkd.**

Designs: 2s, Charioteer and chariot. 3s, Trumpeters. 5s, Woman carrying tray with food. 13s, Man holding bowl. 20s, Woman in armchair. Designs are from a Thracian tomb at Kazanlik.

1300	A594	1s gray, org & dk red	5	5
1301	A594	2s gray, ocher & pur	5	5
1302	A594	3s gray, dl yel & sl grn	8	5
1303	A594	5s pale grn, ocher & brn	15	6
1304	A594	13s pale grn, bis & blk	50	15
1305	A594	20s pale grn, org & dk car	90	30
		Nos. 1300-1305 (6)	1.73	66

World Map and Emblem
A595

Designs: 2s, Blood transfusion. 3s, Nurse bandaging injured wrist. 5s, Red Cross nurse. 13s, Henri Dunant.

1964, Jan. 27 **Perf. 10½**

1306	A595	1s lem, blk & red	5	5
1307	A595	2s ultra, blk & red	5	5
1308	A595	3s gray, sl, blk & red	6	5
1309	A595	5s brt bl, blk & red	15	6
1310	A595	13s org yel, blk & red	45	18
		Nos. 1306-1310 (5)	76	39

Centenary of International Red Cross.

Speed Skating—A596

Sports: 2s, 50s, Women's figure skating. 3s, Cross-country skiing. 5s, Ski jump. 10s, Ice hockey goalkeeper. 13s, Ice hockey players.

1964, Feb. 21 **Perf. 10½** **Unwmkd.**

1311	A596	1s grnsh bl, ind & ocher	5	5
1312	A596	2s brt pink, ol grn & dk sl grn	5	5
1313	A596	3s dl grn, dk grn & brn	8	5
1314	A596	5s bl, blk & yel brn	20	5
1315	A596	10s gray, org & blk	45	15
1316	A596	13s lil, blk & lil rose	75	25
		Nos. 1311-1316 (6)	1.58	60

Miniature Sheet

Imperf.

1317	A596	50s gray, Prus grn & pink	5.50	4.00

Issued to commemorate 9th Winter Olympic Games, Innsbruck, Jan. 29—Feb. 9, 1964.

No. 1317 measures 64x67½mm.

Mask of Nobleman, 2nd Century
A597

Designs: 2s, Thracian horseman. 3s, Ceramic jug. 5s, Clasp and belt. 6s, Copper kettle. 8s, Angel. 10s, Lioness. 13s, Scrub woman, contemporary sculpture.

1964, Mar. 14 Photo. **Perf. 10½**

Gray Frame

1318	A597	1s dp grn & red	5	5
1319	A597	2s ol gray & red	5	5
1320	A597	3s bis & red	10	6
1321	A597	5s ind & red	20	6
1322	A597	6s org brn & red	25	8
1323	A597	8s brn red & red	45	10
1324	A597	10s ol & red	50	15
1325	A597	13s gray ol & red	75	25
		Nos. 1318-1325 (8)	2.35	80

2,500 years of Bulgarian art.

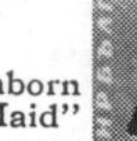

"The Unborn Maid"
A598

Fairy Tales: 2s, Grandfather's Glove. 3s, The Big Turnip. 5s, The Wolf and the Seven Kids. 8s, Cunning Peter. 13s, The Wheat Cake.

1964, Apr. 17 **Perf. 10½** **Unwmkd.**

1326	A598	1s bl grn, red & org brn	5	5
1327	A598	2s ultra, ocher & blk	5	5
1328	A598	3s cit, red & blk	6	5
1329	A598	5s dp rose, brn & blk	10	5
1330	A598	8s yel grn, red & blk	25	15
1331	A598	13s lt vio bl, grn & blk	80	30
		Nos. 1326-1331 (6)	1.31	65

Ascalaphus Otomanus
A599

Insects: 2s, Nemoptera coa. (vert.). 3s, Saga natalia (grasshopper). 5s, Rosalia alpina (vert.). 13s, Anisoplia austriaca (vert.). 20s, Scolia flavitrons.

1964, May 16 Photo. **Perf. 11½**

1332	A599	1s brn org, yel & blk	5	5
1333	A599	2s dl bl grn, bis & blk	6	5
1334	A599	3s gray, grn & blk	10	8
1335	A599	5s lt ol grn, blk & vio	15	10
1336	A599	13s vio, bis & blk	60	18
1337	A599	20s gray bl, yel & blk	90	30
		Nos. 1332-1337 (6)	1.86	76

Soccer
A600

Designs: 13s, Women's volleyball. 60s, Map of Europe and European Women's Volleyball Championship Cup (rectangular, size: 60x69mm.).

1964, June 8 **Perf. 11½** **Unwmkd.**

1338	A600	2s bl, dk bl, ocher & red	20	10
1339	A600	13s bl, dk bl, ocher & red	75	30

Miniature Sheet

Imperf.

1340	A600	60s ultra, ocher, red & gray	3.25	2.50

Issued to commemorate the 50th anniversary of the Levski Physical Culture Association.

Peter Beron and Title Page of Primer—A601

1964, June 22 **Perf. 11½**

1341	A601	20s red brn & dk brn, grysh	1.25	1.00

Issued to commemorate the 140th anniversary of the publication of the first Bulgarian primer.

Robert Stephenson's "Rocket" Locomotive, 1825
A602

Designs: 2s, Modern steam locomotive. 3s, Diesel locomotive. 5s, Electric locomotive. 8s, Freight train on bridge. 13s, Diesel locomotive and tunnel.

1964, July 1 Photo. **Perf. 11½**

1342	A602	1s org brn, blk, bis & gray	5	5
1343	A602	2s org brn, blk, Prus bl & ol	5	5
1344	A602	3s org brn, blk, grn & gray	6	5
1345	A602	5s org brn, blk & bl	15	5
1346	A602	8s org brn, blk, bl & gray	30	10
1347	A602	13s org brn, blk, yel & gray	75	25
		Nos. 1342-1347 (6)	1.36	55

German Shepherd
A603

1964, Aug. 22 Photogravure

Multicolored

1348	A603	1s *shown*	5	5
1349	A603	2s *Setter*	5	5
1350	A603	3s *Poodle*	6	5
1351	A603	4s *Pomeranian*	15	5
1352	A603	5s *St. Bernard*	18	5
1353	A603	6s *Terrier*	25	10
1354	A603	10s *Pointer*	1.25	40
1355	A603	13s *Dachshund*	2.50	75
		Nos. 1348-1355 (8)	4.49	1.50

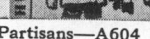

Partisans—A604

Designs: 2s, People welcoming Soviet army. 3s, Russian aid to Bulgaria. 4s, Blast furnace, Kremikovski. 5s, Combine. 6s, Peace demonstration. 8s, Sentry. 13s, Demeter Blagoev and George Dimitrov.

1964, Sept. 9 **Perf. 11½** **Unwmkd.**

Flag in Red

1356	A604	1s lt & dp ultra	5	5
1357	A604	2s ol bis & dp ol	5	5

1358 A604 3s rose lil & mar 6 5
1359 A604 4s lt vio & vio 6 5
1360 A604 5s org & red brn 15 5
1361 A604 6s bl & dp bl 20 5
1362 A604 8s lt grn & grn 30 10
1363 A604 13s fawn & red brn 65 20
Nos. 1356-1363 (8) 1.52 60

Issued to commemorate the 20th anniversary of People's Government of Bulgaria.

No. 967 Surcharged

ММ панаир
ПЛОВДИВ - 1964
ST 20

1964, Sept. 13 ***Perf. 13***

1364 A476 20s on 44s org yel 1.00 30

International Plovdiv Fair.

Gymnast on Parallel Bars
A606

Vratcata Mountain Road
A607

Sports: 2s, Long jump. 3s, Woman diver. 5s, Soccer. 13s, Women's volleyball. 20s, Wrestling.

1964, Oct. 10 ***Perf. 11½***

1366 A606 1s pale grn, grn & red 5 5
1367 A606 2s pale vio, vio bl & red 5 5
1368 A606 3s bl grn, brn & red 6 5
1369 A606 5s pink, pur & red 15 8
1370 A606 13s bl, Prus grn & red 50 15
1371 A606 20s yel, grn & red 90 25
Nos. 1366-1371 (6) 1.71 63

Issued for the 18th Olympic Games, Tokyo. Oct. 10–25. See No. B27.

1964, Oct. 26 Photo. ***Perf. 12½x13***

Bulgarian Views: 2s, Ritlite mountain road. 3s, Pines, Malovica peak. 4s, Pobitite rocks. 5s, Erkupria. 6s, Rhodope mountain road.

1372 A607 1s dk sl grn 5 5
1373 A607 2s brown 5 5
1374 A607 3s grnsh bl 8 5
1375 A607 4s dk red brn 15 5
1376 A607 5s dp grn 25 5
1377 A607 6s bl vio 40 5
Nos. 1372-1377 (6) 98 30

Mail Coach, Plane and Rocket
A608

1964, Oct. 3 ***Perf. 11½*** **Unwmkd.**

1378 A608 20s grnsh bl 1.75 80

Issued to commemorate the first national stamp exhibition, Sofia, Oct. 3–18. Issued in sheets of 12 stamps and 12 labels (woman's head and inscription, 5x5) arranged around one central label showing stylized bird design.

Students Holding Book
A609

1964, Dec. 30 **Photogravure**

1379 A609 13s lt bl & blk 50 15

Issued to commemorate the 8th International Students' Congress, Sofia.

500-Year-Old Walnut Tree at Golemo Drenovo—A610

Designs: Various Old Trees.

1964, Dec. 28

1380 A610 1s blk, buff & cl brn 5 5
1381 A610 2s blk, pink & dp cl 5 5
1382 A610 3s blk, yel & dk brn 6 5
1383 A610 4s blk, lt bl & Prus bl 8 5
1384 A610 10s blk, pale grn & grn 35 10
1385 A610 13s blk, pale bis & dk ol grn 65 20
Nos. 1380-1385 (6) 1.24 50

Soldiers' Monument
A611

1965, Jan. 1 **Unwmkd.**

1386 A611 2s red & blk 20 10

Issued to honor Bulgarian-Soviet friendship.

Olympic Medal Inscribed "Olympic Glory"
A612

1965, Jan. 27 **Photo.** ***Perf. 11½***

1387 A612 20s org brn, gold & blk 90 30

Issued to commemorate Bulgarian victories in the 1964 Olympic Games.

"Victory Over Fascism"
A613

Design: 13s, "Fight for Peace" (dove and globe).

1965, Apr. 16 ***Perf. 11½***

1388 A613 5s gray, blk & ol bis 15 5
1389 A613 13s gray, blk & bl 40 20

Issued to commemorate the 20th anniversary of victory over Fascism, May 9, 1945.

Vladimir M. Komarov and Section of Globe
A614

Designs: 2s, Konstantin Feoktistov. 5s, Boris B. Yegorov. 13s, Komarov, Feoktistov and Yegorov. 20s, Spaceship Voskhod.

1965, Feb. 15 **Photogravure**

1390 A614 1s pale lil & dk bl 5 5
1391 A614 2s lt bl, ind & dl vio 5 5
1392 A614 5s pale grn, grn & ol grn 15 5
1393 A614 13s pale pink, dp rose & mar 45 15
1394 A614 20s lt bl, vio bl, grnsh bl & yel 80 25
Nos. 1390-1394 (5) 1.50 55

Russian 3-man space flight, Oct. 12-13, 1964.

Imperfs. in changed colors. Four low values se-tenant.

Price, set $3 unused, $1.50 canceled.

Bullfinch
A615

Birds: 2s, European golden oriole. 3s, Common rock thrush. 5s, Barn swallow. 8s, European roller. 10s, European goldfinch. 13s, Rosy pastor starling. 20s, Nightingale.

1965, Apr. 20 ***Perf. 11½*** **Unwmkd.**

Birds in Natural Colors

1395 A615 1s bl grn 5 5
1396 A615 2s rose lil 5 5
1397 A615 3s rose 5 5
1398 A615 5s brt bl 10 5
1399 A615 8s citron 35 6
1400 A615 10s gray 1.25 20
1401 A615 13s lt vio bl 1.25 35
1402 A615 20s emerald 2.50 65
Nos. 1395-1402 (8) 5.60 1.46

Sting Ray
A616

Black Sea Fish: 2s, Belted bonito. 3s, Hogfish. 5s, Gurnard. 10s, Scad. 13s, Turbot.

1965, June 10 **Photo.** ***Perf. 11½***

Gray Frames

1403 A616 1s org, blk & gold 5 5
1404 A616 2s ultra, ind & sil 5 5
1405 A616 3s emer, blk & gold 12 5
1406 A616 5s dp car, blk & gold 20 10
1407 A616 10s grnsh bl, blk & sil 85 25
1408 A616 13s red brn, blk & gold 1.25 40
Nos. 1403-1408 (6) 2.52 90

Plane, Bus, Train, Ship and Whale
A617

ITU Emblem and Communications Symbols
A618

1965, Apr. 30

1409 A617 13s multi 50 15

Issued to publicize the fourth International Conference of Transport, Dock and Fishery Workers, Sofia, May 10–14.

1965, May 17

1410 A618 20s multi 70 25

Issued to commemorate the centenary of the International Telecommunication Union.

Col. Pavel Belyayev and Lt. Col. Alexei Leonov
A619

Design: 20s, Leonov floating in space.

1965, May 20 **Unwmkd.**

1411 A619 2s gray, dl bl & dk brn 10 8
1412 A619 20s multi 1.75 60

Space flight of Voskhod 2 and the first man floating in space, Lt. Col. Alexei Leonov.

ICY Emblem
A620

1965, May 15 **Photogravure**

1413 A620 20s org, ol & blk 70 20

International Cooperation Year, 1965.

Corn
A621

Marx and Lenin
A622

Designs: 2s, Wheat. 3s, Sunflowers. 4s, Sugar beet. 5s, Clover. 10s, Cotton. 13s, Tobacco.

1965, Apr. 1 ***Perf. 12½x13***

1414	A621	1s org yel	5	5
1415	A621	2s brt grn	5	5
1416	A621	3s dp org	8	5
1417	A621	4s olive	15	5
1418	A621	5s brt rose	25	5
1419	A621	10s grnsh bl	70	10
1420	A621	13s bister	1.00	20
		Nos. 1414-1420 (7)	2.28	55

1965, June ***Perf. 10½***

1421 A622 13s red & dk brn 60 20

Issued to commemorate the 6th Conference of Postal Ministers of Communist Countries, Peking, June 21–July 15.

Film and UNESCO Emblem
A623

1965, June 30

1422 A623 13s dp bl, blk & lt gray 50 20

Balkan Film Festival, Varna.

Ballerina
A624

1965, July 10 **Photogravure**

1423 A624 5s dp lil rose & blk 60 30

Issued to publicize the Second International Ballet Competition, Varna.

Map of Balkan Peninsula and Dove with Letter—A625

Col. Pavel Belyayev and Lt. Col. Alexei Leonov—A626

Designs: 2s, Sailboat and modern buildings. 3s, Fish and plants. 13s, Symbolic sun and rocket. 40s, Map of Balkan Peninsula and dove with letter (like 1s).

1965, July 23–Aug. 7 ***Perf. 10½***

1424	A625	1s sil, dp ultra & yel	5	5
1425	A625	2s sil, pur & yel	6	5
1426	A625	3s gold, grn & yel	15	8
1427	A625	13s gold, hn brn & yel	75	50
1428	A626	20s sil, bl & brn	90	55
		Nos. 1424-1428 (5)	1.91	1.23

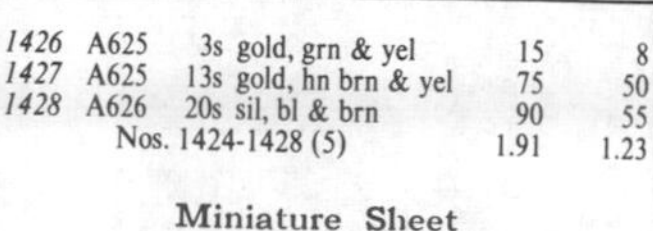

Miniature Sheet
Imperf.

1429 A625 40s gold & brt bl 2.75 1.50

Balkanphila 1965 Philatelic Exhibition, Varna, Aug. 7-15, and visit of Russian astronauts Belyayev and Leonov. The 20s and 40s were issued Aug. 7.

No. 1429 has gold denomination and inscription in margin. Size: 69x61½mm.

Price, #1428 imperf. in changed colors, 90 cents.

Woman Gymnast
A627

Designs: 2s, Woman gymnast on parallel bars. 3s, Weight lifter. 5s, Automobile and chart. 10s, Women basketball players. 13s, Automobile and map of rally.

1965, Aug. 14 ***Perf. 10½***

1430	A627	1s crim, brn & blk	5	5
1431	A627	2s rose vio, dp cl & blk	5	5
1432	A627	3s dp car, brn & blk	6	5
1433	A627	5s fawn, red brn & blk	20	5
1434	A627	10s dp lil rose, dp cl & blk	75	20
1435	A627	13s lil, cl & blk	90	25
		Nos. 1430-1435 (6)	2.01	65

Issued to commemorate various sports events in Bulgaria during May–June, 1965.

No. 989 Surcharged

2 Ст

ПЪРВИ НАЦИОНАЛЕН
СЪБОР НА НАРОДНОТО
ТВОРЧЕСТВО
12-15-VIII
1965

1965, Aug. 12 ***Perf. 13***

1436 A499 2s on 8s org brn 75 40

Issued to publicize the First National Folklore Competition, Aug. 12–15.

Escaping Prisoners
A628

Apples
A629

1965, July 23 ***Perf. 10½***

1437 A628 2s slate 20 10

Issued to commemorate the 40th anniversary of the escape of political prisoners from Bolshevik Island.

1965, July 1 ***Perf. 13***

Fruit: 2s, Grapes. 3s, Pears. 4s, Peaches. 5s, Strawberries. 6s, Walnuts.

1438	A629	1s dp org	5	5
1439	A629	2s lt ol grn	5	5
1440	A629	3s bister	5	5
1441	A629	4s orange	6	5
1442	A629	5s car rose	30	5
1443	A629	6s yel brn	50	15
		Nos. 1438-1443 (6)	1.01	40

Dressage—A630

Horsemanship: 2s, Three-day test. 3s, Jumping. 5s, Race. 10s, Steeplechase. 13s, Hurdle race.

1965, Sept. 30 ***Perf. 10½*** **Unwmkd.**

1444	A630	1s bluish gray, blk & dk vio	5	5
1445	A630	2s buff, blk & hn brn	5	5
1446	A630	3s gray, blk & dk car rose	5	5
1447	A630	5s gray ol, dk grn & red brn	8	5
1448	A630	10s lt gray, blk & dk red brn	65	25
1449	A630	13s sal, dk grn & dk red brn	1.10	35
		Nos. 1444-1449 (6)	1.98	80

See also No. B28.

Smiling Children
A631

Designs: 2s, Two girl Pioneers. 3s, Bugler. 5s, Pioneer with model plane. 8s, Two singing girls in national costume. 13s, Running boy.

1965, Oct. 24 **Photogravure**

1450	A631	1s dk bl grn & yel grn	5	5
1451	A631	2s vio & dp rose	5	5
1452	A631	3s ol & lem	10	5
1453	A631	5s dp bl & bis	15	6
1454	A631	8s ol bis & org	35	15
1455	A631	13s rose car & vio	85	30
		Nos. 1450-1455 (6)	1.55	66

Issued to honor the Dimitrov Pioneer Organization.

U-52 Plane over Trnovo
A632

Designs: 2c, IL-14 over Plovdiv. 3s, Mi-4 Helicopter over Dimitrovgrad. 5s, Tu-104 over Ruse. 13s, IL-18 over Varna. 20s, Tu-114 over Sofia.

1965, Nov. 25 ***Perf. 10½***

1456	A632	1s gray, bl & red	5	5
1457	A632	2s gray, lil & red	5	5
1458	A632	3s gray, grnsh bl & red	7	5
1459	A632	5s gray, org & red	10	8
1460	A632	13s gray, bis & red	65	15
1461	A632	20s gray, lt grn & red	90	40
		Nos. 1456-1461 (6)	1.82	78

Issued to publicize the development of Bulgarian Civil Air Transport.

IQSY Emblem, and Earth Radiation Zones
A633

Designs (IQSY Emblem and): 2s, Sun with corona. 13s, Solar eclipse.

1965, Dec. 15 **Photo.** ***Perf. 10½***

1462	A633	1s grn, yel & ultra	5	5
1463	A633	2s yel, red lil & red	5	5
1464	A633	13s bl, yel & blk	45	20

International Quiet Sun Year, 1964–65.

"North and South Bulgaria"
A634

"Martenitsa" Emblem
A635

1965, Dec. 6

1465 A634 13s brt yel grn & blk 55 25

Issued to commemorate the centenary of the Union of North and South Bulgaria.

1966, Jan. 10 **Photo.** ***Perf. 10½***

"Spring" in Folklore: 2s, Drummer. 3s, Bird ornaments. 5s, Dancer "Lazarka." 8s, Vase with flowers. 13s, Bagpiper.

1466	A635	1s rose lil, vio bl & gray	5	5
1467	A635	2s gray, blk & crim	5	5
1468	A635	3s red, vio & gray	5	5
1469	A635	5s lil, blk & crim	9	5
1470	A635	8s rose lil, brn & pur	25	7
1471	A635	13s bl, blk & rose lil	55	20
		Nos. 1466-1471 (6)	1.04	47

Church of St. John the Baptist, Nessebr—A636

Designs: 1s, Christ, fresco from Bojana Church. 2s, Ikon "Destruction of Idols" (horiz.). 3s, Bratchkovo Monastery. 4s, Zemen Monastery (horiz.). 13s, Nativity, ikon from Arbanassi. 20s, Ikon "Virgin and Child," 1342.

1966, Feb. 25 **Litho.** ***Perf. 11½***

1472	A636	1s gray & multi	*3.00*	*2.50*
1473	A636	2s gray & multi	20	15
1474	A636	3s multi	20	15
1475	A636	4s multi	20	15
1476	A636	5s multi	25	20
1477	A636	13s gray & multi	40	25
1478	A636	20s multi	75	60
		Nos. 1472-1478 (7)	*5.00*	*4.00*

2,500 years of art in Bulgaria.

Georgi Benkovski and T. Kableshkov—A637

Designs: 1s, Proclamation of April Uprising, Koprivstitsa. 3s, Dedication of flag, Panagurište. 5s, V. Petleshkov and Z. Dyustabanov. 10s, Botev landing at Kozlodui. 13s, P. Volov and Ilarion Dragostinov.

1966, March 3 Photo. *Perf. 10½*

Center in Black

1479	A637	1s red brn & gold	5	5
1480	A637	2s brt red & gold	5	5
1481	A637	3s ol grn & gold	6	5
1482	A637	5s stl bl & gold	10	5
1483	A637	10s brt rose lil & gold	25	5
1484	A637	13s lt vio & gold	55	15
		Nos. 1479-1484 (6)	1.06	40

Issued to commemorate the 90th anniversary of the April Uprising against the Turks.

Elephant A638

Animals from Sofia Zoo: 2s, Tiger. 3s, Chimpanzee. 4s, Siberian ibex. 5s, Polar bear. 8s, Lion. 13s, Bison. 20s, Kangaroo.

1966, May 23 Lithographed

1485	A638	1s yel, blk & gray	5	5
1486	A638	2s dl yel, org yel & blk	5	5
1487	A638	3s pale grn, bis & blk	6	5
1488	A638	4s tan, brn & blk	15	5
1489	A638	5s lt bl & blk	20	5
1490	A638	8s pale rose, bis & blk	20	15
1491	A638	13s cit, brn & blk	65	30
1492	A638	20s pale lil, bis & blk	1.25	45
		Nos. 1485-1492 (8)	2.61	1.15

WHO Headquarters, Geneva A639

1966, May 3 Photogravure

1493	A639	13s dp bl & sil	75	20

Issued to commemorate the inauguration of the World Health Organization Headquarters, Geneva.

Worker A640

1966, May 9 Photo. *Perf. 10½*

1494	A640	20s gray & rose	65	20

Sixth Trade Union Congress.

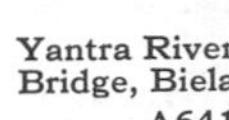

Yantra River Bridge, Biela A641

Designs: No. 1496, Maritsa River Bridge, Svilengrad. No. 1497, Fountain, Samokov. No. 1498, Ruins of Fort, Kaskovo. 8s, Old Fort, Ruse. 13s, House, Gabrovo.

1966, Feb. 10 Photo. *Perf. 13*

1495	A641	1s Prus bl	5	5
1496	A641	1s brt grn	5	5
1497	A641	2s ol grn	5	5
1498	A641	2s dk red brn	5	5
1499	A641	8s red brn	30	10
1500	A641	13s dk bl	50	15
		Nos. 1495-1500 (6)	1.00	45

Souvenir Sheet

Moon Allegory—A642

1966, Apr. 29 *Imperf.*

1501	A642	60s blk, plum & sil	3.00	2.00

Issued to commemorate the first Russian soft landing on the moon by Luna 9, Feb. 3, 1966. Size: 70x50mm.

Steamer Radetzky and Bugler—A643

1966, May 28 *Perf. 10½*

1502	A643	2s multi	20	5

Issued to commemorate the 90th anniversary of the participation of the Danube steamer Radetzky in the uprising against the Turks.

Standard Bearer Nicola Simov-Kuruto A644

1966, May 30

1503	A644	5s bis, grn & ol	25	12

Issued to honor Nicola Simov-Kuruto, hero of the Turkish War.

UNESCO Emblem A645

1966, June 8

1504	A645	20s gold, blk & ver	70	25

Issued to commemorate the 20th anniversary of UNESCO (United Nations Educational, Scientific and Cultural Organization).

Youth Federation Badge—A646

1966, June 6 Photo. *Perf. 10½*

1505	A646	13s sil, bl & blk	40	15

Issued to publicize the 7th Assembly of the International Youth Federation.

Soccer—A647

Designs: Various soccer scenes. 50s, Jules Rimet Cup.

1966, June 27

1506	A647	1s gray, yel brn & blk	5	5
1507	A647	2s gray, crim & blk	5	5
1508	A647	5s gray, ol bis & blk	15	5
1509	A647	13s gray, ultra & blk	40	15
1510	A647	20s gray, Prus bl & blk	70	30
		Nos. 1506-1510 (5)	1.35	60

Miniature Sheet

Imperf.

1511	A647	50s gray, dp lil rose & gold	3.00	1.50

Issued to commemorate the World Soccer Cup Championship, Wembley, England, July 11–30. Size of No. 1511: 60x64mm.

Woman Javelin Thrower—A648

Designs: No. 1513, Runner. No. 1514, Young man and woman carrying banners (vert.).

1966 Photo. *Perf. 10½*

1512	A648	2s grn, yel & ver	5	5
1513	A648	13s dp grn, yel & sal pink	45	15
1514	A648	13s bl, lt bl & sal	45	20

Nos. 1512–1513 commemorate the 3rd Spartacist Games; issued Aug. 10. No. 1514 commemorates the 3rd congress of the Bulgarian Youth Federation; issued May 25.

Wrestlers Nicolas Petrov and Dan Kolov—A649

1966, July 29

1515	A649	13s bis brn, dk brn & lt ol grn	60	20

3rd International Wrestling Championships.

Map of Balkan Countries, Globe and UNESCO Emblem A650

1966, Aug. 26 *Perf. 10½x11½*

1516	A650	13s ultra, lt grn & pink	30	15

First Congress of Balkanologists.

Children with Building Blocks A651

Designs: 2s, Bunny and teddy bear with book. 3s, Children as astronauts. 13s, Children with pails and shovel.

1966, Sept. 1 *Perf. 10½*

1517	A651	1s dk car, org & blk	5	5
1518	A651	2s emer, blk & red brn	5	5
1519	A651	3s ultra, org & blk	10	5
1520	A651	13s bl, rose & blk	75	20

Issued for Children's Day.

Yuri A. Gagarin and Vostok 1 A652

Designs: 2s, Gherman S. Titov and Vostok 2. 3s, Andrian G. Nikolayev, Pavel R. Popovich, and Vostoks 3 & 4. 5s, Valentina Tereshkova, Valeri Bykovski and Vostoks 5 and 6. 8s, Vladimir M. Komarov, Boris B. Yegorov, Konstantin Feoktistov and Voskhod 1. 13s, Pavel Belyayev, Alexei Leonov and Voskhod 2.

1966, Sept. 29 Photo. *Perf. 11½x11*

1521	A652	1s sl & gray	5	5
1522	A652	2s plum & gray	5	5
1523	A652	3s yel brn & gray	6	5
1524	A652	5s brn red & gray	8	6
1525	A652	8s ultra & gray	10	10
1526	A652	13s Prus bl & gray	45	15
		Nos. 1521-1526, B29 (7)	1.89	96

Russian space explorations.

St. Clement, 14th Century Wood Sculpture A653

1966, Oct. 27 Photo. *Perf. 11½x11*

1527	A653	5s red, buff & brn	25	5

Issued to commemorate the 1050th anniversary of the birth of St. Clement of Ochrida.

Metodi Shatorov A654

Portraits: 3s, Vladimir Trichkov. 5s, Valcho Ivanov. 10s, Raiko Daskalov. 13s, General Vladimir Zaimov.

1966, Nov. 8 *Perf. 11x11½*

Gold Frame, Black Denomination

1528	A654	2s crim & bl vio	5	5
1529	A654	3s mag & blk	5	5
1530	A654	5s car rose & dk bl	10	5
1531	A654	10s org & ol	35	10
1532	A654	13s red & brn	45	15
		Nos. 1528-1532 (5)	1.00	40

Issued to honor fighters against fascism.

George Dimitrov A655

Steel Worker A656

1966, Nov. 14 Photo. *Perf. 11½x11*

1533	A655	2s mag & blk	5	5
1534	A656	20s fawn, gray & blk	50	20

Bulgarian Communist Party, 9th Congress.

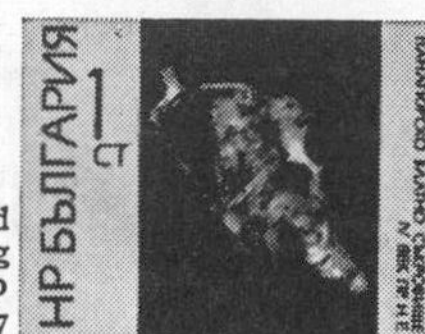

Deer's Head Drinking Cup A667

Gold Treasure: 2s, 6s, 10s, Various Amazon's head jugs. 3s, Ram's head cup. 5s, Circular plate. 8s, Deer's head cup. 13s, Amphora. 20s, Ram drinking horn.

1966, Nov. 28 *Perf. 12x11½*

Vessels in Gold and Brown; Black Inscriptions

1535	A667	1s gray & vio	5	5
1536	A667	2s gray & grn	7	5
1537	A667	3s gray & dk bl	10	5
1538	A667	5s gray & red brn	15	5
1539	A667	6s gray & Prus bl	18	5
1540	A667	8s gray & brn ol	1.10	15
1541	A667	10s gray & sep	1.10	20
1542	A667	13s gray & dk vio bl	1.10	30
1543	A667	20s gray & vio brn	1.25	35
		Nos. 1535-1543 (9)	5.10	1.25

The gold treasure from the 4th century B.C. was found near Panagyurishte in 1949.

Tourist House, Bansko A668

Tourist Houses: No. 1545, Belogradchik. No. 1546, Triavna. 20s, Rila.

1966, Nov. 29 Photo. *Perf. 11x11½*

1544	A668	1s dk bl	5	5
1545	A668	2s dk grn	5	5
1546	A668	2s brn red	5	5
1547	A668	20s lilac	50	15

Decorated Tree A669

Design: 13s, Jug with bird design.

1966, Dec. 12 *Perf. 11*

1548	A669	2s grn, pink & gold	5	5
1549	A669	13s brn lake, rose, emer & gold	45	15

Issued for New Year, 1967.

Pencho Slavikov, Author A670

Dahlia A671

Portraits: 2s, Dimcho Debeljanov, author. 3s, P. H. Todorov, author. 5s, Dimitri Dobrovich, painter. 8s, Ivan Markvichka, painter. 13s, Ilya Bezhkov, painter.

1966, Dec. 15 *Perf. 10½x11*

1550	A670	1s bl, ol & org	5	5
1551	A670	2s org, brn & gray	5	5
1552	A670	3s ol, bl & org	5	5
1553	A670	5s gray, red brn & org	8	5
1554	A670	8s lil, dk gray & bl	35	8
1555	A670	13s bl, vio & lil	45	15
		Nos. 1550-1555 (6)	1.03	43

1966, Dec. 29

Flowers: No. 1557, Clematis. No. 1558, Foxglove. No. 1559, Narcissus. 3s, Snowdrop. 5s, Petunia. 13s, Tiger lily. 20s, Bellflower.

Flowers in Natural Colors

1556	A671	1s gray & lt brn	5	5
1557	A671	1s gray & dl bl	5	5
1558	A671	2s gray & dl lil	5	5
1559	A671	2s gray & brn	5	5
1560	A671	3s gray & dk grn	15	6
1561	A671	5s gray & dp ultra	20	12
1562	A671	13s gray & brn	55	15
1563	A671	20s gray & ultra	90	25
		Nos. 1556-1563 (8)	2.00	78

Ring-necked Pheasant A672

Game: 2s, Rock partridge. 3s, Gray partridge. 5s, Hare. 8s, Roe deer. 13s, Red deer.

1967, Jan. 28 *Perf. 11x10½*

1564	A672	1s lt ultra, dk brn & ocher	5	5
1565	A672	2s pale yel grn & dk grn	5	5
1566	A672	3s lt bl, blk & cr	15	5
1567	A672	5s lt grn & blk	15	5
1568	A672	8s pale bl, dk brn & ocher	75	15
1569	A672	13s bl & dk brn	1.35	35
		Nos. 1564-1569 (6)	2.50	70

Bulgaria No. 1, 1879 A673

Thracian Coin, 6th Century, B.C. A674

1967, Feb. 4 Photo. *Perf. 10½*

1570	A673	10s emer, blk & yel	85	35

Issued to publicize the 10th Congress of the Bulgarian Philatelic Union.

1967, March 30 *Perf. 11½x11*

Coins: 2s, Macedonian tetradrachma, 2nd century, B.C. 3s, Tetradrachma of Odessus, 2nd century, B.C. 5s, Philip II of Macedonia, 4th century, B.C. 13s, Thracian King Seuthus VII, 4th century, B.C., obverse and reverse. 20s, Apollonian coin, 5th century, B.C., obverse and reverse.

Size: 25x25mm.

1571	A674	1s brn, blk & sil	5	5
1572	A674	2s red lil, blk & sil	5	5
1573	A674	3s grn, blk & sil	10	5
1574	A674	5s brn org, blk & sil	20	5

Size: 37½x25mm.

1575	A674	13s brt bl, blk & brnz	85	40
1576	A674	20s vio, blk & sil	1.50	75
		Nos. 1571-1576 (6)	2.75	1.35

Partisans Listening to Radio A675

Design: 20s, George Dimitrov addressing crowd and Bulgarian flag.

1967, Apr. 20 *Perf. 11x11½*

1577	A675	1s red, gold, buff & sl grn	5	5
1578	A675	20s red, gold, dl red, grn & blk	60	20

Issued to commemorate the 25th anniversary of the Union of Patriotic Front Organizations.

Nikolas Kofardjiev A676

Portraits: 2s, Petko Napetov. 5s, Petko D. Petkov. 10s, Emil Markov. 13s, Traitcho Kostov.

1967, Apr. 24 *Perf. 11½x11*

1579	A676	1s brn red, gray & blk	5	5
1580	A676	2s ol grn, gray & blk	5	5
1581	A676	5s brn, gray & blk	8	5
1582	A676	10s dp bl, gray & blk	17	10
1583	A676	13s mag, gray & blk	40	12
		Nos. 1579-1583 (5)	75	37

Issued to honor fighters against fascism.

Symbolic Flower and Flame A677

1967, May 18 Photo. *Perf. 11x11½*

1584	A677	13s gold, yel & lt grn	50	1

First Cultural Congress, May 18–19.

Gold Sand Beach and ITY Emblem A678

Designs: 20s, Hotel, Pamporovo. 40s, Nessebr Church.

1967, June 12 Photo. *Perf. 11x11½*

1585	A678	13s ultra, yel & blk	25	15
1586	A678	20s Prus bl, blk & buff	35	20
1587	A678	40s brt grn, blk & ocher	90	45

Issued for International Tourist Year, 1967.

Angora Cat A679

Cats: 2s, Siamese (horiz.). 3s, Abyssinian. 5s, Black European. 13s, Persian (horiz.). 20s, Striped domestic.

Perf. 11½x11, 11x11½

1967, June 19

1588	A679	1s dl vio, dk brn & buff	5	5
1589	A679	2s ol, sl & brt bl	10	5
1590	A679	3s dl bl & brn	10	5
1591	A679	5s grn, blk & yel	15	5
1592	A679	13s dl red brn, sl & org	70	20
1593	A679	20s gray grn, brn & buff	1.25	40
		Nos. 1588-1593 (6)	2.35	80

Scene from Opera "The Master of Boyana" by K. Iliev A680

Songbird on Keyboard A681

1967, June 19

1594	A680	5s gray, vio bl & dp car	15	5
1595	A681	13s gray, dp car & dk bl	45	15

Issued to commemorate the 3rd International Competition for Young Opera Singers.

George Kirkov A682

1967, June 24 ***Perf. 11x11½***

1596	A682	2s rose red & dk brn	15	5

Issued to commemorate the centenary of the birth of George Kirkov (1867–1919), revolutionist.

Symbolic Tree and Stars
A683

1967, July 28 Photo. ***Perf. 11½x11***

1597	A683	13s dp bl, car & blk	45	15

Issued to commemorate the 11th Congress of Dimitrov's Union of the People's Youth.

Roses and Distillery
A684

Designs: No. 1599, Chick and incubator. No. 1600, Cucumbers and hothouse. No. 1601, Lamb and sheep farm. 3s, Sunflower and oil mill. 4s, Pigs and pig farm. 5s, Hops and hop farm. 6s, Corn and irrigation system. 8s, Grapes and Bolgar tractor. 10s, Apples and cultivated tree. 13s, Bees and honey. 20s, Bee, blossoms and beehives.

1967 ***Perf. 11x11½***

1598	A684	1s multi	5	5
1599	A684	1s dk car, yel & blk	5	5
1600	A684	2s vio, lt grn & blk	5	5
1601	A684	2s brt grn, gray & blk	5	5
1602	A684	3s yel grn, yel & blk	5	5
1603	A684	4s brt pur, yel & blk	7	5
1604	A684	5s ol bis, yel grn & blk	10	8
1605	A684	6s ol, brt grn & blk	15	10
1606	A684	8s grn, bis & blk	15	10
1607	A684	10s multi	30	10
1608	A684	13s grn, bis brn & blk	45	15
1609	A684	20s grnsh bl, brt pink & blk	60	20
		Nos. 1598-1609 (12)	2.07	1.03

Issue dates: Nos. 1598–1601, 1607 and 1609, July 15; Nos. 1602–1606 and 1608, July 24.

Map of Communist Countries, Spasski Tower
A685

Designs: 2s, Lenin speaking to soldiers. 3s, Fighting at Wlodaja, 1918. 5s, Marx, Engels and Lenin. 13s, Oil refinery. 20s, Molniya communication satellite.

1967, Aug. 25 ***Perf. 11***

1610	A685	1s multi	5	5
1611	A685	2s mag & ol	5	5
1612	A685	3s mag & dl vio	5	5
1613	A685	5s mag & red	8	5
1614	A685	13s mag & ultra	25	12
1615	A685	20s mag & bl	55	15
		Nos. 1610-1615 (6)	1.03	47

Issued to commemorate the 50th anniversary of the Russian October Revolution.

Rod, "Fish" and Varna
A686

1967, Aug. 29 Photo. ***Perf. 11***

1616	A686	10s multi	50	20

7th World Angling Championships, Varna.

Skiers and Winter Olympics' Emblem—A687

Sports and Emblem: 2s, Ski jump. 3s, Biathlon. 5s, Ice hockey. 13s, Figure skating couple.

1967, Sept. 20 Photo. ***Perf. 11***

1617	A687	1s dk bl grn, red & blk	5	5
1618	A687	2s ultra, blk & ol	5	5
1619	A687	3s vio brn, bl & blk	5	5
1620	A687	5s grn, yel & blk	10	5
1621	A687	13s vio bl, blk & buff	40	15
		Nos. 1617-1621, B31 (6)	2.00	86

Issued to publicize the 10th Winter Olympic Games, Grenoble, France, Feb. 6–18, 1968.

Bogdan Mountain
A688

Mountain Peaks: 2s, Czerny. 3s, Ruen (vert.). 5s, Persenk. 10s, Botev. 13s, Rila (vert.). 20s, Vihren.

1967, Sept. 25 Engr. ***Perf. 11½***

1622	A688	1s sl grn & yel	5	5
1623	A688	2s sep & pale bl	5	5
1624	A688	3s ind & lt bl	5	5
1625	A688	5s sl grn & lt bl	10	5
1626	A688	10s dp cl & lt bl	15	6
1627	A688	13s dk gray & lt bl	30	10
1628	A688	20s ind & rose	60	20
		Nos. 1622-1628 (7)	1.30	56

George Rakovski
A689

1967, Oct. 20 Photo. ***Perf. 11***

1629	A689	13s yel grn & blk	45	15

Issued to commemorate the centenary of the death of George Rakovski, revolutionary against Turkish rule.

Yuri A. Gagarin, Valentina Tereshkova and Alexei Leonov
A690

Designs: 2s, Lt. Col. John H. Glenn, Jr., and Maj. Edward H. White. 5s, Earth and Molniya 1. 10s, Gemini 6 and 7. 13s, Luna 13 moon probe. 20s, Gemini 10 and Agena rocket.

1967, Nov. 25

1630	A690	1s Prus bl, blk & yel	5	5
1631	A690	2s dl bl, blk & dl yel	5	5
1632	A690	5s vio bl, grnsh bl & blk	8	5
1633	A690	10s dk bl, blk & red	25	10
1634	A690	13s grnsh bl, brt yel & blk	40	12
1635	A690	20s dl bl, blk & red	55	30
		Nos. 1630-1635 (6)	1.38	67

Achievements in space exploration.

View of Trnovo
A691

Various Views of Trnovo

1967, Dec. 5 Photogravure ***Perf. 11***

1636	A691	1s multi	5	5
1637	A691	2s multi	5	5
1638	A691	3s multi	5	5
1639	A691	5s multi	15	5
1640	A691	13s multi	35	15
1641	A691	20s multi	50	20
		Nos. 1636-1641 (6)	1.15	55

Issued to publicize the restoration of the ancient capital Veliko Trnovo.

Ratchenitza Folk Dance, by Ivan Markvichka
A692

1967, Dec. 9

1642	A692	20s gold & gray grn	1.25	1.00

Issued to commemorate the Belgo-Bulgarian Philatelic Exposition, Brussels, Dec. 9–10. Printed in sheets of 8 stamps and 8 labels.

Canceled-to-order stamps are often from remainders. Most collectors of canceled stamps prefer postally used specimens.

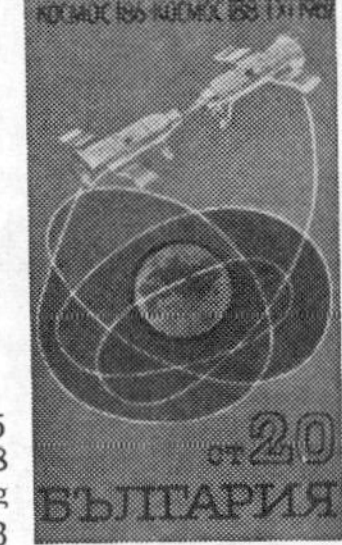

Cosmos 186 and 188 Docking
A693

Design: 40s, Venus 4 and orbits around Venus (horiz.).

1968, Jan.

1643	A693	20s vio, gray & pink	55	20
1644	A693	40s rose car, gray, sil & blk	1.10	40

Issued to commemorate the docking maneuvers of the Russian spaceships Cosmos 186 and Cosmos 188, Nov. 1, 1967, and the flight to Venus of Venus 4, June 12–Nov. 18, 1967.

Crossing the Danube, by Orenburgski
A694

Paintings: 2s, Flag of Samara, by J. Veschin (vert.). 3s, Battle of Pleven by Orenburgski. 13s, Battle of Orlovo Gnezdo, by N. Popov (vert.). 20s, Welcome for Russian Soldiers, by D. Gudienov.

1968, Jan. 25 Photo. ***Perf. 11***

1645	A694	1s gold & dk grn	5	5
1646	A694	2s gold & dk bl	5	5
1647	A694	3s gold & cl brn	5	5
1648	A694	13s gold & dk vio	45	20
1649	A694	20s gold & Prus grn	65	30
		Nos. 1645-1649 (5)	1.25	65

Issued to commemorate the 90th anniversary of the liberation from Turkey.

Shepherds, by Zlatyn Boyadjiev
A695

Paintings: 2s, Wedding dance, by V. Dimitrov. (vert.). 3s, Partisans' Song, by Ilya Petrov. 5s, Portrait of Anna Penchovich, by Nikolai Pavlovich (vert.). 13s, Self-portrait, by Zachary Zograf (vert.). 20s, View of Old Plovdiv, by T. Lavrenov. 60s, St. Clement of Ochrida, by A. Mitov.

1967, Dec. Litho. ***Perf. 11½***

Size: 45x38mm., 38x45mm.

1650	A695	1s gray & multi	8	5
1651	A695	2s gray & multi	10	5

Size: 55x35mm.

1652	A695	3s gray & multi	20	10

Size: 38x45mm., 45x38mm.

1653	A695	5s gray & multi	40	15
1654	A695	13s gray & multi	90	35
1655	A695	20s gray & multi	1.25	60
		Nos. 1650-1655 (6)	2.93	1.30

Miniature Sheet

Imperf.

Size: 65x84mm.

1656	A695	60s multi	4.00	3.00

Marx Statue, Sofia
A696

Maxim Gorky
A697

1968, Feb. 20 Photo. *Perf. 11*

1657	A696	13s blk & red	35	10

150th anniversary of birth of Karl Marx.

1968, Feb. 20

1658	A697	13s ver & grnsh blk	40	15

Issued to commemorate the centenary of the birth of Maxim Gorky (1868–1936), Russian writer.

Folk Dancers—A698

Designs: 5s, Runners. 13s, Doves. 20s, Festival poster, (head, flowers and birds). 40s, Globe and Bulgaria No. 1 under magnifying glass.

1968, Mar. 20

1659	A698	2s multi	5	5
1660	A698	5s multi	10	5
1661	A698	13s multi	20	10
1662	A698	20s multi	45	25
1663	A698	40s multi	1.00	50
		Nos. 1659-1663 (5)	1.80	95

Issued to publicize the 9th Youth Festival for Peace and Friendship, Sofia, July 28–Aug. 6.

Bellflower
A699

Flowers: 2s, Gentian. 3s, Crocus. 5s, Iris. 10s, Dog-tooth violet. 13s, Sempervivum. 20s, Dictamnus.

1968, Apr. 25 *Perf. 11*

Flowers in Natural Colors

1664	A699	1s dl bl & blk	5	5
1665	A699	2s yel grn & blk	5	5
1666	A699	3s gray grn & blk	5	5
1667	A699	5s brn org & blk	15	5
1668	A699	10s ultra & blk	20	10
1669	A699	13s rose lil & blk	65	15
1670	A699	20s ol & blk	90	30
		Nos. 1664-1670 (7)	2.05	75

"The Unknown Hero," Tale by Ran Bosilek
A700

Design: 20s, The Witch and the Young Man (Hans Christian Andersen fairy tale.)

1968, Apr. 25 Photo. *Perf. 10½*

1671	A700	13s blk & multi	40	20
1672	A700	20s blk & multi	50	30

Bulgarian-Danish Philatelic Exhibition.

Memorial Church, Shipka
A701

Steeplechase
A702

1968, May 3

1673	A701	13s multi	75	30

Bulgarian Stamp Exhibition in West Berlin.

1968, June 24 Photo. *Perf. 10½*

Designs (Olympic Rings and): 1s, Gymnast on bar. 3s, Fencer. 10s, Boxer. 13s, Woman discus thrower.

1674	A702	1s red & blk	5	5
1675	A702	2s gray, blk & rose brn	5	5
1676	A702	3s mag, gray & blk	5	5
1677	A702	10s grnsh bl, blk & lem	20	5
1678	A702	13s vio bl, gray & pink	55	20
		Nos. 1674-1678, B33 (6)	1.90	75

Issued to publicize the 19th Olympic Games, Mexico City, Oct. 12–27.

Battle of Buzluja
A703

Design: 13s, Haji Dimitr and Stefan Karaja.

1968, July 1

1679	A703	2s sil & red brn	5	5
1680	A703	13s gold & sl grn	35	15

Issued to commemorate the centenary of the death of the patriots Haji Dimitr and Stefan Karaja.

Lakes of Smolian
A704

Cinereous Vulture
A705

Bulgarian Scenes: 2s, Ropotamo Lake. 3s, Erma-Idreloto mountain pass. 8s, Isker River dam. 10s, Slanchev Breg (sailing ship). 13s, Cape Caliacra. 40s, Old houses, Sozopol. 2 l, Chudnite Skali ("Strange Mountains").

1968 Photogravure *Perf. 13*

1681	A704	1s Prus grn	5	5
1682	A704	2s dk grn	5	5
1683	A704	3s dk brn	5	5
1684	A704	8s ol grn	15	8
1685	A704	10s redsh brn	20	10
1686	A704	13s dk ol grn	30	10
1687	A704	40s Prus bl	80	35
1688	A704	2 l sepia	5.00	1.25
		Nos. 1681-1688 (8)	6.60	2.03

1968, July 29 *Perf. 10½*

Designs: 2s, Crowned crane. 3s, Zebra. 5s, Leopard. 13s, Indian python. 20s, African crocodile.

1689	A705	1s ultra, blk & tan	5	5
1690	A705	2s org brn, blk & yel	5	5
1691	A705	3s yel grn & blk	15	5
1692	A705	5s brn red, blk & yel	25	6
1693	A705	13s dp grn, blk & tan	45	15
1694	A705	20s dl bl, blk & gray grn	80	30
		Nos. 1689-1694 (6)	1.75	66

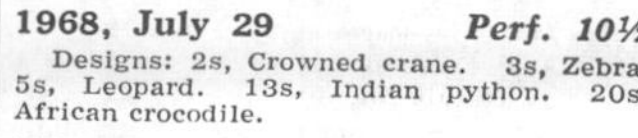

Centenary of the Sofia Zoo.

Human Rights Flame
A706

1968, July 8

1695	A706	20s dp bl & gold	50	20

International Human Rights Year, 1968.

Congress Hall, Varna, and Emblem
A707

1968, Sept. 17 Photo. *Perf. 10½*

1696	A707	20s bis, grn & red	45	15

Issued to publicize the 56th International Dental Congress, Varna.

Flying Swans
A708

Rose
A709

Stag Beetle
A710

Designs: 2s, Jug. 20s, Five Viking ships.

1968 Photogravure *Perf. 10½*

1697	A709	2s grn & ocher	1.00	1.00
1698	A708	5s dp bl & gray	1.00	1.00
1699	A709	13s dp plum & lil rose	1.00	1.00
1700	A708	20s dp vio & gray	1.00	1.00

Issued to publicize cooperation with the Scandinavian countries. Nos. 1697 and 1700 are printed with connecting label showing bridge made of flags of Scandinavian countries.

Issue dates: 5s, 13s, Sept. 12. Others, Nov. 22.

Perf. 12½x13, 13x12½

1968, Aug. 26

Insects: No. 1702, Ground beetle (Procerus scabrosus). No. 1703, Ground beetle (Calosoma sycophania). No. 1704, Scarab beetle (horiz.). No. 1705, Saturnid moth (horiz.).

1701	A710	1s brn ol	5	5
1702	A710	1s dk bl	5	5
1703	A710	1s dk grn	5	5
1704	A710	1s org brn	5	5
1705	A710	1s magenta	5	5
		Nos. 1701-1705 (5)	25	25

Turks Fighting Insurgents, 1688
A711

1968, Aug. 22 *Perf. 10½*

1706	A711	13s multi	50	10

Issued to commemorate the 280th anniversary of the Tchiprovtzi insurrection.

Christo Smirnenski—A712

1968, Sept. 28 Litho. *Perf. 10½*

1707	A712	13s gold, red org & blk	40	10

Issued to commemorate the 70th birthday of Christo Smirnenski (1898–1923), poet.

Dalmatian Pelican
A713

Birds: 2s, Little egret. 3s, Crested grebe. 5s, Common tern. 13s, European spoonbill. 20s, Glossy ibis.

1968, Oct. 28 Photogravure

1708	A713	1s sil & multi	5	5
1709	A713	2s sil & multi	5	5
1710	A713	3s sil & multi	8	5
1711	A713	5s sil & multi	10	8
1712	A713	13s sil & multi	40	10
1713	A713	20s sil & multi	85	35
		Nos. 1708-1713 (6)	1.53	68

Issued to publicize the Srebirna wild life reservation.

Carrier Pigeon
A714

1968, Oct. 19

1714	A714	20s emerald	70	35
a.		Sheet of 4 + labels	3.50	2.00

Issued to publicize the 2nd National Stamp Exhibition in Sofia, Oct. 25–Nov. 15. No. 1714a contains 4 No. 1714 and 5 decorative labels of two types with commemorative inscriptions. Gold frame. Size: 133x161½mm. No. 1714 was issued only as sheet No. 1714a.

Man and Woman from Lovetch
A715

Regional Costumes: 1s, Silistra. 3s, Jambol. 13s, Chirpan. 20s, Razgrad. 40s, Ihtiman.

1968, Nov. 20 Litho. *Perf. 13½*

1715	A715	1s dp org & multi	5	5
1716	A715	2s Prus bl & multi	6	5
1717	A715	3s multi	15	5
1718	A715	13s multi	25	8
1719	A715	20s multi	50	25
1720	A715	40s grn & multi	1.25	45
		Nos. 1715-1720 (6)	2.26	93

St. Arsenius
A716

Designs (10th century Murals and Icons): 2s, Procession with relics of St. Ivan Rilsky (horiz.). 3s, St. Michael Torturing the Soul of the Rich Man. 13s, St. Ivan Rilsky. 20s, St. John. 40s, St. George. 1 l, Procession meeting relics of St. Ivan Rilsky (horiz.).

Perf. 11½x12½, 12½x11½

1968, Nov. 25 Photogravure

1721	A716	1s gold & multi	5	5
1722	A716	2s gold & multi	5	5
1723	A716	3s gold & multi	15	5
1724	A716	13s gold & multi	50	15
1725	A716	20s gold & multi	1.00	30
1726	A716	40s gold & multi	1.50	65
		Nos. 1721-1726 (6)	3.25	1.25

Souvenir Sheet

Imperf.

1727	A716	1 l gold & multi	4.50	3.50

Issued to commemorate the millenium of Rila Monastery. No. 1727 also publicizes "Sofia 1969," International Philatelic Exhibition, May 31–June 8, 1969. No. 1727 contains one stamp (size: 57x51mm.), gray margin with emblems of Philatelic Exhibition. Size: 100x75mm.

Medlar
A717

Herbs: No. 1729, Camomile. 2s, Lily-of-the-valley. 3s, Belladonna. 5s, Mallow. 10s, Buttercup. 13s, Poppies. 20s, Thyme.

1969, Jan. 2 Litho. *Perf. 10½*

1728	A717	1s blk, grn & org red	5	5
1729	A717	1s blk, grn & yel	5	5
1730	A717	2s blk, emer & grn	5	5
1731	A717	3s blk & multi	5	5
1732	A717	5s blk & multi	10	5
1733	A717	10s blk, grn & yel	16	8
1734	A717	13s blk & multi	30	15
1735	A717	20s blk, lil & grn	65	20
		Nos. 1728-1735 (8)	1.41	68

Silkworms and Spindles
A718

Designs: 2s, Silkworm, cocoons and pattern. 3s, Cocoons and spinning wheel. 5s, Cocoons, woof-and-warp diagram. 13s, Silk moth, cocoon and spinning frame. 20s, Silk moth, eggs and shuttle.

1969, Jan. 30 Photo. *Perf. 10½*

1736	A718	1s bl, grn, sl & blk	5	5
1737	A718	2s dp car, sil & blk	5	5
1738	A718	3s Prus bl, sil & blk	5	5
1739	A718	5s pur, ver, sil & blk	8	6
1740	A718	13s red lil, ocher, sil & blk	30	15
1741	A718	20s grn, org, sil & blk	50	20
		Nos. 1736-1741 (6)	1.03	56

Bulgarian silk industry.

Attack and Capture of Emperor Nicephorus
A719

Sts. Cyril and Methodius, Mural, Troian Monastery
A720

Designs (Manasses Chronicle): No. 1742, Death of Ivan Asen. 3s, Khan Kroum feasting after victory. No. 1748, Invasion of Bulgaria by Prince Sviatoslav of Kiev. No. 1750, Russian invasion and campaigns of Emperor John I Zimisces, c. 972 A.D. 40s, Tsar Ivan Alexander, Jesus and Constantine Manasses.

Horizontal designs: No. 1743, Kings Nebuchadnezzar, Balthazar, Darius and Cyrus. No. 1745, Kings Cambyses, Gyges and Darius. 5s, King David and Tsar Ivan Alexander. No. 1749, Persecution of Byzantine army after battle of July 26, 811. No. 1751, Christening of Bulgarian Tsar Boris, 865. 60s, Arrival of Tsar Simeon in Constantinople and his succeeding surprise attack on that city.

1969 Photo. *Perf. 14x13½, 13½x14*

Gold Frame

1742	A719	1s multi	5	5
1743	A719	1s multi	5	5
1744	A719	2s multi	5	5
1745	A719	2s multi	5	5
1746	A719	3s multi	10	5
1747	A719	5s multi	10	5
1748	A719	13s multi	30	8
1749	A719	13s multi	30	10
1750	A719	20s multi	60	20
1751	A719	20s multi	60	20
1752	A719	40s multi	1.00	50
1753	A719	60s multi	1.75	60
		Nos. 1742-1753 (12)	4.95	1.98

1969, Mar. 23

1754	A720	28s gold & multi	85	40

Post Horn
A721

Designs: 13s, Bulgaria Nos. 1 and 534. 20s, Street fighting at Stačkata, 1919.

1969, Apr. 15 Photo. *Perf. 10½*

1755	A721	2s grn & yel	5	5
1756	A721	13s multi	40	10
1757	A721	20s dk bl & lt bl	50	20

Issued to commemorate the 90th anniversary of the Bulgarian postal administration.

The Fox and the Rabbit
A722

Children's Drawings: 2s, Boy reading to wolf and fox. 13s, Two birds and cat singing together.

1969, Apr. 21

1758	A722	1s emer, org & blk	5	5
1759	A722	2s org, lt bl & blk	5	5
1760	A722	13s lt bl, ol & blk	50	15

Issued for Children's Week.

ILO Emblem
A723

1969, Apr. 28

1761	A723	13s dl grn & blk	30	15

Issued to commemorate the 50th anniversary of the International Labor Organization.

St. George and SOPHIA 69 Emblem
A724

Designs: 2s, Virgin Mary and St. John Bogoslov. 3s, Archangel Michael. 5s, Three Saints. 8s, Jesus Christ. 13s, Sts. George and Dimitrie. 20s, Christ, the Almighty. 40s, St. Dimitrie. 60s, The 40 Martyrs. 80s, The Transfiguration.

1969, Apr. 30 *Perf. 11x12*

1762	A724	1s gold & multi	5	5
1763	A724	2s gold & multi	5	5
1764	A724	3s gold & multi	5	5
1765	A724	5s gold & multi	10	5
1766	A724	8s gold & multi	15	5
1767	A724	13s gold & multi	30	10
1768	A724	20s gold & multi	60	20
1769	A724	40s gold & multi	1.25	40
	a.	Sheet of four	5.00	3.50
1770	A724	60s gold & multi	1.75	80
1771	A724	80s gold & multi	2.50	90
		Nos. 1762-1771 (10)	6.80	2.65

Old Bulgarian art from the National Art Gallery. No. 1769a contains 4 of No. 1769 with center gutter showing Alexander Nevski Shrine. See note on SOPHIA 69 after Nos. C112-C120.

St. Cyril Preaching
A725

St. Sophia Church
A726

Design: 28s, St. Cyril and followers.

1969, June 20 Litho. *Perf. 10½*

1772	A725	2s sil, grn & red	15	5
1773	A725	28s sil, dk bl & red	65	35

Issued to commemorate the 1100th anniversary of the death of St. Cyril (827–869), apostle to the Slavs, inventor of Cyrillic alphabet. Issued in sheets of 25 with se-tenant labels; Cyrillic inscription on label of 2s, Glagolitic inscription on label of 28s.

1969, May 25 *Perf. 13x12½*

Sofia Through the Ages: 1s, Roman coin with inscription "Ulpia Serdica." 2s, Roman coin with Aesculapius Temple. 4s, Bojana Church. 5s, Sobranie Parliament. 13s, Vasov National Theater. 20s, Alexander Nevski Shrine. 40s, Clement Ochrida University. 1 l, Coat of arms.

1774	A726	1s gold & bl	5	5
1775	A726	2s gold & ol grn	5	5
1776	A726	3s gold & red brn	5	5
1777	A726	4s gold & pur	7	5
1778	A726	5s gold & plum	10	5
1779	A726	13s gold & brt grn	25	10
1780	A726	20s gold & vio bl	45	15
1781	A726	40s gold & dp car	1.10	35
		Nos. 1774-1781 (8)	2.12	85

Souvenir Sheet

Imperf.

1782	A726	1 l grn, gold & red	2.50	2.50

Issued to show historic Sofia in connection with the International Philatelic Exhibition. Sofia, May 31–June 8.

No. 1782 contains one stamp (size: 43½x43½mm.). Emblems of 8 preceding philatelic exhibitions in metallic ink in margin; gold inscription. Size: 80x72mm.

No. 1782 was overprinted in green "IBRA '73" and various symbols, and released May 4, 1973, for the Munich Philatelic Exhibition. The overprint also exists in gray.

St. George
A727

1969, June 9 Litho. *Perf. 11½*

1783	A727	40s sil, blk & pale rose	1.10	50

Issued to commemorate the 38th FIP (Féderation Internationale de Philatelie) Congress, June 9–11.

Hand Planting Sapling
A728

1969, Apr. 28 Photo. ***Perf. 11***

1784	A728	2s ol grn, blk & lil	10	5

Issued to publicize 25 years of the reforestation campaign.

Partisans
A729

Designs: 2s, Combine harvester. 3s, Dam. 5s, Flutist and singers. 13s, Factory. 20s, Lenin, Dimitrov, Russian and Bulgarian flags.

1969, Sept. 9

1785	A729	1s blk, pur & org	5	5
1786	A729	2s blk, ol bis & org	5	5
1787	A729	3s blk, bl grn & org	5	5
1788	A729	5s blk, brn red & org	10	5
1789	A729	13s blk, bl & org	30	10
1790	A729	20s blk, brn & org	55	20
		Nos. 1785-1790 (6)	1.10	50

25th anniversary of People's Republic.

Women Gymnasts
A730

Design: 20s, Wrestlers.

1969, Sept. Photo. ***Perf. 11***

1791	A730	2s bl, blk & pale brn	5	5
1792	A730	20s red org & multi	60	25

Third National Spartakiad.

Tchanko Bakalov Tcherkovski
A731

1969, Sept.

1793	A731	13s multi	30	10

Birth centenary of Tchanko Bakalov Techerkovski, poet.

Woman Gymnast
A732

Designs: 2s, Two women with hoops. 3s, Woman with hoop. 5s, Two women with spheres.

1969, Oct.

Gymnasts in Light Gray

1794	A732	1s grn & dk bl	5	5
1795	A732	2s bl & dk bl	5	5
1796	A732	3s emer & sl grn	8	5
1797	A732	5s org & pur	12	8
		Nos. 1794-1797, B35-B36(6)	1.51	1.06

Issued to publicize the World Championships for Artistic Gymnastics, Varna.

The Priest Rilski, by Zachary Zograf
A733

Paintings from the National Art Gallery. 2s, Woman at Window, by Vasil Stoilov. 3s, Workers at Rest, by Nenko Balkanski (horiz.). 4s, Woman Dressing (Nude), by Ivan Nenov. 5s, Portrait of a Woman, by N. Pavlovich. 13s, Falstaff, by Duzunov Kr. Sarafov. No. 1804, Portrait of a Woman, by N. Mihajlov (horiz.). No. 1805, Workers at Mealtime, by Stojan Sotirov (horiz.). 40s, Self-portrait, by Tcheno Togorov.

Perf. 11½x12, 12x11½

1969, Nov. 10

1798	A733	1s gold & multi	5	5
1799	A733	2s gold & multi	5	5
1800	A733	3s gold & multi	5	5
1801	A733	4s gold & multi	7	5
1802	A733	5s gold & multi	10	5
1803	A733	13s gold & multi	40	10
1804	A733	20s gold & multi	80	25
1805	A733	20s gold & multi	80	25
1806	A733	40s gold & multi	1.50	70
		Nos. 1798-1806 (9)	3.82	1.55

Roman Bronze Wolf—A734

Design: 2s, Roman statue of woman, found at Silistra (vert.).

1969, Oct. Photogravure ***Perf. 11***

1807	A734	2s sil, ultra & gray	10	5
1808	A734	13s sil, dk grn & gray	45	15

City of Silistra's 1,800th anniversary.

Worker and Factory
A735

1969 ***Perf. 13***

1809	A735	6s ultra & blk	15	8

25th anniversary of the factory militia.

European Hake—A736

Designs: No. 1811, Deep-sea fishing trawler. Fish: 2s, Atlantic horse mackerel. 3s, Pilchard. 5s, Dentex macrophthalmus. 10s, Chub mackerel. 13s, Otolithes macrognathus. 20s, Lichia vadigo.

1969 ***Perf. 11***

1810	A736	1s ol grn & blk	5	5
1811	A736	1s ultra, ind & gray	5	5
1812	A736	2s lil & blk	5	5
1813	A736	3s vio bl & blk	5	5
1814	A736	5s rose cl, pink & blk	15	6
1815	A736	10s gray & blk	30	10
1816	A736	13s ver, sal & blk	40	12
1817	A736	20s ocher & blk	75	25
		Nos. 1810-1817 (8)	1.80	73

Marin Drinov
A737

1969, Nov. 10 Litho. ***Perf. 11***

1818	A737	20s blk & red org	40	15

Issued to commemorate the centenary of the Bulgarian Academy of Science, founded by Marin Drinov.

Trapeze Artists
A738

Pavel Bania Sanatorium
A739

Circus Performers: 2s, Jugglers. 3s, Jugglers with loops. 5s, Juggler and bear on bicycle. 13s, Woman and performing horse. 20s, Musical clowns.

1969 Photogravure ***Perf. 11***

1819	A738	1s dk bl & multi	5	5
1820	A738	2s dk grn & multi	5	5
1821	A738	3s dk vio & multi	8	5
1822	A738	5s multi	8	5
1823	A738	13s multi	40	15
1824	A738	20s multi	75	30
		Nos. 1819-1824 (6)	1.41	65

1969, Dec. Photogravure ***Perf. 10½***

Health Resorts: 5s, Chisar Sanatorium. 6s, Kotel Children's Sanatorium. 20s, Narechen Polyclinic.

1825	A739	2s blue	5	5
1826	A739	5s ultra	9	6
1827	A739	6s green	15	10
1828	A739	20s emerald	45	10

G. S. Shonin, V. N. Kubasov and Spacecraft
A740

Designs: 2s, A. V. Filipchenko, V. N. Volkov, V. V. Gorbatko and spacecraft. 3s, Vladimir A. Shatalov, Alexei S. Yeliseyev and spacecraft. 28s, Three spacecraft in orbit.

1970, Jan. Photo. ***Perf. 11***

1829	A740	1s rose car, ol grn & blk	5	5
1830	A740	2s bl, dl cl & blk	5	5
1831	A740	3s grnsh bl, vio & blk	5	
1832	A740	28s vio bl, lil rose & lt bl	75	2

Issued to commemorate the Russian space flights of Soyuz 6, 7 and 8, Oct. 11–13, 1969.

Khan Krum and Defeat of Emperor Nicephorus, 811
A741

Bulgarian History: 1s, Khan Asparuch and Bulgars crossing the Danube (679). 3s, Conversion of Prince Boris to Christianity, 865. 5s, Tsar Simeon and battle of Akhelo, 917. 8s, Tsar Samuel defeating the Byzantines, 976. 10s, Tsar Kaloyan defeating Emperor Baldwin, 1205. 13s, Tsar Ivan Assen II defeating Greek King Theodore Komnine, 1230. 20s, Coronation of Tsar Ivailo, 1277.

1970, Feb. ***Perf. 10½***

1833	A741	1s gold & multi	5	5
1834	A741	2s gold & multi	5	5
1835	A741	3s gold & multi	5	5
1836	A741	5s gold & multi	5	5
1837	A741	8s gold & multi	14	6
1838	A741	10s gold & multi	25	10
1839	A741	13s gold & multi	35	15
1840	A741	20s gold & multi	60	20
		Nos. 1833-1840 (8)	1.54	71

See also Nos. 2126–2133.

Bulgarian Pavilion, EXPO '70
A742

1970 ***Perf. 12½***

1841	A742	20s brn, sil & org	65	45

Issued to publicize EXPO '70 International Exposition, Osaka, Japan, Mar. 15–Sept. 13, 1970.

Soccer
A743

Designs: Various views of soccer game.

1970, Mar. 4 Photo. ***Perf. 12½***

1842	A743	1s bl & multi	5	5
1843	A743	2s rose car & multi	5	5
1844	A743	3s ultra & multi	7	5
1845	A743	5s grn & multi	12	10
1846	A743	20s emer & multi	50	10
1847	A743	40s red & multi	1.10	30
		Nos. 1842-1847 (6)	1.89	65

Issued to publicize the 9th World Soccer Championships for the Jules Rimet Cup, Mexico City, May 30–June 21, 1970. See No. B37.

Lenin
A744

Designs: 13s, Lenin portrait. 20s, Lenin writing.

1970, Apr. 22

1848	A744	2s vio bl & multi	5	5
1849	A744	13s brn & multi	35	10
1850	A744	20s multi	75	20

Centenary of birth of Lenin (1870–1924).

Tephrocactus Alexanderi V. Bruchii
A745

Cacti: 2s, Opuntia drummondii. 3s, Hatiora cilindrica. 5s, Gymnocalycium vatteri. 8s, Helianthо cereus grandiflorus. 10s, Neochilenia andreaeana. 13s, Peireskia vargasii v. longispina. 20s, Neobesseya rosiflora.

1970 Photogravure *Perf. 12½*

1851	A745	1s multi	5	5
1852	A745	2s dk grn & multi	5	5
1853	A745	3s multi	5	5
1854	A745	5s bl & multi	10	5
1855	A745	8s brn & multi	25	5
1856	A745	10s vio bl & multi	95	20
1857	A745	13s brn red & multi	95	20
1858	A745	20s pur & multi	1.25	40
		Nos. 1851-1858 (8)	3.65	1.05

Rose
A746

Designs: Various Roses.

1970, June 8 Litho. *Perf. 13½*

1859	A746	1s gray & multi	5	5
1860	A746	2s gray & multi	5	5
1861	A746	3s gray & multi	5	5
1862	A746	4s gray & multi	7	5
1863	A746	5s gray & multi	10	5
1864	A746	13s gray & multi	30	15
1865	A746	20s gray & multi	90	35
1866	A746	28s gray & multi	1.50	55
		Nos. 1859-1866 (8)	3.02	1.30

Gold Bowl
A747

Designs: Various bowls and art objects from Gold Treasure of Thrace.

1970, June 15 Photo. *Perf. 12½*

1867	A747	1s blk, bl & gold	5	5
1868	A747	2s blk, lt vio & gold	5	5
1869	A747	3s blk, ver & gold	7	5
1870	A747	5s blk, yel grn & gold	10	6
1871	A747	13s blk, org & gold	70	15
1872	A747	20s blk, lil & gold	85	25
		Nos. 1867-1872 (6)	1.82	61

EXPO Emblem, Rose and Bulgarian Woman
A748

Designs (EXPO Emblem and): 2s, Three women. 3s, Woman and fruit. 28s, Dancers. 40s, Mt. Fuji and pavilions.

1970, June 20

1873	A748	1s gold & multi	10	5
1874	A748	2s gold & multi	10	5
1875	A748	3s gold & multi	12	5
1876	A748	28s gold & multi	80	25

Miniature Sheet

Imperf.

1877	A748	40s gold & multi	1.25	75

Issued to publicize EXPO '70 International Exposition, Osaka, Japan, Mar. 15–Sept. 13. No. 1877 contains one stamp with simulated perforations; gray margin with blue border and roses. Size: 75½x90mm.

Ivan Vasov
A749

1970, Aug. 1 Photo. *Perf. 12½*

1878	A749	13s vio bl	40	10

Issued to commemorate the 120th anniversary of the birth of Ivan Vasov, author.

U.N. Emblem—A750

1970, Aug. 1

1879	A750	20s Prus bl & gold	45	15

25th anniversary of the United Nations.

George Dimitrov
A751

Retriever
A752

1970, Aug.

1880	A751	20s blk, gold & org	55	20

Issued to commemorate the 70th anniversary of BZNC (Bulgarian Communist Party).

1970 Photo. *Perf. 12½*

Dogs: 1s, Golden retriever (horiz.). 3s, Great Dane. 4s, Boxer. 5s, Cocker spaniel. 13s, Doberman pinscher. 20s, Scottish terrier. 28s, Russian greyhound (horiz.).

1881	A752	1s multi	5	5
1882	A752	2s multi	5	5
1883	A752	3s multi	7	5
1884	A752	4s multi	10	6
1885	A752	5s multi	10	8
1886	A752	13s multi	50	15
1887	A752	20s multi	1.00	35
1888	A752	28s multi	1.50	45
		Nos. 1881-1888 (8)	3.37	1.24

Volleyball
A753

Designs: No. 1890, Two women players. No. 1891, Woman player. No. 1892, Man player.

1970, Sept. Photo. *Perf. 12½*

1889	A753	2s dk red brn, bl & blk	10	5
1890	A753	2s ultra, org & blk	15	5
1891	A753	20s Prus bl, yel & blk	80	20
1892	A753	20s grn, yel & blk	80	20

World Volleyball Championships.

Enrico Caruso and "I Pagliacci" by Ruggiero Leoncavallo
A754

Opera Singers and Operas: 2s, Christina Morfova and "The Bartered Bride" by Bedrich Smetana. 3s, Peter Reitchev and "Tosca" by Giacomo Puccini. 10s, Svetana Tabakova and "The Flying Dutchman" by Richard Wagner. 13s, Katia Popova and "The Masters" by Paroshkev Hadjev. 20s, Feodor Chaliapin and "Boris Godunov" by Modest Musorgski.

1970, Oct. 15 Photo. *Perf. 14*

1893	A754	1s blk & multi	8	8
1894	A754	2s blk & multi	8	8
1895	A754	3s blk & multi	8	8
1896	A754	10s blk & multi	18	12
1897	A754	13s blk & multi	25	15
1898	A754	20s blk & multi	95	25
		Nos. 1893-1898 (6)	1.62	76

Issued to honor opera singers in their best roles.

Ivan Assen II Coin—A755

Coins from 14th Century with Ruler's Portrait: 2s, Theodor Svetoslav. 3s, Mikhail Chichman. 13s, Ivan Alexander and Mikhail Assen. 20s, Ivan Sratsimir. 28s, Ivan Chichman (initials).

1970, Nov. *Perf. 12½*

1899	A755	1s buff & multi	5	5
1900	A755	2s gray & multi	5	5
1901	A755	3s multi	8	5
1902	A755	13s multi	25	12
1903	A755	20s lt bl & multi	70	15
1904	A755	28s multi	90	25
		Nos. 1899-1904 (6)	2.03	67

Fireman
A756

Design: 3s, Fire engine.

1970 Lithographed *Perf. 12½*

1905	A756	1s blk, gray & yel	5	5
1906	A756	3s blk, gray & red	10	5

Fire protection publicity.

Bicyclists
A757

Congress Emblem
A758

1970 Photogravure

1907	A757	20s grn, yel & pink	60	15

For the 20th Bulgarian bicycle race.

1970

1908	A758	13s gold & multi	40	10

For the 7th World Congress of Sociology, Varna, Sept. 14–19.

Beethoven
A759

Friedrich Engels
A760

1970

1909	A759	28s lil rose & dk bl	75	25

Bicentenary of the birth of Ludwig van Beethoven (1770–1827), composer.

1970 Photogravure *Perf. 12½*

1910	A760	13s ver, tan & brn	40	15

Sesquicentennial of the birth of Friedrich Engels (1820–1895), German socialist, collaborator of Karl Marx.

Miniature Sheets

Luna 16
A761

Design (Russian moon mission): 80s, Lunokhod 1, unmanned vehicle on moon (horiz.).

1970 Photogravure *Imperf.*

1911	A761	80s plum, sil, blk & bl	2.50	2.00
1912	A761	1 l vio bl, sil & red	4.00	2.50

No. 1911 commemorates Lunokhod 1, Nov. 10–17. Size: 60x72mm. No. 1912, Luna 16 mission, Sept. 12–24. Size: 50x68mm.

Issue dates: 80s, Dec. 18; 1 lev, Nov. 10.

Snowflake
A762

1970, Dec. 15 Photo. *Perf. 12½x13*

1913	A762	2s ultra & multi	8	5

New Year 1971.

Birds and Flowers
A763

Folk Art: 2s, Bird and flowers. 3s, Flying birds. 5s, Birds and flowers. 13s, Sun. 20s, Tulips and pansies.

1971, Jan. 25 *Perf. 12½x13½*

1914	A763	1s multi	5	5
1915	A763	2s multi	5	5
1916	A763	3s multi	5	5
1917	A763	5s multi	5	5
1918	A763	13s multi	20	10
1919	A763	20s multi	70	15
		Nos. 1914-1919 (6)	1.10	45

Spring 1971.

Girl, by Zeko Spiridonov
A764

Modern Bulgarian Sculpture: 2s, Third Class (people looking through train window), by Ivan Funev. 3s, Bust of Elin Pelin, by Marko Markov. 13s, Bust of Nina, by Andrej Nikolov. 20s, Monument to P. K. Yavorov (kneeling woman), by Ivan Lazarov. 28s, Engineer, by Ivan Funev. 1 l, Refugees, by Sekul Krimov (horiz.).

1971, Feb. *Perf. 12½*

1920	A764	1s gold & vio	6	6
1921	A764	2s gold & dk ol grn	6	6
1922	A764	3s gold & rose brn	10	8
1923	A764	13s gold & dk grn	30	15
1924	A764	20s gold & red brn	55	15
1925	A764	28s gold & dk brn	80	25
		Nos. 1920-1925 (6)	1.87	75

Souvenir Sheet

Imperf.

1926	A764	1 l gold, dk brn & buff	2.50	2.00

No. 1926 has green marginal inscription. Size: 60x72mm.

Runner
A765

Design: 20s, Woman putting the shot.

1971, Mar. 13 Photo. *Perf. 12½x13*

1927	A765	2s brn & multi	10	5
1928	A765	20s dp grn, org & blk	1.25	25

2nd European Indoor Track and Field Championships.

Bulgarian Secondary School, Bolgrad
A766

Educators: 20s, Dimiter Mitev, Prince Bogoridi and Sava Radoulov.

1971, March 16 *Perf. 12½*

1929	A766	2s sil, brn & grn	5	5
1930	A766	20s sil, brn & vio	55	20

First Bulgarian secondary school, 1858, in Bolgrad, USSR.

Communards
A767

1971, Mar. 18 Photo. *Perf. 12½x13*

1931	A767	20s rose mag & blk	60	20

Centenary of the Paris Commune.

Dimitrov Facing Goering, Quotation, FIR Emblem
A768

1971, Apr. 11 *Perf. 12½*

1932	A768	2s grn, gold, blk & red	5	5
1933	A768	13s plum, gold, blk & red	70	15

International Federation of Resistance Fighters (FIR), 20th anniversary.

George S. Rakovski
A769

1971, Apr. 14

1934	A769	13s ol & blk brn	30	10

150th anniversary of birth of George S. Rakovski (1821–1867), revolutionary against Turkish rule.

Edelweiss Hotel, Borovets
A770

Designs: 2s, Panorama Hotel, Pamporovo. 4s, Boats at Albena, Black Sea. 8s, Boats at Rousalka. 10s, Shtastlivetsa Hotel, Mt. Vitosha.

1971 *Perf. 13*

1935	A770	1s brt grn	5	5
1936	A770	2s ol gray	5	5
1937	A770	4s brt bl	7	5
1938	A770	8s blue	15	5
1939	A770	10s bluish grn	25	6
		Nos. 1935-1939 (5)	57	26

Technological Progress—A771

Designs: 1s, Mason with banner (vert.). 13s, Two men and doves (vert.).

1971, Apr. 20 Photo. *Perf. 12½*

1940	A771	1s gold & multi	5	5
1941	A771	2s gray bl & multi	5	5
1942	A771	13s lt grn & multi	40	15

Tenth Congress of Bulgarian Communist Party.

Panayot Pipkov and Anthem
A772

1971, May 20

1943	A772	13s sil, blk & brt grn	40	15

Birth centenary of Panayot Pipkov, composer.

Mammoth
A773

Prehistoric Animals: 2s, Bear (vert.). 3s, Hipparion (horse). 13s, Platybelodon. 20s, Dinotherium (vert.). 28s, Saber-tooth tiger.

1971, May 29 *Perf. 12½*

1944	A773	1s dl bl & multi	6	5
1945	A773	2s lil & multi	6	5
1946	A773	3s multi	10	8
1947	A773	13s multi	50	10
1948	A773	20s dp grn & multi	90	20
1949	A773	28s multi	1.50	30
		Nos. 1944-1949 (6)	3.12	78

Khan Asparuch Crossing Danube, 679 A.D., by Boris Angelushev—A774

Historical Paintings: 3s, Reception at Trnovo, by Ilya Petrov. 5s, Chevartov's Troops at Benkovsky, by P. Morozov. 8s, Russian Gen. Gurko and People in Sofia, 1878, by D. Gudjenko. 28s, People Greeting Red Army, by S. Venov.

1971, Mar. 6 *Perf. 13½x14*

1950	A774	2s gold & multi	5	5
1951	A774	3s gold & multi	5	5
1952	A774	5s gold & multi	15	6
1953	A774	8s gold & multi	30	10
a.		Souv. sheet of 4	1.00	75
1954	A774	28s gold & multi	2.50	85
		Nos. 1950-1954 (5)	3.05	1.11

No. 1953a contains one each of Nos. 1950–1953. Gold decoration in gutter between stamps. Size: 137½x130mm.

In 1973, No. 1953a was surcharged 1 lev and overprinted "Visitez la Bulgarie", airline initials and emblems, and, on the 5s stamp, "Par Avion".

Freed Black, White and Yellow Men
A775

1971, May 20 Photo. *Perf. 12½*

1955	A775	13s bl, blk & yel	40	15

International Year against Racial Discrimination.

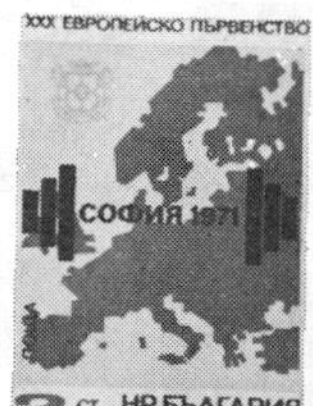

Map of Europe, Championship Emblem
A776

"XXX" Supporting Barbell
A777

1971, June 19

1956	A776	2s lt bl & multi	5	5
1957	A777	13s yel & multi	70	15

30th European Weight Lifting Championships, Sofia, June 19–27.

Facade, Old House, Koprivnica
A778

Designs: Decorated facades of various old houses in Koprivnica.

1971, July 10 Photo. *Perf. 12½*

1958	A778	1s grn & multi	5	5
1959	A778	2s brn & multi	5	5
1960	A778	6s vio & multi	10	8
1961	A778	13s dk red & multi	55	15

Frontier Guard and German Shepherd
A779

1971, July 31 *Perf. 13*

1962	A779	2s grn & ol grn	10	5

25th anniversary of the Frontier Guards.

Congress of Busludja, Bas-relief
A780

1971, July 31 *Perf. 12½*

1963	A780	2s dk red & ol grn	10	5

80th anniversary of the first Congress of the Bulgarian Social Democratic party.

Young Woman, by Ivan Nenov
A781

Paintings: 2s, Lazarova in Evening Gown, by Stefan Ivanov. 3s, Performer in Dress Suit, by Kyril Zonev. 13s, Portrait of a Woman, by Detchko Uzunov. 20s, Woman from Kalotina, by Vladimir Dimitrov. 40s, Gorjanin (Mountain Man), by Stoyan Venev.

1971, Aug. 2 *Perf. 14x13½*

1964	A781	1s grn & multi	5	5
1965	A781	2s grn & multi	5	5
1966	A781	3s grn & multi	5	5
1967	A781	13s grn & multi	35	10
1968	A781	20s grn & multi	75	35
1969	A781	40s grn & multi	1.50	55
		Nos. 1964-1969 (6)	2.75	1.15

National Art Gallery.

Wrestlers
A782

Designs: 13s, Wrestlers.

1971, Aug. 27 *Perf. 12½*

1970	A782	2s grn, blk & bl	5	5
1971	A782	13s red org, blk & bl	55	10

European Wrestling Championships.

Young Workers
A783

Post Horn Emblem
A784

1971 **Photogravure** *Perf. 13*

1972	A783	2s dk bl	10	5

25th anniversary of the Young People's Brigade.

1971, Sept. 15 *Perf. 12½*

1973	A784	20s dp grn & gold	50	20

8th meeting of postal administrations of socialist countries, Varna.

FEBS Waves Emblem—A785

1971, Sept. 20

1974	A785	13s blk, red & mar	50	20

7th Congress of European Biochemical Association (FEBS), Varna.

Statue of Republic
A786

Design: 13s, Bulgarian flag.

1971, Sept. 20 *Perf. 13x12½*

1975	A786	2s gold, yel & dk red	5	5
1976	A786	13s gold, grn & red	45	20

25th anniversary of the Bulgarian People's Republic.

Cross Country Skiing and Winter Olympics Emblem
A787

Sport and Winter Olympics Emblem: 2s, Downhill skiing. 3s, Ski jump and skiing. 4s, Women's figure skating. 13s, Ice hockey. 28s, Slalom skiing. 1 l, Torch and stadium.

1971, Sept. 25 *Perf. 12½*

1977	A787	1s dk grn & multi	6	5
1978	A787	2s vio bl & multi	6	5
1979	A787	3s ultra & multi	6	5
1980	A787	4s dp plum & multi	9	5
1981	A787	13s dk bl & multi	60	10
1982	A787	28s multi	1.35	35
		Nos. 1977-1982 (6)	2.22	65

Miniature Sheet

Imperf.

1983	A787	1 l multi	4.50	2.75

11th Winter Olympic Games, Sapporo, Japan, Feb. 3–13, 1972.
Size of No. 1983: 70x80mm.

Factory, Botevgrad
A788

Industrial Buildings: 2s, Petro-chemical works, Pleven (vert.). 10s, Chemical works, Vratsa. 13s, Maritsa-Istok Power Station, Dimitrovgrad. 40s, Electronics works, Sofia.

1971 **Photogravure** *Perf. 13*

1984	A788	1s violet	5	5
1985	A788	2s orange	6	5
1986	A788	10s dp pur	20	9
1987	A788	13s lil rose	25	10
1988	A788	40s dp brn	75	15
		Nos. 1984-1988 (5)	1.31	44

UNESCO Emblem
A789

1971, Nov. 4 *Perf. 12½*

1989	A789	20s lt bl, blk, gold & red	60	20

25th anniversary of the United Nations Educational, Scientific and Cultural Organization (UNESCO).

Soccer Player, by Kyril Zonev (1896–1971)
A790

Paintings by Kyril Zonev: 2s, Landscape (horiz.). 3s, Self-portrait. 13s, Lilies. 20s, Landscape (horiz.). 40s, Portrait of a Young Woman.

1971, Nov. 10 *Perf. 11x12*

1990	A790	1s gold & multi	8	8
1991	A790	2s gold & multi	8	8
1992	A790	3s gold & multi	8	8
1993	A790	13s gold & multi	25	10
1994	A790	20s gold & multi	90	25
1995	A790	40s gold & multi	1.25	40
		Nos. 1990-1995 (6)	2.64	99

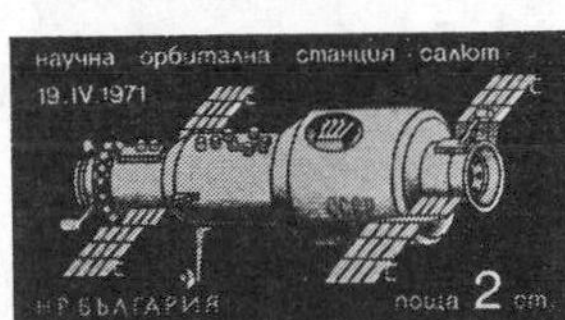

Salyut Space Station—A791

Astronauts Dobrovolsky, Volkov and Patsayev—A792

Designs: 13s, Soyuz 11 space transport. 40s, Salyut and Soyuz 11 joined.

1971, Dec. 20 *Perf. 12½*

1996	A791	2s dk grn, yel & red	5	5
1997	A791	13s multi	25	15
1998	A791	40s dk bl & multi	1.25	35

Souvenir Sheet

Imperf.

1999	A792	80s multi	2.00	1.75

Salyut-Soyuz 11 space mission, and in memory of the Russian astronauts Lt. Col. Georgi T. Dobrovolsky, Vladislav N. Volkov and Victor I. Patsayev, who died during the Soyuz 11 space mission, June 6–30, 1971. Size of No. 1999: 70x73½mm.

Oil Tanker Vihren—A793

1972, Jan. 8 **Photo.** *Perf. 12½*

2000	A793	18s lil rose, vio & blk	70	20

Bulgarian shipbuilding industry.

Goce Delchev
A794

Portraits: 5s, Jan Sandanski. 13s, Damjan Gruev.

1972, Jan. 21 **Photo.** *Perf. 12½*

2001	A794	2s brick red & blk	5	5
2002	A794	5s grn & blk	11	6
2003	A794	13s lem & blk	40	15

Centenary of the births of Bulgarian patriots Delchev (1872–1903) and Sandanski, and of Macedonian Gruev (1871–1906).

Gymnast with Ball, Medals—A795

Designs: 18s, Gymnast with hoop, and medals. 70s, Gymnasts with hoops, and medals.

1972, Feb. 10

2004	A795	13s grn, brn, red & gold	65	15
2005	A795	18s brn, grn, red & gold	85	25

Miniature Sheet

Imperf.

2006	A795	70s gold, brn, grn & red	3.00	2.00

5th World Women's Gymnastic Championships, Havana, Cuba.
Size of No. 2006: 61½x73mm.

View of Melnik, by Petar Mladenov
A796

Paintings from National Art Gallery: 2s, Plower, by Pencho Georgiev. 3s, Funeral, by Alexander Djendov. 13s, Husband and Wife, by Vladimir Dimitrov. 20s, Nursing Mother, by Nenko Balkanski. 40s, Paisii Hilendarski Writing History, by Koio Denchev.

1972, Feb. 20 *Perf. 13½x14*

2007	A796	1s grn & multi	6	5
2008	A796	2s grn & multi	6	5
2009	A796	3s grn & multi	10	8
2010	A796	13s grn & multi	40	12
2011	A796	20s grn & multi	70	20
2012	A796	40s grn & multi	1.25	35
		Nos. 2007-2012 (6)	2.57	85

Paintings from National Art Gallery.

Worker
A797

Singing Harvesters
A798

1972, Mar. 7 ***Perf. 12½***

2013	A797	13s sil & multi	30	10

7th Bulgarian Trade Union Congress.

Perf. 11½x12, 12x11½

1972, Mar. 31

Designs: Paintings by Vladimir Dimitrov.

Olive Brown & Multicolored

2014	A798	1s *shown*	8	5
2015	A798	2s *Harvester*	8	5
2016	A798	3s *Women Diggers*	12	10
2017	A798	13s *Fabric Dyers*	35	10
2018	A798	20s *"My Mother"*	75	15
2019	A798	40s *Self-portrait*	1.50	35
		Nos. 2014-2019 (6)	2.88	80

90th anniversary of birth of Vladimir Dimitrov, painter.

"Your Heart is your Health"

A799

St. Mark's Basilica and Wave

A800

1972, Apr. 30 ***Perf. 12½***

2020	A799	13s red, blk & grn	60	15

World Health Day.

1972, May 6 ***Perf. 13x12½***

Design: 13s, Ca' D'Oro and wave.

2021	A800	2s ol grn, bl grn & lt bl	5	5
2022	A800	13s red brn, vio & lt grn	60	15

UNESCO campaign to save Venice.

Dimitrov in Print Shop, 1901—A801

Designs: Life of George Dimitrov.

1972, May 8 Photo. ***Perf. 12½***

Gold and Multicolored

2023	A801	1s *shown*	6	5
2024	A801	2s *Dimitrov as leader of 1923 uprising*	6	5
2025	A801	3s *Leipzig trial, 1933*	6	5
2026	A801	5s *as Communist functionary, 1935*	9	6
2027	A801	13s *as leader and teacher, 1948*	15	9
2028	A801	18s *addressing youth rally, 1948*	65	15
2029	A801	28s *with Pioneers, 1948*	1.00	25
2030	A801	40s *Mausoleum*	1.50	50
2031	A801	80s *Portrait*	2.50	70
a.		Souvenir sheet	5.00	3.50
		Nos. 2023-2031 (9)	6.07	1.90

90th anniversary of the birth of George Dimitrov (1882–1949), communist leader.
No. 2031a contains one imperf. stamp similar to No. 2031, but in different colors. Gold marginal inscription. Size: 86x82mm.

Price, #2031 imperf. in slightly changed colors, $4.

A802

Design: 2s, Flame and quotation.

1972, May 12

2032	A802	2s gold, grn & brn	5	5
2033	A802	13s gold, grn & brn	40	15

250th anniversary of the birth of the monk Paisii Hilendarski (1722–1798), writer of Bulgarian-Slavic history.

Canoeing, Motion and Olympic Emblems—A803

Designs (Motion and Olympic emblems and): 2s, Gymnastics. 3s, Swimming, women's. 13s, Volleyball. 18s, Jumping. 40s, Wrestling. 80s, Stadium and sports.

1972, June 25

Figures of Athletes in Silver & Black

2034	A803	1s lt bl & multi	5	5
2035	A803	2s org & multi	8	8
2036	A803	3s multi	10	10
2037	A803	13s yel & multi	20	10
2038	A803	18s multi	55	25
2039	A803	40s pink & multi	1.60	40
		Nos. 2034-2039 (6)	2.58	98

Miniature Sheet

Imperf.

Size: 62x60mm.

2040	A803	80s gold, ver & yel	2.50	1.50

20th Olympic Games, Munich, Aug. 26–Sept. 11.

Angel Kunchev

A804

1972, June 30 Photo. ***Perf. 12½***

2041	A804	2s mag, dk pur & gold	10	5

Centenary of the death of Angel Kunchev, patriot and revolutionist.

Zlatni Pyassatsi
A805

1972, Sept. 16 **Multicolored**

2042	A805	1s *shown*	5	5
2043	A805	2s *Drouzhba*	5	5
2044	A805	3s *Slunchev Bryag*	8	5
2045	A805	13s *Primorsko*	15	10
2046	A805	28s *Roussalka*	55	30
2047	A805	40s *Albena*	90	35
		Nos. 2042-2047 (6)	1.78	90

Bulgarian Black Sea resorts.

Bronze Medal, Olympic Emblems, Canoeing
A806

Designs (Olympic Emblems and): 2s, Silver medal, broad jump. 3s, Gold medal, boxing. 18s, Gold medal, wrestling. 40s, Gold medal, weight lifting.

1972, Sept. 29

2048	A806	1s Prus bl & multi	5	5
2049	A806	2s dk grn & multi	5	5
2050	A806	3s org brn & multi	5	5
2051	A806	18s ol & multi	50	20
2052	A806	40s multi	1.00	35
		Nos. 2048-2052 (5)	1.65	70

Bulgarian victories in 20th Olympic Games.

Stoj Dimitrov
A807

Resistance Fighters: 2s, Cvetko Radoinov. 3s, Bogdan Stivrodski. 5s, Mirko Laiev. 13s, Nedelyo Nikolov.

1972, Oct. 30 Photo. ***Perf. 12½x13***

2053	A807	1s ol & multi	5	5
2054	A807	2s multi	5	5
2055	A807	3s multi	6	6
2056	A807	5s multi	10	8
2057	A807	13s multi	25	10
		Nos. 2053-2057 (5)	51	34

"50 Years USSR"
A808

1972, Nov. 3 Photo. ***Perf. 12½x13***

2058	A808	13s gold, red & yel	25	10

50th anniversary of Soviet Union.

Turk's-cap Lily
A809

Protected Plants: 2s, Gentian. 3s, Sea daffodil. 4s, Globe flower. 18s, Primrose. 23s, Pulsatilla vernalis. 40s, Snake's-head.

1972, Nov. 25 ***Perf. 12½***

Flowers in Natural Colors

2059	A809	1s ol bis	5	5
2060	A809	2s ol bis	5	5
2061	A809	3s ol bis	8	5
2062	A809	4s ol bis	10	8
2063	A809	18s ol bis	25	10
2064	A809	23s ol bis	70	25
2065	A809	40s ol bis	1.35	45
		Nos. 2059-2065 (7)	2.58	1.03

No. 2052 Overprinted in Red СВЕТОВЕН ПЪРВЕНЕЦ

1972, Nov. 27

2066	A806	40s multi	1.10	35

Bulgarian weight lifting Olympic gold medalists.

Dobri Chintulov—A810

1972, Nov. 28 Photo. ***Perf. 12½***

2067	A810	2s gray, dk & lt grn	20	5

Dobri Chintulov, writer, 150th birth anniversary.

Forehead Band—A811

Designs (14th–19th Century Jewelry): 2s, Belt buckles. 3s, Amulet. 8s, Pendant. 23s, Earrings. 40s, Necklace.

1972, Dec. 27 Engr. ***Perf. 14x13½***

2068	A811	1s red brn & blk	5	5
2069	A811	2s emer & blk	5	5
2070	A811	3s Prus bl & blk	7	5
2071	A811	8s dk red & blk	16	12
2072	A811	23s red org & multi	60	25
2073	A811	40s vio & blk	1.35	55
		Nos. 2068-2073 (6)	2.28	1.07

Skin Divers—A812

Designs: 2s, Shelf-1 underwater house and divers. 18s, Diving bell and diver (vert.). 40s, Elevation balloon and divers (vert.).

1973, Jan. 24 Photo. ***Perf. 12½***

2074	A812	1s lt bl, blk & yel	5	5
2075	A812	2s blk, bl & org yel	5	5
2076	A812	18s blk, Prus bl & dl org	60	20
2077	A812	40s blk, ultra & bis	1.35	45

Bulgarian deep-sea research in the Black Sea.
A souvenir sheet of four contains imperf. 20s stamps in designs of Nos. 2074–2077 with colors changed. Gray marginal inscriptions. Size: 118x99mm. Sold for 1 lev. Price $4 unused, $2.50 canceled.

Execution of Levski, by Boris Angelushev
A813

Design: 20s, Vassil Levski, by Georgi Danchev.

1973, Feb. 10 *Perf. 13x12½*

No.	Type	Description	Unused	Used
2078	A813	2s dl rose & Prus grn	5	5
2079	A813	20s dl grn & brn	95	25

Centenary of the death of Vassil Levski (1837–1873), patriot, executed by the Turks.

Kukersky Mask, Elhovo Region
A814

Nicolaus Copernicus
A815

Kukersky Masks at pre-Spring Festival: 2s, Breznik. 3s, Hissar. 13s, Radomir. 20s, Karnobat. 40s, Pernik.

1973, Feb. 26 *Perf. 12½*

No.	Type	Description	Unused	Used
2080	A814	1s dp rose & multi	8	8
2081	A814	2s emer & multi	8	8
2082	A814	3s vio & multi	8	8
2083	A814	13s multi	40	15
2084	A814	20s multi	45	20
2085	A814	40s multi	2.50	1.75
		Nos. 2080-2085 (6)	3.59	2.34

1973, Mar. 21 Photo. *Perf. 12½*

No.	Type	Description	Unused	Used
2086	A815	28s ocher, blk & cl	1.25	60

500th anniversary of the birth of Nicolaus Copernicus (1473–1543), Polish astronomer.

Vietnamese Worker and Rainbow
A816

1973, Apr. 16

No.	Type	Description	Unused	Used
2087	A816	18s lt bl & multi	40	15

Peace in Viet Nam.

Poppy
A817

Designs: Wild flowers.

1973, May Photo. *Perf. 13*

Multicolored

No.	Type	Description	Unused	Used
2088	A817	1s *shown*	5	5
2089	A817	2s *Daisy*	6	5
2090	A817	3s *Peony*	7	5
2091	A817	13s *Centaury*	25	10
2092	A817	18s *Corn cockle*	2.50	1.65
2093	A817	28s *Ranunculus*	60	35
		Nos. 2088-2093 (6)	3.53	2.25

Christo Botev
A818

1973, June 2

No.	Type	Description	Unused	Used
2094	A818	2s pale grn, buff & brn	6	5
2095	A818	18s pale brn, gray & grn	70	45

125th anniversary of the birth of Christo Botev (1848–1876), poet.

"Suffering Worker"—A819

Design: 1s, Asen Halachev and revolutionists.

1973, June 6 Photo. *Perf. 13*

No.	Type	Description	Unused	Used
2096	A819	1s gold, red & blk	5	5
2097	A819	2s gold, org & dk brn	5	5

50th anniversary of Pleven uprising.

Muskrat
A820

Perf. 12½x13, 13x12½

1973, June 29 Lithographed

Multicolored

No.	Type	Description	Unused	Used
2098	A820	1s *shown*	5	5
2099	A820	2s *Racoon*	5	5
2100	A820	3s *Mouflon (vert.)*	7	5
2101	A820	12s *Fallow deer* (vert.)	20	15
2102	A820	18s *European bison*	45	20
2103	A820	40s *Elk*	2.25	1.50
		Nos. 2098-2103 (6)	3.07	2.00

Aleksandr Stamboliski—A821

1973, June 14 Photo. *Perf. 12½*

No.	Type	Description	Unused	Used
2104	A821	18s dp brn & org	50	30
a.		18s org	2.75	1.25

50th anniversary of the death of Aleksandr Stamboliski (1879–1923), leader of Peasants' Party and premier.

Trade Union Emblem
A822

Stylized Sun, Olympic Rings
A823

1973, Aug. 27 Photo. *Perf. 12½*

No.	Type	Description	Unused	Used
2105	A822	2s yel & multi	8	5

8th Congress of World Federation of Trade Unions, Varna, Oct. 15–22.

1973, Aug. 29 *Perf. 13*

Designs: 28s, Emblem of Bulgarian Olympic Committee and Olympic rings. 80s, Soccer, emblems of Innsbruck and Montreal 1976 Games (horiz.).

No.	Type	Description	Unused	Used
2106	A823	13s multi	65	45
2107	A823	28s multi	1.10	55

Souvenir Sheet

No.	Type	Description	Unused	Used
2108	A823	80s multi	3.50	2.50

Olympic Congress, Varna. No. 2108 contains one stamp. Blue and gray green margin shows emblems of various Olympic committees and games. Size: 60x77½ mm. It also exists imperf.; also with violet margin, imperf.

Revolutionists with Communist Flag
A824

Designs: 5s, Revolutionists on flatcar blocking train. 13s, Raising Communist flag (vert.). 18s, George Dimitrov and Vassil Kolarov.

1973, Sept. 22 Photo. *Perf. 12½*

No.	Type	Description	Unused	Used
2109	A824	2s mag & multi	5	5
2110	A824	5s mag & multi	8	6
2111	A824	13s mag & multi	30	15
2112	A824	18s mag & multi	80	50

50th anniversary of the September Revolution.

Warrior Saint
A825

Murals from Boyana Church: 1s, Tsar Kaloyan and 2s, his wife Dessislava. 5s, "St. Wystratti." 10s, Tsar Constantine Assen. 13s, Deacon Laurentius. 18s, Virgin Mary. 20s, St. Ephraim. 28s, Jesus. 80s, Jesus in the Temple (horiz.).

1973, Sept. 24

No.	Type	Description	Unused	Used
2113	A825	1s gold & multi	10	8
2114	A825	2s gold & multi	10	8
2115	A825	3s gold & multi	10	8
2116	A825	5s gold & multi	10	8
2117	A825	10s gold & multi	25	10
2118	A825	13s gold & multi	35	10
2119	A825	18s gold & multi	50	25
2120	A825	20s gold & multi	70	30
2121	A825	28s gold & multi	2.50	60
		Nos. 2113-2121 (9)	4.70	1.67

Miniature Sheet

Imperf.

No.	Type	Description	Unused	Used
2122	A825	80s gold & multi	5.00	3.50

No. 2122 contains one stamp with simulated perforations. Gold margin with view of Boyana Church. Size: 56x76½mm.

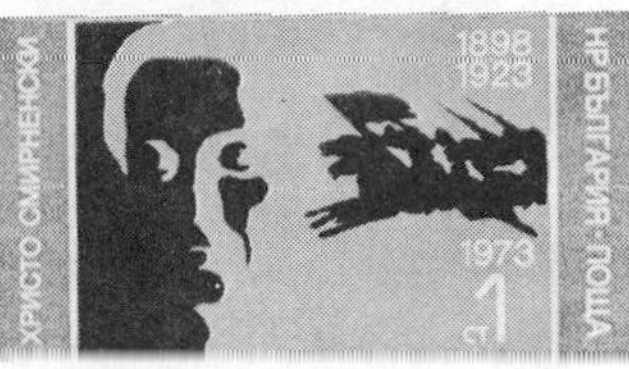

Christo Smirnenski—A826

1973, Sept. 29 Photo. *Perf. 12½*

No.	Type	Description	Unused	Used
2123	A826	1s multi	5	5
2124	A826	2s vio bl & multi	20	5

75th anniversary of the birth of Christo Smirnenski (1898–1923), poet.

Human Rights Flame
A827

1973, Oct. 10

No.	Type	Description	Unused	Used
2125	A827	13s dk bl, red & gold	30	20

25th anniversary of the Universal Declaration of Human Rights.

Type of 1970

History of Bulgaria: 1s, Tsar Theodor Svetoslav receiving Byzantine envoys. 2s, Tsar Mihail Shishman's army in battle with Byzantines. 3s, Tsar Ivan Alexander's victory at Russocastro. 4s, Patriarch Euthimius at the defense of Turnovo. 5s, Tsar Ivan Shishman leading horsemen against the Turks. 13s, Momchil attacking Turks at Umour. 18s, Tsar Ivan Stratsimir meeting King Sigismund's crusaders. 28s, The Boyars Balik, Theodor and Dobrotitsa, meeting ship bringing envoys from Anne of Savoy.

1973, Oct. 23 *Perf. 13*

Silver and Black Vignettes

No.	Type	Description	Unused	Used
2126	A741	1s ol bis	8	8
2127	A741	2s Prus bl	8	8
2128	A741	3s lilac	10	8
2129	A741	4s green	10	8
2130	A741	5s violet	10	8
2131	A741	13s org & brn	20	10
2132	A741	18s ol grn	35	15
2133	A741	28s yel brn & brn	1.00	45
		Nos. 2126-2133 (8)	2.01	1.10

Fin Class
A828

1973, Oct. 29 Lithographed *Perf. 13*

Sailboats: 2s, Flying Dutchman. 3s, Soling class. 13s, Tempest class. 20s, Class 470. 40s, Tornado class.

No.	Type	Description	Unused	Used
2134	A828	1s ultra & multi	8	8
2135	A828	2s grn & multi	8	8
2136	A828	3s dk bl & multi	10	8
2137	A828	13s dl vio & multi	30	10

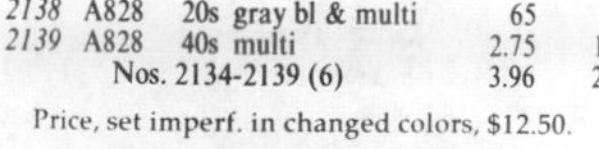

2138	A828	20s gray bl & multi	65	25
2139	A828	40s multi	2.75	1.50
		Nos. 2134-2139 (6)	3.96	2.09

Price, set imperf. in changed colors, $12.50.

Village, by Bencho Obreshkov
A829

Paintings: 2s, Mother and Child, by Stoyan Venev. 3s, Rest (woman), by Tsenko Boyadjiev. 13s, Flowers in Vase, by Sirak Skitnik. 18s, Meri Kuneva (portrait), by Ilya Petrov. 40s, Winter in Plovdiv, by Zlatyu Boyadjiev. 13s, 18s, 40s, vertical.

Perf. 12½x12, 12x12½

1973, Nov. 10

2140	A829	1s gold & multi	8	8
2141	A829	2s gold & multi	8	8
2142	A829	3s gold & multi	8	8
2143	A829	13s gold & multi	20	15
2144	A829	18s gold & multi	40	25
2145	A829	40s gold & multi	2.00	1.00
		Nos. 2140-2145 (6)	2.84	1.64

Souvenir Sheet

Paintings by Stanislav Dospevski: No. 2146a, Domnica Lambreva. No. 2146b, Self-portrait. Both vertical.

2146	A829	Sheet of 2	4.00	2.50
a.		50s gold & multi	1.00	75
b.		50s gold & multi	1.00	75

Bulgarian paintings. No. 2146 commemorates the 150th birth anniv. of Stanislav Dospevski; gold margin and brown inscription. Size: 100x96mm.

Souvenir Sheet

Soccer—A830

1973, Dec. 10 Photo. *Perf. 13*

2147	A830	28s multi	5.00	3.50

No. 2147 sold for 1 l. Size: 65x100mm. Exists overprinted for Argentina 78.

Angel and Ornaments
A831

Designs: 1s, Attendant facing right. 2s, Passover table and lamb. 3s, Attendant facing left. 8s, Abraham and ornaments. 13s, Adam and Eve. 28s, Expulsion from Garden of Eden.

1974, Jan. 21 Photo. *Perf. 13*

2148	A831	1s fawn, yel & brn	10	8
2149	A831	2s fawn, yel & brn	10	8
2150	A831	3s fawn, yel & brn	10	8
2151	A831	5s sl grn & yel	10	8
2152	A831	8s sl grn & yel	25	10
2153	A831	13s lt brn, yel & ol	35	20
2154	A831	28s lt brn, yel & ol	70	30
		Nos. 2148-2154 (7)	1.70	92

Woodcarvings from Rozhen Monastery, 19th century. Nos. 2148–2150, 2151–2152, 2153–2154 printed se-tenant.

Lenin, by N. Mirtchev—A832

Design: 18s, Lenin visiting Workers, by W. A. Serov.

1974, Jan. 28 Litho. *Perf. 12½x12*

2155	A832	2s ocher & multi	5	5
2156	A832	18s ocher & multi	45	20

50th anniversary of the death of Lenin.

1974, Jan. 28

Design: Demeter Blagoev at Rally, by G. Kowachev.

2157	A832	2s multi	8	5

50th anniversary of the death of Demeter Blagoev, founder of Bulgarian Communist Party.

Sheep
A833

Designs: Domestic animals.

1974, Feb. 1 Photo. *Perf. 13*

Multicolored

2158	A833	1s *shown*	8	8
2159	A833	2s *Goat*	8	8
2160	A833	3s *Pig*	8	8
2161	A833	5s *Cow*	12	8
2162	A833	13s *Buffalo cow*	30	10
2163	A833	20s *Horse*	80	25
		Nos. 2158-2163 (6)	1.46	67

Comecon Emblem
A834

1974, Feb. 11 Photo. *Perf. 13*

2164	A834	13s sil & multi	40	10

25th anniversary of the Council of Mutual Economic Assistance.

Soccer—A835

Designs: Various soccer action scenes.

1974, Mar. Photo. *Perf. 13*

2165	A835	1s dl grn & multi	8	8
2166	A835	2s brt grn & multi	8	8
2167	A835	3s sl grn & multi	8	8
2168	A835	13s ol & multi	10	10
2169	A835	28s bl grn & multi	60	25
2170	A835	40s emer & multi	1.35	40
		Nos. 2165-2170 (6)	2.29	99

Souvenir Sheet

2171	A835	1 l grn & multi	4.00	2.50

World Soccer Championship, Munich, June 13–July 7. No. 2171 contains one stamp. Red margin with emblem and inscription in white; soccer cup in yellow and gold. Size: 67x78½mm. No. 2171 exists imperf.

Salt Production
A836

Children's Paintings: 1s, Cosmic Research for Peaceful Purposes. 3s, Fire Dancers. 28s, Russian-Bulgarian Friendship (train and children). 60s, Spring (birds).

1974, Apr. 15 Photo. *Perf. 13*

2172	A836	1s lil & multi	8	8
2173	A836	2s lt grn & multi	8	8
2174	A836	3s bl & multi	15	8
2175	A836	28s sl & multi	1.75	1.00

Souvenir Sheet
Imperf.

2176	A836	60s bl & multi	2.50	1.75

Third World Youth Philatelic Exhibition, Sofia, May 23–30. No. 2176 contains one stamp with simulated perforations, rose and lilac border. Size: 70x70mm.

Folk Singers
A837

Designs: 2s, Folk dancers (men). 3s, Bagpiper and drummer. 5s, Wrestlers. 13s, Runners (women). 18s, Gymnast.

1974, Apr. 25 *Perf. 13*

2178	A837	1s ver & multi	5	5
2179	A837	2s org brn & multi	5	5
2180	A837	3s brn red & multi	5	5
2181	A837	5s bl & multi	15	5
2182	A837	13s ultra & multi	90	35
2183	A837	18s vio bl & multi	55	20
		Nos. 2178-2183 (6)	1.75	75

4th Amateur Arts and Sports Festival

Aster
A838

Flowers: 2s, Petunia. 3s, Fuchsia. 18s, Tulip. 20s, Carnation. 28s, Pansy. 80s, Sunflower.

1974, May Photogravure *Perf. 13*

2184	A838	1s grn & multi	5	5
2185	A838	2s vio bl & multi	5	5
2186	A838	3s ol & multi	5	5
2187	A838	18s brn & multi	20	10
2188	A838	20s multi	40	20
2189	A838	28s dl bl & multi	1.00	55
		Nos. 2184-2189 (6)	1.75	1.00

Souvenir Sheet

2190	A838	80s multi	2.00	1.2

No. 2190 contains one stamp. Deep ultramarine margin with white inscription and flower design. Size: 78x60mm.

Automobiles and Emblems
A839

1974, May 15 Photo. *Perf. 13*

2191	A839	13s multi	35	1

International Automobile Federation (FIA) Spring Congress, Sofia, May 20–24.

Old and New Buildings, UNESCO Emblem
A840

1974, June 15

2192	A840	18s multi	35	15

UNESCO Executive Council, 94th Session, Varna.

Postrider
A841

Designs: 18s, First Bulgarian mail coach. 28s, UPU Monument, Bern.

1974, Aug. 5

2193	A841	2s ocher, blk & vio	5	5
2194	A841	18s ocher, blk & grn	40	20

Souvenir Sheet

2195	A841	28s ocher, blk & bl	2.00	1.25

Centenary of Universal Postal Union. No. 2195 contains one stamp, multicolored marginal inscription. Size: 79x58mm. Exists imperf.

Pioneer and Komsomol Girl
A842

"Bulgarian Communist Party"
A843

Designs: 2s, Pioneer and birds. 60s, Emblem with portrait of George Dimitrov.

1974, Aug. 12

2196	A842	1s grn & multi	5	5
2197	A842	2s bl & multi	5	5

Souvenir Sheet

2198	A842	60s red & multi	2.00	1.75

30th anniversary of Dimitrov Pioneer Organization, Sepremvriiche. No. 2198 contains one stamp, gold margin with black inscription. Size: 60x83mm.

1974, Aug. 20

Symbolic Designs: 2s, Russian liberators. 5s, Industrialization. 13s, Advanced agriculture and husbandry. 18s, Scientific and technical progress.

2199	A843	1s bl gray & multi	5	5
2200	A843	2s bl gray & multi	5	5

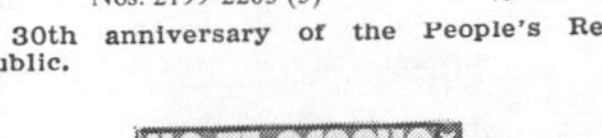

2201 A843 5s gray & multi 9 5
2202 A843 13s gray & multi 25 10
2203 A843 18s gray & multi 35 15
Nos. 2199-2203 (5) 79 40

30th anniversary of the People's Republic.

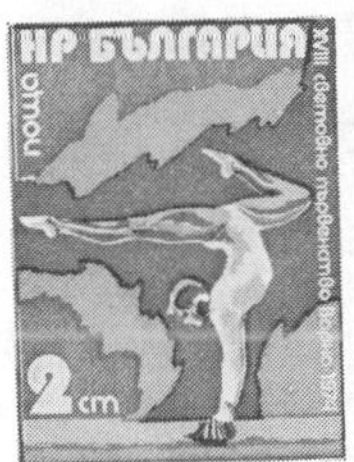

Gymnast on Parallel Bars
A844

Design: 13s, Gymnast on vaulting horse.

1974, Oct. 18 Photo. *Perf. 13*

2204 A844 2s multi 8 5
2205 A844 13s multi 35 20

18th Gymnastic Championships, Varna.

Souvenir Sheet

Symbols of Peace—A845

1974, Oct. 29 Photo. *Perf. 13*

2206 A845 Sheet of 4, multi 2.50 1.50
a. 13s *Doves* 25 15
b. 13s *Map of Europe* 25 15
c. 13s *Olive Branch* 25 15
d. 13s *Inscription* 25 15

1974 European Peace Conference. "Peace" in various languages written on Nos. 2206a–2206c. No. 2206 has yellow, brown and lilac margin. Size: 97½x117 mm. Sold for 60s. Exists imperf.

Nib and Envelope
A846

1974, Nov. 20

2207 A846 2s yel, blk & grn 10 5

Introduction of postal zone numbers.

Flowers
A847

1974, Dec. 5

2208 A847 2s emer & multi 8 5

St. Todor, Ceramic Icon
A848

Apricot Blossoms
A849

Designs: 2s, Medallion, Veliko Turnovo. 3s, Carved capital. 5s, Silver bowl. 8s, Goblet. 13s, Lion's head finial. 18s, Gold plate with Cross. 28s, Breastplate with eagle.

1974, Dec. 18 Photogravure *Perf. 13*

2209 A848 1s org & multi 5 5
2210 A848 2s pink & multi 5 5
2211 A848 3s bl & multi 5 5
2212 A848 5s lt vio & multi 8 5
2213 A848 8s brn & multi 15 8
2214 A848 13s multi 25 10
2215 A848 18s red & multi 35 15
2216 A848 28s ultra & multi 1.10 55
Nos. 2209-2216 (8) 2.08 1.08

Art works from 9th–12th centuries.

1975, Jan. Photogravure *Perf. 13*

Fruit Tree Blossoms: 2s, Apple. 3s, Cherry. 19s, Pear. 28s, Peach.

2217 A849 1s org & multi 5 5
2218 A849 2s multi 5 5
2219 A849 3s car & multi 5 5
2220 A849 19s lem & multi 35 15
2221 A849 28s ver & multi 90 30
Nos.2217-2221 (5) 1.40 60

Tree and Book
A850

1975, Mar. 25 Photo. *Perf. 13*

2222 A850 2s gold & multi 12 5

Forestry High School, 50th anniversary.

Souvenir Sheet

Farmers' Activities (Woodcuts)—A851

1975, Mar. 25

2223 A851 Sheet of 4 multi 1.00 75
a. 2s *Farmer with ax and flag*
b. 5s *Farmers on guard*
c. 13s *Dancing couple*
d. 18s *Woman picking fruit*

Bulgarian Agrarian Peoples' Union, 75th anniversary. No. 2223 has orange and green margin. Size: 102x95mm.

Michelangelo, Self-portrait
A852

Designs: 13s, Night (horiz.). 18s, Day (horiz.). Both designs after sculptures from Medici Tomb, Florence.

1975

2224 A852 2s plum & dk bl 5 5
2225 A852 13s vio bl & plum 25 10
2226 A852 18s brn & grn 55 18

Souvenir Sheet

2227 A852 2s ol & red 1.50 1.50

500th birth anniversary of Michelangelo Buonarotti (1475–1564), Italian sculptor, painter and architect. No. 2227 issued to publicize ARPHILA 75 International Philatelic Exhibition, Paris, June 6–16. Marginal inscriptions and border in gold, red and green. Sheet sold for 60s. Size: 69x83mm.

Issue dates: Nos. 2224–2226, Mar. 28. No. 2227, Mar. 31.

Souvenir Sheet

Spain No. 1 and España 75 Emblem—A853

1975, Apr. 4

2228 A853 40s multi 4.50 3.00

España 75 International Philatelic Exhibition, Madrid, Apr. 4–13. No. 2228 contains one stamp; bright ultramarine margin with white design and inscription, bister post horn. Size: 70x102mm.

Gabrov Costume
A854

Regional Costumes: 3s, Trnsk. 5s, Vidin. 13s, Gocedelchev. 18s, Risen.

1975, Apr. Photogravure *Perf. 13*

2229 A854 2s bl & multi 5 5
2230 A854 3s emer & multi 5 5
2231 A854 5s org & multi 12 8
2232 A854 13s ol & multi 30 12
2233 A854 18s multi 70 30
Nos. 2229-2233 (5) 1.22 60

Red Star and Arrow
A855

Standard Kilogram and Meter
A856

Design: 13s, Dove and broken sword.

1975, May 9

2234 A855 2s red, blk & gold 5 5
2235 A855 13s bl, blk & gold 40 18

Victory over Fascism, 30th anniversary.

1975, May 9 *Perf. 13x13½*

2236 A856 13s sil, lil & blk 25 10

Centenary of International Meter Convention, Paris, 1875.

IWY Emblem, Woman's Head
A857

Ivan Vasov
A858

1975, May 20 Photo. *Perf. 13*

2237 A857 13s multi 25 10

International Women's Year 1975.

1975, May

Design: 13s, Ivan Vasov, seated.

2238 A858 2s buff & multi 5 5
2239 A858 13s gray & multi 25 10

125th birth anniversary of Ivan Vasov.

Nikolov and Sava Kokarechkov
A859

Designs: 2s, Mitko Palaouzov and Ivan Vassilev. 5s, Nicolas Nakev and Stevtcho Kraychev. 13s, Ivanka Pachkoulova and Detelina Mintcheva.

1975, May 30

2240 A859 1s multi 5 5
2241 A859 2s multi 5 5
2242 A859 5s multi 9 5
2243 A859 13s multi 30 15

Teen-age resistance fighters, killed during World War II.

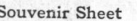

Mother Feeding Child, by John E. Millais
A861

Etchings: 2s, The Dead Daughter, by Goya. 3s, Reunion, by Beshkov. 13s, Seated Nude, by Renoir. 20s, Man in a Fur Hat, by Rembrandt. 40s, The Dream, by Daumier (horiz.). 1 l, Temptation, by Dürer.

Photogravure and Engraved

1975, Aug. Perf. 12x11½, 11½x12

2248	A861	1s yel grn & multi	5	5
2249	A861	2s org & multi	5	5
2250	A861	3s lil & multi	5	5
2251	A861	13s lt bl & multi	30	10
2252	A861	20s ocher & multi	40	20
2253	A861	40s rose & multi	1.25	35
		Nos. 2248-2253 (6)	2.10	80

Souvenir Sheet

2254	A861	1 l emer & multi	2.50	1.75

World Graphics Exhibition. No. 2254 contains one stamp; gray green marginal inscription and border. Size: 80x95mm.

Letter "Z" from 12th Century Manuscript
A862

Whimsical Globe
A863

Initials from Illuminated Manuscripts: 2s, "B" from 17th century prayerbook. 3s, "V" from 16th century Bouhovo Gospel. 8s, "B" from 14th century Turnovo collection. 13s, "V" from Dobreisho's Gospel, 13th century. 18s, "E" from 11th century Enina book of the Apostles.

1975, Aug. Litho. Perf. 11½

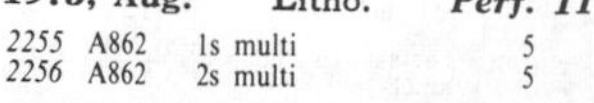

2255	A862	1s multi	5	5
2256	A862	2s multi	5	5
2257	A862	3s multi	5	5
2258	A862	8s multi	15	5
2259	A862	13s multi	25	10
2260	A862	18s multi	65	18
		Nos. 2255-2260(6)	1.20	48

Bulgarian art.

1975, Aug. Photo. Perf. 13

2261	A863	2s multi	12	5

Festival of Humor and Satire.

Lifeboat Dju IV and Gibraltar-Cuba Route
A864

1975, Aug. 5 Photo. Perf. 13

2262	A864	13s multi	25	15

Oceanexpo 75, First International Ocean Exhibition, Okinawa, July 20, 1975–Jan. 18, 1976.

Sts. Cyril and Methodius
A865

Sts. Constantine and Helena
A866

St. Sophia Church, Sofia, Woodcut by V. Zahriev—A867

1975, Aug. 21

2263	A865	2s ver, yel & brn	5	5
2264	A866	13s grn, yel & brn	30	15

Souvenir Sheet

2265	A867	50s org & multi	1.50	1.25

Balkanphila V, philatelic exhibition, Sofia, Sept. 27–Oct. 5. No. 2265 has bluish gray and orange margin. Size: 89x85mm.

Peace Dove and Map of Europe
A868

1975, Nov. Photogravure Perf. 13

2266	A868	18s ultra, rose & yel	55	30

European Security and Cooperation Conference, Helsinki, Finland, July 30–Aug. 1. No. 2266 printed in sheets of 5 stamps and 4 labels, arranged checkerwise.

Acherontia Atropos
A869

Designs: Moths.

1975 Photo. Perf. 13

2267	A869	1s *shown*	5	5
2268	A869	2s *Daphnis nerii*	5	5
2269	A869	3s *Smerinthus ocellata*	5	5
2270	A869	10s *Deilephila nicea*	20	8
2271	A869	13s *Choerocampa elpenor*	25	10
2272	A869	18s *Macroglossum fuciformis*	90	30
		Nos. 2267-2272 (6)	1.50	63

Soccer Player
A870

1975, Sept. 21

2273	A870	2s multi	12	5

8th Inter-Toto (soccer pool) Soccer Championships, Varna.

Constantine's Rebellion Against the Turks, 1403—A871

Designs (Woodcuts): 2s, Campaign of Vladislav III, 1443–1444. 3s, Battles of Turnovo, 1598 and 1686. 10s, Battle of Liprovsko, 1688. 13s, Guerrillas, 17th century. 18s, Return of exiled peasants.

1975, Nov. 27 Photo. Perf. 13

2274	A871	1s bis, grn & blk	5	5
2275	A871	2s bl, car & blk	5	5
2276	A871	3s yel, lil & blk	8	6
2277	A871	10s org, grn & blk	20	8
2278	A871	13s grn, lil & blk	25	10
2279	A871	18s pink, grn & blk	55	25
		Nos. 2274-2279 (6)	1.18	59

Bulgarian history.

Red Cross and First Aid—A872

Design: 13s, Red Cross and dove.

1975, Dec. 1

2280	A872	2s red brn, red & blk	5	5
2281	A872	13s bl grn, red & blk	25	10

90th anniversary of Bulgarian Red Cross.

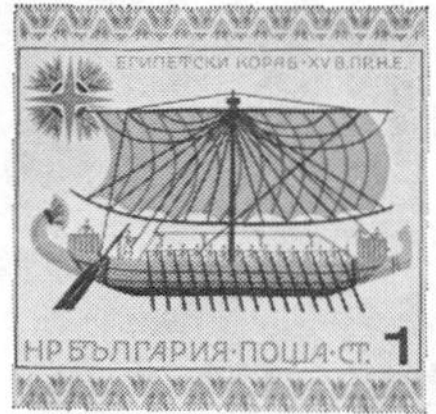

Egyptian Galley
A873

Historic Ships: 2s, Phoenician galley. 3s, Greek trireme. 5s, Roman galley. 13s, Viking longship. 18s, Venetian galley.

1975, Dec. 15 Photo. Perf. 13

2282	A873	1s multi	5	5
2283	A873	2s multi	5	5
2284	A873	3s multi	5	6
2285	A873	5s multi	12	6
2286	A873	13s multi	35	15
2287	A873	18s multi	65	25
		Nos. 2282-2287 (6)	1.27	62

See Nos. 2431-2436, 2700-2705.

Souvenir Sheet

Ethnographical Museum, Plovdiv
A874

1975, Dec. 17

2288	A874	Sheet of 3	4.25	4.00
a.		80s grn, yel & dk brn	1.25	1.00

European Architectural Heritage Year. No. 2288 contains 3 stamps and 3 labels showing stylized bird. Olive margin and inscription. Size: 160x96½mm.

Dobri Hristov
A875

1975, Dec. Perf. 13

2289	A875	5s brt grn, yel & brn	12	5

Dobri Hristov, musician, birth centenary.

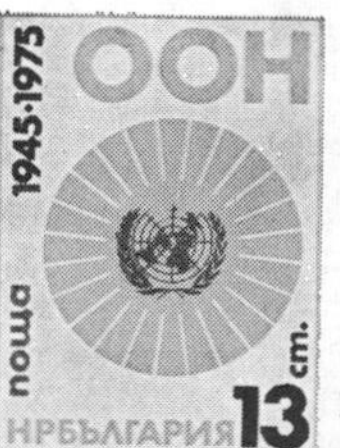

United Nations Emblem
A876

1975, Dec.

2290	A876	13s gold, blk & mag	25	10

United Nations, 30th anniversary.

Glass Ornaments
A877

Design: 13s, Peace dove, decorated ornament.

1975, Dec. 22 Photo. *Perf. 13*

2291	A877	2s brt vio & multi	5	5
2292	A877	13s gray & multi	25	10

New Year 1976.

Downhill Skiing—A878

Designs (Winter Olympic Games Emblem and): 2s, Cross country skier (vert.). 3s, Ski jump. 13s, Biathlon (vert.). 18s, Ice hockey (vert.). 23s, Speed skating (vert.). 80s, Figure skating, pair (vert.).

1976, Jan. 30 *Perf. 13½*

2293	A878	1s sil & multi	5	5
2294	A878	2s sil & multi	5	5
2295	A878	3s sil & multi	5	5
2296	A878	13s sil & multi	25	9
2297	A878	18s sil & multi	35	20
2298	A878	23s sil & multi	85	40
		Nos. 2293-2298 (6)	1.60	84

Souvenir Sheet

2299	A878	80s sil & multi	2.25	1.50

12th Winter Olympic Games, Innsbruck, Austria, Feb. 4–15. No. 2299 has light blue margin with white inscription. Size: 71x80mm.

Electric Streetcar, Sofia, 1976
A879

Design: 13s, Streetcar and trailer, 1901.

1976, Jan. 12 Photo. *Perf. 13½x13*

2300	A879	2s gray & multi	5	5
2301	A879	13s gray & multi	25	10

75th anniversary of Sofia streetcars.

Stylized Bird
A880

Designs: 5s, Dates "1976" and "1956" and star. 13s, Hammer and sickle. 50s, George Dimitrov.

1976, Mar. 1 *Perf. 13*

2302	A880	2s gold & multi	5	5
2303	A880	5s gold & multi	15	5
2304	A880	13s gold & multi	25	10

Souvenir Sheet

2305	A880	50s gold & multi	1.00	70

11th Bulgarian Communist Party Congress. No. 2305 contains one stamp; crimson margin. Size: 56x64mm.

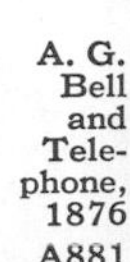

A. G. Bell and Telephone, 1876
A881

1976, Mar. 10

2306	A881	18s dk brn, yel & ocher	40	20

Centenary of first telephone call by Alexander Graham Bell, Mar. 10, 1876.

Mute Swan—A882

Waterfowl: 2s, Ruddy shelduck. 3s, Common shelduck. 5s, Garganey teal. 13s, Mallard. 18s, Red-crested pochard.

1976, Mar. 27 Litho. *Perf. 11½*

2307	A882	1s vio bl & multi	5	5
2308	A882	2s yel grn & multi	5	5
2309	A882	3s bl & multi	5	5
2310	A882	5s multi	18	5
2311	A882	13s pur & multi	50	15
2312	A882	18s grn & multi	75	15
		Nos. 2307-2312 (6)	1.58	50

Guerrillas—A883

Designs (Woodcuts by Stoev): 2s, Peasants with rifle and proclamation. 5s, Raina Knaginia with horse and guerrilla. 13s, Insurgents with cherrywood cannon.

1976, Apr. 5 Photo. *Perf. 13*

2313	A883	1s multi	5	5
2314	A883	2s multi	5	5
2315	A883	5s multi	9	5
2316	A883	13s multi	25	10

Centenary of uprising against Turkey.

Guard and Dog
A884

Design: 13s, Men on horseback, observation tower.

1976, May 15

2317	A884	2s multi	5	5
2318	A884	13s multi	25	12

30th anniversary of Border Guards.

Construction Worker
A885

1976, May 20

2319	A885	2s multi	12	5

Young Workers Brigade, 30th anniversary.

Busludja, Bas-relief
A886

AES Complex
A887

Design: 5s, Memorial building.

1976, May 28 Photo. *Perf. 13*

2320	A886	2s grn & multi	5	5
2321	A886	5s vio bl & multi	12	5

First Congress of Bulgarian Social Democratic Party, 85th anniversary.

1976, Apr. 7

Designs: 8s, Factory. 10s, Apartment houses. 13s, Refinery. 20s, Hydroelectric station.

2322	A887	5s green	10	5
2323	A887	8s maroon	13	5
2324	A887	10s green	18	8
2325	A887	13s violet	30	12
2326	A887	20s brt grn	40	16
		Nos. 2322-2326 (5)	1.11	46

Five-year plan accomplishments.

Children Playing Around Table
A888

Designs (Kindergarten Children): 2s, with doll carriage and hobby horse. 5s, playing ball. 23s, in costume.

1976, June 15

2327	A888	1s grn & multi	5	5
2328	A888	2s yel & multi	5	5
2329	A888	5s lil & multi	10	5
2330	A888	23s rose & multi	45	18

Demeter Blagoev
A889

Christo Botev
A890

1976, May 28

2331	A889	13s bluish blk, red & gold	30	15

Demeter Blagoev (1856–1924), writer, political leader, 120th birth anniversary.

1976, May 25

2332	A890	13s ocher & sl grn	30	15

Christo Botev (1848–1876), poet, death centenary. Printed se-tenant with yellow green and ocher label, inscribed with poem.

Boxing, Montreal Olympic Emblem
A891

Belt Buckle
A892

Designs (Montreal Olympic Emblem): 1s, Wrestling (horiz.). 3s, 1 l, Weight lifting. 13s, One-man kayak. 18s, Woman gymnast. 28s, Woman diver. 40s, Woman runner.

1976, June 25

2333	A891	1s org & multi	5	5
2334	A891	2s multi	5	5
2335	A891	3s lil & multi	5	5
2336	A891	13s multi	25	8
2337	A891	18s multi	35	15
2338	A891	28s bl & multi	50	25
2339	A891	40s lem & multi	1.00	45
		Nos. 2333-2339 (7)	2.25	1.08

Souvenir Sheet

2340	A891	1 l org & multi	2.25	1.50

21st Olympic Games, Montreal, Canada, July 17–Aug. 1. No. 2340 contains one stamp; multicolored margin. Size: 69x79mm.

1976, July 30 Photo. *Perf. 13*

Thracian Art (8th–4th Centuries): 2s, Brooch. 3s, Mirror handle. 5s, Helmet cheek cover. 13s, Gold ornament. 18s, Lion's head (harness decoration). 20s, Knee guard. 28s, Jeweled pendant.

2341	A892	1s brn & multi	5	5
2342	A892	2s bl & multi	5	5
2343	A892	3s multi	5	5
2344	A892	5s cl & multi	10	5
2345	A892	13s pur & multi	25	12
2346	A892	18s multi	35	15
2347	A892	20s multi	40	16
2348	A892	28s multi	60	25
		Nos. 2341-2348 (8)	1.85	88

Composite of Bulgarian Stamp Designs—A893

1976, June 5

2349	A893	50s red & multi	1.25	1.00

International Federation of Philately (F.I.P.), 50th anniversary and 12th Congress. No. 2349 has multicolored margin. Size: 73x102mm.

Partisans at Night, by Ilya Petrov—A894

Paintings: 5s, Old Town, by Tsanko Lavenov. 13s, Seated Woman by Petrov (vert.). 18s, Seated Boy, by Petrov (vert.). 28s, Old Plovdiv, by Lavenov (vert.). 80s, Ilya Petrov, self-portrait (vert.).

1976, Aug. 11 Photo. *Perf. 14*

2350	A894	2s multi	5	5
2351	A894	5s multi	10	5
2352	A894	13s ultra & multi	25	12
2353	A894	18s multi	35	15
2354	A894	28s multi	55	25
		Nos. 2350-2354 (5)	1.30	62

Souvenir Sheet

2354A	A894	80s multi	1.50	1.35

No. 2354A has green border. Size: 60x 83mm.

Souvenir Sheet

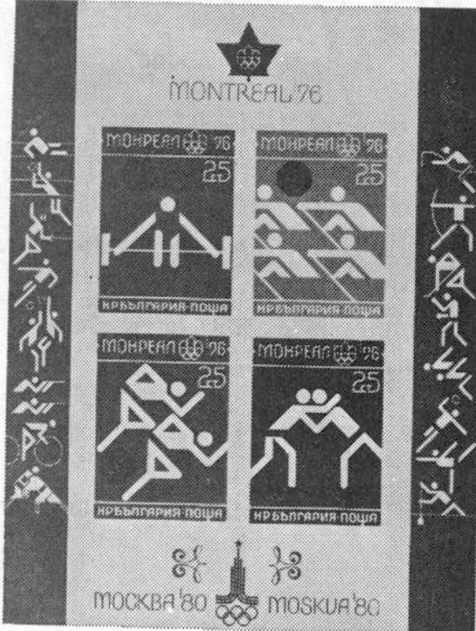

Olympic Sports and Emblems
A895

1976, Sept. 6 Photo. *Perf. 13*

Multicolored

2355	A895	Sheet of 4	1.75	1.35
a.		25s *Weight Lifting*	40	25
b.		25s *Rowing*	40	25
c.		25s *Running*	40	25
d.		25s *Wrestling*	40	25

Medalists, 21st Olympic Games, Montreal. No. 2355 has gold margin, green and red inscription. Size: 98x117mm.

Souvenir Sheet

Fresco and UNESCO Emblem—A896

1976, Dec. 3

2356	A896	50s red & multi	1.25	80

U.N. Educational, Scientific and Cultural Organization, 30th anniversary. No. 2356 has brown and orange margin. Size: 71x 80mm.

"The Pianist" by Jendov
A897

Fish and Hook
A898

Designs (Caricatures by Jendov): 5s, Imperialist "Trick or Treat." 13s, The Leader, 1931.

1976, Sept. 30 Photo. *Perf. 13*

2357	A897	2s grn & multi	5	5
2358	A897	5s pur & multi	10	5
2359	A897	13s mag & multi	30	12

Alex Jendov (1901–1953), caricaturist.

1976, Sept. 21 Photo. *Perf. 13*

2360	A898	5s multi	18	5

World Sport Fishing Congress, Varna.

St. Theodore
A899

Frescoes: 3s, St. Paul. 5s, St. Joachim. 13s, Melchizedek. 19s, St. Porphyrius. 28s, Queen. 1 l, The Last Supper.

1976, Oct. 4 Litho. *Perf. 12x12½*

2361	A899	2s gold & multi	5	5
2362	A899	3s gold & multi	5	5
2363	A899	5s gold & multi	10	5
2364	A899	13s gold & multi	35	12
2365	A899	19s gold & multi	40	20
2366	A899	28s gold & multi	75	30
		Nos. 2361-2366 (6)	1.70	77

Miniature Sheet

Perf. 12

2367	A899	1 l gold & multi	2.00	1.35

Frescoes from Zemen Monastery, 14th century. No. 2367 has gold and vermilion border. Size: 60x75mm.

Document
A900

1976, Oct. 5

2368	A900	5s multi	15	5

State Archives, 25th anniversary.

Cinquefoil
A901

Designs: 1s, Chestnut. 5s, Holly. 8s, Yew. 13s, Daphne. 23s, Judas tree.

1976, Oct. 14 Photo. *Perf. 13*

2369	A901	1s car & grn	5	5
2370	A901	2s grn & multi	5	5
2371	A901	5s multi	10	5
2372	A901	8s multi	18	5
2373	A901	13s brn & multi	30	12
2374	A901	23s multi	65	25
		Nos. 2369-2374 (6)	1.33	57

Dimitri Polianov
A902

1976, Nov. 19

2375	A902	2s dk pur & ocher	12	5

Dimitri Polianov (1876–1953), poet, birth centenary.

Christo Boteff, by Zlatyu Boyadjiev
A903

Paintings: 2s, Partisan Carrying Cherrywood Cannon, by Ilya Petrov. 3s, "Necklace of Immortality" (man's portrait), by Detchko Uzunov. 13s, "April 1876," by Georgi Popoff. 18s, Partisans, by Stoyan Venev. 60s, The Oath, by Svetlin Ruseff.

1976, Dec. 8

2376	A903	1s bis & multi	5	5
2377	A903	2s bis & multi	5	5
2378	A903	3s bis & multi	5	5
2379	A903	13s bis & multi	25	10
2380	A903	18s bis & multi	40	15
		Nos. 2376-2380 (5)	80	40

Souvenir Sheet

Imperf.

2381	A903	60s gold & multi	1.25	80

Uprising against Turkish rule, centenary. No. 2381 contains one stamp; gold border. Size: 44x82mm.

"Pollution" and Tree—A904

Design: 18s, "Pollution" obscuring sun.

1976, Nov. 10 *Perf. 13*

2382	A904	2s ultra & multi	5	5
2383	A904	18s bl & multi	35	15

Protection of the environment.

Congress Emblem
A904a

Flags
A904b

1976, Nov. 28 Photo. *Perf. 13*

2384	A904a	2s multi	5	5
2384A	A904b	13s multi	25	15

33rd BSIS Congress (Bulgarian Socialist Party).

Tobacco Workers, by Stajkov
A905

Paintings by Stajkov: 2s, View of Melnik. 13s, Shipbuilder.

1976, Dec. 16 Photo. *Perf. 13*

2385	A905	1s multi	5	5
2386	A905	2s multi	5	5
2387	A905	13s multi	35	15

Veselin Stajkov (1906–1970), painter, 70th birth anniversary.

Snowflake
A906

1976, Dec. 20

2388	A906	2s sil & multi	12	5

New Year 1977.

Zachary Stoyanov
A907

1976, Dec. 30

2389	A907	2s multi	12	5

Zachary Stoyanov (1851–1889), historian, 125th birth anniversary.

Bronze Coin of Septimus Severus
A908

Roman Coins: 2s, 13s, 18s, Bronze coins of Caracalla (diff.). 23s, Copper coin of Diocletian.

1977, Jan. 28 Photo. *Perf. 13½x13*

2390	A908	1s gold & multi	5	5
2391	A908	2s gold & multi	5	5

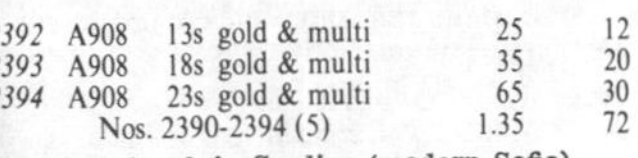

2392	A908	13s gold & multi	25	12
2393	A908	18s gold & multi	35	20
2394	A908	23s gold & multi	65	30
		Nos. 2390-2394 (5)	1.35	72

Coins struck in Serdica (modern Sofia).

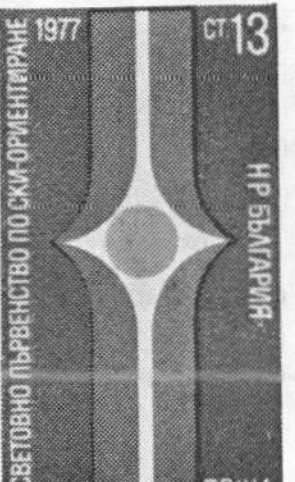

Skis and Compass
A909

Tourist Congress Emblem
A910

1977, Feb. 14 *Perf. 13*

2395	A909	13s ultra, red & lt bl	30	15

2nd World Ski Orienteering Championships.

1977, Feb. 24 Photo. *Perf. 13*

2396	A910	2s multi	12	5

5th Congress of Bulgarian Tourist Organization.

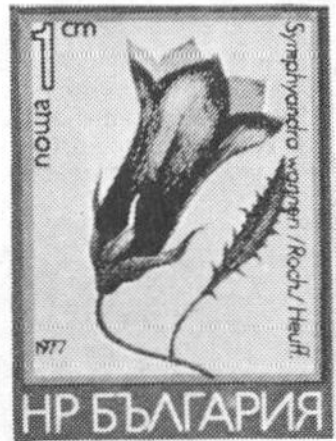

Bellflower
A911

Designs: Various bellflowers.

1977, Mar. 2

2397	A911	1s yel & multi	5	5
2398	A911	2s rose & multi	5	5
2399	A911	3s lt bl & multi	5	5
2400	A911	13s multi	25	12
2401	A911	43s yel & multi	90	40
		Nos. 2397-2401 (5)	1.30	67

Vasil Kolarov
A912

Union Congress Emblem
A913

1977, Mar. 21 Photo. *Perf. 13*

2402	A912	2s bl & blk	12	5

Vasil Kolarov (1877–1950), politician.

1977, Mar. 25

2403	A913	2s multi	12	5

8th Bulgarian Trade Union Congress, Apr. 4–7.

Wolf—A914

Wild Animals: 2s, Red fox. 10s, Weasel. 13s, European wildcat. 23s, Jackal.

1977, May 16 Litho. *Perf. 12½x12*

2404	A914	1s multi	5	5
2405	A914	2s multi	5	5
2406	A914	10s multi	20	6
2407	A914	13s multi	35	10
2408	A914	23s multi	65	25
		Nos. 2404-2408 (5)	1.30	51

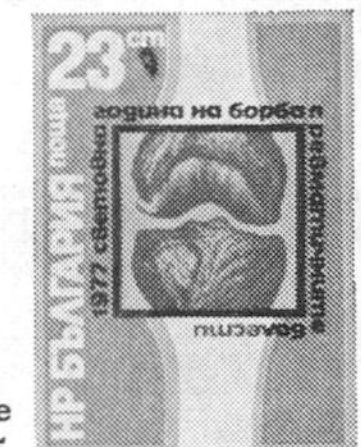

Diseased Knee
A915

1977, Mar. 31 Photo. *Perf. 13*

2409	A915	23s multi	45	20

World Rheumatism Year.

Writers' Congress Emblem
A916

1977, June 7

2410	A916	23s lt bl & yel grn	80	30

International Writers Congress: "Peace, the Hope of the Planet." No. 2410 printed in sheets of 8 stamps and 4 labels with signatures of participating writers.

Old Testament Trinity, Sofia, 16th Century
A917

Icons: 1s, St. Nicholas, Nessebur, 13th century. 3s, Annunciation, Royal Gates, Veliko Turnovo, 16th century. 5s, Christ Enthroned, Nessebur, 17th century. 13s, St. Nicholas, Elena, 18th century. 23s, Presentation of the Virgin, Rila Monastery, 18th century. 35s, Virgin and Child, Tryavna, 19th century. 40s, St. Demetrius on Horseback, Provadia, 19th century. 1 l, The 12 Holidays, Rila Monastery, 18th century.

1977, May 10 Photo. *Perf. 13*

2411	A917	1s blk & multi	5	5
2412	A917	2s grn & multi	5	5
2413	A917	3s brn & multi	5	5
2414	A917	5s bl & multi	10	5
2415	A917	13s ol & multi	25	12
2416	A917	23s mar & multi	45	18
2417	A917	35s grn & multi	70	30
2418	A917	40s dp ultra & multi	90	50
		Nos. 2411-2418 (8)	2.55	1.30

Miniature Sheet
Imperf.

2419	A917	1 l gold & multi	2.25	1.75

Bulgarian icons. No. 2419 has decorative orange border. Size: 101x100mm.

Souvenir Sheet

St. Cyril
A918

1977, June 7 Photo. *Perf. 13*

2420	A918	1 l gold & multi	2.00	1.50

1150th anniversary of the birth of St. Cyril (827–869), reputed inventor of Cyrillic alphabet. No. 2420 has violet blue and gold margin showing ancient Cyrillic writing. Size: 103x87mm.

Congress Emblem
A919

1977, May 9

2421	A919	2s red, gold & grn	12	5

13th Komsomol Congress.

Newspaper Masthead—A920

1977, June 3 Photo. *Perf. 13*

2422	A920	2s multi	12	5

Centenary of Bulgarian daily press and 50th anniversary of Rabotnichesko Delo newspaper.

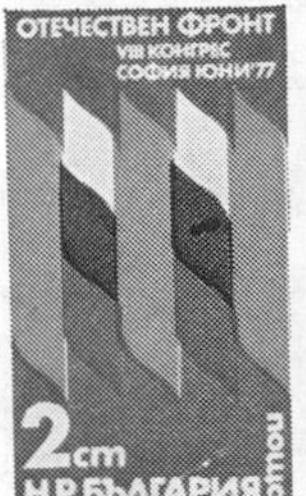

Patriotic Front Emblem
A921

Weight Lifting
A922

1977, May 26

2423	A921	2s gold & multi	12	5

8th Congress of Patriotic Front.

1977, June 15

2424	A922	13s dp brn & multi	20	12

European Youth Weight Lifting Championships, Sofia, June.

Women Basketball Players
A923

1977, June 15 *Perf. 13*

2425	A923	23s multi	50	25

7th European Women's Basketball Championships.

Wrestling—A924

Designs (Games' Emblem and): 13s, Running. 23s, Basketball. 43s, Women's gymnastics.

1977, Apr. 15

2426	A924	2s multi	5	5
2427	A924	13s multi	25	12
2428	A924	23s multi	45	18
2429	A924	43s multi	90	40

UNIVERSIADE '77, University Games, Sofia, Aug. 18–27.

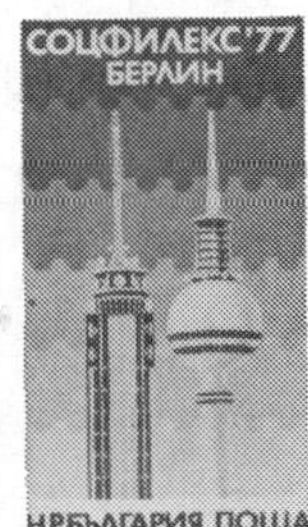

TV Tower, Berlin
A925

1977, Aug. 12 Litho. *Perf. 13*

2430	A925	25s bl & dk bl	55	25

SOZPHILEX 77 Philatelic Exhibition, Berlin, Aug. 19–28.

Ship Type of 1975

Historic Ships: 1s, Hansa cog. 2s, Santa Maria, caravelle. 3s, Golden Hind, frigate. 12s, Santa Catherina, carrack. 13s, La Corone, galleon. 43s, Mediterranean galleass.

1977, Aug. 29 Photo. *Perf. 13*

2431	A873	1s multi	5	5
2432	A873	2s multi	5	5
2433	A873	3s multi	5	5
2434	A873	12s multi	25	6
2435	A873	13s multi	25	10
2436	A873	43s multi	1.00	40
		Nos. 2431-2436 (6)	1.65	71

Ivan Vasov National Theater
A926

Buildings, Sofia: 13s, Party Headquarters. 23s, House of the People's Army. 30s, Clement Ochrida University. 80s, National Gallery. 1 l, National Assembly.

1977, Apr. 30 Photogravure *Perf. 13*

2437	A926	12s red, *gray*	25	8
2438	A926	13s red brn, *gray*	25	9
2439	A926	23s bl, *gray*	45	18
2440	A926	30s ol, *gray*	60	25
2441	A926	80s vio, *gray*	1.60	70
2442	A926	1 l cl, *gray*	2.00	85
		Nos. 2437-2442 (6)	5.15	2.15

Map of Europe A927

1977 June10

2443	A927	23s brn, bl & grn	50	25

21st Congress of the European Organization for Quality Control, Varna.

Union of Earth and Water, by Rubens A928

Rubens Paintings: 23s, Venus and Adonis. 40s, Pastoral Scene (man and woman). 1 l, Portrait of a Lady in Waiting.

1977, Sept. 23 Litho. *Perf. 12*

2444	A928	13s gold & multi	30	10
2445	A928	23s gold & multi	45	18
2446	A928	40s gold & multi	80	35

Souvenir Sheet

2447	A928	1 l gold & multi	2.00	1.50

Peter Paul Rubens (1577–1640), 400th birth anniversary. No. 2447 has gold border. Size: 72x88mm.

George Dimitrov A929

1977, June 17 Photo. *Perf. 13*

2448	A929	13s red & dp cl	30	12

George Dimitrov (1882–1947), first Prime Minister of Bulgaria.

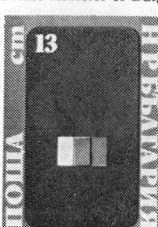

Flame with Star A930

Smart Pete on Donkey, by Ilya Beshkov A931

1977, May 17

2449	A930	13s gold & multi	25	12

3rd Bulgarian Culture Congress.

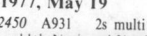

1977, May 19

2450	A931	2s multi	12	5

11th National Festival of Humor and Satire, Gabrovo.

Elin Pelin A932 Dr. Pirogov A934

13th Canoe World Championships A933

Albena, Black Sea—A933a

Writers: 2s, Pelin (Dimitur Ivanov Stojanov, 1877-1949). 5s Peju K. Jaworov (1878-1914). Artists: 13s, Boris Angelushev (1902-1966). 23s, Ceno Todorov (Ceno Todorov Dikov, 1877-1953). Each printed with label showing scenes from authors' works or illustrations by the artists.

1977, Aug. 26 Photo. *Perf. 13*

2451	A932	2s gold & brn	5	5
2452	A932	5s gold & gray grn	10	5
2453	A932	13s gold & cl	25	10
2454	A932	23s gold & bl	60	18

1977, Sept. 1 Photo. *Perf. 13*

2455	A933	2s shown	5	5
2456	A933	23s 2-man canoe	45	18

1977, Oct. 5 Photo. *Perf. 13*

2456A	A933a	35s shown	80	30
2456B	A933a	43s Rila Monastery	90	35

Sheet contains 4 each plus label.

1977, Oct. 14 Photo. *Perf. 13*

2457	A934	13s ol, ocher & brn	25	12

Centenary of visit by Russian physician N. J. Pirogov during war of liberation from Turkey.

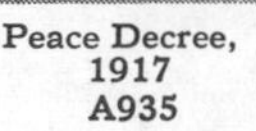

Peace Decree, 1917 A935

Old Soldier with Grandchild A936

Designs: 13s, Lenin, 1917. 23s, "1917" as a flame.

1977, Oct. 21

2458	A935	2s blk, buff & red	5	5
2459	A935	13s multi	25	10
2460	A935	23s multi	45	18

60th anniversary of Russian October Revolution.

1977, Sept. 30

Designs (Festival Posters): 13s, "The Bugler." 23s, Liberation Monument, Sofia (detail). 25s, Samara flag.

2461	A936	2s multi	5	5
2462	A936	13s multi	25	10
2463	A936	23s multi	45	18
2464	A936	25s multi	55	25

Liberation from Turkish rule, centenary.

Souvenir Sheet

Games' and Sports Emblems—A937

1977, Aug. 10 Photo. *Perf. 13½x13*

2465	A937	1 l multi	2.00	1.25

University Games '77, Sofia. No. 2465 has multicolored margin. Size: 83x75mm.

Conference Building—A938

1977, Sept. 12 *Perf. 13½*

2466	A938	23s multi	50	25

64th Interparliamentary Union Conference, Sofia.

Ornament A940

Design: 13s, Different ornament.

1977, Dec. 1

2468	A940	2s gold & multi	5	
2469	A940	13s sil & multi	25	1

New Year 1978.

Railroad Bridge—A941

1977, Nov. 9

2470	A941	13s grn, yel & gray	35	15

Transport Organization, 50th anniversary.

Petko Ratchev Slaveikov A942

1977, Nov. 15

2471	A942	8s gold & vio brn	16	5

Petko Ratchev Slaveikov (1827–95), poet, birth sesquicentennial. No. 2471 printed in sheets of 8 stamps and 8 labels in 4 alternating vertical rows. Pink and black label shows woman rocking cradle.

Soccer Player A943

Design: 23s, Soccer player and Games' emblem. 50s, Soccer players.

1978, Jan. 30 Photo. *Perf. 13*

2472	A943	13s multi	25	10
2473	A943	23s multi	50	18

Souvenir Sheet

2474	A943	50s ultra & multi	1.35	1.00

11th World Cup Soccer Championship, Argentina, June 1–25.

No. 2474 contains one stamp; cup and Argentina '78 emblem in margin. Size: 75x62mm.

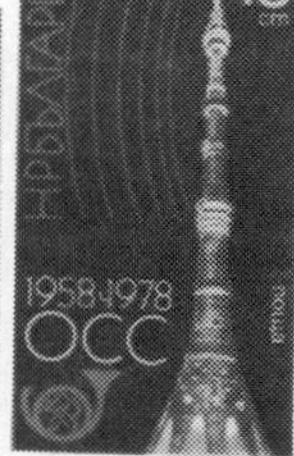

Todor Zhivkov and Leonid I. Brezhnev A944

Ostankino Tower, Moscow, Bulgarian Post Emblem A945

1977, Sept. 7 Photo. *Perf. 13*

475	A944	18s gold, car & brn	35	18

Bulgarian-Soviet Friendship. No. 2475 ssued in sheets of 3 stamps and 3 labels.

1978, Mar. 1

476	A945	13s multi	25	10

20th anniversary of the Comecon Postal)rganization (Council of Mutual Economic Assistance).

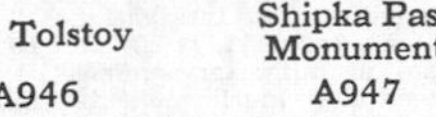

Leo Tolstoy A946 — Shipka Pass Monument A947

Portraits: 5s, Fedor Dostoevski. 13s, Ivan Sergeevich Turgenev. 23s, Vasili Vasilievich Vershchagin. 25s, Giuseppe Garibaldi. 35s, Victor Hugo.

1978, Mar. 28 Photo. *Perf. 13*

2477	A946	2s yel & dk grn	5	5
2478	A946	5s lem & brn	10	5
2479	A946	13s tan & sl grn	25	10
2480	A946	23s gray & vio brn	45	12
2481	A946	25s yel grn & blk	50	15
2482	A946	35s lt bl & vio bl	90	40
		Nos. 2477-2482 (6)	2.25	87

Souvenir Sheet

2483	A947	50s multi	1.00	60

Centenary of Bulgaria's liberation from Ottoman rule. No. 2483 has yellow ornaments in margin. Size: 55x73mm.

Bulgarian and Russian Colors A948

1978, Mar. 18

2484	A948	2s multi	12	5

30th anniversary of Russo-Bulgarian cooperation.

Heart and WHO Emblem A949

1978, May 12

2485	A949	23s gray, red & org	45	18

World Health Day, fight against hypertension.

Goddess A950

Ceramics (2nd–4th Centuries) and Exhibition Emblem: 5s, Mask of bearded man. 13s, Vase. 23s, Vase. 35s, Head of Silenus. 53s, Cock.

1978, Apr. 26

2486	A950	2s grn & multi	5	5
2487	A950	5s multi	10	5
2488	A950	13s multi	25	12
2489	A950	23s multi	45	25
2490	A950	35s multi	70	35
2491	A950	53s car & multi	1.10	50
		Nos. 2486-2491 (6)	2.65	1.32

Philaserdica Philatelic Exhibition.

Nikolai Roerich, by Svyatoslav Roerich A951 — "Mind and Matter," by Andrei Nikolov A952

1978, Apr. 5

2492	A951	8s multi	15	6
2493	A952	13s multi	25	12

Nikolai K. Roerich (1874–1947) and Andrei Nikolov (1878–1959), artists.

Bulgarian Flag and Red Star—A953

1978, Apr. 18

2494	A953	2s vio bl & multi	12	5

Bulgarian Communist Party Congress.

Young Man, by Albrecht Dürer A954

Paintings: 23s, Bathsheba at Fountain, by Rubens. 25s, Portrait of a Man, by Hans Holbein the Younger. 35s, Rembrandt and Saskia, by Rembrandt. 43s, Lady in Mourning, by Tintoretto. 60s, Old Man with Beard, by Rembrandt. 80s, Knight in Armor, by Van Dyck.

1978, June 19 Photo. *Perf. 13*

2495	A954	13s multi	25	8
2496	A954	23s multi	45	10
2497	A954	25s multi	50	15
2498	A954	35s multi	70	18
2499	A954	43s multi	85	30
2500	A954	60s multi	1.25	40
2501	A954	80s multi	1.60	55
		Nos. 2495-2501 (7)	5.60	1.76

Dresden Art Gallery paintings.

Doves and Festival Emblem—A955

1978, May 31

2502	A955	13s multi	25	12

11th World Youth Festival, Havana, July 28–Aug. 5.

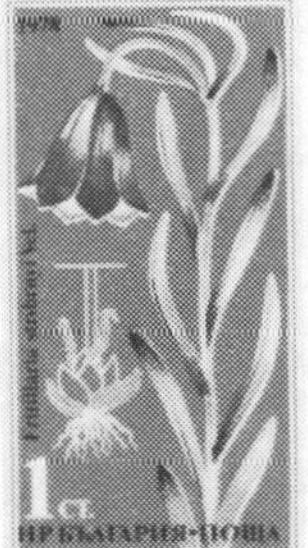

Fritillaria Stribrnyi A956

Rare Flowers: 2s, Fritillaria drenovskyi. 3s, Lilium rhodopaeum. 13s, Tulipa urumoffii. 23s, Lilium jankae. 43s, Tulipa rhodopaea.

1978, June 27

2503	A956	1s multi	5	5
2504	A956	2s multi	5	5
2505	A956	3s multi	10	5
2506	A956	13s multi	30	10
2507	A956	23s multi	50	18
2508	A956	43s multi	1.00	40
		Nos. 2503-2508 (6)	2.00	83

Yacht Cor Caroli and Map of Voyage A957

1978, May 19 Photo. *Perf. 13*

2509	A957	23s multi	50	25

First Bulgarian around-the-world voyage, Capt. Georgi Georgiev, Dec. 20, 1976–Dec. 20, 1977.

Market, by Naiden Petkov—A958

Views of Sofia: 5s, Street, by Emil Stoichev. 13s, Street, by Boris Ivanov. 23s, Tolbukhin Boulevard, by Nikola Tanev. 35s, National Theater, by Nikola Petrov. 53s, Market, by Anton Mitov.

1978, Aug. 28 Litho. *Perf. 12½x12*

2510	A958	2s multi	5	5
2511	A958	5s multi	10	5
2512	A958	13s multi	25	10
2513	A958	23s multi	45	15
2514	A958	35s multi	70	25
2515	A958	53s multi	1.10	40
		Nos. 2510-2515 (6)	2.65	1.00

Miniature Sheet

Sleeping Venus, by Giorgione—A959

1978, Aug. 7 Photo. *Imperf.*

2516	A959	1l multi	2.00	1.00

No. 2516 has light green decorative margin. Size: 71x71mm.

View of Varna—A960

1978, July 13 Photo. *Perf. 13*

2517	A960	13s multi	30	15

63rd Esperanto Congress, Varna, July 29–Aug. 5.

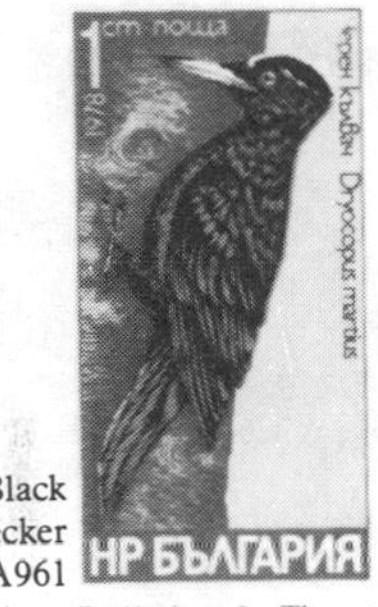

Black Woodpecker A961

Woodpeckers: 2s, Syrian. 3s, Three-toed. 13s, Middle spotted. 23s, Lesser spotted. 43s, Green

1978, Sept. 1

2518	A961	1s multi	5	5
2519	A961	2s multi	5	5
2520	A961	3s multi	5	5
2521	A961	13s multi	25	10
2522	A961	23s multi	45	18
2523	A961	43s multi	1.00	35
		Nos. 2518-2523 (6)	1.85	78

"September 1923" A962

1978, Sept. 5

2524	A962	2s red & brn	12	5

55th anniversary of September uprising.

Souvenir Sheet

National Theater, Sofia A963

Photogravure and Engraved

1978, Sept. 1 *Perf. 12x11½*

Multicolored

2525		Sheet of 4	3.25	1.50
a.	A963	40s *shown*	80	25
b.	A963	40s *Festival Hall, Sofia*	80	25
c.	A963	40s *Charles Bridge, Prague*	80	25
d.	A963	40s *Belvedere Palace, Prague*	80	25

PRAGA '78 and PHILASERDICA '79 Philatelic Exhibitions. No. 2525 has pink marginal inscriptions and PRAGA and PHILASERDICA emblems. Size: 153x112mm.

Black and White Hands, Human Rights Emblem
A964

1978, Oct. 3 Photo. *Perf. 13x13½*

2526 A964 13s multi 25 12

Anti-Apartheid Year.

Gotse Deltchev
A965

Bulgarian Calculator
A966

1978, Aug. 1 Photo. *Perf. 13*

2527 A965 13s multi 25 10

Gotse Deltchev (1872–1903), patriot.

1978, Sept. 3

2528 A966 2s multi 12 5

International Sample Fair, Plovdiv.

Guerrillas—A967

1978, Aug. 1

2529 A967 5s blk & rose red 12 5

75th anniversary of the Ilinden and Preobrazhene revolts.

"Pipe Line" and Flags
A968

1978, Oct. 3

2530 A968 13s multi 30 12

Construction of gas pipe line from Orenburg to Russian border.

Three Acrobats
A969

1978, Oct. 4 *Perf. 13x13½*

2531 A969 13s multi 25 12

3rd World Acrobatic Championships, Sofia, Oct. 6-8.

Christo G. Danov
A970

1978, Sept. 18 Photo. *Perf. 13*

2532 A970 2s dp cl & ocher 12 5

Christo G. Danov (1828–1911), 1st Bulgarian publisher. No. 2532 printed with se-tenant label showing early printing press.

Insurgents, by Todor Panajotov
A971

1978, Sept. 20

2533 A971 2s multi 12 5

Vladaja mutiny, 60th anniversary.

Salvador Allende
A972

Human Rights Flame
A973

1978, Oct. 11 Photo. *Perf. 13*

2534 A972 13s dk brn & org red 25 12

Salvador Allende (1908–1973), president of Chile.

1978, Oct. 18

2535 A973 23s multi 45 15

Universal Declaration of Human Rights, 30th anniversary.

"Strength for my Arm" by Zlatyu Boyadjiev
A974

Bulgarian Paintings: 1s, Levski and Matei Mitkaloto, by Kalina Tasseva. 3s, Rumena, woman military leader, by Nikola Mirchev (horiz.). 13s, Kolju Ficeto, by Elza Goeva. 23s, Family, National Revival Period, by Naiden Petkov.

Perf. 12x12½, 12½x12

1978, Oct. 25 Lithographed

2536 A974 1s multi 5 5
2537 A974 2s multi 5 5
2538 A974 3s multi 5 2
2539 A974 13s multi 25 10
2540 A974 23s multi 45 12
Nos. 2536-2540 (5) 85 34

1300th anniversary of Bulgaria (in 1981).

Souvenir Sheet

Tourism Building, Plovdiv
A975

Design: No. 2541b, Chrelo Tower, Rila Cloister.

1978, Nov. 1 Photo. *Perf. 13*

2541 Sheet of 5 4.50 3.00
a. A975 43s multi 85 40
b. A975 43s multi 85 40

Conservation of European architectural heritage. No. 2541 contains 3 No. 2541a, 2 No. 2541b and ornamental label. Lilac marginal inscription. Size: 116x116mm.

Ferry, Map of Black Sea with Route
A976

1978, Nov. 1 Photo. *Perf. 13*

2542 A976 13s multi 30 15

Opening of Ilychovsk-Varna Ferry.

Bird, from Marble Floor, St. Sofia Church
A977

1978, Nov. 20

2543 A977 5s multi 15 5

3rd Bulgaria '78, National Philatelic Exhibition, Sofia. Printed se-tenant with label showing emblems of Bulgaria '78 and Philaserdica '79.

Initial, 13th Century Gospel
A978

Designs: 13s, St. Cyril, miniature, 1567. 23s, Book cover, 16th century. 80s, St. Methodius, miniature, 13th century.

1978, Dec. 15 Photo. *Perf. 13*

2544 A978 2s multi 5 5
2545 A978 13s multi 25 10
2546 A978 23s multi 45 18

Souvenir Sheet

2547 A978 80s multi 1.60 85

Centenary of the Cyril and Methodius National Library. No. 2547 shows Gospel page. Size: 63x95mm.

Bulgaria No. 53
A979

Bulgarian Stamps: 13s, No. 534. 23s, No. 968. 35s, No. 1176 (vert.). 53s, No. 1223 (vert.). 1 l, No. 1.

1978, Dec. 30

2548 A979 2s ol grn & red 5 5
2549 A979 13s ultra & rose car 25 10
2550 A979 23s rose lil & ol grn 45 15
2551 A979 35s brt bl & blk 70 30
2552 A979 53s ver & sl grn 1.25 50
Nos. 2548-2552 (5) 2.70 1.10

Souvenir Sheet

2553 A979 1 l multi 2.00 1.25

Philaserdica '79, International Philatelic Exhibition, Sofia, May 18–27, 1979, and centenary of Bulgarian stamps. No. 2553 has green and black marginal inscription and UPU emblem. Size: 62x88mm. See Nos. 2560–2564.

No. 2553 exists imperf.

St. Clement of Ochrida
A980

1978, Dec. 8

2554 A980 2s multi 12 5

Clement of Ochrida University, 90th anniversary.

Ballet Dancers
A981

1978, Dec. 22

2555 A981 13s multi 30 15

Bulgarian ballet, 50th anniversary.

Nikola Karastojanov
A982

1978, Dec. 12

2556 A982 2s multi 12 5

Nikola Karastojanov (1778–1874), printer. No. 2556 printed se-tenant with label showing printing press.

Christmas Tree Made of Birds
A983

Design: 13s, Post horn.

1978, Dec. 22

No.	Type	Value	Unused	Used
2557	A983	2s multi	5	5
2558	A983	13s multi	25	12

New Year 1979.

COMECON Building, Moscow, Members' Flags—A984

1979, Jan. 25 Photo. *Perf. 13*

No.	Type	Value	Unused	Used
2559	A984	13s multi	25	12

Council for Mutual Economic Aid (COMECON), 30th anniversary.

Philaserdica Type of 1978
Designs as Before

1979, Jan. 30

No.	Type	Value	Unused	Used
2560	A979	2s brt bl & red	5	5
2561	A979	13s grn & dk car	25	10
2562	A979	23s org brn & multi	45	15
2563	A979	35s dl red & blk	70	30
2564	A979	53s vio & dk ol	1.25	50
		Nos. 2560-2564 (5)	2.70	1.10

Philaserdica '79.

Bank Building, Commemorative Coin
A985

1979, Feb. 13

No.	Type	Value	Unused	Used
2565	A985	2s yel, gray & sil	12	5

Centenary of Bulgarian People's Bank.

Aleksander Stamboliski
A986

1979, Feb. 28

No.	Type	Value	Unused	Used
2566	A986	2s org & dk brn	12	5

Aleksander Stamboliski (1879–1923), leader of peasant's party and premier.

Flower with Child's Face, IYC Emblem
A987

Stylized Heads, World Association Emblem
A988

1979, Mar. 8

No.	Type	Value	Unused	Used
2568	A987	23s multi	45	18

International Year of the Child.

1979, Mar. 20

No.	Type	Value	Unused	Used
2569	A988	13s multi	25	12

8th World Congress for the Deaf, Varna, June 20–27.

"75" and Trade Union Emblem
A989

1979, Mar. 20

No.	Type	Value	Unused	Used
2570	A989	2s sl grn & org	12	5

75th anniversary of Bulgarian Trade Unions.

Souvenir Sheet

Sculptures in Sofia—A990

Designs: 2s, Soviet Army Monument (detail). 5s, Mother and Child, Central Railroad Station. 13s, 23s, 25s, Bas-relief from Monument of the Liberators.

1979, Apr. 2 Photo. *Perf. 13*

No.	Type	Value	Unused	Used
2571	A990	Sheet of 5 + label	1.50	75
a.		2s multi	5	
b.		5s multi	10	
c.		13s multi	25	
d.		23s multi	45	
e.		25s multi	50	

Centenary of Sofia as capital. No. 2571 has ultramarine and red border. Size: 106x103mm.

Rocket Launch, Space Flight Emblems
A991

Designs (Intercosmos and Bulgarian-USSR Flight Emblems and): 25s, Link-up (horiz.). 35s, Parachute descent. 1 l, Globe, emblems and orbit (horiz.).

1979, Apr. 11

No.	Type	Value	Unused	Used
2572	A991	12s multi	25	12
2573	A991	25s multi	50	20
2574	A991	35s multi	70	30

Souvenir Sheet

No.	Type	Value	Unused	Used
2575	A991	1 l multi	2.00	1.10

First Bulgarian cosmonaut on Russian space flight. No. 2575 has space emblems in margin. Size: 68x85mm.

Nicolai Rukavishnikov
A992

Design: 13s, Rukavishnikov and Soviet cosmonaut Georgi Ivanov.

1979, May 14 Photo. *Perf. 13*

No.	Type	Value	Unused	Used
2576	A992	2s multi	5	5
2577	A992	13s multi	25	12

Col. Nicolai Rukavishnikov, first Bulgarian astronaut.

Souvenir Sheet

Thracian Gold-leaf Collar—A993

1979, May 16

No.	Type	Value	Unused	Used
2578	A993	1 l multi	2.00	1.25

48th International Philatelic Federation Congress, Sofia, May 16–17. No. 2578 has ultramarine and carmine decorative margin. Size: 77x86mm.

Post Horn, Carrier Pigeon, Jet, Globes and UPU Emblem—A994

Designs (Post Horn, Globes and ITU Emblem): 5s, 1st Bulgarian and modern telephones. 13s, Morse key and teleprinter. 23s, Old radio transmitter and radio towers. 35s, Bulgarian TV tower and satellite.

1979, May 8 *Perf. 13½x13*

No.	Type	Value	Unused	Used
2579	A994	2s multi	5	5
2580	A994	5s multi	10	5
2581	A994	13s multi	25	10
2582	A994	23s multi	45	15
2583	A994	35s multi	70	30
		Nos. 2579-2583 (5)	1.55	65

Souvenir Sheet

Design: 50s, Ground receiving station.

Perf. 13

No.	Type	Value	Unused	Used
2584	A994	50s vio, blk & gray	1.25	90

International Telecommunications Day and centenary of Bulgarian Postal and Telegraph Services. No. 2584 has ocher marginal inscription and emblems. Size of stamp: 39x28mm. Size of sheet: 65x70mm. No. 2584 exists imperf.

Hotel Vitosha—New Otani
A996

1979, May 20

No.	Type	Value	Unused	Used
2586	A996	2s ultra & pink	12	5

Philaserdica '79 Day.

Horseman Receiving Gifts, by Karellia and Boris Kuklievi—A997

1979, May 23

No.	Type	Value	Unused	Used
2587	A997	2s multi	12	5

Bulgarian-Russian Friendship Day.

Man on Donkey, by Boris Angeloushev
A998

Four Women, by Albrecht Dürer
A999

1979, May 23 Photo. *Perf. 13½*

No.	Type	Value	Unused	Used
2588	A998	2s multi	12	5

12th National Festival of Humor and Satire, Gabrovo.

Lithographed and Engraved

1979, May 31 *Perf. 14x13½*

Dürer Engravings: 23s, Three Peasants. 25s, The Cook and his Wife. 35s, Portrait of Helius Eobanus Hessus. 80s, Rhinoceros (horiz.).

No.	Type	Value	Unused	Used
2589	A999	13s multi	25	10
2590	A999	23s multi	45	15
2591	A999	25s multi	50	20
2592	A999	35s multi	70	25

Souvenir Sheet

Imperf.

No.	Type	Value	Unused	Used
2593	A999	80s multi	1.60	1.25

Albrecht Dürer (1471–1528), German engraver and painter. No. 2593 has lilac and brown decorative margin. Size: 81x81mm.

Unused Prices

Catalogue prices for unused stamps through 1960 are for hinged copies in fine condition.

R. Todorov (1879–1916)
A1000

Bulgarian Writers: No. 2595, Dimitri Dymov (1909–1966). No. 2596, S. A. Kostov (1879–1939).

1979, June 26 **Photo.** ***Perf. 13***

2594	A1000	2s multi	8	5
2595	A1000	2s sl grn & yel grn	8	5
2596	A1000	2s dp cl & yel	8	5

Nos. 2594–2596 each printed se-tenant with label showing title page or character from writer's work.

Moscow '80 Emblem, Runners—A1001

Moscow '80 Emblem and: 13s, Pole vault (horiz.). 25s, Discus. 35s, Hurdles (horiz.). 43s, High jump (horiz.). 1 l, Long jump.

1979, May 15 ***Perf. 13***

2597	A1001	2s multi	5	5
2598	A1001	13s multi	25	15
2599	A1001	25s multi	50	20
2600	A1001	35s multi	1.00	40
2601	A1001	43s multi	1.25	50
2602	A1001	1 l multi	2.75	1.10
		Nos. 2597-2602 (6)	5.80	2.40

Souvenir Sheet

2602A	A1001	2 l multi	6.75	5.00

22nd Summer Olympic Games, Moscow, July 19-Aug. 3, 1980.

Rocket—A1002

1979, Sept. 4 **Photogravure**

Designs: 5s, Flags of U.S.S.R. and Bulgaria. 13s, "35."

2603	A1002	2s multi	5	5
2604	A1002	5s multi	10	5
2605	A1002	13s multi	25	12

35th anniversary of liberation.

Moscow '80 Emblem, Gymnast—A1003

Designs: Moscow '80 Emblem and gymnasts. 13s horiz.

1979, July 31 **Photo.** ***Perf. 13***

2606	A1003	2s multi	5	5
2607	A1003	13s multi	25	15
2608	A1003	25s multi	60	20
2609	A1003	35s multi	90	35
2610	A1003	43s multi	1.25	40
2611	A1003	1 l multi	2.75	1.25
		Nos. 2606-2611 (6)	5.80	2.40

Souvenir Sheet

2612	A1003	2 l multi	6.75	5.00

22nd Summer Olympic Games, Moscow, July 19-Aug. 3, 1980. No. 2612 has light and dark blue margin showing Moscow '80 emblem; black control number. Size: 67×89mm.

Theater Institute, 18th Congress
A1004

1979, July 8 **Photo.** ***Perf. 13***

2613	A1004	13s ultra & blk	25	10

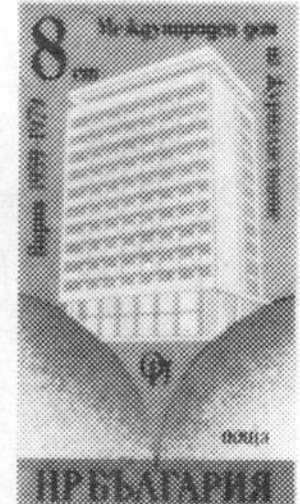

Journalists' Vacation House, Varna, 20th Anniversary—A1005

1979, July 17

2614	A1005	8s multi	16	5

Icon Type of 1977

Virgin and Child by: 13s, 23s, Nesebar, 16th century (diff.). 35s, 43s, Sozopol, 16th century (diff.). 53s, Samokov, 19th century. Inscribed 1979.

1979, Aug. 7 **Litho.** ***Perf. 12½***

2615	A917	13s multi	25	10
2616	A917	23s multi	45	15
2617	A917	35s multi	70	18
2618	A917	43s multi	85	25
2619	A917	53s multi	1.10	35
		Nos. 2615-2619 (5)	3.35	1.03

Anton Besenschek—A1006

1979, Aug. 9 **Photo.** ***Perf. 13x13½***

2620	A1006	2s dk ol grn & pale yel	12	5

Bulgarian stenography centenary.

Bulgarian Alpine Club, 50th Anniversary—A1007

1979, Aug. 28 ***Perf. 13***

2621	A1007	2s multi	12	5

Public Health Ordinance—A1008

1979, Aug. 31 ***Perf. 13½***

2622	A1008	2s multi	12	5

Public Health Service centenary. No. 2622 printed with label showing Dimitar Mollov, founder.

Isotope Measuring Device—A1009

1979, Sept. 8 ***Perf. 13½x13***

2623	A1009	2s multi	12	5

International Sample Fair, Plovdiv.

Games' Emblem—A1010

1979, Sept. 20 ***Perf. 13***

2624	A1010	5s multi	12	5

Universiada '79, World University Games, Mexico City, Sept.

Sofia Locomotive Sports Club, 50th Anniversary—A1011

1979, Oct. 2

2625	A1011	2s bl & org red	12	5

Ljuben Karavelov—A1012

1979, Oct. 4 **Photo.** ***Perf. 13***

2626	A1012	2s bl & sl grn	12	5

Ljuben Karavelov (1837-1879), poet and freedom fighter.

Biathlon, Lake Placid '80 Emblem—A1013

1979, Oct. 20

2627	A1013	2s *shown*	5	5
2628	A1013	13s *Speed skating*	25	10
2629	A1013	23s *Downhill skiing*	45	15
2630	A1013	43s *Luge*	85	30

Souvenir Sheet

Imperf.

2631	A1013	1 l *Slalom*	2.00	1.75

13th Winter Olympic Games, Lake Placid, N.Y., Feb. 12-24. No. 2631 has gold and bluish green margin showing Lake Placid '80 emblem. Size: 70x78mm.

Woman from Thrace, by Decko Uzunov—A1014

ecko Uzunov, 80th Birthday: 12s, Apparition in ed. 23s, Composition.

979, Oct. 31 *Perf. 14*

632	A1014	12s multi	25	8
633	A1014	13s multi	25	10
634	A1014	23s multi	45	15

Swimming, Moscow '80 Emblem—A1016

979, Nov. 30 **Photo.** *Perf. 13*

2636	A1016	2s *Two-man kayak*, vert.	5	5
2637	A1016	13s *Swimming*, vert.	25	15
2638	A1016	25s *shown*	50	20
2639	A1016	35s *One-man kayak*	1.00	30
2640	A1016	43s *Diving*, vert	1.25	60
2641	A1016	1 l *Diving*, vert. (diff.)	2.75	1.10
		Nos. 2636-2641 (6)	5.80	2.40

Souvenir Sheet

2642	A1016	2 l *Water polo*, vert.	6.75	5.00

22nd Summer Olympic Games, Moscow, July 19-Aug. 3, 1980. No. 2642 has multicolored margin showing Moscow '80 emblem; black control number. Size: 66x88mm.

Nikola Vapzarov—A1017

1979, Dec. 7 **Photo.** *Perf. 13*

2643	A1017	2s cl & rose	12	5

Vapzarov (1909-1942), poet and freedom fighter. No. 2643 printed with label showing smokestacks.

The First Socialists, by Bojan Petrov A1018

Paintings: 13s, Demeter Blagoev Reading Newspaper, by Demeter Gjudshenov, 1892. 25s, Workers' Party March, by Sotir Sotirov, 1917. 35s, Dawn in Plovdiv, by Johann Leviev (vert.).

1979, Dec. 10 Litho. *Perf. 12½x12, 12x12½*

2644	A1018	2s multi	5	5
2645	A1018	13s multi	25	10
2646	A1018	25s multi	50	15
2647	A1018	35s multi	70	20

Sharpshooting, Moscow '80 Emblem A1019

1979, Dec. 22 **Photo.** *Perf.13*

2648	A1019	2s *shown*	5	5
2649	A1019	13s *Judo*, horiz.	25	15
2650	A1019	25s *Wrestling*, horiz.	50	20
2651	A1019	35s *Archery*	1.00	30
2652	A1019	43s *Fencing*, horiz.	1.25	60
2653	A1019	1 l *Fencing*	2.75	1.10
		Nos. 2687-2692 (6)	5.80	2.40

Souvenir Sheet

2654	A1019	2 l *Boxing*	6.75	5.00

Procession with Relics, 11th Century Fresco—A1020

Frescoes of Sts. Cyril and Methodius, St. Clement's Basilica, Rome: 13s, Reception by Pope Hadrian II. 23s, Burial of Cyril the Philosopher, 18th century. 25s, St. Cyril. 35s, St. Methodius.

1979, Dec. 25

2655	A1020	2s multi	5	5
2656	A1020	13s multi	25	10
2657	A1020	23s multi	45	12
2658	A1020	25s multi	50	15
2659	A1020	35s multi	70	25
		Nos. 2655-2659 (5)	1.95	67

Bulgarian Television Emblem—A1021

1979, Dec. 29 *Perf. 13½*

2660	A1021	5s vio bl & lt bl	12	5

Bulgarian television, 25th anniversary. No. 2660 printed with label showing Sofia television tower.

Doves in Girl's Hair—A1022

Design: 2s, Children's heads, mosaic (vert.).

1979 *Perf. 13*

2661	A1022	2s multi	12	5
2662	A1022	13s multi	25	10

International Year of the Child. Issue dates: 2s, July 17; 13s, Dec. 14.

Puppet on Horseback, IYC Emblem A1023

Thracian Rider, Votive Tablet, 3rd Century A1024

1980, Jan. 22 **Photo.** *Perf. 13*

2663	A1023	2s multi	12	5

UNIMA, International Puppet Theater Organization, 50th anniversary (1979); International Year of the Child (1979).

1980, Jan. 29 **Photo.** *Perf. 13x13½*

National Archaeological Museum Centenary; 13s, Deines stele, 5th century B.C.

2664	A1024	2s brn & gold	5	5
2665	A1024	13s multi	25	10

Dimitrov Meeting Lenin in Moscow, by Alexander Poplilov A1026

1980, Mar. 28 *Perf. 12x12½*

2667	A1026	13s multi	25	10

Lenin, 110th birth anniversary.

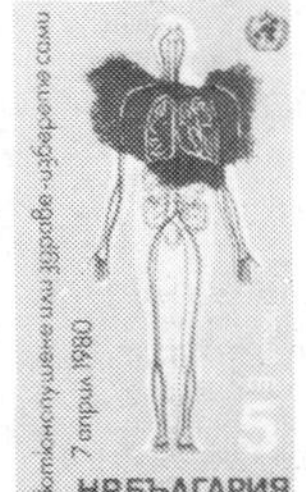

Circulatory System, Lungs Enveloped in Smoke—A1027

1980, Apr. 7 *Perf. 13*

2668	A1027	5s multi	12	5

World Health Day fight against cigarette smoking.

Basketball Moscow '80 Emblem A1027a

1980, Apr. 10 **Photo.** *Perf. 13*

2669	A1027a	2s shown	5	5
2670	A1027a	13s soccer	25	15
2671	A1027a	25s hockey	50	20
2672	A1027a	35s cycling	1.00	30
2673	A1027a	43s handball	1.25	60
2674	A1027a	1 l volleyball	2.75	1.10
		Nos. 2669-2674 (6)	5.80	2.40

Souvenir Sheet

2675	A1027a	2 l weightlifting	6.75	5.00

Souvenir Sheet

Intercosmos Emblem, Cosmonauts—A1028

1980, Apr. 22 *Perf. 12*

2676	A1028	50s multi	1.00	70

Intercosmos cooperative space program. Multicolored margin shows planets, stars and emblems. Size: 111x102mm.

Penio Penev (1930-1959), Poet—A1029

1980, Apr. 22 **Photo.** *Perf. 13*

2677	A1029	5s multi	12	5

Se-tenant with label showing quote from author's work.

Penny Black A1030

1980, Apr. 24 *Perf. 13*

2678	A1030	25s dk red & sep	50	20

London 1980 International Stamp Exhibition, May 6-14; printed se-tenant with label showing Rowland Hill between every two stamps.

Dimiter H. Tchorbadjiiski, Self-portrait—A1031

1980, Apr. 29

2679	A1031	5s *shown*	10	5
2680	A1031	13s *"Our People"*	25	10

Nikolai Giaurov

A1032

Raising Red Flag Reichstag Building, Berlin
A1033

1980, Apr. 30

2681	A1032	5s multi	12	5

Nikolai Giaurov (b. 1930), opera singer; printed se-tenant with label showing Boris Godunov.

1980, May 6 ***Perf. 13x13½***

Armistice, 35th Anniversary: 13s, Soviet Army memorial, Berlin-Treptow.

2682	A1033	5s multi	10	5
2683	A1033	13s multi	25	10

Numeral—A1034

1979 ***Perf. 14***

2684	A1034	2s ultra	5	5
2685	A1034	5s rose car	12	5

75th Anniv. of Teachers' Union—A1034a

1980, May 12 **Photo.** ***Perf. 13***

2685A	A1034a	5s multi	10	5

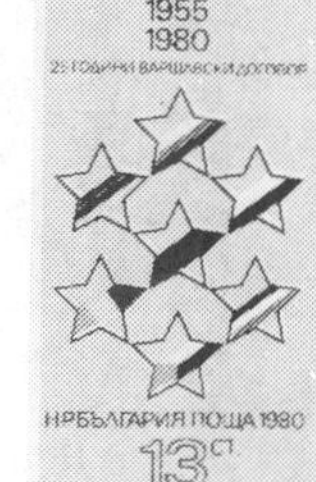

Warsaw Pact, 25th Anniversary
A1035

1980, May 14 **Photo.** ***Perf. 13***

2686	A1035	13s multi	25	10

A1036

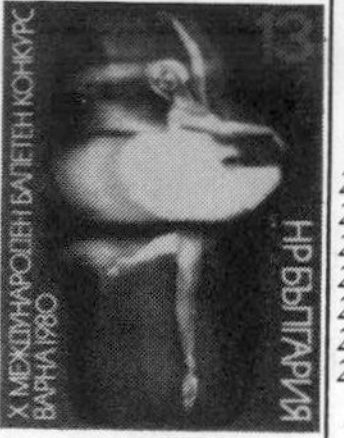

10th Intl. Ballet Competition, Varna—A1037

1980, June 10

2687	A1036	2s multi	5	5
2688	A1036	13s multi	25	15
2689	A1036	25s multi	50	20
2690	A1036	35s multi	1.00	30
2691	A1036	43s multi	1.25	60
2692	A1036	1 l multi	2.75	1.10
		No. 2687-2692 (6)	5.80	2.40

Souvenir Sheet

2693	A1036	2 l multi	6.75	5.00

22nd Summer Olympic Games, Moscow, July 19-Aug. 3.

1980, Sept. **Photo.** ***Perf. 13***

2694	A1037	13s multi	30	12

Hotel Europa, Sofia—A1038

Hotels: No. 2696, Bulgaria, Burgas, vert. No. 2697, Plovdiv, Plovdiv. No. 2698, Riga, Russe, vert. No. 2699, Varna, Djuba.

1980, July 11

2695	A1038	23s lt ultra & multi	45	18
2696	A1038	23s org & multi	45	18
2697	A1038	23s gray & multi	45	18
2698	A1038	23s bl & multi	45	18
2699	A1038	23s yel & multi	45	18
		Nos. 2695-2699 (5)	2.25	90

See No. 2766.

Ship Type of 1975

Ships of 16th, 17th Centuries: 5s, Christ of Lubeck, galleon. 8s, Roman galley. 13s, Eagle, Russian galleon. 23s, Mayflower. 35c, Maltese galley. 53, Royal Louis, galleon.

1980, July 14

2700	A873	5s multi	10	5
2701	A873	8s multi	15	5
2702	A873	13s multi	25	10
2703	A873	23s multi	45	18
2704	A873	35s multi	70	20
2705	A873	53s multi	1.10	35
		Nos. 2700-2705 (6)	2.75	93

Int'l Year of the Child, 1979—A1040

Designs: Children's drawings and IYC emblem. 43s, Tower. 5s, 25s, 43s, vert.

Perf. 12½x12, 12x12½

1980 **Lithographed**

2708	A1040	3s multi	5	5
2709	A1040	5s multi	10	5
2710	A1040	8s multi	15	5
2711	A1040	13s multi	25	10
2712	A1040	25s multi	50	15
2713	A1040	35s multi	70	20
2714	A1040	43s multi	85	25
		Nos. 2708-2714 (7)	2.60	85

Helicopter, Missile Transport, Tank—A1041

1980, Sept. 23 **Photo.** ***Perf. 13***

2715	A1041	3s *shown*	5	5
2716	A1041	5s *Jet, radar, rocket*	12	5
2717	A1041	8s *Helicopter, ships*	15	5

Bulgarian People's Army, 35th anniversary.

St. Anne, by Leonardo da Vinci—A1042

Da Vinci Paintings: 8s, 13s, Annunciation (diff.). 25s, Adoration of the Kings. 35s, Lady with the Ermine. 50s, Mona Lisa.

1980, Nov.

2718	A1042	5s multi	10	5
2719	A1042	8s multi	15	5
2720	A1042	13s multi	25	10
2721	A1042	25s multi	50	15
2722	A1042	35s multi	70	25
		Nos. 2718-2722 (5)	1.70	60

Souvenir Sheet
Imperf.

2723	A1042	50s multi	1.00	55

No. 2723 has multicolored margin showing human figure. Size: 57½x81mm.

International Peace Conference, Sofia—A1043

1980, Sept. 4 **Photo.** ***Perf. 13***

2724	A1043	25s multi	50	20

Jordan Jowkov (1880-1937), Writer—A1044

1980, Sept. 19

2725	A1044	5s multi	12	5

Se-tenant with label showing scene from Jowkov's work.

International Samples Fair, Plovdiv—A1045

1980, Sept. 24 ***Perf. 13½x13***

2726	A1045	5s multi	12	5

Blooming Cacti—A1045a

1980, Nov. 4 **Photo.** ***Perf. 13***

2726A	A1045a	5s multi	10	5
2726B	A1045a	13s multi	25	10
2726C	A1045a	25s multi	50	20
2726D	A1045a	35s multi	70	28
2726E	A1045a	53s multi	1.10	35
		Nos. 2726A-2726E (5)	2.65	98

Souvenir Sheet

25th Anniv. of Bulgarian UN Membership
A1045b

1980, Nov. 25

2726F	A1045a	60s multi	3.00	3.00

World Ski Racing Championship, Velingrad—A1046

1981, Jan. 17 **Photo.** ***Perf. 13***

2727	A1046	43s multi	85	30

ławthorn—A1047 Slalom—A1048

Designs: Medicinal herbs.

981, Jan.

'28	A1047	3s shown	5	5
'29	A1047	5s St. John's wort	10	5
'30	A1047	13s Common elder	25	10
'31	A1047	25s Blackberries	50	20
'32	A1047	35s Lime	70	30
'33	A1047	43s Wild briar	85	35
		Nos. 2728-2733 (6)	2.45	1.05

981, Feb. 27 **Photo.** ***Perf. 13***

734	A1048	43s multi	85	35

Evian Alpine World Ski Cup Championship, orovets.

Nuclear Traces, Research Institute—A1049

1981, Mar. 10 ***Perf. 13½x13***

735	A1049	13s gray & blk	25	10

Nuclear Research Institute, Dubna, USSR, 25th anniversary.

Congress Emblem—A1050

1981, Mar. 12 ***Perf. 13½***

736	A1050	5s shown	10	5
737	A1050	13s Stars	25	10
738	A1050	23s Teletape	45	18

Souvenir Sheet

'739	A1050	50s Demeter Blagoev, George Dimitrov	1.00	75

12th Bulgarian Communist Party Congress. Nos. 2736-2738 each printed se-tenant with label. No. 2739 has red marginal inscription. Size: 55x87mm.

Paintings by Zachary Zograf—A1050a

Nos. 2739A-2739C are vert.

1981, Mar. 23 **Photo.** ***Perf. 12x12½***

2739A	A1050a	5s multi	10	5
2739B	A1050a	13s multi	25	10
2739C	A1050a	23s multi	45	18
2739D	A1050a	25s multi	50	20
2739E	A1050a	35s multi	70	28
		Nos. 2739A-2739E (5)	2.00	81

EXPO '81, Plovdiv—A1050b

1981, Apr. 7

2739F	A1050b	5s multi	10	5
2739G	A1050b	8s multi	15	5
2739H	A1050b	13s multi	25	10
2739J	A1050b	25s multi	50	20
2739K	A1050b	53s multi	1.10	35
		Nos. 2739F-2739K (5)	2.10	75

Centenary of Bulgarian Shipbuilding—A1050c

1981, Apr. 15 **Photo.** ***Perf. 13***

2739L	A1050c	35s Georgi Dimitrov, liner	70	28
2739M	A1050c	43s 5th from RMS, freighter	85	35
2739N	A1050c	53s Khan Asparuch, tanker	1.10	40

Arabian Horse A1051

1980, Nov. 27 **Litho.** ***Perf. 12½x12***

2740	A1051	3s multi	5	5
2741	A1051	5s multi	10	5
2742	A1051	13s multi	25	10
2743	A1051	23s multi	45	18
2744	A1051	35s multi	70	28
		Nos. 2740-2744 (5)	1.55	66

Vassil Stoin, Ethnologist, Birth Centenary—A1052

1980, Dec. 5 **Photo.** ***Perf. 13½x13***

2745	A1052	5s multi	12	5

12th Bulgarian Communist Party Congress—A1052a

1980, Dec. 26 **Photo.** ***Perf. 13x13½***

2745A	A1052a	5s Party symbols	12	5

New Year—A1053

1980, Dec. 8 ***Perf. 13***

2746	A1053	5s shown	10	5
2747	A1053	13s Cup, date	25	12

Culture Palace, Sofia—A1053a

1981, Mar. 13 **Photo.** ***Perf. 13***

2747A	A1053a	5s multi	10	5

Vienna Hofburg Palace—A1054

1981, May 15 **Photo.** ***Perf. 13***

2748	A1054	35s multi	70	28

WIPA 1981 Intl. Philatelic Exhibition, Vienna, May 22-31.

34th Farmers' Union Congress—A1055

1981, May 18 ***Perf. 13½***

2749	A1055	5s shown	10	5
2750	A1055	8s Flags	15	6
2751	A1055	13s Flags, diff.	25	12

Wild Cat A1056

1981, May 27

2752	A1056	5s shown	10	5
2753	A1056	13s Boar	25	12
2754	A1056	23s Mouflon	45	18
2755	A1056	25s Mountain goat	50	20
2756	A1056	35s Stag	70	28
2757	A1056	53s Roe deer	1.10	40
		Nos. 2752-2757 (6)	3.10	1.23

Souvenir Sheet
Perf. 13½x13

2758	A1056	1 l Stag (diff.)	2.00	1.25

EXPO '81 Intl. Hunting Exhibition, Plovdiv. Nos. 2752-2757 each se-tenant with labels showing various hunting rifles. No. 2758 contains one stamp (48½x39mm.); multicolored margin shows hunter with bird. Size: 79x104mm.

25th Anniv. of UNESCO Membership A1057

1981, June 11 ***Perf. 13***

2759	A1057	13s multi	25	12

Hotel Type of 1980

1981, July 13 **Photo.** ***Perf. 13***

2766	A1038	23s Veliko Tirnovo Hotel	45	18

Flying Figure, Sculpture by Velichko Minekov—A1059

Bulgarian Social Democratic Party Buzludja Congress, 90th Anniv. (Minkov Sculpture): 13s, Advancing Female Figure.

1981, July 16 ***Perf. 13½***

2767	A1059	5s multi	10	5
2768	A1059	13s multi	25	12

Kukeri, by Georg Tschapkanov A1060

Statistics Office Centenary A1061

1981, May 28 **Photo.** ***Perf. 13***

2769	A1060	5s multi	12	5

13th Natl. Festival of Humor and Satire.

1981, June 9

2770	A1061	5s multi	12	5

Gold Dish—A1063

Designs: Goldsmiths' works, 7th-9th cent.

1981, July 21

2772	A1063	5s multi	10	5
2773	A1063	13s multi	25	12
2774	A1063	23s multi	45	18
2775	A1063	25s multi	50	20
2776	A1063	35s multi	70	28
2777	A1063	53s multi	1.10	40
		Nos. 2772-2777 (6)	3.10	1.23

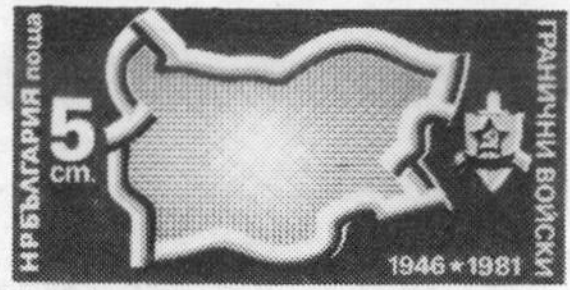

35th Anniv. of Frontier Force—A1064

1981, July 28 *Perf. 13½x13*

2778	A1064	5s multi	12	5

1300th Anniv. of First Bulgarian State—A1065

Designs: No. 2779, Sts. Cyril and Methodius. No. 2780, 9th cent. bas-relief. 8s, Floor plan, Round Church, Preslav, 10th cent. 12s, Four Evangelists of King Ivan Alexander, miniature, 1356. No. 2783, King Ivan Asen II memorial column. No. 2784, Warriors on horseback. 16s, April uprising, 1876. 23s, Russian liberators, Tirnovo. 25s, Social Democratic Party founding, 1891. 35s, September uprising, 1923. 41s, Fatherland Front. 43s, Prime Minister George Dimitrov, 5th Communist Party Congress, 1948. 50s, Lion, 10th cent. bas-relief. 53s, 10th Communist Party Congress. 55s, Kremikovski Metalurgical Plant, 1 l, Brezhnev, Gen. Todor Jovkov.

1981, Aug. 10

2779	A1065	5s multi	10	5
2780	A1065	5s multi	10	5
2781	A1065	8s multi	15	6
2782	A1065	12s multi	25	10
2783	A1065	13s multi	25	12
2784	A1065	13s multi	25	12
2785	A1065	16s multi	32	15
2786	A1065	23s multi	45	18
2787	A1065	25s multi	50	20
2788	A1065	35s multi	70	30
2789	A1065	41s multi	85	35
2790	A1065	43s multi	85	35
2791	A1065	53s multi	1.10	45
2792	A1065	55s multi	1.10	50
		Nos. 2779-2792 (14)	6.97	2.98

Souvenir Sheets

2793	A1065	50s multi	1.00	70
2794	A1065	1 l multi	2.00	1.25

Nos. 2791-2794 have multicolored margins showing flags and arms. Size: 83x75mm.

European Volleyball Championship A1066

1981, Sept. 16 *Perf. 13*

2795	A1066	13s multi	25	12

Pegasus, Bronze Sculpture (Word Day) A1067

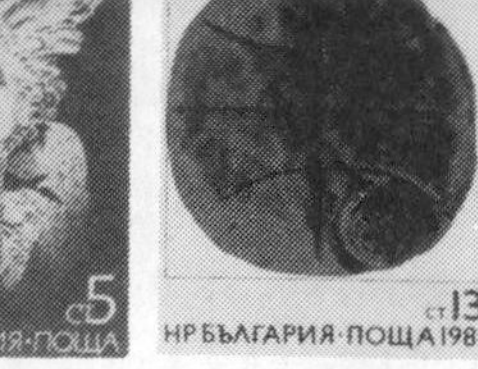

World Food Day A1068

1981, Oct. 2

2796	A1067	5s ol & cr	12	5

1981, Oct. 16

2797	A1068	13s multi	25	12

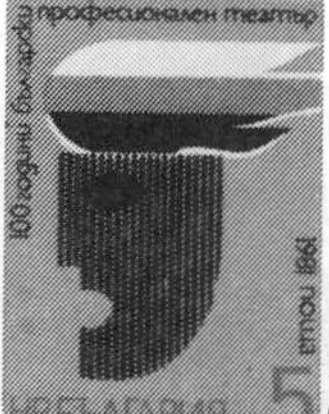

Professional Theater Centenary—A1069

1981, Oct. 30

2798	A1069	5s multi	12	5

Anti-Apartheid Year—A1070

1981, Dec. 2

2799	A1070	5s multi	12	5

Espana '82 World Cup Soccer—A1071

Designs: Various soccer players.

1981, Dec.

2800	A1071	5s multi	12	12
2801	A1071	13s multi	25	25
2802	A1071	43s multi	85	35
2803	A1071	53s multi	1.10	50

Heritage Day—A1072

1981, Nov. 21 **Photo.** *Perf. 13*

2804	A1072	13s multi	25	12

Souvenir Sheet

2804A	A1072	60s multi	1.50	1.50

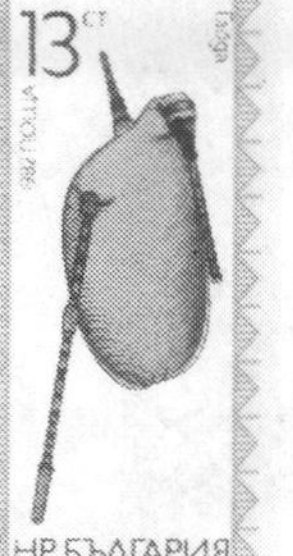

Bagpipe A1073

Public Libraries and Reading Rooms, 125th Anniv A1074

1982, Jan. 14

2805	A1073	13s shown	25	12
2806	A1073	25s Flutes	50	25
2807	A1073	30s Rebec	60	30
2808	A1073	35s Flute, recorder	70	35
2809	A1073	44s Mandolin	90	45
		Nos. 2805-2809 (5)	2.95	1.47

1982, Jan. 20

2810	A1074	5s dk grn	12	5

Souvenir Sheet

Intl. Decade for Women (1975-1985)—A1075

1982, Mar. 8

2811	A1075	1 l multi	2.00	1.50

Size: 65x78mm.

New Year 1982—A1076

1981, Dec. 22 **Photo.** *Perf. 13*

2812	A1076	5s Ornament	10	5
2813	A1076	13s Ornament, diff.	25	12

The Sofia Plains, by Nicolas Petrov (1881-1916)—A1077

1982, Feb. 10 *Perf. 12½*

2814	A1077	5s shown	10	5
2815	A1077	13s Girl Embroidering	25	12
2816	A1077	30s Fields of Peshtera	60	30

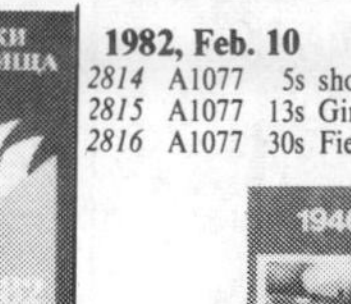

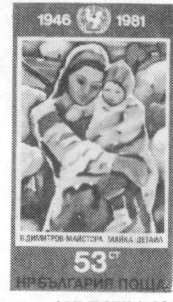

25th Anniv. of UNICEF (1981)—A1078

Mother and Child Paintings.

1982, Feb. 25 *Perf. 14*

2817	A1078	53s Vladimir Dimitrov	1.10	50
2818	A1078	53s Basil Stoilov	1.10	50
2819	A1078	53s Ivan Milev	1.10	50
2820	A1078	53s Liliana Russeva	1.10	50

Figures, by Vladamir Dimitrov (1882-1961)—A1079

1982, Mar. 8 **Litho.**

2821	A1079	5s shown	10	5
2822	A1079	8s Landscape	15	6
2823	A1079	13s View of Istanbul	25	12
2824	A1079	25s Harvesters, vert.	50	25
2825	A1079	30s Woman in a Landscape, vert.	60	30
2826	A1079	35s Peasant Woman, vert.	70	40
		Nos. 2821-2826 (6)	2.30	1.18

Souvenir Sheet

2827	A1079	50s Self-portrait	1.00	75

No. 2827 contains one stamp (54x32mm.); olive green and brown margin. Size: 65x58mm.

Trade Union Congress—A1080

1982, Apr. 8 **Photo.** *Perf. 13½*

2828	A1080	5s Dimitrov reading union paper	10	5
2829	A1080	5s Culture Palace	10	5

Nos. 2828-2829 se-tenant with label showing text.

Marsh Snowdrop A1081

Designs: Medicinal plants.

982, Apr. 10 **Photo.** ***Perf. 13***

30 A1081 3s shown 6 5
31 A1081 5s Chicory 10 5
32 A1081 8s Chamaenerium angustifolium 15 6
33 A1081 13s Solomon's seal 25 12
34 A1081 25s Violets 50 25
35 A1081 35s Centaury 70 35
Nos. 2830-2835 (6) 1.76 88

Cosmonauts' Day
A1082

982, Apr. 12 ***Perf. 13½***

36 A1082 13s Salyut-Soyuz link-up 25 12

Se-tenant with label showing K.E. Tsiolkovsky pace pioneer).

Souvenir Sheet

SOZFILEX Stamp Exhibition—A1083

1982, May 7 ***Perf. 13***

2837 A1083 50s Dimitrov, emblems 1.00 70

Size: 62x82mm.

14th Komsomol Congress (Youth Communists)—A1084

1982, May 25

2838 A1084 5s multi 12 5

PHILEXFRANCE '82 Intl. Stamp Exhibition, Paris, June 11-21—A1085

1982, May 28

2839 A1085 42s France #1, Bulgaria #1 85 35

19th Cent. Fresco—A1086

Designs: Various floral pattern frescoes.

1982, June 8 ***Perf. 11½***

2840 A1086 5s red & multi 10 5
2841 A1086 13s grn & multi 25 10
2842 A1086 25s vio & multi 50 20
2843 A1086 30s ol grn & multi 60 30
2844 A1086 42s bl & multi 85 35
2845 A1086 60s brn & multi 1.25 55
Nos. 2840-2845 (6) 3.55 1.55

Souvenir Sheet

George Dimitrov (1882-1949), First Prime Minister—A1087

1982, June 15 ***Perf. 13***

2846 A1087 50s multi 1.00 70

Multicolored margin shows natl. colors, olive branch. Size: 77x52mm.

9th Congress of the National Front—A1088

1982, June 21 **Photo.** ***Perf. 13***

2847 A1088 5s Dimitrov 12 5

35th Anniv. of Balkan Bulgarian Airline—A1089

1982, June 28 ***Perf. 13½x13***

2848 A1089 42s multi 85 35

Nuclear Disarmament—A1090

1982, July 15 ***Perf. 13***

2849 A1090 13s multi 25 12

Ludmila Jirkova (b. 1942), Artist—A1091

1982, July **Photo.** ***Perf. 13***

2850 A1091 5s multi 10 5
2851 A1091 13s multi 24 10

Souvenir Sheet

2852 A1091 1l multi 2.00 1.00

No. 2852 has multicolored margin showing Jirkova's paintings. Size: 62x67mm.

5th Congress of Bulgarian Painters—A1092

1982, July 27 ***Perf. 13½***

2853 A1092 5s multi 10 5

Se-tenant with label showing text.

Flag of Peace Youth Assembly—A1092a

Various children's drawings.

1982, Aug. 10 ***Perf. 14***

2853A A1092a 3s multi 6 5
2853B A1092a 5s multi 10 5
2853C A1092a 8s multi 16 8
2853D A1092a 13s multi 26 10

Souvenir Sheet

Perf. 14, Imperf.

2853E A1092a 50s In balloon 1.00 50

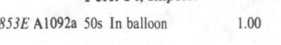

10th Anniv. of UN Conference on Human Environment, Stockholm—A1093

1982, Nov. 10 ***Perf. 13***

2854 A1093 13s dk bl & grn 24 10

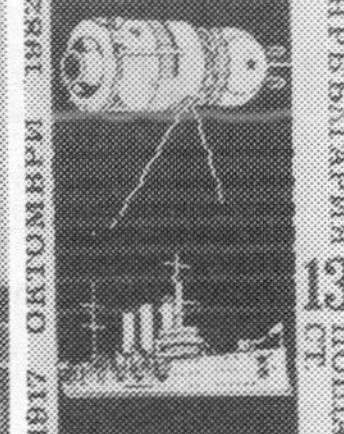

Park Hotel Moskva, Sofia
A1094

October Revolution, 65th Anniv.
A1095

Design: No. 2856, Tchernomore, Varna.

1982, Oct. 20 **Photo.** ***Perf. 13***

2855 A1094 32s 55 25
2856 A1094 32s lt bl & multi 55 25

1982, Nov. 4

2857 A1095 13s Cruiser Aurora, Sputnik II 24 10

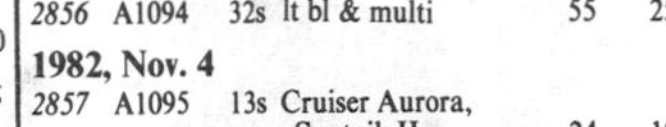

60th Anniv. of Institute of Communications—A1096

1982, Dec. 9

2858 A1096 5s ultra 10 5

60th Anniv. of USSR—A1097

1982, Dec. 9

2859 A1097 13s multi 24 10

The Piano, by Pablo Picasso (1881-1973)—A1098

1982, Dec. 24 **Litho.** ***Perf. 11½x12½***

2860	A1098	13s shown	24	10
2861	A1098	30s Portrait of Jacqueline	50	25
2862	A1098	42s Maternity	70	35

Souvenir Sheet

2863	A1098	1 l Self-portrait	2.00	1.00

Size of No. 2863: 62x80mm.

2nd Flag of Peace Youth Assembly—A1099

Various children's drawings. 8s, 13s, 50s vert.

1982, Dec. 28 ***Perf. 14***

2864	A1099	3s multi	6	5
2865	A1099	5s multi	10	5
2866	A1099	8s multi	16	8
2867	A1099	13s multi	24	10
2868	A1099	25s multi	45	20
2869	A1099	30s multi	50	25
		Nos. 2864-2869 (6)	1.51	73

Souvenir Sheet

Perf. 14, Imperf.

2870	A1099	50s Shaking hands	1.00	50

New Year 1983—A1100

1982, Dec. 28 **Photo.** ***Perf. 13***

2872	A1100	5s multi	10	5
2873	A1100	13s multi	24	10

Robert Koch (TB Bacillus Centenary)—A1101

1982, Dec. 28

2874	A1101	25s shown	45	20
2875	A1101	30s Simon Bolivar (1783-1830)	50	25
2876	A1101	30s Rabindranath Tagore (1861-1941)	50	25

Vassil Levski (1837-1873), Revolutionary—A1102

1983, Jan. 10 **Photo.** ***Perf. 13x13½***

2877	A1102	5s ol & brn	10	5

Universiade Games—A1103

1983, Feb. 15 ***Perf. 13***

2878	A1103	30s Downhill skiing	50	25

Fresh-water Fish—A1104

1983, Mar. 24 **Photo.** ***Perf. 13½x13***

2879	A1104	3s Pike	6	5
2880	A1104	5s Sturgeon	10	5
2881	A1104	13s Chub	25	12
2882	A1104	25s Perch	45	22
2883	A1104	30s Catfish	50	25
2884	A1104	42s Trout	70	35
		Nos. 2879-2884 (6)	2.06	1.04

Karl Marx (1818-1883)—A1105

1983, Apr. 5 ***Perf. 13x13½***

2885	A1105	13s multi	25	12

Jaroslav Hasek (1883-1923)—A1106

1983, Apr. 20 **Photo.** ***Perf. 13***

2886	A1106	13s multi	25	12

Martin Luther (1483-1546)—A1107

1983, May 10

2887	A1107	13s multi	25	12

55th Anniv. of Komsomol Youth Movement—A1108

1983, May 13

2888	A1108	5s "PMC"	10	5

National Costumes—A1109

1983, May 17 **Litho.** ***Perf. 14***

2889	A1109	5s Chaskovov	10	5
2890	A1109	8s Pernik	16	8
2891	A1109	13s Burgas	25	12
2892	A1109	25s Tolbukhin	45	22
2893	A1109	30s Blagoevgrad	50	25
2894	A1109	42s Topolovgrad	70	35
		Nos. 2889-2894 (6)	2.16	1.07

6th Satire and Humor Biennale, Gabrovo—A1111

1983, May 20

2900	A1111	5s Old Man Feeding Chickens	10	5

Christo Smirnensky (1898-1983), Poet—A1112

1983, May 25

2901	A1112	5s multi	10	5

17th Intl. Geodesists' Congress—A1113

1983, May 27

2902	A1113	30s Emblem	60	30

Interarch '83 Architecture Exhibition, Sofia—A1114

1983, June 6

2903	A1114	30s multi	60	30

8th European Chess Championships, Plovdiv—A1115

1983, June 20 **Photo.** ***Perf. 13***

2904	A1115	13s Chess pieces, map of Europe	25	12

Souvenir Sheets

BRASILIANA '83 Philatelic Exhibition—A1116

1983, June 24

2905	A1116	1 l Brazilian and Bulgarian stamps	2.00	1.00

Multicolored margin shows symbols and text. Size: 75x104mm.

Social Democratic Party Congress of Russia, 80th Anniv.—A1118

1983, July 29 **Photo.** ***Perf. 13***

2907	A1118	5s Lenin addressing congress	10	5

Ilinden-Preobrazhensky Insurrection, 80th Anniv. A1119

983, July 29

908	A1119	5s Gun, dagger, book	10	5

Institute of Mining and Geology, Sofia, 30th Anniv.—A1120

983, Aug. 10

909	A1120	5s multi	10	5

60th Anniv. of September 1923 Uprising—A1121

983, Aug. 19

910	A1121	5s multi	10	5
911	A1121	13s multi	25	12

Angora Cat—A1123

983, Sept. 26 *Perf. 13*

917	A1123	5s shown	10	5
918	A1123	13s Siamese	26	10
919	A1123	20s Abyssinian, vert.	40	20
920	A1123	25s Persian	50	25
921	A1123	30s European, vert.	60	30
922	A1123	42s Indochinese	85	42
		Nos. 2917-2922 (6)	2.71	1.32

Animated Film Festival—A1124

1983, Sept. 15 **Photo.** *Perf. 14x13½*

2923	A1124	5s Articulation layout	10	5

Trevethick's Engine, 1804—A1125

Locomotives: 13s, Blenkinsop's Prince Royal, 1810. 42s, Hedley's Puffing Billy, 1812. 60s, Adler (first German locomotive), 1835.

1983, Oct. 20 *Perf. 13*

2924	A1125	5s multi	10	5
2925	A1125	13s multi	26	10
2926	A1125	42s multi	85	42
2927	A1125	60s multi	1.20	60

See Nos. 2983-2987.

Souvenir Sheet

Liberation Monument, Plovdiv—A1126

1983, Nov. 4

2928	A1126	50s multi	1.00	50

Philatelic Federation, 90th anniv. Gold marginal inscription. Size: 66x79mm.

Sofia Opera, 75th Anniv. A1127

Composers' Assoc., 50th Anniv. A1128

1983, Dec. 2 *Perf. 13x13½*

2929	A1127	5s Mask, lyre, laurel	10	5

1983, Dec. 5

Composers: 5s, Ioan Kukuzel (14th cent.) 8s, Atanasov. 13s, Petko Stainov. 20s, Veselin Stodiov. 25s, Liubomir Pipkov. 30s, Pancho Vladigerov. Se-tenant with labels showing compositions.

2930	A1128	5s multi	10	5
2931	A1128	8s multi	16	8
2932	A1128	13s multi	26	10
2933	A1128	20s multi	40	20
2934	A1128	25s multi	50	25
2935	A1128	30s multi	60	30
		Nos. 2930-2935 (6)	2.02	98

New Year 1984—A1129

1983, Dec. 10 *Perf. 13*

2936	A1129	5s multi	10	5

Angelo Donni, by Raphael—A1130

1983, Dec. 22 *Perf. 14*

2937	A1130	5s shown	10	5
2938	A1130	13s Cardinal	26	10
2939	A1130	30s Baldassare Castiglioni	60	30
2940	A1130	42s Donna Belata	85	42

Souvenir Sheet

2941	A1130	1 l Sistine Madonna	2.00	1.00

No. 2941 has silver marginal inscription. Size: 60x98mm.

Bat, World Wildlife Emblem—A1131

Various bats and rodents.

1983, Dec. 30 *Perf. 13*

2942	A1131	12s multi	24	8
2943	A1131	13s multi	26	10
2944	A1131	20s multi	40	20
2945	A1131	30s multi	60	30
2946	A1131	42s multi	85	42
		Nos. 2942-2946 (5)	2.35	1.10

Dmitri Mendeleev (1834-1907), Russian Chemist—A1132

1984, Mar. 14

2947	A1132	13s multi	26	10

Ljuben Karavelov, Poet and Freedom Fighter, Birth Sesquicentenary—A1133

1984, Jan. 31 *Perf. 13x13½*

2948	A1133	5s multi	10	5

Tanker Gen. V.I. Zaimov—A1137

1984, Mar. 22 *Perf. 13½*

2959	A1137	5s shown	10	5
2960	A1137	13s Mesta	26	10
2961	A1137	25s Veleka	50	25
2962	A1137	32s Ferry	65	32
2963	A1137	42s Cargo ship Rossen	85	42
		Nos. 2959-2963 (5)	2.36	1.14

Souvenir Sheet

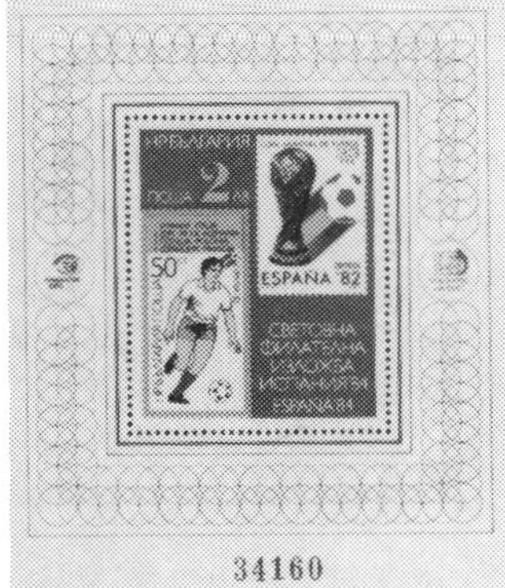

World Cup Soccer Commemorative of 1982, Spain No. 2281—A1137a

1984, Apr. 18 **Photo.** *Perf. 13x13½*

2963A	A1137a	2 l multi	4.00	2.00

ESPANA '84. No. 2963A has multicolored decorative margin containing exhibition and FIP emblems; black control number. Size: 89x110mm.

Dove with Letter over Globe A1138

Berries A1139

1984, Apr. 24 *Perf. 13*
2964 A1138 5s multi 10 5

World Youth Stamp Exhibition, Pleven, Oct. 5-11.

1984, May 5

2965	A1139	5s Cherries	10	5
2966	A1139	8s Strawberries	16	8
2967	A1139	13s Blackberries	26	10
2968	A1139	20s Raspberries	40	20
2969	A1139	42s Currants	85	42
		Nos. 2965-2969 (5)	1.77	85

6th Republican Spartikiade Games—A1140

1984, May 23
2970 A1140 13s Athlete, doves 26 10

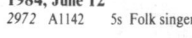

6th Amateur Art Festival—A1142

1984, June 12
2972 A1142 5s Folk singer, drum 10 5

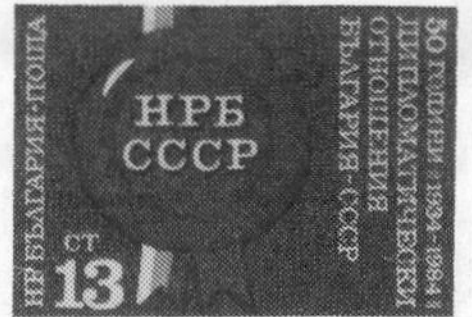

Bulgarian-Soviet Relations, 50th Anniv.—A1143

1984, June 27
2973 A1143 13s Initialed seal 26 10

Doves and Pigeons—A1144

1984, July 6 **Litho.** *Perf. 14*

2974	A1144	5s Rock dove	10	5
2975	A1144	13s Stock dove	26	10
2976	A1144	20s Wood pigeon	40	20
2977	A1144	30s Turtle dove	60	30
2978	A1144	42s Domestic pigeon	85	42
		Nos. 2974-2978 (5)	2.21	1.07

1st Natl. Communist Party Congress, 60th Anniv.—A1145

1984, May 18 **Photo.** *Perf. 13½x13*
2979 A1145 5s multi 10 5

Souvenir Sheet

Intl. Stamp Exhibition, Essen, May 26-31—A1146

Europa Conference stamps: No. 2980a, 1980. No. 2980b, 1981.

1984, May 22 *Perf. 13x13½*
2980 Sheet of 2 6.00 3.00
a.-b. A1146 1.50 l multi 3.00 1.50

No. 2980 has multicolored margin picturing exhibition emblem; black control number. Size: 94x147mm.

Mount Everest—A1147

1984, May 31 *Perf. 13*
2981 A1147 5s multi 10 5

1st Bulgarian Everest climbing expedition, Apr. 20-May 9.

Souvenir Sheet

UPU Congress, Hamburg—A1148

1984, June 11 *Perf. 13½x13*
2982 A1148 3 l Sailing ship 6.00 3.00

No. 2982 has multicolored decorative margin picturing figureheads, congress and association emblems; black control number. Size: 100x107mm.

Locomotives Type of 1983

1984, July 31 *Perf. 13*

2983	A1125	13s Best Friend of Charleston, 1830, USA	28	14
2984	A1125	25s Saxonia, 1836, Dresden	50	25
2985	A1125	30s Lafayette, 1837, USA	60	30
2986	A1125	42s Borsig, 1841, Germany	85	42
2987	A1125	60s Philadelphia, 1843, Austria	1.25	65
		Nos. 2983-2987 (5)	3.48	1.76

September 9 Revolution, 40th Anniv.—A1149

1984, Aug. 4

2988	A1149	5s K, production quality emblem	10	5
2989	A1149	20s Victory Monument, Sofia	40	20
2990	A1149	30s Star, "9"	60	30

Paintings by Nenko Balkanski (1907-1977)—A1150

1984, Sept. 17 *Perf. 1*

2991	A1150	5s Boy Playing Harmonica, vert.	10	
2992	A1150	30s A Paris Window, vert.	60	3
2993	A1150	42s Double Portrait	85	4

Souvenir Sheet

2994 A1150 1 l Self-portrait, vert. 2.00 1.0

No. 2994 has multicolored decorative margin Size: 65x110mm.

MLADPOST '84 International Youth Stamp Exhibition, Pleven—A1151

Buildings in Pleven: 5s, Mausoleum to Russian soldiers, 1877-78 Russo-Turkish War. 13s Panorama Building.

1984, Sept. 20 *Perf. 13*
2995 A1151 5s multi 10
2996 A1151 13 multi 28 1

Septembrist Young Pioneers Org., 40th Anniv.—A1152

1984, Sept. 21 **Photo.** *Perf. 13*
2997 A1152 5s multi 10 5

Nikola Vapzarov—A1153

1984, Oct. 2
2998 A1153 5s mar & pale yel 10 5

Natl. Soccer, 75th Anniv.—A1154

1984, Oct. 3
2999 A1154 42s multi 85 42

Souvenir Sheet

MLADPOST '84—A1152

1984, Oct. 5 **Photo.** *Perf. 13*
3000 A1155 50s multi 1.00 50

Bridges and Maps—A1156

1984, Oct. 5 **Photo.** *Perf. 13½x13*
3001 A1156 5s Devil's Bridge, Arda River 10 5
3002 A1156 13s Koljo-Fitscheto, Bjala 28 14
3003 A1156 30s Asparuchow, Warna 65 32
3004 A1156 42s Bebresch Highway Bridge, Botevgrad 90 45

Intl. Olympic Committee, 90th Anniv.—A1158

1984, Oct. 24 **Photo.** *Perf. 13*
3007 A1158 13s multi 28 14

Pelecanus Crispus—A1159

1984, Nov. 2
3008 A1159 5s Adult, young 10 5
3009 A1159 13s Two adults 28 14
3010 A1159 20s Adult in water 40 20
3011 A1159 32s In flight 65 32

World Wildlife Fund.

Anton Ivanov (1884-1942), Labor Leader—A1160

1984, Nov. 2
3012 A1160 5s multi 10 5

Women's Socialist Movement, 70th Anniv.—A1161

1984, Nov. 9
3013 A1161 5s multi 10 5

Telecommunication Towers—A1162

1984, Nov. 23
3014 A1162 5s Snezhanka 10 5
3015 A1162 1 l Orelek 2.00 1.00

Snowflakes, New Year 1985—A1163

1984, Dec. 5
3016 A1163 5s Doves, posthorns 10 5
3017 A1163 13s Doves, blossom 28 14

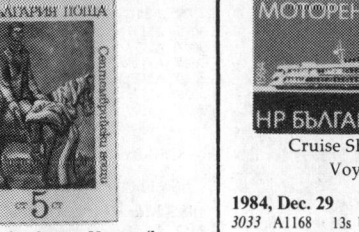

Paintings by Stoyan Venev (b. 1904)—A1164

1984, Dec. 10 **Litho.**
3018 A1164 5s September Nights 10 5
3019 A1164 30s Man with Three Medals 60 30
3020 A1164 42s The Best 85 42

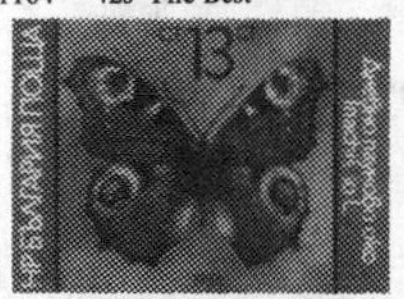

Butterflies—A1165

1984, Dec. 14 *Perf. 11½*
3021 A1165 13s Inachis io 28 14
3022 A1165 25s Papilio machaon 50 25
3023 A1165 30s Brintesia circe 60 30
3024 A1165 42s Anthocaris cardamines 85 42
3025 A1165 60s Vanessa atalanta 1.20 60
Nos. 3021-3025 (5) 3.43 1.71

Souvenir Sheet

3026 A1165 1 l Limenitis populi 2.00 1.00

No. 3026 has multicolored margin picturing Limenitis populi. Size: 75x60mm.

Cesar Augusto Sandino (1895-1934), Nicaraguan Freedom Fighter A1166

Raphael, 500th Birth Anniv. (1983) A1167

1984, Dec. 18 **Photo.** *Perf. 13x13½*
3027 A1166 13s multi 28 14

1984, Dec. 28 **Litho.** *Perf. 14*
3028 A1167 5s The Three Graces 10 5
3029 A1167 13s Cupid and the Graces 28 14
3030 A1167 30s Original Sin 60 30
3031 A1167 42s La Fornarina 85 42

Souvenir Sheet

3032 A1167 1 l Galatea 2.00 1.00

No. 3032 has multicolored margin continuing design. Size: 106x95mm.

Cruise Ship Sofia, Maiden Voyage—A1168

1984, Dec. 29 **Photo.** *Perf. 13*
3033 A1168 13s bl, dk bl & yel 28 14

Predators—A1170

1985, Jan. 17
3035 A1170 13s Conepatus leuconotus 28 14
3036 A1170 25s Prionodon linsang 50 25
3037 A1170 30s Ictonix striatus 60 30
3038 A1170 42s Hemigalus derbyanus 85 42
3039 A1170 60s Galidictis fasciata 1.20 60
Nos. 3035-3039 (5) 3.43 1.71

Nikolai Liliev (1885-1960), Poet, UNESCO Emblem—A1171

1985, Jan. 25
3040 A1171 30s multi 60 30

Zviatko Radojnov (1895-1942), Labor Leader—A1172

1985, Jan. 29
3041 A1172 5s dk red & dk brn 10 5

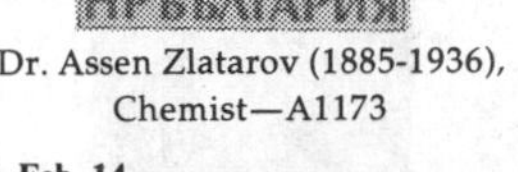

Dr. Assen Zlatarov (1885-1936), Chemist—A1173

1985, Feb. 14
3042 A1173 5s multi 10 5

Souvenir Sheet

Akademik, Research Vessel—A1174

1985, Mar. 1

3043 A1174 80s multi 1.60 80

UNESCO Intl. Oceanographic Commission, 25th anniv. No. 3043 has multicolored inscribed margin picturing UN and commission emblems and marine life. Size: 90x60mm.

Souvenir Sheet

Lenin—A1175

1985, Mar. 12

3044 A1175 50s multi 1.00 50

No. 3044 has tan, dark red and silver margin continuing the design. Size: 56x88mm.

Warsaw Treaty Org., 30th Anniv.—A1176

1985, Mar. 19

3045 A1176 13s multi 28 14

Composers—A1177

1985, Mar. 25

3046 A1177 42s Bach 85 42
3047 A1177 42s Mozart 85 42
3048 A1177 42s Tchaikovsky 85 42
3049 A1177 42s Mussorgsky 85 42
3050 A1177 42s Verdi 85 42
3051 A1177 42s Tenev 85 42
Nos. 3046-3051 (6) 5.10 2.52

Children's Drawings Type of 1982

Inscribed 1985. Various children's drawings.

1985, Mar. 26 **Litho.** ***Perf. 14***

3052 A1099 5s multi 10 5
3053 A1099 8s multi 16 8
3054 A1099 13s multi 28 14
3055 A1099 20s multi 40 20
3056 A1099 25s multi 50 25
3057 A1099 30s multi 60 30
Nos. 3052-3057 (6) 2.04 1.02

Souvenir Sheet

3058 A1099 50s Children dancing, vert. 1.00 50

3rd Banner of Peace Intl. Assembly, Sofia. No. 3058 has multicolored decorative margin. Exists with and without blue control number. Size: 71x111mm.

St. Methodius, 1100th Death Anniv.—A1179

1985, Apr. 6 **Photo.** ***Perf. 13***

3059 A1179 13s multi 28 14

Victory Parade, Moscow, 1945—A1180

Designs: 13s, 11th Infantry on parade, Sofia. 30s, Soviet soldier, orphan. 50s, Soviet flag-raising, Berlin.

1985, Apr. 30 ***Perf. 13½***

3060 A1180 5s multi 10 5
3061 A1180 13s multi 28 14
3062 A1180 30s multi 60 30

Souvenir Sheet
Perf. 13

3063 A1180 50s multi 1.00 50

Defeat of Nazi Germany, end of World War II, 40th anniv. Nos. 3060-3062 printed se-tenant with labels picturing Soviet (5s, 30s) and Bulgarian medals of honor. No. 3063 has multicolored decorative margin picturing postwar scenes, Soviet Orders of the Patriotic War and Victory. Size: 90x124mm.

7th Intl. Humor and Satire Biennale—A1181

1985, Apr. 30 ***Perf. 13½***

3064 A1181 13s yel, sage grn & red 28 14

No. 3064 printed se-tenant with label picturing Gabrovo Cat emblem.

Intl. Youth Year—A1182

1985, May 21 ***Perf. 13***

3065 A1182 13s multi 28 14

Ivan Vasov (1850-1921), Poet—A1183

1985, May 30 ***Perf. 13½***

3066 A1183 5s tan & sep 10 5

No. 3066 printed se-tenant with label picturing Vasov's birthplace in Sopot.

Soviet War Memorial, Haskovo City Arms—A1184

1985, June 1 ***Perf. 13***

3067 A1184 5s multi 10 5

Haskovo millennium.

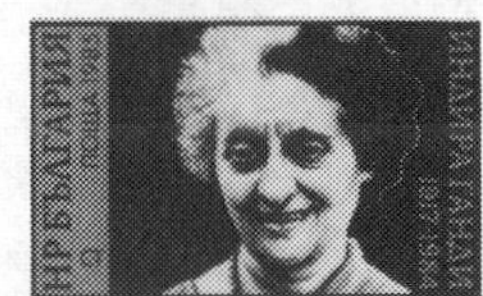

12th World Youth Festival, Moscow—A1185

1985, June 25

3068 A1185 13s multi 28 14

Indira Gandhi (1917-1984), Prime Minister of India—A1186

1985, June 26

3069 A1186 30s org yel, sep & ver 60 30

Vasil Aprilov, Founder—A1187

1985, June 30

3070 A1187 5s multi 10

1st secular school, Gabrovo, 150th anniv.

INTERSTENO '85—A1188

1985, June 30

3071 A1188 13s multi 28 1

Congress for the Intl. Union of Stenographers and Typists, Sofia.

Alexander Nevski Cathedral—A1189

1985, July 9

3072 A1189 42s multi 85 4

World Tourism Org., general assembly, Sofia.

UN, 40th Anniv.—A1190

1985, July 16

3073 A1190 13s multi 28 14

Admission of Bulgaria to UN, 30th Anniv.—A1191

1985, July 16

3074 A1191 13s multi 28 14

Roses—A1192

1985, July 20 **Litho.**

3075	A1192	5s	Rosa damascena	10	5
3076	A1192	13s	Rosa trakijka	28	14
3077	A1192	20s	Rosa radiman	40	20
3078	A1192	30s	Rosa marista	60	30
3079	A1192	42s	Rosa valentina	85	42
3080	A1192	60s	Rosa maria	1.20	60
			Nos. 3075-3080 (6)	3.43	1.71

Helsinki Conference, 10th Anniv.—A1193

1985, Aug. 1 **Photo.**

3081	A1193	13s	multi	28	14

European Swimming Championships, Sofia—A1194

1985, Aug. 2 **Litho.** ***Perf. 12½***

3082	A1194	5s	Butterfly stroke	10	5
3083	A1194	13s	Water polo, vert.	28	14
3084	A1194	42s	Diving, vert.	85	42
3085	A1194	60s	Synchronized swimming	1.20	50

Natl. Tourism Assoc., 90th Anniv.—A1195

1985, Aug. 15 **Photo.** ***Perf. 13***

3086	A1195	5s	multi	10	5

1986 World Cup Soccer Championships, Mexico—A1196

Various soccer plays.

1985, Aug. 29 ***Perf. 13***

3087	A1196	5s	multi	10	5
3088	A1196	13s	multi	28	14
3089	A1196	30s	multi	60	30
3090	A1196	42s	multi	85	42

Souvenir Sheet

3091	A1196	1 l	multi	2.00	1.00

No. 3091 has multicolored margin picturing soccer cup, emblem and stadium. Size: 55x77mm.

Union of Eastern Rumelia and Bulgaria, 1885—A1197

1985, Aug. 29 ***Perf. 14x13½***

3092	A1197	5s	multi	10	5

Computer Design Portraits—A1198

1985, Sept. 23 ***Perf. 13***

3093	A1198	5s	Boy	10	5
3094	A1198	13s	Youth	28	14
3095	A1198	30s	Cosmonaut	60	30

Intl. Exhibition of the Works of Youth Inventors, Plovdiv.

St. John the Baptist Church, Nessebar—A1199

Natl. restoration projects: 13s, Tyrant Hreljo Tower, Rila Monastery. 35s, Soldier, fresco, Ivanovo Rock Church. 42s, Archangel Gabriel, fresco, Bojana Church. 60s, Thracian Woman, fresco, Tomb of Kasanlak, 3rd century B.C. 1 l, The Horseman of Madara, bas-relief.

1985, Sept. 25 **Litho.** ***Perf. 12½***

3096	A1199	5s	multi	10	5
3097	A1199	13s	multi	28	14
3098	A1199	35s	multi	70	35
3099	A1199	42s	multi	85	42
3100	A1199	60s	multi	1.25	65
			Nos. 3096-3100 (5)	3.18	1.61

Souvenir Sheet
Imperf.

3101	A1199	1 l	multi	2.00	1.00

UNESCO, 40th anniv. No. 3101 has multicolored margin picturing the site and UNESCO emblem. Size: 100x83mm.

Souvenir Sheet

Ludmila Zhishkova Cultural Palace, Sofia—A1200

1985, Oct. 8 ***Perf. 13***

3102	A1200	1 l	multi	2.00	1.00

UNESCO 23rd General Assembly, Sofia. No. 3102 has multicolored margin showing the assembly site; UNESCO emblem. Size: 62x96mm.

Colosseum, Rome—A1201

1985, Oct. 15 **Photo.** ***Perf. 13½***

3103	A1201	42s	multi	85	42

ITALIA '85. No. 3103 printed se-tenant with label picturing the exhibition emblem.

Souvenir Sheet

Cultural Congress, Budapest—A1202

Designs: No. 3104a, St. Cyril, patron saint of Europe. No. 3104b, Map of Europe. No. 3104c, St. Methodius, patron saint of Europe.

Perf. 13, 13 Vert. (#3104b)

1985, Oct. 22 **Photo.**

3104		Sheet of 3	3.00	1.50
a.-c.	A1202	50s, any single	1.00	50

Helsinki Congress, 10th anniv. No. 3104 has blue and green inscribed margin. Size: 105x93mm.

Flowers—A1203

1985, Oct. 22 **Photo.** ***Perf. 13x13½***

3105	A1203	5s	Gladiolus hybridy	10	5
3106	A1203	5s	Iris germanica	10	5
3107	A1203	5s	Convolvulus tricolor	10	5

Historic Sailing Ships—A1204

1985, Oct. 28 **Photo.** ***Perf. 13***

3108	A1204	5s	Dutch	10	5
3109	A1204	12s	Sea Sovereign, Britain	24	12
3110	A1204	20s	Mediterranean	40	20
3111	A1204	25s	Royal Prince, Britain	50	25
3112	A1204	42s	Mediterranean	85	42
3113	A1204	60s	British battleship	1.20	60
			Nos. 3108-3113 (6)	3.29	1.64

Souvenir Sheet

PHILATELIA '85, Cologne—A1205

Designs: No. 3114a, Cologne Cathedral. No. 3114b, Alexander Nevski Cathedral, Sofia.

1985, Nov. 4 ***Imperf.***

3114		Sheet of 2	1.25	62
a.-b.	A1205	30s, any single	60	30

No. 3114 has pale yellow green margin picturing exhibition emblem. Size: 110x55mm.

Conspiracy to Liberate Bulgaria from Turkish Rule, 150th Anniv.—A1206

Freedom fighters and symbols: No. 3115, Georgi Stojkov Rakowski (1820-1876). No. 3116, Batscho Kiro (1835-1876). No. 3117, Sword, Bible and hands.

1985, Nov. 6 ***Perf. 13***

3115	A1206	5s	multi	10	5
3116	A1206	5s	multi	10	5
3117	A1206	13s	multi	25	12

Liberation from Byzantine Rule, 800th Anniv.—A1207

Paintings: 5s, The Revolt 1185, by G. Bogdanov. 13s, The Revolt 1185, by Alexander Tersiev. 30s, Battle Near Kiokotnitza, by B. Grigorov and M. Ganowski. 42s, Velika Tarnovo Town Wall, by Zanko Lawrenov.

1985, Nov. 15 **Litho.**

3118	A1207	5s multi	10	5
3119	A1207	13s multi	25	12
3120	A1207	30s multi	60	30
3121	A1207	42s multi	85	42

Souvenir Sheet
Imperf.

3122	A1207	1 l St. Dimitriev Church, 12th cent.	2.00	1.00

No. 3122 has buff, olive bister and dark green margin picturing city arms of Velika Tarnovo. Size: 74x80mm.

Souvenir Sheet

BALKANPHILA '85—A1208

1985, Nov. 29 **Photo.** ***Perf. 13***

3123	A1208	40s Dove, posthorn	80	40

No. 3123 has blue and violet blue inscribed margin picturing exhibition emblem. Size: 55x80mm.

Intl. Post and Telecommunications Development Program—A1209

1985, Dec. 2

3124	A1209	13s multi	28	14

Anton Popov (1915-1942), Freedom Fighter—A1210

1985, Dec. 11 **Photo.** ***Perf. 13***

3125	A1210	5s lake	10	5

New Year 1986—A1211

1985, Dec. 11 **Photo.** ***Perf. 13***

3126	A1211	5s Doves, snowflake	10	5
3127	A1211	13s Doves	28	14

Hunting Dogs and Prey—A1212

Designs: 5s, Pointer and partridge. 8s, Irish setter and pochard. 13s, English setter and mallard. 20s, Cocker spaniel and woodcock. 25s, German pointer and rabbit. 30s, Bulgarian bloodhound and boar. 42s, Shorthaired dachshund and fox.

1985, Dec. 27 **Litho.** ***Perf. 13x12½***

3128	A1212	5s multi	10	5
3129	A1212	8s multi	16	8
3130	A1212	13s multi	28	14
3131	A1212	20s multi	40	20
3132	A1212	25s multi	50	25
3133	A1212	30s multi	60	30
3134	A1212	42s multi	85	42
		Nos. 3128-3134 (7)	2.89	1.44

Intl. Year of the Handicapped—A1213

1985, Dec. 30 **Photo.** ***Perf. 13***

3135	A1213	5s multi	10	5

George Dimitrov (1882-1949)—A1214

1985, Dec. 30 **Photo.** ***Perf. 13***

3136	A1214	13s brn lake	25	12

7th Intl. Communist Congress, Moscow.

UN Child Survival Campaign—A1215

1986, Jan. 21 **Photo.** ***Perf. 13***

3137	A1215	13s multi	28	14

UNICEF, 40th anniv.

Demeter Blagoev (1856-1924)—A1216

1986, Jan. 28 **Photo.** ***Perf. 13***

3138	A1216	5s dk lake, car & dk red	10	5

Intl. Peace Year—A1217

1986, Jan. 31 ***Perf. 13½***

3139	A1217	5s multi	10	5

Orchids—A1218

1986, Feb. 12 **Litho.** ***Perf. 13x12½***

3140	A1218	5s Dactylorhiza romana	10	5
3141	A1218	13s Epipactis palustris	25	12
3142	A1218	30s Ophrys cornuta	60	30
3143	A1218	32s Limodorum abortivum	65	32
3144	A1218	42s Cypripedium calceolus	85	42
3145	A1218	60s Orchis papilionacea	1.20	60
a.		Miniature sheet of 6	3.75	1.75
		Nos. 3140-3145 (6)	3.65	1.81

Size: 177x109mm.

Hares and Rabbits—A1219

1986, Feb. 24 ***Perf. 12½x12***

3146	A1219	5s multi	10	5
3147	A1219	25s multi	50	25
3148	A1219	30s multi	60	30
3149	A1219	32s multi	65	32
3150	A1219	42s multi	85	42
3151	A1219	60s multi	1.20	60
		Nos. 3146-3151 (6)	3.90	1.94

Bulgarian Eagle, Newspaper, 140th Anniv.—A1220

Design: Front page of first issue and Ivan Bogorov, journalist.

1986, Feb. 2 **Photo.** ***Perf. 13***

3152	A1220	5s multi	10	5

Souvenir Sheet

Halley's Comet—A1221

Comet's orbit in the Solar System: No. 3153a, 1980. No. 3153b, 1910-1986. No. 3153c, 1916-1970. No. 3153d, 1911.

1986, Mar. 7 ***Perf. 13½x13***

3153		Sheet of 4	2.00	1.00
a.-d.	A1221	25s, any single	50	25

No. 3153 has violet black and violet gray margin picturing Edmond Halley, Planet-A, Vega, Giotto and Pioneer space probes, and Bulgarian observatory telescope. Size: 121x115mm.

Vladimir Bachev (1935-1967), Poet—A1222

1986, Mar. 12 ***Perf. 13x13½***

3154	A1222	5s dp bl & bl	10	5

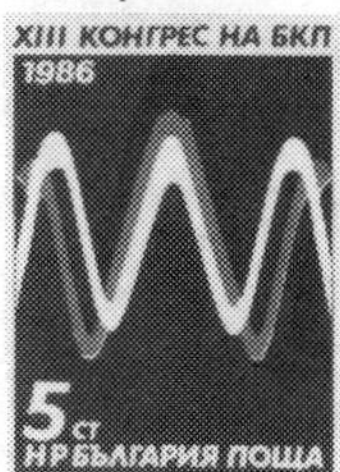

13th Natl. Communist Party Congress—A1223

1986, Mar. 17 ***Perf. 13***

3155	A1223	5s Wavy lines	10	5
3156	A1223	8s Star	16	8
3157	A1223	13s Worker	28	14

Souvenir Sheet
Imperf.

3158	A1223	50s Scaffold, flags	1.00	50

No. 3158 has dark red inscribed margin. Size: 60x78mm.

Souvenir Sheet

1st Manned Space Flight, 25th Anniv.—A1224

Designs: No. 3159a, Vostok I, 1961. No. 3159b, Yuri Gagarin (1934-1968), Russian cosmonaut.

1986, Mar. 28 *Perf. 13½x13*

3159		Sheet of 2	2.00	1.00
a.-b.	A1224	50s, any single	1.00	50

No. 3159 has greenish black and greenish blue margin picturing star chart, Soyuz-Salyut space lab, Vostok 6, Intercosmos emblem and Apollo 11. Size: 105x101mm.

April Uprising against the Turks, 110th Anniv.—A1225

Monuments: 5s, 1876 Uprising monument, Panagjuriste. 13s, Christo Botev, Vraca.

1986, Mar. 30 *Perf. 13*

3160	A1225	5s multi	10	5
3161	A1225	13s multi	28	14

Souvenir Sheet

Levsky-Spartak Sports Club, 75th Anniv.—A1226

1986, May 12 ***Imperf.***

3162	A1226	50s Rhythmic gymnastics	1.00	50

No. 3162 has dull grayish violet and gray margin picturing athletes. Size: 80x65mm.

35th Congress of Bulgarian Farmers, Sofia—A1227

1986, May 19 *Perf. 13*

3163	A1227	5s Congress emblem	10	5
3164	A1227	8s Emblem on globe	16	8
3165	A1227	13s Flags	28	14

Conference of Transport Ministers from Socialist Countries—A1228

1986, May 27 *Perf. 13x13½*

3166	A1228	13s multi	28	14

17th Intl. Book Fair, Sofia—A1229

1986, May 28

3167	A1229	13s blk, brt red & grysh blk	28	14

1986 World Cup Soccer Championships, Mexico—A1230

Various soccer plays; attached labels picture Mexican landmarks.

1986, May 30 *Perf. 13½*

3168	A1230	5s multi, vert.	10	5
3169	A1230	13s multi	28	14
3170	A1230	20s multi	40	20
3171	A1230	30s multi	60	30
3172	A1230	42s multi	85	42
3173	A1230	60s multi, vert.	1.20	60
		Nos. 3168-3173 (6)	3.43	1.71

Souvenir Sheet
Perf. 13

3174	A1230	1 l Azteca Stadium	2.00	1.00

Treasures of Preslav—A1231

Gold artifacts: 5s, Embossed brooch. 13s, Pendant with pearl cross, vert. 20s, Crystal and pearl pendant. 30s, Embossed shield. 42s, Pearl and enamel pendant, vert. 60s, Enamel shield.

1986, June 7 *Perf. 13½x13, 13x13½*

3175	A1231	5s multi	10	5
3176	A1231	13s multi	28	14
3177	A1231	20s multi	40	20
3178	A1231	30s multi	60	30
3179	A1231	42s multi	85	42
3180	A1231	60s multi	1.20	60
		Nos. 3175-3180 (6)	3.43	1.71

World Fencing Championships, Sofia, July 25-Aug. 3—A1232

1986, July 25 **Photo.** *Perf. 13*

3181	A1232	5s Heat cut, lunge	10	5
3182	A1232	13s Touche	28	14
3183	A1232	25s Lunge, parry	50	25

Flower Type of 1985

1986, July 29 *Perf. 13x13½*

3184	A1203	8s Ipomoea tricolor	16	8
3185	A1203	8s Anemone coronaria	16	8
3186	A1203	32s Lilium auratum	65	32

STOCKHOLMIA '86—A1233

1986, Aug. 25

3187	A1233	42s sep, sal brn & lake	85	42

No. 3187 printed in sheets of 3 plus 3 labels picturing folk art.

Miniature Sheet

Environmental Conservation—A1234

Designs: No. 3188a, Ciconia ciconia. No. 3188b, Nuphar lutea. No. 3188c, Salamandra salamandra. No. 3188d, Nymphaea alba.

1986, Aug. 25 **Litho.** *Perf. 14*

3188		Sheet of 4 + label	1.80	90
a.-d.	A1234	30s, any single	60	30

No. 3188 contains center label picturing the oldest oak tree in Bulgaria, Granit Village. Size: 139x90mm.

Natl. Arms, Building of the Sobranie—A1235

1986, Sept. 13 **Photo.** *Perf. 13*

3189	A1235	5s Prus grn, yel grn & red	10	5

People's Republic of Bulgaria, 40th anniv.

15th Postal Union Congress—A1236

1986, Sept. 24

3190	A1236	13s multi	28	14

Natl. Youth Brigade Movement, 40th Anniv. A1237

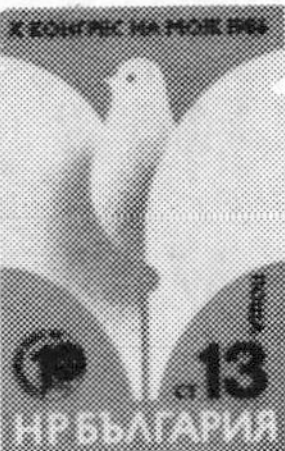

Intl. Organization of Journalists, 10th Congress A1238

1986, Oct. 4

3191	A1237	5s multi	10	5

1986, Oct. 13

3192	A1238	13s bl & dk bl	28	14

Sts. Cyril and Methodius, Disciples—A1239

1986, Oct. 23 *Perf. 13½*

3193	A1239	13s dk brn & buff	28	14

Sts. Cyril and Methodius in Bulgaria, 1100th anniv. No. 3193 printed se-tenant with inscribed label.

Telephones in Bulgaria, Cent.—A1240

1986, Nov. 5 *Perf. 13*

3194	A1240	5s multi	10	5

World Weight Lifting Championships—A1241

1986, Nov. 6

3195	A1241	13s multi	28	14

Ships—A1242

1986, Nov. 20

3196	A1242	5s King of Prussia	10	5
3197	A1242	13s East Indiaman, 18th cent.	28	14
3198	A1242	25s Shebek, 18th cent.	50	25
3199	A1242	30s St. Paul	60	30
3200	A1242	32s Topsail schooner, 18th cent.	65	32
3201	A1242	42s Victory	85	42
		Nos. 3196-3201 (6)	2.98	1.48

Souvenir Sheet

European Security and Cooperation Congress, Vienna—A1243

Various buildings and emblems: No. 3202a, Bulgaria. No. 3202b, Austria. No. 3202c, Donau Park, UN.

Perf. 13, Imperf. x13 (#3202b)

1986, Nov. 27

3202		Sheet of 3	3.00	1.50
a.-c.	A1243	50s, any single	1.00	50

No. 3202 has blue and yellow-green inscribed margin. Exists imperf. bearing control number. Size: 106x90mm.

Rogozen Thracian Pitchers—A1244

1986, Dec. 5 ***Perf. 13***

3203	A1244	10s Facing left	20	10
3204	A1244	10s Facing right	20	10

Union of Bulgarian Philatelists, 14th Congress. Nos. 3203-3204 printed se-tenant with labels picturing carved figures on pitchers in blocks of 4.

New Year 1987—A1245

1986, Dec. 9

3205	A1245	5s shown	10	5
3206	A1245	13s Snow flakes	28	14

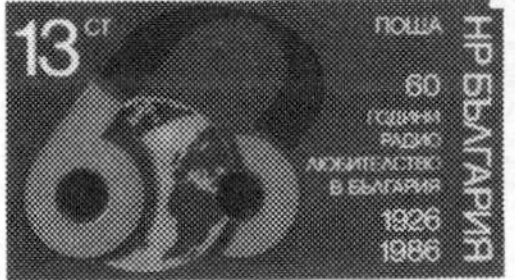

Home Amateur Radio Operators in Bulgaria, 60th Anniv.—A1246

1986, Dec. 10

3207	A1246	13s multi	28	14

Miniature Sheet

Paintings by Bulgarian Artists—A1247

Designs: No. 3208a, Red Tree, by Danail Dechev (1891-1962). No. 3208b, Troopers Confront Two Men, by Ilya Beshkov (1901-1958). No. 3208c, View of Melnik, by Veselin Stajkov (1906-1970). No. 3208d, View of Houses through Trees, by Kyril Zonev (1896-1961).

1986, Dec. 10 **Litho.** ***Perf. 14***

3208		Sheet of 4	2.25	1.10
a.-b.	A1247	25s, any single	50	25
c.-d.	A1247	30s, any single	60	30

Size: 146x102mm.

Augusto Cesar Sandino (1893-1934), Nicaraguan Revolutionary, and Flag—A1248

1986, Dec. 16 **Photo.** ***Perf. 13***

3209	A1248	13s multi	28	14

Sandinista movement in Nicaragua, 25th anniv.

Smoyan Mihylovsky (b. 1856), Writer A1249

Ran Bossilek (b. 1886) A1250

Title Page from Bulgarian Folk Songs of the Miladinov Brothers—A1251

Annivs. and events: No. 3211, Pentcho Slaveyckov (b. 1886), writer. No. 3212, Nickola Atanassov (b. 1886), musician.

1986, Dec. 17

3210	A1249	5s multi	10	5
3211	A1249	5s multi	10	5
3212	A1249	8s multi	16	8
3213	A1250	8s multi	16	8
3214	A1251	10s multi	20	10
		Nos. 3210-3214 (5)	72	36

A1252

Paintings by Titian—A1253

Various portraits.

1986, Dec. 23 **Litho.** ***Perf. 14***

3215	A1253	5s multi	10	5
3216	A1253	13s multi	28	14
3217	A1253	20s multi	40	20
3218	A1253	30s multi	60	30
3219	A1253	32s multi	65	32
3220	A1253	42s multi	85	42
a.		Min. sheet of 6, #3215-3220	3.00	1.50
		Nos. 3215-3220 (6)	2.88	1.43

Souvenir Sheet

3221	A1253	1 l multi	2.00	1.00

Size of No. 3220a: 150x166mm. No. 3221 has inscribed multicolored margin continuing the design and bearing black control number. Size: 106x76mm.

Sports Cars—A1255

1986, Dec. 30 **Litho.** ***Perf. 13½***

3223	A1255	5s 1905 Fiat	10	5
3224	A1255	10s 1928 Bugatti	20	10
3225	A1255	25s 1936 Mercedes	50	25
3226	A1255	32s 1952 Ferrari	65	32
3227	A1255	40s 1985 Lotus	80	40
3228	A1255	42s 1986 McLaren	85	42
		Nos. 3223-3228 (6)	3.10	1.54

Varna Railway Inauguration, 120th Anniv.—A1257

1987, Jan. **Photo.**

3229	A1257	5s multi	15	6

SEMI-POSTAL STAMPS

Regular Issues of 1911-20 Surcharged:

ЗА НАШИТѢ ПЛѢННИЦИ

1

a

ЗА НАШИТѢ ПЛѢННИЦИ

5

b

ЗА НАШИТѢ ПЛѢННИЦИ

50

c

Perf. 11½x12, 12x11½.

1920, June 20 **Unwmkd.**

B1	A43 (a)	2s	+1s ol grn	5	5
B2	A44 (b)	5s	+2½s grn	5	5
B3	A44 (b)	10s	+5s rose	5	5
B4	A44 (b)	15s	+7½s vio	5	5
B5	A44 (b)	25s	+12½s dp bl	5	5
B6	A44 (b)	30s	+15s choc	5	5
B7	A44 (b)	50s	+25s yel brn	5	5
B8	A29 (c)	1 l	+50s dk brn	15	15
B9	A37a (a)	2 l	+1 l brn org	30	30
B10	A38 (a)	3 l	+1½ l cl	60	60
			Nos. B1-B10 (10)	1.40	1.40

Surtax aided ex-prisoners of war.
Price, #B1-B7 imperf., $12.50.

Souvenir Sheet

SP1

1937, Nov. 22 **Photo.** ***Imperf.***

B11	SP1	2 l +18 l ultra	5.00	5.00

Issued to commemorate the 19th anniversary of the accession of Tsar Boris III to the throne. Size: 80x115mm.

Stamps of 1917-21 Surcharged in Black

Наводненнето
1939
1+1
лсва

1939, Oct. 22 ***Perf. 12½, 12***

B12	A34	1 l +1 l on 15s sl	10	10
B13	A69	2 l +1 l on 1½ l ol grn	12	12
B14	A69	4 l +2 l on 2 l dp grn	18	18
B15	A69	7 l +4 l on 3 l Prus bl	50	50
B16	A69	14 l +7 l on 5 l red brn	85	85
		Nos. B12-B16 (5)	1.75	1.75

The surtax aided victims of the Sevlievo flood.

The surcharge on Nos. B13–B16 omits "leva."

Map of Bulgaria SP2

1947, June 6 Typo. *Perf. 11½*

B17	SP2	20 l + 10 l dk brn red & grn	45	45

Issued to commemorate the 30th Jubilee Esperanto Congress, Sofia, 1947.

Postman
SP3

Radio Towers
SP6

Designs: 10 l+5 l, Lineman. 20 l+10 l, Telephone operators.

1947, Nov. 5

B18	SP3	4 l + 2 l ol brn	6	6
B19	SP3	10 l + 5 l brt red	15	15
B20	SP3	20 l + 10 l dp ultra	15	15
B21	SP6	40 l + 20 l choc	75	75

Christo Ganchev
SP7

Actors' Portraits: 10 l+6 l, Adriana Budevska. 15 l+7 l, Vasil Kirkov. 20 l+15 l, Sava Ognianov. 30 l+20 l, Krostyu Sarafov.

1947, Dec. 8 Litho. *Perf. 10½*

B22	SP7	9 l + 5 l Prus grn	10	10
B23	SP7	10 l + 6 l car lake	20	20
B24	SP7	15 l + 7 l rose vio	20	20
B25	SP7	20 l + 15 l ultra	20	20
B26	SP7	30 l + 20 l vio brn	50	50
		Nos. B22-B26 (5)	1.20	1.20

National Theater, 50th anniversary.

Souvenir Sheet

Olympic Emblem—SP8

1964, Oct. 10 Litho. *Imperf.*

B27	SP8	40s + 20s bis, red & bl	3.50	2.25

Issued to commemorate the 18th Olympic Games, Tokyo, Oct. 10–25. No. B27 measures 60x68mm.

Horsemanship Type of 1965
Miniature Sheet

Design: 40s+20s, Hurdle race.

1965, Sept. 30 Photo. *Imperf.*

B28	A630	40s + 20s bluish gray, gold & vio blk	3.00	1.50

No. B28 measures 80x79mm.

Space Exploration Type of 1966

Designs: 20s+10s, Yuri A. Gagarin, Alexei Leonov and Valentina Tereshkova. 30s+10s, Rocket and globe.

1966, Sept. 29 Photo. *Perf. 11½x11*

B29	A652	20s + 10s pur & gray	1.00	50

Miniature Sheet
Imperf.

B30	A652	30s + 10s gray, fawn & blk	2.00	1.25

Issued to publicize Russian space explorations. No. B30 measures 59x51mm.

Winter Olympic Games Type of 1967

Sports and Emblem: 20s+10s, Slalom. 40s+10s, Figure skating couple.

1967, Sept. Photo. *Perf. 11*

B31	A687	20s + 10s multi	1.35	45

Souvenir Sheet
Imperf.

B32	A687	40s + 10s multi	2.50	1.25

Issued to publicize the 10th Winter Olympic Games, Grenoble, France, Feb. 6–8, 1968. No. B32 has silver and bister marginal design. Size: 68x68mm.

Type of Olympic Games Issue, 1968

Designs: 20s+10s, Rowing. 50s+10s, Stadium, Mexico City, and communications satellite.

1968, June 24 Photo. *Perf. 10½*

B33	A702	20s + 10s vio bl, gray & pink	1.00	35

Miniature Sheet
Imperf.

B34	A702	50s + 10s gray, blk & Prus bl	2.50	1.50

Issued to publicize the 19th Olympic Games, Mexico City, Oct. 12–27. No. B34 measures 75x75mm.

Sports Type of Regular Issue, 1969

Designs: 13s+5s, Woman with ball. 20s+10s, Acrobatic jump.

1969, Oct. Photo. *Perf. 11*

Gymnasts in Light Gray

B35	A732	13s + 5s brt rose & vio	50	15
B36	A732	20s + 10s cit & bl grn	90	35

Issued to publicize the Championships for Artistic Gymnastics in Varna.

Miniature Sheet

Soccer Ball
SP9

1970, Mar. 4 Photo. *Imperf.*

B37	SP9	80s + 20s org, blk, sil & bl	2.75	2.00

Issued to publicize the 9th World Soccer Championships for the Jules Rimet Cup, Mexico City, May 30–June 21, 1970. No. B37 measures 55x73½mm.

Souvenir Sheet

Yuri A. Gagarin—SP10

1971, Apr. 12 Photo. *Imperf.*

B38	SP10	40s + 20s multi	2.25	1.75

10th anniversary of the first man in space. No. B38 measures 80x53mm.

Bulgarian Lion, Magnifying Glass, Stamp Tongs
SP11

1971, July 10 Photo. *Perf. 12½*

B39	SP11	20s + 10s brn org, blk & gold	1.00	50

11th Congress of Bulgarian Philatelists, Sofia, July, 1971.

AIR POST STAMPS.

Regular Issues of 1925-26
Overprinted in Various Colors

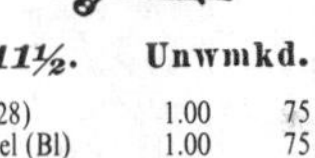

1927-28 *Perf. 11½.* Unwmkd.

C1	A76	2 l ol (R) ('28)	1.00	75
C2	A74	4 l lake & yel (Bl)	1.00	75
C3	A77	10 l brn blk & brn org (G) ('28)	15.00	14.00

Overprinted Vertically and Surcharged with New Value.

C4	A77	1(l) on 6 l dp bl & pale lem (C)	1.00	75
a.		Inverted surcharge	*450.00*	*400.00*
b.		Pair, one without surcharge	*600.00*	

Nos. C2-C4 overprinted in changed colors were not issued, price set $17.50.

Dove Delivering Message
AP1

Junkers Plane, Rila Monastery
AP2

1931, Oct. 28 Typographed.

C5	AP1	1(l) dk grn	25	10
C6	AP1	2(l) maroon	25	10
C7	AP1	6(l) dp bl	40	20
C8	AP1	12(l) carmine	40	30
C9	AP1	20(l) dk vio	1.00	60
C10	AP1	30(l) dp org	1.50	1.25
C11	AP1	50(l) org brn	3.00	1.50
		Nos. C5-C11 (7)	6.80	4.05

Counterfeits exist.

1932, May 9

C12	AP2	18 l bl grn	15.00	15.00
C13	AP2	24 l dp red	15.00	15.00
C14	AP2	28 l ultra	15.00	15.00

1938, Dec. 27

C15	AP1	1(l) vio brn	20	10
C16	AP1	2(l) green	20	15
C17	AP1	6(l) dp rose	75	30
C18	AP1	12(l) pck bl	90	35

Counterfeits exist.

Mail Plane
AP3

Plane over Tsar Assen's Tower
AP4

Designs: 4 l, Plane over Bachkovski Monastery. 6 l, Bojurishte Airport, Sofia. 10 l, Plane, train and motorcycle. 12 l, Planes over Sofia Palace. 16 l, Plane over Pirin Valley. 19 l, Plane over Rila Monastery. 30 l, Plane and Swallow. 45 l, Plane over Sofia Cathedral. 70 l, Plane over Shipka Monument. 100 l, Plane and Royal Cipher.

Photogravure.

1940, Jan. 15 *Perf. 13.*

C19	AP3	1 l dk grn	8	6
C20	AP4	2 l crimson	1.00	6
C21	AP4	4 l red org	10	8
C22	AP3	6 l dp bl	15	10
C23	AP4	10 l dk brn	25	15
C24	AP3	12 l dl brn	50	30
C25	AP3	16 l brt bl vio	55	40
C26	AP3	19 l sapphire	70	55
C27	AP4	30 l rose lake	1.00	80
C28	AP4	45 l gray vio	2.75	1.60
C29	AP4	70 l rose pink	2.75	2.00
C30	AP4	100 l dp sl bl	8.50	6.50
		Nos. C19-C30 (12)	18.33	12.60

Nos. 368 and 370 Overprinted in Black

О.Ф.

1945, Jan. 26

C31	A181	1 l brt grn	5	5
C32	A181	4 l red org	5	5

A similar overprint on Nos. O4, O5, O7 and O8 was privately applied.

Type of Parcel Post Stamps of 1944 Surcharged or Overprinted in Various Colors

О.Ф.

10 10

Imperf.

C37	PP5	10 l on 100 l dl yel (Bl)	12	10
C38	PP5	45 l on 100 l dl yel (C)	18	15
C39	PP5	75 l on 100 l dl yel (G)	30	25
C40	PP5	100 l dl yel (V)	50	35

Plane and Sun
AP16

Pigeon with Letter
AP17

Plane and Letter
AP18

Wings and Posthorn
AP19

Winged Letter
AP20

Plane and Sun
AP21

Pigeon and Posthorn
AP22

Mail Plane
AP23

Conventionalized Figure Holding Pigeon
AP24

1946, July 15 Litho. *Perf. 13*

C41	AP16	1 l dl lil	5	5
C42	AP16	2 l sl gray	5	5
C43	AP17	4 l vio blk	6	5
C44	AP18	6 l blue	6	5
C45	AP19	10 l turq grn	6	5
C46	AP19	12 l yel brn	8	6
C47	AP20	16 l rose vio	8	6
C48	AP19	19 l carmine	12	6
C49	AP21	30 l orange	15	6
C50	AP22	45 l lt ol grn	20	10
C51	AP22	75 l red brn	25	10
C52	AP23	100 l sl blk	75	25
C53	AP24	100 l red	75	25
		Nos. C41-C53 (13)	2.66	1.19

No. C47 exists imperf. Price $90.

People's Republic

Plane over Plovdiv
AP25

1947, Aug. 31 Photo. *Imperf.*

C54	AP25	40 l dl ol grn	70	70

Plovdiv International Fair, 1947.

Baldwin's Tower
AP26

1948, May 23 Litho. *Perf. 11½*

C55	AP26	50 l ol brn, *cr*	1.10	90

Issued to commemorate Stamp Day and the 10th Congress of Bulgarian Philatelic Societies, June 1948.

Romanian and Bulgarian Parliament Buildings
AP27

Romanian and Bulgarian Flags, Bridge over Danube
AP28

1948, Nov. 3 Photogravure

Cream Paper

C56	AP27	40 l ol gray	30	15
C57	AP28	100 l red vio	70	50

Issued to publicize Romanian-Bulgarian friendship.

Mausoleum of Pleven
AP29

1949, June 26

C58	AP29	50 l brown	2.25	2.25

Issued to commemorate the 7th Congress of Bulgarian Philatelic Associations, June 26–27, 1949.

Symbols of the U.P.U.
AP30

Frontier Guard and Dog
AP31

1949, Oct. 10 *Perf. 11½*

C59	AP30	50 l vio bl	1.50	85

Issued to commemorate the 75th anniversary of the formation of the Universal Postal Union.

1949, Oct. 31

C60	AP31	60 l ol blk	1.50	1.25

Dimitrov Mausoleum
AP32

1950, July 3 *Perf. 10½.*

C61	AP32	40 l ol brn	3.50	1.50

Issued to commemorate the first anniversary of the death of George Dimitrov, statesman.

Belogradchic Rocks
AP33

Air View of Plovdiv Fair
AP34

Designs: 16s, Beach, Varna. 20s, Harvesting grain. 28s, Rila monastery. 44s, Studena dam. 60s, View of Dimitrovgrad. 80s, View of Trnovo. 1 l, University building, Sofia. 4 l, Partisans' Monument.

1954, Apr. 1 *Perf. 13* Unwmkd.

C62	AP33	8s ol blk	6	5
C63	AP34	12s rose brn	6	5
C64	AP33	16s brown	10	5
C65	AP33	20s brn red, *cr*	15	5
C66	AP33	28s dp bl, *cr*	20	5
C67	AP33	44s vio brn, *cr*	20	5
C68	AP33	60s red brn, *cr*	35	8
C69	AP34	80s dk grn, *cr*	35	25
C70	AP33	1 l dk bl grn, *cr*	1.75	50
C71	AP34	4 l dp bl	3.75	1.10
		Nos. C62-C71 (10)	6.97	2.23

Glider on Mountainside
AP35

Designs:
60s, Glider over airport. 80s, Three gliders.

1956, Oct. 15 Photogravure

C72	AP35	44s brt bl	20	10
C73	AP35	60s purple	40	15
C74	AP35	80s dk bl grn	60	20

Issued to commemorate the 30th anniversary of glider flights in Bulgaria.

Passenger Plane
AP36

1957, May 21 *Perf. 13* Unwmkd.

C75	AP36	80s dp bl	80	50

Issued to commemorate the tenth anniversary of civil aviation in Bulgaria.

Sputnik 3 over Earth
AP37

1958, Nov. 28 *Perf. 11*

C76	AP37	80s brt grnsh bl	3.50	3.00

International Geophysical Year, 1957-58.
Price, imperf. $7.50.

Lunik 1 Leaving Earth for Moon
AP38

1959, Feb. 28 *Perf. 10½*

C77	AP38	2 l brt bl & ocher	5.50	5.00

Launching of 1st man-made satellite to orbit moon.

Price, imperf. in slightly different colors, $8.50 unused, $7.50 canceled.

Statue of Liberty and Tu-110 Airliner
AP39

Perf. 10½

1959, Nov. 11 Photo. Unwmkd.

C78	AP39	1 l vio bl & pink	2.00	1.50

Visit of Khrushchev to U.S.
Price, imperf. $6 unused, $5 canceled.

Lunik 2 and Moon
AP40

1960, June 23 Litho. *Perf. 11*

C79	AP40	1.25 l bl, blk & yel	4.00	2.50

Russian rocket to the Moon, Sept. 12, 1959.

Sputnik 5 and Dogs Belka and Strelka
AP41

1961, Jan. 14 Photo. *Perf. 11*

C80	AP41	1.25 l brt grnsh bl & org	4.50	3.75

Russian rocket flight of Aug. 19, 1970.

Maj. Yuri A. Gagarin and Vostok 1—AP42

1961, Apr. 26 **Unwmkd.**

C81	AP42	4 l grnsh bl, blk & red	4.50	2.50

First manned space flight, Apr. 12, 1961.

Soviet Space Dogs
AP43

1961, June 28 ***Perf. 11***

C82	AP43	2 l sl & dk car	2.75	1.50

Venus-bound Rocket
AP44

1961, June 28

C83	AP44	2 l brt bl, yel & org	4.50	2.50

Issued to commemorate the Soviet launching of the Venus space probe, Feb. 12, 1961.

Maj. Gherman Titov
AP45

Design: 1.25 l, Spaceship Vostok 2.

1961, Nov. 20 **Photo.** ***Perf. 11x10½***

C84	AP45	75s dk ol grn & gray grn	2.75	1.50
C85	AP45	1.25 l vio bl, lt bl & pink	3.25	2.25

Issued to commemorate the first manned space flight around the world, Maj. Gherman Titov of Russia, Aug. 6–7, 1961.

Iskar River Narrows
AP46

Designs: 2s, Varna and sailboat. 3s, Melnik. 10s, Trnovo. 40s, Pirin mountains.

1962, Feb. 3 ***Perf. 13*** **Unwmkd.**

C86	AP46	1s bl grn & gray bl	5	5
C87	AP46	2s bl & pink	10	5
C88	AP46	3s brn & ocher	30	5
C89	AP46	10s blk & lem	60	6
C90	AP46	40s dk grn & grn	1.50	40
		Nos. C86-C90 (5)	2.55	61

Ilyushin Turboprop Airliner
AP47

1962, Aug. 18 ***Perf. 11***

C91	AP47	13s bl & blk	60	25

15th anniversary of TABSO airline.

Konstantin E. Tsiolkovsky and Rocket Launching—AP48

Design: 13s, Earth, moon and rocket on future flight to the moon.

1962, Sept. 24 ***Perf. 11***

C92	AP48	5s dp grn & gray	2.25	1.00
C93	AP48	13s ultra & yel	1.25	40

13th meeting of the International Astronautical Federation.

Maj. Andrian G. Nikolayev
AP49

Designs: 2s, Lt. Col. Pavel R. Popovich. 40s, Vostoks 3 and 4 in orbit.

1962, Dec. 9 **Photo.** **Unwmkd.**

C94	AP49	1s bl, sl grn & blk	15	5
C95	AP49	2s bl grn, grn & blk	30	5
C96	AP49	40s dk bl grn, pink & blk	2.00	1.00

First Russian group space flight of Vostoks 3 and 4, Aug. 12–15, 1962.

Spacecraft "Mars 1" Approaching Mars—AP50

Design: 13s, Rocket launching spacecraft, Earth, Moon and Mars.

1963, Feb. 25 ***Perf. 11*** **Unwmkd.**

C97	AP50	5s multi	75	25
C98	AP50	13s multi	1.50	40

Issued to commemorate the launching of the Russian spacecraft "Mars 1," Nov. 1, 1962.

Lt. Col. Valeri F. Bykovski
AP51

Designs: 2s, Lt. Valentina Tereshkova. 5s, Globe and trajectories.

1963, Aug. 26 ***Perf. 11½*** **Unwmkd.**

C99	AP51	1s pale vio & Prus bl	10	5
C100	AP51	2s cit & red brn	10	5
C101	AP51	5s rose & dk red	20	6

Issued to commemorate the space flights of Valeri Bykovski, June 14–19, and Valentina Tereshkova, first woman cosmonaut, June 16–19, 1963. An imperf. souvenir sheet contains one 50s stamp showing Spasski tower and globe in lilac and red brown. Light blue border with red brown inscription. Size: 77x67mm. Price $1.50.

See also No. CB3.

Nos. C99–C100 Surcharged in Magenta or Green

МЕЖДУНАРОДНА
КОСМИЧЕСКА
ИЗЛОЖБА
РИЧИОНЕ·1964
ST 10

1964, Aug. 22

C102	AP51	10s on 1s pale vio & Prus bl (M)	40	20
C103	AP51	20s on 2s cit & red brn (G)	80	25

Issued to commemorate the International Space Exhibition in Riccione, Italy. Overprint in Italian on No. C103.

St. John's Monastery, Rila
AP52

Design: 13s, Notre Dame, Paris; French inscription.

1964, Dec. 22 **Photo.** ***Perf. 11½***

C104	AP52	5s pale brn & blk	20	10
C105	AP52	13s lt ultra & sl bl	80	30

Issued to commemorate the philatelic exhibition at St. Ouen (Seine) organized by the Franco-Russian Philatelic Circle and philatelic organizations in various People's Democracies.

Paper Mill, Bukijovtz
AP53

Designs: 10s, Metal works, Plovdiv. 13s, Metal works, Kremikovtsi. 20s, Oil refinery, Stara-Zagora. 40s, Fertilizer plant, Stara-Zagora. 1 l, Rest home, Meded.

1964–68 ***Perf. 13*** **Unwmkd.**

C106	AP53	8s grnsh bl	15	5
C107	AP53	10s red lil	20	6
C108	AP53	13s brt vio	30	8
C109	AP53	20s sl bl	1.00	15
C110	AP53	40s dk ol grn	1.50	25
C111	AP53	1 l red ('68)	2.50	45
		Nos. C106-C111 (6)	5.65	1.04

Three-master
AP54

Veliko Turnovo
AP55

Means of Communication: 2s, Postal coach. 3s, Old steam locomotive. 5s, Early cars. 10s, Montgolfier balloon. 13s, Early plane. 20s, Jet planes. 40s, Rocket and satellites. 1 l, Postrider.

1969, Mar. 31 **Photo.** ***Perf. 13x12½***

C112	AP54	1s gray & multi	5	5
C113	AP54	2s gray & multi	5	5
C114	AP54	3s gray & multi	5	5
C115	AP54	5s gray & multi	8	5
C116	AP54	10s gray & multi	15	10
C117	AP54	13s gray & multi	25	10
C118	AP54	20s gray & multi	50	25
C119	AP54	40s gray & multi	90	45
		Nos. C112-C119 (8)	2.03	1.10

Miniature Sheet

Imperf.

C120	AP54	1 l gold & org	2.25	2.00

Issued to publicize SOFIA 1969 Philatelic Exhibition, Sofia, May 31–June 8. No. C120 contains one stamp, silver marginal inscription. Size: 57x54mm.

1973, July 30 **Photo.** ***Perf. 13***

Designs: Historic buildings in various cities.

Multicolored

C121	AP55	2s *shown*	5	5
C122	AP55	13s *Roussalka*	30	15
C123	AP55	20s *Plovdiv*	1.75	1.25
C124	AP55	28s *Sofia*	65	30

Aleksei A. Leonov and Soyuz
AP56

Designs: 18s, Thomas P. Stafford and Apollo. 28s, Apollo and Soyuz over earth. 1 l, Apollo Soyuz link-up.

1975, July 15

C125	AP56	13s bl & multi	25	10
C126	AP56	18s pur & multi	35	15
C127	AP56	28s multi	80	35

Souvenir Sheet

C128	AP56	1 l vio & multi	2.50	1.75

Apollo Soyuz space test project (Russo-American cooperation), launching July 15; link-up July 17.

Balloon Over Plovdiv
AP57

1977, Sept. 3

C129	AP57	25s yel, brn & red	50	25

Alexei Leonov Floating in Space—AP58

Designs: 25s, Mariner 6, US spacecraft. 35s, Venera 4, USSR Venus probe.

1977, Oct. 14 **Photo.** ***Perf. 13½***

C130	AP58	12s multi	25	8
C131	AP58	25s multi	50	20
C132	AP58	35s multi	75	30

Space era, 20 years.

TU-154, Balkanair Emblem
AP59

1977 ***Perf. 13***

C133	AP59	35s ultra & multi	90	50

30th anniversary of Bulgarian airline, Balkanair. No. C133 issued in sheets of 6 stamps and 3 labels (in lilac) with commemorative inscription and Balkanair emblem.

Baba Vida Fortress
AP60

Design: 35s, Peace Bridge, connecting Rousse, Bulgaria, with Giurgiu, Romania.

1978 **Photo.** ***Perf. 13***

C134	AP60	25s multi	50	20
C135	AP60	35s multi	70	28

The Danube, European Intercontinental Waterway. Issued in sheets containing 5 each of Nos. C134-C135 and 2 labels, one showing course of Danube, the other hydrofoil and fish.

Red Cross
AP61

1978, Mar. **Photo.** ***Perf. 13***

C136	AP61	25s multi	50	20

Centenary of Bulgarian Red Cross.

Clock Tower, Byalla Cherkva
AP62

Clock Towers: 23s, Botevgrad. 25s, Pazardgick. 35s, Grabovo. 53s, Tryavna.

1979, June 5 **Litho.** ***Perf. 12x12½***

C137	AP62	13s multi	22	10
C138	AP62	23s multi	40	18
C139	AP62	25s multi	45	20
C140	AP62	35s multi	60	28
C141	AP62	53s multi	95	45
		Nos. C137-C141 (5)	2.62	1.21

1980, Oct. 22 **Photo.** ***Perf. 12x12½***

C142	AP62	12s Bjala	26	12
C143	AP62	23s Rasgrad	46	22
C144	AP62	25s Karnabat	50	25
C145	AP62	35s Serlievo	70	35
C146	AP62	53s Berkovitza	1.05	50
		Nos. C142-C146 (5)	2.97	1.44

15th World Parachute Championships, Kazanluk—AP63

1980

C147	AP63	13s *shown*	25	10
C148	AP63	25s *Parachutist*	50	20

DWVY-1 Aircraft—AP64

1981, June 24 **Litho.** ***Perf. 12½***

C149	AP64	5s shown	10	5
C150	AP64	12s LAS-7	25	10
C151	AP64	25s LAS-8	50	20
C152	AP64	35s DAR-1	70	28
C153	AP64	45s DAR-3	90	38
C154	AP64	55s DAR-9	1.10	45
		Nos. C149-C154 (6)	3.55	1.46

Women in Space, 20th Anniv.—AP65

1983, June 28

C155	Sheet of 2	2.00	1.00
a.	AP65 50s Valentina Tereshkova	1.00	50
b.	AP65 50s Svetlana Savitskava	1.00	50

Multicolored margin shows Vostok 6, Soyuz T-7 and stars. Size: 122x76mm.

World Communications Year—AP66

1983, July 20 **Photo.** ***Perf. 13***

C156	AP63	5s TV tower, Tolbukhin	10	5
C157	AP63	13s Postwoman	25	12
C158	AP61	30s TV tower, Mt. Botev	60	30
a.		Strip of 3 (#C156-C158)	95	50

Emblems of World Communications Year, Bulgarian Post, UPU and ITU on attached margins.

Souvenir Sheet

Geophysical Map of the Moon, Russia's Luna I, II and III Satellites—AP64

1984, Oct. 24 **Photo.** ***Perf. 13***

C159	AP64	1 l multi	2.00	1.00

Conquest of Space. No. C159 has multicolored margin picturing moon walker, cosmonaut and lunar surface. Size: 79x57mm.

Intl. Civil Aviation Org., 40th Anniv.—AP65

1984, Dec. 21 **Photo.** ***Perf. 13***

C160	AP65	42s Balkan Airlines jet	85	42

AIR POST SEMI-POSTAL STAMPS.

Statue of Liberty, Plane and Bridge
SPAP1

Lithographed.

1947, May 24 *Perf. 11½.* Unwmkd.

CB1	SPAP1	70 l +30 l red brn	1.50	1.25

Issued to honor the 5th Philatelic Congress, Trnovo, and the Centenary International Philatelic Exhibition, New York, May, 1947.

Bulgarian Worker
SPAP2

Photogravure.

1948, Feb. 28 *Perf. 12x11½.*

CB2	SPAP2	60 l (+16 l) hn brn, *cr*	60	35

Issued to commemorate the 2nd Bulgarian Workers' Congress, and sold by subscription only, at a premium of 16 levas over face value.

Type of Air Post Stamps, 1963

Design: Valeri Bykovski and Valentina Tereshkova.

1963, Aug. 26 *Perf. 11½* Unwmkd.

CB3	AP51	20s +10s pale bluish grn & dk grn	1.35	60

See note after No. C101.

SPECIAL DELIVERY STAMPS.

Postman on Bicycle
SD1

Postman on Motorcycle
SD3

Mail Car
SD2

Photogravure.

1939 *Perf. 13* Unwmkd.

E1	SD1	5 l dp bl	60	20
E2	SD2	6 l cop brn	25	20
E3	SD3	7 l gldn brn	35	25
E4	SD2	8 l red org	60	25
E5	SD1	20 l brt rose	1.25	60
		Nos. E1-E5 (5)	3.05	1.50

POSTAGE DUE STAMPS.

D1

D2

Large Lozenge Perf. 5½ to 6½.

1884 Typographed. Unwmkd.

J1	D1	5s orange	200.00	22.50
J2	D1	25s lake	100.00	16.00
J3	D1	50s blue	8.00	7.50

1886 *Imperf.*

J4	D1	5s orange	100.00	5.00
J5	D1	25s lake	160.00	5.00
J6	D1	50s blue	5.50	5.00

1887 *Perf. 11½.*

J7	D1	5s orange	12.50	1.75
J8	D1	25s lake	12.50	1.75
J9	D1	50s blue	5.00	1.75

Same, Redrawn.

24 horizontal lines of shading in upper part instead of 30 lines.

1892 *Perf. 10½, 11½*

J10	D1	5s orange	12.50	2.00
J11	D1	25s lake	12.50	2.00

1893 Pelure Paper.

J12	D2	5s orange	13.50	5.50

D3

D4

Imperf.

1895 Ordinary Paper

J13	D3	30s on 50s bl	7.50	3.00

Perf. 10½, 11½

J14	D3	30s on 50s bl	7.50	3.50

Wmkd. Coat of Arms in the Sheet.

1896 *Perf. 13*

J15	D4	5s orange	4.25	1.00
J16	D4	10s purple	2.75	1.00
J17	D4	30s green	2.00	60

Nos. J15–J17 are also known on unwatermarked paper from the edges of sheets.

In 1901 a cancellation, "T" in circle, was applied to Nos. 60–65 and used provisionally as postage dues.

D5

D6

1901–04 *Perf. 11½* Unwmkd.

J19	D5	5s dl rose	30	15
J20	D5	10s yel grn	65	15
J21	D5	20s dl bl ('04)	5.00	20
J22	D5	30s vio brn	55	20
J23	D5	50s org ('02)	8.50	5.00
		Nos. J19-J23 (5)	15.00	5.70

Nos. J19–J23 exist imperf. and in pairs imperf. between. Price, imperf., $250.

Thin Semi-Transparent Paper.

1915 *Perf. 11½* Unwmkd.

J24	D6	5s green	15	5
J25	D6	10s purple	20	5
J26	D6	20s dl rose	20	8
J27	D6	30s dp org	1.10	25
J28	D6	50s dp bl	35	20
		Nos. J24-J28 (5)	2.00	63

1919–21 *Perf. 11½, 12x11½*

J29	D6	5s emerald	10	6
a.		5s gray grn ('21)	30	15
J30	D6	10s violet	10	6
J31	D6	20s salmon	10	6
a.		20s yel	10	6
J32		30s orange	10	8
a.		30s red org ('21)	65	65
J33	D6	50s blue	10	6
J34	D6	1 l emer ('21)	15	5
J35	D6	2 l rose ('21)	15	5
J36	D6	3 l brn org ('21)	25	5
		Nos. J29-J36 (8)	1.05	47

Stotinki values of the above series surcharged 10s or 20s were used as ordinary postage stamps. See Nos. 182–185.

The 1919 printings are on thicker white paper with clean-cut perforations, the 1921 printings on thicker grayish paper with rough perforations.

Most of this series exist imperforate and in pairs imperforate between.

Heraldic Lion
D7

Lion of Trnovo
D8

National Arms
D9

1932, Aug. 15 Thin Paper

J37	D7	1 l ol bis	40	30
J38	D7	2 l rose brn	40	30
J39	D7	6 l brn vio	1.25	50

1933, Apr. 10

J40	D8	20s dk brn	5	5
J41	D8	40s dp bl	5	5
J42	D8	80s car rose	5	5
J43	D9	1 l org brn	25	20
J44	D9	2 l olive	35	30
J45	D9	6 l dl vio	15	10
J46	D9	14 l ultra	25	15
		Nos. J40-J46 (7)	1.15	90

National Arms
D10

Arms of the People's Republic
D11

1947, June Typo. *Perf. 10½*

J47	D10	1 l chocolate	5	5
J48	D10	2 l dp cl	5	5
J49	D10	8 l dp org	10	6
J50	D10	20 l blue	20	10

1951 *Perf. 11½x10½*

J51	D11	1 l chocolate	5	5
J52	D11	2 l claret	5	5
J53	D11	8 l red org	20	15
J54	D11	20 l dp bl	60	50

OFFICIAL STAMPS.

Bulgarian Coat of Arms
O1 O2

Typographed

1942 *Perf. 13* Unwmkd.

O1	O1	10s yel grn	5	5
O2	O1	30s red	5	5
O3	O1	50s bister	5	5
O4	O2	1 l vio bl	5	5
O5	O2	2 l dk grn	5	5
O6	O2	3 l lilac	6	5
O7	O2	4 l rose	8	5
O8	O2	5 l carmine	10	5
		Nos. O1-O8 (8)	49	40

1944 *Perf. 10½x11½*

O9	O2	1 l blue	20	15
O10	O2	2 l brt red	20	15

Lion Rampant
O3 O4

O5

1945 *Imperf.*

O11	O5	1 l pink	5	5

Perf. 10½x11½, Imperf.

O12	O3	2 l bl grn	5	5
O13	O4	3 l bis brn	5	5
O14	O4	4 l lt ultra	5	5
O15	O5	5 l brn lake	5	5
		Nos. O11-O15 (5)	25	25

In 1950, four stamps prepared for official use were issued as regular postage stamps. See Nos. 724–727.

PARCEL POST STAMPS.

Weighing Packages
PP1

Parcel Post
PP2

Designs: 3 l, 8 l, 20 l, Parcel post truck. 4 l, 6 l, 10 l, Motorcycle.

Perf. 12½x13½, 13½x12½.

1941-42 Photogravure. Unwmkd.

Q1	PP1	1 l sl grn	5	5
Q2	PP2	2 l crimson	5	5
Q3	PP2	3 l dl brn	5	5
Q4	PP2	4 l red org	5	5
Q5	PP1	5 l dp bl	5	5
Q6	PP1	5 l sl grn ('42)	5	5
Q7	PP2	6 l red vio	5	5
Q8	PP2	6 l hn brn ('42)	5	5
Q9	PP1	7 l dk bl	5	5
Q10	PP1	7 l dk brn ('42)	6	5
Q11	PP2	8 l brt bl grn	6	5
Q12	PP2	8 l grn ('42)	6	5
Q13	PP2	9 l ol gray	10	5
Q14	PP2	9 l dp ol ('42)	10	5
Q15	PP2	10 l orange	10	5
Q16	PP2	20 l gray vio	35	6
Q17	PP2	30 l dl blk	50	10
Q18	PP2	30 l sep ('42)	45	10
		Nos. Q1-Q18 (18)	2.23	1.01

Arms of Bulgaria
PP5

1944 Lithographed. *Imperf.*

Q21	PP5	1 l dk car	5	5
Q22	PP5	3 l bl grn	5	5
Q23	PP5	5 l dl bl grn	5	5
Q24	PP5	7 l rose lil	6	5
Q25	PP5	10 l dp bl	6	5
Q26	PP5	20 l org brn	12	5
Q27	PP5	30 l dk brn car	15	5
Q28	PP5	50 l red org	30	12
Q29	PP5	100 l blue	55	25
		Nos. Q21-Q29 (9)	1.39	72

POSTAL TAX STAMPS.

The use of stamps Nos. RA1 to RA18 was compulsory on letters, etc., to be delivered on Sundays and holidays. The money received from their sale was used toward maintaining a sanatorium for employees of the post, telegraph and telephone services.

View of Sanatorium
PT1

Sanatorium, Peshtera
PT2

Typographed.

1925–29 *Perf. 11½* Unwmkd.

RA1	PT1	1 l *grnsh bl*	3.00	15
RA2	PT1	1 l choc ('26)	3.00	10
RA3	PT1	1 l org ('27)	3.50	15
RA4	PT1	1 l pink ('28)	5.00	15
RA5	PT1	1 l vio, *pnksh* ('29)	4.50	15
RA6	PT2	2 l bl grn	40	15
RA7	PT2	2 l vio ('27)	40	20
RA8	PT2	5 l dp bl	3.25	1.00
RA9	PT2	5 l rose ('27)	4.00	50
		Nos. RA1-RA9 (9)	27.05	2.55

St. Constantine Sanatorium
PT3

1930–33

RA10	PT3	1 l red brn & ol grn	6.00	15
RA11	PT3	1 l ol grn & yel ('31)	75	15
RA12	PT3	1 l red vio & ol brn ('33)	75	15

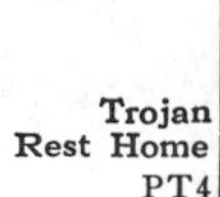

Trojan Rest Home
PT4

Sanatorium
PT5

Wmkd. Wavy Lines. (145)

1935 *Perf. 11, 11½.*

RA13	PT4	1 l choc & red org	45	10
RA14	PT4	1 l emer & ind	45	10
RA15	PT5	5 l red brn & ind	2.00	45

St. Constantine Sanatorium
PT6

Children at Seashore
PT7

Rest Home
PT8

Photogravure.

1941 *Perf. 13* Unwmkd.

RA16	PT6	1 l dk ol grn	5	5
RA17	PT7	2 l red org	15	5
RA18	PT8	5 l dp bl	30	15

BURMA

See British Commonwealth Section of Vol. I.

BURUNDI

LOCATION — Central Africa, adjoining the ex-Belgian Congo Republic, Rwanda and Tanzania.
GOVT.—Republic.
AREA—10,759 sq. mi.
POP.—4,920,000 (est. 1983).
CAPITAL—Bujumbura.

Burundi was established as an independent country on July 1, 1962. With Rwanda, it had been a U.N. trusteeship territory (Ruanda-Urundi) administered by Belgium. A military coup overthrew the monarchy November 28, 1966.

100 Centimes = 1 Franc

Flower Issue of Ruanda-Urundi, 1953 Overprinted:

Royaume du Burundi

Photogravure

1962, July 1 *Perf. 11½* Unwmkd.

Flowers in Natural Colors

1	A27	25c dk grn & dl org	20	15
2	A27	40c grn & sal	20	15
3	A27	60c bl grn & pink	40	30
4	A27	1.25fr dk grn & bl	21.00	20.00
5	A27	1.50fr vio & ap grn	90	75
6	A27	5fr dp plum & lt bl grn	1.25	90
7	A27	7fr dk grn & fawn	2.50	1.75
8	A27	10fr dp plum & pale ol	3.50	2.50
		Nos. 1-8 (8)	29.95	26.50

Animal Issue of Ruanda-Urundi, 1959–61 with Similar Overprint or Surcharge in Black or Violet Blue.

Size: 23x33mm., 33x23mm.

9	A29	10c brn, crim & blk brn	5	5
10	A30	20c gray, ap grn & blk	5	5
11	A29	40c mag, blk & gray grn	5	5
12	A30	50c grn, org yel & brn	6	5
a.		Larger ovpt. and bar	10	10
13	A29	1fr brn, ultra & blk	15	15
14	A30	1.50fr blk, gray & org (VB)	15	15
15	A29	2fr grnsh bl, ind & brn	15	15
16	A30	3fr brn, dp car & blk	15	15
17	A30	3.50fr on 3fr brn, dp car & blk	20	20
18	A30	4fr on 10fr multi ("XX" 6 mm wide)	30	30
a.		"XX" 4 mm wide	90	90
19	A30	5fr multi	30	30
20	A30	6.50fr red, org yel & brn	50	35
21	A30	8fr bl, mag & blk	60	45
a.		vio bl ovpt.	1.25	1.25
22	A30	10fr multi	60	60

Size: 45x26½mm.

23	A30	20fr multi	1.25	1.25
24	A30	50fr red, org, dp bl & brn (ovpt. bars 2mm wide)	2.50	2.25
a.		Ovpt. bars 4mm wide	3.75	2.25
		Nos. 9-24 (16)	7.06	6.50

On No. 12a, "Burundi" is 13mm. long; bar is continuous line across sheet. On No. 12, "Burundi" is 10mm.; bar is 29mm. No. 12a was issued in 1963.

Two types of overprint exist on 10c, 40c, 1fr and 2fr: I, "du" is below "me"; bar 22½mm. II, "du" below "oy"; bar 20 mm.

The 50c and 3fr exist in two types, besides the larger 50c overprint listed as No. 12: I, "du" is closer to "Royaume" than to "Burundi"; bar is less than 29mm; wording is centered above bar. II, "du" is closer to "Burundi"; bar is more than 30mm.; wording is off-center leftward.

King Mwami Mwambutsa IV and Royal Drummers—A1

Flag and Arms of Burundi
A2

Design: 2fr, 8fr, 50fr, Map of Burundi and King.

Photogravure

1962, Sept. 27 *Perf. 14* Unwmkd.

25	A1	50c dl rose car & dk brn	10	5
26	A2	1fr dk grn, red & emer	15	5
27	A1	2fr brn ol & dk brn	20	5
28	A1	3fr ver & dk brn	45	20
29	A2	4fr Prus bl, red & emer	35	5
30	A1	8fr vio & dk brn	65	12
31	A1	10fr brt grn & dk brn	80	18
32	A2	20fr brn, red & emer	2.00	38
33	A1	50fr brt pink & dk brn	3.50	75
		Nos. 25-33 (9)	8.20	1.83

Issued to commemorate Burundi's independence, July 1, 1962.

Ruanda-Urundi Nos. 151–152 Surcharged:

HOMMAGE A
DAG HAMMARSKJÖLD
3.50F
ROYAUME DU BURUNDI

Photogravure, Surcharge Engraved

1962, Oct. 31 *Perf. 11½*

Inscription in French

34	A31	3.50fr on 3fr ultra & red	33	25
35	A31	6.50fr on 3fr ultra & red	60	50
36	A31	10fr on 3fr ultra & red	90	75

Inscription in Flemish

37	A31	3.50fr on 3fr ultra & red	33	25
38	A31	6.50fr on 3fr ultra & red	60	50
39	A31	10fr on 3fr ultra & red	90	75
		Nos. 34-39 (6)	3.66	3.00

Issued in memory of Dag Hammarskjold, Secretary General of the United Nations, 1953–61.

King Mwami Mwambutsa IV, Map of Burundi and Emblem—A3

1962, Dec. 10 Photo. *Perf. 14*

40	A3	8fr yel, bl grn & blk brn	1.00	30
41	A3	50fr gray grn, bl grn & blk brn	2.75	70

Issued for the World Health Organization drive to eradicate malaria.

Stamps of type A3 without anti-malaria emblem are listed as Nos. 27, 30 and 33.

Sowing Seed over Africa
A4

1963, Mar. 21 *Perf. 14x13*

42	A4	4fr ol & dl pur	15	10
43	A4	8fr dp org & dl pur	35	25

44	A4	15fr emer & dl pur	50	40

Issued for the "Freedom from Hunger" campaign of the U.N. Food and Agriculture Organization.

Nos. 27 and 33 Overprinted in Dark Green

1963, June 19 *Perf. 14* Unwmkd.

45	A1	2fr brn ol & dk brn	3.75	3.00
46	A1	50fr brt pink & dk brn	4.25	3.00

Conquest and peaceful use of outer space.

Types of 1962 Inscribed: "Premier Anniversaire" in Red or Magenta

1963, July 1 Photogravure

47	A2	4fr ol, red & emer (R)	25	8
48	A1	8fr org & dk brn (M)	40	15
49	A1	10fr lil & dk brn (M)	65	25
50	A2	20fr gray, red & emer (R)	1.65	50

First anniversary of independence.

Nos. 26 and 32 Surcharged in Brown

1963, Sept. 24 *Perf. 14* Unwmkd.

51	A2	6.50fr on 1fr dk grn, red & emer	75	20
52	A2	15fr on 20fr brn, red & emer	1.50	50

Red Cross Flag over Globe with Map of Africa
A5

1963, Sept. 26 *Perf. 14x13*

53	A5	4fr emer, car & gray	30	12
54	A5	8fr brn ol, car & gray	60	25
55	A5	10fr bl, car & gray	90	35
56	A5	20fr lil, car & gray	1.85	60

Centenary of International Red Cross.

"1962", Arms of Burundi, U.N. and UNESCO Emblems
A6

U.N. Agency Emblems: 8fr, International Telecommunications Union. 10fr, World Meteorological Organization. 20fr, Universal Postal Union. 50fr, Food and Agriculture Organization.

1963, Nov. 4 *Perf. 14* Unwmkd.

57	A6	4fr yel, ol grn & blk	25	10
58	A6	8fr pale lil, Prus bl & blk	45	12
59	A6	10fr bl, lil & blk	60	18
60	A6	20fr yel grn, grn & blk	1.10	30
61	A6	50fr yel, red brn & blk	2.75	60
a.		Souv. sheet of 2	6.75	6.75
		Nos. 57-61 (5)	5.15	1.30

Issued to commemorate the first anniversary of Burundi's admission to the United Nations. No. 61a contains two imperf. stamps with simulated perforations similar to Nos. 60–61. The 20fr stamp shows the FAO and the 50fr the WMO emblems. Gray margin with black inscription. Size: 111x73½mm.

UNESCO Emblem, Scales and Map—A7

Designs: 3.50fr, 6.50fr, Scroll, scales and "UNESCO". 10fr, 20fr, Abraham Lincoln, broken chain and scales.

Lithographed

1963, Dec. 10 *Perf. 14x13½*

62	A7	50c pink, lt bl & blk	5	5
63	A7	1.50fr org, lt bl & blk	7	5
64	A7	3.50fr fawn, lt grn & blk	18	15
65	A7	6.50fr lt vio, lt grn & blk	35	18
66	A7	10fr bl, bis & blk	60	20
67	A7	20fr pale brn, ocher, bl & blk	1.20	35
		Nos. 62-67 (6)	2.45	98

Issued to commemorate the 15th anniversary of the Universal Declaration of Human Rights and the centenary of the American Emancipation Proclamation (Nos. 66–67).

Ice Hockey
A8

Impala
A9

Designs; 3.50 fr, Women's figure skating. 6.50fr, Torch. 10fr, Men's speed skating. 20fr, Slalom.

Photogravure

1964, Jan 25 *Perf. 14* Unwmkd.

68	A8	50c ol, blk & gold	10	5
69	A8	3.50fr lt brn, blk & gold	30	10
70	A8	6.50fr pale gray, blk & gold	60	20
71	A8	10fr gray, blk & gold	90	27
72	A8	20fr tan, blk & gold	1.75	65
		Nos. 68-72 (5)	3.65	1.27

Issued to publicize the 9th Winter Olympic Games, Innsbruck, Jan. 29–Feb. 9, 1964.

A souvenir sheet contains two stamps (10fr+5fr and 20fr+5fr) in tan, black and gold. Size: 121x65mm.

Canceled to Order

Starting about 1964, prices in the used column are for "canceled to order" stamps. Postally used copies sell for much more.

1964 Lithographed

Animals: 1fr, 5fr, Hippopotamus (horiz.). 1.50fr, 10fr, Giraffe. 2fr, 8fr, Cape buffalo (horiz.). 3fr, 6.50fr, Zebra (horiz.). 3.50fr, 15fr, Defassa waterbuck. 20fr, Cheetah. 50fr, Elephant. 100fr, Lion.

Perf. 14x13, 13x14

Size: 21½x35mm., 35x21½mm.

73	A9	50c multi	10	5
74	A9	1fr multi	15	5
75	A9	1.50fr multi	20	5
76	A9	2fr multi	25	5
77	A9	3fr multi	30	6
78	A9	3.50fr multi	35	7

Size: 26x42mm., 42x26mm.

79	A9	4fr multi	40	8
80	A9	5fr multi	50	10
81	A9	6.50fr multi	60	10
82	A9	8fr multi	75	20
83	A9	10fr multi	90	20
84	A9	15fr multi	1.10	33

Perf. 14

Size: 53x33mm.

85	A9	20fr multi	1.50	40
86	A9	50fr multi	4.00	65
87	A9	100fr multi	7.00	1.35
		Nos. 73-87 (15)	18.10	3.74

See also Nos. C1–C7.

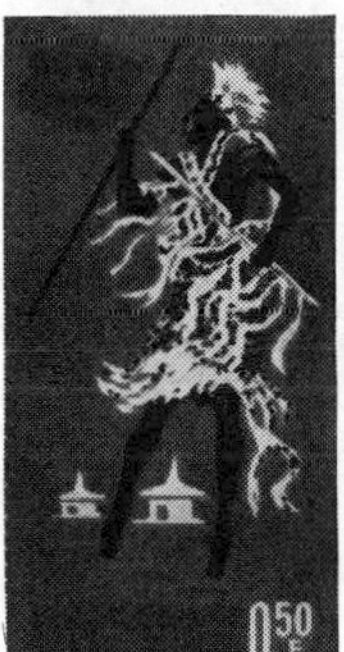

Burundi Dancer
A10

Designs: Various Dancers and Drummers.

Lithographed

1964, Aug. 21 *Perf. 14* Unwmkd.

Dancers Multicolored

88	A10	50c gold & emer	8	5
89	A10	1fr gold & vio bl	10	5
90	A10	4fr gold & brt bl	25	10
91	A10	6.50fr gold & red	40	18
92	A10	10fr gold & brt bl	60	25
93	A10	15fr gold & emer	90	30
94	A10	20fr gold & red	1.25	45
a.		Souv. sheet of 3	5.00	5.00
		Nos. 88-94 (7)	3.58	1.38

1965, Sept. 10

Dancers Multicolored

88a	A10	50c sil & emer	8	5
89a	A10	1fr sil & vio bl	8	5
90a	A10	4fr sil & brt bl	20	10
91a	A10	6.50fr sil & red	30	15
92a	A10	10fr sil & brt bl	50	20
93a	A10	15fr sil & emer	60	35
94b	A10	20fr sil & red	90	60
c.		Souv. sheet of 3	4.00	4.00
		Nos. 88a-94b (7)	2.66	1.50

Issued to commemorate the New York World's Fair, 1964–65. No. 94a contains one each of Nos. 92–94, gold background and bright blue border. No. 94c, dated "1965" in yellow, contains one each of Nos. 92a–94b, silver background and bright blue border. Size of souvenir sheets: 120x100mm.

Pope Paul VI and King Mwami Mwambutsa IV—A11

22 Sainted Martyrs
A12

Designs: 4fr, 14fr, Pope John XXIII and King Mwami.

1964, Nov. 12 Photo. *Perf. 12*

95	A11	50c brt bl, gold & red brn	10	5
96	A12	1fr mag, gold & sl	10	5
97	A11	4fr pale rose lil, gold & brn	50	8
98	A12	8fr red, gold & brn	50	15
99	A11	14fr lt grn, gold & brn	1.25	30
100	A11	20fr red brn, gold & grn	2.00	60
		Nos. 95-100 (6)	4.45	1.23

Issued to commemorate the canonization of 22 African martyrs, Oct. 18, 1964.

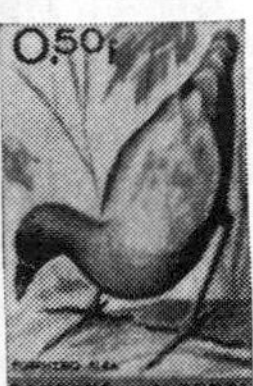

Shot Put
A13

African Purple Gallinule
A14

Sports: 1fr, Discus. 3fr, Swimming (horiz.). 4fr, Running. 6.50fr, Javelin, woman. 8fr, Hurdling (horiz.). 10fr, Broad jump (horiz.). 14fr, Diving, woman. 18fr, High jump (horiz.). 20fr, Vaulting (horiz.).

1964, Nov. 18 Litho. *Perf. 14*

101	A13	50c ol & multi	5	5
102	A13	1fr brt pink & multi	6	5
103	A13	3fr multi	15	10
104	A13	4fr multi	18	12
105	A13	6.50fr multi	30	18
106	A13	8fr lt bl & multi	40	20
107	A13	10fr multi	50	25
108	A13	14fr multi	75	30
109	A13	18fr bis & multi	90	40
110	A13	20fr gray & multi	1.00	50
		Nos. 101-110 (10)	4.29	2.15

Issued to commemorate the 18th Olympic Games, Tokyo, Oct. 10–25, 1964. See also No. B8.

1965 *Perf. 14* Unwmkd.

Birds: 1fr, 5fr, Little bee eater. 1.50fr, 6.50fr, Secretary bird. 2fr, 8fr, Yellow-billed stork. 3fr, 10fr, Congo peacock. 3.50fr, 15fr, African anhinga. 20fr, Saddle-billed stork. 50fr, Abyssinian ground hornbill. 100fr, Crowned crane.

Birds in Natural Colors

Size: 21x35mm.

111	A14	50c tan, grn & blk	5	5

112	A14	1fr	pink, mag & blk	5	5
113	A14	1.50fr	bl & blk	6	5
114	A14	2fr	yel grn, dk grn & blk	8	5
115	A14	3fr	yel, brn & blk	10	5
116	A14	3.50fr	yel grn, dk grn & blk	10	6

Size: 26x43mm.

117	A14	4fr	tan, grn & blk	12	8
118	A14	5fr	pink, mag & blk	15	8
119	A14	6.50fr	bl & blk	20	10
120	A14	8fr	yel grn, dk grn & blk	25	10
121	A14	10fr	yel, brn & blk	35	12
122	A14	15fr	yel grn, dk grn & blk	60	15

Size: 33x53mm.

123	A14	20fr	rose lil & blk	75	60
124	A14	50fr	yel, brn & blk	2.00	40
125	A14	100fr	grn, yel & blk	4.25	80
			Nos. 111-125 (15)	9.11	2.74

Issue dates: Nos. 111–116, Mar. 31. Nos. 117–122, Apr. 16. Nos. 123–125, Apr. 30.

See also Nos. C8–C16.

Relay Satellite and Morse Key
A15

Designs: 3fr, Telstar and old telephone handpiece. 4fr, Relay satellite and old wall telephone. 6.50fr, Orbiting Geophysical Observatory and radar screen. 8fr, Telstar II and headphones. 10fr, Sputnik II and radar aerial. 14fr, Syncom and transmission aerial. 20fr, Interplanetary Explorer and tracking aerial.

1965, July 3 Litho. *Perf. 13*

126	A15	1fr	multi	5	5
127	A15	3fr	multi	10	5
128	A15	4fr	multi	10	10
129	A15	6.50fr	multi	20	15
130	A15	8fr	multi	30	18
131	A15	10fr	multi	35	20
132	A15	14fr	multi	50	28
133	A15	20fr	multi	60	35
			Nos. 126-133 (8)	2.20	1.36

Issued to commemorate the centenary of the International Telecommunication Union. Perf. and imperf. souvenir sheets of two contain one each of Nos. 131 and 133. Bluish black margin and gold inscription. Size: 120x86mm. Price, both sheets, $7.50.

Globe and ICY Emblem—A16

Designs: 4fr, Map of Africa and U.N. development emblem. 8fr, Map of Asia and Colombo Plan emblem. 10fr, Globe and U.N. emblem. 18fr, Map of the Americas and Alliance for Progress emblem. 25fr, Map of Europe and EUROPA emblems. 40fr, Map of Outer Space and satellite with U.N. wreath.

1965, Oct. 1 Litho. *Perf. 13*

134	A16	1fr	ol grn & multi	5	5
135	A16	4fr	dl bl & multi	15	5
136	A16	8fr	pale yel & multi	30	12
137	A16	10fr	lil & multi	40	12
138	A16	18fr	sal & multi	65	20
139	A16	25fr	gray & multi	1.00	20
140	A16	40fr	bl & multi	1.60	25
a.			Souv. sheet of 3	4.50	4.50
			Nos. 134-140 (7)	4.15	99

Issued for the International Cooperation Year. No. 140a contains one each of Nos. 138–140. Gray margin with multicolored inscription. Size: 101½x100mm.

Protea
A17

Flowers: 1fr, 5fr, Crossandra. 1.50fr, 6.50fr, Ansellia. 2fr, 8fr, Thunbergia. 3fr, 10fr, Schizoglossum. 3.50fr, 15fr, Dissotis. 4fr, 20fr, Protea. 50fr, Gazania. 100fr, Hibiscus. 150fr, Markhamia.

1966 *Perf. 13½* Unwmkd.

Size: 26x26mm.

141	A17	50c	multi	5	5
142	A17	1fr	multi	5	5
143	A17	1.50fr	multi	5	5
144	A17	2fr	multi	7	5
145	A17	3fr	multi	10	5
146	A17	3.50fr	multi	10	5

Size: 31x31mm.

147	A17	4fr	multi	12	5
148	A17	5fr	multi	15	8
149	A17	6.50fr	multi	20	10
150	A17	8fr	multi	25	12
151	A17	10fr	multi	30	15
152	A17	15fr	multi	60	20

Size: 39x39mm.

153	A17	20fr	multi	75	20
154	A17	50fr	multi	2.00	50
155	A17	100fr	multi	3.75	75
156	A17	150fr	multi	5.50	1.10
			Nos. 141-156 (16)	14.04	3.55

Issue dates: Nos. 141–147, Feb. 28; Nos. 148–153, May 18; Nos. 154–156, June 15.

See also Nos. C17–C25.

Souvenir Sheets

Allegory of Prosperity and Equality Tapestry by Peter Colfs—A18

1966, Nov. 4 Litho. *Perf. 13½*

157	A18	Sheet of 7 (1.50fr)	2.00	75
158	A18	Sheet of 7 (4fr)	5.00	2.00

Issued to commemorate the 20th anniversary of UNESCO (United Nations Educational, Scientific and Cultural Organization). Each sheet contains 6 stamps showing a reproduction of the Colfs tapestry from the lobby of the General Assembly Building, New York, and one stamp with the UNESCO emblem plus a label. The labels on Nos. 157–158 and C26 are inscribed in French or English. The 3 sheets with French inscription have light blue marginal border. The 3 sheets with English inscription have pink border. Size: 203x124mm. See also No. C26.

Republic

Nos. 141–152, 154–156 Overprinted

REPUBLIQUE
DU
BURUNDI

1967 Lithographed *Perf. 13½*

Size: 26x26mm.

159	A17	50c	multi	5	5
160	A17	1fr	multi	5	5
161	A17	1.50fr	multi	6	5
162	A17	2fr	multi	8	5
163	A17	3fr	multi	12	5
164	A17	3.50fr	multi	15	5

Size: 31x31mm.

165	A17	4fr	multi	1.25	60
166	A17	5fr	multi	25	5
167	A17	6.50fr	multi	30	5
168	A17	8fr	multi	40	5
169	A17	10fr	multi	50	7
170	A17	15fr	multi	60	10

Size: 39x39mm.

171	A17	50fr	multi	6.00	2.00
172	A17	100fr	multi	10.00	4.00
173	A17	150fr	multi	8.50	3.50
			Nos. 159-173 (15)	28.31	10.72

Nos. 111, 113, 116, 118–125 Overprinted "REPUBLIQUE DU BURUNDI" and Horizontal Bar.

1967 Lithographed *Perf. 14*

Birds in Natural Colors

Size: 21x35mm.

174	A14	50c	multi	2.00	1.00
175	A14	1.50fr	bl & blk	5	5
176	A14	3.50fr	multi	12	5

Size: 26x43mm.

177	A14	5fr	multi	15	5
178	A14	6.50fr	bl & blk	18	5
179	A14	8fr	multi	25	5
180	A14	10fr	yel, brn & blk	50	7
181	A14	15fr	multi	90	10

Size: 33x53mm.

182	A14	20fr	multi	3.00	75
183	A14	50fr	multi	6.00	2.25
184	A14	100fr	multi	9.00	4.50
			Nos. 174-184 (11)	22.15	8.92

Haplochromis Multicolor
A19

Various Tropical Fish.

1967 Photogravure *Perf. 13½*

Size: 42x19mm.

186	A19	50c	multi	6	5
187	A19	1fr	multi	6	5
188	A19	1.50fr	multi	8	5
189	A19	2fr	multi	10	5
190	A19	3fr	multi	15	5
191	A19	3.50fr	multi	18	5

Size: 50x25mm.

192	A19	4fr	multi	28	5
193	A19	5fr	multi	35	5
194	A19	6.50fr	multi	42	5
195	A19	8fr	multi	50	5
196	A19	10fr	multi	60	7
197	A19	15fr	multi	85	10

Size: 59x30mm.

198	A19	20fr	multi	1.00	20
199	A19	50fr	multi	2.50	35
200	A19	100fr	multi	5.25	60
201	A19	150fr	multi	7.50	85
			Nos. 186-201 (16)	19.88	2.67

Issue Dates: Nos. 186–191, Apr. 4; Nos. 192–197, Apr. 28; Nos. 198–201, May 18.

See also Nos. C46–C54.

Ancestor Figures, Ivory Coast
A20

African Art: 1fr, Seat of Honor, Southeast Congo. 1.50fr, Antelope head, Aribinda Region. 2fr, Buffalo mask, Upper Volta. 4fr, Funeral figures, Southwest Ethiopia.

1967, June 5 Photo. *Perf. 13½*

202	A20	50c	sil & multi	5	5
203	A20	1fr	sil & multi	5	5
204	A20	1.50fr	sil & multi	10	5
205	A20	2fr	sil & multi	12	5
206	A20	4fr	sil & multi	18	5
			Nos. 202-206, C36-C40 (10)	3.50	2.00

Scouts on Hiking Trip
A21

Designs: 1fr, Cooking at campfire. 1.50fr, Lord Baden-Powell. 2fr, Boy Scout and Cub Scout giving Scout sign. 4fr, First aid.

1967, Aug. 9 Photo. *Perf. 13½*

207	A21	50c	sil & multi	5	5
208	A21	1fr	sil & multi	8	6
209	A21	1.50fr	sil & multi	10	6
210	A21	2fr	sil & multi	12	8
211	A21	4fr	sil & multi	18	8
			Nos. 207-211, C41-C45 (10)	4.08	1.63

Issued to commemorate the 60th anniversary of the Boy Scouts and the 12th Boy Scout World Jamboree, Farragut State Park, Idaho, Aug. 1–9.

The Gleaners, by Francois Millet
A22

Paintings Exhibited at EXPO '67: 8fr, The Water Carrier of Seville, by Velazquez. 14fr, The Triumph of Neptune and Amphitrite, by Nicolas Poussin. 18fr, Acrobat Standing on a Ball, by Picasso. 25fr, Marguerite van Eyck, by Jan van Eyck. 40fr, St. Peter Denying Christ, by Rembrandt.

1967, Oct. 12 Photo. ***Perf. 13½***

212	A22	4fr multi	25	8
213	A22	8fr multi	35	10
214	A22	14fr multi	50	12
215	A22	18fr multi	65	20
216	A22	25fr multi	1.00	35
217	A22	40fr multi	1.50	50
a.		Souv. sheet of 2	2.50	2.00
		Nos. 212-217 (6)	4.25	1.35

Issued to commemorate EXPO '67 International Exhibition, Montreal, Apr. 28–Oct. 27. Printed in sheets of 10 stamps and 2 labels inscribed in French or English. No. 217a contains one each of Nos. 216–217. Blue margin with black and red inscription. Size: 105x105mm. Exists imperf.

Place de la Revolution and Pres. Michel Micombero
A23

Designs: 5fr, President Michel Micombero and flag. 14fr, Formal garden and coat of arms. 20fr, Modern building and coat of arms.

1967, Nov. 23 ***Perf. 13½***

218	A23	5fr multi	25	10
219	A23	14fr multi	60	20
220	A23	20fr multi	90	20
221	A23	30fr multi	1.20	45

First anniversary of the Republic.

Madonna by Carlo Crivelli
A24

Designs: 1fr, Adoration of the Shepherds by Juan Bautista Mayno. 4fr, Holy Family by Anthony Van Dyck. 14fr, Nativity by Maitre de Moulins.

1967, Dec. 7 Photo. ***Perf. 13½***

222	A24	1fr multi	6	5
223	A24	4fr multi	15	10
224	A24	14fr multi	50	30
225	A24	26fr multi	1.20	50

Christmas 1967.

Printed in sheets of 25 and one corner label inscribed "Noel 1967" and giving name of painting and painter.

Slalom
A25

Designs: 10fr, Ice hockey. 14fr, Women's skating. 17fr, Bobsled. 26fr, Ski jump. 40fr, Speed skating. 60fr, Hand holding torch, and Winter Olympics emblem.

1968, Feb. 16 Photo. ***Perf. 13½***

226	A25	5fr sil & multi	30	5
227	A25	10fr sil & multi	45	5
228	A25	14fr sil & multi	60	10
229	A25	17fr sil & multi	75	10
230	A25	26fr sil & multi	1.10	15
231	A25	40fr sil & multi	1.75	25
232	A25	60fr sil & multi	3.00	40
		Nos. 226-232 (7)	7.95	1.10

Issued to publicize the 10th Winter Olympic Games, Grenoble, France, Feb. 6–18. Issued in sheets of 10 stamps and label.

The Lacemaker, by Vermeer
A26

Paintings: 1.50fr, Portrait of a Young Man, by Botticelli. 2fr, Maja Vestida, by Goya (horiz.).

1968, Mar. 29 Photo. ***Perf. 13½***

233	A26	1.50fr gold & multi	8	5
234	A26	2fr gold & multi	12	8
235	A26	4fr gold & multi	25	12
		Nos. 233-235, C59-C61 (6)	3.15	1.30

Issued in sheets of 6.

Moon Probe
A27

Designs: 6fr, Russian astronaut walking in space. 8fr, Weather satellite. 10fr, American astronaut walking in space.

1968, May 15 Photo. ***Perf. 13½***

Size: 35x35mm.

236	A27	4fr sil & multi	20	10
237	A27	6fr sil & multi	30	10
238	A27	8fr sil & multi	40	10
239	A27	10fr sil & multi	45	15
		Nos. 236-239, C62-C65 (8)	4.75	1.28

Issued to publicize peaceful space explorations.

A souvenir sheet contains one 25fr stamp in Moon Probe design and one 40fr in Weather Satellite design. Margin in silver and deep red lilac; black inscription. Stamp size: 41x41mm. Sheet size: 109x83mm. Price $2.

Sheet exists imperf. Price $3.

Salamis Aethiops
A28

Butterflies: 1fr, 5fr, Graphium ridleyanus. 1.50fr, 6.50fr, Cymothoe. 2fr, 8fr, Charaxes eupale. 3fr, 10fr, Papilio bromius. 3.50fr, 15fr, Teracolus annae. 20fr, Salamis aethiops. 50fr, Papilio zonobia. 100fr, Danais chrysippus. 150fr, Salamis temora.

1968

Size: 30x33½mm.

240	A28	50c gold & multi	5	5
241	A28	1fr gold & multi	5	5
242	A28	1.50fr gold & multi	6	5
243	A28	2fr gold & multi	8	5
244	A28	3fr gold & multi	10	6
245		3.50fr gold & multi	12	6

Size: 33½x37½mm.

246	A28	4fr gold & multi	20	8
247	A28	5fr gold & multi	25	8
248	A28	6.50fr gold & multi	55	8
249	A28	8fr gold & multi	65	8
250	A28	10fr gold & multi	75	10
251	A28	15fr gold & multi	85	15

Size: 41x46mm.

252	A28	20fr gold & multi	1.50	20
253	A28	50fr gold & multi	3.00	25
254	A28	100fr gold & multi	5.00	55
255	A28	150fr gold & multi	7.50	80
		Nos. 240-255 (16)	20.71	2.69

Issue dates: Nos. 240–245, June 7; Nos. 246–251, June 28. Nos. 252–255, July 19.

See also Nos. C66–C74.

Women, Along the Manzanares, by Goya
A29

Paintings: 7fr, The Letter, by Pieter de Hooch. 11fr, Woman Reading a Letter, by Gerard Terborch. 14fr, Man Writing a Letter, by Gabriel Metsu.

1968, Sept. 30 Photo. ***Perf. 13½***

256	A29	4fr multi	15	8
257	A29	7fr multi	25	12
258	A29	11fr multi	40	18
259	A29	14fr multi	60	25
		Nos. 256-259, C84-C87 (8)	5.25	1.58

International Letter Writing Week.

Soccer
A30

Designs: 7fr, Basketball. 13fr, High jump. 24fr, Relay race. 40fr, Javelin.

1968, Oct. 24

260	A30	4fr gold & multi	10	5
261	A30	7fr gold & multi	18	6
262	A30	13fr gold & multi	35	10
263	A30	24fr gold & multi	70	20
264	A30	40fr gold & multi	1.15	30
		260-264, C88-C92 (10)	7.43	2.11

Issued to commemorate the 19th Olympic Games, Mexico City, Oct. 12–27. Printed in sheets of 8.

Virgin and Child, by Fra Filippo Lippi
A31

Paintings: 5fr, The Magnificat, by Sandro Botticelli. 6fr, Virgin and Child, by Albrecht Durer. 11fr, Madonna del Gran Duca, by Raphael.

1968, Nov. 26 Photo. ***Perf. 13½***

265	A31	3fr multi	15	8
266	A31	5fr multi	20	10
267	A31	6fr multi	24	15
268	A31	11fr multi	45	25
a.		Souv. sheet of 4	1.50	1.50
		Nos. 265-268, C93-C96 (8)	3.14	1.48

Christmas 1968.

No. 268a contains one each of Nos. 265–268, decorative border and inscription. Size: 120x120mm. See Nos. C93–C96.

WHO Emblem and Map of Africa
A32

1969, Jan. 22

269	A32	5fr gold, dk grn & yel	18	8
270	A32	6fr gold, vio & ver	28	12
271	A32	11fr gold, pur & red lil	45	20

Issued to commemorate the 20th anniversary of the World Health Organization in Africa.

Nos. 265–268 Overprinted in Silver

1969, Feb. 17 Photo. ***Perf. 13½***

272	A31	3fr multi	15	8
273	A31	5fr multi	20	10
274	A31	6fr multi	25	15
275	A31	11fr multi	45	25
		Nos. 272-275, C100-C103 (8)	3.70	1.71

Issued to commemorate man's first flight around the moon by the U.S.A. spacecraft Apollo 8, Dec. 21–27, 1968.

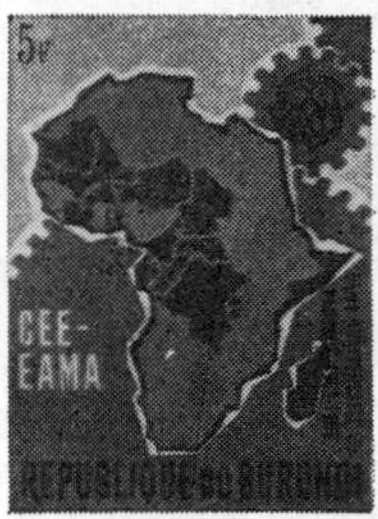

Map of Africa, and CEPT Emblem
A33

Designs: 14fr, Plowing with tractor. 17fr, Teacher and pupil. 26fr, Maps of Europe and Africa and CEPT (Conference of European Postal and Telecommunications Administrations) emblem (horiz.).

1969, Mar. 12 Photo. ***Perf. 13***

276	A33	5fr multi	20	8
277	A33	14fr multi	60	20

278	A33	17fr multi	75	25
279	A33	26fr multi	1.00	30

Issued to commemorate the 5th anniversary of the Yaoundé (Cameroun) Agreement, creating the European and African-Malgache Economic Community.

Resurrection, by Gaspard Isenmann
A34

Paintings: 14fr, Resurrection by Antoine Caron. 17fr, Noli me Tangere, by Martin Schongauer. 26fr, Resurrection, by El Greco.

1969, Mar. 24

280	A34	11fr gold & multi	45	15
281	A34	14fr gold & multi	55	20
282	A34	17fr gold & multi	75	25
283	A34	26fr gold & multi	1.10	30
a.		Souv. sheet of 4	3.00	3.00

Easter 1969.
No. 283a contains one each of Nos. 280–283; gold and blue border and inscription. Size: 100½x125mm.

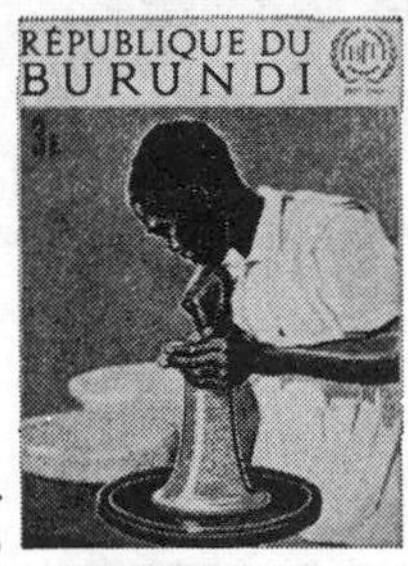

Potter
A35

Designs (BIT Emblem and): 5fr, Farm workers. 7fr, Foundry worker. 10fr, Woman testing corn crop.

1969, May 17 Photo. ***Perf. 13½***

284	A35	3fr multi	12	6
285	A35	5fr multi	20	6
286	A35	7fr multi	30	12
287	A35	10fr multi	40	18

Issued to commemorate the 50th anniversary of the International Labor Organization.

Industry and Bank's Emblem
A36

Designs (African Development Bank Emblem and): 17fr, Communications. 30fr, Education. 50fr, Agriculture.

1969, July 29 Photo. ***Perf. 13½***

288	A36	10fr gold & multi	35	10
289	A36	17fr gold & multi	60	20
290	A36	30fr gold & multi	1.00	30
291	A36	50fr gold & multi	1.60	50
a.		Souv. sheet of 4	3.75	3.75

Issued to publicize the 5th anniversary of the African Development Bank. No. 291a contains one each of Nos. 288–291, gold decorative border. Size: 103x124mm.

Girl Reading Letter, by Vermeer
A37

Paintings: 7fr, Graziella (young woman), by Auguste Renoir. 14fr, Woman writing a letter, by Gerard Terborch. 26fr, Galileo Galilei, painter unknown. 40fr, Ludwig van Beethoven, painter unknown.

1969, Oct. 24 Photo. ***Perf. 13½***

292	A37	4fr multi	18	5
293	A37	7fr multi	30	10
294	A37	14fr multi	65	18
295	A37	26fr multi	1.10	28
296	A37	40fr multi	1.50	40
a.		Souv. sheet of 2	3.50	3.50
		Nos. 292-296 (5)	3.73	1.01

Issued for International Letter Writing Week, Oct. 7–13.
No. 296a contains one each of Nos. 295–296. Buff decorative margin with commemorative inscription. Size: 133x75mm.

Moon Landing Issue

Rocket Launching
A38

Designs: 6.50fr, Rocket in space. 7fr, Separation of landing module from capsule. 14fr, 26fr, Landing module landing on moon. 17fr, Capsule in space. 40fr, Neil A. Armstrong leaving landing module. 50fr, Astronaut on moon.

1969, Nov. 6 Photo. ***Perf. 13½***

297	38	4fr bl & multi	30	10
298	38	6.50fr vio bl & multi	42	25
299	38	7fr vio bl & multi	42	25
300	38	14fr blk & multi	70	38
301	38	17fr vio bl & multi	1.10	50
		Nos. 297-301, C104-C106 (8)	7.24	3.58

Souvenir Sheet

302	A38	Souvenir sheet of 3	6.00	6.00
a.		26fr multi	1.00	1.00
b.		40fr multi	1.50	1.50
c.		50fr multi	2.00	2.00

See note after Algeria No. 427.
On. No. 302 stamp designs extend into inscribed margin. Size: 140x88mm.

Madonna and Child, by Rubens
A39

Paintings: 6fr, Madonna and Child with St. John, by Giulio Romano. 10fr, Magnificat Madonna, by Botticelli.

1969, Dec. 2 Photogravure

303	A39	5fr gold & multi	15	8
304	A39	6fr gold & multi	25	10
305	A39	10fr gold & multi	50	15
a.		Souvenir sheet of 3	1.50	1.50
		Nos. 303-305, C107-C109 (6)	4.45	1.28

Christmas 1969.
No. 305a contains one each of Nos. 303–305. Gold frame with inscription. Size: 110x87mm.

Sternotomis Bohemani
A40

Designs: Various Beetles and Weevils.

1970 ***Perf. 13½***

Size: 39x28mm.

306	A40	50c sil & multi	5	5
307	A40	1fr sil & multi	5	5
308	A40	1.50fr sil & multi	5	5
309	A40	2fr sil & multi	5	5
310	A40	3fr sil & multi	8	5
311	A40	3.50fr sil & multi	9	5

Size: 46x32mm.

312	A40	4fr sl & multi	18	5
313	A40	5fr sl & multi	22	5
314	A40	6.50fr sl & multi	30	5
315	A40	8fr sl & multi	40	5
316	A40	10fr sl & multi	50	5
317	A40	15fr sl & multi	75	5

Size: 52x36mm.

318	A40	20fr sl & multi	1.00	6
319	A40	50fr sl & multi	2.00	35
320	A40	100fr sl & multi	3.75	70
321	A40	150fr sl & multi	5.50	1.00
		Nos. 306-321, C110-C118 (25)	31.37	4.85

Issue dates: Nos. 306–313, Jan. 20; Nos. 314–318, Feb. 17; Nos. 319–321, Apr. 3.

Jesus Condemned to Death
A41

Stations of the Cross, by Juan de Aranoa y Carredano: 1.50fr, Jesus carries His Cross. 2fr, Jesus falls the first time. 3fr, Jesus meets His mother. 3.50fr, Simon of Cyrene helps carry the cross. 4fr, Veronica wipes the face of Jesus. 5fr, Jesus falls the second time.

1970, Mar. 16 Photo. ***Perf. 13½***

322	A41	1fr gold & multi	5	5
323	A41	1.50fr gold & multi	6	6
324	A41	2fr gold & multi	8	6
325	A41	3fr gold & multi	15	6
326	A41	3.50fr gold & multi	18	8
327	A41	4fr gold & multi	22	10
328	A41	5fr gold & multi	30	10
a.		Souv. sheet of 7 + label	1.10	1.10
		Nos. 322-328, C119-C125 (14)	5.09	2.18

Easter 1970.
No. 328a contains one each of Nos. 322–328 and label showing three crosses. Gold decorative border. Size: 154x123mm.

Parade and EXPO '70 Emblem
A42

Designs (EXPO '70 Emblem and): 6.50fr, Aerial view. 7fr, African pavilions. 14fr, Pagoda (vert.). 26fr, Recording pavilion and pool. 40fr, Tower of the Sun (vert.). 50fr, Flags of participating nations.

1970, May 5 Photo. ***Perf. 13½***

329	A42	4fr gold & multi	15	5
330	A42	6.50fr gold & multi	25	5
331	A42	7fr gold & multi	30	6
332	A42	14fr gold & multi	50	12
333	A42	26fr gold & multi	80	18
334	A42	40fr gold & multi	1.25	30
335	A42	50fr gold & multi	1.75	40
		Nos. 329-335 (7)	5.00	1.16

Issued to publicize EXPO '70 International Exhibition, Osaka, Japan, March 15–Sept. 13, 1970. See No. C126.

White Rhinoceros—A43

Designs, FAUNA: Camel, dromedary, okapi, addax, Burundi cow (2 stamps of each animal in 2 different poses). MAP OF THE NILE: Delta and pyramids, dhow, cataract, Blue Nile and crowned crane, Victoria Nile and secretary bird, Lake Victoria and source of Nile on Mt. Gikizi.

1970, July 8 Photo. ***Perf. 13½***

336	A43	7fr multi	75	10
a.		Sheet of 18	14.00	2.75

Issued in sheets of 18 (3x6) stamps of different designs, to publicize the southernmost source of the Nile on Mt. Gikizi in Burundi. See No. C127.

Winter Wren, Firecrest, Skylark and Crested Lark—A44

Birds: 2fr, 3.50fr and 5fr, vertical; others horizontal.

1970, Sept. 30 Photo. ***Perf. 13½***

Stamp Size: 44x33mm.

Gold Frame & Multicolored; Birds in Natural Colors

337	A44	2fr Block of four	75	20
a.		*Northern shrike*	18	
b.		*European starling*	18	
c.		*Yellow wagtail*	18	
d.		*Bank swallow*	18	
338	A44	3fr Block of four	1.10	20
a.		*Winter wren*	25	
b.		*Firecrest*	25	
c.		*Skylark*	25	
d.		*Crested lark*	25	
339	A44	3.50fr Block of four	1.40	20
a.		*Woodchat shrike*	35	
b.		*Common rock thrush*	35	
c.		*Black redstart*	35	
d.		*Ring ouzel*	35	
340	A44	4fr Block of four	1.65	20
a.		*European Redstart*	40	
b.		*Hedge sparrow*	40	
c.		*Gray wagtail*	40	
d.		*Meadow pipit*	40	

341	A44	5fr Block of four	2.00	20
a.		*Eurasian hoopoe*	50	
b.		*Pied flycatcher*	50	
c.		*Great reed warbler*	50	
d.		*Eurasian kingfisher*	50	
342	A44	6.50fr Block of four	2.50	25
a.		*House martin*	60	
b.		*Sedge warbler*	60	
c.		*Fieldfare*	60	
d.		*European Golden oriole*	60	
		Nos. 337-342, C132-C137 (12 blocks of 4)	40.90	5.80

Nos. 337–342 are printed in sheets of 16 containing 4 blocks of 4.

Library, U.N. Emblem—A45

Designs: 5fr, Students taking test, and emblem of University of Bujumbura. 7fr, Students in laboratory and emblem of Ecole Normale Supérieure of Burundi. 10fr, Students with electron-microscope and Education Year emblem.

1970, Oct. 23

343	A45	3fr gold & multi	12	5
344	A45	5fr gold & multi	20	5
345	A45	7fr gold & multi	30	8
346	A45	10fr gold & multi	40	10

Issued for International Education Year.

Pres. and Mrs. Michel Micombero
A46

Designs: 7fr, Pres. Michel Micombero and Burundi flag. 11fr, Pres. Micombero and Revolution Memorial.

1970, Nov. 28 Photo. *Perf. 13½*

347	A46	4fr gold & multi	15	6
348	A46	7fr gold & multi	25	12
349	A46	11fr gold & multi	40	17
a.		Souvenir sheet of 3	1.00	1.00

Issued to commemorate the 4th anniversary of independence. No. 349a contains 3 stamps similar to Nos. 347–349, but inscribed "Poste Aerienne." Dark gray and gold margin with commemorative inscription. Size: 125x143mm. Exists imperf.

See Nos. C140–C142.

Lenin with Delegates
A47

Designs (Lenin, Paintings): 5fr, addressing crowd. 6.50fr, with soldier and sailor. 15fr, speaking from balcony. 50fr, Portrait.

1970, Dec. 31 Photo. *Perf. 13½*
Gold Frame

350	A47	3.50fr dk red brn	14	6
351	A47	5fr dk red brn	20	8
352	A47	6.50fr dk red brn	28	12
353	A47	15fr dk red brn	60	25
354	A47	50fr dk red brn	2.00	35
		Nos. 350-354 (5)	3.22	86

Lenin's birth centenary (1870–1924).

Lion
A48

1971, March 19 Photo. *Perf. 13½*
Multicolored
Size: 38x38mm.

355	A48	1fr Strip of four	32	20
a.		*Lion*	8	
b.		*Cape buffalo*	8	
c.		*Hippopotamus*	8	
d.		*Giraffe*	8	
356	A48	2fr Strip of four	48	20
a.		*Hartebeest*	12	
b.		*Black rhinoceros*	12	
c.		*Zebra*	12	
d.		*Leopard*	12	
357	48	3fr Strip of four	60	25
a.		*Grant's gazelles*	15	
b.		*Cheetah*	15	
c.		*African white-backed vultures*	15	
d.		*Johnston's okapi*	15	
358	A48	5fr Strip of four	1.00	40
a.		*Chimpanzee*	25	
b.		*Elephant*	25	
c.		*Spotted hyenas*	25	
d.		*Beisa*	25	
359	A48	6fr Strip of four	1.25	45
a.		*Gorilla*	30	
b.		*Gnu*	30	
c.		*Wart hog*	30	
d.		*Cape hunting dog*	30	
360	A48	11fr Strip of four	2.75	90
a.		*Sable antelope*	65	
b.		*Caracal lynx*	65	
c.		*Ostriches*	65	
d.		*Bongo*	65	
		Nos. 355-360, C146-C151 (12 strips of 4)	24.15	5.95

The Resurrection, by Il Sodoma
A49

Paintings: 6fr, Resurrection, by Andrea del Castagno. 11fr, Noli me Tangere, by Correggio.

1971, Apr. 2

361	A49	3fr gold & multi	15	5
362	A49	6fr gold & multi	30	10
363	A49	11fr gold & multi	55	15
a.		Souvenir sheet of 3	1.10	1.10
		Nos. 361-363, C143-C145 (6)	2.80	88

Easter 1971. No. 363a contains one each of Nos. 361–363. Red and gold margin. Size: 120x85mm. Sheet exists imperf.

The indexes in each volume of the Scott Catalogue contain many listings which help to identify stamps.

Young Venetian Woman, by Dürer
A50

Dürer Paintings: 11fr, Hieronymus Holzschuher. 14fr, Emperor Maximilian I. 17fr, Holy Family, from Paumgartner Altar. 26fr, Haller Madonna. 31fr, Self-portrait, 1498.

1971, Sept. 20

364	A50	6fr multi	25	12
365	A50	11fr multi	45	22
366	A50	14fr multi	55	28
367	A50	17fr multi	70	35
368	A50	26fr multi	1.00	50
369	A50	31fr multi	1.25	60
a.		Souvenir sheet of 2	2.50	2.50
		Nos. 364-369 (6)	4.20	2.07

International Letter Writing Week. Paintings by Dürer. 500th anniversary of the birth of Albrecht Dürer (1471–1528), German painter and engraver. No. 369a contains one each of Nos. 368–369. Tan margin with portrait of Erasmus. Size: 137x80mm. Exists imperf.

Nos. 364–369, 369a Overprinted in Black and Gold:

"VIème CONGRES / DE L'INSTITUT INTERNATIONAL / DE DROIT D'EXPRESSION FRANCAISE"

1971, Oct. 8

370	A50	6fr multi	25	6
371	A50	11fr multi	45	12
372	A50	14fr multi	55	15
373	A50	17fr multi	70	20
374	A50	26fr multi	1.00	30
375	A50	31fr multi	1.25	35
a.		Souvenir sheet of 2	2.50	2.50
		Nos. 370-375 (6)	4.20	1.18

6th Congress of the International Legal Institute of the French-speaking Area, Usumbura, Aug. 10–19.

Madonna and Child, by Il Perugino
A51

Paintings of the Madonna and Child by: 5fr, Andrea del Sarto. 6fr, Luis de Morales.

1971, Nov. 2 Photo. *Perf. 13½*

376	A51	3fr dk grn & multi	12	5
377	A51	5fr dk grn & multi	20	6
378	A51	6fr dk grn & multi	27	8
a.		Souvenir sheet of 3	75	75
		Nos. 376-378,C153-C155 (6)	2.79	1.14

Christmas 1971. No. 378a contains one each of Nos. 376–378. Multicolored border. Size: 125x81mm. Sheet exists imperf.

Lunar Orbiter
A52

Designs: 11fr, Vostok. 14fr, Luna 1. 17fr, Apollo 11 astronaut on moon. 26fr, Soyuz 11. 40fr, Lunar Rover (Apollo 15).

1972, Jan. 15

379	A52	6fr gold & multi	35	18
380	A52	11fr gold & multi	45	22
381	A52	14fr gold & multi	55	28
382	A52	17fr gold & multi	80	40
383	A52	26fr gold & multi	80	65
384	A52	40fr gold & multi	1.25	65
a.		Souvenir sheet of 6	4.25	4.25
		Nos. 379-384 (6)	4.20	2.38

Conquest of space. See No. C156.

No. 384a contains one each of Nos. 379–384 inscribed "APOLLO 16." Multicolored margin inscribed "La Conquête de l'Espace." Size: 134x135mm.

Slalom and Sapporo '72 Emblem
A53

Designs (Sapporo '72 Emblem and): 6fr, Figure skating, pairs. 11fr, Figure skating, women's. 14fr, Ski jump. 17fr, Ice hockey. 24fr, Speed skating, men's. 26fr, Snow scooter. 31fr, Downhill skiing. 50fr, Bobsledding.

1972, Feb. 3

385	A53	5fr sil & multi	15	5
386	A53	6fr sil & multi	20	7
387	A53	11fr sil & multi	35	10
388	A53	14fr sil & multi	45	15
389	A53	17fr sil & multi	55	15
390	A53	24fr sil & multi	75	18
391	A53	26fr sil & multi	80	20
392	A53	31fr sil & multi	1.00	25
393	A53	50fr sil & multi	1.60	40
		Nos. 385-393 (9)	5.85	1.55

11th Winter Olympic Games, Sapporo, Japan, Feb. 3–13. Printed in sheets of 12. See No. C157.

Issue dates: Nos. 385–390, Feb. 1; Nos. 391–393, Feb. 21.

Ecce Homo, by Quentin Massys
A54

Paintings: 6.50fr, Crucifixion, by Rubens. 10fr, Descent from the Cross, by Jacopo da Pontormo. 18fr, Pietà, by Ferdinand Gallegos. 27fr, Trinity, by El Greco.

1972, Mar. 20 Photo. *Perf. 13½*

394	A54	3.50fr gold & multi	8	5
395	A54	6.50fr gold & multi	25	8
396	A54	10fr gold & multi	35	12
397	A54	18fr gold & multi	65	20

398 A54 27fr gold & multi 1.50 30
a. Souvenir sheet of 5+label 3.00 2.50
Nos. 394-398 (5) 2.83 75

Easter 1972. Printed in sheets of 8 with label. No. 398a contains one each of Nos. 394–398 and decorative label. Dark brown and gold margin. Size: 120x157mm. Exists imperf.

Gymnastics, Olympic Rings and "Motion"
A55

1972, May 19

Gold and Multicolored

399 A55 5fr *shown* 18 6
400 A55 6fr *Javelin* 20 7
401 A55 11fr *Fencing* 42 13
402 A55 14fr *Bicycling* 52 17
403 A55 17fr *Pole vault* 65 20
Nos. 399-403, C158-C161 (9) 5.62 1.81

Souvenir Sheet

404 A55 Souv. sheeet of 2 3.50 2.50
a. 31fr *Discus* 90 90
b. 40fr *Soccer* 1.20 1.20

20th Olympic Games, Munich, Aug. 26–Sept. 11. No. 404 has multicolored margin with Olympic flag, "Motion" and commemorative inscription. Size: 126x80mm.

Prince Rwagasore, Pres. Micombero, Burundi Flag, Drummers
A56

Designs: 7fr, Rwagasore, Micombero, flag, map of Africa, globe. 13fr, Micombero, flag, globe.

1972, Aug. 24 Photo. *Perf. 13½*

405 A56 5fr sil & multi 15 5
406 A56 7fr sil & multi 25 8
407 A56 13fr sil & multi 45 15
a. Souvenir sheet of 3 1.00
Nos. 405-407, C162-C164 (6) 2.85 95

10th anniversary of independence.
No. 407a contains one each of Nos. 405–407. Silver and light blue margin with black inscription. Size: 146x80mm.

Madonna and Child, by Andrea Solario
A57

Paintings of the Madonna and Child by: 10fr, Raphael. 15fr, Botticelli.

1972, Nov. 2

408 A57 5fr lt bl & multi 15 5
409 A57 10fr lt bl & multi 30 10
410 A57 15fr lt bl & multi 45 15
a. Souvenir sheet of 3 1.00
Nos. 408-410, C165-C167 (6) 3.45 1.07

Christmas 1972. Sheets of 20 stamps and one label. No. 410a contains one each of Nos. 408–410. Deep carmine and gold border. Size: 128x81mm.

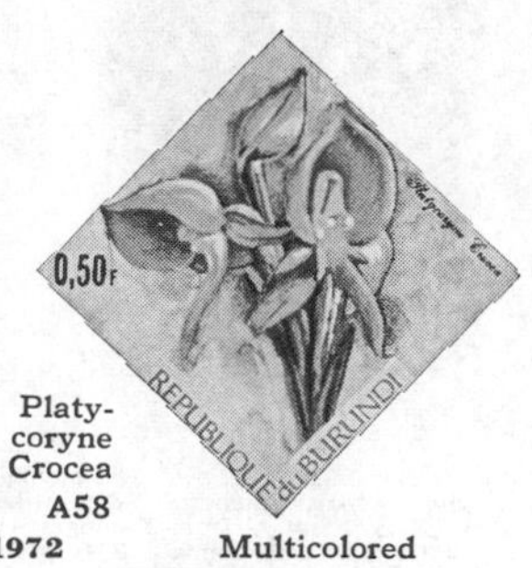

Platycoryne Crocea
A58

1972 Multicolored

Size: 33x33mm.

411 A58 50c *shown* 5 5
412 A58 1fr *Cattleya trianaei* 5 5
413 A58 2fr *Eulophia cucullata* 7 5
414 A58 3fr *Cymbidium hamsey* 10 5
415 A58 4fr *Thelymitra pauciflora* 13 6
416 A58 5fr *Miltassia* 17 8
417 A58 6fr *Miltonia* 20 10

Size: 38x38mm.

418 A58 7fr Like 50c 23 12
419 A58 8fr Like 1fr 27 13
420 A58 9fr Like 2fr 30 15
421 A58 10fr Like 3fr 35 17
Nos. 411-421, C168-C174 (18) 6.39 2.15

Orchids. Issue dates: Nos. 411–417, Nov. 6; Nos. 418–421, Nov. 29.

Henry Morton Stanley—A59

Designs: 7fr, Porters, Stanley's expedition. 13fr, Stanley entering Ujiji.

1973, Mar. 19 Photo. *Perf. 13½*

422 A59 5fr gold & multi 15 5
423 A59 7fr gold & multi 20 7
424 A59 13fr gold & multi 40 13
Nos. 422-424, C175-C177 (6) 2.55 85

Exploration of Africa by David Livingstone (1813–1873) and Henry Morton Stanley (John Rowlands; 1841–1904).

Crucifixion, by Roger van der Weyden
A60

Paintings: 5fr, Flagellation of Christ, by Caravaggio. 13fr, The Burial of Christ, by Raphael.

1973, Apr. 10

425 A60 5fr gold & multi 15 5
426 A60 7fr gold & multi 20 7
427 A60 13fr gold & multi 40 13
a. Souvenir sheet of 3 1.00 1.00
Nos. 425-427, C178-C180 (6) 3.00 85

Easter 1973. No. 427a contains one each of Nos. 425–427. Multicolored margin. Size: 121x73mm.

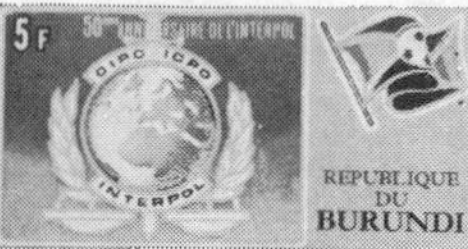

INTERPOL Emblem, Flag—A61

Design: 10fr, INTERPOL flag and emblem. 18fr, INTERPOL Headquarters and emblem.

1973, May 19 Photo. *Perf. 13½*

428 A61 5fr sil & multi 15 5
429 A61 10fr sil & multi 30 12
430 A61 18fr sil & multi 55 22
Nos. 428-430, C181-C182 (5) 2.75 1.09

50th anniversary of International Criminal Police Organization (INTERPOL).

Signs of the Zodiac, Babylon—A62

Designs: 5fr, Greek and Roman gods representing planets. 7fr, Ptolemy (No. 433a) and Ptolemaic solar system. 13fr, Copernicus (No. 434a) and heliocentric system.

1973, July 27 Photo. *Perf. 13½*

Gold and Multicolored

431 A62 3fr Block of four 40 20
a. 3fr in UL 10 5
b. 3fr in UR 10 5
c. 3fr in LL 10 5
d. 3fr in LR 10 5
432 A62 5fr Block of four 75 20
a. 5fr in UL 18 5
b. 5fr in UR 18 5
c. 5fr in LL 18 5
d. 5fr in LR 18 5
433 A62 7fr Block of four 1.00 20
a. 7fr in UL 25 5
b. 7fr in UR 25 5
c. 7fr in LL 25 5
d. 7fr in LR 25 5
434 A62 13fr Block of four 2.25 40
a. 13fr in UL 55 10
b. 13fr in UR 55 10
c. 13fr in LL 55 10
d. 13fr in LR 55 10
e. Souvenir sheet of 4 6.50 3.50
Nos. 431-434, C183-C186 (8 blocks of 4) 27.40 4.70

500th anniversary of the birth of Nicolaus Copernicus (1473–1543), Polish astronomer.

Nos. 431–434 are printed in sheets of 32 containing 8 blocks of 4. No. 434e contains one each of Nos. 431–434. Gold and multicolored margin. Size: 136x136mm.

Flowers and Butterflies—A63

Designs: Each block of 4 contains 2 flower and 2 butterfly designs. The 1fr, 2fr, 5fr and 11fr have flower designs listed as "a" and "d" numbers, butterflies as "b" and "c" numbers; the arrangement is reversed for the 3fr and 6fr.

1973, Sept. 3 Photo. *Perf. 13*

Stamp Size: 34x41½mm.

Gold and Multicolored

435 A63 1fr Block of 4 32 20
a. *Protea cynaroides* 8 5
b. *Precis octavia* 8 5
c. *Epiphora bauhiniae* 8 5
d. *Gazania longiscapa* 8 5
436 A63 2fr Block of 4 32 20
a. *Kniphofia* 8 5
b. *Cymothoe coccinata* 8 5
c. *Nudaurelia zambesina* 8 5
d. *Freesia refracta* 8 5
437 A63 3fr Block of 4 48 20
a. *Calotis eupompe* 12 5
b. *Narcissus* 12 5
c. *Cineraria hybrida* 12 5
d. *Cyrestis camillus* 12 5
438 A63 5fr Block of 4 80 20
a. *Iris tingitana* 20 5
b. *Pappilio demodocus* 20 5
c. *Catopsilia avelaneda* 20 5
d. *Nerine sarniensis* 20 5
439 A63 6fr Block of 4 1.00 25
a. *Hypolimnas dexithea* 25 6
b. *Zantedeschia tropicalis* 25 6
c. *Sandersonia aurantiaca* 25 6
d. *Drurya antimachus* 25 6
440 A63 11fr Block of 4 2.00 45
a. *Nymphaea capensis* 50 10
b. *Pandoriana pandora* 50 10
c. *Precis orythia* 50 10
d. *Pelargonium domestica* 50 10
Nos. 435-440, C187-C192 (12 blocks of 4) 37.76 6.37

Virgin and Child, by Giovanni Bellini
A64

Virgin and Child by: 10fr, Jan van Eyck. 15fr, Giovanni Boltraffio.

1973, Nov. 13 Photo. *Perf. 13*

441 A64 5fr gold & multi 15 5
442 A64 10fr gold & multi 30 8
443 A64 15fr gold & multi 45 12
a. Souvenir sheet of 3 1.00 1.00
Nos. 441-443, C193-C195 (6) 3.45 95

Christmas 1973. No. 443a contains one each of Nos. 441–443 with multicolored margin. Size: 143x79mm.

Pietá, by Paolo Veronese
A65

Paintings: 10fr, Virgin and St. John, by van der Weyden. 18fr, Crucifixion, by van der Weyden. 27fr, Burial of Christ, by Titian. 40fr, Pietá, by El Greco.

1974, Apr. 19 Photo. *Perf. 14x13½*

444 A65 5fr gold & multi 15 5
445 A65 10fr gold & multi 30 10
446 A65 18fr gold & multi 55 18
447 A65 27fr gold & multi 85 25
448 A65 40fr gold & multi 1.35 30
a. Souvenir sheet of 5 3.25 3.25
Nos. 444-448 (5) 3.20 88

Easter 1974. No. 448a contains one each of Nos. 444–448, rose brown and gold margin. Size: 145x120mm.

Fish—A66

Designs: Fish.

1974, May 30 Photo. *Perf. 13*

Stamp Size: 35x35mm.

Multicolored

449 A66 1fr Block of 4 20 20
 a. *Haplochromis multicolor* 5 5
 b. *Pantodon buchholzi* 5 5
 c. *Tropheus duboisi* 5 5
 d. *Distichodus sexfasciatus* 5 5
450 A66 2fr Block of 4 24 20
 a. *Pelmatochromis kribensis* 6 5
 b. *Nannaethiops tritaeniatus* 6 5
 c. *Polycentropsis abbreviata* 6 5
 d. *Hemichromis bimaculatus* 6 5
451 A66 3fr Block of 4 36 20
 a. *Ctenopoma acutirostre* 9 5
 b. *Synodontis angelicus* 9 5
 c. *Tilapia melanopleura* 9 5
 d. *Aphyosemion bivittatum* 9 5
452 A66 5fr Block of 4 60 20
 a. *Monodactylus argenteus* 15 5
 b. *Zanclus canescens* 15 5
 c. *Pygoplites diacanthus* 15 5
 d. *Cephalopholis argus* 15 5
453 A66 6fr Block of 4 72 20
 a. *Priacanthus arenatus* 18 5
 b. *Pomacanthus arcuatus* 18 5
 c. *Scarus guacamaia* 18 5
 d. *Zeus faber* 18 5
454 A66 11fr Block of 4 1.32 32
 a. *Lactophrys quadricornis* 33 8
 b. *Balistes vetula* 33 8
 c. *Acanthurus bahianus* 33 8
 d. *Holocanthus ciliaris* 33 8
 Nos. 449-454, C207-C212 (12 blocks of 4) 23.69 4.42

Soccer and Cup
A67

Designs: Various soccer scenes and cup.

1974, July 4 Photogravure *Perf. 13*

455 A67 5fr gold & multi 15
456 A67 6fr gold & multi 18
457 A67 11fr gold & multi 33
458 A67 14fr gold & multi 42
459 A67 17fr gold & multi 50
 a. Souvenir sheet of 3 2.75 2.75
 Nos. 455-459, C196-C198 (8) 4.16

World Soccer Championship, Munich, June 13–July 7. No. 459a contains 3 stamps similar to Nos. C196–C198 without "Poste Aerienne." Gold and multicolored margin with picture of Munich City Hall. Size: 88x142mm.

Nos. 455–459 and 459a exist imperf.

Flags over UPU Headquarters, Bern
A68

Designs: No. 461, G.P.O., Usumbura. No. 462, Mailmen ("11F" in UR). No. 463, Mailmen ("11F" in UL). No. 464, UPU emblem. No. 465, Means of transportation. No. 466, Pigeon over globe showing Burundi. No. 467, Swiss flag, pigeon over map showing Bern.

1974, July 23

460 A68 6fr gold & multi 35
461 A68 6fr gold & multi 35
462 A68 11fr gold & multi 60
463 A68 11fr gold & multi 60
464 A68 14fr gold & multi 75
465 A68 14fr gold & multi 75
466 A68 17fr gold & multi 95
467 A68 17fr gold & multi 95
 a. Souvenir sheet of 8 5.50 4.25
 Nos. 460-467, C199-C206 (16) 17.30 2.00

Centenary of Universal Postal Union. Stamps of same denomination printed se-tenant (continuous design) in sheets of 40.

No. 467a contains one each of Nos. 460–467. Violet, gold and light blue margin. Size: 96x162mm.

St. Ildefonso Writing Letter, by El Greco
A69

Paintings: 11fr, Lady Sealing Letter, by Chardin. 14fr, Titus at Desk, by Rembrandt. 17fr, The Love Letter, by Vermeer. 26fr, The Merchant G. Gisze, by Holbein. 31fr, Portrait of Alexandre Lenoir, by David.

1974, Oct. 1 Photo. *Perf. 13*

468 A69 6fr gold & multi 18
469 A69 11fr gold & multi 33
470 A69 14fr gold & multi 42
471 A69 17fr gold & multi 50
472 A69 26fr gold & multi 78
473 A69 31fr gold & multi 93
 a. Souvenir sheet of 2 2.00 2.00
 Nos. 468-473 (6) 3.14

International Letter Writing Week, Oct. 6–12. No. 473a contains one each of Nos. 472–473. Multicolored margin. Size: 95x105mm. Sheet exists imperf.

Virgin and Child, by Bernaert van Orley
A70

Paintings of the Virgin and Child: 10fr, by Hans Memling. 15fr, by Botticelli.

1974, Nov. 7 Photo. *Perf. 13*

474 A70 5fr gold & multi 15
475 A70 10fr gold & multi 30
476 A70 15fr gold & multi 45
 a. Souvenir sheet of 3 1.00 1.00
 Nos. 474-476, C213-C215 (6) 3.45 2.50

Christmas 1974. Sheets of 20 stamps and one label. No. 476a contains one each of Nos. 474–476, gold and multicolored margin. Size: 137x90mm. Sheet exists imperf.

Apollo-Soyuz Space Mission and Emblem—A71

1975, July 10 Photo. *Perf. 13*

Multicolored

477 A71 26fr Block of 4 1.60
 a. *A.A. Leonov, V.N. Kubasov, Soviet flag* 40
 b. *Soyuz and Soviet flag* 40
 c. *Apollo and American flag* 40
 d. *D.K. Slayton, V.D. Brand, T.P. Stafford, American flag* 40
478 A71 31fr Block of 4 2.20
 a. *Apollo-Soyuz link-up* 55
 b. *Apollo, blast-off* 55
 c. *Soyuz, blast-off* 55
 d. *Kubasov, Leonov, Slayton, Brand, Stafford* 55
 Nos.477-478, C216-C217 (4 blocks of 4) 8.20 2.00

Apollo Soyuz space test project (Russo-American cooperation), launching July 15; link-up, July 17. Nos. 477–478 are printed in sheets of 32 containing 8 blocks of 4.

Addax
A72

1975, July 31 Photo. *Perf. 13½*

Multicolored

479 A72 1fr Strip of four 20
 a. *shown* 5
 b. *Roan antelope* 5
 c. *Nyala* 5
 d. *White rhinoceros* 5
480 A72 2fr Strip of four 24
 a. *Mandrill* 6
 b. *Eland* 6
 c. *Salt's dik-dik* 6
 d. *Thomson's gazelles* 6
481 A72 3fr Strip of four 36
 a. *African small-clawed otter* 9
 b. *Reed buck* 9
 c. *Indian civet* 9
 d. *Cape buffalo* 9
482 A72 5fr Strip of four 60
 a. *White-tailed gnu* 15
 b. *African wild asses* 15
 c. *Black-and-white colobus monkey* 15
 d. *Gerenuk* 15
483 A72 6fr Strip of four 72
 a. *Dama gazelle* 18
 b. *Black-backed jackal* 18
 c. *Sitatungas* 18
 d. *Zebra antelope* 18
484 A72 11fr Strip of four 1.32
 a. *Fennec* 33
 b. *Lesser kudus* 33
 c. *Blesbok* 33
 d. *Serval* 33
 Nos. 479-484, C218-C223 (12 strips of 4) 24.44 2.25

Jonah, by Michelangelo
A73

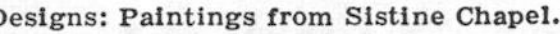
Designs: Paintings from Sistine Chapel.

1975, Dec. 3 Photo. *Perf. 13*

Multicolored

485 A73 5fr *shown* 15
486 A73 5fr *Libyan Sybil* 15
487 A73 13fr *Prophet Isaiah* 40
488 A73 13fr *Delphic Sybil* 40
489 A73 27fr *Daniel* 80
490 A73 27fr *Cumaean Sybil* 80
 a. Souvenir sheet of 6 3.00 3.00
 Nos. 485-490, C228-C233 (12) 8.04 1.25

Michelangelo Buonarotti (1475–1564), Italian sculptor, painter and architect. Stamps of same denominations printed se-tenant in sheets of 18 stamps and 2 labels. No. 490a contains one each of Nos. 485–490; brown & gold margin, black inscription. Size: 137x111mm.

Speed Skating
A74

Basketball
A75

Designs (Innsbruck Games Emblem and): 24fr, Figure skating, women's. 26fr, Two-man bobsled. 31fr, Cross-country skiing.

1976, Jan. 23 Photo. *Perf. 14x13½*

491 A74 17fr dp bl & multi 50
492 A74 24fr multi 72
493 A74 26fr multi 76
494 A74 31fr plum & multi 93
 a. Souvenir sheet of 3 3.25 3.25
 Nos. 491-494, C234-C236 (7) 6.03 75

12th Winter Olympic Games, Innsbruck, Austria, Feb. 4–15.

No. 494a contains 3 stamps similar to Nos. C234–C236, perf. 13½, without "POSTE AERIENNE." Multicolored margin with snowflakes and Games' emblem. Size: 130x62½mm.

1976, May 3 Litho. *Perf. 13½*

Designs (Montreal Games Emblem and): Nos. 496, 499, 503b, Pole vault. Nos. 497, 500, 503d, Running. Nos. 498, 501, 503a, Soccer. No. 502, 503c, Basketball.

495 A75 14fr bl & multi 42
496 A75 14fr ol & multi 42
497 A75 17fr mag & multi 50
498 A75 17fr ver & multi 50
499 A75 28fr ol & multi 80
500 A75 28fr mag & multi 80
501 A75 40fr ver & multi 1.20
502 A75 40fr bl & multi 1.20
 Nos. 495-502, C237-C242 (14) 12.26 1.75

Souvenir Sheet

503 A75 Sheet of 4 3.20 60
 a. 14fr red & multi 42
 b. 17fr ol & multi 50
 c. 28fr bl & multi 80
 d. 40fr mag & multi 1.20

21st Olympic Games, Montreal, Canada, July 17–Aug. 1. Stamps of same denomination printed se-tenant in sheets of 20.

No. 503 has gold inscription, black Montreal Olympic emblem and multicolored band in margin. Size: 115x120mm.

Virgin and Child, by Dirk Bouts
A76

Virgin and Child by: 13fr, Giovanni Bellini. 27fr, Carlo Crivelli.

1976, Oct. 18 Photo. *Perf. 13½*

504 A76 5fr gold & multi 15
505 A76 13fr gold & multi 40
506 A76 27fr gold & multi 80
a. Souvenir sheet of 3 1.50
Nos. 504-506, C250-C252 (6) 4.03 80

Christmas 1976. Sheets of 20 stamps and descriptive label. No. 506a contains one each of Nos. 504–506; multicolored margin. Size: 123x80mm.

St. Veronica, by Rubens
A77

Paintings by Rubens: 21fr, Christ on the Cross. 27fr, Descent from the Cross. 35fr, The Deposition.

1977, Apr. 5 Photo. *Perf. 13*

507 A77 10fr gold & multi 30
508 A77 21fr gold & multi 62
509 A77 27fr gold & multi 80
510 A77 35fr gold & multi 1.05
a. Souvenir sheet of 4 3.00

Easter 1977. Sheets of 30 stamps and descriptive label. No. 510a contains 4 stamps similar to Nos. 507–510 inscribed "POSTE AERIENNE." Multicolored margin. Size: 111x85mm.

Alexander Graham Bell
A78

Intelsat Satellite, Modern and Old Telephones
A79

Designs: No. 513, Switchboard operator, c. 1910, and wall telephone. No. 514, Intelsat and radar. No. 515, A.G. Bell and first telephone. No. 516, Satellites around globe and videophone.

1977, May 17 Photo. *Perf. 13*

511 A78 10fr multi 16
512 A79 10fr multi 16
513 A78 17fr multi 28
514 A79 17fr multi 28
515 A78 26fr multi 45
516 A79 26fr multi 45
Nos. 511-516, C253-C256 (10) 3.44

Centenary of first telephone call by Alexander Graham Bell, Mar. 10, 1876. Stamps of same denomination printed se-tenant in sheets of 32.

Buffon's Kob
A80

1977, Aug. 22 Photo. *Perf. 14x14½*

Multicolored

517 A80 2fr Strip of four 24
a. *shown* 6
b. *Marabous* 6
c. *Brindled gnu* 6
d. *River hog* 6
518 A80 5fr Strip of four 60
a. *Zebras* 15
b. *Shoebill* 15
c. *Striped hyenas* 15
d. *Chimpanzee* 15
519 A80 8fr Strip of four 96
a. *Flamingos* 24
b. *Nile crocodiles* 24
c. *Green mamba* 24
d. *Greater kudus* 24
520 A80 11fr Strip of four 1.36
a. *Hyrax* 34
b. *Cobra* 34
c. *Jackals* 34
d. *Verreaux's eagles* 34
521 A80 21fr Strip of four 2.56
a. *Honey badger* 64
b. *Harnessed antelopes* 64
c. *Secretary bird* 64
d. *Klipspringer* 64
522 A80 27fr Strip of four 2.80
a. *African big-eared fox* 70
b. *Elephants* 70
c. *Vulturine guineafowl* 70
d. *Impalas* 70
Nos. 517-522, C258-C263 (12 strips of 4) 37.52

The Goose Girl, by Grimm
A81

Fairy Tales: 5fr, by Grimm Brothers. 11fr, by Aesop. 14fr, by Hans Christian Andersen. 17fr, by Jean de La Fontaine. 26fr, English fairy tales.

1977, Sept. 14 *Perf. 14*

Multicolored

523 A81 5fr Block of four 75
a. *shown* 18
b. *The Two Wanderers* 18
c. *The Man of Iron* 18
d. *Snow White and Rose Red* 18
524 A81 11fr Block of four 1.65
a. *The Quarreling Cats* 40
b. *The Blind and the Lame* 40
c. *The Hermit and the Bear* 40
d. *The Fox and the Stork* 40
525 A81 14fr Block of four 2.00
a. *The Princess and the Pea* 50
b. *The Old Tree Mother* 50
c. *The Ice Maiden* 50
d. *The Old House* 50
526 A81 17fr Block of four 2.50
a. *The Oyster and the Suitors* 60
b. *The Wolf and the Lamb* 60
c. *Hen with the Golden Egg* 60
d. *The Wolf as Shepherd* 60
527 A81 26fr Block of four 4.00
a. *Three Heads in the Well* 1.00
b. *Mother Goose* 1.00
c. *Jack and the Beanstalk* 1.00
d. *Alice in Wonderland* 1.00
Nos. 523-527 (5 blocks of four) 10.90

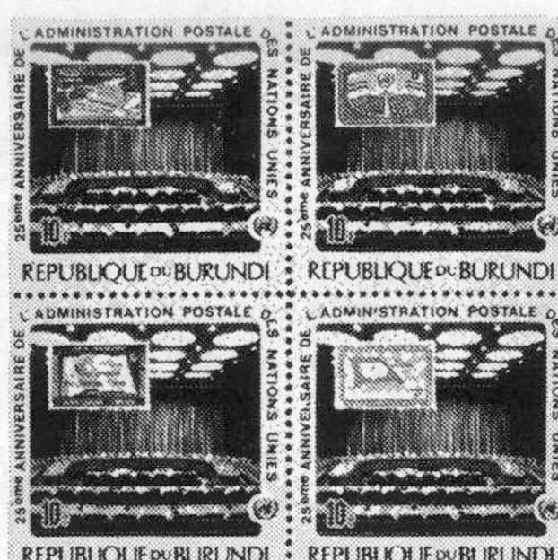

Security Council Chamber, UN Nos. 28, 46, 37, C7—A82

Designs (UN Stamps and): 8fr, UN General Assembly, interior. 21fr, UN Meeting Hall.

1977, Oct. 10 Photo. *Perf. 13½*

528 A82 8fr Block of four 96
a. No. 25 24
b. No. C5 24
c. No. 23 24
d. No. 2 24
529 A82 10fr Block of four 1.20
a. No. 28 30
b. No. 46 30
c. No. 37 30
d. No. C7 30
530 A82 21fr Block of four 2.48
a. No. 45 62
b. No. 42 62
c. No. 17 62
d. No. 13 62
e. Souvenir sheet of 3 1.30
Nos. 528-530, C264-C266 (6 blocks of 4) 14.92

25th anniversary (in 1976) of the United Nations Postal Administration. No. 530e contains 8fr in design of No. 529d, 10fr in design of No. 530b, 21fr in design of No. 528c; silver margin. Size: 128x76mm.

Virgin and Child
A83

Designs: Paintings of the Virgin and Child.

1977, Oct. 31 Photo. *Perf. 14x13*

531 A83 5fr By Meliore Toscano 15
532 A83 13fr By J. Lombardos 40
1610-1680 80
a. Souvenir sheet of 3 1.50
Nos. 531-533, C267-C269 (6) 4.05

Christmas 1977. Sheets of 24 stamps with descriptive label. No. 533a contains one each of Nos. 531–533; gold and multicolored margin. Size: 130x72mm.

Cruiser Aurora, Russia Nos. 211, 303, 1252, 187—A84

Designs (Russian Stamps and): 8fr, Kremlin, Moscow. 11fr, Pokrovski Cathedral, Moscow. 13fr, Labor Day parade, 1977 and 1980 Olympic Games emblem.

1977, Nov. 14 Photo. *Perf. 13*

534 A84 5fr Block of four 60
a. No. 211 15
b. No. 303 15
c. No. 1252 15
d. No. 187 15
535 A84 8fr Block of four 96
a. No. 856 24
b. No. 1986 24
c. No. 908 24
d. No. 2551 24
536 A84 11fr Block of four 1.36
a. No. 3844b 34
b. No. 3452 34
c. No. 3382 34
d. No. 3837 34
537 A84 13fr Block of four 1.60
a. No. 4446 40
b. No. 3497 40
c. No. 2926 40
d. No. 2365 40
Nos. 534-537 (4 blocks of 4) 4.52

60th anniversary of Russian October Revolution.

Ship at Dock, Arms and Flag—A85

Burundi Arms and Flag and: 5fr, Men at lathes. 11fr, Male leopard dance. 14fr, Coffee harvest. 17fr, Government Palace.

1977, Nov. 25 Photo. *Perf. 13½*

538 A85 1fr sil & multi 5
539 A85 5fr sil & multi 15
540 A85 11fr sil & multi 35
541 A85 14fr sil & multi 42
542 A85 17fr sil & multi 50
Nos. 538-542 (5) 1.47

15th anniversary of independence.

Virgin and Child, by Rubens
A86

Paintings of the Virgin and Child by: 13fr, Rubens. 17fr, Solario. 27fr, Tiepolo. 31fr, Gerard David. 40fr, Bellini.

1979, Feb. Photo. *Perf. 14x13*

543	A86	13fr multi	40
544	A86	17fr multi	50
545	A86	27fr multi	80
546	A86	31fr multi	95
547	A86	40fr multi	1.20
		Nos. 543-547 (5)	3.85

Christmas 1978. See No. C270.

Abyssinian Hornbill—A87

1979 Photo. *Perf. 13½×13*

Multicolored

548	A87	1fr *shown*	5
549	A87	2fr *Snakebird*	6
550	A87	3fr *Melittophagus pusillus*	10
551	A87	5fr *Flamingo*	15
552	A87	8fr *Afropavo congenis*	25
553	A87	10fr *Gallinule*	30
554	A87	20fr *Martial eagle*	60
555	A87	27fr *Ibis*	80
556	A87	50fr *Saddle-billed stork*	1.50
		Nos. 548-556 (9)	3.81

See Nos. C273-C281.

Mother and Infant, IYC Emblem—A88

IYC Emblem and: 20fr, Infant. 27fr, Girl with doll. 50fr, Children in Children's Village.

1979, July 19 Photo. *Perf. 14*

557	A88	10fr multi	50
558	A88	20fr multi	80
559	A88	27fr multi	1.00
560	A88	50fr multi	1.65

International Year of the Child. See No. B82.

Rowland Hill, Penny Black—A90

Stamps of Burundi: 27fr, German East Africa Nos. 17, N17. 31fr, Nos. 4, 24. 40fr, Nos. 29, 294. 60fr, Heinrich von Stephan, Nos. 464-465.

1979, Nov. 6

565	A90	20fr multi	60
566	A90	27fr multi	80
567	A90	31fr multi	95
568	A90	40fr multi	1.20
569	A90	60fr multi	1.80
		Nos. 565-569 (5)	5.35

Sir Rowland Hill (1795-1879), originator of penny postage. See No. C272.

A91

1980, Oct. 24 Photo. *Perf. 13x13½*

570	A91	20fr 110-meter hurdles	75
571	A91	20fr Hurdles, Thomas Munkelt	75
572	A91	20fr Hurdles, R.D.A.	75
573	A91	30fr Discus	1.10
574	A91	30fr Discus, V. Rasshchupkin	1.10
575	A91	30fr Discus, U.R.S.S.	1.10
576	A91	40fr Soccer, Tchecoslovaquie	1.50
577	A91	40fr "Football"	1.50
578	A91	40fr shown	1.50
		Nos. 570-578 (9)	10.05

22nd Summer Olympic Games, Moscow, July 19-Aug. 3. Stamps of same denomination se-tenant.

UPRONA Party National Congress, 1979—A93

Johannes Kepler, Dish Antenna—A94

1981, Feb. 12 *Perf. 14*

586	A94	10fr shown	30
587	A94	40fr Satellite	1.20
588	A94	45fr Satellite, diff.	1.35
a.		Souvenir sheet of 3	3.00

350th death anniversary of Johannes Kepler and first earth satellite station in Burundi. No. 588a contains Nos. 586-588; gold and red margin shows trajectory. Size: 78x109mm.

Lion—A95

1983, Apr. 22 Photo. *Perf. 13*

589	A95	2fr shown	6
590	A95	3fr Giraffes	10
591	A95	5fr Rhinoceros	15
592	A95	10fr Water buffalo	30
593	A95	20fr Elephant	60
594	A95	25fr Hippopotamus	75
595	A95	30fr Zebra	90
596	A95	50fr Warthog	1.50
597	A95	60fr Oryx	1.80
598	A95	65fr Wild dog	2.00
599	A95	70fr Leopard	2.10
600	A95	75fr Wildebeest	2.25
601	A95	85fr Hyena	2.50
		Nos. 589-601 (13)	15.01

Nos. 589-601 Overprinted in Silver with World Wildlife Fund Emblem.

1983 Photo. *Perf. 13*

589a	A95	2fr multi	6
590a	A95	3fr multi	10
591a	A95	5fr multi	15
592a	A95	10fr multi	30
593a	A95	20fr multi	60
594a	A95	25fr multi	75
595a	A95	30fr multi	90
596a	A95	50fr multi	1.50
597a	A95	60fr multi	1.80
598a	A95	65fr multi	2.00
599a	A95	70fr multi	2.10
600a	A95	75fr multi	2.25
601a	A95	85fr multi	2.50
		Nos. 589a-601a (13)	15.01

20th Anniv. of Independence, July 1, 1982—A96

Flags, various arms, map or portrait.

1983 *Perf. 14*

602	A96	10fr multi	30
603	A96	25fr multi	75
604	A96	30fr multi	90
605	A96	50fr multi	1.50
606	A96	65fr multi	2.00
		Nos. 602-606 (5)	5.45

Christmas 1983—A97

Virgin and Child paintings: 10fr, by Luca Signorelli (1450-1523). 25fr, by Esteban Murillo (1617-1682). 30fr, by Carlo Crivelli (1430-1495). 50fr, by Nicolas Poussin (1594-1665).

1983, Oct. 3 Litho. *Perf. 14½x13½*

607	A97	10fr multi	30
608	A97	25fr multi	75
609	A97	30fr multi	90
610	A97	50fr multi	1.50
		Nos. 607-610, B91-B94 (8)	7.00

See Nos. C285, CB50.

Butterflies—A98

1984, June 29 Photo. *Perf. 13*

611	A98	5fr Cymothoe coccinata	15
612	A98	5fr Papilio zalmoxis	15
613	A98	10fr Asterope pechueli	30
614	A98	10fr Papilio antimachus	30
615	A98	30fr Papilio hesperus	90
616	A98	30fr Bebearia mardania	90
617	A98	35fr Euphaedra neophron	1.00
618	A98	35fr Euphaedra perseis	1.00
619	A98	65fr Euphaedra imperialis	2.00
620	A98	65fr Pseudocraea striata	2.00
		Nos. 611-620 (10)	8.70

Stamps of the same denomination printed horizontally se-tenant.

19th UPU Congress, Hamburg—A99

UPU emblem and: 10fr, German East Africa, Nos. 17, N17. 30fr, Nos. 4, 24. 35fr, Nos. 294, 595. 65fr, Dr. Heinrich von Stephan, Nos. 464-465.

1984, July 14 Litho. *Perf. 13x13½*

621	A99	10fr multi	30
622	A99	30fr multi	90
623	A99	35fr multi	1.00
624	A99	65fr multi	2.00

See No. C286.

1984 Summer Olympics—A100

Virgin and Child, by del Garbo—A89

Virgin and Child by: 27fr, Giovanni Penni. 31fr, G. Romano. 50fr, Jacopo Bassano.

1979, Oct. 12

561	A89	20fr multi	60
562	A89	27fr multi	80
563	A89	31fr multi	95
564	A89	50fr multi	1.50
		Nos. 561-564, B83-B86 (8)	7.85

Christmas 1979. See Nos. C271, CB48.

Virgin and Child, by Mainardi—A92

Christmas 1980 (Paintings): 30fr, Holy Family, by Michelangelo. 40fr, Virgin and Child, by di Cosimo. 45fr, Holy Family, by Fra Bartolomeo.

1980, Dec. 12 Photo. *Perf. 13½x13*

579	A92	10fr multi	30
580	A92	30fr multi	90
581	A92	40fr multi	1.20
582	A92	45fr multi	1.35
		Nos. 579-582, B87-B90 (8)	7.85

1980, Dec. 29 *Perf. 14x13½*

583	A93	10fr multi	30
584	A93	40fr multi	1.20
585	A93	45fr multi	1.35

Gold medalists: 10fr, Jesse Owens (USA), track and field, Berlin, 1936. 30fr, Rafer Johnson (USA), decathlon, 1960. 35fr, Bob Beamon (USA), long jump, 1968. 65fr, Kipchoge Keino (Kenya), 3000-meter steeplechase, 1972.

1984, Aug. 6 ***Perf. 13½x13***

625	A100	10fr multi	30
626	A100	30fr multi	90
627	A100	35fr multi	1.00
628	A100	65fr multi	2.00

See No. C287.

Christmas 1984—A101

Paintings: 10fr, Rest During the Flight into Egypt, by Murillo (1617-1682). 25fr, Virgin and Child, by R. del Garbo. 30fr, Virgin and Child, by Botticelli (1445-1510). 50fr, The Adoration of the Shepherds, by Giacomo da Bassano (1517-1592).

1984, Dec. 15 ***Perf. 13½***

629	A101	10fr multi	30
630	A101	25fr multi	75
631	A101	30fr multi	90
632	A101	50fr multi	1.50
		Nos. 629-632, B95-B98 (8)	7.00

See Nos. C288, CB51.

Flowers—A102

1986, July 31 **Photo.** ***Perf. 13x13½***

633	A102	2fr Thunbergia	5
634	A102	3fr Saintpaulia	5
635	A102	5fr Clivia	8
636	A102	10fr Cassia	16
637	A102	20fr Strelitzia	32
638	A102	35fr Gloriosa	55
		Nos. 633-638, C289-C294 (12)	10.21

SEMI-POSTAL STAMPS

Prince Louis Rwagasore
SP1

Prince and Stadium—SP2

Design: 1.50fr+75c, 6.50fr+3fr, Prince and memorial monument.

Perf. 14x13, 13x14

1963, Feb. 15 Photo. Unwmkd.

B1	SP1	50c +25c brt vio	5	5
B2	SP2	1fr +50c red org & dk bl	6	6
B3	SP2	1.50fr +75c lem & dk vio	10	8
B4	SP1	3.50fr +1.50fr lil rose	15	12
B5	SP2	5fr +2fr rose pink & dk bl	25	15
B6	SP2	6.50fr +3fr gray ol & dk vio	30	20
		Nos. B1-B6 (6)	91	66

Issued in memory of Prince Louis Rwagasore (1932–61), son of King Mwami Mwambutsa IV and Prime Minister. The surtax was for the stadium and monument in his honor.

Red Cross Type of Regular Issue
Souvenir Sheet

1963, Sept. 26 Litho. *Imperf.*

B7	A5	Sheet of four	4.00	4.00
a.		4fr+2fr fawn, red & blk	65	65
b.		8fr+2fr grn, red & blk	75	75
c.		10fr+2fr gray, red & blk	85	85
d.		20fr+2fr ultra, red & blk	1.25	1.25

Issued to commemorate the centenary of the International Red Cross. The surtax was for Red Cross work in Burundi. Pale yellow margin with black and red inscription. Size: 90x140mm.

Olympic Type of Regular Issue
Souvenir Sheet

Designs: 18fr+2fr, Hurdling (horiz.). 20fr+5fr, Vaulting (horiz.).

1964, Nov. 18 *Perf. 13½*

B8	A13	Sheet of two	5.00	4.50
a.		18fr+2fr yel grn & multi	2.00	1.75
b.		20fr+5fr brt pink & multi	2.00	1.75

Issued to commemorate the 18th Olympic Games, Tokyo, Oct. 10–25, 1964. No. B8 has ornamental red brown border and black and blue marginal inscriptions. Size: 115x71mm.

Scientist with Microscope and Map of Burundi—SP3

Lithographed and Photogravure

1965, Jan. 28 *Perf. 14½* Unwmkd.

B9	SP3	2fr +50c tan, red & dk brn	12	8
B10	SP3	4fr +1.50fr pink, red & grn	28	12
B11	SP3	5fr +2.50fr ocher, red & vio	40	16
B12	SP3	8fr +3fr gray, red & dk bl	50	25
B13	SP3	10fr +5fr grnsh gray, red & red brn	75	32
		Nos. B9-B13 (5)	2.05	93

Souvenir Sheet

Perf. 13x13½

B14	SP3	10fr +10fr pale ol, red & dk brn	1.75	1.75

Issued for the fight against tuberculosis. No. B14 contains one stamp. Tan, red & dark brown margin. Size: 100x71mm.

Coat of Arms, 10fr Coin, Reverse
SP4

Designs (Coins of Various Denominations): 4fr+50c, 8fr+50c, 15fr+50c, 40fr+50c, King Mwambutsa IV, obverse.

Litho.; Embossed on Gilt Foil

1965, Aug. 9 *Imperf.*

Diameter: 39mm.

B15	SP4	2fr +50c crim & org	10	10
B16	SP4	4fr +50c ultra & ver	15	15

Diameter: 45mm.

B17	SP4	6fr +50c org & gray	20	20
B18	SP4	8fr +50c bl & mag	30	30

Diameter: 56mm.

B19	SP4	12fr +50c lt grn & red lil	50	50
B20	SP4	15fr +50c yel grn & lt lil	60	60

Diameter: 67mm.

B21	SP4	25fr +50c vio bl & buff	1.00	1.00
B22	SP4	40fr +50c brt pink & red brn	1.50	1.50
		Nos. B15-B22 (8)	4.35	4.35

Stamps are backed with patterned paper in blue, orange and pink engine-turned design.

Prince Louis Rwagasore and Pres. John F. Kennedy
SP5

Designs: 4fr+1fr, 20fr+5fr, Prince Louis and memorial. 20fr+2fr, 40fr+5fr, Pres. John F. Kennedy and library shelves. 40fr+2fr, King Mwambutsa IV at Kennedy grave, Arlington (vert.).

1966, Jan. 21 Photo. *Perf 13½*

B23	SP5	4fr +1fr gray bl & dk brn	20	5
B24	SP5	10fr +1fr pale grn, ind & brn	35	10
B25	SP5	20fr +2fr lil & dp grn	75	15
B26	SP5	40fr +2fr gray grn & dk brn	1.25	20

Souvenir Sheet

B27	SP5	Sheet of two	4.00	3.00
a.		20fr+5fr gray bl & dk brn	1.50	1.20
b.		40fr+5fr lil & dp grn	2.00	1.50

Issued in memory of Prince Louis Rwagasore and President John F. Kennedy. No. B27 has brown margin with picture of King Mwambutsa IV and inscription. Size: 75x90mm.

Republic

Winston Churchill and St. Paul's, London
SP6

Designs: 15fr+2fr, Tower of London and Churchill. 20fr+3fr, Big Ben and Churchill.

1967, March 23 Photo. *Perf.13½*

B28	SP6	4fr +1fr multi	20	6
B29	SP6	15fr +2fr multi	70	20
B30	SP6	20fr +3fr multi	90	35

Issued in memory of Sir Winston Churchill (1874–1965), statesman and World War II leader.

A souvenir sheet contains one airmail stamp, 50fr+5fr, with Churchill portrait centered, marginal decorations and inscriptions. Size: 80x80mm. Exists perf. and imperf. Price, each sheet, $3.50.

Nos. B28–B30 Overprinted

1967, July 14 Photo. *Perf. 13½*

B31	SP6	4fr +1fr multi	30	12
B32	SP6	15fr +2fr multi	85	40
B33	SP6	20fr +3fr multi	1.25	60

50th anniversary of Lions International. Exist with dates transposed.

The souvenir sheets described below No. B30 also received this Lions overprint. Price, each $3.50.

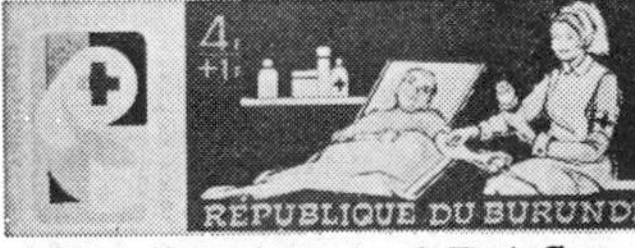

Blood Transfusion and Red Cross
SP7

Designs: 7fr+1fr, Stretcher bearers and wounded man. 11fr+1fr, Surgical team. 17fr+1fr, Nurses tending blood bank.

1969, June 26 Photo. *Perf. 13½*

B34	SP7	4fr +1fr multi	20	5
B35	SP7	7fr +1fr multi	30	8
B36	SP7	11fr +1fr multi	60	8
B37	SP7	17fr +1fr multi	65	15
		Nos. B34-B37, CB9-CB11 (7)	4.95	1.24

Issued to commemorate the 50th anniversary of the League of Red Cross Societies.

Pope Paul VI and Map of Africa—SP8

Designs: 3fr+2fr, 17fr+2fr, Pope Paul VI (vert.). 10fr+2fr, Flag made of flags of African Nations. 14fr+2fr, View of St. Peter's, Rome. 40fr+2fr, 40fr+5fr, Martyrs of Uganda. 50fr+2fr, 50fr+5fr, Pope on Throne. All designs include portrait of Pope Paul VI.

1969, Sept. 12 Photo. *Perf. 13½*

B38	SP8	3fr +2fr multi	15	5
B39	SP8	5fr +2fr multi	30	5
B40	SP8	10fr +2fr multi	45	10
B41	SP8	14fr +2fr multi	65	12
B42	SP8	17fr +2fr multi	75	15
B43	SP8	40fr +2fr multi	1.50	35
B44	SP8	50fr +2fr multi	1.75	40
		Nos. B38-B44 (7)	5.55	1.22

Souvenir Sheet

B45	SP8	Sheet of 2	4.00	3.50
a.		40fr+5fr multi	1.75	1.50
b.		50fr+5fr multi	2.00	1.75

Issued to commemorate the visit of Pope Paul VI to Uganda, July 31–Aug. 2. No. B45 contains 2 stamps, yellow margin with black inscription and church window design. Size: 80x102mm.

Virgin and Child, by Albrecht Dürer
SP9

Paintings: 11fr+1fr, Madonna of the Eucharist, by Sandro Botticelli. 20fr+1fr, Holy Family, by El Greco.

1970, Dec. 14 Photo. *Perf. 13½*

Gold Frame

B46	SP9	6.50fr +1fr multi	30	10
B47	SP9	11fr +1fr multi	45	15
B48	SP9	20fr +1fr multi	85	28
a.		Souvenir sheet of 3	1.75	1.75
		Nos. B46-B48, CB12-CB14 (6)	4.30	1.42

Christmas 1970. No. B48a contains one each of Nos. B46–B48 with ornamental border and inscription. Size: 135x75mm.

Nos. 376–378 Surcharged in Gold and Black

1971, Nov. 27

B49	A51	3fr +1fr multi	22	10
B50	A51	5fr +1fr multi	30	15
B51	A51	6fr +1fr multi	38	18
a.		Souvenir sheet of 3	1.10	1.10
		Nos. B49-B51, CB19-CB21 (6)	3.00	1.11

25th anniversary of the United Nations International Children's Fund (UNICEF). No. B51a contains 3 stamps similar to Nos. B49–B51 with 2fr surtax each. Size: 125 x81mm.

"La Polenta," by Pietro Longhi
SP10

Designs: 3fr+1fr, Archangel Michael, Byzantine icon from St. Mark's 6fr+1fr, "Gossip," by Pietro Longhi. 11fr+1fr, "Diana's Bath," by Giovanni Batista Pittoni. All stamps inscribed UNESCO.

1971, Dec. 27

B52	SP10	3fr +1fr gold & multi	15	6
B53	SP10	5fr +1fr gold & multi	24	10
B54	SP10	6fr +1fr gold & multi	28	12
B55	SP10	11fr +1fr gold & multi	48	20
a.		Souvenir sheet of 4	1.20	1.00
		Nos. B52-B55, CB22-CB25 (8)	3.68	1.48

The surtax was for the UNESCO campaign to save the treasures of Venice. No. B55a contains 4 stamps similar to Nos. B52–B55, but with 2fr surtax instead 1f. Gold and black ornamental margin. Size: 113x131½mm. Sheet exists imperf.

Nos. 408–410 Surcharged "+1F" in Silver

1972, Dec. 12 Photo. *Perf. 13½*

B56	A57	5fr +1fr multi	20	7
B57	A57	10fr +1fr multi	40	13
B58	A57	15fr +1fr multi	60	20
a.		Souvenir sheet of 3	1.40	1.40
		Nos. B56-B58, CB26-CB28 (6)	3.65	1.17

Christmas 1972. No. B58a contains 3 stamps similar to Nos. B56–B58, but with 2fr surtax. Deep carmine and gold border. Size: 128x81mm.

Nos. 441–443 Surcharged "+1F" in Silver

1973, Dec. 14 Photo. *Perf. 13*

B59	A64	5fr +1fr multi	20	6
B60	A64	10fr +1fr multi	40	12
B61	A64	15fr +1fr multi	60	18
a.		Souvenir sheet of 3	1.25	1.25
		Nos. B59-B61, CB29-CB31 (6)	3.80	1.18

Christmas 1973. No. B61a contains 3 stamps similar to Nos. B59–B61 with 2fr surtax each. Size: 143x79mm.

Christmas Type of 1974

1974, Dec. 2 Photogravure *Perf. 13*

B62	A70	5fr +1fr multi	25	15
B63	A70	10fr +1fr multi	40	25
B64	A70	15fr +1fr multi	60	38
a.		Souvenir sheet of 3	1.50	1.50
		Nos. B62-B64, CB32-CB34 (6)	4.30	1.35

No. B64a contains 3 stamps similar to Nos. B62–B64 with 2fr surtax each. Size: 137x90mm.

Nos. 485–490 Surcharged "+1 F" in Silver and Black

1975, Dec. 22 Photo. *Perf. 13*

Multicolored

B65	A73	5fr +1fr #485	20	
B66	A73	5fr +1fr #486	20	
B67	A73	13fr +1fr #487	45	
B68	A73	13fr +1fr #488	45	
B69	A73	27fr +1fr #489	85	
B70	A73	27fr +1fr #490	85	
a.		Souvenir sheet of 6	3.50	3.50
		Nos. B65-B70, CB35-CB40 (12)	8.60	1.75

Michelangelo Buonarroti (1475–1564), 500th birth anniversary. No. B70a contains 6 stamps similar to Nos. B65–B70 with 2fr surcharge each. Size: 132x106 mm.

Nos. 504–506 Surcharged "+1f" in Silver and Black

1976, Nov. 25 Photo. *Perf. 13½*

B71	A76	5fr +1fr multi	18	
B72	A76	13fr +1fr multi	45	
B73	A76	27fr +1fr multi	85	
a.		Souvenir sheet of 3	1.75	1.75
		Nos. B71-B73, CB41-CB43 (6)	4.33	1.50

Christmas 1976. No. B73a contains 3 stamps similar to Nos. B71–B73 with 2fr surtax each. Size: 123x80mm.

Nos. 531–533 Surcharged "+1fr" in Silver and Black

1977 Photo. *Perf. 14x13*

B74	A83	5fr +1fr multi	18	
B75	A83	13fr +1fr multi	45	
B76	A83	27fr +1fr multi	85	
a.		Souvenir sheet of 3	1.75	1.75
		Nos. B74-B76, CB44-CB46 (6)	4.31	

Christmas 1977. No. B76a contains 3 stamps similar to Nos. B74–B76 with 2fr surtax each. Size: 130x71mm.

Christmas Type of 1979

1979, Feb. Photo. *Perf. 14x13*

B77	A86	13fr +1fr multi	45	
B78	A86	17fr +1fr multi	55	
B79	A86	27fr +1fr multi	85	
B80	A86	31fr +1fr multi	1.00	
B81	A86	40fr +1fr multi	1.25	
		Nos. B77-B81 (5)	4.10	

Christmas 1978.

IYC Type of 1979

1979, July 19 Photo. *Perf. 14*

B82		Sheet of 4, multi	3.75	3.00
a.		A88 10fr+2fr *like #557*	35	25
b.		A88 20fr+2fr *like #558*	65	45
c.		A88 27fr+2fr *like #559*	88	60
d.		A88 50fr+2fr *like #560*	1.50	1.00

International Year of the Child. No. B82 has multicolored margin showing detail from Virgin and Child by Rubens, IYC emblem. Size: 131x85mm.

Christmas Type of 1979

1979, Dec. 10 Photo *Perf. 13½*

B83	A89	20fr +1fr *like #561*	65	
B84	A89	27fr +1fr *like #562*	85	
B85	A89	31fr +1fr *like #563*	95	
B86	A89	50fr +2fr *like #564*	1.55	

Christmas Type of 1980

1981, Jan. 16 Photo. *Perf. 13½x13*

B87	A92	10fr +1fr *like #579*	35	
B88	A92	30fr +1fr *like #580*	95	
B89	A92	40fr +1fr *like #581*	1.25	
B90	A92	50fr +1fr *like #582*	1.55	

Christmas 1980.

Christmas Type of 1983

1983, Nov. 2 Litho. *Perf. 14½x13½*

B91	A97	10fr +1fr like #607	32	
B92	A97	25fr +1fr like #608	78	
B93	A97	30fr +1fr like #609	95	
B94	A97	50fr +1fr like #610	1.50	

Christmas Type of 1984

1984, Dec. 15 *Perf. 13½*

B95	A101	10fr +1fr like #629	32	
B96	A101	25fr +1fr like #630	78	
B97	A101	30fr +1fr like #631	95	
B98	A101	50fr +1fr like #632	1.50	

AIR POST STAMPS

Animal Type of Regular Issue.

Animals: 6fr, Zebra. 8fr, Cape buffalo (bubalis). 10fr, Impala (vert.). 14fr, Hippopotamus. 15fr, Defassa waterbuck (vert.). 20fr, Cheetah. 50fr, Elephant.

Lithographed

1964, July 2 *Perf. 14* Unwmkd.

Border in Gold

Size: 42x21mm., 21x42mm.

C1	A9	6fr multi	40	5
C2	A9	8fr multi	50	8
C3	A9	10fr multi	65	10
C4	A9	14fr multi	90	15
C5	A9	15fr multi	1.00	18

Size: 53x32½mm.

C6	A9	20fr multi	1.35	30
C7	A9	50fr multi	3.50	75
		Nos. C1-C7 (7)	8.30	1.61

Bird Type of Regular Issue

Birds: 6fr, Secretary bird. 8fr, African anhinga. 10fr, African peacock. 14fr, Bee eater. 15fr, Yellow-billed stork. 20fr, Saddle-billed stork. 50fr, Abyssinian ground hornbill. 75fr, Martial eagle. 130fr, Lesser flamingo.

1965, June 10 Litho. *Perf. 14*

Birds in Natural Colors, Border in Gold.

Size: 26x43mm.

C8	A14	6fr multi	25	5
C9	A14	8fr multi	30	8
C10	A14	10fr multi	40	10
C11	A14	14fr multi	50	12
C12	A14	15fr multi	60	15

Size: 33x53mm.

C13	A14	20fr multi	70	13
C14	A14	50fr multi	1.75	40
C15	A14	75fr multi	2.50	50
C16	A14	130fr multi	4.50	75
		Nos. C8-C16 (9)	11.50	2.28

Flower Type of Regular Issue

Flowers: 6fr, Dissotis. 8fr, Crossandra. 10fr, Ansellia. 14fr, Thunbergia. 15fr, Schizoglossum. 20fr, Gazania. 50fr, Protea. 75fr, Hibiscus. 130fr, Markhamia.

1966, Oct. 10 *Perf. 13½* Unwmkd.

Gold Background.

Size: 31x31mm.

C17	A17	6fr multi	22	5
C18	A17	8fr multi	30	8
C19	A17	10fr multi	40	10
C20	A17	14fr multi	50	12
C21	A17	15fr multi	50	15

Size: 39x39mm.

C22	A17	20fr multi	50	18
C23	A17	50fr multi	1.25	40
C24	A17	75fr multi	1.85	50
C25	A17	130fr multi	3.35	75
		Nos. C17-C25 (9)	8.87	2.33

Souvenir Sheet

Tapestry Type of Regular Issue

1966, Nov. 4 *Perf. 13½* Unwmkd.

C26	A18	Sheet of 7 (14fr)	3.50	2.00

See note after No. 158.

Republic

Nos. C17–C25, Overprinted

REPUBLIQUE
DU
BURUNDI

1967 Lithographed *Perf. 13½*

Size: 31x31mm.

Gold Background

C27	A17	6fr multi	38	13
C28	A17	8fr multi	45	15
C29	A17	10fr multi	50	17
C30	A17	14fr multi	75	25
C31	A17	15fr multi	75	25

Size: 39x39mm.

C32	A17	20fr multi	1.10	35
C33	A17	50fr multi	3.00	1.00
C34	A17	75fr multi	4.75	1.00
C35	A17	130fr multi	6.50	2.10
		Nos. C27-C35 (9)	18.18	5.40

Nos. C8–C16 Overprinted "REPUBLIQUE / DU / BURUNDI" and Horizontal Bar

1967 Lithographed *Perf. 14*

Birds in Natural Colors, Border in Gold

Size: 26x43mm.

C35A	A14	6fr multi	*30*	
C35B	A14	8fr multi	*35*	
C35C	A14	10fr multi	*40*	
C35D	A14	14fr multi	*60*	
C35E	A14	15fr multi	*75*	

Size: 33x53mm

C35F	A14	20fr multi	*1.20*	
C35G	A14	50fr multi	*3.00*	
C35H	A14	75fr multi	*4.75*	
C35I	A14	130fr multi	*5.50*	
		Nos. C35A-C35I (9)	*16.85*	

African Art Type of Regular Issue

African Art: 10fr, Spirit of Bakutu figurine, Equatorial Africa. 14fr, Pearl throne of Sultan of the Bamum, Cameroun. 17fr, Bronze head of Mother Queen of Benin, Nigeria. 24fr, Statue of 109th Bakouba king, Kata-Mbula, Central Congo. 26fr, Baskets and lances, Burundi.

1967, June 5 Photo. *Perf. 13½*

C36	A20	10fr gold & multi	30	20
C37	A20	14fr gold & multi	40	20
C38	A20	17fr gold & multi	45	20
C39	A20	24fr gold & multi	65	40
C40	A20	26fr gold & multi	1.20	75
		Nos. C36-C40 (5)	3.00	1.75

Boy Scout Type of Regular Issue

Designs: 10fr, Scouts on hiking trip. 14fr, Cooking at campfire. 17fr, Lord Baden-Powell. 24fr, Boy Scout and Cub Scout giving Scout sign. 26fr, First aid.

1967, Aug. 9 *Perf. 13½*

C41	A21	10fr gold & multi	30	20
C42	A21	14fr gold & multi	45	20
C43	A21	17fr gold & multi	55	20
C44	A21	24fr gold & multi	85	35
C45	A21	26fr gold & multi	1.40	35
		Nos. C41-C45 (5)	3.55	1.30

Issued to commemorate the 60th anniversary of the Boy Scouts and the 12th Boy Scout World Jamboree, Farragut State Park, Idaho, Aug. 1–9.

A souvenir sheet of 2 contains one each of Nos. C44–C45 and 2 labels in the designs of Nos. 208–209 with commemorative inscriptions was issued Jan. 8, 1968. Size: 100x100mm.

Fish Type of Regular Issue

Designs: Various Tropical Fish

1967, Sept. 8 Photo. *Perf. 13½*

Size: 50x23mm.

C46	A19	6fr multi	25	5
C47	A19	8fr multi	35	6
C48	A19	10fr multi	40	8
C49	A19	14fr multi	55	10
C50	A19	15fr multi	55	12

Size: 58x27mm.

C51	A19	20fr multi	75	14
C52	A19	50fr multi	1.75	25
C53	A19	75fr multi	2.75	35
C54	A19	130fr multi	4.50	60
		Nos. C46-C54 (9)	11.85	1.75

Boeing 707 of Air Congo and ITY Emblem

AP1

Designs: 14fr, Boeing 727 of Sabena over lake. 17fr, Vickers VC10 of East African Airways over lake. 26fr, Boeing 727 of Sabena over airport.

1967, Nov. 3 Photo. *Perf. 13*

No.	Type	Description	Unused	Used
C55	AP1	10fr blk, yel brn & sil	25	10
C56	AP1	14fr blk, org & sil	40	15
C57	AP1	17fr blk, brt bl & sil	50	20
C58	AP1	26fr blk, brt rose lil & sil	85	30

Issued to commemorate the opening of the jet airport at Bujumbura and for International Tourist Year, 1967.

Paintings Type of Regular Issue

Paintings: 17fr, Woman with Cat, by Renoir. 24fr, The Jewish Bride, by Rembrandt (horiz.). 26fr, Pope Innocent X, by Velazquez.

1968, Mar. 29 Photo. *Perf. 13½*

Light Green and Gold Frame

No.	Type	Description	Unused	Used
C59	A26	17fr multi	70	30
C60	A26	24fr multi	90	35
C61	A26	26fr multi	1.10	40

Issued in sheets of 6.

Space Type of Regular Issue

Designs: 14fr, Moon Probe. 18fr, Russian astronaut walking in space. 25fr, Weather satellite. 40fr, American astronaut walking in space.

1968, May 15 Photo. *Perf. 13½*

Size: 41x41mm.

No.	Type	Description	Unused	Used
C62	A27	14fr sil & multi	50	10
C63	A27	18fr sil & multi	60	18
C64	A27	25fr sil & multi	90	20
C65	A27	40fr sil & multi	1.40	35

Issued to publicize peaceful space explorations.

Butterfly Type of Regular Issue

Butterflies: 6fr, Teracolus annae. 8fr, Graphium ridleyanus. 10fr, Cymothoe. 14fr, Charaxes eupale. 15fr, Papilio bromius. 20fr, Papilio zenobia. 50fr, Salamis aethiops. 75fr, Danais chrysippus. 130fr, Salamis temora.

1968, Sept. 9 Photo. *Perf. 13½*

Size: 38x42mm.

No.	Type	Description	Unused	Used
C66	A28	6fr gold & multi	25	5
C67	A28	8fr gold & multi	30	5
C68	A28	10fr gold & multi	35	5
C69	A28	14fr gold & multi	50	5
C70	A28	15fr gold & multi	50	8

Size: 44x49mm.

No.	Type	Description	Unused	Used
C71	A28	20fr gold & multi	75	12
C72	A28	50fr gold & multi	1.75	18
C73	A28	75fr gold & multi	3.00	25
C74	A28	130fr gold & multi	5.00	40
		Nos. C66-C74 (9)	12.40	1.23

Painting Type of Regular Issue

Paintings: 17fr, The Letter, by Jean H. Fragonard. 26fr, Young Woman Reading Letter, by Jan Vermeer. 40fr, Lady Folding Letter, by Elisabeth Vigée-Lebrun. 50fr, Mademoiselle Lavergne, by Jean Etienne Liotard.

1968, Sept. 30 Photo. *Perf. 13½*

No.	Type	Description	Unused	Used
C84	A29	17fr multi	45	12
C85	A29	26fr multi	85	20
C86	A29	40fr multi	1.15	28
C87	A29	50fr multi	1.40	35

Issued for International Letter Writing Week, Oct. 7–13.

Olympic Games Type of 1968

Designs: 10fr, Shot put. 17fr, Running. 26fr, Hammer throw. 50fr, Hurdling. 75fr, Broad jump.

1968, Oct. 24

No.	Type	Description	Unused	Used
C88	A30	10fr gold & multi	25	8
C89	A30	17fr gold & multi	45	12
C90	A30	26fr gold & multi	75	20
C91	A30	50fr gold & multi	1.40	40
C92	A30	75fr gold & multi	2.10	60
		Nos. C88-C92 (5)	4.95	1.40

Issued to commemorate the 19th Olympic Games, Mexico City, Oct. 12–27.

Christmas Type of 1968

Paintings: 10fr, Virgin and Child, by Correggio. 14fr, Nativity, by Federigo Baroccio. 17fr, Holy Family, by El Greco. 26fr, Adoration of the Magi, by Maino.

1968, Nov. 26 Photo. *Perf. 13½*

No.	Type	Description	Unused	Used
C93	A31	10fr multi	30	15
C94	A31	14fr multi	45	20
C95	A31	17fr multi	55	25
C96	A31	26fr multi	80	30
a.		Souv. sheet of 4	2.25	

No. C96a contains one each of Nos. C93–C96, decorative border and inscriptions. Size: 120x120mm.

Human Rights Flame, Hand and Globe
AP2

1969, Jan. 22

No.	Type	Description	Unused	Used
C97	AP2	10fr multi	30	10
C98	AP2	14fr multi	42	10
C99	AP2	26fr lil & multi	80	25

International Human Rights Year, 1968.

Nos. C93–C96 Overprinted in Silver

1969, Feb. 17 Photo. *Perf. 13½*

No.	Type	Description	Unused	Used
C100	A31	10fr multi	40	15
C101	A31	14fr multi	55	25
C102	A31	17fr multi	70	28
C103	A31	26fr multi	1.00	45

Issued to commemorate man's first flight around the moon by the U.S. spacecraft Apollo 8, Dec. 21–27, 1968.

Moon Landing Type of 1969

Designs: 26fr, Neil A. Armstrong leaving landing module. 40fr, Astronaut on moon. 50fr, Splashdown in the Pacific.

1969, Nov. 6 Photo. *Perf. 13½*

No.	Type	Description	Unused	Used
C104	A38	26fr gold & multi	1.00	50
C105	A38	40fr gold & multi	1.50	75
C106	A38	50fr gold & multi	1.80	85

See note after Algeria No. 427.

Christmas Type of 1969

Paintings: 17fr, Madonna and Child, by Benvenuto da Garofalo. 26fr, Madonna and Child, by Jacopo Negretti. 50fr, Madonna and Child, by Il Giorgione. All horizontal.

1969, Dec. 2 Photogravure

No.	Type	Description	Unused	Used
C107	A39	17fr gold & multi	75	15
C108	A39	26fr gold & multi	1.00	25
C109	A39	50fr gold & multi	1.80	55
a.		Souvenir sheet of 3	3.00	3.00

No. C109a contains one each of Nos. C107–C109. Gold frame with black and red inscription. Size: 87x110mm.

Insect Type of Regular Issue

Designs: Various Beetles and Weevils.

1970 *Perf. 13½*

Size: 46x32mm.

No.	Type	Description	Unused	Used
C110	A40	6fr gold & multi	20	5
C111	A40	8fr gold & multi	25	5
C112	A40	10fr gold & multi	35	5
C113	A40	14fr gold & multi	50	5
C114	A40	15fr gold & multi	60	5

Size: 52x36mm.

No.	Type	Description	Unused	Used
C115	A40	20fr gold & multi	1.00	6
C116	A40	50fr gold & multi	3.00	50
C117	A40	75fr gold & multi	4.00	50
C118	A40	130fr gold & multi	6.50	80
		Nos. C110-C118 (9)	16.40	2.11

Issue dates: Nos. C110–C115, Jan. 20. Nos. C116–C118, Feb. 27.

Easter Type of 1970

Stations of the Cross, by Juan de Aranoa y Carredano: 8fr, Jesus meets the women of Jerusalem. 10fr, Jesus falls a third time. 14fr, Jesus stripped. 15fr, Jesus nailed to the cross. 18fr, Jesus dies on the cross. 20fr, Descent from the cross. 50fr, Jesus laid in the tomb.

1970, Mar. 16 Photo. *Perf. 13½*

No.	Type	Description	Unused	Used
C119	A41	8fr gold & multi	25	10
C120	A41	10fr gold & multi	30	12
C121	A41	14fr gold & multi	45	18
C122	A41	15fr gold & multi	50	20
C123	A41	18fr gold & multi	55	22
C124	A41	20fr gold & multi	60	25
C125	A41	50fr gold & multi	1.40	60
a.		Souv. sheet of 7 + label	3.50	3.50
		Nos. C119-C125 (7)	4.05	1.67

No. C125a contains one each of Nos. C119–C125 and label showing Ascension. [illegible]

EXPO '70 Type of Regular Issue

Souvenir Sheet

Designs: 40fr, Tower of the Sun (vert.). 50fr, Flags of participating nations (vert.).

1970, May 5 Photo. *Perf. 13½*

No.	Type	Description	Unused	Used
C126	A42	Souv. sheet of 2	2.75	2.75
a.		40fr multi	95	95
b.		50f multi	1.20	1.20

Issued to publicize EXPO '70 International Exhibition, Osaka, Japan, March 15–Sept. 13, 1970. No. C126 has gold and black decorative border. Size: 104½x80mm.

Rhinoceros Type of Regular Issue

Designs, FAUNA: Camel, dromedary, okapi, rhinoceros, addax, Burundi cow (2 stamps of each animal in 2 different poses). MAP OF THE NILE: Delta and pyramids, dhow, cataract, Blue Nile and crowned crane, Victoria Nile and secretary bird, Lake Victoria and source of Nile on Mt. Gikizi.

1970, July 8 Photo. *Perf. 13½*

No.	Type	Description	Unused	Used
C127	A43	14fr multi	56	20
a.		Sheet of 18	10.50	

Issued in sheets of 18 (3x6) stamps of different designs, to publicize the southernmost source of the Nile on Mt. Gikizi in Burundi.

U.N. Emblem and Headquarters, N.Y.
AP3

Designs (U.N. Emblem and): 11fr, Security Council and mural by Per Krohg. 26fr, Pope Paul VI and U Thant. 40fr, Flags in front of U.N. Headquarters, N.Y.

1970, Oct. 23 Photo. *Perf. 13½*

No.	Type	Description	Unused	Used
C128	AP3	7fr gold & multi	20	5
C129	AP3	11fr gold & multi	35	8
C130	AP3	26fr gold & multi	75	15
C131	AP3	40fr gold & multi	1.20	25
a.		Souvenir sheet of 2	2.00	1.75

Issued to commemorate the 25th anniversary of the United Nations. No. C131a contains 2 stamps similar to Nos. C130–C131 but without "Poste Aerienne"; blue margin with gold ornament, black inscription and U.N. emblem. Size: 123x80mm. Exists imperf.

Bird Type of Regular Issue

Birds: 8fr, 14fr, 30fr, vertical; 10fr, 20fr, 50fr, horizontal.

1970 Photogravure *Perf. 13½*

Gold Frame & Multicolored; Birds in Natural Colors

Stamp size: 52x44mm.

No.	Type	Description	Unused	Used
C132	A44	8fr Block of four	2.00	25
a.		*Northern shrike*	50	6
b.		*European starling*	50	6
c.		*Yellow wagtail*	50	6
d.		*Bank swallow*	50	6
C133	A44	10fr Block of four	2.50	35
a.		*Winter wren*	60	8
b.		*Firecrest*	60	8
c.		*Skylark*	60	8
d.		*Crested lark*	60	8
C134	A44	14fr Block of four	3.00	50
a.		*Woodchat shrike*	75	12
b.		*Common rock thrush*	75	12
c.		*Black redstart*	75	12
d.		*Ring ouzel*	75	12
C135	A44	20fr Block of four	5.00	65
a.		*European redstart*	1.25	15
b.		*Hedge sparrow*	1.25	15
c.		*Gray wagtail*	1.25	15
d.		*Meadow pipit*	1.25	15
C136	A44	30fr Block of four	7.00	1.05
a.		*Eurasian hoopoe*	1.75	25
b.		*Pied flycatcher*	1.75	25
c.		*Great reed warbler*	1.75	25
d.		*Eurasian kingfisher*	1.75	25
C137	A44	50fr Block of four	12.00	1.75
a.		*House martin*	3.00	40
b.		*Sedge warbler*	3.00	40
c.		*Fieldfare*	3.00	40
d.		*European Golden oriole*	3.00	40
		Nos. C132-C137 (6 blocks of 4)	31.50	4.55

Nos. C132–C137 are printed in sheets of 16 containing 4 blocks of 4.

Queen Fabiola and King Baudouin of Belgium
AP4

Designs: 20fr, Pres. Michel Micombero and King Baudouin. 40fr, Pres. Micombero and coats of arms of Burundi and Belgium.

1970, Nov. 28 Photo. *Perf. 13½*

No.	Type	Description	Unused	Used
C140	AP4	6fr gold, dp brn & dp plum	30	10
C141	AP4	20fr gold, dp brn & dp plum	90	30
C142	AP4	40fr gold, dp brn & dp plum	1.85	60
a.		Souvenir sheet of 3	3.00	3.00

Issued to commemorate the visit of the King and Queen of Belgium. No. C142a contains 3 stamps similar to Nos. C140–C142, but without "Poste Aerienne." Deep plum and gold margin with commemorative inscription. Size: 143½x108mm.

Easter Type of Regular Issue

Paintings of the Resurrection: 14fr, by Louis Borrassá. 17fr, Piero della Francesca. 26fr, Michel Wohlgemuth.

1971, Apr. 2 Photo. *Perf. 13½*

No.	Type	Description	Unused	Used
C143	A49	14fr gold & multi	50	15
C144	A49	17fr gold & multi	55	18
C145	A49	26fr gold & multi	75	25
a.		Souvenir sheet of 3	1.90	1.50

Easter 1971. No. C145a contains one each of Nos. C143–C145. Red and gold margin. Size: 120x85mm. Sheet exists imperf.

Animal Type of Regular Issue

1971 Photogravure *Perf. 13½*

Multicolored

Size: 44x44mm.

No.	Type	Description	Unused	Used
C146	A48	10fr Strip of four	1.25	25
a.		*Lion*	30	6
b.		*Cape buffalo*	30	6
c.		*Hippopotamus*	30	6
d.		*Giraffe*	30	6
C147	A48	14fr Strip of four	2.25	45
a.		*Hartebeest*	50	10
b.		*Black rhinoceros*	50	10
c.		*Zebra*	50	10
d.		*Leopard*	50	10
C148	A48	17fr Strip of four	2.50	50
a.		*Grant's gazelles*	60	12
b.		*Cheetah*	60	12
c.		*African white-backed vultures*	60	12
d.		*Johnston's okapi*	60	12
C149	A48	24fr Strip of four	3.25	65
a.		*Chimpanzee*	75	15
b.		*Elephant*	75	15
c.		*Spotted Hyenas*	75	15
d.		*Beisa*	75	15

C150 A48 26fr Strip of four 4.00 80
a. Gorilla 90 20
b. Gnu 90 20
c. Warthog 90 20
d. Cape hunting dog 90 20
C151 A48 31fr Strip of four 4.50 90
a. Sable antelope 1.00 22
b. Caracal lynx 1.00 22
c. Ostriches 1.00 22
d. Bongo 1.00 22
Nos. C146-C151 (6 strips of 4) 17.75 3.55

No. C146 Overprinted in Gold and Black

LUTTE CONTRE LE RACISME ET
LA DISCRIMINATION RACIALE

1971, July 20 Photo. *Perf. 13½*

C152 A48 10fr Strip of four 1.20 24
a. Lion 30 5
b. Cape buffalo 30 5
c. Hippopotamus 30 5
d. Giraffe 30 5

International Year Against Racial Discrimination.

Christmas Type of Regular Issue

Paintings of the Madonna and Child by: 14fr, Cima de Conegliano. 17fr, Fra Filippo Lippi. 31fr, Leonardo da Vinci.

1971, Nov. 2 Photo. *Perf. 13½*

C153 A51 14fr red & multi 55 25
C154 A51 17fr red & multi 65 30
C155 A51 31fr red & multi 1.00 40
a. Souvenir sheet of 3 2.25 2.25

Christmas 1971. No. C155a contains one each of Nos. C153-C155. Multicolored margin. Size: 125x81mm. Sheet exists imperf.

Spacecraft Type of Regular Issue
Souvenir Sheet

1972, Jan. 15 Photo. *Perf. 13½*

C156 A52 Sheet of 6, multi 3.00 2.00
a. 6fr Lunar Orbiter 15 8
b. 11fr Vostok 30 15
c. 14fr Luna I 35 18
d. 17fr Apollo 11 astronaut on moon 42 20
e. 26fr Soyuz 11 70 35
f. 40fr Lunar rover (Apollo 15) 95 50

Conquest of space. No. C156 has dark blue and multicolored margin. Size: 134x 135mm.

Sapporo '72 Type of Regular Issue
Souvenir Sheet

Designs (Sapporo '72 Emblem and): 26fr, Snow scooter. 31fr, Downhill skiing. 50fr, Bobsledding.

1972, Feb. 3

C157 A53 Sheet of 3 3.00 2.50
a. 26fr sil & multi 70 50
b. 31fr sil & multi 80 60
c. 50fr sil & multi 1.25 80

11th Winter Olympic Games, Sapporo, Japan, Feb. 3-13. No. C157 contains 3 stamps, arranged vertically. Silver decorative margin with blue and black inscription. Size: 106x125mm.

Olympic Games Type of 1972

1972, July 24 Photo. *Perf. 13½*

Gold and Multicolored

C158 A55 24fr Weight lifting 72 23
C159 A55 26fr Hurdles 78 25
C160 A55 31fr Discus 95 30
C161 A55 40fr Soccer 1.20 40

20th Olympic Games, Munich, Aug. 26-Sept. 11.

Independence Type of 1972

Designs: 15fr, Prince Rwagasore, Pres. Micombero, Burundi flag, drummers. 18fr, Rwagasore, Micombero, flag, map of Africa, globe. 27fr, Micombero, flag, globe.

1972, Aug. 24 Photo. *Perf. 13½*

C162 A56 15fr gold & multi 50 17
C163 A56 18fr gold & multi 60 20
C164 A56 27fr gold & multi 90 30
a. Souvenir sheet of 3 2.25 2.25

10th anniversary of independence.
No. C164a contains one each of Nos. C162-C164. Gold and light blue margin with black inscription. Size: 146x80mm.

Christmas Type of 1972

Paintings of the Madonna and Child by: 18fr, Sebastiano Mainardi. 27fr, Hans Memling. 40fr, Lorenzo Lotto.

1972, Nov. 2 Photo. *Perf. 13½*

C165 A57 18fr dk car & multi 55 17
C166 A57 27fr dk car & multi 80 25
C167 A57 40fr dk car & multi 1.20 35
a. Souvenir sheet of 3 2.75 2.75

Christmas 1972. No. C167a contains one each of Nos. C165-C167, slate green and gold border. Size: 128x81mm.

Orchid Type of Regular Issue

1973, Jan. 18 Photo. *Perf. 13½*

Multicolored

Size: 38x38mm.

C168 A58 13fr Thelymitra pauciflora 42 10
C169 A58 14fr Miltassia 45 12
C170 A58 15fr Miltonia 50 13
C171 A58 18fr Platycoryne crocea 55 15
C172 A58 20fr Cattleya trinaei 60 17
C173 A58 27fr Eulophia cucullata 85 20
C174 A58 36fr Cymbidium hamsey 1.10 27
Nos. C168-C174 (7) 4.47 1.14

African Exploration Type of 1973

Designs: 15fr, Livingstone writing his diary. 18fr, "Dr. Livingstone, I presume." 27fr, Livingstone and Stanley discussing expedition.

1973, Mar. 19 Photo. *Perf. 13½*

C175 A59 15fr gold & multi 45 15
C176 A59 18fr gold & multi 55 18
C177 A59 27fr gold & multi 80 27
a. Souvenir sheet of 3 2.10 2.10

Exploration of Africa by David Livingstone and Henry Morton Stanley. No. C177a contains 3 stamps similar to Nos. C175-C177, but without "Poste Aerienne." Gold and violet decorative margin. Size: 100x140mm.

Easter Type of 1973

Paintings: 15fr, Christ at the Pillar, by Guido Reni. 18fr, Crucifixion, by Mathias Grunewald. 27fr, Descent from the Cross, by Caravaggio.

1973, Apr. 10

C178 A60 15fr gold & multi 55 15
C179 A60 18fr gold & multi 70 18
C180 A60 27fr gold & multi 1.00 27
a. Souvenir sheet of 3 2.10 2.10

Easter 1973. No. C180a contains one each of Nos. C178-C180. Multicolored margin. Size: 121x73mm.

INTERPOL Type of Regular Issue

Designs: 27fr, INTERPOL emblem and flag. 40fr, INTERPOL flag and emblem.

1973, May 19 Photo. *Perf. 13½*

C181 A61 27fr gold & multi 80 32
C182 A61 40fr gold & multi 95 38

50th anniversary of International Criminal Police Organization (INTERPOL).

Copernicus Type of Regular Issue

Designs: 15fr, Copernicus (C183a), Earth, Pluto, and Jupiter. 18fr, Copernicus (No. C184a), Venus, Saturn, Mars. 27fr, Copernicus (No. C185a), Uranus, Neptune, Mercury. 36fr, Earth and various spacecrafts.

1973, July 27 Photo. *Perf. 13½*

Gold and Multicolored

C183 A62 15fr Block of four 4.00 60
a. 15fr in UL 1.00 15
b. 15fr in UR 1.00 15
c. 15fr in LL 1.00 15
d. 15fr in LR 1.00 15
C184 A62 18fr Block of four 4.50 70
a. 18fr in UL 1.10 16
b. 18fr in UR 1.10 16
c. 18fr in LL 1.10 16
d. 18fr in LR 1.10 16
C185 A62 27fr Block of four 6.50 1.00
a. 27fr in UL 1.60 25
b. 27fr in UR 1.60 25
c. 27fr in LL 1.60 25
d. 27fr in LR 1.60 25
C186 A62 36fr Block of four 8.00 1.40
a. 36fr in UL 2.00 35
b. 36fr in UR 2.00 35
c. 36fr in LL 2.00 35
d. 36fr in LR 2.00 35
e. Souvenir sheet of 4 17.50 17.50

500th anniversary of the birth of Nicolaus Copernicus (1473-1543), Polish astronomer. Nos. C183-C186 are printed in sheets of 32 containing 8 blocks of 4. No. C186e contains one each of Nos. C183-C186. Gold and multicolored margin. Size: 136x136mm.

Flower-Butterfly Type of 1973

Designs: Each block of 4 contains 2 flower and 2 butterfly designs. The 10fr, 14fr, 24fr and 31fr have flower designs listed as "a" and "d" numbers, butterflies as "b" and "c" numbers; the arrangement is reversed for the 17fr and 26fr.

1973, Sept. 28 Photo. *Perf. 13*

Stamp Size: 35x45mm.

Gold and Multicolored

C187 A63 10fr Block of 4 3.00 40
a. Protea cynaroides 75 10
b. Precis octavia 75 10
c. Epiphora bauhiniae 75 10
d. Gazania longiscapa 75 10
C188 A63 14fr Block of 4 4.00 55
a. Kniphofia 1.00 13
b. Cymothoe coccinata 1.00 13
c. Nudaurelia zambesina 1.00 13
d. Freesia refracta 1.00 13
C189 A63 17fr Block of 4 5.00 65
a. Calotis eupompe 1.25 15
b. Narcissus 1.25 15
c. Cineraria hybrida 1.25 15
d. Cyrestis camillus 1.25 15
C190 A63 24fr Block of 4 6.00 95
a. Iris tingitana 1.50 23
b. Papilio demodocus 1.50 23
c. Catopsilia avelaneda 1.50 23
d. Nerine sarniensis 1.50 23
C191 A63 26fr Block of 4 7.00 1.10
a. Hypolimnas dexithea 1.75 25
b. Zantedeschia tropicalis 1.75 25
c. Sandersonia aurantiaca 1.75 25
d. Drurya antimachus 1.75 25
C192 A63 31fr Block of 4 8.00 1.30
a. Nymphaea capensis 2.00 30
b. Pandoriana pandora 2.00 30
c. Precis orythia 2.00 30
d. Pelargonium domestica 2.00 30
Nos. C187-C192 (6 blocks of 4) 33.00 4.95

Christmas Type of 1973

Virgin and Child by: 18fr, Raphael. 27fr, Pietro Perugino. 40fr, Titian.

1973, Nov. 19

C193 A64 18fr gold & multi 55 15
C194 A64 27fr gold & multi 80 22
C195 A64 40fr gold & multi 1.20 33
a. Souvenir sheet of 3 2.75 2.75

Christmas 1973. No. C195a contains one each of Nos. C193-C195 with multicolored margin. Size: 143x79mm.

Soccer Type of Regular Issue

Designs: Various soccer scenes and cup.

1974, July 4 Photogravure *Perf. 13*

C196 A67 20fr gold & multi 60
C197 A67 26fr gold & multi 78
C198 A67 40fr gold & multi 1.20

World Cup Soccer Championships, Munich, June 13-July 7. For souvenir sheet see No. 459a.

UPU Type of 1974

Designs: No. C199, Flags over UPU Headquarters, Bern. No. C200, G.P.O., Usumbura. No. C201, Mailmen ("26F" in UR). No. C202, Mailmen ("26F" in UL). No. C203, UPU emblem. No. C204, Means of transportation. No. C205, Pigeon over globe showing Burundi. No. C206, Swiss flag, pigeon over map showing Bern.

1974, July 23

C199 A68 24fr gold & multi 1.00
C200 A68 24fr gold & multi 1.00
C201 A68 26fr gold & multi 1.25
C202 A68 26fr gold & multi 1.25
C203 A68 31fr gold & multi 1.75
C204 A68 31fr gold & multi 1.75
C205 A68 40fr gold & multi 2.00
C206 A68 40fr gold & multi 2.00
a. Souvenir sheet of 8 12.00 12.00
Nos. C199-C206 (8) 12.00

Centenary of Universal Postal Union. Stamps of same denomination printed se-tenant (continuous design) in sheets of 40. No. C206a contains one each of Nos. C199-C206. Violet, gold and light blue margin. Size: 96x162mm.

Fish Type of 1974

1974, Sept. 9 Photo. *Perf. 13*

Size: 35x35mm.

Multicolored

C207 A66 10fr Block of 4 2.00 25
a. Haplochromis multicolor 50 6
b. Pantodon buchholzi 50 6
c. Tropheus duboisi 50 6
d. Distichodus sexfasciatus 50 6
C208 A66 14fr Block of 4 2.50 35
a. Pelmatochromis kribensis 60 8
b. Nannaethiops tritaeniatus 60 8
c. Polycentropsis abbreviata 60 8
d. Hemichromis bimaculatus 60 8
C209 A66 17fr Block of 4 3.00 40
a. Ctenopoma acutirostre 75 10
b. Synodontis angelicus 75 10
c. Tilapia melanopleura 75 10
d. Aphyosemion bivittatum 75 10
C210 A66 24fr Block of four 3.75 60
a. Monodactylus argenteus 90 15
b. Zanclus canescens 90 15
c. Pygoplites diacanthus 90 15
d. Cephalopholis argus 90 15
C211 A66 26fr Block of 4 4.00 70
a. Priacanthus arenatus 1.00 17
b. Pomacanthus arcutus 1.00 17
c. Scarus guacamaia 1.00 17
d. Zeus faber 1.00 17
C212 A66 31fr Block of 4 5.00 80
a. Lactophrys quadricornis 1.25 20
b. Balistes vetula 1.25 20
c. Acanthurus bahianus 1.25 20
d. Holocanthus ciliaris 1.25 20
Nos. C207-C212 (6 blocks of 4) 20.25 3.10

Christmas Type of 1974

Paintings of the Virgin and Child: 18fr, by Hans Memling. 27fr, by Filippino Lippi. 40fr, by Lorenzo di Gredi.

1974, Nov. 7 Photo. *Perf. 13*

C213 A70 18fr gold & multi 55 45
C214 A70 27fr gold & multi 80 65
C215 A70 40fr gold & multi 1.20 95
a. Souvenir sheet of 3 3.00 3.00

Christmas 1974. Sheets of 20 stamps and one label. No. C215a contains one each of Nos. C213-C215, gold and multicolored border. Size: 137x90mm. Sheet exists imperf.

Apollo-Soyuz Type of 1975.

1975, July 10 Photo. *Perf. 13*

Multicolored

C216 A71 27fr Block of 4 1.80
a. A.A. Leonov, V.N. Kubasov, Soviet flag 45
b. Soyuz and Soviet flag 45
c. Apollo and American flag 45
d. Slayton, Brand, Stafford, American flag 45
C217 A71 40fr Block of 4 2.60
a. Apollo-Soyuz link-up 65
b. Apollo, blast-off 65
c. Soyuz, blast-off 65
d. Kubasov, Leonov, Slayton, Brand, Stafford 65

Apollo Soyuz space test project (Russo-American cooperation), launching July 15; link-up, July 17. Nos. C216-C217 are printed in sheets of 32 containing 8 blocks of 4.

Animal Type of 1975

1975, Sept. 17 Photo. *Perf. 13½*

Multicolored

C218 A72 10fr Strip of four 1.75
a. Addax 42
b. Roan antelope 42
c. Nyala 42
d. White rhinoceros 42
C219 A72 14fr Strip of four 2.50
a. Mandrill 60
b. Eland 60
c. Salt's dik-dik 60
d. Thomson's gazelles 60
C220 A72 17fr Strip of four 3.00
a. African small-clawed otter 75
b. Reed buck 75
c. Indian civet 75
d. Cape buffalo 75

C221 A72 24fr Strip of four 4.00
a. *White-tailed gnu* 1.00
b. *African wild asses* 1.00
c. *Black-and-white colobus monkey* 1.00
d. *Gerenuk* 1.00
C222 A72 26fr Strip of four 4.50
a. *Dama gazelle* 1.10
b. *Black-backed jackal* 1.10
c. *Sitatungas* 1.10
d. *Zebra antelope* 1.10
C223 A72 31fr Strip of four 5.25
a. *Fennec* 1.30
b. *Lesser kudus* 1.30
c. *Blesbok* 1.30
d. *Serval* 1.30
Nos. C218-C223 (6 strips of 4) 21.00

Nos. C218–C219 Overprinted in Black and Silver with IWY Emblem and: "ANNEE INTERNATIONALE / DE LA FEMME"

1975, Nov. 19 Photo. Perf. 13½

C224 A72 10fr Strip of four 1.20 24
a. *Addax* 30 5
b. *Roan antelope* 30 5
c. *Nyala* 30 5
d. *White rhinoceros* 30 5
C225 A72 14fr Strip of four 1.68 35
a. *Mandrill* 42 8
b. *Oryx* 42 8
c. *Dik-dik* 42 8
d. *Thomson's gazelles* 42 8

International Women's Year 1975.

Nos. C222–C223 Overprinted in Black and Silver with U.N. Emblem and: "30ème ANNIVERSAIRE DES/ NATIONS UNIES"

1975, Nov. 19

C226 A72 26fr Strip of four 3.15 60
a. *Dama gazelle* 76 15
b. *Wild dog* 76 15
c. *Sitatungas* 76 15
d. *Striped duiker* 76 15
C227 A72 31fr Strip of four 3.75 65
a. *Fennec* 93 15
b. *Lesser kudus* 93 15
c. *Blesbok* 93 15
d. *Serval* 93 15

United Nations, 30th anniversary.

Michelangelo Type of 1975

Designs: Paintings from Sistine Chapel.

1975, Dec. 3 Photo. Perf. 13

C228 A73 18fr *Zachariah* 54
C229 A73 18fr *Joel* 54
C230 A73 31fr *Erythrean Sybil* 93
C231 A73 31fr *Prophet Ezekiel* 93
C232 A73 40fr *Persian Sybil* 1.20
C233 A73 40fr *Prophet Jeremiah* 1.20
a. Souvenir sheet of 6 5.50
Nos. C228-C233 (6) 5.34

Michelangelo Buonarotti (1475–1564), Italian sculptor, painter and architect. Stamps of same denominations printed se-tenant in sheets of 18 stamps and 2 labels. No. C233a contains one each of Nos. C228–C233, green & gold margin, black inscription. Size: 137x111mm.

Olympic Games Type, 1976

Designs (Olympic Games Emblem and): 18fr, Ski jump. 36fr, Slalom. 50fr, Ice hockey.

1976, Jan. 23 Photo. Perf. 14x13½

C234 A74 18fr ol brn & multi 54
C235 A74 36fr grn & multi 1.08
C236 A74 50fr pur & multi 1.50
a. Souvenir sheet of 4 3.10 2.00

12th Winter Olympic Games, Innsbruck, Austria, Feb. 4–15.
No. C236a contains 4 stamps similar to Nos. 491–494, perf. 13½, inscribed "POSTE AERIENNE." Multicolored margin with snowflakes and Games' emblem. Size: 100x103mm.

Hurdles—AP5

Designs (Montreal Games Emblem and): Nos. C238, C241, C243b, High jump. Nos. C239, C242, C243a, Athlete on rings. No. C240, C243c, Hurdles.

1976, May 3 Litho. Perf. 13½

C237 AP5 27fr grn & multi 78
C238 AP5 27fr dk bl & multi 78
C239 AP5 31fr ocher & multi 93
C240 AP5 31fr grn & multi 93
C241 AP5 50fr dk bl & multi 1.50
C242 AP5 50fr ocher & multi 1.50
Nos. C237-C242 (6) 6.42

Souvenir Sheet

C243 AP5 Sheet of 3 3.40 60
a. 27fr ocher & multi 78
b. 31fr dk bl & multi 95
c. 50fr grn & multi 1.50

21st Olympic Games, Montreal, Canada, July 17–Aug. 1. Stamps of same denomination printed se-tenant in sheets of 20.
No. C243 has gold inscription, Montreal Olympic emblem and multicolored band in margin. Size: 100x120mm.

Battle of Bunker Hill, by John Trumbull
AP6 AP7

Paintings: 26fr, Franklin, Jefferson and John Adams. 36fr, Declaration of Independence, by John Trumbull.

1976, July 16 Photo. Perf. 13

C244 AP6 18fr gold & multi 70
C245 AP7 18fr gold & multi 70
C246 AP6 26fr gold & multi 90
C247 AP7 26fr gold & multi 90
C248 AP6 36fr gold & multi 1.50
C249 AP7 36fr gold & multi 1.50
a. Souvenir sheet of 6 5.00 3.00
Nos. C244-C249 (6) 6.20

American Bicentennial. Stamps of same denomination printed se-tenant in sheets of 50. No. C249a contains one each of Nos. C244–C249 with Bicentennial emblem in margin. Size: 102x148mm.

Christmas Type of 1976

Paintings: 18fr, Virgin and Child with St. Anne, by Leonardo da Vinci. 31fr, Holy Family with Lamb, by Raphael. 40fr, Madonna of the Basket, by Correggio.

1976, Oct. 18 Photo. Perf. 13½

C250 A76 18fr gold & multi 54
C251 A76 31fr gold & multi 94
C252 A76 40fr gold & multi 1.20
a. Souvenir sheet of 3 2.80 1.75

Christmas 1976. Sheets of 20 stamps and descriptive label. No. C252a contains one each of Nos. C250–C252; multicolored margin. Size: 123x80mm.

A.G. Bell Type 1977

Designs: 10fr, A.G. Bell and first telephone. Nos. C253, 17fr, A.G. Bell speaking into microphone. Nos. C254, C257e, Satellites around globe and videophone. No. C255, Switchboard operator, c.1910, and wall telephone. Nos. C256, 26fr, Intelsat satellite, modern and old telephones. No. C257c, Intelsat and radar.

1977, May 17 Photo. Perf. 13

C253 A78 18fr multi 28
C254 A79 18fr multi 28
C255 A78 36fr multi 55
C256 A79 36fr multi 55

Souvenir Sheet

C257 Sheet of 5 3.50 2.00
a. A78 10fr multi 30 14
b. A78 17fr multi 50 22
c. A79 18fr multi 54 25
d. A79 26fr multi 80 45
e. A79 36fr multi 1.05 50

Centenary of first telephone call by Alexander Graham Bell, Mar. 10, 1876. No. C257 contains 3 postage (10fr, 17fr, 26fr) and 2 air post stamps (18fr, 36fr). Multicolored margin with ITU emblem and old telephone. Size: 120x135mm.

Animal Type of 1977

1977, Aug. 22 Photo. Perf. 14x14½

Multicolored

C258 A80 9fr Strip of four 1.50
a. *Buffon's kob* 35
b. *Marabous* 35
c. *Brindled gnu* 35
d. *River hog* 35
C259 A80 13fr Strip of four 2.00
a. *Zebras* 50
b. *Shoebill* 50
c. *Striped hyenas* 50
d. *Chimpanzee* 50
C260 A80 30fr Strip of four 4.00
a. *Flamingos* 1.00
b. *Nile Crocodiles* 1.00
c. *Green mamba* 1.00
d. *Greater kudus* 1.00
C261 A80 35fr Strip of four 5.00
a. *Hyrax* 1.25
b. *Cobra* 1.25
c. *Jackals* 1.25
d. *Verreaux's eagles* 1.25
C262 A80 54fr Strip of four 7.50
a. *Honey badger* 1.75
b. *Harnessed antelopes* 1.75
c. *Secretary bird* 1.75
d. *Klipspringer* 1.75
C263 A80 70fr Strip of four 9.00
a. *African big-eared fox* 2.25
b. *Elephants* 2.25
c. *Vulturine guineafowl* 2.25
d. *Impalas* 2.25
Nos. C258-C263 (6 strips of 4) 29.00

UN Type of 1977

Designs (UN Stamps and): 24fr, UN buildings by night. 27fr, UN buildings and view of Manhattan. 35fr, UN buildings by day.

1977, Oct. 10 Photo. Perf. 13½

C264 A82 24fr Block of four 2.88
a. No. 77 72
b. No. 78 72
c. No. 40 72
d. No. 32 72
C265 A82 27fr Block of four 3.20
a. No. 50 80
b. No. 21 80
c. No. 30 80
d. No. 44 80
C266 A82 35fr Block of four 4.20
a. No. C6 1.05
b. No. 105 1.05
c. No. 4 1.05
d. No. 1 1.05
e. Souvenir sheet of 3 2.75

25th anniversary (in 1976) of the United Nations Postal Administration. No. C266e contains 24fr in design of No. C265b, 27fr in design of No. C266a, 35fr in design of No. C264c; silver margin. Size: 128x76 mm.

Christmas Type of 1977

Designs: Paintings of the Virgin and Child.

1977, Oct. 31 Photo. Perf. 14x13

C267 A83 18fr Master of Moulins 55
C268 A83 31fr Workshop of Lorenzo de Credi 95
C269 A83 40fr Palma Vecchio 1.20
a. Souvenir sheet of 3 (#C267-C269) 3.00 2.00

Sheets of 24 stamps and descriptive label.

Souvenir Sheet

Type of 1979

1979, Feb. Photo. Perf. 14x13½

C270 Sheet of 5, multi 4.00
a. A86 13fr *like* #543 40
b. A86 17fr *like* #544 50
c. A86 27fr *like* #545 80
d. A 86 31fr *like* #546 95
e. A86 40fr *like* #547 1.20

Christmas 1978. No. C270 has green, gold and black margin. Size: 114x120mm.

Christmas Type of 1979

Souvenir Sheet

1979, Oct. 12 Perf. 13½

C271 Sheet of 4, multi 4.00 2.50
a. A89 20fr *like* #561 60 32
b. A89 27fr *like* #562 80 45
c. A89 31fr *like* #563 95 55
d. A89 50fr *like* #564 1.50 85

Christmas 1979.

Hill Type of 1979

Souvenir Sheet

1979, Nov.6

C272 Sheet of 5, multi 7.00 3.50
a. A90 20fr *like* #565 80 32
b. A90 27fr *like* #566 1.10 45
c. A90 31fr *like* #567 1.25 55
d. A90 40fr *like* #568 1.65 70
e. A90 50fr *like* #569 2.00 1.00

Sir Rowland Hill (1795-1879), originator of penny postage.

Bird Type of 1979

1979 Photo. Perf. 13½×13

Multicolored

C273 A87 6fr *like* #548 18
C274 A87 13fr *like* #549 40
C275 A87 18fr *like* #550 55
C276 A87 26fr *like* #551 78
C277 A87 31fr *like* #552 95
C278 A87 36fr *like* #553 1.10
C279 A87 40fr *like* #554 1.20
C280 A87 54fr *like* #555 1.65
C281 A87 70fr *like* #556 2.10
Nos. C273-C281 (9) 8.91

Olympic Type of 1980

Souvenir Sheet

1980, Oct. 24 Photo. Perf. 13½

C282 Sheet of 9 8.50
a. A91 20fr like #570 60
b. A91 20fr like #571 60
c. A91 20fr like #572 60
d. A91 30fr like #573 90
e. A91 30fr like #574 90
f. A91 30fr like #575 90
g. A91 40fr like #576 1.20
h. A91 40fr like #577 1.20
i. A91 40fr like #578 1.20

22nd Summer Olympic Games, Moscow, July 19-Aug. 3. No. C282 has multicolored margin showing Moscow '80 emblem. Size: 144½x 112mm.

Christmas Type of 1980

Souvenir Sheet

1980, Dec. 12 Photo. Perf. 13½x13

C283 Sheet of 4 3.75 2.75
a. A92 10fr *like* #579 30 20
b. A92 30 fr *like* #580 90 60
c. A92 40fr *like* #581 1.20 80
d. A92 45fr *like* #582 1.35 90

Multicolored decorative margin. Size: 133½x104mm.

UPRONA Type of 1980

Souvenir Sheet

1980, Dec. 29 Perf. 14½x13½

C284 Sheet of 3 3.00
a. A93 10fr like #583 30
b. A93 40fr like #584 1.20
c. A93 45fr like #585 1.35

No. C284 has light blue and gold decorative margin. Size: 109x68mm.

Christmas Type of 1983

Souvenir Sheet

1983, Oct. 3 Litho. Perf. 14½x13½

C285 Souvenir sheet of 4 3.50
a. A97 10fr like #607 30
b. A97 25fr like #608 75
c. A97 30fr like #609 90
d. A97 50fr like #610 1.50

No. C285 has gold and deep lilac-rose decorative margin. Size: 106x152mm.

UPU Congress Type of 1984

1984, July 14 *Perf. 13x13½*

C286	Souvenir sheet of 4	4.25
a.	A99 10fr like #621	30
b.	A99 30fr like #622	90
c.	A99 35fr like #623	1.00
d.	A99 65fr like #624	2.00

No. C286 has multicolored margin picturing the Conference Center, Hamburg. Size: 148x84mm.

Summer Olympics Type of 1984

1984, Aug. 6 *Perf. 13½x13*

C287	Souvenir sheet of 4	4.25
a.	A100 10fr like #625	30
b.	A100 30fr like #626	90
c.	A100 35fr like #627	1.00
d.	A100 65fr like #628	2.00

No. C287 has multicolored decorative margin. Size: 119x99mm.

Christmas Type of 1984

1984, Dec. 15 *Perf. 13½*

C288	Souvenir sheet of 4	3.50
a.	A101 10fr like #629	30
b.	A101 25fr like #630	75
c.	A101 30fr like #631	90
d.	A101 50fr like #632	1.50

Size: 126x92mm.

Flower Type of 1986 with Dull Lilac Border.

1986, July 31 **Photo.** *Perf. 13x13½*

C289	A102	70fr like #633	1.10
C290	A102	75fr like #634	1.20
C291	A102	80fr like #635	1.30
C292	A102	85fr like #636	1.40
C293	A102	100fr like #637	1.60
C294	A102	150fr like #638	2.40
		Nos. C289-C294 (6)	9.00

AIR POST SEMI-POSTAL STAMPS

Coin Type of Semi-Postal Issue

Designs (Coins of Various Denominations): 3fr+1fr, 11fr+1fr, 20fr+1fr, 50fr+1fr, Coat of Arms, reverse. 5fr+1fr, 14fr+1fr, 30fr+1fr, 100fr+1fr, King Mwambutsa IV, obverse.

1965, Nov. 15 *Imperf.*

Lithographed; Embossed on Gilt Foil

Diameter: 39mm.

CB1	SP4	3fr +1fr lt & dk vio	10	10
CB2	SP4	5fr +1fr pale grn & red	15	15

Diameter: 45mm.

CB3	SP4	11fr +1fr org & lil	25	25
CB4	SP4	14fr +1fr red & emer	30	30

Diameter: 56mm.

CB5	SP4	20fr +1fr ultra & blk	40	40
CB6	SP4	30fr +1fr dp org & mar	60	60

Diameter: 67mm.

CB7	SP4	50fr +1fr bl & vio bl	1.00	1.00
CB8	SP4	100fr +1fr rose & dp cl	2.25	2.25
		Nos. CB1-CB8 (8)	5.05	5.05

Stamps are backed with patterned paper in blue, orange, and pink engine-turned design.

Red Cross Type of Semi-Postal Issue

Designs: 26fr+3fr, Laboratory. 40fr+3fr, Ambulance and thatched huts. 50fr+3fr, Red Cross nurse with patient.

1969, June 26 Photo. *Perf. 13½*

CB9	SP7	26fr +3fr multi	75	20
CB10	SP7	40fr +3fr multi	1.10	30
CB11	SP7	50fr +3fr multi	1.35	40

Issued to commemorate the 50th anniversary of the League of Red Cross Societies. Perf. and imperf. souvenir sheets exist containing 3 stamps similar to Nos. CB9–CB11, but without "Poste Aerienne." Gold frame with green commemorative inscription. Size: 90½x97mm.

Christmas Type of Semi-Postal Issue

Paintings: 14fr+3fr, Virgin and Child, by Velázquez. 26fr+3fr, Holy Family, by Joos van Cleve. 40fr+3fr, Virgin and Child, by Rogier van der Weyden.

1970, Dec. 14 Photo. *Perf. 13½*

CB12	SP9	14fr +3fr multi	50	17
CB13	SP9	26fr +3fr multi	90	30
CB14	SP9	40fr +3fr multi	1.30	42
a.		Souvenir sheet of 3	3.00	3.00

No. CB14a contains one each of Nos. CB12–CB14 with ornamental border and inscription. Size: 135x75mm.

No. C147 Surcharged in Gold and Black

+2F

LUTTE CONTRE L'ANALPHABETISME

1971, Aug. 9 Photo. *Perf. 13½*

CB15	A48	14fr +2fr Strip of four	1.60	32
a.		*Hartebeest*	40	8
b.		*Black rhinoceros*	40	8
c.		*Zebra*	40	8
d.		*Leopard*	40	8

UNESCO campaign against illiteracy.

No. C148 Surcharged in Gold and Black

+1F

AIDE INTERNATIONALE AUX REFUGIES

1971, Aug. 9 **Multicolored**

CB16	A48	17fr +1fr Strip of four	1.85	35
a.		*Grant's gazelles*	45	8
b.		*Cheetah*	45	8
c.		*African white-backed vultures*	45	8
d.		*Johnston's okapi*	45	8

International help for refugees.

Nos. C150–C151 Surcharged in Black and Gold

+1F

75eme ANNIVERSAIRE DES JEUX OLYMPIQUES MODERNES (1896-1971)

a

+1F

JEUX PRE-OLYMPIQUES MUNICH 1972

b

1971, Aug. 16

CB17	A48(a)	26fr +1fr Strip of four	4.50	90
a.		*Gorilla*	1.10	22
b.		*Gnu*	1.10	22
c.		*Warthog*	1.10	22
d.		*Cape hunting dog*	1.10	22
CB18	A48(b)	31fr +1fr Strip of four	6.00	1.20
a.		*Sable antelope*	1.50	30
b.		*Caracal lynx*	1.50	30
c.		*Ostriches*	1.50	30
d.		*Bongo*	1.50	30

75th anniversary of modern Olympic Games (No. CB17); Olympic Games, Munich, 1972 (No. CB18).

Nos. C153–C155 Surcharged

1971, Nov. 27 Photo. *Perf. 13½*

CB19	A51	14fr +1fr multi	50	15
CB20	A51	17fr +1fr multi	60	20
CB21	A51	31fr +1fr multi	1.00	33

25th anniversary of the United Nations International Children's Fund (UNICEF).

Casa D'Oro, Venice SPAP1

Views in Venice: 17fr+1fr, Doge's Palace. 24fr+1fr, Church of Sts. John and Paul. 31fr+1fr, Doge's Palace and Piazzetta at Feast of Ascension, by Canaletto.

1971, Dec. 27

CB22	SPAP1	10fr +1fr gold & multi	33	15
CB23	SPAP1	17fr +1fr gold & multi	55	22
CB24	SPAP1	24fr +1fr gold & multi	75	30
CB25	SPAP1	31fr +1fr gold & multi	90	35
a.		Souvenir sheet of 4	3.00	3.00

The surtax was for the UNESCO campaign to save the treasures of Venice. No. CB25a contains 4 stamps similar to Nos. CB22–CB25, but with 2fr surtax instead 1fr. Gold and black ornamental margin. Size: 113x131½mm. Sheet exists imperf.

Nos. C165–C167 Surcharged "+1F" in Silver

1972, Dec. 12 Photo. *Perf. 13½*

CB26	A57	18fr +1fr multi	50	17
CB27	A57	27fr +1fr multi	85	25
CB28	A57	40fr +1fr multi	1.10	35
a.		Souvenir sheet of 3	2.50	2.50

Christmas 1972. No. CB28a contains 3 stamps similar to Nos. CB26–CB28 but with 2fr surtax. Slate green and gold border. Size: 128x81mm.

Nos. C193–C195 Surcharged "+1F" in Silver

1973, Dec. 14 Photo. *Perf. 13*

CB29	A64	18fr +1fr multi	55	17
CB30	A64	27fr +1fr multi	80	25
CB31	A64	40fr +1fr multi	1.25	40
a.		Souvenir sheet of 3	3.00	3.00

Christmas 1973. No. CB31 contains 3 stamps similar to Nos. CB29–CB31 with 2fr surtax each. Size: 143x79mm.

Christmas Type of 1974

1974, Dec. 2 Photogravure *Perf. 13*

CB32	A70	18fr +1fr multi	65	40
CB33	A70	27fr +1fr multi	1.00	60
CB34	A70	40fr +1fr multi	1.40	85
a.		Souvenir sheet of 3	3.50	3.50

Christmas 1974. No. CB34a contains 3 stamps similar to Nos. CB32–CB34 with 2fr surtax. Size: 137x90mm.

Nos. C228–C233 Surcharged "+ 1 F" in Silver and Black

1975, Dec. 22 Photo. *Perf. 13*

Multicolored

CB35	A73	18fr +1fr #C228	60	
CB36	A73	18fr +1fr #C229	60	
CB37	A73	31fr +1fr #C230	95	
CB38	A73	31fr +1fr #C231	95	
CB39	A73	40fr +1fr #C232	1.25	
CB40	A73	40fr +1fr #C233	1.25	
a.		Souvenir sheet of 6	6.00	6.00
		Nos. CB35-CB40 (6)	5.60	

Michelangelo Buonarroti (1475–1564), 500th birth anniversary. No. CB40a contains 6 stamps similar to Nos. CB35–CB40 with 2fr surtax each. Size: 132x106mm.

Nos. C250–C252 Surcharged "+1f" in Silver and Black

1976, Nov. 25 Photo. *Perf. 13½*

CB41	A76	18fr +1fr multi	60	
CB42	A76	31fr +1fr multi	1.00	
CB43	A76	40fr +1fr multi	1.25	
a.		Souvenir sheet of 3	3.00	3.00

Christmas 1976. No. CB43a contains 3 stamps similar to Nos. CB41–CB43 with 2fr surtax each. Size: 123x80mm.

Nos. C267–C269 Surcharged "+1fr" in Silver and Black

1977 Photo. *Perf. 14x13*

CB44	A83	18fr +1fr multi	58	
CB45	A83	31fr +1fr multi	1.00	
CB46	A83	40fr +1fr multi	1.25	
a.		Souvenir sheet of 3	3.00	3.00

Christmas 1977. No. CB46a contains 3 stamps similar to Nos. CB44–CB46 with 2fr surtax each. Size: 130x71mm.

Type of 1979

Souvenir Sheet

1979, Feb. Photo. *Perf. 14x13*

CB47		Sheet of 5	6.00
a.	A86	13fr +2fr multi	60
b.	A86	17fr +2fr multi	75
c.	A86	27fr +2fr multi	1.10
d.	A86	31fr +2fr multi	1.40
e.	A86	40fr +2fr multi	1.75

Christmas 1978. No. CB47 has gold, black and blue border. Size: 115x121mm.

Christmas Type of 1979

Souvenir Sheet

1979, Dec. 10 Photo. *Perf. 13½*

CB48		Sheet of 4	5.50
a.	A89	20fr +2fr *like* #561	90
b.	A89	27fr +2fr *like* #562	1.10
c.	A89	31fr +2fr *like* #563	1.40
d.	A89	50fr +2fr *like* #564	2.00

No. CB48 has multicolored decorative margin. Size: 86x110mm.

Christmas Type of 1980

Souvenir Sheet

1981, Jan. 16 Photo. *Perf. 13½x13*

CB49		Sheet of 4	5.00
a.	A92	10fr +2fr *like* #579	42
b.	A92	30fr +2fr *like* #580	1.10
c.	A92	40fr +2fr *like* #581	1.50
d.	A92	50fr +2fr *like* #582	1.90

Christmas 1980. Multicolored decorative margin. Size: 133x104mm.

Christmas Type of 1983

1983, Nov. 2 Litho. *Perf. 14½x13½*

CB50		Souvenir sheet of 4	3.60
a.	A97	10fr +1fr like #607	32
b.	A97	25fr +1fr like #608	78
c.	A97	30fr +1fr like #609	1.00
d.	A97	50fr +1fr like #610	1.50

No. CB50 has gold and bright blue decorative margin. Size: 106x152mm.

Christmas Type of 1984

1984, Dec. 15 *Perf. 13½*

CB51		Souvenir sheet of 4	3.60
a.	A101	10fr +1fr like #629	32
b.	A101	25fr +1fr like #630	78
c.	A101	30fr +1fr like #631	1.00
d.	A101	50fr +1fr like #632	1.50

Size: 126x92mm.

CAMBODIA

(kăm·bō′dĭ·ȧ)

Khmer Republic

LOCATION—Southern Indo-China.
GOVT.—Republic
AREA—69,866 sq. mi.
POP.—7,640,000 (est. 1974).
CAPITAL—Phnom Penh.

Before 1951, Cambodia used stamps of Indo-China. In October, 1970, the Kingdom of Cambodia became the Khmer Republic.

100 Cents = 1 Piaster
100 Cents = 1 Riel (1955)

Imperforates

Most Cambodia stamps exist imperforate in issued and trial colors, and also in small presentation sheets in issued colors.

Apsaras
A1

King Norodom Sihanouk
A3

Enthronement Hall
A2

Engraved.

1951–52 ***Perf. 13*** **Unwmkd.**

No.	Type	Description	Unused	Used
1	A1	10c dk bl grn	55	55
2	A1	20c cl & org brn	35	20
3	A1	30c pur & ind	35	20
4	A1	40c ultra & brt bl grn	35	20
5	A2	50c dk grn & dk ol grn	35	20
6	A3	80c bl blk & dk bl grn	70	70
7	A2	1pi ind & pur	90	90
8	A3	1.10pi dp car & brt red	90	90
9	A3	1.50pi blk brn & red brn ('51)	1.25	90
10	A1	1.50pi dp car & cer	1.25	90
11	A2	1.50pi ind & dp ultra	1.25	1.10
12	A3	1.90pi ind & dp ultra	1.75	1.60
13	A2	2pi dp car & org brn	1.60	1.00
14	A3	3pi dp car & org brn	2.25	1.60
15	A1	5pi ind & pur	9.00	4.00
a.		Souvenir sheet of 1	27.50	
16	A2	10pi pur & ind	16.50	8.50
a.		Souvenir sheet of 1	27.50	
17	A3	15pi dk pur & pur	22.50	12.00
a.		Souvenir sheet of 1	32.50	
		Nos. 1-17 (17)	61.80	35.45

Nos. 15a, 16a, 17a sold in a booklet for 30pi.

Phnom Daun Penh
A4

East Gate, Angkor Thom
A5

Arms of Cambodia
A6

Methods of Mail Transport
A7

1954–55 ***Perf. 13*** **Unwmkd.**

No.	Type	Description	Unused	Used
18	A4	10c rose car	6	6
a.		Souvenir sheet of 5 ('55)	27.50	
19	A4	20c dk grn	6	6
20	A4	30c indigo	6	6
21	A4	40c dk pur	6	6
22	A4	50c dk vio brn	6	6
23	A5	70c chocolate	20	20
a.		Souvenir sheet of 5 ('55)	27.50	
24	A5	1pi red vio	20	20
25	A5	1.50pi red	20	20
26	A6	2pi rose red	40	40
a.		Souvenir sheet of 5 ('55)	27.50	
27	A6	2.50pi green	60	60
28	A7	2.50pi bl grn	80	60
a.		Souvenir sheet of 5 ('55)	27.50	
29	A6	3pi ultra	90	75
30	A7	4pi blk brn	1.00	1.00
31	A6	4.50pi purple	1.20	1.00
32	A7	5pi rose red	1.25	1.00
33	A6	6pi chocolate	1.50	1.00
34	A7	10pi purple	1.50	1.50
35	A7	15pi dp bl	2.00	1.85
36	A5	20pi ultra	4.00	2.50
37	A5	30pi bl grn	6.00	5.00
		Nos. 18-37 (20)	22.05	18.10

The four souvenir sheets each contain five different stamps: No. 18a (10c, 20c, 30c, 40c, 50c); No. 23a (70c, 1pi, 1.50pi, 20pi, 30pi); No. 26a (2pi, 2.50pi green, 3pi, 4.50pi, 6pi); No. 28a (2.50pi blue green, 4pi, 5pi, 10pi, 15pi). Size of Nos. 18a, 26a and 28a: 120x120mm. Size of No. 23a: 160x92mm.

King Norodom Suramarit
A8

King Norodom Suramarit and Queen Kossamak Nearirat Serey Vathana
A9

Portraits: 50c (No. 39), 2.50r, 4r, 6r, 15r, Queen Kossamak Nearirat Serey Vathana.

Perf. 14x13(A8), 13(A9)

1955, Nov. 24 **Engr.** **Unwmkd.**

No.	Type	Description	Unused	Used
38	A8	50c violet	10	10
39	A8	50c indigo	10	10
40	A8	1r car lake	15	15
41	A9	1.50r dk brn	40	40
42	A9	2r blk & ind	40	30
43	A8	2r dp ultra	25	40
44	A8	2.50r dk vio brn	40	40
45	A9	3r brn org & car	40	40
46	A8	4r dk grn	60	60
47	A9	5r blk & dk grn	60	60
48	A8	6r dp plum	1.00	75
49	A8	7r dk brn	1.25	75
50	A9	10r brn car & vio	1.00	1.00
51	A8	15r purple	1.75	1.25
52	A8	20r dp grn	2.25	2.00
		Nos. 38-52 (15)	10.65	9.20

Issued to commemorate the coronation of King Norodom Suramarit and Queen Kossamak Nearirat Serey Vathana.

See also Nos. 74–75.

King Norodom Suramarit
A10

Prince Sihanouk, Globe and Flags
A11

Portrait: 3r, 5r, 50r, Queen Kossamak Nearirat Serey Vathana.

1956, Mar. 8 ***Perf. 13***

No.	Type	Description	Unused	Used
53	A10	2r dk red	1.00	1.00
54	A10	3r dk bl	1.50	1.50
55	A10	5r yel grn	2.25	2.25
56	A10	10r dk grn	5.50	5.50
57	A10	30r dk vio	12.00	12.00
58	A10	50r rose lil	22.50	22.50
		Nos. 53-58 (6)	44.75	44.75

Issued to commemorate the coronation of King Norodom Suramarit and Queen Kossamak Nearirat Serey Vathana.

1957, Mar. 1

No.	Type	Description	Unused	Used
59	A11	2r grn, ultra & car	60	45
60	A11	4.50r ultra	60	45
61	A11	8.50r carmine	60	45

Issued to commemorate the first anniversary of Cambodia's admission to the United Nations (in 1956).

Type of Semi-Postal Stamps, 1957.

1957, May 12 ***Perf. 13*** **Unwmkd.**

No.	Type	Description	Unused	Used
62	SP1	1.50r vermilion	55	55
63	SP1	6.50r bluish vio	70	70
64	SP1	8r dk grn	70	70

Issued to commemorate the 2500th anniversary of the birth of Buddha.

King Ang Duong
A12

1958, Mar. 4

No.	Type	Description	Unused	Used
65	A12	1.50r pur & brn	20	20
66	A12	5r ol gray & ol	50	40
67	A12	10r cl & dl brn	1.00	60
a.		Souvenir sheet of 3	3.50	3.50

Issued to honor King Ang Duong (1795–1860).

No. 67a contains one each of Nos. 65–67. Sold for 25r. Size: 155x93mm.

King Norodom I
A13

1958–59 **Engraved** ***Perf. 12½x13***

No.	Type	Description	Unused	Used
68	A13	2r ultra & ol	40	40
69	A13	6r org & sl grn	80	80
70	A13	15r grn & ol gray	1.20	1.20
a.		Souvenir sheet of 3 ('59)	3.50	3.50

Issued in honor of King Norodom I (1835–1904).

No. 70a contains one each of Nos. 68–70. Sold for 32r. Size: 155x93mm.

Issue dates: Nos. 68–70, Nov. 3, 1958. No. 70a, Jan. 31, 1959.

Children of the World
A14

1959, Dec. 9 ***Perf. 13*** **Unwmkd.**

No.	Type	Description	Unused	Used
71	A14	20c rose vio	6	6
72	A14	50c blue	12	12
73	A14	80c rose car	20	20

Issued to promote friendship among the children of the world.

Nos. 49 and 52 with Black Border.

1960 ***Perf. 14x13***

No.	Type	Description	Unused	Used
74	A8	7r dk brn & blk	1.25	1.25
75	A8	20r dp grn & blk	1.25	1.25

Issued to commemorate the death of King Norodom Suramarit.

Port of Sihanoukville, Prince Sihanouk and Serpent Naga
A15

(double size)
20r

1960, Apr. ***Perf. 13x12½***

No.	Type	Description	Unused	Used
76	A15	2r car & sep	40	40
a.		Cambodian 20r	1.20	1.20
77	A15	5r ultra & dp brn	40	40
a.		Cambodian 20r	1.60	1.60
78	A15	20r lil & dk bl	1.40	1.00

Issued to commemorate the opening of the port of Sihanoukville. By error the denomination in Cambodian on the 2r and 5r was engraved as 20r; it was corrected later.

Ceremonial Plow
A16

1960				***Perf. 12***
79	A16	1r magenta	10	10
80	A16	2r brown	40	40
81	A16	3r bluish grn	40	40

Feast of the Sacred Furrow.

Works of Sangkum Issue

Fight Against Illiteracy
A17

Water Conservation, Dam at Chhouksar
A18

Dove, Factory and Books
A19

Buddhist Ceremony
A20

Designs: 6r, Workman and house. 10r, Woman in rice field.

1960, Sept. 1		**Engraved**		***Perf. 13***
82	A17	2r dk grn, brn & dk bl	22	18
a.		Souvenir sheet of 3	3.50	3.50
83	A18	3r brn & grn	32	27
a.		Souvenir sheet of 3	3.50	3.50
84	A19	4r rose car, vio & grn	35	32
85	A17	6r brn, org & grn	45	40
86	A17	10r ultra, grn & bis	90	80
87	A20	25r dk car, red & mag	2.25	1.65
		Nos. 82-87 (6)	4.49	3.62

No. 82a contains one each of Nos. 82, 85 and 87, and sold for 42r. No. 83a contains one each of Nos. 83, 84 and 86, and sold for 23r. Marginal inscriptions in bister. Size: 149x100mm. Nos. 82a–83a were issued Dec. 5, 1960.

Cambodian Flag and Dove
A21

Frangipani
A22

1960, Dec. 24		**Engraved**		***Perf. 13***
Flag in Ultramarine and Red				
88	A21	1.50r brn & grn	25	25
89	A21	5r org red	35	35
90	A21	7r grn & ultra	85	85
a.		Souvenir sheet of 3	3.50	3.50
b.		Souvenir sheet of 3 (colors changed)	6.25	6.25

Issued as peace propaganda.

No. 90a contains one each of Nos. 88–90 and sold for 16r. No. 90b contains one of each denomination with colors changed to: 1.50r orange red, 5r green & ultramarine, 7r brown & green. No. 90b sold for 20r. Marginal inscriptions in bistre. Size: 146½x93mm.

1961, July 1		***Perf. 13***		**Unwmkd.**
Flowers: 5r, Oleander. 10r, Amaryllis.				
91	A22	2r lil rose, yel & grn	30	30
92	A22	5r ultra, lil rose & grn	50	50
93	A22	10r vio, car & grn	1.25	1.25
a.		Souv. sheet of 3	3.50	3.50

No. 93a contains one each of Nos. 91–93. Gold marginal inscription. Size: 130x100mm. Sold for 20r.

Krishna in Chariot, Khmer Frieze
A23

Independence Monument
A24

1961–63		**Typo.**		***Perf. 14x13½***
94	A23	1r lilac	10	10
94A	A23	2r bl ('63)	1.25	75
95	A23	3r emerald	25	25
96	A23	6r orange	45	25
a.		Souv. sheet of 3	7.00	7.00

Issued to honor Cambodian armed forces.

No. 94A issued in coils. No. 96a contains one each of Nos. 94, 95, 96. Orange marginal inscriptions. Size: 149x85mm. Sold for 12r.

1961, Nov. 9		**Engr.**		***Perf. 13x12½***
97	A24	2r green	30	30
98	A24	4r gray brn	30	30
a.		Souvenir sheet of 2	1.20	1.20
		Nos. 97-98, C15-C17 (5)	6.85	5.10

Issued to commemorate the tenth anniversary of Independence. No. 98a contains one each of Nos. 97–98 with gold marginal inscription. Size: 150x85mm.

Nos. 27 and 31 Overprinted in Red:
"VIe CONFERENCE MONDIALE BOUDDIQUE 12-11-1961"

1961, Nov. 11				***Perf. 13***
99	A6	2.50pi (r) grn	35	35
100	A6	4.50pi (r) pur	50	50

Sixth World Conference of Buddhism.

Highway (American Aid)
A25

Foreign Aid: 2r, Power station (Czech aid). 4r, Textile factory (Chinese aid). 5r, Hospital (Russian aid). 6r, Airport (French aid).

1961, Dec.		**Engraved**		***Perf. 13***
101	A25	2r org & rose car	20	12
102	A25	3r bl, grn & org brn	30	20
103	A25	4r dl bl, org brn & mag	35	22
104	A25	5r dl grn & lil rose	40	35
105	A25	6r dk bl & org brn	55	40
a.		Souvenir sheet of 5	3.25	3.25
		Nos. 101-105 (5)	1.80	1.29

Issued to publicize foreign aid to Cambodia. No. 105a contains one each of Nos. 101–105 with bistre marginal inscription. Size: 148x84mm.

Malaria Eradication Emblem
A26

1962, Apr. 7		***Perf. 13***		**Unwmkd.**
106	A26	2r mag & brn	25	18
107	A26	4r grn & dk brn	38	32
108	A26	6r vio & ol bis	45	38

Issued for the World Health Organization drive to eradicate malaria.

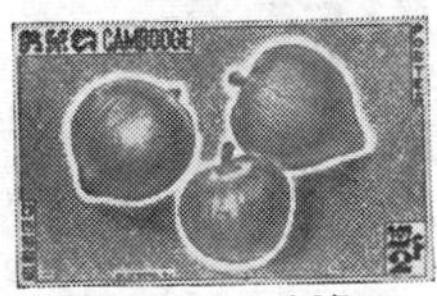

Turmeric—A27

Fruits: 4r, Cinnamon. 6r, Mangosteens.

1962, June 4				**Engraved**
109	A27	2r gray & bis	45	40
110	A27	4r dk bl grn & ol gray	45	40
111	A27	6r dk bl, grn & mag	70	60
a.		Souv. sheet of 3	3.00	3.00

Nos. 111a contains one each of Nos. 109–111 with marginal inscription in gray. Size: 149x84mm. Sold for 15r.

Pineapples
A28

Designs: 5r, Sugar cane. 9r, Sugar palms.

1962		***Perf. 13***		**Unwmkd.**
112	A28	2r bluish grn & brn	40	35
113	A28	5r brn & grn	50	40
114	A28	9r Prus grn & brn	75	50

No. 73 Surcharged

1962, Nov. 9				***Perf. 13***
115	A14	50c on 80c rose car	30	30

No. 97 Surcharged with New Value in Red and Overprinted in Black with Two Bars and:
"INAUGURATION / DU / MONUMENT"

1962				
116	A24	3r on 2r grn	25	18

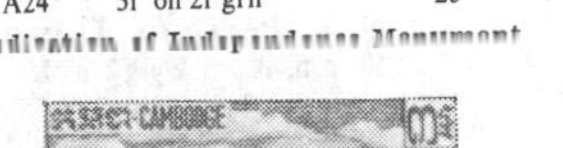

Dedication of Independence Monument

Corn, Rice and FAO Emblem
A29

1963, Mar. 21		**Engraved**		***Perf. 13***
117	A29	3r multi	55	45
118	A29	6r org red, vio bl & ocher	55	45

Issued for the "Freedom from Hunger" campaign of the U.N. Food and Agriculture Organization.

Preah Vihear, Ancient Temple
A30

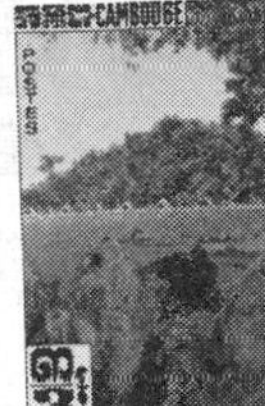

Tonsay Lake
A31

1963, June 15				***Perf. 12½x13***
119	A30	3r cl, brn & sl grn	25	25
120	A30	6r org, sl grn & grnsh blk	50	38
121	A30	15r bl, choc & grn	1.00	85

Return by Thailand of Preah Vihear on the Mekong River.

No. 44 Surcharged with New Value and Bars

1963		**Engraved**		***Perf. 14x13***
122	A8	3r on 2½r dk vio brn	35	35

		Perf. 12x12½, 12½x12		
1963, Aug. 1				**Photogravure**
Designs: 7r, Popokvil Falls. 20r, Beach (horiz.).				
123	A31	3r multi	20	20
124	A31	7r multi	45	30
125	A31	20r multi	1.20	70

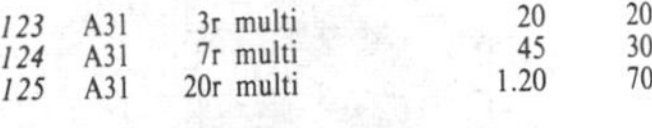

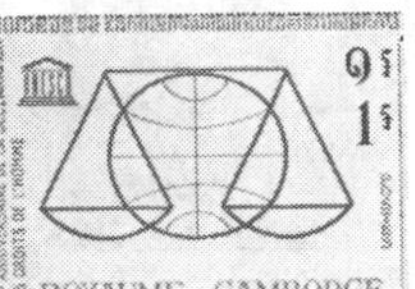

UNESCO Emblem, Scales and Globe
A32

1963, Dec. 10		**Engraved**		***Perf. 13***
126	A32	1r vio bl, rose cl & grn	20	20

127 A32 3r yel grn, vio bl & rose cl 35 35
128 A32 12r rose cl, yel grn & vio bl 75 75

Issued to commemorate the 15th anniversary of the Universal Declaration of Human Rights.

Kouprey
A33

1964, March 3 ***Perf. 13*** **Unwmkd.**

129 A33 50c grn, dk brn & org brn 15 15
130 A33 3r org, brn, dk brn & grn 25 25
131 A33 6r bl, dk brn & grn 40 30

Black-billed Magpie
A34

Birds: 6r, Kingfisher. 12r, Gray heron.

1964, May 2 **Engraved** ***Perf. 13***

132 A34 3r dk bl, ind & grn 30 20
133 A34 6r ind, org & brn 75 40
134 A34 12r Prus grn, ind & red brn 1.25 85

Emblem of Royal Cambodian Airline
A35

1964 ***Perf. 13x12½*** **Unwmkd.**

135 A35 1.50r rose car & pur 20 20
136 A35 3r ver & dk bl 25 20
137 A35 7.50r ultra & car 60 50

Issued to commemorate the 8th anniversary of the Royal Cambodian Airline.

Prince Norodom Sihanouk
A36

1964 **Engraved** ***Perf. 12½x13***

138 A36 2r purple 18 18
139 A36 3r red brn 25 25
140 A36 10r dk bl 70 60

Issued to commemorate the 10th anniversary of the Sangkum (political party).

Woman Weaver
A37

Khmer Handicrafts: 3r, Metal worker. 5r, Basket maker.

1965, Feb. 1 ***Perf. 13x12½***

141 A37 1r multi 15 15
142 A37 3r red lil, red brn & gray ol 35 25
143 A37 5r grn, dk brn & car 40 30

Nos. 139-140 Overprinted in Black or Red:
"CONFERENCE / DES PEUPLES / INDOCHINOIS"

1965, Mar. 1 ***Perf. 12½x13***

144 A36 3r red brn 40 40
145 A36 10r dk bl (R) 60 40

Conference of the people of Indo-China.

ITU Emblem, Old and New Communication Equipment
A38

1965, May 17 **Engraved** ***Perf. 13***

146 A38 3r grn & ol bis 30 30
147 A38 4r red & bl 40 30
148 A38 10r vio & rose lil 70 60

Issued to commemorate the centenary of the International Telecommunication Union.

Cotton Plant
A39

Designs: 3r, Peanut plant. 7.50r, Coconut palm.

1965, Aug. 2 ***Perf. 12½x13***

149 A39 1.50r org, sl grn & pur 25 25
150 A39 3r bl, yel, grn & brn 38 38
151 A39 7.50r org brn & sl grn 70 70

Preah Ko Temple, Rolouoh
A40

Temples at Angkor: 5r, Baksei Chamkrong, Rolouoh. 7r, Banteay Srei (Citadel of Women). 9r, Angkor Wat. 12r, Bayon, Angkor Thom.

1966, Feb. 1 **Engraved** ***Perf. 13***

152 A40 3r gray ol, sal & dl grn 45 28
153 A40 5r lil, dk grn & redsh brn 50 40
154 A40 7r dk grn, redsh brn & bis 60 45
155 A40 9r vio bl, pur & dk grn 1.00 55
156 A40 12r dk grn, rose car & ver 1.25 75
Nos. 152-156 (5) 3.80 2.43

WHO Headquarters, Geneva
A41

1966, July 1 **Photo.** ***Perf. 12½x13***
WHO Emblem in Blue and Yellow

157 A41 2r blk & pale rose 20 15
158 A41 3r blk & yel grn 25 20
159 A41 5r blk & lt bl 35 25

Issued to commemorate the inauguration of World Health Headquarters, Geneva.

Tree Planting
A42

UNESCO Emblem
A43

1966, July 22 **Engr.** ***Perf. 12½x13***

160 A42 1r brn, dl brn & brt grn 15 10
161 A42 3r org, dl brn & brt grn 25 20
162 A42 7r gray, dl brn & brt grn 50 30

Issued for Arbor Day.

1966 **Photogravure** ***Perf. 13***

163 A43 3r multi 30 30
164 A43 7r multi 50 30

Issued to commemorate the 20th anniversary of UNESCO (United Nations Educational, Scientific and Cultural Organization).

Wrestlers and Games' Emblem
A44

Designs (Games Emblem and): 3r, Stadium, Phnom Penh. 7r, Swordsmen. 10r, Indian club swingers. Bas-reliefs from Angkor Wat.

1966, Nov. 25 **Engraved** ***Perf. 13***

165 A44 3r vio bl 25 20
166 A44 4r green 30 20
167 A44 7r dk car rose 45 25
168 A44 10r dk brn 60 40

Issued to commemorate the GANEFO Games.

Indian Wild Boar
A45

Designs: 5r, Muntjac (vert.). 7r, Elephant.

Perf. 13x12½, 12½x13

1967, Feb. 20 **Engraved**

169 A45 3r brt bl, grn & blk 25 20
170 A45 5r multi 35 20
171 A45 7r multi 50 30

Nos. 152-153, 155-156 and 121 Overprinted in Red:
"ANNEE INTERNATIONALE DU TOURISME 1967"

1967, Apr. 27 **Engr.** ***Perf. 13***

172 A40 3r multi 30 30
173 A40 5r multi 40 30
174 A40 9r multi 60 55
175 A40 12r multi 70 70
176 A30 15r multi 85 85
Nos. 172-176 (5) 2.85 2.70

International Tourist Year, 1967.

No. 154 Overprinted in Red:
"MILLENAIRE / DE BANTEAY SREI / 967-1967"

1967, Apr. 27

177 A40 7r multi 65 35

Issued to commemorate the millennium of the Banteay Srei Temple at Angkor.

Royal Ballet Dancer
A46

Various Dancers

1967, June **Engraved** ***Perf. 13***

178 A46 1r orange 15 15
179 A46 3r Prus bl 30 25
180 A46 5r ultra 45 35
181 A46 7r car rose 60 55
182 A46 10r multi 90 70
Nos. 178-182 (5) 2.40 2.00

Issued to publicize the Cambodian Royal Ballet.

Nos. 128 and 70 Surcharged in Red

Journée Internationale
de l'Alphabétisation
8-9-67
6r

1967, Sept. 8 **Engraved**

183 A32 6r on 12r multi 50 40
184 A13 7r on 15r grn & ol gray 60 45

Issued for International Literacy Day, Sept. 8. The surcharge on No. 184 is adapted to fit the shape of the stamp.

Symbolic Water Cycle
A47

1967, Nov. 1 **Typo.** ***Perf. 13x14***

185 A47 1r blk, bl & org 15 15
186 A47 6r lil, lt bl & org 40 25
187 A47 10r dk bl, emer & org 65 40

Hydrological Decade (UNESCO), 1965-74.

Royal University, Kompong Cham
A48

Designs: 6r, Engineering School, Pnompenh. 9r, University Center, Sangkum Reastr Niyum.

1968, Mar. 1 Engraved *Perf. 13*

188 A48 4r vio bl & multi 30 30
189 A48 6r sl & multi 45 45
190 A48 9r Prus bl & multi 65 45

Vaccination and WHO Emblem
A49

Design: 7r, Malaria control and WHO emblem (man spraying DDT).

1968, July 8 Engraved *Perf. 13*

191 A49 3r ultra 20 18
192 A49 7r dp bl 45 30

Issued for the 20th anniversary of the World Health Organization.

Stadium, Mexico City
A50

Designs: 2r, Wrestling. 3r, Bicycling. 5r, Boxing (vert.). 7.50r, Torch bearer (vert.).

1968, Oct. 12 Engraved *Perf. 13*

193 A50 1r brn ol, grn & brn red 17 15
194 A50 2r brn, dk bl & rose cl 20 17
195 A50 3r plum, Prus bl & sep 30 25
196 A50 5r dk pur 38 30
197 A50 7.50r multi 42 38
Nos. 193-197 (5) 1.47 1.25

Issued to commemorate the 19th Olympic Games, Mexico City, Oct. 12–27.

Red Cross Team
A51

1968, Nov. 1 Engraved *Perf. 13*

198 A51 3r Prus bl, grn & red 30 15

Issued to honor the Cambodian Red Cross.

Prince Norodom Sihanouk
A52

Design: 8r, Soldiers wading through swamp.

1968, Nov. 9

199 A52 7r emer, ultra & pur 50 30
200 A52 8r bl, grn & dp brn 60 30

15th anniversary of independence.

Human Rights Flame and Prince Sihanouk
A53

1968, Dec. 10 Engraved *Perf. 13*

201 A53 3r blue 25 18
202 A53 5r brt plum 40 25
203 A53 7r multi 50 30

International Human Rights Year.

ILO Emblem
A54

1969, May 1 Engraved *Perf. 13*

204 A54 3r ultra 22 18
205 A54 6r dp car 35 25
206 A54 9r bl grn 50 30

Issued to commemorate the 50th anniversary of the International Labor Organization.

Globe, Red Cross, Crescent, Lion and Sun Emblems
A55

1969, May 8

207 A55 1r bl, red & yel 15 15
208 A55 3r sl grn, red & vio brn 22 20
209 A55 10r brt lil, red & brn 60 30

Issued to commemorate the 50th anniversary of the League of Red Cross Societies.

Papilio Oeacus—A56

Butterflies: 4r, Papilio agamenon. 8r, Danaus plexippus.

1969, Oct. 10 Engraved *Perf. 13*

210 A56 3r lil, blk & yel 60 25
211 A56 4r ver, blk & grn 80 35
212 A56 8r yel grn, dk brn & org 1.25 45

Map of Cambodia and Diesel Engine
A57

Designs: Various railroad stations and trains.

1969, Nov. 27 Engraved *Perf. 13*

213 A57 3r multi 55 20
214 A57 6r sl grn & lt brn 75 28
215 A57 8r black 1.00 38
216 A57 9r dk grn & bl 1.25 38

Issued to publicize the new rail link between Phnom Penh and Sihanoukville.

Tripletail
A58

Fish: 7r, Sleeper goby. 9r, Snakehead.

1970, Jan. 29 Photo. *Perf. 13*

217 A58 3r multi 40 12
218 A58 7r multi 65 27
219 A58 9r multi 90 35

Wat Maniratanaram
A59

Monasteries: 2r, Wat Tepthidaram (vert.). 6r, Wat Patumavati. 8r, Wat Unnalom.

1970, Apr. 29 Photo. *Perf. 13*

220 A59 2r multi 12 10
221 A59 3r multi 25 15
222 A59 6r multi 38 25
223 A59 8r multi 50 38

U.P.U. Headquarters and Monument, Bern—A60

1970, May 20

224 A60 1r grn & multi 5 5
225 A60 3r scar & multi 6 6
226 A60 4r dp bl & multi 10 8
227 A60 10r brn & multi 18 15

Issued to commemorate the inauguration of the new Universal Postal Union Headquarters in Bern.

Open Book and Satellite Earth Receiving Station
A61

1970, May 17 Photo. *Perf. 13*

228 A61 3r dk vio bl & multi 10 5
229 A61 4r sl grn & multi 12 8
230 A61 9r brn ol & multi 18 15

World Telecommunications Day.

Nelumbium Speciosum
A62

Flowers: 4r, Eichhornia crassipes. 13r, Nymphea lotus.

1970, Aug. 17 Photo. *Perf. 13*

231 A62 3r multi 8 8
a. Cambodian and Arabic 3's transposed 1.25
232 A62 4r multi 12 12
233 A62 13r multi 20 20

Elephant God, Bas-relief at Banteay Srei
A63

1970, Sept. 21 Engraved *Perf. 13*

234 A63 3r lil rose & dp grn 10 6
235 A63 4r bl grn, grn & lil rose 12 7
236 A63 7r bl grn, dk brn & grn 18 10

Issued for World Meteorological Day.

Khmer Republic

Globe, Rocket, Dove and U.N. Emblem—A64

1970, Nov. 9 Photo. *Perf. 12½x12*

237 A64 3r blk & multi 10 7
238 A64 5r brn red & multi 12 10
239 A64 10r dp vio & multi 18 10

25th anniversary of the United Nations.

Education Year Emblem
A65

1970, Nov. 9 Engr. *Perf. 13x12½*

240 A65 1r blue 5 5
241 A65 3r brt rose lil 10 6
242 A65 8r bl grn 20 10

Issued for International Education Year.

Chuon-Nath—A66

1971, Jan. 27 Photo. *Perf. 13*

243 A66 3r ol grn & multi 7 5
244 A66 8r pur & multi 12 8
245 A66 9r vio & multi 18 10

In memory of Chuon-Nath (1883–1969), Cambodian language expert.

Soldiers in Battle
A67

1971, March 18 Photo. *Perf. 13*

246 A67 1r gray & multi 5 5
247 A67 3r bis & multi 15 10
248 A67 10r bl & multi 50 25

National territorial defense.

U.N. Emblem, Men of Four Races
A68

1971, March 21

249	A68	3r bl & multi	6	5
250	A68	7r grn & multi	12	10
251	A68	8r brt rose & multi	18	12

International year against racial discrimination.

General Post Office, Phnom Penh
A69

1971, Apr. 19

252	A69	3r bl & multi	15	10
253	A69	9r lil rose & multi	45	20
254	A69	10r blk & multi	50	25

Symbolic Globe and Waves—A70

Design: 7r, 8r, ITU emblem and waves.

1971, May 17 Photo. *Perf. 13*

255	A70	3r grn, blk & bl	5	5
256	A70	4r yel & multi	13	5
257	A70	7r lil, blk & red	8	8
258	A70	8r sal pink, blk & red	15	10

3rd World Telecommunications Day.

Erythrina Indica
A71

Wild Flowers: 3r, Bauhinia variegata. 6r, Butea frondosa. 10r, Lagerstroemia floribunda (vert.).

1971, July 5 *Perf. 13x12½, 12½x13*

259	A71	2r lt ultra & multi	8	5
260	A71	3r yel grn & multi	10	8
261	A71	6r bl & multi	18	12
262	A71	10r brn & multi	30	25

Khmer Coat of Arms
A72

Flag and Square of the Republic
A73

1971, Oct. 9 Engraved *Perf. 13*

263	A72	3r brt grn & bis	8	5
264	A73	3r pur & multi	8	5
265	A73	4r dp cl & multi	8	5
266	A72	8r org & bis	10	7
267	A72	10r lt brn & bis	15	8
a.		Souvenir sheet of 3	1.00	1.00

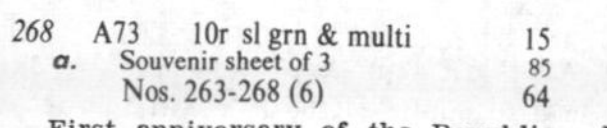

268	A73	10r sl grn & multi	15	8
a.		Souvenir sheet of 3	85	85
		Nos. 263-268 (6)	64	38

First anniversary of the Republic. No. 267a contains one each of Nos. 263, 266–267 with olive marginal inscriptions. Sold for 25r. No. 268a contains one each of Nos. 264–265 and 268 with purple marginal inscription. Sold for 20r. Size of sheets: 129x100mm.

UNICEF Emblem
A74

1971, Dec. 11

269	A74	3r blk brn	6	5
270	A74	5r ultra	10	6
271	A74	9r dk pur & brn red	18	10

25th anniversary of the United Nations International Children's Fund (UNICEF).

Book Year Emblem
A75

1972, Feb. 7

272	A75	3r bl, grn & vio	8	5
273	A75	8r vio, grn & bl	15	8
274	A75	9r emer & multi	18	10
a.		Souvenir sheet of 3	90	90

International Book Year 1972. No. 274a contains one each of Nos. 272–274 with emerald marginal inscription. Size: 159x99mm. Sold for 23r.

Lion of St. Mark
A76

Designs: 5r, Waves engulfing St. Mark's Basilica. 10r, Bridge of Sighs (vert.).

1972, Feb. 7 Engraved *Perf. 13*

275	A76	3r lil rose & org brn	8	5
276	A76	5r yel grn & org brn	15	7
277	A76	10r org brn, bl & yel grn	25	18
a.		Souvenir sheet of 3	85	85

UNESCO campaign to save Venice. No. 277a contains one each of Nos. 275–277. Yellow green marginal inscription. Size: 140x99mm. Sold for 23r.

U.N. Emblem
A77

1972, Mar. 28

278	A77	3r dp car	8	5
279	A77	6r dp bl	18	12
280	A77	9r dp org	20	17
a.		Souvenir sheet of 3	90	90

25th anniversary. United Nations Economic Commission for Asia and the Far East (ECAFE), No. 280a contains one each of Nos. 278–280. Deep blue marginal inscription. Size: 138x100mm. Sold for 23r.

Dancing Apsarases
A78

"UIT"
A79

1972, May 5 Engraved *Perf. 13*

281	A78	1r gldn brn	5	5
282	A78	3r violet	8	6
283	A78	7r rose cl	18	15
284	A78	8r ol brn	20	15
285	A78	9r bl grn	22	18
286	A78	10r ultra	25	20
287	A78	12r purple	28	25
288	A78	14r Prus bl	35	28
		Nos. 281-288 (8)	1.61	1.32

1972, May 17 Lithographed

Size: 35½x22mm.

289	A79	3r blk, yel & grnsh bl	10	5
290	A79	9r blk, dp lil rose & bl grn	25	13
291	A79	14r blk, brn & bl grn	35	25

4th World Telecommunications Day.

"Human Environment"
A80

1972, June 5 Engraved

292	A80	3r org, plum & grn	10	7
293	A80	12r brt grn & plum	40	25
294	A80	15r plum & brt grn	48	32
a.		Souv. sheet of 3	1.10	1.10

U.N. Conference on Human Environment, Stockholm, June 5–16. No. 294a contains one each of Nos. 292–294. Green marginal inscription. Size: 129x100mm. Sold for 35r.

Javan Rhinoceros
A81

1972, Aug. 1 Engraved *Perf. 13*

Multicolored

295	A81	3r *shown*	6	5
296	A81	4r *Serow*	6	5
297	A81	6r *Malayan sambar*	10	7
298	A81	7r *Banteng*	12	8
299	A81	8r *Water buffalo*	12	8
300	A81	10r *Gaur*	15	10
		Nos. 295-300 (6)	61	43

Nos. 263, 267, 134, 293, 294 Overprinted in Red

XXe JEUX OLYMPIQUES
MUNICH 1972

1972, Sept. 9 Engr. *Perf. 13*

301	A72	3r brt grn & bis	30	10
302	A72	10r org & bis	60	30
303	A34	12r multi	90	35
304	A80	12r brt grn & plum	90	35
305	A80	15r plum & brt grn	1.10	50
		Nos. 301-305 (5)	3.80	1.60

20th Olympic Games, Munich, Aug. 26–Sept. 11.

Raising Khmer Flag
A82

1972, Oct. 9 Photo. *Perf. 12½x13*

306	A82	3r multi	8	5
307	A82	5r brt rose & multi	16	6
308	A82	9r yel grn & multi	16	10

2nd anniversary of the establishment of the Khmer Republic.

Stupa and Crest
A83

Apsaras
A84

1973, May 12 Engraved *Perf. 13*

309	A83	3r ocher & multi	7	5
310	A83	12r yel grn & multi	15	18
311	A83	14r bl & multi	20	23
a.		Souvenir sheet of 3	90	90

New Constitution. No. 311a contains one each of Nos. 309–311 with brown marginal inscription. Size: 128½x99mm. Sold for 34r.

1973, July 23 Engraved *Perf. 13*

Sculptures from Angkor Wat: 8r, 10r, Devata (different).

312	A84	3r brn blk	7	5
313	A84	8r Prus grn	13	13
314	A84	10r ol bis	17	17
a.		Souvenir sheet of 3	75	75

No. 314a contains one each of Nos. 312–314 with black marginal inscription. Size: 130x100mm. Sold for 25r.

INTERPOL Emblem
A85

Marshal Lon Nol
A86

1973, Oct. 2 Engraved *Perf. 13*

315	A85	3r grn & multi	8	5
316	A85	7r red brn & multi	15	13
317	A85	10r ol & multi	20	20
a.		Souvenir sheet of 3	80	80

50th anniversary of the International Criminal Police Organization. No. 317a contains one each of Nos. 315–317; black marginal inscription. Size: 123x100mm. Sold for 30r.

1973, Oct. 9

318	A86	3r lt grn, blk & brn	12	7
319	A86	8r brn, ol & blk	25	15
320	A86	14r blk & brn	42	25
a.		Souvenir sheet of 3	1.10	1.10

Marshal Lon Nol, first president of the Republic. No. 320a contains stamps similar to Nos. 318–320 in changed colors; greenish black marginal inscription. Size: 129x99mm. Sold for 50r.

Nos. 248, 243 and 307 Surcharged with New Value, 2 Bars and Overprinted in Red or Silver: "4th ANNIVERSAIRE/DE LA REPUBLIQUE"

1974 Photo. *Perf. 13, 12½x13*

321	A67	10r multi (R)	5	5
322	A66	50r on 3r multi (S)	20	15
323	A82	100r on 5r multi (S)	45	30

4th anniversary of independence.

Copernicus and "Nerva"—A87

Designs: Copernicus, various spacecraft and events.

1974, Sept. 10 Litho. *Perf. 13*

Multicolored

324	A87	1r *shown*		
325	A87	5r *Mariner II*		
326	A87	10r *Apollo*		
327	A87	25r *Telstar*		
328	A87	50r *Space walk*		
329	A87	100r *Moon landing*		
330	A87	150r *Separation of spaceship and module*		
		Nos. 324-330, C32-C33 (9)	*19.00*	*19.00*

500th anniversary of the birth of Nicolaus Copernicus (1473–1543), Polish astronomer.

Carrier Pigeon and UPU Emblem

A88

Design: 60r, Sailing ship and UPU emblem.

1974, Nov. 2

331	A88	10r multi	5	5
332	A88	60r multi	25	15

Centenary of Universal Postal Union. A souvenir sheet containing one No. 332 exists. See No. C34.

Importation Prohibited

The U.S. Treasury Department prohibited the importation of stamps of Cambodia (Khmer Republic) as of Apr. 17, 1975.

SEMI-POSTAL STAMPS.

Nos. 8, 12, 14 and 15 Surcharged in Black

+60c
AIDE A L'ÉTUDIANT

1952, Oct. 20 *Perf. 13* Unwmkd.

B1	A3	1.10pi	+40c dp car & brt red	3.25	3.25
B2	A3	1.90pi	+60c ind & dp ultra	3.25	3.25
B3	A3	3pi	+1pi dp car & org brn	3.25	3.25
B4	A1	5pi	+2pi ind & pur	3.25	3.25

Preah Stupa

SP1

1957, Mar. 15 Engraved *Perf. 13*

B5	SP1	1.50r	+50c ind, ol & red	60	60
B6	SP1	6.50r	+1.50r red lil, ol & red	1.00	1.00
B7	SP1	8r	+2r bl, ol & red	1.50	1.50

Issued to commemorate the 2500th anniversary of the birth of Buddha. See Nos. 62–64.

Type of Regular Issue, 1959, with Red Typographed Surcharge

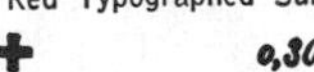

1959, Dec. 9

B8	A14	20c	+20c rose vio	6	6
B9	A14	50c	+30c bl	12	12
B10	A14	80c	+50c rose car	18	18

The surtax was for the Red Cross.

Nos. 107–108 Surcharged and Overprinted in Red: "1863–1963 CENTENAIRE DE LA CROIX ROUGE"

1963, Oct. 1 *Perf. 13* Unwmkd.

B11	A26	4r	+40c grn & dk brn	60	60
B12	A26	6r	+60c vio & ol bis	75	75

Centenary of International Red Cross.

Nos. 263, 267, 293–294, 134 Surcharged in Red

SECOURS AUX
VICTIMES DE GUERRE

1972, Nov. 15 Engr. *Perf. 13*

B13	A72	3r	+2r multi	20	20
B14	A72	10r	+6r multi	50	30
B15	A80	12r	+7r multi	60	35
B16	A34	12r	+7r multi	60	35
B17	A80	15r	+8r multi	1.00	65
			Nos. B13-B17 (5)	2.90	1.85

Surtax was for war victims. Surcharge arranged differently on Nos. B15–B17.

AIR POST STAMPS.

Kinnari

AP1

Engraved

1953, Apr. 16 *Perf. 13* Unwmkd.

C1	AP1	50c	dp grn	55	55
a.			Souvenir sheet of 4	50.00	50.00
C2	AP1	3pi	red brn	65	55
a.			Souvenir sheet of 3	50.00	50.00
C3	AP1	3.30pi	rose vio	90	65
C4	AP1	4pi	dk brn & dp bl	1.10	65
C5	AP1	5.10pi	brn, red & org	1.35	90
C6	AP1	6.50pi	dk brn & lil rose	1.35	1.50
a.			Souvenir sheet of 2	50.00	50.00
C7	AP1	9pi	lil rose & dp grn	2.00	2.00
C8	AP1	11.50pi	multi	3.75	3.00
C9	AP1	30pi	dk brn, bl grn & org	5.75	3.50
			Nos. C1-C9 (9)	17.40	13.30

No. C1a contains one each of the 50c, 3.30pi, 5.10pi and 30pi, and sold for 50pi. No. C2a contains one each of the 3pi, 4pi and 11.50pi, and sold for 25pi. No C6a contains one each of the 6.50pi and 9pi, and sold for 20pi. Marginal inscriptions in brown. Size: 129x100mm.

AP2

1957, Dec. 11

C10	AP2	50c maroon	12	8
C11	AP2	1r emerald	20	15
C12	AP2	4r ultra	90	55
C13	AP2	50r car rose	5.00	4.50
C14	AP2	100r grn, bl & car	8.00	6.00
a.		Souvenir sheet of 5	20.00	20.00
		Nos. C10-C14 (5)	14.22	11.28

No. C14a contains one each of Nos. C10–C14, and sold for 160r. Size: 159x93mm.

Independence Type of 1961

1961, Nov. 9 *Perf. 13x12½*

C15	A24	7r multi	75	40
C16	A24	30r grn, car & ultra	2.00	1.60
C17	A24	50r ind, grn & ol	3.50	2.50
a.		Souvenir sheet of 3	8.00	8.00

Issued to commemorate the tenth anniversary of Independence. No. C17a contains one each of Nos. C15–C17 with gold marginal inscription. Size: 150x85mm.

No. C15 Surcharged with New Value in Red and Overprinted in Black with Two Bars and: "INAUGURATION DU MONUMENT"

1962, Nov. 9

C18	A24	12r on 7r multi	1.10	90

Dedication of Independence Monument.

Hanuman, Monkey God

AP3

1964, Sept. 1 Engraved *Perf. 13*

C19	AP3	5r multi	50	27
C20	AP3	10r ol bis, lil rose & grn	70	35
C21	AP3	20r vio, bl & ol bis	1.10	55
C22	AP3	40r bl, ol bis & dk bl	2.50	1.10
C23	AP3	80r multi	4.00	3.25
		Nos. C19-C23 (5)	8.80	5.52

Nos. C19–C22 Surcharged in Red

1964, Oct.

C24	AP3	3r on 5r multi	40	32
C25	AP3	6r on 10r multi	55	50
C26	AP3	9r on 20r multi	80	70
C27	AP3	12r on 40r multi	1.20	1.00

18th Olympic Games, Tokyo, Oct. 10–25.

Certain unlisted issues of Cambodia, starting in 1972, are mentioned and briefly described in "For the Record" at the back of this volume.

Garuda, 12th Century, Angkor Thom

AP4

1973, Jan. 18 Engraved *Perf. 13*

C28	AP4	3r carmine	8	6
C29	AP4	30r vio bl	65	50
C30	AP4	50r dl pur	1.10	80
C31	AP4	100r dl grn	2.25	1.50

Copernicus Type of 1974

Designs: 200r, Copernicus and Skylab III. 250r, Copernicus, Concorde and solar eclipse.

1974, Sept. 10 Litho. *Perf. 13*

C32	A87	200r multi		
C33	A87	250r multi		

500th anniversary of the birth of Nicolaus Copernicus (1473–1543), Polish astronomer.
A souvenir sheet containing No. C32 is perf., size 110x82mm. A souvenir sheet containing No. C33 is imperf., size 83x111 mm.

UPU Type of 1974

Design: 700r, Rocket, globe and UPU emblem.

1974, Nov. 2

C34	A88	700r gold & multi	2.80	2.00

Centenary of Universal Postal Union. A souvenir sheet containing one No. C34 exists.

POSTAGE DUE STAMPS

Frieze, Angkor Wat

D1

D2

Typographed.

1957 *Perf. 13½* Unwmkd.

Denomination in Black.

J1	D1	10c ver & pale bl	12	12
J2	D1	50c ver & pale bl	18	18
J3	D1	1r ver & pale bl	22	22
J4	D1	3r ver & pale bl	33	33
J5	D1	5r ver & pale bl	60	60
		Nos. J1-J5 (5)	1.45	1.45

1974, Feb. 18 Engr. *Perf. 12½x13*

J6	D2	2r ocher	8	6
J7	D2	6r green	13	10
J8	D2	8r dp car	20	15
J9	D2	10r vio bl	27	20

CAMEROUN

(kăm′ēr·ōōn)

(Kamerun)

LOCATION — On the west coast of Africa, north of the equator.
GOVT.—Republic.
AREA—456,054 sq. mi.
POP.—9,060,000 (est. 1983).
CAPITAL—Yaounde.

Before World War I, Cameroun (Kamerun) was a German Protectorate. It was occupied during the war by Great Britain and France and in 1922 was mandated to these countries by the League of Nations. The French-mandated part became the independent State of Cameroun on January 1, 1960. The Southern Cameroons, a United Kingdom Trust Territory, joined this state to form the Federal Republic of Cameroun on October 1, 1961. The name was changed to United Republic of Cameroon on May 20, 1972.

Stamps of Southern Cameroons are listed under Cameroons in Volume 1.

100 Pfennig = 1 Mark
12 Pence = 1 Shilling
100 Centimes = 1 Franc

Issued under German Dominion.

A1

A2

Stamps of Germany, 1889-1900, Overprinted in Black.

1897 *Perf. 13½x14½* Unwmkd.

1	A1	3pf yel brn	15.00	22.50
a.		3pf red brn	27.50	50.00
b.		3pf dk brn	8.75	37.50
2	A1	5pf green	7.50	5.00
3	A2	10pf carmine	5.50	5.50
4	A2	20pf ultra	6.50	10.00
5	A2	25pf orange	30.00	50.00
6	A2	50pf red brn	25.00	42.50
		Nos. 1-6 (6)	89.50	135.50

Kaiser's Yacht "Hohenzollern"
A3 A4

Typographed.

1900 *Perf. 14* Unwmkd.

7	A3	3pf brown	1.75	1.75
8	A3	5pf green	25.00	1.00
9	A3	10pf carmine	60.00	1.50
10	A3	20pf ultra	40.00	2.50
11	A3	25pf org & blk, *yel*	1.75	*7.50*
12	A3	30pf org & blk, *sal*	2.25	*6.00*
13	A3	40pf lake & blk	2.25	*6.00*
14	A3	50pf pur & blk, *sal*	2.75	*7.50*
15	A3	80pf lake & blk, *rose*	3.50	*17.50*

Engraved.

Perf. 14½x14

16	A4	1m carmine	100.00	87.50
17	A4	2m blue	7.50	*87.50*
18	A4	3m blk vio	8.00	*150.00*
19	A4	5m sl & car	150.00	*650.00*
		Nos. 7-19 (13)	404.75	*1,026.25*

Wmk. 125

Typographed.

1905-18 Wmkd. Lozenges. (125)

20	A3	3pf brn ('18)	1.00	
21	A3	5pf grn ('06)	1.00	2.00
b.		Booklet pane of 6,(2 No. 21+4 No. 22)	77.50	
c.		Booklet pane of 5 + label	375.00	
22	A3	10pf carmine	1.00	1.00
b.		Booklet pane of 5 + label	550.00	
23	A3	20pf ultra ('14)	3.00	*200.00*
24	A4	1m car ('15)	3.00	
25	A4	5m sl & car ('13)	25.00	*5,000.*

The 3pf and 1m were not placed in use.

Issued under British Occupation.

Stamps of German Cameroun Surcharged — C. E. F. ½d.

Wmkd. Lozenges (125) (#54-56, 65)
Unwmkd. (Other Values.)

1915 *Perf. 14, 14½*

Blue Surcharge.

53	A3	½p on 3pf brn	11.50	17.50
54	A3	½p on 5pf grn	4.50	7.50
a.		Double surcharge	600.00	300.00
b.		blk surcharge	8.00	10.00
55	A3	1p on 10pf car	4.50	7.50
a.		"l" with thin serifs	16.00	20.00
b.		Double surcharge	300.00	300.00
c.		Black surcharge	35.00	50.00
d.		"C.E.F." omitted	*2,750.*	
e.		"1d" double	*2,500.*	

Black Surcharge.

56	A3	2p on 20pf ultra	5.00	*15.00*
57	A3	2½p on 25pf org & blk, *yel*	22.50	32.50
a.		Double surcharge	*3,500.*	
58	A3	3p on 30pf org & blk, *sal*	17.50	*32.50*
59	A3	4p on 40pf lake & blk	17.50	*32.50*
60	A3	6p on 50pf pur & blk, *sal*	17.50	*32.50*
61	A3	8p on 80pf lake & blk, *rose*	17.50	32.50

Surcharged — C. E. F. 1s.

62	A4	1sh on 1m car	300.00	*400.00*
a.		"S" inverted	1,000.	*1,500.*
63	A4	2sh on 2m bl	300.00	*400.00*
a.		"S" inverted	1,000.	*1,500.*
64	A4	3sh on 3m blk vio	300.00	*400.00*
a.		"S" inverted	1,000.	*1,500.*
b.		Double surcharge	*5,000.*	
65	A4	5sh on 5m sl & car	300.00	*400.00*
a.		"S" inverted	1,000.	*1,500.*
		Nos. 53-65 (13)	1,318.	*1,810.*

The letters "C. E. F." are the initials of "Cameroons Expeditionary Force."

Issued under French Occupation.

Stamps of Gabon, 1910, Overprinted

Corps Expéditionnaire
Franco-Anglais
CAMEROUN

1915 *Perf. 13½x14.* Unwmkd.

101	A10	10c red & car	25.00	12.00
102	A13	1c choc & org	75.00	25.00
103	A13	2c blk & choc	125.00	100.00
104	A13	4c vio & dp bl	125.00	100.00
105	A13	5c ol gray & grn	25.00	12.00
105A	A13	10c red & car	*16,000.*	*17,500.*
106	A13	20c ol brn & dk vio	125.00	120.00
107	A14	25c dp bl & choc	47.50	20.00
108	A14	30c gray blk & red	125.00	110.00
109	A14	35c dk vio & grn	37.50	20.00
a.		Double ovpt.	1,400.	1,400.
110	A14	40c choc & ultra	125.00	110.00
111	A14	45c car & vio	130.00	110.00
112	A14	50c bl grn & gray	130.00	120.00
113	A14	75c org & choc	190.00	120.00
114	A15	1fr dk brn & bis	175.00	130.00
115	A15	2fr car & brn	200.00	160.00
		Nos. 101-105, 106-115 (15)	1,660.	1,269.

The overprint is vertical, reading up, on Nos. 101–106, 114–115, and horizontal on Nos. 107–113.

Stamps of Middle Congo, Issue of 1907, Overprinted

Occupation
Francaise
du Cameroun

1916 Unwmkd.

116	A1	1c ol gray & brn	60.00	60.00
117	A1	2c vio & brn	77.50	65.00
118	A1	4c bl & brn	77.50	65.00
119	A1	5c dk grn & bl	21.00	19.00
120	A2	35c vio brn & bl	87.50	60.00
121	A2	45c vio & red	52.50	47.50

The overprint is horizontal on Nos. 116–119, and vertical, reading down, on Nos. 120–121.

Same Overprint
On Stamps of French Congo, 1900.
Wmkd. Branch of Thistle. (122)

122	A4	15c dl vio & ol grn	77.50	75.00
a.		Inverted overprint	100.00	100.00

Wmkd. Branch of Rose Tree. (123)

123	A5	20c yel grn & org	135.00	75.00
124	A5	30c car rose & org	70.00	47.50
125	A5	40c org brn & brt grn	52.50	47.50
126	A5	50c gray vio & lil	70.00	52.50
127	A5	75c red vio & org	70.00	47.50

Wmkd. Branch of Olive. (124)

128	A6	1fr gray lil & ol	95.00	60.00
129	A6	2fr car & brn	95.00	60.00
		Nos. 116-129 (14)	1,041.	781.50

The overprint is horizontal on No. 122; vertical, reading down or up, on Nos. 123–129.

Counterfeits exist of Nos. 101–129.

Stamps of Middle Congo, Issue of 1907 Overprinted

CAMEROUN
Occupation
Française

1916-17 Unwmkd.

130	A1	1c ol gray & brn	6	6
131	A1	2c vio & brn	8	6
132	A1	4c bl & brn	14	8
133	A1	5c dk grn & bl	22	10
134	A1	10c car & bl	75	42
135	A1	15c brn vio & rose ('17)	75	35
136	A1	20c brn & bl	42	25
137	A2	25c bl & grn	52	35
a.		Triple ovpt.	425.00	
138	A2	30c scar & grn	30	30
a.		Double ovpt.	300.00	
139	A2	35c vio brn & bl	52	40
140	A2	40c dl grn & brn	1.00	42
141	A2	45c vio & red	1.00	48
142	A2	50c bl grn & red	1.00	60
143	A2	75c brn & bl	1.10	60
144	A3	1fr dp grn & vio	95	60
145	A3	2fr vio & gray grn	5.75	3.50
146	A3	5fr bl & rose	7.00	4.25
		Nos. 130-146 (17)	21.56	12.82

Nos. 130 to 146 exist on ordinary paper and, with the exception of No. 132, on chalk surfaced paper. Nos. 137 to 146 are known with inverted "S" in "Francaise."

On Nos. 137 to 146 there is a space of 7mm. between "Cameroun" and "Occupation."

Provisional French Mandate.

Types of Middle Congo, 1907, Overprinted — CAMEROUN

1921

147	A1	1c ol grn & org	5	5
148	A1	2c brn & rose	5	5
149	A1	4c gray & lt grn	15	15
150	A1	5c dl red & org	15	15
a.		Double overprint	600.00	
151	A1	10c bl grn & lt grn	25	22
152	A1	15c bl & org	25	22
153	A1	20c red brn & ol	30	22
154	A2	25c sl & org	30	22
155	A2	30c rose & ver	35	22
156	A2	35c gray & ultra	42	40
157	A2	40c ol grn & org	35	30
158	A2	45c brn & rose	35	22
159	A2	50c bl & ultra	35	30
160	A2	75c red brn & lt grn	42	30
161	A3	1fr sl & org	1.25	1.00
162	A3	2fr ol grn & rose	4.25	3.50
163	A3	5fr dl red & gray	5.25	5.00
		Nos. 147-163 (17)	14.49	12.52

The 2c, 4c, 15c, 25c and 50c exist with overprint omitted.

Nos. 152, 162, 163, 158, 160 Surcharged with New Value and Bars.

1924-25

164	A1	25c on 15c bl & org ('25)	42	42
165	A3	25c on 2fr ol grn & rose	42	42
166	A3	25c on 5fr red & gray	55	55
a.		Pair, one without new value and bars		
167	A2	65c on 45c brn & rose ('25)	1.25	1.25
168	A2	85c on 75c red brn & lt grn ('25)	1.25	1.25
		Nos. 164-168 (5)	3.89	3.89

French Mandate

Herder and Cattle Crossing Sanaga River—A5

Tapping Rubber Tree
A6

Rope Suspension Bridge
A7

1925-38 Typo. *Perf. 14x13½*

170	A5	1c ol grn & brn vio, *lav*	5	5
171	A5	2c rose & grn, *grnsh*	5	5
172	A5	4c bl & blk	6	6
173	A5	5c org & red vio, *lav*	6	5
174	A5	10c red brn & org, *yel*	8	8
175	A5	15c sl grn & grn	10	10
176	A5	15c lil & red ('27)	52	40

Perf. 13½x14.

177	A6	20c ol brn & red brn	25	22
178	A6	20c grn ('26)	25	22
179	A6	20c brn red & ol brn ('27)	30	18
180	A6	25c lt grn & blk	52	22
181	A6	30c bluish grn & ver	25	22
182	A6	30c dk grn & grn ('27)	30	18
183	A6	35c brn & blk	25	22
184	A6	35c dl grn & grn ('38)	85	48
185	A6	40c org & vio	1.00	60
186	A6	45c dp rose & cer	25	22
187	A6	45c vio & org brn ('27)	1.50	1.10
188	A6	50c lt grn & cer	25	5
189	A6	55c ultra & car ('38)	1.00	80
190	A6	60c red vio & blk	25	22
191	A6	60c brn red ('26)	15	15
192	A6	65c ind & brn	15	15
193	A6	75c ind & dp bl	42	30
194	A6	75c org brn & red vio ('27)	42	25
195	A6	80c car & brn ('38)	85	60
196	A6	85c dp rose & bl	52	25
197	A6	90c brn red & cer ('27)	1.50	80

Perf. 14x13½.

198	A7	1fr ind & brn	65	42
199	A7	1fr dl bl ('26)	35	30
200	A7	1fr ol brn & red vio ('27)	60	35
201	A7	1fr grn & dk brn ('29)	1.00	70
202	A7	1.10fr rose red & dk brn ('28)	3.00	2.50
203	A7	1.25fr gray & dp bl ('33)	4.25	2.00
204	A7	1.50fr dl bl ('27)	55	30
205	A7	1.75fr brn & org ('33)	75	55
206	A7	1.75fr dk bl & lt bl ('38)	75	48
207	A7	2fr dl grn & brn org	1.25	52
208	A7	3fr ol brn & red vio ('27)	4.75	95
209	A7	5fr brn & blk, *bluish*	2.25	95
a.		Cliché of 2fr in plate of 5fr	1,300.	
210	A7	10fr org & vio ('27)	8.50	4.25
211	A7	20fr rose & ol grn ('27)	14.00	7.75
		Nos. 170-211 (42)	54.80	30.24

Common Design Types pictured in section at front of book.

No. 199 Surcharged with New Value and Bars in Red.

1926

212	A7	1.25fr on 1fr dl bl	35	35

Colonial Exposition Issue.
Common Design Types
Name of Country in Black.

1931 Engraved. *Perf. 12½.*

213	CD70	40c dp grn	2.25	1.90
214	CD71	50c violet	3.25	2.75
215	CD72	90c red org	3.25	2.75
216	CD73	1.50fr dl bl	4.00	3.25

Paris International Exposition Issue.
Common Design Types

1937 *Perf. 13.*

217	CD74	20c dp vio	1.25	1.25
218	CD75	30c dk grn	90	90
219	CD76	40c car rose	90	90
220	CD77	50c dk brn	90	90
221	CD78	90c red	1.25	1.25
222	CD79	1.50fr ultra	1.25	1.25
		Nos. 217-222 (6)	6.45	6.45

French Colonial Art Exhibition.
Common Design Type
Souvenir Sheet.

1937 *Imperf.*

222A	CD77	3fr org red & blk	3.50	3.50

Size: 118x99mm.

New York World's Fair Issue.
Common Design Type

1939 *Perf. 12½x12.*

223	CD82	1.25fr car lake	90	90
224	CD82	2.25fr ultra	90	90

Mandara Woman
A19

Falls on M'bam River near Banyo
A20

Elephants
A21

Man in Yaré
A22

1939-40 Engraved *Perf. 13*

225	A19	2c blk brn	5	5
226	A19	3c magenta	5	5
227	A19	4c dp ultra	6	6
228	A19	5c red brn	6	6
229	A19	10c dp bl grn	5	5
230	A19	15c rose red	18	6
231	A19	20c plum	18	6
232	A20	25c blk brn	30	30
233	A20	30c dk red	30	25
234	A20	40c ultra	42	40
235	A20	45c sl grn	1.50	1.10
236	A20	50c brn car	42	30
237	A20	60c pck bl	48	35
238	A20	70c plum	2.00	1.75
239	A21	80c Prus bl	1.50	1.25
240	A21	90c Prus bl	65	40
241	A21	1fr car rose	90	48
242	A21	1fr choc ('40)	90	42
243	A21	1.25fr car rose	3.00	2.00
244	A21	1.40fr org red	90	70
245	A21	1.50fr chocolate	70	52
246	A21	1.60fr blk brn	1.50	1.50
247	A21	1.75fr dk bl	65	48
248	A21	2fr dk grn	75	65
249	A21	2.25fr dk bl	65	42
250	A21	2.50fr brt red vio	90	65
251	A21	3fr dk vio	52	35
252	A22	5fr blk brn	65	42
253	A22	10fr brt red vio	1.25	1.00
254	A22	20fr dk grn	2.50	1.75
		Nos. 225-254 (30)	23.97	17.83

Stamps of 1925-40 Overprinted in Black or Orange "CAMEROUN FRANCAIS 27.8.40."

1940 *Perf. 14x13½, 13½x14, 13.*

255	A19	2c blk brn (O)	42	42
256	A19	3c magenta	42	42
257	A19	4c dp ultra (O)	52	52
258	A19	5c red brn	1.75	1.75
259	A19	10c dp bl grn (O)	42	42
260	A19	15c rose red	65	65
260A	A19	20c plum (O)	6.00	4.75
261	A20	25c blk brn	52	42
b.		Inverted ovpt.	175.00	175.00
261A	A20	30c dk red	5.75	4.75
262	A20	40c ultra	2.25	1.50
263	A20	45c sl grn	1.75	1.25
264	A6	50c lt grn & cer	90	42
a.		Inverted ovpt.	160.00	
265	A20	60c pck bl	2.25	1.50
266	A20	70c plum	80	80
267	A21	80c Prus bl (O)	2.25	1.90
268	A21	90c Prus bl (O)	52	52
269	A21	1.25fr car rose	80	52
270	A21	1.40fr org red	1.25	90
271	A21	1.50fr chocolate	52	52
272	A21	1.60fr blk brn (O)	90	52
273	A21	1.75fr dk bl (O)	1.25	1.25
274	A21	2.25fr dk bl (O)	65	65
275	A21	2.50fr brt red vio	65	65
276	A7	5fr brn & blk, *bluish*	10.50	7.75
277	A22	5fr blk brn	12.00	11.00
278	A7	10fr org & vio	15.00	11.00
278A	A22	10fr brt red vio	30.00	22.50
279	A7	20fr rose & ol grn	32.50	25.00
279A	A22	20fr dk grn	165.00	150.00

Same Overprint on Stamps of 1939.

Perf. 12½x12.

280	CD82	1.25fr car lake	2.25	2.25
281	CD82	2.25fr ultra	2.25	2.25
		Nos. 255-281 (31)	302.69	258.75

Issued to note Cameroun's affiliation with General de Gaulle's "Free France" movement.

Cattle Fording Sanaga River and Marshal Petain
A22a

1941 Engraved *Perf. 12½x12*

281A	A22a	1fr green	65	
281B	A22a	2.50fr dk bl	65	

Nos. 281A-281B were issued by the Vichy government, and were not placed on sale in Cameroun.

Lorraine Cross and Joan of Arc Shield
A23

1941 Photo. *Perf. 14x14½*

282	A23	5c brown	5	5
283	A23	10c dk bl	5	5
284	A23	25c emerald	6	6
285	A23	30c dp org	6	6
286	A23	40c dk sl grn	5	5
287	A23	80c red brn	12	5
288	A23	1fr dp red lil	5	5
289	A23	1.50fr brt red	10	5
290	A23	2fr gray blk	30	12
291	A23	2.50fr brt ultra	35	18
292	A23	4fr dl vio	65	52
293	A23	5fr bister	70	65
294	A23	10fr dp brn	75	65
295	A23	20fr dp grn	1.50	1.00
		Nos. 282-295 (14)	4.79	3.54

Eboue Issue
Common Design Type
Engraved.

1945 *Perf. 13.* Unwmkd.

296	CD91	2fr black	30	30
297	CD91	25fr Prus grn	1.00	1.00

Surcharged with New Values and Bars in Red, Carmine or Black.

1946 *Perf. 14x14½.*

297A	A23	50c on 5c brn (R)	25	25
298	A23	60c on 5c brn (R)	40	40
a.		Inverted surcharge	87.50	
299	A23	70c on 5c brn (R)	40	40
300	A23	1.20fr on 5c brn (C)	40	40
301	A23	2.40fr on 25c emer	30	30
302	A23	3fr on 25c emer	60	60
302A	A23	4.50fr on 25c emer	1.00	1.00
303	A23	15fr on 2.50fr brt ultra (C)	1.00	1.00
		Nos. 297A-303 (8)	4.35	4.35

Zebu and Herder
A25

Tikar Women
A26

Porters Carrying Bananas
A27

Bowman

A28

Lamido Horsemen

A29

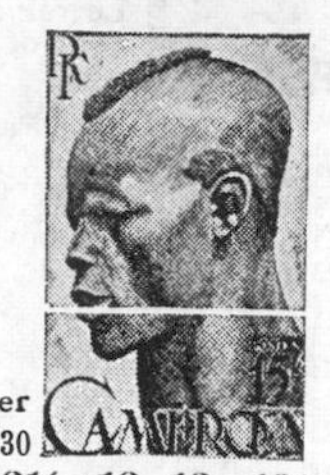

Farmer
A30

Perf. 12½x12, 12x12½.

1946		Engraved.		
304	A25	10c bl grn	5	5
305	A25	30c brn org	5	5
306	A25	40c brt ultra	5	5
307	A26	50c ol brn	5	5
308	A26	60c dp plum	6	6
309	A26	80c chnt brn	30	8
310	A27	1fr org red	6	6
311	A27	1.20fr dp grn	40	25
312	A27	1.50fr dk car	1.25	95
313	A28	2fr black	6	6
314	A28	3fr dk car	12	5
314A	A28	3.60fr red brn	65	48
315	A28	4fr dp bl	30	22
316	A29	5fr brn car	65	22
317	A29	6fr ultra	65	10
318	A29	10fr sl grn	70	12
319	A30	15fr grnsh bl	1.10	48
320	A30	20fr dk grn	1.40	35
321	A30	25fr black	1.90	70
		Nos. 304-321 (19)	9.80	4.38

Imperforates

Most Cameroun stamps from 1952 onward exist imperforate in issued and trial colors, and also in small presentation sheets in issued colors.

Military Medal Issue.

Common Design Type

Engraved and Typographed.

1952		*Perf. 13.*	Unwmkd.	
322	CD101	15fr multi	3.75	2.50

Issued to commemorate the centenary of the creation of the French Military Medal.

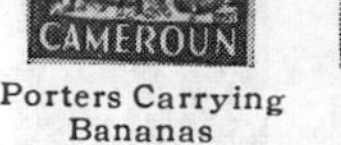

Porters Carrying Bananas

A32

Picking Coffee Beans

A33

1954		Engraved		
323	A32	8fr red vio, org brn & vio bl	52	25
324	A32	15fr brn red, yel & blk brn	90	42
325	A33	40fr blk brn, org brn & lil rose	90	42

FIDES Issue

Common Design Type

Designs: 5fr, Plowmen. 15fr, Wouri bridge. 20fr, Technical instruction. 25fr, Mobile medical station.

1956		*Perf. 13*	Unwmkd.	
326	CD103	5fr org brn & dk brn	52	40
327	CD103	15fr aqua, sl & blk	85	60
328	CD103	20fr grnsh bl & dp ultra	85	60
329	CD103	25fr dp ultra	1.25	95

Coffee Issue

Coffee—A35

1956		Engraved	*Perf. 13*	
330	A35	15fr car & brt red	75	40

Autonomous Government

Flag and Woman Holding Child

A36

1958				
331	A36	20fr multi	45	10

Issued to commemorate the anniversary of the installation of the first autonomous government of Cameroun.

Men Looking to the Sun

A37

1958				
332	A37	20fr sep & brn red	50	40

Issued to commemorate the tenth anniversary of the signing of the Universal Declaration of Human Rights.

Flower Issue

Common Design Type

Design: 20fr, *Randia malleifera.*

1959		Photogravure	*Perf. 12½x12*	
333	CD104	20fr dp grn, yel & rose	40	20

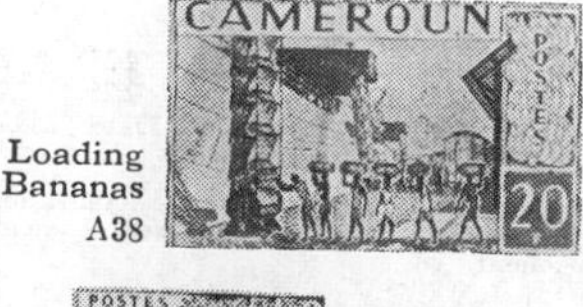

Loading Bananas

A38

Harvesting Bananas

A39

1959		Engraved.	*Perf. 13*	
334	A38	20fr dk grn & org	30	8
335	A39	25fr mar & sl grn	40	10

Independent State

Map and Flag of Cameroun

A40

Prime Minister Ahmadou Ahidjo

A41

Engraved.

1960		*Perf. 13*	Unwmkd.	
336	A40	20fr multi	40	10
337	A41	25fr blk, grn & pale lem	45	15

Declaration of independence, Jan. 1, 1960.

Uprooted Oak Emblem

A42

1960				
338	A42	30fr red brn, ultra & yel grn	60	55

Issued to publicize World Refugee Year, July 1, 1959–June 30, 1960.

C.C.T.A. Issue

Common Design Type

1960				
339	CD106	50fr dl cl & sl	1.00	60

U.N. Headquarters, New York, and Flag—A43

1961, May 20 ***Perf. 13***

Flag in Green, Red and Yellow

340	A43	15fr grn, dk bl & brn	40	35
341	A43	25fr dk bl & grn	45	35
342	A43	85fr red, dk bl & vio brn	1.35	1.20

Issued to commemorate Cameroun's admission to the United Nations, Sept. 20, 1960.

Federal Republic

Stamps of 1946-60 Surcharged in Red or Black:

REPUBLIQUE
FEDERALE
2 d

Two types of 2sh6p:

I. Large figures. "2/6" measures 8x3¾mm.

II. Small figures. "2/6" measures 6x2½mm.

Engraved

1961, Oct. 1		*Perf. 12x12½, 13*		
343	A27	½p on 1fr org red (#310)	25	25
344	A28	1p on 2fr blk (#313)	35	25
345	CD103	1½p on 5fr org brn & dk brn (#326)	35	25
346	A29	2p on 10fr sl grn (#318)	40	30
347	CD103	3p on 15fr aqua, sl & blk (#327)	45	35
348	A35	4p on 15fr car & brt red (Bk) (#330)	60	45
349	A38	6p on 20fr dk grn & org (#334)	75	50
350	A41	1sh on 25fr blk, grn & pale lem (#337)	1.50	1.25
351	A42	2sh6p on 30fr red brn, ultra & yel grn (#338) (I)	2.50	2.50
a.		Type II	6.50	6.50
		Nos. 343-351 (9)	7.15	6.10

Issued for use in the former United Kingdom Trust Territory of Southern Cameroons.

The "Republique Federale" overprint is in one line on Nos. 345, 347–349, in two vertical lines on No. 350. See Nos. C38–C40.

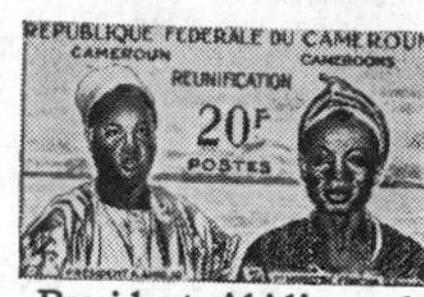

President Ahidjo and Prime Minister Foncha

A45

Engraved

1962, Jan. 1		*Perf. 13*	Unwmkd.	
352	A45	20fr vio & choc	7.50	6.50
353	A45	25fr dk grn & brn	12.50	10.00
354	A45	60fr car & dl grn	35.00	32.50

Same Surcharged for Use in Southern Cameroons

=
3 d

355	A45	3p on 20fr vio & choc	140.00	140.00
356	A45	6p on 25fr dk grn & brn	140.00	140.00
357	A45	2sh6p on 60fr car & dl grn	140.00	140.00

Issued to commemorate the reunification of the former French and British Sections of Cameroun. It is reported that Nos. 352–357 were withdrawn after a few days and destroyed.

Mustache Monkey

A46

Designs: 1fr, 4fr, Elephant, Ntem Falls. 1.50fr, 3fr, Buffon's kob, Dschang. 2fr, 5fr, Hippopotamus. 6fr, 15fr, Mustache monkey. 8fr, 30fr, Manatee, Lake Ossa. 10fr, 25fr, Buffalo, Batouri. 20fr, 40fr, Giraffes, Waza Reservation (vert.).

Engraved

1962		*Perf. 12*	Unwmkd.	
358	A46	50c brn, brt grn & bl	10	5
359	A46	1fr gray brn, bl grn & org	10	5
360	A46	1.50fr brn, lt grn & sl grn	10	5
361	A46	2fr dk gray, grnsh bl & grn	10	5

362	A46	3fr brn, org & lil rose	10	6
363	A46	4fr brn, yel grn & bl grn	12	6
364	A46	5fr gray brn, grn & sal	15	8
365	A46	6fr brn, yel & bl	18	10
366	A46	8fr dk bl, red & grn	25	15
367	A46	10fr ol blk, org & brt bl	25	8
368	A46	15fr brn, Prus bl & bl	30	8
369	A46	20fr brn & gray	40	12
370	A46	25fr red brn, grn & yel	60	30
371	A46	30fr blk, org & bl	85	40
372	A46	40fr dp cl, yel grn & blk	1.20	60
		Nos. 358-372 (15)	4.80	2.23

See also Nos. 396–397.

African and Malgasy Union Issue

Common Design Type

1962, Sept. 8 Photo. *Perf. 12½x12*

373	CD110	30fr multi	1.00	70

Issued to commemorate the first anniversary of the African and Malgasy Union.

Village and Map of Cameroun
A48

Designs: 20fr, 25fr, Sun rising over city. 50fr, Hands holding scroll.

1962, Oct. 1 Engr. *Perf. 13*

374	A48	9fr pur, ol & dk brn	20	20
375	A48	18fr grn, org brn & dk bl	35	25
376	A48	20fr lil rose, ol bis & ind	35	25
377	A48	25fr bl, red org & sep	50	30
378	A48	50fr dk red, sep & bl	1.00	75
		Nos. 374-378 (5)	2.40	1.75

Issued to commemorate the first anniversary of the reunification of Cameroun.

"School under the Trees"
A49

1962, Nov. 5 Photo. *Perf. 12x12½*

379	A49	20fr ver, emer & yel	40	20

Literacy and popular education campaign.

Telstar and Globe
A50

1963, Feb. 9 Engraved *Perf. 13*

Size: 36x22mm.

380	A50	1fr dk bl, ol & pur	5	5
381	A50	2fr dk bl, cl & grn	8	8
382	A50	3fr dk grn, ol & dp cl	12	12
383	A50	25fr grn, dp cl & brt bl	70	60

Issued to commemorate the first television connection of the United States and Europe through the Telstar satellite, July 11–12, 1962. See No. C45.

High Frequency Transmission Station, Mt. Bankolo
A51

"Yaoundé—Regional Center of Textbook Production"
A52

Design: 20fr, Station and wiring plan.

1963, May 18 Photo. *Perf. 12x12½*

384	A51	15fr multi	25	20
385	A51	20fr multi	35	25

Issued to publicize the high frequency telegraph connection Douala-Yaounde. See No. C46.

1963, Aug. 10 *Perf. 12½* Unwmkd.

386	A52	20fr emer, blk & red	35	20
387	A52	25fr org, blk & red	45	25
388	A52	100fr gold, blk & red	1.75	1.00

Issued to publicize the UNESCO regional center for the production of school books at Yaounde.

Pres. Ahmadou Ahidjo and Flag
A53

Design: 18fr, Flag and map of Cameroun.

1963, Oct. 1 *Perf. 12x12½*

Flag in Green, Red and Yellow

389	A53	9fr grn, bl & dk brn	15	15
390	A53	18fr grn, bl & lil	30	25
391	A53	20fr grn, blk & yel grn	35	30

Second anniversary of reunification.

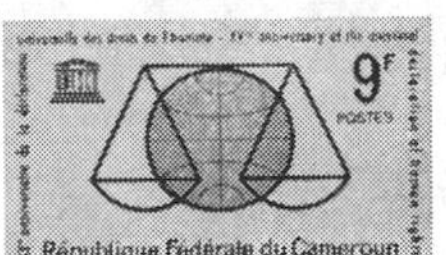

Scales, Globe, UNESCO Emblem
A54

1963, Dec. 10 Photo. *Perf. 12½x12*

392	A54	9fr ultra, blk & sal	15	12
393	A54	18fr brt yel grn, blk & rose red	30	20
394	A54	25fr rose red, blk & brt yel grn	40	30
395	A54	75fr yel, blk & ultra	1.35	75

Issued to commemorate the 15th anniversary of the Universal Declaration of Human Rights.

Animal Type of 1962

Design: 10fr, 25fr, Lion, Waza National Park, North Cameroun.

1964, June 20 Engr. *Perf. 13*

396	A46	10fr red brn, bis & grn	25	10
397	A46	25fr grn & bis	50	25

Soccer Game in Stadium
A55

Designs: 18fr, Pile of sports equipment. 30fr, Stadium (outside), flags and map of Africa.

1964, July 11 Engraved *Perf. 13*

398	A55	10fr grn, bl & red brn	20	10
399	A55	18fr car, grn & vio	30	20
400	A55	30fr blk, dk bl & org brn	50	30

Tropics Cup Games, Yaounde, July 11–18.

Europafrica Issue, 1964

Common Design Type and

Palace of Justice, Yaounde
A56

Design: 40fr, Emblems of Science, Agriculture, Industry and Education and two sunbursts.

1964, July 20 Photo. *Perf. 12x13*

401	A56	15fr multi	50	40
402	CD116	40fr multi	1.00	85

Issued to commemorate the first anniversary of the economic agreement between the European Economic Community and the African and Malgache Union.

Hurdling and Olympic Flame
A57

Design: 10fr, Runners (vert.).

1964, Oct. 10 Engraved *Perf. 13*

403	A57	9fr red, yel grn & blk	85	60
404	A57	10fr red, vio & ol gray	85	60

18th Olympic Games, Tokyo, Oct. 10–25. See Nos. C49, C49a.

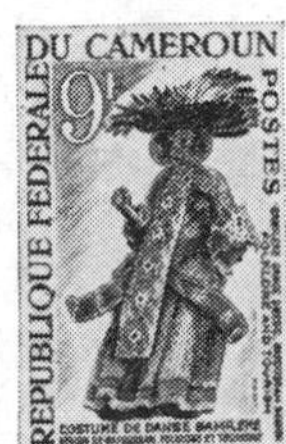

Bamileke Dance Dress
A58

Ntem Falls, Ebolowa Region
A59

Designs: 18fr, Dance mask, Bamenda region. 25fr, Fulani horseman, North Cameroun (horiz.).

1964 *Perf. 13* Unwmkd.

405	A58	9fr red, yel grn & bl	15	10
406	A58	18fr bl, red & brn	30	20
407	A59	20fr dk car, grn & ol	35	20
408	A58	25fr dk brn, org & car	45	30

See also No. C50.

Cooperation Issue

Common Design Type

1964, Nov. 7 Engraved

409	CD119	18fr dk bl, yel grn & dk brn	35	20
410	CD119	30fr red brn, bl grn & dk brn	60	25

Memorial Stone
A60

Diesel Train
A61

1965, Jan. 1 Engraved *Perf. 13*

411	A60	12fr bl, ind & grn	25	15

Typographed

Perf. 14x13

412	A61	20fr rose car, yel & grn	40	20

Issued to commemorate the laying of the first rail of the Mbanga-Kumba Railroad, March 28, 1964.

Red Cross Station and Ambulance
A62

Design: 50fr, Red Cross nurse and infant (vert.).

1965, May 8 Engraved *Perf. 13*

413	A62	25fr car, sl grn & ocher	45	25
414	A62	50fr gray, red & red brn	90	45

Issued for the Cameroun Red Cross.

Coins Inserted in Map of Cameroun, and Bankbook
A63

Savings Bank Building
A64

Design: 20fr, Bankbook and coins inserted in cacao pod-shaped bank (horiz.).

1965, June 10

Size: 22x37mm.

415 A63 9fr grn, red & org 20 20

Size: 48x27mm., 27x48mm

416 A64 15fr choc, ultra & grn 30 25
417 A63 20fr ocher, brt grn & brn 35 30

Federal Postal Savings Banks.

Soccer Players and Africa Cup
A65

Engraved

1965, June 26 *Perf. 13* **Unwmkd.**

418 A65 9fr car, brn & yel 20 15
419 A65 20fr car, sl bl & yel 35 25

Issued to honor the Cameroun Oryx Club, winner of the club champions' Africa Cup, February 1965.

Symbolic Map of Europe and Africa
A66

Designs: 40fr, Delegates around conference table.

1965, July 20 Photo. *Perf. 12x12½*

420 A66 5fr car, blk & lil 10 10
421 A66 40fr brn, buff, grn & ultra 70 50

Issued to commemorate the second anniversary of the economic agreement between the European Economic Community and the African and Malgache Union.

UPU Monument, Bern
A67

1965, July 26 Engraved *Perf. 13*

422 A67 30fr blk & red 55 40

Issued to commemorate the fifth anniversary of Cameroun's admission to the UPU.

ICY Emblem—A68

1965, Sept. 11 *Perf. 13* **Unwmkd.**

423 A68 10fr dk bl & car rose 25 25

Issued for the International Cooperation Year, 1964-65. See also No. C57.

Pres. Ahidjo and Government House
A69

Design: 9fr, 20fr, Pres. Ahidjo and Government House (vert.).

Perf. 12x12½, 12½x12

1965, Oct. 1 Photo. **Unwmkd.**

Portrait in Dark Brown; Building in Gray

424 A69 9fr dp red, brt pink, & brt bl 15 12
425 A69 18fr brt yel & blk 30 18
426 A69 20fr vio bl, brt bl & org 35 20
427 A69 25fr yel grn & blk 45 25

Reelection of Pres. Ahmadou Ahidjo.

National Tourist Office, Yaoundé
A70

Designs: 9fr, Pouss Musgum houses. 18fr, Great Calao's dance (North Cameroun). 20fr, Gate of Sultan's Palace, Foumban (vert.).

1965 Engraved *Perf. 13*

428 A70 9fr brn, rose red & grn 15 10
429 A70 18fr brt bl, brn & grn 30 25
430 A70 20fr bl, brn & choc 35 20
431 A70 25fr mar, emer & gray 35 20

See also No. C58.

Mountain Hotel, Buea—A71

Designs: 20fr, Hotel of the Deputies, Yaoundé. 35fr, Dschang Health Center.

1966

432 A71 9fr sl grn, rose cl & brn 20 15
433 A71 20fr brt bl, sl grn & blk 35 20
434 A71 35fr brn, sl grn & car 60 45
Nos. 432-434, C63-C69 (10) 8.55 4.75

Issue dates: Nos. 432-433, Apr. 6; No. 434, June 4.

Bas-relief, Foumban
A72

Designs: 18fr, Ekoi mask (vert.). 20fr, Mother and child, carving, Bamiléké (vert.). 25fr, Ceremonial stool, Bamoun.

1966, Apr. 15 **Unwmkd.**

435 A72 9fr red & blk 25 15
436 A72 18fr brt grn, org brn & choc 35 25
437 A72 20fr brt bl, red brn & pur 45 25
438 A72 25fr pur & dk brn 50 30

Issued to commemorate the International Negro Arts Festival, Dakar, Senegal, Apr. 1-24.

WHO Headquarters, Geneva
A73

1966, May 3 Photo. *Perf. 12½x13*

439 A73 50fr ultra, red brn & yel 85 50

Issued to commemorate the inauguration of the World Health Organization Headquarters, Geneva.

ITU Headquarters, Geneva
A74

1966, May 3 Photo. *Perf. 12½x13*

440 A74 50fr ultra & yel 85 50

Issued to publicize the International Telecommunication Union Headquarters, Geneva.

Phaeomeria Magnifica
A75

"6" and Men Dancing around U.N. Emblem
A76

Flowers: 18fr, Hibiscus (rose of China). 20fr, Mountain rose.

1966, May 20 *Perf. 12x12½*

Flowers in Natural Colors

Size: 22x36mm.

441 A75 9fr red brn 15 10
442 A75 18fr green 30 15
443 A75 20fr dk grn 35 15
Nos. 441-443, C70-C72 (6) 3.60 1.15

See also No. 469.

1966, Sept. 20 Engraved *Perf. 13*

Design: 50fr, U.N. General Assembly (horiz.).

444 A76 50fr ultra, grn & vio brn 85 20
445 A76 100fr red brn, grn & ultra 1.75 75

Issued to commemorate the 6th anniversary of Cameroun's admission to the United Nations.

Prime Minister's Residence, Buea
A77

Designs (Prime Minister's Residences): 18fr, at Yaoundé, front view. 20fr, at Yaoundé, side view. 25fr, at Buea, front view.

1966, Oct. 1 Photogravure

446 A77 9fr multi 15 12
447 A77 18fr multi 30 18
448 A77 20fr multi 35 15
449 A77 25fr multi 40 25

5th anniversary of re-unification.

Learning to Write and UNESCO Emblem
A78

Design: No. 451, Children's heads and UNICEF emblem.

1966, Nov. 24 Engraved *Perf. 13*

450 A78 50fr red lil, bl & brn 85 45
451 A78 50fr red lil, blk & brt bl 85 45

No. 450 commemorates the 20th anniversary of UNESCO (United Nations Educational, Scientific and Cultural Organization), No. 451 commemorates the 20th anniversary of UNICEF (United Nations International Children's Emergency Fund).

Independence Proclamation
A79

1967, Jan. 1 Engraved *Perf. 13*

452 A79 20fr grn, red & yel 45 35

7th anniversary of independence.

Map of Africa and Madagascar, Railroad Tracks and Symbols
A80

Design: 25fr, Map of Africa and Madagascar and train.

1967, Feb. 21 Photo. *Perf. 13*

453 A80 20fr multi 35 25
454 A80 25fr multi 45 25

Issued to commemorate the 5th Conference of African and Madagascan Railroad Technicians.

Lions Emblem and Forest—A81

Design: 100fr, Lions emblem and palms.

1967, Mar. 3

455 A81 50fr multi 85 50
456 A81 100fr multi 1.75 1.00

Lions International, 50th anniversary.

Jet and I.C.A.O. Emblem
A82

Dove and I.A.E.A. Emblem
A83

Perf. 13x12½, 12½x13

1967, March 15 **Photogravure**

457	A82	50fr ultra, lt bl, brn & gold	85	50
458	A83	50fr ultra & emer	85	50

Issued to honor United Nations agencies: No. 457, the International Civil Aviation Organization; No. 458, the International Atomic Energy Agency.

Rotary International Emblem
A84

1967, Apr. 17 **Photo.** ***Perf. 12½***

459	A84	25fr crim, vio bl & gold	45	25

Issued to commemorate the 10th anniversary of the Douala, Cameroun, branch of Rotary International.

Pomelo
A85

Bird-of-Paradise Flower
A86

Fruit: 2fr, Papaya. 3fr, Custard apple. 4fr, Breadfruit. 5fr, Coconut. 6fr, Mango. 8fr, Avocado. 10fr, Pineapple. 30fr, Bananas.

1967, May 10 **Photo.** ***Perf. 12x12½***

460	A85	1fr multi	7	5
461	A85	2fr multi	7	5
462	A85	3fr multi	12	5
463	A85	4fr multi	12	5
464	A85	5fr multi	15	6
465	A85	6fr multi	20	6
466	A85	8fr multi	25	10
467	A85	10fr multi	30	12
468	A85	30fr multi	70	30
		Nos. 460-468 (9)	1.98	84

1967, June 22 **Photo.** ***Perf. 12x12½***

Size: 22x36mm.

469	A86	15fr lt bl & multi	25	10

Sanaga Falls and ITY Emblem
A87

1967, Aug. 14 **Photo.** ***Perf. 13x12½***

470	A87	30fr multi	50	30

Issued for International Tourist Year 1967.

Art of Cameroun: Coconut Harvest
A88

Designs (Carved Bas-reliefs): 20fr, Lion hunt. 30fr, Women carrying baskets. 100fr, Carved chest.

1967, Sept. 22 ***Perf. 12½x13***

471	A88	10fr brn, bl & car	15	10
472	A88	20fr brn, yel & grn	35	20
473	A88	30fr emer, brn & car	50	20
474	A88	100fr red org, brn & emer	1.75	70

Coat of Arms
A89

1968, Jan. 1 **Litho.** ***Perf. 12½x13***

475	A89	30fr gold & multi	60	30

Spiny Lobster
A90

Designs (Fish and Crustaceans): 10fr, River crayfish. 15fr, Nile mouth-breeder. 20fr, Sole. 25fr, Common pike. 30fr, Crab. 40fr, Spadefish (vert.). 50fr, Shrimp (vert.). 55fr, African snakehead. 60fr, Threadfin.

1968, July 25 **Engraved** ***Perf. 13***

476	A90	5fr brn, vio bl & dl grn	10	5
477	A90	10fr ultra, brn ol & sl	15	6
478	A90	15fr sal, red lil & sep	20	10
479	A90	20fr red brn, dp bl & sep	25	12
480	A90	25fr lt brn, emer & sl	40	15
481	A90	30fr mag, dk bl & dk brn	50	15
482	A90	40fr sl bl & org	60	20
483	A90	50fr emer, gray & rose car	75	30
484	A90	55fr lt brn, Prus bl & dk brn	85	40
485	A90	60fr brn, bl grn & ind	1.00	50
		Nos. 476-485 (10)	4.80	2.03

Tanker, Refinery and Map of Area Served—A91

1968, July 30 **Photo.** ***Perf. 12½***

486	A91	30fr multi	45	20

Issued to commemorate the opening of the Port Gentil (Gabon) Refinery, June 12, 1968.

Human Rights Flame
A92

1968, Sept. 14 **Photo.** ***Perf. 12½x13***

487	A92	15fr bl & sal	25	12

Issued for International Human Rights Year. See also No. C110.

Pres. Ahmadou Ahidjo
A93

1969, Apr. 10 **Photo.** ***Perf. 12½x12***

488	A93	30fr car & multi	45	20

Chocolate Vat
A94

Designs: 30fr, Chocolate factory. 50fr, Candy making (vert.).

1969, Apr. 24 **Engraved** ***Perf. 13***

489	A94	15fr red brn, ind & choc	25	10
490	A94	30fr grn, blk & red brn	45	20
491	A94	50fr brn & multi	75	30

Cameroun chocolate industry.

Fertility Symbol, Abbia
A95

Diesel Train on Bridge
A96

Art and Folklore from Abbia: 10fr, Two toucans (horiz.). 15fr, Forest symbol. 30fr, Vulture attacking monkey (horiz.). 70fr, Oliphant player.

1969, May 30 **Engraved** ***Perf. 13***

492	A95	5fr ultra, Prus bl & brt rose lil	10	6
493	A95	10fr bl, ol gray & org	18	8
494	A95	15fr ultra, dk red & blk	20	15
495	A95	30fr brt bl, lem & grn	45	18
496	A95	70fr brt bl, dk grn & ver	1.10	50
		Nos. 492-496 (5)	2.03	97

Perf. 12½x13, 13x12½

1969, July 11 **Photogravure**

Design: 30fr, Kumba Railroad station (horiz.).

497	A96	30fr bl & multi	45	20
498	A96	50fr blk & multi	85	40

Opening of Mbanga-Kumba Railroad.

Development Bank Issue

Common Design Type

1969, Sept. 10 **Engraved** ***Perf. 13***

499	CD130	30fr vio bl, grn & ocher	50	20

Issued to commemorate the 5th anniversary of the African Development Bank.

ASECNA Issue

Common Design Type

1969, Dec. 12 **Engraved** ***Perf. 13***

500	CD132	100fr sl grn	1.50	90

Red Sage
A99

Design: 30fr, Passionflower.

1970, Mar. 24 **Photo.** ***Perf. 12x12½***

Size: 22x36½mm.

501	A99	15fr yel grn & multi	25	15
502	A99	30fr multi	40	15

See Nos. C140-C141.

U.P.U. Headquarters Issue

Common Design Type

1970, May 20 **Engraved** ***Perf. 13***

503	CD133	30fr bl, pur & grn	45	18
504	CD133	50fr gray, red & bl	75	25

Brewery
A100

Design: 30fr, Cellar with barrels.

1970, July 9 **Engraved** ***Perf. 13***

505	A100	15fr brn, gray & dk grn	20	15
506	A100	30fr bl grn, dk brn & brn red	40	15

Cameroun brewing industry.

Ozila Dancers A101 — Cameroun Doll A102

Design: 50fr, Ozila dancer and drummer.

1970, Oct. 19 Engraved *Perf. 13*

507 A101 30fr multi 40 15
508 A101 50fr red & multi 75 30

1970, Nov. 2

Designs: 15fr, Doll in short skirt. 30fr, Doll with basket on back.

509 A102 10fr car & multi 20 12
510 A102 15fr dk grn & multi 28 15
511 A102 30fr brn red & multi 50 20

Cogwheels and Grain A103

1970, Feb. 9 Photo. *Perf. 13*

512 A103 30fr multi 40 20

Europafrica Economic Conference.

Federal University, Yaoundé A104

1971, Jan. 19 Engraved

513 A104 50fr multi 60 20

Inauguration of Federal University at Yaoundé.

Presidents Ahidjo and Pompidou, Flags of Cameroun and France A105

1971, Feb. 9 Photogravure *Perf. 13*

514 A105 30fr multi 60 50

Visit of Georges Pompidou, President of France.

Young People, Globe, Map of Cameroun A106

1971, Feb. 11

515 A106 30fr bl & multi 35 13

Fifth National Youth Festival, Feb. 11.

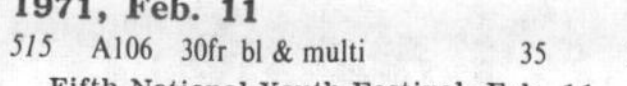

Gerbera Hybrida A107 — Men of Four Races—A108

Designs: 40fr, Opuntia polyantha (cactus). 50fr, Hemerocallis hybrida (lily).

1971, Mar. 14 Photogravure

516 A107 20fr multi 27 10
517 A107 40fr grn & multi 45 22
518 A107 50fr bl & multi 60 20

1971, March 21 *Perf. 13x12½*

Design: 30fr, Hands and globe.

519 A108 20fr grn & multi 25 7
520 A108 30fr ultra & multi 40 13

International year against racial discrimination.

Crowned Cranes at Waza Camp A109

Designs: 20fr, Canoe on Sanaga River. 30fr, Sanaga River.

1971, Apr. 9. Engraved *Perf. 13*

521 A109 10fr red, grn & blk 12 8
522 A109 20fr dk grn, brn & red 27 8
523 A109 30fr red, dk grn & brt bl 35 12

International Court, The Hague A110

1971, June 14 Engr. *Perf. 13*

524 A110 50fr ultra, org brn & sl grn 60 25

25th anniversary of the International Court in The Hague, Netherlands.

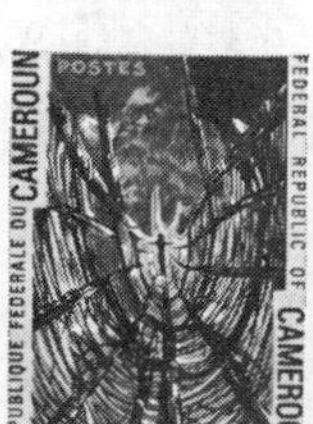

Liana Bridge A111 — Bamoun Horseman A113

Local Market A112

1971, Aug. 16 Photo. *Perf. 13*

525 A111 40fr multi 50 20
526 A112 45fr multi 55 20

1971, Sept. 18

African Art: 15fr, Animal fetish statuette.

527 A113 10fr brn & yel 12 5
528 A113 15fr dp brn & org yel 18 8

Communications Satellite and Globe A114

1971, Oct. 14 *Perf. 13x12½*

529 A114 40fr Prus bl, sl grn & org 45 18

Pan-African telecommunications system.

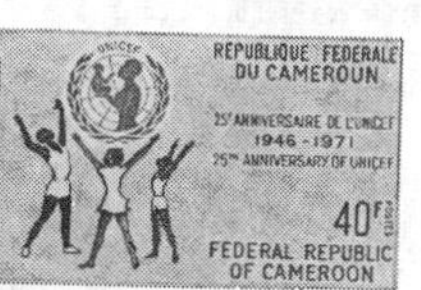

UNICEF Emblem A115

Design: 50fr, UNICEF emblem and grain (vert.).

1971, Dec. 11 Engraved *Perf. 13*

530 A115 40fr sl grn, bl grn & plum 60 30
531 A115 50fr dp bl, dk red & lt grn 85 40

25th anniversary of the United Nations International Children's Fund (UNICEF).

Houses from South-Central Region A116

Design: 15fr, Adamaua round houses.

1972, Jan. 15 Photo. *Perf. 13*

532 A116 10fr dk bl & multi 10 8
533 A116 15fr blk & multi 20 12

Giraffe A117

Designs: 5fr, Home industries. 10fr, Smith (horiz.). 15fr, Women carrying burdens.

Perf. 13x13½, 13½x13

1972, Feb. 18 Lithographed

534 A117 2fr multi 8 5
535 A117 5fr blk, org & red 12 5
536 A117 10fr multi 20 5
537 A117 15fr multi 25 10

Youth Day 1972.

Soccer Players and Field—A118

1972, Feb. 22 *Perf. 13½*

Designs: 20fr, African Soccer Cup (vert.). 45fr, Team captains shaking hands (vert.).

538 A118 20fr gray & multi 25 15
539 A118 40fr gray & multi 50 30
540 A118 45fr yel & multi 60 35

African Soccer Cup, Yaoundé, Feb. 23–Mar. 5.

Government Building, Yaoundé, and Laurel A119

1972, Apr. 6 Photo. *Perf. 12½x12*

541 A119 40fr multi 35 20

110th session of Inter-Parliamentary Council, Yaoundé, Apr. 1972.

"Fantasia," North Cameroun A120

Bororo Woman A121

Design: 40fr, Boat on Wouri River and Mt. Cameroun.

Perf. 13x12½, 12½x13

1972, Apr. 24

542 A120 15fr dk vio & multi 25 10
543 A121 20fr multi 25 10
544 A120 40fr multi 40 20

Chemical Apparatus A122

1972, May 15 Engraved *Perf. 13*

545 A122 40fr lil, red & grn 35 18

President Ahmadou Ahidjo Prize.

United Republic

Solanum Macranthum A123

Design: 45fr, Wax plant.

1972, July 20 Photo. *Perf. 13*

546 A123 40fr multi 40 18
547 A123 45fr yel & multi 42 20

Charaxes Ameliae
A124

Design: 45fr, Papilio tynderaeus.

1972, Aug. 20 Photo. *Perf. 13*

548 A124 40fr bl, dk bl & gold 50 25
549 A124 45fr lt grn, blk & gold 55 30

No. 468 Surcharged

=
40 F

1972, Aug. 30 Photo. *Perf. 12x12½*

550 A85 40fr on 30fr multi 40 20

Resurrection Lily
A125

Great Blue Touraco
A126

Flowers: 45fr, Candlestick cassia. 50fr, Amaryllis.

1972, Sept. 16 *Perf. 13*

551 A125 40fr lt grn & multi 40 20
552 A125 45fr multi 45 25
553 A125 50fr lt bl & multi 55 30

Perf. 12½x13, 13x12½

1972, Nov. 20 Lithographed

Design: 45fr, Red-faced lovebirds (horiz.).

554 A126 10fr yel & multi 10 7
555 A126 45fr yel & multi 45 20

Cotton (North)
A127

Designs: 10fr, Cacao (south central). 15fr, Logging (southeast and southern coast). 20fr, Coffee (west). 45fr, Tea (northwest and southwest).

1973, Mar. 26 Photo. *Perf. 12½x13*

556 A127 5fr blk & multi 6 6
557 A127 10fr blk & multi 8 8
558 A127 15fr blk & multi 13 10
559 A127 20fr blk & multi 18 15
560 A127 45fr blk & multi 45 20
Nos. 556-560 (5) 90 59

Third 5-Year Plan.

Flag and Map of Cameroun, Pres. Ahidjo and No. 331—A128

Design: 20fr, Proclamation of independence, Pres. Ahidjo and No. 336.

1973, May 20 Engr. *Perf. 13*

561 A128 10fr ultra & multi 10 10
562 A128 20fr multi 20 12

First anniversary of the United Republic of Cameroun. See Nos. C200–C201.

Bamoun Mask
A129

Dr. Hansen
A130

Designs: Various Bamoun masks.

1973, July 10 Engraved *Perf. 13*

563 A129 5fr grn, brn & blk 5 5
564 A129 10fr lil, brn & blk 10 6
565 A129 45fr red, brn & blk 35 20
566 A129 100fr ultra, brn & blk 80 50

1973, July 25 Engraved *Perf. 13*

567 A130 45fr multi 40 20

Centenary of the discovery by Dr. Armauer G. Hansen of the Hansen bacillus, the cause of leprosy.

No. 556 Surcharged with New Value, 2 Bars, and Overprinted in Ultramarine: "SECHERESSE/SOLIDARITE AFRICAINE"

1973, Aug. 16 Photo. *Perf. 12½x13*

568 A127 100fr on 5fr multi 80 60

African solidarity in drought emergency.

Dancers, South West Africa
A131

WMO Emblem
A132

Designs: Southwest African dances.

1973, Aug. 17 *Perf. 13*

569 A131 10fr multi 8 6
570 A131 25fr multi 20 15
571 A131 45fr multi 45 20

1973, Sept. 1 Engraved *Perf. 13*

572 A132 45fr grn & ultra 40 25

Centenary of international meteorological cooperation.

Garoua Party Headquarters—A133

1973, Sept. 1 Photogravure

573 A133 40fr multi 40 25

7th anniversary of Cameroun National Union.

African Postal Union Issue, 1973
Common Design Type

1973, Sept. 12 Engraved

574 CD137 100fr brt bl, bl & sl grn 90 60

11th anniversary of African and Malagasy Posts and Telecommunications Union (UAMPT).

Avocados
A135

1973, Sept. 20
Multicolored

575 A135 10fr *shown* 15 6
576 A135 20fr *Mangos* 25 13
577 A135 45fr *Plums* 45 20
578 A135 50fr *Custard apple* 65 25

Kirdi Village
A136

Views: 45fr, Mabas village. 50fr, Fishing village.

1973, Oct. 25 Engraved *Perf. 13*

579 A136 15fr blk, bis & grn 20 10
580 A136 45fr mag, brn & org 45 25
581 A136 50fr grn, blk & org 50 30

Handshake on Map of Africa
A137

1974, May 15 Engr. *Perf. 12½x13*

582 A137 40fr car & multi 35 18
583 A137 45fr ind & multi 40 20

10th anniversary of the Organization for African Unity.

Spinning Mill
A138

1974, May 25 Engr. *Perf. 13x12½*

584 A138 45fr multi 40 25

CICAM Industrial Complex.

Carved Panel from Bilinga
A139

Cameroun Art (Carvings): 40fr, Detail from Bubinga chair. 45fr, Detail Acajou Ngollon panel.

1974, May 30

585 A139 10fr brt grn & ocher 10 6
586 A139 40fr red & brn 35 20
587 A139 45fr bl & rose brn 40 25

Zebu
A140

1974, June 1 *Perf. 13½*

588 A140 40fr multi 35 23

North Cameroun cattle raising. See No. C210.

Laying Rail Section
A141

Designs: 5fr, Map showing line Yaoundé to Ngaoundéré (vert.). 40fr, Welding rail joint (vert.). 100fr, Train on Djerem River Bridge.

Perf. 12½x13, 13x12½

1974, June 10 Engraved

589 A141 5fr multi 8 5
590 A141 20fr multi 18 10
591 A141 40fr multi 35 20
592 A141 100fr multi 85 65

Opening of Yaoundé-Ngaoundéré railroad line.

No. 466 Surcharged

1974, June 1 Photo. *Perf. 12x12½*

593 A85 40fr on 8fr multi 40 20

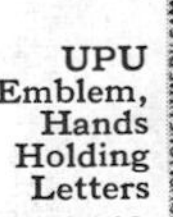

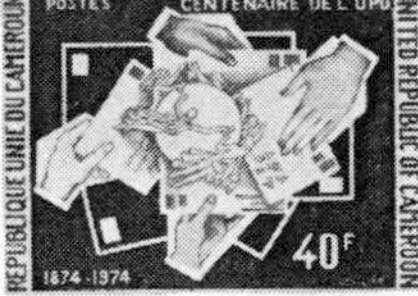

UPU Emblem, Hands Holding Letters
A142

1974, Oct. 8 Engraved *Perf. 13*

594 A142 40fr multi 35 20

Centenary of Universal Postal Union. See Nos. C218–C219.

Presidents and Flags of Cameroun, CAR, Congo, Gabon and Meeting Center—A143

1974, Dec. 8 Photogravure *Perf. 13*

595 A143 40fr gold & multi 35 20

10th anniversary of Central African Customs and Economic Union (Union Douanière et Economique de l'Afrique Centrale, UDEAC). See also No. C223.

═ 100F

No. 589 Surcharged in Violet Blue

10 DECEMBRE 1974

1974, Dec. 10 Engr. *Perf. 12½x13*

596 A141 100fr on 5fr multi 80 70

Virgin of Autun, 15th Century Sculpture
A144

Design: 45fr, Virgin and Child, by Luis de Morales (c. 1509–1586).

1974, Dec. 20 Photogravure *Perf. 13*

597 A144 40fr gold & multi 35 25
598 A144 45fr gold & multi 40 30

Christmas 1974.

Cockscomb
A145

1975, Mar. 10 Photo. *Perf. 13*
Multicolored

599 A145 5fr *shown* 8 5
600 A145 40fr *Costus spectabilis* 35 20
601 A145 45fr *Mussaenda erythrophylla* 38 25

Tropical plants.

Fishing by Night—A146

Design: 45fr, Fishing by day.

1975, Apr. 1 Engr. *Perf. 13*

602 A146 40fr bl & multi 35 20
603 A146 45fr bl & multi 40 25

Afo Akom Statue and Chief's Stool
A147

1975, Apr. 1 Photogravure

604 A147 40fr multi 30 20
605 A147 45fr multi 35 20
606 A147 200fr multi 1.60 1.10

Tree Fungus
A148

Design: 40fr, Chrysalis.

1975, Apr. 14

607 A148 15fr brn & multi 15 10
608 A148 40fr blk & multi 40 23

Ministry of Posts and Telecommunications
A149

1975, July 21 Engraved *Perf. 13*

609 A149 40fr brn, grn & Prus bl 35 25
610 A149 45fr Prus bl, brn & grn 40 30

Presbyterian Church, Elat
A150

Designs: No. 612, Foumban Mosque. 45fr, Catholic Church, Ngaoundere.

1975, Aug. 20 Engr. *Perf. 13*

611 A150 40fr multi 32 20
612 A150 40fr multi 32 20
613 A150 45fr multi 38 25

Plowing
A151

Design: No. 615, Corn harvest (vert.).

Perf. 13x12½, 12½x13
1975, Dec. 15 Photogravure

614 A151 40fr dp grn & multi 32 20
615 A151 40fr dp grn & multi 32 20

Green revolution.

Zamengoe Satellite Monitoring Station—A152

Design: 100fr, Radar (vert.).

1976, May 20 Litho. *Perf. 13*

616 A152 40fr multi 30 25
617 A152 100fr multi 85 60

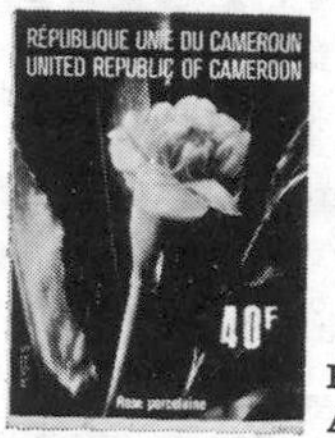

Porcelain Rose
A153

Design: 50fr, Flower of North Cameroun.

1976, July 20 Litho. *Perf. 12½*

618 A153 40fr multi 30 20
619 A153 50fr multi 40 25

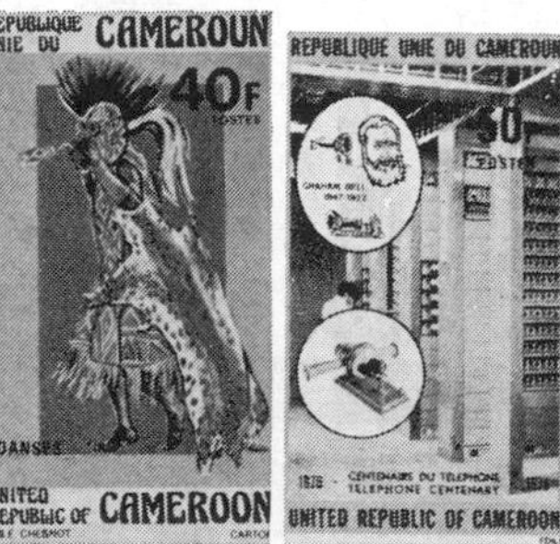

Leopard Dance
A154

Telephone Exchange
A155

1976, Sept. 15 Litho. *Perf. 12*

620 A154 40fr gray & multi 32 25

See Nos. C233–C234.

1976, Oct. 5 *Perf. 13*

621 A155 50fr multi 45 30

Centenary of first telephone call by Alexander Graham Bell, Mar. 10, 1876.

Young Men Building House—A156

Design: 45fr, Young women working in field.

1976, Oct. 10 Litho. *Perf. 12*

622 A156 40fr multi 32 25
623 A156 45fr multi 40 25

10th National Youth Day.

Konrad Adenauer, Cologne Cathedral
A157

1976, Oct. 20

624 A157 100fr multi 85 60

Konrad Adenauer (1876–1967), German chancellor, birth centenary.

Party Headquarters, Douala—A158

Design: No. 626, Party Headquarters, Yaoundé.

1976, Dec. 28 Litho. *Perf*

625 A158 50fr org & multi 40 30
626 A158 50fr bl & multi 40 30

10th anniversary of the Cameroun National Union.

Bamoun Copper Pipe
A159

Ostrich
A160

1977, Feb. 4 Litho. *Perf. 12½*

627 A159 50fr multi 40 30

2nd World Black and African Festival, Lagos, Nigeria, Jan. 15–Feb. 12. See No. C239.

1977, Mar. 20 Litho. *Perf. 12*

Design: 50fr, Crowned cranes.

628 A160 30fr multi 25 15
629 A160 50fr multi 40 25

Cameroun No. 609 and Switzerland No. 3L1—A161

1977, June 5 Litho. *Perf. 12*

630 A161 50fr multi 40 30

Jufilex Philatelic Exhibition, Bern, Switzerland. See Nos. C252–C253.

No. 617 Overprinted in French and English in Red:
"To the Welfare of the / families of martyrs and / freedom fighters of Palestine."

1977, Aug. 22 Litho. *Perf. 13*

635 A152 100fr multi 85 60

Palestinian fighters and their families.

Chairman Mao and Great Wall
A164

1977, Sept. 9 Engr. *Perf. 13*

636 A164 100fr ol & brn 85 60

Mao Tse-tung (1893–1976), Chinese communist leader, first death anniversary.

Nativity, by Albrecht Altdorfer
A165

Design: 50fr, Madonna of the Grand Duke, by Raphael.

1977, Dec. 15 Litho. *Perf. 12½x12*

637	A165	30fr multi	25	20
638	A165	50fr multi	40	30

Christmas 1977. See Nos. C264–C265.

Gazelle and Rotary Emblem
A166

Pres. Ahidjo, Flag and Map of Cameroun
A167

1978, Feb. 11 Litho. *Perf. 12*

639	A166	50fr org & multi	40	30

Rotary Club of Yaoundé, 20th anniversary.

1978, Apr. 3 Litho. *Perf. 12½*

640	A167	50fr multi	40	20

New flag of Cameroun. See No. C266.

Cardioglossa Escalerae
A168

Design: 60fr, Cardioglossa elegans.

1978, Apr. 5

641	A168	50fr multi	40	25
642	A168	60fr multi	50	35

See No. C267.

Jules Verne and "From Earth to Moon"
A169

1978, Oct. 10 Litho. *Perf. 12*

643	A169	250fr multi	2.50	2.00

Jules Verne (1828–1905), science fiction writer, birth sesquicentennial. See No. C276.

Hypolimnas Salmacis Drury—A170

Butterflies: 25fr, Euxanthe trajanus ward. 30fr, Euphaedra cyparissa cramer.

1978, Oct. 15

644	A170	20fr multi	20	15
645	A170	25fr multi	25	20
646	A170	30fr multi	30	20

Men Planting Seedlings
A171

1978, Oct. 30 *Perf. 12½*

647	A171	10fr multi	10	8
648	A171	15fr multi	15	10

Green barrier against the desert.

Carved Bamun Drum
A172

Designs: 60fr, String instrument (Gueguerou; horiz.).

1978, Nov. 20 Litho. *Perf. 12½*

649	A172	50fr multi	50	30
650	A172	60fr multi	60	40

See No. C277.

Pres. Ahidjo, Giscard D'Estaing, Flags of Cameroun and France—A173

1979, Feb. 8 Photo. *Perf. 13*

651	A173	60fr multi	60	40

Visit of Pres. Valery Giscard D'Estaing of France to Cameroun.

Human Rights Emblem, Globe, Scroll and African—A174

1979, Feb. 11 Litho. *Perf. 12x12½*

652	A174	5fr multi	5	5

Universal Declaration of Human Rights, 30th anniversary (in 1978). See No. C278. See No. 803.

Boy and Girl Greeting Sun
A175

1979, Aug. 15 Litho. *Perf. 12*

653	A175	50fr multi	50	30

International Year of the Child.

Rhinoceros
A176

Protected Animals: No. 655, Giraffe (vert.). No. 656, Gorilla. No. 657, Leopard. No. 658, Elephant (vert.).

1979, Sept. 20 *Perf. 12½*

654	A176	50fr multi	50	30
655	A176	60fr multi	60	40
656	A176	60fr multi	60	40
657	A176	100fr multi	1.00	60
658	A176	100fr multi	1.00	60
		Nos. 654-658 (5)	3.70	2.30

Eugene Jamot, Map of Cameroun, Tsetse Fly—A177

1979, Nov. 5 Engr. *Perf. 13*

659	A177	50fr multi	50	30

Eugene Jamot (1879-1937), discoverer of sleeping sickness cure.

Annunciation, by Fra Filippo Lippi
A178

Paintings; 50fr, Rest During the Flight to Egypt, C. 1620. No. 622, Flight into Egypt, by Jan Joest. No. 663, Nativity, by Joest. 100fr, Nativity, by Botticelli.

1979, Dec. 6 Litho. *Perf. 12½×12*

660	A178	10fr multi	10	6
661	A178	50fr multi	50	30
662	A178	60fr multi	60	40
663	A178	60fr multi	60	40
664	A178	100fr multi	1.00	60
		Nos. 660-664 (5)	2.80	1.76

Christmas 1979. Nos. 662-663 printed se-tenant.

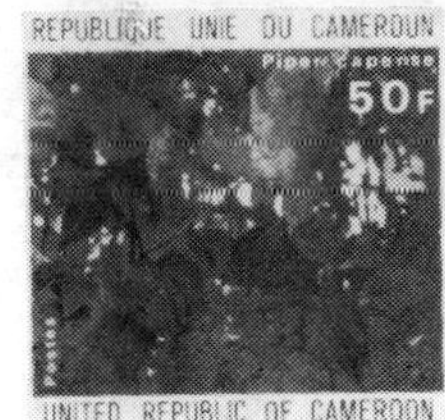

Pepper Capense—A179

Medicinal Plants: 60fr, Bracken fern.

1979, Dec. 15 Litho. *Perf. 12½*

665	A179	50fr multi	50	30
666	A179	60fr multi	60	40

Pres. Ahidjo, Cameroun Map, Arms and No. 331—A180

1980, Feb. 12 Litho. *Perf. 12½*

667	A180	50fr multi	50	30

Independence, 20th anniversary.

Congress Building, Bafoussam—A181

1980, Feb. 12

668	A181	50fr multi	50	30

Cameroun National Union, 3rd Ordinary Congress, Bafoussam, Feb. 12-17.

Rotary Emblem, Map of Cameroun—A182

Rotary International, 75th Anniversary: No. 670, Anniversary emblem.

1980, Mar. 15 **Litho.** ***Perf. 12½***

669	A182	200fr multi	2.00	1.20
670	A182	200fr multi	2.00	1.20
a.		Souvenir sheet of 2	4.00	2.50

No. 670a contains Nos. 669-670; multicolored margin shows emblems of various Rotary clubs. Size: 175x140mm.

Voacanga Medicinal Beans—A183

1980, Dec. 3 **Litho.** ***Perf. 12½***

671	A183	50fr *shown*	50	30
672	A183	60fr *Voacanga tree*, vert.	60	40
673	A183	100fr *Voacanga flower*, vert.	1.00	60

Violet Mellowstone—A184

1980, Dec. 5

674	A184	50fr *shown*	50	30
675	A184	60fr *Patula*	60	40
676	A184	100fr *Cashmere bouquet*	1.00	60

Occupation of Mecca by Mohammed, 1350th Anniversary—A185

1980, Dec. 9

677	A185	50fr multi	50	30

African Slender-snouted Crocodile (Endangered Species)—A186

1980, Dec. 24

678	A186	200fr *shown*	2.00	1.20
679	A186	300fr *Buffon's antelope*, vert.	3.00	1.80

Bororo Girls and Roumsiki Peaks—A187

1980, Dec. 29

680	A187	50fr *shown*	50	30
681	A187	60fr *Dschang tourist center*	60	40

Banana Tree—A188

1981, Feb. 5

682	A188	50fr *shown*	50	30
683	A188	60fr *Cattle*, vert	60	40

Girl on Crutches—A189

1981, Feb. 20 **Litho.** ***Perf. 12½***

684	A189	60fr shown	60	40
685	A189	150fr Boy in motorized wheelchair	1.50	1.00

International Year of the Disabled.

Air Terminal, Douala Airport—A190

1981, Apr. 4 **Litho.** ***Perf. 12½***

686	A190	100fr shown	1.00	65
687	A190	200fr Boeing 747	2.00	1.40
688	A190	300fr Douala Intl. Airport	3.00	2.00

Cameroun Airlines, 10th anniv.

Pres. Ahidjo Presenting Trophy to Canon Soccer Team—A191

1981, Apr. 20

689	A191	60fr shown	60	40
690	A191	60fr Union team captain	60	40

1979 African Soccer Cup champions.

Scaly Anteater A192

Designs: Endangered species.

1981, July 20 **Litho.** ***Perf. 12½***

691	A192	50fr Moutourou	50	32
692	A192	50fr Tortoise	50	32
693	A192	100fr shown	1.00	65

Prince Charles and Lady Diana, St. Paul's Cathedral—A193

1981, July 29 **Litho.** ***Perf. 12½***

694	A193	500fr shown	5.00	3.25
695	A193	500fr Couple, royal coach	5.00	3.25
a.		Souvenir sheet of 2	10.00	6.50

Royal wedding. No. 695a contains Nos. 694-695; multicolored margin shows flowers. Size: 145x94mm.

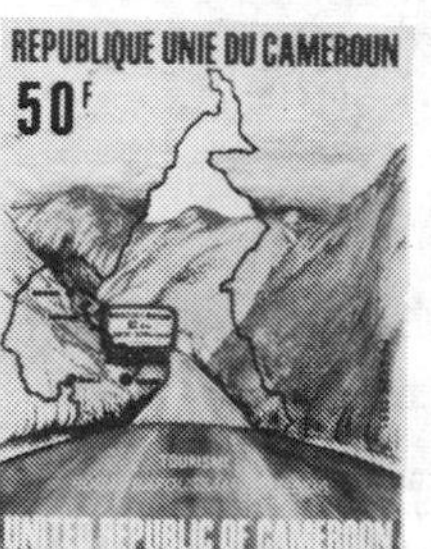

Bafoussam-Bamenda Highway A194

1981, Sept. 10 **Litho.** ***Perf. 12½***

696	A194	50fr multi	50	32

Freighter Cam Iroko (Cameroun Shipping Line)—A195

1981, Sept. 25

697	A195	60fr multi	60	40

20th Anniv. of Reunification—A196

1981, Oct. 10 ***Perf. 12½x13***

698	A196	50fr multi	50	32

Medicinal Plants—A197

1981, Dec. 31 **Litho.** ***Perf. 12½***

699	A197	60fr Voacanga thouarsii	60	40
700	A197	70fr Cassia alata	70	45

Easter 1982—A198

Paintings: 100fr, Christ in the Garden of Olives, by Delacroix. 200fr, Descent from the Cross, by Giotto. 250fr, Pieta in the Countryside, by Bellini.

1982, Apr. 10 **Litho.** ***Perf. 13***

701	A198	100fr multi	1.00	65
702	A198	200fr multi	2.00	1.20
703	A198	250fr multi	2.50	1.55

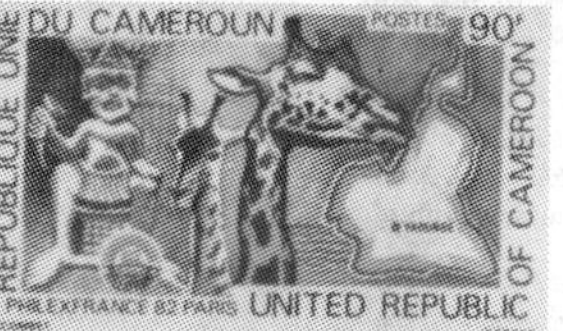

PHILEXFRANCE '82 Stamp Exhibition, Paris, June 11-21—A199

1982, Apr. 25 ***Perf. 12***

704	A199	90fr multi	90	60

Snakeskin Handbag—A200

1982, Apr. 30 ***Perf. 12½***

705	A200	60fr shown	60	40
706	A200	70fr Clay water jug	70	50

10th Anniv. of Republic—A201

1982, May 20 ***Perf. 13***

707	A201	500fr multi	5.00	3.00

Town Hall, Douala—A202

1982, June 15 **Litho.** ***Perf. 12½***

708	A202	40fr shown	40	30
709	A202	60fr Yaounde	60	40

See Nos. 730-731, 757-758, 790-791.

1982 World Cup—A203

1982, July 10 ***Perf. 13***

710	A203	100fr Natl. team	1.00	65
711	A203	200fr Semi-finalists	2.00	1.20
712	A203	300fr Players, vert.	3.00	1.90
713	A203	400fr Natl. team 2nd lineup	4.00	2.50
a.		Souvenir sheet of 2	8.00	5.00

No. 713a contains 2 Nos. 713; multicolored margin. Size: 217x95mm.

Partridge—A204

1982 ***Perf. 12½x13***

714	A204	10fr shown	10	6
715	A204	15fr Turtle dove	15	10
716	A204	20fr Swallow	20	12
717	A204	200fr Bongo antelope	2.00	1.20
718	A204	300fr Black colobus	3.00	1.90
		Nos. 714-718 (5)	5.45	3.38

Issue dates: 200fr, 300fr, July 20; others Aug. 10.

Scouting Year—A205

1982, Sept. 30 **Litho.** ***Perf. 13x12½***

719	A205	200fr Campfire	2.00	1.20
720	A205	400fr Baden-Powell	4.00	2.50

25th Anniv. of the Presbyterian Church in Cameroun—A206

1982, Oct. 30 ***Perf. 13x12½, 12½x13***

721	A206	45fr Buea Chapel	45	45
722	A206	60fr Nyasoso Chapel, vert.	60	40

ITU Plenipotentiaries Conference, Nairobi, Sept.—A207

1982, Oct. 5 **Litho.** ***Perf. 12½x13***

723	A207	70fr multi	70	45

Italy's Victory in 1982 World Cup—A208

1982, Nov. ***Perf. 13***

724	A208	500fr Cup, globe	5.00	3.00
725	A208	1000fr	10.00	6.00

30th Anniv. of Customs Cooperation Council—A209

1983, Jan. 10 ***Perf. 12½x13***

726	A209	250fr Emblem	2.50	1.50
727	A209	250fr Headquarters, Brussels	2.50	1.50

2nd Yaounde Medical Conference—A210

1983, Jan. 23 **Litho.** ***Perf. 13***

728	A210	60fr grn & multi	60	30
729	A210	70fr brn & multi	70	35

City Hall Type of 1982

1983, Feb. 25 **Litho.** ***Perf. 12½***

730	A202	60fr Bafoussam	60	40
731	A202	70fr Garoua	70	45

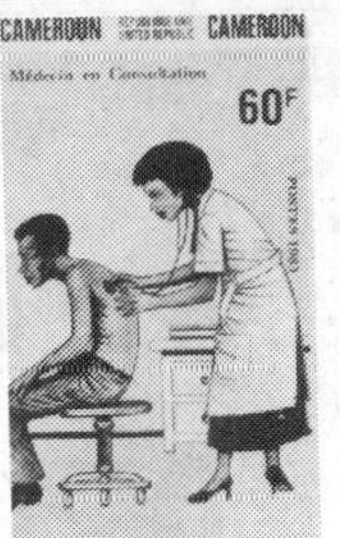

Homage to Women—A211

1983, Apr. 25 **Litho.** ***Perf. 12½***

733	A211	60fr Nurse	60	30
734	A211	70fr Lawyer	70	35

11th Anniv. of Independence—A212

Flag and Pres. Paul Biya.

1983, May 18 **Litho.** ***Perf. 13***

735	A212	60fr dk grn & multi	60	40
736	A212	70fr dk bl & multi	70	45

25th Anniv. of Intl. Maritime Org.—A213

1983, May 23 ***Perf. 13x12½***

737	A213	500fr multi	5.00	3.00

Eagle—A214

1983, June 15 **Litho.** **perf. 12½x13**

738	A214	25fr shown	25	15
739	A214	30fr Sparrowhawk	30	20
740	A214	50fr Purple heron	50	30

Pearl Mask, by Wery-Nwen-Nto, 1899—A215

1983, July 25 **Litho.** ***Perf. 12***

741	A215	60fr shown	60	40
742	A215	70fr Basket with lid	70	45

World Communications Year—A216

1983, Aug. 20 **Litho.** ***Perf. 12***

743	A216	90fr Mobile Post Office (horiz.)	45	30
744	A216	150fr Telegraph Operator	75	50
745	A216	250fr Tom-Tom	1.25	80

Endangered Species—A217

1983, Sept. 22 ***Perf. 12***

746	A217	200fr Civet Cat	1.00	65
747	A217	200fr Gorilla (vert.)	1.00	65
748	A217	350fr Cobaya (vert.)	1.75	1.25

Lake Tizon—A218

1983, Nov. 25 **Litho.** ***Perf. 13***

749	A218	60fr shown	30	22
750	A218	70fr Mt. Cameroon	35	25

Human Rights Declaration, 35th Anniv—A219

1983, Dec. 20 **Litho.** ***Perf. 12½x13***

751	A219	60fr multi	30	22
752	A219	70fr multi	35	25

Christmas 1983—A220

Designs: 60fr, Christmas tree. 200fr, Stained-glass window, Yaounde Cathedral. No. 755, Rest during Flight into Egypt, by Philipp Otto Runge. No. 756, Angel of the Annunciation. 60fr, 200fr, No. 756 vert.

1983, Dec. 20 **Litho.** ***Perf. 12½***
753 A220 60fr multi 30 22
754 A220 200fr multi 1.00 65
755 A220 500fr multi 2.50 1.60
756 A220 500fr multi 2.50 1.60
a. Souvenir sheet of 3 6.00 4.00

No. 756a contains Nos. 754-756. Size: 140x90mm.

City Hall Type of 1982

1984, Apr. 20 **Litho.** ***Perf. 12½***
757 A202 60fr Bamenda 30 20
758 A202 70fr Mbalmayo 35 22

Catholic Church, Zoetele—A221

1984, July 25 **Litho.** ***Perf. 13***
759 A221 60fr shown 30 22
760 A221 70fr Protestant Church, Yaounde 35 25

Endangered Species—A222

1984, Aug. 15
761 A222 250fr Wild pig 1.25 80
762 A222 250fr Deer 1.25 80

1984, Oct. 10 **Litho.** ***Perf. 13½***
763 A222 60fr Nightingale 28 20
764 A222 60fr Vultures 28 20

Bamenda Farming Fair—A223

1984, Dec. 10 **Litho.** ***Perf. 13***
765 A223 60fr Corn 28 20
766 A223 70fr Cattle 32 22
767 A223 300fr Potatoes 1.35 90

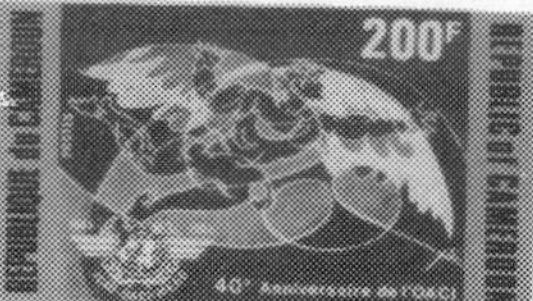

International Civil Aviation Organization, 40th Anniv.—A224

1984, Dec. 20 **Litho.** ***Perf. 12½***
768 A224 200fr Icarus 90 60
769 A224 200fr ICAO emblem, vert. 90 60
770 A224 300fr Boeing 747 1.35 90
771 A224 300fr Solar Princess painting 1.35 90

Olymphilex '85, Lausanne—A225

1985, Apr. 5 **Photo.** ***Perf. 13***
772 A225 150fr Wrestlers, exhibition emblem 65 65

Domestic Musical Instruments—A226

1985, Apr. 23 ***Perf. 13½***
773 A226 60fr Balafons (xylophone) 25 25
774 A226 70fr Guitar 28 28
775 A226 100fr Flute 42 42

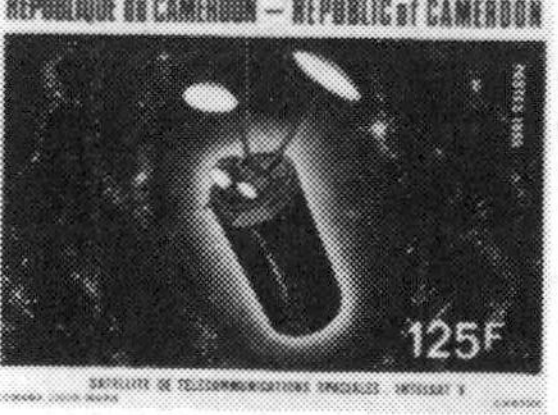

INTELSAT Org., 20th Anniv.—A227

1985, May 8 ***Perf. 13***
776 A227 125fr Intelsat V 52 52
777 A227 200fr Intelcam, Yaounde 85 85

New York Headquarters—A228

UN, 40th Anniv.

1985, May 30
778 A228 250fr multi 1.10 1.10
779 A228 500fr multi 2.25 2.25

Pres. Mitterand, Biya—A229

1985, June 20
780 A229 60fr multi 28 28
781 A229 70fr multi 32 32

Visit of Pres. Mitterand of France.

UNICEF—A230

UN Infant Survival Campaign—A231

1985, July 15
782 A230 60fr multi 28 28
783 A231 300fr multi 1.40 1.40

Visit of Pope John Paul II, Aug. 10-14—A232

1985, Aug. 9 ***Perf. 13x12½***
784 A232 60fr Pope, papal arms 28 2
785 A232 70fr Pope, crosier 32 3

Size: 60x40mm.
786 A232 300fr Pres. Biya, John Paul II 1.40 1.4
a. Souvenir sheet of 3 2.00 2.0

No. 786a contains Nos. 784-786; margin contains inscriptions. Size: 138x100mm.

Landscapes—A233

1985, July 25 **Litho.** ***Perf. 12½***
787 A233 60fr Lake Barumbi, Kumba 25 25
788 A233 70fr Bonando Pygmy Village, Doume 28 28
789 A233 150fr Cameroun River 62 62

City Hall Type of 1982

1985, July 30
790 A202 60fr Ngaoundere 25 25
791 A202 60fr D'Ebolowa 25 25

Wildlife A234

Wood Sculptures A235

1985, Aug. 20 ***Perf. 13½***
792 A234 125fr Porcupine 52 52
793 A234 200fr Squirrel 85 85
794 A234 350fr Hedgehog 1.40 1.40

1985, Sept. 15
795 A235 60fr Mask 25 25
796 A235 70fr Mask, diff. 28 28
797 A235 100fr Wood bas-relief, horiz. 42 42

Birds—A236

1985, Nov. 10

798	A236	140fr	Toucans	58	58
799	A236	150fr	Rooster	62	62
800	A236	200fr	Red-throated bee-eater	85	85

American Peace Corps in Cameroun, 25th Anniv.—A237

1986, Jan. 1 **Litho.** ***Perf. 12½***

801	A237	70fr	multi	38	38
802	A237	100fr	multi	55	55

Stamps of 1979-1982 Redrawn.

1986, Mar. ***Perf. 13, 13½***

803	A174	5fr	multi	5	5
804	A204	10fr	multi	6	6

Nos. 803-804 inscribed "Republic of Cameroon" instead of "United Republic of Cameroon."

Easter A238

Insects A239

Paintings: 210fr, Head of the Virgin, by Pierre-Paul Prud'Hon (1758-1823). 350fr, The Stoning of St. Steven, by Van Scorel (1495-1562).

1986, Apr. 15 ***Perf. 13½***

805	A238	210fr	multi	1.15	1.15
806	A238	350fr	multi	1.90	1.90

1986, Apr. 20

807	A239	70fr	Honeybee	38	38
808	A239	70fr	Dragonfly	38	38
809	A239	100fr	Grasshopper	55	55

Nos. 808-809 horiz.

Flags, Conference Center—A240

1986, Apr. 25 **Litho.** ***Perf. 13***

810	A240	100fr	Map, vert.	55	55
811	A240	175fr	shown	95	95

Conference of Ministers of the Economic Commission for Africa, Apr. 9-29.

Statues—A241

1986, July 5 **Litho.** ***Perf. 13½***

812	A241	70fr	Bronze earth mother	40	40
813	A241	100fr	Wood funerary figure	55	55
814	A241	130fr	Wood equestrian figure	70	70

Queen Elizabeth II, 60th Birthday—A242

1986, July 15 **Litho.** ***Perf. 13***

815	A242	100fr	Elizabeth	55	55
816	A242	175fr	Elizabeth, Pres. Biya	95	95
817	A242	210fr	Elizabeth, diff.	1.15	1.15

Natl. Democratic Party, 1st Anniv.—A243

1986, July 25 ***Perf. 12½***

818	A243	70fr	Party headquarters, Bamenda	38	38
819	A243	70fr	Pres. Biya, vert.	38	38
820	A243	100fr	Presidential address, vert.	55	55

Kwem Mask Dancers of the Northeast—A244

1986, Aug. 1 ***Perf. 13½***

821	A244	100fr	multi	55	55
822	A244	130fr	multi	70	70

Endangered Species—A245

1986, Aug. 20

823	A245	300fr	Varanus niloticus	1.65	1.65
824	A245	300fr	Panthera pardus	1.65	1.65

Intl. Peace Year—A246

Designs: 175fr, 200fr, Desmond Tutu, South Africa, Nobel Peace Prize winner. 250fr, UN and IPY emblems.

1986, Sept. 25 **Litho.** ***Perf. 13½***

825	A246	175fr	multi	95	95
826	A246	200fr	multi	1.10	1.10
827	A246	250fr	multi	1.40	1.40

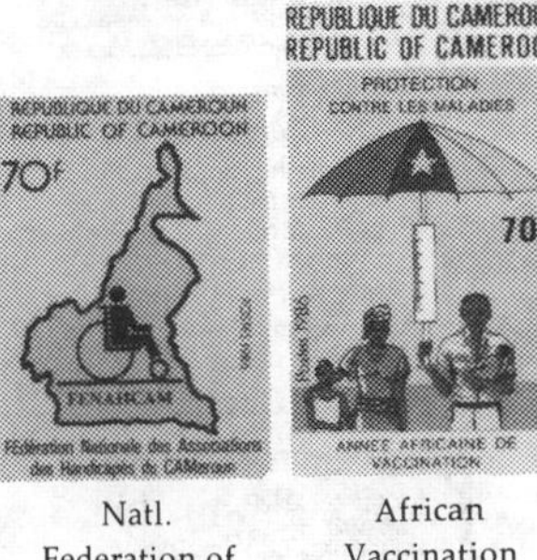

Natl. Federation of Associations for the Handicapped A247

African Vaccination Year A248

1986, Oct. 30 **Litho.** ***Perf. 13½***

828	A247	70fr	multi	40	40

1986, Nov. 9

829	A248	70fr	Family under umbrella	40	40
830	A248	100fr	Child immunization	55	55

Arbor Day A249

1986, Dec. 20 **Litho.** ***Perf. 13½***

831	A249	70fr	Afforestation map	40	40
832	A249	100fr	Hands, seedling	55	55

Agricultural Development A250

1986, Dec. 24

833	A250	70fr	ONCPB seminar	40	40
834	A250	70fr	Coconut farming, Dibombari	40	40
835	A250	200fr	Pineapple farm	1.10	1.10

SEMI-POSTAL STAMPS.

Curie Issue

Common Design Type

1938 *Perf. 13* **Unwmkd.**

B1	CD80	1.75fr +50c brt ultra	4.50	4.00

French Revolution Issue

Common Design Type

1939 **Photogravure.**

Name and Value Typo. in Black.

B2	CD83	45(c) +25(c) grn	5.00	5.00
B3	CD83	70(c) +30(c) brn	5.00	5.00
B4	CD83	90(c) +35(c) red org	5.00	5.00
B5	CD83	1.25fr +1fr rose pink	5.25	5.25
B6	CD83	2.25fr +2fr bl	6.25	6.25
		Nos. B2-B6 (5)	26.50	26.50

Stamps of 1925–33 Surcharged in Black

OEUVRES DE GUERRE

+ 2 frs.

1940 *Perf. 14x13½.*

B7	A7	1.25fr +2fr gray & dp bl	7.50	7.50
B8	A7	1.75fr +3fr brn & org	7.50	7.50
B9	A7	2fr +5fr dl grn & brn org	7.50	7.50

The surtax was used for war relief work.

Regular Stamps of 1939 Surcharged in Black **+ 5 Frs. SPITFIRE**

1940 *Perf. 13.*

B10	A20	25c +5fr blk brn	75.00	70.00
B11	A20	45c +5fr sl grn	75.00	70.00
B12	A20	60c +5fr pck bl	90.00	82.50
B13	A20	70c +5fr plum	90.00	82.50

The surtax was used to purchase Spitfire planes for the Free French army.

Common Design Type and

Military Doctor
SP2

Cameroun Militiaman
SP4

1941 **Photogravure** *Perf. 13½*

B13A	SP2	1fr +1fr red	75
B13B	CD86	1.50fr +3fr mar	75
B13C	SP4	2.50fr +1fr dk bl	75

Nos. B13A–B13C were issued by the Vichy government, and were not placed on sale in Cameroun.

Nos. 281A–281B were surcharged "OEUVRES COLONIALES" and surtax (including change of denomination of the 2.50fr to 50c). These were issued in 1944 by the Vichy government, and not placed on sale in Cameroun.

New York World's Fair Stamps, 1939 Surcharged in Black

+ SPITFIRE 10fr. Général de GAULLE

1941 *Perf. 12½x12.*

B14	CD82	1.25fr +10fr car lake	62.50	55.00
B15	CD82	2.25fr +10fr ultra	62.50	55.00

New York World's Fair Stamps, 1939, Surcharged in Black or Blue **+ 10 Frs. AMBULANCE LAQUINTINIE**

1941

B16	CD82	1.25fr +10fr car lake (Bl)	12.00	9.50
B17	CD82	2.25fr +10fr ultra (Bk)	12.00	9.50

The surtax was used to purchase ambulances for the Free French army.

Regular Stamps of 1933–39 Surcharged in Black **Valmy + 100 frs.**

1943

Perf. 14x13½, 13, 12½x12.

B21	A7	1.25fr +100 gray & dp bl	6.00	6.00
B22	A21	1.25fr +100fr car rose	6.00	6.00
B23	CD82	1.25fr +100fr car lake	6.00	6.00
B24	A21	1.50fr +100fr choc	6.00	6.00
B25	CD82	2.25fr +100fr ultra	6.00	6.00
		Nos. B21-B25 (5)	30.00	30.00

Red Cross Issue

Common Design Type

1944 Photogravure. *Perf. 14½x14.*

B28	CD90	5fr +20fr rose	1.25	1.10

The surtax was for the French Red Cross and national relief.

Tropical Medicine Issue

Common Design Type

1950 **Engraved** *Perf. 13*

B29	CD100	10fr +2fr dk bl grn & dk grn	2.50	2.50

The surtax was for charitable work.

Independent State

Map and Flag
SP7

Engraved

1961, Mar. 25 *Perf. 13* **Unwmkd.**

B30	SP7	20fr +5fr grn, car & yel	65	65
B31	SP7	25fr +10fr multi	75	75
B32	SP7	30fr +15fr car, yel & grn	1.10	1.10

The surtax was for the Red Cross.

Federal Republic

Map of Cameroun, Lions Emblem and Physician Helping Leper
SP8

1962, Jan. 28

B33	SP8	20fr +5fr blk, mar & red brn	60	60
B34	SP8	25fr +10fr ultra, mar & red brn	70	70
B35	SP8	50fr +15fr grn, mar & red brn	1.25	1.25

Issued for leprosy relief work.

Anti-Malaria Issue

Common Design Type

1962, Apr. 7 *Perf. 12½x12*

B36	CD108	25fr +5fr rose lil	75	70

Issued for the World Health Organization drive to eradicate malaria.

Freedom from Hunger Issue

Common Design Type

1963, Mar. 21 **Engraved** *Perf. 13*

B37	CD112	18fr +5fr grn, dk ultra & brn	65	50
B38	CD112	25fr +5fr red brn & grn	80	60

AIR POST STAMPS.

Common Design Type

Photogravure.

1942 *Perf. 14½x14.* **Unwmkd.**

C1	CD87	1fr dk org	18	18
C2	CD87	1.50fr brt red	18	18
C3	CD87	5fr brn red	18	18
C4	CD87	10fr black	38	38
C5	CD87	25fr ultra	45	45
C6	CD87	50fr dk grn	65	65
C7	CD87	100fr plum	90	90
		Nos. C1-C7 (7)	2.92	2.92

Victory Issue

Common Design Type

1946, May 8 **Engraved** *Perf. 12½*

C8	CD92	8fr dk vio brn	38	38

Issued to commemorate the European victory of the Allied Nations in World War II.

Chad to Rhine Issue

Common Design Types

1946, June 6

C9	CD93	5fr dk bl grn	50	50
C10	CD94	10fr dk rose vio	50	50
C11	CD95	15fr red	60	60
C12	CD96	20fr brt bl	60	60
C13	CD97	25fr org red	75	75
C14	CD98	50fr gray	95	95
		Nos. C9-C14 (6)	3.90	3.90

Plane and Map
AP9

Seaplane Alighting
AP10

Plane and Freighters
AP11

1946 **Photogravure** *Perf. 13, 13½*

C15	AP9	25c brn red	5	5
C16	AP9	50c green	5	5
C17	AP9	1fr brt vio	5	5
C18	AP10	2fr ol grn	18	18
C19	AP10	3fr chocolate	18	18
C20	AP10	4fr dp ultra	15	15
C21	AP10	6fr bl grn	18	18
C22	AP10	7fr brt vio	22	22
C23	AP10	12fr orange	2.75	2.75
C24	AP10	20fr crimson	65	65
C25	AP11	50fr dk ultra	70	70
		Nos. C15-C25 (11)	5.16	5.16

Nos. C15 to C25 were "issued" in 1941 in France by the Vichy Government, but were not sold in Cameroun until 1946.

V8

This 100fr stamp and eight denominations of types AP9, AP10 and AP11 without "RF" monogram were issued by the Vichy Government in 1943-44, but were not on sale in Cameroun.

Birds over Mountains
AP12

Cavalry and Plane
AP13

Warrior, Dance Mask and Nose of Plane
AP14

Engraved

1947, Feb. 10 *Perf. 12½.* **Unwmkd.**

C26	AP12	50fr dk grn	90	50
C27	AP13	100fr brn red	1.90	30
C28	AP14	200fr black	3.75	90

U.P.U. Issue

Common Design Type

1949, July *Perf. 13.*

C29	CD99	25fr multi	2.75	2.25

Issued to commemorate the 75th anniversary of the Universal Postal Union.

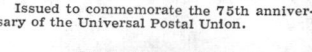

Humsiki Peak
AP16

1953, Feb. 16

C30 AP16 500fr grnsh blk, dk vio & vio bl 10.00 2.00

Edéa Dam and Sacred Ibis
AP17

1953, Nov. 18

C31 AP17 15fr choc, brn lake & ultra 1.20 50

Issued to publicize the official dedication of Edea Dam on the Sanaga River.

Liberation Issue
Common Design Type

1954, June 6

C32 CD102 15fr dk grnsh bl & bl grn 2.25 1.75

10th anniversary of the liberation of France.

Dr. Eugene Jamot, Research Laboratory and Tsetse Flies
AP19

1954, Nov. 29

C33 AP19 15fr dk grn, ind & dk brn 1.40 1.25

Issued to commemorate the 75th anniversary of the birth of Dr. Eugene Jamot.

Logging—AP20

Designs: 100fr, Giraffes. 200fr, Port of Douala.

1955, Jan. 24

C34 AP20 50fr ol grn, brn & vio brn 70 15

C35 AP20 100fr grnsh bl, brn & dk brn 2.00 30

C36 AP20 200fr dk grn, choc & dp ultra 2.75 50

Federal Republic

Air Afrique Issue
Common Design Type
Engraved

1962, Feb. 17 *Perf. 13* Unwmkd.

C37 CD107 25fr mar, pur & lt grn 60 55

Founding of Air Afrique (African Airlines).

The lack of a price for a listed item does not necessarily indicate rarity.

Nos. C35–C36 and C30 Surcharged in Red with New Value, Bars and: "REPUBLIQUE FEDERALE"

Two types of 5sh:
I. "5/-" measures 6½x4mm.
II. "5/" measures 3¾x3mm. No dash after diagonal line.

Three types of 10sh:
I. "10/-" measures 9x3¾mm.
II. "10/-" measures 7x2½–3mm.
III. "1" of "10/" vertically in line with last "E" of "FEDERALE".

Two types of £1:
I. "REPUBLIQUE / FEDERALE" 17¼ mm. wide.
II. "REPUBLIQUE / FEDERALE" 22mm. wide.

1961, Oct. 1 Engraved *Perf. 13*

C38 AP20 5sh on 100fr (I) 4.00 4.00
a. Type II 10.00 10.00

C39 AP20 10sh on 200fr (I) 8.00 8.00
a. Type II 35.00 35.00
b. Type III 8.00 8.00

C40 AP16 £1 on 500fr (I) 15.00 15.00
a. Type II 22.50 22.50

Issued for use in the former United Kingdom Trust Territory of Southern Cameroons.

Kapsikis Mokolo—AP21

Designs: 50fr, Cocotieres Hotel, Douala. 100fr, Cymothoe sangaris butterflies. 200fr, Ostriches, Waza Reservation.

1962, June 15

C41 AP21 50fr sl grn, bl & dl red 75 45

C42 AP21 100fr multi 1.65 60

C43 AP21 200fr dk grn, blk & bis 3.50 1.00

C44 AP21 500fr vio brn, bl & ocher 7.50 2.50

Telstar Type of Regular Issue

1963, Feb. 9

Size: 48x27mm.

C45 A50 100fr dk grn & red brn 1.75 1.00

See note after No. 383.

Edéa Relay Station
AP22

1963, May 18 Photo. *Perf. 12x12½*

C46 AP22 100fr multi 1.75 1.00

Issued to publicize the high frequency telegraph connection Douala-Yaounde.

African Postal Union Issue
Common Design Type

1963, Sept. 8 *Perf. 12½* Unwmkd.

C47 CD114 85fr ultra, ocher & red 1.75 1.50

Air Afrique Issue, 1963
Common Design Type

1963, Nov. 19 *Perf. 13x12*

C48 CD115 50fr pink, gray, blk & grn 85 60

Olympic Games Type of 1964

Design: 300fr, Greco-Roman wrestlers (ancient).

1964, Oct. 10 Engraved *Perf. 13*

C49 A57 300fr red, dk brn & dl grn 5.00 3.00
a. Sheet of 3 6.50 6.50

Issued to commemorate the 18th Olympic Games, Tokyo, Oct. 10–25. No. C49a contains one each of Nos. 403–404 and C49. Size: 168x99mm.

Kribi Port—AP25

1964, Oct. 26 *Perf. 13* Unwmkd.

C50 AP25 50fr red brn, ultra & grn 85 50

Black Rhinoceros—AP26

1965, Dec. 15 Engraved *Perf. 13*

C51 AP26 250fr brn red, grn & dk brn 4.50 1.75

Pres. John F. Kennedy—AP27

1964, Dec. 8 Photogravure *Perf. 12½*

C52 AP27 100fr grn, yel grn & brn 1.75 1.75
a. Souv. sheet of 4 7.00 7.00

Issued in memory of Pres. John F. Kennedy (1917–63). No. C52a contains 4 No. C52; green marginal inscription. Size: 128x90mm.

Abraham Lincoln—AP28

1965, Apr. 20 *Perf. 13* Unwmkd.

C53 AP28 100fr multi 1.65 1.25

Abraham Lincoln, death centenary.

Syncom Satellite and ITU Emblem
AP29

1965, May 17 Engraved

C54 AP29 70fr red, dk bl, & blk 1.25 90

Centenary of International Telecommunication Union.

Winston Churchill
AP30

Design: 18fr, Churchill, battleship and oak leaves with acorns.

Perf. 13x12½

1965, May 28 Photo. Unwmkd.

C55 AP30 12fr org, dk brn & ultra 1.00 75

C56 AP30 18fr org, dk brn, & ultra 1.00 75
a. Strip of 2 + label 2.50 2.00

Issued in memory of Sir Winston Spencer Churchill, statesman and World War II leader. No. C56a contains Nos. C55–C56 and label between inscribed "Sir Winston Churchill 1874 1965."

ICY Type of Regular Issue

1965, Sept. 11 Engraved *Perf. 13*

C57 A68 100fr dk red & dk bl 1.65 1.10

International Cooperation Year, 1964–65.

Racing Boat, Sanaga River, Edéa
AP31

1965, Oct. 27 *Perf. 13* Unwmkd.

C58 AP31 50fr brn, dk grn & sl 90 50

Edward H. White Floating in Space and Gemini IV—AP32

Designs: 50fr, Vostok 6. 200fr, Gemini V and REP (rendezvous evaluation pod). 500fr, Gemini VI & VII rendezvous.

1966, March 30 Engraved *Perf. 13*

C59 AP32 50fr car rose & dk sl grn 85 50

C60 AP32 100fr red lil & vio bl 1.65 1.00

C61 AP32 200fr ultra & dk pur 3.00 2.00

C62 AP32 500fr brt bl & ind 8.00 4.50

Man's conquest of space.

Hotel Type of Regular Issue

Designs: 18fr, Mountain Hotel, Buea. 25fr, Hotel Akwa Palace, Douala. 50fr, Terminus Hotel, Yaoundé. 60fr, Imperial Hotel, Yaoundé. 85fr, Independence Hotel, Yaoundé. 100fr, Hunting Lodge, Mora (vert.). 150fr, Boukarous (round huts), Waza Camp.

1966

C63 A71 18fr sl grn, brt bl & blk 25 20

C64 A71 25fr car, ultra & sl 40 25

C65 A71 50fr choc, grn & ocher 85 50

C66	A71	60fr choc, grn & brt bl	90	50
C67	A71	85fr dk car rose, dl bl & grn	1.25	75
C68	A71	100fr brn, grn & sl	1.65	75
C69	A71	150fr brn, dl bl & ocher	2.10	1.00
		Nos. C63-C69 (7)	7.40	3.95

Issue dates: Nos. C63–C64, Apr. 6; Nos. C65–C69, June 4.

Flower Type of Regular Issue

Flowers: 25fr, Hibiscus mutabilis. 50fr, Delonix regia. 100fr, Bougainvillea.

1966, May 20 Photo. *Perf. 12½*

Flowers in Natural Colors

Size: 26x45mm.

C70	A75	25fr sl grn	40	15
C71	A75	50fr brt grnsh bl	75	20
C72	A75	100fr gold	1.65	40

Military Police—AP33

Design: 25fr, "Army," soldier, tanks and parachutes. 60fr, "Navy," and "Vigilante." 100fr, "Air Force," plane.

1966, June 21 Engraved *Perf. 13*

C73	AP33	20fr vio bl, org brn & dl pur	30	20
C74	AP33	25fr dk grn, dl pur & brn	40	25
C75	AP33	60fr bl grn, bl & ind	1.00	45
C76	AP33	100fr brn, Prus bl & car rose	1.65	1.00

Issued to honor Cameroun's armed forces.

Wembley Stadium, London
AP34

Design: 200fr, Soccer.

1966, July 20

C77	AP34	50fr grn, cop red & sl	85	40
C78	AP34	200fr red, bl & grn	3.00	1.75

Issued to commemorate the 8th World Cup Soccer Championship, Wembley, England, July 11–30.

Air Afrique Issue, 1966

Common Design Type

1966, Aug. 31 Photo. *Perf. 13*

C79	CD123	25fr red lil, blk & gray	40	20

Issued to commemorate the introduction of DC-8F planes by Air Afrique.

Yaoundé Cathedral—AP35

Designs: 18fr, Buea Cathedral. 30fr, Orthodox Church, Yaoundé. 60fr, Mosque, Garoua.

1966, Dec. 19 Engraved *Perf. 13*

C80	AP35	18fr choc, bl & grn	30	25
C81	AP35	25fr brn, grn & brt vio	40	25
C82	AP35	30fr lil, grn & dl red	45	30
C83	AP35	60fr mar, brt grn & grn	1.00	50

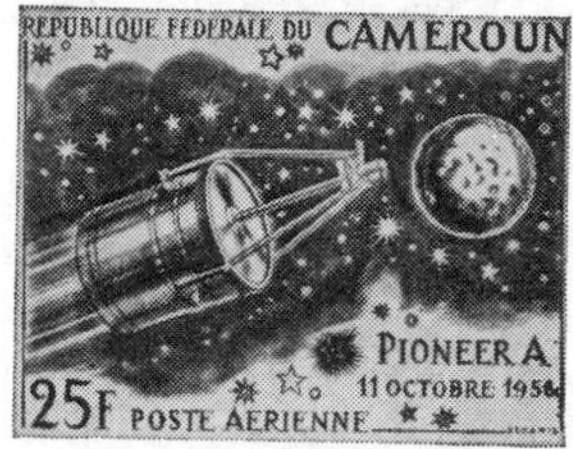

Pioneer A and Moon—AP36

Designs: 50fr, Ranger 6. 100fr, Luna 9. 250fr, Luna 10.

1967, Apr. 30 Engraved *Perf. 13*

C84	AP36	25fr grn, bl & bis	40	25
C85	AP36	50fr grn, dk pur & brn	85	50
C86	AP36	100fr red brn, brt bl & lil	1.75	1.00
C87	AP36	250fr red brn, sl & brn	4.00	3.00

"Conquest of the Moon."

Flower Type of Regular Issue

Flowers: 200fr, Thevetia Peruviana. 250fr, Amaryllis.

1967, June 22 Photo. *Perf. 12½*

Size: 26x46mm.

C88	A86	200fr multi	3.00	1.35
C89	A86	250fr multi	4.00	1.75

African Postal Union Issue, 1967

Common Design Type

1967, Sept. 9 Engraved *Perf. 13*

C90	CD124	100fr red brn, Prus bl & brt lil	1.60	1.00

Skis, Ice Skates, Olympic Flame and Emblem
AP38

1967, Oct. 11 Engr. *Perf. 13*

C91	AP38	30fr ultra & sep	55	30

Issued to publicize the 10th Winter Olympic Games, Grenoble, Feb. 6–8, 1968.

Cameroun Exhibit, EXPO '67
AP39

Designs: 100fr, Bangwa house poles carved with ancestor figures. 200fr, Canadian Pavilions.

1967, Oct. 18

C92	AP39	50fr mag, ol & mar	75	35
C93	AP39	100fr dk grn, mar & dk brn	1.75	80
C94	AP39	200fr brn, lil rose & sl grn	3.50	1.75

Issued to commemorate EXPO '70, International Exhibition, Montreal, Apr. 28–Oct. 27, 1967.

See note after No. C116 regarding 1969 moon overprint.

Konrad Adenauer and Cologne Cathedral
AP40

Design: 70fr, Adenauer and Chancellery, Bonn.

1967, Dec. 1 Photo. *Perf. 12½*

C95	AP40	30fr multi	50	30
C96	AP40	70fr multi	1.25	60
a.		Strip of 2 + label	1.80	1.00

Issued in memory of Konrad Adenauer (1876–1967), chancellor of West Germany (1949–63). No. C96a contains Nos. C95–C96 and label between showing the CEPT design of the 1967 Europa issues.

Pres. Ahidjo, King Faisal and View of Mecca—AP41

Design: 60fr, Pres. Ahidjo, Pope Paul VI and view of Rome.

1968, Feb. 18 Photo. *Perf. 12½*

C97	AP41	30fr multi	45	25
C98	AP41	60fr multi	90	45

Issued to commemorate President Ahidjo's pilgrimage to Mecca and visit to Rome.

Earth on Television Transmitted by Explorer VI—AP42

Designs: 30fr, Molniya spacecraft. 40fr, Earth on television screen transmitted by Molniya.

1968, Apr. 20 Engraved *Perf. 13*

C99	AP42	20fr multi	30	15
C100	AP42	30fr multi	45	25
C101	AP42	40fr multi	60	30

Telecommunication by satellite.

Forge—AP43 Boxing—AP44

Designs: No. C103, Tea harvest. No. C104, Trans-Cameroun railroad (diesel train emerging from tunnel). 40fr, Rubber harvest. 60fr, Douala Harbor (horiz.).

1968, June 5 Engraved *Perf. 13*

C102	AP43	20fr red brn, dk grn & ind	30	15
C103	AP43	30fr dk brn, grn & ultra	45	25
C104	AP43	30fr ind, sl grn & bis brn	45	25
C105	AP43	40fr ol bis, dk grn & bl grn	50	30
C106	AP43	60fr ultra, dk brn & sl	90	60
		Nos. C102-C106 (5)	2.60	1.55

Issued to publicize the Second Economic Development Five-Year Plan.

1968, Aug. 19 Engraved *Perf. 13*

Design: 50fr, Broad jump. 60fr, Athlete on rings.

C107	AP44	30fr brt grn, dk grn & choc	45	25
C108	AP44	50fr brt grn, brn red & choc	75	45
C109	AP44	60fr brt grn, ultra & choc	90	50
a.		Min. sheet of 3	2.25	2.25

Issued to commemorate the 19th Olympic Games, Mexico City, Oct. 12–27. No. C109a contains one each of Nos. C107–C109. Size: 128x99mm.

Human Rights Type of Regular Issue

1968, Sept. 14 Photo. *Perf. 12½x13*

C110	A92	30fr grn & brt pink	40	22

International Human Rights Year, 1968.

Martin Luther King, Jr.
AP45

Portraits: No. C112, Mahatma Gandhi and map of India. 40fr, John F. Kennedy. 60fr, Robert F. Kennedy. No. C115, Rev. Martin Luther King, Jr. No. C116, Mahatma Gandhi.

1968, Dec. 5 Photo. *Perf. 12½*

C111	AP45	30fr bl & blk	50	30
C112	AP45	30fr multi	50	30
C113	AP45	40fr pink & blk	60	40
C114	AP45	60fr bluish lil & blk	90	60
C115	AP45	70fr yel grn & blk	1.00	70
a.		Souv. sheet of 4	3.00	3.00

C116	AP45 70fr multi	1.00	70
	Nos. C111-C116 (6)	4.50	3.00

Issued to honor exponents of non-violence. The 2 King stamps (Nos. C111 and C115), the 2 Gandhi stamps (Nos. C112 and C116) and the 2 Kennedy stamps (Nos. C113–C114) are each printed as triptychs with a descriptive label between. No. C115a contains one each of Nos. C112–C115; black marginal inscription. Size: 122x160mm.

In 1969 Nos. C111–C116 and C94 were overprinted in carmine capitals: "Premier Homme / sur la Lune / 20 Juillet 1969" and "First Man / Landing on Moon / 20 July 1969".

PHILEXAFRIQUE Issue

The Letter, by Armand Cambon
AP46

1968, Dec. 10

C117	AP46 100fr multi	1.65	1.25

Issued to publicize PHILEXAFRIQUE, Philatelic Exhibition in Abidjan, Feb. 14–23, 1969. Printed with alternating light green label.

2nd PHILEXAFRIQUE Issue
Common Design Type

Design: 50fr, Cameroun No. 199 and Wouri Bridge.

1969, Feb. 14 Engraved *Perf. 13*

C118	CD128 50fr sl grn, ol & dl bl	85	85

Issued to commemorate the opening of PHILEXAFRIQUE, Abidjan, Feb. 14.

Caladium Bicolor
AP47

Flowers: 50fr, Aristolochia elegans. 100fr, Gloriosa simplex.

1969, May 14 Photo. *Perf. 12½*

C119	AP47 30fr lil & multi	45	30
C120	AP47 50fr grn & multi	85	50
C121	AP47 100fr brn & multi	1.50	80

Issued to publicize the 3rd International Flower Show, Paris, Apr. 23–Oct. 5.

Douala Post Office—AP48

Designs: 50fr, Buèa Post Office. 100fr, Bafoussam Post Office.

1969, June 19 Engraved *Perf. 13*

C122	AP48 30fr grn, vio bl & brn	35	20
C123	AP48 50fr sl, emer & red brn	70	40
C124	AP48 100fr dk brn, brt grn & brn	1.40	75

Coronation of Napoleon I, by Jacques Louis David
AP49

Napoleon Crossing Saint Bernard, after J. L. David
AP50

1969, July 4 Photo. *Perf. 12x12½*

C125	AP49 30fr vio bl & multi	75	30

Embossed on Gold Foil
Die-cut Perf. 10

C126	AP50 1000fr gold	25.00	25.00

Bicentenary of birth of Napoleon I.

William E. B. Dubois (1868–1963), American Writer—AP51

Portraits: 15fr, Dr. Price Mars, Haiti (1876–1969). No. C128, Aimé Cesaire, Martinique (1913–). No. C130, Langston Hughes, U.S. (1902–1967). No. C131, Marcus Garvey, Jamaica (1887–1940). 100fr, René Maran, Martinique (1887–1960).

1969, Sept. 25 Photo. *Perf. 12½*

C127	AP51 15fr lt bl & blk	20	10
C128	AP51 30fr lem & blk	40	20
C129	AP51 30fr rose brn & blk	40	20
C130	AP51 50fr gray & blk	65	35
C131	AP51 50fr emer & blk	65	35
C132	AP51 100fr yel & blk	1.35	85
a.	Min. sheet of 6	4.00	4.00
	Nos. C127-C132 (6)	3.65	2.05

Issued to honor Negro writers.

No. C132a contains one each of Nos. C127–C132. Size: 114x125mm.

ILO Emblem
AP52

1969, Oct. 29 Photo. *Perf. 13*

C133	AP52 30fr blk, bl grn & gray	50	20
C134	AP52 50fr blk, dp lil rose & gray	85	40

Issued to commemorate the 50th anniversary of the International Labor Organization.

Armstrong, Collins and Aldrin Splashdown in the Pacific
AP53

Design: 500fr, Landing module and Neil A. Armstrong's first step on moon.

1969, Nov. 29 Photo. *Perf. 12½*

C135	AP53 200fr multi	3.00	1.50
C136	AP53 500fr multi	6.50	3.75

See note after Algeria No. 427.

Pres. Ahidjo, Arms and Map of Cameroun—AP54

Embossed on Gold Foil

1970, Jan. 1 *Die-cut Perf. 10*

C137	AP54 1000fr gold & multi	12.50	12.50

10th anniversary of independence.

Hotel Mont Fébé, Yaoundé
AP55

1970, Jan. 15 Engraved *Perf. 13*

C138	AP55 30fr lt brn, sl grn & gray	50	20

Lenin
AP56

1970, Jan. 25 Photo. *Perf. 12½*

C139	AP56 50fr org & blk	70	40

Issued to commemorate the centenary of the birth of Nikolai Lenin (1870–1924), Russian Communist leader.

Plant Type of Regular Issue

Designs: 50fr, Cleome speciosa (caper). 100fr, Mussaenda erythrophylla (madder).

1970, Mar. 24 Photo. *Perf. 12½*
Size: 26x46mm.

C140	A99 50fr blk & multi	60	40
C141	A99 100fr multi	1.20	60

Map of Africa and Lions Emblem Pinpointing Yaoundé—AP57

1970, May 2 Photo. *Perf. 12½*

C142	AP57 100fr multi	1.35	75

Issued to commemorate the 13th Lions International Congress of District 13, Yaoundé, May 2, 1970.

U.N. Emblem and Doves—AP58

Design: 50fr, U.N. emblem and dove (vert.).

1970, June 26 Engraved *Perf. 13*

C143	AP58 30fr brn & org	40	25
C144	AP58 50fr Prus bl & sl bl	65	35

25th anniversary of the United Nations.

Japanese Pavilion and EXPO Emblem—AP59

Designs (EXPO Emblem and): 100fr, Map of Japan (vert.). 150fr, Australian pavilion.

1970, Aug. 1 Engraved *Perf. 13*

C145	AP59 50fr ind, lt grn & ver	65	35
C146	AP59 100fr bl, lt grn & red	1.35	65
C147	AP59 150fr choc, bl & gray	2.00	1.00

Issued to commemorate EXPO '70 International Exhibition, Osaka, Japan, Mar. 15–Sept. 13.

Charles de Gaulle AP60 **Pelé and Team AP61**

Design: 200fr, de Gaulle in uniform.

1970, Aug. 27

C148 AP60 100fr grn, vio bl & ol brn 1.50 75
C149 AP60 200fr ol brn, vio bl & grn 3.00 1.40
a. Strip of 2 + label 5.00 2.50

Issued to commemorate the 30th anniversary of the rallying of the Free French.

Nos. C148–C149 were printed in same sheet flanking a label showing maps of Cameroun and France, and Cross of Lorraine.

1970, Oct. 14 Photo. *Perf. 12½*

Designs: 50fr, Aztec Stadium, Mexico City (horiz.). 100fr, Mexican soccer team (horiz.).

C150 AP61 50fr multi 75 35
C151 AP61 100fr multi 1.50 75
C152 AP61 200fr multi 3.00 1.50

Issued to publicize the 9th World Soccer Championships for the Jules Rimet Cup, Mexico City, May 30–June 21, and the final victory of Brazil over Italy.

Ludwig van Beethoven AP62

1970, Nov. 23 Engraved *Perf. 13*

C153 AP62 250fr multi 2.75 1.50

Issued to commemorate the bicentenary of the birth of Ludwig van Beethoven (1770–1827), composer.

Christ at Emmaus, by Rembrandt AP63

Design: 150fr, The Anatomy Lesson, by Rembrandt.

1970, Dec. 5 Photo. *Perf. 12x12½*

C154 AP63 70fr grn & multi 80 40
C155 AP63 150fr multi 1.80 90

Charles Dickens AP64

Designs: 50fr, Scenes from David Copperfield. 100fr, Dickens holding quill.

1970, Dec. 22 *Perf. 13*

C156 AP64 40fr blk & rose 50 25
C157 AP64 50fr bis & multi 60 30
C158 AP64 100fr rose & multi 1.20 60

Death centenary of Charles Dickens (1812–1870), English novelist. Nos. C156–C158 printed se-tenant.

De Gaulle Type of 1970 Overprinted with Black Border and: "IN MEMORIAM / 1890–1970"

1971, Jan. 15 Engraved *Perf. 13*

C159 AP60 100fr vio bl, emer & brn red 1.20 60
C160 AP60 200fr brn red, emer & vio bl 2.40 1.20
a. Strip of 2 + label 4.25 2.00

In memory of Gen. Charles de Gaulle (1890–1970), President of France.

Timber Storage, Douala—AP65

Designs (Industrialization): 70fr, ALUCAM aluminum plant, Edea (vert.). 100fr, Mbakaou Dam.

1971, Feb. 14 Engraved *Perf. 13*

C161 AP65 40fr dk red, bl grn & ol brn 50 20
C162 AP65 70fr ol brn, sl grn & brt bl 80 40
C163 AP65 100fr Prus bl, yel grn & red brn 1.20 60

Relay Race—AP66

Designs: 50fr, Torch bearer (vert.). 100fr, Discus.

1971, Apr. 24 Engraved *Perf. 13*

C164 AP66 30fr dk brn, ver & ind 40 20
C165 AP66 50fr blk, bl & choc 70 35
C166 AP66 100fr multi 1.25 50

75th anniversary of revival of Olympic Games.

Fishing Trawler—AP67

Designs: 40fr, Local fishermen, Northern Cameroun. 70fr, Fishing harbor, Douala. 150fr, Shrimp boats, Douala.

1971, May 14 Engraved *Perf. 13*

C167 AP67 30fr lt brn, bl & grn 35 20
C168 AP67 40fr sl grn, bl & dk brn 45 25
C169 AP67 70fr dk brn, bl & red org 85 40
C170 AP67 150fr multi 1.80 90

Cameroun fishing industry.

Cameroun No. 123 and War Memorial, Yaoundé—AP68

Designs (Cameroun Stamps): 25fr, No. C33 and Jamot memorial. 40fr, No. 431 and government buildings, Yaoundé. 50fr, No. 19 and Imperial German postal emblem. 100fr, No. 101 and World War II memorial.

1971, Aug. 1 Engraved *Perf. 13*

C171 AP68 20fr grn, ocher & dk brn 25 10
C172 AP68 25fr dk brn, vio bl & sl grn 30 15
C173 AP68 40fr grn, mar & sl 45 25
C174 AP68 50fr dk brn, blk & ver 60 30
C175 AP68 100fr mar, sl grn & org 1.20 60
Nos. C171-C175 (5) 2.80 1.40

PHILATECAM 1971 Philatelic Exhibition.

Cameroun Flag, Pres. Ahidjo and Reunification Highway—AP69

Typo., Silk Screen, Embossed

1971, Oct. 1 *Perf. 12½*

C176 AP69 250fr gold & multi 3.75 3.00

PHILATECAM Philatelic Exhibition, Yaoundé-Douala.

African Postal Union Issue, 1971

Common Design Type

1971, Nov. 13 Photo. *Perf. 13x13½*

C177 CD135 100fr bl & multi 1.35 65

Annunciation, by Fra Angelico AP71

Paintings: 45fr, Virgin and Child, by Andrea del Sarto. 150fr, Christ Child with Lamb, detail from Holy Family, by Raphael (vert.).

Perf. 13x13½, 13½x13

1971, Dec. 19

Brown Inscriptions

C178 AP71 40fr multi 40 20
C179 AP71 45fr multi 60 30
C180 AP71 150fr multi 2.00 90

Christmas 1971.

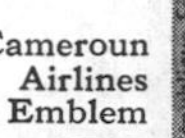

Cameroun Airlines Emblem AP72

1972, Feb. 2 Photo. *Perf. 12½x12*

C181 AP72 50fr lt bl & multi 60 30

Inauguration of Cameroun Airlines.

Doge's Palace, by Ippolito Caffi AP73

Paintings: 100fr, 200fr, Details from "Regatta on the Grand Canal," by School of Canaletto.

1972 Photogravure *Perf. 13*

C182 AP73 40fr gold & multi 50 25
C183 AP73 100fr gold & multi 1.20 60
C184 AP73 200fr gold & multi 2.50 1.20

UNESCO campaign to save Venice.

Astronauts Patsayev, Dobrovolsky and Volkov—AP74

1972, May 1 Photo. *Perf. 13x13½*

C185 AP74 50fr multi 60 25

Salute-Soyuz 11 space mission, and in memory of the Russian astronauts Victor I. Patsayev, Georgi T. Dobrovolsky and Vladislav N. Volkov, who died during Soyuz 11 space mission, June 6–30, 1971.

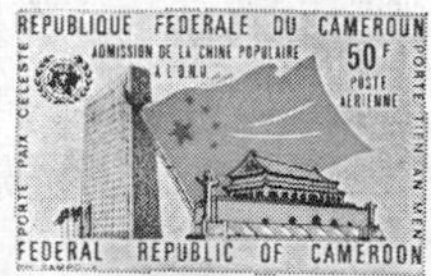

U.N. Headquarters, Chinese Flag and Gate of Heavenly Peace AP75

1972, May 19 *Perf. 13*

C186 AP75 50fr blk, scar & gold 50 25

Admission of People's Republic of China to United Nations.

United Republic

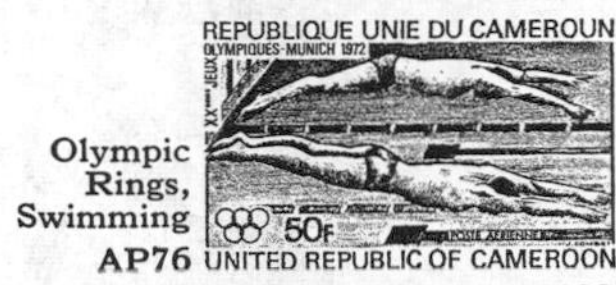

Olympic Rings, Swimming
AP76

Designs (Olympic Rings and): No. C188, Boxing (vert.). 200fr, Equestrian.

1972, Aug. 1 Engraved *Perf. 13*

C187	AP76	50fr lake & sl grn	60	30
C188	AP76	50fr choc & sl	60	30
C189	AP76	200fr cl, gray & dk brn	2.25	1.10
a.		Min. sheet of 3	3.25	3.25

20th Olympic Games, Munich, Aug. 26–Sept. 11. No. C189a contains stamps similar to Nos. C187–C189, but in changed colors. The 50fr (swimming) is Prussian blue, violet & brown; the 50c (boxing) lilac, Prussian blue & brown; the 200fr, Prussian blue & brown. Size: 139x99mm.

Nos. C187–C189 Overprinted in Red or Black

NATATION MARK SPITZ
MEDAILLES D'OR
a

SUPER WELTER
KOTTYSCH
MEDAILLE D'OR
b

CONCOURS COMPLET
MEADE
MEDAILLE D'OR
c

1972, Oct. 23 Engraved *Perf. 13*

C190	AP76 (a)	50fr lake & sl grn (R)	60	30
C191	AP76 (b)	50fr choc & sl	60	30
C192	AP76	200fr cl, gray & dk brn	2.50	1.20

Gold Medal Winners in 20th Olympic Games: Mark Spitz, USA, swimming (C190); Dieter Kottysch, West Germany, light middleweight boxing (C191); Richard Meade, Great Britain, 3-day equestrian (C192).

Madonna with Angels, by Cimabue
AP77

Design: 140fr, Madonna of the Rose Arbor, by Stefan Lochner.

1972, Dec. 21 Photo. *Perf. 13*

C193	AP77	45fr gold & multi	60	30
C194	AP77	140fr gold & multi	1.40	70

Christmas 1972.

St. Teresa, the Little Flower
AP78

Design: 100fr, Lisieux Cathedral and St. Teresa.

1973, Jan. 2 Engraved

C195	AP78	45fr vio bl, pur & mar	50	25
C196	AP78	100fr mag, ultra & brn	1.00	55

Centenary of the birth of St. Teresa of Lisieux (1873–1897), Carmelite nun.

African Unity Hall, Addis Ababa and Emperor Haile Selassie—AP79

1973, Mar. 14 Photo. *Perf. 13*

C197	AP79	45fr yel & multi	40	25

80th birthday of Emperor Haile Selassie of Ethiopia.

Corn, Grain, Healthy and Starving People—AP80

1973, Apr. 10 Typo. *Perf. 13*

C198	AP80	45fr multi	40	20

World Food Program, 10th anniversary.

Hearts and Blood Vessels
AP81

1973, May 5 Engraved

C199	AP81	50fr dk car rose & dk vio bl	40	25

"Your Heart is Your Health" and for the 25th anniversary of the World Health Organization.

Type of Regular Issue

Designs: 45fr, Map of Cameroun, Pres. Ahidjo and No. C176. 70fr, National colors and commemorative inscriptions.

1973, May 20 Engr. *Perf. 13*

C200	A128	45fr grn & multi	40	25
C201	A128	70fr red & multi	60	40

First anniversary of the United Republic of Cameroun.

Scout Emblem and Flags
AP82

1973, July 31 Typo. *Perf. 13*

C202	AP82	40fr multi	40	25
C203	AP82	45fr multi	45	30
C204	AP82	100fr multi	85	65

Cameroun's admission to the World Scout Conference, Mar. 26, 1971.

African Weeks Issue

Head and City Hall, Brussels
AP83

1973, Sept. 17 Engraved *Perf. 13*

C205	AP83	40fr dp brn & rose cl	40	25

African Weeks, Brussels, Sept. 15–30.

Map of Africa with Cameroun
AP84

1973, Sept. 29 Engraved *Perf. 13*

C206	AP84	40fr blk, red & grn	50	25

Help for handicapped children.

Zamengoe Radar Station
AP85

1973, Dec. 8 Engraved *Perf. 13*

C207	AP85	100fr bl, lt brn & grn	85	60

Chancellor Rolin Madonna, by Van Eyck
AP86

Design: 140fr, Nativity, by Federigo Barocci.

1973, Dec. 11 Photo. *Perf. 13*

C208	AP86	45fr gold & multi	45	30
C209	AP86	140fr gold & multi	1.50	1.10

Christmas 1973.

Zebu Type of 1974

Design: Zebu herd.

1974, June 1 Lithographed *Perf. 13*

C210	A140	45fr multi	40	20

North Cameroun cattle raising.

Churchill and Union Jack
AP87

1974, July 10 Engraved *Perf. 13*

C211	AP87	100fr blk, bl & red	90	60

Birth centenary of Winston Churchill (1874–1965).

Soccer, Arms of Frankfurt, Dortmund, Gelsenkirchen and Stuttgart—AP88

Designs: 100fr, Soccer and arms of Berlin, Hamburg, Hanover and Düsseldorf. 200fr, Soccer cup and game.

1974, Aug. 5 Photo. *Perf. 13*

C212	AP88	45fr gray, sl & org	40	20
C213	AP88	100fr gray, sl & org	85	60
C214	AP88	200fr org, sl & bl	1.65	1.00
		Strip of 3, Nos. C212-C214	3.25	2.00

World Cup Soccer Championship, Munich, June 13–July 7. Nos. C212–C214 printed se-tenant in sheets containing 5 triptychs.

Nos. C212–C214 Overprinted in Dark Blue:
"7th JULY 1974 / R.F.A. 2 HOLLANDE 1 / 7 JUILLET 1974"

1974, Sept. 16 Photo. *Perf. 13*

C215	AP88	45fr multi	40	25
C216	AP88	100fr multi	85	65
C217	AP88	200fr multi	1.65	1.20
		Strip of 3, Nos. C215-C217	3.25	2.25

World Cup Soccer Championship, 1974, victory of German Federal Republic.

UPU Type of 1974

Designs: 100fr, Cameroun No. 503. 200fr, Cameroun No. C29.

1974, Oct. 8 Engraved *Perf. 13*

C218	A142	100fr bl & multi	80	60
C219	A142	200fr red & multi	1.65	1.10

Centenary of Universal Postal Union.

Copernicus and Planets Circling Sun
AP89

1974, Oct. 15 Engraved *Perf. 13*

C220	AP89	250fr multi	2.00	1.50

500th anniversary of the birth of Nicolaus Copernicus (1473–1543), Polish astronomer.

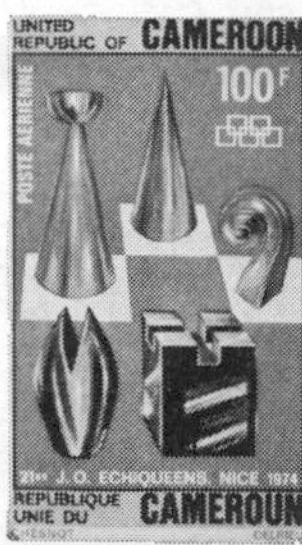

Chess Pieces
AP90

1974, Nov. 3 Photo. *Perf. 13x12½*

C221 AP90 100fr multi 75 65

21st Chess Olympiad, Nice, France, June 6–30.

Mask and ARPHILA Emblem—AP91

1974, Nov. 30 Engraved *Perf. 13*

C222 AP91 50fr choc & mag 40 25

ARPHILA 75, Paris, June 6–16, 1975.

Presidents and Flags of Cameroun, CAR, Gabon and Congo—AP92

1974, Dec. 8 Photogravure

C223 AP92 100fr gold & multi 80 60

See note after No. 595.

Man Landing on Moon—AP93

1974, Dec. 15 Engraved

C224 AP93 200fr brn, bl & car 1.60 1.20

5th anniversary of man's first landing on the moon.

Charles de Gaulle and Félix Eboué—AP94

1975, Feb. 24 Typo. *Perf. 13*

C225 AP94 45fr multi 50 25
C226 AP94 200fr multi 2.10 1.20

Félix A. Eboué (1884–1944), Governor of Chad, first colonial governor to join Free French in WWII, 30th death anniversary.

Marquis de Lafayette
AP95

Designs: 140fr, George Washington and soldiers. 500fr, Benjamin Franklin and Independence Hall.

1975, Oct. 20 Engr. *Perf. 13*

C227 AP95 100fr vio bl & multi 80 60
C228 AP95 140fr brn & multi 1.10 90
C229 AP95 500fr grn & multi 4.00 2.50

American Bicentennial.

The Burning Bush, by Nicolas Froment
AP96

Painting: 500fr, Adoration of the Kings, by Gentile da Fabriano (horiz.).

1975, Dec. 25 Photo. *Perf. 13*

C230 AP96 50fr gold & multi 50 25
C231 AP96 500fr gold & multi 4.75 2.50

Christmas 1975.

Concorde and Route: Paris–Dakar–Rio de Janeiro—AP97

1976, July 20 Litho. *Perf. 13*

C232 AP97 500fr lt bl & multi 4.50 2.50
a. Souvenir sheeet 5.50 5.50

First commercial flight of supersonic jet Concorde from Paris to Rio de Janeiro, Jan. 21. No. C232a contains one stamp; black marginal inscription giving specifications of Concorde. Size: 130x93mm. Sold for 600fr.

Dance Type of 1976

Designs: 50fr, Dancers and drummer. 100fr, Woman dancer.

1976, Sept. 15 Litho. *Perf. 12*

C233 A154 50fr gray & multi 40 30
C234 A154 100fr gray & multi 80 50

Virgin and Child, by Giovanni Bellini—AP98

Paintings: 30fr, Adoration of the Shepherds, by Le Brun. 60fr, Adoration of the Kings, by Rubens. 500fr, The Newborn, by Georges de la Tour.

1976, Dec. 15 Litho. *Perf. 12½*

C235 AP98 30fr gold & multi 25 15
C236 AP98 60fr gold & multi 50 35
C237 AP98 70fr gold & multi 55 40
C238 AP98 500fr gold & multi 4.00 2.50
a. Souvenir sheet of 4 5.50 5.50

Christmas 1976. No. C238a contains one each of Nos. C235–C238; black and gold marginal inscription. Size: 150x120 mm.

Festival Type of 1977

Design: 60fr, Traditional Chief on his throne, sculpture.

1977, Feb. 4 Litho. *Perf. 12½*

C239 A159 60fr multi 50 35

2nd World Black and African Festival, Lagos, Nigeria, Jan. 15–Feb. 12.

Crucifixion, by Matthias Grunewald—AP99

Paintings: 125fr, Christ on the Cross, by Velazquez (vert.). 150fr, The Deposition, by Titian.

1977, Apr. 2 Litho. *Perf. 12½*

C240 AP99 50fr gold & multi 40 30
C241 AP99 125fr gold & multi 1.00 60
C242 AP99 150fr gold & multi 1.25 80
a. Souvenir sheet of 3 2.75 2.75

Easter 1977. No. C242a contains one each of Nos. C240–C242, perf. 12; black and gold marginal inscription and black control number. Size: 210x115mm. Sold for 350fr.

Lions Emblem, Map of Africa
AP100

Rotary Emblem
AP101

1977, Apr. 29 Litho. *Perf. 12½*

C243 AP100 250fr multi 2.00 1.50

Lions Club of Douala, 19th Congress, Apr. 29–30.

1977, May 18

C244 AP101 60fr multi 50 35

Rotary Club of Douala, 20th anniversary.

Antoine de Saint-Exupéry
AP102

Charles Lindbergh and Spirit of St. Louis—AP103

Designs: 50fr, Jean Mermoz and his plane. 80fr, Maryse Bastié and her plane. 100fr, Sikorsky S-43. 300fr, Concorde.

1977, May 20 Engr. *Perf. 13*

C245 AP103 50fr org & bl 40 30
C246 AP102 60fr mag & org 50 35
C247 AP103 80fr mag & bl 60 45
a. Souvenir sheet of 3 1.75 1.75
C248 AP103 100fr grn & yel 80 60
C249 AP103 300fr multi 2.50 1.85
C250 AP103 500fr multi 4.00 2.75
a. Souvenir sheet of 3 8.50 8.50
Nos. C245-C250 (6) 8.80 6.30

Aviation pioneers and events. No. C247a contains one each of Nos. C245–C247; blue marginal inscription. Size: 170x100mm. Sold for 200fr. No. C250a contains one each of Nos. C248–C250; blue marginal inscription. Size: 190x100mm. Sold for 1000fr.

Sassenage Castle, Grenoble—AP104

1977, May 21 Litho. *Perf. 12½*

C251 AP104 70fr multi 55 40

10th anniversary of International French Language Council.

Jufilex Type of 1977

Designs: 70fr, Switzerland (Zurich) No. 1L1 and Cameroun No. 16. 100fr, Switzerland (Geneva) No. 2L1 and Cameroun No. 254.

1977, June 5 Litho. *Perf. 12*

C252 A161 70fr multi 55 40
C253 A161 100fr multi 80 60

Jufilex Philatelic Exhibition, Bern, Switzerland.

Diseased Knee, WHO Emblem
AP105

1977, Oct. 15 Engr. *Perf. 13*

C260 AP105 70fr multi 55 40

World Rheumatism Year.

Nos. C249 and C232 Overprinted in Red: "PREMIER VOL PARIS – NEW YORK / FIRST FLIGHT PARIS – NEW YORK / 22 Nov. 1977–22nd Nov. 1977"

Perf. 13

1977, Nov. 22 **Engr., Litho.**

C262	AP103	300fr multi	2.50	1.85
C263	AP97	500fr multi	4.00	3.00

Concorde, first commercial flight Paris to New York.

Christmas Type of 1977

Paintings: 60fr, Virgin and Child with 4 Saints, by Bellini (horiz.). 400fr, Adoration of the Shepherds, by George de la Tour (horiz.).

1977, Dec. 15 **Litho.** ***Perf. 12x12½***

C264	A165	60fr multi	50	35
C265	A165	400fr multi	3.50	2.50

Christmas 1977.

Flag Type of 1978

Design: 60fr, New flag, Pres. Ahidjo and spear.

1978, Apr. 3 **Litho.** ***Perf. 12½***

C266	A167	60fr multi	50	25

New flag of Cameroun.

Frog Type of 1978

Design: 100fr, Cardioglossa trifasciata.

1978, Apr. 5

C267	A168	100fr multi	85	60

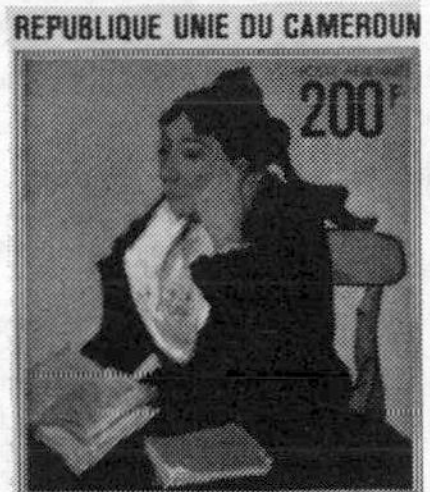

L'Arlesienne, by Van Gogh AP106

Painting: No. C269, Burial of Christ, by Albrecht Dürer.

1978, May 15 **Litho.** ***Perf. 12½***

C268	AP106	200fr multi	2.00	1.60
C269	AP106	200fr multi	2.00	1.60

Vincent Van Gogh (1853–1890), 125th birth anniversary and Albrecht Dürer (1471–1528), 450th death anniversary.

Leprosy Distribution on World Map, Raoul Follereau—AP107

1978, June 6 **Litho.** ***Perf. 12***

C270	AP107	100fr multi	1.00	80

25th World Leprosy Day.

Capt. Cook and Siege of Quebec AP108

Design: 250fr, Capt. Cook, Adventure and Resolution, map of voyages.

1978, July 26 **Engr.** ***Perf. 13***

C271	AP108	100fr multi	1.00	80
C272	AP108	250fr multi	2.50	2.00

Capt. James Cook (1728–1779), explorer.

Argentine Soccer Team, Coat of Arms and Rimet Cup—AP109

Designs: 200fr, Two soccer players (vert.). 1000fr, Soccer ball illuminating world map (vert.).

1978, Sept. 1 **Litho.** ***Perf. 13***

C273	AP109	100fr multi	1.00	80
C274	AP109	200fr multi	2.00	1.60
C275	AP109	1000fr multi	10.00	8.00

11th World Cup Soccer Championship, Argentina, June 1–25.

Jules Verne Type of 1978

Design: 400fr, Jules Verne and "20,000 Leagues Under the Sea" (horiz.).

1978, Oct. 10 **Litho.** ***Perf. 12***

C276	A169	400fr multi	4.00	3.20

Jules Verne (1828–1905), science fiction writer, birth sesquicentennial.

Musical Instrument Type of 1978

Design: 100fr, Man playing Mvet zither.

1978, Nov. 20 **Litho.** ***Perf. 12½***

C277	A172	100fr multi	1.00	60

Human Rights Type of 1979

1979, Feb. 11 **Litho.** ***Perf. 12x12½***

C278	A174	500fr multi	5.00	4.00

Universal Declaration of Human Rights, 30th anniversary (in 1978).

Lions Emblem, Map of District 403 AP110

1979, Apr. 26 **Litho.** ***Perf. 12½***

C279	AP110	60fr multi	60	40

21st Congress of Lions Club of Yaounde.

Penny Black, Hill, Cameroun No. 9 AP111

1979, Aug. 30 **Engraved** ***Perf. 13***

C280	AP111	100fr multi	1.00	60

Sir Rowland Hill (1795–1879), originator of penny postage.

See "Special Notices" at the front of this volume for data on the listing methods of this Catalogue, abbreviations, condition, prices and examination.

"TELECOM 79" AP112

1979, Sept. 26 **Litho.** ***Perf. 13x12½***

C281	AP112	100fr multi	1.00	60

3rd World Telecommunications Exhibition, Geneva, Sept. 20–26.

Pope Paul VI—AP113

1979, Oct. 23 **Engraved** ***Perf. 12½x13***

Multicolored

C282	AP113	100fr *shown*	1.00	65
C283	AP113	100fr *John Paul I*	1.00	65
C284	AP113	100fr *John Paul II*	1.00	65

"Double Eagle" over French Coastline AP114

Design: No. C286, Balloonists and balloon.

1979, Dec. 15 **Litho.** ***Perf. 12½***

C285	AP114	500fr multi	5.00	3.00
C286	AP114	500fr multi	5.00	3.00

First Transatlantic balloon crossing.

100-Meter Race—AP115

Designs: 150fr, Figure skating pairs. 200fr, Javelin. 300fr, Wrestling.

1980, Dec. 18 **Litho.** ***Perf. 12½***

C287	AP115	100fr yel brn & brn	1.00	60
C288	AP115	150fr bl & brn	1.50	90
C289	AP115	200fr grn & brn	2.00	1.20
C290	AP115	300fr red & brn	3.00	1.80

22nd Summer Olympic Games, Moscow, July 19-Aug. 3; 13th Winter Olympic Games, Lake Placid, Feb. 12-24 (150fr).

Alan Shepard and Freedom 7—AP116

1981, Sept. 15 **Litho.** ***Perf. 12½***

C291	AP116	500fr shown	5.00	3.00
C292	AP116	500fr Yuri Gagarin, Vostok I	5.00	3.00

Manned space flight, 20th anniv.

4th African Scouting Conference, Abidjan, June AP117

1981, Oct. 5

C293	AP117	100fr Emblem, salute, badge	1.00	65
C294	AP117	500fr Scout saluting	5.00	3.00

Guernica (detail), by Pablo Picasso (1881-1973)—AP118

Design: No. C296, Landscape, by Paul Cezanne (1839-1906).

1981, Nov. 10 **Litho.** ***Perf. 12½***

C295	AP118	500fr multi	5.00	3.00
C296	AP118	500fr multi	5.00	3.00

Christmas 1981—AP119

Designs: 50fr, Virgin and Child, by Froment (vert.). 60fr, San Zeno Altarpiece, by Mantegna (vert.). 400fr, Flight into Egypt, by Giotto.

1981, Dec. 1 **Litho.** ***Perf. 12½***

C297	AP119	50fr multi	50	30
C298	AP119	60fr multi	60	40
C299	AP119	400fr multi	4.00	2.40
a.		Souvenir sheet of 3	5.25	3.25

No. C299a contains Nos. C297-C299 (perf. 13x13½); green and gold marginal inscription. Size: 190x112mm.

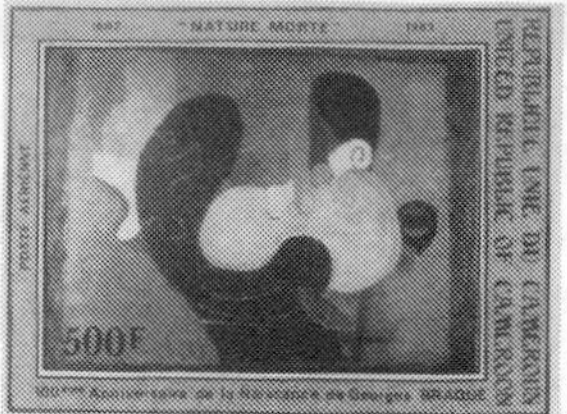

Still Life, by Georges Braque (1882-1963)—AP120

Paintings: No. C301, Olympia, by Edouard Manet (1832-1883).

1982, Dec. 5 **Litho.** ***Perf. 13***

C300	AP120	500fr multi	5.00	3.00
C301	AP120	500fr multi	5.00	3.00

Pres. John F. Kennedy (1917-1963)—AP121

1983, Mar. 15 **Litho.** ***Perf. 13***

C302	AP121	500fr multi	5.00	3.00

Lions District 403 (Douala), 2nd Convention, May—AP122

1983, May 5 **Litho.** ***Perf. 12½***

C303	AP122	70fr multi	70	45
C304	AP122	150fr multi	1.50	1.00

Jeanne of Aragon by Raphael—AP123

Design: No. C306, Massacre of Scio by Delacroix.

1983, Oct. 15 **Litho.** ***Perf. 13***

C305	AP123	500fr multi	2.50	1.50
C306	AP123	500fr multi	2.50	1.50

Easter 1984—AP124

Designs: 200fr, Pieta, by G. Hernandez. 500fr, Martyrdom of St. John the Evangelist, by C. Le Brun.

1984, Mar. 30 **Litho.** ***Perf. 13***

C307	AP124	200fr multi	1.00	65
C308	AP124	500fr multi	2.50	1.60
a.		Souvenir sheet of 2	3.50	2.25

No. C308a contains Nos. C307-C308. Size: 160x106mm.

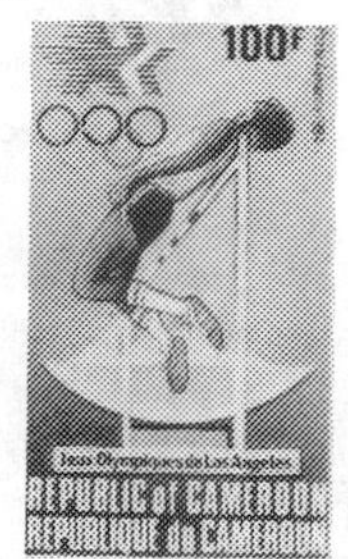

1984 Summer Olympics—AP125

1984, Apr. 30 ***Perf. 12½***

C309	AP125	100fr High jump	50	32
C310	AP125	150fr Volleyball	75	48
C311	AP125	250fr Handball	1.25	80
C312	AP125	500fr Bicycling	2.50	1.60

European Soccer Championship, June 12-27—AP126

1984, June 5 **Litho.** ***Perf. 12½***

C313	AP126	250fr Player in red shorts	1.25	80
C314	AP126	250fr Yellow shorts	1.25	80
C315	AP126	500fr Players	2.50	1.50
a.		Souvenir sheet of 3	5.00	2.50

No. C315a contains Nos. C313-C315 in changed panel colors. Size: 131x85mm.

Presidential Oath—AP127

1984 **Litho.** ***Perf. 13***

C316	AP127	60fr French inscription	28	20
a.		English inscription	28	20
C317	AP127	70fr French inscription	32	22
a.		English inscription	32	22
C318	AP127	200fr French inscription	90	60
a.		English inscription	90	60

Issue dates: French, Sept. 15; English, Nov.

Famous Men—AP128

Paintings: C316, Diana in the Bath, by Watteau (1684-1721). C317, Portrait of Diderot (1713-1784).

1984, Sept. 20 **Litho.** ***Perf. 13***

C319	AP128	500fr Witteau	2.25	1.50
C320	AP128	500fr Diderot, vert.	2.25	1.50

Nos. C309-C312 in Changed Colors with Added Inscriptions as Noted

1984, Sept. 25 **Litho.** ***Perf. 12½***

C321	AP125	100fr MOEGENBURG (R.F.A.) 11-08-84	45	30
C322	AP125	150fr U.S.A. 11-08-84	68	45
C323	AP125	250fr YOUGOSLAVIE 9-08-84	1.15	80
C324	AP125	500fr GORSKI (U.S.A.) 3-08-84	2.25	1.50

Moon Landing, 15th Anniv.—AP129

1984, Nov. 15 **Litho.** ***Perf. 12½***

C325	AP129	500fr Neil Armstrong	2.25	1.50
C326	AP129	500fr Apollo 12 launching	2.25	1.50

Louis Pasteur (1822-1895), Chemist, Microbiologist—AP130

Designs: No. 328, Mourning Woman (detail), Mausoleum of Henri Claude d'Harcourt, by sculptor Jean Baptiste Pigalle (1714-1785).

1985, Oct. 10 **Litho.** ***Perf. 13***

C327	AP130	500fr multi	2.00	2.00
C328	AP130	500fr multi	2.00	2.00

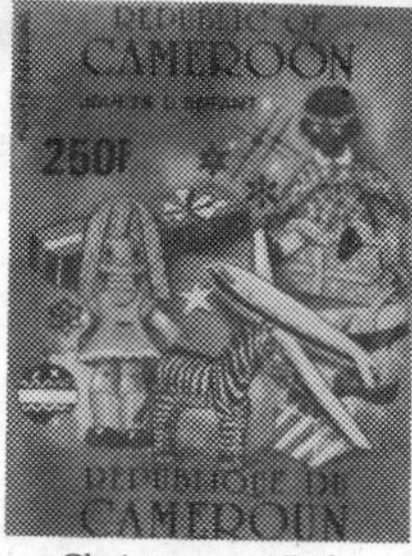

Christmas—AP131

Designs: 250fr, Children's gifts. 300fr, Akono Church. 400fr, Holy Family and drummer boy. 500fr, The Virgin with the Blue Diadem, by Raphael.

1985, Dec. 20 **Litho.** ***Perf. 13***

C329	AP131	250fr multi	1.40	1.40
C330	AP131	300fr multi	1.65	1.65
C331	AP131	400fr multi	2.25	2.25
C332	AP131	500fr multi	2.75	2.75

1986 World Cup Soccer Championships, Mexico—AP132

1986 ***Perf. 13½***

C333	AP132	250fr Argentina, winner	1.40	1.40
C334	AP132	300fr Stadium	1.65	1.65
C335	AP132	400fr Mexican team	2.25	2.25

Famous Men—AP133

Designs: No. C336, Pierre Curie (1859-1906), chemist, atom and elements. No. C337, Jean Mermoz (1901-1936), aviator, and aircraft.

1986, Oct. 22 **Litho.** ***Perf. 12½***

C336	AP133	500fr multi	2.75	2.75
C337	AP133	500fr multi	2.75	2.75

AIR POST SEMI-POSTAL STAMPS.

V9

V10

Stamps of the designs shown above were issued in 1942 by the Vichy Government, but were not placed on sale in Cameroun.

POSTAGE DUE STAMPS.

Man Felling Tree
D1

Typographed.

1925–27 ***Perf. 14x13½*** **Unwmkd.**

J1	D1	2c lt bl & blk	15	15
J2	D1	4c ol bis & red vio	15	15
J3	D1	5c vio & blk	28	28
J4	D1	10c red & blk	28	28
J5	D1	15c gray & blk	38	38
J6	D1	20c ol grn & blk	45	45
J7	D1	25c yel & blk	50	50
J8	D1	30c bl & org	60	60
J9	D1	50c brn & blk	75	75
J10	D1	60c bl grn & rose red	90	90
J11	D1	1fr dl red & grn, *grnsh*	1.25	1.25
J12	D1	2fr red & vio ('27)	2.25	2.25
J13	D1	3fr org brn & ultra ('27)	3.25	3.25
		Nos. J1-J13 (13)	11.19	11.19

Carved Figures
D2 D3

1939 **Engraved** ***Perf. 14x13***

J14	D2	5c brt red vio	6	6
J15	D2	10c Prus bl	50	50
J16	D2	15c car rose	6	6
J17	D2	20c blk brn	6	6
J18	D2	30c ultra	6	6
J19	D2	50c dk grn	22	22
J20	D2	60c brn vio	22	22
J21	D2	1fr dk vio	45	45
J22	D2	2fr org red	80	80
J23	D2	3fr dk bl	1.25	1.25
		Nos. J14-J23 (10)	3.68	3.68

A 10c stamp, type D2, without "RF" was issued in 1944 by the Vichy Government, but was not placed on sale in Cameroun.

1947 ***Perf. 13.*** **Unwmkd.**

J24	D3	10c dk red	5	5
J25	D3	30c dp org	5	5
J26	D3	50c grnsh blk	6	6
J27	D3	1fr dk car	15	15
J28	D3	2fr dp yel grn	30	30
J29	D3	3fr dp red lil	32	32
J30	D3	4fr dp ultra	32	32
J31	D3	5fr red brn	38	38
J32	D3	10fr pck bl	60	60
J33	D3	20fr sepia	1.00	1.00
		Nos. J24-J33 (10)	3.23	3.23

Federal Republic

Hibiscus
D4

Flowers: No. J35, Erythrine. No. J36, Plumeria lutea. No. J37, Ipomoea. No. J38, Hoodia gordonii. No. J39, Grinum. No. J40, Ochna. No. J41, Gloriosa. No. J42, Costus spectabilis. No. J43, Bougainvillea spectabilis. No. J44, Delonix regia. No. J45, Haemanthus. No. J46, Ophthalmophyllum. No. J47, Titanopsis. No. J48, Amorphophallus. No. J49, Zingiberacee.

Engraved

1963, Apr. 10 ***Perf. 11*** **Unwmkd.**

J34	D4	50c car, bl, grn & yel	5	5
J35	D4	50c car, bl, grn & yel	5	5
J36	D4	1fr mag, grn & yel	6	6
J37	D4	1fr mag, grn & yel	6	6
J38	D4	1.50fr dk grn, lil & yel	5	5
J39	D4	1.50fr dk grn, lil & yel	5	5
J40	D4	2fr org ver, yel & grn	12	12
J41	D4	2fr org ver, yel & grn	12	12
J42	D4	5fr mag, grn & yel	15	15
J43	D4	5fr mag, grn & yel	15	15
J44	D4	10fr crim, grn & yel	32	32
J45	D4	10fr crim, grn & yel	32	32
J46	D4	20fr grn, yel & lil	70	70
J47	D4	20fr grn, yel & lil	70	70
J48	D4	40fr lil & yel	1.25	1.25
J49	D4	40fr lil & yel	1.25	1.25
		Nos. J34-J49 (16)	5.40	5.40

The two types of each value in Nos. J34–J49 were printed tête bêche, se-tenant at the base.

MILITARY STAMP

M1

Typographed

1963, July 1 ***Perf. 13*** **Unwmkd.**

M1	M1	rose cl	2.25	2.25

CAMPIONE D'ITALIA

The 1944 issues of this Italian enclave within the borders of Switzerland are not listed because of their local nature. These stamps were valid only on mail going from Campione d'Italia to Switzerland. Letters going to other countries required Swiss stamps in addition.

CAPE JUBY

(kāp jōō'bī)

LOCATION — Northwest coast of Africa in Spanish Sahara.

GOVT.—Spanish administration.

AREA—12,700 sq. mi.

POP.—9,836.

CAPITAL—Villa Bens (Cape Juby).

By agreement with France, Spain's Sahara possessions were extended to include Cape Juby and in 1916 Spanish troops occupied the territory. It is attached for administrative purposes to Spanish Sahara.

100 Centimos = 1 Peseta

Stamps of Rio de Oro, 1914 Surcharged in Violet, Red or Green

CABO JUBI 5 CÉNTIMOS

1916 *Perf. 13.* **Unwmkd.**

No.	Type	Description	Unused	Used
1	A6	5c on 4p rose (V)	115.00	20.00
2	A6	10c on 10p dl vio (R)	42.50	20.00
3	A6	15c on 50c dk brn (G)	57.50	37.50
4	A6	15c on 50c dk brn (R)	42.50	20.00
5	A6	40c on 1p red vio (G)	90.00	45.00
6	A6	40c on 1p red vio (R)	75.00	25.00
		Nos. 1-6 (6)	422.50	167.50

Nos. 1-6 exist with inverted surcharge. Prices about twice those quoted.

Stamps of Spain, 1876-1917, Overprinted in Red or Black

CABO JUBY

1919 *Imperf.*

No.	Type	Description	Unused	Used
7	A21	¼c bl grn (R)	25	6

Perf. 13x12½, 14.

No.	Type	Description	Unused	Used
8	A46	2c dk brn (Bk)	25	6
a.		Double overprint	20.00	9.00
b.		Double overprint (Bk+R)	55.00	37.50
9	A46	5c grn (R)	55	6
a.		Double overprint	20.00	9.00
b.		Inverted overprint	28.50	18.50
10	A46	10c car (Bk)	65	10
a.		Double overprint (Bk+R)	55.00	37.50
11	A46	15c ocher (Bk)	3.00	20
b.		Double overprint	20.00	9.00
c.		Red control #	4.50	4.50
d.		As "c," inverted ovpt.	15.00	
12	A46	20c ol grn (R)	16.50	3.00
13	A46	25c dp bl (R)	2.75	30
a.		Double overprint	20.00	9.00
14	A46	30c bl grn (R)	2.75	40
15	A46	40c rose (Bk)	2.75	40
16	A46	50c sl bl (R)	3.25	40
17	A46	1p lake (Bk)	9.00	3.00
18	A46	4p dp vio (R)	35.00	14.00
19	A46	10p org (Bk)	47.50	15.00
		Nos. 7-19 (13)	124.20	36.98

Nos. 8-19 have blue control number on back.
Nos. 8-13, 15, 17-19 exist imperf.

Same Overprint on Stamps of Spain, 1920-21.

1922 *Imperf.*

No.	Type	Description	Unused	Used
20	A47	1c bl grn (R)	25.00	13.00

Perf. 13x12½.
Engraved.
Blue Control Number on Back.

No.	Type	Description	Unused	Used
23	A46	20c violet	125.00	42.50

A 2c litho. exists, price $300.

Same Overprint on Stamps of Spain, 1922-23.

1925 *Perf. 13½x13.*

No.	Type	Description	Unused	Used
25	A49	5c red vio	5.50	2.50
26	A49	10c bl grn	16.00	2.50
28	A49	20c violet	35.00	8.00

Spain #331, 2c ol grn, exists.

Price $300 unused, $80 canceled

Seville-Barcelona Exposition Issue.

Stamps of Spain, 1929, Overprinted CABO JUBY in Red or Blue.

1929 *Perf. 11.*

No.	Type	Description	Unused	Used
29	A52	5c rose lake (Bl)	25	20
30	A53	10c grn (R)	25	20
31	A50	15c Prus bl (R)	25	20
32	A51	20c pur (R)	25	20
33	A50	25c brt rose (Bl)	25	20
34	A52	30c blk brn (Bl)	30	40
35	A53	40c dk bl (R)	30	40
36	A51	50c dp org (Bl)	50	60
37	A52	1p bl blk (R)	14.00	8.50
38	A53	4p dp rose (Bl)	17.50	17.50
39	A53	10p brn (Bl)	17.50	12.50
		Nos. 29-39 (11)	51.35	40.90

Stamps of Spanish Morocco, 1928-33, Overprinted in Black or Red

Cabo Juby

1934 *Perf. 14.*

No.	Type	Description	Unused	Used
40	A7	1c brt rose (Bk)	35	40
41	A2	2c dk vio (R)	3.25	45
42	A2	5c dp bl (R)	3.25	65
43	A2	10c dk grn (Bk)	7.00	1.25
43A	A10	10c dk grn (R)	2.25	1.90
44	A2	15c org brn (Bk)	16.00	6.00
45	A7	20c sl grn (R)	6.50	3.75
46	A3	25c cop red (Bk)	3.25	3.25
47	A10	30c red brn (Bk)	6.50	3.75
48	A13	40c dp bl (R)	22.50	14.00
49	A13	50c red org (Bk)	42.50	22.50
50	A4	1p yel grn (Bk)	26.00	12.50
51	A5	2.50p red vio (Bk)	57.50	27.50
52	A6	4p ultra (R)	75.00	35.00

No. 43A and 1c, 20c, 30c, 40c, 50c, with control numbers.

Same Overprint in Black on Stamp of Spanish Morocco, 1932.

No.	Type	Description	Unused	Used
53	A2	1c car rose ("Ct")	1.40	65
		Nos. 40-53 (15)	273.25	133.55

Stamps of Spanish Morocco, 1933-35, Overprinted in Black, Blue or Red

CABO JUBY

1935-36

No.	Type	Description	Unused	Used
54	A8	2c grn (R)	55	15
55	A9	5c mag (Bk)	2.25	20
55A	A10	10c dk grn (R) ('36)	12.50	2.25
56	A11	15c yel (Bl)	5.00	1.50
57	A12	25c crim (Bk)	42.50	22.50
58	A8	1p sl blk (R)	7.50	3.75
59	A9	2.50p brn (Bl)	30.00	14.00
60	A11	4p yel grn (R)	40.00	17.00
61	A12	5p blk (R)	40.00	22.50
		Nos. 54-61 (9)	180.30	83.85

Same Overprint in Black or Red on Stamps of Spanish Morocco, 1935.

1935 *Perf. 13½.*

No.	Type	Description	Unused	Used
62	A14	25c vio (R)	3.50	1.50
63	A15	30c crim (Bk)	3.50	1.25
64	A14	40c org (Bk)	4.75	1.50
65	A15	50c brt bl (R)	9.25	1.50
66	A14	60c dk bl grn (R)	11.00	3.50
67	A15	2p brn lake (Bk)	60.00	22.50

Same Overprint on Stamps of Spanish Morocco, 1933.

Perf. 13½, 14.

No.	Type	Description	Unused	Used
68	A7	1c brt rose (Bk)	20	10

Perf. 14

No.	Type	Description	Unused	Used
69	A7	20c sl grn (R)	4.75	2.25
		Nos. 62-69 (8)	96.95	34.10

Same Overprint on Stamps of Spanish Morocco, 1937.

1937 *Perf. 13½.*

No.	Type	Description	Unused	Used
70	A21	1c dk bl (Bk)	25	10
71	A21	2c org brn (Bk)	25	10
72	A21	5c cer (Bk)	25	10
73	A21	10c emer (Bk)	25	10
74	A21	15c brt bl (Bk)	30	15
75	A21	20c red brn (Bk)	30	15
76	A21	25c mag (Bk)	30	15
77	A21	30c red org (Bk)	30	15
78	A21	40c org (Bk)	1.00	60
79	A21	50c ultra (R)	1.00	60
80	A21	60c yel grn (Bk)	1.00	60
81	A21	1p bl vio (Bk)	1.00	60
82	A21	2p Prus bl (Bk)	55.00	50.00
83	A21	2.50p gray blk (R)	55.00	50.00
84	A21	4p dk brn (Bk)	55.00	50.00
85	A22	10p vio blk (R)	55.00	50.00
		Nos. 70-85 (16)	226.20	203.40

Issued in commemoration of the First Year of the Revolution.

Same Overprint in Black on Types of Spanish Morocco, 1939.

Designs: 5c, Spanish quarter. 10c, Moroccan quarter. 15c, Street scene, Larache. 20c, Tetuan.

1939 **Photogravure.** *Perf. 13½.*

No.	Type	Description	Unused	Used
86	A25	5c vermilion	60	45
87	A25	10c dp grn	60	45
88	A25	15c brn lake	60	55
89	A25	20c brt bl	60	55

Same Overprint in Black or Red on Stamps of Spanish Morocco, 1940.

1940 *Perf. 11½x11.*

No.	Type	Description	Unused	Used
90	A26	1c dk brn (Bk)	15	6
91	A27	2c ol grn (R)	15	6
92	A28	5c dk bl (R)	15	6
93	A29	10c dk red lil (Bk)	20	6
94	A30	15c dk grn (R)	20	6
95	A31	20c pur (R)	20	6
96	A32	25c blk brn (R)	20	15
97	A33	30c brt grn (Bk)	20	15
98	A34	40c sl grn (R)	60	25
99	A35	45c org ver (Bk)	60	25
100	A36	50c brn org (Bk)	60	25
101	A37	70c saph (R)	1.50	60
102	A38	1p ind & brn (Bk)	3.50	60
103	A39	2.50p choc & dk grn (Bk)	8.25	4.25
104	A40	5p dk cer & sep (Bk)	8.25	4.25
105	A41	10p dk ol grn & brn org (Bk)	25.00	16.00
		Nos. 90-105 (16)	49.75	27.11

Stamps of Spanish Morocco, 1944, Overprinted in Black or Red

CABO JUBY

1944 *Perf. 12½.* **Unwmkd.**

No.	Type	Description	Unused	Used
106	A47	1c choc & lt bl	10	10
107	A48	2c sl grn & lt grn	10	10
108	A49	5c choc & grnsh blk (R)	10	10
109	A50	10c brt ultra & red org	10	10
110	A51	15c sl grn & lt grn	10	10
111	A52	20c dp cl & blk (R)	10	10
112	A53	25c lt bl & choc	10	10
113	A47	30c yel grn & brt ultra (R)	10	10
114	A48	40c choc & red vio	10	10
115	A49	50c brt ultra, & red brn	10	10
116	A50	75c yel grn & brt ultra (R)	90	40
117	A51	1p brt ultra & choc	90	40
118	A52	2.50p blk & brt ultra (R)	2.50	2.00
119	A53	10p sal & gray blk (R)	17.50	14.00
		Nos. 106-119 (14)	22.80	17.80

Same Overprint on Stamps of Spanish Morocco, 1946.

1946 *Perf. 10½x10.*

No.	Type	Description	Unused	Used
120	A54	1c pur & brn	10	10
121	A55	2c dk Prus grn & vio blk (R)	10	10
122	A54	10c dp org & vio bl	10	10
123	A55	15c dk bl & bl grn	10	10
124	A54	25c yel grn & ultra	10	10
125	A56	40c dk bl & brn (R)	10	10
126	A55	45c blk & rose	20	20
127	A57	1p dk Prus grn & dp bl	1.00	45
128	A58	2.50p dp org & grnsh gray (R)	3.00	2.25
129	A59	10p dk bl & gray (R)	10.00	6.75
		Nos. 120-129 (10)	14.80	10.25

Same Overprint in Carmine, Black or Brown on Stamps of Spanish Morocco, 1948.

1948 *Perf. 10, 10x10½*

No.	Type	Description	Unused	Used
130	A64	2c pur & brn	8	8
131	A65	5c dp cl & vio	8	8
132	A66	15c brt ultra & bl grn (Bk)	8	8
133	A67	25c blk & Prus grn	8	8
134	A65	35c brt ultra & gray blk	10	10
135	A68	50c red & vio (Br)	10	10
136	A66	70c dk gray grn & ultra (Bk)	10	10
137	A67	90c cer & dk gray grn (Bk)	10	10
138	A68	1p brt ultra & vio (Br)	25	25
139	A64	2.50p vio brn & sl grn	1.00	60
140	A69	10p blk & dp ultra	3.25	2.50
		Nos. 130-140 (11)	5.22	4.07

SEMI-POSTAL STAMPS.

Types of Semi-Postal Stamps of Spain, 1926, Overprinted

CABO-JUBY

1926 *Perf. 12½, 13* **Unwmkd.**

No.	Type	Description	Unused	Used
B1	SP1	1c orange	9.00	5.00
B2	SP2	2c rose	9.00	5.00
B3	SP3	5c blk brn	2.50	2.00
B4	SP4	10c dk grn	1.40	1.10
B5	SP1	15c dk vio	75	75
B6	SP4	20c vio brn	75	75
B7	SP5	25c dp car	75	75
B8	SP1	30c ol grn	75	75
B9	SP3	40c ultra	8	8
B10	SP2	50c red brn	8	8
B11	SP4	1p vermilion	8	8
B12	SP3	4p bister	90	65
B13	SP5	10p lt vio	1.65	1.40
		Nos. B1-B13 (13)	27.69	18.39

AIR POST STAMPS.

Spanish Morocco, Nos. C1 to C10
Overprinted in Black CABO JUBY

1938, June 1 *Perf. 13½.* Unwmkd.

C1	AP1	5c brown	20	8
C2	AP1	10c brt grn	20	8
C3	AP1	25c crimson	15	8
C4	AP1	40c lt bl	2.25	1.25
C5	AP2	50c brt mag	20	8
C6	AP2	75c dk bl	20	30
C7	AP1	1p sepia	20	30
C8	AP1	1.50p dp vio	1.25	65
C9	AP1	2p dp red brn	3.00	1.65
C10	AP1	3p brn blk	8.00	5.50
		Nos. C1-C10 (10)	15.65	9.97

Strait of Gibraltar
AP3

Designs: 5c, Ketama landscape. 10c, Mosque, Tangier. 15c, Velez. 90c, Sanjurjo.

1942, Apr. 1 Photo. *Perf. 12½*

C11	AP3	5c dp bl	10	10
C12	AP3	10c org brn	10	10
C13	AP3	15c grnsh blk	10	10
C14	AP3	90c dk rose	60	45
C15	AP3	5p black	2.25	1.65
		Nos. C11-C15 (5)	3.15	2.40

SPECIAL DELIVERY STAMPS.

Special Delivery Stamp of Spain Overprinted "CABO JUBY" as on Nos. 7-28.

1919 *Perf. 14* Unwmkd.

E1	SD1	20c red (Bk)	1.60	1.00
b.		Double overprint	28.50	16.50

Spanish Morocco No. E4 Overprinted in Red

Cabo Juby

1934

E2	SD2	20c black	7.00	6.75

Spanish Morocco No. E5 Overprinted in Black

CABO JUBY

1935

E3	SD3	20c vermilion	3.50	1.00

Same Overprint on Spanish Morocco, No. E6.

1937 *Perf. 13½.*

E4	SD4	20c brt car	1.00	60

Issued in commemoration of the First Year of the Revolution.

Same Overprint on Spanish Morocco, No. E8.

1940 *Perf. 11½x11.*

E5	SD5	25c scarlet	45	30

SEMI-POSTAL SPECIAL DELIVERY STAMP.

Type of Semi-Postal Special Delivery Stamp of Spain, 1926, Overprinted CABO-JUBY

1926 *Perf. 12½, 13.* Unwmkd.

EB1	SPSD1	20c ultra & blk	2.50	1.75

CAPE VERDE

LOCATION — A group of 10 islands and five islets in the Atlantic Ocean, about 500 miles due west of Senegal.
GOVT.—Republic.
AREA—1,557 sq. mi.
POP.—296,093 (1980).
CAPITAL—Praia.

The Portuguese territory of Cape Verde became independent on July 5, 1975.

1000 Reis = 1 Milreis
100 Centavos = 1 Escudo (1913)

Crown of Portugal
A1

King Luiz
A2

Typographed.

1877 *Perf. 12½, 13½.* Unwmkd.

1	A1	5r black	2.00	1.50
2	A1	10r yellow	17.50	8.00
3	A1	20r bister	1.50	1.25
4	A1	25r rose	1.75	1.25
a.		Perf. 13½	7.00	5.00
5	A1	40r blue	65.00	30.00
a.		Cliche of Mozambique in Cape Verde plate, in pair with #5	1,250.	1,000.
b.		As "a," perf. 13½	1,900.	1,900.
6	A1	50r green	65.00	42.50
7	A1	100r lilac	7.00	2.50
8	A1	200r orange	3.00	2.50
a.		Perf. 13½	7.00	5.00
9	A1	300r brown	4.00	3.00

1881-85

10	A1	10r green	2.00	1.75
11	A1	20r car ('85)	4.50	3.00
a.		Perf. 13½	40.00	30.00
12	A1	25r vio ('85)	3.25	2.50
13	A1	40r yel buff	2.00	1.75
a.		Imperf.	1.00	
b.		Cliche of Mozambique in Cape Verde plate, in pair with #13	90.00	90.00
c.		As "b," imperf.	30.00	
14	A1	50r blue	5.50	4.00

Reprints of the 1877-85 issues are on smooth white chalky paper, ungummed, and on thin white paper with shiny white gum. They are perf. 13½.

Price, $2.75 each.

Embossed.
Chalk-Surfaced Paper.

1886 *Perf. 12½, 13½*

15	A2	5r black	3.00	2.00
16	A2	10r green	3.25	2.25
17	A2	20r carmine	4.50	3.00
a.		Perf.13½	5.50	4.50
18	A2	25r violet	4.50	2.25
19	A2	40r chocolate	5.00	2.50
a.		Perf. 13½	7.50	5.00
20	A2	50r blue	5.00	2.50
21	A2	100r yel brn	5.25	3.00
22	A2	200r gray lil	12.00	8.00
23	A2	300r orange	14.00	10.00

The 25, 50 and 100r have been reprinted in aniline colors with clean-cut

Perf. 13½. Price $3.50 each.

King Carlos
A3 A4

Typographed.

1894-95 *Perf. 11½, 12½, 13½.*

24	A3	5r orange	1.20	90
25	A3	10r redsh vio	1.25	1.00
26	A3	15r chocolate	2.75	2.00
a.		Perf. 12½	125.00	85.00
27	A3	20r lavender	2.75	1.75
28	A3	25r dp grn	2.50	2.00
a.		Perf. 12½	3.00	2.00
29	A3	50r lt bl	2.50	2.00
a.		Perf. 13½	7.00	2.50
30	A3	75r car ('95)	10.00	5.50
a.		Perf. 13½	25.00	15.00
31	A3	80r yel grn ('95)	11.00	7.00
a.		Perf. 13½	16.50	11.00
32	A3	100r brn, *buff* ('95)	7.50	2.50
a.		Perf. 12½	37.50	15.00
33	A3	150r car, *rose* ('95)	15.00	11.00
a.		Perf. 12½	110.00	90.00
b.		Perf. 11½	37.50	25.00
34	A3	200r dk bl, *lt bl* ('95)	12.50	8.00
a.		Perf. 12½	100.00	80.00
35	A3	300r dk bl, *sal* ('95)	22.50	13.50

1898-1903 *Perf. 11½.*

Name and Value in Black except 500r

36	A4	2½r gray	30	20
37	A4	5r orange	30	20
38	A4	10r lt grn	30	20
39	A4	15r brown	3.75	1.50
40	A4	15r gray grn ('03)	1.25	1.00
41	A4	20r gray vio	1.25	50
42	A4	25r sea grn	2.50	1.00
a.		Perf. 12½	60.00	25.00
43	A4	25r car ('03)	80	30
44	A4	50r dk bl	2.50	1.00
45	A4	50r brn ('03)	2.50	2.00
46	A4	65r sl bl ('03)	12.50	*12.50*
47	A4	75r rose	6.00	3.00
48	A4	75r lil ('03)	2.25	1.75
49	A4	80r violet	6.00	3.50
50	A4	100r dk bl, *bl*	2.00	1.25
51	A4	115r org brn, *pink* ('03)	10.00	*10.00*
52	A4	130r brn, *straw* ('03)	10.00	*10.00*
53	A4	150r brn, *straw*	6.00	4.00
54	A4	200r red vio, *pnksh*	2.50	2.00
55	A4	300r dk bl, *rose*	7.50	3.75
56	A4	400r dl bl, *straw* ('03)	7.50	6.00
57	A4	500r blk & red, *bl* ('01)	7.50	3.75
58	A4	700r vio, *yelsh* ('01)	20.00	12.50
		Nos. 36-58 (23)	115.20	*81.90*

Regular Issues Surcharged in Red or Black

65
RÉIS

Two spacing types of surcharge. See note above Angola No. 61.

On Issue of 1886.

1902, Dec. 1 *Perf. 12½, 13½*

59	A2	65r on 5r blk (R)	4.00	3.00
60	A2	65r on 200r gray lil	4.00	3.00
61	A2	65r on 300r org	4.00	3.00
62	A2	115r on 10r grn	4.00	3.00
63	A2	115r on 20r rose	4.00	3.00
a.		Perf. 13½	30.00	20.00
64	A2	130r on 50r bl	4.00	3.00
65	A2	130r on 100r brn	4.00	3.00
66	A2	400r on 25r vio	2.25	1.75
67	A2	400r on 40r choc	3.00	2.75
a.		Perf. 13½	30.00	22.50

On Issue of 1894.

Perf. 11½, 12½, 13½.

68	A3	65r on 10r red vio	6.50	4.00
69	A3	65r on 20r lav	6.00	3.00
70	A3	65r on 100r brn, *buff*	6.00	4.00
a.		Perf 12½	15.00	10.00
71	A3	115r on 5r org	3.25	2.50
a.		Inverted surcharge	15.00	15.00
72	A3	115r on 25r bl grn	3.00	2.40
a.		Perf. 11½	17.50	8.00
73	A3	115r on 150r car, *rose*	6.00	5.00
a.		Perf. 13½	25.00	15.00
74	A3	130r on 75r car	3.25	2.75
a.		Perf. 13½	37.50	25.00
75	A3	130r on 80r yel grn	3.00	2.75
76	A3	130r on 200r dk bl, *bl*	4.00	2.50
77	A3	400r on 50r lt bl	4.50	3.00
a.		Inverted surcharge	40.00	40.00
b.		Perf. 13½	50.00	40.00
78	A3	400r on 300r dk bl, *sal*	2.00	1.50

On Newspaper Stamp of 1893.

79	N1	400r on 2½r brn	1.75	1.50
a.		Inverted surcharge	12.50	
b.		Perf. 12½	37.50	25.00
		Nos. 59-79 (21)	82.50	60.40

Reprints of Nos. 59, 66, 67, and 77 have shiny white gum and clean-cut perforation 13½. Price $1 each.

Overprinted in Black PROVISORIO

On Nos. 39, 42, 44, 47

1902-03 *Perf. 11½*

80	A4	15r brown	1.50	1.25
81	A4	25r sea grn	1.50	1.25
82	A4	50r bl ('03)	1.75	1.40
83	A4	75r rose ('03)	2.50	2.00
a.		Invtd. ovpt.	20.00	20.00

No. 46 Surcharged in Black

50
RÉIS

1905, July 1

84	A4	50r on 65r sl bl	2.50	2.25

Stamps of 1898-1903 Overprinted in Carmine or Green

REPUBLICA

1911, Aug. 20

85	A4	2½r gray	35	25
86	A4	5r orange	35	25
87	A4	10r lt grn	1.00	80
88	A4	15r gray grn	70	35
89	A4	20r gray vio	1.00	1.00
90	A4	25r car (G)	1.00	50
91	A4	50r brown	6.50	4.50
92	A4	75r red lil	1.25	75
93	A4	100r dk bl, *bl*	1.25	1.00
94	A4	115r org brn, *pink*	90	*2.00*
95	A4	130r brn, *straw*	90	*2.00*
96	A4	200r red vio, *pnksh*	5.00	5.00
97	A4	400r dl bl, *straw*	2.00	2.00
98	A4	500r blk & red, *bl*	2.25	1.75
99	A4	700r vio, *straw*	2.25	1.75
		Nos. 85-99 (15)	26.70	*23.90*

King Manuel II
A5

Overprinted in Carmine or Green.

1912 *Perf. 11½x12*

100	A5	2½r violet	20	*2.00*
101	A5	5r black	20	18
102	A5	10r gray grn	25	25
103	A5	20r car (G)	2.00	1.25
104	A5	25r vio brn	40	30
105	A5	50r dk bl	3.50	2.50
106	A5	75r bis brn	90	60
107	A5	100r brn, *lt grn*	90	60
108	A5	200r dk grn, *sal*	1.25	90
109	A5	300r *azure*	1.25	90

Perf. 14½x15.

110	A5	400r blk & bl	3.00	2.50
111	A5	500r ol grn & vio brn	3.00	2.50
		Nos. 100-111(12)	16.85	*14.48*

Vasco da Gama Issue of Various Portuguese Colonies. Common Design Types CD20–CD27 Surcharged

REPUBLICA
CABO VERDE
¼ C.

On Stamps of Macao.

1913, Feb. 13 ***Perf. 12½ to 16***

No.	Description	Unused	Used
112	¼c on ½a bl grn	1.25	1.25
113	½c on 1a red	1.25	1.25
114	1c on 2a red vio	1.25	1.25
115	2½c on 4a yel grn	1.25	1.25
116	5c on 8a dk bl	6.00	6.00
117	7½c on 12a vio brn	5.50	5.50
118	10c on 16a bis brn	2.50	2.50
119	15c on 24a bis	5.00	5.00
	Nos. 112-119 (8)	24.00	24.00

On Stamps of Portuguese Africa.

Perf. 14 to 15.

No.	Description	Unused	Used
120	¼c on 2½r bl grn	1.00	1.00
121	½c on 5r red	1.00	1.00
122	1c on 10r red vio	1.00	1.00
123	2½c on 25r yel grn	1.00	1.00
124	5c on 50r dk bl	2.00	2.00
125	7½c on 75r vio brn	3.00	3.00
126	10c on 100r bis brn	2.50	2.50
127	15c on 150r bis	3.00	3.00
	Nos. 120-127 (8)	14.50	14.50

On Stamps of Timor.

No.	Description	Unused	Used
128	¼c on ½a bl grn	1.25	1.25
129	½c on 1a red	1.25	1.25
130	1c on 2a red vio	1.25	1.25
131	2½c on 4a yel grn	1.25	1.25
132	5c on 8a dk bl	5.50	5.50
133	7½c On 12a vio brn	5.50	5.50
134	10c on 16a bis brn	2.75	2.75
135	15c on 24a bis	3.00	3.00
	Nos. 128-135 (8)	21.75	21.75

No. 75 Overprinted in Red

REPUBLICA

1913 ***Perf. 11½, 12½, 13½.***

No.	Type	Description	Unused	Used
137	A3	130r on 80r yel grn	3.50	2.75

Nos. 73 and 76 overprinted but not issued. Prices, $10, $12.

Same Overprint on No. 83 in Green

1914 ***Perf. 12***

No.	Type	Description	Unused	Used
139	A4	75r rose	3.50	2.75
a.		"PROVISORIO" double (G and R)	30.00	27.50

Ceres
A6

Perf. 11½, 12x11½, 15x14.

1914-26 **Typographed.**

Name and Value in Black.

No.	Type	Description	Unused	Used
144	A6	¼c ol brn	10	10
a.		Imperf.		
145	A6	½c black	10	10
146	A6	1c bl grn	1.25	1.00
147	A6	1c yel grn ('22)	10	10
148	A6	1½c lil brn	10	10
149	A6	2c carmine	18	15
150	A6	2c gray ('26)	25	*3.00*
151	A6	2½c lt vio	10	5
152	A6	3c org ('22)	35	25
153	A6	4c rose ('22)	12	*2.00*
154	A6	4½c gray ('22)	20	*3.00*
155	A6	5c dp bl	1.25	60
156	A6	5c brt bl ('22)	20	20
157	A6	6c lil ('22)	20	*3.00*
158	A6	7c ultra ('22)	20	*3.00*
159	A6	7½c yel brn	20	*3.00*
160	A6	8c slate	65	50
161	A6	10c org brn	20	15
162	A6	12c bl grn ('22)	35	25
163	A6	15c plum	7.50	5.50
164	A6	15c brn rose ('22)	25	15
165	A6	20c yel grn	20	15
166	A6	24c ultra ('26)	1.50	1.50
167	A6	25c choc ('26)	1.50	1.50
168	A6	30c brn, *grn*	5.00	5.00
169	A6	30c gray grn ('22)	35	25
170	A6	40c brn, *pink*	5.00	5.00
171	A6	40c turq bl ('22)	75	22
172	A6	50c org, *sal*	5.00	5.00
173	A6	50c vio ('26)	1.00	40
174	A6	60c dk bl ('22)	90	60
175	A6	60c rose ('26)	1.00	75
176	A6	80c brt rose ('22)	3.50	1.50
177	A6	1e grn *bl*	5.00	5.00
178	A6	1e rose ('22)	5.00	3.00
179	A6	1e dp bl ('26)	4.00	2.00
180	A6	2e dk vio ('22)	5.00	3.00
181	A6	5e buff ('26)	9.00	6.50
182	A6	10e pink ('26)	17.50	12.00
183	A6	20e pale turq ('26)	50.00	25.00
		Nos. 144-183 (40)	135.05	*104.57*

Provisional Issue of 1902 Overprinted in Carmine

REPUBLICA

1915 ***Perf. 11½, 12½, 13½***

No.	Type	Description	Unused	Used
184	A2	115r on 10r grn	1.75	1.75
a.		Perf. 13½	20.00	20.00
185	A2	115r on 20r rose	2.00	2.00
a.		Perf. 13½	20.00	20.00
186	A2	130r on 50r bl	1.75	1.75
187	A2	130r on 100r brn	1.25	1.25
188	A3	115r on 5r org	75	50
a.		Invtd. ovpt.	22.50	
189	A3	115r on 25r bl grn	1.25	1.10
a.		Perf. 11½	20.00	20.00
190	A3	115r on 150r car, *rose*	75	50
191	A3	130r on 75r car	1.25	1.25
192	A3	130r on 80r yel grn	1.25	1.25
a.		Inverted overprint	22.50	
193	A3	130r on 200r bl, *bl*	1.25	1.25
a.		Perf. 12½	55.00	45.00
		Nos. 184-193 (10)	13.25	12.60

War Tax Stamps of Portuguese Africa Surcharged

CABO VERDE
CORREIOS
½ C.

1921, Feb. 3 ***Perf. 15x14, 11½***

No.	Type	Description	Unused	Used
194	WT1	¼c on 1c grn	30	30
195	WT1	½c on 1c grn	45	30
a.		"1/2" instead of "½"	8.50	8.50
196	WT1	1c green	45	35

Nos. 127 and 126 Surcharged

Perf. 14 to 15.

No.	Type	Description	Unused	Used
197	CD27	2c on 15c on 150r bis	1.50	1.50
198	CD26	4c on 10c on 100r bis brn	1.75	1.50
a.		On No. 118(error)	110.00	110.00

No. 50 Surcharged

6 C.
REPUBLICA

Perf. 12.

No.	Type	Description	Unused	Used
200	A4	6c on 100r dk bl, *bl*	1.75	1.00
a.		Accent on "U" of surch.	7.50	7.50

Stamps of 1913-15 Surcharged

$04

1922, Apr. ***Perf. 11½, 12½, 13½***

On No. 137

No.	Type	Description	Unused	Used
201	A3	4c on 130r on 80r yel grn	2.00	2.00

On Nos. 191–193

No.	Type	Description	Unused	Used
202	A3	4c on 130r on 75r car	2.50	2.50
203	A3	4c on 130r on 80r yel grn	2.00	2.00
204	A3	4c on 130r on 200r bl, *bl*	1.25	90
a.		Perf. 12½	20.00	20.00

Surcharge of Nos. 201–204 with smaller $ occurs once in sheet of 28. Price eight times normal.

Nos. 78–79 Surcharged

República
40 C.

1925 ***Perf. 13½, 11½***

No.	Type	Description	Unused	Used
205	A3	40c on 400r on 300r bl, *sal*	90	60
206	N1	40c on 400r on 2½r brn	65	60

No. 176 Surcharged

70 C.

1931, Nov. ***Perf. 12x11½***

No.	Type	Description	Unused	Used
214	A6	70c on 80c brt rose	3.00	2.25

Ceres
A7

Wmkd. Maltese Cross. (232)

1934, May 1 ***Perf. 12x11½***

No.	Type	Description	Unused	Used
215	A7	1c bister	10	*1.00*
216	A7	5c ol brn	10	10
217	A7	10c violet	10	10
218	A7	5c black	10	10
219	A7	20c gray	10	10
220	A7	30c dk grn	13	10
221	A7	40c red org	40	25
222	A7	45c brt bl	75	50
223	A7	50c brown	60	40
224	A7	60c ol grn	60	40
225	A7	70c brn org	60	40
226	A7	80c emerald	60	40
227	A7	85c dp rose	2.50	2.00
228	A7	1e maroon	2.00	40
229	A7	1.40e dk bl	2.75	2.00
230	A7	2e dk vio	3.50	1.50
231	A7	5e ap grn	15.00	4.50
232	A7	10e ol bis	25.00	13.00
233	A7	20e orange	55.00	25.00
		Nos. 215-233 (19)	109.93	*52.25*

Vasco da Gama Issue

Common Design Types

1938 ***Perf. 13½x13.*** **Unwmkd.**

Name and Value in Black.

No.	Type	Description	Unused	Used
234	CD34	1c gray grn	5	*1.0*
235	CD34	5c org brn	10	*1.0*
236	CD34	10c dk car	10	1
237	CD34	15c dk vio brn	75	4
238	CD34	20c slate	35	2
239	CD35	30c rose vio	30	2
240	CD35	35c brt grn	40	3
241	CD35	40c brown	30	2
242	CD35	50c brt red vio	30	2
243	CD36	60c gray blk	45	4
244	CD36	70c brn vio	45	3
245	CD36	80c orange	45	3
246	CD36	1e red	60	3
247	CD37	1.75e blue	1.50	8
248	CD37	2e dk bl grn	2.25	1.0
249	CD37	5e ol grn	6.50	2.0
250	CD38	10e bl vio	9.00	2.0
251	CD38	20e red brn	25.00	5.0
		Nos. 234-251 (18)	48.85	*16.0*

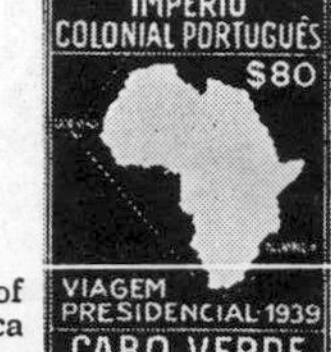

Outline Map of Africa
A8

1939, June 23 Litho. ***Perf. 11½x12***

No.	Type	Description	Unused	Used
252	A8	80c vio, *pale rose*	4.00	2.00
253	A8	1.75e bl, *pale bl*	20.00	17.50
254	A8	20e brn, *buff*	60.00	20.00

Issued to commemorate the visit of the President of Portugal to this colony in 1939.

Nos. 239 and 221 Surcharged with New Value and Bars in Black.

1948 ***Perf. 13½x13*** **Unwmkd.**

No.	Type	Description	Unused	Used
255	CD35	10c on 30c rose vio	1.50	2.00

Perf. 12x11½ **Wmk. 232**

No.	Type	Description	Unused	Used
256	A7	25c on 40c red org	1.50	2.00

Machado Pt., Sao Vicente
A9

Brava Creek, Sao Nicoláo
A10

Designs: 10c, Ribeira Grande. 1e, Harbor, Sao Vicente. 1.75e, Mindelo, distant view. 2e, Joao de Evora Beach. 5e, Mindelo. 10e, Volcano, Fire Island. 20e, Mt. Paul.

Perf. 14½

1948, Oct. 1 **Litho.** **Unwmkd.**

No.	Type	Description	Unused	Used
257	A9	5c vio brn & bis	40	40
258	A9	10c ol grn & pale grn	40	25
259	A10	50c mag & lil rose	60	30
260	A10	1e brn vio & rose lil	2.00	1.00
261	A10	1.75e ultra & grnsh bl	2.50	1.50
262	A10	2e dk brn & buff	12.00	1.50
263	A10	5e ol grn & yel	17.50	7.00
264	A10	10e red & cr	22.50	12.00
265	A10	20e dk vio & bis	55.00	20.00
		Nos. 257-265 (9)	112.90	43.95

Common Design Types pictured in section at front of book

Lady of Fatima Issue.
Common Design Type

1948, Dec.

266 CD40 50c dk bl 10.00 6.00

U.P.U Symbols
A10a

1949, Oct. ***Perf. 14***

267 A10a 1e red vio & pink 4.00 1.00

U.P.U., 75th anniversary

Holy Year Issue
Common Design Types

1950, May ***Perf. 13x13½***

268 CD41 1e org brn 70 50
269 CD42 2e slate 3.50 2.00

Holy Year Conclusion Issue
Common Design Type

1951, Oct. ***Perf. 14*** **Unwmkd.**

270 CD43 2e pur & lil 1.25 1.00

Stamps of 1938 Surcharged with New Value and Bars in Black.

Perf. 13½x13

1951, May 21 **Unwmkd.**

271 CD35 10c on 35c brt grn 50 *1.50*
272 CD36 20c on 70c brn vio 75 *1.50*
273 CD36 40c on 70c brn vio 1.50 *2.00*
274 CD36 50c on 80c org 2.50 *3.00*
275 CD37 1e on 1.75e bl 3.00 *4.00*
276 CD38 2e on 10e bl vio 5.00 *7.50*
a. 1e on 10e bl vio 100.00 100.00
Nos. 271-276 (6) 13.25 *19.50*

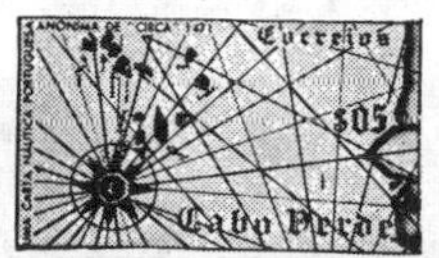

Map of Cape Verde Islands, 1502
A11

Vicente Dias and Gonçalo de Cintra
A12

Portraits: 30c, Diogo Alfonso and Alvaro Fernandes. 50c, Lançarote and Soeiro da Costa. 1e, Diogo Gomes and Antonio da Nola. 2e, Prince Fernando and Prince Henry the Navigator. 3e, Antao Gonçalves and Dinis Dias. 5e, Alfonso Gonçalves Baldaia and Joao Fernandes. 10e, Dinis Eanes da Gra and Alvaro de Freitas. 20e, Map of Cape Verde Islands, 1502.

1952, Feb. 24 ***Perf. 14***

277 A11 5c multi 10 10
278 A12 10c multi 10 10
279 A12 30c multi 10 10
280 A12 50c multi 13 10
281 A12 1e multi 20 13
282 A12 2e multi 1.00 20
283 A12 3e multi 6.00 1.00
284 A12 5e multi 3.00 60
285 A12 10e multi 4.50 1.25
286 A11 20e multi 10.00 1.50
Nos. 277-286 (10) 25.13 5.08

Medical Congress Issue.
Common Design Type

Design: Hypodermic Injection.

1952, June ***Perf. 13½***

287 CD44 20c ol grn & dk brn 50 40

No. 247 Surcharged with New Values and "X" in Black.

1952, Jan. 25 ***Perf. 13½x13***

288 CD37 10c on 1.75e bl 1.75 1.75
289 CD37 20c on 1.75e bl 1.75 1.75
290 CD37 50c on 1.75e bl 6.00 6.00
291 CD37 1e on 1.75e bl 75 75
292 CD37 1.50e on 1.75e bl 75 75
Nos. 288-292 (5) 11.00 11.00

Facade of Jeronymos Convent
A13

Lithographed.

1953, Jan. ***Perf. 13½*** **Unwmkd.**

293 A13 10c brn & pale ol 10 10
294 A13 50c pur & fawn 50 30
295 A13 1e dk grn & fawn 1.10 75

Issued to commemorate the Exhibition of Sacred Missionary Art held at Lisbon in 1951.

Stamp of Portugal and Arms of Colonies
A13a

1953 **Photogravure**

Stamp and Arms Multicolored.

296 A13a 50c lil rose & gray 1.00 60

Centenary of Portuguese stamps.

Sao Paulo Issue
Common Design Type

1954 **Lithographed.** ***Perf. 13½***

297 CD46 1e grn, cr & gray 35 20

Belem Tower, Lisbon, and Colonial Arms
A14

Arms of Praia
A15

1955, May 15 **Litho.** ***Perf. 13½***

298 A14 1e multi 30 20
299 A14 1.60e buff & multi 50 30

Issued to publicize the visit of Pres. Francisco H. C. Lopes.

1958, June 14 ***Perf. 12x11½***

300 A15 1e multi 30 20
301 A15 2.50e pink & multi 60 30

Centenary of city of Praia.

Fair Emblem, Globe and Arms
A15a

1958 ***Perf. 12x11½***

302 A15a 2e multi 50 40

World's Fair, Brussels, Apr. 17–Oct. 19.

Tropical Medicine Congress Issue
Common Design Type

Design: Aloe vera.

1958, Sept. 5 ***Perf. 13½***

303 CD47 3e multi 3.50 2.00

Prince Henry
A16

Antonio da Nola
A17

1960, June 25 **Litho.** ***Perf. 13½***

304 A16 2e multi 30 20

Issued to commemorate the 500th anniversary of the death of Prince Henry the Navigator.

1960, Oct. ***Perf. 14½*** **Unwmkd.**

Design: 2.50e, Diogo Gomes.

305 A17 1e multi 45 30
306 A17 2.50e multi 1.00 65

Discovery of Cape Verde, 500th anniversary.

School Children
A18

1960

307 A18 2.50e multi 75 50

Issued to commemorate the 10th anniversary of the Commission for Technical Cooperation in Africa South of the Sahara (C.C.T.A.).

Arms of Praia
A19

Designs: Arms of various cities and towns of Cape Verde.

1961, July **Litho.** ***Perf. 13½***

Multicolored

308 A19 5c *shown* 5 5
309 A19 15c *Nova Sintra* 5 5
310 A19 20c *Ribeira Brava* 5 5
311 A19 30c *Assomada* 10 10
312 A19 1e *Maio* 60 13
313 A19 2e *Mindelo* 50 13
314 A19 2.50e *Santa Maria* 90 18
315 A19 3e *Pombas* 1.50 30
316 A19 5e *Sal-Rei* 1.50 30
317 A19 7.50e *Tarrafal* 1.00 40
318 A19 15e *Maria Pia* 1.50 60
319 A19 30e *San Felipe* 3.50 1.35
Nos. 308-319 (12) 11.25 3.64

Sports Issue
Common Design Type

Sports: 50c, Throwing javelin. 1e, Discus throwing. 1.50e, Cricket. 2.50e, Boxing. 4.50e, Hurding. 12.50e, Golf.

1962, Jan. 18 ***Perf. 13½***

Multicolored Design

320 CD48 50c lt brn 10 10
321 CD48 1e lt grn 70 25
322 CD48 1.50e lt bl grn 40 20
323 CD48 2.50e pale vio bl 60 30
324 CD48 4.50e orange 1.00 60
325 CD48 12.50e beige 2.25 1.50
Nos. 320-325 (6) 5.05 2.95

Anti-Malaria Issue
Common Design Type

Design: Anopheles pretoriensis.

1962 **Lithographed** ***Perf. 13½***

326 CD49 2.50e multi 1.00 70

Issued for the World Health Organization drive to eradicate malaria.

Airline Anniversary Issue
Common Design Type

1963, Oct. ***Perf. 14½*** **Unwmkd.**

327 CD50 2.50e gray & multi 60 40

Issued to commemorate the 10th anniversary of Transportes Aéreos Portugueses.

National Overseas Bank Issue
Common Design Type

Design: 1.50e, José da Silva Mendes Leal.

1964, May 16 ***Perf. 13½***

328 CD51 1.50e multi 60 50

Issued to commemorate the centenary of the National Overseas Bank of Portugal.

ITU Issue
Common Design Type

1965, May 17 **Litho.** ***Perf. 14½***

329 CD52 2.50e buff & multi 1.50 1.00

Issued to commemorate the centenary of the International Telecommunication Union.

Militia Drummer, 1806
A20

Designs: 1e, Soldier, Militia, 1806. 1.50e, Grenadier officer, 1833. 2.50e, Grenadier, 1833. 3e, Cavalry officer, 1834. 4e, Grenadier, 1835. 5e, Artillery officer, 1848. 10e, Drum major, infantry, 1856.

1965, Dec. 1 **Litho.** ***Perf. 14½***

330 A20 50c multi 12 12
331 A20 1e multi 30 18
332 A20 1.50e multi 45 18
333 A20 2.50e multi 1.00 30
334 A20 3e multi 1.50 50
335 A20 4e multi 1.00 50
336 A20 5e multi 1.00 60
337 A20 10e multi 2.00 1.50
Nos. 330-337 (8) 7.37 3.88

National Revolution Issue
Common Design Type

Design: 1e, Dr. Adriano Moreira School and Health Center.

1966, May 28 **Litho.** ***Perf. 12***

338 CD53 1e multi 30 30

National Revolution, 40th anniversary.

Navy Club Issue
Common Design Type

Designs: 1e, Capt. Fontoura da Costa and gunboat Mandovy. 1.50e, Capt. Carvalho Araujo and minesweeper Augusto Castilho.

1967, Jan. 31 **Litho.** ***Perf. 13***

339 CD54 1e multi 60 30
340 CD54 1.50e multi 1.00 40

Centenary of Portugal's Navy Club.

Virgin Mary Statue
A21

Pres. Rodrigues Thomaz
A22

1967, May 13 Litho. *Perf. 12½x13*

341	A21	1e multi	20	15

Issued to commemorate the 50th anniversary of the apparition of the Virgin Mary to 3 shepherd children at Fatima.

1968, Feb. 9 Litho. *Perf. 13½*

342	A22	1e multi	20	20

Issued to commemorate the 1968 visit of Pres. Americo de Deus Rodrigues Thomaz.

Cabral Issue

Pedro Alvares Cabral
A23

Design: 1e, Cantino's world map, 1502 (horiz.).

1968, Apr. 22 Litho. *Perf. 14*

343	A23	1e multi	70	40
344	A23	1.50e multi	80	40

See note after Angola No. 545.

São Vicente Harbor
A24

Physic Nut
A25

Designs: 1.50e, Peanut plant. 2.50e, Castor-oil plant. 3.50e, Yams. 4e, Date palm. 4.50e, Guavas. 5e, Tamarind. 10e, Bitter cassava. 30e, Woman carrying fruit baskets.

1968, Oct. 15 Litho. *Perf. 14*

345	A24	50c multi	6	5
346	A25	1e multi	10	5
347	A25	1.50e multi	15	15
348	A25	2.50e multi	25	12
349	A25	3.50e multi	30	15
350	A25	4e multi	30	18
351	A25	4.50e multi	40	18
352	A25	5e multi	40	18
353	A25	10e multi	80	35
354	A25	30e multi	3.00	1.35
		Nos. 345-354 (10)	5.76	2.76

Admiral Coutinho Issue

Common Design Type

Design: 30c, Adm. Coutinho and map showing route of first flight from Lisbon to Rio de Janeiro (vert.).

1969, Feb. 17 Litho. *Perf. 14*

355	CD55	30c multi	20	10

Issued to commemorate the centenary of the birth of Admiral Carlos Viegas Gago Coutinho (1869–1959), explorer and aviation pioneer.

Vasco da Gama
A26

King Manuel I
A27

Vasco da Gama Issue

1969, Aug. 29 Litho. *Perf. 14*

356	A26	1.50e multi	20	10

Issued to commemorate the 500th anniversary of the birth of Vasco da Gama (1469–1524), navigator.

Administration Reform Issue

Common Design Type

1969, Sept. 25 Litho. *Perf. 14*

357	CD56	2e multi	20	20

King Manuel I Issue

1969, Dec. 1 Litho. *Perf. 14*

358	A27	3e multi	30	20

Issued to commemorate the 500th anniversary of the birth of King Manuel I.

Marshal Carmona Issue

Common Design Type

Design: 2.50e, Antonio Oscar Carmona in marshal's uniform.

1970, Nov. 15 Litho. *Perf. 14*

359	CD57	2.50e multi	30	20

Galleons on Sanaga River
A28

1972, May 25 Litho. *Perf. 13*

360	A28	5e lil rose & multi	30	20

4th centenary of the publication of The Lusiads by Luiz Camoëns.

Olympic Games Issue

Common Design Type

Design: 4e, Basketball and boxing, Olympic emblem.

1972, June 20 *Perf. 14x13½*

361	CD59	4e multi	30	20

20th Olympic Games, Munich, Aug. 26–Sept. 11.

Lisbon-Rio de Janeiro Flight Issue

Common Design Type

Design: 3.50e, "Lusitania" landing at San Vicente.

1972, Sept. 20 Litho. *Perf. 13½*

362	CD60	3.50e multi	40	20

WMO Centenary Issue

Common Design Type

1973, Dec. 15 Litho. *Perf. 13*

363	CD61	2.50e ultra & multi	40	20

Centenary of international meteorological cooperation.

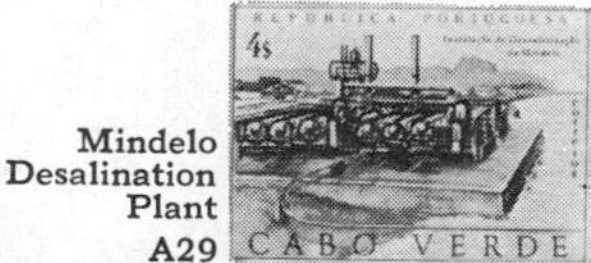

Mindelo Desalination Plant
A29

1974 Lithographed *Perf. 13½*

364	A29	4e multi	75	45

Opening of the Mindelo desalination plant.

Republic

No. 343 Overprinted: "INDEPENDENCIA / 5-Julho-75"

1975, Dec. 19 Litho. *Perf. 14*

365	A23	1e multi	25	15

Proclamation of Independence.

Amilcar Cabral, Flag and Crowd
A30

1976, Jan. 20

366	A30	5e multi	50	20

3rd anniversary of the assassination of Amilcar Cabral (1924–1973), revolutionary leader.

Rising Sun, Coat of Arms, Liberated People—A31

1976, July 5 Litho. *Perf. 14*

367	A31	50c multi	10	10
368	A31	3e multi	45	20
369	A31	15e multi	1.25	60
370	A31	50e multi	4.00	2.00
	a.	Miniature sheet of 4	*20.00*	*20.00*

First anniversary of independence. No. 370a contains one each of Nos. 367–370. Size: 154x110mm.

No. 351 Overprinted with Row of Stars and: "REPUBLICA / DE"

1976 Litho. *Perf. 14*

372	A25	4.50e multi	3.00	2.25

Amilcar Cabral, Map and Flag of Cape Verde—A32

1976, Sept. 19 *Perf. 14*

373	A32	1e multi	20	20

Party of International Action (PAICC), 20th anniversary.

Electronic Tree and ITU Emblem
A33

Ashtray
A34

1977, May 17 Litho. *Perf. 13½x13*

374	A33	5.50e multi	40	20

World Telecommunications Day.

1977, July 5 Litho. *Perf. 14*

Carved Coconut Shells: 30c, Bell on stand. 50c, Lamp with Adam and Eve. 1e, Hollow shell with Nativity. 1.50e, Desk lamp. 5e, Jar. 10e, Jar with hinged cover. 20e, Tobacco jar with palms. 30e, Stringed instrument.

375	A34	20c lil & multi	12	5
376	A34	30c rose & multi	20	5
377	A34	50c sal & multi	12	8
378	A34	1e lt grn & multi	20	12
379	A34	1.50e org yel & multi	25	20
380	A34	5e gray & multi	40	12
381	A34	10e lt bl & multi	80	20
382	A34	20e yel & multi	1.50	80
383	A34	30e rose lil & multi	2.50	1.25
		Nos. 375-383 (9)	6.09	2.87

Cape Verde No. 1 and Coat of Arms
A35

Congress Emblem
A36

1977, Sept. 12 Litho. *Perf. 13½*

384	A35	4e bl & multi	30	12
385	A35	8e lil & multi	70	28

Centenary of Cape Verde stamps.

1977, Nov. 15 *Perf. 14*

386	A36	3.50e multi	30	10

African Party of Independence of Guinea-Bissau and Cape Verde (PAIGC), 3rd congress, Nov. 15–20.

No. 363 Overprinted with Row of Stars and: "REPUBLICA / DE"

1978, May 1 *Perf. 12*

387	CD61	2.50e ultra & multi	30	10

No. 355 Surcharged with New Value and Bars

1978, May 1 *Perf. 14*

388	CD55	3e on 30c multi	30	12

Antenna and ITU Emblem—A37

1978, May 17 Litho. *Perf. 14*

389	A37	3.50e sil & multi	30	15

10th World Telecommunications Day.

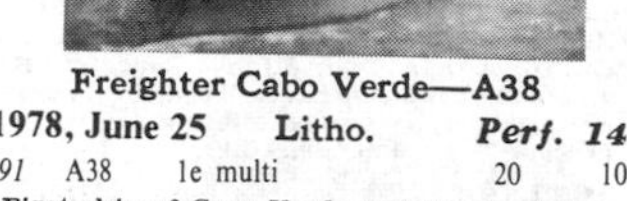

Freighter Cabo Verde—A38

1978, June 25 Litho. *Perf. 14*

391	A38	1e multi	20	10

First ship of Cape Verde merchant marine.

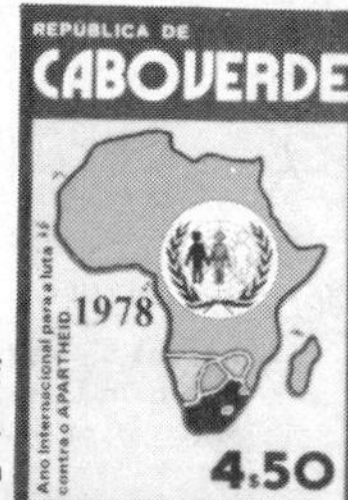

Map of Africa and Equality Emblem
A39

1978, June 21
392 A39 4.50e multi 40 20
Anti-Apartheid Year.

Human Rights Emblem
A40

1978, Dec. 10 **Litho.** ***Perf. 14***
393 A40 1.50e multi 20 5
394 A40 2e multi 30 15
Universal Declaration of Human Rights, 30th anniversary.

Children and Balloons, IYC Emblem
A41

IYC Emblem and Child's Drawing: 3.50e, Children and flowers.

1979, June 1 **Litho.** ***Perf. 14***
395 A41 1.50e multi 20 5
396 A41 3.50e multi 30 15

International Year of the Child.

Pindjiguiti Massacre Monument—A42
Natl. Youth Week—A42a

1979, Aug. 3 ***Perf. 13***
397 A42 4.50e multi 40 15

Massacre of Pindjiguiti, 20th anniversary.

1979, Sept. 1 **Litho.** ***Perf. 14***
397A A42a 3.50e Poster 70 15

Centenary of Mindelo—A43

1980, Apr. 23 **Litho.** ***Perf. 12½***
398 A43 4e multi 30 15

Flag of Cape Verde
A44

Stylized Bird, "V"
A45

1980 **Litho.** ***Perf. 12½***
399 A44 4e multi 30 15
400 A45 4e multi 30 15
401 A45 7e multi 60 20
402 A45 11e multi 90 30

5th anniversary of independence No. 399 issued June 1, others July 5.

1980 Natl. Census—A45a

1980, May 13
402A A45a 3.50e multi 70
402B A45a 4.50e multi 90

Running—A46

1980, June 6
403 A46 1e *shown* 20 15
404 A46 2.50e *Boxing* 20 10
405 A46 3e *Basketball* 20 15
406 A46 4e *Volleyball* 30 15
407 A46 20e *Swimming* 1.75 40
408 A46 50e *Tennis* 4.00 1.00
Nos. 403-408 (6) 6.65 1.95

Souvenir Sheet
Perf. 13
409 A46 30e *Soccer*, horiz. *10.00*

22nd Summer Olympic Games, Moscow, July 19-Aug. 3. No. 409 has multicolored margin showing Misha, the bear, and Olympic flame. Size: 99x67mm.

Thunnus Alalunga—A47

1980, Nov. 11 **Litho.** ***Perf. 13***
410 A47 50c shown 10 10
411 A47 4.50e Trachurus trachurus 30 15
412 A47 8e Muraena helena 60 20
413 A47 10e Corvina nigra 80 20
414 A47 12e Katsuwonus pelamis 1.00 30
415 A47 50e Prionace glauca 4.00 1.00
Nos. 410-415 (6) 6.80 1.95

Lochnera Rosea
A48

1980, Dec. 29
416 A48 50c shown 10 10
417 A48 4.50e Poinciana regia-bojer 30 15
418 A48 8e Mirabilis jalapa 60 20
419 A48 10e Nerium oleander 80 20
420 A48 12e Bougainvillia litoralis 1.00 30
421 A48 30e Hibiscus 2.50 60
Nos. 416-421 (6) 5.30 1.55

WHO Anti-smoking Campaign—A48a

1980, Sept. 19 ***Perf. 12½***
421A A48a 4e multi 80
421B A48a 7e multi 1.40

Arca Verde—A49

1980, Nov. 30 **Litho.** ***Perf. 12½x12***
422 A49 3e shown 20 10
423 A49 5.50e Ilha do Maio 40 20
424 A49 7.50e Ilha de Komo 60 20
425 A49 9e Boa Vista 70 20
426 A49 12e Santo Antao 1.00 30
427 A49 30e Santiago 2.50 60
Nos. 422-427 (6) 5.40 1.60

Hand-woven Bag, Map—A49a

Various hand-woven articles. 10e vert.

1978, May 21 **Litho.** ***Perf. 14***
427A A49a 50c multi 10
427B A49a 1.50e multi 30
427C A49a 2e multi 40
427D A49a 3e multi 60
427E A49a 10e multi 2.00
Nos. 427A-427E (5) 3.40

Desert Erosion Prevention Campaign—A50

1981, Mar. 30 **Litho.** ***Perf. 13***
428 A50 4.50e multi 40 20
429 A50 10.50e multi 80 30

6th Anniv. of Constitution
A51

1981, Apr. 15
430 A51 4.50e multi 40 20

Souvenir Sheet

Austria No. B336
A52

1981, May 18
431 A52 50e multi 4.00

WIPA '81 Philatelic Exhibition, Vienna, Austria, May 22-31. No. 431 has multicolored margin showing Prince Eugene statue, exhibition emblem. Size: 108x63mm.

Antenna—A53

1981, Aug. 25 **Litho.** ***Perf. 12½***
432 A53 4.50e shown 40 20
433 A53 8e Dish antenna 60 20
434 A53 20e Dish antenna, diff. 1.75 50

Intl. Year of the Disabled—A54

1981, Dec. 25 **Litho.** ***Perf. 12½***
435 A54 4.50e multi 30 15

Purple Gallinule—A55

1981, Dec. 30

436	A55	1e Egret, vert.	10	10
437	A55	4.50e Barn owl, vert.	30	15
438	A55	8e Passerine, vert.	55	15
439	A55	10e shown	60	15
440	A55	12e Guinea fowl	75	20
		Nos. 436-440 (5)	2.30	75

Souvenir Sheet
Perf. 13

441	A55	50e Razo. Isld. lark	3.00	2.00

No. 441 contains one stamp (31x39mm.); multicolored margin continues design. Size: 80x56mm.

CILSS Congress, Praia, Jan. 17—A56

1982, Jan. 17 ***Perf. 13x12½***

442	A56	11.50e multi	65	30

Amilcar Cabral Soccer Championship—A57

Designs: Soccer players and flags.

1982, Feb. 10 **Litho.** ***Perf. 12½***

443	A57	4.50e multi	30	15
444	A57	7.50e multi	45	15
445	A57	11.50e multi	75	20

1982 World Cup—A58

Designs: Soccer players and ball.

1982, Apr. 25

446	A58	1.50e multi	10	10
447	A58	4.50e multi	30	15
448	A58	8e multi	55	15
449	A58	10.50e multi	60	20
450	A58	12e multi	75	20
451	A58	20e multi	1.25	30
		Nos. 446-451 (6)	3.55	1.10

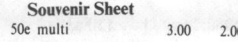

Souvenir Sheet

452	A58	50e multi	3.00	2.00

No. 452 has multicolored margin continuing design. Size: 83x91mm.

First Anniv of Women's Organization—A59

1982, Apr. 15 **Litho.** ***Perf. 12½x12***

453	A59	4.50e Marching	30	15
454	A59	8e Farming	55	15
455	A59	12e Child care	75	20

Estaleiros Navais Port, St. Vincent—A59a

1982 **Litho.** ***Perf. 13x12½***

455A	A59a	10.50e multi	60	20

Natl. independence, 7th anniv.

Return of Barque Morrissey-Ernestina—A60

1982, July 5 **Litho.** ***Perf. 13***

456	A60	12e multi	75	20

Butterflies—A61

1982, July 27 **Litho.**

457	A61	2e Hypolimnas misippus	8	
458	A61	4.50e Melanitis lede	18	
459	A61	8e Catopsilia florella	30	
460	A61	10.50e Colias electo	42	
461	A61	11.50e Danaus chrysippus	48	
462	A61	12e Papilio demodecus	50	
		Nos. 457-462 (6)	1.96	

Francisco Xavier da Cruz (1905-1958), Composer—A62

Design: 14e, Eugenio Tavares (1867-1930), poet.

1983, Feb. 20 **Litho.** ***Perf. 13***

463	A62	7e multi	28	
464	A62	14e multi	55	

World Communications Year—A63

1983, Oct. 10 **Litho.**

465	A63	13e multi	52	

Local Seashells—A64

1983, Nov. 30 ***Perf. 13½***

466	A64	50c Conus ateralbus	5	
467	A64	1e Conus decoratus	5	
468	A64	3e Conus salreiensis	12	
469	A64	10e Conus verdensis	40	
470	A64	50e Conus cuneolus	2.00	
		Nos. 466-470 (5)	2.62	

40th Anniv. of Intl. Civil Aviation Org.—A65

Airplanes: 50c, Ogma-Auster D5/160, 1966. 2e, De Havilland DH-104 Dove, 1945. 10e, Hawker Siddeley 748-200, 1972. 13e, De Havilland Dragon Rapide, 1945. 20e, De Havilland Twin Otter, 1977. 50e, Britten-Norman Islander, 1971.

1984, Feb. 15 **Litho.**

471	A65	50c multi	5	
472	A65	2e multi	8	
473	A65	10e multi	40	
474	A65	13e multi	52	
475	A65	20e multi	80	
476	A65	50e multi	2.00	
		Nos. 471-476 (6)	3.85	

Amilcar Cabral—A66

1983, Jan. 17 **Litho.** ***Perf. 14½***

477	A66	7e multi	25	
478	A66	10.50e multi	36	
a.		Souvenir sheet of 2, #477-478	1.05	

Amilcar Cabral Symposium, Jan. 17-20.

No. 478a has pale green and bluish greer inscribed margin picturing Cabral quote. Sold fo 30e. Size: 130x70mm.

Christianity in Cape Verde, 450th Anniv.—A67

1983 **Photo.** ***Perf. 14½***

479	A67	7e Cross overshadowing islands	18	

Natl. Solidarity Campaign—A68

1984, Dec. ***Perf. 13½***

480	A68	6.50e multi	35	12
481	A68	13.50e multi	75	25

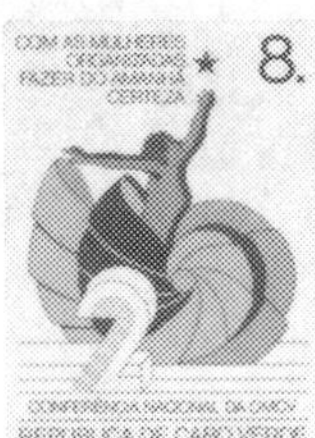

2nd Conference of Natl. Women's Orgs., Mar. 23-27—A69

1985, Mar. 27 **Litho.** ***Perf. 13½***

482	A69	8e multi	20	

Miniature Sheet

483	A69	30e multi	75	

Size: 99x80mm.

Natl. Independence, 10th Anniv.—A70

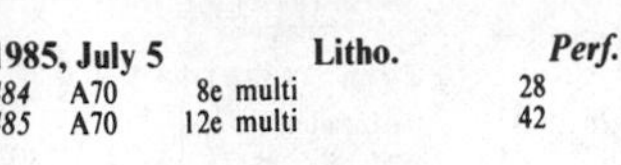

1985, July 5 **Litho.** ***Perf.***

484	A70	8e multi	28
485	A70	12e multi	42

Vapor, by Hundertwasser—A72

1985, Oct. 30 **Photo. & Engr.** ***Perf. 14***

Black Surcharge

487	A72	30e on 10e multi	1.05

Souvenir Sheets
Background Color

488	Sheet of 4	7.00
a.	A72 50e yel & multi	1.75
489	Sheet of 4	7.00
a.	A72 50e red & multi	1.75
490	Sheet of 4	7.00
a.	A72 50e grn & multi	1.75

Nos. 488-490 have gray decorative margins; dark gray control numbers. Sizes: 190x259mm.

World Wildlife Fund—A73

1986, June 15 **Litho.** ***Perf. 13½x14½***

491	A73	8e Mabuya vaillanti	28
492	A73	10e Tarentola gigas brancoensis	35
493	A73	15e Tarentola gigas gigas	52
494	A73	30e Hemidactylus bouvieri	1.05

Souvenir Sheet

495	Sheet of 2	3.50
a.	A73 50e Mabuya vaillanti	1.75
b.	A73 50e Hemidactylus bouvieri	1.75

No. 495 printed with center label picturing progress union emblem. Nos. 495a-495b have bister margin; printed without WWF emblem. Size: 130x60mm.

World Food Day—A74

1986, June 20 ***Perf. 14***

496	A74	8e Caldron	28
497	A74	12e Mortar & pestle	42
498	A74	15e Quern stone	52

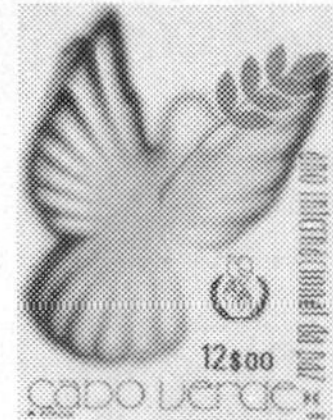

Intl. Peace Year—A75

1986, Dec. 24 **Litho.** ***Perf. 14***

499	A75	12e multi	42
500	A75	30e multi	1.05

AIR POST STAMPS.

Common Design Type
Name and Value in Black
Perf. 13½x13.

1938, July 26 **Unwmkd.**

C1	CD39	10c scarlet	50	45
C2	CD39	20c purple	50	45
C3	CD39	50c orange	50	45
C4	CD39	1e ultra	50	45
C5	CD39	2e lil brn	1.10	70
C6	CD39	3e dk grn	2.00	1.50
C7	CD39	5e red brn	6.00	1.50
C8	CD39	9e rose car	10.00	3.00
C9	CD39	10e magenta	14.00	4.50
		Nos. C1-C9 (9)	35.10	13.00

No. C7 exists with overprint "Exposicao Internacional de Nova York, 1939–1940" and Trylon and Perisphere.

POSTAGE DUE STAMPS.

D1

D2

Typographed.
1904 *Perf. 12.* **Unwmkd.**

J1	D1	5r yel grn	28	50
J2	D1	10r slate	28	50
J3	D1	20r yel brn	50	60
J4	D1	30r red org	90	1.00
J5	D1	50r gray brn	50	1.00
J6	D1	60r red brn	6.50	6.50
J7	D1	100r lilac	1.50	1.75
J8	D1	130r dl bl	1.50	1.75
J9	D1	200r carmine	1.75	2.00
J10	D1	500r dl vio	4.50	5.00
		Nos. J1-J10 (10)	18.21	20.60

Overprinted in Carmine or Green

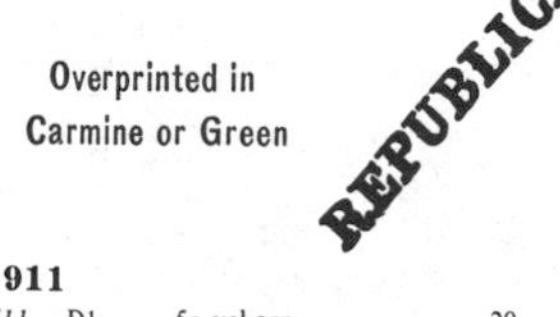

1911

J11	D1	5r yel grn	20	20
J12	D1	10r slate	20	20
J13	D1	20r yel brn	30	25
J14	D1	30r orange	30	25
J15	D1	50r gray brn	30	25
J16	D1	60r red brn	60	40
J17	D1	100r lilac	60	40
J18	D1	130r dl bl	70	50
J19	D1	200r car (G)	1.25	75
J20	D1	500r dl vio	1.75	1.75
		Nos. J11-J20 (10)	6.20	4.95

1921 *Perf. 11½.*

J21	D2	½c yel grn	12	25
J22	D2	1c slate	12	25
J23	D2	2c red brn	12	25
J24	D2	3c orange	12	25
J25	D2	5c gray brn	12	25
J26	D2	6c lt brn	12	12
J27	D2	10c red vio	12	12
J28	D2	13c dl bl	50	75
J29	D2	20c carmine	50	75
J30	D2	50c gray	1.25	1.50
		Nos. J21-J30 (10)	3.09	4.49

Common Design Type
Photogravure and Typographed.
1952 *Perf. 14.* **Unwmkd.**
Numeral in Red, Frame Multicolored.

J31	CD45	10c chocolate	8	8
J32	CD45	30c blk brn	12	12
J33	CD45	50c dk bl	15	15
J34	CD45	1e dk bl	20	20
J35	CD45	2e red brn	20	20
J36	CD45	5e ol grn	40	40
		Nos. J31-J36 (6)	1.15	1.15

NEWSPAPER STAMP.

N1

1893 Typo. *Perf. 11½* **Unwmkd.**

P1	N1	2½r brown	1.00	60
a.		Perf. 12½	2.00	1.25
b.		Perf. 13½	5.75	2.50

POSTAL TAX STAMPS.

Pombal Issue
Common Design Types
Engraved.
1925 *Perf. 12½.* **Unwmkd.**

RA1	CD28	15c dl vio & blk	50	50
RA2	CD29	15c dl vio & blk	50	50
RA3	CD30	15c dl vio & blk	50	50

St. Isabel
PT1

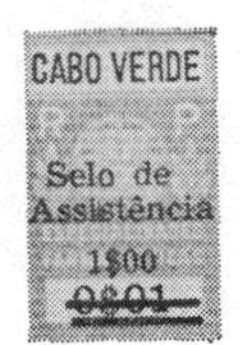

PT2

1948 Lithographed *Perf. 11*

RA4	PT1	50c dk grn	2.50	2.00
RA5	PT1	1e hn brn	5.50	3.00

No. RA5 Surcharged with New Value and Bars

1959

RA6	PT1	50c on 1e hn brn	1.00	75

Perf. 14

RA7	PT1	50c car rose	1.50	80
RA8	PT1	1e blue	1.50	80

St. Isabel Type Redrawn
1967–72 Lithographed *Perf. 14*
Multicolored

RA9	PT1	30c (bl panel)	20	20
RA10	PT1	50c (lil rose panel)	50	50
RA11	PT1	50c (red panel) ('72)	*2.50*	*2.50*
RA12	PT1	1e (brn panel)	60	60
RA13	PT1	1e (red lil panel) ('72)	*2.50*	*2.50*
		Nos. RA9-RA13 (5)	*6.30*	*6.30*

Nos. RA9–RA13 are inscribed "ASSISTENCIA" in large letters in bottom panel and "PORTUGAL" and "CABO VERDE" in small letters in upper left corner.

Revenue Stamps Surcharged in Green, Blue or Black

1967–72 Typographed *Perf. 12*
Black "CABO VERDE" & Value
Pale Green Burelage

RA14	PT2	50c on 1c org (Bl) ('71)	1.50	60
a.		Black surcharge ('68?)	*10.00*	*8.75*
RA15	PT2	50c on 2c org (G) ('69)	*1.75*	*1.00*
a.		Blue surcharge	1.50	60
b.		Black surcharge ('68?)	*10.00*	*8.00*
c.		Inverted surcharge (Bk)		
RA16	PT2	50c on 3c org (G) ('72)	80	60
RA17	PT2	50c on 5c org (G) ('72)	80	60
RA18	PT2	50c on 10c org (G) ('71)	1.00	1.00
RA19	PT2	1e on 1c org (Bk)	5.00	4.00
RA20	PT2	1e on 2c org (G) ('71)	1.75	1.75
a.		Blue surcharge ('71)	1.50	60
b.		Black surcharge	5.00	4.00
		Nos. RA14-RA20 (7)	*12.60*	*9.55*

POSTAL TAX DUE STAMPS.

Pombal Issue.
Common Design Types
1925 *Perf. 12½.* **Unwmkd.**

RAJ1	CD31	30c dl vio & blk	50	50
RAJ2	CD32	30c dl vio & blk	50	50
RAJ3	CD33	30c dl vio & blk	50	50

CARINTHIA

See Austria and Jugoslavia.

CAROLINE ISLANDS

(kăr'ō·līn)

LOCATION—A group of about 549 small islands in the West Pacific Ocean, north of the Equator.
GOVT.—Former German colony.
AREA—550 sq. mi.
POP.—40,000 (approx. 1915.)

100 Pfennig = 1 Mark

Stamps of Germany 1889–90 Overprinted in Black

Overprinted at 56° Angle.
1900 *Perf. 13½x14½.* **Unwmkd.**

1	A9	3pf dk brn	17.50	20.00
2	A9	5pf green	22.50	20.00
3	A10	10pf carmine	25.00	25.00
4	A10	20pf ultra	30.00	35.00
5	A10	25pf orange	75.00	80.00
6	A10	50pf red brn	75.00	80.00
		Nos. 1-6 (6)	245.00	260.00

1899 Overprinted at 48° Angle.

1a	A9	3pf lt brn	700.00	1,000.
2a	A9	5pf green	850.00	750.00
3a	A10	10pf carmine	110.00	200.00
4a	A10	20pf ultra	110.00	200.00
5a	A10	25pf orange	*2,000.*	*4,000.*
6a	A10	50pf red brn	*1,250.*	*2,400.*

Kaiser's Yacht "Hohenzollern"
A3 A4

1900–10 Typographed *Perf. 14*

7	A3	3pf brown	1.25	1.50
8	A3	5pf green	1.25	2.25
9	A3	10pf carmine	1.25	*6.00*
a.		Half used as 5pf on cover, back-stamped in Jaluit ('05)		*150.00*
10	A3	20pf ultra	1.75	*10.00*
a.		Half used as 10pf on cover ('10)		*8,500.*
11	A3	25pf org & blk, *yel*	2.25	*17.50*
12	A3	30pf org & blk, *sal*	2.25	*17.50*
13	A3	40pf lake & blk	2.25	*20.00*
14	A3	50pf pur & blk, *sal*	2.75	*25.00*
15	A3	80pf lake & blk, *rose*	4.00	*32.50*

Engraved.
Perf. 14½x14

16	A4	1m carmine	5.50	*75.0*
17	A4	2m blue	9.25	*100.0*
18	A4	3m blk vio	14.00	*200.0*
19	A4	5m sl & car	225.00	*700.0*
		Nos. 7-19 (13)	272.75	

No. 9a is known as the "typhoon provisional" the stock of 5pf stamps having been destroyed during a typhoon. Covers (cards) without backstamp, price about $90.

Forged cancellations are found on Nos. 7–19.

No. 7 Handstamp Surcharged **5 Pf**

1910, July 12

20	A3	5pf on 3pf brn	*6,500*

Price is for stamp tied to cover. Stamps on piece sell for about one-third less.

Wmk. 125

Typographed
1915–19 **Wmkd. Lozenges. (125)**

21	A3	3pf brn ('19)	1.25
22	A3	5pf green	20.00

Engraved.

23	A4	5m sl & car	25.00

Nos. 21–23 were never placed in use.

CARPATHO-UKRAINE

(Listed under Czechoslovakia).

CASTELLORIZO

(käs·tĕl'lō·rē'tsō)
(Castelrosso)

LOCATION—A Mediterranean island in the Dodecanese group lying close to the coast of Asia Minor and about 60 miles east of Rhodes.
GOVT.—Former Italian Colony.
AREA—4 sq. mi.
POP.—2,238 (1936).

Formerly a Turkish possession, Castellorizo was occupied by the French in 1915 and ceded to Italy after World War I.

Issued under French Occupation.

25 Centimes = 1 Piastre
100 Centimes = 1 Franc

Stamps of French Offices in Turkey Overprinted **B. N. F. CASTELLORIZO**

1920 *Perf. 14x13½* **Unwmkd.**

1	A2	1c gray	30.00	30.00
a.		Inverted ovpt.	60.00	60.00
b.		Double ovpt.	77.50	77.50
2	A2	2c vio brn	30.00	30.00
3	A2	3c red org	30.00	30.00
a.		Inverted overprint	60.00	60.00
4	A2	5c green	30.00	30.00
a.		Inverted overprint	60.00	60.00
5	A3	10c rose	35.00	35.00
6	A3	15c pale red	50.00	50.00
a.		Inverted overprint	125.00	125.00
7	A3	20c brn vio	55.00	55.00
8	A5	1pi on 25c bl	55.00	55.00

9	A3	30c lilac	55.00	55.00
10	A4	40c red & pale bl	125.00	125.00
a.		Inverted ovpt.	375.00	375.00
11	A6	2pi on 50c bis brn & lav	125.00	125.00
a.		Inverted ovpt.	375.00	375.00
12	A6	4pi on 1fr cl & ol grn	160.00	160.00
a.		Double ovpt.	475.00	475.00
b.		Inverted ovpt.	475.00	475.00
13	A6	20pi on 5fr dk bl & buff	475.00	475.00
a.		Double overprint	825.00	825.00
		Nos. 1-13 (13)	1,255.	1,255.

On Nos. 10–13 the overprint is placed vertically.

No. 1–9 were overprinted in blocks of 25. Position 4 had "CASTELLORIZO" inverted and Positions 8 and 18 had "CASTELLORISO". The later variety also occurred in the setting of the form for Nos. 10–13.

"B. N. F." are the initials of "Base Navale Francaise".

Overprinted in Black or Red — O. N. F. Castellorizo

1920

On Stamps of French Offices in Turkey

14	A2	1c gray	14.00	14.00
15	A2	2c vio brn	14.00	14.00
16	A2	3c red org	16.00	16.00
17	A2	5c grn (R)	16.00	16.00
19	A3	10c rose	16.00	16.00
20	A3	15c pale red	22.50	22.50
21	A3	20c brn vio	45.00	45.00
22	A5	1pi on 25c bl (R)	40.00	40.00
23	A3	30c lil (R)	40.00	40.00
24	A4	40c red & pale bl	40.00	40.00
25	A6	2pi on 50c bis brn & lav	40.00	40.00
26	A6	4pi on 1fr cl & ol grn	45.00	45.00
28	A6	20pi on 5fr dk bl & buff	225.00	225.00
		Nos. 14-28 (13)	573.50	573.50

On Nos. 25, 26 and 28 the two lines of the overprint are set wider apart than on the lower values.

"O.N.F." are the initials of "Occupation Navale Francaise."

Overprint on 8pi on 2fr (#37), price $700.

On Stamps of France.

30	A22	10c red	17.50	13.00
a.		Inverted ovpt.		87.50
31	A22	25c bl (R)	17.50	13.00
a.		Inverted ovpt.		87.50

This overprint exists on 8 other 1900–1907 denominations of France (5c, 15c, 20c, 30c, 40c, 50c, 1fr, 5fr). These are believed not to have been issued or postally used.

Stamps of France, 1900-1907, Handstamped in Black or Violet — CASTELLORISO O F

1920

33	A22	5c green	110.00	110.00
34	A22	10c red	110.00	110.00
35	A22	20c vio brn	110.00	110.00
36	A22	25c blue	110.00	110.00
37	A18	50c bis brn & lav	775.00	775.00
38	A18	1fr cl & ol grn (V)	775.00	775.00
		Nos. 33-38 (6)	1,990.	1,990.

Nos. 1–38 are considered speculative.

Forgeries of overprints on Nos. 1–38 exist. They abound of Nos. 33–38.

Stamps of French Offices in Turkey handstamped "Occupation Francaise Castellorizo" were made privately.

Issued under Italian Dominion.

100 Centesimi = 1 Lira

Italian Stamps of 1906-20 Overprinted — CASTELROSSO

Wmkd. Crown. (140)

1922 *Perf. 14*

51	A48	5c green	90	4.50
52	A48	10c claret	38	4.50
53	A48	15c slate	38	4.50
54	A50	20c brn org	38	4.50
a.		Double ovpt.	90.00	
55	A49	25c blue	38	4.50
56	A49	40c brown	7.50	4.50
57	A49	50c violet	7.50	1.50
58	A49	60c carmine	7.50	4.50
59	A49	85c chocolate	90	4.50
		Nos. 51-59 (9)	25.82	

Map of Castellorizo; Flag of Italy
A1

1923

60	A1	5c gray grn	32	3.75
61	A1	10c dl rose	32	3.75
62	A1	25c dl bl	32	3.75
63	A1	50c gray lil	32	3.75
64	A1	1 l brown	32	3.75
		Nos. 60-64 (5)	1.60	

Italian Stamps of 1901-20 Overprinted

1924

65	A48	5c green	45	15.00
66	A48	10c claret	45	15.00
67	A48	15c slate	45	15.00
68	A50	20c brn org	45	15.00
69	A49	25c blue	45	15.00
70	A49	40c brown	45	15.00
71	A49	50c violet	45	15.00
72	A49	60c carmine	45	15.00
a.		Double ovpt.	90.00	
73	A49	85c red brn	45	15.00
74	A46	1 l brn & grn	45	15.00
		Nos. 65-74 (10)	4.50	

Ferrucci Issue.

Types of Italian Stamps of 1930, Overprinted in Red or Blue — CASTELROSSO

1930 **Wmkd. Crowns. (140)**

75	A102	20c violet	1.10	2.00
76	A103	25c dk grn	1.10	2.00
77	A103	50c black	1.10	2.00
78	A103	1.25 l dp bl	1.10	2.00
79	A104	5 l +2 l dp car (Bl)	4.75	10.50
		Nos. 75-79 (5)	9.15	

Garibaldi Issue.

Types of Italian Stamps of 1932, Overprinted in Red or Blue — CASTELROSSO

1932

80	A138	10c brown	5.50	11.00
81	A138	20c red brn (Bl)	5.50	11.00
82	A138	25c dp grn	5.50	11.00
83	A138	30c bluish sl	5.50	11.00
84	A138	50c red vio (Bl)	5.50	11.00
85	A141	75c cop red (Bl)	5.50	11.00
86	A141	1.25 l dl bl	5.50	11.00
87	A141	1.75 l +25c brn	5.50	11.00
88	A144	2.55 l +50c org (Bl)	5.50	11.00
89	A145	5 l +1 l dl vio	5.50	11.00
		Nos. 80-89 (10)	55.00	

CENTRAL AFRICA

LOCATION—Western Africa, north of equator.
GOVT.—Empire.
AREA—241,313 sq. mi.
POP.—2,610,000 (est. 1974).
CAPITAL—Bangui.

The former French colony of Ubangi-Shari, a unit in French Equatorial Africa, proclaimed itself the Central African Republic Dec. 1, 1958. It became the Central African Empire Dec. 4, 1976.

100 Centimes = 1 Franc

Central African Republic

Premier Barthélemy Boganda and Flag
A1

Design: 25fr, Barthélemy Boganda and flag (horiz.).

Engraved.

1959 *Perf. 13* **Unwmkd.**

1	A1	15fr multi	25	20
2	A1	25fr multi	40	20

Issued to commemorate the first anniversary of the establishment of the Republic and to honor Premier Barthélemy Boganda (1910–1959).

Imperforates

Most stamps of Central African Republic exist imperforate in issued and trial colors, and also in small presentation sheets in issued colors.

C.C.T.A. Issue

Common Design Type

1960 *Perf. 13* **Unwmkd.**

3	CD106	50fr lt grn & dk bl	1.15	85

Dactyloceras Widenmanni—A2

Designs: Various butterflies.

1960–61

4	A2	50c bl grn & dk red ('61)	5	5
5	A2	1fr multi	5	5
6	A2	2fr dk grn & brn ('61)	6	5
7	A2	3fr yel grn & dk red ('61)	6	6
8	A2	5fr dk sl grn, pale grn & ol brn	8	8
9	A2	10fr multi	20	10
10	A2	20fr multi	35	18
11	A2	85fr multi	1.35	80
		Nos. 4-11 (8)	2.20	1.37

No. 2 Overprinted:
"FETE NATIONALE 1-12-1960"

1960

12	A1	25fr multi	1.10	1.10

National Holiday, Dec. 1, 1960.

Common Design Types pictured in section at front of book.

Louis Pasteur and Pasteur Institute, Bangui
A3

1961, Feb. 25 *Perf. 13* **Unwmkd.**

13	A3	20fr multi	65	65

Opening of Pasteur Institute at Bangui.

Flag, Map, and U.N. Emblem
A4

1961, Mar. 4 **Engraved**

14	A4	15fr multi	30	20
15	A4	25fr multi	40	30
16	A4	85fr multi	1.35	1.10

Issued to commemorate the admission of Central African Republic to the United Nations.

No. 15 Overprinted in Green:
"FETE NATIONALE 1-12-61" and Star

1961, Dec. 1

17	A4	25fr multi	1.40	1.40

National Holiday, Dec. 1.

No. 16 Surcharged in Red Brown:
"U.A.M. CONFERENCE DE BANGUI 25-27 Mars 1962"

1962, March 25

18	A4	50fr on 85fr multi	1.20	1.20

Issued to commemorate the conference of the African and Malgache Union at Bangui, March 25–27.

Abidjan Games Issue

Common Design Type

Designs: 20fr, Hurdling. 50fr, Bicycling.

1962, July 21 Photo. *Perf. 12½x12*

19	CD109	20fr multi	30	25
20	CD109	50fr multi	80	55

See No. C6.

African-Malgache Union Issue

Common Design Type

1962, Sept. 8 **Unwmkd.**

21	CD110	30fr multi	55	45

Issued to commemorate the first anniversary of the African and Malgache Union.

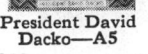

President David Dacko—A5

Soldiers with Flag—A6

1962 *Perf. 12*

22	A5	20fr multi	30	12
23	A5	25fr multi	35	15

1963, Aug. 13 Photogravure

24	A6	20fr blk & multi	30	20

National Army, third anniversary.

Waves Around Globe
A6a

Design: 100fr, Orbit patterns around globe.

1963, Sept. 19 *Perf. 12½* Unwmkd.

25 A6a 25fr plum & grn 45 40
26 A6a 100fr org, bl & grn 1.75 1.65

Issued to publicize space communications.

Young Pioneers
A7

1963, Oct. 14 Engr. *Perf. 12½*

27 A7 50fr grnsh bl, vio bl & brn 70 50

Issued to honor Young Pioneers.

Boali Falls
A8

1963, Oct. 28 *Perf. 13*

28 A8 30fr bl, grn & red brn 45 30

Colotis Evippe
A9

Designs: Various butterflies.

1963, Nov. 18 Photo. *Perf. 12½x13*

29 A9 1fr multi 15 15
30 A9 3fr multi 20 20
31 A9 4fr multi 25 25
32 A9 60fr multi 1.00 1.00

UNESCO Emblem, Scales and Tree—A9a

1963, Dec. 10 *Perf. 13*

33 A9a 25fr grn, ol & red brn 45 35

Issued to commemorate the 15th anniversary of the Universal Declaration of Human Rights.

Leaves and IQSY Emblem
A10

1964, Apr. 20 Engr. *Perf. 13*

34 A10 25fr org, Prus grn & bis 1.10 1.00

International Quiet Sun Year, 1964–65.

Child
A11

"All Men Are Men"
A12

Designs: Heads of Children.

1964, Aug. 13 *Perf. 13* Unwmkd.

35 A11 20fr rose lil, red brn & lt ol grn 35 25
36 A11 25fr brick red, red brn & bl 40 30
37 A11 40fr lt ol grn, red brn & rose lil 60 45
38 A11 50fr dl cl, red brn & lt grn 80 50
a. Min. sheet of 4 2.25 2.25

No. 38a contains one each of Nos. 35–38. Size: 144x99mm.

Cooperation Issue
Common Design Type

1964, Nov. 7 Engraved

39 CD119 25fr grn, mag & dk brn 45 30

1964, Dec. 1 Litho. *Perf. 13x12½*

40 A12 25fr multi 42 20

Issued to publicize National Unity.

Putting Yoke on Oxen
A13

Designs: 50fr, Ox pulling harrow. 85fr, Team of oxen in field. 100fr, Hay wagon.

1965, Apr. 28 Engr. *Perf. 13*

41 A13 25fr sl grn, sep & rose 40 30
42 A13 50fr sl grn, lt bl & brn 75 45
43 A13 85fr bl, grn & red brn 1.25 75
44 A13 100fr multi 1.50 1.00

Telegraph Receiver by Pouget-Maisonneuve—A14

Designs: 30fr, Chappe telegraph (vert.). 50fr, Doignon regulator (vert.). 85fr, Pouillet telegraph transcriber.

1965, May 17 Unwmkd.

45 A14 25fr red, grn & ultra 40 30
46 A14 30fr lake & grn 50 35
47 A14 50fr car & vio 85 50
48 A14 85fr red lil & sl 1.25 80

Issued to commemorate the centenary of the International Telecommunication Union.

"Health"
A15

Designs: 25fr, "Clothes;" shuttle, cloth and women. 60fr, "Teaching;" student and school. 85fr, "Food;" mother feeding child, tractor in wheat field.

1965, June 10 Engr. *Perf. 13*

49 A15 25fr ultra, brt grn & brn 40 30
50 A15 50fr ultra, brn & grn 75 50
51 A15 60fr grn, ultra & brn 90 65
52 A15 85fr multi 1.35 75

Issued to publicize the slogans and aims of "M.E.S.A.N." (Mouvement d'Evolution Sociale de l'Afrique Noire). See No. C30.

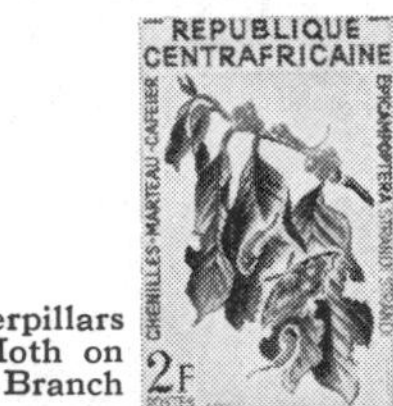

Caterpillars and Moth on Coffee Branch
A16

Designs: 3fr, Hawk moth and caterpillar on coffee leaves (horiz.). 30fr, Platyedra moth and larvae on cotton plant.

1965, Aug. 25 Engr. *Perf. 13*

53 A16 2fr dk pur, dp org & sl grn 5 5
54 A16 3fr blk, sl grn & red 8 8
55 A16 30fr red lil, red & sl grn 1.00 40

Issued to publicize plant protection.

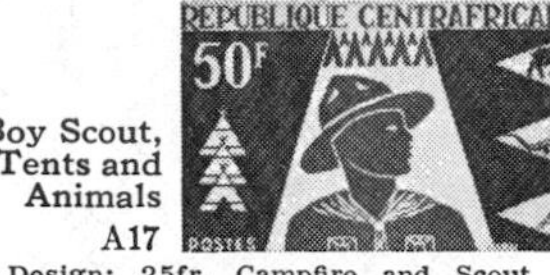

Boy Scout, Tents and Animals
A17

Design: 25fr, Campfire and Scout emblem.

1965, Sept. 27 *Perf. 13* Unwmkd.

56 A17 25fr red org, bl & red lil 40 22
57 A17 50fr brn & Prus bl 80 55

Issued to honor the Boy Scouts.

Nos. 30, 1 and 22 Surcharged in Black or Brown

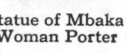

5 F

Engraved; Photogravure
Perf. 13, 12, 12½x13

1965, Aug. 26 Unwmkd.

58 A9 2fr on 3fr multi 1.75 1.75
59 A1 5fr on 15fr multi 1.75 1.75
60 A5 10fr on 20fr multi (Br) 2.00 2.00

The surcharges are adjusted to shape of stamps.

U.N. Emblem and Wheat
A18

1965, Oct. 16 Engraved *Perf. 13*

61 A18 50fr ocher, sl grn & brt bl 90 60

Issued for the "Freedom from Hunger Campaign" of the United Nations Food and Agriculture Organization.

Diamond Cutter
A19

1966, March 14 Engraved *Perf. 13*

62 A19 25fr car rose, dk pur & brn 40 25

Nos. 43–44 Surcharged

5 F

1966, Feb.

63 A13 5fr on 85fr multi 25 25
64 A13 10fr on 100fr multi 45 45

Issue dates: No. 63, Feb. 17. No. 64, Feb. 15.

Statue of Mbaka Woman Porter
A20

WHO Headquarters, Geneva
A21

1966, Apr. 9 Photo. *Perf. 13x12½*

65 A20 25fr multi 40 25

Issued to commemorate the International Negro Arts Festival. Dakar, Senegal, Apr. 1–24.

1966, May 3 Photo. Unwmkd.

66 A21 25fr pur, bl & yel 40 25

Issued to commemorate the inauguration of the World Health Organization Headquarters, Geneva.

Eulophia Cucullata
A22

Orchids: 5fr, Lissochilus horsfalii. 10fr, Tridactyle bicaudata. 15fr, Polystachya. 20fr, Eulophia alta. 25fr, Microcelia macrorrhynchium.

1966, May 16 Photo. *Perf. 12x12½*

Orchids in Natural Colors

67 A22 2fr dk red 8 5
68 A22 5fr brn org & vio 10 8
69 A22 10fr bl grn & blk 15 10
70 A22 15fr lt grn & dk brn 25 15
71 A22 20fr dk grn 35 20
72 A22 25fr lt ultra & brn 45 20
Nos. 67-72 (6) 1.38 78

Congo Forest Mouse
A23

Rodents: 10fr, One-stripe mouse. 20fr, Dollman's tree mouse (vert.).

1966, Sept. 15 Photo. *Perf. 12½x12*

73 A23 5fr yel & multi 12 10
74 A23 10fr tan & multi 18 10
75 A23 20fr lt grn & multi 35 25

UNESCO Emblem A24

Pres. Jean Bedel Bokassa A25

1966, Dec. 5 Photo. Perf. 13

76 A24 30fr multi 45 25

Issued to commemorate the 20th anniversary of UNESCO (United Nations Educational, Scientific and Cultural Organization).

1967, Jan. 1 Perf. 12x12½

77 A25 30fr yel grn, blk & bis brn 50 25

No. 72 Surcharged with New Value and "XX"

1967, May 8 Photo. Perf. 12x12½

78 A22 10fr on 25fr multi 20 10

See also No. C43.

Central Market, Bangui A26

1967, Aug. 8 Photo. Perf. 12½x13

79 A26 30fr multi 50 30

Safari Hotel, Bangui A27

1967, Sept. 26 Photo. Perf. 12½x13

80 A27 30fr multi 50 30

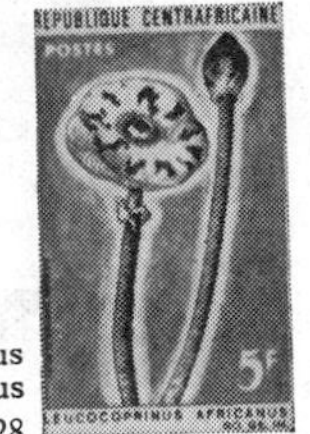

Leucocoprinus Africanus A28

Various Mushrooms

1967, Oct. 3 Engraved Perf. 13

81 A28 5fr dk brn, ol & ocher 12 10
82 A28 10fr dk brn, ultra & yel 18 13
83 A28 15fr dk brn, sl grn & yel 25 17
84 A28 30fr multi 60 25
85 A28 50fr multi 85 50
Nos. 81-85 (5) 2.00 1.15

Map, Radio Tower, Projector and People—A29

1967, Oct. 31

86 A29 30fr emer, ocher & ind 50 30

Radiovision service.

African Hair Style A30

Various African Hair Styles.

1967, Nov. 7 Engraved Perf. 13

87 A30 5fr ultra, dk brn & bis brn 10 8
88 A30 10fr car, dk brn & bis brn 20 12
89 A30 15fr dp grn, dk brn & bis brn 25 15
90 A30 20fr org, dk brn & bis brn 35 15
91 A30 30fr red lil, dk brn & bis brn 50 25
Nos. 87-91 (5) 1.40 75

Nurse Vaccinating Children A31

1967, Nov. 14

92 A31 30fr dk red brn & brt grn 50 25

Vaccination campaign, 1967–70.

Douglas DC-3 A32

Designs: 2fr, Beechcraft Baron. 5fr, Douglas DC-4.

1967, Nov. 24

93 A32 1fr brn red, ind & grn 6 6
94 A32 2fr brt bl, blk & brt pink 6 6
95 A32 5fr grnsh bl, blk & emer 13 12
Nos. 93-95, C47-C49 (6) 11.85 6.14

Pierced Stone, Kwe Tribe A33

Designs: 30fr, Primitive dwelling at Toulou (horiz.). 100fr, Megaliths, Bouar. 130fr, Rock painting (people), Toulou (horiz.).

1967, Dec. 26 Engraved Perf. 13

96 A33 30fr crim, ind & mar 50 30
97 A33 50fr ol brn, ocher & dk grn 80 40
98 A33 100fr dk brn, brt bl & brn 1.60 70
99 A33 130fr dk red, brn & dk grn 2.00 90

Issued to publicize the 6th Pan-African Prehistoric Congress, Dakar.

Tanker, Refinery and Map of Area Served—A33a

1968, July 30 Photo. Perf. 12½

100 A33a 30fr multi 40 20

Issued to commemorate the opening of the Port Gentil (Gabon) Refinery, June 12, 1968.

Bulldozer Clearing Land A34

Designs: 10fr, Baoule cattle. 20fr, 15,000-spindle spinning machine. No. 104, Automatic Diederichs looms. No. 105, Bulldozer.

1968, Oct. 1 Engraved Perf. 13

101 A34 5fr blk, grn & dk brn 7 5
102 A34 10fr blk, pale grn & bis brn 18 15
103 A34 20fr grn, red brn & yel 30 18
104 A34 30fr brn, ol & ultra 50 20
105 A34 30fr ind, red brn & sl grn 50 20
Nos. 101-105 (5) 1.55 78

Issued to publicize "Operation Bokassa."

Bangui Mosque A35

1968, Oct. 14

106 A35 30fr grn, bl & ocher 45 20

Hunting Knife of Baya and Boufi Tribes—A36

Designs: 20fr, Hunting knife of Nzakara tribe. 30fr, Crossbow of Babinga and Babenzele (pygmy) tribes.

1968, Nov. 19 Engraved Perf. 13

107 A36 10fr lem, Prus bl & ultra 15 12
108 A36 20fr ultra, dk ol & sl grn 30 17
109 A36 30fr sl grn, ultra & brn org 45 17

"Ville de Bangui," 1958 A37

River Boats: 30fr, "J. B. Gouandjia," 1968. 50fr, "Lamblin," 1944.

1968, Dec. 10 Engraved Perf. 13

Size: 36x22mm.

110 A37 10fr mag, brt grn & vio bl 15 10
111 A37 30fr bl, grn & brn 50 20
112 A37 50fr brn, sl & ol grn 85 40
Nos. 110-112, C62-C63 (5) 5.00 2.40

Woman Javelin Thrower A38

Sport Designs: 10fr, Women runners. 15fr, Soccer.

1969, Mar. 18 Photo. Perf. 13x12½

113 A38 5fr multi 10 6
114 A38 10fr multi 17 10
115 A38 15fr multi 25 12
Nos. 113-115, C71-C72 (5) 2.77 1.23

BIT and ILO Emblems and Worker A39

1969, May 20 Photo. Perf. 12½x13

116 A39 30fr dp bl, grn & ol brn 40 15
117 A39 50fr dp car, grn & ol brn 75 35

Issued to commemorate the 50th anniversary of the International Labor Organization.

Pres. Jean Bedel Bokassa A40

Garayah A41

1969, Dec. 1 Litho. Perf. 13x13½

118 A40 30fr ver & multi 40 20

ASECNA Issue

Common Design Type

1969, Dec. 12 Engraved Perf. 13

119 CD132 100fr dp bl 1.50 70

1970, Jan. 6 Engraved Perf. 13

Musical Instuments: 15fr, Ngombi (harp; horiz.). 30fr, Xylophone (horiz.). 50fr, Ndala (lute; horiz.). 130fr, Gatta and babyon (drums).

120 A41 10fr yel grn, dk grn & ocher 15 12
121 A41 15fr bl grn, ocher & dk brn 25 15
122 A41 30fr mar, ocher & dk brn 45 20
123 A41 50fr rose car & ind 75 45
124 A41 130fr brt bl, brn & ol 2.00 70
Nos. 120-124 (5) 3.60 1.62

U.P.U. Headquarters Issue

Common Design Type

1970, May 20 Engraved Perf. 13

125 CD133 100fr ultra, ver & red brn 1.00 50

Loading Platform and Flour Storage Bins
A42

Designs: 50fr, Flour milling machinery. 100fr, View of mill.

1970, Feb. 24 Litho. *Perf. 14*

126	A42	25fr sl & multi	35	18
127	A42	50fr lil & multi	70	32
128	A42	100fr red & multi	1.40	75

Inauguration of SICPAD (Société Industrielle Centrafricaine des Produits Alimentaires et Dérivés, a part of Operation Bokassa, Feb. 22, 1968.

Pres. Bokassa
A43

1970, Aug. 13 Litho. *Perf. 14*

129	A43	30fr multi	3.25	2.75
130	A43	40fr multi	4.75	3.50

Cheese Factory, Sarki—A44

Silk Worm
A45

Designs: 10fr, M'Bali Ranch. 20fr, Zebu (vert.).

Perf. 13x13½, 13½x13

1970, Sept. 15

131	A44	5fr red & multi	20	10
132	A44	10fr red & multi	4.00	3.50
133	A44	20fr red & multi	65	45
134	A45	40fr red & multi	1.10	75
		Nos. 131-134, C83 (5)	7.95	5.90

Issued to publicize Operation Bokassa, a national development plan.

Gnathonemus Monteiri—A46

River Fish: 20fr, Mormyrus proboscirostris. 30fr, Marcusenius wilverthi. 40fr, Gnathonemus elephas. 50fr, Gnathonemus curvirostris.

1971, Apr. 6 Photo. *Perf. 12½*

135	A46	10fr multi	15	10
136	A46	20fr multi	30	20
137	A46	30fr multi	50	25
138	A46	40fr multi	65	25
139	A46	50fr multi	80	40
		Nos. 135-139 (5)	2.40	1.20

Berberati Cathedral
A47

1971, July 20 Litho. *Perf. 13½*

140	A47	5fr grn & multi	10	8

New Roman Catholic Cathedral at Berberati.

Charles de Gaulle
A48

Gray Galago
A49

1971, Aug. 20 *Perf. 13½x13*

141	A48	100fr brt bl & multi	1.50	1.10

In memory of Gen. Charles de Gaulle (1890–1970), president of France.

1971, Oct. 25 Photo. *Perf. 13*

Designs: 40fr, Elegant galago. 100fr, Calabar potto (horiz.). 150fr, Bosman's potto (horiz.). 200fr, Oustalet's colobo (horiz.).

142	A49	30fr pink & multi	50	40
143	A49	40fr lt bl & multi	70	50
144	A49	100fr multi	1.40	1.00
145	A49	150fr multi	2.25	1.25
146	A49	200fr multi	3.25	1.50
		Nos. 142-146 (5)	8.10	4.65

Alan B. Shepard
A50

Designs: No. 148, Yuri Gagarin. No. 149, Edwin E. Aldrin, Jr. No. 150, Alexei Leonov. No. 151, Neil A. Armstrong on moon. No. 152, Lunokhod I on moon.

1971, Nov. 19 Litho. *Perf. 14*

147	A50	40fr vio & multi	50	25
148	A50	40fr vio & multi	50	25
149	A50	100fr multi	1.35	60
150	A50	100fr multi	1.35	60
151	A50	200fr red & multi	2.50	1.00
152	A50	200fr red & multi	2.50	1.00
		Nos. 147-152 (6)	8.70	3.70

Space achievements of United States and Russia.

"Operation Bokassa" and Pres. Bokassa
A51

1971, Dec. 1 Photo. *Perf. 13*

153	A51	40fr red & multi	60	22

12th anniversary of independence.

Racial Equality Emblem
A52

1971, Dec. 6 Lithographed

154	A52	50fr multi	60	25

International Year Against Racial Discrimination.

Bokassa School Emblem and Cadets—A53

Book Year Emblem
A54

1972, Jan. 1 Photogravure

155	A53	30fr gold & multi	45	20

J. B. Bokassa Military School.

1972, Mar. 11 Photo. *Perf. 12½x13*

156	A54	100fr red brn, gold & org	1.10	65

International Book Year 1972.

"Your Heart is your Health"
A55

1972, Apr. 7 Photo. *Perf. 13x12½*

157	A55	100fr yel, blk & car	1.10	65

World Health Day.

Red Cross Workers in Village
A56

1972, May 8 *Perf. 13*

158	A56	150fr multi	2.00	90

25th World Red Cross Day.

Globe
A57

1972, May 17 Lithographed

159	A57	50fr yel, blk & dp org	60	30

4th World Telecommunications Day.

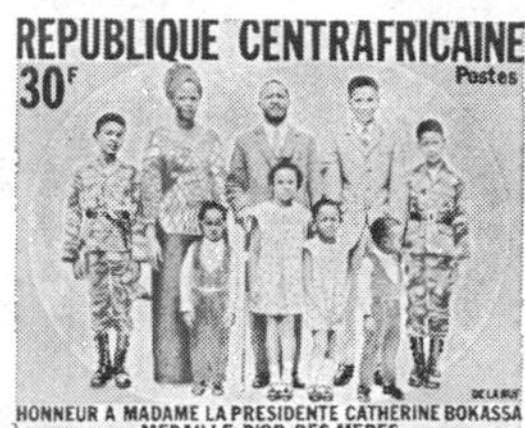

Pres. and Mrs. Bokassa and Family—A58

1972, May 28 *Perf. 14*

160	A58	30fr yel & multi	40	15

Mother's Day. Mothers' gold medal awarded to Catherine Bokassa.

Pres. Bokassa Planting Cotton, Map of Africa
A59

1972, June 5 Photo. *Perf. 13*

161	A59	40fr yel & multi	50	25

Operation Bokassa, a national development plan.

Postal Checking and Savings Center
A60

1972, June 21

162	A60	30fr yel org & multi	40	18

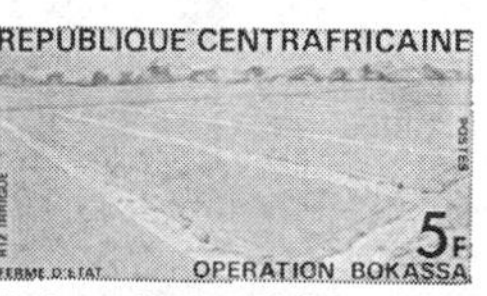

Irrigated Rice Fields—A61

"Le Pacifique" Apartment House
A62

Designs: 25fr, Plowing rice field. No. 166, Swimming pool, Hotel St. Sylvestre. No. 167, Entrance, Hotel St. Sylvestre. No. 168, J. B. Bokassa University.

1972 Lithographed *Perf. 13x13½*

163	A61	5fr multi	7	6
164	A61	25fr multi	32	15

Engraved *Perf. 13*

165	A62	30fr multi	35	15
166	A62	30fr multi	35	15
167	A62	40fr multi	45	25
168	A62	40fr multi	45	20
		Nos. 163-168 (6)	1.99	96

Operation Bokassa. Issue dates: 5fr, 25fr, Nov. 10; No. 165, June 27; Nos. 166–167, Dec. 9; No. 168, Aug. 26.

Bull Chasing Woman on Clock Face
A63

Designs (Scenes Painted on Clock Faces): 10fr, Men and open cooking fire. 20fr, Fishermen. 30fr, Palms, monkeys and giraffe. 40fr, Warriors.

1972, July 31 **Photo.** *Perf. 12½*

169	A63	5fr dk red & multi	8	5
170	A63	10fr brt bl & multi	10	6
171	A63	20fr grn & multi	25	10
172	A63	30fr yel & multi	45	20
173	A63	40fr vio & multi	50	30
		Nos. 169-173 (5)	1.38	71

HORCEN Central African clock and watch factory.

Protestant Youth Center—A64

Design: 10fr, Postal runner carrying mail in cleft stick (vert.).

1972, Aug. 12 *Perf. 13*

174	A64	10fr multi	15	8
175	A64	20fr multi	25	10
		Nos. 174-175, C95-C98 (6)	5.50	2.48

Centraphilex 1972, Central African Philatelic Exhibition, Bangui.

Mail Truck
A65

1972, Oct. 23 **Photo.** *Perf. 13*

176	A65	100fr ocher & multi	1.35	50

Universal Postal Union Day.

Mother Teaching Child to Write
A66

Central African Mothers: 10fr, Caring for infant. 15fr, Combing child's hair. 20fr, Teaching to read. 180fr, Nursing. 190fr, Teaching to walk.

1972, Dec. 27 *Perf. 13½x13*

177	A66	5fr multi	8	5
178	A66	10fr lil & multi	12	7
179	A66	15fr dl org & multi	20	8
180	A66	20fr yel grn & multi	25	12
181	A66	180fr multi	2.25	75
182	A66	190fr pink & multi	2.25	1.10
		Nos. 177-182 (6)	5.15	2.17

Farmer Carrying Sheaf—A67

1973, May 30 **Photo.** *Perf. 13*

183	A67	50fr vio bl & multi	55	35

10th anniversary of the World Food Program.

Garcinia Punctata
A68

African Flora: 20fr, Bertiera racemosa. 30fr, Corynanthe pachyceras. 40fr, Combretodendron africanum. 50fr, Xylopia Villosa (vert.).

1973, June 8

184	A68	10fr pale bl & multi	10	7
185	A68	20fr multi	20	10
186	A68	30fr lt gray & multi	40	15
187	A68	40fr multi	40	30
188	A68	50fr multi	50	35
		Nos. 184-188 (5)	1.60	97

Pygmy Chameleon
A69

1973, June 26 **Photo.** *Perf. 13*

189	A69	15fr multi	20	10

Caterpillar—A70

Designs: Various caterpillars.

1973, Aug. 6 **Photo.** *Perf. 13*

190	A70	3fr multi	5	5
191	A70	5fr multi	8	5
192	A70	25fr multi	30	15

No. 184 Surcharged with New Value, 2 Bars, and Overprinted in Red: "SECHERESSE SOLIDARITE AFRICAINE"

1973, Aug. 16

193	A68	100fr on 10fr multi	90	75

African solidarity in drought emergency.

African Postal Union Issue
Common Design Type

1973, Sept. 12 **Engraved** *Perf. 13*

194	CD137	100fr dk brn, red org & ol	90	65

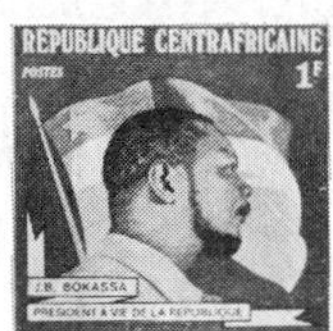

Pres. Bokassa and CAR Flag
A71

1973, Nov. 30 **Photo.** *Perf. 12½*

195	A71	1fr brn & multi	5	5
196	A71	2fr pur & multi	5	5
197	A71	3fr vio bl & multi	5	5
198	A71	5fr ocher & multi	5	5
199	A71	10fr multi	10	7
200	A71	15fr org & multi	15	10
201	A71	20fr multi	20	15
202	A71	30fr dk grn & multi	30	20
203	A71	40fr dk brn & multi	40	30
		Nos. 195-203, C117-C118 (11)	2.85	2.07

INTERPOL Emblem
A72

1973, Dec. 20 *Perf. 13x12½*

204	A72	50fr yel & multi	50	40

50th anniversary of the International Criminal Police Organization.

Catherine Bokassa Center
A73

Design: 40fr, Ambulance in front of Catherine Bokassa Center.

1974, Jan. 24 **Engraved** *Perf. 13*

205	A73	30fr multi	25	18
206	A73	40fr multi	32	25

Catherine Bokassa Center for Mothers and Children.

Cigarette-making Machine
A74

Designs: 10fr, Cigarette in ashtray, and factory. 30fr, Hand lighting cigarette, and Administration Building.

1974, Jan. 29

207	A74	5fr sl grn & multi	7	5
208	A74	10fr sl grn & multi	10	10
209	A74	30fr sl grn & multi	25	15

Publicity for Centra cigarettes.

"Communications"
A75

1974, June 8 **Photo.** *Perf. 12½x13*

210	A75	100fr multi	1.00	70

World Telecommunications Day.

People and WPY Emblem
A76

1974, June 20 **Engraved** *Perf. 13*

211	A76	100fr red, sl grn & brn	1.00	70

World Population Year.

Mother, Child, WHO Emblem
A77

1974, July 10

212	A77	100fr multi	1.00	45

26th anniversary of World Health Organization.

Hoeing—A78

Designs: 10fr, Battle scene ("yesterday"). 15fr, Pastoral scene ("today"). 20fr, Rice planting. 25fr, Storehouse. 40fr, Veterans Headquarters. Borders show tanks and tractors.

1974, Nov. 15 **Litho.** *Perf. 13*

213	A78	10fr multi	10	7
214	A78	15fr multi	12	8
215	A78	20fr multi	18	10
216	A78	25fr multi	22	15
217	A78	30fr multi	25	15
218	A78	40fr multi	35	15
		Nos. 213-218 (6)	1.22	70

Veterans' activities.

Presidents and Flags of Cameroun, CAR, Congo, Gabon and Meeting Center—A79

1974, Dec. 8 **Photogravure** *Perf. 13*

219	A79	40fr gold & multi	40	22

See No. C126 and note after Cameroun No. 595.

House in OCAM City
A80

Designs: Scenes in housing development, OCAM City.

1975, Feb. 1 **Photo.** *Perf. 13*

220	A80	30fr multi	30	17
221	A80	40fr multi	40	22
222	A80	50fr multi	45	30
223	A80	100fr multi	90	65

1975, Feb. 22

Designs: Cottage scenes in J. B. Bokassa "pilot village."

224	A80	25fr multi	20	12
225	A80	30fr multi	25	15
226	A80	40fr multi	40	20

Foreign Ministry
A81

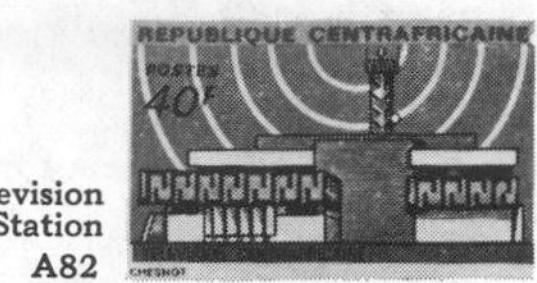

Television Station
A82

1975, Feb. 28 ***Perf. 13x12½***

227	A81	40fr multi	40	18

Perf. 13

228	A82	40fr multi	40	18

Public buildings, Bangui.

Bokassa's Saber—A83

Design: 40fr, Bokassa's baton.

1975, Feb. 22 **Photo.** ***Perf. 13***

229	A83	30fr dp bl & multi	25	17
230	A83	40fr vio bl & multi	35	20

Jean Bedel Bokassa, President for Life and Marshal of the Republic. See Nos. C127-C128.

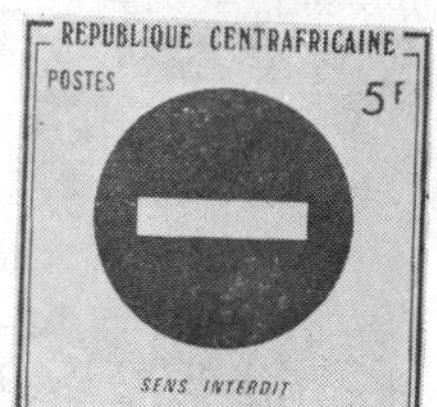

Do Not Enter
A84

Traffic Signs: 10fr, Stop. 20fr, No parking. 30fr, School. 40fr, Intersection.

1975, Mar. 20

231	A84	5fr ultra & red	5	5
232	A84	10fr ultra & red	10	8
233	A84	20fr ultra & red	15	10
234	A84	30fr ultra & multi	20	17
235	A84	40fr ultra & multi	40	20
		Nos. 231-235 (5)	90	60

Buffon's Kob
A85

Designs: 15fr, Wart hog. 20fr, Waterbuck. 30fr, Lion.

1975, June 24 **Photo.** ***Perf. 13***

236	A85	10fr dl grn & multi	10	7
237	A85	15fr lem & multi	15	8
238	A85	20fr yel grn & multi	20	13
239	A85	30fr lt bl & multi	30	17

Crane Lifting Log onto Truck
A86

Designs: 10fr, Forest (vert.). 15fr, Tree felling (vert.). 100fr, Log pile. 150fr, Logs transported by raft. 200fr, Lumberyard.

1975, Nov. 28 **Engr.** ***Perf. 13***

240	A86	10fr multi	8	5
241	A86	15fr multi	12	8
242	A86	50fr multi	40	25
243	A86	100fr multi	75	55
244	A86	150fr multi	1.10	90
245	A86	200fr multi	1.50	1.10
		Nos. 240-245 (6)	3.95	2.93

Promotion of Central African wood.

Women's Heads and Various Occupations—A87

1975, Dec. 10 **Photogravure**

246	A87	40fr multi	35	20
247	A87	100fr multi	75	55

International Women's Year 1975.

Alexander Graham Bell
A88

1976, Mar. 25 **Litho.** ***Perf. 12½x13***

248	A88	100fr yel & blk	75	50

Centenary of first telephone call by Alexander Graham Bell, Mar. 10, 1876.

Satellite and ITU Emblem—A89

Design: No. 250, UPU emblem, various forms of mail transport.

1976 **Engr.** ***Perf. 13***

249	A89	100fr vio bl, cl & grn	75	50
250	A89	100fr car, grn & ocher	90	70

World Telecommunications Day (No. 249); Universal Postal Union Day (No. 250).

Soyuz on Launching Pad—A90

Design: 50fr, Apollo rocket.

1976, June 14 **Litho.** ***Perf. 14x13½***

251	A90	40fr multi	42	18
252	A90	50fr multi	55	25
		Nos. 251-252, C135-C137 (5)	6.97	2.91

Apollo Soyuz space test project, Russo-American cooperation, launched July 15, link-up July 17, 1975.

Drurya Antimachus—A91

Butterfly: 40fr, Argema mittrei (vert.).

1976, Sept. 20 **Litho.** ***Perf. 12½***

253	A91	30fr ocher & multi	25	15
254	A91	40fr ultra & multi	35	20

See Nos. C145-C146.

Slalom, Piero Gros—A92

Design: 60fr, Karl Schnabel and Toni Innauer.

1976, Sept. 23 ***Perf. 13½***

255	A92	40fr multi	42	20
256	A92	60fr multi	65	32
		Nos. 255-256, C147-C149 (5)	6.92	3.17

12th Winter Olympic Games winners, Innsbruck.

Viking Components
A93

Design: 60fr, Viking take-off.

1976, Dec.

257	A93	40fr multi	42	18
258	A93	60fr multi	65	30
		Nos. 257-258, C151-C153 (5)	6.92	2.88

Viking Mars project.

Empire

Stamps of 1973–76 Overprinted with Bars and "EMPIRE CENTRAFRICAIN" in Black, Green, Violet Blue, Silver, Carmine, Brown or Red

Printing and Perforations as Before

1977, March

Multicolored

259	A70	3fr (#190; B)	5	5
260	A78	10fr (#213;B)	12	10
261	A84	10fr (#232;VB)	12	10
262	A85	10fr (#236;C)	15	12
263	A85	15fr (#237;C)	20	15
264	A86	15fr (#241;B)	17	12
265	A78	20fr (#215;B)	20	18
266	A85	20fr (#238;C)	20	18
267	A78	25fr (#216;B)	25	20
268	A80	25fr (#224;B)	25	20
269	A80	30fr (#220;VB)	30	25
270	A80	30fr (#225;B)	30	25
271	A85	30fr (#239;C)	30	25
272	A79	40fr (#219;B)	35	30
273	A80	40fr (#221;VB)	40	30
274	A80	40fr (#226;B)	35	30
275	A81	40fr (#227;B & S)	35	30
276	A82	40fr (#228;B)	35	30
277	A84	40fr (#235;VB)	30	25
278	A91	40fr (#254;B)	30	25
279	A86	50fr (#242;Br)	45	35
280	A75	100fr (#210;B)	90	70
281	A76	100fr (#211;B)	90	70
282	A77	100fr (#212;G)	1.00	80
283	A88	100fr (#248;R)	1.00	80
284	A89	100fr (#249;B)	1.00	80
285	A89	100fr (#250;B)	1.00	80
		Nos. 259-285 (27)	11.26	9.10

Stamps of 1975–76 Overprinted "EMPIRE CENTRAFRICAIN" in Black on Silver Panel

1977, Apr. 1

286	A83	40fr multi (#230)	30	25
287	A90	40fr multi (#251)	40	30
288	A92	40fr multi (#255)	30	25
289	A93	40fr multi (#257)	30	25
290	A90	50fr multi (#252)	50	35
291	A92	60fr multi (#256)	50	35
292	A93	60fr multi (#258)	50	35
		Nos. 286-292 (7)	2.80	2.10

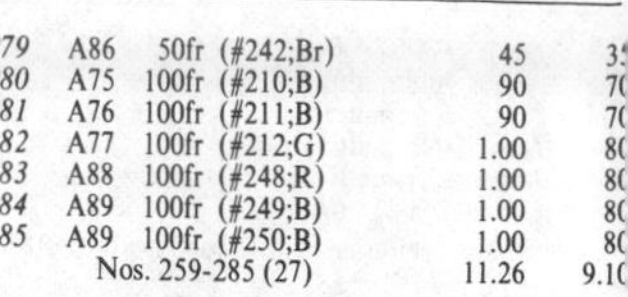

Pierre and Marie Curie—A94

Design: 60fr, Wilhelm C. Roentgen.

1977, Apr. 1 **Litho.** ***Perf. 13½***

293	A94	40fr multi	35	18
294	A94	60fr multi	60	30
		Nos. 293-294, C180-C182 (5)	6.80	2.88

Nobel Prize winners.

Italy No. C42 and Faustine Temple, Rome—A95

Design: 60fr, Russia No. C12 and St. Basil's Cathedral, Moscow.

1977, Apr. 11 **Litho.** ***Perf. 11***

295	A95	40fr multi	35	18
296	A95	60fr multi	60	30
		Nos. 295-296, C184-C186 (5)	6.80	2.88

75th anniversary of the Zeppelin.

Lindbergh over Paris—A96

Designs: 60fr, Santos Dumont and "14 bis." 100fr, Bleriot and monoplane. 200fr, Roald Amundsen and "N24." 300fr, Concorde. 500fr, Lindbergh and Spirit of St. Louis.

1977, Sept. 30 **Litho.** ***Perf. 13½***

297	A96	50fr multi	50	25
298	A96	60fr multi	60	30
299	A96	100fr multi	95	38
300	A96	200fr multi	1.90	80
301	A96	300fr multi	3.00	1.20
		Nos. 297-301 (5)	6.95	2.93

Souvenir Sheet

302	A96	500fr multi	4.75	2.25

History of aviation, famous fliers. No. 302 has multicolored margin showing Spirit of St. Louis and Concorde. Size: 117x91½mm.

Shot on Goal—A97

Designs: 60fr, Heading ball in net. 100fr, Backfield defense. 200fr, Argentina '78 poster. 300fr, Mario Zagalo and stadium. 500fr, Ferenc Puskas.

1977, Nov. 18 Litho. *Perf. 13½*

303	A97	50fr	multi	50	25
304	A97	60fr	multi	60	30
305	A97	100fr	multi	95	35
306	A97	200fr	multi	1.90	80
307	A97	300fr	multi	3.00	1.20
		Nos. 303-307 (5)		6.95	2.90

Souvenir Sheet

308	A97	500fr	multi	4.75	2.25

World Soccer Championships, Argentina, June 1–25, 1978. No. 308 has multicolored margin showing Argentina '78 emblem, World Cup and Stadium. Size: 120x81mm.

Emperor Bokassa I, Central African Flag
A98

1977, Dec. 4 Litho. *Perf. 13½*

309	A98	40fr	multi	30	25
310	A98	60fr	multi	50	35
311	A98	100fr	multi	80	60
312	A98	150fr	multi	1.20	90
		Nos. 309-312, C188-C189 (6)		6.90	4.60

Coronation of Emperor Bokassa I, Dec. 4.

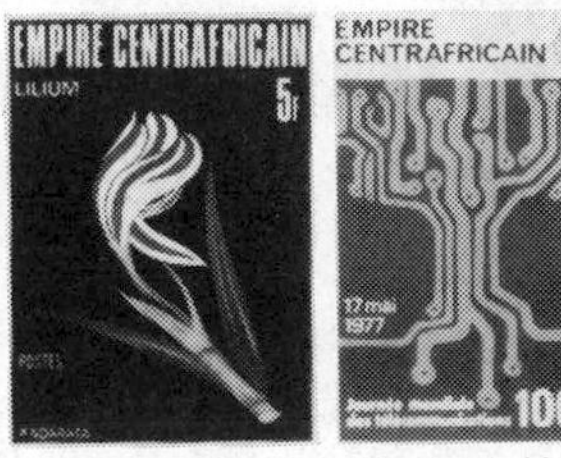

Lilium
A99

Electronic Tree, ITU Emblem
A100

Design: 10fr, Hibiscus.

1977 Litho. *Perf. 13½x14*

313	A99	5fr	multi	5	5
314	A99	10fr	multi	10	5

1977

315	A100	100fr	blk, org & brn	1.20	90

World Telecommunications Day.

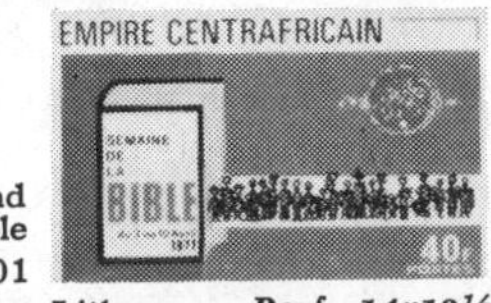

Bible and People
A101

1977 Litho. *Perf. 14x13½*

316	A101	40fr	multi	40	20

Bible Week.

People and Rotary Emblem
A102

1977

317	A102	60fr	multi	60	30

Rotary Club of Bangui, 20th anniversary.

Holy Family, by Rubens
A103

Rubens Paintings: 150fr, Marie de Medicis. 200fr, Son of artist. 300fr, Neptune. 500fr, Marie de Medicis (different).

1978, Jan. 26

318	A103	60fr	multi	60	30
319	A103	150fr	multi	1.40	60
320	A103	200fr	multi	1.90	80
321	A103	300fr	multi	3.00	1.20

Souvenir Sheet

322	A103	500fr	gold & multi	4.75	2.25

Peter Paul Rubens (1577–1640), 400th birth anniversary. No. 322 contains one stamp; multicolored margin shows entire painting. Size: 89x116mm.

Rhinoceros—A104

Endangered Animals and Wildlife Fund Emblem: 50fr, Slender-nosed crocodile. 60fr, Leopard (vert.). 100fr, Giraffe (vert.). 200fr, Elephant. 300fr, Gorilla (vert.).

1978, Feb. 21 Litho. *Perf. 13½*

323	A104	40fr	multi	35	18
324	A104	50fr	multi	50	25
325	A104	60fr	multi	60	30
326	A104	100fr	multi	95	42
327	A104	200fr	multi	1.90	80
328	A104	300fr	multi	3.00	1.25
		Nos. 323-328 (6)		7.30	3.20

Bokassa Sports Palace
A105

Design: 60fr, Sports Palace, side view.

1978 *Perf. 14*

329	A105	40fr	multi	32	25
330	A105	60fr	multi	50	35

Automatic Telephone Exchange, Bangui—A106

1978

331	A106	40fr	multi	40	20
332	A106	60fr	multi	60	30

Diligence and Satellite—A107

Designs (UPU Emblem and): 50fr, Steam locomotive and communications via satellite. 60fr, Paddle-wheel steamer and ship-to-shore communication via satellite. 80fr, Old mail truck and satellite.

1978, May 17 *Perf. 13½*

333	A107	40fr	multi	40	20
334	A107	50fr	multi	50	25
335	A107	60fr	multi	60	30
336	A107	80fr	multi	80	40
		Nos. 333-336, C191-C192 (6)		5.30	2.65

Century of progress of posts and telecommunications.

Mask
A108

Capt. Cook on "Endeavour"
A109

Designs: 30fr, Mask. 60fr, Women dancers (horiz.). 100fr, Men dancers (horiz.).

Perf. 13½x14, 14x13½

1978, July 11 Lithographed

337	A108	20fr	blk & yel	20	10
338	A108	30fr	blk & brt bl	30	15
339	A108	60fr	blk & multi	60	30
340	A108	100fr	blk & multi	1.00	50

Black-African World Arts Festival, Lagos.

1978, Aug. 30 *Perf. 14½*

Designs: 60fr, Resolution off Hawaii (horiz.). 200fr, Hawaiians welcoming Capt. Cook (horiz.). 350fr, Masked rowers in Hawaiian boat (horiz.).

341	A109	60fr	multi	60	30
342	A109	80fr	multi	80	40
343	A109	200fr	multi	2.00	1.00
344	A109	350fr	multi	3.50	1.75

Capt. James Cook (1728–1779), explorer.

Dürer, Self-portrait
A110

Dürer Paintings: 80fr, The Four Apostles. 200fr, Virgin and Child. 350fr, Emperor Maximilian I.

1978, Oct. 24 Litho. *Perf. 13½*

345	A110	60fr	multi	60	30
346	A110	80fr	multi	80	40
347	A110	200fr	multi	2.00	1.00
348	A110	350fr	multi	3.50	1.75

Albrecht Dürer (1471–1528), German painter.

Tutankhamen's Gold Mask
A111

Treasures of Tutankhamen: 60fr, King and Queen, gold back panel of throne. 80fr, Gilt folding chair. 100fr, King wearing crowns of Upper and Lower Egypt, painted wood sculpture. 120fr, Lion's head. 150fr, Tutankhamen, wood stature. 180fr, Gold throne. 250fr, Gold miniature coffin.

1978, Nov. 22

349	A111	40fr	multi	40	20
350	A111	60fr	multi	60	30
351	A111	80fr	multi	80	40
352	A111	100fr	multi	1.00	50
353	A111	120fr	multi	1.20	60
354	A111	150fr	multi	1.50	75
355	A111	180fr	multi	1.80	90
356	A111	250fr	multi	2.50	1.25
		Nos. 349-356 (8)		9.80	4.90

Tutankhamen, c. 1358 B.C., King of Egypt.

Lenin at Smolny Institute
A112

Designs: 60fr, 200fr, 300fr, Various Lenin portraits. 100fr, Ulyanov family (horiz.). 150fr, Lenin, Cruiser "Aurora" and flag (horiz.). 500fr, "Aurora" and star.

1978, Nov. *Perf. 14*

357	A112	40fr	multi	40	20
358	A112	60fr	multi	60	30
359	A112	100fr	blk & gold	1.00	50
360	A112	150fr	blk, gold & red	1.50	75
361	A112	200fr	multi	2.00	1.00
362	A112	300fr	multi	3.00	1.50
		Nos. 357-362 (6)		8.50	4.25

Souvenir Sheet

363	A112	500fr	multi	5.25

60th anniversary of the Soviet Union. No. 363 has red marginal inscription and hammer and sickle emblem. Size: 78x110mm.

Catherine Bokassa A113

Design: 60fr, Emperor Bokassa.

1978, Dec. 4 Litho. *Perf. 13*

364	A113	40fr multi	40	20
365	A113	60fr multi	60	30

First anniversary of coronation. See No. C202.

Rowland Hill, Letter Scale and G.B. No. 1—A114

Designs (Rowland Hill and): 50fr, U.S. No. 1, mailman on bicycle. 60fr, Austria No. P4 and 19th century mailman. 80fr, Switzerland No. 2L1, postilion and mail-coach.

1978, Dec. 9 Litho. *Perf. 13½*

366	A114	40fr multi	40	20
367	A114	50fr multi	50	25
368	A114	60fr multi	60	30
369	A114	80fr multi	80	40
		Nos. 366-369, C203-C204 (6)	5.30	2.65

Sir Rowland Hill (1795–1879), originator of penny postage.

Nos. 303–307 Overprinted in Silver: "VAINQUEUR : ARGENTINE"

1978, Dec. 27

370	A97	50fr multi	50	25
371	A97	60fr multi	60	30
372	A97	100fr multi	1.00	50
373	A97	200fr multi	2.00	1.00
374	A97	300fr multi	3.00	1.50
		Nos. 370-374 (5)	7.10	3.55

Souvenir Sheet

No. 308 Overprinted in Silver: "ARGENTINE – PAYS BAS 3–1 / 25 juin 1978"

375	A97	500fr multi	5.00	2.50

Argentina's victory in World Cup Soccer Championship 1978.

Children Painting and Dutch Portrait—A115

Designs (UNICEF, Eagle Emblems and): 50fr, Eskimo children skiing, and ski jump. 60fr, Children with toy racing car, and Carl Benz with early car model. 80fr, Children launching rocket, and Intelsat.

1979, Mar. 6 Litho. *Perf. 13½*

376	A115	40fr multi	40	20
377	A115	50fr multi	50	25
378	A115	60fr multi	60	30
379	A115	80fr multi	80	40
		Nos. 376-379, C206-C207 (6)	5.30	2.65

International Year of the Child.

High Jump, Moscow '80 Emblem and "M" A116

Designs (Moscow '80 Emblem, Various Sports and): 50fr, Bicycling and "O". 60fr, Weight lifting and "C". 80fr, Judo and "K".

1979, Mar. 16 Litho. *Perf. 13*

380	A116	40fr multi	32	15
381	A116	50fr multi	40	20
382	A116	60fr multi	48	25
383	A116	80fr multi	65	30
		Nos. 380-383, C209-C210 (6)	4.25	2.10

22nd Olympic Games, Moscow, July 19–Aug. 3, 1980. Background letters on Nos. 380–383, C209–C210 spell "Mockba." A 1500fr gold embossed stamp showing emblems and Discobolus exists.

Memorial, Bangui, Butterfly, Hibiscus—A117

Design: 150fr, Canoe, truck and letters.

1979, June 8 Litho. *Perf. 12x12½*

384	A117	60fr multi	48	25
385	A117	150fr multi	1.20	60

Philexafrique II, Libreville, Gabon, June 8–17. No. 384, 385 each printed in sheets of 10 with 5 labels showing exhibition emblem.

Schoolgirl A118

1979, July 25 Litho. *Perf. 12½x12*

386	A118	70fr multi	55	22

International Bureau of Education, Geneva, 50th anniversary.

Chicken A119

Designs: 20fr, Bull. 40fr, Sheep.

1979, Aug. *Perf. 13*

387	A119	10fr multi	8	5
388	A119	20fr multi	16	8
389	A119	40fr multi	32	15

National Husbandry Association. See No. C211.

Souvenir Sheet

Virgin and Child, by Dürer A120

1979, Aug. *Perf. 13½*

390	A120	500fr lt grn & dl red	4.00	1.85

Albrecht Dürer (1471–1528), German engraver and printer. No. 390 has dull red and light green margin showing entire etching. Size: 90x115mm.

Nos. 257-258 Overprinted "ALUNISSAGE/APOLLO XI/ JUILLET 1969" and Emblem

1979, Nov. 11 Litho. *Perf. 13½*

391	A93	40fr multi	32	15
392	A93	60fr multi	48	25
		Nos. 391-392, C212-C214 (5)	5.60	2.80

Apollo 11 moon landing, 10th anniversary.

Girl and Rose—A121

1979, Dec. 15 Multicolored

393	A121	30fr *Butterfly and girl*, vert.	24	12
394	A121	40fr *shown*	32	16
395	A121	60fr *Hansel and Gretel*, vert.	48	24
396	A121	200fr *Cinderella*	1.60	80
397	A121	250fr *Mermaid*, vert.	2.00	1.00
		Nos. 393-397 (5)	4.64	2.32

International Year of the Child.

Locomotive, U.S. Type A27, Hill—A122

Locomotives, Hill and Stamps: 100fr, France No. 1. 150fr, Germany type A11. 250fr, Great Britain No. 32. 500fr, CAR No. 2.

1979, Dec. 20

398	A122	60fr multi	48	24
399	A122	100fr multi	80	40
400	A122	150fr multi	1.20	60
401	A122	250fr multi	2.00	1.00

Souvenir Sheet

402	A122	500fr multi	4.25	2.25

Sir Rowland Hill (1795-1879), originator of penny postage. No. 402 has multicolored margin showing Hill and Penny Black. Size: 116×78½mm.

Basketball, Moscow '80 Emblem—A123

Pre-Olympic Year: Men's or women's basketball.

1979, Dec. 28 Litho. *Perf. 14½*

403	A123	50fr multi	40	20
404	A123	125fr multi	1.00	50
405	A123	200fr multi	1.60	80
406	A123	300fr multi	2.40	1.20
407	A123	500fr multi	4.00	2.00
		Nos. 403-407 (5)	9.40	4.70

Nos. 313-314, 337-338 Overprinted "REPUBLIQUE CENTRAFRICAINE" in Black on Silver Panel and

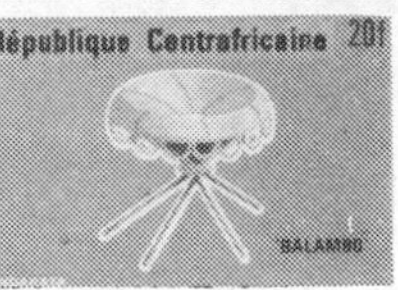

Balambo Chair—A124

1980, Mar. 20 Litho. *Perf. 13½x14, 14x13½*

408	A99	5fr multi	5	5
409	A99	10fr multi	8	5
410	A124	20fr multi	16	8
411	A108	20fr multi	16	8
412	A108	30fr multi	24	12
		Nos. 408-412 (5)	69	38

Viking Satellite—A125

1980, Apr. 8 *Perf. 13½*

413	A125	40fr *shown*	32	16
414	A125	50fr *Apollo-Soyuz*	40	20
415	A125	60fr *Voyager*	48	24
416	A125	100fr *European Space Agency emblem, flags*	80	40
		Nos. 413-416, C221-C222 (6)	4.80	2.40

Walking, Olympic Medal, Moscow '80 Emblem—A126

1980, July 25 Litho. *Perf. 13½*

417	A126	30fr *shown*	24	12
418	A126	40fr *Relay race*	32	16
419	A126	70fr *Running*	55	25
420	A126	80fr *High jump*	65	32
		Nos. 417-420, C231-C232 (6)	3.76	1.85

Agricultural Development—A127

1980, Nov. 4 **Litho.** *Perf. 13½*

421	A127	30fr *shown*	24	12
422	A127	40fr *Telecommunications*	32	16
423	A127	70fr *Engineering*	55	25
424	A127	100fr *Civil engineering*	80	40
		Nos. 421-424, C234-C235 (6)	4.71	2.33

Europe-Africa cooperation.

Nos. 403-407 Overprinted with Medal and Country

1980, Nov. 12 *Perf. 14½*

425	A123	50fr multi	40	20
426	A123	125fr multi	1.00	50
427	A123	200fr multi	1.60	80
428	A123	300fr multi	2.40	1.20
429	A123	500fr multi	4.00	2.00
		Nos. 425-429 (5)	9.40	4.70

Virgin and Child, by Raphael A128

African Postal Union, 5th Anniversary A129

Christmas 1980: Virgin and Child paintings by Raphael.

1980, Dec. 20 *Perf. 12½*

430	A128	60fr multi	50	25
431	A128	150fr multi	1.20	60
432	A128	250fr multi	2.00	1.00

1980, Dec. 24 **Photo.** *Perf. 13½*

433	A129	70fr multi	55	25

Peruvian Soccer Team, Soccer Cup—A130

1981, Jan. 13 **Litho.** *Perf. 13½*

434	A130	10fr shown	8	5
435	A130	15fr Scotland	12	6
436	A130	20fr Mexico	16	8
437	A130	25fr Sweden	20	10
438	A130	30fr Austria	25	12
439	A130	40fr Poland	32	16
440	A130	50fr France	40	20
441	A130	60fr Italy	50	25
442	A130	70fr Germany	60	30
443	A130	80fr Brazil	65	32
		Nos. 434-443, C237-C238 (12)	5.68	2.84

ESPANA '82 World Cup Soccer Championship.

13th World Telecommunications Day—A131

1981, May 17 **Litho.** *Perf. 12½*

444	A131	150fr multi	1.20	60

Apollo 15 Crew on Moon—A132

Space Exploration: Columbia space shuttle.

1981, June 10 **Litho.** *Perf. 14*

445	A132	100fr multi	80	40
446	A132	150fr multi	1.20	60
447	A132	200fr multi	1.60	80
448	A132	300fr multi	2.40	1.20

Souvenir Sheet

449	A132	500fr multi	4.00	2.00

No. 449 has multicolored margin continuing design of stamp. Size: 103x78mm.

Family of Acrobats with Monkey, by Picasso—A133

Picasso Birth Centenary: 50fr, The Balcony. 80fr, The Artist's Son as Pierrot. 100fr, The Three Dancers.

1981, June 30 *Perf. 13½*

450	A133	40fr multi	32	16
451	A133	50fr multi	40	20
452	A133	80fr multi	65	32
453	A133	100fr multi	80	40
		Nos. 450-453, C245-C246 (6)	4.97	2.48

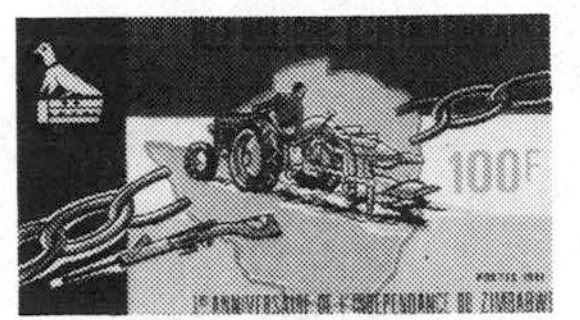

First Anniv. of Zimbabwe's Independence—A134

1981, July 9 **Litho.** *Perf. 12½*

454	A134	100fr multi	80	80
455	A134	150fr multi	1.20	60
456	A134	200fr multi	1.60	80

Prince Charles and Lady Diana—A135

1981, July, 24 *Perf. 14*

457	A135	75fr Charles	60	30
458	A135	100fr Diana	80	40
459	A135	150fr St. Paul's Cathedral	1.20	60
460	A135	175fr shown	1.40	70

Souvenir Sheet

461	A135	500fr Couple	4.00	2.00

Royal Wedding. No. 461 has multicolored margin showing flowers. Size: 70x91mm.

Nos. 417-420 Overprinted with Event, Winner and Country in Gold.

1981 **Litho.** *Perf. 13½*

462	A126	30fr multi	24	12
463	A126	40fr multi	32	16
464	A126	70fr multi	55	25
465	A126	80fr multi	65	32
		Nos. 462-465, C248-C249 (6)	3.76	1.85

Prince Charles and Lady Diana—A136

1981, Aug. 20 **Litho.** *Perf. 13½*

466	A136	40fr shown	32	16
467	A136	50fr Crowned Prince of Wales	40	20
468	A136	80fr Diana	65	32
469	A136	100fr Naval training	80	40
		Nos. 466-469, C251-C252 (6)	4.97	2.48

Royal wedding.

1906 Renault—A137

1981, Sept. 22 **Litho.** *Perf. 12½*

470	A137	20fr shown	16	8
471	A137	40fr Mercedes-Benz, 1937	32	16
472	A137	50fr Matra-Ford, 1969	40	20
473	A137	110fr Tazio Nuvolari, 1927	90	45
474	A137	150fr Jackie Stewart, 1965	1.20	60
		Nos. 470-474 (5)	2.98	1.49

Souvenir Sheet
Perf. 10

475	A137	450fr Finish line, 1914	3.75	2.00

Grand Prix of France, 75th anniv. No. 475 has multicolored margin continuing design. Size: 104x80mm.

World Food Day—A138

1981, Oct. 16

476	A138	90fr multi	72	36
477	A138	110fr multi	90	45

Navigators and their Ships—A139

1981, Sept. 4 **Litho.** *Perf. 13½*

478	A139	40fr C.V. Rietschoten	32	16
479	A139	50fr M. Pajot	40	20
480	A139	60fr K. Jaworski	50	25
481	A139	80fr M. Birch	65	32
		Nos. 478-481, C254-C255 (6)	4.27	2.13

Downfall of Empire—A140

1981, Oct. 6

482	A140	5fr Sword through crown	5	5
483	A140	10fr like #482	8	5
484	A140	25fr Victory holding map	20	10
485	A140	60fr like #484	50	25
486	A140	90fr Toppled Bokassa statue	72	36
487	A140	500fr like #486	4.00	2.00
		Nos. 482-487 (6)	5.55	2.81

Komba A141

1981, Nov. 17

488	A141	50fr shown	40	20
489	A141	90fr Dodoro, horiz.	72	36
490	A141	140fr Kaya, horiz.	1.15	60

Central African States Bank—A142

1981, Dec. 12 **Litho.** *Perf. 12½x13*

491	A142	90fr multi	72	36
492	A142	110fr multi	90	45

Christmas 1981
A143

Virgin and Child Paintings.

1981, Dec. 24

493	A143	50fr Fra Angelico, 1430	40	20
494	A143	60fr Cosimo Tura, 1484	50	25
495	A143	90fr Bramantino	72	36
496	A143	110fr Memling	90	45
		Nos. 493-496, C260-C261 (6)	5.27	2.66

Scouting Year—A144

1982, Jan. 13 *Perf. 12½*

497	A144	100fr Hiking	80	40
498	A144	150fr Scouts, horiz.	1.20	60
499	A144	200fr Hiking	1.60	80
500	A144	300fr Salute, flag, vert.	2.40	1.20

Souvenir Sheet

501	A144	500fr Scout, Baden-Powell, vert.	4.00	2.00

No. 501 contains one stamp (perf. 13); multicolored margin shows hike, emblem. Size: 84x113mm.

Elephant—A145

1982, Jan. 22 *Perf. 13½*

502	A145	60fr shown	50	25
503	A145	90fr Giraffes	72	36
504	A145	100fr Addaxes	80	40
505	A145	110fr Okapi	90	45
		Nos. 502-505, C263-C264 (6)	9.32	4.66

Norman Rockwell Illustrations—A146

1982, Feb. 17 *Perf. 13½x14*

506	A146	30fr Grandfather snowman	25	12
507	A146	60fr Croquet players	50	25
508	A146	110fr Women talking	90	45
509	A146	150fr Searching	1.20	60

AT 16 Dirigible—A147

1982, Feb. 27 **Litho.** *Perf. 13½*

510	A147	5fr shown	5	5
511	A147	10fr Beyer-Garrat locomotive	8	5
512	A147	20fr Bugatti 24 "Royale," 1924	16	8
513	A147	110fr Vickers "Valentia," 1928	90	45
		Nos. 510-513, C266-C267 (6)	7.59	3.88

Bellvue Garden, by Edouard Manet (1832-1883)—A148

Anniversaries: 400fr, Goethe (1749-1832) (vert.). Nos. 519-520, Princess Diana, 21st birthday, July 1 (vert.). 300fr, George Washington (1732-1799) (vert.).

1982, Apr. 6 **Litho.** *Perf. 13*

517	A148	200fr multi	1.60	80
517A	A148	300fr multi	2.40	1.25
518	A148	400fr multi	3.25	1.60
519	A148	500fr multi	4.00	2.00

Souvenir Sheet

520	A148	500fr multi	4.00	2.00

No. 520 has multicolored margin showing flowers. Size: 80x104mm.

23rd Olympic Games, Los Angeles, 1984—A149

1982, July 24 **Litho.** *Perf. 13½*

521	A149	5fr Soccer	5	5
522	A149	10fr Boxing	8	5
523	A149	20fr Running	16	8
524	A149	110fr Long jump	90	45
		Nos. 521-524, C269-C270 (6)	7.69	3.88

21st Birthday of Princess Diana—A150

Portraits.

1982, July 20 **Litho.** *Perf. 13½*

525	A150	5fr multi	5	5
526	A150	10fr multi	8	5
527	A150	20fr multi	16	8
528	A150	110fr multi	90	45
		Nos. 525-528, C272-C273 (6)	7.69	3.88

Nos. 457-461 Overprinted in Blue: "NAISSANCE ROYALE 1982"

1982, Aug. 20 *Perf. 14*

529	A135	75fr multi	60	30
530	A135	110fr multi	90	45
531	A135	150fr multi	1.25	60
532	A135	175fr multi	1.40	70

Souvenir Sheet

533	A135	500fr multi	4.00	2.00

Birth of Prince William of Wales, June 21.

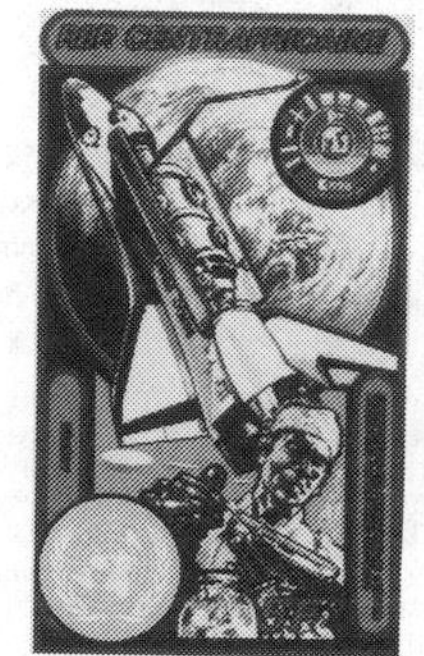

2nd UN Conference on Peaceful Uses of Outer Space, Vienna, Aug. 9-21—A151

Various satellites and space scenes.

1982, Aug. 15 **Litho.** *Perf. 13½*

534	A151	5fr multi	5	5
535	A151	10fr multi	8	5
536	A151	20fr multi	16	8
537	A151	110fr multi	90	45
		Nos. 534-537, C277-C278 (6)	7.68	3.85

Sakpa Basket—A152

Baskets and bowls.

1982, Sept. 2 *Perf. 13*

538	A152	5fr shown	5	5
539	A152	10fr like 5fr	8	5
540	A152	25fr Ngbenda gourd, vert.	20	10
541	A152	60fr like 25fr	48	24
542	A152	120fr Ta ti ngou jugs	1.00	50
543	A152	175fr Kangu bowls	1.60	80
544	A152	300fr Kolongo bowls, vert.	2.50	1.25
		Nos. 538-544 (7)	5.91	2.99

13th World UPU Day—A153

1982, Oct. 9

549	A153	60fr multi	48	24
550	A153	120fr multi	1.00	50

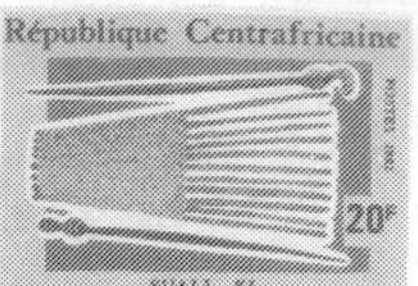

Comb and Hairpins—A154

1982, Oct. 20 *Perf. 13x12½*

551	A154	20fr multi	16	8
552	A154	30fr multi	24	12
553	A154	60fr multi	48	24
554	A154	80fr multi	65	32
555	A154	120fr multi	1.00	50
		Nos. 551-555 (5)	2.53	1.26

Artist Pierre Ndarata and No. 69—A155

1982, Oct. *Perf. 13*

556	A155	40fr Jean Tubind at easel, vert.	32	16
557	A155	70fr shown	56	28
558	A155	90fr like 70fr	72	36
559	A155	140fr like 40fr	1.35	68

TB Bacillus Centenary—A156

1982, Nov. 30 *Perf. 13½x13*

560	A156	100fr vio & blk	80	40
561	A156	120fr red org & blk	1.00	50
562	A156	175fr bl & blk	1.60	80

10th Anniv. of UN Conference on Human Environment—A157

1982, Dec. 8

563	A157	120fr multi	1.00	50
564	A157	150fr multi	1.20	60
565	A157	300fr multi	2.50	1.25

Granary—A158

1982, Dec. 15 *Perf. 13*

566	A158	60fr multi	48	24
567	A158	80fr multi	65	32
568	A158	120fr multi	1.00	50
569	A158	200fr multi	1.60	80

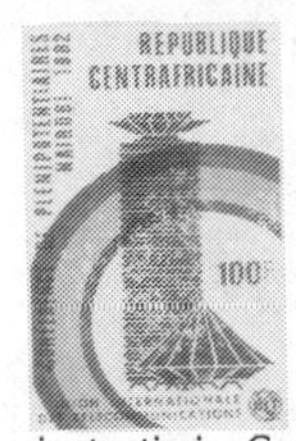

ITU Plenipotentiaries Conference, Nairobi, Sept.—A159

1982, Dec.

570 A159 100fr multi 00 10
571 A159 120fr multi 1.00 50

UN Decade for African Transportation and Communication, 1978-88—A160

1983, Jan. 31 **Litho.** ***Perf. 13½x13***

572 A160 5fr Modes of communication 5 5
573 A160 60fr like 5fr 50 25
574 A160 120fr Map, jet 1.00 50
575 A160 175fr like 120fr 1.60 80

Chess Champions—A161

Men and Chess Pieces: 5fr, Steinitz, first world champion, 1886. 10fr, Aaron Niemzovitch, castle. 20fr, Alexander Alekhine, knights. 110fr, Botvinnik. 300fr, Boris Spassky, glass pieces. 500fr, Bobby Fischer, king, knight. 600fr, Korchnoi, Karpov, pawn.

1983, Jan. 15

576 A161 5fr multi 5 5
577 A161 10fr multi 8 5
578 A161 20fr multi 16 8
579 A161 110fr multi 90 45
580 A161 300fr multi 2.50 1.25
581 A161 500fr multi 4.00 2.00
Nos. 576-581 (6) 7.69 3.88

Souvenir Sheet

582 A161 600fr multi 5.00 2.50

No. 582 contains one stamp (56x33mm.); multicolored margin shows 18th cent. chess set. 300fr, 500fr, 600fr air mail.

Marshal Tito (1892-1980) A162

1983, Jan. 22

583 A162 20fr George Washington 16 8
a. Souvenir sheet 25 15
584 A162 110fr shown 90 45
a. Souvenir sheet 1.00 50

Size of Nos. 583a-584a: 62x98mm.

Easter 1983 A163

Rembrandt Paintings.

1983, Apr. 16

585 A163 100fr Entombment 80 40
586 A163 300fr Crucifixion 2.50 1.25
587 A163 400fr Descent from the Cross 3.25 1.75

Vintage Cars and their Makers—A164

Designs: 10fr, Emile Levassor, Rene Panhard, 1895 car. 20fr, Henry Ford, 1896 car. 30fr, Louis Renault, 1899 car. 80fr, Ettore Bugatti, type 37, 1925. 400fr, Enzo Ferrari, 815 sport, 1940. 500fr, Ferdinand Porsche, 356 coupe, 1951. 600fr, Karl Benz, velociped, 1886. 400fr, 500fr, 600fr airmail.

1983, June 3 **Litho.** ***Perf. 13½***

588 A164 10fr multi 8 5
589 A164 20fr multi 16 8
590 A164 30fr multi 24 12
591 A164 80fr multi 65 32
592 A164 400fr multi 3.25 1.75
593 A164 500fr multi 4.00 2.00
Nos. 588-593 (6) 8.38 4.32

Souvenir Sheet

594 A164 600fr multi 5.00 2.50

No. 594 has multicolored margin showing cars. Size: 77x87mm.

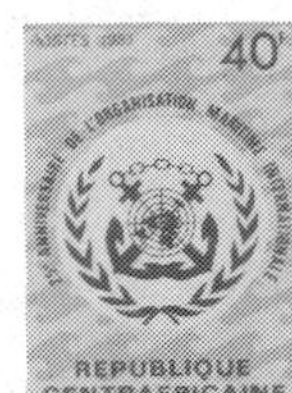

25th Anniv. of Intl. Maritime Org.—A165

1983, July 8 **Litho.** ***Perf. 12½x13***

595 A165 40fr multi 32 16
596 A165 100fr multi 80 40

World Communications Year—A166

1983, July 22

597 A166 50fr multi 40 20
598 A166 130fr multi 1.05 52

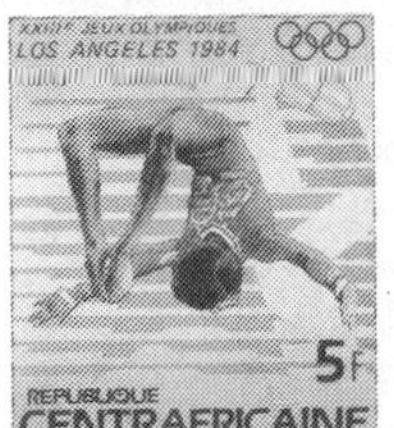

Pre-Olympics, Los Angeles—A167

1983, Aug. 3 **Litho.** ***Perf. 13***

599 A167 5fr Gymnast 5 5
600 A167 40fr Javelin throwing 32 16
601 A167 60fr Pole vault 48 24
602 A167 120fr Fencing 96 48
603 A167 200fr Cycling 1.60 80
604 A167 300fr Sailing 2.40 1.25
Nos. 599-604 (6) 5.81 2.98

Souvenir Sheet

605 A167 600fr Handball 5.00 2.50

Multicolored margin shows various players. Size: 109x81mm.

Namibia Day—A168

1983, Sept. 16 **Litho.** ***Perf. 13***

606 A168 100fr multi 80 40
607 A168 200fr multi 1.60 80

Manned Flight Bicentenary—A169

Designs: 50fr, J. Montgolfier and his balloon, 1783. 100fr, J.P. Blanchard, English Channel crossing, 1785. 200fr, L.-J. Gay-Lussac, 4000-meter balloon ascent, 1804. 300fr, Giffard and his dirigible, 1852. 400fr, Santos Dumont, dirigible, Eiffel Tower. 500fr, A. Laquot, captive observation balloon, 1914. 600fr, J.A. Charles, first gas balloon; G. Tissandier, dirigible, 1883.

1983, Sept. 30 **Litho.** ***Perf. 13½***

608 A169 50fr multi 25 12
609 A169 100fr multi 50 25
610 A169 200fr multi 1.00 50
611 A169 300fr multi 1.50 75
612 A169 400fr multi 2.00 1.00
613 A169 500fr multi 2.50 1.25
Nos. 608-613 (6) 7.75 3.87

Souvenir Sheet

614 A169 600fr multi 3.00 1.50

No. 614 has multicolored margin continuing design. Size: 79x85mm. 400fr, 500fr, 600fr airmail.

Black Rhinoceros and World Wildlife Emblem—A170

Various black rhinoceroses.

1983, Nov. 14

615 A170 10fr multi 5 5
616 A170 40fr multi 20 10
617 A170 70fr multi 35 18
618 A170 180fr multi 90 45

UPU Day, World Communications Year—A171

1983, Nov. 2 **Litho.** ***Perf. 13***

619 A171 205fr multi 1.65 85

2nd Anniv. of the Natl. Military Committee—A172

Gen. Andre Kolingba, head of state.

1983, Sept. 1 ***Perf. 12½***

620 A172 65fr sil & multi 32 16
621 A172 130fr gold & multi 65 32

Earth Satellite Receiving Station, Bangui M'Poko—A173

1983 ***Perf. 13***

622 A173 130fr multi 65 32

Natl. Day of the Handicapped and the Elderly—A174

1983, Dec. 20		Engr.	Perf. 13x12½		
623	A174	65fr vio & org		32	16
624	A174	130fr ultra & org		65	32
625	A174	205fr dk grn & org		1.05	52

Fishing Resources—A175

1983, Dec. 31		Litho.	Perf. 12½		
626	A175	25fr Breeding tank		12	6
627	A175	65fr Net fishing		32	16
628	A175	100fr Dam fishing		50	25
629	A175	130fr Still life with fish		65	32
630	A175	205fr Basket trap		1.05	52
		Nos. 626-630 (5)		2.64	1.31

Wildlife Protection—A176

1984, Jan. 25			Perf. 13		
631	A176	30fr Forest fire		15	8
632	A176	130fr Hunters		65	32

Packet Ship Pericles—A177

1984, June		Litho.	Perf. 12½		
633	A177	65fr shown		32	16
634	A177	110fr CC-1500 locomotive		55	28
635	A177	120fr Three-master Pereire		60	30
636	A177	240fr PLM series 210, 1868		1.20	60
637	A177	250fr Admella		1.25	62
638	A177	350fr 231-726 locomotive, 1937		1.75	90
639	A177	400fr Royal William		2.00	1.00
640	A177	440fr Pacific S3/6, 1908		2.20	1.10
641	A177	500fr Great Britain		2.50	1.25
642	A177	500fr Henschel 151 series 45, 1937		2.50	1.25
		Nos. 633-642 (10)		14.87	7.46

J. W. Goethe, Scene from Faust—A178

Designs: 100fr, Henri Dunant, Red Cross Founder, Battle of Solferino, 125th anniv. 200fr, Alfred Nobel, Nobel Foundation headquarters. 300fr, Lord Baden-Powell, World Scouting Jamboree, Alberta, 1983. 400fr, John F. Kennedy, first man on the Moon, 1969. 500fr, 600fr, wedding of Prince and Princess of Wales.

1984, Feb. 25		Litho.	Perf. 13½		
643	A178	50fr multi		20	10
644	A178	100fr multi		40	20
645	A178	200fr multi		80	40
646	A178	300fr multi		1.15	60
647	A178	400fr multi		1.50	75
648	A178	500fr multi		2.00	1.00
		Nos. 643-648 (6)		6.05	3.05

Souvenir Sheet

649	A178	600fr multi		2.50	1.25

No. 649 has multicolored decorative margin. Size: . 400fr, 500fr, airmail.

Old Masters—A179

Paintings: 50fr, Madonna and Child, by Raphael. 100fr, Madonna with Pear, by Durer. 200fr, Aldobrandini Madonna, by Raphael. 300fr, Madonna with Carnation, by Durer. 400fr, Virgin and Child, by Correggio. 500fr, La Bohemienne, by Modigliani. 600fr, Madonna and Child on the Throne, by Raphael.

1984, Mar. 30		Litho.	Perf. 13½		
650	A179	50fr multi		24	12
651	A179	100fr multi		48	24
652	A179	200fr multi		95	48
653	A179	300fr multi		1.40	70
654	A179	400fr multi		1.90	95
655	A179	500fr multi		2.35	1.20
		Nos. 650-655 (6)		7.32	3.69

Miniature Sheet

656	A179	600fr multi		2.85	1.45

No. 656 contains 1 stamp, size 30 x 59mm, with design continuing into margin. Size: 80x111mm. 400fr, 500fr and 600fr are airmail.

Space—A180

1984, Aug. 6		Litho.	Perf. 13½		
657	A180	20fr Galileo, Ariane rocket		10	5
658	A180	70fr Piccard, X-15, balloon		35	18
659	A180	150fr Oberth, satellite		75	38
660	A180	205fr Einstein, satellites		1.05	55
661	A180	300fr Curie, Viking vehicle		1.50	75
662	A180	500fr Merbold, Spacelab		2.50	1.25
		Nos. 657-662 (6)		6.25	3.16

Miniature Sheet

663	A180	600fr Armstrong, Apollo 11, horiz.		3.00	1.50

No. 663 contains 1 stamp, size 42x36mm, with design continuing into margin. Size: 75x60mm. 300fr, 500fr and 600fr are airmail.

Forestry Resources A181

UNICEF A182

1984, Oct. 9		Litho.	Perf. 13x12½		
664	A181	70fr Forest		35	18
665	A181	130fr Logging		65	32

1984, Oct. 27		Litho.	Perf. 13x12½		
666	A182	10fr Weighing child		5	5
667	A182	30fr Vaccinating child		15	8
668	A182	65fr Giving liquids		35	18
669	A182	100fr Balancing diet		50	25

Fishing Traps—A183

1984, Nov. 6		Litho.	Perf. 13		
670	A183	50fr Bangui-Kette		25	12
671	A183	80fr Mbres		40	20
672	A183	150fr Bangui-Kette		75	38

Mushrooms—A184

1984, Nov. 15		Litho.	Perf. 13½		
673	A184	5fr Leptoporus lignosus		5	5
674	A184	10fr Phlebopus sudanicus		5	5
675	A184	40fr Termitomyces letestui		16	8
676	A184	130fr Lepiota esculenta		52	25
677	A184	300fr Termitomyces aurantiacus		1.25	62
678	A184	500fr Termitomyces robustus		2.00	1.00
		Nos. 673-678 (6)		4.03	2.05

Souvenir Sheet

679	A184	600fr Tricholoma lobayensis		2.50	1.25

Nos. 677-679 are airmail. No. 679 has multicolored margin continuing the design. Size: 68x90mm.

Flowers—A185

1984, Nov. 22		Litho.	Perf. 13½		
680	A185	65fr Hibiscus		35	18
681	A185	130fr Canna Indica		65	32
682	A185	205fr Eichlornia Crassipes		1.05	52

Economic Campaign—A186

1984, Dec. 3		Litho.	Perf. 13½		
683	A186	25fr Cotton planting		12	6
684	A186	40fr Selling cotton crop		18	10
685	A186	130fr Cotton market		55	28

World Food Day—A187

1984, Dec. 10		Litho.	Perf. 13½		
686	A187	205fr Picking corn		90	45

Anniversaries and Events—A189

Famous men: 50fr, Abraham Lincoln, American Civil War soldiers. 90fr, Auguste Piccard (1884-1962), inventor, bathyscaphe Trieste. 120fr, Gottlieb Daimler (1834-1900), 1938 Mercedes Type 540. 200fr, Louis Bleriot (1872-1936), inventor, plane. 350fr, Anatoly Karpov, world chess champion. 400fr, Jean Henri Dunant (1828-1910) Red Cross founder, worker caring for wounded soldier.

1984, Dec. 22		Litho.	Perf. 13½		
694	A189	50fr multi		20	10
695	A189	90fr multi		38	20
696	A189	120fr multi		50	25
697	A189	200fr multi		82	40
698	A189	350fr multi		1.40	70
698A	A189	400fr multi		1.75	90
		Nos. 694-698A (6)		5.05	2.55

Nos. 698-698A are airmail.

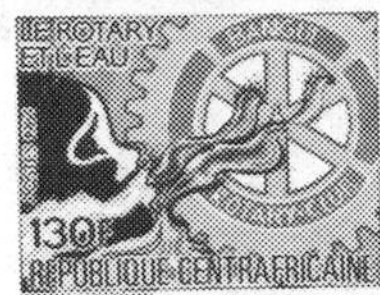

Bangui Rotary Club and Water—A190

1984, Dec. 29

699	A190	130fr	multi	52	25
700	A190	205fr	multi	85	42

Nos. 637-640, C302A Overprinted with Exhibitions in Red.

1985, Mar. 13 **Litho.** ***Perf. 12½***

701	A177	250fr	Argentina '85, Buenos Aires	1.00	50
702	A177	350fr	Tsukuba Expo '85	1.40	70
703	A177	400fr	Italia '85, Rome	1.60	80
704	A177	440fr	Mophila '85, Hamburg	1.75	90

Souvenir Sheet ***Perf. 13½x13***

705	AP89	500fr	Olymphilex '85, Lausanne	2.00	1.00

500fr airmail.

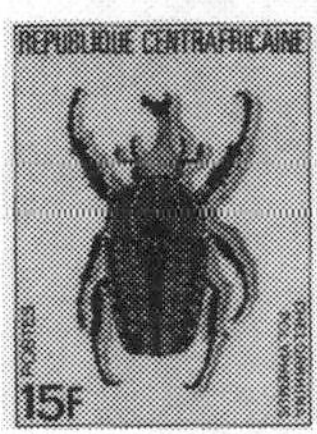

Beetles—A191

1985, Mar. **Litho.** ***Perf. 13½***

706	A191	15fr	Chelorrhina polyphemus	6	5
707	A191	20fr	Fornasinius russus	8	5
708	A191	25fr	Goliathus giganteus	10	5
709	A191	65fr	Goliathus meleagris	25	12

Audubon Birth Bicentenary—A192

Illustrations of North American bird species by John Audubon.

1985, Mar. 25 **Litho.** ***Perf. 13½***

710	A192	40fr	Cyanocitta cristata	18	10
711	A192	80fr	Caprimulgus carolinensis	32	16
712	A192	130fr	Campephilus principales	52	25
713	A192	250fr	Calocitta formosa	1.00	50
714	A192	300fr	Coccizus minor, horiz.	1.25	62
715	A192	500fr	Hirundo rustica, horiz.	2.00	1.00
			Nos. 710-715 (6)	5.27	2.63

Souvenir Sheet

716	A192	600fr	Dryocopus pileatus, horiz.	2.50	1.25

Nos. 714-716 are airmail. No. 716 has multicolored margin continuing the design. Size: 69x104mm.

Intl. Youth Year—A193

Famous children's book authors and scenes from their best-known novels: 100fr, The Jungle Book, 1894, by Rudyard Kipling (1865-1936), vert. 200fr, Les Cavaliers, 1967, by Joseph Kessel (1898-1979). 300fr, Twenty-Thousand Leagues Under the Sea, 1873, by Jules Verne (1828-1905). 400fr, The Adventures of Tom Sawyer, 1876, by Mark Twain (1835-1910).

1985, Apr. **Litho.** ***Perf. 13***

718	A193	100fr	multi	40	20
719	A193	200fr	multi	80	40
720	A193	300fr	multi	1.20	60
721	A193	400fr	multi	1.60	80

Philexafrica '85, Lome—A194

Designs: No. 722, UPU emblem, Postmen unloading parcel post van. No. 723, Exhibition emblem, scout troop.

1985, May 15 ***Perf. 13x12½***

722	A194	200fr	multi	80	40
723	A194	200fr	multi	80	40

Nos. 722-723 se-tenant with center label picturing a map of Africa or the UAPT emblem.

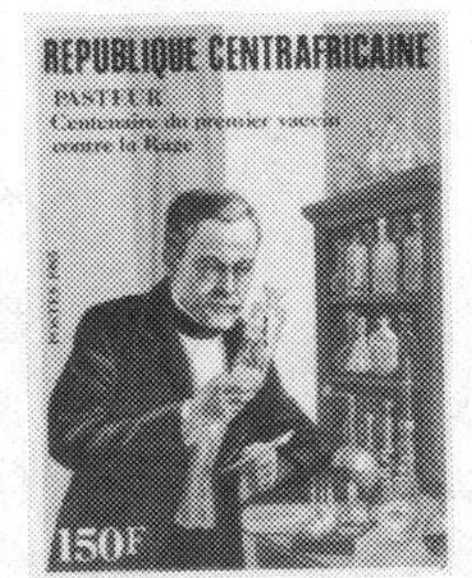

Battle of Solferino, Founding of the Red Cross, 125th Anniv., Founder Jean-Henri Dunant (1828-1910)—A195

Anniversaries and events: 150fr, Rabies vaccine centenary, Louis Pasteur (1822-1895), chemist, microbiologist, vert. 300fr, Girl Guides, 75th anniv., vert. 450fr, Elizabeth, the Queen Mother, 85th birthday, vert. 500fr, Statue of Liberty, cent., vert.

1985, June ***Perf. 13***

724	A195	150fr	multi	60	30
725	A195	200fr	multi	80	40
726	A195	300fr	multi	1.20	60
727	A195	450fr	multi	1.80	90
728	A195	500fr	multi	2.00	1.00
			Nos. 724-728 (5)	6.40	3.20

1986 World Cup Soccer Championships, Mexico—A196

Famous soccer players and match scenes.

1985, July 24 **Litho.** ***Perf. 13½***

730	A196	5fr	Pele	5	5
731	A196	10fr	Tony Schumacher	5	5
732	A196	20fr	Paolo Rossi	10	5
733	A196	350fr	Kevin Keegan	1.40	70
734	A196	400fr	Michel Platini	1.75	90
735	A196	500fr	Karl Heinz Rummenigge	2.00	1.00
			Nos. 730-735 (6)	5.35	2.75

Souvenir Sheet

736	A196	600fr	Diego Armando Maradona	2.50	1.25

Nos. 734-736 are airmail. No. 736 has multicolored margin picturing bullfight scenes. Size: 95x64mm.

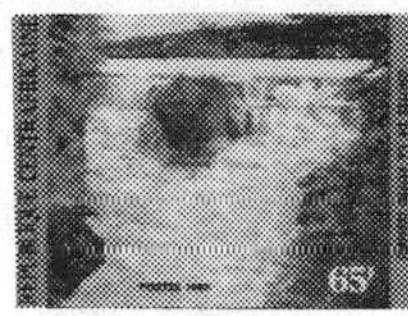

Kotto Waterfalls—A197

1985, July 27 **Litho.** ***Perf. 13½***

737	A197	65fr	multi	25	14
738	A197	90fr	multi	36	18
739	A197	130fr	multi	55	28

State Visit of Pope John Paul II—A198

Portraits.

1985, Aug. 14

740	A198	65fr	multi	25	14
741	A198	130fr	multi	55	28

Natl. Economic Development Campaign—A199

Designs: 5fr, Troops plowing. 60fr, Soldier preparing field for planting, vert. 130fr, Planting cotton seeds, vert.

1985, Sept. 1 ***Perf. 13***

742	A199	5fr	multi	5	5
743	A199	60fr	multi	22	12
744	A199	130fr	multi	55	28

Queen Mother, 85th Birthday—A200

1985, Sept. 16 **Litho.** ***Perf. 13½***

745	A200	100fr	Age 4, with brother	42	20
746	A200	200fr	Duchess of York, 1923	82	40
747	A200	300fr	Reviewing Irish Guards, 1928	1.25	62
748	A200	350fr	Family portrait, 1936	1.40	70
749	A200	400fr	George VI coronation, 1937	1.75	90
750	A200	500fr	Wedding anniv., 1948	2.00	1.00
			Nos. 745-750 (6)	7.64	3.82

Souvenir Sheet

751	A200	600fr	Christening Prince Charles, 1948	2.50	1.25

Nos. 749-751 are airmail. No. 751 has multicolored margin picturing baptism of Prince Henry, Dec. 21, 1984. Size: 75x87mm.

Dr. Rene Labusquiere (1919-1977), Promoter of Preventive Medicine—A201

1985, Sept. 22 **Litho.** ***Perf. 13½***

752	A201	10fr	multi	5	5
753	A201	45fr	multi	18	10
754	A201	110fr	multi	45	22

Natl. Postal Service—A202

1985, Oct. 9 ***Perf. 12½***

755	A202	15fr	Loading mail van	6	5
756	A202	60fr	Bangui P.O., van	22	12
757	A202	150fr	Hdqtrs, Bangui, and vans	62	32

Space Research—A203

Designs: 40fr, Yuri Gagarin and Sergei Korolev, Soviet cosmonauts. 110fr, Nicolaus Copernicus, Cassini probe. 240fr, Galileo, Viking orbiter. 300fr, Theodor von Karman (1881-1963), American aeronautical engineer, and space shuttle recovering Palapa B satellite. 450fr, Percival Lowell (1855-1916), American astronomer, and Viking probe. 500fr, Dr. U. Merbold and orbiting space station project Colombo. 600fr, Apollo 11 Project, first step on Moon by Neil Armstrong.

1985, Oct. 31 Litho. *Perf. 13½*

758	A203	40fr	multi	18	10
759	A203	110fr	multi	45	22
760	A203	240fr	multi	1.00	50
761	A203	300fr	multi	1.25	62
762	A203	450fr	multi	1.85	95
763	A203	500fr	multi	2.00	1.00
			Nos. 758-763 (6)	6.73	3.39

Souvenir Sheet
Imperf.

764	A203	600fr	multi	2.50	1.25

Nos. 762-764 are airmail. No. 764 has multicolored margin continuing the design. Size: 96x68mm.

Solar Energy Apparatus, Damara—A204

1985, Nov. 4 Litho. *Perf. 13½*

765	A204	65fr	multi	25	12
766	A204	130fr	multi	55	28

Girl Guides Nature Study—A205

1985, Nov. 16 *Perf. 13*

767	A205	250fr	shown	1.00	50
768	A205	250fr	Ouaka Sugar Refinery	1.00	50

PHILEXAFRICA '85, Lome, Togo, Nov. 16-24. Nos. 767-768 se-tenant with center labels picturing map of Africa or UAPT emblem.

State Visit of Pres. Mitterand of France, Dec. 12-13—A206

1985, Dec. 12 Litho. *Perf. 13x12½*

769	A206	65fr	multi	25	12
770	A206	130fr	multi	52	25
770A	A206	160fr	multi ('86)	65	32

UN 40th Anniv., Central Africa Admission, 25th Anniv.—A207

1985, Dec. 18 *Perf. 13½*

771	A207	140fr	multi	58	30

Intl. Youth Year—A208

Designs: 40fr, Madonna with the Carnation, 1470, by Leonardo da Vinci. 80fr, Johann Sebastian Bach. 100fr, St. John at Patmos, 1619, by Velazquez. 250fr, The Erl King score, by Franz Schubert. 400fr, Portrait of Vicente Osorio de Moscoso, by Goya. 500fr, The Young Mozart Playing in Paris, 1764. 600fr, Woman in a Plumed Hat, 1901, by Picasso.

1985, Dec. 28

772	A208	40fr	multi	18	10
773	A208	80fr	multi	32	16
774	A208	100fr	multi	42	20
775	A208	250fr	multi	1.00	50
776	A208	400fr	multi	1.75	90
777	A208	500fr	multi	2.00	1.00
			Nos. 772-777 (6)	5.67	2.86

Souvenir Sheet

778	A208	600fr	multi	2.50	1.25

Nos. 776-778 are airmail. No. 778 has multicolored margin picturing Picasso, his studio and Paris residence. Size: 79x79mm.

Halley's Comet—A209

Designs: 100fr, Edmond Halley, British astronomer. 200fr, Sir Isaac Newton's telescope and comet sighting. 300fr, Halley and Newton observing comet. 350fr, US probe. 400fr, Soviet probe plotting comet's perihelion. 500fr, Isodensity photograph of comet. 600fr, Comet, Earth, Sun and probe.

1985, Dec. 29

779	A209	100fr	multi	42	20
780	A209	200fr	multi	85	42
781	A209	300fr	multi	1.25	62
782	A209	350fr	multi	1.40	70
783	A209	400fr	multi	1.75	90
784	A209	500fr	multi	2.00	1.00
			Nos. 779-784 (6)	7.67	3.84

Souvenir Sheet

785	A209	600fr	multi	2.50	1.25

Nos. 783-785 are airmail. No. 785 has multicolored margin continuing the design. Size: 70x101mm.

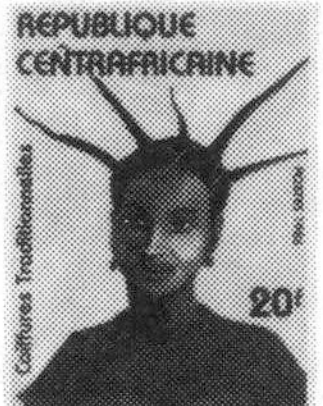

Christopher Columbus (1451-1506)—A210

Various events leading to the discovery of America and beyond.

1986

786	A210	90fr	Plotting course	38	20
787	A210	110fr	Receiving blessing	45	22
788	A210	240fr	Fleet in port	1.00	50
789	A210	300fr	Trade with natives	1.25	62
790	A210	400fr	Storm at sea	1.75	90
791	A210	500fr	Fleet at sea	2.00	1.00
			Nos. 779-784 (6)	6.83	3.44

Souvenir Sheet

792	A210	600fr	Portrait	2.50	1.25

Nos. 790-792 are airmail. No. 792 has multicolored margin picturing exotic birds and flagship. Size: 71x101mm.

Hairstyles A211 France-Central Africa Week A212

1986, May 21 Litho. *Perf. 13x12½*

793	A211	20fr	multi	10	5
794	A211	30fr	multi	14	6
795	A211	65fr	multi	25	12
796	A211	160fr	multi	65	32

1986, May 26 *Perf. 12½*

797	A212	40fr	Communications, horiz.	18	10
798	A212	60fr	Youth, horiz.	25	12
799	A212	100fr	Basket maker	42	20
800	A212	130fr	Bicycling	52	25

Centrapalm Palm Oil—A213

Designs: 25fr, 65fr, Refinery, Bossongo, and palm tree. 120fr, 160fr, Refinery and palm tree, vert.

1986, Aug. 12 Litho. *Perf. 13½*

801	A213	25fr	multi	14	8
802	A213	65fr	multi	35	18
803	A213	120fr	multi	65	32
804	A213	160fr	multi	88	45

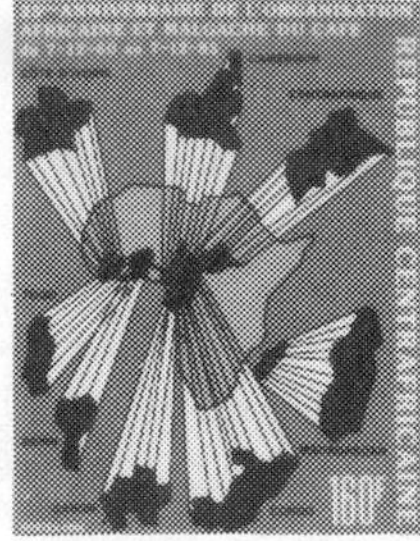

Dogs and Cats—A214

1986, Sept. 9

805	A214	10fr	Pointer	6	5
806	A214	20fr	Egyptian mau	12	6
807	A214	200fr	Newfoundland	1.10	55
808	A214	300fr	Borzoi	1.65	82
809	A214	400fr	Persian red	2.20	1.10
			Nos. 805-809 (5)	5.13	2.58

Souvenir Sheet

810	A214	500fr	Spaniel, Burmese-Malayan	2.75	1.40

Nos. 808-810 are airmail. No. 810 has dark olive bister margin picturing King Charles spaniel, Burmese zibeline and kitten. Size: 95x60mm.

African Coffee Producers Organization, 25th Anniv.—A215

1986, Sept. 25 Litho. *Perf. 13*

811	A215	160fr	multi	90	45

1986 World Cup Soccer Championships, Mexico—A216

Satellites, final scores, World Cup and athletes: 30fr, Muller, Socrates. 110fr, Scifo, Ceulemans. 160fr, Stopyra, Platini. 350fr, Brehme, Schumacher. 450fr, Maradona. 500fr, Schumacher, Burruchaga.

1986, Nov. 12 *Perf. 13½*

812	A216	30fr	multi	18	10
813	A216	110fr	multi	60	30
814	A216	160fr	multi	90	45
815	A216	350fr	multi	2.00	1.00
816	A216	450fr	multi	2.50	1.25
			Nos. 812-816 (5)	6.18	3.10

Souvenir Sheet

817	A216	500fr	multi	2.75	1.40

Nos. 816-817 are airmail. No. 817 has multicolored margin continuing the design, picturing Maradona, Burruchaga, Briegel, stadium and final scores. Size: 110x68mm.

15F

US Anniversaries and Events—A217

Designs: 15fr, Judith Resnik. 25fr, Frederic Auguste Bartholdi. 70fr, Elvis Presley. 300fr, Ronald McNair. 450fr, Christa McAuliffe. 500fr, McAuliffe, Scobee, Smith, Resnik, Onizuka, McNair, Jarvis.

1986, Nov. 19

818	A217	15fr	multi	10	5
819	A217	25fr	multi	14	8
820	A217	70fr	multi	40	20
821	A217	300fr	multi	1.65	80
822	A217	450fr	multi	2.50	1.25
			Nos. 818-822 (5)	4.79	2.38

Souvenir Sheet

823	A217	500fr	multi	2.75	1.50

US space shuttle Challenger explosion; Statue of Liberty, cent. Nos. 822-823 are airmail. No. 823 has multicolored decorative margin. Size: 86x86mm.

Flora and Fauna—A218

1986, May 30 Litho. *Perf. 13½*

824	A218	25fr	Allamanda neriifolia	14	6
825	A218	65fr	Taurotragus eurycerus	38	18
826	A218	160fr	Plumieria acuminata	88	45
827	A218	300fr	Acinonyx jubatus	1.65	58
828	A218	400fr	Eulophia erthoplata	2.20	1.10
829	A218	500fr	Leopard	2.75	1.40
			Nos. 824-829 (6)	8.00	3.77

Souvenir Sheet

830	A218	600fr	Derby's eland, eulophia cucullata	3.25	1.65

Nos. 824, 826, 828 vert. Nos. 828-830 are airmail. No. 830 contains one stamp (size: 51x30mm); multicolored margin continues the design, picturing eland and orchids in habitat. Size: 100x69mm.

Intl. Peace Year
A219

Air Africa, 25th Anniv.
A220

1986, Nov. 29

831	A219	160fr	multi	88	45

1986, Dec. 15

832	A220	200fr	multi	1.10	55

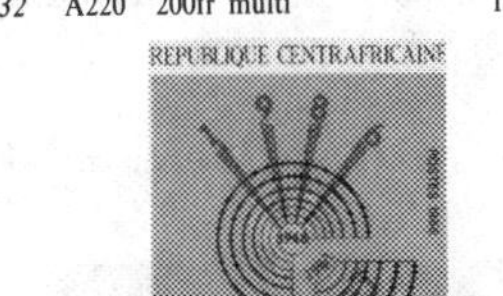

UNICEF, 40th Anniv.—A221

1986, Dec. 24

833	A221	15fr	shown	8	5
834	A221	130fr	Child immunization	70	35
835	A221	160fr	Youth, food, map	88	45

German Railways Sesquicentenary—A222

Inventors and locomotives: 40fr, Alfred de Glehn, Prussian Railways DH2 Green Elephant. 70fr, Rudolf Diesel, S3/6 No. 1829 Rheingold. 160fr, Carl Golsdorf, Trans-Europe Express train Type 103. 300fr, Wilhelm Schmidt, Beyer Garratt locomotive. 400fr, Monsieur de Bousquet, Series 3500 compound locomotive. 500fr, Werner von Siemens, 1980s electric locomotive.

1986, Dec. 31

836	A222	40fr	multi	22	10
837	A222	70fr	multi	38	18
838	A222	160fr	multi	88	45
839	A222	300fr	multi	1.65	58
840	A222	400fr	multi	2.20	1.10
			Nos. 836-840 (5)	5.33	2.41

Souvenir Sheet

841	A222	500fr	multi	2.75	1.40

Nos. 840-841 are airmail. No. 841 contains one stamp (size: 42x36mm); multicolored decorative margin pictures 19th century Locomotive 220. Size: 83x67mm.

Agriculture Radio Project—A223

1986, Dec. 27 Litho. *Perf. 13½*

842	A223	170fr	shown	1.00	50
843	A223	265fr	Satellite communication	1.55	78

Pan-African Telecommunications Union congress, Dec. 7, 1986.

Space—A224

Scientists and inventions: 25fr, Sir William Herschel (1738-1822), British astronomer, and Miranda satellite. 65fr, Wernher von Braun (1912-1977), American engineer, and Mars rover. 160fr, Rudolf Hanel, Mariner Mark II and Titan. 300fr, Patrick Baudry, Hermes shuttle and Eureka platform. 400fr, U. Keller, Halley's Comet and Giotto probe. 500fr, Wubbo Ockels, Ulf Merbold and Columbus European Space Station. 600fr, Wilhelm Obers (1758-1840) and Mariner Mark II surveying asteroids. Nos. 844-849 vert.

1987, Jan. 27

844	A224	25fr	multi	15	8
845	A224	65fr	multi	38	20
846	A224	160fr	multi	95	48
847	A224	300fr	multi	1.75	90
848	A224	400fr	multi	2.50	1.25
849	A224	500fr	multi	3.00	1.50
			Nos. 844-849 (6)	8.73	4.41

Souvenir Sheet

850	A224	600fr	multi	3.50	1.75

Nos. 848-850 are airmail. No. 850 has multicolored margin picturing man-made and natural satellites and La Genese. Size: 106x66mm.

SEMI-POSTAL STAMPS

Central African Republic

Anti-Malaria Issue

Common Design Type

Perf. 12½x12

1962, Apr. 7 Engraved Unwmkd.

B1	CD108	25fr + 5fr sl	70	70

Issued for the World Health Organization drive to eradicate malaria.

Freedom from Hunger Issue

Common Design Type

1963, Mar. 21 ***Perf. 13***

B2	CD112	25fr + 5fr bis, Prus grn & brn	65	65

Guinea Fowl and Partridge
SP1

Designs: 10fr+5fr, Yellow-backed duiker and snail. 20fr+5fr, Elephant, tortoise and hippopotamus playing tug-of-war. 30fr+10fr, Cuckoo and tortoise. 50fr+20fr, Patas monkey and leopard.

1971, Feb. 9 Photo. ***Perf. 12½x12***

B3	SP1	5fr + 5fr multi	1.20	60
B4	SP1	10fr + 5fr multi	1.75	1.25
B5	SP1	20fr + 5fr multi	2.50	1.75
B6	SP1	30fr + 10fr multi	3.50	2.50
B7	SP1	50fr + 20fr multi	7.00	5.00
		Nos. B3-B7 (5)	15.95	11.10

Lengué Dancer
SP2

Dancers: 40fr+10fr, Le Lengué. 100fr+40fr, Teke. 140fr+40fr, Englabolo.

1971 Lithographed ***Perf. 13***

B8	SP2	20fr + 5fr multi	35	20
B9	SP2	40fr + 10fr multi	65	40
B10	SP2	100fr + 40fr multi	1.75	90
B11	SP2	140fr + 40fr multi	2.25	1.20

AIR POST STAMPS

Central African Republic

Abyssinian Roller—AP1

Birds: 200fr, Gold Coast touraco. 500fr, African fish eagle.

Engraved

1960, Sept. 3 ***Perf. 13*** **Unwmkd.**

C1	AP1	100fr vio bl, org brn & emer	1.50	65
C2	AP1	200fr multi	3.00	1.25
C3	AP1	500fr Prus bl, emer & red brn	7.50	3.00

Olympic Games Issue

French Equatorial Africa No. C37 Surcharged in Red Like Chad No. C1.

1960, Dec. 15 ***Perf. 13***

C4	AP8	250fr on 500fr grnsh blk, blk & sl	6.50	6.50

Issued to commemorate the 17th Olympic Games, Rome, Aug. 25–Sept. 11.

Air Afrique Issue

Common Design Type

1962, Feb. 17 ***Perf. 13*** **Unwmkd.**

C5	CD107	50fr vio, lt grn & red brn	75	70

Founding of Air Afrique airline.

Pole Vault
AP1a

1962, July 21 Photo. ***Perf. 12x12½***

C6	AP1a	100fr grn, yel, brn & blk	1.50	1.00

Abidjan games.

Red-faced Lovebirds—AP2

Bird: 50fr, Great blue touraco.

1962–63 Engraved ***Perf. 13***

C7	AP2	50fr sl grn, bl grn & org	75	35
C8	AP2	250fr multi ('63)	3.75	2.10

Issue dates: 50fr, Nov. 15, 1962; 250fr, Mar. 11, 1963.

Runner with Torch and Palm Branch
AP3

1962, Dec. 24

C9	AP3	100fr gray grn, brn & car	1.50	1.00

Tropics Cup Games, Bangui, Dec. 24–31.

African Postal Union Issue

Common Design Type

1963, Sept. 8 Photo. ***Perf. 12½***

C10	CD114	85fr emer, ocher & red	1.25	85

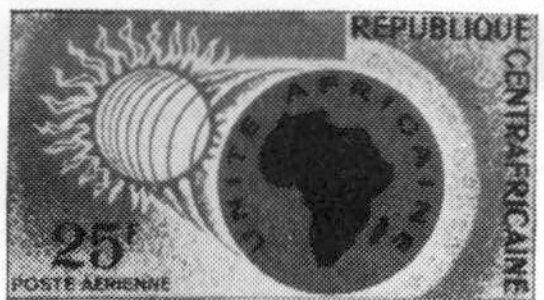

Sun Shining on Africa—AP4

1963, Nov. 9 ***Perf. 13x12***

C11	AP4	25fr bl, yel & vio bl	40	30

Issued for African unity.

Europafrica Issue

Common Design Type

1963, Nov. 30 ***Perf. 12x13***

C12	CD116	50fr ultra, yel & dk brn	1.35	1.10

Diesel Engine—AP5

Designs: Various Locomotives; 25fr, 50fr, vertical.

1963, Dec. 1 Engraved ***Perf. 13***

C13	AP5	20fr brn, cl & dk grn	30	30
C14	AP5	25fr brn, bl & choc	40	30
C15	AP5	50r brn, red lil & vio	80	60
C16	AP5	100fr brn, grn & dl red brn	1.65	1.20
a.		Min. sheet of 4	3.25	3.25

Bangui-Douala railroad project.
No. C16a contains one each of Nos. C13–C16. Size: 189x99mm.

Bangui Cathedral—AP6

1964, Jan. 21 ***Perf. 13*** **Unwmkd.**

C17	AP6	100fr yel grn, org brn & bl	1.50	90

Radar Tracking Station and WMO Emblem—AP7

1964, Mar. 23 Engr. ***Perf. 13***

C18	AP7	50fr org brn, bl & pur	75	65

World Meteorological Day.

Map and Presidents of Chad, Congo, Gabon and Central African Republic
AP8

1964, June 23 Photo. ***Perf. 12½***

C19	AP8	100fr multi	1.50	1.00

Issued to commemorate the 5th anniversary of the Conference of Chiefs of State of Equatorial Africa.

Javelin Throwers—AP9

Designs: 50fr, Basketball game. 100fr, Four runners. 250fr, Swimmers, one in water.

1964, June 23 Engraved ***Perf. 13***

C20	AP9	25fr grn, dk brn & lt vio bl	40	20
C21	AP9	50fr blk, car & grn	75	40
C22	AP9	100fr grn, vio bl & dk brn	1.50	80
C23	AP9	250fr grn, blk & car	3.75	2.25
a.		Min. sheet	6.50	6.50

Issued for the 18th Olympic Games, Tokyo, Oct. 10–25, 1964.
No. C23a contains one each of Nos. C20–C23. Size: 128½x99mm.

John F. Kennedy
AP10

1964, July 4 Photo. ***Perf. 12½***

C24	AP10	100fr lil, brn & blk	1.65	1.35
a.		Min. sheet of 4	7.50	7.50

Issued in memory of President John F. Kennedy.

Industrial Symbols, Maps of Africa and Europe
AP11

1964, Dec. 19 ***Perf. 13x12*** **Unwmkd.**

C25	AP11	50fr yel, org & grn	75	70

See note after Cameroun No. 402.

International Cooperation Year Emblem—AP12

1965, Jan. 2 ***Perf. 13***

C26	AP12	100fr red brn, yel & bl	1.50	90

International Cooperation Year.

Nimbus Weather Satellite
AP13

1965, Mar. 23 Engraved *Perf. 13*

C27 AP13 100fr org brn, ultra & blk 1.60 1.00

Fifth World Meteorological Day.

Lincoln and Statue of Liberty
AP14

1965, Apr. 15 Photo. *Perf. 13*

C28 AP14 100fr bluish grn, ind & bis 1.60 90

Centenary of death of Abraham Lincoln.

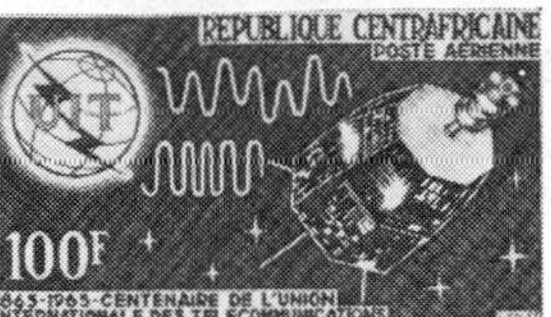

ITU Emblem and Relay Satellite
AP15

1965, May 17 Engr. *Perf. 13*

C29 AP15 100fr dk grn vio bl & brn 1.60 90

Issued to commemorate the centenary of the International Telecommunication Union.

"Housing," New Home in Village
AP16

1965, June 10 Unwmkd.

C30 AP16 100fr ultra, brn & sl grn 1.50 90

See note after No. 52.

Europafrica Issue

Tractor, Cotton Picker, Cotton, Sun and Emblem
AP17

1965, Nov. 7 Photo. *Perf. 12x13*

C31 AP17 50fr multi 70 50

See note after Chad No. C11.

Mercury by Antoine Coysevox
AP18

Father Holding Sick Child
AP19

1965, Dec. 5 Engraved *Perf. 13*

C32 AP18 100fr red brn, bl & blk 1.60 1.00

Issued to commemorate the fifth anniversary of Central African Republic's admission to the Universal Postal Union.

1965, Dec. 12

Design: 100fr, Mother and child.

C33 AP19 50fr dk bl, car & blk 75 50
C34 AP19 100fr red brn, red & brt grn 1.50 1.00

Issued to honor the Red Cross.

Air Afrique Issue
Common Design Type

1966, Aug. 31 Photo. *Perf. 13*

C35 CD123 25fr bl, blk & lem 40 15

Issued to commemorate the introduction of DC-8F planes by Air Afrique.

Surveyor Spacecraft on Moon
AP20

Designs: No. C37, Luna 9 on Moon and Earth. 200fr, Rocket take-off, Jules Verne's "From the Earth to the Moon."

1966, Oct. 24 Photo. *Perf. 12x12½*

C36 AP20 130fr multi 2.00 1.20
C37 AP20 130fr multi 2.00 1.20
C38 AP20 200fr multi 3.00 1.80
a. Souv. sheet of 3 8.00 8.00

Issued to commemorate the conquest of the Moon. No. C38a contains one each of Nos. C36–C38, black marginal inscription and control number. Size: 132x158mm.

Eugene A. Cernan, Gemini 9 and Agena Rocket
AP21

Design: No. C40, Pavel R. Popovich and rocket.

1966, Nov. 14 Photo. *Perf. 13*

C39 AP21 50fr multi 75 35
C40 AP21 50fr multi 75 35

Issued to honor American and Russian astronauts.

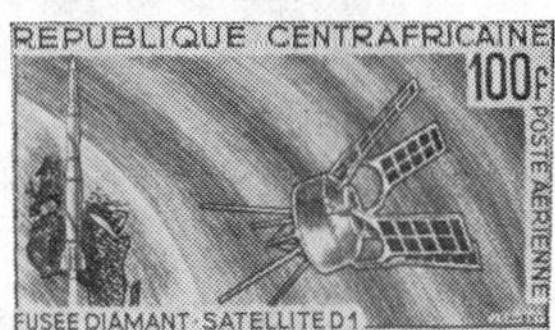

Diamant Rocket, D-1 Satellite and Globe with Map of Africa
AP22

1966, Nov. 14 Engraved

C41 AP22 100fr brt rose lil & brn 1.60 70

Issued to commemorate the launching of France's first satellite, Nov. 26, 1965, and the launching of the D-1 satellite, Feb. 17, 1966.

Exchange of Agricultural and Industrial Products between Africa and Europe
AP23

1966, Dec. 5 Photo. *Perf. 12x13*

C42 AP23 50fr multi 75 45

See note after Gabon No. C46.

No. C35 Surcharged

1967, May 8 *Perf. 13*

C43 CD123 5fr on 25fr multi 15 10

The surcharge obliterates the "2" of the original 25fr denomination.

DC-8F Over M'Poko Airport, Bangui—AP24

1967, July 3 Engraved *Perf. 13*

C44 AP24 100fr sl, dk grn & brn 1.60 75

View of EXPO '67, Montreal
AP25

1967, July 17

C45 AP25 100fr vio bl, dk red brn & dk grn 1.50 70

Issued to commemorate the International Exposition, EXPO '67, Montreal, Apr. 28–Oct. 27.

African Postal Union Issue, 1967
Common Design Type

1967, Sept. 9 Engraved *Perf. 13*

C46 CD124 100fr brt grn, dk car rose & plum 1.50 70

Potez 25 TOE—AP26

Designs: 200fr, Junkers 52. 500fr, Caravelle 11R.

1967, Nov. 24 Engraved *Perf. 13*

C47 AP26 100fr brt bl, brn & gray grn 1.60 65
C48 AP26 200fr dk brn, grn & ind 2.75 1.25
C49 AP26 500fr bl, ind & org brn 7.25 4.00

Presidents Boganda and Bokassa
AP27

1967, Dec. 1 Photo. *Perf. 12½*

C50 AP27 130fr org, red, lt bl & blk 2.00 1.35

9th anniversary of the republic.

Pres. Jean Bedel Bokassa
AP28

1968, Jan. 1 *Perf. 12½x12*

C51 AP28 30fr multi 50 30

Human Rights Flame, Men and Globe—AP29

1968, Mar. 26 Photo. *Perf. 13*

C52 AP29 200fr brt grn, vio & ver 3.00 1.50

International Human Rights Year.

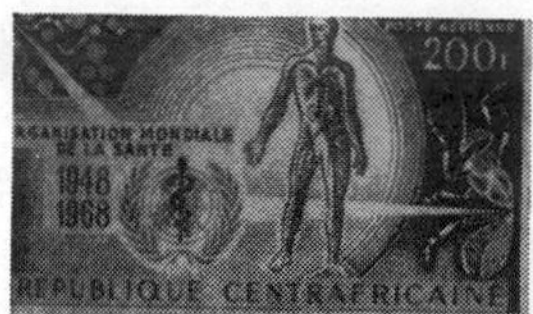

Man, WHO Emblem and Tsetse Fly—AP30

1968, Apr. 8 **Engraved**

C53	AP30 200fr multi	3.00	1.50

Issued to commemorate the 20th anniversary of the World Health Organization.

Javelin Thrower AP31

Space Probe Landing on Venus AP32

Design: No. C55, Downhill skier.

1968, Apr. 16 **Engraved** ***Perf. 13***

C54	AP31 200fr choc, dk red & Prus bl	3.00	1.60
C55	AP31 200fr dk red, choc & Prus bl	3.00	1.60

The 1968 Olympic Games.

1968, Apr. 23

C56	AP32 100fr ultra, dk & brt grn	1.50	70

Issued to commemorate the Venus exploration by Venus IV, Oct. 18, 1967.

Marie Curie and "Cancer Destroyed"—AP33

1968, Apr. 30

C57	AP33 100fr vio, brt bl & brn	1.50	70

Issued to commemorate the centenary of the birth of Marie Curie (1867–1934), scientist.

Nos. C36–C37 and C47–C48 Surcharged with New Value

Photogravure; Engraved

1968, Sept. 16 ***Perf. 12x12½, 13***

C58	AP20 5fr on 130fr multi	10	8
C59	AP26 10fr on 100fr multi	15	10
C60	AP26 20fr on 200fr multi	30	12
C61	AP20 50fr on 130fr multi	80	55

On No. C58 the old denomination has been obliterated with "XIX", on No. C61 the obliteration is a rectangular bar. On Nos. C59–C60 the last zero of the old denomination has been obliterated with a black square.

River Boat Type of Regular Issue

Craft: 100fr, "Pie X," Bangui, 1894. 130fr, "Ballay," Bangui, 1891.

1968, Dec. 10 **Engraved** ***Perf. 13***

Size: 48x27mm.

C62	A37 100fr bl, dk brn & ol	1.50	70
C63	A37 130fr brt pink, sl grn & sl	2.00	1.00

PHILEXAFRIQUE Issue

Mme. de Sévigné, French School, 17th Century AP34

1968, Dec. 17 **Photo.** ***Perf. 12½***

C64	AP34 100fr brn & multi	1.60	1.40

Issued to publicize PHILEXAFRIQUE, Philatelic Exhibition in Abidjan, Feb. 14–23. Printed with alternating brown label.

2nd PHILEXAFRIQUE Issue

Common Design Type

Design: 50fr, Ubangi No. J16, cotton field and Pres. Bokassa.

1969, Feb. 14 **Engraved** ***Perf. 13***

C65	CD128 50fr bis brn, blk & dk grn	90	90

Issued to commemorate the opening of PHILEXAFRIQUE, Abidjan, Feb. 14.

Holocerina Angulata Aur.—AP35

Butterflies and Moths: 20fr, Nudaurelia dione fabr. 30fr, Eustera troglophylla hamp. (vert.). 50fr, Aurivillius aratus west. 100fr, Epiphora albida druce.

1969, Feb. 25 **Photogravure**

C66	AP35 10fr yel & multi	15	6
C67	AP35 20fr vio & multi	30	15
C68	AP35 30fr multi	45	20
C69	AP35 50fr multi	85	40
C70	AP35 100fr multi	1.65	80
	Nos. C66-C70 (5)	3.40	1.61

Boxing—AP36

Sport Design: 100fr, Basketball.

1969, Mar. 18 **Photo.** ***Perf. 13***

C71	AP36 50fr multi	75	35
C72	AP36 100fr yel & multi	1.50	60

Apollo 8 over Moonscape—AP37

1969, May 27 **Photo.** ***Perf. 13***

C73	AP37 200fr dp bl, gray & yel	3.00	1.35

Issued to commemorate the U.S. Apollo 8 mission, the first men in orbit around the moon, Dec. 21–27, 1968.

Market Cross, Nuremberg, and Toys—AP38

1969, June 3

C74	AP38 100fr blk, brt rose lil & emer	1.50	1.00

Issued to publicize the International Toy Fair in Nuremberg, Germany.

Napoleon as First Consul, by Anne-Louis Girodet-Trioson AP39

Designs: 130fr, Napoleon meeting Emperor Francis II, by Antoine Jean Gros (horiz.). 200fr, The Wedding of Napoleon and Marie-Louise, by Georges Rouget (horiz.).

1969, Nov. 4 **Photo.** ***Perf. 12½***

C75	AP39 100fr multi	1.75	1.25
C76	AP39 130fr brn & multi	2.50	1.50
C77	AP39 200fr multi	4.00	3.00

Issued to commemorate the bicentenary of the birth of Napoleon Bonaparte (1769–1821).

Pres. Bokassa, Map of Africa and Flag AP40

Franklin Delano Roosevelt AP41

1970, Jan. 1 ***Die-cut*** ***Perf. 10½***

Embossed on Gold Foil

C78	AP40 2000fr gold	25.00	25.00

1970 **Lithographed** ***Perf. 13½x14***

Design: No. C80, Lenin.

C79	AP41 100fr gold, yel, blk & bl	1.35	80
C80	AP41 100fr gold, yel, blk & red	1.25	70

No. C79 issued to commemorate the 25th anniversary of the death of Pres. Franklin Delano Roosevelt (1882–1945); Nos. C80 commemorates the centenary of the birth of Lenin (1870–1924).

Issue dates: No. C79, Apr. 29; No. C80, Apr. 22.

No. C73 Overprinted in Red:

ATTERRISSAGE
d'APOLLO 12
19 novembre 1969

1970, June 1 **Photogravure** ***Perf. 13***

C81	AP37 200fr multi	8.50	6.50

Issued to commemorate the moon landing mission of Apollo 12, Nov. 14–24, 1969.

AP42

1970, Sept. 15 **Litho.** ***Perf. 10***

C82	AP42 Triptych	2.50	1.25
a.	100fr *Dancer*	1.25	50
b.	100fr *Still life*	1.25	50

Issued to publicize Knokphila 70, 6th International Philatelic Exhibition at Knokke, Belgium, July 4–10. The two stamps and violet blue label are printed se-tenant and imperf. between stamps and label.

Sericulture Type of Regular Issue

1970, Sept. 15 ***Perf. 10***

C83	A45 140fr multi	2.00	1.10

Issued to publicize Operation Bokassa, a plan for the development of the country.

C.A.R. Flag, EXPO Emblem and Pavilion AP43

1970, Dec. 18 **Litho.** ***Perf. 13½x13***

C84	AP43 200fr red & multi	2.75	1.35

International Exposition EXPO '70, Osaka, Japan.

Soccer AP44

1970, Dec. 8 ***Perf. 13x13½***

C85	AP44 200fr multi	2.75	1.35

World Soccer Championships, Mexico, May 30–June 21, 1970.

Dove AP45

1970, Dec. 31

C86	AP45 200fr bl, yel & blk	2.75	1.35

25th anniversary of the United Nations.

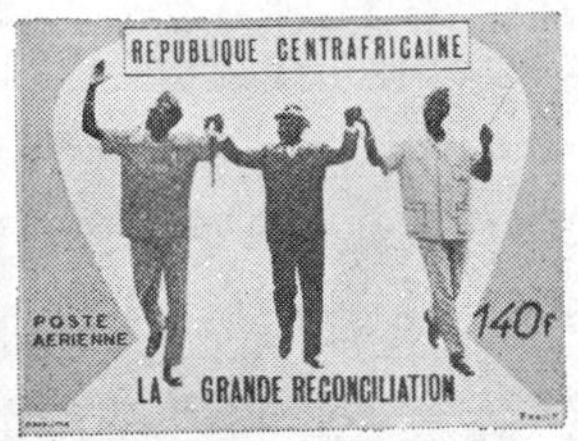

Presidents Mobutu, Bokassa, and Tombalbaye—AP46

1971, Jan. 10

C87	AP46	140fr multi	2.00	90

Return of Central African Republic to the United States of Central Africa which also includes Congo Democratic Republic and Chad.

Satellite over Globe—AP47

1971, May 17 Photo. *Perf. 12½*

C88	AP47	100fr multi	1.35	65

3rd World Telecommunications Day.

African Postal Union Issue, 1971

Common Design Type

Design: 100fr, Carved head and UAMPT building, Brazzaville, Congo.

1971, Nov. 13 Photo. *Perf. 13x13½*

C89	CD135	100fr bl & multi	1.35	65

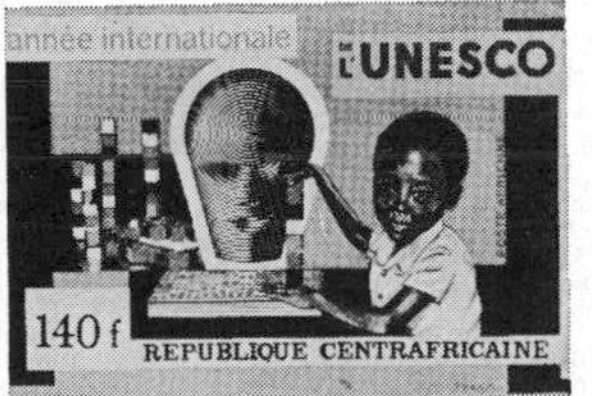

Child and Education Year Emblem—AP48

1971, Nov. 11 Litho. *Perf. 13x13½*

C90	AP48	140fr multi	1.75	75

25th anniversary of the United Nations Educational, Scientific and Cultural Organization (UNESCO).

Fight Against Cancer AP49 — Gamal Abdel Nasser AP50

1971, Nov. 20 Photo. *Perf. 12½*

C91	AP49	100fr grn & multi	1.35	60

1972, Jan. 15

C92	AP50	100fr dk red, blk & bis	1.25	60

In memory of Gamal Abdel Nasser (1918–1970), president of Egypt.

Olympic Rings and Boxing—AP51

Design: No. C94, Track and Olympic rings (vert.).

1972, May 26 Engraved *Perf. 13*

C93	AP51	100fr brn org & sep	1.50	60
C94	AP51	100fr grn & vio	1.50	60
a.		Miniature sheet of 2	3.00	3.00

20th Olympic Games, Munich, Aug. 26–Sept. 10. No. C94a contains 2 stamps similar to Nos. C93–C94, but in changed colors. The boxing stamp is red lilac and green, the track stamp ocher and red lilac. Size: 129x98mm.

Tiling's Mail Rocket, 1931, and Mailman—AP52

Designs: 50fr, DC-3 and mailman riding camel (vert.). 150fr, Sirio satellite and rocket (vert.). 200fr, Intelsat 4 and rocket.

1972, Aug. 12

C95	AP52	40fr bl, org & ind	50	25
C96	AP52	50fr bl, brn & org	60	25
C97	AP52	150fr brn, org & gray	1.75	80
C98	AP52	200fr brn, bl & org	2.25	1.00
a.		Souv. sheet of 4	5.25	5.25

Centraphilex 1972, Central African Philatelic Exhibition, Bangui. No. C98a contains one each of Nos. C95–C98. Brown marginal inscription. Size: 200x99½mm.

Europafrica Issue

Arrows with Symbols of Agriculture and Industry AP53

1972, Nov. 17 Litho. *Perf. 13*

C99	AP53	100fr multi	1.10	60

Nos. C93–C94, C94a Overprinted

a. POIDS-MOYEN / LEMECHEV MEDAILLE D'OR

b. LONGUER / WILLIAMS MEDAILLE D'OR

1972, Nov. 24 Engraved

C100	AP51 (a)	100fr brn org & sep	1.35	60
C101	AP51 (b)	100fr grn & vio	1.35	60
a.		Miniature sheet of 2	3.00	3.00

Gold Medal Winners in 20th Olympic Games: Viatschesiav Lemechev, USSR, middleweight boxing (C100); Randy Williams, USA, broad jump (C101).

Lunar Rover and Module—AP54

1972, Dec. 18 Engr. *Perf. 13*

C102	AP54	100fr sl grn, bl & gray	1.20	65

Apollo 16 U.S. moon mission, Apr. 15–27, 1972.

Virgin and Child, by Francesco Pesellino AP55

Design: 150fr, Adoration of the Child with St. John the Baptist and St. Romuald, by Fra Filippo Lippi.

1972, Dec. 25 Photogravure

C103	AP55	100fr gold & multi	1.25	65
C104	AP55	150fr gold & multi	1.85	1.00

Christmas 1972.

Parthenon, Athens, Spyridon Louis, Marathon, 1896—AP56

Designs (Olympic Rings and): 40fr, Arc de Triomphe, Paris, H. Barrelet, single scull, 1900. 50fr, Old Courthouse and Western Arch, St. Louis, Myer Prinstein, triple jump, 1904. 100fr, Tower, London, Henry Taylor, swimming, 1908. 150fr, City Hall, Stockholm, Greco-Roman wrestling, 1912.

1972, Dec. 28 Engraved

C105	AP56	30fr brt grn, mag & brn	40	12
C106	AP56	40fr vio bl, emer & brn	50	18
C107	AP56	50fr car rose, vio bl & Prus bl	60	25
C108	AP56	100fr sl, red lil & brn	1.25	55
C109	AP56	150fr red lil, blk & Prus bl	1.85	90
		Nos. C105-C109 (5)	4.60	2.00

Olympic Games 1896–1912.

WHO Emblem, Surgeon and Nurse—AP57

1973, Apr. 7 Photo. *Perf. 13*

C110	AP57	100fr multi	1.25	70

World Health Organization, 25th anniversary.

World Map, Arrows, Waves AP58

1973, May 17 Litho. *Perf. 12½*

C111	AP58	200fr lt bl, dp org & blk	2.00	1.20

5th International Telecommunications Day.

Head and City Hall, Brussels AP58a

1973, Sept. 17 Engr. *Perf. 13*

C112	AP58a	100fr pur, ocher & brn	1.25	70

African Weeks, Brussels, Sept. 15–30, 1973.

Europafrica Issue

Map of Central African Republic with Industry and Agriculture, Young Man—AP59

1973, Sept. 28 Engraved *Perf. 13*

C113	AP59	100fr sep, grn & org	1.10	70

Carrier Pigeon with Letter and UPU Emblem—AP60

1973, Oct. 9 Photogravure

C114	AP60	200fr multi	2.25	1.40

Universal Postal Union Day.

WMO Emblem, Weather Map—AP61

1973, Oct. 20 Engraved *Perf. 13*

C115	AP61	150fr brt ultra & sl grn	1.50	75

Centenary of international meteorological cooperation.

Copernicus, Heliocentric System
AP62

1973, Nov. 2 Photogravure

C116	AP62	100fr gold & multi	1.15	70

500th anniversary of the birth of Nicolaus Copernicus (1473–1543), Polish astronomer.

Pres. Bokassa
AP63

Pres. Bokassa
AP64

Rocket Launch and Apollo 17 Badge
AP65

1973, Nov. 30 Photo. *Perf. 12½*

C117	AP63	50fr multi	50	35
C118	AP64	100fr multi	1.00	70

1973, Dec. 15 Engraved *Perf. 13*

Designs: 65fr, Capsule over moonscape (horiz.). 100fr, Moon landing (horiz.). 150fr, Astronauts on moon. 200fr, Splash-down with parachutes and badge.

C119	AP65	50fr ver, gray grn & brn	50	40
C120	AP65	65fr dk brn, brn red & sl grn	60	50
C121	AP65	100fr ver, sl & choc	1.00	70
C122	AP65	150fr brn, ol & sl grn	1.40	1.00
C123	AP65	200fr red, bl & sl grn	2.00	1.40
		Nos. C119-C123 (5)	5.50	4.00

Apollo 17 U.S. moon mission, Dec. 7–19, 1972.

St. Teresa
AP66

UPU Emblem, Letter
AP67

1973, Dec. 25

C124	AP66	500fr vio bl & grnsh bl	5.00	3.00

Centenary of the birth of St. Teresa of the Infant Jesus, the Little Flower (1873–1897), Carmelite nun.

1974, Oct. 9 Engraved *Perf. 13*

C125	AP67	500fr multi	5.00	3.50

Centenary of Universal Postal Union.

Presidents and Flags of Cameroun, CAR, Gabon and Congo
AP68

1974, Dec. 8 Photogravure *Perf. 13*

C126	AP68	100fr gold & multi	90	65

See note after Cameroun No. 595.

Marshal Bokassa
AP69

Design: 100fr, Bokassa in Marshal's uniform with cape.

1975, Feb. 22 Photo. *Perf. 13*

C127	AP69	50fr tan & multi	40	30
C128	AP69	100fr tan & multi	80	60

Jean Bedel Bokassa, President for Life and Marshal of the Republic.

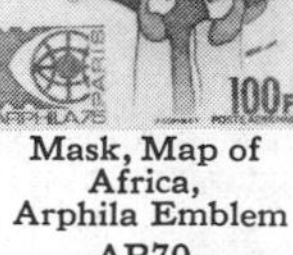

Mask, Map of Africa, Arphila Emblem
AP70

Albert Schweitzer and Dugout, Lambarene
AP71

1975, Aug. 25 Engr. *Perf. 13*

C129	AP70	100fr brt bl, red brn & red	1.00	50

ARPHILA 75 International Philatelic Exhibition, Paris, June 6–16.

1975, Sept. 30 Engr. *Perf. 13*

C130	AP71	200fr blk, ultra & ol	2.00	1.00

Dr. Albert Schweitzer (1875–1965), medical missionary and musician.

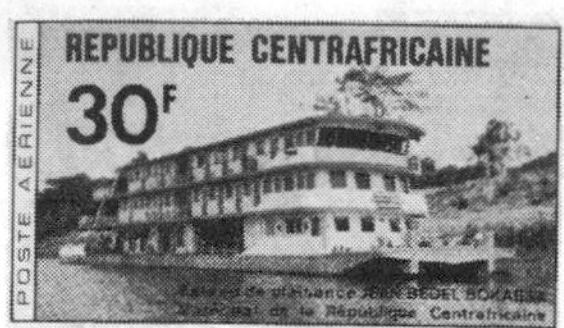

Pres. Bokassa's Houseboat, Bow—AP72

Design: 40fr, Pres. Bokassa's houseboat, stern.

1976, Feb. 22 Litho. *Perf. 13*

C131	AP72	30fr multi	25	15
C132	AP72	40fr multi	35	20

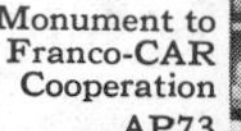

Monument to Franco-CAR Cooperation
AP73

Presidents and Flags of France and CAR
AP74

1976, Mar. 5

C133	AP73	100fr multi	80	50
C134	AP74	200fr multi	1.60	1.00

Official visit of Pres. Valery Giscard d'Estaing to Central African Republic, Mar. 5–8.

Apollo Soyuz Type, 1976

Designs: 100fr, Soyuz space ship. 200fr, Apollo space ship. 300fr, Astronauts and cosmonauts in cabin. 500fr, Apollo and Soyuz after link-up.

1976, June 14 Litho. *Perf. 14x13½*

C135	A90	100fr multi	1.00	38
C136	A90	200fr multi	2.00	85
C137	A90	300fr multi	3.00	1.25

Souvenir Sheet

C138	A90	500fr multi	4.75	2.25

Apollo Soyuz space test project, Russo-American cooperation, launched July 15, link-up July 17. No. C138 has multicolored margin showing Apollo Soyuz insignia. Size: 103½x78mm.

French Hussar
AP75

Uniforms: 125fr, Scottish "Black Watch." 150fr, German dragoon. 200fr, British grenadier. 250fr, American ranger. 450fr, American dragoon.

1976, July 4 *Perf. 13½*

C139	AP75	100fr multi	95	30
C140	AP75	125fr multi	1.20	50
C141	AP75	150fr multi	1.50	60
C142	AP75	200fr multi	1.90	70
C143	AP75	250fr multi	2.25	90
		Nos. C139-C143 (5)	7.80	3.00

Souvenir Sheet

C144	AP75	450fr multi	4.25	1.90

American Bicentennial. No. C144 has U.S. Bicentennial emblem in tri-color in margin, black inscription. Size: 118x80 mm.

Acherontia Atropos—AP76

Design: 100fr, Papilio nireus and heniocha marnois.

1976, Sept. 20 Litho. *Perf. 12½*

C145	AP76	50fr multi	40	25
C146	AP76	100fr multi	80	50

Olympic Winners Type, 1976

Designs: 100fr, Women's figure skating, Dorothy Hamill (vert.). 200fr, Ice skating, Alexander Gorshkov and Ludmilla Pakhomova. 300fr, Men's figure skating, John Curry (vert.). 500fr, Down-hill skiing, Rosi Mittermaier (vert.).

1976, Sept. 23 Litho. *Perf. 13½*

C147	A92	100fr multi	95	40
C148	A92	200fr multi	1.90	90
C149	A92	300fr multi	3.00	1.35

Souvenir Sheet

C150	A92	500fr multi	4.75	2.25

12th Winter Olympic Games winners, Innsbruck. No. C150 has multicolored margin showing Olympic flags and eternal flame, black inscriptions. Size: 103x78 mm.

Viking Mars Type, 1976

Designs: 100fr, Phases of Mars landing. 200fr, Viking descending on Mars (horiz.). 300fr, Viking probe. 500fr, Viking flight to Mars (horiz.).

1976, Dec.

C151	A93	100fr multi	95	35
C152	A93	200fr multi	1.90	85
C153	A93	300fr multi	3.00	1.20

Souvenir Sheet

C154	A93	500fr multi	4.75	2.25

Viking Mars project. No. C154 has multicolored margin showing flight control room. Size: 102x77mm.

Empire

Stamps of 1973–76 Overprinted with Bars and "EMPIRE CENTRAFRICAIN" in Black, Violet Blue or Gold

Printing and Perforations as Before

1977, March

Multicolored

C155	AP68	100fr (#C126;B)	90	70
C156	AP70	100fr (#C129;VB)	90	70
C157	AP73	100fr (#C133;G)	90	70
C158	AP71	200fr (#C130;B)	2.00	1.50
C159	AP67	500fr (#C125;B)	5.50	4.00
		Nos. C155-C159 (5)	10.20	7.60

No bar on No. C159.

Stamps of 1976 Overprinted "EMPIRE CENTRAFRICAIN" in Black on Silver Panel

1977, Apr. 1

C160	AP76	50fr multi (#C145)	50	30
C161	A90	100fr multi (#C135)	90	70
C162	AP75	100fr multi (#C139)	80	60
C163	AP76	100fr multi (#C146)	80	60

C164	A92	100fr multi (#C147)	80	60
C165	A93	100fr multi (#C151)	80	60
C166	AP75	125fr multi (#C140)	1.00	80
C167	AP75	150fr multi (#C141)	1.20	90
C168	A90	200fr multi (#C136)	2.00	1.50
C169	AP75	200fr multi (#C142)	1.60	1.20
C170	A92	200fr multi (#C148)	1.60	1.20
C171	A93	200fr multi (#C152)	1.60	1.20
C172	AP75	250fr multi (#C143)	2.00	1.50
C173	A90	300fr multi (#C137)	3.00	2.25
C174	A92	300fr multi (#C149)	2.50	1.85
C175	A93	300fr multi (#C153)	2.50	1.85
		Nos. C160-C175 (16)	23.60	17.65

Souvenir Sheets

C176	AP75	450fr multi (#C144)	3.75	3.75
C177	A90	500fr multi (#C138)	4.00	4.00
C178	A92	500fr multi (#C150)	4.00	4.00
C179	A93	500fr multi (#C154)	4.00	4.00

Overprint on type AP75 is in upper and lower case letters.

Nobel Prize Type, 1977

Designs: 100fr, Rudyard Kipling. 200fr, Ernest Hemingway. 300fr, Luigi Pirandello. 500fr, Rabindranath Tagore.

1977, Apr. 1 Litho. *Perf. 13½*

C180	A94	100fr multi	95	35
C181	A94	200fr multi	1.90	85
C182	A94	300fr multi	3.00	1.20

Souvenir Sheet

C183	A94	500fr multi	4.75	2.25

Nobel Prize winners. No. C183 has multicolored margin with black inscription. Size: 118x80mm.

Zeppelin Type of 1977

Designs: 100fr, Germany No. C42 and North Pole. 200fr, Germany No. C44 and Science and Industry Building, Chicago. 300fr, Germany No. C35 and Brandenburg Gate, Berlin. 500fr, U.S. No. C14 and U.S. Capitol, Washington, D.C.

1977, Apr. 11 Litho. *Perf. 11*

C184	A95	100fr multi	95	35
C185	A95	200fr multi	1.90	85
C186	A95	300fr multi	3.00	1.20

Souvenir Sheet

C187	A95	500fr multi	4.75	2.25

75th anniversary of Zeppelin. No. C187 has multicolored margin showing early Zeppelin and 15 Zeppelin stamps from various countries. Size: 129x90mm.

Bokassa Type of 1977

1977, Dec. 4 Litho. *Perf. 13½*

C188	A98	200fr multi	1.60	1.00
C189	A98	300fr multi	2.50	1.50
a.		Souvenir sheet, 500fr	4.00	3.00

Coronation of Emperor Bokassa I, Dec. 4. No. C189a contains a horizontal stamp in similar design; multicolored margin with eagle and government buildings. Size: 112x80mm. A 2500fr gold embossed horizontal stamp in similar design exists.

Vaccination AP77

1977 Litho. *Perf. 14x13½*

C190	AP77	150fr multi	1.50	75

World Health Day.

Communications Type of 1978

Designs: 100fr, Balloon and spaceships docking in space. 200fr, Hydrofoil and Concorde. 500fr, Tom-tom and Zeppelin.

1978, May 17 Litho. *Perf. 13½*

C191	A107	100fr multi	1.00	50
C192	A107	200fr multi	2.00	1.00

Souvenir Sheet

C193	A107	500fr multi	5.50	3.50

Century of progress of posts and telecommunications. No. C193 contains one stamp (53x35mm.); multicolored margin shows allegory of posts. Size: 104x70mm.

Clement Ader and his Plane—AP78

Designs: 50fr, Wilbur and Orville Wright and plane. 60fr, John W. Alcock, Arthur W. Brown and plane. 100fr, Alan Cobham and plane 150fr, Claude Dornier and hydroplane. 500fr, Wilbur and Orville Wright and plane.

1978, Sept. 19 *Perf. 14*

C194	AP78	40fr multi	45	20
C195	AP78	50fr multi	55	25
C196	AP78	60fr multi	65	30
C197	AP78	100fr multi	1.10	50
C198	AP78	150fr multi	1.60	75
		Nos. C194-C198 (5)	4.35	2.00

Souvenir Sheet

C199	AP78	500fr multi	5.50	2.75

History of aviation. No. C199 has multicolored margin showing Concorde. Size: 116x80mm.

Philexafrique II—Essen Issue
Common Design Types

Designs: No. C200, Crocodile and Central African Rep. No. C3. No. C201, Birds and Mecklenburg-Schwerin No. 1.

1978, Nov. 1 Litho. *Perf. 12½*

C200	CD138	100fr multi	1.00	50
C201	CD139	100fr multi	1.00	50

Nos. C200-C201 printed se-tenant.

Bokassa Type 1978

Design: 150fr, Catherine and Jean Bedel Bokassa (horiz.).

1978, Dec. 4 Litho. *Perf. 13*

C202	A113	150fr multi	1.50	75

First anniversary of coronation. A 1000fr gold embossed souvenir sheet showing Emperor Bokassa exists.

Rowland Hill Type of 1978

Designs (Rowland Hill and): 100fr, Mailman and Tuscany No. 23. 200fr, Balloon and France No. 1. 500fr, Central Africa Nos. 1-2.

1978, Dec. 27

C203	A114	100fr multi	1.00	50
C204	A114	200fr multi	2.00	1.00

Souvenir Sheet

C205	A114	500fr multi	5.00	2.50

Sir Rowland Hill (1795-1879), originator of penny postage. No. C205 contains one stamp (37½x39mm.); multicolored margin shows Penny Black. Size: 83x85mm. 1500fr gold embossed stamp and souvenir sheet exist.

IYC Type of 1979

Designs (UNICEF, Eagle Emblems and): 100fr, Chinese girl flying kites and German Do-X flying boat, 1929. 200fr, Boys playing leapfrog, hurdler and Olympic emblem. 500fr, Child with abacus and Albert Einstein with his equation.

1979, Mar. 6 *Perf. 13½*

C206	A115	100fr multi	1.00	50
C207	A115	200fr multi	2.00	1.00

Souvenir Sheet

C208	A115	500fr multi	5.00	2.50

International Year of the Child. No. C208 contains one stamp (56x33mm.); multicolored margin shows various spacecraft. Size: 110x79mm. 1500fr gold embossed stamp and souvenir sheet exist.

Olympic Type of 1979

Designs (Moscow '80 Emblem, various Sports and): 100fr, Hurdles and "B". 200fr, Broad jump and "A".

1979, Mar. 16 Litho. *Perf. 13*

C209	A116	100fr multi	1.00	50
C210	A116	200fr multi	2.00	1.00

22nd Olympic Games, Moscow, July 19-Aug. 3, 1980. A 1500fr gold embossed souvenir sheet exists showing diver, runner and javelin.

Type of 1979

Design: 60fr, Horse.

1979, Aug. Litho. *Perf. 13*

C211	A119	60fr multi	48	25

National Husbandry Association.

Nos. C151-C154 Overprinted "ALUNISSAGE/APOLLO XI/ JUILLET 1969" and Emblem in Black or Silver

1979, Oct. Litho. *Perf. 14×13½*

C212	A93	100fr multi	80	40
C213	A93	200fr multi	1.60	80
C214	A93	300fr multi	2.40	1.20

Souvenir Sheet

C215	A93	500fr multi (S)	4.25	2.25

Apollo 11 moon landing, 10th anniversary.

Ski Jump, Lake Placid '80 Emblem AP79

Lake Placid Emblem and: 100fr, Downhill skiing. 200fr, Hockey. 300fr, Slalom. 500fr, Bobsledding.

1979, Nov. 11 Litho. *Perf. 13½*

C216	AP79	60fr multi	48	25
C217	AP79	100fr multi	80	40
C218	AP79	200fr multi	1.60	80
C219	AP79	300fr multi	2.40	1.20

Souvenir Sheet

C220	AP79	500fr multi	4.25	2.25

13th Winter Olympics Games, Lake Placid, N.Y., Feb. 12-24, 1980. No.C 220 has multicolored margin showing skiers. Size 113×78mm.

Space Type of 1980

1980, Apr. 8 Litho. *Perf. 13½*

C221	A125	150fr *Early satellites*	1.20	60
C222	A125	200fr *Space shuttle*	1.60	80

Souvenir Sheet

C223	A125	500fr *Apollo 11, Armstrong*	4.00	2.00

Space explorations No. C223 has multicolored margin showing Neil Armstrong on moon. Size: 85x58½mm.

Nos. C216-C220 Overprinted:

a. VAINQUEUR / INNAVER / AUTRICHE
b. VAINQUEUR / MOSER-PROELL / AUTRICHE
c. VAINQUEUR / ETATS-UNIS
d. VAINQUEUR / STENMARK / SUEDE
e. VAINQUEURS / SCHAERER-BENZ / SUISSE

1980, May 12 Litho. *Perf. 13½*

C224	AP79 (a)	60fr multi	48	25
C225	AP79 (b)	100fr multi	80	40
C226	AP79 (c)	200fr multi	1.60	80
C227	AP79 (d)	300fr multi	2.40	1.20

Souvenir Sheet

C228	AP79 (e)	500fr multi	4.00	2.00

World Telecommunications Day—AP80

1980, June 26 Litho. *Perf. 12½*

C229	AP80	100fr multi	80	40
C230	AP80	150fr multi, vert.	1.20	60

Olympic Type of 1980

1980, July 25 Litho. *Perf. 13½*

C231	A126	100fr *Boxing*	80	40
C232	A126	150fr *Hurdles*	1.20	60

Souvenir Sheet

C233	A126	250fr *Long jump*	2.00	1.00

22nd Summer Olympic Games, Moscow, July 19-Aug. 3. No. C233 contains one stamp (39x36mm); multicolored margin shows satellite, Olympic rings, Moscow '80 emblem, Kremlin. Size: 87x84mm.

Europe-Africa Type of 1980

1980, Nov. 4 Litho. *Perf. 13½*

C234	A127	150fr *Meteorology*	1.20	60
C235	A127	200fr *Aviation*	1.60	80

Souvenir Sheet

C236	A127	500fr *Concorde jet*	4.00	2.00

No. C236 contains one stamp (41½x29mm.); multicolored margin showing jet, flags and maps. Size: 89x64½mm.

Soccer Type of 1981

1981, Jan. 13 Litho. *Perf. 13½*

C237	A130	100fr Netherlands	80	40
C238	A130	200fr Spain	1.60	80

Souvenir Sheet

C239	A130	500fr Argentina	4.00	2.00

ESPANA '82 World Cup Soccer Championship. No. C239 has multicolored margin showing soccer scenes and teams. Size: 119x87mm.

Jacob Wrestling with the Angel, by Rembrandt—AP81

Rembrandt Paintings: 90fr, Christ during the Storm. 150fr, Jeremiah Mourning the Destruction of Jerusalem. 250fr, Tobit Accusing Anne of Theft of a Goat. 500fr, Belshazzar's Feast (horiz.).

1981, Feb. 20 *Perf. 12½*

C240	AP81	60fr multi	50	25
C241	AP81	90fr multi	70	35
C242	AP81	150fr multi	1.20	60
C243	AP81	250fr multi	2.00	1.00

Souvenir Sheet

C244	AP81	500fr multi	4.00	2.00

No. C244 has gray and light brown margin showing figures by Rembrandt. Size: 105x80mm.

Picasso Type of 1981

Paintings: 150fr, Woman in Mirror with Self-portrait. 200fr, Woman Sleeping, The Dream. 500fr, Portrait of Maia (the Artist's Daughter).

1981, June 30 Litho. *Perf. 13½*

C245 A133 150fr multi 1.20 60
C246 A133 200fr multi 1.60 80

Souvenir Sheet

C247 A133 500fr multi 4.00 2.00

No. C247 contains one stamp (42x46mm.); multicolored margin shows entire painting. Size: 78½x113½mm.

Nos. C231-C233 Overprinted with Event, Winner and Country in Gold.

1981 Litho. *Perf. 13½*

C248 A126 100fr multi 80 40
C249 A126 150fr multi 1.20 60

Souvenir Sheet

C250 A126 250fr multi 2.00 1.00

Royal Wedding Type of 1981

1981, Aug. 20 Litho. *Perf. 13½*

C251 A136 150fr Prince of Wales arms 1.20 60
C252 A136 200fr Palace 1.60 80

Souvenir Sheet

C253 A136 500fr St. Paul's Cathedral 4.00 2.00

No. C253 contains one stamp (60x32mm.); multicolored margin shows arms. Size: 120x70mm.

Navigator Type of 1981

1981, Sept. 4 Litho. *Perf. 13½*

C254 A139 100fr O. Kersauson 80 40
C255 A139 200fr Chichester 1.60 80

Souvenir Sheet

C256 A139 500fr A. Colas 4.00 2.00

No. C256 has multicolored margin showing ships. Size: 100x80mm.

Lizard—AP82

1981, Oct. 30 *Perf. 12½x13*

C257 AP82 30fr shown 25 12
C258 AP82 60fr Snake 50 25
C259 AP82 110fr Crocodile 90 45

Christmas Type of 1981

1981, Dec. 24 *Perf. 13½*

C260 A143 140fr Correggio 1.15 60
C261 A143 200fr Gentileschi, 1610 1.60 80

Souvenir Sheet

C262 A143 500fr Holy Family, by Cranach 4.00 2.00

No. C262 contains one stamp (41x50mm.); multicolored margin shows entire painting. Size: 81x98mm.

Animal Type of 1982

1982, Jan. 22 Litho. *Perf. 13½*

C263 A145 300fr Mandrill 2.40 1.20
C264 A145 500fr Lion 4.00 2.00

Souvenir Sheet

C265 A145 600fr Nile crocodiles 5.00 2.50

No. C265 contains one stamp (47x38mm.); multicolored margin shows crocodiles. Size: 100x80mm.

Transportation Type of 1982

1982, Feb. 27 Litho. *Perf. 13½*

C266 A147 300fr Savannah cargo ship 2.40 1.25
C267 A147 500fr Columbia space shuttle 4.00 2.00

Souvenir Sheet

C268 A147 600fr Spirit of Locomotion emblem 5.00 2.50

No. C268 contains one stamp (39x43mm.); multicolored margin shows modes of transportation. Size: 101x81mm.

Olympic Type of 1982

1982, July 24 Litho. *Perf. 13½*

C269 A149 300fr Diving 2.50 1.25
C270 A149 500fr Equestrian 4.00 2.00

Souvenir Sheet

C271 A149 600fr Basketball 5.00 2.50

No. C271 contains one stamp (38x56mm.); multicolored margin shows city views. Size: 80x108mm.

Diana Type of 1982

1982, July 20 Litho. *Perf. 13½*

C272 A150 300fr multi 2.50 1.25
C273 A150 500fr multi 4.00 2.00

Souvenir Sheet

C274 A150 600fr multi 5.00 2.50

No. C274 contains one stamp (56x32mm.). Size: 120x75mm.

Christmas 1982—AP83

Raphael Paintings.

1982, Dec. *Perf. 13*

C275 AP83 150fr Beautiful Gardener 1.20 60
C276 AP83 500fr Holy Family 4.00 2.00

Space Type of 1982

Various satellites and space scenes.

1982, Aug. 15 Litho. *Perf. 13½*

C277 A151 300fr multi 2.50 1.25
C278 A151 500fr multi 4.00 2.00

Souvenir Sheet

C279 A151 600fr multi 5.00 2.50

No. C279 has multicolored margin showing planets, satellite. Size: 105x67mm.

Birth of Prince William of Wales, June 21, 1982—AP84

1983, Jan. 22

C280 AP84 500fr Diana, William 4.00 2.00

Souvenir Sheet

C281 AP84 600fr Family 5.00 2.50

Size of No. C281: 120x70mm.

Manned Flight Bicentenary—AP85

1983, Apr.

C282 AP85 65fr Robert's & Hullin's balloon 52 25
C283 AP85 130fr John Wise's, 1859 1.05 52
C284 AP85 350fr Mail balloon, 1870 2.75 1.35
C285 AP85 400fr Dirigible Underberg 3.25 1.65

Souvenir Sheet

C286 AP85 500fr Montgolfiere, 1783 4.00 2.00

No. C286 has multicolored margin continuing design. Size: 117x91mm.

Pre-Olympics—AP86

Various equestrian events.

1983, July Litho. *Perf. 13*

C287 AP86 100fr multi 80 40
C288 AP86 200fr multi 1.60 80
C289 AP86 300fr multi 2.50 1.25
C290 AP86 400fr multi 3.25 1.65

Souvenir Sheet

C291 AP86 500fr multi 4.00 2.00

Multicolored margin continues design. Size: 104x81mm.

Endangered Animals, Rotary Emblem—AP87

1983, Nov. 14 Litho. *Perf. 13½*

C292 AP87 500fr Lions, gray parrot, deer, elephant 2.50 1.25

Souvenir Sheet

C293 AP87 600fr Leopard 3.00 1.50

No. C293 contains one stamp (47x32mm.); multicolored margin shows Rotary emblem, rhinoceros, map, bird. Size: 112x75mm.

Christmas 1983—AP88

Paintings: 130fr, Annunciation, by da Vinci. 205fr, Virgin of the Rocks, by da Vinci. 350fr, Adoration of the Shepherds, by Rubens. 500fr, Virgin and Child with Donor, by Rubens.

1984, Jan. 3 Litho. *Perf.13*

C294 AP88 130fr multi 65 32
C295 AP88 205fr multi 1.05 52
C296 AP88 350fr multi 1.75 85
C297 AP88 500fr multi 2.50 1.25

1984 Summer Olympics—AP89

Various gymnastic and rhythmic gymnastic events. 65fr, 100fr, 205fr, 350fr vert.

1984, Mar. 13 Litho. *Perf. 13*

C298 AP89 65fr multi 32 16
C299 AP89 100fr multi 50 25
C300 AP89 130fr multi 65 32
C301 AP89 205fr multi 1.05 52
C302 AP89 350fr multi 1.75 85
Nos. C298-C302 (5) 4.27 2.10

Souvenir Sheet

1984, Mar. 13 Litho. *Perf. 13½x13*

C302A AP89 500fr Rhythmic formation 2.50 1.25

No. C302A has multicolored margin showing the Los Angeles skyline. Size: 103x78mm.

Summer Olympics Winners—AP90

1985, Jan. 7 Litho. *Perf. 14*

C303 AP90 60fr 400 meter relay 25 14
C304 AP90 140fr 400 meter hurdles 58 30
C305 AP90 300fr 5000 meter race 1.25 65
C306 AP90 440fr Decathlon 1.80 90

Souvenir Sheet

C307 AP90 500fr 800 meter race, horiz. 2.10 1.05

Size: 102x76mm.

Christmas 1984—AP91

Paintings by Titian: 130fr, Virgin and Infant Jesus. 350fr, Virgin with Rabbit. 400fr, Virgin and Child.

1985, Jan. 17 **Litho.** ***Perf. 13***

C308	AP91	130fr multi	55	28
C309	AP91	350fr multi	1.45	75
C310	AP91	400fr multi	1.65	85

Audubon Bicentenary—AP92

1985, Jan. 25 **Litho.** ***Perf. 13***

C311	AP92	60fr Otus asio	25	14
C312	AP92	110fr Coccizus minor, vert.	48	24
C313	AP92	200fr Zenaidura macroura, vert.	85	42
C314	AP92	500fr Aix sponsa	2.10	1.05

Christmas 1985—AP93

Religious paintings: 100fr, Virgin with Angels, by the Master of Burgo de Osma. 200fr, Nativity, by Louis Le Nain (1593-1648). 400fr, Virgin and Child with Dove, by Piero de Cosimo (1462-1521).

1985, Dec. 24 **Litho.** ***Perf. 13***

C315	AP93	100fr multi	42	20
C316	AP93	200fr multi	85	42
C317	AP93	400fr multi	1.75	90

Halley's Comet—AP94

1986, Mar. 8

C318	AP94	110fr Edmond Halley	45	22
C319	AP94	130fr Giotto probe	52	25
C320	AP94	200fr Comet, planet	85	42
C321	AP94	300fr Vega probe	1.25	62
C322	AP94	400fr Space shuttle	1.75	90
		Nos. C318-C322 (5)	4.82	2.41

Christmas—AP95

Painting details: 250fr, Nativity, by Giotto. 440fr, Adoration of the Magi, by Botticelli, vert. 500fr, Nativity, by Giotto, diff.

1986, Dec. 24 **Litho.** ***Perf. 13½***

C323	AP95	250fr multi	1.40	70
C324	AP95	440fr multi	2.40	1.20
C325	AP95	500fr multi	2.75	1.40

Tennis at the 1988 Olympics—AP96

Various plays.

1986, Dec. 31 ***Perf. 12½***

C326	AP96	150fr multi	82	40
C327	AP96	250fr multi, vert.	1.40	70
C328	AP96	440fr multi, vert.	2.40	1.20
C329	AP96	600fr multi	3.25	1.65

AIR POST SEMI-POSTAL STAMPS

Central African Republic

Isis of Kalabsha
SPAP1

Engraved

1964, March 7 ***Perf. 13*** **Unwmkd.**

CB1	SPAP1	25fr	+10fr ol, ultra & brt pink	1.00	1.00
CB2	SPAP1	50fr	+10fr dk bl grn, ol & red brn	1.50	1.50
CB3	SPAP1	100fr	+10fr ol gray, lil & mar	2.50	2.50

Issued to publicize the UNESCO world campaign to save historic monuments in Nubia.

African Infants and Globe—SPAP2

1971, Dec. 11 Litho. ***Perf. 13x13½***

CB4	SPAP2 140fr	+50fr multi	2.50	1.50

25th anniversary of the United Nations International Children's Fund (UNICEF), and Children's Day.

POSTAGE DUE STAMPS

Central African Republic

Sternotomis Virescens—D1

Beetles: No. J2, Sternotomis gama. No. J3, Augosoma centaurus. No. J4, Phosphorus virescens and ceroplesis carabarica. No. J5, Cetoine scaraboidae. No. J6, Ceroplesis S.P. No. J7, Macrorhina S.P. No. J8, Cetoine scaraboidae. No. J9, Phryneta leprosa. No. J10, Taurina longiceps. J11, Monohamus griseoplagiatus. J12, Jambonus trifasciatus.

Engraved

1962, Oct. 15 ***Perf. 11*** **Unwmkd.**

J1	D1	50c grn & dp org	5	5
J2	D1	50c grn & dp org	5	5
J3	D1	1fr blk, brn & lt grn	10	10
J4	D1	1fr blk, brn & lt grn	10	10
J5	D1	2fr blk, org & yel grn	10	10
J6	D1	2fr blk & red org	10	10
J7	D1	5fr brn, org & grn	18	18
J8	D1	5fr brn, org, grn & red	18	18
J9	D1	10fr blk, grn & brn	45	45
J10	D1	10fr blk, brn & grn	45	45
J11	D1	25fr blk, bl grn & brn	70	70
J12	D1	25fr blk, brn & bl grn	70	70
		Nos. J1-J12 (12)	3.16	3.16

Each two stamps of the same denomination are printed together in the sheet, se-tenant at the base.

MILITARY STAMPS

Central African Republic

No. 1 Overprinted **FM**

Engraved

1962, Jan. 1 ***Perf. 13*** **Unwmkd.**

M1	A1	bl, car, grn & yel	12.50	12.50

No. 1 Overprinted **FM**

1963

M2	A1	bl, car, grn & yel	13.50	13.50

OFFICIAL STAMPS

Central African Republic

Coat of Arms
O1

Imprint: "d'après G. RICHER SO.GE.IM."

Perf. 13x12½

1965–69 Litho. Unwmkd.

Arms in Original Colors

O1	O1	1fr blk & brn org	6	6
O2	O1	2fr blk & vio	7	6
O3	O1	5fr blk & gray	10	6
O4	O1	10fr blk & grn	28	12
O5	O1	20fr blk & red brn	45	32
O6	O1	30fr blk & emer ('69)	80	60
O7	O1	50fr blk & dk bl	1.00	80
O8	O1	100fr blk & bis	2.10	1.25
O9	O1	130fr blk & ver ('69)	3.25	2.50
O10	O1	200fr blk & cl	4.50	3.00
		Nos. O1-O10 (10)	12.61	8.77

Redrawn

Imprint: "d'après G. RICHER DELRIEU"

1971 Photo. ***Perf. 12x12½***

Arms in Original Colors

O11	O1	5fr blk & gray	18	18
O12	O1	30fr blk & emer	45	28
O13	O1	40fr blk & dp cl	60	35
O14	O1	100fr blk & bis	1.40	70
O15	O1	140fr blk & lt bl	2.50	1.00
O16	O1	200fr blk & cl	3.25	1.60
		Nos. O11-O16 (6)	8.38	4.11

Empire

Nos. O11, O13–O16 Overprinted with Bar and "EMPIRE CENTRAFRICAIN"

1977 Lithographed ***Perf. 12x12½***

O17	O1	5fr multi	18	15
O18	O1	40fr multi	35	28
O19	O1	100fr multi	80	55
O20	O1	140fr multi	1.20	85
O21	O1	200fr multi	1.85	1.35
		Nos. O17-O21 (5)	4.38	3.18

Type of 1965 Inscribed: "EMPIRE CENTRAFRICAIN"

1978, July Litho. ***Perf. 12½***

O22	O1	1fr multi	5	5
O23	O1	2fr multi	5	5
O24	O1	5fr multi	5	5
O25	O1	10fr multi	12	12
O26	O1	15fr multi	15	15
O27	O1	20fr multi	20	20
O28	O1	30fr multi	30	30
O29	O1	40fr multi	40	40
O30	O1	50fr multi	50	50
O31	O1	60fr multi	60	60
O32	O1	100fr multi	1.00	1.00
O33	O1	130fr multi	1.30	1.30
O34	O1	140fr multi	1.40	1.40
O35	O1	200fr multi	2.00	2.00
		Nos. O22-O35 (14)	8.12	8.12

CENTRAL LITHUANIA

(lĭth'û-ā'nĭ-ȧ)

LOCATION—North of Poland and east of Lithuania.

CAPITAL—Vilnius.

At one time Central Lithuania was a grand duchy of Lithuania but at the end of the 18th Century it fell under Russian rule. After World War I, Lithuania regained her sovereignty but certain areas were occupied by Poland. During the Russo-Polish war this territory was seized by Lithuania whose claim was promptly recognized by the Soviet Government. Under the leadership of the Polish General Zeligowski the territory was recaptured and it was during this occupation the stamps of Central Lithuania came into being. Subsequently the territory became a part of Poland.

100 Fennigi = 1 Markka

Coat of Arms
A1

Perf. 11½, Imperf.

1920-21 Typo. Unwmkd.

1	A1	25f red	40	75
2	A1	25f dk grn ('21)	40	75
3	A1	1m blue	40	75
4	A1	1m dk brn ('21)	40	75
5	A1	2m violet	50	75
6	A1	2m org ('21)	50	75
		Nos. 1-6 (6)	2.60	4.50

Lithuanian Stamps of 1919 Surcharged in Blue or Black

Wmkd. Wavy Lines. (145)

Perf. 11½x12, 12½x11½, 14

1920, Nov. 23

13	A5	2m on 15sk lil	10.00	10.00
a.		Invtd surch.	*250.00*	
14	A5	4m on 10sk red	10.00	10.00
a.		Invtd surch.	*250.00*	
15	A5	4m on 20sk dl bl (Bk)	10.00	10.00
a.		Invtd surch.	*250.00*	
16	A5	4m on 30sk buff	10.00	10.00
a.		Invtd surch.	*250.00*	
17	A6	6m on 50sk lt grn	10.00	10.00
a.		4m on 50sk lt grn (error)	*250.00*	
b.		10m on 50sk lt grn (error)	*250.00*	
18	A6	6m on 60sk vio & red	10.00	10.00
a.		4m on 60sk vio & red (error)	*250.00*	
b.		10m on 60sk vio & red (error)	*250.00*	
19	A6	6m on 75sk bis & red	10.00	10.00
a.		4m on 75sk bis & red (error)	*250.00*	
b.		10m on 75sk bis & red (error)	*250.00*	
20	A8	10m on 1auk gray & red	15.00	15.00
a.		Invtd. surch.	*375.00*	
21	A8	10m on 3auk lt brn & red	*500.00*	*550.00*
22	A8	10m on 5auk bl grn & red	*500.00*	*550.00*
		Nos. 13-22 (10)	*1,085.*	*1,185.*

Reprints of Nos. 17a, 17b, 18a, 18b, 19a, 19b. Price, each $75.

Counterfeits of Nos. 21-22 exist.

Lithuanian Girl
A2

Warrior
A3

Holy Gate of Vilnius
A4

Tower and Cathedral, Vilnius
A5

Rector's Insignia
A6

Gen. Lucien Zeligowski
A7

Perf. 11½, Imperf.

1920 Litho. Unwmkd.

23	A2	25f gray	25	50
24	A3	1m orange	25	50
25	A4	2m claret	50	1.00
26	A5	4m gray grn & buff	75	1.00
27	A6	6m rose & gray	1.50	1.25
28	A7	10m brn & yel	2.50	3.00
		Nos. 23-28 (6)	5.75	7.25

St. Anne's Church, Vilnius
A8

White Eagle and White Knight Vytis
A10

St. Stanislas Cathedral, Vilnius
A9

Queen Hedwig and King Ladislas II Jagello
A11

Coat of Arms of Vilnius
A12

Poczobut Astronomical Observatory
A13

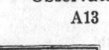

Union of Lithuania and Poland
A14

Tadeusz Kosciuszko and Adam Mickiewicz
A15

1921 ***Perf. 11½, 13½, 14, Imperf.***

35	A8	1(m) dk gray & yel	50	75
36	A9	2(m) rose & grn	50	75
37	A10	3(m) dk grn	50	75
38	A11	4(m) brn & buff	50	75
39	A12	5(m) red brn	50	75
40	A13	6(m) sl & buff	50	1.00
41	A14	10(m) red vio & buff	1.25	1.75
42	A15	20(m) blk brn & buff	1.50	1.75
		Nos. 35-42 (8)	5.75	8.25

Peasant Girl Sowing
A16

Allegory: Peace and Industry
A19

White Eagle and Vytis
A17

Great Theater at Vilnius
A18

Gen. Zeligowski Entering Vilnius
A20

Gen. Zeligowski
A21

1921-22 ***Perf. 11½, Imperf.***

53	A16	10m brn ('22)	3.50	4.00
54	A17	25m red & yel ('22)	3.50	3.50
55	A18	50m dk bl ('22)	4.00	4.00
56	A19	75m vio ('22)	5.50	5.50
57	A20	100m bl & bis	3.75	5.00
58	A21	150m ol grn & brn	4.00	5.00
		Nos. 53-58 (6)	24.25	27.00

Nos. 53-56 commemorate the opening of the National Parliament; Nos. 57-58, the anniversary of the entry of General Zeligowski into Vilnius.

SEMI-POSTAL STAMPS.

Nos. 1-6 Surcharged in Black or Red

NA
ŚLĄSK
2 M.

1921 ***Perf. 11½, Imperf.*** **Unwmkd.**

B1	A1	25f +2m red (Bk)	90	1.50
B2	A1	25f +2m dk grn	90	1.50
B3	A1	1m +2m bl	1.25	2.00
B4	A1	1m +2m dk brn	1.25	2.00
B5	A1	2m +2m vio	1.50	2.00
B6	A1	2m +2m org	1.25	2.00
		Nos. B1-B6 (6)	7.05	11.00

The surcharge means "For Silesia 2 marks." The stamps were intended to provide a fund to assist the plebiscite in Upper Silesia.

Nos. 25, 26 Surcharged:

a b

Perf. 11½, Imperf.

B13	A4 (a)	2m +1(m) cl	2.50	3.00
B14	A5 (b)	4m +1m gray grn & buff	2.50	3.00

Nos. 25-26, 28 with inset

10M

Perf. 11½, Imperf.

B17	A4	2m +1m cl	1.50	1.50
B18	A5	4m +1m gray grn & buff	1.50	1.50
B19	A7	10m +2m brn & yel	1.50	1.50
		Nos. B13-B19 (5)	9.50	10.50

POSTAGE DUE STAMPS.

University, Vilnius
D1

Castle Ruins, Troki
D3

Castle Hill, Vilnius
D2

Holy Gate, Vilnius
D4

St. Stanislas Cathedral
D5

St. Anne's Church, Vilnius
D6

Perf. 11½, Imperf.

1920-21 Unwmkd.

J1	D1	50f red vio	40	75
J2	D2	1m green	40	75
J3	D3	2m red vio	40	75
J4	D4	3m red vio	60	1.00
J5	D5	5m red vio	1.00	1.50
J6	D6	20m scarlet	3.00	3.50
		Nos. J1-J6 (6)	5.80	8.25

CHAD

(chäd)

(Tchad)

LOCATION — Central Africa, south of Libya.
GOVT.—Republic.
AREA—495,572 sq. mi.
POP.—5,122,000 (est. 1984).
CAPITAL—N'djamena.

A former dependency of Ubangi-Shari, Chad became a separate French colony in 1920. In 1934, the colonies of Chad, Gabon, Middle Congo and Ubangi-Shari were grouped in a single administrative unit known as French Equatorial Africa, with the capital at Brazzaville. The Republic of Chad was proclaimed November 28, 1958.

100 Centimes = 1 Franc

Types of Middle Congo, 1907-17, Overprinted **TCHAD**

Perf. 14x13½, 13½x14.

1922 **Unwmkd.**

No.	Type	Description	Unused	Used
1	A1	1c red & vio	15	15
a.		Overprint omitted	100.00	
2	A1	2c ol brn & sal	35	35
a.		Ovpt. omitted	160.00	
3	A1	4c ind & vio	42	42
4	A1	5c choc & grn	65	65
5	A1	10c dp grn & gray grn	1.00	1.00
6	A1	15c vio & red	1.25	1.25
7	A1	20c grn & vio	3.25	3.25
8	A2	25c ol brn & brn	6.50	6.50
9	A2	30c rose & pale rose	80	80
10	A2	35c dl bl & dl rose	1.50	1.50
11	A2	40c choc & grn	1.50	1.50
12	A2	45c vio & grn	1.50	1.50
13	A2	50c dk bl & pale bl	1.65	1.65
14	A2	60c on 75c vio, *pnksh*	2.75	2.75
a.		"TCHAD" omitted	150.00	
b.		"60" omitted	150.00	
15	A1	75c red & vio	1.40	1.40
16	A3	1fr ind & sal	7.00	7.00
17	A3	2fr ind & vio	11.00	11.00
18	A3	5fr ind & ol brn	9.25	9.25
		Nos. 1-18 (18)	51.77	51.77

Stamps of 1922 Overprinted in Various Colors:

AFRIQUE EQUATORIALE FRANÇAISE (a)

AFRIQUE EQUATORIALE FRANÇAISE (b)

1924-33

No.	Type	Description	Unused	Used
19	A1 (a)	1c red & vio	5	5
a.		"TCHAD" omitted	95.00	
b.		Dbl. ovpt.	87.50	
20	A1 (a)	2c ol brn & sal	5	5
a.		"TCHAD" omitted	95.00	
b.		Dbl. ovpt.	100.00	
21	A1 (a)	4c ind & vio	5	5
a.		"TCHAD" omitted	525.00	
22	A1 (a)	5c choc & grn (Bl)	70	42
a.		"TCHAD" omitted	95.00	
23	A1 (a)	5c choc & grn	42	40
a.		"TCHAD" omitted	125.00	
24	A1 (a)	10c dp grn & gray grn (Bl)	42	40
25	A1 (a)	10c dp grn & gray grn	42	40
26	A1 (a)	10c red org & blk ('25)	30	30
27	A1 (a)	15c vio & red	42	40
28	A1 (a)	20c grn & vio	42	40
29	A2 (b)	25c ol brn & brn	42	40
30	A2 (b)	30c rose & pale rose	22	22
31	A2 (b)	30c gray & bl (R) ('25)	22	22
32	A2 (b)	30c dk grn & grn ('27)	70	70
a.		"Afrique Equatoriale Francaise" omitted	150.00	
33	A2 (b)	35c ind & dl rose	25	25
34	A2 (b)	40c choc & grn	70	70
a.		Dbl. overprint (R + Bk)	150.00	
35	A2 (b)	45c vio & grn	52	52
a.		Dbl. overprint (R + Bk)	150.00	
36	A2 (b)	50c dk bl & pale bl	52	52
a.		Inverted overprint	87.50	
37	A2 (b)	50c grn & vio ('25)	70	70
38	A2 (b)	65c org brn & bl ('28)	1.40	1.40
39	A2 (b)	75c red & vio	48	42
40	A2 (b)	75c dp bl & lt bl (R) ('25)	30	30
a.		"TCHAD" omitted	100.00	
41	A2 (b)	75c rose & dk brn ('28)	1.40	1.40
42	A2 (b)	90c brn red & pink ('30)	4.25	4.25
43	A3 (b)	1fr ind & sal	1.00	1.00
44	A3 (b)	1.10fr dl grn & bl ('28)	1.50	1.50
45	A3 (b)	1.25fr org brn & lt bl ('33)	4.25	4.25
46	A3 (b)	1.50fr ultra & bl ('30)	4.25	4.25
47	A3 (b)	1.75fr ol brn & vio ('33)	32.50	32.50
48	A3 (b)	2fr ind & vio	1.65	1.40
49	A3 (b)	3fr red vio ('30)	7.00	7.00
50	A3 (b)	5fr ind & ol brn	1.75	1.40
		Nos. 19-50 (32)	69.23	68.17

Types of 1922 Overprinted Type "b" and Surcharged with New Values.

1924-27

No.	Type	Description	Unused	Used
51	A2	60c on 75c dk vio, *pnksh*	42	42
a.		"60" omitted	100.00	
52	A3	65c on 1fr brn & ol grn ('25)	1.00	1.00
53	A3	85c on 1fr brn & ol grn ('25)	1.00	1.00
54	A2	90c on 75c brn red & rose red ('27)	1.00	1.00
55	A3	1.25fr on 1fr dk bl & ultra (R) ('26)	30	30
a.		"Afrique Equatoriale Francaise" omitted	100.00	
56	A3	1.50fr on 1fr ultra & bl ('27)	1.00	1.00
57	A3	3fr on 5fr org brn & dl red ('27)	3.00	3.00
58	A3	10fr on 5fr ol grn & cer ('27)	7.00	7.00
59	A3	20fr on 5fr vio & ver ('27)	11.00	11.00
		Nos. 51-59 (9)	25.72	25.72

Colonial Exposition Issue.

Common Design Types

Name of Country in Black.

1931 **Engraved** ***Perf. 12½***

No.	Type	Description	Unused	Used
60	CD70	40c dp grn	3.00	3.00
61	CD71	50c violet	3.00	3.00
62	CD72	90c red org	3.00	3.00
63	CD73	1.50fr dl bl	3.00	3.00

Common Design Types

pictured in section at front of book.

Republic

"Birth of the Republic"
A1

"Solidarity of the Community"
A2

Engraved.

1959 ***Perf. 13*** **Unwmkd.**

No.	Type	Description	Unused	Used
64	A1	15fr ultra, grn & mar	27	15
65	A2	25fr dk grn & dp cl	40	15

Issued to commemorate the first anniversary of the proclamation of the Republic.

Imperforates

Most Chad stamps from 1959 onward exist imperforate in issued and trial colors, and also in small presentation sheets in issued colors.

C.C.T.A. Issue

Common Design Type

1960

No.	Type	Description	Unused	Used
66	CD106	50fr rose lil & dk pur	90	80

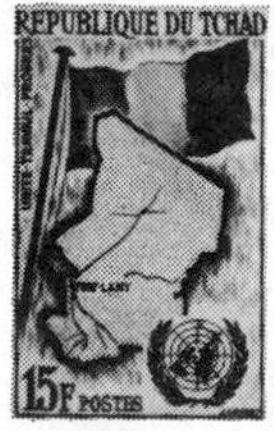

Flag and Map of Chad and U.N. Emblem
A3

Engraved

1961, Jan. 11 ***Perf. 13*** **Unwmkd.**

Flag in blue, yellow and carmine.

No.	Type	Description	Unused	Used
67	A3	15fr brn & dk bl	35	25
68	A3	25fr org brn & dk bl	45	25
69	A3	85fr sl grn & dk bl	1.50	85

Admission of Chad to United Nations.

Chari Bridge and Hippopotamus
A4

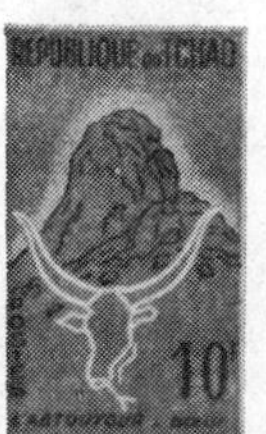

Abtouyoua Mountain and Ox
A5

Designs: 50c, Biltine and dorcas gazelle. 1fr, Logone and elephant. 2fr, Batha and lion. 3fr, Salamat and buffalo. 4fr, Ouaddai and Kudu. 15fr, Bessada and giant eland. 20fr, Tibesti mountains and mouflon. 25fr, Rocherg and antelope. 30fr, Kanem and cheetah. 60fr, Borkou and oryx. 85fr, Gorge of Archet and addax.

Typographed

1961-62 ***Perf. 13½x14, 14x13½***

No.	Type	Description	Unused	Used
70	A5	50c yel grn & dk grn ('62)	5	5
71	A5	1fr bl grn & dk bl grn ('62)	5	5
72	A5	2fr dk red brn & blk ('62)	5	5
73	A5	3fr ocher & dl grn ('62)	6	6
74	A5	4fr dk crim & blk ('62)	8	8
75	A4	5fr yel & blk	10	10
76	A5	10fr pink & blk	15	10
77	A5	15fr lil & blk ('62)	25	8
78	A5	20fr red & blk	30	15
79	A5	25fr bl & blk ('62)	40	15
80	A5	30fr ultra & blk ('62)	50	20
81	A5	60fr yel & ol grn ('62)	90	30
82	A5	85fr org & blk	1.20	50
		Nos. 70-82 (13)	4.09	1.87

First anniversary of Independence.

Abidjan Games Issue

Common Design Type

Designs: 20fr, Relay race. 50fr, High jump.

1962, July 21 **Photo.** ***Perf. 12½x12***

No.	Type	Description	Unused	Used
83	CD109	20fr brn, lt grn & blk	35	20
84	CD109	50fr brn, lt grn & blk	75	50

See No. C8.

African-Malgache Union Issue

Common Design Type

1962, Sept. 8 **Unwmkd.**

No.	Type	Description	Unused	Used
85	CD110	30fr dk bl, bluish grn, red & gold	50	45

Issued to commemorate the first anniversary of the African and Malgache Union.

Pres. Ngarta Tombalbaye
A7

1963, Apr. 22 ***Perf. 12x12½***

No.	Type	Description	Unused	Used
86	A7	20fr multi	30	15
87	A7	85fr multi	1.20	45

Space Communciations Issue

Waves Around Globe
A8

Design: 100fr, Orbit patterns around globe.

Photogravure

1963, Sept. 19 ***Perf. 12½*** **Unwmkd.**

No.	Type	Description	Unused	Used
88	A8	25fr grn & pur	40	35
89	A8	100fr pink & ultra	1.50	1.10

Ancestral Mask
A9

Excavated Sao Art: 5fr, Clay weight. 25fr, Ancestral clay statuette. 60fr, Gazelle, bronze. 80fr, Bronze pectoral.

1963, Dec. 2 Engraved *Perf. 13*

90	A9	5fr brt grn & red brn	10	5
91	A9	15fr gray, dl cl & red	25	15
92	A9	25fr dk bl & org brn	40	25
93	A9	60fr org brn & sl grn	90	40
94	A9	80fr org red & ol	1.20	40
		Nos. 90-94 (5)	2.85	1.25

UNESCO Emblem, Scales and Tree—A10

1963, Dec. 10

95	A10	25fr grn & mar	40	30

Issued to commemorate the 15th anniversary of the Universal Declaration of Human Rights.

Potter
A11

Designs: 30fr, Boatmaker. 50fr, Weaver. 85fr, Smiths.

Engraved

1964, Feb. 5 *Perf. 12½* Unwmkd.

96	A11	10fr bl, blk & org	15	10
97	A11	30fr yel, blk & car	45	20
98	A11	50fr grn, blk & car	75	30
99	A11	85fr pur, blk & yel	85	50

Barograph and WMO Emblem
A12

1964, March 23 *Perf. 13*

100	A12	50fr red lil, pur & ultra	85	45

Fourth World Meteorological Day.

Cotton
A13

Design: 25fr, Royal poinciana.

1964, Apr. 6 Photo. *Perf. 12½x13*

101	A13	20fr multi	40	20
102	A13	25fr multi	40	20

Co-operation Issue
Common Design Type

1964, Nov. 7 Engraved *Perf. 13*

103	CD119	25fr ver, dk bl & dk brn	40	30

National Guard and Map of Chad
A14

Design: 25fr, Infantry, flag and map (vert.).

Perf. 12½x13, 13x12½

1964, Dec. 11 Photogravure

104	A14	20fr multi	35	20
105	A14	25fr lt bl & multi	40	20

Issued to honor the army of Chad.

Aoudad or Barbary Sheep
A15

Animals: 10fr, Addax. 20fr, Oryx. 25fr, Derby's eland (vert.). 30fr, Giraffe, buffalo and lion, Zakouma Park (vert.). 85fr, Great kudu at water hole. (vert.).

Perf. 12½x12, 12x12½

1965, Jan. 11 Unwmkd.

106	A15	5fr dk brn, ultra & yel	7	5
107	A15	10fr ultra, org & blk	18	12
108	A15	20fr multi	30	15
109	A15	25fr multi	40	20
110	A15	30fr multi	45	25
111	A15	85fr multi	1.25	65
		Nos. 106-111 (6)	2.65	1.42

Olsen Perforator
A16

Designs: 60fr, Mildé telephone (vert.). 100fr, Distributor of Baudot telegraph.

1965, May 17 Engraved *Perf. 13*

112	A16	30fr choc, red, grn & ver	45	30
113	A16	60fr red brn, sl grn & ver	90	60
114	A16	100fr sl grn, red brn & ver	1.40	1.00

Issued to commemorate the centenary of the International Telecommunication Union.

Motorized Police
A17

Perf. 12½x12

1965, June 22 Photo. Unwmkd.

115	A17	25fr ol, dk grn, gold & brn	40	25

Issued to honor the national police.

Guitar
A18

Musical Instruments from National Museum: 1fr, Drum and stool (vert.). 3fr, Shoulder drums (vert.). 15fr, Viol. 60fr, Harp (vert.).

1965, Oct. 26 Engraved *Perf. 13*

Size: 22x36, 36x22mm.

116	A18	1fr car, emer & brn	6	5
117	A18	2fr red, brt lil & brn	6	5
118	A18	3fr red & sep	6	6
119	A18	15fr red, ocher & sl grn	25	15
120	A18	60fr mar & sl grn	90	40
		Nos. 116-120, C23 (6)	2.68	1.16

Head and Bowl
A19

WHO Headquarters, Geneva
A20

Sao Art: 20fr, Head. 60fr, Head with crown. 80fr, Circlet with human head. From excavations at Bouta Kebira and Gawi.

1966, Apr. 1 Engr. *Perf. 13*

121	A19	15fr ol, choc & ultra	20	15
122	A19	20fr dk red, brn & bl grn	30	20
123	A19	60fr brt bl, choc & ver	90	50
124	A19	80fr brn org, grn & pur	1.20	60

Issued to publicize the International Negro Arts Festival, Dakar, Senegal, Apr. 1–24.

No. 86 Surcharged with New Value and Two Bars in Orange

1966, Apr. 15 Photo. *Perf. 12x12½*

125	A7	25fr on 20fr multi	40	20

1966, May 3

126	A20	25fr car, lt ultra & yel	40	30
127	A20	32fr emer, ultra & yel	45	35

Issued to commemorate the inauguration of the World Health Organization Headquarters, Geneva.

Staff of Mercury and Map of Africa
A21

1966, May 24 *Perf. 12½x12*

128	A21	30fr multi	45	20

Central African Customs and Economic Union (Union Douaniere et Economique de l'Afrique Centrale, UDEAC).

Soccer Player
A22

Design: 60fr, Soccer player facing left.

1966, July 12 Engraved *Perf. 13*

129	A22	30fr grn, bl grn & mar	45	25
130	A22	60fr dk bl, gray & car	90	50

Issued to commemorate the 8th World Cup Soccer Championship, Wembley, England, July 11–30.

Young Men, Flag and Emblem
A23

Photogravure

1966, Aug. 11 *Perf. 12½x13*

131	A23	25fr dk bl & multi	40	25

Chad Youth Movement.

Greek Columns and UNESCO Emblem
A24

1966, Aug. 23 Engr. *Perf. 13*

132	A24	32fr sl bl, vio & car rose	50	30

Issued to commemorate the 20th anniversary of UNESCO (United Nations Educational, Scientific and Cultural Organization).

Reconstructed Skull of Chadanthropus
A25

1966, Sept. 20 Engraved *Perf. 13*

133	A25	30fr gray, red & ocher	45	20

Issued to commemorate Yves Coppens' discovery of Lake Chad man.

Stone Axe
A26

Prehistoric Tools: 30fr, Flint arrow head. 85fr, Bone harpoon. 100fr, Sandstone millstone with grinder.

1966, Dec. 11 Engraved *Perf. 13*

134	A26	25fr dp bl, red & dk brn	32	18
135	A26	30fr brn, dp bl & blk	45	22
136	A26	85fr dk red, brt bl & brn	1.20	55
137	A26	100fr Prus grn, dk brn & bis brn	1.40	70
	a.	Min. sheet of 4	3.75	3.75

No. 137a contains one each of Nos. 134–137. Size: 128x99mm.

Map of Chad and Various Sports
A27

1967, Apr. 10 Photo. *Perf. 12x12½*

138	A27	25fr multi	40	25

Issued for Sports Day, Apr. 10, 1967.

Colotis Protomedia
A28

Various Butterflies.

1967, May 23 Photo. *Perf. 12½x12*

139	A28	5fr bl & multi	10	8
140	A28	10fr emer & multi	20	12
141	A28	20fr org & multi	30	20
142	A28	130fr red & multi	1.75	90

WHO Headquarters, Brazzaville
A29

1967, Sept. 23 Photo. *Perf. 12½x13*

143	A29	30fr vio bl & multi	45	25

Issued to commemorate the opening of the Regional Office of the United Nations World Health Organization, Brazzaville.

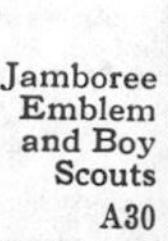

Jamboree Emblem and Boy Scouts
A30

Design: 32fr, Jamboree emblem and Boy Scout.

1967, Oct. 17 Photo. *Perf. 12½x13*

144	A30	25fr multi	35	15
145	A30	32fr multi	50	25

Issued to publicize the 12th Boy Scout World Jamboree, Farragut State Park, Idaho, Aug. 1–9.

Great Mills of Chad
A31

Design: 30fr, Lake reclamation project, grain fields.

1967, Nov. 14 Engraved *Perf. 13*

146	A31	25fr brt bl, ind & sep	35	15
147	A31	30fr ultra, emer & ol brn	40	25

Economic development of Chad.

Woman and Harp Player
A32

Rock Paintings: 30fr, Giraffes. 50fr, Camel rider hunting ostrich.

1967, Dec. 19 Engraved *Perf. 13*

Size: 36x22mm.

148	A32	15fr bl, sal & mar	20	12
149	A32	30fr grnsh bl, sal & mar	45	25
150	A32	50fr emer, sal & mar	75	32
		Nos. 148-150, C38-C39 (5)	4.75	2.24

Issued to commemorate the Balloud expedition in the Ennedi Mountains. See also Nos. 163–166.

Rotary Emblem
A33

Map of Chad, WHO Emblem, Well, Physicians, Mother and Child
A34

1968, Jan. 9 Photo. *Perf. 13x12½*

151	A33	50fr multi	75	35

Rotary Club of Chad, 10th anniversary.

1968, Apr. 6 *Perf. 13x12½*

152	A34	25fr multi	35	20
153	A34	32fr multi	50	30

Issued to commemorate the 20th anniversary of the World Health Organization.

"Water" Aiding Agriculture and Industry—A35

1968, Apr. 23 Engraved *Perf. 13*

154	A35	50fr grnsh bl, brn & brt grn	70	30

Hydrological Decade (UNESCO), 1965–74.

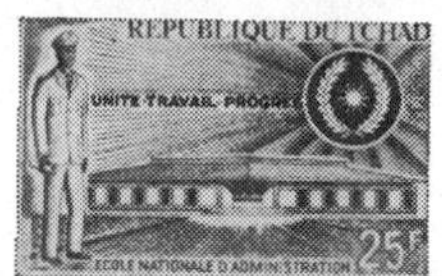

National Administration School
A36

1968, Aug. 20 Engraved *Perf. 13*

155	A36	25fr sl, brn red & rose vio	35	20

Boy Learning to Write
A37

1968, Sept. 10

156	A37	60fr dk bl, dk brn & blk	75	35

Issued for National Literacy Day.

Cotton Harvest
A38

Loom, Fort Archambault Factory
A39

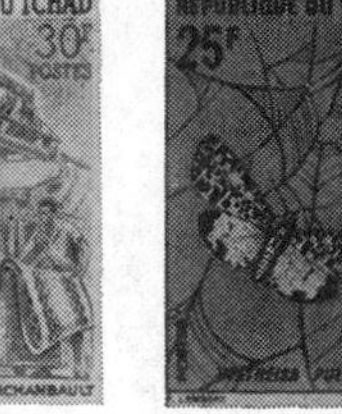

Tiger Moth
A40

1968, Sept. 24 Engraved *Perf. 13*

157	A38	25fr Prus bl, choc & dk grn	35	13
158	A39	30fr brt grn, ol & ultra	45	20

Issued to publicize the cotton industry.

1968, Oct. 1 Photogravure

Designs (Moths): 30fr, Owlet. 50fr, Saturnid (Gynanisa maja). 100fr, Saturnid (Epiphora bauhiniae).

159	A40	25fr multi	30	15
160	A40	30fr multi	40	20
161	A40	50fr multi	70	35
162	A40	100fr multi	1.25	50

Rock Paintings Type of 1967

Rock Paintings: 2fr, Archers. 10fr, Costumes (4 women, 1 man). 20fr, Funeral vigil. 25fr, Dispute.

1968, Nov. 19 Engraved *Perf. 13*

Size: 36x22mm.

163	A32	2fr scar, sal & brn	6	5
164	A32	10fr pur, sal & dk red	15	6
165	A32	20fr grn, sal & mar	30	15
166	A32	25fr bl, sal & mar	40	20

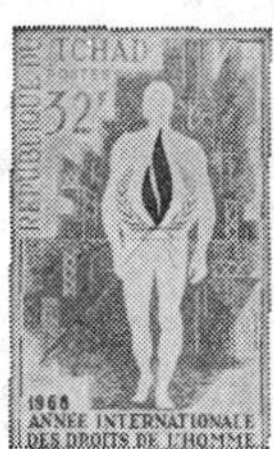

Man and Human Rights Flame
A41

St. Paul
A42

1968, Dec. 10 Engraved *Perf. 13*

167	A41	32fr grn, brt bl & red	50	30

International Human Rights Year.

1969, May 6 Litho. *Perf. 12½x13*

Apostles: 1fr, St. Peter. 2fr, St. Thomas. 5fr, St. John the Evangelist. 10fr, St. Bartholomew. 20fr, St. Matthew. 25fr, St. James the Less. 30fr, St. Andrew. 40fr, St. Jude. 50fr, St. James the Greater. 85fr, St. Philip. 100fr, St. Simon.

168	A42	50c multi	5	5
169	A42	1fr multi	5	5
170	A42	2fr multi	5	5
171	A42	5fr multi	8	5
172	A42	10fr multi	15	8
173	A42	20fr multi	28	15

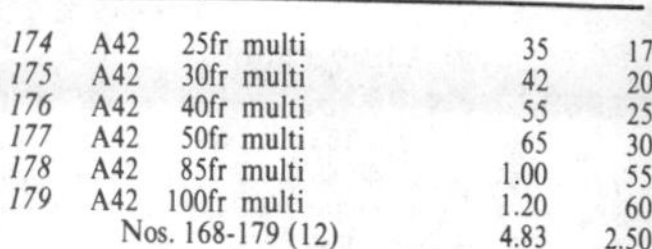

174	A42	25fr multi	35	17
175	A42	30fr multi	42	20
176	A42	40fr multi	55	25
177	A42	50fr multi	65	30
178	A42	85fr multi	1.00	55
179	A42	100fr multi	1.20	60
		Nos. 168-179 (12)	4.83	2.50

Issued to commemorate the Jubilee Year of the Catholic Church in Chad. Nos. 168–179 printed se-tenant in sheets of 12 (4x3).

Tractors and Trucks
A43

1969, June 19 Engraved *Perf. 13*

180	A43	32fr grn, red brn & ind	40	25

Issued to commemorate the 50th anniversary of the International Labor Organization.

Deborah Meyer, U.S., 200 Meter Freestyle
A44

Woman with Flowers, by Veneto
A45

Winners of 1968 Olympic Games: No. 182, Roland Matthes, East Germany, 100 meter backstroke. No. 183, Klaus DiBiasi, Italy, springboard diving. No. 184, Bruno Cipolla, Primo Baran and Renzo Sambo, Italy, pair with coxswain. No. 185, Annemarie Zimmermann and Rosewitha Esser, West Germany, women's kayak tandem. No. 186, Sailing, Great Britain. No. 187, Pierre Trentin, France, 1000 meter bicycling. No. 188, Pier Franco Vianelli, Italy, 196 kilometer bicycle road race. No. 189, Daniel Morelon and Pierre Trentin, France, tandem. No. 190, Daniel R. Rebillard, France, 4000 meter pursuit (bicycle). No. 191, Ingrid Becker, West Germany, pentathlon. No. 192, Jean J. Guyon, France, equestrian. No. 193, Olympic dressage team, West Germany. No. 194, Bernd Klinger, West Germany, small bore rifle. No. 195, Manfred Wolke, East Germany, welterweight. No. 196, Randy Matson, U.S., shot put. No. 197, Colette Besson, France, 400 meter run. No. 198, Mohammed Gammoudi, Tunisia, 5,000 meter run. No. 199, Tommie Smith, U.S., 200 meter run. No. 200, David Hemery, Great Britain, 200 meter hurdles. No. 201, Willie Davenport, U.S., 110 meter hurdles. No. 202, Bob Beamon, U.S., broad jump. No. 203, Sawao Kato, Japan, all around gymnastics. No. 204, Dick Fosbury, U.S., high jump.

Paintings: No. 206, Holy Family, by Murillo (horiz.). No. 207, Adoration of the Kings, by Rubens. No. 208, Portrait of an African Woman, by Bezombes. No. 209, Three Negroes, by Rubens. No. 210, Mother and Child, by Gauguin.

Lithographed

1969, June 30 ***Perf. 12½x13***

Multicolored

No.	Type	Description	Unused	Used
181	A44	1fr *Meyer*	35	35
182	A44	1fr *Matthes*	35	35
183	A44	1fr *DiBiasi*	35	35
184	A44	1fr *Cipolla, Baran & Sambo*	35	35
185	A44	1fr *Zimmermann & Esser*	35	35
186	A44	1fr *Sailing, Great Britain*	35	35
187	A44	1fr *Trentin*	35	35
188	A44	1fr *Vianelli*	35	35
189	A44	1fr *Morelon & Trentin*	35	35
190	A44	1fr *Rebillard*	35	35
191	A44	1fr *Becker*	35	35
192	A44	1fr *Guyon*	35	35
193	A44	1fr *Dressage, Germ.*	35	35
194	A44	1fr *Klinger*	35	35
195	A44	1fr *Wolke*	35	35
196	A44	1fr *Matson*	35	35
197	A44	1fr *Besson*	35	35
198	A44	1fr *Gammoudi*	35	35
199	A44	1fr *Smith*	35	35
200	A44	1fr *Hemery*	35	35
201	A44	1fr *Davenport*	35	35
202	A44	1fr *Beamon*	35	35
203	A44	1fr *Kato*	35	35
204	A44	1fr *Fosbury*	35	35

Perf. 12½x13, 13x12½

No.	Type	Description	Unused	Used
205	A45	1fr *Veneto*	35	35
206	A45	1fr *Murillo*	35	35
207	A45	1fr *Rubens*	35	35
208	A45	1fr *Bezombes*	35	35
209	A45	1fr *Rubens*	35	35
210	A45	1fr *Gauguin*	35	35
		Nos. 181-210 (30)	10.50	10.50

Issued to stress the brotherhood of mankind.

Cochlospermum Tinctorium A46

Flowers: 4fr, Parkia biglobosa. 10fr, Pancratium trianthum. 15fr, Morning glory.

1969, July 8 **Photo.** ***Perf. 12½x13***

No.	Type	Description	Unused	Used
211	A46	1fr pink, yel & blk	5	5
212	A46	4fr dk grn, yel & red	5	5
213	A46	10fr dk grn, yel & gray	15	8
214	A46	15fr vio bl & multi	20	10

Meat Freezer, Farcha A47

Design: 30fr, Cattle at Farcha slaughter-house.

1969, Aug. 19 **Engraved** ***Perf. 13***

No.	Type	Description	Unused	Used
215	A47	25fr sl grn, ocher & red brn	32	18
216	A47	30fr red brn, sl grn & gray	38	25

Economic development in Chad.

Development Bank Issue

Common Design Type

1969, Sept. 10

No.	Type	Description	Unused	Used
217	CD130	30fr dl red, grn & ocher	40	20

Issued to commemorate the 5th anniversary of the African Development Bank.

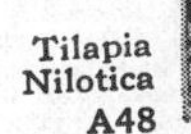

Tilapia Nilotica A48

Fish: 3fr, Citharinus latus. 5fr, Tetraodon fahaka strigosus. 20fr, Hydrocyon forskali.

1969, Nov. 25 **Engraved** ***Perf. 13***

No.	Type	Description	Unused	Used
218	A48	2fr choc, grn & gray	5	5
219	A48	3fr gray, red & bl	8	5
220	A48	5fr ocher, blk & yel	10	8
221	A48	20fr blk, red & grn	32	18

ASECNA Issue

Common Design Type

1969, Dec. 12 **Engraved** ***Perf. 13***

No.	Type	Description	Unused	Used
222	CD132	30fr orange	30	15

Pres. François Tombalbaye A49

Lenin A50

1970, Jan. 11 **Litho.** ***Perf. 14***

No.	Type	Description	Unused	Used
223	A49	25fr multi	38	20

1970, Apr. 22 **Photo.** ***Perf. 11½***

No.	Type	Description	Unused	Used
224	A50	150fr gold, blk & buff	1.85	1.00

Issued to commemorate the centenary of the birth of Lenin (1870–1924), Russian communist leader.

U.P.U. Headquarters Issue

Common Design Type

1970, May 20 **Engraved** ***Perf. 13***

No.	Type	Description	Unused	Used
225	CD133	30fr dk red, pur & brn	40	12

Adult Education Class and U.N. Emblem A52

1970, June 16 **Litho.** ***Perf. 14***

No.	Type	Description	Unused	Used
226	A52	100fr bl & multi	1.20	30

Issued for International Education Year.

Bull's Head, Symbols of Weather and Agriculture—A53

Ahmed Mangue A54

1970, July 22 **Engr.** ***Perf. 13***

No.	Type	Description	Unused	Used
227	A53	50fr org, gray & grn	55	15

Issued for World Meteorological Day.

Lithographed and Engraved

1970, Sept. 15 ***Perf. 13***

No.	Type	Description	Unused	Used
228	A54	100fr gold, car & blk	1.10	25

Issued in memory of Ahmed Mangue, Minister of Education.

Tanner A55

Designs: 2fr, Cloth dyer (vert.). 3fr, Camel turning oil press (horiz.). 4fr, Water carrier. 5fr, Copper worker (horiz.).

1970, Oct. 10 **Engraved** ***Perf. 13***

No.	Type	Description	Unused	Used
229	A55	1fr ol brn, bl & brn	5	5
230	A55	2fr dk brn, ol & ind	5	5
231	A55	3fr pur, ol brn & rose car	5	5
232	A55	4fr choc, lem & bl grn	6	6
233	A55	5fr red, choc & sl grn	5	5
		Nos. 229-233 (5)	26	26

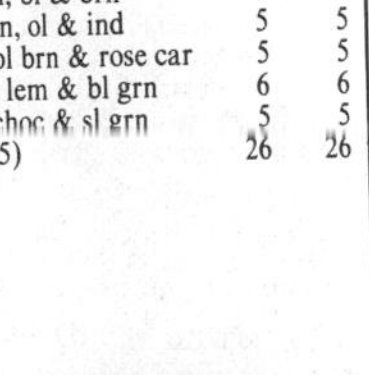

U.N. Emblem, Grain and Dove A56

1970, Oct. 24 **Photo.** ***Perf. 12x12½***

No.	Type	Description	Unused	Used
234	A56	32fr dk bl & multi	40	25

25th anniversary of United Nations.

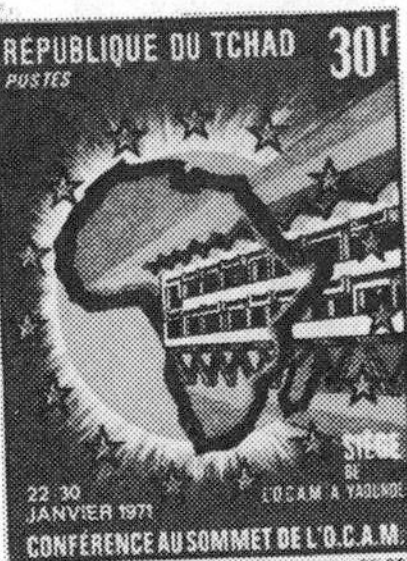

OCAM Headquarters, Map of Africa, Stars A57

1971, Jan. 23 **Photo.** ***Perf. 12½x12***

No.	Type	Description	Unused	Used
235	A57	30fr dk grn & multi	40	25

OCAM (Organisation Commune Africaine, Malgache et Mauricienne) Summit Conference, N'djamena, Jan. 22–30.

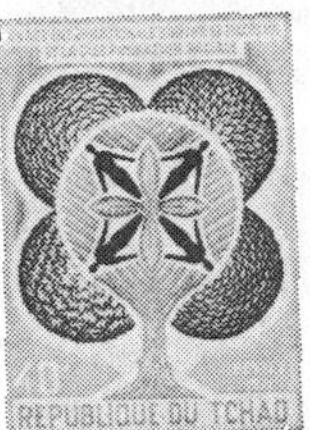

Symbolic Tree A58

1971, March 21 **Engraved** ***Perf. 13***

No.	Type	Description	Unused	Used
236	A58	40fr bl grn, dk red & grn	50	25

International year against racial discrimination.

Map of Africa, Radar Antenna A59

Designs (Map of Africa and): 40fr, Communications tower. 50fr, Communications satellite.

1971, May 17 **Engraved** ***Perf. 13***

No.	Type	Description	Unused	Used
237	A59	5fr ultra, org & dk red	10	8
238	A59	40fr pur, emer & brn	40	20
239	A59	50fr dk red, blk & brn	60	30

3rd World Telecommunications Day.

UNICEF Emblem and Children A60

1971, Dec. 11

No.	Type	Description	Unused	Used
240	A60	50fr Prus bl, emer & brt pink	60	30

25th anniversary of the United Nations International Children's Fund (UNICEF).

Gorane Nangara Dancers A61

Dancers: 15fr, Girls' initiation dance, Yondo. 30fr, Women of M'Boum (vert.). 40fr, Men of Sara Kaba (vert.).

1971, Dec. 18 **Litho.** ***Perf. 13***

No.	Type	Description	Unused	Used
241	A61	10fr blk & multi	15	5
242	A61	15fr brn org & multi	25	8
243	A61	30fr bl & multi	50	15
244	A61	40fr yel grn & multi	65	18

Presidents Pompidou and Tombalbaye, Map with Paris and Fort Lamy—A62

1972, Jan. 25 **Photo.** ***Perf. 13***

No.	Type	Description	Unused	Used
245	A62	40fr bl & multi	50	30

Visit of Pres. Georges Pompidou of France, Jan. 1972.

Examination

The Catalogue editors cannot undertake to appraise, identify or pass upon genuineness or condition of stamps.

Canceled-to-order stamps are often from remainders. Most collectors of canceled stamps prefer postally used specimens.

President Tombalbaye A63

1972, Apr. 13 Litho. *Perf. 13*

246	A63	30fr multi	30	15
247	A63	40fr multi	40	20

See Nos. C112-C113.

Downhill Skiing—A64

Designs: 75fr, Women's figure skating. 150fr, Luge.

1972, Apr. 13 *Perf. 13½*

248	A64	25fr multi	25	13
249	A64	75fr multi	75	38
250	A64	150fr multi	1.50	75
		Nos. 248-250, C114-C115 (5)	5.80	2.91

11th Winter Olympic Games, Sapporo, Japan.

Heart A65

Gorrizia Dubiosa A66

1972, Apr. 25 Engraved *Perf. 13*

251	A65	100fr pur, bl & car	1.20	25

"Your heart is your health," World Health Month.

1972, May 6 Photogravure

Insects: 2fr, Spider (argiope sector). 3fr, Silk spider (nephila senegalense). 4fr, Beetle (oryctes boas). 5fr, Dragonfly (hemistigma albipunctata).

252	A66	1fr grn & multi	8	6
253	A66	2fr bl & multi	8	6
254	A66	3fr car rose & multi	8	6
255	A66	4fr yel grn & multi	8	6
256	A66	5fr dp grn & multi	8	6
		Nos. 252-256 (5)	40	30

Scout Greeting—A67

Designs: 70fr, Mountain climbing. 80fr, Canoeing.

1972, May 15

257	A67	30fr multi	30	15
258	A67	70fr multi	70	35
259	A67	80fr multi	80	40
		Nos. 257-259, C118-C119 (5)	4.00	2.25

Scout Jamboree.

Hurdles, Motion and Olympic Emblems A68

Designs (Motion and Olympic Emblems and): 130fr, Gymnast on rings. 150fr, Swimming. 300fr, Bicycling.

1972, June 9 Litho. *Perf. 13½*

260	A68	50fr blk & multi	60	18
261	A68	130fr blk & multi	1.40	38
262	A68	150fr blk & multi	1.80	45

Souvenir Sheet

263	A68	300fr blk & multi	3.50	3.00

20th Olympic Games, Munich, Aug. 26-Sept. 10. No. 263 contains one stamp. Black marginal inscription and multicolored torch. Size: 101x86mm.

Ski Jump, Kasaya, Japan—A69

Designs: 75fr, Cross-country skiing, P. Tyldum, Sweden. 100fr, Figure-skating, pairs, L. Rodnina and A. Ulanov, USSR. 130fr, Men's speed skating, A. Schenk, Netherlands.

1972, June 15 *Perf. 14½*

264	A69	25fr gold & multi	25	13
265	A69	75fr gold & multi	75	38
266	A69	100fr gold & multi	1.00	50
267	A69	130fr gold & multi	1.30	65
		Nos. 264-267, C130-C131, (6)	6.80	3.41

11th Winter Olympic Games, gold-medal winners. Nos. 264-267 exist se-tenant with label showing earth satellite.

TV Tower and Weight-lifting—A70

Designs (TV Tower, Munich and): 40fr, Woman sprinter. 60fr, Soccer goalkeeper.

1972, Aug. 15 Litho. *Perf. 14½*

268	A70	20fr gold & multi	20	10
269	A70	40fr gold & multi	40	20
270	A70	60fr gold & multi	60	30
		Nos. 268-270, C135-C137 (6)	4.90	2.45

20th Summer Olympic Games, Munich. Nos. 268-270 exist se-tenant with label showing arms of Munich.

Dromedary A71

Domestic Animals: 30fr, Horse. 40fr, Dog. 45fr, Goat.

1972, Aug. 29 Engraved *Perf. 13*

271	A71	25fr pur & bis	35	12
272	A71	30fr red lil & ind	40	15
273	A71	40fr emer & lt brn	50	15
274	A71	45fr dk bl & brn	55	20

Tobacco Cultivation A72

Design: 50fr, Plowing.

1972, Oct. 24 Engraved *Perf. 13*

275	A72	40fr dk brn, dk car & sl grn	40	20
276	A72	50fr ultra, brn & sl grn	50	25

Massa Warrior A73

Design: 20fr, Moundang warrior.

1972, Nov. 15 Photo. *Perf. 14x13*

277	A73	15fr org & multi	25	20
278	A73	20fr yel & multi	30	25

King Faisal and Pres. Tombalbaye A74

1972, Nov. 17 Litho. *Perf. 13*

279	A74	100fr gold & multi	1.00	60

Visit of King Faisal of Saudi Arabia. See No. C143.

Gen. Gowon and Pres. Tombalbaye A75

1972, Dec. 7

280	A75	70fr multi	75	40

Visit of Gen. Yakubu Gowon of Nigeria.

Olympic Emblem and 100-meter Sprint, Valeri Borzov, USSR—A76

Designs (Olympic Emblem and): 20fr, Shotput, Komar, Poland. 40fr, Hammer throw, Bondartchuk, USSR. 60fr, Discus, Danek, Czechoslovakia.

1972, Dec. 22 *Perf. 11*

281	A76	10fr multi	10	5
282	A76	20fr multi	20	10
283	A76	40fr multi	40	20
284	A76	60fr multi	60	30
		Nos. 281-284, C148-C149 (6)	5.30	2.65

20th Summer Olympic Games, winners.

Olympic Emblem and Fencing, Woyda, Poland—A77

Designs (Olympic Emblem and): 30fr, 3-day equestrian event, Richard Meade, Gt. Britain. 50fr, Two-man sculls, Brietzke-Mager, East Germany.

1972, Dec. 22

285	A77	20fr gold & multi	20	10
286	A77	30fr gold & multi	30	15
287	A77	50fr gold & multi	50	25
		Nos. 285-287, C151-C152 (5)	5.00	2.50

20th Summer Olympic Games, winners.

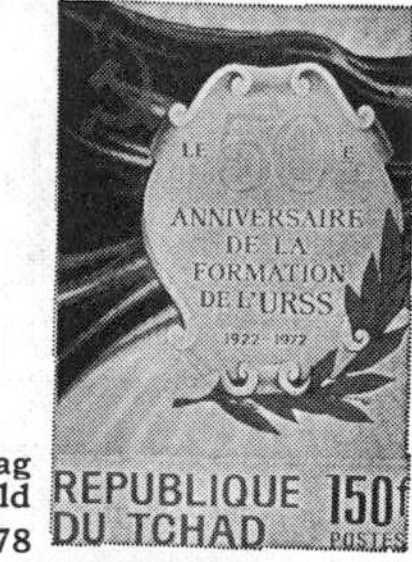

Soviet Flag and Shield A78

1972, Dec. 30 Lithographed *Perf. 12*

288	A78	150fr red & multi	1.35	65

50th anniversary of the Soviet Union.

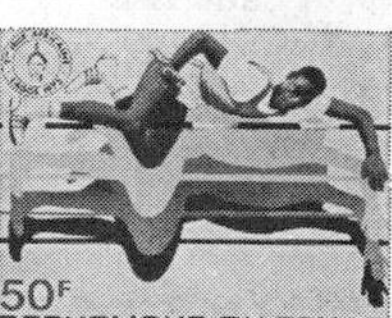

High Jump A79

Designs (Games Emblem and): 125fr, Running. 200fr, Shot put. 250fr, Discus.

1973, Jan. 17 Litho. *Perf. 13½x13*

289	A79	50fr vio bl & multi	50	22
290	A79	125fr ol & multi	1.20	60
291	A79	200fr lil & multi	2.00	1.00

Souvenir Sheet

292 A79 250fr brn & multi 3.00 3.00

2nd African Games, Lagos, Nigeria, Jan. 7-18. No. 292 contains one stamp. Ultramarine margin with inscription and black Games emblems. Size: 101½x 85mm.

No. 271 Surcharged with New Value, 2 Bars, and Overprinted In Red: "SECHERESSE SOLIDARITE AFRICAINE"

1973, Aug. 16 Engr. *Perf. 13*

293 A71 100fr on 25fr multi 1.00 65

African solidarity in drought emergency.

African Postal Union Issue
Common Design Type

1973, Sept. 17 Engraved *Perf. 13*

294 CD137 100fr cl, sl grn & brn ol 1.00 60

Dinothrombium Tinctorium
A80

Rotary Emblem
A81

1974, Sept. 3 Photogravure *Perf. 13*
Multicolored

295	A80	25fr *shown*	22	12
296	A80	30fr *Bupreste sternocera*	25	15
297	A80	40fr *Diptere hyperechia*	35	20
298	A80	50fr *Chrysis*	45	27
299	A80	100fr *Longicorn beetle*	85	40
300	A80	130fr *Spider*	1.10	50
		Nos. 295-300 (6)	3.22	1.64

1975, Apr. 11 Typo. *Perf. 13*

301 A81 50fr multi 45 25

Rotary International, 70th anniversary.

Craterostigma Plantagineum
A82

Flowers: 10fr, Tapinanthus globiferus. 15fr, Commelina forskalaei (vert.). 20fr, Adenium obesum. 25fr, Yellow hibiscus. 30fr, Red hibiscus. 40fr, Kigelia africana.

1975, Sept. 25 Photo. *Perf. 13*

302	A82	5fr org & multi	5	5
303	A82	10fr gray bl & multi	8	5
304	A82	15fr yel grn & multi	13	8
305	A82	20fr lt brn & multi	17	10
306	A82	25fr lil & multi	20	12
307	A82	30fr bis & multi	25	13
308	A82	40fr ultra & multi	32	18
		Nos. 302-308 (7)	1.20	71

A. G. Bell, Satellite and Waves
A83

1976, June 10 Litho. *Perf. 12½*

309	A83	100fr bl, brn & ocher	80	50
310	A83	125fr lt grn, brn & ocher	1.00	60

Centenary of first telephone call by Alexander Graham Bell, Mar. 10, 1876.

Ice Hockey, USSR—A84

Design: 90fr, Ski jump, Karl Schnabl, Austria.

1976, June 21 *Perf. 14*

311	A84	60fr multi	60	30
312	A84	90fr multi	85	35

12th Winter Olympic Games, winners. See Nos. C178-C180.

High Hurdles—A85

1976, July 12 Litho. *Perf. 13½*

313 A85 45fr multi 45 25

21st Summer Olympic Games, Montreal, Canada.
See Nos. C187—C190.

Mars Landing and Viking Rocket
A86

Design (Mars Landing and): 90fr, Viking trajectory, Earth to Mars.

1976, July 23 *Perf. 14*

314	A86	45fr multi	42	25
315	A86	90fr multi	85	42
		Nos. 314-315, C191-C193 (5)	6.52	2.97

Viking Mars project.

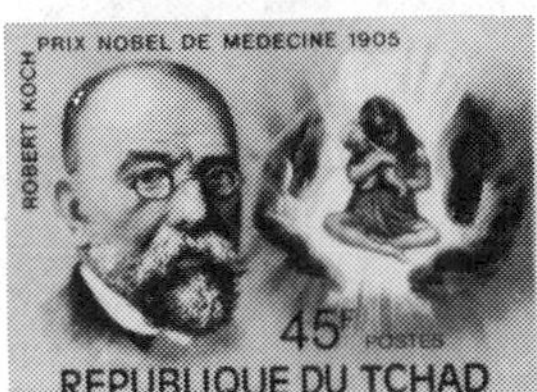

Robert Koch, Medicine—A87

Design: 90fr, Anatole France, literature.

1976, Dec. 15

316	A87	45fr multi	50	25
317	A87	90fr multi	85	42
		Nos. 316-317, C196-C198 (5)	7.05	3.12

Nobel Prize winners.

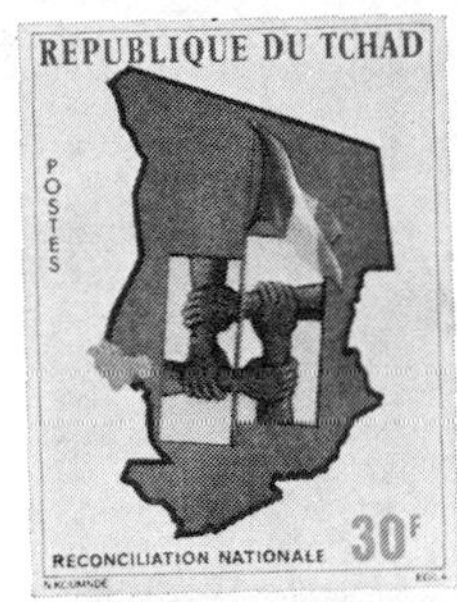

Map and Flag of Chad, Clasped Hands
A88

Designs: 60fr, like 30fr. 120fr, Map of Chad, people and various occupations.

1976, Sept. 15 Litho. *Perf. 12½x13*

318	A88	30fr multi	25	18
319	A88	60fr org & multi	50	30
320	A88	120fr brn & multi	1.00	65

National reconciliation.

Freed Political Prisoners—A89

Designs: 60fr, Parade of cadets. 120fr, like 30fr.

1976, Sept. 25 Litho. *Perf. 12½*

321	A89	30fr bl & multi	25	18
322	A89	60fr blk & multi	50	30
323	A89	120fr red & multi	1.00	65

Revolution of Apr. 13, 1975, first anniversary.

Decorated Calabashes—A90

Designs: Various pyrographed calabashes.

1976, Nov. Litho. *Perf. 12½x13*

324	A90	30fr multi	25	18
325	A90	60fr multi	50	30
326	A90	120fr multi	1.00	65

Germany No. C57 and Friedrichshafen, Germany—A91

1977, Mar. 30 *Perf. 14*

327	A91	100fr multi	95	42
		Nos. 327, C206-C209 (5)	7.20	3.07

75th anniversary of the Zeppelin.

Elizabeth II in Coronation Regalia and Clergy—A92

Design: 450fr, Elizabeth II and Prince Philip.

1977, June 15 Litho. *Perf. 14x13½*

328 A92 250fr multi 2.35 70

Souvenir Sheet

329 A92 450fr multi 4.25 2.00

25th anniversary of the reign of Elizabeth II. No. 329 has multicolored margin showing Buckingham Palace and heraldic supporters. Size: 110x91mm.

Simon Bolivar—A93

Famous Personalities: 175fr, Joseph J. Roberts. No. 332, Queen Wihelmina of Netherlands. No. 333, Charles de Gaulle. 325fr, King Baudouin and Queen Fabiola of Belgium.

1977, June 15 *Perf. 13½x14*

330	A93	150fr multi	1.40	50
331	A93	175fr multi	1.60	60
332	A93	200fr multi	1.85	65
333	A93	200fr multi	1.85	65
334	A93	325fr multi	3.25	1.00
		Nos. 330-334 (5)	9.95	3.40

Post and Telecommunications Emblem—A94

Map of Chad and Waves
A95

Society Emblem
A96

Perf. 13 (A94); 12½ (A95); 13½x13 (A96)

1977, Aug. 15 Lithographed

335	A94	30fr yel & blk	25	18
336	A95	60fr multi	50	30
337	A96	120fr multi	1.00	65

Telecommunications (30fr); National Telecommunications School, 10th anniversary (60fr); International Telecommunication Society of Chad (120fr).

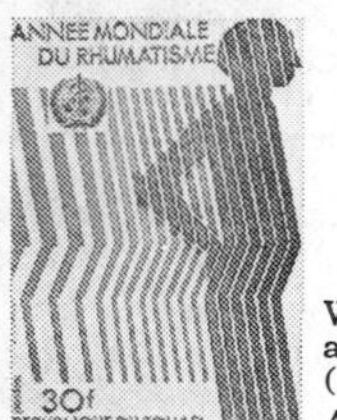

WHO Emblem and Man (Back Pain)
A97

Designs (WHO Emblem and): 60fr, Woman's head (neck pain; horiz.). 120fr, Leg (knee pain).

Perf. 12½x13, 13x12½

1977, Nov. 10 Engraved

338	A97	30fr multi	25	18
339	A97	60fr multi	50	30
340	A97	120fr multi	1.00	65

World Rheumatism Year.

World Cup Emblems and Saving a Goal—A98

Designs (Argentina '78, World Cup Emblems and): 60fr, Heading the ball. 100fr, Referee whistling a goal. 200fr, World Cup poster. 300fr, Pelé. 500fr, Helmut Schoen and Munich stadium.

1977, Nov. 25 Litho. ***Perf. 13½***

341	A98	40fr multi	35	15
342	A98	60fr multi	60	27
343	A98	100fr multi	95	42
344	A98	200fr multi	1.90	75
345	A98	300fr multi	3.00	1.15
		Nos. 341-345 (5)	6.80	2.74

Souvenir Sheet

346	A98	500fr multi	4.75	1.85

World Cup Soccer Championship, Argentina '78. No. 346 has multicolored margin showing Argentina '78 emblem and stadium. Size: 119x80½mm.

Nos. 328–329 Overprinted in Silver: "ANNIVERSAIRE DU COURONNEMENT 1953–1978"

1978, Sept. 13 ***Perf. 14x13½***

347	A92	250fr multi	2.00	1.00

Souvenir Sheet

348	A92	450fr multi	4.00	2.00

25th anniversary of coronation of Queen Elizabeth II. Size of No. 348: 111x92mm.

Abraham and Melchisedek, by Rubens—A99

Rubens Paintings: 120fr, Helene Fourment (vert.). 200fr, David and the Elders of Israel. 300fr, Anne of Austria (vert.). 500fr, Marie de Medicis (vert.).

1978, Nov. 23 Litho. ***Perf. 13½***

349	A99	60fr multi	60	30
350	A99	120fr multi	1.20	60
351	A99	200fr multi	2.00	1.00
352	A99	300fr multi	3.00	1.50

Souvenir Sheet

353	A99	500fr multi	5.50	2.75

Peter Paul Rubens (1577–1640). No. 353 has multicolored margin showing entire painting. Size: 78x103mm.

Dürer Portrait
A100

Dürer Paintings: 150fr, Jacob Muffel. 250fr, Young Woman. 350fr, Oswolt Krel.

1978, Nov. 23

354	A100	60fr multi	60	30
355	A100	150fr multi	1.50	75
356	A100	250fr multi	2.50	1.25
357	A100	350fr multi	3.50	1.75

Albrecht Dürer (1471–1528), German painter.

Head, Village and Fly
A101

1978, Nov. 28 ***Perf. 13***

358	A101	60f multi	60	30

National Health Day.

Nos. 341–346 Overprinted in Silver:

a. 1962 BRESIL–TCHECOSLOVAQUIE / 3–1
b. 1966 / GRANDE BRETAGNE / – ALLEMAGNE (RFA) / 4–2
c. 1970 BRESIL–ITALIE 4–1
d. 1974 ALLEMAGNE (RFA)– / PAY BAS 2–1
e. 1978 / ARGENTINE –/ PAY BAS / 3–1
f. ARGENTINE –PAYS BAS / 3–1

1978, Dec. 30 Litho. ***Perf. 13½***

359	A98(a)	40fr multi	40	20
360	A98(b)	60fr multi	60	30
361	A98(c)	100fr multi	1.00	50
362	A98(d)	200fr multi	2.00	1.00
363	A98(e)	300fr multi	3.00	1.50
		Nos. 359-363 (5)	7.00	3.50

Souvenir Sheet

364	A98(f)	500fr multi	5.00	2.50

World Soccer Championship winners. Size of No. 364: 119x80½mm.

UPU Emblems, Camel Caravan, Satellites—A102

Design: 150fr, Obus woman and houses, Massa Territory, hibiscus.

1979, June 8 Litho. ***Perf. 12x12½***

365	A102	60fr multi	60	30
366	A102	150fr multi	1.50	75

Philexafrique II, Libreville, Gabon, June 8–17. Nos. 365, 366 each printed in sheets of 10 with 5 labels showing exhibition emblem.

Wildlife Fund Emblem and Gazelle
A103

Protected Animals: 50fr, Addax. 60fr, Oryx antelope. 100fr, Cheetah. 150fr, Zebra. 300fr, Rhinoceros.

1979, Sept. 15 Litho. ***Perf. 14½***

367	A103	40fr multi	40	20
368	A103	50fr multi	50	25
369	A103	60fr multi	60	30
370	A103	100fr multi	1.00	50
371	A103	150fr multi	1.50	75
372	A103	300fr multi	3.00	1.50
		Nos. 367-372 (6)	7.00	3.50

Souvenir Sheet

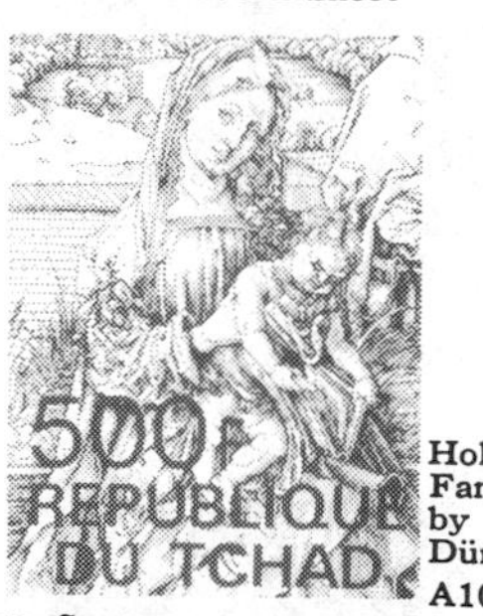

Holy Family, by Dürer
A104

1979, Sept. 1 ***Perf. 13½***

373	A104	500fr brn & dl red	5.50	2.75

Albrecht Dürer (1471–1528), German engraver and painter. No. 373 has brown and dull red margin showing entire etching. Size: 90x115mm.

See "Special Notices" at the front of this volume for data on the listing methods of this Catalogue, abbreviations, condition, prices and examination.

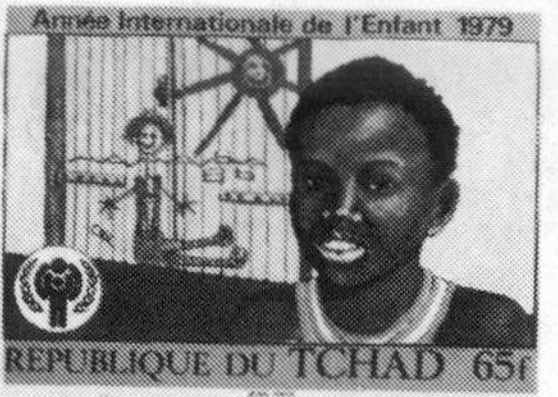

Boy and Handpainted Doors—A105

IYC Emblem and: 75fr, Oriental girl. 100fr, Caucasian girl, doves. 150fr, African boys. 250fr, Pencil and outlines of child's hands.

1979, Sept. 19 Litho. ***Perf. 13½***

374	A105	65fr multi	65	32
375	A105	75fr multi	75	38
376	A105	100fr multi	1.00	50
377	A105	150fr multi	1.50	75

Souvenir Sheet

378	A105	250fr multi	2.75	1.40

International Year of the Child. No. 378 has multicolored margin showing IYC emblem, children and trains. Size: 103x78mm.

Nos. 314-315 Overprinted "ALUNISSAGE/APOLLO XI/ JUILLET 1969" and Emblem

1979, Nov. 26 Litho. ***Perf. 13½×14***

379	A86	45fr multi	45	22
380	A86	90fr multi	90	45
		Nos. 379-380, C240-C242 (5)	6.85	3.42

Apollo 11 moon landing, 10th anniversary.

Ski Jump, Lake Placid '80 Emblem
A106

Lake Placid '80 Emblem and: 20fr, Slalom (vert.). 40fr, Biathlon (vert.). 150fr, Women's slalom (vert.). 350fr, Cross-country skiing. 500fr, Downhill skiing.

1979, Dec. 18 ***Perf. 14½***

381	A106	20fr multi	20	10
382	A106	40fr multi	40	20
383	A106	60fr multi	60	30
384	A106	150fr multi	1.50	75
385	A106	350fr multi	3.50	1.75
386	A106	500fr multi	5.00	2.50
		Nos. 381-386 (6)	11.20	5.60

13th Winter Olympic Games, Lake Placid, N.Y., Feb. 12-24, 1980.

Jet over Map of Africa—A107

1980, Feb. 20 Litho. ***Perf. 12½***

387	A107	15fr yel & multi	15	8
388	A107	30fr bl & multi	30	15
389	A107	60fr red & multi	60	30

ASECNA (Air Safety Board), 20th anniversary.

21st Birthday of Princess Diana—A109

1982, July 2 Litho. *Perf. 13½*

395	A109	30fr 1961	30	15
396	A109	40fr 1965	40	20
397	A109	50fr 1967	50	25
398	A109	60fr 1975	60	30
		Nos. 395-398, C260-C261 (6)	5.60	2.80

1984 Olympic Games, Los Angeles—A110

1982, Aug. 2 Litho. *Perf. 13½*

399	A110	30fr Gymnast	30	15
400	A110	40fr Equestrian	40	20
401	A110	50fr Judeo	50	25
402	A110	60fr High jump	60	30
403	A110	80fr Hurdles	80	40
404	A110	300fr Woman gymnast	3.00	1.50
		Nos. 399-404(6)	5.60	2.80

Souvenir Sheet

405	A110	500fr Relay race	5.00	2.50

No. 405 contains one stamp (56x39mm.); multicolored margin continues design. Size: 110x82mm. Nos. 403-405 airmail.

Scouting Year—A111

Scouts from various countries.

1982, July 15

406	A111	30fr West Germany	30	15
407	A111	40fr Upper Volta	40	20
408	A111	50fr Mali	50	25
409	A111	60fr Scotland	60	30
410	A111	80fr Kuwait	80	40
411	A111	300fr Chad	3.00	1.50
		Nos. 401-411 (6)	5.60	2.80

Souvenir Sheet

412	A111	500fr Chad, diff.	5.00	2.50

No. 412 contains one stamp (53x35mm.); multicolored margin shows banner around globe. Size: 110x75mm. Nos. 410-412 airmail.

Nos. 395-398, C260-C262 Overprinted: "21 JUIN 1982 / WILLIAM ARTHUR PHILIP LOUIS / PRINCE DE GALLES"

1982, Oct. 4 Litho. *Perf. 13½*

413	A109	30fr multi	30	15
414	A109	40fr multi	40	20
415	A109	50fr multi	50	25
416	A109	60fr multi	60	30
417	A109	80fr multi	80	40
418	A109	300fr multi	3.00	1.50
		Nos. 413-418 (6)	5.60	2.80

Souvenir Sheet

419	A109	500fr multi	5.00	2.50

Birth of Prince William of Wales, June 21. Nos. 417-419 airmail.

1982 World Cup—A112

Various players and flags.

1982, Nov. 30

420	A112	30fr multi	30	15
421	A112	40fr multi	40	20
422	A112	50fr multi	50	25
423	A112	60fr multi	60	30
424	A112	80fr multi	80	40
425	A112	300fr multi	3.00	1.50
		Nos. 420-425 (6)	5.60	2.80

Souvenir Sheet

426	A112	500fr multi	5.00	2.50

No. 426 contains one stamp (56x32mm.). Size: 110x80mm. Nos. 424-426 airmail.

Chess Champions—A113

1982, Dec. 24

427	A113	30fr Philidor	30	15
428	A113	40fr Paul Morphy	40	20
429	A113	50fr Howard Staunton	50	25
430	A113	60fr Jean-Paul Capablanca	60	30
431	A113	80fr Boris Spassky	80	40
432	A113	300fr Anatole Karpov	3.00	1.50
		Nos. 427-432 (6)	5.60	2.80

Souvenir Sheet

433	A113	500fr Victor Korchnoi	5.00	2.50

No. 433 contains one stamp (53x35mm.). Size: 98x80mm. Nos. 431-433 airmail.

2nd UN Conference on Peaceful Uses of Outer Space, Vienna, Aug. 9-21—A114

Inventors and Satellites 30fr, K.E. Tsiolkovsky, Soyuz. 40fr, RH Goddard, space telescope design. 50fr, Korolev, ultraviolet telescope. 60fr, von Braun, Columbia space shuttle. 80fr, Esnault Pelterie, Ariana rocket. 300fr, H. Oberth, orbital space station. 500fr, Pres. Kennedy, Apollo 11 badge, lunar rover.

1983, Jan. 31 Litho. *Perf. 13½*

434	A114	30fr multi	30	15
435	A114	40fr multi	40	20
436	A114	50fr multi	50	25
437	A114	60fr multi	60	30
438	A114	80fr multi	80	40
439	A114	300fr multi	3.00	1.50
		Nos. 434-439 (6)	5.60	2.80

Souvenir Sheet

440	A114	500fr multi	5.00	2.50

No. 440 contains one stamp ([illegible]x50mm.); multicolored margin continues design. Size: 85x85mm. Nos. 438-440 airmail.

Bobsledding—A115

1983, Apr. 25 Litho. *Perf. 13½*

441	A115	30fr shown	30	15
442	A115	40fr Speed skating	40	20
443	A115	50fr Cross-country skiing	50	25
444	A115	60fr Hockey	60	30
445	A115	80fr Ski jumping	80	40
446	A115	300fr Downhill skiing	3.00	1.50
		Nos. 441-446 (6)	5.60	2.80

Souvenir Sheet

447	A115	500fr Figure skating	5.00	2.50

14th Winter Olympic Games, Sarajevo, Jugoslavia, Feb. 8-19, 1984. Nos. 445-447 airmail No. 447 has multicolored margin showing figure skating scenes. Size: 100x80mm.

First Manned Balloon Flight, 200th Anniv.—A116

Designs: 25fr, Hot air balloon, Montgolfier Brothers. 45fr, Captive balloon, Pilatre De Rozier. 50fr, First parachute descent, Jacques Garnerin. 60fr, Chelsea balloon, J.P. Blanchard.

1983, May 30 Litho. *Perf. 13½*

448	A116	25fr multi	25	12
449	A116	45fr multi	45	22
450	A116	50fr multi	50	25
451	A116	60fr multi	60	30
		Nos. 448-451, C268-C269 (6)	3.60	1.77

1984 Olympics. Los Angeles—A117

1983, Nov. 15 Litho. *Perf. 13½*

452	A117	25fr Kayak	10	5
453	A117	45fr Long jump	18	10
454	A117	50fr Boxing	20	10
455	A117	60fr Discus	24	12
456	A117	80fr Running	32	16
457	A117	350fr Equestrian	1.40	70
		Nos. 452-457 (6)	2.44	1.23

Souvenir Sheet

458	A117	500fr Gymnastics	2.00	1.00

No. 458 has multicolored margin showing various gymnastics. Size: 90x93mm. 80fr, 350fr, 500fr airmail.

Nos. 427-433 Overprinted: "60e ANNIVERSAIRE FEDERATION / MONDIALE D'ECHECS 1924-1984"

1983, Dec. 27 Litho. *Perf. 13½*

459	A113	30fr multi	12	6
460	A113	40fr multi	16	8
461	A113	50fr multi	20	10
462	A113	60fr multi	24	12
463	A113	80fr multi	32	16
464	A113	300fr multi	1.20	60
		Nos. 459-464 (6)	2.24	1.12

Souvenir Sheet

465	A113	500fr multi	2.00	1.00

World Chess Fedn., 60th anniv.

Nos. 406-412 Ovptd. with Emblem for the 15th World Scout Jamboree, Alberta, Canada, 1983.

1983, Dec. 27 Litho. *Perf. 13½*

466	A111	30fr multi	12	6
467	A111	40fr multi	16	8
468	A111	50fr multi	20	10
469	A111	60fr multi	25	12
470	A111	80fr multi	32	16
471	A111	300fr multi	1.25	62
		Nos. 466-471 (6)	2.30	1.14

Souvenir Sheet

472	A111	500fr multi	2.25	1.10

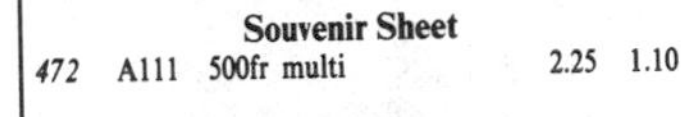

Locomotive "Lady," 1879—A118

1984, Mar. 15

473	A118	50fr shown	20	10
474	A118	200fr Sailboat, Lake Chad	80	40
475	A118	300fr Graf Zeppelin	1.20	60
476	A118	350fr Renault desert transport, 1930	1.40	70
477	A118	400fr Bloch 120 monoplane	1.60	80
478	A118	500fr Air Africa DC-8	2.00	1.00
		Nos. 473-478 (6)	7.20	3.60

Souvenir Sheet

479	A118	600fr Intelsat V satellite	2.50	1.25

Nos. 477-479 airmail. No. 479 has multicolored margin continuing design. Size: 85x110mm.

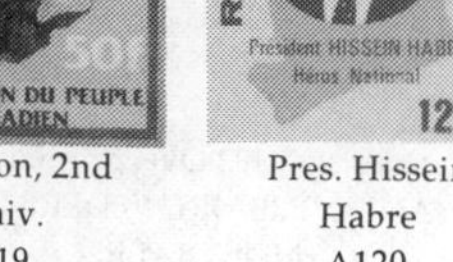

Liberation, 2nd Anniv. A119

Pres. Hissein Habre A120

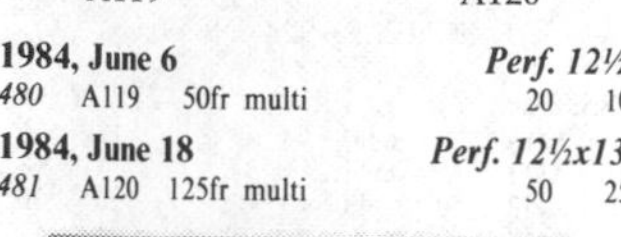

1984, June 6			Perf. 12½		
480	A119	50fr multi		20	10

1984, June 18			Perf. 12½x13		
481	A120	125fr multi		50	25

Anniversaries and Events—A121

Designs: 50fr, Pres. Habre, civil war martyrs. 200fr, Paul Harris, Rotary Intl. headquarters, Illinois. 300fr, Alfred Nobel, will establishing fund for Prizes. 350fr, Raphael, detail from Virgin with Child and St. John the Baptist. 400fr, Rembrandt, detail from The Holy Family. 500fr, J.W. Goethe, scene from Faust. 600fr, Rubens, detail from Helene Forement and Her Two Children.

1984, Jan. 16		Litho.	Perf. 13½	
482	A121	50fr multi	20	10
483	A121	200fr multi	85	42
484	A121	300fr multi	1.25	62
485	A121	350fr multi	1.40	70
486	A121	400fr multi	1.75	85
487	A121	500fr multi	2.25	1.10
		Nos. 482-487 (6)	7.70	3.79

Souvenir Sheet

488	A121	600fr multi	2.75	1.40

Nos. 486-488 are airmail. No. 488 has multicolored margin picturing Rubens painting crucifixion. Size: 79x87mm.

Homage to Our Martyred Dead—A122

1984, Feb. 22		Litho.	Perf. 13½	
500	A122	50fr multi	15	8
501	A122	80fr multi	24	12
502	A122	120fr multi	36	18
503	A122	200fr multi	60	30
504	A122	250fr multi	75	35
		Nos. 500-504 (5)	2.10	1.03

Nos. 503-504 airmail.

World Communications Year—A123

1984, Feb. 29		Litho.	Perf. 13½	
505	A123	50fr sil & multi	15	8
506	A123	60fr sil & multi	18	10
507	A123	70fr sil & multi	22	12
508	A123	125fr sil & multi	38	20
509	A123	250fr sil & multi	75	35
		Nos. 505-509 (5)	1.68	85

Nos. 508-509 airmail.

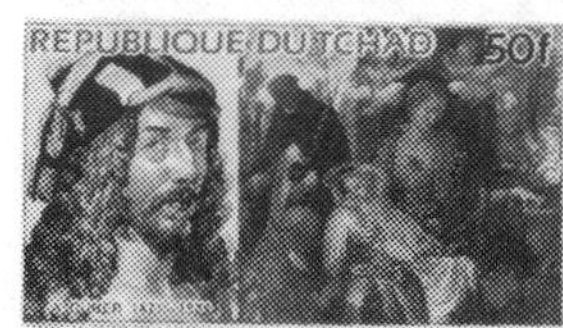

Anniversaries and Events—A123a

Designs: 50fr, Durer, detail from Madonna of the Rosary. 200fr, Henri Dunant, Red Cross founder, Battle of Solferino. 300fr, Early telephone, Goonhilly Downs Satellite Station, Britain. 350fr, J.F. Kennedy, Neil Armstrong's first step on Moon, 1969. 400fr, Europe-Africa Satellite infrared photograph. 500fr, Prince Charles and Lady Diana.

1984				
510	A123a	50fr multi	20	10
511	A123a	200fr multi	85	42
512	A123a	300fr multi	1.25	62
513	A123a	350fr multi	1.40	70
514	A123a	400fr multi	1.75	85
515	A123a	500fr multi	2.25	1.40
a.		Souvenir sheet of one	3.50	1.75
		Nos. 510-515 (6)	7.70	4.09

Nos. 514-515 are airmail. No. 515a has multicolored decorative margin picturing cherubs. Size: 110x60mm. A 600fr souvenir sheet picturing a wedding photograph of Prince Charles and Lady Diana exists.

Development of Communications—A123b

Ships and locomotives.

1984, Aug. 1		Litho.	Perf. 12½	
517	A123b	90fr Indiaman, East India Co.	28	14
518	A123b	100fr Nord 701, 1885	30	15
519	A123b	125fr Vera Cruz	38	20
520	A123b	150fr Columbia, 1888	45	24
521	A123b	200fr Carlisle Castle	60	30
522	A123b	250fr Rete Mediterranea, 1900	75	35
523	A123b	300fr Britannia	90	45
524	A123b	350fr Mav 114	1.05	55
		Nos. 517-524 (8)	4.71	2.38

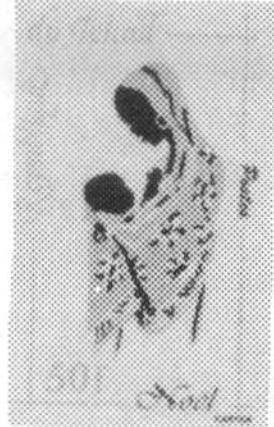

Christmas—A124

1984, Dec. 28		Litho.	Perf. 13	
525	A124	50fr lt bl & org brn	22	12
526	A124	60fr ver & org brn	25	14
527	A124	80fr emer & org brn	34	18
528	A124	85fr rose lil & org brn	35	18
529	A124	100fr org yel & org brn	42	22
530	A124	135fr dp bl vio & org brn	58	30
		Nos. 525-530 (6)	2.16	1.14

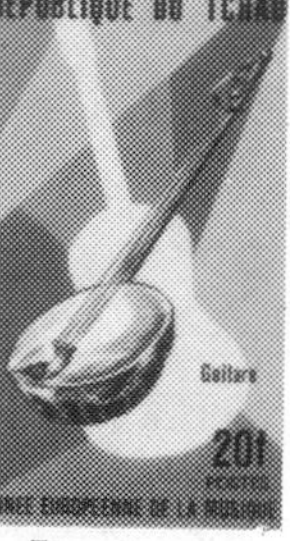

European Music Year A125

Mushrooms A126

Instruments.

1985, Apr. 30		Litho.	Perf. 12x12½	
531	A125	20fr Guitar	6	5
532	A125	25fr Harp	8	5
533	A125	30fr Xylophone	10	5
534	A125	50fr Shoulder drum	15	8
535	A125	70fr like #534	22	12
536	A125	80fr like #532	24	12
537	A125	100fr like #531	30	15
538	A125	250fr like #533	75	35
		Nos. 531-538 (8)	1.90	97

1985, May 15		Litho.	Perf. 12½	
539	A126	25fr Chlorophyllum molybdites	8	5
540	A126	30fr Tulostoma volvulatum	10	5
541	A126	50fr Lentinus tuber-regium	15	8
542	A126	70fr like #541	22	12
543	A126	80fr Podaxis pistillaris	24	12
544	A126	100fr like #539	30	15
		Nos. 539-544 (6)	1.09	57

Anniversaries and Events—A127

Designs: 25fr, Abraham Lincoln. 45fr, Henri Dunant, Geneva birthplace and red cross. 50fr, Gottlieb Daimler, 1887 Motor Carriage. 60fr, Louis Bleriot, Bleriot XI monoplane, 1909. 80fr, Paul Harris, Chicago site of Rotary Intl. founding. 350fr, Auguste Piccard, bathyscaphe Trieste, 1953. 600fr, Anatoly Karpov, 1981 world chess champion. 1500fr, Paul Harris commemorative medal.

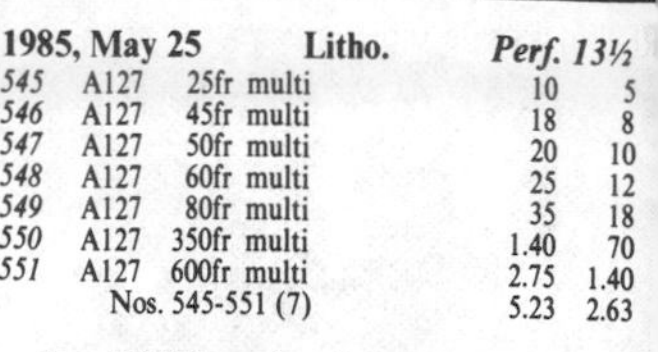

1985, May 25		Litho.	Perf. 13½	
545	A127	25fr multi	10	5
546	A127	45fr multi	18	8
547	A127	50fr multi	20	10
548	A127	60fr multi	25	12
549	A127	80fr multi	35	18
550	A127	350fr multi	1.40	70
551	A127	600fr multi	2.75	1.40
		Nos. 545-551 (7)	5.23	2.63

Nos. 548-551 are airmail.

Souvenir sheets of one exist for Nos. 545-551.

Intl. Youth Year—A128

1985, May 30		Litho.	Perf. 13	
552	A128	70fr Development levels, vert.	22	12
553	A128	200fr Globe	60	30

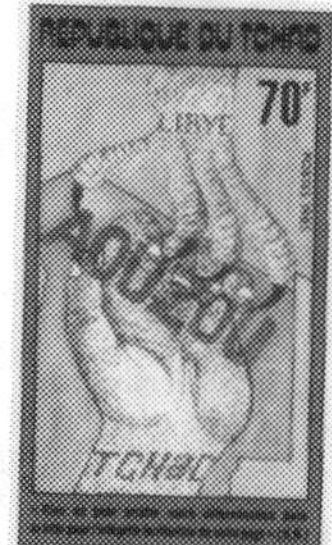

A129

3rd Anniv. of the Republic—A130

1985, June 7		Litho.	Perf. 13, 12½x13	
554	A129	70fr Hand, claw	22	12
555	A129	70fr Hands, map	22	12
556	A130	70fr Pres. Hissein Habre	22	12
557	A129	110fr like #554	35	18
558	A129	110fr like #555	35	18
559	A130	110fr like #556	35	18
		Nos. 554-559 (6)	1.71	90

Audubon Birth Bicent. A131

Mammals A132

1985, July 20		Engr.	Perf. 13	
560	A131	70fr Stork	30	15
561	A131	110fr Ostrich	45	22
562	A131	150fr Marabou	62	30
563	A131	200fr Snake eagle	85	42

Souvenir Sheet

564	A131	500fr like 200fr	2.25	1.10

No. 564 has sepia and olive green margin picturing various species. Size: 130x100mm.

1985, Oct. 1

565	A132	50fr Waterbuck	20	10
566	A132	70fr Kudus, horiz.	58	28
567	A132	250fr Shaggy mouflon	1.10	55

Souvenir Sheet

568	A132	500fr White rhinoceros	2.25	1.10

No. 568 has Prussian blue, henna brown and sepia margin continuing the design. Size: 130x100mm.

UN, 40th Anniv.—A133

1985, Oct. 24

569	A133	200fr brt bl, red & brn	85	42

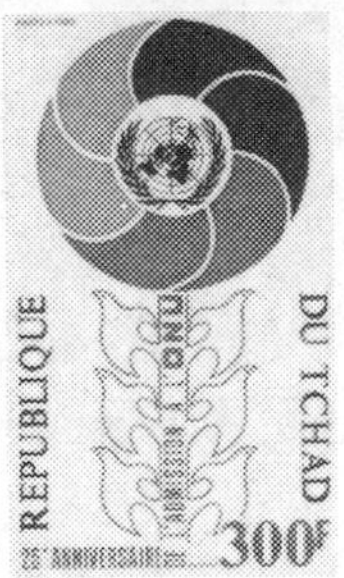

Chad Admission to UN, 25th Anniv.—A134

1985, Oct. 24

570	A134	300fr red, brt bl & yel	1.25	62

President's Visit to the Nation's Interior—A135

1986, June 7		Litho.	Perf. 12½x13	
571	A135	100fr multi	42	20
572	A135	170fr multi	70	35
573	A135	200fr multi	85	42

SEMI-POSTAL STAMPS

Anti-Malaria Issue

Common Design Type

Perf. 12½x12

1962, Apr. 7 Engraved Unwmkd.

B1 CD108 25fr +5fr org 65 65

Issued for the World Health Organization drive to eradicate malaria.

Freedom from Hunger Issue

Common Design Type

1963, Mar. 21 ***Perf. 13***

B2 CD112 25fr +5fr dk grn, dk bl & brn 65 65

Red Cross, Mother and Children
SP1

1974, Oct. 2 Photo. ***Perf. 12½x13***

B3 SP1 30fr +10fr multi 35 30

Red Cross of Chad, first anniversary.

AIR POST STAMPS

Olympic Games Issue

French Equatorial Africa No. C37 Surcharged in Red

XVII° OLYMPIADE 1960 250F REPUBLIQUE DU TCHAD

Engraved

1960, Dec. 15 ***Perf. 13*** **Unwmkd.**

C1 AP8 250fr on 500fr grnsh blk, blk & sl 8.50 8.50

Issued to commemorate the 17th Olympic Games, Rome, Aug. 25–Sept. 11. Surcharge 46mm. wide; illustration reduced.

Red Bishops AP1 Discus Thrower AP2

Designs (birds in pairs): 100fr, Scarlet-chested sunbird. 200fr, African paradise flycatcher. 250fr, Malachite kingfisher. 500fr, Nubian carmine bee-eater.

Engraved

1961-63 ***Perf. 13*** **Unwmkd.**

C2 AP1 50fr dk grn, mag & blk 60 25
C3 AP1 100fr multi 1.50 70
C4 AP1 200fr multi 3.00 1.25
C5 AP1 250fr dk bl, grn & dp org ('63) 4.00 2.00
C6 AP1 500fr multi 8.50 4.00
Nos. C2-C6 (5) 17.60 8.20

Air Afrique Issue

Common Design Type

1962, Feb. 17 ***Perf. 13*** **Unwmkd.**

C7 CD107 25fr lt bl, org brn & blk 40 18

Issued to commemorate the founding of Air Afrique (African Airlines).

Abidjan Games Issue

Photogravure

1962, July 21 ***Perf. 12x12½***

C8 AP2 100fr brn, lt grn & blk 1.50 85

African Postal Union Issue

Common Design Type

1963, Sept. 8 ***Perf. 12½*** **Unwmkd.**

C9 CD114 85fr dk bl, ocher & red 1.00 45

Air Afrique Issue, 1963

Common Design Type

1963, Nov. 19 ***Perf. 13x12***

C10 CD115 50fr multi 90 60

Europafrica Issue

Common Design Type

1963, Nov. 30 Photo. ***Perf. 12x13***

C11 CD116 50fr dp grn, yel & dk brn 75 55

Mail Truck and Broussard Plane
AP4

Engraved

1963, Dec. 16 ***Perf. 13*** **Unwmkd.**

C12 AP4 100fr sl grn, ultra & red brn 1.50 50

Chiefs of State Issue

Map and Presidents of Chad, Congo, Gabon and Central African Republic
AP4a

1964, June 23 Photo. ***Perf. 12½***

C13 AP4a 100fr multi 1.35 65

See note after Central African Republic No. C19.

Europafrica Issue, 1964

Globe and Emblems of Industry and Agriculture—AP5

1964, July 20 ***Perf. 13x12***

C14 AP5 50fr brn, pur & dp org 65 45

See note after Cameroun No. 402.

Soccer—AP6

Designs: 50fr, Javelin throw (vert.). 100fr, High jump (vert.). 200fr, Runners.

1964, Aug. 12 Engr. ***Perf. 13***

C15 AP6 25fr yel grn, sl grn & org brn 35 25
C16 AP6 50fr org brn, ind & brt bl 75 50
C17 AP6 100fr blk, red & brt grn 1.50 1.00
C18 AP6 200fr bis, blk & car 3.00 1.65
a. Min. sheet of 4 6.00 6.00

Issued for the 18th Olympic Games, Tokyo, Oct. 10–25, 1964. No. C18a contains one each of Nos. C15–C18. Size: 191x99mm.

Communications Symbols
AP7

1964, Nov. 2 Litho. ***Perf. 12½x13***

C19 AP7 25fr lil, dk brn & lt red brn 40 20

Issued to commemorate the Pan-African and Malagasy Posts and Telecommunications Congress, Cairo, Oct. 24–Nov. 6.

President John F. Kennedy
AP8

1964, Nov. 3 Photo. ***Perf. 12½***

C20 AP8 100fr multi 1.75 1.25
a. Souv. sheet of 4 7.00 7.00

Issued in memory of Pres. John F. Kennedy (1917–1963). No. C20a contains 4 No. C20; black marginal inscription. Size: 90x129mm.

ICY Emblem
AP9

1965, July 5 Photo. ***Perf. 13***

C21 AP9 100fr multi 1.50 85

International Cooperation Year, 1965.

Abraham Lincoln—AP10

1965, Sept. 7 ***Perf. 13*** **Unwmkd.**

C22 AP10 100fr multi 1.50 85

Centenary of death of Abraham Lincoln.

Musical Instrument Type of Regular Issue

Design: 100fr, Xylophone (marimba).

1965, Oct. 26 Engraved ***Perf. 13***

Size: 48x27mm.

C23 A18 100fr ocher, brt bl & vio bl 1.35 45

Winston Churchill
AP11

1965, Nov. 23 Engraved ***Perf. 13***

C24 AP11 50fr dk grn & blk 75 35

Issued in memory of Sir Winston Spencer Churchill (1874–1965), statesman and World War II leader.

Dr. Albert Schweitzer and Outstretched Hands
AP12

1966, Feb. 15 Photo. ***Perf. 12½***

C25 AP12 100fr multi 1.50 75

Issued in memory of Dr. Albert Schweitzer (1875–1965), medical missionary, theologian and musician.

Air Afrique Issue, 1966

Common Design Type

1966, Aug. 31 Photo. ***Perf. 13***

C26 CD123 30fr yel grn, blk & gray 45 25

Issued to commemorate the introduction of DC-8F planes by Air Afrique.

White-throated Bee-eater—AP13

Birds: 50fr, Blue-eared glossy starling. 200fr, African pygmy kingfisher. 250fr, Red-throated bee-eater. 500fr, Little green bee-eater.

1966–67 Photo. *Perf. 13x12½*

C27	AP13	50fr gold & multi	50	25
C28	AP13	100fr bluish gray & multi	1.00	45
C29	AP13	200fr grnsh gray & multi	2.00	1.00
C30	AP13	250fr pale bl & multi	2.50	1.20
C31	AP13	500fr pale sal & multi	5.00	2.50
		Nos. C27-C31 (5)	11.00	5.40

Issue dates: 100fr, 200fr, 500fr, Oct. 18, 1966. Others, Mar. 21, 1967.

Congress Hall—AP14

1967, Jan. 5 Photo. *Perf. 12½*

C32	AP14	25fr multi	40	20

Opening of the new Congress Hall.

Breguet 19 Biplane—AP15

Planes: 30fr, Latécoère 631 hydroplane. 50fr, Douglas DC-3. 100fr, Piper Cherokee 6.

1967, Aug. 1 Engr. *Perf. 13*

C33	AP15	25fr sky bl, sl grn & lt brn	40	20
C34	AP15	30fr sky bl, ind & grn	45	25
C35	AP15	50fr sky bl, ol bis & sl grn	75	40
C36	AP15	100fr dk bl, sl grn & dk red	1.50	75

First anniversary of Air Chad.

African Postal Union Issue, 1967

Common Design Type

1967, Sept. 9 Engraved *Perf. 13*

C37	CD124	100fr ol, brt pink & red brn	1.35	70

Rock Painting Type of Regular Issue

Rock Paintings: 100fr, Masked dancers. 125fr, Rabbit hunt.

1967, Dec. 19 Engraved *Perf. 13*

Size: 48x27mm.

C38	A32	100fr brt grn, sal & mar	1.50	65
C39	A32	125fr ultra, sal & mar	1.85	90

Issued to commemorate the Balloud expedition in the Ennedi Mountains.

Downhill Skiing—AP16

Design: 100fr, Ski jump (vert.).

1968, Feb. 5 Engraved *Perf. 13*

C40	AP16	30fr red lil, brt grn & dk ol	45	25
C41	AP16	100fr vio bl, brt bl & sl grn	1.50	85

Issued to commemorate the 10th Winter Olympic Games, Grenoble, France, Feb. 6–18.

Konrad Adenauer AP17

1968, Mar. 19 Photo. *Perf. 12½*

C42	AP17	52fr grn, dk brn & lt lil	80	45
a.		Souv. sheet of 4	3.25	3.25

Issued in memory of Konrad Adenauer (1876–1967), chancellor of West Germany (1949–63). No. C42a contains four No. C42. Margin with black inscription and 1967 CEPT (Europa) emblem. Size: 120½x169mm.

The Snake Charmer, by Henri Rousseau—AP18

Design: 130fr, "War" by Henri Rousseau.

1968, May 14 Photo. *Perf. 13½*

Size: 41x41mm.

C43	AP18	100fr ultra & multi	1.50	60

Size: 48x35mm. ***Perf. 12½***

C44	AP18	130fr brn & multi	1.80	80

Hurdlers—AP19

Design: 80fr, Relay race.

1968, Oct. 16 Engraved *Perf. 13*

C45	AP19	32fr cop red, grn & choc	50	20
C46	AP19	80fr ultra, choc & car	1.00	30

Issued to commemorate the 19th Olympic Games, Mexico City, Oct. 12–27.

PHILEXAFRIQUE Issue

The Actor Wolf (Bernard), by Jacques L. David AP20

1969, Jan. 15 Photo. *Perf. 12½*

C47	AP20	100fr multi	1.50	90

Issued to publicize PHILEXAFRIQUE, Philatelic Exhibition in Abidjan, Feb. 14–23. Printed with alternating lilac rose label.

2nd PHILEXAFRIQUE Issue

Common Design Type

Design: 50fr, Chad No. J12 and Moundang Dancers.

1969, Feb. 14 Engraved *Perf. 13*

C48	CD128	50fr red, brt bl, brn & grn	75	50

Issued to commemorate the opening of PHILEXAFRIQUE, Abidjan, Feb. 14.

Gustav Nachtigal and Tibesti Gorge, 1869 AP21

Design: No. C50, Heinrich Barth and Lake Chad, 1851.

1969, Feb. 17

C49	AP21	100fr vio bl, dk brn & brn	1.25	35
C50	AP21	100fr grn, pur & bl	1.25	35

Issued to honor the German explorers Gustav Nachtigal (1834–1885) and Heinrich Barth (1821–1865), and to commemorate the state visit of the President of West Germany Heinrich Lubke.

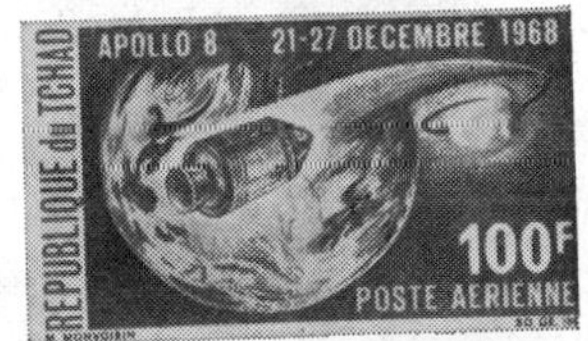

Apollo 8, Earth and Moon AP22

1969, Apr. 10 Photo. *Perf. 13*

C51	AP22	100fr multi	1.25	65

Issued to commemorate the U.S. Apollo 8 mission, the first men in orbit around the moon, Dec. 21–27, 1968.

Mahatma Gandhi AP23

Portraits: No. C53, John F. Kennedy. No. C54, Rev. Dr. Martin Luther King, Jr. No. C55, Robert F. Kennedy.

1969, May 20 Photo. *Perf. 12½*

C52	AP23	50fr blk & lt grn	65	35
C53	AP23	50fr blk & tan	65	35
C54	AP23	50fr blk & pink	65	35
C55	AP23	50fr blk & lt vio bl	65	35
a.		Souv. sheet of 4	3.00	3.00

Issued to honor exponents of non-violence. No. C55a contains one each of Nos. C52–C55. Black marginal inscription. Size: 120x159mm.

Presidents Tombalbaye and Mobutu, Map and Flags of Chad and Congo—AP24

Embossed on Gold Foil

1969 *Die-cut Perf. 13½*

C56	AP24	1000fr gold, dk bl & red	16.00	16.00

Issued to commemorate the first anniversary of the establishment of the Union of Central African States, comprising Chad, Congo Democratic Republic and Central African Republic.

Napoleon Visiting Hospital, by Alexandre Veron-Bellecourt AP25

Paintings: 85fr, Battle of Wagram, by Horace Vernet. 130fr, Battle of Austerlitz, by Francois Pascal Gerard.

1969, July 23 Photo. *Perf. 12x12½*

C57	AP25	30fr multi	60	45
C58	AP25	85fr multi	1.50	1.10
C59	AP25	130fr multi	2.50	1.75

Bicentenary of birth of Napoleon I.

Apollo 11 Issue

Astronaut on Moon—AP26

Embossed on Gold Foil

1969, Oct. 17 *Die-cut Perf. 13½*

C60	AP26	1000fr gold	16.00	16.00

See note after Algeria No. 427.

Village Life, by Goto Narcisse AP27

Designs: No. C62, Women at the Market, by Iba N'Diaye. No. C63, Woman with Flowers, by Iba N'Diaye (vert.).

Perf. 12x12½, 12½x12

1970 Photogravure

C61	AP27	100fr multi	1.10	30
C62	AP27	250fr grn & multi	3.00	70
C63	AP27	250fr brn & multi	3.00	70

Issue dates: Mar. 17, 100fr. Aug. 28, Nos. C62–C63.

EXPO Emblem and Osaka Print
AP28

Designs (EXPO Emblem and): 100fr, Tower of the Sun. 125fr, Osaka print (diff. design).

1970, June 30 Engraved *Perf. 13*

C64	AP28	50fr bl, red brn & sl grn	70	18
C65	AP28	100fr red, yel grn & Prus bl	1.35	28
C66	AP28	125fr blk, dk red & bis	1.60	40

Issued to publicize EXPO '70 International Exhibition, Osaka, Japan, Mar. 15–Sept. 13.

Nos. C28–C30 Surcharged in Carmine with New Value and Bars and Overprinted:
a. "APOLLO XI / 1er débarquement sur la lune / 20 juillet 1969"
b. "APOLLO XII / Exploration de la lune / 19 novembre 1969"
c. "APOLLO XIII / Exploit spatial / 11–17 avril 1970"

1970, July 9 Photo. *Perf. 13x12½*

C67	AP13 (a)	50fr on 100fr multi	65	40
C68	AP13 (b)	100fr on 200fr multi	1.30	60
C69	AP13 (c)	125fr on 250fr multi	1.60	80

Space missions of Apollo 11, 12 and 13.

DC-8 "Fort Lamy" over Airport
AP29

1970, Aug. 5 *Perf. 12½*

C70	AP29	30fr dk sl grn & multi	40	15

The Visitation, Venetian School, 15th Century
AP30

Paintings, Venetian School: 25fr, Nativity, 15th century. 30fr, Virgin and Child, c. 1350.

1970, Dec. 15 Photo. *Perf. 12½x12*

C71	AP30	20fr gold & multi	30	15
C72	AP30	25fr gold & multi	32	20
C73	AP30	30fr gold & multi	40	25

Christmas 1970. See Nos. C105–C108.

Post Office Mauritius and Emblem
AP31

Designs (PHILEXOCAM Emblem and): 20fr, Tuscany No. 23. 30fr, France No. 8. 60fr, United States No. 2. 80fr, Japan No. 8. 100fr, Saxony No. 1.

1971, Jan. 23 Engraved *Perf. 13*

C74	AP31	10fr lt bl grn, bis & dk bl	15	5
C75	AP31	20fr brt grn, blk & bis	25	8
C76	AP31	30fr mar, blk & org brn	40	15
C77	AP31	60fr car lake, org brn & blk	70	25
C78	AP31	80fr bl, bis brn & dl bl	90	38
C79	AP31	100fr bl, dl bl & bis brn	1.35	45
a.		Souvenir sheet of 6	4.00	4.00
		Nos. C74-C79 (6)	3.75	1.36

Publicity for PHILEXOCAM, philatelic exhibition, Fort Lamy, Jan. 23–30. No. C79a contains one each of Nos. C74–C79 with orange brown marginal inscription. Size: 158x130mm.

Gamal Abdel Nasser
AP32

1971, Feb. 16 Photo. *Perf. 12½*

C80	AP32	75fr multi	75	20

In memory of Gamal Abdel Nasser (1918–1970), President of Egypt.

Presidents Mobutu, Bokassa and Tombalbaye—AP33

1971, Apr. 28 Photo. *Perf. 13*

C81	AP33	100fr multi	1.00	50

Return of Central African Republic to the United States of Central Africa which also includes Congo Democratic Republic and Chad.

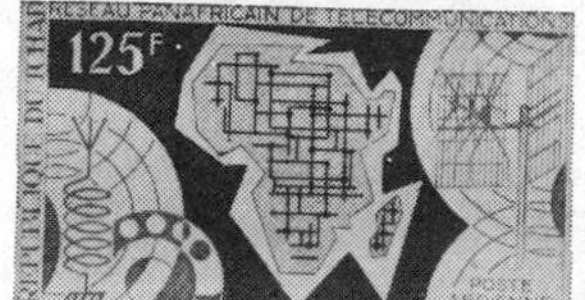

Map of Africa, Communications Network and Symbols—AP34

1971, May 17 Engraved *Perf. 13*

C82	AP34	125fr ultra, sl grn & brn red	1.40	30

Pan-African telecommunications system.

Boys Around Campfire, Torii
AP35

1971, Aug. 24 Photo. *Perf. 12½*

C83	AP35	250fr multi	2.75	85

13th Boy Scout World Jamboree, Asagiri Plain, Japan, Aug. 2–10.

White Egret—AP36

1971, Sept. 28 Photo. *Perf. 13x12½*

C84	AP36	1000fr blk, dk bl & ocher	10.00	7.00

Greek Marathon Runners—AP37

Designs: 45fr, Ancient Olympic Stadium. 75fr, Greek wrestlers. 130fr, Olympic Stadium, Athens, 1896.

1971, Oct. 5 *Perf. 12½*

C85	AP37	40fr multi	50	25
C86	AP37	45fr multi	55	35
C87	AP37	75fr multi	85	40
C88	AP37	130fr multi	1.40	75

75th anniversary of modern Olympic Games.

Duke Ellington
AP38

Portraits: 50fr, Sidney Bechet. 100fr, Louis Armstrong.

1971, Oct. 20 Lithographed *Perf. 13*

C89	AP38	50fr multi	65	18
C90	AP38	75fr lt bl & multi	90	23
C91	AP38	100fr multi	1.25	35

Famous American jazz musicians.

Charles de Gaulle
AP39

Design: No. C93, Félix Eboué.

Lithographed and Embossed

1971, Nov. 9 *Perf. 12½*

C92	AP39	200fr grn, yel grn & gold	3.50	3.50
C93	AP39	200fr bl, lt bl & gold	3.50	3.50
a.		Souvenir sheet of 2	7.50	7.50

First anniversary of the death of Charles de Gaulle (1890–1970), president of France. No. C93a contains one each of Nos. C92–C93 with brown and ocher label carrying commemorative inscription and de Gaulle's signature. Size: 110x70mm.

African Postal Union Issue, 1971

Common Design Type

Design: 100fr, Sao antelope head and UAMPT building, Brazzaville, Congo.

1971, Nov. 13 Photo. *Perf. 13x13½*

C94	CD135	100fr bl & multi	1.10	35

Apollo 15 Rocket
AP40

Designs: 80fr, Apollo 15 capsule (horiz.). 150fr, Lunar module on Moon (horiz.). 250fr, Astronaut making tests. 300fr, Moon-buggy. No. C100, Successful splash-down (horiz.). No. C101, Apollo 15 insignia.

1972, Jan. 5 Litho. *Perf. 13½*

C95	AP40	40fr multi	32	15
C96	AP40	80fr multi	65	33
C97	AP40	150fr multi	1.20	60
C98	AP40	250fr multi	2.00	1.00
C99	AP40	300fr multi	2.40	1.20
C100	AP40	500fr multi	4.00	2.00
		Nos. C95-C100 (6)	10.57	5.28

Souvenir Sheet

C101	AP40	500fr multi	4.00	1.85

Apollo 15 moon landing. No. C101 has multicolored margin with American flag, and portraits of the families of astronauts Scott, Worden and Irwin. Size: 103x84 mm.

Soyuz 2 Link-up—AP41

Designs: 30fr, Soyuz 2 on launching pad (vert.). 50fr, No. C108, Cosmonauts in uniform. 200fr, V. I. Patzaev. No. C106, V. N. Volkov. 400fr, G. L. Dobrovolsky. No. C109, Three cosmonauts.

1972, Jan. 5 *Perf. 13½x13*

C102	AP41	30fr multi	25	13
C103	AP41	50fr multi	40	20
C104	AP41	100fr multi	80	40
C105	AP41	200fr multi	1.60	80
C106	AP41	300fr multi	2.40	1.20
C107	AP41	400fr multi	3.25	1.60
		Nos. C102-C107 (6)	8.70	4.33

Souvenir Sheets

C108	AP41	300fr multi	3.00	1.50
C109	AP41	400fr multi	4.00	2.00

Soyuz 2 link-up project. No. C108 has multicolored margin depicting launching pad, No. C109, Moscow sky-line. Size: 100x79mm.

Bobsledding—AP42

Design: 100fr, Slalom.

1972, Feb. 24 Engraved *Perf. 13*

C110	AP42	50fr Prus bl & rose red	60	20
C111	AP42	100fr red lil & sl grn	1.20	35

11th Winter Olympic Games, Sapporo, Japan, Feb. 3–13.

Pres. Tombalbaye Type, 1972

1972, Apr. 13 Litho. *Perf. 13*

C112	A63	70fr multi	70	35
C113	A63	80fr multi	80	40

11th Winter Olympic Type, 1972

Designs: 130fr, Speed skating. No. C115, Ice hockey. No. C116, Ski jumping. 250fr, 4-man bobsled.

1972, Apr. 13 *Perf. 13½*

C114	A64	130fr multi	1.30	65
C115	A64	200fr multi	2.00	1.00

Souvenir Sheets

C116	A64	200fr multi	2.00	1.00
C117	A64	250fr multi	2.50	1.25

11th Winter Olympic Games, Sapporo, Japan. Nos. C116 and C117 have multicolored margins showing Japanese religious figures. Size: 99x79mm.

Scout Jamboree Type, 1972

Designs: 100fr, Cooking preparation. 120fr, Lord Baden Powell. 250fr, Hiking.

1972, May 15

C118	A67	100fr multi	1.00	60
C119	A67	120fr multi	1.20	75

Souvenir Sheet

C120	A67	250fr multi	2.50	1.50

Scout Jamboree. No. C120 has multicolored margin showing African veldt and ostrich. Size: 102x81mm.

Zebras—AP43

Designs: 30fr, Mandrills. 100fr, African elephants. 130fr, Gazelles. 150fr, Hippopotamuses. 200fr, Lion cub.

1972, May 15 Litho. *Perf. 13*

C121	AP43	20fr multi	20	10
C122	AP43	30fr multi	30	15
C123	AP43	100fr multi	1.00	50
C124	AP43	130fr multi	1.30	65
C125	AP43	150fr multi	1.50	75
		Nos. C121-C125 (5)	4.30	2.15

Souvenir Sheet

C126	AP43	200fr multi	2.00	1.00

African wild animals. No. C126 has multicolored margin showing map of Africa, sun and various animals. Size: 102½x79 mm.

See "Special Notices" at the front of this volume for data on the listing methods of this Catalogue, abbreviations, condition, prices and examination.

View of Venice, by Caffi—AP44

Paintings by Ippolito Caffi: 40fr, Sailing ship and Doge's Palace (vert.). 140fr, Grand Canal (vert.).

1972, May 23 Photo.

C127	AP44	40fr gold & multi	50	15
C128	AP44	45fr gold & multi	60	20
C129	AP44	140fr gold & multi	1.50	1.00

UNESCO campaign to save Venice.

11th Winter Olympic Winners Type, 1972

Designs: 150fr, Slalom, B. Cochran, U.S. 200fr, Women's figure skating, B. Schuba, Austria. 250fr, Ice hockey, USSR. 300fr, 2-man bobsled. W. Zimmerer and P. Utzschneider, West Germany.

1972, June 15 *Perf. 14½*

C130	A69	150fr gold & multi	1.50	75
C131	A69	200fr gold & multi	2.00	1.00

Souvenir Sheets

C132	A69	250fr gold & multi	2.00	1.25
C133	A69	300fr gold & multi	3.00	1.75

11th Winter Olympic gold medal winners. Nos. C130–C131 exist se-tenant with label showing earth satellite. Nos. C132–C133 have multicolored margins showing satellite orbiting earth. Size: 127x89mm.

Daudet, "Tartarin de Tarascon," Book Year Emblem—AP45

1972, July 22 Engraved *Perf. 13*

C134	AP45	100fr dk red, lil & dk brn	1.20	30

International Book Year, 1972, and to honor Alphonse Daudet (1840–1897), French writer.

20th Summer Olympics Type, 1972

Designs (TV Tower, Munich and): 100fr, Gymnast. 120fr, Pole vault. 150fr, Fencing. 250fr, Hammer throw. 300fr, Boxing.

1972, Aug. 15

C135	A70	100fr gold & multi	1.00	50
C136	A70	120fr gold & multi	1.20	60
C137	A70	150fr gold & multi	1.50	75

Souvenir Sheets

C138	A70	250fr gold & multi	2.50	1.25
C139	A70	300fr gold & multi	3.00	1.50

20th Summer Olympic Games, Munich, Nos. C135–C137 exist se-tenant with label showing arms of Munich. Nos. C138–C139 have multicolored margin with Munich views. Size: 127x89mm.

Lunokhod on Moon—AP46

Design: 100fr, Luna 16 on moon and rocket in flight (vert.).

1972, Sept. 19

C140	AP46	100fr dk bl, pur & bis	1.20	50
C141	AP46	150fr sl, brn & lil	1.80	75

Russian moon missions.

Farcha Laboratory, Cattle, Scientist—AP47

1972, Nov. 11 Photo. *Perf. 13*

C142	AP47	75fr yel & multi	70	35

20th anniversary of the Farcha Laboratory for veterinary research.

King Faisal and Holy Kaaba, Mecca—AP48

1972, Nov. 17

C143	AP48	75fr multi	75	40

Visit of King Faisal of Saudi Arabia.

Christmas Type of 1970

Designs: 40fr, Virgin and Child, by Giovanni Bellini. 75fr, Virgin and Child, by Dall'Occhio. 80fr, Nativity, by Fra Angelico (horiz.). 95fr, Adoration of the Kings, by Il Perugino.

1972, Dec. 15 Photo. *Perf. 13*

C144	AP30	40fr gold & multi	50	15
C145	AP30	75fr gold & multi	85	25
C146	AP30	80fr gold & multi	1.00	28
C147	AP30	95fr gold & multi	1.10	38

Christmas 1972.

20th Summer Olympic Winners Type, 1972

Designs (Olympic Emblems and): 150fr, Pole vault, Nordwig, East Germany. 250fr, Hurdles, Milburn, U.S. 300fr, Javelin, Wolfermann, West Germany.

1972, Dec. 22

C148	A76	150fr multi	1.50	75
C149	A76	250fr multi	2.50	1.25

Souvenir Sheet

C150	A76	300fr multi	3.00	1.50

20th Summer Olympic Games winners. No. C150 has multicolored margin showing Olympic emblems. Size: 111½x82 mm.

Summer Olympic Winners Type, 1972

Designs (Olympic Emblem and): 150fr, Dressage, Mancinelli, Italy. No. C152; Finn class sailing, Serge Maury, France. No. C153, Swimming, Mark Spitz.

1972, Dec. 22 Litho. *Perf. 11*

C151	A77	150fr gold & multi	1.50	75
C152	A77	250fr gold & multi	2.50	1.25

Souvenir Sheet

C153	A77	250fr multi	2.50	1.25

20th Summer Olympic Games, winners. No. C153 has gold and multicolored margin showing Olympic emblem and flame. Size: 111x82½mm.

Copernicus and Solar System AP49

1973, Mar. 31 Engraved *Perf. 13*

C154	AP49	250fr gray, mag & brn	2.75	1.50

500th anniversary of the birth of Nicolaus Copernicus (1473–1543), Polish astronomer.

Skylab over Africa—AP50

Design: 150fr, Skylab.

1974, Aug. 6 Engraved *Perf. 13*

C155	AP50	100fr mar, bl & ol	1.00	55
C156	AP50	150fr brn, bl & sl grn	1.40	75

Exploits of Skylab, U.S. manned space station.

Soccer—AP51

Designs: 125fr, 150fr, Soccer players; 125fr, vertical.

1974, Oct. 22 Engraved *Perf. 13*

C157	AP51	50fr dl red & choc	45	25
C158	AP51	125fr red & dp grn	1.10	65
C159	AP51	150fr grn & rose red	1.35	75

World Cup Soccer Championship, Munich, June 13–July 7.

Family and WPY Emblem AP52

1974, Nov. 11

C160 AP52 250fr multi 2.25 1.40

World Population Year.

Mail Delivery by Canoe—AP53

Designs (UPU Emblem and): 40fr, Diesel train. 100fr, Jet. 150fr, Spacecraft.

1974, Dec. 20 Engraved *Perf. 13*

C161 AP53 30fr car & multi 28 18
C162 AP53 40fr ultra & blk 35 20
C163 AP53 100fr brn, ultra & blk 90 55
C164 AP53 150fr grn, lil & ol 1.40 85

Centenary of Universal Postal Union.

Women of Different Races, IWY Emblem—AP54

1975, June 25 Photo. *Perf. 13*

C165 AP54 250fr bl & multi 2.10 1.25

International Women's Year 1975.

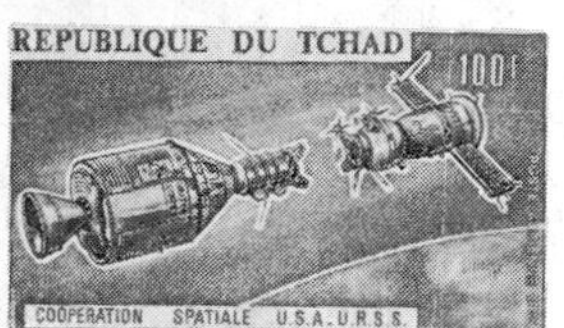

Apollo and Soyuz Before Link-up—AP55

Design: 130fr, Apollo and Soyuz after link-up.

1975, July 15 Engr. *Perf. 13*

C166 AP55 100fr ultra, choc & grn 1.00 50
C167 AP55 130fr vio bl, brn & grn 1.20 75

Apollo Soyuz space test project (Russo-American space cooperation), launching July 15; link-up July 17.

Soccer Player, View of Montreal AP56

Designs (Olympic Rings, Montreal Skyline): 100fr, Discus thrower. 125fr, Runner.

1975, Oct. 14 Engr. *Perf. 13*

C168 AP56 75fr car & sl grn 70 38
C169 AP56 100fr car, choc & bl grn 1.00 50
C170 AP56 125fr brn, bl & car 1.25 75

Pre-Olympic Year 1975.

Nos. C166-C167 Overprinted: "JONCTION / 17 JUILLET 1975"

1975, Nov. 4 Engr. *Perf. 13*

C171 AP55 100fr multi 1.00 50
C172 AP55 130fr multi 1.20 70

Apollo-Soyuz link-up in space, July 17.

Stylized British and American Flags, "200"—AP57

1975, Dec. 5 Engr. *Perf. 13*

C173 AP57 150fr vio bl, car & ol bis 1.35 75

American Bicentennial.

Adoration of the Shepherds, by Murillo—AP58

Paintings: 75fr, Adoration of the Shepherds, by Georges de La Tour. 80fr, Virgin and Child with Bible, by Rogier van der Weyden (vert.). 100fr, Holy Family, by Raphael (vert.).

1975, Dec. 15 Litho. *Perf. 13x12½*

C174 AP58 40fr yel & multi 40 20
C175 AP58 75fr yel & multi 70 38
C176 AP58 80fr yel & multi 80 40
C177 AP58 100fr yel & multi 1.00 45

Christmas 1975.

12th Winter Olympic Winners Type, 1976

Designs: 250fr, 4-man bobsled, West Germany. 300fr, Speed skating, J. E. Storholt, Norway. 500fr, Downhill skiing, F. Klammer, Austria.

1976, June 21 *Perf. 14*

C178 A84 250fr multi 2.40 1.10
C179 A84 300fr multi 2.85 1.35

Souvenir Sheet

C180 A84 500fr multi 4.75 2.00

12th Winter Olympic Games winners, Innsbruck. No. C180 has multicolored margin showing snowflakes. Size: 114x78mm.

Paul Revere's Ride and Portrait by Copley—AP59

Designs: 125fr, George Washington crossing Delaware. 150fr, Lafayette offering his services to America. 200fr, Rochambeau at Yorktown with Washington. 250fr, Benjamin Franklin presenting Declaration of Independence. 400fr, Count de Grasse's victory at Cape Charles.

1976, July 4 Litho. *Perf. 14*

C181 AP59 100fr multi 95 45
C182 AP59 125fr multi 1.20 60
C183 AP59 150fr multi 1.40 70
C184 AP59 200fr multi 1.90 85
C185 AP59 250fr multi 2.50 95
Nos. C181-C185 (5) 7.95 3.55

Souvenir Sheet

C186 AP59 400fr multi 4.00 1.85

American Bicentennial. No. C186 has multicolored margin showing George Washington and his staff. Size: 113x78mm.

Summer Olympics Type, 1976

Designs: 100fr, Boxing. 200fr, Pole vault. 300fr, Shot put. 500fr, Sprint.

1976, July 12

C187 A85 100fr multi 90 50
C188 A85 200fr multi 1.85 85
C189 A85 300fr multi 2.75 1.10

Souvenir Sheet

C190 A85 500fr multi 4.00 2.00

21st Summer Olympic Games, Montreal. No. C190 has multicolored margin showing Olympic stadium. Size: 103x77mm.

Viking Mars Project Type, 1976

Designs (Mars Lander and): 100fr, Viking landing on Mars. 200fr, Capsule over Mars. 250fr, Lander over Mars. 450fr, Lander and probe.

1976, July 23 Litho. *Perf. 14*

C191 A86 100fr multi 95 50
C192 A86 200fr multi 1.90 85
C193 A86 250fr multi 2.40 95

Souvenir Sheet

C194 A86 450fr multi 4.25 2.00

Viking Mars project, No. C194 has multicolored margin showing Viking probe. Size: 114x89mm.

Concorde—AP60

1976, Oct. 15 Litho. *Perf. 12½*

C195 AP60 250fr bl, blk & ver 2.00 75

First commercial flight of supersonic jet Concorde, Jan. 21.

Nobel Prize Type, 1976

Designs: 100fr, Albert Einstein, physics. 200fr, Dag Hammarskjold, peace. 300fr, Shinichiro Tomanaga, physics. 500fr, Alexander Fleming, medicine.

1976, Dec. 15

C196 A87 100fr multi 95 50
C197 A87 200fr multi 1.90 85
C198 A87 300fr multi 2.85 1.10

Souvenir Sheet

C199 A87 500fr multi 4.75 2.00

Nobel Prize winners. No. C199 has multicolored margin showing reverse and obverse of Nobel medal. Size: 116x79mm.

Adoration of the Shepherds, by Gerard van Honthorst—AP61

Paintings: 30fr, Nativity, by Albrecht Altdorfer (vert.). 60fr, Nativity, by Hans Holbein (vert.). 150fr, Adoration of the Kings, by Gerard David.

1976, Dec. 22 Litho. *Perf. 12½*

C200 AP61 30fr gold & multi 25 15
C201 AP61 60fr gold & multi 50 30
C202 AP61 120fr gold & blk 1.00 60
C203 AP61 150fr gold & blk 1.20 70

Christmas 1976.

Lesdiguières Bridge, by Jongkind—AP62

Design: 120fr, Sailing Ship and Boats, by Johan Barthold Jongkind (1819–1891).

1976, Dec. 27 Photo. *Perf. 13*

C204 AP62 100fr multi 80 45
C205 AP62 120fr multi 1.00 60

Centenary of impressionism.

Zeppelin Type of 1977

Designs: 125fr, Germany No. C40 and North Pole. 150fr, Germany No. C45 and Chicago department store. 175fr, Germany No. C38 and scenes of New York and London. 200fr, 500fr, U.S. No. C15 and New York.

1977, Mar. 30 *Perf. 11*

C206 A91 125fr multi 1.20 50
C207 A91 150fr multi 1.40 60
C208 A91 175fr multi 1.65 70
C209 A91 200fr multi 2.00 85

Souvenir Sheet

C210 A91 500fr multi 4.75 2.00

75th anniversary of the Zeppelin. No. C210 has multicolored margin showing world map with cancellations of Zeppelin flights. Size: 130x91mm.

Sassenage Castle, Grenoble—AP63

1977, May 21 Litho. *Perf. 12½*

C211 AP63 100fr multi 80 45

10th anniversary of the International French Language Council.

Lafayette and Ships—AP64

Designs: 120fr, Abraham Lincoln, eagle and flags (vert.). 150fr, James Madison and family.

1977, July 30 Engr. *Perf. 13*

C212 AP64 100fr multi 80 60
C213 AP64 120fr multi 1.00 70
C214 AP64 150fr multi 1.20 90

American Bicentennial.

Lindbergh and Spirit of St. Louis—AP65

Designs: 100fr, Concorde. 150fr, 200fr, 300fr, Various Lindbergh portraits and Spirit of St. Louis.

1977, Sept. 27

C215	AP65	100fr multi	80	60
C216	AP65	120fr multi	1.00	70
C217	AP65	150fr multi	1.20	90
C218	AP65	200fr multi	1.60	1.10
C219	AP65	300fr multi	2.40	1.65
		Nos. C215-C219 (5)	7.00	4.95

Charles A. Lindbergh's solo transatlantic flight from New York to Paris, 50th anniversary, and first supersonic transatlantic flight of Concorde.

Mariner 10—AP66

Spacecraft: 200fr, Lunokhod on moon, Luna 21. 300fr, Viking on Mars.

1977, Oct. 10 Engr. *Perf. 13*

C220	AP66	100fr multi	80	60
C221	AP66	200fr multi	1.60	1.20
C222	AP66	300fr multi	2.40	1.60

Running AP67

Designs: 60fr, Volleyball. 120fr, Soccer. 125fr, Basketball.

1977, Oct. 24 Engr. *Perf. 13*

C223	AP67	30fr multi	25	20
C224	AP67	60fr multi	50	35
C225	AP67	120fr multi	1.00	70
C226	AP67	125fr multi	1.00	75

No. C215 Overprinted:
"PARIS NEW – YORK / 22.11.77"

1977, Nov. 22

C227	AP65	100fr multi	80	60

Concorde, first commercial flight Paris to New York.

Virgin and Child, by Rubens AP68

Rubens Paintings: 60fr, Virgin and Child and Two Donors. 100fr, Adoration of the Shepherds. 125fr, Adoration of the Kings.

1977, Dec. 20 Litho. *Perf. 12½x12*

C228	AP68	30fr multi	25	20
C229	AP68	60fr multi	50	35
C230	AP68	100fr multi	80	60
C231	AP68	125fr multi	1.00	75

Christmas 1977.

Antoine de Saint-Exupéry—AP69

Designs: 50fr, Wilbur and Orville Wright and Flyer. 80fr, Hugo Junkers and his plane. 100fr, Gen. Italo Balbo and his plane. 120fr, Concorde. 500fr, Wilbur and Orville Wright and Flyer.

1978, Oct. 25 Litho. *Perf. 13½*

C232	AP69	40fr multi	40	20
C233	AP69	50fr multi	50	25
C234	AP69	80fr multi	80	40
C235	AP69	100fr multi	1.00	50
C236	AP69	120fr multi	1.20	60
		Nos. C232-C236 (5)	3.90	1.95

Souvenir Sheet

C237	AP69	500fr multi	5.50	2.75

History of aviation and 75th anniversary of 1st powered flight. No. C237 has multicolored margin showing Concorde in flight. Size: 104x99mm.

Philexafrique II—Essen Issue
Common Design Types

Designs: No. C238, Rhinoceros and Chad No. C6. No. C239, Kingfisher and Mecklenburg-Strelitz No. 1.

1978, Nov. 1 *Perf. 12½*

C238	CD138	100fr multi	1.00	50
C239	CD139	100fr multi	1.00	50

Nos. C238–C239 printed se-tenant.

Nos. C191-C194 Overprinted
"ALUNISSAGE/APOLLO XI/ JUILLET 1969"

1979, Nov. 26 Litho. *Perf. 13½×14*

C240	A86	100fr multi	1.00	50
C241	A86	200fr multi	2.00	1.00
C242	A86	250fr multi	2.50	1.25

Souvenir Sheet

C243	A86	450fr multi	4.75	2.50

Apollo 11 moon landing, 10th anniversary.

Hurdles, Moscow '80 Emblem—AP70

Moscow '80 Emblem and: 30fr, Field hockey. 250fr, Swimming. 350fr, Running. 500fr, Yachting.

1979, Nov. 30 *Perf. 13½*

C244	AP70	15fr multi	15	8
C245	AP70	30fr multi	30	15
C246	AP70	250fr multi	2.50	1.25
C247	AP70	350fr multi	3.50	1.75

Souvenir Sheet

C248	AP70	500fr multi	5.25	2.75

Pre-Olympic Year. No. C248 has multicolored margin showing Moscow '80 emblem. Size: 118×80mm.

Austria Jubilee Issue of 1910, Canoe, Hill AP71

Hill, Stamps and Vessels: 100fr, U.S. type A97, dhow. 200fr, France No. 21, Sidewheeler. 300fr, Holstein No. 16, ocean liner. 500fr, Chad No. J13, ocean liner.

1979, Dec. 3 *Perf. 14×13½*

C249	AP71	65fr multi	65	35
C250	AP71	100fr multi	1.00	50
C251	AP71	200fr multi	2.00	1.00
C252	AP71	300fr multi	3.00	1.50

Souvenir Sheet

C253	AP71	500fr multi	5.25	2.75

Sir Rowland Hill (1795-1879), originator of penny postage. No. C253 has multicolored margin showing early stamps. Size: 114×91mm.

Nos. C244-C245, C249-C250 Overprinted: "POSTES 1981" in Red or Overprinted and Surcharged Silver on Red.

1981, Nov. 15 Litho. *Perf. 13½, 14x13½*

C254	AP70	30fr on 15fr multi	30	15
C255	AP70	30fr multi	30	15
C256	AP71	60fr on 65fr multi	60	30
C257	AP71	60fr on 100fr multi	60	30

Soccer Type of 1982

1982 Litho. *Perf. 13½*

C258	A108	80fr Brazil	32	16
C259	A108	300fr Spain	1.25	62

Souvenir Sheet

C259A	A108	500fr like 300fr	2.25	1.10

No. C259A contains one stamp (size: 42x51mm); multicolored margin pictures Spanish cultural attractions. Size: 77x100mm.

Diana Type of 1982

1982, July 2 Litho. *Perf. 13½*

C260	A109	80fr 1977	80	40
C261	A109	300fr 1980	3.00	1.50

Souvenir Sheet

C262	A109	500fr 1981	5.00	2.50

No. C262 has multicolored margin showing family tree. Size: 78x75mm.

Manned Flight Bicentenary—AP72

Balloons: 100fr, Charles' and Roberts', 1783 (vert.). 200fr, J.P. Blanchard, Berlin, 1788 (vert.). 300fr, Charles Green, London, 1837. 400fr, Modern blimp. 500fr, Montgolfiere, 1783 (vert.).

1983, Apr. Litho. *Perf. 13*

C263	AP72	100fr multi	1.00	50
C264	AP72	200fr multi	2.00	1.00
C265	AP72	300fr multi	3.00	1.50
C266	AP72	400fr multi	4.00	2.00

Souvenir Sheet

C267	AP72	500fr multi	5.00	2.50

No. C267 has multicolored margin continuing design. Size: 80x98mm.

Balloon Type

Designs: 80fr, Steam Powered Airship, H. Giffard. 250fr, Graf Zeppelin; Airship L-1, first flight. 300fr, 1st Balloon Flight, Montgolfier and Rozier.

1983, May 30 Litho. *Perf. 13*

C268	A116	80fr multi	80	40
C269	A116	250fr multi	1.25	60

Souvenir Sheet

C270	A116	300fr multi	3.00	1.50

Multicolored margin depicts crowd watching balloon ascent. Size: 57x95mm.

1984 Summer Olympics—AP73

Various kayak scenes.

1984, Mar. 1 Litho. *Perf. 13*

C271	AP73	100fr multi	40	20
C272	AP73	200fr multi	80	40
C273	AP73	300fr multi	1.20	60
C274	AP73	400fr multi	1.60	80

Souvenir Sheet

C275	AP73	500fr multi	2.00	1.00

No. C275 has multicolored margin continuing design. Size: 105x81mm.

IYY, PHILEXAFRICA '85—AP74

1985, May 2 Litho. *Perf. 13*

C280	AP74	200fr Boy scout, tree	60	30
C281	AP74	200fr Air Chad Fokker 27	60	30

Printed se-tenant with center label.

IYY, PHILEXAFRICA Type of 1985

1985, Nov. 1 **Litho.** ***Perf. 13x12½***

C283	AP74	250fr	Girl, Scout ceremony	1.10	55
C284	AP74	250fr	Communications and transportation	1.10	55

Nos. C283-C284 printed se-tenant with center labels picturing map of Africa or UAPT emblem.

ASCENA Airlines, 25th Anniv.—AP75

1985, Aug. 15 ***Perf. 12½***

C285	AP75	70fr	bl & multi	30	15
C286	AP75	110fr	org & multi	45	22
C287	AP75	250fr	yel & multi	1.10	55

Victor Hugo (1802-1885), French Novelist—AP76

Scene from Les. Miserables.

1985, Nov. 24 **Engr.** ***Perf. 13***

C288	AP76	70fr	org brn, chlky bl & dp brn	30	15
C289	AP76	110fr	lake, dk brn & dk grn	45	20
C290	AP76	250fr	brt org, blk & dk red	1.10	55
C291	AP76	300fr	dk red, cl & sl bl	1.25	62

Christmas 1985—AP77

1985, Dec. 22 **Litho.** ***Perf. 13½***

C292	AP77	250fr	Adoration of the Magi	1.10	55

AIR POST SEMI-POSTAL STAMPS

Ramses II Battling the Hittites (from Abu Simbel)
SPAP1

Engraved

1964, March 9 *Perf. 13* Unwmkd.

CB1	SPAP1 10fr	+5fr red, grn & vio	35	30
CB2	SPAP1 25fr	+5fr red, grn & vio brn	50	40
CB3	SPAP1 50fr	+5fr red, grn & sl grn	1.00	90

Issued to publicize the UNESCO world campaign to save historic monuments in Nubia.

Lions Emblem
SPAP2

1967, July 5 Photo. *Perf. 13*

CB4	SPAP2 50fr	+10fr multi	90	35

Issued to commemorate the 50th anniversary of Lions International and to publicize the Lions work for the blind.

POSTAGE DUE STAMPS

Postage Due Stamps of France Overprinted **TCHAD** **A. E. F.**

1928 *Perf. 14x13½* Unwmkd.

J1	D2	5c lt bl	18	18
J2	D2	10c gray brn	18	18
J3	D2	20c ol grn	25	25
J4	D2	25c brt rose	52	52
J5	D2	30c lt red	60	60
J6	D2	45c bl grn	80	80
J7	D2	50c brn vio	95	95
J8	D2	60c yel brn	1.10	1.10
J9	D2	1fr red brn	1.10	1.10
J10	D2	2fr org red	3.75	3.75
J11	D2	3fr brt vio	1.90	1.90
		Nos. J1-J11 (11)	11.33	11.33

Huts
D3

Canoe
D4

Typographed.

1930 *Perf. 14x13½, 13½x14.*

J12	D3	5c dp bl & ol	30	30
J13	D3	10c dk red & brn	40	40
J14	D3	20c grn & brn	70	70
J15	D3	25c lt bl & brn	90	90
J16	D3	30c bis brn & Prus bl	90	90
J17	D3	45c Prus bl & ol	1.00	1.00
J18	D3	50c red vio & brn	1.40	1.40
J19	D3	60c gray lil & bl blk	2.00	2.00
J20	D4	1fr bis brn & bl blk	2.00	2.00
J21	D4	2fr vio & brn	4.25	4.25
J22	D4	3fr dp red & brn	30.00	30.00
		Nos. J12-J22 (11)	43.85	43.85

In 1934 stamps of Chad were superseded by those of French Equatorial Africa.

Republic

Rhinoceros—D5

Tibesti Pictographs: No. J24, Kudu. No. J25, Two antelopes. No. J26, Three antelopes. No. J27, Ostrich. No. J28, Horned bull. No. J29, Bull. No. J30, Wild swine. No. J31, Elephant. No. J32, Rhinoceros. No. J33, Warrior with spear and shield. No. J34, Masked archer.

Engraved

1962, Apr. 20 *Perf. 13* Unwmkd.

J23	D5	50c ol bis	6	6
J24	D5	50c brn red	6	6
J25	D5	1fr blue	8	8
J26	D5	1fr green	8	8
J27	D5	2fr vermilion	12	12
J28	D5	2fr maroon	12	12
J29	D5	5fr sl grn	22	22
J30	D5	5fr vio bl	22	22
J31	D5	10fr brown	50	50
J32	D5	10fr org brn	50	50
J33	D5	25fr car rose	1.25	1.25
J34	D5	25fr violet	1.25	1.25
		Nos. J23-J34 (12)	4.46	4.46

The two designs of the same denomination are printed se-tenant.

Kanem Doll
D6

Dolls: 2fr, Kotoko. 5fr, Leather doll. 10fr, Kotoko. 25fr, Guera.

1969, Sept. 19 Engr. *Perf. 14x13*

J35	D6	1fr grn, ver & brn	5	5
J36	D6	2fr ver, yel grn & brn	5	5
J37	D6	5fr grn, brn & sl grn	10	5
J38	D6	10fr grn, lil & brn	18	18
J39	D6	25fr rose, bl & brn	38	22
		Nos. J35-J39 (5)	76	55

MILITARY STAMPS

Flag Bearer and Map of Chad
M1

1st Regiment Emblem
M2

No. 78 Overprinted "F.M."

1965 Typo. *Perf. 14x13½*

M1	A5	20fr red & blk	135.00	135.00

Lithographed

1968 *Perf. 13x12½* Unwmkd.

M2	M1	tan & multi	1.40	90

1972, Jan. 21 Photo. *Perf. 13*

M3	M2	bl & multi	65	40

OFFICIAL STAMPS

Flag and Map of Chad
O1

Perf. 13½x14

1966–71 Typographed Unwmkd.

Flag in blue, yellow and carmine.

O1	O1	1fr lt bl	6	5
O2	O1	2fr gray	6	5
O3	O1	5fr black	7	6
O4	O1	10fr vio bl	10	8
O5	O1	25fr orange	25	12
O6	O1	30fr brt grn	38	18
O7	O1	40fr car ('71)	45	18
O8	O1	50fr red lil	60	25
O9	O1	85fr green	90	45
O10	O1	100fr brown	1.40	50
O11	O1	200fr red	2.50	90
		Nos. O1-O11 (11)	6.77	2.82

CHILE

LOCATION — Southwest corner of South America.
GOVT.—Republic.
AREA—292,135 sq. mi.
POP.—11,682,260 (est. 1982).
CAPITAL—Santiago.

100 Centavos = 1 Peso
1000 Milésimos = 100 Centésimos = 1 Escudo (1960)
100 Centavos = 1 Peso (1975)

> **Prices of early Chile stamps vary according to condition. Quotations for Nos. 1–14 are for fine copies. Very fine to superb specimens sell at much higher prices, and inferior or poor copies sell at reduced prices, depending on the condition of the individual specimen.**
> **Pen cancellations are common on the 1862–67 issues. Such stamps sell for much less than the quoted prices which are for those with handstamped postal cancellations.**

Christopher Columbus
A1

Wmkd.

1 5 5 5
a b c d

10 10 20
e f g

London Prints.
Engraved.

1853 ***Imperf.*** **Wmk. b.**
Blued Paper.

1 A1 5c brn red 500.00 55.00
a. White paper 90.00

Wmk. e.
White Paper.

2 A1 10c dp brt bl 800.00 110.00
a. Blued paper 650.00
b. Diagonal half used as 5c on cover 600.00

Santiago Prints.
Impressions Fine and Clear.
White Paper.

1854 **Wmks. b and e.**

3 A1 5c pale red brn 450.00 45.00
a. 5c dp red brn 500.00 50.00
b. 5c chnt 800.00 150.00
4 A1 5c brnt sien 1,500. 225.00
a. 5c dl choc 2,750. 1,200.
5 A1 10c dp bl 1,250. 125.00
a. 10c sl bl 125.00
b. 10c grnsh bl 1,200.
c. Half used as 5c on cover 550.00
6 A1 10c lt dl bl 1,250. 125.00
a. 10c pale bl 125.00
b. Diagonal half used as 5c on cover 400.00

Lithographed.

7 A1 5c red brn 2,250. 300.00
a. 5c pale brn 1,600. 250.00

London Print.
Engraved.

1855 **Blued Paper** **Wmk. c.**

8 A1 5c brn red 175.00 12.50

Santiago Prints.
Impressions Worn and Blurred.
White Paper.

1856-62 **Wmks. b and e.**

9 A1 5c rose red ('58) 40.00 6.00
a. 5c car red ('62) 100.00 20.00
b. 5c org red ('61) 250.00 150.00
c. 5c dl redsh brn ('57) 250.00 25.00
d. Printed on both sides 650.00
e. Double impression
10 A1 10c dp bl 200.00 25.00
a. 10c sky bl ('57) 200.00 25.00
b. 10c lt bl 200.00 25.00
c. 10c ind bl 250.00 75.00
d. Half used as 5c on cover 175.00

London Prints.

1862 **Wmks. a, f and g.**

11 A1 1c lem yel 30.00 37.50
a. Double impression 950.00
12 A1 10c brt bl 50.00 10.00
a. 10c dp bl 50.00 10.00
b. Blued paper 125.00 25.00
c. Wmkd. "20" (error) 4,000. 2,000.
d. Half used as 5c on cover 150.00
13 A1 20c green 75.00 45.00
a. 20c emer

Santiago Print.

1865 **Wmk. d.**

14 A1 5c rose red 30.00 12.50
a. 5c car red 35.00 12.50
b. Printed on both sides 250.00
c. Laid paper 225.00
d. Double impression 225.00

The 5c rose red (shades) on unwatermarked paper, either wove or ribbed, and on paper watermarked Chilean arms in the sheet are reprints made about 1870.

No. 13 has been reprinted in the color of issue and in fancy colors, both from the original engraved plate and from lithographic transfers. The reprints are on paper without watermark or with watermark CHILE and Star.

A2 A3

1867 ***Perf. 12*** **Unwmkd.**

15 A2 1c orange 17.50 2.50
Pen cancellation 25
16 A2 2c black 25.00 3.75
Pen cancellation 40
17 A2 5c red 17.50 1.25
Pen cancellation 10
18 A2 10c blue 17.50 2.50
Pen cancellation 25
19 A2 20c green 25.00 3.75
Pen cancellation 35

Unused prices for Nos. 15-19 are for stamps with original gum.

1877 ***Rouletted***

20 A3 1c gray 2.50 1.25
21 A3 2c orange 15.00 3.75
22 A3 5c dl lake 17.50 1.00
23 A3 10c blue 15.00 2.50
a. Diagonal half used as 5c on cover
24 A3 20c green 16.00 3.75

The panel inscribed "CENTAVO" is straight on No. 22.

A4 A5

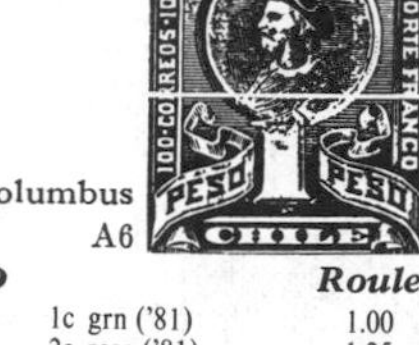

Columbus
A6

1878-99 ***Rouletted***

25 A4 1c grn ('81) 1.00 20
26 A4 2c rose ('81) 1.25 20
27 A5 5c dl lake ('78) 5.00 50
28 A5 5c ultra ('83) 1.25 10
29 A5 10c org ('85) 2.00 40
a. 10c yel 8.00 1.00
30 A5 15c dk grn ('92) 1.50 50
31 A5 20c gray ('86) 1.25 50
32 A5 25c org brn ('92) 2.00 50
33 A5 30c rose car ('99) 5.00 2.00
34 A5 50c lil ('78) 50.00 10.00
35 A5 50c vio ('85) 2.50 1.00
36 A6 1p dk brn & blk ('92) 25.00 2.00
a. Imperf. horiz. or vert. pair 125.00
Nos. 25-36 (12) 97.75 17.90

Columbus
A7 A8

1894 **Re-engraved.**

37 A7 1c bl grn 1.00 20
38 A7 2c car lake 1.00 20

In type A4 there is a small colorless ornament at each side of the base of the numeral, above the "E" and "V" of "CENTAVO". In type A7 these ornaments are missing, the figure "1" is broader than in type A4 and the head of the figure "2" is formed by a curved line instead of a ball.

1900–01

Type I. There is a heavy shading of short horizontal lines below "Chile" and the adjacent ornaments.
Type II. There is practically no shading below "Chile" and the ornaments.

Type I.

39 A8 1c yel grn 1.00 20
40 A8 2c brn rose 2.00 20
41 A8 5c dp bl 12.50 20
42 A8 10c violet 7.50 40
a. Horizontal pair, imperf. between
43 A8 20c gray 5.00 1.00
44 A8 30c dp org ('01) 6.00 1.00
45 A8 50c red brn 7.50 1.75
a. Horiz. pair, imperf. btwn. 75.00
Nos. 39-45 (7) 41.50 4.75

Type II.

46 A8 1c yel grn ('01) 1.00 20
47 A8 2c rose ('01) 1.00 20
48 A8 5c dl bl ('01) 5.00 20
a. Printed on both sides
49 A8 10c vio ('01) 6.00 50

Columbus
A9 A10

1900 Black Surcharge

50 A9 5c on 30c rose car 1.00 20
a. Inverted surcharge 37.50 20.00
b. Double surcharge 125.00 80.00
c. Double surcharge, both inverted 125.00 80.00
d. Double surcharge, one inverted 125.00 80.00
e. Surcharged on front and back 125.00 80.00

1901–02 ***Perf. 12***

51 A10 1c green 35 20
52 A10 2c carmine 50 20
53 A10 5c ultra 1.00 10
54 A10 10c red & blk 2.50 40
55 A10 30c vio & blk 7.50 40
56 A10 50c red org & blk 9.00 3.00
Nos. 51-56 (6) 20.85 4.30

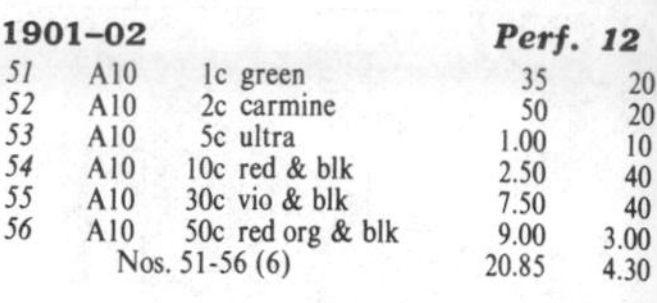

No. 44 Surcharged in Dark Blue

1903 ***Rouletted.***

57 A8 10c on 30c org 2.50 50
a. Inverted surcharge 25.00 15.00
b. Double surcharge 30.00 15.00
c. Double surch., one inverted 30.00 15.00
d. Double surch., both inverted 30.00 15.00
e. Stamp design printed on both sides

Pedro de Valdivia Coat of Arms
A11 A12

A13

Telegraph Stamps Surcharged or Overprinted in Black

Type I. Animal at left has neither mane nor tail.
Type II. Animal at left has mane and tail.

1904 ***Perf. 12.***

58 A11 1c on 20c ultra 35 20
a. Imperf. horiz. pair 50.00 50.00
b. Inverted surcharge 60.00 60.00
59 A13 2c yel brn, I 35 20
a. Inverted overprint 25.00 25.00
b. Pair, one without overprint 60.00 60.00
60 A13 5c red, I 60 20
a. Inverted overprint 25.00 25.00
c. Pair, one without overprint 60.00 60.00
61 A13 10c ol grn, I 2.00 60
a. Inverted overprint 60.00 60.00

Perf. 12½ to 16.

62 A13 2c yel, brn, II 6.00 4.00
63 A11 3c on 5c brn red 60.00 55.00
a. Inverted surcharge
64 A12 3c on 1p brn, II 50 30
a. Double surcharge 60.00 60.00
65 A13 5c red, II 10.00 7.50
a. Inverted overprint
66 A13 10c ol grn, II 22.50 13.00
67 A11 12c on 5c brn red 1.25 50
a. No star at left of "Centavos" 2.50 1.50
b. Inverted surcharge 50.00 50.00
c. Double surcharge 60.00 60.00
Nos. 62-67 (6) 100.25 80.30

Counterfeits exist of the overprint and surcharge varieties of Nos. 57–67.

Columbus
A14 A15

Columbus
A16

1905-09 *Perf. 12.*

No.	Type	Description	Unused	Used
68	A14	1c green	30	20
69	A14	2c carmine	30	20
70	A14	3c yel brn	75	30
71	A14	5c ultra	75	10
72	A15	10c gray & blk	1.50	20
73	A15	12c lake & blk	7.50	2.50
74	A15	15c vio & blk	1.50	20
75	A15	20c org brn & blk	3.50	20
76	A15	30c bl grn & blk	4.50	30
77	A15	50c ultra & blk	5.00	30
78	A16	1p gold, grn & gray	17.50	9.00
		Nos. 68-78 (11)	43.10	13.50

A 20c dull red and black, type A15, was prepared but not issued. Price $125. "Specimen" copies of Nos. 74, 76-78 exist, punched to prevent postal use.

Nos. 73, 78 Surcharged in Blue or Red

ISLAS DE
JUAN FERNANDEZ
5
a

ISLAS DE
JUAN FERNANDEZ
10 Cts.
b

1910

No.	Type	Description	Unused	Used
79	A15 (a)	5c on 12c lake & blk (Bl)	60	20
80	A16 (b)	10c on 1p gold, grn & gray (R)	1.50	40
81	A16 (b)	20c on 1p gold, grn & gray (R)	2.00	80
82	A16 (b)	1p gold, grn & gray (R)	4.00	1.50

The 1p is overprinted "ISLAS DE JUAN FERNANDEZ" only. The use of these stamps throughout Chile was authorized.

Independence Centenary Issue.

Oath of Independence
A17

Monument to O'Higgins
A26

Gen. Manuel Blanco Encalada
A29

Designs: 2c, Battle of Chacabuco. 3c, Battle of Roble. 5c, Battle of Maipû. 10c, Naval Engagement of "Lautaro" and "Esmeralda." 12c, Capturing the "Maria Isabel." 15c, First Sortie of Liberating Forces. 20c, Abdication of O'Higgins. 25c, Chile's First Congress. 50c, Monument to José M. Carrera. 1p, Monument to San Martin. 5p, Gen. José Ignacio Zenteno. 10p, Adm. Lord Thomas Cochrane.

1910 Center in Black.

No.	Type	Description	Unused	Used
83	A17	1c dk grn	40	20
a.		Center inverted	7,000.	
84	A17	2c lake	40	20
85	A17	3c red brn	1.25	60
86	A17	5c dp bl	75	10
87	A17	10c gray brn	1.25	40
88	A17	12c vermilion	3.00	1.20
89	A17	15c slate	3.00	60
90	A17	20c red org	4.00	1.00
91	A17	25c ultra	5.00	2.00
92	A26	30c violet	4.00	1.00
93	A26	50c ol grn	9.00	3.00
94	A26	1p yel org	20.00	7.50
95	A29	2p red	20.00	7.50
96	A29	5p yel grn	55.00	25.00
97	A29	10p dk vio	50.00	22.50
		Nos. 83-97 (15)	177.05	72.80

Columbus
A32

De Valdivia
A33

Mateo de Toro Zambrano
A34

Bernardo O'Higgins
A35

Ramón Freire
A36

F. A. Pinto
A37

Joaquín Prieto
A38

Manuel Bulnes
A39

Manuel Montt
A40

José Joaquín Pérez
A41

Federico Errázuriz Zanartu
A42

Aníbal Pinto
A43

Designs: 2p, Domingo Santa María. 5p, José de Balmaceda. 10p, Federico Errázuriz Echaurren.

Outer backgrounds consist of horizontal and diagonal lines.

1911 Engraved. *Perf. 12.*

No.	Type	Description	Unused	Used
98	A32	1c dp grn	30	10
99	A33	2c scarlet	30	10
100	A34	3c sepia	1.00	40
101	A35	5c dk bl	30	5
102	A36	10c gray & blk	1.00	20
a.		Center inverted	1,100.	800.00
103	A37	12c car & blk	1.50	20
104	A38	15c vio & blk	1.20	20
a.		Center inverted	1,100.	
105	A39	20c org red & blk	2.50	20
a.		Center inverted	90.00	85.00
106	A40	25c lt bl & blk	3.00	75
107	A41	30c bis brn & blk	4.50	30
108	A42	50c myr grn & blk	5.50	30
109	A43	1p grn & blk	10.00	40
110	A43	2p ver & blk	17.50	1.50
111	A43	5p ol grn & blk	65.00	10.00
112	A43	10p org yel & blk	55.00	8.00
		Nos. 98-112 (15)	168.60	22.70

See also Nos. 117, 121, 123, 127-128, 133-141, 143, 155A, 157-161, 165-169, 171-172.

Columbus
A47

Toro Z.
A48

Freire
A49

O'Higgins
A50

1912-13 Engraved. *Perf. 12.*

No.	Type	Description	Unused	Used
113	A47	2c scarlet	25	10
114	A48	4c blk brn	35	10
115	A49	8c gray	1.40	20
116	A50	10c bl & blk	1.40	10
a.		Center inverted	700.00	600.00
b.		Imperf. horizontally or vertically, pair	70.00	
117	A37	14c car & blk	1.50	20
121	A38	40c vio & blk	6.50	60
123	A40	60c lt bl & blk	14.00	1.75
		Nos. 112-123 (7)	25.40	3.05

See also Nos. 125-126, 131, 164, 170, 173.

Cochrane
A52

Columbus
A53

1915 Engraved. *Perf. 13½x14.*

No.	Type	Description	Unused	Used
124	A52	5c sl bl	75	10
a.		Imperf., pair	16.00	

See also Nos. 155, 162-163.

1918

No.	Type	Description	Unused	Used
125	A49	8c slate	14.00	60

No. 125 is from a plate made in Chile to resemble No. 115. The top of the head is further from the oval, the spots of color enclosed in the figures "8" are oval instead of round, and there are many small differences in the design.

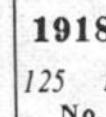
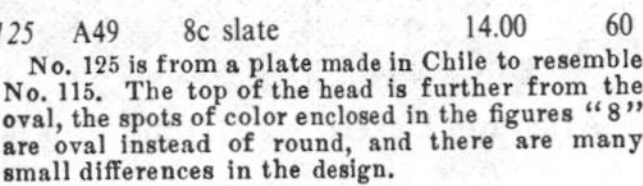

1921 Worn Plate.

No.	Type	Description	Unused	Used
126	A49	8c gray	37.50	9.00

No. 126 differs from No. 125 in not having diagonal lines in the frame and only a few diagonal lines above the shoulders (due to wear), while No. 125 has diagonal lines in the oval up to the level of the forehead.

1915-25 Typo. *Perf. 13½x14½*

No.	Type	Description	Unused	Used
127	A32	1c gray grn	30	10
128	A33	2c red	30	10
129	A53	4c brn ('18)	40	10

Frame Litho.; Head Engraved

No.	Type	Description	Unused	Used
131	A50	10c bl & blk	2.00	5
a.		10c dk bl & blk	2.00	
b.		Imperf., pair	150.00	
c.		Center inverted	450.00	
133	A38	15c vio & blk	1.50	10
134	A39	20c org red & blk	2.75	10
a.		20c brn org & blk	2.75	10
135	A40	25c dl bl & blk	1.00	20
136	A41	30c bis brn & blk	3.00	20
137	A42	50c dp grn & blk	3.00	20

Perf. 14

No.	Type	Description	Unused	Used
138	A43	1p grn & blk	15.00	30
139	A43	2p red & blk	17.50	20
a.		2p ver & blk	35.00	1.00
140	A43	5p ol grn & blk ('20)	45.00	1.00
141	A43	10p org & blk ('25)	50.00	2.50
		Nos. 127-141 (13)	141.75	5.15

The frames have crosshatching on the 15c, 20c, 30c, 2p, 5p and 10p. They have no crosshatching on the 10c, 25c, 50c and 1p.

Nos. 131a and 134a are printed from new head plates which give blacker and heavier impressions. No. 131a exists with; (a) frame lithographed and head engraved; (b) frame typographed and head engraved; (c) frame typographed and head lithographed. No. 134a is with frame typographed and head engraved.

A 4c stamp with portrait of Balmaceda and a 14c with portrait of Manuel de Salas were prepared but not placed in use. Both stamps were sent to the paper mill at Puente Alto for destruction. They were not all destroyed as some were privately preserved and sold. Price $7.50 each.

Columbus
A54

Manuel Rengifo
A55

Types of 1915-20 Re-drawn.

1918-20 *Perf. 13½x14½*

No.	Type	Description	Unused	Used
143	A32	1c gray grn ('20)	40	20
144	A54	4c brown	75	20

No. 143 has all the lines much finer and clearer than No. 127. The white shirt front is also much less shaded.

1921

No.	Type	Description	Unused	Used
145	A55	40c dk vio & blk	3.00	20

Pan-American Congress Building
A56

Admiral Juan José Latorre
A57

1923, Apr. 25 Typo. *Perf. 14½x14*

No.	Type	Description	Unused	Used
146	A56	2c red	25	15
147	A56	4c brown	25	15

Typographed; Center Engraved.

No.	Type	Description	Unused	Used
148	A56	10c bl & blk	25	15
149	A56	20c org & blk	60	20
150	A56	40c dl vio & blk	1.00	30
151	A56	1p grn & blk	1.25	50
152	A56	2p red & blk	5.00	60
153	A56	5p dk grn & blk	17.50	4.00
		Nos. 146-153 (8)	26.10	6.05

Fifth Pan-American Congress.

Typographed; Head Engraved.

1927 *Perf. 13½x14½*

No.	Type	Description	Unused	Used
154	A57	80c dk brn & blk	3.50	80

Wmk. 215 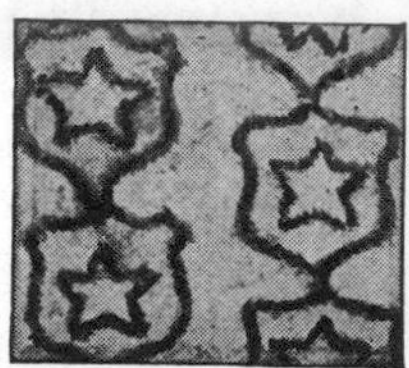

Wmkd.
Small Star in Shield, Multiple. (215)

Types of 1915-25 Issues. Inscribed: "Chile Correos".

1928–31 Engr. *Perf. 13½x14½*

155	A52	5c sl bl	1.40	30

Frame Typo.; Center Engraved

155A	A38	15c vio & blk		*500.00*
156	A55	40c dk vio & blk	85	10
157	A42	50c dp grn & blk	3.00	10

Perf. 14

158	A43	1p grn & blk	1.40	10
159	A43	2p red & blk	5.00	20
160	A43	5p ol grn & blk	11.00	40
161	A43	10p org & blk	11.00	1.50
		Nos. 155, 156-161 (7)	33.65	2.70

Paper of Nos. 155-161 varies from thin to thick.

Types of 1915-25 Issues. Inscribed: "Correos de Chile"
Perf. 13½x14½

1928 Engraved.

162	A52	5c dp bl	60	10

1929 Lithographed.

163	A52	5c lt grn	60	10

Frame Litho.; Center Engraved

164	A50	10c bl & blk	2.50	10
165	A38	15c vio & blk	2.75	10
166	A39	20c org red & blk	6.50	12
167	A40	25c bl & blk	1.25	10
168	A41	30c brn & blk	90	30
169	A42	50c dp grn & blk	75	10
		Nos. 163-169 (7)	15.25	92

Redrawn.
Frame Typo.; Center Litho.

1929

170	A50	10c bl & blk	3.00	6
171	A38	15c vio & blk	2.50	20
172	A39	20c org red & blk	4.00	25

1931 Unwmkd.

173	A50	10c bl & blk	1.00	30

In the redrawn stamps the lines behind the portraits are heavier and completely fill the ovals. There are strong diagonal lines above the shoulders. On No. 170 the head is larger than on Nos. 164 and 173.

A58

Prosperity of Saltpeter Trade
A59 A60

Perf. 13½x14

1930, July 21 Litho. Wmk. 215

Size: 20x25 mm.

175	A58	5c yel grn	50	20
176	A58	10c red brn	50	20
177	A58	15c violet	50	20
178	A59	25c dp gray	2.00	60
179	A60	70c dk bl	5.00	1.50

Perf. 14

Size: 24½x30 mm.

180	A60	1p dk gray grn	3.75	75
		Nos. 175-180 (6)	12.25	3.45

Issued to commemorate the centenary of the first shipment of saltpeter from Chile, July 21, 1830.

Manuel Bulnes
A61

Bernardo O'Higgins
A62

1931 *Perf. 13½, 14*

181	A61	20c dk brn	1.25	10

1932

182	A62	10c dp bl	1.50	10

Mariano Egana
A63

Joaquín Tocornal
A64

1934 *Perf. 13½x14*

183	A63	30c magenta	75	20

Perf. 14

184	A64	1.20p brt bl	1.25	30

Centenary of the constitution.

José Joaquín Pérez
A65

1934 *Perf. 13½x14*

185	A65	30c brt pink	2.00	10

Atacama Desert
A66

Fishing Boats
A67

Coquito Palms
A68

Sheep
A69

Mining
A70

Lonquimay Forest
A71

Colliery at Port Lota
A72

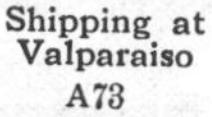

Shipping at Valparaiso
A73

Puntiagudo Volcano—A74

Diego de Almagro—A75

Cattle
A76

Mining Saltpeter
A77

Perf. 14

1936, Mar. 1 Litho. Wmk. 215

186	A66	5c vermilion	35	20
187	A67	10c violet	25	15
188	A68	20c magenta	25	15
189	A69	25c grnsh bl	2.50	80
190	A70	30c lt grn	25	15
191	A71	40c blk, *cr*	2.50	75
192	A72	50c bl, *bluish*	1.25	30

Engraved.

193	A73	1p dk grn	1.25	50
194	A74	1.20p dp bl	1.50	70
195	A75	2p dk brn	1.50	85
196	A76	5p cop red	4.00	2.00
197	A77	10p dk vio	10.00	7.00
		Nos. 186-197 (12)	25.60	13.55

Issued in commemoration of the 400th anniversary of the discovery of Chile by Diego de Almagro.

Laja Waterfall
A78

Agriculture
A79

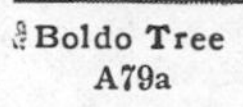

Boldo Tree
A79a

Nitrate Industry
A80

Mineral Spas
A81

Copper Mine
A82

Mining
A83

Fishing in Chiloé
A84

Osorno Volcano
A85

Mercantile Marine
A86

Lake Villarrica
A87

State Railways
A88

Perf. 13½x14

1938–40 Lithographed Wmk. 215

198	A78	5c brn car ('39)	25	10
199	A79	10c sal pink ('39)	25	10
200	A79a	15c brn org ('40)	25	10
201	A80	20c lt bl	25	10
202	A81	30c brt pink	25	10
203	A82	40c lt grn ('39)	25	6
204	A83	50c violet	25	10

Perf. 14

Engraved.

205	A84	1p org brn	25	10
206	A85	1.80p dp bl	65	30
207	A86	2p car lake	25	10
208	A87	5p dk sl grn	50	10
209	A88	10p rose vio ('40)	1.25	10
		Nos. 198-209 (12)	4.65	1.36

See also Nos. 217–227.

Map of the Americas
A89

Perf. 14

1940, Sept. 11 Litho. Unwmkd.

210 A89 40c dl grn & yel grn 25 10

Pan American Union, 50th anniversary.

Camilo Henríquez
A90

Founding of Santiago
A93

Designs: 40c, Pedro de Valdivia. 1.10p, Benjamin Vicuna Mackenna. 3.60p, Diego Barros Arana.

Perf. 14½x14, 14½.

1941, Jan. 23 Engraved Wmk. 215

211 A90 10c car lake 25 15
212 A90 40c green 40 12
213 A90 1.10p red 1.25 75
214 A93 1.80p blue 1.25 75
215 A90 3.60p indigo 3.75 2.50
Nos. 211-215 (5) 6.90 4.27

400th anniversary of Santiago.

Types of 1938.
Lithographed.

1942-46 *Perf. 13½x14.* Unwmkd.

217 A79 10c sal pink ('43) 25 10
218 A79a 15c brn org ('43) 25 10
219 A80 20c lt bl ('43) 25 10
220 A81 30c brt pink ('43) 30 10
221 A82 40c yel grn 1.00 10
222 A83 50c vio ('43) 25 10

Engraved.
Perf. 14.

223 A84 1p brn org 2.00 10
225 A86 2p car lake ('43) 25 10
226 A87 5p dk sl grn ('43) 65 10
227 A88 10p rose vio ('46) 1.00 10
Nos. 217-227 (10) 6.20 1.00

Valentin Letelier
A95

University of Chile
A98

Designs: 40c, Andrés Bello. 90c, Manuel Bulnes. 1.80p, Manuel Montt.

1942, Nov. 1 *Perf. 14x14½, 14 (1p)*

228 A95 30c rose red 25 10
229 A95 40c dp grn 25 10
230 A95 90c rose vio 1.50 1.00
231 A98 1p dp brn 1.00 60
232 A95 1.80p dk bl 3.00 2.00
Nos. 228-232 (5) 6.00 3.80

University of Chile centenary. See also No. C89.

Manuel Bulnes
A100

Map Showing Strait of Magellan
A104

Designs: 30c, Juan Williams Wilson. 40c, Diego Duble Almeida. 1p, José Mardones.

1944, Mar. 3 Litho Perf. 14

233 A100 15c black 25 15
234 A100 30c dp rose 25 15
235 A100 40c yel grn 25 15
236 A100 1p brn car 1.25 40
237 A104 1.80p ultra 1.75 1.00
Nos. 233-237 (5) 3.75 1.85

Issued to commemorate the 100th anniversary of the occupation of the Strait of Magellan.

Red Cross and Lamp of Life
A105

Serpent and Cup
A106

1944, Oct. 18 Unwmkd.

238 A105 40c grn, red & blk 35 15
239 A106 1.80p ultra & red 90 50

Issued to commemorate the 80th anniversary of the International Red Cross Society.

Bernardo O'Higgins
A107

"Embrace of Maipú"
(O'Higgins Joining San Martin)
A108

Designs: 40c, Abdication of O'Higgins. 1.80p, Battle of Rancagua.

1945 Engr. *Perf. 14 (15c), 14½*

Center in Black.

240 A107 15c carmine 25 15
241 A108 30c brown 35 15
242 A108 40c dp grn 35 15
243 A108 1.80p dk bl 1.75 1.20

Issued to commemorate the centenary of the death of Bernardo O'Higgins in 1842.

Proposed Columbus Lighthouse
A111

Perf. 14

1945, Sept. 10 Litho. Wmk. 215

244 A111 40c lt grn 30 20

Issued in honor of the discovery of America by Columbus and the Memorial Lighthouse to be erected in his memory.

Andrés Bello
A112

1946 Engraved

245 A112 40c dk grn 20 10
246 A112 1.80p dk bl 20 15

Issued to commemorate the 80th anniversary of the death of Andrés Bello, poet and educator.

Map Showing Chile's Claims of Antarctic Territory
A113

1947, May 12 Litho. *Perf. 14½*

247 A113 40c carmine 50 15
248 A113 2.50p dp bl 1.00 40

Eusebio Lillo and Ramon Carnicer
A114

1947, Sept. 18 Engraved

249 A114 40c dk grn 20 12

Centenary of national anthem.

Miguel de Cervantes Saavedra
A115

1947, Oct. 11 Wmk. 215

250 A115 40c dk car 30 20

Issued to commemorate the 400th anniversary of the birth of Miguel de Cervantes Saavedra, novelist, playwright and poet.

Arturo Prat Chacón and Iquique Naval Battle
A116

1948, Dec. 24 *Perf. 14½*

251 A116 40c dp bl 20 8

Issued to commemorate the centenary of the birth of Arturo Prat Chacon, Chilean naval hero.

Bernardo O'Higgins
A117

Lithographed.

1948 *Perf. 13½x14.* Wmk. 215

252 A117 60c black 10 10

See also No. 262.

No. 203 Surcharged in Black

VEINTE
CTS.

1948

253 A82 20c on 40c lt grn 10 10

Chilean Pigeons
A118

American Skunk
A119

Designs not illustrated, FAUNA: Chilean Otter. Southern sea lions. Sugar-cane borer moth. Emperor penguins. Bat. Chinchilla. Grant's stag beetle. Trevally (fish). Chilean slender lizard. Crested caracara. Red-gartered coot. Chilean guemal (deer). Spiny rock lobster. Tilefish. Praying mantis. Torrent duck. Red conger. FLORA: Araucarian pine (monkey puzzle tree). Evening primrose. Chilean red bell flower. Loxodon (flower). Boldo tree. Coquito palm trees.

Lithographed.

1948, Dec. 6 *Perf. 14* Wmk. 215

254 A118 60c ultra 35 20
a. Block of 25 10.00
255 A119 2.60p green 50 35
a. Block of 25 15.00

Issued in panes of 100 stamps, divisible into four blocks of 25 different designs.

The stamps commemorate the centenary (in 1944) of the publication of the first volume of Claudio Gay's Natural History of Chile. See also No. C124.

Benjamin Vicuna Mackenna
A121

1949, Mar. 22 Engr. *Perf. 13½x14*

257 A121 60c dp bl 10 10

See also No. C126.

Symbols of Arts and Crafts Education
A122

Heinrich von Stephan
A123

Design: 2.60p, Badge and book.

Lithographed.

1949, Nov. 11 ***Perf. 14*** **Unwmkd.**

258	A122	60c lil rose	20	10
259	A122	2.60p vio bl	50	30

Issued to commemorate the centenary of the foundation of Chile's School of Arts and Crafts. See also Nos. C127–C128.

1950, Jan. 6 **Engraved**

260	A123	60c dp car	20	10
261	A123	2.50p dp bl	50	30

Issued to commemorate the 75th anniversary of the formation of the Universal Postal Union. See also Nos. C129–C130.

O'Higgins Type of 1948.

1950 **Lithographed** ***Perf. 13x14***

262	A117	60c black	10	8

Gen. José de San Martín
A124

Queen Isabella I
A125

Perf. 14

1951, Mar. 16 **Engr.** **Wmk. 215**

263	A124	60c dp bl	10	8

Issued to commemorate the centenary of the death of Gen. José de San Martin. See also No. C165.

1952, Mar. 20

264	A125	60c brt bl	10	8

Issued to commemorate the 500th anniversary of the birth of Queen Isabella I of Spain. See also No. C166.

Bernardo O'Higgins
A126

Mateo de Toro Zambrano
A127

Lithographed.

1952 ***Perf. 13½x14*** **Unwmkd.**

265	A126	1p dk bl grn	10	8

See also No. 275.

Nos.252 and 262 Surcharged "40 Ctvs." in Red.

1952, Sept.

266	A117	40c on 60c blk	10	8

Wmk. 215

267	A117	40c on 60c blk	10	8

1953, Mar. 13 **Wmk. 215**

268	A127	80c green	10	8

See also No. 285.

Valdivia Arms
A128

Old Fort
A129

Designs: 3p, Modern Valdivia. 5p, Street in ancient Valdivia.

1953, May ***Perf. 14***

269	A128	1p brt ultra	20	10
270	A129	2p dl rose vio	20	10
271	A129	3p bl grn	30	20
272	A129	5p dp brn	30	20
		Nos. 269-272, C167 (5)	2.00	85

Issued to commemorate the 4th centenary of the founding of Valdivia, capital of Valdivia province.

José Toribio Medina
A130

1953, June **Engraved** ***Perf. 14½***

273	A130	1p brown	15	15
274	A130	2.50p dp bl	30	20

Issued to commemorate the centenary of the birth of Jose Toribio Medina (1852–1930), historian and bibliographer.

O'Higgins Type of 1952.
Lithographed.

1953, Oct. ***Perf. 13½x14*** **Wmk. 215**

275	A126	1p dk bl grn	10	8

Stamp of 1853
A131

1953, Oct. 15 **Engr.** ***Perf. 14½***

276	A131	1p chocolate	20	15

Centenary of Chile's first postage stamps. Souvenir sheet including No. 276 is noted below No. C168.

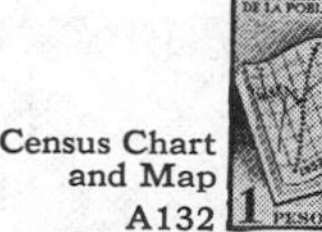

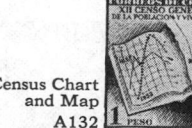

Census Chart and Map
A132

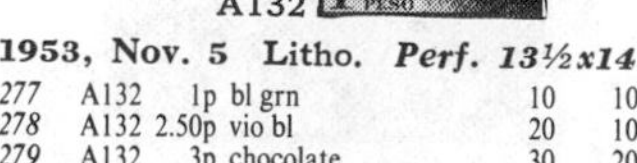

1953, Nov. 5 **Litho.** ***Perf. 13½x14***

277	A132	1p bl grn	10	10
278	A132	2.50p vio bl	20	10
279	A132	3p chocolate	30	20
280	A132	4p carmine	40	20

Issued to publicize the 12th general census of population and housing.

Arms of Angol
A133

Ignacio Domeyko
A134

1954, May 28 ***Perf. 14*** **Unwmkd.**

281	A133	2p dp car	15	8

Issued to commemorate the 400th anniversary of the founding of Angol, capital of Malleco province.

1954, Aug. 16 **Engr.** ***Perf. 13½x14***

282	A134	1p grnsh bl	10	5

Issued to commemorate the 150th anniversary of the birth of Ignacio Domeyko (1802–1889), mineralogist and educator. See also No. C171.

Early Steam Locomotive—A135

Perf. 14½

1954, Sept. 10 **Wmk. 215**

283	A135	1p red	15	10

Issued to commemorate the centenary (in 1951) of the first South American railroad. See also No. C172.

Adm. Arturo Prat Chacón
A136

Arms of Viña del Mar
A137

Lithographed.

1954 ***Perf. 14*** **Unwmkd.**

284	A136	2p dk vio bl	10	8

Issued to commemorate the 75th anniversary of the naval Battle of Iquique.

Toro Zambrano Type of 1953

1954, Nov. 6 ***Perf. 13½x14***

285	A127	80c green	10	5

1955, Mar. 5 ***Perf. 14*** **Wmk. 215**

Design: 2p, Arms of Valparaiso.

286	A137	1p vio bl	10	8
287	A137	2p carmine	10	8

Issued to publicize the first International Philatelic Exhibition, Valparaiso, March 1955.

Dr. Alejandro del Rio
A138

1955, May 24 ***Perf. 13½x14***

288	A138	2p vio bl	10	8

14th Pan-American Sanitary Conference.

Christ of the Andes, Emblems of Chile, Argentina
A139

1955, Aug. 31 ***Perf. 14½*** **Unwmkd.**

289	A139	1p vio bl	15	10

Issued to publicize the reciprocal visits of Presidents Juan D. Peron and Carlos Ibanez del Campo. See also No. C173.

Manuel Rengifo
A140

Portraits: 5p, Mariano Egana. 50p, Diego Portales.

1955–56 ***Perf. 14x14½*** **Unwmkd.**

290	A140	3p vio bl	10	8
291	A140	5p dk car rose	15	8
292	A140	50p rose lil ('56)	1.75	40

Issued to commemorate the centenary of the death of Joaquin Prieto (1786–1854), soldier and political leader; president, 1831–41. See No. QRA1.

Jose M. Carrera
A141

Ramón Freire
A142

Portraits: 5p, Manuel Bulnes. 10p, Pres. Francisco A. Pinto. 50p, Manuel Montt.

Lithographed

1956–58 ***Perf. 14x14½*** **Unwmkd.**

293	A141	2p purple	10	5
293A	A142	3p lt vio bl	10	5
294	A141	5p redsh brn (19½x23mm)	10	5
a.		Size 19x22mm	10	8
295	A142	10p vio (19x22¼mm)	15	5
a.		Perf. 13½x14 (19¼x22½mm) ('58)	50	8
296	A141	50p rose red	35	10
		Nos. 293-296 (5)	80	30

No. 294 has yellow gum; No. 294a, white gum.

Wmk. 215

297	A141	2p dl pur	10	8
298	A142	3p vio bl	10	8

Federico Santa Maria
A143

Gabriela Mistral
A144

Engraved.

1957, Jan. 31 ***Perf. 14*** **Unwmkd.**

299	A143	5p dk red brn	15	8

Issued to commemorate the 25th anniversary of the Federico Santa Maria Technical University. See Nos. C190–C191.

Souvenir sheet including No. 299 is noted below No. C191.

1958, Jan. 10

300 A144 10p red brn 15 5

Issued in honor of Gabriela Mistral, poet and educator. See also No. C192.

Arms of Osorno A145 — Arms of Santiago A146

Design: 50p, García Hdo. de Mendoza.

1958, Mar. 23 Lithographed *Perf. 14*

301 A145 10p carmine 15 10

Engraved

302 A145 50p green 40 15

Issued to commemorate the 400th anniversary of the founding of the city of Osorno, capital of Osorno province.
Souvenir sheet including No. 302 in red brown is noted below No. C193.

1958, Oct. 18 *Perf. 14* Unwmkd.

303 A146 10p dk vio 15 5

Issued to publicize the National Philatelic Exposition, Santiago, Oct. 18–26.
Souvenir sheet including No. 303 in deep red is noted below No. C194.

Symbolical Savings Bank A147 — Modern Map of Antarctica A148

1958, Dec. 18

304 A147 10p dk bl 15 5

Issued to commemorate the centenary of the Savings Bank for Public Employees.
Souvenir sheet including No. 304 in violet is noted below No. C195.

1958, Aug. 28 *Perf. 14* Unwmkd.

305 A148 40p rose car 20 10

Issued to commemorate the International Geophysical Year, 1957–1958. See No. C214.

Antarctic Map and 'La Araucana' A149 — Map of Strait of Magellan, 1588 A150

1958 Lithographed. *Perf. 14*

310 A149 10p vio bl 15 10

Engraved.

311 A150 200p dl pur 2.25 75

See also Nos. C199–C200.

Valdivia River Bridge A153

1959, Feb. 9 Engraved *Perf. 14*

319 A153 40p green 20 10

Issued to commemorate the centenary of the German School in Valdivia and to publicize the Valdivia Philatelic Exhibition, Feb. 9–18.
Souvenir sheet including No. 319 is noted below No. C213.

Strait of Magellan, Map by Pedro Sarmiento de Gamboa, c. 1582 A154

1959, Aug. 27 Lithographed

320 A154 10p dl pur 20 10

Issued to commemorate the 400th anniversary of the Juan Ladrillero expedition to explore the Strait of Magellan, 1557–1558. See also No. C215.

Diego Barros Arana A155 — Henri Dunant A156

1959, Aug. 27

321 A155 40p ultra 20 10

Issued to commemorate the 50th anniversary of the death of Diego Barros Arana (1830–1907), historian. See No. C216.

1959, Oct. 6 *Perf. 14* Unwmkd.

322 A156 20p red & red brn 15 5

Issued to commemorate the centenary of the Red Cross idea. See No. C217.

Manuel Bulnes A157 — Francisco A. Pinto A158

Choshuenco Volcano A159

Designs: No. 326, Choshuenco volcano, redrawn. 5c, Manuel Montt. 10c, Maule River Valley. 20c, 1e, Inca Lake.

1960–67 Lithographed *Perf. 13x14*

323 A157 5m bluish grn 5 5
324 A158 1c carmine 5 5

Perf. 14

Size: 29x25mm.

325 A159 2c ultra ('61) 10 5

Perf. 14x13

Size: 23½x18mm.

326 A159 2c ultra ('62) 5 5

Perf. 13x14

327 A157 5c blue 10 5

Perf. 14

Size: 29x25mm.

328 A159 10c grn ('62) 25 10
329 A159 20c Prus bl ('62) 40 15
329A A159 1e bluish grn ('67) 50 25
Nos. 323-329A (8) 1.50 75

On No. 325 "Volcan Choshuenco" is at upper left, below "Correos." On No. 326, it is at bottom, above "Centesimos."

Refugee Family A160

1960, Apr. 7 *Perf. 14½*

330 A160 1c green 15 10

Issued to publicize World Refugee Year, July 1, 1959–June 30, 1960. A souvenir sheet is noted below No. C218.

Type of Air Post Issue, 1962, and

Arms of Chile A161

José M. Carrera A162

Designs: No. 332, Palace of Justice. 5c, National Memorial. 10c, Manuel de Toro y Zambrano and Martinez de Rozas. 20c, Manuel de Salas and Juan Egana. 50c, Manuel Rodriguez and Juan Mackenna.

Wmk. 215 (#331, 1e); Unwmkd.

1960–65 Engraved *Perf. 14½*

331 A161 1c mar & sep 20 10
332 A161 1c brn & cl ('62) 15 5
333 A162 5c grn & Prus grn ('61) 15 5
334 AP54 10c brn & vio brn ('64) 20 5
334A AP54 20c ind & bl grn ('65) 20 5
335 AP54 50c red brn & mar ('65) 35 15
336 A162 1e gray ol & brn 1.25 50
Nos.331-336, C218A-C220D (14) 5.00 2.05

Issued to commemorate the 150th anniversary of the formation of the first National Government. A souvenir sheet is noted below No. C220B. See also No. C285.

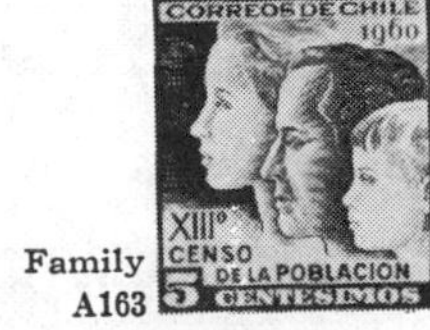

Family A163

Design: 10c, Various buildings.

Lithographed

1960, Jan. 18 *Perf. 14* Unwmkd.

337 A163 5c green 20 8
338 A163 10c brt vio 20 8

Issued to publicize the 13th population census (No. 337) and the second housing census (No. 338).

Chamber of Deputies A164

1961, Aug. 14 *Perf. 14½* Unwmkd.

339 A164 2c red brn 60 10

Issued to commemorate the 150th anniversary of the first National Congress. See also No. C245.

Soccer Players and Globe A165

Design: 5c, Goalkeeper and stadium (vert.).

1962, May 30 Engr. *Perf. 14½*

340 A165 2c blue 20 10
341 A165 5c green 30 10

Issued to commemorate the World Soccer Championship, Chile, May 30–June 17.
Note on souvenir sheet follows No. C247.

Mother and Child A166 — Centenary Emblem A167

1963, Mar. 21 Litho. *Perf. 14*

342 A166 3c maroon 10 5

Issued for the "Freedom from Hunger" campaign of the U.N. Food and Agriculture Organization. See also No. C248.

1963, Aug. 23 *Perf. 14* Unwmkd.

343 A167 3c red & gray 15 8

Issued to commemorate the centenary of the International Red Cross. See No. C249.

Fireman Carrying Woman A168 — Enrique Molina A169

1963, Dec. 20 *Perf. 14* Unwmkd.

344 A168 3c violet 10 8

Issued to commemorate the centenary of the Santiago Fire Brigade. See No. C250.

1964, Nov. 14 Litho. *Perf. 14*

Design: No. 346, Msgr. Carlos Casanueva.

345 A169 4c bis brn 15 5
346 A169 4c rose cl 10 5

Issued to honor Enrique Molina, founder of the University of Concepcion, and Msgr. Carlos Casanueva, rector of the Catholic University, 1920–53. See Nos. C257–C258.

Easter Island Statue A170 — Copihue, National Flower A171

Design: 30c, Robinson Crusoe.

1965–69 Litho. *Perf. 14x14½*

347 A170 6c rose lil 10 6
347A A170 10c rose pink ('68) 10 6

Perf. 14

348 A171 15c yel grn & rose red 15 8
348A A171 20c yel grn & rose red ('69) 10 6

Perf. 14x14½

349 A170 30c rose cl 20 15

Skier A172 — Lorenzo Sazie A173

1965, Aug. 30 *Perf. 14*

350 A172 4c bl grn 10 5

World Skiing Championships, Chile, 1966.

1966, Feb. 9 Litho. *Perf. 14x14½*

351 A173 1e green 60 10

Issued to commemorate the centenary of the death of Dr. Lorenzo Sazie, dean of the Faculty of Medicine, University of Santiago.

German Riesco, President in 1901–1906
A174

Portrait: 30c, Jorge Montt (1847–1922), president in 1891–1896.

1966 *Perf. 13x14* Unwmkd.

354 A174 30c violet 10 5
355 A174 50c dl brn 10 5

William Wheelwright and S.S. Chile
A175

1966, Aug. 2 *Perf. 14½*

358 A175 10c ultra & lt bl 10 8

Issued to commemorate the 125th anniversary (in 1965) of the arrival of the paddle steamers "Chile" and "Peru." See also No. C268.

Learning to Read
A176

1966, Aug. 13 Litho. *Perf. 14*

359 A176 10c red brn 10 8

Literacy campaign.

U.N. and ICY Emblems
A177

1966, Oct. 28 *Perf. 14½* Unwmkd.

360 A177 1e grn & brn 1.00 20

International Cooperation Year, 1965. See No. C269.

Capt. Luis Pardo and Ship in Antarctica—A178

1967, Jan. Litho. *Perf. 14½*

361 A178 20c turq bl 10 10

Issued to commemorate the 50th anniversary of the rescue of the Shackleton South Pole expedition by Capt. Luis Pardo of Chile. See also No. C271.

Family A179 — Trees and Mountains A180

1967, Apr. 13 *Perf. 14* Unwmkd.

362 A179 10c mag & blk 5 5

Issued to publicize the 8th International Conference for Family Planning, Santiago, April 1967. See also No. C272.

1967, June 9 Litho. *Perf. 14½*

363 A180 10c bl grn & lt bl 5 5

Reforestation Campaign. See No. C274.

Lions Emblem
A181

1967, July 12 Litho. *Perf. 14*

364 A181 20c Prus bl & yel 15 10

Issued to commemorate the 50th anniversary of Lions International. See also Nos. C275–C276.

Chilean Flag
A182

1967, Oct. 20 *Perf. 14½* Unwmkd.

365 A182 80c crim & ultra 15 10

Issued to commemorate the sesquicentennial of the national flag. See No. C277.

José Maria Cardinal Caro
A183

1967, Dec. 4 Engraved *Perf. 14½*

366 A183 20c dp car 60 20

Issued to commemorate the centenary of the birth of José Maria Cardinal Caro, the first Chilean cardinal. See No. C279.

San Martin and O'Higgins
A184

1968, Apr. 23 Litho. Unwmkd.

367 A184 3e blue 10 6

Issued to commemorate the sesquicentennial of the Battles of Chacabuco and Maipu. See No. C280.

Farm Couple
A185

1968, June 18 *Perf. 14½*

368 A185 20c blk, org & grn 20 10

Agrarian reforms. See No. C281.

Juan I. Molina
A186

1968, Aug. 27 Litho. *Perf. 14½*

369 A186 2e red lil 10 6

Issued to honor Juan I. Molina, educator and scientist. See also No. C282.

Hand Holding Cogwheel
A187

1968, Sept. *Perf. 14x14½*

370 A187 30c dp car 10 6

Fourth census of manufacturers.

Map of Chiloé Province, Sailing Ship and Coastal Vessel
A188

1968, Oct. 7 *Perf. 14½*

371 A188 30c ultra 10 6

Issued to commemorate the anniversaries of the founding of five towns in Chiloé Province. See also No. C283.

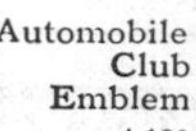

Automobile Club Emblem
A189

1968, Nov. 10 Engr. *Perf. 14½x14*

372 A189 1e car rose 10 6

Issued to commemorate the 40th anniversary of the Automobile Club of Chile. See No. C284.

Francisco Garcia Huidobro
A190

Design: 5e, King Philip V of Spain.

1968, Dec. 31 Litho. *Perf. 14½*

373 A190 2e pale rose & ultra 10 6
374 A190 5e brn & yel grn 15 8

Issued to commemorate the 225th anniversary of the founding of the State Mint (Casa de Moneda de Chile). See Nos. C288–C289.

Satellite and Radar Station
A191

1969, May 20 Litho. *Perf. 14½*

375 A191 30c blue 10 5

Issued to publicize the inauguration of ENTEL-Chile, the first commercial satellite communications ground station, Longovilo. See No. C290.

Red Cross, Crescent and Lion and Sun Emblems—A192

1969, Sept. Lithographed *Perf. 14½*

376 A192 2e vio bl & red 10 6

Issued to commemorate the 50th anniversary of the League of Red Cross Societies. See No. C291.

Rapel Hydro-electric Plant
A193

1969, Nov. 18 Litho. *Perf. 14½*

377 A193 40c green 10 8

See No. C292.

Col. Rodriguez Monument
A194

1969, Nov. 24

378 A194 2e rose cl 10 6

Issued to commemorate the 150th anniversary of the death of Col. Manuel Rodriguez. See No. C293.

EXPO '70 Emblem
A195

1969, Dec. 2 Litho. *Perf. 14*

379 A195 3e blue 8 5

Issued to publicize EXPO '70 International Exhibition, Osaka, Japan, March 15–Sept. 13, 1970. See No. C294.

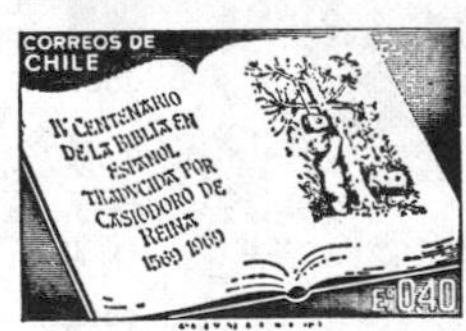

Open Book
A196

1969, Dec. 3 *Perf. 14½*

380 A196 40c red brn 5 5

Issued to commemorate the 400th anniversary of the translation of the Bible into Spanish by Casiodoro de Reina. See No. C295.

Globes and ILO Emblem
A197

1969, Dec. 17 *Perf. 14½*

381 A197 1e grn & blk 8 5

Issued to commemorate the 50th anniversary of the International Labor Organization. See No. C296.

Human Rights Flame
A198

1969, Dec. 18

382 A198 4e bl & red 8 5

Human Rights Year, 1968. See No. C297.

Policarpo Toro and Easter Island
A199

1970, Jan. 26 *Perf. 14½*

383 A199 5e lilac 8 5

Issued to commemorate the 80th anniversary of the acquisition of Easter Island. See No. C298.

Sailing Ship and Arms of Valdivia
A200

1970, Feb. 4 Litho. *Perf. 14½*

384 A200 40c dk car 10 5

Issued to commemorate the 150th anniversary of the capture of Valdivia during Chile's war of independence by Thomas Cochrane (1775–1860), naval commander. See No. C299.

Paul Harris and Rotary Emblem
A201

1970, Mar. 18 Lithographed *Perf. 14*

385 A201 10e vio bl 10 5

Issued to commemorate the centenary of the birth of Paul Harris (1868–1947), founder of Rotary International. See No. C300.

Mahatma Gandhi
A202

Santo Domingo Church, Santiago, Chile
A203

1970, Apr. 1 Litho. *Perf. 14½*

386 A202 40c bl grn 10 5

Issued to commemorate the centenary of the birth of Mohandas K. Gandhi (1869–1948), leader in India's fight for independence. See No. C301.

1970, Apr. 30 Engraved

Designs: 2e, Casa de Moneda de Chile (horiz.). 3e, Pedro de Valdivia. 5e, Bridge (horiz.). 10e, Ambrosio O'Higgins.

387 A203 2e vio brn 10 5
388 A203 3e dk red 8 5
389 A203 4e dk bl 8 5
390 A203 5e brown 10 5
391 A203 10e green 10 8
Nos. 387-391 (5) 46 28

Issued to commemorate the exploration and development of Chile by Spanish explorers.

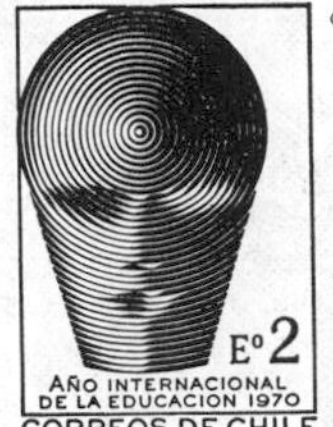

Education Year Emblem
A204

Virgin and Child
A205

1970, July 17 Litho. *Perf. 14½*

392 A204 2e claret 8 5

Issued for International Education Year. See No. C302.

1970, July 28

393 A205 40c green 8 5

Issued to publicize the O'Higgins National Shrine at Maipu. See No. C303.

Torch and Snake—A206

Copper Symbol, Chile Arms
A207

1970, Aug. 11

394 A206 40c cl & lt bl 5 5

Issued to commemorate the International Cancer Congress, Houston, Texas, May 22–29. See No. C304.

1970, Oct. 21 Litho. *Perf. 14½*

395 A207 40c car & lt red brn 5 5

Issued to commemorate the nationalization of the copper industry. See No. C305.

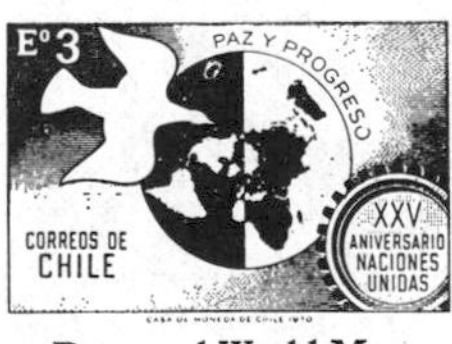

Dove and World Map
A208

1970, Oct. 22

396 A208 3e rose mag & pur 8 5

Issued to commemorate the 25th anniversary of the United Nations. See No. C306.

No. 375 Surcharged in Red

1970, Dec. 24 Litho. *Perf. 14½*

397 A191 52c on 30c bl 10 8

Freighter and Ship's Wheel
A209

1971, Jan. 18 Litho. *Perf. 14*

398 A209 52c dp car 8 5

National Maritime Commission. See No. C307.

Bernardo O'Higgins and Ship
A210

1971, Feb. 3 *Perf. 14½*

399 A210 5e grnsh bl & grn 8 5

The 150th anniversary of the expedition to liberate Peru from Spanish rule. See No. C309.

Youth, Girl and U.N. Emblem
A211

1971, Feb. 11 Litho. *Perf. 14½*

400 A211 52c dk bl & brn 8 5

First meeting in Latin America of the Executive Council of UNICEF (U.N. Children's Fund), Santiago, May 20–31, 1969. See No. C310.

Chilean Boy Scout Emblem
A212

1971, Feb. 10 *Perf. 14*

401 A212 1e grn & brn 8 5

Founding of Chilean Boy Scouts, 60th anniversary. See No. C311.

Satellite and Radar Station
A213

1971, May 25 Litho. *Perf. 14½*

402 A213 40c dl grn 10 5

First commercial Chilean satellite communications ground station, Longovilo. See No. C312.

Diver with Harpoon Gun
A214

1971, Sept. 1

403 A214 1.15e lt & dk grn 10 5
404 A214 2.35e vio bl & dp vio bl 8 5

10th World Championship of Underwater Fishing.

Ferdinand Magellan and Sailing Ship
A215

1971, Nov. 3

405 A215 35c lt vio & brn vio 8 5

450th anniversary of first trip through and discovery of the Strait of Magellan, Oct. 21–Nov. 28, 1520.

Dagoberto Godoy and Plane over Andes
A216

1971, Nov. 4

406	A216	1.15e bl & grn	8	5

First trans-Andean flight, Dec. 12, 1918.

Virgin of San Cristobal
A217

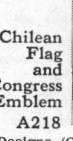

Chilean Flag and Congress Emblem
A218

Designs (Congress Emblem and): 4.35e, Church of San Francisco. 9.35e, Central post office (horiz.). 18.35e, La Posada (Inn) del Corregidor (horiz.).

1971

407	A217	1.15e dk bl	15	8
408	A218	2.35e ultra & car	10	5
409	A217	4.35e brn red	10	5
410	A217	9.35e violet	10	5
411	A217	18.35e lil rose	15	8
		Nos. 407-411 (5)	60	31

10th Congress of the Postal Union of the Americas and Spain, Santiago. Issue dates: 2.35e, 4.35e, Nov. 5; 1.15e, Nov. 11; 9.35e, Nov. 18; 18.35e, Nov. 19.

Observation Dome, Cerro el Tololo Observatory
A219

1971, Dec. 18

412	A219	1.95e lt & dk bl	8	5

Boeing 707 over Easter Island
A220

1971, Dec. 18

413	A220	2.35e dk brn & yel	8	5

Inauguration of flights to Easter Island.

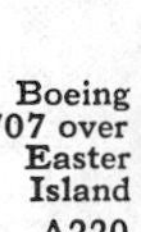

Alonso de Ercilla y Zuniga
A221

1972, Mar. 20 Engraved *Perf. 14*

414	A221	1e dk red	8	5

4th centenary (in 1969) of "La Araucana," by Alonso de Ercilla y Zuniga (1533–1596), Spanish author. See No. C313.

Map of Antarctica and Dog Sled
A222

1972, Mar. 20 Litho. *Perf. 14½x15*

415	A222	1.15e vio bl & blk	10	5
416	A222	3.50e bl grn & grn	8	5

10th anniversary (in 1971) of the Antarctic Treaty pledging peaceful uses of and scientific cooperation in Antarctica.

"Your Heart is your Health"
A223

1972, Apr. 2 Litho. *Perf. 14½*

417	A223	1.15e blk & car	8	5

World Health Day.

People and Statement by Pres. Allende
A224

Conference Hall and U.N. Emblem
A225

1972, Apr. 13 Litho. *Perf. 14½*

418	A224	35c dl grn & buff	10	8
419	A225	1.15e ultra & pur	8	5
420	A224	4e dk pur & pale rose	10	8
421	A225	6e org & vio bl	10	5

3rd United Nations Conference on Trade and Development (UNCTAD III), Santiago, Apr.–May 1972. Design A224 is perforated horizontally in the middle.

Soldier, 1822, Andes, Military College Emblem
A226

1972, June 9

422	A226	1.15e bl & yel	8	5

Sesquicentennial of Bernardo O'Higgins Military College.

Miner Holding Copper Ingot, Chilean Flag
A227

Sailing Ship
A228

1972, July 11 Litho. *Perf. 15x14½*

423	A227	1.15e bl & rose red	8	5
424	A227	5e bl, blk & rose red	10	5

Nationalization of copper industry.

1972, Aug. 4

425	A228	1.15e vio brn	8	5

Sesquicentennial of the Arturo Pratt Naval Training School.

Mt. Calan Observatory
A229

1972, Aug. 31 Litho. *Perf. 14½*

426	A229	50c ultra	10	5

University of Chile Mt. Calan Observatory.

Carrier Pigeon
A230

1972, Oct. 9 Litho. *Perf. 14½*

427	A230	1.15e red lil & vio	8	5

International Letter Writing Week, Oct. 9–15.

René Schneider and Army Flag—A231

1972, Oct. 25 *Perf. 14*

428	A231	2.30e multi	8	5

2nd anniversary of the death of Gen. René Schneider. No. 428 is perforated vertically in the middle.

Book and Young People
A232

1972, Oct. 31 *Perf. 14½*

429	A232	50c blk & dp org	8	5

International Book Year 1972.

Guitar and Earthen Jar
A233

Designs: 2.65e, Fish and produce. 3.50e, Stove, pots and rug (vert.).

1972, Nov. 20 Litho. *Perf. 14½*

430	A233	1.15e red & blk	8	5
431	A233	2.65e ultra & rose lake	8	5
432	A233	3.50e red & red brn	8	5

Tourism Year of the Americas.

José M. Carrera Before Execution
A234

Map of Antarctica, Flag at O'Higgins Base
A235

1973, Feb. 1 Litho. *Perf. 14½*

433	A234	2.30e lt ultra	8	5

Sesquicentennial of the death of José Miguel Carrera (1785–1821), Chilean revolutionist and dictator.

1973, Feb. 8

434	A235	10e ultra & red	8	5

25th anniversary of the Bernardo O'Higgins Antarctic Base.

Naval Air Service Emblem, Destroyer
A236

La Silla Observatory
A237

1973, Mar. 16 Litho. *Perf. 14½*

435	A236	20e brt bl & ocher	8	5

Chilean Naval Aviation, 50th anniversary.

1973, Apr. 25 Litho. *Perf. 14½*

436	A237	2.30e ultra & blk	8	5

INTERPOL Emblem
A238

Designs: 50e, Fingerprint over globe.

1973, Sept. 23 Litho. *Perf. 14½*

437	A238	30e bis & ultra	10	8
438	A238	50e blk & red	25	8

50th anniversary of International Criminal Police Organization.

Grapes
A239

Design: 100e, Globe inscribed "Chile Exporta Vino."

1973, Dec. 10 Litho. *Perf. 14½*

No.	Type	Description	Unused	Used
439	A239	20e buff & lil	10	8
440	A239	100e bl & cl	10	8

Chilean wine export.

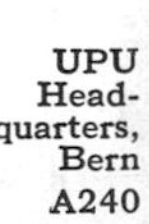

UPU Headquarters, Bern
A240

1974, Apr. 4

No.	Type	Description	Unused	Used
441	A240	500e on 45c grn	8	5

Centenary of Universal Postal Union. No. 441 was not issued without dark green surcharge and overprint.

Bernardo O'Higgins, Armed Forces Emblems—A241

1974, Apr. 11 Litho. *Perf. 14½*

Multicolored

No.	Type	Description	Unused	Used
442	A241	30e *shown*	8	5
443	A241	30e *Soldiers with mortar*	8	5
444	A241	30e *Navy anti-aircraft gunners*	8	5
445	A241	30e *Pilot in cockpit*	8	5
446	A241	30e *Mounted policeman*	8	5
		Nos. 442-446 (5)	40	25

Honoring the Armed Forces.

Soccer Ball and Globe
A242

Traffic Police
A243

Design: 1000e, Soccer ball and stadium (horiz.).

1974 Lithographed *Perf. 14*

No.	Type	Description	Unused	Used
447	A242	500e dk red & org	10	5
448	A242	1000e bl & ind	20	10

World Cup Soccer Championship, Munich, June 13—July 7.

A souvenir sheet contains 2 imperf. stamps similar to Nos. 447—448, with blue marginal inscription. Printed on thin card. Size: 90x119mm.

Nos. 386, 355 Surcharged

1974, June Litho. *Perf. 14½*

No.	Type	Description	Unused	Used
449	A202	100e on 40c bl grn	10	5

Perf. 13x14

No.	Type	Description	Unused	Used
450	A174	300e on 50c dl brn	10	5

1974, June 20 *Perf. 14½*

No.	Type	Description	Unused	Used
451	A243	30e red brn & grn	10	5

Traffic safety.

Santiago-Fiji Air Service—A244

1974, Sept. 5 Litho. *Perf. 14½x14*

Brown & Green

No.	Type	Description	Unused	Used
452	A244	Block of 4	1.00	50
a.		200e *Easter Island turtle*	20	10
b.		200e *Polynesian dancer*	20	10
c.		200e *Map of Fiji Islands*	20	10
d.		200e *Kangaroo*	20	10

Inauguration of air service by LAN (Chile's national airline) from Santiago to Easter Island, Tahiti, Fiji, Australia.

Globe Cut to Show Mantle and Core
A245

1974, Sept. 9 *Perf. 14x14½*

No.	Type	Description	Unused	Used
453	A245	500e red brn & org	10	5

International Volcanology Congress, Santiago, Sept. 9—14.

No. 393 Surcharged in Brown

E°100

24 OCTUBRE 1974

INAUGURACION TEMPLO VOTIVO

1974, Oct. 24 Litho. *Perf. 14½*

No.	Type	Description	Unused	Used
454	A205	100e on 40c grn	10	8

Inauguration of the O'Higgins National Shrine at Maipu, Oct. 24, 1974.

Juan Fernandez Archipelago—A246

1974, Nov. 22 Litho. *Perf. 14½x14*

Blue & Brick Red

No.	Type	Description	Unused	Used
455	A246	Block of 4	75	50
a.		200e *Robinson Crusoe Island*	15	10
b.		200e *Chonta palms*	15	10
c.		200e *Mountain goat*	15	10
d.		200e *Crayfish*	15	10

400th anniversary of discovery of Juan Fernandez Archipelago.

O'Higgins and Bolivar
A247

1974, Dec. 9 *Perf. 14½*

No.	Type	Description	Unused	Used
456	A247	100e red brn & buff	8	5

Sesquicentennial of the Battles of Junin and Ayacucho.

F. Vidal Gormaz and Institute Seal
A248

Albert Schweitzer
A249

1975, Jan. 22 Litho. *Perf. 14½*

No.	Type	Description	Unused	Used
457	A248	100e rose cl & bl	10	6

Centenary of the Naval Hydrographic Institute; F. Vidal Gormaz was first commandant.

1975, Apr. 7 Litho. *Perf. 14x14½*

No.	Type	Description	Unused	Used
458	A249	500e yel & red brn	12	6

Dr. Albert Schweitzer (1875—1965), medical missionary, birth centenary.

E° 70.-

No. 395 Surcharged in Red

Revalorizada
1975

1975, Apr. 7 *Perf. 14½*

No.	Type	Description	Unused	Used
459	A207	70e on 40c car & lt red brn	10	6

Volunteer Lifeboat Service—A250

1975, Apr. 15 Litho. *Perf. 14½x14*

Dark Blue & Gray Olive

No.	Type	Description	Unused	Used
460	A250	Block of 4	75	50
a.		150e *Lighthouse*	15	10
b.		150e *Shipwreck*	15	10
c.		150e *Lifeboat*	15	10
d.		150e *Sailor reaching for life preserver*	15	10

Valparaiso Volunteer Lifeboat service, 50th anniversary.

Frigate Lautaro
A251

1975, May 21 Photo. & Engr.

Emerald & Black

No.	Type	Description	Unused	Used
461	A251	500e *shown*	20	10
462	A251	500e *Corvette Baquedano*	20	10
463	A251	500e *Cruiser Chacabuco*	20	10
464	A251	500e *Brigantine Goleta Esmeralda*	20	10

Orange & Black

No.	Type	Description	Unused	Used
465	A251	800e *Frigate Lautaro*	25	10
466	A251	800e *Corvette Baquedano*	25	10
467	A251	800e *Cruiser Chacabuco*	25	10
468	A251	800e *Brigantine Goleta Esmeralda*	25	10

Ultramarine & Black

No.	Type	Description	Unused	Used
469	A251	1000e *Frigate Lautaro*	35	12
470	A251	1000e *Corvette Baquedano*	35	12
471	A251	1000e *Cruiser Chacabuco*	35	12
472	A251	1000e *Brigantine Goleta Esmeralda*	35	12
		Nos.461-472 (12)	3.20	1.28

Shipwreck of training frigate Lautaro, 30th anniversary. Stamps of same denomination printed se-tenant in sheets of 25 (5x5) with 7 Lautaro stamps and 6 each of the others.

A souvenir card contains impressions of Nos. 469—472 with ultramarine and orange marginal inscription and decoration. Size: 118x150mm.

Happy Mother, by Alfredo Valenzuela P.
A252

Diego Portales, Finance Minister
A253

Paintings: No. 474, Young Girl, by Francisco Javier Mandiola. No. 475, Lucia Guzman, by Pedro Lira Rencoret. No. 476, Woman, by Magdalena Mira Mena.

1975, Oct. 13 Litho. *Perf. 14½*

No.	Type	Description	Unused	Used
473	A252	50c multi	12	8
474	A252	50c multi	12	8
475	A252	50c multi	12	8
476	A252	50c multi	12	8

International Women's Year 1975. Gray inscription on back, printed beneath gum, gives details about painting shown.

A souvenir card contains impressions of Nos. 473—476 with black and blue marginal inscription and decoration. Size: 149x120 mm.

Inscribed D. Portales

1975-78 Litho. *Perf. 13x14*

No.	Type	Description	Unused	Used
477	A253	10c gray grn	8	5
478	A253	20c vio ('76)	8	5
479	A253	30c org ('76)	8	5
480	A253	50c lt brn	8	5
481	A253	1p blue	8	5
482	A253	1.50p ocher ('76)	10	5
483	A253	2p gray ('77)	10	5
483A	A253	2.50p cit ('78)	10	5
483B	A253	3.50p pnksh rose ('78)	20	5
484	A253	5p rose cl	20	5
		Nos. 477-484 (10)	1.10	50

See Nos. 635-639.

Cochrane and Liberating Squadron, 1820—A254

Designs: No. 486, Capture of Valdivia, 1820. No. 487, Capture of Three-master Esmeralda, 1820. No. 488, Cruiser Cochrane, 1874. No. 489, Destroyer Cochrane, 1962.

1976, Jan. 6 ***Perf. 14½***

485 A254 1p multi 12 8
486 A254 1p multi 12 8
487 A254 1p multi 12 8
488 A254 1p multi 12 8
489 A254 1p multi 12 8
Nos. 485-489 (5) 60 40

Lord Thomas Cochrane, first commander of Chilean Navy, birth bicentenary. Nos. 485–489 printed se-tenant.

Flags of Chile and Bolivia A255

1976, May 25 **Litho.** ***Perf. 14½***

490 A255 1.50p multi 15 8

Sesquicentennial of Bolivia's independence.

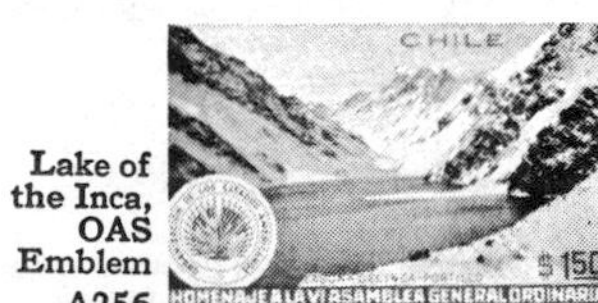

Lake of the Inca, OAS Emblem A256

1976, June 11

491 A256 1.50p multi 12 8

6th General Assembly of the Organization of American States.

George Washington A257

1976, July

492 A257 5p multi 35 15

American Bicentennial.

Minerva and Academy Emblem A258

1976, July

493 A258 2.50p multi 12 8

Polytechnic Military Academy, 50th anniversary.

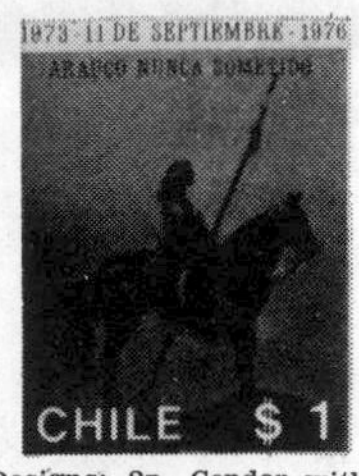

Araucan Indian A259

Designs: 2p, Condor with broken chain. 3p, Winged woman, symbolizing rebirth.

1976, Sept. 20 **Litho.** ***Perf. 14½***

494 A259 1p bl & multi 12 8
495 A259 2p bl & multi 15 8
496 A259 3p yel & multi 25 12

3rd anniversary of the Military Junta. Nos. 494–496 printed se-tenant.

View, Antarctica A260

1977, Feb. 10 **Litho.** ***Perf. 14½***

497 A260 2p multi 12 6

Visit of President Augusto Pinochet to Antarctica.

School Emblem, Planted Field A261

Justice A262

1977, Mar. 10 ***Perf. 14½***

498 A261 2p multi 12 6

Centenary of advanced agricultural education.

1977, Mar. 30 **Litho.** ***Perf. 14½***

499 A262 2p brn & sl 12 6

Supreme Court of Justice, sesquicentennial.

Eye with Globe, Caduceus A263

1977, Mar. 30 **Litho.** ***Perf. 14½***

500 A263 2p multi 12 6

11th Pan-American Ophthalmological Congress.

Mounted Policeman A264

Designs: No. 502, Policewoman with children. No. 503, Paine Peaks and Osorno Volcano, crossed rifle emblem. No. 504, Crossed rifle emblem, mounted and motorcycle policemen, helicopter and automobile. (horiz.).

1977, Apr. 27

501 A264 2p multi 12 6
502 A264 2p multi 12 6
503 A264 2p multi 12 6
504 A264 2p multi 12 6

Chilean police organization, 50th anniversary.

Intelsat Satellite over Globe A265

1977, May 17 **Litho.** ***Perf. 14½***

505 A265 2p multi 12 6

World Telecommunications Day.

El Mercurio's First Front Page, Press and Ship—A266

1977, July 5 **Litho.** ***Perf. 14½***

506 A266 2p multi 12 6

El Mercurio de Valparaiso, first Chilean newspaper, 150th anniversary.

St. Francis, Birds and Cross A267

Science and Technology A268

1977, July 26 **Litho.** ***Perf. 14½***

507 A267 5p multi 25 12

St. Francis of Assisi, 750th death anniversary.

1977, Aug. 26 **Litho.** ***Perf. 14½***

508 A268 4p multi 20 10

Young Mother Weaving A269

Designs: No. 510, Handicapped boy in wheelchair and nurse. No. 511, Children dancing in circle (horiz.). No. 512, Old man and home (horiz.).

1977, Sept. 13 **Litho.** ***Perf. 14½***

509 A269 5p multi 25 8
510 A269 5p multi 25 8
511 A269 10p multi 50 12
512 A269 10p multi 50 12

4th anniversary of Government Junta and social services of armed forces.

Diego de Almagro A270

1977, Oct. 31 **Engr.** ***Perf. 14½***

513 A270 5p rose & car 25 6

Diego de Almagro (1475–1538), leader of Spanish expedition to Chile.

Bell, Letters, Dove and Child A271

1977, Dec. 12 **Litho.** ***Perf. 14½***

514 A271 2.50p multi 12 6

Christmas 1977.

Loading Timber A272

1978 **Litho.** ***Perf. 15***

515 A272 10p multi 50 12
516 A272 20p multi 1.00 12

No. 516 inscribed "CORREOS," ship is flying Chilean flag.

Papal Arms and Globe A273

University A274

1978 **Litho.** ***Perf. 14½***

521 A273 10p multi 50 12
522 A274 25p multi 1.25 20

World Peace Day (10p); Catholic University of Valparaiso, 50th anniversary (25p). Issue dates: 10p, July 28; 25p, July 31.

O'Higgins, by Gil de Castro A275

1978, Aug. 20 Litho. *Perf. 15*

523 A275 10p multi 50 12

Bernardo O'Higgins (1778–1842), soldier and statesman.

Chacabuco Victory Monument
A276

1978, Sept. 11

524 A276 10p multi 50 12

160th anniversary of O'Higgins victory at Chacabuco, and 5th anniversary of military government.

Teacher Writing on Blackboard
A277

1978, Sept. 21

525 A277 15p multi 75 12

10th anniversary and 9th Reunion of Interamerican Council for Education, Science and Culture (C.I.E.C.C.), Sept. 21–29.

First National Fleet, by Thomas Somerscales—A278

Design: 30p, Last Moments of Rancagua Battle, by Pedro Subercaseaux.

1978 Litho. *Perf. 15*

526 A278 20p multi 1.00 12
527 A278 30p multi 1.50 20

Bernardo O'Higgins (1778–1842), soldier and statesman.
Issue dates: 20p, Oct. 9; 30p, Oct. 2.

San Martin-O'Higgins Medal, by Rene Thenot, 1942—A279

1978, Oct. 20

528 A279 7p multi 35 8

José de San Martin and Bernardo O'Higgins, 200th birth anniversaries.

A particular stamp may be scarce, but if few want it, its market potential may remain relatively low.

Council Emblem
A280

1978, Nov. 27 Litho. *Perf. 14½*

529 A280 50p multi 3.00 50

International Council of Military Sports, 30th anniversary.

Three Kings A281 **Virgin and Child A282**

1978, Dec. 14 Litho. *Perf. 14½*

530 A281 3p multi 15 8
531 A282 11p multi 60 25

Christmas 1978.

Philippi Brothers
A283

1978, Dec. 29 Litho. *Perf. 14½x15*

532 A283 3.50p multi 20 8

Bernardo E. Philippi (1811–1852) and Rodulfo A. Philippi (1808–1904), scientists and travelers.

No. 477 Surcharged in Bright Green

1979 Litho. *Perf. 13x14*

533 A253 3.50p on 10c gray grn 25 15

Flags of Chile and Salvation Army
A284

1979, Mar. 17 Litho. *Perf. 14½*

534 A284 10p multi 75 50

Salvation Army in Chile, 70th anniversary.

Pope Paul VI
A285

1979, Mar. 30

535 A285 11p multi 80 50

In memory of Pope Paul VI (1897–1978).

Battle of Maipu Monument
A286

1979, Apr. 17 Litho. *Perf. 14½*

536 A286 8.50p multi 65 40

Bernardo O'Higgins (1778–1842), Liberator of Chile.

Battle of Angamos
A287

Naval Battles: No. 538, Iquique. No. 539, Punta Gruesa.

1979, May 21 Litho. *Perf. 14½*

537 A287 3.50p multi 25 15
538 A287 3.50p multi 25 15
539 A287 3.50p multi 25 15

Centenary of victorious naval battles against Peru.

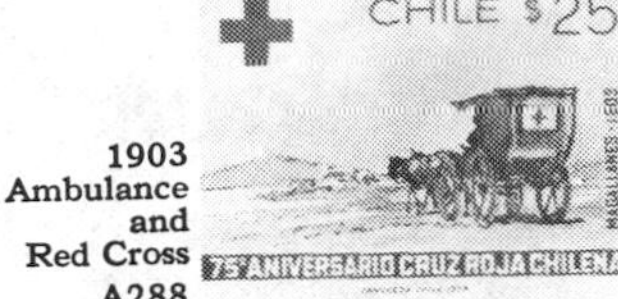

1903 Ambulance and Red Cross
A288

1979, June 29 Litho. *Perf. 14½*

540 A288 25p multi 1.50 90

75th anniversary of Chilean Red Cross.

Inscribed Diego Portales

A289

1979-86 Litho. *Perf. 13½*

542	A289	1.50p ocher	10	5
543	A289	2p gray ('81)	12	10
545	A289	3.50p red	20	10
546	A289	4.50p bl grn ('81)	25	15
547	A289	5p rose cl	30	15
548	A289	6p emerald	35	20
549	A289	7p yel ('82)	30	20
550	A289	10p bl ('82)	45	20
550A	A289	12p org ('86)	14	8
		Nos. 542-550A (9)	2.21	1.23

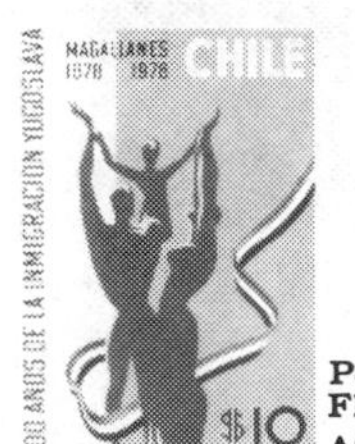

People and Flag
A290

1979, Aug. 28 Litho. *Perf. 14½*

551 A290 10p multi 60 35

Jugoslavian immigration, centenary.

Coat of Arms and Mt. Castillo—A290a

1979, Oct. 12 Litho. *Perf. 14½*

552 A290a 20p multi 1.20 75

Coyhaique 50th anniv.

IYC Emblem, Playground—A291

IYC Emblem, Children's Drawings: 11p, Girl and shadow (vert.). 12p, Dancing.

1979, Oct. 9 *Perf. 14½*

553 A291 9.50p multi 60 35
554 A291 11p multi 65 40
555 A291 12p multi 70 40

International Year of the Child.

Telecom 79—A292

1979, Oct. 26 Litho. *Perf. 14½*

556 A292 15p multi 90 50

3rd World Telecommunications Exhibition, Geneva, Sept. 20-26.

Puerto Williams, 25th Anniversary
A293

1979, Nov. 21

557 A293 3.50p multi 20 10

Adoration of the Kings—A294

1979, Dec. 4 Litho. *Perf. 15*

558 A294 3.50p multi 20 10

Christmas 1979.

Rafael Sotomayor, Minister of War
A295

Military Heroes: No. 560, Erasmo Escala. No. 561, Emilio Sotomayor. No. 562, Eleuterio Ramirez

1979, Dec. 29 *Perf. 13½*

559 A295 3.50p ocher & brn 20 10
560 A295 3.50p ocher & brn 20 10
561 A295 3.50p ocher & brn 20 10
562 A295 3.50p ocher & brn 20 10

Nos. 559-562 printed se-tenant in blocks of four.

Bell UH-1 Rescue Helicopter at Tinguiririca Volcano, by S.O. Mococain—A296

Air Force, 50th Anniversary: No. 564, Flying boat Catalina Skua over Antarctic, by E.F. Alvarez. No. 565, F5-E Tiger II over Andes, by M.M. Barria.

1980, Mar. 21 **Litho.** *Perf. 13½*

563 A296 3.50p *shown* 20 10
564 A296 3.50p *Jet* 20 10
565 A296 3.50p *Sea plane* 20 10

The Death of Bueras, by Pedro Leon Carmona—A297

1980, Apr. 14 **Litho.** *Perf. 13½*

566 A297 12p multi 70 40

Charge of Bueras, Battle of Maipo, 1818.

Rotary International, 75th Anniversary—A298

1980, Apr. 15

567 A298 10p multi 60 30

Gen. Manuel Baquedano, by Pedro Subercaseaux—A299

Gen. Pedro Lagos, Battle Scene, by Subercaseaux—A300

Battle of Morro de Arica Centenary (Subercaseaux Paintings): No. 570, Commander Juan J. San Martin, battle scene.

1980, June 7 **Litho.** *Perf. 13½*

568 A299 3.50p multi 20 10
569 A300 3.50p multi 20 10
570 A300 3.50p multi 20 10

Score and Perez's Silhouette—A301

1980, June 27 **Litho.** *Perf. 13½*

571 A301 6p multi 35 20

Osman Perez Freire (1880-1930), composer, and fragment from his song "Ay, Ay, Ay."

Mt. Gasherbrum II, Chilean Flag, Ice Pick—A302

1980, July 9

572 A302 15p multi 90 50

Chilean Himalayan expedition, June 1979.

"Charity," Stained-glass Window—A303

1980, July 18

573 A303 10p multi 60 30

Daughters of Charity, 125th anniversary in Chile.

Condor, Colors of Chile—A304

1980, Sept. 11 **Litho.** *Perf. 13½*

574 A304 3.50p multi 20 10

17th anniversary of constitution.

Inca Child Mummy

A305

Pablo Burchard, by Pedro Lira

A306

1980, Sept. 14

575 A305 5p *shown* 30 15
576 A305 5p *Claudio Gay* 30 15

National Museum of Natural History (founded by Claudio Gay, 1800-1873) sesquicentennial. Nos. 575-576 se-tenant with gutter between giving history of museums and mummy.

1980, Sept. 27 **Litho.** *Perf. 13½*

577 A306 3.50p multi 20 10

Museum of Fine Art centenary (directed by Burchard, 1932).

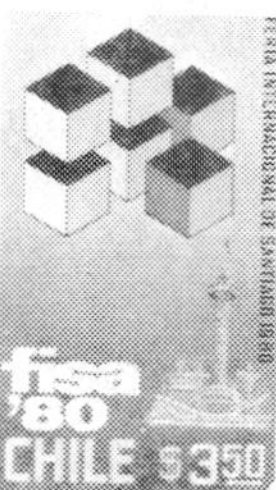

Santiago International Fair
A307

1980, Oct. 30

578 A307 3.50p multi 20 10

Nativity—A308

Christmas 1980: 3.50p, Family (vert.).

1980, Nov. 25 **Litho.** *Perf. 13½*

579 A308 3.50p multi 20 10
580 A308 10.50p multi 65

Infantryman 1879
A309

Congress Emblem
A310

Designs: Pacific War period uniforms, 1879. Nos. 581-584 se-tenant.

1980, Nov. 27

581 A309 3.50p *shown* 20 10
582 A309 3.50p *Cavalry officer* 20 10
583 A309 3.50p *Artillery officer* 20 10
584 A309 3.50p *Engineer colonel* 20 10

1980, Dec. 1

585 A310 11.50p multi 70 40

23rd International Congress of Military Medicine and Pharmacy.

Successful Eradication of Hoof and Mouth Disease—A311

1981, Jan. 16 **Litho.** *Perf. 13½*

586 A311 9.50p multi 45 15

Maoi Statues, Easter Island—A312

1981, Jan. 28 **Litho.** *Perf. 13½*

587 A312 3.50p shown 16 10
588 A312 3.50p Robinson Crusoe Island 16 10
589 A312 10.50p Penguins, Antarctic Territory 65 50

National Heroine Javiera Carrera, by O.M. Pizarro, Birth Bicentenary—A313

1981, Mar. 20

590 A313 3.50p multi 16 10

UPU Membership Centenary—A314

1981, Apr. 1

591 A314 3.50p multi 16 10

C130 Hercules Air Force Transport Plane Unloading Cargo—A315

1981, Apr. 21

592 A315 3.50p multi 16 10

Lieutenant Marsh Air Force Base, first anniversary.

13th World Telecom—munications Day—A316

1981, May 17 **Litho.** ***Perf. 13½***

593 A316 3.50p multi 16 10

Arturo Prat Naval Base A317

1981, June 23 **Litho.** ***Perf. 13½***

594 A317 3.50p multi 16 10

Capt. Jose Luis Araneda—A318

1981, June 26

595 A318 3.50p multi 16 10

Battle of Sangrar centenary.

Philatelic Society of Chile, 90th Anniv.—A319

1981, July 29 **Litho.** ***Perf. 13½***

596 A319 4.50p multi 20 10

Minister Recabarren and Chief Conuepan Giving Speeches, by Hector Robles Acuna—A320

1981, Aug. 7

597 A320 4.50p multi 20 10

Temuco city centenary.

Exports—A321

1981, Aug. 31 **Litho.** ***Perf. 13½***

598 A321 14p multi 65 35

Palacio de Moneda (Govt. Mint)—A322

1981, Sept. 11

599 A322 4.50p multi 20 15

Natl. liberation, 8th anniv.

St. Vincent de Paul, 400th Birth Anniv.—A323

1981, Sept. 27 **Litho.** ***Perf. 13½***

600 A323 4.50p multi 25 10

Andres Bello, Statesman, Birth Bicentenary

A324

1981, Sept. 29

601 A324 4.50p Coin 25 10
602 A324 9.50p Bust, books 50 15
603 A324 11.50p Statue, arms 60 25

2nd Congress of South American Uniformed Police—A325

1981, Oct. 15

604 A325 4.50p multi 25 10

World Food Day—A326

1981, Oct. 16

605 A326 5.50p multi 30 10

Uniform Type of 1980

1879 Parade Uniforms. Nos. 544-547 se-tenant.

1981, Nov. 6 ***Perf. 13½***

606 A309 5.50p Infantry private 30 10
607 A309 5.50p Cadet 30 10
608 A309 5.50p Cavalryman 30 10
609 A309 5.50p Artilleryman 30 10

Intl. Year of the Disabled—A327

1981, Nov. 11

610 A327 5.50p multi 30 10

Christmas 1981—A328

1981, Nov. 25

611 A328 5.50p Nativity 30 10
612 A328 11.50p Three Kings 60 25

50th Anniv. of Federico Santa Maria Technical University—A329

1981, Dec. 1 **Litho.** ***Perf. 13½***

613 A329 5.50p multi 30 10

Dario Salas (1881-1941), Educator—A330

1981, Dec. 4

614 A330 5.50p multi 30 10

FIDA '82, 2nd Natl. Air Force Fair—A331

1982, Mar. 6 **Litho.** ***Perf. 13½***

615 A331 4.50p multi 25

1982 Constitution—A332

1982, Mar. 11

616 A332 4.50p Cardinal Caro, family 25
617 A332 11p Diego Portales 65
618 A332 30p Bernardo O'Higgins 1.80

Panamerican Institute of Geography and History, 12th General Assembly—A333

1982, Mar. 22 Litho. *Perf. 13½*
619 A333 4.50p multi 25

American Air Forces Cooperation System—A334

1982, Apr. 12
620 A334 4.50p multi 25

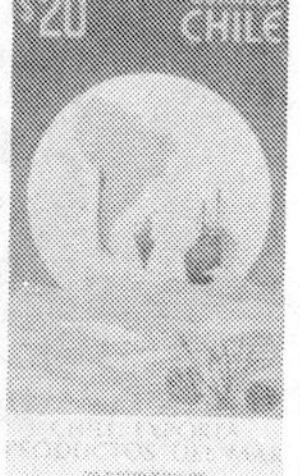

Pedro Montt—A335 Fish Exports—A336

1982
621 A335 4.50p lt vio 25

1982, May 3 Litho. *Perf. 13½*
622 A336 20p multi 1.20

Scouting Year—A337

1982, May 21 Litho. *Perf. 13*
623 Pair 50
a.-b. A337 4.50p multi 25

Battle of Concepcion Centenary—A338

Designs: Chacabuco Regiment officers killed in battle.

1982, June 18 Litho. *Perf. 13½*
624 Block of 4 1.00
a. A338 4.50p I. Carrera Pinto 25
b. A338 4.50p A. Perez Canto 25
c. A338 4.50p J. Montt Salamanca 25
d. A338 4.50p L. Cruz Martinez 25

UN World Assembly on Aging, July 26—Aug 6—A339

1982, Aug. 5
625 A339 4.50p multi 25

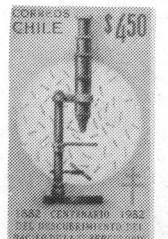

TB Bacillus Centenary—A340

1982, Aug. 31
626 A340 4.50p multi 20

9th Anniv. of National Liberation—A341

1982, Sept. 11 Litho. *Perf. 13½*
627 A341 4.50p multi 20

Christmas 1982—A342

Children's drawings.

1982, Nov. 2
628 A342 10p multi 45
629 A342 25p multi, vert. 1.00

Nos. 416-417 Surcharged in Green or Black.

1982, Nov. *Perf. 14½x15, 14½*
630 A222 1p on 3.50p bl grn & grn (G) 5
631 A223 2p on 1.15p blk & car 8

Marist Alumni, 9th World Congress—A342a

Design: 7p, Virgin Mary and Marcellus Champagnat (founder of Marist Brotherhood), stained glass window, Church of the Sacred Heart of Jesus, Barcelona.

1982, Nov. 11 Litho. *Perf. 13½*
631A A342a 7p multi 30

El Sur Newspaper Centenary—A342b

1982, Nov. 15
631B A342b 7p Wooden handpress, masthead 30

110th Anniv. of South American Steamship Co.—A342c

1982, Dec. 20
631C A342c 7p Steamer Copiapo 30

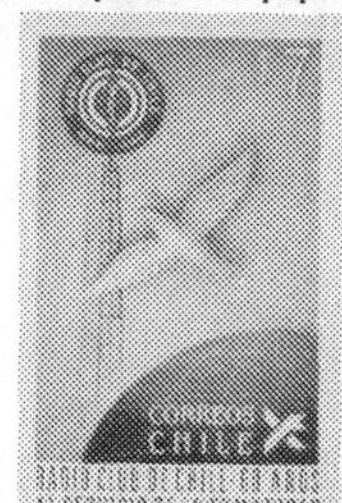

60th Anniv. of Radio Club of Chile—A342d

1982, Dec. 29
631D A342d 7p multi 30

First Anniv. of Postal Agreement with Order of Malta—A343

1983, Mar. 30 Litho. *Perf. 13½*
632 A343 25p Arms of Order of Malta 1.00
633 A343 50p Chile 2.00

Se-tenant.

D. Portales Type of 1975 Inscribed Diego Portales and:

Ramon Barros Luco—A344

Juan Luis Sanfuentes—A344a

1983-84 Litho. *Perf. 13½*

634	A344	1p	grnsh bl	5	5
635	A253	1p	chlky bl	5	5
636	A253	1.50p	ocher	6	5
636A	A344	2p	dl vio ('84)	5	5
637	A253	2p	ol gray	8	5
638	A253	2.50p	lemon	10	5
640	A253	3.50p	pink ('84)	8	5
641	A344	5p	crim rose	12	5
642	A344a	5p	red ('84)	10	5
643	A344	7p	ultra	28	8
645	A344	9p	brn ('84)	22	8
646	A344	9p	grn ('84)	22	8
647	A344	10p	black	25	8
			Nos. 634-647 (13)	1.66	77

50th Anniv. of Bureau of Investigation—A345

1983, June 19 Litho. *Perf. 13½*
649 A345 20p multi 80

Antonio Cardinal Samore (1905-1983)—A346

1983, June 26
650 A346 30p multi 1.20

Centenary of Cliff Elevators in Valparaiso—A347

1983, Aug. 19 Litho. *Perf. 13½*
651 A347 40p multi 1.00

Pucara de Quitor Settlement Ruins, San Pedro de Atacama—A348

Designs: No. 653, Llamas, rock painting, Rio Ibanez, Aisen. No. 654, Duck-shaped jug with human head, Diaguita cultures. No. 655, Puoko Tangata carved stone head, Easter Isld. (vert.).

1983, Aug. 26

652	A348	7p multi	18
653	A348	7p multi	18
654	A348	7p multi	18
655	A348	7p multi	18

10th Anniv. of National Liberation—A349

1983, Sept. 11 Litho. *Perf. 13½*

656	A349	7p Angel with broken chains	18
657	A349	7p Couple, flag	18
658	A349	10p Family, torch	25
659	A349	40p Coat of arms, "10"	1.00

Nos. 656-659 se-tenant.

Famous Hondurans—A350

Designs: No. 660, Francisco Morazan (1792-1842), Advocate of United Central America. No. 661, Jose Cecilio Del Valle (1777-1834), Scholar and Leader of Pan Americanism.

1983, Oct. 3 Litho. *Perf. 13½*

660	A350	7p multi	18
661	A350	7p multi	18

World Communications Year

A351 A352

1983, Oct. 13 Litho. *Perf. 13½*

662	A351	7p Central P.O.	18
663	A352	7p Challenger spaceship	18

Nos. 662-663 printed se-tenant.

Christmas 1983—A353

Childrens' Drawings: 10p Chilean Peasant, Hanny Chacon. 30p, Holy Family. Lucrecia Cardenas, vert.

1983, Nov. 14 Litho. *Perf. 13*

664	A353	10p multi	25
665	A353	30p multi	75

Design descriptions printed on back on top of gum.

State Railways Centenary—A354

Train Cars: a. Presidential coach, 1911. b. Service coach, 1910; tender, 1929. c. Locomotive Type 80, 1929.

1984, Jan. 4 Litho. *Perf. 13½*

666		Strip of 3	70
a.-c.	A354	9p, any single	22

3rd Intl. Air Fair, Santiago, Mar. 3-11—A355

1984, Jan. 31 Litho. *Perf. 13½*

667	A355	9p Flags, plane	22

20th Anniv. of Nuclear Energy Commission—A356

1984, Apr. 16 Litho. *Perf. 13*

668	A356	9p multi	22

Nos. 656-657 Surcharged in Purple.

1984, June 11 Litho. *Perf. 13½*

669	A349	9p on 7p #656	18
670	A349	9p on 7p #657	18

Antarctic Colonization—A357

1984, June 18

671	A357	15p Women's expedition	30
672	A357	15p Villa las Estrellas Station	30
673	A357	15p Scouts, flag, Air Force base	30

Nos. 671-673 se-tenant.

10th Anniv. of Regionalization—A358

Designs: a. Parinacota Church, Tarapaca. b. El Tatio geyser, Antofagasta. c. Copper mining, Atacama. d. Tololo Observatory, Coquimbo. e. Valparaiso Harbor, Valparaiso. f. Ahu Akivi head sculptures, Easter Isld. g. St. Francis Church, Santiago. h. El Hunique House, O'Higgins. i. Colburn Machicura Dam and Hydroelectric Power Station, Maule. j. Sta. Juana de Guadalcazar Fort, Bio-Bio. k. Indian woman, Araucania. l. Cuar Isld. Church, Los Lagos. m. Main road, Gen. del Campo. n. Shepherds' Monument, Magellanes and Antarctic. o. Family, Villa las Estrellas Station, Antarctic.

1984, July 11

674		Sheet of 15	2.75
a.-o.	A358	9p multi, any single	18

Capt. Pedro Sarmiento de Gamboa, Map, 1584—A359

1984, July 31 Litho. *Perf. 13*

675	A359	100p multi	2.00

400th anniv. of Spanish presence in Straits of Magellan.

State Bank of Chile Centenary—A360

1984, Sept. 6 Litho. *Perf. 13½*

676	A360	35p Founder Antonio Varas de la Barra, coin	70

11th Anniv. of Liberation—A361

1984, Sept. 11

677	A361	20p Monument to O'Higgins	40

Circus Centenary—A362

1984, Sept. 28 Litho. *Perf. 13½*

678	A362	45p Clown	90

Endangered Species, World Wildlife Emblem—A363

1985, July Litho. *Perf. 13½*

679	A363	9p Chinchilla	18
680	A363	9p Blue whale	18
681	A363	9p Sea lions	18
682	A363	9p Chilean huemuls	18

Nos. 679-682 se-tenant.

Christmas 1984—A364

Children's drawings.

1984, Nov. 20 Litho. *Perf. 13½*

683	A364	9p Shepherds	18
684	A364	40p Bethlehem	80

Santiago University Planetarium Opening—A365

1984, Dec. 29

685	A365	10p multi	20

Flora and Fauna—A366

Wildlife: a. Conepatus chinga. b. Leucocoryne purpurea. c. Himantopus himantopus. d. Lutra felina. e. Balbisia peduncularis. f. Psittacus cyanalysias. g. Pudu Pudu. h. Fuschia magellanica. i. Diuca diuca. j. Dusicyon griseus. k. Alstroemeria sierrae. l. Glaucidium nanum.

1985, Feb.

686		Block of 12	2.40
a.-l.	A366	10p, Any single	20

American Airforces Cooperation System, 25th Anniv.—A367

1985, Mar. 26

687 A367 45p Emblem, flags 90

Chile—Argentina Peace Treaty—A368

1985, May 2 **Litho.** ***Perf. 13½***

688 A368 20p Papal arms, flags 25

Fr. Joseph Kentenich (1885-1968), Founder, Intl. Schonstatt Movement of Catholic Laymen—A369

1985, May 19 **Litho.** ***Perf. 13½***

689 A369 40p Portrait, La Florida Sanctuary, Santiago 48

Antarctic Treaty, 25th Anniv.—A370

Resources, research: 15p, Krill, pack ice, map. 20p, Seismological Station, O'Higgin's Base. 35p, Georeception Station, dish receiver.

1985, June 21

690 A370 15p multi 18
691 A370 20p multi 24
692 A370 35p multi 42

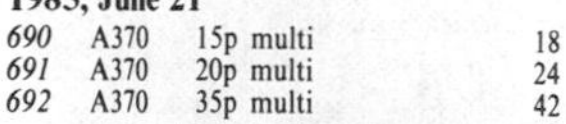

Canis Fulvipes—A371

Endangered wildlife: No. 693b, Phoenicoparrus jamesi. No. 693c, Fulica gigantea. No. 693d, Lutra provocax.

1985, Aug. 9 **Litho.** ***Perf. 13½***

693 Block of 4 1.00
a.-d. A371 20p, any single 25

Intl. Youth Year—A372

UN, 40th Anniv.—A373

1985, Aug. 31

694 A372 15p multi 18
695 A373 15p multi 18

Nos. 694-695 printed se-tenant.

Gen. Jose Miguel Carrera Verdugo (1785-1821)—A374

1985, Oct. 8 **Litho.** ***Perf. 13½***

696 A374 40p multi 45

Farmer and Ox-drawn Hay Cart—A375

Folklore: No. 697b, Street photographer, wet plate camera. No. 697c, One-man band. No. 697d, Basket maker.

1985, Oct.

697 Block of 4 40
a.-d. A375 10p, any single 10

Christmas 1985—A376

Winning children's drawings, 7th natl. design contest.

1985, Nov. 4

698 A376 15p Nativity 16
699 A376 100p Father Christmas, vert. 1.10

Nos. 698-699 inscribed in black on gummed side with child's name, age, school and region.

16th Armed Forces Conference—A377

Designs: 20p, Cavalryman, Directorial Escort, 1818. 35p, Officer, Grand Guard, 1813.

1985, Nov. 15 **Litho.** ***Perf. 13½***

700 A377 20p multi 22
701 A377 35p multi 38

Halley's Comet—A378

1985, Nov. 29 **Litho.** ***Perf. 13½***

702 A378 45p multi 48
a. Souvenir sheet

No. 702a has multicolored margin picturing US space shuttle during take-off; black control number. Exists imperf. Size: 90x105mm.

Natl. Solidarity Campaign—A379

1985

703 A379 5p red & bl 5

Campaign for Prevention of Forest Fires—A380

1985, Dec. 27

704 A380 40p Forest 45
705 A380 40p Fire destruction 45

Nos. 704-705 printed se-tenant in continuous design.

Dungeness Point Lighthouse, Straits of Magellan—A381

1986, Jan. 26

706 A381 45p shown 50
707 A381 45p Evangelistas Lighthouse 50

Nos. 706-707 printed se-tenant in a continuous design.

View of Santiago, Mackenna—A382

1986, Jan. 28

708 A382 30p multi 35

Benjamin Vicuna Mackenna (d. 1886), municipal superintendent of Santiago, 1872-1875.

Diego Portales, Natl. Crest, Text—A382a

1986, Feb. **Litho.** ***Perf. 13½***

708A A382a 12p on 3.50p multi 14

No. 708A not issued without surcharge.

1986 World Cup Soccer Championships, Mexico—A383

Host stadiums: 15p, Natl. Stadium, Chile, 1962. 20p, Aztec Stadium, Mexico, 1970. 35p, Maracana Stadium, Brazil, 1950. 50p, Wembley Stadium, Great Britain, 1966.

1986, Feb. 18

709 A383 15p multi 18
710 A383 20p multi 22
711 A383 35p multi 40
712 A383 50p multi 55

Environmental Conservation—A384

1986, Feb. 28

713 A384 20p Water 24
714 A384 20p Air 24
715 A384 20p Soil 24

Sailing Ship Santiaguillo, Flags—A385

1986, Mar. 20

716 A385 40p multi 48

Discovery of Valparaiso Bay, 450th anniv.

Interamerican Development Bank, 25th Anniv.—A386

1986, Apr. 9

717 A386 45p multi 55

St. Rosa de Lima (1586-1617), Sanctuary at Pelequen—A387

1986, Apr. 30 **Litho.** ***Perf. 13½***

718 A387 15p multi 18

Maoi Statues, Easter Is.—A388

1986, May 15

719 A388 60p Raraku Volcano 65
a. Souv. sheet 1.15
720 A388 100p Tongariki Ruins 1.10
a. Souv. sheet 1.90

Nos. 719a-720a have multicolored margins continuing the designs and bearing black control numbers. Sizes: 90x105mm, 104x90mm (100p).

AMERIPEX '86—A389

1986, May 23

721 A389 100p multi 1.10

Historic Naval Ships—A390

1986, May 30

722 A390 35p Schooner Ancud, 1843 38
723 A390 35p Armed merchantman Aguilar, 1830 38
724 A390 35p Corvette Esmeralda, 1856 38
725 A390 35p Frigate O'Higgins, 1834 38

Printed se-tenant.

Paintings by Juan Francisco Gonzalez (1853-1933)—A391

1986, June 24

726 A391 30p Rush and Chrysanthemums 32
727 A391 30p Gate of La Serena 32

Exports—A392

Designs: No. 728a, Saltpeter. No. 728b, Iron. No. 728c, Copper. No. 728d, Molybdenum.

1986 **Litho.** ***Perf. 13½***

728 Block of 4 56
a.-d. A392 12p, any single 14

Antarctic Fauna—A393

Designs: No. 729a, Sterna vittata. No. 729b, Phalacrocorax atriceps. No. 729c, Aptenodytes forsteri. No. 729d, Catharacta lonnberg.

1986, July 16 **Litho.** ***Perf. 13½***

729 Block of 4 1.80
a.-d. A393 40p, any single 45

Writers—A394

Designs: No. 730, Pedro de Oña (1570-1643). No. 731, Vicente Huidobro (1893-1948).

1986, Aug. 19

730 A394 20p multi 22
731 A394 20p multi 22

Printed se-tenant in a continuous design.

Military Academy, Cent.—A395

1986, Sept. 8 **Litho.** ***Perf. 13½***

732 A395 45p Major-General, 1878 48
733 A395 45p Major, 1950 48

Nos. 732-733 printed se-tenant.

Art—A396

1986, Oct. 17 ***Perf. 13½***

734 A396 30p Diaguita urn, duck jug 30
735 A396 30p Mapuche silver ornament, embroidery 30

Nos. 734-735 printed se-tenant.

Christmas—A397

8th Natl. design contest-winning children's drawings.

1986, Nov. 19 **Litho.** ***Perf. 13½***

736 A397 15p multi 16
737 A397 105p multi 1.10

Nos. 736-737 inscribed in black on gummed side with child's name, age, school and region.

Intl. Peace Year—A398

1986, Nov. 26

738 A398 85p multi 00

Natl. Women Volunteers—A399

1986, Dec. 15 **Litho.** ***Perf. 13½***

739 A399 15p multi 16

Crowning of Our Lady of Mt. Carmel, Patron of Chile, by Pius XI, 60th Anniv.—A400

1986, Dec. 19

740 A400 25p multi 28

Andean Railways Kitson-Meyer No. 59, 1907, designed by Robert Sterling—A401

1987, Jan. 27 **Litho.** ***Perf. 13½***

741 A401 95p multi 1.05

Arturo Prat Naval Base, Greenwich Island, the Antarctic, 40th Anniv.—A402

1987, Feb. 6

742 A402 100p Storage and power supplies 1.15
743 A402 100p Working and living quarters 1.15

Nos. 742-743 printed se-tenant in continuous design.

SEMI-POSTAL STAMPS.

S. S. Abtao and Captain Policarpo Toro—SP1

S. S. Abtao and Brother Eugenio Eyraud SP2

Perf. 14½x15

1940, Mar. 1 Engr. Unwmkd.

B1	SP1	80c +2.20p dk grn & lake	2.00	1.75
B2	SP2	3.60p +6.40p lake & dk grn	2.00	1.75

Issued in commemoration of the 50th anniversary of Chilean ownership of Easter Island. The surtax was used for charitable institutions.

These stamps were printed together in a sheet containing fifteen of each value, of which nine pairs are se-tenant.

Pedro de Valdivia SP3

Portraits: 10c+10c, Jose Toribio Medina.

1961, Apr. 29 Photo. *Perf. 13x12½*

B3	SP3	5c +5c pale brn & sl grn	1.00	25
B4	SP3	10c +10c buff & vio blk	75	25

Printed without charge by the Spanish Mint as a gift to Chile. The surtax was to aid the 1960 earthquake victims and to increase teachers' salaries. See also Nos. CB1-CB2.

No. 402 Surcharged in Dark Green

E° 27+3

"Centenario de la Organización Meteorológica Mundial IMO-W-MO 1973"

1974, Mar. 25 Litho. *Perf. 14½*

B5	A213	27e +3e on 40c dl grn	8	5

Centenary of international meteorological cooperation.

The 3e surtax of Nos. B5-B10 was for modernization of the postal system.

E° 27+3

No. 412 Surcharged in Dark Blue

"V Centenario del Nacimiento de Copérnico 1473 - 1973"

1974, Apr. 25 Litho. *Perf. 14½*

B6	A219	27e +3e on 1.95e lt & dk bl	8	5

500th anniversary of the birth of Nicolaus Copernicus (1473-1534), Polish astronomer.

E° 27+3

No. 329A Surcharged

"Centenario de la ciudad de Viña del Mar 1874 - 1974"

1974, May 2 Litho. *Perf. 14*

B7	A159	27e +3e on 1e bluish grn	8	5

Centenary of the city of Viña del Mar.

No. 377 Surcharged

1974, June 7 Litho. *Perf. 14½*

B8	A193	47e +3e on 40c grn	8	5

Nos. 395 and 380 Surcharged in Red

1974

B9	A207	67e +3e on 40c multi	8	5
B10	A196	97e +3e on 40c red brn	8	5

Issue dates: No. B9, July 9; No. B10, June 20.

AIR POST STAMPS.

Bernardo O'Higgins AP1

Lithographed; Center Engraved

Black Surcharge.

1927 *Perf. 13½x14.* Unwmkd.

C1	AP1	40c on 10c blk brn & bl	325.00	35.00
C2	AP1	80c on 10c blk brn & bl	325.00	60.00
C3	AP1	1.20p on 10c blk brn & bl	325.00	60.00
C4	AP1	1.60p on 10c blk brn & bl	325.00	60.00
C5	AP1	2p on 10c blk brn & bl	325.00	60.00
		Nos. C1-C5 (5)	1,625.	275.00

Nos. C1 to C5 were issued for air post service between Santiago and Valparaiso, and are not known without surcharge.

Regular Issues of 1915-28 Overprinted or Surcharged in Black, Red or Blue

Inscribed: "Chile Correos".

1928-29 *Perf. 13½x14, 14*

C6	A39	20c brn org & blk (Bk)	50	20
C6A	A55	40c dk vio & blk (R)	50	20
C6B	A43	1p grn & blk (Bl)	1.50	60
C6C	A43	2p red & blk (Bl)	2.50	40
f.		2p ver & blk (Bl)	110.00	27.50
C6D	A43	5p ol grn & blk (Bl)	3.75	1.00
C6E	A50	6p on 10c dp bl & blk (R)	60.00	32.50
C7	A43	10p org & blk (Bk) ('29)	12.50	4.00
C8	A43	10p org & blk (Bl)	55.00	32.50
		Nos.C6-C8 (8)	136.25	71.40

On Nos. C6B to C6D, C7 and C8 the overprint is larger than on the other stamps of the issue.

Same Overprint or Surcharge on Nos. 155, 156, 158-161.

Inscribed: "Chile Correos".

1928-32 Wmk. 215

C9	A55	40c vio & blk (R)	60	30
C10	A43	1p grn & blk (Bl)	1.75	50
C11	A43	2p red & blk (Bl)	10.00	2.00
C12	A52	3p on 5c sl bl (R)	40.00	27.50
C13	A43	5p ol grn & blk (Bl)	7.50	2.00
C14	A43	10p org & blk (Bk)	40.00	10.00
		Nos. C9-C14 (6)	99.85	42.30

Same Overprint on Nos. 166-169, 172 and 158 in Black, Red or Blue.

Inscribed: "Correos de Chile"

1928-30

C15	A39	20c org red & blk (#166) (Bk) ('29)	1.25	60
C16	A39	20c org red & blk (#172) (Bk) ('30)	40	20
C17	A40	25c bl & blk (R)	60	20
C18	A41	30c brn & blk (Bk)	35	20
a.		Double ovpt., one inverted	350.00	350.00
C19	A42	50c dp grn & blk (R)	50	20
		Nos. C15-C19 (5)	3.10	1.40

Inscribed: "Chile Correos".

1932 *Perf. 13½x14, 14.*

C21	A43	1p yel grn & blk (Bk)	3.75	2.00

Condor on Andes AP1a

Airplane Crossing Andes AP3

Los Cerrillos Airport AP2

Lithographed.

1931 *Perf. 13½x14, 14½x14*

C22	AP1a	5c yel grn	35	20
C23	AP1a	10c yel brn	35	20
C24	AP1a	20c rose	35	20
C25	AP2	50c dk bl	1.75	50
C26	AP3	50c blk brn	85	40
C27	AP3	1p purple	75	30
C28	AP3	2p bl blk	1.50	40
a.		2p bluish sl	1.50	40
C29	AP2	5p lt red	3.75	35
		Nos. C22-C29 (8)	9.65	2.55

Airplane over City AP4

Wings over Chile AP5

Condor AP6

Airplane and Star of Chile AP7

Condor and Statue of Canpolican AP8

Two Airplanes over Globe AP9

Seaplane AP10

Airplane AP11

Airplane and Southern Cross AP12

Airplane and Symbols of Space AP13

Perf. 13½x14

1934-39 Engraved Wmk. 215

Size: 21x25 mm.

C30	AP4	10c yel grn ('35)	25	10
C31	AP4	15c dk grn ('35)	35	20
C32	AP4	20c dp bl ('36)	20	12
C33	AP5	30c blk brn ('35)	20	12
C34	AP5	40c ind ('38)	20	12
C35	AP5	50c dk brn ('36)	20	12
C36	AP6	60c vio blk ('35)	20	12
C37	AP7	70c bl ('35)	35	20
C38	AP8	80c ol blk ('35)	20	12

Perf. 14

Size: 24½x29 mm.

C39	AP9	1p sl blk	20	12
C40	AP9	2p grnsh bl	20	12
C41	AP10	3p org brn ('35)	25	15
C42	AP10	4p brn ('35)	25	15
C43	AP10	5p org red	25	15
C44	AP11	6p yel brn ('35)	35	20
a.		6p brn ('39)	3.75	2.00
C45	AP11	8p grn ('35)	30	15
C46	AP11	10p brn lake	35	20
C47	AP12	20p olive	35	20
C48	AP12	30p gray blk	35	20
C49	AP13	40p gray vio	1.00	60
C50	AP13	50p brn vio	1.00	60
		Nos. C30-C50 (21)	7.00	4.06

Nos. C30-C50 have been re-issued in slightly different colors, with white gum. The first printings are considerably scarcer.

See also Nos. C90-C107B, C148-C154.

Types of 1931 Surcharged in Black or Red

Cts.80

Perf. 13½x14, 14½x14.

1940 Wmk. 215

C51	AP1a	80c on 20c lt rose	60	20
C52	AP2	1.60p on 5p lt red	3.75	1.25
C53	AP3	5.10p on 2p sl bl (R)	3.00	1.50

The surcharge on No. C52 measures 21½mm.

Plane and Weather Vane
AP14

Plane and Caravel
AP23

Designs (Plane and): 20c, Globe. 30c, Chilean flag. 40c, Map of Chile and Southern Cross. 50c, Mountains. 60c, Tree. 70c, Lakes. 80c, Shore. 90c, Sunrise. 2p, Compass. 3p, Telegraph lines. 4p, Rainbow. 5p, Factory. 10p, Snow-capped mountain.

Lithographed

1941-42 ***Perf. 14.*** **Wmk. 215**

C54 AP14 10c ol gray 25 15
C55 AP14 20c dp rose 25 15
C56 AP14 30c bl vio 25 15
C57 AP14 40c dl red brn 25 15
C58 AP14 50c red org ('42) 65 20
C59 AP14 60c dp grn 25 15
C60 AP14 70c rose 50 30
C61 AP14 80c ultra ('42) 3.00 50
C62 AP14 90c dk brn 75 30
C63 AP23 1p brt bl 50 30
C64 AP23 2p rose lake 75 40
C65 AP23 3p dk bl grn & yel grn 1.10 65
C66 AP23 4p bl vio & buff 1.65 85
C67 AP23 5p dk org red ('42) 15.00 6.00
C68 AP23 10p gray grn & bl grn 8.50 5.00
Nos. C54-C68 (15) 33.65 15.25

The 1p, dated "1541–1941", commemorates the 400th anniversary of Santiago.

1942-46 **Unwmkd.**

C69 AP14 10c ultra ('43) 25 15
C70 AP14 10c rose lil ('45) 25 15
C71 AP14 20c dl grn ('43) 25 15
C72 AP14 20c cop brn ('45) 25 15
C73 AP14 30c dl vio ('44) 25 15
C74 AP14 30c ol blk ('45) 25 15
C75 AP14 40c red brn ('44) 50 20
C76 AP14 40c ultra ('45) 25 15
C77 AP14 50c rose ('43) 25 15
C78 AP14 50c org red ('45) 25 15
C79 AP14 60c orange 25 15
C79B AP14 60c dp grn ('46) 25 15
C80 AP14 70c rose ('45) 75 40
C81 AP14 80c sl grn 25 15
C82 AP14 90c brn ('45) 75 40
C83 AP23 1p gray grn & lt bl ('43) 35 20
C84 AP23 2p org red ('43) 75 20
C85 AP23 3p dk pur & pale org ('43) 75 20
C86 AP23 4p bl grn & yel grn 75 40
C87 AP23 5p dk rose car ('43) 65 30
a. 5p dk car rose ('44) 30 20
C88 AP23 10p saph ('43) 75 40
Nos. C69-C88 (21) 8.25 4.10

No. C83 is without dates "1541–1941." See Nos. C109–C123, C145–C147.

Coat of Arms and Plane
AP29

1942, Nov. 5 **Engr.** ***Perf. 14½***

C89 AP29 100p car lake 35.00 25.00

University of Chile centenary.

Types of 1934-39.
Engraved.

1944-55 ***Perf. 13½x14.*** **Unwmkd.**

C90 AP4 10c yel grn ('55) 35 25
C92 AP4 20c dp bl 20 12
C93 AP5 30c blk brn 20 12
C94 AP5 40c indigo 20 12
C95 AP5 50c dk brn ('47) 20 12
C96 AP6 60c sl vio 20 12
C97 AP7 70c bl ('48) 20 12
C98 AP8 80c ol blk 20 12

Perf. 14

C99 AP9 1p sl blk 20 12
C100 AP9 2p grnsh bl 35 15
C101 AP10 3p org brn ('45) 20 12
C102 AP10 4p brown 20 12
C103 AP10 5p org red 50 20
C104 AP11 6p yel brn ('46) 50 20
C105 AP11 8p green 50 20
C106 AP11 10p brn lake 1.25 20
C107 AP12 20p ol gray ('45) 1.00 20
a. Imperf., pair 100.00
C107B AP13 50p rose vio ('50) 25.00 4.00
Nos. C90-C107B (18) 31.45 6.60

Plane and Radio Tower
AP30

Lithographed.

1945 ***Perf. 14*** **Unwmkd.**

C108 AP30 1.60p brt vio 75 30

Types of 1941–42.

1946-48 **Wmk. 215**

C109 AP14 10c rose lil ('47) 20 12
C110 AP14 20c dk red brn ('48) 20 12
C111 AP14 20c dl grn ('48) 2.50 40
C112 AP14 30c blk ('48) 20 12
C113 AP14 40c ultra ('48) 20 12
C114 AP14 60c ol grn ('48) 20 12
C115 AP14 80c ol blk ('48) 20 12
C116 AP14 90c choc ('48) 25 15
C117 AP23 1p gray grn & lt bl ('48) 25 12
C118 AP30 1.60p brt vio 25 12
C119 AP30 1.80p brt vio ('48) 25 12
C119A AP23 2p org red 50 15
C120 AP23 3p dk pur & pale org ('47) 2.00 40
C121 AP23 4p bl grn & yel grn ('48) 1.50 60
C122 AP23 5p rose car ('47) 1.00 30
C123 AP23 10p saph ('47) 1.25 30
Nos. C109-C123 (16) 10.95 3.38

No. C117 is without dates "1541–1941."

Araucarian Pine
AP31

1948

C124 AP31 3p carmine 60 60
a. Block of 25 20.00

Issued in panes of 100 stamps, divisible into four blocks of 25 different designs, the same animals, insects, birds, fish, flowers and trees of Chile as illustrated and described for Nos. 254–255.

The stamps commemorate the centenary (in 1944) of the publication of the first volume of Claudio Gay's Natural History of Chile.

Air Line Emblem and Planes
AP32

Lithographed.

1949 ***Perf. 14.*** **Wmk. 215**

C125 AP32 2p ultra 40 25

Issued to commemorate the 20th anniversary of the establishment of Chile's National Air Line.

Benjamin Vicuna Mackenna
AP33

Factory, Badge and Book
AP34

1949, Mar. 22 **Engr.** ***Perf. 13½x14***

C126 AP33 3p dk car rose 20 12

Lithographed.

1949, Nov. 11 ***Perf. 14*** **Unwmkd.**

Design: 10p, Column and cogwheel.

C127 AP34 5p green 60 40
C128 AP34 10p red brn 1.00 60

Issued to commemorate the centenary of the founding of Chile's School of Arts and Crafts.

Plane and Globe—AP35

1950, Jan. **Engraved**

C129 AP35 5p green 25 20
C130 AP35 10p red brn 60 40

Issued to commemorate the 75th anniversary of the formation of the Universal Postal Union.

Plane over Snow-capped Mountain
AP36

Plane over Fishing Boat—AP37

Araucarian Pine and Plane
AP38

Plane Above River
AP39

Plane and: 40c, Coast and Sunrise. 2p, Chilean flag. 3p, Dock crane. 5p, Blast furnace. 10p, Mountain lake. 20p, Cable cars.

Imprint: "Especies Valoradas-Chile"
Lithographed.

1950–54 ***Perf. 14*** **Wmk. 215**

C135 AP36 20c yel brn ('54) 20 10
C136 AP36 40c pur ('52) 20 10
C137 AP37 60c lt bl ('53) 1.50 60
C138 AP38 1p dl grn 20 10
C139 AP38 2p brn red 20 10
C140 AP38 3p vio bl 20 10
C141 AP39 4p red org ('54) 20 10
C142 AP38 5p violet 20 10
C143 AP39 10p yel grn ('53) 20 10
C144 AP39 20p red brn ('54) 40 10
Nos. C135-C144 (10) 3.50 1.50

See also Nos. C155–C164, C207–C212.

Nos. C115, C81 and C116 Surcharged with New Value in Carmine or Black.

1951–52 **Wmk. 215**

C145 AP14 40c on 80c ol blk (C) ('52) 20 10

Unwmkd.

C146 AP14 40c on 80c sl grn (C) ('52) 5.00 3.00

Wmk. 215

C147 AP14 1p on 90c choc 20 10

Types of 1934–39.
Engraved.

1951–53 ***Perf. 14*** **Unwmkd.**

C148 AP9 1p dp bl 20 12
C149 AP9 2p blue 35 15
C150 AP11 6p bis brn ('52) 50 20
C151 AP12 30p dk gray ('53) 5.00 75
C152 AP13 40p dk pur brn 15.00 2.00
C153 AP13 50p dk pur 25.00 8.00
Nos. C148-C153 (6) 46.05 11.22

Wmk. 215

C154 AP13 50p dk pur ('52) 1.00 50

Types of 1950–54.
Designs as Before.
Imprint: "Especies Valoradas-Chile"
Lithographed.

1951–55 ***Perf. 14*** **Unwmkd.**

C155 AP36 20c yel brn ('54) 20 10
C156 AP36 40c purple 20 10
C157 AP37 60c lt bl ('53) 25 15
C158 AP38 1p dk bl grn ('55) 20 10
C159 AP38 2p brn red 20 10
C160 AP38 3p vio bl 20 10
C161 AP39 4p red org ('52) 35 20
C162 AP38 5p violet 35 20
C163 AP39 10p emerald 35 10
C164 AP39 20p brown 50 15
Nos. C155-C164 (10) 2.80 1.30

San Martin Crossing Andes—AP40

Engraved.

1951, Mar. 16 *Perf. 14½*. Wmk. 215

C165	AP40	5p red vio	40	25

Issued to commemorate the centenary of the death of Gen. José de San Martín.

Isabella Type of Regular Issue, 1952.

1952, Mar. 21 *Perf. 14*

C166	A125	10p carmine	50	30

Issued for the 500th anniversary of the birth of Queen Isabella I of Spain.

A souvenir card without franking value was issued for the Hispano-Chilean Philatelic Exhibition at Santiago, Oct. 12, 1969. It contains 2 imperf. stamps similar to Nos. 264 and C166—60c green and 10p rose red. Size: 115x137½mm. Price $12.50.

Ancient Fortress
AP42

1953, Apr. 28

C167	AP42	10p brn car	1.00	25

4th centenary of the founding of Valdivia.

Stamp Centenary Type of 1953.

1953, Oct. 15 Engraved *Perf. 14½*

C168	A131	100p dp grnsh bl	1.50	1.00

Issued to commemorate the centenary of Chile's first postage stamps.

An imperf. souvenir sheet contains one each of Nos. 276 and C168, with inscriptions in black at top and bottom center. Sheet measures 178x229mm. It is stated that this sheet was not valid for postage. Price $425.

Early Plane and Stylized Modern Version
AP44

Engraved.

1954, May 26 *Perf. 14* Unwmkd.

C170	AP44	3p dp bl	15	10

Issued to commemorate the 25th anniversary of the founding of Chile's National Air Line.

Domeyko Type of Regular Issue, 1954.

1954, Aug. 16 *Perf. 13½x14*

C171	A134	5p org brn	20	10

Issued to commemorate the 150th anniversary (in 1952) of the birth of Ignacio Domeyko.

Railroad Type of Regular Issue, 1954.

1954, Sept. 10 *Perf. 14½* Wmk. 215

C172	A135	10p dk pur	40	20

Issued to commemorate the centenary (in 1951) of the first South American railroad.

An imperforate souvenir sheet contains one each of Nos. 283 and C172. Size: 174x232mm. Price, $300.

Presidential Visits Type of 1955

1955, May 24

C173	A139	100p red	1.25	1.00

Issued to publicize the reciprocal visits of Presidents Juan D. Peron and Carlos Ibanez del Campo.

Jet Plane in Clouds
AP48

Comet Air Liner
AP49

Designs: 2p, Helicopter over bridge. 10p, Oil derricks and plane. 50p, Control tower and plane. 200p, Beechcraft monoplane. 500p, Douglas DC-6.

***Perf. 14½x14, 14x13½* (AP49)**

1955-56 Engraved. Wmk. 215

C174	AP48	1p dp red lil ('56)	20	10
C175	AP48	2p pale brn ('56)	10	5
C176	AP48	10p bluish grn ('56)	10	5
C177	AP48	50p rose ('56)	60	25
C178	AP49	100p green	75	15
C179	AP49	200p dp ultra	5.00	75
C180	AP49	500p dk car	6.00	75
		Nos. C174-C180 (7)	12.75	2.10

Stamps similar to type AP49, but inscribed in escudo currency, are listed as type AP58.

1956-58 Unwmkd.

Designs: 5p, Train and plane. 20p, Jet plane and Easter Island statue.

C183	AP48	5p violet	10	5
C184	AP48	10p grn ('57)	10	5
C185	AP48	20p ultra	10	5
C186	AP48	50p rose ('57)	10	5
C187	AP49	100p bl grn ('57)	40	15
a.		Litho. ('60)	40	20
C188	AP49	200p dp ultra ('57)	40	15
C189	AP49	500p car ('58)	60	20
		Nos. C183-C189 (7)	1.80	70

Symbols of University Departments
AP50

Design: 100p, View of the University.

1956, Dec. 15 *Perf. 14½* Unwmkd.

C190	AP50	20p green	25	15
C191	AP50	100p dk vio bl	1.00	60

Issued to commemorate the 25th anniversary of the Federico Santa Maria Technical University, Valparaiso.

A souvenir sheet contains one each of Nos. 299, C190-C191, imperf. It was not issued for postal use, though some served postally. Size: 127x160mm. Price, $30.

Mistral Type of Regular Issue, 1958

1958, Jan. 10 Engraved *Perf. 14*

C192	A144	100p green	20	10

Issued in honor of Gabriela Mistral, poet and educator.

Ambrosio O'Higgins
AP51

1958, March 23

C193	AP51	100p lt bl	25	15

Issued to commemorate the 400th anniversary of the founding of the city of Osorno.

A souvenir sheet contains one each of Nos. 302 and C193, imperf. and printed in red brown. It was not issued for postal use, though some served postally. Size: 155x138mm. Price, $20.

Exhibition Type of Regular Issue

1958, Oct. 18 Unwmkd.

C194	A146	50p dl grn	15	10

Issued to publicize the National Philatelic Exhibition, Santiago, Oct. 18-26.

A souvenir sheet contains one each of Nos. 303 and C194, imperf. and printed in deep red. It was not issued for postal use, though some served postally. Size: 188x 220mm. Price, $20.

Bank Type of Regular Issue, 1958.

1958, Dec. 18 Engraved. *Perf. 14*

C195	A147	50p redsh brn	15	10

Issued to commemorate the centenary of the Savings Bank for Public Employees.

A souvenir sheet contains one each of Nos. 304 and C195, printed in dull violet, imperf. It was not issued for postal use, though some served postally. Price, $17.50.

Antarctic Types of Regular Issue

1958 Lithographed. *Perf. 14*

C199	A149	20p violet	20	10

Engraved.

C200	A150	500p dk bl	2.50	1.25

Symbols of Various Religions
AP52

Engraved.

1959, Jan. 28 *Perf. 14½* Unwmkd.

C206	AP52	50p dk car rose	15	10

Issued to commemorate the 10th anniversary of the Universal Declaration of Human Rights.

Types of 1950-54.

Imprint: "Casa de Moneda de Chile."

Designs: 1p, Araucarian pine and plane. 10p, Plane over mountain lake. 20p, Plane and cable cars. 50p, Plane silhouette over shore. 100p, Plane over map of Antarctica. 200p, Plane over natural arch rock.

1959 Lithographed. *Perf. 14*

C207	AP38	1p dk bl grn	60	30
a.		Wmk. 215	30.00	
C208	AP39	10p emerald	40	10
C209	AP39	20p red brn	25	10
C210	AP39	50p yel grn	25	10
C211	AP39	100p car rose	25	10
C212	AP39	200p brt bl	40	10
		Nos. C207-C212 (6)	2.15	80

Carlos Anwandter
AP53

1959, June 18 Engraved. *Perf. 14*

C213	AP53	20p rose car	20	10

Issued to commemorate the centenary of the German School in Valdivia, founded by Carlos Anwandter.

A souvenir sheet contains one each of Nos. 319 and C213, imperf. It was not issued for postal use, though some served postally. Price, $25.

IGY Type of Regular Issue, 1958.

1959, Aug. 28 *Perf. 14* Unwmkd.

C214	A148	50p green	20	10

Issued to commemorate the International Geophysical Year, 1957-58.

Ladrillero Type of Regular Issue.

1959, Aug. 28 Lithographed.

C215	A154	50p green	20	10

Issued to commemorate the 400th anniversary (in 1957) of the Juan Ladrillero expedition.

Barros Arana Type of Regular Issue.

1959, Aug. 28

C216	A155	100p purple	40	20

Issued to commemorate the 50th anniversary of the death of Diego Barros Arana (1830-1907), historian.

Red Cross Type of Regular Issue.

1959, Oct. 6

C217	A156	50p red & blk	25	15

Centenary of Red Cross idea.

WRY Type of Regular Issue, 1960.

1960, Apr. 7 *Perf. 14½* Unwmkd.

C218	A160	10c violet	25	15

Issued to publicize World Refugee Year, July 1, 1959-June 30, 1960.

A souvenir sheet contains two stamps similar to Nos. 330 and C218, the 1c printed in blue, the 10c airmail in maroon. The sheet is imperf., printed on thin cardboard and has border, inscriptions and WRY emblems in dark green with drab background. Size: 160x204mm. Price, $110.

Type of Regular Issue, 1960-62, and

José Agustin Eyzaguirre and José Miguel Infante—AP54

Designs: 2c, Palace of Justice. 5c, National memorial. No. C220, Arms of Chile. No. C220A, José Gaspar Marin and J. Gregorio Argomedo. 50c, Archbishop J. I. Cienfuegos and Brother Camilo Henriquez. 1e, Bernardo O'Higgins.

Engraved

1960-65 *Perf. 14½* Unwmkd.

C218A	AP54	2c mar & gray vio ('62)	15	10
C219	A162	5c vio bl & dl pur ('61)	20	10

Wmk. 215

C220	A161	10c dk brn & red brn	20	10

Unwmkd.

C220A	AP54	10c vio brn & brn ('64)	20	10
C220B	AP54	20c dk bl & dl pur ('64)	25	10
C220C	AP54	50c bl grn & ind ('65)	50	20
C220D	A162	1e dk red & red brn ('63)	1.00	40
		Nos. C218A-C220D (7)	2.50	1.10

Issued to commemorate the 150th anniversary of the formation of the first National Government.

A souvenir sheet contains two airmail stamps: a 5c brown similar to No. C219 (National Memorial) and a 10c green, type A161. The sheet is imperf., printed on heavy paper with papermaker's watermark, and has green inscriptions. Size: 120x 168mm. Price, $40.

Map and Rotary Emblem
AP55

Lithographed

1960, Dec. 1 *Perf. 14* Unwmkd.

C221	AP55	10c blue	25	15

Issued to commemorate the South American Rotary Regional Conference, Santiago, 1960.

A souvenir sheet contains one 10c maroon, type AP55, with brown marginal inscription. Size: 118x158mm. Price, $17.50.

The souvenir sheet was overprinted in green "El Mundo Unida Contra la Malaria" and the outline of a mosquito, and released in October, 1962. Price, $35.

Plane over Mountain Lake
AP56

Designs: 1m, Araucarian pine and plane. 2m, Chilean flag and plane. 3m, Plane and dock crane. 4m, Plane above river (vignette like AP39). 5m, Blast furnace. 2c, Plane over cable cars. 5c, Plane silhouette over shore. 10c, Plane over map of Antarctica. 20c, Plane over natural arch rock.

Imprint: "Casa de Moneda de Chile."

1960–62 Lithographed *Perf. 14*

C222	AP56	1m orange	10	10
C223	AP56	2m yel grn	10	5
C224	AP56	3m violet	10	5
C225	AP56	4m gray ol	10	5
C226	AP56	5m brt bl grn	10	5
C227	AP56	1c ultra	10	5
C228	AP56	2c red brn ('61)	20	5
C229	AP56	5c yel grn ('61)	1.25	10
C230	AP56	10c car rose ('62)	30	10
C231	AP56	20c brt bl ('62)	30	10
		Nos. C222-C231 (10)	2.65	70

Oil Derricks and Douglas DC-6
AP57

Beechcraft Monoplane
AP58

Designs: 5m, Train and plane. 2c, Jet plane and Easter Island statue. 5c, Control tower and plane. 10c, Comet airliner. 50c, Douglas DC-6.

Lithographed

1960–67 *Perf. 14x13½* Unwmkd.

C234	AP57	5m red brn	5	5
C235	AP57	1c dl bl	5	5
C236	AP57	2c ultra ('62)	5	5
C237	AP57	5c rose red ('64)	5	5
C238	AP58	10c ultra ('67)	5	6
C239	AP58	20c car ('62)	5	5
C240	AP58	50c grn ('63)	5	5
		Nos. C234-C240 (7)	35	36

Stamps similar to type AP58, but inscribed in peso ($) currency, are listed as type AP49.

Congress Type of Regular Issue.

1961, Oct. 5 *Perf. 14½*

C245	A164	10c gray grn	75	25

Issued to commemorate the 150th anniversary of the first National Congress.

Soccer Type of Regular Issue, 1962.

Designs: 5c, Goalkeeper and stadium (vert.). 10c, Soccer players and globe.

Engraved

1962, May 30 *Perf. 14½* Unwmkd.

C246	A165	5c rose lil	15	10
C247	A165	10c dk car	25	15

Issued to commemorate the World Soccer Championship, Chile, May 30–June 17.

A souvenir sheet of four contains one each of Nos. 340–341, C246–C247, imperf., with light brown marginal inscriptions. Size: 123x194mm. Sold for 7.50 escudos (face value, 22 centavos). Price, $7.50.

Hunger Type of Regular Issue.

Design: 20c, Mother with empty bowl (horiz.).

1963, Mar. 21 Litho. *Perf. 14*

C248	A166	20c green	10	5

Issued for the "Freedom from Hunger" campaign of the U.N. Food and Agriculture Organization.

Red Cross Type of Regular Issue.

Design: 20c, Centenary emblem and plane silhouette (horiz.).

1963, Sept. 6 *Perf. 14* Unwmkd.

C249	A167	20c gray & red	15	10

Centenary of International Red Cross.

Fire Engine of 1860's
AP59

1963, Dec. 20 Litho. *Perf. 14½*

C250	AP59	30c red	15	10

Centenary of the Santiago Fire Brigade.

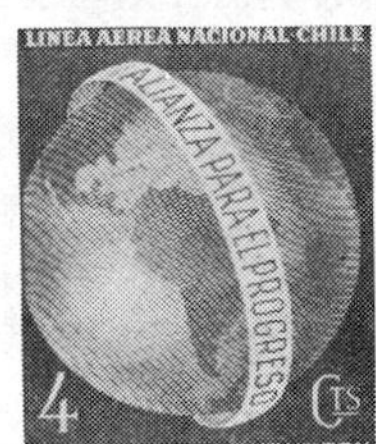

Western Hemisphere
AP60

1964, Apr. 9 *Perf. 14½* Unwmkd.

C254	AP60	4c ultra	10	5

Issued in memory of President John F. Kennedy and to honor the Alliance for Progress.

Battle of Rancagua
AP61

1965, May 7 Engraved *Perf. 14½*

C255	AP61	5c dl grn & sep	10	5

Issued to commemorate the sesquicentennial of the Battle of Rancagua, Oct. 7, 1814.

ITU Emblem, Old and New Communication Equipment
AP62

1965, May 7 Litho. *Perf. 14½x14*

C256	AP62	40c red & mar	10	5

Issued to commemorate the centenary of the International Telecommunication Union.

Portrait Type of 1964

Portraits: No. C257, Enrique Molina. No. C258, Msgr. Carlos Casanueva.

1965, June Litho. *Perf. 14*

C257	A169	60c brt vio	10	5
C258	A169	60c green	10	5

See note after No. 346.

Skier Type of Regular Issue 1965

Design: 20c, Skier (horiz.).

1965, Aug. 30 *Perf. 14* Unwmkd.

C259	A172	20c ultra	10	5

World Skiing Championships, Chile, 1966.

Fishing Boats, Angelmo Harbor
AP63

Aviators' Monument
AP64

1965

C260	AP63	40c brown	10	5

Perf. 14x14½

C262	AP64	1e car rose	15	5

Andrés Bello
AP65

1965, Nov. 29 Engraved Unwmkd.

C263	AP65	10c dk car rose	15	10

Issued to commemorate the centenary of the death of Andrés Bello (1780?–1865), Venezuela-born writer and educator.

Skiers
AP66

Basketball
AP67

1966, Apr. 6 Litho. *Perf. 14*

C264	AP66	4e dk bl & red brn	60	15

World Skiing Championships, Partillo, Aug. 1966.

1966, Apr. 28

C265	AP67	13c rose car	10	5

International Basketball Championships.

Slalom
AP68

Perf. 14½x15

1966, July 20 Litho. Unwmkd.

C266	AP68	75c rose car & lil	10	5
C267	AP68	3e ultra & lt bl	20	10

International Skiing Championships, Partillo, August 1966. A souvenir sheet of 2 contains imperf. stamps similar to Nos. C266–C267. Marginal inscription in ultramarine and rose carmine. No gum. Size: 109x140mm. Price $3.50.

Ship Type of Regular Issue

1966 Lithographed *Perf. 14½*

C268	A175	70c Prus grn & yel grn	10	10

See note below No. 358.

ICY Type of Regular Issue

1966, Oct. 28 *Perf. 14½* Unwmkd.

C269	A177	3e bl & car	50	20

International Cooperation Year, 1965.

A souvenir sheet of 2 contains imperf. stamps similar to Nos. 360 and C269. Brown marginal inscription. No gum. Size: 111x140mm. Price $3.

Chilean Flag and Ships
AP69

1966, Nov. 21 Litho. *Perf. 14*

C270	AP69	13c dl red brn	10	5

Centenary of the city of Antofagasta.

Pardo Type of Regular Issue

Design: 40c, Pardo and map of Chile's claim to Antarctica.

1967, Jan. 6 *Perf. 14½* Unwmkd.

C271	A178	40c ultra	10	5

See note below No. 361.

Family Type of Regular Issue

1967, Apr. 13 Litho. *Perf. 14*

C272	A179	80c brt bl & blk	10	5

Issued to publicize the 8th International Conference for Family Planning, Santiago, April 1967.

Ruben Dario and Title Page of "Azul"
AP70

1967, May 15 Engr. *Perf. 14½*

C273	AP70	10c dk bl	10	5

Issued to commemorate the centenary of the birth of Ruben Dario (pen name of Felix Ruben Garcia Sarmiento, 1867–1916), Nicaraguan poet, newspaper correspondent and diplomat.

Tree Type of Regular Issue

1967, June 9 Lithographed

C274	A180	75c grn & pale rose	10	5

Reforestation Campaign.

Lions Type of Regular Issue

1967 Lithographed *Perf. 14*

C275	A181	1e pur & yel	10	5
C276	A181	5e bl & yel	1.00	15

Issued to commemorate the 50th anniversary of Lions International. A souvenir sheet without franking value contains 3 imperf. stamps, 20c, 1e and 5e, in violet blue and yellow. Marginal inscription and design in violet blue and yellow. Size: 110x140mm. Price, $10.

Issue dates: 1e, July 12; 5e, Aug. 11.

Flag Type of Regular Issue

1967, Oct. 20 *Perf. 14½* Unwmkd.

C277	A182	50c ultra & crim	10	10

Sesquicentennial of the national flag.

ITY Emblem
AP71

1967, Nov. 22 Litho. *Perf. 14½*

C278 AP71 30c lt vio bl & blk 10 5

Issued for International Tourist Year, 1967.

Caro Type of Regular Issue, 1967.

1967, Dec. 4 Engraved *Perf. 14½*

C279 A183 40c violet 60 25

Issued to commemorate the centenary of the birth of José Maria Cardinal Caro.

Type of Regular Issue, 1968

1968, Apr. 23 Litho. *Perf. 14½*

C280 A184 2e brt vio 10 5

Issued to commemorate the sesquicentennial of the Battles of Chacabuco and Maipu. A souvenir sheet of 2 contains imperf. stamps similar to Nos. 367 and C280. Gold marginal inscription commemorates the battles and the First Trans-Andes Philatelic Week, Apr. 4–10. Price, $5. A second sheet exists with the 2e in green and the 3e in brown. Size: 139½x100mm. Price, $5.

Farm Type of Regular Issue

1968, June 18 Unwmkd.

C281 A185 50c blk, org & grn 10 5

Issued to publicize the agrarian reforms.

Juan I. Molina
AP72

1968, Aug. 27 Litho. *Perf. 14½*

C282 AP72 1e brt grn 10 5

Issued to honor Juan I. Molina, educator and scientist.

Map of Chiloé Province AP73 — **British Crown and Map of Chile AP74**

Lithographed

1968, Oct. 7 *Perf. 14½* Unwmkd.

C283 AP73 1e rose cl 10 5

Issued to commemorate the anniversaries of the founding of five towns in Chiloé Province.

Auto Club Type of Regular Issue

1968, Nov. 10 Engr. *Perf. 14½x14*

C284 A189 5e ultra 20 10

Issued to commemorate the 40th anniversary of the Automobile Club of Chile.

1968, Nov. 12 Litho. *Perf. 14½*

Designs: 50c, Chilean coat of arms (horiz.; similar to type A161). 3e, British coat of arms (horiz.).

C285 AP74 50c grn & brn 20 10
C286 AP74 3e bl & org brn 10 5

Engraved

C287 AP74 5e pur & mag 20 10

Visit of Queen Elizabeth II of Great Britain, Nov. 11–18. A souvenir sheet of 3 contains imperf., lithographed stamps similar to Nos. C285–C287. Dark blue marginal inscription. Size: 124½x190mm. The souvenir sheet also publicizes the British-Chilean Philatelic Exhibition. Price, $10.

First Coin Minted in Chile and Coin Press
AP75

Design: 1e, Chile No. 128.

1968, Dec. 31 Litho. *Perf. 14½*

C288 AP75 50c ocher & vio brn 10 5
C289 AP75 1e lt bl & dp org 10 5

Issued to commemorate the 225th anniversary of the founding of the State Mint (Casa de Moneda de Chile).

A souvenir sheet of 4 contains imperf. stamps similar to Nos. 373–374, C288–C289. Brown marginal inscription. Size: 150x119mm. Price, $2.50.

Satellite Type of Regular Issue

1969, May 20 Litho. *Perf. 14½*

C290 A191 2e rose lil 10 5

Issued to publicize the inauguration of ENTEL-Chile, the first commercial satellite communications ground station, Longovilo.

Red Cross Type of Regular Issue

1969, Sept. Litho. *Perf. 14½*

C291 A192 5e blk & red 10 5

Issued for the 50th anniversary of the League of Red Cross Societies.

A souvenir card contains 2 imperf. stamps similar to Nos. 376 and C291, with red marginal inscription. Size: 109x140 mm. Price $4.

Dam Type of Regular Issue

1969, Nov. 18 Litho. *Perf. 14½*

C292 A193 3e blue 10 5

Rodriguez Type of Regular Issue

1969, Nov. 24

C293 A194 30c brown 10 5

Issued to commemorate the 150th anniversary of the death of Col. Manuel Rodriguez.

EXPO '70 Type of Regular Issue

1969, Dec. 1 Litho. *Perf. 14*

C294 A195 5e red 15 10

Issued to publicize EXPO '70 International Exposition, Osaka, Japan, March 15–Sept. 13, 1970.

Bible Type of 1969

1969, Dec. 2 *Perf. 14½*

C295 A196 1e green 10 5

Issued to commemorate the 400th anniversary of the translation of the Bible into Spanish by Casiodoro de Reina.

ILO Type of Regular Issue

1969, Dec. 17 *Perf. 14½*

C296 A197 2e rose lil & blk 10 5

Issued to commemorate the 50th anniversary of the International Labor Organization.

Human Rights Year Type of 1969

1969, Dec. 18

C297 A198 4e brn & red 10 5

Human Rights Year, 1968.

A souvenir sheet of 2 contains imperf. stamps similar to Nos. 382 and C297. Blue commemorative marginal inscription. Size: 110x140mm. Price, $4.50.

Easter Island Type of 1970

1970, Jan. 26

C298 A199 50c dl grnsh bl 10 5

Issued to commemorate the 80th anniversary of the acquisition of Easter Island.

Ship Type of Regular Issue

1970, Feb. 4 Litho. *Perf. 14½*

C299 A200 2e dp ultra 20 5

Issued to commemorate the 150th anniversary of the capture of Valdivia during Chile's war of independence by Thomas Cochrane (1775–1860), naval commander.

Rotary Type of Regular Issue

1970, Mar. 18 Lithographed *Perf. 14*

C300 A201 1e rose cl 10 5

Issued to commemorate the centenary of the birth of Paul Harris (1868–1947), founder of Rotary International.

Gandhi Type of Regular Issue

1970, Apr. 1 Litho. *Perf. 14½*

C301 A202 1e red brn 10 5

Issued to commemorate the centenary of the birth of Mohandas K. Gandhi (1869–1948), leader in India's fight for independence.

Education Year Type of 1970

1970, July 17 Litho. *Perf. 14½*

C302 A204 4e red brn 10 5

Issued for International Education Year.

National Shrine Type of 1970

1970, July 28 Litho. *Perf. 14½*

C303 A205 1e ultra 10 5

Issued to publicize the O'Higgins National Shrine at Maipu.

Cancer Type of Regular Issue

1970, Aug. 11

C304 A206 2e brn & lt ol 10 10

Issued to commemorate the International Cancer Congress, Houston, Texas, May 22–29.

Copper Type of Regular Issue

1970, Oct. 21 Litho. *Perf. 14½*

C305 A207 3e grn & lt red brn 10 5

Nationalization of the copper industry.

United Nations Type of 1970

1970, Oct. 22

C306 A208 5e dk car & grn 40 5

United Nations, 25th anniversary.

Freighter Type of Regular Issue

1971, Jan. 18 Litho. *Perf. 14*

C307 A209 5e lt red brn 10 5

National Maritime Commission.

No. C290 Surcharged in Red

1971, Jan. 21 Litho. *Perf. 14½*

C308 A191 52c on 2e rose lil 20 5

Liberation Type of Regular Issue

1971, Feb. 3 *Perf. 14½*

C309 A210 1e gray bl & brn 5 5

The 150th anniversary of the expedition to liberate Peru.

UNICEF Type of Regular Issue

1971, Feb. 11 Litho. *Perf. 14½*

C310 A211 2e bl & grn 5 5

First meeting in Latin America of the Executive Council of UNICEF, Santiago, May 20–31, 1969.

Boy Scout Type of Regular Issue

1971, Feb. 10 *Perf. 14*

C311 A212 5c dk car & ol 10 5

Founding of Chilean Boy Scouts, 60th anniversary.

Satellite Type of Regular Issue

1971, May 25 Litho. *Perf. 14½*

C312 A213 2e brown 10 5

First commercial Chilean satellite communications ground station, Longovilo.

De Ercilla Type of Regular Issue

1972, Mar. 20 Engraved *Perf. 14*

C313 A221 2e Prus bl 10 5

4th centenary (in 1969) of "La Araucana," by Alonso de Ercilla y Zuniga (1533–1596).

A souvenir card contains impressions of Nos. 414 and C313 with black marginal inscription commemorating España 75 Philatelic Exhibition. Size: 165x220mm.

AIR POST SEMI-POSTAL STAMPS

Type of Semi-Postal Stamps, 1961.

Portraits: 10c+10c, Alonso de Ercilla. 20c+20c, Gabriela Mistral.

Perf. 13x12½

1961, Apr. 29 Photo. Unwmkd.

CB1 SP3 10c +10c sal & choc 75 25
CB2 SP3 20c +20c gray & dp cl 75 25

Printed without charge by the Spanish Mint as a gift to Chile. The surtax was to aid the 1960 earthquake victims and to increase teachers' salaries.

ACKNOWLEDGMENT OF RECEIPT STAMPS.

AR1

1894 *Perf. 11½.* Unwmkd.

H1 AR1 5c brown 50 50
a. Imperf., pair 3.00

The black stamp of design similar to AR1 inscribed "Avis de Paiement" was prepared for use on notices of payment of funds but was not regularly issued.

POSTAGE DUE STAMPS.

D1 **D2**

Handstamped

1894 *Perf. 13* Unwmkd.

J1	D1	2c blk, *straw*	15.00	7.00
J2	D1	4c blk, *straw*	15.00	7.00
J3	D1	6c blk, *straw*	15.00	7.00
J4	D1	8c blk, *straw*	15.00	7.00
J5	D2	10c blk, *straw*	15.00	7.00
J6	D1	16c blk, *straw*	15.00	7.00
J7	D1	20c blk, *straw*	15.00	7.00
J8	D1	30c blk, *straw*	15.00	7.00
J9	D1	40c blk, *straw*	15.00	7.00
		Nos. J1-J9 (9)	135.00	63.00
J1a	D1	2c blk, *yel*	62.50	60.00
J2a	D1	4c blk, *yel*	50.00	40.00
J3a	D1	6c blk, *yel*	37.50	35.00
J4a	D1	8c blk, *yel*	15.00	12.50
J5a	D2	10c blk, *yel*	15.00	12.50
J6a	D1	16c blk, *yel*	15.00	12.50
J7a	D1	20c blk, *yel*	15.00	12.50
J8a	D1	30c blk, *yel*	15.00	12.50
J9a	D1	40c blk, *yel*	15.00	12.50
		Nos. J1a-J9a (9)	240.00	210.00

Counterfeits exist.

D3

1895 Lithographed. *Perf. 11.*

J19	D3	1c red, *yel*	5.00	2.00
J20	D3	2c red, *yel*	5.00	2.00
J21	D3	4c red, *yel*	4.00	2.00
J22	D3	6c red, *yel*	5.00	2.00
J23	D3	8c red, *yel*	3.00	2.00
J24	D3	10c red, *yel*	3.00	2.00
J25	D3	20c red, *yel*	2.00	1.25
J26	D3	40c red, *yel*	3.00	2.00
J27	D3	50c red, *yel*	3.00	2.00
J28	D3	60c red, *yel*	6.00	3.00
J29	D3	80c red, *yel*	6.00	3.50
J30	D3	1p red, *yel*	6.00	3.50
		Nos. J19-J30 (12)	51.00	27.25

Nos. J19–J30 were printed in sheets of 100 (10x10) containing all 12 denominations.

Counterfeits of Nos. J19–J42 exist.

1896 *Perf. 13½.*

J31	D3	1c red, *straw*	85	50
J32	D3	2c red, *straw*	85	50
J33	D3	4c red, *straw*	85	50
J34	D3	6c red, *straw*	2.00	75
J35	D3	8c red, *straw*	85	50
J36	D3	10c red, *straw*	85	50
J37	D3	20c red, *straw*	85	50
J38	D3	40c red, *straw*	12.50	10.00
J39	D3	50c red, *straw*	12.50	10.00
J40	D3	60c red, *straw*	12.50	10.00
J41	D3	80c red, *straw*	12.50	10.00
J42	D3	100c red, *straw*	25.00	20.00
		Nos. J31-J42 (12)	82.10	63.75

D4

D5

1898 *Perf. 13.*

J43	D4	1c scarlet	50	30
J44	D4	2c scarlet	1.25	60
J45	D4	4c scarlet	50	30
J46	D4	10c scarlet	50	30
J47	D4	20c scarlet	50	30
		Nos. J43-J47 (5)	3.25	1.80

1924 *Perf. 11½, 12½.*

J48	D5	2c bl & red	75	50
J49	D5	4c bl & red	75	50
J50	D5	8c bl & red	75	50
J51	D5	10c bl & red	75	50
J52	D5	20c bl & red	75	30
J53	D5	40c bl & red	75	50
J54	D5	60c bl & red	75	50
J55	D5	80c bl & red	75	50
J56	D5	1p bl & red	1.00	60
J57	D5	2p bl & red	2.00	1.25
J58	D5	5p bl & red	2.00	1.25
		Nos. J48-J58 (11)	11.00	6.90

Nos. J48–J58 were printed in sheets of 150 containing all 11 denominations, and in sheets of 50 containing the five lower denominations, providing various se-tenants.

All values of this issue exist imperforate, also with center inverted, but are not believed to have been regularly issued. Those with inverted centers sell for about 10 times normal stamps.

OFFICIAL STAMPS.

For Domestic Postage.

O1

Single-lined frame.

Control number in violet.

1907 *Imperf.* Unwmkd.

O1	O1	dl bl, "CARTA" in org	30.00	22.50
O2	O1	red, "OFICIO" in bl	30.00	22.50
O3	O1	vio, "PAQUETE" in red	30.00	22.50
O4	O1	org, *bl*, "EP" in vio	30.00	22.50

The diagonal inscription in differing color indicates type of usage: CARTA for letters of ordinary weight; OFICIO, heavy letters to 100 grams; PAQUETE, parcels to 100 grams; E P (Encomienda Postal), heavier parcels; C (Certificado), as on No. O8, registration including postage.

Varieties include CARTA, PAQUETE and E P inverted, OFICIO omitted, etc.

Double-lined frame.

Large control number in black.

Perf. 11.

O5	O1	bl, "CARTA" in yel	7.50	6.25
O6	O1	red, "OFICIO" in bl	7.50	5.00
O7	O1	brn, "PAQUETE" in grn	7.50	5.00
O8	O1	grn, "C" in red	150.00	110.00

Nos. O5–O8 exist in tête bêche pairs; with CARTA, OFICIO or PAQUETE double or inverted, and other varieties.

Counterfeits of Nos. O1–O8 exist.

For Foreign Postage.

Regular Issues of 1892-1909 Overprinted in Red

a

On Stamps of 1904-09.

1907 *Perf. 12.*

O9	A14	1c green	7.50	7.50
a.		Inverted ovpt.	25.00	
O10	A12	3c on 1p brn	20.00	20.00
a.		Inverted ovpt.	75.00	
O11	A14	5c ultra	15.00	15.00
a.		Inverted ovpt.	50.00	
O12	A15	10c gray & blk	15.00	15.00
O13	A15	15c vio & blk	20.00	20.00
O14	A15	20c org brn & blk	20.00	20.00
O15	A15	50c ultra & blk	62.50	62.50

On Stamp of 1892.

Rouletted.

O16	A6	1p dk brn & blk	150.00	125.00

Counterfeits of Nos. O9–O16 exist.

Regular Issues of 1915–25 Overprinted in Red or Blue

b

1926 *Perf. 13½x14, 14.*

O17	A52	5c sl bl (R)	1.75	40
O18	A50	10c bl & blk (R)	2.75	60
O19	A39	20c org red & blk (Bl)	1.25	30
O20	A42	50c dp grn & blk (Bl)	1.25	30
O21	A43	1p grn & blk (R)	4.00	50
O22	A43	2p ver & blk (Bl)	2.75	80
		Nos. O17-O22 (6)	13.75	2.90

Nos. O21 and O22 are overprinted vertically at each side.

Nos. O17 to O22 were for the use of the Biblioteca Nacional.

Regular Issue of 1915-25 Overprinted in Red

Servicio del

ESTADO

c

1928 *Perf. 13½x14, 14.*

O23	A50	10c bl & blk	6.00	1.50
O24	A39	20c brn org & blk	2.75	75
O25	A40	25c dl bl & blk	7.00	75
O26	A42	50c dp grn & blk	4.00	75
O27	A43	1p grn & blk	4.50	1.00
		Nos. O23-O27 (5)	24.25	4.75

The overprint on Nos. O23 to O26 is 16½mm. high; on No. O27 it is 20mm.

Regular Issues of 1928-30 Overprinted in Red

Servicio del

ESTADO

d

On Stamp Inscribed: "Correos de Chile".

1930-31

O28	A50	10c bl & blk	2.75	1.00

Wmkd.

Small Star in Shield, Multiple. (215)

On Stamps Inscribed: "Correos de Chile".

O29	A50	10c bl & blk	6.00	2.00
O30	A39	20c org red & blk	75	35
O31	A40	25c bl & blk	75	35
O32	A42	50c dp grn & blk	1.50	50

On Stamps Inscribed: "Chile Correos".

O33	A42	50c dp grn & blk	1.50	50
O34	A43	1p grn & blk	1.50	75
		Nos.O28-O34 (7)	14.75	5.45

Same Overprint on No. 181.

1933 *Perf. 13½x14.*

O35	A61	20c dk brn	75	35

Same Overprint in Red on No. 182.

1935 Wmk. 215

O36	A62	10c dp bl	75	50

No. 163 Overprinted Type "b" in Red.

Inscribed: "Correos de Chile".

1934

O37	A52	5c lt grn	65	50

Overprint "b" on No. 182.

1935

O38	A62	10c dp bl	65	50

Same Overprint in Black on No. 181.

1936 *Perf. 13½x14.* Wmk. 215

O39	A61	20c dk brn	10.00	50

Overprint "b" in Red on No. 158.

1938 *Perf. 14.*

O40	A43	1p grn & blk	2.50	1.00

Nos. 204 and 205 Overprinted Type "d" in Black.

1939 *Perf. 13½x14, 14.*

O41	A83	50c violet	3.75	1.25
O42	A84	1p org brn	5.00	3.50

Stamps of 1938-40 Overprinted Type "b" in Black, Red or Blue.

1940-46 *Perf. 13½x14, 14.*

O43	A79	10c sal pink ('45)	2.00	1.50
O44	A79a	15c brn org	1.00	35
O45	A80	20c lt bl (R) ('42)	1.25	50
O46	A81	30c brn pink (Bl)	65	35
O47	A82	40c lt grn	65	35
O48	A83	50c vio ('45)	3.75	75
O49	A84	1p org brn ('42)	2.50	75
O50	A85	1.80p dp bl (R) ('45)	10.00	6.25
O51	A86	2p car lake ('42)	2.00	1.25
		Nos. O43-O51 (9)	23.80	12.05

Overprint "b" in Black on Nos. 223, 225.

Unwmkd.

O58	A84	1p brn org	2.50	1.25
O59	A86	2p car lake ('46)	4.50	1.50

Regular Issues of 1938–43 Overprinted Diagonally in Carmine, Black or Blue

e

1948-54 Unwmkd., Wmk. 215

Perf. 13½x14, 14.

O60	A80	20c lt bl, #219 (C)	65	35
O61	A81	30c brt pink, #202 (Bl) ('54)	1.25	50
O62	A82	40c brt grn, #203 ('54)	2.50	1.25
O63	A83	50c vio #222 ('49)	75	35
O64	A84	1p org brn, #205	2.50	1.00
O65	A86	2p car lake, #207 ('54)	1.00	50
O66	A87	5p dk sl grn, #208 (C) ('51)	2.50	1.00
		Nos.O60-O66 (7)	11.15	4.95

Overprint "e" Diagonally on Nos. 265 and 275 in Red or Black.

1953-55 Unwmkd., Wmk. 215

Perf. 13½x14, 13x14

O67	A126	1p dk bl grn, #265 (R)	1.00	50
O68	A126	1p dk bl grn, #265 (Bk) ('55)	75	50
O69	A126	1p dk bl grn, #275 (R) ('55)	75	50

Overprint "e" Horizontally on Nos. 207, 209 in Black or Blue

1955-56 *Perf. 14.* Wmk. 215

O70	A86	2p car lake ('56)	2.50	75
O71	A88	10p rose vio (Bl)	3.00	1.75

Overprint "e" Horizontally on Nos. 293–295 and Types of 1956 Regular Issue in Black or Red.

1956 *Perf. 14x14½.* Unwmkd.

O72	A141	2p purple	1.00	60
O73	A142	3p lt vio bl (R)	3.00	2.00
O74	A141	5p redsh brn	75	30
O75	A142	10p vio (19x22¼mm) (R)	3.00	1.75
a.		Perf. 13½x14 (19½x22½mm) ('58)	50	30
O76	A141	50p rose red	2.50	1.00

No. 310 Overprinted in Red Vertically, Reading Down, Similar to Type "e."

Size of Overprint: 21x2½mm.

1958 Lithographed *Perf. 14*

O77	A149	10p vio bl	*275.00*	*30.00*

Overprint "e" Horizontally on No. 327 in Red.

1960 *Perf. 13x14* Unwmkd.

O79	A157	5c blue	2.50	1.00

Methods and style of listing are detailed in "Special Notices" at the front of this volume.

POSTAL TAX STAMPS

Talca Issue.

A 10c blue postal tax stamp, inscribed "Bicentenario de Talca" and picturing a coat of arms, was issued in 1942. It was sold only in Talca and was required for a time on all domestic letters sent from that city. The tax helped pay for Talca's bicentenary celebration. Price 10 cents.

Nos. 326 and 347 Surcharged

Eº 0,10
Art. 77
LEY
17272

Lithographed

1970 ***Perf. 14x13*** **Unwmkd.**

RA1	A159	10c on 2c ultra	10	8
		Perf. 14x14½		
RA2	A170	10c on 6c rose lil	10	8

Chilean Arms
PT1

Perf. 14½x14

1970, Apr. 23 Litho. Unwmkd.

RA3	PT1	10c blue	15	8

No. RA3 Surcharged in Red

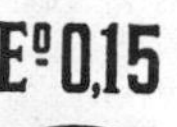

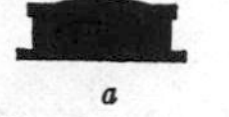

a

b

1971-72

RA4	PT1 (a)	15c on 10c bl	5	5
RA5	PT1 (b)	15c on 10c bl ('72)	10	8

Type of 1970

1972, July Litho. ***Perf. 14½x14***

RA6	PT1	15c rose red	15	8

No. RA6 Surcharged in Ultramarine

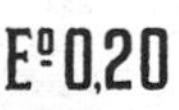

1972-73

RA7	PT1	20c on 15c rose red	12	6
RA8	PT1	50c on 15c rose red ('73)	15	8

No. RA8 has 9 bars instead of 8.

The surtax on Nos. RA1-RA8 was for modernization of postal system. Compulsory on all inland mail.

PARCEL POST POSTAL TAX STAMP

Pres. J. J. Prieto V.
PPT1

Lithographed

1957, Apr. 8 ***Perf. 14*** **Unwmkd.**

QRA1	PPT1	15p green	25	15

The surtax aided the Prieto Foundation. No. QRA1 was required on parcel post entering or leaving Chile.

CHINA

(chī'nȧ)

LOCATION—Eastern Asia.
GOVT.—Republic.
AREA—2,903,475 sq. mi.
POP.—462,798,093 (1948).

10 Candareen = 1 Mace
10 Mace = 1 Tael
100 Cents = 1 Dollar (Yuan) (1897)

Issues of the Imperial Maritime Customs Post.

Imperial Dragon
A1

Typographed

1878 ***Perf. 12½*** **Unwmkd.**

Thin Paper.

Stamps printed 2½ mm. apart.

1	A1	1c green	80.00	30.00
a.		Imperf. (pair)	600.00	
2	A1	3c brn red	45.00	12.00
a.		Imperf. (pair)	500.00	
3	A1	5c orange	80.00	15.00
a.		Imperf. (pair)	600.00	

Imperforate proofs of Nos. 1-3 have an extra circle near the dragon's lower left foot.

1882

Thin or Pelure Paper.

Stamps printed 4½ mm apart.

4	A1	1c green	125.00	55.00
5	A1	3c brn red	175.00	16.00
6	A1	5c org yel	1,900.	375.00

1883

Rough to smooth Perf. 12½.

Medium to Thick Opaque Paper.

Stamps printed 2 to 3¼ mm. apart.

7	A1	1c green	75.00	16.00
a.		Vertical pair, imperf. between	1,700.	
8	A1	3c brn red	95.00	11.00
a.		Vertical pair, imperf. between		*1,600.*
9	A1	5c yellow	135.00	11.00

Nos. 1 to 9 were printed from plates of 25, 20 or 15 individual copper dies, but only No. 5 exists in the 15-die setting. Many different printings and plate settings exist. All values occur in a wide variety of shades and papers. The effect of climate on certain papers has produced the varieties on so-called toned papers in Nos. 1 to 15.

Counterfeits, frequently with forged cancellations, occur in all early Chinese issues.

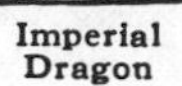

Imperial Dragon
A2

Wmk. 103

Wmkd. Yin-Yang Symbol. (103)

1885 ***Perf. 12½***

10	A2	1c green	12.50	2.50
a.		Vertical pair, imperf. between	500.00	
b.		Horiz. pair, imperf. between		
11	A2	3c lilac	15.00	3.50
a.		Horizontal pair, imperf. between		250.00
b.		Vertical pair, imperf. between		300.00
12	A2	5c grnsh yel	25.00	5.00
a.		5c bis brn	35.00	8.00
b.		Vertical pair, imperf. between	600.00	
c.		Horizontal pair, imperf. between		525.00

1888 ***Perf. 11½-12***

13	A2	1c green	3.00	1.00
14	A2	3c lilac	5.00	1.25
b.		Double impression		
15	A2	5c grnsh yel	7.00	1.25
b.		Horiz. pair, imperf. vert.		400.00
c.		Double impression	250.00	150.00

Nos. 10 to 15 were printed from plates made of 40 individual copper dies, arranged in two panes of 20 each. Several different settings exist of all values.

Imperforates of Nos. 13-15 are considered proofs by most authorities.

Stamps overprinted "Formosa" in English or Chinese are proofs.

"Shou" and "Wu Fu"
A3

Dragon and Hydrangea Leaves
A4

"Pa Kua" Signs in Corners
A5

Dragon and Peony
A6

Carp, the Messenger Fish
A7

Dragon, "Pa Kua" and Immortelle
A8

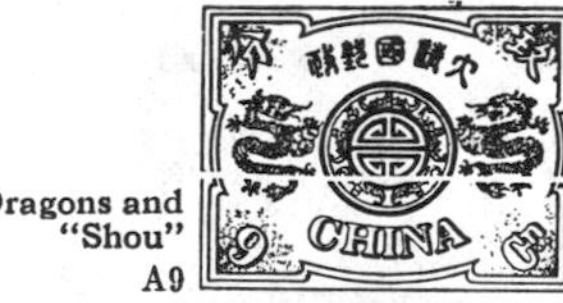

Dragons and "Shou"
A9

Dragons and Giant Peony
A10

Junk on the Yangtse
A11

Lithographed in Shanghai.

1894

16	A3	1c org red	4.50	2.00
a.		Vertical pair, imperf. between	250.00	200.00
b.		Horizontal pair, imperf. between	250.00	250.00
c.		Imperf. horizontally (pair)	150.00	150.00
17	A4	2c green	4.50	2.00
a.		Horizontal pair, imperf. between	225.00	
18	A5	3c org yel	4.00	1.25
a.		Vertical pair, imperf. between	200.00	200.00
b.		Horizontal pair, imperf. between	200.00	200.00
19	A6	4c rose pink	19.00	6.50
a.		Horizontal pair, imperf. between	300.00	
20	A7	5c dl org	30.00	12.50
a.		Horizontal pair, imperf. between	250.00	
21	A8	6c brown	8.00	2.50
a.		Vertical pair, imperf. between	200.00	
b.		Horizontal pair, imperf. between	200.00	
22	A9	9c dl grn	25.00	6.00
a.		Imperf., pair	200.00	
b.		Imperf. vert., pair	250.00	
c.		Imperf. horiz., pair	200.00	
d.		Vertical pair, imperf. between	250.00	
e.		Tête bêche pair	150.00	150.00
f.		Tête bêche pair, imperf. horizontally	750.00	
g.		Tête bêche pair, imperf. vertically	600.00	
h.		Vert. strip of 3, imperf. between	300.00	
23	A10	12c orange	50.00	12.50
24	A11	24c carmine	75.00	25.00
a.		Vertical pair, imperf. between	650.00	

Nos. 16 to 24 were issued to commemorate the 60th birthday of Tsz'e Hsi, the Empress Dowager. All values exist in several distinct shades.

On March 20, 1896, the Customs Post was changed, by Imperial Edict, to a National Post and the dollar was adopted as the unit of currency. The effective date of the Imperial Edict was January 1, 1897 and until that date the Customs Post continued operating.

Time was required to work out details of the Imperial Post and design new stamps. As a provisional measure, stocks of Nos. 16 to 24 were ordered surcharged with new values in dollars and cents. It is believed that only the Shanghai office stock of Nos. 16 to 24 (plus any reserve stock at the printer's) was surcharged with small figures of value. Other post offices throughout China were instructed to return all unoverprinted stocks on receipt of the new surcharges.

Early in the year it was apparent that all stamps would be exhausted before the new issues were ready (Nos. 86 to 97), and since the stones from which Nos. 16 to 24 had been printed no longer existed, new stones were made from the original transfers. A printing from the new stones was made early in 1897 and surcharged with large figures of value spaced 2½mm. below the Chinese characters. During the surcharging, sheets from the 1894 (original) printing were received from outlying post offices and surcharged as they arrived. A small quantity of the 1897 printing reached the public without surcharge (Nos. 16n to 24n).

Additional stamps were still required and another printing was made from the new stones and surcharged with large figures, but in a new setting with 1½mm. between the Chinese characters and the value. Additional sheets of the 1894 printing were received from the most distant post offices and were also surcharged with the 1½mm. setting. Thus there are four different sets of the large-figure surcharges. All these stamps were regularly issued but no attempt was made by the post office to separate printings. Some values are difficult to distinguish as to printing, particularly in used condition.

1897 Lithographed in Shanghai.

16n	A3	1c red org	150.00
17n	A4	2c yel grn	100.00
18n	A5	3c chr yel	95.00
p.		3c yel buff	300.00
19n	A6	4c pale rose	150.00
20n	A7	5c yellow	90.00
21n	A8	6c red brn	200.00
22n	A9	9c yelsh grn	250.00
23n	A10	12c pale org yel	300.00
24n	A11	24c rose red	275.00

Nos. 16n to 24n were new printings from new stones. These stamps were prepared solely for surcharging and were not regularly issued without surcharge. The colors of the 1897 printings are pale or dull; the gum is thin and white. The 1894 printing has a thicker, yellowish gum.

The set of nine values on thick unwatermarked paper is a special printing ordered by P. G. von Mollendorf, a Customs official, for presentation purposes. Price, set, $100.

Issues of the Chinese Government Post.

Preceding Issues Surcharged in Black

貳洋暫
分銀作
2
cents.

Small Numerals.

Surcharged on Nos. 13–15.

1897, Jan. 2 ***Perf. 11½–12.***

No.	Type	Description	Unused	Used
25	A2	1c on 1c grn	7.50	2.00
26	A2	2c on 3c lil	22.50	5.00
27	A2	5c on 5c grnsh yel	20.00	4.00

Surcharged on Nos. 16–24.

No.	Type	Description	Unused	Used
28	A5	½c on 3c org yel	5.00	1.75
a.		'1' instead of '½'	100.00	100.00
b.		Horizontal pair, imperf.between	250.00	
c.		Imperf. horizontally (pair)	125.00	125.00
d.		Double surcharge	300.00	
e.		Vert. pair, imperf. between	300.00	
29	A3	1c on 1c org red	2.25	1.25
a.		Inverted surcharge	600.00	500.00
30	A4	2c on 2c grn	2.50	1.25
a.		Imperf. vertically (pair)	200.00	
b.		Vertical pair, imperf. between	250.00	
c.		Double surcharge	300.00	
d.		Inverted surcharge	600.00	
e.		Horizontal pair, imperf. between	225.00	
31	A6	4c on 4c rose pink	2.50	1.50
a.		Double surch.	300.00	300.00
b.		Vertical pair, imperf. between	225.00	225.00
c.		Horizontal pair, imperf. between	225.00	225.00
32	A7	5c on 5c dl org	3.50	1.50
a.		Vertical pair, imperf. between	300.00	
33	A8	8c on 6c brn	4.00	2.00
a.		Vertical pair, imperf. between	175.00	175.00
b.		Vertical strip of three, imperf. between	250.00	250.00
c.		Horizontal pair, imperf. between	225.00	225.00
34	A8	10c on 6c brn	12.00	6.00
a.		10c on 6c choc	12.00	6.00
b.		Vertical pair, imperf. between	175.00	175.00
c.		Imperf. vertically (pair)	250.00	
35	A9	10c on 9c dl grn	17.50	8.00
a.		Double surcharge	400.00	400.00
b.		Invtd. surch.	750.00	750.00
36	A10	10c on 12c org	30.00	15.00
a.		Imperf. horizontally (pair)	150.00	
37	A11	30c on 24c car	45.00	25.00
a.		Vert. pair, imperf. between	*1,250.*	

Preceding Issues Surcharged in Black

貳洋暫
分銀作
2
cents.

Large Numerals

Numerals 2½mm. below Chinese characters.

1897, March

Surcharged on Nos. 16 to 24.

No.	Type	Description	Unused	Used
38	A5	½c on 3c org yel	375.00	100.00
b.		Inverted surch.		400.00
39	A3	1c on 1c org red	55.00	40.00
40	A4	2c on 2c grn	100.00	60.00
41	A6	4c on 4c rose pink	110.00	45.00
b.		Horiz. pair, imperf. between	*1,750.*	
42	A7	5c on 5c dl org	32.50	22.50
43	A8	8c on 6c brn	375.00	375.00
44	A9	10c on 9c dl grn	125.00	60.00
45	A10	10c on 12c org	1,200.	250.00
46	A11	30c on 24c car	275.00	250.00
b.		2mm spacing between '30' and 'cents.'	*1,250.*	

Same Surcharge on Nos. 16n to 24n.

No.	Type	Description	Unused	Used
47	A5	½c on 3c chr yel	1.40	75
a.		'cen' for 'cent'	150.00	135.00
b.		Vertical pair, imperf. between	135.00	135.00
c.		Imperf. horizontally (pair)	75.00	75.00
d.		As 'a,' imperf. horiz. (pair)	750.00	750.00
48	A3	1c on 1c red org	2.75	1.75
a.		Horiz. pair, imperf. between	250.00	
49	A4	2c on 2c yel grn	2.25	1.00
50	A6	4c on 4c pale rose	3.25	2.00
a.		Horizontal pair, imperf. between	150.00	150.00
51	A7	5c on 5c yel	4.50	2.75
52	A8	8c on 6c red brn	20.00	12.00
53	A9	10c on 9c yelsh grn	25.00	11.00
a.		10c on 9c emer	25.00	12.50
54	A10	10c on 12c pale org yel	20.00	12.50
55	A11	30c on 24c rose red	60.00	30.00
a.		2mm spacing between '30' and 'cents'	300.00	150.00
b.		Vertical pair, imperf. between	*2,000.*	

Numerals 1⅛mm. below Chinese characters.

1897, May

Surcharged on Nos. 16 to 24.

No.	Type	Description	Unused	Used
56	A5	½c on 3c org yel	50.00	35.00
57	A3	1c on 1c org red	60.00	50.00
58	A4	2c on 2c grn	*6,000.*	100.00
59	A6	4c on 4c rose pink	40.00	35.00
60	A7	5c on 5c dl org	30.00	27.50
61	A8	8c on 6c brn	225.00	200.00
62	A9	10c on 9c dl grn	40.00	25.00
63	A10	10c on 12c org	200.00	175.00
64	A11	30c on 24c car	*2,000.*	

Same Surcharge on Nos. 16n to 24n.

No.	Type	Description	Unused	Used
65	A5	½c on 3c yel	75	60
a.		Invtd. surch.	250.00	200.00
b.		½mm spacing	800.00	700.00
66	A3	1c on 1c red org	1.50	1.00
67	A4	2c on 2c yel grn	2.50	1.50
a.		Inverted surcharge	700.00	
68	A6	4c on 4c pale rose	45.00	30.00
a.		Inverted surcharge	200.00	200.00
69	A7	5c on 5c yel	50.00	30.00
70	A9	10c on 9c gray grn	35.00	15.00
a.		Inverted surcharge	150.00	125.00
71	A10	10c on 12c brn org	75.00	25.00
72	A11	30c on 24c pale rose	1,500.	600.00

Same Surcharge (1½mm. Spacing) on Type A12, and

A12

A12a

Redrawn Designs. Printed from New Stones.

1897

No.	Type	Description	Unused	Used
73	A12	½c on 3c yel	85.00	35.00
a.		½mm spacing	300.00	250.00
74	A12a	2c on 2c yel grn	16.00	2.00
a.		Horizontal pair, imperf. between	300.00	

Nos. 73 and 74 were surcharged on stamps printed from new stones, which differ slightly from the originals. On No. 73 the numeral "3" and symbols in the four corner panels have been enlarged and strengthened. On No. 74, the numeral "2" has a thick, flat base.

Surcharged on 1888 Issue.

No.	Type	Description	Unused	Used
75	A2	1c on 1c grn	75.00	
76	A2	2c on 3c lil	150.00	
77	A2	5c on 5c grnsh yel	40.00	

Nos. 75–77 were not regularly issued.

Type A13 Surcharged in Black:

A13

政郵清大
分 壹 當
one cent
a

政郵清大
貳洋暫
分銀作
2 cents
b

政郵清大
貳洋暫
分銀作
2
cents
c

政郵清大
肆洋暫
分銀作
4
cents.
d

政郵清大
肆洋暫
分銀作
4
cents.
e

政郵清大
當
壹
圓
1 dollar.
f

政郵清大
當
壹
圓
1 dollar
g

1897 ***Perf. 12 to 15.*** **Unwmkd.**

No.	Type	Description	Unused	Used
78	A13 (a)	1c on 3c red	11.00	2.50
a.		No period after 'cent'	35.00	25.00
b.		Central character with large 'box'	16.00	10.00
79	A13 (b)	2c on 3c red	35.00	12.50
a.		Invtd. surch.	300.00	250.00
b.		Inverted 'S' in 'CENTS'	70.00	35.00
c.		No period after 'CENTS'	70.00	35.00
d.		Comma after 'CENTS'	70.00	35.00
e.		Double surch.	1,000.	
f.		Double surcharge, both inverted	*2,000.*	
g.		Double surch. (blk. & grn.)	*2,250.*	
80	A13 (c)	2c on 3c red	11.00	4.00
81	A13 (d)	4c on 3c red	1,500.	1,250.
a.		Double surch. (blk. & vio.)	3,000.	2,000.
82	A13 (e)	4c on 3c red	65.00	17.50
83	A13 (f)	$1 on 3c red	*60,000.*	
a.		No period after 'r'		
84	A13 (g)	$1 on 3c red	200.00	85.00
85	A13 (g)	$5 on 3c red	2,500.	1,750.
a.		Inverted surcharge	*3,250.*	*3,250.*

A few copies of the 3c red exist without surcharge; one cancelled. No. 79 with green surcharge is a trial printing.

Dragon
A14

Carp
A15

Wild Goose
A16

"Imperial Chinese Post".

Lithographed in Japan.

Perf. 11, 11½, 12.

1897, Aug. 16 **Wmk. 103**

No.	Type	Description	Unused	Used
86	A14	½c pur brn	1.50	75
a.		Horizontal pair, imperf. between	175.00	
87	A14	1c yellow	1.75	60
88	A14	2c orange	1.25	40
a.		Imperf. horizontally (pair)	200.00	
89	A14	4c brown	2.25	75
a.		Horizontal pair, imperf. between	300.00	
90	A14	5c rosc rcd	3.50	1.00
91	A14	10c dk grn	8.00	85
92	A15	20c maroon	15.00	4.00
93	A15	30c red	18.00	8.00
94	A15	50c yel grn	22.00	10.00
a.		50c blk grn	175.00	
b.		[illegible]	[illegible]	
95	A16	$1 car & rose	65.00	32.50
a.		Imperf. vertically (pair)	1,000.	
96	A16	$2 org & yel	325.00	300.00
a.		Imperf. vertically (pair)	1,100.	
97	A16	$5 yel grn & pink	200.00	185.00

The inner circular frames and outer frames of Nos. 86 to 91 differ for each denomination.

No. 97 imperforate was not regularly issued. Copies have been privately perforated and offered as No. 97. Shades occur in most values of this issue.

Dragon
A17

Carp
A18

Wild Goose
A19

Engraved in London.

"Chinese Imperial Post".

1898 ***Perf. 12 to 16.*** **Wmk. 103**

No.	Type	Description	Unused	Used
98	A17	½c chocolate	40	10
a.		Vertical pair, imperf. between		150.00
99	A17	1c ocher	40	10
a.		Vertical pair, imperf. between	60.00	60.00
b.		Horizontal pair, imperf. between	110.00	110.00
100	A17	2c scarlet	60	10
a.		Vertical pair, imperf. between	35.00	35.00
b.		Imperf. vertically (pair)		
101	A17	4c org brn	1.50	10
a.		Vertical pair, imperf. between	85.00	
b.		Imperf. vertically (pair)	50.00	50.00
c.		Horiz. pair, imperf. between	135.00	135.00
d.		Horiz. strip of 3, imperf. between	160.00	160.00
102	A17	5c salmon	2.00	50
a.		Vertical pair, imperf. between	70.00	70.00
b.		Horizontal pair, imperf. between	75.00	75.00
103	A17	10c dk bl grn	2.00	20
a.		Vert. or horiz. pair, imperf. between	75.00	75.00
104	A18	20c claret	7.00	85
a.		Horizontal pair, imperf. between	165.00	
b.		Imperf. horiz. (pair)	110.00	110.00
105	A18	30c dl rose	8.00	60
a.		Horizontal pair, imperf. between	160.00	
b.		Imperf. horizontally (pair)	160.00	
106	A18	50c lt grn	15.00	2.00
a.		Vertical pair, imperf. between	225.00	
107	A19	$1 red & pale rose	65.00	5.00

No.	Type	Description	Unused	Used
108	A19	$2 brn, red & yel	110.00	20.00
109	A19	$5 dp grn & sal	190.00	40.00
a.		Horizontal pair, imperf. between	1,250.	
b.		Vert. pair, imperf. between	1,500.	

No. 98 surcharged "B. R. A.—5—Five Cents" in three lines in black or green, was surcharged by British military authorities shortly after the Boxer riots for use from military posts in an occupied area along the Peking-Mukden railway. Usually canceled in violet.

1902–03 *Perf. 12 to 16* Unwmkd.

No.	Type	Description	Unused	Used
110	A17	½c brown	30	8
a.		Horiz. or vert. pair, imperf. between	70.00	70.00
111	A17	1c ocher	30	8
a.		Horizontal pair, imperf. between	35.00	35.00
b.		Vertical pair, imperf. between	40.00	40.00
c.		Vert. pair, imperf. horiz.	30.00	30.00
112	A17	2c scarlet	60	8
a.		Horiz. or vert. pair, imperf. between	35.00	35.00
c.		Vert. pair, imperf. horiz.	30.00	30.00
d.		Horiz. pair, imperf. vert.	30.00	30.00
e.		Vert. strip of 3 imperf. between	45.00	45.00
113	A17	4c org brn	1.00	20
a.		Horiz. or vert. pair, imperf. between	50.00	50.00
114	A17	5c rose red	7.00	1.00
a.		Vertical pair, imperf. between	110.00	
b.		Vert. pair, imperf. horiz.	60.00	
115	A17	5c orange	7.50	1.00
a.		5c yel	60.00	10.00
b.		Vertical pair, imperf. between	80.00	
c.		Horizontal pair, imperf. between	100.00	
116	A17	10c green	6.00	15
a.		Vertical pair, imperf. between	40.00	
b.		Horizontal pair, imperf. between	45.00	
c.		Vert. pair, imperf. horiz.	40.00	
d.		Vert. strip of 3, imperf. between	95.00	
117	A18	20c red brn	5.00	25
a.		Horizontal pair, imperf. between	100.00	
b.		Vertical pair, imperf. between	85.00	
118	A18	30c dl red	7.50	35
a.		Vertical pair, imperf. between	150.00	
119	A18	50c yel grn	10.00	50
120	A19	$1 red & pale rose	37.50	1.50
121	A19	$2 brn red & yel	85.00	7.50
122	A19	$5 dp grn & sal	125.00	30.00
		Nos. 110-122 (13)	292.70	42.69

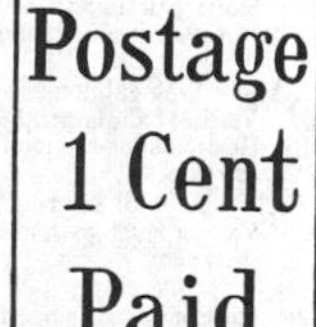

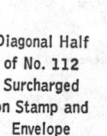

Diagonal Half of No. 112 Surcharged on Stamp and Envelope

1903

No.	Type	Description	Unused	Used
123	A17	1c on half of 2c scar, on cover		300.00

Excellent forgeries of No. 123 are plentiful, particularly on pieces of cover.

1905-10

No.	Type	Description	Unused	Used
124	A17	2c grn ('08)	50	5
a.		Horizontal pair, imperf. between	55.00	55.00
b.		Vertical pair, imperf. between	65.00	65.00
c.		Imperf. vertically (pair)	55.00	
d.		Horiz. strip of 4, imperf. between	135.00	
125	A17	3c sl grn ('10)	75	6
a.		Horiz. or vert. pair, imperf. between	70.00	
126	A17	4c ver ('09)	1.25	12
127	A17	5c violet	1.75	12
a.		5c lil	2.25	12
b.		Horiz. or vert. pair, imperf. between	70.00	
d.		Vert. pair, imperf. horiz.	40.00	
128	A17	7c mar ('10)	5.00	70
129	A17	10c ultra ('08)	3.00	10
a.		Horiz. or vert. pair, imperf. between	110.00	
c.		Vert. pair, imperf. horiz.	85.00	60.00
130	A18	16c ol grn ('07)	16.50	1.50
		Nos. 124-130 (7)	28.75	2.65

Temple of Heaven, Peking
A20

1909 *Perf. 14*

No.	Type	Description	Unused	Used
131	A20	2c org & grn	1.00	35
132	A20	3c org & bl	1.25	50
133	A20	7c org & brn vio	1.50	50

Issued to commemorate the first year of the reign of Hsuan T'ung, who later became Henry Pu-yi and then Emperor Kang Teh of Manchukuo.

Stamps of 1902-10 Overprinted with Chinese Characters.

1912 *Perf. 12 to 16*

Foochow Issue.

Overprinted in Red or Black 臨時中立

No.	Type	Description	Unused	Used
134	A17	3c sl grn (R)	65.00	32.50
135	A19	$1 red & pale rose (Bk)	600.00	500.00
136	A19	$2 brn red & yel (Bk)	800.00	625.00
137	A19	$5 dp grn & sal (Bk)	900.00	650.00

The overprint "Ling Shih Chung Li" or "Provisional Neutrality," signified that the Post Office was conducted neutrally by agreement between the Manchu and opposing forces.

Nanking Issue

Overprinted in Red or Black

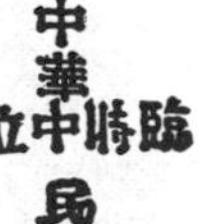

No.	Type	Description	Unused	Used
138	A17	1c ocher (R)	32.50	27.50
139	A17	3c sl grn (R)	27.50	22.50
140	A17	7c mar (Bk)	140.00	110.00
141	A18	16c ol grn (R)	525.00	400.00
142	A18	50c yel grn (R)	900.00	750.00
143	A19	$1 red & pale rose (Bk)	800.00	650.00
144	A19	$2 brn red & yel (Bk)	1,500.	1,500.
145	A19	$5 dp grn & sal (Bk)	3,000.	3,000.

Vertical overprint reads: "Chung Hwa Min Kuo" (Republic of China).
Stamps of this issue were also used in Shanghai and Hankow.
Additional values were overprinted but not issued. Excellent forgeries of the overprints of Nos. 134–145 exist.

Issues of the Republic

Overprinted in Black or Red 中華民國 *a*

Overprinted by the Maritime Customs Statistical Department, Shanghai.

No.	Type	Description	Unused	Used
146	A17	½c brn (Bk)	35	6
a.		Inverted overprint	3.50	3.00
b.		Double overprint	35.00	
147	A17	1c ocher (R)	40	6
a.		Vert. pair, imperf. horiz.	40.00	40.00
b.		Invtd. ovpt.	35.00	25.00
c.		Double overprint	40.00	40.00
d.		Horizontal pair, imperf. between	40.00	40.00
e.		Horiz. pair, imperf. vert.	25.00	
f.		Pair, one without overprint	25.00	
148	A17	2c grn (R)	50	5
a.		Vertical pair, imperf. between	50.00	50.00
149	A17	3c sl grn (R)	80	5
a.		Inverted overprint	45.00	20.00
b.		Horiz. or vert. pair, imperf. between	60.00	60.00
d.		Horiz. pair, imperf. vert.	45.00	
150	A17	4c ver (Bk)	85	10
a.		Vertical pair, imperf. between	350.00	
151	A17	5c vio (R)	1.40	12
a.		Horizontal pair, imperf. between		
152	A17	7c mar (Bk)	2.00	40
153	A17	10c ultra (R)	1.75	10
a.		Double overprint	75.00	
b.		Pair, one without overprint	300.00	
c.		Brnsh red overprint	6.00	4.00
d.		Inverted overprint	100.00	100.00
154	A18	16c ol grn (R)	3.50	1.00
155	A18	20c red brn (Bk)	4.00	30
156	A18	30c rose red (Bk)	5.00	50
157	A18	50c yel grn (R)	7.00	40
158	A19	$1 red & pale rose (Bk)	35.00	1.25
a.		Inverted overprint		*2,000.*
159	A19	$2 brn red & yel (Bk)	50.00	6.00
a.		Inverted overprint	135.00	135.00
160	A19	$5 dp grn & sal (Bk)	135.00	110.00
		Nos. 146-160 (15)	247.55	120.39

Stamps with blue overprint similar to the preceding were not an official issue but were privately made by a printer in Tientsin.

Overprinted in Red 中華民國 *b*

Overprinted by the Commercial Press, Shanghai

Type "b" differs from "a" in that the top character is shifted slightly to right and the bottom character is larger and has small "legs".

No.	Type	Description	Unused	Used
161	A17	1c ocher (R)	1.50	12
a.		Inverted overprint	40.00	40.00
b.		Vertical pair, imperf. between	60.00	
c.		Double ovpt.	55.00	
162	A17	2c grn (R)	15.00	12
a.		Inverted overprint	650.00	400.00
b.		Vertical pair, imperf. between	85.00	
c.		Horizontal pair, imperf. between	100.00	
d.		Horiz. strip of 3, imperf. btwn.	250.00	

Overprinted in Blue, Carmine or Black

Overprinted by Waterlow & Sons, London.

No.	Type	Description	Unused	Used
163	A17	½c brn (Bl)	20	5
a.		Vertical pair, imperf. between	350.00	350.00
164	A17	1c ocher (C)	20	5
a.		Horizontal pair, imperf. between	55.00	
165	A17	2c grn (C)	30	5
166	A17	3c sl grn (C)	60	5
a.		Inverted overprint		450.00
167	A17	4c ver (Bk)	90	15
168	A17	5c vio (C)	1.00	20
169	A17	7c mar (Bk)	4.50	1.50
170	A17	10c ultra (C)	1.25	12
a.		Vertical pair, imperf. between	175.00	150.00
171	A18	16c ol grn (R)	4.50	1.00
172	A18	20c red brn (Bk)	4.00	50
173	A18	30c dl red (Bk)	5.00	50
174	A18	50c yel grn (R)	9.00	1.25
175	A19	$1 red & pale rose (Bk)	27.50	2.00
176	A19	$2 brn red & yel (Bk)	65.00	42.50
177	A19	$5 dp grn & sal (C)	130.00	100.00
		Nos. 163-177 (15)	253.95	149.92

Due to instructions issued to postmasters throughout China at the time of the Revolution, a number of them prepared unauthorized overprints using the same characters as the overprints prepared by the government. While many were made in good faith, some, like the blue overprints from Tientsin, were bogus, and the status of certain others is extremely dubious.

Dr. Sun Yat-sen
A21

1912, Dec. 14 *Perf. 14½*

No.	Type	Description	Unused	Used
178	A21	1c orange	90	60
179	A21	2c yel grn	90	60
180	A21	3c sl grn	90	60
181	A21	5c rose lil	1.50	75
182	A21	8c dp brn	2.00	1.25
183	A21	10c dl bl	1.75	1.25
184	A21	16c ol grn	5.00	2.25
185	A21	20c maroon	6.00	1.75
186	A21	50c dk grn	17.50	10.00
187	A21	$1 brn red	50.00	20.00
188	A21	$2 yel brn	250.00	150.00
189	A21	$5 gray	110.00	60.00
		Nos. 178-189 (12)	446.45	249.05

Issued in honor of the leader of the Revolution.

President Yuan Shih-kai
A22

1912, Dec. 14

No.	Type	Description	Unused	Used
190	A22	1c orange	60	50
191	A22	2c yel grn	60	50
192	A22	3c sl grn	60	50
193	A22	5c rose lil	75	60
194	A22	8c dp brn	2.50	1.50
195	A22	10c dl bl	1.50	1.25
196	A22	16c ol grn	3.00	2.50
197	A22	20c maroon	4.00	2.50
198	A22	50c dk grn	20.00	11.00
199	A22	$1 brn red	30.00	16.00
200	A22	$2 yel brn	45.00	22.50

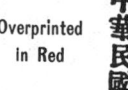

No.	Type	Description	Unused	Used
201	A22	$5 gray	95.00	65.00
		Nos. 190-201 (12)	203.55	124.35

Issued in honor of the first president of the Republic.

Junk
A24

Reaping Rice
A25

Gateway, Hall of Classics, Peking
A26

DESIGN A24.

London Printing: Vertical shading lines under top panel fine, junk with clear diagonal shading lines on sails, right pennant of junk usually long, lines in water weak except directly under junk.

Peking Printing: Vertical shading lines under top panel and inner vertical frame line much heavier, water and sails of junk more evenly and strongly colored, white wave over "H" of "CHINA" pointed upward, touching the junk.

DESIGN A25.

London: Front hat brim thick and nearly straight, left foot touches shadow.

Peking: Front hat brim thin and strongly upturned, left foot and sickle clearly outlined in white, shadow of middle tree lighter than those of the right and left trees.

DESIGN A26.

London: Light colored walk clearly defined almost to the doorway, figure in right doorway "T" shaped with strong horizontal cross-bar, white panel in base of central tower rectangular, vertical stroke in top left character uniformly thick at its base, tree to right of doorway ends in minute dots.

Peking: Walk more heavily shaded near doorway, especially at right; figure in right doorway more like a "Y", white panel at base of central tower is a long oval, right vertical stroke in top left character incurved near its base, tree at right has five prominent dots at top.

London Printing: By Waterlow & Sons, London, perforated 14 to 15.

Peking Printing: By the Chinese Bureau of Engraving and Printing, Peking, perforated 14.

London Printing.

1913, May 5 *Perf. 14–15.*

No.	Type	Description	Unused	Used
202	A24	½c blk brn	25	5
a.		Horiz. or vert. pair, imperf. btwn.	90.00	
203	A24	1c orange	25	5
a.		Horizontal pair, imperf. between	90.00	
b.		Vertical pair, imperf. between	80.00	
c.		Horiz. strip of 5, imperf. between	225.00	
204	A24	2c yel grn	60	5
a.		Horizontal pair, imperf. between	125.00	
205	A24	3c bl grn	90	5
a.		Horizontal pair, imperf. between	90.00	
b.		Vertical pair, imperf. between		225.00
206	A24	4c scarlet	1.50	5
207	A24	5c rose lil	2.50	6
208	A24	6c gray	1.50	10
209	A24	7c violet	2.50	75
210	A24	8c brn org	2.75	20
211	A24	10c dk bl	2.75	6
a.		Horizontal pair, imperf. between	200.00	200.00
b.		Vertical pair, imperf. between	225.00	175.00
212	A25	15c brown	10.00	50
213	A25	16c ol grn	3.00	50
214	A25	20c brn red	5.00	15
215	A25	30c brn vio	7.00	20
a.		Horiz. pair, imperf. between	225.00	175.00
216	A25	50c green	11.00	20
217	A26	$1 ocher & blk	35.00	35
218	A26	$2 bl & blk	45.00	2.50
219	A26	$5 scar & blk	75.00	20.00
220	A26	$10 yel grn & blk	425.00	350.00
		Nos. 202-220 (19)	631.50	375.82

First Peking Printing.

1915 *Perf. 14.*

No.	Type	Description	Unused	Used
221	A24	½c blk brn	25	5
222	A24	1c orange	25	5
223	A24	2c yel grn	35	5
224	A24	3c bl grn	50	5
225	A24	4c scarlet	1.20	5
226	A24	5c rose lil	1.20	5
a.		Bklt. pane of 4	100.00	
227	A24	6c gray	1.50	12
228	A24	7c violet	1.75	50
229	A24	8c brn org	1.50	6
230	A24	10c dk bl	1.50	5
a.		Bklt. pane of 4	100.00	
231	A25	15c brown	10.00	75
232	A25	16c ol grn	3.50	20
233	A25	20c brn red	3.00	5
234	A25	30c brn vio	3.00	8
235	A25	50c green	5.00	6
236	A26	$1 ocher & blk	14.00	20
237	A26	$2 bl & blk	20.00	50
a.		Center invtd.	4,500.	5,000.
238	A26	$5 scar & blk	45.00	3.50
239	A26	$10 yel grn & blk	250.00	70.00
		Nos. 221-239 (19)	363.50	76.37

1919

No.	Type	Description	Unused	Used
240	A24	1½c violet	35	8
241	A25	13c brown	60	6
242	A26	$20 yel & blk	1,350.	1,100.

Nos. 226 and 230 overprinted in red with five characters in vertical column were for postal savings use.

The higher values of the 1913–19 issues are often overprinted with Chinese characters, which are the names of various postal districts. Stamps were frequently stolen while in transit to post offices. The overprints served to protect them, since the stamps could only be used in the districts for which they were overprinted.

Yeh Kung-cho, Hsu Shi-chang and Chin Yun-peng
A27

1921, Oct. 10

No.	Type	Description	Unused	Used
243	A27	1c orange	4.00	75
244	A27	3c bl grn	4.00	75
245	A27	6c gray	4.00	75
246	A27	10c blue	4.00	75

National Post Office, 25th anniversary.

A28

1923 Red Surcharge.

No.	Type	Description	Unused	Used
247	A28	2c on 3c bl grn	1.00	10
a.		Inverted surcharge	1,000.	900.00

Second Peking Printing.

A29

A30

A31

Types of 1913-19 Issues.

Re-engraved.

Type A29: Most of the whitecaps in front of the junk have been removed and the water made darker. The shading lines have been removed from the arabesques and pearls above the top inscription. The inner shadings at the top and sides of the picture have been cut away.

Type A30: The heads of rice in the side panels have a background of crossed lines instead of horizontal lines. The Temple of Heaven is strongly shaded and has a door. There are rows of pearls below the Chinese characters in the upper corners. The arabesques above the top inscription have been altered and are without shading lines.

Type A31: The curved line under the inscription at top is single instead of double. There are four vertical lines, instead of eight, at each side of the picture. The trees at the sides of the temple had foliage in the 1913-19 issues, but now the branches are bare. There are numerous other alterations in the design.

1923 *Perf. 14.*

No.	Type	Description	Unused	Used
248	A29	½c blk brn	25	5
a.		Horizontal pair, imperf. between	75.00	75.00
b.		Horiz. pair, imperf. vert.	60.00	60.00
249	A29	1c orange	25	5
a.		Imperf., pair	35.00	
b.		Horiz. pair, imperf. vert.	50.00	
c.		Booklet pane of 6	60.00	
d.		Booklet pane of 4	30.00	
250	A29	1½c violet	30	20
251	A29	2c yel grn	40	5
252	A29	3c bl grn	35	5
a.		Bklt. pane of 6	50.00	
253	A29	4c gray	5.00	5
254	A29	5c claret	80	5
a.		Bklt. pane of 4	100.00	
255	A29	6c scarlet	1.00	5
256	A29	7c violet	1.50	15
257	A29	8c orange	1.25	5
258	A29	10c blue	1.25	5
a.		Bklt. pane of 6	75.00	
b.		Bklt. pane of 2	90.00	
259	A30	13c brown	5.00	8
260	A30	15c dp bl	2.00	5
261	A30	16c ol grn	3.00	10
262	A30	20c brn red	3.00	5
263	A30	30c purple	4.00	6
264	A30	50c dp grn	14.00	6
265	A31	$1 org brn & sep	15.00	10
266	A31	$2 bl & red brn	22.50	15
267	A31	$5 red & sl	40.00	35
268	A31	$10 grn & cl	100.00	12.50
269	A31	$20 plum & bl	225.00	25.00
		Nos. 248-269 (22)	445.85	39.30

Nos. 249 and 275 exist with webbing watermark from experimental printing.

To prevent speculation and theft, the dollar denominations were overprinted with single characters in red for use in Kwangsi ($1–$20) and Kweichow ($1–$5).

See also Nos. 275, 324.

Temple of Heaven, Peking
A32

1923, Oct. 17 *Perf. 14*

No.	Type	Description	Unused	Used
270	A32	1c orange	1.75	30
271	A32	3c bl grn	2.00	50
272	A32	4c red	3.00	50
273	A32	10c blue	7.00	1.25

Adoption of Constitution, October, 1923.

No. 253 Surcharged in Red

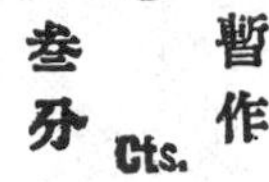

1925

No.	Type	Description	Unused	Used
274	A29	3c on 4c gray	2.00	10
a.		Invtd. surch.	1,000.	1,000.
b.		Vertical pair, imperf. between		

Junk Type of 1923

1926

No.	Type	Description	Unused	Used
275	A29	4c ol grn	1.00	10
a.		Imperf. vertically (pair)	75.00	
b.		Horiz. pair, imperf. between	90.00	
c.		Horiz. strip of 3, imperf. between	100.00	

Marshal Chang Tso-lin
A34

President Chiang Kai-shek
A35

1928, Mar. 1 *Perf. 14*

No.	Type	Description	Unused	Used
276	A34	1c brn org	75	25
277	A34	4c ol grn	1.50	35
278	A34	10c dl bl	7.00	1.25
279	A34	$1 red	37.50	19.00

Issued to commemorate the assumption of office by Marshal Chang Tso-lin. The stamps of this issue were only available for postage in the Provinces of Chihli and Shantung and at the Offices in Manchuria and Sinkiang.

1929, May

No.	Type	Description	Unused	Used
280	A35	1c brn org	1.25	35
281	A35	4c ol grn	1.50	50
282	A35	10c dk bl	19.00	1.50
283	A35	$1 dk red	90.00	32.50

Issued to commemorate the unification of China.

Sun Yat-sen Mausoleum, Nanking
A36

1929, May 30 *Perf. 14*

No.	Type	Description	Unused	Used
284	A36	1c brn org	50	35
285	A36	4c ol grn	75	35
286	A36	10c dk bl	6.00	1.25
287	A36	$1 dk red	47.50	26.00

Issued in commemoration of Dr. Sun Yat-sen on the occasion of the transfer of his remains from Peiping to the mausoleum at Nanking.

Nos. 224 and 252 Surcharged in Red

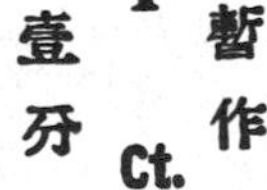

1930

No.	Type	Description	Unused	Used
288	A24	1c on 3c bl grn	1.50	1.50
289	A29	1c on 3c bl grn	40	5
a.		No period after "Ct"	12.50	8.00

See Nos. 311, 325, 330.

Dr. Sun Yat-sen—A37

Type I. Double-lined circle in the sun.
Type II. Heavy, single-lined circle in the sun.

Engraved

Perf.

11½x12½, 12½x13, 12½, 13½.

Printed by De la Rue & Co., Ltd., London.

1931 **Type I.**

No.	Type	Description	Unused	Used
290	A37	1c orange	35	5
291	A37	2c ol grn	35	5

292	A37	4c green	40	5
293	A37	20c ultra	40	5
294	A37	$1 org brn & dk brn	3.00	8
295	A37	$2 bl & org brn	6.00	20
296	A37	$5 dl red & blk	10.00	75
		Nos. 290-296 (7)	20.50	1.23

Stamps issued prior to 1933 were printed by a wet-paper process, and owing to shrinkage such stamps are 1—1½ mm. narrower than the later dry-printed stamps. Early printings are perf. 12½x13. Nos. 304, 305 and 306 were later perf. 11½x12½.

1931-37 Type II.

297	A37	2c ol grn	15	5
298	A37	4c green	15	5
299	A37	5c grn ('33)	15	5
300	A37	15c dk grn	2.75	40
301	A37	15c scar ('34)	20	5
302	A37	20c ultra ('37)	50	5
303	A37	25c ultra	50	5
304	A37	$1 org brn & dk brn	3.50	5
305	A37	$2 bl & org brn	7.00	25
306	A37	$5 dl red & blk	12.00	50
		Nos. 297-306 (10)	26.90	1.50

See Nos. 631 to 635 for other stamps of type A37.

"Nomads in the Desert"
A38

1932 Perf. 14 Unwmkd.

307	A38	1c dp org	17.50	12.50
308	A38	4c ol grn	17.50	12.50
309	A38	5c claret	17.50	12.50
310	A38	10c dp bl	17.50	12.50

Issued to commemorate the Northwest Scientific Expedition of Sven Hedin. A small quantity of this issue was sold at face at Peking and several other cities. The bulk of the issue was given to Hedin and sold at $5 (Chinese) a set for funds to finance the expedition. Letters franked with these stamps were carried without additional charge.

No. 252 Surcharged in Black Like No. 288.

1932

311	A29	1c on 3c bl grn	1.00	10

Martyrs Issue.

Teng Keng
A39

Ch'en Ying-shih
A40

Chu Chih-hsin
A45

Sung Chiao-jen
A46

Huang Hsing
A47

Liao Chung-kai
A48

1932-34 Perf. 14

312	A39	½c blk brn	5	8
313	A40	1c org ('34)	5	8
314	A39	2½c rose lil ('33)	5	8
315	A48	3c dp brn ('33)	5	8
316	A45	8c brn org	15	8
317	A46	10c dl vio	20	8
318	A45	13c bl grn	15	8
319	A46	17c brn ol	15	8
320	A47	20c brn red	15	8
321	A48	30c brn vio	15	8
322	A47	40c orange	15	8
323	A40	50c grn ('34)	20	8
		Nos. 312-323 (12)	1.50	96

Perfs. 12 to 13 and compound and with secret marks are listed as Nos. 402-439. No. 316 re-drawn is No. 485.

Junk Type of 1923 Issue.

1933 Perf. 14.

324	A29	6c brown	15.00	25

No. 275 Surcharged in Red Like No. 288.

325	A29	1c on 4c ol grn	1.00	10
a.		No period after Ct		

Tan Yuan-chang
A49

1933, Jan. 9

326	A49	2c ol grn	1.00	30
327	A49	5c green	1.25	35
328	A49	25c ultra	6.00	1.00
329	A49	$1 red	40.00	20.00

Issued in commemoration of Tan Yuan-chang, more commonly known as Tan Yen-kai, a prominent statesman in China since the revolution of 1912 and President of the Executive Department of the National Government. The stamps were placed on sale January 9, 1933, the date of the ceremony in celebration of the completion of the Tan Yuan-chang Memorial Hall and Tomb at Mukden.

No. 251 Surcharged in Red Like No. 288.

1935 Perf. 14

330	A29	1c on 2c yel grn	85	6

Emblem of New Life Movement
A50

Four Virtues of New Life
A51

Lighthouse
A52

1936, Jan. 1

331	A50	2c ol grn	75	25
332	A50	5c green	1.25	25
333	A51	20c dk bl	6.00	1.00
334	A52	$1 rose red	20.00	4.00

"New Life" movement.

Methods of Mail Transportation
A53

Maritime Scene
A54

Shanghai General Post Office
A55

Ministry of Communications, Nanking
A56

1936, Oct. 10

335	A53	2c orange	60	25
336	A54	5c green	75	20
337	A55	25c blue	5.00	60
338	A56	$1 dk car	20.00	2.50

Issued in commemoration of the 40th anniversary of the founding of the Chinese Post Office.

Nos. 260 and 261 Surcharged in Red

伍 暫
5
分 作

339	A30	5c on 15c dp bl	1.25	5
340	A30	5c on 16c ol grn	1.40	5

No. 298 Surcharged in Red

壹 暫
分 1 作

1937 Type II.

341	A37	1c on 4c grn	40	5
a.		Upper left character missing		

Nos. 322 and 303 Surcharged in Black or Red

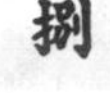

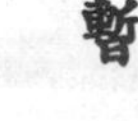

分 8 作

1938 Perf. 12½, 14.

342	A47	8c on 40c org (Bk)	70	5
343	A37	10c on 25c ultra (R)	70	5

Dr. Sun Yat-sen
A57

Type I. Coat button half circle. Six lines of shading above head. Top frame partially shaded with vertical lines.

Type II. Coat button complete circle. Nine lines of shading above head. Top frame partially shaded with vertical lines.

Type III. Coat button complete circle. Nine lines of shading above head. Top frame line fully shaded with vertical lines.

Engraved.

1938 Perf. 12½ Unwmkd.

Printed by the Chung Hwa Book Co.

Type I.

344	A57	$1 hn & dk brn	20.00	2.50
345	A57	$2 dp bl & org brn	8.00	80
346	A57	$5 red & grnsh blk	35.00	9.00

1939 Type II.

347	A57	$1 hn & dk brn	5.00	50
348	A57	$2 dp bl & org brn	7.00	1.00

1939-41 Type III.

349	A57	2c ol grn	10	10
350	A57	3c dl cl	10	5
351	A57	5c green	10	5
352	A57	5c ol grn	10	5
353	A57	8c ol grn	15	5
354	A57	10c green	10	5
355	A57	15c scarlet	15	15
356	A57	15c dk vio brn ('41)	1.75	2.00
357	A57	16c ol gray	25	8
358	A57	25c dk bl	15	15
359	A57	$1 hn & dk brn	1.75	15
360	A57	$2 dp bl & org brn	2.00	15
a.		Imperf., pair	250.00	
361	A57	$5 red & grnsh blk	1.25	15
362	A57	$10 dk grn & dl pur	5.00	60
363	A57	$20 rose lake & dk bl	11.00	3.00
		Nos. 349-363 (15)	23.95	6.78

Several values exist imperforate, but these were not regularly issued. No. 361 imperforate was sold as waste paper.

See also Nos. 368-401, 506-524.

Chinese and American Flags and Map of China
A58

Frame Engr., Center Litho.

1939, July 4 *Perf. 12* Unwmkd.

Printed by American Bank Note Co.

Flag in Deep Rose and Ultramarine.

364	A58	5c dk grn	75	30
365	A58	25c dp bl	1.50	60
366	A58	50c brown	1.75	1.25
367	A58	$1 rose car	3.50	2.25

Issued in commemoration of the 150th anniversary of the Constitution of the United States of America.

Type of 1939-41 Issue. Re-engraved.

2c, 1939-41

Re-engraved.

8c, 1939-41 Re-engraved.

1940 *Perf. 12½.*

368	A57	2c ol grn	15	10
369	A57	8c ol grn	15	10

Type of 1938–41 Issue.

1940 *Perf. 14* Unwmkd.

Type III.

370	A57	2c ol grn	40	40
371	A57	5c green	1.00	35
372	A57	$1 hn & dk brn	30.00	6.00
373	A57	$2 dp bl & org brn	8.00	2.00
374	A57	$5 red & grnsh blk	8.00	2.00
375	A57	$10 dk grn & dl pur	8.00	2.00
		Nos. 370-375 (6)	55.40	12.75

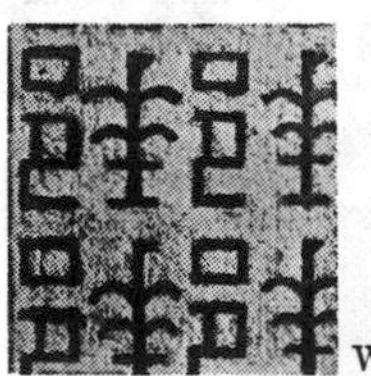
Wmk. 261

Type of 1939-41.

Wmkd.

Character Yu (Post) Multiple. (261)

1940 *Perf. 12½.*

Type III.

376	A57	$1 hn & dk brn	3.00	2.00
377	A57	$2 dp bl & org brn	4.00	1.00
378	A57	$5 red & grnsh blk	4.00	3.00
379	A57	$10 dk grn & dl pur	6.50	3.00
380	A57	$20 rose lake & dp bl	8.00	3.00
		Nos. 376-380 (5)	25.50	12.00

Printed by the Dah Tung Book Co.

Type III with secret marks.

Five Cent.

Type III
Characters joined.

Secret Mark.
Characters not joined.

Eight Cent.

Type III
Characters not joined.

Secret Mark.
Characters joined.

Ten Cent.

Type III
Characters sharp and well-proportioned.

Secret Mark.
Characters coarse and varying in thickness.

Dollar Values.

Type III

Secret Mark.

1940 *Perf. 14.* Unwmkd.

381	A57	5c green	5	5
382	A57	5c ol grn	5	5
383	A57	8c ol grn	35	5
a.		Without 'star' in uniform button	65	65
384	A57	10c green	7	5
385	A57	30c scarlet	7	5
386	A57	50c dk bl	8	5
387	A57	$1 org brn & sep	75	5
388	A57	$2 dp bl & yel brn	75	5
389	A57	$5 red & sl grn	75	12
390	A57	$10 dk grn & dl pur	1.25	25
391	A57	$20 rose lake & dk bl	2.00	50
		Nos. 381-391 (11)	6.17	1.27

Type III with secret marks.

1940 *Perf. 14.* Wmk. 261

392	A57	5c green	5	5
393	A57	5c ol grn	5	5
394	A57	10c green	10	5
395	A57	30c scarlet	10	5
396	A57	50c dk bl	10	5
397	A57	$1 org brn & sep	1.00	25
398	A57	$2 dp bl & yel brn	2.00	1.00
399	A57	$5 red & sl grn	2.00	1.25
400	A57	$10 dk grn & dl pur	6.00	2.50
401	A57	$20 rose lake & dk bl	7.50	3.00
		Nos. 392-401 (10)	18.90	8.25

Nos. 383, 384, 385, 397, 400 and 401 exist perf. 12½, but were not issued with this perforation.

Types of 1932-34.

Martyrs Issue with secret mark.

1932-34 Issue.
In the left Chinese character in bottom row, the two parts are not joined.

Secret Mark, 1940-41 Issue.
The two parts are joined.

Perf. 12½, 13 and Compound.

1940-41 Wmk. 261

402	A39	½c ol blk	6	5
403	A40	1c orange	6	5
404	A46	2c dp bl ('41)	6	12
405	A39	2½c rose lil	6	5
406	A48	3c dp yel brn	6	8
407	A39	4c pale vio ('41)	6	8
408	A48	5c dl red org ('41)	6	8
409	A45	8c dp org	6	8
410	A46	10c dl vio	6	8
411	A45	13c dp yel grn	6	8
412	A48	15c brn car	6	8
413	A46	17c brn ol	6	8
414	A47	20c lt bl	6	8
415	A45	21c ol brn ('41)	6	8
416	A40	25c red vio ('41)	6	8
417	A46	28c ol ('41)	6	12
418	A48	30c brn car	6	8
a.		Vert. pair, imperf. btwn.	125.00	
419	A47	40c orange	6	8
420	A40	50c green	6	8

Unwmkd.

421	A39	½c ol blk	6	5
422	A40	1c orange	6	5
a.		Without secret mark	75	50
b.		Horiz. pair, imperf. vert.	25.00	
423	A46	2c dp bl	6	5
a.		Vert. pair, imperf. horiz.	6.00	
b.		Horiz. pair, imperf. between	125.00	
424	A39	2½c rose lil	6	5
425	A48	3c dp yel brn	6	5
426	A39	4c pale vio	6	5
427	A48	5c dl red org	6	5
428	A45	8c dp org	6	5
429	A46	10c dl vio	6	5
430	A45	13c dp yel grn	6	5
431	A48	15c brn car	6	5
432	A46	17c brn ol	6	5
433	A47	20c lt bl	6	5
a.		Vert. pair, imperf. horiz.	100.00	
b.		Horiz. pair, imperf. vert.	100.00	
434	A45	21c ol brn	6	5
435	A40	25c rose vio	6	5
436	A46	28c olive	6	5
437	A48	30c brn car	1.00	25
438	A47	40c orange	6	5
439	A40	50c green	6	5
		Nos. 402-439 (38)	3.22	2.66

Several values exist imperforate, but they were not regularly issued.

Regional Surcharges.

The regional surcharges, Nos. 440 to 448, 482 to 484, 486 to 491 and 525 to 549, have been given a general listing according to the basic stamps, with black or red surcharges. The surcharges of the individual provinces, plus Hong Kong and Shanghai, are noted in small type beneath each major listing. These surcharges are identified by the following italic letters:

a—Hong Kong
b—Shanghai
bx—Anhwei
c—Hunan
d—Kansu
e—Kiangsi
f—Eastern Szechwan
g—Chekiang
h—Fukien
i—Kwangsi
j—Kwantung
k—Western Szechwan
l—Yunnan
m—Honan
n—Shensi
o—Kweichow
p—Hupeh

The numeral following each italic letter is the surcharge denomination.

In listings that include more than one region, the lowest price is used for the major.

Regional Surcharges on Stamps of 1939-40:

分 4 作 分 3 作

a 4 *b 3*
Hong Kong Shanghai

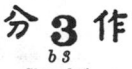

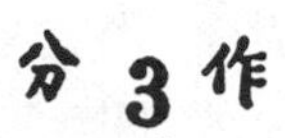

c 3
Hunan

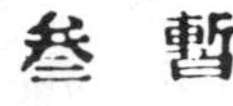

分 3 作

Kansu

叁 暫 叁 暫

分 3 作 分 3 作

e 3 *f 3*
Kiangsi Eastern Szechwan

叁 暫

分 3 作

g 3
Chekiang

1940-41 *Perf. 12½, 14.* Unwmkd.

Parenthetical number indicates basic stamp.

Carmine Surcharge.

440		A57 (a4) 4c on 5c ol grn (#382)	15	15
a.		Lower right character duplicated at left	12.50	14.00

Black Surcharge.

441		A57 (b3) 3c on 5c grn (#351)	15	15
442		A57 (c3) 3c on 5c ol grn (#352)	35	25
		(d3) Kansu	40	40
443		A57 (b3) 3c on 5c grn (#381)	12	15
444	A57	3c on 5c ol grn (#382) (b3, e3)	12	15
		(f3) Eastern Szechwan	15	15
r.		Lower left character duplicated at right (Kiangsi)	30.00	35.00

The Kansu surcharges of No. 442 are of six types. Differences include formation of top part of fen character (at left of "3"), fen with low right hook, height of "3" (5mm. to 4mm.), space between upper and lower characters (6 to 9mm.), etc.

1940-41 *Perf. 14.* Wmk. 261

445	A57	3c on 5c grn (#392) (b3, e3)	12	15
		(c3) Hunan	25	30
r.		Lower left character duplicated at right (Kiangsi)	20.00	20.00
446		A57 (b3) 3c on 5c ol grn (#393)	25	25
		(f3) Eastern Szechwan	40	50
r.		Lower left character duplicated at right (Eastern Szechwan)	30.00	35.00

Red Surcharge.

447		A57 (g3) 3c on 5c grn (#392)	90	30
448		A57 (g3) 3c on 5c ol grn (#393)	2.00	1.75

Dr. Sun Yat-sen
A59

Engraved

1941 *Perf. 12* Unwmkd.

Printed by American Bank Note Co.

449	A59	½c sepia	5	5
450	A59	1c orange	5	5
451	A59	2c brt ultra	5	5
452	A59	5c green	5	5
453	A59	8c red org	5	5
454	A59	8c turq grn	5	5
455	A59	10c brt grn	5	5
456	A59	17c olive	1.25	1.25
457	A59	25c rose vio	5	5
458	A59	30c scarlet	5	5

No.	Type	Description	Unused	Used
459	A59	50c dk bl	6	5
460	A59	$1 brn & blk	10	5
461	A59	$2 bl & blk	10	7
a.		Center invert.	5,000.	
462	A59	$5 scar & blk	20	10
463	A59	$10 grn & blk	2.00	60
464	A59	$20 rose vio & blk	2.00	60
		Nos. 449-464 (16)	6.16	3.17

Industry and Agriculture
A60

1941, June 21 *Perf. 12½*

Printed by Chung Hwa Book Co.

No.	Type	Description	Unused	Used
465	A60	8c green	5	5
466	A60	21c red brn	10	10
467	A60	28c dk ol grn	12	12
468	A60	33c vermilion	18	15
469	A60	50c dp ultra	20	18
470	A60	$1 dk vio	50	40
		Nos. 465-470 (6)	1.15	1.00

Issued to promote the Thrift Movement and its aim to "Save for Reconstruction."

Souvenir Sheet.

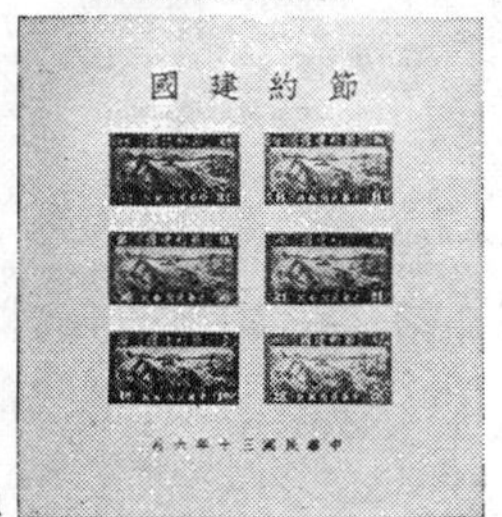

A61

Typographed
Imperf.

No.	Type	Description	Unused	Used
471	A61	Sheet of six	10.00	10.00
a.		8c dl grn	1.00	1.00
b.		21c dk org brn	1.00	1.00
c.		28c dl yel grn	1.00	1.00
d.		33c red	1.00	1.00
e.		50c dl bl	1.00	1.00
f.		$1 dk vio	1.00	1.00

Issued in sheets measuring 155x171mm. without gum.

This sheet exists with additional blue marginal overprints in Russia, French and Chinese reading "Souvenir of the Exhibition of the Russian Philatelic Society in China, Shanghai, China, Feb. 28, 1943."

The overprinting was applied by the society, and when so overprinted this sheet had no franking power.

Stamps of 1939-41 Overprinted in Carmine or Blue

中華民國創立
三十週年紀念
三十年十月十日

1941, Oct. 10 *Perf. 12½, 14, 13*

No.	Type	Description	Unused	Used
472	A40	1c dl org (Bl)	5	5
473	A57	2c ol grn (C)	5	5
474	A39	4c pale vio (C)	5	5
475	A57	8c ol grn (#369) (C)	5	5
476	A57	10c grn (#354) (C)	5	5
477	A57	16c ol gray (#257) (C)	5	5
478	A45	21c ol brn (C)	7	7
479	A46	28c ol (C)	20	15
480	A57	30c scar (Bl)	30	25
481	A57	$1 hn & dk brn (#359) (Bl)	50	40
		Nos. 472-481 (10)	1.37	1.17

Chinese Republic, 30th anniversary.

e7 Kiangsi — f7 Eastern Szechwan

g7 Chekiang — h7 Fukien

1941 *Perf. 12½, 14* **Unwmkd.**

No.	Type	Description	Unused	Used
482	A57	7c on 8c ol grn (#353) (g7, h7)	15	15
483	A57 (f7)	7c on 8c ol grn (#369)	12	12
484	A57	7c on 8c ol grn (#383) (e7, h7)	15	15
		(g7) Chekiang	25	25
a.		Without "star" in uniform button	35.00	

Type of 1932–34 Re-engraved.

1941 *Perf. 14* **Unwmkd.**

No.	Type	Description	Unused	Used
485	A45	8c dp org	5.00	6.00

The original stamps are 19½mm. wide, the re-engraved 21mm.

Eleven other values of the Martyrs Issue and types A37 and A57 exist re-engraved, but were not issued.

c1 Hunan — e1 Kiangsi

h1 Fukien — i1 Kwangsi

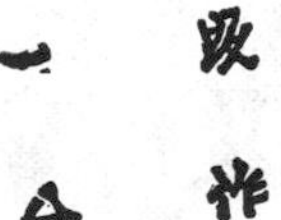

j1
Kwangtung

1942 **Red Surcharge.**

No.	Type	Description	Unused	Used
486	A39	1c on ½c blk brn (#312) (c1, i1)	20	25
487	A39	1c on ½c ol blk (#421) (c1,e1,h1,i1)	20	25
488	A59	1c on ½c sep (#449) (c1,j1)	12	20

c40 Hunan — f40 Eastern Szechwan

k40 Western Szechwan — l40 Yunnan

Red Surcharge.

No.	Type	Description	Unused	Used
489	A57 (f40)	40c on 50c dk bl (#386)	25	25
		(k40) Western Szechwan	1.00	1.00
		(l40) Yunnan	85	85
a.		Inverted surcharge (Yunnan)	75.00	

Wmk. 261.

No.	Type	Description	Unused	Used
490	A40 (c40)	40c on 50c grn (#420)	20	15

Unwmkd.

No.	Type	Description	Unused	Used
491	A59 (e40)	40c on 50c dk bl (#459)	12	8

Dr. Sun Yat-sen
A62

Central Trust Printing.
Perf. 10½–11, 11½–12½, 13 and Compounds

1942-43 **Typo.** **Without Gum**

No.	Type	Description	Unused	Used
492	A62	10c dp grn ('43)	6	6
493	A62	16c dl ol brn	3.75	4.25
a.		Perf. 10½	100.00	75.00
494	A62	20c dk ol grn ('43)	12	10
a.		Perf. 11	3.00	3.00
495	A62	25c brn vio	8	25
496	A62	30c dl ver	8	8
a.		Perf. 11	1.50	1.50
497	A62	40c dk red brn ('43)	25	25
a.		Perf. 11x13	35.00	
b.		Perf. 11	10.00	10.00
498	A62	50c sage grn	6	5
a.		Perf. 11	1.00	1.00
499	A62	$1 rose lake	6	6
a.		Perf. 11	20.00	20.00
500	A62	$1 dl grn ('43)	6	6
501	A62	$1.50 dp bl ('43)	6	6
a.		Perf. 11	200.00	
502	A62	$2 dk bl grn	6	6
503	A62	$3 dk yel ('43)	6	6
504	A62	$4 red brn	6	6
505	A62	$5 cer ('43)	6	6
		Nos. 492-505 (14)	4.82	5.46

Many shades and part-perforate varieties exist. See Nos. 550 to 563 for other stamps of type A62 with secret mark and new values and colors.

Type of 1938.
Thin Paper Without Gum.
Engraved.

1942-44 ***Imperf.*** **Unwmkd.**

No.	Type	Description	Unused	Used
506	A57	$10 red brn	10	8
507	A57	$20 bl grn	15	10
508	A57	$20 rose red ('44)	3.00	50
509	A57	$30 dl vio ('43)	30	25
510	A57	$40 rose red ('43)	10	5
511	A57	$50 blue	75	75
512	A57	$100 org brn ('43)	1.00	75

Rouletted.

No.	Type	Description	Unused	Used
513	A57	$5 lil gray ('44)	1.50	60
a.		Rouletted x perf. 12½	15.00	
514	A57	$10 red brn	1.25	25
515	A57	$50 blue	1.50	60
a.		Rouletted x imperf.		
		Nos. 506-515 (10)	9.65	3.93

1942-45 ***Perf. 12½ to 15.***

No.	Type	Description	Unused	Used
516	A57	$4 dp bl ('43)	10	6
517	A57	$5 lil gray ('43)	10	7
518	A57	$10 red brn	10	7
519	A57	$20 bl grn ('43)	10	10
520	A57	$20 rose red ('45)	22.50	22.50
521	A57	$30 dl vio ('43)	10	10
522	A57	$40 rose ('43)	50	25
523	A57	$50 blue	50	25
524	A57	$100 org brn ('45)	22.50	22.50
		Nos. 516-524 (9)	46.50	45.90

No. 493 Overprinted in Black or Red

國內平信
附加已付

1942

No.	Type	Description	Unused	Used
525	A62 (i)	16c dl ol brn (Bk)	15.00	15.00
		(c) Hunan	175.00	
		(k) Western Szechwan	35.00	35.00
		(m) Honan	300.00	300.00
r.		Perf. 10½ (Kwangsi)	250.00	
		(n) Shensi	50.00	50.00
s.		Inverted ovpt. (Shensi)	85.00	
526	A62 (d)	16c dl ol brn (R)	3.00	4.00
		(bx) Anhwei	125.00	125.00
		(e) Kiangsi	8.50	8.50
		(f) Eastern Szechwan	10.00	10.00
r.		Perf. 10½ (E. Szechwan)	300.00	
		(h) Fukien	35.00	35.00
		(j) Kwangtung	225.00	250.00
		(l) Yunnan	9.00	9.00
		(o) Kweichow	30.00	30.00
		(p) Hupeh, perf. 10½	275.00	275.00
s.		Horiz. pair, imperf. between (Yunnan)	150.00	
t.		Perf. 13 (Hupeh)	600.00	400.00

This overprint means "Domestic Ordinary Letter Surcharge Paid." It was applied in various sizes and types by 14 districts, 9 using red ink, 5 using black. (The Anhwei overprint comes in two types.) These overprinted stamps were briefly sold for $1.16 before the government ordered their sale suspended. The vertical bars and 50c surcharge of Nos. 527–528 were then applied.

bx
Anhwei

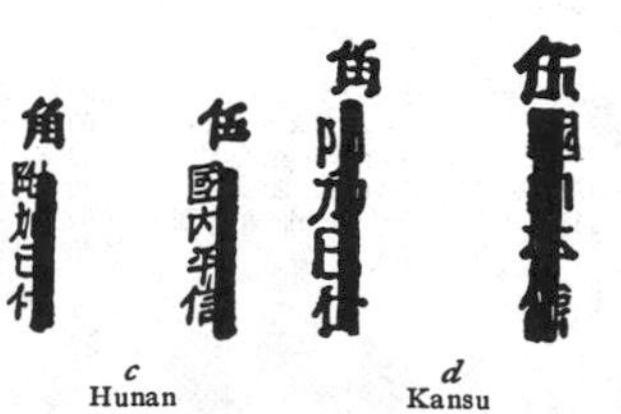

c Hunan — d Kansu

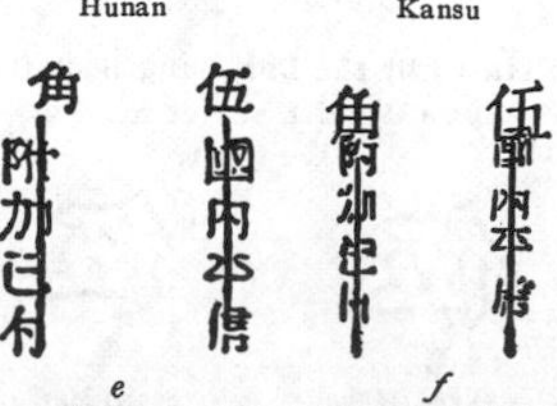

e Kiangsi — f Eastern Szechwan

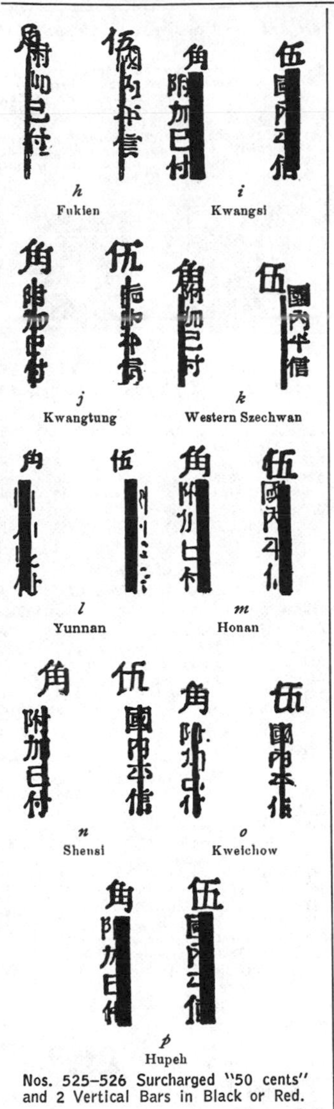

h Fukien — i Kwangsi

j Kwangtung — k Western Szechwan

l Yunnan — m Honan

n Shensi — o Kweichow

p Hupeh

Nos. 525–526 Surcharged "50 cents" and 2 Vertical Bars in Black or Red.

1942 **Unwmkd.**

No.	Type	Description	Unused	Used
527	A62	50c on 16c dl ol brn (Bk) (c,f)	1.00	1.00
		(i) Kwangsi	1.50	1.50
		(k) Western Szechwan	2.50	2.50
r.		Inverted surch. (W. Szech.)	50.00	
s.		"k" surch. on #493	60.00	
		(m) Honan	3.50	3.50
		(n) Shensi	1.50	1.50
528	A62 (d)	50c on 16c dl ol brn (R)	75	75
		(bx) Anhwei	10.00	10.00
		(e) Kiangsi	3.00	2.50
		(h) Fukien	3.00	
		(j) Kwangtung	1.75	1.75
		(l) Yunnan	3.50	
		(o) Kweichow	1.50	1.50
		(p) Hupeh	1.25	1.25
r.		Inverted surch. (Kweichow)	25.00	
s.		"p" surch. on #526f	35.00	35.00

Many varieties of Nos. 527–528 exist, including narrow or wide spacing between the two top characters, or between the vertical bars, or both.

Surcharges on stamps perf. 10½ (basic No. 493a) usually sell at much higher prices."

General Issue — c 50 Hunan

f 50 Eastern Szechwan — g 50 Chekiang

i 50 Kwangsi — j 50 Kwangtung

k 50 Western Szechwan — m 50 Honan

n 50 Shensi — o 50 Kweichow

No. 493 Surcharged in Black, Red or Carmine.

1943 **Unwmkd.**

No.	Type	Description	Unused	Used
529	A62 (n50)	50c on 16c dl ol brn (Bk)	1.00	1.00
		(m50) Honan	1.50	1.50
r.		Perf. 11x13 (Shensi)	50.00	
530	A62	50c on 16c dl ol brn (R, C)	25	25
a.		General Issue (C)	25	25
		General Issue (C) (c50) Hunan	1.00	1.00
r.		Inverted surch. (Hunan)	35.00	
		(f50) Eastern Szechwan	75	75
		(g50) Chekiang	10.00	
		(i50) Kwangsi	1.50	1.50
		(j50) Kwangtung	1.25	1.25
		(k50) Western Szechwan	2.00	2.00
		(m50) Honan	2.50	2.50
		(o50) Kweichow	1.25	1.25
s.		"05" instead of "50" (Kweichow)	250.00	

Many varieties of Nos. 529–530 exist, such as narrow or wide spacing horizontally or vertically between the overprinted Chinese characters.

Surcharges on No. 493a (perf. 10½) usually sell at much higher prices.

The General Issue type, No. 530a, was distributed to all head offices, which in turn supplied the post offices under their direction. It is surcharged in carmine; the other stamps listed under No. 530 are surcharged in red or carmine.

The lack of a price for a listed item does not necessarily indicate rarity.

c 20 Hunan — d 20 Kansu

e 20 Kiangsi — f 20 Eastern Szechwan

h 20 Fukien — i 20 Kwangsi

j 20 Kwangtung — k 20 Western Szechwan

l 20 Yunnan

m 20 Honan — n 20 Shensi

o 20 Kweichow — p 20 Hupeh

1943 **Unwmkd.**

No.	Type	Description	Unused	Used
531	A45 (n20)	20c on 13c bl grn (#318) (Bk)	8	10
		(d20) Kansu	25	30
		(k20) Western Szechwan	10	12
532	A45 (i20)	20c on 13c bl grn (#318) (R)	12	12
		(c20) Hunan	350.00	
		(e20) Kiangsi	35.00	
		(j20) Kwangtung	12.00	12.00
		(p20) Hupeh	20	30

Wmk. 261

No.	Type	Description	Unused	Used
533	A45 (n20)	20c on 13c dp yel grn (#411) (Bk)	10	12
		(d20) Kansu	30	30
		(k20) Western Szechwan	15	15
		(l20) Yunnan	90	90
		(m20) Honan	35.00	
534	A45	20c on 13c dp yel grn (#411) (R) (f20,p20)	10	10
		(c20) Hunan	15	15
		(e20) Kiangsi	12	12
		(h20) Fukien	25	25
		(i20) Kwangsi	20	20
		(j20) Kwangtung	5.00	5.00
		(o20) Kweichow	35	25

Unwmkd.

No.	Type	Description	Unused	Used
535	A45 (n20)	20c on 13c dp yel grn (#430) (Bk)	10	12
		(d20) Kansu	15	20
		(k20) Western Szechwan	8.00	8.00
		(l20) Yunnan	18	20
		(m20) Honan	35	35
536	A45	20c on 13c dp yel grn (#430) (R) (f20,i20,j20,p20)	10	12
		(c20) Hunan	1.25	1.25
		(e20) Kiangsi	15	20
		(o20) Kweichow	20	20
537	A57	20c on 16c ol gray (#357) (Bk) (c20,n20)	8	10
		(d20) Kansu	10	12
		(k20) Western Szechwan	10	12
		(m20) Honan	75	75
538	A57	20c on 16c ol gray (#357) (R) (e20,i20,o20)	15	20
		(c20) Hunan	65	70
		(j20) Kwangtung	15.00	16.50

Wmk. 261.

No.	Type	Description	Unused	Used
539	A46 (i20)	20c on 17c brn ol (#413) (R)	10	12
		(c20) Hunan	25	30
		(j20) Kwangtung	10.00	10.00

Unwmkd.

No.	Type	Description	Unused	Used
540	A46 (k20)	20c on 17c brn ol (#432) (Bk)	12	15
		(d20) Kansu	90	1.00
		(m20) Honan	8.50	9.00
541	A46	20c on 17c brn ol (#432) (R) (e20,j20,o20)	15	20
542	A59 (m20)	20c on 17c ol (#456) (Bk)	60.00	65.00
543	A59 (c20)	20c on 17c ol (#456) (R)	1.25	1.25

Wmk. 261.

No.	Type	Description	Unused	Used
544	A45 (e20)	20c on 21c ol brn (#415) (R)	25	30

Unwmkd.

No.	Type	Description	Unused	Used
545	A45 (c20)	20c on 21c ol brn (#434) (Bk)	8	8
		(d20) Kansu	15	20
		(k20) Western Szechwan	10	12
		(l20) Yunnan	10	12
		(m20) Honan	25	30
546	A45 (f20)	20c on 21c ol brn (#434) (R)	8	8
		(e20) Kiangsi	12	15
		(h20) Fukien	12	15
		(i20) Kwangsi	8	10
		(j20) Kwangtung	8	10
		(o20) Kweichow	15	15
		(p20) Hupeh	12	15

Wmk. 261.

547	A46(e20)	20c on 28c ol (#417) (R)	250.00	275.00

Unwmkd.

548	A46(l20)	20c on 28c (#436) (Bk)	10	12
		(d20) Kansu	6.00	6.00
		(k20) Western Szechwan	10.00	10.00
		(m20) Honan	10.00	10.00
549	A46	20c on 28c ol (#436) (R) (c20,h20)	8	8
		(e20) Kiangsi	10	12
		(i20) Kwangsi	10	12
		(j20) Kwangtung	10	12
		(o20) Kweichow	25	25

Many varieties of Nos. 531-549 exist, such as narrow or wide spacing between the overprinted Chinese characters, and "20" higher or lower than illustrated.

Type of 1942-43.

Pacheng Printing.

1944-46 ***Perf. 12*** **Unwmkd.**

Without Gum

550	A62	30c chocolate	25	2.00
551	A62	$1 green	2.00	1.50
552	A62	$2 dk vio brn	8	8
a.		Imperf., pair	3.50	4.00
553	A62	$2 dk bl grn	15	15
a.		Perf. 10½	75.00	80.00
554	A62	$2 dp bl	10	10
555	A62	$3 lt yel	12	8
556	A62	$4 vio brn	8	8
a.		Imperf., pair	50.00	
557	A62	$5 car ('46)	8	6
a.		Perf. 10½	75.00	80.00
558	A62	$6 gray vio ('45)	8	6
559	A62	$10 red brn ('45)	8	6
a.		Imperf., pair	50.00	
560	A62	$20 dp ultra ('46)	8	6
561	A62	$50 dk grn ('46)	12	6
562	A62	$70 lil ('46)	15	8
563	A62	$100 lt brn ('46)	8	6
		Nos. 550-563 (14)	3.45	4.43

In the Pacheng printing of the Central Trust type stamps, the secret mark "C" has been added below the lower left foliate ornament beneath the sun emblem. On the $3, it is below the right ornament. New values also include a "P" at right of sun emblem on the $6 and $10, and at right of necktie on the $20. Some values of Pacheng printing exist on paper with elephant watermark in sheet.

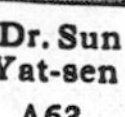

Dr. Sun Yat-sen
A63

Allegory of Savings
A64

Typographed

1944-46 ***Perf. 12½*** **Unwmkd.**

Without Gum.

565	A63	40c brn red	8	5
566	A63	$2 gray brn	8	5
567	A63	$3 red	8	5
a.		$3 org red	1.25	1.00
568	A63	$3 lt red brn ('45)	30	20
569	A63	$6 pale lil gray ('45)	8	5
570	A63	$10 dl lake ('45)	8	5
571	A63	$20 rose ('45)	8	5
a.		Perf. 15½	30.00	
572	A63	$50 lt brn ('46)	15	5
573	A63	$70 rose vio ('46)	10	5
		Nos. 565-573 (9)	1.03	60

1944-45 **Engraved** ***Perf. 13***

Without Gum.

574	A64	$40 ind ('45)	8	5
575	A64	$50 yel grn ('45)	8	5
576	A64	$100 yel brn	8	5
577	A64	$200 dk grn ('45)	15	15

All four values were printed on thick paper; the first three were also printed on thin paper.

Dr. Sun Yat-sen
A65 A66

Lithographed

1944, Dec. 25 **Without Gum**

578	A65	$2 dp grn	12	12
579	A65	$5 fawn	18	18
580	A65	$6 dl rose vio	30	35
581	A65	$10 vio bl	50	60
582	A65	$20 carmine	75	85
		Nos. 578-582 (5)	1.85	2.10

50th anniversary of the Kuomintang.

1945, Mar. 12 **Without Gum**

583	A66	$2 gray grn	8	8
584	A66	$5 red brn	15	15
585	A66	$6 dk vio bl	18	18
586	A66	$10 lt bl	30	30
587	A66	$20 rose	40	40
588	A66	$30 buff	60	60
		Nos. 583-588 (6)	1.71	1.71

Issued to commemorate the 20th anniversary of the death of Dr. Sun Yat-sen.

Dr. Sun Yat-sen
A67

1945-46 **Without Gum** ***Perf. 12½***

589	A67	$2 green	8	10
590	A67	$5 dl grn	8	5
591	A67	$10 dk bl	8	5
a.		Imperf., pair	25.00	
592	A67	$20 car ('46)	8	5
a.		Imperf., pair	50.00	

Statue of Liberty, Map of China, Flags of Great Britain, China and United States, and Chiang Kai-shek
A68

Engraved

1945, July 7 ***Perf. 12*** **Unwmkd.**

Flags in Dark Blue and Red.

593	A68	$1 dp bl	15	15
594	A68	$2 dl grn	30	30
595	A68	$5 ol gray	30	30
596	A68	$6 brown	75	75
597	A68	$10 rose lil	3.00	4.00
598	A68	$20 car rose	2.00	5.00
		Nos. 593-598 (6)	6.50	10.50

Issued to commemorate the signing of a Treaty in 1943 between Great Britain, the United States and China.

President Lin Sen
A69

President Chiang Kai-shek
A70

1945, Aug. ***Perf. 12*** **Unwmkd.**

599	A69	$1 dp ultra & blk	8	8
600	A69	$2 myr grn & blk	8	8
601	A69	$5 red & blk	12	12
602	A69	$6 pur & blk	30	30
603	A69	$10 choc & blk	50	80
604	A69	$20 ol grn & blk	70	1.00
		Nos. 599-604 (6)	1.78	2.38

Issued in memory of President Lin Sen (1864-1943).

1945, Oct. 10

Flag in Rose Red and Violet Blue.

605	A70	$2 green	25	25
606	A70	$4 dk bl	25	25
607	A70	$5 ol gray	25	25
608	A70	$6 bis brn	60	60
609	A70	$10 gray	85	85
610	A70	$20 red vio	1.40	1.40
		Nos. 605-610 (6)	3.60	3.60

Issued to commemorate the inauguration of Chiang Kai-shek as president, October 10, 1943.

President Chiang Kai-shek
A71

1945, Oct. 10 **Typo.** ***Perf. 13***

Without Gum.

Flag in Carmine and Blue.

611	A71	$20 grn & bl	10	8
612	A71	$50 bis brn & bl	20	12
613	A71	$100 blue	18	15
614	A71	$300 rose red & bl	18	15

Issued to commemorate the Victory of the Allied Nations over Japan.

C. N. C. Surcharges.

The green surcharges on Nos. 615 to 621, and the surcharges on Nos. 647 to 721, and 768 to 774 represent Chinese National Currency and were applied at Shanghai.

Stamps of 1938-41 Surcharged in Black with Chinese Characters and New Value in Checkered Rectangle at Bottom, Re-surcharged in Green

臺 國
角 幣

1945 ***Perf. 12, 12½***

615	A57	10c on $20 on 3c dl cl (#350)	6	5
616	A46	15c on $30 on 2c dp bl (#423)	6	10
a.		Horiz. pair, imperf. between	75.00	
b.		Vert. pair, imperf. between	65.00	
617	A59	25c on $50 on 1c org (#450)	6	10
618	A57	50c on $100 on 3c dl cl (#350)	6	10
619	A40	$1 on $200 on 1c org (#422)	6	10
a.		Horiz. pair, imperf. between	90.00	
620	A57	$2 on $400 on 3c dl cl (#350)	6	10
621	A59	$5 on $1000 on 1c org (#450)	6	10

The black (first) surcharges on Nos. 615 to 621 represent Nanking puppet government currency.

In the green surcharge, the characters at the left express the new value and are either two or four in number.

Types of 1932-34, Re-engraved, Overprinted in Black 北 華

and Surcharged in Green with Horizontal Bar and Four or Five Chinese Characters.

Perf. 14.

622	A47	$10 on 20c brn red	2.00	3.00
623	A47	$20 on 40c org	8.00	10.00
a.		Green surcharge inverted	20.00	
624	A48	$50 on 30c vio brn	5.00	7.00

These provisional surcharges were applied in Honan in National currency to stamps of the Hwa Pei (North China) government. The black overprint reads: "Hwa Pei."

The two-character "Hwa Pei" overprint was applied to various stamps in 1941-43 by the North China puppet government. See Nos. 8N1-8N53, 8N60-8N84.

Dr. Sun Yat-sen
A72 A73

1945, Dec. **Typo.** ***Perf. 12***

Without Gum.

625	A72	$20 dp car	6	6
626	A72	$30 dp bl	6	6
627	A72	$40 orange	8	6
628	A72	$50 green	10	6
629	A72	$100 dk brn	10	8
630	A72	$200 brn vio	10	9
		Nos. 625-630 (6)	50	41

Type of 1931-37.

Perf. 12½, 13x12½, 13½.

1946 **Unwmkd.**

631	A37	$1 dk vio	8	8
632	A37	$2 ol grn	8	8
633	A37	$20 brt yel grn	10	8
634	A37	$30 chocolate	10	8
635	A37	$50 red org	12	6
		Nos. 631-635 (5)	48	38

1946-47 **Engraved** ***Perf. 14***

Without Gum.

636	A73	$20 carmine	15	5
637	A73	$30 dk bl ('47)	6	5
638	A73	$50 purple	12	5
639	A73	$70 red org ('47)	6.00	1.00
640	A73	$100 dk car	6	5
641	A73	$200 ol grn ('47)	8	5
642	A73	$500 brt bl grn ('47)	15	5
643	A73	$700 red brn ('47)	15	15
644	A73	$1000 rose lake	15	5
645	A73	$3000 blue	45	5
646	A73	$5000 dp grn & ver	65	8
		Nos. 636-646 (11)	8.02	1.63

Stamps of 1932-41 Surcharged in Black

Perf. 12½, 13, 13x12, 14.

Wmk. 261

647	A45	$20 on 8c dp org (#409)	8	15
648	A39	$30 on ½c ol blk (#402)	700.00	700.00
649	A45	$50 on 21c ol brn (#415)	8	15
650	A45	$70 on 13c dp yel grn (#411)	8	10
651	A46	$100 on 28c ol (#417)	8	15

Unwmkd.

652	A39	$3 on 2½c rose lil (#424)	50	75
653	A48	$10 on 15c brn car (#431)	8	10
654	A45	$20 on 8c dp org (#428)	8	10
655	A47	$20 on 20c lt bl (#433)	8	10
656	A39	$30 on ½c ol blk (#421)	8	10
657	A45	$50 on 21c ol brn (#434)	8	10
657A	A45	$70 on 13c bl grn (#318)	55.00	65.00
658	A45	$70 on 13c dp yel grn (#430)	8	25
659	A46	$100 on 28c ol (#436)	8	10

Stamps of 1931-1946 Surcharged in Black or Carmine

伍拾圓 國幣 50.00

Perf. 12½, 13, 14

1946-47 **Wmk. 261**

No.	Type	Description	Unused	Used
660	A57	$50 on 5c grn (#392)	[illegible]	10
661	A57	$50 on 5c ol grn (#393)	16.00	15.00
662	A48	$50 on 5c dl red org (#408)	5	*30*
663	A40	$100 on 1c org (#403)	5	*25*

Perf. 12, 12½, 12½x13, 13, 14.

1946-47 **Unwmkd.**

No.	Type	Description	Unused	Used
664	A57	$20 on 3c dl cl (#350)	8	*15*
665	A45	$20 on 8c dp org (#428)	8	10
666	A57	$50 on 3c dl cl (#350)	15	10
667	A57	$50 on 5c ol grn (#352)	8	10
668	A57	$50 on 5c ol grn (#382)	8	*20*
669	A48	$50 on 5c dl red org (#427)	8	10
670	A59	$50 on 5c grn (#452)	10	10
671	A62	$50 on $1 dl grn (#500)	8	10
672	A40	$100 on 1c org (#422)	8	10
a.		Without secret mark (No. 422a)	55.00	
673	A57	$100 on 3c dl cl (#350)	8	10
674	A57	$100 on 8c ol grn (#353)	12.00	10.00
675	A57	$100 on 8c ol grn (#369)	10	10
676	A57	$100 on 8c ol grn (#383)	10	10
a.		Without "star" in uniform button (No. 383a)	15.00	15.00
677	A59	$100 on 8c turq grn (#454)	15	10
678	A37	$100 on $1 dk vio (#631)	20	10
679	A73	$100 on $20 car (#636)	85	15
680	A57	$200 on 10c grn (#354)	25	10
681	A57	$200 on 10c grn (#384)	25	10
682	A37	$200 on $4 dl bl	10	10
a.		Double surch.	15.00	
683	A62	$250 on $1.50 dp bl (#501)	8	*20*
a.		Perf. 11	200.00	225.00
684	A37	$250 on $2 ol grn (#632)	20	10
685	A37	$250 on $5 car	10	10
686	A57	$300 on 10c grn (#354)	8	10
687	A59	$300 on 10c brt grn (#455)	8	*15*
688	A57	$500 on 3c dl cl (#350)	15	10
689	A37	$500 on $20 brt yel grn (#633)	8	10
690	A37	$800 on $30 choc (#634)	8	10
691	A37	$1000 on 2c ol grn (#297)	35	20
692	A62	$1000 on $2 dk vio brn (#552)	12	12
a.		Imperf., pair	15.00	15.00
693	A62	$1000 on $2 dk bl grn (#553)	8	8
694	A62	$1000 on $2 dp bl (#554)	8	*12*
695	A67	$1000 on $2 grn (#589)	10	12
696	A62	$2000 on $5 car (#557)	10	12
697	A67	$2000 on $5 dl grn (C) (#590)	15	20
		Nos. 664-697 (34)	16.72	*13.91*

Nos. 682 and 685 wer not issued without surcharge. No. 682 is perf. 13x13½; No. 685, perf. 12x12½.

The characters at the left express the new value and vary in number.

Stamps of 1938-41 Surcharged in Black

伍拾圓 國幣 50.00

Perf. 12, 12½, 13, 14.

1940 **Wmk. 261**

No.	Type	Description	Unused	Used
698	A45	$20 on 8c dp org (#409)	85.00	95.00
699	A57	$50 on 5c grn (#392)	8	*25*
700	A57	$50 on 5c ol grn (#393)	8	*25*

1946-48 **Unwmkd.**

No.	Type	Description	Unused	Used
700A	A57	$20 on 5c grn (#381)	375.00	
701	A57	$20 on 8c ol grn (#353)	6	10
702	A57	$20 on 8c ol grn (#369)	25	30
703	A57	$20 on 8c ol grn (#383)	6	10
a.		Without "star" in uniform button (No. 383a)	4.00	3.50
b.		Inverted surch.	15.00	
c.		Double surcharge, one on back	25.00	20.00
d.		Double surch.	25.00	
704	A45	$20 on 8c dp org (#428)	6	*15*
a.		Double surch.	12.50	
705	A59	$20 on 8c red org (#453)	10	15
706	A59	$20 on 8c turq grn (#454)	6	10
a.		Inverted surch.	12.50	
b.		Double surcharge	12.50	
707	A57	$50 on 5c grn (#351)	2.00	2.00
708	A57	$50 on 5c ol grn (#352)	6	10
a.		Inverted surch.	20.00	
709	A57	$50 on 5c grn (#381)	6	*15*
710	A57	$50 on 5c ol grn (#382)	10	10
711	A48	$50 on 5c dl red org (#427)	10	10
a.		Inverted surch.	25.00	
712	A59	$50 on 5c grn (#452)	10	10
a.		Double surch.	20.00	

Stamps of 1939-41 Surcharged in Blue or Red

拾圓 國幣 10.00

1946 *Perf. 12½.* **Wmk. 261**

No.	Type	Description	Unused	Used
713	A40	$10 on 1c org (Bl) (#403)	5	10
a.		Inverted surch.	35.00	
714	A48	$20 on 3c dp yel brn (#406) (Bl)	250.00	150.00

1946 *Perf. 12, 12½, 13* **Unwmkd.**

No.	Type	Description	Unused	Used
715	A40	$10 on 1c org (Bl) (#422)	5	10
a.		Without secret mark (No. 422a)	5.00	6.00
b.		Inverted surcharge	7.50	9.00
716	A59	$10 on 1c org (Bl) (#450)	5	10
a.		Double surch.	20.00	
717	A57	$20 on 2c ol grn (R) (#368)	5	10
718	A59	$20 on 2c brt ultra (R) (#451)	5	10
a.		Inverted surch.	12.50	
b.		Double surch.	12.50	
719	A57	$20 on 3c dl cl (Bl) (#350)	5	10
a.		Double surch.	20.00	
720	A48	$20 on 3c dp yel brn (Bl) (#425)	5	15
721	A39	$30 on 4c pale vio (R) (#426)	5	15
a.		Inverted surch.	8.00	

President Chiang Kai-shek
A74

Perf. 14, 10½-11½

1946, Oct. 31 **Engraved** **Unwmkd.**

No.	Type	Description	Unused	Used
722	A74	$20 carmine	12	15
723	A74	$30 green	12	15
724	A74	$50 vermilion	12	15
725	A74	$100 yel grn	12	15
726	A74	$200 yel org	12	15
727	A74	$300 magenta	12	15
		Nos. 722-727 (6)	72	90

60th birthday of Chiang Kai-shek.

Perf. 14 stamps were printed by Dah Tung Book Co. and have no gum. Perf. 10½-11½ stamps were printed by Dah Yeh Printing Co.; the earlier ones are gumless, the later ones gummed.

Assembly House, Nanking—A75

1946, Nov. 15 **Litho.** ***Perf. 14***

Without Gum

No.	Type	Description	Unused	Used
728	A75	$20 green	6	10
729	A75	$30 blue	6	10
730	A75	$50 dk brn	6	10
a.		Horiz. pair, imperf. between	50.00	60.00
731	A75	$100 carmine	6	10

Convening of National Assembly.

Entrance to Dr. Sun Yat-sen Mausoleum
A76

Dr. Sun Yat-sen
A77

1947, May 1 **Engraved**

No.	Type	Description	Unused	Used
732	A76	$100 dp grn	10	12
733	A76	$200 dp bl	10	12
734	A76	$250 carmine	10	12
735	A76	$350 lt brn	10	12
736	A76	$400 dp cl	10	12
		Nos. 732-736 (5)	50	60

First anniversary of return of Chinese National Government to Nanking.

1947 ***Perf. 12½, 11½x12½***

No.	Type	Description	Unused	Used
737	A77	$500 ol grn	10	5
738	A77	$1000 grn & car	15	5
739	A77	$2000 dp bl & red brn	15	6
740	A77	$5000 org red & blk	15	6

Confucius
A78

Confucius' Lecturing School
A79

Tomb of Confucius
A80

Temple of Confucius
A81

1947, Aug. 27 **Litho.** ***Perf. 14***

Without Gum

No.	Type	Description	Unused	Used
741	A78	$500 car rose	8	*10*

Engraved.

No.	Type	Description	Unused	Used
742	A79	$800 yel brn	8	*15*
743	A80	$1250 bl grn	8	*15*
744	A81	$1800 blue	8	*15*

Sun Yat-sen and Plum Blossoms
A82

Chinese Flag and Map of Taiwan
A83

1947-48 **Engraved** ***Perf. 14***

Without Gum

No.	Type	Description	Unused	Used
745	A82	$150 dk bl	8	*15*
746	A82	$250 dp lil	20	10
747	A82	$500 bl grn	6	10
748	A82	$1000 red	6	6
749	A82	$2000 vermilion	15	6
750	A82	$3000 blue	5	6
751	A82	$4000 gray ('48)	15	6
752	A82	$5000 dk brn	6	6
753	A82	$6000 rose lil ('48)	15	6
754	A82	$7000 lt red brn ('48)	15	6
755	A82	$10,000 dp bl & car	50	6
756	A82	$20,000 car & yel grn	35	6
757	A82	$50,000 grn & dk bl	50	6
758	A82	$100,000 dl yel & ol grn ('48)	75	6
759	A82	$200,000 vio brn & dp bl ('48)	1.00	25
760	A82	$300,000 sep & org brn ('48)	1.00	25
761	A82	$500,000 dk Prus grn & sep ('48)	1.25	25
		Nos. 745-761 (17)	6.46	*1.76*

See also Nos. 788-799.

1947, Oct. 25 **With Gum**

No.	Type	Description	Unused	Used
762	A83	$500 carmine	10	*20*
763	A83	$1250 dp grn	10	*20*

Second anniversary, restoration of Taiwan to China.

Mobile Post Office
A84

Street-Corner Branch Post Office
A85

1947, Nov. 5

764 A84 $500 carmine 8 15
765 A85 $1000 lilac 8 15
766 A85 $1250 green 8 15
767 A84 $1800 dp bl 8 15

Stamps and Type of 1943-47 Surcharged in Black or Green

國幣 伍佰圓 500.00

Perf. 12½, 13, 14.

1947-48 **Unwmkd.**

768 A37 $500 on $20 brt yel grn (#633) 8 6
769 A73 $1250 on $70 red org(#639) 8 15
770 A82 $1800 on $350 yel org 8 12
771 A62 $2000 on $3 dk yel ('48) (#503) 8 10
772 A63 $2000 on $3 red (#567) 8 10
a. On #567a 2.50 1.00
773 A62 $3000 on $3 lt yel ('48) (#555) 8 10
774 A63 $3000 on $3 lt red brn (G) ('48) (#568) 8 10
Nos. 768-774 (7) 56 73

The characters at the left express the new value and vary in number.

No. 640 Surcharged

國幣 伍千圓 5000

1948, Aug. *Perf. 14*

775 A73 $5000 on $100 dk car 3.50 5.50

No. 775 received its surcharge in Kwangsi for use in that province.

Map of China and Mail-carrying Vehicles—A86

Rural Mail Delivery—A87

Early and Modern Mail Transportation
A88

1947, Dec. 16 **Engraved** *Perf. 12*

776 A86 $100 violet 5 10
777 A87 $200 brt grn 5 10
778 A87 $300 red brn 5 10
779 A88 $400 scarlet 5 10
780 A88 $500 brt vio bl 5 10
Nos. 776-780 (5) 25 50

Issued to commemorate the 50th anniversary of the Chinese Postal Administration.

National Assembly Building and New Constitution
A89

1947, Dec. 25 *Perf. 14*

Without Gum.

781 A89 $2000 brt red 8 10
782 A89 $3000 blue 8 10
783 A89 $5000 dp grn 8 10

Issued to commemorate the first anniversary of the adoption of China's new constitution, Dec. 25, 1946.

Chinese Stamps of 1947 and 1912
A90

Lithographed

1948, Mar. 20 *Perf. 14, Imperf.*

Without Gum

784 A90 $5000 dk car rose 20 30
a. Vert. pair, imperf. between 30.00
785 A90 $5000 dk grn 20 30
a. Vert. pair, imperf. between 20.00

Issued to commemorate stamp exhibitions at Nanking, Mar. 20 (No. 784), and at Shanghai, May 19 (No. 785).

Sun Yat-sen Memorial Hall, Taipei
A91

1948, Apr. 28 **Engraved** *Perf. 14*

786 A91 $5000 violet 12 20
787 A91 $10000 red 12 20

Issued to commemorate the third anniversary of the restoration of Formosa to China.

Sun Yat-sen Type of 1947–48

1948 **Without Gum**

788 A82 $20000 rose pink 15 15
789 A82 $30000 chocolate 10 15
790 A82 $40000 green 8 5
791 A82 $50000 dp bl 10 5
792 A82 $100000 dl grn 10 5
793 A82 $200000 brn vio 15 5
794 A82 $300000 yel grn 30 5
795 A82 $500000 lil rose 30 8
796 A82 $1000000 claret 25 8
797 A82 $2000000 vermilion 60 15
798 A82 $3000000 ol bis 1.00 25
799 A82 $5000000 ultra 1.75 50
Nos. 788-799 (12) 4.88 1.61

Zeros for "cents" omitted.

Early Ship and Modern Hai Tien
A92

Passenger Ship Kiang Ya
A93

1948, Aug. 16 **Without Gum**

800 A92 $20000 blue 6 10
801 A92 $30000 rose lil 6 10
802 A93 $40000 yel brn 6 15
803 A93 $60000 vermilion 6 15

Issued to commemorate the 75th anniversary of the China Merchants' Steam Navigation Company.

Type of 1947-48 Surcharged in Black

改作伍仟圓 ☆ 5000.00 ☆☆

1948 *Perf. 14* **Unwmkd.**

804 A82 $4000 on $100 car 10 2.00
805 A82 $5000 on $100 car 6 8
806 A82 $8000 on $700 red brn 10 8

Stamps of 1942-46 Surcharged in Black or Red

改作伍仟圓 5000.00

1948 *Perf. 12½, 13*

807 A62 $5000 on $1 dl grn (#500) 8 8
808 A62 $5000 on $1 grn (#551) 2.50 3.25
809 A62 $5000 on $2 dk bl grn (#502) 8 10
810 A72 $10000 on $20 dp car (#625) 8 10
811 A62 $20000 on 10c dp grn (#492) 8 10
812 A62 $20000 on 50c sage grn (R) (#498) 8 10
813 A62 $30000 on 30c dl ver (#496) 8 10
a. Perf. 10½ 15.00 15.00
Nos. 807-813 (7) 2.98 3.83

Nos. 492, 556 and 558 Surcharged in Black or Carmine

改作壹萬伍仟圓 15000

1948

814 A62 $15,000 on 10c dp grn 12 15
815 A62 $15,000 on $4 vio brn 12 15
816 A62 $15,000 on $6 gray vio (C) 12 15

No. 498, 494 and 504 Surcharged in Black

改作肆萬圓 40000

1948 *Perf. 11½, 13.* **Unwmkd.**

817 A62 $15,000 on 50c sage grn 12 15
818 A62 $40,000 on 20c dk ol grn 12 15
a. Perf. 11 5.00 5.00
819 A62 $60,000 on $4 red brn 12 15

Gold Yuan Surcharges (Nos. 820–885E)

Stamps of 1942-47 Surcharged in Black, Carmine or Red

1/2 分

1948 *Perf. 14, 13, 11*

820 A62 ½c on 30c dl ver (#496) 8 20
821 A82 ½c on $500 bl grn (Bk) (#747) 8 10
822 A82 ½c on $500 bl grn (C) (#747) 8 10
823 A73 1c on $20 car (#636) 8 50
824 A62 2c on $1.50 dp bl (R) (#501) 8 25
825 A62 3c on $5 cer (#505) 8 25
826 A62 4c on $1 rose lake (#499) 8 20
827 A62 5c on 50c sage grn (#498) 8 10
a. Perf. 11 3.00 3.00
Nos. 820-827 (8) 64 1.70

On No. 820–827, the position of the surcharged denomination and "Gold Yuan" characters varies, the aim being to obliterate the original denomination.

Stamps of 1940-48 Surcharged in Black, Violet, Carmine, Blue or Green

金圓 壹角 10

Perf. 12, 12½, 13, 14, 12½x13.

1948–49

828 A63 5c on $20 rose (#571) 8 15
829 A72 5c on $30 dp bl (C) (#626) 8 50
a. Double surch. 10.00
830 A57 10c on 2c ol grn (#368) 8 10
831 A39 10c on 2½c rose lil (#424) 8 12
832 A62 10c on 25c brn vio (V) (#495) 8 10
833 A63 10c on 40c brn red (#565) 6 15
834 A62 10c on $1 dl grn (#500) 6 10
834A A62 10c on $1 grn (#551) 30.00 30.00
835 A63 10c on $2 gray brn (#566) 8 10
836 A62 10c on $20 ultra (C) (#560) 8 12
836A A63 10c on $20 rose (#571) 30.00 30.00
837 A67 10c on $20 car (#592) 12 12
837A A73 10c on $20 car (#636) 50 75
838 A72 10c on $30 dp bl (C) (#626) 8 25
839 A63 10c on $70 rose vio (#573) 8 10
a. Double surch. 8.00
840 A82 10c on $7000 lt red brn (#754) 20 20
841 A82 10c on $20,000 rose pink (#788) 8 50
842 A63 20c on $6 pale lil gray (#569) 8 10
843 A37 20c on $30 choc (#634) 8 30
844 A73 20c on $30 dk bl (C) (#637) 8 50
845 A73 20c on $100 dk car (#640) 8 40
a. Inverted surch. 11.00
b. Double surch. 12.50
846 A39 50c on ½c blk brn (#312) 17.50 18.00
847 A39 50c on ½c ol blk (#421) 8 10
a. Inverted surch. 17.50
848 A62 50c on 20c dk ol grn (#494) 8 10
849 A62 50c on 30c dl ver (Bl) (#496) 8 30
850 A62 50c on 40c dk red brn (V) (#497) 8 30
a. Perf. 11 3.00 3.50
851 A63 50c on 40c brn red (V) (#565) 8 10
852 A62 50c on $4 vio brn (#556) 8 15
853 A62 50c on $4 vio brn (Bl) (#556) 8 30
854 A62 50c on $20 dp ultra (C) (#560) 8 10
855 A67 50c on $20 car (V) (#592) 8 20
856 A73 50c on $20 car (#636) 8 10
857 A62 50c on $70 lil (C) (#562) 8 10
858 A82 50c on $6000 rose lil (#753) 20 25
859 A82 50c on $6000 rose lil (Bl) (#753) 12 15
860 A62 $1 on 30c choc (#550) 10 12
a. Perf. 11 30.00
861 A62 $1 on 40c dk red brn (#497) 8 12
a. Perf. 11 2.50 3.00
862 A62 $1 on $1 rose lake (#499) 8 10
863 A62 $1 on $5 car (#557) 8 10

864 A63 $2 on $2 gray brn (R) (#566) 8 10
865 A72 $2 on $20 dp car (#625) 8 10
866 A73 $2 on $100 dk car (#640) 8 10
867 A46 $5 on 17c brn ol (#432) 8 10
868 A63 $5 on $2 gray brn (#566) 10 12
869 A82 $5 on $3000 bl (C) (#750) 8 10
870 A47 $8 on 20c lt bl (#433) 8 15
871 A82 $8 on $30,000 choc (C) (#789) 10 12
872 A47 $10 on 40c org (#438) 20 10
873 A63 $10 on $2 gray brn (G) (#566) 8 10
874 A63 $10 on $2 gray brn (C) (#566) 10 12
875 A63 $20 on $2 gray brn (C) (#566) 10 12
875A A73 $20 on $20 car (#636) 1.00 60
876 A62 $50 on 30c dl ver (#496) 8 10
877 A63 $50 on $2 gray brn (Bl) (#566) 12 15
878 A73 $80 on $20 car (#636) 15 20
879 A62 $100 on $1 grn (#551) 15 20
a. Perf. 11 30.00
880 A63 $100 on $2 gray brn (C) (#566) 15 20
880A A82 $50,000 on $20,000 rose pink (#788) 35 30
880B A82 $100,000 on $30,000 choc (V) (#789) 40 30

Wmk. 261.

881 A39 10c on 2½c rose lil (#405) 8 50
882 A39 50c on ½c ol blk (#402) 8 50
Nos. 828-882 (61) 84.82 89.73

Characters at left express the new value. Style of characters and numerals varies.

Nos. Q7 to Q9 Surcharged in Black or Carmine

改作郵票
500⁰⁰

1948 ***Perf. 12½*** **Unwmkd.**

883 PP2 $200 on $3000 red org 10 10
884 PP2 $500 on $5000 dk bl (C) 10 12
885 PP2 $1000 on $10,000 vio 20 20

Nos. 788-791 Surcharged in Gold Yuan in Red or Black at Foochow

200000

1949, Apr. 30 ***Perf. 14*** **Unwmkd.**

885A A82 $20,000 on $40,000 grn 3.00 3.00
885B A82 $50,000 on $30,000 choc (B) 3.00 3.75
885C A82 $100,000 on $20,000 rose pink (B) 3.00 3.00
885D A82 $200,000 on $40,000 grn 3.00 3.00
885E A82 $200,000 on $50,000 dp bl 3.00 3.75
Nos. 883A-885E (5) 15.00 16.50

Nos. 885A-885E were issued in Fukien Postal District.

Dr. Sun Yat-sen
A94

Engraved.

1949 ***Perf. 14*** **Unwmkd.**

Without Gum.

886 A94 $1 orange 5 5
887 A94 $10 green 5 5
888 A94 $20 vio brn 5 10
889 A94 $50 dk Prus grn 8 10
890 A94 $100 org brn 5 5
891 A94 $200 red org 6 6
892 A94 $500 rose lil 5 5
893 A94 $800 car rose 20 30
894 A94 $1000 blue 5 5

Redrawn. Engraved.

Perf. 12½

894A A94 $10 green 20 1.50
b. Perf. 14 2.00 2.50
894C A94 $20 vio brn 10 10
d. Perf. 14 40 1.25
Nos. 886-894C (11) 94 2.41

Small "T" at left of necktie on Nos. 894A-894d.

Redrawn.

1949 **Lithographed** ***Perf. 12½***

Without Gum

895 A94 $50 grnsh gray 10 1.00
896 A94 $100 dk org brn 5 15
897 A94 $200 org red 10 1.00
898 A94 $1000 dp bl 6 20
899 A94 $5000 lt bl 6 10
900 A94 $10,000 sepia 6 10
Nos. 895-900 (6) 43 2.55

Diagonal lines have been added to the background of the redrawn design. See also Nos. 945-958, 973-981.

50

Plane, Train and Ship
A95

Two types, 50c on $20:
I. Thick numerals in "20." Vertical stroke in lower right corner of vignette. (Dah Tung Book Co.)
II. Thin "20." No vertical stroke in corner. (Central Trust.)

Two types, $2 on $50, $10 on $30, $100 on $50 and $300 on $50:
III. "Y" in lower right corner of vignette. (Dah Yeh Printing Co.)
IV. No "Y" in corner. (Dah Tung, Central Trust or Chung Ming.)

Two types, $50 on $300 and $1000 on $100:
V. Projection on left frame column below foliate ornament. (Dah Yeh Printing Co.)
VI. No projection. (Dah Tung Book Co.)

Gold Yuan Surcharge in Various Colors on Revenue Stamps.

Lithographed;

Nos. 923, 933, 935-936 Engraved.

1949 ***Perf. 12½, 13, 14***

Without Gum.

915 A95 50c on $20 red brn, I (Bk) 8 5
a. 50c on $20 brn, II (Bk) 8 5
916 A95 $1 on $15 red org (Bk) 10 30
917 A95 $2 on $50 dk bl, IV (C) 8 10
d. Type III 25 50
917A A95 $3 on $50 dk bl (Bl) 7 6
917C A95 $3 on $50 dk bl (Bk) 8 5
918 A95 $5 on $500 brn (Dk Br) 8 5
919 A95 $10 on $30 dk vio, III (Bl) 8 5
a. Type IV 40 15
b. Dbl. surch., IV
920 A95 $15 on $20 org brn (Bl) 8 5
921 A95 $25 on $20 org brn (G) 8 5
922 A95 $50 on $50 dk bl (R O) 8 5
923 A95 $50 on $300 grn, VI (C) 8 5
a. $50 on $300 yel grn, V (C) 10 10
924 A95 $80 on $50 dk bl (Dk Br) 8 20
925 A95 $100 on $50 dk bl, IV (Bk) 8 5
a. Type III 75 1.50
926 A95 $200 on $50 dk bl (Bk) 8 5
927 A95 $200 on $500 brn (Bl) 20 15
928 A95 $300 on $50 dk bl, III (C) 13 20
a. Type IV 40 40
929 A95 $300 on $50 dk bl (Br) 50 45
930 A95 $500 on $15 red org (Bl) 20 20
931 A95 $500 on $30 dk vio (Bk) 20 20
932 A95 $1000 on $50 dk bl (C) 25 30
933 A95 $1000 on $100 ol grn, V (Bk) 25 50
a. Type VI 2.50 2.50
934 A95 $1500 on $50 dk bl (Bl) 1.00 1.00
935 A95 $2000 on $300 grn (Bl) 25 10
936 A95 $5000 on $100 ol grn (C) 125.00
Nos. 915-935 (23) 4.13 4.26

No. 936 was officially authorized, but never issued.

Key pattern of overprinted border inverted and in 2 or 3 detached sections at top and bottom.

Hankow Prints.

Lithographed.

Without Gum.

937 A95 $50 on $10 sl grn (Bk) 2.00 2.00
938 A95 $100 on $10 sl grn (Bl) 3.00 3.00
939 A95 $500 on $10 sl grn (Bk) 3.00 2.50
940 A95 $1000 on $10 sl grn (Bl) 1.50 1.50
941 A95 $5000 on $20 red brn (Bl) 3.00 3.00
942 A95 $10,000 on $20 red brn (Bk) 3.00 3.00
943 A95 $50,000 on $20 red brn (Bl) 3.50 3.50
944 A95 $100,000 on $20 red brn (Bk) 4.00 4.00
944A A95 $500,000 on $20 red brn (Bl) 150.00 75.00
944B A95 $2,000,000 on $20 red brn (G) 250.00 100.00
944C A95 $5,000,000 on $20 red brn (Bl) 500.00 200.00
Nos. 937-944C (11) 923.00 397.50

The basic revenue stamps of Nos. 915-944C were the work of several printers. There are three main types, differing in the bottom label. Nos. 922 and 925 are in a second type: Nos. 923 and 930 in a third. Varieties of paper, color and overprint exist.

Counterfeits exist of Nos. 944A-944C.

Type of 1949 Redrawn.

1949 **Without Gum** ***Perf. 12½***

945 A94 $500 rose lil 7 12
946 A94 $2000 violet 8 15
947 A94 $20,000 ap grn 8 15
948 A94 $50,000 rose pink 15 25
949 A94 $80,000 brn red 60 75
950 A94 $100,000 bl grn 50 40
Nos. 945-950 (6) 1.48 1.82

Zeros for "cents" omitted on No. 950.

Redrawn Coarse Impression

1949 **Litho.** **Without Gum**

Size: 18¼x20¾ mm.

951 A94 $50 green 50 1.00
952 A94 $1000 dp bl 40 50
953 A94 $5000 carmine 50 50
954 A94 $10,000 brown 60 1.00
955 A94 $20,000 orange 50 75
956 A94 $50,000 blue 50 40
957 A94 $200,000 violet 60 1.00
958 A94 $500,000 vio brn 60 40
Nos. 951-958 (8) 4.20 5.55

Zeros for "cents" omitted on Nos. 957-958.

Locomotive and Ship
A96

1949, May 1 **Litho.** ***Perf. 12½***

Without Gum

959 A96 orange 85 40
a. Rouletted 2.50 1.50

Nos. 959, C62, E12 and F2 were printed without denomination and sold at the daily rate of the yuan. This was necessitated by the gold yuan inflation.

Revenue Stamps Overprinted in Black

中華民國郵政

1949, May ***Perf. 12½, 13, 14***

Without Gum

960 A95 $30 dk vio 70.00 40.00

Engraved.

961 A95 $200 vio brn 8.00 5.00
962 A95 $500 dk grn 10.00 5.00

A similar overprint appears on Nos. C63, E13 and F3, differing in second and third characters of bottom row.

Silver Yuan Surcharge in Various Colors

中華郵政
銀圓壹角
10

1949 **Lithographed**

963 A95 1c on $5000 brn (G) 60 70
964 A95 4c on $100 ol grn (Bl) 25 30
965 A95 4c on $3000 org (Bk) 25 30
966 A95 10c on $50 dk bl (RV) 40 50
967 A95 10c on $1000 car (Bk) 40 25
a. Inverted surch. 55.00
968 A95 20c on $1000 red (V) 40 80
b. Inverted surch. 20.00
968A A95 50c on $30 dk vio (C) 50 80
969 A95 50c on $50 dk bl (C) 1.25 80
970 A95 $1 on $50 dk bl (Bk) 1.00 75
Nos. 963-970 (9) 5.05 5.20

Nos. 963-965 and 967 are engraved.

Sun Type of 1949 Redrawn.

Coarse Impression.

Perf. 12½, 13 or Compound

1949

973 A94 1c ap grn 1.50 50
974 A94 2c orange 75 50
975 A94 4c bl grn 10 10
976 A94 10c dp lil 10 25
977 A94 16c org red 50 1.50
978 A94 20c blue 30 30
979 A94 50c dk brn 1.50 2.50

980	A94	100c dp bl	110.00	100.00
981	A94	500c scarlet	135.00	125.00
		Nos. 973-981 (9)	249.75	230.65

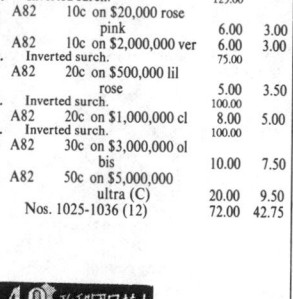

Flying Geese Over Globe A97

Pigeons, Globe and Wreath A98

1949, May Litho. *Perf. 12½*

Without Gum

984	A97	$1 brn org	3.00	2.00
985	A97	$2 blue	6.00	2.50
986	A97	$5 car rose	9.00	5.00
987	A97	$10 bl grn	17.50	6.50

Five other denominations—10c, 16c, 50c, $20 and $50—were also printed at Shanghai, but were not issued.

Engraved and Typographed.

1949, Aug. 1 Without Gum *Imperf.*

988	A98	$1 org red & blk	2.50	3.00

Issued to commemorate the 75th anniversary of the formation of the Universal Postal Union.

Exists with black denomination omitted.

Summer Palace, Peiping A99

Bronze Bull and Kunming Lake A100

Engraved and Typographed.

1949, Aug. *Rouletted*

Without Gum

989	A99	15c org brn & grn	25	1.00
990	A100	40c dl grn & car	35	1.00
a.		2nd and 3rd characters at top transposed	40.00	50.00

Silver Yuan Surcharge in Black on 1949 Sun Yat-sen Issues

1 壹分

1949 *Perf. 12½, 14*

991	A94	1c on $100 org brn (890)	2.50	2.50
992	A94	1c on $100 dk org brn (896)	2.50	2.50
993	A94	2½c on $500 rose lil (892)	3.00	3.00
a.		Inverted surch.	15.00	
994	A94	2½c on $500 rose lil (945)	3.00	3.00
995	A94	15c on $10 grn (887)	6.00	4.00
a.		Inverted surch.	15.00	
996	A94	15c on $20 vio brn (894C)	9.00	6.00
		Nos. 991-996 (6)	26.00	21.00

Silver Yuan Surcharge in Black or Carmine

5 伍分

997	A94	2½c on $50 grn (951)	75	50
998	A94	2½c on $50,000 bl (956)	75	50
999	A94	5c on $1000 dp bl (952) (C)	1.00	75
1000	A94	5c on $20,000 org (955)	1.00	75
1001	A94	5c on $200,000 vio (957) (C)	1.00	1.00
1002	A94	5c on $500,000 vio brn (958)	1.00	1.00
1003	A94	10c on $5000 car (953)	1.50	1.75
1004	A94	10c on $10,000 brn (954)	1.50	1.50
1005	A94	15c on $200 red org (891)	2.50	2.50
1006	A94	25c on $100 dk org brn (896)	5.50	4.00
		Nos. 997-1006 (10)	16.50	14.25

Republic of China (Taiwan)

LOCATION (since 1949)—Taiwan (Formosa).

GOVT.—Republic.

AREA—13,892 sq. mi.

POP.—16,700,000 (est. 1978).

CAPITAL—Taipei.

Stamps issued and used in Taiwan after Communist forces occupied the Chinese mainland include Taiwan Nos. 91–96, 101–103, J10–J17.

Type of 1949 with Value Omitted Surcharged in Various Colors

壹臺 圓幣 1 00

1950, Jan. 1 *Perf. 12½* Unwmkd.

1007	A97	$1 grn (Bk)	15.00	1.50
1008	A97	$2 grn (C)	20.00	5.00
1009	A97	$5 grn (V)	400.00	20.00
1010	A97	$10 grn (Br)	300.00	75.00
1011	A97	$20 grn (Dk Bl)	750.00	350.00
		Nos. 1007-1011 (5)	1,485.	451.50

Two printings of the $1 and $2 show minor differences.

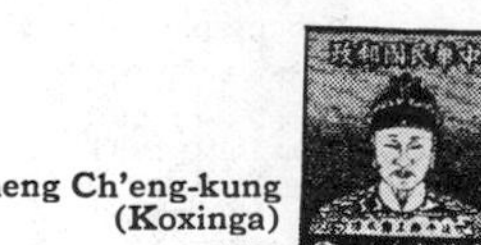

Cheng Ch'eng-kung (Koxinga) A101

1950, June 26 Typo. *Rouletted*

Without Gum.

1012	A101	3c dk gray grn	50	20
1013	A101	10c org brn	50	10
1014	A101	15c org yel	5.00	1.00
1015	A101	20c emerald	1.00	15
1016	A101	30c claret	12.50	6.00
1017	A101	40c red org	1.50	15
1018	A101	50c chocolate	3.00	25
1019	A101	80c carmine	3.00	1.25
1020	A101	$1 ultra	3.50	15
1021	A101	$1.50 green	10.00	1.00
1022	A101	$1.60 blue	12.50	75
1023	A101	$2 red vio	17.50	75
1024	A101	$5 aqua	50.00	5.00
		Nos. 1012-1024 (13)	120.50	16.75

Part perforate pairs exist of the 10c, 20c, and 80c.

Stamps of 1947-48 Surcharged in Carmine or Black

3 臺幣叁分

1950, Mar. 25 *Perf. 14*

1025	A82	3c on $30,000 choc	1.50	1.50
1026	A82	3c on $40,000 grn (C)	1.50	1.50
1027	A82	3c on $50,000 dp bl (C)	2.00	2.00
1028	A82	5c on $200,000 brn vio	2.00	1.25
1029	A82	10c on $4000 gray	4.00	3.00
a.		Inverted surch.	50.00	
1030	A82	10c on $6000 rose lil	6.00	2.00
a.		Inverted surch.	125.00	
1031	A82	10c on $20,000 rose pink	6.00	3.00
1032	A82	10c on $2,000,000 ver	6.00	3.00
a.		Inverted surch.	75.00	
1033	A82	20c on $500,000 lil rose	5.00	3.50
a.		Inverted surch.	100.00	
1034	A82	20c on $1,000,000 cl	8.00	5.00
a.		Inverted surch.	100.00	
1035	A82	30c on $3,000,000 ol bis	10.00	7.50
1036	A82	50c on $5,000,000 ultra (C)	20.00	9.50
		Nos. 1025-1036 (12)	72.00	42.75

Allegory of Election A102

Perf. 12x12½, Imperf.

1951, Mar. 20 Engraved Unwmkd.

Without Gum

1037	A102	40c carmine	3.00	35
a.		Horiz. pair, imperf. btwn.	60.00	
1038	A102	$1 dp bl	6.00	1.25
1039	A102	$1.60 purple	9.00	1.50
1040	A102	$2 brown	14.00	3.00

Adoption of local self-government in Taiwan.

Souvenir Sheet.

Imperf.

1041	A102	$2 dp bl grn	40.00	40.00

Marginal inscriptions publicize Postal Commemorative Day, Mar. 20, 1951. Size: 100x71 mm.

Type A97 Surcharged A103

Farmer and Scroll Announcing Tax Reduction A104

Surcharge in Various Colors.

1951, July 19 *Perf. 12½*

Without Gum

1042	A103	$5 grn (R Br)	14.00	3.00
1043	A103	$10 grn (Bk)	37.50	4.00
1044	A103	$20 grn (R)	150.00	17.50
1045	A103	$50 grn (P)	300.00	35.00

1952, Jan. 1 *Imperf., Perf. 14*

Without Gum

1046	A104	20c red org	3.00	1.75
1047	A104	40c dk grn	6.00	2.25
1048	A104	$1 brown	8.00	6.00
1049	A104	$1.40 dp bl	15.00	5.00
1050	A104	$2 dk gray	20.00	12.00
1051	A104	$5 brn car	30.00	9.00
		Nos. 1046-1051 (6)	82.00	36.00

Land tax reduction of 37.5% in Taiwan.

Pres. Chiang Kai-shek, Flag and Followers A105

Imperf., Perf. 14

1952, Mar. 1 Unwmkd.

Without Gum

Flag in Violet Blue and Carmine.

1052	A105	40c rose car	4.00	60
a.		Vert. pair, imperf. btwn.	40.00	
1053	A105	$1 dp grn	7.00	2.00
1054	A105	$1.60 brn org	15.00	1.25
a.		Horiz. pair, imperf. btwn.	100.00	
1055	A105	$2 brt bl	20.00	5.00
1056	A105	$5 vio brn	25.00	3.00
		Nos. 1052-1056 (5)	71.00	11.85

Issued to commemorate the 2nd anniversary of Chiang Kai-shek's return to the presidency.

See Nos. 1064 - 1069.

Nos. 975, 976, 978 and 979 Surcharged in Black

叁臺 分幣 3

1952 *Perf. 12½.*

1057	A94	3c on 4c bl grn	1.75	75
1058	A94	3c on 10c dp lil	1.75	75
a.		Inverted surch.		
1059	A94	3c on 20c bl	1.75	75
1060	A94	3c on 50c dk brn	1.75	75

Geese Type of 1949 with Value Omitted Surcharged

圓拾壹臺幣 10.00

1952, Dec. 8

1061	A97	$10 grn (P)	40.00	7.50
1062	A97	$20 grn (R)	150.00	15.00
1063	A97	$50 grn (Bk)	800.00	600.00

Chiang Type of 1952 Redrawn.

Perf. 12½

1953, Mar. 1 Engraved Unwmkd.

Without Gum

Flag in Dark Blue & Carmine.

1064	A105	10c red org	5.00	50
1065	A105	20c green	5.00	50
1066	A105	40c rose pink	9.00	75
1067	A105	$1.40 blue	16.50	1.00
1068	A105	$2 brown	22.50	2.00
1069	A105	$5 rose vio	45.00	3.00
		Nos. 1064-1069 (6)	103.00	7.75

Third anniversary of Chiang Kai-shek's return to presidency.

Many differences in redrawn design.

Price, imperf. set, $103

Nos. 1020, 1014, 1016 and 1022 Surcharged in Various Colors

3 cts. 叁分

1953–54 *Rouletted.*

1070	A101	3c on $1 ultra (C)	1.50	25
1070A	A101	10c on 15c org yel (G) ('54)	13.00	50
1071	A101	10c on 30c cl (Bl)	1.50	30
1072	A101	20c on $1.60 bl (Bk)	1.50	30

Chinese characters and ornamental device at bottom differ on each value.

Nurse and Patients A106

1953, July 1 Litho. *Perf. 12½*

Without Gum

Cross in Red, Burelage Color in Italics.

1073	A106	40c brn, *buff*	6.00	1.00
1074	A106	$1.60 bl, *bl*	9.00	80
1075	A106	$2 grn, *yel*	22.50	1.25
1076	A106	$5 red org, *org*	30.00	3.50

Issued to honor the Chinese Anti-Tuberculosis Association.

Pres. Chiang Kai-shek
A107

1953, Oct. 31 Engraved

Without Gum

1077	A107	10c dk brn	55	25
1078	A107	20c lilac	1.75	25
1079	A107	40c dp grn	1.75	15
1080	A107	50c dp pink	1.75	40
1081	A107	80c brn bis	11.00	5.50
1082	A107	$1 dp ol grn	4.50	35
1083	A107	$1.40 dp bl	8.50	70
1084	A107	$1.60 dp car	11.00	55
1085	A107	$1.70 ap grn	5.50	5.00
1086	A107	$2 brown	6.50	35
1087	A107	$3 dk bl	40.00	12.50
1088	A107	$4 aqua	16.00	1.10
1089	A107	$5 red org	9.00	1.40
1090	A107	$10 dk grn	14.00	2.25
1091	A107	$20 dk brn lake	40.00	5.00
a.		Souvenir folder	45.00	
		Nos. 1077-1091 (15)	171.80	35.75

67th birthday of Pres. Chiang Kai-shek.
No. 1091a contains Nos. 1077–1091 imperf., arranged in 3 sheets of 5 stamps each.

Silo Highway Bridge
A108

Forest of Evergreens
A109

Design: $1.60 and $5, Silo bridge, side view.

Without Gum

1954, Jan. 28 *Perf. 12½* Unwmkd.

Various Frames.

1092	A108	40c vermilion	2.00	50
1093	A108	$1.60 bl vio	27.50	75
1094	A108	$3.60 sepia	11.00	1.75
1095	A108	$5 magenta	35.00	2.25
a.		Souv. sheet	40.00	

Opening of Silo bridge, 1st anniversary.
No. 1095a contains one each of Nos. 1092–1095 imperforate.

1954, Mar. 12 *Perf. 12x12½*

Design: $10, Nursery.

Without Gum

1096	A109	40c bl grn	12.00	60
1097	A109	$10 red vio	30.00	3.50

Issued to publicize forest conservation.

Runner
A110

Globe, Bridge and Ship
A111

1954, Mar. 29 Without Gum

1098	A110	40c dp ultra	15.00	1.25
1099	A110	$5 carmine	30.00	5.00

Issued to publicize 11th Youth Day, March 29, 1954.

1954, Oct. 21 *Perf. 12*

Without Gum

1100	A111	40c red org	11.00	30
1101	A111	$5 dp bl	7.00	1.50

Issued to publicize the second Overseas Chinese Day, October 21, 1954.

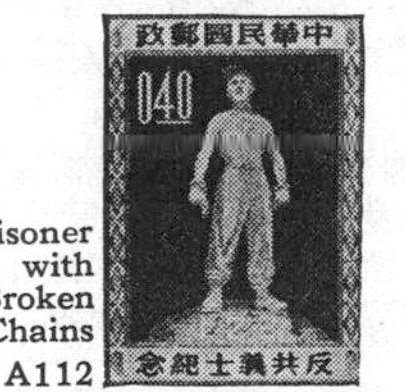

Ex-Prisoner with Broken Chains
A112

Designs: $1, Ex-prisoner with torch and flag, UN emblem. $1.60, Torch and date.

1955, Jan. 23

1102	A112	40c bl grn	1.75	40
a.		Vert. pair, imperf. btwn.	150.00	
1103	A112	$1 sepia	14.00	1.75
1104	A112	$1.60 lake	17.50	1.60

Issued to honor anti-Communist Chinese prisoners who fought with the North Korean army, released January 23, 1955.

Nos. 1019–1021, 1017 Surcharged in Brown, Blue or Green:

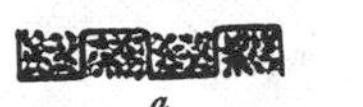

a

0.10

b

角 貳

0.20

c

1955 *Rouletted*

1105	A101 (a)	3c on $1 ultra (Br)	2.00	60
1106	A101 (b)	10c on 80c car (Bl)	2.00	60
1107	A101 (b)	10c on $1.50 grn (Bl)	2.00	60
1108	A101 (c)	20c on 40c red org (G)	2.00	60

Hand Planting Evergreen Tree
A113

Chiang Kai-shek, Flags, Building
A114

Design: $50, Seedling and map of Taiwan.

1955, Apr. 1 *Perf. 12*

Without Gum

1109	A113	$20 dp car	14.00	1.50
1110	A113	$50 blue	25.00	5.50

Issued to publicize forest conservation.

1955, May 20 Engraved *Perf. 12*

Without Gum

1111	A114	20c olive	1.50	10
1112	A114	40c bl grn	2.00	10
1113	A114	$2 car rose	4.00	60
1114	A114	$7 dp ultra	8.50	1.25
a.		Souvenir sheet of 4	20.00	20.00

No. 1114a contains one each of Nos. 1111–1114, imperforate, with ornamental border typographed in red.
First anniversary of Pres. Chiang Kai-shek's re-election.

Armed Forces Emblem
A115

1955, Sept. 3 Without Gum

1115	A115	40c dk bl	1.75	20
1116	A115	$2 org ver	12.50	60
1117	A115	$7 bl grn	11.50	1.25
a.		Sheet of three	32.50	32.50

Armed Forces Day, Sept. 3.
No. 1117a measures 147x104mm. and contains one each of Nos. 1115–1117.

Nos. 1017, 1018 and C64 Surcharged in Magenta

1955 Typographed *Rouletted*

1118	A101	20c on 40c red org	2.25	60
1119	A101	20c on 50c choc	2.25	60
1120	AP6	20c on 60c dp bl	2.25	60

Flags of U.N. and China
A116

1955, Oct. 24 Engraved *Perf. 11½*

Without Gum.

1121	A116	40c dk bl	1.75	20
1122	A116	$2 dk car rose	6.00	60
1123	A116	$7 sl grn	5.25	1.25

Issued to commemorate the tenth anniversary of the United Nations, Oct. 24, 1955.

Pres. Chiang Kai-shek
A117

Birthplace of Sun Yat-sen
A118

1955, Oct. 31 Photo. *Perf. 13½*

1124	A117	40c dk bl, red & brn	1.75	20
1125	A117	$2 grn, red & dk bl	4.50	60
1126	A117	$7 brn, red & grn	6.00	1.25
a.		Souvenir sheet of 3	13.00	13.00

69th birthday of Pres. Chiang Kai-shek.
No. 1126a measures 147x105 mm. and contains one each of Nos. 1124–1126, imperf.

1955, Nov. 12 Engraved *Perf. 12*

Without Gum

1127	A118	40c blue	1.75	20
1128	A118	$2 red brn	4.00	75
1129	A118	$7 rose lake	6.00	1.25

90th anniversary, birth of Sun Yat-sen.

No. 959a Surcharged in Bright Green

角貳

0.20

1956 Litho. *Rouletted*

1130	A96	20c on org	40	15

See also No. 1213.

China Map and Transportation Methods
A119

Wmk. 281

Wmkd. Wavy Lines (281).

1956, Mar. 20 Engraved *Perf. 12*

Without Gum

1131	A119	40c dk car	40	15
1132	A119	$1 int blk	75	40
1133	A119	$1.60 chocolate	1.50	20
1134	A119	$2 dk grn	2.00	40

Issued to commemorate the 60th anniversary of the founding of the modern Chinese postal system.

Souvenir Sheets

Imperf.

1135	A119	$2 magenta	4.50	4.50
1136	A119	$2 red	4.50	4.50

Issued for the exhibition for the 60th anniversary of the modern Chinese postal system, March 20, 1956.
Nos. 1135-36 measure 148x103mm. Marginal floral design and inscription in red and silver (No. 1135), and red and gold (No. 1136).

Children at Play
A120

Early and Modern Locomotives
A121

1956, Apr. 4 *Perf. 12* Unwmkd.

Without Gum.

1137	A120	40c emerald	50	10
1138	A120	$1.60 dk bl	1.25	20
1139	A120	$2 dk car	1.75	70

Children's Day, Apr. 4, 1956.

1956, June 9 Wmk. 281 (vert.)

Without Gum

1140	A121	40c rose car	1.25	10
1141	A121	$2 blue	1.25	15
1142	A121	$8 green	3.75	75

75th anniversary of Chinese Railroads.

Pres. Chiang Kai-shek
A122 A123

A124
Various Portraits of Chiang

Perf. 14½x13½,
14½*(A123), *13½x14½

1956, Oct. 31 Photo. Unwmkd.

1143	A122	20c red org	40	10
1144	A122	40c car rose	1.20	10
1145	A123	$1 brt ultra	90	20
1146	A123	$1.60 red lil	1.50	20
1147	A124	$2 red brn	3.50	25
1148	A124	$8 brt grnsh bl	8.00	1.00
		Nos. 1143-1148 (6)	15.50	1.85

Issued in honor of the 70th birthday of Pres. Chiang Kai-shek.

Types of Special Delivery, Air Post and Registration Stamps of 1949 Surcharged in Black or Maroon

分叁

a

分叁 角壹

b

0.10

c

Lithographed.

1956 *Rouletted* Unwmkd.

Without Gum.

1150	SD2 (a)	3c red vio	85	20
a.		Perf. 12½	1.50	60
1151	AP5 (b)	3c bl grn (M)	85	20
1152	R2 (c)	10c brt red	85	20

Telecommunications Emblem and Radio Tower
A125

Engraved.

1956, Dec. 28 *Perf. 12* Wmk. 281

Without Gum.

1153	A125	40c dp ultra	18	10
1154	A125	$1.40 carmine	30	10
1155	A125	$1.60 dk grn	45	10
1156	A125	$2 chocolate	2.50	30

Issued to commemorate the 75th anniversary of the founding of the Chinese telegraph service.

Map of China
A126

Mother Instructing Mencius
A127

Pin Perf., Perf. 12x12½

1957 Lithographed. Wmk. 281

Without Gum.

1157	A126	3c brt bl	35	6
1158	A126	10c violet	35	10
1159	A126	20c red org	35	10
1160	A126	40c rose red	35	10

Unwmkd.

1161	A126	$1 org brn	60	10
1162	A126	$1.60 green	90	20
		Nos. 1157-1162 (6)	2.90	66

Map inscription reads: "Recovery of Mainland."

See also Nos. 1177-82.

Engraved

1957, May 12 *Perf. 12* Unwmkd.

Design: $3, Mother tattooing Yueh Fei.

Without Gum

1163	A127	40c green	50	20
1164	A127	$3 redsh brn	1.25	35

Issued to honor Mother's Day, 1957.

Badge of Chinese Boy Scouts
A128

1957, Aug. 11 Without Gum

1165	A128	40c lilac	25	10
1166	A128	$1 green	45	15
1167	A128	$1.60 dk bl	65	20

Issued to commemorate the centenary of the birth of Lord Baden-Powell and to publicize the World Scout Jubilee Jamboree, England, Aug. 1-12.

Globe, Radio Tower and Microphone—A129

1957, Sept. 16 Without Gum

1168	A129	40c vermilion	25	10
1169	A129	50c brt rose lil	45	20
1170	A129	$3.50 dk bl	1.10	35

Issued to commemorate the 30th anniversary of Chinese broadcasting.

Map of Taiwan
A130

1957, Oct. 26 Without Gum

1171	A130	40c bl grn	45	10
1172	A130	$1.40 lt ultra	1.15	35
1173	A130	$2 gray	1.50	40

Issued to commemorate the start of construction on the Cross Island Highway, Taiwan.

Freighter "Hai Min" and River Boat "Kiang Foo"
A131

1957, Dec. 16 Engraved *Perf. 12*

Without Gum.

1174	A131	40c dp ultra	25	10
1175	A131	80c rose lake	60	15
1176	A131	$2.80 vermilion	1.50	50

Issued to commemorate the 85th anniversary of the establishment of the China Merchants Steam Navigation Co.

Type of 1957.

1957, Dec. 25 Typo. Unwmkd.

Pin Perf., Perf. 12x12½

Without Gum.

Dark Blue Frames.

1177	A126	3c brt bl	30	10
1178	A126	10c violet	30	15
1179	A126	20c brick red	30	15
1180	A126	40c rose red	70	25
1181	A126	$1 dp org brn	70	15
1182	A126	$1.60 dp grn	1.00	15
		Nos. 1177-1182 (6)	3.30	95

Butterfly
A132

Mme. Chiang Kai-shek Orchid
A133

Photogravure.

1958, Mar. 20 *Perf. 13½* Unwmkd.

Various Insects in Natural Colors

1183	A132	10c pale grn, grn & blk	30	10
1184	A132	40c lem, pink, grn & blk	30	15
1185	A132	$1 yel grn & mar	45	15
1186	A132	$1.40 yel, org & blk	60	20
1187	A132	$1.60 pale brn & dk pur	70	20
1188	A132	$2 brt yel, org & blk	90	30
		Nos.1183-1188 (6)	3.25	1.10

1958, Mar. 20

Orchids: 20c, Formosan Wilson (horiz.). $1.40, Klotzsch. $3, Fitzgerald (horiz.).

Orchids in Natural Colors.

1189	A133	20c chocolate	30	15
1190	A133	40c purple	45	15
1191	A133	$1.40 dk vio brn	60	25
1192	A133	$3 dk bl	90	50

World Health Organization Emblem
A134

1958, May 28 Engraved *Perf. 12*

Without Gum.

1193	A134	40c dk bl	15	10
1194	A134	$1.60 brick red	40	10
1195	A134	$2 dp red lil	75	30

Issued to commemorate the 10th anniversary of the World Health Organization.

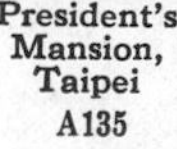

President's Mansion, Taipei
A135

Wmk. 323
Wmk. 323 is found with "Yu" in various arrangements.

Wmkd.

Seal Character 'Yu' (323)

1958, Sept. 20 Engraved *Perf. 12*

Without Gum

1196	A135	$10 bl grn	3.50	10
a.		Granite paper ('63)	3.00	10
1197	A135	$20 car rose	5.00	30
a.		Granite paper ('63)	4.50	10
1198	A135	$50 red brn	20.00	1.75
1199	A135	$100 dk bl	35.00	3.50

See also Nos. 1349-1351.

Taiwan Farm Scene
A136

1958, Oct. 1 Unwmkd.

Without Gum

1200	A136	20c emerald	15	8
1201	A136	40c black	15	8
1202	A136	$1.40 brt mag	60	10
1203	A136	$3 ultra	1.40	40

Issued to commemorate the tenth anniversary of the Joint Commission on Rural Reconstruction.

Pres. Chiang Kai-shek
A137

1958, Oct. 31 Photo. *Perf. 13½*

Without Gum.

1204	A137	40c multi	40	15

Issued to honor Pres. Chiang Kai-shek on his 72nd birthday.

UNESCO Building, Paris
A138

1958, Nov. 3 Engraved *Perf. 12*
Without Gum.

1205	A138	20c	dk bl	12	8
1206	A138	40c	green	18	8
1207	A138	$1.40	org ver	70	10
1208	A138	$3	red lil	1.00	40

Issued to commemorate the opening of UNESCO (U. N. Educational, Scientific and Cultural Organization) Headquarters in Paris, Nov. 3.

Flame from Liberty Torch Encircling Globe
A139

1958, Dec. 10 Unwmkd.
Without Gum

1209	A139	40c	green	12	8
1210	A139	60c	gray brn	18	8
1211	A139	$1	carmine	50	15
1212	A139	$3	ultra	1.00	40

Issued to commemorate the tenth anniversary of the signing of the Universal Declaration of Human Rights.

No. 959a Surcharged in Bright Green

0.20
角貳

Rouletted
1958, Dec. 11 Litho. Unwmkd.
Without Gum

1213	A96	20c	on org	30	10

Ballot Box, Scales and Constitution
A140

1958, Dec. 25 Engraved *Perf. 12*
Without Gum.

1214	A140	40c	green	18	8
1215	A140	50c	dl pur	25	8
1216	A140	$1.40	car rose	75	15
1217	A140	$3.50	dk bl	1.25	50

Issued to commemorate the 10th anniversary of the adoption of the constitution.

Chu Kwang Tower, Quemoy
A141

Lithographed.
1959–60 *Perf. 12* Wmk. 323
Without Gum.

1218	A141	3c	orange	12	5
1218A	A141	5c	lt yel grn ('60)	12	8
1219	A141	10c	lilac	12	5
1220	A141	20c	ultra	12	5
1221	A141	40c	brown	18	5
1222	A141	50c	bluish grn	30	5
1223	A141	$1	rose red	50	5
1224	A141	$1.40	yel grn	70	5
1225	A141	$2	gray grn	70	8
1226	A141	$2.80	rose pink	1.20	8
1227	A141	$3	sl bl	1.20	9
			Nos. 1218-1227 (11)	5.26	68

See also Nos. 1270–1283.

ILO Emblem and Headquarters, Geneva
A142

1959, June 15 Engraved *Perf. 12*
Without Gum

1228	A142	40c	blue	12	6
1229	A142	$1.60	dk brn	30	6
1230	A142	$3	brt bl grn	60	15
1231	A142	$5	org ver	1.50	40

Issued to commemorate the 40th anniversary of the International Labor Organization.

Bugler and Tents
A143

1959, July 8 Unwmkd.
Without Gum

1232	A143	40c	carmine	20	10
1233	A143	50c	dk bl	60	15
1234	A143	$5	green	1.50	50

Issued to publicize the 10th World Boy Scout Jamboree, at Makiling National Park, Philippines, July 17–26.

Inscribed Stone, Mt. Tai-wu, Quemoy
A144

Map of Taiwan Straits
A145

1959, Sept. 3 Engraved *Perf. 12*
Without Gum.

1235	A144	40c	brown	20	10
1236	A145	$1.40	ultra	50	15
1237	A145	$2	green	1.10	30
1238	A144	$3	dk bl	1.40	40

Defense of Quemoy and Matsu islands.

Pigeons Circling Globe
A146

1959, Oct. 4 Without Gum

1239	A146	40c	blue	15	10
1240	A146	$1	rose car	30	15
1241	A146	$2	gray brn	50	10
1242	A146	$3.50	red org	1.10	40

Issued for International Letter Writing Week, Oct. 4–10.

National Taiwan Science Hall, Taipei—A147

Design: $3, Front view.

1959, Nov. 12 Photo. *Perf. 13x13½*

1243	A147	40c	multi	85	15
1244	A147	$3	multi	1.75	45

Emblem
A148

1959, Dec. 7 Engraved *Perf. 12*
Without Gum

1245	A148	40c	bl grn	25	10
1246	A148	$1.60	red lil	60	15
1247	A148	$3	orange	1.00	30

Issued to commemorate the 10th anniversary of the International Confederation of Free Trade Unions.

Sun Yat-sen, Lincoln and Flags
A149

Perf. 13½, 12
1959, Dec. 25 Photo. Unwmkd.

1248	A149	40c	multi	30	15
1249	A149	$3	multi	40	25

Issued to honor Sun Yat-sen and Abraham Lincoln as "Leaders of Democracy."

Mailman on Motorcycle Delivering Night Mail
A150

Postal Launch
A151

1960, Mar. 20 Engraved *Perf. 11½*
Without Gum

1250	A150	$1.40	dk vio brn	65	15
1251	A151	$1.60	ultra	85	20

Issued to publicize the Prompt Delivery Service.

WRY Uprooted Oak Emblem
A152

1960, Apr. 7 Photo. *Perf. 13*

1252	A152	40c	blk, red brn & emer	25	10
1253	A152	$3	blk, red org & grn	65	30

Issued to publicize World Refugee Year, July 1, 1959–June 30, 1960.

Cross Island Highway, Taiwan
A153

Design: $1, $2, Road through tunnel (vert.).

Perf. 11½
1960, May 9 Engr. Unwmkd.
Without Gum

1254	A153	40c	green	30	10
1255	A153	$1	dk bl	95	40
1256	A153	$2	brn vio	40	20
1257	A153	$3	brown	1.25	25
a.			Souv. sheet of 2, wmk. 323	22.50	22.50

Issued to commemorate the opening of the Cross Island Highway, Taiwan.

No. 1257a contains imperf. copies of Nos. 1255 and 1257, with multicolored pictorial background and marginal inscriptions in red. Size: 144x103mm.

Red Overprint on Nos. 1237–1238
Chinese and English:
"Welcome U.S. President
Dwight D. Eisenhower 1960"

1960, June 18 *Perf. 12* Unwmkd.

1258	A145	$2	green	50	15
a.			Invtd. ovpt.	135.00	135.00
1259	A144	$3	dk bl	1.00	40

Issued to commemorate President Eisenhower's visit to China, June 18, 1960.

Phonopost
A154

1960, June 27 Without Gum

1260	A154	$2	red org	70	20

Issued to publicize the Phonopost Service of the Chinese armed forces.

Two Horses and Groom, by Han Kan
A155

Paintings from Palace Museum, Taichung: $1, Two Riders, by Wei Yen. $1.60, Flowers and Birds by Hsiao Yung (vert.). $2, Pair of Mandarin Ducks by Monk Hui Ch'ung.

1960, Aug. 4 Photo. *Perf. 13*

1261	A155	$1	ol gray, blk & brn	85	30
1262	A155	$1.40	bis brn, blk & fawn	1.00	30
1263	A155	$1.60	multi	1.40	40
1264	A155	$2	beige, blk & gray grn	2.50	75

Chinese paintings, 7th–11th centuries.

Youth Corps Flag and Summer Activities **A156**
Reforestation **A157**

Design: $3, similar to 50c (horiz.).

1960, Aug. 20 Engraved *Perf. 12*
Without Gum

1265	A156	50c	sl grn	40	10
1266	A156	$3	cop brn	1.40	40

Summer activities of China Youth Corps.

1960, Aug. 29 Photo. *Perf. 13½x13*

Designs: $2, Protection of forest. $3, Timber industry.

1267	A157	$1	multi	50	10
1268	A157	$2	multi	1.20	40
1269	A157	$3	multi	1.20	40
a.			Souvenir sheet of 3	1.75	1.75

Issued to commemorate the Fifth World Forestry Congress, Seattle, Washington, Aug. 29–Sept. 10.

No. 1269a contains Nos. 1267–1269 assembled as a triptych, 65½x40mm. and imperf., but with simulated black perforations. Marginal inscriptions in carmine. Size of sheet: 99x144½mm.

Chu Kwang Tower, Quemoy **A158**
Diver **A159**

Lithographed
1960–61 *Perf. 12* Wmk. 323
Without Gum

1270	A158	3c	lt red brn	15	5
1271	A158	40c	pale vio	15	5
1272	A158	50c	org ('61)	15	5
1273	A158	60c	rose lil	15	5
1274	A158	80c	pale grn	20	5
1275	A158	$1	gray grn ('61)	1.25	5
1276	A158	$1.20	gray ol	60	5
1277	A158	$1.50	ultra	60	6
1278	A158	$2	car rose ('61)	1.35	8
1279	A158	$2.50	pale bl	1.35	8
1280	A158	$3	bluish grn	90	8
1281	A158	$3.20	lt red brn	2.25	8
1282	A158	$3.60	vio bl ('61)	2.00	18
1283	A158	$4.50	vermilion	3.50	25
			Nos. 1270-1283 (14)	14.60	1.16

1962–64 Granite Paper
Without Gum

1270a	A158	3c	lt red brn	30	5
1270B	A158	10c	emer ('63)	75	5
1271a	A158	40c	pale vio	30	5
1274a	A158	80c	pale grn	50	5
1275a	A158	$1	gray grn ('63)	2.00	5
1278a	A158	$2	car rose	2.25	7
1281a	A158	$3.20	red brn ('64)	2.25	6
1282A	A158	$4	brt bl grn	4.00	15
1283a	A158	$4.50	vermilion	2.25	20
			Nos. 1270a-1283a (9)	14.60	73

Two types of No. 1271a: I. Seven lines in "0" of "40." II. Eight lines in "0."

Perf. 12½
1960, Oct. 25 Photo. Unwmkd.

Sports: 80c, Discus thrower. $2, Basketball. $2.50, Soccer. $3, Hurdling. $3.20, Runner.

1284	A159	50c	ultra, yel & org	35	10
1285	A159	80c	rose cl, pur & yel	35	15
1286	A159	$2	blk, red org & yel	60	25
1287	A159	$2.50	org & blk	90	30
1288	A159	$3	multi	1.00	50
1289	A159	$3.20	multi	1.65	60
			Nos. 1284-1289 (6)	4.85	1.90

Bronze Wine Container, 1751–1111 B.C.
A160

Flat Bowl, 1111–771 B.C.
A161

Designs: $1, Cauldron, 1111–771 B.C. $1.20, Porcelain vase, 960–1126 A.D. $1.50, Perforated tube, 1111–771 B.C. $2, Jug in shape of monk's cap, 1368–1661 A.D. $2.50, Jade flower vase, 1368–1661, A.D.

Art Series I
1961–62 Photo. *Perf. 13*

1290	A160	80c	lt ol, blk & dk vio	60	12
1291	A160	$1	sal, bl & blk	65	15
1292	A160	$1.20	yel, brn & ultra	85	30
1293	A160	$1.50	lil, bl & sep	85	40
1294	A160	$2	pale grn, dk grn & red brn	1.20	30
1295	A160	$2.50	grnsh bl & dk vio	1.50	35
			Nos. 1290-1295 (6)	5.65	1.62

Art Series II

Designs: 80c, Palace perfumer, 1662–1911. $1, Corn vase, 770–221 B.C. $2, Jade tankard, 960–1126 A.D. $4, Glazed washer, 1127–1279 A.D. $4.50, Jade chimera, 8 B.C.–206 A.D.

1296	A160	80c	pink, brn, bl & yel	40	10
1297	A160	$1	cit, blk & brn	1.20	20
1298	A161	$1.50	sal & ind	1.20	50
1299	A160	$2	bl, blk & rose	1.20	40
1300	A161	$4	red, blk & bluish gray	4.00	40
1301	A161	$4.50	grnsh bl, blk & brn	3.75	1.00
			Nos. 1296-1301 (6)	11.75	2.60

Art Series III
(1962)

Designs: 80c, Topaz twin wine vessels, 1662–1911 A.D. $1, Squat pouring vase, 1751–1111 B.C. $2.40, Vase, 1368–1661 A.D. $3, Wine vase, 1751–1111 B.C. $3.20, Covered porcelain jar, 1662–1911 A.D. $3.60, Perforated disc, 206 B.C.–8 A.D.

1302	A160	80c	crim, blk & ocher	30	10
1303	A160	$1	bl & vio blk	40	10
1304	A160	$2.40	hn brn, blk & bl	1.35	40
1305	A160	$3	bl, blk & pink	3.00	1.25
1306	A160	$3.20	ultra, lt grn & red	4.00	25
1307	A160	$3.60	yel, blk & brn	3.00	75
			Nos. 1302-1307 (6)	12.05	2.85

Issued to publicize ancient Chinese art treasures.

Farmer with Mechanized Plow **A162**
Madame Chiang Kai-shek and League Emblem **A163**

1961, Feb. 4 Engraved *Perf. 12*
Without Gum

1308	A162	80c	rose vio	25	10
1309	A162	$2	green	85	40
1310	A162	$3.20	vermilion	85	20

Issued to publicize the 1961 agricultural census.

Photogravure
1961, March 8 *Perf. 13* Unwmkd.
Portrait in Black

1311	A163	80c	lt grn & car rose	60	10
1312	A163	$1	yel grn & car rose	1.50	25
1313	A163	$2	org brn & car rose	1.50	25
1314	A163	$3.20	lil & car rose	3.25	50

Issued to commemorate the 10th anniversary of the Chinese Women's Anti-Aggression League.

Spiny Lobster and Mail Order Service Emblem **A164**
Jeme Tien-yow and Pataling Tunnel **A165**

1961, Mar. 20 Engraved *Perf. 11½*
Without Gum

1315	A164	$3	sl grn	1.20	25

Issued to publicize the mail order service for consumer goods.

1961, Apr. 26 *Perf. 11½*
Without Gum

Design: $2, Jeme Tien-yow and 1909 locomotive (horiz.).

1316	A165	80c	lilac	25	10
1317	A165	$2	black	1.25	40

Issued to commemorate the centenary of the birth of Jeme Tien-yow, builder of the Peking-Kalgan railroad.

Map of China inscribed: "Recovery of the Mainland"
A166

Pres. Chiang Kai-shek
A167

1961, May 20 Photo. *Perf. 13½*

1318	A166	80c	multi	60	15
1319	A167	$2	multi	2.00	75
a.			Souvenir sheet of 2	1.50	1.50

Issued to commemorate the first anniversary of Pres. Chiang Kai-shek's 3rd term inauguration.

No. 1319a contains one each of Nos. 1318–1319, imperf. with simulated perforations and red marginal inscription. Without gum. Size: 135x100mm.

Convair 880-M, Biplane of 1921 and Flag
A168

1961, July 1 *Perf. 13x12½*

1320	A168	$10	multi	3.00	40

40th anniversary of civil air service.

Sun Yat-sen and Chiang Kai-shek
A169

Flag and Map of China
A170

Photogravure

1961, Oct. 10 *Perf. 13½* Unwmkd.

1321	A169	80c gray, lt brn & sl	75	10
1322	A170	$5 gray, ultra, red & beige	2.75	90
a.		Souvenir sheet of 2	2.00	2.00

Issued to commemorate the 50th anniversary of the Republic of China. No. 1322a contains one each of Nos. 1321–1322, imperf. with simulated perforations and red marginal inscription. No gum. Size of sheet: 135x99mm.

Lotus Pond
A172

Green Lake
A171

Oil Refinery
A173

Taiwan Scenery: $2, Sun-Moon Lake. $3.20, Wulai waterfalls.

Perf. 13½x14, 14x13½

1961, Oct. 31 Unwmkd.

1323	A171	80c multi	50	15
1324	A172	$1 multi	1.50	50
1325	A172	$2 multi	1.50	50
1326	A171	$3.20 multi	3.00	75

1961, Nov. 14 *Perf. 11½*

Designs: $1.50, Steel works. $2.50, Aluminum plant. $3.20, Fertilizer plant (horiz.).

1327	A173	80c multi	50	10
1328	A173	$1.50 multi	1.50	80
1329	A173	$2.50 multi	1.50	80
1330	A173	$3.20 multi	3.00	70

Issued to publicize Chinese industrial development and in connection with the Golden Jubilee Convention of the Chinese Institute of Engineers, Nov. 13–16.

Atomic Reactor, Tsing-Hwa University
A174

Atomic Reactor in Operation
A175

Design: $3.20, Atomic symbol and laboratory, Tsing-Hwa (horiz.).

1961–62 Photogravure *Perf. 12½*

1331	A174	80c multi	1.00	10
1332	A175	$2 multi ('62)	2.25	1.40
1333	A175	$3.20 multi ('62)	3.25	90

Issued to commemorate the inauguration on Apr. 13, 1961, of the first Chinese atomic reactor at the National Tsing-Hwa University Institute of Nuclear Science.

Microwave Reflector and Telegraph Wires
A176

Design: $3.20, Microwave parabolic antenna and mountains (horiz.).

1961, Dec. 28 *Perf. 12½*

1334	A176	80c multi	50	12
1335	A176	$3.20 multi	2.75	90

Issued to commemorate the 80th anniversary of Chinese telecommunications.

Mechanical Postal Equipment and Twine Tying Machine—A176a

Perf. 11½

1962, Mar. 20 Engraved Wmk. 323

Without Gum

1336	A176a	80c chocolate	1.00	15

Yu Shan Observatory
A177

Observation Balloon, Earth and Cumulus Clouds
A178

Design: $1, Map showing route of typhoon Pamela, Sept. 1961 (horiz.).

1962 Without Gum

1337	A177	80c brown	30	10
1338	A178	$1 bluish blk	2.25	40
1339	A178	$2 green	2.25	80

Issue dates: 80c, $2, Mar. 23; $1, May 7. World Meteorological Day, Mar. 23.

Child Receiving Milk, U.N. Emblem—A179

1962, Apr. 4 Without Gum

1340	A179	80c rose red	25	10
1341	A179	$3.20 green	1.75	75
a.		Souvenir sheet of 2	1.50	1.50

Issued to commemorate the 15th anniversary of UNICEF (United Nations Children's Emergency Fund.) No. 1341a contains one each of Nos. 1340–1341 imperf. with simulated perforations and red marginal inscription. Size: 135x100mm.

Malaria Eradication Emblem
A180

Photogravure

1962, Apr. 7 *Perf. 12½* Unwmkd.

1342	A180	80c dk bl, red & lt grn	60	10
1343	A180	$3.60 brn, pink & grn	1.40	75

Issued for the World Health Organization drive to eradicate malaria.

Yu Yu-jen
A181

Cheng Ch'eng-kung (Koxinga)
A182

1962, Apr. 24 *Perf. 13*

1344	A181	80c gray, blk & pink	65	10

Issued to honor Yu Yu-jen, newspaper reporter, revolutionary leader and co-worker of Sun Yat-sen, on his 84th birthday.

1962, Apr. 29

1345	A182	80c dp cl	50	10
1346	A182	$2 dk grn	1.10	25

Issued to commemorate the 300th anniversary (in 1961) of the recovery of Taiwan from the Dutch by Koxinga.

Emblem of International Cooperative Alliance
A183

Clasped Hands Across Globe
A184

Engraved

1962, July 7 *Perf. 12* Wmk. 323

Without Gum

1347	A183	80c brown	60	10
1348	A184	$2 violet	1.75	50

Issued to publicize the International Cooperative Movement and to commemorate the 40th International Cooperative Day, July 7, 1962.

Mansion Type of 1958

1962, July 20 Without Gum

1349	A135	$5 gray grn	2.00	6
a.		Granite paper ('63)	2.25	10
1350	A135	$5.60 violet	2.50	8
a.		Granite paper ('63)	3.50	10
1351	A135	$6 orange	2.75	10
a.		Granite paper ('63)	3.75	10

"Art and Science"
A185

Designs: $2, "Education," book and UNESCO emblem (horiz.). $3.20, "Communications," globes (horiz.).

1962, Aug. 28 *Perf. 12* Wmk. 323

Without Gum

1352	A185	80c lil rose	25	15
1353	A185	$2 rose cl	1.00	60
1354	A185	$3.20 yel grn	1.25	40

Issued to publicize the activities of UNESCO in China.

Emperor T'ai Tsung, T'ang Dynasty, 627–649—A186

Emperors: $2, T'ai Tsu, Sung dynasty, 960–975. $3.20, T'ai Tsu, Yuan dynasty (Genghis Khan), 1206–27. $4, T'ai Tsu, Ming dynasty, 1368–98.

1962, Sept. 20 Photo. Unwmkd.

1355	A186	80c multi	1.00	20
1356	A186	$2 multi	4.50	1.35
1357	A186	$3.20 multi	5.00	1.10
1358	A186	$4 multi	4.50	1.65

Lions International Emblem
A187

1962, Oct. 8 *Perf. 13*

1359	A187	80c multi	75	10
1360	A187	$3.60 multi	2.25	85
a.		Souvenir sheet of 2	2.00	2.00

Issued to commemorate the 45th anniversary of Lions International. No. 1360a contains one each of Nos. 1359–1360, imperf. with simulated perforations and gold marginal inscription. Size: 100x75mm.

Pole Vaulting
A188

Shooting
A189

1962, Oct. 25 *Perf. 13* Unwmkd.

1361	A188	80c multi	85	15
1362	A189	$3.20 multi	1.65	40

Sports meet.

Young Farmers and 4-H Emblem
A190

Flag and Liner of China Merchants' Steam Navigation Co.
A191

Design: $3.20, 4-H emblem and rice.

Engraved

1962, Dec. 7 *Perf. 12* Wmk. 323

Without Gum

1363	A190	80c carmine	40	10
1364	A190	$3.20 green	1.00	50
a.		Souvenir sheet of 2	1.25	1.25

Issued to commemorate the 10th anniversary of the 4-H Club in China. No. 1364a contains one each of Nos. 1363-1364, imperf. with simulated perforations and red lithographed marginal inscription. Size: 135x100mm.

Photogravure

1962, Dec. 16 *Perf. 13½* Unwmkd.

Design: $3.60, Company's Pacific navigation chart and freighter (horiz.).

1365	A191	80c multi	75	10
1366	A191	$3.60 multi	2.25	85

Issued to commemorate the 90th anniversary of the China Merchants' Steam Navigation Co., Ltd.

Farm Woman, Tractor and Plane Dropping Food over Mainland
A192

Photogravure

1963, Mar. 21 *Perf. 12½* Unwmkd.

1367	A192	$10 multi	3.50	90

Issued for the "Freedom from Hunger" campaign of the U.N. Food and Agriculture Organization.

Torch, Young Couple and Martyrs' Monument, Canton
A193

Engraved

1963, Mar. 29 *Perf. 11½* Wmk. 323

Without Gum

1368	A193	80c purple	35	8
1369	A193	$3.20 green	1.75	40

Issued for the 20th Youth Day.

Swallows, Pagoda and AOPU Emblem
A194

Designs: $2, Northern gannet (horiz.). $6, Japanese crane and pine.

Photogravure

1963, Apr. 1 *Perf. 13* Unwmkd.

1370	A194	80c multi	1.50	15
1371	A194	$2 multi	1.50	15
1372	A194	$6 multi	5.00	1.75

Issued to commemorate the first anniversary of the formation of the Asian-Oceanic Postal Union, AOPU.

Refugee Girl (Li Ying) and Map of China
A195

Refugees Fleeing Mainland
A196

Engraved

1963, June 27 *Perf. 11½* Wmk. 323

Without Gum

1373	A195	80c bluish blk	75	15
1374	A196	$3.20 dp cl	1.65	25

Issued to commemorate the first anniversary of the evacuation of Chinese mainland refugees from Hong Kong to Taiwan. Designs from photographs of refugees.

Nurse and Red Cross
A197

Basketball Player, Stadium and Asian Cup
A198

Design: $10, Globe and Red Cross.

Photogravure

1963, Sept. 1 *Perf. 12½* Unwmkd.

1375	A197	80c blk & car	1.50	20
1376	A197	$10 sl, gray & car	5.50	2.00

Centenary of International Red Cross.

Engraved

1963, Nov. 20 *Perf. 12* Wmk. 323

Without Gum

Design: $2, Hands reaching for ball and Asian cup.

1377	A198	80c lil rose	35	10
1378	A198	$2 violet	2.25	75

Issued to commemorate the 2nd Asian Basketball Championship, Taipei, Nov. 20.

U.N. Emblem, Torch and Men
A199

Scales and Men of Various Races
A200

1963, Dec. 10 *Perf. 11½* Wmk. 323

Without Gum

1379	A199	80c brt grn	25	8
1380	A200	$3.20 maroon	75	20

Universal Declaration of Human Rights, 15th anniversary.

Village and Orchids
A201

"Kindle the Fire of Conscience"
A202

Perf. 13½x13

1963, Dec. 17 Photo. Unwmkd.

1381	A201	40c multi	80	10
1382	A202	$4.50 multi	2.75	75

Issued to commemorate the contribution of the Good-People-Good-Deeds campaign to improve ethical standards.

Sun Yat-sen and Book, "Three Principles of the People"
A203

1963, Dec. 25 *Perf. 13*

1383	A203	$5 bl & multi	2.50	30

"Land-to-the-Tillers" program, 10th anniversary.

Torch
A204

Hands Unchained
A205

Engraved

1964, Jan. 23 *Perf. 11½* Wmk. 323

Without Gum

1384	A204	80c red org	20	8
1385	A205	$3.20 indigo	1.00	15

Liberty Day, 10th anniversary.

Broadleaf Cactus
A206

Wu Chih-hwei
A207

Designs: $1, Crab cactus. $3.20, Nopalxochia. $5, Grizzly bear cactus.

Photogravure

1964, Feb. 27 *Perf. 12½* Unwmkd.

Plants in Original Colors

1386	A206	80c dp plum & fawn	40	10
1387	A206	$1 dk bl & car	1.00	40
1388	A206	$3.20 green	1.50	10
1389	A206	$5 lil & yel	2.00	40

Perf. 11½

1964, Mar. 25 Engraved Wmk. 323

Without Gum

1390	A207	80c blk brn	65	12

Issued to commemorate the centenary of the birth of Wu Chih-hwei (1865-1953), politician and leader of the Kuomintang.

Chu Kwang Tower, Quemoy
A208

Lithographed

1964-66 *Perf. 13x12½* Wmk. 323

Granite Paper; Without Gum

1391	A208	3c sepia	10	5
1392	A208	5c brt yel grn ('65)	10	5
1393	A208	10c yel grn	10	5
1394	A208	20c sl grn ('65)	10	5
1395	A208	40c rose red	10	5
1396	A208	50c brown	10	5
1397	A208	80c org ('65)	20	5
1398	A208	$1 vio ('65)	25	5
1399	A208	$1.50 brt lil ('66)	35	15
1400	A208	$2 lil rose	35	6
1401	A208	$2.50 ultra ('65)	35	6
1402	A208	$3 slate	60	10
1403	A208	$3.20 brt bl	75	6
1404	A208	$4 brt grn	90	8
		Nos. 1391-1404 (14)	4.35	91

Nurses Holding Candles
A209

Florence Nightingale and Student Nurse
A210

1964, May 12 Engr. *Perf. 11½*

Without Gum

1406	A209	80c vio bl	50	8
1407	A210	$4 red	1.50	25

Issued for Nurses Day.

Shihmen Reservoir
A211

Designs: $1, Irrigation system. $3.20, Main dam and power plant. $5, Spillway.

Photogravure

1964, June 14 *Perf. 12½* Unwmkd.

1408	A211	80c multi	60	10
1409	A211	$1 multi	60	10
1410	A211	$3.20 multi	1.20	15
1411	A211	$5 multi	3.00	75

Completion of Shihmen Reservoir.

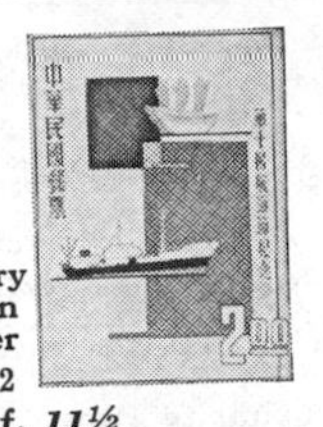

15th Century Ship, Modern Liner
A212

Perf. 11½

1964, July 11 Engr. Wmk. 323
Without Gum

1412	A212	$2 orange	45	8
1413	A212	$3.60 brt grn	85	20

China's 10th Navigation Day.

Bananas
A213

Photogravure

1964, July 25 *Perf. 14* Unwmkd.
Multicolored

1414	A213	80c *shown*	60	8
1415	A213	$1 *Oranges*	1.20	40
1416	A213	$3.20 *Pineapple*	1.50	25
1417	A213	$4 *Watermelon*	2.50	65

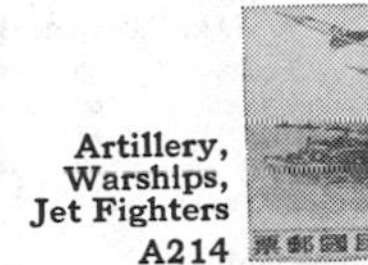

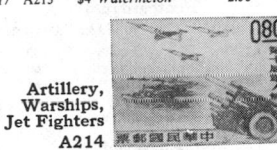

Artillery, Warships, Jet Fighters
A214

Engraved

1964, Sept. 3 *Perf. 11½* Wmk. 323
Without Gum

1418	A214	80c dk bl	30	8
1419	A214	$6 vio brn	1.65	40

Issued for the 10th Armed Forces Day.

Unisphere, Flags of China and U.S.
A215

Chinese Pavilion, N.Y. World's Fair
A216

1964, Sept. 10 Photo. Unwmkd.

1420	A215	80c vio & multi	60	8
1421	A216	$5 bl & multi	2.75	45

New York World's Fair, 1964-65. See also Nos. 1450-1451.

Cowboy Carrying Calf, and Ranch
A217

Bicycling
A218

Engraved

1964, Sept. 24 *Perf. 11½* Wmk. 323
Without Gum

1422	A217	$2 brn lake	75	10
1423	A217	$4 dk vio bl	1.75	40

Animal Protection Week, Sept. 24-30.

1964, Oct. 10 Without Gum

Sports: $1, Runner. $3.20, Gymnast on rings. $10, High jump.

1424	A218	80c vio bl	35	6
1425	A218	$1 rose red	65	10
1426	A218	$3.20 dl bl grn	1.20	10
1427	A218	$10 lilac	3.50	1.50

18th Olympic Games, Tokyo, Oct. 10-25.

Hsü Kuang-chi
A219

Pharmaceutical Industry
A220

Textile Industry
A221

1964, Nov. 8 Engraved *Perf. 11½*
Without Gum

1428	A219	80c indigo	75	10

Issued to honor Hsü Kuang-chi (1562-1633), scholar and statesman.

1964, Nov. 11 Photo. Unwmkd.

Designs: $2, Chemical industry. $3.60, Cement industry.

1429	A220	40c multi	50	8
1430	A221	$1.50 multi	1.25	40
1431	A220	$2 multi	1.50	15
1432	A221	$3.60 multi	2.50	30

Dr. Sun Yat-sen
A222

Eleanor Roosevelt and Scales of Justice
A223

1964, Nov. 24 Engraved Wmk. 323
Without Gum

1433	A222	80c green	60	8
1434	A222	$3.60 purple	1.20	25

Founding of the Kuomintang by Sun Yat-sen, 70th anniversary.

Photogravure

1964, Dec. 10 *Perf. 13* Unwmkd.

1435	A223	$10 vio & brn	1.65	40

Issued to honor Eleanor Roosevelt (1884-1962) on the 16th anniversary of the Universal Declaration of Human Rights.

Scales, Code Book and Plum Blossom
A224

Rotary Emblem and Mainspring
A225

Engraved

1965, Jan. 11 *Perf. 11½* Wmk. 323
Without Gum

1436	A224	80c car rose	25	8
1437	A224	$3.20 dl sl grn	75	20

The 20th Judicial Day.

1965, Feb. 23 *Perf. 11½* Wmk. 323
Without Gum

1438	A225	$1.50 vermilion	30	8
1439	A225	$2 emerald	85	15
1440	A225	$2.50 blue	1.00	25

Rotary International, 60th anniversary.

Double Carp Design
A226

Madame Chiang Kai-shek
A227

Engraved

1965, Mar. 29 *Perf. 11½* Wmk. 323
Granite Paper; Without Gum

1441	A226	$5 purple	4.00	25
1442	A226	$5.60 dp bl	2.50	2.00
1443	A226	$6 brown	2.00	50
1444	A226	$10 lil rose	4.00	20
1445	A226	$20 rose car	5.00	40
1446	A226	$50 green	10.00	1.25
1447	A226	$100 crim rose	22.50	2.25
		Nos. 1441-1447 (7)	50.00	6.85

1965, Apr. 17 Photo. Unwmkd.

1448	A227	$2 multi	1.75	10
1449	A227	$6 sal & multi	4.50	1.00

Chinese Women's Anti-Aggression League, 15th anniversary.

Unisphere and Chinese Pavilion
A228

"100 Birds Paying Homage to Queen Phoenix" and Unisphere
A229

1965, May 8

1450	A228	$2 bl & multi	1.25	10
1451	A229	$10 red, ocher & bis	5.00	75

New York World's Fair, 1964-65.

ITU Emblem, Old and New Communication Equipment—A230

Design: $5, similar to 80c (vert.).

Perf. 13½x13, 13x13½

1965, May 17 Photo. Unwmkd.

1452	A230	80c multi	30	8
1453	A230	$5 multi	1.90	50

Issued to commemorate the centenary of the International Telecommunication Union.

Red Sea Bream
A231

Fish: 80c, White pomfret. $2, Skip-jack (vert.). $4, Moonfish.

1965, July 1 *Perf. 13*

1454	A231	40c multi	25	6
1455	A231	80c multi	50	6
1456	A231	$2 multi	75	8
1457	A231	$4 multi	1.50	30

Issued for Fishermen's Day.

Confucius
A232

ICY Emblem
A233

Portraits: $2.50, Yueh Fei. $3.50, Wen Tien-hsiang. $3.60, Mencius.

Engraved

1965-66 *Perf. 11½* Wmk. 323
Without Gum

1458	A232	$1 dp car	50	6
1459	A232	$2.50 blk brn	50	8
1460	A232	$3.50 dk red	1.00	15
1461	A232	$3.60 dk bl	1.50	20

Issue dates: Nos. 1458, 1461, Sept. 28, 1965. Nos. 1459-1460, Sept. 3, 1966.
The $2.50 and $3.50 have colored background.
See also Nos. 1507-1508.

Photogravure

1965, Oct. 24 *Perf. 13* Unwmkd.

Design: $6, ICY emblem (horiz.).

1462	A233	$2 brn, blk & gold	65	8
1463	A233	$6 brt grn, red & gold	2.50	1.00

International Cooperation Year, 1965.

Street Crossing and Traffic Light
A234

Sun Yat-sen
A235

Engraved

1965, Nov. 1 *Perf. 11½* Wmk. 323
Without Gum

1464	A234	$1 brn vio	80	8
1465	A234	$4 crim rose	1.40	20

Issued to publicize traffic safety.

Photogravure

1965, Nov. 12 *Perf. 13½* Unwmkd.

Designs: $4, Dr. Sun Yat-sen, portrait at right. $5, Sun Yat-sen and flags (horiz.).

1466	A235	$1 multi	50	8
1467	A235	$4 multi	1.00	25
1468	A235	$5 multi	2.50	1.00

A little time given to study of the arrangement of the Scott Catalogue can make it easier to use effectively.

Children with New Year's Firecrackers
A236

Dragon Dance, "Dragon Playing Ball"
A237

1965, Dec. 1 Photo. ***Perf. 13***

1469 A236 $1 multi 1.30 10
1470 A237 $4.50 multi 1.50 75

Lien Po from "Marshal and Prime Minister Reconciled"
A238

Facial Paintings for Chinese Operas: $3, Kuan Yü from "Reunion at Ku City." $4, Gen. Chang Fei from "The Battle of Chang Pan Hill." $6, Buddha from "The Flower-Scattering Angel."

1966, Feb. 15 ***Perf. 11½*** **Unwmkd.**

1471 A238 $1 ol & multi 2.25 30
1472 A238 $3 multi 2.00 25
1473 A238 $4 multi 2.25 30
1474 A238 $6 ver & multi 3.50 2.00

Postal Service Emblem Held by Carrier Pigeon
A239

Stone, Mt. Tai-wu, Quemoy, and Mailman
A240

Designs (postal service emblem and): $3, Postal Museum. $4, Mailman climbing symbolic slope.

1966, Mar. 20 Photo. ***Perf. 12½***

1475 A239 $1 grn & multi 50 8
1476 A240 $2 multi 50 8
1477 A240 $3 multi 75 15
1478 A239 $4 multi 1.50 50

China postal service, 70th anniversary.

Fishing on a Snowy Day, "Five Dynasties" (907–960)
A241

Paintings from Palace Museum: $3.50, Calves on the Plain, Sung artist (960–1126). $4.50, Winter landscape, Sung artist (960–1126). $5, Magpies, by Lin Ch'un, Southern Sung dynasty (1127–1279).

1966, May 20 Photo. ***Perf. 13***

1479 A241 $2.50 blk, brn & red 1.00 8
1480 A241 $3.50 bis brn, blk & gray 75 10
1481 A241 $4.50 blk, buff & sl 75 40
1482 A241 $5 multi 2.25 50

Issued to commemorate the inauguration of Pres. Chiang Kai-shek for a fourth term.

Dragon Boat Race
A242

Lion Dance
A243

Design: $4, Lady Chang O flying to the Moon.

1966 **Unwmkd.**

1483 A242 $2.50 multi 1.75 8
1484 A242 $4 multi 1.25 8
1485 A243 $6 multi 1.00 25

Issued for the Dragon Boat, Mid-Autumn and Lunar New Year Festivals. Issue dates: $2.50, June 23; $4, Sept. 29; $6, Nov. 26.

Flags of China and Argentina
A244

1966, July 9 Photogravure ***Perf. 13***

1486 A244 $10 multi 1.75 25

Issued to commemorate the 150th anniversary of Argentina's Independence.

Lin Sen
A245

Flying Geese
A246

Engraved

1966, Aug. 1 ***Perf. 11½*** **Wmk. 323**

Without Gum

1487 A245 $1 dk brn 60 8

Issued to commemorate the centenary of the birth of Lin Sen (1867–1943), Chairman of the Nationalist Government of China (1931–43).

1966–67 ***Perf. 11½ rough***

Granite Paper; Without Gum

1496 A246 $3.50 brown 30 5
1497 A246 $4 vermilion 40 5
1498 A246 $4.50 brt grn 50 15
1499 A246 $5 rose lil 50 5
1500 A246 $5.50 yel grn ('67) 50 15
1501 A246 $6 brt bl 1.50 40
1502 A246 $6.50 violet 1.00 25
1503 A246 $7 black 85 5
1504 A246 $8 car rose ('67) 1.00 15
Nos. 1496-1504 (9) 6.55 1.30

The $4.50, $5, $6, $7 and $8 were reissued with gum in 1970–71.

Pres. Chiang Kai-shek in Chung San Robe
A247

Design: $5, Chiang Kai-shek in marshal's uniform.

Photogravure

1966, Oct. 31 ***Perf. 13*** **Unwmkd.**

1505 A247 $1 multi 60 10
1506 A247 $5 multi 2.40 50

Issued to commemorate Chiang Kai-shek's inauguration for a fourth term as president, May 20, 1966.

Famous Men Type of 1965–66 with Frame Line

Portraits: No. 1507, Tsai Yuan-pei (1868–1940), educator. No. 1508, Chiu Ching (1875–1907), woman educator and revolutionist.

Engraved

1967 ***Perf. 11½*** **Wmk. 323**

Without Gum

1507 A232 $1 vio bl 60 15
1508 A232 $1 black 60 15

Issue dates: No. 1507, Jan. 11. No. 1508, July 15.
No. 1507 is on granite paper.

Motorized Mailman and Microwave Station
A248

"Transportation" and Radar Weather Station
A249

Photogravure

1967, Mar. 15 ***Perf. 13*** **Unwmkd.**

1511 A248 $1 multi 60 5
1512 A249 $5 multi 1.20 20

Issued to publicize the progress in communication and transportation services.

Pres. Chiang Kai-shek and Chinese Flag
A250

Chu Yuan, 332–295 B.C.
A251

Design: $4, Different frame.

1967, May 20 Lithographed ***Perf. 13***

1513 A250 $1 multi 90 10
1514 A250 $4 multi 1.85 20

First anniversary of President Chiang Kai-shek's 4th-term inauguration.

Engraved

1967, June 12 ***Perf. 11½*** **Wmk. 323**

Portraits: $2, Li Po (705–760). $2.50, Tu Fu (712–770). $3, Po Chu-i (772–846).

Granite Paper; Without Gum

1515 A251 $1 black 50 5
1516 A251 $2 brown 75 8
1517 A251 $2.50 brn blk 90 20
1518 A251 $3 grnsh blk 90 15

Issued for Poets' Day.

Hotei, Wood Carving
A252

World Map
A253

Handicrafts: $2.50, Vase and plate. $3, Dolls. $5, Palace lanterns.

Photogravure

1967, Aug. 12 ***Perf. 11½*** **Unwmkd.**

1519 A252 $1 gray & multi 30 8
1520 A252 $2.50 multi 60 8
1521 A252 $3 multi 85 15
1522 A252 $5 multi 1.40 40

Taiwan handicraft industry.

Engraved

1967, Sept. 25 ***Perf. 11½*** **Wmk. 323**

Granite Paper; Without Gum

1523 A253 $1 vermilion 10 6
1524 A253 $5 blue 50 25

Issued to commemorate the first Conference of the World Anti-Communist League, WACL, Taipei, Sept. 25–29.

Players on Stilts: "The Fisherman and the Woodcutter"
A254

Photogravure

1967, Oct. 10 ***Perf. 13*** **Unwmkd.**

1525 A254 $4.50 multi 50 25

Issued for the 56th National Day.

Maroon Oriole—A255

Formosan Birds: $1, Formosan barbet (vert.). $2.50, Formosan green pigeon. $3, Formosan blue magpie. $5, Crested serpent eagle (vert.). $8, Mikado pheasants.

1967, Nov. 25 Photo. ***Perf. 11***

Granite Paper

1526 A255 $1 multi 20 15
1527 A255 $2 multi 40 15
1528 A255 $2.50 multi 40 20
1529 A255 $3 multi 50 20
1530 A255 $5 multi 1.00 30
1531 A255 $8 multi 1.50 75
Nos. 1526-1531 (6) 4.00 1.75

Chung Hsing Pagoda
A256

Buddha, Changhua
A257

Designs: $2.50, Seashore, Yeh Liu Park. $5, National Palace Museum, Taipei.

Photogravure

1967, Dec. 10 ***Perf. 13*** **Unwmkd.**

1532	A256	$1 multi		25	8
1533	A257	$2.50 multi		75	30
1534	A257	$4 multi		1.00	20
1535	A257	$5 multi		1.75	50

Issued for International Tourist Year 1967.

China Park, Manila, and Flags
A258

1967, Dec. 30 ***Perf. 13½***

1536	A258	$1 multi	35	6
1537	A258	$5 multi	1.10	25

Sino-Philippine Friendship Year 1966–67.

Sun Yat-sen Building, Yangmingshan
A259 A259a

Perf. 13x12½

1968–75 Lithographed Wmk. 323

Granite Paper

1538	A259	5c lt brn	10	5
1539	A259	10c grnsh blk	10	5
1540	A259	50c brt rose lil	10	5
1541	A259	$1 vermilion	20	5
1542	A259	$1.50 emerald	30	10
1543	A259	$2 plum	30	5
1544	A259	$2.50 blue	30	5
1545	A259	$3 grnsh bl	60	10
		Nos. 1538-1545 (8)	2.00	50

Coil Stamps

Perf. 13 Horiz.

Photo. Unwmkd.

1546	A259a	$1 car rose ('70)	25	15
1547	A259a	$1 ver ('75)	20	10

Issue dates: 50c, $1, $2.50, Jan. 23, 1968; No. 1546, Mar. 20, 1970; No. 1547, Jan. 28, 1975; others July 11, 1968.

Inscription on No. 1546 is in color with white background. On No. 1547 it is white with colored background.

Harvesting Sugar Cane
A260

Jade Cabbage, 1662–1911
A261

Photogravure

1968, Mar. 1 ***Perf. 13*** **Unwmkd.**

1548	A260	$1 ol & multi	40	10
1549	A260	$4 multi	60	30

1968, Mar. 29 ***Perf. 13*** **Unwmkd.**

Ancient Art Treasures: $1.50, Jade battle axe. $2, Porcelain flower bowl, 960–1126 A.D. (horiz.). $2.50, Cloisonné enamel vase, 1723–1736 A.D. $4, Agate flower holder in shape of finger citrus, 1662–1911 A.D. (horiz.). $5, Sacrificial kettle, 1111–771 B.C.

1550	A261	$1 rose & multi	25	8
1551	A261	$1.50 bl & multi	50	25
1552	A261	$2 bl & multi	60	10
1553	A261	$2.50 dl rose & multi	60	25
1554	A261	$4 pink & multi	65	30
1555	A261	$5 bl & multi	1.00	40
		Nos. 1550-1555 (6)	3.60	1.38

View of City in Cathay (1)—A262

Views: No. 1557, City and wall of Forbidden City (2). No. 1558, Wall at right, bridge at left (3). No. 1559, Queen's ship landing at left (4). No. 1560, Palace (5). $5, City wall and gate. $8, Suburb around Great Bridge. Design from scroll "A City in Cathay," painted 1736.

1968, June 18 Photo. ***Perf. 13½***

Size: 50x29mm.

1556	A262	$1 multi	25	9
1557	A262	$1 multi	25	9
1558	A262	$1 multi	25	9
1559	A262	$1 multi	25	9
1560	A262	$1 multi	25	9

Size: 60x31mm. ***Perf. 13x13½***

1561	A262	$5 multi	1.50	80
1562	A262	$8 multi	2.25	90
		Nos. 1556-1562 (7)	5.00	2.15

Nos. 1556–1560 printed se-tenant in sheet of 50 with horizontal strips of five containing one of each.

See also Nos. 1610–1614.

Entrance Gate, Taroko Gorge
A263

Design: $8, Sun Yat-sen Building, Yangmingshan.

1968, Feb. 12 Photo. ***Perf. 13***

1563	A263	$5 multi	1.00	25
1564	A263	$8 multi	1.00	25

The 17th Annual Conference of the Pacific Area Travel Association.

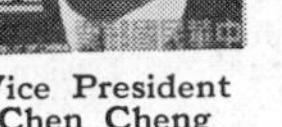

Vice President Chen Cheng
A264

Flying Geese
A265

1968, Mar. 5

1565	A264	$1 brn & multi	50	10

Issued in memory of Vice President Chen Cheng (1898–1965).

Lithographed

1968, Mar. 20 ***Perf. 12*** **Wmk. 323**

Granite Paper

1566	A265	$1 vermilion	30	12

Souvenir Sheet

Imperf.

1567	A265	$3 green	60	60

Issued to commemorate the 90th anniversary of Chinese postage stamps. No. 1567 contains one stamp with simulated perforations, yellow decorative margin with red inscription. Size: 75x100mm.

WHO Emblem and "20"
A266

Symbolic Water Cycle
A267

1968, Apr. 7 Engraved ***Perf. 12***

Granite Paper

1568	A266	$1 green	30	5
1569	A266	$5 scarlet	75	30

Issued to commemorate the 20th anniversary of the World Health Organization.

Lithographed

1968, June 6 ***Perf. 11½*** **Wmk. 323**

Granite Paper

1570	A267	$1 grn & org	35	8
1571	A267	$4 brt bl & org	75	8

Hydrological Decade (UNESCO) 1965–74.

Broadcasting to Mainland China
A268

Dual Carriers for F.M. Broadcasting
A269

Lithographed

1968, Aug. 1 ***Perf. 12*** **Wmk. 323**

Granite Paper

1572	A268	$1 bl, vio bl & gray	35	8
1573	A269	$4 lt ultra & ver	75	15

Issued to commemorate the 40th anniversary of the Broadcasting Corporation of China, and the inauguration of frequency modulation broadcasting.

Human Rights Flame
A270

Crop Improvement and Extension Work
A271

1968, Sept. 3 **Granite Paper**

1574	A270	$1 multi	30	15
1575	A270	$5 multi	60	15

International Human Rights Year 1968.

Lithographed

1968, Sept. 30 ***Perf. 12*** **Wmk. 323**

Granite Paper

1576	A271	$1 yel, bis & dk brn	25	5
1577	A271	$5 yel, emer & dk grn	75	50

Joint Commission on Rural Reconstruction, 20th anniversary.

Javelin
A272

Designs: $2.50, Weight lifting. $5, Pole vault (horiz.). $8, Woman hurdling (horiz.).

Photogravure

1968, Oct. 12 ***Perf. 13*** **Unwmkd.**

1578	A272	$1 multi	25	5
1579	A272	$2.50 multi	35	15
1580	A272	$5 multi	60	10
1581	A272	$8 pink & multi	85	30

Issued to commemorate the 19th Olympic Games, Mexico City, Oct. 12–27.

Pres. Chiang Kai-shek and Whampoa Military Academy
A273

Designs: $2, Pres. Chiang Kai-shek reviewing forces of the Northern Expedition. $2.50, Suppression of bandits, reconstruction work and New Life Movement emblem. $3.50, Marco Polo Bridge near Peking and victory parade, Nanking. $4, Original copy of Constitution of Republic of China. $5, Nationalist Chinese flag flying over mainland China.

1968, Oct. 31 ***Perf. 11½x12***

1582	A273	$1 multi	35	8
1583	A273	$2 multi	50	20
1584	A273	$2.50 multi	50	20
1585	A273	$3.50 multi	60	20
1586	A273	$4 multi	75	40
1587	A273	$5 multi	1.00	40
		Nos. 1582-1587 (6)	3.70	1.48

Chiang Kai-shek's achievements for China.

Cock
A274

1968, Nov. 12 Litho. *Perf. 12*

Granite Paper

1588	A274	$1 pink & multi	4.50	15
1589	A274	$4.50 lil & multi	4.50	2.25

Issued for use on New Year's greetings.

Flag
A275

1968, Dec. 25 *Perf. 12½* Wmk. 323

Granite Paper

1590	A275	$1 multi	35	6
1591	A275	$5 lt bl & multi	75	20

Constitution of the Republic of China, 20th anniversary.

Jade Belt Buckle, 1662–1911
A276

Ancient Art Treasures: $1.50, Yellow jade vase, 960–1126 A.D. (vert.). $2, Cloisonné enamel square teapot, 1662–1911 A.D. $2.50, Kuei, sacrificial bronze vessel, 722–481 B.C. $4, Heavenly ball vase, 1368–1661 A.D. (vert.). $5, Gourd-shaped vase, 1662–1911 A.D. (vert.).

Photogravure

1969, Jan. 15 *Perf. 13* Unwmkd.

1592	A276	$1 dl rose & multi	25	5
1593	A276	$1.50 rose & multi	30	15
1594	A276	$2 brt rose & multi	30	10
1595	A276	$2.50 lt bl & multi	50	20
1596	A276	$4 tan & multi	65	20
1597	A276	$5 pale bl & multi	90	40
		Nos. 1592-1597 (6)	2.90	1.10

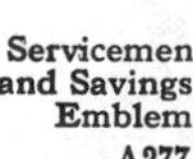

Servicemen and Savings Emblem
A277

Engraved

1969, Feb. 1 *Perf. 12* Wmk. 323

Granite Paper

1598	A277	$1 dl red brn	30	8
1599	A277	$4 dp bl	85	15

Issued to commemorate the 10th anniversary of the Military Savings Program.

Ti (Flute)
A278

Musical Instruments: $2.50, Sheng (13 bamboo pipes connected at the base). $4, P'i p'a (lute). $5, Cheng (zither).

Photogravure

1969, Mar. 16 *Perf. 13* Unwmkd.

1600	A278	$1 buff & multi	20	5
1601	A278	$2.50 lt ap grn & multi	35	10
1602	A278	$4 pink & multi	75	40
1603	A278	$5 lt grnsh bl & multi	75	25

Sun Yat-sen Building and Kuomintang Emblem—A279

Double Carp Design
A280

1969, Mar. 29 Litho. *Perf. 13½*

1604	A279	$1 multi	25	5

Issued to commemorate the 10th National Congress of the Chinese Nationalist Party (Kuomintang), Mar. 29. A $2.50 stamp portraying Sun Yat-sen and Chiang Kai-shek was prepared but not issued.

Perf. 13½x12½

1969–74 Engr. Wmk. 323

Granite Paper

1606	A280	$10 dk bl ('74)	1.00	20
a.		Perf. 11½	1.75	15
1607	A280	$20 dk brn ('74)	2.00	20
a.		Perf. 11½	2.50	20
1608	A280	$50 grn ('74)	5.00	75
a.		Perf. 11½	6.50	75
1609	A280	$100 brt red ('74)	8.00	2.00
a.		Perf. 11½	10.00	2.50

The 1969 issue is 27mm. high; 1974, 28mm. See No. 1980.

Bridal Procession—A281

Designs: No. 1610, Musicians and standard bearer from bridal procession. $2.50, Emigrant farm family in oxcart. $5, Art gallery. $8, Roadside food stands. Designs from scroll "A City in Cathay," painted in 1736. Nos. 1610–1611 printed se-tenant in sheets of 30 (6x5).

Photogravure

1969, May 20 *Perf. 13½* Unwmkd.

1610	A281	$1 multi	25	10
1611	A281	$1 multi	25	10
1612	A281	$2.50 multi	65	40
1613	A281	$5 multi	75	50
1614	A281	$8 multi	1.25	80
		Nos. 1610-1614 (5)	3.15	1.90

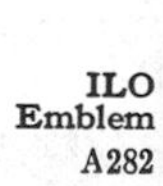

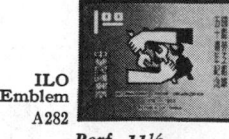

ILO Emblem
A282

Perf. 11½

1969, June 15 Engr. Wmk. 323

Granite Paper

1615	A282	$1 dk bl	25	5
1616	A282	$8 dk car	85	30

International Labor Organization, 50th anniversary.

Family at Dinner Table and Dressing
A283

Pupils in Laboratory and Playing
A284

Designs: $2.50, Housecleaning and obeying traffic rules. $4, Recreation (music, fishing, basketball) and education.

Perf. 11½

1969, July 15 Engr. Wmk. 323

1617	A283	$1 brick red	20	5
1618	A283	$2.50 blue	75	25
1619	A283	$4 green	75	20

Model Citizen's Life Movement.

1969, Sept. 1 *Perf. 11½* Wmk. 323

Design: $1, $5, Pupils with book and various school activities (horiz.).

Granite Paper

1620	A284	$1 brt red	20	8
1621	A284	$2.50 brt grn	35	10
1622	A284	$4 dk bl	50	15
1623	A284	$5 brown	65	25

Issued to commemorate the first anniversary of the free 9-year education system.

Wild Flowers and Pheasants, by Lu Chih (Ming)
A285

Paintings: $2.50, Bamboo and birds, Sung dynasty. $5, Flowers and Birds, Sung dynasty. $8, Cranes and Flowers, by G. Castiglione, S.J. (1688–1766).

1969, Oct. 9 Photo. *Perf. 13½*

1624	A285	$1 multi	20	8
1625	A285	$2.50 multi	40	15
1626	A285	$5 multi	80	25
1627	A285	$8 multi	1.25	40

Golden Scepter Rose
A286

Rocket and Radar Station
A287

Roses: $1, "Charles Mollerin," called black rose. $5, Peace. $8, Josephine Bruce.

1969, Oct. 31 Litho. *Perf. 14*

1628	A286	$1 lt vio & multi	30	10
1629	A286	$2.50 lt bl & multi	50	20
1630	A286	$5 dl org & multi	85	50
1631	A286	$8 ap grn & multi	1.00	40

Engraved

1969, Nov. 21 *Perf. 11½* Wmk. 323

1632	A287	$1 rose cl	25	10

The 30th Air Defense Day.

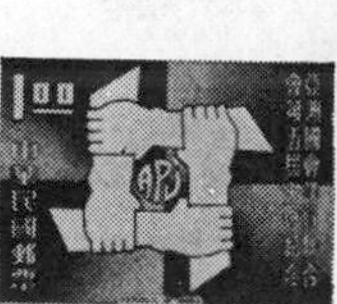

Symbol of International Cooperation
A288

Pekingese
A289

1969, Nov. 25

1633	A288	$1 rose cl	35	8
1634	A288	$5 green	70	20

Issued to commemorate the 5th General Assembly of the Asian Parliamentary Union, Taipei, Nov. 24–28.

1969, Dec. 1 Lithographed *Perf. 12*

Granite Paper

1635	A289	50c red & multi	40	8
1636	A289	$4.50 grn & multi	2.50	60

Issued for use on New Year's greetings.

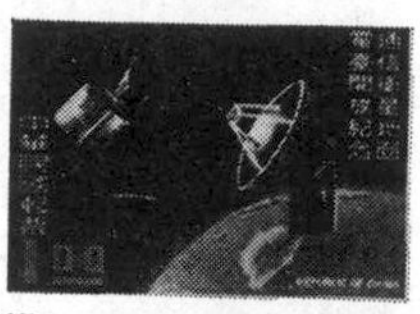

Satellite, Earth Station and Map of Taiwan
A290

Photogravure

1969, Dec. 28 *Perf. 13* Unwmkd.

1637	A290	$1 brn & multi	25	10
1638	A290	$5 vio bl & multi	70	30
1639	A290	$8 pur & multi	1.15	50

Issued to commemorate the inauguration of the Communication Satellite Earth Station at Chin-Shan-Li, Dec. 28.

Agate Grinding Stone, 1662–1911
A291

Ancient Art Treasures: $1, Carved lacquer ware vase, 1662–1911 (vert.). $2, White jade Chin-li-chih melons, 1662–1911. $2.50, Black jade shepherd and ram, 206 B.C.–220 A.D. $4, Chien-lung twin porcelain vase, 1736–1796 (vert.). $5, Ju porcelain vase with 3 bulls, 960–1126 (vert.).

1970, Jan. 23

1640	A291	$1 lt grnsh bl & multi	18	8
1641	A291	$1.50 pale bl & multi	30	15
1642	A291	$2 grn & multi	30	15
1643	A291	$2.50 pink & multi	40	15
1644	A291	$4 ol bis & multi	70	15
1645	A291	$5 ultra & multi	90	30
		Nos. 1640-1645 (6)	2.78	98

Hsuan Chuang
A292

Chu Hsi
A293

Design: $2.50, Hua To.

Engraved

1970, Feb. 20 *Perf. 11½* Wmk. 323

Granite Paper

1646	A292	$1 car rose	30	10
1647	A293	$2.50 bl grn	50	15
1648	A293	$4 blue	60	20

Issued in memory of Hsuan Chuang (602–664), who propagated Buddhism in China; Chu Hsi (1130–1200), who developed Neo-Confucianism, and Hua To (3rd century A.D.) physician and surgeon.

EXPO '70 Pavilion, Emblem and Flags of Participants
A294

Design: $5, Chinese pavilion, EXPO '70 emblem, exhibition and Chinese flags.

Photogravure

1970, Mar. 13 *Perf. 13* Unwmkd.

1649	A294	$5 org red & multi	60	25
1650	A294	$8 lt bl & multi	85	40

EXPO '70 International Exhibition, Osaka, Japan, Mar. 15-Sept. 13.

Nimbus III and WMO Emblem
A295

Design: $1, Agricultural meteorological station and tropical landscape (vert.).

Perf. 14x13½, 13½x14

1970, Mar. 23 Litho. Wmk. 323

Granite Paper

1651	A295	$1 grn & multi	30	8
1652	A295	$8 bl & multi	90	40

10th Annual World Meteorological Day.

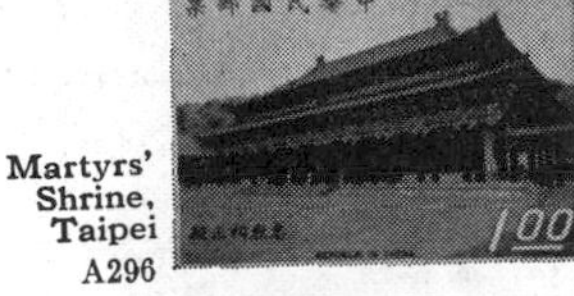

Martyrs' Shrine, Taipei
A296

Shrine's Gate
A297

Photogravure

1970, Mar. 29 *Perf. 13* Unwmkd.

1653	A296	$1 multi	30	8
1654	A297	$8 multi	90	40

Issued to commemorate the completion of the Martyrs' Shrine in Northern Taipei, dedicated to the memory of 72 young revolutionaries who died March 29, 1911.

Yueh Fei Fighting for Lost Territories
A298

Characters from Chinese Operas: $2.50, Emperor Shun and stepmother. $5, The Lady Warrior Chin Liang-yu. $8, Kuan Yu and groom.

1970, May 4 *Perf. 13½* Unwmkd.

1655	A298	$1 multi	30	10
1656	A298	$2.50 multi	50	25
1657	A298	$5 multi	75	30
1658	A298	$8 multi	1.25	50

"One Hundred Horses" (Detail) by Lang Shih-ning—A299

Three Horses Playing—A300

Designs (Horses): No. 1660, Trees in left background. No. 1661, Tree trunk in lower left corner. No. 1662, Group of trees at right. No. 1663, Barren tree at right. $8, Groom roping horses. Designs from scroll "One Hundred Horses" by Lang Shih-ning (Giuseppe Castiglione, 1688-1766). Nos. 1659-1663 printed se-tenant in sheets of 50 (5x10).

Photogravure

1970, June 18 *Perf. 13½* Unwmkd.

1659	A299	$1 multi	20	8
1660	A299	$1 multi	20	8
1661	A299	$1 multi	20	8
1662	A299	$1 multi	20	8
1663	A299	$1 multi	20	8
1664	A300	$5 bis & multi	85	60
1665	A300	$8 dl yel & multi	1.25	75
		Nos. 1659-1665 (7)	3.10	1.75

Lai-tsu Amusing his Old Parents
A301

Chinese Fairy Tales: No. 1667, Man disguised as deer, and hunters. No. 1668, Boy cooling his father's bed. No. 1669, Boy fishing through ice. No. 1670, Son reunited with old mother. No. 1671, Emperor tasting mother's medicine. No. 1672, Boy saving oranges for mother. No. 1673, Boy saving father from tiger.

Lithographed

1970, July 10 *Perf. 13½* Wmk. 323

Granite Paper

1666	A301	10c red & multi	5	5
1667	A301	10c car rose & multi	5	5
1668	A301	10c lt vio & multi	5	5
1669	A301	10c gray & multi	5	5
1670	A301	10c emer & multi	5	5
1671	A301	50c bis & multi	10	5
1672	A301	$1 sky bl & multi	20	5
1673	A301	$1 dp bl & multi	20	5
		Nos. 1666-1673 (8)	75	40

See also Nos. 1726-1733.

Man's First Step onto Moon
A302

Designs: $1, Pres. Chiang Kai-shek's message brought to the moon. $5, Neil A. Armstrong, Michael Collins, Edwin E. Aldrin, Jr., and moon (horiz.).

Perf. 13½x13, 13x13½

1970, July 21 Photo. Unwmkd.

1674	A302	$1 yel & multi	35	10
1675	A302	$5 lt yel grn & multi	65	25
1676	A302	$8 bl & multi	1.00	50

Issued to commemorate the first anniversary of man's first landing on the moon.

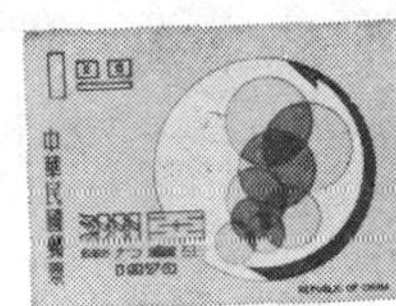

Asian Productivity Year Symbol
A303

Lithographed

1970, Aug. 18 *Perf. 13½* Wmk. 323

Granite Paper

1677	A303	$1 emer & multi	30	5
1678	A303	$5 bl & multi	65	20

Issued to publicize Asian Productivity Year.

Flags of China and U.N.
A304

1970, Sept. 19 *Perf. 12* Wmk. 323

Granite Paper

1679	A304	$5 bl, car & blk	75	25

Issued to commemorate the 25th anniversary of the United Nations.

Postal Zone Map of Taiwan—A305 **Postal Code Emblem—A306**

1970, Oct. 8 Lithographed

1680	A305	$1 lt bl & multi	25	8
1681	A306	$2.50 grn & multi	60	25

Issued to publicize the postal code system.

Eleventh Month Scroll
A307

Designs: A scroll series, "Activities of the 12 Months," painted on silk by a group of painters of the Ch'ien Lung court (1736-1796). Chinese number in parenthesis at right of denomination tells month.

Perf. 13½x13

1970-71 Photo. Unwmkd.

Jan., Feb., Mar. Scrolls

(一) (二) (三)

1682	A307	$1 multi	1.00	20
1683	A307	$2.50 multi	1.50	30
1684	A307	$5 multi	2.50	50

Apr., May, June Scrolls

(四) (五) (六)

1685	A307	$1 multi	20	8
1686	A307	$2.50 multi	50	20
1687	A307	$5 multi	70	40

July, Aug., Sept. Scrolls

(七) (八) (九)

1688	A307	$1 multi	20	8
1689	A307	$2.50 multi	50	20
1690	A307	$5 multi	70	30

Oct., Nov., Dec. Scrolls

(十) (一十) (二十)

1691	A307	$1 multi	20	8
1692	A307	$2.50 multi	50	20
1693	A307	$5 multi	70	30
		Nos. 1682-1693 (12)	9.20	2.84

Issue dates: Nos. 1691-1693, Oct. 21, 1970. Nos. 1682-1684, Jan. 14, 1971. Nos. 1685-1687, Apr. 26, 1971. Nos. 1688-1690, Aug. 27, 1971.

Family at Home
A308

Piggy Bank
A309

Design: $4, Family of 5 going on an excursion (vert.).

Perf. 13½x14, 14x13½

1970, Nov. 11 Litho. Wmk. 323

Granite Paper

1694	A308	$1 multi	20	8
1695	A308	$4 yel grn & multi	60	20

Issued to publicize family planning.

1970, Dec. 1 *Perf. 12½x12*

Granite Paper

1696	A309	50c multi	35	8
1697	A309	$4.50 bl & multi	1.50	40

Issued for use on New Year's greetings.

Tibia Fusus Shells
A310

Rare Taiwan Shells: $2.50, Harpeola kurodai. $5, Conus stupa kuroda. $8, Entemnotrochus rumphii.

1971, Feb. 25 *Perf. 13x13½*

1698	A310	$1 vio & multi	20	8
1699	A310	$2.50 multi	25	20
1700	A310	$5 org & multi	60	40
1701	A310	$8 grn & multi	1.00	25

Sun Yat-sen Building, Yangmingshan
A311

Passbook and Postal Savings Certificate
A312

Perf. 13½x12½

1971 **Lithographed** **Wmk. 323**

Granite Paper

1702	A311	5c brown	8	5
1703	A311	10c dk gray	8	5
1704	A311	50c brt rose lil	10	5
1705	A311	$1 vermilion	10	5
1706	A311	$1.50 ultra	25	5
1707	A311	$2 plum	25	5
1708	A311	$2.50 emerald	50	5
1709	A311	$3 aqua	50	5
		Nos. 1702-1709 (8)	1.86	40

Perf. 13½x14

1971, Mar. 20 **Litho.** **Wmk. 323**

Design: $4, People and hand dropping coin into bank.

1712	A312	$1 yel grn & multi	15	8
1713	A312	$4 ver & multi	60	20

Publicizing Chinese Postal Savings Service.

Cooperation Emblem, Farmers
A313

Rock Monkey
A314

Design: $8, Chinese teaching rice farming to Africans (horiz.).

Photogravure

1971, May 20 *Perf. 13* **Unwmkd.**

1714	A313	$1 multi	20	8
1715	A313	$8 multi	90	40

Sino-African Technical Cooperation Committee, 10th anniversary.

1971, June 25 *Perf. 11½*

Taiwan Animals: $2, White-face flying squirrel. $3, Chinese pangolin. $5, Formosan sika deer. ($2, $3, $5 are horiz.).

1716	A314	$1 gold & multi	25	15
1717	A314	$2 gold & multi	25	20
1718	A314	$3 gold & multi	50	20
1719	A314	$5 gold & multi	50	40

Pitcher
A315

Designs: $2.50, Players at base (horiz.). $4, Hitter and catcher.

1971, July 29 **Photo.** *Perf. 13*

1720	A315	$1 multi	25	8
1721	A315	$2.50 multi	35	20
1722	A315	$4 multi	60	20

Pacific Regional competition for the 1971 Little League World Series.

中華少年棒球世界冠軍紀念

Nos. 1541, 1544-1545 Overprinted in Magenta or Red

Perf. 13x12½

1971, Sept. 9 **Litho.** **Wmk. 323**

Granite Paper

1723	A259	$1 ver (M)	20	8
1724	A259	$2.50 bl (R)	50	25
1725	A259	$3 grnsh bl (R)	40	30

Chinese victory in 1971 Little League World Series, Williamsport, Pa., Aug. 24.

Fairy Tale Type of 1970

Chinese Fairy Tales (Filial Piety): No. 1726, Birds and elephant helping in rice field. No. 1727, Son gathering mulberries for mother. No. 1728, Son gathering firewood. No. 1729, Son, mother and bandits. No. 1730, Son carrying heavy burden. 50c, Son digging for bamboo shoots in winter. No. 1732, Man and wife working as slaves. No. 1733, Father, son and carriage.

1971, Sept. 22 *Perf. 13½*

Granite Paper

1726	A301	10c dp org & multi	8	5
1727	A301	10c lil & multi	8	5
1728	A301	10c ocher & multi	8	5
1729	A301	10c dp car & multi	8	5
1730	A301	10c lt ultra & multi	8	5
1731	A301	50c multi	10	5
1732	A301	$1 emer & multi	20	5
1733	A301	$1 lt red brn & multi	20	5
		Nos. 1726-1733 (8)	90	40

Flag of China, "Double Ten" and Anniversary Emblems
A316

Designs (Flag of China and): $2.50, National anthem. $5, Gen. Chiang Kai-shek. $8, Sun Yat-sen.

1971, Oct. 10 **Photo.** *Perf. 13*

1734	A316	$1 org & multi	20	8
1735	A316	$2.50 multi	30	15
1736	A316	$5 grn & multi	60	40
1737	A316	$8 ol & multi	75	40

60th National Day.

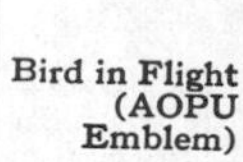

Bird in Flight (AOPU Emblem)
A317

Perf. 13½x14

1971, Nov. 8 **Litho.** **Wmk. 323**

1738	A317	$2.50 yel & multi	70	20
1739	A317	$5 org & multi	70	20

Asian-Oceanic Postal Union Executive Committee Session, Taipei, Nov. 8-15.

"White Frost Hawk," by Lang Shih-ning
A318

Dog Series I

Designs: $2, "Star-Glancing Wolf." $2.50, "Golden-Winged Face." $5, "Young Black Dragon." $8, "Young Gray Dragon."

Designs from painting series "Ten Prized Dogs," by Lang Shih-ning (Giuseppe Castiglione, 1688-1766).

Perf. 13½x13

1971, Nov. 16 **Litho.** **Unwmkd.**

Multicolored

1740	A318	$1 *Facing left*	25	8
1741	A318	$2 *Lying down*	30	10
1742	A318	$2.50 *Scratching*	35	20
1743	A318	$5 *Facing right*	70	30
1744	A318	$8 *Looking back*	1.20	60
		Nos. 1740-1744 (5)	2.80	1.28

Dog Series II

Designs: $1, "Black with Snow-white Paws." $2, "Yellow Leopard." $2.50, "Flying Magpie." $5, "Heavenly Lion." $8, "Mottled Tiger."

1972, Jan. 12

1745	A318	$1 *Facing right*	25	10
1746	A318	$2 *Walking*	30	10
1747	A318	$2.50 *Sleeping*	35	20
1748	A318	$5 *Facing left*	70	30
1749	A318	$8 *Sitting*	1.50	50
		Nos. 1745-1749 (5)	3.10	1.20

Squirrels—A319

Perf. 13½x12½

1971, Dec. 1 **Wmk. 323**

1750	A319	Block of 4, multi	60	40
a.		50c in UL corner	10	5
b.		50c in UR corner	10	5
c.		50c in LL corner	10	5
d.		50c in LR corner	10	5
1751	A319	Block of 4, multi	3.25	2.25
a.		$4.50 in UL corner	60	30
b.		$4.50 in UR corner	60	30
c.		$4.50 in LL corner	60	30
d.		$4.50 in LR corner	60	30

New Year 1972.

Flags of China and Jordan
A320

1971, Dec. 16 *Perf. 13½*

Granite Paper

1752	A320	$5 multi	70	20

50th anniversary of the founding of the Hashemite Kingdom of Jordan.

Cargo Ship "Hai King"
A321

Design: $7, Ocean liner and map of Pacific Ocean (vert.).

1971, Dec. 16 *Perf. 12½*

1753	A321	$4 grn, dk bl & red	45	20
1754	A321	$7 ocher & multi	70	20

Centenary of China Merchants Steam Navigation Co.

Downhill Skiing, Olympic Rings
A322

Designs: $5, Cross-country skiing. $8, Giant slalom.

1972, Feb. 3 *Perf. 13½*

1755	A322	$1 org, blk & bl	20	8
1756	A322	$5 yel grn, dp org & blk	60	20
1757	A322	$8 red, gray & blk	70	20

11th Winter Olympic Games, Sapporo, Japan, Feb. 3-13.

Vase, 18th Century
A323

Porcelain Series I

Porcelain Masterworks of Ching Dynasty: $2, Covered jar. $2.50, Pitcher. $5, Vase with 5 openings and dragon design. $8, Covered jar with children design.

Perf. 11½

1972, Mar. 20 **Photo.** **Unwmkd.**

1758	A323	$1 vio & multi	30	8
1759	A323	$2 plum & bl	30	15
1760	A323	$2.50 org ver & bl	30	15
1761	A323	$5 bis brn & bl	60	25
1762	A323	$8 sl grn & multi	90	40
		Nos. 1758-1762 (5)	2.40	1.03

See also Nos. 1812-1821, 1864-1868.

Nine Flying Doves
A324

Perf. 13½x14

1972, Apr. 1 Litho. Wmk. 323

1763	A324	$1	lt bl & blk	20	8
1764	A324	$5	lt vio & blk	60	20

Asian-Oceanic Postal Union, 10th anniversary.

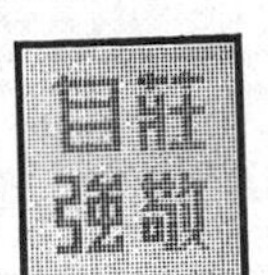

"Dignity with Self-reliance"
A325

Perf. 13½x12½

1972–75 Litho. Wmk. 323

1765	A325	5c	brn & yel	5	5
1766	A325	10c	bl & org	5	5
1767	A325	20c	cl & yel grn ('75)	5	5
1768	A325	50c	lil & lil rose	5	5
1769	A325	$1	red & brt bl	10	5
1770	A325	$1.50	yel & dk bl	20	5
1771	A325	$2	mar & org	20	6
1772	A325	$2.50	emer & ver	20	7
1773	A325	$3	red & lt grn	25	8
			Nos. 1765-1773 (9)	1.15	51

Souvenir Sheet

Imperf.

1775	A325		Sheet of 2	1.00	1.00

No. 1775 commemorates ROCPEX '72 Philatelic Exhibition, Taipei, Oct. 24–Nov. 2. It contains 2 stamps similar to Nos. 1771 and 1773 with simulated perforations. Orange brown margin with white inscriptions. Size: 69x100mm.

Issue dates: $1, $1.50, $2, $3, May 20, 1972; 5c, 10c, 50c, $2.50, No. 1775, Oct. 24, 1972; 20c, 1975.

Emperor Shih-tsung's Procession
A326

Messengers on Horseback—A327

Designs from scrolls depicting Emperor Shih-tsung's (reigned 1522–1566) journey to and from tombs at Cheng-tien. No. 1776 shows land journey and is designed from right to left. No. 1779 shows return trip by boat and is designed from left to right. The five stamps of Nos. 1776 and 1780 are numbered 1 to 5 in Chinese (see illustrations with Nos. 1682–1686 for numerals).

1972 Photo. *Perf. 13½* Unwmkd.

Multicolored

1776	A326		Strip of 5, *Departure*	70	35
a.		$1	*shown* (1)	10	5
b.		$1	*Seven carriages* (2)	10	5
c.		$1	*Carriage drawn by 23 horses* (3)	10	5
d.		$1	*Procession* (4)	10	5
e.		$1	*Emperor under 2 canopies* (5)	10	5
1777	A327	$2.50	*shown*	40	8
1778	A327	$5	*Guards with flags, fans & spears*	60	20
1779	A327	$8	*Sedan chair carried by 28 men*	1.00	40
1780	A326		Strip of 5, *Return trip*	70	35
a.		$1	*Three barges* (1)	10	5
b.		$1	*Procession, sedan chairs* (2)	10	5
c.		$1	*Two barges with trunks* (3)	10	5
d.		$1	*Procession on land* (4)	10	5
e.		$1	*Procession, 2 sedan chairs* (5)	10	5
1781	A327	$2.50	*Courtiers at city welcoming Emperor*	40	8
1782	A327	$5	*Orchestra on horseback*	60	20
1783	A327	$8	*Barges*	90	40
			Nos. 1776-1783 (8)	5.30	2.06

Issue dates: No. 1776–1779, June 14; Nos. 1780–1783, July 12.

First Day Covers
A328

Magnifying Glass, Tongs, Gauge
A329

Design: $2.50, Sun Yat-sen stamp of 1971 (type A311) under magnifying glass.

Wmk. 323

1972, Aug. 9 Engr. *Perf. 12*

1784	A328	$1	dk vio bl	20	5
1785	A328	$2.50	brt brn	25	8
1786	A329	$8	scarlet	75	20

Promotion of philately. Printed in sheets of 40. Each sheet contains 4 blocks of 10 stamps surrounded by margins with inscriptions.

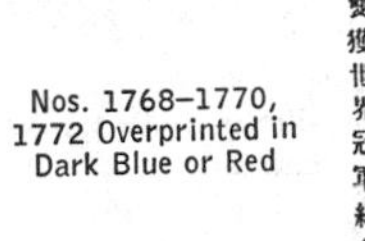

Nos. 1768–1770, 1772 Overprinted in Dark Blue or Red

Perf. 13½x12½

1972, Sept. 9 Litho. Wmk. 323

1787	A325	$1	red & brt bl (DB)	20	8
1788	A325	$1.50	yel & dk bl (R)	40	20
1789	A325	$2	mar & org (R)	40	8
1790	A325	$3	red & lt grn (DB)	40	15

China's championship victories in the Little League World Series, Gary, Ind., and in the Senior League World Series, Williamsport, Pa., Aug. 1972.

Emperor Yao (2357–2258 B.C.)
A330

Mountain Climbing
A331

Rulers: $4, Emperor Shun (ruled 2255–2208 B.C.). $4.50, Yü, the Great (ruled 2205–2198 B.C.). $5, King T'ang (ruled 1783–1754 B.C.). $5.50, King Wen (ruled 1171–1122 B.C.). $6, King Wu (ruled 1121–1114 B.C.). $7, Chou Kung (died 1105 B.C.). $8, Confucius (551–479 B.C.).

1972–73 Engraved *Perf. 12*

Granite Paper

1791	A330	$3.50	dk bl	25	20
1792	A330	$4	rose red	25	20
1793	A330	$4.50	bluish lil	30	20
1794	A330	$5	brt grn	35	20
1795	A330	$5.50	dp org ('73)	50	20
1796	A330	$6	dp cl ('73)	50	25
a.			Perf. 13½x12½ ('76)	50	25
1797	A330	$7	sep ('73)	50	25
a.			Perf. 13½x12½ ('76)	50	25
1798	A330	$8	ind ('73)	75	30
a.			gray, perf. 13½x12½ ('76)	75	30
			Nos. 1791-1798 (8)	3.40	1.80

In the first printing, Nos. 1791-1794, 1796-1798 measure 32mm. high. In a 1974 reissue they are 33mm.

Photogravure

1972, Oct. 31 *Perf. 12* Unwmkd.

Designs (China Youth Corps emblem and): $2.50, Skiing (skiers forming circle). $4, Diving. $8, Parachute jumping.

1800	A331	$1	grn & multi	15	8
1801	A331	$2.50	bl & multi	30	8
1802	A331	$4	org & multi	40	20
1803	A331	$8	multi	90	40

China Youth Corps, 20th anniversary.

JCI Emblem
A332

1972, Nov. 12 Litho. Wmk. 323

1804	A332	$1	multi	20	8
1805	A332	$5	org & multi	50	15
1806	A332	$8	multi	75	40

27th Junior Chamber International (JCI) World Congress, Taipei, Nov. 12–19.

Electronic Mail Sorter
A333

Plane, Ship and Pier
A334

Design: $5, Highway overpass over railroad.

Engraved

1972, Nov. 12 *Perf. 11½* Wmk. 323

1807	A333	$1	red	20	8
1808	A334	$2.50	blue	35	15
1809	A334	$5	dk vio & brn	75	30

Progress of communications system on Taiwan.

Cow and Calf (Parental Love)
A335

1972, Dec. 1 Litho. *Perf. 12*

1810	A335	50c	red & blk	30	8
1811	A335	$4.50	yel, red & brn	80	30

New Year 1973. Printed in sheets of 80, divided into 4 panes of 20, separated by vertical and horizontal gutters 2 rows wide. 20 red chops meaning "Happy New Year" are printed in the gutters.

Porcelain Type of 1972 and

Stem Bowl with Dragons
A336

Porcelain Series II

1973 Photogravure *Perf. 11½*

Porcelain Masterworks of Ming Dynasty: $1, Covered vase with fruits and flowers. $2, Vase with ornamental and floral design. $2.50, Vase imitating ancient bronze. $5, Flask with flowers of 4 seasons. $8, Garlic head vase.

1812	A323	$1	gray & multi	15	5
1813	A323	$2	lt brn & multi	20	8
1814	A323	$2.50	brt grn & multi	30	10
1815	A323	$5	ultra & multi	50	25
1816	A323	$8	ol & multi	75	40
			Nos. 1812-1816 (5)	1.90	88

Porcelain Series III

Ming Porcelain: $2, Refuse container with dragons. $2.50, Covered jar with lotus. $5, Covered jar with horses. $8, Bowl with figures of immortals.

1817	A336	$1	gray & multi	15	5
1818	A336	$2	lt vio & multi	20	8
1819	A336	$2.50	dk red & multi	40	10
1820	A336	$5	bl & multi	40	20
1821	A336	$8	dp org & multi	75	30
			Nos. 1817-1821 (5)	1.90	73

Issue dates: Nos. 1812–1816, Jan. 10; Nos. 1817–1821, Mar. 24.

See also Nos. 1865–1868.

Oyster Fairy and Fisherman's Dance—A337

1973, Feb. 7 Photo. *Perf. 11½*

Granite Paper

Multicolored

1822	A337	$1	*Kicking shuttlecock* (vert.)	35	5
1823	A337	$4	*shown*	60	20
1824	A337	$5	*Rowing boat over land*	60	20
1825	A337	$8	*Old man carrying young lady* (vert.)	90	30

Chinese folklore popular entertainment.

Bamboo Boat
A338

Taiwanese Handicrafts: $2.50, Painted marble vase (vert.). $5, Painted glass plate. $8, Doll, bridegroom carrying bride on back (vert.).

Perf. 13½x14½, 14½x13½

1973, Mar. 9 Photogravure

1826	A338	$1	multi	20	5
1827	A338	$2.50	multi	35	10
1828	A338	$5	multi	60	20
1829	A338	$8	multi	85	30

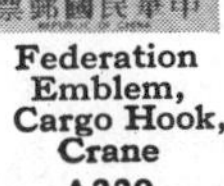

Federation Emblem, Cargo Hook, Crane
A339

Emblem, Tractor, New Buildings
A340

Perf. 12½

1973, Apr. 2 Litho. Wmk. 323

1830 A339 $1 sal & multi 10 5
1831 A340 $5 bl & blk 40 20

12th convention of International Federation of Asian and Western Pacific Contractors Association, Taipei, Apr. 2–10.

Pres. Chiang Kai-shek, Flag of China A341 — Lin Tse-hsü A342

Design: $4, like $1 with different border.

Perf. 12

1973, May 20 Photo. Unwmkd.

1832 A341 $1 yel & multi 30 5
1833 A341 $4 dk grn & multi 65 20

First anniversary of Pres. Chiang Kai-shek's inauguration for a fifth term.

Engraved

1973, June 3 *Perf. 12* Wmk. 323

1834 A342 $1 sepia 15 6

Lin Tse-hsü (1785–1850), Governor of Hunan and Kwantung, who destroyed large quantity of opium at Humen, Kwantung, June 3, 1839.

Willows and Palace Gate in the Morning—A343

Lady Watering Peonies, Stone Ornament A344

Design from scroll "Spring Morning in the Han Palace," by Chiu Ying. The five stamps of No. 1835 are numbered 1 to 5 and the five stamps of No. 1838 are numbered 6–10 in Chinese (see illustrations with Nos. 1682–1691 for numerals). The stamps are numbered and listed from right to left.

Perf. 11½

1973 Photogravure Unwmkd.

Multicolored; Granite Paper

1835 A343 Strip of 5 60 25
a. $1 *shown* (1) 8 5
b. $1 *Ladies feeding peacocks* (2) 8 5
c. $1 *Lady watering peonies* (3) 8 5
d. $1 *Pear tree in bloom* (4) 8 5
e. $1 *Lady musicians* (5) 8 5
1836 A344 $5 *shown* 50 20
1837 A344 $8 *Lady musicians* 70 30
1838 A343 Strip of 5 60 25
a. $1 *Ladies playing go* (6) 8 5
b. $1 *Various games* (7) 8 5
c. $1 *Talking and playing music* (8) 8 5
d. $1 *Artist painting portrait* (9) 8 5
e. $1 *Sentries guarding wall* (10) 8 5
1839 A344 $5 *Ladies playing go* 50 20
1840 A344 $8 *Girl chasing butterfly* 70 30
Nos. 1835-1840 (6) 3.60 1.50

Issue dates: Nos. 1835–1837, June 20; Nos. 1838–1840, July 18.

Fan, Bamboo Design, by Hsiang Te-hsin—A345

Wmk. 368

Wmkd. JEZ Multiple (368)

Designs: Painted fans, Ming dynasty.

1973, Aug. 15 Photo. *Perf. 12½x13*

1841 A345 $1 bis & multi 15 6
1842 A345 $2.50 bis & multi 30 8
1843 A345 $5 bis & multi 50 20
1844 A345 $8 bis & multi 80 30

See also Nos. 1934–1937.

Little League Emblem A346 — INTERPOL Emblem A347

Wmk. 370

Wmkd. Geometrical Design (370)

1973, Sept. 9 Litho. *Perf. 13½*

1845 A346 $1 yel, car & dk bl 20 6
1846 A346 $4 yel, grn & dk bl 40 20

Chinese victory in Little League Twin Championships, Gary, Ind., and Williamsport, Pa.

1973, Sept. 11 Litho. Wmk. 370

Perf. 12

1847 A347 $1 bl & org 10 5
1848 A347 $5 grn & org 40 20
1849 A347 $8 mag & org 60 30

50th anniversary of International Criminal Police Organization.

Ch'iu Feng-chia A348

Engraved

1973, Oct. 5 *Perf. 11½* Wmk. 323

1850 A348 $1 vio blk 20 8

2nd meeting of overseas Hakkas, Taipei, Oct. 5–7, and to honor Ch'iu Feng-chia (1864–1912), Hakka scholar, poet and revolutionist.

Tseng-wen Reservoir A349

Tsengwen Dam A350

Perf. 13½

1973, Oct. 31 Photo. Unwmkd.

Multicolored

1851 A349 Strip of 3 40 15
a. $1 *Upper shore* 8 5
b. $1 *shown* 8 5
c. $1 *Lower shore* 8 5

Perf. 12x11½

1852 A350 $5 *shown* 50 20
1853 A350 $8 *Spillway* 70 30

Inauguration of Tsengwen Reservoir. No. 1851 printed se-tenant in sheets of 15.

Tiger A351

Wmk. 370

1973, Dec. 1 Litho. *Perf. 12½*

1854 A351 50c multi 20 6
1855 A351 $4.50 multi 60 20

New Year 1974.

"Snow-dotted Eagle," by Lang Shih-ning—A352

Designs: No. 1857, "Comfortable Ride." No. 1858, "Red Flower Eagle." No. 1859, "Cloud-running Steed." No. 1860, "Sky-running steed." $2.50, "Red Jade Seat." $5, "Thunderclap Steed." $8, "Arabian Champion." Designs from painting series "Ten Prized Horses," by Lang Shih-ning (Giuseppe Castiglione, 1688–1766).

Perf. 13

1973 Lithographed Unwmkd.

Multicolored; Without Gum

1856 A352 50c *shown* 8 5
1857 A352 $1 *Pinto, blk tail* 18 5
1858 A352 $1 Facing left 18 5
1859 A352 $1 *Facing right* 18 5
1860 A352 $1 *Pinto, white tail* 18 5
1861 A352 $2.50 *Palomino* 40 8
1862 A352 $5 *Grazing* 60 20
a. Souvenir sheet of 4 90
1863 A352 $8 *Brown stallion* 1.00 25
Nos. 1856-1863 (8) 2.80 78

Nos. 1857–1860 printed se-tenant in sheets of 50. No. 1862a contains 4 stamps with simulated perforations similar to Nos. 1856–1857, 1861–1862. Bluish green ornamental margin, black inscription. Size: 150x120mm.

Issue dates: 50c, $2.50, $5, Nov. 21; others Dec. 21.

Porcelain Types of 1972–73

Porcelain Series IV

Porcelain Masterworks of Sung Dynasty: $1, Vase. $2, Three-tiered vase. $2.50, Lotus-shaped bowl. $5, Incense burner. $8, Incense burner on stand.

1974, Jan. 16 Photo. *Perf. 11½*

1864 A323 $1 ultra & multi 12 5
1865 A336 $2 multi 25 8
1866 A336 $2.50 red & multi 30 8
1867 A336 $5 lil & multi 50 20
1868 A336 $8 grn & multi 70 30
Nos. 1864-1868 (5) 1.87 71

Juggler A353 — Taroko Gorge, Hualien A354

Design: $8, Magician producing dishes from his robe (horiz.).

1974, Feb. 6 Photo. *Perf. 11½*

1869 A353 $1 yel & multi 15 5
1870 A353 $8 yel & multi 60 30

1974, Mar. 22 Photo. *Perf. 12*

Designs: $2.50, Luce Chapel, Tunghai University. $5, Tzu En Pagoda, Sun Moon Lake. $8, Goddess of Mercy, Keelung.

1871 A354 $1 multi 12 5
1872 A354 $2.50 multi 30 7
1873 A354 $5 multi 45 15
1874 A354 $8 multi 75 25

Taiwan landmarks.

Fighting Cocks (Brass) A355

Designs: $2.50, Grapes and bowl with fruit (imitation jade). $5, Fisherman (wood carving; vert.). $8, Basket with plastic roses (vert.).

Perf. 13½x14½, 14½x13½

1974, Apr. 10

1875 A355 $1 bl grn & multi 12 5
1876 A355 $2.50 brn & multi 30 8
1877 A355 $5 crim & multi 40 15
1878 A355 $8 multi 75 25

Taiwanese handicraft products.

Sun Yat-sen Memorial Hall
A356

Designs: $2.50, Reaching-moon Tower, Cheng Ching Lake. $5, Orchid Island (boats). $8, Penghu Interisland Bridge.

1974, May 15 Photo. *Perf. 11½*

Granite Paper

1879	A356	$1 bl & multi	12	5
1880	A356	$2.50 bl & multi	[illegible]	8
1881	A356	$5 bl & multi	40	15
1882	A356	$8 bl & multi	75	25

Taiwan landmarks.

Pres. Chiang and Gate of Whampoa Military Academy
A357

Marching Cadets and Entrance Gate
A358

Perf. 11½

1974, June 16 Engraved Wmk. 323

1883	A357	$1 car rose	30	5
1884	A358	$14 vio bl	1.20	50

50th anniversary of the founding of the Whampoa Military Academy.

Long-distance Runner and Olympic Rings
A359

The Boy Wang Ch'i Fighting Invaders
A360

Design: $8, Women's relay race and Olympic rings.

1974, June 23 Litho. *Perf. 12½*

1885	A359	$1 bl, blk & red	12	5
1886	A359	$8 pink, blk & red	65	25

80th anniversary of International Olympic Committee.

1974, July 15 *Perf. 13½* Wmk. 370

Folk Tales: No. 1888, T'i Ying pleading for her father before the Emperor. No. 1889, Wen Yen-po flushing out ball caught in tree. No. 1890, Boy Wang Hua returning gold piece he found. No. 1891, Pu Shih, a rich sheep raiser and benefactor. No. 1892, K'ung Yung as a child choosing smallest pear. No. 1893, Tung Yu studying. No. 1894, Szu Ma-kuang saving playmate from drowning in water jar.

1887	A360	50c ol & multi	5	5
1888	A360	50c ultra & multi	5	5
1889	A360	50c ocher & multi	5	5
1890	A360	50c red brn & multi	5	5
1891	A360	$1 grn & multi	10	5
1892	A360	$1 lil & multi	10	5
1893	A360	$1 bl & multi	10	5
1894	A360	$1 car & multi	10	5
		Nos. 1887-1894 (8)	60	40

Same denominations printed in blocks of four in sheets of 100.

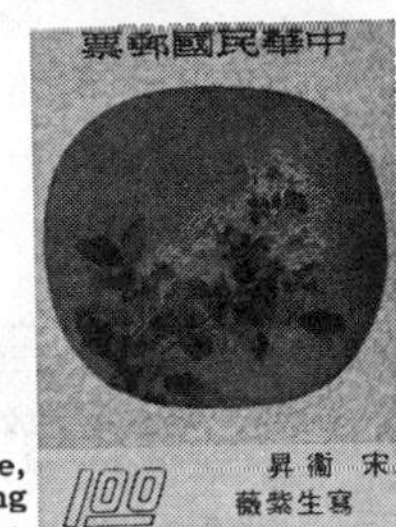

Myrtle, by Wei Sheng
A361

Silk Fan Paintings, Sung Dynasty (960–1279 A.D.): $2.50, Cabbage and Insects, by Hsu Ti. $5, Hibiscus, Cat and Dog, by Li Ti. $8, Pomegranate and Birds, by Wu Ping. Fans from National Palace Museum.

Perf. 13x12½

1974, Aug. 14 Photo. Wmk. 368

1895	A361	$1 multi	15	5
1896	A361	$2.50 multi	35	7
1897	A361	$5 multi	60	15
1898	A361	$8 multi	90	25

See Nos. 1950–1953.

Battle at Marco Polo Bridge, July 7, 1937
A362

Perf. 13½

1974, Sept. 3 Litho. Wmk. 370

1899	A362	$1 multi	10	5

Souvenir Sheet
Wmk. 323
Without Gum; Granite Paper

1900		Sheet of 8	80
a.		A362 $1, Single stamp	10

20th Armed Forces Day. No. 1900 commemorates Armed Forces Stamp Exhibition, Sun Yat-sen Memorial Hall, Sept. 3–9. Sheet has yellow ornamental margin with black inscription. Size: 106x146mm.

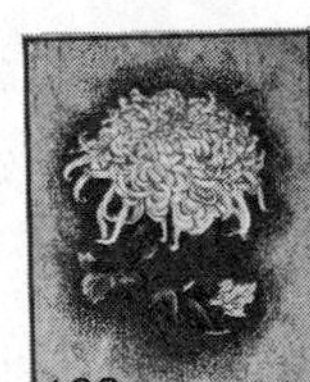

Chrysanthemum
A363

Designs: Various chrysanthemums.

Perf. 12

1974, Sept. 30 Photo. Unwmkd.

Granite Paper

1901	A363	$1 lil & multi	12	5
1902	A363	$2.50 multi	30	8
1903	A363	$5 org & multi	45	15
1904	A363	$8 multi	75	25

Rep. of China Pavilion, EXPO Emblem
A364

Map of Fair Grounds, Chinese Flag
A364a

Perf. 13

1974, Oct. 10 Litho. Wmk. 370

1905	A364	$1 multi	15	5
1906	A364a	$8 multi	60	25

EXPO '74, Spokane, Wash., May 4–Nov. 4. Theme, "Preserve the Environment."

Steel Mill, Kaohsiung
A365

Taichung Harbor
A366

Designs: $1, Taiwan North Link Railroad and map. $2, Oil refinery. $2.50, Electric train. $3.50, Taoyuan International Airport. $4, Taiwan North-South Highway and map. $4.50, Kaohsiung shipyard. $5, Su-ao Port.

Perf. 13x12½, 12½x13

1974, Oct. 31 Wmk. 323

1907	A365	50c lil, yel & brn	5	5
1908	A365	$1 grn & org	10	5
1909	A365	$2 bl & yel	15	5
1910	A365	$2.50 emer & org	15	8
1911	A366	$3 ocher & ultra	20	10
1912	A366	$3.50 sl grn & yel	25	12
1913	A366	$4 brn & yel	30	14
1914	A366	$4.50 ver & bl	30	15
1915	A366	$5 sep & dk bl	40	16
		Nos. 1907-1915 (9)	1.90	90

Major construction projects.
See Nos. 2009–2017, 2068–2076.

Agaricus Bisporus
A367

Edible Mushrooms: $2.50, Pleurotus ostreatus. $5, Dictyophora indusiata. $8, Flammulina velutipes.

Photogravure

1974, Nov. 15 *Perf. 11½* Unwmkd.

1916	A367	$1 multi	10	5
1917	A367	$2.50 multi	35	8
1918	A367	$5 multi	60	16
1919	A367	$8 multi	75	25

9th International Scientific Congress on the Cultivation of Edible Fungi, Taipei, Nov. 1974.

Batters and World Map
A368

Pitcher and Championship Banners
A369

Lithographed

1974, Nov. 24 *Perf. 13½* Wmk. 323

1920	A368	$1 multi	15	5
1921	A369	$8 multi	60	25

China's victory in 1974 Little League Baseball World Series Triple Championships.

Rabbit
A370

Acrobat with Iron Rod
A371

Perf. 12½

1974, Dec. 10 Photo. Wmk. 323

1922	A370	50c org & multi	10	5
1923	A370	$4.50 brn & multi	40	15

New Year 1975.

1975, Jan. 15 *Perf. 11½* Unwmkd.

Design: $5, Two acrobats spinning tops (horiz.).

Granite Paper

1924	A371	$4 yel & multi	30	15
1925	A371	$5 yel & multi	45	20

Children Watching Puppet Show—A372

Ceremonial New Year Greetings—A373

Designs from scroll "Festivals for the New Year," by Ting Kuan-p'eng. Nos. 1926a–1926e are numbered 1–5 in Chinese.

1975, Feb. 25 Photo. *Perf. 11½*

Multicolored; Granite Paper

1926	A372	Strip of 5	50	20
a.		$1 *Ceremonial New Year Greetings* (1)	8	5
b.		$1 *Man with trained monkey* (2)	8	5
c.		$1 *Crowd and musicians* (3)	8	5
d.		$1 *Picnic under a tree* (4)	8	5
e.		$1 *shown* (5)	8	5
1927	A373	$2.50 *shown*	35	8
1928	A373	$5 *Children buying firecrackers*	50	20
1929	A373	$8 *Children and man with trained monkey*	1.20	60

Sun Yat-sen Memorial Hall, Taipei
A374

Sun Yat-sen's Handwriting
A375

Sun Yat-sen, Bronze Statue in Memorial Hall
A376

Sun Yat-sen Memorial Hall, St. John's University, N.Y.
A377

Perf. 13½x14, 14x13½

1975, Mar. 12 Lithographed

1930	A374	$1 grn & multi	12	5
1931	A375	$4 yel grn & multi	35	15
1932	A376	$5 yel & multi	45	20
1933	A377	$8 gray & multi	75	30

Dr. Sun Yat-sen (1866–1925), statesman and revolutionary leader, 50th death anniversary.

Fan Type of 1973 Inscribed: "Landscape" (1st Characters, 水 山 2nd Row)

Designs: Painted fans, Ming Dynasty. Second row of inscription gives design description.

Perf. 12½x13

1975, Apr. 16 Photo. Wmk. 368

1934	A345	$1 bis & multi	12	5
1935	A345	$2.50 bis & multi	30	8
1936	A345	$5 bis & multi	45	20
1937	A345	$8 bis & multi	75	30

Yuan-chin coin, 1122–221 B.C.
A378

Ancient Chinese Coins: $4, Pan-liang, 221–207 B.C. $5, Five chu, 206 B.C.–220 A.D. $8, Five chu, 502–557 A.D.

Perf. 13

1975, May 20 Litho. Wmk. 323

1938	A378	$1 sal & multi	12	5
1939	A378	$4 yel & multi	30	15
1940	A378	$5 dl yel & multi	45	20
1941	A378	$8 lt vio & multi	75	30

The Cloth-bag Monk, by Chang Hung (1577–1668)
A379

Chinese Paintings: $4, Lao-tzu Riding Buffalo, by Chao Pu-chih (1053–1110). $5, Portrait of Shih-te, by Wang Wen (1497–1576). $8, Splashed-ink Immortal, by Liang K'ai (early 13th century).

Perf. 11½

1975, June 18 Photo. Unwmkd.

Granite Paper

1942	A379	$2 blk, buff & ver	15	8
1943	A379	$4 blk, gray & red	30	15
1944	A379	$5 blk, yel & ver	40	20
1945	A379	$8 tan, red & blk	75	30

Chu Yin Reading by the Light of Fireflies
A380

Folk Tales: No. 1947, Hua Mu-lan going to war for her father. No. 1948, King Kou Chien tasting gall. $5, Chou Ch'u killing tiger.

Perf. 14x13½

1975, July 16 Litho. Wmk. 368

1946	A380	$1 ol & multi	12	5
1947	A380	$2 bis brn & multi	18	8
1948	A380	$2 lt grn & multi	18	8
1949	A380	$5 bl & multi	50	16

See Nos. 2108–2111.

Cherry-Apple Blossoms, by Lin Ch'un
A381

Silk Fan Paintings, Sung Dynasty: $2, Spring Blossoms and Butterfly, by Ma K'uei. $5, Monkeys and Deer, by I Yüan-chih. $8, Tame Sparrow among Bamboo.

Perf. 13x12½

1975, Aug. 15 Litho. Wmk. 323

1950	A381	$1 multi	12	5
1951	A381	$2 multi	25	8
1952	A381	$5 multi	50	16
1953	A381	$8 multi	70	30

See Nos. 2001–2004.

Gen. Chang Tzu-chung (1891–1940)
A382

Portraits: No. 1955, Maj. Gen. Kao Chih-hong (1908–1937). No. 1956, Capt. Sha Shih-chiun (1896–1938). No. 1957, Maj. Gen. Hsieh Chin-yuan (1905–1941). No. 1958, Lt. Yen Hai-wen (1916–1937). No. 1959, Lt. Gen. Tai An-lan (1905–1942).

Perf. 12

1975, Sept. 3 Engr. Wmk. 323

1954	A382	$2 carmine	25	8
1955	A382	$2 sepia	25	8
1956	A382	$2 dl grn	25	8
1957	A382	$5 vio blk	60	20
1958	A382	$5 vio bl	60	20
1959	A382	$5 dk bl	60	20
		Nos. 1954-1959 (6)	2.55	84

Martyrs of the resistance fight against Japan.

Lotus Pond with Willows, by Madame Chiang—A383

Paintings by Madame Chiang Kai-shek: $5, Sun Breaks through Mountain Clouds. $8, A Pair of Pine Trees. $10, Fishing and Farming.

Perf. 13½

1975, Oct. 31 Litho. Unwmkd.

1960	A383	$2 multi	20	10
1961	A383	$5 multi	40	25
1962	A383	$8 multi	60	40
1963	A383	$10 multi	75	50

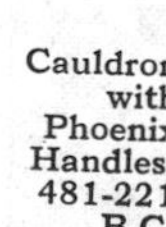

Cauldron with Phoenix Handles, 481-221 B.C.
A384

Ancient Bronzes: $2, Rectangular cauldron, 1122–722 B.C. (vert.). $8, Flat jar, 481–221 B.C. $10, 3-legged wine vessel, 1766–1122 B.C. (vert.).

1975, Nov. 12 Photo. *Perf. 12*

1964	A384	$2 pink & multi	15	10
1965	A384	$5 lt bl & multi	40	25
1966	A384	$8 yel & multi	60	40
1967	A384	$10 lil & multi	75	50

Dragon, Nine-Dragon Wall, Peihai
A385

Techi Dam
A386

Perf. 12½

1975, Dec. 1 Litho. Wmk. 323

1968	A385	$1 org & multi	10	5
1969	A385	$5 grn & multi	40	20

New Year 1976.

1975, Dec. 17 *Perf. 13½* Unwmkd.

Design: $10, Panoramic view of Techi Dam.

1970	A386	$2 grn & multi	20	
1971	A386	$10 bl & multi	85	4

Completion of Techi Dam, Tachia River.

Biathlon and Olympic Rings
A387

Designs (Olympic Rings and): $5, Luge. $8, Skiing.

1976, Jan. 15 Litho. *Perf. 13½*

1972	A387	$2 bl & multi	20	8
1973	A387	$5 bl & multi	40	16
1974	A387	$8 bl & multi	60	25

12th Winter Olympic Games, Innsbruck, Austria, Feb. 4–15.

Chin, Oldest Chinese Instrument
A388

Musical Instruments: $5, Se, c. 2900 B.C. $8, Standing kong-ho (harp). $10, Sleeping kong-ho.

1976, Feb. 11 *Perf. 14* Unwmkd.

1975	A388	$2 yel & multi	20	8
1976	A388	$5 org & multi	40	16
1977	A388	$8 grnsh bl & multi	60	25
1978	A388	$10 multi	75	32

Double Carp Type of 1969.

Perf. 13½x12½

1976, Dec. 15 Engraved Unwmkd.

1980	A280	$14 car rose	1.00	25

Mail Collecting
A389

Mail Sorting
A390

Designs: $8, Mail transport. $10, Mail delivery.

Perf. 13½

1976, Mar. 20 Litho. Wmk. 323

1984	A389	$2 yel & multi	20	8
1985	A390	$5 grn & multi	40	16
1986	A390	$8 bl & multi	60	25
1987	A389	$10 org & multi	75	32
a.		Souvenir sheet of 4	2.25	2.25

80th anniversary of postal service. No. 1987a contains one each of Nos. 1984–1987; buff margin with red inscription. Size: 130x100mm.

Pres. Chiang Kai-shek
A391

People Paying Homage—A392

Designs: No. 1990, Pres. Chiang lying in state. No. 1991, Hearse leaving funeral chapel. $5, People along funeral route. $8, Spirit tablet in Tzuhu Guest House. $10, Tzuhu Guest House, Pres. Chiang's burial place.

1976, Apr. 4

1988	A391	$2 gray & multi	20	8
1989	A392	$2 gray & multi	20	8
1990	A392	$2 gray & multi	20	8
1991	A392	$2 gray & multi	20	8
1992	A392	$5 gray & multi	35	20
1993	A392	$8 gray & multi	60	30
1994	A392	$10 gray & multi	65	40
		Nos. 1988-1994 (7)	2.40	1.22

Pres. Chiang Kai-shek (1887–1975), first death anniversary.

Flags of China and USA
A393

Perf. 13½

1976, May 29 Litho. Wmk. 323

1995	A393	$2 multi	20	8
1996	A393	$10 yel & multi	70	40

American Bicentennial.

Coin, 12th Century B.C.
A394

Cauldron, Shang Dynasty
A395

Bronze Shovel Coins (pu): $5, Pointed-feet coin, 481–221 B.C. $8, Round-feet coin, 722–481 B.C. $10, Square-feet coin, 3rd–2nd centuries B.C.

1976, June 16

1997	A394	$2 sal & multi	15	8
1998	A394	$5 lt bl & multi	40	16
1999	A394	$8 gray & multi	60	25
2000	A394	$10 multi	75	32

Fan Painting Type of 1975

Silk Fan Paintings, Sung Dynasty: $2, Hibiscus, by Li Tung. $5, Lilies, by Lin Ch'un. $8, Deer and Pine, by Mou Chung-fu. $10, Quail and Wild Flowers, by Li An-chung.

Perf. 13x12½

1976, July 14 Litho. Wmk. 323

2001	A381	$2 multi	20	8
2002	A381	$5 multi	40	20
2003	A381	$8 multi	60	30
2004	A381	$10 multi	75	35

1976, Aug. 25 Photo. *Perf. 11½*

Granite Paper

Ancient Bronzes: $5, 3-legged cauldron, Chou Dynasty (1122–722 B.C.). $8, Wine container, Chou Dynasty. $10, Wine vessel with spout, Shang Dynasty (1766–1122 B.C.).

2005	A395	$2 rose & multi	20	8
2006	A395	$5 lt bl & multi	40	16
2007	A395	$8 yel & multi	60	25
2008	A395	$10 lil & multi	75	32

Construction Types of 1974

Designs: $1, Taiwan North Link railroad and map. $2, Railroad electrification. $3, Taichung Harbor. $4, Taiwan North-South Highway and map. $5, Steel Mill, Kaohsiung. $6, Taoyuan International Airport. $7, Kao-hsiung shipyard. $8, Oil refinery. $9, Su-ao Port.

Perf. 13½x12½, 12½x13½

1976 Lithographed Wmk. 323

2009	A365	$1 car & grn	10	5
2010	A365	$2 org & multi	15	5
2011	A366	$3 vio & multi	20	10
2012	A366	$4 car & multi	25	15
2013	A365	$5 grn & brn	30	20
2014	A366	$6 brn & multi	35	20
2015	A366	$7 brn & multi	40	25
2016	A365	$8 car & grn	50	30
2017	A366	$9 ol & bl	50	30
		Nos. 2009-2017 (9)	2.75	1.60

Chiang Kai-shek and Mother
A396

Sun Yat-sen and Chiang Kai-shek at Canton Station—A397

Design: $5, Chiang Kai-shek, portrait.

1976, Oct. 31 Litho. *Perf. 13½*

2023	A396	$2 multi	20	8
2024	A396	$5 multi	40	20
2025	A397	$10 multi	75	40

Pres. Chiang Kai-shek, 90th anniversary of birth.

Flags of Kuomintang and China
A398

Sun Yat-sen and Chiang Kai-shek
A399

1976, Nov. 12 *Perf. 13½x14*

2026	A398	$2 multi	20	8
2027	A399	$10 multi	75	40
a.		Souvenir sheet of 2	1.00	1.00

11th National Kuomintang Congress, Taipei.

No. 2027a contains one each of Nos. 2026–2027; yellow margin with red inscription. Size: 110x87mm.

Brazen Serpent
A400

1976, Dec. 15 Wmk. 323 *Perf. 12½*

2028	A400	$1 red, lil & gold	10	5
2029	A400	$5 plum, yel & gold	40	16

New Year 1977.

Bird and Plum Blossoms, by Ch'en Hung-shou
A401

Chinese Paintings: $8, "Wintry Days" (pine), by Yang Wei-chen. $10, Rock and Bamboo, by Hsia Ch'ang.

Unwmkd.

1977, Jan. 12 Photo. *Perf. 11½*

Granite Paper

2030	A401	$2 multi	20	8
2031	A401	$8 multi	50	30
2032	A401	$10 multi	75	35

Black-naped Orioles—A402

Birds of Taiwan: $8, Common Kingfisher. $10, Chinese pheasant-tailed jacana.

1977, Feb. 16 Lithographed

2033	A402	$2 multi	20	8
2034	A402	$8 multi	50	30
2035	A402	$10 multi	75	35

See Nos. 2163-2165.

Census Emblem, Industry and Commerce
A403

Unwmkd.

1977, Mar. 16 Litho. *Perf. 13½*

2036	A403	$2 red & multi	20	8
2037	A403	$10 pur & multi	75	35

Industry and Commerce Census.

Green Mountains Rising into Clouds, by Madame Chiang—A404

Landscapes, by Madame Chiang Kai-shek: $5, Boat in the Beauty of Spring. $8, Scholar beside Waterfall. $10, Water Rises to Meet the Bridge.

Photogravure

1977, Mar. 31 *Perf. 11½* Unwmkd.

Granite Paper

2038	A404	$2 multi	20	5
2039	A404	$5 multi	40	12
2040	A404	$8 multi	60	20
2041	A404	$10 multi	75	25

League Emblem
A405

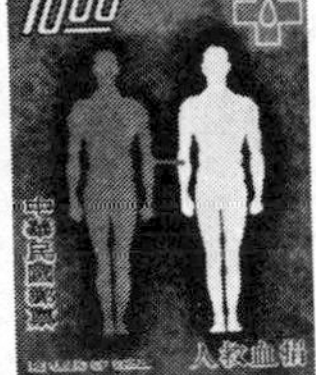

Blood Donation
A406

1977, Apr. 18 Litho. *Perf. 12½*

2042	A405	$2 car & multi	25	5
2043	A405	$10 grn & multi	80	25

10th World Anti-Communist League Conference.

1977, May 5 *Perf. 13½* Wmk. 323

Design: $2, Donating blood (horiz).

2044	A406	$2 red & blk	20	5
2045	A406	$10 red & blk	70	25

Blood donation movement.

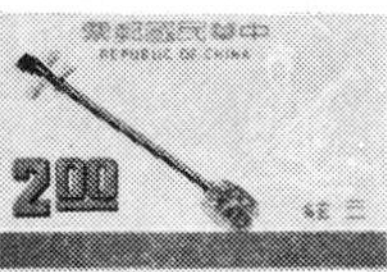

San-hsien
A407

Musical Instruments: $5, Tung-hsiao (bamboo flute). $8, Yang-chin (butterfly harpsichord). $10, Pai-hsiao (pipes). Background shows musician playing instrument.

Unwmkd.

1977, June 21 Photo. *Perf. 14*

2046	A407	$2 multi	20	5
2047	A407	$5 multi	40	12
2048	A407	$8 multi	60	20
2049	A407	$10 multi	75	25

Idea Leuconoe
A408

Protected Butterflies: $4, Hebomoia glaucippe formosana. $6, Stichophthalma howqua formosana. $10, Atrophaneura horishana.

1977, July 20 Litho. *Perf. 13½*

2050	A408	$2 ver & multi	20	5
2051	A408	$4 lt grn & multi	40	10
2052	A408	$6 lt bl & multi	60	15
2053	A408	$10 yel & multi	75	25

National Palace Museum
A409

Temple
A410

Children's Drawings: $2, Sea Goddess Festival. $4, Boats on Shore of Lan-yu.

Perf. 13½

1977, Aug. 27 Litho. Wmk. 323

2054	A409	$1 multi	10	5
2055	A409	$2 multi	20	5
2056	A409	$4 multi	30	10
2057	A410	$5 multi	40	12

8th Exhibition of World School Children's Art.

Carved Lacquer Plate, Wan-li Ware
A411

Ancient Carved Lacquer Ware: $5, Bowl, Ching dynasty. $8, Round box, Ming dynasty. $10, Four-tiered box, Ching dynasty.

Perf. 13x14

1977, Sept. 28 Photo. Wmk. 368

2058	A411	$2 multi	20	5
2059	A411	$5 multi	40	12
2060	A411	$8 multi	60	20
2061	A411	$10 multi	75	25

Lions International, Emblem and Activities
A412

Unwmkd.

1977, Oct. 8 Litho. *Perf. 13*

2062	A412	$2 multi	20	5
2063	A412	$10 multi	70	25

International Association of Lions Clubs, 60th anniversary.

Nos. 2069 and 2075 Overprinted in Claret

1977
中華民國青
年、青少年
及少年棒球
隊再獲世界
三冠軍紀念

Perf. 13½x12½

1977, Sept. 9 Litho. Unwmkd.

2064	A365	$2 org & multi	20	5
2065	A365	$8 car & grn	60	20

Little League baseball championship.

Chinese Quality Mark
A413

Unwmkd.

1977, Oct. 14 Litho. *Perf. 13x12½*

2066	A413	$2 red & multi	20	5
2067	A413	$10 bl & multi	70	25

International Standardization Day.

Construction Types of 1974

Redrawn: Numerals Outlined

Designs as 1976 Issue.

Perf. 13½x12½, 12½x13½

1977 Lithographed Unwmkd.

Granite Paper

2068	A365	$1 car & dp grn	10	5
2069	A365	$2 ver & multi	15	5
2070	A366	$3 vio & multi	20	7
2071	A366	$4 car & multi	25	10
2072	A365	$5 grn & multi	30	12
2073	A366	$6 sep & multi	35	15
2074	A366	$7 sep & multi	40	18
2075	A365	$8 red lil & multi	50	20
2076	A366	$9 ol & multi	50	22
		Nos. 2068-2076 (9)	2.75	1.14

Numerals are in solid color on Nos. 1907–1915, 2009–2017; in outline on Nos. 2068–2076.

Man and Heart
A414

Wmk. 323

1977, Nov. 12 Litho. *Perf. 13½x12½*

2077	A414	$2 multi	20	5
2078	A414	$10 multi	70	25

Physical health, cardiac care.

White Stallion
A415

Design: $5, Two horses (horiz.). Designs from painting "100 Horses," by Lang Shih-ning.

Lithographed

1977, Dec. 1 *Perf. 12½* Unwmkd.

2079	A415	$1 red & multi	10	5
2080	A415	$5 emer & multi	40	15

New Year 1978.

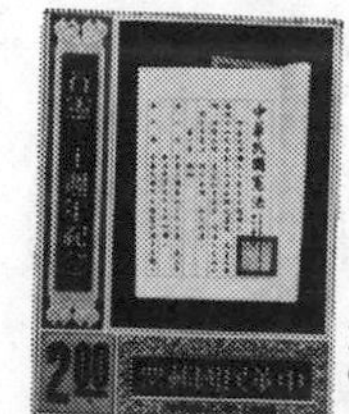

First Page of Constitution
A416

Pres. Chiang Accepting Constitution, 1946
A417

1977, Dec. 25 Litho. *Perf. 13½*

2081	A416	$2 multi	20	6
2082	A417	$10 multi	70	30

30th anniversary of the Constitution.

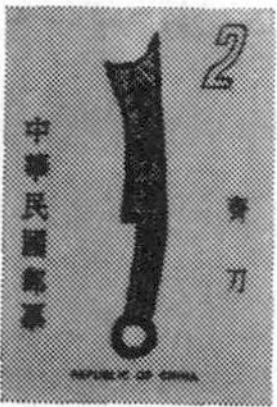

Knife Coin with 3 Characters, 403–221 B.C.
A418

Designs: Ancient knife coins.

1978, Jan. 18 *Perf. 13½* Wmk. 323

2083	A418	$2 sal & multi	20	5
2084	A418	$5 lt bl & blk	40	16
2085	A418	$8 lt gray & multi	60	25
2086	A418	$10 tan & multi	75	32

China No. 1 and Flag of China
A419

Designs: $5, No. 464 (Sun Yat-sen). $10, No. 1204 (Chiang Kai-shek).

1978, Feb. 21 Litho. *Perf. 13½*

2087	A419	$2 brn & multi	20	8
2088	A419	$5 bl & multi	40	16
2089	A419	$10 org & multi	75	32
a.		Souvenir sheet of 3	1.50	

Centenary of Chinese postage stamps. No. 2089a contains one each of Nos. 2087–2089; orange and dark carmine margin. Size: 143x101mm.

Sun Yat-Sen Memorial Hall
A420

China Nos. 2079 and 2
A421

Perf. 14x12½, 12½x14

1978, Mar. 20 Wmk. 323

2090	A420	$2 multi	25	8
2091	A421	$10 multi	75	32

ROCPEX '78 Philatelic Exhibition, Taipei, Mar. 20–29.

Chiang Kai-shek with Revolutionary Army—A422

Designs (Chiang Kai-shek); $2, as young man, 1912 (vert.). $8, Making speech at Mt. Lu, July 17, 1937. $10, Reviewing Armed Forces on National Day, 1956, and Chinese flags (vert.).

1978, Apr. 5 *Perf. 13½* Wmk. 323

2092	A422	$2 vio & multi	20	8
2093	A422	$5 grn & multi	40	16
2094	A422	$8 bl & multi	60	25
2095	A422	$10 vio bl & multi	75	32

Pres. Chiang Kai-shek (1887–1975).

Nuclear Reactor and Plant
A423

Poem by Wen Cheng-ming (1470–1559)
A424

Perf. 13½x12½

1978, Apr. 28 Unwmkd.

2096	A423	$10 multi	65	32

First nuclear power plant on Taiwan.

Lithographed

1978, May 20 *Perf. 13½* Wmk. 323

Chinese Calligraphy: $2, Letter by Wang Hsi-chih (307–365). $4, Eulogy by Chu Sui-liang (596–658). $8, From Autobiography of Huai-su, Tang Dynasty. $10, Poem by Ch'ang Piao, Sung Dynasty.

2097	A424	$2 multi	15	8
2098	A424	$4 multi	25	16
2099	A424	$6 multi	35	24
2100	A424	$8 multi	50	32
2101	A424	$10 multi	60	40
		Nos. 2097-2101 (5)	1.85	1.20

Head and Dao Cancer Fund Emblem
A425

Carved Lacquer Vase, Ming Dynasty
A426

1978, June 15 Litho. *Perf. 13½*

2102 A425 $2 red, org & ol 15 8
2103 A425 $10 dk & lt bl & grn 60 40

Cancer prevention.

1978, July 12

Ancient Carved Lacquer Ware: $2, Box with dragon and cloud design, Ch'ing dynasty (horiz.). $5, Double box on legs, Ch'ing dynasty (horiz.). $8, Round box with peonies, Ming dynasty (horiz.).

2104 A426 $2 gray ol & multi 15 8
2105 A426 $5 gray ol & multi 30 16
2106 A426 $8 gray ol & multi 50 25
2107 A426 $10 gray ol & multi 60 32

Tsu Ti Practicing with his Sword
A427

Folk Tales: No. 2109, Pan Ch'ao, diplomat and governor. No. 2110, Tien Tan's "Fire Bull Battle." $5, Liang Hung-yu, a general's wife, who served as drummer in battle.

Perf. 13½

1978, Aug. 16 Litho. Wmk. 323

2108 A427 $1 multi 10 5
2109 A427 $2 bis & multi 15 8
2110 A427 $2 gray & multi 15 8
2111 A427 $5 multi 30 16

Nos. 2012 and 2014 Overprinted in Red

1978 中華民國青年青少年及少年棒球隊三榮世界三冠軍紀念

1978, Sept. 9 *Perf. 12½x13*

2112 A366 $4 multi 25 16
2113 A366 $6 multi 40 25

Triple championships won by Chinese teams in Little League World Series. "1978" overprint on $4 at left, on $6 at right.

Ixias Pyrene
A428

Protected Butterflies: $4, Euploea sylvestor swinhoei. $6, Cyrestis thyodamas formosana. $10, Byasa polyeuctes termessus.

1978, Sept. 20

2114 A428 $2 multi 15 8
2115 A428 $4 multi 25 16
2116 A428 $6 multi 35 25
2117 A428 $10 multi 60 40

Scout Symbols
A429

Tropical Tomatoes
A430

1978, Oct. 5 Litho. *Perf. 13½*

2118 A429 $2 multi 25 8
2119 A429 $10 multi 40 40

5th Chinese Boy Scout Jamboree, Cheng Ching Lake, Oct. 5–12.

1978, Oct. 23 Wmk. 323

Design: $10, Tropical tomatoes (horiz.).

2120 A430 $2 multi 10 8
2121 A430 $10 multi 50 40

International Symposium on Tropical Tomatoes, Taiwan, Oct. 23–28.

Sino-Saudi Bridge
A431

Design: $6, Buttresses of bridge, flags of Taiwan and Saudi Arabia (horiz.).

1978, Oct. 31

2122 A431 $2 multi 10 8
2123 A431 $6 multi 30 25

Completion of Sino-Saudi Bridge over Cho-Shui River.

National Flag
A432

1978-80 *Perf. 13½*

2124 A432 $1 red & dk bl 8 5
a. Bklt. pane of 16 ($5, $6, $8, $10, 3 $1, 9 $2) 3.00
2125 A432 $2 red & dk bl 12 8
a. Bklt. pane of 15 + label 2.00
2126 A432 $3 lt grn & multi ('80) 30 12
2127 A432 $4 bis & multi ('80) 35 15
2128 A432 $5 lt grn & multi 25 20
2129 A432 $6 brn org & multi 30 24
2130 A432 $7 dk brn & multi ('80) 35 28
2131 A432 $8 dk grn & multi 45 32
2132 A432 $10 brt bl & multi ('79) 60 40
2133 A432 $12 brt rose lil & multi ('80) 60 45
Nos. 2124-2133 (10) 3.40 2.29

Two types exist: 1. Second line (red) below flag is same width as blue line. 2. Second line is a hairline, notably thinner. The $3, $4, $7 and $12 were issued only in type 2; Nos. 2129, 2132, 2134, 2124a, only in type 1; others in both types.

Nos. 2129-2133 have colorless inscriptions and denomination in a panel of solid color.

Coil Stamp

1980, Jan. 15 *Perf. 12 Horiz.*

2134 A432 $2 multi 10 6

See Nos. 2288-2300.

Three Rams, by Emperor Hsuan-tsung
A433

Taoyuan International Airport
A434

Wmk. 323

1978, Dec. 1 Litho. *Perf. 12½*

2135 A433 $1 multi 5 5
2136 A433 $5 multi 25 20

New Year 1979.

1978, Dec. 31 *Perf. 13½*

Design: $10, Passenger terminal and control tower (horiz.).

2137 A434 $2 multi 10 8
2138 A434 $10 multi 50 40

Completion of Taoyuan International Airport.

Oracle Bones and Inscription, 1766–1123 B.C.—A435

Antiquities and Inscriptions: $5, Leh-chi cauldron, 722–481 B.C. $8, Small seal (turtle), 206 B.C.–8 A.D. $10, Inscribed stone tablet, 175–183 A.D.

1979, Jan. 17

2139 A435 $2 multi 10 8
2140 A435 $5 multi 25 20
2141 A435 $8 multi 40 32
2142 A435 $10 multi 50 40

Origin and development of Chinese characters.

Chihkan Tower, 1653
A436

Taiwan Scenery: $5, Shrine of Confucius, 1665. $8, Shrine of Koxinga, 1661. $10, Eternal Castle and moat.

1979, Feb. 11 Litho. *Perf. 13½*

2143 A436 $2 multi 10 8
2144 A436 $5 multi 25 20
2145 A436 $8 multi 40 32
2146 A436 $10 multi 50 40

Children Playing on Winter Day, Sung Dynasty—A437

1979, Mar. 8

Multicolored

2147 A437 Block of four 1.00 60
a. $5 in UL corner 25 15
b. $5 in UR corner 25 15
c. $5 in LL corner 25 15
d. $5 in LR corner 25 15
e. Souvenir sheet of 4 1.25 1.00

No. 2147e contains No. 2147; pink and black margin. Size: 101x145mm.

Lu Hao-tung
A438

Yellow Jade Brush Holder
A439

Wmk. 323

1979, Mar. 29 Engr. *Perf. 13x12½*

2148 A438 $2 blue 10 8

Lu Hao-tung (1868–1895), revolutionist.

Unwmkd.

1979, Apr. 12 Photo. *Perf. 12*

Ancient Brush Washers: $5, White jade, Ming Dynasty. $8, Dark green jade, Ch'ing Dynasty. $10, Bluish jade, Ch'ing Dynasty. All horiz.

Granite Paper

2149 A439 $2 multi 10 8
2150 A439 $5 multi 25 20
2151 A439 $8 multi 40 32
2152 A439 $10 multi 50 40

Plum Blossoms, National Flower
A440

City Houses and Garden
A441

Plum Blossoms—A440a

Wmk. 323

1979-85 Engr. *Perf. 13x12½*

Granite Paper

2153 A440 $10 dk bl 50 40
2154 A440 $20 brown 1.00 80
2154A A440 $40 brt car ('85) 2.00 1.25
2155 A440 $50 dl grn 2.50 2.00
2156 A440 $100 vermilion 5.00 4.00

Perf. 14x13½

2156A A440a $300 pur & red org ('83) 15.00 10.00
2156B A440a $500 ver & brn ('82) 25.00 15.00

See No. 2510

Perf. 13x12½, 12½x13

1979, June 5 Lithographed

Design: $10, Rural landscape (horiz.).

2157 A441 $2 multi 10 8
2158 A441 $10 multi 50 40

Protection of the Environment.

Bankbook and Computer Department
A442

Designs: $2, Children at counter (vert.). $5, People standing in line (vert.). $10, Hand putting coin in savings bank, symbolic tree.

1979, July 1 *Perf. 13½* Wmk. 323

2159 A442 $2 multi 15 8
2160 A442 $5 multi 35 20
2161 A442 $8 multi 50 32
2162 A442 $10 multi 60 40

Postal savings, 60th anniversary.

Bird Type of 1977

Birds of Taiwan: $2, Swinoe's pheasant. $8, Steere's babbler. $10, Formosan yuhina.

1979, Aug. 8 *Perf. 11½*

2163 A402 $2 multi 10 8
2164 A402 $8 multi 40 32
2165 A402 $10 multi 50 40

Rowland Hill, Penny Black A443

Perf. 13½x13

1979, Aug. 27 Litho. Wmk. 323

2166	A443	$10 multi	50	40

Sir Rowland Hill (1795—1879), originator of penny postage.

Jar with Rope Design, Shang Dynasty A444

Ancient Chinese Pottery: $5, Two-handled jar, Shang dynasty. $8, Red jar with "ears," Han dynasty. $10, Green glazed jar, Han dynasty.

1979, Sept. 12 ***Perf. 13½***

2167	A444	$2 multi	12	8
2168	A444	$5 multi	30	20
2169	A444	$8 multi	45	32
2170	A444	$10 multi	60	40

Children and IYC Emblem A445

1979, Sept. 28 Litho. ***Perf. 13½***

2171	A445	$2 multi	10	8
2172	A445	$10 multi	50	40

International Year of the Child.

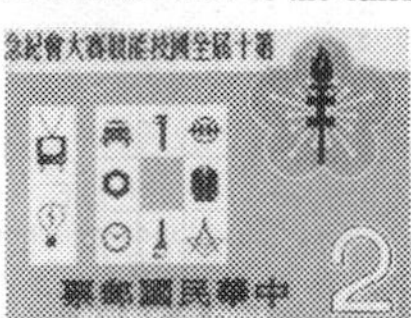

Trade Symbols, Competition Emblem A446

1979, Nov. 11 Litho. ***Perf. 13½***

2173	A446	$2 bl & multi	10	8
2174	A446	$10 grn & multi	50	40

10th National Vocational Training Competition, Taichung, Nov. 11.

Trees on a Winter Plain, by Li Ch'eng A447

Paintings: $5, Bamboo, Wen T'ung. $8, Old tree, bamboo and rock, by Chao Meng-fu. $10, Twin Pines, by Li K'an.

1979, Nov. 21

2175	A447	$2 multi	10	8
2176	A447	$5 multi	25	20
2177	A447	$8 multi	40	32
2178	A447	$10 multi	50	40

Monkey-A448

1979, Dec. 1 ***Perf. 12½***

2179	A448	$1 yel & multi	5	5
2180	A448	$6 tan & multi	30	25

New Year 1980.

Rotary Emblem and "75"—A449

Rotary International, 75th Anniversary. $12, Anniversary emblem (vert.).

1980, Feb. 23 Wmk. 323 Litho. ***Perf. 13½***

2181	A449	$2 multi	10	6
2182	A449	$12 multi	60	50

Mt. Hohuan—A450

Taiwan Landscapes (East-West Cross-Island Highway): $2, Tunnel of Nine Turns (vert.). $12, Bridge, Tien Hsiang (vert.).

1980, Mar. 1

2183	A450	$2 multi	10	6
2184	A450	$8 multi	40	24
2185	A450	$12 multi	60	50

Shih Chien-Ju—A451

1980, Mar. 29 Engr. ***Perf. 13½×12½***

Granite Paper

2186	A451	$2 red brn	10	6

Shih Chien-Ju (1879-1900), revolutionist.

Chung-cheng Memorial Hall—A452

1980, Apr. 4 Litho. ***Perf. 13½***

2187	A452	$2 *shown*	15	6
2188	A452	$8 *Quotation*	50	24
2189	A452	$12 *Bronze statue*	75	50

Chiang Kai-shek (1887-1975), 5th anniversary of death.

Melon-shaped Jade Brush Washer, Ming Dynasty—A453

Jade Pottery: $2, Jar with dragons, Sung dynasty (vert.). $8, Monk's alms bowl, Ch'ing dynasty. $10, Yellow jade brush washer, Ch'ing dynasty.

1980, May 20 Photo. ***Perf. 12***

Granite Paper

2190	A453	$2 multi	10	6
2191	A453	$5 multi	25	20
2192	A453	$8 multi	40	32
2193	A453	$10 multi	50	40

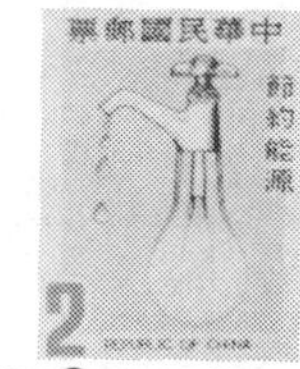

Energy Conservation—A454

1980, July 15 Litho. ***Perf. 13½***

2194	A454	$2 multi	10	6
2195	A454	$12 multi	60	50

Soldier, T'ang Dynasty Pottery—A455

1980, Aug. 18 Litho. ***Perf. 13½***

2196	A455	$2 *shown*	10	6
2197	A455	$5 *Roosters*	25	20
2198	A455	$8 *Horse*	40	32
2199	A455	$10 *Camel*	50	40

Confucius Returning Lost Article—A456

Folk Tales: $1, Grinding mortar into a needle. No. 2202, Wen Tien-hsiang in jail. $5, Sending coal in snow.

1980, Sept. 23 Wmk. 323 Litho. ***Perf. 14x13½***

2200	A456	$1 multi	5	5
2201	A456	$2 multi	10	6
2202	A456	$2 multi	10	6
2203	A456	$5 multi	25	20

Railroad Electrification—A457

1980, Oct. 10 ***Perf. 13½x14***

2204	A457	$2 *shown*	10	6
2205	A457	$2 *Taichung Harbor*	10	6
2206	A457	$2 *Chiang Kai-shek Airport*	10	6
2207	A457	$2 *Steel Mill*	10	6
2208	A457	$2 *Sun Yat-sen Freeway*	10	6
2209	A457	$2 *Nuclear power plant*	10	6
2210	A457	$2 *Petrochemical plants*	10	6
2211	A457	$2 *Su-ao Harbor*	10	6
2212	A457	$2 *Kaohsiung shipyard*	10	6
2213	A457	$2 *North link railroad*	10	6
a.		Souvenir sheet of 10	1.25	
		Nos. 2204-2213 (10)	1.00	60

Completion of major construction projects. Nos. 2204-2213 se-tenant. No. 2213a contains one each of Nos. 2204-2213. Size: 218x100mm.

10th National Savings Day—A458

1980, Oct. 25 Wmk. 323 Litho. ***Perf. 13½***

2214	A458	$2 *Ancient coin and coin banks*	10	6
2215	A458	$12 *shown*	60	35

Landscape, by Ch'iu Ying, Ming Dynasty—A459

1980, Nov. 12 **Litho.** ***Perf. 13½***

2216	A459	Block of 4	1.00	80
a.		$5 in UL corner	25	20
b.		$5 in UR corner	25	20
c.		$5 in LL corner	25	20
d.		$5 in LR corner	25	20
e.		Souvenir sheet	1.25	1.00

No. 2216e contains No. 2216a-2216d; yellow and brown decorative margin. Size: 102x145½mm.

Cock A460

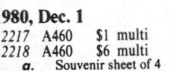

Faces, Flag, Census Form A461

1980, Dec. 1 ***Perf. 12½***

2217	A460	$1 multi	5	5
2218	A460	$6 multi	30	24
a.		Souvenir sheet of 4	75	

New Year 1980. No. 2218a contains 2 each Nos. 2217-2218; black marginal inscription. Size: 77x102mm.

1980, Dec. 13 ***Perf. 13½***

2219	A461	$2 *shown*	10	6
2220	A461	$12 *Buildings*, horiz.	60	50

1980 population and housing census.

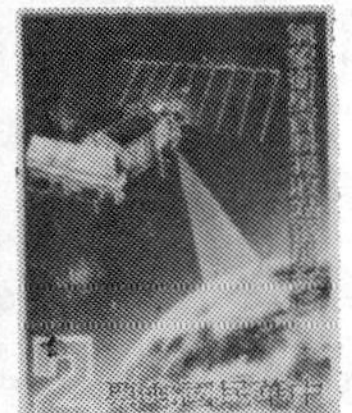

TIROS-N Satellite A462

Design: $10, Central weather bureau (horiz.).

1981, Jan. 28 **Litho.** ***Perf. 13½***

2221	A462	$2 multi	10	6
2222	A462	$10 multi	50	50

Completion of meteorological satellite ground station, Taipei.

"Happiness" A463

1981, Feb. 3 ***Perf. 13½x12½***

New Year 1981 (Calligraphy): No. 2224, Wealth. No. 2225, Longevity. No. 2226, Joy. Nos. 2223-2226 se-tenant.

2223	A463	$5 multi, 5 at B	25	15
2224	A463	$5 multi, 5 at R	25	15
2225	A463	$5 multi, 5 at L	25	15
2226	A463	$5 multi, 5 at T	25	15

International Year of the Disabled—A464

1981, Feb. 19 **Litho.** ***Perf. 13½***

2227	A464	$2 multi	10	6
2228	A464	$12 multi	60	55

Mt. Ali—A465

1981, Mar. 1

2229	A465	$2 shown	10	6
2230	A465	$7 Oluanpi Beach	35	28
2231	A465	$12 Sun Moon Lake	60	35

A $2 multicolored stamp for the 12th National Kuomintang Congress at Taipei was prepared for release Mar. 29, 1981, but not issued. It showed Sun Yat-sen, Chiang Kai-shek, flags of China and the Koumintang and a map of China.

Children in Forest—A467

Children's Day: Drawings.

1981, Apr. 4

2233	A467	$1 multi	5	5
2234	A467	$2 multi	10	6
2235	A467	$5 multi	25	20
2236	A467	$7 multi	35	28

Chiang Kai-shek Memorial Hall—A468

1981, Apr. 5 ***Perf. 12½x13½***

2237	A468	20c bluish lil	5	5
2238	A468	40c crim rose	5	5
2239	A468	50c dl red brn	5	5

Chiang Kai-shek (1887-1975), 6th anniversary of death.

Cloisonne Enamel Brush Washer, 15th Cent.—A469

Cloisonne Enamel: $5, Ritual vessel, 15th cent. (vert.). $8, Plate, 17th cent. $10, Vase, Ming Dynasty (vert.).

1981, May 20 **Photo.** ***Perf. 12***
Granite Paper

2240	A469	$2 multi	10	6
2241	A469	$5 multi	25	20
2242	A469	$8 multi	40	32
2243	A469	$10 multi	50	40

Early and Modern Locomotives A470

Linnaeus Crab A471

Wmk. 323
1981, June 9 **Litho.** ***Perf. 12½***

2244	A470	$2 shown	10	6
2245	A470	$14 Trains, horiz.	70	52

Railroad service centenary.

1981, June 14 ***Perf. 13½***

2246	A471	$2 De Haan crab, horiz.	10	6
2247	A471	$5 shown	25	20
2248	A471	$8 Miers crab, horiz.	40	32
2249	A471	$14 Rathbun crab	70	52

Central Weather Bureau, 40th Anniv.—A472

1981, July 1 **Litho.** ***Perf. 13½***

2250	A472	$2 multi	10	6
2251	A472	$14 multi	70	50

Scene from The Cowherd and the Weaving Maid—A473

Designs: Scenes from the Cowherd and the Weaving Maid.

1981, Aug. 6 **Litho.** ***Perf. 13½x14***

2252	A473	$2 multi	10	6
2253	A473	$4 multi	20	12
2254	A473	$8 multi	40	24
2255	A473	$14 multi	70	42

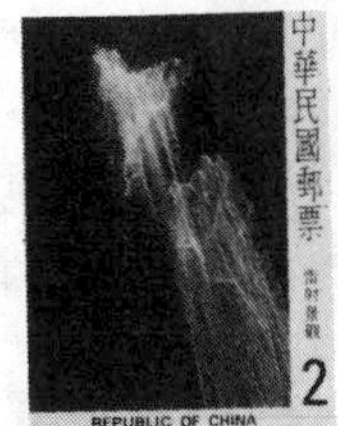

First Lasography Exhibition—A474

Lasography Designs.

1981, Aug. 15 ***Perf. 13½***

2256	A474	$2 multi	10	6
2257	A474	$5 multi	25	15
2258	A474	$8 multi	40	24
2259	A474	$14 multi	70	42

Soccer Players

A475 A476

1981, Sept. 9 **Litho.** ***Perf. 13½***

2260	A475	$5 multi	25	15
2261	A476	$5 multi	25	15

Sports Day. Se-tenant.

70th Anniv. of Republic: No. 2263, Eastward Expedition (soldiers on Hill). No. 2264, Northward Expedition (Chiang on horse). No. 2265, Resistance War with Japan (Chiang, fist raised). No. 2266, Suppression of Communist Rebels (Battle scene). No. 2267, Counter-offensive and unification. $8, Chiang Kai-shek. $14, Sun Yat-sen.

Wmk. 323
1981 **Litho.** ***Perf. 13½***

2262	A477	$2 multi	10	6
2263	A477	$2 multi	10	6
2264	A477	$2 multi	10	6
2265	A477	$2 multi	10	6
2266	A477	$3 multi	15	10
2267	A477	$3 multi	15	10
2268	A477	$8 multi	40	25
2269	A477	$14 multi	70	40
a.		Souvenir sheet of 8	2.00	1.25
		Nos. 2262-2269 (8)	1.80	1.09

No. 2269a contains Nos. 2262-2269; multicolored decorative margin. Size: 117x168mm. Nos. 2262-2269 issued Oct. 10; No. 2269a, Oct. 25.

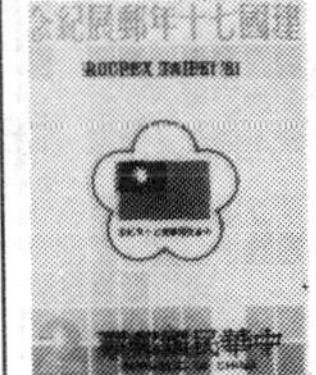

ROCPEX TAIPEI '81 Intl. Philatelic Exhibition, Taipei, Oct. 25-Nov. 2 A478

1981, Oct. 25

2270	A478	$2 multi	10	6
2271	A478	$14 multi	70	40

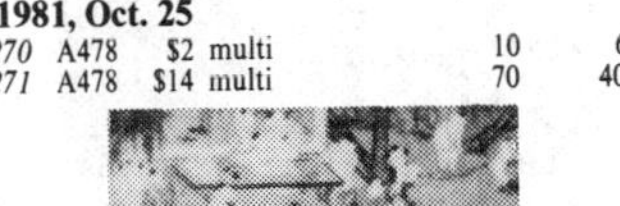

Boys Playing Games (#2272a)—A479

Design: "One Hundred Boys," Sung Dynasty scroll. Two strips of 5 each in continuous design.

1981, Nov. 12

2272	Block of 10	1.00	60
a.-e.	A479 $2 single (top)	10	6
f.-j.	A479 $2 single (bottom)	10	6

New Year 1982 (Year of the Dog) A480

Information Week, Dec. 6-12 A481

Wmk. 323
1981, Dec. 1 **Litho.** ***Perf. 12½***

2273	A480	$1 multi	5	5
2274	A480	$10 multi	50	30
a.		Souvenir sheet of 4	1.25	75

No. 2274a contains 2 each Nos. 2273-2274;black marginal inscription. Size: 78x103mm.

1981, Dec. 7 ***Perf. 14x13½***

2275	A481	$2 multi	10	6

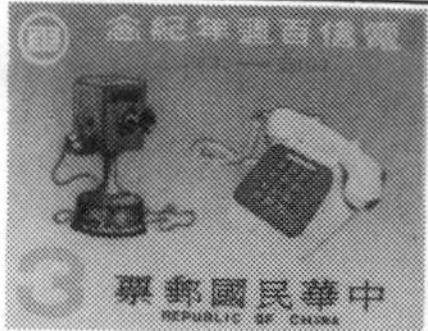

Telecommunications Centenary—A482

1981, Dec. 28 ***Perf. 14x13½, 13½x14***

2276	A482	$2	Telephone, vert.	10	6
2277	A482	$3	Old, new phones	15	10
2278	A482	$8	Submarine cable	40	25
2279	A482	$18	Computers, vert.	90	65

Floral Arrangement—A483

Designs: Various floral arrangements in Ming vases.

Wmk. 323

1982, Jan. 23 **Litho.** ***Perf. 13½***

2280	A483	$2	multi	10	6
2281	A483	$3	multi	15	10
2282	A483	$8	multi	40	25
2283	A483	$18	multi	90	65

The Ku Cheng Reunion—A484

Designs: Opera scenes.

Wmk. 323

1982, Feb. 15 **Litho.** ***Perf. 13½***

2284	A484	$2	multi	10	6
2285	A484	$3	multi	15	10
2286	A484	$4	multi	20	12
2287	A484	$18	multi	90	65

Flag Type of 1978
Value Colorless in Colored Panel

1981 **Litho.** ***Perf. 13½***

Panel Color

2288	A432	$1	dk bl	5	5
2289	A432	$1.50	lt ol	8	5
2290	A432	$2	dk ol bis	10	6
2291	A432	$3	red	15	10
2292	A432	$4	blue	20	12
2293	A432	$5	sepia	25	15
2294	A432	$6	orange	30	20
2295	A432	$7	green	35	22
2296	A432	$8	magenta	40	25
2297	A432	$9	ol grn	45	28
2298	A432	$10	dk pur	50	30
2299	A432	$12	lilac	60	40
2300	A432	$14	dk grn	70	45
			Nos. 2288-2300 (13)	4.13	2.63

Second line (red) below flag is a hairline, notably thinner.

Tubercle Bacillus Centenary A485

Cheng Shih-liang, Revolutionary A486

Wmk.323

1982, Mar. 24 **Litho.** ***Perf. 13½***

2309	A485	$2	multi	10	6

1982, Mar. 29 **Engr.** ***Perf. 13½x12½***

Granite Paper

2310	A486	$2	car rose	10	6

Children's Day—A487

Designs: Various children's drawings. $2 vert.

1982, Apr. 4 **Litho.**

2311	A487	$2	multi	10	6
2312	A487	$3	multi	15	10
2313	A487	$5	multi	25	15
2314	A487	$8	multi	40	25

Dentists' Day—A488

1982, May 4 **Litho.** ***Perf. 13½***

2315	A488	$2	Tooth, boy	10	6
2316	A488	$3	Flossing, brushing	15	10
2317	A488	$10	Examination	50	30

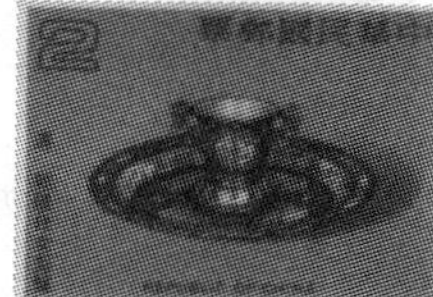

Champleve Enamel Cup and Saucer, 18th Cent.—A489

Painted Enamelware: $5, Cloisonne gold-plated duck Ch'ien-lung period (1736-1795) (vert.). $8, Incense burner, K'ang-hsi period (1662-1722). $12, Cloisonne pitcher, Ch'ien-lung period (vert.).

1982, May 20 **Photo.** ***Perf. 12***

Granite Paper

2318	A489	$2	multi	10	6
2319	A489	$5	multi	25	16
2320	A489	$8	multi	40	26
2321	A489	$12	multi	60	40

See Nos. 2348-2351.

Poets' Day—A490

Tang Dynasty Poetry Illustrations (618-906): $2, Spring Dawn, by Meng Hao-Jan. $3, On Looking for a Hermit and Not Finding Him, by Chia Tao. $5, Summer Dying, by Liu Yu-Hsi. $18, Looking at the Snow Drifts on South Mountain, by Tsu Yung.

Wmk. 323

1982, June 25 **Litho.** ***Perf. 13½***

2322	A490	$2	multi	10	6
2323	A490	$3	multi	15	10
2324	A490	$5	multi	25	16
2325	A490	$18	multi	90	60

See Nos. 2352-2355.

5th World Women's Softball Championship, Taipei, July 1-12—A491

1982, July 2

2326	A491	$2	lt grn & multi	10	6
2327	A491	$18	tan & multi	90	60

Scouting Year—A492

1982, July 18

2328	A492	$2	Crossing bridge, Baden-Powell	10	6
2329	A492	$18	Emblem, camp	90	60

Stamp in Tongs—A493

1982, Aug. 9

2330	A493	$2	shown	10	6
2331	A493	$18	Album stamps magnified	90	60

Carved Lion, Tsu Shih Temple A494

Hsun Kuan Saving Hsiang-cheng City A495

Tsu Shih Temple of Sanhsia Architecture: $3, Lion brackets (horiz.). $5, Sub-lintels. $18, Tiled roof (horiz.).

1982, Sept. 1 **Litho.** ***Perf. 13½***

2332	A494	$2	multi	10	6
2333	A494	$3	multi	15	10
2334	A494	$5	multi	25	15
2335	A494	$18	multi	90	60

1982, Oct. 15 ***Perf. 14x13½***

Designs: Scenes from The Thirty-Six Examples of Filial Piety, Folk Tale collection by Wu Yen-huan.

2336	A495	$1	multi	5	5
2337	A495	$2	multi	10	6
2338	A495	$3	multi	15	10
2339	A495	$5	multi	25	15

30th Anniv. of China Youth Corps—A496

1982, Oct. 31

2340	A496	$2	Riding	10	6
2341	A496	$3	Raising flag, vert.	15	10
2342	A496	$18	Mountain climbing	90	60

Seated Lohan (Buddhist Saint) A497

New Year 1983 (Year of the Boar) A498

Paintings of Lohan, Hanging Scrolls by Liu Sung-nien, 13th cent.

Wmk. 323

1982, Nov. 12 **Litho.** ***Perf. 13x12½***

2343	A497	$2	multi	10	6
2344	A497	$3	multi	15	10
2345	A497	$18	multi	90	60
a.			Souvenir sheet of 3	1.25	75

No. 2345a contains Nos. 2343-2345; marginal inscription. Size: 140x102mm.

1982, Dec. 1 ***Perf. 12½***

2346	A498	$1	multi	5	5
2347	A498	$10	multi	50	30
a.			Souvenir sheet of 4	1.25	75

No. 2347a contains 2 each Nos. 2346-2347; marginal inscription. Size: 78x102mm.

Enamelware Type of 1982

Designs: $2, Square basin, Ch'ing Dynasty (1644-1911). $3, Vase, Ch'ien-lung period (1736-1795) (vert.). $4, Tea pot, Ch'ien-lung period. $18, Elephant vase, Ch'ing Dynasty (vert.).

1983, Jan. 5 **Photo.** ***Perf. 12***

Granite Paper

2348	A489	$2	multi	10	6
2349	A489	$3	multi	15	10
2350	A489	$4	multi	20	12
2351	A489	$18	multi	90	60

Poetry Illustration Type of 1982

Sung Dynasty Poetry: $2, Seeing the Flowers Fade Away. $3, River. $5, Freckled with Clouds is the Azure Sky. $11, Yielding Fine Fragrance in the Snow. Nos. 2352-2355 vert.

Wmk. 323

1983, Feb. 10 **Litho.** ***Perf. 13½***

2352	A490	$2	multi	10	6
2353	A490	$3	multi	15	8
2354	A490	$5	multi	25	16
2355	A490	$11	multi	55	30

Mt. Jade, Taiwan—A499

983, Mar. 1

356	A499	$2	Wawa Valley, vert.	10	6
357	A499	$3	University Pond, vert.	15	8
358	A499	$18	shown	90	60

400th Anniv. of Arrival of Matteo Ricci (1552-1610), Italian Missionary—A500

Wmk. 323

1983, Apr. 3 **Litho.** ***Perf. 14x13½***

2359	A500	$2	Globe	10	6
2360	A500	$18	Great Wall	90	60

Mandarin Phonetic Symbols, 70th Anniv.
A501

Scenes from Lady White Snake Fairytale
A502

Wmk. 323

1983, May 22 **Litho.** ***Perf. 13½***

2361	A501	$2	Wu Ching-heng, inventor	10	6
2362	A501	$18	Children writing	90	60

1983, June 15 ***Perf. 14x13½***

2363	A502	$2	multi	10	6
2364	A502	$3	lt bl & multi	15	10
2365	A502	$3	org & multi	15	10
2366	A502	$18	multi	90	60

Bamboo Jug—A503

Various bamboo carved objects. Nos. 2367-2369 Ch'ing dynasty.

Wmk. 323

1983, July 14 **Litho.** ***Perf. 13½***

2367	A503	$2	shown	10	6
2368	A503	$3	Tao-t'ieh motif vase	15	10
2369	A503	$4	Landscape sculpture	20	12
2370	A503	$18	Brush holder, Ming dynasty	90	60

World Communications Year—A504

Wmk. 323

1983, Aug. 5 **Litho.** ***Perf. 13½***

2371	A504	$2	Globe	10	6
2372	A504	$18	Emblem	90	60

Fishing Industry (Local Fish)—A505

1983, Aug. 20

2373	A505	$2	Epinephelus tauvina	10	6
2374	A505	$18	Saurida undosquamis	90	60

40th Journalists' Day—A506

1983, Sept. 1

2375	A506	$2	multi	10	6

Views of Mongolia and Tibet—A507

1983, Sept. 15

2376	A507	$2	Village	10	6
2377	A507	$3	Potala Palace	15	10
2378	A507	$5	Sheep grazing	25	15
2379	A507	$11	Camel caravan	55	32

2nd East Asian Bird Protection Conference, Oct.—A508

1983, Oct. 8 **Litho.** ***Perf. 13½***

2380	A508	$2	Lanius cristatus, vert.	10	6
2381	A508	$18	Butastur indicus	90	60

Plum Blossoms, Photography by Hu Ch'ung-hsien—A509

1983, Oct. 31 **Litho.** ***Perf. 14x13½***

2382	A509	$2	multi	10	6
2383	A509	$3	multi	15	10
2384	A509	$5	multi	25	15
2385	A509	$11	multi	55	32

Jaycees Intl., 38th World Congress, Taipei—A510

1983, Nov. 6 ***Perf. 13x13½, 13½x13***

2386	A510	$2	JCI and Congress emblems	10	6
2387	A510	$18	Globe and emblems (horiz.)	90	60

8th Asian-Pacific Cardiology Congress—A511

1983, Nov. 27 **Litho.** ***Perf. 13½***

2388	A511	$2	shown	10	6
2389	A511	$18	Electrocardiogram	90	60

New Year 1984 (Year of the Rat)—A512

1983, Dec. 1 **Litho.** ***Perf. 12½***

2390	A512	$1	multi	5	5
2391	A512	$10	multi	50	30
	a.		Souvenir sheet of 4	1.10	65

No. 2391a contains 2 each Nos. 2390-2391; marginal inscription. Size: 78x102mm.

Literacy Week—A513

1983, Dec. 17 **Litho.** ***Perf. 13½***

2392	A513	$2	shown	10	6
2393	A513	$18	Modern family, vert.	90	60

World Freedom Day—A514

1984, Jan. 23 **Litho.** ***Perf. 13½***

2394	A514	$2	Korean War Patriots	10	6
2395	A514	$18	Intl. support	90	60

Drama Day—A515

Yuan Dynasty Poetry Illustrations by Tien-shih Lin (Poems by): $2, Kuan Yun-shih. $3, Po Pu. $5, Chang Ko-chiu. $18, Shang Cheng-shu.

1984, Feb. 15 **Litho.** ***Perf. 13½***

2396	A515	$2	multi	10	6
2397	A515	$3	multi	15	10
2398	A515	$5	multi	25	16
2399	A515	$18	multi	90	60

A516

A517

A518

A519

Arbor Day

1984, Mar. 12 **Litho.** ***Perf. 13½x14***

2400	A516	$2	multi	10	6
2401	A517	$2	multi	10	6
2402	A518	$2	multi	10	6
2403	A519	$2	multi	10	6

Nos. 2400-2403 se-tenant.

Lin Chueh-min—A520

1984, Mar. 29 **Engr.** ***Perf. 13x12½***
Granite Paper

2404	A520	$2 dk grn	10	6

Central News Agency, 60th Anniv.—A521

Wmk.
1984, Apr. 1 **Litho.** ***Perf. 14x13½***

2405	A521	$2 Emblem	10	6
2406	A521	$10 Emblem, satellite, dish antenna	50	30

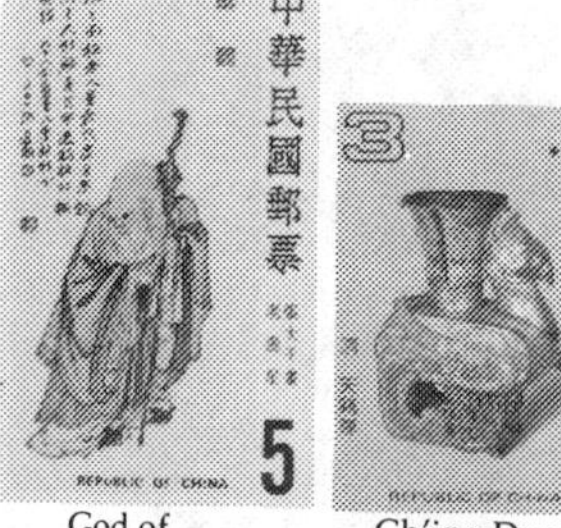

God of Longevity, A522 — Ch'ing Dynasty Enamelware A523

Paintings by Chang Ta-chien (1899-1983): $2, Five Auspicious Tokens. $18, Lotus Blossoms in Ink Splash.

Wmk. 323
1984, Apr. 20 **Litho.** ***Perf. 11½***

2407	A522	$2 multi	10	6
2408	A522	$5 multi	25	15
2409	A522	$18 multi	90	60

1984, May 20 **Photo.** ***Perf. 12***
Granite Paper

2410	A523	$2 Cup, pot, plate, horiz.	10	6
2411	A523	$3 Wine jug	15	10
2412	A523	$4 Teapot	20	12
2413	A523	$18 Candle holder	90	60

China Airlines World-wide Service Inauguration—A524

1984, May 31 **Litho.** ***Perf. 13½x14***

2414	A524	$2 Jet circling globe	10	6
2415	A524	$7 Globe, jet	35	28
2416	A524	$11 New York City	55	45
2417	A524	$18 Amsterdam	90	60

30th Navigation Day—A525

Wmk. 323
1984, July 11 **Litho.** ***Perf. 13½x13***

2418	A525	$2 Container ship	10	6
2419	A525	$18 Oil tanker	90	60

1984 Summer Olympics A526 — Alpine Plants A527

1984, July 28 ***Perf. 13½x14, 14x13½***

2420	A526	$2 Judo, horiz.	10	6
2421	A526	$5 Archery	25	15
2422	A526	$18 Swimming, horiz.	90	60

1984, Aug. 8 ***Perf. 13***

2423	A527	$2 Gentiana arisanensis	10	6
2424	A527	$3 Epilobium nankotaizanense	15	10
2425	A527	$5 Adenophora uehatae	25	15
2426	A527	$18 Aconitum fukutomei	90	60

The Eighteen Scholars, Sung Dynasty Hanging Scroll—A528

Details.

Wmk. 323
1984, Aug. 20 **Litho.** ***Perf. 13***

2427	A528	$2 Playing instruments	10	6
2428	A528	$3 Playing chess	15	10
2429	A528	$5 Practicing calligraphy	25	15
2430	A528	$18 Painting	90	60

Athletics Day

A529 A530

1984, Sept. 9

2431	A529	$5 Two players	25	15
2432	A530	$5 One player	25	15

Asian-Pacific Parliamentarians' Union, 20th Anniv.—A531

1984, Sept. 9

2433	A531	$10 "20," map of Asia	50	30

Postal Museum Opening—A532

1984, Oct. 10 **Litho.** ***Perf. 12½***

2434	A532	$2 No. 1458	10	6
2435	A532	$5 No. 296	25	15
2436	A532	$18 Museum	90	60
a.		Souvenir sheet of 3	1.25	1.00

No. 2436a contains Nos. 2434-2436. Size: 129x91mm.

Flag, Alliance Emblem—A533

1984, Oct. 16 ***Perf. 13½***

2437	A533	$2 multi	10	6

Grand Alliance for China's Reunification Under the Three Principles of the People Convention, Taipei, Oct. 16-17.

Veteran's Assistance A534

Pine Tree A535

1984, Nov. 1 **Litho.** ***Perf. 13½***

2438	A534	$2 Vignettes	10	6

1984, Nov. 12

2439	A535	$2 shown	10	6
2440	A535	$8 Bamboo	40	25
2441	A535	$10 Plum	50	30

See Nos. 2495-2497.

New Year 1985 (Year of the Ox)—A536

1984, Dec. 1 ***Perf. 12x12½***

2442	A536	$1 multi	5	
2443	A536	$10 multi	50	3
a.		Miniature sheet of 4 (2 each #2442-2443)	1.25	7

Size of No. 2443a: 78x102mm.

Judicial Day 1985—A537

1985, Jan. 11 **Litho.** ***Perf. 13½***

2444	A537	$5 Scales, legal codes	25	15

Quemoy and Matsu Scenes—A538

1985, Jan. 23 **Litho.** ***Perf. 13½x14***

2445	A538	$2 Ku-kang Lake, Quemoy	10	6
2446	A538	$5 Kuang-hai Stone, Quemoy	25	15
2447	A538	$8 Sheng-li Reservoir, Matsu	40	25
2448	A538	$10 Tung-chu Lighthouse, Matsu	50	30

Sir Robert Hart (1835-1911)—A539

1985, Feb. 15 **Litho.** ***Perf. 14x13½***

2449	A539	$2 No. 1	10	6

Inspector General of Chinese Customs, 1863-1908, and founder of the Chinese Postal Service.

Lo Fu-hsing (1886-1914)—A540

1985, Feb. 24 ***Perf. 13x13½***

2450	A540	$2 multi	10	6

Tsou Jung (1882-1905)—A541

985, Mar. 29 Engr. *Perf. 13½x12½*
Granite Paper

451	A541	$3 green	15	10

Chung-cheng Memorial Hall Main Gate—A542

1985, Apr. 5 Litho. *Perf. 13*

2452	A542	$2 shown	10	6
2453	A542	$8 Tzuhu Memorial	40	24
2454	A542	$10 Chiang Kai-shek, vert.	50	30

Tenth death anniv. of Chiang Kai-shek (1887-1975).

Mother's Day—A543

1985, May 8 Litho. *Perf. 13½*

2455	A543	$2 Carnation	10	6
2456	A543	$2 Day lily	10	6
a.		Se-tenant pair	20	12

Kaohsiung Cross-Harbor Tunnel, 1st Anniv.—A544

1985, May 18

2457	A544	$5 Tunnel to Chi-chin Island	25	15

Girl Scouts, 75th Anniv.—A545

Wmk. 323
1985, June 1 Litho. *Perf. 13½*

2458	A545	$2 multi	10	6
2459	A545	$18 multi	90	36

Poetry Illustration Type of 1982

Designs from The Book of Odes, Confucius.

Wmk. 323
1985, June 22 Litho. *Perf.*

2460	A490	$2 Spring	10	6
2461	A490	$5 Summer	25	15
2462	A490	$8 Fall	40	24
2463	A490	$10 Winter	50	30

Fruit—A546

Wmk. 323
1985, July 5 Litho. *Perf. 13½x14*

2464	A546	$2 Wax Jambo	12	8
2465	A546	$3 Guava	15	10
2466	A546	$5 Carambola	25	15
2467	A546	$8 Litchi nut	42	25

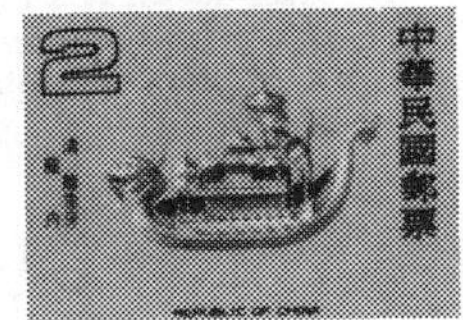

Ch'ing Dynasty (1644-1911) Ivory Carvings—A547

1985, July 18 Wmk. 323 *Perf. 13½*

2468	A547	$2 Dragon Boat	12	8
2469	A547	$3 Landscape	15	10
2470	A547	$5 Melon, water container	25	15
2471	A547	$18 Brush holder, vert.	95	58

T'ang Dynasty (618-907) Aristocrat—A548

Designs: $5, Sung Dynasty (960-1280) palace woman. $8, Yuan Dynasty (1280-1368) aristocrat. $11, Ming Dynasty (1368-1644) aristocrat.

1985, Aug. 1 Wmk. 323 *Perf. 13½*

2472	A548	$2 multi	12	8
2473	A548	$5 multi	25	15
2474	A548	$8 multi	42	25
2475	A548	$11 multi	55	32

4th Asian Conference on Costume, Aug. 3.

Social Welfare Program—A549

1985, Aug. 1 Wmk. 323 *Perf. 13½x14*

2476	A549	$2 Heart, bird feeding young	12	8

Historic Sites—A550

Wmk. 323
1985, Sept. 3 Litho. *Perf. 13½*

2477	A550	$2 Taipei North Gate	12	8
2478	A550	$5 San Domingo Fort, Tamsui	25	15
2479	A550	$8 Lung Shun Temple, Lukang	42	25
2480	A550	$10 Confucius Temple, Changhua	52	30

Bonsai A551

Trade Shows A552

Wmk. 323
1985, Sept. 22 *Perf. 13½x14*

2481	A551	$2 Oak	10	6
2482	A551	$5 Five-leaf pine	25	15
2483	A551	$8 Lohan pine	40	24
2484	A551	$18 Banyan	90	55

1985, Oct. 5 *Perf. 13½*

Taipei World Trade Center and show emblems: No. 2485a, Sporting goods. No. 2485b, Toys and gifts. No. 2485c, Electronics. No. 2485d, Machinery. Se-tenant in continuous design.

2485	Strip of 4	40	24
a.-d.	A552 $2, Any single	10	6

Scenes of Modern Taiwan, Map, Flag—A553

1985, Oct. 25

2486	A553	$2 shown	10	6
2487	A553	$18 Chiang Kai-shek, Triumphal Arch	90	55

Defeat of Japanese army, end of World War II, and return of Taiwan to control of the Republic, 40th anniv.

7th Asian Conference on Mental Retardation A554

Sun Yat-sen and Birthplace A555

1985, Nov. 8 *Perf. 14x13½*

2488	A554	$2 multi	10	6
2489	A554	$11 multi	55	32

1985, Nov. 12 *Perf. 13½*

2490	A555	$2 multi	10	6
2491	A555	$18 multi	90	55

Postal Life Insurance, 50th Anniv. A556

New Year 1986 (Year of the Tiger) A557

1985, Dec. 1

2492	A556	$2 multi	10	6

1985, Dec. 1 *Perf. 12½*

2493	A557	$1 multi	5	5
2494	A557	$10 multi	50	30
a.		Miniature sheet of 4 (2 each #2493-2494)	1.10	1.10

Flora Type of 1984

1986, Jan. 10 Litho. *Perf. 13½*

2495	A535	$1 Pine	5	5
2496	A535	$11 Bamboo	55	32
2497	A535	$18 Plum	90	55

Cultural Renaissance Movement—A558

Painting: Hermit Anglers on a Mountain Stream, Ming Dynasty, 1386-1644. Se-tenant in a continuous design.

1986, Jan. 28 Litho. *Perf. 13½*

2507	Strip of 5	50	30
a.-e.	A558 $2, any single	10	6

Plum Blossom Type of 1979

Wmk. 323

1986, Jan. 10 Engr. *Perf. 13½x12½*

2510	A440	$40	car rose	2.50	1.75

Floral Arrangements—A559

Wmk. 323

1986, Feb. 20 Litho. *Perf. 13½*

2517	A559	$2	multi	12	8
2518	A559	$5	multi	30	20
2519	A559	$8	multi	50	35
2520	A559	$10	multi	62	42

Natl. Postal Service, 90th Anniv.—A560

Designs: $2, Unloading express mail at airport. $5, Motorcycle delivery, vert. $8, Technological innovations, vert. $10, Electronic sorting machine.

1986, Mar. 20

2521	A560	$2	multi	12	8
2522	A560	$5	multi	30	20
2523	A560	$8	multi	50	35
2524	A560	$10	multi	62	42
a.			Souvenir sheet of 4, #2521-2524	1.55	1.05

No. 2524a has pale salmon and red decorative margin. Size: 130x100mm.

Chen Tien-hua (1875-1905), Revolutionary—A561

1986, Mar. 29 Engr. *Perf. 13½x12½*
Granite Paper

2525	A561	$2	violet	12	8

Yushan Natl. Park—A562

Various views.

1986, Apr. 10 Litho. *Perf. 13½*

2526	A562	$2	multi	12	8
2527	A562	$5	multi	30	20
2528	A562	$8	multi	50	35
2529	A562	$10	multi	62	42

Power Plants—A563

1986, Apr. 29

2530	A563	$2	Hydro-electric	12	8
2531	A563	$8	Thermo-electric	50	35
2532	A563	$10	Nuclear	62	42

Economic prosperity through energy development.

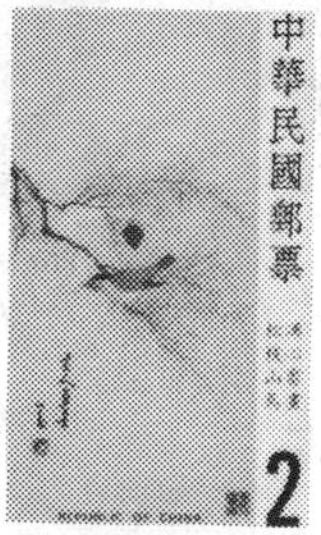

Paintings by P'u Hsin-yu (1896-1963)—A564

1986, May 22 *Perf. 11½*

2533	A564	$2	Bird	12	8
2534	A564	$8	Landscape	50	35
2535	A564	$10	Woman in forest	62	42

Asian Productivity Org., 25th Anniv.—A565

1986, June 3 *Perf. 13x13½*

2536	A565	$2	multi	12	8
2537	A565	$11	multi	68	45

Natl. Productivity Center, 30th anniv.

Coral-reef Fish—A566

Designs: No. 2538a, Chrysiptera starcki. No. 2538b, Chelmon rostratus. No. 2538c, Chaetodon xanthurus. No. 2538d, Chaetodon quadrimaculatus. No. 2538e, Chaetodon meyeri. No. 2538f, Genicanthus semifasciatus. No. 2538g, Genicanthus semifasciatus. No. 2538h, Pomacanthus annularis. No. 2538i, Lienardella fasciata. No. 2538j, Balistapus undulatus.

1986, June 3 *Perf. 13½*

2538	Block of 10	1.25	80
a.-j.	A566 $2, any single	12	8

Protection of Intellectual Property Rights—A567

1986, June 12

2539	A567	$2	Macaw	12	8

Nos. 2294 and 2297 Ovptd. "60th ANNIVERSARY OF NORTHWARD EXPEDITION BY THE NATIONAL REVOLUTIONARY ARMY" in Chinese and Surcharged with Fleur-de-lis and New Value.

1986, July 9 Litho. *Perf. 13½*

2540	A432	$2	on $6 multi	12	8
2541	A432	$8	on $9 multi	48	32

Bridges—A568

1986, July 30

2542	A568	$2	Tzu Mu, 1965	12	8
2543	A568	$5	Chang Hung, 1968	30	20
2544	A568	$8	Kuan Fu, 1977	48	32
2545	A568	$10	Kuan Tu, 1983	60	40

Love between Liang Shanpo and Chu Yingtai, Folk Tale—A569

Cartoons by Huang Mu-ts'un: No. 2546a, Yingtai disguised to go to school. No. 2546b, Yingtai and Shanpo meet in class. No. 2546c, The friends at pond. No. 2546d, Yingtai summoned home for arranged marriage. No. 2546e, Yingtai and Shanpo ascend to heaven as butterflies.

1986, Aug. 12 *Perf. 12½*

2546	Strip of 5	1.50	1.0
a.-e.	A569 $5, any single	30	2

Social Awareness Campaign—A570

1986, Sept. 12 Litho. *Perf. 13½*

2547	A570	$2	Rainbow, children	12	8
2548	A570	$8	Children, adults	48	32

Folk Costumes—A571

Designs: $2, Shang Dynasty (1766-1122 B.C.) aristocrat. $5, Warring States (403-221 B.C.) aristocrat. $8, Later Han Dynasty (A.D. 25-221) empress. $10, Flying ribbons gown, Wei and Tsin Dynasties (A.D. 221-420) aristocrat.

1986, Sept. 23 Litho. *Perf. 13½*

2549	A571	$2	multi	12	8
2550	A571	$5	multi	30	20
2551	A571	$8	multi	50	35
2552	A571	$10	multi	62	42

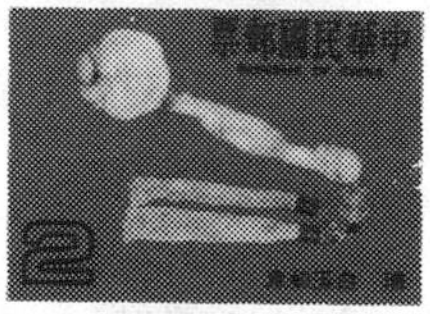

Ch'ing Dynasty Ju-i Scepters—A572

1986, Oct. 10 Photo. *Perf. 14½x15*

2553	A572	$2	White jade	12	8
2554	A572	$3	Red coral	18	12
2555	A572	$4	Redwood and gems	24	16
2556	A572	$18	Gilded wood	1.10	75

Chiang Kai-Shek—A573

Portrait and: $5, Map and flag. $8, Emblem. $10, Flags on globe.

1986, Oct. 31 Litho. *Perf. 13½*

2557	A573	$2	multi	12	8
2558	A573	$5	multi	30	20
2559	A573	$8	multi	48	32
2560	A573	$10	multi	60	40
a.			Souv. sheet of 4, #2557-2560	1.50	1.00

No. 2560a has pale orange inscribed margin. Size: 120x90mm.

Cultural Heritage—A574

Architecture: $2, Chin-Kuang Fu land development and defense fund building, 1826. $5, h-sha-wan Gun Emplacement, Keelung, 1841, stored 1979. $8, Fort Hsi T'ai, 1886. $10, Matsu mple, Peng-hu, renovated 1563-1624.

986, Nov. 14 Litho. ***Perf. 13½***

[illegible]	A574	$2 multi	12	8
62	A574	$5 multi	30	20
63	A574	$8 multi	48	32
64	A574	$10 multi	60	40

New Year 1987 (Year of the Hare)—A575

986, Dec. 1 ***Perf. 12½***

65	A575	$1 dl pink & multi	6	5
66	A575	$10 pale grn & multi	60	40
a.		Souv. sheet of 4, 2 each #2565-2566	1.35	1.35

No. 2566a has inscribed margin. Size: 3x102mm.

Kenting, 1st Natl. Park—A576

1987, Jan. 8 Litho. ***Perf. 13½***

2567	A576	$2 Garden	14	6
2568	A576	$5 Shore rocks	32	14
2569	A576	$8 Shore and hill	52	22
2570	A576	$10 Shore and rocks, diff.	65	28

Folk Art—A577

Puppets: $2, Hand puppet. $5, Marionette. $18, Shadow puppet.

1987, Feb. 12 Litho. ***Perf. 14x13½***

2571	A577	$2 multi	14	6
2572	A577	$5 multi	32	14
2573	A577	$18 multi	1.20	80

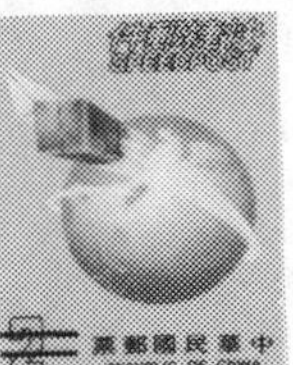

Speedpost

A578

Wu Yueh (1878-1905), Revolutionary A579

1987, Mar. 20 Litho. ***Perf. 14x13½***

2574	A578	$2 multi	14	6
2575	A578	$18 multi	1.20	80

Stamp Day.

1987, Mar. 29 Engr. ***Perf. 13½x12½***

2576	A579	$2 orange	14	6

SEMI-POSTAL STAMPS.

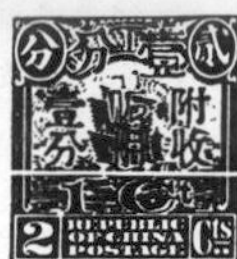

SP1

Red or Blue Surcharge.

1920, Dec. 1 *Perf. 14, 15* Unwmkd.

B1	SP1	1c on 2c grn	7.00	1.75
B2	SP1	3c on 4c scar (B)	9.00	2.75
B3	SP1	5c on 6c gray	14.00	4.00

The surcharge represents the actual franking value. The extra cent helped victims of the 1919 Yellow River flood.

War Refugees
SP2

Black Surcharge.

1944, Oct. 10 Engraved *Perf. 12*

B4	SP2	$2+$2 on 50c+50c brt ultra	25	25
B5	SP2	$4+$4 on 8c+8c brt grn	25	25
B6	SP2	$5+$5 on 21c+21c red brn	75	75
B7	SP2	$6+$6 on 28c+28c ol grn	1.25	1.25
B8	SP2	$10+$10 on 33c+33c red	1.75	1.75
B9	SP2	$20+$20 on $1+$1 vio	3.50	3.50
a.		Sheet of six	12.50	12.50
		Nos. B4-B9 (6)	7.75	7.75

The borders of each stamp differ slightly in design.

The surtax was for war refugees.

No. B9a measures 191x112mm. and contains one each of Nos. B4 to B9 with marginal inscriptions in olive green, red brown and bright green.

Nos. B4–B8 exist without surcharge, but were not regularly issued.

Great Wall of China
SP4

Chinese Refugee Family
SP5

Lithographed.

1948, July 5 *Perf. 14, Imperf.*

Without Gum.

Cross in Carmine.

B11	SP4	$5000 +$2000 vio	12	12
B12	SP4	$10,000 +$2000 brn	12	12
B13	SP4	$15,000 +$2000 gray	12	12
a.		Cross omitted		

The surtax was for anti-tuberculosis work.

Republic of China (Taiwan)

1954, Oct. 1 Engraved *Perf. 12*

Without Gum

B14	SP5	40c +10c dp bl	8.00	1.25
B15	SP5	$1.60 +40c lil rose	16.00	3.00
B16	SP5	$5 +$1 red	37.50	22.50

The surtax was used to aid in the evacuation of Chinese from North Viet Nam.

AIR POST STAMPS.

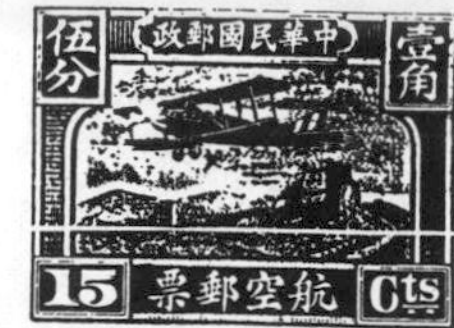

Curtiss "Jenny" over Great Wall
(Bars of Republic flag on tail.)
AP1

Engraved

1921, July 1 *Perf. 14* Unwmkd.

C1	AP1	15c bl grn & blk	17.50	8.50
C2	AP1	30c scar & blk	12.50	7.50
C3	AP1	45c dl vio & blk	12.50	7.50
C4	AP1	60c dk bl & blk	17.50	8.50
C5	AP1	90c ol grn & blk	20.00	10.00
		Nos. C1-C5 (5)	80.00	42.00

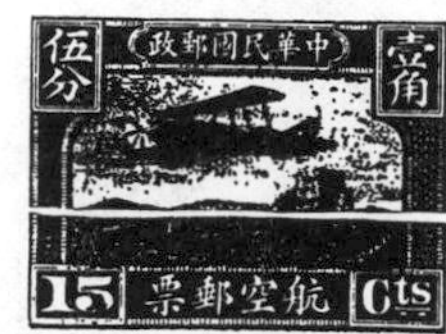

(Nationalist sun emblem on tail.)
AP2

1929, July 5

C6	AP2	15c bl grn & blk	2.50	50
C7	AP2	30c dk red & blk	4.00	1.00
C8	AP2	45c dk vio & blk	7.50	3.00
C9	AP2	60c dk bl & blk	7.50	3.00
C10	AP2	90c ol grn & blk	10.00	5.00
		Nos. C6-C10 (5)	31.50	12.50

Junkers F-13 over Great Wall
AP3

1932-37

C11	AP3	15c gray grn	10	6
C12	AP3	25c org ('33)	10	5
C13	AP3	30c red	25	10
C14	AP3	45c brn vio	10	8
C15	AP3	50c dk brn ('33)	10	8
C16	AP3	60c dk bl	10	8
C17	AP3	90c ol grn	25	10
C18	AP3	$1 yel grn ('33)	25	10
C19	AP3	$2 brn ('37)	25	10
C20	AP3	$5 brn car ('37)	1.00	75
		Nos. C11-C20 (10)	2.50	1.50

Type of 1932–37, with secret mark

1932–37 Issue. Lower part of left character joined.

Secret Mark, 1940–41 Issue. Separated.

Wmkd. Character Yu (Post) Multiple. (261)

Perf. 12, 12½, 12½x13, 13.

1940-41

C21	AP3	15c gray grn	10	*20*
C22	AP3	25c yel org	15	25
C23	AP3	30c red	10	10
a.		Vert. pair, imperf. between	150.00	
C24	AP3	45c dl rose vio ('41)	8	*25*
C25	AP3	50c brown	8	*25*
C26	AP3	60c dp bl ('41)	10	*30*
C27	AP3	90c ol ('41)	10	*30*
C28	AP3	$1 ap grn ('41)	12	*30*
C29	AP3	$2 lt brn ('41)	12	*30*
C30	AP3	$5 lake	12	*25*
		Nos. C21-C30 (10)	1.07	*2.50*

Unwmkd.

Perf. 12½, 13, 13½.

C31	AP3	15c gray grn ('41)	6	6
C32	AP3	25c lt org ('41)	6	6
C33	AP3	30c lt red ('41)	6	6
C34	AP3	45c dl rose vio ('41)	8	8
C35	AP3	50c brown	6	6
C36	AP3	60c bl ('41)	6	6
C37	AP3	90c lt ol ('41)	6	6
C38	AP3	$1 ap grn ('41)	10	10
C39	AP3	$2 lt brn ('41)	15	15
C40	AP3	$5 lake ('41)	12	12
		Nos. C31-C40 (10)	81	81

Nos. C11 and C12 Surcharged in Black

圓叁拾伍幣國

5300

1946, May 2 *Perf. 14* Unwmkd.

C41	AP3	$53 on 15c gray grn	20	*35*
C42	AP3	$73 on 25c org	650.00	700.00

Forgeries of No. C42 exist.

On Nos. C23, C21, C22, C29 and C30.

Perf. 13, 13x12, 12½.

Wmk. 261

C43	AP3	$23 on 30c red	10	*40*
C44	AP3	$53 on 15c gray grn	7.00	*9.00*
C45	AP3	$73 on 25c yel org	30	*50*
C46	AP3	$100 on $2 lt brn	10	*40*
C47	AP3	$200 on $5 lake	15	*45*

On Nos. C33, C31, C32, C39 and C40.

Perf. 13, 13x12, 13x12½, 12½.

Unwmkd.

C48	AP3	$23 on 30c lt red	5	5
a.		Inverted surcharge	100.00	
b.		"2300" omitted	50.00	
c.		Last character (kuo) of surch. omitted	50.00	
C49	AP3	$53 on 15c gray grn	5	5
a.		Horiz. pair, imperf. between		750.00
C50	AP3	$73 on 25c lt org	5	5
a.		Inverted surcharge	750.00	
C51	AP3	$100 on $2 lt brn	5	5
C52	AP3	$200 on $5 lake	5	5
a.		Inverted surcharge	75.00	

The surcharges on Nos. C41–C52 represent Chinese national currency and were applied at Shanghai.

Douglas DC-4 over Sun Yat-sen Mausoleum, Nanking
AP4

1946, Sept. 10 Litho. *Perf. 14*

Without Gum.

C53	AP4	$27 blue	15	10

No. C23 Surcharged in Black

圓萬壹作改

Perf. 13x12

1948, May 18 Wmk. 261

C54	AP3	$10,000 on 30c red	10	*50*

Same, in Black or Carmine, on Nos. C33, C32, C37, C36, C18 and C38.

Perf. 12½, 13x12½, 14

Unwmkd.

C55	AP3	$10,000 on 30c lt red	7	*1*
C56	AP3	$20,000 on 25c lt org	8	*1.*
C57	AP3	$30,000 on 90c lt ol (C)	8	*1.*
C58	AP3	$50,000 on 60c bl (C)	10	*2*
C59	AP3	$50,000 on $1 yel grn (C)	40.00	40.0
C60	AP3	$50,000 on $1 ap grn (C)	10	*2*

No. C53 Surcharged in Black

改作壹萬圓

Perf. 14.

C61	AP4	$10,000 on $27 bl	8	*15*
		Nos. C54-C61 (8)	40.61	*41.42*

Douglas DC-4 and Arrow
AP5

Lithographed

1949, May 2 *Perf. 12½* Unwmkd.

Without Gum.

C62	AP5	bl grn	1.25	1.25
a.		Rouletted	3.50	3.50

See note after No. 959.

Revenue Stamp Overprinted in Blue

政郵國民華中
費空航內國

1949, May Engraved *Perf. 14*

C63	A95	$100 ol grn	17.50	19.00

See note after No. 962.

Republic of China (Taiwan)

Cheng Ch'eng-kung (Koxinga)
AP6

Typographed.

Rouletted.

1950, Sept. 26 Unwmkd.

Without Gum.

C64	AP6	60c dp bl	11.00	2.00

Plane over City Gate, Taipei
AP7

Jet Planes above Chung Shan Bridge
AP8

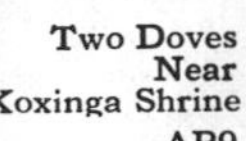

Two Doves Near Koxinga Shrine
AP9

1954 **Engraved** ***Perf. 11½***

Without Gum

C65	AP7	$1 dk brn	7.00	50
a.	Vert. pair, imperf. btwn.			300.00
C66	AP8	$1.60 ol blk	4.50	40
a.	Vert. pair, imperf. btwn.		200.00	
b.	Horiz. pair, imperf. between		150.00	175.00
C67	AP9	$5 grnsh bl	5.50	50

No. C67 Surcharged in Red.

1958, Dec. 11

C68	AP9	$3.50 on $5 grnsh bl	1.25	25

Sea Gull
AP10

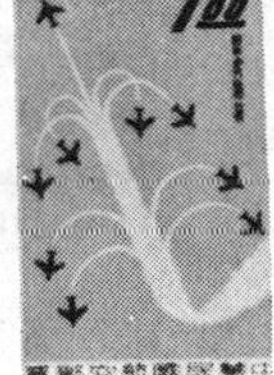

Sabre Jets in Bomb Burst Formation
AP11

1959, Mar. 20 Photo. ***Perf. 13***

C69	AP10	$8 bl, gray & blk	1.20	25

1960, Feb. 29 ***Perf. 13*** **Unwmkd.**

Plane Formations: $2, Loop (horiz.). $5, Diamond formation passing over grounded plane (horiz.).

C70	AP11	$1 multi	1.50	40
C71	AP11	$2 multi	1.50	25
C72	AP11	$5 multi	3.00	50

Issued to honor the Chinese Air Force and the "Thunder Tiger" aerobatic team.

Jet Airliner over Pitan Bridge
AP12

Designs: $6, Jet over Tropic of Cancer monument, Kiai (vert.). $10, Jet over Lion Head mountain, Sinchu (vert.).

1963, Aug. 14 Photo. ***Perf. 13***

C73	AP12	$2.50 multi	1.00	8
C74	AP12	$6 multi	1.75	12
C75	AP12	$10 multi	3.50	1.00

Boeing 727 over Chilin Pavilion, Grand Hotel
AP13

Design: $8, Boeing 727 over National Palace Museum, Taipei.

1967, Apr. 1 ***Perf. 13*** **Unwmkd.**

C76	AP13	$5 multi	90	10
C77	AP13	$8 multi	1.25	30

Wild Geese Flying over Mountains
AP14

Designs (Wild Geese flying over): $5, The sea. $8, The land (horiz.).

1969, Aug. 14 Photo. ***Perf. 13***

C78	AP14	$2.50 multi	50	10
C79	AP14	$5 multi	75	20
C80	AP14	$8 multi	1.00	30

Presidental Palace and Tzu-Ch'iang Squadron—AP15

1980, June 18 **Litho.** ***Perf. 13½***

C81	AP15	$5 *shown*	25	20
C82	AP15	$7 *China Airlines jet*	35	32
C83	AP15	$12 *China flag, jet*	60	50

Civil Aeronautics Administration, 37th Anniv.—AP16

Jet Airliners over: $7, Chiang Kai-shek Intl. Airport, vert. $11, Chung Cheng Memorial Hall. $18, Sun Yat-sen Memorial Hall.

1984, Jan. 20 Litho. ***Perf. 14x13½, 13½x14***

C84	AP16	$7 multi	35	22
C85	AP16	$11 multi	55	32
C86	AP16	$18 multi	90	60

SPECIAL DELIVERY STAMPS.

Design: Dragon in irregular oval. Stamp 8x2½ inches, divided into four parts by perforation or serrate rouletting. Prices of Nos. E1–E8 are for used parts. Complete unused strips of four are exceptionally scarce.

"Chinese Imperial Post Office" in lines, repeated to form the background which is usually lighter in color than the rest of the design.

Dragon's head facing downward. Background with period after "POSTOFFICE".

No Date.

1905 *Perf. 11.* **Unwmkd.**

E1	10c grass grn	125.00	

Serrate Roulette in Black.

E2	10c dp grn	85.00	

1907-10

Dragon's head facing forward. Background with no period after "POSTOFFICE".

No Date.

E3	10c lt bluish grn	55.00	

1909-11

Background with date at bottom.

E4	10c grn (Feb. 1909)	22.50	
E5	10c bl grn (Jan. 1911)	15.00	

1912

"Imperial Post Office" in serifed letters repeated to form the background.

No Date. No Border. Background of 30 or 28 lines.

E6	10c grn (30 lines)	22.50	
a.	28 lines	27.50	

Background of 35 lines of sans-serif letters. Colored Border

E8	10c green	27.50	

On No. E8 the medallion in the third section has Chinese characters in the background instead of the usual English inscriptions. E6 and E8 occur with many types of four-character overprints reading "Republic of China," applied locally but unofficially at various post offices.

1913

Design: Wild Goose. Stamp 7½x2¾ inches, divided into five parts.

"Chinese Post Office" in sans-serif letters, repeated to form the background of 28 lines. With border.

Serrate Roulette in Black.

E9	10c green	150.00	12.50

Unused prices for Nos. E9–E10 are for complete strips of five parts. Used prices are for single parts.

1914

"Chinese Post Office" in antique letters, forming a background of 29 or 30 lines. No border.

Serrate Roulette in Green.

E10	10c green	40.00	1.25

On No. E9 the background is in sans-serif capitals, the Chinese and English inscriptions are on white tablets and the serial numbers are in black.

On No. E10 the background is in antique capitals and extends under the inscriptions. The serial numbers are in green.

NOTE:

In February, 1916, the Special Delivery Stamps were demonetized and became merely receipts without franking value. To mark this, four of the five sections of the stamp had the letters A, B, C, D either handstamped or printed on them.

SD1

Typographed.

1941 ***Rouletted*** **Unwmkd.**

Without Gum.

E11	SD1	($2) car & yel	11.00	3.00

Motorcycle Messenger SD2

1949, July Litho. ***Perf. 12½***

Without Gum.

E12	SD2	red vio	1.25	1.50
a.		Rouletted	2.75	4.75

See note after No. 959.

Revenue Stamp Overprinted in Purple Brown 中華民國郵政 國內快遞費

1949 Without Gum

E13	A95	$10 grnsh gray	10.00	10.00

See note after No. 962.

REGISTRATION STAMPS.

R1

Typographed.

1941 ***Rouletted.*** **Unwmkd.**

Without Gum.

F1	R1	($1.50) grn & buff	9.00	2.25

Mountain Scene R2

1949, July Litho. ***Perf. 12½***

Without Gum.

F2	R2	carmine	1.40	1.40
a.		Rouletted	2.50	3.50

See note after No. 959.

Revenue Stamp Overprinted in Carmine 中華民國郵政 國內掛號費

1949

F3	A95	$50 dk bl	7.50	7.50

See note after No. 962.

POSTAGE DUE STAMPS.

Regular Issue of 1902-03 Overprinted in Black POSTAGE DUE 欠資

1904 ***Perf. 14 to 15.*** **Unwmkd.**

J1	A17	½c chocolate	6.00	1.25
J2	A17	1c ocher	6.00	1.00
J3	A17	2c scarlet	6.00	1.75
J4	A17	4c red brn	6.00	1.75
J5	A17	5c salmon	10.00	1.75
J6	A17	10c dk bl grn	12.00	2.00
a.		Vertical pair, imperf. between	250.00	
		Nos. J1-J6 (6)	46.00	9.50

D1 D2 D3

1904 **Engraved**

J7	D1	½c blue	2.25	15
a.		Horizontal pair, imperf. between	150.00	150.00
J8	D1	1c blue	3.50	15
J9	D1	2c blue	2.00	15
a.		Horizontal pair, imperf. between	150.00	150.00
J10	D1	4c blue	5.00	35
J11	D1	5c blue	6.00	40
J12	D1	10c blue	6.00	75
J13	D1	20c blue	15.00	2.50
J14	D1	30c blue	20.00	3.00
		Nos. J7-J14 (8)	59.75	7.45

Arabic numeral of value at left on Nos. J12 to J14.

1911

J15	D1	1c brown	5.00	1.00
J16	D1	2c brown	7.00	1.50

The ½c, 4c, 5c and 20c in brown exist but were not issued as they arrived in China after the downfall of the Ching dynasty.

Issue of 1904 Overprinted in Red 臨時中立

1912

J19	D1	½c blue	300.00	275.00
J20	D1	4c blue	475.00	375.00
J21	D1	5c blue	500.00	475.00
J22	D1	10c blue	500.00	475.00
J23	D1	20c blue	1,400.	1,200.
J24	D1	30c blue	1,400.	1,200.

Nos. J15–J16 exist with this overprint, but were not regularly issued.

1912 Overprinted in Red.

J25	D2	½c blue	25	15
J26	D2	1c brown	30	20
a.		Horizontal pair, imperf. between	175.00	
b.		Inverted overprint	150.00	
J27	D2	2c brown	50	30
J28	D2	4c blue	1.50	40
J29	D2	5c blue	85.00	80.00
J30	D2	5c brown	1.50	50
a.		Inverted overprint	110.00	90.00
J31	D2	10c blue	4.00	65
J32	D2	20c blue	6.00	1.50
J33	D2	30c blue	11.00	4.00
		Nos. J25-J33 (9)	110.05	87.70

1912 Overprinted in Black.

J34	D3	½c blue	6.00	2.00
J35	D3	½c brown	1.00	35
J36	D3	1c brown	75	3
a.		Inverted overprint	135.00	
J37	D3	2c brown	2.00	6
J38	D3	4c blue	4.00	1.
J39	D3	5c brown	4.00	1.2
a.		Horizontal pair, imperf. between	225.00	
J40	D3	10c blue	11.00	2.
J41	D3	20c brown	22.50	7.
J42	D3	30c blue	27.50	8.
		Nos. J34-J42 (9)	78.75	22.6

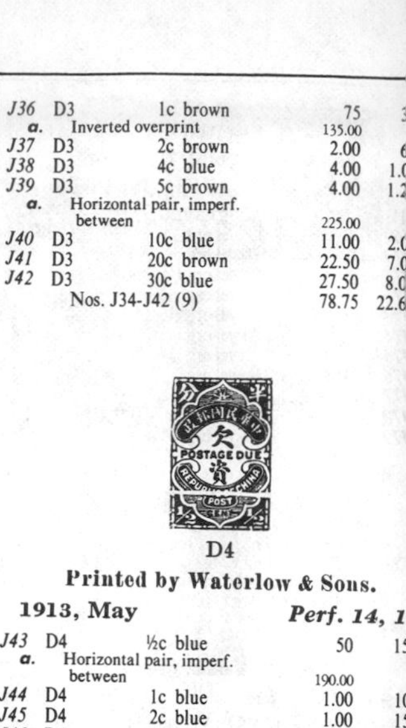

D4

Printed by Waterlow & Sons.

1913, May ***Perf. 14, 1***

J43	D4	½c blue	50	15
a.		Horizontal pair, imperf. between	190.00	
J44	D4	1c blue	1.00	10
J45	D4	2c blue	1.00	15
J46	D4	4c blue	2.50	20
J47	D4	5c blue	3.00	20
J48	D4	10c blue	5.00	50
J49	D4	20c blue	7.50	80
J50	D4	30c blue	10.00	2.00
		Nos. J43-J50 (8)	30.50	4.10

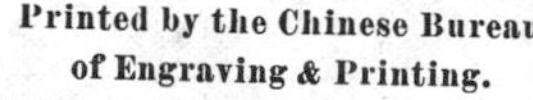

Printed by the Chinese Bureau of Engraving & Printing.

1915 **Re-engraved** ***Perf. 14***

J51	D4	½c blue	60	10
J52	D4	1c blue	1.25	10
J53	D4	2c blue	1.25	10
J54	D4	4c blue	1.25	10
J55	D4	5c blue	1.75	25
J56	D4	10c blue	2.50	35
J57	D4	20c blue	7.00	40
J58	D4	30c blue	20.00	1.50
		Nos. J51-J58 (8)	35.60	2.90

In the upper part of the stamps of type D4 there is an ornament of five marks like the letter "V" Below this is a curved label with an inscription in Chinese characters. On the 1913 stamps there are two complete background lines between the ornament and the label. The 1915 stamps show only one unbroken line at this place. There are other minute differences in the engraving of the stamps of the two issues.

D5

1932 ***Perf. 14.***

J59	D5	½c orange	12	8
J60	D5	1c orange	12	8
J61	D5	2c orange	12	8
J62	D5	4c orange	25	25
J63	D5	5c orange	25	25
J64	D5	10c orange	60	35
J65	D5	20c orange	60	35
J66	D5	30c orange	60	35
		Nos. J59-J66 (8)	2.66	1.79

1940

Regular Stamps of 1939 Overprinted in Black or Red 暫作欠資

J67	A57	$1 hn & dk brn (Bk)	1.50	1.50
J68	A57	$2 dl bl & org brn (R)	2.00	2.00

Type of 1932.
Printed by
The Commercial Press, Ltd.
Perf. 12½, 12½x13, 13.

1940-41 **Engraved.**

J69	D5	½c yel org	6	8
J70	D5	1c yel org	15	20
J71	D5	2c yel org ('41)	6	8
J72	D5	4c yel org	6	8
J73	D5	5c yel org ('41)	10	12
J74	D5	10c yel org ('41)	10	12
J75	D5	20c yel org ('41)	10	12
J76	D5	30c yel org	10	12
J77	D5	50c yel org	10	12
J78	D5	$1 yel org	10	12
J79	D5	$2 yel org	20	25
		Nos. J69-J79 (11)	1.13	1.41

D6

Thin Paper Without Gum.

1944 **Typographed** ***Perf. 13***

J80	D6	10c bluish grn	5	5
J81	D6	20c lt chlky bl	5	5
J82	D6	40c dl rose	5	5
J83	D6	50c bluish grn	5	5
J84	D6	60c dl bl	5	5
J85	D6	$1 dl rose	10	10
J86	D6	$2 lil brn	12	15
		Nos. J80-J86 (7)	47	50

D7

1945 **Without Gum** **Unwmkd.**

J87	D7	$2 rose car	5	6
J88	D7	$6 rose car	5	6
J89	D7	$8 rose car	5	6
J90	D7	$10 rose car	6	8
J91	D7	$20 rose car	6	8
J92	D7	$30 rose car	6	8
		Nos. J87-J92 (6)	33	42

D8

Thin Paper Without Gum.

1947 **Lithographed** ***Perf. 14***

J93	D8	$50 plum	8	8
J94	D8	$80 plum	8	8
J95	D8	$100 plum	8	8
J96	D8	$160 plum	8	8
J97	D8	$200 plum	8	8
J98	D8	$400 vio brn	8	8
J99	D8	$500 vio brn	8	8
a.		Vert. pair, imperf. between	10.00	
J100	D8	$800 vio brn	8	8
J101	D8	$2000 vio brn	8	8
		Nos. J93-J101 (9)	72	72

Type of 1945, Redrawn.
Surcharged with New Value in Black.

1948 **Engraved.** ***Perf. 13½x14.***

Without Gum

J102	D7	$1000 on $20 dp cl	10	12
J103	D7	$2000 on $30 dp cl	10	12
J104	D7	$3000 on $50 dp cl	10	12
J105	D7	$4000 on $100 dp cl	10	12
J106	D7	$5000 on $200 dp cl	10	12
J107	D7	$10,000 on $300 dp cl	12	15
J108	D7	$20,000 on $500 dp cl	12	15
J109	D7	$30,000 on $1000 dp cl	15	20
		Nos. J102-J109 (8)	89	1.10

There are many differences in the redrawn design.

資欠作改
壹 金
分 圓
1

No. 627
Surcharged
in Black

1949 ***Perf. 12***

J110	A72	1 (c) on $40 org	10	12
J111	A72	2 (c) on $40 org	10	12
J112	A72	5 (c) on $40 org	10	12
J113	A72	10 (c) on $40 org	10	12
J114	A72	20 (c) on $40 org	10	12
J115	A72	50 (c) on $40 org	12	15
J116	A72	$1 on $40 org	12	15
J117	A72	$2 on $40 org	12	15
J118	A72	$5 on $40 org	12	15
J119	A72	$10 on $40 org	20	25
		Nos. J110-J119 (10)	1.18	1.45

Republic of China (Taiwan)

肆 臺
角 幣
資 欠
40 40

No. 438
Surcharged
in Green or Black

1951 ***Perf. 12½.*** **Unwmkd.**

J120	A47	40c on 40c org (G)	7.50	6.00
J121	A47	80c on 40c org (G)	7.50	6.00

Revenue Stamps Surcharged in Various Colors

政郵國民華中
角壹幣台資欠
10

Without Gum

1953 ***Perf. 12½, 14.*** **Unwmkd.**

J122	A95	10c on $50 dk bl (O)	6.00	2.50
J123	A95	20c on $100 ol grn (Dk Br)	6.00	2.50
J124	A95	40c on $20 org brn	7.50	75
J125	A95	80c on $500 sl grn (Dk Bl)	12.50	1.50
J126	A95	$1 on $30 dk vio (G)	12.50	5.00
		Nos. J122-J126 (5)	44.50	12.25

D9

Lithographed

1956 ***Perf. 12½*** **Unwmkd.**

Without Gum

J127	D9	20c rose car, & lt bl	25	10
J128	D9	40c grn & buff	25	10
J129	D9	80c brn & gray	50	10
J130	D9	$1 ultra & pink	50	15

5.00
資 欠
伍
圓

No. 1197
Surcharged
in Dark Violet

Engraved

1961, Dec. 28 ***Perf. 12*** **Wmk. 323**

Without Gum

J131	A135	$5 on $20 car rose	1.50	1.00

0.10
資 欠
壹
角

Nos. 1274, 1282-1283
Surcharged in Black,
Carmine Rose
or Blue

1964-65 **Lithographed**

J132	A158	10c on 80c pale grn	15	10
J133	A158	20c on $3.60 vio bl (CR) ('65)	15	10
J134	A158	40c on $4.50 ver (B) ('65)	25	10

D10

1966-76 ***Perf. 12½*** **Wmk. 323**

Granite Paper; Without Gum

J135	D10	10c dk brn & lil	10	8
J136	D10	20c bl & yel	10	8
J137	D10	50c vio bl & lt bl ('70)	25	8
J138	D10	$1 pur & sal	20	8
J139	D10	$2 grn & lt bl	25	8
J140	D10	$5 red & sal	50	30
a.		org red & pale yel	50	30
J141	D10	$10 lil rose & pink ('76)	1.00	60

The 50c, $10 and No. J140a are gummed. The $1 and $2 were reissued with gum in 1968 and 1973 respectively. No. J140a and the $10 are on ordinary paper.

D11

1984, Mar. 15 **Litho.** ***Perf. 12½***

J142	D11	$1 rose & vio	5	5
J143	D11	$2 yel & bl	10	8
J144	D11	$5 bl & yel	25	16
J145	D11	$10 yel & lil rose	50	32

PARCEL POST STAMPS

PP1

PP2

PP3

Engraved

1945-48 ***Perf. 13*** **Unwmkd.**

Without Gum.

Q1	PP1	$500 green	40	8
Q2	PP1	$1000 blue	40	8

Q3	PP1	$3000 rose red	1.00	13
Q4	PP1	$5000 brown	20.00	2.00
Q5	PP1	$10,000 lil gray	30.00	2.50
Q6	PP1	$20,000 red org	*650.00*	
		Nos. Q1-Q5 (5)	51.80	4.79

No. Q6 was prepared but not issued.

Perf. 12½.

Q7	PP2	$3000 red org	60	10
Q8	PP2	$5000 dk bl	70	12
Q9	PP2	$10,000 violet	70	20
Q10	PP2	$20,000 dk red	70	20

Perf. 13½

Q11	PP3	$1000 org yel	70	25
Q12	PP3	$3000 bl grn	90	25
Q13	PP3	$5000 org red	90	25
Q14	PP3	$7000 dl bl	90	25
Q15	PP3	$10,000 car rose	1.00	25
Q16	PP3	$30,000 olive	1.00	25
Q17	PP3	$50,000 indigo	1.00	25
Q18	PP3	$70,000 org brn	1.25	25
Q19	PP3	$100,000 dp plum	1.25	25

Denomination Tablet Without Inner Frame.

Q20	PP3	$200,000 dk grn	1.75	40
Q21	PP3	$300,000 pink	1.75	40
Q22	PP3	$500,000 vio brn	1.75	50
Q23	PP3	$3,000,000 sl bl	2.00	75
Q24	PP3	$5,000,000 lilac	2.00	75
Q25	PP3	$6,000,000 ol gray	2.25	85
Q26	PP3	$8,000,000 scarlet	2.25	1.00
Q27	PP3	$10,000,000 sage grn	3.50	1.25
		Nos. Q11-Q27 (17)	26.15	8.15

Zeros for "cents" omitted on Nos. Q23-Q27.

Parcel Post Stamps of 1945-48 Surcharged in Black or Carmine

金圓拾圓
10
金圓拾圓

1949 ***Perf. 13½.*** **Unwmkd.**

Q32	PP3	$10 on $3000 bl grn	40	10
Q33	PP3	$20 on $5000 org red	40	10
Q34	PP3	$50 on $10,000 car rose	40	10
Q35	PP3	$100 on $3,000,000 sl bl (C)	60	15
Q36	PP3	$200 on $5,000,000 lil	1.00	15
Q37	PP3	$500 on $1000 org yel	2.00	25
Q38	PP3	$1000 on $7500 dl bl	2.00	40
		Nos. Q32-Q38 (7)	6.80	1.25

Five characters in each line on Nos. Q33 to Q38.

MILITARY STAMPS.

No. 454 Overprinted in Dull Red 郵 軍

1943-44 ***Perf. 12.*** **Unwmkd.**

M1	A59	8c turq grn	1.25	1.25

Nos. 383, 453-454 Overprinted in Red 郵 軍

6mm. between characters.

Perf. 14, 12½.

M2	A57	8c ol grn	1.00	1.00
a.		8mm between characters	1.50	1.50
M3	A59	8c red org	150.00	
M4	A59	8c turq grn	2.50	2.50

No. 493 Overprinted in Red 郵 軍

Perf. 13.

M5	A62	16c dl ol brn	1.25	1.25
a.		Perf. 10½-11	85.00	

No. M5 overprinted in black is a proof.

Stamps of 1942-44 Overprinted in Carmine or Black 郵 軍

M6	A62	50c sage grn (C)	1.25	1.25
M7	A62	$1 rose lake (Bk)	1.25	1.25
M8	A62	$1 dl grn (Bk)	1.50	1.50
M9	A62	$2 dk bl grn (C)	3.00	3.00
M10	A62	$2 dk vio brn ('44) (Bk)	13.00	17.00

Nos. 383 and 357 Overprinted in Red 郵 軍

1944 ***Perf. 12, 14.***

M11	A57	8c ol grn	1.50	1.75
a.		Right character inverted	85.00	
M12	A57	16c ol gray	7.50	7.50

Anti-Aircraft Guns
M1

Thin Paper Without Gum.

1945, Jan. 1 **Typo.** ***Perf. 12½***

M13	M1	rose	70	1.50

Taiwan (Formosa)

100 Sen = 1 Yen
100 Cents = 1 Dollar

Stamps and Types of Japan (Taiwan) Overprinted in Black

中華民國
臺灣省

Lithographed.
Values in Sen and Yen.
Black Overprint.

1945 ***Imperf.*** **Unwmkd.**

Stamps Divided by Lines of Colored Dashes.

1	A1	3s carmine	50	40
2	A1	5s bl grn	60	30
3	A1	10s pale bl	75	30
a.		Inverted ovpt.	35.00	
b.		Double ovpt.	40.00	
4	A1	30s dk bl	1.00	1.00
5	A1	40s violet	1.25	75
6	A1	50s gray brn	75	75
7	A1	1y ol grn	85	1.00

Same Overprint on Types of Japan A99 and A100.

8	A99	5y gray grn	4.00	2.50
9	A100	10y brn vio	6.00	3.50
a.		Invtd. ovpt.	135.00	
		Nos. 1-9 (9)	15.70	10.50

The basic stamps of this issue were prepared by Japanese authorities for Taiwan use before the end of World War II when the island reverted to Chinese control. They are printed on crude buff or white wove paper. The overprint translates: "For Use in Taiwan, Chinese Republic."

A second overprinting of Nos. 2-3 was made with a different font.

China, Nos. 728-731, Surcharged in Black

限臺灣省貼用
70 錢拾柒

1946 ***Perf. 14.***

10	A75	70s on $20 grn	10	7
a.		Inverted surcharge	135.00	
11	A75	1y on $30 bl	20	15
12	A75	2y on $50 dk brn	30	25
13	A75	3y on $100 car	30	25

Issued to commemorate the convening of the Chinese National Assembly.

China Issues and Types of 1940-1946 Surcharged in Black

用貼灣臺限
錢 拾
a

Perf.
12½, 12½x13, 13, 13x12½, 14.

1946-47

14	A46	2s on 2c dp bl ('47)	5	5
15	A48	5s on 5c dl red org	5	5
16	A39	10s on 4c pale vio	5	5
17	A48	30s on 15c brn car	5	5
18	A73	50s on $20 car ('47)	5	5
19	A37	65s on $20 brt yel grn ('47)	5	5
20	A47	1y on 20c lt bl	5	5
a.		Inverted surch.	65.00	
21	A37	1y on $30 choc ('47)	5	5
22	A37	2y on $50 red org ('47)	5	5
23	A73	3y on $100 dk car ('47)	10	10
24	A73	5y on $200 ol grn ('47)	10	10
25	A73	10y on $500 brt bl grn ('47)	10	10
26	A73	20y on $700 red brn ('47)	25	25
27	A73	50y on $1000 rose lake ('47)	50	50
28	A73	100y on $3000 bl ('47)	75	75
		Nos. 14-28 (15)	2.25	2.25

The bottom line of the surcharge expresses the new value and consists of 2, 3 or 4 characters.

Same Surcharge on China No. 412.

1947 ***Perf. 13.*** **Wmk. 261**

28A	A48	30s on 15c brn car	30.00	35.00

Type of China, 1946. Inscribed:

臺 灣
貼 用

Engraved

1947 ***Perf. 11, 11½.*** **Unwmkd.**

29	A74	70c carmine	15	15
30	A74	$1 green	15	15
31	A74	$2 vermilion	15	15
32	A74	$3 yel grn	15	15
33	A74	$7 yel org	25	25
34	A74	$10 magenta	25	25
		Nos. 29-34 (6)	1.10	1.10

60th birthday of Chiang Kai-shek.

Type of China, 1947.

Inscribed: 用貼灣臺限

1947 ***Perf. 14***

35	A76	50c dp grn	15	15
36	A76	$3 dp bl	15	15
37	A76	$7.50 carmine	15	15
38	A76	$10 lt brn	15	15
39	A76	$20 dp cl	15	15
		Nos. 35-39 (5)	75	75

First anniversary of return of Chinese National Government to Nanking.

Dr. Sun Yat-sen
A1

1947, July 10 **Without Gum**

40	A1	$1 dk brn	5	5
41	A1	$2 org brn	5	5
42	A1	$3 bl grn	5	5
43	A1	$5 vermilion	5	5
44	A1	$9 dp bl	5	5
45	A1	$10 brt rose car	5	5
46	A1	$20 dp grn	5	5
47	A1	$50 rose lil	10	1[illegible]
48	A1	$100 blue	18	1[illegible]
49	A1	$200 dk red	15	1[illegible]
		Nos. 40-49 (10)	78	7[illegible]

The 30c gray and $7.50 orange were not regularly issued without surcharge.

Type of 1947 Surcharged in Black

改作伍佰圓
500.00
b

1948 ***Perf. 14*** **Unwmkd.**

51	A1	$25 on $100 bl	60	25
52	A1	$500 on $7.50 org	75	50
53	A1	$1000 on 30c gray	3.00	1.25

Stamps of China, 1943-48, Surcharged Type "a" in Black or Carmine.

1948-49 ***Perf. 12½, 14***

54	A73	$5 on $70 red org	15	15
55	A62	$10 on $3 dk yel	20	20
56	A82	$10 on $150 dk bl (C)	15	15
57	A82	$20 on $250 dp lil (C)	15	15
58	A67	$100 on $20 car	125.00	125.00
59	A82	$1000 on $20,000 rose pink ('49)	1.00	50
		Nos. 54-59 (6)	126.65	126.15

The bottom line of the surcharge expresses the new value and consists of 2 or 3 characters.

Type of 1947.

1949 **Engraved.** ***Perf. 14.***

63	A1	$25 ol grn	15	12
64	A1	$5000 ocher	25	15
65	A1	$10,000 ap grn	25	15
66	A1	$20,000 ol bis	25	15
67	A1	$30,000 indigo	25	15
68	A1	$40,000 vio brn	25	15
		Nos. 63-68 (6)	1.40	87

No. 42 and Type of 1947 Surcharged Type "b" in Black, Carmine Violet or Red Violet.

1949

69	A1	$300 on $3 bl grn	25	20
70	A1	$1000 on $3 bl grn (C)	75	20
71	A1	$2000 on $3 bl grn (V)	50	40
72	A1	$3000 on $3 bl grn (RV)	2.00	30
73	A1	$3000 on $7.50 org	16.50	1.50
		Nos. 69-73 (5)	20.00	2.60

Stamps of China, 1940-47, Surcharged Type "a" in Black or Carmine.

Perf. 12½, 13x13½, 14.

74	A39	$2 on 2½c rose lil (#424)	10	10
75	A72	$5 on $40 org (#627)	10	10
76	A73	$5 on $50 pur (C) (#638)	10	10
77	A73	$5 on $100 dk car (#640)	10	10
78	A57	$20 on 2c ol grn (#368)	15	15
81	A63	$100 on $20 rose (#571)	15	10
82	A67	$200 on $10 dk bl (C) (#591)	25	25
84	A57	$500 on $30 dl vio (#521)	20	20
86	A62	$800 on $4 red brn (#504)	50	50

87	A67	$5000 on $10 dk bl (#591)	85	85
88	A67	$10,000 on $20 car (#592)	2.00	1.50
89	A82	$200,000 on $3000 bl (C) (#750)	37.50	17.50
		Nos. 74-89 (12)	42.00	21.45

Northeastern Provinces No. 47, Surcharged in Green, Red Violet, Black or Blue

2 ★★★ 2

1949–50

91	A2	2c on $44 dk car rose (G)	2.25	1.00
92	A2	5c on $44 dk car rose (RV) ('50)	2.50	1.50
a.		vio surcharge	2.50	2.00
93	A2	10c on $44 dk car rose (RV) ('50)	8.00	90
94	A2	20c on $44 dk car rose (Bk) ('50)	8.00	2.35
a.		Double surcharge	30.00	
95	A2	30c on $44 dk car rose (Bl) ('50)	9.00	2.65
96	A2	50c on $44 dk car rose (Bl) ('50)	14.00	5.25
		Nos. 91-96 (6)	43.75	13.65

China 959a, Overprinted in Black 用貼灣臺限

Ovpt. 15mm. Wide.

1949 ***Rouletted 9½.*** **Unwmkd.**

97	A96	orange	40	20

China Nos. 567, 498 and 640 Surcharged Type "a" in Black.

1948–49 ***Perf. 12½, 13, 14*** **Unwmkd.**

98	A63	$20 on $3 red	75	30
99	A62	$50 on 50c sage grn	30	10
a.		Perf. 11	12.00	12.00
100	A73	$600 on $100 dk car	1.50	60

Bottom line of surcharge consists of 3 characters.
No. 99 has two settings of surcharge: I. Spacing 10mm. between rows of characters. II. Spacing 12mm.

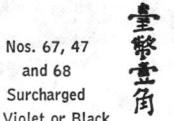

Nos. 67, 47 and 68 Surcharged in Violet or Black 臺幣壹角 10

1949 ***Perf. 14.***

101	A1	2c on $30,000 ind (V)	2.00	2.00
102	A1	10c on $50 rose lil	3.00	1.25
103	A1	10c on $40,000 vio brn	2.50	2.50

Numerals slightly larger on Nos. 101 and 103.
For similar surcharges on China type A82 see China Nos. 1025–1036.

AIR POST STAMP.

China No. C62a, Overprinted in Black 用貼灣臺限

Ovpt. 15mm. Wide.

1949 ***Rouletted 9½*** **Unwmkd.**

C1	AP5	bl grn	60	50

SPECIAL DELIVERY STAMP.

China No. E12a, Overprinted in Black 用貼灣臺限

Ovpt. 12½mm. Wide.

1950 ***Rouletted 9½.*** **Unwmkd.**

E1	SD2	red vio	60	1.00

REGISTRATION STAMP.

China No. F2a Overprinted in Black 用貼灣臺限

Ovpt. 12mm. Wide.

1950 ***Rouletted 9½*** **Unwmkd.**

F1	R2	carmine	60	50

POSTAGE DUE STAMPS.

D1

Lithographed.

1948, Feb. 10 ***Perf. 14*** **Unwmkd.**

Without Gum

J1	D1	$1 blue	10	40
J2	D1	$3 blue	10	40
J3	D1	$5 blue	10	40
J4	D1	$10 blue	10	40
J5	D1	$20 blue	10	40
		Nos. J1-J5(5)	50	2.00

Nos. J1–J4 Surcharged in Carmine 作改 伍拾圓 50.00

1948, Dec. 4

J6	D1	$50 on $1 bl	2.00	2.50
J7	D1	$100 on $3 bl	2.00	2.50
J8	D1	$300 on $5 bl	2.00	2.50
J9	D1	$500 on $10 bl	2.00	2.50

Nos. 70, 72 and 64 Handstamped in Violet 資 欠

1949, Aug. 5

J10	A1	$1000 on $3 bl grn	5.00	5.50
J11	A1	$3000 on $3 bl grn	5.00	5.50
J12	A1	$5000 ocher	5.00	5.50

No. 48 Surcharged in Various Colors 臺幣肆分 資 欠 4

1950

J13	A1	4c on $100 bl (Br)	2.00	2.50
J14	A1	10c on $100 bl (RV)	2.25	2.25
J15	A1	20c on $100 bl (Bk)	2.25	2.25
J16	A1	40c on $100 bl (C)	6.00	6.00
J17	A1	$1 on $100 bl (Bl)	11.00	8.00
		Nos. J13-J17 (5)	23.50	21.00

The indexes in each volume of the Scott Catalogue contain many listings which help to identify stamps.

PARCEL POST STAMPS.

Type of China, Parcel Post Stamps of 1945–48 With Added Inscription:

Engraved.

1949 ***Perf. 14.*** **Unwmkd.**

Q1	PP3	$100 bluish grn	60.00	20
Q2	PP3	$300 rose car	60.00	20
Q3	PP3	$500 ol grn	60.00	20
Q4	PP3	$1000 slate	60.00	20
Q5	PP3	$3000 dp plum	60.00	20
		Nos. Q1-Q5 (5)	300.00	1.00

Chinese characters in lower corners have colorless background; denomination tablet in color.

OCCUPATION STAMPS.

Issued Under Japanese Occupation.

Kwangtung.

(kwäng'dōōng')

China No. 297 Overprinted in Black 用特區省

1942 ***Perf. 12½*** **Unwmkd.**

1N1	A37	2c ol grn	1.00	1.00
a.		Inverted ovpt.	35.00	

Same Overprint in Red or Black on Stamps of China, 1939-41.

Perf. 12½, 14.

1N2	A57	3c dl cl (#350)	60	60
1N3	A57	8c ol grn (#383)	60	60
1N4	A57	10c grn (#354) (R)	60	60
1N5	A57	10c grn (#384) (R)	60	60
1N6	A57	16c ol gray (#357)	1.00	1.00
1N7	A57	30c scar (#385)	60	60
1N8	A57	50c dk bl (#386) (R)	60	60
1N9	A57	$1 org brn & sep (#387)	2.00	2.00
1N10	A57	$2 dp bl & yel brn (#388)	1.00	1.00
1N11	A57	$5 red & sl grn (#389)	1.75	1.75
1N12	A57	$10 dk grn & dl pur (#390)	4.00	4.00
1N13	A57	$20 rose lake & dk bl (#391)	1.75	1.75

Same Overprint on China Nos. 422 and 433.

Perf. 12½.

1N14	A40	1c orange	50	50
a.		Inverted ovpt.	37.50	37.50
1N15	A47	20c lt bl	1.00	1.00

Same Overprint on Stamps of China, 1941.

Perf. 12.

1N16	A59	1c orange	50	50
1N17	A59	5c green	50	50
1N18	A59	8c turq grn	50	50
1N19	A59	10c brt grn	50	50
1N20	A59	17c olive	1.00	1.00
1N21	A59	30c scarlet	1.00	1.00
1N22	A59	50c dk bl	1.00	1.00
		Nos.1N1-1N22 (22)	22.60	22.60

Stamps of China, 1939-41 Overprinted in Black 貼 粵 用 省

1942 ***Perf. 12½, 14***

1N23	A57	2c ol grn (#368)	50	50
1N24	A57	3c dl cl (#350)	50	50
1N25	A57	5c ol grn (#352)	50	50
1N26	A57	8c ol grn (#353)	140.00	
1N27	A57	8c ol grn (#369)	60	60
1N28	A57	10c grn (#354)	90	90
1N29	A57	16c ol gray (#357)	90	90
1N30	A57	25c dk bl (#358)	90	90
1N31	A57	30c scar (#385)	50	50
1N32	A57	50c dk bl (#386)	50	50
1N33	A57	$1 org brn & sep (#387)	1.50	1.50
1N34	A57	$2 dp bl & yel brn (#388)	1.50	1.50
1N35	A57	$5 red & sl grn (#389)	2.50	2.50
1N36	A57	$10 dk grn & dl pur (#390)	3.50	3.50
1N37	A57	$20 rose lake & dk bl (#391)	5.00	5.00
		Nos. 1N23-1N25, 1N27-1N37 (14)	19.80	19.80

Same Overprint on China Nos. 397–401.

1942 ***Perf. 14.*** **Wmk. 261**

1N38	A57	$1 org brn & sep	4.00	4.00
1N39	A57	$2 dp bl & yel brn	4.00	4.00
1N40	A57	$5 red & sl grn	5.00	4.00
1N41	A57	$10 dk grn & dl pur	5.00	4.00
1N42	A57	$20 rose lake & dk bl	8.00	7.00
		Nos. 1N38-1N42 (5)	26.00	23.00

Same Overprint on Stamps of China, 1941.

1942 ***Perf. 12.*** **Unwmkd.**

1N43	A59	2c brt ultra	25	25
1N44	A59	5c green	25	25
1N45	A59	8c red org	25	25
1N46	A59	8c turq grn	25	25
1N47	A59	10c brt grn	60	60
1N48	A59	17c olive	60	60
1N49	A59	25c rose vio	60	60
1N50	A59	30c scarlet	60	60
1N51	A59	50c dk bl	50	50
1N52	A59	$1 brn & blk	1.00	1.00
1N53	A59	$2 bl & blk	1.00	1.00
1N54	A59	$5 scar & blk	1.00	1.00
1N55	A59	$10 grn & blk	2.25	2.25
1N56	A59	$20 rose vio & blk	3.00	3.00
		Nos. 1N43-1N56 (14)	12.15	12.15

China Nos. 354 and 369 Surcharged in Black

用 省

圓佰貳售暫

1945 ***Perf. 12½*** **Unwmkd.**

1N57	A57	$200 on 10c grn	60.00	35.00
1N58	A57	$400 on 8c ol grn	60.00	35.00

China No. 422 Surcharged in Black

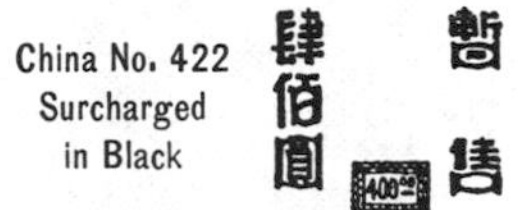

1945

1N59	A40	$400 on 1c org	400.00	400.00

POSTAGE DUE STAMP.

China, No. J79 Surcharged Diagonally with New Value Between Parallel Lines in Black.

1945 ***Perf. 12½.*** **Unwmkd.**

1NJ1	D5	$100 on $2 yel org	400.00	400.00
a.		Inverted surch.	550.00	

MENG CHIANG (Inner Mongolia)

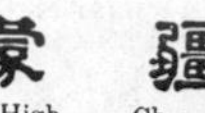
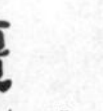
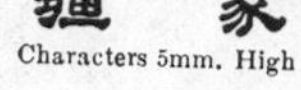

Characters 4mm. High — I

Characters 5mm. High — II

Nos. 297-298, 301-303 Overprinted

1941 Engraved Unwmkd.

No.	Type	Description	Unused	Used
2N1	A37	2c #297, I	50	50
a.		Type II	60	60
2N2	A37	4c #298, II	9.00	9.00
a.		Type I	15.00	15.00
2N3	A37	15c #301, I	50	50
a.		Type II	1.00	1.00
2N4	A37	20c #302, II	1.50	1.00
a.		Type I	1.50	1.50
2N5	A37	25c #303, II	1.50	1.00
a.		Type I	14.00	14.00
		Type I, set of 5	31.50	31.50
		Type II, set of 5	13.60	12.60

On Nos. 312, 314, 318, 321

1941 *Perf. 14*

No.	Type	Description	Unused	Used
2N6	A39	½c #312, I	90	90
a.		Type II	6.00	6.00
2N7	A39	2½c #314, II	35	30
a.		Type I	40	40
2N8	A45	13c #318, II	1.25	1.00
a.		Type I	32.50	32.50
2N9	A48	30c #321, II	27.50	27.50

On Stamps of 1939-41

1941 *Perf. 12½*

No.	Type	Description	Unused	Used
2N10	A57	2c #368, II	35	35
2N11	A57	3c #350, I	25	25
a.		Type II	35	35
2N12	A57	5c #352, I	25	25
a.		Type II	35	35
2N13	A57	8c #353, I	25	25
a.		Type II	35	35
2N14	A57	8c #369, II	2.25	1.75
2N15	A57	10c #354, II	60	40
2N16	A57	16c #357, II	85	75
2N17	A57	$1 #359, II	3.50	3.50
a.		Type I	250.00	250.00
b.		#347, I	37.50	37.50
2N18	A57	$5 #361, II	20.00	20.00
		Type I, set of 5	288.25	288.25
		Type II, set of 9	28.60	27.80

On Stamps of 1940 with Secret Marks

1941 *Perf. 14* Unwmkd.

No.	Type	Description	Unused	Used
2N19	A57	5c #382, II	30	30
2N20	A57	8c #383, I	35	30
a.		Type II	16.50	16.50
2N21	A57	10c #384, I	35	30
a.		Type II	50	40
2N22	A57	30c #385, I	90	35
a.		Type II	1.25	90
2N23	A57	50c #386, I	1.25	75
a.		Type II	1.25	90
2N24	A57	$1 #387, I	3.50	3.50
a.		Type II	6.00	6.00
2N25	A57	$2 #388, I	4.00	4.00
a.		Type II	12.00	8.00
2N26	A57	$5 #389, I	14.00	14.00
a.		Type II	22.50	22.50
2N27	A57	$10 #390, II	22.50	22.50
a.		Type I	27.50	27.50
2N28	A57	$20 #391, II	32.50	32.50
a.		Type I	37.50	37.50
		Type I, set of 9	89.35	88.20
		Type II, set of 10	115.30	110.50

On Stamps of 1940 with Secret Marks

1941 *Perf. 14* Wmk. 261

No.	Type	Description	Unused	Used
2N29	A57	10c #394, II	1.25	90
2N30	A57	30c #395, II	1.75	1.75
a.		Type I	32.50	32.50
2N31	A57	50c #396, II	1.75	1.75

On Stamps of 1940-41 (Martyrs) with Secret Marks

1941 *Perf. 12½, 13 & Comp.* Wmk. 261

No.	Type	Description	Unused	Used
2N32	A39	½c #402, II	5.00	3.00
2N33	A40	1c #403, I	30	25
a.		Type II	30	30
2N34	A39	2½c #405, II	20.00	20.00
a.		Type I	22.50	22.50
2N35	A48	3c #406, II	30	30
2N36	A46	10c #410, II	2.00	1.75
a.		Type I	2.25	1.75
2N37	A46	17c #413, II	13.50	13.50
a.		Type I	22.50	22.50
2N38	A40	25c #416, II	1.75	60
2N39	A48	30c #418, II	16.50	14.00
a.		Type I	22.50	22.50
2N40	A47	40c #419, II	60	35
a.		Type I	1.75	1.75
2N41	A40	50c #420, I	3.50	1.75
a.		Type II	13.50	13.50
		Type I, set of 7	75.30	73.00
		Type II, set of 10	73.45	67.30

Unwmkd.

No.	Type	Description	Unused	Used
2N42	A39	½c #421, I	30	30
a.		Type II	30	30
2N43	A40	1c #422, I	30	30
a.		Type II	90	30
2N44	A46	2c #423, I	30	30
2N45	A48	3c #425, I	40	40
a.		Type II	50	30
2N46	A39	4c #426, II	60	30
2N47	A45	8c #428, II	4.00	4.00
a.		Type I	37.50	37.50
2N48	A46	10c #429, I	6.00	4.00
a.		Type II	16.50	16.50
2N49	A45	13c #430, I	1.75	90
a.		Type II	3.00	2.25
2N50	A48	15c #431, II	1.00	1.00
2N51	A46	17c #432, I	90	75
a.		Type II	1.00	75
2N52	A47	20c #433, II	1.00	50
a.		Type I	1.25	1.25
2N53	A45	21c #434, II	1.00	1.00
2N54	A40	25c #435, I	1.25	1.25
2N55	A46	28c #436, II	1.00	1.00
2N56	A40	50c #439, II	2.00	2.00
a.		Type I	3.50	1.75
		Type I, set of 11	53.45	48.70
		Type II, set of 13	32.80	30.20

China Nos. 297-298, 302 Surcharged in Black

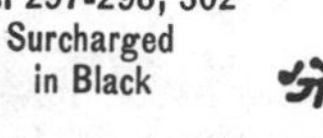
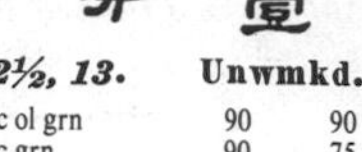

1942 *Perf. 12½, 13.* Unwmkd.

No.	Type	Description	Unused	Used
2N57	A37	1c on 2c ol grn	90	90
2N58	A37	2c on 4c grn	90	75
2N59	A37	10c on 20c ultra	12.00	12.00

Same, on China No. 313.

Perf. 14.

No.	Type	Description	Unused	Used
2N60	A40	½c on 1c org	2.00	

Same, on Stamps of China, 1938-41

Perf. 12½.

No.	Type	Description	Unused	Used
2N61	A57	1c on 2c ol grn (#368)	50	30
2N62	A57	4c on 8c ol grn (#353)	2.50	2.00
a.		Inverted surch.	50.00	50.00
2N63	A57	4c on 8c ol grn (#369)	75	75
2N64	A57	5c on 10c grn (#354)	50	35
2N65	A57	8c on 16c ol gray (#357)	1.00	60
2N66	A57	50c on $1 hn & dk brn (#359)	2.50	2.50
a.		50c on $1 hn & dk brn (#347)	20.00	20.00
b.		50c on $1 hn & dk brn (#344)	200.00	200.00
2N67	A57	$1 on $2 dp bl & org brn (#360)	12.50	12.50

No. 2N66b was issued without gum.

Same, on Stamps of China, 1940.

Perf. 14.

No.	Type	Description	Unused	Used
2N68	A57	4c on 8c ol grn (#383)	25	25
2N69	A57	15c on 30c scar (#385)	60	60
a.		Inverted surch.	50.00	50.00
2N70	A57	25c on 50c dk bl (#386)	1.00	1.00
2N71	A57	50c on $1 org brn & sep (#387)	1.50	1.00
2N72	A57	$1 on $2 dp bl & yel brn (#388)	3.00	2.50
2N73	A57	$5 on $10 dk grn & dl pur (#390)	10.00	10.00
2N74	A57	$10 on $20 rose lake & dk bl (#391)	37.50	37.50

Same, on China No. 395.

1942 *Perf. 14.* Wmk. 261

No.	Type	Description	Unused	Used
2N75	A57	15c on 30c scar	25.00	25.00

Same, on China Nos. 418 and 419.

Perf. 12½, 13.

No.	Type	Description	Unused	Used
2N76	A48	15c on 30c brn car	12.00	12.00
2N77	A47	20c on 40c org	2.50	2.50

Same, on Stamps of China, 1940-41.

1942 Unwmkd.

No.	Type	Description	Unused	Used
2N78	A40	½c on 1c org	20	20
2N79	A39	2c on 4c pale vio	40	35
2N80	A47	10c on 20c lt bl	75	60
2N81	A47	20c on 40c org	3.00	2.50
2N82	A40	25c on 50c grn	7.00	7.00

Same Surcharge on "New Peking" Prints.

Perf. 14.

No.	Type	Description	Unused	Used
2N83	A37	1c on 2c ol grn	15	15
2N84	A37	2c on 4c dl grn	15	15
2N85	A46	5c on 10c dl vio	30	30
2N86	A57	8c on 16c ol gray	30	30
2N87	A47	10c on 20c red brn	50	50
2N88	A48	15c on 30c brn car	75	75
2N89	A47	20c on 40c org	75	75
2N90	A40	25c on 50c grn	1.00	1.00
2N91	A57	50c on $1 org brn & sep	2.00	2.00
2N92	A57	$1 on $2 dp bl & org brn	14.00	14.00
2N93	A57	$5 on $10 dk grn & dl pur	17.50	17.50

The "New Peking" printings were made by the Chinese Bureau of Engraving and Printing for use in Japanese controlled areas of North China. They are on thin, poor quality paper, with dull gum or without gum and there are slight alterations in the designs.

Dragon-Carved Pillar and Doves
A1

Mining Coal
A2

Wmkd.

Characters in Circle in Sheet.

Perf. 12 x Pin-Perf. 12.

1943 Engraved

No.	Type	Description	Unused	Used
2N94	A1	4f dp org	15	*30*
2N95	A1	8f dk bl	25	*50*

Issued to commemorate the 5th anniversary of the Inner Mongolia post and telegraph service.

The watermark, which is 40mm. in diameter and covers four stamps, occurs three times in the sheet.

Photogravure.

1943 *Perf. 12.* Unwmkd.

No.	Type	Description	Unused	Used
2N96	A2	8f Prus grn	12	*30*
2N97	A2	8f brn red	25	*50*

Issued to commemorate the 2nd anniversary of the "Greater East Asia War".

Flying Horse
A3

Yun Wang
A4

1944 *Perf. 12½x12, 12x12½.*

No.	Type	Description	Unused	Used
2N98	A3	4f rose	15	*30*
2N99	A4	8f dl bl	25	*50*

Issued to commemorate the 5th anniversary of the founding of the Federal Autonomous Government of Mongolia, September 1, 1939.

Industrial Plant
A5

1944, Dec. 8 Photo. *Perf. 12x12½*

No.	Type	Description	Unused	Used
2N100	A5	8f red brn	10	*50*

Issued to commemorate the 3rd anniversary of the "Greater East Asia War" and to encourage production increase.

New Peking Printings of 1942 Overprinted in Black 疆 蒙

Engraved

1945 *Perf. 14.* Unwmkd.

Without Gum.

2N101 A37 2c ol grn 10 10
2N102 A37 4c dl grn 1.25 1.25
2N103 A37 5c green 10 10
2N104 A57 $1 org brn & sep 75 75
2N105 A57 $2 dp bl & org brn 3.00 3.00
2N106 A57 $5 red & grnsh blk 10.00 10.00

Same Overprint on New Peking Printings of Martyrs Issue

2N107 A40 1c orange 10 10
2N108 A45 8c dp org 10 10
2N109 A46 10c dl vio 15 15
2N110 A47 20c red brn 15 15
2N111 A48 30c brn car 10 10
2N112 A47 40c orange 10 10
2N113 A40 50c green 35 35
Nos. 2N101-2N113 (13) 16.25 16.25

Stamps of Meng Chiang, 1941 With Additional Surcharge in Red or Black 角 伍

1945

2N114 A39 10c on ½c ol blk (#2N42) (R) 25 25
a. 10c on ½c ol blk (#2N42a) 75
2N115 A40 10c on 1c org (#2N43a) (R) 25 25
a. Without secret mark (China #313) 20.00 20.00
2N116 A37 50c on 2c ol grn (#2N1a) (Bk) 40 40
2N117 A57 50c on 2c ol grn (#2N10) (Bk) 10 10
2N118 A39 50c on 4c pale vio (#2N46) (R) 25 25
2N119 A57 50c on 5c ol grn (#2N12a) (R) 15 15
a. On #2N12
2N120 A57 50c on 5c ol grn (#2N19) (R) 25 25
Nos. 2N114-2N120 (7) 1.65 1.65

Same Surcharge on Nos. 2N32, 2N33a

1945 Wmk. 261

2N121 A39 10c on ½c ol blk (R) 7.50 7.50
2N122 A40 10c on 1c org (R) 50 50

Same Surcharge on Nos. 2N107 2N101-2N103 and 2N108

1945 Unwmkd.

2N123 A40 10c on 1c org (R) 20 20
2N124 A37 50c on 2c ol grn (Bk) 15 15
2N125 A37 50c on 4c dl grn (R) 2.50 2.50
2N126 A37 50c on 5c grn 20 20
2N127 A45 $1 on 8c dp org (R) 35 35
Nos. 2N123-2N127 (5) 3.40 3.40

NORTH CHINA

Honan

南 河 南 河

I II

Nos. 297-298, 301-303 Overprinted

1941 Engraved Unwmkd.

3N1 A37 2c #297, II 60 60
a. Type I 1.50 1.50
3N2 A37 4c #298, I 2.25 1.75
a. Type II 7.00 7.00
3N3 A37 15c #301, II 50 50
a. Type I 60 50
3N4 A37 20c #302, I 2.50 50
3N5 A37 25c #303, II 7.00 7.00

1941 *Perf. 14*

3N6 A39 ½c #312, I 30 30
a. Type II 4.00 4.00
3N7 A39 2½c #314, II 25 25
a. Type I 30 30
3N8 A45 13c #318, II 50 30
a. Type I 37.50 37.50
3N9 A48 30c #321, II 4.00 2.00
3N10 A47 40c #322, II 37.50 37.50

On Stamps of 1939-41

1941 *Perf. 12½*

3N11 A57 2c #368, II 25 25
3N12 A57 3c #350, II 25 25
a. Type I 30 30
3N13 A57 5c #352, II 25 25
a. Type I 30 30
3N14 A57 8c #353, II 25 25
a. Type I 60 60
3N15 A57 10c #354, II 25 25
3N16 A57 16c #357, II 25 25
3N17 A57 $1 #359, II 4.00 3.25
a. Type I 165.00 165.00
b. On #347, I 30.00 30.00
3N18 A57 $5 #361, II 32.50 32.50

On Stamps of 1940 with Secret Marks

1941 *Perf. 14* Unwmkd.

3N20 A57 5c #382, II 90 25
3N21 A57 8c #383, II 25 25
3N22 A57 10c #384, II 25 25
3N23 A57 30c #385, II 1.25 40
a. Type I 1.50 1.00
3N24 A57 50c #386, I 1.50 1.25
a. Type II 3.50 2.25
3N25 A57 $1 #387, I 3.50 1.75
a. Type II 27.50 25.00
3N26 A57 $2 #388, I 5.00 4.00
a. Type II 6.00 3.50
3N27 A57 $5 #389, I 7.00 7.00
a. Type II 22.50 22.50
3N28 A57 $10 #390, II 20.00 20.00
a. Type I 65.00 65.00
3N29 A57 $20 #391, II 32.50 32.50
a. Type I 35.00 35.00
Type I, set of 7 73.50 70.00
Type II, set of 10 159.65 151.90

On Stamps of 1940 with Secret Marks

1941 *Perf. 14* Wmk. 261

3N30 A57 5c #392, II 7.00 1.25
3N31 A57 5c #393, II 3.50 50
3N32 A57 30c #395, II 4.00 1.75
a. Type I 7.00 3.50
3N33 A57 50c #396, II 7.00 7.00

On Stamps of 1940-41 (Martyrs) with Secret Marks

1941 *Perf. 12½, 13 & Comp.* Wmk. 261

3N34 A39 ½c #402, II 25 25
3N35 A40 1c #403, II 25 25
a. Type I 25 25
3N36 A39 2½c #405, II 6.00 3.50
3N37 A46 10c #410, I 90 30
a. Type II 2.25 1.75
3N38 A45 13c #411, II 25 25
3N39 A46 17c #413, II 50 25
a. Type I 4.00 1.75
3N40 A40 25c #416, II 50 25
3N41 A47 40c #419, II 75 25
a. Type I 6.00 1.50

Unwmkd.

3N42 A39 ½c #421, II 25 25
a. Type I 25 25
3N43 A40 1c #422, I 25 25
a. Type II 50 25
3N44 A46 2c #423, I 3.00 60
3N45 A48 3c #425, I 50 50
3N46 A39 4c #426, II 25 25
3N47 A46 10c #429, I 13.50 7.00
3N48 A45 13c #430, II 75 25
a. Type I 5.00 1.75
3N49 A48 15c #431, II 25 25
3N50 A46 17c #432, II 25 25
a. Type I 5.00 1.50
3N51 A47 20c #433, II 25 25
a. Type I 13.50 4.00
3N52 A45 21c #434, II 25 25
3N53 A40 25c #435, I 1.25 90
3N54 A46 28c #436, II 25 25
Type I, set of 9 42.25 16.75
Type II, set of 9 3.00 2.25

Overprinted in Red

坡 嘉 新
念 紀 落 陷

1942

3N55 A39 4c #3N46 90 90
3N56 A57 8c #3N14 8.00 8.00
3N57 A57 8c #369, II 3.00 3.00

The fall of Singapore.

Overprinted in Red

國 建 國 洲 滿
念 紀 年 週 十

1942

3N58 A57 2c #3N11 2.50 2.50
3N59 A39 4c #3N46 3.50 3.50
3N60 A57 8c #369, II 15.00 15.00
3N61 A57 8c #3N14 15.00 15.00

Tenth Anniv. of the formation of Manchukuo.

Hopei

北 河 北 河

I II

Nos. 297-298, 301-303 Overprinted

1941 Engraved Unwmkd.

4N1 A37 2c #297, II 40 40
a. Type I 60 60
4N2 A37 4c #298, I 75 60
a. Type II 27.50 27.50
4N3 A37 15c #301, II 40 40
a. Type I 1.50 90
4N4 A37 20c #302, II 60 60
4N5 A37 25c #303, II 2.25 1.75
a. Type I 37.50 37.50

On Nos. 312, 314, 318, 321

1941 *Perf. 14*

4N6 A39 ½c #312, II 25 25
a. Type I 50 50
4N7 A39 2½c #314, II 25 25
a. Type I 35 25
4N8 A45 13c #318, II 75 50
a. Type I 1.25 1.25
4N9 A48 30c #321, II 1.75 1.25

On Stamps of 1939-41

1941 *Perf. 12½*

4N10 A57 2c #368, II 25 25
4N11 A57 2c #349, II 25 25
4N12 A57 3c #350, II 25 25
a. Type I 90 60
4N13 A57 5c #352, II 25 25
a. Type I 50 50
4N14 A57 8c #353, II 25 25
a. Type I 60 60
4N15 A57 8c #369, II 75 30
4N16 A57 10c #354, II 25 25
4N17 A57 16c #357, II 25 25
4N18 A57 $1 #359, II 2.25 2.25
a. On #347, I 135.00 135.00
4N19 A57 $2 #360, II 2.25 2.25
a. Type I 25.00 25.00
4N20 A57 $5 #361, II 16.50 16.50
a. Type I 20.00 20.00
4N21 A57 $10 #362, II 55.00 55.00
4N22 A57 $20 #363, II 160.00 160.00
Type II, set of 13 238.50 238.05
Type I, set of 6 182.00 181.70

On Stamps of 1940 with Secret Marks

1941 *Perf. 14* Unwmkd.

4N24 A57 5c #382, II 25 25
a. Type I 25 25
4N25 A57 8c #383, II 25 25
a. Type I 27.50 27.50
4N26 A57 10c #384, II 25 25
a. Type I 60 50
4N27 A57 30c #385, II 25 25
4N28 A57 50c #386, II 75 25
a. Type I 90 75
4N29 A57 $1 #387, II 1.75 90
a. Type I 2.25 1.75
4N30 A57 $2 #388, II 6.00 1.75
a. Type I 11.00 7.00
4N31 A57 $5 #389, II 12.00 12.00
a. Type I 17.50 17.50
4N32 A57 $10 #390, II 16.50 16.50
a. Type I 22.50 22.50
4N33 A57 $20 #391, II 27.50 27.50
a. Type I 32.50 32.50
Type II, set of 10 65.50 59.90
Type I, set of 9 115.00 110.25

On Stamps of 1940 with Secret Marks

1941 *Perf. 14* Wmk. 261

4N34 A57 5c #392, II 25 25
4N35 A57 5c #393, II 25 25
4N36 A57 10c #394, II 25 25
4N37 A57 30c #395, II 50 50
a. Type I 1.50 1.25
4N38 A57 50c #396, II 75 60

On Stamps of 1940-41 (Martyrs) with Secret Marks

1941 *Perf. 12½, 13 & Comp.* Wmk. 261

4N39 A39 ½c #402, II 25 25
4N40 A40 1c #403, II 25 25
a. Type I 25 25
4N41 A46 2c #404, II 25 25
4N42 A39 2½c #405, II 25 25
4N43 A48 3c #406, II 25 25
4N44 A46 10c #410, II 50 50
a. Type I 50 30
4N45 A45 13c #411, II 50 50
4N46 A46 17c #413, II 50 50
a. Type I 90 75
4N47 A40 25c #416, II 60 50
4N48 A48 30c #418, II 60 50
a. Type I 9.00 9.00
4N49 A47 40c #419, II 60 50
a. Type I 1.75 1.50
Nos. 4N39-4N49 (11) 4.55 4.25

Unwmkd.

4N50 A39 ½c #421, II 25 25
a. Type I 25 25
4N51 A40 1c #422, II 25 25
a. Type I 25 25
4N52 A46 2c #423, I 50 50
4N53 A48 3c #425, II 25 25
a. Type I 50 50
4N54 A39 4c #426, II 50 50
4N55 A45 8c #428, II 50 50
a. Type I 75 60
4N56 A46 10c #429, II 50 50
4N57 A45 13c #430, II 75 75
a. Type I 75 60
4N58 A48 15c #431, II 50 50
4N59 A46 17c #432, II 60 50
a. Type I 1.50 1.00
4N60 A47 20c #433, II 50 50
a. Type I 1.50 1.00
4N61 A45 21c #434, II 50 50
4N62 A40 25c #435, II 75 50
a. Type I 1.50 1.00
4N63 A46 28c #436, II 50 50
Type II, set of 13 6.35 6.00
Type I, set of 9 7.50 5.70

Honan Singapore Overprint in Red

1942

4N64 A39 4c #4N54 50 50
4N65 A57 8c #4N25 1.50 1.50
4N66 A57 8c #4N14 1.75 1.75
4N67 A57 8c #4N15 2.00 2.00

Honan Anniv. of Manchukuo Overprint in Red

1942

4N68 A57 2c #4N10 3.00 3.00
4N69 A39 4c #4N54 1.25 1.25
4N70 A57 8c #4N14 25.00 25.00
4N71 A57 8c #4N25 3.00 3.00

Shansi

西 山 西 山

I II

Nos. 297-298, 301, 303
Overprinted

1941 **Engraved** **Unwmkd.**
5N1 A37 2c #297, II 90 50
a. Type I 1.50 75
5N2 A37 4c #298, I 5.00 1.25
a. Type II 55.00 32.50
5N3 A37 15c #301, I 75 50
a. Type II 75 50
5N4 A37 25c #303, II 1.50 60
a. Type I 22.50 22.50

On Nos. 312, 314, 318, 321

1941 ***Perf. 14***
5N5 A39 ½c #312, II 25 25
a. Type I 60 30
5N6 A39 2½c #314, II 25 25
a. Type I 50 50
5N7 A45 13c #318, II 60 60
a. Type I 55.00 55.00
5N8 A48 30c #321, II 3.50 3.50

On Stamps of 1939-41

1941 ***Perf. 12½***
5N9 A57 2c #368, II 50 50
5N10 A57 3c #350, II 50 50
a. Type I 3.50 1.00
5N11 A57 5c #352, II 50 50
a. Type I 90 40
5N12 A57 8c #353, II 50 50
a. Type I 90 50
5N13 A57 8c #369, II 16.50 11.00
5N14 A57 10c #354, II 50 30
5N15 A57 16c #357, II 90 90
5N16 A57 $1 #359, II 4.00 2.25
5N17 A57 $2 #360, II 14.00 14.00
5N18 A57 $5 #361, II 25.00 25.00
Nos. 5N9-5N18 (10) 62.90 55.45

On Stamps of 1940
with Secret Marks

1941 ***Perf. 14*** **Unwmkd.**
5N19 A57 5c #382, II 25 25
5N20 A57 8c #383, II 50 50
5N21 A57 10c #384, II 50 50
a. Type I 60 30
5N22 A57 30c #385, I 75 50
a. Type II 75 75
5N23 A57 50c #386, I 90 75
a. Type II 90 90
5N24 A57 $1 #387, I 5.00 2.50
a. Type II 14.00 5.00
5N25 A57 $2 #388, I 7.00 2.50
a. Type II 7.00 5.00
5N26 A57 $5 #389, II 9.00 9.00
a. Type I 27.50 27.50
5N27 A57 $10 #390, II 14.00 14.00
a. Type I 16.50 16.50
5N28 A57 $20 #391, II 25.00 25.00
a. Type I 27.50 27.50
Type II, set of 10 71.90 60.90
Type I, set of 8 85.75 78.05

On Stamps of 1940
with Secret Marks

1941 ***Perf. 14*** **Wmk. 261**
5N29 A57 5c #392, II 40 40
5N30 A57 5c #393, II 40 40
5N31 A57 10c #394, II 75 75
5N32 A57 30c #395, I 30.00 30.00
5N33 A57 50c #396, I 2.50 1.50
Nos. 5N29-5N33 (5) 34.05 33.05

On Stamps of 1940-41
(Martyrs) with Secret Marks

1941 ***Perf. 12½, 13 & Comp.*** **Wmk. 261**
5N34 A39 ½c #402, II 25 25
5N35 A40 1c #403, II 25 25
a. Type I 25 25
5N36 A46 2c #404, II 50 50
5N37 A39 2½c #405, I 1.50 1.50
5N38 A46 10c #410, I 1.75 1.25
5N39 A45 13c #411, II 35 35
5N40 A46 17c #413, I 11.00 8.00
5N41 A40 25c #416, II 60 60
5N42 A48 30c #418, II 27.50 27.50
a. Type I 27.50 27.50
5N43 A47 40c #419, II 60 60
a. Type I 12.00 7.00
5N44 A40 50c #420, II 90 75
a. Type I 15.00 9.00
Type II, set of 8 30.95 30.80
Type I, set of 7 69.00 54.50

Unwmkd.
5N45 A39 ½c #421, II 25 25
a. Type I 25 25
5N46 A40 1c #422, II 25 25
a. Type I 25 25
5N47 A46 2c #423, II 25 25
5N48 A48 3c #425, I 2.00 1.25
5N49 A39 4c #426, II 25 25
5N50 A45 8c #428, I 5.00 1.75
a. Type II 5.00 2.25
5N51 A46 10c #429, I 11.00 10.00
a. Type II 20.00 20.00
5N52 A45 13c #430, I 6.50 1.25
a. Type II 6.00 4.00
5N53 A48 15c #431, II 75 60
5N54 A46 17c #432, II 75 60
a. Type I 90 90
5N55 A47 20c #433, II 75 60
a. Type I 90 90
5N56 A45 21c #434, II 75 60
5N57 A40 25c #435, I 1.25 75
5N58 A46 28c #436, II 90 75
5N59 A40 50c #439, II 3.00 1.75
Type I, set of 9 38.90 32.15
Type II, set of 13 28.05 17.30

Honan Singapore
Overprint in Red

1942
5N60 A39 4c #5N49 90 90
5N61 A57 8c #5N20 3.00 3.00
5N62 A57 8c #5N12 3.00 3.00
5N63 A57 8c #5N13 10.00 10.00

Honan Anniv. of Manchukuo
Overprint in Red

1942
5N64 A57 2c #5N9 1.50 1.50
5N65 A39 4c #5N49 1.50 1.50
5N66 A57 8c #5N12 15.00 15.00
5N67 A57 8c #5N13 18.00 18.00
5N68 A57 8c #5N20 15.00 15.00
Nos. 5N64-5N68 (5) 51.00 51.00

Shantung

東 山 東 山

I II

Nos. 297-298, 301-303
Overprinted

1941 **Engraved** **Unwmkd.**
6N1 A37 2c #297, II 25 25
a. Type I 50 40
6N2 A37 4c #298, I 1.75 90
a. Type II 1.75 1.25
6N3 A37 15c #301, II 25 25
a. Type I 90 50
6N4 A37 20c #302, II 50 25
6N5 A37 25c #303, II 1.50 1.25
a. Type I 80.00 80.00

On Nos. 312, 314, 318

1941 ***Perf. 14***
6N6 A39 ½c #312, II 25 25
a. Type I 40 25
6N7 A39 2½c #314, II 25 25
a. Type I 25 25
6N8 A45 13c #318, II 25 25
a. Type I 9.00 7.00

On Stamps of 1939-41

1941 ***Perf. 12½***
6N9 A57 2c #349, II 25 25
6N10 A57 2c #368, II 25 25
6N11 A57 3c #350, II 25 25
a. Type I 50 25
6N12 A57 5c #352, II 25 25
a. Type I 25 25
6N13 A57 8c #353, II 25 25
a. Type I 25 25
6N14 A57 8c #369, II 25 25
6N15 A57 10c #354, II 25 25
6N16 A57 16c #357, II 60 60
6N17 A57 $1 #359, II 4.00 4.00
a. Type I 135.00 135.00
b. On No. 347, I 25.00 25.00
6N18 A57 $5 #361, II 20.00 20.00
Nos. 6N9-6N18 (10) 26.35 26.35

On Stamps of 1940
with Secret Marks

1941 ***Perf. 14*** **Unwmkd.**
6N20 A57 5c #382, II 25 25
6N21 A57 8c #383, I 20 20
a. Type II 25 25
6N22 A57 10c #384, II 25 25
6N23 A57 30c #385, II 50 25
a. Type I 1.25 1.25
6N24 A57 50c #386, II 90 75
a. Type I 1.25 90
6N25 A57 $1 #387, II 90 75
a. Type I 3.00 3.00
6N26 A57 $2 #388, II 2.50 2.00
a. Type I 6.00 5.00
6N27 A57 $5 #389, II 7.00 6.00
a. Type I 14.00 14.00
6N28 A57 $10 #390, II 16.50 16.50
a. Type I 22.50 22.50
6N29 A57 $20 #391, II 25.00 25.00
a. Type I 32.50 32.50
Type II, set of 10 54.05 52.00
Type I, set of 8 80.70 79.35

On Stamps of 1940
with Secret Marks

1941 ***Perf. 14*** **Wmk. 261**
6N30 A57 5c #392, II 25 25
6N31 A57 5c #393, II 25 25
6N32 A57 10c #394, II 2.00 1.75
6N33 A57 30c #395, II 2.00 1.00
a. Type I 7.00 6.00
6N34 A57 50c #396, II 1.50 75
a. Type I 2.25 1.75
Nos. 6N30-6N34 (5) 6.00 4.00

On Stamps of 1940-41
(Martyrs) with Secret Marks

1941 ***Perf. 12½, 13 & Comp.*** **Wmk. 261**
6N35 A39 ½c #402, II 25 25
6N36 A40 1c #403, II 25 25
a. Type I 25 25
6N37 A39 2½c #405, II 1.75 1.50
6N38 A46 10c #410, I 90 40
6N39 A45 13c #411, II 50 25
6N40 A46 17c #413, II 1.50 50
a. Type I 3.00 1.25
6N41 A40 25c #416, II 50 50
6N42 A48 30c #418, I 9.00 9.00
6N43 A47 40c #419, II 50 50
a. Type I 9.00 9.00
6N44 A40 50c #420, II 1.00 60
Nos. 6N35-6N44 (10) 16.15 13.75

Unwmkd.
6N45 A39 ½c #421, II 25 25
a. Type I 25 25
6N46 A40 1c #422, II 25 25
a. Type I 25 25
b. On No. 422a, II 32.50 32.50
6N48 A46 2c #423, II 25 25
6N49 A48 3c #425, I 50 50
a. Type II 75 50
6N50 A39 4c #426, II 25 25
6N51 A45 8c #428, II 25 25
a. Type I 6.00 6.00
6N52 A46 10c #429, I 2.50 1.75
6N53 A45 13c #430, II 25 25
a. Type I 60 60
6N54 A48 15c #431, II 25 25
6N55 A46 17c #432, II 25 25
a. Type I 60 60
6N56 A47 20c #433, II 25 25
a. Type I 60 60
6N57 A45 21c #434, II 25 25
6N58 A40 25c #435, I 90 75
6N59 A46 28c #436, II 50 30
6N60 A40 50c #439, II 3.00 3.00
Type II, set of 13 6.75 6.30
Type I, set of 9 12.20 11.30

Honan Singapore
Overprint in Red

1942
6N61 A39 4c #6N50 50 50
6N62 A57 8c #6N13 3.00 3.00
6N63 A57 8c #6N21a 1.75 1.75
6N64 A57 8c #6N14 7.00 7.00

Honan Anniv. of Manchukuo
Overprint in Red

1942
6N65 A57 2c #6N10 1.50 1.50
6N66 A39 4c #6N50 1.25 1.25
6N67 A57 8c #6N13 10.00 10.00
6N68 A57 8c #6N14 16.50 16.50
6N69 A57 8c #6N21a 1.50 1.50
Nos. 6N65-6N69 (5) 30.75 30.75

Supeh

北 蘇 北 蘇

I II

Nos. 297-298, 301-302
Overprinted

1941 **Engraved** **Unwmkd.**
7N1 A37 2c #297, I 2.25 2.25
a. Type II 5.00 5.00
7N2 A37 4c #298, I 15.00 15.00
7N3 A37 15c #301, I 60 50
a. Type II 75 60
7N4 A37 20c #302, II 75 60

On Nos. 312, 314, 318

1941 ***Perf. 14***
7N5 A39 ½c #312, I 60 60
7N6 A39 2½c #314, II 50 50
a. Type I 50 50
7N7 A45 13c #318, II 50 50
a. Type I 55.00 55.00

On Stamps of 1939-41

1941 ***Perf. 12½***
7N8 A57 2c #368, II 50 50
7N9 A57 3c #350, II 50 50
a. Type I 7.00 6.00
7N10 A57 5c #352, II 50 50
a. Type I 50 50
7N11 A57 8c #353, I 50 50
a. Type II 1.75 1.75
7N12 A57 8c #369, II 16.50 16.50
7N13 A57 10c #354, II 50 50
7N14 A57 16c #357, II 50 50
7N15 A57 $1 #359, II 6.00 6.00
a. On No. 347, I 100.00 100.00
Nos. 7N8-7N15 (8) 25.50 25.50

On Stamps of 1940
with Secret Marks

1941 ***Perf. 14*** **Unwmkd.**
7N17 A57 5c #382, II 20 20
7N18 A57 8c #383, II 20 20
7N19 A57 10c #384, I 50 40
a. Type II 60 40
7N20 A57 30c #385, II 75 40
a. Type I 75 60
7N21 A57 50c #386, II 75 40
a. Type I 1.25 75
7N22 A57 $1 #387, I 7.00 4.00
a. Type II 14.00 14.00
7N23 A57 $2 #388, I 8.00 7.00
a. Type II 8.00 8.00
7N24 A57 $5 #389, I 14.00 14.00
a. Type II 37.50 37.50
7N25 A57 $10 #390, II 22.50 22.50
a. Type I 27.50 27.50
7N26 A57 $20 #391, II 32.50 32.50
a. Type I 32.50 32.50
Type II, set of 10 117.00 116.10
Type I, set of 8 91.50 86.75

On Stamps of 1940
with Secret Marks

1941 ***Perf. 14*** **Wmk. 261**
7N27 A57 10c #394, II 50 30
7N28 A57 30c #395, I 3.00 2.25
7N29 A57 50c #396, I 3.00 2.25

On Stamps of 1940-41 (Martyrs) with Secret Marks

941 *Perf. 12½, 13 & Comp.* **Wmk. 261**

N30	A39	½c #402, II	25	25
N31	A40	1c #403, II	25	25
a.		Type I	25	25
N32	A46	2c #404, II	25	25
N33	A39	2½c #405, I	10.00	10.00
N34	A46	10c #410, I	3.50	3.00
N35	A45	13c #411, II	1.50	1.00
N36	A46	17c #413, II	75	30
a.		Type I	27.50	27.50
N37	A40	25c #416, II	75	50
N38	A48	30c #418, I	3.50	3.00
N39	A47	40c #419, II	60	40
a.		Type I	2.25	2.25
N40	A40	50c #420, I	32.50	32.50
		Nos. 7N30-7N40 (11)	33.85	31.43

Unwmkd.

7N41	A39	½c #421, II	20	20
a.		Type I	25	25
7N42	A40	1c #422, II	20	20
7N43	A46	2c #423, I	2.25	1.75
7N44	A48	3c #425, I	50	50
7N45	A39	4c #426, II	25	25
7N46	A46	10c #429, I	16.50	16.50
7N47	A45	13c #430, I	60	60
7N48	A48	15c #431, II	60	30
7N49	A46	17c #432, II	75	50
a.		Type I	75	75
7N50	A47	20c #433, II	50	30
a.		Type I	1.50	1.25
7N51	A45	21c #434, II	50	30
7N52	A40	25c #435, I	1.50	1.25
a.		Type II	1.75	1.50
7N53	A46	28c #436, II	40	40
		Nos. 7N41-7N53 (13)	24.75	23.05

Honan Singapore Overprint in Red

942

7N54	A37	4c #298, II	32.50	32.50
7N55	A39	4c #7N45	1.50	1.50
7N56	A57	8c #7N11a	3.00	3.00
7N57	A57	8c #7N12	7.00	7.00

Honan Anniv. of Manchukuo Overprint in Red

1942

7N58	A57	2c #7N8	1.75	1.75
7N59	A39	4c #7N45	1.25	1.25
7N60	A57	8c #7N11a	37.50	37.50
7N61	A57	8c #7N12	20.00	20.00

North China

For use in:
Honan, Hopei, Shansi, Shantung and Supeh (Northern Kiangsu).

Stamps of China, 1931-37 Surcharged North China (Hwa Pei) and Half of Original Value

北 華
分 壹

1942 *Perf. 14, 12½* **Unwmkd.**

8N1	A40	½c on 1c org (#313)	15	15
8N2	A37	1c on 2c ol grn (#297)	25	20
8N3	A37	2c on 4c grn (#298)	50	20
8N4	A45	10c on 0c brn org (#316)	90.00	

Same Surcharge on Stamps of 1938-41.
Perf. 12½

8N5	A57	1c on 2c ol grn (#349)	1.25	1.25
8N6	A57	1c on 2c ol grn (#368)	30	15
8N7	A57	4c on 8c ol grn (#353)	75	40
8N8	A57	4c on 8c ol grn (#369)	15	15
8N9	A57	5c on 10c grn	15	15
8N10	A57	8c on 16c ol gray	50	20
8N11	A57	50c on $1 hn & dk brn (#359)	1.25	1.25
8N12	A57	50c on $1 hn & dk brn (#344)	200.00	200.00
8N13	A57	50c on $1 hn & dk brn (#347)	22.50	22.50
8N14	A57	$1 on $2 dp bl & org brn (#360)	3.00	3.00
8N15	A57	$1 on $2 dp bl & org brn (#345)	9.00	9.00
8N16	A57	$1 on $2 dp bl & org brn (#348)	50.00	50.00

No. 8N12 was issued without gum.

Same Surcharge on China Nos. 383-388, 390-391.
Perf. 14

8N17	A57	4c on 8c ol grn	10	10
8N18	A57	5c on 10c grn	10	10
8N19	A57	15c on 30c scar	10	10
a.		Invtd. surch.	60.00	60.00
8N20	A57	25c on 50c dk bl	15	10
8N21	A57	50c on $1 org brn & sep	65	50
8N22	A57	$1 on $2 dp bl & yel brn	1.50	1.00
8N23	A57	$5 on $10 dk grn & dl pur	20.00	20.00
8N24	A57	$10 on $20 rose lake & dk bl	12.50	12.50

Same Surcharge on China Nos. 394-396.
Wmk. 261

8N25	A57	5c on 10c grn	20	20
8N26	A57	15c on 30c scar	50	40
8N27	A57	25c on 50c dk bl	30	20

Same Surcharge on Stamps of 1940-41.
1942 *Perf. 12½, 13* **Wmk. 261**

8N28	A40	½c on 1c org	10	10
8N29	A46	1c on 2c dp bl	10	10
8N30	A45	4c on 8c dp org	7.00	7.00
8N31	A46	5c on 10c dl vio	10	10
8N32	A48	15c on 30c brn car	35	20
8N33	A47	20c on 40c org	20	10
8N34	A40	25c on 50c grn	50	30

Unwmkd.

8N35	A40	½c on 1c org (#422)	10	10
a.		½c on 1c org (#422a)	2.00	2.00
8N36	A46	1c on 2c dp bl	10	10
8N37	A39	2c on 4c pale vio	10	10
8N38	A45	4c on 8c dp org	10	10
8N39	A46	5c on 10c dl vio	10	10
8N40	A47	10c on 20c lt bl	10	10
8N41	A47	20c on 40c org	20	15
8N42	A40	25c on 50c grn	1.25	1.00

Same Surcharge on "New Peking" Prints.
Perf. 14

8N43	A37	1c on 2c ol grn	10	10
8N44	A37	2c on 4c dl grn	10	10
a.		Inverted surch.	30.00	
8N45	A45	4c on 8c dp org	10	10
8N46	A57	8c on 16c ol gray	10	10
8N47	A47	10c on 20c red brn	15	10
8N48	A48	15c on 30c brn car	25	10
8N49	A47	20c on 40c org	20	10
a.		Inverted surch.	35.00	
8N50	A40	25c on 50c grn	30	15
8N51	A57	50c on $1 org brn & sep	20	10
8N52	A57	$1 on $2 dp bl & org brn	1.50	1.00
8N53	A57	$5 on $10 dk grn & dl pur	6.00	6.00

See note after No. 2N93.

Nos. 8N44, 8N17 and 8N46 with Additional Overprint in Red

邦友
界租 還交
念紀

1943 *Perf. 14* **Unwmkd.**

8N54	A37	2c on 4c dl grn	10	10
8N55	A57	4c on 8c ol grn	10	10
8N56	A57	8c on 16c ol gray	20	20

Issued to commemorate the return of the Foreign Concessions to China.

Nos. 8N44, 8N7 and 8N46 with Additional Overprint in Red

局總 政郵
立成
念紀年週五

1943, Aug. 15 *Perf. 14, 12½*

8N57	A37	2c on 4c dl grn	10	10
8N58	A57	4c on 8c ol grn	15	15
8N59	A57	8c on 16c ol gray	30	30

Issued to commemorate the fifth anniversary of the North China Postal Service.

Stamps of China, 1934-41, Overprinted in Black

北 華

1943, Nov. 1

8N60	A40	1c org (#313)	10	10
8N61	A40	1c org (#422)	10	10
8N62	A57	10c grn (#354)	10	10
8N63	A57	$2 dp bl & yel brn (#388)	12.00	10.00
8N64	A57	$5 red & grnsh blk (#361)	3.50	3.00
8N65	A57	$5 red & sl grn (#389)	3.00	2.50
8N66	A57	$10 dk grn & dl pur (#390)	10.00	9.00
8N67	A57	$20 rose lake & dk bl (#391)	70.00	60.00
		Nos. 8N60-8N67 (8)	98.80	84.80

Same Overprint on "New Peking" Prints.

8N68	A40	1c orange	10	10
8N69	A37	2c ol grn	10	10
8N70	A37	4c dl grn	10	10
8N71	A37	5c green	10	10
8N72	A57	9c ol grn	10	10
8N73	A46	10c dl vio	10	10
8N74	A57	16c ol gray	10	10
8N75	A57	18c ol gray	10	10
8N76	A47	20c henna	15	10
8N77	A48	30c brn car	15	10
8N78	A47	40c brt org	20	10
a.		Inverted ovpt.	30.00	30.00
8N79	A40	50c green	20	10
8N80	A57	$1 org brn & sep	50	25
8N81	A57	$2 bl & org brn	60	30
8N82	A57	$5 red & sl grn	1.25	1.00
8N83	A57	$10 dk grn & dl pur	2.50	2.50
8N84	A57	$20 rose lake & dk bl	5.00	5.00
		Nos. 8N68-8N84 (17)	11.35	10.25

See note after No. 2N93.

Nos. 8N70 and 8N62 with Additional Overprint in Red

戰 參
念紀年週一

1944, Jan. 9

8N85	A37	4c dl grn	15	15
8N86	A57	10c green	15	15

Issued to commemorate the first anniversary of the declaration of war against the Allies by North China.

Nos. 8N72, 8N75, 8N79 and 8N80 with Additional Overprint in Red

會員委務政
念紀年週四

1944, Mar. 30

8N87	A57	9c ol grn	15	15
8N88	A57	18c ol gray	20	20
8N89	A40	50c green	40	40
8N90	A57	$1 org brn & sep	75	75
a.		red ovpt. inverted	25.00	25.00

Issued to commemorate the fourth anniversary of the North China Political Council.

Shanghai-Nanking Nos. 9N101-9N104 Surcharged North China (Hwa Pei) and New Value in Red or Black

(a) 華北玖分
(b) 華北壹角捌分
(c) 華北叁角陸分
(d) 華北玖角

1944 *Perf. 12½x12, 12x12½*

8N91	OS1 (a)	9c on 50c org	10	10
8N92	OS1 (b)	18c on $1 grn (R)	15	15
a.		Dble. surch.	25.00	25.00
8N93	OS2 (c)	36c on $2 dp bl (R)	15	15
8N94	OS2 (d)	90c on $5 car rose	25	25

Nos. 8N72, 8N75, 8N79 and 8N80 Overprinted in Red or Blue

立成局總政郵
念紀年週六

1944, Aug. 15

8N95	A57	9c ol grn	10	10
8N96	A57	18c ol gray	10	10
8N97	A40	50c green	20	20
8N98	A57	$1 org brn & sep (Bl)	35	35

Issued to commemorate the sixth anniversary of the General Post Office Department of North China.

North China Nos. 8N76, 8N79-8N81 Overprinted in Blue or Black

席 主 汪
念 紀 典 葬

1944, Dec. 5

8N99	A47	20c hn (Bl)	12	12
8N100	A40	50c grn (Bl)	12	12
8N101	A57	$1 org brn & sep (Bl)	18	18
8N102	A57	$2 bl & org brn	18	18

Issued to commemorate the death of Wang Ching-wei, puppet ruler of China.

North China Nos. 8N76, 8N79-8N81 Overprinted in Red or Black

年週二戰參
念 紀

1945

8N103	A47	20c henna	12	12
8N104	A40	50c grn (R)	20	20
8N105	A57	$1 org brn & sep	20	20
8N106	A57	$2 bl & org brn	35	35

Issued to commemorate the second anniversary of the declaration of war.

Shanghai-Nanking Nos. 9N105-9N106 Surcharged in Red

華北伍角

1945 ***Perf. 12x12½***

8N107	OS3	50c on $3 lt org	10	10
8N108	OS3	$1 on $6 bl	15	15

Issued to commemorate the return of the foreign concessions in Shanghai.

Dragon Pillar
OS1

Dr. Sun Yat-sen
OS2

Designs: $2, Long Bridge and White Pagoda. $5, Tower in Imperial City. $10, Marble Boat, Summer Palace.

Lithographed.

1945 ***Perf. 14*** **Unwmkd.**

Various Papers.

8N109	OS1	$1 dl yel	8	8
8N110	OS1	$2 dp bl	6	6
8N111	OS1	$5 carmine	15	15
8N112	OS1	$10 dl grn	15	15

Issued to commemorate the fifth anniversary of the North China Political Council.

1945

Without Gum; Various Papers.

8N113	OS2	$1 bister	15	10
8N114	OS2	$2 dk bl	18	10
8N115	OS2	$5 fawn	25	15
8N116	OS2	$10 sage grn	40	25
8N117	OS2	$20 dl vio	50	30
8N118	OS2	$50 brown	12.50	6.00
		Nos. 8N113-8N118 (6)	13.98	6.90

Nos. 8N113–8N118 without "Hwa Pei" overprint are proofs.

Wutai Mountain, Shansi
OS3

Designs: $10, Kaifeng Iron Pagoda. $20, International Bridge, Tientsin. $30, Taishan Mountain, Shantung. $50, General Post Office, Peking.

1945, Aug. 15

Without Gum; Various Papers.

8N119	OS3	$5 gray grn	5	5
8N120	OS3	$10 dl brn	5	5
8N121	OS3	$20 dl pur	7	7
8N122	OS3	$30 sl bl	8	8
8N123	OS3	$50 carmine	15	15
		Nos. 8N119-8N123 (5)	40	40

Issued to commemorate the seventh anniversary of the North China Postal Directorate.

Shanghai and Nanking

China Nos. 299-303 Surcharged

貳角伍分 暫售 25

a

暫售 陸圓 6.00

b

1942-45 ***Perf. 12½, 13½*** **Unwmkd.**

9N1	A37 (b)	$6 on 5c grn	10	10
9N2	A37 (b)	$20 on 15c scar	10	10
9N3		$500 on 15c dk grn	15	15
9N4	A37 (b)	$1000 on 20c ultra	15	15
9N5	A37 (b)	$1000 on 25c ultra	15	15

A $1000 on 20c ultramarine, No. 293, exists. Price $200.

Same Surcharge on Stamps of 1939–41.

Perf. 12½

9N6	A57 (a)	25c on 5c ol grn (#352)	10	10
9N7	A57 (a)	30c on 2c ol grn (#368)	10	10
9N8	A57 (a)	50c on 3c dl cl (#350)	10	10
9N9	A57 (a)	50c on 5c ol grn (#352)	10	10
9N10	A57 (a)	50c on 8c ol grn (#353)	10	10
9N11	A57 (b)	$1 on 8c ol grn (#353)	10	10
9N12	A57 (b)	$1 on 8c ol grn (#369)	5.00	5.00
9N13	A57 (b)	$1 on 15c dk vio brn (#356)	10	10
9N14	A57 (b)	$1.30 on 16c ol gray (#357)	10	10
9N15	A57 (b)	$1.50 on 3c dl cl (#350)	10	10
9N16	A57 (b)	$2 on 5c ol grn (#352)	10	10
9N17	A57 (b)	$2 on 10c grn (#354)	10	10
9N18	A57 (b)	$3 on 15c dk vio brn (#356)	10	10
9N19	A57 (b)	$4 on 16c ol gray (#357)	10	10
9N20	A57 (b)	$5 on 15c dk vio brn (#356)	10	10
9N21	A57 (b)	$6 on 5c grn (#351)	10	10
a.		Perf. 14 (#371)	15.00	15.00
9N22	A57 (b)	$6 on 5c ol grn (#352)	10	10
9N23	A57 (b)	$6 on 8c ol grn (#353)	10	10
9N24	A57 (b)	$6 on 8c ol grn (#369)	450.00	450.00
9N25	A57 (b)	$6 on 10c grn (#354)	10	10
9N26	A57 (b)	$10 on 10c grn (#354)	10	10
9N27	A57 (b)	$10 on 16c ol gray (#357)	10	10
9N28	A57 (b)	$20 on 3c dl cl (#350)	10	10
9N29	A57 (b)	$20 on 15c scar (#355)	10	10
9N30	A57 (b)	$20 on 15c dk vio brn (#356)	10	10
9N31	A57 (b)	$20 on $2 dp bl & org brn (#360)	50	50
9N32	A57 (b)	$100 on 3c dl cl (#350)	10	10
9N33	A57 (b)	$500 on 8c ol grn (#353)	40	40
9N34	A57 (b)	$500 on 8c ol grn (#369)	12.50	12.50
9N35	A57 (b)	$500 on 10c grn (#354)	10	10
9N36	A57 (b)	$500 on 15c scar (#355)	10	10
9N37	A57 (b)	$500 on 15c dk vio brn (#356)	10	10
9N38	A57 (b)	$500 on 16c ol gray (#357)	10	10
9N39	A57 (b)	$1000 on 25c dk bl (#358)	10	10
9N40	A57 (b)	$2000 on $5 red & grnsh blk (#361)	25	25
		Nos. 9N1-9N23, 9N25-9N40 (39)	22.20	22.20

Nos. 381–391 Surcharged with Type "b."

Perf. 14

9N41	A57	$1 on 8c ol grn	10	10
9N42	A57	$1.70 on 30c scar	10	10
a.		Perf. 12½	15	15
9N43	A57	$2 on 5c ol grn	10	10
9N44	A57	$2 on $1 org brn & sep	35	35
9N45	A57	$3 on 8c ol grn	10	10
a.		$3 on 8c ol grn (#383a)		
b.		"3" with flat top	10	10
9N46	A57	$6 on 5c grn	10	10
9N47	A57	$6 on 5c ol grn	10	10
9N48	A57	$6 on 8c ol grn	10	10
9N49	A57	$10 on 10c grn	10	10
a.		Perf. 12½	25	25
9N50	A57	$20 on $2 dp bl & yel brn	15	15
9N51	A57	$50 on 30c scar	10	10
9N52	A57	$50 on 50c dk bl	10	10
9N53	A57	$50 on $5 red & sl grn	15	15
9N54	A57	$50 on $20 rose lake & dk bl	60	60
9N55	A57	$100 on $10 dk grn & dl pur	30	30
9N56	A57	$200 on $20 rose lake & dk bl	10	10
9N57	A57	$500 on 8c ol grn	3.00	3.00
a.		$500 on 8c ol grn (#383a)	12.50	12.50
9N58	A57	$500 on 10c grn	15	15
9N59	A57	$1000 on 30c scar	15	15
9N60	A57	$1000 on 50c dk bl	15	15
9N61	A57	$1000 on $2 dp bl & yel brn	75	75
9N62	A57	$2000 on $5 red & sl grn	30	30

China Nos. 392–395 and 399–401 Surcharged with Type "b."

1942-45 ***Perf. 14*** **Wmk. 261**

9N63	A57	$2 on $1 org brn & sep, perf. 12½	30	30
9N64	A57	$6 on 5c grn	10	10
9N65	A57	$6 on 5c ol grn	10	10
9N66	A57	$50 on $5 red & sl grn	10	10
a.		Numeral tablet vio	10	10
9N67	A57	$100 on $10 dk grn & dl pur	15	15
9N68	A57	$200 on $20 rose lake & dk bl	15	15
9N69	A57	$500 on 10c grn	25	25
9N70	A57	$1000 on 30c scar	50	50
9N71	A57	$5000 on $10 dk grn & dl pur, perf. 12½	3.50	3.50
a.		Perf. 14	30.00	30.00
		Nos. 9N41-9N71 (31)	12.30	12.30

Nos. 9N63 and 9N71 were not issued without surcharge. A $50 on 30c scarlet exists.

Same Surcharge on Stamps of 1940-41.

Wmk. 261

Perf. 12½, 13

9N72	A46	$30 on 2c dp bl	35.00	35.00

A $7.50 on ½c and a $15 on 1c are known.

Unwmkd.

9N73	A39	$7.50 on ½c ol blk	10	10
9N74	A40	$15 on 1c org	10	10
a.		Without secret mark	30.00	30.00
9N75	A46	$30 on 2c dp bl	10	10
9N76	A40	$200 on 1c org	10	10
9N77	A45	$200 on 8c dp org	10	10
		Nos. 9N73-9N77 (5)	50	50

Same Surcharge on Stamps of 1941.

Perf. 12

9N78	A59 (a)	5c on ½c sep	10	10
9N79	A59 (a)	10c on 1c org	10	10
9N80	A59 (a)	20c on 1c org	10	10
9N81	A59 (a)	40c on 5c grn	10	10
9N82	A59 (b)	$5 on 5c grn	10	10
9N83	A59 (b)	$10 on 10c brt grn	10	10
9N84	A59 (b)	$50 on ½c sep	10	10
9N85	A59 (b)	$50 on 1c org	10	1
9N86	A59 (b)	$50 on 17c ol	10	1
9N87	A59 (b)	$200 on 5c grn	10	1
9N88	A59 (b)	$200 on 8c turq grn	10	1
9N89	A59 (b)	$200 on 8c red org	10	1
9N90	A59 (b)	$500 on $5 scar & blk	15	1
9N91	A59 (b)	$1000 on 1c org	15	1
9N92	A59 (b)	$1000 on 25c rose vio	25	2
9N93	A59 (b)	$1000 on 30c scar	25	2
9N94	A59 (b)	$1000 on $2 bl & blk	40	4
9N95	A59 (b)	$1000 on $10 grn & blk	25	2
9N96	A59 (b)	$2000 on $5 scar & blk	50	5
		Nos. 9N78-9N96 (19)	3.15	3.1

Stamps of China 1939-41 Surcharged in Red or Blue

收回租界紀念 三十二年 八月一日 貳角伍分

1943 ***Perf. 12, 12½*** **Unwmkd.**

9N97	A57	25c on 5c grn	5	5
9N98	A59	50c on 8c red org (Bl)	5	5
9N99	A57	$1 on 16c ol gray	10	10
9N100	A59	$2 on 50c dk bl	10	10

Issued to commemorate the return of the foreign concessions in Shanghai.

Wheat and Cotton
OS1

Purple Mountain, Nanking
OS2

Perf. 12½x12, 12x12½

1944 **Engraved.** **Unwmkd.**

9N101	OS1	50c orange	5	5
9N102	OS1	$1 green	5	5
9N103	OS2	$2 dp bl	5	5
9N104	OS2	$5 car rose	10	5

Issued to commemorate the fourth anniversary of the establishment of the puppet government at Nanking.

Map of Foreign Concessions in Shanghai
OS3

1944 ***Perf. 12x12½***

9N105	OS3	$3 lt org	5	10
9N106	OS3	$6 blue	5	10

Issued to commemorate the first anniversary of the return of the foreign concessions in Shanghai.

Nos. 9N101-9N104 Surcharged in Black with Type "b."

1945, Mar. 30

9N107	OS1	$15 on 50c org	5	5
9N108	OS1	$30 on $1 grn	5	5
9N109	OS2	$60 on $2 dp bl	5	5
9N110	OS2	$200 on $5 car rose	10	10

China Nos. C31, C32, C36 and C38 Surcharged in Red, Green, Orange or Carmine

壹暫
仟
圓售

1945 *Perf. 12½, 13.*

9N111	AP3	$150 on 15c gray grn (R)	5	5
9N112	AP3	$250 on 25c yel org (G)	5	5
9N113	AP3	$600 on 60c dp bl (O)	10	10
9N114	AP3	$1,000 on $1 ap grn (C)	15	15

Issued as air raid precaution propaganda.

AIR POST STAMPS

China Nos. C35 and C38 Surcharged in Black

10

付已費空航之片明內國

The surcharges on Nos. 9NC1–9NC7 were in Japanese currency because all air mail then was carried by Japanese planes.

1941 *Perf. 12½* **Unwmkd.**

The surcharges translate: (10c) "Airmail fee for postcard within the nation has been paid." (20c) "Airmail fee for letter within the nation has been paid."

9NC1	AP3	10(s) on 50c brn	10	10
9NC2	AP3	20(s) on $1 ap grn	10	10

Two types of surcharge exist on No. 9NC1.

Similar Surcharge on No. C28.

1941 *Perf. 13* **Wmk. 261**

9NC3	AP3	20(s) on $1 ap grn	7.50	7.50

Nos. C37 and C39 Surcharged

35

付已費空航函信本日寄

1941 *Perf. 12½, 13* **Unwmkd.**

The surcharges translate: (18c and 25c) "Airmail fee for postcard to Japan has been paid." (35c) "Airmail fee for letter to Japan has been paid."

9NC4	AP3	18(s) on 90c lt ol	10	10
9NC5	AP3	25(s) on 90c lt ol	10	10
9NC6	AP3	35(s) on $2 lt brn	10	10

No. 9NC6 with Additional Surcharge in Red *Perf. 12½.*

9NC7	AP3	60(s) on 35 (s) on $2 lt brn	10	10

POSTAGE DUE STAMPS

Postage Due Stamps of China 1932 Surcharged in Black

壹 改
圓 作
100

1945 *Perf. 14* **Unwmkd.**

9NJ1	D5	$1 on 2c org	10	10
9NJ2	D5	$2 on 5c org	10	10
9NJ3	D5	$5 on 10c org	10	10
9NJ4	D5	$10 on 20c org	10	10

Northeastern Provinces.

民中
國華

With the end of World War II and the collapse of Manchukuo, the Northeastern Provinces reverted to China. In many Manchurian towns and cities, the Manchukuo stamps were locally handstamped in ideograms: "Republic of China," "China Postal Service" or "Temporary Use for China." A typical example is shown above.

Dr. Sun Yat-sen
A1 A2

Typographed.

Black Surcharge.

1946, Feb. *Perf. 14* **Unwmkd.**

1	A1	50c on $5 red	6	5
2	A1	50c on $10 grn	6	5
3	A1	$1 on $10 grn	6	5
4	A1	$2 on $20 brn vio	6	5
5	A1	$4 on $50 brn	12	10
		Nos. 1-5 (5)	36	30

The two characters at left express the new value.

Stamps of China, 1938–41 Overprinted 用貼北東限

1946, Apr. *Perf. 12½, 13, 13½, 14*

6	A40	1c org (#422)	8	5
7	A48	3c dp yel brn (#425)	8	5
8	A48	5c dl red org (#427)	8	5
9	A57	10c grn (#354)	8	5
10	A57	10c grn (#384)	8	5
11	A47	20c lt bl (#433)	8	5
a.		Horiz. pair, imperf. between	45.00	
		Nos. 6-11 (6)	48	30

Without Gum.

1946, July **Engraved** *Perf. 14*

12	A2	5c lake	12	8
13	A2	10c orange	12	8
14	A2	20c yel grn	12	8
15	A2	25c blk brn	12	8
16	A2	50c red org	12	8
17	A2	$1 blue	12	8
18	A2	$2 dk vio	12	8
19	A2	$2.50 indigo	12	8
20	A2	$3 brown	12	8
21	A2	$4 org brn	12	8
22	A2	$5 dk grn	12	8
23	A2	$10 crimson	12	8
24	A2	$20 olive	12	8
25	A2	$50 bl vio	12	8
		Nos. 12-25 (14)	1.68	1.12

Two types of $4, $10, $20 and $50: I. Character *kuo* directly left of sun emblem is open at upper and lower left corners of "box." Diagonal stroke from top center to lower right has no hook at bottom. II. Character is closed at left corners. Diagonal stroke has hook at bottom.

See also Nos. 47–52, 61–63.

China Nos. 728–731 Surcharged in Black

限東北貼用
2.00 圓貳

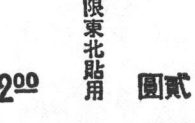

1946

26	A75	$2 on $20 grn	12	12
27	A75	$3 on $30 bl	12	12
28	A75	$5 on $50 dk brr	12	12
29	A75	$10 on $100 car	12	12

Convening of Chinese National Assembly.

Type of China, 1946. Inscribed:

貼 東
用 北

1947 **Engraved** *Perf. 11, 11½*

30	A74	$2 carmine	10	10
31	A74	$3 green	10	10
32	A74	$5 vermilion	10	10
33	A74	$10 yel grn	12	12
34	A74	$20 yel org	12	12
35	A74	$30 magenta	12	12
		Nos. 30-35 (6)	66	66

60th birthday of Chiang Kai-shek.

Type of China, 1947.

Inscribed: 用貼北東

Engraved.

1947 *Perf. 14* **Unwmkd.**

36	A76	$2 dp grn	10	10
37	A76	$4 dp bl	10	10
38	A76	$6 carmine	10	10
39	A76	$10 lt brn	10	10
40	A76	$20 dp cl	10	10
		Nos. 36-40 (5)	50	50

First anniversary of return of Chinese National Government to Nanking.

China Nos. 644 to 646 and 634 Surcharged in Black

用貼北東限
叁 改
佰
圓 300 作

1947 *Perf. 12½, 14.*

41	A73	$100 on $1000 rose lake	10	7
42	A73	$300 on $3000 bl	12	8
43	A73	$500 on $5000 dp grn & ver	15	8
44	A37	$500 on $30 choc	15	12

Type of 1946.

Without Gum.

1947 **Engraved** *Perf. 14*

47	A2	$44 dk car rose	17.50	17.50
48	A2	$100 dp grn	5	5
49	A2	$200 rose brn	5	5
50	A2	$300 bluish grn	6	6
51	A2	$500 rose car	6	6
52	A2	$1000 dp org	8	8
		Nos. 47-52 (6)	17.80	17.80

Stamps and Types of 1946-47 Surcharged in Black or Red

1948 *Perf. 14* **Unwmkd.**

53	A2	$1500 on 20c yel grn	25	25
54	A2	$3000 on $1 bl	10	10
55	A2	$4000 on 25c blk brn (R)	10	10
56	A2	$8000 on 50c red org	10	10
57	A2	$10,000 on 10c org	15	15
58	A2	$50,000 on $109 dk grn (R)	30	33
59	A2	$100,000 on $65 dl grn	30	40
60	A2	$500,000 on $22 gray (R)	30	40
		Nos. 53-60 (8)	1.60	1.83

Type of 1946.

Without Gum

1949

61	A2	$22 gray	20.00	
62	A2	$65 dl grn	25.00	
63	A2	$109 dk grn	35.00	

POSTAGE DUE STAMPS.

D1

Engraved.

Without Gum.

1947 *Perf. 14* **Unwmkd.**

J1	D1	10c dk bl	5	15
J2	D1	20c dk bl	5	15
J3	D1	50c dk bl	5	15
J4	D1	$1 dk bl	5	15
J5	D1	$2 dk bl	5	15
J6	D1	$5 dk bl	5	15
		Nos. J1-J6 (6)	30	90

Nos. J1 to J3 Surcharged in Red

拾 改
圓 作

1948

J7	D1	$10 on 10c dk bl	5	15
J8	D1	$20 on 20c dk bl	5	15
J9	D1	$50 on 50c dk bl	5	15

The surcharge reads "Changed to . . . . dollars." Characters at the left express the new value and vary on each denomination.

MILITARY STAMPS

No. 16 Surcharged in Black

郵 軍
作暫
圓肆拾肆

1947 *Perf. 14.* **Unwmkd.**

M1	A2	$44 on 50c red org	1.75	1.75

The surcharge reads: "Army Post. Temporarily for 44 dollars."

China No. M13 Overprinted in Black 用貼北東限

Thin Paper Without Gum.

Perf. 12½.

M2	M1	rose	25	25

China No. M13 Overprinted in Black 用貼北東限

M3	M1	rose	3.50	3.00

PARCEL POST STAMP.

China No. Q25 Surcharged in Black

用貼北東限
伍 改
拾
萬
圓 作

Engraved.

1948 *Perf. 13½* **Unwmkd.**

Without Gum.

Q1	PP3	$500,000 on $5,000,000 lil	40.00	

Anhwei Province

(ăn·(h)wā)

China Type A95 Handstamp Surcharged

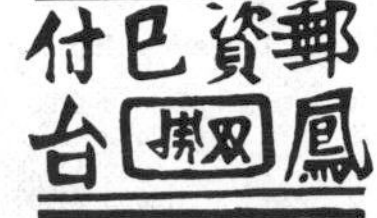

1949, Mar. 16 **Lithographed**

1	A95	On $1000 car	30.00	

SPECIAL DELIVERY STAMP

China Type A95 with Similar Surcharge

1949, Mar 16 — **Lithographed**

E1	A95	On $500 brn	30.00

REGISTRATION STAMP

China Type A95 with Similar Surcharge

1949, Mar. 16 — **Lithographed**

F1	A95	On $3000 org	30.00

ACKNOWLEDGMENT OF RECEIPT STAMP

China Type A95 with Similar Surcharge

1949, Mar. 16 — **Lithographed**

H1	A95	On $20 red brn	30.00

Fukien Province

(fü·kyen)

Stamps of China, 1945–49, Surcharged

壹 郵
分 1 資

Without Gum

1949 — **Engraved** — ***Perf. 14***

1	A82	1c on $500 bl grn	4.00	4.00
2	A82	1c on $7000 lt red brn	7.50	7.50
3	A82	2c on $2,000,000 ver	1.75	1.75
4	A82	2½c on $50,000 dp bl	2.50	2.50
5	A73	4c on $100 dk car	1.75	1.75
6	A73	10c on $200 ol grn	1.75	1.75
7	A82	10c on $3000 bl	1.25	1.25
8	A82	10c on $4000 gray	1.50	1.50
9	A82	10c on $6000 rose lil	1.25	1.25
10	A82	10c on $100,000 dl grn	1.25	1.25
11	A82	10c on $1,000,000 cl	1.25	1.25
12	A82	40c on $200,000 brn vio	3.00	3.00

The surcharge on No. 2 is handstamped and in slightly larger characters.
Issue dates: No. 2, May 10; others, June.

China Nos. 973, 975–978 Overprinted

州 福

1949, June — **Litho.** — ***Perf. 12½, 13***

13	A94	1c ap grn	3.50	2.50
14	A94	4c bl grn	1.25	75
15	A94	10c dp lil	15.00	6.00
16	A94	16c org red	3.00	3.00
17	A94	20c blue	7.50	5.00

Same Overprint on China No. 959, 959a

Perf. 12½, Rouletted

1949, July — **Lithographed**

18	A96	orange	5.00	5.00

Same Overprint on Fukien Nos. 1, 3–4, 11 in Black or Red

1949, June — **Engraved** — ***Perf. 14***

19	A82	1c on $500 bl grn	30.00	22.50
20	A82	2c on $2,000,000 ver	5.00	4.00
21	A82	2½c on $50,000 dp bl	5.00	4.00
22	A82	10c on $4000 gray	10.00	8.00
23	A82	10c on $1,000,000 cl	30.00	22.50

AIR POST STAMP

China No. C62 Overprinted as Nos. 13–17

Perf. 12½, Rouletted

1949, July — **Lithographed**

C1	AP5	bl grn	5.00	5.00

SPECIAL DELIVERY STAMP

China No. E12 Overprinted as Nos. 13–17

Perf. 12½, Rouletted

1949, July — **Lithographed**

E1	SD2	red vio	5.00	5.00

REGISTRATION STAMP

China No. F2 Overprinted as Nos. 13–17

Perf. 12½, Rouletted

1949, July — **Lithographed**

F1	R2	carmine	5.00	5.00

Hunan Province

(hü·nän)

China No. 640 Surcharged

郵資已付 湘 國內平信

1949, May — **Engr.** — ***Perf. 14***

1	A73	On $100 dk car	1.75	1.75

The first printing of surcharge on No. 1 is in smaller characters.

China Nos. 797, 788, 750, 747 Surcharged

伍分
湘

1949, May — **Engr.** — ***Perf. 14***

2	A82	1c on $2,000,000 ver	3.00	3.00
3	A82	2c on $20,000 rose pink	3.00	3.00
4	A82	5c on $3000 bl	3.00	3.00
5	A82	10c on $500 bl grn	3.00	3.00

AIR POST STAMP

China No. 790 Surcharged

湘 國內航空
付已資郵

1949, May — **Engr.** — ***Perf. 14***

C1	A82	On $40,000 grn	1.75	1.75

SPECIAL DELIVERY STAMP

China No. 637 Surcharged as No. F1 in Red

1949, May — **Engr.** — ***Perf. 14***

E1	A73	On $30 dk bl	1.00	1.00

REGISTRATION STAMP

China No. 754 Surcharged

號掛內國
湘
付已資郵

1949, May — **Engr.** — ***Perf. 14***

F1	A73	On $7000 lt red brn	1.50	1.50

Hupeh Province

(hü·pā, -be)

China Type A95 Surcharged

限起華中
分壹資郵
1

1949, May — **Lithographed**

1	A95	1c on $20 red brn	6.50	6.50
2	A95	10c on $20 red brn	6.50	6.50

Kansu Province

(kan·sü, gän·sü)

China No. 959 Handstamped in Purple

區青寧甘限
用貼

1949, Aug. — **Litho.** — ***Perf. 12½***

1	A96	orange	125.00

AIR POST STAMP

Same Handstamp Overprinted on China No. C62 in Red

1949, Aug. — **Litho.** — ***Perf. 12½***

C1	AP5	bl grn	125.00

Counterfeits exist.

Kiangsi Province

(kyang·sē, jyäng·sē)

China Nos. 789–791 Surcharged

郵資已付 國內平信
贛

1949 — **Engraved** — ***Perf. 14***

1	A82	On $30,000 choc	3.00	3.00
2	A82	On $40,000 grn	5.00	5.00
3	A82	On $50,000 dp bl	5.00	5.00

AIR POST STAMP

Similar Surcharge on China No. 754

1949 — **Engraved** — ***Perf. 14***

C1	A82	On $7000 lt red brn	10.00	10.00

Third and fourth characters in right column of surcharge read "Air Mail" in Chinese on No. C1, "Registered" on Nos. F1–F2.

SPECIAL DELIVERY STAMP

Similar Surcharge on China No. 750

1949 — **Engraved** — ***Perf. 14***

E1	A82	On $3000 bl	4.00	4.00

See note below No. C1.

REGISTRATION STAMPS

Similar Surcharge on China Nos. 747 and 754

1949 — **Engraved** — ***Perf. 14***

F1	A82	On $500 bl grn	5.00	5.00
F2	A82	On $7000 lt red brn	6.00	6.00

Kwangsi Province

(kwäng·sē, gwäng·sē)

China Nos. 811 and 818 Also Surcharged in Red

伍銀桂
分圓區

1949, May 21 — **Typographed**

6	A62	5c on $20,000 on 10c dp grn	4.00	4.00
7	A62	5c on $40,000 on 20c dk ol grn	7.50	7.50

China Stamps of 1946–48 Surcharged in Black or Red

a: 桂區 分2圓銀

b: 桂區 銀圓壹角貳分

1949 — **Engraved** — ***Perf. 14***

Type "a" Surcharge

8	A82	½c on $500,000 lil rose	7.50	7.50
9	A82	1c on $200,000 brn vio	2.25	2.25
10	A82	2c on $300,000 yel grn	15.00	15.00
11	A73	5c on $3000 bl	2.25	2.25
12	A82	5c on $3000 bl	2.25	2.25
13	A82	5c on $40,000 grn	3.00	3.00

Type "b" Surcharge

14	A82	13c on $50,000 dp bl (R)	3.00	3.00
15	A82	13c on $50,000 dp bl	7.00	7.00
16	A82	17c on $7000 lt red brn	3.00	3.00
17	A82	21c on $100,000 dl grn	3.00	3.00

Shensi Province

(shen·sē)

China Nos. 747, 750 Surcharged

郵資已付 (陝) 國內平信

1949, May — **Engraved** — ***Perf. 14***

1	A82	On $500 bl grn	3.50	3.50
2	A82	On $3000 bl	3.50	3.50

AIR POST STAMP

Similar Surcharge on China No. 754

1949, May — **Engraved** — ***Perf. 14***

C1	A82	On $7000 lt red brn	4.50	4.50

SPECIAL DELIVERY STAMP

Similar Surcharge on China No. 746 in Red

1949, May — **Engraved** — ***Perf. 14***

E1	A82	On $250 dp lil	3.50	3.50

REGISTRATION STAMPS

Similar Surcharge on China Nos. 626, 637 in Red

1949, May — **Typo.** — ***Perf. 12***

F1	A72	On $30 dp bl	7.00	7.00
F2	A73	On $30 dk bl	3.50	3.50

Szechwan Province.

(se'chwän', sŭ'chwän')

Re-engraved Issue of China, 1923, Overprinted 用貼川四限

•33	*Perf. 14.*		**Unwmkd.**	
	A29	1c orange	1.00	15
	A29	5c claret	1.00	15
	A30	50c dp grn	3.75	90

The overprint reads "For use in Szechwan ovince exclusively".

Same Overprint on Sun Yat-sen Issue of 1931-37.

Type II.

•33-34	*Perf. 12½.*			
	A37	2c ol grn	15	20
	A37	5c green	15	15
	A37	15c dk grn	90	30
	A37	15c scar ('34)	75	1.00
	A37	25c ultra	75	20
	A37	$1 org brn & dk brn	5.00	1.00
)	A37	$2 bl & org brn	10.00	2.00
	A37	$5 dl red & blk	30.00	8.00
		Nos. 4-11 (8)	47.70	12.85

Same Overprint on Martyrs Issue of 1932-34.

933		*Perf. 14*		
2	A39	½c blk brn	30	15
3	A40	1c orange	15	15
4	A39	2½c rose lil	1.00	50
5	A48	3c dp brn	60	15
6	A45	8c brn org	75	15
7	A46	10c dl vio	1.50	15
8	A45	13c bl grn	1.50	15
9	A46	17c brn ol	2.00	75
0	A47	20c brn red	2.00	15
1	A48	30c brn vio	2.00	15
2	A47	40c orange	5.00	40
3	A40	50c green	10.00	50
		Nos. 12-23 (12)	26.80	3.35

Stamps of China, 1947-48, Surcharged 國內平信郵資 每重貳拾公分 蓉

1949		**Engraved**	*Perf. 14*	
24	A82	On $150 dk bl	10.00	10.00
25	A82	On $250 dp lil	10.00	10.00
26	A82	On $500 bl grn	2.00	2.00
27	A82	On $1000 red	6.00	6.00
28	A82	On $2000 ver	2.00	2.00
29	A82	On $3000 bl	2.00	2.00
30	A82	On $4000 gray	2.00	2.00
31	A82	On $5000 dk brn	10.00	10.00
32	A82	On $6000 rose lil	2.00	2.00
33	A82	On $7000 lt red brn	10.00	10.00
34	A82	On $10,000 dk bl & car	2.00	2.00
35	A82	On $20,000 rose pink	4.00	4.00
36	A82	On $30,000 choc	2.00	2.00
37	A82	On $50,000 grn & dk bl	2.00	2.00
38	A82	On $50,000 dp bl	3.00	3.00
39	A82	On $100,000 dl yel & ol	3.50	3.50
40	A82	On $100,000 dl grn	4.00	4.00
41	A82	On $200,000 vio brn & dp bl	4.00	4.00
42	A82	On $200,000 brn vio	4.00	4.00
43	A82	On $300,000 sep & org brn		
44	A82	On $300,000 yel grn	7.50	7.50
45	A82	On $500,000 dk Prus grn & sep	2.00	2.00
46	A82	On $1,000,000 cl	6.50	6.50
47	A82	On $2,000,000 ver	4.00	4.00
48	A82	On $3,000,000 ol bis	4.00	4.00
49	A82	On $5,000,000 ultra	15.00	15.00

Several of Nos. 24-49 exist with inverted surcharge and a few with bottom character of left row repeated in right row, same position.
Counterfeits exist.

China No. 737 Surcharged in Purple 蓉 貳分 郵資 2

1949			*Perf. 12½*	
50	A77	2c on $500 ol grn	7.00	7.00

China No. 975 Handstamp Surcharged in Purple 蓉 2½ 半分貳

1949			**Lithographed**	
51	A94	2½c on 4c bl grn	6.00	6.00

AIR POST STAMPS

China No. C55-C59, C61 Surcharged 國內航空 郵資 每重貳拾公分 蓉

Perf. 12½, 13x12½, 14

1949, July			**Unwmkd.**	
C1	AP3	On $10,000 on 30c lt red	2.00	2.00
a.		On #C54		500.00
C2	AP4	On $10,000 on $27 bl	3.50	3.50
a.		Second surch. invtd.	125.00	
b.		On #C53	100.00	
C3	AP3	On $20,000 on 25c lt org	3.50	3.50
C4	AP3	On $30,000 on 90c lt ol	4.50	4.50
C5	AP3	On $50,000 on 60c bl	30.00	30.00
C6	AP3	On $50,000 on $1 yel grn	5.00	5.00
		Nos. C1-C6 (6)	48.50	48.50

On No. C2 characters of overprint are arranged in two horizontal rows, and two of four lines are vertical.

REGISTRATION STAMPS

Stamps of China, 1944-47, Surcharged 國內信函 掛號郵資 蓉

Engr.; Typo. (A72)

1949			*Perf. 12, 13, 14*	
F1	A64	On $100 yel brn	20.00	
F2	A72	On $100 dk brn	30.00	
F3	A64	On $200 dk grn	10.00	
F4	A72	On $200 brn vio	10.00	
F5	A73	On $200 ol grn	60.00	
F6	A73	On $500 brt bl grn	60.00	
F7	A73	On $700 red brn	85.00	
F8	A73	On $5000 dp grn & ver	50.00	
		Nos. F1-F8 (8)	325.00	

PARCEL POST STAMP

China No. Q10 Surcharged 蓉 壹分

1949		**Engr.**	*Perf. 12½*	
Q1	PP2	1c on $20,000 dk red	75.00	

No. Q1 is also found with surcharged value repeated in 5 characters at top of stamp.

Tsingtau

(tsing·tou, ching·dou)

China Nos. 890, 899, 945, 894 Handstamp Surcharged in Purple Blue or Red 銀圓 壹分 (青島)

Engr.; Litho.

1949, May			*Perf. 14, 12½*	
1	A94	1c on $100 org brn (P)	10.00	10.00
2	A94	4c on $5000 lt bl (P)	8.00	7.00
3	A94	6c on $500 rose lil (B)	7.00	6.00
4	A94	10c on $1000 bl (R)	7.00	6.00

Yunnan Province.

(yōōn'nän'; yün'-)

Stamps of China, 1923-26, Overprinted 用貼省滇限

The overprint reads "For exclusive use in the Province of Yunnan". It was applied to prevent stamps being purchased in the depreciated currency of Yunnan and used elsewhere.

1926	*Perf. 14.*		**Unwmkd.**	
1	A29	½c blk brn	15	10
2	A29	1c orange	20	10
3	A29	1½c violet	25	20
4	A29	2c yel grn	40	20
5	A29	3c bl grn	30	15
6	A29	4c ol grn	30	15
7	A29	5c claret	50	15
8	A29	6c red	40	25
9	A29	7c violet	40	30
10	A29	8c brn org	50	40
11	A29	10c dk bl	50	15
12	A30	13c brown	85	60
13	A30	15c dk bl	75	60
14	A30	16c ol grn	85	60
15	A30	20c brn red	1.25	25
16	A30	30c brn vio	2.00	60
17	A30	50c dp grn	1.75	75
18	A31	$1 org brn & sep	7.00	2.00
19	A31	$2 bl & red brn	14.00	6.00
20	A31	$5 red & sl	90.00	75.00
		Nos. 1-20 (20)	122.35	88.55

Unification Issue of China, 1929, Overprinted in Red 滇省 貼用

1929			*Perf. 14*	
21	A35	1c brn org	75	30
22	A35	4c ol grn	1.00	50
23	A35	10c dk bl	2.25	1.25
24	A35	$1 dk red	40.00	32.50

Similar Overprint in Black on Sun Yat-sen Mausoleum Issue.

Characters 15½-16mm. apart.

25	A36	1c brn org	60	25
26	A36	4c ol grn	90	50
27	A36	10c dk bl	2.50	1.25
28	A36	$1 dk red	27.50	15.00

London Print Issue of China, 1931-37, Overprinted 用貼省滇限

1932-34	*Perf. 12½.*		**Unwmkd.**	
	Type I (double circle).			
29	A37	1c orange	50	50
30	A37	2c ol grn	75	75
31	A37	4c green	85	85
32	A37	20c ultra	1.25	1.25
33	A37	$1 org brn & dk brn	17.50	12.50
34	A37	$2 bl & org brn	35.00	22.50
35	A37	$5 dl red & blk	100.00	75.00
		Nos. 29-35 (7)	155.85	113.35

Type II (single circle).

36	A37	2c ol grn	40	20
37	A37	4c green	75	75
38	A37	5c green	50	50
39	A37	15c dk grn	2.50	1.75
40	A37	15c scar ('34)	1.50	1.50
41	A37	25c ultra	1.75	1.75
42	A37	$1 org brn & dk brn	20.00	12.50
43	A37	$2 bl & org brn	40.00	20.00
44	A37	$5 dl red & blk	90.00	75.00
		Nos. 36-44 (9)	157.40	113.95

Nos. 36-39, 41-44 were overprinted in London as well as in Peiping. The overprints differ in minor details. Price of London overprints (8), $350.

Tan Yuan-chang Issue of China, 1933, Overprinted 滇省 貼用

1933			*Perf. 14.*	
45	A49	2c ol grn	75	40
46	A49	5c green	90	60
47	A49	25c ultra	2.00	1.25
48	A49	$1 red	25.00	18.00

Martyrs Issue of China, 1932-34 Overprinted 用貼省滇限

1933				
49	A39	½c blk brn	25	20
50	A40	1c orange	30	20
51	A39	2½c rose lil	50	30
52	A48	3c dp brn	60	40
53	A45	8c brn org	1.25	75
54	A46	10c dl vio	85	40
55	A45	13c bl grn	1.00	40
56	A46	17c brn ol	2.00	75
57	A47	20c brn red	1.00	60
58	A48	30c brn vio	2.00	75
59	A47	40c orange	15.00	12.00
60	A40	50c green	15.00	12.00
		Nos. 49-60 (12)	39.75	28.75

China No. 324 was overprinted with characters arranged vertically, like Sinkiang No. 114, but was not issued.

China Stamps of 1945-49 Surcharged in Black or Blue 滇省貼用 壹角10

Engr.; Litho.; Typo.

1949			*Perf. 12, 12½, 14*	
61	A82	1c on $200,000 brn vio	1.25	1.25
62	A82	1.2c on $40,000 grn	1.75	1.75
63	A94	6c on $200 red org	1.00	1.00
64	A94	10c on $20,000 org	1.00	1.00
65	A94	12c on $50 dk Prus grn (Bl)	1.25	1.25
66	A72	12c on $50 grnsh gray (Bl)	1.50	1.50
67	A72	12c on $200 brn vio (Bl)	75	75
68	A94	30c on $20 vio brn	1.00	1.00
69	A82	$1.20 on $100,000 dl grn	3.00	3.00

China No. 888 and 630 Surcharged 4 郵資 肆分 滇

1949		**Engr.**	*Perf. 14*	
70	A94	4c on $20 vio brn	75.00	
		Typo.	*Perf. 12*	
71	A72	12c on $200 brn vio	100.00	

Manchuria.

(măn·chŏŏr'ĭ·*ȧ*)

Kirin and Heilungkiang Issue.

Stamps of China, 1923-26, Overprinted 用貼黑吉限

The overprint reads: "For use in Ki-Hei District" the two names being abbreviated.

The intention of the overprint was to prevent the purchase of stamps in Manchuria, where the currency was depreciated, and their resale elsewhere.

1927 ***Perf. 14.*** **Unwmkd.**

1	A29	½c blk brn	10	10
2	A29	1c orange	10	10
3	A29	1½c violet	20	20
4	A29	2c yel grn	25	15
5	A29	3c bl grn	20	20
6	A29	4c ol grn	25	10
7	A29	5c claret	25	15
8	A29	6c red	35	20
9	A29	7c violet	35	25
10	A29	8c brn org	35	20
11	A29	10c dk bl	35	10
12	A30	13c brown	1.25	50
13	A30	15c dk bl	75	30
14	A30	16c ol grn	75	30
15	A30	20c brn red	1.25	50
16	A30	30c brn vio	1.25	50
17	A30	50c dp grn	4.00	50
18	A31	$1 org brn & sep	12.00	2.00
19	A31	$2 bl & red brn	17.50	10.00
20	A31	$5 red & sl	90.00	75.00
		Nos. 1-20 (20)	131.50	91.35

Several values of this issue exist with inverted overprint, double overprint and in pairs with one overprint omitted. These "errors" were not regularly issued. Forgeries also exist.

Chang Tso-lin Stamps of 1928 Overprinted in Red or Blue 貼 吉 用 黑

1928 ***Perf. 14***

21	A34	1c brn org (R)	40	30
22	A34	4c ol grn (R)	75	50
23	A34	10c dl bl (R)	2.00	1.25
24	A34	$1 red (Bl)	22.50	15.00

Unification Issue of China, 1929, Overprinted in Red as in 1928.

1929

25	A35	1c brn org	75	40
26	A35	4c ol grn	1.00	60
27	A35	10c dk bl	3.00	1.75
28	A35	$1 dk red	40.00	25.00

Similar Overprint in Black on Sun Yat-sen Mausoleum Issue of China.

Characters 15-16mm. apart.

1929 ***Perf. 14***

29	A36	1c brn org	75	75
30	A36	4c ol grn	75	75
31	A36	10c dk bl	2.00	1.50
32	A36	$1 dk red	25.00	15.00

Sinkiang.

(sĭn'kyäng'; shĭn'jyäng',-gyäng')

Stamps of China, 1913-19, Overprinted in Black or Red 限新省貼用 *a*

The first character of overprint "a" is ½ mm. out of alignment, to the left, and the overprint measures 16mm.

1915 ***Perf. 14, 15.*** **Unwmkd.**

1	A24	½c blk brn	35	25
2	A24	1c orange	35	15
3	A24	2c yel grn	40	25
4	A24	3c sl grn	40	25
5	A24	4c scarlet	50	30
6	A24	5c rose lil	60	50
7	A24	6c gray	75	50
8	A24	7c violet	1.00	90
9	A24	8c brn org	75	60
10	A24	10c dk bl	1.40	1.25
11	A25	15c brown	1.25	1.25
12	A25	16c ol grn	3.00	2.00
13	A25	20c brn red	3.00	2.00
14	A25	30c brn vio	4.00	2.00
15	A25	50c dp grn	10.00	7.50
16	A26	$1 ocher & blk (R)	60.00	25.00
a.		Second & third characters of ovpt. transposed	*1,000.*	
		Nos. 1-16 (16)	87.75	44.70

Stamps of China, 1913-19, Overprinted in Black or Red 限新省貼用 *b*

The five characters of overprint "b" are correctly aligned and measure 15½mm.

1916-19

17	A24	½c blk brn	40	15
18	A24	1c orange	40	15
19	A24	1½c violet	40	30
20	A24	2c yel grn	40	15
21	A24	3c sl grn	40	15
22	A24	4c scarlet	40	30
23	A24	5c rose lil	50	30
24	A24	6c gray	60	25
25	A24	7c violet	1.00	75
26	A24	8c brn org	35	15
27	A24	10c dk bl	25	15
28	A25	13c brown	1.00	40
29	A25	15c brown	1.00	50
30	A25	16c ol grn	60	30
31	A25	20c brn red	40	30
32	A25	30c brn vio	75	50
33	A25	50c dp grn	1.00	50
34	A26	$1 ocher & blk (R)	6.00	1.50
35	A26	$2 dk bl & blk (R)	12.50	4.00
36	A26	$5 scar & blk (R)	35.00	15.00
37	A26	$10 yel grn & blk (R)	110.00	75.00
38	A26	$20 yel & blk (R)	350.00	275.00
		Nos. 17-38 (22)	523.35	375.80

China Nos. 243-246 Overprinted 用貼省新限

1921 ***Perf. 14***

39	A27	1c orange	75	60
40	A27	3c bl grn	1.00	1.00
41	A27	6c gray	3.00	2.00
42	A27	10c blue	25.00	20.00

Constitution Issue of China, 1923, Overprinted 貼 新 疆 用 省

1923

43	A32	1c orange	1.75	35
44	A32	3c bl grn	1.75	50
45	A32	4c red	5.00	75
46	A32	10c blue	12.50	5.00

Stamps of China, 1923-26, Overprinted Type "b" as in 1916-19, in Black or Red.

1924 **Re-engraved**

47	A29	½c blk brn	20	8
48	A29	1c orange	20	8
49	A29	1½c violet	20	8
50	A29	2c yel grn	20	8
51	A29	3c bl grn	25	8
52	A29	4c gray	2.00	1.25
53	A29	5c claret	35	8
54	A29	6c red	40	15
55	A29	7c violet	35	15
56	A29	8c org brn	*5.00*	*2.00*
57	A29	10c dk bl	35	15
58	A30	13c red brn	50	25
59	A30	15c dp bl	50	30
60	A30	16c ol grn	60	30
61	A30	20c brn red	60	20
62	A30	30c brn vio	1.00	25
63	A30	50c dp grn	1.25	40
64	A31	$1 org brn & sep (R)	5.00	75
65	A31	$2 bl & red brn (R)	10.00	2.00
66	A31	$5 red & sl (R)	35.00	5.00
67	A31	$10 grn & cl (R)	100.00	60.00
68	A31	$20 plum & bl (R)	150.00	100.00
		Nos. 47-68 (22)	*313.95*	*173.63*

See also Nos. 69, 114.

Same Overprint on China No. 275.

1926

69	A29	4c ol grn	40	12

Chang Tso-lin Stamps of China, 1928 Overprinted in Red or Blue 貼 新 用 疆

1928 ***Perf. 14***

70	A34	1c brn org (R)	50	30
71	A34	4c ol grn (R)	1.00	60
72	A34	10c dl bl (R)	2.50	1.50
73	A34	$1 red (Bl)	22.50	15.00

Unification Issue of China, 1929, Overprinted in Red as in 1928.

1929

74	A35	1c brn org	75	50
75	A35	4c ol grn	1.25	1.00
76	A35	10c dk bl	3.00	2.00
77	A35	$1 dk red	42.50	25.00

Similar Overprint in Black on Sun Yat-sen Mausoleum Issue of China.

Characters 15mm. apart

1929 ***Perf. 14***

78	A36	1c brn org	1.25	50
79	A36	4c ol grn	1.75	75
80	A36	10c dk bl	5.00	1.50
81	A36	$1 dk red	32.50	15.00

Stamps of Sun Yat-sen Issue of 1931-37 Overprinted 用貼省新限

1932 **Type I** ***Perf. 12½***

82	A37	1c orange	50	60
83	A37	2c ol grn	1.00	1.25
84	A37	4c green	75	75
85	A37	20c ultra	1.00	1.25
86	A37	$1 org brn & dk brn	4.00	4.00
87	A37	$2 bl & org brn	6.00	5.00
88	A37	$5 dl red & blk	14.00	12.50
		Nos. 82-88 (7)	27.25	25.35

No. 83 was overprinted in Shanghai in 1938. The overprint differs in minor details.

1932-38 **Type II**

89	A37	2c ol grn	15	15
90	A37	4c green	15	15
91	A37	5c green	15	15
92	A37	15c dk grn	40	35
93	A37	15c scar ('34)	35	30
93A	A37	20c ultra ('38)	30	50
94	A37	25c ultra	35	30
95	A37	$1 org brn & dk brn	2.00	1.75
96	A37	$2 bl & org brn	3.00	3.00
97	A37	$5 dl red & blk	12.00	10.00
		Nos. 89-97 (10)	18.85	16.65

Nos. 89, 90 and 94 were overprinted in London, Peiping and Shanghai. Nos. 92, 95–97 exist with London and Peiping overprints. Nos. 91 and 93 exist with Peiping and Shanghai overprints. No. 93A is a Shanghai overprint. The overprints differ in minor details.

Tan Yuan-chang Issue of China, 1933, Overprinted as in 1928.

1933 ***Perf. 14.***

98	A49	2c ol grn	40	30
99	A49	5c green	1.00	75
100	A49	25c ultra	2.00	1.50
101	A49	$1 red	25.00	20.00

Stamps of China Martyrs Issue of 1932-34 Overprinted 用貼省新限

1933-34

102	A39	½c blk brn	10	
103	A40	1c orange	10	
104	A39	2½c rose lil	10	
105	A48	3c dp brn	10	
106	A45	8c brn org	10	
107	A46	10c dl vio	10	
108	A45	13c bl grn	15	
109	A46	17c brn ol	15	
110	A47	20c brn red	25	
111	A48	30c brn vio	25	
112	A47	40c orange	35	
113	A40	50c green	40	
		Nos. 102-113 (12)	2.15	2.

Nos. 102–113 were originally over printed in Peiping. In 1938, Nos. 103 105, 108–112 were overprinted in Shang hai. The two overprints differ in mino details. No. 105, Shanghai overprint, scarce. Price $35.

China No. 324 Overprinted Type "b" as in 1924.

1936 ***Perf. 14***

114	A29	6c brown	9.00	8.

Stamps of China, 1939-40 Overprinted in Black.

1940-45 ***Perf. 12½*** **Unwmkd**

Type III.

115	A57	2c ol grn	8	
116	A57	3c dl cl ('41)	8	
117	A57	5c green	8	
118	A57	5c ol grn	8	
119	A57	8c ol grn ('41)	8	
120	A57	10c grn ('41)	8	
121	A57	15c scarlet	8	
122	A57	16c ol gray ('41)	15	
123	A57	25c dk bl	8	
124	A57	$1 hn & dk brn (type II)	2.50	2.5
125	A57	$2 dp bl & org brn (type I)	3.00	2.5
126	A57	$5 red & grnsh blk	10.00	10.0
		Nos. 115-126 (12)	16.29	15.4

Perf. 14.

With Secret Marks.

127	A57	8c ol grn (#383a)	8	
a.		On #383	4.00	4.0
128	A57	10c grn ('41)	90	7.
129	A57	30c scar ('45)	8	
130	A57	50c dk bl ('45)	8	
131	A57	$1 org brn & sep	15	1
132	A57	$2 dp bl & org brn	30	2
133	A57	$5 red & sl grn	45	4
134	A57	$10 dk grn & dl pur	1.00	1.0
135	A57	$20 rose lake & dk bl	1.75	1.5
		Nos. 127-135 (9)	4.79	4.1

Wmkd. Character Yu (Post). (261)

Perf. 14.

136	A57	5c ol grn	8	8
137	A57	10c green	15	1
138	A57	30c scarlet	15	1
139	A57	50c dk bl	18	18

Martyrs Issue, 1940-41, Overprinted in Black 用貼省新限

Perf. 12, 12½, 13, 13x12, 13½x13.

1941-45 **Wmk. 261**

140	A40	1c orange	15	10
141	A39	2½c rose lil	15	10
142	A45	8c dp org ('45)	90	75
143	A46	10c dl vio	15	10
144	A45	13c dp yel grn	40	30
145	A46	17c brn ol	50	40
146	A40	25c red vio ('45)	60	50
147	A47	40c org ('45)	90	75
		Nos. 140-147 (8)	3.75	3.00

Unwmkd.

148	A39	½c ol blk	8	5
149	A40	1c org ('45)	8	5
150	A46	2c dp bl ('45)	8	5

151	A48	3c dp yel brn	8	5
152	A39	4c pale vio ('45)	8	5
153	A45	8c dp org	8	5
154	A45	13c dp yel grn ('45)	12	10
155	A48	15c brn car ('45)	12	10
156	A46	17c brn ol ('45)	30	25
157	A47	20c lt bl ('45)	15	10
158	A45	21c ol brn ('45)	25	20
159	A46	28c ol ('45)	25	20
160	A47	40c org ('45)	1.50	1.25
161	A40	50c grn ('45)	25	20
		Nos. 148-161 (14)	3.42	2.70

Stamps of China, 1942–43 Overprinted in armine, Black or Red 用貼省新限

Without Gum.

944 *Perf. 12½, 13.*

162	A62	10c dp grn (C)	6	5
163	A62	20c dk ol grn (C)	6	5
164	A62	25c vio brn	6	5
165	A62	30c dk org	6	5
166	A62	40c red brn	6	5
167	A62	50c sage grn	6	5
a.		Perf. 11	1.00	1.00
168	A62	$1 rose lake	6	5
169	A62	$1 dl grn	6	5
170	A62	$1.50 dp bl (C)	6	5
171	A62	$2 dk bl grn (R)	6	5
172	A62	$3 yellow	6	5
173	A62	$5 cerise	6	5
		Nos. 162-173 (12)	72	60

Same Overprint on Stamps of China, 1942-43, in Black.

1944-46 *Imperf.*

174	A57	$10 red brn	20.00	20.00
175	A57	$20 rose red	25	25
176	A57	$30 dl vio	40	35
177	A57	$40 rose red	45	40
178	A57	$50 bl ('46)	350.00	400.00
179	A57	$100 org brn	90	75

Perf. 13½.

180	A57	$4 dp bl	8	5
181	A57	$5 lil gray	8	5
182	A57	$10 red brn	8	5
183	A57	$20 bl grn	50	50
184	A57	$20 rose red	25.00	25.00
185	A57	$30 dl vio	65	60
186	A57	$40 rose	75	75
187	A57	$50 blue	1.00	1.00
188	A57	$100 org brn	25.00	25.00
		Nos. 174-177, 179-188 (14)	75.14	74.75

Nos. 162 and 164 Surcharged in Black 改作壹 角貳分

1944, Aug. 1

194	A62	12c on 10c dp grn	15	8
195	A62	24c on 25c brn vio	20	10

Stamps of China, 1940–41, Overprinted in Black at Chengtu, Szechwan 用貼省新限

1943

196	A57	10c grn (#354)	1.50	1.50
197	A47	20c lt bl (#433)	1.50	1.50

Perf. 14 **Wmk. 261**

198	A57	50c dk bl (#396)	1.50	1.50

China Nos. 565 and 567 Overprinted in Black 用貼省新限

1945 *Perf. 12½* **Unwmkd.**

200	A63	40c brn red	8	8
201	A63	$3 red	8	8

China Nos. 640–642, 788, 750, 753 Surcharged in Black or Red 改作 伍分 用貼省新限

1949 **Engraved** *Perf. 14*

202	A73	1c on $100 dk car	2.00	2.00
203	A73	3c on $200 ol grn (R)	2.00	2.00
204	A73	5c on $500 brt bl grn (R)	2.00	2.00
205	A82	10c on $20,000 rose pink	3.50	3.50
206	A82	50c on $4000 gray (R)	4.00	4.00
207	A82	$1 on $6000 rose lil	10.00	10.00
		Nos. 202-207 (6)	23.50	23.50

AIR POST STAMPS.

Sinkiang Nos. 53, 57, 59, 32 Overprinted in Red 空航

1932-33 *Perf. 14.* **Unwmkd.**

C1	A29	5c cl ('33)	125.00	75.00
C2	A29	10c dk bl ('33)	125.00	60.00
C3	A30	15c dp bl	1,000.	250.00
C4	A25	30c brn vio	375.00	275.00

Counterfeits exist of Nos. C1–C19.

Air Post Stamps of China, 1932–37 Handstamped in Dull Red

用貼省新限

1942

C5	AP3	15c gray grn	1.00	75
C6	AP3	25c orange	200.00	200.00
C7	AP3	30c red	60	60
C8	AP3	45c brn vio	1.00	75
C9	AP3	50c dk brn	8.00	8.00
C10	AP3	60c dk bl	1.00	75
C11	AP3	90c ol grn	12.50	12.50
C12	AP3	$1 yel grn	1.00	75
		Nos. C5-C12 (8)	225.10	224.10

Same Handstamped Overprint on Air Post Stamps of China, 1940–41.

1942 *Perf. 12½, 13, 13½* **Wmk. 261**

C13	AP3	15c gray grn	65	50
C14	AP3	25c yel org	65	50

1942 **Unwmkd.**

C15	AP3	25c lt org	75	60
C16	AP3	30c lt red	75	75
C17	AP3	50c brown	1.00	75
C18	AP3	$2 lt brn	8.00	8.00
C19	AP3	$5 lake	8.00	8.00
		Nos. C15-C19 (5)	18.50	18.10

Twelve values exist with this overprint in black. Their status has not been determined. Inverted overprints exist in both red and black.

Official Perforated Characters

For use on official mail, various Sinkiang stamps were perforated with an arrangement of four Chinese characters ("For Official Business Only"). These include Nos. 1–38, 47—69, 114.

Offices in Tibet.

(tĭ·bĕt'; tĭb'ĕt)

12 Pies = 1 Anna

16 Annas = 1 Rupee

Stamps of China, Issues of 1902-10, Surcharged

1911 *Perf. 12 to 16.* **Unwmkd.**

1	A17	3p on 1c ocher	3.00	3.50
a.		Inverted surcharge	375.00	
2	A17	½a on 2c grn	3.00	3.50
3	A17	1a on 4c ver	3.00	3.50
4	A17	2a on 7c mar	4.00	5.00
5	A17	2½a on 10c ultra	7.00	8.00
6	A18	3a on 16c ol grn	12.00	14.00
a.		Large "S" in "Annas"	375.00	
7	A18	4a on 20c red brn	12.00	14.00
8	A18	6a on 30c rose red	20.00	22.50
9	A18	12a on 50c yel grn	45.00	50.00
10	A19	1r on $1 red & pale rose	160.00	185.00
11	A19	2r on $2 red & yel	400.00	450.00
		Nos. 1-11	669.00	759.00

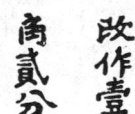

CHINA,
People's Republic of

LOCATION — Eastern Asia.
GOVT.—Communist Republic.
POP.—1,015,400,000 (est. 1983).
CAPITAL—Beijing (Peking).

The communists completed their conquest of all mainland China in 1949. They established the Central Government and General Postal Administration in Peking. They ordered all but two regions to stop selling regional issues by June 30, 1950, extending validity one year from that date. The Northeast and Port Arthur-Dairen regions were exempted because their currency had a different value. These two regions stopped using separate issues at the end of 1950. Thereafter unified issues were used throughout mainland China.

After currency revaluation Mar. 1, 1955, reprints were prepared and put on sale by the Philatelic Agency in order to supply stocks of exhausted issues for collectors. Minor differences in design or paper distinguish the reprints. They are of commemorative and special issues up to the gymnastics set of 1952. Many exist canceled to order. Reprints are plentiful and inexpensive. Prices are for original issues. Reprint distinctions are footnoted.

Commemorative issues, beginning in 1949, and special issues, beginning in 1951, bear 4 numbers in lower margin: 1. Issue number. 2. Total of stamps in set. 3. Position of stamp in set. 4. Cumulative number of stamp (usually in parenthesis). A fifth number, the year of issue, was added in 1952.

The numbering system varies at times, with all numbers omitted on Nos. 938–1046.

In certain sets listings include parenthetically the position-in-set number. During some periods the parentheses in listings hold the stamp's cumulative number.

All stamps to the beginning of 1960 were issued without gum, except as noted. After that date, most stamps have gum, which is translucent and almost invisible. All issues are unwatermarked, unless otherwise noted.

100 fen = 1 yuan ($)

Prices fluctuate for most P.R.C. issues, and for Communist Regional issues. Information is inadequate or lacking about quantities printed and issued, existence of large stocks, and possible release of remainders.

Prices quoted represent averages and indicate relative values.

Lantern and Gate of Heavenly Peace
A1

Globe and Hand Holding Hammer
A2

1949, Oct. 8 Litho. Perf. 12½

1 A1 $30 blue 1.25 1.50
2 A1 $50 rose red 1.25 1.50
3 A1 $100 green 1.25 1.50
4 A1 $200 maroon 1.25 1.50

First session of Chinese People's Political Conference. See also Nos. 1L121–1L124.

Original Reprint

Reprints have altered ornament on lantern base. On originals, it is a full oval; in reprints, only a partial circle. Price, set, 40 cents.

1949, Nov. 16

5 A2 $100 carmine 4.00 2.50
6 A2 $300 sl grn 4.00 1.50
7 A2 $500 dk bl 4.00 4.00

Asiatic and Australasian Congress of the World Federation of Trade Unions, Peking. The $100, imperf., is of dubious status. See also Nos. 1L133–1L135.

Original

Reprint

Reprints show heavier shading on index finger and thumb. Price, set 75 cents.

Conference Hall, Peking
A3

Mao Tse-tung on Rostrum
A4

1950, Feb. 1 Engraved Perf. 14

8 A3 $50 red 3.00 3.00
9 A3 $100 blue 3.00 3.00
10 A4 $300 red brn 3.00 2.00
11 A4 $500 green 3.00 2.00

Chinese People's Political Conference. See also Nos. 1L136–1L139.

Original

Reprint

Nos. 8-9: First character in top inscription shows a square, reprints an oblong.

Nos. 10-11: Originals have heavy crosshatching and lines which touch back of head and top of rostrum. Reprints have lighter lines which do not touch head or top of rostrum.

Reprints, price set $1.25.

Gate of Heavenly Peace
(same size)
A5

First Issue: Top line of shading broken at right.

1950, Feb. 10 Litho. Perf. 12½

12 A5 $200 green 1.00 1.00
13 A5 $300 brn red 10 30
14 A5 $500 red 15 12
15 A5 $800 orange 11.00 12
16 A5 $1000 dl vio 15 10
17 A5 $2000 olive 1.00 50
18 A5 $5000 brt pink 15 1.00
19 A5 $8000 blue 15 3.00
20 A5 $10,000 brown 15 1.50
Nos. 12-20 (9) 13.85 7.64

1950, June 9 Typographed

Second Issue: Top line of shading extends to frame line at right.

21 A5 $1000 dl vio 15 10
22 A5 $3000 red brn 15 10
23 A5 $10,000 brown 15 10

1949 Unit Issue of China Surcharged in Blue, Black, Green or Red

中國人民郵政
貳佰圓
200

1950, Mar. Litho. Perf. 12½

24 SD2 $100 on red vio (Bl) 3.00 3.00
a. Rouletted 20 40
25 R2 $200 on red (Bk) 13.00 2.00
a. Rouletted 1.50 50
26 AP5 $300 on bl grn (Bk) 20 85
a. Rouletted 10 75
27 A96 $500 on org (G) 10 30
a. Perf. 14 75.00 60.00
28 A96 $800 on org (R) 8.00 75
a. Rouletted 1.50 20
b. Perf. 14 100.00 50.00
29 A96 $1000 on org (Bk) 5 25
a. Perf. 14 10 20
Nos. 24a, 25a, 26a, 27, 28a, 29 (6) 3.45 2.40

Harvesters with Ox
A6

1950, May

30 A6 $20,000 on $10,000 red 200.00 20.00

No. 30 is surcharged on an unissued stamp of East China.

Flag, Mao Tse-tung, Gate of Heavenly Peace
A7

1950, July 1 Perf. 14

Yellow Stars

31 A7 $800 grn & red 14.00 2.50
32 A7 $1000 brn & red 14.00 5.00
33 A7 $2000 dk brn & red 14.00 6.00
34 A7 $3000 dk bl & red 14.00 7.00

Inauguration of the People's Republic, Oct. 1, 1949. See also Nos. 1L150–1L153.

Original

Reprint

Originals have a single curved line in jacket button, reprints have an extra dot in button. Price, set $1.50.

Sun Yat-sen Stamps of Northeastern Provinces Surcharged in Red, Black or Blue

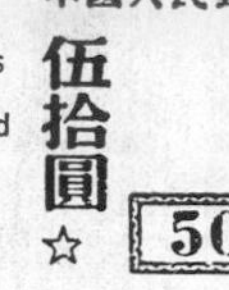

1950, July 1 Engraved

35 A2 $50 on 20c yel grn (R) 50 4.00
36 A2 $50 on 25c blk brn (R) 1.50 1.75
37 A2 $50 on 50c red org (Bk) 15 50
38 A2 $100 on $2.50 ind (R) 35 50
39 A2 $100 on $3 brn (Bk) 6.00 50
40 A2 $100 on $4 org brn, Type II (Bl) 4.00 2.75
a. Type I 40.00 40.00
41 A2 $100 on $5 dk grn (Bk) 6.00 50
42 A2 $100 on $10 crim (Bl) 6.00 4.00
43 A2 $400 on $20 ol, Type II (Bl) 6.00 4.00
a. Type I 95.00 75.00
44 A2 $400 on $44 dk car rose (Bl) 20 2.50
45 A2 $400 on $65 dl grn (R) 20.00 8.00
46 A2 $400 on $100 dp grn (R) 6.00 2.50
47 A2 $400 on $200 rose brn (Bk) 30.00 3.50
48 A2 $400 on $300 bluish grn (R) 30.00 3.50
Nos. 35-48 (14) 116.70 38.50

Flying Geese Type of China Surcharged in Red, Blue, Green, Brown or Black

中國人民郵政
貳佰圓
★★ 200

1950, Aug. 1 Perf. 12½, Imperf.

49 A97 $50 on 10c dk bl (R) 5 25
50 A97 $100 on 16c ol, imperf. (Bl) 5 25
51 A97 $100 on 50c dl grn, imperf. (Bl) 5 12
52 A97 $200 on $1 org (G) 10 12
53 A97 $200 on $2 bl (Br) 1.75 20
54 A97 $400 on $5 car rose (Bk) 15 25
55 A97 $400 on $10 bl grn (Bk) 15 80
56 A97 $400 on $20 pur (Bk) 20 1.00
Nos. 49-58 (8) 2.50 2.99

Dove of Peace, by Picasso
A8

Chinese Flag and "1"
A9

1950, Aug. 1 Engraved Perf. 14

57 A8 $400 brown 5.00 3.00
58 A8 $800 green 5.00 3.00
59 A8 $2000 blue 5.00 3.00

World Peace Campaign. See also Nos. 1L154–1L156.

Paper of originals appears bright under ultraviolet lamp. That of reprints looks dull. Price, set 75 cents.

1950 Engraved & Litho.

Flag in Red & Yellow

60 A9 $100 purple 8.00 4.00
61 A9 $400 red brn 8.00 7.00

62	A9	$800 green	8.00	4.00
63	A9	$1000 lt ol	8.00	5.00
64	A9	$2000 blue	8.00	7.00
		Nos. 60-64 (5)	40.00	27.00

First anniversary of the Chinese People's Republic. Size of $800: 38x46 mm.; others 26x32 mm.

Issue dates: No. 62, Oct. 1; others Oct. 31. See also Nos. 1L157–1L161.

Original ($800) Reprint

Reprints are a brighter red, leaves beside "1" are gray brown instead of reddish brown. On the $800 the arrangement of dots in background differs in relationship to large star. Price, set 90 cents.

(same size)

Gate of Heavenly Peace
A10

"Communication" and Map of China
A11

Third Issue: Cloud almost touches character at upper left. Cloud breaks inner frame line at top.

1950 Lithographed

65	A10	$100 lt grnsh bl	40.00	8.00
66	A10	$200 green	140.00	10.00
67	A10	$300 dk car	1.00	*5.00*
68	A10	$400 grnsh gray	40	*5.00*
69	A10	$500 carmine	25	*6.00*
70	A10	$800 orange	2.00	35
71	A10	$2000 gray ol	50	60
		Nos. 65-71 (7)	184.15	*34.95*

Issue dates: $800, Oct. 8; $500, $2000, Dec. 1; others, Oct. 6.

1950, Nov. 1 Lithographed

72	A11	$400 grn & brn	4.00	4.00
73	A11	$800 car & grn	4.00	3.00

First All-China Postal Conference, Peking.

Original Reprint

Originals have 3 lines below horizontal bar between 1st & 2nd character; reprints have four. Price, set 50 cents.

Stalin and Mao Tse-tung—A12

1950, Dec. 1 Engraved *Perf. 14*

74	A12	$400 red	6.00	4.00
75	A12	$800 dp grn	6.00	3.00
76	A12	$2000 dk bl	6.00	4.00

Signing of Sino-Soviet Treaty of Friendship, Alliance and Mutual Assistance. See also Nos. 1L176–1L178.

Paper of originals appears bright under ultraviolet lamp. That of reprints looks dull. Price, set $1.50.

East China Issue of 1949 Surcharged In Red, Black, Brown or Blue

Train and Postal Runner
A12a

1950, Dec. Litho. *Perf. 12½*

77	A12a	$50 on $10 dp ultra (R)	5	10
78	A12a	$100 on $15 org ver (Bk)	6	10
a.		$100 on $15 red (Bk), perf. 14	10	10
79	A12a	$300 on $50 car (Bk)	5	20
80	A12a	$400 on $1600 vio bl (Br)	50	15
81	A12a	$400 on $2000 brn vio (Bl)	20	15
		Nos. 77-81 (5)	86	70

East China Issue of 1949 Surcharged in Red or Black

Chairman Mao
A12b

1950, Dec.

82	A12b	$50 on $10 ultra (R)	15	10
83	A12b	$400 on $15 ver (Bk)	15	10
84	A12b	$400 on $2000 grn (Bk)	75	10

(same size)

Gate of Heavenly Peace
A13 A14

Fourth Issue: Similar to 3rd issue, but large cloud does not break inner frame line at top.

1950–51 Lithographed

85	A13	$100 lt bl	1.00	1.00
86	A13	$200 dl grn	1.20	1.20
87	A13	$300 dl lil	25	*7.00*
88	A13	$400 gray grn	25	1.00
89	A13	$500 carmine	5	*1.50*
90	A13	$800 orange	40.00	1.25
a.		Imperf., pair	*1,000.*	
91	A13	$1000 violet	35	1.00
92	A13	$2000 olive	120.00	4.00
93	A13	$3000 brown	5	*8.00*
94	A13	$5000 pink	5	*8.00*
		Nos. 85-94 (10)	163.20	*33.95*

Issue dates: $200, $300, $500, $800, $2000, $5000, Dec. 22, 1950; others June 8, 1951.

1951, Jan. 18 Engraved *Perf. 14*

Fifth Issue: Colored network on surface in salmon.

95	A14	$10,000 brown	50	*10.00*
96	A14	$20,000 olive	50	*7.50*
97	A14	$30,000 green	12.00	*18.00*
98	A14	$50,000 violet	50.00	12.50
99	A14	$100,000 scarlet	900.00	75.00
100	A14	$200,000 blue	900.00	75.00
		Nos. 95-100 (6)	1,863.	*198.00*

Unit Issue of China Surcharged

中國人民郵政
伍
圓
5

1951, May 2 Litho. *Perf. 12½*

101	SD2	$5 on rose lil	3.00	25
102	AP5	$10 on brt grn	15	8
103	R2	$15 on red	10	8
104	A96	$25 on org	40	8

Issued for use in Northeast China, but available for use throughout China. Nos. 101–104 rouletted were sold for philatelic purposes only.

Price, set $1.

Chairman Mao Tse-tung
A15

1951, July 1 Engraved *Perf. 14*

105	A15	$400 chestnut	3.00	2.00
106	A15	$500 dp grn	3.00	2.00
107	A15	$800 crimson	3.00	2.00

30th anniversary of the Chinese Communist Party.

Reprints are on whiter, thinner and harder paper.

Price, set 60 cents.

Picasso Dove—A16

1951, Aug. 15 *Perf. 12½*

108	A16	$400 org brn	5.00	2.50
109	A16	$800 bl grn	5.00	1.50
110	A16	$1000 dl vio	5.00	2.50

Reprints are perf. 14.
Price, set $1.50.

Remittance Stamp of China Surcharged in Carmine or Black

(same size)

A17

Engraved, Commercial Press

1951, Sept. *Perf. 12½*

111	A17	$50 on $2 bl grn (C)	20	75

Typo. Kang Hwa Printing Co.
Roul. 9½

112	A17	$50 on $2 gray bl (C)	50	75
113	A17	$50 on $5 red org (Bk)	5	75
114	A17	$50 on $50 gray (C)	4.00	75

Litho., Central Trust Co.
Perf. 13

115	A17	$50 on $50 gray blk (C)	5	75

Litho., Chung Hwa Book Co.
Perf. 11½

116	A17	$50 on $50 gray (C)	1.50	75
a.		Perf. 11½x10	50	50
		Nos. 111-116 (6)	6.30	4.50

National Emblem
A18

1951, Oct. 1 *Perf. 14*

Engraved; Background Network Lithographed in Yellow.

117	A18	$100 Prus bl	5.00	2.00
118	A18	$200 brown	5.00	1.50
119	A18	$400 orange	5.00	2.00
120	A18	$500 green	5.00	1.50
121	A18	$800 carmine	5.00	1.50
		Nos. 117-121 (5)	25.00	8.50

Reprints exist but difficult to distinguish; paper whiter, and colors slightly brighter.

Price, set $1.

Lu Hsun and Quotation
A19

1951, Oct. 19 Litho. *Perf. 12½*

122	A19	$400 lilac	4.00	3.00
123	A19	$800 green	4.00	3.00

15th anniversary of the death of Lu Hsun (1881–1936), writer.

Original Reprint

Reprints have dot in triangle at lower right; no dot in original. Price, set, 30 cents.

Peasant Uprising, Chintien—A20

Design: Nos. 126–127, Coin of Taiping Regime and decrees of peasant government.

1951, Dec. 15 Engraved *Perf. 14*

124	A20	$400 green	5.00	2.00
125	A20	$800 scarlet	5.00	2.00
126	A20	$800 orange	5.00	2.00
127	A20	$1000 dp bl	5.00	3.00

Centenary of Taiping Peasant Rebellion.

Original

Reprint

Reprints of Nos. 124-125 have additional short stroke at upper left.

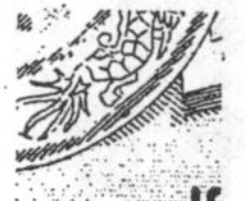
Original

Reprint

Reprints of Nos. 126-127 have two short strokes on scale near tail of right dragon on coin.

Price, Nos. 124-127, 35 cents.

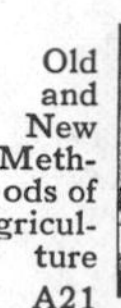

Old and New Methods of Agriculture
A21

1952, Jan. 1

No.	Type	Value	Unused	Used
128	A21	$100 scarlet	3.00	3.00
129	A21	$200 brt bl	3.00	3.00
130	A21	$400 dp brn	3.00	2.00
131	A21	$800 green	3.00	2.00

Agrarian reform.

Original

Reprint

One short horizontal line between legs of plower; 2 lines in reprints.

Price, set 50 cents.

Potala Monastery, Lhasa
A22

Designs: Nos. 134-135, Farmer plowing with yaks.

1952, Mar. 15 ***Perf. 12½***

No.	Type	Value	Unused	Used
132	A22	$400 vermilion	4.00	3.00
133	A22	$800 claret	4.00	3.00
134	A22	$800 bl grn	4.00	2.00
135	A22	$1000 dl vio	4.00	2.00

Liberation of Tibet.

Reprints, perf. 14, have a small Chinese character at lower left of the vignette which is missing in the original.

Price, set 50 cents.

Children of Four Races
A23

Hammer and Sickle on Numeral 1
A24

1952, Apr. 12 **Lithographed**

No.	Type	Value	Unused	Used
136	A23	$400 dl grn	15	5
137	A23	$800 vio bl	15	5

International Child Protection Conference, Vienna.

1952, May 1

Designs: No. 139, Dove rising from worker's hand. No. 140, Dove, hammer, wheat and chimneys.

No.	Type	Value	Unused	Used
138	A24	$800 scarlet	5	5
139	A24	$800 bl grn	5	5
140	A24	$800 org brn	15	5

Labor Day.

Physical Exercises—A25

Stamps printed in blocks of four for each color, each block representing a specific setting-up exercise; exercises coincided with a national radio program. Where exercise positions are identical within the block, the serial number (in parenthesis) is the only means of differentiation.

1952, June 20

No.	Type	Value	Unused	Used
141	A25	$400 ver, blk. of 4	15.00	15.00
a.		*Right arm forward (1)*	2.00	1.00
b.		*Left arm forward (2)*	2.00	1.00
c.		*as "a" (3)*	2.00	1.00
d.		*as "b" (4)*	2.00	1.00
142	A25	$400 bl, blk. of 4	15.00	15.00
a.		*Arms outstretched (5)*	2.00	1.00
b.		*Knee-bend (6)*	2.00	1.00
c.		*as "a" (7)*	2.00	1.00
d.		*Rest (8)*	2.00	1.00
143	A25	$400 brn red, blk. of 4	15.00	15.00
a.		*Arms forward (9)*	2.00	1.00
b.		*Arms outstretched (10)*	2.00	1.00
c.		*as "b" (11)*	2.00	1.00
d.		*Rest (12)*	2.00	1.00
144	A25	$400 yel grn, blk. of 4	15.00	15.00
a.		*Arms outstretched (13)*	2.00	1.00
b.		*Sideways bend (14)*	2.00	1.00
c.		*as "a" (15)*	2.00	1.00
d.		*Hands on hips (16)*	2.00	1.00
145	A25	$400 red org, blk. of 4	15.00	15.00
a.		*as 144a (17)*	2.00	1.00
b.		*Alternate toe touch (18)*	2.00	1.00
c.		*as "a" (19)*	2.00	1.00
d.		*Rest (20)*	2.00	1.00
146	A25	$400 dl bl, blk. of 4	15.00	15.00
a.		*Stretch (21)*	2.00	1.00
b.		*Toe touch (22)*	2.00	1.00
c.		*Hands on floor (23)*	2.00	1.00
d.		*Rest (24)*	2.00	1.00
147	A25	$400 org, block of 4	15.00	15.00
a.		*Leg forward (25)*	2.00	1.00
b.		*Leg extended back (26)*	2.00	1.00
c.		*as "a" (27)*	2.00	1.00
d.		*Rest (28)*	2.00	1.00
148	A25	$400 dl pur, block of 4	15.00	15.00
a.		*Jumping jack (29)*	2.00	1.00
b.		*Rest (30)*	2.00	1.00
c.		*as "a" (31)*	2.00	1.00
d.		*as "b" (32)*	2.00	1.00
149	A25	$400 yel bis, blk. of 4	15.00	15.00
a.		*Left leg raised (33)*	2.00	1.00
b.		*Hands on hips (34)*	2.00	1.00
c.		*Right leg raised (35)*	2.00	1.00
d.		*as "b" (36)*	2.00	1.00
150	A25	$400 sky bl, blk. of 4	15.00	15.00
a.		*Arms raised forward (37)*	2.00	1.00
b.		*Arms above head (38)*	2.00	1.00
c.		*Arms outstretched (39)*	2.00	1.00
d.		*Rest (40)*	2.00	1.00
		Nos. 141-150 (10 blocks of 4)	150.00	150.00

Originals are on thin gray paper, colors darker. Reprints on thicker white paper, colors brighter.

Price, set $7.

Hunting, Wei Dynasty, A.D. 386-580—A26

Designs from Murals in Cave Temples at Tunhuang, Kansu Province: No. 152, Lady attendants, Sui Dynasty, 581-617 A.D. No. 153, Gandharvas (mythology), Tang Dynasty, 618-906. No. 154, Dragon, Tang Dynasty.

1952, July 1 **Engraved**

No.	Type	Value	Unused	Used
151	A26	$800 sl grn (1)	12	6
152	A26	$800 choc (2)	12	6
153	A26	$800 ind (3)	12	6
154	A26	$800 blk (4)	12	6

"Glorious Mother Country," 1st series.

Marco Polo Bridge, near Peking
A27

Designs: No. 156, Cavalry passing through Great Wall. No. 157, Departure of New Fourth Army. No. 158, Mao Tse-tung and Gen. Chu Teh planning counter-attack.

1952, July 7 **Litho.** ***Perf. 14***

No.	Type	Value	Unused	Used
155	A27	$800 brt bl	10	6
156	A27	$800 bl grn	30	6
157	A27	$800 plum	10	6
158	A27	$800 scarlet	5	6

15th anniversary of war against Japan.

Soldier and Tanks
A28

Designs: No. 159, Soldier, sailor and airman (vert.). No. 161, Sailor and warships. No. 162, Airman and planes.

1952, Aug. 1 **Engraved** ***Perf. 12½***

No.	Type	Value	Unused	Used
159	A28	$800 carmine	10	6
160	A28	$800 dp grn	20	6
161	A28	$800 purple	10	6
162	A28	$800 org brn	10	6

25th anniversary of People's Liberation Army.

Huai River Sluice Dam—A29

Designs: No. 164, Train on the Chengtu-Chungking Railway. No. 165, Oil refinery and derricks in the Northwest. No. 166, Mechanized state farm.

1952, Oct. 1 ***Perf. 14***

No.	Type	Value	Unused	Used
163	A29	$800 dk vio	10	6
164	A29	$800 red	10	6
165	A29	$800 dk vio brn	10	6
166	A29	$800 dp grn	10	6

"Glorious Mother Country," 2nd series.

Doves and Globe
A30

Designs: Nos. 167-168, Picasso dove over Pacific (vert.). $2500, as No. 169.

1952, Oct. 2 ***Perf. 14***

No.	Type	Value	Unused	Used
167	A30	$400 maroon	10	5
168	A30	$800 red	10	5
169	A30	$800 brn org	10	6
170	A30	$2500 dp grn	30	15

Peace Conference of the Asian and Pacific Regions.

Volunteers on the March—A31

Designs: No. 172, Chinese peasants loading supplies. No. 173, Volunteers attacking across river. No. 174, Meeting of Chinese and Korean troops.

1952, Oct. 25

No.	Type	Value	Unused	Used
171	A31	$800 bl grn (1)	10	6
172	A31	$800 ver (2)	10	6
173	A31	$800 vio (3)	15	6
174	A31	$800 lake brn (4)	20	6

2nd anniversary of Chinese Volunteers in Korea.

Woman Textile Worker
A32

Design: No. 176, Farm woman with sickle.

1953, Mar. 10

No.	Type	Value	Unused	Used
175	A32	$800 carmine	10	9
176	A32	$800 emerald	20	9

International Women's Day.

Textile Worker
A33

Karl Marx
A34

Designs: $200, Shepherdess. $250, Stone lion. $800, Lathe operator. $1600, Coal miners. $2000, Corner tower of Forbidden City, Peking.

1953 **Litho.** ***Perf. 14; 12½*** **($250)**

No.	Type	Value	Unused	Used
177	A33	$50 magenta	10	8
178	A33	$200 emerald	8	10
179	A33	$250 ultra	60	10
180	A33	$800 bl grn	5	6
181	A33	$1600 gray	10	25
182	A33	$2000 red org	5	15
		Nos. 177-182 (6)	98	74

Issue dates: Nos. 177-181, Mar. 25; No. 182, May 23.

1953, May 20 **Engraved** ***Perf. 14***

No.	Type	Value	Unused	Used
183	A34	$400 dk brn	10	8
184	A34	$800 sl grn	20	8

135th anniversary of the birth of Karl Marx (1818-1883).

Workers and Banners
A35

1953, June 25

No.	Type	Value	Color	Unused	Used
185	A35	$400	Prus bl	15	5
186	A35	$800	carmine	10	5

7th All-China Trade Union Congress.

Picasso Dove
A36

1953, July 25

No.	Type	Value	Color	Unused	Used
187	A36	$250	bl grn	20	7
188	A36	$400	org brn	10	10
189	A36	$800	purple	15	10

World Peace.

Groom, Wei Dynasty, 386–580
A37

Scenes from Tunhuang Murals: No. 191, Court Players, Wei Dynasty. No. 192, Battle Scene, Sui Dynasty, 581–617. No. 193, Ox-drawn palanquin, Tang Dynasty, 618–906.

1953, Sept. 1

No.	Type	Value	Color	Unused	Used
190	A37	$800	dp grn (1)	20	6
191	A37	$800	red org (2)	5	6
192	A37	$800	Prus bl (3)	12	6
193	A37	$800	car (4)	5	6

"Glorious Mother Country," 3rd series.

Stalin and Mao on Kremlin Terrace—A38

Statue of Stalin at Volga-Don Canal
A39

Designs: No. 195, Lenin proclaiming Soviet power. No. 197, Stalin as orator.

1953, Oct. 5

No.	Type	Value	Color	Unused	Used
194	A38	$800	grn (1)	20	8
195	A38	$800	car (2)	15	8
196	A39	$800	brt bl (3)	12	8
197	A39	$800	org brn (4)	10	8

35th anniversary of the Russian October Revolution.

Stamps in same designs with two additional characters meaning "Soviet" in the single-line Chinese inscription, and in different colors, were unofficially released at several small post offices in Hunan, Fukien and Canton areas in February, 1953, but were withdrawn after only a small number had been sold.

Price, set $3500 unused, $2000 canceled.

Compass, 3rd Century B.C.
A40

Designs: No. 199, Seismoscope, later Han Dynasty. No. 200, Drum cart to measure distance, Chin Dynasty. No. 201, Armillary sphere, Ming Dynasty.

1953, Dec. 1

No.	Type	Value	Color	Unused	Used
198	A40	$800	ind (1)	12	6
199	A40	$800	dk grn (2)	5	6
200	A40	$800	dk sl grn (3)	8	6
201	A40	$800	choc (4)	8	6

Major inventions by ancient and medieval Chinese scientists.
"Glorious Mother Country," 4th series.

(same size)

Francois Rabelais
A41

Gate of Heavenly Peace
A42

Designs: $400, José Marti, Cuban revolutionary. $800, Chu Yuan (350–275 B.C.), philosopher. $2200, Nicolaus Copernicus, astronomer.

1953, Dec. 30

No.	Type	Value	Color	Unused	Used
202	A41	$250	sl grn (3)	20	5
203	A41	$400	brn blk (4)	10	5
204	A41	$800	ind (1)	10	5
205	A41	$2200	choc (2)	10	10

1954, April 16 — Lithographed

Sixth Issue: Inscription at upper right.

No.	Type	Value	Color	Unused	Used
206	A42	$50	carmine	5	5
207	A42	$100	lt bl	5	6
208	A42	$200	green	5	6
209	A42	$250	ultra	75	8
210	A42	$400	gray grn	5	8
211	A42	$800	orange	5	6
212	A42	$1600	gray	5	40
213	A42	$2000	olive	5	20
			Nos. 206-213 (8)	1.10	99

Textile Plant, Harbin
A43

Lenin
A44

1954, May 1 — Engraved

Designs: $200, Tangku Harbor. $250, Tienshui-Lanchow railroad bridge, Kansu Province. $400, Heavy machine-building plant, Taiyuan, Shansi. No. 218, Automatic blast, furnace, Anshan, Manchuria. No. 219, Fushun open-cut coal mine. $2000, Automatic power plant, Northeast. $3200, Prospecting in Tayeh district, Hupeh.

No.	Type	Value	Color	Unused	Used
214	A43	$100	brn ol	10	5
215	A43	$200	bl grn	10	5
216	A43	$250	violet	5	5
217	A43	$400	black	10	5
218	A43	$800	claret	5	5
219	A43	$800	indigo	5	5
220	A43	$2000	red	5	15
221	A43	$3200	dk brn	15	25
			Nos. 214-221 (8)	65	70

Economic progress.

1954, June 30 — Engraved

Designs: $400, Lenin and Stalin Monument, Gorki (horiz.). $2000, Lenin proclaiming Soviet power.

No.	Type	Value	Color	Unused	Used
222	A44	$400	dp grn	10	8
223	A44	$800	dk brn	5	12
224	A44	$2000	dp car	40	12

30th anniversary of the death of Lenin.

Pottery Vessels, Neolithic Period, 2000 B. C.—A45

Archeological Treasures: No. 226, Stone chime, Shang Dynasty, c. 1200 B.C. No. 227, Kuo Chi Tsu-pai bronze basin, Middle Chou Dynasty, 816 B.C. No. 228, Lacquered box and wine cup, Warring States Period, 403–221 B.C.

1954, Aug. 25

No.	Type	Value	Color	Unused	Used
225	A45	$800	brown	9	6
226	A45	$800	indigo	9	6
227	A45	$800	Prus bl	9	6
228	A45	$800	dk car	9	6

"Glorious Mother Country," 5th series.

Pipe Production, Anshan Steel Mill
A46

Stalin Statue, by Tomsky
A47

Design: $800, Rolling mill, Anshan.

1954, Oct. 1

No.	Type	Value	Color	Unused	Used
229	A46	$400	Prus grn	30	15
230	A46	$800	vio brn	30	15

1954, Oct. 15

Designs: $800, Stalin portrait. $2000, Stalin viewing hydroelectric plant.

Size: 21x45mm.

No.	Type	Value	Color	Unused	Used
231	A47	$400	black	50	12

Size: 26x37mm.

No.	Type	Value	Color	Unused	Used
232	A47	$800	blk brn	10	12

Size: 42x26mm.

No.	Type	Value	Color	Unused	Used
233	A47	$2000	dp red	10	12

First anniversary of the death of Stalin.

Exhibition Building, Peking—A48

1954, Nov. 7

No.	Type	Value	Color	Unused	Used
234	A48	$800	brn, *cr*	7.50	4.00

Russian Economic and Cultural Exhibition, Peking. No. 234 measures 52½x24½mm. It also exists 53½x24mm.

Apprentices and Lathe
A49

Design: $800, Heavy machinery and workers.

1954, Dec. 15

No.	Type	Value	Color	Unused	Used
235	A49	$400	dk ol grn	15	10
236	A49	$800	brt red	10	10

Progress in technology.

Woman Worker Voting
A50

People Celebrating Opening of Congress—A51

1954, Dec. 30

No.	Type	Value	Color	Unused	Used
237	A50	$400	dp cl	5	12
238	A51	$800	brt red	15	10

First National Congress.

Flags, Worker and Woman Holding Constitution—A52

1954, Dec. 30

No.	Type	Value	Color	Unused	Used
239	A52	$400	brn, *buff*	15	7
240	A52	$800	brt red, *yel*	15	10

Adoption of Constitution.

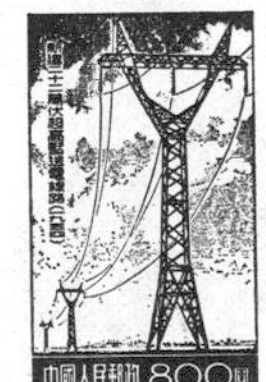

High-tension Pylon
A53

1955, Feb. 25

No.	Type	Value	Color	Unused	Used
241	A53	$800	dk Prus bl	25	15

Development of electric power.

Factory Health Workers and Red Cross—A54

1955, June 25

Engraved; Cross Typographed

No.	Type	Value	Color	Unused	Used
242	A54	8f	dp grn & red	10.50	25

50th anniversary of Chinese Red Cross.

Stalin and Mao in Kremlin
A55

Soviet Specialist and Chinese Worker
A56

1955, July 25 **Engraved**

243 A55 8f brn red 6.50 15
244 A56 20f ol blk 6.50 40

5th anniversary of Sino-Soviet Friendship Treaty.

Chang Heng (78–139), Astronomer
A57

Portraits of Scientists: No. 246, Tsu Chung-chih (429–500), mathematician. No. 247, Chang Sui (683–727), astronomer. No. 248, Li Shih-chen (1518–1593), physician and pharmacologist.

1955, Aug. 25 ***Perf. 14***

245 A57 8f sep, *buff* 40 5
a. Min. sheet, sep, *white* 2.50 1.00
246 A57 8f dp grn, *buff* 40 5
a. Min. sheet, dp grn, *white* 2.50 1.00
247 A57 8f blk, *buff* 40 5
a. Min. sheet, blk, *white* 2.50 1.00
248 A57 8f cl, *buff* 40 5
a. Min. sheet, cl, *white* 2.50 1.00

Miniature sheets contain one imperf. stamp each. Size: 63x90mm.

Steel Pouring Ladle
A58

1955–56 **Lithographed**

Bluish Black Frames, Multicolored Centers.

Position-in-set number in ( ).

249 A58 8f *shown* (1) 25 5
250 A58 8f *High tension line* (2) 25 5
251 A58 8f *Mechanized coal mining* (3) 25 5
252 A58 8f *Tank cars and derricks* (4) 25 5
253 A58 8f *Heavy machine shop* (5) 25 5
254 A58 8f *Soldier on guard* (6) 25 5
255 A58 8f *Spinning machine* (7) 25 5
256 A58 8f *Workers discussing 5-year plan* (8) 25 5
257 A58 8f *Combine harvester* (9) 25 5
258 A58 8f *Milk production* (10) 25 5
259 A58 8f *Dam* (11) 25 5

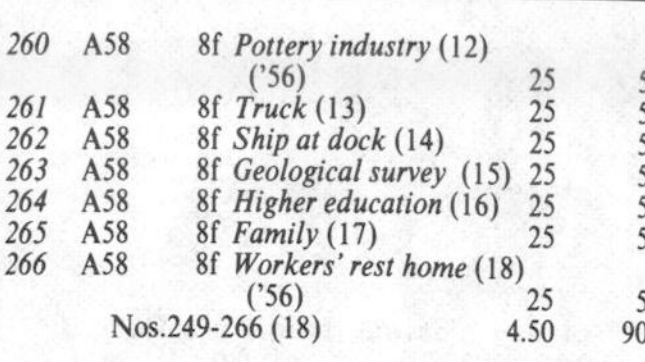

260 A58 8f *Pottery industry* (12) ('56) 25 5
261 A58 8f *Truck* (13) 25 5
262 A58 8f *Ship at dock* (14) 25 5
263 A58 8f *Geological survey* (15) 25 5
264 A58 8f *Higher education* (16) 25 5
265 A58 8f *Family* (17) 25 5
266 A58 8f *Workers' rest home* (18) ('56) 25 5
Nos. 249-266 (18) 4.50 90

First Five Year Plan.
Issue dates: Nos. 249–257, Oct. 1, 1955; Nos. 258–259, 261–265, Dec. 15, 1955; Nos. 260, 266, Feb. 24, 1956.

Lenin
A59

Engels
A60

1955, Dec. 15 **Engraved** ***Perf. 14***

267 A59 8f dk bl grn 6.00 10
268 A59 20f dk rose car 6.00 1.00

85th anniversary of the birth of Lenin.

1955, Dec. 15

269 A60 8f dp org 6.00 10
270 A60 20f brown 6.00 1.00

135th anniversary of the birth of Friedrich Engels (1820–1895), German socialist.

Storming Lu Ting Bridge
A61

Crossing Great Snow Mountains
A62

1955, Dec. 30

271 A61 8f dk red 5.00 25
272 A62 8f dk bl 5.00 75

Long March of Chinese Communist army, 20th anniversary.

Miner
A63

Gate of Heavenly Peace
A64

Designs: 1f, Machinist. 2f, Airman. 2½f, Nurse. 4f, Soldier. 8f, Steel worker. 10f, Scientist. 20f, Farm woman. 50f, Sailor.

1955–56 **Lithographed** ***Perf. 14***

273 A63 ½f org brn 3.00 5
274 A63 1f purple 3.00 10
275 A63 2f green 3.00 5
276 A63 2½f bl ('56) 3.00 5
277 A63 4f gray ol 3.00 10
278 A63 8f red org (Peking printing) 3.00 35
a. Perf. 12½ (Shanghai printing) 80.00 20.00
279 A63 10f cl ('56) 25.00 5
280 A63 20f dp bl 5.00 5
281 A63 50f gray 5.00 5
Nos. 273-281 (9) 53.00 85

Engraved

282 A64 $1 cl ('56) 1.50 25
283 A64 $2 sep ('55) 2.75 25
284 A64 $5 ind ('56) 6.75 40
285 A64 $10 dp org ('56) 14.00 4.00
286 A64 $20 gray vio ('56) 27.50 16.00
Nos. 282-286 (5) 52.50 20.90

Nos. 282–286 are the 7th Gate Issue.

Trucks, Mountains, Highway Map
A65

Suspension Bridge over Tatu River
A66

Design: No. 289, First truck arriving in Lhasa, and the Potala.

1956, Mar. 10 **Engraved**

287 A65 4f dp bl 40 10
288 A66 8f dk brn 40 10
289 A65 8f carmine 40 10

Completion of Sikang-Tibet and Chinghai-Tibet Highways.

Summer Palace and Marble Boat
A67

Famous Views of Imperial Peking: No. 291, Peihai Park with Jade Belt Marble Bridge. No. 292, Gate of Heavenly Peace. No. 293, Temple of Heaven. No. 294, Great Throne Hall, Forbidden City.

1956–57

290 A67 4f car rose (1) 50 10
291 A67 4f bl grn (2) 50 10
292 A67 8f red org (3) ('57) 50 10
293 A67 8f Prus bl (4) 50 10
294 A67 8f yel brn (5) 50 10
Nos. 290-294 (5) 2.50 50

Issue dates: No. 292, Feb. 20, 1957; others, June 15, 1956.
No. 292 exists with sun rays in background.

Salt Making
A68

Designs: No. 296, Dwelling of the Eastern Han period. No. 297, Duck hunting and harvesting. No. 298, Carriage crossing bridge.

1956, Oct. 1

295 A68 4f gray ol 20 5
296 A68 4f sl bl 20 5
297 A68 8f gray brn 20 5
298 A68 8f sepia 20 5

Murals, Tung Han Dynasty, 250 B.C.–220 A.D., found near Chengtu.

Ancient Coins and "Save"
A69

1956, Oct. 1

299 A69 4f yel brn 4.00 12
300 A69 8f rose red 4.00 12

Promotion of saving.

Gate of Heavenly Peace
A70

Sun Yat-sen
A71

1956, Nov. 10

301 A70 4f dk grn 4.00 10
302 A70 8f brt red 4.00 10
303 A70 16f dk car 4.00 15

8th National Congress of the Communist Party of China.

1956, Nov. 12

304 A71 4f brn, *cr* 6.00 5
305 A71 8f dp bl, *cr* 6.00 80

90th anniversary of birth of Sun Yat-sen.

Weight Lifting
A72

Designs: No. 306, Shot put. No. 308, Track. No. 309, Soccer. No. 310, Bicycling.

1957, Mar. 20 **Litho.** ***Perf. 12½***

Hibiscus red and green; inscription in brown.

306 A72 4f dp car (2) 40 5
307 A72 4f red lil (5) 40 5
308 A72 8f dk bl grn (1) 40 5
309 A72 8f dp bl (3) 40 5
310 A72 8f dp yel brn (4) 40 5
Nos. 306-310 (5) 2.00 25

First National Workers' Sports Meeting.

Truck Factory No. 1, Changchun
A73

Designs: 8f, Trucks rolling off assembly line.

1957, May 1 **Engraved** ***Perf. 14***

311 A73 4f lt brn 20 5
312 A73 8f sl grn 20 5

China's truck industry.

Nanchang Uprising—A74

Designs: No. 314, Mao and Chu Teh at Chingkanshan. No. 315, Crossing Yellow River. No. 316, Liberation of Nanking, Apr. 23, 1949.

1957

313	A74	4f blk vio (1)	4.00	15
314	A74	4f sl grn (2)	4.00	25
315	A74	8f red brn (3)	4.00	10
316	A74	8f dp bl (4)	4.00	10

30th anniversary of People's Liberation Army.

Issue dates: Nos. 313, 315, Aug. 10; No. 314, Aug. 30; No. 316, Dec. 30.

Congress Emblem A75

1957, Sept. 30

317	A75	8f chocolate	5.00	12
318	A75	22f indigo	5.00	20

4th International Trade Union Congress, Leipzig, Oct. 4-15.

Yangtze River Bridge A76

Design: 20f, Road leading to and over bridge.

1957, Oct. 1

319	A76	8f scarlet	40	10
320	A76	20f sl bl	40	5

Completion of Yangtze River Bridge at Wuhan.

Fireworks over Kremlin A77

Designs: 8f, Hammer and sickle over globe and broken chain. 20f, Stylized dove and olive branch. 22f, Hands of three races holding book with Marx and Lenin. 32f, Star and pylon.

1957, Nov. 7

321	A77	4f brt red	5.00	10
322	A77	8f chocolate	5.00	10
323	A77	20f dp grn	5.00	10
324	A77	22f red brn	5.00	10
325	A77	32f dp bl	5.00	75
		Nos. 321-325 (5)	25.00	1.15

40th anniversary of Russian October Revolution.

Map of Yellow River Basin—A78

Designs: No. 327, Sanmen Gorge dam and powerhouse. No. 328, Ocean liner on Yellow River. No. 329, Dam, irrigation canals and tree-bordered fields.

1957, Dec. 30

326	A78	4f dp org (1)	4.50	20
327	A78	4f dp bl (2)	4.50	25
328	A78	8f dp lake (3)	4.50	10
329	A78	8f bl grn (4)	4.50	10

Yellow River control plan.

Old Man and Young Drummer A79

Crane, Dove and Flowers A80

1957, Dec. 30 **Lithographed**

Multicolored

330	A79	8f *shown* (1)	20	10
331	A79	8f *Plowman* (2)	20	5
332	A79	8f *Woman planting tree* (3)	20	5
333	A79	8f *Harvest* (4)	20	5

Agricultural cooperation.

1958, Jan. 30 **Engraved**

Designs (Congratulatory Banner and): 8f, Crane with hot ingots, cotton bolls and wheat. 16f, Train on bridge, ship and plane.

334	A80	4f emer, *cr*	35	5
335	A80	8f red, *cr*	35	10
336	A80	16f ultra, *cr*	35	5

Fulfillment of First Five-Year Plan.

Sungyu Pagoda, Honan A81

Trilobite, Kaoli A82

Ancient Pagodas: No. 338, Chienhsun Pagoda, Yunnan. No. 339, Sakyamuni Pagoda, Shansi. No. 340, Flying Rainbow Pagoda, Shansi.

1958, Mar. 15 **Engraved**

337	A81	8f sep (1)	40	5
338	A81	8f Prus bl (2)	40	5
339	A81	8f mar (3)	40	5
340	A81	8f dp grn (4)	40	10

1958, Apr. 15

Designs: 8f, Lufeng dinosaur. 16f, Choukoutien sino-megaceros.

341	A82	4f black	35	8
342	A82	8f sepia	35	12
343	A82	16f sl grn	35	8

Prehistoric animals of China.

Heroes Monument A83

1958, May 1

344	A83	8f scarlet	9.00	80
	a.	Souvenir sheet	16.00	9.00

Unveiling of People's Heroes Monument, Peking. No. 344a contains one imperf. stamp, scarlet marginal inscription. Size: 87x137mm. Issued May 30.

Karl Marx A84

Cogwheels and Factories—A85

Design: 22f, Marx Speaking to German Workers' Educational Association, London, painting by Zhukow.

1958, May 5

345	A84	8f chocolate	8.00	30
346	A84	22f dk grn	8.00	60

140th anniversary of the birth of Karl Marx (1818-1883).

1958, May 25

347	A85	4f brt grnsh bl	7.00	*4.00*
348	A85	8f red lil	7.00	1.00

8th All-China Trade Union Congress, Peking.

Dove over Globe A86

Mother and Child A87

1958, June 1

349	A86	8f vio bl	7.00	10
350	A86	20f bl grn	7.00	1.40

4th Congress of the International Democratic Women's Federation, Vienna, Austria, June 1958.

1958, June 1 **Lithographed**

Designs (Children): No. 352, Watering sunflowers. No. 353, Playing hide-and-seek. No. 354, Sailing toy boat.

351	A87	8f grn & multi (1)	5.00	25
352	A87	8f grn & multi (2)	5.00	25
353	A87	8f grn & multi (3)	5.00	25
354	A87	8f grn & multi (4)	5.00	25

Children's Day.

Kuan Han-ching A88

Designs (Operas): 4f, "Dream of Butterflies." 20f, "The Riverside Pavilion."

1958, June 20 **Engraved**

355	A88	4f ind, *cr*	8.00	*1.00*
356	A88	8f brn, *cr*	8.00	25
357	A88	20f blk, *cr*	8.00	35
	a.	Souvenir sheet of 3, *white*	125.00	35.00

700th anniversary of publication of works of Kuan Han-ching (1210-1280), dramatist. No. 357a contains 3 imperf. stamps similar to Nos. 355-357. Dark brown marginal inscription. Size: 130x100mm. Issued June 28.

Planetarium A89

Design: 20f, Telescope and stars over Peking.

1958, June 25

358	A89	8f dk grn	7.50	15
359	A89	20f indigo	7.50	35

First Chinese planetarium, Peking.

Marx and Engels A90

Wild Goose and Broadcasting Tower A91

Design: 8f, Cover of first edition of the Communist Manifesto.

1958, July 1

360	A90	4f dk red vio	6.50	1.75
361	A90	8f Prus bl	6.50	15

110th anniversary of publication of the Communist Manifesto.

1958, July 10

362	A91	4f ultra	6.50	15
363	A91	8f dp grn	6.50	45

1st Conference of the Ministers of Posts and Telecommunications of Socialist Countries, Moscow, Dec. 3-17, 1957.

Peony and Doves A92

Bronze Weather Vane A93

Designs: 8f, Olive branch with ribbon and clouds. 22f, Atomic energy symbol over factories.

1958, July 20

364	A92	4f red	11.00	1.00
365	A92	8f green	11.00	12.00
366	A92	22f red brn	11.00	4.00

Congress for Disarmament and International Cooperation, Stockholm, July 17-22.

1958, Aug. 25

Designs: No. 368, Weather balloon. No. 369, Typhoon tower and weather map of Asia.

367	A93	8f yel bis & blk (1)	40	10
368	A93	8f bl & blk (2)	40	10
369	A93	8f brt grn & blk (3)	40	10

Meteorological services in ancient and modern China.

"5" Encircling IUS Emblem A94

1958, Sept. 4

370	A94	8f rose lil	7.50	15
371	A94	22f dp bl grn	7.50	25

5th Congress of the International Union of Students, Peking, Sept. 4-13.

Telegraph Building, Peking
A95

1958, Sept. 29

372 A95 4f grnsh blk 75 8
373 A95 8f rose red 75 8

Opening of Telegraph Building, Peking.

Exhibition Emblem and Exhortation
A96

Designs: No. 375, Dragon over clouds signifying "aiming high." No. 376, Flying horses, signifying "great leap forward" in production.

1958, Oct. 1

374 A96 8f sl grn (1) 6.00 15
375 A96 8f rose car (2) 6.00 15
376 A96 8f red brn (3) 6.00 40

National Exhibition of Industry and Communications, Peking.

Worker and Excavator
A97

Design: 8f, Completed dam and pylon.

1958, Oct. 25

377 A97 4f dk brn 15 10
378 A97 8f dp Prus bl 25 5

Completion of the 13 Ming Tombs Reservoir.

Sputnik over Armillary Sphere
A98

Designs: 8f, Sputnik 3 in orbit. 10f, Trajectories of 3 Sputniks over earth.

1958, Oct. 30

379 A98 4f scarlet 3.00 10
380 A98 8f dp vio bl 3.00 10
381 A98 10f dp grn 3.00 40

Anniversary of first earth satellite launched by the USSR.

Chinese and North Korean Soldiers
A99

Designs: No. 383, Chinese soldier embracing Korean woman. No. 384, Chinese girl presenting flowers to returning soldier.

1958, Nov. 20

382 A99 8f brt pur (1) 60 20
383 A99 8f chnt (2) 60 10
384 A99 8f rose car (3) 60 10

Return of the Chinese Volunteers from Korea.

Forest and Mountains
A100

Peony
A101

Designs: No. 386, Mounted forest patrol. No. 387, Mechanized lumbering (horiz.). No. 388, Tree-planting: "Turning the Country Green" (horiz.).

1958, Dec. 15

385 A100 8f dp bl grn (1) 85 30
386 A100 8f sl grn (2) 85 10
387 A100 8f dk pur (3) 85 10
388 A100 8f ind (4) 85 20

Afforestation.

1958, Sept. 25 **Lithographed**

Designs: 3f, Lotus. 5f, Chrysanthemums.

389 A101 1½f lil rose 7.00 15
390 A101 3f bl grn 7.00 50
391 A101 5f dp org 7.00 5

Atomic Reactor
A102

Design: 20f, Cyclotron.

1958, Dec. 30 **Engraved**

392 A102 8f dp bl 7.00 *1.00*
393 A102 20f dp brn 7.00 15

Inauguration of China's first atomic reactor and cyclotron, Peking.

Children Launching Model Planes
A103

Camel Carrying Load
A104

Designs: 8f, Gliders over trees. 10f, Parachutists descending. 20f, Small monoplanes in mid-air.

1958, Dec. 30

394 A103 4f carmine 45 10
395 A103 8f dp sl grn 45 5
396 A103 10f dk brn 45 5
397 A103 20f Prus bl 45 5

Sports-aviation publicity.

1959, Jan. 1

Designs: No. 399, Pomegranates. No. 400, Rooster. No. 401, Theatrical figure.

398 A104 8f vio & blk (1) 5.00 5
399 A104 8f dp bl grn & blk (2) 5.00 15
400 A104 8f red & blk (3) 5.00 15
401 A104 8f dp bl & blk (4) 5.00 25

Paper cut-outs (folk art).

Red Flag, Mao and Workers
A105

Women Workers and Atomic Model
A106

Designs: 8f, Traditional and modern blast furnaces. 10f, Steel works and workers.

1959

402 A105 4f brt red 8.00 30
403 A105 8f lake 8.00 30
404 A105 10f dp red 8.00 30

"Great Leap Forward" in steel production.

Issue dates: 4f, 8f, Feb. 19; 10f, May 25.

1959, Mar. 8

Design: 22f, Chinese and Soviet women holding banners dated "3.8".

405 A106 8f emer, *cr* 50 15
406 A106 22f mag, *cr* 50 5

International Women's Day.

Natural History Museum
A107

1959, Apr. 1

407 A107 4f grnsh bl 25 10
408 A107 8f ol brn 25 10

Opening of Museum of Natural History, Peking.

Wheat
A108

Designs on Chinese Flag: No. 410, Rice. No. 411, Cotton bolls. No. 412, Soybeans, rapeseed and peanuts.

1959, Apr. 25

409 A108 8f red (1) 40 10
410 A108 8f red (2) 40 10
411 A108 8f red (3) 40 10
412 A108 8f red (4) 40 10
Block of 4 (Nos. 409-412) 3.50 50

Successful harvest, 1958. Printed se-tenant in blocks of four.

Marx, Lenin and Workers
A109

Designs: 8f, Black, yellow and white fists holding banner. 22f, Steel workers parading with banners dated "5.1."

1959, May 1

413 A109 4f ultra 7.50 30
414 A109 8f red 7.50 30
415 A109 22f emerald 7.50 30

International Labor Day.

Peking Airport
A110

Design: 10f, Plane loading on runway.

1959, June 20

416 A110 8f lil & blk 7.00 20
417 A110 10f ol gray & blk 7.00 20

Opening of new Peking Airport.

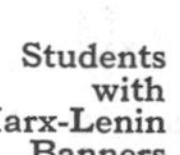

Students with Marx-Lenin Banners
A111

Design: 8f, Workers with banners of Mao.

1959, July 1 **Photo.** ***Perf. 11x11½***

418 A111 4f gray, red & dk brn 10.00 3.00
419 A111 8f bis, red & dk brn 10.00 3.00

40th anniversary of the May 4th students' uprising.

Frederick Joliot-Curie
A112

Design: 22f, Three races, dove and olive branch.

1959, July 25 **Engraved** ***Perf. 11½***

420 A112 8f vio brn 8.00 *1.25*
421 A112 22f dk vio 8.00 5

10th anniversary of the World Peace Movement.

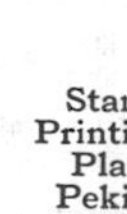

Stamp Printing Plant, Peking
A113

1959, Aug. 15 ***Perf. 11x11½***

422 A113 8f dp bl grn 8.50 90

Sino-Czechoslovak cooperation in stamp production.

Table Tennis
A114

1959, Aug. 30 **Litho.** ***Perf. 14***

423 A114 4f blk & bl 75 15
424 A114 8f blk & red 75 10

25th World Table Tennis Championships, Dortmund, German Democratic Republic.

Soviet Space Rocket
A115

1959, Sept. 10 **Photo.** ***Perf. 11½***

425 A115 8f Prus bl, red & blk 16.00 1.00

Launching of first Russian space rocket, Jan. 2, 1959.

Backyard Steel Production A116 — Mao and Gate of Heavenly Peace A117

Designs: No. 426, Sun rising over "industry and agriculture." No. 428, Farming. No. 429, Trade. No. 430, Education. No. 431, Militia. No. 432, Communal dining. No. 433, Nursery. No. 434, Care for the aged. No. 435, Health services. No. 436, Flutist; culture and sports. No. 437, Flower symbolizing unity of industry, agriculture, trade, education and armed forces.

Position-in-set number in ( ).

1959, Sept. 25 **Engraved**

426	A116	8f rose (1)	30	8
427	A116	8f vio brn (2)	30	8
428	A116	8f dp org (3)	30	8
429	A116	8f sl grn (4)	30	8
430	A116	8f dp bl (5)	30	8
431	A116	8f ol (6)	30	8
432	A116	8f ind (7)	30	8
433	A116	8f lil rose (8)	30	8
434	A116	8f gray blk (9)	30	8
435	A116	8f emer (10)	30	8
436	A116	8f dk vio (11)	30	8
437	A116	8f red (12)	30	8
		Nos. 426-437 (12)	3.60	96

First anniversary of Peoples' Communes.

1959, Sept. 28 Photo. *Perf. 11½x11*

Designs: 8f, Marx, Lenin and Kremlin. 22f, Dove over globe.

With Gum

438	A117	8f lt brn & red	9.00	3.00
439	A117	8f dl bl & red	9.00	1.00
440	A117	22f bl grn & red	9.00	50

See note after No. 456.

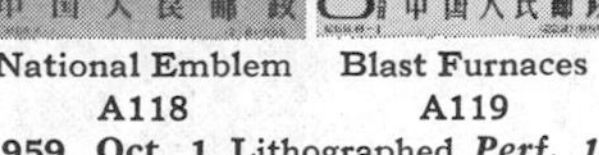

National Emblem A118 — Blast Furnaces A119

1959, Oct. 1 Lithographed *Perf. 14*

441	A118	4f pale grn, red & gold	5.25	6.00
442	A118	8f gray, red & gold	5.25	50
443	A118	10f lt bl, red & gold	5.25	50
444	A118	20f pale brn, red & gold	5.25	2.00

Engraved and Photogravure

1959, Oct. 1 ***Perf. 11½x11***

Designs: No. 446, Large coal mine. No. 447, Planer, Wuhan heavy machinery plant. No. 448, Wuhan Yangtze River Bridge. No. 449, Combine harvester. No. 450, Hsinankiang hydroelectric station. No. 451, Spinning machine. No. 452, Kirin chemical fertilizer plant.

With Gum

445	A119	8f brn & rose red (1)	35	10
446	A119	8f brn & gray (2)	35	10
447	A119	8f brn & yel brn (3)	35	10
448	A119	8f brn & stl bl (4)	35	10
449	A119	8f brn & org (5)	35	10
450	A119	8f brn & ol (6)	35	10
451	A119	8f brn & bl grn (7)	35	15
452	A119	8f brn & vio (8)	35	15
		Nos. 445-452 (8)	2.80	90

Celebration at Gate of Heavenly Peace A120

Mao Proclaiming Republic—A121

Designs: 10f, Workers and factory (vert.). No. 455, People rejoicing (vert.).

1959, Oct. 1 Lithographed *Perf. 14*

Inscribed: 1949–1959.

453	A120	8f cr & multi	3.50	35
454	A120	10f cr & multi	3.50	35
455	A120	20f cr & multi	3.50	35

Engraved

456	A121	20f dp car	20.00	8.50

Nos. 438–456 commemorate 10th anniversary of the Proclamation of the People's Republic of China.

Pioneer Bugler A122 — Exhibition Emblem, Communications Symbols A123

Designs: No. 457, Pioneers' emblem. No. 459, Schoolgirl. No. 460, Girl using rain gauge. No. 461, Boy planting tree. No. 462, Girl figure skater.

1959, Nov. 10 Photo. *Perf. 11½*

457	A122	4f red yel & blk (1)	1.75	15
458	A122	4f Prus bl & red (2)	1.75	15
459	A122	8f brn & red (3)	1.75	15
460	A122	8f dk bl & red (4)	1.75	15
461	A122	8f red & grn (5)	1.75	15
462	A122	8f mag & red (6)	1.75	15
		Nos. 457-462 (6)	10.50	90

10th anniversary of the Young Pioneers. Black inscription on No. 457 engraved.

1959, Dec. 1 **Engraved**

Design: 8f, Exhibition emblem and chimneys.

463	A123	4f dk bl	35	12
464	A123	8f red	35	8

Exhibition of Industry and Communications, Peking.

Palace of Nationalities A124

Engraved, Frame Litho.

1959, Dec. 10 ***Perf. 14***

465	A124	4f red & blk	1.85	10
466	A124	8f brt grn & blk	1.85	15

Inauguration of the Cultural Palace of Nationalities, Peking.

Athletes' Monument and Track A125

Designs: No. 468, Parachuting. No. 469, Marksmanship. No. 470, Diving. No. 471, Table tennis. No. 472, Weight lifting. No. 473, High jump. No. 474, Rowing. No. 475, Track. No. 476, Basketball. No. 477, Traditional Chinese fencing. No. 478, Motorcycling. No. 479, Gymnastics. No. 480, Bicycling. No. 481, Horsemanship. No. 482, Soccer.

1959, Dec. 28 **Lithographed**

467	A125	8f bis, blk & gray (1)	60	15
468	A125	8f dl bl, blk & gray (2)	60	15
469	A125	8f red brn & blk (3)	60	15
470	A125	8f grn, blk & brn (4)	60	15
471	A125	8f brt grn, blk, brn & gray (5)	60	15
472	A125	8f gray, blk & brn (6)	60	15
473	A125	8f dl bl, blk & brn (7)	60	15
474	A125	8f Prus grn, blk & brn (8)	60	15
475	A125	8f org, blk & brn (9)	60	15
476	A125	8f dl vio, blk & brn (10)	60	15
477	A125	8f lt ol, blk & brn (11)	60	15
478	A125	8f bl, blk & gray (12)	60	15
479	A125	8f gray bl, blk, brn, & bl (13)	60	15
480	A125	8f gray, blk, brn, & vio (14)	60	15
481	A125	8f red org, blk, brn, & gray (15)	60	15
482	A125	8f lt gray, blk, brn, & red (16)	60	15
		Nos. 467-482 (16)	9.60	2.40

First National Sports Meeting, Peking.

Wheat and Main Pavilion A126

Designs (Pavilion and): 8f, Meteorological symbols. 10f, Domestic animals. 20f, Fish.

1960, Jan. 20 **Engr. and Litho.**

Cream Background

483	A126	4f blk & org	45	10
484	A126	8f blk & dl bl	45	10
485	A126	10f blk & org brn	45	10
486	A126	20f blk & grnsh bl	45	20

Opening of the National Agricultural Exhibition Halls, Peking.

With Gum

From No. 487 onward all stamps were issued with gum except as noted.

Conference Hall, Tsunyi A127

Designs: 8f, Mao addressing conference. 10f, Crossing Chinsha River.

Engr. (4f, 10f); Photo. (8f)

1960, Jan. 25 ***Perf. 11x11½***

487	A127	4f vio & bl	9.00	1.00
488	A127	8f red & multi	9.00	*5.00*
489	A127	10f sl grn	9.00	2.00

25th anniversary of the Communist Party Conference at Tsunyi.

Clara Zetkin (1857–1933) A128 — Chinese and Russian Workers A129

Designs: 8f, Mother, child and dove. 10f, Woman tractor driver. 22f, Women of three races.

1960, Mar. 8 Photo. *Perf. 11½x11*

490	A128	4f blk & multi	85	15
491	A128	8f blk & multi	85	15
492	A128	10f blk & multi	85	15
493	A128	22f blk & multi	85	15

50th anniversary of International Women's Day.

1960, Mar. 10

Designs: 8f, Chinese and Russian flags. 10f, Chinese and Russian soldiers.

494	A129	4f dk brn	9.00	1.50
495	A129	8f red, yel & blk	9.00	1.50
496	A129	10f dp bl	9.00	5.00

10th anniversary of Sino-Soviet Treaty of Friendship. Black inscription engraved on No. 495.

Flags of Hungary and China A130

Design: 8f, Parliament Building, Budapest.

1960, Apr. 4 ***Perf. 11x11½***

497	A130	8f yel, blk, red & grn	8.00	1.00
498	A130	8f bl, red & blk	8.00	4.00

15th anniversary of the liberation of Hungary.

Lenin Speaking A131 — Lunik 2, Earth and Russian Arms A132

Designs: 8f, Portrait of Lenin. 20f, Lenin talking with Smolny Palace guard.

Engr. (4f, 20f); Engr. & Photo. (8f).

1960, April 22 ***Perf. 11½x11***

499	A131	4f vio brn	8.25	2.00
500	A131	8f org red & blk	8.25	6.00
501	A131	20f dk brn	8.25	2.00

90th anniversary of the birth of Lenin.

1960, Apr. 30 Engraved *Perf. 11½*

Design: 10f, Lunik 3 over earth.

502	A132	8f red	3.00	35
503	A132	10f green	3.00	35

Russian space flights.

Pioneers and Flags of Czechoslovakia and China
A133

View of Prague with Charles Bridge
A134

Perf. 11½x11; 11x11½

1960, May 9 Photogravure

504	A133	8f yel & multi	8.00	2.50
505	A134	8f dp grn	8.00	2.50

15th anniversary of the liberation of Czechoslovakia.

Nostril Bouquet
A135

Designs: Various goldfish.
Position-in-set number in ( ).

1960, June 1 *Perf. 11x11½*

Multicolored

506	A135	4f *shown* (1)	6.50	50
507	A135	4f *Black-back dragon eye* (2)	6.50	50
508	A135	4f *Bubble eye* (3)	6.50	50
509	A135	4f *Red tiger head* (4)	6.50	50
510	A135	8f *Pearl scale* (5)	6.50	50
511	A135	8f *Blue dragon eye* (6)	6.50	50
512	A135	8f *Skyward eye* (7)	6.50	50
513	A135	8f *Red cap*(8)	6.50	50
514	A135	8f *Purple cap* (9)	6.50	4.00
515	A135	8f *Red head* (10)	6.50	4.00
516	A135	8f *Red and white dragon eye* (11)	6.50	4.00
517	A135	8f *Red dragon eye* (12)	6.50	4.00
		Nos. 506-517 (12)	78.00	20.00

Sow with Litter
A136

Designs: No. 519, Pig being inoculated. No. 520, Pigs. No. 521, Pig and mechanized feeding. No. 522, Pig and bales.

1960, June 15

518	A136	8f red & blk (1)	5.50	50
519	A136	8f dp grn & blk (2)	5.50	50
520	A136	8f lil rose & blk (3)	5.50	50
521	A136	8f lt yel grn & blk (4)	5.50	50
522	A136	8f org & blk (5)	5.50	1.75
		Nos. 518-522 (5)	27.50	3.75

Flag Inscribed "Serving the Workers"
A137

Flowers, Flags of North Korea and China
A138

Design: 8f, Inscribed stone seal.

Photogravure

1960, July 30 *Perf. 11½x11*

523	A137	4f lt grn, red, pink & brn	8.00	2.50

Engraved and Photogravure

524	A137	8f pale bl, red & bis	8.00	2.50

3rd National Congress for Literature and Arts, Peking.

1960, Aug. 15 Photogravure

Design: 8f, Flying horse of Korea.

525	A138	8f red & multi	9.00	3.00
526	A138	8f ultra, red & ind	9.00	3.00

15th anniversary of the liberation of Korea.

Railroad Station, Peking—A139

Design: 10f, Train arriving at station.

1960, Aug. 30 *Perf. 11½*

527	A139	8f bl, cr & brn	4.00	2.50
528	A139	10f bluish grn, cr & ind	4.00	2.50

Opening of new Peking Railroad Station.

Girls and Flags of North Viet Nam and China
A140

Lake of the Returning Sword, Hanoi
A141

Worker and Fresh-air Installation
A142

1960, Sept. 2 *Perf. 11x11½, 11½x11*

529	A140	8f red & multi	2.50	60
530	A141	8f red, gray grn & gray	2.50	40

15th anniversary of the Democratic Republic of North Viet Nam.

1960, Sept. 10 *Perf. 11½*

Designs: No. 532, Exterminator. No. 533, Window cleaning. No. 534, Medical examination of child. No. 535, Physical exercise.

531	A142	8f blk & org (1)	1.00	10
532	A142	8f ind & sl (2)	1.00	15
533	A142	8f brn & bl (3)	1.00	20
534	A142	8f mar & ocher (4)	1.00	30
535	A142	8f ind & brt grn (5)	1.00	25
		Nos. 531-535 (5)	5.00	1.00

National health campaign.

Great Hall of the People—A143

Design: 10fr, Inside view.

1960, Oct. 1

536	A143	8f yel & multi	4.50	2.50
537	A143	10f brn & multi	4.50	2.50

Completion of the Great Hall of the People, Peking.

Dr. Norman Bethune
A144

Engels Addressing Congress at The Hague—A145

Design: No. 539, Dr. Bethune operating on a soldier.

Photo. (No. 538); Engr. (No. 539)

1960, Nov. 20 *Perf. 11½x11*

538	A144	8f red & multi	1.50	15
539	A144	8f sepia	1.50	15

Dr. Norman Bethune (1890–1939), Canadian surgeon with 8th Army.

Engr. (No. 540); Photo. (No. 541).

1960, Nov. 28

Designs: 10f, Portrait of Engels.

540	A145	8f brown	8.00	5.50
541	A145	10f bl & multi	8.00	5.50

140th anniversary of the birth of Friedrich Engels (1820–1895), German Socialist.

"Hwang Shi Ba"
A146

Freighter
A147

1960–61 Photogravure

Various Chrysanthemums in Natural Colors.

542	A146	4f bl gray (1)	5.00	75
543	A146	4f pink (2)	5.00	75
544	A146	8f dk gray (3)	5.00	75
545	A146	8f dp bl (4)	5.00	75
546	A146	8f grn (5)	5.00	75
547	A146	8f mag (6)	5.00	75
548	A146	8f ol (7)	5.00	75
549	A146	8f grnsh bl (8)	5.00	75
550	A146	10f gray (9)	5.00	75
551	A146	10f choc (10)	5.00	75
552	A146	20f dp bl (11)	5.00	75
553	A146	20f brt red (12)	5.00	75
554	A146	22f ol bis (13)	5.00	75
555	A146	22f car (14)	5.00	75
556	A146	30f grnsh gray (15)	5.00	75
557	A146	30f brt pink (16)	5.00	75
558	A146	35f dp grn (17)	5.00	75
559	A146	52f brt lil rose (18)	5.00	75
		Nos. 542-559 (18)	90.00	13.50

Issue dates: Nos. 548–550, 557–559, Dec. 10, 1960; Nos. 545–547, 554–556, Jan. 18, 1961; Nos. 542–544, Feb. 24, 1961.

1960, Dec. 15 *Perf. 11½*

Without Gum

560	A147	8f dp bl	8.00	1.50

Launching of first 10,000-ton Chinese-built freighter.

Pantheon, Paris
A148

Design: 8f, Proclamation of the Commune.

Engraved and Photogravure

1961, Mar. 18 *Perf. 11½x11*

561	A148	8f gray blk & red	4.00	1.00
562	A148	8f brn & red	4.00	1.00

90th anniversary of the Paris Commune.

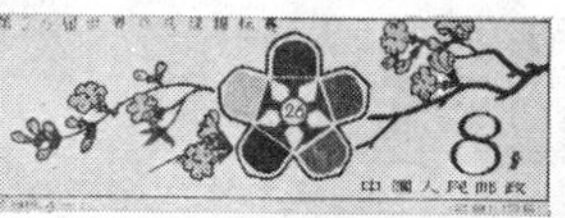

Championship Symbol and Jasmine—A149

Designs: 10f, Table tennis racket and ball; Temple of Heaven. 20f, Table tennis match. 22f, Peking workers' gymnasium.

1961, Apr. 5 Photo. *Perf. 11*

563	A149	8f multi	60	15
564	A149	10f multi	60	10
565	A149	20f multi	60	10
566	A149	22f multi	60	25
a.		Souv. sheet of 4	90.00	75.00

26th World Table Tennis Championships, Peking. No. 566a contains one each of Nos. 563–566. Red and bister marginal inscription and decoration. Size: 150x100 mm.

Jeme Tien-yow
A150

Design: 10f, Train and tunnel, Peking-Changchow Railroad.

1961, June 20 *Perf. 11½x11*

567	A150	8f ol grn & blk	1.50	15
568	A150	10f org brn & brn	1.50	15

Centenary of the birth of Jeme Tien-yow, railroad construction engineer.

Congress Building, Shanghai—A151

Designs: 8f, August 1st Building, Nanchang. 10f, Provisional Central Government Office, Juikin. 20f, Pagoda Hill, Yenan. 30f, Gate of Heavenly Peace, Peking.

1961, July 1 ***Perf. 11½***

569	A151	4f gold, red & cl	7.50	50
570	A151	8f gold, red & bl grn	7.50	50
571	A151	10f gold, red & yel brn	7.50	1.00
572	A151	20f gold, red & ultra	7.50	50
573	A151	30f gold, red & org red	7.50	60
		Nos. 569-573 (5)	37.50	3.10

40th anniversary of the Chinese Communist Party.

August 1 Building, Nanchang
A152

Designs: 1½f, 2f, as 1f. 3f, 4f, 5f, Trees and Sha Cho Pa Building, Juikin. 8f, 10f, 20f, Pagoda Hill, Yenan. 22f, 30f, 50f, Gate of Heavenly Peace, Peking.

1961-62 **Engraved** ***Perf. 11***

Without Gum

Size: 24x16mm

574	A152	1f vio bl	2.25	50
575	A152	1½f maroon	2.25	10
576	A152	2f indigo	2.25	50
577	A152	3f dl vio	2.25	10
578	A152	4f green	2.25	10
579	A152	5f gray	2.25	50
580	A152	8f sepia	2.25	5
581	A152	10f brt lil rose	2.25	5
582	A152	20f grnsh bl	2.25	5
583	A152	22f brown	2.25	5
584	A152	30f blue	2.25	5
585	A152	50f vermilion	2.25	5
		Nos. 574-585 (12)	27.00	2.10

Issue dates: 1f, 1½f, 5f, July 20, 1962; others July 20, 1961. See Nos. 647-654, 1059-1064.

Flowers, Flags of Mongolia and China
A153

Design: 10f, Parliament, Ulan Bator, and statue of Sukhe Bator.

1961, July 11 **Photo.** ***Perf. 11x11½***

586	A153	8f crim, ultra & yel	9.00	1.00
587	A153	10f org, blk & yel	9.00	7.00

40th anniversary of the Mongolian People's Republic.

Military Museum—A154

1961, Aug. 1 ***Perf. 11½***

Engraved and Photogravure

588	A154	8f gray bl, brn & grn	8.50	60
589	A154	10f gray, blk & grn	8.50	15

Opening of the People's Revolutionary Military Museum.

Uprising at Wuchang
A155

Sun Yat-sen
A156

Perf. 11x11½, 11½x11

1961, Oct. 10 **Photogravure**

590	A155	8f gray & blk	8.50	*1.75*
591	A156	10f tan & blk	8.50	25

50th anniversary of the 1911 Revolution.

Donkey
A157

Rejoicing Tibetans
A158

Designs: 8f, 10f, 20f, 22f, Horses; 30f, 50f, Camels. Ceramic statuettes from Tang Dynasty (618-906) graves.

1961, Nov. 10 ***Perf. 11½x11***

Statuettes in Original Colors

592	A157	4f dl bl	1.25	25
593	A157	8f gray grn	1.25	25
594	A157	8f dp pur	1.25	25
595	A157	10f dp bl	1.25	20
596	A157	20f olive	1.25	25
597	A157	22f bl grn	1.25	10
598	A157	30f red brn	1.25	25
599	A157	50f slate	1.25	25
		Nos. 592-599 (8)	10.00	1.80

1961, Nov. 25

Designs: 8f, Woman sower. 10f, Celebration of bumper crop. 20f, People's representatives. 30f, Tibetan children.

600	A158	4f brn & ocher	9.00	5
601	A158	8f brn & lt bl grn	9.00	20
602	A158	10f brn & yel	9.00	5
603	A158	20f brn & rose	9.00	1.50
604	A158	30f brn & bluish gray	9.00	1.50
		Nos. 600-604 (5)	45.00	3.30

Rebirth of the Tibetan people.

Lu Hsun
A159

1962, Feb. 26

605	A159	8f red brn & blk	50	15

80th anniversary of the birth of Lu Hsun, writer.

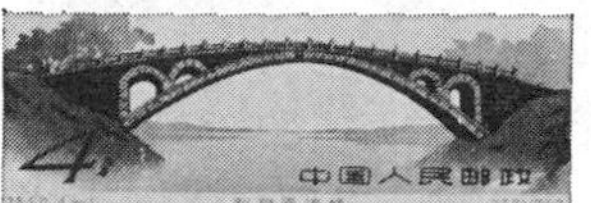

An Chi Bridge, Chao Hsien—A160

Bridges of Ancient China: 8f, Pao Tai, Soochow. 10f, Chu Pu, Kwan Hsien. 20f, Chen Yang, San Kiang.

1962, May 15 ***Perf. 11***

606	A160	4f dk gray bl	1.00	10
607	A160	8f dp grn	1.00	10
608	A160	10f brown	1.00	5
609	A160	20f grnsh bl	1.00	45

Tu Fu
A161

Cranes and Bamboo
A162

Design: 4f, Tu Fu memorial pavilion, Chengtu.

1962, May 25 ***Perf. 11½x11***

610	A161	4f ol bis & blk	9.00	25
611	A161	8f grnsh bl & blk	9.00	50

Poet Tu Fu, 1,250th anniversary of birth.

1962, June 10

Designs: 10f, Two cranes in flight. 20f, Crane on rock.

612	A162	8f tan & multi	4.00	1.25
613	A162	10f bl & multi	4.00	70
614	A162	20f bis & multi	4.00	70

"The Sacred Crane," from paintings by Chen Chi-fo.

Cuban Soldier and Flag
A163

Designs: 10f, Sugar cane worker. 22f, Militiaman and woman.

1962, July 10 ***Perf. 11x11½***

615	A163	8f car, rose & blk	12.00	1.50
616	A163	10f grn & blk	12.00	50
617	A163	22f ultra & blk	12.00	9.00

Support of Cuba.

Torch and Map of Algeria
A164

Mei Lan-fang
A165

Design: 22f, Algerian soldiers and flag.

1962, July 10 ***Perf. 11½x11***

618	A164	8f dp brn & red org	45	20
619	A164	22f ocher & dp brn	45	30

Support of Algeria.

1962 ***Perf. 11½x11, 11x11½***

Designs (Mei Lan-fang in Women's Roles): No. 621, Beating drum. No. 622, With fan. 10f, Lady Yu with swords. 20f, With bag. 22f, Heavenly Maiden (horiz.). 30f, With spinning wheel (horiz.). 50f, Kneeling (horiz.). $3, Scene from opera "Drunken Beauty."

620	A165	4f tan & multi	8.00	1.00
621	A165	8f tan & multi	8.00	1.00
622	A165	8f gray & multi	8.00	10
623	A165	10f gray & multi	8.00	1.00
624	A165	20f lt grn & multi	8.00	50
625	A165	22f cr & multi	8.00	4.00
626	A165	30f lt bl & multi	8.00	5.00
627	A165	50f buff & multi	8.00	6.00
		Nos. 620-627 (8)	64.00	18.60

Souvenir Sheet

Perf. 11

628	A165	$3 brn & multi	450.00	325.00

Stage art of Mei Lan-fang, actor.

Issue dates: 4f, 8f, 10f, Aug. 8; $3, Sept. 15; others Sept. 1. Imperfs. exist. *Price, set $300.*

No. 628 contains one stamp (48x58mm); Prussian blue margin with white ornamental design. Size: 108x147mm.

Flower Drum Dance, Han
A166

Folk Dances: 8f, Ordos, Mongolia. 10f, Catching shrimp, Chuang. 20f, Friend, Yi. 30f, Fiddle dance, Tibet. 50f, Tambourine dance, Uighur.

Cumulative numbers 246-251 at lower right.

1962, Oct. 15 **Litho.** ***Perf. 12½***

Without Gum

629	A166	4f cr & multi	40	5
630	A166	8f cr & multi	40	5
631	A166	10f cr & multi	40	10
632	A166	20f cr & multi	40	40
633	A166	30f cr & multi	40	30
634	A166	50f cr & multi	40	40
		Nos. 629-634 (6)	2.40	1.30

See Nos. 696-707.

Soldiers Storming Winter Palace—A167

Design: 8f, Lenin leading soldiers (vert.).

1962, Nov. 7 **Photo.** ***Perf. 11½***

635	A167	8f blk & red	13.00	20
636	A167	20f sl grn & red	13.00	60

45th anniversary of the Russian Revolution.

Monument and Map of Albania
A168

Tsai Lun, Inventor of Papermaking
A169

Design: 10f, Albanian flag and Girl Pioneer.

1962, Nov. 28 ***Perf. 11½x11***

637	A168	8f Prus bl & sep	1.00	30
638	A168	10f red, yel, & blk	1.00	30

50th anniversary of Albanian independence.

1962, Dec. 1 ***Perf. 11½x11***

Designs: No. 640, Paper making. No. 641, Sun Szu-miao, physician. No. 642, Writing medical treatise. No. 643, Shen Ko, geologist. No. 644, Making field notes. No. 645, Kuo Shou-chin, astronomer. No. 646, Astronomical instrument. Cumulative numbers 297–304 at lower right.

639	A169	4f multi	40	20
640	A169	4f multi	40	10
641	A169	8f multi	40	15
642	A169	8f multi	40	20
643	A169	10f multi	40	10
644	A169	10f multi	40	25
645	A169	20f multi	40	25
646	A169	20f multi	40	25
		Nos. 639-646 (8)	3.20	1.50

Scientists of ancient China.

Building Type of 1961

Designs: 1f, 2f, Building, Nanchang. 3f, 4f, Trees and Sha Cho Pa Building. 8f, 10f, 20f, Pagoda Hill, Yenan. 30f, Gate of Heavenly Peace, Peking.

Rough Perf. 12½

1962, Jan. **Lithographed**

Size: 21x16mm.

647	A152	1f ultra	40	10
648	A152	2f grnsh gray	40	10
649	A152	3f vio gray	40	10
650	A152	4f green	40	10
651	A152	8f dk ol, perf. 14	40	10
a.		Perf. 12½		50
652	A152	10f brt rose lil	40	10
653	A152	20f sl bl	40	10
654	A152	30f dl bl	40	10
		Nos. 647-654 (8)	3.20	80

Tank Monument, Havana
A170

Crowd in Havana—A171

Designs: No. 656, Cuban revolutionaries. No. 658, Crowd in Peking. No. 659, Cuban soldier. No. 660, Castro and Cuban flag.

Perf. 11½, 11x11½

1963, Jan. 1 **Photogravure**

655	A170	4f red & blk brn	8.50	15
656	A170	4f grn & blk	8.50	15
657	A171	8f dl red & brn	8.50	1.00
658	A171	8f dl red & brn	8.50	20
659	A170	10f ocher & blk	8.50	3.00
660	A170	10f red, bl & blk	8.50	*10.00*
		Nos. 655-660 (6)	51.00	*14.50*

4th anniversary of the Cuban revolution.

Green Dragontail
A172

Karl Marx
A173

Position-in-set number in ( ).

1963 **Without Gum** ***Perf. 11***

Butterflies in Natural Colors.

661	A172	4f *Tibetan clouded yel* (1)	1.25	15
662	A172	4f *Tritailed glory* (2)	1.25	15
663	A172	4f *Neumogeni jungle queen* (3)	1.25	15
664	A172	4f *Washan swordtail* (4)	1.25	40
665	A172	4f *Striped ringlet* (5)	1.25	15
666	A172	8f *shown* (6)	1.25	10
667	A172	8f *Dilunulated peacock* (7)	1.25	15
668	A172	8f *Yamfly* (8)	1.25	5
669	A172	8f *Golden kaiser-i-hind* (9)	1.25	5
670	A172	8f *Mushaell hairstreak* (10)	1.25	5
671	A172	10f *Yellow orange-tip* (11)	1.25	5
672	A172	10f *Great jay* (12)	1.25	10
673	A172	10f *Striped punch* (13)	1.25	5
674	A172	10f *Hainan violet-beak* (14)	1.25	5
675	A172	10f *Omeiskipper* (15)	1.25	5
676	A172	20f *Philippines birdwing* (16)	1.25	15
677	A172	20f *Richtofenis red apollo* (17)	1.25	15
678	A172	22f *Blue-banded king crow* (18)	1.25	20
679	A172	30f *Solskyi copper* (19)	1.25	50
680	A172	50f *Yunnan clipper* (20)	1.25	1.25
		Nos. 661-680 (20)	25.00	3.95

Issue dates: Nos. 666–675, July 15; others Apr. 5.

1963, May 5 ***Perf. 11½***

Designs: No. 682, "Workers of the World, Unite" on cover of first edition of Communist Manifesto. No. 683, Marx and Engels.

Without Gum

681	A173	8f blk, gold & sal (1)	7.50	3.00
682	A173	8f gold & red (2)	7.50	3.00
683	A173	8f gold & choc (3)	7.50	3.00

145th anniversary of birth of Karl Marx (1818–1883), German political philosopher.

Child with Top
A174

Designs (Child): No. 685, eating berries. No. 686, as traffic policeman. No. 687, with windmill. No. 688, listening to caged cricket. No. 689, with sword. No. 690, embroidering. No. 691, with umbrella. No. 692, playing with sand. No. 693, playing table tennis. No. 694, learning to add. No. 695, with kite.

1963, June 1 **Litho.** ***Perf. 12½***

Without Gum

Multicolored Designs

684	A174	4f grnsh gray (1)	45	5
685	A174	4f tan (2)	45	5
686	A174	8f gray (3)	45	5
687	A174	8f bl (4)	45	5
688	A174	8f tan (5)	45	5
689	A174	8f dp gray (6)	45	5
690	A174	8f cit (7)	45	5
691	A174	8f gray (8)	45	5
692	A174	10f grn (9)	45	15
693	A174	10f vio (10)	45	15
694	A174	20f bis (11)	45	40
695	A174	20f grn (12)	45	40
		Nos. 684-695 (12)	5.40	1.50

Children's Day.
Price, imperf set $11.

Dance Type of 1962

Folk Dances: 4f, Weavers' dance, Puyi. 8f, Kazakh. 10f, Olunchun. 20f, Labor dance, Kaochan. 30f, Reed pipe dance, Miao. 50f, Fan dance, Korea.
Cumulative numbers 261–266 at lower right.

1963, June 15 ***Perf. 12½***

Without Gum

696	A166	4f cr & multi	40	5
697	A166	8f cr & multi	40	5
698	A166	10f cr & multi	40	10
699	A166	20f cr & multi	40	25
700	A166	30f cr & multi	40	30
701	A166	50f cr & multi	40	50
		Nos. 696-701 (6)	2.40	1.25

1963, June 30 **Without Gum**

Folk Dances: 4f, "Wedding Ceremony," Yu. 8f, "Encircling Mountain Forest," Pai. 10f, Long drum dance, Yao. 20f, Third day of the third month dance, Li. 30f, Knife dance, Kawa. 50f, Peacock dance, Thai.
Cumulative numbers 279–284 at lower right.

702	A166	4f cr & multi	40	5
703	A166	8f cr & multi	40	5
704	A166	10f cr & multi	40	10
705	A166	20f cr & multi	40	30
706	A166	30f cr & multi	40	30
707	A166	50f cr & multi	40	40
		Nos. 702-707 (6)	2.40	1.20

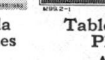

Giant Panda Eating Apples
A175

Table Tennis Player
A176

Designs: No. 709, Giant panda eating bamboo shoots. 10f, Two pandas (horiz.).

1963, Aug. 5 **Photo.** ***Perf. 11½x11***

Size: 28x38mm.

708	A175	8f pale bl & blk	5.00	15
709	A175	8f pale bl & blk	5.00	2.00

Size: 50x29mm. ***Perf. 11½***

710	A175	10f ol & blk	5.00	10

Price, imperf set $18.

1963, Sept. 10 **Engr.** ***Perf. 11½***

Design: No. 712, Trophies won by Chinese team.

711	A176	8f dk ol grn	9.00	70
712	A176	8f brown	9.00	5

27th World Table Tennis Championships.

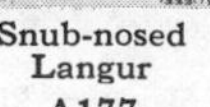

Snub-nosed Langur
A177

Jade-green Screen Mountain
A178

Designs: 10f, Two monkeys playing. 22f, Two monkeys grooming.

Photogravure

1963, Sept. 23 ***Perf. 11½x11***

713	A177	8f gray & multi	1.50	10
714	A177	10f gray & multi	1.50	10
715	A177	22f gray & multi	1.50	1.50

Price, imperf set $12.

Engraved and Photogravure

1963, Oct. 15 ***Perf. 11½***

Hwang Shan Landscapes (Yellow Mountains), Anhwei Province. Nos. 724–731 horizontal.

Multicolored

716	A178	4f *shown* (1)	1.50	20
717	A178	4f *'Guests Welcoming Pines'* (2)	1.50	35
718	A178	4f *Pines and Rock Behind the Sea* (3)	1.50	25
719	A178	4f *Terrace of Keeping Cool* (4)	1.50	10
720	A178	8f *Mount of Heavenly Capital* (5)	1.50	20
721	A178	8f *Mount of Scissors* (6)	1.50	20
722	A178	8f *Forest of Ten Thousand Pines* (7)	1.50	20
723	A178	8f *'Brush Blooming in Dream'* (8)	1.50	20
724	A178	10f *Mount of Lotus Flower* (9)	1.50	20
725	A178	10f *Cumulus Cloud over West Sea* (10)	1.50	20
726	A178	10f *Old Pines of Hwang Shan* (11)	1.50	20
727	A178	10f *'Watching the Clouds over West Sea'*	1.50	10
728	A178	20f *Mount of Stalagmites* (13)	1.50	30
729	A178	22f *'Stone Monkey Watching the Sea'* (14)	1.50	25
730	A178	30f *Forest of Lions* (15)	1.50	*4.00*
731	A178	50f *Three Fairy Tales of Pen Lai* (16)	1.50	20
		Nos. 716-731 (16)	24.00	*7.15*

Soccer Player
A179

Athletes and Banners—A180

Designs: No. 733, Discus, women's. No. 734, Diving, men's. No. 735, Gymnastics, women's.

Engraved and Photogravure

1963, Nov. 17 ***Perf. 11***

732	A179	8f gray, red & blk (1)	6.75	20
733	A179	8f gray, ultra & blk (2)	6.75	20
734	A179	8f lt grn, brn & blk (3)	6.75	20
735	A179	8f gray, lil rose & blk (4)	6.75	20

Photogravure ***Perf. 11½***

736	A180	10f red & multi (5)	6.75	40
		Nos. 732-736 (5)	33.75	1.20

Games of the Newly Emerging Forces, Djakarta.

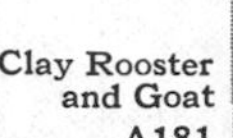

Clay Rooster and Goat
A181

Chinese Folk Toys: No. 738, Cloth camel. No. 739, Cloth tigers. No. 740, Clay ox and rider. No. 741, Cloth rabbit, wooden doll, clay roosters. No. 742, Straw rooster. No. 743, Cloth donkey and bird. No. 744, Clay lion. No. 745, Cloth tiger and tumbler doll.

1963, Dec. 10 Litho. *Perf. 11½*

Toys Multicolored; Without Gum

737	A181	4f bis (1)	25	8
738	A181	4f gray (4)	25	8
739	A181	4f lt bl (7)	25	8
740	A181	8f bis (2)	25	8
741	A181	8f gray (5)	25	8
742	A181	8f lt bl (8)	25	8
743	A181	10f bis (3)	25	8
744	A181	10f gray (6)	25	8
745	A181	10f lt bl (9)	25	8
		Nos. 737-745 (9)	2.25	72

Armed Vietnamese Family
A182

Flags of Cuba and China
A183

Design: No. 747, Militia with Vietnamese flag.

Photogravure

1963, Dec. 20 *Perf. 11½x11*

746	A182	8f tan, blk & red	2.00	15
747	A182	8f red & multi	2.00	25

Liberation of South Viet Nam.

1964, Jan. 1

Design: No. 749, Boy waving Cuban flag.

748	A183	8f red, yel, bl & ind	9.25	50
749	A183	8f multi	9.25	2.50

5th anniversary of the liberation of Cuba.

Woman Driving Tractor
A184

Women of the People's Commune: No. 751, harvesting. No. 752, picking cotton. No. 753, picking fruit. No. 754, reading book. No. 755, on guard duty.

1964, Mar. 8

750	A184	8f ol, pink & brn (1)	50	10
751	A184	8f brn yel & org (2)	50	10
752	A184	8f gray & multi (3)	50	10
753	A184	8f blk, org & bl (4)	50	10
754	A184	8f grn & multi (5)	50	10
755	A184	8f lil & multi (6)	50	10
		Nos. 750-755 (6)	3.00	60

Helpful notes abound in the "Information for Collectors" section at the front of this volume.

Chinese and African Men
A185

Design: No. 757, African drummer.

1964, Apr. 12 Photo. *Perf. 11*

756	A185	8f red & multi	1.25	10
757	A185	8f blk & dk brn	1.25	10

African Freedom Day.

Marx, Engels, Lenin and Stalin
A186

Design: No. 759, Banners and workers.

1964, May 1 *Perf. 11½*

758	A186	8f gold, red & blk	12.00	*5.00*
759	A186	8f gold, red & blk	12.00	*4.00*

Labor Day.

Orchard, Yenan
A187

Yenan, Shrine of the Chinese Revolution: No. 761, Central Auditorium, Yang Chia Ling. No. 762, Mao's office and residence. No. 763, Auditorium, Wang Chia Ping. No. 764, Border Region Assembly Hall. No. 765, Pagoda Hill and Bridge.

1964, July 1 Photo. *Perf. 11x11½*

760	A187	8f multi (1)	1.75	20
761	A187	8f multi (2)	1.75	20
762	A187	8f multi (3)	1.75	20
763	A187	8f multi (4)	1.75	20
764	A187	8f multi (5)	1.75	20
765	A187	52f multi (6)	1.75	85
		Nos. 760-765 (6)	10.50	1.85

Map and Flag of Viet Nam
A188

Alchemist's Glowing Crucible
A189

1964, July 20 *Perf. 11½*

766	A188	8f multi	18.00	1.25

Victory in South Viet Nam.

1964, Aug. 5 *Perf. 11½x11*

Position-in-set number in ( ).

Peonies in Natural Colors

767	A189	4f *shown* (1)	1.25	10
768	A189	4f *Night-shining jade* (2)	1.25	10
769	A189	8f *Pur. Kuo's cap* (3)	1.25	5
770	A189	8f *Chao pink* (4)	1.25	5
771	A189	8f *Yao yel* (5)	1.25	10
772	A189	8f *Twin beauty* (6)	1.25	5
773	A189	8f *Ice-veiled ruby* (7)	1.25	5
774	A189	10f *Gold-sprinkled Chinese ink* (8)	1.25	8
775	A189	10f *Cinnabar jar* (9)	1.25	8
776	A189	10f *Lan Tien jade* (10)	1.25	5
777	A189	10f *Imperial robe yel* (11)	1.25	8
778	A189	10f *Hu red* (12)	1.25	8
779	A189	20f *Pea green* (13)	1.25	1.50
780	A189	43f *Wei purple* (14)	1.25	1.50
781	A189	52f *Intoxicated celestial peach* (15)	1.25	1.50
		Nos. 767-781 (15)	18.75	5.37

Souvenir Sheet

Perf. 11½

Without Gum

782	A189	$2 *Glorious crimson & great gold pink*	90.00	60.00

No. 782 contains one stamp (48x59mm.). Bluish gray and silver border. Size: 77x136mm.

Wine Cup
A190

Grain Harvest
A191

Designs: Sacrificial bronze vessels of Yin dynasty, prior to 1050 B.C.

Engraved and Photogravure

1964, Aug. 25 *Perf. 11½x11*

Frames & Inscriptions Black, Vessels Multicolored

783	A190	4f *shown* (1)	1.00	60
784	A190	4f *Ku beaker* (2)	1.00	60
785	A190	8f *Kuang wine urn* (3)	1.00	8
786	A190	8f *Chia wine cup* (4)	1.00	8
787	A190	10f *Tsun wine vessel* (5)	1.00	10
788	A190	10f *Yu wine urn* (6)	1.00	10
789	A190	20f *Tsun wine vessel* (7)	1.00	20
790	A190	20f *Ceremonial cauldron* (8)	1.00	20
		Nos. 783-790 (8)	8.00	1.96

1964, Sept. 26 Photogravure

Designs: No. 792, Students planting trees. No. 793, Study period. No. 794, Scientific experimentation.

791	A191	8f multi (1)	40	10
792	A191	8f multi (2)	40	10
793	A191	8f multi (3)	40	10
794	A191	8f multi (4)	40	10

Youth helping in agriculture.

Marx, Engels, Trafalgar Square, London
A192

People with Banners
A193

1964, Sept. 28 *Perf. 11½*

795	A192	8f red, gold & red brn	35.00	14.00

Centenary of the First International.

1964, Oct. 1

Designs: No. 797, Gate of Heavenly Peace and Chinese flag. No. 798, People with banners, facing left.

796	A193	8f cr & multi (1)	7.00	25
797	A193	8f cr & multi (2)	7.00	25
798	A193	8f cr & multi (3)	7.00	25
a.		Souv. sheet of three	150.00	75.00
		Strip of three, Nos. 796-798	27.50	3.00

15th anniversary of the People's Republic. Nos. 796–798 printed se-tenant. No. 798a contains Nos. 796–798 as continuous design without separating perfs. Red and gold marginal inscription. Size: 153x114mm.

Oil Derricks
A194

Designs: 4f, Geological surveyors and truck (horiz.). 8f, "Christmas tree" and extraction accessories. 10f, Oil refinery. 20f, Tank cars (horiz.).

1964, Oct. 1

799	A194	4f lt bl & multi	9.50	10
800	A194	8f lt bl & multi	9.50	5
801	A194	8f lil & multi	9.50	15
802	A194	10f sl & multi	9.50	5
803	A194	20f brn & multi	9.50	*8.00*
		Nos. 799-803 (5)	47.50	*8.35*

Oil industry.

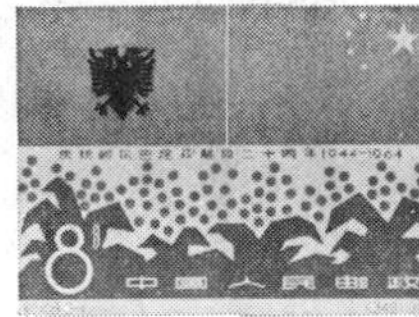

Albanian and Chinese Flags
A195

Design: 10f, Enver Hoxha and Albanian coat of arms.

1964, Nov. 29 *Perf. 11x11½*

804	A195	8f red & multi	13.00	*75*
805	A195	10f red, yel & blk	13.00	7.50

20th anniversary of the liberation of Albania.

Power Dam Construction
A196

Designs: No. 807, Installation of turbo-generator rotor. No. 808, Main dam. 20f, Pylon.

1964, Dec. 15 *Perf. 11½*

806	A196	4f multi	12.00	10
807	A196	8f multi	12.00	10
808	A196	8f multi	12.00	5
809	A196	20f multi	12.00	7.50

Hsin An Kiang Dam and hydroelectric power station.

Fertilizer Industry—A197

Designs (Chemical Industry): No. 811, Plastics. No. 812, Medicines. No. 813, Rubber. No. 814, Insecticides. No. 815, Industrial acids. No. 816, Industrial alkalies. No. 817, Synthetic fibers.

1964, Dec. 30 **Engr. & Photo.**

810	A197	8f red & blk (1)	50	15
811	A197	8f yel grn & blk (2)	50	10
812	A197	8f brn & blk (3)	50	10
813	A197	8f lil rose & blk (4)	50	10
814	A197	8f bl & blk (5)	50	10
815	A197	8f org & blk (6)	50	20
816	A197	8f vio & blk (7)	50	20
817	A197	8f brt grn & blk (8)	50	20
		Nos. 810-817 (8)	4.00	1.15

Mao Studying Map
A198

Mao Tse-tung
A199

Design: No. 819, Victory at Lushan Pass.

1965, Jan. 31 **Photo.** ***Perf. 11***

818	A198	8f red & multi	11.00	4.00
819	A198	8f red & multi	11.00	4.00

Perf. 11½x11

820	A199	8f gold & multi	11.00	4.00

Tsunyi Conference, 30th anniversary.

Conference Hall, Bandung—A200

Lenin
A201

1965, Apr. 18 ***Perf. 11½x11***

Design: No. 822, Asians and Africans applauding.

821	A200	8f cr & multi	25	7
822	A200	8f cr & multi	25	8

10th anniversary of the Bandung, Indonesia, Conference, Apr. 1955.

1965, Apr. 25 ***Perf. 11½***

823	A201	8f red, choc & sal	16.00	6.00

95th anniversary of the birth of Lenin.

Chinese Player
A202

1965, Apr. 25 ***Perf. 11½***

Emerald, Gold, Red & Black

824	A202	8f *shown* (1)	10	8
825	A202	8f *European woman* (2)	10	8
826	A202	8f *Chinese woman* (3)	10	8
827	A202	8f *European man* (4)	10	8

28th World Table Tennis Championships, Ljubljana, Jugoslavia, Apr. 15-25. Nos. 824-827 printed se-tenant.

Climbers on Mt. Minya Konka
A203

Marx and Lenin
A204

Mountain Climbers: No. 829, on Muztagh Ata. No. 830, on Mt. Jolmo Lungma (Mt. Everest). No. 831, Women camping on Kongur Tiubie Tagh. No. 832, on Shisha Pangma.

1965, May 25 **Engr. & Photo.**

828	A203	8f bl, blk & ol (1)	90	20
829	A203	8f bl, blk & ol (2)	90	20
830	A203	8f ultra, blk & gray (3)	90	20
831	A203	8f lt bl, blk & yel gray (4)	90	20
832	A203	8f ultra, blk & gray (5)	90	20
		Nos.828-832 (5)	4.50	1.00

Chinese mountaineering achievements, 1957-64.

1965, June 21 **Photo.** ***Perf. 11½x11***

833	A204	8f red, yel & blk	16.00	6.00

Postal Ministers' Congress, Peking.

Tseping Valley
A205

Chingkang Mountains, Cradle of the Chinese Revolution.

1965, July 1 ***Perf. 11x11½***

Multicolored

834	A205	4f *shown* (1)	2.50	10
835	A205	8f *San Wan Tsun* (2)	2.50	10
836	A205	8f *Octagon Bldg., Mao Ping* (3)	2.50	15
837	A205	8f *River and Bridge at Lung Shih* (4)	2.50	85
838	A205	8f *Ta Ching Tsun* (5)	2.50	8
839	A205	10f *Bridge across the Lung Yuan* (6)	2.50	8
840	A205	10f *Hwang Yang Mountain* (7)	2.50	2.00
841	A205	52f *Chingkang peaks* (8)	2.50	2.00
		Nos. 834-841 (8)	20.00	5.36

Soldiers with Books—A206

1965, Aug. 1 ***Perf. 11½***

Without Gum
Multicolored

842	A206	8f *shown* (1)	4.50	2.50
843	A206	8f *Soldiers reading Little Red Books* (2)	4.50	2.50
844	A206	8f *With shell and artillery* (3)	4.50	30
845	A206	8f *Rifle instruction* (4)	4.50	30
846	A206	8f *Sewing jacket* (5)	4.50	30
847	A206	8f *Bayonet charge*(6)	4.50	3.50
848	A206	8f *With banner* (7)	4.50	3.50
849	A206	8f *Military band* (8)	4.50	3.50
		Nos. 842-849 (8)	36.00	16.40

People's Liberation Army. Nos. 846-849 vertical.

"Welcome to Peking"
A207

Designs: No. 851, Chinese and Japanese young men. No. 852, Chinese and Japanese girls. No. 853, Musical entertainment. No. 854, Emblem of meeting.

1965, Aug. 25 ***Perf. 11½x11***

850	A207	4f yel & multi	60	10
851	A207	8f pink & multi	60	12
852	A207	8f multi	60	12
853	A207	10f multi	60	12
854	A207	22f lt bl & multi	60	25
		Nos. 850-854 (5)	3.00	71

Chinese-Japanese Youth Meeting, Peking.

North Vietnamese Soldier
A208

Peoples of the World—A209

Designs: No. 856, Soldier with guns. No. 857, Soldier giving victory salute.

1965, Sept. 2 ***Perf. 11½x11***

855	A208	8f red & red brn (1)	50	15
856	A208	8f red & blk (2)	50	15
857	A208	8f red & vio brn (3)	50	15

Perf. 11½

858	A209	8f blk & red (4)	50	15

Struggle of the people of Viet Nam.

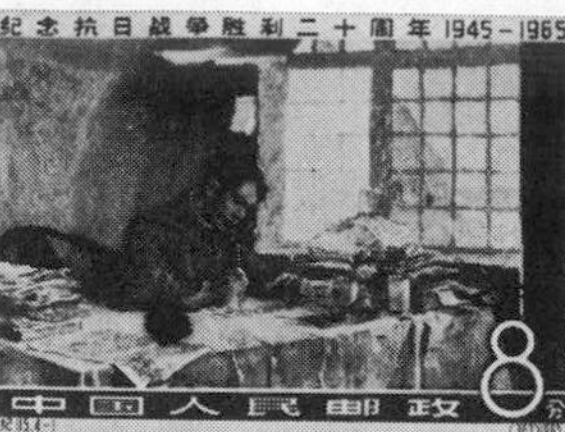

Mao Tse-tung at His Desk—A210

Crossing Yellow River
A211

Victory Monument
A212

Design: No. 862, Recruits in cart.

1965, Sept. 3 ***Perf. 11***

859	A210	8f red & multi (1)	5.75	2.00

Perf. 11x11½, 11½x11

860	A211	8f red & dk grn (2)	5.75	6.00
861	A212	8f red & dk brn (3)	5.75	50
862	A211	8f red & dk grn (4)	5.75	50

20th anniversary of victory over Japan.

Soccer
A213

National Games Opening Ceremonies—A214

Designs: No. 864, Archery. No. 865, Javelin. No. 866, Gymnastics. No. 867, Volleyball. No. 869, Bicycling. 20f, Diving. 22f, Hurdles. 30f, Weight lifting. 43f, Basketball.

Position-in-set number in ( ).

Perf. 11½x11, 11 (A214)

1965, Sept. 28

863	A213	4f red & multi (1)	4.50	20
864	A213	4f gray & multi (2)	4.50	20
865	A213	8f dk grn & multi (3)	4.50	20
866	A213	8f lil rose & multi (4)	4.50	20
867	A213	8f dp grn & multi (5)	4.50	20

868	A214	10f red, gold & multi (6)	4.50	20
869	A213	10f ol & multi (7)	4.50	20
870	A213	20f ultra & multi (8)	4.50	50
871	A213	22f org & multi (9)	4.50	60
872	A213	30f dp bl & multi (10)	4.50	1.00
873	A213	43f red lil & multi (11)	4.50	2.00
		Nos. 863-873 (11)	49.50	5.50

2nd National Games.

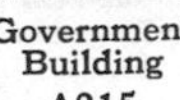

Government Building A215 — Textile Workers A216

Designs: 4f, 20f, as 1f. 1½f, 5f, 22f, Gate of Heavenly Peace. 2f, 8f, 30f, People's Hall. 3f, 10f, 50f, Military Museum.

1965-66 ***Perf. 11½x11***

Without Gum

874	A215	1f brown	10	5
875	A215	1½f red lil	10	30
876	A215	2f green	10	5
877	A215	3f bl grn	10	5
878	A215	4f brt bl	10	5
879	A215	5f vio brn ('66)	15	5
880	A215	8f rose red	15	5
881	A215	10f gray ol	15	5
882	A215	20f violet	15	6
883	A215	22f orange	75	6
884	A215	30f yel grn	75	5
885	A215	50f dp bl ('66)	75	60
		Nos. 874-885 (12)	3.35	1.42

1965, Nov. 30

Multicolored

886	A216	8f *shown* (1)	8.50	5
887	A216	8f *Machine shop* (2)	8.50	10
888	A216	8f *Welder* (3)	8.50	5
889	A216	8f *Students* (4)	8.50	1.50
890	A216	8f *Militia* (5)	8.50	1.50
		Nos. 886-890 (5)	42.50	3.20

Women workers.

Soccer—A217

Children's Sports: No. 892, Racing. No. 893, Tobogganing and skating. No. 894, Gymnastics. No. 895, Swimming. No. 896, Rifle practice. No. 897, Jumping rope. No. 898, Table tennis.

1966, Feb. 25 ***Perf. 11***

891	A217	4f emer & multi (1)	7	5
892	A217	4f yel brn & multi (2)	7	5
893	A217	8f bl & multi (3)	15	10
894	A217	8f yel & multi (4)	15	10
895	A217	8f grnsh bl & multi (5)	15	10
896	A217	8f grn & multi (6)	15	10
897	A217	10f org & multi (7)	20	12
898	A217	52f grnsh gray & multi (8)	1.10	60
		Nos. 891-898 (8)	2.04	1.22

Mobile Transformer A218

New Industrial Machinery: No. 900, Electron microscope (vert.). No. 901, Lathe. No. 902, Vertical boring and turning machine (vert.). No. 903, Gear-grinding machine. No. 904, Hydraulic press. No. 905, Milling machine. No. 906, Electron accelerator (vert.).

Perf. 11x11½, 11½x11

1966, Mar. 30 **Engr. and Photo.**

899	A218	4f yel & blk (1)	5.50	15
900	A218	8f blk & lt ultra (2)	5.50	15
901	A218	8f sal pink & blk (3)	5.50	15
902	A218	8f ol & blk (4)	5.50	15
903	A218	8f rose lil & blk (5)	5.50	15
904	A218	10f gray & blk (6)	5.50	1.00
905	A218	10f bl grn & blk (7)	5.50	1.00
906	A218	22f lil & blk (8)	5.50	1.00
		Nos. 899-906 (8)	44.00	3.75

Military and Civilian Workers A219

Women in Various Occupations: No. 908, Train conductor. No. 909, Red Cross worker. No. 910, Kindergarten teacher. No. 911, Road sweeper. No. 912, Hairdresser. No. 913, Bus conductor. No. 914, Traveling saleswoman. No. 915, Canteen worker. No. 916, Rural mail carrier.

1966, May 10 ***Perf. 11x11½***

907	A219	8f red & multi (1)	25	12
908	A219	8f pale grn & multi (2)	25	12
909	A219	8f yel & multi (3)	25	12
910	A219	8f grn & multi (4)	25	12
911	A219	8f sal & multi (5)	25	12
912	A219	8f pale bl & bl (6)	25	12
913	A219	8f yel & multi (7)	25	12
914	A219	8f tan & multi (8)	25	12
915	A219	8f yel grn & multi (9)	25	12
916	A219	8f grn & multi (10)	25	12
		Nos. 907-916 (10)	2.50	1.20

Statue "Thunder-storm" A220

Design: 22f, Open book and association emblem.

1966, June 27 **With Gum** ***Perf. 11***

917	A220	8f red & blk	1.00	10
918	A220	22f red, gold & yel	1.50	20

Afro-Asian Writers' Association Conference, Peking.

Sun Yat-sen A221

1966, Nov. 12 ***Perf. 11½x11***

919	A221	8f sep & lt buff	12.50	5.00

Birth centenary of Sun Yat-sen.

Athletes Holding Portrait of Mao A222

Two Women Athletes with Little Red Book A223

Designs: No. 921, Athletes holding Little Red Books. No. 923, Athletes reading Mao texts.

1966, Dec. 31 ***Perf. 11***

920	A222	8f red & multi (1)	7.50	2.50
921	A222	8f red & multi (2)	7.50	2.50

Perf. 11x11½

922	A223	8f bl & multi (3)	7.50	2.50
923	A223	8f bl & multi (4)	7.50	2.50

1st Athletic Games of the New Emerging Nations.

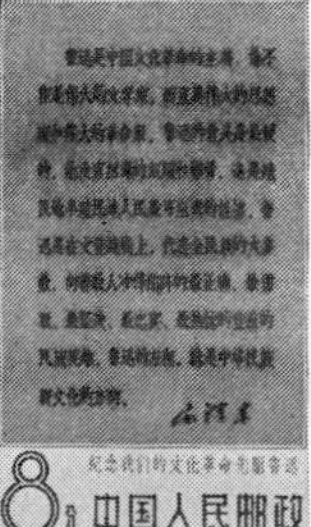

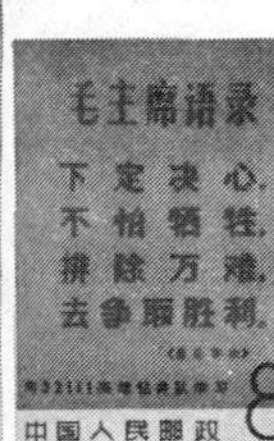

Appreciation of Lu Hsun by Mao A224 — "Be Resolute . . . ," by Mao Tse-tung A225

Designs: No. 925, Portrait of Lu Hsun. No. 926, Lu Hsun's handwriting (3 vert. rows).

Engr. & Photo.; Photo. (No. 925)

1966, Dec. 31 ***Perf. 11½***

924	A224	8f red & blk (1)	8.00	3.00
925	A224	8f red & multi (2)	8.00	3.00
926	A224	8f red & blk (3)	8.00	3.00

Lu Hsun, Revolutionary writer (1881-1936).

Perf. 11½x11, 11½ (No. 928)

1967, Mar. 10 **Photogravure**

Designs: No. 928, Drilling crew fighting natural gas fire (horiz.). No. 929, Attempt to close fire-engulfed valve.

Sizes: Nos. 927, 929, 26x38mm.; No. 928, 49x29mm.

927	A225	8f red, gold & blk	6.00	3.00
928	A225	8f brick red & blk	6.00	3.00
929	A225	8f brick red & blk	6.00	3.00

Heroic oil well firefighters.

Liu Ying-chun A226

1967, Mar. 25 ***Perf. 11½x11***

Multicolored

930	A226	8f *shown* (1)	5.00	2.00
931	A226	8f *With book by Mao* (2)	5.00	2.00
932	A226	8f *Holding bridle of horse* (3)	5.00	2.00
933	A226	8f *With film slide* (4)	5.00	2.00
934	A226	8f *Lecturing* (5)	5.00	2.00
935	A226	8f *Fatal attempt to stop runaway horse* (6)	5.00	2.00
		Nos. 930-935 (6)	30.00	12.00

In memory of soldier Liu Ying-chun, hero.

Industrial Growth—A227

Design: No. 937, Banners and people facing left: agricultural growth.

1967, Apr. 15 ***Perf. 11***

936	A227	8f red & multi	6.25	2.50
937	A227	8f red & multi	6.25	2.50

Third Five-Year Plan.

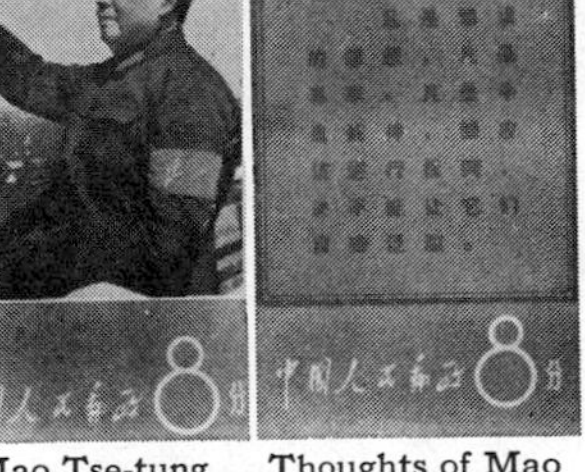

Mao Tse-tung A228 — Thoughts of Mao A229

1967, Apr. 20 ***Perf. 11½***

938	A228	8f red & multi	8.00	3.00

Red & Gold

939	A229	8f *39 characters*	8.00	3.00
940	A229	8f *50 characters*	8.00	3.00
941	A229	8f *39 characters in 6 lines*	8.00	3.00
942	A229	8f *53 characters*	8.00	3.00
943	A229	8f *46 characters*	8.00	3.00
		Strip of five	60.00	30.00

Gold & Red

944	A229	8f *41 characters*	8.00	3.00
945	A229	8f *49 characters*	8.00	3.00
946	A229	8f *35 characters*	8.00	3.00
947	A229	8f *22 characters*	8.00	3.00
948	A229	8f *29 characters*	8.00	3.00
		Strip of five	60.00	30.00
		Nos. 938-948 (11)	88.00	33.00

Thoughts of Mao Tse-tung. Nos. 939-943, Nos. 944-948 printed se-tenant in strips of 5 each.

No numbers appear below design on Nos. 938-1046.

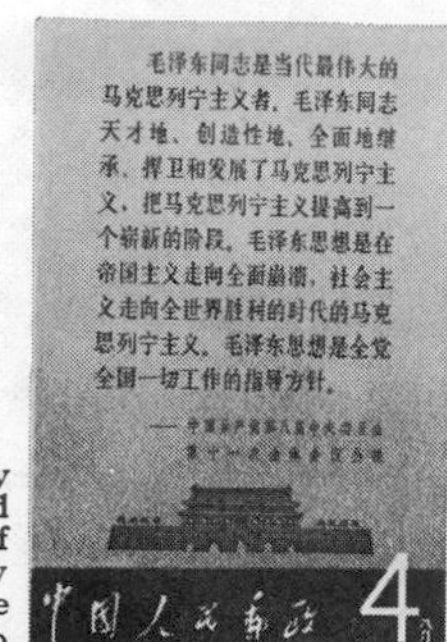

Text by Mao and Gate of Heavenly Peace
A230

Mao and Lin Piao
A231

Designs: No. 950, Mao and poem. No. 951, Mao among people of various races. No. 952, Mao facing left and Red Guards with books. No. 953, Mao with upraised right hand. No. 954, Mao leaning on rail (horiz.). 10f, Mao and Lin Piao in discussion (horiz.).

Engraved and Photogravure

1967 ***Perf. 11x11½***

Size: 36x56mm.

949	A230	4f yel, red & mar	8.00	2.00

Photogravure

950	A230	8f yel, brn, & red	8.00	2.00
951	A230	8f yel, red & multi	8.00	2.00
952	A230	8f yel, red & multi	8.00	2.00

Perf. 11

Size: 36x50, 50x36mm.

953	A231	8f blk & multi	8.00	2.00
954	A231	8f blk & multi	42.50	17.00
955	A231	8f lt bl & multi	15.00	17.00
956	A231	10f blk & multi	32.50	17.00
		Nos. 949-956 (8)	130.00	61.00

"Mao Tse-tung Our Great Teacher."
Issue dates: Nos. 949-953, May 1; Nos. 954-956, Sept. 20.

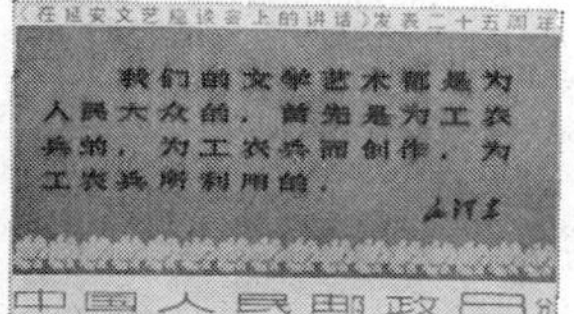

Mao Text (4 lines)—A232

Parade of Supporters—A233

Design: No. 958, Mao text (5 lines).

Engraved and Photogravure

1967, May 23 ***Perf. 11½***

957	A232	8f blk, red & yel	12.00	5.50
958	A232	8f blk, red & yel	12.00	5.50

Photogravure ***Perf. 11***

959	A233	8f multi	12.00	5.50

25th anniversary of Mao Tse-tung's "Talks on Literature and Art" in Yenan.

Mao Tse-tung
A234

1967 **Engraved** ***Perf. 11***

960	A234	4f brown	20.00	7.50
961	A234	8f carmine	20.00	7.50
962	A234	35f dk brn	20.00	7.50
963	A234	43f vermilion	20.00	7.50
964	A234	52f carmine	20.00	7.50
		Nos. 960-964 (5)	100.00	37.50

46th anniversary of Chinese Communist Party.
Issue dates: 8f, July 1, others September.

Mao, "Sun of the Revolution"—A235

Design: No. 966, Mao and people of various races.

1967, Oct. 1 ***Perf. 11½x11***

965	A235	8f multi	13.00	6.50
966	A235	8f multi	13.00	6.50

18th anniversary of the People's Republic of China.

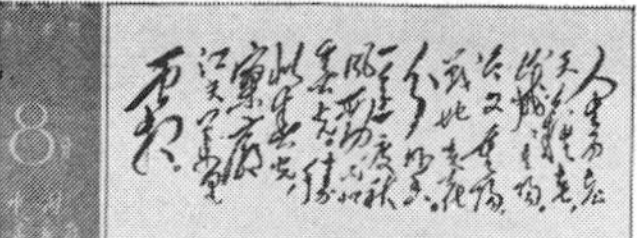

"September 9"—A236

"Huichang" A237 "Peitaiho" A238

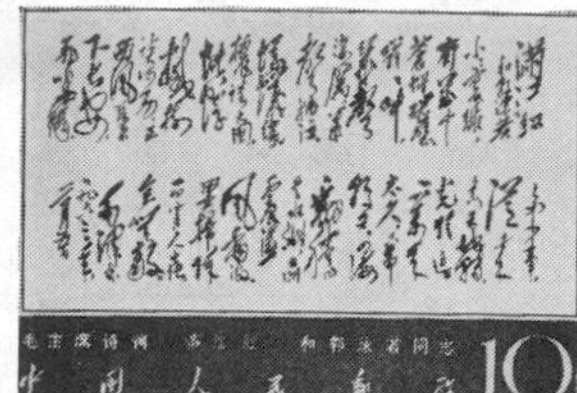

Reply to Comrade Kuo Mo-jo—A239

Mao Tse-tung Writing Poems—A240

Designs (Poems by Mao): No. 967, "The Long March." No. 968, "Liupanshan." No. 969, shown. No. 970, "The Cave of the Fairies." No. 971, "Snow." No. 972, "Lushan Pass." Nos. 973-974, shown. No. 975, "Conquest of Nanking." No. 976, "The Yellow Crane Pavilion." No. 977, "Swimming." No. 978, shown. No. 979, "Changsha."

1967-68 **Photogravure** ***Perf. 11***

Red and Yellow Frame; Poem Written in Black

Size: 79x18½mm.

967	A236	4f *9 characters, UL panel* ('68)	12.00	6.00
968	A236	4f *11 characters, UL panel* ('68)	12.00	6.00

Size: 60x24mm. ***Perf. 11½***

969	A236	8f *shown, 10 characters in UL panel*	7.00	2.00
970	A236	8f *21 characters in UL panel*	7.00	2.00
971	A236	8f *11 characters in UL panel*	12.00	6.00
972	A236	8f *9 characters in UL panel*	12.00	6.00

Size: 29x50mm.

973	A237	8f *shown*	7.00	2.00
974	A238	8f *shown*	12.00	6.00
975	A238	8f *3 rows in bottom panel*	7.00	2.00
976	A238	8f *2 rows in bottom panel*	12.00	6.00

Size: 52x38mm. ***Perf. 11***

977	A239	8f *3 short vert. rows, at left of poem*	12.00	6.00
978	A239	10f *shown*	12.00	6.00
979	A239	10f *undivided text*	7.00	2.00
980	A240	10f red, yel & multi	9.00	6.00
		Nos. 967-980 (14)	140.00	64.00

Poems by Mao Tse-tung.
Issue dates: Nos. 969-970, 980, Oct. 1, 1967; Nos. 973-974, 977, May 20, 1968; others July 20, 1968.

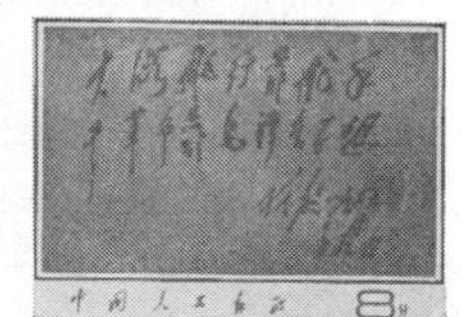

Lin Piao's Epigram on Mao Tse-tung
A241

1967, Dec. 26 Photo. ***Perf. 11x11½***

981	A241	8f red & gold	17.50	8.00

Mao and Parade of Artists—A242

"Raid on White Tiger Regiment"
A243

"Red Detachment of Women"—A244

1968 ***Perf. 11½x11; 11 (983, 990)***

Multicolored

982	A242	8f *shown (56x36mm)*	5.00	2.00
983	A242	8f *"The Red Lantern" (vert.)*	5.00	2.00
984	A243	8f *shown*	5.00	2.00
985	A243	8f *"Shachiapang" (women & soldier)*	5.00	2.00
986	A243	8f *"On the Dock"*	5.00	2.00
987	A243	8f *"Taking Bandits' Fort"if*	5.00	2.00
988	A244	8f *shown*	10.00	7.00
989	A244	8f *"The White-haired Girl"*	10.00	7.00
990	A242	8f *Mao with Orchestra & Chorus (50x36mm)*	8.00	5.00
		Nos. 982-990 (9)	58.00	31.00

Mao's direction for revolutionary literature and art.
Issue dates: Nos. 982-987, Jan. 30; Nos. 988-990, May 1.

"Unite still more closely. . ."—A245

1968, May 31 **Photo.** ***Perf. 11***

991	A245	8f red, gold & red brn	22.50	8.00

Mao Tse-tung's statement of support of Afro-Americans.

Statement about Cultural Revolution
A246

Directives of Chairman Mao: No. 993, Experiences of Revolutionary Committee. No. 994, Leadership role of Revolutionary Committee. No. 995, Basic principle of reform. No. 996, Purpose of Cultural Revolution.

1968, July 20 Photo. *Perf. 11½*
Red, Yellow & Brown

992	A246	8f *shown*	15.00	4.00
993	A246	8f *5 lines over signature*	15.00	4.00
994	A246	8f *4½ lines over signature*	15.00	4.00
995	A246	8f *4 lines over signature*	15.00	4.00
996	A246	8f *8 lines over signature*	15.00	4.00
		Strip of five	125.00	90.00

Printed se-tenant in horizontal strips of 5 within sheet.

Lin Piao's Statement, July 26, 1965
A247

1968, Aug. 1 Engr. and Photo.

997	A247	8f red, gold & blk	7.50	5.00

41st anniversary of the Chinese People's Liberation Army.

Mao Tse-tung Going to An Yuan, 1921
A248

1968, Aug. 1 *Perf. 11x11½*

998	A248	8f multi	9.00	6.00

Shade varieties include varying amount of red in clouds.

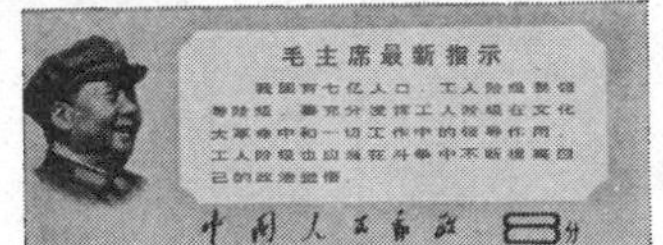

Directive of Chairman Mao—A249

1968, Nov. 30 *Perf. 11½*

999	A249	8f red & blk brn	25.00	8.00

China Map, Worker, Farmer and Soldier
A249a

1968, Nov. Photo. *Perf. 11½x11*

999A	A249a	8f red, bl & bis	*4,500.*	*2,500.*

Map inscribed: "The entire nation is red." Issued in Canton and quickly withdrawn because Taiwan appears white instead of red.

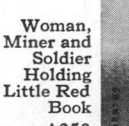

Woman, Miner and Soldier Holding Little Red Book
A250

1968, Dec. 26 *Perf. 11x11½*

1000	A250	8f multi	12.00	1.50

Yangtze Bridge, Nanking
A251

Road across Bridge—A252

Designs: No. 1003, Side view. 10f, Aerial view.

Litho., *Perf. 11½x11 (A251)*;
Photo., *Perf. 11½ (A252)*

1969 Without Gum

1001	A251	4f multi	3.00	2.00
1002	A252	8f multi	3.00	4.00
1003	A252	8f multi	3.00	2.00
1004	A251	10f multi	3.00	2.00

Inauguration of Yangtze Bridge at Nanking on Dec. 29, 1968.

Singer and Pianist
A253

Designs (Piano Music from the Opera, "The Red Lantern"): No. 1006, Woman singer and pianist.

1969, Aug. Photo. *Perf. 11x11½*
Without Gum

1005	A253	8f multi	3.00	2.00
1006	A253	8f multi	3.00	2.00

Harvest
A254

1969, Oct.
Multicolored

1007	A254	4f *shown*	2.00	2.00
a.		Brown omitted	20.00	10.00
1008	A254	8f *Two harvesters*	2.00	2.00
1009	A254	8f *Harvesters with Little Red Books*	5.50	3.00
1010	A254	10f *Red Cross worker examining baby*	2.00	1.00

Agriculture students.

Armed Forces and Slogan—A255

Guarding the Coast—A256

Designs: No. 1013, 43f, Snow patrol (vert.).

1969, Oct. *Perf. 11½*

1011	A255	8f red & multi	2.50	*2.00*
a.		Bayonets omitted	90.00	50.00
1012	A256	8f bl & multi	2.50	*2.00*
1013	A256	8f bl & multi	2.50	*2.00*
1014	A256	35f blk & multi	2.50	*3.00*
1015	A256	43f blk & multi	2.50	*3.00*
		Nos. 1011-1015 (5)	12.50	*12.00*

Defense of Chen Pao-tao (Damansky Islands) in Ussuri River.

Farm Woman
A257

Designs: 8f, Foundry worker. 10f, Soldier.

1969, Dec. *Perf. 10; 11½* (*1017)
Without Gum

1016	A257	4f ver & dk pur	50	1.25
1017	A257	8f ver & dk brn	50	1.25
1018	A257	10f ver & blk	50	1.25

Perforation

Nos. 1016–1018 and some succeeding issues bear two kinds of perforation: clean (Peking) and rough (Shanghai).

Building

A258

Communist Party Building, Shanghai
A259

Agriculture Building, Canton
A260

Foundry Worker
A261

Two types of 8f Gate of Heavenly Peace:
I. Strong, definite halo around sun.
II. Halo missing, white shades gradually into red.

1969-72 Photo. *Perf. 10, 11½*
Multicolored; Without Gum

1019	A258	1f *shown*	5	*25*
1020	A259	1½f *shown*	1.00	1.00
a.		Perf. 11½	6.00	5.00
1021	A260	2f *shown*	5	*15*
1022	A260	3f *1929 Party Day House, PuTien*	8	5
1023	A260	4f *Mao's Home and Office, Yunnan*	10	*20*
1024	A261	5f *Woman Tractor Driver*	1.50	75
1025	A260	8f *Gate of Heavenly Peace*, type II	1.50	50
a.		Type I	1.50	60
1026	A259	8f *Heroes Monument*	1.50	1.00
a.		Perf. 11½	5.00	4.00
1027	A260	8f *Pagoda Hill, Yenan*	1.50	5.00
1028	A260	8f *Gate of Heavenly Peace* (*no sun*)	15	10
1029	A260	10f *Monument, Tsu Ping*	20	*30*
1030	A259	20f *Conference Hall, Tsunyi*	1.50	2.00
a.		Perf. 11½	4.00	4.00
1031	A260	20f *Highway* ('72)	30	30
1032	A260	22f *Shao Shan Village, Birthplace of Mao*	35	*50*
1033	A260	35f *Conference Hall*	50	50
1034	A260	43f *Chingkang Peaks*	60	50
1035	A259	50f *as 4f, different view*	3.00	2.00
1036	A260	52f *People's Hall, Peking*	80	50
1037	A261	$1 *shown* ('70)	3.00	4.00
a.		Perf. 11		
b.		Perf. 11½		
		Nos. 1019-1037 (19)	17.68	*19.60*

Kin Hsün-hua **Mounted Patrol**
A262 **A263**

1970, Jan. Without Gum *Perf. 11½*

1045	A262	8f red & gray brn	4.00	4.00
a.		8f red & blk	4.00	*8.00*

Death of Kin Hsün-hua in Kirin border flood.

1970, Aug. 1 Without Gum

1046	A263	8f yel grn & multi	4.00	4.00

43rd anniversary of the People's Liberation Army.

Beginning with No. 1047 commemorative stamps carry a cumulative number in parenthesis at lower left and the year at lower right. Where such numbers help to identify, they are quoted in parenthesis.

Cpl. Yang Tse-jung
A264

Ensemble
A265

1970, Aug. 1

Perf. 11½x11, 11x11½

1047	A264	8f *shown* (1)	70	70
1048	A264	8f *Armed guards* (2)	70	70
1049	A264	8f *Yang leaping through forest* (3)	70	70
1050	A265	8f *shown* (4)	70	70
1051	A265	8f *Yang in folk costume* (5)	70	70
1052	A265	8f *Four actors* (6)	50	50
		Nos. 1047-1052 (6)	4.00	4.00

Scenes from opera "Taking Tiger Mountain by Strategy." Nos. 1048, 1052, horizontal.

Frontier Guard
A266

1971, Jan. Litho. *Perf. 11½*

Without Gum

1053	A266	4f multi	2.00	75
a.		Perf. 10	60	1.00
b.		Perf. 11½x10	5.00	
c.		Perf. 10x11½	5.00	

Banner of the Commune
A267

Street Battle, Paris, 1871
A268

Designs: 10f, Proclamation of the Commune. 22f, Rally.

1971, Mar. 18 Litho. and Engr.

Perf. 11½x11, 11x11½

1054	A267	4f sal & multi	1.50	1.50
1055	A268	8f ver, pink & brn	1.50	1.50
1056	A267	10f ver, pink & dk brn	1.50	1.50
1057	A268	22f ver, pink & dk brn	1.50	1.50

Centenary of the Paris Commune.

Redrawn Building Type of 1961

Designs: 2f, 3f, August 1 building, Nanchang. 4f, 52f, Gate of Heavenly Peace, Peking. 10f, 20f, Pagoda Hill, Yenan.

1971 Litho. *Perf. 11x11½*

Size: 21x16mm.

1059	A152	2f sl grn	2.00	3.00
1060	A152	3f sepia	2.00	3.00
1061	A152	4f brt pink	2.00	3.00
1062	A152	10f brt rose lil	2.00	3.00
1063	A152	20f dk bl grn	2.00	3.00
1064	A152	52f orange	2.00	3.00
		Nos. 1059-1064 (6)	12.00	18.00

Paper of Nos. 1059–1064 is white. That of Nos. 647–654 is toned.

Communist Party Building, Shanghai—A269

People and Factories
A270

Designs: No. 1068, Peasant Movement Training Institute. No 1069, Ching Kang Peaks. No. 1070, Conference Building, Tsunyi. No. 1071, Pagoda Hill, Yenan. No. 1073, People and People's Hall, Peking. No. 1074, People and Pagoda Hill, Yenan. 22f, Gate of Heavenly Peace, Peking.

Red and Gold Frame

1971, July 1 Photo. *Perf. 11½*

1067	A269	4f ver (12)	40	40
1068	A269	4f brt grn (13)	40	40
1069	A269	8f grnsh bl & red (14)	40	40
1070	A269	8f ol blk (15)	40	40
1071	A269	8f bis, grn & red (16)	40	40
1072	A270	8f yel, red & multi (18)	40	40
1073	A270	8f yel, red & multi (19)	40	40
1074	A270	8f yel, red & multi (20)	40	40
a.		Strip of 3 (#1072-1074)	1.50	1.50
1075	A269	22f red, gold & brn (17)	40	40
		Nos. 1067-1075 (9)	3.60	3.60

50th anniversary of the Chinese Communist Party. Nos. 1072–1074 printed se-tenant with continuous design.

Chinese Welcome
A271

Enver Hoxha
A272

Designs: No. 1077, Chinese and African players. No. 1078, Chinese and African girl players. 43f, Games' emblem.

1971, Nov. 3 Litho. *Perf. 11½*

1076	A271	8f lil rose & multi	20	20
1077	A271	8f lt yel & multi	20	20
1078	A271	8f dk grn & multi	20	20
1079	A271	43f grn, gold & org	1.00	1.00

Afro-Asian Table Tennis Games, Peking.

1971, Nov. 3 Photo. *Perf. 11*

Designs: No. 1081, Party's birthplace. No. 1082, Albanian flag. 52f, Albanian partisans (horiz.).

1080	A272	8f Prus bl & multi	3.00	3.00
1081	A272	8f buff & multi	3.00	3.00
1082	A272	8f red, yel & multi	3.00	3.00
1083	A272	52f lt bl & multi	3.00	3.00

30th anniversary of the founding of Albanian Communist Party.

Yenan Pagoda and 1942 Meeting House
A273

1972, May 23 Photogravure *Perf. 11*

Cumulative numbers in parenthesis.

Multicolored

1084	A273	8f *shown* (33)	75	75
1085	A273	8f *Uniformed choir* (34)	75	75
1086	A273	8f *"Brother & Sister"* (35)	75	75
1087	A273	8f *Outdoor performance* (36)	75	75
1088	A273	8f *"The Red Signal Lantern"* (37)	75	75
1089	A273	8f *Dancer from "The Red Company of Women"* (38)	75	75
		Nos. 1084-1089 (6)	4.50	4.50

30th anniversary of the publication of the Discussions on Literature and Art at the Yenan Forum.

Various Ball Games—A274

Workers' Gymnastics
A275

1972, June 10 Multicolored

1090	A274	8f *shown* (39)	20	20
1091	A275	8f *shown* (40)	20	20
1092	A275	8f *Tug of war* (41)	20	20
1093	A275	8f *Mountain climbers and tents* (42)	20	20
1094	A275	8f *Children diving & swimming* (43)	20	20
		Nos. 1090-1094 (5)	1.00	1.00

10th anniversary of Mao Tse-tung's edict on physical culture.

Ocean Freighter Fenglei—A276

1972, July 10 Photo. *Perf. 11½*

Multicolored

1095	A276	8f *shown* (29)	50	50
1096	A276	8f *Tanker Taching No. 30* (30)	50	50
1097	A276	8f *Cargo-passenger ship Changzeng* (31)	50	50
1098	A276	8f *Dredger Xienfeng* (32)	50	50

Table Tennis Players' Welcome
A277

Perf. 11½x11, 11x11½

1972, Sept. 2

1099	A277	8f *Championship emblem* (vert.) (45)	25	14
1100	A277	8f *shown* (46)	25	14
1101	A277	8f *Table tennis* (47)	25	14
1102	A277	22f *Women from different countries* (vert.) (48)	1.00	65

First Asian table tennis championships.

Wang Chin-hsi
A278

Workers on Cliffs along Canal
A279

Engraved and Photogravure

1972, Dec. 25 *Perf. 11½x11*

1103	A278	8f multi (44)	75	75

Wang Chin-hsi, the Iron Man, fighter for the working class.

1972, Dec. 30

Designs: No. 1105, Canal flowing through tunnel. No. 1106, Bridge. No. 1107, Canal along cliffs.

1104	A279	8f multi (49)	25	25
1105	A279	8f multi (50)	25	25
1106	A279	8f multi (51)	25	25
1107	A279	8f multi (52)	25	25

Construction of Red Flag Canal, Linhsien county, Honan.

Giant Panda
A280

Woman Coal Miner
A281

Designs: Pandas in various positions. The 8f stamps are horizontal.

Perf. 11½x11, 11x11½

1973, Jan. 15 Photogravure

Designs in Black and Red

1108	A280	4f lt yel grn (61)	1.50	1.50
1109	A280	8f buff (59)	1.50	1.50
1110	A280	8f lt tan (60)	1.50	1.50
1111	A280	10f pale grn (58)	1.50	1.50
1112	A280	20f pale bl gray (57)	1.50	1.50
1113	A280	43f pale lil (62)	1.50	1.50
		Nos. 1108-1113 (6)	9.00	9.00

1973, Mar. 8 Photo. **Perf. 11½x11**

Multicolored

1114	A281	8f *shown* (63)	30	30
1115	A281	8f *Committee member* (64)	30	30
1116	A281	8f *Telephone line worker* (65)	30	30

International Working Women's Day. Designs are after paintings from an exhibition for 30th anniversary of the Yenan Forum on Literature and Art.

Dancing Girl A282

Tournament Emblem A283

1973, June 1 Photo. **Perf. 11**

Yellow & Multicolored

1117	A282	8f *shown* (86)	20	20
1118	A282	8f *Musician, boy* (87)	20	20
1119	A282	8f *Girl with scarf* (88)	20	20
1120	A282	8f *Boy with tambourine* (89)	20	20
1121	A282	8f *Girl with drum* (90)	20	20
		Nos. 1117-1121 (5)	1.00	1.00

Nos. 1117–1121 printed se-tenant.

1973, Aug. 25 Photo. **Perf. 11½**

Designs: No. 1123, Visitors from Asia, Africa and Latin America arriving by plane. No. 1124, Woman player. 22f, African, Asian and Latin American women.

1122	A283	8f multi (91)	30	30
1123	A283	8f multi (92)	30	30
1124	A283	8f multi (93)	30	30
1125	A283	22f multi (94)	30	30

Asian, African and Latin American Table Tennis Friendship Invitational Tournament.

The White-haired Girl A284

Designs: Scenes from the ballet "The White-haired Girl." Nos. 1126 and 1129 vertical.

1973, Sept. 25 Photo. **Perf. 11½**

1126	A284	8f multi (53)	35	35
1127	A284	8f multi (54)	35	35
1128	A284	8f multi (55)	35	35
1129	A284	8f multi (56)	35	35

Fair Building, Canton—A285

1973, Oct. 15 Photo. **Perf. 11**

1130	A285	8f multi (95)	60	60

Export Commodities Fall Fair, Canton.

Teapot with Blue Phoenix Design A286

Designs: No. 1132, Silver pot with horse design. No. 1133, Black pottery horse. No. 1134, Woman, clay figurine. No. 1135, Carved stone pillar base. No. 1136, Galloping bronze horse. No. 1137, Bronze inkwell (toad). No. 1138, Bronze lamp, Chang Hsin Palace. No. 1139, Bronze tripod. No. 1140, Square bronze pot. 20f, Bronze wine vessel. 52f, Painted red clay tripod.

1973, Nov. 20 **Perf. 11½**

1131	A286	4f ol bis & multi (66)	20	20
1132	A286	4f ver & multi (67)	20	20
1133	A286	8f yel grn & multi (68)	20	20
1134	A286	8f brt rose & multi (69)	20	20
1135	A286	8f lt vio & multi (70)	20	20
1136	A286	8f yel bis & multi (71)	20	20
1137	A286	8f lt bl & multi (72)	20	20
1138	A286	8f gray & multi (73)	20	20
1139	A286	10f yel bis & multi (74)	20	20
1140	A286	10f dp org & multi (75)	20	20
1141	A286	20f lil & multi (76)	40	40
1142	A286	52f grn & multi (77)	1.00	1.00
		Nos. 1131-1142 (12)	3.40	3.40

Excavated works of art.

Marginal Markings

Marginal inscriptions on stamps of 1974 start at lower left with "J" for commemoratives and "T" for "special issues," followed by three numbers indicating (a) set sequence for the year, (b) total of stamps in set, and (c) number of stamp within set. At right appears the year date. Listings include the "c" number parenthetically.

Woman Gymnast A287

Designs: No. 1144, Gymnast on rings. No. 1145, Aerial split over balance beam, woman. No. 1146, Gymnast on parallel bars. No. 1147, Uneven bars, woman. No. 1148, Gymnast on horse.

1974, Jan. 1 Photo. **Perf. 11½x11**

1143	A287	8f lt grn & multi (1)	25	25
1144	A287	8f lt vio & multi (2)	25	25
1145	A287	8f lt bl & multi (3)	25	25
1146	A287	8f sal & multi (4)	25	25
1147	A287	8f yel & multi (5)	25	25
1148	A287	8f lil rose & multi (6)	25	25
		Nos. 1143-1148 (6)	1.50	1.50

Girls Twirling Bamboo Diabolos—A288

Designs: No. 1149, Lion Dance (vert.). No. 1150, Handstand on chairs (vert.). No. 1152, Men balancing jar. No. 1153, Plate spinning (vert.). No. 1154, Twirling umbrella (vert.).

1974, Jan. 21 **Perf. 11**

1149	A288	8f brn & multi (1)	25	25
1150	A288	8f Prus bl & multi (2)	25	25
1151	A288	8f lil & multi (3)	25	25
1152	A288	8f dl bl & multi (4)	25	25
1153	A288	8f ol grn & multi (5)	25	25
1154	A288	8f gray & multi (6)	25	25
		Nos. 1149-1154 (6)	1.50	1.50

Traditional acrobatics.

Shao Shan A289

Transportation by Railroad A290

Designs: 1½f, Site of 1st National Communist Party Congress. 2f, Peasant Movement Institute, Kwangchow. 3f, Headquarters of Nanchang Uprising. 4f, Great Hall of the People, Peking. 5f, View of Wen Chia Shih. 8f, Tien An Men. 10f, Tzeping in Chingkang Mountains. 20f Site of Kutien Meeting. 22f, Tsunyi Conference site. 35f, Yenan (bridge). 43f, Hsi Pai Ho, Communist Party meeting site. 50f, Fairy Cave, Lushan. 52f, Monument to People's Heroes. $2, Trucks on mountain road.

1974 Litho. **Perf. 11**

Without Gum

1163	A289	1f sl grn & pale grn	5	5
1164	A289	1½f car & buff	5	50
1165	A289	2f dk bl & pale grn	5	5
1166	A289	3f dk ol & yel	5	5
1167	A289	4f red & yel	8	8
1168	A289	5f brn & lt yel	10	10
1169	A289	8f dl mag & buff	15	15
1170	A289	10f bl & pink	20	20
1171	A289	20f dk red & buff	40	40
1172	A289	22f vio & lt yel	45	45
1173	A289	35f mar & lt yel	60	60
1174	A289	43f red brn & buff	85	*1.50*
1175	A289	50f dk bl & pink	*5.00*	*1.00*
1176	A289	52f sep & buff	1.00	1.00

Photogravure & Engraved

1177	A290	$1 multi	2.00	75
1178	A290	$2 multi	4.00	1.25
		Nos. 1163-1178 (16)	*15.03*	*8.13*

Capital Stadium A290a

Design: 8f, Hotel Peking.

1974, Dec. 1 Photo. **Perf. 11**

Without Gum

1179	A290a	4f blk & yel grn	15	*20*
1180	A290a	8f blk & ultra	25	25

"Veteran Secretary" A291

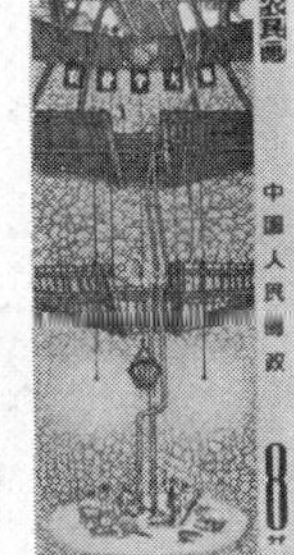

Well Diggers A292

Designs: Nos. 1183–1186 horizontal.

1974, Apr. 20 Photo. **Perf. 11**

Multicolored

1181	A291	8f *shown* (1)	30	30
1182	A292	8f *shown* (2)	30	30
1183	A291	8f *Spring hoeing* (3)	30	30
1184	A291	8f *Farmers* (4)	30	30
1185	A292	8f *Farm* (5)	30	30
1186	A291	8f *Bumper crops* (6)	30	30
		Nos. 1181-1186 (6)	1.80	1.80

Paintings by farmers of Huhsien County, shown at exhibition in Peking.

Mailman on Motorcycle—A293

1974, May 15 Photo. **Perf. 11**

Multicolored

1187	A293	8f *shown* (1)	45	45
1188	A293	8f *People of the world* (2)	45	45
1189	A293	8f *Great Wall* (3)	45	45

Centenary of the Universal Postal Union.

Barefoot Doctor Inocculating Children—A294

Designs (Barefoot Doctors): No. 1191, Crossing stream at night to reach patient (vert.). No. 1192, Gathering herbs (vert.). No. 1193, Acupuncture treatment for farmer in the field.

Perf. 11x11½, 11½x11

1974, June 26 Photogravure

1190	A294	8f multi (82)	25	25
1191	A294	8f multi (83)	25	25
1192	A294	8f multi (84)	25	25
1193	A294	8f multi (85)	25	25

Steel Worker Wang Chin-hsi—A295

1974, Sept. 30 Photo. *Perf. 11*

Designs: No. 1195, Workers studying Mao's writings around campfire. No. 1196, Drilling for oil in winter. No. 1197, Scientific industrial management. No. 1198, Oil derricks and farms. Numbered T.4.

1194	A295	8f multi (5-1)	25	25
1195	A295	8f multi (5-2)	25	25
1196	A295	8f multi (5-3)	25	25
1197	A295	8f multi (5-4)	25	25
1198	A295	8f multi (5-5)	25	25
		Nos. 1194-1198 (5)	1.25	1.25

The workers of Taching as examples of achievement.

Members of Tachai Commune—A296

Designs: No. 1200, Farmers leveling mountains and fields in winter. No. 1201, Scientific farming. No. 1202, Trucks carrying surplus harvest. No. 1203, Young workers with banner. Numbered T.5.

1974, Sept. 30

1199	A296	8f multi (5-1)	30	30
1200	A296	8f multi (5-2)	30	30
1201	A296	8f multi (5-3)	30	30
1202	A296	8f multi (5-4)	30	30
1203	A296	8f multi (5-5)	30	30
		Nos. 1199-1203 (5)	1.50	1.50

The farmers of Tachai as examples of achievement.

Arms of Republic and Members of Ethnic Grops—A297

Taching Steel Worker A298

Designs: No. 1206, Tachai farm woman. No. 1207, Soldier, planes and ships. Numbered J.3.

1974, Oct. 1

1204	A297	8f multi (1-1)	1.25	1.25
1205	A298	8f multi (3-1)	30	30
1206	A298	8f multi (3-2)	30	30
1207	A298	8f multi (3-3)	30	30

People's Republic of China, 25th anniversary. Nos. 1205–1207 printed se-tenant.

Export Commodities Fair Building, Canton—A299

1974, Oct. 15

1208	A299	8f multi	50	50

Chinese Export Commodities Fair, Canton.

Guerrillas' Monument, Permet, Albania A300

Albanian Patriots and Coat of Arms A301

1974, Nov. 29 Photo. *Perf. 11½x11*

1209	A300	8f multi	1.50	1.50
1210	A301	8f multi	1.50	1.50

Albania's liberation, 30th anniversary.

Water-cooled Generator—A302

Designs: No. 1212, Motorized rice sprouts transplanter. No. 1213, Universal cylindrical grinding machine. No. 1214, Open-air rock drill (vert.). All dated 1973.

Photogravure and Engraved

1974, Dec. 23 *Perf. 11*

1211	A302	8f vio & multi (78)	35	35
1212	A302	8f yel grn & multi (79)	35	35
1213	A302	8f ver & multi (80)	35	35
1214	A302	8f bl & multi (81)	35	35

Industrial products.

Congress Delegates—A303

Designs: No. 1216, Red flags, constitution and flowers. No. 1217, Worker, farmer and soldier, agriculture and industry. Numbered J.5.

1975, Jan. 25 Photo. *Perf. 11½*

1215	A303	8f gold & multi (3-1)	50	50
1216	A303	8f gold & multi (3-2)	50	50
1217	A303	8f gold & multi (3-3)	50	50

Fourth National People's Congress, Peking.

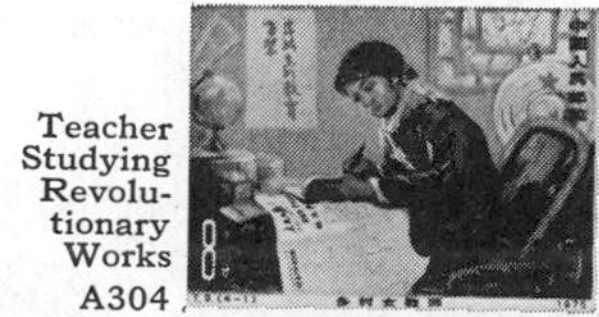

Teacher Studying Revolutionary Works A304

Designs: No. 1219, Teacher, children and horse. No. 1220, Outdoors class. No. 1221, Class held in boat. Numbered T.9.

1975, Mar. 8 Photo. *Perf. 11*

1218	A304	8f multi (4-1)	25	25
1219	A304	8f multi (4-2)	25	25
1220	A304	8f multi (4-3)	25	25
1221	A304	8f multi (4-4)	25	25

Rural women teachers and for International Working Women's Day.

"Broadsword," Encounter Position A305

Designs: No. 1223, Exercise with 2 swords (woman). No. 1224, Graceful boxing (woman). No. 1225, Man leaping with spear. No. 1226, Woman holding cudgel. 43f, Two women with spears against man with cudgel.

1975, June 10 Photo. *Perf. 11x11½*

Size: 39x29mm.

1222	A305	8f red & multi (6-1)	50	50
1223	A305	8f red & multi (6-2)	50	50
1224	A305	8f red & multi (6-3)	50	50
1225	A305	8f red & multi (6-4)	50	50
1226	A305	8f red & multi (6-5)	50	50

Size: 59x29mm.

1227	A305	43f red & multi (6-6)	1.00	1.00
		Nos. 1222-1227 (6)	3.50	3.50

Wushu ("Kung Fu"), self-defense exercises. Tête bêche in sheets of 50 (5x10).

Mass Judgment and Criticisms A306

Designs: No. 1229, Brigade leader writing wall newspaper. No. 1230, Study and criticism on battlefield (horiz.). No. 1231, Former "slave" led into battle by criticism of Lin Piao and Confucius (horiz.). Numbered T. 8.

Perf. 11½x11, 11x11½

1975, Aug. 20 Photogravure

1228	A306	8f red & multi (4-1)	60	60
1229	A306	8f red & multi (4-2)	60	60
1230	A306	8f red & multi (4-3)	60	60
1231	A306	8f red & multi (4-4)	60	60

Campaign to encourage criticism of Lin Piao and Confucius.

Athletes Studying Theory of Dictatorship of Proletariat—A307

Designs: No. 1232, Women athletes leading parade (vert.). No. 1234, Women volleyball players. No. 1235, Runner, soldier, farmer and worker (vert.). No. 1236, Young athlete and various sports. No. 1237, Athletes of various races and horse race. 35f, Children and diving tower (vert.). Numbered J. 6.

1975, Sept. 12 Photo. *Perf. 11½*

1232	A307	8f multi (7-1)	20	20
1233	A307	8f multi (7-2)	20	20
1234	A307	8f multi (7-3)	20	20
1235	A307	8f multi (7-4)	20	20
1236	A307	8f multi (7-5)	20	20
1237	A307	8f multi (7-6)	20	20
1238	A307	35f multi (7-7)	90	90
		Nos. 1232-1238 (7)	2.10	2.10

3rd National Sports Meet.

Mountaineers A308

Mt. Everest A309

Design: No. 1240, Mountaineers raising Chinese flag on summit (horiz.). Numbered T.15.

Perf. 11½x11, 11x11½

1975 Photogravure

1239	A308	8f multi (3-2)	25	25
1240	A308	8f multi (3-3)	25	25
1241	A309	43f multi (3-1)	1.00	1.00

Chinese Mt. Everest expedition.

Agricultural Workers with Book—A310

Designs: No. 1243, Workers carrying load. No. 1244, Woman driving harvester combine. Numbered J.7.

1975, Oct. 1 *Perf. 11½*

1242	A310	8f multi (3-1)	70	70
1243	A310	8f multi (3-2)	70	70
1244	A310	8f multi (3-3)	70	70

National Conference to promote learning from Tachai's achievements in agriculture.

Girl Giving Boy Red Scarf A311

Designs (Children): No. 1246, Putting up wall posters criticizing Lin Piao and Confucius. No. 1247, Studying. No. 1248, Harvesting. 52f, Physical training. Numbered T.14.

1975, Dec. 1 Photo. *Perf. 11½*

1245	A311	8f multi (5-1)	20	20
1246	A311	8f multi (5-2)	20	20
1247	A311	8f multi (5-3)	20	20
1248	A311	8f multi (5-4)	20	20
1249	A311	52f multi (5-5)	1.25	1.25
		Nos. 1245-1249 (5)	2.05	2.05

Moral, intellectual and physical progress of Chinese children.

Woman Plowing Rice Field A312

Designs: No. 1251, Mechanized rice planting. No. 1252, Drainage and irrigation. No. 1253, Woman spraying insecticide over cotton field. No. 1254, Combine. Numbered T.13.

1975, Dec. 15 *Perf. 11*

1250	A312	8f multi (5-1)	25	25
1251	A312	8f multi (5-2)	25	25
1252	A312	8f multi (5-3)	25	25
1253	A312	8f multi (5-4)	25	25
1254	A312	8f multi (5-5)	25	25
		Nos. 1250-1254 (5)	1.25	1.25

Priority program of farm mechanization.

Farmland and Irrigation Canal
A313

Designs of Nos. 1255–1270 numbered J.8.

1976, Feb. 20 Photo. *Perf. 11½*

Multicolored

1255	A313	8f *shown* (16-1)	25	25
1256	A313	8f *Irrigation canal* (16-2)	25	25
1257	A313	8f *Fertilizer plant* (16-3)	25	25
1258	A313	8f *Textile plant* (16-4)	25	25
1259	A313	8f *Anshan Iron and Steel Co.* (16-5)	25	25

Nos. 1255–1270 commemorate fulfillment of 4th Five-year Plan.

1976, Apr. 9

Multicolored

1260	A313	8f *Coal freight trains* (16-6)	25	25
1261	A313	8f *Hydroelectric station* (16-7)	25	25
1262	A313	8f *Ship building* (16-8)	25	25
1263	A313	8f *Oil industry* (16-9)	25	25
1264	A313	8f *Pipe line and port* (16-10)	25	25

1976, June 12

Multicolored

1265	A313	8f *Train on viaduct* (16-11)	25	25
1266	A313	8f *Scientific research* (16-12)	25	25
1267	A313	8f *Classroom* (16-13)	25	25
1268	A313	8f *Health Center* (16-14)	25	25
1269	A313	8f *Apartment houses* (16-15)	25	25
1270	A313	8f *Department store* (16-16)	25	25
		Nos. 1255-1270 (16)	4.00	4.00

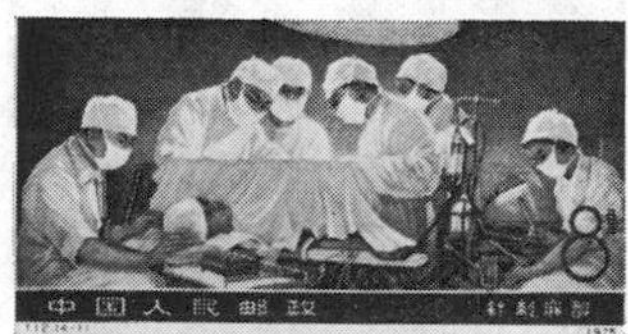

Heart Surgery with Acupuncture Anesthesia—A314

Designs (Operating Room and): No. 1272, Man driving tractor with severed arm restored. No. 1273, Man exercising broken arm in cast. No. 1274, Patient threading needle after cataract operation. Numbered T.12.

1976, Apr. 9 Photo. *Perf. 11½*

1271	A314	8f brn & multi (4-1)	30	30
1272	A314	8f yel grn & multi (4-2)	30	30
1273	A314	8f bl grn & multi (4-3)	30	30
1274	A314	8f vio bl & multi (4-4)	30	30

Achievements in medical and health services.

Students in May 7 School—A315

Designs: No. 1276, Students as farm workers. No. 1277, Production brigade. Numbered J.9.

1976, May 7 Photo. *Perf. 11½*

1275	A315	8f multi (3-1)	40	40
1276	A315	8f multi (3-2)	40	40
1277	A315	8f multi (3-3)	40	40

10th anniversary of Chairman Mao's May 7 Directive.

Mass Training in Swimming—A316

Designs: No. 1279, Swimmers crossing Yangtze River. No. 1280, Swimmers walking into the surf. Numbered J.10.

1976, July 16 Photo. *Perf. 11½*

Size: 47x27mm.

1278	A316	8f multi (3-1)	40	40

Size: 35x27mm.

1279	A316	8f multi (3-2)	40	40
1280	A316	8f multi (3-3)	40	40

Chairman Mao's swim in Yangtze River, 10th anniversary.

Workers, Peasants and Soldiers Going to College—A317

Designs: No. 1282, Classroom. No. 1283, Instruction on construction site. No. 1284, Computer room. No. 1285, Graduates returning home. Numbered T.18.

1976, Sept. 6 Photo. *Perf. 11½*

1281	A317	8f multi (5-1)	30	30
1282	A317	8f multi (5-2)	30	30
1283	A317	8f multi (5-3)	30	30
1284	A317	8f multi (5-4)	30	30
1285	A317	8f multi (5-5)	30	30
		Nos. 1281-1285 (5)	1.50	1.50

Success of proletarian education system.

Power Line Repair by Woman
A318

Designs: No. 1287, Insulator repair. No. 1288, Cherry picker. No. 1289, Transformer repair. Numbered T.16.

1976, Sept. 15

1286	A318	8f multi (4-1)	30	30
1287	A318	8f multi (4-2)	30	30
1288	A318	8f multi (4-3)	30	30
1289	A318	8f multi (4-4)	30	30

Maintenance of high power lines.

Lu Hsun
A319

Designs: No. 1291, Lu Hsun sick, writing in bed. No. 1292, Lu Hsun with worker, soldier and peasant. Numbered J.11.

Photogravure and Engraved

1976, Oct. 19 *Perf. 11x11½*

1290	A319	8f multi (3-1)	60	60
1291	A319	8f multi (3-2)	60	60
1292	A319	8f multi (3-3)	60	60

Lu Hsun (1881–1936), writer and revolutionary leader.

Old Farmer Tying Towel on Student's Head
A320

Designs: No. 1294, Student teaching farm woman (horiz.). No. 1295, Students climbing mountain for new water resources. No. 1296, Student testing wheat (horiz.). 10f, Student feeding lamb. 20f, Frontier guards (horiz.). Numbered T.17.

1976, Dec. 22 Photo. *Perf. 11½*

1293	A320	4f multi (6-1)	25	25
1294	A320	8f multi (6-2)	25	25
1295	A320	8f multi (6-3)	25	25
1296	A320	8f multi (6-4)	25	25
1297	A320	10f multi (6-5)	25	25
1298	A320	20f multi (6-6)	1.00	1.00
		Nos. 1293-1298 (6)	2.25	2.25

Students' efforts to help poor country people.

Mao's Home, Shaoshan—A321

Designs: No. 1300, School building. No. 1301, Farmers' Association building. 10f, Railroad station. All in Shaoshan. Numbered T.11.

1976, Dec. 26 *Perf. 11*

1299	A321	4f multi (4-1)	30	30
1300	A321	8f multi (4-2)	30	30
1301	A321	8f multi (4-3)	30	30
1302	A321	10f multi (4-4)	30	30

Shaoshan, Mao's birthplace.

Chou En-lai
A322

Designs: No. 1304, Chou giving report at 10th Party Congress. No. 1305, Chou with Wang Chin-hsi, famous oil worker (horiz.). No. 1306, Chou with people of Tachai, 1973 (horiz.). Numbered J.13.

1977, Jan. 8 Photo. *Perf. 11½*

1303	A322	8f multi (4-1)	20	20
1304	A322	8f multi (4-2)	20	20
1305	A322	8f multi (4-3)	20	20
1306	A322	8f multi (4-4)	20	20

Premier Chou En-lai (1898–1976), a founder of Chinese Communist Party, 1st death anniversary.

Liu Hu-lan, an Inspiration
A323

Designs: No. 1307, Liu Hu-lan monument. No. 1308, Mao Tse-tung quotation: "A great life—a glorious death." Numbered J.12.

1977, Jan. 31

1307	A323	8f multi (3-1)	25	25
1308	A323	8f multi (3-2)	25	25
1309	A323	8f multi (3-3)	25	25

Liu Hu-lan, Chinese heroine.

Uprising in Taiwan
A324

Design: 10f, Gate of Heavenly Peace, Peking; Sun Moon Lake, Taiwan, Taiwanese people holding PRC flag. Numbered J.14.

1977, Feb. 28 Photo. *Perf. 11*

1310	A324	8f multi (2-1)	35	35
1311	A324	10f multi (2-2)	35	35

Uprising of the people of Taiwan, Feb. 28, 1947.

Sharpshooters—A325

Designs: No. 1313, Women horseback riders. No. 1314, Underground defense tunnel. Numbered T.10.

1977, Mar. 8 *Perf. 11½*

1312	A325	8f multi (3-1)	25	25
1313	A325	8f multi (3-2)	25	25
1314	A325	8f multi (3-3)	25	25

Militia women.

Forestry
A326

Designs: 1f, Coal mining. 1½f, Sheep-herding. 2f, Export (loading railroad car onto ship). 4f, Hydroelectric station. 5f, Fishery. 8f, Combine in field. 10f, Radio tower and mail truck. 20f, Steel production. 30f, Trucks on mountain road. 40f, Textiles. 50f, Tractor assembly line. 60f, Offshore oil rigs and birds, setting sun. 70f, Railroad bridge, Yangtze Gorge. No numbers.

1977 Photogravure *Perf. 11½*

1315	A326	1f yel grn, red & blk	15	5
1316	A326	1½f bl grn, yel grn & brn	15	*50*
1317	A326	2f org, bl & blk	15	7
1318	A326	3f ol & dk grn	15	9
1319	A326	4f lil, org & blk	15	10
1320	A326	5f lt ol & ultra	25	10
1321	A326	8f red & yel	25	10
1322	A326	10f lt grn, org & bl	25	5
1323	A326	20f org, yel & brn	45	5
1324	A326	30f bl, lt grn & blk	55	10
1325	A326	40f multi	65	40
1326	A326	50f cit, red & blk	75	20
1327	A326	60f pur, yel & org	1.00	30
1328	A326	70f bl & multi	1.25	50
		Nos. 1315-1328 (14)	6.15	*2.61*

Address by Party Committee
A327

Designs: No. 1330, Planting new rice fields. No. 1331, Farmers reading wall newspaper. No. 1332, Land reclamation. Numbered T.22.

1977, Apr. 9 *Perf. 11x11½*

1329	A327	8f multi (4-1)	20	20
1330	A327	8f multi (4-2)	20	20
1331	A327	8f multi (4-3)	20	20
1332	A327	8f multi (4-4)	20	20

Building Tachai-type communities throughout China.

Worker at Microphone—A328

Designs: No. 1334, Drilling for oil during snowstorm. No. 1335, Crowd advancing under Red banner. No. 1336, Workers, industrial complex, rocket blast-off. Numbered J.15.

1977, Apr. 25 *Perf. 11*

1333	A328	8f multi (4-1)	20	20
1334	A328	8f multi (4-2)	20	20
1335	A328	8f multi (4-3)	20	20
1336	A328	8f multi (4-4)	20	20

Conference on learning from Taching workers in industry.

Mongolians Hailing Anniversary
A329

Designs: 10f, Iron and steel complex, iron ore train. 20f, Cattle grazing in improved pasture. Numbered J.16.

1977, May 1 *Perf. 11x11½*

1337	A329	8f multi (3-1)	25	25
1338	A329	10f multi (3-2)	25	25
1339	A329	20f multi (3-3)	50	50

30th anniversary of Inner Mongolian Autonomous Region.

1877 Flag of Romania and Oak Leaves
A330

Mihai Viteazu Memorial (16th Century Hero)
A331

Design: 10f, Battle of Smirdan, by N. Grigorescu. Numbered J.17.

1977, May 9 Photo. *Perf. 11*

1340	A330	8f multi (3-1)	25	25
1341	A331	10f multi (3-2)	25	25
1342	A331	20f multi (3-3)	50	50

Centenary of Romanian independence.

Yenan "Let 100 Flowers Bloom"
A332

Design: No. 1344, Hammer, sickle, gun and flowers; "Proletarian revolutionary literature will prosper." Numbered J.18.

1977, May, 23

1343	A332	8f grn, red & gold	25	25
1344	A332	8f lt brn, red & gold	25	25

Yenan Forum on Literature and Art, 35th anniversary.

Chu Teh
A333

Designs: No. 1346, Chu Teh, last address to Congress. No. 1347, Chu Teh at his desk (horiz.). No. 1348, Chu Teh on horseback as commander of Red Army. Numbered J.19.

1977, July 6 Photo. *Perf. 11½*

1345	A333	8f multi (4-1)	20	20
1346	A333	8f multi (4-2)	20	20
1347	A333	8f multi (4-3)	20	20
1348	A333	8f multi (4-4)	20	20

Chu Teh (1886–1976), Commander of Red Army, Chairman of National People's Congress.

Military under Mao's Banner
A334

Designs: No. 1350, Red Flag, Soldiers, Chingkang Mountains. No. 1351, Guerrilla fighters returning to base. No. 1352, Guerrillas crossing Yangtze. No. 1353, National defense. Numbered J.20.

1977, Aug. 1

1349	A334	8f multi (5-1)	25	25
1350	A334	8f multi (5-2)	25	25
1351	A334	8f multi (5-3)	25	25
1352	A334	8f multi (5-4)	25	25
1353	A334	8f multi (5-5)	25	25
		Nos. 1349-1353 (5)	1.25	1.25

Liberation Army Day, 50th anniversary of People's Army.

Gate of Heavenly Peace, People and Red Flags—A335

Designs: No. 1355, People marching under Red Flag with Mao's portrait. No. 1356, People marching under Red Flag with hammer and sickle. Numbered J.23.

1977, Aug. 22 Photo. *Perf. 11½x11*

1354	A335	8f multi (3-1)	50	50
1355	A335	8f multi (3-2)	50	50
1356	A335	8f multi (3-3)	50	50

11th National Congress of the Communist Party of China.

Chairman Mao
A336

Designs (Mao Portraits): No. 1358, as young man in Shansi. No. 1359, addressing Communist Party in Plenary Session. No. 1360, Proclaiming People's Republic at Gate of Heavenly Peace. No. 1361, at airport with Chou En-lai and Chu Teh (horiz.). No. 1362, Reviewing Army as old man. Numbered J.21.

1977, Sept. 9 Photo. *Perf. 11½*

1357	A336	8f multi (6-1)	20	20
1358	A336	8f multi (6-2)	20	20
1359	A336	8f multi (6-3)	20	20
1360	A336	8f multi (6-4)	20	20
1361	A336	8f multi (6-5)	20	20
1362	A336	8f multi (6-6)	20	20
		Nos. 1357-1362 (6)	1.20	1.20

Mao-Tse-tung (1893–1976), first death anniversary.

Mao Memorial Hall—A337

Design: No. 1364, Chairman Hua's inscription. Numbered J.22.

1977, Sept. 9

1363	A337	8f lt ultra & multi	70	70
1364	A337	8f lt grn, tan & gold	70	70

Completion of Mao Memorial Hall.

Tractors Moving Drilling Tower
A338

Designs: No. 1366, Shui Pow Tsi oil well and women workers. No. 1367, Construction of oil pipe line, Taching, and silos. No. 1368, Tung Fang Hung oil refinery, Peking. No. 1369, Taching oil loaded into tanker in harbor. 20f, Off-shore drilling platform "Pohai No. 1." Numbered T.19.

1978, Jan. 31 Photo. *Perf. 11*

1365	A338	8f multi (6-1)	25	25
1366	A338	8f multi (6-2)	25	25
1367	A338	8f multi (6-3)	25	25
1368	A338	8f multi (6-4)	25	25
1369	A338	8f multi (6-5)	25	25
1370	A338	20f multi (6-6)	50	50
		Nos. 1365-1370 (6)	1.75	1.75

Development of Chinese oil industry.

"Army Teaching Militia"—A339

Design: No. 1372, "Army helping with rice planting." Numbered T.23.

1978, Feb. 5 Photo. *Perf. 11*

1371	A339	8f multi (2-1)	20	20
1372	A339	8f multi (2-2)	20	20

Army and people working as a family.

Red Flags, Mao Tse-tung
A340

Constitution and Red Flags
A341

Design: No. 1375, Atom symbol over symbols of agriculture and industry. All designs include Great Hall of the People, Peking, and flowers. Numbered J.24.

1978, Feb. 26

1373	A340	8f multi (3-1)	25	25
1374	A341	8f multi (3-2)	25	25
1375	A340	8f multi (3-3)	25	25

5th National People's Congress.

Mao's Eulogy for Lei Feng
A342

Lei Feng, Studying Mao's Works
A343

Design: No. 1377, Chairman Hua's thoughts (5 lines). Numbered J.26.

1978, Mar. 5

1376	A342	8f gold & red (3-1)	40	40
1377	A342	8f gold & red (3-2)	40	40
1378	A343	8f multi (3-3)	40	40

Lei Feng (1940–1962), communist fighter; 15th anniversary of Chairman Mao's eulogy "Learn from Comrade Feng."

Hsiang Ching-yu A344 Yang Kai-hui A345

Numbered J.27.

1978, Mar. 8

1379	A344	8f multi (2-1)	25	25
1380	A345	8f multi (2-2)	25	25

Hsiang Ching-yu, pioneer of Women's Movement, executed 1928; Yang Kai-hui, communist fighter, executed 1930.

Conference Emblem A346

Designs: No. 1382, Banners symbolizing industry, agriculture, defense and science. No. 1383, Red flag, atom symbol and globe. Numbered J.25.

1978, Mar. 18 Litho. *Perf. 11½x11*

1381	A346	8f gold & red (3-1)	25	25
1382	A346	8f multi (3-2)	25	25
1383	A346	8f multi (3-3)	25	25
a.		Souvenir sheet of 3	35.00	

National Science Conference. No. 1383a contains one each of Nos. 1381–1383 with simulated perforations; olive margin with atom symbols and inscription. Size: 140x105mm. Sold for 50fen.

Release of Weather Balloon A347

Weather Observations: No. 1385, Radar station, typhoon watch. No. 1386, Computer, weather maps. No. 1387, Local weather observers. No. 1388, Rockets intercepting hail clouds. Numbered T.24.

1978, Apr. 25 Photo. *Perf. 11x11½*

1384	A347	8f multi (5-1)	25	25
1385	A347	8f multi (5-2)	25	25
1386	A347	8f multi (5-3)	25	25
1387	A347	8f multi (5-4)	16	16
1388	A347	8f multi (5-5)	16	16
		Nos. 1384-1388 (5)	1.07	1.07

Galloping Horse A348 Children Playing Soccer A349

Designs: Galloping Horses, by Hsu Pei-hung (1895–1953). 40f, 50f, 60f, 70f, $5, horiz. Numbered T.28.

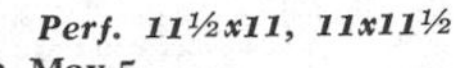

Perf. 11½x11, 11x11½

1978, May 5

1389	A348	4f multi (10-1)	20	20
1390	A348	8f multi (10-2)	20	20
1391	A348	8f multi (10-3)	20	20
1392	A348	10f multi (10-4)	20	20
1393	A348	20f multi (10-5)	50	50
1394	A348	30f multi (10-6)	60	60
1395	A348	40f multi (10-7)	80	80
1396	A348	50f multi (10-8)	1.00	1.00
1397	A348	60f multi (10-9)	1.25	1.25
1398	A348	70f multi (10-10)	1.65	1.65
		Nos. 1389-1398 (10)	6.60	6.60

Souvenir Sheet

1399	A348	$5 multi	22.50

No. 1399 contains one stamp showing 4 horses (89x39mm.); black and silver margin shows floral damask pattern. Size: 147x98mm.

1978, June 1 ***Perf. 11½***

Designs: No. 1401, Children on the beach. No. 1402, Little girls dancing. No. 1403, Children taking long walks. 20f, Children exercising for good health. Numbered T.21.

Size: 22x27mm.

1400	A349	8f multi (5-2)	25	25
1401	A349	8f multi (5-3)	25	25
1402	A349	8f multi (5-4)	25	25
1403	A349	8f multi (5-5)	25	25

Size: 48x28mm.

1404	A349	20f multi (5-1)	25	25
		Nos. 1400-1404 (5)	1.25	1.25

Build up your health while young.

Synthetic Fiber Feeder A350

Designs: No. 1406, Drawing out threads. No. 1407, Weaving. No. 1408, Dyeing and printing. No. 1409, Finished products. Numbered T.25.

1978, June 15 Photo. *Perf. 11½*

1405	A350	8f multi (5-1)	16	16
1406	A350	8f multi (5-2)	16	16
1407	A350	8f multi (5-3)	16	16
1408	A350	8f multi (5-4)	16	16
1409	A350	8f multi (5-5)	16	16
		Nos. 1405-1409 (5)	80	80

Chemical fiber industry. Nos. 1405–1409 printed se-tenant in continuous design.

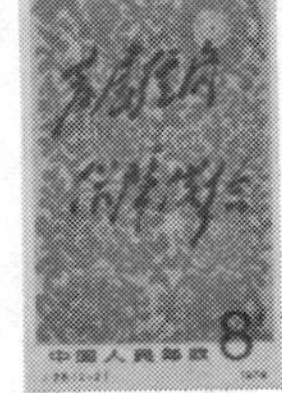

Conference Emblem A351 "Develop Economy and Ensure Supplies" A352

Numbered J.28.

1978, June 20 ***Perf. 13***

1410	A351	8f multi (2-1)	20	20
1411	A352	8f multi (2-2)	20	20

National Conference on Learning from Taching and Tachai in Finance and Trade.

New Pastures, Mongolia A353

Designs: No. 1412, Kazakh shepherds selecting sheep for breeding. No. 1414, Mechanized shearing of sheep, Tibet, Numbered T.27.

1978, June 30 Photo. *Perf. 11½*

1412	A353	8f multi (3-1)	25	25
1413	A353	8f multi (3-2)	25	25
1414	A353	8f multi (3-3)	25	25

Learning from Tachai in developing animal husbandry and new pastoral areas.

Coke Oven—A354

Designs: No. 1416, Iron furnace. No. 1417, Pouring steel. No. 1418, Steel rolling. No. 1419, Finished iron and steel products. Numbered T.26.

1978, July 22

1415	A354	8f multi (5-1)	20	20
1416	A354	8f multi (5-2)	20	20
1417	A354	8f multi (5-3)	20	20
1418	A354	8f multi (5-4)	20	20
1419	A354	8f multi (5-5)	20	20
		Nos. 1415-1419 (5)	1.00	1.00

Iron and steel industry.

Iron Fist to Prevent Revisionism A355 Jug in Shape of Sheep A356

Designs: No. 1421, "Carrying forward revolutionary tradition." No. 1422, "Strenuous training in military skills to wipe out enemy." Numbered T.32.

1978, Aug. 1 Photo. *Perf. 11½*

1420	A355	8f multi (3-1)	20	20
1421	A355	8f multi (3-2)	20	20
1422	A355	8f multi (3-3)	20	20

"Learn from Hard-boned 6th Company." (A military unit since 1939).

1978, Aug. 26

Arts and Crafts: 4f, Giant lion (toy; horiz.). No. 1425, Rhinoceros (lacquer ware; horiz). 10f, Cat (embroidery). 20f, Bag (weaving; horiz.). 30f, Teapot in shape of peacock (cloisonné). 40f, Plate with lotus, and swan-shaped box (lacquer ware; horiz.). 50f, Dragon flying in sky (ivory). 60f, Sun rising (jade; horiz.). 70f, Flight to human world (ivory). $3, Flying fairies (arts and crafts; horiz.). Numbered T.29.

1423	A356	4f multi (10-1)	20	20
1424	A356	8f multi (10-2)	20	20
1425	A356	8f multi (10-3)	20	20
1426	A356	10f multi (10-4)	20	20
1427	A356	20f multi (10-5)	50	50
1428	A356	30f multi (10-6)	60	60
1429	A356	40f multi (10-7)	80	80
1430	A356	50f multi (10-8)	1.00	1.00
1431	A356	60f multi (10-9)	1.25	1.25
1432	A356	70f multi (10-10)	1.65	1.65
		Nos. 1423-1432 (10)	6.60	6.60

Souvenir Sheet

1433	A356	$3 multi	20.00

No. 1433 contains one stamp (85x36 mm.). Gold decorative margin. Size: 139x90mm.

Women, Atom Symbol, Rootrot and Wheat A357

1978, Sept. 8 Photo. *Perf. 11*

1434	A357	8f multi	50	30

4th National Women's Congress.

Ginseng A358 Flag, Wheat, Cogwheel, Plane, Atom Symbols A359

Medicinal Plants: No. 1436, Horn of plenty. No. 1437, Blackberry lily. No. 1438, Balloonflower. 55f, Rhododendron dauricum. Numbered T.30.

1978, Sept. 15

1435	A358	8f multi (5-1)	16	16
1436	A358	8f multi (5-2)	16	16
1437	A358	8f multi (5-3)	16	16
1438	A358	8f multi (5-4)	16	16
1439	A358	55f multi (5-5)	1.10	1.10
		Nos. 1435-1439 (5)	1.74	1.74

1978, Oct. 11 Photo. *Perf. 11*

1440	A359	8f multi	50	50

9th National Trade Union Congress.

Youth League Emblem A360

1978, Oct. 16

1441	A360	8f multi	50	50

10th National Communist Youth League Congress.

Chinese and Japanese Girls Exchanging Gifts A361

Great Wall and Mt. Fuji A362

1978, Oct. 22

1442 A361 8f multi 25 25
1443 A362 55f multi 1.25 1.25

Signing of Sino-Japanese Peace and Friendship Treaty.

Moslem, Chinese and Mongolian People
A363

Chinsha River Bridge, West Szechuan
A364

Designs: No. 1445, Loading coal at Holan Mountain. 10f, Irrigated rice fields and boxthorn. Numbered J.29.

1978, Oct. 25

1444 A363 8f multi (3-1) 20 20
1445 A363 8f multi (3-2) 20 20
1446 A363 10f multi (3-3) 20 20

20th anniversary of founding of Ningsia Moslem Autonomous Region.

1978, Nov. 1 Photo. *Perf. 11½x11*

Highway Bridges: No. 1448, Hsinhong bridge, Wuhsi. No. 1449, Chiuhsikou bridge, Fengdu. No. 1450, Chinsha River bridge, West Szechuan. 60f, Shangyeh bridge, Sanmen. $2, Hsiang-kiang River bridge. Numbered T.31.

1447 A364 8f multi (5-1) 16 16
1448 A364 8f multi (5-2) 16 16
1449 A364 8f multi (5-3) 16 16
1450 A364 8f multi (5-4) 16 16
1451 A364 60f multi (5-5) 1.20 1.20
Nos. 1447-1451 (5) 1.84 1.84

Souvenir Sheet

1452 A364 $2 multi 20.00

No. 1452 contains one stamp (86x37 mm.). Ultramarine, white and gold margin shows tiny boats. Size: 145x69mm.

Mechanical Transplanting of Rice Seedlings
A365

Paintings: No. 1454, Spraying fields. No. 1455, Seed selection. No. 1456, Trade. No. 1457, Delivery of public grain in city. Numbered T.34.

1978, Nov. 30 *Perf. 11½*

1453 A365 8f multi (5-1) 20 20
1454 A365 8f multi (5-2) 20 20
1455 A365 8f multi (5-3) 20 20
1456 A365 8f multi (5-4) 20 20
1457 A365 8f multi (5-5) 20 20
Strip of 5 (#1453-1457) 1.25 1.25

Agricultural progress. Nos. 1453–1457 printed se-tenant in continuous design.

Dancers and Fireworks—A366

Designs: No. 1459, Industry (vert.). 10f, Agriculture (vert.). Numbered J.33.

1978, Dec. 11 Photo. *Perf. 11*

1458 A366 8f multi (3-1) 20 20
1459 A366 8f multi (3-2) 20 20
1460 A366 10f multi (3-3) 20 20

20th anniversary of Kwangsi Chuang Autonomous Region.

Miners with Pneumatic Drill
A367

Mine Development: 4f, Old Tibetan peasant reporting to surveyor. 10f, Open-cut mining with power shovel. 20f, Loaded electric train in pit. Numbered T.20.

1978, Dec. 29 Photo. & Engr.

1461 A367 4f multi (4-1) 8 8
1462 A367 8f multi (4-2) 16 16
1463 A367 10f multi (4-3) 20 20
1464 A367 20f multi (4-4) 40 40

Golden Pheasants Roosting on Rock
A368

Golden Pheasants: 8f, In flight. 45f, Seeking food. Numbered T.35.

1979, Jan. 25 Photo. *Perf. 11½*

1465 A368 4f multi (3-1) 20 20
1466 A368 8f multi (3-2) 20 20
1467 A368 45f multi (3-3) 75 75

Albert Einstein and his Equation
A369

1979, Mar. 14 Photo. *Perf. 11½x11*

1468 A369 8f brn gold & blk 35 35

Albert Einstein (1879–1955), theoretical physicist.

Phoenix Battling Monster, Praying Woman
A370

Design: 60f, Man riding dragon to heaven. Designs from silk paintings found in Changsha tomb, Warring States Period (475–221 B.C.). Numbered T.33.

1979, Mar. 29 *Perf. 11*

1469 A370 8f multi (2-1) 25 25
1470 A370 60f multi (2-2) 1.40 1.40

Summer Palace
A371

Photo., Photo. & Engr. ($5)

1979-80 *Perf. 13*

1471 A371 $1 *Pagoda* ('80) 1.00 50
1472 A371 $2 *Shown* 2.00 1.00
1473 A371 $5 *Temple, Beihai Park* ('80) 7.00 2.50

Hammer and Sickle "5 1" and Bars from "International"
A372

1979, May 1 Photo. *Perf. 11*

1474 A372 8f multi 35 25

International Labor Day, 90th anniv.

"Tradition of May 4th Movement"
A373

Young Woman, Rocket, Antenna, Nuclear Reactor
A374

1979, May 4

1475 A373 8f multi 25 25
1476 A374 8f multi 25 25

60th anniversary of May 4th Movement.

IYC Emblem, Children Holding Balloons
A375

Children of Three Races, IYC Emblem
A376

1979, May 25 *Perf. 11½*

1477 A375 8f multi 20 20
1478 A376 60f multi 1.25 1.25

International Year of the Child.

Great Wall in Spring
A377

Designs (The Great Wall): No. 1480, in summer. No. 1481, in autumn. 60f, in winter. $2, Guard tower. Numbered T.38.

1979, June 25 Photo. *Perf. 11*

1479 A377 8f multi (4-1) 20 20
1480 A377 8f multi (4-2) 20 20
1481 A377 8f multi (4-3) 20 20
1482 A377 60f multi (4-4) 1.25 1.25

Souvenir Sheet

1483 A377 $2 multi 10.00

No. 1483 has blue gray and gold margin showing Great Wall and towers. Size: 140x78mm.

Roaring Tiger
A379

Manchurian Tiger: 8f, Two young tigers. 60f, Tiger at rest. Numbered T.40.

1979, July 20 *Perf. 11½x11*

1484 A379 4f multi (3-1) 20 20
1485 A379 8f multi (3-2) 20 20
1486 A379 60f multi (3-3) 1.25 1.25

Mechanical Harvesting—A380

Work of the Communes: No. 1488, Forestry. No. 1489, Raising ducks. No. 1490, Women weaving baskets. 10f, Fishing. Numbered T.39.

1979, Aug. 10 *Perf. 11½*

1487 A380 4f multi (5-1) 15 15
1488 A380 8f multi (5-2) 15 15
1489 A380 8f multi (5-3) 15 15
1490 A380 8f multi (5-4) 15 15
1491 A380 10f multi (5-5) 15 15
Nos. 1487-1491 (5) 75 75

Souvenir Sheet

No. 1483 Overprinted with Gold Inscription and "1979"

1979, Aug. 25 Photo. *Perf. 11*

1492 A377 $2 multi 60.00

31st International Stamp Exhibition, Riccione, Italy. Size: 140x78mm. Numbered J41 (1-1).

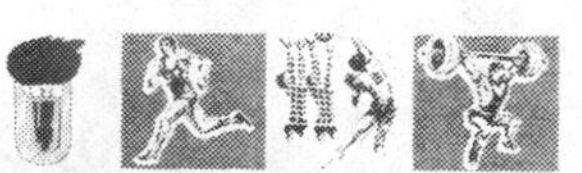

Games Emblem, Sports—A381

Emblem and: No. 1494, Soccer, badminton, high jump, speed skating. No. 1495, Fencing, skiing, gymnastics, diving. No. 1496, Motorcycling, table tennis, basketball, archery. No. 1497, Emblem only (vert.). Numbered J.43.

1979, Sept. 15 *Perf. 11½x11*

1493 A381 8f multi (4-1) 20 20
1494 A381 8f multi (4-2) 20 20
1495 A381 8f multi (4-3) 20 20
1496 A381 8f multi (4-4) 20 20

Souvenir Sheet
Perf. 11½

1497	A381	$2 multi	7.00

4th National Games. Nos. 1493–1496 printed se-tenant. No. 1497 has gray olive margin showing symbols of various sports. Size of stamp: 22x26mm., size of sheet: 57x62mm.

Flag and Rainbow—A382

National Emblem A383

National Anthem A384

Dancers A385

Tractor, Aerial Crop Spraying, Irrigation A386

Designs: No. 1499, Flag and mountains. Nos. 1503–1505, various dances (numbered J.47). No. 1507, Atom symbol. No. 1509, Rocket, submarine, jets (Nos. 1506–1509 numbered J.48). No. 1510, National Emblem.

1979, Oct. 1 Photo. *Perf. 11½*

1498	A382	8f multi	20
1499	A382	8f multi	20
1500	A383	8f multi	25

Engraved *Perf. 11*

1501	A384	8f multi	25

Photogravure *Perf. 11½*

1502	A385	8f multi (4-1)	20
1503	A385	8f multi (4-2)	20
1504	A385	8f multi (4-3)	20
1505	A385	8f multi (4-4)	20
		Block of 4 (#1502-1505)	1.25
1506	A386	8f multi (4-1)	20
1507	A386	8f multi (4-2)	20
1508	A386	8f multi (4-3)	20
1509	A386	8f multi (4-4)	20

Souvenir Sheet

1510	A383	$1 multi	6.50

People's Republic of China, 30th anniversary. Nos. 1502–1505 printed in blocks of 4. No. 1510 has multicolored decorative margin. Size: 67x75mm.

Exhibition Emblem A387

Children Flying Model Planes A388

1979, Oct. 3

1511	A387	8f multi	35

Junior National Scientific and Technological Exhibition.

1979, Oct. 3

Designs: No. 1513, Girls and microscope. No. 1514, Children and telescope. No. 1515, Boy catching butterflies. No. 1516, Girl taking meteorological readings. No. 1517, Boys sailing model boat. No. 1518, Girl with book. Numbered T.41.

1512	A388	8f multi (6-1)	20
1513	A388	8f multi (6-2)	20
1514	A388	8f multi (6-3)	20
1515	A388	8f multi (6-4)	20
1516	A388	8f multi (6-5)	16
1517	A388	60f multi (6-6)	70
		Nos. 1512-1517 (6)	1.66

Souvenir Sheet
Perf. 11

1518	A388	$2 multi	55.00

Study Science from Childhood. No. 1518 contains one stamp (90x40mm.). Light blue margin shows fish. Size: 148x 90mm.

Yu Shan Mountain—A389

Taiwan Landscapes: No. 1520, Sun and Moon Lake. No. 1521, Chihkan Tower. No. 1522, Suao-Hualien Highway. 55f, Tian Xiang Falls. 60f, Banping Mountain. Numbered T.42.

1979, Oct. 20 Photo. *Perf. 11×11½*

1519	A389	8f multi (6-1)	20
1520	A389	8f multi (6-2)	20
1521	A389	8f multi (6-3)	20
1522	A389	8f multi (6-4)	20
1523	A389	55f multi (6-5)	80
1524	A389	60f multi (6-6)	90
		Nos. 1519-1524 (6)	2.50

Arts Symbols—A390

Design: 8f, Seals and modernization symbols. Numbered J.39.

1979, Oct. 30

1525	A390	4f multi	15
1526	A390	8f multi	30

4th National Congress of Literary and Art Workers.

Train in Tunnel—A391

Railroads: No. 1520, Mountain bridge. No. 1521, Freight train. Numbered T.36.

Photogravure and Engraved

1979, Oct. 30

1527	A391	8f multi (3-1)	15
1528	A391	8f multi (3-2)	15
1529	A391	8f multi (3-3)	15

Chrysanthemum Petal—A392

Camellias: No. 1531, Lion head. No. 1532, Camellia chryantha. 10f, Small osmanthus leaf. 20f, Baby face. 30f, Cornelian. 40f, Peony camellia. 50f, Purple gown. 60f, Dwarf rose. 70f, Willow leaf spinel pink. $2, Red jewelry. Numbered T.37.

1979, Nov. 10 Photo. *Perf. 11×11½*

1530	A392	4f multi (10-1)	20
1531	A392	8f multi (10-2)	20
1532	A392	8f multi (10-3)	20
1533	A392	10f multi (10-4)	20
1534	A392	20f multi (10-5)	40
1535	A392	30f multi (10-6)	55
1536	A392	40f multi (10-7)	75
1537	A392	50f multi (10-8)	90
1538	A392	60f multi (10-9)	1.10
1539	A392	70f multi (10-10)	1.25
		Nos. 1530-1539 (10)	5.75

Souvenir Sheet
Perf. 11½×11

1540	A392	$2 multi	10.00

No. 1540 contains one stamp (86×36mm.), gold margin with white inscription. Size: 135×90mm.

Souvenir Sheet

No. 1540 Overprinted and Numbered in Gold in Margin.

1979, Nov. 10

1541	A392	$2 multi	40.00

People's Republic of China Philatelic Exhibition, Hong Kong, 1979. Numbered J.42 (1-1).

Norman Bethune Treating Soldier A393

Design: 70f, Bethune statue.

1979, Nov. 12

1542	A393	8f multi (2-2)	20
1543	A393	70f multi (2-1)	1.25

Dr. Norman Bethune, 40th death anniversary. Numbered J.50.

Central Archives Hall—A394

International Archives Weeks: No. 1545, Gold archive cabinet (vert.). 60f, Pavilion. Numbered J.51.

Perf. 11×11½, 11½×11

1979, Nov. 26 Photo.

1544	A394	8f multi (3-1)	25
1545	A394	8f multi (3-2)	25
1546	A394	60f multi (3-3)	1.10

Monkey King in Waterfall Cave—A395

Monkey King, Scenes from Pilgrimage to the West (Novel): No. 1548, Fighting Necha, son of Prince Li. No. 1549, In Mother Queen's peach orchard. No. 1550, In the alchemy furnace. 10f, Subduing the white bone demon. 20f, With palm leaf fan. 60f, In cobweb cave. 70f, Walking on scripture-seeking route. Numbered T.43.

1979, Dec. 1 *Perf. 11½×11*

1547	A395	8f multi (8-1)	20
1548	A395	8f multi (8-2)	20
1549	A395	8f multi (8-3)	20
1550	A395	8f multi (8-4)	20
1551	A395	10f multi (8-5)	20
1552	A395	20f multi (8-6)	30
1553	A395	60f multi (8-7)	1.00
1554	A395	70f multi (8-8)	1.10
		Nos. 1547-1554 (8)	3.40

Stalin Delivering Speech—A396

Design: No. 1555, Portrait of Stalin (vert.). Numbered J. 49.

Perf. 11×11½, 11½×11

1979, Dec. 21 Engraved

1555	A396	8f brn (2-1)	30
1556	A396	8f blk (2-2)	30

Joseph Stalin (1879-1953).

See "Special Notices" at the front of this volume for data on the listing methods of this Catalogue, abbreviations, condition, prices and examination.

Peony, by Qi Baishi—A397

1980 Photo. *Perf. 11½*

1557	A397	4f *shown* (16-1)	20
1558	A397	4f *Squirrels and grapes* (16-2)	20
1559	A397	8f *Crabs candle and wine* (16-3)	20
1560	A397	8f *Tadpoles in mountain spring* (16-4)	20
1561	A397	8f *Chicks* (16-5)	20
1562	A397	8f *Lotus* (16-6)	20
1563	A397	8f *Red plum* (16-7)	20
1564	A397	8f *Kingfisher* (16-8)	20
1565	A397	10f *Bottle gourd* (16-9)	20
1566	A397	20f *Voice of autumn* (16-10)	32
1567	A397	30f *Wisteria* (16-11)	45
1568	A397	40f *Chrysanthemums* (16-12)	60
1569	A397	50f *Shrimp* (16-13)	75
1570	A397	55f *Litchi* (16-14)	80
1571	A397	60f *Cabbages, mushrooms* (16-15)	90
1572	A397	70f *Peaches* (16-16)	1.10
		Nos. 1557-1572 (16)	6.72

Souvenir Sheet

1980, May 20 Photo. *Perf. 11½*

1573	A397	$2 Evergreen	7.00

Qi Baishi paintings. Issue dates: Nos. 1557-1560, 1569-1572, Jan. 15; others, May 20. Numbered T. 44.

No. 1573 contains one stamp (37½x61mm); brown and tan margin shows portrait of Qi Baishi and inscription. Size: 120x86mm.

Meng Liang Mask from Hongyang Cave Opera—A398

Opera Masks. No. 1575, Li Kui, from Black Whirlwind. No. 1576, Huang Gai, from Meeting of Heroes. No. 1577, 10f, Lu Zhishen, from Wild Boar Forest. 20f, Lian Po, from Reconciliation between the General and Minister. 60f, Zhang Fei, from Reed Marsh. 70f, Dou Erdun, from Stealing the Emperor's Horse, Numbered T. 45.

1980, Jan. 25 *Perf. 11½×11*

1574	A398	4f multi (8-1)	15
1575	A398	4f multi (8-2)	15
1576	A398	8f multi (8-3)	15
1577	A398	8f multi (8-4)	15
1578	A398	10f multi (8-5)	15
1579	A398	20f multi (8-6)	30
1580	A398	60f multi (8-7)	90
1581	A398	70f multi (8-8)	1.00
		Nos. 1574-1581 (8)	2.95

Speed Skating, Olympic Rings A399

Monkey, New Year A400

Olympic Rings and: No. 1582, Chinese flag. No. 1584, Figure skating. 60f, Downhill skiing. Numbered J. 54.

1980, Feb. 13

1582	A399	8f multi (4-1)	20
1583	A399	8f multi (4-2)	20
1584	A399	8f multi (4-3)	20
1585	A399	60f multi (4-4)	1.10

13th Winter Olympic Games, Lake Placid, N.Y., Feb. 12-24.

Engraved & Photogravure

1980, Feb. 15 *Perf. 11½*

1586	A400	8f multi	8.00

Clara Zetkin—A401

1980, Mar. 8 Photo. & Engr. *Perf. 11½x11*

1587	A401	8f blk & yel	35

International Working Women's Day, 70th anniversary, founded by Clara Zetkin (1857-1933).

Orchard—A402

Afforestation: 8f, Trees lining highway. 10f, Aerial seeding. 20f, Trees surrounding factory. Numbered T.48.

1980, Mar. 12 *Perf. 11x11½*

1588	A402	4f multi (4-1)	10
1589	A402	8f multi (4-2)	15
1590	A402	10f multi (4-3)	20
1591	A402	20f multi (4-4)	40

Apsaras, Symbols of Modernization—A403

1980, Mar. 15 Photo. *Perf. 11½*

1592	A403	8f multi	35

2nd National Conference of the Scientific and Technical Association of China.

Mail Transport by Ship—A404

1980, Mar. 20 *Perf. 11x11½*

1593	A404	2f *shown* (4-1)	5
1594	A404	4f *Bus* (4-2)	6
1595	A404	8f *Train* (4-3)	15
1596	A404	10f *Jet* (4-4)	15

Numbered T.49.

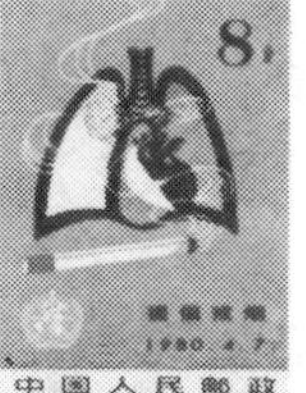

Lungs, Heart, Cigarette, WHO Emblem A405

Statue of Chien Chen (688-763) A406

1980, Apr. 7 *Perf. 11½x11*

1597	A405	8f *shown* (2-1)	15
1598	A405	60f *Faces* (2-2)	90

Fight against cigarette smoking. Numbered J.56.

1980, Apr. 13 *Perf. 11x11½, 11½x11*

Loan to China by Japan of statue of Chien Chen (Jian Zhen), Buddhist missionary to Japan (754-763): No. 1600, Chien Chen Memorial Hall, Yangchou (horiz.). 60f, Chien Chen's ship (horiz.). His name in Japan is Ganjin. Numbered J.55.

1599	A406	8f multi (3-1)	15
1600	A406	8f multi (3-2)	15
1601	A406	60f multi (3-3)	1.00

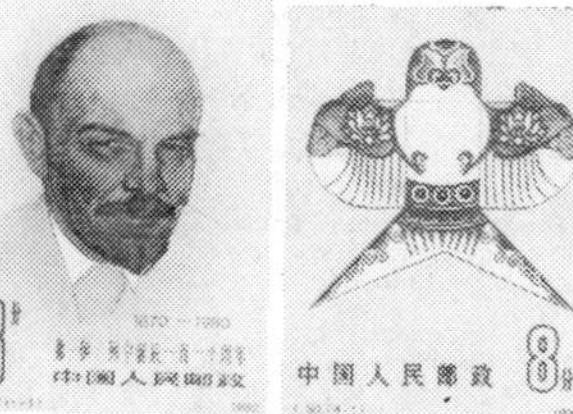

Lenin's 110th Birthday—A407

Swallow Chick Kite—A408

Photo. & Engr.

1980, Apr. 22 *Perf. 11½x11*

1602	A407	8f multi	35

1980, May 10 Photo. *Perf. 11½*

Designs: Kites. Numbered T.50.

1603	A408	8f *Shown* (4-1)	20
1604	A408	8f *Slender-swallow* (4-2)	20
1605	A408	8f *Semi-slender swallow* (4-3)	20
1606	A408	70f *Dual swallows* (4-4)	1.25

Hare Running from Fallen Papaya—A409

1980, June 1 Photo. *Perf. 11x11½*

1607		Strip of 4	60
a.		A409 8f *Shown* (4-1)	12
b.		A409 8f *Hare fox, monkey running away* (4-2)	12
c.		A409 8f *Lion instructing animals* (4-3)	12
d.		A409 8f *Discovery of fallen papaya* (4-4)	12

Gu Dong fairy tale. Nos. 1607a-1607d se-tenant with label telling story. Numbered T.51.

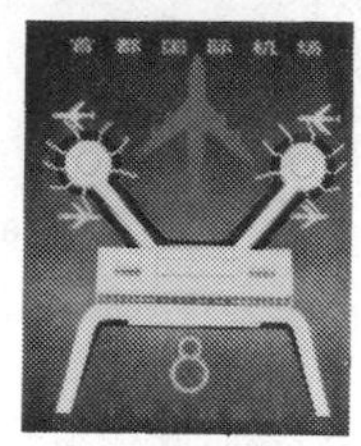

Terminal Building, Jets—A410

1980, June 20 *Perf. 11½*

1608	A410	8f *Shown* (2-1)	15
1609	A410	10f *Runways, jets* (2-2)	20

Peking International Airport opening. Numbered T.47.

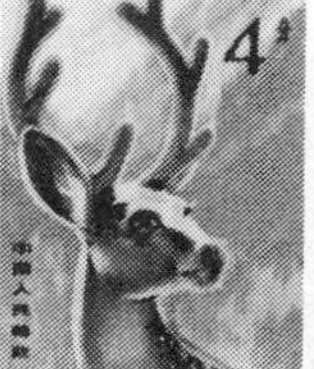

Sika Stag A411

White Lotus A412

1980, July 18 Photo. *Perf. 11½*

1610	A411	4f *Shown* (3-1)	10
1611	A411	8f *Doe and fawn* (3-2)	15
1612	A411	60f *Herd* (3-3)	90

Numbered T.52.

1980, Aug. 4

1613	A412	8f *Shown* (4-1)	15
1614	A412	8f *Rose-tipped snow* (4-2)	15
1615	A412	8f *Buddha's seat* (4-3)	15
1616	A413	70f *Variable charming face* (4-4)	1.25

Souvenir Sheet

1617	A412	$1 *Fresh lotus on rippling water*	11.00

Numbered T.54. No. 1617 contains one stamp (48x88mm); light gray decorative margin. Size: 70x145½mm.

Pearl Cave, Sword-cut Stone Sculptures—A413

Guilin Landscapes: No. 1619, Three mountains, distant views. No. 1620, Nine-horse fresco hill. No. 1621, Egrets around aged banyan. No. 1622, Western hills at sunset (vert.). No. 1623, Moonlight on Lijiang River (vert.). 60f, Springhead, ancient ferry (vert.). 70f, Scenic path, Yangshue (vert.). Numbered T.53.

1980, Aug. 30 Photo. *Perf. 11½*

1618	A413	8f multi (8-1)	12
1619	A413	8f multi (8-2)	12
1620	A413	8f multi (8-3)	12
1621	A413	8f multi (8-4)	12
1622	A413	8f multi (8-5)	12
1623	A413	8f multi (8-6)	12
1624	A413	60f multi (8-7)	90
1625	A413	70f multi (8-8)	1.05
		Nos. 1618-1625 (8)	2.67

Entrance Gate and Good Fairies—A414

Great Wall, Symbols of Chicago, San Francisco and New York—A415

1980, Sept. 13 Photo. *Perf. 11x11½*

1626 A414 8f multi 12
1627 A415 70f multi 1.05

Exhibitions of the People's Republic of China in San Francisco, Chicago and New York, Sept.-Dec.

Sheets of 12 were sold only at U.S. exhibitions.

Romanian Flag, Warrior and Scroll—A416

1980, Sept. 20 Photo. *Perf. 11½x11*

1628 A416 8f multi 40

2050th anniversary of Dacia, first independent Romanian state.

UNESCO Exhibition of Drawings and Paintings—A417
Numbered J.60.

1980, Oct. 8 *Perf. 11½*

1629 A417 8f *Sea of Clouds, by Liu Haisu,* (3-1) 15 25
1630 A417 8f *Oriole and Magnolia, by Yu Feian,* vert., (3-2) 15 25
1631 A417 8f *Camels, by Wu Zuoren,* (3-3) 15 25

Quxi Tower, Tarrying Garden—A418

Designs: Scenes from Tarrying Garden. Numbered T.56.

1980, Oct. 25 Photo. *Perf. 11½*

1632 A418 8f *shown* (4-1) 12
1633 A418 8f *Yuancui Pavilion* (4-2) 12
1634 A418 10f *Hanbi Shanfang* (4-3) 15
1635 A418 60f *Guanyun Peak* (4-4) 90

Xu Guangpi (1562-1633), Agronomist
A419

Shooting, Olympic Rings
A420

Scientists of Ancient China: No. 1637, Li Bing, hydraulic engineer, 3rd century B.C. No. 1638, Jia Sixie, agronomist, 5th century. 60f, Huang Daopo, textile expert, 13th century. Numbered J.58.

Photo. & Engr.

1980, Nov. 20 *Perf. 11½x11*

1636 A419 8f multi (4-1) 15
1637 A419 8f multi (4-2) 15
1638 A419 8f multi (4-3) 15
1639 A419 60f multi (4-4) 1.00

1980, Nov. 26 Photo.

1640 A420 4f *shown* (5-1) 6
1641 A420 8f *Gymnastics* (5-2) 12
1642 A420 8f *Diving* (5-3) 12
1643 A420 10f *Volleyball* (5-4) 15
1644 A420 60f *Archery* (5-5) 90
Nos. 1640-1644 (5) 1.35

Return to International Olympic Committee, 1st anniversary. Numbered J.62.

Chinese River Dolphin—A421

1980, Dec. 25 Photo. & Engr. *Perf. 11x11½*

1645 A421 8f *shown* (2-1) 15
a. Booklet pane of 6 90
1646 A421 60f *Dolphins* (2-2) 1.00
a. Booklet pane of 1 2.00

Cock—A422

1981, Jan. 5 Photo. & Engr. *Perf. 11½*

1647 A422 8f multi 1.25
a. Bklt. pane of 12 3.50

New Year 1981. Numbered T.58.

Early Morning in Xishuang Bana—A423

Photo.

1981, Jan. 20 *Perf. 11x11½, 11½x11*

1648 A423 4f *shown* (6-1) 6
1649 A423 4f *Dai mountain village* (6-2) 6
1650 A423 8f *Rainbow over Lanchang River* (6-3) 12
1651 A423 8f *Ancient temple,* vert. (6-4) 12
1652 A423 8f *Moonlit night,* vert. (6-5) 12
1653 A423 60f *Phoenix tree,* vert. (6-6) 90
Nos. 1648-1653 (6) 1.38

Flower Basket Palace Lantern—A424

Designs: Palace lanterns. Numbered T.60.

1981, Feb. 19 Photo. *Perf. 11½*

1654 A424 4f multi (6-1) 6
1655 A424 8f multi (6-2) 12
1656 A424 8f multi (6-3) 12
1657 A424 8f multi (6-4) 12
1658 A424 20f multi (6-5) 30
1659 A424 60f multi (6-6) 90
Nos. 1654-1659 (6) 1.62

Crossing River, Scene from Marking the Gunwale—A425

Designs: Scenes from Marking the Gunwale fable.

1981, Mar. 10 Photo. *Perf. 11x11½*

1660 A425 8f Text (5-1) 12
1661 A425 8f shown (5-2) 12
1662 A425 8f Dropping sword in water (5-3) 12
1663 A425 8f Marking gunwale (5-4) 12
1664 A425 8f Searching for sword (5-5) 12
a. Bklt. pane of 10 (2 each #1660-1664) 1.75
Nos. 1660-1664 (5) 60

Nos. 1660-1664 se-tenant. Numbered T.59.

Chinese Juniper—A426

Designs: Miniature landscapes. Numbered T.61.

1981, Mar. 31 *Perf. 11½*

1665 A426 4f Chinese elm, vert. (6-1) 6
1666 A426 8f Juniper, vert. (6-2) 12
1667 A426 8f Maidenhair tree, vert. (6-3) 12
1668 A426 10f shown (6-4) 15
1669 A426 20f Persimmon (6-5) 30
1670 A426 60f Juniper (6-6) 90
Nos. 1665-1670 (6) 1.65

Vase with Tiger-shaped Handles—A427

Cizhou Kiln Ceramic Pottery: 4f, Vase with two tigers, Song Dynasty (vert.). No. 1672, Black glazed jar, Jin Dynasty. No. 1673, Amphora (vert.). No. 1674, Jar with two phoenixes (Yuan Dynasty). 10f, Flat flask, Yuan Dynasty. Numbered T.62.

1981, Apr. 15 Photo. *Perf. 11½x11*

1671 A427 4f multi (6-1) 6
1672 A427 8f multi (6-2) 12
1673 A427 8f multi (6-3) 12
1674 A427 8f multi (6-4) 12
1675 A427 10f multi (6-5) 15
1676 A427 60f multi (6-6) 90
Nos. 1671-1676 (6) 1.47

Panda Bear and Colored Stamps
A428

1981, Apr. 29 Photo. *Perf. 11½x11*

1677 A428 8f shown (2-1) 12
1678 A428 60f Boat, bird (2-2) 90
a. Booklet (8 #1677, 1677-1678 se-tenant) 2.00

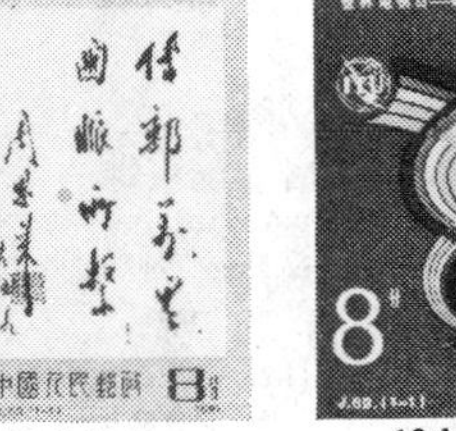

Qinchuan Steer—A429

Cattle Breeds: No. 1680, Binhu buffalo. No. 1681, Yak. No. 1682, Black and white dairy cows. 10f, Pasture red cow. 55f, Simmental cross-breed. Numbered T.63.

1981, May 5 *Perf. 11x11½*

1679 A429 4f multi (6-1) 6
1680 A429 8f multi (6-2) 12
1681 A429 8f multi (6-3) 12
1682 A429 8f multi (6-4) 12
1683 A429 10f multi (6-5) 15
1684 A429 55f multi (6-6) 85
Nos. 1679-1684 (6) 1.42

Mail Delivery Slogan
A430

13th World Telecommunications Day
A431

1981, May 9 *Perf. 11*

1685 A430 8f multi 25

Numbered J.70.

1981, May 17 *Perf. 11½x11*

1686 A431 8f multi 25

Numbered J.69.

Construction Worker
A432

Telephone Building, Peking—A433

1981, May 20 *Perf. 11½*

1687 A432 8f shown (4-1) 15
1688 A432 8f Miner (4-2) 15
1689 A432 8f Children crossing street (4-3) 15
1690 A432 8f Farm worker (4-4) 15

National Safety Month. Numbered J.65.

1981, June 5 Engr. *Perf. 11½x11*

1691 A433 8f vio brn 20

Swaythling Cup, Men's Team Table Tennis—A434

36th World Table Tennis Championships Victory: No. 1692a, St. Bride Vase, men's singles (7-3). No. 1692b, Iran Cup, men's doubles (7-4). No. 1692c, G. Geist Prize, women's singles (7-5). No. 1692d, W.J. Pope Trophy, women's doubles (7-6). No. 1692e, Heydusek Prize, mixed doubles (7-7). No. 1694, Marcel Corbillon Cup, women's team. Nos. 1693-1694 printed in sheets of 16 (8 each) with 2 labels. Numbered J.71.

1981, June 30 Photo. *Perf. 11½x11*

No.	Type	Description	Value
1692		Strip of 5	60
a.-e.	A434	8f multi	12
1693	A434	20f multi (7-1)	30
1694	A434	20f multi (7-2)	30

Chinese Communist Party, 60th Anniv.—A435

1981, July 1 Photo. *Perf. 11x11½*

No.	Type	Description	Value
1695	A435	8f multi	35

Hanpo Pass, Lushan Mountains—A436

1981, July 20 Photo. & Engr. *Perf. 12½x12,*

No.	Type	Description	Value
1696	A436	8f Five-veteran Peak, vert. (7-1)	12
1697	A436	8f shown (7-2)	12
1698	A436	8f Yellow Dragon Pool, vert. (7-3)	12
1699	A436	8f Sunlit Peak (7-4)	12
1700	A436	8f Three-layer Spring, vert. (7-5)	12
1701	A436	8f Stone and pines (7-6)	12
1702	A436	60f Dragon-head Cliff, vert. (7-7)	90
		Nos. 1696-1702 (7)	1.62

Numbered T.67.

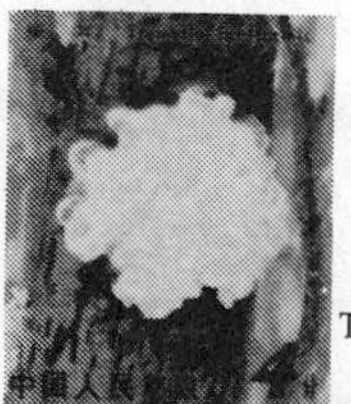

Tremella Fuciformis A437

Designs: Edible mushrooms. Numbered T.66.

1981, Aug. 6 Photo. Perf 11½

No.	Type	Description	Value
1703	A437	4f shown (6-1)	6
1704	A437	8f Dictyophora indusiata (6-2)	12
1705	A437	8f Hericium erinaceus (6-3)	12
1706	A437	8f Russula rubra (6-4)	12
1707	A437	10f Lentinus edodes (6-5)	15
1708	A437	70f Agaricus bisporus (6-6)	1.05
		Nos. 1703-1708 (6)	1.62

Quality Month A438

Lunan Stone Forest, Yunn A439

1981, Sept. 1 Photo. *Perf. 11½x11*

No.	Type	Description	Value
1709	A438	8f Silver medal (2-1)	20
1710	A438	8f Gold medal (2-2)	20

Numbered J.66.

1981, Sept. 18 *Perf. 11½*

Designs: Views of limestone formations, Lunan Stone Forest. Nos. 1711-1713 horiz. Numbered T.64.

No.	Type	Description	Value
1711	A439	8f multi (5-1)	12
1712	A439	8f multi (5-2)	12
1713	A439	8f multi (5-3)	12
1714	A439	10f multi (5-4)	15
1715	A439	70f multi (5-5)	1.05
		Nos. 1711-1715 (5)	1.56

Lu Xun, Writer, Birth Centenary A440

1981, Sept. 25

No.	Type	Description	Value
1716	A440	8f shown (2-1)	12
1717	A440	20f Portrait (diff.) (2-2)	30

Numbered J.67.

Sun Yat-sen and Text—A441

70th Anniv. of 1911 Revolution: No. 1719, 72 Martyrs Grave, Huang Hua Gang. No. 1720, Hubei Provincial Government Headquarters, 1911. Numbered J.68.

1981, Oct. 10 Photo. *Perf. 11x11½*

No.	Type	Description	Value
1718	A441	8f multi (3-1)	15
1719	A441	8f multi (3-2)	15
1720	A441	8f multi (3-3)	15

Asian Conference of Parliamentarians on Population and Development, Peking, Oct. 27—A442

1981, Oct. 27 *Perf. 11½x11, 11x11½*

No.	Type	Description	Value
1721	A442	8f Tree, vert. (2-1)	12
1722	A442	70f shown (2-2)	1.05

Numbered J.73.

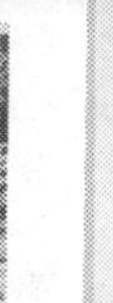

Huang Guo Shu Falls A443

Cowrie Shell and Shell-shaped Coin A444

Perf. 13x13½, 11½(Photo.)

1981-83 Engr., Photo.

No.	Type	Description	Value
1723	A443	1f Xishuang Banna	5
1724	A443	1½f Mt. Hua	5
1725	A443	2f Mt. Tai	5
1726	A443	3f shown	5
a.		Photo.	5
1727	A443	4f Hainan Isld.	6
a.		Photo.	6
1728	A443	5f Tiger Hill, Suzhou	8
1729	A443	8f Great Wall	12
a.		Photo.	12
1730	A443	10f Immense Forest	15
a.		Photo.	15
1731	A443	20f Mt. Tian	30
a.		Photo.	30
1732	A443	30f Grassland, Inner Mongolia	45
1733	A443	40f Stone Forest	60
1734	A443	50f Banping Mountain	75
1735	A443	70f Mt. Qomolangma	1.05
1736	A443	80f Seven-Star Crag	1.20
1737	A443	$1 Three Gorges, Changjiang River	1.50
1738	A443	$2 Guilin landscape	3.00
1739	A443	$5 Mt. Huangshan	7.50
		Nos. 1723-1739 (17)	16.96
		Nos. 1726a-1731a (5)	68

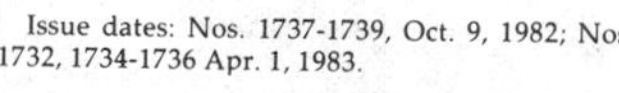

Issue dates: Nos. 1737-1739, Oct. 9, 1982; Nos. 1732, 1734-1736 Apr. 1, 1983.

1981, Oct. 29 Photo. & Engr. *Perf. 11½x11*

Ancient Coins. Numbered T.65.

No.	Type	Description	Value
1740	A444	4f shown (8-1)	6
1741	A444	4f Shovel (8-2)	6
1742	A444	8f Shovel, diff. (8-3)	12
1743	A444	8f Shovel, diff. (8-4)	12
1744	A444	8f Knife (8-5)	12
1745	A444	8f Knife (8-6)	12
1746	A444	60f Knife, diff. (8-7)	90
1747	A444	70f Gong (8-8)	1.05
		Nos. 1740-1747 (8)	2.55

See Nos. 1765-1772.

Intl. Year of the Disabled—A445

1981, Nov. 10 Photo. *Perf. 11½x11*

No.	Type	Description	Value
1748	A445	8f multi	25

Numbered J.72.

Twelve Beauties, from The Dream of Red Mansions, by Cao Xueqin—A446

1981-82 Photo. *Perf. 11*

No.	Type	Description	Value
1749	A446	4f Daiyu (12-1)	6
1750	A446	4f Baochai (12-2)	6
1751	A446	8f Yuanchun (12-3)	12
1752	A446	8f Yingchun (12-4)	12
1753	A446	8f Tanchun (12-5)	12
1754	A446	8f Xichun (12-6)	12
1755	A446	8f Xiangyun (12-7)	12
1756	A446	10f Liwan (12-8)	15
1757	A446	20f Xifeng (12-9)	30
1758	A446	30f Sister Qiao (12-10)	45
1759	A446	40f Keqing (12-11)	60
1760	A446	80f Miaoyu (12-12)	1.20
		Nos. 1749-1760 (12)	3.42

Souvenir Sheet

No.	Type	Description	Value
1761	A446	$2 Baoyu, Daiyu	6.00

No. 1761 contains one stamp (59x39mm.); multicolored margin continues design. Size: 140x78mm. Issue dates: Nos. 1749, 1751, 1753, 1755, 1757, 1759, 1761, Nov. 20, 1981; others, Apr. 24, 1982. Numbered T.69.

Women's Team Victory in 3rd World Cup Volleyball Championship—A447

1981, Dec. 21 Photo.

No.	Type	Description	Value
1762	A447	8f Girl playing volleyball (2-1)	25
1763	A447	20f Girl holding trophy (2-2)	50

Numbered J.76.

New Year 1982 (Year of the Dog) A448

1982, Jan. 5 Photo. & Engr. *Perf. 11½*

No.	Type	Description	Value
1764	A448	8f multi	50
a.		Bklt. pane of 10 plus label	2.00

Numbered T.70.

Coin Type of 1981

1982, Feb. 12 Photo. & Engr.

No.	Type	Description	Value
1765	A444	4f Guilian mask (8-1)	6
1766	A444	4f Shu shovel (8-2)	6
1767	A444	8f Xia zhuan shovel (8-3)	12
1768	A444	8f Han Dan shovel (8-4)	12
1769	A444	8f Knife (8-5)	12
1770	A444	8f Ming knife (8-6)	12
1771	A444	70f Jin hua knife (8-7)	1.05
1772	A444	80f Yi Liu Hua coin (8-8)	1.20
		Nos. 1765-1772 (8)	2.85

Numbered T.71.

Nie Er (1912-1935), Natl. Anthem Composer—A449

1982, Feb. 15 *Perf. 11x11½*

1773 A449 8f multi 25

Numbered J.75.

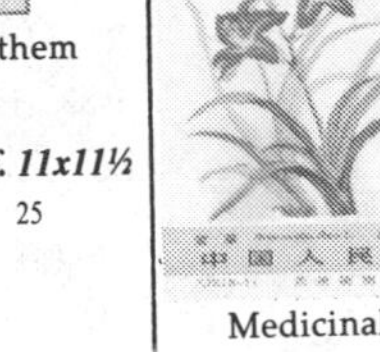

Intl. Drinking Water and Sanitation Decade, 1981-1990—A450

1982, Mar. 1 *Perf. 11½x11*

1774 A450 8f multi 20

Numbered J.77.

TB Bacillus Centenary—A451

1982, Mar. 24 *Perf. 11x11½*

1775 A451 8f multi 25

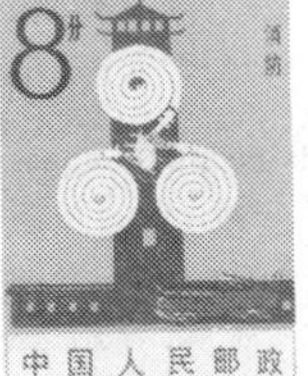

Fire Control—A452

1982, May 8 **Photo.** *Perf. 11½x11*

1776 A452 8f Water hoses (2-1) 12
1777 A452 8f Chemical extinguisher (2-2) 12

Numbered T.76.

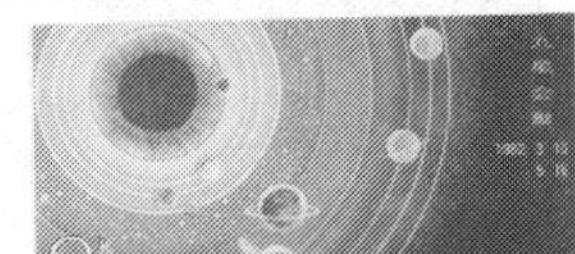

Syzygy of the Nine Planets, Mar. 10 and May 16—A453

1982, May 16 *Perf. 11½*

1778 A453 8f multi 25

Numbered T.78.

Medicinal Herbs

A454

Soong Ching Ling (1893-1981), Sun Yat-sens' Widow

A455

1982, May 20 *Perf. 11½x11*

1779 A454 4f Hemerocallis flava (6-1) 6
1780 A454 8f Fritillaria unibracteata (6-2) 12
1781 A454 8f Aconitum carmichaeli (6-3) 12
1782 A454 10f Lilium brownii (6-4) 15
1783 A454 20f Arisaema ... (6-5) 30
1784 A454 70f Paeonia lactiflora (6-6) 1.05
Nos. 1779-1784 (6) 1.80

Souvenir Sheet

1785 A454 $2 Iris tectorum maxim 3.00

No. 1785 contains one stamp (89x39mm.); gold and gray decorative margin. Size: 138x70mm. Nos. 1779-1784 numbered T.72.

1982, May 29 *Perf. 11½*

1786 A455 8f Addressing Consultative Conference (2-1) 15
1787 A455 20f Portrait (2-2) 35

Numbered J.82.

Sable—A456

1982, June 20 **Photo.** *Perf. 11½*

1788 A456 8f shown (2-1) 25
1789 A456 80f Sable, diff. (2-2) 1.50
a. Bklt. pane of 8: 6x8f plus sheetlet of 2 (8f, 80f) 1.75

Numbered T.68.

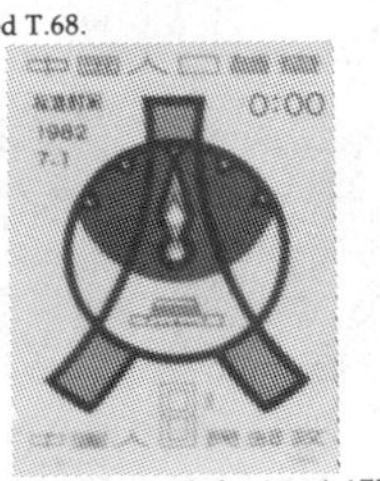

Natl. Census, July 1—A457

1982, June 30 *Perf. 11½x11*

1790 A457 8f multi 15

Numbered J.78.

2nd UN Conference on Peaceful Uses of Outer Space, Vienna, Aug. 9-21—A458

1982, July 25 **Photo.** *Perf. 11½x11*

1791 A458 8f multi 15

Numbered J.81.

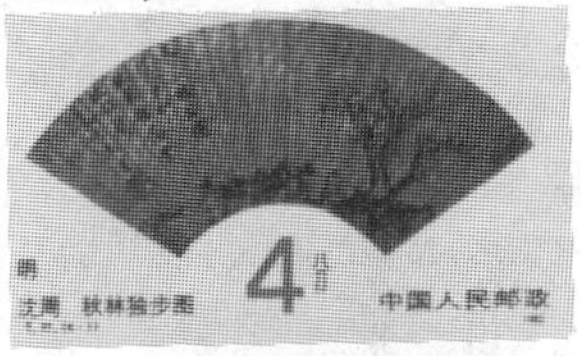

Strolling in Autumn Woods, by Shen Zhou, Ming Dynasty—A459

Fan Paintings (Ming or Qing Dynasty): No. 1793, Jackdaw on Withered Tree, by Tang Yin. No. 1794, Bamboo and Sparrows, by Zhou Zhimian. 10f, Writing Poem under Pine, by Chen Hongshou and Bai Han. 20f, Chrysanthemums, by Yun Shouping, Qing. 70f, Birds, Crape Myrtle and Chinese Parasol, by Wang Wu, Qing.

1982, July 31 *Perf. 11½*

1792 A459 4f multi (6-1) 6
1793 A459 8f multi (6-2) 12
1794 A459 8f multi (6-3) 12
1795 A459 10f multi (6-4) 15
1796 A459 20f multi (6-5) 30
1797 A459 70f multi (6-6) 1.05
Nos. 1792-1797 (6) 1.80

Numbered T.77.

60th Anniv. of Chinese Geological Society—A460

1982, Aug. 25 *Perf. 11½x11*

1798 A460 8f multi 15

Numbered J.79.

Orpiment—A461

1982, Aug. 25 **Photo.** *Perf. 11½x11*

1799 A461 4f shown (4-1) 6
1800 A461 8f Stibnite (4-2) 12
1801 A461 10f Cinnabar (4-3) 15
1802 A461 20f Wolframite (4-4) 30

Numbered T.73.

Souvenir Sheet

Messenger, Tomb Mural, Jiayu Pass, Wei-Jin Period—A462

1982, Aug. 25

1803 A462 $1 multi 4.75

All-China Philatelic Federation, First Congress. Pale green margin, black inscription. Size: 136x80mm. Numbered J.85.

12th Natl. Communist Party Congress

A463

Hoopoe

A464

1982, Sept. 1 *Perf. 11½*

1804 A463 8f multi 25

Numbered J.86.

1982, Sept. 10 *Perf. 11½x11*

1805 A464 8f shown (5-1) 12
1806 A464 8f Swallows (5-2) 12
1807 A464 8f Oriole (5-3) 12
1808 A464 20f Swifts (5-4) 30
1809 A464 70f Woodpecker (5-5) 1.05
Nos. 1805-1809 (5) 1.71

Souvenir Sheet

1810 A464 $2 Cuckoos 4.75

No. 1810 contains one stamp (56x36mm.); gray blue margin shows tree; black inscription. Size: 136x80mm. Numbered T.79.

Japan-China Relations Normalization, 10th Anniv.

A465

World Food Day

A466

Flower Paintings: 8f, Plum blossoms, by Guan Shanyue. 70f, Hibiscus, by Xiao Shufang.

1982, Sept. 29 ***Perf. 11***

1811	A465	8f J.84 (2-1)	12
1812	A465	70f J.84 (2-2)	1.05

1982, Oct. 16 ***Perf. 11½***

1813	A466	8f J.80	15

Guo Morou (1892-1978), Acad. of Sciences Pres. A467

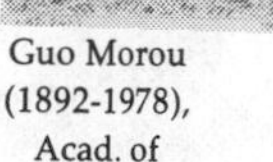

Bodhisattva, 11th Cent. Sculpture A468

Designs: Portraits. Numbered J.87.

1982, Nov. 16 **Photo.** ***Perf. 11½x11***

1814	A467	8f multi (2-1)	15
1815	A467	20f multi (2-2)	30

1982, Nov. 19 ***Perf. 11***

Liao Dynasty Buddha Sculptures, Lower Huayan Monastery. Numbered T.74.

1816	A468	8f multi (4-1)	12
1817	A468	8f multi (4-2)	12
1818	A468	8f multi (4-3)	12
1819	A468	70f multi (4-4)	1.05

Souvenir Sheet

Perf. 11x11½

1820	A468	$2 multi	4.75

No. 1820 contains one stamp (36x55mm.); marginal inscription. Size: 130x80mm.

Dr. D.S. Kotnis, Indian Physician in 8th Army—A469

1982, Dec. 9 Photo. ***Perf. 11½x11, 11x11½***

1821	A469	8f Portrait, vert. (2-1)	12
1822	A469	70f Riding horse (2-2)	1.05

Numbered J.83.

11th Communist Youth League Natl. Congress—A470

1982, Dec. 20 ***Perf. 11x11½***

1823	A470	8f multi	15

Numbered J.88.

Bronze Wine Container—A471

Western Zhou Dynasty Bronze (1200-771 B.C.): No. 1825, Three-legged cooking pot. No. 1826, Food bowl. No. 1827, Three-legged cooking pot (diff.). No. 1828, Animal-shaped wine container. 10f, Wine container with lid. 20f, Round food bowl. 70f, Square wine container. Numbered T.75.

1982, Dec. 25 **Photo. & Engr.** ***Perf. 11***

1824	A471	4f multi (8-1)	6
1825	A471	4f multi (8-2)	6
1826	A471	8f multi (8-3)	12
1827	A471	8f multi (8-4)	12
1828	A471	8f multi (8-5)	12
1829	A471	10f multi (8-6)	15
1830	A471	20f multi (8-7)	30
1831	A471	70f multi (8-8)	1.05
		Nos. 1824-1831 (8)	1.98

New Year 1983 (Year of the Pig)—A472

1983, Jan. 5 ***Perf. 11½***

1832	A472	8f multi	1.00
a.		Bklt. pane of 12	

Numbered T.80.

Stringed Instruments—A473

1983, Jan. 20 ***Perf. 11½x11, 11x11½***

1833	A473	4f Konghou (5-1)	6
1834	A473	8f Ruan (5-2)	15
1835	A473	8f Qin, horiz. (5-3)	15
1836	A473	10f Piba (5-4)	20
1837	A473	70f Sanxian (5-5)	1.40
		Nos. 1833-1837 (5)	1.96

Numbered T.81.

60th Anniv. of Peking-Hankow Railroad Workers' Strike—A474

1983, Feb. 7 **Photo.** ***Perf. 11½x11***

1838	A474	8f Memorial Tower, Zhengzhou (2-1)	20
1839	A474	8f Monument, Jiangan (2-2)	20

Numbered J.89.

The Western Chamber, Traditional Opera, by Wang Shifu (1271-1368)—A475

Scenes from the opera.

1983, Feb. 21 **Photo.** ***Perf. 11x11½***

1840	A475	8f multi (4-1)	12
1841	A475	8f multi (4-2)	12
1842	A475	10f multi (4-3)	15
1843	A475	80f multi (4-4)	1.25

Souvenir Sheet

Photo. & Engr. ***Perf. 12***

1844	A475	$2 multi	3.75

No. 1844 contains one stamp (27x48mm.). Size: 130x80mm. Numbered T.82.

Karl Marx (1818-1883)—A476

1983, Mar. 14Photo. & Engr.*Perf. 11½x11*

1845	A476	8f Portrait (2-1)	15
1846	A476	20f Making speech (2-2)	30

Numbered J.90.

Tomb of the Yellow Emperor—A477

1983, Apr. 5 **Photo. & Engr.** ***Perf. 11½***

1847	A477	8f Tomb, vert. (3-1)	12
1848	A477	10f Hall of Founder of Chinese Culture (3-2)	15
1849	A477	20f Cypress tree, vert. (3-3)	30

Numbered T.84.

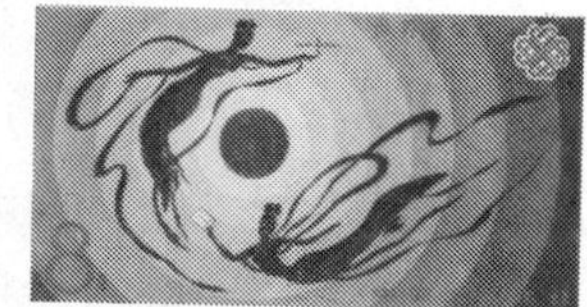

World Communications Year—A478

1983, Apr. 28 **Photo.** ***Perf. 11½***

1850	A478	8f multi	25

Numbered J.91.

Male Chinese Alligator—A479

1983, May 24 **Photo. & Engr.** ***Perf. 11***

1851	A479	8f shown (2-1)	12
1852	A479	20f Female, hatching eggs (2-2)	30

Numbered T.85.

Kitten, by Tan Arxi—A480

Various children's drawings. Numbered T.86.

1983, June 1 ***Perf. 11½x11***

1853	A480	8f multi (4-1)	12
1854	A480	8f multi (4-2)	12
1855	A480	8f multi (4-3)	12
1856	A480	8f multi (4-4)	12

6th Natl. People's Congress—A481

Perf. 11x11½

1983, June 6 **Photo. & Engr.**

1857	A481	8f Hall (2-1)	12
1858	A481	20f Natl. anthem score (2-2)	30

Numbered J.94.

Terra Cotta Figures, Qin Dynasty (221-207 BC)—A482

1983, June 30

1859	A482	8f Soldiers (4-1)	12
1860	A482	8f Heads (4-2)	12
1861	A482	10f Soldiers, horses (4-3)	15
1862	A482	70f Excavation site (4-4)	1.05
a.		Bklt. pane of 8 (#1859, 3 #1860, 3 #1861, #1862)	2.00

Souvenir Sheet

1863	A482	$2 Soldier leading horse	3.00
a.		Blkt. pane	3.00

No. 1863 contains one stamp (59x39mm., perf. 11½x11); multicolored margin continues design. Size: 100x86mm. Numbered T.88.

Female Roles in Peking Opera—A483

1983, July 20 **Photo.** ***Perf. 11***

1864	A483	4f Sun Yujiao (8-1)	6
1865	A483	8f Chen Miaochang (8-2)	12
1866	A483	8f Bai Suzhen (8-3)	12
1867	A483	8f Sister Thirteen (8-4)	12
1868	A483	10f Qin Xianglian (8-5)	15
1869	A483	20f Yang Yuhuan (8-6)	30
1870	A483	50f Cui Yingying (8-7)	75
1871	A483	80f Mu Guiying (8-8)	1.25
		Nos. 1864-1871 (8)	2.87

Numbered T.87.

Poets and Philosophers of Ancient China—A484

Paintings by Liu Lingcang.

1983, Aug. 10 **Photo.** ***Perf. 11½***

1872	A484	8f Li Bai (4-1)	12
1873	A484	8f Du Fu (4-2)	12
1874	A484	8f Han Yu (4-3)	12
1875	A484	70f Liu Zongyuan (4-4)	1.05

Numbered J.92.

5th Natl. Women's Congress—A485

1983, Sept. 1 **Photo.** ***Perf. 11½***

1876	A485	8f multi (1-1)	20

Numbered J.95.

5th National Games—A486

1983, Sept. 16 **Photo.** ***Perf. 11½***

1877	A486	4f Emblem (6-1)	6
1878	A486	8f Gymnast (6-2)	12
1879	A486	8f Badminton (6-3)	12
1880	A486	8f Diving (6-4)	12
1881	A486	20f High jump (6-5)	30
1882	A486	70f Wind surfing (6-6)	1.05
		Nos. 1877-1882 (6)	1.77

Numbered J.93.

Family Planning—A487

1983, Sept. 19 ***Perf. 11x11½***

1883	A487	8f One child (2-1)	12
1884	A487	8f Cultivated land (2-2)	12

Numbered T.91.

10th Intl. Trade Union Congress—A488

1983, Oct. 18 **Litho.** ***Perf. 11½***

1885	A488	8f multi (1-1)	20

Numbered J. 98

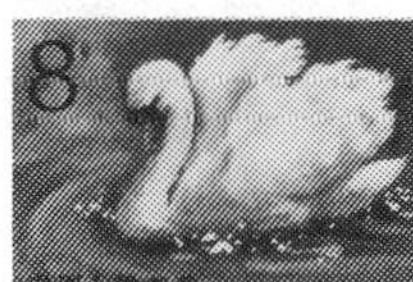

Swans—A489

1983, Nov. 18 ***Perf. 11x11½ on 3 sides*** **Photo.**

1886	A489	8f (4-1)	15
1887	A489	8f (4-2)	15
1888	A489	10f (4-3)	20
1889	A489	80f (4-4)	1.25
a.		Booklet pane, 7 #1886, 1 each #1887-1889	2.50

Numbered T.83.

85th Birth Anniv. of Liu Shaoqi, Political Leader—A490

Various photos. Numbered J.96.

1983, Nov. 24 **Photo.** ***Perf. 11½***

1890	A490	8f multi (4-1)	12
1891	A490	8f multi (4-2)	12
1892	A490	8f multi (4-3)	12
1893	A490	8f multi (4-4)	12

CHINAPEX '83 Natl. Philatelic Exhibition—A491

1983, Nov. 29 **Photo.** ***Perf. 11½***

1894	A491	8f No. 117 (2-1)	12
1895	A491	20f No. 4L1 (2-2)	30

Numbered J.99.

90th Birth Anniv. of Mao Tse-tung—A492

Various portraits. Numbered J.97.

1983, Dec. 26 **Photo.** ***Perf. 11½***

1896	A492	8f 1925 (4-1)	12
1897	A492	8f 1945 (4-2)	12
1898	A492	10f 1952 (4-3)	15
1899	A492	20f 1961 (4-4)	40

New Year 1984 (Year of the Rat)—A493

1984, Jan. 5 **Photo. & Engr.** ***Perf. 11½***

1900	A493	8f multi	45
a.		Bklt. pane of 12	2.00

Numbered T90.

Beauties Wearing Flowers—A494

Portions of painting by Zhou Fang (Tang Dynasty). Numbered T.89.

1984, Mar. 24 **Photo.** ***Perf. 11***

1901	A494	8f multi (3-1)	12
1902	A494	10f multi (3-2)	15
1903	A494	70f multi (3-3)	1.05

Souvenir Sheet

1904	A494	$2 Entire painting	4.75

No. 1904 contains one stamp (162x40mm.). Size: 176x66mm.

Chinese Roses—A495

1984, Apr. 20 **Photo.** ***Perf. 11½***

1905	A495	4f Spring of Shanghai (6-1)	6
1906	A495	8f Rosy Dawn of Pujiang River (6-2)	12
1907	A495	8f Pearl (6-3)	12
1908	A495	10f Black whirlwind (6-4)	15
1909	A495	20f Yellow flower in battlefield (6-5)	30
1910	A495	70f Blue Phoenix (6-6)	1.05
		Nos. 1905-1910 (6)	1.80

Numbered T.93.

Ren Bishi (1904-50), Statesman—A496

1984, Apr. 30 ***Perf. 11½x11***

1911	A496	8f multi	15

Numbered J.100.

Crested Ibis—A497

1984, May 15 **Photo.** ***Perf. 11x11½***

1912	A497	8f Flying (3-1)	12
1913	A497	8f Wading (3-2)	12
1914	A497	80f Perching (3-3)	1.25

Numbered T.94.

Chinese Red Cross Society, 80th Anniv.—A498

1984, May 29 ***Perf. 11½***

1915	A498	8f multi	15

Numbered J.102.

Gezhou Dam, Yangtze River—A499

1984, June 15 **Photo.**

1916	A499	8f Dam (3-1)	12
1917	A499	10f Bridge, vert. (3-2)	15
1918	A499	20f Lock Gate No. 2 (3-3)	30

Numbered T.95.

Zhuo Zheng Garden, Suzhou—A500

Perf. 11½x11

1984, June 30 **Photo. & Engr.**

1919	A500	8f Inverted Image Tower (4-1)	12
1920	A500	8f Loquat Garden (4-2)	12
1921	A500	10f Water Court, Xiao Cang Lang (4-3)	15
1922	A500	70f Yuanxiang Hall, Yiyu Study (4-4)	1.05

Numbered T.96.

1984 Summer Olympics—A501

1984, July 28 **Photo.** *Perf. 11½*

1923	A501	4f Shooting (6-1)	6
1924	A501	8f High jump (6-2)	12
1925	A501	8f Weight lifting (6-3)	12
1926	A501	10f Gymnastics (6-4)	15
1927	A501	20f Volleyball (6-5)	30
1928	A501	80f Diving (6-6)	1.20
		Nos. 1923-1928 (6)	1.95

Souvenir Sheet

1929	A501	$2 Athletes, rings	3.00

No. 1929 contains one stamp (61x38mm.); multicolored decorative margin. Size: 96x70mm. Numbered J.103.

Calligraphy

A502

Luanhe River Water Diversion Project A503

Artworks by Wu Changshuo. Numbered T.98.

1984, Aug. 27 **Photo.** *Perf. 11½*

1930	A502	4f shown (8-1)	5
1931	A502	4f A Pair of Peaches (8-2)	5
1932	A502	8f Lotus (8-3)	10
1933	A502	8f Wistaria (8-4)	10
1934	A502	8f Peony (8-5)	10
1935	A502	10f Chrysanthemum (8-6)	12
1936	A502	20f Plum Blossom (8-7)	25
1937	A502	70f Seal Cutting (8-8)	88
		Nos. 1930-1937 (8)	1.65

Perf. 11½x11, 11 (#1939)

1984, Sept. 11 **Photo.**

1938	A503	8f multi (3-1)	10
1939	A503	10f multi, horiz. (3-2)	12
1940	A503	20f multi (3-3)	25

Numbered T.97.

Chinese-Japanese Youth—A504

1984, Sept. 24 **Photo.** *Perf. 11½*

1941	A504	8f Neighbors (3-1)	10
1942	A504	20f Planting tree (3-2)	25
1943	A504	80f Dancing (3-3)	1.00

Numbered J.104.

People's Republic, 35th Anniv.—A505

1984, Oct. 1 **Photo.** *Perf. 11½x11*

Size: 26x35mm.

1944	A505	8f Engineer (5-1)	10
1945	A505	8f Farm woman (5-2)	10
1946	A505	8f Scientist (5-4)	10
1947	A505	8f Soldier (5-5)	10

Size: 36x48mm. *Perf. 11*

1948	A505	20f Birds (5-3)	25
		Nos. 1944-1948 (5)	65

Numbered J.105.

110th Birth Anniv. of Chen Jiageng—A506

1984, Oct. 21 **Photo.** *Perf. 12½x12*

1949	A506	8f Chen Jiageng (2-1)	10
1950	A506	80f Jimei School (2-2)	1.00

Numbered J.106.

The Maiden's Study—A507

Scenes from The Peony Pavilion, by Tang Xianzu. Numbered T.99.

1984, Oct. 30 **Photo. & Engr.** *Perf. 11*

1951	A507	8f shown (4-1)	10
1952	A507	8f In the dreamland (4-2)	10
1953	A507	20f Du Liniang drawing self-portrait (4-3)	25
1954	A507	70f Married to Liu Mengmai (4-4)	88

Souvenir Sheet

1955	A507	$2 Playing in the garden	2.50

No. 1955 contains one stamp (90x60mm, perf. 11½); multicolored decorative margin continues design. Size: 136x80mm.

Emei Shan Mountain Scenery—A508

1984, Nov. 16

1956	A508	4f Baoguo Temple (6-1)	5
1957	A508	8f Leiyin Temple (6-2)	10
1958	A508	8f Hongchun Lawn (6-3)	10
1959	A508	10f Elephant bath (6-4)	12
1960	A508	20f Woyun Temple (6-5)	25
1961	A508	80f Shining Cloud Sea at Jinding (6-6)	1.00
		Nos. 1956-1961 (6)	1.62

Numbered T.100.

Former Party Secretary Ren Bishi (1904-1950)—A509

Portraits.

1984, Dec. 15 **Photo** *Perf. 11½x11*

1962	A509	8f During the Long March (3-1)	10
1963	A509	10f At 7th Natl. Party Congress (3-2)	12
1964	A509	20f In motorcade (3-3)	25

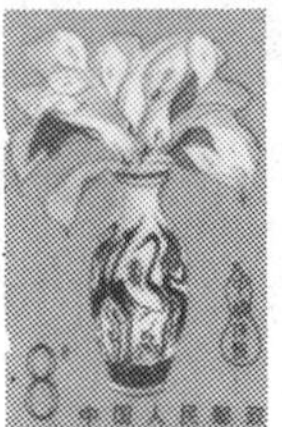

Chinese Insurance Industry—A510

1984, Dec. 25 *Perf. 11*

1965	A510	8f Flower arrangement	15

Numbered T.101.

New Year 1985 (Year of the Ox)—A511

1985, Jan. 5 **Photo. & Engr.** *Perf. 11½*

1966	A511	8f multi	15
a.		Bklt. pane of 4 + 8 plus label	2.00

Numbered T.102.

Zunyi Meeting, 50th Anniv.—A512

Paintings: 8f, The Zunyi Meeting, by Liu Xiangping. 20f, The Red Army Successfully Arrived in Northern Shaanxi, by Zhao Yu. Numbered J.107.

1985, Jan. 15 **Photo.** *Perf. 11x11½*

1967	A512	8f multi (2-1)	10
1968	A512	20f multi (2-2)	25

Lotus of Good Luck—A513

Lantern Folk Festival: No. 1970, Auspicious dragon and phoenix. No. 1971, A hundred flowers blossoming. 70f, Prosperity and affluence. Numbered T.104.

1985, Feb. 28 *Perf. 11½*

1969	A513	8f multi (4-1)	10
1970	A513	8f multi (4-2)	10
1971	A513	8f multi (4-3)	10
1972	A513	70f multi (4-4)	88

UN Decade for Women (1976-1985)—A514

1985, Mar. 8

1973	A514	20f multi	25

Numbered J.108.

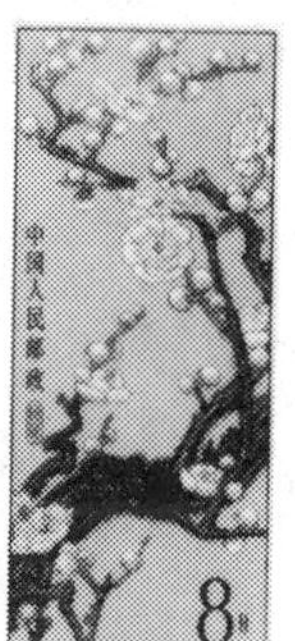

Mei (Prunus mume)—A515

1985, Apr. 5 *Perf. 11*

1974	A515	8f Green calyx (6-1)	10
1975	A515	8f Pendant mei (6-2)	10
1976	A515	8f Contorted dragon (6-3)	10
1977	A515	10f Cinnabar (6-4)	12
1978	A515	20f Versicolor mei (6-5)	25
1979	A515	80f Apricot mei (6-6)	1.00
		Nos. 1974-1979 (6)	1.67

Souvenir Sheet

1980	A515	$2 Duplicate and condensed fragrance mei	2.50

No. 1980 contains one stamp (93x52mm, perf. 11½); multicolored margin pictures floral design. Size: 130x70mm. Numbered T.103.

All-China Fed. of Trade Unions—A516

1985, May 1 **Photo.** *Perf. 11*

1981	A516	8f Huizo Guild Hall, Guangzhou	10

Numbered J.109.

Intl. Youth Year—A517

1985, May 4 **Photo.**

1982	A517	20f multi	25

Numbered J.110.

Giant Pandas—A518

Paintings of pandas: 8f, 20f, 50f, 80f, by Han Meilin; $3, by Wu Zuoren.

1985, May 24 *Perf. 11½*

1983	A518	8f multi (4-1), vert.	10
1984	A518	20f multi (4-2)	25
1985	A518	50f multi (4-3), vert.	65
1986	A518	80f multi (4-4)	1.00

Souvenir Sheet

1987	A518	$3 multi, vert.	3.75

No. 1987 contains one stamp (39x59mm, perf. 11x11½); multicolored margin contains inscriptions. Size: 74x80mm. Numbered T.106.

Xian Xinghai (1905-1945), Composer A519

Agnes Smedley, 1892-1950 (3-1) A520

Design: Bust, by Cao Chongen and music from The Yellow River Cantata. Numbered J.111.

1985, June 13 **Photo.** *Perf. 11½x11*

1988	A519	8f multi	10

1985, June 25

American journalists: 20f, Anna Louise Strong, 1885-1970 (3-2). 80f, Edgar Snow, 1905-1972 (3-3). Numbered J.112.

1989	A520	8f multi	10
1990	A520	20f multi	25
1991	A520	80f multi	1.00

Zheng He's West Seas Expedition, 580th Anniv.—A521

Designs: No. 1992, Portrait of the navigator (4-1). No. 1993, Peace envoy (4-2). 20f, Trade, cultural exchange (4-3). 80f, Honored for navigational feats (4-4). Numbered J.113.

1985, July 11 *Perf. 11½*

1992	A521	8f multi	10
1993	A521	8f multi	10
1994	A521	20f multi	25
1995	A521	80f multi	1.00

Xu Beihong, 1895-1953, Painter (2-2)—A522

1985, July 19 *Perf. 11½x11, 11x11½*

1996	A522	8f Self-portrait (2-1), vert.	10
1997	A522	20f shown	25

Numbered J.114.

Lin Zexu, 1785-1850, Statesman, Patriot (2-1)—A523

Design: 80f, Burning opium at Humen, bas-relief (2-2).

1985, Aug. 30 *Perf. 11*

1998	A523	8f multi	10

Size: 51x22mm.

1999	A523	80f multi	1.00

Lin Zexu's ban of the opium trade catalyzed the Anglo-Chinese Opium Wars. Numbered J.115.

Tibet Autonomous Region, 20th Anniv.—A524

1985, Sept. 1 *Perf. 11½x11*

2000	A524	8f Prosperity (3-1)	10
2001	A524	10f Celebration (3-2)	12
2002	A524	20f Abundant Harvest (3-3)	25

Numbered J.116.

End of World War II, 40th Anniv.—A525

Woodcuts by Wu Biduan: 8f, The Chinese Army Rose Against the Japanese Agressors at Logouqiao (2-1). 80f, The Eighth Route Army and Militia Fought Around the Great Wall (2-2). Numbered J.117.

1985, Sept. 3 *Perf. 11*

2003	A525	8f multi	10
2004	A525	80f multi	1.00

2nd Natl. Worker's Games, Sept. 8-15, Beijing—A526

Competitors from various events and: 8f, Men's bicycling (2-1). 20f, Women hurdlers (2-2). Numbered J.118.

1985, Sept. 8 *Perf. 11x11½*

2005	A526	8f multi	10
2006	A526	20f multi	25

Xinjiang Uygur Autonomous Region, 30th Anniv.—A527

1985, Oct. 1 **Photo.** *Perf. 11½*

2007	A527	8f Oasis in the Gobi, woman (3-1)	10
2008	A527	10f Oil field, Lake Tianchi (3-2)	14
2009	A527	20f Tianshan pasture, woman (3-3)	25

Numbered J.119. Size of No. 2008, 60x30mm.

1st Natl. Youth Games, Oct. 6-15, Zhengzhou—A528

1985, Oct. 6 *Perf. 11½x11*

2010	A528	8f Girls' track & field (2-1)	10
2011	A528	20f Boys' basketball (2-2)	25

Numbered J.121

Forbidden City Main Buildings—A529

1985, Oct. 10 *Perf. 11½*

2012	A529	8f multi (4-1)	10
2013	A529	8f multi (4-2)	10
2014	A529	20f multi (4-3)	25
2015	A529	80f multi (4-4)	1.00

Palace Museum, 60th anniv. Numbered J.120.

Zou Taofen (1895-1935), Journalist—A530

1985, Nov. 5 *Perf. 11½x11*

2016	A530	8f Portrait (2-1)	10
2017	A530	20f Epitaph by Zhou Enlai (2-2)	25

Se-tenant. Numbered J.122.

December 9th Revolution, 50th Anniv.—A531

1985, Dec. 9 *Perf. 11½*
2018 A531 8f Memorial Pavilion 10

Numbered J.125

New Year 1986 A532

Natl. Space Industry A533

1986, Jan. 5 Photo. & Engr. *Perf. 11½*
2019 A532 8f multi 10
a. Bklt. pane of 4 + 8 with label between 1.25

Numbered T.107.

1986, Feb. 1 **Photo.**

Designs: 4f, 1st experimental satellite. No. 2021, Recoverable satellite. No. 2022, Underwater rocket launch. 10f, Rocket launch. 20f, Earth satellite receiver. 70f, Satellite trajectory diagram. Numbered T.108.

2020 A533 4f multi (6-1) 5
2021 A533 8f multi (6-2) 10
2022 A533 8f multi (6-3) 10
2023 A533 10f multi (6-4) 12
2024 A533 20f multi (6-5) 25
2025 A533 70f multi (6-6) 90
Nos. 2020-2025 (6) 1.52

Dong Biwu (1886-1975), Party Founder A534

Lin Boqu (1886-1960), Party Leader A535

1986, Mar. 5 Photo. & Engr. *Perf. 11½x11*
2026 A534 8f Portrait, 1975 (2-1) 10
2027 A534 20f Portrait, 1945 (2-2) 25

Numbered J.123.

1986, Mar. 20
2028 A535 8f shown (2-1) 10
2029 A535 20f Boqu standing (2-2) 25

Nos. 2028-2029 printed se-tenant. Numbered J.124.

He Long (1896-1969), Revolution Leader—A536

1986, Mar. 22 *Perf. 11x11½*
2030 A536 8f shown (2-1) 10
2031 A536 20f Long on horseback (2-2) 25

Nos. 2030-2031 printed se-tenant. Numbered J.126.

Halley's Comet—A537

1986, Apr. 11 **Photo.** *Perf. 11½*
2032 A537 20f dk bl & gray 15

Numbered T.109.

White Crane—A538

1986, May 22 *Perf. 11x11½, 11½x11*
2033 A538 8f Two cranes (3-1) 6
2034 A538 10f One flying (3-2), vert. 8
2035 A538 70f Four cranes (3-3), vert. 52

Souvenir Sheet

2036 A538 $2 Flock 1.50

Numbered T.110. No. 2036 contains one stamp (size:); beige inscribed margin. Size: 160x52mm.

Li Weihan (1896-1984), Party Leader—A539

1986, June 2 *Perf. 11x11½*
2037 A539 8f Portrait (2-1) 6
2038 A539 20f Writing (2-2) 15

Numbered J.127.

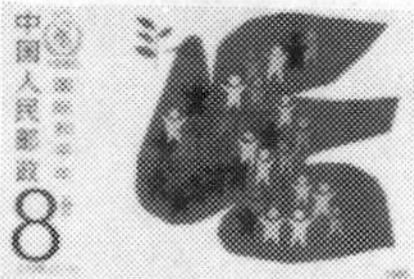

Intl. Peace Year—A540

1986, June 16 *Perf. 11*
2039 A540 8f multi 6

Numbered J.128.

Mao Dun (1896-1981), Writer—A541

1986, July 4 *Perf. 11x11½*
2040 A541 8f Portrait (2-1) 6
2041 A541 20f Portrait, diff. (2-2) 15

Numbered J.129.

Wang Jiaxiang (1906-1974), Party Leader—A542

1986, Aug. 15
2042 A542 8f Portrait (2-1) 6
2043 A542 20f Portrait, diff. (2-2) 15

Numbered J.130.

Teacher's Day—A543

1986, Sept. 10 *Perf. 11*
2044 A543 8f multi 6

Numbered J.131.

Magnolia Liliflora—A544

1986, Sept. 23 *Perf. 11x11½*
2045 A544 8f Blossom (3-1) 6
2046 A544 8f Two blossoms (3-2) 6
2047 A544 70f Blossom, diff. (3-3) 52

Souvenir Sheet

2048 A544 $2 Three blossoms 1.50

Numbered T.111. No. 2048 contains one stamp (size: 132x70mm).

Folk Houses—A545

Perf. 13x13½, 11x11½ (1½f, 30f, 90f, $1.10)

1986, Apr. 1 **Photo.**
2049 A545 1f Inner Mongolia 5
2050 A545 1½f Tibet 5
2051 A545 2f Northeastern China 5
2054 A545 8f Yunnan 10
2055 A545 10f Shanghai 12
2057 A545 30f Anhui 35
2060 A545 90f Taiwan 1.05
2062 A545 $1.10 Zhejiang 1.30
Nos. 2049-2062 (8) 3.07

Souvenir Sheet

All-China Philatelic Federation, 2nd Congress—A546

1986, Oct. 17 **Litho.** *Perf. 11½*
2063 A546 $2 Jade lion 2.50

Numbered J.135. No. 2063 has yellow bister, red and black decorative margin.

Leaders of the 1911 Revolution—A547

1986, Oct. 10 **Photo.** *Perf. 11x11½*
2064 A547 8f Sun Yat-sen (3-1) 10
2065 A547 10f Huang Xing (3-2) 12
2066 A547 40f Zhang Taiyan (3-3) 48

Numbered J.132

Souvenir Sheet

Sun Yat-sen (1866-1925)—A548

1986, Nov. 12			*Perf. 11½*
2067	A548	$2 multi	2.25

No. 2067 has black and gold decorative margin. Size: 82x137mm. Numbered J.133

Marshal Zhu De (1886-1976)—A549

Designs: 20f, Orating.

1986, Dec. 1		**Engr.**	*Perf. 11½x11*
2068	A549	8f sep (2-1)	10
2069	A549	20f myr grn (2-2)	24

Numbered J.134.

Sports of Ancient China—A550

Stone carvings. Numbered T.113.

1986, Dec. 20		**Photo.** *Perf. 11½x11, 11x11½*	
2070	A550	8f Archery (4-1), vert.	10
2071	A550	8f Weiqi (4-2)	10
2072	A550	10f Golf (4-3)	12
2073	A550	50f Soccer (4-4), vert.	60

New Year 1987 (Year of the Hare)—A551

1987, Jan. 5		**Photo. & Engr.**	*Perf. 11½*
2074	A551	8f blk, dk pink & yel grn	10
	a	Bklt. pane of 4+8+label	1.20

Numbered T.112.

SEMI-POSTAL STAMPS

Girl Holding Ball—SP1

1984, Feb. 16		**Photo.**	*Perf. 11½*
B1	SP1	8 +2f shown (2-1)	15
B2	SP1	8 +2f Boy, panda (2-2)	15

Numbered T.92. Surtax was for China Children's Fund.

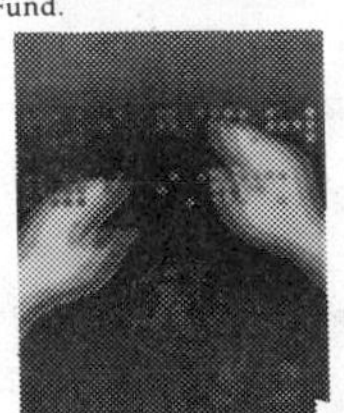

Hands Reading Braille—SP2

1985, Mar. 15		**Photo.**	*Perf. 11½*
B3	SP2	8f +2f shown (4-1)	12
B4	SP2	8f +2f Sign language, lip reading (4-2)	12
B5	SP2	8f +2f Artificial limb (4-3)	12
B6	SP2	8f +2f Handicapped person in wheelchair (4-4)	12

Surtax for China Welfare Fund. Numbered T.105.

AIR POST STAMPS

Mail Plane and Temple of Heaven
AP1

1951, May 1 Engraved *Perf. 12½*

C1	AP1	$1000 carmine	5	10
C2	AP1	$3000 green	10	10
C3	AP1	$5000 orange	5	15
C4	AP1	$10,000 vio brn & grn	8	25
C5	AP1	$30,000 dk bl & brn	1.50	75
		Nos. C1-C5 (5)	1.78	1.35

Planes at Airport
AP2

Designs: 28f, Plane over winding mountain highway. 35f, Plane over railroad yard. 52f, Plane over ship.

1957–58 *Perf. 14*

C6	AP2	16f indigo	16.00	5
C7	AP2	28f ol blk	16.00	10
C8	AP2	35f slate	16.00	4.00
C9	AP2	52f Prus bl ('58)	16.00	50

POSTAGE DUE STAMPS

Grain and Cogwheel
D1

Numeral
D2

1950, Sept. 1 Typo. *Perf. 12½*

J1	D1	$100 stl bl	5	10
J2	D1	$200 stl bl	5	10
J3	D1	$500 stl bl	5	10
J4	D1	$800 stl bl	10.00	10
J5	D1	$1000 stl bl	15	40
J6	D1	$2000 stl bl	15	40
J7	D1	$5000 stl bl	10	60
J8	D1	$8000 stl bl	10	1.00
J9	D1	$10,000 stl bl	20	2.00
		Nos. J1-J9 (9)	10.85	4.80

1954, Aug. 18 Litho. *Perf. 14*

J10	D2	$100 red	50	8
J11	D2	$200 red	15	8
J12	D2	$500 red	50	8
J13	D2	$800 red	5	8
J14	D2	$1600 red	5	15
		Nos. J10-J14 (5)	1.25	47

MILITARY STAMPS

Red Star, 8-1 in Center
M1

1953, Aug. 1 Lithographed *Perf. 14*

M1	M1	$800 yel, org & red (Army)	9.00	15.00
M2	M1	$800 dp pur, org & red (Air Force)	70.00	
M3	M1	$800 bl, org & red (Navy)	6,000.	

NORTHEAST CHINA

The Northeast Liberation Area included the provinces of Liaoning, Kirin, Jehol and Heilungkiang—the area generally known as Manchuria under the Japanese. The first postwar issues were local overprints on stamps of Manchukuo. In early 1946, a Ministry of Posts and Telegraphs served the areas already liberated, and in August, 1946, a Communications Committee of the Political Council was established. In June, 1947, these postal services were subordinated to the Harbin General Post Office, and this was extended to Changchun on Oct. 22, 1948, and to Mukden on Nov. 4, 1948. It was rapidly extended to cover all Manchuria.

All Stamps Issued without Gum

Mao Tse-tung
A1 A2

Lithographed

1946, Feb. *Perf. 11* Unwmkd.

1L1	A1	$1 violet	9.00	9.00
1L2	A2	$2 vermilion	60	1.00
1L3	A2	$5 orange	60	1.00
a.		Booklet pane of 6	150.00	
1L4	A2	$10 blue	60	1.00
a.		Booklet pane of 6	150.00	

Price, imperf set $35.

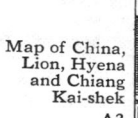

Map of China, Lion, Hyena and Chiang Kai-shek
A3

1946, Dec. 12 *Perf. 10½*

1L5	A3	$1 violet	1.50	1.50
1L6	A3	$2 orange	1.50	1.50
1L7	A3	$5 org brn	7.00	7.00
1L8	A3	$10 lt grn	11.00	11.00
a.		Imperf. pair	30.00	

10th anniversary of the capture of Chiang Kai-shek at Sian.

Railroad Workers, Chengchow
A4

1947, Feb. 7 *Perf. 10½*

1L9	A4	$1 pink	25	*1.00*
1L10	A4	$2 dl grn	25	*1.00*
1L11	A4	$5 pink	1.00	1.00
1L12	A4	$10 dl grn	2.50	2.50

24th anniversary of the Chengchow railroad workers' strike and massacre.

Women (Worker, Soldier and Farmer)
A5

Wmkd. Chinese Characters in Sheet

1947, Mar. 8 *Perf. 10½x11*

1L13	A5	$5 brick red	65	65
1L14	A5	$10 brown	65	65

International Women's Day, March 8.

Same Overprinted in Green ("Northeast Postal Service")

北 政

1947, Mar. 18

1L15	A5	$5 brick red	2.50	3.25
1L16	A5	$10 brown	2.50	3.25

Children Carrying Banner
A6

1947, Apr. 4 *Perf. 11x10½*

Granite Paper

1L17	A6	$5 rose red	3.00	3.00
1L18	A6	$10 lt grn	3.00	4.00
1L19	A6	$30 orange	3.00	5.00

Children's Day.

Nos. 1L1–1L2 Surcharged in Red, Brown, Black, Blue or Green

伍 政 拾 作 圓 5000

1947, Apr. *Perf. 11* Unwmkd.

1L20	A1	$50 on $1 vio (R)	19.00	19.00
a.		Brown surcharge	19.00	19.00
1L21	A2	$50 on $2 ver	19.00	19.00
a.		Brown surcharge	19.00	19.00
1L22	A1	$100 on $1 vio	19.00	19.00
a.		Green surcharge	19.00	19.00
1L23	A2	$100 on $2 ver (Bl)	19.00	19.00
a.		Green surcharge	19.00	19.00

Farmer and Worker
A7

Ax Severing Chain
A8

Wmkd. Chinese Characters in Sheet

1947, May 1 *Perf. 10½x11*

Granite Paper

1L24	A7	$10 org red	1.00	1.00
1L25	A7	$30 ultra	1.50	1.50
1L26	A7	$50 gray grn	2.50	2.50

Labor Day. Price, imperf pairs, set $200.

1947, May 4 *Perf. 11*

1L27	A8	$10 brt grn	2.50	2.50
1L28	A8	$30 brown	2.50	2.50
1L29	A8	$50 violet	3.00	3.00

28th anniversary of the students' revolt at Peking University against the 1918 peace treaty.

Price, imperf pairs, set $200.

Workers with Banner: "Oppose Imperialist Aggression"
A9

1947, May 30 *Perf. 10½x11*

Banner in Red

1L30	A9	$2 brt lil	2.50	2.50
1L31	A9	$5 brt grn	2.50	2.50
1L32	A9	$10 yellow	2.50	2.50
1L33	A9	$20 violet	2.50	2.50
1L34	A9	$30 red brn	2.50	2.50
1L35	A9	$50 dk bl	2.50	2.50
1L36	A9	$100 brown	2.50	2.50
a.		Souvenir sheet of 7	60.00	
		Nos. 1L30-1L36 (7)	17.50	17.50

22nd anniversary of the Shanghai-Nanking Road incident. No. 1L36a is on granite paper and contains 7 imperf. stamps similar to Nos. 1L30–1L36. Multicolored marginal inscription. Size: 215x158mm.

Price, imperf pairs, ordinary paper, set $500.

Mao and Communist Flag
A10

1947, July 1 *Perf. 10½x11*

1L37	A10	$10 red	4.00	4.00
1L38	A10	$30 brt lil	4.00	4.00
1L39	A10	$50 rose brn	11.00	11.00
1L40	A10	$100 vermilion	13.00	13.00

26th anniversary of the founding of the Chinese Communist Party.

Hand Holding Rifle
A11

1947, July 7 *Perf. 10½*

1L41	A11	$10 orange	4.00	4.00
1L42	A11	$30 green	4.00	4.00
1L43	A11	$50 dl bl	3.75	3.75
1L44	A11	$100 brown	3.75	3.75
a.		Souvenir sheet of 4	45.00	50.00

10th anniversary of the start of Sino-Japanese War. No. 1L44a contains 4 imperf. stamps similar to Nos. 1L41–1L44. Brown marginal inscription. Size: 149x107mm.

Exist imperf. Price set of pairs $600.

White Mountain and Black Water, Northeast China
A12

Wmkd. Zigzag Lines (141)

1947, Aug. 15 *Perf. 10½*

1L45	A12	$10 brn org	13.00	10.00
1L46	A12	$30 lt ol grn	1.50	10.00
1L47	A12	$50 bl grn	1.50	10.00
1L48	A12	$100 sepia	13.00	10.00

2nd anniversary of the reoccupation of Northeast China and the surrender of Japan.

Nos. 1L1–1L2 Surcharged in Black, Red, Green or Blue

圓 作 1000

1947, Aug. 29 *Perf. 11* Unwmkd.

1L49	A1	$5 on $1 vio	20.00	20.00
a.		Red surcharge	20.00	20.00
b.		Green surcharge	20.00	20.00
1L50	A2	$10 on $2 ver	20.00	20.00
a.		Blue surcharge	20.00	20.00
b.		Green surcharge	20.00	20.00

Map of Manchuria
A13

1947, Sept. 18 **Unwmkd.**

White Paper

1L51	A13	$10 gray grn	8.00	8.00
1L52	A13	$20 rose lil	8.00	8.00
1L53	A13	$30 blk brn	8.00	8.00
1L54	A13	$50 carmine	8.00	8.00

16th anniversary of Japanese attack on Mukden, Sept. 18, 1931.

Northeast Political Council Offices
A14

Mao Tse-tung
(Value figures repeated)
A15

1947, Oct. 10 ***Perf. 10½***

1L55	A14	$10 yel org	25.00	25.00
1L56	A14	$20 rose red	25.00	25.00
1L57	A14	$100 brown	70.00	70.00

35th anniversary of the founding of the Chinese Republic.

1947, Oct. 10 White Paper ***Perf. 11***

1L58	A15	$1 brown	20	1.50
1L59	A15	$5 gray grn	4.00	1.50
1L60	A15	$10 brt grn	12.00	8.00
1L61	A15	$15 bluish lil	12.00	8.00
1L62	A15	$20 brt rose	10	1.50
1L63	A15	$30 green	15	2.00
1L64	A15	$50 blk brn	15.00	10.00
1L65	A15	$90 blue	4.00	4.00
1L66	A15	$100 red	2.00	2.00
1L67	A15	$500 red org	30.00	15.00
		Nos. 1L58-1L67 (10)	79.45	53.50

Type A22 resembles A15, but has "YUAN" at upper right.

1947, Nov. **Redrawn**

White Paper

1L68	A15	$50 lt grn	75	1.50
1L69	A15	$150 red org	1.00	1.50
a.		Wmkd. Chinese characters	2.50	
1L70	A15	$250 bluish lil	25	1.50
a.		Wmkd. Chinese characters	1.00	1.50

1947, Dec. **Unwmkd.**

Newsprint

1L71	A15	$300 green	40.00	25.00
1L72	A15	$1,000 yellow	1.00	1.00
		Nos. 1L68-1L72 (5)	43.00	30.50

Panel below portrait 8½x3mm. on Nos. 1L68–1L70; 7x3mm. on No. 1L58–1L67. Nos. 1L68–1L70 have different ornamental border.

Nos. 1L71–1L72 without zeros for cents.

The $1, $90, $100 and $500 were also printed on newsprint; the $1,000 also on white paper.

Hand Holding Torch
A16

1947, Dec. 12 ***Perf. 11*** **Unwmkd.**

White Paper

1L73	A16	$30 rose red	7.00	7.00
1L74	A16	$90 dk bl	7.00	7.00
1L75	A16	$150 green	7.00	7.00

11th anniversary of the capture of Chiang Kai-shek at Sian.

Tomb of Gen. Li Chao-lin
A17

Globe and Banner
A18

Perf. 10½x11

1948, Mar. 9 **Unwmkd.**

1L76	A17	$30 green	10.00	10.00
a.		Granite paper, wmkd.	9.00	9.00
1L77	A17	$150 vio gray	10.00	10.00
a.		Granite paper, wmkd.	9.00	9.00

2nd anniversary of the assassination of Gen. Li Chao-lin, Commander of 3rd Army.

Wmkd. Chinese Characters in Sheet

1948, May 1 ***Perf. 11x10½***

1L78	A18	$50 red	8.00	10.00
1L79	A18	$150 green	1.00	15.00
1L80	A18	$250 lilac	1.00	30.00

Labor Day.

Student, Torch and Banner
A19

Perf. 10½x11

1948, May 4 **Unwmkd.**

Granite paper

1L81	A19	$50 green	10.00	10.00
1L82	A19	$150 brown	10.00	10.00
1L83	A19	$250 red	10.00	10.00

Youth Day, May 4.

Nos. 1L58, 1L61, 1L59, 1L63, 1L65, 1L2–1L4, 1L68–1L69, 1L71 Surcharged in Black, Blue, Red or Green

壹佰圓 10000 改作

1948–49 ***Perf. 11***

1L84	A15	$100 on $1 brn pur	60.00	45.00
a.		Blue surcharge	40.00	40.00
1L85	A15	$100 on $15 bluish lil	17.50	17.50
a.		Blue surcharge	40.00	40.00
1L86	A15	$300 on $5 gray grn (R)	55.00	25.00
1L87	A15	$300 on $30 grn (R)	8.50	10.00
1L88	A15	$300 on $90 bl (R)	8.50	10.00
1L89	A2	$500 on $2 ver	5.00	5.00
1L90	A15	$500 on $50 lt grn (R, '49)	27.50	20.00
1L91	A2	$1500 on $5 org (bl)	5.00	5.00
1L92	A15	$1500 on $150 red org (Gr, '49)	6.00	6.00
1L93	A2	$2500 on $10 bl (R)	5.00	5.00
1L94	A15	$2500 on $300 grn ('49)	5.00	5.00
		Nos. 1L84-1L94 (11)	203.00	153.50

Crane Operator
A20

Wmkd. Chinese Characters in Sheet

1948, May ***Perf. 11***

1L95	A20	$100 red & pink	50	50
1L96	A20	$300 vio brn & yel	1.50	1.50
1L97	A20	$500 bl & grn	1.50	1.50

6th All-China Labor Conference, Harbin.

Farmer, Worker and Soldier Saluting
A21

Mao Tse-tung
("YUAN" at upper right)
A22

Perf. 11x10½

1948, Dec. 3 **Unwmkd.**

White paper

1L98	A21	$500 vermilion	3.50	3.50
1L99	A21	$1500 brt grn	7.00	7.00
1L100	A21	$2500 brown	11.00	11.00

Liberation of Northeast China.

1949, Feb. ***Perf. 11***

1L101	A22	$300 olive	40	60
1L102	A22	$500 orange	1.00	1.00
1L103	A22	$1500 bl grn	40	60
1L104	A22	$4500 brown	40	60
1L105	A22	$6500 dk bl	40	70
		Nos. 1L101-1L105 (5)	2.60	3.50

See also type A15.

Workers, Globe and Flag
A23

Fields and Factories
A24

1949, May 1 ***Perf. 11½***

1L106	A23	$1000 red & dl bl	15	30
1L107	A23	$1500 red & pale bl	10	30
1L108	A23	$4500 rose & ol brn	15	40
1L109	A23	$6500 dl org & grn	60	50
1L110	A23	$10,000 mar & ultra	60	60
		Nos. 1L106-1L110 (5)	1.60	2.10

Labor Day.

1949 ***Perf. 10, 11***

1L111	A24	$5000 Prus bl	4.00	1.00
1L112	A24	$10,000 org brn	50	50
1L113	A24	$50,000 green	10	2.00
1L114	A24	$100,000 violet	15	8.00

Production in agriculture and industry.

Workers with Flags
A25

Heroes' Monument, Harbin
A26

1949, July 1 ***Perf. 11***

1L115	A25	$1500 vio, lt bl & red	5	25
1L116	A25	$4500 dk brn, lt bl & ver	1.00	30
1L117	A25	$6500 gray, lt bl & rose red	10	50

28th anniversary of the founding of the Chinese Communist Party.

1949, Aug. 15 ***Perf. 11½x11***

1L118	A26	$1500 brick red	10	50
1L119	A26	$4500 yel grn	25	50
1L120	A26	$6500 lt bl	1.25	50

4th anniversary of the Reoccupation, and the surrender of Japan.

東北貼用

(enlarged)

"Northeast Postal Service"

The following commemorative issues are similar to those of the People's Republic of China, with the 4 characters shown added in different sizes and various arrangements. Reprints were also issued similar to those of the PRC.

Chinese Lantern Type of PRC, 1949

1949, Sept. 12 **Litho.** ***Perf. 12½***

1L121	A1	$1000 dp bl	4.00	5.00
1L122	A1	$1500 scarlet	4.00	5.00
1L123	A1	$3000 green	4.00	5.00
1L124	A1	$4500 maroon	4.00	5.00

First session of Chinese People's Political Conference.

Reprints exist. Price, set 60 cents.

Factory
A27

1949, Oct. ***Perf. 11x10½***

1L125	A27	$1500 orange	25	40

Nos. 1L101, 1L103–1L105, 1L125 Surcharged in Black or Green

1949, Nov. 20

1L126	A22	$2000 on $300 ol	35.00	2.50
1L127	A22	$2000 on $4500 pur brn (G)	20.00	15.00
1L128	A22	$2500 on $1500 bl grn	75	3.00
1L129	A22	$2500 on $6500 bl	20.00	10.00
1L130	A27	$5000 on $1500 org	50	70
1L131	A22	$20,000 on $4500 pur brn	30	3.00
1L132	A22	$35,000 on $300 ol	45	4.00
		Nos. 1L126-1L132(7)	77.00	38.20

Globe and Hammer Type of PRC

1949, Nov. 15 ***Perf. 12½***

1L133	A2	$5000 crimson	60.00	60.00
1L134	A2	$20,000 dp grn	60.00	60.00
1L135	A2	$35,000 vio bl	60.00	60.00

Asiatic and Australasian Congress of the World Federation of Trade Unions, Peking.

Reprints, price, set $25.

Mao and Conference Hall Types of PRC

1950, Feb. 1 ***Perf. 14***

1L136	A3	$1000 vermilion	11.00	11.00
1L137	A3	$1500 dp bl	11.00	11.00
1L138	A4	$5000 dk vio brn	11.00	11.00
1L139	A4	$20,000 green	11.00	11.00

First session of Chinese People's Political Conference.

Reprints exist. Price, set $1.25.

Gate of Heavenly Peace (same size)
A28

1950 ***Perf. 10½***

Narrow horizontal shading

1L140 A28	$500 olive	25	50
1L141 A28	$1000 orange	25	50
1L142 A28	$1000 lil rose	1.00	50
1L143 A28	$2000 gray grn	10	15
1L144 A28	$2500 yellow	50	15
1L145 A28	$5000 dp org	10.00	20
1L146 A28	$10,000 brn org	50	50
1L147 A28	$20,000 vio brn	10	20
1L148 A28	$35,000 dp bl	10	35
1L149 A28	$50,000 brt grn	25	70
	Nos. 1L140-1L149 (10)	13.05	3.75

Flag and Mao Type of PRC

1950, July 1 ***Perf. 14***

Yellow Stars

1L150 A7	$5000 grn & red	11.00	11.00
1L151 A7	$10,000 brn & red	11.00	11.00
1L152 A7	$20,000 dk brn & red	11.00	11.00
1L153 A7	$30,000 dk vio bl & red	12.50	12.50

Inauguration of the People's Republic, Oct. 1, 1949.

Reprints exist. Price, set $1.50.

Picasso Dove Type of PRC

1950, Aug. 1 **Engraved** ***Perf. 14***

1L154 A8	$2500 brown	9.00	9.00
1L155 A8	$5000 green	9.00	9.00
1L156 A8	$20,000 blue	9.00	9.00

World Peace Campaign.

Reprints exist. Price, set $1.25.

Flag Type of PRC

1950, Oct. 1 **Engraved & Litho.**

Flag in Red & Yellow

1L157 A9	$1000 purple	10.00	10.00
1L158 A9	$2500 org brn	10.00	10.00
1L159 A9	$5000 dp grn	10.00	10.00
1L160 A9	$10,000 olive	10.00	10.00
1L161 A9	$20,000 blue	10.00	10.00
	Nos. 1L157-1L161 (5)	50.00	50.00

First anniversary of the Chinese People's Republic. Size of No. 1L159: 38x47mm., others 26x33mm. Reprints exist. Price, set, 35 cents.

Reprints exist. Price, set $1.

Postal Conference Type of PRC

1950, Nov. 1 **Lithographed**

1L162 A11	$2500 grn & dp org	4.00	4.00
1L163 A11	$5000 car & grn	4.00	4.00

All-China Postal Conference, Peking.

Reprints exist. Price, set, 40 cents.

Gate of Heavenly Peace (same size)
A29

1950 ***Perf. 10½***

Wide horizontal shading

1L164 A29	$5000 orange	40	1.25
1L165 A29	$30,000 scarlet	25	*3.00*
1L166 A29	$100,000 violet	2.50	3.25

Wmkd. Zigzag Lines (141)

1L167 A29	$250 brown	20	30
1L168 A29	$500 olive	20	30
1L169 A29	$1000 lil rose	25	50
1L170 A29	$2000 dl grn ('51)	10	50
1L171 A29	$2500 yellow	15	50
1L172 A29	$5000 orange	20	50
1L173 A29	$10,000 brn org ('51)	30	50
1L174 A29	$12,500 maroon	10	50
1L175 A29	$20,000 dp brn ('51)	30	1.00
	Nos. 1L164-1L175 (12)	4.95	*12.10*

A $50,000 grn was prepared, but not issued. Price $7.50.

Stalin and Mao Tse-tung Type of PRC

Engraved

1950, Dec. 1 ***Perf. 14*** **Unwmkd.**

1L176 A12	$2500 red	2.00	2.00
1L177 A12	$5000 dp grn	2.00	2.00
1L178 A12	$20,000 dk bl	2.00	2.00

Signing of the Sino-Soviet Treaty of Friendship, Alliance and Mutual Assistance.

Reprints exist. Price, set $1.50.

PARCEL POST STAMPS

Locomotive
PP1

Lithographed

1951 ***Imperf., perf. 10½***

1LQ1 PP1	$100,000 pur (P)	40.00
1LQ2 PP1	$300,000 brn (P, I)	150.00
1LQ3 PP1	$500,000 grnsh bl (P, I)	250.00
1LQ4 PP1	$1,000,000 ver (P, I)	400.00

PORT ARTHUR AND DAIREN

The Liaoning Postal Administration was established on April 1, 1946, in accordance with the Sino-Soviet Treaty, but was renamed one week later the Port Arthur and Dairen Postal Administration. On Apr. 3, 1947, it was combined with telecommunications and renamed the Kwantung Post and Telegraph General Administration. On May 1, 1949, the name was again changed to Port Arthur and Dairen Post and Telegraph Administration. Postal tariffs were based on local currency and both Manchukuo and Japanese stamps were overprinted for use.

With Gum

Manchukuo Nos. 162 and 94 Handstamp Surcharged in Violet ("Liaoning Post")

遼寧郵政
暫作
五圓

1946, Mar. 15

2L1	A19	20f on 30f buff	70.00	70.00
2L2	A18	1y on 12f org	40.00	40.00

Same Surcharge on Japan Nos. 260, 337, 195, 244, 263, 342 in Violet, Red or Black

1946, Apr. 1

2L3	A85	20f on 3s grn (V)	15.00	15.00
2L4	A151	1y on 17s gray vio (R)	12.00	12.00
2L5	A57	5y on 6s car	30.00	30.00
2L6	A57	5y on 6s crim	30.00	30.00
2L7	A88	5y on 6s org	20.00	20.00
2L8	A154	15y on 40s dk vio	90.00	90.00
		Nos. 2L1-2L8 (8)	307.00	307.00

Surcharge sideways on Nos. 2L5–2L6.

Japan Nos. 260 and 263 Surcharged

暫作
伍圓

1946, Apr.

2L9	A85	1y on 3s grn	*350.00*	
2L10	A88	5y on 6s org	*230.00*	

Sha Ho Kow (suburb of Dairen) issue.

Manchukuo Nos. 84, 88 and 98 Handstamp Surcharged in Green, Red or Black

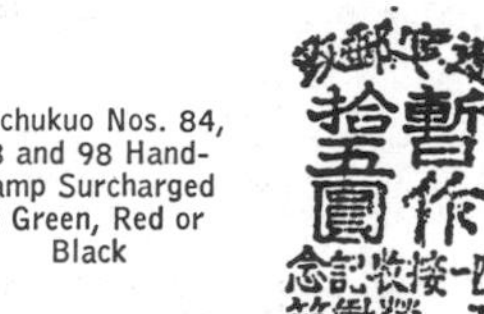

1946, May 1

2L11	A16	1y on 1f red brn (G)	18.00	18.00
2L12	A18	5y on 4f lt ol grn (R)	25.00	25.00
2L13	A19	15y on 30f chnt brn	50.00	50.00

Transfer of postal administration and Labor Day.

Manchukuo Nos. 159, 86 and 94 Surcharged in Green, Red or Black

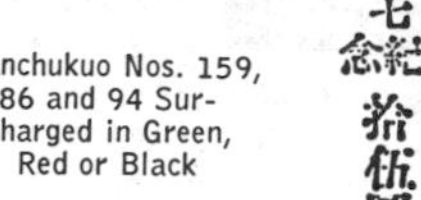

1946, July 7

2L14	A17	1y on 6f crim rose (G)	15.00	15.00
2L15	A17	5y on 2f lt grn (R)	65.00	65.00
2L16	A18	15y on 12f dp org	90.00	90.00

9th anniversary of the outbreak of war with Japan.

Manchukuo Nos. 94, 84 and 158 Surcharged in Black, Green or Red

中華民國光復
一週年紀念
暫作
壹圓
八•一五

1946, Aug. 15

2L17	A18	1y on 12f dp org (B)	27.50	27.50
2L18	A16	5y on 1f red brn (G)	50.00	50.00
2L19	A10	15y on 5f gray blk (R)	100.00	100.00

Surrender of Japan, first anniversary.

Manchukuo Nos. 159, 94 and 86 Surcharged in Green, Black or Red

中華民國
雙十節紀念
暫作
五圓

1946, Oct. 10

2L20	A17	1y on 6f crim rose (G)	27.50	27.50
2L21	A18	5y on 12f dp org (B)	50.00	50.00
2L22	A17	15y on 2f lt grn (R)	100.00	100.00

35th anniversary of Chinese revolution.

Manchukuo Nos. 84, 159 and 94 Surcharged in Black, Green or Blue

中華民國
魯迅逝世
十週年紀念
暫作
拾五圓

1946, Oct. 19

2L23	A16	1y on 1f red brn (B)	45.00	45.00
2L24	A17	5y on 6f crim rose (G)	70.00	70.00
2L25	A18	15y on 12f dp org (Bl)	110.00	110.00

10th anniversary of the death of Lu Hsun (1881–1936), writer.

Manchukuo Nos. 86, 159 and 95 Surcharged in Red, Green or Black

慶祝蘇聯建
軍節第二十
九週年紀念
暫作
五圓

1947, Feb. 20

2L26	A16	1y on 2f lt grn (R)	45.00	45.00
2L27	A17	5y on 6f crim rose (G)	85.00	85.00
2L28	A10	15y on 13f dk red brn	140.00	140.00

29th anniversary of the Red (USSR) Army.

Manchukuo Nos. 86, 159 and 162 Surcharged in Red, Green or Black

中國
關東郵政
暫作
拾五圓
紀念
五一勞動節

1947, May 1

2L29	A17	1y on 2f lt grn (R)	22.50	22.50
2L30	A17	5y on 6f crim rose (G)	65.00	65.00
2L31	A19	15y on 30f buff	100.00	100.00

Labor Day.

Manchukuo Nos. 86, 88, 98 and 162 Surcharged ("Kwantung Postal Service, China")

中國關東郵政
暫作
五圓

1947, Sept. 15

2L32	A17	5y on 2f lt grn	30.00	25.00
2L33	A18	15y on 4f lt ol grn	50.00	40.00
2L34	A19	20y on 30f red brn	75.00	60.00
2L35	A19	20y on 30f buff	80.00	75.00

Manchukuo Nos. 86 and 159 Surcharged in Red and Green

慶祝蘇聯建軍
節卅週年紀念
暫作
貳拾圓
關東郵政

Sacred Golden Kite (same size)
A1

1948, Feb. 20

2L36	A17	10y on 2f lt grn (R)	100.00	100.00
2L37	A17	20y on 6f crim rose (G)	120.00	120.00
2L38	A1	100y on bl & red brn	500.00	500.00

30th anniversary of the Red (USSR) Army. No. 2L38 is on an ungummed label commemorating the 2600th anniversary of the Japanese Empire.

政郵華中
五 暫
圓 作
電郵東關

Japan No. 260 and Manchukuo Nos. 84, 86 and 88 Surcharged in Red, Blue or Black

1948, July

2L39	A85	5y on 3s grn (R)	80.00	80.00
2L40	A16	10y on 1f red brn (Bl)	145.00	145.00
2L41	A17	50y on 2f lt grn	250.00	250.00
2L42	A18	100y on 4f lt ol grn (R)	600.00	400.00

Smaller Characters on Bottom Line

2L43	A17	10y on 2f lt grn (R)	200.00	145.00
2L44	A16	50y on 1f red brn	250.00	180.00

政郵東關
年週一卄念紀
壹 暫
佰
圓 作
節命革月十

Stamps of Manchukuo Nos. 84, 86 and 88 Surcharged in Blue, Red or Black

1948, Nov. 1

2L45	A16	10y on 1f red brn (Bl)	500.00	500.00
2L46	A17	50y on 2f lt grn (R)	500.00	500.00
2L47	A18	100y on 4f lt ol grn	450.00	450.00

31st anniversary of the Russian Revolution.

年八四祝慶
換勞業農東關
念紀會大覽展
拾 暫
圓 作
電郵東關

Manchukuo Nos. 86 and 161 Surcharged in Red or Green

1948, Nov. 15

2L48	A17	10y on 2f lt grn (R)	700.00	400.00
2L49	A17	50y on 20f brn (G)	700.00	700.00

Kwantung Agricultural and Industrial Exhibition.

政郵東關
貳 暫
拾
圓 作

Manchukuo Nos. 86, 88 and 161 Surcharged in Red, Black or Green

1949, Jan.

2L50	A17	20y on 2f lt grn (R)	500.00	
2L51	A18	50y on 4f lt ol grn	700.00	
2L52	A17	100y on 20f brn (G)	700.00	

Without Gum

From No. 2L56 onward all stamps were issued without gum except as noted.

Farmer and Worker
A2

Train and Ship
A3

Ship at Dock
(No. 2L55)
A4

(No. 2L56)

1949 Litho. *Perf. 11, 11½*

2L53	A2	5y pale grn	1.50	2.50
2L54	A3	10y orange	10.00	7.00
2L55	A4	50y vermilion	15.00	10.00
2L56	A4	50y red (redrawn)	20.00	15.00

Issue dates: Nos. 2L56, July 7; others Apr. 1.

Worker, Flag and Means of Transport
A5

1949, May 1 *Perf. 11*

2L57	A5	10y rose pink	8.00	8.00
a.		10y ver	75.00	75.00

Labor Day. No. 2L57a is from a worn plate.

Mao Tse-tung and Red Flag
A6

Heroes' Monument, Dairen
A7

1949, July 1

2L59	A6	50y red	24.00	24.00

28th anniversary of the founding of the Chinese Communist Party.

1949, Sept.

2L60	A7	10y red, bl & ol	15.00	15.00
a.		10y red, bl & pale bl	100.00	100.00

4th anniversary of victory over Japan and opening of the Dairen Industrial Fair.

Nos. 2L53–2L54 Surcharged in Red or Black

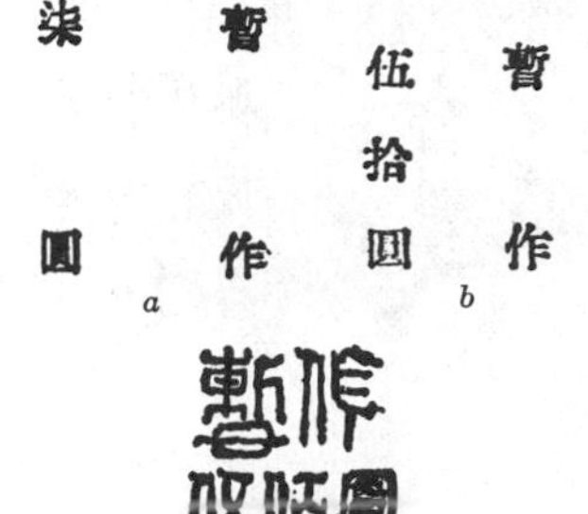

a *b*

c

With Gum

1949, Sept.

2L62	A2(a)	7y on 5y lt grn (R)	30.00	25.00
2L63	A2(a)	7y on 5y lt grn	30.00	25.00
2L64	A2(b)	50y on 5y lt grn (R)	85.00	70.00
2L65	A3(b)	100y on 10y org	450.00	350.00
2L66	A3(c)	500y on 10y org (R)	600.00	400.00
		Nos. 2L62-2L66 (5)	1,195.	870.00

Size of surcharge on No. 2L63: 16x19mm.

A 500y on 5y light green with red surcharge "c", and a 500y on 10y orange with surcharge "b" were prepared but not issued.

Stalin and Lenin
A8

1949, Nov. 7 *Perf. 11x11½*

2L68	A8	10y dl bl grn (shades)	8.00	8.00

32nd anniversary of the Russian Revolution.

Workers Saluting Mao, Star and Flag
A9

1949, Nov. 16 *Perf. 11*

2L69	A9	35y dk bl, red, & yel	9.00	10.00

Founding of the People's Republic of China.

(same size)

Stalin
A10

Gate of Heavenly Peace
A11

1949, Dec. 20 *Perf. 11½*

2L70	A10	20y dl mag	21.00	21.00
2L71	A10	35y rose red	21.00	21.00

70th birthday of Stalin.

1950, Mar. 10 Typo. *Perf. 10½*

2L72	A11	10y Prus bl	50	3.00
2L73	A11	20y dl grn	11.00	10.00
2L74	A11	35y red	50	3.00
2L75	A11	50y dp pur	30	4.00
2L76	A11	100y lil rose	50	7.00
		Nos. 2L72-2L76 (5)	12.80	27.00

NORTH CHINA

The North China Liberation Area included the provinces of Hopeh, Chahar, Shansi and Suiyuan. The original postal service, begun in the Shansi-Hopeh-Chahar Border Area in December, 1937, became the North China Postal and Telegraph Administration in May, 1949.

All Stamps Issued without Gum

Large Victory Issue

Cavalry Man Holding Nationalist Flag
A1

Perf. 10½

1946, Mar. **Wmk. Wavy Lines**

Granite Paper

Size: 34½x42mm.

3L1	A1	$1 red brn	1.00	1.00
a.		Newsprint	12.00	12.00
3L2	A1	$2 gray grn	1.00	1.00
3L3	A1	$4 vermilion	1.25	1.00
3L4	A1	$5 vio brn	1.25	1.00
3L5	A1	$8 vio bl	1.25	1.00
3L6	A1	$10 dp car	1.25	1.00
3L7	A1	$12 yellow	3.00	3.00
3L8	A1	$20 lt grn	7.00	7.00
		Nos. 3L1-3L8 (8)	17.00	16.00

Defeat of Japan.

Small Victory Issue

Perf. 10½x10, 9½ rough

1946, May **Unwmkd.**

Granite paper

Size: 20x21mm.

3L9	A1	$1 red org	1.00	1.00
3L10	A1	$2 green	1.50	1.00
3L11	A1	$3 lt lil	3.00	4.00
3L12	A1	$5 dl pur	4.00	10
3L13	A1	$8 dk bl	6.00	8.00
3L14	A1	$10 rose red	1.50	2.00
3L15	A1	$15 purple	30.00	20.00
3L16	A1	$20 green	3.00	3.00
3L17	A1	$30 brt grnsh bl	2.50	3.50
3L18	A1	$40 brt rose lil	3.00	3.00
3L19	A1	$50 brown	20.00	25
3L20	A1	$60 myr grn	30.00	75

Wmkd. Wavy Lines

3L21	A1	$100 orange	1.00	2.00
3L22	A1	$200 dl bl	1.00	2.00
3L23	A1	$500 rose	10.00	25.00
		Nos. 3L9-3L23 (15)	117.50	75.60

North China Postal and Telegraph Administration

Charging Infantrymen
A2

Agriculture and Industry
A3

1949, Jan. *Imperf.* **Unwmkd.**

White Paper

3L24	A2	50c brn lake	1.25	30
3L25	A2	$1 Prus bl	1.25	30

Newsprint

3L26	A2	$2 ap grn	1.25	30
3L27	A2	$3 dl vio	1.25	30

3L28	A2	$5 brown	1.25	30
3L29	A3	$6 dp rose	1.25	80
a.		White paper	1.25	80
3L30	A2	$10 bl grn	20	80
3L31	A2	$12 dp car	1.25	30
		Nos. 3L24-3L31 (8)	8.95	3.40

No. 3L29 issued in Peking, others in Tientsin.

Remittance Stamps of China Surcharged

壹 $1

叁 $3

A4

1949, Jan. Engraved Perf. 13

Small Central Characters

3L32	A4	50c on $50 brn blk	4.00	1.00
3L33	A4	$1 on $50 gray blk	3.00	1.00
3L34	A4	$3 on $50 gray	3.00	1.50

Large Central Characters

3L35	A4	50c on $50 blk	2.00	1.50
3L36	A4	$6 on $20 dk vio brn	2.00	1.50

Issued in Tientsin.

Sun Yat-sen Type A2 of Northeastern Provinces and China No. 640 Surcharged in Black, Red, Green or Blue

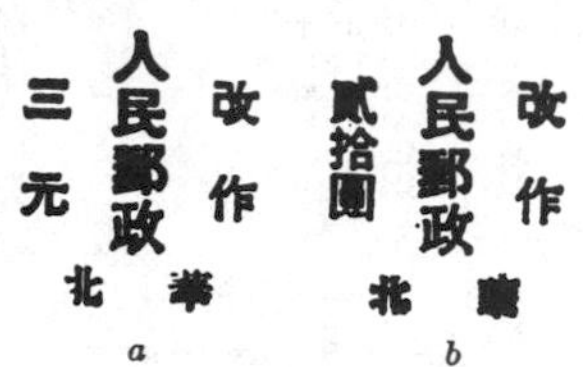

a b

c

Type "b," bottom character of left vertical row (yuan) differs. Type "c," top character of right vertical row differs.

1949, March 7 Perf. 14

3L37	A2 (a)	50c on 5c lake	25	3.00
3L38	A2 (a)	$1 on 10c org	25	1.00
3L39	A2 (a)	$2 on 20c yel grn	40.00	1.25
a.		Surch. inverted	140.00	
3L40	A2 (a)	$3 on 50c red org	25	3.00
3L41	A2 (a)	$4 on $5 dk grn	4.00	1.50
3L42	A2 (a)	$6 on $10 crim	1.00	1.00
3L43	A2 (a)	$10 on $300 bluish grn	1.25	2.00
3L44	A2 (a)	$12 on $1 bl	1.25	1.50
3L45	A2 (a)	$18 on $3 brn	1.25	75
3L46	A2 (b)	$20 on 50c red org (Bl)	1.25	25
3L47	A2 (a)	$20 on $20 ol, II	1.25	50
a.		Type I	10.00	10.00
3L48	A2 (a)	$30 on $2.50 ind (R)	1.25	2.00
3L49	A2 (a)	$40 on 25c blk brn (R)	4.00	1.00
3L50	A2 (a)	$50 on $109 dk grn (R)	9.00	2.00
3L51	A2 (b)	$80 on $1 bl (R)	15.00	1.00
3L52	A2 (a)	$100 on $65 dl grn (R)	18.00	1.50
3L53	A73 (b)	$100 on $100 dk car, surch. 16mm. wide (Bl)	25.00	1.30
a.		Surch. 14mm. wide	24.00	18.00

1949, Apr.

3L55	A2 (c)	$2 on 20c yel grn	1.25	1.50
3L56	A2 (c)	$3 on 50c red org	20	1.00
3L57	A2 (c)	$4 on $5 dk grn	8.00	2.00
3L58	A2 (c)	$6 on $10 crim, II	4.00	1.00
a.		Type I	9.00	1.00
3L59	A2 (c)	$12 on $1 bl	75	75

d e

1949, Apr.

3L60	A2 (d)	$1 on 25c blk brn (G)	15	2.50
3L61	A2 (d)	$10 on $300 bluish grn (R)	9.00	2.75
3L62	A2 (d)	$20 on 50c red org (G)	12.00	2.00
3L63	A2 (d)	$20 on $20 ol (R)	6.00	40
3L64	A2 (d)	$40 on 25c blk brn (R)	6.00	1.25
3L65	A2 (d)	$50 on $109 dk grn, surch. 15mm. wide (R)	9.00	1.25
a.		Surch. 13mm. wide	30.00	8.00
3L66	A2 (d)	$80 on $1 bl (R)	6.00	1.25

On Stamps of China

3L67	A73 (d)	$100 on $100 dk car (G)	50.00	4.00
3L68	A73 (d)	$300 on $700 red brn (Bl)	10.00	1.15
3L69	A82 (d)	$500 on $500 bl grn (R)	7.50	1.00
3L70	A82 (d)	$3000 on $3000 bl (R)	10.00	1.25

On Stamps of Northeastern Provinces

1949, Aug.

3L71	A2 (e)	$10 on $10 crim (Bl), II	6.00	1.15
a.		Type I	12.00	12.00
3L72	A2 (e)	$30 on 20c yel grn (R)	6.00	1.00
3L73	A2 (e)	$50 on $44 dk car rose (Bl)	6.00	50
3L74	A2 (e)	$100 on $3 brn (Bl)	10.00	1.25
3L75	A2 (e)	$200 on $4 org brn (Bl), II	18.00	4.00
a.		Type I	300.00	150.00

On China No. 754

3L76	A82	$10 on $7000 lt red brn (Bl)	10.00	4.00
		Nos. 3L37-3L76 (39)	320.10	61.50

Overprints on Nos. 3L71 and 3L76 have 2 characters in center row.

Farmer and Worker on Globe
A5

1949, May 1 Engraved Perf. 14

3L77	A5	$20 crimson	1.75	65
3L78	A5	$40 dk bl	1.75	80
3L79	A5	$60 brn org	1.75	65
3L80	A5	$80 dk grn	1.75	1.25
3L81	A5	$100 purple	1.75	1.00
		Nos. 3L77-3L81 (5)	8.75	4.35

Labor day. Exists imperf. Price, set $12.50. Also issued in blocks of 4, imperf between.

Mao Tse-tung (Chinese Numeral)
A6

Mao Tse-tung (Arabic Numeral)
A7

1949, July 1 Perf. 14

3L82	A6	$10 red	25	60
3L83	A7	$20 dk bl	25	60
3L84	A6	$50 orange	2.00	60
3L85	A7	$80 dk grn	30	1.00
3L86	A6	$100 purple	2.00	1.00
3L87	A7	$120 olive	20	1.00
3L88	A6	$140 vio brn	2.00	1.00
		Nos. 3L82-3L88 (7)	7.00	5.80

28th anniversary of the founding of the Chinese Communist Party.

Price, imperf set $30.

(same size)
Gate of Heavenly Peace
A8

Farmers and Factory
A9

1949, Nov. 26 Litho. Perf. 12½

3L89	A8	$50 orange	20	3.00
3L90	A8	$100 crimson	5	40
3L91	A8	$200 green	50	50
3L92	A8	$300 rose brn	9.00	1.00
3L93	A8	$400 blue	9.00	1.00
3L94	A8	$500 brown	9.00	60
3L95	A8	$700 violet	3.00	3.00
		Nos. 3L89-3L95 (7)	30.75	9.50

1949, Dec. Engraved Perf. 14

3L96	A9	$1000 orange	2.50	50
3L97	A9	$3000 dk bl	5	40
3L98	A9	$5000 crimson	10	75
3L99	A9	$10,000 red brn	10	1.50

PARCEL POST STAMPS

Parcel Post Stamps of China Nos. Q23-Q27 Surcharged in Red, Black or Blue

a b

1949, June

3LQ1	PP3 (a)	$300 on $6,000,000 ol gray (R)	15.00
3LQ2	PP3 (a)	$400 on $8,000,000 scar (Bl)	15.00
3LQ3	PP3 (a)	$500 on $10,000,000 sage grn (R)	18.00
3LQ4	PP3 (a)	$800 on $5,000,000 lil (R)	25.00
3LQ5	PP3 (a)	$1000 on $3,000,000 sl bl (R)	35.00

Surcharged Type "b"

3LQ6	PP3	$500 on $3,000,000 dk bl	25.00
3LQ7	PP3	$1000 on $5,000,000 vio gray	40.00
3LQ8	PP3	$3000 on $8,000,000 ver	75.00
3LQ9	PP3	$5000 on $10,000,000 dl grn	140.00
		Nos. 3LQ1-3LQ9 (9)	388.00

Nos. 3LQ8-3LQ9 have large numerals unboxed.

Remittance Stamps of China (like North China Type A4) Surcharged in Black or Red

a b

Peking Surcharge (a)

1949, June Litho. Perf. 13

3LQ10	$6 on $5 ver	5.00
3LQ11	$20 on $50 gray	5.00
3LQ12	$50 on $20 dk vio brn	5.00
3LQ13	$100 on $10 ol grn	10.00

Tientsin Surcharge (b)

Engraved Perf. 14

3LQ14	$20 on $1 brn org	12.00	6.00
a.	Perf. 12½	20.00	7.00
3LQ15	$30 on $2 dk grn	12.00	4.00
a.	Red surcharge	20.00	7.00
3LQ16	$30 on $10 ol grn	90.00	45.00
3LQ17	$100 on $10 gray grn (R)	12.00	6.00

Lithographed Perf. 13

3LQ18	$50 on $5 red	12.00	6.00

Engraved Perf. 12½

3LQ19	$20 on $1 org brn	35.00	18.00
3LQ20	$100 on $10 yel grn (R)	60.00	30.00

Typographed Roulette 9½

3LQ21	$30 on $2 bl grn (R)	45.00	22.50

The surcharge on No. 3LQ19 is without first and last lines.

Locomotive
PP1

1949, Nov. Engraved Perf. 14

3LQ22	PP1	$500 crimson	5.00	6.00
3LQ23	PP1	$1000 dp bl		10.00
3LQ24	PP1	$2000 green		15.00
3LQ25	PP1	$5000 dp ol		30.00
3LQ26	PP1	$10,000 orange		60.00
3LQ27	PP1	$20,000 red brn		150.00
3LQ28	PP1	$50,000 brn pur		300.00
		Nos. 3LQ22-3LQ28 (7)		571.00

NORTHWEST CHINA

The Northwest China Liberation Area consisted of the provinces of Sinkiang, Tsinghai, Ningsia and the western part of Shensi. The area was first established as the Shensi-Kansu-Ningsia Border Area in October, 1936, after the Long March to Yenan. Remote Sinkiang was not included until late 1949.

All Stamps Issued without Gum

Pagoda on Yenan Hill
A1

1945, Mar. Lithographed Imperf.

4L1	A1	$1 green	15.00
a.		Rouletted 9	80.00
4L2	A1	$5 dk bl	100.00
a.		Rouletted 9	115.00
4L3	A1	$10 rose red	14.00
a.		Rouletted 9	80.00
4L4	A1	$50 dl pur	10.00
4L5	A1	$100 yel org	14.00
		Nos. 4L1-4L5 (5)	153.00

First issue; denomination in Chinese and Arabic. Heavy shading at top of vignette. Columns at sides.

Nos. 4L1–4L2 Surcharged in Red:

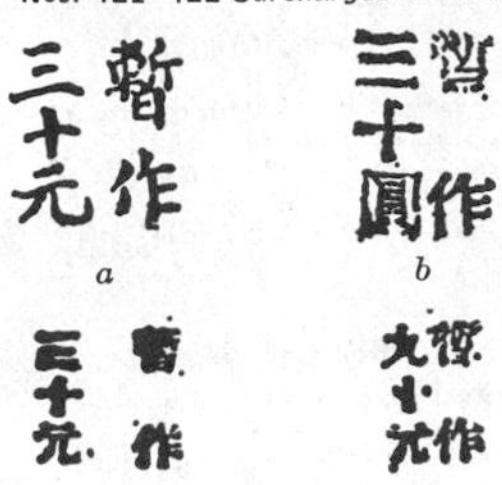

1946, Nov.

No.	Type	Description	Unused	Used
4L6	A1 (a)	$30 on $1 grn	30.00	
4L7	A1 (b)	$30 on $1 grn	125.00	
a.		Rectangular lower left character	600.00	
4L8	A1 (c)	$30 on $1 grn	15.00	
4L9	A1 (b)	$60 on $1 grn		
4L10	A1 (d)	$90 on $5 dk bl	20.00	

Surcharges on Nos. 4L7a and 4L9 are type "b" as illustrated. Surcharge on No. 4L7 differs from "b," having lower left character as in type "a."

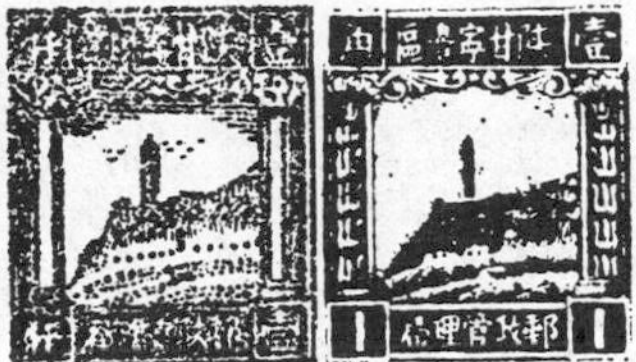

(same size)

Pagoda on Yenan Hill

A2 A3

1948, June

No.	Type	Description	Unused	Used
4L11	A2	$100 buff	140.00	
4L12	A2	$300 rose pink	1.00	
4L13	A2	$500 red	3.50	
4L14	A2	$1000 blue	3.50	
4L15	A2	$2000 yel grn	24.00	
4L16	A2	$5000 dl pur	10.00	
		Nos. 4L11-4L16 (6)	182.00	

Second issue; denominations in Chinese only. Many shades and proofs exist.

1948, Dec.

No.	Type	Description	Unused	Used
4L17	A3	10c yel org	1.50	
4L18	A3	20c lemon	1.50	
4L19	A3	$1 dk bl	1.50	
4L20	A3	$2 vermilion	1.50	
4L21	A3	$5 pale bl grn	9.00	
4L22	A3	$10 violet	13.50	
		Nos. 4L17-4L22 (6)	28.50	

Third issue; ornamental border at sides. Many shades exist.

Nos. 4L2 and 4L13 Surcharged in Red or Black

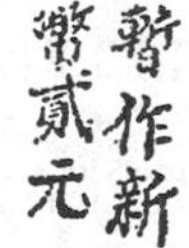

1949, Jan.

No.	Type	Description	Unused	Used
4L23	A1	$1 on $5 dk bl	45.00	
4L24	A2	$2 on $500 red	20.00	

Pagoda on Yenan Hill

A4

1949, May 1

No.	Type	Description	Unused	Used
4L25	A4	50c yel to ol	10	20
4L26	A4	$1 dl bl to ind	15	20
4L27	A4	$3 ol yel to org yel	10	20
4L28	A4	$5 bl grn	50	20
4L29	A4	$10 vio to dp vio	6.00	5.00
4L30	A4	$20 pink to rose red	1.50	2.00
		Nos. 4L25-4L30 (6)	8.35	7.80

Fourth issue; light shading at top of vignette, columns without ornaments at sides. Many shades exist.

China Nos. 959, F2 and E12 Overprinted ("People's Post, Shensi")

人民郵政(陝)

1949, June 13 Engr. *Perf. 12½*

No.	Type	Description	Unused	Used
4L31	A96	orange	18.00	18.00
4L32	R2	carmine	25.00	25.00
4L33	SD2	red vio	25.00	25.00

Stamps of China, Sun Yat-sen Type of 1949, Overprinted in Black or Red ("People's Post, Shensi")

西 人民郵政 陝

Lithographed; Engraved

1949, July 1 *Perf. 14, 12½*

No.	Type	Description	Unused	Used
4L34	A94	$10 grn (887)	1.00	1.00
4L35	A94	$20 vio brn (888)	2.00	2.00
4L36	A94	$20 vio brn (894C)	1.00	1.00
4L37	A94	$50 dk Prus grn (889; R)	5.00	5.00
4L38	A94	$50 grn (951)	5.00	5.00
4L39	A94	$100 org brn (890)	12.00	6.00
4L40	A94	$500 ros lil (892)	18.00	6.00
4L41	A94	$1000 dp bl (952; R)	25.00	8.00
4L42	A94	$2000 vio (946;R)	25.00	8.00
4L43	A94	$5000 car (953)	34.00	15.00
4L44	A94	$10,000 brn (954)	65.00	32.00
		Nos. 4L34-4L44 (11)	193.00	89.00

Kansu-Ningsia-Tsinghai Area, Lanchow Overprints

China Nos. 959a, F2 and E12 Overprinted ("People's Post, Kansu")

人民郵政(甘)

1949, Oct. Engr. *Rouletted*

No.	Type	Description	Unused	Used
4L45	A96	orange	18.00	18.00

Perf. 12½

No.	Type	Description	Unused	Used
4L46	R2	carmine	25.00	25.00
4L47	SD2	red vio	25.00	25.00

Stamps of China, Sun Yat-sen Type of 1949, Overprinted ("People's Post, Kansu")

人民郵政(甘)

Engraved; Lithographed

1949, Oct. *Perf. 14, 12½*

No.	Type	Description	Unused	Used
4L48	A94	$10 grn (887)	3.25	1.50
4L49	A94	$20 vio brn (888)	3.25	3.00
4L50	A94	$50 dk Prus grn (889)	9.00	8.00
4L51	A94	$100 org brn (890)	3.25	3.00
4L52	A94	$100 dk org brn (896)	5.00	4.00
4L53	A94	$200 red org (891)	6.50	5.00
4L54	A94	$500 rose lil (892)	6.50	5.00
4L55	A94	$1000 bl (894)	3.25	3.00
4L56	A94	$1000 dp bl (898)	6.50	5.00
4L57	A94	$2000 vio (946)	11.00	9.00
4L58	A94	$5000 lt bl (899)	22.00	18.00
4L59	A94	$10,000 sep (900)	30.00	25.00
4L60	A94	$20,000 ap grn (947)	60.00	50.00
		Nos. 4L48-4L60 (13)	169.50	139.50

China Nos. 959, F2 and 791–792 Surcharged in Black or Red ("People's Post, Sinkiang")

政郵民人 (新) 圓壹

1949, Oct.

No.	Type	Description	Unused	Used
4L61	A96	$1 on org	25.00	25.00
4L62	R2	$3 on car	25.00	25.00
4L63	A82	10c on $50,000 dp bl (R)	25.00	25.00
4L64	A82	$1.50 on $100,000 dl grn (R)	25.00	30.00

Northwest People's Post

Mao Tse-tung

A5

Great Wall

A6

1949, Oct. 15 Litho. *Imperf.*

No.	Type	Description	Unused	Used
4L65	A5	$50 rose	2.50	2.00
a.		$200 cliche in $50 plate	120.00	
4L66	A6	$100 dk bl	15	15
4L67	A5	$200 orange	15	75
4L68	A6	$400 sepia	2.50	1.25

EAST CHINA

The East China Liberation Area included the provinces of Shantung, Kiangsu, Chekiang, Anhwei and Fukien. The original postal service established in Shantung in 1941, became the East China Posts and Telegraph General Office in July, 1948.

All Stamps Issued without Gum

Mao Tse-tung

A1

Transportation and Tower

A2

1948, Mar. Litho. *Perf. 10½*

No.	Type	Description	Unused	Used
5L1	A1	$50 yel org	1.50	1.00
5L2	A1	$100 dp rose	5.00	3.50
5L3	A1	$200 dk vio bl	5.00	3.50
5L4	A1	$300 brt grn	5.00	3.50
5L5	A1	$500 dp bl	2.00	1.50
5L6	A1	$800 vermilion	5.00	4.00
5L7	A1	$1000 dk bl	10.00	8.00
5L8	A1	$5000 rose	20.00	15.00
5L9	A1	$10,000 dp car	35.00	25.00
		Nos. 5L1-5L9 (9)	88.50	65.00

Many varieties, including unissued imperforates exist.

Perf. 9 to 11 and comp.

1949, Apr. Lithographed

No.	Type	Description	Unused	Used
5L10	A2	$1 yel grn	10	10
5L11	A2	$2 bl grn	10	10
5L12	A2	$3 dl red	10	10
5L13	A2	$5 pale brn (ovpt. 4x4 mm)	10	10
a.		Without overprint	60.00	60.00
b.		Overprint 3x3 mm	1.00	1.00
5L14	A2	$10 ultra	15	15
5L15	A2	$13 brt vio	15	15
5L16	A2	$18 brt bl	15	15
5L17	A2	$21 vermilion	20	20
5L18	A2	$30 gray	20	20
5L19	A2	$50 crimson	25	35
5L20	A2	$100 olive	12.00	9.00
		Nos. 5L10-5L20 (11)	13.50	10.60

Seventh anniv. of Shantung Communist Postal Administration. The overprint on the $5, character "yu" meaning "Posts," obliterates Japanese flag on tower, erroneously included in design.

Price, imperfs of Nos. 5L10-5L12, 5L13a, 5L14-5L20 on different paper, set $75.

Train and Postal Runner (1949.2.7)

A3

Mao, Soldiers, Map

A4

Perf. 8 to 11

1949, Apr. Lithographed

No.	Type	Description	Unused	Used
5L21	A3	$1 brt emer	10	10
5L22	A3	$2 bl grn	10	10
5L23	A3	$3 dk red	5	10
5L24	A3	$5 brown	5	10
5L25	A3	$10 ultra	40	10
5L26	A3	$13 brt vio	5	10
5L27	A3	$18 brt bl	5	10
5L28	A3	$21 vermilion	5	10
5L29	A3	$30 slate	15	25
5L30	A3	$50 crimson	25	25
5L31	A3	$100 olive	50	50
		Nos. 5L21-5L31 (11)	1.75	1.80

Seventh anniversary of Shantung Post Office, Feb. 7. Imperf. sets were sold by the Philatelic Dept., Tientsin P.O. Price $25. See Nos. 5L69-5L76.

Perf. 9½ to 11 comp.

1949, Apr.

No.	Type	Description	Unused	Used
5L32	A4	$1 brt emer	5	5
5L33	A4	$2 bl grn	5	5
5L34	A4	$3 dl red	5	5
5L35	A4	$5 brown	5	5
5L36	A4	$10 ultra	5	5
5L37	A4	$13 brt vio	5	5
5L38	A4	$18 brt bl	10	10
5L39	A4	$21 vermilion	10	10
5L40	A4	$30 gray	10	10
5L41	A4	$50 crimson	10	10
5L42	A4	$100 olive	1.50	1.50
		Nos. 5L32-5L42 (11)	2.20	2.20

Victory of Hwai-Hai (Hwaiying and Haichow). Imperf. sets were sold by the Philatelic Dept., Tientsin P.O.

Price, set $60.

Stamps of China, Sun Yat-sen Type of 1949, Surcharged in Red or Black

政郵東華 京 圓壹作暫

(Nanking)

a

人民券 伍拾圓 東華 ═

(Wuhu)

b

1949, May 4 Engr. *Perf. 12½*

No.	Type	Description	Unused	Used
5L43	A94 (a)	$1 on $10 grn (894A, R)	50	50
a.		Perf. 13	3.00	3.00
5L44	A94 (a)	$3 on $20 vio brn (894C)	50	50
a.		Perf. 13	75	2.00
b.		Perf. 14	6.00	6.00
c.		Surch. inverted	165.00	

Perf. 12½, 14

1949, May Lithographed, Engraved

No.	Type	Description	Unused	Used
5L45	A94 (b)	$30 on $1000 dp bl (898)	7.50	5.00
5L46	A94 (b)	$30 on $1000 bl (894)	7.50	5.00
5L47	A94 (b)	$50 on $200 org red (897)	7.50	5.00
5L48	A94 (b)	$100 on $5000 lt bl (899,R)	16.00	13.00
5L49	A94 (b)	$300 on $10,000 sep (900,R)	50.00	40.00
5L50	A94 (b)	$500 on $200 org red (897)	75.00	60.00
		Nos. 5L45-5L50 (6)	163.50	128.00

Many varieties exist.

China Nos. 915a and 915 Surcharged in Blue, Green, Black or Red

(East China)

1949, May Litho. *Perf. 12½*

No.	Type	Description	Unused	Used
5L51	A95	$5 on 50c on $20 brn, II (B)	14.00	16.00
a.		grn surcharge	50.00	*25.00*
5L52	A95	$10 on 50c on $20 brn, II	14.00	16.00
5L53	A95	$20 on 50c on $20 red brn, II (R)	14.00	16.00
a.		Type I (R)	18.00	18.00

Stamps of China, Sun Yat-sen Type of 1949, Surcharged in Black or Red

政郵東華
杭
圓叁拾作暫

(Hangchow)

Engr., No. 5L57 Litho.

1949, June 25 *Perf. 14, 12½*

No.	Type	Description	Unused	Used
5L54	A94	$1 on $1 org (886)	1.50	1.50
5L55	A94	$3 on $20 vio brn (894C,R)	85	85
5L56	A94	$5 on $100 org brn (890)	4.00	2.00
5L57	A94	$5 on $100 dk org brn (896)	2.00	60
5L58	A94	$10 on $50 dk Prus grn (889,R)	14.00	12.00
5L59	A94	$13 on $10 grn (894A)	30	*70*
		Nos. 5L54-5L59 (6)	22.65	*17.65*

East China Liberation Area

Maps of Shanghai and Nanking
A5

1949, May 30 Litho. *Perf. 8½ to 11*

No.	Type	Description	Unused	Used
5L60	A5	$1 org ver	10	*20*
5L61	A5	$2 bl grn	10	*20*
5L62	A5	$3 brt vio	5	*10*
5L63	A5	$5 vio brn	6	*10*
5L64	A5	$10 ultra	10	10
5L65	A5	$30 slate	6	*20*
5L66	A5	$50 carmine	15	*40*
5L67	A5	$100 olive	15	*20*
5L68	A5	$500 orange	1.50	1.50
		Nos. 5L60-5L68 (9)	2.27	*3.00*

Liberation of Shanghai and Nanking. Many shades, paper and perforation varieties and imperfs. exist.

Train and Postal Runner Type Dated "1949"

1949, July–1950, Feb. *Perf. 12½, 14*

No.	Type	Description	Unused	Used
5L69	A3	$10 dp ultra	5	*10*
5L70	A3	$15 org ver	5	*40*
a.		$15 red, perf. 14	40	10
5L71	A3	$30 sl grn	5	10
a.		Perf. 12½	5	10
5L72	A3	$50 carmine	10	*40*
5L73	A3	$60 bl grn, perf. 14	5	*1.00*
5L74	A3	$100 ol, perf. 14	3.00	40
5L75	A3	$1600 vio bl ('50)	75	*3.00*
5L76	A3	$2000 brn vio ('50)	1.00	*3.00*
		Nos. 5L69-5L76 (8)	5.05	*8.40*

Chu Teh, Mao, Troops with Flags
A7

Mao Tse-tung
A8

1949, Aug. 17 *Perf. 12½*

No.	Type	Description	Unused	Used
5L77	A7	$70 orange	5	*10*
5L78	A7	$270 crimson	5	*10*
5L79	A7	$370 emerald	40	30
5L80	A7	$470 vio brn	65	40
5L81	A7	$570 blue	10	*30*
		Nos. 5L77-5L81 (5)	1.25	*1.20*

22nd anniversary of the People's Liberation Army.

1949, Oct.

No.	Type	Description	Unused	Used
5L82	A8	$10 dk bl	2.00	5.00
5L83	A8	$15 vermilion	2.50	2.50
5L84	A8	$70 brown	5	5
5L85	A8	$100 vio brn	10	5
5L86	A8	$150 orange	5	5
5L87	A8	$200 grnsh gray	10	5
5L88	A8	$500 gray bl	10	5
5L89	A8	$1000 rose	5	5
5L90	A8	$2000 emerald	5	10
		Nos. 5L82-5L90 (9)	5.00	7.90

Stamps of China, Sun Yat-sen Type of 1949 Surcharged in Black or Red

政郵民人華中
肆佰圓 華東區
★★★★★

1949, Nov. Litho. *Perf. 12½*

No.	Type	Description	Unused	Used
5L91	A94	$400 on $200 org red (897)	24.00	80
5L92	A94	$1000 on $50 grnsh gray (895, R)	2.00	80
5L93	A94	$1200 on $100 dk org brn (896)	5	*2.00*
5L94	A94	$1600 on $20,000 ap grn (947)	5	*80*
5L95	A94	$2000 on $1000 dp bl (952,R)	5	*80*
a.		Perf. 14	90.00	25.00
		Nos. 5L91-5L95 (5)	26.15	*5.20*

PARCEL POST STAMPS

Parcel Post Stamps of China 1945–48 Surcharged

20000
山東 郵政
貳百圓

(Shantung)

1949, Aug. 1 Engraved *Perf. 13*

No.	Type	Description	Unused	Used
5LQ1	PP1	$200 on $500 grn	8.00	8.00
5LQ2	PP1	$500 on $1000 Bl	8.00	8.00

Perf. 13½

No.	Type	Description	Unused	Used
5LQ3	PP3	$200 on $200,000 dk grn	40.00	30.00
5LQ4	PP3	$200 on $10,000,000 sage grn	8.00	8.00
5LQ5	PP3	$500 on $7000 dl bl	70.00	50.00
5LQ6	PP3	$500 on $50,000 ind	8.00	8.00
5LQ7	PP3	$1000 on $10,000 car rose	8.00	8.00
5LQ8	PP3	$1000 on $100,000 dk rose brn	8.00	8.00
5LQ9	PP3	$1000 on $300,000 pink	6.00	6.00
5LQ10	PP3	$1000 on $500,000 vio brn	50.00	45.00
5LQ11	PP3	$1000 on $8,000,000 org ver	8.00	8.00
5LQ12	PP3	$2000 on $5,000,000 dl vio	12.00	12.00
5LQ13	PP3	$2000 on $6,000,000 brn blk	12.00	12.00
5LQ14	PP3	$3000 on $30,000 ol	20.00	17.50
5LQ15	PP3	$3000 on $70,000 org brn	20.00	17.50
5LQ16	PP3	$5000 on $3,000,000 dl bl	25.00	22.50
		Nos. 5LQ1-5LQ16 (16)	311.00	268.50

China No. 987 Surcharged

紙印裹包 圓萬壹
政郵東華
圓萬壹 紙印裹包

$200 $500
$1000 $2000
$5000 $10,000

1949, Sept. 7 Litho. *Perf. 12½*

No.	Type	Description	Unused	Used
5LQ17	A97	$200 on $10 bl grn	30.00	15.00
5LQ18	A97	$500 on $10 bl grn	30.00	15.00
5LQ19	A97	$1000 on $10 bl grn	30.00	15.00
5LQ20	A97	$2000 on $10 bl grn	30.00	15.00
5LQ21	A97	$5000 on $10 bl grn	30.00	15.00
5LQ22	A97	$10,000 on $10 bl grn	30.00	15.00
		Nos. 5LQ17-5LQ22 (6)	180.00	90.00

Flying Geese Type of China, 1949, and China Nos. 984–986 Surcharged in Red or Black

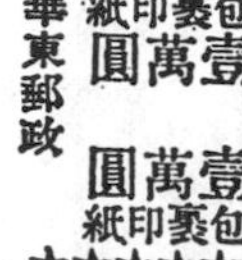

1950, Jan. 28

No.	Type	Description	Unused	Used
5LQ23	A97	$5000 on 10c bl vio (R)	90.00	50.00
5LQ24	A97	$10,000 on $1 brn org	90.00	50.00
5LQ25	A97	$20,000 on $2 bl	90.00	50.00
5LQ26	A97	$50,000 on $5 car rose	90.00	50.00

Parcel Post Stamps of China Nos. Q1–Q4 Surcharged in Red or Black

紙印裹包
圓萬貳
政郵東華
圓萬貳

1950, Jan. 28 Engraved *Perf. 13*

No.	Type	Description	Unused	Used
5LQ27	PP1	$5000 on $500 grn (R)	20	*50.00*
5LQ28	PP1	$10,000 on $1000 bl (R)	120.00	50.00
5LQ29	PP1	$20,000 on $3000 bl grn	120.00	50.00
5LQ30	PP1	$50,000 on $5000 org red	20.00	50.00

CENTRAL CHINA

The Central Chinese Liberation Area included the provinces of Honan, Hupeh, Hunan and Kiangsi. The area was established between August and September, 1949, following the liberation of Hankow.

All Stamps Issued without Gum

Hupeh Postal and Telegraph Administration

Stamps of China, Sun Yat-sen Type of 1949, Surcharged ("Chinese P.O., Temporary Use")

政郵中華
用暫
100 圓壹

Engraved; Lithographed

1949, June 4 *Perf. 14, 12½*

Thin parallel lines.

No.	Type	Description	Unused	Used
6L1	A94	$1 on $200 red org (891)	75	75
6L2	A94	$6 on 10,000 sep (900)	75	75
6L3	A94	$15 on $1 org (886)	75	75
6L4	A94	$30 on $100 org brn (890)	3.50	3.50
6L5	A94	$30 on $100 dk org brn (896)	75	75
6L6	A94	$50 on $20 vio brn (894C)	12.00	12.00
6L7	A94	$80 on $1000 dp bl (898)	2.25	2.25

Thick parallel lines.

No.	Type	Description	Unused	Used
6L8	A94	$1 on $200 red org (891)	3.50	3.50
6L9	A94	$3 on $5000 lt bl (899)	50	50
6L10	A94	$10 on $500 rose lil (892)	50	50
6L11	A94	$10 on $500 rose lil (945)	3.50	3.50
6L12	A94	$50 on $20 vio brn (888)	3.50	3.50
6L13	A94	$50 on $20 vio brn (894C)	1.00	1.00
6L14	A94	$80 on $1000 bl (894)	3.50	3.50
6L15	A94	$80 on $1000 dp bl (898)	12.00	12.00
6L16	A94	$100 on $50 dk Prus grn (899)	1.50	1.50
		Nos. 6L1-6L16 (16)	50.25	50.25

Kiangsi Postal and Telegraph Administration

Central Trust Revenue Stamps of China Surcharged ("People's Post, Kiangsi")

(same size)
A1

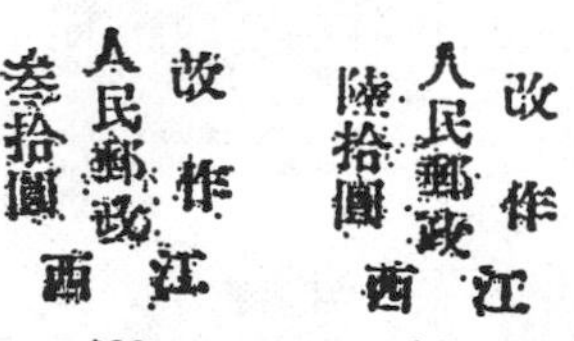

$30 $60

1949, June 20 Engr. *Perf. 12½*

No.	Type	Description	Unused	Used
6L17	A1	$3 on $30 pur	1.00	1.00
6L18	A1	$15 on $15 red org	1.00	1.00
6L19	A1	$30 on $50 dk bl	1.00	1.00
6L20	A1	$60 on $50 dk bl	1.00	1.00
6L21	A1	$130 on $15 red org	1.00	1.00

The $15 surcharge has 3 characters in left vertical row, the $130 surcharge has 5.

Same Surcharge on Sun Yat-sen Issues of China, 1945–49

Engraved, Litho. *Perf. 14, 12½*

No.	Type	Description	Unused	Used
6L22	A82	$1 on $250 dp lil (746)	3.00	3.00
6L23	A94	$5 on $1000 dp bl (898)	3.00	3.00
6L24	A94	$5 on $2000 vio (946)	3.00	3.00
6L25	A94	$5 on $5000 lt bl (899)	1.00	1.00
6L26	A94	$10 on $1000 bl (894)	3.00	3.00
6L27	A82	$20 on $4000 gray	1.00	1.00
6L28	A73	$30 on $100 dk car	3.00	3.00
6L29	A82	$30 on $20,000 rose pink	1.00	1.00
6L30	A94	$80 on $500 rose lil (945)	1.00	1.00
6L31	A94	$100 on $1000 dp bl (898)	1.00	1.00
6L32	A82	$200 on $250 dp lil	2.00	2.00
		Nos. 6L17-6L32 (16)	27.00	27.00

Central China Posts and Telegraph Administration

Farmer, Soldier and Worker
A2 A3

I. Top white line of square character (yuan) at upper left does not touch left vertical stroke. No gap in shading between soldier's feet.
II. Top line connects with left vertical stroke. Gap in shading between feet.

Perf. 10 to 11½ & Comp.

1949 **Lithographed**

6L33	A2	$1 orange	9.00	9.00
6L34	A2	$3 brn org	3.00	3.00
6L35	A2	$6 emerald	3.00	3.00
6L36	A3	$7 yel brn	50	50
6L37	A2	$10 bl grn	15	30
6L38	A3	$14 org brn	18.00	9.00
6L39	A2	$15 ultra	40	15
6L40	A2	$30 grn, I	10	15
a.		Type II	10	15
6L41	A3	$35 gray bl	12.00	9.00
6L42	A2	$50 rose vio	10.00	6.00
6L43	A3	$70 dp grn	15	15
6L44	A2	$80 pink	50	50
6L45	A3	$100 bl grn	30	30
6L46	A3	$220 rose red	4.00	4.00
		Nos. 6L33-6L46 (14)	61.10	45.05

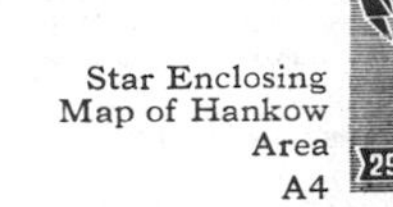

Star Enclosing Map of Hankow Area
A4

Two types of $500:
I. Thick numerals of "500". No period after "500".
II. Thin numerals and period.
Two types of $1000:
I. No period after "1000".
II. Period after "1000".

1949, July

6L48	A4	$110 org brn	25	25
6L49	A4	$130 violet	5.00	25
6L50	A4	$200 dp org	10	25
6L51	A4	$290 brown	2.00	75
6L52	A4	$370 dk bl	2.00	50
6L53	A4	$500 lt bl, I	5.00	1.00
a.		$500 bl, II	25.00	6.00
6L54	A4	$1000 dk red, I	35.00	2.50
a.		$1000 dl red, II	25.00	4.50
6L55	A4	$5000 brown	1.00	2.00
6L56	A4	$10,000 brt pink	2.00	3.00
		Nos. 6L48-6L56 (9)	52.35	10.50

Hankow River Customs Building
A5

River Wall, Wuchang
A6

Design: $290, $370, River scene, Hanyang.

1949, Aug. 16 ***Perf. 11, Imperf.***

6L57	A5	$70 green	60	80
6L58	A5	$220 crimson	60	80
6L59	A5	$290 brown	60	80
6L60	A5	$370 brt bl	60	80
6L61	A6	$500 purple	60	1.00
6L62	A6	$1000 vermilion	60	1.50
		Nos. 6L57-6L62 (6)	3.60	5.70

Liberation of Hankow, Wuchang and Hanyang.

Nos. 6L35, 6L39 and 6L40 Surcharged in Red ("Honan People's Post")

柒拾圓 人民幣
河南省

1949, July

6L63	A2	$7 on $6 emer	8.50	8.50
6L64	A2	$14 on $15 ultra	10.00	10.00
6L65	A2	$70 on $30 grn	15.00	15.00

Surcharge shown is for $70. The $7 has 5 characters in left column and no bottom line.

Issues of 1949 Overprinted ("Honan People's Post")

人民幣 河南省

1949, Aug.

6L66	A2	$3 brn org	1.00	1.00
6L67	A3	$7 yel brn	1.00	1.00
6L68	A2	$10 bl grn	2.00	2.00
6L69	A3	$14 org brn	2.00	2.00
6L70	A2	$30 yel grn (6L40a)	2.00	2.00
6L71	A3	$35 gray bl	1.00	1.00
6L72	A2	$50 rose vio	7.50	7.50
6L73	A3	$70 dp grn	2.00	2.00
6L74	A4	$110 org brn	14.00	14.00
6L75	A3	$220 rose red	4.00	4.00
6L76	A4	$290 brown	14.00	14.00
6L77	A4	$370 blue	16.00	16.00
6L78	A4	$500 bl, II	24.00	24.00
6L79	A4	$1000 dk red, I	32.00	32.00
6L80	A4	$5000 brown	90.00	90.00
6L81	A4	$10,000 brt pink	200.00	200.00
		Nos. 6L66-6L81 (16)	412.50	412.50

Width of the overprint varies slightly.

Nos. 6L57-6L62 Overprinted ("Honan People's Post")

人民幣 河南省

1949, Aug. ***Perf. 11, Imperf.***

6L82	A5	$70 green	4.50	4.50
6L83	A5	$220 crimson	4.50	4.50
6L84	A5	$290 brown	4.50	4.50
6L85	A5	$370 brt bl	4.50	4.50
6L86	A6	$500 purple	4.50	4.50
6L87	A6	$1000 vermilion	4.50	4.50
		Nos. 6L82-6L87 (6)	27.00	27.00

Width of overprint on Nos. 6L82-6L85, 7mm.; on Nos. 6L86-6L87, 12mm.

Changchow Issue Surcharged in Red ("Honan Post")

(same size)
Mao Tse-tung
A7

1949, Sept. ***Perf. 10***

6L88	A7	$290 on $30 yel grn	50.00	30.00
6L89	A7	$370 on $30 yel grn	70.00	40.00

Issues of 1949 Surcharged

政作
貳佰圓
200.00

1950, Jan.

6L90	A2	$200 on $1 org	50	2.00
6L91	A2	$200 on $3 brn org	3.00	2.00
6L92	A2	$200 on $6 emer	50	2.00
6L93	A3	$200 on $7 yel brn	3.00	2.00
6L94	A3	$200 on $14 org brn	3.00	2.00
6L95	A3	$200 on $35 gray bl	3.00	2.00
6L96	A3	$200 on $70 dp grn	3.00	2.00
6L97	A2	$200 on $80 pink	3.00	2.00
6L98	A3	$200 on $220 rose red	3.00	2.00
6L99	A4	$200 on $370 bl	50	2.00
6L100	A3	$300 on $70 dp grn	50	2.00
6L101	A2	$300 on $80 pink	50	2.00
6L102	A3	$300 on $220 rose red	10	2.00
6L103	A2	$1200 on $3 brn org	30.00	15.00
6L104	A3	$1200 on $7 yel brn	6.00	3.00
6L105	A3	$1500 on $14 org brn	9.00	2.00
6L106	A2	$2100 on $1 org	35.00	15.00
6L107	A2	$2100 on $6 emer	35.00	15.00
6L108	A3	$2100 on $35 gray bl	13.00	2.50
6L109	A4	$5000 on $370 bl	5.00	3.00
		Nos. 6L90-6L109 (20)	156.60	81.50

Two types of surcharge exist, differing in spacing of characters in top row.

PARCEL POST STAMPS

Star and Map of Hankow
PP1

1949, Nov. **Litho.** ***Perf. 11, 11½***

6LQ1	PP1	$5000 brown	1.00	2.00
6LQ2	PP1	$10,000 scarlet	7.00	4.00
6LQ3	PP1	$20,000 dk sl grn	2.50	6.00
6LQ4	PP1	$50,000 vermilion	1.00	20.00

SOUTH CHINA

The South China Liberation Area included the provinces of Kwantung and Kwangsi and Hainan Island. The South China Postal and Telegraph Administration was organized on or about Nov. 4, 1949.

All Stamps Issued without Gum

Pearl River Bridge, Canton
A1

1949, Nov. 4 **Litho.** ***Imperf.***

7L1	A1	$10 green	5	5
7L2	A1	$20 sepia	15	5
7L3	A1	$30 violet	5	5
7L4	A1	$50 carmine	5	5
7L5	A1	$100 ultra	25	15
		Nos. 7L1-7L5 (5)	55	35

China Nos. 993-995 With Additional Overprint in Red ("Liberation of Swatow")

解放
暫用

1949, Nov. 9

7L6	A94	2½c on $500 rose lil (993)	12.50	12.50
a.		Handstamped	30.00	30.00
7L7	A94	2½c on $500 rose lil (994)	20.00	20.00
a.		Handstamped	30.00	30.00
7L8	A94	15c on $10 grn (995)	15.00	15.00
a.		Handstamped	40.00	40.00

On Unit Issues of China, 1949

7L9	A96	org (959)	15.00	12.00
7L10	AP5	bl grn (C62)	15.00	12.00
7L11	SD2	red vio (E12)	15.00	12.00
7L12	R2	car (F2)	15.00	12.00

On Sun Yat-sen and Flying Geese Issues of China

7L13	A94	2c org (974)	30.00	30.00
7L14	A94	4c bl grn (975)	350.00	250.00
7L15	A94	10c dp lil (976)	18.00	14.00
7L16	A94	20c bl (978)	18.00	14.00
7L17	A97	$1 brn org (984)	18.00	14.00
7L18	A97	$10 bl grn (987)	230.00	190.00
		Nos. 7L6-7L18 (13)	771.50	607.50

Nos. 7L1-7L3 Surcharged in Red or Green

300
政作參佰圓

1950, Jan.

7L19	A1	$300 on $30 vio (R)	3.50	1.00
7L20	A1	$500 on $20 brn (R)	3.50	1.00
7L21	A1	$800 on $30 vio (G)	3.50	1.25
7L22	A1	$1000 on $10 gray grn (R)	3.50	1.00
7L23	A1	$1000 on $20 brn (R)	3.50	1.00
		Nos. 7L19-7L23 (5)	17.50	5.25

SOUTHWEST CHINA

The Southwest China Liberation Area included the provinces of Kweichow, Szechwan, Yunnan, Sikang and Tibet. The Southwest Postal and Telegraph Administration was organized on or about Nov. 15, 1949 after the liberation of Kweiyang, capital of Kweichow Province.

All Stamps Issued without Gum

Chu Teh, Mao and Troops
A1

1949, Dec. **Litho.** ***Perf. 12½***

8L1	A1	$10 dp bl	2.00	1.50
8L2	A1	$20 rose cl	15	1.00
8L3	A1	$30 dp org	10	50
8L4	A1	$50 gray grn	35	50
8L5	A1	$100 carmine	10	50
8L6	A1	$200 blue	50	60
8L7	A1	$300 bl vio	1.00	1.50
8L8	A1	$500 dk gray	2.50	2.50
8L9	A1	$1000 pale pur	5.00	5.00
8L10	A1	$2000 green	15.00	15.00
8L11	A1	$5000 orange	40.00	40.00
		Nos. 8L1-8L11 (11)	66.70	68.60

China Nos. 974-975, 984, 986-987 Surcharged ("Kweichow People's Post")

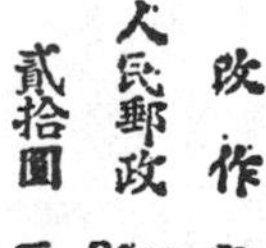

1949, Dec. 1 ***Perf. 12½***

8L12	A94	$20 on 2c org	5.00	5.00
8L13	A94	$50 on 4c bl grn	5.00	5.00
8L14	A97	$100 on $1 brn org	8.00	8.00
8L15	A97	$400 on $5 car rose	25.00	25.00
8L16	A97	$2000 on $10 bl grn	60.00	60.00
		Nos. 8L12-8L16 (5)	103.00	103.00

Map of China, Flag Planted in Southwest
A2

1950, Jan. **Litho.** ***Perf. 9 to 11½***

8L17	A2	$20 dk bl	10	40
8L18	A2	$30 green	50	40
8L19	A2	$50 red	20	60
8L20	A2	$100 brown	20	60

Liberation of the Southwest.

Nos. 8L5–8L6 Surcharged 圓仟貳作改

Perf. 12½

8L21 A1 $300 on $100 car 15.00 5.00
8L22 A1 $500 on $100 car 15 1.50
8L23 A1 $1200 on $100 car 1.00 3.00
8L24 A1 $1500 on $200 bl 1.00 3.00
8L25 A1 $2000 on $200 bl 25.00 15.00
Nos. 8L21-8L25 (5) 42.15 27.50

Nos. 8L5–8L6 Overprinted ("East Szechwan") （川東）

1950, Jan.

8L26 A1 $100 carmine 5.00 5.00
8L27 A1 $200 blue 5.00 5.00

Nos. 8L5–8L6 Handstamp Surcharged 壹仟伍百 改作

1950, Jan.

8L28 A1 $1200 on $100 car 30.00 20.00
8L29 A1 $1500 on $200 bl 45.00 20.00

Many varieties, including wide and narrow settings, exist.

Nos. 8L17–8L20 Surcharged in Black or Red

叁仟圓 改作 伍仟圓
$3000 $5000
壹萬圓 貳萬圓 伍萬圓
$10,000 $20,000 $50,000

1950 *Perf. 9 to 11½*

8L30 A2 $60 on $30 grn 20.00 6.00
8L31 A2 $150 on $30 grn 20.00 6.00
8L32 A2 $300 on $20 dk bl (R) 2.00 2.50
8L33 A2 $300 on $100 brn 20.00 6.00
8L34 A2 $1500 on $100 brn 24.00 15.00
8L35 A2 $3000 on $50 red 6.00 10.00
8L36 A2 $5000 on $50 red 5.00 12.00
8L37 A2 $10,000 on $50 red 50.00 25.00
8L38 A2 $20,000 on $50 red 3.00 20.00
8L39 A2 $50,000 on $50 red 5.00 30.00
Nos. 8L30-8L39 (10) 155.00 132.50

Nos. 8L5–8L7 Overprinted ("West Szechwan") 川 西

1950, Jan. *Perf. 12½*

8L40 A1 $100 carmine 20.00 20.00
8L41 A1 $200 pale bl 20.00 20.00
8L42 A1 $300 bl vio 20.00 20.00

Nos. 8L4–8L7 Surcharged 圓仟貳作改 $2000

1950, Jan.

8L43 A1 $500 on $100 car 8.00 6.00
a. Narrow spacing 70.00 60.00
8L44 A1 $800 on $100 car 8.00 6.00
8L45 A1 $1000 on $50 gray grn 10.00 8.00
8L46 A1 $2000 on $200 pale bl 17.50 15.00
8L47 A1 $3000 on $300 gray vio 32.50 27.50
Nos. 8L43-8L47 (5) 76.00 62.50

Two lines of surcharge 7mm. apart on No. 8L43, 4mm. on No. 8L43a.

China Nos. 975 and 977 Surcharged

政郵民人 政郵民人
圓百貳 $200 圓仟壹 $1000

Perf. 12½, 13 or Compound

1950, Jan.

8L48 A94 $100 on 4c bl grn 12.00 12.00
8L49 A94 $200 on 4c bl grn 25.00 25.00
8L50 A94 $800 on 16c org red 80.00 80.00
8L51 A94 $1000 on 16c org red 225.00 225.00

Unit Issue of China Overprinted ("Southwest People's Post") 人民郵政 西南

1950, Jan. **Engraved** ***Perf. 12½***

8L52 A96 orange 125.00 100.00
a. Rouletted 125.00 120.00
8L53 SD2 red vio 125.00 120.00
8L54 R2 carmine 125.00 120.00

On No. 8L54, space between overprint columns is 3mm. and right column is raised to height of left.

Nos. 8L3, 8L17–8L20 Surcharged in Black or Red

改作 捌百元

1950, Mar. ***Perf. 12½, 9 to 11½***

8L55 A1 $800 on $30 dp org 42.00 35.00
8L56 A2 $1000 on $50 red 9.00 7.50
8L57 A2 $2000 on $100 brn 12.00 9.00
8L58 A2 $4000 on $20 dk bl (R) 35.00 25.00
8L59 A2 $5000 on $30 gray grn 55.00 45.00
Nos. 8L55-8L59 (5) 153.00 121.50

SHANGHAI

(See Vol. IV.)

CILICIA

(sĭ-lĭsh'ĭ-ȧ ; -lĭsh'ȧ)

LOCATION—A territory of Turkey, in southeastern Asia Minor.

GOVT.—Former French occupation.

AREA—6,238 sq. mi.

POP.—383,645.

PRINCIPAL TOWN—Seyhan.

British and French forces occupied Cilicia in 1918 and in 1919 its control was transferred to the French. Eventually part of Cilicia was assigned to the French Mandated Territory of Syria but by the Lausanne Treaty of 1923 which fixed the boundary between Syria and Turkey, Cilicia reverted to Turkey.

40 Paras = 1 Piaster

Issued under French Occupation.

The overprint on Nos. 2–93 is often found inverted, double, etc.
Numbers in parentheses are those of basic Turkish stamps.

Turkish Stamps of 1913–19 Handstamped CILICIE

Perf. 11½, 12, 12½, 13½.

1919 **Unwmkd.**

On Pictorial Issue of 1913.

2 A24 2pa red lil (254) 1.00 1.00
3 A25 4pa dk brn (255) 90 90
4 A27 6pa dk bl (257) 5.00 3.00
5 A32 1¾pi sl & red brn (262) 1.50 1.40

On Issue of 1915.

6 A17 1pi bl (300) 75 75
7 A21 20pa car rose (318) 75 75
9 A22 20pa car rose (330) 1.75 1.75

On Commemorative Issue of 1916.

10 A41 20pa ultra (347) 90 90
11 A41 1pi vio & blk (348) 1.00 1.00
12 A41 5pi yel brn & blk (349) 90 90

On Issue of 1916-18.

13 A44 10pa grn (424) 1.10 1.10
14 A47 50pa ultra (428) 3.75 1.85
15 A51 25pi car, *straw* (434) 1.25 1.25
16 A52 50pi car (437) 90 90
17 A52 50pi ind (438) 12.00 12.00

On Issue of 1917.

18 A53 5pi on 2pa Prus bl (547) 3.75 3.00

On Issue of 1919.

19 A47 50pa ultra (555) 3.00 1.75
20 A48 2pi org brn & ind (556) 1.25 1.00
21 A49 5pi pale bl & blk (557) 3.75 1.85

On Newspaper Stamp of 1916.

22 N3 5pa on 10pa gray grn (P137) 90 90

On Semi-Postal Stamps of 1916.

23 A17 1pi bl (B19) 75 75
24 A21 20pa car rose (B28) 90 90
25 A21 1pi ultra (B29) 3.75 3.00

Turkish Stamps of 1913–18 Handstamped CILICIE

1919

On Pictorial Issue of 1913.

31 A24 2pa red lil (254) 60 60
32 A25 4pa dk brn (255) 1.25 1.25

On Issue of 1915.

33 A17 1pi bl (300) 90 90
34 A22 20pa car rose (330) 75 75

On Commemorative Issue of 1916.

35 A41 20pa ultra (347) 1.00 1.00
36 A41 1pi vio & blk (348) 75 75

On Issue of 1917.

40 A53 5pi on 2pa Prus bl (547) 90 90

On Newspaper Stamp of 1916.

41 N3 5pa on 10pa gray grn (P137) 90 90

On Semi-Postal Stamps of 1916.

42 A17 1pi bl (B19) 1.25 1.10
43 A21 20pa car rose (B28) 75 75

Turkish Stamps of 1913-19 Handstamped *Cilicie*

1919

On Pictorial Issue of 1913.

51 A24 2pa red lil (254) 75 75
52 A25 4pa dk brn (255) 75 75

On Issue of 1915.

53 A17 1pi bl (300) 38 38
55 A22 5pa ocher (328) 1.75 1.50
56 A22 20pa car rose (330) 90 90

On Commemorative Issue of 1916.

57 A41 20pa ultra (347) 80 80
58 A41 1pi vio & blk (348) 90 90
59 A41 5pi yel brn & blk (349) 90 90

On Issue of 1916

59A A17 1pi bl (372) 35.00 35.00

On Issue of 1916-18.

60 A43 5pa org (421) 1.50 1.40
61 A46 1pi dl vio (426) 1.20 1.00
63 A52 50pi grn *straw* (439) 20.00 9.00

On Issue of 1917

64 A53 5pi on 2pa Prus bl (547) 3.50 2.75

On Newspaper Stamp of 1916.

65 N3 5pa on 10pa gray grn (P137) 90 90

On Semi-Postal Stamps of 1916.

66 A17 1pi bl (B19) 1.10 1.00
67 A19 20pa car (B26) 3.00 3.00
68 A21 20pa car rose (B28) 75.00 35.00
69 A21 20pa car rose (B31) 1.00 1.00

Turkey No. 424 Handstamped *T.E.O. Cilicie*

1919

71 A44 10pa green 60 60

Turkish Stamps of 1913-19 Overprinted in Black, Red or Blue T. E. O. Cilicie

1919

In this setting there are various broken and wrong font letters and the letter "i" is sometimes replaced by a "t."

On Pictorial Issue of 1913.

75 A30 1pi bl (R) (260) 55 38

On Issue of 1915.

76 A21 20pa car rose (318) 80 80

On Commemorative Issue of 1916.

77 A41 20pa ultra (347) 75 65
78 A41 1pi vio & blk (348) 55 38

On Issue of 1916-18.

79 A43 5pa org (Bl) (421) 38 38
80 A44 10pa grn (424) 38 38

No.	Type	Description	Unused	Used
81	A45	20pa dp rose (Bk) (425)	85	85
82	A45	20pa dp rose (Bl) (425)	38	38
83	A48	2pi org brn & ind (429)	55	38
83C	A49	5pi pale bl & blk (R) (430)	60	38
84	A51	25pi car, *straw* (434)	5.00	2.50
85	A52	50pi grn, *straw* (439)	50.00	32.50

On Issue of 1917.

No.	Type	Description	Unused	Used
85A	A53	5pi on 2pa Prus bl (547)		
86	A53	5pi on 2pa Prus bl (548)	2.75	2.50

On Newspaper Stamps of 1916–19

No.	Type	Description	Unused	Used
87	N3	5pa on 10pa gray grn (P137)	1.00	1.00
88	N4	5pa on 2pa ol grn (P173)	30	30

On Semi-Postal Stamps of 1915–17

No.	Type	Description	Unused	Used
90	A21	20pa car rose (B28)	80	80
91	A41	10pa car (B42)	45	38
92	A11	10pa on 20pa vio brn (B38)	38	38
93	SP1	10pa red vio (B46)	75	65

It is understood that the Newspaper and Semi-Postal stamps overprinted "Cilicie" were used as ordinary postage stamps.

A1

Blue Surcharge.

1920 ***Perf. 11½.***

No.	Type	Description	Unused	Used
98	A1	70pa on 5pa red	45	45
99	A1	3½pi on 5pa red	45	45

Nos. 98-99 exist with surcharge double, inverted, double with one inverted, "OCCUPTTION," etc. Price, $1 to $2 each.

French Offices in Turkey No. 26 Surcharged — T. E. O 20 PARAS

1920 ***Perf. 14x13½***

No.	Type	Description	Unused	Used
100	A3	20pa on 10c rose red	45	45
a.		'PARAS' omitted	13.00	13.00
b.		Surcharged on back	2.50	2.50

Three types of "20" exist on No. 100.

Stamps of France, 1900-17, Surcharged — O. M. F. Cilicie 5 PARAS

1920

No.	Type	Description	Unused	Used
101	A16	5pa on 2c vio brn	38	38
102	A22	10pa on 5c grn	45	45
103	A22	20pa on 10c red	75	75
104	A22	1pi on 25c bl	90	90
105	A20	2pi on 15c gray grn	5.50	5.50
106	A18	5pi on 40c red & gray bl	9.00	9.00
107	A18	10pi on 50c bis brn & lav	10.00	10.00
108	A18	50pi on 1fr cl & ol grn	50.00	50.00
109	A18	100pi on 5fr dk bl & buff	650.00	650.00
		Nos. 101-109 (9)	726.98	726.98

Nos. 106 to 109 surcharged in four lines.

Stamps of France, 1917, Surcharged — O. M. F. Cilicie SAND. EST 20 PARAS

1920

No.	Type	Description	Unused	Used
110	A16	5pa on 2c vio brn	3.00	
111	A22	10pa on 5c grn	3.00	
112	A22	20pa on 10c red	2.00	
113	A22	1pi on 25c bl	2.00	
114	A20	2pi on 15c gray grn	10.00	
115	A18	5pi on 40c red & gray bl	40.00	
116	A18	20pi on 1fr cl & ol grn	80.00	
		Nos. 110-116 (7)	140.00	

On Nos. 115 and 116 "SAND. EST" is placed vertically. "Sand. Est" is an abbreviation of Sandjak de l'Est (Eastern County).

Nos. 110–116 were prepared for use, but never issued.

Stamps of France, 1900-17, Surcharged — O. M. F. Cilicie 10 PARAS

1920

No.	Type	Description	Unused	Used
117	A16	5pa on 2c vio brn	22	22
a.		Inverted surch.	7.50	6.75
b.		Double surcharge	9.00	
c.		"Cililie"	7.25	7.25
d.		Surch. 5 pi (error)	15.00	15.00
119	A22	10pa on 5c grn	25	25
a.		Inverted surcharge	7.50	6.75
b.		Surch. 5pa (error)	15.00	15.00
121	A22	20pa on 10c red	30	30
a.		Inverted surcharge	7.50	6.75
b.		Surch. 10pa (error)	16.50	16.50
122	A22	1pi on 25c bl	30	30
a.		Double surcharge	12.00	
b.		Inverted surcharge	7.50	6.75
123	A20	2pi on 15c gray grn	40	40
a.		Double surcharge	12.00	
b.		Inverted surcharge	7.50	6.75
124	A18	5pi on 40c red & gray bl	75	75
a.		Double surcharge	17.50	
b.		Inverted surcharge	11.50	10.00
c.		"PIASRTES"	15.00	15.00
125	A18	10pi on 50c bis brn & lav	2.00	2.00
a.		"PIASRTES"	15.00	15.00
126	A18	50pi on 1fr cl & ol grn	2.50	2.50
a.		"PIASRTES"	18.50	18.50
b.		Inverted surch.	20.00	18.00
127	A18	100pi on 5fr dk bl & buff	8.00	8.00
a.		"PIASRTES"	40.00	40.00
		Nos.117-127 (9)	14.72	14.72

This surcharge has "O.M.F." in thicker letters than the preceding issues.

There were two printings of this surcharge which may be distinguished by the space of 1 or 2mm. between "Cilicie" and the numeral.

The surcharge on Nos. 119b and 121b is always inverted.

AIR POST STAMPS.

Nos. 123 and 124 Handstamped — POSTE PAR AVION

Perf. 14x13½

1920, July 15 **Unwmkd.**

No.	Type	Description	Unused	Used
C1	A20	2pi on 15c gray grn	*5,250.*	
C2	A18	5pi on 40c red & gray bl	*5,250.*	
a.		"PIASRTES"		

A very limited number of Nos. C1 and C2 were used on two air mail flights between Adana and Aleppo. At a later date impressions from a new handstamp were struck "to oblige" on stamps of the regular issue of 1920 (Nos. 123, 124, 125 and 126) that were in stock at the Adana Post Office.

Counterfeits exist.

POSTAGE DUE STAMPS.

Turkish Postage Due Stamps of 1914 Handstamped.

1919 ***Perf. 12.*** **Unwmkd.**

Handstamped CILICIE

No.	Type	Description	Unused	Used
J1	D1	5pa claret	2.50	2.50
J2	D2	20pa red	2.50	2.50
J3	D3	1pi dk bl	5.75	5.75
J4	D4	2pi slate	5.75	5.75

Handstamped CILICIE

No.	Type	Description	Unused	Used
J5	D1	5pa claret	2.50	2.50
J6	D2	20pa red	2.50	2.50
J7	D3	1pi dk bl	5.75	5.75
J8	D4	2pi slate	5.75	5.75

Handstamped *Cilicie*

No.	Type	Description	Unused	Used
J9	D1	5pa claret	2.50	2.50
J10	D2	20pa red	2.50	2.50
J11	D3	1pi dk bl	5.75	5.75
J12	D4	2pi slate	5.75	5.75

Postage Due Stamps of France Surcharged — O. M. F. Cilicie 2 PIASTRES

1921

No.	Type	Description	Unused	Used
J13	D2	1pi on 10c choc	4.50	4.50
J14	D2	2pi on 20c ol grn	4.50	4.50
J15	D2	3pi on 30c red	4.50	4.50
J16	D2	4pi on 50c vio brn	4.50	4.50

COCHIN CHINA

(kō′chĭn chī′nȧ; kŏch′ĭn)

LOCATION — The southernmost state of French Indo-China in the Cambodian Peninsula.

GOVT.—French Colony.

AREA—26,476 sq. mi.

POP.—4,615,968.

CAPITAL—Saigon.

100 Centimes = 1 Franc

Surcharged in Black on Stamps of French Colonies:

5 (*a*) 5 C. CH. (*b*) 5 (*c*)

1886-87 ***Perf. 14x13½*** **Unwmkd.**

No.	Type	Description	Unused	Used
1	A9 (a)	5c on 25c yel, *straw*	140.00	100.00
2	A9 (b)	5c on 2c brn, *buff*	9.50	9.50
3	A9 (b)	5c on 25c yel, *straw*	10.50	10.50
4	A9 (c)	5c on 25c *rose* ('87)	30.00	27.50
a.		Double surcharge, one of type b	*2,500.*	*1,200.*
b.		Triple surcharge, two of type b		
c.		Inverted surcharge		

15 / 15 (*d*)

1888

No.	Type	Description	Unused	Used
5	A9 (d)	15c on half of 30c brn, *bis*		26.00

No. 5 was prepared but not issued.

The so-called Postage Due stamps were never issued.

Stamps of Cochin China were superseded by those of Indo-China in 1892.

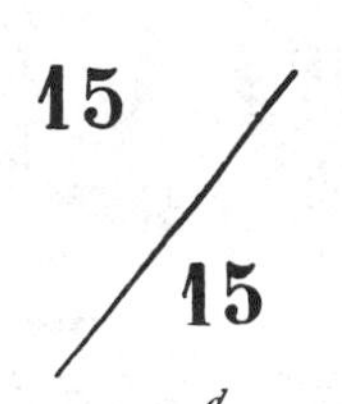

COLOMBIA

(kô·lôm′bē·ä)

LOCATION — On the northwest coast of South America, bordering on the Caribbean Sea and the Pacific Ocean.

GOVT.—Republic.

AREA—456,535 sq. mi.

POP.—28,240,000 (est. 1984).

CAPITAL—Bogota.

In 1810 the Spanish Viceroyalty of New Grenada gained its independence and with Venezuela and Ecuador formed the State of Greater Colombia. In 1832 this state split into three independent units as Venezuela, Ecuador and the Republic of New Grenada. The name of the country has been, successively, Granadine Confederation (1858-61), United States of New Grenada (1861), United States of Colombia (1861-65), and the Republic of Colombia (1885 to date).

100 Centavos = 1 Peso

Prices of early Colombia stamps vary according to condition. Quotations for Nos. 1–34 are for fine copies. Very fine to superb specimens sell at much higher prices, and inferior or poor copies sell at reduced prices, depending on the condition of the individual specimen.

In the earlier days many towns did not have handstamps for canceling and stamps were canceled with pen and ink. Pen cancellations, therefore, do not indicate fiscal use. (Postage stamps were not used for revenue purposes.) Prices of Nos. 1–128 are for pen-canceled specimens. Those with handstamped cancellations sell for considerably more.

Fractions of many Colombian stamps of both early and late issues are found canceled, their use to pay postage having been tolerated even though forbidden by the postal laws and regulations. Many are known to have been made for philatelic purposes.

Granadine Confederation

Coat of Arms

A1 A2

Type A1: Asterisks in frame. Wavy lines in background.

Type A2: Diamond-shaped ornaments in frame. Straight lines in background. Numerals larger.

Lithographed.

1859 ***Imperf.*** **Unwmkd.**

Wove Paper.

No.	Type	Description	Unused	Used
1	A1	2½c green	100.00	110.00
a.		2½c yel grn	100.00	110.00
2	A1	5c blue	140.00	90.00
a.		Tête bêche pair	*3,000.*	*6,500.*
3	A1	5c violet	250.00	110.00
b.		"50" instead of "5"		*12,500.*
4	A1	10c red brn	110.00	80.00
a.		10c buff	110.00	80.00
6	A1	20c blue	110.00	70.00
a.		20c gray bl	110.00	70.00
b.		Se-tenant with 5c	*40,000.*	
c.		Tête bêche pair	*25,000.*	*25,000.*
7	A1	1p carmine	70.00	125.00
a.		1p rose	70.00	125.00
8	A1	1p rose, *bluish*	350.00	

The 10c green is an essay.

Reprints of No. 7 are in brown rose or brown red. Wavy lines of background are much broken; no dividing lines between stamps.

1860 **Laid Paper.**

No.	Type	Description	Unused	Used
9	A2	5c lilac	300.00	225.00

Wove Paper.

No.	Type	Description	Unused	Used
10	A2	5c gray lil	80.00	65.00
a.		5c lil	80.00	65.00
11	A2	10c yel buff	70.00	60.00
a.		Tête bêche pair	6,000.	
12	A2	20c blue	175.00	140.00

United States of New Granada

Arms of New Granada
A3

1861

No.	Type	Description	Unused	Used
13	A3	2½c black	1,100.	525.00
14	A3	5c yellow	240.00	150.00
a.		5c buff	240.00	150.00
16	A3	10c blue	725.00	175.00
17	A3	20c red	425.00	225.00
18	A3	1p pink	950.00	425.00

There are 54 varieties of the 5c, 20c, and 1 peso.

Forgeries exist of Nos. 13–18.

United States of Colombia

Coat of Arms
A4 A5 A6

1862

No.	Type	Description	Unused	Used
19	A4	10c blue	225.00	125.00
20	A4	20c red	*3,000.*	725.00
21	A4	50c green	225.00	160.00
22	A4	1p red lil	550.00	275.00
23	A4	1p red lil, *bluish*	*3,500.*	*1,500.*

No. 23 is on a thinner, coarser wove paper than Nos. 19-22.

1863

No.	Type	Description	Unused	Used
24	A5	5c orange	85.00	65.00
a.		Star after "Cent"	100.00	75.00
25	A5	10c blue	200.00	25.00
a.		Period after "10"	225.00	30.00
26	A5	20c red	200.00	80.00
a.		Star after "Cent"	225.00	90.00
b.		Transfer of 50c in stone of 20c	*16,500.*	*5,000.*

Bluish Paper.

No.	Type	Description	Unused	Used
28	A5	10c blue	150.00	35.00
a.		Period after "10"	165.00	37.50
29	A5	50c green	175.00	80.00
a.		Star after "Cent"	185.00	90.00

Ten varieties of each.

1864 **Wove Paper.**

No.	Type	Description	Unused	Used
30	A6	5c orange	65.00	40.00
a.		Tête bêche	475.00	400.00
31	A6	10c blue	50.00	16.00
a.		Period after 10	50.00	16.00
32	A6	20c scarlet	90.00	55.00
33	A6	50c green	75.00	55.00
34	A6	1p red vio	325.00	175.00

Two varieties of each.

Arms of Colombia
A7 A9

A8

1865

No.	Type	Description	Unused	Used
35	A7	1c rose	12.50	12.50
a.		bluish pelure paper	17.50	15.00
36	A8	2½c *lilac*	21.00	13.00
37	A9	5c yellow	40.00	20.00
a.		5c org	40.00	20.00
38	A9	10c violet	60.00	6.50
39	A9	20c blue	60.00	21.00
40	A9	50c green	100.00	55.00
41	A9	50c grn (small figures)	100.00	55.00
42	A9	1p vermilion	110.00	17.50
a.		1p rose red	110.00	17.50
b.		Period after "PESO"	120.00	20.00

Ten varieties of each of the 5c, 10c, 20c, and 50c, and six varieties of the 1 peso.

No. 36 was used as a carrier stamp.

A10 A11 A12

A13 A14

A15 A16

1866 **White Wove Paper.**

No.	Type	Description	Unused	Used
45	A10	5c orange	62.50	30.00
46	A11	10c lilac	13.00	7.50
a.		Pelure paper	20.00	13.00
47	A12	20c lt bl	37.50	22.50
a.		Pelure paper	57.50	47.50
48	A13	50c green	16.00	13.50
49	A14	1p rose red, *bluish*	85.00	32.50
a.		1p ver	85.00	32.50
51	A15	5p *green*	425.00	225.00
52	A16	10p *vermilion*	325.00	200.00

There are several varieties of the 1 peso having the letters "U", "N", "S" and "O" smaller.

A17

A18 A19

A20 A21

TEN CENTAVOS:

Type I: "B" of "COLOMBIA" over "V" of "CENTAVOS".

Type II: "B" of "COLOMBIA" over "VO" of "CENTAVOS".

ONE PESO:

Type I: Long thin spear heads Diagonal lines in lower part of shield.

Type II: Short thick spear heads. Horizontal and a few diagonal lines in lower part of shield.

Type III: Short thick spear heads. Crossed lines in lower part of shield. Ornaments at each side of circle are broken. (See No. 97.)

1868

No.	Type	Description	Unused	Used
53	A17	5c orange	62.50	55.00
54	A18	10c lil (I)	2.50	1.10
a.		10c red vio (I)	2.50	1.10
b.		10c lil (II)	2.50	1.10
c.		10c red vio (II)	2.50	1.10
d.		Printed on both sides	5.00	2.50
55	A19	20c blue	2.50	1.25
56	A20	50c yel grn	3.00	2.10
57	A21	1p ver (II)	3.00	2.25
a.		Tête bêche pair	250.00	225.00
b.		1p rose red (I)	52.50	35.00
c.		1p rose red (II)	3.00	2.25

See also Nos. 83–84, 96–97.

Counterfeits or reprints.

10c. There is a large white dot at the upper left between the circle enclosing the "X" and the ornament below.

50c. There is a shading of dots instead of dashes below the ribbon with motto. There are crossed lines in the lowest section of the shield instead of diagonal or horizontal ones.

1p. The ornaments in the lettered circle are broken. There are crossed lines in the lowest section of the shield.

These counterfeits, or reprints, are on white paper, wove and laid, on colored wove paper and in fancy colors.

A22

Two varieties.

1869–70 **Wove Paper**

No.	Type	Description	Unused	Used
59	A22	2½c *violet*	4.00	2.50
a.		Laid paper ('70)	275.00	275.00
b.		Laid batonné paper ('70)	25.00	25.00

Nos. 59, 59a and 59b were used as carrier stamps.

Counterfeits, or reprints, are on magenta paper wove or ribbed.

A23 A24

1870 **Wove Paper.**

No.	Type	Description	Unused	Used
62	A23	5c orange	1.50	1.50
a.		5c yel	1.50	1.50
63	A24	25c *blue*	14.00	14.00

See also No. 89.

In the counterfeits, or reprints, of No. 63, the top of the "2" of "25" does not touch the down stroke. The counterfeits are on paper of various colors.

A25 A26

5 pesos. The ornament at the left of the "C" of "Cinco" cuts into the "C", and the shading of the flag is formed of diagonal lines.

10 pesos. The stars have extra rays between the points, and the central part of the shield has some horizontal lines of shading at each end.

1870 **Surface Colored, Chalky Paper**

No.	Type	Description	Unused	Used
64	A25	5p *green*	90.00	70.00
65	A26	10p *vermilion*	100.00	70.00

See Nos. 77-79.

A27

A28 A29

TEN CENTAVOS:

Type I: "S" of "CORREOS" 2¼ mm. high. First "N" of "NACIONALES" small.

Type II: "S" of "CORREOS" 2 mm. high. First "N" of "NACIONALES" wide.

1871–74 **Thin Porous Paper**

No.	Type	Description	Unused	Used
66	A27	1c grn ('72)	3.25	3.25
67	A27	1c rose ('73)	3.25	3.25
a.		1c car ('73)	3.25	3.25
68	A28	2c brown	1.50	1.50
a.		2c red brn	1.50	1.50
69	A29	10c vio (I) ('74)	1.60	1.75
a.		10c lil (I) ('74)	1.60	1.75
b.		10c vio (II) ('74)	1.60	1.75
c.		10c lil (II) ('74)	1.60	1.75
d.		Laid paper, as #69 ('72)	125.00	125.00
e.		Laid paper, as "b" ('72)	125.00	125.00

Counterfeits or reprints.

1c. The outer frame of the shield is broken near the upper left corner and the "A" of "Colombia" has no cross-bar.

2c. There are scratches across "DOS" and many white marks around the letters on the large "2".

The counterfeits, or reprints, are on white wove and bluish white laid paper.

Condor
A30

Liberty Head
A31 A32

Wove Paper.

5 pesos, re-drawn: The ornament at the left of the "C" only touches the "C", and the shading of the flag is formed of vertical and diagonal lines.

10 pesos, re-drawn: The stars are distinctly five pointed, and there is no shading in the central part of the shield.

1877

No.	Type	Description	Unused	Used
73	A30	5c purple	6.25	2.50
a.		5c lil	6.25	2.50
74	A31	10c bis brn	2.25	1.00
a.		10c red brn	2.25	1.00
b.		10c vio brn	2.25	1.00
75	A32	20c blue	3.00	1.35
a.		20c vio bl	7.50	3.75

77	A26	10p *rose*	100.00	70.00
78	A25	5p *lt grn*, redrawn	35.00	35.00
79	A26	10p *rose*, redrawn	12.00	3.00

Stamps of the issues of 1871-77 are known with private perforations of various gauges, also with sewing machine perforation.

In the counterfeits, or reprints, of the 5 pesos the ornament at the left of the "C" of "Cinco" is separated from the "C" by a black line.

In the counterfeits, or reprints, of the 10 pesos the outer line of the double circle containing "10" is broken at the top, below "OS" of "Unidos", and the vertical lines of shading contained in the double circle are very indistinct. There is a colorless dash below the loop of the "P" of "Pesos".

1876-79 Laid Paper.

80	A30	5c lilac	72.50	72.50
81	A31	10c brown	40.00	30.00
82	A32	20c blue	85.00	72.50
83	A20	50c grn ('79)	90.00	70.00
84	A21	1p pale red (II) ('79)	60.00	16.50

1879 Wove Paper.

89	A24	25c green	35.00	37.50

1881 Blue Wove Paper.

93	A30	5c violet	17.50	12.00
a.		5c lil	17.50	12.00
94	A31	10c brown	10.00	2.75
95	A32	20c blue	10.00	4.00
96	A20	50c yel grn	11.00	8.00
97	A21	1p ver (III)	15.00	8.00

For types of 1p, see note over No. 53.

Reprints of the 10c and 20c are much worn. On the 10c the letters "TAVOS" of "CENTAVOS" often touch. On the 20c the letters "NT" of "VEINTE" touch and the left arm of the "T" is too long. Reprints of the 25c, 50c and 1p have the characteristics previously described. The reprints are on white wove or laid paper, on colored papers, and in fancy colors. Stamps on green paper exist only as reprints.

A34

A35

A36

White Wove Paper.

1 centavo: The period before "UNION" is round and there are rays between the stars and the condors.
2 centavos: The "2"s and "C"s in the corners are placed upright.
5 centavos: The last star at the right almost touches the frame.
10 centavos: The letters of the inscription are thin; there are rays between the stars and the condor.

1881 Imperf.

103	A34	1c green	4.50	4.50
104	A35	2c vermilion	1.75	1.75
a.		2c rose	1.75	1.75
106	A34	5c blue	4.00	1.50
a.		Printed on both sides		
107	A36	10c violet	3.50	1.25
108	A34	20c black	4.00	2.00
		Nos. 103-108 (5)	17.75	11.00

The stamps of this issue are found with perforations of various gauges, also sewing machine perforation, all of which are unofficial.

Liberty Head
A37

A37a

1881 Imperf.

109	A37	1c *green*	3.00	5.00
110	A37	2c *lil rose*	3.00	5.00
111	A37	5c *lilac*	5.00	2.50

Nos. 109 to 111 are found with regular or sewing machine perforation, unofficial.

Reprints:

1c. The top line of the stamp and the top frame extend to the left.

2c. There is a curved line over the scroll below the "AV" of "CENTAVOS".

5c. There are scratches across the "5" in the upper left corner.

All three values were reprinted on the three colors of paper of the originals.

Redrawn.

1 centavo: The period before "UNION" is square and the rays between the stars and the condor have been wholly or partly erased.
2 centavos: The "2"s and "C"s in the corners are placed diagonally.
5 centavos: The last star at the right touches the wing of the condor.
10 centavos: The letters of the inscription are thick; there are no rays under the stars; the last star at the right touches the wing of the condor and this wing touches the frame.

1883 Imperf.

112	A34	1c green	6.50	6.50
113	A37a	2c rose	1.75	1.75
114	A34	5c blue	3.50	1.25
a.		5c ultra	3.50	1.25
b.		Printed on both sides, reverse ultra	30.00	25.00
115	A36	10c violet	3.50	1.90

The stamps of this issue are found with regular or sewing machine perforation, privately applied.

A38

A39

1883 Perf. 10½, 12, 13½

116	A38	1c gray grn, *grn*	1.00	1.00
a.		Imperf., pair	5.00	5.00
117	A39	2c red, *rose*	1.00	1.50
a.		2c org red, rose	1.00	1.50
b.		2c red, *buff*	7.50	7.50
c.		Imperf., pair (#117 or 117a)	5.00	5.00
d.		"DE LOS" in very small caps	10.00	10.00
118	A38	5c bl, *bluish*	2.00	1.75
a.		5c dk bl, *bluish*	2.00	1.25
b.		5c bl	2.50	2.50
c.		Imperf., pair (#118 or 118a)	8.50	8.50
d.		As "b," imperf., pair	12.00	12.00
119	A39	10c org, *yel*	1.25	1.65
a.		"DE LOS" in large caps	62.50	27.50
b.		Imperf., pair	7.50	7.50
120	A39	20c vio, *lil*	1.25	1.60
a.		Imperf., pair	5.00	5.00
122	A38	50c brn, *buff*	3.00	3.50
a.		Perf. 12	3.00	3.50
123	A38	1p cl, *bluish*	5.25	2.25
a.		Imperf., pair	17.50	17.50
		Nos. 116-123 (7)	14.75	13.25

1886 Perf. 10½, 11½, 12.

127	A38	5p brn, *straw*	8.00	8.00
a.		Imperf., pair	35.00	35.00
128	A38	10p *rose*	9.50	9.50
a.		Imperf., pair	35.00	35.00

Republic of Colombia

A40

Simón Bolívar
A41

President Rafael Núñez
A42

1886 Perf. 10½ and 13½

129	A40	1c grn, *grn*	1.75	90
a.		Imperf., pair	7.50	7.50
130	A41	5c bl, *bl*	1.75	50
a.		5c ultra, *bl*	1.75	50
b.		Imperf., pair (#130)	7.50	7.50
131	A42	10c orange	4.00	90
a.		Imperf., pair	10.00	10.00
b.		Pelure paper	5.00	1.25

General Antonio José de Sucre y Alcala
A43

General Antonio Nariño
A44

1887

133	A43	2c org red, *rose*	2.50	1.25
a.		2c org red, *yel*	6.25	6.25
b.		2c org red	7.25	7.25
c.		Imperf., pair (#133)	11.00	11.00
134	A44	20c pur, *grysh*	3.25	1.25
a.		Imperf., pair	9.00	9.00
b.		Pelure paper	4.00	2.50

Impressions of No. 134 on white, blue or greenish blue paper were not regularly issued.

Arms
A45

Nariño
A46

1888

135	A45	50c brn, *buff*	2.00	2.00
a.		Imperf., pair	6.50	6.50
136	A45	1p cl, *bluish*	7.50	2.50
137	A45	1p claret	3.50	1.75
138	A45	5p org brn	9.00	6.00
139	A45	5p black	16.00	10.00
140	A45	10p *rose*	18.50	7.50
		Nos. 135-140 (6)	56.50	29.75

1889

141	A46	20c pur, *grysh*	2.00	1.50
a.		Imperf., pair	10.00	10.00

Impressions on white, blue or greenish blue paper were not regularly issued.

A47

A48

A49

A50

A51

1890-91 Perf. 10½, 13½, 11

142	A47	1c grn, *grn*	2.00	1.65
143	A48	2c org red, *rose*	90	1.00
144	A49	5c bl, *grnsh bl*	1.50	50
a.		5c dp bl, *bl*	1.25	50
b.		Imperf., pair	6.00	6.00
146	A50	10c brn, *yel*	90	50
147	A51	20c vio, pelure paper	4.00	5.00
		Nos. 142-147 (5)	9.30	8.65

A52

A53

A54

Perf. 10½, 12, 13½, 14 to 15½.

1892 Ordinary Paper.

148	A47	1c red, *yel*	80	40
149	A52	2c red, *rose*	40.00	40.00
150	A52	2c green	50	30
a.		2c yel grn	50	30
151	A49	5c blk, *buff*	6.25	40
152	A50	10c bis brn, *rose*	75	40
153	A53	20c brn, *bl*	75	45
154	A45	50c vio, *vio*	1.25	75
155	A54	1p bl, *grnsh*	2.00	50
156	A45	5p red, *pale rose*	8.00	3.25
157	A45	10p blue	15.00	3.50
a.		Thin, pale rose paper	30.00	8.00
		Nos. 148-157 (10)	75.30	49.95

Nos. 148, 150-155 and 157 exist imperf. Price per pair, $5-$7.50.

A55

A55a

1895–99

158 A55 5c org brn, *pale buff* 85 30
a. Imperf., pair 6.00 6.00
159 A55 5c red brn, *sal* ('97) 85 30
a. Imperf., pair 6.00 6.00
160 A53 20c yel brn, *grnsh bl* ('97) 5.00 13.00
160A A53 20c brn, *buff* ('97) 17.50 13.00
161 A55a 50c red vio, *vio* ('99) 1.50 1.40

Type A55a is a redrawing of type A45. The letters of the inscriptions are slightly larger and the numerals "50" slightly smaller than in type A45.

The 20c brown on white paper is believed to be a chemical changeling.

A56

1899

162 A56 1c red, *yel* 75 45
163 A56 5c red brn, *sal* 75 45
164 A56 10c brn, *lil rose* 2.50 2.25
165 A56 50c bl, *lil* 1.40 1.40

Cartagena Issues.

A57

1899 Blue Overprint. *Imperf.*

167 A57 5c red, *buff* 30.00 30.00
a. Sewing machine perf. 30.00 30.00
168 A57 10c ultra, *buff* 30.00 30.00
a. Sewing machine perf. 30.00 30.00

Nos. 168 and 168a differ slightly from the illustration.

A58

A59

A60

A61

Purple Overprint.

1899 *Sewing Machine Perf.*

170 A58 1c brn, *buff* 25.00 25.00
a. Altered from 10c 30.00 30.00
171 A59 2c blk, *buff* 25.00 25.00
a. Altered from 10c 30.00 30.00
172 A60 5c mar, *grnsh bl* 20.00 20.00
a. Perf. 12 20.00 20.00
b. Without ovpt. 12.50 12.50
173 A61 10c red, *sal* 20.00 20.00
a. perf. 12 20.00 20.00

Types A58 and A59 illustrate Nos. 170a and 171a, which were made from altered plates of the 10c (No. 168). Nos. 170 and 171 were made from altered plate of the 5c denomination (No. 167), show part of the top flag of the "5" and differ slightly from the illustrations.

Nos. 170–173 exist imperf. Prices about same as perf.

A62

1900 *Imperf.*

Purple Overprint

174 A62 5c red 30.00 30.00
a. Perf. 12 40.00 40.00

A63 A64

Sewing Machine Perf.

1901 Purple Overprint.

175 A63 1c black 1.25 1.25
a. Without overprint 2.75 2.75
b. Double overprint 3.00 3.00
c. Imperf., pair 3.00 3.00
d. Inverted overprint 1.50 1.50
176 A64 2c *rose* 1.25 1.25
a. Imperf., pair 3.00 3.00
b. Without overprint 2.75 2.75
c. Double overprint 3.00 3.00

A65

A66

1901 Rose Overprint

177 A65 1c blue 1.25 1.25
a. Imperf., pair 3.50 3.50
178 A66 2c brown 1.25 1.25
a. Imperf., pair 3.50 3.50
b. Without overprint 1.25 1.25

A67

A68

Sewing Machine or Regular Perf. 12, 12½

1902 Magenta Overprint.

179 A67 5c violet 2.50 2.50
a. Without overprint 2.50 2.50
b. Double overprint 2.50 2.50
c. Imperf., pair 5.50 5.50
180 A68 10c yel brn 2.50 2.50
a. Double overprint 2.50 2.50
b. Imperf., pair 5.50 5.50
c. Without overprint 2.50 2.50
d. Printed on both sides 3.50 3.50

A69

A70

1902 Magenta Overprint

181 A69 5c yel brn 2.50 2.50
a. Without overprint 2.25 2.25
b. Imperf., pair 5.50 5.50
182 A69 10c black 1.75 1.75
a. Without overprint 1.50 1.50
b. Imperf., pair 8.50 8.50
183 A70 20c maroon 6.00 3.50
b. Imperf., pair 15.00 15.00

Nos. 181–183 exist tête bêche. Price of 10c and 20c, each $17.50.

Washed copies of Nos. 167–183 are offered as "without overprint."

Barranquilla Issues.

Magdalena River
A75

Iron Quay at Sabanilla
A76

La Popa Hill
A77

1902–03 *Imperf.*

184 A75 2c green 3.00 2.75
185 A75 2c dk bl 2.00 2.00
186 A75 2c rose 22.50 22.50
187 A76 10c scarlet 1.25 1.00
188 A76 10c orange 10.00 9.00
189 A76 10c rose 1.25 1.00
190 A76 10c maroon 2.00 2.00
191 A76 10c claret 2.00 2.00
192 A77 20c violet 4.00 4.00
a. Laid paper
193 A77 20c dl bl 5.00 5.00
194 A77 20c dl bl, *pink* *150.00* *150.00*
195 A77 20c car rose 22.50 22.50
Nos. 184-195 (12) *225.50* *223.75*

Sewing Machine Perf. and Perf. 12.

184a A75 2c green 7.50 7.50
185a A75 2c dk bl 6.00 6.00
186a A75 2c carmine *40.00* *40.00*
187a A76 10c scarlet 4.00 4.00
188a A76 10c orange *30.00* *30.00*
189a A76 10c rose 6.00 6.00
190a A76 10c maroon 6.00 6.00
191a A76 10c claret 6.00 6.00
192b A77 20c purple 60 60
c. 20c lil 60 60
193a A77 20c dl bl 5.00 5.00
194a A77 20c dl bl, *rose* *150.00* *150.00*
195b A77 20c car rose *60.00* *60.00*
Nos. 184a-195b (12) *321.10* *321.10*

See also Nos. 240–245.

Cruiser "Cartagena"
A78

Bolívar
A79

General Próspero Pinzón
A80

A81

A82

1903-04 *Imperf.*

209 A78 5c blue 3.00 3.00
210 A78 5c bister 3.00 4.00
211 A79 50c yellow 4.50 4.50
212 A79 50c green 5.00 5.00
213 A79 50c scarlet 5.00 5.00
214 A79 50c carmine 5.00 5.00
a. 50c rose 5.00 5.00
215 A79 50c pale brn 5.00 5.00
216 A80 1p yel brn 1.90 1.90
217 A80 1p rose 3.00 3.00
218 A80 1p blue 3.00 3.00
219 A80 1p violet 30.00 30.00
220 A81 5p claret 6.00 6.00
221 A81 5p pale brn 8.00 8.00
222 A81 5p bl grn 7.00 7.00
223 A82 10p pale grn 9.00 9.00
224 A82 10p claret 30.00 30.00
Nos. 209-224 (16) 129.40 129.40

Nos. 216 and 217 measure 20½x26½mm. and No. 218, 18x24 mm.

Stamps of this issue exist with forged perforations.

Perf. 12.

209a A78 5c blue 7.00 6.00
210a A78 5c bister 7.50 7.50
211a A79 50c yellow 11.50 10.00
b. 50c org 11.50 10.00
212a A79 50c green 20.00 20.00
213a A79 50c scarlet 9.00 9.00
214b A79 50c rose 9.00 9.00
215a A79 50c pale brn 9.00 9.00
216a A80 1p yel brn 4.00 4.00
217a A80 1p rose 5.50 5.50
218a A80 1p blue 5.50 5.50
219a A80 1p violet 50.00 50.00
220a A81 5p claret 16.00 16.00
221a A81 5p pale brn 17.50 17.50
222a A81 5p bl grn 15.00 15.00
223a A82 10p pale grn 25.00 25.00
224a A82 10p claret 60.00 60.00
Nos. 209a-224a (16) 271.50 269.00

Imperf.

Laid Paper.

240 A76 10c dk bl, *lil* 4.50 4.50
241 A76 10c dk bl, *bluish* 4.50 4.50
242 A76 10c dk bl, *brn* 4.50 4.50
243 A76 10c dk bl, *sal* 9.00 9.00
244 A76 10c dk bl, *grnsh bl* 8.00 8.00
245 A76 10c dk bl, *dp rose* 4.50 4.50
Nos. 240-245 (6) 35.00 35.00

Perf. 12.

240a A76 10c dk bl, *lil* 13.00 13.00
241a A76 10c dk bl, *bluish* 8.00 8.00
242a A76 10c dk bl, *brn* 8.00 8.00
243a A76 10c dk bl, *sal* 70.00 70.00
244a A76 10c dk bl, *grnsh bl* 20.00 20.00
245a A76 10c dk bl, *dp rose* 8.00 8.00
Nos. 240a-245a (6) 127.00 127.00

Medellin Issue.

A83

1902

257 A83 1c grn, *straw* 30 60
a. Imperf., pair 12.00 12.00
258 A83 2c sal, *rose* 30 60
a. Imperf., pair 12.00 12.00
259 A83 5c dp bl, *grnsh* 30 60
a. Imperf., pair 12.00 12.00
260 A83 10c pale brn, *straw* 30 60
a. Imperf., pair 12.00 12.00
261 A83 20c pur, *rose* 50 60
a. Imperf., pair 12.00 12.00
262 A83 50c dl rose, *grnsh* 2.50 3.75
a. Imperf., pair 12.00 12.00
263 A83 1p *yellow* 5.00 7.50
a. Imperf., pair 32.50 32.50
264 A83 5p sl, *bl* 40.00 40.00
a. Imperf., pair 90.00 90.00
265 A83 10p dk brn, *rose* 25.00 25.00
a. Imperf., pair 70.00 70.00
Nos. 257-265 (9) 74.20 79.25

Regular Issue.

A84

A85

A86

A87

A88

A89

A90

A91

A92

1902 ***Imperf.***

No.	Type	Description	Unused	Used
266	A84	2c *rose*	25	25
267	A85	4c red, *grn*	30	30
268	A86	5c grn, *bl*	30	30
269	A87	10c *pink*	30	30
270	A88	20c brn, *buff*	30	30
271	A89	50c dk grn, *rose*	1.50	1.50
272	A90	1p pur, *buff*	60	60
273	A91	5p grn, *bl*	4.50	4.50
274	A92	10p grn, *pale grn*	12.00	7.00
		Nos. 266-274 (9)	20.05	15.05

Sewing Machine Perf.

No.	Type	Description	Unused	Used
266a	A84	2c *rose*	1.75	1.75
267a	A85	4c red, *grn*	1.75	1.75
268a	A86	5c grn, *bl*	2.00	2.00
269a	A87	10c *pink*	2.00	2.00
270a	A88	20c brn, *buff*	2.00	2.00
271a	A89	50c dk grn, *rose*	4.00	3.00
272a	A90	1p pur, *buff*	4.00	4.00
273a	A91	5p grn, *bl*	30.00	30.00
274a	A92	10p grn, *pale grn*	60.00	50.00
		Nos. 266a-274a(9)	107.50	96.50

1903 ***Perf. 12***

No.	Type	Description	Unused	Used
266b	A84	2c *rose*	1.75	1.75
269b	A87	10c *pink*	2.00	2.00
270b	A88	20c brn, *buff*	2.00	2.00
272b	A90	1p pur, *buff*	4.00	4.00
273b	A91	5p grn, *bl*	30.00	30.00
274b	A92	10p grn, *pale grn*	60.00	50.00
		Nos. 266b-274b (6)	99.75	89.75

1903 ***Imperf.***

No.	Type	Description	Unused	Used
284	A85	4c bl, *grn*	30	30
285	A86	5c bl, *bl*	30	30
286	A88	20c bl, *buff*	30	30
288	A89	50c bl, *rose*	2.00	2.00

Sewing Machine Perf.

No.	Type	Description	Unused	Used
284a	A85	4c bl, *grn*	2.00	2.00
285a	A86	5c bl, *bl*	2.00	2.00
286a	A88	20c bl, *buff*	2.00	2.00
288a	A89	50c bl, *rose*	6.00	5.00

Perf. 12

No.	Type	Description	Unused	Used
284b	A85	4c bl, *grn*	2.00	2.00
285b	A86	5c bl, *bl*	2.00	2.00
286b	A88	20c bl, *buff*	2.00	2.00
288b	A89	50c bl, *rose*	6.00	5.00

A93

1904 **Pelure Paper** ***Imperf.***

No.	Type	Description	Unused	Used
303	A93	½c yel brn	1.40	1.40
304	A90	1c bl grn	1.50	1.50
a.		1c yel grn	1.50	1.50
306	A84	2c blue	1.25	90
307	A86	5c carmine	1.40	1.40
308	A87	10c violet	1.50	1.25
		Nos. 303-308 (5)	7.05	6.45

1904 ***Perf. 13***

No.	Type	Description	Unused	Used
303a	A93	½c yel brn	3.00	3.00
304b	A90	1c bl grn	4.00	4.00
c.		1c yel grn	5.00	5.00
306a	A84	2c blue	3.00	3.00

Perf. 12

No.	Type	Description	Unused	Used
307a	A86	5c carmine	3.50	3.00
308a	A87	10c violet	3.50	3.00
		Nos. 303a-308a (5)	17.00	16.00

Pres. José Manuel Marroquín

A94 A95 A96

Imprint: "Lit. J. L. Arango Medellin. Col."

1904 **Wove Paper** ***Perf. 12***

No.	Type	Description	Unused	Used
314	A94	½c yellow	90	15
a.		Redrawn	90	15
b.		Imperf., pair	3.75	3.75
315	A94	1c green	90	6
a.		Redrawn	90	6
b.		Imperf. pair	3.00	3.00
316	A94	2c rose	90	5
a.		Redrawn	90	5
b.		Imperf., pair	3.75	3.75
317	A94	5c blue	1.50	15
a.		Redrawn	1.50	15
b.		Imperf., pair	3.75	3.75
318	A94	10c violet	1.90	22
a.		Imperf., pair	4.75	4.75
319	A94	20c black	2.00	30
a.		Redrawn	2.00	30
b.		Imperf., pair	8.50	8.50
320	A95	1p brown	20.00	3.50
a.		Imperf., pair	47.50	47.50
321	A96	5p red & blk, *yel*	65.00	65.00
322	A96	10p bl & blk, *grnsh*	65.00	65.00
		Nos. 314-322 (9)	158.10	134.43

On the redrawn types, the imprint is close to the base of the design instead of being spaced from it. On the redrawn 2c and 5c, the lower end of the vertical white line below "OR" of "CORREOS" forms a hook which turns to the right instead of to the left as in the originals.

See also Nos. 325–330.

A97

A98

1905 ***Imperf.***

No.	Type	Description	Unused	Used
323	A97	50p org yel, *pale pink*	100.00	100.00
324	A98	100p dk bl, *dk rose*	90.00	90.00

Imprint: "Lit. Nacional".

Perf. 10, 13, 13½ and Compound.

1908

No.	Type	Description	Unused	Used
325	A94	½c orange	90	15
a.		½c yel	90	15
b.		Imperf., pair	2.25	2.25
c.		Without imprint	6.00	6.00
326	A94	1c yel grn	90	6
a.		Without imprint	90	6
d.		Imperf., pair	3.75	3.75
327	A94	2c red	90	6
a.		2c car	90	6
b.		Imperf., pair	3.75	3.75
328	A94	5c blue	80	15
a.		Imperf., pair	6.00	6.00
329	A94	10c violet	*55.00*	1.00
330	A94	20c gray blk	*55.00*	70
		Nos. 325-330 (6)	*113.50*	2.12

The above stamps may be easily distinguished from those of 1904 by the perforation, by the height of the design, 24mm. instead of 23mm., and by the "Lit. Nacional" imprint.

Camilo Torres
A99

Policarpa Salavarrieta
A100

Nariño
A101

Bolívar
A102

Francisco José de Caldas
A103

Francisco de Paula Santander
A104

Bolívar Demanding Liberation of Slaves
A105

Bolívar Resigning
A106

1910, Aug. **Engraved** ***Perf. 12***

No.	Type	Description	Unused	Used
331	A99	½c vio & blk	1.10	70
a.		Center inverted	425.00	425.00
332	A100	1c dp grn	90	70
333	A101	2c scarlet	75	45
334	A102	5c dp bl	1.90	65
335	A103	10c plum	15.00	7.25
336	A104	20c blk brn	22.50	8.00
337	A105	1p dk vio	75.00	27.50
338	A106	10p claret	300.00	210.00
		Nos. 331-338 (8)	417.15	255.25

Colombian independence centenary.

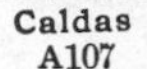
Caldas
A107

Torres
A108

Nariño
A109

Santander
A110

Bolívar
A111

José María Córdoba
A112

Monument to Battle of Boyacá
A113

View of Cartagena
A114

Sucre
A115

Rufino Cuervo
A116

Antonio Ricaurte y Lozano
A117

Coat of Arms
A118

1917 **Engraved.** ***Perf. 14***

No.	Type	Description	Unused	Used
339	A107	½c bister	45	15
340	A108	1c green	40	8
341	A109	2c car rose	40	8
342	A110	4c violet	1.20	45
343	A111	5c dl bl	2.25	25
344	A112	10c gray	2.00	25
345	A113	20c red	3.25	25
346	A114	50c carmine	2.25	25
347	A115	1p brt bl	15.00	60
348	A116	2p orange	12.00	65
349	A117	5p gray	27.50	7.50
350	A118	10p dk brn	55.00	15.00
		Nos. 339-350 (12)	121.70	25.51

The 1c, 5c, 10c, 50c, 2p, 5p and 10p also exist perf. 11½ and 11½ compounded with 14.

Lithographed varieties of Nos. 343, 345 and 346 are counterfeits made to defraud the government.

Imperforate copies of Nos. 339–350 are not known to have been regularly issued.

See Nos. 373–374, 400–405.

Nos. 318–319, 329–330 Surcharged in Red

Especie Provisional
$ 0.00½

1918 **On Issue of 1904.**

No.	Type	Description	Unused	Used
351	A94	½c on 20c blk	1.50	35
352	A94	3c on 10c vio	3.00	1.00

On Issue of 1908.

No.	Type	Description	Unused	Used
353	A94	½c on 20c gray blk	10.00	7.00
354	A94	3c on 10c vio	15.00	6.25

Nos. 351 to 354 inclusive exist with surcharge reading upward or downward. On one stamp in each sheet the letter "S" in "Especie" is omitted. All denominations exist with a small zero before the decimal in the surcharge.

A119

A120

1918 **Lithographed.** ***Perf. 13½.***

No.	Type	Description	Unused	Used
358	A119	3c red	75	15
a.		Imperf., pair	6.00	6.00

1920 **Engraved.** ***Perf. 14.***

No.	Type	Description	Unused	Used
359	A120	3c red, *org*	45	10
a.		Imperf., pair	4.50	4.50

See also Nos. 371–372.

A121

A122

A123

Perf. 10, 13½ and Compound

1920-21 **Lithographed.**

No.	Type	Description	Unused	Used
360	A121	½c yellow	80	35
361	A121	1c green	1.25	20
362	A121	2c red	90	22
363	A122	3c green	80	22
a.		3c yel grn	80	22
364	A121	5c blue	1.40	30
365	A121	10c violet	4.50	2.25
366	A121	20c dp grn	12.00	5.25
367	A123	50c dk red	12.00	5.50
		Nos. 360-367 (8)	33.65	14.29

The tablet with "PROVISIONAL" was added separately to each design on the various lithographic stones and its position varies slightly on different stamps in the sheet. For some values there were two or more stones, on which the tablet was placed at various angles.

Nos. 360–366 exist imperf.

See also No. 375.

No. 342 Surcharged in Red

PROVICIONAL
$003
a

PROVISIONAL
$0.03
(15mm. wide)
b

1921

No.	Type	Description	Unused	Used
369	A110(a)	3c on 4c vio	1.10	32
a.		Dbl. surcharge	17.50	
370	A110(b)	3c on 4c vio	5.00	3.00

See also No. 377.

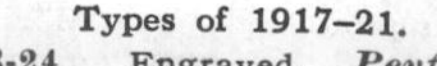

Types of 1917–21.

1923-24 **Engraved.** ***Perf. 13½.***

No.	Type	Description	Unused	Used
371	A120	1½c chocolate	1.25	75
372	A120	3c blue	70	18
373	A111	5c cl ('24)	3.00	25
374	A112	10c blue	8.50	60

Lithographed.

No.	Type	Description	Unused	Used
375	A121	10c dk bl	12.00	7.50
		Nos. 371-375 (5)	25.45	9.28

No. 342 Surcharged in Red

PROVISIONAL
$003
(18mm. wide)

1924

No.	Type	Description	Unused	Used
377	A110	3c on 4c vio	3.75	1.90
a.		Double surcharge	17.50	
b.		Double surcharge, one inverted	17.50	
c.		With added surch. "3cs." in red		

A124

1924–25 **Litho.** ***Perf. 10, 10x13½***

No.	Type	Description	Unused	Used
379	A124	1c red	1.00	25
380	A124	3c dp bl ('25)	1.00	25

Exist imperf. Price, each pair $5.

A125

A126

Black, Red or Green Surcharge and Overprint.

Imprint of Waterlow & Sons.

1925 ***Perf. 14, 14½.***

No.	Type	Description	Unused	Used
382	A125	1c on 3c bis brn (Bk)	45	15
383	A126	4c vio (R)	55	30
a.		Inverted surch.	10.00	10.00

Imprint of American Bank Note Co.

Perf. 12.

No.	Type	Description	Unused	Used
384	A125	1c on 3c bis brn (Bk)	6.00	5.00
a.		Inverted surcharge	15.00	15.00
385	A126	4c vio (G)	60	45
a.		Inverted overprint	8.00	8.00

Correos
Provisional

Revenue stamps of basic types A125 and A126 were handstamped as above in violet or blue by the Cali post office in 1925, but were not authorized by the government. Denominations so overprinted are 1c, 2c, 3c, 4c and 5c.

A127

A128

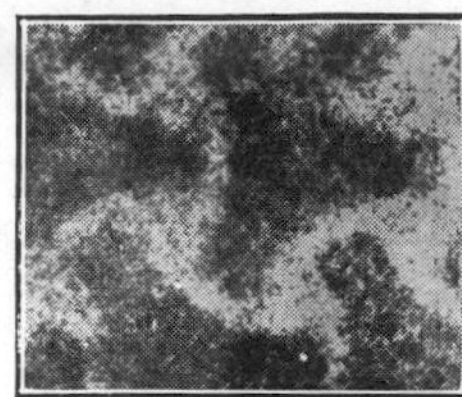
Wmk. 194

Wmkd.

Multiple Curvilinear Triangles. (194)

1926 **Litho.** ***Perf. 10, 13½x10***

No.	Type	Description	Unused	Used
395	A127	1c gray grn	50	22
396	A128	4c dp bl	50	22

Exist imperf. Price, each pair $4.

Types of 1917 and

Sabana Station
A129

Engraved.

1926–29 ***Perf. 14*** **Unwmkd.**

No.	Type	Description	Unused	Used
400	A110	4c dp bl	60	5
401	A120	8c dk bl	75	12
402	A107	30c ol bis	7.00	90
403	A129	40c brn & yel brn	11.00	1.50
404	A117	5p violet	9.00	1.00
a.		Perf. 11 ('29)	9.00	1.50
405	A118	10p green	18.50	3.00
a.		Perf. 11 ('29)	37.50	6.00
		Nos. 400-405 (6)	46.85	6.57

Death of Bolívar
A130

1930, Dec. 17 ***Perf. 12½***

No.	Type	Description	Unused	Used
408	A130	4c dk bl & blk	40	35

Issued to commemorate the centenary of the death of Gen. Simón Bolívar. See also Nos. C80–C82.

Nos. 400 and 402 Surcharged in Red or Dark Blue

1932, Jan. 20 ***Perf. 14***

No.	Type	Description	Unused	Used
409	A110	1c on 4c dp bl (R)	45	12
a.		Inverted surcharge	8.00	8.00
410	A107	20c on 30c ol bis (Bl)	12.00	1.00
a.		Inv. surcharge	25.00	
b.		Dbl. surcharge	25.00	

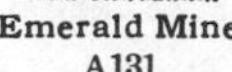
Emerald Mine
A131

Oil Wells
A132

Coffee Cultivation
A133

Platinum Mine
A134

Gold Mining
A135

Christopher Columbus
A136

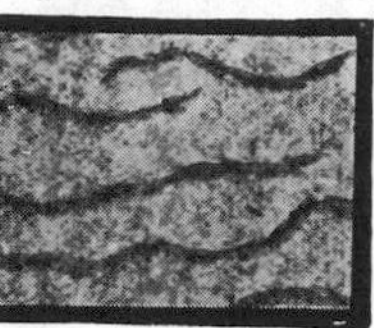
Wmk. 229

Wmkd. Wavy Lines. (229)

Imprint: "Waterlow & Sons Ltd. Londres"

1932 **Engraved** ***Perf. 12½***

No.	Type	Description	Unused	Used
411	A131	1c green	90	5
412	A132	2c red	90	5
413	A133	5c brown	1.00	5
414	A134	8c bl blk	5.50	70
415	A135	10c yellow	5.00	12
416	A136	20c dk bl	12.00	50
		Nos. 411-416 (6)	25.30	1.47

See Nos. 441–442, 464–466a, 517.

Pedro de Heredia
A137

Coffee Picking
A138

Lithographed.

1934, Jan. 10 ***Perf. 11½*** **Unwmkd.**

No.	Type	Description	Unused	Used
417	A137	1c dk grn	3.00	90
418	A137	5c chocolate	4.00	75
419	A137	8c dk bl	3.00	90

400th anniversary of Cartagena. See also Nos. C111–C114.

1934, Dec. **Engraved** ***Perf. 12***

No.	Type	Description	Unused	Used
420	A138	5c brown	3.25	5

Discus Thrower
A139

Post and Telegraph Building
A145

Allegory of Olympic Games at Barranquilla—A140

Foot Race—A141

Tennis—A142

Pier at Puerto Colombia—A143

View of the Bay—A144

Designs: 2c, Soccer. 10c, Hurdling. 15c, Athlete in stadium. 18c, Baseball. 24c, Swimming. 50c, View of Barranquilla. 2p, Monument to Flag. 5p, Coat of Arms. 10p, Condor.

1935, Jan. 26 Litho. *Perf. 11½*

No.	Type	Description	Unused	Used
421	A139	2c bluish grn & buff	1.75	75
422	A139	4c dp grn	1.75	75
423	A140	5c dk brn & yel	1.75	75
a.		Horizontal pair, imperf. btwn.	300.00	
424	A141	7c dk car	2.50	2.25
425	A142	8c blk & pink	2.75	2.75
426	A141	10c brn & bl	4.25	2.25
427	A143	12c indigo	4.75	3.75
428	A141	15c bl & red brn	8.50	6.25
429	A141	18c dk vio & buff	10.00	10.00
430	A144	20c pur & grn	10.00	7.50
431	A144	24c bluish grn & ultra	10.00	10.00
432	A144	50c ultra & buff	15.00	12.50
433	A145	1p db & bl	135.00	75.00
434	A145	2p dl grn & gray	185.00	135.00
435	A145	5p pur blk & bl	600.00	450.00
436	A145	10p blk & gray	725.00	600.00
		Nos. 421-436 (16)	1,718.	1,319.50

3rd National Olympic Games, Barranquilla. Counterfeits of 10p exist.

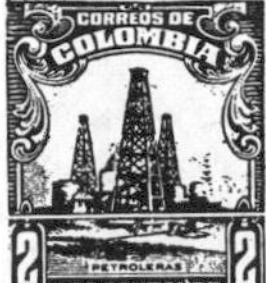
Oil Wells
A155

Gold Mining
A157

Imprint:
"American Bank Note Co."
Engraved

1935, Mar. *Perf. 12* Unwmkd.

No.	Type	Description	Unused	Used
437	A155	2c car rose	45	5
439	A157	10c dp org	27.50	15

See also Nos. 468, 470, 498, 516.

No. 347 Surcharged in Black — 12 CENTAVOS

1935, Aug. *Perf. 14*

No.	Type	Description	Unused	Used
440	A115	12c on 1p brt bl	4.75	2.25

Types of 1932
Lithographed.
Imprint: "Lit. Nacional Bogotá"

1935–36 *Perf. 11, 11½, 12½*

No.	Type	Description	Unused	Used
441	A131	1c lt grn	15	5
a.		Imperf. (pair)	5.00	
442	A133	5c brn ('36)	80	12
a.		Imperf. (pair)	6.00	6.00

Simón Bolívar
A159

Tequendama Falls
A160

Wmkd. Wavy Lines. (229)

1937 Engraved *Perf. 12½*

No.	Type	Description	Unused	Used
443	A159	1c dp grn	25	5
a.		Perf. 14		
444	A160	12c dp bl	3.75	1.40

See also No. 570.

Soccer Player
A161

Discus Thrower
A162

Runner
A163

1937, Jan. 4 Photo. Unwmkd.

No.	Type	Description	Unused	Used
445	A161	3c lt grn	2.25	1.40
446	A162	10c car rose	4.00	2.50
447	A163	1p black	50.00	45.00

National Olympic Games, Manizales.

Exposition Palace
A164

Stadium at Barranquilla
A165

Monument to the Colors
A166

1937, Jan. 4

No.	Type	Description	Unused	Used
448	A164	5c vio brn	75	45
449	A165	15c blue	6.25	5.00
450	A166	50c org brn	16.00	8.50

Barranquilla National Exposition.

Stamps of 1926-37 Surcharged in Black — 1 CENTAVO

1937-38 *Perf. 12½.* Unwmkd.

No.	Type	Description	Unused	Used
452	A161	1c on 3c lt grn	1.10	1.10
a.		Invtd. surcharge	2.50	2.50
453	A120	5c on 8c dk bl	55	50
a.		Invtd. surcharge	2.50	2.50

Wmkd. Wavy Lines. (229)

No.	Type	Description	Unused	Used
454	A160	2c on 12c dp bl	55	50
455	A134	5c on 8c bl blk	60	60
a.		Invtd. surcharge	2.25	2.25
456	A160	10c on 12c dp bl ('38)	6.25	1.25
a.		Dbl. surcharge	12.00	12.00
		Nos. 452-456 (5)	9.05	3.95

Calle del Arco
A168

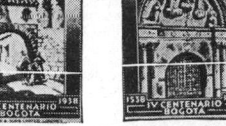

Entrance to Church of the Rosary
A169

Arms of Bogotá
A170

Gonzálo Jiménez de Quesada
A171

Bochica
A172

Santo Domingo Convent
A173

Mass of the Conquistadors—A174

1938, July 27 *Perf. 12½* Unwmkd.

No.	Type	Description	Unused	Used
457	A168	1c yel grn	18	18
458	A169	2c scarlet	20	18
459	A170	5c brn blk	25	18
460	A171	10c brown	70	35
461	A172	15c brt bl	3.25	1.85
462	A173	20c brt red vio	3.25	1.85
463	A174	1p red brn	42.50	32.50
		Nos. 457-463 (7)	50.33	37.09

Bogotá, 400th anniversary.

Types of 1932.
Imprint:
"Litografia Nacional Bogotá".

1938, Dec. 5 Litho. *Perf. 10½, 11*

No.	Type	Description	Unused	Used
464	A132	2c rose	1.10	40
465	A135	10c yellow	3.00	45
466	A136	20c dl bl	6.25	1.50
a.		20c dk bl, perf. 12½ ('44)	60.00	7.50

Simón Bolívar
A175

Coffee Picking
A176

Arms of Colombia
A177

Christopher Columbus
A178

Caldas
A179

Sabana Station
A180

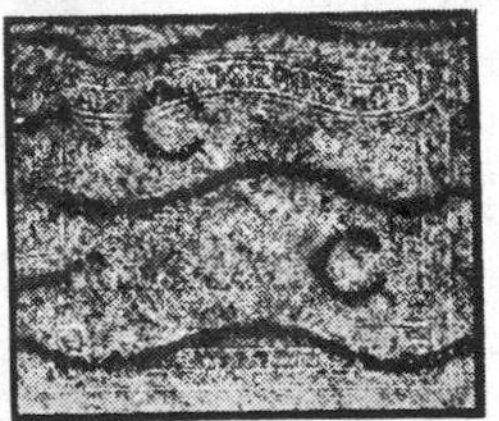
Wmk. 255

Wmkd.
Wavy Lines and C Multiple. (255)

Imprint:
"American Bank Note Co."

1939, Mar. 3 Engr. *Perf. 12*

No.	Type	Description	Unused	Used
467	A175	1c green	18	5
468	A155	2c car rose	25	5
469	A176	5c dl brn	25	5
470	A157	10c dp org	1.25	5
471	A177	15c dl bl	3.00	22
472	A178	20c vio blk	5.25	30
473	A179	30c ol bis	5.25	45
474	A180	40c bis brn	15.00	4.25
		Nos. 467-474 (8)	30.43	5.42

See also Nos. 497–499, 515, 518, 574.

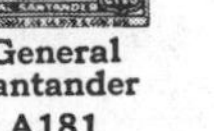
General Santander
A181

Allegory
A182

General Santander
A183

Statue at Cúcuta
A184

Church at Rosario
A186

Birthplace of Santander
A185

Paya
A187

Bridge at Boyacá
A188

Death of General Santander
A189

Invasion of the Liberators
A190

Perf. 13½x13, 13½x13

Wmkd. Wavy Lines. (229)

1940, May 6 **Engraved**

475	A181	1c ol grn	30	25
476	A182	2c dk car	60	45
477	A183	5c sepia	30	22
478	A184	8c carmine	2.25	1.50
479	A185	10c org yel	1.00	75
480	A186	15c dk bl	2.75	1.65
481	A187	20c green	3.50	2.00
482	A188	50c violet	8.00	6.00
483	A189	1p dp rose	25.00	25.00
484	A190	2p orange	80.00	80.00
		Nos. 475-484 (10)	123.70	117.82

Issued in commemoration of the centenary of the death of General Francisco Santander.

Tobacco Plant
A194

General Santander
A195

Garcia Rovira
A196

R. Galan
A197

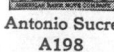

Antonio Sucre
A198

Arms of Palmira
A199

Wmkd.

Wavy Lines and C Multiple. (255)

1940-43 **Engraved.** ***Perf. 12.***

488	A194	8c rose car & grn	1.50	85
489	A195	15c dp bl ('43)	1.60	35
490	A196	20c gray blk ('41)	4.00	55
491	A197	40c brn bis ('41)	2.75	55
492	A198	1p black	9.50	80
		Nos. 488-492 (5)	19.35	3.10

See also Nos. 500, 554.

Lithographed.

1942, July 4 ***Perf. 11*** **Unwmkd.**

493	A199	30c claret	2.50	90

Issued to commemorate the 8th National Agricultural Exposition, held at Palmira.

Paradise of Isaacs, Palmira
A200

Signing Treaty of the Wisconsin
A201

1942, July 4

494	A200	50c lt bl grn	3.25	1.25

Issued in honor of the writer, Jorge Isaacs.

1942, Nov. 21 ***Perf. 10½***

495	A201	10c dl org	1.60	75
a.		"2. XI.1902" instead of "21. XI. 1902"	21.00	22.50
b.		Perf. 12	4.50	4.50

Issued in commemoration of the 40th anniversary of the signing of the Treaty of the Wisconsin, November 21, 1902.

No. 470 Surcharged in Black

5
Centavos

1944 ***Perf. 12.*** **Wmk. 255**

496	A157	5c on 10c dp org	20	15

Counterfeits exist of No. 496 with inverted or double surcharge.

Types of 1935-41 and

National Shrine
A202

San Pedro Alejandrino
A203

Engraved.

Imprint:

"Columbian Bank Note Co."

1944-45 ***Perf. 11*** **Unwmkd.**

497	A175	1c green	20	10
498	A155	2c rose	20	10
499	A176	5c dl brn	20	5
500	A196	20c gray blk	3.75	1.10
501	A202	30c dl ol grn ('45)	2.00	1.40
502	A203	50c rose	2.50	1.40
		Nos. 497-502 (6)	8.85	4.15

No. 499 Surcharged in Black

1
CENTAVO

1944, Oct.

506	A176	1c on 5c dl brn	12	12
507	A176	2c on 5c dl brn	12	12

Nos. 506 and 507 exist with inverted or double surcharge, created by favor.

Flag—A204

Arms—A205

Murillo Toro
A206

Hospital of St. John of God
A207

Virrey Solis
A208

A209

1944, Oct. 10 **Lithographed**

508	A204	2c ultra & bis	40	40
a.		Sheet of 18	12.00	
b.		Imperf., pair	12.50	
509	A205	5c ultra & bis	40	40
a.		Sheet of 22	15.00	
b.		Imperf., pair	12.50	
510	A206	20c blk & bluish grn	1.10	1.10
a.		Sheet of 8	12.00	
b.		Imperf., pair	18.50	
511	A207	40c blk & red	5.00	4.50
a.		Sheet of 4	20.00	
512	A208	1p blk & red	13.00	13.00
a.		Sheet of 2	27.50	
		Nos. 508-512 (5)	19.90	19.40

Souvenir Sheet.

Perforated 11x11½ all around, Stamps Imperf.

513	A209	Sheet of five	20.00	20.00

75th anniversary of General Benevolent Association of Cundinamarca. Size of No. 513: 100x87mm.

Nos. 508-513 were printed in composite sheets containing one each of Nos. 508a, 509a, 510a, 511a and 512a, and two of 513. Fifty of these were presented to government officials.

Murillo Toro
A210

San Pedro Alejandrino
A211

1944, Nov. 10 ***Perf. 11***

514	A210	5c lt brn	40	22

Types of 1932-39 and A211.

Imprint:

"Litografia Nacional Bogota".

1944 **Lithographed.** ***Perf. 12½.***

515	A175	1c dp grn	45	20
a.		1c ol grn	45	20
b.		Imperf., pair	3.00	3.00
516	A155	2c dk car	45	20
a.		Imperf., pair	3.00	3.00
517	A135	10c yel org	2.50	75
518	A179	30c gray ol	12.00	5.25
a.		Imperf., pair	40.00	
519	A211	50c rose	13.00	6.00
		Nos. 515-519 (5)	28.40	12.40

No. 469 Overprinted in Green, Blue or Red

Engraved.

1945, July 19 ***Perf. 12*** **Wmk. 255**

520	A176	5c dl brn (G)	25	12
521	A176	5c dl brn (R)	25	12
522	A176	5c dl brn (Bl)	25	12

Portraits are Joseph Stalin, Franklin D. Roosevelt and Winston Churchill.

Clock Tower, Cartagena
A212

1945, Nov. 15

523	A212	50c ol blk	5.75	1.75

Sierra Nevada of Santa Marta
A213

Designs: 30c, Seaplane Tolima. 50c, San Sebastian Fort, Cartagena.

Lithographed.

1945, Dec. 14 ***Perf. 11*** **Unwmkd.**

524	A213	20c lt grn	2.25	1.50
525	A213	30c pale bl	2.25	1.50
526	A213	50c sal pink	2.25	1.50

Issued to commemorate the 25th anniversary of the first airmail service in America, according to the inscription, but earlier services are known to have existed.

No. 442 Surcharged in Black

1
UN CENTAVO

1946, Mar. 8 ***Perf. 11x11½, 12½***

527	A133	1c on 5c brn	10	10
a.		Inverted surcharge	1.25	

Gen. Antonio José de Sucre
A216

Engraved.

1946, Apr. 16 ***Perf. 12*** **Wmk. 255**

Size: 19x26½mm.

528	A216	1c brn & turq grn	22	12
529	A216	2c vio & rose car	22	12

Size: 23x31mm.

530	A216	5c sep & bl	22	12
531	A216	9c dk grn & red	90	90
532	A216	10c ultra & org	80	70

533	A216	20c blk & dp org	80	45
534	A216	30c brn red & grn	1.40	45
535	A216	40c ol blk & red vio	1.40	60
536	A216	50c dp brn & vio	1.40	60
		Nos. 528-536 (9)	7.36	4.06

Map of South America
A217

National Observatory
A218

Lithographed.

1946, June 7 Perf. 11 Unwmkd.

537	A217	15c ultra	75	45
a.		Imperf. (pair)	6.00	

1946, Aug.

538	A218	5c fawn	35	12
a.		Imperf. (pair)	6.00	

See No. 565.

Andrés Bello
A219

Joaquín de Cayzedo y Cuero
A220

Engraved.

1946, Sept. 3 Perf. 12 Wmk. 255

539	A219	3c sepia	22	15
540	A219	10c orange	75	45
541	A219	15c sl blk	85	45

Issued to commemorate the 80th anniversary of the death of Andrés Bello (1781-1865), poet and educator. See also No. C145.

1946, Sept. 20 Perf. 12½ Wmk. 229

542	A220	2p bluish grn	6.75	1.75

See also No. 568.

Type of 1945, Overprinted in Black or Green

V JUEGOS C.
A. Y DEL C.
1946

1946, Dec. 6 Perf. 12 Wmk. 255

543	A212	50c red (Bk)	4.75	3.25
a.		Dbl. overprint	32.50	
544	A212	50c red (G)	4.75	3.25
a.		Dbl. overprint	32.50	

Issued to commemorate the fifth Central American and Caribbean Championship Games.

Coffee
A221

Engraved and Lithographed.

1947, Jan. 10 Perf. 12½ Wmk. 229

545	A221	5c multi	60	12

Colombian Orchid: Masdevallia Nycterina
A222

Designs (Orchids): 2c, Miltonia vexillaria. No. 548, Cattleya chocoensis. No. 549, Odontoglossum crispum. No. 550, Cattleya dowiana aurea. 10c, Cattleya labiata trianae.

Engraved and Lithographed.

1947, Feb. 7 Perf. 12 Wmk. 255

546	A222	1c multi	45	18
547	A222	2c multi	45	18
548	A222	5c multi	1.40	18
549	A222	5c multi	1.40	18
550	A222	5c multi	1.40	18
551	A222	10c multi	2.25	60
		Nos. 546-551 (6)	7.35	1.50

Antonio Nariño
A228

Alberto Urdaneta y Urdaneta
A229

Perf. 12½

1947, May 9 Litho. Unwmkd.

552	A228	5c bl, *grnsh*	40	22
553	A229	10c red brn, *grnsh*	50	22

Issued to commemorate the 4th Pan-American Press Congress, 1946. See also Nos. C146-C147.

Sucre Type of 1940.

Engraved.

1947 Perf. 12. Wmk. 255

554	A198	1p violet	3.25	1.50

José Celestino Mutis and José Jerónimo Triana
A230

Miguel A. Caro and Rufino J. Cuervo
A231

1947 Perf. 12½ Wmk. 229

555	A230	25c ol grn	85	40
556	A231	3p dk pur	5.75	4.00

See also Nos. 567, 569.

Metropolitan Cathedral, Plaza Bolívar, Bogotá
A232

National Capitol
A233

Ministry of Foreign Affairs
A234

A235

1948, Apr. 2

557	A232	5c blk brn	15	5
558	A233	10c orange	85	75
559	A234	15c dk bl	85	75
		Nos. 557-559, C148-C149 (5)	2.40	2.85

Miniature Sheet

Imperf.

560	A235	50c slate	2.25	2.25

Nos. 557-560 commemorate the 9th Pan-American Conference, Bogotá. No. 560 measures 90½x90½mm.

No. RA5A Overprinted in Black

Without Gum.

1948 Perf. 12½ Unwmkd.

561	PT3	1c yel org	10	5

The letter "C" is the initial of "CORREOS".

Nos. RA33, RA24 and RA25 Overprinted in Black

CORREOS

With Gum.

1948 Perf. 12. Wmk. 255

562	PT6	1c olive	6	5
563	PT6	2c green	6	5
564	PT6	20c brown	25	5

Nos. 561-564 exist with inverted and double overprints.

Observatory Type of 1946.

Lithographed

1948, June 30 Perf. 11 Unwmkd.

565	A218	5c blue	30	6

Simón Bolívar
A236

Carlos Martinez Silva
A237

Engraved.

1948, May 29 Perf. 12 Wmk. 255

566	A236	15c green	60	25

Types of 1946-47.

1948 Perf. 12½ Unwmkd.

567	A230	25c green	30	12
568	A220	2p dp grn	80	18
569	A231	3p dp red vio	1.00	22

Falls Type of 1937.

1948 Wmk. 229

570	A160	10c red	15	5

Lithographed.

1948, Dec. 21 Perf. 13½ Unwmkd.

571	A237	40c carmine	60	35

Juan de Dios Carrasquilla
A238

1949, May 20 Perf. 12½ Wmk. 229

572	A238	5c bister	22	12

Issued to commemorate the 75th anniversary of the foundation of the Colombian Society of Agriculture.

Julio Garavito Armero
A239

Arms of Colombia
A240

Engraved.

1949, Apr. 24 Perf. 12 Wmk. 229

573	A239	4c green	45	22

Issued to honor Julio Garavito Armero (1865-1920), mathematician.

Coffee Type of 1939.

Imprint: "American Bank Note Co."

1949, Aug. 4 Wmk. 255

574	A176	5c blue	15	5

1949, Oct. 7 Perf. 13 Unwmkd.

575	A240	15c blue	25	6

Issued to honor the new Constitution. See also Nos. C164-C165.

Shield and Tree
A241

Francisco Javier Cisneros
A242

1949, Oct. 13 Perf. 12½ Wmk. 229

576	A241	5c olive	15	5

Issued to commemorate the 4th anniversary of Colombia's first Forestry Congress and as propaganda for the government's reforestation program.

1949, Dec. 15 Photo. Unwmkd.

577	A242	50c red vio & yel	1.50	85
578	A242	50c grn & vio	1.50	85
579	A242	50c brn & lt bl	1.50	85

Issued to commemorate the 50th anniversary (in 1948) of the death of Francisco Javier Cisneros.

Masdevallia Chimaera
A243

Odontoglossum Crispum
A244

Eastern Hemisphere
A245

Designs: 3c, Cattleya labiata trianae. 4c, Masdevallia nycterina. 5c, Cattleya dowiana aurea. 11c, Miltonia vexillaria. 18c, Santo Domingo post office.

1950, Aug. 22 Photo. *Perf. 13*

580	A243	1c brown	22	15
581	A244	2c violet	22	15
582	A243	3c rose lil	28	15
583	A243	4c emerald	40	15
584	A243	5c red org	1.10	15
585	A244	11c red	2.50	2.10
586	A244	18c ultra	2.00	90
		Nos. 580-586 (7)	6.72	3.75

Miniature Sheet

Imperf.

587	A245	50c org yel	1.85	1.85

Nos. 580–587 commemorate the 75th anniversary (in 1949) of the formation of the Universal Postal Union. No. 587 measures 91x90mm.

See No. C199.

Antonio Baraya
A246

Engraved

1950, Nov. 27 *Perf. 12½* Unwmkd.

588	A246	2c red	10	5

Colombian Farm
A247

1950, Dec. 28 Photo. *Perf. 11½*

589	A247	5c dp car & buff	30	10
590	A247	5c bl grn & gray	30	10
591	A247	5c vio bl & gray	30	10

Issued to publicize rural life.

Arms of Bogotá
A248

Arms of Colombia
A249

Perf. 12x12½

1950, Dec. 28 Engr. Wmkd. 255

592	A248	5p dp grn	3.75	55
593	A249	10p red org	11.00	65

Map and Badge
A250

Guillermo Valencia
A251

Perf. 12½x13

1951, Jan. 30 Photo. Unwmkd.

594	A250	20c red, yel & bl	60	22

Issued to commemorate the 60th anniversary (in 1947) of the formation of the Colombian Society of Engineers.

1951, Oct. 20 Engr. *Perf. 13x13½*

595	A251	25c black	1.40	30

Issued to honor Guillermo Valencia (1873–1943), newspaper founder, governor of Cauca, presidential candidate, author.

No. 468 Overprinted in Black

REVERSION
CONCESION MARES
25 Agosto 1951

1951, Dec. 11 *Perf. 12* Wmk. 255

596	A155	2c car rose	10	6

Issued to publicize the reversion of the Mares oil concession to Colombia.

Nicolas Osorio
A252

Portraits: No. 598, Pompilio Martinez. No. 599, Ezequiel Uriocoechea. No. 600, Jose M. Lombana.

Engraved.

1952, Aug. 6 *Perf. 11½* Unwmkd.

Various Frames.

597	A252	1c dp bl	10	6
598	A252	1c dp bl	10	6
599	A252	1c dp bl	10	6
600	A252	1c dp bl	10	6

Nos. 597-600 were printed in a single sheet containing four panes of twenty-five each, separated by double rows of ornamental tabs. Although inscribed "sobretasa," the stamps were for ordinary postage.

Types of Postal Tax Stamps of 1945–50 and

Communications Building
A253 A253a

1952 *Perf. 12*

601	A253	5c ultra	22	6

Wmk. 255.

602	PT10	20c brown	6.75	22
603	PT6	25c dk gray	7.50	2.25
604	PT10	25c bl grn	60	10
605	A253a	50c org yel	26.00	12.00
606	A253a	1p rose car	2.00	45
607	A253a	2p lil rose	25.00	6.50
608	A253a	2p violet	1.50	70
		Nos. 601-608 (8)	69.57	22.28

Although inscribed "sobretasa," Nos. 601–608 were issued for ordinary postage.

Cathedral of Manizales
A254

Perf. 11½

1952, Oct. 10 Photo. Unwmkd.

609	A254	23c bl & gray blk	40	30

Centenary of city of Manizales.

No. 555 Surcharged in Blue

1ª CONFERENCIA 19 52 SIDERURGICA
LATINO-AMERICANA.
15

1952, Oct. 30 *Perf. 12½* Wmk. 229

610	A230	15c on 25c ol grn	45	30

Issued to publicize the Latin American Siderurgical Conference, 1952. See also No. C226.

Queen Isabella I and Monument
A255

Engraved

1953, Mar. 10 *Perf. 12½* Unwmkd.

611	A255	23c bl & blk	90	75

Issued to commemorate the fifth centenary of the birth of Queen Isabella I of Spain.

Nos. 606 and 568 Surcharged with New Values in Dark Blue

1953, Oct. 19 Wmk. 255

612	A253a	40c on 1p rose car	1.40	22
613	A220	50c on 2p dp grn	1.40	22

Manuel Ancizar
A256

Portraits: 23c, José Jeronimo Triana. 30c, Manuel Ponce de Leon. 1p, Agustin Codazzi.

Perf. 12½x13

1953, Nov. Engraved Unwmkd.

Frames in Black.

614	A256	14c rose red	50	50
615	A256	23c ultra	50	30
616	A256	30c chocolate	45	20
617	A256	1p emerald	45	15

Issued to commemorate the centenary (in 1950) of the establishment of the Chorographic Commission.

See also Nos. 687, 690, 692.

Murillo Toro and Map
A257

Engraved and Lithographed.

1953, Dec. 12 *Perf. 12* Wmk. 255

Black Surcharge.

618	A257	5c on 5p multi	38	22

Issued to publicize the 2nd National Philatelic Exhibition, Bogotá, December 1953. See also No. C237.

Nos. 609 and 614 Surcharged with New Value or New Value and Ornaments.

Perf. 11½, 12½x13.

1953 Unwmkd.

619	A254	5c on 23c bl & gray blk (C)	45	30
620	A256	5c on 14c blk & rose red (Bk)	45	40

No. 614 surcharged "CINCO" in blue is listed as No. 687.

Symbolical of St. Francis Receiving Christ's Wounds
A258

1954, Apr. 23 Photo. *Perf. 11½*

621	A258	5c sep & grn	25	10

Issued to commemorate the 400th anniversary of the establishment of Colombia's first Franciscan community.

Soldier, Map and Arms
A259

1954, June 13 Engraved *Perf. 13*

622	A259	5c dl bl	25	10

Issued to commemorate the first anniversary of the assumption of the presidency by Gen. Gustavo Rojas Pinilla. See also Nos. C255, 637a.

Sports Emblem
A260

Design: 10c, Stadium and athlete holding arms of Colombia.

1954, July 18 **Unwmkd.**

623	A260	5c dp bl	50	22
624	A260	10c red	85	22

Issued to publicize the 7th National Athletic Games, Cali, July 1954. See also Nos. C256–C257.

History Academy Seal
A261

1954, July 24

625	A261	5c ultra & grn	22	10

Issued to commemorate the 50th anniversary (in 1952) of the Colombian Academy of History.

Convent and Cell of St. Peter Claver
A262

1954, Sept. 9

627	A262	5c dk grn	20	10
a.		Souvenir sheet	3.25	3.25

Issued to commemorate the 300th anniversary of the death of St. Peter Claver.

No. 627a contains one stamp similar to No. 627, but printed in greenish black. Marginal inscriptions in black. Sheet size: 121x129½mm. See also Nos. C258–C258a.

Mercury
A263

1954, Oct. 29

628	A263	5c orange	40	10

Issued to publicize the first International Fair and Exhibition, Bogotá, 1954. See Nos. C259–C260.

Tapestry Madonna
A264

College Cloister—A265

Designs: 10c, Brother Cristobal de Torres. 20c, College chapel and arms.

Perf. 12½x11½, 11½x12½

1954, Dec. 6

629	A264	5c org & blk	40	18
630	A264	10c blue	40	18
631	A265	15c vio brn	45	18
632	A265	20c blk & brn	90	35
a.		Souvenir sheet	6.25	6.25
		Nos. 629-632, C263-C266 (8)	5.83	2.51

Issued to commemorate the 300th anniversary (in 1953) of the founding of the Senior College of Our Lady of the Rosary, Bogota.

No. 632a contains four stamps similar to Nos. 629–632, but printed in different colors: 5c yellow and black, 10c green, 15c dull violet, 20c black and light-blue. Marginal inscriptions in black. Sheet size: 124½x130½mm.

Steel Mill
A266

José Marti
A267

1954, Dec. 12 ***Perf. 12½x13***

633	A266	5c ultra & blk	30	10

Issued to mark the opening of the Paz del Rio steel mill, October 1954. See No. C267.

1955, Jan. 28 ***Perf. 13½x13***

634	A267	5c dp car	20	10

Issued to commemorate the centenary of the birth of José Marti (1853–1895), Cuban patriot. See No. C268.

Arms, Flags and Soldiers Building Bridge
A268

1955, Mar. 23 ***Perf. 12½***

635	A268	10c claret	25	10

Issued to honor Colombian soldiers who served in Korea, 1951–53. See Nos. 637a, C269.

Fleet Emblem
A269

M. S. City of Manizales and New York Skyline
A270

1955, Apr. 12 **Unwmkd.**

636	A269	15c dp grn	25	10
637	A270	20c violet	25	10
a.		Souvenir sheet	6.25	6.25

Issued to honor the Grand-Colombian Merchant Fleet. See Nos. C270–C271a.

No. 637a contains four stamps similar to Nos. 622, 635–637, but printed in different colors: 5c blue, 10c dark carmine, 15c green, 20c purple. Marginal inscriptions in black. Sheet size: 125x131mm.

Hotel Tequendama and Church of San Diego
A271

1955, May 16 Photo. ***Perf. 11½x12***

638	A271	5c blue	15	5

See also No. C273.

Bolivar's Country Estate, Bogotá
A272

1955, Sept. 28 Engr. ***Perf. 12½***

639	A272	5c dp ultra	15	5

Issued to commemorate the 50th anniversary of Rotary International. See No. C274.

Belalcazar, Jiménez de Quesada and Balboa
A273

Caravels and Columbus
A274

Design: 5c, San Martin, Bolivar and Washington.

Engraved and Photogravure.

1955, Oct. 29 ***Perf. 13x12½***

640	A273	2c yel grn & brn	10	6
641	A273	5c brt bl & brn	22	6
642	A274	23c lt ultra & blk	25	22
a.		Souvenir sheet	7.25	7.25
		Nos. 640-642, C275-C280 (9)	16.62	10.59

Issued to publicize the seventh Congress of the Postal Union of the Americas and Spain, Bogota, Oct. 12.-Nov. 9, 1955.

No. 642a contains one each of Nos. 640-642, printed in slightly different shades. It measures 120x132 mm. and is inscribed in black: "Ministerio de Comunicaciones. III Exposicion Filatelica Nacional Bogota 1955."

José Eusebio Caro
A275

1955, Nov. 29 **Engr.** ***Perf. 13½x13***

643	A275	5c brown	12	6

Issued to commemorate the centenary of the death of José Eusebio Caro (1817–1853), poet. See also No. C281.

Departmental Issue

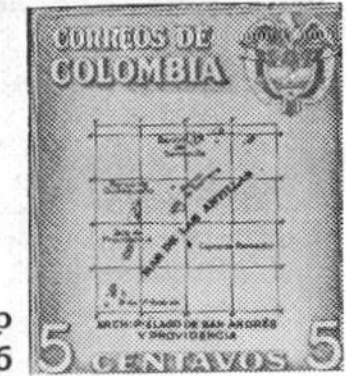

Map
A276

View of San Andres Harbor
A277

Cattle at Waterhole—A278

Designs: 2c, Docks, Atlantico. 3c, "Industry," Antioquia. 4c, Cartagena Harbor, Bolivar. No. 647, Steel Mill, Boyaca. No. 648, Cattle, Cordoba. No. 649, Map. No. 650, San Andres Harbor. No. 651, Cacao picker, Cauca. 10c, Coffee picker, Caldas. 15c, Salt Mine Chapel, Zipaquira, Cundinamarca. 20c, Tropical plants and map, Choco. 23c, Harvester, Huila. 25c, Banana Plantation, Magdalena. 30c, Gold mining, Nariño. 40c, Tobacco plantation, Santander. 50c, Oil wells, North Santander. 60c, Cotton plantation, Tolima. 1p, Sugar industry, Cauca. 3p, Amazon river at Leticia, Amazonas. 5p, Windmills and panoramic view, La Guajira. 10p, Rubber plantation, Vaupes.

Engraved; Engraved and Lithographed.

Perf. 13½x13, 13x13½, 13

1956 **Engraved.** **Unwmkd.**

Various Frames.

644	A277	2c car & grn	10	5
645	A276	3c brn vio & blk	10	5

646	A277	4c grn & blk	10	5
647	A276	5c dk brn & bl	20	6
648	A277	5c ol & dk vio brn	35	5
649	A276	5c bl & blk	30	5
650	A277	5c car & grnsh bl	25	5
651	A277	5c ol grn & red brn	25	5
652	A276	10c org & blk	25	6
653	A276	15c ultra & blk	30	10
654	A276	20c dk brn & bl	25	10
655	A277	23c ultra & ver	30	25
656	A276	25c ol grn & blk	30	25
657	A277	30c ultra & brn	25	5
658	A277	40c dl pur & red brn	25	5
659	A277	50c dk grn & blk	25	5
660	A277	60c pale brn & grn	25	5
661	A278	1p mag & grnsh bl	2.00	25
662	A278	2p grn & red brn	2.50	30
663	A278	3p car & blk	3.25	50
664	A278	5p brn & lt ultra	5.00	1.25
665	A276	10p red brn & grn	14.00	6.25
		Nos. 644-665 (22)	30.80	9.92

Nos. 645, 647, 649, 652–654 measure 27x32mm. No. 665 measures 27x37 mm. See also Nos. 681–684, 685, 688–689.

Columbus and Proposed Lighthouse—A279

1956, Oct. 12 Photo. *Perf. 12*

666	A279	3c gray blk	15	10

Issued in honor of Christopher Columbus. See also Nos. C285, C306.

Altar of St. Elizabeth and Tomb of Jimenez de Quesada
A280

1956, Nov. 19 Unwmkd.

667	A280	5c red lil	15	10

Issued to commemorate the 7th centenary of St. Elizabeth of Hungary, patron saint of Sante Fé de Bogotá. See No. C286.

St. Ignatius of Loyola
A281

Javier Pereira
A282

1956, Nov. 26 Engr. *Perf. 12½x13*

668	A281	5c blue	25	8

Issued to commemorate the 400th anniversary of the death of St. Ignatius of Loyola. See No. C287.

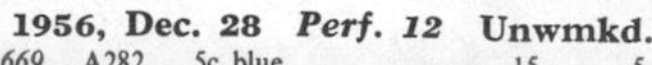

1956, Dec. 28 *Perf. 12* Unwmkd.

669	A282	5c blue	15	5

Issued to honor 167-year-old Javier Pereira. See No. C288.

Emblem and Dairy Farm
A283

Designs: 2c, Emblem and tractor. 5c, Emblem, coffee and corn.

1957, Mar. 5 Photo. *Perf. 14x13½*

670	A283	1c lt ol grn	6	5
671	A283	2c lt brn	6	5
672	A283	5c lt bl	15	7
		Nos. 670-672, C292-C296 (8)	2.77	1.83

25th anniversary of the Agrarian Savings Bank of Colombia.

Arms of Military Academy and Gen. Rafael Reyes—A284

Design: 10c, Arms and Academy.

1957, July 20 Engr. *Perf. 12½*

673	A284	5c blue	15	5
674	A284	10c orange	15	5
a.		Souv. sheet of 2	15.00	15.00

Issued to commemorate the 50th anniversary of the Colombian Military Academy. See Nos. C299–C300.

No. 674a contains one each of Nos. 673–674 in slightly different shades. It measures 120x131½mm. with marginal inscriptions in black.

Statue of José Matias Delgado
A285

1957, Sept. 16 Photo. *Perf. 12*

675	A285	2c rose brn	6	5

Issued in honor of Jose Matias Delgado, liberator of El Salvador. See No. C301.

Santo Michelena, Marcos V. Crespo, P. Alcantara Herran and UPU Monument—A286

1957, Oct. 10 Unwmkd.

676	A286	5c green	15	10
677	A286	10c gray	15	5

Issued for International Letter Writing Week and the 14th UPU Congress. See Nos. C302–C303.

St. Vincent de Paul and Children
A287

1957, Oct. 18

678	A287	1c dk ol grn	5	5

Issued to commemorate the centenary of the Colombian Society of St. Vincent de Paul. See No. C304.

Fencer
A288

1957, Nov. 22 Photo. *Perf. 12*

679	A288	4c lilac	15	10

Issued to commemorate the third South American Fencing Championship. See No. C305.

Francisco José de Caldas and Hypsometer
A289

1958, May 12 *Perf. 12* Unwmkd.

680	A289	10c black	35	10

Issued for the International Geophysical Year, 1957–58. See Nos. C309–C310.

Departmental Issue.
Type of 1956,
Designs as Before.

1958 Engraved. *Perf. 13*

681	A276	3c ultra & brn	10	5
682	A276	3c ol grn & pur	10	5
683	A276	10c grn & brn	20	5
684	A276	10c dk bl & brn	20	5

Nos. 646, C291, 614, 653, 655, 616, C308, 615 and 611 Surcharged with New Value, and Old Value Obliterated, or Overprinted in Dark Blue or Green.

Perf. 12½, 12½x13, 13.

1958-59 Unwmkd.

685	A277	2c on 4c grn & blk	15	5
686	AP48	5c dp plum & multi ('59)	15	10
687	A256	5c on 14c blk & rose red ("CINCO") ('59)	45	38
688	A276	5c on 15c ultra & blk	15	5
689	A277	5c on 23c ultra & ver (G)	35	25
690	A256	5c on 30c blk & choc	15	10
691	AP40	10c on 25c rose vio	15	5
692	A256	20c on 23c blk & ultra (G) ('59)	35	30
693	A255	20c on 23c bl & blk ('59)	35	30
		Nos. 685-693 (9)	2.25	1.58

On No. 686 the words "Correo Extra Rapido" are obliterated in dark blue.

Father Rafael Almanza and Church of San Diego, Bogota
A290

1958, Oct. 23 Photo. *Perf. 14x13*

695	A290	10c purple	15	5

See also Nos. C313–C314.

Msgr. R. M. Carrasquilla and Church
A291

1959, Jan. 22 *Perf. 14x13*

696	A291	10c dk red brn	20	5

Issued to commemorate the centenary of the birth of Msgr. R. M. Carrasquilla (1857–1930), rector of Our Lady of the Rosary Seminary, Bogotá. See Nos. C315–C316.

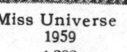

Miss Universe 1959
A292

Jorge Eliecer Gaitan
A293

1959, June 26 Photo. *Perf. 11½*

697	A292	10c multi	10	5

Issued to honor Luz Marina Zuluaga, Miss Universe, 1959. See Nos. C317–C318.

Engraved

1959, July 28 *Perf. 12x13½*

698	A293	10c on 3c gray bl (Bl)	20	5
699	A293	30c rose vio	50	20

Issued in honor of Jorge Elieccr Gaitan (1898–1948), lawyer and politician.

No. 698 exists without blue surcharge.

See also Nos. C319–C320.

Gen. Francisco de Paula Santander
A294

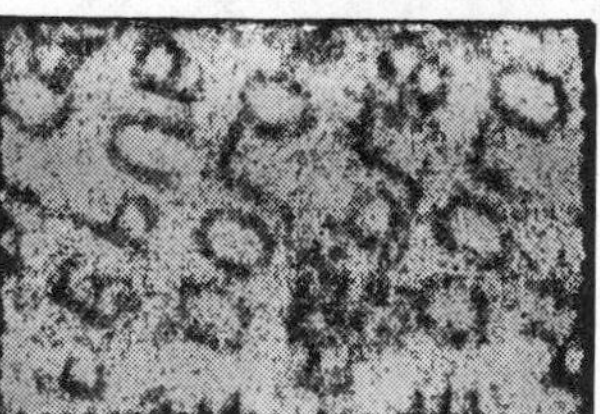

Wmk. 331

Designs: Nos. 701, 703, Simon Bolivar.

Wmkd. "REPÚBLICA DE COLOMBIA". (331)

1959 Lithographed *Perf. 12½*

700	A294	5c brn & yel	15	10
701	A294	5c ultra & bl	15	10
702	A294	10c gray & grn	20	10
703	A294	10c gray & red	20	10

See also No. C389.

Capitol, Bogota
A295

1959

704	A295	2c dk bl & red brn	12	10
705	A295	3c blk brn & lil	12	10

Stamp of 1859 and Mail Transport by Mule
A296

Two-Toed Sloth
A297

Designs (various stamps of 1859 and): 10c, Mail boat on the Magdalena river. 25c, Train.

Photogravure

1959, Dec. 1 ***Perf. 12*** **Unwmkd.**

709	A296	5c org & grn	20	15
710	A296	10c rose cl & bl	20	15
711	A296	15c car rose & grn	45	45
712	A296	25c bl & red brn	60	55
		Nos. 709-712, C351-C354 (8)	6.00	4.85

Centenary of Colombian postage stamps.

1960, Feb. 12 ***Perf. 12***

Designs: 10c, Alexander von Humboldt. 20c, Spider monkey.

713	A297	5c grnsh bl & brn	20	10
714	A297	10c blk & dp car	25	5
715	A297	20c cit & gray brn	20	5
		Nos. 713-715, C357-C359 (6)	6.40	6.45

Issued to commemorate the centenary of the death of Alexander von Humboldt (1769–1859), German naturalist and geographer.

Anthurium Andreanum
A298

Lincoln Statue, Washington
A299

Flower: 20c, Espeletia grandiflora.

1960, May 10

716	A298	5c multi	15	15
717	A298	20c brn, yel & gray ol	10	10
		Nos. 716-717, C360-C370 (13)	18.20	25.18

See also Nos. C420–C425.

Perf. 10½

1960, June 10 Litho. Wmk. 331

718	A299	20c rose lil & blk	30	20

Issued to commemorate the sesquicentennial of the birth of Abraham Lincoln (1809–1865). See also Nos. C375–C376.

Floredo House, Cradle of the Republic
A300

Arms of Santa Cruz de Mompox
A301

Design: 5c, First coins of Republic.

Perf. 12

1960, July 19 Photo. Unwmkd.

719	A301	5c grn & ocher	10	10
720	A300	20c ol bis & mar	10	10
721	A301	20c multi	20	30
		Nos. 719-721, C377-C385 (12)	5.60	3.85

Issued to commemorate the 150th anniversary of Colombia's independence.

St. Isidro and Farm Animals
A302

Design: 20c, Nativity by Gregorio de Arce Vasquez y Ceballos.

1960, Sept. 26 ***Perf. 12***

722	A302	10c multi	15	10
723	A302	20c multi	22	10

Issued to honor St. Isidro the Farmer, patron saint of the rural people.

See also Nos. 747, C387–C388, C439–C440.

U.N. Headquarters and Emblem
A303

Perf. 11

1960, Oct. 24 Litho. Wmk. 331

724	A303	20c blk & pink	22	15

Souvenir Sheet

Imperf.

725	A303	50c dk brn, brt grn & blk	3.50	3.50

15th anniversary of the United Nations. No. 725 contains one stamp and has dark brown marginal inscription and black number. Size: 55x48½mm.

Pan-American Highway through Colombia
A304

Alfonso Lopez
A305

Perf. 10½x11

1961, Mar. 7 Unwmkd.

726	A304	20c brn & grnsh bl	90	80
		Nos. 726, C390-C393 (5)	4.30	3.80

Issued to commemorate the 8th Pan-American Highway Congress, Bogota, May 20–29, 1960.

1961, Mar. 22 Photo. ***Perf. 12½***

727	A305	10c brt rose & brn	25	15
728	A305	20c vio & brn	25	15

Issued to honor Alfonso Lopez (1886–1959), President of Colombia.

See Nos. C394–C396.

Cauca River Bridge, Cali
A306

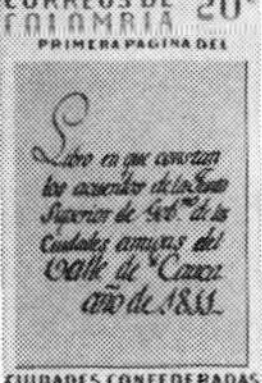

Page from Resolutions of Confederated Cities
A307

1961-62 ***Perf. 12½x13, 13½x13***

729	A306	10c red brn, bl, grn & red ('62)	15	6
730	A307	20c pale brn & blk	20	7
		Nos. 729-730, C397-C401 (7)	4.00	1.67

Issued to commemorate the 50th anniversary (in 1960) of the Department of Valle del Cauca.

View of Cucuta and Arms
A308

Design: No. 732, Arms of Ocana and Pamplona.

1961, Aug. 29 ***Perf. 13x13½***

731	A308	20c bl, blk, yel & red	15	6
732	A308	20c ocher, ultra & red	15	6

Issued to commemorate the 50th anniversary (in 1960) of the Department of North Santander. See Nos. C402–C403.

Arms of Popayan
A309

Basketball
A310

Designs: No. 734, Arms of Barranquilla. No. 735, Arms of Bucaramanga.

Perf. 12½x13

1961, Oct. 10 Unwmkd.

Arms in Multicolor

733	A309	10c bl & sil	15	7
734	A309	20c bl & yel	15	7
735	A309	20c bl & gold	15	7
		Nos. 733-735, C404-C408 (8)	3.40	88

Issued to honor Atlantico Department.

1961, Dec. 16 Litho. ***Perf. 13½x14***

Multicolored

736	A310	20c *shown*	10	5
737	A310	20c *Runners*	10	5
738	A310	20c *Boxers*	35	15
739	A310	25c *Soccer*	20	7
		Nos. 736-739, C414-C418 (9)	3.90	1.32

4th Bolivarian Games, Barranquilla, 1961.

Colombian Anti-Malaria Emblem
A311

Engineers Society Emblem
A312

Design: 50c, Malaria eradication emblem and mosquito in swamp.

1962, Apr. 12 ***Perf. 12*** **Unwmkd.**

740	A311	20c lt bis & red	22	20
741	A311	50c bis & ultra	25	15
		Nos. 740-741, C426-C428 (5)	6.72	6.45

Issued for the World Health Organization drive to eradicate malaria.

1962, June 12 Photo. ***Perf. 11½x12***

742	A312	10c multi	30	30
		Nos. 742, C429-C432 (5)	3.50	3.30

Issued to commemorate the 75th anniversary of the Colombian Society of Engineers.

Flags of American Nations
A313

Woman Casting Ballot and Statue of Policarpa Salavarrieta
A314

1962, June 28 ***Perf. 13***

Flags in National Colors

743	A313	25c blk & org ver	15	5

Souvenir Sheet

744	A313	2.50p blk & yel	4.50	4.50

Issued to commemorate the 70th anniversary of the founding of the Organization of American States.

No. 744 contains one stamp, black marginal inscription. Size: 45x55mm.

See also No. C433.

Perf. 12x12½

1962, July 20 Litho. Wmk. 229

745	A314	10c lt bl, gray & blk	10	5

Issued to publicize women's political rights. See also Nos. 752, C434, C448–C450.

Scouts at Campfire and Tents
A315

Railroad Map of Colombia
A316

Perf. 11½x12

1962, July 28 Photo. **Unwmkd.**

746	A315	10c brt grnsh bl & brn	45	38
		Nos. 746, C435-C438 (5)	7.85	6.85

Issued to commemorate the 30th anniversary of the Colombian Boy Scouts.

St. Isidro Type of 1960 Redrawn

1962, Aug. 28 *Perf. 12*

747	A302	10c pink & multi	15	8

The frame on No. 747 is solid color with white inscription similar to type AP82. See also Nos. C439-C440.

1962, Sept. 28 *Perf. 12½*

748	A316	10c blk, gray, grn & red	15	5
		Nos. 748, C441-C444 (5)	8.15	2.95

Issued to publicize the progress of Colombian railroads and to commemorate the completion of the Atlantic Line from Santa Marta to Bogota.

Post Horn
A317

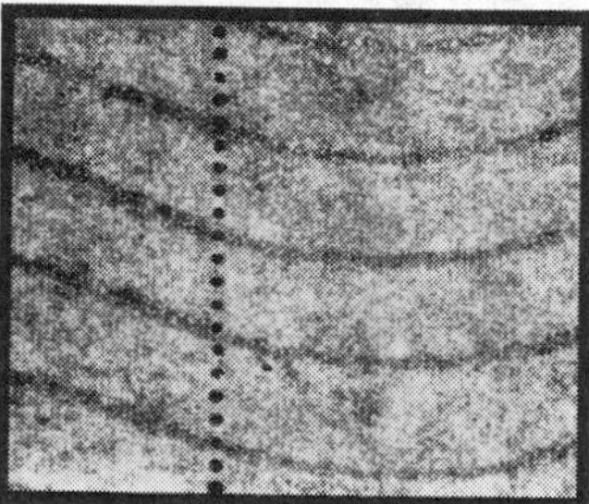

Wmk. 346

Wmkd. Parallel Curved Lines. (346)

1962, Oct. 18 Litho. *Perf. 13½x14*

749	A317	20c gold, dl gray vio & blk	22	5

Issued to commemorate the 50th anniversary of the founding of the Postal Union of the Americas and Spain, UPAE.
See also Nos. C445-C446.

"Virgin of the Rock"
A318

Red Cross Centenary Emblem
A319

1963, Mar. 11 **Wmk. 346**

750	A318	60c multi	25	5

Issued to commemorate Vatican II, the 21st Ecumenical Council of the Roman Catholic Church. See also No. C447.

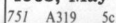

1963, May 1 *Perf. 12x12½*

751	A319	5c ol bis & red	10	5

Centenary of International Red Cross.

Women's Rights Type of 1962

1963, July 11 **Wmk. 346**

752	A314	5c org, gray & blk	6	5

See also Nos. C448-C450.

Manuel Mejia J. and Flag of National Coffee Growers Assn.
A320

Perf. 12½x13

1965, Feb. 10 Engraved Unwmkd.

753	A320	25c rose & blk	25	5

Issued to honor Manuel Mejia J. (1887–1958), banker and manager of the National Coffee Growers Association. See Nos. C464-C466.

Julio Arboleda
A321

1966, Mar. 9 Litho. *Perf. 14x13½*

754	A321	5c lt brn, lt yel grn & blk	5	5

Issued to honor Julio Arboleda (1817–1862), writer, soldier and statesman.

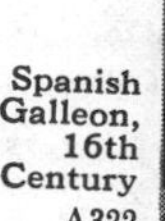

Spanish Galleon, 16th Century
A322

History of Maritime Mail: 15c, Rio Hacha brigantine, 1850. 20c, Uraba canoe. 40c, Magdalena River steamship and barge, 1900. 50c, Modern motor ship and sea gull.

1966, June 16 Photo. **Unwmkd.**

755	A322	5c org & multi	10	6
756	A322	15c car rose, blk & brn	15	6
757	A322	20c brt grn, org & blk	15	6
758	A322	40c dp bl & multi	25	10
759	A322	50c pale bl & multi	65	35
		Nos. 755-759 (5)	1.30	63

Plumed Hogfish
A323

Design: 10p, Bat ray and brittle starfish.

1966, Aug. 25 Photo. *Perf. 12½x13*

760	A323	80c multi	25	10
761	A323	10p multi	7.25	6.75
		Nos. 760-761, C481-C483 (5)	22.00	21.05

Arms of Venezuela, Colombia and Chile
A324

1966, Oct. 11 Litho. *Perf. 14x13½*

762	A324	40c yel & multi	15	7

Issued to commemorate the visits of Eduardo Frei and Raul Leoni, presidents of Chile and Venezuela. See Nos. C484-C485.

Camilo Torres, 1766–1816, Lawyer
A325

Portraits: 60c, Jorge Tadeo Lozano (1771–1816), naturalist. 1p, Francisco Antonio Zea (1776–1822), naturalist and politician.

Perf. 13½x14

1967, Jan. 18 Litho. **Unwmkd.**

763	A325	25c vio & bis	5	5
764	A325	60c dk red brn & bis	10	5
765	A325	1p grn & bis	50	25
		Nos. 763-765, C486-C487 (5)	1.15	55

Issued to honor famous men of Colombia.

Map of South America and Arms
A326

1967, Feb. 2 Litho. *Perf. 14x13½*

766	A326	40c multi	20	10
767	A326	60c multi	20	5

Issued to publicize the Declaration of Bogota for cooperation and world peace, signed by Colombia, Chile, Ecuador, Peru and Venezuela. See No. C488.

Monochaetum Orchid and Bee
A327

Orchid: 2p, Passiflora vitifolia and butterfly.

1967, May 23 Litho. *Perf. 14*

768	A327	25c multi	10	6
769	A327	2p multi	1.25	1.25
		Nos. 768-769, C489-C491 (5)	4.53	2.06

Issued to commemorate the First National Orchid Exhibition and the Topical Philatelic Flora and Fauna Exhibition, Medellin, Apr. 1967.

Lions Emblem
A328

SENA Emblem
A329

1967, July 12 Litho. *Perf. 13½x14*

770	A328	10p multi	4.00	85

Issued to commemorate the 50th anniversary of Lions International. See No. C492.

Lithographed and Embossed

1967, Sept. 20 **Unwmkd.**

771	A329	5p gold, brt grn & blk	1.50	22

Issued to commemorate the 10th anniversary of National Apprenticeship Service, SENA. See No. C494.

Gold Diadem in Calima Style
A330

Radar Installation
A331

Pre-Columbian Art: 3p, Gold statuette, ornamental globe and bird (horiz.).

Perf. 13½x14, 14x13½

1967, Oct. 13 Photogravure

772	A330	1.60p brt rose lil, gold & brn	70	20
773	A330	3p dk bl, gold & brn	1.00	40
		Nos. 772-773, C495-C497 (5)	17.40	12.75

Issued to commemorate the meeting of the Universal Postal Union Committee on Postal Studies, Bogota, October, 1967.

1968, May 14 Litho. *Perf. 13½x14*

Design: 1p, Map of communications network.

774	A331	50c brt yel grn, blk & org brn	15	5
775	A331	1p multi	30	5

Issued to commemorate the 20th anniversary of the National Telecommunications Service (TELECOM). See Nos. C498-C499.

The Eucharist
A332

St. Augustin, by Gregorio Vasquez
A333

1968, June 6 Litho. *Perf. 13½x14*

776	A332	60c multi	15	5

Issued to publicize the 39th Eucharistic Congress, Bogotá, Aug. 18–25. See Nos. C500-C501.

1968, Aug. 13 Photo. *Perf. 13*

Designs: 60c, The Gathering of Manna, by Gregorio Vasquez. 1p, The Marriage of the Virgin, by Baltazar de Figueroa. 5p, Jeweled monstrance, c. 1700. 10p, Pope Paul VI, painting by Roman Franciscan nuns.

777	A333	25c multi	5	5
778	A333	60c multi	5	5
779	A333	1p multi	15	6
780	A333	5p multi	80	10
781	A333	10p multi	1.65	50
a.		Souv. sheet of 2	2.75	1.40
		Nos. 777-781, C502-C506 (10)	10.50	4.06

Issued to commemorate the 39th Eucharistic Congress, Bogotá, Aug. 18–25. No. 781a contains two imperf. stamps similar to Nos. 780–781. Black inscription, Congress emblem in crimson and red control number in margin. Size: 90x89½mm.

Pope Paul VI
A334

Arms of National University
A335

1968, Aug. 22 Litho. ***Perf. 13½x14***

782 A334 25c multi 10 5

Issued to commemorate the visit of Pope Paul VI to Colombia, Aug. 22–24. See Nos. C507–C509.

1968, Oct. 29 Litho. ***Perf. 13½x14***

783 A335 80c multi 15 5

Issued to commemorate the centenary of the founding of the National University. See No. C510.

Stamp of Antioquia, 1868
A336

Institute Emblem
A337

1968, Nov. 20 Litho. ***Perf. 12x12½***

784 A336 30c emer & bl 20 5

Souvenir Sheet

785 A336 5p lt ol & bl 3.75 3.00

Issued to commemorate the centenary of the first postage stamps of Antioquia and to publicize the 7th National Philatelic Exhibition, Medellin, Nov. 20–29. No. 785 contains one stamp; vermilion margin with white inscription and blue coat of arms and control number. Size: 59x79mm.

1969, Mar. 5 Litho. ***Perf. 13½x14***

786 A337 20c multi 15 5

Issued to commemorate the 25th anniversary (in 1967) of the Inter-American Agricultural Sciences Institute. See No. C511.

Battle of Boyaca (Detail), by José Maria Espinosa—A338

Design: 30c, Army of liberation crossing Pisba Pass, by Francisco Antonio Caro.

1969, July 24 Litho. ***Perf. 13½x14***

787 A338 20c gold & multi 15 5
788 A338 30c gold & multi 20 5

Issued to commemorate the sesquicentennial of the fight for independence. See No. C517.

"Poverty"
A339

1970, Mar. 1 Litho. ***Perf. 14***

789 A339 30c bl & multi 15 5

Issued to publicize the Colombian Institute for Family Welfare and to commemorate the 10th anniversary of the Children's Rights Law.

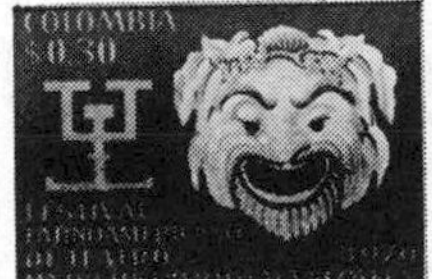

Greek Mask and Pre-Columbian Symbol of Literary Contest
A340

1970, Sept. 12 Litho. ***Perf. 14x13½***

790 A340 30c dk brn, red org & ocher 10 5

Issued to publicize the 3rd Latin American Theatrical Festival of the Universities, Manizales, Sept. 12–20.

Colombian Stamps, Envelope and Emblem
A341

1970, Sept. 24 Litho. ***Perf. 14x13½***

791 A341 2p brt bl & multi 40 5

Issued to publicize Philatelic Week.

Arms of Ibague and Discobolus
A342

1970, Oct. 13

792 A342 80c buff, emer & sep 30 5

9th National Games in Ibague.

St. Theresa, by Baltazar de Figueroa
A343

1970, Oct. 28 Litho. ***Perf. 13½x14***

793 A343 2p multi 50 5

Elevation of St. Theresa (1515–1582), to Doctor of the Church. See No. C568.

Casa Cural
A344

1971, May 20 Litho. ***Perf. 14x13½***

794 A344 1.10p multi 40 10

Fourth centenary (in 1970) of the founding of Guacari, Valle. See also No. 809.

Dancers and Music, Currulao
A345

1971 Litho. ***Perf. 13½x14***

Design: 1p, Chicha Maya dancers and music.

795 A345 1p pink & multi 30 8
796 A345 1.10p lt bl & multi 40 8

Souvenir Sheets

Imperf.

797 A345 Sheet of 3, multi 4.75 4.25
a. 2.50p Napanga 50 50
b. 2.50p Joropo 50 50
c. 5p Guabina 1.00 1.00
798 A345 Sheet of 3, multi 4.75 4.25
a. 4p Bambuco 80 80
b. 4p Cumbia 80 80
c. 4p Currulao 80 80

Size of Nos. 797–798: 78x110mm. Issue dates: No. 795, Dec. 20; No. 796, Aug. 5; Nos. 797–798, Aug. 10.

Constitutional Assembly, by Delgado
A346

1971, Oct. 2 ***Perf. 14***

801 A346 80c multi 22 5

Sequicentennial of Gran Colombian Constitutional Assembly in Rosario del Cucuta. See No. C589.

Arrows Emblem
A347

1972, Feb. 24 ***Perf. 13½x14***

802 A347 60c blk & gray 40 5

Inter-Governmental Committee on European Migration, 20th anniversary.

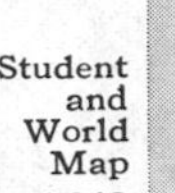

Student and World Map
A348

1972, Mar. 15 ***Perf. 14x13½***

803 A348 1.10p lt grn & brn 25 5

20th anniversary of ICETEX, an organization which furnishes financial help for educational purposes and for technical studies abroad.

U.N. Emblem, Soldier and Frigate
A349

1972, Apr. 7

804 A349 1.20p lt bl & multi 25 6

20th anniversary of the Colombian Battalion in Korea.

Mother Francisca Josefa del Castillo
A350

Handicraft
A351

1972, Apr. 6 ***Perf. 13½x14***

805 A350 1.20p brn & multi 25 6

Tercentenary (in 1971) of the birth of Mother Francisca Josefa del Castillo, Poor Clare abbess and writer.

1972, Apr. 11

806 A351 1.10p multi 40 15

Colombian artisans. See Nos. C569–C571.

Maxillaria Triloris
A352

Emeralds
A353

1972, Apr. 20

807 A352 20p grn & multi 5.25 65

10th National Philatelic Exhibition, Medellin.

1972, June 16 Litho. ***Perf. 13½x14***

808 A353 1.10p multi 70 15

Type of 1971

Design: Antonio Nariño House.

1972, June 17 ***Perf. 14x13½***

809 A344 1.10p multi 60 10

4th centenary, town of Leyva.

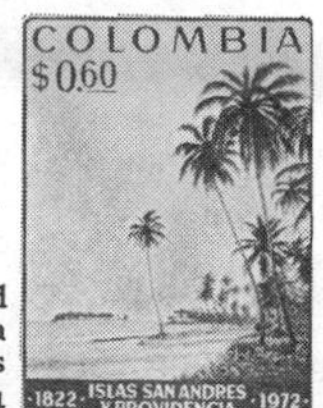

San Andres and Providencia Islands
A354

1972, June 24 ***Perf. 13½x14***

810 A354 60c bl & multi 20 5

Sesquicentennial of annexation by Colombia of San Andres and Providencia Islands.

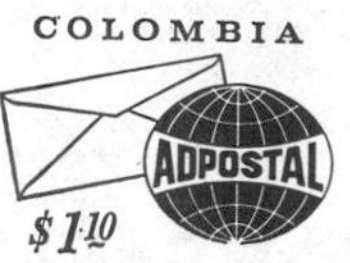

Postal Service Emblem
A355

1972, Nov. 15 Litho. ***Perf. 12½x12***

811 A355 1.10p emerald 15 6

Family
A356

1972, Nov. 23

812 A356 60c orange 15 6

Social progress.

Radio League Emblem
A357

Human Figure, Tamalameque
A358

1973, Apr. 6 Litho. ***Perf. 12x12½***

813 A357 60c lt bl, ultra & red 25 6

40th anniversary of the Colombian Radio Amateurs' League.

1973, June 15 Litho. ***Perf. 13½x14***

Excavated Ceramic Artifacts: 1p, Winged urn, Tairona. 1.10p, Jug, Muisca.

814 A358 60c lt bl & multi 35 10
815 A358 1p org & multi 65 10
816 A358 1.10p vio bl & multi 45 5
Nos. 814-816, C583-C586 (7) 6.00 2.30

Antonio Nariño, by José M. Espinosa
A359

Child
A360

1973, Dec. 13 Litho. ***Perf. 13½x14***

817 A359 60c multi 15 6

Sesquicentennial of the death of General Antonio Nariño (1765–1823).

1973, Dec. 17

818 A360 1.10p multi 22 5

National Campaign for Children's Welfare.

Symbols of Financial Controls
A361

1973, Dec. 20 Litho. ***Perf. 14x13½***

819 A361 80c ultra, ocher & blk 15 5

50th anniversary of Comptroller-general's Office.

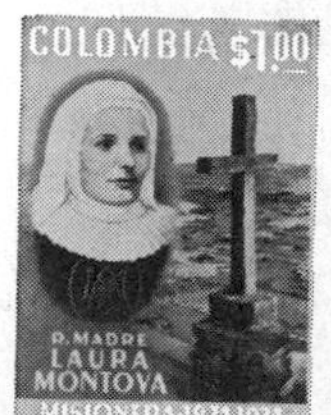

Mother Laura Montoya
A362

1974, June 18 Litho. ***Perf. 13½x14***

820 A362 1p multi 20 5

Centenary of the birth of Mother Laura Montoya (1874–1949), founder and Mother Superior of the Missionaries of Mary Immaculata and St. Catherine of Siena.

Runner and Games' Emblem
A363

1974, July 18 Litho. ***Perf. 14x13½***

821 A363 2p ver, yel & brn 25 10

10th National Games, Pereira.

José Rivera
A364

1974, Aug. 3 Litho. ***Perf. 14x13½***

822 A364 10p grn & multi 1.65 15

50th anniversary of the publication of "La Voragine" (The Whirlpool) by José Eustasio Rivera.

Abstract Pattern
A365

Train Emerging from Tunnel
A366

1974, Oct. 24 Litho. ***Perf. 13½x14***

823 A365 1.10p multi 30 5

Centenary of National Insurance Co. See No. C610.

1974, Nov. 27 Litho. ***Perf. 13½x14***

824 A366 1.10p multi 25 5

Centenary of the Antioquia railroad.

Boy, Puppy and Soccer Ball
A367

Design: 1p, Girl with racket and kitten.

1974, Dec. 9

825 A367 80c multi 20 5
826 A367 1p multi 25 10

Christmas 1974.

Gold Animal
A368

Design: 1.10p, Gold necklace.

1975, Apr. 11 Litho. ***Perf. 14x13½***

827 A368 80c ultra, gold & brn 30 6
828 A368 1.10p red, gold & brn 30 6

Pre-Columbian Sinu culture artifacts. See Nos. C621–C622.

Guglielmo Marconi
A369

Santa Maria Cathedral
A370

1975, June 2 Litho. ***Perf. 13½x14***

829 A369 3p multi 25 10

Birth centenary of Guglielmo Marconi (1874–1937), Italian electrical engineer and inventor.

1975, July 26

830 A370 80c multi 15 5

400th anniversary of Santa Maria City. See No. C623.

Rafael Nuñez
A371

Arms of Medellin
A372

1975, Sept. 28 Litho. ***Perf. 13½x14***

831 A371 1.10p multi 22 6

Rafael Nuñez (1825–1894), philosopher, poet, political leader, birth sesquicentenary.

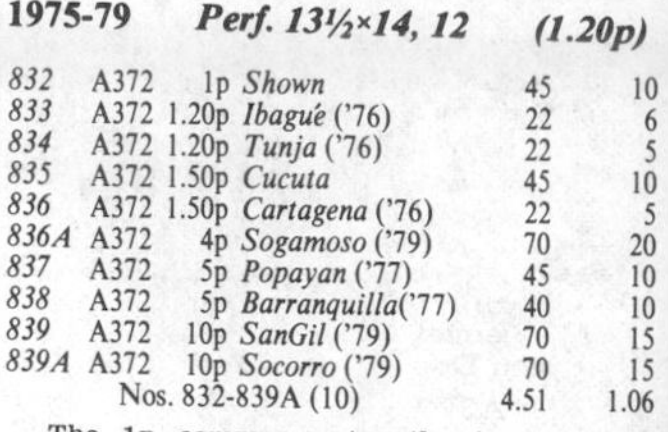

1975-79 ***Perf. 13½×14, 12*** ***(1.20p)***

832 A372 1p *Shown* 45 10
833 A372 1.20p *Ibagué ('76)* 22 6
834 A372 1.20p *Tunja ('76)* 22 5
835 A372 1.50p *Cucuta* 45 10
836 A372 1.50p *Cartagena ('76)* 22 5
836A A372 4p *Sogamoso ('79)* 70 20
837 A372 5p *Popayan ('77)* 45 10
838 A372 5p *Barranquilla('77)* 40 10
839 A372 10p *SanGil ('79)* 70 15
839A A372 10p *Socorro ('79)* 70 15
Nos. 832-839A (10) 4.51 1.06

The 1p commemorates the tercentenary of Medellin; No. 835, the centenary of Cucuta's reconstruction.

No. 827 Surcharged **$ 1.20**

1975 ***Perf. 14x13½***

840 A368 1.20p on 80c multi 15 6

Purace Indians, Cauca
A373

1976, Nov. 10 Litho. ***Perf. 13½x14***

841 A373 1.50p multi 15 5

Callicore
A374

Designs: 5p, Morpho (butterfly). 20p, Anthurium.

1976, Nov. 17 ***Perf. 12***

842 A374 3p multi 50 10
843 A374 5p multi 70 15
844 A374 20p multi 2.25 50

Rotary Emblem
A375

1976, Dec. 3 Litho. ***Perf. 12***

845 A375 1p multi 15 6

Rotary Club of Colombia, 50th anniversary.

Declaration of Independence, by John Trumbull—A376

1976, Dec. 21 Litho. ***Perf. 12***

846 A376 Strip of 3, multi 13.00 15.00
a. 30p, single stamp 4.00 2.00

American Bicentennial. No. 846 printed in sheets of 4 triptychs; black control number in margin showing Bicentennial emblems and personalities of the American Revolution.

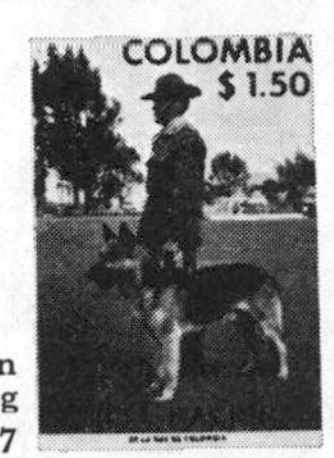

Policeman with Dog
A377

1976, Dec. 29 *Perf. 13½x14*

847	A377	1.50p multi	25	5

Honoring the National Police.

Nos. 831, 834, 847 Surcharged in Light Brown

1977, June Litho. *Perf. 13½x14, 12*

848	A371	2p on 1.10p multi	30	5
849	A372	2p on 1.20p multi	22	5
850	A377	2p on 1.50p multi	22	5

Souvenir Sheet

Postal Museum, Bogota—A378

1977, July 27 **Litho.** *Perf. 14*

855	A378	25p multi	3.25	3.25

Postal Museum, Bogota. No. 855 contains one stamp (50x40mm.); multicolored margin shows Colombian stamps; black control number. Size: 130x105mm.

Mother and Child
A379

1977–78 **Litho.** *Perf. 12*

856	A379	2p multi	20	5
857	A379	2.50p multi ('78)	1.25	10

National good nutrition plan.
Issue dates: 2p, Aug. 30. 2.50p, Jan. 26.

Jacana and Eichhornia
A380

Fidel Cano, by Francisco Cano
A381

Design: 20p, Mayan cotinga and pyrostegia venusta.

1977, Sept. 6 **Litho.** *Perf. 14*

858	A380	10p multi	1.00	25
859	A380	20p multi	1.65	38
		Nos. 858-859, C644-C647 (6)	5.35	1.37

1977, Sept. 16 *Perf. 14*

860	A381	4p multi	30	5

90th anniversary of El Espectador, newspaper founded by Fidel Cano.

Abacus and Alphabet
A382

Cattleya Triannae
A383

1977, Sept. 16 *Perf. 13½x14*

861	A382	3p multi	22	6

Popular education.

1978, Apr. 18 **Litho.** *Perf. 12*

862	A383	2.50p multi	22	5

1979, May 10 **Litho.** *Perf. 12*

863	A383	3p multi	25	5

Sprinting and Games Emblem
A384

1978, June 27 **Litho.** *Perf. 14*

Multicolored

868		Sheet of 16	21.00	3.50
a.	A384 10p	*shown*	1.25	20
b.	A384 10p	*Basketball*	1.25	20
c.	A384 10p	*Baseball*	1.25	20
d.	A384 10p	*Boxing*	1.25	20
e.	A384 10p	*Bicycling*	1.25	20
f.	A384 10p	*Fencing*	1.25	20
g.	A384 10p	*Soccer*	1.25	20
h.	A384 10p	*Gymnastics*	1.25	20
i.	A384 10p	*Judo*	1.25	20
j.	A384 10p	*Weight lifting*	1.25	20
k.	A384 10p	*Wrestling*	1.25	20
l.	A384 10p	*Swimming*	1.25	20
m.	A384 10p	*Tennis*	1.25	20
n.	A184 10p	*Target shooting*	1.25	20
o.	A384 10p	*Volleyball*	1.25	20
p.	A384 10p	*Water polo*	1.25	20

13th Central American and Caribbean Games, Medellin. No. 863 has black marginal inscription and control number. Size: 200x160mm.

"Sigma 2" by Alvaro Herrán
A385

1978, June 30

869	A385	8p multi	50	25

Chamber of Commerce, Bogota, centenary.

Gen. Tomás Cipriano de Mosquera
A386

1978, Oct. 6 **Litho.** *Perf. 12*

870	A386	6p multi	60	22

Gen. Tomás Cipriano de Mosquera (1778–1878), statesman.

Anthurium Narinenses
A387

1979, July 23 *Perf. 12*

871	A387	3p red & multi	25	6
872	A387	3p pur & multi	25	6
873	A387	3p rose & pur	25	6
874	A387	3p white & multi	25	6

Nos. 871–874 printed in blocks of four, sheets of 100.

Gen. Rafael Uribe, by Acevedo Bernal
A388

1979, Oct. 31 **Litho.** *Perf. 12*

875	A388	8p multi	50	20

Gen. Rafael Uribe, statesman, 60th death anniversary.

Village, by Leonor Alarcon—A389

1979, Nov. 22 *Perf. 14*

876	A389	15p multi	1.50	50

Community Work Boards, 20th anniversary.

Introduction of Color Television—A390

1980, Mar. 4 **Litho.** *Perf. 14*

877	A390	5p multi	40	10

Bullfight, Arms of Cali—A391

1980, Mar. 25

878	A391	5p multi	60	15

Cali Tourist Festival, Dec. 25, 1979-Jan. 2, 1980.

"Learn to Write"—A392

1980, Apr. 25 **Litho.** *Perf. 12½*

879		Block of 30	9.00	9.00
a.		A392 4p, any single	30	8

Each stamp shows letter of alphabet and corresponding animal. Issued in sheets of 90 (30x3).

Villavicencio Festival—A393

Design: 9p, Vallenato festival.

1980 **Litho.** *Perf. 14*

880	A393	5p multi	45	20
881	A393	9p multi	45	20

Issue dates: 5p, July 15; 9p, June 17.

Gustavo Uribe Ramirez and Tree—A394

1980, Aug. 5 **Litho.** *Perf. 12*

882	A394	10p multi	45	20

Gustavo Uribe Ramirez (1893-1968), ecologist.

Narino Palace (Former Presidential Residence)—A395

1980, Sept. 19 **Litho.** *Perf. 14*

883	A396	5p multi	60	10

Monument to First Pioneers of 1819, Armenia—A396

1980, Oct. 14

884	A396	5p multi	50	10

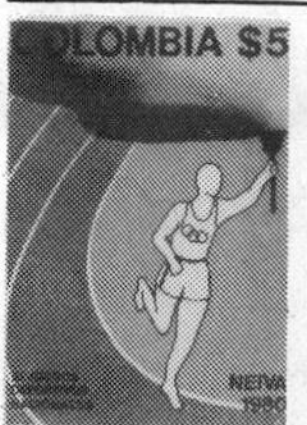

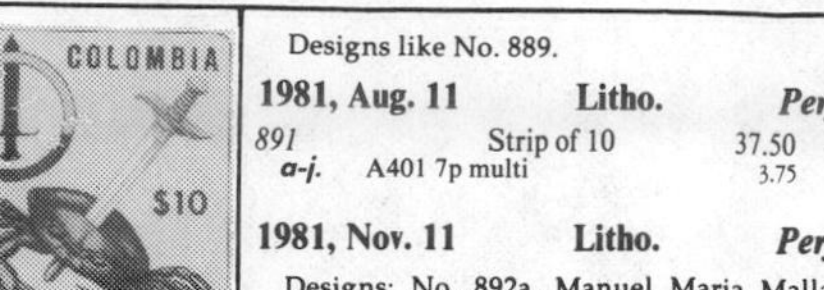

11th National Games, Neiva
A397

Fight against Cancer
A398

1980, Nov. 28 *Perf. 13½x14*

885 A397 5p multi 65 6

1980, Dec. 9

886 A398 10p multi 45 15

Xavier Universary Law Faculty, 50th Anniversary—A399

1980, Dec. 16 **Litho.** *Perf. 14½*

887 A399 20p multi 80 20

Death of Bolivar—A400

1980, Dec. 17 *Perf. 12*

888 A400 25p multi 1.40 45

Simon Bolivar, death sesquicentennial. See No. C696.

José Maria Obando, President of Colombia
A401

115th Anniv. of Constitution (Former Presidents): No. 889b, Jose Hilario Lopez. No. 889c, Manuel Murillo Toro. No. 889d, Santiago Perez. No. 889e, Rafael Reyes. No. 889f, Carlos E. Restrepo. No. 889g, Jose Vicente Concha. No. 889h, Miguel Abadia Mendez. No. 889i, Eduardo Santos. No. 889j, Mariano Ospina Perez.

1981, June 9 **Litho.** *Perf. 12*

889 Strip of 10 2.25 90
a-j. A401 5p multi 22 6

1981, Sept. 23 **Litho.** *Perf. 12*

Designs: No. 890a, Rafael Nunez (1825-1894). No. 890b, Marco Fidel Suarez (1855-1927). No. 890c, Pedro Nel Ospina (1858-1927). No. 890d, Enrique Olaya Herrera (1880-1937). No. 890e, Alfonso Lopez Pumarejo (1886-1959). No. 890f, Aquileo Parra (1825-1900). No. 890g, Santos Gutierrez (1820-1872). No. 890h, Tomas Cipriano de Mosquera (1789-1878). No. 890i, Mariano Ospina Rodriguez. No. 890j, Pedro Alcantara Herran (1800-1872).

890 Strip of 10 25.00
a-j. A401 7p multi 2.50 40

Designs like No. 889.

1981, Aug. 11 **Litho.** *Perf. 12*

891 Strip of 10 37.50
a-j. A401 7p multi 3.75 1.25

1981, Nov. 11 **Litho.** *Perf. 12*

Designs: No. 892a, Manuel Maria Mallarino. No. 892b, Santos Acosta. No. 892c, Eustorgio Salgar. No. 892d, Julian Trujillo. No. 892e, Francisco Javier Zaldua. No. 892f, Guillermo Leon Valencia. No. 892g, Laureano Gomez. No. 892h, Manuel A. Sanclemente. No. 892i, Miguel Antonio Caro. No. 892j, Jose Eusebio Otalora.e

892 Strip of 10 16.00
a.-j. A401 7p multi 1.50 30

1981, Dec. 15 **Litho.** *Perf. 12*

Designs: No. 893a, Ruben Piedrahita Arango. No. 893b, Jorge Holguin. No. 893c, Ramon Gonzalez Valencia. No. 893d, Jose Manuel Marroquin. No. 893e, Carlos Holguin. No. 893f, Bartolome Calvo. No. 893g, Sergio Camargo. No. 893h, Jose Maria Rojas Garrido. No. 893i, J.M. Campo Serrano. No. 893j, Eliseo Payan.

893 Strip of 10 12.00
a.-j. A401 7p multi 1.10 20

1982, May 3 *Perf. 12*

Designs: a. Simon Bolivar. b. Francisco de Paula Santander. c. Joaquin Mosquera. d. Domingo Caicedo. e. Jose Ignacio de Marquez. f. Roberto Urdaneta Arbelaez. g. Carlos Lozano y Lozano. h. Guillermo Quintero Calderon. i. Jose de Obaldia. j. Juan de Dios Aranzazu.

894 Strip of 10 11.00
a-j. A401 7p multi 1.10 20

Jose Maria Villa and West Bridge over Cauca River A404

1981, Nov. 25 **Litho.** *Perf. 14x13½*

895 A404 60p multi 1.50 30

Agrarian, Mineral and Industrial Credit Bank, 50th Anniv.
A405

Los Nevados Park
A406

1981, Dec. 9 **Litho.** *Perf. 14*

896 A405 15p multi 50 10

1981, Dec. 10 **Litho.** *Perf. 13½x14*

897 A406 20p multi 90 15

Girl Sitting on Fence—A407

1982, Feb. 22 **Litho.** *Perf. 12½x12*

898 Strip of 3 3.00 1.65
a. A407 30p shown 90 30
b. A407 30p Girl, basket 90 30
c. A407 30p Boy, wheelbarrow 90 30

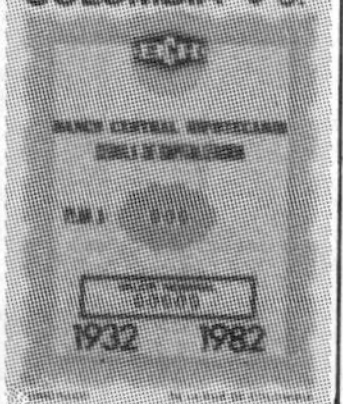

Floral Bouquet
A408

Hipotecario Bank, 50th Anniv.
A409

Designs: Various floral arrangements.

1982, July 28

900 Strip of 10 4.00 2.50
a. A408 7p, any single 35 10

1982, July 29 *Perf. 14*

901 A409 9p blk & grn 30 10

St. Thomas Aquinas (1225-1274)—A410

Paintings by Zurbaran.

1982, Aug. 6 **Litho.** *Perf. 12*

902 A410 5p multi 20 6
903 A410 5p St. Teresa of Avila (1515-1582) 20 6
904 A410 5p St. Francis of Assisi (1182-1226) 20 6

Issue dates: No. 903, Sept. 28; No. 904, Oct. 4.

Arms of Buga City
A411

Gabriel Marquez, 1982 Nobel Prize, Literature
A412

1982 **Litho.** *Perf. 14*

905 A411 10p shown 35 10
905A A411 10p San Juan de Pasto 35 10
906 A411 16p Rionegro 60 20
907 A411 20p Santa Fe de Bogota 60 20
907A A411 20p Santiago de Cali ('86) 24 8
908 A411 23p Honda 80 30
913 A411 55p Antioquia ('86) 60 20
Nos. 905-913 (7) 3.54 1.18

1982, Dec. 10 *Perf. 13½x14*

917 A412 7p gray & grn 30 10

See No. C731-C732.

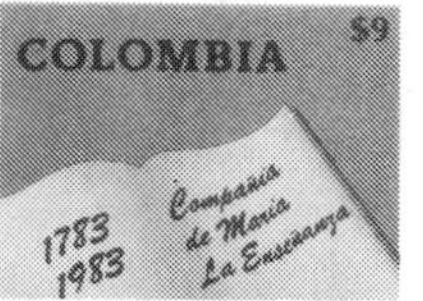

Public Education Bicentenary (Society of Mary for Education)—A413

1983, May 6

918 A413 9p gold & blk 50 25

José Maria Espinosa Prieto, Painter—A414

1983, June 3 *Perf. 12*

919 A414 9p Self-portrait, 1860 25 10

250th Anniv. of City of Cucuta—A415

1983, June 23 **Litho.** *Perf. 12*

920 A415 9p multi 25 6

Porfirio Barba-Jacob (1883-1942), Poet—A416

1983, July 29 **Litho.** *Perf. 13½ x14*

921 A416 9p Portrait 25 6

Simon Bolivar, 200th Birth Anniv.—A417

1983, July 24 *Perf. 12*

922	A417	9p multi	30	10

See Nos. C736-C737.

Royal Spanish Botanical Exhibition, 200th Anniv.—A418

1983, Aug. 18 *Perf. 14*

923	A418	9p Cinchona Lancefolia	25	10
924	A418	9p Passiflora Laurifolia L.	25	10
925	A418	60p Cinchona Cordiflora	1.65	70
		Nos. 923-925, C738-C740 (6)	2.50	1.55

Dawn in the Andes, by Alejandro Obregon—A420

1983, Oct. 5 **Litho.** *Perf. 12*

928	A420	20p multi	50	15

See No. C741.

Francisco de Paula Santander (1792-1840), General—A421

1984, Mar. 6 **Litho.** *Perf. 14½x14*

929	A421	12p lt ol grn	28	10
930	A421	12p pale car	28	10
931	A421	12p lt ultra	28	10

Admiral Jose Prudencio Padilla (1784-1831)—A423

1984, May 17 **Litho.** *Perf. 12*

933	A423	10p multi	25	8

Luis Antonio Calvo (1882-1945) Composer—A424

1984, Jul 26

934	A424	18p multi	45	15

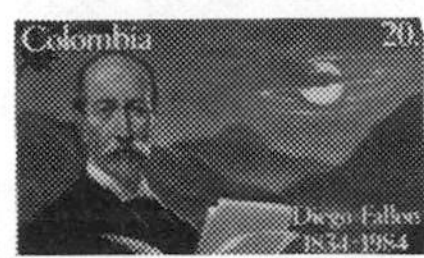

Diego Fallon (1834-1905), Educator, Musician, Poet—A425

1984, Aug. 31 *Perf. 12*

935	A425	20p multi	45	15

Candelario Obeso (1849-1884), Writer—A426

1984, Sept. 4 *Perf. 14x13½*

936	A426	20p multi	45	15

Site of Marandua, Future City—A427

1984, Sept. 28 *Perf. 12*

937	A427	15p multi	32	10

See No. C744.

Christmas 1984—A428

Nativity and Children Playing, by Jose Uriel Sierra, Age 7.

1984, Dec. 14

938	A428	12p multi	28	10

See No. C746.

Dr. Luis Eduardo Lopez, Education Minister—A429

1984, Dec. 21

939	A429	22p multi	50	16

Independence War Heroine—A430

Maria Concepcion Loperena de Fernandez de Castro.

1985, Jan. 6

940	A430	12p multi	22	8

Gonzalo Mejia (1885-1956)—A431

1985, Feb. 25

941	A431	12p Portrait, biplane, camera	20	8

Aviation, motion picture and meat exporting industrialist.

Self-portrait with Wife—A432

1985, Feb. 25

942	A432	37p multi	62	20

Pedro Nel Gomez (1899-1984), painter. See No. C748.

Fauna—A433

1985 *Perf. 14 (12p), 13*

943	A433	12p Hydrochaeris hydrochaeris	16	6
944	A433	15p Felis pardalis	20	8
945	A433	15p Tremarctos ornatus, vert.	20	8
946	A433	20p Tapirus pinchaque	28	10

Issued dates: 12p, Apr. 12. No. 944, 20p, Aug. 6. No. 945, Aug. 29.

Carlos Gardel (1890-1935), Entertainer A434

Camina Literacy Program A435

1985, June 23 *Perf. 14*

947	A434	15p Portrait, Fokker F-31 Trimotor	20	8

1985, Nov. 25 *Perf. 13½x14*

948	A435	15p Tree, alphabet	20	8

Christmas 1985—A436

1985, Dec. 4 **Litho.** *Perf. 13*

949	A436	15p multi	20	8

Rafael Pombo Children's Foundation. See No. C755.

Eduardo Carranza (b. 1913), Poet A437

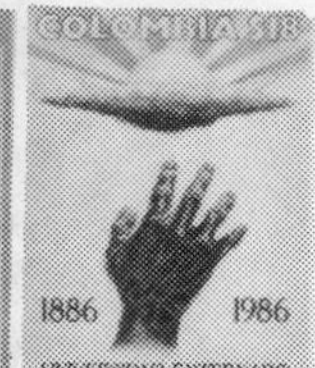

Colombian Free University, Cent. A438

1986, Feb. 13
950 A437 18p multi 24 8

1986, Feb. 14
951 A438 18p multi 24 8

Gen. Antonio Ricaurte (b. 1786), Liberator—A439

1986, May 7 **Litho.** ***Perf. 13***
952 A439 18p Leiva birthplace 24 8

Jose Asuncion Silva (1865-1896), Poet, and Scene from Nocturno—A440

1986, May 30 **Litho.** ***Perf. 12***
953 A440 18p multi 22 8

Fernando Gomez Martinez (1897-1985), Journalist—A441

1986, June 19
954 A441 24p multi 30 10

Santiago de Cali, 450th Anniv.—A442

1986, July 25 **Litho.** ***Perf. 13***
955 A442 25p La Merced 30 10

Monsignor Jose Vicente Castro Silva (1885-1968), Rector of the Mayor del Rosario School—A443

Portrait by Ricardo Gomez.

1986, Aug. 4 **Litho.** ***Perf. 12***
956 A443 20p multi 22 8

Natl. University—A444

1986, Oct. 14 **Litho.** ***Perf. 12***
957 A444 40p multi 45 15

Faculties: Fine Arts, cent., and Architecture, 50th anniv.

Rafael Maya (1897-1980), Poet, and Salamanca University Entrance—A445

1986, Oct. 15
958 A445 25p multi 28 10

See No. C772.

Condor in Flight—A446

1986, Nov. 6
963 A446 20p ultra 22 8

SEMI-POSTAL STAMP

Girl Giving First Aid
SP1

Perf. 13½x14

1966, Apr. 26 Litho. Unwmkd.

B1	SP1	5c + 5c multi	10	6

Issued for the Red Cross.

AIR POST STAMPS.

No. 341 Overprinted

1er.
Servicio
Postal
Aereo
6-18-19

1919 *Perf. 14.* **Unwmkd.**

C1	A109	2c car rose	3,000.	1,850.
a.		Numerals "1" with serifs	*7,000.*	*4,000.*

Used for the first experimental flight from Barranquilla to Puerto Colombia, June 18, 1919.

Issued by Compania Colombiana de Navegacion Aerea.

From 1920 to 1932 the internal airmail service of Colombia was handled by the Compania Colombiana de Navegacion Aerea (1920) and the Sociedad Colombo-Alemana de Transportes Aéreos, known familiarly as "SCADTA" (1920-1932). These organizations under government contracts operated and maintained their own post offices, and issued stamps which were the only legal franking for airmail service during this period, both in the internal and international mails. All letters had to bear government stamps as well.

Woman and Boy Watching Plane
AP1

Designs: No. C3, Clouds and small biplane at top. No. C4, Tilted plane viewed close-up from above. No. C5, Flier in plane watching biplane. No. C6, Lighthouse. No. C7, Fuselage and tail of biplane. No. C8, Condor on cliff. No. C9, Plane at rest; pilot foreground. No. C10, Ocean liner.

Lithographed.

1920, Feb. *Imperf.* **Unwmkd.**

Without Gum.

C2	AP1	10c grn, red, bl, yel & blk	2,750.	2,250.
C3	AP1	10c bl, red & blk	3,250.	2,250.
C4	AP1	10c yel, red, bl & blk	3,250.	2,250.
C5	AP1	10c bl, red, yel & blk	2,750.	2,250.
C6	AP1	10c bl, grn, red, yel, & blk	2,750.	2,250.
C7	AP1	10c grn, red, bl, red brn & blk	11,000.	4,750.
C8	AP1	10c brn, grn, bl, red & blk	4,750.	3,750.
a.		Without overprint		
C9	AP1	10c grn, bl, red, yel, red brn & blk	3,250.	2,250.
C10	AP1	10c bl, yel, grn, red & blk	5,250.	3,250.

Flier in Plane Watching Biplane
AP2

1920, March

C11	AP2	10c green	62.50	*100.00*

Four other 10c stamps, similar to No. C11, have two designs showing plane, mountains and water. They are printed in deep green or light brown red. Some authorities state that these four were not used regularly.

Issued by Sociedad Colombo-Alemana de Transportes Aereos (SCADTA)

Seaplane over Magdalena River
AP3

1920-21 Lithographed. *Perf. 12*

C12	AP3	10c yel ('21)	47.50	37.50
C13	AP3	15c bl ('21)	47.50	40.00
C14	AP3	30c blk, *rose*	21.00	15.00
C15	AP3	30c rose ('21)	42.50	35.00
C16	AP3	50c pale grn	47.50	42.50
		Nos. C12-C16 (5)	206.00	170.00

No. C16 Handstamp Surcharged in Violet or Black:
(Illustrations of types "a" to "e" are reduced in size.)

VALOR 10 CENTAVOS
a

VALOR 10 CENTAVOS
b

Valor 10 Céntavos
c

VALOR 30 Ctvos
S.C.A.T.A
d

30¢ 30¢
e

$030
f

$030¢
g

1921

C17	AP3 (a) 10c on 50c		650.00	650.00
C18	AP3 (b) 10c on 50c		575.00	575.00
C19	AP3 (c) 10c on 50c		*1,250.*	*1,000.*
C20	AP3 (b) 30c on 50c		650.00	650.00
C21	AP3 (d) 30c on 50c		850.00	800.00
C22	AP3 (e) 30c on 50c		1,350.	1,000.
C23	AP3 (f) 30c on 50c		1,100.	950.00
C24	AP3 (g) 30c on 50c		1,100.	950.00

Plane over Magdalena River
AP4

Plane over Bogota Cathedral
AP5

1921 *Perf. 11½*

C25	AP4	5c org yel	6.25	6.25
C26	AP4	10c sl grn	2.25	1.50
C27	AP4	15c org brn	2.25	1.60
C28	AP4	20c red brn	3.50	2.25
a.		Imperf. vert., pair	*200.00*	
C29	AP4	30c green	2.75	75
C30	AP4	50c blue	3.50	1.20
C31	AP4	60c vermilion	17.50	12.50
C32	AP5	1p gray blk	20.00	12.50
C33	AP5	2p rose	37.50	25.00
C34	AP5	3p violet	85.00	70.00
C35	AP5	5p ol grn	500.00	475.00
		Nos. C25-C35 (11)	680.50	608.55

Exist imperf.

Nos. C16 and C12 Handstamp Surcharged
(Illustration of type "h" is reduced in size.)

VALOR 20 Ctvs.
h

30 cent.
i

1921-22 *Perf. 12*

C36	AP3 (h) 20c on 50c		1,650.	1,400.
C37	AP3 (i) 30c on 10c		700.00	475.00

Seaplane over Magdalena River
AP6

Plane over Bogota Cathedral
AP7

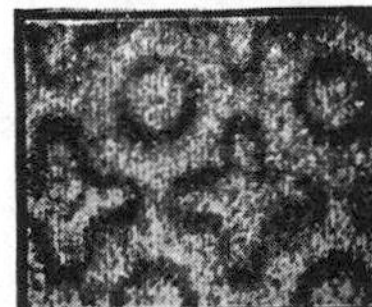

Wmk. 116

Wmkd. Crosses and Circles (116)

1923-28 *Perf. 14x14½*

C38	AP6	5c org yel	1.25	30
C39	AP6	10c green	1.25	25
C40	AP6	15c carmine	1.25	25
C41	AP6	20c gray	1.25	15
C42	AP6	30c blue	1.25	15
C43	AP6	40c pur ('28)	11.00	6.00
C44	AP6	50c green	2.00	30
C45	AP6	60c brown	3.00	30
C46	AP6	80c ol grn ('28)	30.00	30.00
C47	AP7	1p black	12.00	3.00
C48	AP7	2p red org	21.00	7.50
C49	AP7	3p violet	45.00	25.00
C50	AP7	5p ol grn	72.50	35.00
		Nos. C38-C50 (13)	202.75	108.20

Nos. C41 and C31 Surcharged in Carmine and Dark Blue:

30 30 30 30
j *k*

1923

C51	AP6 (j) 30c on 20c gray (C)		85.00	50.00
C52	AP4 (k) 30c on 60c ver (Bl)		72.50	40.00

Nos. C41-C42 Overprinted in Black

1928 *Perf. 14x14½* **Wmk. 116**

C53	AP6	20c gray	75.00	75.00
C54	AP6	30c blue	75.00	75.00

Issued to commemorate the goodwill flight of Lt. Benjamin Mendez from New York to Bogota.

Magdalena River and Tolima Volcano
AP8

Columbus' Ship and Plane
AP9

Wmk. 127

Wmkd. Quatrefoils. (127)

1929, June 1 *Perf. 14*

C55	AP8	5c yel org	1.25	50
C56	AP8	10c red brn	1.25	40
C57	AP8	15c dp grn	1.25	50
C58	AP8	20c carmine	1.25	20
C59	AP8	30c gray bl	1.25	40
C60	AP8	40c dl vio	1.50	40
C61	AP8	50c dk ol grn	3.00	60
C62	AP8	60c org brn	3.00	60
C63	AP8	80c green	10.00	6.00
C64	AP9	1p blue	12.00	3.50
C65	AP9	2p brn org	18.50	6.00
C66	AP9	3p pale rose vio	37.50	30.00
C67	AP9	5p ol grn	90.00	60.00
		Nos. C55-C67 (13)	181.75	109.10

For International Airmail.

AP10

AP11

1929, June 1 *Perf. 14* **Wmk. 127**

C68	AP10	5c yel org	7.25	7.25
C69	AP10	10c red brn	1.25	3.50
C70	AP10	15c dp grn	1.25	3.50

C71	AP10	20c carmine	1.25	4.00
C72	AP10	25c vio bl	1.25	1.10
C73	AP10	30c gray bl	1.25	1.10
C74	AP10	50c dk ol grn	1.25	2.00
C75	AP10	60c brown	3.25	3.50
C76	AP11	1p blue	6.00	9.00
C77	AP11	2p red org	9.00	12.00
C78	AP11	3p violet	110.00	100.00
C79	AP11	5p ol grn	140.00	150.00
		Nos. C68-79 (12)	283.00	296.95

This issue was sold abroad for use on correspondence to be flown from coastal to interior points of Colombia. Cancellations are those of the country of origin rather than Colombia.

Nos. C63, C66 and C64 Surcharged in Black:

10 10
1830 — 1930

m

1830 1930
SIMON BOLIVAR
30 30
cts. cts.

n

1930, Dec. 15

C80	AP8(m)	10c on 80c grn	6.25	6.75
C81	AP9(n)	20c on 3p pale rose vio	12.00	13.00
C82	AP9(n)	30c on 1p bl	13.00	13.00

Issued to commemorate the centenary of the death of Simon Bolivar (1783-1830).

Colombian Government Issues.

Nos. C55-C67 Overprinted in Black:

CORREO AEREO

o

CORREO AEREO

p

Typographed.

1932, Jan. 1 *Perf. 14* Wmk. 127

C83	AP8(o)	5c yel org	12.00	12.00
C84	AP8(o)	10c red brn	2.50	70
C85	AP8(o)	15c dp grn	4.25	4.25
C86	AP8(o)	20c carmine	2.00	45
C87	AP8(o)	30c gray bl	2.00	75
C88	AP8(o)	40c dl vio	3.00	1.40
C89	AP8(o)	50c dk ol grn	4.75	4.25
C90	AP8(o)	60c org brn	3.75	4.25
C91	AP8(o)	80c green	20.00	20.00
C92	AP9(p)	1p blue	16.00	13.00
C93	AP9(p)	2p brn org	45.00	40.00
C94	AP9(p)	3p pale rose vio	85.00	75.00
C95	AP9(p)	5p ol grn	150.00	160.00
		Nos. C83-C95 (13)	350.25	336.05

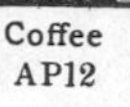

Coffee
AP12

Cattle
AP13

Petroleum
AP14

Bananas
AP15

Gold
AP16

Emerald
AP17

Photogravure.

1932-39 *Perf. 14* Wmk. 127

C96	AP12	5c org & blk brn	1.40	40
C97	AP13	10c lake & blk	1.50	35
C98	AP14	15c bl grn & vio blk	70	25
C99	AP14	15c ver & vio blk ('39)	4.00	20
C100	AP15	20c car & ol blk	1.10	5
C101	AP15	20c turq grn & ol blk ('39)	5.50	50
C102	AP12	30c dk bl & blk brn	2.25	25
C103	AP15	40c dk vio & ol bis	1.25	22
C104	AP13	50c dk grn & brnsh blk	5.50	2.00
C105	AP14	60c dk brn & blk vio	1.75	40
C106	AP12	80c grn & blk brn	8.50	3.25
C107	AP16	1p dk bl & ol bis	14.00	2.00
C108	AP16	2p org brn & ol bis	15.00	3.50
C109	AP17	3p dk vio & emer	26.00	9.50
C110	AP17	5p gray blk & emer	72.50	30.00
		Nos. C96-C110 (15)	160.95	52.87

Nos. C104, C106-C108 Surcharged:

1533
CARTAGENA
1933
10 10

a

1533 1933
CARTAGENA
20 centavos 20

b

1934, Jan. 5

C111	AP13(a)	10(c) on 50c	6.00	6.00
C112	AP12(a)	15(c) on 80c	8.00	8.00
C113	AP16(b)	20c on 1p	9.00	9.00
C114	AP16(b)	30c on 2p	10.00	10.00

400th anniversary of Cartagena.

Nos. C100 and C103 Surcharged in Black or Carmine:

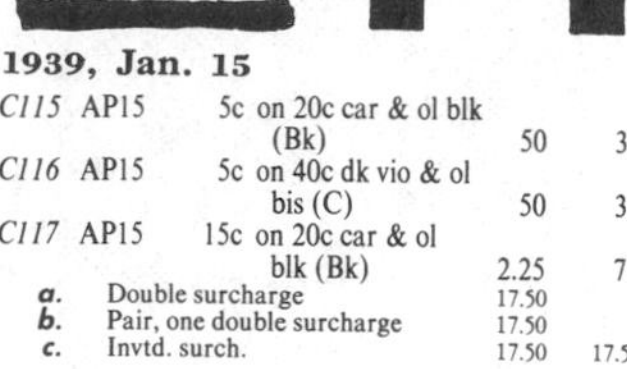

1939, Jan. 15

C115	AP15	5c on 20c car & ol blk (Bk)	50	35
C116	AP15	5c on 40c dk vio & ol bis (C)	50	35
C117	AP15	15c on 20c car & ol blk (Bk)	2.25	75
a.		Double surcharge	17.50	
b.		Pair, one double surcharge	17.50	
c.		Invtd. surch.	17.50	17.50

No. CF5 Surcharged in Black.

C118	AP15	5c on 20c car & ol blk	1.00	1.00

Nos. C102-C103 Surcharged in Black or Red

15
cts

1940, Oct. 20

C119	AP12	15c on 30c dk bl & blk brn	1.75	70
a.		Invtd. surch.	17.50	
C120	AP15	15c on 40c dk vio & ol bis (R)	3.75	1.25
a.		Double surcharge	17.50	

Pre-Columbian Monument
AP18

Symbol of Legend of El Dorado
AP19

Spanish Fortifications, Cartagena
AP20

Colonial Bogotá
AP21

Proclamation of Independence
AP22

National Library, Bogotá
AP23

Engraved.

1941, Jan. 28 *Perf. 12* Unwmkd.

C121	AP18	5c gray blk	20	10
C122	AP19	10c yel org	20	6
C123	AP20	15c car rose	25	5
C124	AP21	20c yel grn	50	10
a.		Imperf. vert., pair	125.00	
C125	AP18	30c dp bl	50	10
C126	AP19	40c rose lake	1.00	10
C127	AP20	50c turq grn	1.00	10
C128	AP21	60c sepia	1.00	10
C129	AP18	80c ol blk	2.75	70
C130	AP22	1p bl & blk	4.50	70
C131	AP23	2p red org & blk	7.50	3.00
C132	AP22	3p vio & blk	20.00	9.00
C133	AP23	5p lt grn & blk	40.00	30.00
		Nos. C121-C133 (13)	79.40	44.11

See also Nos. C151-C163, C217-C225.

San Sebastian Fort, Cartagena
AP24

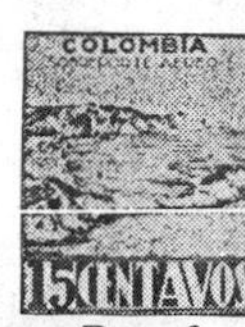

Bay of Santa Marta
AP25

Tequendama Waterfall
AP26

National Capitol, Bogotá
AP27

Lithographed.

1945, Nov. 3 *Perf. 11* Unwmkd.

C134	AP24	5c bl gray	20	10
a.		Imperf., pair	12.00	
C135	AP26	10c yel org	20	10
a.		Imperf., pair	12.00	
C136	AP25	15c rose	20	5
a.		Imperf., pair	12.00	
C137	AP24	20c lt yel grn	45	10
a.		Imperf., pair	12.00	
C138	AP26	30c ultra	45	10
a.		Imperf., pair	12.00	
C139	AP25	40c claret	75	22
a.		Imperf., pair	12.00	
C140	AP24	50c bluish grn	80	25
a.		Imperf., pair	12.00	
C141	AP26	60c lt vio brn	3.25	1.25
a.		Imperf., pair	12.00	
C142	AP25	80c dk sl grn	5.00	1.20
a.		Imperf., pair	15.00	
C143	AP27	1p dk bl	7.00	1.25
a.		Imperf., pair	25.00	
C144	AP27	2p red org	10.00	4.75
a.		Imperf., pair	85.00	
		Nos. C134-C144 (11)	28.30	9.37

Part-perforate varieties exist for all denominations except 80c.

Bello Type of Regular Issue, 1946.

Engraved.

1946, Sept. 3 *Perf. 12* Wmk. 255

C145	A219	5c dp bl	25	20

Issued to commemorate the 80th anniversary of the death of Andrés Bello, poet and educator.

Francisco José de Caldas
AP29

Manuel del Socorro Rodriguez
AP30

Perf. 12½

1947, May 9 Litho. Unwmkd.

C146	AP29	5c dp bl, *grnsh*	50	30
C147	AP30	10c red org, *grnsh*	75	65

4th Pan-American Press Congress (1946).

Chancellery Patio
AP31

Capitol, Patio Rafael Nunez
AP32

AP33

1948, Apr. 2 Engraved Wmk. 229

C148	AP31	5c dk brn	15	5
C149	AP32	15c dp bl	1.40	1.25

Miniature Sheet

Imperf.

C150	AP33	50c brown	2.25	2.25

Nos. C148–C150 commemorate the 9th Pan-American Conference, Bogotá. No. C150 measures 90½x90½mm.

Types of 1941.

1948, July 21 *Perf. 12* Unwmkd.

C151	AP18	5c org yel	25	5
C152	AP19	10c scarlet	25	5
C153	AP20	15c dp bl	25	5
C154	AP21	20c violet	25	5
C155	AP18	30c yel grn	60	22
C156	AP19	40c gray	70	20
C157	AP20	50c rose lake	75	20
C158	AP21	60c ol gray	1.25	20
C159	AP18	80c red brn	1.50	25
C160	AP22	1p ol grn & vio brn	2.50	50
C161	AP23	2p dp grn & brt bl	4.50	1.00
C162	AP22	3p rose car & blk	9.50	5.50
C163	AP23	5p lt brn & turq grn	25.00	12.00
		Nos. C151-C163 (13)	47.30	20.27

"Air Week" 5c Blue

The War and Air Department issued a 5c blue stamp in May, 1949, to publicize Air Week (Semana de Aviacion). The design shows a coat-of-arms, inscribed "FAC," superimposed upon an outline map of Colombia. This stamp had no franking value and its use was optional during May 16-23.

Justice and Liberty
AP34

Wing
AP35

Design: 10c, Liberty holding tablet of laws.

1949, Oct. 7 *Perf. 13* Unwmkd.

C164	AP34	5c bl grn	15	5
C165	AP34	10c orange	15	5

Issued to honor the new Constitution.

For Domestic Postage.

1950, June 22 Litho. *Perf. 12*

C166	AP35	5c org yel	40	35
C167	AP35	10c brn red	50	40
C168	AP35	15c lt bl	60	40
C169	AP35	20c lt grn	1.10	75
C170	AP35	30c lil gray	2.50	2.50
C171	AP35	60c chocolate	3.25	3.50

With Network as in Parenthesis.

C172	AP35	1p gray (buff)	25.00	25.00
C173	AP35	2p bl (pale grn)	25.00	25.00
C174	AP35	5p red brn (red brn)	70.00	70.00
		Nos. C166-C174 (9)	128.35	127.90

No. C172 was issued both with and without network.

Nos. C151–C157 and C160–C163 Overprinted in Black L

1950, July 18

C175	AP18	5c org yel	25	15
C176	AP19	10c scarlet	25	15
C177	AP20	15c dp bl	25	15
C178	AP21	20c violet	35	20
C179	AP18	30c yel grn	60	30
C180	AP19	40c gray	1.25	50
C181	AP20	50c rose lake	75	40
C182	AP22	1p ol grn & vio brn	4.50	3.50
C183	AP23	2p dp grn & brt bl	7.00	5.00
C184	AP22	3p rose car & blk	20.00	20.00
C185	AP23	5p lt brn & turq grn	42.50	42.50
		Nos. C175-C185 (11)	77.70	72.85

Nos. C151-C163 Overprinted in Black

1950, July 12

C186	AP18	5c org yel	25	7
C187	AP19	10c scarlet	25	7
C188	AP20	15c dp bl	25	5
C189	AP21	20c violet	35	5
C190	AP18	30c yel grn	35	5
C191	AP19	40c gray	75	15
C192	AP20	50c rose lake	75	15
C193	AP21	60c ol gray	1.25	25
C194	AP18	80c red brn	1.90	65
C195	AP22	1p ol grn & vio brn	2.00	80
C196	AP23	2p dp grn & brt bl	5.50	2.25
C197	AP22	3p rose car & blk	13.00	12.00
C198	AP23	5p lt brn & turq grn	30.00	25.00
		Nos. C186-C198 (13)	56.60	41.54

On Nos. C175–C198, "L" stands for LANSA, "A" for AVIANCA.

Miniature Sheet

Western Hemisphere
AP36

Imperf.

1950, Aug. 22 Photo. Unwmkd.

C199	AP36	50c gray	1.50	1.50

Issued to commemorate the 75th anniversary (in 1949) of the formation of the Universal Postal Union.

Types of 1941 Overprinted at Lower Right in Black L

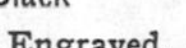

Engraved.

1951, Sept. 15 *Perf. 12* Unwmkd.

C200	AP19	40c org yel	2.50	2.00
C201	AP20	50c ultra	2.50	2.00
C202	AP21	60c gray	2.50	2.00
C203	AP18	80c car rose	1.75	1.50
C204	AP22	1p red org & red brn	6.00	5.00
C205	AP23	2p rose car & bl	6.50	5.00
C206	AP22	3p choc & emer	16.00	13.00
C207	AP23	5p org & gray	47.50	47.50
		Nos. C200-C207 (8)	85.25	78.00

Types of 1941 Overprinted at Lower Right in Black A

1951–54

C208	AP19	40c org yel	5.00	80
C209	AP20	50c ultra	6.00	90
C210	AP21	60c gray	4.50	65
a.		Overprint centered	2.50	75
C211	AP18	80c car rose	1.25	45
C212	AP22	1p red org & red brn	5.00	70
C213	AP22	1p ol grn & vio brn ('54)	6.00	1.10
C214	AP23	2p rose car & bl	5.00	75
C215	AP22	3p choc & emer	7.50	2.00
C216	AP23	5p org & gray	15.00	2.75
		Nos. C208-C216 (9)	55.25	10.10

All values except the 2p and 3p exist without overprint.

Types of 1941.

1952, May 10 Engraved

C217	AP18	5c ultra	45	20
C218	AP19	10c ultra	45	25
C219	AP20	15c ultra	45	25
C220	AP21	20c ultra	1.00	40
C221	AP18	30c ultra	2.50	90
C222	AP18	5c car rose	45	20
C223	AP19	10c car rose	45	25
C224	AP21	20c car rose	1.00	30
C225	AP18	30c car rose	2.00	45
		Nos. C217-C225 (9)	8.75	3.20

Type of 1941 Surcharged in Blue

1º CONFERENCIA 1952 SIDERURGICA LATINO AMERICANA 70 Ctvos.

1952, Oct. 30

C226	AP18	70c on 80c car rose	2.25	1.00

Issued to publicize the Latin American Siderurgical Conference, 1952.

Type of Postal Tax Stamps, 1948–50, Nos. 602 and 604 Surcharged or Overprinted in Black

CORREO 5 AEREO

1953 *Perf. 12.* Wmk. 255

C227	PT10	5c on 8c bl	15	5
C228	PT10	15c on 20c brn	35	5
C229	PT10	15c on 25c bl grn	1.50	10
C230	PT10	25c bl grn	50	10

Many varieties of overprint or surcharge exist on Nos. C227–C231.

No. 570 Overprinted "AEREO" in Blue.

1953, Aug. *Perf. 12½* Wmk. 229

C231	A160	10c red	22	5

"Extra Rapido"

Stamps inscribed "Extra Rapido" are for use on domestic airmail carried by airlines other than AVIANCA.

No. 585 Surcharged and Overprinted "Extra Rapido" in Dark Blue

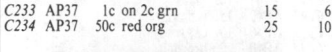

CORREO 5 EXTRA RAPIDO 5

1953 *Perf. 13* Unwmkd.

C232	A244	5c on 11c red	50	45

Capitol and Arms
AP37

Revenue Stamps Overprinted "Correo Extra-Rapido"

Gray Security Paper.

Engraved.

1953 *Perf. 12* Wmk. 255

C233	AP37	1c on 2c grn	15	6
C234	AP37	50c red org	25	10

AP38

Real Estate Tax Stamps Overprinted "Correo Extra-Rapido" in Black or Carmine

1953

C235	AP38	5c red org	20	6
C236	AP38	20c brn (C)	30	10

On 20c, overprint is at bottom of stamp and two lines of ornaments cover real estate tax inscription at top.

Castillo y Rada and Map
AP39

Real Estate Tax Stamp Surcharged "Correo Aereo, II Exposicion Filatelica Nacional, Bogota Dicbre 1953, 15 Centavos"

Engraved and Lithographed.

1953, Dec. 12

C237	AP39	15c on 10p multi	50	25

Issued to publicize the second National Philatelic Exhibition, Bogota, Dec. 1953.

No. RA45 Overprinted in Black — CORREO EXTRA-RAPIDO

1953

C238	PT10	10c purple	15	6

Galeras Volcano
AP40

Retreat of San Diego
AP41

Designs: 15c (C241), Las Lajas Shrine, Narino. 15c (C242), 50c, Bolivar monument. 20c, 80c, Ruiz mountain, Manizales. 40c, George Isaacs monument, Cali. 60c, Monkey Fountain, Tunja. 1p, Stadium, Medellin. 2p, Pastelillo Fort, Cartagena. 3p, Santo Domingo University gate. 5p, Las Lajas Shrine. 10p, Map of Colombia.

Perf. 13½x13, 13.

1954, Jan. 15 Engraved. **Unwmkd.**

C239	AP40	5c dp red vio	20	10
C240	AP41	10c black	20	10
C241	AP40	15c red org	25	5
C242	AP40	15c car rose	25	5
C243	AP40	20c brown	25	5
C244	AP40	30c brn org	25	5
C245	AP40	40c blue	25	10
C246	AP40	50c dk vio brn	30	10
C247	AP40	60c dk brn	40	10
C248	AP40	80c red brn	90	20

Size: 37x27mm.
Center in Black.

C249	AP41	1p dp bl	3.00	30
C250	AP41	2p dk grn	4.75	45
C251	AP41	3p car rose	11.00	1.50

Size: 38x32mm., 32x38mm.

C252	AP41	5p dk grn & red brn	12.00	3.75
C253	AP40	10p gray grn & red org	15.00	8.50
		Nos. C239-C253 (15)	49.00	15.40

See also Nos. C307–C308.

Condor Carrying Shield
AP42

Inscribed: "Correo Extra-Rapido"
Lithographed.

1954, Apr. 23 ***Perf. 12½.***

C254	AP42	5c lil rose	90	40

Soldier-Map-Arms Type of Regular Issue, 1954.

1954, June 13 Engraved ***Perf. 13***

C255	A259	15c carmine	40	10

Issued to commemorate the first anniversary of the assumption of the presidency by General Rojas Pinilla.

See also No. C271a.

Games Type of Regular Issue, 1954.

Design: 20c, Stadium and Athlete holding arms of Colombia.

1954, July 18

C256	A260	15c chocolate	80	20
C257	A260	20c dp bl grn	1.50	50

7th National Games, Cali, July 1954.

Church of St. Peter Claver, Cartagena
AP45

1954, Sept. 9

C258	AP45	15c brown	35	10
a.		Souvenir sheet	3.25	3.25

Issued to commemorate the 300th anniversary of the death of St. Peter Claver.

No. C258a contains one stamp similar to No. C258, but printed in red brown. Marginal inscriptions in black. Sheet size: 120½x127mm.

Mercury Type of Regular Issue, 1954.

1954, Oct. 29

C259	A263	15c dp bl	45	10

Inscribed "Extra Rapido"

C260	A263	50c scarlet	40	10

Issued to publicize the first International Fair and Exhibition, Bogotá, 1954.

Archbishop Manuel José Mosquera
AP47

Inscribed: "Correo Extra Rapido"

1954, Nov. 17

C261	AP47	2c yel grn	10	8

Issued to commemorate the centenary of the death of Archbishop Manuel José Mosquera.

Virgin of Chiquinquira
AP48

Inscribed: "Correo Extra Rapido"
Engraved and Lithographed

1954, Dec. 4

C262	AP48	5c org brn & multi	10	5

See also No. C291.

College Types of Regular Issue, 1954.

Designs: 20c, Brother Cristobal de Torres. 50c, College chapel and arms.

Perf. 12½x11½, 11½x12½

1954, Dec. 6 Engraved **Unwmkd.**

C263	A264	15c org & blk	40	20
C264	A264	20c ultra	60	20
C265	A265	25c dk brn	80	22
C266	A265	50c blk & car	1.90	1.00
a.		Souvenir sheet	6.00	6.00

Issued to commemorate the 300th anniversary (in 1953) of the founding of the Senior College of Our Lady of the Rosary, Bogotá.

No. C266a contains four stamps similar to Nos. C263–C266, but printed in different colors: 15c red and black, 20c pale purple, 25c brown, 50c black and olive green. Marginal inscriptions in black. Sheet size: 124½x130½mm.

Steel Mill Type of Regular Issue.

1954, Dec. 12 ***Perf. 12½x13***

C267	A266	20c grn & blk	1.50	90

Issued to mark the opening of the Paz del Rio steel mill, October 1954.

Marti Type of Regular Issue, 1955

1955, Jan. 28 ***Perf. 13½x13***

C268	A267	15c dp grn	40	15

Issued to commemorate the centenary (in 1953) of the birth of José Marti.

Korean Veterans Type of Regular Issue, 1955.

1955, Mar. 23 ***Perf. 12½***

C269	A268	20c dk grn	75	25

Issued to honor Colombian soldiers who served in Korea.

Merchant Fleet Types of Regular Issue, 1955.

1955, Apr. 12 ***Perf. 12½***

C270	A269	25c black	40	10
C271	A270	50c dk grn	80	45
a.		Souvenir sheet	6.00	6.00

Issued to honor the Grand-Colombian Merchant Fleet.

No. C271a contains four stamps similar to Nos. C255, C269–C271, but printed in different colors; 15c lilac red, 20c olive, 25c bluish black, 50c bluish green. Marginal inscriptions in black. Sheet size: 125x131mm.

Pres. Marco Fidel Suarez
AP56

Inscribed: "Correo Extra Rapido"

1955, April 23 ***Perf. 13***

C272	AP56	10c dp bl	15	5

Issued to commemorate the centenary of the birth of Marco Fidel Suarez (1855–1927), president in 1918–1921.

Hotel-Church Type of Regular Issue, 1955.

1955, May 16 Photo. ***Perf. 11½x12***

C273	A271	15c rose brn	40	10

Rotary Type of Regular Issue, 1955.
Engraved.

1955, Oct. 17 ***Perf. 13*** **Unwmkd.**

C274	A272	15c dk car rose	40	10

Rotary International, 50th anniversary.

O'Higgins, Santander and Sucre
AP59

Ferdinand the Catholic and Queen Isabella I
AP60

Designs: 2c, Atahualpa, Tisquesuza and Montezuma. 20c, Marti, Hidalgo and Petion. 1p, Artigas, Solano Lopez and Murillo. 2p, Abdon Calderon, Baron de Rio Branco and José de La Mar.

1955, Oct. 12 **Engr. & Photo.**

Inscribed: "Extra Rapido"

C275	AP59	2c dl brn & blk	10	5
C276	AP60	5c dk brn & yel	20	15

Regular Air Post

C277	AP59	15c rose car & blk	30	15
C278	AP59	20c pale brn & blk	45	15
a.		Souvenir sheet of 2	9.50	9.50

Inscribed: "Extra Rapido"

C279	AP60	1p ol gray & brn	9.00	5.25
C280	AP60	2p vio & blk	6.00	4.50
		Nos. C275-C280 (6)	16.05	10.25

Issued to publicize the 7th Congress of the Postal Union of the Americas and Spain, Bogota, Oct. 12–Nov. 9, 1955.

No. C278a contains one each of Nos. C277–C278 printed in different shades. It measures 120x132mm. with marginal inscription in black: "Ministerio de Comunicaciones. III Exposicion Filatelica Nacional Bogota 1955."

Caro Type of Regular Issue, 1955.

1955, Nov. 29 Engr. ***Perf. 13½x13***

C281	A275	15c gray grn	35	5

Issued to commemorate the centenary of the death of José Eusebio Caro, poet.

University of Salamanca
AP62

Inscribed: "Extra Rapido"

1955, Nov. 29 ***Perf. 13*** **Unwmkd.**

C282	AP62	20c dk brn	15	5

University of Salamanca, 7th centenary.

Type of Postal Tax Stamp of 1948-50

Surcharged in Black CORREO EXTRA-RAPIDO

Engraved.

1956 *Perf. 12* Wmk. 255

C283	PT10	2c on 8c bl	6	5

No. 617 Overprinted in Black EXTRA-RAPIDO

1956 *Perf. 12½x13* Unwmkd.

C284	A256	1p blk & emer	25	5

Columbus Type of Regular Issue.

1956, Oct. 11 Photo. *Perf. 12*

C285	A279	15c int bl	50	15

Issued in honor of Christopher Columbus. See also No. C306.

St. Elizabeth Type of Regular Issue

1956, Nov. 19

C286	A280	15c red brn	40	20

Issued to commemorate the 7th centenary of St. Elizabeth of Hungary, patron saint of Santa Fé de Bogota.

St. Ignatius Type of Regular Issue

1956, Nov. 26 Engr. *Perf. 12½x13*

C287	A281	5c brown	25	5

Issued to commemorate the 400th anniversary of the death of St. Ignatius of Loyola.

Javier Pereira
AP63

1956, Dec. 28 *Perf. 12* Unwmkd.

C288	AP63	20c rose car	15	10

Issued to honor 167-year-old Javier Pereira.

No. 649 and Type of 1941 Overprinted in Red "EXTRA RAPIDO."

1957 *Perf. 13½x13*

C289	A276	5c bl & blk	9.50	5.50
		Perf. 12		
C290	AP23	5p org & gray	8.50	6.00

The overprint measures 14mm.

Virgin Type of 1954.

Engraved and Lithographed

1957, May 23 *Perf. 13* Unwmkd.

C291	AP48	5c dp plum & multi	8	6

Bank Type of Regular Issue, 1957.

Designs: C292, 20c, Emblem and dairy farm. 10c, Emblem and tractor. 15c, Emblem, coffee and corn. C293, Emblem, cow, horse and herd.

1957 Photo. *Perf. 14x13½*

C292	A283	5c chocolate	20	5
C293	A283	5c orange	15	5
C294	A283	10c green	70	55
C295	A283	15c black	40	8
C296	A283	20c dl red	25	25
		Nos. C292-C296 (5)	1.70	98

Nos. C292–C296 issued to commemorate the 25th anniversary of the founding of the Agrarian Savings Bank of Colombia.

No. C292 is inscribed "Extra Rapido."

No. C292 issued Mar. 5, others May 23.

Cyclist
AP64

1957, July 6 *Perf. 12* Unwmkd.

C297	AP64	2c brown	15	15
C298	AP64	5c ultra	25	25

Seventh Bicycle Tour of Colombia.

Academy Type of Regular Issue.

Designs: 15c, Coat of arms and Gen. Rafael Reyes. 20c, Coat of arms and Academy.

1957, July 20 Engraved *Perf. 12½*

C299	A284	15c rose car	22	5
C300	A284	20c brown	40	8

Issued to commemorate the 50th anniversary of the Colombian Military Academy.

Delgado Type of Regular Issue, 1957.

1957, Sept. 15 Photo. *Perf. 12*

C301	A285	10c sl bl	25	10

Issued in honor of José Matias Delgado, liberator of El Salvador.

UPU Type of Regular Issue, 1957.

1957, Oct. 10

C302	A286	15c dk red brn	25	15
C303	A286	25c dk bl	25	5

Issued for International Letter Writing Week and the 14th UPU Congress.

St. Vincent de Paul Type of Regular Issue, 1957.

1957, Oct. 18

C304	A287	5c rose brn	25	15

Issued to commemorate the centenary of the Colombian Society of St. Vincent de Paul.

Fencing Type of Regular Issue, 1957.

1957, Nov. 23 *Perf. 12*

C305	A288	20c dk red brn	40	35

Issued to commemorate the third South American Fencing Championship.

Columbus Type of Regular Issue, 1956, Inscribed "Extra Rapido."

1958, Jan. 8 *Perf. 12* Unwmkd.

C306	A279	3c dk grn	10	7

Scenic Type of 1954.

Design: 25c, Las Lajas Shrine.

1958, June 20 Engr. *Perf. 13*

C307	AP40	25c dk bl	40	7
C308	AP40	25c rose vio	40	7

IGY Type of Regular Issue, 1958.

1958, May 12 Photo. *Perf. 12*

C309	A289	25c green	70	10
		Inscribed "Extra Rapido."		
C310	A289	1p purple	50	10

Nos. C309–C310 issued for the International Geophysical Year, 1957–58.

No. 659 Overprinted "AEREO" in Carmine.

1958, Oct. 16 Engraved *Perf. 13*

C312	A277	50c dk grn & blk	60	15

Almanza Type of Regular Issue, 1958.

1958, Oct. 23 Photo. *Perf. 14x13*

C313	A290	25c dk gray	40	10
		Inscribed "Extra Rapido"		
C314	A290	10c ol grn	15	5

Carrasquilla Type of Regular Issue, 1959.

1959, Jan. 22 Photo. *Perf. 14x13*

C315	A291	25c car rose	30	5
C316	A291	1p dk bl	90	25

Issued to commemorate the centenary of the birth (in 1857) of Msgr. R. M. Carrasquilla, rector of Our Lady of the Rosary Seminary, Bogota.

Miss Universe Type of Regular Issue, 1959.

1959, June 26 *Perf. 11½* Unwmkd.

C317	A292	1.20p multi	2.00	1.65
C318	A292	5p multi	47.50	47.50

Issued to honor Luz Marina Zuluaga, Miss Universe, 1959.

Gaitan Type of Regular Issue, 1959, Inscribed "Extra Rapido" and Surcharged in Black or Blue.

1959, July 28 Engr. *Perf. 12x13½*

C319	A293	2p on 1p blk	1.50	1.40
C320	A293	2p on 1p blk (Bl)	1.75	1.65

Issued in honor of Jorge Eliecer Gaitan, (1898–1948), lawyer and politician.

The 1p black, type A293, exists without surcharge.

No. C247 Surcharged with New Value in Dark Blue; Old Value Obliterated.

1959, Aug. 24 *Perf. 13* Unwmkd.

C321	AP40	50c on 60c dk brn	1.75	55

Regular and Air Post Issues of 1948–1959 Overprinted in Black or Red (UNIFICADO)

1959–60

C322	A283	5c orange	45	40
C323	A287	5c rose brn ('60)	60	60
C324	A281	5c brn (R)	55	45
C325	AP41	10c black	22	8
a.		Double ovpt.	3.50	3.50
C326	A160	10c red	50	10
a.		Double ovpt.	2.00	2.00
C328	A284	15c rose car	35	5
a.		Inverted ovpt.	4.50	4.50
C330	AP40	20c brown	20	5
a.		Double ovpt.	2.00	2.00
C331	A284	20c brown	30	30
C332	A288	20c dk red brn ('60)	25	20
C333	AP40	25c rose vio ('60)	25	5
C334	AP40	25c dk bl	25	5
C335	A291	25c car rose	30	10
C336	A290	25c dk gray	25	7
C338	AP40	30c brn org	20	5
C340	AP40	50c on 60c dk brn	50	18
C341	A291	1p dk bl	90	20
a.		Double ovpt.	3.50	3.50
C342	A292	1.20p brn, ultra, car & ol	1.50	1.25
C343	AP41	2p dk grn & blk	2.00	30
C344	AP41	3p car rose & blk	5.50	75
a.		Double ovpt.	12.00	12.00
C345	AP41	5p dk grn & red brn	7.50	1.65
a.		Double ovpt.	12.00	12.00
b.		Invert. ovpt.	12.00	12.00
C346	AP40	10p gray grn & red org	9.50	3.50
		Nos. C322-C346 (21)	32.07	10.38

Issued following agreement between the Colombian government and AVIANCA to unify the air postage used on all mail carried by AVIANCA.

Vertical overprint on Nos. C342 and C346.

Airmail Stamp of 1919 and Planes
AP66

Designs: 60c, No. C350a, Planes of 1919 and 1959. C349b, C350b, Stamp of 1919 and Planes.

Photogravure.

1959, Dec. 5 *Perf. 12* Unwmkd.

C347	AP66	35c lt bl, blk & red	75	10
C348	AP66	60c yel grn & gray	40	10

Souvenir Sheets.

C349	AP66	Sheet of two	6.75	6.75
a.		1p org & gray	1.00	1.00
b.		1p lil, gray & red	1.00	1.00

Inscribed "Extra Rapido"

1960, May 17

C350	AP66	Sheet of two	6.75	6.75
a.		1.50p red org & gray	1.25	1.25
b.		1.50p ol, gray & rose	1.25	1.25

Nos. C347–C350 issued to commemorate the 40th anniversary of air post service and of the AVIANCA company.

Nos. C349–C350 measure 90x49½mm. with black marginal inscriptions.

Type of Regular Issue, 1959 and

1859 Stamp and Seaplane
AP67

Designs (various stamps of 1859 and): 10c, Map of Colombia. 25c, Pres. Mariano Ospina. 1.20p, Plane over mountains.

1959, Dec. 1 Photo. *Perf. 12*

C351	A296	25c choc & red	50	35
C352	AP67	50c ver & ultra	1.25	75
C353	AP67	1.20p yel grn & car	2.75	1.65

Inscribed "Extra Rapido"

C354	A296	10c lem & vio	15	5

Souvenir Sheet

Tête Bêche 5c Stamps of 1859
AP68

Wmkd. "REPUBLICA DE COLOMBIA". (331)

1959, Dec. 23 Litho. *Imperf.*

C355	AP68	5p bl, *pink*	16.50	16.50

Nos. C351–C355 issued to commemorate the centenary of Colombian postage stamps.

No. C355 contains a tête bêche pair simulating the 5c blue of 1859, No. 2. Sheet sold for 5p. Size: 74½x70mm.

No. C355 exists with inscription "VALOR $5.10" instead of "VALOR $5."

Eldorado Airport, Bogota
AP69

1960, Jan. 5 *Perf. 12½* Wmk. 331

C356	AP69	35c blk & ocher	75	35
C356A	AP69	60c ver & gray	90	60

Inscribed "Extra Rapido"

C356B	AP69	1p Prus bl & gray	1.25	60

Ant Bear
AP70

Designs: 1.30p, Armadillo. 1.45p, Parrot fish.

Photogravure

1960, Feb. 12 Perf. 12 Unwmkd.

C357	AP70	35c sepia	1.25	15
C358	AP70	1.30p rose car & dk brn	2.50	2.25
C359	AP70	1.45p lt bl, bl & yel	2.00	1.90

Issued to commemorate the centenary of the death of Alexander von Humboldt, German naturalist and geographer (1769–1859).

Flower Type of Regular Issue, 1960

Flowers: Nos. C360, C362, C366, Passiflora mollissima. Nos. C361, C364, C367, Odontoglossum luteo purpureum. Nos. C363, C369, Anthurium andreanum. Nos. C365, C370, Stanhopea tigrina. No. C368, Espeletia grandiflora.

1960, May 10 Photo. Perf. 12

Flowers in Natural Colors.

C360	A298	5c dk bl	15	12
C361	A298	35c maroon	60	7
C362	A298	60c dk bl	1.25	80
C363	A298	1.45p dk brn	1.25	1.25

Inscribed "Extra Rapido"

C364	A298	5c maroon	10	10
C365	A298	10c brown	10	10
C366	A298	1p dk bl	2.50	2.50
C367	A298	1p maroon	2.50	2.50
C368	A298	1p brown	2.50	2.50
C369	A298	1p brown	2.50	2.50
C370	A298	1p brown	2.50	2.50
		Nos. C360-C370 (11)	15.95	14.94

See also Nos. C420–C425.

Fleeing Family and Uprooted Oak Emblem
AP71

Perf. 10, 11

1960, May 24 Litho. Wmk. 331

C371	AP71	60c bl grn & gray	45	30

Issued to publicize World Refugee Year, July 1, 1959–June 30, 1960.

Souvenir Sheet

Pan-American Highway Through Colombia
AP72

1960, May 28 Lithographed *Imperf.*

C372	AP72	2.50p brn & aqua	7.50	7.50

Issued to commemorate the 8th Pan-American Highway Congress, Bogota, May 20–29.

No. C372 measures 44x54mm. with brown marginal inscription and black control number.

Lincoln Type of Regular Issue.

1960, June 6 Perf. 10½

C375	A299	40c dl red brn & blk	1.25	90
C376	A299	60c rose red & blk	35	10

Issued to commemorate the sesquicentennial (in 1959) of the birth of Abraham Lincoln.

Type of Regular Issue and

Joaquin Camacho, Jorge Tadeo Lozano and Jose Miguel Pey
AP73

Designs: No. C378, Arms of Cartagena. 35c, 1.45p, Colombian flag. 60c, Andres Rosillo, Antonio Villavicencio and Joaquin Caicedo. 1p, Manuel de Bernardo Alvarez and Joaquin Gutierrez. 1.20p, Jose Antonio Galan statue. 1.30p, Front page of newspaper La Bagatela, 1811. 1.65p, Antonia Santos, Jose Acevedo y Gomez and Liborio Mejia.

Photogravure

1960, July 20 Perf. 12 Unwmkd.

C377	AP73	5c lil & brn	15	10
C378	A301	5c dp bl grn & multi	15	10
C379	AP73	35c multi	25	5
C380	AP73	60c red brn & grn	60	20
C381	AP73	1p ver & sl grn	1.25	90
C382	A301	1.20p ultra & ind	1.25	90
C383	AP73	1.30p org & blk	1.25	90
C384	AP73	1.45p multi	1.65	1.25
C385	AP73	1.65p grn & brn	1.25	1.25
		Nos. C377-C385 (9)	7.80	5.65

Souvenir Sheet

Stamps Inscribed "Extra Rapido"

Flag, Coins and Arms of Mompox and Cartagena
AP74

C386	AP74	Sheet of four	5.50	5.50
a.		50c dp cl & multi	85	85
b.		50c grn & multi	85	85
c.		1p brn ol, yel, bl & car	85	85
d.		1p lil & gray	85	85

Nos. C377–C386 issued to commemorate the 150th anniversary of Colombia's independence.

No. C386 measures 90x75mm.

St. Isidro Type of Regular Issue, 1960.

Designs: 35c, No. C388a, St. Isidro and farm animals. No. C388b, Nativity.

Photogravure

1960, Sept. 26 Perf. 12 Unwmkd.

C387	A302	35c multi	25	10

Souvenir Sheet

Stamps Inscribed "Extra Rapido"

C388	A302	Sheet of two	9.00	9.00
a.		1.50p multi	3.00	3.00
b.		1.50p multi	3.00	3.00

Issued to honor St. Isidro the Farmer, patron saint of the rural people. Black marginal inscription on No. C388. Size: 89½x60mm.

See also Nos. C439–C440.

Type of Regular Issue, 1959

Portrait: 35c, Simon Bolivar.

Perf. 12½

1960, Nov. 23 Litho. Wmk. 331

C389	A294	35c gray	4.50	60

Type of Regular Issue, 1961 (Pan-American Highway)

Perf. 10½x11

1961, Mar. 7 Unwmkd.

C390	A304	10c rose lil & emer	85	75
C391	A304	20c ver & lt bl	85	75
C392	A304	30c blk & emer	85	75

Inscribed "Extra Rapido"

C393	A304	10c dk bl & emer	85	75

Issued to commemorate the 8th Pan-American Highway Congress, Bogota, May 20–29, 1960.

Lopez Type of Regular Issue, 1961

1961, Mar. 22 Photo. Perf. 12½

C394	A305	35c bl & brn	75	10

Inscribed "Extra Rapido"

C395	A305	10c emer & brn	25	15

Souvenir Sheet

C396	A305	1p lil & brn	5.00	5.00

Issued to honor Alfonso Lopez (1886–1959), President of Colombia.

No. C396 contains one stamp with margin solidly printed in brown and lilac; colorless inscriptions, and black control number. Size: 60x75mm.

Brother Damian and San Francisco Church, Cali
AP75

Designs: No. 398, Emblem of University del Valle (vert.). 1.30p, Fine Arts School, Cali. 1.45p, Agricultural College, Palmira.

Perf. 13x13½, 13½x13

1961, Aug. 17 Photo. Unwmkd.

C397	AP75	35c vio brn & ol	45	7
C398	AP75	35c ol & grn	45	7
C399	AP75	1.30p sep & pink	1.25	65
C400	AP75	1.45p multi	1.25	65

Inscribed: "Extra Rapido"

Design: 10c, View of Cali (vert.).

C401	AP75	10c brn & yel grn	25	10
		Nos. C397-C401 (5)	3.65	1.54

Issued to commemorate the 50th anniversary (in 1960) of the department of Valle del Cauca.

View of Cucuta
AP76

1961, Aug. 29

C402	AP76	35c brn ol & grn	90	10

Inscribed: "Extra Rapido"

Design: 10c, Church of the Rosary, Cucuta (vert.).

C403	AP76	10c dk brn & gray grn	15	6

Issued to commemorate the 50th anniversary (in 1960) of the department of North Santander.

Old and New Ships at Barranquilla
AP77

Arms and View of San Gil
AP78

Hotel, Popayan
AP79

Statue of Christ in Procession
AP80

Design: 1.45p, View of Velez.

Perf. 12½x13, 13x12½

1961, Oct. 10 Photo. Unwmkd.

C404	AP77	35c gold & bl	70	10
C405	AP78	35c bl grn, yel & red	70	10
C406	AP79	35c car & brn	70	10
C407	AP78	1.45p brn & grn	70	30

Inscribed: "Extra Rapido."

C408	AP80	10c brn & yel	15	7
		Nos. C404-C408 (5)	2.95	67

Souvenir Sheets

Types of Regular and Air Post Issues

Designs, No. C409: 35c, Barranquilla arms. 40c, Popayan arms. "c," Arms and view of San Gil. "d," Holy Week in Popayan. No. C410: "a," Old and new ships at Barranquilla. "b," Hotel, Popayan. "c," Bucaramanga arms. "d," Holy Week in Popayan.

C409		Sheet of four	7.50	7.50
a.	A309	35c gold & multi	50	50
b.	A309	40c gold & multi	50	50
c.	AP78	1p bl, yel & red	1.10	1.10
d.	AP80	1p car rose & yel	1.10	1.10

Stamps Inscribed: "Extra Rapido."

C410		Sheet of four	7.50	7.50
a.	AP77	50c gold & car rose	85	85
b.	AP79	50c gold & bl	85	85
c.	A309	50c pink & multi	85	85
d.	AP80	50c bl & yel	85	85

Nos. C404–C408 are in honor of the Atlantico Department. Nos. C409–C410 are in honor of the Departments of Atlantico, Cauca and Santander. The sheets have blue marginal inscriptions, black control numbers. Size: 90x75mm.

Nos. 713, 716 and 715 Overprinted and Surcharged AEREO

1961, Sept. ***Perf. 12***

C411	A297	5c grnsh bl & brn	15	10
C412	A298	5c multi	15	8
C413	A297	10c on 20c cit & gray brn	15	8

"Aereo" in script on No. C412.
See also Nos. C420–425.

Sports Type of Regular Issue, 1961

Designs: No. C414, Women divers. No. C415, Tennis, mixed doubles. 1.45p, C419b, Baseball. No. C417, Torch bearer. No. C418, C419a, Bolivar statue and flags of six participating nations. No. C419c, Soccer. No. C419d, Basketball.

1961, Dec. 16 Litho. ***Perf. 13½x14***

C414	A310	35c ultra, yel & brn	85	5
C415	A310	35c car, yel & brn	85	5
C416	A310	1.45p Prus grn, yel & brn	1.25	80

Inscribed: "Extra Rapido"

C417	A310	10c car lake, yel & brn	15	5
C418	A310	10c ol, yel, bl & red	15	5
		Nos. C414-C418 (5)	3.25	1.00

Souvenir Sheet
Stamps Inscribed: "Extra Rapido."
Imperf.

C419		Sheet of four	7.25	7.25
a.	A310	50c multi	60	60
b.	A310	50c multi	60	60
c.	A310	1p multi	1.20	1.20
d.	A310	1p multi	1.20	1.20

Issued to publicize the 4th Bolivarian Games, Barranquilla, 1961. No. C419 has black marginal inscription and control number. Size: 74x106mm.

Flower Type of 1960

Flowers: 5c, Passiflora mollissima. 10c, Espeletia grandiflora. 20c, 2p, Odontoglossum luteo purpureum. 25c, Stanhopea tigrina. 60c, Anthurium Andreanum.

Photogravure

1962, Jan. 30 ***Perf. 12*** **Unwmkd.**

Flowers in Natural Colors

C420	A298	5c gray	15	10
C421	A298	10c gray bl	15	10
C422	A298	20c rose lil	15	10
C423	A298	25c citron	40	10
C424	A298	60c lt brn	40	40

Inscribed "Extra Rapido"

C425	A298	2p sal pink	2.75	2.00
		Nos. C420-C425 (6)	4.00	2.80

Anti-Malaria Type of Regular Issue.

Designs: 40c, Colombian anti-malaria emblem. 1p, 1.45p, Malaria eradication emblem and mosquito in swamp.

1962, Apr. 12 Litho. ***Perf. 12***

C426	A311	40c yel & red	25	20
C427	A311	1.45p gray & ultra	75	65

Inscribed "Extra Rapido"

C428	A311	1p yel grn & ultra	5.25	5.25

Issued for the World Health Organization drive to eradicate malaria.

Type of Regular Issue, 1962 and

Abelardo Ramos and Engineering School, Cauca
AP81

Designs: 10c, Miguel Triana, Andres A. Arroyo and Monserrate shrine with cable cars. 15c, Diodoro Sanchez and first meeting place of Engineers Society. 2p, Engineers Society emblem.

1962, June 12 Photo. ***Perf. 11½x12***

C429	AP81	5c bl & dp rose	10	10
C430	AP81	10c grn & sep	20	15
C431	AP81	15c lil & sep	40	25

Inscribed: "Extra Rapido"

C432	A312	2p blk, yel, red & bl	2.50	2.50

Issued to commemorate the 75th anniversary of the founding of the Colombian Society of Engineers and to publicize the Sixth National Congress of Engineers.

American States Type of 1962.

1962, June 28 Photo. ***Perf. 13***

Flags in National Colors

C433	A313	35c blk & bl	50	5

Type of Regular Issue, 1962 (Women's Rights)
Perf. 12x12½

1962, July 20 Litho. Wmk. 229

C434	A314	35c ocher, gray & blk	30	5

Issued to publicize women's political rights. See also Nos. C448–C450.

Scout Type of 1962.

Designs: 15c, No. C438, Scouts at campfire and tents. 40c and No. C437, Girl Scouts.

Perf. 11½x12

1962, July 26 Photo. Unwmkd.

C435	A315	15c brn & rose	30	25
C436	A315	40c dp cl & pink	35	30
C437	A315	1p bl & buff	1.40	50

Inscribed "Extra Rapido"

C438	A315	1p pur & yel	5.50	5.50

Nos. C435 and C438 issued to commemorate the 30th anniversary of the Colombian Boy Scouts. Nos. C436 and C437 commemorate the 25th anniversary of the Girl Scouts.

Nativity by Gregorio Vasquez
AP82

Design: 2p, St. Isidro, similar to type A302.

Inscribed "Extra Rapido"

Photogravure

1962, Aug. 28 ***Perf. 12*** **Unwmkd.**

C439	AP82	10c gray & multi	15	5
C440	AP82	2p gray & multi	4.75	4.75

See also Nos. C387–C388.

Type of Regular Issue, 1962 and

Pres. Aquileo Parra and Magdalena River Bridge
AP83

Design: 5c, Locomotives of 1854 and 1961. 10c, Railroad map of Colombia.

1962, Sept. 28 Photo. ***Perf. 12½***

C441	AP83	5c sep & sl grn	20	5
C442	A316	10c multi	15	5

Engraved

C443	AP83	1p dl pur & brn	2.00	20

Inscribed: "Extra Rapido."

C444	AP83	5p bl, brn & dl grn	5.25	2.50

Issued to publicize the progress of Colombian railroads and to commemorate the completion of the Atlantic Line from Santa Maria to Bogota.

UPAE Type of Regular Issue

Designs: 50c, Map of Americas and carrier pigeon. 60c, Post horn.

Perf. 13½x14

1962, Oct. 18 Litho. Wmk. 346

C445	A317	50c sl grn & gold	40	10
C446	A317	60c gold & plum	30	5

Issued to commemorate the 50th anniversary of the founding of the Postal Union of the Americas and Spain, UPAE.

Pope John XXIII
AP84

1963, Mar. 11

C447	AP84	60c gold, red brn, buff & red	30	5

Issued to commemorate Vatican II, the 21st Ecumenical Council of the Roman Catholic Church.

Type of Regular Issue, 1962 (Women's Rights)

1963–64 ***Perf. 12x12½***

C448	A314	5c sal, gray & blk ('64)	6	5
C449	A314	45c pale grn, gray & blk	50	5
C450	A314	45c brt pink, gray & blk	50	5

Games Emblem
AP85

Perf. 13x14

1963, Aug. 12 Wmk. 346

C451	AP85	20c gray & multi	20	7
C452	AP85	80c buff & multi	20	5

Issued to commemorate the South American Athletic Championships (22nd for men, 12th for women), Cali, June 30–July 7.

Bolivar Statue by Arenas-Betancourt
AP86

Perf. 14x13½

1963, Aug. 30 Unwmkd.

C453	AP86	1.90p ol bis & bl	30	5

Centenary of the city of Pereira.

Tennis Player
AP87

1963, Oct. 11 ***Perf. 13½x14***

C454	AP87	55c multi	15	5

Issued to commemorate the 30th South American Tennis Championships, Medellin, Oct. 3–13.

Pres. John F. Kennedy and Alliance for Progress Emblem
AP88

1963, Dec. 17 Litho. ***Perf. 14x13½***

C455	AP88	10c multi	5	5

Issued to honor President John F. Kennedy (1917–1963).

Church of the True Cross, National Pantheon, Bogota
AP89

Design: 2p, Christ of the Martyrs, bell and tomb.

Perf. 13½x14

1964, Mar. 10 Photo. Unwmkd.

C459	AP89	1p multi	40	10
C460	AP89	2p multi	50	25

View of Cartagena AP90

1964, Mar. 18 Litho. *Perf. 14x13½*

C461	AP90	3p vio, bl, ocher & brn	2.00	85

Issued to commemorate Cartagena's independence in 1811, Simon Bolivar's visit in 1812 and the siege of 1815.

Eleanor Roosevelt AP91

1964, Nov. 10 Photo. *Perf. 12*

C462	AP91	20c ol & dl red brn	10	5

Issued to honor Eleanor Roosevelt (1884–1962).

Alberto Castilla and Score of "El Bunde" AP92

1964, Nov. 10 Unwmkd.

C463	AP92	30c ol bis & Prus grn	10	5

Issued to honor the Department of Tolima and Maestro Alberto Castilla (1878–1937) who in 1906 founded the Tolima Conservatory of Music in Ibague.

Mejia Type of Regular Issue

Designs (Mejia portrait and): 45c, Women picking coffee. 5p, Mules carrying coffee bags. 10p, Loading coffee on freighter "Manuel Mejia."

1965, Feb. 10 Engr. *Perf. 12½x13*

C464	A320	45c brn & blk	25	5
C465	A320	5p gray grn & blk	3.00	45
C466	A320	10p ultra & blk	4.00	40

Issued to honor Manuel Mejia J. (1887–1958), banker and manager of the National Coffee Growers Association.

ITU Emblem AP93

1965, Oct. 25 Photo. *Perf. 12*

C467	AP93	80c Prus bl, lt bl & red	20	8

Issued to commemorate the centenary of the International Telecommunication Union.

Cattleya Truanae AP94

Pres. Manuel Murillo Toro Statue, Telegraph and Orbits AP95

1965, Oct. 3 Litho. *Perf. 13½x14*

C468	AP94	20c yel & multi	10	6

Fifth Philatelic Exhibition.

1965, Nov. 1 *Perf. 13½x14, 14x13½*

Design: No. C470, Telegraph and satellites over South America (horiz.).

C469	AP95	60c multi	20	5
C470	AP95	60c multi	20	5

Centenary of the telegraph in Colombia.

Junkers F-13 Seaplane, 1920 AP96

History of Colombian Aviation: 10c, Dornier Wal, 1924. 20c, Dornier Mercur, 1926. 50c, Trimotor Ford, 1932. 60c, De Havilland biplane, 1930. 1p, Douglas DC-4, 1947. 1.40p, Douglas DC-3, 1944. 2.80p, Superconstellation 1049, 1951. 3p, Boeing 720B jet, 1961.

Perf. 14x13½

1965-66 Photo. Unwmkd.

C471	AP96	5c multi	10	5
C472	AP96	10c multi	10	5
C473	AP96	20c multi	15	5
C474	AP96	50c multi	15	5
C475	AP96	60c multi	30	5
C476	AP96	1p multi	50	15
C477	AP96	1.40p multi	60	20
C478	AP96	2.80p multi	1.25	90
C479	AP96	3p multi	1.90	1.25
		Nos. C471-C479 (9)	5.05	2.75

Issue dates: 5c, 60c, 3p, Dec. 13, 1965; 10c, 1p, 1.40p, July 15, 1966; 20c, 50c, 2.80p, Dec. 14, 1966.

Automobile Club Emblem and Car on Road AP97

1966, Feb. 16 Litho. *Perf. 14x13½*

C480	AP97	20c multi	10	6

Issued to commemorate the 25th anniversary (in 1965) of the Automobile Club of Colombia.

Fish Type of Regular Issue, 1966.

Fish: 2p, Flying fish. 2.80p, Queen angelfish. 20p, King mackerel.

1966, Aug. 25 Photo. *Perf. 12½x13*

C481	A323	2p multi	50	20
C482	A323	2.80p multi	1.50	1.50
C483	A323	20p multi	12.50	12.50

Coat of Arms Type of Regular Issue, 1966

1966, Oct. 11 Litho. *Perf. 14x13½*

C484	A324	1p ultra & multi	35	10
C485	A324	1.40p red & multi	30	10

Issued to commemorate the visits of Eduardo Frei and Raul Leoni, presidents of Chile and Venezuela.

Portrait Type of Regular Issue

Portraits: 80c, Father Felix Restrepo Mejia, S.J. (1887—1965), theologian and scholar. 1.70p, José Joaquin Casas (1866–1951), educator and diplomat.

Perf. 13½x14

1967, Jan. 18 Litho. Unwmkd.

C486	A325	80c dk bl & bis	15	5
C487	A325	1.70p blk & bis	35	15

Famous men of Colombia.

Declaration of Bogota Type of Regular Issue

1967, Feb. 2 Litho. *Perf. 14x13½*

C488	A326	3p multi	50	25

See note after No. 767.

Orchid Type of Regular Issue

Orchids: 1p, Cattleya dowiana aurea (vert.). 1.20p, Masdevallia coccinea (vert.). 5p, Catasetum macrocarpum and bee.

1967, May 23 Litho. *Perf. 14*

C489	A327	1p multi	55	20
C490	A327	1.20p multi	38	10
C491	A327	5p multi	2.25	50
a.		Souv. sheet of 3	3.50	3.50

Issued to commemorate the First National Orchid Exhibition and the Topical Philatelic Flora and Fauna Exhibition, Medellin, Apr. 1967. No. C491a contains one each of Nos. C489–C491. Gray margin with black inscription and red control number. Size: 99x149mm.

Lions Type of Regular Issue

1967, July 12 Litho. *Perf. 13½x14*

C492	A328	25c multi	20	5

Lions International, 50th anniversary.

"First Caesarean Section" by Grau AP98

Perf. 14x13½

1967, Sept. 7 Litho. Unwmkd.

C493	AP98	80c multi	10	5

Issued to publicize the 6th Congress of Colombian Surgeons, Bogota, Sept. 25.

SENA Type of Regular Issue
Lithographed and Embossed

1967, Sept. 20 *Perf. 13½x14*

C494	A329	2p gold, ver & blk	70	15

Issued to commemorate the 10th anniversary of National Apprenticeship Service, SENA.

Pre-Columbian Art Type of Regular Issue

Designs: 30c, Bird pectoral. 5p Ornamental pectoral. 20p, Pitcher.

Photogravure

1967, Oct. 13 *Perf. 13½x14*

C495	A330	30c ver, gold & brn	20	5
C496	A330	5p red, gold & brn	2.50	50
a.		Souvenir sheet of 2	3.00	2.50
C497	A330	20p vio, gold & brn	13.00	11.00

Issued to commemorate the meeting of the Universal Postal Union Committee on Postal Studies, Bogota, October, 1967; No. C496a also commemorates the 6th National Philatelic Exhibition. No. C496a contains 2 imperf. stamps in changed colors similar to Nos. C495–C496 (30c has green background and 5 p maroon background). Gray margin with red control number. Size: 92x91mm.

Telecommunications Type of Regular Issue

Designs: 50c, Signal lights. 1p, Early Bird satellite, Southern Cross and radar.

Perf. 13½x14

1968, May 14 Litho. Unwmkd.

C498	A331	50c blk, ver & emer	15	5
C499	A331	1p ultra, yel & gray	25	5

Issued to commemorate the 20th anniversary of the National Telecommunications Service (TELECOM).

Eucharist Type of Regular Issue

1968, June 6 Litho. *Perf. 13½x14*

C500	A332	80c rose lil, red, yel & blk	15	5
C501	A332	3p bl, red, yel & blk	45	15

Issued to publicize the 39th Eucharistic Congress, Bogotá, Aug. 18–25.

Eucharistic Congress Type of Regular Issue

Designs: 80c, The Last Supper, by Gregorio Vasquez (horiz.). 1p, St. Francis Xavier Preaching, by Gregorio Vasquez. 2p, The Dream of the Prophet Elias, by Gregorio Vasquez. 3p, Monstrance, c. 1700. 20p, Pope Paul VI, painting by Roman Franciscan nuns.

1968, Aug. 13 Photo. *Perf. 13*

C502	A333	80c multi	25	5
C503	A333	1p multi	35	5
C504	A333	2p multi	50	10
C505	A333	3p lil & multi	90	10
C506	A333	20p gold & multi	5.75	3.00
		Nos. C502-C506 (5)	7.75	3.30

Issued to commemorate the 39th Eucharistic Congress, Bogotá, Aug. 18–25.

Shrine of the Eucharist, Bogotá AP99

Designs: 1.20p, Pope Paul VI giving blessing and Papal arms (vert.). 1.80p, Cathedral of Bogotá (vert.).

Perf. 14x13½, 13½x14

1968, Aug. 22 Lithographed

C507	AP99	80c multi	15	5
C508	AP99	1.20p multi	30	10
C509	AP99	1.80p multi	45	20

Visit of Pope Paul VI to Colombia.

Computer Symbols AP100

1968, Oct. 29 Litho. *Perf. 13½x14*

C510	AP100	20c buff, car & grn	10	5

Issued to commemorate the centenary of the National University and the First Data Processing Congress in 1967 at the University.

Agriculture Institute Type of Regular Issue

1968, Mar. 5 Litho. *Perf. 13½x14*

C511	A337	1p gray & multi	25	5

Issued to commemorate the 25th anniversary (in 1967) of the Inter-American Agricultural Sciences Institute.

Microscope and Pen—AP101

1969, Mar. 24 Litho. *Perf. 14*

C512	AP101	5p blk, yel, ver & pur	1.65	15

Issued to commemorate the 20th anniversary (in 1968) of the University of the Andes.

Alexander von Humboldt and Andes
AP102

1969, May 3 Litho. *Perf. 14x13½*

C513	AP102	1p grn & brn	20	5

Issued to commemorate the bicentenary of the birth of Alexander von Humboldt (1769–1859), German naturalist and traveler.

Map of Colombia, Amphibian Plane and Letter
AP103

Design: 1.50p, No. C516b, Globe, letter, and jet of Avianca airlines.

1969, June 18 Litho. *Perf. 14x13½*

C514	AP103	1p multi	25	6
C515	AP103	1.50p multi	35	15

Souvenir Sheet

Imperf.

C516	AP103	Sheet of 2	5.25	5.25
a.		5p grn & multi	1.00	1.00
b.		5p vio & multi	1.00	1.00

Issued to commemorate the 50th anniversary of the first air post flight in Colombia. No. C516 also publicizes the 8th National Philatelic Exhibition, EXFILBA 69, Barranquilla, June 18–22. No. C516 contains 2 stamps in the designs of the 1p and 1.50p; gray margin with commemorative inscription, coats of arms and red control number. Size: 92x92mm.

Independence Type of Regular Issue

1969, July 24 Litho. *Perf. 13½x14*

Design: 2.30p, Simon Bolivar, José Antonio Anzoategui, Francisco de Paula Santander and victorious army entering Bogotá, Sept. 18, 1819; painting by Ignacio Castillo Cervantes.

C517	A338	2.30p gold & multi	70	25

Issued to commemorate the sesquicentennial of the fight for independence.

Social Security Emblem
AP104

Neurosurgeons' Congress Emblem
AP105

1969, Oct. 29 Litho. *Perf. 13½x14*

C518	AP104	20c emer & blk	10	5

Issued to commemorate the 20th anniversary of the Colombian Institute of Social Security.

1969, Oct. 29

C519	AP105	70c vio, red & yel	30	10

Issued to publicize the 13th Congress of Latin-American Neurosurgeons, Bogotá.

Junkers F-13
AP106

Designs: No. C521, C522b, Globe with airlines from Bogota and Boeing jet. No. C522a, like No. C520.

1969, Nov. 28 Litho. *Perf. 14x13½*

C520	AP106	2p grn & multi	50	15
C521	AP106	3.50p ultra & multi	70	40

Souvenir Sheet

Imperf.

C522	AP106	Sheet of 2	5.25	5.25
a.		3.50p lt grn & multi	75	75
b.		5p ultra & multi	1.10	1.10

Issued to commemorate the 50th anniversary of AVIANCA; No. C522 also publicizes the First Interamerican Philatelic Exhibition, Bogota, Nov. 28–Dec. 7.

No. C522 contains 2 imperf. stamps. Multicolored inscriptions, coat of arms, medals and red control number on light olive margin. Size: 92x90mm.

Child Mailing Letter
AP107

Design: 1.50p, Praying child and gifts.

1969, Dec. 16 Litho. *Perf. 13½x14*

C523	AP107	60c ocher & multi	60	25
C524	AP107	1p multi	60	10
C525	AP107	1.50p multi	70	25

Christmas 1969.

Radar Station and Pre-Columbian Head
AP108

1970, Mar. 25 Litho. *Perf. 14x13½*

C526	AP108	1p dl grn, blk & brick red	40	5

Issued to publicize the opening of the communications satellite earth station at Chocontá in Cundinamarca Province.

Emblem of Colombian Youth Sports Institute
AP109

Art Exhibition Emblem
AP110

Design: 2.30p, Games' emblem (dove and 3 rings).

1970, Apr. 6 Litho. *Perf. 13½x14*

C527	AP109	1.50p dk ol grn, yel & blk	40	25
C528	AP109	2.30p red & multi	60	25

Issued to publicize the 9th National Youth Games, Ibague, July 10–20.

1970, Apr. 30 Litho. *Perf. 13½x14*

C529	AP110	30c multi	10	5

Issued to publicize the 2nd Biennial Art Exhibition, Medellin, May 1–June 14.

Eduardo Santos, Rural and Urban Buildings
AP111

1970, June 18 Litho. *Perf. 14x13½*

C530	AP111	1p grn, yel & blk	25	5

Issued to commemorate the founding (in 1939) of the Territorial Credit Institute.

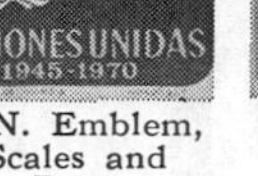

U.N. Emblem, Scales and Dove
AP112

EXFILCA Emblem
AP113

1970, June 26 *Perf. 13½x14*

C531	AP112	1.50p dk bl, lt bl & yel	25	5

25th anniversary of United Nations.

1970, Nov. Litho. *Perf. 13½x14*

C532	AP113	10p bl, gold & blk	5.00	38

Issued to publicize EXFILCA 70, 2nd Interamerican Philatelic Exhibition. Caracas, Venezuela, Nov. 27–Dec. 6.

Mother Juana Ruperta in Napanga Costume and Music by Efrain Orozco
AP114

Athlete and Games Emblem
AP115

Designs: 1p, Dancers from Eastern Plains and music by Alejandro Wills. No. C535, Guabina man, woman and folk song. No. C536, Bambuco man and woman, and music. No. C537, Man and woman dancing the Cumbia, and music.

1970–71 Litho. *Perf. 13½x14*

C533	AP114	60c dp lil rose & multi	70	20
C534	AP114	1p ultra & multi	50	8
C535	AP114	1.30p bl & multi	65	10
C536	AP114	1.30p emer & multi ('71)	65	10
C537	AP114	1.30p lil & multi ('71)	50	10
		Nos. C533-C537 (5)	3.00	58

1971, Mar. 11

Design: 2p, Games emblem.

C542	AP115	1.50p multi	1.30	90
C543	AP115	2p blk, org & grn	1.20	80

6th Pan-American Games, Cali, July 30–Aug. 13.

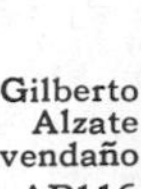

Gilberto Alzate Avendaño
AP116

1971, Apr. 29 Litho. *Perf. 14x13½*

C544	AP116	1p bl & multi	60	38

Gilberto Alzate Avendaño (1910–1960), journalist and popular leader, 10th anniversary of death.

Commemorative Medal
AP117

Lithographed and Embossed

1971, June 21 *Perf. 14x13½*

C545	AP117	1p sl grn & gold	70	40

Centenary (in 1970) of the Bank of Bogota.

Olympic Center
AP118

Soccer
AP119

Designs (Games Emblem and): Nos. C546–C546c, Olympic Center. No. 547, Soccer. No. C548, Wrestling. No. C549, Bicycling. No. C550, Volleyball. No. C551, Diving (women). No. C552, Fencing. No. C553, Sailing. No. C554, Equestrian. No. C555, Jumping. No. C556, Rowing. No. C557, Cali emblem. No. C558, Basketball (women). No. C559, Stadium. No. C560, Baseball. No. C561, Hockey. No. C562, Weight lifting. No. C563, Medals. No. C564, Boxing. No. C565, Gymnastics (women). No. C566, Sharpshooting.

1971, July 16 Litho. *Perf. 13½x14*

C546	AP118	1.30p yel & multi	1.75	30
a.		1.30p grn & multi	1.75	30
b.		1.30p bl & multi	1.75	30
c.		1.30p car & multi	1.75	30
C547	AP119	1.30p emer & multi	1.75	30
C548	AP119	1.30p lil & multi	1.75	30
C549	AP119	1.30p bl & multi	1.75	30
C550	AP119	1.30p car & multi	1.75	30
C551	AP119	1.30p bl & multi	1.75	30
C552	AP119	1.30p car & multi	1.75	30
C553	AP119	1.30p bl & multi	1.75	30
C554	AP119	1.30p gray & multi	1.75	30
C555	AP119	1.30p grn & multi	1.75	30
C556	AP119	1.30p bl & multi	1.75	30
C557	AP118	1.30p org & multi	1.75	30
C558	AP119	1.30p car & multi	1.75	30
C559	AP118	1.30p lt bl & multi	1.75	30
C560	AP119	1.30p plum & multi	1.75	30
C561	AP119	1.30p yel grn & multi	1.75	30
C562	AP119	1.30p pink & multi	1.75	30

C563 AP118 1.30p dp org & multi 1.75 30
C564 AP119 1.30p plum & multi 1.75 30
C565 AP119 1.30p lil rose & multi 1.75 30
C566 AP119 1.30p grn & multi 1.75 30
a. Sheet of 25 (Nos. C546-C566) 45.00 7.25

6th Pan American Athletic Games, Cali. First color in listings is color of emblem. No. C546b appears twice in sheet. No. C566a has marginal multicolored inscription commemorating EXFILCALI 71 Philatelic Exhibition.

Battle of Carabobo, by Martin Tovar y Tovar—AP120

1971, Nov. 25 Litho. *Perf. 13½x14*

C567 AP120 1.50p multi 1.50 25

Sesquicentennial of the Battle of Carabobo.

St. Theresa Type of Regular Issue Overprinted "AEREO"

1972 Lithographed *Perf. 13½x14*

C568 A343 2p multi 45 5

See note after No. 793.

Vendor AP121

Designs: 50c, Woman wearing shawl, and woven shawl. 3p, Fruit vendor (puppet).

1971, Apr. 11 Litho. *Perf. 13½x14*

C569 AP121 50c multi 38 25
C570 AP121 1p multi 40 15
C571 AP121 3p multi 50 35

Colombian artisans.

Mormodes Rolfeanum AP122

1972, Apr. 20 *Perf. 14x13½*

C572 AP122 1.30p multi 40 5

7th World Orchidology Congress, Medellin.

Congo Grande Dancer AP123

Pres. Laureano Gomez, by Ridriguez Cubillos AP124

1972, June 21 Litho. *Perf. 13½x14*

C573 AP123 1.30p multi 60 7

International Carnival of Barranquilla.

No. C453 Surcharged in Brown **$ 1.30**

1972, Oct. 5 Litho. *Perf. 14x13½*

C574 AP86 1.30p on 1.90p ol bis & bl 80 25

1972, Oct. 17 *Perf. 13½x14*

C575 AP124 1.30p multi 20 5

Laureano Gomez (1898–1966), President of Colombia.

1972, Nov. 28

Design: 1.30p, Guillermo León Valencia Muñoz.

C576 AP124 1.30p multi 25 5

Guillermo León Valencia Muñoz (1909–1971), President of Colombia.

Benito Juarez AP125  — Rebecca Fountain AP126

1972, Dec. 12 *Perf. 13½x14*

C577 AP125 1.50p multi 30 10

Centenary of the death of Benito Juarez (1806–1872), revolutionary leader and president of Mexico.

1972, Dec. 19 Lithographed

C578 AP126 80c multi 70 40
C579 AP126 1p multi 60 15

"Bucaramanga" AP127

1972, Dec. 22 *Perf. 14x13¼*

C580 AP127 5p multi 1.25 10

350th anniversary of the founding of Bucaramanga.

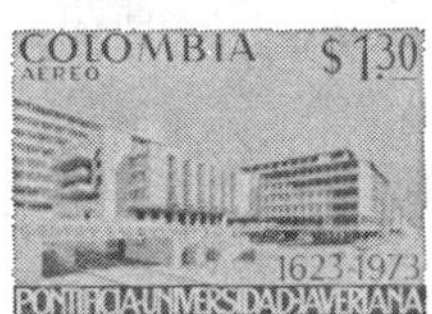

Xavier University AP128

1973, May 8 Litho. *Perf. 14x13½*

C581 AP128 1.30p lt grn & sep 35 8
C582 AP128 1.50p lt bl & sep 35 8

350th anniversary of the founding of Xavier University in Bogotá.

Ceramic Type of Regular Issue

Excavated Ceramic Artifacts: 1p, Winged urn, Tairona. 1.30p, Woman and child, Sinu. 1.70p, Two-headed figure, Quimbaya. 3.50p, Man, Tumaco.

1973 Lithographed *Perf. 13½x14*

C583 A358 1p multi 1.40 1.25
C584 A358 1.30p multi 70 5
C585 A358 1.70p multi 80 35
C586 A358 3.50p multi 1.65 40

Issue dates: 1p, Oct. 11; others, June 15.

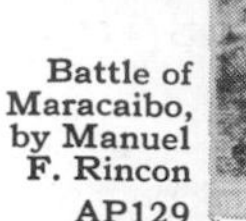

Battle of Maracaibo, by Manuel F. Rincon AP129

1973, July 24 Litho. *Perf. 14x13½*

C587 AP129 10p bl & multi 3.00 25

Battle of Maracaibo, sesquicentennial.

Bank Emblem AP130

1973, Oct. 1 Litho. *Perf. 14x13½*

C588 AP130 2p multi 30 5

50th anniversary of the Bank of the Republic.

No. 801 Overprinted "AEREO"

1973, Oct. 11 *Perf. 14*

C589 A346 80c multi 40 10

Pres. Pedro Nel Ospina, by Coroleano Leudo AP131  — Arms of Toro AP132

1973, Nov. 9 *Perf. 13½x14*

C590 AP131 1.50p multi 30 8

50th anniversary of the Ministry of Communications founded under Pres. Ospina.

1973, Dec. 1

C591 AP132 1p multi 20 5

4th centenary of the founding of Toro, Valle del Cauca.

Bolivar, Battle of Bombona AP133

1973, Dec. 7 Litho. *Perf. 14x13½*

C592 AP133 1.30p multi 20 6

Sesquicentennial (in 1972) of the Battle of Bombona.

Nicolaus Copernicus AP134 — Andes, Map of South America AP135

1974, Feb. 19 Litho. *Perf. 13½x14*

C593 AP134 2.50p multi 70 25

500th anniversary of the birth of Nicolaus Copernicus (1473–1543), Polish astronomer.

1974, May 11 Litho. *Perf. 14*

C594 AP135 2p multi 40 10

Meeting of Communications Ministers of Members of the Andean Group, Cali, May 7–11, 1974.

Television Set AP136

1974, July 16 Litho. *Perf. 14x13½*

C595 AP136 1.30p org, blk & brn 25 5

20th anniversary of Colombian television and 10th anniversary of INRAVISION, the National Institute of Radio and Television.

Championship Emblem AP137

1974, Aug. 5 Litho. *Perf. 14x13½*

C596 AP137 4.50p multi 45 20

2nd World Swimming Championships, Cali.

Condor—AP138

1974, Aug. 28 *Perf. 14*

C597 AP138 1.50p multi 25 10

Bank of Colombia centenary.

UPU Envelope AP139

1974, Sept. 9 Litho. *Perf. 14*

C598 AP139 20p multi 3.50 40

Centenary of Universal Postal Union.

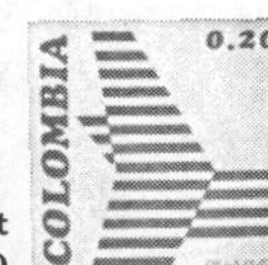

Symbol of Flight AP140

1974, Sept. *Perf. 12x12½*

C599 AP140 20c olive 8 5

Gen. José Maria Cordoba
AP141

White-tailed Trogon, Letter
AP142

1974, Oct. 14 Litho. *Perf. 13½x14*

C609 AP141 1.30p multi 25 5

Sesquicentennial of the Battles of Junin and Ayacucho.

Insurance Type of 1974

Design: 3p, Abstract pattern.

1974, Oct. 24 Litho. *Perf. 13½x14*

C610 A365 3p multi 40 10

Centenary of National Insurance Company.

Perf. 13½x14, 14x13½

1974, Nov. 14

Designs (UPU Letter and): 1.30p, Keel-billed Toucan (horiz.). 2p, Peruvian cock-of-the-rock (horiz.). 2.50p, Scarlet macaw.

C611 AP142 1p multi 25 8
C612 AP142 1.30p multi 30 5
C613 AP142 2p multi 40 10
C614 AP142 2.50p multi 45 15

Centenary of Universal Postal Union.

Forest No. 1, by Roman Roncancio—AP143

Boy with Thorn in Finger, by Gregorio Vazquez
AP144

Paintings: 3p, Women Fruit Vendors, by Miguel Diaz Vargas (1886–1956). 5p, Annunciation, Santafereña School, 17th–18th centuries.

Perf. 13½x14, 14x13½

1975, Mar. 12 Lithographed

C615 AP143 2p multi 80 10
C616 AP144 3p multi 55 10
C617 AP144 4p multi 70 25
C618 AP144 5p multi 1.25 40

Modern and Colonial Colombian paintings.

Trees and Lake
AP145

Design: 6p, Victoria regia, Amazon River.

1975, Mar. 12 *Perf. 14x13½*

C619 AP145 1p yel & multi 22 5
C620 AP145 6p yel & multi 65 10

Nature conservation of trees and Amazon Region.

Gold Treasure Type of 1975

Designs: 2p, Nose pendant. 10p, Alligator-shaped staff ornament.

1975, Apr. 11 Litho. *Perf. 14x13½*

C621 A368 2p grn, gold & brn 60 6
C622 A368 10p multi 3.25 85

Pre-Columbian Sinu Culture artifacts.

El Rodadero, Santa Maria
AP146

1975, July 26 Litho. *Perf. 14x13½*

C623 AP146 2p multi 20 5

400th anniversary of Santa Maria City.

Maria de J. Paramo
AP147

1975, Aug. 31 Litho. *Perf. 13½x14*

C624 AP147 4p multi 30 5

International Women's Year 1975. Maria de Jesus Paramo de Collazos founded first normal school for women in Bucaramanga in 1875.

"Sugar Cane"
AP148

1976, Mar. 12 Litho. *Perf. 13½x14*

C625 AP148 5p blk & emer 1.25 15

4th Congress of Latin-American and Caribbean sugar-exporting countries, Cali, Mar. 8–12.

View of Bogota—AP149

1976, July 2 Litho. *Perf. 12*

Blue and Multicolored

C626 AP149 10p *shown* 1.75 80
C627 AP149 10p *Barranquilla* 1.75 80
C628 AP149 10p *Cali* 1.75 80
C629 AP149 10p *Medellin* 1.75 80

Habitat, U.N. Conference on Human Settlements, Vancouver, Canada, May 31–June 11. Nos. C626–C629 printed se-tenant in blocks of 4, sheets of 60.

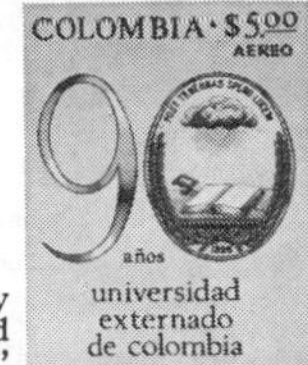

University Emblem and "90"
AP150

1976, Aug. 6 Litho. *Perf. 13½x14*

C630 AP150 5p lt bl & multi 75 15

University of Colombia, 90th anniversary.

Miguel Samper
AP151

Telephone, 1895
AP152

1976, Oct. 29 Litho. *Perf. 13½x14*

C631 AP151 2p multi 30 5

Miguel Samper (1825–1899), economist and writer.

1976, Nov. 2

C632 AP152 3p multi 25 5

Centenary of first telephone call by Alexander Graham Bell, Mar. 10, 1876.

747 Jumbo Jet
AP153

1976, Dec. 3 Litho. *Perf. 12*

C633 AP153 2p multi 20 5

Inauguration of 747 jumbo jet service by Avianca.

Convent, Church and Plaza de San Francisco—AP154

1976, Dec. 29 Litho. *Perf. 14*

C634 AP154 6p multi 75 20

150th anniversary of the Congress of Panama.

Souvenir Sheet

Bank of the Republic Emblem—AP155

1977, June 6 Litho. *Perf. 14*

C635 AP155 25p multi 8.00 8.00

Opening of Philatelic Museum of Medellin under auspices of Banco de la Republica. No. C635 contains one stamp (50x40mm.); multicolored margin shows various orchids; black control number. Size: 130x105mm.

No. C633 Surcharged in Light Brown

1977, June Litho. *Perf. 12*

C636 AP153 3p on 2p multi 20 5

Coffee
AP156

Coffee Grower, Pack Mule
AP157

1977–78 Litho. *Perf. 12½*

C640 AP156 3p multi 20 5
C641 AP156 3.50p multi ('78) 25 5

Colombian coffee.

1977, Aug. 9 Litho. *Perf. 13½x14*

C642 AP157 10p multi 75 7

National Federation of Coffee Growers, 50th anniversary.

Beethoven and 9th Symphony
AP158

Games' Emblem
AP159

1977, Aug. 17

C643 AP158 8p multi 75 10

Sesquicentennial of the death of Ludwig van Beethoven (1770–1827).

Bird Type of 1977

Tropical Birds and Plants: No. C644, Woodpecker and meriania. C645, Purple gallinule and water lilies. No. C646, Xipholaena punicea and cochlospermum orinocense. No. C647, Crowned flycatcher and jacaranda copaia.

1977, Sept. 6 Litho. *Perf. 14*

C644 A380 5p multi 60 15
C645 A380 5p multi 60 15
C646 A380 10p multi 75 22
C647 A380 10p multi 75 22

1977, Sept. 9 *Perf. 12x12½*

C648 AP159 6p multi 35 10

13th Central American and Caribbean Games, Medellin, 1978.

La Cayetana, by Enrique Grau
AP160

Design: No. C650, Water Nymphs, by Beatriz Gonzalez.

1977, Sept. 13 *Perf. 14x13½*

C649	AP160	8p multi	65	22
C650	AP160	8p multi	65	22

Women's suffrage, 20th anniversary.

Judge Francisco Antonio Moreno by, Joaquin Gutierrez
AP161

Design: 25p, Viceroy Manuel de Guirior.

1977, Sept. 13 *Perf. 12*

C651	AP161	20p multi	1.75	80
C652	AP161	25p multi	2.50	1.25

Bicentenary of National Library.

Federico Lleras Acosta
AP162

Cauca University Arms
AP163

1977, Sept. 27 Litho. *Perf. 14*

C653	AP162	5p multi	38	10

Dr. Federico Lleras Acosta, veterinarian and bacteriologist; birth centenary.

1977, Oct. 14

C654	AP163	5p multi	40	15

Sesquicentennial of the University of Cauca.

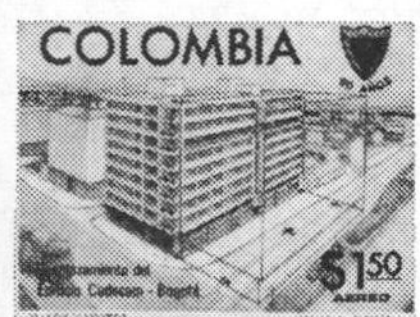

CUDECOM Building, Bogota
AP164

1977, Oct. 14

C655	AP164	1.50p multi	15	6

Colombian Society of Engineers, 90th anniversary.

No. C612 Surcharged with New Value and Bars in Brown

1977, Dec. 3 Litho. *Perf. 14x13½*

C656	AP142	2p on 1.30p multi	40	15

Lost City, Tayrona Culture
AP165

Creator of Energy, by Arenas Betancourt
AP166

1978, Apr. 18 Litho. *Perf. 12½*

C657	AP165	3.50p multi	30	5

1978, Apr. 25 *Perf. 12*

C658	AP166	4p bl & multi	35	15

Sesquicentennial of Antioquia University Law School.

Column of the Slaves
AP167

Statue of Catalina, Cartagena
AP168

1978, May 9

C659	AP167	2.50p multi	35	15

Sesquicentennial of Ocaña Convention (meeting of various political groups).

1978, May 30 Litho. *Perf. 12*

C660	AP168	4p blk & lt bl	35	15

Sesquicentennial of University of Cartagena.

Gold Pendant, Tolima
AP169

1978, July 11 Litho. *Perf. 12x12½*

C661	AP169	3.50p multi	30	5

Apotheosis of Spanish Language, by Luis Alberto Acuña—AP170

1978, Aug. 9 *Perf. 14*

C662	AP170	Strip of 3, multi	6.75	6.75
a.		11p, single stamp	1.65	1.65

Millennium of Spanish language. No. C662 printed in sheets of 15 (3x5). Black control number.

Presidential Guard
AP171

Figure, Muisca Culture
AP172

1978, Aug. 16 *Perf. 13½x14*

C663	AP171	9p multi	60	60

Presidential Guard Battalion, 50th anniversary.

1978, Sept. 12 Litho. *Perf. 12½*

C664	AP172	3.50p multi	30	5

Apse of Carmelite Church
AP173

1978, Oct. 12 *Perf. 13*

C665	AP173	30p multi	3.50	60

Souvenir Sheet

Perf. 13½x14

C666	AP173	50p multi	4.50	4.50

ESPAMER '78 Philatelic Exhibition, Bogota, Oct. 12–21. No. C666 contains one stamp; multicolored margin shows enlarged stamp design, ESPAMER emblem and black control number. Size: 125x95mm.

Owl, Gold Ornament, Calima
AP174

Virgin and Child, by Gregorio Vasquez
AP175

1978-80 Litho. *Perf. 12½*

Designs: No. C669, Gold frog, Quimbaya culture. No. C670, Gold nose pendant, Tairona, horiz.

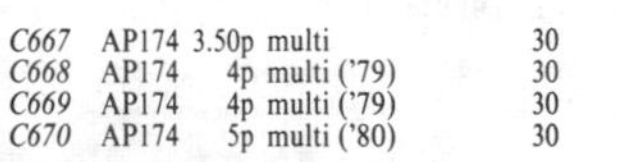

C667	AP174	3.50p multi	30	5
C668	AP174	4p multi ('79)	30	5
C669	AP174	4p multi ('79)	30	5
C670	AP174	5p multi ('80)	30	8

1978, Nov. 28 *Perf. 13½x14*

C671	AP175	2.50p multi	20	5

Christmas 1978.

Bull Ring, Cathedral, Manizales
AP176

1979, Jan. 6 Litho. *Perf. 14*

C672	AP176	7p multi	90	20

Manizales Fair.

Children Playing Hopscotch, and IYC Emblem
AP177

Designs: No. C674, Child at blackboard and UNESCO emblem (horiz.). No. C675, The Paper Collector, by Omar Gordillo, and U.N. emblem.

Perf. 13½x14, 14x13½

1979, July 19

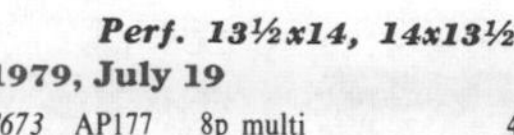

C673	AP177	8p multi	45	25
C674	AP177	12p multi	65	30
C675	AP177	12p multi	65	30

International Year of the Child.

Rio Prado Hydroelectric Station
AP178

1979, Aug. 24 *Perf. 13½x14*

C676	AP178	5p multi	70	15

Tomb, 6th Century—AP179

1979, Sept. 25 Litho. *Perf. 14*

C677	AP179	8p multi	75	25

San Augustin Archaeological Park.

Gonzalo Jimenez de Quesada, by C. Leudo—AP180

1979, Oct. 11 *Perf. 12*

C678	AP180	20p multi	2.25	70

Gonzalo Jimenez de Quesada (1500-1579), Spanish conquistador.

Hill, Penny Black, Colombia No. 1
AP181

1979, Oct. 23 *Perf. 13½x14*

C679	AP181	15p multi	90	30

Sir Rowland Hill (1795-1879), originator of penny postage.

Amazon Region—AP182

Tourism: 14p, San Fernando Fortress.

1979 **Litho.** ***Perf. 13½×14***

C680	AP182	7p multi	50	20
C681	AP182	14p multi	1.25	50

Issue dates: 7p, Nov. 16; 14p, Nov. 9.

Nativity—AP183

Creche Sculptures: No. C682, Three Kings and soldiers. No. C684, Shepherds.

1979, Nov. 30 ***Perf. 12***

C682	AP183	3p multi	50	45
C683	AP183	3p multi	50	45
C684	AP183	3p multi	50	45

Christmas 1979. Nos. C682-C684 se-tenant in continuous design.

Magdalena Bridge, Avianca Emblem AP184

1979, Dec. 5 ***Perf. 14***

C685	AP184	15p multi	90	25

Barranquilla, 350th anniversary; Avianca National Airline, 60th anniversary.

Boy Playing Flute, by Judith Leyster AP185

1980, Feb. 15 ***Perf. 13½x14***

C686	AP185	6p multi	38	15

2nd International Music Competition, Ibague, Dec. 1979.

Gen. Antonio José de Sucre, 150th Death Anniversary—AP186

1980, Feb. 15 **Litho.** ***Perf. 12½x12***

C687	AP186	12p multi	65	25

The Watchman, by Edgar Negret AP187

1980, Feb. 26 ***Perf. 12x12½***

C688	AP187	25p multi	2.00	90

Virgin Mary, by Real del Sarte, 1929—AP188

1980, May 23 **Litho.** ***Perf. 14x13½***

C689	AP188	12p multi	45	18

Apparition of the Virgin Mary to Sister Catalina Labouri Gontard, 150th anniversary.

San Gil Produce Market, by Luis Roncancio—AP189

1980, May 27 ***Perf. 13½x14***

C690	AP189	12p multi	45	20

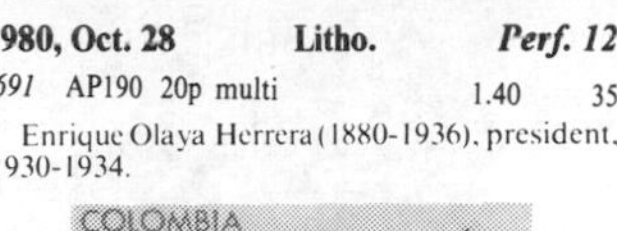

Pres. Enrique Olaya Herrera, by Miguel Diaz Vargas—AP190

1980, Oct. 28 **Litho.** ***Perf. 12***

C691	AP190	20p multi	1.40	35

Enrique Olaya Herrera (1880-1936), president, 1930-1934.

The Boy Fishing in a Bucket—AP191

Christmas 1980 (Christmas Stories by Rafael Pombo): No. C693, The Frog and the Mouse. No. C694, The Seven Lives of the Cat.

1980, Nov. 21 **Litho.** ***Perf. 14½***

C692	AP191	4p multi	30	25
C693	AP191	4p multi	30	25
C694	AP191	4p multi	30	25

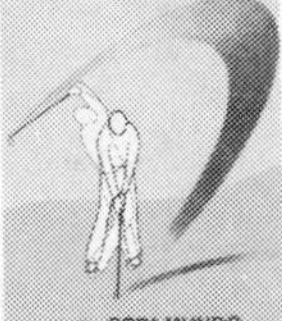

28th World Golf Cup, Cajica—AP192

1980, Dec. 9 **Litho.** ***Perf. 13½x14***

C695	AP192	30p multi	2.00	60

Bolivar Type of 1980

Simon Bolivar Death Sesquicentennial: 6p, Portrait, last words to Colombia (vert.).

1980, Dec. 17 ***Perf. 12***

C696	A400	6p multi	90	35

St. Peter Claver Holding Cross—AP193

1981, Jan. 13 ***Perf. 14½***

C697	AP193	15p multi	70	25

St. Peter Claver (1580-1654), helped American Indians.

Sculptured Bird, San Augustin AP194

Archaeological Finds: No. C699, Funeral chamber, Tierradentro. No. C700, Chamber hallway, Tierradentro. No. C701, Statue of man, San Augustin. Nos. C698-C701 se-tenant.

1981, May 12 **Litho.** ***Perf. 14***

C698	AP194	7p multi	40	15
C699	AP194	7p multi	40	15
C700	AP194	7p multi	40	15
C701	AP194	7p multi	40	15

See Nos. C707-C710.

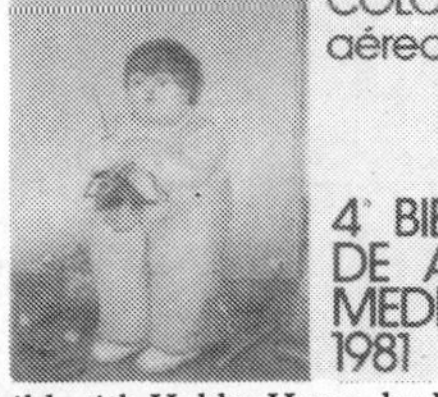

Child with Hobby Horse, by Fernando Botero—AP195

4th Biennial Arts show, Medellin: 20p, Square Abstract, by Omar Rayo. 25p, Flowers, by Alejandro Obregon.

1981, May 15 ***Perf. 12***

C702	AP195	20p multi	1.25	25
C703	AP195	25p multi	1.40	40
C704	AP195	50p multi	2.50	75

8th South American Swimming Championships, Medellin—AP196

1981, June 5

C705	AP196	15p multi	75	22

Santamaria Bull Ring, 50th Anniv.—AP197

1981, June 9 **Litho.** ***Perf. 12***

C706	AP197	30p multi	3.00	1.00

Archaeological Type of 1981

Quimbaya Culture: Nos. C707-C710 se-tenant.

1981, Sept. 23 **Litho.** ***Perf. 14***

C707	AP194	9p Man	55	15
C708	AP194	9p Seated man	55	15
C709	AP194	9p Seal, print	55	15
C710	AP194	9p Jug	55	15

1981, Dec. 17 **Litho.** ***Perf. 14***

Calima Culture: Nos. C710A-C710D se-tenant.

C710A	**AP194**	**9p Anthropomorphic container**	55	15
C710B	**AP194**	**9p Jar**	55	15
C710C	**AP194**	**9p Anthropomorphic jar**	55	15
C710D	**AP194**	**9p Urn**	55	15

Fruit—AP198

1981, Nov. 3 **Litho.** ***Perf. 14***

C711	Block of 6	12.00	9.00
a.-f.	AP198 25p, any single	1.75	70

Revolt of the Comuneros, 200th Anniv.—AP199

1981, Nov. 21 **Litho.** ***Perf. 12***

C712 AP199 20p multi 80 40

Jose Manuel Restrepo, Historian, 1775?-1860? AP200

Andres Bello, 1780?-1865 AP201

1981, Dec. 1 **Litho.** ***Perf. 12***

C713 AP200 35p multi 1.25 30

1981, Dec. 11 **Litho.** ***Perf. 12***

C714 AP201 18p multi 70 20

Colombia's Admission to UPU, 100th Anniv. AP202

1981 **Litho.** ***Perf. 12 (30p), Imperf.***

C715 AP202 30p No. 103 1.00 25
C716 AP202 50p Hemispheres, Nos. 104-108 2.00 1.00

No. C716 has red control number. Size: 100x70mm. Dates of issue: No. C715, Dec. 18. No. C716, Dec. 28.

Tourism Type of 1979

1982 **Litho.** ***Perf. 12***

C717 AP182 20p Solano Bay 70 18
C718 AP182 20p Tota Lake, Boyaca 70 18
C719 AP182 20p Corrales, Boyaca 70 18

Issue dates: No. C717, June 2; others, June 16.

1982 World Cup—AP202a

Designs: Players and team emblems.

1982, June 21 ***Perf. 14***

C720 Sheet of 15 6.00 3.00
a. AP202a 9p any single 40 15

No. C720 has black control number. Size: 181x150mm.

Bogota Gun Club Centenary—AP202b

1982, July 16 ***Perf. 12***

C721 AP202b 20p multi 60 20

Gold Crocodile Figure, Tairona Culture—AP202c

Tairona Culture Exhibit, Gold Museum: Various figures. Nos. C723-C727 vert.

1982, July 28

C722 AP202c 25p lt brn, gold & blk 1.00 40
C723 AP202c 25p brt pink, gold & blk 1.00 40
C724 AP202c 25p grn, gold & blk 1.00 40
C725 AP202c 25p dk bl, gold, & blk 1.00 40
C726 AP202c 25p vio. gold & blk 1.00 40
C727 AP202c 25p red, gold & blk 1.00 40
Nos. C722-C727 (6) 6.00 2.40

Government Buildings, Pereira—AP203

1982, Aug. 4 **Litho.** ***Perf. 12***

C728 AP203 35p multi 1.25 35

Bi-plane in Flight, by Edgar Antonio Bustos—AP204

1982, Aug. 5 ***Perf. 14***

C729 AP204 18p multi 60 20

American Air Forces Cooperation System.

Magdalena River—AP205

1982, Oct. 21 **Litho.** ***Perf. 12***

C730 AP205 30p multi 1.00 30

Marquez Type of 1982

1982, Dec. 10 ***Perf. 13½x14***

C731 A412 25p gray & bl 90 25
C732 A412 30p gray & brn 1.25 30

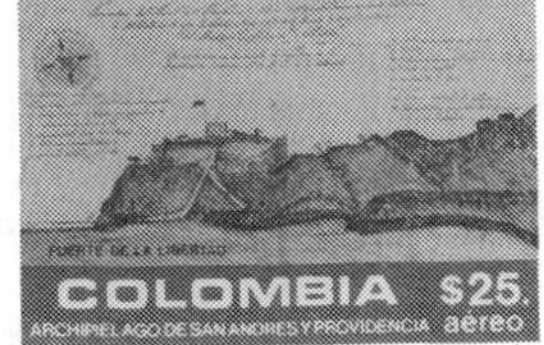

San Andres Archipelago—AP206

1983, Apr. 9 **Litho.** ***Perf. 12***

C733 AP206 25p Liberty Fort 70 15

Opening of Las Gaviotas (The Seagulls) Ecological Center, Bogota—AP207

1983, June 1 **Litho.**

C734 AP207 12p multi 40 15

50th Anniv. of Radio Amateurs League—AP208

1983, June 11 ***Perf. 14x13½***

C735 AP208 12p multi 45 15

Bolivar Type of 1983

1983, July 24 ***Perf. 12***

C736 A417 30p multi 90 30
C737 A417 100p multi 3.00 1.25

Botanical Exhibition Type of 1983

1983, Aug. 18 ***Perf. 14***

C738 A418 12p Begonia Guaduensis H.B.K. 35 15
C739 A418 12p Chinchona Ovaliflora 35 15
C740 A418 40p Begonia Urticae L.F. 1.25 35

Cartagena, 450th Anniv.—AP208a

1983, Sept. 9 **Litho.** ***Perf. 12***

C740A AP208a 12p Customs Square 35 15
C740B AP208a 35p Historic sites, Cartagena 1.00 45

Painting Type of 1983

1983, Oct. 5 **Litho.** ***Perf. 12***

C741 A420 30p multi 75 18

Scouting Year—AP209

1983, Oct. 24

C742 AP209 12p multi 30 8

Coffee beans—AP210

1984, Mar. 28 **Litho.** ***Perf. 14½x14***

C743 AP210 14p multi 30 10

Marandua City Type of 1984

1984, Sept. 28 ***Perf. 12***

C744 A427 30p multi 68 22

45th Congress of Americanists, Bogota, 1985—AP211

1984, Nov. 2

C745 AP211 45p multi 1.00 32

Christmas Type of 1984

1984, Dec. 14

C746 A428 14p multi 32 10

Contadora Group of Latin American Countries—AP212

Design: Dove, map and flags of Colombia, Mexico, Costa Rica and Venezuela.

1985, Feb. 15

C747 AP212 40p multi 68 32

Gomez Type of 1985

1985, Feb. 25

C748 A432 40p multi 68 32

Birds—AP213

1985

C749	AP213	14p Dryocopus lineatus nuperus	20	6
C750	AP213	20p Xiphorhynchus picus	78	10
C751	AP213	50p Eriocnemis cupreoventris	70	22
C752	AP213	55p Momotus momota	78	25

Issue dates: 14p, Apr. 12. 20p, 50p, Aug. 6. 55p, Aug. 29.

Almirante Padilla Naval School, 50th Anniv.—AP214

1985, July 15

C753 AP214 20p multi 28 10

1985 Census—AP215

1985, Oct. 15 ***Perf. 12***

C754 AP215 20p multi 28 10

Christmas Type of 1985

1985, Dec. 4 **Litho.** ***Perf. 13***

C755 A436 20p Girl, Christmas tree 28 10

Alfonso Lopez Pumarejo (1886-1959), President, 1934-38, 1942-45—AP216

1986, Jan. 31

C756 AP216 24p multi 30 10

Coffee Berries, Natl. Cycling Team—AP217

1986, Feb. 4

C757 AP217 60p multi 75 25

Natl. Coffee Producers Assoc. sponsorship of natl. cycling team, 25th anniv.

Fauna Type of 1985

1986, Feb. 18

C758 A433 50p Pudu mephistophiles 65 22

World Communications Day—AP218

1986, May 17 **Litho.** ***Perf. 13***

C759 AP218 50p multi 65 22

Intl. Peace Year—AP219

1986, June 13 **Litho.** ***Perf. 13***

C760 AP219 55p multi 65 22

Visit of Pope John Paul II—AP220

1986, July 1 **Litho.** ***Perf. 13***

C761	AP220	24p Portrait, papal arms	32	10
C762	AP220	55p Portrait, Medellin cathedral, horiz.	65	22
C763	AP220	60p Blessing crowd, horiz.	70	24

Souvenir Sheet

C764 AP220 200p Praying, Madonna of Bogota 1.40 1.40

Nos. C762-C763 each printed in sheets of 20 with se-tenant labels picturing religious symbols.

Enrique Santos Montejo (1886-1971), Journalist—AP221

1986, July 15 ***Perf. 12***

C765 AP221 25p multi 30 10

Bach, Handel and Schutz, Composers—AP222

1986, July 17 ***Perf. 13***

C766	AP222	70p Bach	82	28
C767	AP222	100p Text, music	1.15	38

Salesian Order Education in Colombia, Cent.—AP223

1986, July 23 ***Perf. 12***

C768 AP223 25p De La Salle, founder 30 10

Completion of Coal Mining Complex, El Cerrejon—AP224

1986, July 29 **Litho.** ***Perf. 12***

C769 AP224 55p multi 62 20

AP225

Natl. Constitution, Cent.—AP226

Designs: 25p, The Five Signators, by R. Vasquez, detail, and Bogota Cathedral. 200p, Pres. Nunez and Miguel Antonio Caro, Natl. Council of Delegates chairman, and Presidential Palace, constitution.

1986, Aug. 5 **Litho.** ***Perf. 14***

C770 AP225 25p multi 28 10

Souvenir Sheet

Perf. 12

C771 AP226 200p multi 2.25 75

No. C771 has multicolored margin continuing the design and showing black control number. Size: 120x80mm.

Poet Type of 1986

Design: Federico Garcia Lorca (1898-1936), poet, and birthplace, Fuentevaqueros, Granada, Spain.

1986, Sept. 26 **Litho.** ***Perf. 12***

C772 A445 60p multi 68 24

Gratitude for Intl. Aid after the Armero Mudslide Disaster—AP227

1986, Nov. 13

C773 AP227 50p multi 55 18

Christmas—AP228

Wood sculpture: Virgin Mestiza, Nerina.

1986, Dec. 19 **Litho.** ***Perf. 12***

C774 AP228 25p multi 28 10

The Apotheosis of Papayan, by Ephrain Martinez Zambrano (1898-1956)—AP229

1987, Jan. 13

C775	AP229	100p Papayan riding horse	1.10	35
C776	AP229	100p Onlookers	1.10	35

Nos. C775-C776 printed se-tenant in continuous design.

AIR POST SPECIAL DELIVERY STAMPS

Post Horn and Wings
APSD1

Lithographed

1958, May 19 ***Perf. 12*** **Unwmkd.**

CE1 APSD1 25c dk bl & red 60 20

Same Overprinted Vertically in Red

1959

CE2 APSD1 25c dk bl & red 50 20

Jet Plane and Envelope
APSD2

1963, Oct. 4 ***Perf. 14***

CE3 APSD2 50c red & blk 30 10

Aviation Type of Air Post Issue

History of Colombian Aviation: 80c, Boeing 727 jet, 1966.

Perf. 14x13½

1966, Dec. 14 Photo. **Unwmkd.**

CE4 AP96 80c crim & multi 45 20

AIR POST REGISTRATION STAMPS.

Issued by Sociedad Colombo-Alemana de Transportes Aereos (SCADTA)

No. C41 Overprinted in Red

1923 ***Perf. 14x14½*** **Wmk. 116**

CF1 AP6 20c gray 4.00 1.75

No. C58 Overprinted in Black

1929 ***Perf. 14*** **Wmk. 127**

CF2 AP8 20c carmine 5.50 1.75

Same Overprint on No. C71.

CF3 AP10 20c carmine 9.00 9.00

Colombian Government Issues.

Same Overprint on No. C86.

1932

CF4 AP8 20c carmine 10.00 8.00

No. C100 Overprinted

CF5 AP15 20c car & ol blk 6.25 2.00

SPECIAL DELIVERY STAMP.

Special Delivery Messenger
SD1

Engraved.

1917 ***Perf. 14.*** **Unwmkd.**

E1 SD1 5c gray grn 3.25 4.50

REGISTRATION STAMPS.

R1  R2

Lithographed.

1865 ***Imperf.*** **Unwmkd.**

F1 R1 5c black 100.00 57.50
F2 R2 5c black 85.00 55.00

R3 R4

1870 White Paper.

Vertical Lines in Background.

F3 R3 5c black 2.50 2.50
F4 R4 5c black 2.50 2.50

Horizontal Lines in Background.

F5 R3 5c black 5.00 5.00
F6 R4 5c black 2.50 2.50

Reprints of Nos. F3 to F6 show either crossed lines or traces of lines in background.

R5

1881 ***Imperf.***

F7 R5 10c violet 55.00 60.00
 a. Sewing machine perf. 62.50 67.50
 b. Perf. 11 67.50 70.00

R6

1883 ***Perf. 12, 13½***

F8 R6 10c red, *org* 2.00 2.50

R7

1889-95 ***Perf. 12, 13½***

F9 R7 10c red, *grysh* 7.50 3.50
F10 R7 10c red, *yelsh* 7.50 3.50
F11 R7 10c dp brn, *rose buff* ('95) 2.00 1.65
F12 R7 10c yel brn, *lt buff* ('92) 2.00 1.65

Nos. F9-F12 exist imperf. Prices same as for perf.

R9

1902 ***Imperf.***

F13 R9 20c red brn, *bl* 2.00 2.00
 a. Sewing machine perf. 5.25 5.25
 b. Perf. 12 5.25 5.25

Medellin Issue.

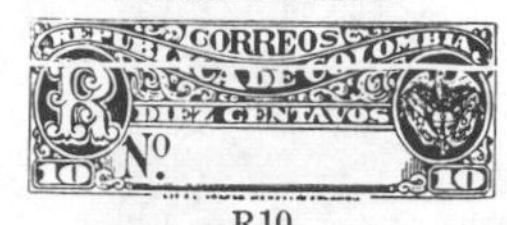

R10

1902 ***Perf. 12.***

Wove Paper.

F16 R10 10c blk vio 21.00 21.00
 a. Laid paper 17.50 17.50

Regular Issue.

1903 ***Imperf.***

F17 R9 20c bl, *bl* 1.90 1.90
 a. Sewing machine perf. 5.50 5.50
 b. Perf. 12 5.50 5.50

R11

1904 Pelure Paper. ***Imperf.***

F19 R11 10c purple 4.25 4.25
 a. Sewing machine perf. 4.25 4.25
 b. Perf. 12 5.75 5.75

R12

Wove Paper.

Imprint: "J. L. Arango".

1904 ***Perf. 12***

F20 R12 10c purple 3.00 75
 a. Imperf., pair 9.00 9.00

1909 ***Perf. 10, 14, 10x14, 14x10***

Imprint: "Lit. Nacional".

F21 R12 10c purple 3.25 1.00
 a. Imperf., pair 7.50 7.50

Execution at Cartagena in 1816
R13

1910, July 20 Engr. ***Perf. 12***

F22 R13 10c red & blk 25.00 90.00

Centenary of National Independence.

Pier at Puerto Colombia
R14

Tequendama Falls—R15

Perf. 11, 11½, 14, 11½x14

1917, Aug. 25

F23 R14 4c grn & ultra 75 3.50
 a. Center inverted 650.00 650.00
F24 R15 10c dp bl 2.75 90

R16

1925 Lithographed. ***Perf. 10x13½***

F25 R16 (10c) blue 3.50 2.25
 a. Imperf., pair 10.00 10.00
 b. Perf. 13½x10 5.50 5.50

ACKNOWLEDGMENT OF RECEIPT STAMPS.

AR1 AR2

Lithographed.

1893 ***Perf. 13½.*** **Unwmkd.**

H1 AR1 5c ver, *bl* 6.00 6.00

1894 ***Perf. 12.***

H2 AR1 5c vermilion 5.00 5.00

1902-03 ***Imperf.***

H3 AR2 10c bl, *bl* 4.00 4.00
 a. 10c bl, *grnsh bl* 4.00 4.00
 b. Sewing machine perf. 4.00 4.00
 c. Perf. 12 4.00 4.00

The handstamp "AR" in circle is believed to be a postmark.

AR3 AR4

1904 Pelure Paper ***Imperf.***

H12 AR3 5c pale bl 15.00 15.00
 a. Perf. 12 15.00 15.00

No. 307 Overprinted in Black, Green or Volet

H13 A86 5c carmine 25.00 25.00

1904 ***Perf. 12.***

H16 AR4 5c blue 4.75 4.00
 a. Imperf., pair 12.50 12.50

General José Acevedo y Gómez
AR5

1910, July 20 — *Engraved*

H17	AR5	5c org & grn	8.50	*22.50*

Centenary of National Independence.

Sabana Station AR6 — Map of Colombia AR7

1917 — ***Perf. 14.***

H18	AR6	4c bis brn	2.50	3.00
H19	AR7	5c org brn	2.10	2.50
a.		Imperf., pair	13.50	

LATE FEE STAMPS.

LF1 LF2

Lithographed.

1886 ***Perf. 10½.*** **Unwmkd.**

I1	LF1	2½c *lilac*	4.50	3.50
a.		Imperf., pair	15.00	15.00

1892 ***Perf. 12, 13½.***

I2	LF2	2½c dk bl, *rose*	4.00	3.00
a.		Imperf., pair	15.00	
I3	LF2	2½c ultra, *pink*	4.00	3.00

LF3 LF4

1902 ***Imperf.***

I4	LF3	5c pur, *rose*	1.25	1.25
a.		Perf. 12	2.50	2.50

1914 ***Perf. 10, 13½.***

I6	LF4	2c vio brn	6.00	4.25
I7	LF4	5c bl grn	6.00	4.25

Retardo — Refardo 1921

Overprints illustrated above are unauthorized and of private origin.

POSTAGE DUE STAMPS.

These are not, strictly speaking, postage due stamps but were issued to cover an additional fee, "Sobreporte", charged on mail to foreign countries with which Colombia had no postal conventions.

D1 D2 D3

Lithographed.

1866 ***Imperf.*** **Unwmkd.**

J1	D1	25c *blue*	50.00	50.00
J2	D2	50c *yellow*	50.00	50.00
J3	D3	1p *rose*	135.00	110.00

DEPARTMENT STAMPS.

These stamps are said to be for interior postage, to supersede the separate issues for the various departments.

Regular Issues Handstamped in Black, Violet, Blue or Green

Correos Departamentales
a

On Stamps of 1904.

1909 ***Perf. 12.*** **Unwmkd.**

L1	A94	½c yellow	3.00	3.00
a.		Imperf., pair	8.50	8.50
L2	A94	1c yel grn	3.00	3.00
L3	A94	2c red	3.75	3.75
a.		Imperf., pair	14.00	14.00
L4	A94	5c blue	4.75	4.75
L5	A94	10c violet	8.00	8.00
L6	A94	20c black	14.00	14.00
L7	A95	1p brown	24.00	24.00

On Stamp of 1902.

L8	A83	10p dk brn, *rose*	22.50	22.50
		Nos. L1-L8 (8)	83.00	83.00

On Stamps of 1908.

Perf. 10, 13, 13½ and Compound.

L9	A94	½c orange	3.00	3.00
a.		Imperf., pair	6.50	6.50
L10	A94	1c green	4.75	4.75
a.		Without imprint	5.50	5.50
L11	A94	2c red	4.75	4.75
a.		Imperf., pair		
L12	A94	5c blue	4.75	4.75
a.		Imperf., pair	10.00	10.00
L13	A94	10c violet	7.50	7.50

On Tolima Stamp of 1888.

Perf. 10½.

L14	A23	1p red brn	12.00	12.00
		Nos. L9-L14 (6)	36.75	36.75

Regular Issues Handstamped

b

On Stamps of 1904.

Perf. 12.

L15	A94	½c yellow	3.00	3.00
L16	A94	1c yel grn	3.00	3.00
L17	A94	2c red	4.75	4.75
L18	A94	5c blue	4.75	4.75
L19	A94	10c violet	7.50	7.50
L20	A94	20c black	13.00	13.00
L21	A94	1p brown	24.00	24.00
		Nos. L15-L21 (7)	60.00	60.00

On Stamps of 1908.

Perf. 10, 13, 13½.

L22	A94	½c orange	3.00	3.00
L23	A94	1c yel grn	9.00	9.00
L24	A94	2c red	4.50	4.50
a.		Imperf., pair	10.00	10.00
L25	A94	5c lt bl	4.50	4.50

The handstamps on Nos. L1 to L25 are, as usual, found inverted and double.

DEPARTMENT REGISTRATION STAMPS.

Registration Stamps Handstamped like Nos. L1 to L25.

On Registration Stamp of 1904.

1909 ***Perf. 12.*** **Unwmkd.**

LF1	R12(a)	10c purple	30.00	30.00
LF2	R12(b)	10c purple	30.00	30.00

On Registration Stamp of 1909.

Perf. 10, 13.

LF3	R12(a)	10c purple	30.00	30.00
LF4	R12(b)	10c purple	30.00	30.00

Nos. LF1–LF4 exist imperf. Price per pair, $20.

DEPARTMENT ACKNOWLEDGMENT OF RECEIPT STAMPS.

Acknowledgment of Receipt Stamp of 1904 Handstamped like Nos. L1 to L25.

1909 ***Perf. 12.*** **Unwmkd.**

LH1	AR4(a)	5c blue	30.00	30.00
a.		Imperf., pair	45.00	
LH2	AR4(b)	5c blue	30.00	30.00
a.		Imperf., pair	45.00	

Local Stamps for the City of Bogota.

(bō'gō-tä')

A1

Lithographed.

Pelure Paper.

1889 ***Perf. 12*** **Unwmkd.**

LX1	A1	½c black	1.25	1.25
a.		Imperf., pair	6.00	6.00

Impressions on bright blue and blue-gray paper were not regularly issued

A2 A3

White Wove Paper.

1896 ***Perf. 12, 13½***

LX2	A2	½c black	1.25	1.25

1903 ***Imperf.***

LX3	A3	10c *pink*	1.75	1.75
a.		Perf. 12	6.00	6.00

OFFICIAL STAMPS.

Stamps of 1917-1937 Overprinted in Black or Red:

OFICIAL *a* — OFICIAL *b*

Perf. 11, 12, 13½.

1937 **Unwmkd.**

O1	A131(a)	1c grn (Bk)	10	5
O2	A157(a)	10c dp org (Bk)	15	15
O3	A107(b)	30c ol bis (Bk)	2.50	1.40
O4	A129(b)	40c brn & yel brn (Bk)	1.50	1.10
O5	A114(b)	50c car (Bk)	1.40	70
O6	A115(b)	1p lt bl (Bk)	6.50	4.00
O7	A116(b)	2p org (Bk)	13.00	6.50
O8	A117(b)	5p gray (Bk)	55.00	35.00
O9	A118(b)	10p dk brn (Bk)	160.00	125.00

Wmkd. Wavy Lines. (229)

Perf. 12½.

O10	A132(a)	2c red (Bk)	15	15
O11	A133(a)	5c brn (Bk)	10	10
O12	A160(a)	12c dp bl (R)	1.40	60
O13	A136(b)	20c dk bl (R)	2.25	85
		Nos. O1-O13 (13)	244.05	175.60

Tall, wrong font "I's" in OFICIAL exist on all stamps with "a" overprint.

POSTAL TAX STAMPS.

"Greatest Mother"
PT1

Lithographed.

1935, May 27 ***Perf. 11½*** **Unwmkd.**

RA1	PT1	5c ol blk & scar	3.00	1.10

This stamp was required on all mail during Red Cross Week in 1935 (May 27–June 3) and in 1936.

Mother and Child
PT2

Perf. 10½, 10½x11.

1937, May 24 **Unwmkd.**

RA2	PT2	5c red	1.00	40

This stamp was required on all mail during Red Cross Week. The tax was for the Red Cross.

Ministry of Posts and Telegraphs Building
PT3 PT4

1939–45 **Litho.** ***Perf. 10½, 12½***

RA3	PT3	¼c dp bl	5	5
RA3A	PT3	¼c dk vio brn ('45)	8	5
RA4	PT3	½c pink	10	5
RA5	PT3	1c violet	55	15
RA5A	PT3	1c yel org ('45)	2.50	90
RA6	PT3	2c pck grn	50	20
RA7	PT3	20c lt brn	3.50	1.00
		Nos. RA3-RA7 (7)	7.28	2.40

These stamps were obligatory on all mail. The tax was for the construction of the new Communications Building.

The 25c of type PT3 and PT4 were not usable on postal matter.

See also No. 561.

Wmkd. Wavy Lines (229)

1940, Jan. 20 **Engr.** ***Perf. 12½x13***

RA8	PT4	¼c ultra	6	5
RA9	PT4	½c carmine	6	5
RA10	PT4	1c violet	6	5
RA11	PT4	2c bl grn	35	5
RA12	PT4	20c brown	1.40	35
		Nos. RA8-RA12 (5)	1.92	55

See note after No. RA7.

"Protection"
PT5

Wmkd.
Wavy Lines and C Multiple. (255)

1940, Apr. 25 ***Perf. 12***
RA13 PT5 5c rose car 30 15

See also No. RA17.

Postal Tax Stamps of 1939 Surcharged in Black — $ 0,0½ MEDIO CENTAVO

1943 ***Perf. 10½.*** **Unwmkd.**
RA14 PT3 ½c on 1c vio 5 5
a. Inverted surcharge 2.25
RA15 PT3 ½c on 2c pck grn 5 5
RA16 PT3 ½c on 20c lt brn 15 15

Types of 1940.
Imprint:
"Litografia Colombia Bogota S. A."

1944 **Lithographed.** ***Perf. 11.***
RA17 PT5 5c dk rose 45 22

Imprint:
"Lito-Colombia Bogota-Colombia"
RA18 PT4 ¼c ultra 8 6

Ministry of Posts and Telegraphs Building
PT6

Engraved.

1945-48 ***Perf. 12.*** **Wmk. 255**
RA19 PT6 ¼c ultra 5 5
RA20 PT6 ¼c sep ('46) 5 5
RA21 PT6 ½c car rose 5 5
RA22 PT6 ½c dp mag ('46) 5 5
RA23 PT6 1c vio ('46) 5 5
RA23A PT6 1c red org ('46) 5 5
RA24 PT6 2c grn ('46) 8 6
RA25 PT6 20c brn ('46) 1.25 30
a. 20c red brn ('48) 90 15
Nos. RA19-RA25 (8) 1.63 66

These stamps were obligatory on all mail. The surtax was for the construction of the new Communications Building. See also Nos. 603, RA33.

No. 469 Overprinted in Carmine

1946, May 25
RA26 A176 5c dl brn 50 22

The surtax was for the Red Cross.

Ministry of Posts and Telegraphs Building
PT7

Lithographed.

1946 ***Perf. 11*** **Unwmkd.**
RA27 PT7 3c blue 15 8

No. 490 Overprinted in Carmine — SOBRETASA
c

1947 ***Perf. 12*** **Wmk. 255**
RA28 A196 20c gray blk 2.00 1.40

Arms of Colombia and Red Cross
PT8 **PT9**

Engraved

1947, Sept. ***Perf. 12½*** **Unwmkd.**
RA29 PT8 5c car lake 22 15

The surtax of Nos. RA29 and RA40 was for the Red Cross. See also No. RA40.

No. 466 Overprinted Type "c" in Carmine.
RA30 A136 20c dk bl 6.00 4.50

Type of 1945.
Engraved.

1947 ***Perf. 12*** **Wmk. 255**
RA33 PT6 1c ol bis 6 5

Lithographed.
Black Surcharge.

1948 ***Perf. 11.*** **Unwmkd.**
RA36 PT9 1c on 5c lt brn 8 5
RA37 PT9 1c on 10c lt vio 8 5
RA38 PT9 1c on 25c red 8 5
RA39 PT9 1c on 50c ultra 8 5

Type of 1947.

1948 ***Perf. 10½***
RA40 PT8 5c vermilion 22 15

Ministry of Posts and Telegraphs Building **Mother and Child**
PT10 **PT11**

Engraved

1948-50 ***Perf. 12*** **Wmk. 255**
RA41 PT10 1c rose car ('49) 5 5
RA42 PT10 2c grn ('50) 8 5
RA43 PT10 3c blue 10 5
RA44 PT10 5c gray 10 6
RA45 PT10 10c purple 30 7
Nos. RA41-RA45 (5) 63 28

A 25c stamp of type PT10 was for use on telegrams, later for regular postage. See Nos. 602, 604.

Lithographed.

1950, May 25 ***Perf. 11*** **Unwmkd.**
Dark Blue Surcharge.
RA46 PT11 5c on 2c gray, red, blk & yel 1.10 45
a. "195" instead of "1950" 2.00 2.00
b. Top bar and "19" of "1950" omit. 2.00 2.00

Marginal perforations omitted, creating 26 straight-edged copies in each sheet of 44. Surtax for Red Cross.

No. 574 Overprinted in Black — SOBRETASA

1950, May 26 ***Perf. 12*** **Wmk. 255**
RA47 A176 5c blue 22 8
a. Inverted ovpt. 1.25

Telegraph Stamp Surcharged in Black.
RA48 A253a 8c on 50c org yel 15 8

Fiscal stamps of type A253a were available for postal use after May 9, 1952. See Nos. 605-608.

Arms and Cross **Bartolome de Las Casas Aiding Youth**
PT12 **PT13**

Engraved.

1951, May ***Perf. 12½*** **Unwmkd.**
RA49 PT12 5c red 30 10
RA50 PT13 5c carmine 30 10

The surtax was for the Red Cross.

No. RA43 Surcharged with New Value in Black.

1951 ***Perf. 12.*** **Wmk. 255**
RA51 PT10 1c on 3c bl 8 5

Type of 1951.
Engraved; Cross Lithographed.

1953 ***Perf. 12½.*** **Unwmkd.**
RA52 PT13 5c grn & car 30 10

The surtax of Nos. RA52-RA60 was for the Red Cross.

No. C254 Overprinted with Cross and Bar in Carmine.

1954
RA53 AP42 5c lil rose 90 55

St. Peter Claver Offering Gifts to Slaves
PT14

Engraved; Cross Typographed

1955, May 2 ***Perf. 13*** **Unwmkd.**
RA54 PT14 5c dp plum & red 30 10

Issued to commemorate the 300th anniversary of the death of St. Peter Claver.

Jean Henri Dunant and Santiago Samper Brush
PT15

Photogravure;
Red Cross and "Cruz Roja" Engraved.

1956, June 1 ***Perf. 13*** **Unwmkd.**
RA55 PT15 5c brn & red 30 10

Nurses and Ambulances
PT16

1958, June 2 **Photo.** ***Perf. 12***
RA56 PT16 5c gray & red 15 8

St. Louisa de Marillac and Church
PT17

Design: No. RA58, Henri Dunant and battle scene.

1960, Sept. 1 **Litho.** ***Perf. 11***
RA57 PT17 5c brn & rose 30 12
RA58 PT17 5c vio bl & rose 30 12

No. RA57 issued to commemorate the 3rd centenary of the Sisters of Charity. No. RA58 issued to commemorate the centenary (in 1959) of the Red Cross idea.

Manuelita de la Cruz **Red Cross Worker and Patient**
PT18 **PT19**

1961, Nov. 2 **Engraved** ***Perf. 13***
RA59 PT18 5c dl pur & red 22 8
RA60 PT18 5c brn & red 22 8

Issued in memory of Red Cross Nurse Manuelita de la Cruz, who died in the line of duty during the floods of 1955. Obligatory on domestic mail for a month.

1965, Apr. 30 **Photo.** ***Perf. 12***
RA61 PT19 5c bl gray & red 8 6

Obligatory on domestic mail during May.

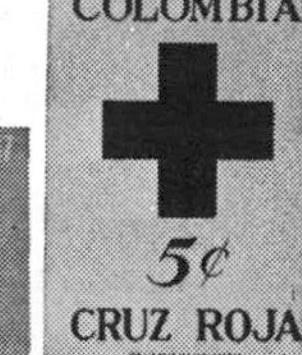

Nurse's Cap **Red Cross**
PT20 **PT21**

1967, June 1 **Litho.** ***Perf. 12***
RA62 PT20 5c brt bl & red 8 6

1969, July 1 **Litho.** ***Perf. 12x12½***
RA63 PT21 5c vio bl & red 8 6

Child Care
PT22

1970, July 1 **Litho.** ***Perf. 12½x12***
RA64 PT22 5c lt bl & red 5 5

Antioquia

(än'tē-ō'kyä)

Originally a State, now a Department of the Republic of Colombia. Until the revolution of 1885, the separate states making up the United States of Colombia were sovereign governments in their own right. On August 4, 1886, the National Council of Bogotá, composed of two delegates from each state, adopted a new constitution which abolished the sovereign rights of states, which then became departments with governors appointed by the President of the Republic. The nine original states represented at the Bogotá Convention retained some of their previous rights, as management of their own finances, and all issued postage stamps until as late as 1904. For Panama's issues, see Panama Nos. 1-30.

Coat of Arms

A1 A2

A3 A4

Lithographed.

Wove Paper.

1868 ***Imperf.*** **Unwmkd.**

1	A1	2½c blue	*600.00*	*400.00*
2	A2	5c green	*450.00*	*300.00*
3	A3	10c lilac	*1,350.*	*600.00*
4	A4	1p red	*350.00*	*275.00*

Reprints of Nos. 1, 3 and 4 are on a bluish white paper and all but No. 3 have scratches across the design.

A5 A6

A7 A8

A9 A10

1869

5	A5	2½c blue	3.00	3.00
6	A6	5c green	3.75	3.75
7	A7	5c green	3.75	3.75
8	A8	10c lilac	5.25	2.00
9	A9	20c brown	5.25	3.75
10	A10	1p rose red	10.00	10.00
a.		1p ver	22.50	22.50

Reprints of Nos. 7, 8 and 10 are on a bluish white paper; reprints of Nos. 5 and 10a on white paper. The 10c blue is believed to be a reprint.

A11

A12 A13

A14 A15

A16 A17

A18

1873

12	A11	1c yel grn	4.50	4.00
a.		1c grn	4.50	4.00
13	A12	5c green	5.25	4.00
14	A13	10c lilac	20.00	20.00
15	A14	20c yel brn	5.25	5.25
a.		20c dk brn	5.25	5.25
16	A15	50c blue	1.75	1.75
17	A16	1p vermilion	3.00	3.00
18	A17	2p *yellow*	7.50	7.50
19	A18	5p *rose*	67.50	60.00

A19 A20

Liberty Head

A21 A22

Pedro Justo Berrio

A23

1875–85

20	A19	1c *grn*, unglazed ('76)	1.50	1.50
a.		Glazed paper	2.25	2.25
b.		1c *lt grn*, laid paper ('85)	3.50	3.00
21	A19	1c blk ('76)	1.10	70
a.		Laid paper	125.00	100.00
22	A19	1c bl grn ('85)	2.25	2.25
23	A19	1c red lil, laid paper ('85)	2.25	2.25
24	A20	2½c blue	2.25	2.25
a.		Pelure paper ('78)	*1,850.*	*1,650.*
25	A21	5c green	15.00	14.00
a.		Laid paper	120.00	80.00
26	A22	5c green	15.00	14.00
a.		Laid paper	120.00	80.00
27	A23	10c lilac	22.50	21.00
a.		Laid paper	120.00	110.00
28	A20	10c vio, pelure paper ('78)	*525.00*	450.00

Arms Liberty

A24 A25

A26 A27

1878–85

29	A24	2½c bl, pelure paper	2.25	2.25
30	A24	2½c grn ('83)	2.25	2.25
a.		Laid paper ('83)	60.00	45.00
31	A24	2½c *buff* ('85)	4.50	4.50
32	A25	5c grn ('83)	2.25	2.25
a.		Pelure paper	24.00	21.00
b.		Laid paper ('82)	30.00	9.00
33	A25	5c vio ('83)	5.25	5.25
a.		5c bl vio ('83)	5.25	5.00
34	A26	10c vio, laid paper ('82)	110.00	45.00
35	A26	10c scar ('83)	2.25	2.25
a.		Tete beche pair	50.00	50.00
36	A27	20c brn ('83)	2.25	2.25
a.		Laid paper ('82)	4.50	4.50

A28 A29

Liberty

A30

1883–85

37	A28	5c brown	4.50	3.25
a.		Laid paper	135.00	75.00
38	A28	5c grn ('85)	90.00	45.00
a.		Laid paper ('85)	100.00	67.50
39	A28	5c yel, laid paper ('85)	4.50	4.50
40	A29	10c bl grn, laid paper	4.50	4.50
41	A29	10c bl, *bl* ('85)	4.50	4.50
42	A29	10c lil, laid paper ('85)	6.00	6.00
a.		Wove paper ('85)	90.00	45.00
43	A30	20c bl, laid paper ('85)	4.50	4.50

Coat of Arms

A31

1886 **Wove Paper.**

55	A31	1c grn, *pink*	65	65
56	A31	2½c *orange*	65	65
57	A31	5c ultra, *buff*	1.75	1.75
a.		5c bl, *buff*	3.00	3.00
58	A31	10c rose, *buff*	85	75
a.		Transfer of 50c in stone of 10c	72.50	72.50
59	A31	20c dk vio, *buff*	1.50	1.50
61	A31	50c yel brn, *buff*	2.75	2.75
62	A31	1p yel, *grn*	4.50	4.50
63	A31	2p grn, *vio*	4.50	4.50

1887-88

64	A31	1c red, *vio*	45	45
65	A31	2½c lil, *pale lil*	65	65
66	A31	5c car, *buff*	75	75
67	A31	5c red, *grn*	2.25	2.25
68	A31	10c brn, *grn*	65	65

Medellin Issue.

A32

A33 A34

1888 **Type-set.**

69	A32	2½c *yellow*	14.00	14.00
70	A33	5c *yellow*	4.50	4.50
71	A34	5c red, *yel*	4.50	4.50

Two varieties of No. 69, six of No. 70 and ten of No. 71.

A35

1889

72	A35	2½c red	4.50	4.50

Ten varieties including "eentavos".

Regular Issue.

Coat of Arms

A36 A37

A38

A39

A40

A41

1889–90 Litho. *Perf. 13½*

73	A36	1c *rose*	30	30
74	A36	2½c *blue*	30	30
75	A36	5c *yellow*	38	38
76	A36	10c *green*	38	38
78	A37	20c bl ('90)	1.50	1.50
79	A38	50c vio brn ('90)	3.00	3.00
a.		Transfer of 20c in stone of 50c	90.00	90.00
80	A38	50c grn ('90)	2.50	2.50
81	A39	1p red ('90)	2.25	2.25
82	A40	2p *mag* ('90)	13.00	13.00
83	A41	5p *org red* ('90)	18.50	18.50

Nos. 73–76, 82–83 exist imperf.

The so-called "errors" of Nos. 73 to 76, printed on paper of wrong colors, are essays or, possibly, reprints. They exist perforated and imperforate.

See also No. 96.

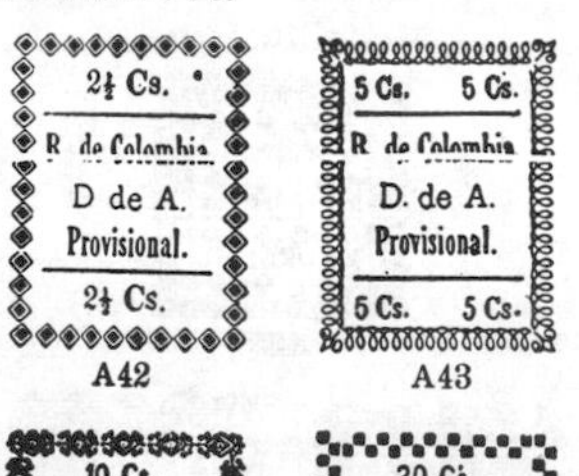

A42 A43

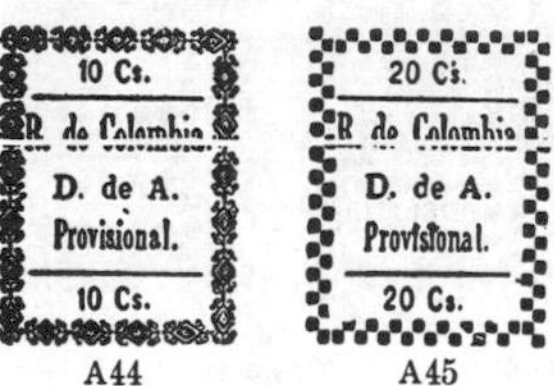

A44 A45

1890 Type-set. *Perf. 14.*

84	A42	2½c *buff*	1.75	1.75
85	A43	5c *orange*	1.75	1.75
86	A44	10c *buff*	6.00	6.00
87	A44	10c *rose*	6.75	6.75
88	A45	20c *orange*	6.75	6.75

Twenty varieties of the 5c, ten of each of the other values.

A46

A47

1892 Lithographed *Perf. 13½*

89	A46	1c brn, *brnsh*	45	45
90	A46	2½c pur, *lil*	45	45
92	A46	5c *gray*	90	90
a.		Transfer of 2½c in stone of 5c	150.00	

1893

93	A46	1c blue	30	30
94	A46	2½c green	45	45
95	A46	5c vermilion	30	30
96	A36	10c pale brn	30	30

1896 *Perf. 14*

97	A47	2c gray	30	30
98	A47	2c lil rose	30	30
99	A47	2½c brown	30	30
100	A47	2½c stl bl	30	30
101	A47	3c orange	30	30
102	A47	3c ol grn	30	30
103	A47	5c green	30	30
104	A47	5c yel buff	30	30
105	A47	10c brn vio	60	60
106	A47	10c violet	60	60
107	A47	20c brn org	60	60
108	A47	20c blue	1.00	1.00
109	A47	50c gray brn	1.00	1.00
110	A47	50c rose	1.40	1.40
111	A47	1p bl & blk	18.50	18.50
112	A47	1p rose red & blk	18.50	18.50
113	A47	2p org & blk	60.00	60.00
114	A47	2p dk grn & blk	60.00	60.00
115	A47	5p red vio & blk	90.00	90.00
116	A47	5p pur & blk	90.00	90.00

Nos. 115–116 with centers omitted are proofs.

General José María Córdoba

A48

1899 *Perf. 11.*

117	A48	½c grnsh bl	7	12
118	A48	1c sl bl	7	12
119	A48	2c sl brn	7	12
120	A48	3c red	7	12
121	A48	4c bis brn	7	12
122	A48	5c green	7	12
123	A48	10c scarlet	7	12
124	A48	20c gray vio	7	12
125	A48	50c ol bis	7	12
126	A48	1p grnsh blk	7	12
127	A48	2p ol gray	7	12
		Nos. 117-127 (11)	77	1.32

Numerous part-perf. and imperf. varieties of Nos. 117-127 exist.

A49

A50 A50a

1901 Type-set *Perf. 12*

128	A49	1c red	30	30
129	A50	1c ultra	75	75
130	A50	1c bister	75	75
130A	A50a	1c dl red	75	75
130B	A50a	1c ultra	6.00	6.00

Eight varieties of No. 128, four varieties of Nos. 129–130B.

A51

A52

Atanasio Girardot

A53

Dr. José Félix Restrepo

A54

1902 Lithographed Wove Paper

131	A51	1c brt rose	22	15
a.		Laid paper	75	75
b.		Imperf., pair	3.00	
132	A51	2c blue	15	15
a.		Transfer of 3c in stone of 2c	6.25	6.25
133	A51	3c green	15	15
a.		Imperf., pair	3.50	
134	A51	4c dl vio	15	15
135	A52	5c rose red	22	22
136	A53	10c rose lil	15	15
a.		Small head	6.25	6.25
b.		10c rose	15	15
137	A53	20c gray grn	22	22
138	A53	30c brt rose	22	22
139	A53	40c blue	22	22
140	A53	50c brn, *yel*	22	22

Laid Paper.

141	A54	1p pur & blk	90	90
142	A54	2p rose & blk	90	90
143	A54	5p sl bl & blk	1.50	1.50
		Nos. 131-143 (13)	5.22	5.15

1903 Wove Paper.

143A	A51	1c blue	15	15
144	A51	2c violet	15	15
a.		Imperf.	3.00	

A55

A56

Francisco Antonio Zea A57 — Custodio García Rovira A58 — La Pola (Policarpa Salavarrieta) A59

J. M. Restrepo

A60

José Fernández Madrid

A61

Juan del Corral

A62

1903–04

145	A55	4c yel brn	22	22
146	A55	5c blue	22	22
147	A56	10c yellow	22	22
148	A56	20c purple	22	22
149	A56	30c brown	75	75
150	A56	40c green	75	75
151	A56	50c rose	22	22
152	A57	1p ol gray	75	75
153	A58	2p purple	75	75
154	A59	3p dk bl	75	75
155	A60	4p dl red	1.10	1.10
156	A61	5p red brn	1.10	1.10
157	A62	10p scarlet	4.50	4.50
		Nos. 145-157 (13)	11.55	11.55

Nos. 145–146, 151, 153–157 exist imperf. Price by pair, $3 to $4.

Manizales Issue.

Stamps of these designs are local private post issues.

OFFICIAL STAMPS.

Stamps of 1903–04 with overprint "OFICIAL" were never issued.

REGISTRATION STAMPS.

R1

Lithographed.

1896 *Perf. 14* Unwmkd.

F1	R1	2½c rose	1.40	1.40
F2	R1	2½c dl bl	1.40	1.40

Córdoba

R2

R3

1899 *Perf. 11*

F3	R2	2½c dl bl	30	30
F4	R3	10c red lil	30	30

R4

1902 *Perf. 12*

F5	R4	10c pur, *bl*	38	38
a.		Imperf.		

ACKNOWLEDGMENT OF RECEIPT STAMPS.

AR1

Lithographed.

1902–03 *Perf. 12* Unwmkd.

H1	AR1	5c *rose*	1.10	1.10
H2	AR1	5c sl ('03)	38	38

AR2

Purple Handstamp.

1903 *Imperf.*

H3 AR2 10c *pink* 21.00 21.00

LATE FEE STAMPS.

Córdoba
LF1

Lithographed.

1899 *Perf. 11* Unwmkd.

11 LF1 2½c dk grn 30 30
a. Imperf., pair 3.50

LF2 LF3

1901 Type-set. *Perf. 12.*

12 LF2 2½c red vio 65 65
a. 2½c pur 65 65

1902 Lithographed

13 LF3 2½c violet 22 22

City of Medellin

(mä'thē·yĕn')

Stamps of the designs shown were not issued by any governmental agency but by the Sociedad de Mejoras Publicas.

Bolivar

(bô·lē'vär)

Originally a State, now a Department of the Republic of Colombia. (See Antioquia.)

A1

Lithographed.

1863–66 *Imperf.* Unwmkd.

1 A1 10c green *850.00* *500.00*
a. Five stars below shield *1,850.* *1,500.*
2 A1 10c red ('66) 30.00 30.00
a. Diagonal half used as 5c on cover 55.00
b. Five stars below shield 75.00 75.00
3 A1 1p red 10.00 10.00

Fourteen varieties of each. Counterfeits of Nos. 1 and 1a exist.

Coat of Arms
A2 A3

A4 A5

1873

4 A2 5c blue 6.75 6.75
5 A3 10c violet 6.75 6.75
6 A4 20c yel grn 27.50 27.50
7 A5 80c vermilion 60.00 60.00

A6

A7 A8

1874–78

8 A6 5c blue 25.00 25.00
9 A7 5c bl ('78) 7.50 7.50
10 A8 10c vio ('77) 3.75 3.75

Simón Bolívar
A9

Dated "1879".
White Wove Paper.

1879 *Perf. 12½*

11 A9 5c blue 30 30
a. Imperf., pair 1.00
12 A9 10c violet 22 22
13 A9 20c red 30 30
a. 20c grn (error) 12.50 12.50

Bluish Laid Paper.

15 A9 5c blue 30 30
a. Imperf., pair 2.50
16 A9 10c violet 2.00 2.00
a. Imperf., pair 5.00
17 A9 20c red 40 40
a. Imperf., pair 2.25

Stamps of 80c and 1p on white wove paper and 1p on bluish laid paper were prepared but not placed in use.

Dated "1880".
White Wove Paper

1880 *Perf. 12½*

19 A9 5c blue 30 30
a. Imperf., pair 2.00
20 A9 10c violet 40 40
a. Imperf., pair 2.00
21 A9 20c red 40 40
a. 20c grn (error) 16.00 16.00
23 A9 80c green 2.75 2.75
24 A9 1p orange 2.75 2.75
a. Imperf., pair 7.00

Bluish Laid Paper.

25 A9 5c blue 30 30
a. Imperf., pair 1.50
26 A9 10c violet 2.75 2.75
27 A9 20c red 40 40
a. Imperf., pair 3.50
28 A9 1p orange 500.00
a. Imperf. *600.00*

A11 A12

A13 A15

A16

Dated "1882".
White Wove Paper.

1882 *Perf. 12, 16x12*

29 A11 5c blue 40 40
30 A12 10c lilac 30 30
31 A13 20c red 40 40
33 A15 80c green 80 80
34 A16 1p orange 80 80

Nos. 29, 30 and 34 are known imperforate. They are printer's waste and were not issued through post offices.

Bolívar Bolívar
A17 A18

1882 Engraved *Perf. 12*

35 A17 5p bl & rose red 75 75
a. Imperf., pair 6.00
b. Perf. 16 7.50 7.50
c. Perf. 14 7.50 7.50
36 A17 10p brn & bl 2.00 2.00
a. Imperf., pair 10.00
b. Perf. 16 6.75 6.75
c. Rouletted 10.00 10.00

Dated "1883".

1883 Litho. *Perf. 12, 16x12*

37 A11 5c blue 22 22
a. Imperf., pair 1.00
b. Perf. 12 2.75 1.25
38 A12 10c lilac 30 30
39 A13 20c red 30 30
41 A15 80c green 40 40
42 A16 1p orange 75 75
a. Perf. 16x12 2.50 2.50

1884 Dated "1884"

43 A11 5c blue 40 40
a. Perf. 12 11.50 11.50
44 A12 10c lilac 22 22
45 A13 20c red 22 22
a. Perf. 12 5.25 5.25
47 A15 80c green 30 30
a. Perf. 12 2.50 2.50
48 A16 1p orange 40 40

1885 Dated "1885"

49 A11 5c blue 18 18
50 A12 10c lilac 18 18
51 A13 20c red 18 18
53 A15 80c green 30 30
54 A16 1p orange 40 40

The note after No. 34 will also apply to imperforate stamps of the 1884-85 issues.

1891 *Perf. 14.*

55 A18 1c black 10 10
56 A18 5c orange 40 40
a. Imperf., pair 1.00
57 A18 10c carmine 40 40
58 A18 20c blue 75 75
59 A18 50c green 1.10 1.10
60 A18 1p purple 1.10 1.10
Nos. 55-60 (6) 4.15 4.15

Overprinted with 7 Parallel Wavy Lines in Purple

1899

61 A18 1c black 55.00 55.00

The overprint is a control mark.

Bolívar José Fernández Madrid
A19 A20

Manuel Rodriguez Torices José María García de Toledo
A21 A22

1903 Laid Paper *Imperf.*

62 A19 50c dk bl, *pink* 75 75
a. bluish paper 75 75
63 A19 50c sl grn, *pink* 75 75
a. rose paper 1.10 1.10
b. grnsh bl paper 2.25 2.25
c. yel paper 2.75 2.75
d. brn paper 2.75 2.75
e. sal paper 6.00 6.00
64 A19 50c pur, *pink* 1.10 1.10
a. white paper 2.50 2.50
b. brn paper 2.50 2.50
c. grnsh bl paper 2.50 2.50
d. lil paper 2.50 2.50
e. rose paper 2.25 2.25
f. yel paper 2.50 2.50
g. sal paper 4.50 4.50
h. As "a," wove paper 8.50 8.50
65 A20 1p org, *sal* 75 75
a. yel paper 4.50 4.50
b. grnsh bl paper 15.00 15.00
66 A20 1p gray grn, *lil* 1.75 1.75
a. yel paper 6.75 6.75
b. sal paper 7.50 7.50
c. grn paper 7.50 7.50
d. white wove paper 10.00
67 A21 5p car rose, *lil* 75 75
a. brn paper 75 75
b. yel paper 1.40 1.40
c. grnsh bl paper 4.50 4.50
d. bluish paper 6.00 6.00
e. sal paper 7.50 7.50
f. rose paper 9.00 9.00
68 A22 10p dk bl, *bluish* 1.50 1.50
a. grnsh bl paper 1.50 1.50
b. rose paper 7.50 7.50
c. sal paper 7.50 7.50
d. yel paper 7.50 7.50
e. brn paper 9.00 9.00
f. lil paper 10.00 10.00
g. white paper 9.00 9.00

69 A22 10p pur, *grnsh bl* 4.50 4.50
a. bluish paper 7.50 7.50
b. rose paper 6.75 6.75
c. yel paper 7.50 7.50
d. brn paper 7.50 7.50

Sewing Machine Perf.

Laid Paper

70 A19 50c dk bl, *pink* 75 75
a. bluish paper 75 75
71 A19 50c sl grn, *pink* 1.75 1.75
72 A19 50c pur, *grnsh bl* 2.50 2.50
a. white paper 2.50 2.50
b. white wove paper 7.50
73 A20 1p org, *sal* 1.75 1.75
74 A20 1p gray grn, *lil* 9.00 9.00
a. yel paper 9.00 9.00
75 A21 5p car rose, *lil* 2.50 2.50
a. yel paper 1.75 1.75
b. brn paper 2.50 2.50
c. bluish paper 5.25 5.25
d. white wove paper 9.00
76 A22 10p dk bl, *bluish* 6.75 6.75
a. grnsh bl paper 4.50 4.50
b. yel paper 9.00 9.00
c. As "b," wove paper 10.00
77 A22 10p pur, *grnsh bl* 6.75 6.75
a. bluish paper 11.00 11.00
b. rose paper 8.25 8.25
c. yel paper 11.00 11.00

José María del Castillo y Rada
A23

Manuel Anguiano
A24

Pantaleón C. Ribón
A25

1904 ***Sewing Machine Perf.***

89 A23 5c black 30 30
a. Imperf., pair 4.25 4.25
90 A24 10c brown 30 30
a. Imperf., pair 3.50 3.50
91 A25 20c red 38 38
a. Imperf., pair 8.00 8.00
92 A25 20c red brn 75 75
a. Imperf., pair 8.00 8.00

A26

A28

A27

1904 ***Imperf.***

93 A26 ½c black 75 75
a. Tête bêche pair 4.50 4.50
94 A27 1c blue 1.40 1.40
95 A28 2c purple 1.50 1.50

REGISTRATION STAMPS.

Simón Bolívar
R1 R2

Lithographed.

White Wove Paper.

1879 ***Perf. 12½, 16x12.*** **Unwmkd.**

F1 R1 40c brown 90 90

Bluish Laid Paper.

F2 R1 40c brown 90 90
a. Imperf., pair 4.00

Dated "1880".

1880 **White Wove Paper.**

F3 R1 40c brown 40 40

Bluish Laid Paper.

F4 R1 40c brown 80 80
a. Imperf., pair 4.50

Dated "1882" to "1885".

White Wove Paper.

1882-85 ***Perf. 16x12***

F5 R2 40c brn (1882) 40 40
a. Perf. 12 22.50
F6 R2 40c brn (1883) 30 30
a. Perf. 12 11.50
F7 R2 40c brn (1884) 30 30
a. Perf. 12 12.00
F8 R2 40c brn (1885) 40 40
a. Perf. 12 3.00

R3

Laid Paper.

1903 ***Imperf.***

F9 R3 20c org, *rose* 75 75
a. sal paper 1.40 1.40
b. grnsh bl paper 4.50 4.50

Sewing Machine Perf.

F10 R3 20c org, *rose* 1.50 1.50
a. sal paper 1.50 1.50
b. grnsh bl paper 4.50 4.50

R4

1904 **Wove Paper**

F11 R4 5c black 4.00 4.00

ACKNOWLEDGMENT OF RECEIPT STAMPS.

AR1

Lithographed

1903 ***Imperf.*** **Unwmkd.**

Laid Paper

H1 AR1 20c org, *rose* 1.50 1.50
a. yel paper 1.50 1.50
b. grnsh bl paper 3.75 3.75
H2 AR1 20c dk bl, *yel* 1.75 1.75
a. brn paper 1.75 1.75
b. rose paper 2.00 2.00
c. sal paper 4.75 4.75
d. grnsh bl paper 4.50 4.50

Sewing Machine Perf.

H3 AR1 20c org, *grnsh bl* 7.50 7.50
a. yel paper 9.00 9.00
H4 AR1 20c dk bl, *yel* 9.00 9.00
a. lil paper 9.00

AR2

1904 **Wove Paper.**

H5 AR2 2c red 1.40 1.40

LATE FEE STAMPS.

LF1

Lithographed

1903 ***Imperf.*** **Unwmkd.**

Laid Paper.

I1 LF1 20c car rose, *bluish* 75 75
I2 LF1 20c pur, *bluish* 70 70
a. rose paper 1.50 1.50
b. brn paper 1.50 1.50
c. lil paper 1.75 1.75
d. yel paper 7.50 7.50

Sewing Machine Perf.

I3 LF1 20c car rose, *bluish* 75 75
I4 LF1 20c pur, *bluish* 75 75
a. rose paper 1.50 1.50
b. lil paper 1.75 1.75
c. yel paper 7.50 7.50

Boyaca

(bō′yä·kä′)

Originally a State, now a Department of the Republic of Colombia. (See Antioquia.)

Diego Mendoza Pérez
A1

Lithographed.

1902 ***Perf. 13½*** **Unwmkd.**

Wove Paper.

1 A1 5c bl grn 90 90
a. bluish paper 90.00 90.00
b. Imperf., pair 13.50

Laid Paper.

Perf. 12

2 A1 5c green 100.00 100.00

Coat of Arms
A2 A3

General Próspero Pinzón
A4

Numeral of Value
A5

Monument of Battle of Boyacá
A6

President José Manuel Marroquin
A7

1903 **Lithographed.** ***Imperf.***

4 A2 10c dk gray 30 30
5 A3 20c red brn 40 40
6 A5 1p red 3.75 3.75
a. 1p cl 4.50 4.50
8 A6 5p *rose* 1.40 1.40
a. 5p *buff* 12.00 12.00
9 A7 10p *buff* 1.40 1.40
a. 10p *rose* 12.00 12.00
b. Tête bêche pair 18.50
Nos. 4-9 (5) 7.25 7.25

Perf. 12.

10 A2 10c dk gray 30 30
11 A3 20c red brn 45 45
12 A4 50c green 40 40
13 A4 50c dl bl 2.00 2.00
14 A5 1p red 40 40
a. 1p cl 3.75 3.75
16 A6 5p *rose* 1.40 1.40
a. 5p *buff* 12.00 12.00
17 A7 10p *buff* 1.40 1.40
a. 10p *rose* 12.00 12.00
b. Tête bêche pair 15.00 15.00
Nos. 10-17 (7) 6.35 6.35

Statue of Bolívar
A8

1904

18 A8 10c orange 30 30
a. Imperf., pair 4.50 4.50

Cauca

(kou′kä)

Originally a State, now a Department of the Republic of Colombia. (See Antioquia.)

A1

A2

Handstamped.

1879 (?) ***Imperf.*** **Unwmkd.**

1 A1 (5c) black *4,000.* *3,500.*

1882

2 A2 5c violet 80.00 80.00
a. Figure in lower left corner omitted

A3

A4

1883

3 A3 (5) violet 25.00 25.00
4 A4 (5) violet 60.00 60.00

A5 A7

1890

5	A5	5c red	75.00	75.00

Nos. 1 to 5 were sanctioned, though not authorized, by the national government.

Imperf., Sewing Machine Perf.

1902 **Typeset**

8	A7	10c *rose*	2.25	2.25
9	A7	20c *orange*	1.50	1.50

Stamps of this design are believed to be of private origin and without official sanction.

Items inscribed "No hay estampillas" (No stamps available) and others inscribed "Manuel E. Jiménez" are considered by specialists to be receipt labels, not postage stamps.

Cundinamarca

(kōōn'dē·nä·mär'kä)

Originally a State, now a Department of the Republic of Colombia. (See Antioquia.)

Coat of Arms

A1 A2

Lithographed

1870 ***Imperf.*** **Unwmkd.**

1	A1	5c blue	4.75	4.75
2	A2	10c red	15.00	15.00

The counterfeits, or reprints, show traces of the cuts made to deface the dies.

A3

A4

A5

A6

1877-82

3	A3	10c red ('82)	3.00	3.00
a.		Laid paper ('77)	4.50	4.50
4	A4	20c grn ('82)	6.75	6.75
a.		Laid paper ('77)	7.50	7.50
7	A5	50c pur ('82)	7.50	7.50
8	A6	1p brn ('82)	11.00	11.00

A7

1884

10	A7	5c blue	75	75
11	A7	5c bl (redrawn)	1.50	1.50
a.		Tête bêche pair	75.00	75.00

The redrawn stamp has no period after "COLOMBIA."

A8

A9

A10

A11

1883 **Typeset**

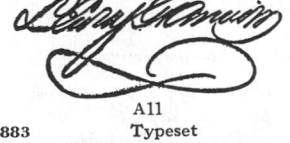

13	A8	10c *yellow*	11.00	11.00
14	A9	50c *rose*	11.00	11.00
15	A10	1p *brown*	30.00	30.00
16	A11	2r *green*	*1,600.*	

Typeset varieties exist: 4 of the 10c, 2 each of 50c and 1p.

Some experts doubt that No. 16 was issued. The variety without signature and watermarked "flowers" is believed to be a proof. Forgeries exist.

A12

1886 **Lithographed.**

17	A12	5c blue	75	75
18	A12	10c red	4.50	4.50
19	A12	10c red, *lil*	2.40	2.40
20	A12	20c green	3.75	3.75
a.		20c yel grn	4.50	4.50
21	A12	50c purple	4.50	4.50
22	A12	1p org brn	5.25	5.25

Nos. 17 to 22 have been reprinted. The colors are aniline and differ from those of the original stamps. The impression is coarse and blurred.

A13

A14

A15

A16

Arms

A17

A18

A19

A20

A21

1904 ***Perf. 10½, 12***

23	A13	1c orange	30	30
24	A14	2c gray bl	30	30
25	A15	3c rose	45	45
26	A15	5c ol grn	45	45
27	A16	10c pale brn	45	45
28	A17	15c pink	45	45
29	A18	20c bl, *grn*	45	45
30	A18	20c blue	75	75
31	A19	40c blue	75	75
32	A19	40c bl, *buff*	17.50	17.50
33	A20	50c red vio	75	75
34	A21	1p gray grn	60	60
		Nos. 23-34 (12)	23.20	23.20

Imperf.

23a	A13	1c orange	90	90
24a	A14	2c blue	90	90
b.		2c sl	6.00	6.00
25a	A15	3c rose	90	90
26a	A15	5c ol grn	1.50	1.50
27a	A16	10c pale brn	2.50	2.50
28a	A17	15c pink	45	45
29a	A18	20c bl, *grn*	2.25	2.25
30a	A18	20c blue	2.25	2.25
31a	A19	40c blue	75	75
32a	A19	40c bl, *buff*	17.50	17.50
33a	A20	50c red vio	75	75
34a	A21	1p gray grn	75	75
		Nos. 23a-34a (12)	31.40	31.40

REGISTRATION STAMPS.

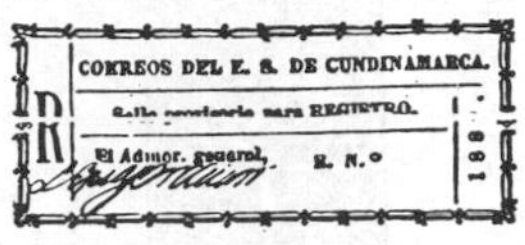

R1

1883 ***Imperf.*** **Unwmkd.**

F1	R1	*orange*	15.00	16.50

R2

1904 ***Perf. 12.***

F2	R2	10c bister	1.00	1.00
a.		Imperf.	4.25	4.25

Magdalena

Items inscribed "No hay estampillas" (No stamps available) are considered by specialists to be not postage stamps but receipt labels.

Panama.

Issues of Panama as a state and later Department of Colombia are listed with the Republic of Panama issues (Nos. 1-30).

Santander

(sän'tän·dâr')

Originally a State, now a Department of the Republic of Colombia. (See Antioquia.)

Coat of Arms

A1 A2

Lithographed.

1884 ***Imperf.*** **Unwmkd.**

1	A1	1c blue	30	30
a.		1c gray bl	50	50
2	A2	5c red	50	50
3	A2	10c bluish pur	1.75	1.75
a.		Tête bêche pair		

No. 2 exists unofficially perforated 14.

A3

A4

1886 ***Imperf.***

4	A3	1c blue	90	90
5	A3	5c red	30	30
6	A3	10c red vio	50	50
a.		10c dp vio	50	50
b.		Inscribed "CINCO CENTAVOS"	25.00	25.00

The numerals in the upper corners are omitted on No. 5, while on No. 6 there are no numerals in the side panels. No. 6 exists unofficially perforated 12.

1887

7	A4	1c blue	22	22
a.		1c ultra	1.50	1.50
8	A4	5c red	1.50	1.50
9	A4	10c violet	3.75	3.75

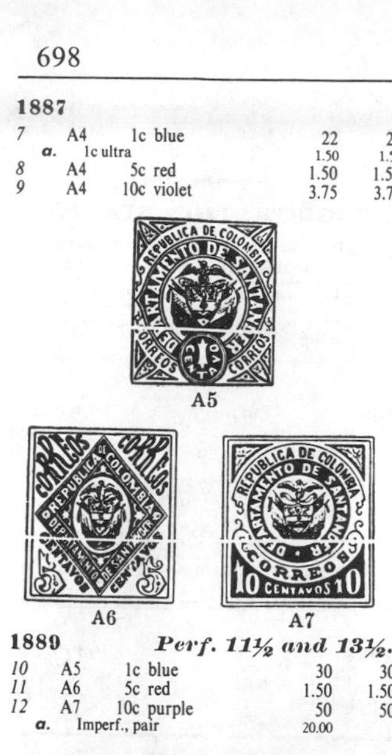

A5

A6 A7

1889 ***Perf. 11½ and 13½.***

10	A5	1c blue	30	30
11	A6	5c red	1.50	1.50
12	A7	10c purple	50	50
a.		Imperf., pair	20.00	

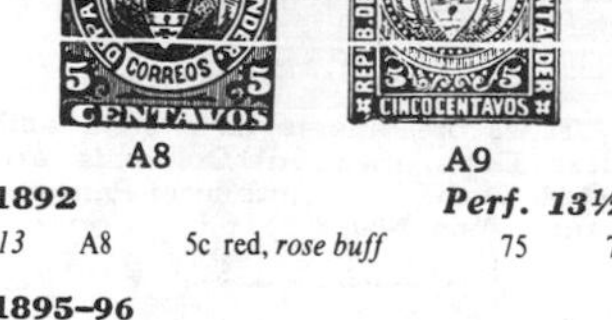

A8 A9

1892 ***Perf. 13½***

13	A8	5c red, *rose buff*	75	75

1895-96

14	A9	5c brown	90	90
15	A9	5c yel grn ('96)	90	90

A10 A11

A12

1899 ***Perf. 10***

16	A10	1c *green*	40	40
17	A11	5c *pink*	40	40

Perf. 13½.

18	A12	10c blue	90	90
a.		Perf. 12	1.25	1.25

A13

1903 ***Imperf.***

19	A13	50c red	65	65
a.		50c rose	65	65
b.		"SANTENDER"	3.00	3.00
c.		"Corrcos"	3.00	3.00
d.		"Corceos"	3.00	3.00
e.		Tête bêche pair	6.00	6.00
f.		Pair, one without overprint	3.50	3.50

The overprint "Correos de Departmento Bucaramanga" on the 50c red revenue stamp has been proved to be a cancellation.

A14 A15

Arms A16 Locomotive A17

A18 A19

A20

1904 ***Imperf.***

22	A14	5c dk grn	30	30
a.		5c yel grn	50	50
24	A15	10c rose	15	15
25	A16	20c brn vio	15	15
26	A17	50c yellow	20	20
27	A18	1p black	20	20
28	A19	5p dk bl	40	40
29	A20	10p carmine	50	50
		Nos. 22-29 (7)	1.90	1.90

1905

30	A14	5c pale bl	50	50
31	A15	10c red brn	50	50
32	A16	20c yel grn	50	50
33	A17	50c red vio	50	50
34	A18	1p dk bl	50	50
35	A19	5p pink	50	50
36	A20	10p red	2.00	2.00
		Nos. 30-36 (7)	5.00	5.00

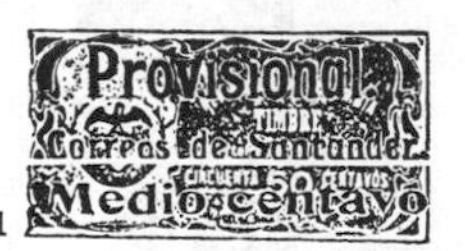

A21

1907 ***Imperf.***

37	A21	½c on 50c rose	65	65

City of Cucuta

(kōō'kōō-tä)

A71 A72

Lithographed.

"Gobierno Provisorio" at Top

1900 ***Perf. 12 Vertically.***

101	A71	1c (ctvo) *bl grn*	4.50	4.50
a.		"cvo."	11.50	11.50
b.		"cvos."	4.50	4.50
c.		"centavo"	5.25	5.25
103	A71	2c black	3.00	3.00
104	A71	5c *pink*	3.00	3.00
a.		Name at side (V)	6.50	6.50
105	A71	10c *pink*	3.00	3.00
a.		Name at side (V)	6.50	6.50
106	A71	20c *yellow*	4.50	4.50
a.		Name at side (G)	9.00	9.00
		Nos. 101-106 (5)	18.00	18.00

"Gobierno Provisional" at Top Name at Side in Black or Green

108	A72	1c (ctvo.) *bl grn* (Bk)	4.50	4.50
a.		"centavo"	17.50	17.50
109	A72	2c *bl grn* (Bk)	2.50	2.50
110	A72	5c blk (G)	2.50	2.50
a.		"ctvos." smaller	5.00	5.00
112	A72	10c *pink* (Bk)	2.50	2.50
113	A72	20c *yel* (G)	4.50	4.50
		Nos. 108-113 (5)	16.50	16.50

Stamps of these and similar designs on white and yellow paper, with and without surcharges of ½c, 1c or 2c, are believed to have been produced without government authorization.

Tolima

(tō-lē'mä)

Originally a State, now a Department of the Republic of Colombia. (See Antioquia.)

A1

Typeset.

1870 ***Imperf.*** **Unwmkd.**

White Wove Paper.

1	A1	5c black	60.00	32.50
2	A1	10c black	60.00	32.50

Printed from two settings. Setting I, ten types of 5c. Setting II, six types of 5c and four types of 10c.

Blue Laid Batonné Paper.

3	A1	5c black	*750.00*	

Buff Laid Batonné Paper.

4	A1	5c black	120.00	80.00

Blue Wove Paper

5	A1	5c black	67.50	45.00

Blue Vertically Laid Paper.

6	A1	5c black	100.00	70.00
a.		Paper with ruled blue vertical lines		

Blue Horizontally Laid Paper

7	A1	5c black	100.00	70.00

Blue Quadrille Paper.

8	A1	5c black	100.00	90.00

Ten varieties each of Nos. 3-5 and 7; 20 varieties each of Nos. 6 and 8.

Official imitations were made in 1886 from new settings of the type. There are only two varieties of each value. They are printed on blue and white paper, wove, batonné, laid, etc.

A2 A3

A4 A5

Yellowish White Wove Paper.

1871 **Lithographed** ***Imperf.***

9	A2	5c dp brn	2.25	2.25
a.		5c red brn	2.25	2.25
b.		Value reads "CINGO"	37.50	37.50
10	A3	10c blue	6.00	6.00
11	A4	50c green	7.50	7.50
12	A5	1p carmine	12.00	12.00

The 5p stamps, type A2, are bogus varieties made from an altered die of the 5c.

The 10c, 50c and 1 peso stamps have been reprinted on bluish white wove paper. They are from new plates and most copies show traces of fine lines with which the dies had been defaced. Reprints of the 5c have a large cross at the top. The 10c on laid batonné paper is known only as a reprint.

A6 A7

A8 A9

1879 **Grayish or White Wove Paper**

14	A6	5c yel brn	45	45
a.		5c pur brn	45	45
15	A7	10c blue	50	50
16	A8	50c grn, *bluish*	50	50
a.		White paper	1.50	1.50
17	A9	1p vermilion	2.25	2.25
a.		1p car rose	9.00	9.00

A10

1883 ***Imperf.***

18	A6	5c orange	45	45
19	A7	10c vermilion	90	90
20	A10	20c violet	1.40	1.40

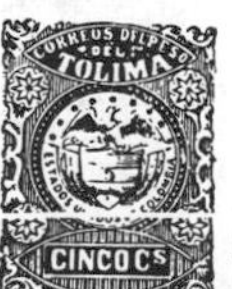

Coat of Arms A12

1884 ***Imperf.***

23	A12	1c gray	15	15
24	A12	2c rose lil	15	15
a.		2c sl	15	15
25	A12	2½c dl org	15	15
26	A12	5c brown	15	15
27	A12	10c blue	38	38
a.		10c sl	22	22
28	A12	20c lemon	38	38
a.		Laid paper	5.00	5.00
29	A12	25c black	30	30
30	A12	50c green	30	30

31	A12	1p vermilion	40	40
32	A12	2p violet	60	60
a.		Value omitted	27.50	27.50
33	A12	5p yellow	40	40
34	A12	10p lil rose	1.10	1.10
a.		Laid paper	27.50	27.50
b.		10p gray	135.00	
		Nos. 23-34 (12)	4.46	4.46

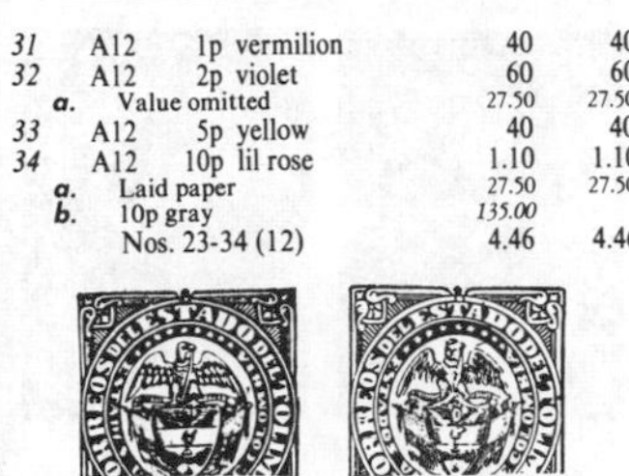

A13 A14

Condor with Long Wings Touching Flagstaffs

A15 A16

1886 Litho. *Perf. 10½, 11*

White Paper

36	A13	5c brown	1.50	1.50
a.		5c yel brn	1.50	1.50
b.		Imperf., pair	20.00	
37	A14	10c blue	4.50	4.50
a.		Imperf., pair	20.00	
38	A15	50c green	1.75	1.75
a.		Imperf., pair	20.00	
39	A16	1p vermilion	3.00	3.00
a.		Imperf., pair	30.00	

No. 38 has been reprinted in pale gray green, perforated 10½, and No. 39 in bright vermilion, perforated 11½. The impressions show many signs of wear.

Lilac Tinted Paper.

36c	A13	5c org brn	13.00	13.00
37b	A14	10c blue	13.00	13.00
38b	A15	50c green	9.00	9.00
39b	A16	1p vermilion	7.50	7.50

A17 A18

Condor with Short Wings

A19 A20

1886 White Paper *Perf. 12*

44	A19	1c gray	7.50	7.50
a.		Imperf., pair	20.00	
45	A17	2c rose lil	8.25	8.25
46	A18	2½c dl org	24.00	24.00
47	A19	5c brown	10.00	10.00
a.		Imperf., pair	32.50	
48	A20	10c blue	10.00	10.00
a.		Imperf., pair	32.50	
49	A20	20c lemon	8.25	8.25
a.		Tête bêche pair	225.00	225.00
50	A20	25c black	7.50	7.50
51	A20	50c green	3.00	3.00
52	A20	1p vermilion	4.50	4.50
a.		Imperf., pair	20.00	
53	A20	2p violet	9.00	9.00
a.		Imperf., pair	25.00	
b.		Tête bêche pair	175.00	175.00
54	A20	5p orange	16.50	16.50
a.		Imperf., pair	40.00	
55	A20	10p lil rose	8.25	8.25
a.		Imperf., pair	20.00	

Condor with Long Wings, Upper Flagstaffs Omitted

A21 A22

1886 *Perf. 12, 12½, 12x11*

56	A15	2½c dl org	75.00	75.00
a.		Imperf., pair		
b.		Transfer of 5c in stone of 2½c		
c.		Transfer of 10c in stone of 2½c		
57	A21	5c brown	7.50	7.50
a.		Imperf., pair	20.00	
b.		Transfer of 10c in stone of 5c		
c.		As "b," imperf.		
58	A14	10c ultra	13.00	13.00
a.		Imperf., pair	32.50	
b.		Transfer of 5c in stone of 10c		
59	A22	2p red vio	15.00	15.00
a.		Imperf., pair	37.50	
b.		Without numerals in corners, colored background, imperf.	27.50	
c.		As "b," white background	27.50	27.50
60	A22	5p pale org	22.50	22.50
a.		Imperf., pair	55.00	
b.		Bottom label inverted	650.00	
c.		Tête bêche pair		
d.		Transfer of 2p in stone of 5p		

Imperf.

61	A13	1c black	150.00	

No. 56 is similar to type A15, and No. 58 similar to type A14, but both have upper flag-staffs omitted.

A23

1888 *Perf. 10½.*

62	A23	5c red	15	15
a.		Imperf., pair	3.50	
63	A23	10c green	38	38
a.		Imperf., pair	4.00	
64	A23	50c blue	1.00	1.00
a.		Imperf., pair	6.00	6.00
65	A23	1p red brn	1.75	1.75
a.		Imperf., pair	9.00	

1895 *Perf. 12, 13½*

66	A23	1c bl, *rose*	30	30
a.		Imperf., pair	9.00	
67	A23	2c grn, *lt grn*	30	30
a.		Imperf., pair	9.00	
68	A23	5c red	15	15
69	A23	10c green	30	30
70	A23	20c bl, *yel*	38	38
a.		Imperf., pair	10.00	
71	A23	1p brown	2.25	2.25
		Nos. 66-71 (6)	3.68	3.68

'No Hay Estampillas'

Items inscribed "No hay estampillas" (No stamps available) are considered by specialists to be not postage stamps but receipt labels.

Honda Issue.

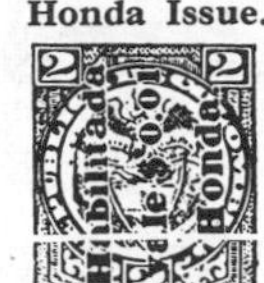

A23a Black Surcharge.

1896 *Perf. 12*

78	A23a	1c on 2c grn	45.00	45.00

Excellent counterfeits exist.

Regular Issue.

A24 A25

A26 A27

A28 A29

A30 A31

Sewing Machine or Regular

Perf. 12

1903-04 Lithographed.

79	A24	4c *green*	30	30
80	A25	10c dl bl	30	30
81	A26	20c orange	60	60
82	A27	50c *rose*	22	22
a.		50c *buff*	22	22
84	A28	1p brown	22	22
85	A29	2p gray	22	22
86	A30	5p red	22	22
a.		Tête bêche pair	6.25	6.25
87	A31	10p *blue*	22	22
a.		10p *lt grn*	22	22
b.		10p *grn glazed*	4.50	4.50
		Nos. 79-87 (8)	2.30	2.30

Imperf.

79a	A24	4c *green*	30	30
80a	A25	10c dl bl	22	22
81a	A26	20c orange	1.40	1.40
82b	A27	50c *rose*	1.75	1.75
c.		50c *buff*	1.75	1.75
84a	A28	1p brown	22	22
85a	A29	2p gray	22	22
86b	A30	5p red	22	22
c.		Tête bêche pair	6.25	6.25
87c	A31	10p *blue*	2.75	2.75
d.		Tête bêche pair		
e.		10p *lt grn*	4.50	4.50
f.		10p *grn glazed*	22.50	22.50
		Nos. 79a-87c (8)	7.08	7.08

COMORO ISLANDS

LOCATION — In Mozambique Channel between Madagascar and Mozambique.

GOVT.—Republic.

AREA—838 sq. mi.

POP.—385,000 (est. 1983).

CAPITAL—Moroni.

The Comoro Archipelago consists of the islands of Mayotte, Anjouan, Grand Comoro (Grande Comore) and Moheli, which issued their own stamps as French protectorates or colonies from 1887-1914. The archipelago was attached to Madagascar from 1914 to 1946, when it became a separate French territory. In July 1975, Anjouan, Grand Comoro and Moheli united to declare independence as the State of Comoro. Mayotte remained French.

100 Centimes = 1 Franc

Anjouan Bay A2

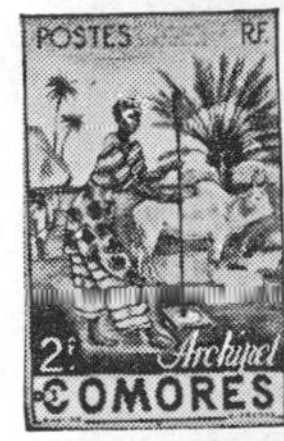

Comoro Woman Grinding Grain A3

Moroni Mosque on Grand Comoro A4

Engraved

1950 *Perf. 13* Unwmkd.

30	A2	10c blue	12	12
31	A2	50c green	15	15
32	A2	1fr dk ol brn	15	15
33	A3	2fr brt grn	30	30
34	A3	5fr purple	30	30
35	A3	6fr vio brn	42	42
36	A4	7fr red	42	42
37	A4	10fr dk grn	50	50
38	A4	11fr dp ultra	65	65
		Nos. 30-38 (9)	3.01	3.01

Imperforates

Most Comoro Islands stamps exist imperforate in issued and trial colors, and also in small presentation sheets in issued colors.

Military Medal Issue.

Common Design Type

1952 Engraved and Typographed

39	CD101	15fr multi	30.00	30.00

Mosque of Ouani, Anjouan A5

Coelacanth A6

1952-54 Engraved

40	A5	15fr dk brn	75	75
41	A5	20fr red brn	85	85
42	A6	40fr aqua & ind ('54)	13.50	10.00

FIDES Issue

Common Design Type

1956 *Perf. 13x12½* Unwmkd.

43	CD103	9fr dp vio	75	60

Human Rights Issue

Common Design Type

1958 Engraved. *Perf. 13*

44	CD105	20fr ol grn & dk bl	5.50	5.50

Flower Issue
Common Design Type

Design: Colvillea.

1959 Photogravure *Perf. 12½x12*

45	CD104	10fr multi	2.50	1.65

View of Dzaoudzi and Radio Symbol
A8

Design: 25fr, Radio tower and radio waves over Islands.

1960, Dec. 23 Engr. *Perf. 13*

46	A8	20fr mar, vio bl & grn	70	60
47	A8	25fr ultra, brn & grn	85	85

Comoro radio station.

Harpa Conoidalis
A9

Sea Shells: 50c, Cypraecassis rufa. 2fr, Murex ramosus. 5fr, Turbo marmoratus. 20fr, Pterocera scorpio. 25fr, Charonia tritonis.

1962, Jan. 13 Photogravure

Shells in Natural Colors

48	A9	50c lil & brn	30	30
49	A9	1fr yel & red	30	30
50	A9	2fr pale grn & pink	40	40
51	A9	5fr yel & grn	80	80
52	A9	20fr sal & brn	1.85	1.85
53	A9	25fr bis & pink	2.50	2.50
		Nos. 48-53, C5-C6 (8)	21.65	20.15

Wheat Emblem and Globe
A10

1963, Mar. 21 Engr. *Perf. 13*

54	A10	20fr choc & dk grn	2.50	2.25

Issued for the "Freedom from Hunger" campaign of the U.N. Food and Agriculture Organization.

Red Cross Centenary Issue
Common Design Type

1963, Sept. 2 *Perf. 13* Unwmkd.

55	CD113	50fr emer, gray & car	4.00	3.50

Centenary of the International Red Cross.

Human Rights Issue
Common Design Type

1963, Dec. 10 Engraved

56	CD117	15fr dk red & yel grn	4.00	3.50

Common Design Types pictured in section at front of book.

Tobacco Pouch A13 — Grand Comoro Canoe A14

Designs: 4fr, Censer. 10fr, Carved lamp.

1963, Dec. 27 *Perf. 13*

Size: 22x36mm.

57	A13	3fr multi	15	15
58	A13	4fr org, dp cl & sl grn	25	25
59	A13	10fr org brn, dk red brn & grn	50	50
		Nos. 57-59, C8-C9 (5)	6.90	4.60

Philatec Issue
Common Design Type

1964, March 31

60	CD118	50fr dk bl, red & grn	1.65	1.65

1964, Aug. 7 Photo. *Perf. 13x12½*

Design: 30fr, Boutre felucca.

Size: 22x37mm.

61	A14	15fr multi	60	60
62	A14	30fr lt grn & multi	1.00	1.00

See Nos. C10-C11.

Spiny Lobster
A15

Designs: 12fr, Hammerhead shark (horiz.). 20fr, Turtle (horiz.). 25fr, Merou fish.

1965, Dec. 20 Engraved *Perf. 13*

63	A15	1fr grn, lil & ocher	20	20
64	A15	12fr org red, sl & gray	50	40
65	A15	20fr org, red & bl grn	60	50
66	A15	25fr bl grn, dk brn & red	70	60

Hotel Itsandra, Moroni
A16

Design: 15fr, Lake Salé, Grand Comoro.

Photogravure

1966, Dec. 19 *Perf. 12½x13*

67	A16	15fr multi	40	30
68	A16	25fr multi	50	30

See Nos. C18-C19.

Comoro Sunbird
A17

Birds: 10fr, Malachite kingfisher. 15fr, Rothschild's fody. 30fr, Cuckoo-roller.

1967, June 20 Photo. *Perf. 12½x13*

Size: 36x23mm.

69	A17	2fr ocher & multi	60	60
70	A17	10fr lil & multi	80	80
71	A17	15fr yel grn & multi	1.00	1.00
72	A17	30fr pink & multi	1.60	1.60
		Nos. 69-72, C20-C21 (6)	7.85	5.50

WHO Anniversary Issue
Common Design Type

1968, May 4 Engraved *Perf. 13*

73	CD126	40fr grn, vio & dp car	80	70

Issued for the 20th anniversary of the World Health Organization.

Surgeonfish
A19

Design: 25fr, Imperial angelfish.

1968, Aug. 1 Engraved *Perf. 13*

Size: 36x22mm.

74	A19	20fr vio bl, yel & red brn	40	40
75	A19	25fr Prus bl, dk bl & org	50	50

See Nos. C23-C24.

Human Rights Year Issue
Common Design Type

1968, Aug. 10 Engraved *Perf. 13*

76	CD127	60fr brn, grn & org	1.20	1.20

Msoila Prayer Rug and Praying Man
A20

Designs: Each stamp shows a different prayer position.

1969, Feb. 27 Engraved *Perf. 13*

77	A20	20fr bl grn, rose red & pur	30	25
78	A20	30fr pur, rose red & bl grn	40	35
79	A20	45fr rose red, pur & bl grn	60	50

Vanilla Flower
A21

Design: 15fr, Flower of ylang-ylang tree. 25fr, Poinsettia (country name in upper right corner).

1969–70 Photo. *Perf. 12½x13*

Size: 36x23mm.

80	A21	10fr multi	25	20
81	A21	15fr multi	32	28
82	A21	25fr multi ('70)	50	35
		Nos. 80-82, C26-C28 (6)	6.32	4.68

Issue dates: Nos. 80–81, Mar. 20, 1969. No. 82, Mar. 5, 1970.

ILO Issue
Common Design Type

1969, Nov. 24 Engraved *Perf. 13*

83	CD131	5fr org, emer & gray	25	20

Issued for 50th anniversary of the International Labor Organization.

U.P.U. Headquarters Issue
Common Design Type

1970, May 20 Engraved *Perf. 13*

84	CD133	65fr pur, bl grn & red brn	1.25	80

Chiromani Costume, Anjouan A22 — Friday Mosque A23

Design: 25fr, Bouiboui costume, Grand Comoro.

1970, Oct. 30 Photo. *Perf. 12½x13*

85	A22	20fr grn, yel & red	40	32
86	A22	25fr brn, yel & dk bl	50	40

1970, Dec. 18 Engraved *Perf. 13*

87	A23	5fr rose car, grn & grnsh bl	25	15
88	A23	10fr dp lil, grn & vio	32	25
89	A23	40fr cop red, grn & dp brn	55	45

Great White Egret A24 — Pyrostegia Venusta A25

Birds: 10fr, Comoro pigeon. 15fr, Green-backed heron. 25fr, Comoro blue pigeon. 35fr, Humblot's flycatcher. 40fr, Allen's gallinule.

Photogravure

1971, March 12 *Perf. 12½x13*

90	A24	5fr multi	20	15
91	A24	10fr yel & multi	28	20
92	A24	15fr bl & multi	30	22
93	A24	25fr org & multi	45	35
94	A24	35fr yel grn & multi	85	60
95	A24	40fr gray & multi	1.00	80
		Nos. 90-95 (6)	3.08	2.32

1971, July 19 Photo. *Perf. 13*

Flowers: 3fr, Dogbane (horiz.). 20fr, Frangipani.

Size: 22x36, 36x22mm.

96	A25	1fr ver & grn	15	15
97	A25	3fr yel, grn & red	25	20
98	A25	20fr ver & grn	70	45
		Nos. 96-98, C37-C38 (5)	3.80	2.30

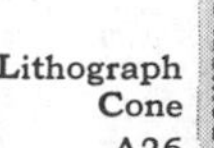

Lithograph Cone
A26

Sea Shells: 10fr, Pacific lettered cone. 20fr, Aulicus cone. 35fr, Polita nerita. 60fr, Snake-head cowrie.

1971, Oct. 4

99	A26	5fr lt ultra & multi	20	15
100	A26	10fr multi	25	20
101	A26	20fr vio & multi	35	30
102	A26	35fr lt bl & multi	60	45
103	A26	60fr lt vio & multi	80	80
		Nos. 99-103 (5)	2.20	1.90

De Gaulle Issue
Common Design Type

Designs: 20fr, Gen. de Gaulle, 1940. 35fr, Pres. de Gaulle, 1970.

104	CD134	20fr dk car & blk	50	25
105	CD134	35fr dk car & blk	70	55

First anniversary of the death of Charles de Gaulle (1890–1970), president of France.

Louis Pasteur, Slides, Microscope A27

1972, Aug. 2

106	A27	65fr ind, org, & ol brn	1.00	75

Sesquicentennial of the birth of Louis Pasteur (1822–1895), chemist.

Type of Air Post Issue 1971

Designs: 10fr, View of Goulaivoini. 20fr, Bay, Mitsamiouli. 35fr, Gate and fountain, Foumbouni. 50fr, View of Moroni.

1973, June 28 Photo. *Perf. 13*

107	AP10	10fr bl & multi	25	20
108	AP10	20fr grn & multi	40	35
109	AP10	35fr bl & multi	70	65
110	AP10	50fr bl & multi	85	75
		Nos. 107-110, C53 (5)	4.45	3.55

Bank of Madagascar and Comoros A28

Buildings in Moroni: 15fr, Post and Telecommunications Administration. 20fr, Prefecture.

1973, July 10 Photo. *Perf. 13x12½*

111	A28	5fr multi	12	10
112	A28	15fr multi	22	20
113	A28	20fr multi	40	35

Salimata Hamissi Mosque A29

Design: 20fr, Zaouiyat Chaduli Mosque (vert.).

Perf. 12½x13, 13x12½

1973, Oct. 20 Photogravure

114	A29	20fr multi	35	30
115	A29	35fr multi	65	60

Cheikh Mausoleum A30

Design: 50fr, Mausoleum of President Said Mohamed Cheikh (different view).

1974, Mar. 16 Engraved *Perf. 13*

116	A30	35fr grn, ol brn & blk	55	45
117	A30	50fr grn, ol brn & blk	75	65

Koran Stand, Anjouan A31

Designs: 15fr, Carved combs (vert.). 20fr, 3-legged table (vert.). 75fr, Sugar press.

1974, May 10 Photo. *Perf. 12½x13*

118	A31	15fr emer & multi	25	20
119	A31	20fr grn & multi	35	25
120	A31	35fr multi	50	40
121	A31	75fr multi	90	75

UPU Emblem, Symbolic Postmark A32

1974, Oct. 9 Engr. *Perf. 13x12½*

122	A32	30fr multi	40	35

Centenary of Universal Postal Union.

Bracelet A33

Designs: 35fr, Diadem. 120fr, Saber. 135fr, Dagger.

1975, Feb. 28 Engr. *Perf. 13*

123	A33	20fr multi	35	30
124	A33	35fr grn & multi	55	50
125	A33	120fr bl & multi	1.75	1.50
126	A33	135fr multi	1.85	1.65

Mohani Village, Moheli—A34

Designs: 50fr, Djoezi Village, Moheli. 55fr, Chirazi tombs.

1975, May 26 Photo. *Perf. 13*

127	A34	30fr vio bl & multi	30	20
128	A34	50fr Prus bl & multi	55	40
129	A34	55fr grn & multi	60	65

Skin Diver Photographing Coelacanth—A35

1975, June 27 Engr. *Perf. 13*

130	A35	50fr multi	80	60

1975 coelacanth expedition.

State of Comoro

AREA—712 sq. mi.

POP.—216,587 (census 1966).

In 1978 the islands' name became the Federal and Islamic Republic of the Comoros.

Issues of 1971–75 Surcharged and Overprinted with Bars and: "ETAT COMORIEN" in Black, Silver or Red.

Tambourine Player—A36

Design: No. 153, Women dancers and tambourine players.

Printing & Perforations as Before.
A36: Photo., *Perf. 13*

1975

Multicolored

131	A25	5fr on 1fr	6	6
132	A25	5fr on 3fr	6	6
133	A17	10fr on 2fr	45	45
134	A28	15fr on 20fr (R)	20	15
135	A29	15fr on 20fr (S)	20	15
136	A33	15fr on 20fr	20	15
137	A31	20fr	28	20
138	A29	25fr on 35fr	35	30
139	A34	30fr	40	35
140	A30	30fr on 35fr	40	35
141	A31	30fr on 35fr	40	35
142	A33	30fr on 35fr	40	35
143	AP10	35fr	45	40
144	SP2	35fr on 35fr + 10fr	45	40
145	A24	40fr	55	45
146	A34	50fr	70	60
147	A35	50fr	70	60
148	A34	50fr on 55fr (S)	70	60
149	A31	75fr	1.10	90
150	A26	75fr on 60fr (S)	1.10	90
151	A33	100fr on 120fr	1.40	1.20
152	A36	100fr bl & multi	1.40	1.20
153	A36	100fr on 150fr (S)	1.40	1.20
154	A33	200fr on 135fr	2.80	2.25
155	A32	500fr on 30fr	7.00	6.00
		Nos. 131-155 (25)	23.15	19.62

Nos. 152–153 exist without overprint or surcharge. No. 155 exists with red surcharge.

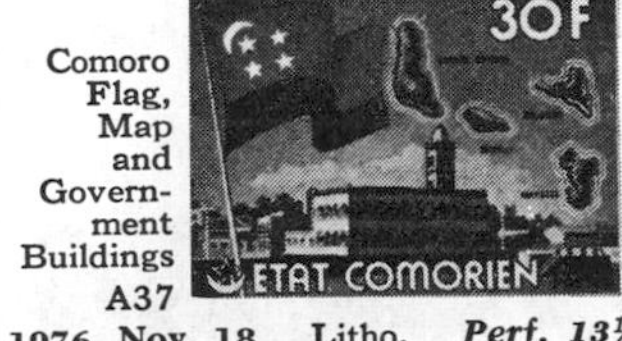

Comoro Flag, Map and Government Buildings A37

1976, Nov. 18 Litho. *Perf. 13½*

156	A37	30fr multi	25	15
157	A37	50fr multi	40	25

1st anniversary of independence.

Comoro Flag, UN Headquarters and Emblem A38

1976, Nov. 25

158	A38	40fr multi	30	20
159	A38	50fr multi	40	25

1st anniversary of United Nations membership.

Islamic Republic

Nos. 156–157 Surcharged and Overprinted with 3 Lines and: "République / Fédérale / et Islamique / des Comores"

1978, July 24 Litho. *Perf. 13½*

160	A37	30fr multi
161	A37	40fr on 30fr multi
162	A37	50fr multi
163	A37	100fr on 30fr multi

Nos. 160 and 162 were also overprinted to commemorate Queen Elizabeth II coronation anniversary; Capt. James Cook; World Cup Soccer winner; Albrecht Dürer; First powered flight; Railroad anniversary; Voyager I and II; Int. Year of the Child; 1980 Olympic Games; World Cup Soccer, Espana '82.

Italian Ball Game, 18th Century, Modern Soccer—A40

Soccer Cup, Argentina '78 Emblem, Soccer Scene and: 2fr, Ball game, London, 14th century. 3fr, Man and boy with ball, Greece, 5th century B.C. 50fr, Ball game, France, 19th century.

1979 Litho. *Perf. 13*

Black Surcharge and Overprint

169	A40	1fr on 100fr multi	5	5
170	A40	2fr on 75fr multi	5	5
171	A40	3fr on 30fr multi	5	5
172	A40	50fr multi	50	50
		Nos. 169-172, C96 (5)	2.40	2.40

Otto Lilienthal and Glider—A41

History of Aviation: No. 174, Wright brothers and Flyer A. No. 175, Louis Bleriot and Bleriot XI. 100fr, Claude Dornier and Dornier-Wall hydrofoil.

1979

Black Overprint and Surcharge

173	A41	30fr multi	22	22
174	A41	50fr multi	60	60
175	A41	50fr on 75fr multi	70	70
176	A41	100fr multi	1.25	1.25

Papilio Dardanus Cenea A42

Butterflies: 15fr, Papilio dardanus. 30fr, Chrysiridia croesus. 50fr, Precis octavia. 75fr, Bunaea alcinoe.

1979

Black Overprint and Surcharge

177	A42	5fr on 20fr multi	5	5
178	A42	15fr multi	15	15
179	A42	30fr multi	35	35
180	A42	50fr multi	60	60
181	A42	75fr multi	1.00	1.00
		Nos. 177-181 (5)	2.15	2.15

For Nos. 169–181 without overprint see "For the Record."

Gallinule A43

Birds: 30fr, Kingfisher. No. 184, Bee-eater. No. 185, Flycatcher. 200fr, Sunbird.

1979 Litho. *Perf. 13*

Black Overprint and Surcharge

182	A43	15fr multi	18	18
183	A43	30fr on 35fr multi	35	35
184	A43	50fr on 20fr multi	75	75
185	A43	50fr on 40fr multi	75	75
186	A43	200fr on 75fr multi	1.90	1.90

Giuseppe Verdi—A44

Composers: 30fr, Johann Sebastian Bach. 40fr, Wolfgang Amadeus Mozart. 50fr, Hector Berlioz.

1979

Black Overprint and Surcharge

187	A44	5fr on 100fr multi	8	8
188	A44	30fr multi	30	30
189	A44	40fr multi	32	32
190	A44	50fr multi	50	50
		Nos. 187-190, C98 (5)	1.90	1.90

For Nos. 182–190, C98 without overprint see "For the Record."

Galileo and Voyager I—A46

Exploration of Solar System: 30fr, Kepler and Voyager II. 40fr, Copernicus and Voyager I, 100fr, Huygens and Voyager II.

1979, Feb. 19

196	A46	20fr multi	10	10
197	A46	30fr multi	22	10
198	A46	40fr multi	32	12
199	A46	100fr multi	70	32
		Nos. 196-199, C99-C100 (6)	5.74	2.44

Philidor, Anderssen, Steinitz and King—A47

Design: 100fr, Chess pieces and board, Venetian chess player.

1979, Feb. 19

200	A47	40fr multi	28	8
201	A47	100fr multi	70	25

Chess Grand Masters. See No. C102.

Satellite and Radar—A48

Design: 100fr, Satellites, earth and radar.

1979, Sept. 15 Litho. *Perf. 13*

Black Overprint

202	A48	75fr multi	75
203	A48	100fr multi	70

See No. C103.

U.N. No. 42, Satellite over Earth—A49

1979, Sept. 15

Black Overprint

204	A49	75fr multi	75

Innsbruck, Olympic Emblems, Skater A50

1979, Sept. 15

Black Overprint

205	A50	35fr multi	35

Philipp Reis, Telephone Operators—A51

1979, Sept. 15

Black Overprint

206	A51	75fr multi	75

For Nos. 202-206 without overprint see "For the Record."

Charaxes Defulvata A52

Birds: 50fr, Leptosomus discolor. 75fr, Bee eater.

1979, Apr. 10 Litho. *Perf. 12½*

207	A52	30fr multi	30	12
208	A52	50fr multi	50	22
209	A52	75fr multi	80	35

Litchi Nuts A53

1979, June 15 Litho. *Perf. 12½*

Fruit: 70fr, Papayas. 100fr, Avocados. 125fr, Bananas.

210	A53	60fr multi	60	30
211	A53	70fr multi	70	35
212	A53	100fr multi	1.00	45
213	A53	125fr multi	1.25	75

Basketball Players A54

1979, Aug. 28 Litho. *Perf. 13*

214	A54	200fr multi	1.65	1.25

Indian Ocean Olympics.

Dugout on Beach A61

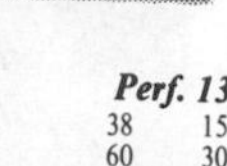

Anjouan Puppet A62

1980, Jan. 4 Litho. *Perf. 13*

232	A61	60fr multi	38	15
233	A62	100fr multi	60	30

Sultan Said Ali—A63

1980, Feb. 20 *Perf. 12½x13*

234	A63	40fr *shown*	28	18
235	A63	60fr *Sultan Ahmed*	38	22

Sherlock Holmes, Doyle—A64

1980, Feb. 25 *Perf. 12½*

236	A64	200fr multi	1.50	1.10

Sir Arthur Conan Doyle (1859-1930), writer.

Grand Mosque, Holy Ka'aba, Mecca—A64a

1980, Mar. 12 *Perf. 13x12½*

237	A64a	75fr multi	45	30

Hegira, 1500th anniv.

Year of the Holy City of Jerusalem—A65

1980, Mar. 12 *Perf. 13x13½*

238	A65	60fr multi	38	22

See "Special Notices" at the front of this volume for data on the listing methods of this Catalogue, abbreviations, condition, prices and examination.

Kepler, Copernicus and Pluto—A66

1980, Apr. 30 **Litho.** ***Perf. 12½***

239 A66 400fr multi 3.00 2.25

Discovery of Pluto, 50th anniversary.

Muscle System, Avicenna—A67

1980, Apr. 30 **Engraved** ***Perf. 13***

240 A67 60fr multi 38 30

Avicenna, Arab physician, birth millennium.

Soccer Players—A69

Designs; Various soccer scenes. 60fr, 150fr, 500fr, vert.

1981, Feb. 20 **Litho.** ***Perf. 12½***

241 A69 60fr multi 40 18
242 A69 75fr multi 45 22
243 A69 90fr multi 60 28
244 A69 100fr multi 75 38
245 A69 150fr multi 1.10 42
Nos. 241-245 (5) 3.30 1.48

Souvenir Sheet

246 A69 500fr multi 3.25 1.40

World Cup Soccer 1982. No. 246 has multicolored margin showing emblems. Size: 104x80mm.

Nos. 236-237, 213, and:

Merops Superciliosus—A70

Perf. 12½, 13x12½ (No. 248)

1981, Feb. **Litho.**

Red, Black or Blue Surcharge

247 A64 15fr on 200fr multi 15 15
248 A64a 20fr on 75fr multi 18 18
249 A53 40fr on 125fr multi (Bk) 40 40
250 A70 60fr on 75fr multi (Bl) 60 60

Space Exploration: 50fr, Apollo program (vert.). 75fr, 100fr, 500fr, Columbia space shuttle.

1981, July 13 **Litho.** ***Perf. 14***

251 A71 50fr multi 32 15
252 A71 75fr multi 45 22
253 A71 100fr multi 65 38
254 A71 450fr multi 3.00 1.50

Souvenir Sheet

255 A71 500fr multi 3.25 1.50

No. 255 has multicolored margin showing Eugene Sanger (1905-1964), and rockets. Size: 104x79mm.

Prince Charles and Lady Diana, Buckingham Palace—A72

1981, Sept. 1 **Litho.** ***Perf. 14½***

256 A72 125fr shown 75 30
257 A72 200fr Highwood House 1.40 60
258 A72 450fr Carnarvon Castle 2.75 1.40
a. Souvenir sheet of 3 5.25 2.25

Royal wedding. No. 258a contains Nos. 256-258 in changed colors. Multicolored margin shows flowers, label shows arms of Prince of Wales. Size: 133x98mm.

Flag Type of 1979

1981, Oct. **Litho.** ***Perf. 13***

259 O1 5fr multi 5 5
260 O1 15fr multi 8 5
261 O1 25fr multi 15 5
262 O1 35fr multi 22 12
263 O1 75fr multi 45 28
Nos. 259-263 (5) 95 55

Nos. 239, 243, 212, 233 Surcharged.

1981, Nov. **Litho.** ***Perf. 12½***

264 A66 5fr on 400fr multi 5 5
265 A69 20fr on 90fr multi 8 5
266 A53 45fr on 100fr multi 28 12
267 A62 45fr on 100fr multi 28 12

75th Anniv. of Grand Prix—A73

Designs: Winners and their Cars.

1981, Dec. 28 **Litho.** ***Perf. 12½***

268 A73 20fr Mercedes, 1914 15 5
269 A73 50fr Delage, 1925 32 15
270 A73 75fr Rudi Caracciola, 1926 50 22
271 A73 90fr Stirling Moss, 1955 55 30
272 A73 150fr Maserati, 1957 95 45
Nos. 268-272 (5) 2.47 1.17

Souvenir Sheet
Perf. 13

273 A73 500fr Changing wheels, vert. 3.25 1.50

No. 273 has multicolored margin continuing design. Size: 107x86mm.

Scouting Year—A74

1982, Jan. 5

274 A74 50fr Climbing rocks 30 15
275 A74 75fr Boating 45 22
276 A74 250fr Sailing 1.50 75
277 A74 350fr Sailing, diff. 2.25 1.10

Souvenir Sheet
Perf. 13

278 A74 500fr Baden-Powell 3.00 1.50

No. 278 has multicolored margin continuing design. Size: 78x102mm.

21st Birthday of Princess of Wales—A75

Designs: Various portraits of Princess Diana.

1982, July 1 **Litho.** ***Perf. 14***

279 A75 200fr multi 1.25 60
280 A75 300fr multi 1.75 90

Souvenir Sheet

281 A75 500fr multi 3.00 1.50

No. 281 has multicolored margin showing portrait. Size: 112x81mm.

Johannes von Goethe (1749-1832)—A76

1982, July

282 A76 75fr multi 45 22
283 A76 350fr multi 2.00 1.00

Nos. 256-258a Overprinted in Blue: "NAISSANCE ROYALE 1982"

1982, July 31 ***Perf. 14½***

284 A72 125fr multi 75 60
285 A72 200fr multi 1.10 90
286 A72 450fr multi 2.75 2.25
a. Souvenir sheet of 3 5.00 5.00

Birth of Prince William of Wales, June 21.

Nos. 241-246 Overprinted with Finalists and Score in Red.

1982, Sept. 20 **Litho.** ***Perf. 12½***

287 A69 60fr multi 38 28
288 A69 75fr multi 45 32
289 A69 90fr multi 50 38
290 A69 100fr multi 60 45

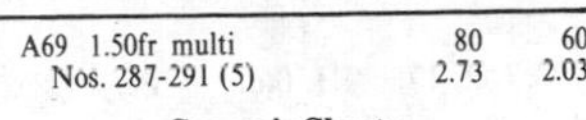
291 A69 1.50fr multi 80 60
Nos. 287-291 (5) 2.73 2.03

Souvenir Sheet

292 A69 500fr multi 3.00 3.00

Italy's victory in 1982 World Cup.

Paintings by Norman Rockwell—A77

1982, Oct. 11 **Litho.** ***Perf. 14***

293 A77 60fr 1931 38 22
294 A77 75fr 1925 45 22
295 A77 100fr 1922 60 30
296 A77 150fr 1919 90 45
297 A77 200fr 1924 1.10 50
298 A77 300fr 1918 1.75 90
Nos. 293-298 (6) 5.18 2.59

Sultans of Anjouan—A78

1982, Dec. ***Perf. 12½x13, 13x12½***

299 A78 30fr Said Mohamed Sidi, vert. 22 15
300 A78 60fr Ahmed Abdallah, vert. 38 22
301 A78 75fr Salim 45 30
302 A78 300fr Sidi, Abdallah 1.75 1.25

Landscapes—A79

1983, Sept. 30 **Litho.** ***Perf. 13***

303 A79 60fr D'Ziani Lake 38 22
304 A79 100fr Sunset 60 38
305 A79 175fr Anjouan, vert. 1.10 60
306 A79 360fr Itsandra 2.00 1.25
307 A79 400fr Anjouan, diff. 2.50 1.65
Nos. 303-307 (5) 6.58 4.10

Woman from Moheli—A80

1983, Oct. 17 Litho. *Perf. 12½x13*

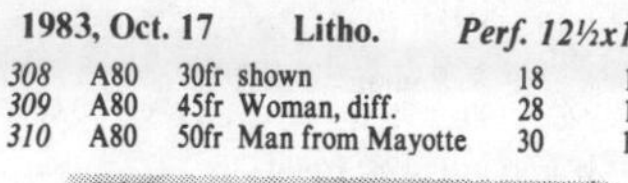

308	A80	30fr	shown	18	15
309	A80	45fr	Woman, diff.	28	18
310	A80	50fr	Man from Mayotte	30	18

Thoroughbred Horses—A81

1983, Nov. 30 Litho. *Perf. 13*

311	A81	75fr	Arabian	45	18
312	A81	100fr	Anglo-Arabian	60	28
313	A81	125fr	Lippizaner	75	30
314	A81	150fr	Tennessee	90	38
315	A81	200fr	Appaloosa	1.25	50
316	A81	300fr	Pure English	1.75	80
317	A81	400fr	Clydesdale	2.50	1.00
318	A81	500fr	Andalusian	3.00	1.40
			Nos. 311-318 (8)	11.20	4.84

Double Portrait, by Raphael—A82

1983, Dec. 30 Litho. *Perf. 13*

319	A82	100fr	shown	60	30
320	A82	200fr	Girl, fresco detail	1.25	45
321	A82	300fr	St. George Killing Dragon	1.75	90
322	A82	400fr	Balthazar Castiglione	2.50	1.10

Ships and Automobiles—A83

1984, Oct. 9 Litho. *Perf. 12½*

323	A83	100fr	William Fawcett	42
324	A83	100fr	De Dion, 1885	42
325	A83	150fr	Lightning	62
326	A83	150fr	Benz Victoria, 1893	62
327	A83	200fr	Rapido	85
328	A83	200fr	Columbia Electric, 1901	85
329	A83	350fr	Sindia	1.25
330	A83	350fr	Fiat, 1902	1.25
			Nos. 323-330 (8)	6.28

Souvenir Sheets

Nos. 255, 273, 278 Ovptd. with Exhibition in Black, Blue or Red.

1985, Mar. 11 *Perf. 14, 13*

335	A71	500fr	'85/HAMBOURG (BK)	2.25
336	A73	500fr	TSUKUBA EXPO '85 (Bl)	2.25
337	A74	500fr	ARGENTINA '85/BUENOS AIRES (R)	2.25

See Nos. C143-C144

Victor Hugo (1802-1885), Author, Pantheon, Paris—A85

Anniversaries and events: 200fr, IYY, Jules Verne (1828-1905), author. 300fr, IYY, Mark Twain (1835-1910), author. 450fr, Queen Mother, 85th birthday, vert. 500fr, Statue of Liberty, cent., vert.

1985, May 27 Litho. *Perf. 13*

338	A85	100fr	multi	40
339	A85	200fr	multi	80
340	A85	300fr	multi	1.15
341	A85	450fr	multi	1.75
342	A85	500fr	multi	2.00
			Nos. 338-342 (5)	6.10

Sea Shells—A86

1985, Oct. 23 *Perf. 14*

343	A86	75fr	Lambis chiragra	30
344	A86	125fr	Strombe lentifinosum	50
345	A86	200fr	Tonna gala	80
346	A86	300fr	Cymbium glans	1.15
347	A86	450fr	Lambis crocata	1.75
			Nos. 343-347 (5)	4.50

Comoros Admission to UN, 10th Anniv.—A87

1985, Nov. 12 Litho. *Perf. 13x12½*

348	A87	5fr	multi	5	5
349	A87	30fr	multi	12	6
350	A87	75fr	multi	30	15
351	A87	125fr	multi	52	25
352	A87	400fr	multi	1.75	90
			Nos. 348-352 (5)	2.74	1.41

Moroni Rotary Club, 20th Anniv.—A88

1985, Nov. 30 *Perf. 13*

353	A88	25fr	multi	10	5
354	A88	75fr	multi	30	15
355	A88	125fr	multi	52	25
356	A88	500fr	multi	2.00	1.00

Mushrooms—A89

1985, Dec. 24 *Perf. 13½*

357	A89	75fr	Boletus edulis	30	15
358	A89	125fr	Sarcoscypha coccinea	52	25
359	A89	200fr	Hypholoma fasciculare	80	40
360	A89	350fr	Astraeus hygrometricus	1.40	70
361	A89	500fr	Armillariella mellea	2.00	1.00
			Nos. 357-361 (5)	5.02	2.50

Health Year—A90

1986, Oct. 2 Litho. *Perf. 15x14½*

362	A90	25fr	Pediatric examination	14	8
363	A90	100fr	Weighing child	55	28
364	A90	200fr	Immunization	1.10	55

Musical Instruments—A91

1986, Dec. 24 Litho. *Perf. 13*

365	A91	75fr	Ndzoumara	40	20
366	A91	125fr	Ndzedze	70	35
367	A91	210fr	Gaboussi	1.15	58
368	A91	500fr	Ngoma	2.75	1.40

SEMI-POSTAL STAMPS

Anti-Malaria Issue

Common Design Type

Perf. 12½x12

1962, Apr. 7 Engraved Unwmkd.

B1	CD108	25fr	+5fr brt pink	1.75	1.75

Issued for the World Health Organization drive to eradicate malaria.

Nurse Feeding Infant
SP1

Mother and Child
SP2

1967, July 3 Engraved *Perf. 13*

B2	SP1	25fr	+5fr red, brt grn & choc	1.10	1.10

For the Red Cross.

1974, Aug. 10 Engraved *Perf. 13*

B3	SP2	35fr	+10fr red & dk brn	80	80

For the Red Cross.

AIR POST STAMPS.

Comoro Village—AP1

Comoro Men and Moroni Mosque
AP2

Design: 200fr, Mosque of Ouani, Anjouan.

Engraved

1950-54 *Perf. 13* Unwmkd.

C1	AP1	50fr grn & red brn	2.25	1.15
C2	AP2	100fr dk brn & red	3.25	1.15
C3	AP1	200fr dk grn, rose brn & pur ('54)	13.50	6.75

Liberation Issue
Common Design Type

1954, June 6

C4	CD102	15fr sep & red	20.00	15.00

10th anniversary of the liberation of France.

Madrepora Fructicosa
AP3

Design: 100fr, Coral, shells and sea anemones.

Photogravure

1962, Jan. 13 *Perf. 12½x13*

C5	AP3	100fr multi	3.00	3.00
C6	AP3	500fr multi	12.50	11.00

Telstar Issue
Common Design Type

1962, Dec. 5 Engraved *Perf. 13*

C7	CD111	25fr dp vio, dl pur & red lil	2.75	1.50

Type of Regular Issue, 1963.

Designs: 65fr, Baskets. 200fr, Pendant.

Engraved

1963, Dec. 27 *Perf. 13* Unwmkd.

Size: 26½x48mm.

C8	A13	65fr car, grn & ocher	2.00	1.20
C9	A13	200fr grnsh bl, rose lake & red	4.00	2.50

Boat Type of Regular Issue

Designs: 50fr, Mayotte pirogue. 85fr, Schooner.

1964, Aug. 7 Photo. *Perf. 13*

Size: 27x48mm.

C10	A14	50fr multi	1.50	60
C11	A14	85fr multi	2.25	1.35

Olympic Torch and Boxers
AP4

Order of Star of Grand Comoro
AP5

1964, Oct. 10 Engraved *Perf. 13*

C12	AP4	100fr red brn, dk brn & gray grn	2.50	2.50

18th Olympic Games, Tokyo, Oct. 10-25.

1964, Dec. 10 Photo. *Perf. 13*

C13	AP5	500fr crim, blk, emer & gold	10.00	6.50

ITU Issue
Common Design Type

1965, May 17 Engraved *Perf. 13*

C14	CD120	50fr gray, grnsh bl & ol	8.50	6.50

International Telecommunication Union centenary.

French Satellite A-1 Issue
Common Design Type

Designs: 25fr, Diamant rocket and launching installations. 30fr, A-1 satellite.

1966, Jan. 17 Engraved *Perf. 13*

C15	CD121	25fr dk pur & ultra	2.00	2.00
C16	CD121	30fr dk pur & ultra	2.50	2.50
a.		Strip of 2 + label	5.00	5.00

Issued to commemorate the launching of France's first satellite, Nov. 26, 1965. No. C16a contains one each of Nos. C15-C16 and dark purple label with commemorative inscription. Each sheet contains 16 triptychs (2x8).

French Satellite D-1 Issue
Common Design Type

1966, May 16 Engraved *Perf. 13*

C17	CD122	30fr dk grn, org & brn	1.75	1.20

Old Gun Battery, Dzaoudzi
AP6

Design: 200fr, Ksar Castle, Mutsamudu (vert.).

1966, Dec. 19 Photo. *Perf. 13*

C18	AP6	50fr multi	1.00	85
C19	AP6	200fr multi	3.50	2.00

Bird Type of Regular Issue

Birds: 75fr, Madagascar paradise flycatchers. 100fr, Blue-cheeked bee eaters.

1967, June 20 Photo. *Perf. 13*

Size: 27x48mm.

C20	A17	75fr yel grn & multi	1.75	65
C21	A17	100fr lt bl & multi	2.10	85

Woman Skier
AP7

1968, Apr. 29 Engraved *Perf. 13*

C22	AP7	70fr brt grn, lt bl & choc	1.20	75

Issued to commemorate the 10th Winter Olympic Games, Grenoble, France, Feb. 6-18, 1968.

Fish Type of Regular Issue

Designs: 50fr, Moorish idol. 90fr, Diagramma lineatus.

1968, Aug. 1 Engraved *Perf. 13*

Size 47½x27mm.

C23	A19	50fr plum blk & yel	1.00	90
C24	A19	90fr brt grn, yel & gray grn	1.75	1.35

Swimmer, Butterfly Stroke
AP8

1969, Jan. 27 Photo. *Perf. 12½*

C25	AP8	65fr ver, grnsh bl & blk	1.35	1.00

Issued to commemorate the 19th Olympic Games, Mexico City, Oct. 12-27.

Flower Type of Regular Issue, 1969.

Designs: 50fr, Heliconia sp. (vert.). 85fr, Tuberose (vert.). 200fr, Orchid (angraecum eburneum; vert.).

1969, Mar. 20 Photo. *Perf. 13*

Size: 27x48mm.

C26	A21	50fr gray & multi	1.00	75
C27	A21	85fr multi	1.50	1.00
C28	A21	200fr dk red & multi	2.75	2.10

Concorde Issue
Common Design Type

1969, Apr. 17 Engraved

C29	CD129	100fr pur & brn org	7.50	6.00

View of EXPO, Globe and Moon
AP9

Design: 90fr, Geisha, map of Japan and EXPO emblem.

1970, Sept. 13 Photo. *Perf. 13*

C30	AP9	60fr sl & multi	1.20	75
C31	AP9	90fr multi	1.20	75

EXPO '70 International Exposition, Osaka, Japan, Mar. 15-Sept. 13.

Sunset over Mutsamudu
AP10

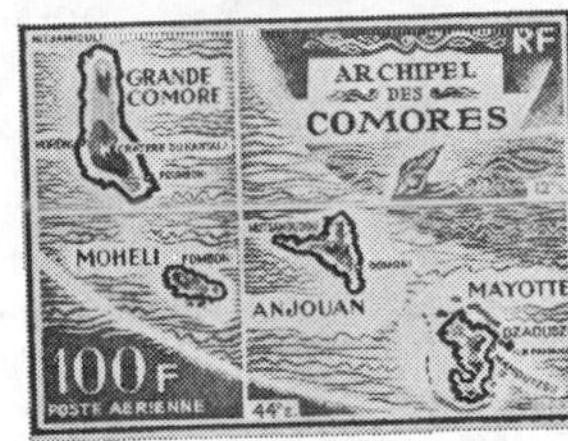

Map of Archipelago
AP11

Designs: 20fr, Sada Village, Mayotte. 65fr, Old Iconi Palace, Grand Comoro. 85fr, Nioumatchoua Island, Moheli.

1971, May 3 Photo. *Perf. 13*

C32	AP10	15fr dk bl & multi	25	10
C33	AP10	20fr multi	45	25
C34	AP10	65fr grn & multi	90	45
C35	AP10	85fr bl & multi	1.10	60

Engraved

C36	AP11	100fr brn red, grn & vio bl	2.00	1.00
		Nos. C32-C36 (5)	4.70	2.40

See Nos. 107-110, C45-C49, C53, C62-C64.

Flower Type of Regular Issue

Flowers: 60fr, Hibiscus schizopetalus. 85fr, Acalypha sanderii.

1971, July 19 Photo. *Perf. 13*

Size: 27x48mm.

C37	A25	60fr grn, ver & yel	1.20	60
C38	A25	85fr grn, red & yel	1.50	90

Mural, Moroni Airport—AP12

Designs: 85fr, Mural in Arrival Hall, Moroni Airport. 100fr, View of Moroni Airport.

1972, Mar. 30 Photo. *Perf. 13*

C39	AP12	65fr gray & multi	60	50
C40	AP12	85fr gray & multi	90	50

Engraved

C41	AP12	100fr brn, bl & sl grn	1.50	75

New airport in Moroni.

Eiffel Tower and Moroni Telephone Exchange—AP13

Design: 75fr, Frenchman and Comoro Islander talking on telephone, radio tower and beacons.

1972, Apr. 24

C42	AP13	35fr dl red & gray	35	20

C43	AP13	75fr dk car, vio & bl	70	35

First radio-telephone connection between France and Comoro Islands.

Underwater Spear-fishing—AP14

1972, July 5 Engraved *Perf. 13*

C44	AP14	70fr vio bl, brt grn & mar	1.10	80

Types of 1971

1972, Nov. 15 Photogravure

Designs: 20fr, Cape Sima. 35fr, Bambao Palace. 40fr, Domoni Palace. 60fr, Gomajou Peninsula. 100fr, Map of Anjouan Island.

C45	AP10	20fr brn & multi	25	20
C46	AP10	35fr dk grn & multi	45	35
C47	AP10	40fr bl & multi	55	40
C48	AP10	60fr grnsh blk & multi	75	60

Engraved

C49	AP11	100fr mar, bl & sl grn	1.50	1.00
		Nos. C45-C49 (5)	3.50	2.55

Pres. Said Mohamed Cheikh AP15

1973, Mar. 16 Photo. *Perf. 13*

C50	AP15	20fr multi	30	25
C51	AP15	35fr multi	50	25

President Said Mohamed Cheikh (1904–1970).

No. C24 Surcharged

120F

Mission Internationale pour l'étude du Cœlacanthe

1973, Apr. 30 Engraved *Perf. 13*

C52	A19	120fr on 90fr multi	1.65	1.25

International Commission for Coelacanth Studies.

Map of Grand Comoro AP16

1973, June 28 Engr. *Perf. 13*

C53	AP16	135fr vio, bl & dk brn	2.25	1.60

See Nos. C65, C68.

Karthala Volcano AP17

1973, July 16 Photo. *Perf. 13x12½*

C54	AP17	120fr multi	1.65	1.25

Eruption of Karthala, Sept. 1972.

Armauer G. Hansen AP18

Design: 150fr, Nicolaus Copernicus.

1973, Sept. 5 Engr. *Perf. 13*

C55	AP18	100fr brn, dk bl & sl grn	1.65	1.25
C56	AP18	150fr grnsh bl, vio bl & choc	2.25	1.50

Centenary of the discovery of the Hansen bacillus, the cause of leprosy (100fr).

500th anniversary of the birth of Nicolaus Copernicus (1473–1543), Polish astronomer (150fr).

Pablo Picasso AP19

1973, Sept. 30 Photogravure

C57	AP19	200fr blk & multi	2.75	2.00

Souvenir Sheet

C58	AP19	100fr blk & multi	1.75	1.75

Pablo Picasso (1881–1973), painter. No. C58 contains one stamp; reddish brown marginal inscription. Size: 100x130mm.

Order of the Star of Anjou AP20

Said Omar ben Soumeth AP21

1974, Jan. 7 Photo. *Perf. 13*

C59	AP20	500fr brn, bl & gold	6.00	5.00

Perf. 13x13½, 13½x13

1974, Jan. 31

Design: 135fr, Grand Mufti Said Omar (horiz.).

C60	AP21	135fr blk & multi	1.60	1.35
C61	AP21	200fr blk & multi	2.75	1.90

Types of 1971–73

1974, Aug. 31 Photo. *Perf. 13*

Designs (Views on Mayotte): 20fr, Moya Beach. 35fr, Chiconi. 90fr, Port Mamutzu. 120fr, Map of Mayotte.

C62	AP10	20fr bl & multi	30	20
C63	AP10	35fr grn & multi	50	40
C64	AP10	90fr multi	1.20	1.00

Engraved

C65	AP16	120fr ultra & grn	1.50	1.20

Jet Take-off—AP22

1975, Jan. 10 Engraved *Perf. 13*

C66	AP22	135fr multi	1.75	1.35

First direct route Moroni-Hahaya-Paris.

ARCHIPEL DES COMORES - RF 250F

Rotary Emblem, Meeting House, Map—AP23

1975, Feb. 23 Photo. *Perf. 13*

C67	AP23	250fr multi	3.25	2.50

Rotary International, 70th anniversary, and Moroni Rotary Club, 10th anniversary.

Map Type of 1973

Design: 230fr, Map of Moheli (horiz.).

1975, May 26 Engr. *Perf. 13*

C68	AP16	230fr ocher, ol grn & bl	3.25	2.50

State of Comoro

Issues of 1968–75 Surcharged and Overprinted with Bars and: "ETAT COMORIEN" in Black, Silver, Red or Orange.

Printing and Perforations as Before.

1975

Multicolored

C69	AP10	10fr on 20fr #C62	12	8
C70	AP15	20fr (S)	28	18
C71	AP10	30fr on 35fr (R) #C63	40	30
C72	AP15	35fr (S)	45	35
C73	AP10	40fr (O)	55	38
C74	A19	50fr	70	45
C75	A25	75fr on 60fr	1.10	70
C76	AP10	75fr on 60fr	1.10	70
C77	AP10	75fr on 65fr (O)	1.10	70
C78	AP14	75fr on 70fr	1.10	70
C79	AP11	100fr #C36	1.40	90
C80	AP11	100fr #C49	1.40	90
C81	AP18	100fr	1.40	90
C82	AP10	100fr on 85fr (O)	1.40	90
C83	A25	100fr on 85fr	1.40	90
C84	AP10	100fr on 90fr	1.40	90
C85	AP21	100fr on 135fr (S)	1.40	90
C86	AP22	100fr on 135fr	1.40	90
C87	AP19	200fr (S)	2.80	1.85
C88	AP21	200fr (S)	2.80	1.85
C89	AP17	200fr on 120fr	2.80	1.85
C90	AP16	200fr on 120fr	2.80	1.85
C91	AP16	200fr on 135fr	2.80	1.85
C92	AP16	200fr on 230fr	2.80	1.85
C93	AP18	400fr on 150fr	5.60	3.75
C94	AP23	400fr on 250fr	5.60	3.75
C95	AP20	500fr	7.00	4.75
		Nos. C69-C95 (27)	53.10	35.09

Surcharged Soccer Type of 1979

Design: 200fr, English soccer game, 19th century, Soccer Cup, Argentina '78 emblem.

1979 Litho. *Perf. 13*

Black Overprint

C96	A40	200fr multi	1.75	1.75

Aviation Type of 1979

Design: 200fr, Charles Lindbergh and Spirit of St. Louis.

1979

Black Overprint

C97	A41	200fr multi	1.75	1.75

For Nos. C96–C97 without overprint see "For the Record."

Composer Type of 1979

Design: 50fr, Peter I. Tchaikovsky.

1979 Litho. *Perf. 13*

Black Surcharge

C98	A44	50fr on 200fr multi	55	55

Space Type of 1979

Exploration of Solar System: 200fr, William Herschel and Voyager II. 400fr, Urbain Leverrier and Voyager II. 500fr, Voyagers I and II, symbolic solar system.

1979, Feb. 19

C99	A46	200fr multi	1.40	55
C100	A46	400fr multi	3.00	1.25

Souvenir Sheet

C101	A46	500fr multi	4.00	1.75

No. C101 has multicolored margin showing symbolic design. Size: 130x80mm.

Chess Masters Type of 1979

Chess Grand Masters Alekhine, Spassky, Fischer, and bishop.

1979, Feb. 19

C102	A47	500fr multi	3.50	1.40

Satellite Type of 1979

Design: 200fr, Satellite (diff.), operator and radar.

1979, Sept. 15 Litho. *Perf. 13*

Black Overprint

C103	A48	200fr multi	2.00	

Gymnasts, Olympic Emblems, Fair Poster-AP24

1979, Sept. 15 Litho. *Perf. 13*

Black Overprint

C104	AP25	250fr multi	2.50	

Unused Prices

Catalogue prices for unused stamps through 1960 are for hinged copies in fine condition.

Never-hinged unused stamps issued before 1961 often sell above Catalogue prices.

Leonid Brezhnev, Pres. Ford, Astronauts
AP25

Design: 200 fr emblem & earth

Black Overprint

1979, Sept. 15.

C105	AP25	100fr multi	1.00	
C106	AP25	200fr multi	2.00	

For Nos. C103-C106 without overprint see "For the Record."

Rotary Emblem, Landscape
AP26

1979, July 31 ***Perf. 13x12½***

C107	AP26	400fr multi	4.50	2.50

Rotary International.

IYC Emblem, Mother and Child
AP27

1979, July 31 Litho. ***Perf. 13x13½***

C108	AP27	250fr multi	2.50	1.90

International Year of the Child. See No. CB1.

Dimadjou Dispensary, Map of Southern Africa, Emblem—AP28

1980, Feb. 23 Litho. ***Perf. 12½***

C109	AP28	100fr *shown*	75	45
C110	AP28	260fr *Globe, Concorde, emblem*	2.00	1.00

Rotary International, 75th anniversary and Moroni Rotary Club, 15th anniversary (100fr).

First Transatlantic Flight, 50th Anniversary—AP29

1980, May 30 Litho. ***Perf. 13***

C111	AP29	200fr multi	1.50	1.10

No. C111 Surcharged in Blue

1981, Feb. Litho. ***Perf. 13***

C112	AP29	30fr on 200fr multi	30	30

The Dove and the Rainbow, by Picasso—AP30

Picasso Birth Centenary: 70fr, Still Life on a Sideboard. 150fr, Studio with Plaster Head. 250fr, Bowl and Pot (vert.). 500fr, The Red Tablecloth.

1981, June 30 Litho. ***Perf. 12½***

C113	AP30	40fr multi	22	12
C114	AP30	70fr multi	38	18
C115	AP30	150fr multi	90	45
C116	AP30	250fr multi	1.50	75
C117	AP30	500fr multi	3.00	1.50
		Nos. C113-C117 (5)	6.00	3.00

Nos. C114, C109-C110, CB1 Surcharged.

1981, Nov. Litho. ***Perf. 12½, 13***

C118	AP30	10fr on 70fr multi	10	6
C119	AP28	10fr on 100fr multi	10	6
C120	AP28	50fr on 260fr multi	30	15
C121	AP27	50fr on 200+30fr multi	30	15

Manned Flight Bicentenary—AP31

Balloons. 100fr, 200fr, 300fr, 500fr vert.

1983, Apr. 20 Litho. ***Perf. 13***

C122	AP31	100fr Montgolfiere, 1783	60	30
C123	AP31	200fr Lunardi, 1784	1.25	60
C124	AP31	300fr Blanchard and Jeffries, 1785	1.75	90
C125	AP31	400fr Giffard, 1852	2.50	1.25

Souvenir Sheet

C126	AP31	500fr Paris Siege, 1870	3.00	1.50

No. C126 has multicolored margin showing aerial view of Paris and ballon monte cover. Size: 80x104mm.

Pre-Olympic Year Sailing—AP32

1983, June 30 Litho. ***Perf. 13***

C127	AP32	150fr Type 470	90	45
C128	AP32	200fr Flying Dutchman	1.25	60
C129	AP32	300fr Type 470, diff.	1.75	80
C130	AP32	400fr Finn	2.50	1.10

Souvenir Sheet

C131	AP32	500fr Solding	3.00	1.50

Multicolored margin continues design. Size: 104x80mm.

1984 Summer Olympics—AP33

1984, July 10 Litho. ***Perf. 13***

C132	AP33	60fr Basketball	38	18
C133	AP33	100fr Basketball, diff.	60	30
C134	AP33	105fr Basketball, diff.	1.00	50
C135	AP33	175fr Baseball, horiz.	1.10	50
C136	AP33	200fr Baseball, horiz.	1.25	60
		Nos. C132-C136 (5)	4.33	2.08

Souvenir Sheet

C137	AP33	500fr Basketball, diff.	3.00	1.50

Nos. C132-C134 vert. Size of No. C137: 104x80mm.

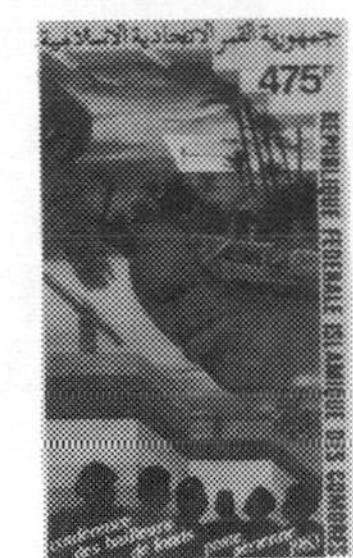

Development Conference—AP34

1984, July 2 Litho. ***Perf. 13***

C138	AP34	475fr Tools for development	2.50	

Audubon Bicentenary—AP35

1985, Jan. 15 Litho. ***Perf. 13***

C139	AP35	100fr Hirundo rustica, vert.	42	
C140	AP35	125fr Icterus galbula, vert.	52	
C141	AP35	150fr Buteo lineatus	62	
C142	AP35	500fr Sphyropicus varius	2.10	

Nos. C126, C131 Ovptd. with Exhibitions in Red or Gold.

1985, Mar. 11 ***Perf. 13***

C143	AP31	500fr Rome, ITALIA '85 emblem (R)	2.25	
C144	AP32	500fr OLYMPHILEX/'85/ LAUSANNE (G)	2.25	

Moroni Port Missile Defense—AP36

Designs: No. C146, Ngome Ntsoudjini Scout troop.

1985, May 20 Litho. ***Perf. 13x12½***

C145	AP36	200fr multi	80	
C146	AP36	200fr multi	80	

PHILEXAFRICA '85, Lome. Nos. C145-C146 printed se-tenant with center labels picturing map of Africa or UAPT emblem.

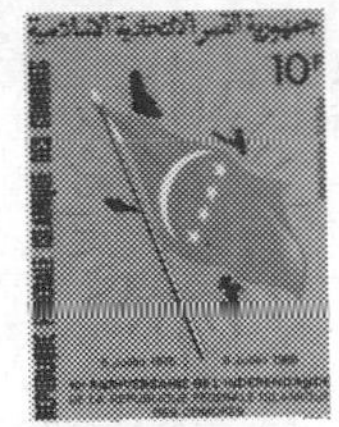

Natl. Flag, Sun, Outline Map of Islands—AP37

1985, July 6

C147	AP37	10fr multi	5	
C148	AP37	15fr multi	6	
C149	AP37	125fr multi	50	
C150	AP37	300fr multi	1.15	

Natl. independence, 10th anniv.

Runners—AP38

1985, Nov. 12

C151	AP38	250fr shown	1.00	
C152	AP38	250fr Mining	1.00	

PHILEXAFRICA '85, Lome, Togo, Nov. 16-24. Nos. C151-C152 printed se-tenant with center label picturing map of Africa or UAPT emblem.

Air Transport Union, UTA, 50th Anniv.—AP39

1985, Dec. 30 Litho. ***Perf. 13***

C153	AP39	25fr F-AOUL seaplane	10	5
C154	AP39	75fr Camel driver, DC-9	30	15
C155	AP39	100fr Noratlas and Heron DC-4s	40	20
a.		Souvenir sheet of 3, #C153-C155, perf. 12½	80	80
C156	AP39	125fr UTA cargo plane	52	25

Size: 40x52mm. ***Perf. 12½x13***

C157	AP39	1000fr Aircraft, 1935-1985	4.00	2.00
a.		Souvenir sheet of 2, #C156-C157, perf. 12½	4.55	4.55
		Nos. C153-C157 (5)	5.32	2.65

No. C155a has multicolored margin picturing world map. No. C157a has multicolored margin picturing airport and UTA jets. Sizes: 132x111mm.

Halley's Comet—AP40

Comets, astronomers and probes.

1986, Mar. 7 ***Perf. 13***

C158	AP40	125fr	Edmond Halley, Giotto probe	52	25
C159	AP40	150fr	Giacobini-Zinner, 1959	62	30
C160	AP40	225fr	Encke, 1961	90	45
C161	AP40	300fr	Bradfield, 1980	1.25	62
C162	AP40	400fr	Planet A probe	1.75	90
			Nos. C158-C162 (5)	5.04	2.52

1986 World Cup Soccer Championships, Mexico—AP41

Various soccer plays.

1986, June 11 **Litho.** ***Perf. 13***

C163	AP41	125fr	multi	52	25
C164	AP41	210fr	multi	88	45
C165	AP41	500fr	multi	2.00	1.00
C166	AP41	600fr	multi	2.40	1.20

Tennis at the 1988 Summer Olympics—AP42

Various players.

1987, Jan. 28 **Litho.** ***Perf. 13½***

C167	AP42	150fr	multi	82	40
C168	AP42	250fr	multi	1.40	70
C169	AP42	500fr	multi	2.75	1.40
C170	AP42	600fr	multi	3.25	1.65

World Wildlife Fund—AP43

Various pictures of the mongoose lemur.

1987, Feb. 18 ***Perf. 13***

C171	AP43	75fr	multi, vert.	40	20
C172	AP43	100fr	multi	55	28
C173	AP43	125fr	multi	70	35
C174	AP43	150fr	multi	82	40

AIR POST SEMI-POSTAL STAMP

Type of Air Post 1979

Design: IYC emblem, mother and son.

1979, July 31 Litho. *Perf. 13½x13*

CB1	AP27	200fr +30fr multi	1.75	1.75

International Year of the Child.

POSTAGE DUE STAMPS

Anjouan Mosque D1

Coelacanth D2

Engraved.

1950 *Perf. 14x13.* Unwmkd.

J1	D1	50c dp grn	38	38
J2	D1	1fr blk brn	38	38

1954

J3	D2	5fr dk brn & grn	42	42
J4	D2	10fr gray & red brn	55	55
J5	D2	20fr ind & bl	85	85

Hibiscus D3

Designs: 2fr, 15fr, 40fr, 50fr, vertical.

1977, Nov. 19 Litho. *Perf. 13½*

Multicolored

J6	D3	1fr *shown*	5	5
J7	D3	2fr *Pineapple*	5	5
J8	D3	5fr *White butterfly*	6	6
J9	D3	10fr *Chameleon*	6	6
J10	D3	15fr *Blooming banana*	8	6
J11	D3	20fr *Orchids*	10	6
J12	D3	30fr *Allamanda cathartica*	15	10
J13	D3	40r *Cashews*	22	12
J14	D3	50fr *Custard apple*	25	15
J15	D3	100fr *Breadfruit*	50	25
J16	D3	200fr *Vanilla*	1.00	50
J17	D3	500fr *Ylang ylang*	2.50	1.25
		Nos. J6-J17 (12)	5.02	2.71

OFFICIAL STAMPS

Comoro Flag O1

Perf. 13x12½

1979-85 Litho. Unwmkd.

O1	O1	5fr multi	5	5
O2	O1	10fr multi	6	6
O3	O1	20fr multi	15	6
O4	O1	30fr multi	28	12
O5	O1	40fr multi	38	25
O6	O1	60fr multi ('80)	32	25
O6A	O1	75fr multi ('85)	30	20
O7	O1	100fr multi	75	50
		Nos. O1-O7 (8)	2.29	1.49

Pres. Said Mohamed Cheikh (1904-1970)-02

1980

O8	O2	100fr multi	50	38
O8A	O2	125fr multi ('85)	50	35
O9	O2	400fr multi	2.00	1.40

CONGO DEMOCRATIC REPUBLIC

(kŏng' gō)

LOCATION — Central Africa.

GOVT.—Republic.

AREA—895,348 sq. mi. (estimated).

POP.—22,480,000 (est. 1971).

CAPITAL—Kinshasa (Leopoldville).

Congo was an independent state, founded by Leopold II of Belgium, until 1908 when it was annexed to Belgium as a colony. Congo became an independent republic in 1960. The name was changed to Republic of Zaire, Oct. 28, 1971. See Zaire in Vol. IV for later issues.

100 Centimes = 1 Franc
100 Sengi = 1 Li-Kuta,
100 Ma-Kuta = 1 Zaire (1967)

Belgian Congo Flower Issue of 1952–53 Overprinted or Surcharged **CONGO**

1960, June 6 Photo. ***Perf. 11½***

Flowers in Natural Colors

Size: 21x25½mm.

Granite Paper

No.	Type	Description	Unused	Used
323	A86	10c dp plum & ocher	6	6
324	A86	10c on 15c red & yel grn	10	10
325	A86	20c grn & gray	6	6
326	A86	40c grn & sal	6	5
327	A86	50c on 60c bl grn & pink	10	10
328	A86	50c on 75c dp plum & gray	10	10
329	A86	1fr car & yel	6	5
330	A86	1.50fr vio & ap grn	8	5
331	A86	2fr ol grn & buff	12	6
332	A86	3fr ol grn & pink	20	8
333	A86	4fr choc & lil	25	20
334	A86	5fr dp plum & lt bl grn	25	10
335	A86	6.50fr dk car & lil	35	10
336	A86	8fr grn & lt yel	50	20
337	A86	10fr dp plum & pale ol	70	20
338	A86	20fr vio bl & dl sal	1.40	55

Overprinted **CONGO**

Size: 22x32mm.

No.	Type	Description	Unused	Used
339	A86	50fr dp plum & gray bl	7.25	3.50
340	A86	100fr grn & buff	12.50	6.00
		Nos. 323-340 (18)	24.14	11.56

Belgian Congo Animal Issue, Nos. 306–317, Overprinted or Surcharged in Red, Blue, Black or Brown **CONGO**

No.	Type	Description	Unused	Used
341	A92	10c bl & brn (R)	6	6
342	A93	20c red org & sl (Bl)	6	6
343	A92	40c brn & bl (Bk)	6	6
344	A93	50c brt ultra, red & sep (R)	5	5
345	A92	1fr brn, grn & blk (Br)	6	5
346	A93	1.50fr blk & org yel (R)	8	6
347	A92	2fr crim, blk & brn (Bl)	10	5
348	A93	3.50fr on 3fr blk, gray & lil rose (Bk)	18	7
349	A92	5fr brn, dk brn & brt grn (Br)	25	10
350	A93	6.50fr bl, brn & org yel (R)	28	10
351	A92	8fr org brn, ol bis & lil (Br)	32	25
352	A93	10fr multi (R)	45	20
		Nos. 341-352 (12)	1.95	1.11

Same Overprint on Belgian Congo No. 318.

1960

No.	Type	Description	Unused	Used
353	A94	50c gldn brn, ocher & red brn	60	60

Same Overprint and Surcharge of New Value on Belgian Congo Nos. 321–322.

Inscription in French

No.	Type	Description	Unused	Used
354	A95	3.50fr on 3fr gray & red	60	50

Inscription in Flemish

No.	Type	Description	Unused	Used
355	A95	3.50fr on 3fr gray & red	60	50

Map of Congo
A93a

1960 **Photogravure** ***Perf. 11½***

No.	Type	Description	Unused	Used
356	A93a	20c brown	8	5
357	A93a	50c rose red	8	5
358	A93a	1fr green	8	6
359	A93a	1.50fr red brn	12	5
360	A93a	2fr rose car	15	5
361	A93a	3.50fr lilac	17	8
362	A93a	5fr brt bl	23	10
363	A93a	6.50fr gray	30	12
364	A93a	10fr orange	50	25
365	A93a	20fr ultra	75	38
		Nos. 356-365 (10)	2.46	1.19

Issued to commemorate Congo's Independence.

Flag, People and Broken Chain
A94

1961 ***Perf. 11½*** **Unwmkd.**

Flag in Blue and Yellow

No.	Type	Description	Unused	Used
366	A94	2fr rose vio	10	6
367	A94	3.50fr vermilion	12	10
368	A94	6.50fr yel brn	25	12
369	A94	10fr brt grn	38	20
370	A94	20fr car rose	65	45
		Nos. 366-370 (5)	1.50	93

Issued to commemorate the signing of the Independence Agreement by Belgium, Jan. 4, 1959.

Nos. 356–365 Overprinted in Blue, Black or Red: "Conference Coquilhatville Avril Mai 1961"

1961

No.	Type	Description	Unused	Used
371	A93a	20c brn (Bl)	60	60
372	A93a	50c rose red (Bk)	60	60
373	A93a	1fr grn (R)	60	60
374	A93a	1.50fr red brn (Bl)	60	60
375	A93a	2fr rose car (Bk)	60	60
376	A93a	3.50fr lil (Bl)	60	60
377	A93a	5fr brt bl (R)	60	60
378	A93a	6.50fr gray (R)	60	60
379	A93a	10fr org (Bk)	60	60
380	A93a	20fr ultra (R)	60	60
		Nos. 371-380 (10)	6.00	6.00

Issued to commemorate the Coquilhatville Conference April–May, 1961.

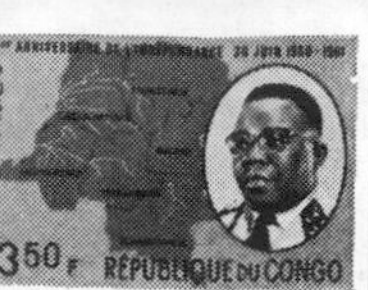

Pres. Joseph Kasavubu
A95

Kasavubu and Map of Congo
A96

Design: 10fr, 20fr, 50fr, 100fr, Kasavubu in uniform and map.

Photogravure

1961, June 30 ***Perf. 11½*** **Unwmkd.**

Portrait and Inscription in Dark Brown

No.	Type	Description	Unused	Used
381	A95	10c yellow	8	8
382	A95	20c dp rose	8	8
383	A95	40c bl grn	8	8
384	A95	50c salmon	8	8
385	A95	1fr lilac	12	8
386	A95	1.50fr lt brn	15	8
387	A95	2fr brt grn	15	8
388	A96	3.50fr rose pink	20	8
389	A96	5fr gray	1.75	18
390	A96	6.50fr ultra	45	8
391	A96	8fr olive	50	15
392	A95	10fr lt vio	1.10	15
393	A95	20fr orange	1.10	18
394	A95	50fr lt bl	1.75	45
395	A95	100fr ap grn	2.50	75
		Nos. 381-395 (15)	10.09	2.58

First anniversary of independence.

Nos. 381–387, 389 and 392 Overprinted: "REOUVERTURE du PARLEMENT JUILLET 1961"

1961

Portrait and Inscription in Dark Brown

No.	Type	Description	Unused	Used
396	A95	10c yellow	10	8
397	A95	20c dp rose	10	8
398	A95	40c bl grn	10	8
399	A95	50c salmon	42	30
400	A95	1fr lilac	42	30
401	A95	1.50fr lt brn	1.10	90
402	A95	2fr brt grn	1.10	90
403	A96	5fr gray	1.10	90
404	A95	10fr lt vio	1.25	1.10
		Nos. 396-404 (9)	5.69	4.64

Issued to commemorate the re-opening of the Congolese parliament, July, 1961.

Dag Hammarskjold and Map of Africa with Congo
A97

Malaria Eradication Emblem and Mosquito
A98

1962, Jan. 20 **Photo.** ***Perf. 11½***

Gray Background

No.	Type	Description	Unused	Used
405	A97	10c dk brn	5	5
406	A97	20c Prus bl	5	5
407	A97	30c brown	7	7
408	A97	40c dk bl	7	7
409	A97	50c brn red	10	10
410	A97	3fr ol grn	2.50	1.65
411	A97	6.50fr dk vio	85	55
412	A97	8fr red brn	95	70
		Nos. 405-412 (8)	4.64	3.24

Souvenir Sheets

Imperf.

No.	Type	Description	Unused	Used
413	A97	25fr blk brn	4.00	4.00
	a.	Ovpt. in grn	1.50	1.50

Nos. 405–413 issued in memory of Dag Hammarskjold, Secretary General of the United Nations, 1953–61.

No. 413 contains one stamp and has gold marginal inscription. Size: 65x90mm.

No 413a is overprinted "30 Juin 1962" on stamp and "2eme Anniversaire de l'Independance" on sheet margin. Issued June 30, 1962.

1962, June 15 **Granite Paper**

No.	Type	Description	Unused	Used
414	A98	1.50fr yel, blk & dk red	8	8
415	A98	2fr yel grn, brn & bl grn	42	20
416	A98	6.50fr ultra, blk & mar	20	15

Issued for the World Health Organization drive to eradicate malaria.

Nos. 405–412 Overprinted in Blue, Purple, Black or Carmine

"Paix, Travail, Austerite .."
C. ADOULA
11 juillet 1962

1962, Oct. 15

Gray Background

No.	Type	Description	Unused	Used
417	A97	10c dk brn (Bl)	7	5
418	A97	20c Prus bl (P)	7	5
419	A97	30c brn (Bk)	7	5
420	A97	40c dk bl (C)	7	5
421	A97	50c brn red (Bl)	1.75	75
422	A97	3fr ol grn (P)	22	7
423	A97	6.50fr dk vio (Bk)	30	12
424	A97	8fr red brn (C)	42	20
		Nos. 417-424 (8)	2.97	1.34

Reorganization of Adoula administration.

Canceled to Order

Starting in 1963, prices in the used column are for "canceled to order" stamps. Postally used copies sell for much more.

A99

1963, Jan. 28 **Engr.** ***Perf. 10½x13***

No.	Type	Description	Unused	Used
425	A99	2fr dl pur	1.40	1.50
426	A99	4fr red	10	8
427	A99	7fr dk bl	15	10
428	A99	20fr sl grn	30	20

Issued to commemorate Congo's first participation at the U.P.U. Congress, New Delhi, March, 1963.

Shoebill
A100

Birds: 10c, Pelicans. 20c, Crested guinea fowl (horiz.). 30c, Openbill. 40c, White-bellied storks (horiz.). 2fr, Marabou. 3fr, Greater flamingos (horiz.). 4fr, Congolese peacock. 5fr, Hartlaub ducks (horiz.). 6fr, Secretary bird. 7fr, Black-casqued hornbill (horiz.). 8fr, Sacred ibis and nest. 10fr, Crowned crane (horiz.). 20fr, Saddle-bill stork (horiz.).

Photogravure

1963 ***Perf. 11½*** **Unwmkd.**

No.	Type	Description	Unused	Used
429	A100	10c pink, ultra & ocher	5	5
430	A100	20c rose red, bl & blk	5	5
431	A100	30c grn, ocher & blk	5	5

432 A100 40c gray, org & blk 5 5
433 A100 1fr brn, emer & gray 5 5
434 A100 2fr gray, red & ind 1.75 50
435 A100 3fr ol grn, blk & rose 8 5
436 A100 4fr car rose, vio bl & grn 8 5
437 A100 5fr lake, lt bl & blk 10 5
438 A100 6fr pur, yel & blk 1.75 50
439 A100 7fr bl grn, blk & ind 15 5
440 A100 8fr yel, org & blk 18 5
441 A100 10fr bl, blk & rose 22 8
442 A100 20fr cit, red & blk 45 10
Nos. 429-442 (14) 5.01 1.68

Cinchona Ledgeriana A101 — Red Cross Nurse A102

Designs: 10c, 30c, 5fr, Strophanthus sarmentosus.

Perf. 12½x13½, 13½x12½

1963, May 25 Engr. Unwmkd.

Cross in Red

443 A101 10c vio & dl grn 5 5
444 A101 20c mag & bl 5 5
445 A101 30c grn & org 5 5
446 A101 40c bl & vio 6 6
447 A101 5fr ol & rose cl 12 5
448 A101 7fr org & blk 12 5
449 A102 9fr gray ol & red 18 8
450 A102 20fr pur & red 1.75 1.00
Nos. 443-450 (8) 2.38 1.39

International Red Cross centenary.

A souvenir sheet of three contains imperf. 5fr, 7fr, and 20fr stamps similar to Nos. 447, 448 and 450, but in changed colors. Marginal inscriptions in violet. Size: 109x75mm. Price $15.

Men Joining Hands and Map of Congo—A103

1963, June 29 Photo. Perf. 11½

451 A103 4fr multi 1.25 45
452 A103 5fr multi 10 5
453 A103 9fr multi 20 8
454 A103 12fr multi 28 12

Issued to celebrate national reconciliation.

Bulldozer and Kabambare Sewer, Leopoldville—A104

Designs: 30c, 5fr, 12fr, Excavator and blueprint. 50c, 9fr, Building Ituri road.

1963, July 1 Engraved Unwmkd.

455 A104 20c multi 5 5
456 A104 30c multi 5 5
457 A104 50c multi 5 5
458 A104 3fr multi 1.25 50
459 A104 5fr multi 10 5
460 A104 9fr multi 18 10
461 A104 12fr multi 22 15
Nos. 455-461 (7) 1.90 95

Issued to publicize aid to Congo by the European Economic Community.

Leopoldville Airport N'Djili A105

Design: 5fr, 7fr, 50fr, Tail assembly and airport.

1963, Nov. 30 Photo. Perf. 11½

462 A105 2fr gray, yel & red brn 5 5
463 A105 5fr mag, vio & yel 8 8
464 A105 6fr bl, yel & dk brn 1.25 55
465 A105 7fr multi 35 22
466 A105 30fr lil, yel & ol 55 38
467 A105 50fr multi 60 40
Nos. 462-467 (6) 2.88 1.68

Issued to publicize Air Congo.

Nos. 425–428 Overprinted with Silver Frame on Three Sides and Black Inscription: "15e anniversaire/10 DECEMBRE 1948/DROITS DE L'HOMME/ 10 DECEMBRE 1963"

Engraved and Typographed

1963, Dec. 10 Perf. 10½x13

468 A99 2fr dl pur 6 6
469 A99 4fr red 8 8
470 A99 7fr dk bl 28 28
471 A99 20fr sl grn 30 30

15th anniversary of Universal Declaration of Human Rights.

Nos. 468–471 exist with side date panels transposed ("1963" at left, "1948" at right). Price, each $5.

Laboratory Technician and Atomic Emblem—A106

Designs: 1.50fr, 60fr, University. 8fr, 75fr, First African nuclear reactor. 25fr, 100fr, University and crest.

1964, Feb. 1 Photo. Perf. 14x12½

472 A106 50c multi 8 8
473 A106 1.50fr multi 8 8
474 A106 8fr multi 2.50 2.25
475 A106 25fr multi 25 20
476 A106 30fr multi 30 25
477 A106 60fr multi 55 45
478 A106 75fr multi 75 70
479 A106 100fr multi 1.00 85
a. Souv. sheet of 3 3.50 3.50
Nos. 472-479 (8) 5.51 4.86

10th anniversary of Lovanium University, Leopoldville.

No. 479a contains 3 imperf. multicolored stamps: 20fr, design as 50c; 30fr, as 8fr; 100fr. Size: 141x70mm.

Belgian Congo Issues of 1952–59 Overprinted "REPUBLIQUE DU CONGO" and Surcharged in Black on Overprinted Metallic Panels.

1964 Perf. 11½

480 A93 1fr on 20c red org & sl (#307) 8 8
481 A86 2fr on 1.50fr multi (#273) 2.10 1.50
482 A93 5fr on 6.50fr multi (#315) 32 20
483 A86 8fr on 6.50fr multi (#278) 40 25

Republic Issues of 1960–61 Surcharged in Black on Overprinted Metallic Rectangles or Ovals.

484 A86 1fr on 6.50fr multi (#335) 8 8
485 A93 1fr on 20c red org & sl (#342) 8 8
486 A86 2fr on 1.50fr multi (#330) 8 8
487 A95 3fr on 20c dp rose & dk brn (#382) 25 20
488 A95 4fr on 40c bl grn & dk brn (#383) 25 20
489 A93 5fr on 6.50fr multi ("Congo" red) (#350) 33 20
a. "Congo" black 33 20
490 A93a 6fr on 6.50fr gray (#363) 33 22
491 A93a 7fr on 20c brn (#356) 50 28
Nos. 480-491 (12) 4.80 3.37

Pole Vault A107

Sports: 7fr, 20fr, Javelin (vert.). 8fr, 100fr, Hurdling.

Photogravure

1964, July 13 Perf. 11½ Unwmkd.

Granite Paper

492 A107 5fr gray, dk brn & car 6 5
493 A107 7fr rose, vio & emer 1.20 55
494 A107 8fr org, yel, red brn & vio bl 10 5
495 A107 10fr bl, vio brn & mag 10 5
496 A107 20fr gray grn, red brn & ver 25 10
497 A107 100fr lil, dk brn & grn 1.20 30
a. Souv. sheet of 3 5.25 5.25
Nos. 492-497 (6) 2.91 1.10

Issued to commemorate the 18th Olympic Games, Tokyo, Oct. 10–25. No. 497a contains 3 imperf. stamps (20fr orange & dark brown, pole vault; 30fr citron and dark brown, hurdling; 100fr dull green and dark brown, javelin). Dark brown marginal inscription and dull green Olympic rings. Size: 134x85mm. Sheet issued Sept. 10.

National Palace, Leopoldville A108

1964, Sept. 15 Granite Paper

498 A108 50c lil rose & bl 5 5
499 A108 1fr bl & lil rose 5 5
500 A108 2fr brn red & vio 5 5
501 A108 3fr emer & red 5 5
502 A108 4fr org & vio bl 5 5
503 A108 5fr gray vio & emer 5 5
504 A108 6fr sep & org 8 5
505 A108 7fr gray ol & red brn 8 5
506 A108 8fr rose red & vio bl 2.50 50
507 A108 9fr vio bl & rose red 7 5
508 A108 10fr brn ol & grn 10 5
509 A108 20fr bl & brn org 15 5
510 A108 30fr dk car rose & grn 22 7
511 A108 40fr ultra & dk car rose 33 7
512 A108 50fr brn org & grn 45 7
513 A108 100fr sl & ver 85 15
Nos. 498-513 (16) 5.13 1.41

Pres. John F. Kennedy—A109

1964, Dec. 8 Photo. Perf. 13½

514 A109 5fr dk bl & blk 8 5
515 A109 6fr rose cl & blk 8 5
516 A109 9fr brn & blk 10 5
517 A109 30fr pur & blk 42 7
518 A109 40fr dl grn & blk 2.50 13
519 A109 60fr red brn & blk 70 30
Nos. 514-519 (6) 3.88 1.27

Souvenir Sheet

520 A109 150fr blk & mar 3.00 3.00

Issued in memory of Pres. John F. Kennedy (1917–63). No. 520 contains one stamp, black marginal inscription. Size: 64x76mm.

Rocket and Unisphere A110 — Basketball A111

Engraved and Typographed

1965, March 1 Perf. 12 Unwmkd.

521 A110 50c lil & blk 5 5
522 A110 1.50fr bl & lil 5 5
523 A110 2fr red brn & brt grn 5 5
524 A110 10fr brt grn & dk red 1.00 60
525 A110 18fr vio bl & brn 15 8
526 A110 27fr rose red & grn 33 12
527 A110 40fr gray & org 50 18
Nos. 521-527 (7) 2.13 1.13

New York World's Fair, 1964–65.

1965, Apr. Photo. Perf. 13½

Designs: 6fr, 40fr, Soccer (horiz.). 15fr, 60fr, Volleyball.

528 A111 5fr blk, grnsh bl & ocher 5 5
529 A111 6fr blk, bl gray & crim 8 5
530 A111 15fr blk, org & yel grn 12 10
531 A111 24fr blk, rose lil & brt grn 30 10
532 A111 40fr blk, brt grn & ultra 1.75 60
533 A111 60fr blk, bl & red lil 55 20
Nos. 528-533 (6) 2.85 1.10

First African Games, Leopoldville, Mar. 31–Apr. 7, 1965.

Earth and Satellites A112

Designs: 9fr, 15fr, 20fr, 40fr, Satellites at left, globe at right.

Perf. 14x14½

1965, June 28 Photo. Unwmkd.

No.	Type	Description	Unused	Used
534	A112	6fr blk, sal & vio	8	5
535	A112	9fr blk, lt grn & gray	8	5
536	A112	12fr org, gray & blk	10	7
537	A112	15fr grn, ultra & blk	13	7
538	A112	18fr blk, lt grn & gray	1.50	42
539	A112	20fr blk, sal & vio	22	8
540	A112	30fr grn, ultra & blk	33	10
541	A112	40fr org, gray & blk	45	15
		Nos. 534-541 (8)	2.89	99

Issued to commemorate the centenary of the International Telecommunication Union.

Congolese Paratrooper and Parachutes A113

1965, July 5 ***Perf. 13x14***

No.	Type	Description	Unused	Used
542	A113	5fr brt bl & brn	5	5
543	A113	6fr org & brn	5	5
544	A113	7fr bl grn & brn	60	28
545	A113	9fr brt pink & brn	10	8
546	A113	18fr lem & brn	18	10
		Nos. 542-546 (5)	98	56

Fifth anniversary of independence.

Matadi Harbor and ICY Emblem
A114

Designs (ICY Emblem and): 8fr, 25fr, Katanga mines. 9fr, 60fr, Tshopo Dam, Stanleyville.

1965, Oct. 25 Photo. ***Perf. 13x14***

No.	Type	Description	Unused	Used
547	A114	6fr ultra, blk & yel	8	5
548	A114	8fr org red, blk & bl	10	5
549	A114	9fr bl grn, blk & brn org	10	5
550	A114	12fr car rose, blk & gray	1.15	45
551	A114	25fr ol, blk & rose red	27	12
552	A114	60fr gray, blk & org	55	15
		Nos. 547-552 (6)	2.25	87

International Cooperation Year, 1965.

Soldiers Giving First Aid
A115

The Army Serving the Country: 7fr, Bridge building. 9fr, Feeding child. 19fr, Maintenance of telegraph lines. 20fr, House building. 30fr, Soldier and flag. (19fr, 20fr, 30fr, vertical.)

Perf. 12½x13, 13x12½

1965, Nov. 17

No.	Type	Description	Unused	Used
553	A115	5fr sal, brn & red	8	5
554	A115	7fr yel & grn	8	5
555	A115	9fr ol & brn	10	5
556	A115	19fr brt grn & brn	90	55
557	A115	20fr lt bl & brn	25	8
558	A115	30fr multi	35	10
		Nos. 553-558 (6)	1.76	88

See also Nos. 582-586.

Nos. 551–552 Overprinted with U.N. Emblem and "6e Journée Météorologique Mondiale / 23.3.66." on Metallic Strip

1966, Mar. 23 Photo. ***Perf. 13x14***

No.	Type	Description	Unused	Used
559	A114	25fr ol & blk	1.10	55
560	A114	60fr gray & blk	1.10	80

6th World Meteorological Day.

Woman's Head and Goat
A116

Designs: 10fr, Sculptured heads. 12fr, Sitting figure and two heads (vert.). 53fr, Figure with earrings and kneeling woman with bowl (vert.).

Perf. 11½x13, 13x11½

1966, Apr. 23 Litho. Unwmkd.

No.	Type	Description	Unused	Used
561	A116	10fr red, blk & gray	12	12
562	A116	12fr grn, blk & bl	15	15
563	A116	15fr dp bl, blk & lil	18	18
564	A116	53fr dp rose, blk & vio bl	1.50	1.25

Issued to commemorate the International Negro Arts Festival, Dakar, Senegal, Apr. 1–24.

Pres. Joseph Desiré Mobutu and Fishing Industry A117

Pres. Mobutu and: 4fr, Pyrethrum harvest. 6fr, Building industry. 8fr, Winnowing rice. 10fr, Cotton harvest. 12fr, Banana harvest. 15fr, Cacao harvest. 24fr, Pineapple harvest.

1966, May 1 Photo. ***Perf. 11½***

No.	Type	Description	Unused	Used
565	A117	2fr dk brn & dk bl	6	6
566	A117	4fr dk brn & org	6	6
567	A117	6fr dk brn & ol	95	85
568	A117	8fr dk brn & brt grnsh bl	7	7
569	A117	10fr dk brn & brn red	10	10
570	A117	12fr dk brn & vio	12	10
571	A117	15fr dk brn & lt ol grn	12	10
572	A117	24fr dk brn & lil rose	30	20
		Nos. 565-572 (8)	1.78	1.54

Souvenir Sheet

Design: Pres. Mobutu without cap, and men rolling up sleeves.

Perf. 11x11½

No.	Type	Description	Unused	Used
573	A117	Sheet of 4	1.10	1.10
a.		15fr red, blk & ultra	25	25

Issued to honor Lt. Gen. Joseph Desiré Mobutu, President of Congo, and to publicize the "Back to Work" campaign. No. 573 contains four stamps and flag of Congo in margin. Size: 127x94½mm.

Nos. 510–513 Overprinted

1966, June 13 ***Perf. 11½***

No.	Type	Description	Unused	Used
574	A108	30fr dk car rose & grn	1.00	1.00
575	A108	40fr ultra & dk car rose	1.00	1.00
576	A108	50fr brn org & grn	1.10	1.10
577	A108	100fr sl & ver	1.10	1.10

Issued to commemorate the inauguration of World Health Organization Headquarters, Geneva.

Soccer Player
A118

Designs: 30fr, Two soccer players. 50fr, Three soccer players. 60fr, Jules Rimet Cup, soccer ball and globe.

1966, July 25 Photo. ***Perf. 14***

No.	Type	Description	Unused	Used
578	A118	10fr ocher, vio & brt grn	10	10
579	A118	30fr brt rose lil, vio & ap grn	35	25
580	A118	50fr ap grn, Prus bl & tan	1.25	1.20
581	A118	60fr brt grn, dk brn & gold	65	55

Issued to commemorate the World Cup Soccer Championship, Wembley, England, July 11–30.

Army Type of 1965

The Army Serving the Country: 2fr, Soldiers giving first aid. 6fr, Feeding child. 10fr, House building (vert.). 18fr, Bridge building. 24fr, Soldier and flag (vert.).

1966, Aug. 8 ***Perf. 12½x13, 13x12½***

No.	Type	Description	Unused	Used
582	A115	2fr ver, ind & red	5	5
583	A115	6fr ultra & red brn	8	8
584	A115	10fr yel grn & red brn	60	55
585	A115	18fr car rose & vio	15	10
586	A115	24fr multi	25	20
		Nos. 582-586 (5)	1.13	98

Nos. 578–581 Overprinted in Black, Carmine or Green: "FINALE / ANGLETERRE-ALLEMAGNE / 4-2"

1966, Nov. 14 Photo. ***Perf. 14***

No.	Type	Description	Unused	Used
587	A118	10fr multi (B or C)	22	22
588	A118	30fr multi (B or G)	70	60
589	A118	50fr multi (B or C)	1.10	90
590	A118	60fr multi (B or C)	1.25	1.00

Issued to commemorate England's victory in the World Soccer Cup Championship. The two colors of the overprint alternate in the sheets.

Souvenir Sheets

Pres. John F. Kennedy—A119

1966, Dec. 28 Engraved ***Perf. 13***

No.	Type	Description	Unused	Used
591	A119	150fr brown	4.00	4.00
592	A119	150fr slate	4.00	4.00

Issued in memory of Pres. John F. Kennedy. No. 591 has slate green, No. 592 deep orange marginal design. Two imperf. sheets exist: 150fr brown with violet blue margin and 150fr slate with lilac margin. Size: 65x76mm. Price $4.25 each.

Nos. 498–503 Surcharged in Black, Red or Maroon

5 K

4e Sommet OUA
KINSHASA
du 11 au 14 - 9 - 67

1967, Sept. 11 Photo. ***Perf. 11½***

No.	Type	Description	Unused	Used
593	A108	1k on 2fr brn red & vio	8	5
a.		Inverted overprint	9.00	
594	A108	3k on 5fr gray vio & emer	15	10
595	A108	5k on 4fr org & vio bl	25	18
596	A108	6.60k on 1fr bl & lil rose (R)	33	25
a.		Inverted overprint	6.50	
597	A108	9.60k on 50c lil rose & bl	55	40
a.		Inverted overprint	6.50	
598	A108	9.80k on 3fr emer & red (M)	75	55
		Nos. 593-598 (6)	2.11	1.53

Souvenir Sheet

Map of Africa, Torch—A120

No.	Type	Description	Unused	Used
599	A120	50k grnsh bl, blk & red	2.25	2.25

Issued to commemorate the 4th meeting of the Organization for African Unity, Kinshasa (Leopoldville), Sept. 9–11. No. 599 has black marginal inscription and design in black and red. Size: 76x90mm.

Souvenir Sheet

Horn Blower and EXPO Emblem
A121

1967, Sept. 28 Engr. ***Perf. 11½***

No.	Type	Description	Unused	Used
600	A121	50k dk brn	2.50	2.50

Issued to commemorate EXPO '67, International Exhibition, Montreal, Apr. 28–Oct. 27, 1967. No. 600 has ultramarine and orange marginal inscription. Size: 90x75mm.

Nos. 565-566 and 582 Overprinted: "NOUVELLE CONSTITUTION 1967" and Surcharged with New Value on Metallic Panel in Magenta or Brown.

Perf. 11½, 12½x13

1967, Oct. 9 **Photogravure**

601 A117 4k on 2fr dk brn & dk bl (M) 25 20
602 A115 5k on 2fr ver, ind & red (B) 30 25
603 A117 21k on 4fr dk brn & org (M) 1.35 1.00

Issued to commemorate the promulgation of the Constitution, June 4, 1967.

Nos. 528 and 530 Surcharged with New Value and Overprinted: "Iere Jeux Congolais / 25/6 au 2/7/1967 / Kinshasa"

1967, Oct. 16 **Photo.** ***Perf. 13½***

604 A111 1k on 5fr multi 12 12
605 A111 9.60k on 15fr multi 75 75

Issued to commemorate the First Congolese Games, Kinshasa, June 25-July 2, 1967.

No. 465 Surcharged with New Value and Overprinted: "Ier VOL BAC / ONE ELEVEN / 14/5/67"

1967, Oct. 16 ***Perf. 11½***

606 A105 9.60k on 7fr multi 1.00 25

Issued to commemorate the first flight of the BAC 111 in the service of Air Congo, May 14, 1967.

Nos. 547 and 549 Surcharged in Red or Black: "JOURNEE MONDIALE / DE L'ENFANCE / 8-10-67"

1968, Feb. 10 **Photo.** ***Perf. 13x14***

607 A114 1k on 6fr ultra, blk & yel (R) 12 12
608 A114 9k on 9fr bl grn, blk & brn org (B) 75 75

Issued for International Children's Day. The surcharge is on a rectangle printed in metallic ink.

Nos. 498, 504 and 501 Surcharged in Blue or Red: "Année Internationale / du Tourisme 24-10-1967"

1968, Feb. 10 ***Perf. 11½***

609 A108 5k on 50c lil rose & bl (Bl) 27 27
610 A108 10k on 6fr sep & org (R) 60 60
611 A108 15k on 3fr emer & red (R) 85 85

Issued for International Tourist Year. The surcharge is on a rectangle printed in metallic ink.

Nos. 500, 498 and 502 Surcharged in Black, Violet Blue or Gold

1968, July **Photo.** ***Perf. 11½***

612 A108 1k on 2fr brn red & vio 7 7
613 A108 2k on 50c lil rose & bl (VBl) 15 15
614 A108 2k on 50c lil rose & bl (G) 15 15
615 A108 9.60k on 4fr org & vio bl 60 60

The surcharge on No. 612 consists of a black rectangle and new denomination in upper right corner; the surcharge on No. 613 has a violet blue rectangle with denomination printed in white on it; on No. 614 the rectangle is gold and the denomination black; on No. 615 the rectangle is black and the denomination white.

No. 565 Surcharged in White on Black Rectangle.

1968, Oct. **Photo.** ***Perf. 11½***

616 A117 10k on 2fr dk brn & dk bl 60 12

Leopard
A122

1968, Nov. 5 **Litho.** ***Perf. 10½***

617 A122 2k brt grnsh bl & blk 12 5
618 A122 9.60k red & blk 60 15

Mobutu Type of 1966 Surcharged

1968, Dec. 20 **Photo.** ***Perf. 11½***

619 A117 15s on 2fr sep & brt bl 5 5
620 A117 1k on 6fr sep & brn 5 5
621 A117 3k on 10fr sep & emer 15 12
622 A117 5k on 12fr sep & org 25 18
623 A117 20k on 15fr sep & brt grn 90 65
624 A117 50k on 24fr sep & brt lil 2.50 1.75
Nos. 619-624 (6) 3.90 2.80

Human Rights Flame
A123

1968, Dec. 30 ***Perf. 12½x13***

625 A123 2k lt ultra & brt grn 12 5
626 A123 9.60k grn & dp car 55 35
627 A123 10k brt lil & brn 55 35
628 A123 40k org brn & pur 2.10 1.50

International Human Rights Year.

Type of 1968 Overprinted in Gold

4EME SOMMET OCAM
27-1-1969 KINSHASA

1969, Jan. 27 **Photo.** ***Perf. 12½x13***

629 A123 2k ap grn & red brn 12 6
630 A123 9.60k rose & emer 55 35
631 A123 10k gray & ultra 55 35
632 A123 40k grnsh bl & pur 2.10 1.50

Issued to publicize the 4th summit meeting of OCAM (Organisation Communitée Afrique et Malgache), Kinshasa, Jan. 27.

Kinshasa Fair Emblem and Cotton Boll—A124

Designs (Fair Emblem and): 6k, Copper. 9.60k, Coffee. 9.80k, Diamond. 11.60k, Oil palm fruits.

1969, May 2 **Photo.** ***Perf. 12½x13***

633 A124 2k brt pur, gold & red lil 12 5
634 A124 6k grn, gold & bl grn 35 35
635 A124 9.60k brn, gold & lt brn 55 25
636 A124 9.80k ultra & gold 55 50
637 A124 11.60k hn brn, gold & brn 70 70
Nos. 633-637 (5) 2.27 1.85

Kinshasa Fair, Limete, June 30-July 21.

Fair Entrance, Emblem—A125

Designs (Fair Emblem and): 3k, Gecomin Mining Co. Pavilion. 10k, Administration Building. 25k, Pavilion of the Organization for African Unity.

1969, June 30 **Photo.** ***Perf. 11½***

Granite Paper

638 A125 2k brt rose lil & gold 10 10
639 A125 3k bl & gold 15 15
640 A125 10k lt ol grn & gold 50 40
641 A125 25k cop red & gold 1.15 1.00

Kinshasa Fair, Limete, June 30-July 21.

Congo Arms
A126

Pres. Mobutu
A127

1969, July-Sept. **Litho.** ***Perf. 14***

642 A126 10s org & blk 5 5
643 A126 15s ultra & blk 5 5
644 A126 30s brt grn & blk 5 5
645 A126 60s brt rose lil & blk 5 5
646 A126 90s dp bis & blk 5 5

Perf. 13

647 A127 1k sky bl & multi 5 5
648 A127 2k org & multi 6 5
649 A127 3k multi 9 6
650 A127 5k brt rose & multi 15 13
651 A127 6k ultra & multi 20 15
652 A127 9.60k multi 35 20
653 A127 10k lt lil & multi 50 25
654 A127 20k yel & multi 1.00 50
655 A127 50k multi 2.50 1.10
656 A127 100k fawn & multi 4.50 2.00
Nos. 642-656 (15) 9.65 4.74

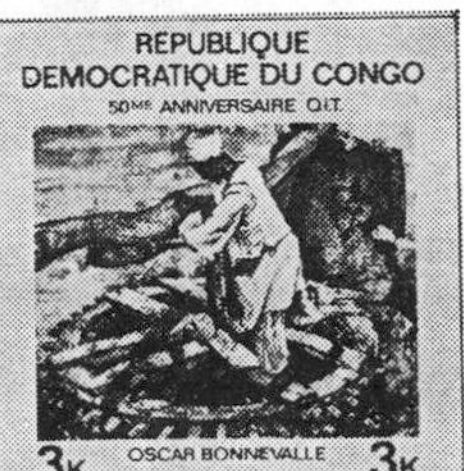

Well Driller, by Oscar Bonnevalle
A128

Paintings: 4k, Preparation of cocoa, by Jean Van Noten. 8k, Dock workers, by Constantin Meunier. 10k, Poultry shop, by Henri Evenepoel. 15k, Steel industry, by Constantin Meunier.

Perf. 13x14, 14x13 (8k)

1969, Dec. 15 **Lithographed**

Size: 41x41mm.

657 A128 3k multi 20 17
658 A128 4k multi 25 20

Size: 28x41mm.

659 A128 8k multi 40 35

Size: 41x41mm.

660 A128 10k multi 65 50
661 A128 15k multi 1.25 75
Nos. 657-661 (5) 2.75 1.97

Issued to commemorate the 50th anniversary of the International Labor Organization.

Souvenir Sheet

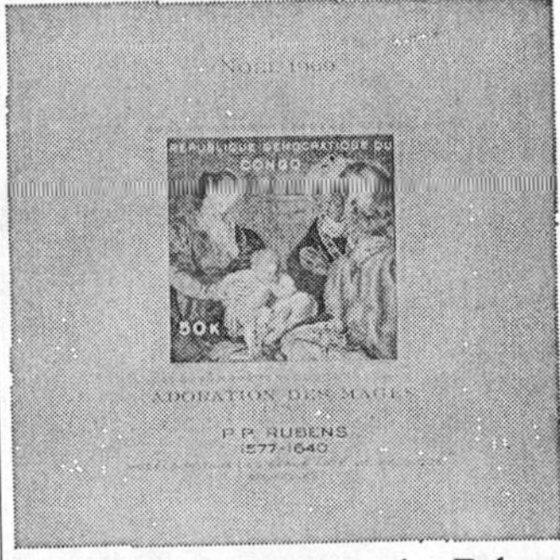

Adoration of the Kings, by Rubens
A129

1969, Dec. **Engraved** ***Perf. 13***

662 A129 50k red lil 2.25 2.25

Issued for Christmas 1969. No. 662 has blue and red lilac marginal inscription. Size: 85x85mm.

Pres. Mobutu, Map and Flag of Congo
A130

1970, June 30 **Litho.** ***Perf. 13½x13***

663 A130 10s multi 5 5
664 A130 90s pur & multi 5 5
665 A130 1k brn & multi 5 5
666 A130 2k multi 9 5
667 A130 7k multi 38 23
668 A130 10k multi 55 35
669 A130 20k multi 1.10 75
Nos. 663-669 (7) 2.27 1.53

10th anniversary of independence.

Issues of 1964-1966 Surcharged

0,20 K

Perf. 11½, 12½x13, 13x12½

1970, Sept. 24 **Photogravure**

670 A108 10s on 1fr bl & lil rose (#499) 8 6
671 A108 20s on 2fr brn red & vio (#500) 8 6
672 A117 20s on 2fr dk brn & dk bl (#565) 15 12
673 A108 30s on 3fr emer & red (#501) 8 6
674 A108 40s on 4fr org & vio bl (#502) 10 8
675 A117 40s on 4fr dk brn & org (#566) 15 12
676 A108 60s on 7fr gray ol & red brn (#505) 1.10 80
677 A108 90s on 9fr vio bl & rose red (#507) 1.10 80
678 A115 90s on 9fr ol & brn (#555) 15 12
679 A115 1k on 7fr yel & grn (#554) 15 12
680 A108 1k on 6fr sep & org (#504) 15 12
681 A117 1k on 12fr dk brn & vio (#570) 1.10 80
682 A117 2k on 24fr dk brn & lil rose (#572) 15 12

683 A115 2k on 24fr multi (#586) 15 12
684 A108 3k on 30fr dk car rose & grn (#510) 1.10 80
685 A108 4k on 40fr ultra & dk car rose (#511) 15 12
686 A108 5k on 50fr brn org & grn (#512) 2.50 1.75
687 A108 10k on 100fr sl & ver (#513) 1.10 75
Nos. 670-687 (18) 9.54 6.92

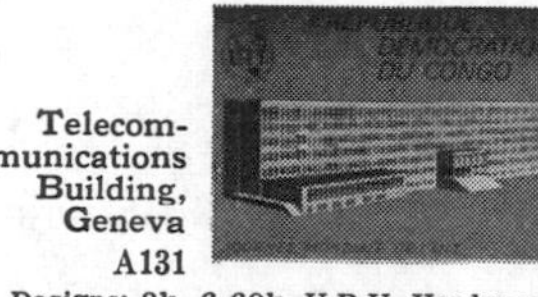

Telecommunications Building, Geneva
A131

Designs: 2k, 6.60k, U.P.U. Headquarters, Bern. 9.80k, 10k, 11k, U.N. Headquarters, New York.

1970, Oct. 24 Photo. *Perf. 11½*

688 A131 1k pink & grn 5 5
689 A131 2k org & grn 10 5
690 A131 6.60k grnsh bl & rose car 35 18
691 A131 9.60k yel & vio bl 45 25
692 A131 9.80k lt ultra & brn 45 25
693 A131 10k lt pur & brn 45 28
694 A131 11k rose & brn 55 32
Nos. 688-694 (7) 2.40 1.38

Issued for International Telecommunications Day (1k, 9.60k); Inauguration of new Universal Postal Union Headquarters, Bern (2k, 6.60k); 25th anniversary of United Nations (9.80k, 10k, 11k).

Pres. Mobutu, Congolese Flag and Arch—A132

1970, Nov. 24 Litho. *Perf. 13*

695 A132 2k yel & multi 12 8
696 A132 10k bl & multi 60 40
697 A132 20k red & multi 1.25 85

Fifth anniversary of new government.

Apollo 11 in Flight
A133

Designs: 2k, Astronaut and spacecraft on moon. 7k, Pres. Mobutu decorating astronauts' wives. 10k, Pres. Mobutu with Neil A. Armstrong, Col. Edwin E. Aldrin, Jr. and Lt. Col. Michael Collins. 30k, Armstrong, Aldrin and Collins in space suits.

1970, Dec. 24 *Perf. 13x13½*

698 A133 1k bl & blk 5 5
699 A133 2k brt pur & blk 12 8
700 A133 7k dl org & blk 45 30
701 A133 10k rose red & blk 50 40
702 A133 30k grn & blk 1.50 1.10
Nos. 698-702 (5) 2.62 1.93

Visit of U.S. Apollo 11 astronauts and their wives to Kinshasa.

Metopodontus 4 Savagei—A134

Designs: Various insects of Congo.

1971, Jan. 25 Photo. *Perf. 11½*

703 A134 10s dl rose & multi 5 5
704 A134 50s gray & multi 5 5
705 A134 90s multi 8 5
706 A134 1k cit & multi 8 5
707 A134 2k gray grn & multi 12 8
708 A134 3k lt vio & multi 22 15
709 A134 5k bl & multi 60 40
710 A134 10k multi 1.00 65
711 A134 30k grn & multi 2.50 1.50
712 A134 40k ocher & multi 3.25 2.00
Nos. 703-712 (10) 7.95 4.98

Colotis Protomedia—A135

Designs: Various butterflies and moths of Congo.

1971, Feb. 24

713 A135 10s lt ultra & multi 5 5
714 A135 20s choc & multi 5 5
715 A135 70s dp org & multi 8 5
716 A135 1k vio bl & multi 8 5
717 A135 3k multi 22 15
718 A135 5k dk grn & multi 50 30
719 A135 10k multi 80 50
720 A135 15k emer & multi 1.25 75
721 A135 25k yel & multi 1.75 1.10
722 A135 40k multi 3.25 1.90
Nos. 713-722 (10) 8.03 4.90

U.N. Emblem, Racial Unity
A136

1971, March 21 Photo. *Perf. 11½*

723 A136 1k lt grn & multi 5 5
724 A136 4k gray & multi 17 10
725 A136 5k lt lil & multi 27 15
726 A136 10k lt bl & multi 50 30

International year against racial discrimination.

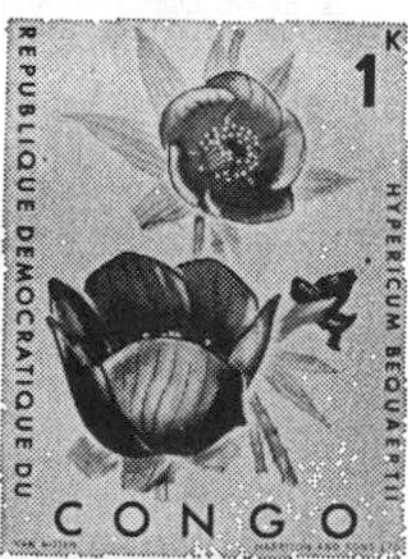

Hypericum Bequaertii
A137

Flowers: 4k, Dissotis brazzae. 20k, Begonia wollastonii. 25k, Cassia alata.

1971, May 24 Litho. *Perf. 14*

727 A137 1k multi 5 5
728 A137 4k multi 30 18
729 A137 20k multi 1.25 50
730 A137 25k multi 1.65 1.00

Obelisk at N'sele, Pres. Mobutu
A138

1971, May 20 Photo. *Perf. 11½*

731 A138 4k gold & multi 22 15

4th anniversary of the People's Revolutionary Movement.

Radar Station
A139

Designs: 1k, Waves. 6k, Map of Africa with telecommunications network.

1971, June 25 Photo. *Perf. 11½*

732 A139 1k rose & multi 5 5
733 A139 3k yel & multi 18 10
734 A139 6k lt bl & multi 40 25

Issued for 3rd World Telecommunications Day, May 17 (1k); opening of satellite telecommunications ground station, Kinshasa, June 30 (3k); Pan-African telecommunication system (6k).

Grass Monkeys
A140

Designs: 20s, Moustached monkeys (vert.). 70s, De Brazza's monkeys. 1k, Yellow baboons. 3k, Pygmy chimpanzee (vert.). 5k, Mangabeys (vert.). 10k, Owl-faced monkeys. 15k, Diana monkeys. 25k, Black-and-white colobus (vert.). 40k, L'Hoest's monkeys (vert.).

1971, Aug.

735 A140 10s vio & multi 10 5
736 A140 20s lt bl & multi 10 5
737 A140 70s ocher & multi 12 5
738 A140 1k gray & multi 12 5
739 A140 3k rose & multi 25 7
740 A140 5k brn & multi 55 12
741 A140 10k multi 90 25
742 A140 15k multi 1.65 50
743 A140 25k brt bl & multi 2.75 75
744 A140 40k red & multi 3.75 1.00
Nos. 735-744 (10) 10.29 2.89

Hotel Inter-Continental, Kinshasa
A141

1971, Oct. 2 Photogravure *Perf. 13*

745 A141 2k sil & multi 10 5
746 A141 12k gold & multi 65 25

Man Reading
A142

Designs: 2.50k, Open book and abacus. 7k, Five letters surrounding symbolic head.

1971, Oct. 24

747 A142 50s gold, red brn, blk & yel 5 5
748 A142 2.50k gold, blk, dk red & tan 15 6
749 A142 7k gold, grn, yel & blk 65 25

Fight against illiteracy.
Succeeding issues are listed in Vol. IV under Zaire.

SEMI-POSTAL STAMPS

Women Carrying Food, Wheat Emblem, and Tractor
SP22

1963, Mar. 21 Photo. *Perf. 14x13*

B48 SP22 5fr +2fr lil, vio & dk bl 18 12
B49 SP22 9fr +4fr ocher, gray & dk grn 45 25
B50 SP22 12fr +6fr bl, dk bl & vio 50 35
B51 SP22 20fr +10fr red, grn & gray 2.50 2.35

Issued for the "Freedom from Hunger" campaign of the U.N. Food and Agriculture Organization.

CONGO PEOPLE'S REPUBLIC (ex-French)

LOCATION — West Africa at equator.
GOVT.—Republic.
AREA—132,046 sq. mi.
POP.—1,740,000 (est. 1984).
CAPITAL—Brazzaville.

The former French colony of Middle Congo became a member state of the French Community on November 28, 1958, and achieved independence on August 15, 1960. For some years before 1958, the colony was joined with three other French territories to form French Equatorial Africa. Issues of Middle Congo (1907-1933) are listed under that heading.

100 Centimes = 1 Franc

Allegory of New Republic
A7

Engraved.

1959 *Perf. 13* Unwmkd.

89 A7 25fr brn, dp cl, org & ol 45 10

Issued to commemorate the first anniversary of the proclamation of the Republic.

Imperforates

Most stamps of the Republic of the Congo exist imperforate in issued and trial colors, and also in small presentation sheets in issued colors.

C.C.T.A. Issue
Common Design Type

1960 ***Perf. 13*** **Unwmkd.**

90 CD106 50fr dl grn & plum 90 80

President Fulbert Youlou
A8

Flag, Map and U.N. Emblem
A9

1960

91 A8 15fr grn, blk & car 25 17
92 A8 85fr ind & car 1.10 50

1961, March 11 ***Perf. 13***
Flag in Green, Yellow & Red

93 A9 5fr vio brn & dk bl 10 6
94 A9 20fr org & dk bl 30 22
95 A9 100fr grn & dk bl 1.50 1.35

Congo's admission to United Nations.

Rainbow Runner
A10

Designs (fish): 50c, 3fr, Rainbow runner. 1fr, 2fr, Sloan's viperfish. 5fr, Hatchet fish. 10fr, A deep-sea fish.

1961, Nov. 28 **Engraved**

96 A10 50c brn, ol grn & sal 6 6
97 A10 1fr bl grn & sep 6 6
98 A10 2fr ultra, sep & dk grn 10 10
99 A10 3fr dk bl, grn & sal 10 10
100 A10 5fr red brn, grn & blk 20 15
101 A10 10fr bl & red brn 25 18
Nos. 96-101 (6) 77 65

Brazzaville Market
A11

1962, March 23 ***Perf. 13*** **Unwmkd.**

102 A11 20fr blk, red & grn 25 12

Common Design Types

pictured in section at front of book.

Abidjan Games Issue
Common Design Type

Designs: 20fr, Boxing. 50fr, Running, finish line.

1962, July 21 **Photo.** ***Perf. 12½x12***

103 CD109 20fr car, brt pink, brn & blk 28 20
104 CD109 50fr car, brt pink, brn & blk 60 45

See No. C7.

African-Malgache Union Issue
Common Design Type

1962, Sept. 8

105 CD110 30fr vio, bluish grn, red & gold 55 55

Waves Around Globe
A11a

Design: 100fr, Orbit patterns around globe.

1963, Sept. 19 ***Perf. 12½***

106 A11a 25fr org, grn & ultra 40 30
107 A11a 100fr lt red brn, bl & plum 1.40 1.10

Issued to publicize space communications.

King Makoko's Collar
A12

Design: 15fr, Kébékébé mask.

Engraved

1963, Oct. 21 ***Perf. 13*** **Unwmkd.**

108 A12 10fr blk & ol bis 15 10
109 A12 15fr brn, blk, bl, yel & red 25 12

UNESCO Emblem, Scales and Tree—A12a

1963, Dec. 10 ***Perf. 13*** **Unwmkd.**

110 A12a 25fr grn, dk bl & brn 35 25

Issued to commemorate the 15th anniversary of the Universal Declaration of Human Rights.

Barograph and WMO Emblem
A12b

1964, Mar. 23 **Engraved**

111 A12b 50fr grn, red brn & ultra 65 65

Fourth World Meteorological Day.

Mechanic with Machine
A13

1964, Apr. 8

112 A13 20fr grnsh bl, mag & dk brn 32 20

Training of technicians.

Corn and Tools
A14

1964, Apr. 24 ***Perf. 13*** **Unwmkd.**

113 A14 80fr brn, grn & brn car 95 50

Importance of manual labor.

Diaboua Ballet
A15

Kébékébé Dance
A16

Carved Figure
A17

1964, May 8 **Engraved**

114 A15 30fr multi 50 30
115 A16 60fr multi 90 60

1964, May 22

116 A17 50fr brn red & sep 65 50

Classroom
A18

1964, May 26

117 A18 25fr dk brn, red & bl 32 20

Issued to publicize education.

Type of Air Post Issue, 1963, Inscribed: "1er ANNIVERSAIRE DE LA REVOLUTION/ FETE NATIONALE/15 AOUT 1964"

1964, Aug. 15 **Photo.** ***Perf. 13x12***

118 AP5 20fr lt bl, red, ocher, dk brn & grn 27 15

Issued to commemorate the first anniversary of the revolution and the National Feast Day, Aug. 15.

Fire Squid
A19

Design: 15fr, Johnson's deep-sea angler (fish).

1964, Oct. 20 **Engraved** ***Perf. 13***

119 A19 2fr ver, lt grn & brn 10 8
120 A19 15fr vio, lt ol grn & dp cl 35 20

Cooperation Issue
Common Design Type

1964, Nov. 7 ***Perf. 13*** **Unwmkd.**

121 CD119 25fr car, brt grn & dk brn 35 25

Communications Emblems
A20

1965, Jan. 1 **Litho.** ***Perf. 12½x13***

122 A20 25fr ol, red brn & blk 40 25

Issued to commemorate the establishment of the national postal administration.

Sitatunga
A21

Dancer on Stilts
A22

Design: 20fr, Elephant (horiz.).

1965, Mar. 15 **Engraved** ***Perf. 13***

123 A21 15fr redsh brn, dl grn & bl 30 15
124 A21 20fr blk, dp bl & sl grn 30 15
125 A22 85fr lil & multi 1.15 90

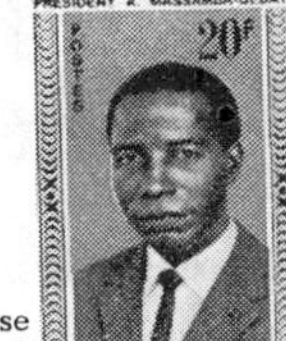

Pres. Alphonse Massamba-Debat
A23

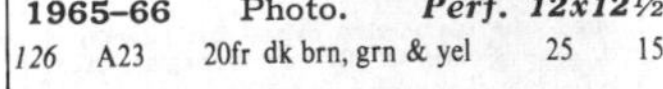

1965–66 **Photo.** ***Perf. 12x12½***

126 A23 20fr dk brn, grn & yel 25 15

127	A23	25fr brn, bl grn, emer & blk ('66)	32	15
128	A23	30fr brn, bl grn, org & blk ('66)	40	20

Soccer Player
A24

Designs: 25fr, Games' emblem (map of Africa and runners). 50fr, Field ball player. 85fr, Runner. 100fr, Bicyclist.

1965, July 17 Photo. *Perf. 12½*

Size: 28x28mm.

129	A24	25fr blk, red, yel & grn	32	20

Size: 34x34mm.

130	A24	40fr yel grn & multi	60	40
131	A24	50fr red & multi	65	40
132	A24	85fr blk & multi	1.10	70
133	A24	100fr yel & multi	1.35	85
a.		Min. sheet of 5	4.75	4.75
		Nos. 129-133 (5)	4.02	2.55

Issued to commemorate the First African Games, Brazzaville, July 18–25. No. 133a contains one each of Nos. 129–133. Size: 136½x169mm.

Arms of Congo
A25

1965, Nov. 15 Litho. *Perf. 12½x13*

134	A25	20fr multi	28	15

Cooperative Village
A26

Design: 30fr, Gymnastic drill team with streamers.

1966, Feb. 18 *Perf. 12½x13*

135	A26	25fr multi	28	15
136	A26	30fr multi	40	25

Sculptured Mask
A27

Designs: 30fr, Weaver, painting. 85fr, String instrument, painting (horiz.).

Perf. 13x12½, 12½x13

1966, Apr. 9 Photogravure

137	A27	30fr multi	40	20
138	A27	85fr multi	1.10	65
139	A27	90fr multi	1.25	70

Issued to publicize the International Negro Arts Festival, Dakar, Senegal, Apr. 1–24.

Men and Clocks
A28

1966, Apr. 15 *Perf. 12½x12*

140	A28	70fr pale brn, ocher & dk brn	1.10	45

Issued to publicize the introduction of the shorter work day (less lunch time, earlier quitting time).

WHO Headquarters, Geneva
A29

1966, May 3 Photo. *Perf. 12½x13*

141	A29	50fr org yel, vio & bl	40	25

Issued to commemorate the inauguration of the World Health Organization Headquarters, Geneva.

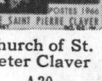

Church of St. Peter Claver
A30

Women's Basketball
A31

1966, June 15 Photo. *Perf. 13x12½*

142	A30	70fr multi	1.10	45

1966, July 15 Engraved *Perf. 13*

Sport: 1fr, Women's volleyball (horiz.). 3fr, Women's field ball (horiz.). 5fr, Athletes of various races. 10fr, Torch bearer. 15fr, Soccer and gold medal of First African Games.

143	A31	1fr ultra, choc & ol	6	6
144	A31	2fr choc, grn & bl	8	6
145	A31	3fr dk grn, dk car & choc	10	8
146	A31	5fr sl, emer & choc	12	10
147	A31	10fr dl bl, dk grn & vio	25	12
148	A31	15fr vio, car & choc	30	18
		Nos. 143-148 (6)	91	60

Jules Rimet Cup and Globe
A32

1966, July 15 Photo. *Perf. 12½x12*

149	A32	30fr brt red, gold, blk & bl	50	27

Issued to commemorate the 8th World Soccer Cup Championship, Wembley, England, July 11–30.

Savorgnan de Brazza School
A33

1966, Sept. 15 Photo. *Perf. 12½x12*

150	A33	30fr dk pur, grn, yel & blk	40	20

Pointe-Noire Railroad Station
A34

1966, Oct. 15 Engraved *Perf. 13*

151	A34	60fr grn, red & brn	85	35

Student with Microscope
A35

Balumbu Mask
A36

1966, Nov. 28 Engraved *Perf. 13*

152	A35	90fr brn, grn & ind	1.20	75

Issued to commemorate the 20th anniversary of UNESCO (United Nations Educational, Scientific and Cultural Organization).

1966, Dec. 12 Engraved *Perf. 13*

Masks: 10fr, Kuyu. 15fr, Bakwélé. 20fr, Batéké.

153	A36	5fr car rose & dk brn	12	8
154	A36	10fr Prus bl & brn	20	12
155	A36	15fr sep, dl org & dk bl	25	13
156	A36	20fr dp bl & multi	28	15

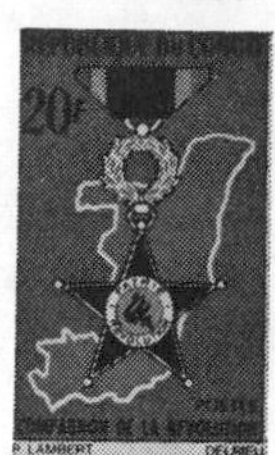

Order of the Revolution and Map
A37

Learning the Alphabet
A38

Design: 45fr, Harvesting and loading sugar cane, and sugar mill.

Perf. 12x12½, 12½x12

1967, March 15 Photogravure

157	A37	20fr org & multi	28	15
158	A38	25fr blk, ocher & dk car	32	20
159	A38	45fr blk, yel grn & lt bl	55	28

Issued to honor the members of the Order of the Revolution (20fr); to publicize the literacy campaign (25fr); to publicize sugar production (45fr).

Mahatma Gandhi
A39

Fruit Vendor
A40

1967, Apr. 21 Engraved *Perf. 13*

160	A39	90fr bl & blk	1.10	60

Issued in memory of Mohandas K. Gandhi (1869–1948), Hindu nationalist leader.

1967, June Photo. *Perf. 13x12½*

Dolls: 5fr, "Elegant Lady." 25fr, Woman pounding saka-saka. 30fr, Mother and child.

161	A40	5fr gold & multi	12	12
162	A40	10fr yel grn & multi	20	15
163	A40	25fr lt ultra & multi	32	20
164	A40	30fr multi	40	25

ITY Emblem, Village and Waterfall
A41

1967, July 5 Engraved *Perf. 13*

165	A41	60fr rose cl, org & ol grn	80	50

Issued for International Tourist Year, 1967.

Symbols of Cooperation
A42

Arms of Brazzaville
A43

Europafrica Issue, 1967

1967, July 20 Photo. *Perf. 12x12½*

166	A42	50fr multi	65	32

1967, Aug. 15 Litho. *Perf. 12½x13*

167	A43	30fr yel & multi	45	20

Fourth anniversary of the revolution.

U.N. Emblem, Dove and People
A44

Boy and UNICEF Emblem
A45

1967, Oct. 24 Photo. *Perf. 13x12½*

168	A44	90fr bl, dk brn, red brn & yel	1.35	70

Issued for United Nations Day, Oct. 24.

1967, Dec. 11 Engraved *Perf. 13*

169 A45 90fr mar, blk & ultra 1.20 65

Issued to commemorate the 21st anniversary of UNICEF (United Nations International Children's Emergency Fund).

Albert Luthuli, Dove and Globe
A46

1968, Jan. 29 Engr. *Perf. 13*

170 A46 30fr brt grn & ol bis 40 25

Issued in memory of Albert Luthuli (1899–1967) of South Africa, winner of 1960 Nobel Peace Prize.

Arms of Pointe Noire
A47

1968, Feb. 20 Litho. *Perf. 12½x13*

171 A47 10fr brt pink & multi 15 12

Motherhood
A48

Mayombe Viaduct
A49

1968, May 25 Engraved *Perf. 13*

172 A48 15fr dk car rose, sky bl & blk 25 15

Issued for Mother's Day.

1968, June 24

173 A49 45fr mar, sl grn & bl 50 25

Daimler, 1889—A50

Antique Cars: 20fr, Berliet, 1897. 60fr, Peugeot, 1898. 80fr, Renault, 1900. 85fr, Fiat, 1902.

1968, July 29 Photo. *Perf. 13x12½*

174 A50 5fr ocher & multi 15 15
175 A50 20fr multi 30 25
176 A50 60fr cit & multi 85 45
177 A50 80fr multi 1.10 60
178 A50 85fr multi 1.20 70
Nos. 174-178 (5) 3.60 2.15

Tanker, Refinery and Map of Area Served—A50a

1968, July 30 *Perf. 12½*

179 A50a 30fr multi 40 18

Issued to commemorate the opening of the Port Gentil (Gabon) Refinery, June 12, 1968.

U.N. Emblem and Tree of Life
A51

1968, Nov. 28 Engraved *Perf. 13*

180 A51 25fr dk grn, red & dp lil 40 18

Issued for the 20th anniversary of the World Health Organization.

Development Bank Issue
Common Design Type

1969, Sept. 10 Engraved *Perf. 13*

181 CD130 25fr car rose, grn & ocher 35 15
182 CD130 30fr bl, grn & ocher 40 15

Issued to commemorate the 5th anniversary of the African Development Bank.

Bicycle
A52

Designs (Bicycles and Motorcycles): 75fr, Hirondelle. 80fr, Folding bicycle. 85fr, Peugeot. 100fr, Excelsior Manxman. 150fr, Norton. 200fr, Brough Superior "Old Bill." 300fr, Matchless and N.L.G.-J.A.P.S.

1969, Oct. 6 Engraved *Perf. 13*

183 A52 50fr dk ol, org & rose lil 65 32
184 A52 75fr org, rose lake & blk 95 40
185 A52 80fr lil, bl & sl grn 1.00 45
186 A52 85fr dk ol, gray & bl grn 1.10 55
187 A52 100fr blk, vio bl, dk brn & car 1.25 65
188 A52 150fr blk, red brn & brn ol 1.60 90
189 A52 200fr bl grn, sl grn & brt rose lil 2.60 1.10
190 A52 300fr blk, brt rose lil & grn 3.50 1.90
Nos. 183-190 (8) 12.65 6.27

Mayombe Train and Tourist Year Emblem
A53

Design: 40fr, Train and Mbamba Tunnel (vert.).

Perf. 13x12½, 12½x13

1969, Oct. 20 Photogravure

191 A53 40fr multi 55 27
192 A53 60fr multi 70 32

Issued for African Tourist Year.

Loutete Cement Works
A54

Designs (Loutete Cement Works): 15fr, Mixing tower (vert.). 25fr, Cable transport (vert.). 30fr, General view of plant.

1969, Dec. 10 Engraved *Perf. 13*

193 A54 10fr dk gray, rose cl & dk ol 13 8
194 A54 15fr Prus bl, red brn & pur 18 13
195 A54 25fr mar, brn & Prus bl 32 18
196 A54 30fr vio brn, ultra & blk 35 22
a. Min. sheet of 4 1.25 1.25

Issued to publicize the cement factory at Loutete. No. 196a contains one each of Nos. 193–196. Size: 170x100mm.

ASECNA ISSUE
Common Design Type

1969, Dec. 12

197 CD132 100fr dl brn 1.35 65

Pineapple Harvest and ILO Emblem
A55

Design: 30fr, Worker at lathe and ILO emblem.

1969, Dec. 20 Engraved *Perf. 13*

198 A55 25fr bl, ol & brn 32 18
199 A55 30fr rose red, choc & sl 35 22

Issued to commemorate the 50th anniversary of the International Labor Organization.

SOTEXCO Textile Plant, Kinsoundi
A56

Designs: 20fr, Women in spinnery. 25fr, Hand-printing textiles. 30fr, Checking woven cloth.

1970, Jan. 20

200 A56 15fr grn, blk & lil 18 13
201 A56 20fr plum, car & sl grn 22 13
202 A56 25fr bl, sl & brn 32 18
203 A56 30fr gray, car rose & brn 40 18

Hotel Cosmos, Brazzaville
A57

1970, Jan. 30

204 A57 90fr sl grn, bl & red brn 1.00 45

Linzolo Church
A58

Diosso Gorge
A59

Design: 90fr, Foulakari waterfall.

1970 Engraved *Perf. 13*

205 A58 25fr multi 32 18
206 A59 70fr multi 80 35
207 A59 90fr multi 1.10 45

Issue dates: 25fr, Feb. 10; others, Feb. 25.

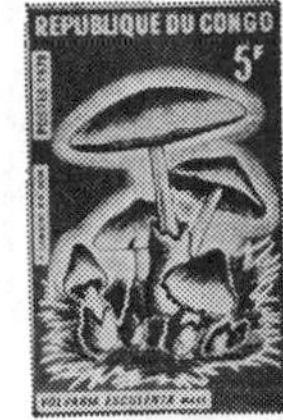

Volvaria Esculenta
A60

Mushrooms: 10fr, Termitomyces entolomoides. 15fr, Termitomyces microcarpus. 25fr, Termitomyces aurantiacus. 30fr, Termitomyces mammiformis. 50fr, Tremella fuciformis.

1970, Mar. 31 Photo. *Perf. 13*

208 A60 5fr Prus bl & multi 13 8
209 A60 10fr brt car rose & multi 15 12
210 A60 15fr vio bl & multi 25 18
211 A60 25fr dk grn & multi 45 22
212 A60 30fr pur & multi 50 27
213 A60 50fr brt bl & multi 70 45
Nos. 208-213 (6) 2.18 1.32

Laying Coaxial Cable
A61

Design: 30fr, Full view of rail car; 3 cable layers on railway roadbed.

1970, Apr. 30 Engraved *Perf. 13*

214 A61 25fr dk brn & multi 32 18
215 A61 30fr brn & multi 40 22

Issued to publicize the laying of the coaxial cable linking Brazzaville and Pointe Noire.

U.P.U. Headquarters Issue
Common Design Type

1970, May 20

216 CD133 30fr dk pur, gray & mag 45 22

Mother Feeding Child
A62

Dag Hammarskjold and U.N. Emblem
A63

Design: 90fr, Mother nursing infant.

1970, May 30 **Photogravure**

217	A62	85fr vio bl & multi	1.00	55
218	A62	90fr lil & multi	1.10	60

Issued for Mother's Day.

1970, June 20 **Engraved** ***Perf. 13***

Designs (U.N. Emblem and): No. 220, Trygve Lie (horiz.). No. 221, U Thant (horiz.).

219	A63	100fr scar, dk red & dk pur	1.25	75
220	A63	100fr dk red, ultra & ind	1.25	75
221	A63	100fr grn, emer & dk red	1.25	75
a.		Souvenir sheet of 3	4.25	4.25

Issued to commemorate the 25th anniversary of the United Nations and to honor its Secretaries General. No. 221a contains one each of Nos. 219–221; U.N. emblem and scarlet inscriptions in margin. Size: 129½x100mm.

Brillantaisia Vogeliana
A64

Sternotomis Variabilis
A65

Designs (Plants and Beetles): 2fr, Plectranthus decurrens. 3fr, Myrianthemum mirabile. 5fr, Connarus griffonianus. 15fr, Chelorrhina polyphemus. 20fr, Metopodontus savagei.

Perf. 12½x12, 12x12½

1970, June 30 **Photogravure**

222	A64	1fr dk grn & multi	5	5
223	A64	2fr multi	8	5
224	A64	3fr ind & multi	10	6
225	A64	5fr lem & multi	12	10
226	A65	10fr lil & multi	15	12
227	A65	15fr org & multi	22	12
228	A65	20fr multi	27	18
		Nos. 222-228 (7)	99	68

Stegosaurus
A66

Prehistoric Fauna: 20fr, Dinotherium (vert.). 60fr, Brachiosaurus (vert.). 80fr, Arsinoitherium.

1970, July 20

229	A66	15fr dl grn, ocher & red brn	25	15
230	A66	20fr lt bl & multi	30	20
231	A66	60fr lt bl & multi	75	28
232	A66	80fr lt bl & multi	1.10	50

Mikado 141, 1932
A67

Locomotives: 60fr, Steam locomotive 130+032, 1947. 75fr, Alsthom BB 1100, 1962. 85fr, Diesel BB BB 302, 1969.

1970, Aug. 20 **Engraved** ***Perf. 13***

233	A67	40fr mag, bl grn & blk	60	30
234	A67	60fr blk, bl & grn	80	40
235	A67	75fr red, bl & blk	1.00	45
236	A67	85fr car, sl grn & ocher	1.25	55

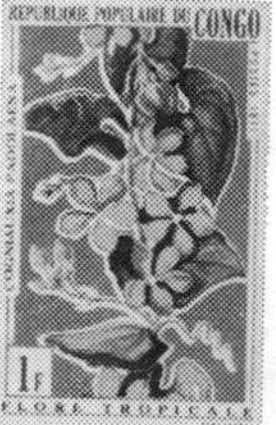

Cogniauxia Padolaena
A68

Green Night Adder
A69

Tropical Flowers: 2fr, Celosia cristata. 5fr, Plumeria acutifolia. 10fr, Bauhinia variegata. 15fr, Poinsettia. 20fr, Thunbergia grandiflora.

1971, Feb. 10 **Photo.** ***Perf. 12x12½***

237	A68	1fr lil & multi	8	7
238	A68	2fr yel & multi	8	7
239	A68	5fr ultra & multi	12	8
240	A68	10fr yel & multi	20	13
241	A68	15fr multi	32	18
242	A68	20fr dk red & multi	40	18
		Nos. 237-242 (6)	1.20	71

Perf. 12x12½, 12½x12

1971, June 26 **Photogravure**

Reptiles: 10fr, African Egg-eating snake (horiz.). 15fr, Flap-necked chameleon. 20fr, Nile crocodile (horiz.). 25fr, Rock python (horiz.). 30fr, Gaboon viper. 40fr, Brown house snake (horiz.). 45fr, Jameson's mamba.

243	A69	5fr multi	8	8
244	A69	10fr multi	15	12
245	A69	15fr multi	25	15
246	A69	20fr red & multi	32	25
247	A69	25fr grn & multi	40	32
248	A69	30fr multi	50	40
249	A69	40fr bis & multi	50	45
250	A69	45fr multi	65	50
		Nos. 243-250 (8)	2.85	2.27

Pseudimbrasia Deyrollei—A70

Caterpillars: 15fr, Bunaea alcinoe (vert.). 20fr, Epiphora vacuna ploetzi. 25fr, Imbrasia eblis. 30fr, Imbrasia dione (vert.). 40fr, Holocera angulata.

1971, July 3 ***Perf. 13***

251	A70	10fr ver, blk & grn	20	15
252	A70	15fr multi	25	20
253	A70	20fr yel grn, blk & ocher	32	28
254	A70	25fr multi	40	32
255	A70	30fr red, blk & yel	50	40
256	A70	40fr bl, blk & org	75	55
		Nos. 251-256 (6)	2.42	1.90

Cymothoe Sangaris
A71

Butterflies and Moths: 40fr, Papilio dardanus (vert.). 75fr, Iolaus timon. 90fr, Papilio phorcas (vert.). 100fr, Euchloron megaera.

Perf. 12½x12, 12x12½

1971, Oct. 15

257	A71	30fr yel & multi	50	32
258	A71	40fr grn & multi	65	45
259	A71	75fr multi	1.10	65
260	A71	90fr multi	1.35	90
261	A71	100fr ultra & multi	1.75	1.25
		Nos. 257-261 (5)	5.35	3.57

Black and White Men Working Together
A72

1971, Oct. 30 ***Perf. 13x12½***

262	A72	50fr org & multi	50	25

International Year Against Racial Discrimination.

REPUBLIQUE POPULAIRE DU CONGO
30F

Nos. 214–215 Surcharged

INAUGURATION DE LA LIAISON COAXIALE 18-11-71

1971, Nov. 18 **Engraved** ***Perf. 13***

263	A61	30fr on 25fr multi	40	25
264	A61	40fr on 30fr multi	50	32

Inauguration of cable service between Brazzaville and Pointe Noire. Words of surcharge arranged differently on No. 264.

Map of Congo
A73

1971, Dec. 31 **Photo.** ***Perf. 12½x13***

265	A73	30fr bl & multi	35	25
266	A73	40fr yel grn & multi	40	20
267	A73	100fr gray & multi	1.10	55

"Labor, Democracy, Peace."

Lion
A74

Animals: 2fr, African elephants. 3fr, Leopard. 4fr, Hippopotamus. 5fr, Gorilla (vert.). 20fr, Potto. 30fr, De Brazza's monkey. 40fr, Pygmy chimpanzee (vert.).

1972, Jan. 31 **Engraved** ***Perf. 13***

268	A74	1fr grn & multi	5	5
269	A74	2fr dk red & multi	5	5
270	A74	3fr red brn & multi	10	8
271	A74	4fr vio & multi	10	8
272	A74	5fr brn & multi	12	12
273	A74	20fr org & multi	32	25
274	A74	30fr ocher & multi	50	28
275	A74	40fr Prus bl & multi	65	45
		Nos. 268-275 (8)	1.89	1.36

WHO Emblem
A75

Design: 50fr, WHO emblem (horiz.).

Perf. 12½x13, 13x12½

1973, June 30 **Typographed**

276	A75	40fr grn & multi	32	15
277	A75	50fr multi	40	20

World Health Organization, 25th anniversary.

Kronenbourg Brewery
A76

Designs (Brewery Trademark and): 40fr, Laboratory. 75fr, Vats and controls. 85fr, Automatic control room. 100fr, Pressure room. 250fr, Bottling plant.

1973, July 15 **Engr.** ***Perf. 13***

278	A76	30fr red & multi	25	15
279	A76	40fr red & multi	32	22
280	A76	75fr red & multi	55	32
281	A76	85fr red & multi	80	40
282	A76	100fr red & multi	1.10	60
283	A76	250fr red & multi	2.10	1.10
		Nos. 278-283 (6)	5.12	2.79

Kronenbourg Brewery, Brazzaville.

Golwe Locomotive, 1935
A77

Locomotives: 40fr, Diesel, 1935. 75fr, Diesel Whithcomb, 1946. 85fr, Diesel CC200.

1973, Aug. 1 **Engr.** ***Perf. 13***

284	A77	30fr ind & multi	40	25
285	A77	40fr vio bl & multi	50	25
286	A77	75fr multi	90	40
287	A77	85fr multi	1.00	50

No. 225 Surcharged with New Value, 2 Bars, and Overprinted in Ultramarine: "SECHERESSE SOLIDARITE AFRICAINE"

1973, Aug. 16 **Photo.** ***Perf. 12½x12***

288	A64	100fr on 5fr multi	80	55

African solidarity in drought emergency.

African Postal Union Issue

Common Design Type

1973, Sept. 12 **Engr.** ***Perf. 13***

289	CD137	100fr bl grn, vio & brn	75	40

Bees, Beehive, Honeycomb
A78

1973, Dec. 10 **Engraved** ***Perf. 13***

290	A78	30fr sl grn, dk red & bl	27	18
291	A78	40fr sl bl, sl grn & lt grn	35	18

"Work and economy."

Family, UN and FAO Emblems
A79

Designs: 40fr, Grain, UN and FAO emblems. 100fr, Grain, UN and FAO emblems (vert.).

1973, Dec. 10

292 A79 30fr dk car & dk brn 27 10
293 A79 40fr dk grn, yel & ind 35 15
294 A79 100fr grn, brn & org 80 50

World Food Program, 10th anniversary.

Amilcar Cabral, Cattle and Child
A80

1974, July 15 Engraved *Perf. 13*

295 A80 100fr multi 75 50

First death anniversary of Amilcar Cabral (1924–1973), leader of anti-Portuguese guerrilla activity in Portuguese Guinea.

Félix Eboué, Cross of Lorraine
A81

1974, Aug. 31 Litho. *Perf. 13*

296 A81 30fr bl & multi 25 15
297 A81 40fr brt pink & multi 35 20

Félix A. Eboué (1884–1944), Governor of Chad, first colonial governor to join Free French in WWII, 30th death anniversary.

Pineapples
A82

1974, Nov. 12

Multicolored

298 A82 30fr *shown* 25 15
299 A82 30fr *Bananas* 25 15
300 A82 30fr *Safous* 25 15
301 A82 40fr *Avocados* 35 20
302 A82 40fr *Mangos* 35 20
303 A82 40fr *Papaya* 35 20
304 A82 40fr *Oranges* 35 20
Nos. 298-304 (7) 2.15 1.25

Charles de Gaulle and Conference Building—A83

1974, Nov. 25 Engraved *Perf. 13*

305 A83 100fr multi 75 50

Brazzaville Conference, 30th anniversary.

George Stephenson and Various Locomotives—A84

1974, Dec. 15

306 A84 75fr sl grn & ol 55 35

George Stephenson (1781–1848), English inventor and railroad founder.

UDEAC Issue

Presidents and Flags of Cameroun, CAR, Congo, Gabon and Meeting Center—A84a

1974, Dec. 8 Photogravure *Perf. 13*

307 A84a 40fr gold & multi 35 20

See note after Cameroun No. 595.
See No. C195.

Irish Setter
A85

Designs: Dogs.

1974, Dec. 15 Photo. *Perf. 13x13½*

Multicolored

308 A85 30fr *shown* 35 18
309 A85 40fr *Borzoi* 45 22
310 A85 75fr *Pointer* 75 35
311 A85 100fr *Great Dane* 1.00 55

1974, Dec. 15

Designs: Cats.

312 A85 30fr *Havana chestnut* 35 15
313 A85 40fr *Red Persian* 45 18
314 A85 75fr *Blue British* 75 35
315 A85 100fr *African serval* 1.00 55

Labor Party Flags and People
A86

Design: 40fr, Hands holding flowers and tools.

1974, Dec. 31 Engr. *Perf. 13x12½*

316 A86 30fr red & multi 25 12
317 A86 40fr red & multi 35 18

5th anniversary of Congolese Labor Party and of introduction of red flag.

Symbols of Development—A87

U Thant and UN Headquarters—A88

Paul G. Hoffman and UN Emblem
A89

Perf. 13x12½, 12½x13

1975, Feb. 28 Lithographed

318 A87 40fr multi 32 18
319 A88 50fr lt bl & multi 35 22
320 A89 50fr yel & multi 35 22

National economic development.

Map of China and Mao Tse-tung—A90

1975, Mar. 9 Engraved *Perf. 13*

321 A90 75fr multi 60 40

25th anniversary of the People's Republic of China.

Woman Breaking Bonds, Women's Activities, Map of Congo
A91

1975, June 20 Litho. *Perf. 12½*

322 A91 40fr gold & multi 40 20

Revolutionary Union of Congolese Women, URFC, 10th anniversary.

CARA Soccer Team—A92

Design: 40fr, Team captain and manager receiving trophy (vert.).

1975, July 15 Litho. *Perf. 12½*

323 A92 30fr multi 27 18
324 A92 40fr multi 35 22

CARA team, winners of African Soccer Cup 1974.

Citroen, 1935—A93

Designs: Early automobiles.

1975, July 17 *Perf. 12*

Multicolored

325 A93 30fr *shown* 25 20
326 A93 40fr *Alfa Romeo, 1911* 35 20
327 A93 50fr *Rolls Royce, 1926* 40 30
328 A93 75fr *Duryea, 1893* 60 45

Tipoye Transport—A94

Design: 40fr, Dugout canoe.

1975, Aug. 5

329 A94 30fr multi 22 13
330 A94 40fr multi 32 18

Traditional means of transportation.

Raising Red Flag—A95

Design: 40fr, National Conference.

1975, Aug. 15

331 A95 30fr multi 25 20
332 A95 40fr multi 35 20

2nd anniversary of installation of popular power (30fr) and 3rd anniversary of National Conference (40fr).

The only foreign revenue stamps listed in this Catalogue are those authorized for prepayment of postage.

Line Fishing A96 — Woman Pounding "Foufou" A97

Traditional Fishing: 30fr, Trap fishing (horiz.). 60fr, Spear fishing. 90fr, Net fishing (horiz.).

1975, Aug. 31 Litho. *Perf. 12*

333	A96	30fr multi	25	20
334	A96	40fr multi	35	20
335	A96	60fr multi	50	30
336	A96	90fr multi	70	50

1975, Sept. 5

Household Tasks: No. 338, Woman chopping wood. 40fr, Woman preparing manioc (horiz.).

337	A97	30fr multi	25	15
338	A97	30fr multi	25	15
339	A97	40fr multi	35	20

Esanga A98

Musical Instruments: 40fr, Kalakwa. 60fr, Likembe. 75fr, Ngongui.

1975, Sept. 20 *Perf. 12½*

340	A98	30fr blk & brn	25	15
341	A98	40fr org & multi	35	20
342	A98	60fr grn & multi	50	35
343	A98	75fr multi	60	40

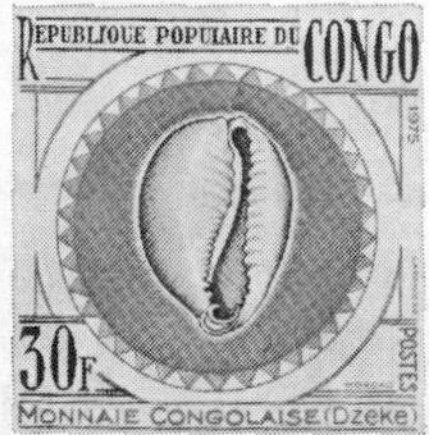

Dzeke (Congolese) Shell Money A99

Ancient Money: No. 346, like No. 344. Nos. 345, 347, Okengo, Congolese, iron bar. 40fr, Gallic coin, c. 60 B.C. 50fr, Roman denarius, 37 B.C. 60fr, Danubian coin, 2nd century B.C. 85fr, Greek stater, 4th century B.C.

1975–76 Engr. *Perf. 13*

344	A99	30fr red & multi	25	20
345	A99	30fr vio & multi	25	20
346	A99	35fr ol & multi	30	20
347	A99	35fr dk car rose & multi	30	20
348	A99	40fr Prus bl & brn	35	20
349	A99	50fr Prus bl & ol	40	25
350	A99	60fr dk grn & brn	50	35
351	A99	85fr mag & sl grn	65	40
		Nos. 344-351 (8)	3.00	2.00

Nos. 346–347 inscribed "1976" and issued Mar. 1976; others issued Oct. 5, 1975.

Moschops—A100

Pre-historic Animals: 75fr, Tyrannosaurus. 95fr, Cryptocleidus. 100fr, Stegosaurus.

1975, Oct. 15 Litho. *Perf. 13*

352	A100	55fr multi	45	30
353	A100	75fr multi	60	35
354	A100	95fr multi	75	50
355	A100	100fr multi	80	55

Albert Schweitzer A101

1975, Oct. 15 Engraved

356	A101	75fr ol, brn & red	60	40

Albert Schweitzer (1875–1965), medical missionary, birth centenary.

Alexander Fleming A102

Designs: No. 358, André Marie Ampère. No. 359, Clement Ader.

1975, Nov. 15 Engr. *Perf. 13*

357	A102	60fr brn, grn & blk	50	30
358	A102	95fr blk, red & grn	75	55
359	A102	95fr red, bl & ind	75	55

Alexander Fleming (1881–1955), developer of penicillin, 20th death anniversary; André Marie Ampère (1775–1836), physicist, bicentenary of birth; Clement Ader (1841–1925), aviation pioneer, 50th death anniversary.

U.N. Emblem "ONU" and "30"—A103

1975, Dec. 20 Engr. *Perf. 13*

360	A103	95fr car, ultra & grn	75	55

United Nations, 30th anniversary.

Women's Broken Chain—A104

Design: 60fr, Equality between man and woman, globe, IWY emblem.

1975, Dec. 20 Litho. *Perf. 12½*

361	A104	35fr mag, ocher & gray	30	20
362	A104	60fr ultra, brn & blk	50	35

International Women's Year, 1975.

Pres. Marien Ngouabi, Flag and Workers—A105

Echo of the P.C.T. A106

Perf. 12½x12, 13x12½

1975, Dec. 31 Lithographed

363	A105	30fr multi	25	15
364	A106	35fr multi	30	15

6th anniversary of the Congolese Labor Party (P.C.T.). See No. C215.

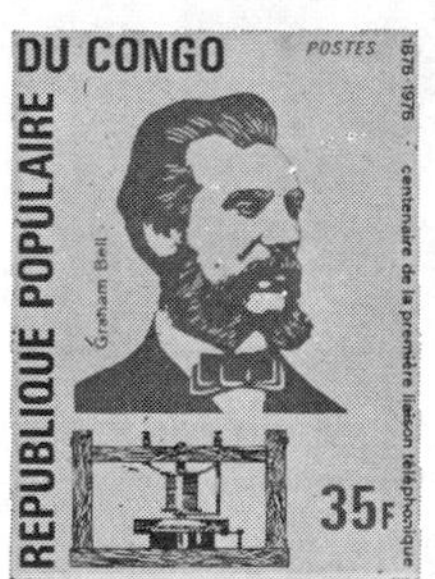

A.G. Bell and 1876 Telephone A107

1976, Apr. 25 Litho. *Perf. 12½x13*

365	A107	35fr yel, brn & org brn	30	20

Centenary of first telephone call by Alexander Graham Bell, Mar. 10, 1876. See No. C229.

Women Selling Fruit and Vegetables A108

Design: 60fr, Market scene.

1976, Sept. 19 Litho. *Perf. 12½x13*

366	A108	35fr multi	30	20
367	A108	60fr multi	50	30

Congolese Coiffure A109

Designs: Various women's hair styles.

1976, Oct. 10 Litho. *Perf. 13*

368	A109	35fr multi	30	20
369	A109	60fr multi	50	35
370	A109	95fr multi	75	50
371	A109	100fr multi	80	55

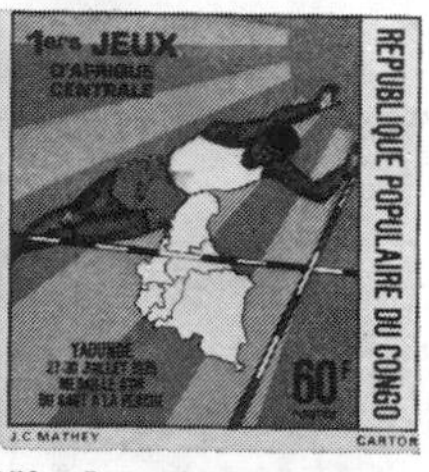

Pole Vault, Map of Central Africa A110

Design: 95fr, Long jump and map of Central Africa.

1976, Oct. 25 *Perf. 12½*

372	A110	60fr yel & multi	50	35
373	A110	95fr yel & multi	75	55

Gold medalists, 1st Central African Games, Yaoundé, July 27–30, 1975. See Nos. C230–C231.

Antelope A111

1976, Oct. 27 Litho. *Perf. 12½*

Multicolored

Size: 36x36mm.

374	A111	5fr *shown*	5	5
375	A111	10fr *Buffalos*	10	5
376	A111	15fr *Hippopotamus*	10	7
377	A111	20fr *Wart hog*	15	10
378	A111	25fr *Elephants*	20	13
		Nos. 374-378 (5)	60	40

1976, Dec. 8

Designs: Birds.

Multicolored

Size: 26x36mm.

379	A111	5fr *Saddle-bill storks*	5	5

Size: 36x36mm.

380	A111	10fr *Malachite kingfisher*	10	8
381	A111	20fr *Crowned cranes*	15	12

Bicycling, Map of Participants A112 — Heliotrope A113

1976, Dec. 21 Photo. ***Perf. 12½x13***

Designs (Map and): 60fr, Fieldball. 80fr, Running. 95fr, Soccer.

382	A112	35fr multi	30	20
383	A112	60fr multi	50	35
384	A112	80fr multi	65	50
385	A112	95fr multi	75	55

First Central African Games, Libreville, Gabon, June–July 1976.

1976, Dec. 23 Photo. ***Perf. 12½x13***

Flowers: 5fr, Water lilies. 15fr, Bird-of-paradise flower.

386	A113	5fr multi	5	5
387	A113	10fr multi	10	5
388	A113	15fr multi	15	10

Torch and Olive Branches
A114

1976, Dec. 25 Litho. ***Perf. 12½x13***

389	A114	35fr multi	20	30

National Pioneer Movement.

The Spirit of '76—A115

Designs: 125fr, Pulling down George III statue. 150fr, Battle of Princeton. 175fr, Generals of Revolutionary War. 200fr, Burgoyne's surrender at Saratoga. 500fr, Battle of Lexington.

1976, Dec. 29 Litho. ***Perf. 14***

390	A115	100fr multi	1.00	38
391	A115	125fr multi	1.25	50
392	A115	150fr multi	1.35	55
393	A115	175fr multi	1.65	75
394	A115	200fr multi	1.85	85
		Nos. 390-394 (5)	7.10	3.03

Souvenir Sheet

395	A115	500fr multi	4.75	2.00

American Bicentennial.

No. 395 has green and blue margin, black marginal inscription. Size: 114x72 mm.

Dugout Canoe Race
A116

Design: 60fr, 2-man dugout canoes.

1977, Mar. 27 Litho. ***Perf. 13x13½***

396	A116	35fr multi	30	20
397	A116	60fr multi	50	35

Dugout canoe races on Congo River.

Lilan Goua
A117

Fresh-water Fish: 15fr, Liko ko. 25fr, Liyan ga. 35fr, Mbessi. 60fr, Mongandza.

1977, June 15 Litho. ***Perf. 12½***

398	A117	10fr multi	10	7
399	A117	15fr multi	15	10
400	A117	25fr multi	20	15
401	A117	35fr multi	30	20
402	A117	60fr multi	50	35
		Nos. 398-402 (5)	1.25	87

Traditional Headdress—A118

Design: 60fr, Leopard cap.

1977, June 30 Litho. ***Perf. 12½***

403	A118	35fr multi	30	20
404	A118	60fr multi	50	35

See Nos. C234–C235.

Bondjo Wrestling
A119

Designs: 40fr, 50fr, Bondjo wrestling (different). 40fr, horiz.

1977, July 15

405	A119	25fr multi	20	15
406	A119	40fr multi	30	25
407	A119	50fr multi	40	30

"Schwaben" LZ 10, 1911
A120

Zeppelins: 60fr, "Viktoria Luise," LZ 11, 1913. 100fr, LZ 120. 200fr, LZ 127. 300fr, "Graf Zeppelin II" LZ 130.

1977, Aug. 5 Litho. ***Perf. 11***

408	A120	40fr multi	35	18
409	A120	60fr multi	60	30
410	A120	100fr multi	95	35
411	A120	200fr multi	1.90	80
412	A120	300fr multi	3.00	1.20
		Nos. 408-412 (5)	6.80	2.83

History of the Zeppelin. Exist imperf. See No. C236.

Coat of Arms and Rising Sun
A121

1977, Aug. 15

413	A121	40fr multi	30	25

14th anniversary of the revolution.

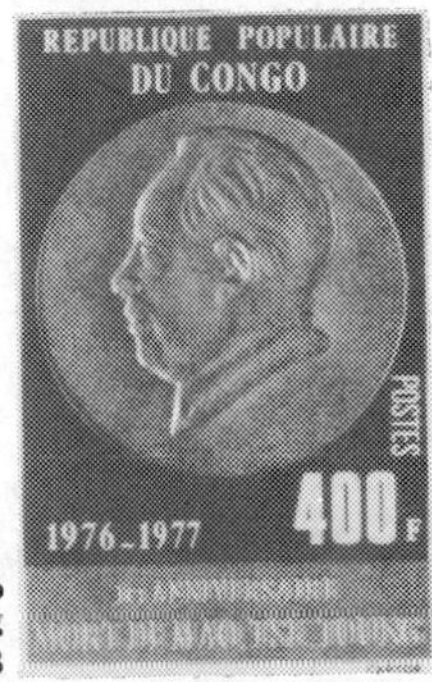

Victor Hugo and The Hunchback of Notre Dame—A122

Designs (Hugo and): 60fr, Les Miserables. 100fr, Les Travailleurs de la Mer (octopus).

1977, Aug. 20 Engr. ***Perf. 13***

414	A122	35fr multi	30	20
415	A122	60fr multi	50	35
416	A122	100fr multi	80	60

Victor Hugo (1802–1885), French novelist.

Mao Tse-tung
A123

Lithographed; Gold Embossed

1977, Sept. 9 ***Perf. 12x12½***

417	A123	400fr red & gold	3.25	2.50

Chairman Mao Tse-tung (1893–1976), Chinese Communist leader, first death anniversary.

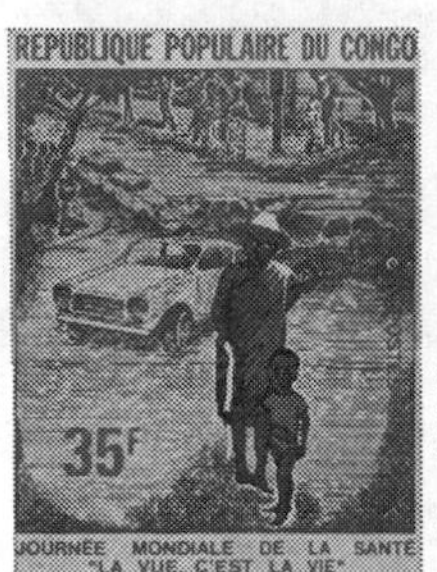

Peter Paul Rubens
A124

1977, Sept. 20 Gold Embossed

418	A124	600fr gold & lt bl	4.75	4.00

Peter Paul Rubens (1577–1640), painter.

Child Leading Blind Woman Across Street
A125

1977, Oct. 22 Litho. ***Perf. 12½x13***

419	A125	35fr multi	30	20

World Health Day: To see is life.

Paul Kamba and Records
A126

1977, Oct. 29

420	A126	100fr multi	80	6

Paul Kamba (1912–1950), musician.

Trajan Vuia and Flying Machine
A127

Designs: 75fr, Louis Bleriot and plane. 100fr, Roland Garros and plane. 200fr, Charles Lindbergh and Spirit of St. Louis. 300fr, Tupolev Tu-144. 500fr, Lindbergh and Spirit of St. Louis over ship in Atlantic.

1977, Nov. 18 Litho. ***Perf. 14***

421	A127	60fr multi	60	35
422	A127	75fr multi	70	42
423	A127	100fr multi	95	42
424	A127	200fr multi	1.90	90
425	A127	300fr multi	3.00	1.40
		Nos. 421-425 (5)	7.15	3.49

Souvenir Sheet

426	A127	500fr multi	4.00	1.85

History of aviation. No. 426 has multicolored margin showing Spirit of St. Louis at Orly Airport, Paris. Size: 117x91mm.

Elizabeth II and Prince Philip
A128

Design: 300fr, Elizabeth II wearing Crown.

1977, Dec. 21

427	A128	250fr multi	2.40	1.30
428	A128	300fr multi	3.00	1.40

25th anniversary of the reign of Queen Elizabeth II. See No. C239.

King Baudouin
A129

Design: No. 430, Charles de Gaulle.

1977, Dec. 21

429	A129	200fr multi	1.90	95
430	A129	200fr multi	1.90	95

King Baudouin of Belgium and Charles de Gaulle, president of France.

Ambete Sculpture
A130

Design: 85fr, Babembe sculpture.

1978, Feb. 18 Engr. *Perf. 13*

431	A130	35fr lt brn & multi	30	20
432	A130	85fr lt grn & multi	70	50

Congolese art.

St. Simon, by Rubens
A131

Rubens Paintings: 140fr, Duke of Lerma. 200fr, Madonna and Saints. 300fr, Rubens and his Wife Helena Fourment. 500fr, Farm at Laeken.

1978, Mar. 7 Litho. *Perf. 13½x14*

433	A131	60fr gold & multi	60	25
434	A131	140fr gold & multi	1.35	45
435	A131	200fr gold & multi	1.90	70
436	A131	300fr gold & multi	3.00	1.00

Souvenir Sheet

437	A131	500fr gold & multi	4.75	2.00

Peter Paul Rubens (1577–1640), 400th birth anniversary. No. 437 contains one stamp; multicolored margin shows entire painting. Size: 106x123mm.

Pres. Ngouabi and Microphones
A132

Designs: 60fr, Ngouabi at his desk (horiz.). 100fr, Portrait.

Perf. 12½x13, 13x12½

1978, Mar. 18 Lithographed

438	A132	35fr multi	30	20
439	A132	60fr multi	50	35
440	A132	100fr multi	80	60

Pres. Marien Ngouabi, first death anniversary.

Ferenc Puskas and Argentina '78 Emblem—A133

Players and Emblem: 75fr, Giacinto Facchetti. 100fr, Bobby Moore. 200fr, Raymond Kopa. 300fr, Pelé. 500fr, Franz Beckenbauer.

1978, Apr. 4 *Perf. 14x13½*

441	A133	60fr multi	60	33
442	A133	75fr multi	70	40
443	A133	100fr multi	90	45
444	A133	200fr multi	2.00	95
445	A133	300fr multi	2.85	1.35
		Nos. 441-445 (5)	7.05	3.48

Souvenir Sheet

446	A133	500fr multi	4.75	2.00

11th World Cup Soccer Championship, Argentina, June 1–25. No. 446 has light and dark blue margin showing soccer ball and net. Size: 136x100mm.

Pearl S. Buck and Chinese Women
A134

Designs: 75fr, Fridtjof Nansen, refugees and Nansen passport. 100fr, Henri Bergson, book and flame. 200fr, Alexander Fleming and Petri dish. 300fr, Gerhart Hauptmann and book. 500fr, Henri Dunant and Red Cross Station.

1978, Apr. 29

447	A134	60fr multi	60	33
448	A134	75fr multi	70	40
449	A134	100fr multi	90	45
450	A134	200fr multi	2.00	95
451	A134	300fr multi	2.85	1.35
		Nos. 447-451 (5)	7.05	3.48

Souvenir Sheet

452	A134	500fr multi	4.75	2.00

Nobel Prize winners. No. 452 has multicolored margin with head of Alfred Nobel and inscribed "Nobel." Size: 119x81mm.

African Buffalos
A135

Animals and Wildlife Fund Emblem: 35fr, Okapi (vert.). 85fr, Rhinoceros. 150fr, Chimpanzee (vert.). 200fr, Hippopotamus. 300fr, Buffon's kob (vert.).

1978 *Perf. 14½*

453	A135	35fr multi	35	25
454	A135	60fr multi	60	30
455	A135	85fr multi	80	42
456	A135	150fr multi	1.40	60
457	A135	200fr multi	2.00	85
458	A135	300fr multi	2.85	1.25
		Nos. 453-458 (6)	8.00	3.67

Endangered animals.
Issue dates: 35fr, Aug. 11. Others, July 11.

Emblem, Young People, Gun and Fist
A136

1978, July 28 *Perf. 12½*

459	A136	35fr multi	30	20

11th World Youth Festival, Havana, July 28–Aug. 5.

Pyramids and Camels—A137

Seven Wonders of the Ancient World: 50fr, Hanging Gardens of Babylon. 60fr, Statue of Zeus, Olympia. 95fr, Colossus of Rhodes. 125fr, Mausoleum of Halicarnassus. 150fr, Temple of Artemis, Ephesus. 200fr, Lighthouse, Alexandria. 300fr, Map of Eastern Mediterranean showing locations. (50fr, 60fr, 95fr, 125fr, 200fr, vertical.)

1978, Aug. 12 Litho. *Perf. 14*

460	A137	35fr multi	35	18
461	A137	50fr multi	50	25
462	A137	60fr multi	60	30
463	A137	95fr multi	90	45
464	A137	125fr multi	1.20	55
465	A137	150fr multi	1.50	70
466	A137	200fr multi	1.90	85
467	A137	300fr multi	3.00	1.20
		Nos. 460-467 (8)	9.95	4.48

Nos. 427–428 Overprinted in Silver:
"ANNIVERSAIRE DU COURONNEMENT 1953–1978"

1978, Sept. Litho. *Perf. 14*

468	A128	250fr multi	2.00	75
469	A128	300fr multi	2.40	1.00

25th anniversary of coronation of Queen Elizabeth II. See No. C244.

Kwame N'Krumah and Map of Africa—A138

1978, Sept. 23 Litho. *Perf. 13x12½*

470	A138	60fr multi	50	25

Kwame N'Krumah (1909–1972), president of Ghana.

Wild Boar Hunt—A139

Designs: 50fr, Fish smoking. 60fr, Hunter with spears and dog (vert.).

1978 Litho. *Perf. 12*

471	A139	35fr multi	35	25
472	A139	50fr multi	50	35
473	A139	60fr multi	60	40

Local hunting and fishing.
Issue dates: 35fr, 60fr, Oct. 5; 50fr, Oct. 10.

View of Kalchreut, by Dürer—A140

Paintings by Dürer: 150fr, Elspeth Tucher (vert.). 250fr, "The Great Piece of Turf" (vert.). 350fr, Self-portrait (vert.).

1978, Nov. 23 Litho. *Perf. 14*

474	A140	65fr multi	65	42
475	A140	150fr multi	1.50	1.05
476	A140	250fr multi	2.50	1.75
477	A140	350fr multi	3.50	2.50

Albrecht Dürer (1471–1528), German painter.

Basketmaker
A141

Productive Labor: 90fr, Woodcarver. 140fr, Women hoeing field.

1978, Nov. 18 Litho. *Perf. 12½*

Size: 25x36mm.

478	A141	85fr multi	85	60
479	A141	90fr multi	90	62

Size: 27x48mm.

Perf. 12

480	A141	140fr multi	1.40	1.00

Nos. 441–446 Overprinted in Silver:

a. "1962 VAINQUEUR:BRESIL"
b. "1966 VAINQUEUR: / GRANDE BRETAGNE"
c. "1970 VAINQUEUR: / BRESIL"
d. "1974 VAINQUEUR: / ALLEMAGNE (RFA)"
e. "1978 VAINQUEUR /: ARGENTINE"
f. "ARGENTINE–PAYS BAS 3–1 / 25 juin 1978"

1978, Nov. *Perf. 14x13½*

481	A133 (a)	60fr multi	60	40
482	A133 (b)	75fr multi	75	50
483	A133 (c)	100fr multi	1.00	70
484	A133 (d)	200fr multi	2.00	1.40
485	A133 (e)	300fr multi	3.00	2.10
		Nos. 481-485(5)	7.35	5.10

Souvenir Sheet

486	A133 (f)	500fr multi	5.25	

Winners, World Soccer Cup Championships 1962–1978.

Heart and Charts
A142

1978, Dec. 16 Engr. *Perf. 13*

487 A142 100fr multi 1.00 70

Fight against hypertension.

Party Emblem and Road—A143

1978, Dec. 31 Litho. *Perf. 12½x12*

488 A143 60fr multi 60 40

Congolese Labor Party, 9th anniversary.

Capt. Cook, Polynesians and House—A144

Designs: 150fr, Island scene. 250fr, Polynesian longboats. 350fr, Capt. Cook's ships off Hawaii.

1979, Jan. *Perf. 14½*

489 A144 65fr multi 55 42
490 A144 150fr multi 1.50 1.05
491 A144 250fr multi 2.50 1.75
492 A144 350fr multi 3.50 2.50

Capt. James Cook (1728–1779), 250th birth anniversary.

Pres. Marien Ngouabi A145

1979, Mar. 18 Litho. *Perf. 12*

493 A145 35fr multi 35 22
494 A145 60fr multi 60 40

2nd anniversary of assassination of President Ngouabi.

"1979," IYC Emblem, Child A146

1979, Apr. 30 Litho. *Perf. 12½x13*

495 A146 45fr multi 45 30
496 A146 75fr multi 75 50

International Year of the Child.

Pottery Vases and Solanum—A147

Design: 150fr, Mail runner, Concorde, train, UPU emblem, envelope.

1979, June 8 Litho. *Perf. 13*

497 A147 60fr multi 60 35

Engraved

498 A147 150fr multi 1.50 90

Philexafrique II, Libreville, Gabon, June 8–17. Nos. 497, 498 each printed in sheets of 10 with 5 labels showing exhibition emblem.

Rowland Hill, Diesel Locomotive, Germany No. 78—A148

Designs (Rowland Hill and): 100fr, Old steam locomotive and France No. B10. 200fr, Diesel locomotive and US No. 245. 300fr, Steam locomotive and England-Australia First Aerialpost vignette, 1919. 500fr, Electric train, Concorde and Middle Congo No. 75.

1979, June *Perf. 14*

499 A148 65fr multi 65 42
500 A148 100fr multi 1.00 70
501 A148 200fr multi 2.00 1.40
502 A148 300fr multi 3.00 2.10

Souvenir Sheet

503 A148 500fr multi 5.25

Sir Rowland Hill (1795–1879), originator of penny postage. No. 503 has multicolored margin showing locomotive and 19th century woman posting letter in pillar box. Size: 102x77mm.

Salvador Allende, Flags, Demonstrators—A149

1979, July 21 Litho. *Perf. 12½*

504 A149 100fr multi 1.00 70

Salvador Allende, president of Chile.

Old Man Telling Stories—A150

1979, July 28

505 A150 45fr multi 45 30

Story telling as education.

Handball Players A151

Designs: 75fr, Players and ball (vert.). 250fr, Pres. Ngouabi, cup on map of Africa, player.

1979, July 31 Litho. *Perf. 12½*

Size: 40x30mm, 30x40mm

506 A151 45fr multi 45 30
507 A151 75fr multi 75 50

Size: 22x40mm *Perf. 12x12½*

508 A151 250fr multi 2.50 1.75

Marien Ngouabi Handball Cup.

Map and Flag of Congo A152

1979, Aug. 15

509 A152 50fr multi 50 35

16th anniversary of revolution.

Souvenir Sheet

Virgin and Child, by Dürer A153

1979, Aug. 13 *Perf. 13½*

510 A153 500fr red brn & lt grn 5.25

Albrecht Dürer (1471–1528), German engraver and painter. No. 510 has light green and red brown margin showing entire etching. Size: 90x115mm.

Bach and Contemporary Instruments A155

1979, Sept. 10 *Perf. 13½*

Design: No. 512, Albert Einstein, astronauts on moon.

511 A155 200fr multi 2.00 1.40
512 A155 200fr multi 2.00 1.40

Yoro Fishing Port—A156

1979, Sept. 26 Litho. *Perf. 12½*

Multicolored

513 A156 45fr *shown* 45 30
514 A156 75fr *Port at night* 75 50

Mukukulu Dam—A157

1979, Oct. 5 *Perf. 12½×12*

515 A157 20fr multi 20 14
516 A157 45fr multi 45 30

Emblem, Control Tower, Jets—A158

1979, Dec. 12 Litho. *Perf. 12½*

517 A158 100fr multi 1.00 75

ASCENA (Air Safety Board), 20th anniversary.

Congolese Labor Party, 10th Anniversary—A159

1979, Dec. 31

518 A159 45fr multi 45 14

Post Office, 15th Anniversary A160

1980, Mar. 30 Litho. *Perf. 12½*

519 A160 45fr multi 45 34
520 A160 95fr multi 95 70

Visit of Pope John Paul II—A161

1980, May 5

521 A161 100fr multi 80 40

Rotary International, 75th Anniversary—A162

1980, May 10 Litho. *Perf. 12½*

522 A162 150fr multi 1.20 60

Pointe Noire Foundry—A163

1980, June 18 **Litho.** ***Perf. 12½***

523	A163	30fr *shown*	24	12
524	A163	35fr *Different view*	28	14

Claude Chappe, Tower—A164

1980, June 21 **Litho.** ***Perf. 12½***

525	A164	200fr multi	1.60	80

Claude Chappe (1763-1805), French engineer.

Mossaka Harbor—A165

1980, June 23

532	A165	45fr *shown*	36	18
533	A165	90fr *Different view*	72	35

Papilio Dardanus (Front and Back) A167

Human Rights Emblem, People A169

July 31st Hospital—A168

1980, July 12 **Litho.** ***Perf. 12½***

534	A167	5fr *shown*	5	5
535	A167	15fr *Kalima aethiops*	12	6
536	A167	20fr *Papilio demodocus*	16	8
537	A167	60fr *Euphaedra*	48	24
538	A167	90fr *Hypolimnas misippus*	72	36
		Nos. 534-538 (5)	1.53	79

Souvenir Sheet

539	A167	300fr *Charaxes smaragdalis*	2.50

Nos. 539 has multicolored margin showing butterflies. Size: 120x80mm.

1980, July 31

540	A168	45fr multi	36	18

1980, Aug. 2

541	A169	350fr *shown*	2.80	1.40
542	A169	500fr *Man breaking chain*	4.00	4.00

Human Rights Convention, 32nd anniversary.

Citizens and Congolese Arms—A170

1980, Aug. 15 ***Perf. 12½***

543	A170	75fr *shown*	60	30
544	A170	95fr *Dove on flag, fists, vert.*	75	38
545	A170	150fr *Dove holding Congolese arms*	1.20	60

August 13-15th Revolution, 17th anniversary.

Coffee and Cocoa Trees on Map of Congo—A171

Coffee and Cocoa Day: 95fr, Branches, map of Congo.

1980, Aug. 18 ***Perf. 13½x13***

546	A171	45fr multi	35	18
547	A171	95fr multi	75	38

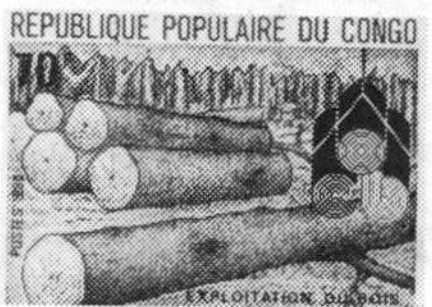

Logging—A172

1980, Aug. 28

548	A172	70fr *shown*	56	28
549	A172	75fr *Wood transport*	60	30

President Neto A173

Lark A174

1980, Sept. 11

550	A173	100fr multi	80	40

1980, Sept. 17

Designs: Birds.

551	A174	45fr multi, horiz.	36	18
552	A174	75fr multi, horiz.	60	30
553	A174	90fr multi, horiz.	72	36
554	A174	150fr multi	1.20	60
555	A174	200fr multi	1.60	80
556	A174	250fr multi	2.00	1.00
a.		Souvenir sheet of 6	6.50	
		Nos. 551-556 (6)	6.48	3.24

No. 556a contains Nos. 551-556. Lilac marginal inscription. Size: 148x105mm.

World Tourism Conference, Manila, Sept. 27—A175

1980, Sept. 27 **Litho.** ***Perf. 13½x13***

557	A175	100fr multi	80	40

First Day of School Term—A176

1980, Oct. 2 **Photo.** ***Perf. 13***

558	A176	50fr multi	40	20

First House in Brazzaville—A177

Brazzaville Centenary: 65fr, First native village. 75fr, Old Town Hall, 1912. 150fr, View from bank of Bacongo, 1912. 200fr, Meeting of explorer Savorgnan de Brazza and chief Makoko, 1880.

1980, Oct. 3 **Litho.** ***Perf. 12½***

559	A177	45fr multi	36	18
560	A177	65fr multi	52	26
561	A177	75fr multi	60	30
562	A177	150fr multi	1.20	60
563	A177	200fr multi	1.60	80
		Nos. 559-563 (5)	4.28	2.14

Boys on Bank of Congo River—A178

1980, Oct. 30

564	A178	80fr *shown*	65	32
565	A178	150fr *Djoue Bridge*	1.20	60

Revolutionary Stadium and Athletes—A179

1980, Nov. 20 ***Perf. 13x12½***

566	A179	60fr multi	50	25

Rebuilt Railroad Bridge over Congo River—A180

1980, Nov. 29 ***Perf. 13x13½***

567	A180	75fr multi	60	30

Mangoes, Loudima Fruit Packing Station—A181

1980, Dec. 2 ***Perf. 13***

568	A181	10fr *shown*	8	5
569	A181	25fr *Oranges*	20	10
570	A181	40fr *Citrons*	32	16
571	A181	85fr *Mandarins*	70	35

African Postal Union, 5th Anniversary—A182

1980, Dec. 24 ***Perf. 13½***

572	A182	100fr multi	80	40

Moungouni Earth Satellite Station—A183

1980, Dec. 30 ***Perf. 12½***

573	A183	75fr multi	60	30

Hertzian Wave Communication, Brazzaville—A184

1980, Dec. 30 ***Perf. 12½x12***

574	A184	150fr multi	1.20	60

1980 African Soccer Champion Team—A185

1981, Jan. 26 Litho. ***Perf. 12½x13, 13x12½***

575 A185 100fr Receiving cup, vert. 80 40
576 A185 150fr shown 1.20 60

Pres. Denis Sassou-Nguesso—A186

1981, Feb. 5 Litho. ***Perf. 12½***

577 A186 45fr multi 36 18
578 A186 75fr multi 60 30
579 A186 100fr multi 80 40

Columbia Space Shuttle Orbiting Earth A187

Space Conquest: 100fr, Luna 17, 1970. 200fr, 300fr, 500fr, Columbia space shuttle, 1981.

1981, May 4 Litho. ***Perf. 14x13½***

580 A187 100fr multi 80 40
581 A187 150fr multi 1.20 60
582 A187 200fr multi 1.60 80
583 A187 300fr multi 2.40 1.20

Souvenir Sheet

584 A187 500fr multi 4.00 2.00

No. 584 has multicolored margin showing space shuttle orbiting earth. Size: 104x79mm.

Fight Against Apartheid A188

Twin Palm Tree of Louingui A189

1981, May 5 Litho. ***Perf. 12½***

585 A188 100fr dp bl 80 40

1981, May 22 ***Perf. 12x12½***

586 A189 75fr multi 60 30

13th World Telecommunications Day—A190

1981, June 6 ***Perf. 12½***

587 A190 120fr multi 95 45

Rubber Extraction—A191

1981, June 27 ***Perf. 13***

588 A191 50fr shown 40 20
589 A191 70fr Sap draining 55 25

Intl. Year of the Disabled—A192

1981, June 29 **Engr.**

590 A192 45fr multi 36 18

See No. B7.

Bird Trap—A194

Designs: Animal traps. 10fr vert.

1981, July

596 A194 5fr multi 5 5
597 A194 10fr multi 8 5
598 A194 15fr multi 12 6
599 A194 20fr multi 16 8
600 A194 30fr multi 24 12
601 A194 35fr multi 28 15
Nos. 596-601 (6) 93 51

Mausoleum of King Maloango—A195

1981, July 4 Litho. ***Perf. 12½***

602 A195 75fr shown 60 30
603 A195 150fr Mausoleum, portrait 1.20 60

Prince Charles and Lady Diana, Coach—A196

Designs: Couple and coaches.

1981, Sept. 1 Litho. ***Perf. 14½***

604 A196 100fr multi 80 40
605 A196 200fr multi 1.60 80
606 A196 300fr multi 2.40 1.20

Souvenir Sheet

607 A196 400fr multi 3.25 1.75

Royal wedding. No. 607 has multicolored margin showing arms of Prince of Wales. Size: 104x78mm.

World Food Day—A197

1981, Oct. 16 Litho. ***Perf. 13½x13***

608 A197 150fr multi 1.20 60

12th World UPU Day—A198

1981, Oct. 24 Engr. ***Perf. 13x12½***

609 A198 90fr multi 72 35

Royal Guard A199

1981, Oct. 31 Litho. ***Perf. 12½x13***

610 A199 45fr multi 35 18

Eradication of Manioc Beetle A200

Natl. Red Cross A201

1981, Nov. 18 Litho. ***Perf. 12½***

611 A200 75fr multi 60 30

1981, Nov. 18 ***Perf. 13***

612 A201 10fr Bandaging patient 8 5
613 A201 35fr Treating child 28 15
614 A201 60fr Drawing well water 50 25

Giant Baobab ("Tree of Savorgnan de Brazza")—A202

1981, Dec. 19 Litho. ***Perf. 13***

615 A202 45fr multi 35 18
616 A202 65fr multi 60 30

Fetish Figure A203

Designs: Various carved figures.

1981, Dec. 19 ***Perf. 13x12½***

617 A203 15fr multi 12 6
618 A203 25fr multi 20 10
619 A203 45fr multi 35 18
620 A203 50fr multi 40 20
621 A203 60fr multi 50 25
Nos. 617-621 (5) 1.57 79

Caves of Bangou—A204

1981, Dec. 29 ***Perf. 13x13½***

622 A204 20fr multi 16 8
623 A204 25fr multi 20 10

King Makoko and His Queen, Ivory Sculptures by R. Engongodzo—A205

1982, Feb. 27 Litho. ***Perf. 13½x13, 13x13½***

No.	Type	Denomination	Design	Unused	Used
624	A205	25fr	Woman, vert.	20	10
625	A205	35fr	Woman, diff., vert.	28	14
626	A205	100fr	shown	80	40

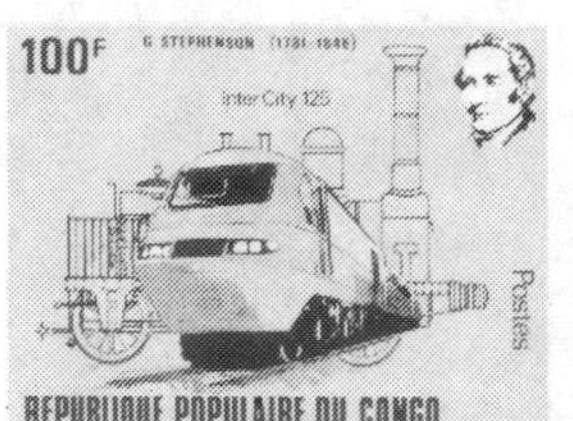

George Stephenson (1781-1848) and Inter City 125, Gt. Britain—A206

Locomotives: 150fr, Sinkansen Bullet Train, Japan. 200fr, Advanced Passenger Train, Gt. Britain. 300fr, TGV-001, France.

1982, Mar. 2 **Litho.** ***Perf. 12½***

No.	Type	Denomination	Design	Unused	Used
627	A206	100fr	multi	80	80
628	A206	150fr	multi	1.20	60
629	A206	200fr	multi	1.60	80
630	A206	300fr	multi	2.40	1.20

Scouting Year—A207

1982, Apr. 13 **Litho.** ***Perf. 13***

No.	Type	Denomination	Design	Unused	Used
631	A207	100fr	Looking through binoculars	80	40
632	A207	150fr	Reading map	1.20	60
633	A207	200fr	Helping woman	1.60	80
634	A207	300fr	Crossing rope bridge	2.40	1.25

Souvenir Sheet

No.	Type	Denomination	Design	Unused	Used
635	A207	500fr	Hiking, horiz.	4.00	2.00

No. 635 has multicolored margin continuing design. Size: 96x71mm.

Franklin Roosevelt (1882-1945)—A208

1982, June 12 **Litho.** ***Perf. 13***

No.	Type	Denomination	Design	Unused	Used
636	A208	150fr	shown	1.20	60
637	A208	250fr	Washington (1732-1799)	2.00	1.00
638	A208	350fr	Goethe (1749-1832)	2.80	1.40

21st Birthday of Princess Diana, July 1—A209

1982, June 12 ***Perf. 14***

No.	Type	Denomination	Design	Unused	Used
639	A209	200fr	Candles	1.60	80
640	A209	300fr	"21"	2.40	1.25

Souvenir Sheet

No.	Type	Denomination	Design	Unused	Used
641	A209	500fr	Diana	4.00	2.00

No. 641 has multicolored margin showing rose. Size: 112x80mm.

5-Year Plan, 1982-1986—A210

1982, June 19 ***Perf. 13x12½, 12½x13***

No.	Type	Denomination	Design	Unused	Used
642	A210	60fr	Road construction	50	25
643	A210	100fr	Communications, vert	80	40
644	A210	125fr	Operating room equipment, vert.	1.00	50
645	A210	150fr	Hydroelectric power, vert.	1.20	60

ITU Plenipotentiary Conference, Nairobi—A211

1982, June 26 ***Perf. 13***

No.	Type	Denomination	Design	Unused	Used
646	A211	300fr	multi	2.40	1.25

Nos. 604-607 Overprinted in Blue: "NAISSANCE ROYALE 1982"

1982, July 30 ***Perf. 14½***

No.	Type	Denomination	Design	Unused	Used
647	A196	100fr	multi	80	40
648	A196	200fr	multi	1.60	80
649	A196	300fr	multi	2.40	1.25

Souvenir Sheet

No.	Type	Denomination	Design	Unused	Used
650	A196	400fr	multi	3.25	1.75

Birth of Prince William of Wales, June 21.

Nutrition Campaign—A212

1982, July 24 **Litho.** ***Perf. 12½***

No.	Type	Denomination	Design	Unused	Used
651	A212	100fr	multi	80	40

WHO African Headquarters, Brazzaville—A213

1982, July 24 **Litho.** ***Perf. 12½***

No.	Type	Denomination	Design	Unused	Used
652	A213	125fr	multi	1.00	50

TB Bacillus Centenary—A214

1982, Aug. 7 ***Perf. 12½x12***

No.	Type	Denomination	Design	Unused	Used
653	A214	250fr	Koch, bacillus	2.00	1.00

Pres. Sassou-Nguesso and 1980 Simba Prize—A215

1982, Oct. 20 **Litho.** ***Perf. 13***

No.	Type	Denomination	Design	Unused	Used
654	A215	100fr	multi	80	40

Turtles—A216

Various turtles and tortoises.

1982, Dec. 1

No.	Type	Denomination	Design	Unused	Used
655	A216	30fr	multi	24	12
656	A216	45fr	multi	35	18
657	A216	55fr	multi	45	22

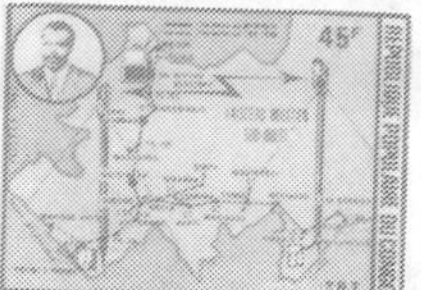

Boy Gathering Coconuts—A217

Nest in Tree Trunk—A218

1982, Dec. 11

No.	Type	Denomination	Design	Unused	Used
658	A217	100fr	multi	80	40

1982, Dec. 29 ***Perf. 12½***

No.	Type	Denomination	Design	Unused	Used
659	A218	40fr	shown	32	16
660	A218	75fr	Nests in palm tree	60	30
661	A218	100fr	Woven nest on thron branch	80	40

Hertzian Wave Communication Network—A219

1982, Dec. 30 ***Perf. 13x12½***

No.	Type	Denomination	Design	Unused	Used
662	A219	45fr	multi	35	18
663	A219	60fr	multi	50	25
664	A219	95fr	multi	75	40

30th Anniv. of Customs Cooperation Council—A220

1983, Jan. 26 **Litho.** ***Perf. 12½x13***

No.	Type	Denomination	Design	Unused	Used
665	A220	100fr	Headquarters	80	40

Mausoleum of Pres. Marien Ngouabi—A221

1983, Feb. 8 ***Perf. 13***

No.	Type	Denomination	Design	Unused	Used
666	A221	60fr	multi	50	25
667	A221	80fr	multi	65	32

Ironsmiths—A222

1983 ***Perf. 12½***

No.	Type	Denomination	Design	Unused	Used
668	A222	45fr	shown	35	18
669	A222	150fr	Weaver, vert.	1.20	62

Issue dates: 45fr, Mar. 5; 150fr, Feb. 24

Carved Chess Pieces, by R. Engongonzo—A223

Various pieces.

1983, Feb. 26 ***Perf. 13***

No.	Type	Denomination	Design	Unused	Used
670	A223	40fr	multi	32	15
671	A223	60fr	multi	50	25
672	A223	95fr	multi	75	38

Easter 1983—A224

Raphael drawings. 200fr, 400fr vert.

1983, Apr. 20 Litho. *Perf. 13*

673	A224	200fr	Transfiguration study	1.60	80
674	A224	300fr	Deposition from Cross	2.40	1.20
675	A224	400fr	Christ in Glory	3.25	1.60

Seashells—A225

Seashells. Dated 1982.

1983 Litho. *Perf. 15x14*

676	A225	35fr	multi	14	8
677	A225	65fr	multi	25	12

Traditional Combs—A226

Various combs.

1983, May *Perf. 14*

678	A226	30fr	multi	12	6
679	A226	70fr	multi	28	14
680	A226	85fr	multi	34	18

20th Anniv. of Revolution—A227

Perf. 12½x13

1983, Aug. 10 Litho. & Engr.

681	A227	60fr	multi	24	12
682	A227	100fr	multi	40	20

Centenary of the Arrival of Christian Missionaries—A228

Churches and Clergymen: 150fr, A. Carrie, Church of the Sacred Heart, Loango (vert.). 250fr, Msgr. Augouard; St. Louis, Liranga; St. Joseph, Linzolo.

1983, Aug. 23 *Perf. 12½*

683	A228	150fr	multi	60	30
684	A228	250fr	multi	1.00	50

Local Flowers—A229

1984, Jan. 20 Litho. *Perf. 12½*

685	A229	5fr	Liana thunderaie, vert.	5	5
686	A229	15fr	Bougainvillea	6	5
687	A229	20fr	Anthurium, vert.	8	5
688	A229	45fr	Allamanda	18	10
689	A229	75fr	Hibiscus, vert.	30	15
			Nos. 685-689 (5)	67	40

35th Anniv. of World Peace Council—A230

1984, Mar. 31 Litho. *Perf. 13x12½*

690	A230	50fr	multi	20	10
691	A230	100fr	multi	40	20

Anti-Nuclear Arms Campaign—A231

1984, May 31 Litho. *Perf. 12x12½*

692	A231	200fr	Explosion, victims	80	40

Agriculture Day—A232

Perf. 13x13½, 13½x13

1984, June 30 Litho.

693	A232	10fr	Rice	5	5
694	A232	15fr	Pineapples	6	5
695	A232	60fr	Manioc, vert.	25	12
696	A232	100fr	Palm tree, map, vert.	40	20

Congress Palace—A233

1984, July 27 *Perf. 13*

697	A233	60fr	multi	25	12
698	A233	100fr	multi	40	20

Chinese-Congolese cooperation.

CFCO - Congo Railways, 50th Anniv.—A234

1984, July 30 *Perf. 13½*

699	A234	10fr	Loulombo Station	5	5
700	A234	25fr	Les Bandas Chinese Labor Camp	10	5
701	A234	125fr	"50"	50	25
702	A234	200fr	Admin. bldg.	80	40

Locomotives—A235

Ships on the Congo River—A236

1984, Aug. 24 *Perf. 12½*

703	A235	100fr	CC 203	40	20
704	A236	100fr	Tugboat	40	20
705	A235	150fr	BB 103	60	30
706	A236	150fr	Pusher tugboat	60	30
707	A235	300fr	BB-BB 301	1.15	55
708	A236	300fr	Dredger	1.15	55
709	A235	500fr	BB 420 L'Eclair	2.00	1.00
710	A236	500fr	Cargo ship	2.00	1.00
			Nos. 703-710 (8)	8.30	4.10

World Fisheries Year—A237

1984, Oct. 16 *Perf. 13½*

711	A237	5fr	Basket of fish	5	5
712	A237	20fr	Net fishermen in boat	8	5
713	A237	25fr	School of fish	10	5
714	A237	40fr	Net fisherman	16	8
715	A237	55fr	Trawler	22	12
			Nos. 711-715 (5)	61	35

Anti-polio Campaign

A238

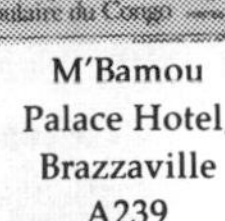

M'Bamou Palace Hotel, Brazzaville

A239

1984, Oct. 30

716	A238	250fr	Disabled men, hand	1.00	50
717	A238	300fr	Target, disabled women, horiz.	1.25	65

1984, Dec. 15 *Perf. 14½*

718	A239	60fr	multi	25	12
719	A239	100fr	multi	40	20

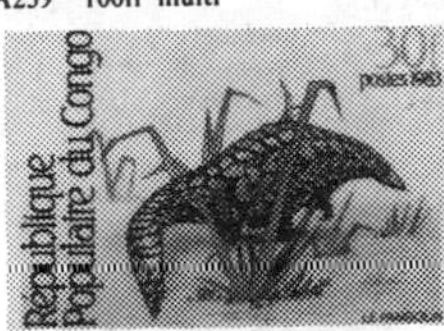

Fauna—A240

1984, Dec. *Perf. 15x14½*

720	A240	30fr	Pangolin	14	8
721	A240	70fr	Bat	30	15
722	A240	85fr	Civet cat	35	18

Congo River Logging—A241

1984, Dec. *Perf. 13½x13*

723	A241	60fr	Log raft, crew hut	25	12
724	A241	100fr	Tugboat pushing logs	40	20

Souvenir Sheets

Nos. 584, 635 Ovptd. with Exhibition in Black or Green.

1985, Mar. 8 *Perf. 14x13½, 13*

725	A187	500fr	TSUKUBA EXPO '85	2.00	1.00
726	A207	500fr	ITALIA '85 emblem, ROME (G)	2.00	1.00

See Nos. C336-C337.

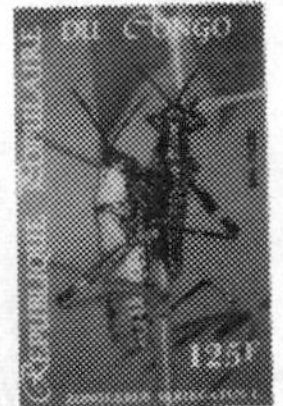

Zonocerus Variegatus—A242

1985, Mar. 15 *Perf. 13*

727	A242	125fr	multi	50	25

Burial of a Teke Chief—A243

1985, Apr. 30 *Perf. 12½*
728 A243 225fr multi 95 48

Edible Fruit—A244

1985, June 15 *Perf. 13½*
729 A244 5fr Trichoscypha acuminata, vert. 5 5
730 A244 10fr Aframomum africanum 5 5
731 A244 125fr Gambeya lacuurtiana 50 25
732 A244 150fr Landolphia jumelei 60 30

Lions Club Intl., 30th Anniv.—A245

1985, June 25 *Perf. 12½*
733 A245 250fr Flag, District 403B 1.00 50

Russian Soldier, Kremlin, Fall of Berlin—A246

1985, July 27 *Perf. 12*
734 A246 60fr multi 25 12

Defeat of Nazi Germany, end of World War II, 40th anniv.

Lady Olave Baden-Powell, Girl Guides Founder—A247

Anniversaries and events: 150fr, Girl Guides, 75th anniv. 250fr, Jacob Grimm, fabulist; Sleeping Beauty. 350fr, Johann Sebastian Bach, composer; European Music Year, St. Thomas Church organ, Leipzig. 450fr, Queen Mother, 85th birthday, vert. 500fr, Statue of Liberty, cent., vert.

1985, Aug. 26 *Perf. 13*
735 A247 150fr multi 60 30
736 A247 250fr multi 1.00 50
737 A247 350fr multi 1.40 70
738 A247 450fr multi 1.75 90
739 A247 500fr multi 2.00 1.00
Nos. 735-739 (5) 6.75 3.40

PHILEXAFRICA '85, Lome, Togo, Nov. 16-24—A248

1985, Oct. 10 *Perf. 13x12½*
740 A248 250fr Silhouettes, cement mixer, skyscrapers 1.00 50
741 A248 250fr Airport, postal van 1.00 50

Nos. 740-741 printed se-tenant with center label picturing map of Africa or UAPT emblem.

Mushrooms—A249

1985, Dec. 14 **Litho.** *Perf. 13*
742 A249 100fr Coprinus, vert. 55 28
743 A249 150fr Cortinarius 82 40
744 A249 200fr Armillariella mellea 1.10 55
745 A249 300fr Dictyophora 1.65 82
746 A249 400fr Crucibulum vulgare 2.25 1.10
Nos. 742-746 (5) 6.37 3.15

Arbor Day — A250

Children's Hoop Races — A251

1986, Mar. 6 *Perf. 13½*
747 A250 60fr Planting sapling 32 16
748 A250 200fr Map, lifecycle diagram 1.10 55

1986, Apr. 30 *Perf. 12½*
749 A251 5fr Two boys 5 5
750 A251 10fr One boy 6 5
751 A251 60fr Three boys, horiz. 32 16
a. Souvenir sheet of 3, #749-751 45 28

No. 751a has blue inscribed margin. Size: 150x100mm.

Intl. Environment Day—A252

1986, June 5 **Litho.** *Perf. 13½*
752 A252 60fr Garbage disposal 32 16
753 A252 125fr Dumping garbage 75 38

Traditional Modes of Transporting Goods—A253

Designs: 5 fr, Basket on head, child in sling carrier. 10fr, Child in carrier on hip, large basket strapped to forehead. 60fr, Man carrying load on shoulder.

1986, July 15 **Litho.** *Perf. 13x12½*
754 A253 5fr multi 5 5
755 A253 10fr multi 6 5
756 A253 60fr multi 32 16

Mission of the Sisters of St. Joseph of Cluny, Cent.—A254

1986, Aug. 19 **Litho.** *Perf. 12½x13*
757 A254 230fr multi 1.25 62

UNESCO Intl. Communications Development Program—A255

1986, Aug. 30 **Litho.** *Perf. 13½*
758 A255 40fr multi 22 10
759 A255 60fr multi 35 18
760 A255 100fr multi 55 28

Intl. Peace Year—A256

1986, Sept. 15 **Litho.** *Perf. 13½*
761 A256 100fr multi 55 28

World Food Day—A257

1986, Oct. 16
762 A257 75fr Food staples 40 20
763 A257 120fr Mother feeding child 65 32

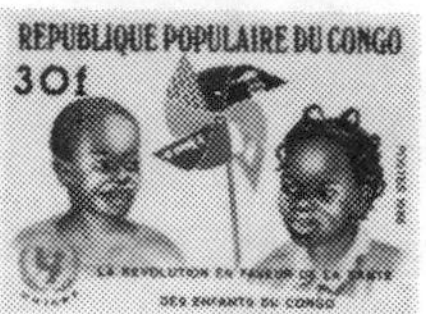

UN Child Survival Campaign—A258

Mothers, children and pinwheels in various designs.

1986, Oct. 27
764 A258 15fr multi, vert. 8 5
765 A258 30fr multi 16 8
766 A258 70fr multi, vert. 38 20

Election of President Sassou-Nguesso, Head of the Organization of African States—A259

1987, Feb. 10 **Litho.** *Perf. 13½*
767 A259 30fr multi 16 8
768 A259 45fr multi 25 12
769 A259 75fr multi 40 20
770 A259 120fr multi 65 32

SEMI-POSTAL STAMPS.

Anti-Malaria Issue

Common Design Type

Engraved

1962, Apr. 7 ***Perf. 12½x12***

B3	CD108 25fr +5fr bis		65	65

Issued for the World Health Organization drive to eradicate malaria.

Freedom from Hunger Issue

Common Design Type

1963, Mar. 21 ***Perf. 13*** **Unwmkd.**

B4	CD112 25fr +5fr vio bl, bl grn & brn		60	60

Boy Suffering from Sleeping Sickness—SP1

Fight Against Communicable Diseases; 40fr+5fr, Examination, treatment (vert.).

1981, June 6 **Litho.** ***Perf. 13***

B5	SP1	40 + 5fr multi	36	18
B6	SP1	65 + 10fr multi	60	30

IYD Type of 1981

1981, June 29 ***Perf. 12½***

B7	A192	75 + 5fr multi	65	32

AIR POST STAMPS

Olympic Games Issue

French Equatorial Africa No. C37 Surcharged in Red Like Chad No. C1.

Engraved

1960 ***Perf. 13*** **Unwmkd.**

C1	AP8	250fr on 500fr grnsh blk, blk & sl	5.50	5.50

Issued to commemorate the 17th Olympic Games, Rome, Aug. 25–Sept. 11.

Helicrysum Mechowiam—AP1

Flowers: 200fr, Cogniauxia podolaena. 500fr, Thesium tencio.

1961, Sept. 28 Engraved ***Perf. 13***

C2	AP1	100fr grn, lil & yel	1.35	95
C3	AP1	200fr bl grn, yel & brn	2.65	1.20
C4	AP1	500fr brn red, yel & sl grn	6.00	2.65

Air Afrique Issue

Common Design Type

1961, Nov. 25 ***Perf. 13*** **Unwmkd.**

C5	CD107	50fr lil rose, sl grn & grn	60	50

Founding of Air Afrique.

Loading Timber, Pointe-Noire Harbor—AP2

1962, June 8 Photo. ***Perf. 12½x12***

C6	AP2	50fr multi	60	50

Issued to commemorate the opening of the International Fair and Exhibition, Pointe-Noire, June 8–11.

Abidjan Games Issue

Basketball AP3

1962, July 21 ***Perf. 12x12½***

C7	AP3	100fr multi	1.35	95

Costus Spectabilis AP4

Design: 250fr, Mountain acanthus.

1963 ***Perf. 13*** **Unwmkd.**

C8	AP4	100fr multi	1.35	80
C9	AP4	250fr multi	3.50	1.85

Brazzaville City Hall and Pres. Fulbert Youlou AP4a

1963, Aug. Photo. ***Perf. 13x12***

C10	AP4a	100fr multi	60.00	60.00

African Postal Union Issue

Common Design Type

1963, Sept. 8 ***Perf. 12½***

C13	CD114	85fr pur, ocher & red	95	65

Air Afrique Issue, 1963

Common Design Type

Photogravure

1963, Nov. 19 ***Perf. 13x12*** **Unwmkd.**

C14	CD115	50fr multi	65	50

Liberty Place, Brazzaville—AP5

1963, Nov. 28

C15	AP5	25fr multi	32	25

See also No. 118.

Europafrica Issue

Common Design Type

1963, Nov. 30 ***Perf. 12x13***

C16	CD116	50fr gray, yel & dk brn	80	55

Timber Industry—AP6

1964, May 12 Engraved ***Perf. 13***

C17	AP6	100fr grn, brn red & blk	1.20	70

Chiefs of State Issue

Map and Presidents of Chad, Congo, Gabon and CAR AP6a

1964, June 23 Photo. ***Perf. 12½***

C18	AP6a	100fr multi	1.25	70

See note after Central African Republic No. C19.

Europafrica Issue, 1964

Sunburst, Wheat, Cogwheel and Globe AP7

1964, July 20 ***Perf. 12x13***

C19	AP7	50fr yel, Prus bl & mar	65	40

See note after Cameroun No. 402.

Hammer Thrower, Olympic Flame and Stadium—AP8

Designs (Olympic flame, stadium) and: 50fr, Weight lifter (vert.). 100fr, Volleyball (vert.). 200fr, High jump.

1964, July 30 ***Perf. 13*** **Engraved**

C20	AP8	25fr vio bl, org & red brn	32	15
C21	AP8	50fr yel grn, org & red lil	65	45
C22	AP8	100fr sl grn, org & red brn	1.25	95
C23	AP8	200fr crim, org & dp grn	2.50	1.90
a.		Min. sheet of 4	5.50	5.50

Issued for the 18th Olympic Games, Tokyo, Oct. 10–25, 1964. No. C23a contains one each of Nos. C20–C23. Size: 191x99mm.

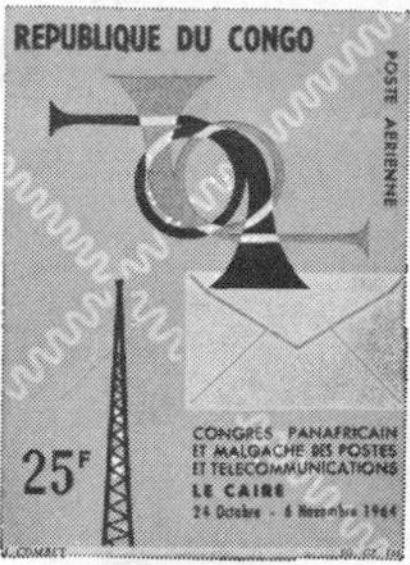

Communications Symbols AP8a

1964, Nov. 2 Litho. ***Perf. 12½x13***

C24	AP8a	25fr dl rose & dk brn	40	30

See note after Chad No. C19.

Town Hall, Brazzaville—AP9

1965, Jan. 30 Photo. ***Perf. 12½***

C25	AP9	100fr multi	1.20	65

Coupling Hooks—AP10

1965, Feb. 27 Photo. ***Perf. 13x12***

C26	AP10	50fr multi	65	40

Economic Europe-Africa Association.

Breguet Dial Telegraph, ITU Emblem and Telstar AP11

1965, May 17 Engraved ***Perf. 13***

C27	AP11	100fr dk bl, ocher & brn	1.35	80

Issued to commemorate the centenary of the International Telecommunication Union.

Pope John XXIII and St. Peter's Cathedral—AP12

Perf. 12½x13

1965, June 26 Photo. Unwmkd.

C28	AP12	100fr gldn brn & multi	1.20	90

Issued in memory of Pope John XXIII (1881–1963).

Pres. John F. Kennedy AP13 — Log Rolling AP14

Portraits: 25fr on 50fr, Patrice Lumumba, premier of Congo Republic (ex-Belgian). 50fr, Sir Winston Churchill. 80fr, Barthélémy Boganda, premier of Central African Republic.

1965, June 25–26 ***Perf. 12½***

C29	AP13	25fr on 50fr dk brn & red	40	40
a.		Surch. omitted	22.50	22.50
C30	AP13	50fr dk brn & yel grn	90	90
C31	AP13	80fr dk brn & bl	1.20	1.20
C32	AP13	100fr dk brn & org yel	1.50	1.50
a.		Min. sheet of 4	6.00	6.00

Issued to honor famous statesmen. No. C32a contains one each of Nos. C29–C32. Size: 106x143 mm.

A second miniature sheet contains one each of Nos. C29a, C30–C32. Price, $30.

1965, Aug. 14 Engraved ***Perf. 13***

C33	AP14	50fr grn, brn & red brn	75	40

Issued to publicize national unity.

World Map and Symbols of Agriculture and Industry AP15

1965, Oct. 18 Engraved ***Perf. 13***

C34	AP15	50fr dk bl, blk, brn & org	75	50

International Cooperation Year, 1965.

Abraham Lincoln—AP16

1965, Dec. 15 Photo. ***Perf. 13***

C35	AP16	90fr pink & multi	1.10	65

Centenary of death of Abraham Lincoln.

Charles de Gaulle, Torch and Map of Africa—AP17

1966, Feb. 28 Engraved ***Perf. 13***

C36	AP17	500fr dk red, dk grn & dk red brn	15.00	12.50

Issued to commemorate the 22nd anniversary of the Brazzaville Conference.

D-1 Satellite over Brazzaville Space Tracking Station AP18 — Grain, Atom Symbol and Map of Africa and Europe AP19

1966, May 15 Engraved ***Perf. 13***

C37	AP18	150fr blk, dl red & bl grn	1.85	95

1966, July 20 Photo. ***Perf. 12x13***

C38	AP19	50fr multi	80	50

See note after Gabon No. C46.

Pres. Massamba-Debat and President's Palace AP20

Designs: 30fr, Robespierre and storming of the Bastille. 50fr, Lenin and storming of the Winter Palace.

1966, Aug. 15 Photo. ***Perf. 12x12½***

C39	AP20	25fr multi	28	15
C40	AP20	30fr multi	35	15
C41	AP20	50fr multi	60	28
a.		Souv. sheet of 3	1.50	1.50

Issued to commemorate the 3rd anniversary of the revolution. No. C41a contains one each of Nos. C39–C41. Black marginal inscription and control number. Size: 131½x160mm.

Air Afrique Issue, 1966

Common Design Type

1966, Aug. 31 Photo. ***Perf. 13***

C42	CD123	30fr lil, lem & blk	45	20

Issued to commemorate the introduction of DC-8F planes by Air Afrique.

Dr. Albert Schweitzer AP21

1966, Sept. 4 Photo. ***Perf. 12½***

C43	AP21	100fr red, blk, bl & lil	1.25	80

Issued to honor Dr. Albert Schweitzer (1875–1965), medical missionary.

Crab, Microscope and Pagoda AP22

1966, Dec. 26 Photo. ***Perf. 13***

C44	AP22	100fr multi	1.20	65

Issued to commemorate the 9th International Anticancer Congress, Tokyo, Oct. 23–29.

Social Weaver AP23

Birds: 75fr, European Bee-eater. 100fr, Lilac-breasted roller. 150fr, Regal sunbird. 200fr, Crowned cranes. 250fr, Secretary bird. 300fr, Knysna touraco.

1967 Photogravure ***Perf. 13***

C45	AP23	50fr multi	1.00	40
C46	AP23	75fr multi	1.35	55
C47	AP23	100fr multi	1.65	80
C48	AP23	150fr multi	2.00	1.10
C49	AP23	200fr multi	2.65	1.35
C50	AP23	250fr multi	3.50	1.75
C51	AP23	300fr multi	4.00	2.25
		Nos. C45-C51 (7)	16.15	8.20

Issue dates: Nos. C45–C47, Feb. 13. Others, June 20.

Shackled Hands AP24

1967, May 24 Photo. ***Perf. 12½x13***

C52	AP24	500fr multi	7.00	3.00

Issued for African Liberation Day.

Sputnik 1, Explorer 6 and Earth AP25

Space Craft: 75fr, Ranger 6, Lunik 2 and moon. 100fr, Mars 1, Mariner 4 and Mars. 200fr, Gemini, Vostok and earth.

1967, Aug. 1 Engr. ***Perf. 13***

C53	AP25	50fr pur, bl & org brn	60	32
C54	AP25	75fr dk car & gray	90	50
C55	AP25	100fr red brn, Prus bl & ultra	1.25	80
C56	AP25	200fr car lake, org & bl	2.50	1.60

Space explorations.

African Postal Union Issue, 1967

Common Design Type

1967, Sept. 9 Engraved ***Perf. 13***

C57	CD124	100fr ver, ol & emer	1.20	70

Boy Scouts, Tents and Jamboree Emblem—AP26

Design: 70c, Borah Peak, Idaho; tents, Scout sign and Jamboree emblem.

1967, Sept. 29

C58	AP26	50fr brt bl, brn org & red brn	55	28
C59	AP26	70fr dl bl, sl grn & red brn	80	40

Issued to commemorate the 12th Boy Scout World Jamboree, Farragut State Park, Idaho, Aug. 1–9.

Sikorsky S-43 and Map of Africa AP27

1967, Oct. 2 Photo. ***Perf. 13***

C60	AP27	30fr multi	45	25

Issued to commemorate the 30th anniversary of the first airmail connection by Aeromaritime Lines from Casablanca to Pointe-Noire.

Men of Four Races Dancing on Globe AP28

1968, Feb 8 Engraved *Perf. 13*

C61 AP28 70fr dk brn, ultra & emer 90 50

Friendship among peoples.

The Oath of the Horatii, by Jacques Louis David—AP29

Paintings: 25fr, On the Barricades, by Delacroix. No. C63, Grandfather and Grandson, by Ghirlandajo (vert.). No. C64, The Demolition of the Bastille, by Hubert Robert. 200fr, Negro Woman Arranging Peonies, by Jean F. Bazille.

Perf. 12x12½, 12½x12

1968 Photogravure

C62 AP29 25fr multi 32 12
C63 AP29 30fr multi 50 32
C64 AP29 30fr multi 35 20
C65 AP29 100fr multi 1.35 80
C66 AP29 200fr multi 3.00 1.75
Nos. C62-C66 (5) 5.52 3.19

Issue dates: Nos. C62, C64, Aug. 15. Nos. C63, C65–C66, Mar. 20.
See also Nos. C78–C81, C111–C115.

Early Automobile Type of Regular Issue

Designs: 150fr, Ford, 1915. 200fr, Citroën, 1922.

1968, July 29 Photo. *Perf. 13x12½*

C67 A50 150fr multi 2.00 1.00
C68 A50 200fr lil & multi 2.50 1.35

Europafrica Issue

Square Knot
AP30

1968, July 20 Photo. *Perf. 13*

C69 AP30 50fr multi 55 25

Issued to commemorate the 5th anniversary of the economic agreement between the European Economic Community and the African and Malgache Union.

Martin Luther King, Jr.
AP31

Robert F. Kennedy
AP32

1968, Aug. 5 *Perf. 12½*

C70 AP31 50fr lt grn, Prus grn & blk 55 25

Issued in memory of the Rev. Dr. Martin Luther King, Jr. (1929–1968), American civil rights leader.

1968, Sept. 30 Photo. *Perf. 13x12½*

C71 AP32 50fr dp car, ap grn & blk 65 32

Issued in memory of Robert F. Kennedy (1925–68), U.S. Senator and Attorney General.

Running
AP33

Olympic Rings and: 20fr, Soccer (vert.). 60fr, Boxing (vert.). 85fr, High jump.

1968, Dec. 27 Engraved *Perf. 13*

C72 AP33 5fr emer, brt bl & choc 7 5
C73 AP33 20fr dk bl, brn & dk grn 25 12
C74 AP33 60fr mar, brt grn & choc 75 40
C75 AP33 85fr blk, car rose & choc 1.00 50

Issued to commemorate the 19th Olympic Games, Mexico City, Oct. 12–27.

PHILEXAFRIQUE Issue

G. De Gueidan, by Nicolas de Largillière
AP34

1968, Dec. 30 Photo. *Perf. 12½*

C76 AP34 100fr pink & multi 1.30 1.10

Issued to publicize PHILEXAFRIQUE, Philatelic Exhibition, in Abidjan, Feb. 14–23. Printed with alternating pink label.
See also Nos. C89–C93.

2nd PHILEXAFRIQUE Issue

Common Design Type

Design: 50fr, Middle Congo No. 72 and Pointe-Noire harbor.

1969, Feb. 14 Engraved *Perf. 13*

C77 CD128 50fr car rose, sl grn & bis brn 75 65

Issued to commemorate the opening of PHILEXAFRIQUE, Abidjan, Feb. 14.

Painting Type of 1968.

Paintings: 25fr, Battle of Rivoli, by Carle Vernet. 50fr, Battle of Marengo, by Jacques Augustin Pajou. 75fr, Battle of Friedland, by Horace Vernet. 100fr, Battle of Jena, by Charles Thevenin.

1969, May 20 Photo. *Perf. 12x12½*

C78 AP29 25fr vio bl & multi 40 25
C79 AP29 50fr cop red & multi 75 50
C80 AP29 75fr grn & multi 1.10 50
C81 AP29 100fr brn & multi 1.60 80

Bicentenary of birth of Napoleon I.

Ernesto Ché Guevara
AP35

1969, June 10 Photo. *Perf. 12½*

C82 AP35 90fr brn, org & blk 1.10 55

Issued in memory of Ernesto Ché Guevara (1928–1967), Cuban revolutionist.

Doll, Train and Space Toy
AP36

1969, June 20 Engraved *Perf. 13*

C83 AP36 100fr mag, org & gray 1.20 65

Issued to publicize the International Toy Fair, Nuremberg, Germany.

Europafrica Issue, 1969

Ribbon Tied Around Bar
AP37

1969, Aug. 5 Photo. *Perf. 13x12*

C84 AP37 50fr bl grn, lil & blk 50 30

See note after Chad No. C11.

Armstrong, Aldrin and Collins
AP38

Painter, Poto-Poto School
AP39

Souvenir Sheet

Design: No. C85b, Blast-off from Moon.

Embossed on Gold Foil

1969, Sept. 15 *Imperf.*

C85 AP38 Sheet of 2 20.00 20.00
a. 1000fr gold 9.00 9.00
b. 1000fr gold 9.00 9.00

See note after Algeria No. 427. No. C85 contains one each of Nos. C85a and C85b with simulated perforations. Size: 65x52mm.

1970, Feb. 20 Engraved *Perf. 13*

Designs: 150fr, Sculpture lesson (man, infant and sculpture). 200fr, Potter working on vase.

C86 AP39 100fr multi 1.10 50
C87 AP39 150fr multi 1.60 80
C88 AP39 200fr multi 1.85 1.25

Painting Type (Philexafrique) of 1968

Paintings: 150fr, Child with Cherries, by John Russell. 200fr, Erasmus, by Hans Holbein the Younger. 250fr, "Silence" (head), by Bernardino Luini. 300fr, Scene from the Massacre of Scio, by Delacroix. 500fr, The Capture of Constantinople by the Crusaders, by Delacroix.

1970 Photogravure *Perf. 12½*

C89 AP34 150fr lil & multi 2.00 95
C90 AP34 200fr multi 2.40 1.20
C91 AP34 250fr brn & multi 2.65 1.50
C92 AP34 300fr multi 3.75 1.75
C93 AP34 500fr brn & multi 5.25 2.65
Nos. C89-C93 (5) 16.05 8.05

Aurichalcite
AP40

Design: 15fr, Dioptase.

1970, Mar. 20

C94 AP40 100fr multi 1.10 55
C95 AP40 150fr multi 1.75 80

Lenin
AP41

Karl Marx
AP42

Design: 75fr, Lenin, seated.

1970, June 25 Photo. *Perf. 12½*

C96 AP41 45fr grn, org & brn 50 20
C97 AP41 75fr vio bl, brn lake & dp cl 75 35

Issued to commemorate the centenary of the birth of Lenin (1870–1924), Russian communist leader.

1970, July 10 Engr. *Perf. 13*

Design: No. C99, Friedrich Engels.

C98 AP42 50fr emer, dk brn & dk red 55 28
C99 AP42 50fr ultra, dk brn & dk red 55 28

Issued in memory of Karl Marx (1818–1883) and Friedrich Engels (1820–1895), German socialist writers.

Otto Lilienthal's Glider, 1891
AP43

Designs: 50fr, "Spirit of St. Louis," Lindbergh's first transatlantic solo flight, 1927. 70fr, Sputnik 1, first satellite in space. 90fr, First man on the moon, Apollo 11, 1969.

1970, Sept. 5 Engraved *Perf. 13*

C100	AP43	45fr dp car, bl & ol bis	55	28
C101	AP43	50fr emer, sl grn & brn	55	32
C102	AP43	70fr brt bl, ol bis & dp car	80	40
C103	AP43	90fr brn, bl & ol gray	1.10	55

Forerunners of space exploration.

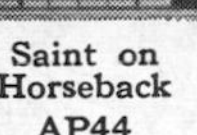

Saint on Horseback
AP44

Marilyn Monroe and New York
AP45

Designs from Stained Glass Windows, Brazzaville Cathedral: 150fr, Saint with staff. 250fr, The Elevation of the Host, from rose window.

1970, Dec. 10 Photo. *Perf. 12½*

C104	AP44	100fr dk vio bl & multi	1.10	55
C105	AP44	150fr dk vio bl & multi	1.75	90
C106	AP44	250fr dk vio bl & multi	3.00	1.60
a.		Souvenir sheet of 3	6.00	6.00

Christmas 1970. No. C106a contains one each of Nos. C104–C106. Black marginal inscription. Size: 150x115mm.

1971, Mar. 16 Engraved *Perf. 13*

Portraits: 150fr, Martine Carol and Paris. 200fr, Erich von Stroheim and Vienna. 250fr, Sergei Eisenstein and Moscow.

C107	AP45	100fr brt grn, red brn & ultra	1.00	40
C108	AP45	150fr brn, brt lil & ultra	1.60	60
C109	AP45	200fr choc & ultra	2.00	90
C110	AP45	250fr brt grn, brn vio & ultra	2.40	1.00

History of motion pictures.

Painting Type of 1968

Paintings: 100fr, Christ Carrying Cross, by Paolo Veronese. 150fr, Christ on the Cross, Burgundian School, 1500 (vert.). 200fr, Descent from the Cross, by Rogier van der Weyden. 250fr, Christ Laid in the Tomb, Flemish School, 1500 (vert.). 500fr, Resurrection, by Hans Memling (vert.).

1971, April 26 Photogravure *Perf. 13*

C111	AP29	100fr grn & multi	1.00	50
C112	AP29	150fr grn & multi	1.40	65
C113	AP29	200fr grn & multi	2.00	1.00
C114	AP29	250fr grn & multi	2.40	1.20
C115	AP29	500fr grn & multi	4.75	2.40
		Nos. C111-C115 (5)	11.55	5.75

Easter 1971.

Examination

The Catalogue editors cannot undertake to appraise, identify or pass upon genuineness or condition of stamps.

Map of Africa and Telecommunications System—AP46

1971, June 18 Photo. *Perf. 12½*

C116	AP46	70fr bl, gray & dk brn	65	32
C117	AP46	85fr bl, lil rose & dk brn	75	40
C118	AP46	90fr grn, yel & dk brn	80	45

Pan-African telecommunications system.

Globe and Waves—AP47

1971, June 19

C119	AP47	65fr lt bl & multi	60	27

3rd World Telecommunications Day.

Japanese Mask and Play
AP48

Olympic Torch and Rings
AP49

Design: 150fr, Japanese and African women, symbolic leaves.

1971, June 28 Engr. *Perf. 13*

C120	AP48	75fr lil, blk & mag	80	40
C121	AP48	150fr dk brn, brn red & red lil	1.50	80

PHILATOKYO '71 International Stamp Exhibition, Tokyo, Apr. 20–30.

1971, July 20 Engraved *Perf. 13*

Design: 350fr, Olympic rings and various sports (horiz.).

C122	AP49	150fr brt rose lil, org & sl grn	1.60	90
C123	AP49	350fr bis, brt grn & vio	3.75	1.75

Pre-Olympic Year, 1971.

Scout Emblem, Japanese Dragon and African Carved Canoe—AP50

Designs (Boy Scout Emblem and): 90fr, Japanese mask and African boy (vert.). 100fr, Japanese woman and African drummer (vert.). 250fr, Congolese mask.

1971, Aug. 25

C124	AP50	85fr brt rose lil, Prus bl & brn	1.00	45
C125	AP50	90fr dk car, brn & vio	1.10	50
C126	AP50	100fr ol gray, rose mag & brt grn	1.25	60
C127	AP50	250fr brt grn, choc & car	3.00	1.40

13th Boy Scout World Jamboree, Asagiri Plain, Japan, Aug. 2–10.

Olympic Rings and Running—AP51

Designs (Olympic Rings and): 85fr, Hurdles. 90fr, Weight lifting, boxing, discus, running, javelin. 100fr, Wrestling. 150fr, Boxing.

1971, Sept. 30

C128	AP51	75fr plum, bl & dk brn	70	32
C129	AP51	85fr scar, sl & dk brn	75	35
C130	AP51	90fr vio bl & dk brn	85	45
C131	AP51	100fr brn & sl	1.00	50
C132	AP51	150fr grn, red & dk brn	1.60	80
		Nos. C128-C132 (5)	4.90	2.42

75th anniversary of the first modern Olympic Games.

Congo No. C36 and de Gaulle
AP52

Pres. Marien Ngouabi's Tribute to de Gaulle—AP53

Design: No. C135, Charles de Gaulle.

1971, Nov. 9

C133	AP52	500fr sl grn & multi	6.50	6.50

Lithographed; Gold Embossed
Perf. 12½

C134	AP53	1000fr gold, grn & red	12.00	12.00
C135	AP53	1000fr gold, grn & red	12.00	12.00

Charles de Gaulle (1890–1970), president of France. Nos. C134–C135 printed se-tenant.

African Postal Union Issue, 1971

Common Design Type

Design: 100fr, Allegory of Congo Republic (woman) and UAMPT Building, Brazzaville.

1971, Nov. 13 Photo. *Perf. 13x13½*

C136	CD135	100fr bl & multi	1.10	55

Flag of Congo Republic and "Revolution"—AP54

1971, Nov. 30

C137	AP54	100fr red & multi	1.00	50

8th anniversary of revolution.

Workers and Flag—AP55

Design: 40fr, Flag of Congo Republic and sun.

1971, Dec 31 Photo. *Perf. 13x12½*

C138	AP55	30fr multi	25	12
C139	AP55	40fr red & multi	35	20

2nd anniversary of founding of Congolese Labor Party (No. C138), and adoption of red flag (No. C139).

Book Year Emblem
AP56

1972, June 3 Litho. *Perf. 12½*

C140	AP56	50fr red, grn & yel	40	20

International Book Year 1972.

Congolese Soccer Team—AP57

Design: No. C142, Captain of winning team and cup (vert.).

1973, Feb. 22 Photogravure *Perf. 13*

C141	AP57	100fr ultra, red & blk	1.10	65
C142	AP57	100fr red, yel & blk	1.10	65

Girl Holding Bird, Environment Emblem
AP58

1973, Mar. 5 **Engraved**

C143 AP58 85fr org, sl grn & bl 65 40

U.N. Conference on Human Environment, Stockholm, Sweden, June 5–16, 1972.

Miles Davis
AP59

Designs: 140fr, Ella Fitzgerald. 160fr, Count Basie. 175fr, John Coltrane.

1973, Mar. 5 **Photo.** ***Perf. 13x13½***

C144 AP59 125fr multi 1.00 50
C145 AP59 140fr multi 1.10 55
C146 AP59 160fr multi 1.30 65
C147 AP59 175fr multi 1.50 75

Black American jazz musicians.

Olympic Rings, Hurdling—AP60

Designs (Olympic Rings and): 150fr, Pole vault (vert.). 250fr, Wrestling.

1973, Mar. 15 **Engraved** ***Perf. 13***

C148 AP60 100fr lil rose & vio 1.00 50
C149 AP60 150fr emer & vio 1.50 75
C150 AP60 250fr bl & mag 2.50 1.35

20th Olympic Games, Munich, Aug. 26–Sept. 11, 1972.

Refinery and Storage Tanks, Djéno—AP61

Designs: 230fr, Off-shore drilling platform (vert.). 240fr, Workers assembling drill (vert.). 260fr, Off-shore drilling installation.

1973, Mar. 20

C151 AP61 180fr red, bl & ind 1.60 80
C152 AP61 230fr red, bl & blk 2.00 1.00
C153 AP61 240fr red, ind & brn 2.25 1.20
C154 AP61 260fr red, bl & blk 2.60 1.40

Oil installations, Pointe-Noire.

Astronauts, Landing Module and Lunar Rover on Moon—AP62

1973, Mar. 31

C155 AP62 250fr multi 2.50 1.50

Apollo 17 U.S. moon mission, Dec. 7–19, 1972.

ITU Emblem, Symbols of Communications
AP63

1973, May 24 **Engr.** ***Perf. 13***

C156 AP63 120fr multi 80 40

5th International Telecommunications Day.

White Horse, by Delacroix—AP64

Designs: Paintings by Eugene Delacroix.

1973, June 30 **Photo.** ***Perf. 13***

Multicolored

C157 AP64 150fr *shown* 1.35 1.35
C158 AP64 250fr *Lion sleeping* 2.25 1.90
C159 AP64 300fr *Lion and tiger* 2.75 2.25

See Nos. C169–C171.

Copernicus and Heliocentric System—AP65

1973, June 30 **Engraved**

C160 AP65 50fr multi 45 35

500th anniversary of the birth of Nicolaus Copernicus (1473–1543), Polish astronomer.

Plane, Ship, Rocket, Village, Sun and Clouds—AP66

1973, July

C161 AP66 50fr red & multi 40 28

Centenary of international meteorological cooperation.

Pres. Marien N'Gouabi
AP67

1973, Aug. 12 **Photo.** ***Perf. 13***

C162 AP67 30fr multi 25 10
C163 AP67 40fr aqua & multi 32 15
C164 AP67 75fr red & multi 65 32

10th anniversary of independence.

Stamps, Album, African Woman
AP68

Designs: 40fr, No. C167, Stamps in shape of map of Congo, album, globe. No. C168, Like 30fr.

1973, Aug. 12

C165 AP68 30fr pur & multi 25 12
C166 AP68 40fr multi 32 15
C167 AP68 100fr dk brn & multi 75 55
C168 AP68 100fr ocher & multi 75 55

Nos. C165 and C168 commemorate the 10th anniversary of the revolution, Nos. C166–C167 the International Philatelic Exhibition, Brazzaville.

Painting Type of 1973 Inscribed "EUROPAFRIQUE"

Designs: Details from "Earth and Paradise," by Jan Brueghel, the Elder.

1973, Oct. 10 **Photo.** ***Perf. 13***

Multicolored

C169 AP64 100fr *Spotted hyena* 1.00 75
C170 AP64 100fr *Leopard and lion* 1.00 75
C171 AP64 100fr *Elephant and creatures* 1.00 75

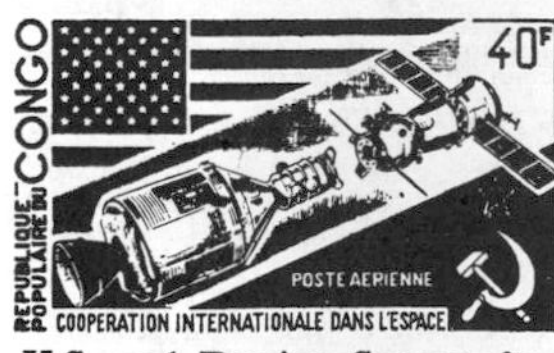

U.S. and Russian Spacecraft Docking—AP69

Design: 80fr, US and USSR spacecraft docked in space and emblems of 1975 joint space mission.

1973, Oct. 15 **Engraved** ***Perf. 13***

C172 AP69 40fr bl, red & brn 35 20
C173 AP69 80fr red, grn & bl 65 40

Planned joint United States and Soviet space missions.

UPU Monument, Satellites, Big Dipper—AP70

1973, Nov. 20 **Engraved** ***Perf. 13***

C174 AP70 80fr vio bl & lt bl 65 35

Universal Postal Union Day.

Astronauts Working in Space—AP71

Design: 40fr, Spacecraft and Skylab docking in space.

1973, Nov. 30

C175 AP71 30fr ultra, sl grn & choc 25 15
C176 AP71 40fr mag, org & sl grn 35 25

Skylab, first space laboratory.

Goalkeeper, Soccer
AP72

Design: 100fr, Soccer player kicking ball.

1973, Dec. 20

C177 AP72 40fr sl grn, sep & brn 32 25
C178 AP72 100fr pur, red & sl grn 1.00 55

World Soccer Cup, Munich, 1974.

John F. Kennedy
AP73

1973, Dec. 20 **Photo.** ***Perf. 12½***

C179 AP73 150fr ultra, gold & blk 1.20 75

10th anniversary of the death of Pres. John F. Kennedy (1917–1963).

Runners
AP74

Flag over Map of Congo
AP75

1973, Dec. 20 **Engraved** ***Perf. 13***

C180 AP74 40fr sl grn, red & brn 32 25
C181 AP74 100fr red, sl grn, & brn 1.00 55

2nd African Games, Lagos, Nigeria.

1973, Dec. 31 **Photogravure**

C182	AP75	40fr dp grn & multi	32	20

4th anniversary of Congolese Labor Party and of the Congo Red Flag.

Soccer and Games Emblem AP76

1974, June 20 Photo. ***Perf. 13***

C183	AP76	250fr multi	2.00	1.30

World Cup Soccer Championship, Munich, June 13–July 7.

Astronauts Yuri A. Gagarin and Alan B. Shepard—AP77

Designs: 30fr, Space, globe, Russian and American flags with names of astronauts who perished in space. 100fr, Alexei Leonov and Neil A. Armstrong in space and on moon.

1974, June 30 Engraved ***Perf. 13***

C184	AP77	30fr red, ultra & brn	25	15
C185	AP77	40fr red, bl & brn	35	20
C186	AP77	100fr car, grn & brn	1.00	60

Soccer Game Superimposed on Ball AP78

Link-up Emblem, Stages of Link-up AP79

1974, July 31 Photo. ***Perf. 13***

C187	AP78	250fr multi	2.00	1.30

Germany's victory in World Cup Soccer Championship.

1974, Aug. 8 Engraved ***Perf. 13***

Design: 300fr, Spacecraft docking over globe (horiz.).

C188	AP79	200fr pur, bl & red	1.60	1.20
C189	AP79	300fr multi	2.40	1.60

Russo-American space cooperation.

Symbols of Communications, UPU Emblem—AP80

1974, Aug. 10

C190	AP80	500fr blk & red	4.00	2.75

Centenary of Universal Postal Union.

Lenin and Pendulum Trace Pattern—AP81

1974, Sept. 16 **Engraved** ***Perf. 13***

C191	AP81	150fr multi	1.20	80

50th death anniversary of Lenin (1870–1924).

Churchill and Order of the Garter AP82

Marconi and Wireless Telegraph AP83

1974, Oct. 1 Litho. ***Perf. 13***

C192	AP82	200fr lt grn & multi	1.60	1.00
C193	AP83	200fr lt ultra & multi	1.60	1.00

Birth centenaries of Sir Winston Churchill (1874–1965), statesman; and of Guglielmo Marconi (1874–1937), Italian electrical engineer and inventor.

No. C190 Surcharged in Violet Blue with New Value, 2 Bars and: "9 OCTOBRE 1974"

1974, Oct. 9

C194	AP80	300fr on 500fr multi	2.40	1.60

Universal Postal Union Day.

UDEAC Issue

Presidents and Flags of Cameroun, CAR, Gabon and Congo—AP83a

1974, Dec. 8 Photogravure ***Perf. 13***

C195	AP83a	100fr gold & multi	80	60

See note after Cameroun No. 595.

Regatta at Argenteuil, by Monet—AP84

Impressionist Paintings: 40fr, Seated Dancer, by Degas. 50fr, Girl on Swing, by Renoir. 75fr, Girl with Straw Hat, by Renoir. All vertical.

1974, Dec. 15

C196	AP84	30fr gold & multi	35	25
C197	AP84	40fr gold & multi	40	30
C198	AP84	50fr gold & multi	65	50
C199	AP84	75fr gold & multi	70	55

National Fair AP85

1974, Dec. 20

C200	AP85	30fr multi	25	15

National Fair, Aug. 24–Sept. 8.

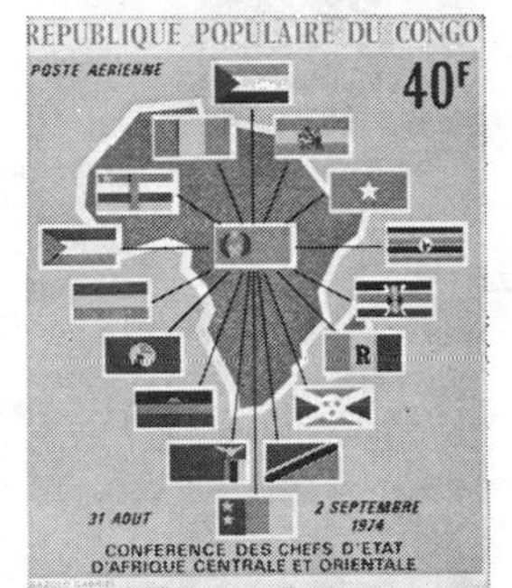

Flags of Participating Nations, Map of Africa—AP86

1974, Dec. 20 ***Perf. 13***

C201	AP86	40fr ultra & multi	40	25

Conference of Chiefs of State of Central and East Africa, Brazzaville, Aug. 31–Sept. 2.

"Five Weeks in a Balloon," by Jules Verne AP87

Design: 50fr, "Around the World in 80 Days," by Jules Verne.

1975, June 30 Litho. ***Perf. 12½***

C202	AP87	40fr multi	35	20
C203	AP87	50fr multi	40	25

Jules Verne (1828–1905), French science fiction writer, 70th death anniversary.

Paris-Brussels Train, 1890—AP88

Design: 75fr, Santa Fe, 1880.

1975, June 30

C204	AP88	50fr ocher & multi	40	25
C205	AP88	75fr lt bl & multi	60	35

Soyuz and Apollo-Soyuz Emblem AP89

Design: 100fr, Apollo and emblem.

1975, July 20 Litho. ***Perf. 12½***

C206	AP89	95fr org, blk & mag	75	50
C207	AP89	100fr vio, bl & blk	80	60

Apollo Soyuz space test project (Russo-American space cooperation), launching July 15; link-up, July 17.

Bicycling and Montreal Olympic Emblem—AP90

Designs (Montreal Olympic Emblem and): 40fr, Boxing (vert.). 50fr, Basketball (vert.). 95fr, High jump. 100fr, Javelin. 150fr, Running.

Perf. 12½x13, 13x12½

1975, Oct. 30 **Photogravure**

C208	AP90	40fr multi	35	20
C209	AP90	50fr red & multi	40	25
C210	AP90	85fr bl & multi	70	50
C211	AP90	95fr org & multi	75	55
C212	AP90	100fr multi	80	60
C213	AP90	150fr multi	1.20	90
		Nos. C208-C213 (6)	4.20	3.00

Pre-Olympic Year 1975.

Map of Africa, Sports and Flags AP91

Workers and Flag AP92

1975, Dec. 20 Litho. ***Perf. 12½***

C214	AP91	30fr multi	25	15

10th anniversary of first African Games, Brazzaville.

1975, Dec. 31 Litho. ***Perf. 12½***

C215	AP92	60fr multi	50	30

6th anniversary of the Congolese Labor Party (P.C.T.).

Alphonse Fondere—AP93

Historic Ships: 5fr, like 30fr. 40fr, Hamburg, 1839. 15fr, 50fr, Gomer, 1831. 20fr, 60fr, Great Eastern, 1858. 95fr, J.M. White II, 1878.

1976 Engraved Perf. 13

C216	AP93	5fr multi	5	5
C217	AP93	10fr multi	8	6
C218	AP93	15fr multi	12	8
C219	AP93	20fr multi	17	12
C220	AP93	30fr multi	25	15
C221	AP93	40fr multi	30	25
C222	AP93	50fr multi	40	30
C223	AP93	60fr multi	50	35
C224	AP93	95fr multi	75	55
		Nos. C216-C224 (9)	2.62	1.91

Issue dates: Nos. C216–C219, May. Nos. C220–C224, Mar. 7.

Europafrica Issue 1976

Peasant Family, by Louis Le Nain AP94

Paintings: 80fr, Boy with Top, by Jean B. Chardin. 95fr, Venus and Aeneas, by Nicolas Poussin. 100fr, The Rape of the Sabine Women, by Jacques Louis David.

1976, Mar. 20 Litho. Perf. 12½

C225	AP94	60fr gold & multi	50	30
C226	AP94	80fr gold & multi	65	45
C227	AP94	95fr gold & multi	75	55
C228	AP94	100fr gold & multi	80	60

Nos. C225–C228 printed in sheets of 8 stamps and horizontal gutter with commemorative inscription. Black control number in margin.

Telephone Type of 1976

1976, Apr. 25 Litho. Perf. 12½x13

C229	A107	60fr pink, mar & crim	50	35

Centenary of first telephone call by Alexander Graham Bell, Mar. 10, 1876.

Sports Type of 1976

Designs: 150fr, Runner and map of Central Africa. 200fr, Discus and map.

1976, Oct. 25 Perf. 12½

C230	A110	150fr multi	1.20	90
C231	A110	200fr multi	1.60	1.10

Gold medalists, 1st Central African Games, Yaoundé, July 27–30, 1975.

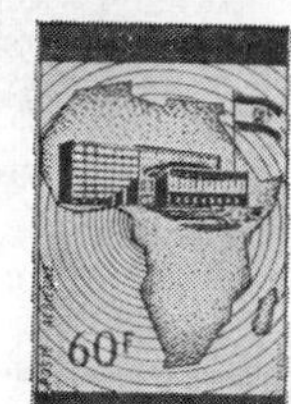

Map of Africa, Flag and OAU Headquarters AP95

1976, Dec. 16 Typo. Perf. 13x14

C232	AP95	60fr multi	50	35

13th anniversary of the Organization for African Unity.

Europafrica Issue

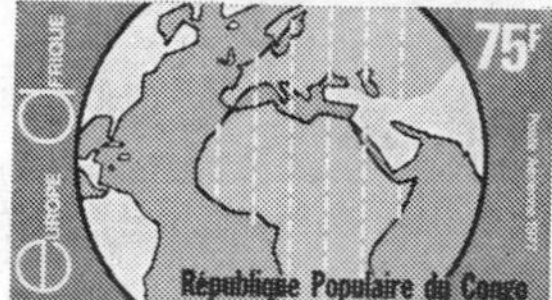

Map of Europe and Africa—AP96

1977, June 28 Litho. Perf. 13

C233	AP96	75fr multi	60	50

Headdress Type of 1977

1977, June 30 Perf. 12½

Designs: 250fr, Two straw caps. 300fr, Beaded cap.

C234	A118	250fr multi	2.00	1.50
C235	A118	300fr multi	2.40	1.80

Zeppelin Type of 1977
Souvenir Sheet

Design: 500fr, LZ 127 over U.S. Capitol.

1977, Aug. 5 Litho. Perf. 11

C236	A120	500fr multi	4.75	2.00

History of the Zeppelin.

No. C236 has multicolored margin showing parts of two Zeppelins. Size: 105x92mm. Exists imperf.

Checkerboard AP97

1977, Aug. 20 Engr. Perf. 13

C237	AP97	60fr red & blk	50	35

Lomé Convention on General Agreement on Tariffs and Trade (GATT).

Newton, Intelsat Satellite and Classical "Planets"—AP98

1977, Aug. 25

C238	AP98	140fr multi	1.10	90

Isaac Newton (1642–1727), natural philosopher and mathematician, 250th death anniversary.

Elizabeth II Type of 1977
Souvenir Sheet

Design: 500fr, Royal family on balcony.

1977, Dec. 21 Litho. Perf. 14

C239	A128	500fr multi	4.75	2.00

25th anniversary of the reign of Queen Elizabeth II.

Mallard AP99

Birds: 75fr, Purple heron (vert.). 150fr, Reed warbler (vert.). 240fr, Hoopoe (vert.).

Perf. 13x12½, 12½x13

1978, May 22

C240	AP99	65fr multi	50	25
C241	AP99	75fr multi	60	30
C242	AP99	150fr multi	1.20	65
C243	AP99	240fr multi	1.90	1.00

Souvenir Sheet

No. C239 Overprinted in Silver: "ANNIVERSAIRE DU / COURONNEMENT / 1953–1978"

1978, Sept. Litho. Perf. 14

C244	A128	500fr multi	4.00	1.85

25th anniversary of coronation of Queen Elizabeth II. Size: 111x92mm.

Philexafrique II—Essen Issue
Common Design Types

Designs: No. C245, Leopard and Congo No. C243. No. C246, Eagle and Wurttemberg No. 1.

1978, Nov. 1 Litho. Perf. 12½

C245	CD138	100fr multi	1.00	60
C246	CD139	100fr multi	1.00	60

Nos. C245–C246 printed se-tenant.

Map of Africa Satellites AP100

1978, Nov. 25 Engr. Perf. 13

C247	AP100	100fr multi	1.00	60

Pan-African Telecommunications Network, PANAFEL.

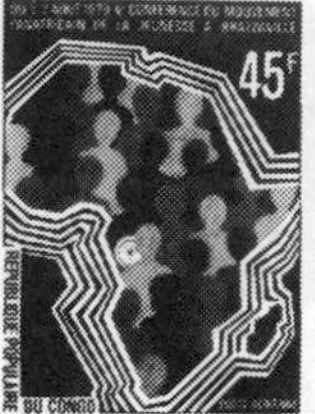

Map of Africa and People AP101

1979, Aug. 2 Litho. Perf. 12½

C248	AP101	45fr multi	45	30
C249	AP101	75fr multi	75	50

5th Conference of Panafrican Youth Movement, Brazzaville, Aug. 2–7.

Abala Peasant Woman AP102

1979, Aug. 20

C250	AP102	150fr multi	1.50	90

Nos. C173, C206-C207, C186, C189 Overprinted "ALUNISSAGE APOLLO XI / JUILLET 1969" and Emblem

Perf. 13, 12½

1979, Nov. 5 Engr., Litho.

C251	AP69	80fr multi	80	52
C252	AP89	95fr multi	95	62
C253	AP89	100fr multi	1.00	65
C254	AP77	100fr multi	1.00	65
C255	AP79	300fr multi	3.00	2.00
		Nos. C251-C255 (5)	6.75	4.44

Apollo 11 moon landing, 10th anniversary.

Runner, Olympic Rings—AP103

Pre-Olympic Year: 100fr, Boxing. 200fr, Fencing (vert.). 300fr, Soccer. 500fr, Moscow '80 emblem (vert.).

1979 Litho. Perf. 13½

C256	AP103	65fr multi	52	26
C257	AP103	100fr multi	80	40
C258	AP103	200fr multi	1.60	80
C259	AP103	300fr multi	2.40	1.20
C260	AP103	500fr multi	4.00	2.00
		Nos. C256-C260 (5)	9.32	4.66

Cross-Country Skiing—AP104

Lake Placid '80 Emblem and: 60fr, Slalom. 200fr, Ski jump, 350fr, Downhill skiing (horiz.). 500fr, Woman skier.

1979, Dec Perf. 14½
Size: 24×42, 42×24mm.

C261	AP104	40fr multi	40	28
C262	AP104	60fr multi	60	42
C263	AP104	200fr multi	2.00	1.40
C264	AP104	350fr multi	3.50	2.50

Size: 31½×46½mm. Perf. 14

C265	AP104	500fr multi	5.00	3.50
		Nos. C261-C265 (5)	11.50	8.10

13th Winter Olympic Games, Lake Placid, N.Y., Feb. 12-24, 1980.

Overprinted with names of winners

1980, Apr. 28

C266	AP104	40fr multi (a)	32	16
C267	AP104	60fr multi (b)	48	24
C268	AP104	200fr multi (c)	1.60	80
C269	AP104	350fr multi (d)	2.80	1.40
C270	AP104	500fr multi (e)	4.00	2.00
		Nos. C266-C270 (5)	9.20	4.60

Long Jump, Olympic Rings—AP105

Olympic rings and long jump scenes. Nos. C266, C268-C269 vert.

1980, May 2 Litho. Perf. 14½

C271	AP105	75fr multi	60	30
C272	AP105	150fr multi	1.20	60
C273	AP105	250fr multi	2.00	1.00
C274	AP105	350fr multi	2.80	1.40

Souvenir Sheet

C275	AP105	500fr multi	4.00	2.00

22nd Summer Olympic Games, Moscow, July 19-Aug. 3. No. C275 has multicolored margin showing Kremlin and runners. Size: 104x78mm.

Stadium, Mascot, Madrid Club Emblem—AP106

Stadium, Mascot and Club Emblem: 75fr, Zaragoza. 100fr, Madrid Athletic Club. 150fr, Valencia. 175fr, Spain. 250fr, Barcelona.

1980, June 23 Litho. *Perf. 14x13½*

C276	AP106	60fr multi	48	24
C277	AP106	75fr multi	60	30
C278	AP106	100fr multi	80	40
C279	AP106	150fr multi	1.20	60
C280	AP106	175fr multi	1.40	70
		Nos. C276-C280 (5)	4.48	2.24

Souvenir Sheet

C281	AP106	250fr multi	2.00	1.00

World Soccer Cup 1982. No. C281 has multicolored margin showing mascot. Size: 104½x79mm.

Adoration of the Shepherds—AP107

Rembrandt Paintings: 100fr, The Burial. 200fr, Christ at Emmaus. 300fr, Annunciation (vert.). 500fr, Crucifixion (vert.).

1980, July 4 *Perf. 12½*

C282	AP107	65fr multi	52	26
C283	AP107	100fr multi	80	40
C284	AP107	200fr multi	1.60	80
C285	AP107	300fr multi	2.40	1.20
C286	AP107	500fr multi	4.00	2.00
		Nos. C282-C286 (5)	9.32	4.66

Albert Camus (1913-1960), Writer—AP108

Design: 150fr, Jacques Offenbach (1819-1880), composer (vert.).

1980, July 5 Engraved *Perf. 13*

C287	AP108	100fr multi	80	40
C288	AP108	150fr multi	1.20	60

Raffia Dancing Skirts—AP109

Traditional Dancing Costumes: 300fr, Tam-tam dancers (vert.). 350fr, Masks.

1980, Aug. 6 Litho. *Perf. 13½*

C289	AP109	250fr multi	2.00	1.00
C290	AP109	300fr multi	2.40	1.20
C291	AP109	350fr multi	2.80	1.40

Nos. C271-C275 Overprinted with Winner and Country

1980, Nov. 14 Litho. *Perf. 14½*

C292	AP105	75fr multi	60	30
C293	AP105	150fr multi	1.20	60
C294	AP105	250fr multi	2.00	1.00
C295	AP105	350fr multi	2.80	1.40

Souvenir Sheet

C296	AP105	500fr multi	4.00	2.00

The Studio by Picasso—AP109a

1981, July 4 *Perf. 12½*

C296A	AP109a	100fr shown	80	40
C296B	AP109a	150fr Landscape	1.20	60
C296C	AP109a	200fr Cannes Studio	1.60	80
C296D	AP109a	300fr Still Life	2.40	1.20
C296E	AP109a	500fr Still Life, diff.	4.00	2.00
		Nos. C296A-C296E (5)	10.00	5.00

1350th Anniv. of Mohamed's Death at Medina—AP110

1982, July 17 Litho. *Perf. 13*

C297	AP110	400fr Medina Mosque minaret	3.25	1.60

Nos. C276-C281 Overprinted with Finalists and/or Scores in Black on Silver.

1982, Oct. 7 Litho. *Perf. 14x13½*

C298	AP106	60fr multi	50	25
C299	AP106	75fr multi	60	30
C300	AP106	100fr multi	80	40
C301	AP106	150fr multi	1.20	60
C302	AP106	175fr multi	1.40	70
		Nos. C298-C302 (5)	4.50	2.25

Souvenir Sheet

C303	AP106	250fr multi	2.00	1.00

30th Anniv. of Amelia Earhart's Transatlantic Flight—AP111

1982, Dec. 4 Engr. *Perf. 13*

C304	AP111	150fr multi	1.20	60

Wind Surfing—AP112

Various wind surfing scenes, 1984 Olympic Games, 100fr, 300fr, 400fr vert.

1983, June 4 Litho. *Perf. 13*

C305	AP112	100fr multi	80	40
C306	AP112	200fr multi	1.60	80
C307	AP112	300fr multi	2.40	1.20
C308	AP112	400fr multi	3.25	1.60

Souvenir Sheet

C309	AP112	500fr multi	4.00	2.00

No. C309 has multicolored margin continuing design. Size: 105x80mm.

Manned Flight Bicentenary—AP113

Various balloons.

1983, June 7

C310	AP113	100fr Montgolfiere, 1783	80	40
C311	AP113	200fr Flesselles, 1784	1.60	80
C312	AP113	300fr Auguste Piccard, 1931	2.40	1.20
C313	AP113	400fr Don Piccard	3.25	1.60

Souvenir Sheet

C314	AP113	500fr Mail transport balloon, 1870	4.00	2.00

No. C314 has multicolored design continuing design and showing balloon cover. Size: 78x100mm.

Christmas 1983—AP114

Various Virgin and Child Paintings by Botticelli.

1984, Jan. 21 Litho. *Perf. 13*

C315	AP114	150fr multi	60	30
C316	AP114	350fr multi	1.40	70
C317	AP114	500fr multi	2.00	1.00

Vase of Flowers, by Manet (1832-83)—AP115

Paintings: 200fr, Small Holy Family, by Raphael. 300fr, La Belle Jardiniere, by Raphael. 400fr, Virgin of Loretto, by Raphael. 500fr, Portrait of Richard Wagner (1813-83), by Giuseppe Tivoli.

1984, Feb. 24 Litho. *Perf. 13*

C318	AP115	100fr multi	40	20
C319	AP115	200fr multi	80	40
C320	AP115	300fr multi	1.20	60
C321	AP115	400fr multi	1.60	80
C322	AP115	500fr multi	2.00	1.00
		Nos. C318-C322 (5)	6.00	3.00

1984 Summer Olympics—AP116

1984, Mar. 31 *Perf. 13*

C323	AP116	45fr Judo, vert.	18	10
C324	AP116	75fr Judo, diff.	30	15
C325	AP116	150fr Wrestling	60	30
C326	AP116	175fr Fencing	70	35
C327	AP116	350fr Fencing, diff.	1.40	70
		Nos. C323-C327 (5)	3.18	1.60

Souvenir Sheet

C328	AP116	500fr Boxing	2.00	1.00

Size of No. C328: 104x80mm.

Virgin and Child, by Giovanni Bellini (c. 1430-1516)—AP118

Religious paintings: 100fr, Holy Family, by Andrea del Sarto (1486-1530), vert. 400fr, Virgin with Angels, by Cimabue (c. 1240-1302), vert.

1985, Feb. 12 Litho. *Perf. 13*

C333	AP118	100fr multi	40	20
C334	AP118	200fr multi	80	40
C335	AP118	400fr multi	1.50	75

Christmas 1984.

Souvenir Sheets

Nos. C309, C314 Ovptd. with Exhibition in Blue or Green.

1985, Mar. 8 *Perf. 13*

C336	AP112	500fr	OLYMPHILEX'85/ LAUSANNE (B)	2.00	1.00
C337	AP113	500fr	MOPHILA '85/ HAMBURG (G)	2.00	1.00

Audubon Birth Bicentenary—AP119

Illustrations of North American bird species by Audubon. Nos. C338-C339 vert.

1985, Apr. 11 *Perf. 13½*

C338	AP119	100fr	Passiformes fringillidae	40	20
C339	AP119	150fr	Eudocimus ruber	60	30
C340	AP119	200fr	Buteo jamaicensis	80	40
C341	AP119	350fr	Camptorhynchus labradorius	1.40	70

PHILEXAFRICA '85, Lome—AP120

Youths in public service activities.

1985, May 20 *Perf. 13*

C342	AP120	200fr	Community health care	80	40
C343	AP120	200fr	Agriculture	80	40

Nos. C342-C343 printed se-tenant with center label picturing map of Africa or UAPT emblem.

Admission to UN, 25th Anniv.—AP121

1985, Aug. 13

C344	AP121	190fr	multi	78	38

UN, 40th Anniv.—AP122

1985, Oct. 25 *Perf. 12½*

C345	AP122	180fr	Rainbow, emblem	75	35

Christmas—AP123

Paintings: 100fr, The Virgin and the Infant Jesus, by David. 200fr, Adoration of the Magi, by Hieronymus Bosch (1450-1516). 400fr, Virgin and Child, by Van Dyck (1599-1641).

1985, Dec. 20 **Litho.** *Perf. 13*

C346	AP123	100fr	multi	55	28
C347	AP123	200fr	multi	1.10	55
C348	AP123	400fr	multi	2.20	1.10

Nos. C346-C347 vert.

Halley's Comet—AP124

1986, Feb. 17

C349	AP124	125fr	Halley, comet	68	35
C350	AP124	150fr	West's Comet, 1976	82	40
C351	AP124	225fr	Ikeya-Seki's Comet, 1965	1.25	62
C352	AP124	300fr	Trajectory diagram	1.65	82
C353	AP124	350fr	Comet, Vega probe	2.00	1.00
			Nos. C349-C353 (5)	6.40	3.19

Nos. C350-C351 vert.

Cosmos-Frantel Hotel—AP125

1986, May 1 *Perf. 13½*

C354	AP125	250fr	multi	1.40	70

1986 World Cup Soccer Championships, Mexico—AP126

Various soccer plays.

1986, July 22 **Litho.** *Perf. 13*

C355	AP126	150fr	multi	80	40
C356	AP126	250fr	multi	1.35	68
C357	AP126	440fr	multi	2.40	1.20
C358	AP126	600fr	multi	3.25	1.60

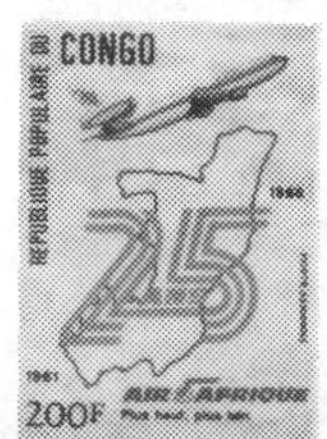

Air Africa, 25th Anniv.—AP127

1986, Nov. 29 **Litho.** *Perf. 13½*

C359	AP127	200fr	multi	1.10	55

1988 Winter Pre-Olympics, Calgary—AP128

1986, Dec. 15 *Perf. 13*

C360	AP128	150fr	Downhill skiing	80	40
C361	AP128	250fr	Bobsled	1.35	68
C362	AP128	440fr	Women's cross-country skiing	2.40	1.20
C363	AP128	600fr	Ski jumping	3.25	1.60

Nos. C361-C362 vert.

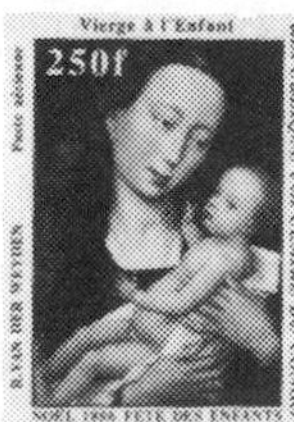

Christmas—AP129

Paintings by Rogier van der Weyden (c. 1399-1464): 250fr, Virgin and Child. 440fr, The Nativity. 500fr, Virgin with Carnation.

1986, Dec. 23 *Perf. 13½*

C364	AP129	250fr	multi	1.35	68
C365	AP129	440fr	multi	2.40	1.20
C366	AP129	500fr	multi	2.75	1.35

Crocodiles, World Wildlife Fund—AP130

1987, Jan. 22 *Perf. 13*

C367	AP130	75fr	Osteolaemus tetraspis	40	20
C368	AP130	100fr	Crocodylus cataphractus	55	28
C369	AP130	125fr	Osteolaemus tetraspis, diff.	68	35
C370	AP130	150fr	Crocodylus cataphractus, diff.	80	40

AIR POST SEMI-POSTAL STAMPS

Hathor Pillar
SPAP1

Engraved

1964, March 9 *Perf. 13* Unwmkd.

CB1	SPAP1	10fr +5fr vio & chnt		28	20
CB2	SPAP1	25fr +5fr org brn & sl grn		45	35
CB3	SPAP1	50fr +5fr sl grn & brn red		80	70

Issued to publicize the UNESCO world campaign to save historic monuments in Nubia.

POSTAGE DUE STAMPS

Messenger—D6

Early Transportation: 1fr, Litter. 2fr, Canoe. 5fr, Bicyclist. 10fr, Steam locomotive. 25fr, Seaplane.

Engraved

1961, Dec. 4 *Perf. 11* Unwmkd.

J34	D6	50c ultra, ol bis & red	5	5
J35	D6	1fr red brn, red & grn	5	5
J36	D6	2fr grn, ultra & brn	8	8
J37	D6	5fr pur & gray brn	12	12
J38	D6	10fr bl, grn & choc	28	28
J39	D6	25fr bl, dk grn & dk brn	65	65

The two types of each value in Nos. J34-J45 (early and modern transportation) were printed tête bêche, se-tenant at the base.

MH. 1521 Broussard Plane—D7

Modern transportation: 1fr, Land Rover. 2fr, River boat transporting barge. 5fr, Trailer-truck. 10fr, Diesel locomotive. 25fr, Boeing 707 jet plane.

J40	D7	50c ultra, ol bis & red	5	5
J41	D7	1fr red & grn	5	5
J42	D7	2fr ultra, grn & brn	8	8
J43	D7	5fr pur & gray brn	12	12
J44	D7	10fr dk grn & choc	28	28
J45	D7	25fr bl, dk grn & sep	65	65
		Nos. J34-J45 (12)	2.46	2.46

See note following No. J39.

Flowers
D8

Flowers: 2fr, Phaeomeria magnifica. 5fr, Millettia laurentii. 10fr, Tuberose. 15fr, Pyrostegia venusta. 20fr, Hibiscus.

1971, Mar. 25 Photo. *Perf. 12x12½*

J46	D8	1fr multi	5	5
J47	D8	2fr multi	8	8
J48	D8	5fr pink & multi	10	10
J49	D8	10fr dk grn & multi	12	12
J50	D8	15fr multi	25	25
J51	D8	20fr multi	40	40
		Nos. J46-51 (6)	1.00	1.00

OFFICIAL STAMPS

Coat of Arms
O1

Typographed

1968–70 *Perf. 14x13* Unwmkd.

O1	O1	1fr multi ('70)	5	5
O2	O1	2fr multi ('70)	5	5
O3	O1	5fr multi ('70)	10	8
O4	O1	10fr multi ('70)	30	18
O5	O1	25fr emer & multi	25	10
O6	O1	30fr red & multi	30	10
O7	O1	50fr multi ('70)	90	45
O8	O1	85fr multi ('70)	1.60	90
O9	O1	100fr multi ('70)	2.00	1.10
O10	O1	200fr multi ('70)	3.00	2.25
		Nos. O1-O10 (10)	8.55	5.26

CORFU

(kôr·foo' ; kôr'fū)

LOCATION—An island in the Ionian Sea opposite the Greek-Albanian border.

GOVT.—A department of Greece.

AREA—245 sq. mi.

POP.—114,620 (1938).

CAPITAL—Corfu.

In 1923 Italy occupied Corfu (Kerkyra) during a controversy with Greece over the assassination of an Italian official in Epirus. Italy again occupied Corfu in 1941–43.

100 Centesimi = 1 Lira

100 Lepta = 1 Drachma

Issued under Italian Occupation

Italian Stamps of 1901-23 Overprinted **CORFÙ**

1923, Sept. 20 ***Perf. 14*** **Wmk. 140**

N1	A48	5c green	75	1.25
N2	A48	10c claret	75	1.25
N3	A48	15c slate	75	1.25
N4	A50	20c brn org	75	1.25
N5	A49	30c org brn	75	1.25
N6	A49	50c violet	75	1.25
N7	A49	60c blue	75	1.25
N8	A46	1 l brn & grn	75	1.25
		Nos. N1-N8 (8)	6.00	10.00

Italian Stamps of 1901-23 Surcharged **CORFÙ Lepta 25**

1923, Sept. 24

N9	A48	25 l on 10c cl	8.00	3.50
N10	A49	60 l on 25c bl	3.00	
N11	A49	70 l on 30c org brn	3.00	
N12	A49	1.20d on 50c vio	6.00	3.50
N13	A49	2.40d on 1 l brn & grn	6.00	3.50
N14	A46	4.75d on 2 l grn & org	3.00	

Nos. 10, 11 and 14 were not placed in use.

Issue for Corfu and Paxos.

Nos. N15–N34, NC1–NC12, NJ1–NJ11 and NRA1–NRA3 have been extensively counterfeited, some with forged cancellations.

Stamps of Greece, 1937-38, Overprinted in Black **CORFU**

Perf. 12x13½, 12½x12, 13½x12.

1941, June 5 **Wmk. 252**

N15	A69	5 l brn red & bl	3.00	3.00
N16	A70	10 l bl & brn red (On 397)	1.00	1.00
N17	A70	10 l bl & brn red (On 413)	75.00	60.00
N18	A71	20 l blk & grn	1.00	1.00
N19	A72	40 l grn & blk	1.50	1.50
N20	A73	50 l brn & blk	4.00	4.00
N21	A74	80 l ind & yel brn	2.00	2.00
N22	A67	1d green	2.50	2.00
N23	A84	1.50d green	12.00	12.00
N24	A75	2d ultra	1.65	1.25
N25	A67	3d red brn	2.25	2.00
N26	A76	5d red	2.50	2.00
N27	A77	6d ol brn	3.75	3.00
N28	A78	7d dk brn	6.00	5.00
N29	A67	8d dp bl	4.75	4.00
N30	A79	10d red brn	150.00	65.00
N31	A80	15d green	10.00	9.00
N32	A81	25d dk bl	8.00	8.00
N33	A84	30d org brn	27.50	22.50
N34	A67	100d car lake	52.50	45.00
		Nos. N15-N34 (20)	370.90	253.25

AIR POST STAMPS.

Greece Nos. C37 and C26 to C35, Overprinted **CORFU**

Perf.

12½x13, 13x12½, 13½x12½.

1941, June 5 **Unwmkd.**

NC1	D3	50 l dk brn	4.00	4.00
NC2	AP16	1d red	165.00	65.00
NC3	AP17	2d gray bl	5.00	5.00
NC4	AP18	5d violet	5.00	5.00
NC5	AP19	7d dp ultra	5.00	5.00
NC6	AP20	10d bis brn (On C26)	165.00	72.50
NC7	AP20	10d brn org (On C35)	22.50	10.00
NC8	AP21	25d rose	30.00	20.00
NC9	AP22	30d dk grn	42.50	37.50
NC10	AP23	50d violet	37.50	30.00
a.		Double overprint		*200.00*
NC11	AP24	100d brown	*900.00*	*400.00*

On No. C36.

Serrate Roulette 13½.

NC12	D3	50 l vio brn	25.00	20.00
a.		On C36a		

POSTAGE DUE STAMPS.

Postage Due Stamps of Greece, 1913-35 Overprinted **CORFU**

1941, June 5 **Unwmkd.**

Serrate Roulette 13½.

NJ1	D3	10 l carmine	2.00	2.00
NJ2	D3	25 l ultra	2.00	2.00
NJ3	D3	80 l lil brn	325.00	90.00

Perf. 12½x13, 13½x12½.

NJ4	D3	1d lt bl (On J80)	*725.00*	*275.00*
NJ5	D3	2d lt red	3.00	2.25
NJ6	D3	5d gray	10.00	9.00
NJ7	D3	10d gray grn	6.00	6.00
NJ8	D3	15d red brn	6.00	6.00
NJ9	D3	25d lt red	6.00	6.00
NJ10	D3	50d orange	8.00	8.00
NJ11	D3	100d sl grn	275.00	175.00

POSTAL TAX STAMPS.

Greece Nos. RA61 to RA63, Overprinted **CORFU**

Perf. 13½x12

1941, June 5 **Unwmkd.**

NRA1	PT7	10 l brt rose, *pale rose*	1.50	1.50
NRA2	PT7	50 l gray grn, *pale grn*	1.50	1.00
NRA3	PT7	1d dl bl, *lt bl*	8.00	7.00

Stamps overprinted "CORFU" were replaced by Italian stamps overprinted "Isole Jonie." (See Ionian Islands.)

COSTA RICA

(kŏs'tȧ rē'kȧ)

LOCATION — Central America between Nicaragua and Panama.

GOVT.—Republic.

AREA—19,344 sq. mi.

POP.—2,450,226 (1984).

CAPITAL—San Jose.

Coat of Arms

A1

Engraved.

1863 ***Perf. 12*** **Unwmkd.**

1	A1	½r blue	75	1.25
a.		½r lt bl	1.50	1.75
b.		Pair, imperf. btwn.	175.00	
2	A1	2r scarlet	1.50	2.25
3	A1	4r green	15.00	17.50
4	A1	1p orange	30.00	35.00

The ½r was printed from two plates. The second is in light blue with little or no sky over the mountains.

Imperforate copies of Nos. 1–2 are corner copies from poorly perforated sheets.

Nos. 1–3 Surcharged in Red or Black:

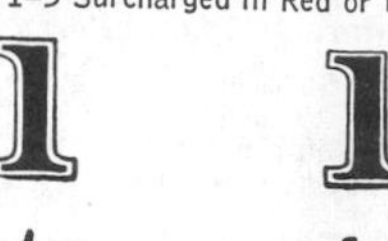

a *b*

5 cts. U.P.U.

c *d*

20 CTS U.P.U.

e

1881–82

Red or Black Surcharge.

7	A1 (a)	1c on ½r bl ('82)	3.00	*12.50*
8	A1 (b)	1c on ½r bl ('82)	15.00	*22.50*
9	A1 (c)	2c on ½r bl	2.50	*6.00*
a.		Double surch.		
b.		"Cts."		
12	A1 (c)	5c on ½r bl	7.50	
a.		Double surch.		
13	A1 (d)	5c on ½r bl ('82)	110.00	*90.00*
14	A1 (d)	10c on 2r scar (Bk) ('82)	70.00	*70.00*
15	A1 (e)	20c on 4r grn ('82)	185.00	*185.00*

The ½r stamps surcharged "DOS CTS" were never placed in use, and are said to have been surcharged to a dealer's order.

Counterfeits exist of surcharges on Nos. 7–15.

Gen. Prospero Fernández

A6

President Bernardo Soto Alfaro

A7

1883, Jan. 1

16	A6	1c green	1.00	60
17	A6	2c carmine	90	70
18	A6	5c bl vio	12.00	60
19	A6	10c orange	45.00	7.50
20	A6	40c blue	1.25	90
		Nos. 16-20 (5)	60.15	10.30

Unused copies of 40c usually lack gum.

1887

21	A7	5c bl vio	8.00	60
22	A7	10c orange	2.25	85

A8

A9

1889 Black Overprint.

23	A8	1c rose	4.50	1.1
24	A9	5c brown	3.50	1.1

President Soto Alfaro

A10 A11

A12

A13

A14

A15

A16

A17

A18

A19

1889 ***Perf. 14–16 & Compound***

25	A10	1c brown	40	50
a.		Horiz. pair, imperf. vert	50.00	
b.		Imperf. pair	60.00	
c.		Horiz. or vert. pair, imperf. between	70.00	
26	A11	2c dk grn	30	50
a.		Imperf., pair	30.00	
b.		Vert. pair, imperf. horiz.	40.00	
c.		Horiz. pair, imperf. btwn.	40.00	
27	A12	5c orange	60	30
a.		Imperf., pair	75.00	
b.		Horiz. pair, imperf. btwn.	60.00	
28	A13	10c red brn	50	40
a.		Vert. or horiz. pair, imperf. btwn.	60.00	
29	A14	20c yel grn	35	30
a.		Vert. pair, imperf. horiz.	50.00	
b.		Horizontal pair, imperf. btwn.	50.00	
30	A15	50c rose red	1.25	
31	A16	1p blue	1.75	
32	A17	2p dl vio	12.00	
a.		2p sl	13.00	

33	A18	5p ol grn	45.00	
34	A19	10p black	80.00	
		Nos. 25-34 (10)	142.15	

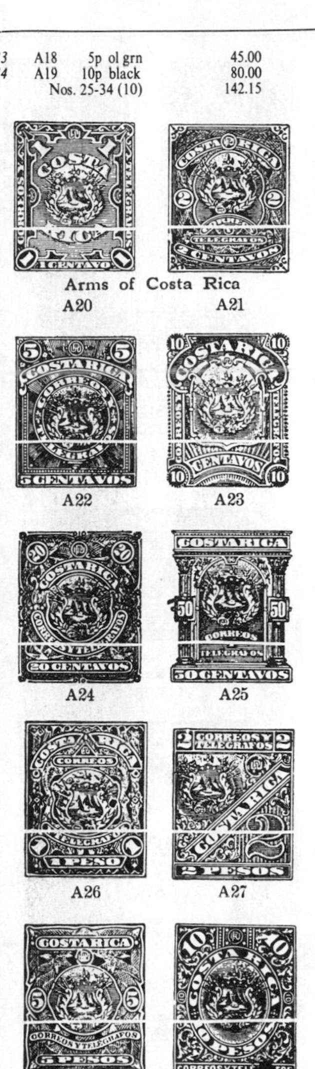

Arms of Costa Rica
A20 A21

A22 A23

A24 A25

A26 A27

A28 A29

1892 ***Perf. 12-15 & Compound***

35	A20	1c grnsh bl	35	50
36	A21	2c yellow	35	50
37	A22	5c red lil	35	20
a.		5c vio	20.00	50
38	A23	10c lt grn	90	40
a.		Horiz. pair, imperf. btwn.	70.00	
39	A24	20c scarlet	12.00	40
a.		Horiz. pair, imperf. btwn.		50.00
40	A25	50c gray bl	8.00	6.00
41	A26	1p grn, *yel*	1.50	1.10
42	A27	2p rose red, *pale lil*	3.50	1.50
a.		2p brn red, *lil*	3.50	1.50
43	A28	5p dk bl, *bl*	3.50	1.50
44	A29	10p brn, *pale buff*	15.00	6.00
a.		10p brn, *yel*	9.00	9.00
		Nos. 35-44 (10)	45.45	18.10

Imperfs. of Nos. 35-44 are proofs.

Statue of Juan Santamaría
A30

Juan Mora Fernández
A31

View of Port Limón
A32

Braulio Carillo
("Branlio" on stamp)
A33

National Theater
A34

José M. Castro
A35

Birris Bridge
A36

Juan Rafael Mora
A37

Jesús Jiménez
A38

Coat of Arms
A39

1901, Jan. ***Perf. 12-15½***

45	A30	1c grn & blk	60	15
a.		Horiz. pair, imperf. btwn.		
46	A31	2c ver & blk	75	25
47	A32	5c gray bl & blk	50	20
a.		Vert. pair, imperf. btwn.		150.00
48	A33	10c ocher & blk	1.50	25
49	A34	20c lake & blk	5.00	40
a.		Vert. pair, imperf. btwn.	150.00	
50	A35	50c dl lil & dk bl	5.00	2.00
51	A36	1col ol bis & blk	45.00	5.00
52	A37	2col car rose & dk grn	18.00	5.00
53	A38	5col brn & blk	35.00	5.00
54	A39	10col yel grn & brn red	30.00	4.00
		Nos. 45-54 (10)	141.35	22.25

The 2c exists with center inverted.

Remainders

In 1914 the government sold a large quantity of stamps at very much less than face value. The lot included most regular issues from 1901 to 1911 inclusive, postage due stamps of 1903 and official stamps of 1901-03. These stamps were cancelled with groups of thin parallel bars. They, of course, sell for much less than the prices quoted which are for stamps with regular postal cancellations.

José M. Cañas
A40

Julián Volio
A41

Eusebio Figueroa Oreamuno
A42

1903 ***Perf. 13½, 14, 15***

55	A40	4c red vio & blk	3.00	1.50
56	A41	6c ol grn & blk	7.50	4.00
57	A42	25c gray lil & brn	15.00	50

No. 49 Surcharged in Black:

1905

58	A34	1c on 20c lake & blk	1.00	1.00
a.		Inverted surcharge	8.50	8.50
b.		Diagonal surcharge	1.00	1.00

Specimens surcharged in other colors are proofs.

Statue of Juan Santamaria
A43

Juan Mora Fernández
A44

José M. Cañas
A45

Mauro Fernández
A46

Braulio Carrillo
A47

Julián Volio
A48

Eusebio Figueroa Oreamuno
A49

José M. Castro
A50

Jesús Jiménez
A51

Juan Rafael Mora
A52

1907 ***Perf. 11x14*** **Unwmkd.**

59	A43	1c red brn & ind	75	30
60	A44	2c yel grn & blk	1.25	30
a.		Perf. 14	1.25	30
61	A45	4c car & ind	8.00	4.00
a.		Perf. 14	250.00	35.00
62	A46	5c yel & dl bl perf 14	90	30
a.		Perf. 11x14	15.00	1.50
63	A47	10c bl & blk	5.00	60
a.		Perf. 14	1.25	60
64	A48	20c ol grn & blk	9.00	4.00
a.		Perf. 14	7.50	3.00
65	A49	25c gray lil & blk, perf. 14	3.00	1.25
a.		Perf. 11x14	40.00	7.50
66	A50	50c red lil & bl	40.00	12.00
a.		Perf. 14	70.00	20.00
67	A51	1col brn & blk	19.00	12.00
a.		Perf. 14	30.00	15.00
68	A52	2col cl & grn	90.00	65.00
a.		Perf. 14	130.00	80.00
		Nos. 59-68 (10)	176.90	99.75

Imperforate copies of the above set are either proofs or from unfinished sheets, which were placed on the market in London. The 1c, 2c, 5c, 20c, 50c, 1 col. and 2 col. exist with center inverted. Price, 5c, $300; others each $500.

Nos. 59-68 exist with papermaker's watermark.

Statue of Juan Santamaria
A53

Juan Mora Fernández
A54

José M. Cañas
A55

Mauro Fernández
A56

Braulio Carrillo
A57

Julián Volio
A58

Eusebio Figueroa Oreamuno
A59

Jesús Jiménez
A60

1910 ***Perf. 12.***

69	A53	1c brown	12	10
70	A54	2c dp grn	30	15
71	A55	4c scarlet	30	15
72	A56	5c orange	30	10
73	A57	10c dp bl	20	10
74	A58	20c ol grn	30	25
75	A59	25c dp vio	8.00	1.00
76	A60	1col dk brn	60	75
		Nos. 69-76 (8)	10.12	2.60

Nos. 69a-73a and 72b-72c ("Cafe" ovpts.) are listed after No. 111.

No. 60a Overprinted in Red *1911*

1911 ***Perf. 14***

77	A44	2c yel grn & blk	1.75	1.10
a.		Inverted overprint	7.00	7.00
b.		Double overprint, both inverted	60.00	

Stamps of 1901-07 Overprinted in Red or Black

*** 1911 ***

78	A30	1c grn & blk (R)	75	50
a.		Black overprint	50.00	25.00
b.		Inverted overprint		
79	A43	1c red brn & ind (Bk)	90	50
a.		Inverted overprint	6.00	5.00
b.		Double overprint	7.00	7.00
80	A44	2c yel grn & blk (Bk)	90	50
a.		Inverted overprint	3.00	3.00
b.		Double overprint, one as on No. 77	27.50	27.50
c.		Double overprint, one inverted	17.50	17.50
d.		Pair, one stamp No. 77	35.00	25.00
e.		Perf. 11x14	1.75	50

Habilitado

No. 55 Overprinted in Black

1911

81	A40	4c red vio & blk	1.50	1.00

Habilitado

Stamps of 1907 Overprinted in Blue, Black or Rose

1911

Perf. 14

82	A46	5c yel & bl (Bl)	60	25
a.		"Habilitada"	4.50	3.50
b.		"2911"	8.00	4.50
c.		Roman "I" in "1911"	2.75	2.00
d.		Double overprint	6.00	4.50
e.		Inverted overprint	8.00	5.50
f.		Black overprint	11.00	3.00
g.		Triple overprint	8.00	
h.		Imperf. horizontally (pair)	55.00	
83	A47	10c bl & blk (Bk)	2.75	2.00
a.		Roman "I" in "1911"	8.00	5.50
c.		Double overprint	27.50	16.50
d.		Perf. 11x14	1.75	1.00
84	A47	10c bl & blk (R), perf. 11x14	8.00	8.00
a.		Roman "I" in "1911"	22.50	20.00
c.		Perf. 14	27.50	16.50

Many counterfeits of overprint exist.

A61

A62

A63

Telegraph Stamps Surcharged in Rose, Blue or Black.

1911 ***Perf. 12, 14, 14x11.***

86	A61	1c on 10c bl (R)	30	20
a.		"Coereos"	11.00	8.00
b.		Inverted surcharge		
87	A61	1c on 10c bl (Bk)	125.00	90.00
a.		"Coereos"		
88	A61	1c on 25c vio (Bk)	30	20
a.		"Coereos"	11.00	8.00
b.		Pair, one without surcharge	27.50	
c.		Double surcharge	11.00	
e.		Double surcharge, one inverted	16.50	
89	A61	1c on 50c red brn (Bl)	60	60
a.		Inverted surcharge	7.00	7.00
b.		Double surcharge	6.00	
90	A61	1c on 1 col brn (R)	60	60
91	A61	1c on 5 col red (Bl)	1.10	85
92	A61	1c on 10 col dk brn (R)	1.35	1.10
93	A62	2c on 5c brn org (Bk)	4.50	3.25
a.		Inverted surcharge	11.00	5.50
b.		"Correos" inverted	22.50	
c.		Double surcharge	11.00	
94	A62	2c on 10c bl (R)	90.00	60.00
a.		Perf. 14	135.00	80.00
b.		"Correos" inverted	200.00	
c.		As "b," perf. 14	550.00	
95	A62	2c on 50c cl (Bk)	60	75
a.		Inverted surcharge	5.50	4.50
b.		Double surcharge	16.50	
96	A62	2c on 1 col brn (Bk)	1.10	1.10
a.		Inverted surcharge	16.50	
b.		Double surcharge	22.50	
97	A62	2c on 2 col car (Bk)	85	85
a.		Inverted surcharge	10.00	7.00
b.		"Correos" inverted	11.00	8.00
c.		Double surcharge		
d.		Perf. 14	18.50	13.00
98	A62	2c on 5 col grn (Bk)	1.10	1.10
a.		Inverted surcharge	11.00	8.00
b.		"Correos" inverted	22.50	6.00
99	A62	2c on 10 col mar (Bk)	1.35	1.10
a.		"Correos" inverted	22.50	
100	A63	5c on 5c org (Bl)	60	25
a.		Double surcharge	8.50	5.50
b.		Inverted surcharge	8.50	5.50
c.		Pair, one without surcharge	25.00	
		Nos. 86-100 (15)	228.75	161.20

Counterfeits exist of Nos. 87, 94 and all minor varieties.

Nos. 93–99 exist with papermaker's watermark.

Coffee Plantation—A64

1921, June 17 **Litho.** ***Perf. 11½***

103	A64	5c bl & blk	1.50	1.25
a.		Tête bêche pair	3.25	3.25
b.		Imperf., pair	15.00	
c.		As "a," imperf.	40.00	

Centenary of coffee raising in Costa Rica.

Liberty with Torch of Freedom
A65

1921 **Typographed.** ***Perf. 11***

104	A65	5c violet	85	50
a.		Imperf.	30.00	

Centenary of Central American independence.

Juan Mora and Julio Acosta—A66

1921, Sept. 15 ***Perf. 11½***

105	A66	2c org & blk	2.00	1.50
106	A66	3c grn & blk	2.00	1.50
107	A66	6c scar & blk	2.50	1.75
108	A66	15c dk bl & blk	6.00	5.00
109	A66	30c org brn & blk	10.00	9.00
		Nos. 105-109 (5)	22.50	18.75

Centenary of Central American independence. Issue requested by Costa Rican Philatelic Society. Authorized by decree calling for 2,000 of 30c and 5,000 each of other values. Many more were printed illegally including imperforates, color changes and inverted centers.

Each sheet of 20 (4x5) contains 5 tête-bêche pairs.

Simón Bolívar
A67

1921 **Engraved.** ***Perf. 12.***

110	A67	15c dp vio	40	20

CORREOS

No. 104 Overprinted

1922

1922 ***Perf. 11***

111	A65	5c violet	60	40
a.		Inverted overprint	5.00	
b.		Double overprint	10.00	

Stamps of 1910–1921 Overprinted in Blue, Red, Black or Gold

CAFE DE COSTARICA

1922 ***Perf. 12***

69a	A53	1c brn (Bl)	15	10
70a	A54	2c dp grn (R)	20	15
71a	A55	4c scarlet	25	20
72a	A56	5c orange	40	25
73a	A57	10c dp bl (R)	50	40
110a	A67	15c dp vio (G)	2.00	1.50
		Nos. 69a-110a (6)	3.50	2.60

Inverted overprints occur on all values. Counterfeits exist.

No. 72 Overprinted with Double-Lined Circle, Inscribed: "Compre Ud. Cafe de Costa Rica"

1923

72b	A56	5c orange	35	25
c.		"VD." for "UD."	60.00	60.00

Jesús Jiménez
A68

1923, June 18 **Litho.** ***Perf. 11½***

112	A68	2c brown	20	20
113	A68	4c green	25	20
114	A68	5c blue	50	20
115	A68	20c carmine	30	30
116	A68	1col violet	50	50
		Nos. 112-116 (5)	1.75	1.40

Issued to commemorate the centenary of the birth of President Jesús Jiménez (1823–1898).

Nos. 112 to 116 exist imperforate but were not regularly issued in that condition.

National Monument
A70

Harvesting Coffee
A71

Banana Growing
A73

General Post Office
A74

Columbus Soliciting Aid of Isabella
A75

Christopher Columbus
A76

Columbus at Cariari
A77

Map of Costa Rica
A78

Manuel M. Gutiérrez
A79

1923–26 **Engraved** ***Perf. 12***

117	A70	1c violet	10	10
118	A71	2c yellow	30	20
119	A73	4c dp grn	60	50
120	A74	5c lt bl	1.00	15
121	A74	5c yel grn ('26)	30	10
122	A75	10c red brn	1.25	25

123	A75	10c car rose ('26)	40	10
124	A76	12c car rose	4.00	3.00
125	A77	20c dp bl	6.00	1.00
126	A78	40c orange	7.50	2.50
127	A79	1col ol grn	2.00	60
		Nos. 117-127 (11)	23.45	8.50

See also Nos. 151–156.

Rodrigo Arias Maldonado
A80

1924 ***Perf. 12½.***

128	A80	2c dk grn	15	10
a.		Perf. 14	25	10

See No. 162.

Map of Guanacaste
A81

Mission at Nicoya
A82

1924 **Lithographed.** ***Perf. 12.***

129	A81	1c car rose	50	30
130	A81	2c violet	50	30
131	A81	5c green	50	30
132	A81	10c orange	3.50	75
133	A82	15c lt bl	1.10	65
134	A82	20c gray blk	1.75	1.10
135	A82	25c lt brn	2.50	2.00
		Nos. 129-135 (7)	10.35	5.40

Centenary of annexation of Province of Guanacaste to Costa Rica.
Exist imperf. Price, set, $40.

1925

Stamps of 1923 Surcharged:

a

b

136	A74 (a)	3c on 5c lt bl	30	25
137	A75 (a)	6c on 10c red brn	40	40
138	A78 (a)	30c on 40c org	75	60
139	A79 (b)	45c on 1 col ol grn	1.25	75
a.		Double surcharge	25.00	

No. 124 Surcharged

═10 10═

1926

140	A76	10c on 12c car rose	1.50	50

College of San Luis, Cartago
A83

Chapui Asylum, San José
A84

Normal School, Heredia
A85

Ruins of Ujarrás
A86

Engraved

1926 ***Perf. 12½.*** **Unwmkd.**

143	A83	3c ultra	25	20
144	A84	6c dk brn	40	30
145	A85	30c dp org	90	40
146	A86	45c blk vio	2.00	1.25

No. 124 Surcharged in Black:

1928, Jan. 7 ***Perf. 12***

147	A76	10c on 12c car rose	10.00	7.50

Issued in honor of Col. Charles A. Lindbergh during his Good Will Tour of Central America.
The surcharge has been counterfeited.

No. 110 Surcharged 5 5

1928

148	A67	5(c) on 15c dp vio	25	15
a.		Inverted surcharge	25.00	

Type I
A88

CORREOS 5 CENTIMOS Type II — CORREOS 5 CENTIMOS Type III

CORREOS 5 CENTIMOS Type IV — CORREOS 5 CENTIMOS Type V

Surcharge Typographed (I–V) and (V) Lithographed.

1929 ***Perf. 12½***

149	A88	5c on 2 col car (I)	25	15
a.		Type II	25	15
b.		Type III	25	15
c.		Type IV	25	15
d.		Type V	25	15

Telegraph Stamp Surcharged for Postage as in 1929, Surcharge Lithographed.

1929

150	A88	13c on 40c dp grn	15	10
a.		Inverted surcharge	1.25	1.00

Excellent counterfeits exist of No. 150a.

Types of 1923–26 Issues Dated "1929"

Imprint of Waterlow & Sons.

1930 Size: 26x21½mm. ***Perf. 12½***

151	A70	1c dk vio	10	8
155	A74	5c green	10	8
156	A75	10c car rose	50	8

Juan Rafael Mora
A89

1931

157	A89	13c car rose	35	25

Seal of Costa Rica Philatelic Society ("Octubre 12 de 1932")
A90

1932, Oct. 12 ***Perf. 12***

158	A90	3c orange	25	25
159	A90	5c dk grn	35	35
160	A90	10c car rose	40	40
161	A90	20c dk bl	50	50

Issued to commemorate the Philatelic Exhibition of Oct. 12, 1932. See also Nos. 179–183.

Maldonado Type of 1924.

1934 ***Perf. 12½***

162	A80	3c dk grn	10	8

Red Cross Nurse—A91

1935, May 31 ***Perf. 12***

163	A91	10c rose car	50	25

Issued in commemoration of the 50th anniversary of the founding of the Costa Rican Red Cross Society.

Air View of Cartago—A92

Miraculous Statuette and View of Cathedral
A93

Vision of 1635
A94

1935, Aug. ***Perf. 12½***

164	A92	5c green	25	15
165	A93	10c carmine	50	25
166	A92	30c orange	75	35
167	A94	45c dk vio	1.75	60
168	A93	50c bl blk	3.00	1.25
		Nos. 164-168 (5)	6.25	2.60

Issued to commemorate the tercentenary of the Patron Saint, Our Lady of the Angels, of Costa Rica.

Map of Cocos Island
A95

1936, Jan. 29 ***Perf. 14, 11½*** **(25c)**

169	A95	4c ocher	35	15
170	A95	8c dk vio	45	25
171	A95	25c orange	50	25
172	A95	35c brn vio	75	25
173	A95	40c brown	1.00	35
174	A95	50c yellow	1.00	1.00
175	A95	2col yel grn	10.00	8.00
176	A95	5col green	27.50	20.00
		Nos. 169-176 (8)	41.55	30.25

Exist imperf. Price, set, $50.

Map of Cocos Island and Ships of Columbus
A96

1936, Dec. 5 ***Perf. 12***

177	A96	5c green	20	6
178	A96	10c car rose	20	6

Seal of Costa Rica Philatelic Society ("Diciembre 1937")—A97

1937

179	A97	2c dk brn	20	20
180	A97	3c black	20	20
181	A97	5c green	25	20
182	A97	10c org red	30	25

Souvenir Sheet.

Imperf.

183	A97	Sheet of four	80	80
a.		2c dk brn	15	15
b.		3c blk	15	15
c.		5c grn	15	15
d.		10c org red	15	15

Issued to commemorate the Philatelic Exhibition, December, 1937. Size of No. 183: 168x101mm.

Purple Guaria Orchid, National Flower—A98

Tuna
A99

Native with Donkey Carrying Bananas
A101

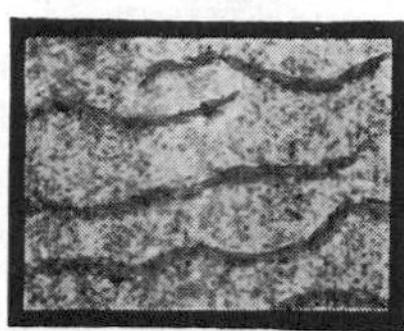

Wmk. 229

Designs: 3c, Cacao pod. 10c, Coffee harvesting.

Wmkd. Wavy Lines. (229)

1937–38			***Perf. 12½***	
184	A98	1c grn & vio ('38)	25	15
185	A98	3c choc ('38)	25	15

Perf. 12

Unwmkd.

186	A99	2c ol gray	30	20
187	A101	5c dk grn	35	15
188	A101	10c car rose	50	30
		Nos. 184-188 (5)	1.65	95

Nos 184–188 were issued to commemorate the National Exposition.

No. 125 Overprinted in Black **1938**

1938		***Perf. 12.***	**Unwmkd.**	
189	A77	20c dp bl	50	25

No. 146 Surcharged in Red:

a

b

c

d

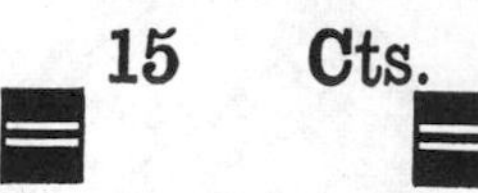

e

1940		***Perf. 12½.***		
190	A86 (a)	15c on 45c blk vio	60	30
190A	A86 (b)	15c on 45c blk vio	60	30
190B	A86 (c)	15c on 45c blk vio	60	30
190C	A86 (d)	15c on 45c blk vio	80	40
190D	A86 (e)	15c on 45c blk vio	60	25
		Nos. 190-190D (5)	3.20	1.55

Allegory—A103

Overprinted "Dia Panamericano de la Salud / 2-Diciembre 1940" and Arc in Black

1940, Dec. 2		**Engraved**	***Perf. 12***	
191	A103	5c green	35	20
192	A103	10c rose car	40	25
193	A103	20c dp bl	1.00	30
194	A103	40c brown	1.50	1.00
195	A103	55c org yel	3.50	1.25
		Nos. 191-195 (5)	6.75	3.00

Pan-American Health Day. See Nos. C46–C54.
Exist without overprint.

Stamps of 1936 Surcharged in Black:

15 CENTIMOS 15

1941			***Perf. 14, 11½***	
196	A95	15c on 25c org	35	30
197	A95	15c on 35c brn vio	35	30
198	A95	15c on 40c brn	35	30
199	A95	15c on 2 col yel grn	35	30
200	A95	15c on 5 col grn	60	55
		Nos. 196-200 (5)	2.00	1.75

Nos. 196–200 exist with surcharge inverted. Price, $5 a set.

National Stadium—A104

Engraved; Flags Typographed in National Colors

1941, May 8			***Perf. 12½***	
201	A104	5c green	1.25	35
	a.	Flags omitted	80.00	
202	A104	10c orange	1.00	35
203	A104	15c car rose	1.50	50
204	A104	25c dk bl	2.50	70
205	A104	40c chestnut	6.00	2.00
206	A104	50c purple	8.00	2.50
207	A104	75c red org	15.00	5.00
208	A104	1col dk car	25.00	10.00
		Nos. 201-208 (8)	60.25	21.40

Issued to commemorate the Caribbean and Central American Soccer Championship. See also Nos. C57–C66, C121–C123.

No. 157 Surcharged in Black **5 Céntimos 5**

1941			***Perf. 12***	
209	A89	5c on 13c car rose	12	8

Cleto González Viquez
A105

1941-45		**Engraved.**	***Perf. 12½.***	
210	A105	3c dp org	25	10
210A	A105	3c dp plum ('43)	25	10
210B	A105	3c car ('45)	25	10
211	A105	5c dp vio (*José Rodriguez*)	30	12
211A	A105	5c brn blk ('43)	30	12
		Nos. 210-211A (5)	1.35	54

See also No. 256.

Old University of Costa Rica
A106

New National University
A107

1941, Aug. 26			***Perf. 12***	
212	A106	5c green	45	15
213	A107	10c yel org	50	15
214	A106	15c lil rose	70	15
215	A107	25c dl bl	1.00	35
216	A106	50c fawn	4.00	2.00
		Nos. 212-216 (5)	6.65	2.80

National University, founded in 1940. See Nos. C74–C80.

Nos. 144, 189 Surcharged in Black or Red

15 CENTIMOS 15

1942			***Perf. 12½, 12***	
217	A84	5c on 6c dk brn	30	20
218	A77	15c on 20c dp bl (R)	40	25

Torch of Freedom, "Victory" and Flags of American Nations
A108

Juan Mora Fernández
A109

1942, Sept. 25			***Perf. 12***	
219	A108	5c rose	30	15
220	A108	5c yel grn	30	15
221	A108	5c purple	30	15
222	A108	5c dp bl	30	15
223	A108	5c red org	30	15
		Nos. 219-223 (5)	1.50	75

1943–47 **Engraved**

Designs: 2c, Bruno Carranza. 3c, Tomas Guardia. 5c, Manuel Aguilar. 15c, Francisco Morazan. 25c, Jose M. Alfaro. 50c, Francisco M. Oreamuno. 1col, Jose M. Castro. 2col, Juan Rafael Mora.

224	A109	1c red lil	6	5
225	A109	2c black	6	6
226	A109	3c dp bl	6	6
227	A109	5c brt bl grn	12	8
	a.	5c brt grn ('47)	12	10
228	A109	15c scarlet	15	6
229	A109	25c brt ultra	35	20
230	A109	50c dp vio	1.00	75
231	A109	1col blk brn	3.00	1.50
232	A109	2col dp org	5.00	3.50
		Nos. 224-232 (9)	9.80	6.26

See Nos. 344-348, C81-C91A, C124-C127, C154-C158, C179-C185, C768-C772, C790-C794, C854-C858.

View of San Ramón
A118

1944, Jan. 19				
233	A118	5c dk grn	20	10
234	A118	10c orange	25	10
235	A118	15c rose pink	40	12
236	A118	40c gray blk	1.50	75
237	A118	50c dp bl	2.50	1.25
		Nos. 233-237 (5)	4.85	2.32

Issued to commemorate the 100th anniversary of the founding of the City of San Ramón. See also Nos. C94–C102.

Nos. 220–223 Overprinted in Red or Black

La entrevista de los Presidentes De la Guardia y Picado contribuirá a afianzar la unidad Continental. 18 setiembre 1944

1944, Sept. 18				
238	A108	5c yel grn (Bk)	15	12
239	A108	5c pur (R)	15	12
240	A108	5c dp bl (R)	15	12
241	A108	5c red org (Bk)	15	12

Issued to commemorate the amicable settlement of a boundary dispute with Panama. This overprint also exists on No. 219.

Mauro Fernández
A119

Engraved.

1945, July 21		***Perf. 14***	**Unwmkd.**	
242	A119	20c dp grn	25	15

Issued to commemorate the centenary of the birth of Mauro Fernandez (1844–1905), statesman.

Coffee Harvesting
A120

1945, Oct. 9			***Perf. 12***	
243	A120	5c dk grn & blk	15	8
244	A120	10c org & blk	25	12
245	A120	20c car rose & blk	30	20

No. 242 Surcharged in Red Brown.

1946		***Perf. 14.***	**Unwmkd.**	
246	A119	15c on 20c dp grn	20	12

No. 080 Overprinted in Red **CORREOS 1947**

1947, Mar. 19			***Perf. 12***	
247	A96	5c green	15	10

Cervantes
A121

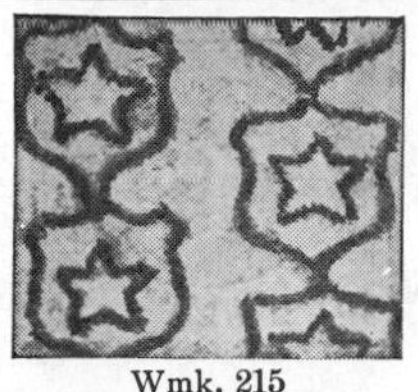

Wmk. 215

Wmkd. Small Star in Shield, Multiple. (215)

1947, Nov. 10 Engraved *Perf. 14*

249	A121	30c dp bl	30	15
250	A121	55c dp car	50	35

Issued to commemorate the 400th anniversary of the birth of Miguel de Cervantes Saavedra, novelist, playwright and poet.

Franklin D. Roosevelt A122

1947, Aug. 26 *Perf. 12* Unwmkd.

251	A122	5c brt grn	10	10
252	A122	10c car rose	15	12
253	A122	15c ultra	20	18
254	A122	25c org red	25	25
255	A122	50c lilac	50	35
		Nos. 251-255, C160-C167 (13)	9.50	8.95

Small Portrait Type of 1941.

1948 *Perf. 12½.*

256	A105	3c dp ultra (*Bishop Bernardo A. Thiel*)	10	8

Old University of Costa Rica A123

1953, June 25 Litho. *Perf. 12*

Black Surcharge.

257	A123	5c on 10c grn	12	6

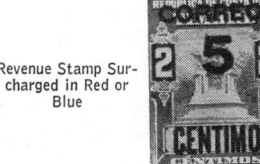

Revenue Stamp Surcharged in Red or Blue

A124

Engraved.

1955-56 *Perf. 12* Unwmkd.

258	A124	5c on 2c emer (R)	8	6
259	A124	15c on 2c emer (Bl)	18	8
260	A124	15c on 2c emer (R) ('56)	18	8
		Nos. 258-260, C341-C344 (7)	1.59	1.17

Justo A. Facio A125

Anglo-Costa Rican Bank A126

1960, Apr. 20 Photo. *Perf. 13½*

261	A125	10c brn red	8	6

Centenary of the birth (in 1859) of Prof. Justo A. Facio. Exists imperf.

1963

Nos. RA12-RA15 Surcharged in Red

10 CENTIMOS

1963, Mar.

262	PT3	10c on 5c dk car	25	20
263	PT3	10c on 5c sep	25	20
264	PT3	10c on 5c dl grn	25	20
265	PT3	10c on 5c bl	25	20

1963 *Perf. 13½* Unwmkd.

266	A126	10c gray	8	6

Centenary of the Anglo-Costa Rican Bank.

Arms of San José A127

Alberto M. Brenes Mora A128

Coats of Arms: 35c, Cartago. 50c, Heredia. 55c, Alajuela. 65c, Guanacaste. 1col, Puntarenas. 2col, Limon.

Lithographed

1969, Sept. 14 *Perf. 14x13½*

267	A127	15c multi	15	10
268	A127	35c multi	15	10
269	A127	50c gray & multi	20	10
270	A127	55c buff & multi	25	20
271	A127	65c multi	35	25
272	A127	1col pink & multi	1.50	25
273	A127	2col multi	1.50	50
		Nos. 267-273 (7)	4.10	1.50

1976, March 1 Litho. *Perf. 10½*

274	A128	1col vio bl	25	20
		Nos. 274, C653-C657 (6)	3.55	2.73

Prof. Alberto Manuel Brenes Mora, botanist, birth centenary.

Map of Costa Rica, Reader with Book A129

1978, July 17 Litho. *Perf. 13½*

275	A129	50c multi	12	10

National five-year literacy plan.

World Communications Year—A130

1983, May 17 Litho. *Perf. 13x13½*

276	A130	10c multi	5	5
277	A130	50c multi	5	5
278	A130	10col multi	70	25

First World Congress of Human Rights, 1982—A131

1983 Litho. *Perf. 10½*

279	A131	20col black	1.40	50

UPU Membership Centenary—A132

1983, June Litho. *Perf. 16*

280	A132	3col No. 17, monument	50	8
281	A132	10col No. 20, headquarters	1.00	28

French Alliance Centenary—A133

1983, July 21 Litho. *Perf. 11*

282	A133	12col Scene in San Jose, by Christina Fournier	85	28

Christmas 1983—A134

Nativity tableau in continuous design.

1983, Dec. 5 Litho. *Perf. 13½*

283	A134	1.50col multi	10	5
284	A134	1.50col multi	10	5
285	A134	1.50col multi	10	5

Costa Rican Gardens Association.

Fishery Development Administration—A135

1983, Dec. 19 Litho. *Perf. 13½*

286	A135	8.50col multi	56	18

Local Birds—A136

1984, Jan. 9 Litho. *Perf. 13½*

287	A136	10c Quetzal	10	5
288	A136	50c Cyanerpes cyaneus	10	5
289	A136	1col Turdus grayi	10	5
290	A136	1.50col Momotus momota	10	5
291	A136	3col Colibri thalassinus	12	5
292	A136	10col Notiochelindon cyanoleuca	50	10
		Nos. 287-292 (6)	1.02	35

Dated 1983. 10c, 1.50col, 3col vert.

José Joaquin Mora, Hero of 1856 Independence Campaign—A137

Paintings, Juan Santamaria Museum, San José: 1.50col, Pancha Carrasco. 3 col, Death of Juan Santamaria (horiz.). 8.50col, Juan Rafael Mora Porras.

1984, Apr. 10 Litho. *Perf. 10½*

293	A137	50c multi	5	5
294	A137	1.50col multi	5	5
295	A137	3col multi	6	5
296	A137	8.50col multi	18	5

Jesus Bonilla Chavarria, Composer—A138

Musicians and Composers: 5col, Benjamin Gutierrez (b. 1937). 12col, Pilar Jimenez (1835-1922). 13col, Jose Daniel Zuniga Zeledon (1889-1981).

1984, May 30 Litho. *Perf. 13½*

297	A138	3.50col blk & lil	8	5
298	A138	5col blk & pink	10	5
299	A138	12col blk & grn	24	6
300	A138	13col blk & yel	26	6

Figurines, Jade Museum A139

1984 Summer Olympics A140

1984, June 27 Litho. *Perf. 13½*

301	A139	4col Man (pendant)	8	5
302	A139	7col Seated man	14	5
303	A139	10col Dish, horiz.	20	5

1984, July 27

304	A140	1col Basketball	5	5
305	A140	8col Swimming	15	5
306	A140	11col Bicycling	22	5
307	A140	14col Running	28	8
308	A140	20col Boxing	40	12
309	A140	30col Soccer	60	16
		Nos. 304-309 (6)	1.70	51

Public Street Lighting Centenary—A141

1984, Aug. 9 Litho. *Perf. 10½*
310 A141 6col Street scene by Luis Chacon 12 5

10th Natl. Stamp Exhibition, Sept. 10-16—A142

1984, Sept. 10 Litho. *Perf. 10½*
311 A142 10col Natl. monument 20 5
312 A142 10col Juan Mora Fernandez monument 20 5
a. Miniature sheet of 4 (2 each #311-312) 80

Size of No. 312a: 117x87mm.

Natl. Arms—A143

1984, Oct. 29 Engr. *Perf. 14x13½*
313 A143 100col dk grn 2.50 2.00
314 A143 100col yel org 2.50 2.00

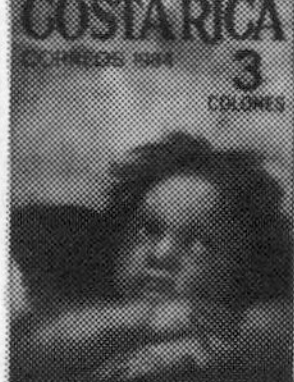

Detail from Sistine Virgin by Raphael
A144 A145

1984, Dec. 7 Litho. *Perf. 10½*
315 A144 3col multi 6 6
316 A145 3col multi 6 6

Nos. 315-316 se-tenant.

20th Intl. Bicycle Race, Costa Rica—A146

1984, Dec. 19 Litho. *Perf. 13½*
317 A146 6col multi 28 28

Intl. Youth Year—A147

1985, Jan. 31 *Perf. 10½*
322 A147 11col IYY emblem, No. C476 45 45

Scouting Movement, 75th anniv.

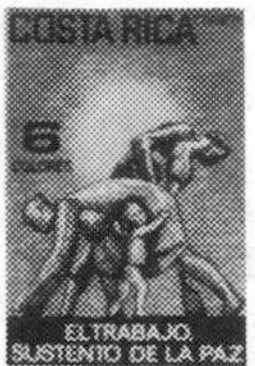

Labor Monument, San Jose—A148

Natl. values: 11col, Freedom of speech—wooden hand printing press. 13col, Neutrality—dove, natl. flag, outline map.

1985, Feb. 28
323 A148 6col multi 28 28
324 A148 11col multi 44 44
325 A148 13col multi 52 52

Size: 68x38mm.
326 A148 30col Nos. 323-325 1.15 1.15

Natl. Red Cross Cent., UN 40th Anniv.—A149

1985, Feb. 19 *Perf. 10½*
327 A149 3col No. 163 14 14
328 A149 5col No. C120, horiz. 25 25

Club Emblem—A150

1st Club Pres., Ricardo Saprissa Ayma—A151

Design: No. 330, Hands holding soccer ball.

1985, July 16 *Perf. 10½*
329 A150 3col multi 14 14
330 A150 3col multi 14 14
331 A151 6col multi 28 28

Saprissa Soccer Club, 50th Anniv. Nos. 329-330 printed se-tenant.

Orchids—A152

1985, Nov. *Perf.*
332 A152 6col Maxillaria especie 28 28
333 A152 6col Encyclia peraltensis 28 28
334 A152 6col Brassia arcuigera 28 28
335 A152 13col Stanhopea ecornuta 60 60
336 A152 13col Trichopilia marginata 60 60
337 A152 13col Oncidium turialbae 60 60
Nos. 332-337 (6) 2.64 2.64

Nos. 332-334 and 335-337 printed se-tenant in sheets of 15.

11th Natl. Philatelic Exposition—A153

1985, Dec. 3 Litho. *Perf. 13½*
338 A153 20col No. C41 80 20

Compulsory Education, Cent. A154 — Agriculture Students A155

Designs: 3col, Primary school, horiz. 30col, Mauro Fernandez Acuna, founder.

1986, Feb. 28 *Perf. 13½*
339 A154 3col pale yel & brn 12 5
340 A154 30col pale pink & brn 1.20 30

1986, Mar. 21 *Perf. 10½*
341 A155 10col shown 40 10
342 A155 10col IDB emblem 40 10
343 A155 10col Capo Bianco fisherman 40 10

Inter-American Development Bank Annual Governors' Assembly, San Jose. Nos. 341-343 printed se-tenant.

Presidents Type of 1943

Design: Francisco J. Orlich Bolmarcich (1907-69), 1962-66.

1986, May 8 *Perf. 10½*
344 A109 3col turq bl 12 5
345 A109 6col yel brn 24 6
346 A109 10col brn org 40 10
347 A109 11col sl gray 45 12
348 A109 13col olive 52 14
Nos. 344-348 (5) 1.73 47

1986 World Cup Soccer Championships, Mexico—A156

1986, May 30 Litho. *Perf. 13½*
369 A156 1col Players 5 5
370 A156 1col Character trademark, vert. 5 5
371 A156 4col As No. 370 16 5
372 A156 6col As No. 369 24 6
373 A156 11col Players, diff. 45 12

Intl. Peace Year—A157

Peace in many languages: No. 374a, "Hoa binh," etc. No. 374b, "Vrede," etc. No. 374c, "Pace," etc.

1986, July Litho. *Perf. 10½*
374 Strip of 3 55 15
a.-c. A157 5col, any single 18 5

Gold Museum, Central Bank of Costa Rica—A158

Pre-Columbian art: No. 375a, Praying mantis. No. 375b, Bird. No. 375c, Frog. No. 375d, Serpent. No. 375e, Two-headed figure. No. 376a, Masked man. No. 376b, Two figures. No. 376c, Serpentine two-legged figure. No. 376d, Bell. No. 376e, Deity.

1986, June 3 *Perf. 13½*
375 Strip of 5 1.10 30
a.-e. A158 6col, any single 22 6
376 Strip of 5 2.25 60
a.-e. A158 13 col, any single 45 12
Nos. 375-376 (10) 3.35 90

A159

Fauna and Flora—A160

1986, Dec. **Litho.** ***Perf. 13x13½***

377	A159	2col	Centurio senex	8	5
378	A159	3col	Glossophaga soricina	12	5
379	A159	4col	Ectophylla alba	14	5
380	A159	5col	Ectophylla alba, diff.	18	5
381	A159	6col	Agalychnis callidryas	22	6
382	A159	10col	Dendrobates pumilio	38	10
383	A159	11col	Hyla ebraccata	40	10
384	A159	20col	Phyllobates lugubris	75	18
			Nos. 377-384 (8)	2.27	64

Miniature Sheet
Perf. 12½x12

385	A160	50col	Agalychnis callidryas, diff.	2.00	50

No. 385 has multicolored margin continuing the design. Size: 60x70mm.

SEMI-POSTAL STAMPS.

No. 72 Surcharged in Red

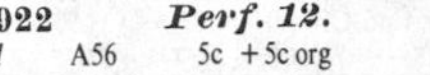

1922 ***Perf. 12.*** **Unwmkd.**

B1	A56	5c +5c org	75	40

Issued for the benefit of the Costa Rican Red Cross Society. In 1928, owing to a temporary shortage of the ordinary 5c stamp, No. B1 was placed on sale as a regular 5c stamp, the surtax being disregarded.

Discus Thrower
SP1

Trophy
SP2

Parthenon
SP3

1924 **Lithographed** ***Imperf.***

B2	SP1	5c dk grn	3.00	4.00
B3	SP2	10c carmine	3.00	4.00
B4	SP3	20c dk bl	7.00	6.00
	a.	Tête bêche pair	18.00	20.00

Perf. 12.

B5	SP1	5c dk grn	3.00	4.00
B6	SP2	10c carmine	3.00	4.00
B7	SP3	20c dk bl	6.00	7.00
	a.	Tête bêche pair	18.00	20.00
		Nos. B2-B7 (6)	25.55	29.15

These stamps were sold at a premium of 10c each, to help defray the expenses of athletic games held at San José in December, 1924.

AIR POST STAMPS.

Airplane
AP1

Engraved

1926, June 4 ***Perf. 12½*** **Unwmkd.**

C1	AP1	20c ultra	2.00	50

No. 123 Overprinted

CORREO AEREO

1930, Mar. 14 ***Perf. 12***

C2	A75	10c car rose	65	20

AP3

1930–32 ***Perf. 12½***

C3	AP3	5c on 10c dk brn ('32)	25	10
	a.	Inverted surcharge	6.00	
C4	AP3	20c on 50c ultra	25	20
C5	AP3	40c on 50c ultra	50	20

Telegraph Stamp Overprinted

Correo Aereo

1930, Mar. 19

C6	AP3	1col orange	2.50	50

No. 079 Surcharged in Red

1930, Mar. 11

C7	O7	8c on 1col lil & blk	75	60
C8	O7	20c on 1col lil & blk	1.00	75
C9	O7	40c on 1col lil & blk	2.00	1.50
C10	O7	1col on 1col lil & blk	3.00	2.00

AP6

AP7

Red Surcharge on Revenue Stamps

1931–32 ***Perf. 12***

C11	AP6	2col on 2col gray grn	27.50	27.50
C12	AP6	3col on 5col lil brn	27.50	27.50
C13	AP6	5col on 10col gray blk	27.50	27.50

There were two printings of this issue which were practically identical in the colors of the stamps and the surcharges.

Nos. C11 and C13 have the date "1929" on the stamp, No. C12 has "1930".

Black Overprint on Telegraph Stamp

1932, Mar. 8 ***Perf. 12½***

C14	AP7	40c green	2.50	50
	a.	Inverted ovpt.	20.00	

Mail Plane about to Land
AP8

Allegory of Flight
AP9

1934, Mar. 14 ***Perf. 12***

C15	AP8	5c green	25	10
C16	AP8	10c car rose	25	8
C17	AP8	15c chocolate	60	15
C18	AP8	20c dp bl	65	12
C19	AP8	25c dp org	85	10
C20	AP8	40c ol blk	1.50	12
C21	AP8	50c gray blk	1.00	25
C22	AP8	60c org yel	2.00	30
C23	AP8	75c dl vio	3.00	75
C24	AP9	1col dp rose	2.25	25
C25	AP9	2col lt bl	2.50	1.00
C26	AP9	5col black	6.50	6.50
C27	AP9	10col red brn	11.00	11.00
		Nos. C15-C27 (13)	32.35	20.72

Stamps Nos. C15 to C27 with holes punched through were for use of government officials.

See also Nos. C216–C219.

Airplane over Poás Volcano
AP10

1937, Feb. 10

No.	Type	Description	Unused	Used
C28	AP10	1c black	12	10
C29	AP10	2c brown	12	10
C30	AP10	3c dk vio	12	10

First Fair of Costa Rica.

Puntarenas
AP11

National Bank
AP12

Perf. 12, 12½

1937, Dec. 15 **Unwmkd.**

No.	Type	Description	Unused	Used
C31	AP11	2c blk gray	8	8
C32	AP11	5c green	15	12
C33	AP11	20c dp bl	50	40
C34	AP11	1.40col ol brn	5.00	5.00

Wmkd. Wavy Lines. (229)

1938, Jan. 11 *Perf. 12½*

No.	Type	Description	Unused	Used
C35	AP12	1c purple	8	6
C36	AP12	3c red org	10	6
C37	AP12	10c car rose	20	15
C38	AP12	75c brown	3.00	3.00

Nos. C31 to C38 were issued to commemorate the National Products Exposition held at San José in December, 1937.

Airport Administration Building, La Sabana—AP13

1940, May 2 **Engraved** **Unwmkd.**

No.	Type	Description	Unused	Used
C39	AP13	5c green	15	10
C40	AP13	10c rose pink	20	15
C41	AP13	25c lt bl	25	20
C42	AP13	35c red brn	45	45
C43	AP13	60c red org	70	70
C44	AP13	85c violet	2.00	1.75
C45	AP13	2.35col turq grn	11.00	11.00
		Nos. C39-C45 (7)	14.75	14.35

Issued to commemorate the opening of the International Airport at La Sabana.

Duran Sanatorium
AP14

Overprinted "Dia Panamericano de la Salud / 2-Diciembre 1940" and Bar in Black

1940, Dec. 2 *Perf. 12*

No.	Type	Description	Unused	Used
C46	AP14	10c scarlet	20	15
C47	AP14	15c purple	25	25
C48	AP14	25c lt bl	45	40
C49	AP14	35c bis brn	70	65
C50	AP14	60c pck grn	90	90
C51	AP14	75c olive	2.00	2.25
C52	AP14	1.35col red org	9.00	9.00
C53	AP14	5col sepia	40.00	40.00
C54	AP14	10col red lil	80.00	90.00
		Nos. C46-C54 (9)	133.50	143.60

Pan-American Health Day. Exist without overprint. Few copies of C53–C54 were sold for postal purposes, nearly all having been obtained by philatelic speculators.

No. 174 Surcharged in Black or Blue

AEREO

Aviación Panamericana

Dic. 17 1940

15 CENTIMOS 15

1940, Dec. 17 *Perf. 14*

No.	Type	Description	Unused	Used
C55	A95	15c on 50c yel (Bk)	75	75
C56	A95	30c on 50c yel (Bl)	75	75

Issued in commemoration of Pan-American Aviation Day, proclaimed by President F. D. Roosevelt.

The 15c surch. exists on #171, price $40.

International Soccer Game at National Stadium—AP15

1941, May 8 *Perf. 12*

No.	Type	Description	Unused	Used
C57	AP15	15c red	1.25	25
C58	AP15	30c dp ultra	1.50	40
C59	AP15	40c red brn	1.50	60
C60	AP15	50c purple	2.00	1.35
C61	AP15	60c brt grn	2.50	1.50
C62	AP15	75c yel org	4.00	2.25
C63	AP15	1col dl vio	7.50	7.50
C64	AP15	1.40col rose	15.00	15.00
C65	AP15	2col bl grn	30.00	30.00
C66	AP15	5col black	65.00	65.00
		Nos. C57-C66 (10)	130.25	123.85

Issued to commemorate the Caribbean and Central American Soccer Championship. See also Nos. C121–C123.

Air Post Stamps of 1934 Overprinted or Surcharged in Black

Mayo 1941

Tratado Limitrofe
Costa Rica - Panamá

with New Values and Bars.

1941, June 2

No.	Type	Description	Unused	Used
C67	AP8	5c on 20c dp bl	30	25
C68	AP8	15c on 20c dp bl	40	30
C69	AP8	40c on 75c dl vio	60	40
C70	AP9	65c on 1col dp rose	1.10	90
C71	AP9	1.40col on 2col lt bl	5.50	5.50
C72	AP9	5col black	20.00	20.00
C73	AP9	10col red brn	22.50	22.50
		Nos. C67-C73 (7)	50.40	49.85

Issued in commemoration of the settlement of the Costa Rica-Panama border dispute.

Nos. C67–C73 are found with hyphen omitted in overprint.

University Types of Regular Issue, 1941.

1941, Aug. 26 *Perf. 12*

No.	Type	Description	Unused	Used
C74	A107	15c salmon	40	20
C75	A106	30c lt bl	60	25
C76	A107	40c orange	70	50
C77	A106	60c turq grn	85	75
C78	A107	1col violet	3.50	3.50
C79	A106	2col black	8.50	8.50
C80	A107	5col sepia	27.50	27.50
		Nos. C74-C80 (7)	42.05	41.20

National University, founded in 1940.

Portrait Type of Regular Issue, 1943–47.

Designs: 40c, Manuel Aguilar. No. C83, Francisco Morazan. No. C83A, Jose R. De Gallegos. 50c, Jose M. Alfaro. 60c, Francisco M. Oreamuno. 65c, Jose M. Castro. 85c, Juan Rafael Mora. 1col, Jose M. Montealegre. 1.05col, Braulio Carrillo. 1.15col, Jesus Jimenez. 1.40 col, Bruno Carranza. 2col, Tomas Guardia.

1943-45 **Engraved.**

No.	Type	Description	Unused	Used
C81	A109	10c rose pink	15	8
C82	A109	40c blue	35	12
C82A	A109	40c car rose ('45)	35	20
C83	A109	45c magenta	50	40
C83A	A109	45c blk ('45)	30	18
C84	A109	50c turq grn	2.50	30
C84A	A109	50c red org ('45)	45	30
C85	A109	60c brt ultra	65	25
C85A	A109	60c brt grn ('45)	30	20
C86	A109	65c scarlet	1.25	40
C86A	A109	65c brt ultra ('45)	35	30
C87	A109	85c dp org	1.50	55
C87A	A109	85c dl pur ('45)	1.75	70
C88	A109	1col black	1.75	75
C88A	A109	1col scar ('45)	75	30
C88B	A109	1.05col bis brn ('45)	1.00	75
C89	A109	1.15col red brn	2.50	2.50
C89A	A109	1.15col grn ('45)	3.50	2.00
C90	A109	1.40col dp vio	3.75	3.50
C90A	A109	1.40col org yel ('45)	2.25	2.25
C91	A109	2col black	6.00	2.00
C91A	A109	2col ol grn ('45)	1.75	50
		Nos. C81-C91A (22)	33.65	18.53

See also Nos. C124–C127, C179–C181.

Nos. C26–C27 Overprinted in Red or Blue

Legislacion Social
15 Setiembre 1943

1943, Sept. 16

No.	Type	Description	Unused	Used
C92	AP9	5col blk (R)	5.00	4.00
C93	AP9	10col red brn (Bl)	10.00	7.50

Mercury and Plane
AP31

1944, Jan. 19

No.	Type	Description	Unused	Used
C94	AP31	10c red org	25	20
C95	AP31	15c dk car	30	20
C96	AP31	40c brt ultra	50	40
C97	AP31	45c dp red lil	60	50
C98	AP31	60c turq grn	85	75
C99	AP31	1col dk red brn	1.75	1.50
C100	AP31	1.40col gray blk	10.00	9.00
C101	AP31	5col violet	27.50	27.50
C102	AP31	10col black	50.00	50.00
		Nos. C94-C102 (9)	91.75	90.05

Issued to commemorate the 100th anniversary of the founding of the City of San Ramón.

Very few copies of the 5col or 10col stamps were sold for postal purposes, nearly all having been obtained by philatelic speculators.

No. CO10 With Additional Overprint in Black **1944**

1944, Nov. 22

No.	Type	Description	Unused	Used
C103	AP9	1col dp rose	1.00	60
a.		Blue ovpt.	65.00	

Nos. CO1-13 Overprinted in Carmine or Black **1945**

1945, Jan. 12 *Perf. 12* **Unwmkd.**

No.	Type	Description	Unused	Used
C104	AP8	5c green	1.00	1.00
C105	AP8	10c car rose (Bk)	1.00	1.00
C106	AP8	15c chocolate	1.00	1.00
C107	AP8	20c dp bl	60	60
C108	AP8	25c dp org (Bk)	1.00	1.00
C109	AP8	40c ol blk	60	60
C110	AP8	50c gray blk	1.00	1.00
C111	AP8	60c org yel (Bk)	1.50	60
C112	AP8	75c dl vio	1.25	1.00
C113	AP9	1col dp rose (Bk)	1.25	60
C114	AP9	2col lt bl	8.00	8.00
C115	AP9	5col black	10.00	10.00
C116	AP9	10col red brn (Bk)	15.00	15.00
		Nos. C104-C116 (13)	43.20	41.40

AP32

Telegraph Stamps Overprinted in Black or Carmine.

Perf. 12½

1945, Feb. 28 **Unwmkd.**

No.	Type	Description	Unused	Used
C117	AP32	40c grn (C)	25	12
C118	AP32	50c ultra (C)	30	12
C119	AP32	1col org (Bk)	65	40

Florence Nightingale and Edith Cavell—AP33

1945 **Engraved.**

No.	Type	Description	Unused	Used
C120	AP33	1col blk & car	75	50

Issued to commemorate the 60th anniversary of the Costa Rican Red Cross Society.

Soccer Type of 1941.

Inscribed: "Febrero 1946."

1946, May 13 *Perf. 12*

No.	Type	Description	Unused	Used
C121	AP15	25c green	1.50	1.10
C122	AP15	30c dl yel	1.50	1.10
C123	AP15	55c dp bl	1.75	1.10

Portrait Type of 1943–47.

Designs: 25c, Aniceto Esquivel. 30c, Vicente Herrera. 55c, Prospero Fernandez. 75c, Bernardo Soto.

1946, May 12

No.	Type	Description	Unused	Used
C124	A109	25c blue	20	12
C125	A109	30c red brn	25	20
C126	A109	55c plum	40	30
C127	A109	75c bl grn	60	40

Hospital of St. John of God
AP38

1946, June 24 *Perf. 12½* **Unwmkd.**

Center in Black.

No.	Type	Description	Unused	Used
C128	AP38	5c yel grn	10	10
C129	AP38	10c dk brn	10	10
C130	AP38	15c carmine	10	10
C131	AP38	25c dk bl	20	20
C132	AP38	30c dp org	40	30
C133	AP38	40c ol grn	20	20
C134	AP38	50c violet	35	35
C135	AP38	60c dk sl grn	75	70
C136	AP38	75c brown	60	50
a.		Horiz. pair, imperf. btwn.	110.00	
C137	AP38	1col blue	75	40
C138	AP38	2col brn org	1.10	90
C139	AP38	3col dk vio brn	2.75	2.75
C140	AP38	5col yellow	3.50	3.50
		Nos. C128-C140 (13)	10.90	10.10

Rafael Iglesias
AP39

Designs: 3col, Ascensión Esquivel. 5col, Cleto González Víquez. 10col, Ricardo Jiménez Oreamuno.

Wmkd.
Small Star in Shield, Multiple. (215)

1947, Jan. 15 Engraved *Perf. 14*

Center in Black.

C141	AP39	2col blue	1.50	1.10
C142	AP39	3col dp car	2.25	1.30
C143	AP39	5col dk grn	3.50	2.25
C144	AP39	10col orange	6.50	4.00

Nos. C121 to C123 Surcharged in Black

Habilitado para

₡ 0.15

Decreto Nº 16 de
28 de abril de 1947

1947, May 5 *Perf. 12* Unwmkd.

C145	AP15	15c on 25c grn	1.25	1.10
C146	AP15	15c on 30c dl yel	1.25	1.10
C147	AP15	15c on 55c dp bl	1.25	1.10

Nos. C145-C147 exist with inverted surcharge;

Columbus in Cariarí
AP43

1947, May 19 Engr. *Perf. 12½*

Center in Black.

C148	AP43	25c green	30	18
C149	AP43	30c dp ultra	30	18
C150	AP43	40c red org	40	20
C151	AP43	45c violet	50	35
C152	AP43	50c brt car	60	30
C153	AP43	65c brn org	1.50	1.00
		Nos. C148-C153 (6)	3.60	2.21

Nos. C84A, C85A, C127, C88A, and C88B Surcharged with New Value in Black or Red.

1947, June 3 *Perf. 12*

C154	A109	15c on 50c red org	25	25
C155	A109	15c on 60c brt grn (R)	25	25
C156	A109	15c on 75c bl grn (R)	25	25
C157	A109	15c on 1col scar	30	30
C158	A109	15c on 1.05col bis brn	25	25
		Nos. C154-C158 (5)	1.30	1.30

Early Steam Locomotive
AP44

Engraved

1947, Nov. 10 *Perf. 12½* Unwmkd.

C159	AP44	35c bl grn & blk	1.00	50

Issued to commemorate the 50th anniversary of the electric railroad to the Pacific coast.

Roosevelt Type of Regular Issue.

1947, Aug. 26 *Perf. 12*

C160	A122	15c green	12	10
C161	A122	30c car rose	18	15
C162	A122	45c red brn	35	35
C163	A122	65c org yel	40	40
C164	A122	75c blue	50	40
C165	A122	1col ol grn	75	70
C166	A122	2col black	2.00	1.85
C167	A122	5col scarlet	4.00	4.00
		Nos. C160-C167 (8)	8.30	7.95

National Theater
AP46

Rafael Iglesias
AP47

1948, Jan. 26 *Perf. 12½*

Center in Black.

C168	AP46	15c brt ultra	20	15
C169	AP46	20c red	25	20
C170	AP47	35c dk grn	35	30
C171	AP46	45c purple	50	35
C172	AP46	50c carmine	50	35
C173	AP46	75c red vio	1.00	1.00
C174	AP46	1col olive	1.85	1.50
C175	AP46	2col red brn	3.00	2.25
C176	AP47	5col org yel	5.00	4.25
C177	AP47	10col brt bl	11.00	8.50
		Nos. C168-C177 (10)	23.65	18.85

50th anniversary of National Theater.

No. C150 Surcharged in Carmine

HABILITADO
PARA
₡ 0.35

1948, Apr. 21

C178	AP43	35c on 40c red org & blk	45	45

Exists with surcharge inverted.

Portrait Type of 1943–47.

Designs: 5c, Salvador Lara. 15c, Carlos Duran.

1948 Engraved *Perf. 12*

C179	A109	5c sepia	15	6
C180	A109	10c ol brn	15	10
C181	A109	15c violet	12	10

Nos. C88B, C120, C89A and C90A Surcharged in Carmine or Black

1824-1949
125 Aniversario
de la Anexión
Guanacaste
₡ 0.55

Perf. 12½, 12

1949, Aug. 28 Unwmkd.

C182	A109	35c on 1.05col bis brn	25	20
C183	AP33	50c on 1col blk & car	40	35
a.		2nd & 3rd lines both read "125 Aniversario"	7.50	7.50
C184	A109	55c on 1.15col grn	65	55
C185	A109	55c on 1.40col org yel (Bk)	65	50

Issued to commemorate the 125th anniversary of the annexation of the province of Guanacaste.

Overprint differs on No. C183, with "Guanacaste" in capitals, and lower case "a" in "Anexión."

The variety "I" for "1" in "Anexion" is found on Nos. C182, C184 and C185.

Symbols of U.P.U.
AP48

1950, Jan. 11 Photo. *Perf. 11½*

C186	AP48	15c lil rose	20	10
C187	AP48	25c chlky bl	25	10
C188	AP48	1col gray grn	50	20

Issued to commemorate the 75th anniversary of the formation of the Universal Postal Union.

Battle of El Tejar, Cartago
AP49

Occupation of Limón
AP50

Bull (Cattle Raising)
AP51

Designs: 25c, Lucha ranch. 35c, Trenches of San Isidro Battalion. 55c and 75c, Observation post. 80c and 1col, Dr. Carlos Luis Valverde.

Inscribed: "Guerra de Liberacion Nacional 1948."

Engraved; Center Photogravure.

1950, July 20 *Perf. 12½*

Center in Black.

C189	AP49	15c brt car	20	10
C190	AP50	20c dl grn	30	20
C191	AP49	25c dl bl	35	25
C192	AP49	35c chestnut	40	25
C193	AP49	55c lilac	80	35
C194	AP49	75c red org	1.25	50
C195	AP50	80c gray	1.25	75
C196	AP50	1col org yel	1.75	85
		Nos. C189-C196 (8)	6.30	3.25

Issued to commemorate the second anniversary of the War for National Liberation.

Inscribed: "Feria Nacional Agricola Ganadera e Industrial Cartago 1950."

1950, July 27

Designs: 1c, 10c, 2col, Bull. 2c, 30c and 3col, Tuna fishing. 3c and 65c, Pineapple. 5c, 50c and 5col, Bananas. 45c, 80c and 10col, Coffee picker.

Center in Black.

C197	AP51	1c brt grn	10	8
C198	AP51	2c brt bl	10	8
C199	AP51	3c chocolate	10	8
C200	AP51	5c dp ultra	10	8
C201	AP51	10c green	15	8
C202	AP51	30c purple	30	18
C203	AP51	45c vermilion	35	25
C204	AP51	50c bl gray	50	15
C205	AP51	65c dk bl	60	35
C206	AP51	80c dp rose	1.25	1.00
C207	AP51	2col org yel	3.50	3.00
C208	AP51	3col blue	5.00	5.00
C209	AP51	5col carmine	11.00	11.00
C210	AP51	10col dp cl	11.00	11.00
		Nos. C197-C210 (14)	34.05	32.33

Issued to publicize the National Agricultural, Livestock and Industrial Fair, Cartago, 1950.

Queen Isabella I and Caravels of Columbus
AP52

Engraved.

1952, Mar. 4 *Perf. 13* Unwmkd.

C211	AP52	15c carmine	20	10
C212	AP52	20c orange	30	15
C213	AP52	25c ultra	40	10
C214	AP52	55c dp grn	1.00	40
C215	AP52	2col violet	2.50	75
		Nos. C211-C215 (5)	4.40	1.50

Issued to commemorate the 500th anniversary of the birth of Queen Isabella I of Spain.

Mail Plane Type of 1934.

1952-53 *Perf. 12.*

C216	AP8	5c blue	25	10
C217	AP8	10c green	25	10
C218	AP8	15c car rose ('53)	30	10
C219	AP8	35c purple	75	20

Nos. C149–C151, C153 Surcharged in Red: "HABILITADO PARA CINCO CENTIMOS 1953"

1953, Apr. 24 *Perf. 12½*

Center in Black.

C220	AP43	5c on 30c dp ultra	1.25	1.10
C221	AP43	5c on 40c red org	10	10
C222	AP43	5c on 45c vio	10	10
C223	AP43	5c on 65c brn org	30	25

Nos. C161-C163 Surcharged in Black

15—o—15

1953, Apr. 11 *Perf. 12*

C224	A122	15c on 30c car rose	25	20
C225	A122	15c on 45c red brn	25	15
C226	A122	15c on 65c org yel	25	15

Refinery of Vegetable Oils and Fats
AP53

Industries: 10c, Pottery. 15c, Sugar. 20c, Soap. 25c, Lumber. 30c, Matches. 35c, Textiles. 40c, Leather. 45c, Tobacco. 50c, Preserving. 55c, Canning. 60c, General. 65c, Metals. 75c, Pharmaceuticals. 1col, Paper. 2col, Rubber. 3col, Airplane maintenance. 5col, Marble. 10col, Beer.

Engraved; Center Photogravure

1954 *Perf. 13x12½* Unwmkd.

Center in Black

C227	AP53	5c red	10	6
C228	AP53	10c dk bl	15	6
C229	AP53	15c green	12	6
C230	AP53	20c violet	15	10
C231	AP53	25c magenta	15	10
C232	AP53	30c purple	45	30
C233	AP53	35c red vio	25	12
C234	AP53	40c black	40	25
C235	AP53	45c dk grn	75	35
C236	AP53	50c vio brn	50	15
C237	AP53	55c yellow	35	12
C238	AP53	60c brown	90	50
C239	AP53	65c carmine	1.10	75
C240	AP53	75c violet	1.65	65
C241	AP53	1col blue	50	30
a.		Imperf., pair	110.00	
C242	AP53	2col rose pink	1.50	90
C243	AP53	3col ol grn	2.25	1.50
C244	AP53	5col black	3.50	1.25
C245	AP53	10col yellow	10.00	8.50
		Nos. C227-C245 (19)	24.77	16.02

See also Nos. C252–C255A.

The indexes in each volume of the Scott Catalogue contain many listings which help to identify stamps.

Globe and Rotary Emblem
AP54

Map of Costa Rica
AP55

Designs: 25c, Hand protecting boy. 40c, 2col, Hospital. 45c, Globe and palm leaves. 60c, Lighthouse.

1956, Feb. 7 Engraved. *Perf. 12*

C246	AP54	10c green	15	6
C247	AP54	25c dk bl	20	18
C248	AP54	40c dk brn	50	40
C249	AP54	45c brt red	35	30
C250	AP54	60c dk red vio	40	35
C251	AP54	2col yel org	1.00	70
		Nos. C246-C251 (6)	2.60	1.99

Issued to commemorate the 50th anniversary of Rotary International (in 1955).

Industries Type of 1954

Engraved; Center Photogravure

Designs: 80c, Pharmaceuticals. Other designs as in 1954.

1956-59 Center in Black *Perf. 12*

C252	AP53	5c ultra	20	6
C253	AP53	10c vio bl	20	6
C254	AP53	15c org yel	20	6
C255	AP53	75c red org	40	25

Perf. 13x12½

C255A	AP53	80c pur & gray ('59)	70	60
		Nos. C252-C255A (5)	1.70	1.03

1957, June 21 Engr. *Perf. 13½x13*

Designs: 10c, Map of Guanacaste. 15c, Inn. 20c, House of Santa Rosa. 25c, Gen. Jose Manuel Quiros. 30c, Old Presidential Palace. 35c, Joaquin Bernardo Calvo. 40c, Luis Molina. 45c, Gen. Jose Joaquin Mora. 50c, Gen. Jose Maria Canas. 55c, Juan Santamaria monument. 60c, National monument. 65c, Antonio Vallerriestra. 70c, Ramon Castilla y Marquesado. 75c, San Carlos fortress. 80c, Francisco Maria Oreamuno. 1col, Pres. Juan Rafael Mora.

C256	AP55	5c lt bl	8	6
C257	AP55	10c green	12	8
C258	AP55	15c dp org	10	8
C259	AP55	20c lt brn	20	12
C260	AP55	25c vio bl	20	15
C261	AP55	30c violet	30	20
C262	AP55	35c car rose	30	20
C263	AP55	40c slate	30	20
C264	AP55	45c rose red	35	25
C265	AP55	50c ultra	35	25
C266	AP55	55c ocher	60	25
C267	AP55	60c brt car	45	35
C268	AP55	65c carmine	50	35
C269	AP55	70c org yel	65	45
C270	AP55	75c emerald	60	40
C271	AP55	80c dk brn	70	50
C272	AP55	1col black	75	50
		Nos. C256-C272 (17)	6.55	4.39

Centenary of War of 1856-57.

Cleto Gonzalez Viquez
AP56

Highway and Gonzalez Viquez
AP57

Designs: 10c, Ricardo Jimenez Oreamuno. 20c, Puntarenas wharf and Jimenez. 35c, Post and Telegraph Bldg. and Jimenez. 55c, Pipeline and Gonzalez Viquez. 80c, National Library and Gonzalez Viquez. 1col, Electric train and Jimenez. 2col, Gonzales and Jimenez.

1959 Engraved. *Perf. 13½*

C274	AP56	5c car & ultra	6	6
C275	AP56	10c red & gray	6	6

Perf. 13½x13

C276	AP57	15c dk bl grn & blk	6	6
C277	AP57	20c car & brn	15	10
C278	AP57	35c rose lil & bl	20	15
C279	AP57	55c ol & vio	40	30
C280	AP57	80c ultra	60	50
C281	AP57	1col org & mar	60	45
C282	AP57	2col gray & mar	1.50	1.25
		Nos. C274-C282 (9)	3.63	2.93

Soccer
AP58

Designs: Various soccer scenes.

Photogravure.

1960, March 7 *Perf. 13½* Unwmkd.

C283	AP58	10c black	10	8
C284	AP58	25c ultra	20	15
C285	AP58	35c red org	25	20
C286	AP58	50c red brn	30	25
C287	AP58	85c Prus grn	1.00	75
C288	AP58	5col dp cl	3.25	3.25
		Nos. C283-C288 (6)	5.10	4.68

Souvenir Sheet.

Imperf.

C289	AP58	2col blue	1.50	1.50

3rd Pan-American Soccer Games, San José, March, 1960.

Nos. C283-C288 exist imperf.

No. C289 measures 137x80mm. with black marginal inscription.

WRY Uprooted Oak Emblem
AP59

1960, Apr. 7 *Perf. 11½* Unwmkd.

Granite Paper

C290	AP59	35c vio bl, blk & yel	30	25
C291	AP59	85c blk & brt pink	60	50

Issued to publicize World Refugee Year, July 1, 1959-June 30, 1960.

Banner and "OEA"
AP60

Designs: 35c, "OEA" in oval. 55c, Clasped hands. 2col, "OEA" and map of Americas. 5col, Flags forming bird. 10col, Map of Costa Rica, flags and "OEA."

1960, Aug. 15 Litho. *Perf. 10*

C292	AP60	25c blk & multi	20	15
	a.	Multi. impression sideways	30.00	
C293	AP60	35c multi	50	45
	a.	Pair, imperf. between	65.00	
C294	AP60	55c multi	75	60
C295	AP60	5col multi	4.50	4.00
C296	AP60	10col blk & multi	7.50	6.00
		Nos. C292-C296 (5)	13.45	11.20

Souvenir Sheet

Imperf.

C297	AP60	2col multi	3.25	3.25

Nos. C292-C297 issued to commemorate the Pan-American Conference, San Jose, Aug. 15.

No. C297 measures 124x76½mm. with flags of American nations forming border.

St. Louisa de Marillac and Orphanage—AP61

St. Vincent de Paul
AP62

Designs: 25c, St. Vincent and old seminary. 50c, St. Louisa and sickroom. 1col, St. Vincent and new seminary.

1960, Oct. 26 Engr. *Perf. 14x13½*

C298	AP61	10c green	10	10
C299	AP61	25c carmine	10	10
C300	AP61	50c dk bl	35	25
C301	AP61	1col brn org	60	50
C302	AP62	5col brown	3.00	2.50
		Nos. C298-C302 (5)	4.15	3.45

Issued to commemorate the 300th anniversary of the deaths of St. Vincent de Paul (1581?-1660) and St. Louisa de Marillac (1591-1660). Exist imperf.

Runner—AP63

Sports: 2c, Woman swimmer. 3c, Bicyclist. 4c, Weight lifter. 5c, Woman tennis player. 10c, Boxers. 25c, Soccer player. 85c, Basketball player. 1col, Baseball batter. 5col, Romulus and Remus statue. 10col, Pistol marksman.

Perf. 13½x14

1960, Dec. 14 Photo. Unwmkd.

Designs in Black

C303	AP63	1c brt yel	5	5
C304	AP63	2c lt ultra	5	5
C305	AP63	3c dp rose	5	5
C306	AP63	4c yellow	5	5
C307	AP63	5c brt yel grn	5	5
C308	AP63	10c pink	8	8
C309	AP63	25c lt bl grn	15	15
C310	AP63	85c lilac	1.50	1.25
C311	AP63	1col gray	1.75	1.50
C312	AP63	10col lt vio	15.00	12.00
		Nos. C303-C312 (10)	18.73	15.23

Souvenir Sheets

Perf. 14x13½, Imperf.

C313	AP63	5col multi	5.50	5.50

17th Olympic Games, Rome, Aug. 25-Sept. 11.

No. C313 has gold marginal inscription. Size: 100x65mm.

Nos. C303-C312 exist imperf.

No. C255 Surcharged and Overprinted in Blue or Ultramarine:

"XV Campeonato Mundial de Beisbol de Aficionados"

Engraved and Photogravure

1961, Apr. 21 *Perf. 1*

Center in Black

C314	AP53	25c on 75c red org (Bl)	30	1.
C315	AP53	75c red org (U)	85	3

15th Amateur Baseball Championships.

Alberto Brenes C.
AP64

Miguel Obregon
AP65

Portraits: No. C317, Manuel Aguilar. No. C318, Agustin Gutierrez L. No. C319, Vicente Herrera.

1961, June 12 Photo. *Perf. 12*

C316	AP64	10c dp cl	10	10
C317	AP64	10c blue	10	10
C318	AP64	25c brt vio	20	15
C319	AP64	25c gray	20	15

First Continental Congress of Lawyers, San José, June 11-15. Exist imperf.

See also Nos. C330-C333.

1961, July 19 Litho. *Perf. 13½*

C320	AP65	10c Prus grn	8	8

Birth centenary of Prof. Miguel Obregon L. Exists imperf.

U.N. Food and Agriculture Organization
AP66

United Nations Organizations: 20c, World Health Organization. 25c, Int. Labor Organization. 30c, Int. Telecommunication Union. 35c, World Meteorological Organization. 45c, UNESCO. 85c, Int. Civil Aviation Organization. 5col, "United Nations" holding the world. 10col, Int. Bank for Reconstruction and Development.

Engraved

1961, Oct. 24 *Perf. 11½* Unwmkd.

C321	AP66	10c lt grn	12	12
C322	AP66	20c orange	25	20
C323	AP66	25c Prus grn	30	25
C324	AP66	30c dk bl	30	25
C325	AP66	35c car rose	1.40	35
C326	AP66	45c violet	50	30
C327	AP66	85c blue	1.10	85
C328	AP66	10col dk sl grn	8.00	6.50
		Nos. C321-C328 (8)	11.97	8.82

Souvenir Sheet

Imperf.

C329	AP66	5col ultra	4.50	4.50

Nos. C321-C329 issued for United Nations Day, Oct. 24.

No. C329 contains one imperf. stamp and has ultramarine border and marginal inscription. Size: 100x65mm.

Portrait Type of 1961

Portraits: No. C330, Dr. José Maria Soto Alfaro. No. C331, Dr. Elias Rojas Roman. No. C332, Dr. Andres Saenz Llorente. No. C333, Dr. Juan José Ulloa Giralt.

1961 Photogravure *Perf. 13½*

C330	AP64	10c bl grn	8	8
C331	AP64	10c violet	10	8

C332	AP64	25c dk gray	20	12
C333	AP64	25c dp cl	20	12

Issued to commemorate the ninth Congress of Physicians of Central America and Panama.

Nos. C229, C236 and C280 Surcharged in Black, Orange or Red.

Engraved; Center Photogravure.

1962 ***Perf. 13x12½, 13½x13***

C334	AP53	10c ("10") on 15c grn & blk	10	10
C334A	AP53	10c ("c0.10") on 15c grn & blk (R)	10	10
C335	AP53	25c on 15c grn & blk	20	12
C336	AP53	35c on 50c vio brn & blk (O)	30	20

Engraved

C337	AP57	85c on 80c ultra (R)	85	65
		Nos. C334-C337 (5)	1.55	1.17

Nos. C324 and C282 Overprinted in Red: "II CONVENCION FILATELICA CENTROAMERICANA SETIEMBRE 1962"

1962, Sept. 12 ***Perf. 11½, 13½x13***

C338	AP66	30c dk bl	65	50
C339	AP57	2col gray & mar	2.00	1.40

Issued to commemorate the second Central American Philatelic Convention.

Revenue Stamp Surcharged with New Values and "CORREO AEREO" in Red

1962 **Engraved** ***Perf. 12***

C341	A124	25c on 2c emer	12	10
C342	A124	35c on 2c emer	20	15
C343	A124	45c on 2c emer	35	30
C344	A124	85c on 2c emer	65	55

Arms and Malaria Eradication Emblem
AP67

1963, Feb. 14 **Photo.** ***Perf. 11½***

C345	AP67	25c brt rose	20	12
C346	AP67	35c brn org	25	20
C347	AP67	45c ultra	40	30
C348	AP67	85c bl grn	65	55
C349	AP67	1col dk bl	85	70
		Nos. C345-C349 (5)	2.35	1.87

Issued for the World Health Organization drive to eradicate malaria.

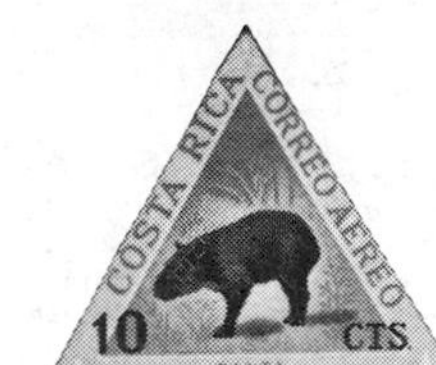

Central American Tapir
AP68

Designs: 5c, Paca. 25c, Jaguar. 30c, Ocelot. 35c, Whitetail deer. 40c, Manatee. 85c, White-throated capuchin monkey. 5col, White-lipped peccary.

Photogravure

1963, May ***Perf. 13½*** **Unwmkd.**

C354	AP68	5c yel ol & brn	8	8
C355	AP68	10c org & sl	8	8
C356	AP68	25c bl & yel	20	10
C357	AP68	30c lt yel grn & brn	35	30
C358	AP68	35c bis & red brn	50	25
C359	AP68	40c emer & sl bl	60	40
C360	AP68	85c grn & blk	90	60
C361	AP68	5col gray grn & choc	5.00	4.00
		Nos. C354-C361 (8)	7.71	5.81

Stamp of 1863 and Packet "William Le Lacheur"
AP69

Issue of 1863 and: 2col, Recaredo Bonilla Carrillo, Postmaster, 1862–63. 3col, Burros, overland mail transport, 1839. 10col, Burro railway car.

1963, June 26 **Lithographed**

C362	AP69	25c dl rose & chlky bl	10	8
C363	AP69	2col gray bl & org	1.75	1.25
C364	AP69	3col bis & emer	3.00	2.25
C365	AP69	10col dl grn & ocher	9.00	6.00

Centenary of Costa Rica's stamps.

Souvenir Sheets

Stamps of 1863 and San José Postmark—AP70

Perf. 13½, Imperf.

1963, June 26 **Unwmkd.**

C366	AP70	5col bl, red, grn & org	5.00	5.00

Issued to commemorate the centenary of Costa Rica's stamps. Orange marginal inscription. Size of stamp: 29x50mm. Size of sheet: 60x100mm.

In 1968 copies of No. C366 were overprinted "2-4 Agosto 1968" and "III Exposicion Filatelica Nacional / 'Costa Rica 68'." Price $6.

Animal Type of 1963 Surcharged in Red

Designs: 10c on 1c, Little anteater. 25c on 2c, Gray fox. 35c on 3c, Armadillo. 85c on 4c, Great anteater.

1963, Sept. 14 **Photo.** ***Perf. 13½***

C367	AP68	10c on 1c brt grn & org brn	25	10
C368	AP68	25c on 2c org yel & ol grn	25	10
C369	AP68	35c on 3c bluish grn & brn	35	15
C370	AP68	85c on 4c dp rose & dk brn	65	30

No. C370 exists without surcharge. Price, $50.

President John F. Kennedy
AP71

Ancestral Figure
AP72

Portraits—Presidents: 25c, Francisco J. Orlich, Costa Rica. 30c, Julio A. Rivera, El Salvador. 35c, Miguel Ydigoras F., Guatemala. 85c, Dr. Ramon Villeda M., Honduras. 1col, Luis A. Somoza, Nicaragua. 3col, Roberto F. Chiari, Panama.

1963, Dec. 7 ***Perf. 14*** **Unwmkd.**

Portraits in Black Brown

C371	AP71	25c vio brn	15	10
C372	AP71	30c brt lil rose	20	15
C373	AP71	35c ocher	25	20
C374	AP71	85c gray bl	60	40
C375	AP71	1col org brn	60	45
C376	AP71	3col lt ol grn	3.00	2.00
C377	AP71	5col gray	4.00	3.00
		Nos. C371-C377 (7)	8.80	6.30

Issued to commemorate the meeting of Central American Presidents with Pres. John F. Kennedy, San José, March 18–20, 1963.

1963–64 **Photo.** ***Perf. 12***

Ancient Art: 5c, Dog (horiz.). 10c, Ornamental stool (horiz.). 25c, Male figure. 30c, Ceremonial dancer. 35c, Ceramic vase. 50c, Frog. 55c, Bell. 75c, Six-limbed figure. 85c, Seated man. 90c, Bird-shaped jug. 1col, Twin human beaker (horiz.). 2col, Alligator (horiz.). 3col, Twin-tailed lizard. 5col, Figure under arch. 10col, Polished stone figure.

C378	AP72	5c lt yel grn & Prus grn	5	5
C379	AP72	10c buff & dk grn	6	6
C380	AP72	25c rose & dk brn	12	9
C381	AP72	30c ocher & Prus grn ('64)	15	8
C382	AP72	35c sal & sl grn	18	12
C383	AP72	45c lt bl & dk brn	20	12
C384	AP72	50c dl bl & dk brn	25	18
C385	AP72	55c yel grn & dk brn	30	18
C386	AP72	75c ocher & dk red brn	30	20
C387	AP72	85c yel & red brn	85	55
C388	AP72	90c cit & red brn	1.10	55
C389	AP72	1col lt bl & dk brn	60	35
C390	AP72	2col buff & dk grn	1.00	65
C391	AP72	3col yel grn & dk brn	1.75	1.10
C392	AP72	5col cit & sep	3.00	2.00
C393	AP72	10col rose lil & sl grn	5.00	4.50
		Nos. C378-C393 (16)	14.91	10.78

Flags of Central American States
AP73

Alfredo Gonzalez F.
AP74

Central American Independence Issue

1964 ***Perf. 14***

C394	AP73	30c bl, gray, red & blk	50	40

Nos. C381, C394 and C387 Surcharged

¢ 0.05

1964, Oct. ***Perf. 12, 14***

C395	AP72	5c on 30c ocher & Prus grn	6	6
C396	AP73	15c on 30c bl, gray, red & blk	6	6
C397	AP72	15c on 85c yel & red brn	10	6

No. C388 Surcharged: "C 0.15 / CONFERENCIA POSTAL / DE PARIS—1864"

1964 ***Perf. 12***

C398	AP72	15c on 90c cit & red brn	12	8

Paris Postal Conference.

1965, June **Photo.** ***Perf. 12***

C399	AP74	35c dk bl grn	15	10

Issued to commemorate the 50th anniversary of the National Bank and to honor Alfredo Gonzalez F., first governor of the bank.

No. C390 Overprinted: "75 ANIVERSARIO / ASILO CHAPUI / 1890 – 1965"

1965, Aug. 14 ***Perf. 12*** **Unwmkd.**

C400	AP72	2col buff & dk grn	1.25	75

Issued to commemorate the 75th anniversary of Chapui Asylum, San José.

Girl, FAO Emblem and Hands Holding Grain
AP75

Church of Nicoya
AP76

Designs (FAO Emblem and): 15c, Map of Costa Rica and silos (horiz.). 50c, World population chart and children. 1 col, Plane over map of Costa Rica (horiz.).

1965 **Lithographed** ***Perf. 14***

C401	AP75	15c lt brn & blk	10	8
C402	AP75	35c blk & yel	20	15
C403	AP75	50c ultra & dk grn	30	20
C404	AP75	1col grn, blk & sil	50	30

Issued for the "Freedom from Hunger" campaign of the U.N. Food and Agriculture Organization.

1965, Dec. 20 ***Perf. 13½x14***

Designs: 5c, Leonidas Briceno B. 15c, Scroll dated "25 de Julio de 1964." 35c, Map of Guanacaste and Nicoya peninsula. 50c, Dancing couple. 1col, Map showing local products.

C405	AP76	5c red brn & blk	5	5
C406	AP76	10c bl & gray	5	5
C407	AP76	15c bis & sl	6	6
C408	AP76	35c bl & sl	15	10
C409	AP76	50c gray & vio bl	25	15
C410	AP76	1col buff & sl	60	40
		Nos. C405-C410 (6)	1.16	81

Acquisition of the Nicoya territory.

Runner and Olympic Rings
AP77

Pres. Kennedy Speaking in San José Cathedral
AP78

1965, Dec. 23 ***Perf. 13x13½***

Olympic Rings and Emblem: 10c, Bicyclists. 40c, Judo. 65c, Basketball. 80c, Soccer. 1col, Hands holding torches, and Mt. Fuji.

C411	AP77	5c bis & multi	6	6
C412	AP77	10c lt lil & multi	6	6

C413	AP77	40c multi	20	15
C414	AP77	65c lem & multi	35	20
C415	AP77	80c tan & multi	50	30
C416	AP77	1col multi	65	40
a.		Souv. sheet of 2	2.25	2.25
		Nos. C411-C416 (6)	1.82	1.17

Issued to commemorate the 18th Olympic Games, Tokyo, Oct. 10–25, 1964. No. C416a contains two 1col stamps, one like No. C416, the other with gray background replacing yellow orange. Dark brown marginal inscription and red control number. Size: 68x93mm. Sheet also exists imperf.

Perf. 13½x13, 13x13½

1965, Dec. 23 Litho. Unwmkd.

Designs: 45c, Friendship 7 capsule circling globe, and Kennedy (horiz.). 85c, Kennedy and John, Jr. 1col, Curtis-Lee Mansion and flame from Kennedy grave, Arlington, Va.

C417	AP78	45c brt bl & lil	25	20
C418	AP78	55c org & brt bl	35	25
C419	AP78	85c gray, dk brn & red brn	55	35
C420	AP78	1col multi	50	40
a.		Souv. sheet of 2	1.50	1.50

Issued in memory of President John F. Kennedy (1917–63). No. C420a contains two 1col stamps, one like No. C420, the other with green background replacing dark blue. Dark gray marginal inscription and red control number. Size: 68x93mm. Sheet also exists imperf.

Firemen with Hoses

AP79

Designs: 5c, Fire engine "Knox" (horiz.). 10c, 1866 fire pump. 35c, Fireman's badge. 50c, Emblem and flags of Confederation of Central American Fire Brigades.

1965, March 12 Litho. *Perf. 11*

C421	AP79	5c blk & red	30	15
C422	AP79	10c bis & red	40	15
C423	AP79	15c blk, red brn & red	50	30
C424	AP79	35c blk & yel	70	40
C425	AP79	50c dk bl & red	1.25	60
		Nos. C421-C425 (5)	3.15	1.60

Centenary of San José Fire Brigade.

Nos. C381, C383, C386 and C418-C419 Surcharged

C0.15
a

C 0.50
b

1966 Photogravure *Perf. 12*

C426	AP72(a)	15c on 30c ocher & Prus grn	10	8
C427	AP72(a)	15c on 45c lt bl & dk brn	10	8
C428	AP72(a)	35c on 75c ocher & dk red brn	20	12

Perf. 13x13½

Lithographed

C429	AP78(a)	35c on 55c org & brt bl	20	12
C430	AP78(b)	50c on 85c multi	35	20
		Nos. C426-C430 (5)	95	60

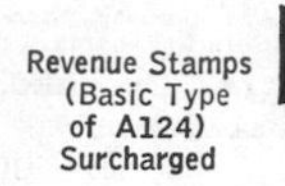

Revenue Stamps (Basic Type of A124) Surcharged

1966, Dec. Engraved *Perf. 12*

C431	A124	15c on 5c bl	10	6
C432	A124	35c on 10c cl	22	12
C433	A124	50c on 20c rose red	35	20

Central Bank of Costa Rica

AP80

1967, Mar. Litho. *Perf. 11*

C434	AP80	5c brt grn	7	5
C435	AP80	15c brown	10	6
C436	AP80	35c scarlet	20	12

Power Lines

AP81

Telecommunications Building, San Pedro

AP82

Designs: 15c, Telephone Central. 25c, La Garita Dam. 35c, Rio Mache Reservoir. 50c, Cachi Dam.

1967, Apr. 24 Litho. *Perf. 11*

C437	AP81	5c dk gray	7	5
C438	AP82	10c brt rose	7	5
C439	AP81	15c brn org	8	6
C440	AP82	25c brt ultra	13	8
C441	AP82	35c brt grn	20	10
C442	AP82	50c red brn	35	20
		Nos. C437-C442 (6)	90	54

Electrification program.

Chondrorhyncha Aromatica

AP83

Institute Emblem

AP84

Orchids: 10c, Miltonia endresii. 15c, Stanhopea cirrhata. 25c, Trichopilia suavis. 35c, Odontoglossum schlieperianum. 50c, Cattleya skinneri. 1col, Cattleya dowiana. 2col, Odontoglossum chiriquense.

1967, June 15 Engr. *Perf. 13x13½*

Orchids in Natural Colors

C443	AP83	5c multi	12	6
C444	AP83	10c ol & multi	20	6
C445	AP83	15c multi	20	8
C446	AP83	25c multi	40	15
C447	AP83	35c dl vio & multi	40	20
C448	AP83	50c brn & multi	50	25
C449	AP83	1col vio & multi	1.00	50
C450	AP83	2col dk ol bis & multi	2.00	1.00
		Nos. C443-C450 (8)	4.82	2.30

Issued for the University Library.

1967, Oct. 6 Litho. *Perf. 13x13½*

C451	AP84	50c vio bl, lt bl & bl	20	18

Issued to commemorate the 25th anniversary of the Inter-American Agriculture Institute.

Church of Solitude

AP85

LACSA Emblem

AP86

Costa Rican Churches: 10c, Basilica of Santo Domingo, Heredia. 15c, Cathedral of Tilaran. 25c, Cathedral of Alajuela. 30c, Mercy Church. 35c, Basilica of Our Lady of Angels. 40c, Church of St. Raphael, Heredia. 45c, Ujarras ruins. 50c, Ruins of parish church, Cartago. 55c, Cathedral of San José. 65c, Parish church, Puntarenas. 75c, Church of Orosi. 80c, Cathedral of St. Isidro, the General. 85c, St. Ramon Church. 90c, Church of the Abandonned. 1col, Coronado Church. 2col, Church of St. Teresita. 3col, Parish Church, Heredia. 5col, Carmelite Church. 10col, Limon Cathedral.

1967, Dec. 15 Engr. *Perf. 12½*

C452	AP85	5c green	5	5
C453	AP85	10c blue	5	5
C454	AP85	15c lilac	6	6
C455	AP85	25c dl yel	10	8
C456	AP85	30c org brn	12	10
C457	AP85	35c lt bl	15	12
C458	AP85	40c dp org	15	12
C459	AP85	45c dl bl grn	16	15
C460	AP85	50c olive	18	18
C461	AP85	55c brown	20	18
C462	AP85	65c car rose	35	30
C463	AP85	75c sepia	40	35
C464	AP85	80c yellow	65	50
C465	AP85	85c vio blk	75	50
C466	AP85	90c emerald	75	60
C467	AP85	1col slate	60	35
C468	AP85	2col brt grn	3.00	2.00
C469	AP85	3col orange	4.00	3.00
C470	AP85	5col vio bl	4.00	3.00
C471	AP85	10col carmine	5.00	4.00
		Nos. C452-C471 (20)	20.72	15.69

See Nos. C561–C576.

Perf. 13x13½, 13½x13

1967, Dec. 12 Litho. & Engraved

Design: 45c, LACSA emblem and jet (horiz.). 50c, Decorated wheel and anniversary emblem.

C472	AP86	40c ultra, grnsh bl & gold	15	15
C473	AP86	45c blk, pale grn, ultra & gold	18	15
C474	AP86	50c bl & multi	20	18

Issued to commemorate the 20th anniversary (in 1966) of Lineas Aereas Costaricenses, LACSA, Costa Rican Airlines.

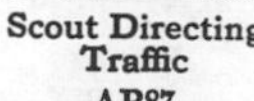

Scout Directing Traffic

AP87

Runner

AP88

Designs: 25c, Campfire under palm tree. 35c, Flag of Costa Rica, Scout flag and emblem. 50c, Encampment (horiz.). 65c, Photograph of first Scout troop (horiz.).

Lithographed and Engraved

1968, Mar. 15 *Perf. 13*

C475	AP87	15c lt bl, blk & lt brn	12	8
C476	AP87	25c lt ultra, vio bl & org	20	12
C477	AP87	35c bl & multi	30	20
C478	AP87	50c multi	35	25
C479	AP87	65c sal, dk bl & brn	50	30
		Nos. C475-C479 (5)	1.47	95

Costa Rican Boy Scouts, 50th anniversary.

1968 Lithographed *Perf. 10x11*

Sports: 40c, Women's running. 55c, Boxing. 65c, Bicycling. 75c, Weight lifting. 1col, High diving. 3col, Rifle shooting.

C481	AP88	30c multi	15	10
C482	AP88	40c multi	25	15
C483	AP88	55c multi	35	25
C484	AP88	65c lil & multi	45	25
C485	AP88	75c multi	45	25
C486	AP88	1col multi	50	35
C487	AP88	3col multi	2.25	1.25
		Nos. C481-C487 (7)	4.40	2.60

Issued to commemorate the 19th Olympic Games, Mexico City, Oct. 12–27.

Philatelic Exhibition Emblem

AP89

1969, June 5 Litho. *Perf. 11x10*

C488	AP89	35c multi	15	10
C489	AP89	40c pink & multi	18	12
C490	AP89	50c lt bl & multi	22	15
C491	AP89	2col multi	80	60

Issued to publicize the 4th National Philatelic Exhibition, San José, June 5–8.

ILO Emblem

AP90

1969, Oct. 29 Litho. *Perf. 10*

C492	AP90	35c bl grn & blk	18	10
C493	AP90	50c scar & blk	27	15

Issued to commemorate the 50th anniversary of the International Labor Organization.

Soccer—AP91

Designs: 65c, Soccer ball, map of North and Central America. 85c, Soccer player. 1 col, Two players in action.

1969, Nov. 23 Litho. *Perf. 11x10*

C494	AP91	65c gray & multi	30	20
C495	AP91	75c multi	30	20
C496	AP91	85c multi	38	25
C497	AP91	1col pink & multi	45	30

Issued to publicize the 4th Soccer Championships (CONCACAF), Nov. 23–Dec. 7.

Stylized Crab—AP92

1970, May 14 Litho. *Perf. 12½*

C498	AP92	10c blk & lil rose	5	5
C499	AP92	15c blk & yel	5	5
C500	AP92	50c blk & brn org	12	10
C501	AP92	1.10col blk & emer	27	20

Issued to publicize the 10th Inter-American Cancer Congress, May 22–29.

Costa Rica No. 124, Magnifying Glass and Stamps AP93

Design: 2col, Father and son with stamps and album.

1970, Sept. 14 Litho. *Perf. 11*

C502	AP93	1col ultra, brn & car rose	40	20
C503	AP93	2col blk, pink & ultra	70	50

The 5th National Philatelic Exhibition.

EXPO Emblem and Costa Rican Cart—AP94

Designs (EXPO Emblem and): 10c, Japanese floral arrangement (vert.). 35c, Pavilion and Tower of the Sun. 40c, Japanese tea ceremony. 45c, Woman picking coffee (vert.). 55c, Earth seen from moon (vert.).

1970, Oct. 22 Litho. *Perf. 13x13½*

C504	AP94	10c multi	6	5
C505	AP94	15c grn & multi	9	6
C506	AP94	35c bl & multi	15	10
C507	AP94	40c gray & multi	20	12
C508	AP94	45c multi	20	15
C509	AP94	55c blk & multi	20	15
		Nos. C504-C509 (6)	90	63

Issued to commemorate EXPO '70 International Exhibition, Osaka, Japan, March 15–Sept. 13.

Escazu Valley, by Margarita Bertheau—AP95

Paintings: 25c, "Irazu," by Rafael A. Garcia (vert.). 80c, Shore landscape, by Teodorico Quiros. 1col, "The Other Face," by Cesar Valverde. 2.50col, Mother and Child, by Luis Daell (vert.).

1970, Nov. 4 Litho. *Perf. 12½*

C510	AP95	25c multi	75	50
C511	AP95	45c multi	75	50
C512	AP95	80c multi	1.00	80
C513	AP95	1col multi	1.00	90
C514	AP95	2.50col multi	2.50	1.50
		Nos. C510-C514 (5)	6.00	4.20

Arms of Costa Rica, 1964 AP96

Various Coats of Arms, dated: 10c, Nov. 27, 1906. 15c, Sept. 29, 1848. 25c, April 21, 1840. 35c, Nov. 22, 1824. 50c, Nov. 2, 1824. 1col, March 6, 1824. 2col, May 10, 1823.

1971, Feb. 10 Litho. *Perf. 14x13½*

C515	AP96	5c buff & multi	25	10
C516	AP96	10c multi	25	10
C517	AP96	15c yel & multi	30	12
C518	AP96	25c pink & multi	35	15
C519	AP96	35c multi	40	20
C520	AP96	50c rose & multi	45	20
C521	AP96	1col beige & multi	50	25
C522	AP96	2col multi	1.00	50
		Nos. C515-C522 (8)	3.50	1.62

National Theater AP97

1971, Apr. Litho. *Perf. 11*

C523	AP97	2col plum	50	40

Organization of American States meeting.

José Matias Delgado, Manuel José Arce AP98

Flag of Costa Rica AP99

Independence Leaders: 10c, Miguel Larreinaga and Manuel Antonio de la Cerda, Nicaragua. 15c, José Cecilio del Valle, Dionisio de Herrera, Honduras. 35c, Pablo Alvarado and Florencio del Castillo, Costa Rica. 50c, Antonio Larrazabal and Pedro Molina, Guatemala. 2col, Costa Rica coat of arms.

1971, Sept. 14 *Perf. 13*

C524	AP98	5c multi	5	5
C525	AP98	10c multi	5	5
C526	AP98	15c gray, brn & blk	6	5
C527	AP98	35c multi	15	12
C528	AP98	50c multi	15	12
C529	AP99	1col multi	25	15
C530	AP99	2col multi	50	40
		Nos. C524-C530 (7)	1.21	94

Sesquicentennial of Central American independence.

Soccer Federation Emblem AP100

Children of the World AP101

1971, Dec.

C531	AP100	50c multi	15	10
C532	AP100	60c multi	15	10

50th anniversary of Soccer Federation of Costa Rica.

1972, Jan. 11 *Perf. 12½*

C533	AP101	50c multi	15	10
C534	AP101	1.10col red & multi	30	25

25th anniversary (in 1971) of the United Nations International Children's Fund (UNICEF).

Tree of Guanacaste AP102

Designs: 40c, Hermitage, Liberia. 55c, Petroglyphs, Rincón Brujo. 60c, Painted head, sculpture from Curubandé (vert.).

1972, Feb. 28 *Perf. 11*

C535	AP102	20c brn, ol & brt grn	10	7
C536	AP102	40c brn & ol	15	10
C537	AP102	55c blk & brn	15	12
C538	AP102	60c blk, buff & ver	20	15

Bicentenary of the founding of the city of Liberia, Guanacaste.

Farm and Family AP103

Inter-American Exhibitions AP104

Designs: 45c, Cattle, dairy products and meat (horiz.). 50c, Kneeling figure with plant. 10col, Farmer and map of Americas.

1972, June 30 Litho. *Perf. 12½*

C539	AP103	20c multi	10	7
C540	AP103	45c multi	15	10
C541	AP103	50c dp yel, grn & blk	15	10
C542	AP103	10col brn, org & blk	2.50	1.50

30th anniversary of the Inter-American Institute of Agricultural Sciences.

1972, Aug. 26 Litho. *Perf. 13*

C543	AP104	50c org & brn	15	10
C544	AP104	2col bl & vio	50	40

4th Interamerican Philatelic Exhibition, EXFILBRA, Rio de Janeiro, Aug. 26–Sept. 2.

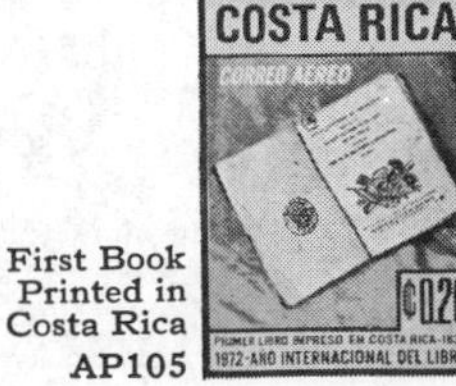

First Book Printed in Costa Rica AP105

Design: 50c, 5col, National Library (horiz.).

1972, Dec. 7 Litho. *Perf. 12½*

C545	AP105	20c brt bl	8	7
C546	AP105	50c gold & multi	15	10
C547	AP105	75c multi	20	15
C548	AP105	5col multi	1.25	1.00

International Book Year 1972.

Road to Irazú Volcano AP106

1972–73 *Perf. 11x11½, 11½x11*

Multicolored

C549	AP106	5c *like 20c*	5	5
C550	AP106	15c *Coco-Culebra Bay*	7	5
C551	AP106	20c *shown*	10	7
C552	AP106	25c *like 15c*	10	8
C553	AP106	40c *Manuel Antonio Beach*	15	10
C554	AP106	45c *Tourist Office emblem*	15	12
C555	AP106	50c *Lindora Lake*	15	12
C556	AP106	60c *San Jose P.O. (vert.)*	20	15
C557	AP106	80c *like 40c*	25	20
C558	AP106	90c *like 45c*	25	20
C559	AP106	1col *like 50c*	25	20
C560	AP106	2col *like 60c*	50	40
		Nos. C549-C560 (12)	2.22	1.74

Tourism year of the Americas.

Issue dates: 20c, 25c, 80c, 90c, 1col and 2col, Dec. 26, 1972. Others, Mar. 21, 1973.

Church Type of 1967

Designs as Before

1973, July 16 Engr. *Perf. 12½*

C561	AP85	5c sl grn	6	5
C562	AP85	10c olive	7	5
C563	AP85	15c orange	8	6
C564	AP85	25c brown	10	8
C565	AP85	30c rose cl	10	8
C566	AP85	35c violet	12	10
C567	AP85	40c brt grn	12	10
C568	AP85	45c dl vel	15	10
C569	AP85	50c rose mag	15	10
C570	AP85	55c blue	15	12
C571	AP85	65c black	20	15
C572	AP85	75c rose red	20	15
C573	AP85	80c yel grn	20	15
C574	AP85	85c lilac	25	20
C575	AP85	90c brt pink	25	20
C576	AP85	1col dk bl	25	20
		Nos. C561-C576 (16)	2.45	1.89

Human Rights Flame AP107

OAS Emblem AP108

1973 Photogravure *Perf. 10½*

C577	AP107	50c blk & red	15	10

25th anniversary of the Universal Declaration of Human Rights.

1973, Dec. 17 Litho. *Perf. 10½*

C578	AP108	20c dk bl & dp car	10	5

25th anniversary of the Organization of American States.

Joaquin Vargas Calvo
AP109

AP110

1974, Jan. 14

Multicolored

C579	AP109	20c	*shown*	10	6
C580	AP109	20c	*Alejandro Monestel*	10	6
C581	AP109	20c	*Julio Mata*	10	6
C582	AP109	60c	*Julio Fonseca*	20	15
C583	AP109	2col	*Rafael A. Chaves*	50	35
C584	AP109	5col	*Manuel M. Gutierrez*	1.25	1.00
			Nos. C579-C584 (6)	2.25	1.68

Costa Rican composers honored by the National Symphony Orchestra.

Revenue Stamps Overprinted "Habilitado para Correo Aereo"

1974, Apr. 5 Engraved *Perf. 12*

C585	AP110	50c	brown	15	10
C586	AP110	1col	violet	25	15
C587	AP110	2col	orange	50	30
C588	AP110	5col	olive	1.25	1.00

Telephone Building, San Pedro
AP111

EXFILMEX 74 Emblem
AP112

Designs: 65c, Rio Macho Control (horiz.). 85c, Turbines, Rio Macho Center. 1.25col, Cachi Dam and reservoir (horiz.). 2col, I.C.E. Headquarters.

1974, July 30 Litho. *Perf. 10½*

C589	AP111	50c	gold & multi	15	10
C590	AP111	65c	gold & multi	20	12
C591	AP111	85c	gold & multi	25	15
C592	AP111	1.25col	gold & multi	30	20
C593	AP111	2col	gold & multi	50	30
			Nos. C589-C593 (5)	1.40	87

25th anniversary of Costa Rican Electrical Institute (I.C.E.).

1974, Aug. 22 *Perf. 13*

C594	AP112	65c	green	20	15
C595	AP112	3col	lil rose	75	50

5th Inter-American Philatelic Exhibition, EXFILMEX-74 UPU, Mexico City, Oct. 26–Nov. 3.

Map of Costa Rica, 4-S Emblem
AP113

Design: 50c, Young harvesters and 4-S emblem.

1974, Oct. 7 Litho. *Perf. 12x11*

C596	AP113	20c	brt grn	10	5
C597	AP113	50c	multi	15	10

25th anniversary of 4-S Clubs of Costa Rica (similar to US 4-H Clubs).

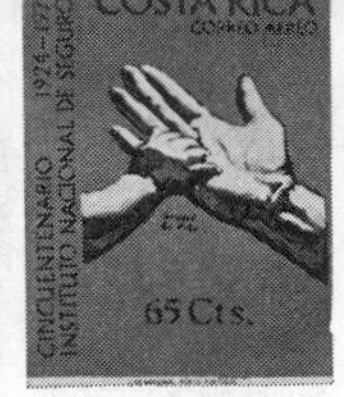

Roberto Brenes Mesen
AP114

"Life Insurance"
AP115

Designs: 85c, "Love and Death," manuscript (horiz.). 5col, Hands of writer.

1974, Oct. 14 Litho. *Perf. 10½*

C598	AP114	20c	blk & brn	10	5
C599	AP114	85c	blk & red	25	20
C600	AP114	5col	blk & red brn	1.25	1.00

Birth centenary of Roberto Brenes Mesen, educator and writer.

1974, Oct. 30 *Perf. 14*

Designs: 20c, Ricardo Jiménez Oreamuno and Tomás Soley Güell (horiz.). 50c, Harvest Insurance (hand holding shovel; horiz.). 85c, Maritime insurance (hand holding paper boat). 1.25col, INS emblem. 2col, Workers rehabilitation (arm with crutch). 2.50col, Workers' Compensation (hand holding wrench). 20col, Fire insurance (hands protecting house).

C601	AP115	20c	multi	9	5
C602	AP115	50c	multi	15	10
C603	AP115	65c	multi	15	10
C604	AP115	85c	multi	20	15
C605	AP115	1.25col	multi	30	20
C606	AP115	2col	multi	50	30
C607	AP115	2.50col	multi	65	50
C608	AP115	20col	multi	5.00	4.00
			Nos. C601-C608 (8)	7.04	5.40

Costa Rican Insurance Institute (Instituto Nacional de Seguros, INS), 50th anniversary.

WPY Emblem
AP116

Oscar J. Pinto F.
AP117

1974, Nov. 13 Litho. *Perf. 11x11½*

C609	AP116	2col	vio bl & red	50	30

World Population Year.

1974, Dec. 2 *Perf. 13*

Designs: 50c, Alberto Montes de Oca D., champion sharpshooter. 1col, Eduardo Garnier, sports promoter. O. J. Pinto, introducer of soccer.

C610	AP117	20c	gray & dk bl	9	5
C611	AP117	50c	gray & dk bl	15	10
C612	AP117	1col	gray & dk bl	25	15

First Central American Olympic Games, held in Guatemala, 1973.

Mormodes Buccinator
AP118

Masdevallia Ephippium
AP119

Designs: Orchids.

1975, Mar. 7 Litho. *Perf. 10½, 13½*

Multicolored

C613	AP118	25c	*shown*	20	10
C614	AP118	25c	*Gongora claviodora*	20	10
C615	AP119	25c	*shown*	20	10
C616	AP119	25c	*Encyclia spondiadum*	20	10
C617	AP118	65c	*Lycaste skinnery alba*	40	20
C618	AP118	65c	*Peristeria elata*	40	20
C619	AP119	65c	*Miltonia roezelii*	40	20
C620	AP119	65c	*Brassavola digbyana*	40	20
C621	AP118	80c	*Epidendrum mirabile*	60	30
C622	AP118	80c	*Barkeria lindleyana*	60	30
C623	AP119	80c	*Cattleya skinneri*	60	30
C624	AP119	80c	*Sobralia macrantha*	60	30
C625	AP118	1.40col	*Lycaste cruenta*	80	35
C626	AP118	1.40col	*Oncidium obryzatum*	80	35
C627	AP119	1.40col	*Gongora armeniaca*	80	35
C628	AP119	1.40col	*Sievekingia suavis*	80	35

Perf. 13½

C629	AP118	1.75col	*Hexisea imbricata*	90	40
C630	AP118	2.15col	*Warcewiczella discolor*	90	40
C631	AP119	2.50col	*Oncidium kramerianum*	1.00	60
C632	AP119	3.25col	*Cattleya dowiana*	1.50	75
			Nos. C613-C632 (20)	12.30	5.95

5th National Flower Exhibition.

Stamps of same denominations printed se-tenant. Nos. C613–C628 were printed in both perforations on two different papers: dull finish and shiny. Nos. C629–C632 were printed on shiny paper.

Radio Club Emblem
AP120

Members' Flags and Emblem
AP121

Design: 2col, Federation emblem.

1975, Apr. 16 Litho. *Perf. 13½*

C633	AP120	1col	blk & red lil	50	15
C634	AP121	1.10col	multi	60	20
C635	AP120	2col	blk & bl	1.00	30

16th Central American Radio Amateurs' Convention, San José, May 2–4.

A little time given to study of the arrangement of the Scott Catalogue can make it easier to use effectively.

Nicoya Beach
AP122

Designs: 75c, Driving cattle. 1col, Colonial Church, Nicoya. 3col, Savannah riders (vert.).

1975, Aug. 1 Litho. *Perf. 13½*

C636	AP122	25c	gray & multi	6	5
C637	AP122	75c	gray & multi	20	20
C638	AP122	1col	gray & multi	25	15
C639	AP122	3col	gray & multi	75	60

Sesquicentennial of annexation of Nicoya District.

Costa Rica No. 158
AP123

Designs (Type A90 of 1932): No. C641, No. 159. No. C642, No. 160. No. C643, No. 161.

1975, Aug. 14 Litho. *Perf. 12*

C640	AP123	2.20col	blk & org	60	50
C641	AP123	2.20col	blk & dk grn	60	50
C642	AP123	2.20col	blk & car rose	60	50
C643	AP123	2.20col	blk & dk bl	60	50

6th National Philatelic Exhibition, San José, Aug. 14–17. Nos. C640–C643 printed se-tenant.

IWY Emblem
AP124

1975, Oct. Litho. *Perf. 10½*

C644	AP124	40c	vio bl & red	10	8
C645	AP124	1.25col	blk & ultra	30	20

International Women's Year 1975.

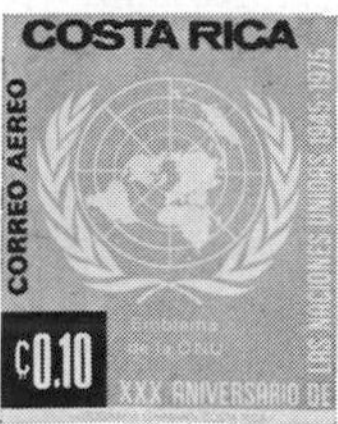

U.N. Emblem
AP125

Designs: 60c, U.N. General Assembly (horiz.). 1.20col, U.N. Headquarters, New York.

1975, Oct. 24 *Perf. 12*

C646	AP125	10c	bl & blk	5	5
C647	AP125	60c	multi	15	12
C648	AP125	1.20col	multi	30	20

30th anniversary of the United Nations.

The Visitation, by Jorge Gallardo
AP126

'20–30' Club Emblem
AP127

Paintings by Jorge Gallardo: 1col, Nativity and Star. 5col, St. Joseph in his Workshop, Virgin and Child.

1975, Nov. ***Perf. 10½***

C649	AP126	50c multi	25	10
C650	AP126	1col multi	40	15
C651	AP126	5col multi	1.50	1.00

Christmas 1975.

1976, Jan. 16 **Litho.** ***Perf. 12***

C652	AP127	1col multi	25	15

'20–30' Club of Costa Rica, 20th anniversary.

Quercus Brenessi Trel
AP128

"Literary Development"
AP129

Plants: 30c, Maxillaria albertii schecht. 55c, Calathea brenesii standl. 2col, Brenesia costaricensis schlecht. 10col, Philodendron brenesii standl.

1976, March 1 ***Perf. 10½***

C653	AP128	5c multi	5	5
C654	AP128	30c multi	10	6
C655	AP128	55c multi	15	12
C656	AP128	2col tan & multi	50	30
C657	AP128	10col multi	2.50	2.00
		Nos. C653-C657 (5)	3.30	2.53

Prof. Alberto Manuel Brenes Mora, botanist, birth centenary.

1976, Apr. 9 **Litho.** ***Perf. 16***

Designs: 1.10col, Man holding book, stylized. 5col, Costa Rican flag emanating from book (horiz.).

C658	AP129	15c multi	6	5
C659	AP129	1.10col multi	25	20
C660	AP129	5col multi	1.25	1.00

Publishing in Costa Rica.

Post-rider, 1839
AP130

Costa Rica No. 13, Post Office
AP131

Designs: 65c, Costa Rica No. 14 and Post Office. 85c, Costa Rica No. 15 and Post Office. 2col, UPU Monument, Bern (vert.).

1976, May 24 ***Perf. 10½***

C661	AP130	20c ap grn & blk	8	5
C662	AP131	50c bis & multi	15	10
C663	AP131	65c multi	20	15
C664	AP131	85c multi	25	20
C665	AP130	2col blk & lt bl	50	40
		Nos. C661-C665 (5)	1.18	90

Centenary of Universal Postal Union (in 1974).

Nos. C662–C664 exist without the surcharges on reproductions of Nos. 13–15.

Telephones, 1876 and 1976
AP132

Designs: 2col, Wall telephone. 5col, Alexander Graham Bell.

1976, June 28

C666	AP132	1.60col lt bl & blk	40	30
C667	AP132	2col multi	50	30
C668	AP132	5col yel & blk	1.25	1.00

Centenary of first telephone call by Alexander Graham Bell, Mar. 10, 1876.

Inverted Center Stamp of 1901 and Association Emblems—AP133

1976, Nov. 11 **Litho.** ***Perf. 10½***

C669	AP133	50c multi	15	10
C670	AP133	1col multi	25	15
C671	AP133	2col multi	50	30

Souvenir Sheet

Design: 5col, 1901 stamp between Costa Rican Philatelic Society and Interamerican Philatelic Federation emblems.

Perf. 12, Imperf.

C672	AP133	5col multi	1.25	1.25

7th National Philatelic Exhibition and 9th Plenary Assembly of the Interamerican Philatelic Federation (FIAF), San José, Nov. 1976. No. C672 has black marginal inscription. Size: 75x60mm.

"Seeing Eye" and Map of Costa Rica
AP134

Amadeo Quiros Blanco
AP135

1976, Nov. 22 ***Perf. 16***

C673	AP134	35c blk & bl	10	8
C674	AP135	2col multi	50	30

General Audit Office, 25th anniversary.

Nurse Attending Child
AP136

LACSA Circling Globe
AP137

Design: 1.10col, National Children's Hospital (horiz.).

1976, Nov. 29

C675	AP136	90c multi	25	20
C676	AP136	1.10col multi	30	25

5th Panamerican Congress of Pediatric Surgery and 12th Congress of Pediatrics.

1976, Dec. 1 ***Perf. 10½***

Designs: 1.20col, Route map. 3col, LACSA emblem and Costa Rican flag.

C677	AP137	1col multi	25	15
C678	AP137	1.20col multi	30	20
C679	AP137	3col multi	75	50

Costa Rican Air Lines (LACSA), 30th anniversary.

Boston Tea Party
AP138

Designs: 5col, Declaration of Independence. 10col, Ringing Liberty Bell to announce Independence (vert.).

1976, Dec. 24

C680	AP138	2.20col multi	55	40
C681	AP138	5col multi	1.25	1.00
C682	AP138	10col multi	2.50	2.00

American Bicentennial.

Tree of Guanacaste
AP139

Felipe J. Alvarado
AP140

Designs (Rotary Emblem and): 60c, Dr. Paul Blanco Cervantes Hospital (horiz.). 3col, Map of Costa Rica (horiz.). 10col, Paul Harris.

1977, Mar. 31 **Litho.** ***Perf. 16***

C683	AP139	40c vio bl & multi	10	8
C684	AP140	50c blk & multi	15	10
C685	AP139	60c vio bl & multi	15	15
C686	AP139	3col vio bl & multi	75	60
C687	AP140	10col blk & multi	2.50	2.00
		Nos. C683-C687 (5)	3.65	2.93

Rotary Club of San José, 50th anniversary.

Boruca Cloth
AP141

Design: 1.50col, Painted wood ornament.

1977, Feb. 22

C688	AP141	75c multi	20	15
C689	AP141	1.50col multi	40	20

National Artisan and Small Industry Program.

Juana Pereira
AP142

Alonso de Anguciana de Gamboa
AP143

Designs: 1col, First Church of Our Lady of the Angels (horiz.). 1.10col, Our Lady of the Angels (gold sculpture). 1.25col, Crown of Our Lady of the Angels.

1977, June 6 **Litho.** ***Perf. 10½***

C690	AP142	50c multi	15	10
C691	AP142	1col multi	25	15
C692	AP142	1.10col multi	30	20
C693	AP142	1.25col multi	35	25

50th anniversary of the coronation of Our Lady of the Angels, patron saint of Costa Rica.

1977, July 4 **Litho.** ***Perf. 10½***

Designs: 75c, Church of Esparza. 1col, Statue of Our Lady of Candlemas. 2col, Statue of Diego de Artieda y Chirino.

C694	AP143	35c multi	10	8
C695	AP143	75c multi	20	15
C696	AP143	1col multi	25	15
C697	AP143	2col multi	50	40

400th anniversary of the founding of Esparza.

CARE Emblem and Child
AP144

Design: 1col, CARE emblem and soybeans (horiz.).

1977, Sept. 14 **Litho.** ***Perf. 16***

C698	AP144	80c multi	20	15
C699	AP144	1col multi	25	15

20th anniversary of CARE (relief organization) in Costa Rica.

Institute's Emblem
AP145

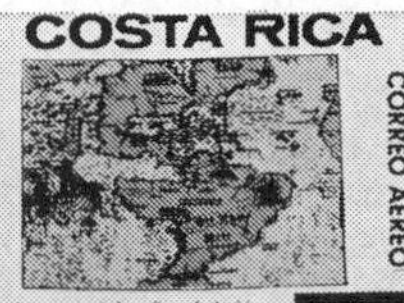

First Map of Americas, 1540
AP146

1977, Oct. 21 Litho. *Perf. 16*

C700	AP145	50c blk & multi	15	10
C701	AP146	1.40col blk & multi	35	30

Hispanic Cultural Institute of Costa Rica, 25th anniversary.

Mercy Church, by Ricardo Ulloa B.
AP147

Health Ministry Emblem
AP148

Paintings: 1col, Christ, by Floria Pinto de Herrero. 5col, St. Francis and the Birds, by Louisa Gonzalez Y Saenz.

1977, Nov. 9 Litho. *Perf. 10½*

C702	AP147	50c multi	15	10
C703	AP147	1col multi	25	15
C704	AP147	5col multi	1.25	1.00

1977, Nov. 16 *Perf. 16*

C705	AP148	1.40col multi	35	30

Creation of Ministry of Health.

Picnic
AP149

José de San Martin
AP150

Designs: 50c, Weaver. 2col, Beach scene. 5col, Fruit and vegetable market. 10col, Swans on lake.

1978, Mar. 21 Litho. *Perf. 10½*

C706	AP149	50c blk & multi	15	10
C707	AP149	1col blk & multi	25	15
C708	AP149	2col blk & multi	50	30
C709	AP149	5col blk & multi	1.25	1.00
C710	AP149	10col blk & multi	2.50	2.00
		Nos. C706-C710 (5)	4.65	3.55

Conference of Latin American Tourist Organizations.

1978, Aug. 7 Litho. *Perf. 10½*

C711	AP150	5col multi	1.25	1.00

Gen. José de San Martin (1778–1850), soldier and statesman, fought for South American independence.

Geographical Institute Emblem
AP151

University Federation Emblem
AP152

1978, Aug. 28 Litho. *Perf. 12½*

C712	AP151	5col multi	1.20	90

Pan-American Geography and History Institute, 50th anniversary.

1978, Sept. 18 *Perf. 11*

C713	AP152	80c ultra	20	15

Central American University Federation, 30th anniversary.

Emblems
AP153

1978, Oct. 24 *Perf. 16*

C714	AP153	2col aqua, blk & gold	48	35

6th Interamerican Philatelic Exhibition, Argentina 78, Buenos Aires, Oct. 1978.

Nos. C629–C631 Overprinted:
"50 Aniversario del / primer vuelo de PAN AM / en Costa Rica / 1928–1978"

1978, Nov. 1 Litho. *Perf. 13½*

C715	AP118	1.75col multi	42	30
C716	AP118	2.15col multi	50	38
C717	AP119	2.50col multi	60	45

First Pan Am flight in Costa Rica, 50th anniversary.

Nos. C629–C631 Overprinted:
"50 Aniversario de la / visita de Lindbergh a / Costa Rica 1928–1978"

1978, Nov. 1

C718	AP118	1.75col multi	42	30
C719	AP118	2.15col multi	50	38
C720	AP119	2.50col multi	60	45

50th anniversary of Lindbergh's visit to Costa Rica.

Nos. C603 and C607 Surcharged with New Value, 4 Bars and:
"Centenario del / Asilo Carlos / Maria Ulloa / 1878–1978"

1978, Nov. 8 *Perf. 14*

C721	AP115	50c on 65c multi	12	10
C722	AP115	2col on 2.50col multi	48	35

Asilo Carlos Maria Ulloa, birth centenary.

No. C617–C620, C630–C631 Surcharged with New Value and 4 Bars.

1978, Nov. 13 Litho. *Perf. 10½, 13½*

C723	AP118	50c on 65c	12	10
C724	AP118	50c on 65c	12	10
C725	AP119	50c on 65c	12	10
C726	AP119	50c on 65c	12	10
C727	AP118	1.20col on 2.15col	30	20
C728	AP119	2col on 2.50col	48	35
		Nos. C723-C728 (6)	1.26	95

Nos. C723–C726 printed se-tenant.

Star over Map of Costa Rica
AP154

"Flying Men", Chorotega
AP155

1978, Nov. 13 *Perf. 10½*

C729	AP154	50c bl & blk	12	10
C730	AP154	1col rose lil & blk	24	18
C731	AP154	5col org & blk	1.20	85

Christmas 1978. Nos. C729–C731 printed in sheets of 100 and se-tenant in sheets of 15 (3x5).

1978, Nov. 20 *Perf. 11½*

Designs: 1.20col, Oviedo giving his History of Indies to Duke of Calabria (horiz.). 10col, Lord of Oviedo's coat of arms.

C732	AP155	85c multi	20	15
C733	AP155	1.20col blk & lt bl	30	20
C734	AP155	10col multi	2.40	1.75

500th birth anniversary of Gonzalo Fernandez de Oviedo, first chronicler of Spanish Indies.

Mgr. Domingo Rivas
AP156

San José Cathedral
AP157

1978, Dec. 6 *Perf. 16*

C735	AP156	1col blk & ind	24	18

Perf. 13½

C736	AP157	20col multi	4.80	3.50

Centenary of the Cathedral of San José.

View of Coco Island
AP158

Designs: 2.10, 3, 5 col, various views of Coco Island. 10col, Installation of memorial plaque, people and flag. 5, 10col (vert.).

1979, Apr. 30 Litho. *Perf. 10½*

C737	AP158	90c multi	22	15
C738	AP158	2.10col multi	50	35
C739	AP158	3col multi	72	55
C740	AP158	5col multi	1.20	90
C741	AP158	10col multi	2.40	1.80
a.		Souvenir sheet of 3	5.25	5.25
		Nos. C737-C741 (5)	5.04	3.75

Visit of Pres. Rodrigo Carazo Odio to Coco Island, June 24, 1978, in the interest of national defense. No. C741a contains Nos. C737–C741. Multicolored margin shows map of Costa Rica. Size: 140x103mm.

Shrimp
AP159

Designs: 85c, Mahogany snapper. 1.80col, Corvina. 3col, Crayfish. 10col, Tuna.

1979, May 14 Litho. *Perf. 13½*

C742	AP159	60c multi	15	10
C743	AP159	85c multi	20	15
C744	AP159	1.80col multi	45	32
C745	AP159	3col multi	72	55
C746	AP159	10col multi	2.40	1.80
		Nos. C742-C746 (5)	3.92	2.92

Marine life protection.

Hungry Nestlings, IYC Emblem
AP160

1979, May 24 *Perf. 11*

C747	AP160	1col multi	50	25
C748	AP160	2col multi	1.00	50
C749	AP160	20col multi	6.00	4.50

International Year of the Child.

Microwave Transmitters, Mt. Irazu
AP161

1979, June 28 Litho. *Perf. 14*

Design: 1col, Arenal Dam (horiz.).

C750	AP161	1col multi	25	18
C751	AP161	5col multi	1.25	90

Costa Rican Electricity Institute, 30th anniversary.

Costa Rica No. 1 and Rowland Hill
AP162

Design: 10col, Penny Black and Hill.

1979, July 16 *Perf. 13*

C752	AP162	5col lil rose & bl gray	1.25	18
C753	AP162	10col dl bl & blk	1.25	90

Sir Rowland Hill (1795–1879), originator of penny postage.

Poverty, by Juan Ramon Bonilla
AP163

Sculptures: 60c, Hope, by Hernan Gonzalez. 2.10col, Cattle, by Victor M. Bermudez (horiz.). 5col, Bust of Clorito Picado, by Juan Rafael Chacon. 20col, Mother and Child, by Francisco Zuniga.

1979, July 16 Litho. *Perf. 12*

C754	AP163	60c multi	15	10
C755	AP163	1col multi	25	18
C756	AP163	2.10col multi	45	32
C757	AP163	5col multi	1.25	90
C758	AP163	20col multi	5.00	1.80
		Nos. C754-C758 (5)	7.10	3.30

National Sculpture Contest.

Danaus Plexippus
AP164

Butterflies: 1col, Phoebis philea. 1.80col, Rothschildia. 2.10col, Prepona omphale. 2.60col, Marpesia marcella. 4.05col, Morpho cypris.

1979, Aug. 31 Litho. *Perf. 13½*

C759	AP164	60c	multi	50	20
C760	AP164	1col	multi	1.00	25
C761	AP164	1.80col	multi	1.25	50
C762	AP164	2.10col	multi	1.50	50
C763	AP164	2.60col	multi	1.50	1.00
C764	AP164	4.05col	multi	2.00	1.25
			Nos. C759-C764 (6)	7.75	3.70

SOS Emblem, Houses AP165

Children's Drawings: 5col, 5.50col, Landscapes (diff.).

1979, Sept. 18

C765	AP165	2.50col	multi	62	45
C766	AP165	5col	multi	1.25	90
C767	AP165	5.50col	multi	1.35	1.00

SOS Children's Villages, 30th anniversary.

President Type of 1943

Presidents of Costa Rica: 60c, Rafael Iglesias C. 85c, Ascension Esquivel Ibarra. 1col, Cleto Gonzalez Viquez. 2col, Ricardo Jimenez Oreamuno.

1979, Oct. 8 Litho. *Perf. 13½*

C768	A109	10c	dk bl	5	5
C769	A109	60c	dl pur	15	10
C770	A109	85c	red org	20	15
C771	A109	1col	red org	25	18
C772	A109	2col	brown	50	35
			Nos. C768-C772 (5)	1.15	83

Nos. C768-C772 printed in sheets of 100 and se-tenant in sheets of 25 (5x5).

See Nos. C790-C794.

Holy Family, Creche—AP167

1979, Nov. 16 Litho. *Perf. 12½*

C773	AP167	1col	multi	25	18
C774	AP167	1.60col	multi	42	30

Christmas 1979.

Reforestation—AP168

1980, Jan. 14 Litho. *Perf. 11*

C775	AP168	1 col	multi	20	15
C776	AP168	3.40 col	multi	70	50

Anatomy Lesson, by Rembrandt—AP169

1980, Feb. 7 Litho. *Perf. 10½*

C777	AP169	10col	multi	2.00	1.50

Legal medicine teaching in Costa Rica, 50th anniversary.

Rotary International, 75th Anniversary—AP170

1980, Feb. 26 *Perf. 16*

C778	AP170	2.10col	multi	40	30
C779	AP170	5col	multi	1.00	75

Gulf of Nicoya, Satellite Photo—AP171

1980, Mar. 10 Litho. *Perf. 12½*

C780	AP171	2.10 col	*Puerto Limon*	40	30
C781	AP171	5 col	*shown*	1.00	75

14th International Symposium on Remote Sensing of the Environment, San José, Apr. 23-30.

Soccer, Moscow '80 Emblem—AP172

1980, Apr. 16 Litho. *Perf. 10½*

C782	AP172	1col	*shown*	20	15
C783	AP172	3col	*Bicycling*	60	40
C784	AP172	4.05col	*Baseball*	80	60
C785	AP172	20col	*Swimming*	4.00	3.00

22nd Summer Olympic Games, Moscow, July 19-Aug. 3.

Poas Volcano—AP173

1980, May 14 Litho. *Perf. 10½*

C786	AP173	1 col	*shown*	20	15
C787	AP173	2.50col	*Cahuita Beach*	50	35

National Parks Service, 10th anniversary.

José Maria Zeledon Brenes, Score—AP174

Design: 10col, Manuel Maria Gutierrez.

1980, June 25 Litho. *Perf. 12½*

C788	AP174	1col	multi	20	15
C789	AP174	10col	multi	2.00	1.50

National anthem composed by Brenes (words) and Gutierrez (music).

President Type of 1943

Presidents of Costa Rica: 1col, Alfredo Gonzalez F. 1.60col, Federico Tinoco G. 1.80col, Francisco Aguilar B. 2.10col, Julio Acosta G. 3col, Leon Cortes C.

1980, Aug. 14 Litho. *Perf. 11*

C790	A109	1col	dk red	20	15
C791	A109	1.60col	sl bl	30	20
C792	A109	1.80col	brown	35	25
C793	A109	2.10col	dl grn	40	30
C794	A109	3col	dk pur	60	40
			Nos. C790-C794 (5)	1.85	1.30

8th National Philatelic Exhibition AP175

Fruits AP176

1980, Sept. 11 *Perf. 13½*

C795	AP175	5col	multi	1.00	75
C796	AP175	20col	multi	4.00	3.50

1980, Sept. 24 *Perf. 10½*

C797	AP176	10c	*shown*	5	5
C798	AP176	60c	*Cacao*	10	28
C799	AP176	1col	*Coffee*	20	15
C800	AP176	2.10col	*Bananas*	40	30
C801	AP176	3.40col	*Flowers*	70	50
C802	AP176	5col	*Sugar cane*	1.00	25
			Nos. C797-C802 (6)	2.45	1.53

COSTA RICA CORREO AEREO ¢1.00

Giant Tree, by Jorge Carvajal AP177

COSTA RICA CORREO AEREO ¢1.00

Virgin and Child, by Raphael AP178

Paintings: 2.10col, Secret Look, by Rolando Cubero. 2.45col, Consuelo, by Fernando Carballo. 3col, Volcano, by Lola Fernandez. 4.05col, attending Mass, by Francisco Amighetti.

1980, Oct. 22 Litho. *Perf. 10½*

C803	AP177	1col	multi	20	15
C804	AP177	2.10 col	multi	40	30

Size: 28x30mm.

C805	AP177	2.45col	multi	50	40

Size: 22x36mm.

C806	AP177	3col	multi	60	45
C807	AP177	4.05col	multi	80	60
			Nos. C803-C807 (5)	2.50	1.90

1980, Nov. 11 *Perf. 13½*

Christmas 1980: 10col, Virgin and Child and St. John, by Raphael.

C808	AP178	1col	multi	20	15
C809	AP178	10col	multi	2.00	1.50

Juan Santamaria International Airport—AP179

1980, Dec. 11 Litho. *Perf. 10½*
Sizes: 30x30mm., 31x25mm. (1.30 col), 25x32mm. (2.60 col)

C810	AP179	1col	*Caldera Harbor*	20	15
C811	AP179	1.30 col	*shown*	25	20
C812	AP179	2.10 col	*Rio Frio Railroad Bridge*	40	30
C813	AP179	2.60 col	*Highway to Colon*	50	40
C814	AP179	5col	*Huetar post office*	1.00	75
			Nos. C810-C814 (5)	2.35	1.80

Paying your taxes means progress.

Repertorio Americano Cover, J. Garcia Monge and Signature—AP180

1981, Jan. 2 Litho. *Perf. 10½*

C815	AP180	1.60col	multi	30	20
C816	AP180	3col	multi	60	40

Birth centenary of J. Garcia Monge, founder of Repertorio Americano journal.

Arms of Aserri (Site of Cornea Bank) AP181

Harpia Harpyja AP182

1981, Jan. 28 Litho. *Perf. 13½*

C817	AP181	1 col	shown	20	15
C818	AP181	1.80col	Eye	35	25
C819	AP181	5 col	Rojas	1.00	75

Establishment of human cornea bank, founded by Abelardo Rojas.

1981 *Perf. 11*

C820	AP182	2.10 col	shown	60	30
C821	AP182	2.50 col	Ara macao	80	40
C822	AP182	3 col	Felis concolor	90	45
C823	AP182	5.50 col	Ateles geoffrovi	2.25	80

Medical and Surgical Clinic—AP183

1981, Apr. 8 **Litho.** ***Perf. 10½***

C824 AP183	5c shown	5	5
C825 AP183	10c Physiology class	5	5
C826 AP183	50c Medical school, A. Chavarria (1st dean)	5	5
C827 AP183	1.30 col Music school	10	6
C828 AP183	3.40 col Carlos Monge Alfaro Library	25	20
C829 AP183	4.05 col R.F. Brenes, rector (1952-1961), vert.	30	25
	Nos. C824-C829 (6)	80	66

University of Costa Rica, 40th anniversary.

Mail Transport by Horse—AP184

1981, May 6 **Litho.** ***Perf. 10½***

C830 AP184	1 col shown	20	15
C831 AP184	2.10 col Train, 1857	40	30
C832 AP184	10 col Mail carriers, 1858	2.00	1.50

Heinrich von Stephan (1831-1897), founder of UPU.

13th World Telecommunications Day—AP185

1981, May 18 ***Perf. 11***

C833 AP185	5 col multi	1.00	75
C834 AP185	25 col multi	5.00	3.50

Bishop Bernardo Thiel AP186

Juan Santamaria AP187

1981, June 8 **Litho.** ***Perf. 10½***

C835	Strip of 5, stained glass windows	50	40
a. AP186	1 col Sts. Peter & Paul	10	6
b. AP186	1 col St. Vincent de Paul	10	6
c. AP186	1 col Death of St. Joseph	10	6
d. AP186	1 col Archangel Michael	10	6
e. AP186	1 col Holy Family	10	6
C836 AP186	2 col shown	20	12

Consecration of Bernardo Augusto Thiel as Bishop of San Jose.

1981, June 26 ***Perf. 13½***

C837 AP187	1 col shown	10	6
C838 AP187	2.45 col Alajuela Cathedral, horiz.	25	15

Alajuela province.

Potters—AP188

1981, July 10 **Litho.** ***Perf. 10½***

C839 AP188	15c shown	5	5
C840 AP188	1.60 col Bricklayers	15	10
C841 AP188	1.80 col Farmers	15	10
C842 AP188	2.50 col Fishermen	20	15
C843 AP188	3 col Nurse, patient	25	20
C844 AP188	5 col Children, traffic policeman	50	30
	Nos. C839-C844 (6)	1.30	90

Model of New Natl. Archives—AP189

Natl. Archives Centenary: 1.40col, Leon Fernandez Bonilla, founder (vert.). 2col, Arms (vert.). 3col, St. Thomas University, former headquarters.

1981, Aug. 24 **Litho.** ***Perf 13½***

C845 AP189	1.40 col multi	15	10
C846 AP189	2 col multi	20	12
C847 AP189	3 col multi	25	20
C848 AP189	3.50 col multi	30	25

Men Reaching for Sun, Map—AP190

1981, Sept. 9 **Litho.** ***Perf. 11***

C849 AP190	1 col Man in wheelchair, stairs, vert.	10	6
C850 AP190	2.60 col Man reaching for scale, vert.	25	15
C851 AP190	10 col shown	90	65

Intl. Year of the Disabled.

World Food Day AP191

1981, Oct. 16 **Litho.** ***Perf. 10½***

C852 AP191	5 col multi	50	30
C853 AP191	10 col multi	90	65

President Type of 1943

President of Costa Rica: 1 col, Rafael A. Calderon Guardia, 1940. 2 col, Teodoro Picado Michalski, 1944. 3 col, José Figueres Ferrer, 1953. 5 col, Otilio Ulate Blanco, 1949. 10 col, Mario Echandi Jimenez, 1958.

1981, Dec. 7 **Litho.** ***Perf. 13½***

C854 A109	1 col pink	10	6
C855 A109	2 col orange	20	12
C856 A109	3 col green	25	20
C857 A109	5 col dk bl	45	30
C858 A109	10 col blue	90	65
	Nos. C854-C858 (5)	1.90	1.33

Bar Assoc. of Costa Rica Centenary (1981) AP192

1982, Mar. 22 **Litho.** ***Perf. 13½***

C859 AP192	1 col Emblem, horiz.	10	5
C860 AP192	2 col E. Figueroa, 1st pres.	15	8
C861 AP192	20 col Bar building, horiz.	1.50	75

National Progress AP193

1982 ***Perf. 10½***

C862 AP193	95c Housing	10	5
C863 AP193	1.15 col Agricultural fair	10	6
C864 AP193	1.45 col Education	15	8
C865 AP193	1.65 col Drinkable water	15	10
C866 AP193	1.80 col Rural medical care	15	12
C867 AP193	2.10 col Recreational areas	15	12
C868 AP193	2.35 col Natl. Theater Square	15	12
C869 AP193	2.60 col Communications	15	12
C870 AP193	3 col Electric railroad	15	12
C871 AP193	4.05 col Irrigation	20	15
	Nos. C862-C871 (10)	1.45	1.04

Issue dates: 1.80 col, 2.10 col, 2.60 col, 3 col, 4.05 col, May 5; others, June 16.

City of Alajuela Bicentenary AP194

Perez Zeledon County, 50th Anniv. (1981) AP195

Designs: 5 col, Central Park Fountain. 10 col, Juan Santamaria Historical and Cultural Museum (horiz.). 15 col, Church of Christ of Esquipulas. 20 col, Monsignor Esteban Lorenzo de Tristan, 25 col, Father Juan Manuel Lopez del Corral.

1982, Aug. 9

C872 AP194	5 col multi	35	20
C873 AP194	10 col multi	70	35
C874 AP194	15 col multi	1.05	75
C875 AP194	20 col multi	1.40	74
C876 AP194	25 col multi	1.75	1.00
	Nos. C872-C876 (5)	5.25	3.04

1982, Aug. 30

Designs: 10c, Saint's Stone. 50c, Monument to Mothers. 1 col, Pedro Perz Zeledon. 1.25 col, St. Isidro Labrador Church. 3.50 col, Municipal Building (horiz.). 4.25 col, Arms.

C877 AP195	10c multi	5	5
C878 AP195	50c multi	6	5
C879 AP195	1 col multi	10	6
C880 AP195	1.25 col multi	12	6
C881 AP195	3.50 col multi	25	15
C882 AP195	4.25 col multi	30	20
	Nos. C877-C882 (6)	88	57

Nos. C695 and C813 Surcharged.

1982, Oct. 28 **Litho.** ***Perf. 10½***

C883 AP143	3col on 75c multi	25	15
C884 AP179	5col on 2.60col multi	40	20

Nos. C640-C643 Surcharged and Overprinted: "IX EXPOSICION FILATELICA—1982."

1982, Oct. 28 ***Perf. 12***

C885 AP123	8.40 on 2.20col #C640	60	50
C886 AP123	8.40 on 2.20col #C641	60	50
C887 AP123	8.40 on 2.20col #C642	60	50
C888 AP123	8.40 on 2.20col #C643	60	50
C889 AP123	9.70 on 2.20col #C640	75	60
C890 AP123	9.70 on 2.20col #C641	75	60
C891 AP123	9.70 on 2.20col #C642	75	60
C892 AP123	9.70 on 2.20col #C643	75	60
	Nos. C885-C892 (8)	5.40	4.40

9th Natl. Stamp Exhibition.

TB Bacillus Centenary AP196

Pan-American Blood Donors' Society, 7th Congress AP197

1982, Nov. 19 ***Perf. 13½***

C893 AP196	1.50col Koch	10	8
C894 AP196	3col Koch, slide	20	15
C895 AP196	3.30col Health Ministry	25	10

1982, Nov. 25 ***Perf. 11***

C896 AP197	30col Natl. Blood Assoc. emblem	2.00	1.25
C897 AP197	50col Congress emblem	3.00	2.00

Inter-Governmental Migration Committee, 30th Anniv. AP198

St. Francis of Assisi, (1182-1226), by El Greco AP199

1982, Dec. 13 **Litho.** ***Perf. 10½***

C898 AP198	8.40col Emblem, horiz.	50	25
C899 AP198	9.70col Emblem, diff.	60	30
C900 AP198	11.70col Handshake, horiz.	75	35
C901 AP198	13.05col Emblem, diff., horiz.	80	40

1983, Jan. 3 ***Perf. 16***

C902 AP199	4.80col shown	30	10
C903 AP199	7.40col Portrait, diff.	45	15

Visit of Pope John Paul II—AP200

1983, Mar. 1 **Litho.** ***Perf. 10½***

C904 AP200	5col multi	75	20
C905 AP200	10col multi	1.00	50
C906 AP200	15col multi	2.00	75

Simon Bolivar (1783-1830), by Francisco Zuniga Chavarria—AP201

1983, July 22 **Litho.** ***Perf. 16***

C907	AP201	10col multi	70	25

Nos. C902-C903 Surcharged.

1983 **Litho.** ***Perf. 16***

C908	AP199	10c on 4.80col	5	5
C909	AP199	50c on 4.80col	5	5
C910	AP199	1.50col on 7.40col	5	5
C911	AP199	3 col on 7.40col	6	5

LACSA Costa Rica Airlines, 40th Anniv.—A161

Various childrens' drawings.

1986, Dec. **Litho.** ***Perf. 13½***

C912	A161	1col Adriana E. Hidalgo	5	5
C913	A161	7col Osvaldo A.G. Vega	28	8
C914	A161	16col David V. Rodriguez	65	18

AIR POST SPECIAL DELIVERY STAMPS

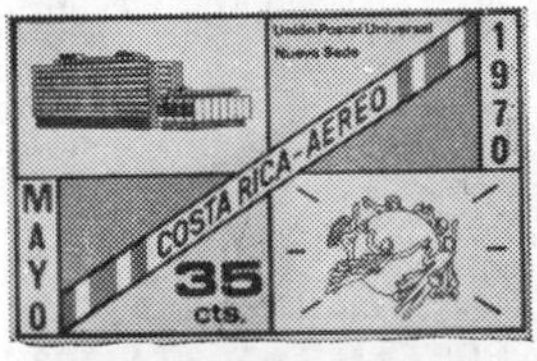

U.P.U. Headquarters and Monument, Bern
APSD1

Perf. 10x11

1970, May 20 **Litho.** **Unwmkd.**

CE1	APSD1	35c multi	20	10
CE2	APSD1	60c multi	30	15

Issued to commemorate the opening of the new Universal Postal Union Headquarters in Bern. The red and black label attached to the 60c is inscribed "EXPRES". Prices are for stamps with label attached.

Stamps with labels removed were used for regular airmail.

AIR POST OFFICIAL STAMPS.

Air Post Stamps of 1934

Overprinted in Red **OFICIAL**

1934 ***Perf. 12.*** **Unwmkd.**

CO1	AP8	5c green	35	35
CO2	AP8	10c car rose	35	35
CO3	AP8	15c chocolate	60	60
CO4	AP8	20c dp bl	90	90
CO5	AP8	25c dp org	90	90
CO6	AP8	40c ol blk	1.00	1.00
CO7	AP8	50c gray blk	1.00	1.00
CO8	AP8	60c org yel	1.25	1.25
CO9	AP8	75c dl vio	1.25	1.25
CO10	AP8	1col dp rose	1.75	1.75
CO11	AP9	2col lt bl	6.00	6.00
CO12	AP9	5col black	11.00	11.00
CO13	AP9	10col red brn	13.00	13.00
		Nos. CO1-CO13 (13)	39.35	39.35

SPECIAL DELIVERY STAMPS

Winged Letter
SD1

Unwmkd.

1972, Mar. 20 **Litho.** ***Perf. 11***

E1	SD1	75c brn & red	25	20
E2	SD1	1.50col bl & red	50	35

1973 ***Perf. 11x12***

E3	SD1	75c grn & red	25	20

1973, Nov. 5 **Litho.** ***Perf. 11x11½***

E4	SD1	75c lil & org	1.25	75

Concorde
SD2

1976, May 17 **Litho.** ***Perf. 16***

E5	SD2	1col ver & multi	25	20

Concorde
SD3

1979, June 15 **Litho.** ***Perf. 12½***

E6	SD3	2col multi	50	35

Concorde—SD4

1980, Dec. 18 **Litho.** ***Perf. 12½***

E7	SD4	2col multi	50	35

1982, Dec. 20 **Litho.** ***Perf. 11***

E8	SD4	4col multi	50	25

POSTAGE DUE STAMPS.

D1

D2

Engraved

1903 ***Perf. 14*** **Unwmkd.**

Numerals in Black.

J1	D1	5c sl bl	7.50	1.35
J2	D1	10c brn org	7.50	1.00
J3	D1	15c yel grn	3.00	2.75
J4	D1	20c carmine	3.50	2.50
J5	D1	25c sl gray	4.50	2.75
J6	D1	30c brown	7.00	3.75
J7	D1	40c ol bis	7.00	3.75
J8	D1	50c red vio	7.00	3.25
		Nos. J1-J8 (8)	47.00	21.10

1915 **Lithographed.** ***Perf. 12.***

J9	D2	2c orange	12	12
J10	D2	4c dk bl	12	12
J11	D2	8c gray grn	50	50
J12	D2	10c violet	20	20
J13	D2	20c brown	25	25
		Nos. J9-J13 (5)	1.19	1.19

OFFICIAL STAMPS.

Official stamps normally were not canceled when affixed to official mail in the 19th century. Occasionally they were canceled in a foreign country of destination. Used prices are for used stamps without cancellation or favor-canceled specimens.

Regular Issues Overprinted.

Overprinted in Red, Black, Blue or Green **Oficial**

1883-85 ***Perf. 12.*** **Unwmkd.**

O1	A6	1c grn (R)	2.00	2.00
O2	A6	1c grn (Bk)	2.00	2.00
O3	A6	2c car (Bk)	2.50	2.50
O4	A6	2c car (Bl)	2.75	2.75
O5	A6	5c bl vio (R)	5.25	5.25
O6	A6	10c org (G)	6.50	6.50
O7	A6	40c bl (R)	6.75	6.75
		Nos. O1-O7 (7)	27.75	27.75

Overprinted **OFICIAL**

1886

O8	A6	1c grn (Bk)	2.00	2.00
O9	A6	2c car (Bk)	3.00	3.00
O10	A6	5c bl vio (R)	19.00	19.00
O11	A6	10c org (Bk)	19.00	19.00

Overprinted **OFICIAL**

O12	A6	1c grn (Bk)	1.50	1.50
O13	A6	2c car (Bk)	2.00	2.00
O14	A6	5c bl vio (R)	15.00	15.00
O15	A6	10c org (Bk)	15.00	15.00

Nos. O8-O11 and O12-O15 exist se-tenant in vertical pairs. Price, each $75.

Overprinted in Black **Oficial**

O16	A6	5c bl vio	50.00	50.00
O17	A6	10c orange	175.00	90.00

Overprinted **OFICIAL.**

1887

O18	A6	1c green	75	75
a.		"OFICAL"	10.00	10.00
b.		Without period	90	90
O19	A6	2c carmine	70	70
a.		"OFICAL"	6.00	6.00
b.		Without period	90	90
O21	A6	10c orange	5.00	5.00
b.		Without period	5.00	
c.		Double overprint	10.00	
O22	A7	5c bl vio	2.75	2.75
a.		"OFICAL"	5.00	
b.		Without period	3.60	3.60
O23	A7	10c orange	70	70
a.		"OFICAL"	3.75	3.75
b.		Without period	1.25	
c.		Double overprint	12.50	
O24	A6	40c blue	70	70
a.		"OFICAL"	4.50	4.50
		Nos. O18-O24 (6)	10.60	10.60

Issues of 1889–1901 Overprinted **OFICIAL**

1889 ***Perf. 14, 15.***

O25	A10	1c brown	30	30
O26	A11	2c dk grn	30	30
O27	A12	5c orange	30	30
O28	A13	10c red brn	30	30
O29	A14	20c yel grn	30	30
O30	A15	50c rose red	1.50	1.50
		Nos. O25-O30 (6)	3.00	3.00

1892

O31	A20	1c grnsh bl	35	35
O32	A21	2c yellow	35	35
O33	A22	5c violet	35	35
O34	A23	10c lt grn	1.50	1.50
O35	A24	20c scarlet	25	22
O36	A25	50c gray bl	70	70
		Nos. O31-O36 (6)	3.50	3.47

1901-02

O37	A30	1c grn & blk	55	55
O38	A31	2c ver & blk	55	55
O39	A32	5c gray bl & blk	55	55
O40	A33	10c ocher & blk	90	90
O41	A34	20c lake & blk	1.20	1.20
O42	A35	50c lil & dk bl	4.25	4.25
O43	A36	1col ol bis & blk	10.00	10.00
		Nos. O37-O43 (7)	18.00	18.00

No. 46 Overprinted in Green **PROVISORIO** **OFICIAL**

1903

O44	A31	2c ver & blk	3.50	3.50
b.		"PROVISIORO"	6.00	6.00
d.		Inverted overprint	6.00	6.00
f.		Same as "b" inverted	12.00	12.00

Regular Issue of 1903 Overprinted **OFICIAL**

1903 ***Perf. 14, 12½ x14.***

O45	A40	4c red vio & blk	1.75	1.75
O46	A41	6c ol grn & blk	2.00	2.00
O47	A42	25c gray lil & brn	9.00	5.00

Regular Issue of 1907 Overprinted **OFICIAL**

1908 ***Perf. 14, 11x14.***

O48	A43	1c red brn & ind	12	12
O49	A44	2c yel grn & blk	12	12
O50	A45	4c car & ind	15	15
O51	A46	5c yel & dl bl	20	20
O52	A47	10c bl & blk	1.25	1.25
O53	A49	25c gray lil & blk	25	25
O54	A50	50c red lil & bl	40	40
O55	A51	1col brn & blk	1.00	1.00
		Nos. O48-O55 (8)	3.49	3.49

The 5c, 10c and 25c exist with inverted overprint, the 4c with double impression of head.

Imperf. examples of Nos. O49 and O53 were found in 1970.

Regular Issue of 1910 Overprinted in Black **OFICIAL** **15 VI-1917**

1917

O56	A56	5c orange	30	30
a.		Inverted overprint	3.50	3.50
O57	A57	10c dp bl	25	25
a.		Inverted overprint		

O2

1920 Red Surcharge. ***Perf. 12.***

O58	O2	15c on 20c ol grn	50	50

O3

O4

O5

O6

1921 Black Surcharge. ***Perf. 12, 14.***

O59	O3	10c on 5c org	50	40
a.		"10 CTS." invert.	22.50	
O60	O4	4c car & ind	45	45
a.		"1291" for "1921"	15.00	
O61	O5	6c on 1c red brn & ind	50	50
O62	O6	20c on 25c gray lil & blk	50	50

Overprinted like No. O60.

O63	A50	50c red lil & bl	2.50	2.50
O64	A51	1col brn & blk	4.50	4.50
		Nos. O59-O64 (6)	8.95	8.85

Nos. O60 to O64 exist with date and new values inverted, often in pairs with the normal varieties. These may be printer's waste but probably were deliberately made.

Regular Issue of 1923 Overprinted **OFICIAL**

1923 ***Perf. 11½.***

O65	A68	2c brown	30	30
O66	A68	4c green	15	15
O67	A68	5c blue	30	30
O68	A68	20c carmine	20	20
O69	A68	1col violet	40	40
		Nos. O65-O69 (5)	1.35	1.35

Nos. O65 to O69 exist imperforate but were not regularly issued in that condition.

O7

Engraved

1926 ***Perf. 12½*** **Unwmkd.**

O70	O7	2c ultra & blk	6	6
O71	O7	3c mag & blk	6	6
O72	O7	4c lt bl & blk	8	8
O73	O7	5c grn & blk	8	8
O74	O7	6c ocher & blk	8	8
O75	O7	10c rose red & blk	8	8
O76	O7	20c ol grn & blk	8	8
O77	O7	30c red org & blk	15	15
O78	O7	45c brn & blk	20	20
O79	O7	1col lil & blk	30	30
		Nos. O70-O79 (10)	1.17	1.17

Regular Issue of 1936 Overprinted in Black **OFICIAL**

1936 ***Perf. 12.*** **Unwmkd.**

O80	A96	5c green	8	8
O81	A96	10c car rose	8	8

Type of 1926.

1937 ***Perf. 12½.***

O82	O7	2c vio & blk	8	8
O83	O7	3c bis brn & blk	8	8
O84	O7	4c rose car & blk	8	8
O85	O7	5c ol grn & blk	8	8
O86	O7	8c blk brn & blk	10	
O87	O7	10c rose lake & blk	10	
O88	O7	20c ind & blk	12	12
O89	O7	40c red org & blk	25	25
O90	O7	55c dk vio & blk	35	
O91	O7	1col brn vio & blk	30	30
O92	O7	2col gray bl & blk	60	60
O93	O7	5col dl yel & blk	3.00	3.00
O94	O7	10col bl & blk	20.00	20.00
		Nos. O82-O94 (13)	25.14	

Nine stamps of this series exist with perforated star (2c, 3c, 4c, 20c, 40c, 1col, 2col, 5col, 10col). These were issued to officials for postal purposes. Unpunched copies were sold to collectors but had no franking power. Prices for unused are for unpunched.

POSTAL TAX STAMPS

Most postal tax issues were to benefit the Children's Village and were obligatory on all mail during December.

No. C198 Surcharged in Red: "Sello de Navidad Pro-Ciudad de Los Niños 5 5"

Engraved; Center Photogravure.

1958 ***Perf. 12½*** **Unwmkd.**

RA1	AP51	5c on 2c brt bl & blk	15	6

Similar Surcharge in Green on Type of 1954.

Design: Like No. C228, pottery.

Perf. 12

RA2	AP53	5c on 10c dk bl & blk	40	8
a.		Inverted surch.		

Father Edward J. Flanagan
PT1

Father Peralta
PT2

Paintings: No. RA4, Boy by El Greco. No. RA5, Boy by Jose Ribera. No. RA6, Girl by Amadeo Modigliani.

Photogravure.

1959, Nov. 25 ***Perf. 13½*** **Unwmkd.**

RA3	PT1	5c green	30	20
RA4	PT1	5c dl gray vio	30	20
RA5	PT1	5c olive	30	20
RA6	PT1	5c lil rose	30	20

Exist imperf.

1960 Lithographed ***Perf. 14***

Designs: No. RA8, Girl by Renoir. No. RA9, Boys with cups by Velazquez. No. RA10, Singing children, sculpture by F. Zuñiga.

RA7	PT2	5c chocolate	30	20
RA8	PT2	5c dp org	30	20
RA9	PT2	5c plum	30	20
RA10	PT2	5c grysh bl	30	20

Exist imperf.

No. C229 Surcharged "Sello de Navidad Pro-Ciudad de los Niños 5 5"

Engraved; Center Photogravure

1961 ***Perf. 13x12½***

RA11	AP53	5c on 15c grn & blk	30	15

Nicolas, Son of Rubens
PT3

Boys in Workshop
PT4

Designs: No. RA13, Madonna by Bellini. RA14, Angel playing stringed instrument by Melozzo. RA15, Msgr. Rubén Odio H.

1962 Photogravure ***Perf. 13½***

RA12	PT3	5c dk car	30	20
RA13	PT3	5c sepia	30	20
RA14	PT3	5c dl grn	30	20
RA15	PT3	5c blue	30	20

Type of 1962, Inscribed "1963" Designs as before

Designs: No. RA16, Rubens' son Nicolas. No. RA17, Madonna, Bellini. No. RA18, Angel, Melozzo. No. RA19, Msgr. Rubén Odio H.

1963 Photogravure ***Perf. 13½***

RA16	PT3	5c sepia	30	15
RA17	PT3	5c ultra	30	15
RA18	PT3	5c dk car	30	15
RA19	PT3	5c black	30	15

1964 Lithographed ***Perf. 12½***

Designs: No. RA21, Two playing boys. No. RA22, Teacher and children. No. RA23, Priest with boys.

RA20	PT4	5c brt grn	30	15
RA21	PT4	5c rose lil	30	15
RA22	PT4	5c blue	30	15
RA23	PT4	5c brown	30	15

Brother Casiano de Madrid
PT5

Christmas Ornaments
PT6

Designs: No. RA25, National Children's Hospital. No. RA26, Poinsettia. No. RA27, Santa Claus with children (diamond).

1965, Dec. 10 Litho. ***Perf. 10***

RA24	PT5	5c red brn	20	15
RA25	PT5	5c green	20	15
RA26	PT5	5c red	20	15
RA27	PT5	5c ultra	20	15

1966 Lithographed ***Perf. 11***

Designs: No. RA29, Angel. No. RA30, Church. No. RA31, Reindeer.

RA28	PT6	5c red	20	8
RA29	PT6	5c lt ultra	20	8
RA30	PT6	5c brt grn	20	8
RA31	PT6	5c brown	20	8

General Post Office, San José
PT7

1967, March Litho. ***Perf. 11***

RA32	PT7	10c blue	10	6

No. RA32 was issued as a postal tax stamp to be used by organizations normally allowed free postage. On Dec. 15, 1972, it was authorized for use as an ordinary postage stamp.

Madonna and Child
PT8

Star of Bethlehem, Mother and Child
PT9

1967 Lithographed ***Perf. 11***

RA33	PT8	5c ol grn	15	10
RA34	PT8	5c dp lil rose	15	10
RA35	PT8	5c brt bl	15	10
RA36	PT8	5c grnsh bl	15	10

1968, Dec. Litho. ***Perf. 12½***

RA37	PT9	5c gray	15	10
RA38	PT9	5c rose red	15	10
RA39	PT9	5c dk rose brn	15	10
RA40	PT9	5c bis brn	15	10

Madonna and Child
PT10

1969, Dec. Lithographed ***Perf. 12½***

RA41 PT10 5c dk bl 5 5
RA42 PT10 5c orange 5 5
RA43 PT10 5c brn red 5 5
RA44 PT10 5c bl grn 5 5

Christ Child and Star
PT11

1970, Dec. Litho. ***Perf. 12½***

RA45 PT11 5c brt pur 5 5
RA46 PT11 5c lil rose 5 5
RA47 PT11 5c olive 5 5
RA48 PT11 5c ocher 5 5

Christ Child and "PAX"
PT12

Madonna and Child
PT13

1971, Nov. 29

RA49 PT12 10c dk bl 7 5
RA50 PT12 10c orange 7 5
RA51 PT12 10c brown 7 5
RA52 PT12 10c green 7 5

1972, Nov. 30 ***Perf. 11x11½***

RA53 PT13 10c dk bl 7 5
RA54 PT13 10c brt red 7 5
RA55 PT13 10c lilac 7 5
RA56 PT13 10c green 7 5

Madonna and Child
PT14

Boys Eating Cake, by Murillo
PT15

1973, Nov. 30 Litho. ***Perf. 12½***

RA57 PT14 10c purple 7 5
RA58 PT14 10c car rose 7 5
RA59 PT14 10c gray 7 5
RA60 PT14 10c org brn 7 5

1974, Nov. 25 ***Perf. 13***

Paintings: No. RA62, Virgin and Child, with St. John, by Raphael. No. RA63, Maternity, by Juan R. Bonilla. No. RA64, Praying Child, by Reynolds.

RA61 PT15 10c brt pink 6 5
RA62 PT15 10c rose lil 6 5
RA63 PT15 10c dk gray 6 5
RA64 PT15 10c vio bl 6 5

"Happy, Dreams, by Sonia Romero
PT16

Virgin and Child, by Hans Memling
PT17

Paintings: No. RA66, Virgin with Carnation, by Leonardo da Vinci. No. RA67, Children with Tortoise, by Francisco Amighetti. No. RA68, Boy with Pigeon, by Picasso.

1975, Nov. 25 Litho. ***Perf. 10½***

RA65 PT16 10c gray 5 5
RA66 PT16 10c red lil 5 5
RA67 PT16 10c org brn 5 5
RA68 PT16 10c brt bl 5 5

Obligatory on all mail during December.

1976, Nov. 24 Litho. ***Perf. 10½***

Paintings: No. RA70, Boy with Sombrero, by Auguste Renoir. No. RA71, Meditation (Boy), by Floria Pinto de Herrero. No. RA72, Gaston de Mezerville (boy), by Lolita Zeller de Peralta.

RA69 PT17 10c rose lil 5 5
RA70 PT17 10c rose car 5 5
RA71 PT17 10c gray 5 5
RA72 PT17 10c vio bl 5 5

Obligatory on all mail during December.

Boy's Head, by Amparo Cruz
PT18

Boy with Kite
PT19

Paintings: No. RA74, Girl's head, by Rubens. No. RA75, Girl and infant, by Cristina Fournier. No. RA76, Mariano Goya, by Goya.

1977, Nov. Litho. ***Perf. 10½***

RA73 PT18 10c gray ol 5 5
RA74 PT18 10c rose red 5 5
RA75 PT18 10c brt ultra 5 5
RA76 PT18 10c brt rose lil 5 5

Obligatory on all mail during December.

1978, Nov. 20 Litho. ***Perf. 12½***

Designs: No. RA77, like No. RA76. Nos. RA78–RA79, Girl flying kite.

RA77 PT19 10c magenta 5 5
RA78 PT19 10c slate 5 5
RA79 PT19 10c lilac 5 5
RA80 PT19 10c vio bl 5 5

Obligatory on all mail during December.

Boy Leaning on Tree—PT20

1979, Nov. 19 Litho. ***Perf. 12½***

RA81 PT20 10c blue 5 5
RA82 PT20 10c orange 5 5
RA83 PT20 10c magenta 5 5
RA84 PT20 10c green 5 5

Obligatory on all mail during December.

Boy on Swing—PT21

1980, Nov. 18 Litho. ***Perf. 12½***

RA85 PT21 10c brt bl 5 5
RA86 PT21 10c brt yel 5 5
RA87 PT21 10c crim rose 5 5
RA88 PT21 10c brt grn 5 5

Obligatory on all mail during December.

Boy Riding Toy Car—PT22

1981, Nov. 19 Litho. ***Perf. 11***

RA89 PT22 10c blue 5 5
RA90 PT22 10c green 5 5
RA91 PT22 10c red 5 5
RA92 PT22 10c orange 5 5

Obligatory on all mail during December.

Youth Running Machine—PT23

1982, Nov. 19 Litho. ***Perf. 10½***

RA93 PT23 10c red 5 5
RA94 PT23 10c gray 5 5
RA95 PT23 10c purple 5 5
RA96 PT23 10c grnsh bl 5 5

Obligatory on all mail during December.

Youths Working on Wheelchair—PT24

1983, Nov. 24 Litho. ***Perf. 16***

RA97 PT24 10c red 5 5
RA98 PT24 10c orange 5 5
RA99 PT24 10c ultra 5 5
RA100 PT24 10c green 5 5

Christmas 1983, Children's Village. Obligatory on all mail during December.

Girl on Bicycle—PT25

1984, Nov. 20 Litho. ***Perf. 10½***

RA101 PT25 10c violet 5 5

Christmas '84, Children's Village. Obligatory on all mail during December.

Depressed Child—PT26

1986, Nov. Litho. ***Perf. 10½***

RA102 PT26 10c lemon 6 5

Christmas stamps, 25th anniv.; Christmas '86. Children's Village. Obligatory on all mail during December.

Guanacaste

(gwä'nä·käs'tā)

(A province of Costa Rica)

LOCATION—On northwestern coast of Central America.

AREA—4,000 sq. mi. (approx.).

POP.—69,531 (estimated).

CAPITAL—Liberia.

Residents of Guanacaste were allowed to buy Costa Rican stamps, overprinted "Guanacaste," at a discount from face value because of the province's isolation and climate, which makes it difficult to keep mint stamps. Use was restricted to the province.

Counterfeits of most Guanacaste overprints are plentiful.

On Issue of 1883.

Overprinted Horizontally in Black **Guanacaste** 16mm.

1885 ***Perf. 12*** **Unwmkd.**

1	A6	1c green	4.00	4.00
a.		"Gnanacaste"	60.00	
2	A6	2C carmine	4.00	4.00
a.		"Gnanacaste"	50.00	
3	A6	10c orange	12.00	12.00
a.		"Gnanacaste"	75.00	

Same Overprint in Red.

4	A6	1c green	4.00	4.00
a.		"Gnanacaste"	45.00	
b.		Overprinted in blk & red	125.00	
5	A6	5c bl vio	12.50	2.75
a.		"Gnanacaste"	75.00	
6	A6	40c blue	20.00	20.00

Overprinted Horizontally in Black **Guanacaste** 17½mm. *b*

7	A6	1c green	7.50	7.50
8	A6	2c carmine	7.50	7.50
9	A6	5c bl vio	17.50	3.00
10	A6	10c orange	13.50	8.50
11	A6	40c blue	45.00	45.00

Same Overprint in Red.

12	A6	5c bl vio	50.00	20.00
13	A6	40c blue	*1,000.*	

Overprinted Horizontally in Black **Guanacaste** 18½mm. *c*

14	A6	2c carmine	8.00	8.00
15	A6	10c orange	40.00	30.00

Same Overprint in Red.

16	A6	1c green	7.00	7.00
a.		Double overprint, one in blk	150.00	
17	A6	5c bl vio	32.50	7.00
18	A6	40c blue	50.00	50.00

Same Overprint, Vertically in Black.

19	A6	1c green	*1,500.*	*1,500.*
20	A6	2c carmine	800.00	600.00
21	A6	5c bl vio	250.00	100.00
22	A6	10c orange	60.00	50.00

Guanacaste *e* GUANACASTE *f* GUANACASTE *g* GUANACASTE *h* GUANACASTE *i*

Overprinted Type e, Vertically.

23	A6	1c green	100.00	100.00
24	A6	2c carmine	110.00	110.00
25	A6	5c bl vio	125.00	62.50
26	A6	10c orange	65.00	60.00

Overprinted Type f, Vertically.

27	A6	1c green	275.00	200.00
28	A6	2c carmine	175.00	175.00
29	A6	5c bl vio	200.00	85.00
30	A6	10c orange	75.00	75.00

Overprinted Type g, Vertically.

31	A6	1c green	300.00	300.00
32	A6	2c carmine	300.00	300.00
33	A6	5c bl vio	300.00	150.00
34	A6	10c orange	150.00	150.00

Overprinted Type h, Vertically.

35	A6	1c green	150.00	150.00
36	A6	2c carmine	90.00	90.00
37	A6	5c bl vio	175.00	85.00
38	A6	10c orange	40.00	40.00

The authenticity of Costa Rica Nos. 16-19 with overprint "i" has not been established.

On Issues of 1883–87

1888-89

Overprinted Horizontally in Black **Guanacaste**

42	A7	5c bl vio	20.00	3.00
a.		"Gnanacaste"		

Overprinted Horizontally in Black **Guanacaste**

43	A7	5c bl vio	20.00	3.00

Overprinted Horizontally in Black **Guanacaste**

44	A6	2c carmine	3.00	
45	A7	10c orange	3.00	
a.		Invtd. ovpt.		

On Issue of 1889.

Overprinted Type b, Horizontally.

1889

47	A8	2c blue	30.00	

Vertically

48	A8	2c bl (c)	150.00	
49	A8	2c bl (e)	75.00	
51	A8	2c bl (f)	90.00	
52	A8	2c bl (g)	300.00	
54	A8	2c bl (h)	135.00	

Nos. 47-54 are overprinted "Correos." Copies without "Correos" are known postally used, and are priced the same as Nos. 47-54, unused.

Dangerous counterfeits exist of Nos. 1–54.

On Nos. 25–33

Overprinted Horizontally in Black **GUANACASTE**

1890 ***Perf. 14 and 15***

55	A10	1c brown	10.00	4.00
56	A11	2c dk grn	4.00	2.50
57	A12	5c orange	6.00	2.50
58	A13	10c red brn	6.00	3.00
59	A14	20c yel grn	1.50	1.50
60	A15	50c rose red	2.50	2.50
a.		"GUAGACASTE"	100.00	
61	A16	1p blue	3.50	3.50
a.		"GUAGACASTE"	100.00	100.00
62	A17	2p violet	7.00	7.00
a.		"GUAGACASTE"	100.00	100.00
63	A18	5p ol grn	35.00	35.00
a.		"GUAGACASTE"	100.00	100.00
		Nos. 55-63 (9)	75.50	61.50

Overprinted Horizontally in Black **GUANACASTE**

64	A10	1c brown	2.25	1.75
a.		Vert. pair, imperf. btwn.		
65	A11	2c dk grn	2.25	1.75
66	A12	5c orange	2.25	1.75
67	A13	10c red brn	2.25	1.75

CRETE

(krēt)

LOCATION — An island in the Mediterranean Sea south of Greece.

GOVT.—A department of Greece.

AREA—3,235 sq. mi.

POP.—336,150 (1913).

CAPITAL—Canea.

Formerly Crete was a province of Turkey. After an extended period of civil wars, France, Great Britain, Italy and Russia intervened and declaring Crete an autonomy, placed it under the administration of Prince George of Greece as High Commissioner. In October, 1908, the Cretan Assembly voted for union with Greece and in 1913 the union was formally effected.

40 Paras = 1 Piaster
4 Metallik = 1 Grosion (1899)
100 Lepta = 1 Drachma (1900)

Issued Under Joint Administration of France, Great Britain, Italy and Russia

British Sphere of Administration. District of Heraklion (Candia).

A1 A2

Handstamped

1898 ***Imperf.*** **Unwmkd.**

1	A1	20pa violet	1,000.	575.00

1898 Lithographed ***Perf. 11½***

2	A2	10pa blue	11.00	15.00
a.		Horizontal pair, imperf. between		
b.		Imperf., pair	500.00	
3	A2	20pa green	11.00	15.00
a.		Imperf., pair	500.00	

1899

4	A2	10pa brown	11.00	15.00
a.		Horizontal pair, imperf. between	500.00	
b.		Imperf., pair	500.00	
5	A2	20pa rose	11.00	15.00
a.		Imperf., pair	500.00	

Counterfeits exist of Nos. 1–5.

Reprints exist of Nos. 2–5.

Russian Sphere of Administration. District of Rethymnon.

Coat of Arms

A3 A4

1899 Handstamped ***Imperf.***

10	A3	1m green	13.00	10.00
11	A3	2m black	13.00	10.00
12	A3	2m rose	70.00	50.00
13	A4	1m blue	25.00	20.00

Nos. 10–13 exist on both wove and laid papers. Counterfeits exist.

Poseidon's Trident

A5 A5a

1899 Lithographed ***Perf. 11½***

With Control Mark Overprinted in Violet.

Without Stars at Sides.

14	A5	1m orange	40.00	32.50
15	A5	2m orange	40.00	32.50
16	A5	1gr orange	40.00	32.50
17	A5	1m green	40.00	32.50
18	A5	2m green	40.00	32.50
19	A5	1gr green	40.00	32.50
20	A5	1m yellow	40.00	32.50
21	A5	2m yellow	40.00	32.50
22	A5	1gr yellow	40.00	32.50
23	A5	1m rose	40.00	32.50
24	A5	2m rose	40.00	32.50
25	A5	1gr rose	40.00	32.50
26	A5	1m violet	40.00	32.50
27	A5	2m violet	40.00	32.50
28	A5	1gr violet	40.00	32.50
29	A5	1m blue	40.00	32.50
30	A5	2m blue	40.00	32.50
31	A5	1gr blue	40.00	32.50
32	A5	1m black	950.00	800.00
33	A5	2m black	950.00	800.00
34	A5	1gr black	950.00	800.00

With Stars at Sides.

35	A5a	1m blue	25.00	13.00
36	A5a	2m blue	13.00	10.00
37	A5a	1gr blue	9.00	8.00
38	A5a	1m rose	25.00	15.00
39	A5a	2m rose	13.00	10.00
40	A5a	1gr rose	9.00	8.00
41	A5a	1m green	25.00	12.50
42	A5a	2m green	13.00	10.00
43	A5a	1gr green	9.00	8.00
44	A5a	1m violet	25.00	12.50
45	A5a	2m violet	13.00	10.00
46	A5a	1gr violet	9.00	8.00
		Nos. 35-46 (12)	188.00	125.00

Nearly all of Nos. 14 to 46 may be found without control mark, with double control marks and in various colors.

Counterfeits exist of Nos. 14–46.

Issued by the Cretan Government.

Hermes

A6

Hera

A7

Prince George of Greece

A8

Talos

A9

Minos

A10

St. George and the Dragon

A11

1900, Mar. 1 Engraved ***Perf. 14***

50	A6	1l vio brn	75	15
51	A7	5l green	1.50	25
52	A8	10l red	2.00	20
53	A7	20l car rose	7.00	2.00

Overprinted ΠΡΟΣΩΡΙΝΟΝ

Red Overprint.

54	A8	25l blue	4.25	2.00
55	A6	50l lilac	5.25	2.75
56	A9	1d gray vio	10.00	5.00
57	A10	2d brown	20.00	12.50
58	A11	5d grn & blk	75.00	75.00
		Nos. 54-58 (5)	114.50	97.25

Black Overprint.

59	A8	25l blue	5.00	2.00
60	A6	50l lilac	6.00	4.00
61	A9	1d gray vio	10.00	5.00
a.		Inverted overprint	750.00	750.00
62	A10	2d brown	20.00	15.00
63	A11	5d grn & blk	75.00	75.00
		Nos. 59-63 (5)	116.00	101.00

1901 Without Overprint.

64	A6	1l bister	50	50
65	A7	20l orange	4.00	75
66	A8	25l blue	15.00	2.00
67	A6	50l lilac	20.00	10.00
68	A6	50l ultra	6.00	6.00
69	A9	1d gray vio	40.00	20.00
70	A10	2d brown	16.50	12.50
71	A11	5d grn & blk	27.50	22.50
		Nos. 64-71 (8)	129.50	74.25

No. 64 is a revenue stamp that was used for postage for a short time. Unused, it can only be considered as a revenue.

Types A6 to A8 in olive yellow, and types A9 to A11 in olive yellow and black are revenue stamps.

No. 66 Overprinted in Black ΠΡΟΣΩΡΙΝΟΝ

1901

72	A8	25l blue	20.00	2.50
a.		First letter of overprint inverted	150.00	150.00

No. 65 Surcharged in Black 5 5

1904, Dec.

73	A7	5l on 20l org	4.00	1.50
a.		Without "5" at right	10.00	10.00

Mycenaean Seal

A12

Britomartis (Cortyna Coin)

A13

Prince George

A14

Kydon and Dog (Cydonia Coin)

A15

Triton (Itanos Coin)

A16

Ariadne (Knossos Coin)

A17

Zeus as Bull Abducting Europa (Cortyna Coin)

A18

Palace of Minos Ruins, Knossos

A19

Arkadi Monastery and Mt. Ida

A20

1905, Feb. 15

74	A12	2l dl vio	1.00	40
75	A13	5l yel grn	4.00	22
76	A14	10l red	4.00	65
77	A15	20l bl grn	9.00	1.50
78	A16	25l ultra	7.50	1.00
79	A17	50l yel brn	8.00	7.50
80	A18	1d rose car & dp brn	110.00	100.00
81	A19	3d org & blk	45.00	40.00
82	A20	5d ol grn & blk	35.00	30.00
		Nos. 74-82 (9)	223.50	181.27

The so-called revolutionary stamps of 1905 were issued for sale to collectors and, so far as can be ascertained, were of no postal value whatever.

A. T. A. Zaimis

A21

Prince George Landing at Suda

A22

1907, Aug. 28

83	A21	25l bl & blk	20.00	2.50
84	A22	1d grn & blk	16.00	12.50

Commemorative of the administration under a High Commissioner.

Stamps of 1900-1907 Overprinted in Black ΕΛΛΑΣ

1908, Sept. 21

85	A6	1 l vio brn	25	25
86	A12	2 l dl vio	75	50
87	A13	5 l yel grn	2.00	38
88	A8	10 l red	2.00	65
89	A15	20 l bl grn	2.50	1.00
90	A21	25 l bl & blk	8.50	3.25
91	A17	50 l yel brn	9.00	7.50
92	A18	1d rose car & dp brn	95.00	85.00
93	A10	2d brown	10.00	9.00
94	A19	3d org & blk	45.00	40.00
95	A20	5d ol grn & blk	35.00	32.50
		Nos. 85-95 (11)	210.00	180.03

This overprint exists inverted and double, as well as with incorrect, reversed, misplaced and omitted letters. Similar errors are found on the Postage Due and Official stamps with this overprint.

Hermes by Praxiteles A23

1908

96	A23	10 l brn red	3.50	1.00
a.		Pair, one without overprint	8.00	
b.		Inverted overprint	15.00	
c.		Double overprint	15.00	

Nos. 96 and 114 were not regularly issued without overprint.

ΕΛΛΑΣ

No. 53 Surcharged

ΠΡΟΣΟΡΙΝΟΝ 5 5

1909

97	A7	5 l on 20 l car rose	150.00	150.00

Forgeries exist of No. 97.

On No. 65

98	A7	5 l on 20 l org	1.00	80
a.		Inverted surcharge		

ΕΛΛΑΣ

Overprinted on Nos. 64, J1

ΠΡΟΣΟΡΙΝΟΝ

99	A6	1 l bister	65	50
100	D1	1 l red	65	50

ΕΛΛΑΣ

No. J4 Surcharged

2

ΠΡΟΣΩΡΙΝΟΝ

101	D1	2 l on 20 l red	1.50	1.50
a.		Double surcharge	10.00	
b.		Inverted surcharge	10.00	
c.		Second letter of surch. "D" instead of "P"	30.00	30.00

ΕΛΛΑΣ

No. J4 Surcharged

2

ΠΡΟΣΩΡΙΝΟΝ

102	D1	2 l on 20 l red	1.00	80

Overprinted in Black:

ΕΛΛΑΣ *a*

ΕΛΛΑΣ *b*

ΕΛΛΑΣ *c*

103	A23(a)	10 l brn red	4.50	75
a.		Inverted overprint	40.00	
104	A15(a)	20 l bl grn	5.00	1.00
105	A21(c)	25 l bl & blk	10.00	5.00
106	A17(a)	50 l yel brn	7.50	6.00
107	A22(b)	1d grn & blk	20.00	17.50
108	A10(a)	2d brown	15.00	15.00
109	A19(b)	3d org & blk	110.00	80.00
110	A20(b)	5d ol grn & blk	35.00	35.00
		Nos. 103-110 (8)	207.00	160.25

Stamps of 1900-08 Overprinted in Red or Black ΕΛΛΑΣ *d*

1909-10

111	A6	1 l vio brn	25	20
112	A12	2 l dl vio	75	35
113	A13	5 l yel grn	38	20
114	A23	10 l brn red (Bk)	70	20
115	A15	20 l bl grn	5.00	50
116	A16	25 l ultra	5.00	75
117	A17	50 l yel brn	9.00	6.00
118	A18	1d rose car & dp brn (Bk)	125.00	110.00
119	A19	3d org & blk	50.00	45.00
120	A20	5d ol grn & blk	85.00	75.00
		Nos. 111-120 (10)	281.08	238.20

POSTAGE DUE STAMPS.

D1

Lithographed.

1901 *Perf. 14* **Unwmkd.**

J1	D1	1 l red	1.10	85
J2	D1	5 l red	2.25	2.00
J3	D1	10 l red	3.25	2.50
J4	D1	20 l red	4.50	2.75
J5	D1	40 l red	6.75	6.75
J6	D1	50 l red	5.50	5.00
J7	D1	1d red	50.00	45.00
J8	D1	2d red	13.00	12.00
		Nos. J1-J8 (8)	86.35	76.85

Surcharged in Black Ι ΔΡΑΧΜΗ

1901

J9	D1	1d on 1d red	20.00	17.50

1908 Overprinted ΕΛΛΑΣ

J10	D1	1 l red	1.00	1.10
a.		Inverted overprint	5.00	5.00
J11	D1	5 l red	3.00	2.50
J12	D1	10 l red	4.00	2.25
J13	D1	20 l red	6.25	5.50
J14	D1	40 l red	10.00	5.50
J15	D1	50 l red	10.00	6.25
J16	D1	1d red	200.00	200.00
J17	D1	1d on 1d red	15.00	10.00
J18	D1	2d red	30.00	20.00
		Nos. J10-J18 (9)	279.25	253.10

Counterfeits of No. J16 exist.

Overprinted ΕΛΛΑΣ

1910

J19	D1	1 l red	75	75
J20	D1	5 l red	2.25	2.25
J21	D1	10 l red	1.65	1.65
J22	D1	20 l red	8.75	7.00
J23	D1	40 l red	6.00	5.00
J24	D1	50 l red	7.50	6.25
J25	D1	1d red	45.00	35.00
J26	D1	2d red	30.00	25.00
		Nos. J19-J26 (8)	101.90	82.90

OFFICIAL STAMPS.

O1

O2

Perf. 14

1908, Jan. 14 Litho. **Unwmkd.**

O1	O1	10 l dl cl	30.00	3.50
O2	O2	30 l blue	37.50	3.75

Nos. O1–O2 exist imperf.

Overprinted ΕΛΛΑΣ

O3	O1	10 l dl cl	30.00	3.50
a.		Inverted overprint	42.50	
O4	O2	30 l blue	37.50	3.50
a.		Inverted overprint	50.00	

1910

Overprinted ΕΛΛΑΣ

O5	O1	10 l dl cl	3.00	1.25
O6	O2	30 l blue	3.00	1.25

CROATIA

(krō-ā'shĭ-ȧ; shȧ)

LOCATION—Southeastern Europe.
GOVT.—Independent state.
AREA—44,453 sq. mi.
POP.—7,000,000 (approx.).
CAPITAL—Zagreb.

The Independent Croatian State of 1941–45 became part of the Jugoslav Federation in 1945.

100 Paras = 1 Dinar
100 Banica = 1 Kuna

Jugoslavia Nos. 143 to 148B Overprinted in Black

NEZAVISNA DRŽAVA HRVATSKA IIIIII

Typographed.

1941, Apr. 12 *Perf. 12½* **Unwmkd.**

1	A16	50p orange	1.65	4.00
2	A16	1d yel grn	1.65	4.00
3	A16	1.50d red	1.65	2.25
4	A16	2d dp mag	1.65	3.25
5	A16	3d dl red brn	3.25	8.25
6	A16	4d ultra	3.25	9.25
7	A16	5d dk bl	4.50	10.00
8	A16	5.50d dk vio brn	4.50	11.00
		Nos. 1-8 (8)	22.10	52.00

The overprint exists inverted on Nos. 1–6; double on Nos. 2, 3 and 5.

Jugoslavia Nos. 142 to 154 Overprinted in Black

NEZAVISNA DRŽAVA HRVATSKA

1941, Apr. 21

9	A16	25p black	22	55
10	A16	50p orange	22	55
11	A16	1d yel grn	22	55
12	A16	1.50d red	22	55
13	A16	2d dp mag	22	1.10
14	A16	3d dl red brn	22	1.65
15	A16	4d ultra	50	1.
16	A16	5d dk bl	80	1
17	A16	5.50d dk vio brn	80	2.
18	A16	6d sl bl	1.00	3.
19	A16	8d sepia	1.65	3.
20	A16	12d brt vio	2.00	4.
21	A16	16d dl vio	2.25	5.
22	A16	20d blue	2.75	6.
23	A16	30d brt pink	4.00	10.
		Nos. 9-23 (15)	17.07	44.

The overprint exists inverted on Nos. 9–11, 17 and 20; double on Nos. 9, 12 and 17.

Jugoslavia Nos. 147, 148 Surcharged in Black

1941, May 16

24	A16	1d on 3d dl red brn	32	5
25	A16	2d on 4d ultra	32	5

The overprint exists inverted and double on Nos. 24–25.

Postage Due Stamps of Jugoslavia, Nos. J28, J30 to J32, Overprinted in Black

NEZAVISNA DRŽAVA HRVATSKA FRANCO

1941, May 17

26	D4	50p violet	22	40
27	D4	2d dp bl	50	90
28	D4	5d orange	50	90
29	D4	10d chocolate	75	1.25

Counterfeit overprints on Nos. 1-29 are plentiful.

Imperforates

Nearly all Croatian stamps, from No. 30 through 80, B3 through B76, J6 through J25, O1 through O24 and RA1 through RA7 exist imperforate.

Ozalj Castle
A1

Designs: 50b, City of Jajce. 75b, Old Warasdin. 1k, Velebit Mountains. 1.50k, Zelanjak. 2k, Zagreb Cathedral. 3k, Osjek Cathedral. 4k, Drina River. No. 38, Konjica. No. 39, Zemun. 6k, Dubrovnik. 7k, Save River. 8k, Sarajevo. 10k, Plitvice. 12k, Klis Fortress, Split. 20k, Hvar. 30k, Syrmia. 50k, Senj. 100k, Banjaluka (without "F.I.").

Photogravure.

1941-43 *Perf. 11.* **Unwmkd.**

Ordinary Paper.

30	A1	25b henna	5	5
a.		Tête bêche pair	22	45
31	A1	50b sl bl	5	5
a.		Tête bêche pair	22	45
32	A1	75b dk ol grn	5	5
33	A1	1k Prus grn	5	5
a.		Tête bêche pair	45	80
34	A1	1.50k dp grn	5	5
a.		Tête bêche pair	45	55
35	A1	2k car lake	5	5
a.		Tête bêche pair	30	45
36	A1	3k brn red	5	8
37	A1	4k dp ultra	5	8
a.		Tête bêche pair	30	55
38	A1	5k black	90	80
a.		Tête bêche pair	2.50	4.50
39	A1	5k blue	8	8
40	A1	6k lt ol brn	8	8
a.		Tête bêche pair	30	55
41	A1	7k org red	8	8
a.		Tête bêche pair	30	55

42 A1 8k chestnut 18 18
a. Tête bêche pair 90 1.40
43 A1 10k dk plum 45 18
a. Tête bêche pair 60 90
44 A1 12k ol brn 60 45
45 A1 20k gldn brn 45 22
a. Tête bêche pair 85 1.50
46 A1 30k blk brn 60 32
a. Tête bêche pair 1.40 2.25
47 A1 50k dk sl grn 1.00 45
a. Tête bêche pair 6.75 12.50
48 A1 100k violet 1.50 2.75
Nos. 30-48 (19) 6.32 6.05

Nos. 31, 35 and 43 exist on thin to pelure paper. Shades of all values exist.

Types of 1941 Overprinted in Brown or Green

1941-1942
10-IV

1942, Apr. 9

49 A1 2k dk brn 18 40
50 A1 5k dk car 38 65
51 A1 10k dk bl grn (G) 55 1.10

First anniversary of Croatian independence.

Banjaluka
("F.I." at upper right)
A20

1942, June 13

52 A20 100k violet 2.75 4.75

Banjaluka Philatelic Exhibition.

No. 35 Surcharged in Red Brown with New Value and Bar.

1942, June 23

53 A1 25b on 2k car lake 15 40
a. Tête bêche pair 45 1.00

Trakoscan Castle
A21

Catherine Zrinski
A23

Design: 12.50k, Citadel of Veliki Tabor.

1943

Pelure Paper

54 A21 3.50k brn car 55 55
55 A21 12.50k vio blk 55 55

No. 54 exists on ordinary paper.

1943, June 7 Engr. *Perf. 12½*

Designs: 2k, Fran Krsto Frankopan. 3.50k, Peter Zrinski.

Various Frames.

56 A23 1k dk bl 15 28
57 A23 2k dk ol grn 15 28
58 A23 3.50k dk red 25 42

Rugjer Boscovich
A26

Ante Pavelich
A27

1943, Dec. 13 *Perf. 11*

59 A26 3.50k cop red 22 42
60 A26 12.50k dk vio brn 38 65

Issued to honor Rugjer Boscovich (1711-1787), Serbo-Croat mathematician and physicist.

1943-44 Litho. *Perf. 12½, 14*

61 A27 25b org ver 10 18
62 A27 50b Prus bl 10 18
63 A27 75b ol grn 10 18
64 A27 1k lt grn 10 18
65 A27 1.50k dl gray vio 10 18
66 A27 2k rose lake 10 18
67 A27 3k rose brn 10 18
68 A27 3.50k brt bl 10 18
a. 3.50k dk bl, perf. 11½ 1.65 3.00
69 A27 4k brt red vio 10 18
70 A27 5k ultra 10 18
71 A27 8k org brn 10 18
72 A27 9k rose pink 18 28
73 A27 10k vio brn 18 28
74 A27 12k dk ol bis 18 28
75 A27 12.50k gray blk 18 28
76 A27 18k dl brn 18 28
77 A27 32k dk brn 18 28
78 A27 50k grnsh bl 18 28
79 A27 70k orange 40 55
80 A27 100k violet 80 90
Nos. 61-80 (20) 3.56 5.39

Nos. 61 and 63 measure 20½x26mm. Nos. 62 and 64-80 measure 22x27½mm.
Issue dates: 2k, 1943; No. 68a, June 13, 1943, Pavelich's birthday; others, 1944.

"Labor Day 1945"
A28

1945 Photogravure. *Perf. 11½*

81 A28 3.50k red brn 25 1.65

SEMI-POSTAL STAMPS.

Types of Jugoslavia, 1941, Overprinted in Gold "NEZAVISNA / DRZAVA / HRVATSKA"

Engraved.

1941, May 10 *Perf. 11½* Unwmkd.

B1 SP80 1.50d +1.50d bl blk 13.00 22.50
B2 SP81 4d +3d choc 13.00 22.50

Five thousand sets of Jugoslavia Nos. 142-154 were overprinted "NEZAVISNA DRZAVA HRVATSKA 10. IV. 1941" and small shield in red or blue, in 1941. Sold for double face value. Price, set, $225.

Costume of Sinj, Dalmatia
SP1

Soldiers with Arms of the Axis States
SP4

Designs (Costumes): 2k+2k, Travnik, Bosnia. 4k+4k, Turopolje, Croatia.

1941, Oct. 12 Photo. *Perf. 10½x10*

B3 SP1 1.50k +1.50k Prus bl & red 32 65
B4 SP1 2k +2k ol brn & red 50 80
B5 SP1 4k +4k brn lake & red 80 2.00

The surtax aided the Croatian Red Cross. Sheets of 20 stamps and 5 labels.

1941, Dec. 3 *Perf. 11*

B6 SP4 4k +2k bl 1.65 3.75

The surtax was used for Croatian Volunteers in the East.

Model Plane
SP5

Model Plane
SP6

Designs: 3k+3k, Boy with model plane. 4k+4k, Model seaplane in flight.

1942, Mar. 25

B7 SP5 2k +2k sep 40 65
B8 SP6 2.50k +2.50k dl grn 50 1.10
B9 SP5 3k +3k brn car 60 1.25
B10 SP6 4k +4k dp bl 90 1.90

The surtax aided the society of Croatian Wings (Hrvatska Krila).
Nos. B7-B10 were issued in sheets of 25 and in sheets of 24 plus label.

Souvenir Sheets.

SP9

Perf. 11.

B11 SP9 Sheet of two 25.00 40.00
a. 2k+8k brn car 9.75 16.00
b. 3k+12k dp bl 9.75 16.00

Imperf.

B12 SP9 Sheet of two 25.00 40.00
a. 2k+8k dp bl 9.75 16.00
b. 3k+12k brn car 9.75 16.00

The sheets measure 125x110mm.
To commemorate the Aviation Exposition of Zagreb. The surtax aided "Croatian Wings."
Nos. B11 and B12 exist with colors of stamps and inscriptions transposed.

Boy Trumpeters
SP10

Mother and Child
SP12

Triumphal Arch
SP11

1942, July 5 *Perf. 11½*

B13 SP10 3k +1k lake 55 1.10
B14 SP11 4k +2k dk brn 70 1.40
B15 SP12 5k +5k dp bl grn 90 1.65

The surtax was for national welfare. Sheets of 25.

Matthew Gubec
SP13

Ante Starcevich
SP14

SP15

1942, Nov. 22 *Perf. 14½*

B16 SP13 3k +6k dk red 28 55
B17 SP14 4k +7k sep 28 55

Souvenir Sheets

Perf. 12, Imperf.

B18 SP15 5k +20k dl bl 13.00 15.00

Issued to commemorate the heroes of Senj, May 9, 1937. Nos. B16-B17 were printed in sheets of 16 plus 9 labels, each bearing a hero's name. Size of No. B18: 80x95mm. The surtax aided the National Youth Society.

Sestine Peasant
SP16

Designs: 3k+1k, Slavonian peasant. 4k+2k, Bosnian peasant. 10k+5k, Dalmatian peasant. 13k+6k, Sestine peasant.

1942, Oct. 4 *Perf. 11½*

B20 SP16 1.50k +50b org brn & red 75 1.40
B21 SP16 3k +1k dl pur & red 75 1.40
B22 SP16 4k +2k dp bl & red 90 1.90
B23 SP16 10k +5k dk ol bis & red 1.25 2.75
B24 SP16 13k +6k rose lake & red 2.75 5.50
Nos. B20-B24 (5) 6.40 12.95

The surtax aided the Croatian Red Cross. Issued in sheets of 24 stamps plus label.

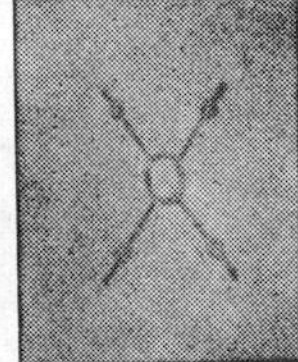

Croatian Labor Corpsman
SP20

Wmk. 278

Designs: 3k+3k, Corpsman with wheelbarrow. 7k+4k, Corpsman plowing.

Wmkd.

Network Connecting Circles. (278)

1943, Jan. 17 *Perf. 11*

B25 SP20 2(k) +1(k) ol gray & sep 1.75 3.50

B26 SP20 3(k) +3(k) brn & sep 1.75 *3.50*
B27 SP20 7(k) +4(k) gray bl & sep 1.75 *3.50*

The surtax aided the State Labor Service (Drzavna Radna Sluzba). Issued in sheets of 9.

Arms of Zagreb and "Golden Bull"
SP23

1943, Mar. 23 **Unwmkd.**

B28 SP23 3.50k (+6.50k) bril ultra 1.10 *3.00*

700th anniversary of Zagreb's "Golden Bull," a Magna Carta of civic rights and privileges granted to the city in 1242 by King Bela because the Croats annihilated Tartar hordes at Grobnik.

Issued in sheets of 8 with marginal inscriptions.

Ante Pavelich
SP24

1943, Apr. 10 ***Perf. 14***

B29 SP24 5k +3k cop red 28 *55*
B30 SP24 7k +5k dk grn 28 *55*

Surtax aided the National Youth Society.

Issued in sheets of 100, and in miniature sheets of 16 stamps and 9 labels.

Souvenir Sheets.

SP25

1943, May 17 ***Perf. 12, Imperf.***

B31 SP25 12k +8k dp ultra 8.25 *13.00*

The sheets measure 79x94mm.

Sailor at Sea of Azov
SP26

Designs: 2k+1k, Flier at Sevastopol and Rzhev. 3.50k+1.50k, Infantrymen at Stalingrad. 9k+4.50k, Panzer Division at Don River.

1943, July 1 ***Perf. 11***

B33 SP26 1k +50b grn 15 *28*
B34 SP26 2k +1k dk red 15 *28*
B35 SP26 3.50k +1.50k dk bl 15 *28*
B36 SP26 9k +4.50k chnt 15 *28*

Issued to honor the Croatian Legion which fought with the Germans in Russia.

Souvenir Sheets.

SP30

Perf. 11, Imperf.

B37 SP30 Sheet of four 1.65 *4.50*
a. 1k+50b dk bl 32 *55*
b. 2k+1k grn 32 *55*
c. 3.50k+1.50k dk red brn 32 *55*
d. 9k+4.50k bluish blk 32 *55*

The sheets measure 105x90mm. The surtax aided the Croatian Legion.

St. Mary's Church and Cistercian Cloister, Zagreb, in 1650
SP31

1943, Sept. 12 **Engr.** ***Perf. 14½***

B39 SP31 18k +9k dl gray vio 1.50 *3.00*

Souvenir Sheet.

Perf. 12½.

B40 SP31 18k +9k blk brn 6.50 *11.00*

Nos. B39–B40 were issued in connection with the Croatian Philatelic Society Exhibition at Zagreb. Size of No. B40: 100x131 mm.

No. B39 Overprinted in Red **HRVATSKO MORE 8. IX. 1943.**

1943, Sept. 12

B41 SP31 18k +9k dl gray vio 5.50 *9.25*

Return to Croatia of the Dalmatian and Croatian coasts.

Mother and Children
SP33

Nurse and Patient
SP34

1943, Oct. 3 **Litho.** ***Perf. 11***

B42 SP33 1k +50b bl grn & red 25 *40*
B43 SP33 2k +1k bril car & red 25 *40*
B44 SP33 3.50k +1.50k brt bl & red 25 *40*
B45 SP34 8k +3k red brn & red 25 *40*
B46 SP34 9k +4k yel grn & red 32 *55*
B47 SP33 10k +5k dp vio & red 40 *65*
B48 SP34 12k +6k brt ultra & red 50 *80*
B49 SP33 12.50k +6k dk brn & red 75 *1.25*
B50 SP34 18k +8k brn org & red 1.00 *1.65*
B51 SP34 32k +12k dk gray & red 1.65 *2.75*
Nos. B42-B51 (10) 5.62 *9.25*

The surtax aided the Croatian Red Cross.

Post Horn and Arms
SP35

Carrier Pigeon and Plane
SP36

Mercury
SP37

Winged Wheel
SP38

1944, Feb. 3

B52 SP35 7k +3.50(k) ol bis & red 12 *22*
B53 SP36 16k +8(k) bl & dk bl 18 *32*
B54 SP37 24k +12(k) red & rose red 28 *50*
B55 SP38 32k +16k gray & red 50 *1.00*

The surtax benefited communications and railway employees. Sheets of 9.

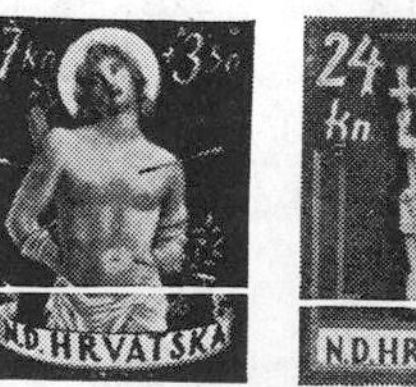

St. Sebastian
SP39

Statue of Ancient Croatian King
SP41

War Invalids
SP40

Death of King Peter Svacic, 1097
SP42

1944, Feb. 15

B56 SP39 7k +3.50(k) org red & rose car 20 *38*
B57 SP40 16k +8k yel grn & dk grn 28 *55*
B58 SP41 24k +12(k) yel brn & red 28 *55*
B59 SP42 32k +16k bl & dk bl 55 *1.10*

The surtax aided wounded war victims.

Issued in sheets of eight stamps, with marginal inscriptions and a central label picturing St. Sebastian.

Black Legion in Combat
SP43

Guarding the Drina
SP44

Jure Francetich
SP45

1944, May 22 **Photo.** ***Imperf.***

B60 SP43 3.50(k) +1.50k brn red 8 *15*
B61 SP44 12.50(k) +6.50k sl bl 8 *15*
B62 SP45 18(k) +9k ol brn 8 *15*

Third anniversary of Croatian independence.

The surtax aided the National Youth Society. Sheets of 20.

Perf. 14½.

B63 SP45 12.50(k) +287.50k int blk 3.25 *16.00*

Issued to commemorate Jure Francetich.

Labor Corpsmen Marching
SP46

Corpsman Digging
SP47

Designs: 18k+9k, Officer instructing corpsman. 32k+16k, Pavelich reviewing Labor Corps.

Perf. 11, 12½, 14½.

1944, Aug. 20 **Engraved**

B65 SP46 3.50(k) +1(k) dk red 10 *15*
B66 SP47 12.50(k) +6(k) sep 12 *28*
B67 SP47 18(k) +9(k) dk bl 12 *32*

B68	SP47	32(k) +16(k) gray grn	18	*32*

The surtax aided the State Labor Service (Drzavna Radna Sluzba).
Issued in sheets of 8 plus label.

Souvenir Sheet.

SP50

Perf. 12½.

B69	SP50	32(k) +16(k) dk brn, *cr*	2.25	4.75

The sheet measures 72x99mm. The surtax aided the State Labor Service.

Palm Leaf
SP51

Lithographed.

1944, Nov. 12 ***Perf. 11***

B70	SP51	2k +1k dl grn & red	10	22
B71	SP51	3.50k +1.50k car lake & red	12	28
B72	SP51	12.50k +6k ind & red	18	32

The surtax aided the Croatian Red Cross. Sheets of 16.

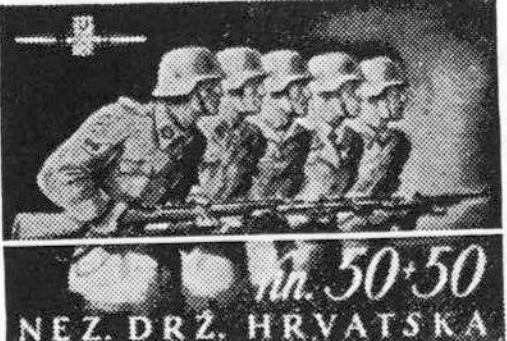

Men of Storm Division
SP52

Designs: 70k+70k, Soldiers of Storm Division in action. 100k+100k, Storm Division emblem.

Lithographed

1944 ***Perf. 11*** **Unwmkd.**

B73	SP52	50k +50k brick red	62.50	*135.00*
B74	SP52	70k +70k sep	62.50	*135.00*
B75	SP52	100k +100k chlky bl, pale bl & dp bl	62.50	*135.00*

The surtax aided the First Croatian Storm Division. Sheets of 20.

Souvenir Sheet.

SP54

B76	SP54	Sheet of three	1,000.	*1,750.*
a.		50k +50k brick red		
b.		70k +70k sep		
c.		100k +100k chlky bl, pale bl & dp bl		

Nos. B76a to B76c are inscribed "O. A." in brick red at right below design. The sheet measures 216x132mm. The surtax aided the First Croatian Storm Division. Counterfeits are plentiful.

Postman
SP55

Telephone Line Repairman
SP56

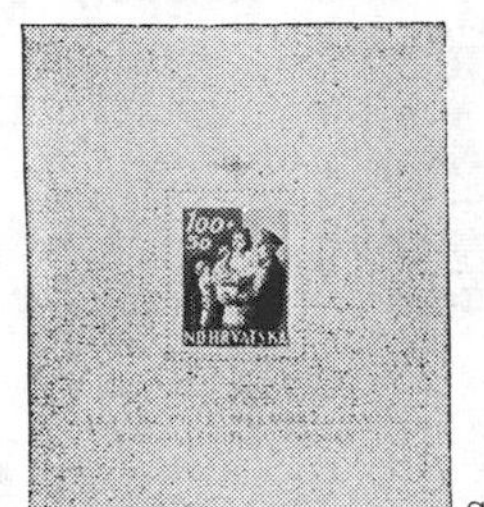

SP59

Designs; 24k+12k, Switchboard operator. 50k+25k, Postman delivering parcel.

1945 Photogravure.

B77	SP55	3.50(k) +1.50(k) sl gray	10	*22*
B78	SP56	12.50(k) +6(k) brn car	12	*28*
B79	SP56	24(k) +12(k) dk grn	18	*32*
B80	SP56	50(k) +25(k) brn vio	28	*55*

Sheets of eight.

Souvenir Sheet.

B81	SP59	100(k) +50(k) dp brn	3.25	*6.50*

The surtax on Nos. B77–B81 aided employees of the P.T.T. Size of No. B81: 100x120mm.

POSTAGE DUE STAMPS.

Jugoslavia Nos. J28–J32 Overprinted in Black

NEZAVISNA
DRZAVA
HRVATSKA

1941, Apr. 26 ***Perf. 12½*** **Unwmkd.**

J1	D4	50p violet	30	*55*
a.		50p rose vio	7.50	*11.00*
J2	D4	1d dp mag	30	*55*
J3	D4	2d dp bl	9.50	*16.00*
J4	D4	5d orange	95	*1.65*
J5	D4	10d chocolate	4.75	*8.25*
		Nos. J1-J5 (5)	15.80	*27.00*

The overprint on the 50p exists inverted. Counterfeit overprints exist.

Numeral of Value
D1 D2

1941, Sept. 12 **Litho.** ***Perf. 11***

J6	D1	50b car lake	18	*32*
J7	D1	1k car lake	18	*32*
J8	D1	2k car lake	28	*70*
J9	D1	5k car lake	40	*80*
J10	D1	10k car lake	65	*1.10*
		Nos. J6-J10 (5)	1.69	*3.24*

Size: 24x24 mm.

1943 ***Perf. 11½, 12x12½, 12½***

J11	D2	50b lt bl & gray	8	*10*
J12	D2	1k lt bl & gray	8	*10*
J13	D2	2k lt bl & gray	12	*22*
J14	D2	4k lt bl & gray	18	*32*
J15	D2	5k lt bl & gray	22	*40*
J16	D2	6k lt bl & gray	18	*32*
J17	D2	10k bl & ind	28	*50*
J18	D2	15k bl & ind	28	*50*
J19	D2	20k bl & ind	90	*1.50*
		Nos. J11-J19 (9)	2.32	*3.96*

Size: 25x24¼ mm.

1942, July 30 ***Perf. 10½, 11½***

J20	D2	50b lt bl & gray	18	*28*
J21	D2	1k lt bl & gray	12	*28*
J22	D2	2k lt bl & gray	30	*50*
J23	D2	5k lt bl & gray	28	*45*
J24	D2	10k lt bl & bl	60	*95*
J25	D2	20k lt bl & bl	1.00	*1.65*
		Nos. J20-J25 (6)	2.48	*4.11*

OFFICIAL STAMPS.

Croatian Coat of Arms
O1 O2

Lithographed.

1942–43 ***Perf. 10½, 11½*** **Unwmkd.**

Ordinary Paper

O1	O1	25b rose lake	5	*8*
O2	O1	50b sl blk	5	*8*
O3	O1	75b gray grn	8	*8*
O4	O1	1k org brn	5	*8*
O5	O1	2k turq bl	8	*18*
O6	O1	3k vermilion	5	*8*
O7	O1	4k brn vio	5	*8*
O8	O1	5k ultra	18	*35*
a.		Thin paper	7.00	*3.00*
O9	O1	6k brt vio	8	*8*
O10	O1	10k lt grn	5	*8*
O11	O1	12k brn rose	18	*25*
O12	O1	20k dk bl	18	*28*
O13	O2	30k brn vio & gray	12	*18*
O14	O2	40k vio blk & gray	18	*28*
O15	O2	50k brn lake & gray	60	*65*
O16	O2	100k blk & pink	60	*65*
		Nos. O1-O16 (16)	2.58	*3.46*

1943–44 Thin Paper ***Perf. 11½***

O17	O1	25b claret	5	*8*
O18	O1	50b gray	5	*8*
O19	O1	75b dl grn	5	*8*
O20	O1	1k org brn	5	*8*
O21	O1	2k sl bl	5	*8*
O22	O1	3.50k car rose	5	*8*
a.		Ordinary paper	7.00	*13.00*
O23	O1	6k brt red vio	5	*8*
O24	O1	12.50k dp org	5	*8*
a.		Ordinary paper	4.50	*8.25*
		Nos. O17-O24 (8)	40	64

POSTAL TAX STAMPS

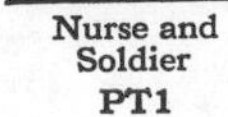

Nurse and Soldier
PT1

Wounded Soldier
PT2

Lithographed.

1942, Oct. 4 ***Perf. 11*** **Unwmkd.**

RA1	PT1	1k ol grn & red	32	*55*

The tax aided the Croatian Red Cross. Issued in sheets of 24 plus label.

1943, Oct. 3

RA2	PT2	2k bl & red	22	*32*

The tax aided the Croatian Red Cross.

Ruins
PT3

Wounded Soldier
PT4

1944, Jan. 1 **Photo.** ***Perf. 12***

RA3	PT3	1k dk sl grn	12	*18*
RA4	PT4	2k car lake	12	*18*
RA5	PT4	5k black	12	*18*
RA6	PT4	10k dp bl	22	*38*
RA7	PT4	20k brown	50	*80*
		Nos. RA3-RA7 (5)	1.08	*1.72*

CUBA

(kū'bȧ)

LOCATION—The largest island of the West Indies; south of Florida.

GOVT.—Former Spanish possession.

AREA—44,206 sq. mi.

POP.—6,743,000 (est. 1960).

CAPITAL—Havana.

Formerly a Spanish possession, Cuba made several unsuccessful attempts to gain her freedom, which finally led to the intervention of the United States in 1898. In that year under the Treaty of Paris, Spain relinquished the island to the U. S. in trust for its inhabitants. In 1902 a republic was established and the Cuban Congress took over the government from the military authorities.

8 Reales Plata = 1 Peso

100 Centesimos = 1 Escudo or Peseta (1867)

1000 Milesimas =

100 Centavos = 1 Peso

Pen cancellations are common on the earlier stamps of Cuba. Stamps so cancelled sell for very much less than those with postmark cancellations.

Issued under Spanish Dominion

Used also in Puerto Rico: Nos. 1–4, 9–14, 18–21, 32–34, 35A–37, 39–41, 43–45, 47–49, 51–53.

Used only in Puerto Rico: Nos. 55–57.

Queen Isabella II
A1

Wmk. 104

Blue Paper.
Wmkd. Loops. (104)

1855 Typographed *Imperf.*

1 A1 ½r p bl grn 40.00 3.00
2 A1 1r p gray grn 40.00 3.00
3 A1 2r p car 160.00 15.00
4 A1 2r p org red 175.00 15.00

Nos. 2-3 also used in Philippines.

Nos. 3-4 Surcharged **Y 1/4**

1855-56

5 A1 ¼r p on 2r p car 825.00 225.00
6 A1 ¼r p on 2r p org red 875.00 325.00

Surcharged **Y 1/4**

7 A1 ¼r p on 2r p car 625.00 110.00
a. Without fraction bar 375.00
8 A1 ¼r p on 2r p org red 825.00 225.00
a. Without fraction bar 525.00

The "Y¼" surcharge met the "Ynterior" rate for delivery within the city of Havana.

Wmk. 105

Rough Yellowish Paper.
1856 Wmkd. Crossed Lines. (105)

9 A1 ½r p on grnsh bl 7.50 1.25
10 A1 1r p grn 425.00 16.00
a. 1r p emer 450.00 22.50
11 A1 2r p org red 300.00 19.00

White Smooth Paper.

1857 **Unwmkd.**

12 A1 ½r p bl 6.00 75
13 A1 1r p gray grn 6.00 75
a. 1r p pale yel grn 9.00 1.75
14 A1 2r p dl rose 14.00 3.75

Surcharged **Y¼**

1860

15 A1 ¼r p on 2r p dl rose 225.00 80.00
a. 1 of ¼ inverted 300.00 160.00

Queen Isabella II
A2 A3

1862-64 *Imperf.*

16 A2 ¼r p blk 27.50 12.00
17 A3 ¼r p *buff* ('64) 27.50 10.00
18 A3 ½r p grn ('64) 6.00 1.00
19 A3 ½r p grn, *pale rose* ('64) 14.00 4.00
20 A3 1r p bl, *sal* ('64) 6.00 1.20
a. Diagonal half used as ½r on cover 100.00
21 A3 2r p ver, *buff* ('64) 40.00 11.00

No. 17 Overprinted in Black **66**

1866

22 A3 ¼r p *buff* 90.00 27.50

A5 A6

1866

23 A5 5c dl vio 70.00 30.00
24 A5 10c blue 3.00 1.50
25 A5 20c green 2.50 1.50
26 A5 40c rose 17.50 12.00

Stamps Dated "1867".

1867 ***Perf. 14.***

27 A5 5c dl vio 50.00 14.00
28 A5 10c blue 8.00 1.50
a. Imperf., pair 45.00 9.00
29 A5 20c green 8.00 1.50
a. Imperf., pair 65.00 100.00
30 A5 40c rose 17.50 10.00

Stamps Dated "1868".

1868

31 A6 5c dl vio 32.50 10.00
32 A6 10c blue 5.00 2.00
a. Diagonal half used as 5c on cover 100.00
33 A6 20c green 10.00 3.75
a. Diagonal half used as 10c on cover 125.00
34 A6 40c rose 20.00 9.00

Nos. 31 to 34 Overprinted in Black **HABILITADO POR LA NACION.** *e*

1868

35 A6 5c dl vio 55.00 25.00
35A A6 10c blue 55.00 25.00
36 A6 20c green 55.00 25.00
37 A6 40c rose 55.00 25.00

Stamps Dated "1869".

1869

38 A6 5c rose 55.00 17.50
39 A6 10c red brn 5.00 2.50
a. Diagonal half used as 5c on cover 75.00
40 A6 20c orange 10.00 3.00
41 A6 40c dl vio 45.00 10.00

Nos. 38-41 Overprinted type "e".

42 A6 5c rose 180.00 52.50
43 A6 10c red brn 65.00 25.00
44 A6 20c orange 55.00 32.50
45 A6 40c dl vio 80.00 32.50

"España"
A8 A9

1870 ***Perf. 14***

46 A8 5c blue 190.00 47.50
47 A8 10c green 3.50 90
a. Diagonal half used as 5c on cover 90.00
48 A8 20c red brn 3.50 90
a. Diagonal half used as 10c on cover 90.00
49 A8 40c rose 170.00 32.50

1871

50 A9 12c red lil 30.00 9.00
a. Imperf., pair 75.00 75.00
51 A9 25c ultra 3.50 1.50
a. Imperf., pair 37.50 37.50
b. Diagonal half used as 12c on cover 125.00
52 A9 50c gray grn 3.50 1.50
a. Imperf., pair 60.00 40.00
b. Diagonal half used as 25c on cover 125.00
53 A9 1p pale brn 35.00 10.00
a. Imperf., pair 60.00 60.00

King Amadeo
A10

1873 ***Perf. 14.***

54 A10 12½c dk grn 47.50 16.00
55 A10 25c gray 3.00 1.50
a. Diagonal half used as 12½c on cover 75.00
56 A10 50c brown 2.00 1.50
a. Imperf., pair 50.00 50.00
b. Half used as 25c on cover 75.00
57 A10 1p red brn 275.00 50.00
a. Diagonal half used as 50c on cover 200.00

Issues for Cuba Only

"España" Coat of Arms
A11 A12

1874

58 A11 12½c brown 17.50 7.50
59 A11 25c ultra 1.50 1.00
a. Diagonal half used as 12½c on cover 75.00
60 A11 50c dp vio 2.25 1.00
61 A11 50c gray 2.25 1.00
a. Diagonal half used as 25c on cover 75.00
62 A11 1p carmine 100.00 35.00
a. Imperf., pair 225.00 225.00

1875

63 A12 12½c lt vio 1.75 75
a. Imperf., pair 55.00
64 A12 25c ultra 90 60
a. Imperf., pair 55.00
b. Diagonal half used as 12½c on cover 75.00
65 A12 50c bl grn 90 60
a. Imperf., pair 55.00
b. Diagonal half used as 25c on cover 45.00
66 A12 1p brown 13.00 6.00
a. 1p dk brn 13.00 6.00
b. Half used as 50c on cover 85.00

King Alfonso XII
A13 A14

1876

67 A13 12½c green 3.00 60
68 A13 25c gray 1.25 50
a. Diagonal half used as 12½c on cover 75.00
69 A13 50c ultra 1.25 60
a. Imperf., pair 17.50
70 A13 1p black 13.00 5.00
a. Imperf., pair 40.00

1877

71 A14 10c lt grn 55.00 27.50
72 A14 12½c gray 10.00 1.50
a. Imperf., pair 27.50
73 A14 25c dk grn 75 50
a. Imperf., pair 27.50
74 A14 50c black 75 50
a. Imperf., pair 27.50
b. Half used as 25c on cover 75.00
75 A14 1p brown 27.50 15.00
Nos. 71-75 (5) 94.00 45.00

Stamps Dated "1878".

1878

76 A14 5c blue 60 50
a. Imperf., pair 27.50
77 A14 10c black 75.00 37.50
a. Imperf., pair 200.00
78 A14 12½c brn bis 3.50 1.50
a. 12½c gray bis 2.50 1.25
b. Imperf., pair 27.50
79 A14 25c dp grn 50 25
a. Imperf., pair 27.50
b. Diagonal half used as 12½c on cover 60.00
80 A14 50c dk bl grn 50 25
a. Imperf., pair 27.50
81 A14 1p carmine 13.00 7.00
a. Imperf., pair 55.00
Nos. 76-81 (6) 93.10 47.00

Stamps Dated "1879"

1879

82 A14 5c sl blk 1.00 50
83 A14 10c orange 175.00 85.00
84 A14 12½c rose 1.00 50
85 A14 25c ultra 75 50
a. Diagonal half used as 12½c on cover 75.00
b. Imperf., pair 55.00 40.00
86 A14 50c gray 60 40
a. Diagonal half used as 25c on cover 75.00
87 A14 1p ol bis 30.00 15.00
Nos. 82-87 (6) 208.35 101.90

A15

A16

A17

1880

88 A15 5c green 50 15
89 A15 10c lake 85.00 42.50
90 A15 12½c gray 50 15
91 A15 25c gray bl 50 15
a. Diagonal half used as 12½c on cover 75.00
92 A15 50c brown 50 20
a. Half used as 25c on cover 75.00
93 A15 1p yel brn 9.00 3.50
Nos. 88-93 (6) 96.00 46.65

1881

94 A16 1c green 50 15
95 A16 2c lake 45.00 22.50
96 A16 2½c ol bis 90 40
97 A16 5c gray bl 50 15
98 A16 10c yel brn 50 15
99 A16 20c dk brn 9.00 7.00
Nos. 94-99 (6) 56.40 30.35

1882

100 A17 1c green 60 40
101 A17 2c lake 3.50 40
102 A17 2½c dk brn 8.00 2.50
103 A17 5c gray bl 3.50 90
a. Diagonal half used as 2½c on cover 75.00
104 A17 10c ol bis 60 15
105 A17 20c red brn 100.00 35.00
Nos. 100-105 (6) 116.20 39.35

See Nos. 121-131.

Issue of 1882 Surcharged or Overprinted in Black, Blue or Red:

a

b

c

d

e

1883

No.	Type	Description	Unused	Used
106	A17 (a)	5 on 5c gray bl (R)	2.25	1.25
a.		Triple surcharge		
b.		Double surcharge	4.00	4.00
c.		Inverted surcharge	3.00	3.00
d.		Without "5" in surcharge	9.00	9.00
e.		Double surcharge, types "a" and "d"		
107	A17 (a)	10 on 10c ol bis (Bl)	2.50	1.50
a.		Inverted surcharge		
b.		Double surcharge	4.00	
108	A17 (a)	20 on 20c red brn (Bk)	35.00	25.00
a.		"10" instead of "20"	75.00	75.00
b.		Double surcharge		
109	A17 (b)	5 on 5c gray bl (R)	2.50	1.25
a.		Inverted surcharge	3.50	3.50
b.		Double surcharge	5.00	
110	A17 (b)	10 on 10c ol bis (Bl)	3.50	1.75
a.		Inverted surcharge	4.50	4.50
b.		Double surcharge		
111	A17 (b)	20 on 20c red brn (Bk)	35.00	25.00
a.		Double surcharge		
b.		Double surcharge, types "b" and "c"		
112	A17 (c)	5 on 5c gray bl (R)	2.50	1.50
a.		Inverted surcharge		
b.		Double surcharge, types "c" and "d"	6.00	
113	A17 (c)	10 on 10c ol bis (Bl)	6.00	2.50
a.		Inverted surcharge		
b.		Double surcharge		
114	A17 (c)	20 on 20c red brn (Bk)	50.00	25.00
a.		"10" instead of "20"	120.00	120.00
b.		Double surcharge		
c.		Double surcharge, types "a" and "c"		
115	A17 (d)	5 on 5c gray bl (R)	2.50	1.50
a.		Inverted surcharge	3.50	3.50
b.		Double surcharge		
116	A17 (d)	10 on 10c ol bis (Bl)	6.00	2.50
a.		Inverted surcharge		
b.		Double surcharge		
117	A17 (d)	20 on 20c red brn (Bk)	80.00	35.00
a.		Double surcharge, types "a" and "d"		
118	A17 (e)	5c gray bl (R)	3.50	2.00
a.		Double overprint	6.00	
119	A17 (e)	10c ol bis (Bl)	6.00	5.00
a.		Double overprint		
120	A17 (e)	20c red brn (Bk)	85.00	40.00
a.		Double overprint		
		Nos. 106-120 (15)	322.25	170.75

No. 120 has been reprinted. The overprint is handstamped instead of being press printed.

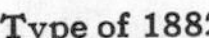

1882

1st retouch

2d retouch

The differences between the stamps of 1882 and the various retouches are as follows :

Original state: The medallion is surrounded by a heavy line of color of nearly even thickness, touching the horizontal line below the word "Cuba" (or "Filipinas", as the case may be); the opening in the hair above the temple is narrow and pointed.

First retouch: The line around the medallion is thin, except at the upper right, and does not touch the horizontal line above it; the opening in the hair is slightly wider and a trifle rounded; the lock of hair above the forehead is shaped like a broad "V" and ends in a point; there is a faint white line below it, which is not found on the stamps in the original state. Owing to wear of the plate the shape of the lock of hair and the width of the white line below it vary.

Second retouch: The opening in the hair forms a semi-circle; the lock above the forehead is nearly straight, having only a slight wave, and the white line is much broader than before.

1883-86

No.	Type	Description	Unused	Used
121	A17	1c grn, 2nd retouch	2.00	25
122	A17	2½c ol bis	50	15
124	A17	2½c violet	50	15
a.		2½c red lil ('85)	60	25
b.		2½c ultra	150.00	70.00
125	A17	5c gray bl, 1st retouch	2.00	15
126	A17	5c gray bl, 2nd retouch	6.00	1.50
a.		Diagonal half used as 2½c on cover		35.00
127	A17	10c brn, 1st retouch	2.50	75
a.		Diagonal half used as 5c on cover		35.00
128	A17	20c ol bis	17.50	4.00
		Nos. 121-128 (7)	31.00	6.95

1888

No.	Type	Description	Unused	Used
129	A17	2½c red brn	4.00	1.50
130	A17	10c blue	2.25	1.00
a.		Diagonal half used as 5c on cover		35.00
131	A17	20c brnsh gray	20.00	6.00

King Alfonso XIII

A18 A19

1890-97

No.	Type	Description	Unused	Used
132	A18	1c gray brn	16.00	6.00
133	A18	1c ol gray ('91)	10.00	1.25
134	A18	1c ultra ('94)	3.50	50
a.		Imperf., pair	75.00	
135	A18	1c dk vio ('96)	1.75	25
136	A18	2c sl bl	6.00	1.50
137	A18	2c lil brn ('91)	1.75	50
138	A18	2c rose ('94)	25.00	3.00
a.		Imperf., pair	110.00	
139	A18	2c cl ('96)	7.50	90
140	A18	2½c emerald	10.00	2.25
141	A18	2½c sal ('91)	30.00	6.00
142	A18	2½c lil ('94)	2.25	35
a.		Imperf., pair	100.00	
143	A18	2½c rose ('96)	1.00	20
144	A18	5c ol gray	1.00	75
145	A18	5c emer ('91)	1.25	60
a.		Imperf., pair	65.00	
146	A18	5c sl bl ('96)	50	20
147	A18	10c brn vio	2.50	90
148	A18	10c cl ('91)	1.75	60
a.		Imperf., pair	65.00	
149	A18	10c emer ('96)	3.50	25
150	A18	20c dk vio	1.00	75
151	A18	20c ultra ('91)	11.00	6.00
152	A18	20c red brn ('94)	25.00	6.00
a.		Imperf. pair	160.00	
153	A18	20c vio ('96)	25.00	7.00
154	A18	40c org brn ('97)	50.00	15.00
155	A18	80c lil brn ('97)	65.00	20.00
		Nos. 132-155 (24)	302.25	80.75

1898

No.	Type	Description	Unused	Used
156	A19	1m org brn	25	20
157	A19	2m org brn	25	20
158	A19	3m org brn	25	20
159	A19	4m org brn	6.00	2.00
160	A19	5m org brn	25	20
161	A19	1c blk vio	25	20
162	A19	2c dk bl grn	25	20
163	A19	3c dk brn	25	20
164	A19	4c orange	17.50	5.00
165	A19	5c car rose	1.25	25
a.		Imperf., pair	60.00	
166	A19	6c dk bl	25	20
a.		Imperf., pair	60.00	
167	A19	8c gray brn	1.25	50
168	A19	10c vermilion	1.25	50
169	A19	15c sl grn	6.00	50
170	A19	20c maroon	75	25
171	A19	40c dk lil	3.00	50
172	A19	60c black	3.00	50
173	A19	80c red brn	20.00	10.00
174	A19	1p yel grn	20.00	10.00
175	A19	2p sl bl	30.00	10.00
		Nos. 156-175 (20)	112.00	41.60

Issued under Administration of the United States.

Puerto Principe Issue.

Issues of Cuba of 1898 and 1896 Surcharged:

HABILITADO 1 cent. — *a*

HABILITADO 1 cents. — *b*

HABILITADO 2 cents. — *c*

HABILITADO 2 cents. — *d*

HABILITADO 3 cents. — *e*

HABILITADO 3 cents. — *f*

HABILITADO 5 cents. — *g*

HABILITADO 5 cents. — *h*

HABILITADO 5 cents. — *i*

HABILITADO 5 cents. — *j*

HABILITADO 3 cents. — *k*

HABILITADO 3 cents. — *l*

HABILITADO 10 cents. — *m*

Types a, c, d, e, f, g and h are 17½mm. high, the others are 19½mm. high.

Black Surcharge

On Nos. 156, 157, 158 and 160.

1898-99

No.	Type	Description	Unused	Used
176	(a)	1c on 1m org brn	55.00	37.50
177	(b)	1c on 1m org brn	45.00	30.00
a.		Broken figure "1"	75.00	60.00
b.		Inverted surcharge		200.00
d.		Same as "a", inverted		250.00
178	(c)	2c on 2m org brn	22.50	15.00
a.		Inverted surcharge	250.00	50.00
179	(d)	2c on 2m org brn	40.00	25.00
a.		Inverted surcharge	350.00	100.00
179B	(k)	3c on 1m org brn	375.00	150.00
c.		Double surcharge	1,500.	750.00
179D	(l)	3c on 1m org brn	1,500.	600.00
e.		Double surcharge		
179F	(e)	3c on 2m org brn		2,000.
179G	(f)	3c on 2m org brn		2,500.
180	(e)	3c on 3m org brn	27.50	22.50
a.		Inverted surcharge		100.00
181	(f)	3c on 3m org brn	75.00	50.00
a.		Inverted surcharge		300.00

182	(g)	5c on 1m org brn	700.00	175.00
a.		Inverted surcharge		500.00
183	(h)	5c on 1m org brn	1,500.	400.00
a.		Inverted surcharge		700.00
184	(g)	5c on 2m org brn	750.00	200.00
185	(h)	5c on 2m org brn	1,500.	400.00
186	(g)	5c on 3m org brn		165.00
a.		Inverted surcharge		700.00
187	(h)	5c on 3m org brn		400.00
a.		Inverted surcharge		1,000.
188	(g)	5c on 5m org brn	70.00	55.00
a.		Inverted surcharge	400.00	175.00
b.		Double surcharge		
189	(h)	5c on 5m org brn	350.00	225.00
a.		Inverted surcharge		400.00
b.		Double surcharge		
189C	(i)	5c on 5m org brn		4,000.

Black Surcharge on No. P25.

190	(g)	5c on ½m bl grn	250.00	75.00
a.		Inverted surcharge	500.00	150.00
b.		Pair, one without surcharge		450.00
191	(h)	5c on ½m bl grn	300.00	90.00
a.		Inverted surcharge		200.00
192	(i)	5c on ½m bl grn	550.00	200.00
a.		Double surcharge, one diagonal		3,000.
193	(j)	5c on ½m bl grn	700.00	300.00

Red Surcharge on No. 161.

196	(k)	3c on 1c blk vio	60.00	25.00
a.		Inverted surcharge		200.00
197	(l)	3c on 1c blk vio	125.00	45.00
a.		Inverted surcharge		300.00
198	(i)	5c on 1c blk vio	20.00	20.00
a.		Inverted surcharge		100.00
b.		Vertical surcharge		2,000.
c.		Double surcharge	400.00	600.00
d.		Double inverted surcharge		
199	(j)	5c on 1c blk vio	50.00	40.00
a.		Inverted surcharge		250.00
b.		Vertical surcharge		2,000.
c.		Double surcharge	1,000.	600.00
200	(m)	10c on 1c blk vio	20.00	50.00
a.		Broken figure "I"	40.00	100.00

Black Surcharge on Nos. P26 - P30.

201	(k)	3c on 1m bl grn	300.00	200.00
a.		Inverted surcharge		400.00
b.		"EENTS"	550.00	400.00
c.		Same as "b", inverted		850.00
202	(l)	3c on 1m bl grn	500.00	400.00
a.		Inverted surcharge		850.00
203	(k)	3c on 2m bl grn	850.00	250.00
a.		"EENTS"	1,200.	450.00
b.		Inverted surcharge		600.00
c.		Same as "a", inverted		750.00
204	(l)	3c on 2m bl grn	1,000.	450.00
a.		Inverted surcharge		750.00
205	(k)	3c on 3m bl grn	900.00	250.00
a.		Inverted surcharge		500.00
b.		"EENTS"	1,200.	375.00
c.		Same as "b", inverted		700.00
206	(l)	3c on 3m bl grn	1,200.	375.00
a.		Invtd. surch.		700.00
211	(i)	5c on 1m bl grn		1,400.
a.		"EENTS"		2,000.
212	(j)	5c on 1m bl grn		2,000.
213	(i)	5c on 2m bl grn		1,250.
a.		"EENTS"		1,750.
214	(j)	5c on 2m bl grn		1,750.
215	(i)	5c on 3m bl grn		500.00
a.		"EENTS"		900.00
216	(j)	5c on 3m bl grn		900.00
217	(i)	5c on 4m bl grn	2,000.	500.00
a.		"EENTS"	2,500.	1,200.
b.		Inverted surcharge		900.00
c.		Same as "a", inverted		1,400.
218	(j)	5c on 4m bl grn		1,100.
a.		Invtd. surch.		1,400.
219	(i)	5c on 8m bl grn	2,500.	1,000.
a.		Inverted surcharge		1,500.
b.		"EENTS"		2,000.
c.		Same as "b", inverted		2,500.
220	(j)	5c on 8m bl grn		2,000.
a.		Invtd. surch.		2,500.

CUBA

United States Nos. 279a, 267, 279B, 268, 281a, 282C and 283a Surcharged in Black

1 c. de PESO.

Wmkd. USPS (191)

1899 *Perf. 12.*

221	A87	1c on 1c yel grn	4.25	60
222	A88	2c on 2c car	4.25	50
a.		2c on 2c red	5.00	40
b.		"CUPA"	120.00	120.00
c.		Invtd. surch.	2,750.	2,750.
223	A88	2½c on 2c red	3.00	60
a.		2½c on 2c car	3.50	2.00
224	A89	3c on 3c pur	8.50	1.25
a.		Period between "B" and "A"	27.50	27.50
225	A91	5c on 5c bl	8.50	1.25
a.		"CUPA"	60.00	50.00
226	A94	10c on 10c brn, type I	22.50	8.00
b.		"CUBA" omitted	2,500.	2,500.
226A	A94	10c on 10c brn, type II	4,500.	
		Nos. 221-226 (6)	51.00	12.20

The 2½c was sold and used as a 2c stamp.

Excellent counterfeits of this and the preceding issue exist, especially inverted and double surcharges.

Issues of the Republic under U. S. Military Rule.

Statue of Columbus
A20

Royal Palms
A21

"Cuba"
A22

Ocean Liner
A23

Cane Field
A24

Wmkd. U S—C. (191C)

1899 **Engraved** *Perf. 12*

227	A20	1c yel grn	3.00	15
228	A21	2c carmine	3.00	15
a.		2c scar	3.00	15
b.		Booklet pane of 6	1,750.	
229	A22	3c purple	3.00	25
230	A23	5c blue	4.50	30
231	A24	10c brown	10.00	75
		Nos. 227-231 (5)	23.50	1.60

Issues of the Republic

No. 229 Surcharged in Carmine

HABILITADO
UN CENTAVO 1 OCTUBRE 1902

1902, Sept. 30

232	A22	1c on 3c pur	1.50	75
a.		Inverted surcharge	20.00	20.00
b.		Surcharge sideways (numeral horizontal)		
c.		Double surcharge	30.00	30.00

Counterfeits of the errors are plentiful.

Re-engraved.

The re-engraved stamps of 1905-07 may be distinguished from the issue of 1899 as follows:

ORIGINAL RE-ENGRAVED

1c: The ends of the label inscribed "Centavo" are rounded instead of square.

2c: The foliate ornaments, inside the oval disks bearing the numerals of value, have been removed.

5c: Two lines forming a right angle have been added in the upper corners of the label bearing the word "Cuba".

10c: A small ball has been added to each of the square ends of the label bearing the word "Cuba".

1905 *Perf. 12* **Unwmkd.**

233	A20	1c green	2.25	15
234	A21	2c rose	1.50	15
a.		Bklt. pane of 6	135.00	
236	A23	5c blue	45.00	1.50
237	A24	10c brown	4.00	60

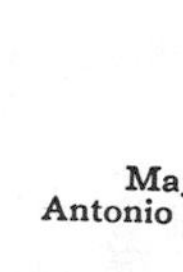

Maj. Gen. Antonio Maceo
A26

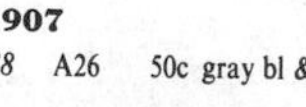

1907

238	A26	50c gray bl & blk	1.50	90

Bartolomé Masó
A27

Máximo Gómez
A28

Julio Sanguily
A29

Ignacio Agramonte
A30

Calixto García
A31

José M. Rodriquez y Rodriquez (Mayia)
A32

Carlos Roloff
A33

1910, Feb. 1

239	A27	1c grn & vio	1.10	10
a.		Center inverted	200.00	200.00
240	A28	2c car & grn	2.25	10
a.		Center inverted	800.00	800.00
241	A29	3c vio & bl	1.50	25
242	A30	5c bl & grn	20.00	1.00
243	A31	8c ol & vio	1.50	40
244	A32	10c brn & bl	9.00	85
a.		Center inverted	1,150.	
245	A26	50c vio & blk	2.25	60
246	A33	1p sl & blk	10.00	5.00
		Nos. 239-246 (8)	47.60	8.30

1911-13

247	A27	1c green	75	10
248	A28	2c car rose	1.00	8
a.		Bklt. pane of 6 ('13)	75.00	
250	A30	5c ultra	2.50	10
251	A31	8c ol grn & blk	1.50	75
252	A33	1p black	7.00	2.50
		Nos. 247-252 (5)	12.75	3.53

Map of Cuba
A34

1914–15

253	A34	1c green	75	6
a.		Booklet pane of 6	80.00	
254	A34	2c car rose	90	5
a.		Booklet pane of 6	80.00	
255	A34	2c red ('15)	1.75	5
a.		Booklet pane of 6	80.00	
256	A34	3c violet	5.00	50
257	A34	5c blue	7.00	25
258	A34	8c ol grn	6.00	1.00
259	A34	10c brown	11.00	50
260	A34	10c ol grn ('15)	13.00	75
261	A34	50c orange	80.00	15.00
262	A34	1p gray	110.00	30.00
		Nos. 253-262 (10)	235.40	48.16

Imperf. pairs, price each $100 to $500.

Gertrudis Gómez de Avellaneda
A34a

1914

263	A34a	5c blue	15.00	6.00

Issued to commemorate the centenary of the birth of the Cuban poetess, Gertrudis Gómez de Avellaneda (1814–1873).

José Martí A35 — Máximo Gómez A36

José de la Luz Caballero A37 — Calixto García A38

Ignacio Agramonte A39 — Tomás Estrada Palma A40

José A. Saco A41 — Antonio Maceo A42

Carlos Manuel de Céspedes A43

1917–18 *Perf. 12.* **Unwmkd.**

264	A35	1c bl grn	1.00	5
a.		Booklet pane of 6	37.50	
b.		Booklet pane of 30	250.00	
265	A36	2c rose	75	5
a.		Booklet pane of 6	50.00	
b.		Booklet pane of 30	250.00	
266	A36	2c lt red ('18)	75	5
a.		Booklet pane of 6	50.00	
267	A37	3c violet	1.25	5
a.		Imperf., pair	325.00	
b.		Booklet pane of 6	50.00	
268	A38	5c dp bl	2.50	6
269	A39	8c red brn	6.00	15
270	A40	10c yel brn	3.00	10
271	A41	20c gray grn	12.00	1.00
272	A42	50c dl rose	14.00	1.00
273	A43	1p black	14.00	1.00
		Nos. 264-273 (10)	55.25	3.51

Wmk. 106

Wmkd. Star. (106)

1925-28 *Perf. 12.*

274	A35	1c bl grn	1.75	6
a.		Booklet pane of 30	325.00	
275	A36	2c brt rose	1.50	5
a.		Booklet pane of 6	70.00	
b.		Booklet pane of 30	325.00	
276	A38	5c dp bl	3.00	10
277	A39	8c red brn ('28)	6.00	50
278	A40	10c yel brn ('27)	7.00	60
279	A41	20c ol grn	11.00	1.00
		Nos. 274-279 (6)	30.25	2.31

1926 *Imperf.*

280	A35	1c bl grn	2.75	1.75
281	A36	2c brt rose	2.50	1.50
282	A38	5c dp bl	4.00	3.00

See also Nos. 304-310.

Arms of Republic A44

1927, May 20 *Perf. 12* **Unwmkd.**

283	A44	25c violet	12.50	6.00

25th anniversary of the Republic.

Tomás Estrada Palma A45

Designs: 2c, Gen. Gerardo Machado. 5c, Morro Castle. 8c, Havana Railway Station. 10c, Presidential Palace. 13c, Tobacco Plantation. 20c, Treasury Building. 30c, Sugar Mill. 50c, Havana Cathedral. 1p, Galician Clubhouse, Havana.

1928, Jan. 2 **Wmk. 106**

284	A45	1c dp grn	60	40
285	A45	2c brt rose	60	40
286	A45	5c dp bl	1.75	60
287	A45	8c lt red brn	2.75	1.50
288	A45	10c bis brn	1.50	1.00
289	A45	13c orange	2.25	1.00
290	A45	20c ol grn	2.75	1.25
291	A45	30c dk vio	5.00	1.00
292	A45	50c car rose	8.00	3.50
293	A45	1p gray blk	16.00	8.00
		Nos. 284-293 (10)	41.20	18.65

Sixth Pan-American Conference.

Capitol, Havana A55

1929, May 18

294	A55	1c green	50	40
295	A55	2c car rose	50	35
296	A55	5c blue	75	50
297	A55	10c bis brn	1.50	60
298	A55	20c violet	5.00	2.50
		Nos. 294-298 (5)	8.25	4.35

Opening of the Capitol, Havana.

Hurdler A56

1930, Mar. 15 **Engraved**

299	A56	1c green	1.00	50
300	A56	2c carmine	1.00	50
301	A56	5c dp bl	1.50	50
302	A56	10c bis brn	2.25	1.00
303	A56	20c violet	10.00	5.00
		Nos. 299-303 (5)	15.75	7.50

Issued to commemorate the second Central American Athletic Games.

Types of 1917 Portrait Issue. Flat Plate Printing. Engraved

1930–45 *Perf. 10* **Wmk. 106**

304	A35	1c bl grn	1.10	25
a.		Booklet pane of 6	50.00	
b.		Booklet pane of 30		
305	A36	2c brt rose	200.00	90.00
a.		Booklet pane of 6	1,400.	
305B	A37	3c dk rose vio ('42)	4.50	60
c.		Booklet pane of 6	50.00	
306	A38	5c dk bl	5.00	40
306A	A39	8c red brn ('45)	5.00	50
307	A40	10c brown	5.00	50
a.		10c yel brn ('35)	7.00	1.00
307B	A41	20c ol grn ('41)	8.00	1.00
		Nos. 304-307B (7)	228.60	93.25

Nos. 305 and 305B were printed for booklet panes and all copies have straight edges.

Rotary Press Printing.

308	A35	1c bl grn	1.75	25
309	A36	2c brt rose	1.75	25
a.		Booklet pane of 50		
310	A37	3c violet	2.50	25
a.		3c dl vio ('38)	1.75	25
b.		3c rose vio ('41)	1.75	25
c.		Bklt. pane of 50		

The flat plate stamps measure 18½x21½mm.; those from the rotary press, 19x22mm.

The Mangos of Baragua A57

War Memorial A61

Battle of Mal Tiempo A58

Battle of Coliseo A59

Maceo, Gómez and Zayas A60

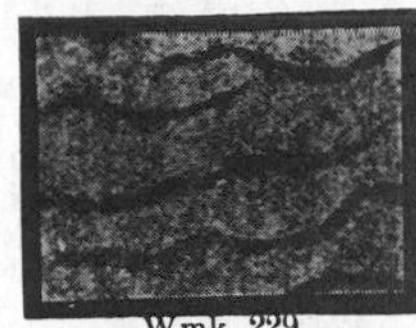

Wmk. 229

Wmkd. Wavy Lines. (229)

1933, Apr. 23 **Photo.** *Perf. 12½*

312	A57	3c dk brn	1.00	25
313	A58	5c dk bl	1.00	50
314	A59	10c emerald	3.00	50
315	A60	13c red	3.00	1.25
316	A61	20c black	6.00	4.00
		Nos. 312-316 (5)	14.00	6.50

Issued in commemoration of the War of Independence and the dedication of the "Soldado Invasor" monument.

Types of 1917 Issues with Carmine or Black Overprint Reading Up or Down

GOBIERNO
REVOLUCIONARIO
4-9-1933

Rotary Press Printing. Engraved

1933, Dec. 23 *Perf. 10* **Wmk. 106**

317	A35	1c bl grn (C)	1.00	35

With Additional Surcharge of New Value and Bars.

318	A37	2c on 3c vio (Bk)	1.00	35

Nos. 317–318 commemorate the establishment of a revolutionary junta.

Dr. Carlos J. Finlay A62

Engraved.

1934, Dec. 3 *Perf. 10* **Wmk. 106**

319	A62	2c dk car	1.00	30
320	A62	5c dk bl	2.25	75

Issued to commemorate the centenary of the birth of Dr. Carlos J. Finlay (1833–1915), physician-biologist who found that a mosquito transmitted yellow fever.

Pres. José Miguel Gómez A63

Gómez Monument A64

1936, May *Perf. 10*

322	A63	1c green	60	30
323	A64	2c carmine	1.50	30

Issued in commemoration of the unveiling of a monument to Gen. José Miguel Gómez, ex-president.

Matanzas Issue.

Map of Cuba A65

Designs: 2c, Map of Free Zone. 4c, S. S. "Rex" in Matanzas Bay. 5c, Ships in Matanzas Bay. 8c, Caves of Bellamar. 10c, Valley of Yumuri. 20c, Yumuri River. 50c, Ships Leaving Port.

Photogravure.
Wmkd. Wavy Lines. (229)

1936, May 5 ***Perf. 12½***

324	A65	1c bl grn	40	25
325	A65	2c red	60	30
326	A65	4c claret	1.25	40
327	A65	5c ultra	1.10	40
328	A65	8c org brn	2.50	1.00
329	A65	10c emerald	2.00	1.00
330	A65	20c brown	5.00	3.50
331	A65	50c slate	8.00	5.00
		Nos. 324-331, C18-C21, CE1, E8 (14)	48.10	27.10

Exist imperf. Price 20% more.

"Peace and Work"
A73

Máximo Gómez Monument
A74

"Independence"
A76

Torch
A75

"Messenger of Peace"
A77

1936, Nov. 18 ***Perf. 12½***

332	A73	1c emerald	50	25
333	A74	2c crimson	60	20
334	A75	4c maroon	75	25
335	A76	5c ultra	2.50	85
336	A77	8c dk grn	4.00	1.75
		Nos. 332-336, C22-C23, E9 (8)	19.85	7.80

Maj. Gen. Máximo Gómez, birth centenary.

Sugar Cane
A78

Primitive Sugar Mill
A79

Modern Sugar Mill
A80

Wmkd. Star. (106)

1937, Oct. 2 **Engraved** ***Perf. 10***

337	A78	1c yel grn	1.00	50
338	A79	2c red	70	30
339	A80	5c brt bl	1.00	60

Issued in commemoration of the 400th anniversary of the sugar cane industry in Cuba.

Argentine Emblem
A81

Mountain Scene (Bolivia)
A82

Arms of Brazil
A83

Canadian Scene
A84

Camilo Henriquez (Chile)
A85

Gen. Francisco de Paula Santander (Colombia)
A86

National Monument (Costa Rica)
A87

Autograph of José Marti (Cuba)
A88

Columbus Lighthouse (Dominican Republic)
A89

Juan Montalvo (Ecuador)
A90

Abraham Lincoln (United States)
A91

Quetzal and Scroll (Guatemala)
A92

Arms of Haiti
A93

Francisco Morazán (Honduras)
A94

Fleet of Columbus
A95

Engraved.

1937, Oct. 13 ***Perf. 10*** **Wmk. 106**

340	A81	1c dp grn	50	50
341	A82	1c green	50	50
342	A83	2c carmine	50	50
343	A84	2c carmine	50	50
344	A85	3c violet	1.50	1.50
345	A86	3c violet	1.50	1.50
346	A87	4c bis brn	1.75	1.75
347	A88	4c bis brn	3.00	3.00
348	A89	5c blue	1.50	1.50
349	A90	5c blue	1.50	1.50
350	A91	8c citron	10.00	10.00
351	A92	8c citron	2.50	2.50
352	A93	10c maroon	2.50	2.50
353	A94	10c maroon	2.50	2.50
354	A95	25c rose lil	25.00	25.00
		Nos. 340-354, C24-C29, E10-E11 (23)	106.75	99.75

Nos. 340 to 354 were sold by the Cuban Post Office for three days, Oct. 13-15, during which no other stamps were sold. They were postally valid for the full face value. Proceeds from their three-day sale above 30,000 pesos were paid by the Cuban Post Office Department to the Association of American Writers and Artists. Remainders were overprinted "SVP" (Without Postal Value).

No. 283 Surcharged in Green

1937, Nov. 19 ***Perf. 12*** **Unwmkd.**

355	A44	10c on 25c vio	10.00	3.00

Centenary of Cuban railroads.

Ciboney Indian and Cigar
A96

Cigar and Globe
A97

Tobacco Plant and Cigars
A98

Wmkd. Star. (106)

1939, Aug. 28 **Engraved** ***Perf. 10***

356	A96	1c yel grn	25	5
357	A97	2c red	50	5
358	A98	5c brt ultra	1.00	20

General Calixto García
A99 A100

1939, Nov. 6 ***Perf. 10, Imperf.***

359	A99	2c dk red	60	20
360	A100	5c dp bl	1.20	60

Birth centenary of General Garcia.

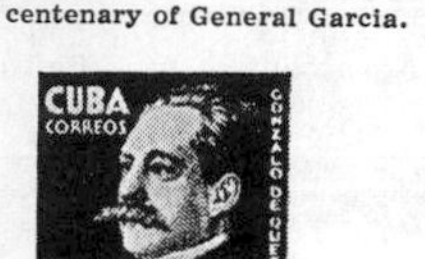

Gonzalo de Quesada
A101

1940, Apr. 30 **Engraved** ***Perf. 10***

361	A101	2c rose red	1.00	50

Pan American Union, 50th anniversary.

Rotary Club Emblem, Cuban Flag and Tobacco Plant
A102

Lions Emblem, Cuban Flag and Royal Palms
A103

1940, May 18 ***Perf. 10*** **Wmk. 106**

362	A102	2c rose red	2.00	1.00

Issued in commemoration of the Rotary International Convention held at Havana.

1940, July 23

363	A103	2c org ver	2.00	1.00

Lions International Convention, Havana.

Dr. Nicolás J. Gutiérrez
A104

1940, Oct. 28

364	A104	2c org ver	1.20	50
365	A104	5c blue	1.50	60
a.		Sheet of four, imperf., unwmkd.	5.00	5.00
b.		As "a," blk overprint ('51)	6.00	6.00

Issued in commemoration of the 100th anniversary of the publication of the first Cuban Medical Review, "El Repertorio Medico Habanero".

No. 365a measures 127x177mm. and contains two each of Nos. 364 and 365 imperforate, and upper and lower marginal inscriptions. The sheet sold for 25c.

In 1951 Nos. 365a was overprinted in black: "50 Aniversario Descubrimiento Agente Transmisor • de la Fiebre Amarilla por el Dr. Carlos J. Finlay • Honor a los Martires de la Ciencia 1901 1951." The overprint is illustrated over No. C43A, but does not include the plane and "Correo Aereo."

Major General Guillermo Moncada
A105

Moncada Riding into Battle
A106

1941, June 25

366	A105	3c dk brn, *buff*	1.20	40
367	A106	5c brt bl	1.50	75

Issued in commemoration of the centenary of the birth of Maj. Gen. Guillermo Moncada (1841-96).

Globe Showing Western Hemisphere
A107

Maceo, Bolívar, Juárez, Lincoln and Arms of Cuba
A108

Tree of Fraternity, Havana
A110

"Labor: Wealth of America"
A109

Statue of Liberty
A111

Perf. 10, Imperf.

1942, Feb. 23 **Wmk. 106**

368	A107	1c emerald	40	12
369	A108	3c org brn	50	15
370	A109	5c blue	90	30
371	A110	10c red vio	2.00	75
372	A111	13c red	2.50	1.25
		Nos. 368-372 (5)	6.30	2.57

Issued to publicize the spirit of Democracy in the Americas.

The imperforate varieties are without gum.

Ignacio Agramonte Loynaz
A112

Rescue of Sanguily by Agramonte
A113

1942, Apr. 10 *Perf. 10*

373	A112	3c bis brn	90	50
374	A113	5c brt bl, *bluish*	1.75	70

Issued in commemoration of the 100th anniversary of the birth of Ignacio Agramonte Loynaz, patriot.

"Unmask the Fifth Columnists"
A114

" Be Careful, The Fifth Column is Spying on You"
A115

" Destroy it. The Fifth Column is like a Serpent"
A116

" Fulfill your Patriotic Duty by Destroying the Fifth Column"
A117

" Don't be Afraid of the Fifth Column. Attack it"
A118

1943, July 5

375	A114	1c dk bl grn	40	18
376	A115	3c red	60	20
377	A116	5c brt bl	70	20
378	A117	10c dl brn	1.75	60
379	A118	13c dl rose vio	3.50	1.75
		Nos. 375-379 (5)	6.95	2.93

General Eloy Alfaro and Flags of Cuba and Ecuador
A119

1943, Sept. 20

380	A119	3c green	1.25	40

Issued to commemorate the 100th anniversary of the birth of General Eloy Alfaro of Ecuador.

Retirement Security
A120

1943, Nov. 8 *Perf. 10* **Wmk. 106**

381	A120	1c yel grn	75	30
382	A120	3c vermilion	90	30
383	A120	5c brt bl	1.00	50

1944, Mar. 18

384	A120	1c brt yel grn	75	30
385	A120	3c salmon	90	30
386	A120	5c lt bl	1.50	75

Half the proceeds from the sale of Nos. 381-386 were used for the Communications Ministry Employees' Retirement Fund.

Portrait of Columbus
A121

Bartolomé de Las Casas
A122

First Statue of Columbus at Cárdenas
A123

Discovery of Tobacco
A124

Columbus Sights Land
A125

1944, May 19

387	A121	1c dk yel grn	30	20
388	A122	3c brown	50	20
389	A123	5c brt bl	70	30
390	A124	10c dk vio	1.75	1.00
391	A125	13c dk red	3.50	1.75
		Nos. 387-391, C36-C37 (7)	9.00	4.15

Issued to commemorate the 450th anniversary of the discovery of America.

Major General Carlos Roloff
A126

Map of the Americas and First Brazilian Postage Stamps
A127

1944, Aug. 21

392	A126	3c violet	75	35

Issued to commemorate the 100th anniversary of the birth of Maj. Gen. Carlos Roloff.

1944, Dec. 20 **Engraved**

393	A127	3c brn org	1.75	75

Issued to commemorate the centenary of the first postage stamps of the Americas, issued by Brazil in 1843.

Seal of the Society
A128

Luis de las Casas and
Luis Maria Penalver
A129

1945, Oct. 5 *Perf. 10* Wmk. 106

394	A128	1c yel grn	30	20
395	A129	2c scarlet	45	20

Issued to commemorate the sesquicentenary of the founding of the Economic Society of Friends of the Country.

Aged Couple—A130

1945, Dec. 27

396	A130	1c dk yel grn	25	10
397	A130	2c scarlet	40	15
398	A130	5c cob bl	75	35

1946, Mar. 26

399	A130	1c brt yel grn	50	25
400	A130	2c sal pink	40	25
401	A130	5c lt bl	60	50

See note after No. 386.

Gabriel de la Concepcion Valdés
Plácido)—A131

1946, Feb. 5

402	A131	2c scarlet	90	30

Issued to commemorate the centenary of the death of the poet Gabriel de la Concepcion Valdés.

Manuel
Marquez Sterling
A132

Globe
and Cross
A133

1946, Apr. 30

403	A132	2c scarlet	90	40

Issued to commemorate the third anniversary of the founding of the Manuel Marquez Sterling Professional School of Journalism.

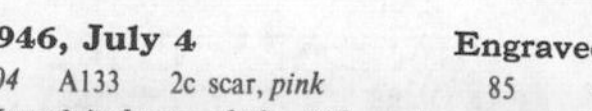

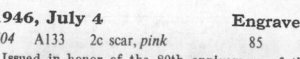

1946, July 4 Engraved

404	A133	2c scar, *pink*	85	40

Issued in honor of the 80th anniversary of the International Red Cross.

Cow and
Milkmaid
A134

Franklin D.
Roosevelt
A135

1947, Feb. 20 *Perf. 10* Wmk. 106

405	A134	2c scarlet	75	30

Issued to commemorate the 1947 National Livestock Exposition.

1947, Apr. 12

406	A135	2c vermilion	50	25

Issued to commemorate the second anniversary of the death of Franklin D. Roosevelt.

Antonio Oms Sarret
and Aged Couple
A136

1947, Oct. 20

407	A136	1c dp yel grn	20	15
408	A136	2c scarlet	35	15
409	A136	5c lt bl	75	40

See note after No. 386.

Marta Abreu
Arenabio
de Estevez
A137

"Charity"
A138

Marta Abreu
Monument,
Santa Clara
A139

"Patriotism"
A140

1947, Nov. 29

410	A137	1c dp yel grn	40	25
411	A138	2c scarlet	60	20
412	A139	5c brt bl	1.00	50
413	A140	10c dk vio	2.00	1.00

Issued to commemorate the centenary of the birth of Marta Abreu Arenabio de Estevez, philanthropist and humanitarian.

Armauer Hansen—A141

1948, Apr. 9

414	A141	2c rose car	75	30

International Leprosy Congress, Havana.

Mother and Child
A142

1948, Oct. 15 Engraved

415	A142	1c yel grn	30	20
416	A142	2c scarlet	40	20
417	A142	5c brt bl	85	40

See note after No. 386.

Death of
José Marti
A143

Marti
Rowing to Shore
A144

Engraved.

1948, Nov. 10 *Perf. 10* Wmk. 106

418	A143	2c scarlet	35	20
419	A144	5c brt bl	80	35

Issued to commemorate (in 1945) the 50th anniversary of the death of José Marti, patriot.

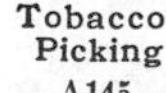

Tobacco
Picking
A145

Liberty Carrying
Flag and Cigars
A146

Cigar and Arms of Cuba
A147

1948, Dec. 6

Size: 22½x26mm.

420	A145	1c green	15	5
421	A146	2c rose car	25	10
422	A147	5c brt bl	35	15

Cuba's tobacco industry.
See Nos. 445–447.

Equestrian Statue
of Gen. Antonio Maceo
A148

Sword Salute to Maceo
A149

Designs: 2c, Portrait of Maceo. 5c, Mausoleum, El Cacahual. 10c, East to West invasion. 20c, Battle of Peralejo. 50c, Declaration of Baragua. 1p, Death of Maceo at San Pedro.

1948, Dec. 15 *Perf. 12½* Wmk. 229

423	A148	1c bl grn	15	10
424	A148	2c red	25	8
425	A148	5c blue	50	25
426	A149	8c blk & brn	75	50
427	A149	10c brn & bl grn	75	35
428	A149	20c bl & car	3.00	1.50
429	A149	50c car & ultra	5.00	3.50
430	A149	1p blk & vio	10.00	5.00
		Nos. 423-430 (8)	20.40	11.28

Issued to commemorate the centenary (in 1945) of the birth of General Antonio Maceo.

Symbol of
Pharmacy
A150

Morro
Lighthouse
A151

1948, Dec. 28 *Perf. 10*

431	A150	2c rose car	75	30

Issued to commemorate the First Pan-American Congress of Pharmacy, Havana, December 1948.

1949, Jan. 17 *Perf. 12½* Wmk. 229

432	A151	2c carmine	50	25

Issued to commemorate the centenary (in 1944) of the erection of the Morro Lighthouse.

Jagua Castle, Cienfuegos
A152

1949, Jan. 27 *Perf. 10* Wmk. 106

433	A152	1c yel grn	40	20
434	A152	2c rose red	80	40

Issued to commemorate the 200th anniversary of the construction of Jagua Castle and the centenary of the publication of the first newspaper in Cienfuegos.

Manuel Sanguily y Garritt
A153

Map of Isle of Pines
A154

1949, Mar. 31

435	A153	2c rose red	35	20
436	A153	5c blue	75	40

Issued to commemorate the centenary of the birth of Manuel Sanguily y Garritt (1848–1925), cabinet member, editor, author.

1949, Apr. 26

437	A154	5c blue	75	35

Issued to commemorate the 20th anniversary of the recognition of Cuban ownership of the Isle of Pines.

Ismael Cespedes
A155

1949, Sept. 28

438	A155	1c yel grn	35	20
439	A155	2c scarlet	35	20
440	A155	5c brt bl	80	40

See note after No. 386.

Gen. Enrique Collazo
A156

Enrique José Varona
A157

1950, Feb. 28 Engraved *Perf. 10*

441	A156	2c scarlet	40	20
442	A156	5c brt bl	80	35

Issued to commemorate the centenary (in 1948) of the birth of General Enrique Collazo.

1950, Feb. 28

443	A157	2c scarlet	40	20
444	A157	5c brt bl	80	40

Issued to commemorate the centenary of the birth of Enrique José Varona, writer and patriot.

Tobacco Types of 1948.

1950, June 20 Re-engraved

Size: 21 x 25 mm.

445	A145	1c green	40	10
446	A146	2c rose red	40	10
447	A147	5c blue	60	35

The re-engraved stamps show slight differences in many minor details.

No. 446 Overprinted in Black

BANCO NACIONAL DE CUBA
INAUGURACION
27 ABRIL
1950

1950, Apr. 27

448	A146	2c rose red	75	35

Issued to commemorate the opening of the National Bank of Cuba, April 27, 1950.

Re-engraved Tobacco Types of 1950 Overprinted in Carmine

U.P.U
1874
1949

1950, May 18

449	A145	1c yel grn	25	15
450	A146	2c lil rose	40	20
451	A147	5c lt bl	75	25

75th anniversary (in 1949) of Universal Postal Union.

No. 451 exists with surcharge inverted.

Manuel Balanzategui, Antonio L. Pausa and Train Wreck
A158

Fernando Figueredo
A159

1950, Sept. 21 Engraved

452	A158	1c yel grn	35	20
453	A158	2c scarlet	35	20
454	A158	5c brt bl	75	40

1951, Mar. 17 *Perf. 10* Wmk. 106

455	A159	1c green	40	15
456	A159	2c scarlet	40	15
457	A159	5c brt bl	75	30

Three-fourths of the proceeds from the sale of these stamps were used for the Communication Ministry Employees' Retirement Fund.

See Nos. 474, C51–C56, E15.

Miguel Teurbe Tolón and Flag
A160

Narciso Lopez
A161

Emilia Teurbe Tolón Sewing Flag
A162

Cuban Flag
A163

Engraved and Lithographed.

1951, July 3 *Perf. 13* Wmk. 229

458	A160	1c Prus grn, ultra & red	40	20
459	A161	2c red & gray blk	60	25
460	A162	5c ultra & red	1.25	50
461	A163	10c rose vio, bl & red	2.00	75
		Nos. 458-461, C41-C43, E13 (8)	15.50	4.70

Centenary of adoption of Cuba's flag.

Clara Louise Maass and Hospitals
A164

Hospitals: Lutheran Memorial, Newark, N.J. and Las Animas, Havana.

Engraved.

1951, Aug. 24 *Perf. 10* Wmk. 106

462	A164	2c scarlet	90	40

Issued to commemorate the 75th anniversary of the birth of Clara Louise Maass, (1876–1901), American nurse and martyr in yellow fever fight.

Airmail Type and

José Raul Capablanca—A165

Capablanca Club, Havana
A166

Design: 2c, Capablanca making "The Exact Play."

Perf. 13

1951, Nov. 1 Photo. Wmk. 229

463	A165	1c bl grn & org	3.50	75
464	AP27	2c rose car & dk brn	4.00	1.50
465	A166	5c blk & dp ultra	8.00	2.50
		Nos. 463-465, C44-C46, E14 (7)	52.00	14.50

Jose Raul Capablanca, World Chess titlist (1921). Imperf., set of 7 pairs, $1,500.

Antonio Guiteras Holmes
A167

Guiteras Preparing Social Legislation
A168

Fort of the Morrillo
A169

Engraved.

1951, Oct. 22 *Perf. 10* Wmk. 106

466	A167	1c yel grn	35	15
467	A168	2c rose car	60	20
468	A169	5c dp bl	1.00	30
		Nos. 466-468, C47-C49 (6)	6.70	2.55

Issued to commemorate the 16th anniversary of the Action of the Morrillo and to honor Antonio Guiteras Holmes, who was killed there.

Souvenir sheets containing stamps similar to Nos. 466-468, but in different colors, are listed as Nos. C49a-C49b.

Poinsettia
A170

Maj. Gen. José Maceo
A171

1951, Dec. 1 Engr. and Typo.

469	A170	1c grn & car	3.00	50
470	A170	2c rose car & grn	3.50	75

See note after No. 457. See also Nos. 498–499.

1952, Feb. 6 Engraved

471	A171	2c yel brn	40	20
472	A171	5c indigo	90	30

Issued to commemorate the centenary of the birth of Major General José Maceo.

See note after No. C49.

Queen Isabella I
A172

Receipt of Autonomy
A173

1952, Feb. 22

473	A172	2c brt red	60	20

Issued to commemorate the 500th anniversary of the birth of Queen Isabella I of Spain.

Souvenir sheets containing 2c stamps of type A172 are listed as Nos. C50a–C50b.

Type of 1951 Surcharged in Green.

1952, Mar. 18

474	A159	10c on 2c yel brn	1.25	50

Engraved.

1952, May 27 *Perf. 12½* Wmk. 106

Designs: 2c, Tomas Estrada Palma and Luis Estevez Romero. 5c, Barnet, Finlay, Guiteras and Nuñez. 8c, Capitol. 20c, Map, Central Highway. 50c, Sugar Mill.

Centers in Black.

475	A173	1c dk grn	40	10
476	A173	2c dk car	50	10
477	A173	5c dk bl	60	20
478	A173	8c dk brn car	1.00	25
479	A173	20c dk ol grn	2.50	75
480	A173	50c dp org	5.00	1.50
		Nos. 475-480, C57-C60, E16 (11)	18.25	5.65

Issued to commemorate the 50th anniversary of the foundation of the Republic of Cuba.

Hands Holding Coffee Beans
A174

Designs: 2c, Map and man picking coffee beans. 5c, Farmer with pan of beans.

1952, Aug. 22 *Perf. 13½* Wmk. 229

481	A174	1c green	40	18
482	A174	2c rose red	75	30
483	A174	5c dk vio bl & aqua	1.00	40

Bicentenary of coffee cultivation.

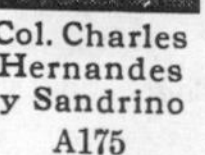

Col. Charles Hernandes y Sandrino
A175

Alonso Alvarez de la Campa
A176

1952, Oct. 7 ***Perf. 10*** **Wmk. 106**

484	A175	1c yel grn	35	20
485	A175	2c scarlet	65	15
486	A175	5c blue	75	25
487	A175	8c black	2.00	60
488	A175	10c brn red	2.00	60
489	A175	20c brown	7.50	5.00
		Nos. 484-489, C63-C72, E17 (17)	47.75	24.55

See note after No. 457.

Frame Engraved; Center Typographed in Black.

1952, Nov. 27

Portraits: 2c, Carlos A. Latorre. 3c, Anacleto Bermudez. 5c, Eladio G. Toledo. 8c, Angel Laborde. 10c, Jose M. Medina. 13c, Pascual Rodriguez. 20c, Carlos Verdugo.

490	A176	1c green	25	10
491	A176	2c carmine	50	25
492	A176	3c purple	60	25
493	A176	5c blue	60	25
494	A176	8c bis brn	1.25	60
495	A176	10c org brn	1.00	50
496	A176	13c lil rose	2.00	75
497	A176	20c ol grn	3.00	1.25
		Nos. 490-497, C73-C74 (10)	12.85	5.55

Issued to commemorate the 81st anniversary of the execution of eight medical students.

Christmas Type of 1951
Dated "1952-1953."
Frame Engraved; Center Typographed.

Centers: Tree.

1952, Dec. 1

498	A170	1c yel grn & car	4.00	1.25
499	A170	3c vio & dk grn	4.00	1.25

Birthplace of José Martí
A177

Marti at St. Lazarus Quarry
A178

Designs: No. 501, Court martial. No. 502, Martiano house, Havana. No. 504, El Abra ranch, Isle of Pines. No. 505, Symbols, "Marti the Poet." No. 506, Marti and Bolivar statue, Caracas. No. 507, At desk in New York. No. 508, House where revolutionary party was formed. No. 509, First issue of "Patria."

1953 **Engraved.** ***Perf. 10.***

500	A177	1c dk grn & red brn	20	10
501	A177	1c dk grn & red brn	20	8
502	A177	3c pur & brn	40	10
503	A178	3c pur & brn	40	8
504	A177	5c dp bl & dk brn	60	25
505	A178	5c ultra & brn	60	25
506	A178	10c red brn & blk	1.50	50
507	A178	10c dk brn & blk	1.50	50
508	A178	13c dk ol grn & dk brn	2.50	1.00
509	A177	13c dk ol grn & brn	2.50	1.25
		Nos. 500-509, C79-C89 (21)	29.00	10.95

Centenary of birth of José Marti.

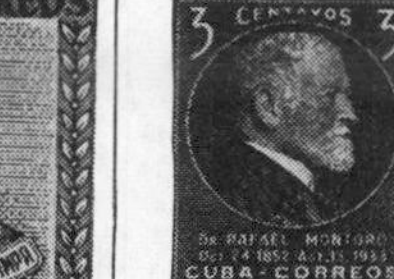

Rafael Montoro Valdez
A179

Francisco Carrera Justiz
A180

1953, Mar. 5

510	A179	3c dk vio	50	20

Issued to commemorate the centenary of the birth of Rafael Montoro Valdez, statesman.

1953, Mar. 9

511	A180	3c rose red	50	20

Issued to honor Francisco Carrera Justiz, educator and statesman.

No. 446 Surcharged with New Value.

1953, June 16

512	A146	3c on 2c rose red	40	15

Board of Accounts Bldg., Havana
A181

1953, Nov. 3 **Engraved**

513	A181	3c blue	40	15

Issued to publicize the First International Congress of Boards of Accounts, Havana, November 2-9, 1953.
See also Nos. C90-C91.

Miguel Coyula Llaguno
A182

Communications Association Flag
A183

Designs: 3c, 8c, Enrique Calleja Hensell. 10c, Antonio Ginard Rojas.

1954 **Dated 1953.**

514	A182	1c green	25	8
515	A182	3c rose red	25	10
516	A183	5c blue	1.00	20
517	A182	8c brn car	1.50	50
518	A182	10c brown	2.50	75
		Nos. 514-518, C92-C95, E19 (10)	19.35	9.13

Nos. 515 and 517 show the same portrait, but inscriptions are arranged differently.
See note after No. 457.

José Marti
A184

Maximo Gomez
A184a

Portraits: 3c, José de la Luz Caballero. 4c, Miguel Aldama. 5c, Calixto Garcia. 8c, Ignacio Agramont. 10c, Tomas Estrada Palma. 13c, Carlos J. Finlay. 14c, Serafin Sanchez. 20c, José Antonio Saco. 50c, Antonio Maceo. 1p, Carlos Manuel de Cespedes.

1954-56 ***Perf. 10.*** **Wmk. 106**

519	A184	1c green	25	5
520	A184a	2c rose car	25	5
521	A184	3c violet	25	5
521A	A184	4c red lil ('55)	30	6
522	A184a	5c sl bl	35	8
523	A184a	8c car lake	50	10
524	A184	10c sepia	50	10
525	A184	13c org red	75	15
525A	A184a	14c gray ('56)	1.00	15
526	A184	20c olive	1.50	25
527	A184a	50c org yel	2.50	50
528	A184a	1p orange	5.00	75
		Nos. 519-528 (12)	13.15	2.29

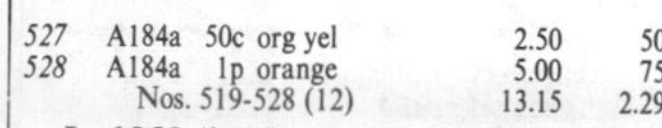

In 1962 the Castro government re-issued Nos. 519-520 in changed colors. On the 2c, "1833" is replaced by "?".

Maj. Gen. José M. Rodriguez
A185

Design: 5c, Gen. Rodriguez on horseback.

1954, June 8 **Engraved** ***Perf. 12½***

Center in Dark Brown

529	A185	2c dk car	50	20
530	A185	5c dp bl	1.00	40

Issued to commemorate the centenary of the birth of Maj. Gen. José Maria Rodriguez (in 1851).

Gen. Batista Sanatorium
A186

1954, Sept. 21 ***Perf. 10*** **Wmk. 106**

531	A186	3c dp bl	50	20

See also No. C107.

Santa Claus
A187

Maria Luisa Dolz
A188

1954, Dec. 15

532	A187	2c dk grn & car	4.00	75
533	A187	4c car & dk grn	3.50	75

Christmas 1954.

1954, Dec. 23

534	A188	4c dp bl	50	20

Issued to commemorate the centenary of the birth of Maria Luisa Dolz, educator and defender of women's rights. See also No. C108.

Cuban Flag and Scouts Saluting
A189

1954, Dec. 27 ***Perf. 12½***

535	A189	4c dk grn	75	30

Issued to publicize the national patrol encampment of the Boy Scouts of Cuba.

Rotary Emblem and Paul P. Harris
A190

1955, Feb. 23 **Engraved** **Wmk. 106**

536	A190	4c blue	75	20

Rotary International, 50th anniversary.
See also No. C109.

Maj. Gen. Francisco Carrillo
A191

Portrait: 5c, Gen. Carrillo standing.

1955, Mar. 8 ***Perf. 10***

537	A191	2c brt red & dk bl	40	15
538	A191	5c dk bl & dk brn	75	25

Issued to commemorate the centenary of the birth of Maj. Gen. Francisco Carrillo (1851-1926).

Stamp of 1885 and Convent of San Francisco—A192

Designs (including 1855 stamp): 4c, Volanta carriage. 10c, Havana, 19th century. 14c, Captain general's residence.

1955, Apr. ***Perf. 12½***

539	A192	2c lil rose & dk grnsh bl	75	25
540	A192	4c ocher & dk grn	1.00	25
541	A192	10c ultra & dk red	2.25	1.25
542	A192	14c grn & dp org	5.50	1.50
		Nos. 539-542,C110-C113 (8)	17.80	7.10

Issued to commemorate the centenary of Cuba's first postage stamps.

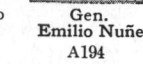

Maj. Gen. Mario G. Menocal
A193

Gen. Emilio Nuñez
A194

Portraits: 10c, J. G. O. Gomez. 14c, A. Sanchez de Bustamente.

1955, June 22

543	A193	2c dk grn	50	6
544	A194	4c lil rose	60	8
545	A193	10c dp bl	1.00	40
546	A194	14c gray vio	2.00	60
		Nos. 543-546, C114-C116, E20 (8)	14.10	6.54

See note after No. 457.

Turkey
A195

Gen. Emilio Nuñez
A196

1955, Dec. 15 **Engraved**

547	A195	2c sl grn & dk car	3.75	75

548 A195 4c rose lake & brt grn 3.75 60

Christmas 1955.

1955, Dec. 27

549 A196 4c claret 50 20

Issued to commemorate the centenary of the birth of Gen. Emilio Nuñez, Cuban revolutionary hero. See also Nos. C127–C128.

Francisco Cagigal de la Vega (1695–1777)
A197

Julian del Casal
A198

1956, Mar. 27 ***Perf. 12½***

552 A197 4c rose brn & sl bl 50 20

Issued to commemorate the bicentenary of the Cuban post. See also No. C129.

1956, May 2

Portraits: 4c, Luisa Perez de Zambrana. 10c, Juan Clemente Zenea. 14c, José Joaquin Palma.

Portraits in Black.

553 A198 2c green 40 10
554 A198 4c rose lil 50 12
555 A198 10c blue 1.00 25
556 A198 14c violet 1.25 35
Nos. 553-556, C131-C133, E21 (8) 9.65 3.32

See note after No. 457.

Victor Muñoz
A199

Masonic Temple, Havana
A200

1956, May 13

557 A199 4c brn & grn 50 20

Issued in honor of Victor Muñoz (1873–1922), founder of Mother's Day in Cuba. See also No. C134.

1956, June 5

558 A200 4c blue 60 20

See also No. C135.

Virgin of Charity, El Cobre
A201

"The Cry of Yara"
A202

1956, Sept. 8 ***Perf. 12½***

559 A201 4c brt bl & yel 75 20

Issued in honor of Our Lady of Charity of Cobre, patroness of Cuba. See also No. C149.

1956, Oct. 10

560 A202 4c dk grn & brn 50 20

Issued to commemorate Cuba's independence from Spain.

Raimundo G. Menocal
A203

The Three Wise Men
A204

1956, Dec. 3 ***Perf. 12½*** **Wmk. 106**

561 A203 4c dk brn 50 20

Issued to commemorate the centenary of the birth of Prof. Raimundo G. Menocal, physician.

1956, Dec. 1

562 A204 2c red & sl grn 4.00 1.00
563 A204 4c sl grn & red 4.00 75

Christmas 1956.

Martin Morua Delgado
A205

Boy Scouts at Campfire
A206

1957, Jan. 30

564 A205 4c dk grn 50 20

Issued to commemorate the centenary of the birth of Martin Morua Delgado, patriot.

1957, Feb. 22 ***Perf. 12½*** **Wmk. 106**

565 A206 4c sl grn & red 90 35

Issued to commemorate the centenary of the birth of Lord Baden-Powell, founder of the Boy Scouts. See also No. C152.

"The Blind," by M. Vega
A207

Paintings: 4c, "The Art Critics" by M. Melero. 10c, "Volanta in Storm" by A. Menocal. 14c, "The Convalescent" by L. Romañach.

1957, Mar. **Engraved** ***Perf. 12½***

Side and Lower Inscriptions in Dark Brown.

566 A207 2c ol grn 40 25
567 A207 4c org red 50 30
568 A207 10c ol grn 75 50
569 A207 14c ultra 1.00 50
Nos. 566-569, C153-C155, E22 (8) 9.60 3.85

See note after No. 457.

Emblem of Philatelic Club of Cuba
A208

Juan F. Steegers
A209

1957, Apr. 24

570 A208 4c ocher, bl & red 60 20

Issued for Stamp Day, Apr. 24, and the National Philatelic Exhibition. See No. C156.

1957, Apr. 30

571 A209 4c blue 50 20

Issued in honor of the centenary of the birth of Juan Francisco Steegers y Perera (1856–1921), dactyloscopy pioneer. See No. C157.

Victoria Bru Sanchez
A210

Joaquin de Aguero in Battle of Jucaral
A211

1957, June 3 ***Perf. 12½*** **Wmk. 106**

572 A210 4c indigo 50 20

1957, July 4

573 A211 4c dk grn 50 20

Issued to honor Joaquin de Aguero, Cuban freedom fighter and patriot. See No. C162.

Boy, Dogs and Cat
A212

Col. Rafael Manduley del Rio
A213

1957, July 17

574 A212 4c Prus grn 75 30

Issued in honor of Mrs. Jeanette Ryder, founder of the Humane Society of Cuba. See Nos. C163–C163a.

1957, July 31

575 A213 4c Prus grn 50 15

Issued to honor Col. Manduley del Rio, patriot, on the centenary of his birth (in 1856).

Palace of Justice
A214

1957, Sept. 2 **Engraved** ***Perf. 12½***

576 A214 4c bl gray 50 20

Issued to commemorate the opening of the new Palace of Justice in Havana. See also No. C165.

Generals of the Liberation
A215

1957, Sept. 26

577 A215 4c dl grn & red brn 50 20
578 A215 4c dl bl & red brn 50 20
579 A215 4c rose & brn 50 20
580 A215 4c org yel & brn 50 20
581 A215 4c lt vio & brn 50 20
Nos. 577-581 (5) 2.50 1.00

Issued to commemorate the Generals of the army of liberation.

First Publication Printed in Cuba
A216

Patio
A217

1957, Oct. 18 ***Perf. 12½*** **Wmk. 106**

582 A216 4c sl bl 50 15

Issued to publicize the José Marti National Library. See Nos. C167–C168.

1957, Nov. 19

583 A217 4c red brn & grn 50 15

Issued to commemorate the centenary of the first Cuban Normal School. See also Nos. C173–C174.

Trinidad, Founded 1514
A218

Fortifications, Havana, 1611
A219

Views: 10c, Padre Pico street, Santiago de Cuba. 14c, Church of Our Lady, Camaguey.

1957, Dec. 17 **Engraved** ***Perf. 12½***

584 A218 2c brn & ind 35 6
585 A219 4c sl grn & brn 50 5
586 A219 10c sep & red 1.50 50
587 A219 14c grn & dk red 1.25 25
Nos. 584-587, C175-C177, E23 (8) 8.85 2.81

See note after No. 457.

Nativity
A220

1957, Dec. 20

Center Multicolored.

588 A220 2c dk brn 3.50 1.00
589 A220 4c dk sl grn 3.50 75

Christmas 1957.

Dayton Hedges and Ariguanabo Textile Factory
A221

1958. Jan. 30 *Perf. 12½* Wmk. 106

590	A221	4c blue	50	15

Issued to honor Dayton Hedges, founder of Cuba's textile industry. See No. C178.

Dr. Francisco Dominguez Roldan
A222

José Ignacio Rivero y Alonso
A223

1958, Feb. 21

591	A222	4c green	50	15

Issued to honor Dr. Francisco Dominguez Roldan (1864–1942), who introduced radiotherapy and physiotherapy to Cuba.

1958, Apr. 1

592	A223	4c lt ol grn	50	15

Issued in honor of José Ignacio Rivero y Alonso, editor of Diario de la Marina, 1919–1944. See also No. C179.

Map of Cuba and Mail Route, 1756
A224

1958, Apr. 24 *Perf. 12½*

593	A224	4c dk grn, aqua & buff	60	20

Issued for Stamp Day, Apr. 24 and the National Philatelic Exhibition. See No. C180.

Maj. Gen. José Miguel Gomez
A225

Nicolas Ruiz Espadero
A226

1958, June 6 *Perf. 12½* Wmk. 106

594	A225	4c slate	50	15

Issued in honor of Maj. Gen. José Miguel Gomez, President of Cuba, 1909–13. See No. C181.

1958, June 27 *Perf. 12½*

Musicians: 4c, Ignacio Cervantes. 10c, José White. 14c, Brindis de Salas.

Indigo Emblem

595	A226	2c brown	50	10
596	A226	4c dk gray	50	20
597	A226	10c ol grn	75	25
598	A226	14c red	1.00	35

Physicians: 2c, Tomas Romay Chacon. 4c, Angel Arturo Aballi. 10c, Fernando Gonzalez del Valle. 14c, Vicente Antonio de Castro.

Green Emblem

599	A226	2c brown	60	10
600	A226	4c gray	1.00	35
601	A226	10c dk car	75	30
602	A226	14c dk bl	1.00	40

Lawyers: 2c, Jose Maria Garcia Montes. 4c, Jose A. Gonzalez Lanuza. 10c, Juan B. Hernandez Barreiro. 14c, Pedro Gonzalez Llorente.

Red Emblem

603	A226	2c sepia	50	10
604	A226	4c gray	75	35
605	A226	10c ol grn	85	25
606	A226	14c sl bl	1.00	35
		Nos. 595-606 (12)	9.20	3.10

Carlos de la Torre
A227

Wmk. 321

Wmkd. "R de C" (321)

1958, Aug. 29 Engraved *Perf. 12½*

607	A227	4c vio bl	60	20

Issued to commemorate the centenary of the birth of Dr. Carlos de la Torre y Huerta (1858–1950), naturalist. See also Nos. C182–C184.

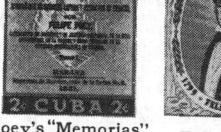

Poey's "Memorias" Title Page
A228

Felipe Poey
A229

1958, Sept. 26 Wmk. 106

608	A228	2c blk & lt vio	35	15
609	A229	4c brn blk	45	15
		Nos. 608-609, C185-C191, E26-E27 (11)	47.30	18.05

Issued in honor of Felipe Poey (1799–1891), naturalist.

Theodore Roosevelt
A230

Cattleyopsis Lindenii Orchid
A231

1958, Oct. 27 *Perf. 12½*

610	A230	4c gray grn	60	15

Issued to commemorate the centenary of the birth of Theodore Roosevelt. See No. C192.

Engraved & Photogravure

1958, Dec. 16 *Perf. 12½* Wmk. 321

Design: 4c, Oncidium Guibertianum Orchid.

611	A231	2c multi	3.50	1.00
612	A231	4c multi	4.00	1.00

Christmas 1958.

Flag and Revolutionary
A232

Gen. Adolfo Flor Crombet
A233

Engraved and Lithographed.

1959, Jan. 28 Wmk. 321

613	A232	2c car rose & gray	30	15

Day of Liberation, Jan. 1, 1959.

1959, Mar. 18 Engr. Wmk. 106

614	A233	4c sl grn	40	15

Issued in honor of General Adolfo Flor Crombet (1848-1895).

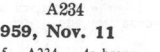

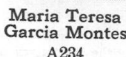

Maria Teresa Garcia Montes
A234

Carlos Manuel de Cespedes
A235

1959, Nov. 11 *Perf. 12½*

615	A234	4c brown	40	15

Issued to honor Maria Teresa Garcia Montes (1880–1930), founder of the Musical Arts Society. See No. C198.

1959, Oct. 10 *Perf. 12½* Wmk. 106

Presidents: No. 617, Salvador Cisneros Betancourt. No. 618, Manuel de Jesus Calvar. No. 619, Bartolomé Maso. No. 620, Juan B. Spotorno. No. 621, Tomas Estrada Palma. No. 622, Francisco Javier de Céspedes. No. 623, Vicente Garcia.

616	A235	2c sl bl	40	10
617	A235	2c green	40	10
618	A235	2c dp vio	40	10
619	A235	2c org brn	40	10
620	A235	4c dk car	50	20
621	A235	4c dp brn	50	20
622	A235	4c dk gray	50	20
623	A235	4c dk vio	50	20
		Nos. 616-623(8)	3.60	1.20

Issued to honor former Cuban presidents.

No. B3 Surcharged in Red: "HABILITADO PARA / 2¢"

1960 Lithographed. Wmk. 321

624	SP2	2c on 2c+1c car & ultra	50	15

See also No. C199.

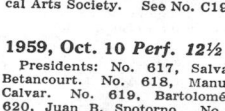

Rebel Attack on Moncada Barracks
A236

Designs: 2c, Rebels disembarking from "Granma." 10c, Battle of the Uvero. 12c, Map of Cuba and rebel ("The Invasion").

Wmkd. Interlacing Lines (320)

1960, Jan. 28 Engr. *Perf. 12½*

625	A236	1c gray ol, bl & ver	20	15
626	A236	2c bl, gray ol & brn	25	20
627	A236	10c bl, gray ol & red	50	20
628	A236	12c brt bl, brn & grn	75	30
		Nos. 625-628, C200-C202 (7)	6.70	2.85

First anniversary of revolution.

Stamps of 1956-59 Surcharged with New Value in Carmine or Silver

1960, Feb. 3

629	A226	1c on 4c dk gray & ind	40	10
630	A226	1c on 4c gray & grn	60	25
631	A226	1c on 4c gray & red	40	10
632	A227	1c on 4c vio bl	40	10
633	A231	1c on 4c multi (S)	1.00	50
634	A233	1c on 4c sl grn	35	10
635	A234	1c on 4c brn	40	10
636	A184a	2c on 14c gray	50	15
		Nos. 629-636, C203-C204 (10)	5.55	2.00

Tomas Estrada Palma Statue, Havana
A237

Sailboats
A238

Statues: 2c, Mambi Victorioso (Battle of San Juan Hill), Santiago de Cuba. 10c, Marta Abreo de Estevez. 12c, Ignacio Agramonte, Camaguey.

Engraved

1960, Mar. 28 *Perf. 12½* Wmk. 321

637	A237	1c brn & dk bl	20	8
638	A237	2c grn & red	30	8
639	A237	10c choc & red	75	25
640	A237	12c gray ol & vio	1.00	40
		Nos. 637-640, C206-C208 (7)	6.10	2.31

See note after No. 386

Nos. 521A, 522 and 525 Surcharged "HABILITADO / PARA / 2¢" in Violet Blue, Red or Black.

1960 *Perf. 10* Wmk. 106

641	A184	2c on 4c red lil (VB)	50	15
642	A184a	2c on 5c sl bl (R)	60	15
643	A184	2c on 13c org red	75	35

No. 307B Surcharged "HABILITADO / 10¢"

644	A41	10c on 20c ol grn	50	20

Perf. 12½

1960, Sept. 22 Engr. Wmk. 321

Design: 2c, Marksman.

645	A238	1c lt vio	30	20
646	A238	2c orange	50	20

Issued to commemorate the 17th Olympic Games, Rome, Aug. 25–Sept. 11. For souvenir sheet see No. C213a.

Camilo Cienfuegos and View of Escolar—A239

1960, Oct. 27 Litho. Unwmkd.

647	A239	2c brn, bl, grn & red	25	10

Issued to commemorate the first anniversary of the death of Camilo Cienfuegos, revolutionary hero.

Morning Glory—A240

Tobacco and Christmas Hymn
A241

1960 Lithographed *Perf. 12½*

Flowers in Natural Colors

648	A240	1c red	1.00	50
649	A241	1c blk & red (*Tobacco*)	1.25	75
650	A241	1c blk & red (*Mariposa*)	1.25	75
651	A241	1c blk & red (*Guaiacum*)	1.25	75
652	A241	1c blk & red (*Coffee*)	1.25	75
a.		Block of four (1 each, #649-652)	6.50	
653	A240	2c ultra	1.25	75
654	A241	2c blk & ultra (*Tobacco*)	3.50	2.00
655	A241	2c blk & ultra (*Mariposa*)	3.50	2.00
656	A241	2c blk & ultra (*Guaiacum*)	3.50	2.00
657	A241	2c blk & ultra (*Coffee*)	3.50	2.00
a.		Block of four (1 each, #654-657)	17.50	
658	A240	10c ocher	4.00	2.00
659	A241	10c blk & ocher (*Tobacco*)	10.00	5.00
660	A241	10c blk & ocher (*Mariposa*)	10.00	5.00
661	A241	10c blk & ocher (*Guaiacum*)	10.00	5.00
662	A241	10c blk & ocher (*Coffee*)	10.00	5.00
a.		Block of four (1 each, #659-662)	50.00	
		Nos. 648-662 (15)	65.25	34.25

Issued for Christmas 1960.

Nos. 648-662 were printed in three sheets of 25. Nine stamps of type A240 form a center cross; stamps of type A241 form a block of four in each corner with the musical bars joined in an oval around the floral designs.

"Public Capital for Economic Benefit"
A242

Designs: 2c, Chart and symbols of agriculture and industry. 6c, Cogwheels.

Photogravure

1961, Jan. 10 *Perf. 11½* Unwmkd.

663	A242	1c yel, blk & org	20	5
664	A242	2c bl, blk & red	20	5
665	A242	6c yel, red org & blk	50	25
		Nos. 663-665, C215-C218 (7)	4.40	2.25

Issued to publicize the conference of underdeveloped countries, Havana.

Jesus Menéndez and Sugar Cane
A243

1961, Jan. 22 Litho. *Perf. 12½*

666	A243	2c dk grn & brn	20	10

Jesus Menéndez, leader in sugar industry.

Same Overprinted in Red:
"PRIMERO DE MAYO 1961
ESTAMOS VENCIENDO"

1961, May 2

667	A243	2c dk grn & brn	60	40

Issued for May Day, 1961.

Dove and U.N. Emblem
A244

1961, Apr. 12 Litho. *Perf. 12½*

668	A244	2c red brn & yel grn	30	10
669	A244	10c emer & rose lil	50	20
a.		Souvenir sheet	2.00	

Issued to commemorate the 15th anniversary (in 1960) of the United Nations.

See also Nos. C222-C223.

No. 669a contains one each of Nos. 668-669, imperf. with red brown marginal inscription. Size: 107x65mm.

Maceo Stamp of 1907 and 1902 Simulated Cancel
A245

Designs: 1c, Revolutionary 10c stamp of 1874 and 1868 "cancel." 10c, Stamp of 1959 (No. 613) and "cancel."

1961, Apr. 24 Unwmkd.

670	A245	1c dl rose & dk grn	35	25
671	A245	2c sal & dk grn	35	25
672	A245	10c pale grn, car rose & blk	75	40

Issued for Stamp Day, Apr. 24.

Hand Releasing Dove
A246

1961, July 26 *Perf. 12½*

673	A246	2c blk, red, yel & gray	30	10

Issued to commemorate the 26th of July (1953) movement, Castro's revolt against Fulgencio Batista.

Burelage on back consisting of wavy lines and diagonal rows of "CUBA CORREOS" in pale salmon.

Importation Prohibited

Cuban stamps issued after No. 673 have not been listed because the embargo on trade with Cuba, proclaimed Feb. 7, 1962, by President Kennedy, prohibits the importation from any country of stamps of Cuban origin, used or unused.

SEMI-POSTAL STAMPS.

Pierre and Marie Curie
SP1

Wmkd. Star. (106)

1938, Nov. 23 Engraved *Perf. 10*

B1	SP1	2c + 1c sal	3.50	1.25
B2	SP1	5c + 1c dp ultra	3.50	1.50

Issued in commemoration of the 40th anniversary of the discovery of radium by Pierre and Marie Curie. The surtax was for the benefit of the International Union for the Control of Cancer.

"Agriculture" Supporting "Industry"
SP2

Perf. 12½

1959, May 7 Litho. Wmk. 321

B3	SP2	2c + 1c car & ultra	35	15

Agricultural reforms. See Nos. 624, CB1.

Nurse—SP3

Perf. 12½, Imperf.

1959, Sept. 22 Wmk. 229

B4	SP3	2c + 1c crim rose	30	15

AIR POST STAMPS.

Seaplane over Havana Harbor
AP1

Wmkd. Star. (106)

1927, Nov. 1 Engraved *Perf. 12*

C1	AP1	5c dk bl	5.00	20

Type of 1927 Issue Overprinted
LINDBERGH
FEBRERO 1928

1928, Feb. 8

C2	AP1	5c car rose	2.50	1.25

No. 283 Surcharged in Red
CORREO AEREO NACIONAL
10¢ 10¢

1930, Oct. 27 Unwmkd.

C3	A44	10c on 25c vio	2.50	1.25

Airplane and Coast of Cuba
AP3

For Foreign Postage.

1931, Feb. 26 *Perf. 10* Wmk. 106

C4	AP3	5c green	50	5
C5	AP3	10c dk bl	50	5
C6	AP3	15c rose	1.00	30
C7	AP3	20c brown	1.00	6
C8	AP3	30c dk vio	1.50	20
C9	AP3	40c dp org	3.50	40
C10	AP3	50c ol grn	4.00	40
C11	AP3	1p black	6.00	1.00
		Nos. C4-C11 (8)	18.00	2.46

See also No. C40.

Airplane
AP4

For Domestic Postage.

1931-46

C12	AP4	5c rose vio ('32)	40	6
a.		5c brn vio ('36)	40	6
C13	AP4	10c gray blk	40	5
C14	AP4	20c car rose	3.00	85
C14A	AP4	20c rose pink ('46)	1.25	20
C15	AP4	50c dk bl	5.00	85
		Nos. C12-C15 (5)	10.05	2.01

See also No. C130.

Type of 1931 Surcharged in Black
PRIMER TREN AEREO
INTERNACIONAL. 1935
O'Meara y du Pont +10cts.

1935, Apr. 24 *Perf. 10*

C16	AP3	10c + 10c red	7.50	6.00

Imperf.

C17	AP3	10c + 10c red	30.00	30.00

Matanzas Issue.

Air View of Matanzas
AP5

Designs: 10c, Airship "Macon." 20c, Airplane "The Four Winds." 50c, Air View of Fort San Severino.

Photogravure.

Wmkd. Wavy Lines. (229)

1936, May 5 *Perf. 12½*

C18	AP5	5c violet	75	50
C19	AP5	10c yel org	1.50	75
C20	AP5	20c green	5.00	3.00
C21	AP5	50c grnsh sl	9.00	6.00

Exist imperf. Price 20% more.

"Lightning"
AP9

Allegory of Flight
AP10

1936, Nov. 18

C22	AP9	5c violet	2.50	50
C23	AP10	10c org brn	3.00	75

Issued in commemoration of the centenary of the birth of Major General Máximo Gómez.

Flat Arch (Panama)
AP11

Carlos Antonio López (Paraguay)
AP12

Inca Gate, Cuzco (Peru)
AP13

Atlacatl (Salvador)
AP14

José Enrique Rodó (Uruguay)
AP15

Simón Bolívar (Venezuela)
AP16

Engraved.

1937. Oct. 13 *Perf. 10* Wmk. 106

C24	AP11	5c red	6.00	5.00
C25	AP12	5c red	6.00	5.00
C26	AP13	10c blue	7.00	6.00
C27	AP14	10c blue	7.00	6.00
C28	AP15	20c green	8.00	7.50
C29	AP16	20c green	8.00	7.50
		Nos. C24-C29 (6)	42.00	37.00

Issued for the benefit of the Association of American Writers and Artists. See note after No. 354.

Type of 1927 Overprinted in Black

1913 1938
ROSILLO
Key West-Habana

1938, May Wmk. 106

C30	AP1	5c dk org	5.00	1.50

Issued in commemoration of the first airplane flight from Key West to Havana, made by Domingo Rosillo, 1913.

Type of 1931–32 Overprinted

EXPERIMENTO DEL
COHETE
Postal
AÑO DE 1939

1939, Oct. 15

C31	AP4	10c emerald	25.00	7.50

Issued in connection with an experimental postal rocket flight held at Havana.

Sir Rowland Hill, Map of Cuba and First Stamps of Britain, Spanish Cuba and Republic of Cuba
AP17

1940, Nov. 28 Engr. Wmk. 106

C32	AP17	10c brown	4.00	1.50

Souvenir Sheet
Imperf.
Unwmkd.

C33	AP17	10c lt brn, sheet of four	12.50	10.00
a.		Single stamp	2.80	2.00

Centenary of the first postage stamp. Sheet measures 128x178mm. Sheet sold for 60c.

No. C33 exists with each of the four stamps overprinted in black: "Exposicion de la ACNU/24 de Octubre de 1951/Dia de las Naciones" and "Historia de la Aviacion" in lower margin.

Price, $70.

Poet José Heredia and Palms
AP18

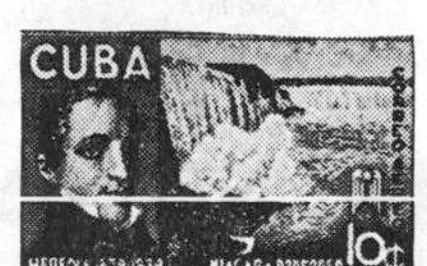

Heredia and Niagara Falls
AP19

1940. Dec. 30 Wmk. 106

C34	AP18	5c emerald	1.50	75
C35	AP19	10c grnsh sl	3.00	1.00

Issued to commemorate the centenary of the death of José Maria Heredia y Campuzano (1803–1839), poet and patriot.

First Cuban Land Sighted by Columbus
AP20

Columbus Lighthouse
AP21

1944, May 19

C36	AP20	5c ol grn	60	15
C37	AP21	10c sl blk	1.25	40

Issued to commemorate the 450th anniversary of the discovery of America.

Conference of La Mejorana (Meceo, Gomez and Marti)
AP22

1948, May 21 *Perf. 12½* Wmk. 229

C38	AP22	8c org yel & blk	2.00	75

Issued to commemorate the 50th anniversary of the start of the War of 1895.

Souvenir Sheet.
No. C33 Overprinted in Ultramarine

CONVENCION
MAYO 21-22-23 1948
AMERICAN AIR MAIL SOCIETY

1948, May 21 *Imperf.* Unwmkd.

C39	AP17	10c lt brn, sheet of four	8.00	7.00

The overprint is applied in the center of the four stamps, so that a portion falls on each.

Issued in honor of the American Air Mail Society Convention, Havana, May 21 to 23, 1948. The sheets sold for 60c each.

Type of 1931.

1948, June 15 *Perf. 10* Wmk. 106

C40	AP3	8c org brn	1.50	20

Narciso Lopez Landing at Cárdenas
AP23

Flag on Cuban Fort
AP24

Flag on Morro Castle, Havana
AP25

Engraved and Lithographed.

1951, July 3 *Perf. 13* Wmk. 229

C41	AP23	5c ol grn, ultra & red	1.25	25
C42	AP24	8c red brn, bl & red	2.00	25
C43	AP25	25c gray blk, bl & red	3.00	1.50

Centenary of adoption of Cuba's flag.

Souvenir Sheet.
No. 365a Overprinted in Green.

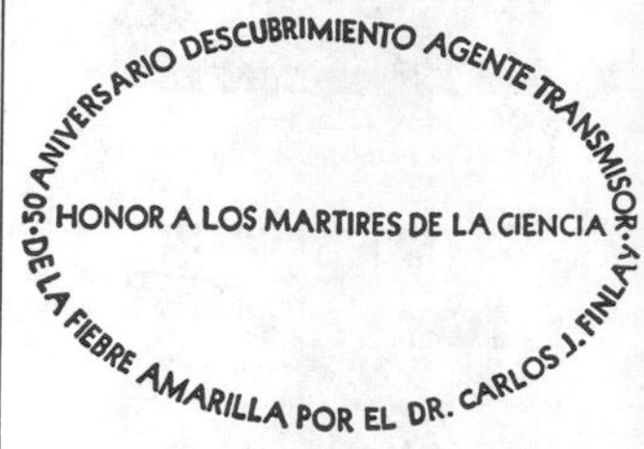

(Reduced Illustration of Overprint)

1951, Aug. 24 *Imperf.* Unwmkd.

C43A		Sheet of four	6.00	5.00

Issued to commemorate the 50th anniversary of the discovery of the cause of yellow fever by Dr. Carlos J. Finlay, and to honor the martyrs of science.

No. C43A measures 127x177 mm. and contains two each of Nos. 364 and 365 imperforate, with upper and lower marginal inscriptions.

Resignation Play of Dr. Lasker
AP26

Capablanca Making "The Exact Play"
AP27

Design: 25c, Capablanca.

Photogravure.

1951, Nov. 1 *Perf. 13* Wmk. 229

C44	AP26	5c bl grn & yel	5.00	1.00
C45	AP27	8c ultra & cl	7.50	1.25
C46	A165	25c brn & dk brn	15.00	4.00

Issued to commemorate the 30th anniversary of the winning of the World Chess title by José Raul Capablanca.

Morrillo Types of Regular Issue, 1951.
Engraved.

1951, Nov. 22 *Perf. 10* Wmk. 106

C47	A167	5c violet	1.00	15
C48	A168	8c dp grn	1.25	25
C49	A169	25c dk brn	2.50	1.50
a.		Souvenir sheet of 6, blk brn, perf. 13	25.00	25.00
b.		Souvenir sheet of 6, grn, imperf.	90.00	90.00

Issued to commemorate the 16th anniversary of the Action of the Morrillo and to honor Antonio Guiteras Holmes who was killed there.

Nos. C49a and C49b contain one each of the 1c, 2c and 5c of types A167-A169 and of the 5c, 8c and 25c airmail stamps of types A167-A169. Marginal inscriptions are typographed in black; coat of arms engraved in color of stamps (black brown or green). Sheets are unwatermarked and measure 124x133mm

Isabella Type of Regular Issue, 1952

1952, Feb. 22

C50	A172	25c purple	3.00	1.00
a.		Souvenir sheet of 2, perf. 11	12.50	10.00
b.		Souvenir sheet of 2, imperf.	15.00	15.00

Issued to commemorate the 500th anniversary of the birth of Queen Isabella I of Spain.

Nos. C50a and C50b contain one each of a 2c of type A172 and a 25c air-mail stamp of type A172. In No. C50a, the 2c and marginal inscriptions are brown carmine; the 25c, dark blue. In No. C50b, the 2c and marginal inscriptions are dark blue; the 25c, brown carmine. Sheets measure 108x108mm.

Type of Regular Issue of 1951 Surcharged in Various Colors

1952, Mar. 18

C51	A159	5c on 2c yel brn	50	15
C52	A159	8c on 2c yel brn (C)	1.00	10
C53	A159	10c on 2c yel brn (Bl)	1.00	15
C54	A159	25c on 2c yel brn (V)	1.50	1.00
C55	A159	50c on 2c yel brn (C)	5.00	2.00
C56	A159	1p on 2c yel brn (Bl)	12.50	7.50
		Nos. C51-C56 (6)	21.50	10.90

Country School
AP32

Entrance, University of Havana
AP33

Designs: 10c, Presidential Mansion. 25c, Banknote.

Engraved.

1952, May 27 ***Perf. 12½*** **Wmk. 106**

Centers Various Shades of Green.

C57	AP32	5c dk pur	50	10
C58	AP33	8c dk red	75	15
C59	AP32	10c dp bl	1.50	25
C60	AP32	25c dk vio brn	2.50	1.25

Issued to commemorate the 50th anniversary of the foundation of the Republic of Cuba.

Plane and Map
AP34

Agustín Parlá
AP35

Engraved

1952, July 22 ***Perf. 10***

C61	AP34	8c black	1.25	50
a.		Souvenir sheet, 8c dp bl	6.00	6.00
b.		Souvenir sheet, 8c dp grn	6.00	6.00
C62	AP35	25c ultra	3.50	1.50
a.		Souvenir sheet, 25c dp bl	6.00	6.00
b.		Souvenir sheet, 25c dp grn	6.00	6.00

Issued to commemorate the 30th anniversary of the Key West-Mariel flight of Agustin Parla.

The four souvenir sheets are perf. 11, measure 107x95mm. and have marginal inscriptions in the same color as the stamp.

Col. Charles Hernandes y Sandrino
AP36

1952, Oct. 7

C63	AP36	5c orange	75	15
C64	AP36	8c brt yel grn	75	10
C65	AP36	10c dk brn	1.00	25
C66	AP36	15c dk Prus grn	2.00	75
C67	AP36	20c aqua	2.50	1.00
C68	AP36	25c crimson	2.00	1.00
C69	AP36	30c dk vio bl	5.00	2.50
C70	AP36	45c rose lil	5.00	3.50
C71	AP36	50c indigo	3.00	2.50
C72	AP36	1p bister	10.00	5.00
		Nos. C63-C72 (10)	32.00	16.75

Three-fourths of the proceeds from the sale of Nos. C63–C72 were used for the Communications Ministry Employees' Retirement Fund.

Entrance, University of Havana
AP37

F. V. Dominguez, M. Estebanez and F. Capdevila—AP38

Engraved; Centers Typographed.

1952, Nov. 27

C73	AP37	5c ind & dk bl	90	35
C74	AP38	25c org & dk grn	2.75	1.25

Issued to commemorate the 81st anniversary of the execution of eight medical students.

AP39

Lockheed Constellation Airliners
AP40

1953, May 22 **Engraved.**

C75	AP39	8c org brn	50	6
C76	AP39	15c scarlet	2.00	30

Typographed and Engraved

C77	AP40	2p dp grn & dk brn	30.00	12.50
C78	AP40	5p bl & dk brn	40.00	20.00

See also Nos. C120-C121.

Page of Manifesto of Montecristi
AP42

House of Maximo Gomez
AP43

Designs: No. C79, Marti in Kingston, Jamaica. No. C80, With Workers in Tampa, Florida. No. C83, Marti addressing liberating army. No. C84, Portrait. No. C85, Dos Rios obelisk. No. C86, Marti's first tomb. No. C87, Present tomb. No. C88, Monument in Havana. No. C89, Martian forge.

1953 **Engraved** ***Perf. 10***

C79	AP42	5c dk car & blk	30	12
C80	AP43	5c dk grn & blk	30	12
C81	AP43	8c dk grn & blk	75	15
C82	AP42	8c dk grn & blk	75	15
C83	AP43	10c dk bl & dk car	1.50	40
C84	AP42	10c dk bl & dk car	1.50	40
C85	AP42	15c vio & gray	1.25	75
C86	AP42	15c vio & gray	1.25	75
C87	AP42	25c brn & car	3.00	1.00
C88	AP42	25c brn & car	3.00	1.00
C89	AP43	50c yel & bl	5.00	2.00
		Nos. C79-C89 (11)	18.60	6.84

Issued to commemorate the centenary of the birth of José Martí.

Board of Accounts Building
AP44

Design: 25c, Plane above Board of Accounts Bldg.

1953, Nov. 3

C90	AP44	8c rose car	1.00	25
C91	AP44	25c dk gray grn	2.00	1.00

Issued to publicize the First International Congress of Boards of Account, Havana, November 2–9, 1953.

Miguel Coyula Llaguno
AP45

Antonio Ginard Rojas
AP46

Designs: 10c, Gregorio Hernandez Saez. 1p, Communications Association Flag.

1954

C92	AP45	5c dk bl	50	15
C93	AP46	8c red vio	60	25
C94	AP46	10c orange	1.25	35
C95	AP45	1p black	8.50	6.00

See note after No. C72.

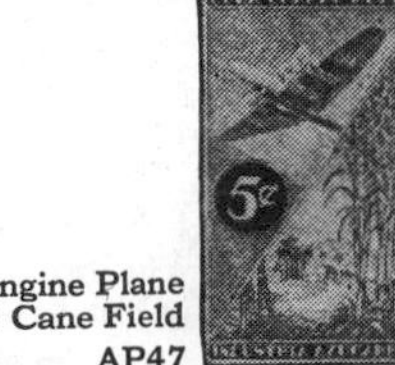

Four-engine Plane and Cane Field
AP47

Plane and Harvesters Cutting Cane
AP48

Designs in Lower Triangle: 10c, Tractor pulling loaded wagons. 15c, Train of sugar cane. 20c, Modern mill. 25c, Evaporators. 30, Sacks of sugar. 40c, Loading sugar on ship. 45c, Ox cart. 50c, Primitive sugar mill. 1p, Alvaro Reinoso.

1954, Apr. 27 **Engraved**

C96	AP47	5c yel grn	60	10
C97	AP48	8c brown	1.25	8
C98	AP48	10c dk grn	1.50	15
C99	AP48	15c hn brn	75	35
C100	AP48	20c blue	1.00	50
C101	AP48	25c scarlet	1.50	50
C102	AP48	30c lil rose	2.50	75
C103	AP48	40c dp bl	3.00	1.00
C104	AP48	45c violet	6.00	2.00
C105	AP48	50c brt bl	4.00	1.25
C106	AP47	1p dk gray bl	8.00	2.50
		Nos. C96-C106 (11)	30.10	9.18

Sanatorium Type of Regular Issue, 1954.

1954, Sept. 21 ***Perf. 10*** **Wmk. 106**

C107	A186	9c dp grn	1.00	50

Dolz Type of Regular Issue, 1954.

1954, Dec. 23

C108	A188	12c carmine	1.00	50

Issued to commemorate the centenary of the birth of Maria Luisa Dolz, educator and defender of women's rights.

Rotary Type of Regular Issue, 1955.

1955, Feb. 23

C109	A190	12c carmine	1.25	40

Issued to commemorate the 50th anniversary of the founding of Rotary International.

Stamps of 1855 and 1905, Palace of Fine Arts
AP52

Designs (including 2 stamps): 12c, Plaza de la Fraternidad. 24c, View of Havana. 30c, Plaza de la Republica.

1955, Apr. 24 ***Perf. 12½***

C110	AP52	8c dk grnsh bl & grn	1.25	50
C111	AP52	12c dk ol grn & red	1.50	35
C112	AP52	24c dk red & ultra	1.75	1.00
C113	AP52	30c dp org & brn	3.75	2.00

Issued to commemorate the centenary of Cuba's first postage stamps.

Mariel Bay—AP53

Views: 12c, Varadero beach. 1p, Vinales valley.

1955, June 22 **Wmk. 106**

C114	AP53	8c dk car & dk grn	75	30
C115	AP53	12c dk ocher & brt bl	1.00	25
C116	AP53	1p dk grn & ocher	6.00	4.00

See note after No. C72.

Map of Crocier's 1914 Flight
AP54

Design: 30c, Jaime Gonzalez Crocier in plane.

1955, July 4 ***Perf. 10***

C117 AP54 12c red & dk grn 60 20
C118 AP54 30c dk grn & mag 2.25 60

Issued to honor Jaime Gonzalez Crocier, aviation pioneer, on the 35th anniversary of his death.

Cuban Museum, Tampa, Fla.
AP55

1955, July 1 Engr. ***Perf. 12½***

C119 AP55 12c red & dk brn 1.10 35

Issued to commemorate the centenary of Tampa's incorporation as a town.

Lockheed Type of 1953
Typographed and Engraved

1955, Sept. 21 **Wmk. 106**

C120 AP40 2p bl & ol grn 17.50 8.50
C121 AP40 5p dp rose & ol grn 37.50 16.50

Wright Brothers' Plane and Stamps
AP56

Designs: 12c, Spirit of St. Louis. 24c, Graf Zeppelin. 30c, Constellation passenger plane. 50c, Convair jet fighter.

Engraved and Photogravure.

1955, Nov. 12 ***Perf. 12½*** **Wmk. 106**

Inscription and Plane in Black.

C122 AP56 8c car & bl 1.00 35
C123 AP56 12c yel grn & car 2.25 70
C124 AP56 24c vio & car 7.00 2.50
C125 AP56 30c bl & red org 6.00 3.25
C126 AP56 50c ol grn & red org 8.00 4.00
a. Souvenir sheet of 5 40.00 45.00
Nos. C122-C126 (5) 24.25 10.80

Issued to commemorate the International Centenary Philatelic Exhibition in Havana, Nov. 12–19, 1955.

No. C126a is printed on thick paper and measures 140x178mm. It contains one each of Nos. C122–C126 with the background of each stamp printed in a different color from the perforated stamps. The sheet is inscribed in black "Republica de Cuba. Souvenir. Exposition Filatelica Internacional Centenario 1955" and "XXXII Convencion de la American Airmail Society."

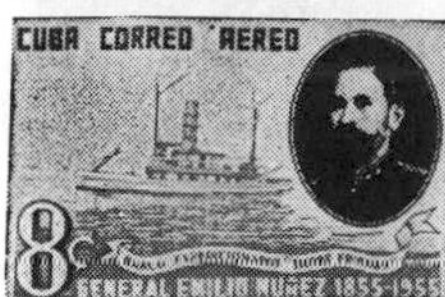

"Three Friends" and Gen. Emilio Nuñez
AP57

Design: 12c, Landing on the Cuban Coast.

1955, Dec. 27 Engraved Unwmkd.

C127 AP57 8c ultra & dk car 1.00 40
C128 AP57 12c grn & dk red brn 1.50 50

Issued to commemorate the centenary of the birth of Gen. Emilio Nuñez, Cuban revolutionary hero.

Post Type of Regular Issue, 1956.

Design: 12c, Bishop P. A. Morell de Santa Cruz (1694–1768).

1956, March 27 **Wmk. 106**

C129 A197 12c dk brn & grn 90 30

Bicentenary of the Cuban post.

Plane Type of 1931–46.

1956 Engraved ***Perf. 10***

C130 AP4 50c grnsh bl 2.00 1.00

Portrait Type of Regular Issue, 1956.

1956, May 2 ***Perf. 12½***

Portraits: 8c, Gen. Julio Sanguily. 12c, Gen. José Maria Aguirre. 30c, Col. Ernesto Ponts Sterling.

Portraits in Black.

C131 A198 8c brown 75 20
C132 A198 12c dl yel 1.25 20
C133 A198 30c indigo 2.25 1.50

See note after No. C72.

Mother and Child
AP60

Masonic Temple Havana
AP61

1956, May 13 ***Perf. 12½*** **Wmk. 106**

C134 AP60 12c ultra & red 80 25

Issued in honor of Mother's Day 1956.

1956, June 5

C135 AP61 12c ol grn 60 20

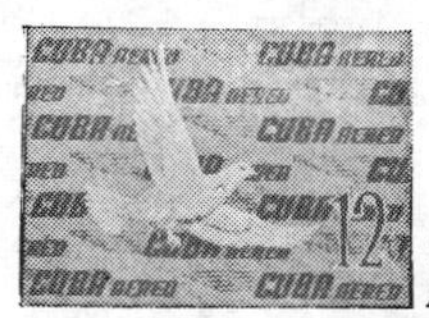

Pigeon
AP62

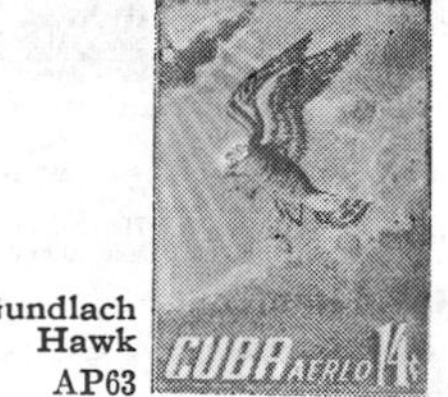

Gundlach Hawk
AP63

Birds: 8c, Wood duck. 19c, Herring gulls. 24c, White pelicans. 29c, Common merganser. 30c, Quail. 50c, Herons (great white, great blue and Wurdemann's). 1p, Northern caracara. 2p, Middle American jacana. 5p, Ivory-billed woodpecker.

1956

C136 AP62 8c blue 50 15
C137 AP62 12c dk bl 7.00 10
C138 AP63 14c green 1.50 25
C139 AP63 19c redsh brn 1.00 50
C140 AP63 24c lil rose 1.25 50
C141 AP62 29c green 1.75 50
C142 AP63 30c dk ol bis 2.00 75
C143 AP63 50c sl blk 4.00 1.00
C144 AP63 1p dk car rose 6.00 2.00
C145 AP62 2p rose vio 12.50 4.00
C146 AP63 5p brt red 30.00 8.00
Nos. C136-C146 (11) 67.50 17.75

See also No. C205.

Type of 1956 Surcharged

Inauguración
Edificio Club
Filatélico de la
República de Cuba
Julio 13 de 1956.

8¢

Design: 24c, White pelicans.

1956, July 13

C147 AP63 8c on 24c dp org 1.00 35

Issued to commemorate the opening of the new building of the Cuba Philatelic Club, Havana, July 14, 1956.

Hubert de Blanck
AP64

Church of Our Lady of Charity
AP65

1956, July 6

C148 AP64 12c ultra 90 25

Issued to commemorate the centenary of the birth of Hubert de Blanck (1856–1932), composer.

1956, Sept. 8

C149 AP65 12c grn & car 90 40
a. Souvenir sheet of 2, imperf. 9.00 8.00

Issued in honor of Our Lady of Charity of Cobre, patroness of Cuba.

No. C149a contains one each of Nos. 559 and C149 with bright blue marginal inscription and coat of arms. Size: 76x77mm. No. C149a exists with yellow of No. 559 omitted.

Benjamin Franklin
AP66

1956, Oct. 5 Engr. ***Perf. 12½***

C150 AP66 12c red brn 1.00 40

Issued to commemorate the 250th anniversary of the birth of Benjamin Franklin.

Type of 1956 Surcharged in Blue

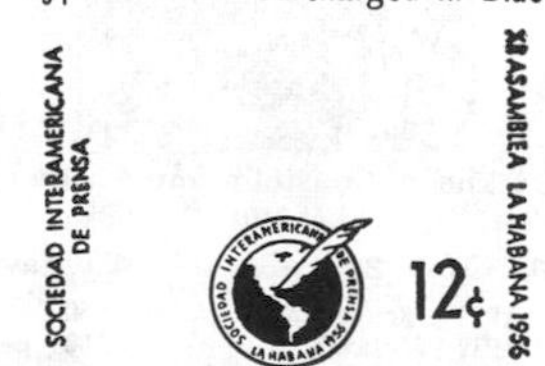

Design: 2p, Middle American Jacana.

1956, Oct. 26 **Wmk. 106**

C151 AP62 12c on 2p dk gray 1.50 75

Issued in honor of the 12th Inter-American Press Association Conference, Havana.

Lord Baden-Powell
AP67

1957, Feb. 22

C152 AP67 12c slate 1.50 35

Issued to commemorate the centenary of the birth of Lord Baden-Powell, founder of the Boy Scouts.

Hanabanilla Waterfall
AP68

Designs: 12c, Sierra de Cubitas. 30c, Puerto Boniato.

1957, March 29

C153 AP68 8c bl & red 75 20
C154 AP68 12c grn & red 1.20 25
C155 AP68 30c ol grn & dk pur 2.00 1.00

See note after No. 457.

Philatelic Club, Havana
AP69

Fingerprint
AP70

1957, Apr. 24 ***Perf. 12½*** **Wmk. 106**

C156 AP69 12c yel, grn & brn 1.00 25

Issued for Stamp Day, Apr. 24, and the National Philatelic Exhibition.

1957, Apr. 30

C157 AP70 12c cl brn 90 20

Issued in honor of the centenary of the birth (in 1856) of Juan Francisco Steegers y Perera, dactyloscopy pioneer.

Baseball Player
AP71

Designs: 12c, Ballerina. 24c, Girl diver. 30c, Boxers.

1957, May 17 ***Perf. 12½*** **Wmk. 106**

C158 AP71 8c ol grn & brn 1.00 35
C159 AP71 12c pale vio & brn 1.75 40
C160 AP71 24c brt bl & brn 2.50 1.00
C161 AP71 30c org & brn 3.50 1.50

Issued to honor young Cuban athletes.

Joaquin de Aguero AP72 — Jeanette Ryder AP73

1957, July 4

C162 AP72 12c indigo 90 25

Issued to honor Joaquin de Aguero, Cuban freedom fighter and patriot.

1957, July 17

C163 AP73 12c dk red brn 90 35
a. Se-tenant with No. 574 2.00 1.00

Printed in sheets of 40, containing alternate copies of Nos. 574 and C163 to honor Mrs. Jeanette Ryder, founder of the Humane Society of Cuba.

José M. de Heredia y Girard AP74 — John Robert Gregg AP75

1957, Aug. 16 Engr. Wmk. 106

C164 AP74 8c dk bl vio 50 25

Issued in honor of the poet José Maria de Heredia y Girard (1842–1905), Cuban-born French poet.

Justice Type of Regular Issue, 1957.

1957, Sept. 2 ***Perf. 12½***

C165 A214 12c green 90 50

Opening of Palace of Justice, Havana.

1957, Oct. 1

C166 AP75 12c dk grn 80 35

Issued to commemorate the 90th anniversary of the birth of John Robert Gregg, inventor of the Gregg shorthand system.

D. Figarola Caneda AP76

José Marti National Library AP77

1957, Oct. 18 ***Perf. 12½*** **Wmk. 106**

C167 AP76 8c ultra 50 20
C168 AP77 12c chocolate 90 25

Issued to publicize the José Marti National Library.

Map of Cuba and U. N. Emblem AP78

1957, Oct. 24

C169 AP78 8c dk grn & brn 75 25
C170 AP78 12c car rose & grn 1.00 50
C171 AP78 30c ind & brt pink 2.50 1.00

Issued for United Nations Day, 1957.

Map of Cuba and Florida AP79

1957, Oct. 28

C172 AP79 12c dk red brn & bl 85 40

Issued to commemorate the 30th anniversary of airmail service from Key West to Havana.

Type of Regular Issue, 1957 and

Stairway and Bell Tower AP80

Design: 12c, Facade of Normal School.

1957, Nov. 19 Engraved. ***Perf. 12½***

C173 A217 12c ind & ocher 85 20
C174 AP80 30c dk car & gray 1.25 60

Issued to commemorate the centenary of the first Cuban Normal School.

View Types of Regular Issue, 1957.

Views: 8c, El Viso Fort, El Caney. 12c, Sancti Spiritus Church. 30c, Concordia Bridge, Matanzas.

1957, Dec. 17 ***Perf. 12½***

C175 A218 8c dk gray & red 75 25
C176 A219 12c brn & gray 1.00 25
C177 A218 30c red brn & bl gray 1.50 85

See note after No. C72.

Hedges Types of Regular Issue, 1958.

Design: 8c, Dayton Hedges and Matanzas rayon factory.

1958, Jan. 30 ***Perf. 12½*** **Wmk. 106**

C178 A221 8c green 80 40

Issued to honor Dayton Hedges, founder of Cuba's textile industry.

Diario de la Marina Building AP81

1958, April 1

C179 AP81 29c black 3.00 2.00

Issued in honor of Jose Ignacio Rivero y Alonso, editor of the newspaper, Diario de la Marina.

Map Showing Sea Mail Route, 1765 AP82

1958, Apr. 24 ***Perf. 12½*** **Wmk. 106**

C180 AP82 29c dk bl aqua & buff 2.25 1.25

Issued for Stamp Day, Apr. 24, and the National Philatelic Exhibition.

Gen. Gomez in Battle AP83 — Snail (Polymita Picta) AP84

1958, June 6 Engraved

C181 AP83 12c sl grn 70 25

Issued in honor of Maj. Gen. José Miguel Gomez, President of Cuba, 1909-13.

1958, Aug. 29 ***Perf. 12½*** **Wmk. 321**

Fossils: 12c, Megalocnus Rodens. 30c, Ammonite.

C182 AP84 8c gray, red & yel 1.50 75
C183 AP84 12c brn, *yel grn* 2.50 1.25
C184 AP84 30c grn, *pink* 3.50 1.75

Issued to commemorate the centenary of the birth of Dr. Carlos de la Torre, naturalist.

Papilio Caiguanabus AP85 — Cuban Sea Bass AP86

Designs: 12c, Teria gundlachia. 14c, Teria ebriola. 19c, Nathalis felicia. 29c, Butter Hamlet. 30c, Tattler.

1958, Sept. 26 ***Perf. 12½*** **Wmk. 106**

C185 AP85 8c multi 1.75 50
C186 AP85 12c emer, blk & org 2.00 50
C187 AP85 14c multi 3.00 75
C188 AP85 19c bl, blk & yel 3.75 1.00
C189 AP86 24c multi 4.50 1.00
C190 AP86 29c blk, brn & ultra 7.00 1.25
C191 AP86 30c blk, yel grn & sep 8.00 1.75
Nos. C185-C191 (7) 30.00 6.75

Issued in honor of Felipe Poey (1799–1891), naturalist.

Battle of San Juan Hill, 1898 AP87

Engraved.

1958, Oct. 27 ***Perf. 12½*** **Wmk. 106**

C192 AP87 12c blk brn 90 30

Birth centenary of Theodore Roosevelt.

UNESCO Building, Paris AP88

Design: 30c, "UNESCO" and map of Cuba.

1958, Nov. 7

C193 AP88 12c dk sl grn 1.00 40
C194 AP88 30c dp ultra 2.25 1.35

Issued to commemorate the opening of UNESCO (U. N. Educational, Scientific and Cultural Organization) Headquarters in Paris, Nov. 3.

Postal Notice of 1765 AP89 — Musical Arts Building AP90

Design: 30c, Administrative postal book of St. Cristobal, Havana, 1765.

1959, Apr. 24 ***Perf. 12½*** **Wmk. 321**

C195 AP89 12c Prus bl & sep 75 25
C196 AP89 30c sep & Prus bl 1.25 85

Issued for Stamp Day, Apr. 24, and the National Philatelic Exhibition.

Type of 1956 Surcharged with New Value, Bar and "ASTA" Emblem in Dark Blue.

1959, Oct. 17 ***Perf. 12½*** **Wmk. 321**

C197 AP63 12c on 1p emer 1.00 40

Issued to publicize the meeting of the American Society of Travel Agents, Oct. 17-23.

Engraved.

1959, Nov. 11 ***Perf. 12½*** **Wmk. 106**

C198 AP90 12c yel grn 90 25

Issued to commemorate the 40th anniversary of the Musical Arts Society.

No. CB1 Surcharged in Red: "HABILITADO PARA / 12c"

Engraved and Lithographed

1960 ***Perf. 12½*** **Wmk. 321**

C199 SPAP1 12c on 12c+3c car & grn 1.50 75

Type of Regular Issue, 1960.

Designs: 8c, Battle of Santa Clara. 12c, Rebel forces entering Havana. 29c, Banknote changing hands ("Clandestine activities in the cities").

Engraved.

1960, Jan. 28 ***Perf. 12½*** **Wmk. 320**

C200 A236 8c bl, gray ol & sal 1.00 25
C201 A236 12c gray ol & ocher 1.50 25
C202 A236 29c gray & car 2.50 1.50

First anniversary of the revolution.

Nos. C9 and C104 Surcharged "12c" in Red

1960, Feb. 3 Wmk. 106

C203 AP3 12c on 40c dp org 75 30
C204 AP48 12c on 45c vio 75 30

Pigeon Type of 1956.

1960, Feb. 12 Wmk. 321

C205 AP62 12c brt bl grn 50 10

Statue Type of Regular Issue, 1960.

Statues: 8c, José Marti, Matanzas. 12c, Heroes of the Cacarajicara, Pinar del Rio. 30c, Cosme de la Torriente, Isle of Pines. (horiz.).

1960, March 28 ***Perf. 12½***

C206 A237 8c gray & car 60 25
C207 A237 12c bl & car 1.00 25
C208 A237 30c vio & brn 2.25 1.00

See note after No. 386.

Type of 1956 and No. C33 Overprinted in Dark Blue

1960, Apr. 24 Perf. 12½ Wmk. 321

C209	AP62	8c org yel	30	20
C210	AP62	12c cerise	50	20

Souvenir Sheet

C211	AP17	Sheet of four	12.00	12.00

Nos. C209-C211 issued for Stamp Day, Apr. 24, 1960, and to publicize the National Philatelic Exhibition.

No. C211 has added marginal inscription in dark blue commemorating the centenary of the ¼r on 2r (No. 15).

Type of Olympic Games Issue, 1960.

Designs: 8c, Boxer. 12c, Runner.

Engraved

1960, Sept. 22 Perf. 12½ Wmk. 321

C212	A238	8c ultra	40	20
C213	A238	12c car rose	60	40
a.		Souvenir sheet of 4	3.50	

Issued to commemorate the 17th Olympic Games, Rome, Aug. 25-Sept. 11. No. C213a contains one each imperf. of types of Nos. 645-646 and Nos. C212-C213 in dark blue. Red marginal inscription. Size: 78x90mm.

Airmail Stamp of 1930 and Flight Symbols of 1930, 1960
AP91

1960, Oct. 30 Litho. Unwmkd.

C214	AP91	8c multi	2.50	1.50

Issued to commemorate the 30th anniversary of national air mail service.

Sword and Sheaf of Wheat
AP92

Designs: 12c, Two workers (horiz.). 30c, Three maps (horiz.). 50c, Hand inscribed "Peace" in 5 languages.

Granite Paper

1961, Jan. 10 Photo. Perf. 11½

C215	AP92	8c multi	30	20
C216	AP92	12c multi	45	20
C217	AP92	30c blk & red	1.25	50
C218	AP92	50c blk, bl & red	1.50	1.00

Issued to publicize the Conference of Underdeveloped Countries, Havana.

José Marti and "Declaration of Havana"
AP93

Background in Spanish, English or French

1961, Jan. 28 Litho. Perf. 12½

C219	AP93	8c pale grn, blk & red	1.00	60
C220	AP93	12c org yel, blk & pale vio	1.50	1.00
C221	AP93	30c pale bl, blk & pale brn	2.50	1.50
a.		Souvenir sheet of 3	7.50	7.50
		Nos. C219-C221 (9)	15.00	9.30

Declaration of Havana, Sept. 1, 1960.

Sheets of 25 are imprinted in margin "E" for Spanish, "I" for English or "F" for French.

No. C221a contains one each of Nos. C219-C221, imperf. The 8c has background in Spanish, the 12c in English and the 30c in French. Black marginal inscription. Size: 102x79mm.

U.N. Type of 1961.

1961, Apr. 12 Perf. 12½ Unwmkd.

C222	A244	8c dp car & yel	30	10
C223	A244	12c brt ultra & org	60	30
a.		Souvenir sheet of 2	2.00	

Issued to commemorate the 15th anniversary (in 1960) of the United Nations.

No. C223a contains one each of Nos. C222-C223, imperf. with marginal bright ultramarine inscription. Size: 107x65mm.

AIR POST SEMI-POSTAL STAMP

Farm Couple and Factory
SPAP1

Engraved and Lithographed

1959, May 7 Perf. 12½ Wmk. 321

CB1	SPAP1	12c +3c car & grn	1.50	60

Agricultural reforms. See also No. C199.

AIR POST SPECIAL DELIVERY STAMP.

Matanzas Issue.

Matanzas Harbor
APSD1

Photogravure.

Wmkd. Wavy Lines. (229)

1936, May 5 Perf. 12½

CE1	APSD1	15c lt bl	5.00	2.50

Exists imperf. Price $5 unused, $2.50 used.

See "Special Notices" at the front of this volume for data on the listing methods of this Catalogue, abbreviations, condition, prices and examination.

SPECIAL DELIVERY STAMPS

Issued under Administration of the United States.

U.S. No. E5 Surcharged in Red

CUBA.
10c.
de PESO

Wmkd. USPS (191)

1899 Perf. 12

E1	SD3	10c on 10c bl	100.00	80.00
a.		No period after "CUBA"	350.00	350.00

Issues of the Republic under U. S. Military Rule.

Special Delivery Messenger
SD2

Engraved.

Inscribed: "Immediata".

1899 Wmkd. U S—C (191C)

E2	SD2	10c orange	45.00	10.00

Issues of the Republic

Inscribed: "Inmediata".

Wmkd. U S-C (191C)

1902 Perf. 12.

E3	SD2	10c orange	1.25	60

J. B. Zayas
SD3

1910 Unwmkd.

E4	SD3	10c org & bl	11.00	2.50
a.		Center inverted	850.00	

Airplane and Morro Castle
SD4

1914, Feb. 24 Perf. 12

E5	SD4	10c dk bl	17.50	1.00

1927 Wmkd. Star. (106)

E6	SD4	10c dp bl	14.00	35

1935 Perf. 10.

E7	SD4	10c blue	14.00	30

Matanzas Issue.

Mercury
SD5

Photogravure.

Wmkd. Wavy Lines. (229)

1936, May 5 Perf. 12½

E8	SD5	10c dp cl	6.00	2.50

Exists imperf. Price $6 unused, $2.50 used.

"Triumph of the Revolution"
SD6

1936, Nov. 18

E9	SD6	10c red org	5.00	2.50

Issued in commemoration of the centenary of the birth of Maj. Gen. Máximo Gómez (1836-1905).

Temple of Quetzalcoatl (Mexico)
SD7

Ruben Dario (Nicaragua)
SD8

Engraved

1937, Oct. 13 Perf. 10 Wmk. 106

E10	SD7	10c dp org	6.00	5.00
E11	SD8	10c dp org	6.00	5.00

Issued for the benefit of the Association of American Writers and Artists. See note after No. 354.

Letter and Symbols of Transportation
SD9

1945, Oct. 30

E12	SD9	10c ol brn	2.00	20

Governor's Building, Cárdenas
SD10

Engraved and Lithographed.

1951, July 3 Perf. 13 Wmk. 229

E13	SD10	10c hn brn, ultra & red	5.00	1.00

Issued to commemorate the centenary of the adoption of Cuba's flag.

Chess Type of Regular Issue, 1951

1951, Nov. 1 Photogravure

E14	A166	10c dk grn & rose brn	10.00	3.50

Issued to commemorate the 30th anniversary of the winning of the World Chess title by José Raul Capablanca.

Type of Regular Issue of 1951 Surcharged in Red Violet

10¢
E. ESPECIAL

Engraved.

1952, Mar. 18 Perf. 10 Wmk. 106

E15	A159	10c on 2c yel brn	2.25	75

Arms and Bars from National Hymn
SD12

Roseate Tern
SD13

1952, May 27 *Perf. 12½*

E16	SD12	10c dp org & bl	3.00	1.00

Issued to commemorate the 50th anniversary of the founding of the Republic of Cuba.

Type of Air Post Stamps of 1952 Inscribed: "Entrega Especial"

1952, Oct. 7 *Perf. 10*

E17	AP36	10c pale ol grn	2.50	1.00

Three-fourths of the proceeds from the sale of No. E17 were used for the Communications Ministry Employees' Retirement Fund.

1953, July 28

E18	SD13	10c blue	2.50	60

Gregorio Hernandez Saez
SD14

Felix Varela
SD15

1954, Feb. 23

E19	SD14	10c ol grn	3.00	75

1955, June 22 *Perf. 12½*

E20	SD15	10c brn car	2.25	85

See note after No. E17.

Portrait Type of Regular Issue, 1956 Inscribed: "Entrega Especial"

Portrait: 10c, Jose Jacinto Milanes.

1956, May 2 **Wmk. 106**

E21	A198	10c dk car rose & blk	2.25	60

See note after No. E17.

Painting Type of Regular Issue, 1957, Inscribed: "Entrega Especial"

Painting: 10c, "Yesterday" by E. Garcia Cabrera.

1957, Mar. 15 Engraved *Perf. 12½*

E22	A207	10c dk brn & turq bl	3.00	85

See note after No. E17.

View Type of Regular Issue, 1957, Inscribed: "Entrega Especial."

View: 10c, Independence square, Pino del Rio.

1957, Dec. 17

E23	A218	10c dk pur & brn	2.00	60

See note after No. E17.

View in Havana and Messenger
SD16

1958, Jan. 10 **Engraved**

E24	SD16	10c blue	1.50	50
E25	SD16	20c green	2.00	60

See also Nos. E28, E31.

Fish Type of Air Post Issue, 1958, Inscribed "Entrega Especial."

Fish: 10c, Blackfish snapper. 20c, Mosquitofish.

1958, Sept. 26 *Perf. 12½* **Wmk. 106**

E26	AP86	10c blk, bl, pink & yel	4.00	2.00
E27	AP86	20c blk, ultra & pink	12.50	9.00

See note after No. C191.

Messenger Type of 1958

1960 *Perf. 12½* **Wmk. 321**

E28	SD16	10c brt vio	1.50	40

Plane Type of Air Post Issue, of 1931–46, Surcharged in Black or Red: "HABILITADO ENTREGA ESPECIAL 10¢"

1960 *Perf. 10* **Wmk. 106**

E29	AP4	10c on 20c car rose	1.25	50
E30	AP4	10c on 50c grnsh bl (R)	1.00	50

Messenger Type of 1958

1961, June 28 *Perf. 12½* **Wmk. 321**

E31	SD16	10c orange	1.50	50

POSTAGE DUE STAMPS

Issued under Administration of the United States

Postage Due Stamps of the United States Nos. J38, J39, J41 and J42 Surcharged in Black Like Regular Issue of Same Date.

Wmkd. USPS (191)

1899 *Perf. 12.*

J1	D2	1c on 1c dp cl	22.50	3.50
J2	D2	2c on 2c dp cl	20.00	3.50
a.		Inverted surcharge		2,000.
J3	D2	5c on 5c dp cl	22.50	3.50
a.		"CUPA"	175.00	160.00
J4	D2	10c on 10c dp cl	20.00	1.25

Issues of the Republic.

D1

Engraved

1914 *Perf. 12* **Unwmkd.**

J5	D1	1c car rose	7.00	1.00
J6	D1	2c car rose	8.00	1.00
J7	D1	5c car rose	14.00	2.00

1927–28

J8	D1	1c rose red	7.00	1.00
J9	D1	2c rose red	11.00	1.00
J10	D1	5c rose red	13.00	1.50

NEWSPAPER STAMPS.

Issued under Spanish Dominion.

N1

N2

Typographed

1888 *Perf. 14* **Unwmkd.**

P1	N1	½m black	25	25
P2	N1	1m black	30	30
P3	N1	2m black	30	30
P4	N1	3m black	2.50	1.00
P5	N1	4m black	3.00	1.75
P6	N1	8m black	12.00	7.50
		Nos. P1-P6 (6)	18.35	11.10

1890

P7	N2	½m red brn	75	60
P8	N2	1m red brn	75	60
P9	N2	2m red brn	1.25	85
P10	N2	3m red brn	1.50	1.00
P11	N2	4m red brn	12.00	5.00
P12	N2	8m red brn	12.00	5.00
		Nos. P7-P12 (6)	28.25	13.05

1892

P13	N2	½m violet	25	25
P14	N2	1m violet	25	25
P15	N2	2m violet	25	25
P16	N2	3m violet	1.50	25
P17	N2	4m violet	6.00	1.50
P18	N2	8m violet	12.00	2.50
		Nos. P13-P18 (6)	20.25	5.00

1894

P19	N2	½m rose	25	25
a.		Imperf., pair	30.00	
P20	N2	1m rose	75	25
P21	N2	2m rose	75	25
P22	N2	3m rose	3.00	1.00
P23	N2	4m rose	5.00	1.25
P24	N2	8m rose	9.00	3.00
		Nos. P19-P24 (6)	18.75	6.00

1896

P25	N2	½m bl grn	25	25
P26	N2	1m bl grn	25	25
P27	N2	2m bl grn	25	25
P28	N2	3m bl grn	4.00	1.25
P29	N2	4m bl grn	9.00	6.00
P30	N2	8m bl grn	16.00	8.00
		Nos. P25-P30 (6)	29.75	16.00

POSTAL TAX STAMPS.

Mother and Child
PT1

Nurse with Child
PT2

Wmkd. Star. (106)

1938, Dec. 1 **Engraved** *Perf. 10*

RA1	PT1	1c brt grn	35	10

The tax benefited the National Council of Tuberculosis fund for children's hospitals. Obligatory on all mail during December and January. This note applies also to Nos. RA2–4, RA7–10, RA12–15, RA17–21.

1939, Dec. 1

RA2	PT2	1c org ver	35	10

"Health" Protecting Children
PT3

Mother and Child
PT4

1940, Dec. 1

RA3	PT3	1c dp bl	35	10

1941, Dec. 1

RA4	PT4	1c ol bis	50	10

Victory
PT5

1942–44

RA5	PT5	½c orange	35	10
RA6	PT5	½c gray ('44)	40	10

Issue dates: No. RA5, July 1, 1942. No. RA6, Oct. 3, 1944.

Type of 1941 Overprinted in Black "1942"

1942, Dec. 1

RA7	PT4	1c salmon	60	20
a.		Inverted ovpt.	60.00	30.00

"Health" Protecting Children
PT6

Mother and Child
PT7

1943, Dec. 1

RA8	PT6	1c brown	35	10

1949, Dec. 9

RA9	PT7	1c blue	35	10

Type of 1949 Inscribed: "1950."

1950, Dec. 1 **Engraved**

RA10	PT7	1c rose red	35	10

Model of Proposed Communications Building
PT8

Woman Holding Child Aloft
PT9

1951, June 5 *Perf. 10* **Wmk. 106**

RA11	PT8	1c violet	50	5

The tax was to help build a new Communications Building. This note applies also to Nos. RA16, RA34, RA43.

1951, Dec. 1

RA12	PT9	1c vio bl	35	5
RA13	PT9	1c brn car	35	5
RA14	PT9	1c ol bis	35	5
RA15	PT9	1c dp grn	35	5

Proposed Communications Building
PT10

Child
PT11

1952, Feb. 8

RA16	PT10	1c dk bl	20	5

See also Nos. RA34, RA43.

1952, Dec. 1

RA17	PT11	1c rose car	50	5
RA18	PT11	1c yel grn	50	5
RA19	PT11	1c blue	50	5
RA20	PT11	1c orange	50	5

Hands reaching for Lorraine Cross
PT12

Child's Head and Lorraine Cross
PT13

1953, Dec. 1 *Perf. 9½*

RA21	PT12	1c rose car	35	5

1954, Nov. 1 *Perf. 9½x10*

RA22	PT13	1c rose red	35	5
RA23	PT13	1c violet	35	5
RA24	PT13	1c brt bl	35	5
RA25	PT13	1c emerald	35	5

The tax benefited the National Council of Tuberculosis fund for children's hospitals. Obligatory on all mail during November, December, January and February. This note applies also to Nos. RA26–33, RA35–42.

Rose and Watering Can
PT14

Child and Protective Hands
PT15

1955, Nov. 1

RA26	PT14	1c red org	50	10
RA27	PT14	1c red lil	50	10
RA28	PT14	1c brt bl	50	10
RA29	PT14	1c org yel	50	10

1956, Nov. 1

RA30	PT15	1c rose red	35	5
RA31	PT15	1c yel brn	35	5
RA32	PT15	1c brt bl	35	5
RA33	PT15	1c emerald	35	5

Building Type of 1952

1957, Jan. 18 *Perf. 10*

RA34	PT10	1c rose red	20	5

Mother and Child by Silvia Arrojo Fernandez
PT16

National Council of Tuberculosis
PT17

Engraved.

1957, Nov. 1 *Perf. 10* **Wmk. 321**

RA35	PT16	1c dl rose	50	5
RA36	PT16	1c brt bl	50	5
RA37	PT16	1c gray	50	5
RA38	PT16	1c emerald	50	5

1958

RA39	PT17	1c rose red	25	5
RA40	PT17	1c red brn	25	5
RA41	PT17	1c gray	25	5
RA42	PT17	1c emerald	25	5

Building Type of 1952

1958 **Wmk. 321**

RA43	PT10	1c rose red	20	5

CURACAO

(See Netherlands Antilles.)

CYRENAICA

(sĭr'ē·nā'ĭ·kȧ)

LOCATION — In northern Africa bordering on the Mediterranean Sea.

GOVT.—Former Italian colony.

AREA—75,340 sq. mi.

POP.—225,000 (approx. 1934).

CAPITAL—Bengasi (Benghazi).

Cyrenaica was incorporated in the kingdom of Libya in 1951.

100 Centesimi = 1 Lira
1000 Milliemes = 1 Pound (1950)

Propaganda of the Faith Issue.

Italy Nos. 143-146 Overprinted
CIRENAICA

Wmkd. Crowns. (140)

1923 *Perf. 14*

1	A68	20c ol grn & brn org	1.65	*8.25*
2	A68	30c cl & brn org	1.65	*8.25*
3	A68	50c vio & brn org	1.25	*6.75*
4	A68	1 l bl & brn org	1.25	*6.75*

Fascisti Issue.

Italy Nos. 159–164 Overprinted CIRENAICA in Red or Black.

1923 *Perf. 14* **Unwmkd.**

5	A69	10c dk grn (R)	1.50	*6.75*
6	A69	30c dk vio (R)	1.50	*6.75*
7	A69	50c brn car	1.50	*6.75*

Wmkd. Crowns. (140)

8	A70	1 l blue	1.50	*6.75*
9	A70	2 l brown	1.50	*6.75*
10	A71	5 l blk & bl (R)	1.50	*11.00*
		Nos. 5-10 (6)	9.00	*44.75*

Manzoni Issue.

Italy Nos. 165-170
Overprinted in Red CIRENAICA

1924 *Perf. 14.*

11	A72	10c brn red & blk	75	*7.50*
12	A72	15c bl grn & blk	75	*7.50*
13	A72	30c blk & sl	75	*7.50*
14	A72	50c org brn & blk	75	*7.50*
15	A72	1 l bl & blk	12.00	*75.00*
a.		Double overprint	250.00	*375.00*
16	A72	5 l vio & blk	275.00	*1,000.*
		Nos. 11-16 (6)	290.00	*1,105.*

Vertical overprints on Nos. 11-14 are essays. On Nos. 15-16 the overprint is vertical at the left.

Victor Emmanuel Issue.

Italy Nos. 175-177
Overprinted CIRENAICA

1925–26 *Perf. 11* **Unwmkd.**

17	A78	60c brn car	26	*3.00*
18	A78	1 l dk bl	26	*3.00*
19	A78	1.25 l dk bl ('26)	75	*9.00*
a.		Perf. 13½	82.50	*225.00*

Saint Francis of Assisi Issue.

Italian Stamps of 1926
Overprinted CIRENAICA

1926 *Perf. 14* **Wmk. 140**

20	A79	20c gray grn	90	*4.50*
21	A80	40c dk vio	90	*4.50*
22	A81	60c red brn	90	*4.50*

Overprinted in Red Cirenaica

Unwmkd.

23	A82	1.25 l dk bl, perf. 11	90	*4.50*
24	A83	5 l + 2.50 l ol grn	2.25	*8.25*
		Nos. 20-24 (5)	5.85	*26.25*

Volta Issue.

Type of Italy 1927,
Overprinted Cirenaica

1927 *Perf. 14.* **Wmkd. Crown. (140)**

25	A84	20c purple	3.00	*11.00*
26	A84	50c dp org	3.75	*7.50*
27	A84	1.25 l brt bl	4.50	*11.00*

No. 25 exists with overprint omitted. Price $75.

Monte Cassino Issue.

Types of 1929 Issue of Italy,
Overprinted in Red or Blue
CIRENAICA

1929

28	A96	20c dk grn (R)	1.65	*7.50*
29	A96	25c red org (Bl)	1.65	*7.50*
30	A98	50c + 10c crim (Bl)	1.65	*11.00*
31	A98	75c + 15c ol brn (R)	1.65	*11.00*
32	A96	1.25 l + 25c dk vio (R)	3.25	*11.00*
33	A98	5 l + 1 l saph (R)	3.25	*11.00*

Overprinted in Red Cirenaica

Unwmkd.

34	A100	10 l + 2 l gray brn	3.25	*15.00*
		Nos. 28-34 (7)	16.35	*74.00*

Royal Wedding Issue.

Type of Italian Stamps of 1930
Overprinted CIRENAICA

1930 **Wmkd. Crowns. (140)**

35	A101	20c yel grn	75	*3.00*
36	A101	50c + 10c dp org	55	*3.75*
37	A101	1.25 l + 25c rose red	55	*4.50*

No. 35 exists with overprint omitted. Price $750.

Ferrucci Issue.

Types of Italian Stamps of 1930,
Overprinted in Red or Blue Cirenaica

1930

38	A102	20c vio (R)	55	*2.25*
39	A103	25c dk grn (R)	55	*2.25*
40	A103	50c blk (R)	55	*2.25*
41	A103	1.25 l dp bl (R)	55	*2.25*
42	A104	5 l + 2 l dp car (Bl)	2.25	*4.50*
		Nos. 38-42 (5)	4.45	*13.50*

Virgil Issue.

Types of Italian Stamps of 1930
Overprinted in Red or Blue
CIRENAICA

1930

43	A106	15c vio blk (R)	38	*2.25*
44	A106	20c org brn (Bl)	38	*2.25*
45	A106	25c dk grn (R)	38	*1.90*
46	A106	30c lt brn (Bl)	38	*2.25*
47	A106	50c dl vio (R)	38	*1.90*
48	A106	75c rose red	38	*2.25*
49	A106	1.25 l gray bl (R)	38	*2.25*

Unwmkd.

50	A106	5 l + 1.50 l dk vio (R)	2.00	*9.00*
51	A106	10 l + 2.50 l ol brn (Bl)	2.00	*9.00*
		Nos. 43-51 (9)	6.66	*33.05*

Saint Anthony of Padua Issue.

Types of Italian Stamps of 1931
Overprinted in Blue or Red CIRENAICA

1931 **Wmkd. Crowns. (140)**

52	A116	20c brn (Bl)	75	*3.25*
53	A116	25c grn (R)	75	*3.25*
54	A118	30c gray brn (Bl)	75	*3.25*
55	A118	50c dl vio (Bl)	75	*2.25*
56	A120	1.25 l sl bl (R)	75	*3.25*

Overprinted in Red or Black Cirenaica

Unwmkd.

57	A121	75c blk (R)	75	*3.25*
58	A122	5 l + 2.50 l dk brn (Bk)	2.25	*11.00*
		Nos. 52-58 (7)	6.75	*29.50*

Carabineer
A1

1934 **Photogravure** **Wmk. 140**

59	A1	5c dk ol grn & brn	1.65	*6.25*
60	A1	10c brn & blk	1.65	*6.25*
61	A1	20c scar & ind	1.65	*6.25*
62	A1	50c pur & brn	1.65	*6.25*
63	A1	60c org brn & ind	1.65	*6.25*
64	A1	1.25 l dk bl & grn	1.65	*6.25*
		Nos. 59-64 (6)	9.90	*37.50*

Issued to commemorate the 2nd Colonial Art Exhibition held at Naples. See also Nos. C24–C29.

Autonomous State

Senussi Warrior
A2 A3

Engraved.

1950 *Perf. 12½* **Unwmkd.**

65	A2	1m dk brn	8	15
66	A2	2m rose car	8	15
67	A2	3m orange	8	15
68	A2	4m dk grn	65	90
69	A2	5m gray	15	15
70	A2	8m red org	18	45
71	A2	10m purple	22	45
72	A2	12m red	22	55
73	A2	20m dp bl	22	45
74	A3	50m choc & ultra	1.50	*4.50*
75	A3	100m bl blk & car rose	4.50	*13.50*
76	A3	200m vio & pur	6.00	*18.00*
77	A3	500m dk grn & org	20.00	*45.00*
		Nos. 65-77 (13)	33.88	*84.40*

SEMI-POSTAL STAMPS

Many issues of Italy and Italian Colonies include one or more semipostal denominations. To avoid splitting sets, these issues are generally listed as regular postage unless all values carry a surtax.

Holy Year Issue.

Italian Semi-Postal Stamps of 1924
Overprinted in Black or Red
CIRENAICA

1925 *Perf. 12* **Wmk. 140**

B1	SP4	20c + 10c dk grn & brn	1.00	*4.50*
B2	SP4	30c + 15c dk brn & brn	1.00	*4.50*
B3	SP4	50c + 25c vio & brn	1.00	*4.50*
B4	SP4	60c + 30c dp rose & brn	1.00	*4.50*
B5	SP8	1 l + 50c dp bl & vio (R)	1.00	*4.50*
B6	SP8	5 l + 2.50 l org brn & vio (R)	1.00	*4.50*
		Nos. B1-B6 (6)	6.00	*27.00*

Colonial Institute Issue.

"Peace" Substituting Spade for Sword—SP1

1926 Typographed. *Perf. 14.*

B7	SP1	5c +5c brn	25	2.50
B8	SP1	10c +5c ol grn	25	2.50
B9	SP1	20c +5c bl grn	25	2.50
B10	SP1	40c +5c brn red	25	2.50
B11	SP1	60c +5c org	25	2.50
B12	SP1	1 l +5c bl	25	2.50
		Nos. B7-B12 (6)	1.50	*15.00*

Surtax for Italian Colonial Institute.

Types of Italian Semi-Postal Stamps of 1926 Overprinted **CIRENAICA**

1927 *Perf. 11.* Unwmkd.

B13	SP10	40c +20c dk brn & blk	1.00	*5.25*
B14	SP10	60c +30c brn red & ol brn	1.00	*5.25*
B15	SP10	1.25 l +60c dp bl & blk	1.00	*5.25*
B16	SP10	5 l +2.50 l dk grn & blk	1.50	*6.75*

The surtax on these stamps was for the charitable work of the Voluntary Militia for Italian National Defense.

Allegory of Fascism and Victory
SP2

1928 *Perf. 14.* Wmk. 140

B17	SP2	20c +5c bl grn	75	*3.75*
B18	SP2	30c +5c red	75	*3.75*
B19	SP2	50c +10c pur	75	*3.75*
B20	SP2	1.25 l +20c dk bl	75	*3.75*

Issued to commemorate the 46th anniversary of the Societa Africana d'Italia. The surtax aided that society.

Types of Italian Semi-Postal Stamps of 1926 Overprinted **CIRENAICA**

1929 *Perf. 11.* Unwmkd.

B21	SP10	30c +10c red & blk	1.25	*5.50*
B22	SP10	50c +20c vio & blk	1.25	*5.50*
B23	SP10	1.25 l +50c brn & bl	1.50	*7.50*
B24	SP10	5 l +2 l ol grn & blk	1.50	*7.50*

The surtax on Nos. B21–B24 was for the charitable work of the Voluntary Militia for Italian National Defense.

Types of Italian Semi-Postal Stamps of 1926 Overprinted in Black or Red **CIRENAICA**

1930 *Perf. 14.*

B25	SP10	30c +10c dk grn & bl grn (Bk)	4.00	*15.00*
B26	SP10	50c +10c dk grn & vio (R)	4.00	*15.00*
B27	SP10	1.25 l +30c ol brn & red brn (R)	4.00	*15.00*
B28	SP10	5 l +1.50 l ind & grn (R)	12.00	*47.50*

The surtax on these stamps was for the charitable work of the Voluntary Militia for Italian National Defense.

Sower
SP3

1930 Photogravure Wmk. 140

B29	SP3	50c +20c ol brn	1.10	*6.00*
B30	SP3	1.25 l +20c dp bl	1.10	*6.00*
B31	SP3	1.75 l +20c grn	1.10	*6.00*
B32	SP3	2.55 l +50c pur	1.65	*6.00*
B33	SP3	5 l +1 l dp car	1.65	*6.00*
		Nos. B29-B33 (5)	6.60	*30.00*

Issued in commemoration of the 25th anniversary of the Italian Colonial Agricultural Institute.

The surtax was for the aid of that institution.

AIR POST STAMPS.

Air Post Stamps of Tripolitania, 1931, Overprinted in Blue **Cirenaica**

1932 *Perf. 14.* Wmk. 140

C1	AP1	50c rose car	38	18
C2	AP1	60c dp org	1.65	*11.00*
C3	AP1	80c dl vio	1.65	*11.00*

Air Post Stamps of Tripolitania, 1931, Overprinted in Blue

1932

C4	AP1	50c rose car	55	38
C5	AP1	80c dl vio	2.25	*15.00*

This overprint was also applied to the 60c, Tripolitania No. C9. The overprinted stamp was never used in Cyrenaica, but was sold at Rome in 1943 by the Postmaster General for the Italian Colonies. Price $4.

Arab on Camel
AP2

Airplane in Flight
AP3

1932 Photogravure.

C6	AP2	50c purple	1.10	18
C7	AP2	75c brn rose	2.50	4.00
C8	AP2	80c dp bl	2.50	4.00
C9	AP3	1 l black	38	18
C10	AP3	2 l green	75	*2.25*
C11	AP3	5 l dp car	1.50	*6.75*
		Nos. C6-C11 (6)	8.73	*17.36*

Graf Zeppelin Issue.

Zeppelin and Clouds forming Pegasus
AP4

Zeppelin and Ancient Galley
AP5

Zeppelin and Giant Bowman
AP6

1933, Apr. 15

C12	AP4	3 l dk brn	6.25	*55.00*
C13	AP5	5 l purple	6.25	*55.00*
C14	AP6	10 l dp grn	6.25	*92.50*
C15	AP5	12 l dp bl	6.25	*130.00*
C16	AP4	15 l carmine	6.25	*110.00*
C17	AP6	20 l black	6.25	*150.00*
		Nos. C12-C17 (6)	37.50	*592.50*

North Atlantic Cruise Issue.

Airplane Squadron and Constellations
AP7

1933, June 1

C18	AP7	19.75 l grn & dp bl	15.00	*375.00*
C19	AP7	44.75 l red & ind	15.00	*375.00*

Type of 1932 Overprinted and Surcharged

1934, Jan. 20

C20	AP3	2 l on 5 l org brn	2.25	*40.00*
C21	AP3	3 l on 5 l yel grn	2.25	*40.00*
C22	AP3	5 l ocher	2.25	*40.00*
C23	AP3	10 l on 5 l rose	2.25	*40.00*

For use on mail to be carried on a special flight from Rome to Buenos Aires.

Transport Plane
AP8

Venus of Cyrene
AP9

1934, Oct. 9

C24	AP8	25c sl bl & org red	1.65	*6.25*
C25	AP8	50c dk grn & ind	1.65	*6.25*
C26	AP8	75c dk brn & org red	1.65	*6.25*
a.		Imperf.	250.00	
C27	AP9	80c org brn & ol grn	1.65	*6.25*
C28	AP9	1 l scar & ol grn	1.65	*6.25*
C29	AP9	2 l dk bl & brn	1.65	*6.25*
		Nos. C24-C29 (6)	9.90	*37.50*

Issued in commemoration of the Second Colonial Arts Exhibition held at Naples.

AIR POST SEMI-POSTAL STAMPS.

King Victor Emmanuel III
SPAP1

Photogravure.

1934 *Perf. 14.* Wmk. 104

CB1	SPAP1	25c +10c gray grn	1.90	*7.50*
CB2	SPAP1	50c +10c brn	1.90	*7.50*
CB3	SPAP1	75c +15c rose red	1.90	*7.50*
CB4	SPAP1	80c +15c brn blk	1.90	*7.50*
CB5	SPAP1	1 l +20c red brn	1.90	*7.50*
CB6	SPAP1	2 l +20c brt bl	1.90	*7.50*
CB7	SPAP1	3 l +25c pur	16.00	*60.00*
CB8	SPAP1	5 l +25c org	16.00	*60.00*
CB9	SPAP1	10 l +30c dp vio	16.00	*60.00*
CB10	SPAP1	25 l +2 l dp grn	16.00	*60.00*
		Nos. CB1-CB10 (10)	75.40	*285.00*

Issued in commemoration of the 65th birthday of King Victor Emmanuel III and the non-stop flight from Rome to Mogadiscio.

AIR POST SEMI-POSTAL OFFICIAL STAMP.

Type of Air Post Semi-Postal Stamps, 1934, Overprinted Crown and "SERVIZIO DI STATO" in Black.

1934, Nov. 5 *Perf. 14* Wmk. 140

CBO1	SPAP1	25 l +2 l cop red	*1,400.*

POSTAGE DUE STAMPS

D1

Engraved

1950 *Perf. 12½* Unwmkd.

J1	D1	2m dk brn	15.00	37.50
J2	D1	4m dp grn	15.00	37.50
J3	D1	8m scarlet	15.00	37.50
J4	D1	10m vermilion	15.00	37.50
J5	D1	20m org yel	15.00	37.50
J6	D1	40m dp bl	15.00	37.50
J7	D1	100m dk gray	15.00	37.50
		Nos. J1-J7 (7)	105.00	262.50

CZECHOSLOVAKIA

(chĕk'ô-slô-vä'kĭ-ȧ)

LOCATION – Central Europe.
GOVT.–Republic.
AREA–49,355 sq. mi.
POP.–15,395,970 (1983).
CAPITAL–Prague.

The Czechoslovakian Republic consists of Bohemia, Moravia and Silesia, Slovakia and Ruthenia (Carpatho-Ukraine). In March 1939, a German protectorate was established over Bohemia and Moravia, as well as over Slovakia which had meanwhile declared its independence. Ruthenia was incorporated in the territory of Hungary. These territories were returned to the Czechoslovak Republic in 1945, except for Ruthenia, which was ceded to Russia. Czechoslovakia became a federal state on January 2, 1969.

100 Haleru = 1 Koruna

Stamps of Austria overprinted "Ceskoslovenska Republika", lion and "Cesko Slovensky Stat", "Provisorni Ceskoslovenska Vlada" and Arms, and "Ceskoslovenska Statni Posta" and Arms were made privately. A few of them were passed through the post but all have been pronounced unofficial and unauthorized by the Postmaster General.

During the occupation of part of Northern Hungary by the Czechoslovak forces, stamps of Hungary were overprinted "Cesko Slovenska Posta", "Ceskoslovenska Statni Posta" and Arms, and "Slovenska Posta" and Arms. These stamps were never officially issued though copies have passed the post.

Hradcany at Prague
A1

Typographed.

1918–19 *Imperf.* **Unwmkd.**

No.	Type	Description	Unused	Used
1	A1	3(h) red vio	5	5
2	A1	5(h) yel grn	10	5
3	A1	10(h) rose	10	5
4	A1	20(h) bluish grn	15	5
5	A1	25(h) dp bl	25	5
a.		25(h) ultra	40.00	
6	A1	30(h) bister	40	5
7	A1	40(h) red org	40	5
8	A1	100(h) brown	1.25	8
9	A1	200(h) ultra	2.00	10
10	A1	400(h) purple	2.50	20

On the 3(h) to 40(h) the words "Posta Ceskoslovenska" are in white on a colored background; on the higher values the words are in color on a white background.
See Nos. 368, 1554, 1600.

Perf. 11½, 13½

No.	Type	Description	Unused	Used
13	A1	5(h) yel grn	50	25
a.		Perf. 11½x10½	1.50	30
14	A1	10(h) rose	35	10
15	A1	20(h) bluish grn	35	10
a.		Perf. 11½	1.50	50
16	A1	25(h) dp bl	40	10
a.		Perf. 11½	2.00	60
20	A1	200(h) ultra	4.00	15
		Nos. 1-10, 13-16, 20 (15)	12.80	1.43

All values of this issue exist with various private perforations and copies have been used on letters.
The 3, 30, 40, 100 and 400h formerly listed are now known to have been privately perforated.

A2

Type II. Sun behind cathedral. Colorless foliage in foreground.
Type III. Without sun. Shaded foliage in foreground.
Type IV. No foliage in foreground. Positions of buildings changed. Letters redrawn.

1919 *Imperf.*

No.	Type	Description	Unused	Used
23	A2	1(h) dk brn (II)	5	5
25	A2	5(h) bl grn (IV)	35	5
27	A2	15(h) red (IV)	25	15
29	A2	25(h) dl vio (IV)	35	5
30	A2	50(h) dl vio (II)	35	5
31	A2	50(h) dk bl (IV)	35	5
32	A2	60(h) org (III)	1.25	15
33	A2	75(h) sl (IV)	1.00	5
34	A2	80(h) ol grn (III)	1.25	8
36	A2	120(h) gray blk (IV)	2.00	20
38	A2	300(h) dk grn (III)	7.50	20
39	A2	500(h) red brn (IV)	4.00	20
40	A2	1000(h) vio (III)	16.00	1.25
a.		1000(h) bluish vio	30.00	2.50
		Nos. 23-40 (13)	34.70	2.53

1919-20

Perf. 11½, 13½, 13½x11½.

No.	Type	Description	Unused	Used
41	A2	1(h) dk brn (II)	5	5
42	A2	5(h) bl grn (IV), perf. 13½	15	5
a.		Perf. 11½	20.00	7.50
43	A2	10(h) yel grn (IV)	30	5
a.		Imperf.	52.50	40.00
b.		Perf. 11½	15.00	1.25
44	A2	15(h) red (IV)	15	5
a.		Perf. 11½x10½	30.00	5.00
b.		Perf. 11½x13½	40.00	10.00
c.		Perf. 13½x10½	75.00	20.00
45	A2	20(h) rose (IV)	35	5
a.		Imperf.	200.00	150.00
46	A2	25(h) dl vio (IV), perf. 11½	60	10
a.		Perf. 11½x10½	4.50	60
b.		Perf. 13½x10½	22.00	14.00
47	A2	30(h) red vio (IV)	25	5
a.		Imperf.	250.00	200.00
b.		Perf. 14x13½	300.00	50.00
c.		30(h) dp vio	25	8
d.		As "c," perf. 14x13½	300.00	50.00
e.		As "c," imperf.	225.00	175.00
50	A2	60(h) org (III)	50	15
a.		Perf. 14x13½	20.00	10.00
53	A2	120(h) gray blk (IV)	7.00	1.65
		Nos. 41-53 (9)	9.35	2.20

Nos. 43a, 45a and 47a were imperforate by accident and not issued in quantities as were Nos. 23 to 40.

Rouletted stamps of the preceding issues are said to have been made by a postmaster in a branch post office at Prague, or by private firms, but without authority from the Post Office Department.

The 50, 75, 80, 300, 500 and 1000h have been privately perforated.

Unlisted color varieties of types A1 and A2 were not officially released, and some are printer's waste.

Pres. Thomas Garrigue Masaryk
A4

1920 *Perf. 13½*

No.	Type	Description	Unused	Used
61	A4	125(h) gray bl	1.75	25
a.		125(h) ultra	40.00	25.00
b.		Imperf. (gray bl)	25.00	
c.		As "a," imperf.	75.00	
62	A4	500(h) sl, *grysh*	8.00	4.00
a.		Imperf.	35.00	
63	A4	1000(h) blk brn, *brnsh*	15.00	7.50
a.		Imperf.	50.00	

Carrier Pigeon with Letter
A5

Czechoslovakia Breaking Chains to Freedom
A6

Hussite Priest
A7

Agriculture and Science
A8

1920 ***Perf. 14***

No.	Type	Description	Unused	Used
65	A5	5(h) dk bl	5	5
a.		Perf. 13½	90.00	25.00
b.		Imperf.	7.50	
66	A5	10(h) bl grn	5	5
a.		Perf. 13½	70.00	30.00
b.		Imperf.	8.00	
67	A5	15(h) red brn	10	5
a.		Imperf.	8.00	
68	A6	20(h) rose	5	5
a.		Imperf.	10.00	
69	A6	25(h) lil brn	8	5
a.		Imperf.	12.00	
70	A6	30(h) red vio	10	5
a.		Imperf.	8.00	
71	A6	40(h) red brn	20	5
a.		Tête bêche pair	3.50	2.00
b.		Perf. 13½	60	20
c.		Imperf.	10.00	
72	A6	50(h) carmine	40	5
a.		Imperf.	6.00	
73	A6	60(h) dk bl	50	5
a.		Tête bêche pair	9.00	5.00
b.		Perf. 13½	4.00	45
c.		Imperf.	7.50	

Photogravure.

No.	Type	Description	Unused	Used
74	A7	80(h) purple	50	25
a.		Imperf.	7.50	
75	A7	90(h) blk brn	80	50
a.		Imperf.	7.50	

Typographed ***Perf. 14***

No.	Type	Description	Unused	Used
76	A8	100(h) dk grn	80	5
a.		Imperf.	6.00	
77	A8	200(h) violet	1.50	5
a.		Imperf.	8.00	
78	A8	300(h) vermilion	3.25	5
a.		Perf. 14x13½	10.00	40
b.		Imperf.	8.50	
79	A8	400(h) brown	10.00	80
a.		Imperf.	45.00	
80	A8	500(h) dp grn	12.00	80
a.		Perf. 14x13½	80.00	7.50
b.		Imperf.	45.00	
81	A8	600(h) dp vio	15.00	80
a.		Perf. 14x13½	250.00	10.00
b.		Imperf.	45.00	
		Nos. 65-81 (17)	45.38	3.75

No. 69 has background of horizontal lines.

1920–25 ***Perf. 14***

No.	Type	Description	Unused	Used
82	A5	5(h) violet	5	5
a.		Tête bêche pair	2.50	1.75
b.		Perf. 13½	35	20
c.		Imperf.	7.50	
83	A5	10(h) ol bis	5	5
a.		Tête bêche pair	3.25	2.00
b.		Perf. 13½	50	20
c.		Imperf.	7.50	
84	A5	20(h) dp org	10	6
a.		Tête bêche pair	40.00	15.00
b.		Perf. 13½	8.50	1.25
c.		Imperf.	9.00	
85	A5	25(h) bl grn	20	5
a.		Imperf.	10.00	
86	A5	30(h) dp vio ('25)	3.25	6
87	A6	50(h) yel grn	50	5
a.		Tête bêche pair	60.00	40.00
b.		Perf. 13½	17.50	4.00
c.		Imperf.	37.50	
88	A6	100(h) dk brn	80	5
a.		Perf. 13½	35.00	40
b.		Imperf.	4.00	

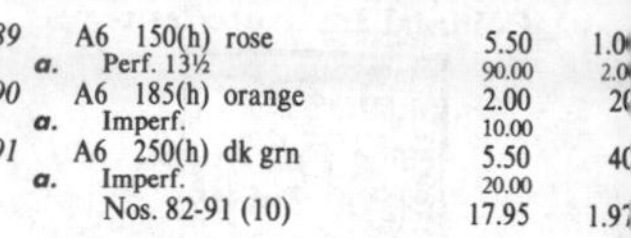

No.	Type	Description	Unused	Used
89	A6	150(h) rose	5.50	1.0
a.		Perf. 13½	90.00	2.0
90	A6	185(h) orange	2.00	2
a.		Imperf.	10.00	
91	A6	250(h) dk grn	5.50	4
a.		Imperf.	20.00	
		Nos. 82-91 (10)	17.95	1.9

Type of 1920 Issue Redrawn.

Type I. Rib of leaf below "O" of POSTA is straight and extends to tip. White triangle above book is entirely at left of twig. "P" has a stubby, abnormal appendage.

Type II. Rib is extremely bent; does not reach tip. Triangle extends at right of twig. "P" like Type I.

Type III. Rib of top left leaf is broken in two. Triangle like Type II. "P" has no appendage.

1923 ***Perf. 14, 14x13½***

No.	Type	Description	Unused	Used
92	A8	100(h) red, *yel*, III, perf. 14x13½	2.50	5
a.		Type I, perf. 14	3.25	5
b.		Type I, perf. 14x13½	4.00	5
c.		Type II, perf. 14	3.25	5
d.		Type II, perf. 14x13½	3.75	5
e.		Type III, perf. 14	20.00	10
93	A8	200(h) bl, *yel*, II, perf. 14	12.00	10
a.		Type II, perf. 14x13½	17.50	35
b.		Type III, perf. 14	13.50	40
c.		Type III, perf. 14x13½	75.00	75
94	A8	300(h) vio, *yel*, I, perf. 14	10.00	10
a.		Type II, perf. 14	60.00	40
b.		Type II, perf. 14x13½	125.00	80
c.		Type III, perf. 14x13½	15.00	8
d.		Type III, perf. 14	35.00	50

President Masaryk
A9 A10

Wmk. 107
(Vertical)

Perf. 14x13½, 13½

Wmkd. Linden Leaves. (107)

1925 Size: 19½x23mm. Photo.

No.	Type	Description	Unused	Used
95	A9	40h brn org	2.00	5
96	A9	50h ol grn	3.50	5
97	A9	60h red vio	4.00	5

Distinctive Marks of the Engravings.

I, II, III: Background of horizontal lines in top and bottom tablets. Inscriptions in Roman letters with serifs.

IV: Crossed horizontal and vertical lines in the tablets. Inscriptions in Antique letters without serifs.

I, II, IV: Shading of crossed diagonal lines on the shoulder at the right.

III. Shading of single lines only.

I: "T" of "Posta" over middle of "V" of "Ceskoslovenska". Three short horizontal lines in lower part of "A" of "Ceskoslovenska".

II: "T" over right arm of "V". One short line in "A".

III: "T" as in II. Blank space in lower part of "A".

IV: "T" over left arm of "V".

Engraved.

I. First Engraving.

Wmkd. Horizontally. (107)

Size: 19¾x22½mm.

No.	Type	Description	Unused	Used
98	A10	1k carmine	2.50	15
99	A10	2k dp bl	6.00	35

100	A10	3k brown	12.00	90
101	A10	5k bl grn	4.00	60

Wmkd. Vertically. (107)

Size: 19¾x23mm.

101A	A10	1k carmine	200.00	7.50
101B	A10	2k dp bl	250.00	25.00
101C	A10	3k brown	750.00	25.00
101D	A10	5k bl grn	8.00	2.75

II. Second Engraving.

Wmkd. Horizontally. (107)

Size: 19x21½mm.

102	A10	1k carmine	80.00	60
103	A10	2k dp bl	9.00	35
104	A10	3k brown	10.00	70

III. Third Engraving

Size: 19-19½x21½-22mm.

Perf. 10.

105	A10	1k car rose	3.00	15
a.		Perf. 14	30.00	15

IV. Fourth Engraving.

Size: 19-19½x21½-22mm.

1926 ***Perf. 10, 14.***

106	A10	1k car rose	2.25	10
108	A10	3k brown	12.50	15

See also No. 130.

Karlstein Castle
A11

1926, June 1 **Engr.** ***Perf. 10***

109	A11	1.20k red vio	1.50	75
110	A11	1.50k car rose	1.25	5
111	A11	2.50k dk bl	7.00	60

See also Nos. 133, 135.

Karlstein Castle
A12

Pernstein Castle
A13

Orava Castle
A14

Masaryk
A15

Strahov Monastery
A16

Hradčany at Prague
A17

Great Tatra
A18

1926–27 **Engraved** **Wmk. 107**

114	A13	30h gray grn	2.50	20
115	A14	40h red brn	1.00	10
116	A15	50h dp grn	1.00	10
117	A15	60h red vio, *lil*	1.75	5
118	A16	1.20k red vio	8.00	2.50

Perf. 13½

119	A17	2k blue	2.00	15
a.		2k ultra	5.00	75
120	A17	3k dp red	4.00	15
121	A18	4k brn vio ('27)	9.00	80
122	A18	5k dk grn ('27)	37.50	5.00
		Nos. 114-122 (9)	66.75	9.05

No. 116 exists in two types. The one with short, straight mustache at left sells for several times as much as that with longer wavy mustache.

See also Nos. 137–140.

Coil Stamps.

Perf. 10 Vertically.

123	A12	20h brick red	1.50	60
a.		Vert. pair, imperf. horiz.	150.00	
124	A13	30h gray grn	1.00	25
a.		Vert. pair, imperf. horiz.	150.00	
125	A15	50h dp grn	50	12

See also No. 141.

1927-31 ***Perf. 10.*** **Unwmkd.**

126	A13	30h gray grn	40	5
127	A14	40h dp brn	1.25	5
128	A15	50h dp grn	35	5
129	A15	60h red vio	1.10	5
130	A10	1k car rose	10.00	20
131	A15	1k dp red	50	5
132	A16	1.20k red vio	70	5
133	A11	1.50k car ('29)	1.00	5
134	A13	2k dp grn ('29)	80	5
135	A11	2.50k dk bl	10.00	40
136	A14	3k red brn ('31)	1.00	5
		Nos. 126-136 (11)	27.10	1.05

No. 130 exists in two types. The one with longer mustache at left sells for several times as much as that with the short mustache.

1927–28 ***Perf. 13½***

137	A17	2k ultra	2.00	10
138	A17	3k dp red ('28)	5.00	95
139	A18	4k brn vio ('28)	12.00	1.50
140	A18	5k dk grn ('28)	14.00	75

Coil Stamp.

1927 ***Perf. 10 Vertically***

141	A12	20h brick red	75	20

Hradec Castle
A19

Town Hall, Levoča
A20

Telephone Exchange, Prague
A21

Town of Jasina
A22

Hluboka Castle
A23

Pilgrims' House at Velehrad
A24

Brno Cathedral
A25

Great Tatra
A26

Masaryk
A27

Old City Square, Prague
A28

1928, Oct. 22 ***Perf. 13½***

142	A19	30h black	15	10
143	A20	40h red brn	25	20
144	A21	50h dk grn	30	8
145	A22	60h org red	[illegible]	[illegible]
146	A23	1k carmine	40	6
147	A24	1.20k brn vio	1.00	90
148	A25	2k ultra	1.25	35
149	A26	2.50k dk bl	3.00	2.25
150	A27	3k dk brn	2.25	50
151	A28	5k dp vio	3.50	3.25
		Nos. 142-151 (10)	12.40	7.77

Issued in commemoration of the tenth anniversary of Czechoslovakian independence.

Coat of Arms
A29

1929–37 ***Perf. 10***

152	A29	5h dk ultra ('31)	5	5
153	A29	10h bis brn ('31)	5	5
154	A29	20h red	5	5
155	A29	25h green	8	5
156	A29	30h red vio	8	5
157	A29	40h dk brn ('37)	35	5
a.		40h red brn ('37)	1.25	12

Coil Stamp.

Perf. 10 Vertically.

158	A29	20h red	30	5
		Nos. 152-158 (7)	96	35

St. Wenceslas
A30

Founding St. Vitus' Cathedral
A31

Design: 3k, 5k, St. Wenceslas martyred.

1929, May 14 ***Perf. 13½***

159	A30	50h gray grn	50	10
160	A30	60h sl vio	80	10
161	A31	2k dl bl	1.75	60
162	A30	3k brown	2.00	30
163	A30	5k brn vio	10.00	4.00
		Nos. 159-163 (5)	15.05	5.10

Millenary of the death of St. Wenceslas.

Statue of St. Wenceslas and National Museum, Prague
A33

1929 ***Perf. 10***

164	A33	2.50k dp bl	85	5

Brno Cathedral
A34

Tatra Mountain Scene
A35

Design: 5k, Old City Square, Prague.

1929, Oct. 15 ***Perf. 13½***

165	A34	3k red brn	4.00	12
166	A35	4k indigo	8.00	85
167	A35	5k gray grn	10.00	50

See also No. 183.

A37

Type I

Type II

Two types of 50h:

I. A white space exists across the bottom of the vignette between the coat, shirt and tie and the "HALERU" frame panel.

II. An extra frame line has been added just above the "HALERU" panel which finishes off the coat and tie shading evenly.

1930, Jan. 2 ***Perf. 10***

168	A37	50h myr grn (II)	25	5
a.		Type I	1.25	5
169	A37	60h brn vio	1.10	5
170	A37	1k brn red	50	5

See also No. 234.

Coil Stamp.

1931 ***Perf. 10 Vertically***

171	A37	1k brn red	2.00	1.00

President Masaryk
A38

St. Nicholas' Church, Prague
A39

1930, Mar. 1 ***Perf. 13½***

175	A38	2k gray grn	1.50	50
176	A38	3k red brn	2.50	45
177	A38	5k sl bl	7.50	3.00
178	A38	10k gray blk	15.00	7.00

Eightieth birthday of President Masaryk.

1931, May 15

183	A39	10k blk vio	14.00	4.00

Krivoklat Castle
A40

Krumlov Castle
A42

Design: 4k, Orlik Castle.

1932, Jan. 2 *Perf. 10*

184	A40	3.50k violet	3.75	1.50
185	A40	4k dp bl	4.25	50
186	A42	5k gray grn	3.75	50

Miroslav Tyrš
A43 A44

1932, Mar. 16

187	A43	50h yel grn	75	8
188	A43	1k brn car	1.25	8
189	A44	2k dk bl	12.00	35
190	A44	3k red brn	20.00	60

Issued to commemorate the centenary of the birth of Miroslav Tyrš (1832–1884), founder of the Sokol movement, and in connection with the 9th Sokol Congress.

Tyrš
A45

1933, Feb. 1

191	A45	60h dl vio	30	5

First Christian Church at Nitra
A46 A47

1933, June 20

192	A46	50h yel grn	60	8
193	A47	1k car rose	6.00	20

Issued in commemoration of Prince Pribina who introduced Christianity into Slovakia and founded there the first Christian church in A. D. 833.

All gutter pairs are vertical.

Friedrich Smetana
A48

1934, Mar. 26 **Engr.** *Perf. 10*

194	A48	50h yel grn	50	5

Issued to commemorate the 50th anniversary of the death of Friedrich Smetana, Czech composer and pianist.

Consecration of Legion Colors at Kiev, Sept. 21, 1914
A49

Ensign Heyduk with Colors
A51

Legionnaires
A52

Design: 1k, Legion receiving battle flag at Bayonne.

1934, Aug. 15 *Perf. 10*

195	A49	50h green	30	6
196	A49	1k rose lake	50	5
197	A51	2k dp bl	2.50	40
198	A52	3k red brn	5.00	40

Issued in commemoration of the 20th anniversary of the Czechoslovakian Legion which fought in World War I.

Antonin Dvořák
A53

1934, Nov. 22

199	A53	50h green	40	5

Issued to commemorate the 30th anniversary of the death of Antonin Dvorák, (1841–1904), composer.

Pastoral Scene
A54

1934, Dec. 17 *Perf. 10*

200	A54	1k claret	80	12
a.		Souvenir sheet of 15	350.00	350.00
b.		As "a," single stamp	13.00	11.00
201	A54	2k blue	2.50	60
a.		Souvenir sheet of 15	1,000.	1,000.
b.		As "a," single stamp	45.00	45.00

Issued in commemoration of the centenary of the National Anthem.

Nos. 200a & 201a were issued in special souvenir sheets of 15 stamps each on thick paper, darker shades, perf. 13½, no gum. Words and music of the anthem at top and bottom of sheet. Forgeries exist.

President Masaryk
A55 A56

1935, Mar. 1

202	A55	50h grn, *buff*	15	5
203	A55	1k cl, *buff*	30	5
204	A56	2k gray bl, *buff*	2.25	45
205	A56	3k brn, *buff*	4.00	45

85th birthday of President Masaryk.

See No. 235.

Monument to Czech Heroes at Arras, France—A57

1935, May 4

206	A57	1k rose	75	5
207	A57	2k dl bl	2.00	30

20th anniversary of the Battle of Arras.

General Milan Stefánik
A58

Sts. Cyril and Methodius
A59

1935, May 18

208	A58	50h green	20	5

1935, June 22

209	A59	50h green	15	8
210	A59	1k claret	60	5
211	A59	2k dp bl	2.00	50

Issued in commemoration of the millenary of the arrival in Moravia of the Apostles Cyril and Methodius.

Masaryk
A60

Statue of Macha, Prague
A61

1935, Oct. 20 *Perf. 12½*

212	A60	1k rose lake	10	5

No. 212 exists imperforate. See No. 256.

1936, Apr. 30

213	A61	50h dp grn	20	8
214	A61	1k rose lake	40	8

Issued to commemorate the centenary of the death of Karel Hynek Macha (1810–1836), Bohemian poet.

Jan Amos Komensky
A61a

President Eduard Beneš
A62

Gen. Milan Stefánik
A63

1936

215	A61a	40h dk bl	10	5
216	A62	50h dl grn	10	5
217	A63	60h dl vio	10	5

See Nos. 252 and 255.

Castle Palanok near Mukacevo
A64

Town of Banska Bystrica
A65

Castle at Zvikov
A66

Ruins of Castle at Strecno
A67

Castle at Cesky Raj
A68

Palace at Slavkov (Austerlitz)
A69

Statue of King George at Podebrad
A70

Town Square at Olomouc
A71

Castle Ruins at Bratislava
A72

1936, Aug. 1

218	A64	1.20k rose lil	12	5
219	A65	1.50k carmine	12	5
220	A66	2k dk bl grn	15	5
221	A67	2.50k dk bl	30	5
222	A68	3k brown	35	6
223	A69	3.50k dk vio	1.75	60
224	A70	4k dk vio	75	10
225	A71	5k green	60	10
226	A72	10k blue	2.00	60
		Nos. 218-226 (9)	6.14	1.66

President Beneš
A73

Soldiers of the Czech Legion
A74

1937, Apr. 26 *Perf. 12½* **Unwmkd.**

227	A73	50h dp grn	10	5

1937, June 15

228	A74	50h dp grn	20	5
229	A74	1k rose lake	35	6

Issued in commemoration of the 20th anniversary of the Battle of Zborov.

Cathedral at Prague
A75

Jan Evangelista Purkyne
A76

1937, July 1

230	A75	2k green	85	15
231	A75	2.50k blue	1.25	50

Issued in commemoration of the 16th anniversary of the founding of the "Little Entente."

1937, Sept. 2

232	A76	50h sl grn	20	5
233	A76	1k dl rose	25	5

Issued in commemoration of the 150th anniversary of the birth of Jan Evangelista Purkyne, Czech physiologist.

Masaryk Types of 1930–35.

1937, Sept. ***Perf. 12½***

234	A37	50h black	20	5

With date "14.IX. 1937" in design.

235	A56	2k black	45	15

Issued in commemoration of the death of former President Thomas G. Masaryk on Sept. 14, 1937.

International Labor Bureau Issue.

Stamps of 1936-37 Overprinted in Violet or Black **B.I.T.1937**

1937, Oct. 6 ***Perf. 12½***

236	A73	50h dp grn (Bk)	40	40
237	A65	1.50k car (V)	50	50
238	A66	2k dp grn (V)	75	75

Bratislava Philatelic Exhibition Issue.

Souvenir Sheet.

A77

1937, Oct. 24 ***Perf. 12½***

239	A77	Sheet of two	1.75	1.75
a.		50h dk bl	75	75
b.		1k brn car	75	75

The sheet measures 149x110mm. The stamps show a view of Poprad Lake (50h) and the tomb of General Milan Stefanik (1k).

No. 239 overprinted "Libération de la Tchéchoslovaquie, 28-X-1945" etc., was sold at a philatelic exhibition in Brussels, Belgium.

St. Barbara's Church, Kutna Hora
A79

Peregrine Falcon, Sokol Emblem
A80

1937, Dec. 4

240	A79	1.60k ol grn	15	5

1938, Jan. 21

241	A80	50h dp grn	40	10
242	A80	1k rose lake	60	15

Issued in commemoration of the 10th International Sokol Games. Imperforate copies of No. 242 are essays. Nos. 241–242 se-tenant with labels sell slightly higher.

Legionnaires
A81

Legionnaires
A82

Legionnaire
A83

1938

243	A81	50h dp grn	15	5
244	A82	50h dp grn	15	5
245	A83	50h dp grn	15	5

Issued to commemorate the 20th anniversary of the Battles of Bachmac, Vouziers and Doss Alto. Nos. 243–245 with label se-tenant sell for more.

Jindrich Fügner, Co-Founder of Sokol Movement
A84

1938, June 18 ***Perf. 12½***

246	A84	50h dp grn	10	5
247	A84	1k rose lake	20	5
248	A84	2k sl bl	70	6

Issued to commemorate the 10th Sokol Summer Games. Nos. 246–248 se-tenant with labels sell slightly higher.

View of Pilsen
A85

Cathedral of Kosice
A86

1938, June 24

249	A85	50h dp grn	15	5

Issued in connection with the Provincial Economic Council meeting at Pilsen.

1938, July 15 ***Perf. 12½***

250	A86	50h dp grn	15	5

Issued in connection with the Kosice Cultural Exhibition.

Prague Philatelic Exhibition Issue.

Souvenir Sheet.

Vysehrad Castle—Hradcany
A87

1938, June 26 ***Perf. 12½***

251	A87	Sheet of two	5.50	5.50
a.		50h dk bl	2.00	2.00
b.		1k dp car	2.00	2.00

Issued in sheets measuring 148½x105mm.

Stefánik Type of 1936.

1938, Nov. 21

252	A63	50h dp grn	10	5

Allegory of the Republic
A89

1938, Dec. 19 **Unwmkd.**

253	A89	2k lt ultra	35	20
254	A89	3k pale brn	75	25

Issued in commemoration of the 20th anniversary of Independence.

"Wir sind frei!"

Stamps of Czechoslovakia, 1918-37, overprinted with a swastika in black or red and "Wir sind frei!" were issued locally and unofficially in 1938 as Czech authorities were evacuating and German authorities arriving. They appeared in the towns of Asch, Karlsbad, Reichenberg - Maffersdorf, Rumburg, etc.

The overprint, sometimes including a surcharge or the town name (as in Karlsbad), exists on many values of postage, air post, semi-postal, postage due and newspaper stamps.

Stefánik Type of 1936.

1939 **Engraved** ***Perf. 12½***

255	A63	60h dk bl	20.00	20.00

Used exclusively in Slovakia.

Masaryk Type of 1935 with hyphen in Cesko - Slovensko.

1939, Apr. 23

256	A60	1k rose lake	15	5

Linden Leaves and Buds
A90

1945 **Photogravure.** ***Perf. 14.***

256A	A90	10(h) black	5	5
257	A90	30(h) yel brn	5	5
258	A90	50(h) dk grn	5	5
258A	A90	60(h) dk red	5	5

Engraved.

(Buds Open.)

Perf. 12½.

259	A90	60(h) blue	5	5
259A	A90	80(h) org ver	6	5
260	A90	1.20(k) rose	5	5
261	A90	3(k) vio brn	5	5
262	A90	5(k) green	5	5
		Nos. 256A-262(9)	46	45

Thomas G. Masaryk
A91

Coat of Arms
A92

1945-46 **Photogravure.** ***Perf. 12.***

262A	A91	5h dl vio ('46)	8	6
262B	A91	10h org yel ('46)	8	6
262C	A91	20h dk brn ('46)	6	5
263	A91	50h brt grn	10	5
264	A91	1k org red	12	6
265	A91	2k chlky bl	30	30
		Nos. 262A-265 (6)	74	58

1945 ***Imperf.***

266	A92	50h ol gray	5	5
267	A92	1k brt red vio	5	5
268	A92	1.50k dk car	6	5
269	A92	2k dp bl	8	5
269A	A92	2.40k hn brn	35	20
270	A92	3k brown	6	5
270A	A92	4k dk sl grn	10	5
271	A92	6k vio bl	30	8
271A	A92	10k sepia	45	10
		Nos. 266-271A (9)	1.50	68

Nos. 266 to 271A exist in two printings. Stamps of the first printing are on thin, hard paper in sheets of 100; those of the second printing on thick, soft wove paper in sheets of 200.

Staff Captain Ridky (British Army)
A93

Dr. Miroslav Novak (French Army)
A94

Captain Otakar Jaros (Russian Army)
A95

Staff Captain Stanislav Zimprich (Foreign Legion)
A96

Second Lieutenant Jiri Kral (French Air Force)
A97

Josef Gabcik (Parachutist)
A98

Staff Captain Alois Vasatko (Royal Air Force)
A99

Private Frantisek Adamek (British Colonial Service)
A100

Engraved

1945, Aug. 18 ***Perf. 11½x12½***

272	A93	5h	int bl	5	5
273	A94	10h	dk brn	5	5
274	A95	20h	brick red	5	5
275	A96	25h	rose red	5	5
276	A97	30h	purple	10	5
277	A98	40h	sepia	5	5
278	A99	50h	dk ol	5	5
279	A100	60h	violet	15	6
280	A93	1k	carmine	5	5
281	A94	1.50k	lake	6	5
282	A95	2k	ultra	8	5
283	A96	2.50k	dp vio	10	5
284	A97	3k	sepia	10	5
285	A98	4k	rose lil	15	6
286	A99	5k	myr grn	27	8
287	A100	10k	brt ultra	80	20
			Nos. 272-287 (16)	2.16	1.00

Flags of Russia, Great Britain, United States and Czechoslovakia
A101

View of Banská Bystrica
A102

Patriot Welcoming Russian Soldier, Turciansky
A103

Ruins of Castle at Sklabina
A104

Czech Patriot, Strecno
A105

1945, Aug. 29 **Photo.** ***Perf. 10***

288	A101	1.50k	brt car	10	15
289	A102	2k	brt bl	10	15
290	A103	4k	dk brn	40	30
291	A104	4.50k	purple	40	30
292	A105	5k	dp grn	1.00	1.00
			Nos. 288-292 (5)	2.00	1.90

National uprising against the Germans.

A card contains one each of Nos. 288—292 with multicolored marginal design, on thin cardboard, ungummed. Size: 148x 210mm. Sold for 50k.

General Milan Stefánik
A106

President Eduard Benes
A107

Thomas G. Masaryk
A108

1945-47 **Engraved** ***Perf. 12, 12½***

293	A106	30h	rose vio	5	5
294	A107	60h	blue	10	5
294A	A106	1k	red org ('47)	10	5
295	A108	1.20k	car rose	12	5
295A	A108	1.20 (k)	rose lil ('46)	10	5
296	A106	2.40(k)	rose	12	5
297	A107	3k	red vio	24	5
297A	A108	4k	dk bl ('46)	15	5
298	A108	5k	Prus grn	24	5
299	A107	7k	gray	30	5
300	A106	10k	gray bl	70	5
300A	A106	20k	sep ('46)	1.50	25
			Nos. 293-300A (12)	3.72	80

1945 **Photogravure.** ***Perf. 14.***

301	A108	50h	brown	5	5
302	A106	80h	dk grn	5	5
303	A107	1.60(k)	ol grn	10	5
304	A108	15k	red vio	90	10

Kozina and Chod Castle, Taus
A109

Red Army Soldier
A110

Engraved.

1945, Nov. 28 ***Perf. 12½***

305	A109	2.40k	rose car	25	20
306	A109	4k	blue	30	20

Issued to commemorate the 250th anniversary of the death of Jan Sladky Kozina, peasant leader.

1945, Mar. 26 **Litho.** ***Imperf.***

307	A110	2k	crim rose	60	60
308	A110	5k	sl blk	2.25	2.25
309	A110	6k	ultra	75	75

Souvenir Sheet.

A111

1945, July 16

Gray Burelage

310	A111		Sheet of three	4.00	4.00
	a.	2k	crim rose	40	40
	b.	5k	sl blk	40	40
	c.	6k	ultra	40	40

Return of President Benes, April, 1945. Size: 137x120mm.

Clasped Hands
A112

Karel Havlícek Borovsky
A113

1945 ***Rouletted 12½***

311	A112	1.50k	brn red	4.25	4.25
312	A112	9k	red org	90	90
313	A112	13k	org brn	1.25	1.25
314	A112	20k	blue	3.25	3.25

1946, July 5 **Engraved**

315	A113	1.20(k)	gray blk	25	25

Issued to commemorate the 90th anniversary of the death of Karel Havlicek Borovsky (1821–1856), editor and writer.

Old Town Hall, Brno
A114

Hodonin Square
A115

Perf. 12½x12, 12x12½.

1946, Aug. 3 **Engraved** **Unwmkd.**

316	A114	2.40(k)	dp rose	30	20
317	A115	7.40(k)	dl vio	50	10

President Eduard Benes
A116

1946, Oct. 28

318	A116	60h	indigo	5	5
319	A116	1.60k	dl grn	6	5
320	A116	3k	red lil	10	5
321	A116	8k	sepia	40	5

Flag and Symbols
A117

Saint Adalbert
A118

1947, Jan. 1 ***Perf. 12½***

322	A117	1.20(k)	Prus grn	20	5
323	A117	2.40(k)	dp rose	20	5
324	A117	4(k)	dp bl	50	15

Issued to publicize Czechoslovakia's two-year reconstruction and rehabilitation program.

1947, Apr. 23

326	A118	1.60(k)	gray	75	40
327	A118	2.40(k)	rose car	1.25	90
328	A118	5(k)	bl grn	1.50	60

Issued to commemorate the 950th anniversary of the death of Saint Adalbert, Bishop of Prague.

Grief
A119

Allegorical Figure
A120

1947, June 10 **Engraved**

329	A119	1.20(k)	black	40	35
330	A119	1.60(k)	sl blk	50	50
331	A120	2.40(k)	brn vio	60	60

Destruction of Lidice, 5th anniversary.

World Federation of Youth Symbol
A121

Thomas G. Masaryk
A122

1947, July 20

332	A121	1.20(k)	vio brn	40	20
333	A121	4k	slate	65	25

Issued to commemorate the World Youth Festival held in Prague, July 20th to August 17, 1947.

1947, Sept. 14

334	A122	1.20(k)	gray blk, *buff*	30	15
335	A122	4k	bl blk, *cr*	70	20

Death of T. G. Masaryk, 10th anniversary.

Msgr. Stefan Moyses
A123

1947, Oct. 24

336	A123	1.20k	rose vio	30	10
337	A123	4k	dp bl	50	30

Issued to commemorate the 150th anniversary of the birth of Stefan Moyses, first Slovakian chairman of the Slavic movement.

"Freedom from Social Oppression"
A124

1947, Oct. 26 **Photo.** ***Perf. 14***

338	A124	2.40k	brt car	30	30
339	A124	4k	brt ultra	60	20

Issued to commemorate the 30th anniversary of the Russian revolution of October, 1917.

President Eduard Benes
A125

"Czechoslovakia" Greeting Sokol Marchers
A126

1948, Feb. 15 **Photogravure**

Size: 17½x21½mm.

340	A125	1.50(k)	brown	6	5

Size: 19x23mm.

341	A125	2k	dp plum	10	5
342	A125	5k	brt ultra	25	5

1948, Mar. 7 **Engr.** ***Perf. 12½***

343	A126	1.50(k)	brown	15	6
344	A126	3k	rose car	15	6
345	A126	5k	blue	50	8

The 11th Sokol Congress.

King Charles IV
A127

St. Wenceslas and King Charles IV
A128

1948, Apr. 7

346	A127	1.50(k) blk brn	20	5
347	A128	2(k) dk brn	25	5
348	A128	3(k) brn red	35	12
349	A127	5(k) dk bl	70	25

Issued to commemorate the 600th anniversary of the foundation of Charles University, Prague.

Czech Peasants in Revolt
A129

Jindrich Vanicek
A130

Photogravure.

1948, May 14 ***Perf. 14*** **Unwmkd.**

350	A129	1.50k dk ol brn	15	10

Centenary of abolition of serfdom.

1948, June 10 Engraved *Perf. 12½*

Designs: 1.50k, 2k, Josef Scheiner.

351	A130	1k dk grn	15	5
352	A130	1.50k sepia	15	5
353	A130	2k gray bl	35	10
354	A130	3k claret	50	15

11th Sokol Congress, Prague, 1948.

Frantisek Palacky and F. L. Rieger
A131

Miloslav Josef Hurban
A132

1948, June 20 **Unwmkd.**

355	A131	1.50k gray	20	8
356	A131	3k brn car	30	8

Issued to commemorate the centenary of the Constituent Assembly at Kromeriz.

1948, Aug. 27 ***Perf. 12½***

Designs: 3k, Ludwig Stur. 5k, Michael M. Hodza.

357	A132	1.50(k) dk brn	15	8
358	A132	3(k) car lake	25	8
359	A132	5(k) indigo	45	20

Centenary of 1848 insurrection against Hungary.

Eduard Benes
A133

Czechoslovak Family
A134

1948, Sept. 28

360	A133	8k black	30	10

Issued in tribute to President Eduard Benes, 1884–1948.

1948, Oct. 28 ***Perf. 12½x12***

361	A134	1.50k dp bl	10	10
362	A134	3k rose car	30	18

Issued to commemorate the 30th anniversary of Czechoslovakia's Independence.

Pres. Klement Gottwald
A135

Gottwald and Presidential Flag
A136

1948–49 ***Perf. 12½.***

Size: 18½x23½mm.

363	A135	1.50(k) dk brn	10	5
364	A135	3(k) car rose	25	5
a.		3(k) rose brn	35	5
365	A135	5(k) gray bl	25	5

Size: 23½x29mm.

366	A135	20(k) purple	1.25	15

See also Nos. 373, 564, 600-604.

Souvenir Sheet.

1948, Nov. 23 ***Imperf.*** **Unwmkd.**

367	A136	30k rose brn	4.75	3.75

52nd birthday of Pres. Klement Gottwald (1896–1953). Size: 67x98½mm.

Souvenir Sheet.

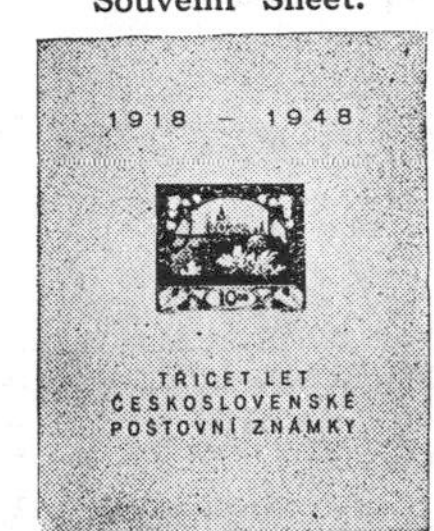

Hradcany Castle
A137

1948, Dec. 18

368	A137	10k dk bl vio	1.50	1.25

30th anniversary of first Czechoslovak postage stamp. Size: 79x90½mm.

Czechoslovak and Russian Workmen Shaking Hands
A138

Lenin
A139

1948, Dec. 12 ***Perf. 12½***

369	A138	3k rose car	24	12

Issued to commemorate the fifth anniversary of the treaty of alliance between Czechoslovakia and Russia.

1949, Jan. 21 Engraved *Perf. 12½*

370	A139	1.50(k) vio brn	30	12
371	A139	5(k) dp bl	50	20

25th anniversary of the death of Lenin.

Gottwald Type of 1948
Inscribed: "UNOR 1948" and

Gottwald Addressing Meeting
A140

1949, Feb. 25 Photo. ***Perf. 14***

372	A140	3k red brn	15	5

Engraved
Perf. 12½
Size: 23½x29mm.

373	A135	10k dp grn	65	20

Nos. 372 and 373 were issued to commemorate the first anniversary of Klement Gottwald's speech announcing the appointment of a new government.

P. O. Hviezdoslav
A141

Stagecoach and Train
A142

Designs (Writers): 80h, V. Vancura. 1k, J. Sverma. 2k, Julius Fucik. 4k, Jiri Wolker. 8k, Alois Jirasek.

1949 Photogravure. ***Perf. 14.***

374	A141	50h vio brn	5	5
375	A141	80h scarlet	10	5
376	A141	1k dk ol grn	10	5
377	A141	2k brt bl	40	5

Engraved
Perf. 12½

378	A141	4k vio brn	40	5
379	A141	8k brn blk	50	5
		Nos. 374-379 (6)	1.55	30

1949, May 20

Designs: 5k, Postrider and post bus. 13k, Sailing ship and plane.

380	A142	3k brn car	4.00	3.00
381	A142	5k dp bl	1.00	60
382	A142	13k dp grn	2.00	90

Issued to commemorate the 75th anniversary of the formation of the Universal Postal Union.

Reaping
A143

Communist Emblem and Workers
A144

Workman, Symbol of Industry
A145

Perf. 12½x12, 12x12½.

1949, May 24 **Unwmkd.**

383	A143	1.50k dp grn	75	45
384	A144	3k brn car	40	30
385	A145	5k dp bl	75	45

No. 384 commemorates the ninth meeting of the Communist Party of Czechoslovakia, May 25, 1949.

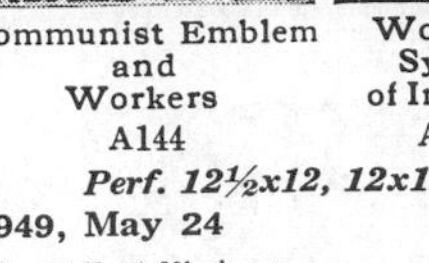

Friedrich Smetana and National Theater, Prague
A146

Aleksander Pushkin
A147

1949, June 4 ***Perf. 12½x12***

386	A146	1.50k dl grn	35	15
387	A146	5k dp bl	75	40

Issued to commemorate the 125th anniversary of the birth of Friedrich Smetana, composer.

1949, June 6 ***Perf. 12x12½***

388	A147	2k ol gray	35	20

Issued to commemorate the 150th anniversary of the birth of Aleksander S. Pushkin.

Frederic Chopin and Conservatory, Warsaw
A148

1949, June 24 ***Perf. 12½x12***

389	A148	3k dk red	50	30
390	A148	8k vio brn	1.25	60

Issued to commemorate the centenary of the death of Frederic F. Chopin.

Globe and Ribbon
A149

Zvolen Castle
A150

1949, Aug. 20 ***Perf. 12½x12***

391	A149	1.50k vio brn	35	30
392	A149	5k ultra	75	50

Issued to publicize the 50th Prague Sample Fair, September 11–18, 1949.

Starting in 1949, commemorative stamps which are priced in italics were issued in smaller quantities than those in the balance of the set and sold at prices higher than face value.

1949, Aug. 28 ***Perf. 12½***

393	A150	10k rose lake	1.00	5

Early Miners
A151

Miner of Today
A152

Design: 5k, Mining Machine.

1949, Sept. 11 ***Perf. 12½x12, 12½***

394	A151	1.50k sepia	1.25	90
395	A152	3k car rose	*7.00*	*2.00*
396	A151	5k dp bl	*5.50*	*2.00*

Issued to commemorate the 700th anniversary of the Czechoslovak mining industry and the 150th anniversary of the miner's laws.

Construction Workers
A153

Joseph V. Stalin
A154

Design: 2k, Machinist.

1949, Dec. 11 *Perf. 12½*

397	A153	1k dk grn	3.50	1.00
398	A153	2k vio brn	2.00	60

2nd Trade Union Congress, Prague, 1949.

Cream Paper.

1949, Dec. 21 **Unwmkd.**

Design: 3k, Stalin facing left.

399	A154	1.50k grnsh gray	2.00	80
400	A154	3k claret	3.00	1.25

70th birthday of Joseph V. Stalin.

Skier
A155

Efficiency Badge
A156

Engraved, 3k Photogravure

1950, Feb. 15 *Perf. 12½, 13½*

401	A155	1.50k gray bl	3.00	1.00
402	A156	3k vio brn, *cr*	3.00	1.75
403	A155	5k ultra	4.00	2.50

Issued to publicize the 51st Ski Championship for the Tatra cup, Feb. 15–26, 1950.

Vladimir V. Mayakovsky
A157

1950, Apr. 14 Engr. *Perf. 12½*

404	A157	1.50k dk brn	3.00	1.75
405	A157	3k brn red	3.00	1.25

Issued to commemorate the 20th anniversary of the death of V. V. Mayakovsky, poet.

See also Nos. 414–417, 422–423, 432–433, 464–465, 477–478.

Soviet Tank Soldier and Hradcany
A158

Designs: 2k, Hero of Labor medal. 3k, Two workers (militiamen) and Town Hall, Prague. 5k, Text of government program and heraldic lion.

1950, May 5

406	A158	1.50k gray grn	50	25
407	A158	2k dk brn	1.25	95
408	A158	3k brn red	40	25
409	A158	5k dk bl	65	20

Issued on the occasion of the fifth anniversary of the Czechoslovak People's Democratic Republic.

Factory and Young Couple with Tools—A159

Designs: 2k, Steam shovel. 3k, Farmer and farm scene. 5k, Three workers leaving factory.

1950, May 9 Engraved

410	A159	1.50k dk grn	1.50	1.00
411	A159	2k dk brn	2.00	1.00
412	A159	3k rose red	75	25
413	A159	5k dp bl	75	25

Canceled to Order

The government philatelic department started about 1950 to sell canceled sets of new issues. Prices in the second ("used") column are for these canceled-to-order stamps. Postally used copies are worth more.

Portrait Type of 1950

Design: S. K. Neumann.

1950, June 5 *Perf. 12½* **Unwmkd.**

414	A157	1.50k dp bl	25	12
415	A157	3k vio brn	1.00	90

Issued to commemorate the 75th anniversary of the birth of Stanislav Kostka Neumann (1875–1947), journalist and poet.

1950, June 21

Design: Bozena Nemcova.

416	A157	1.50k dp bl	1.50	1.25
417	A157	7k dk brn	40	30

Issued to commemorate the 130th anniversary of the birth of Bozena Nemcova (1820–1862), writer.

Liberation of Colonies
A160

Designs: 2k, Allegory, Fight for Peace. 3k, Group of Students. 5k, Marching Students with flags.

1950, Aug. 14

418	A160	1.50k dk grn	15	5
419	A160	2k sepia	1.25	80
420	A160	3k rose car	25	15
421	A160	5k ultra	60	35

Issued to publicize the 2nd International Students World Congress, Prague, August 12–24, 1950.

Portrait Type of 1950.

Design: Zdenek Fibich.

1950, Oct. 15

422	A157	3k rose brn	1.25	90
423	A157	8k gray grn	50	35

Issued to commemorate the centenary of the birth of Zdenek Fibich, musician.

Miner, Soldier and Farmer
A161

Czech and Soviet Soldiers—A162

1950, Oct. 6

424	A161	1.50k slate	75	60
425	A162	3k car rose	40	20

Issued to publicize Czech Army Day.

Prague Castle, 16th Century
A163

Prague, 1493
A164

Designs: 3k, Prague, 1606. 5k, Prague, 1794.

1950, Oct. 21 *Perf. 14*

426	A163	1.50k black	4.50	4.00
427	A164	2k chocolate	4.50	4.00
428	A164	3k brn car	4.50	4.00
429	A164	5k gray	4.50	4.00
	a.	Block of 4	25.00	20.00

Sheets arranged in blocks of four containing one of Nos. 426 to 429. See Nos. 434–435.

Communications Symbols
A165

1950, Oct. 25 *Perf. 12½*

430	A165	1.50k chocolate	12	5
431	A165	3k brn car	75	40

Issued to commemorate first anniversary of the foundation of the International League of P.T.T. Employees.

Portrait Type of 1950.

Design: J. Gregor Tajovsky.

1950, Oct. 26

432	A157	1.50k brown	1.25	75
433	A157	5k dp bl	75	50

Issued to commemorate the 10th anniversary of the death of J. Gregor Tajovsky (1874–1940), Slovakian writer.

Scenic Type of 1950.

Design: Prague, 1950.

1950, Oct. 28

434	A164	1.50k indigo	35	20
	a.	Souvenir sheet of 4, imperf.	17.50	15.00
435	A164	3k brn car	85	75

No. 434a measures 121x100mm. and contains four copies of No. 434, imperforate, with carmine inscription in top margin.

Czech and Soviet Steel Workers
A166

1950, Nov. 4 **Unwmkd.**

436	A166	1.50k chocolate	40	20
437	A166	5k dp bl	95	75

Issued to publicize the 2nd meeting of the Union of Czechoslovak-Soviet Friendship.

Dove by Picasso
A167

1951, Jan. 20 Photo. *Perf. 14*

438	A167	2k dp bl	5.50	2.50
439	A167	3k rose brn	3.00	2.00

Issued to commemorate the first Czechoslovak Congress of Fighters for Peace, held in Prague.

Julius Fucik
A168

1951, Feb. 17 Engr. *Perf. 12½*

440	A168	1.50k gray	70	40
441	A168	5k gray bl	1.75	1.00

Drop Hammer
A169

Installing Gear
A170

1951, Feb. 24

442	A169	1.50k gray blk	10	10
443	A170	3k vio brn	15	10
444	A169	4k gray bl	1.00	75

Women Machinists
A171

Apprentice Miners
A172

Designs: 3k, Woman tractor operator. 5k, Women of different races.

1951, Mar. 8 Photo. *Perf. 14*

445	A171	1.50k ol brn	30	10
446	A171	3k brn car	1.25	75
447	A171	5k blue	50	20

International Women's Day, Mar. 8.

1951, Apr. 12 Engr. *Perf. 12½*

448	A172	1.50k gray	60	35
449	A172	3k red brn	20	10

Plowing
A173

Collective Cattle Breeding
A174

1951, Apr. 28 Photo. ***Perf. 14***

450	A173	1.50k	brown	65	50
451	A174	2k	dk grn	*1.00*	*1.00*

Tatra Mountain Recreation Center—A175

Mountain Recreation Centers: 2k, Beskydy (Beskids). 3k, Krkonose (Carpathians).

1951, May 5 Engr. ***Perf. 12½***

Inscribed: "ROH."

452	A175	1.50k	dp grn	25	10
453	A175	2k	dk brn	*85*	*70*
454	A175	3k	rose brn	1.00	35

Issued to publicize the summer opening of trade union recreation centers.

Klement Gottwald and Joseph Stalin
A176

Factory Militiaman
A177

Red Army Soldier and Partisan
A178

Marx, Engels, Lenin and Stalin
A179

1951 ***Perf. 12½*** **Unwmkd.**

455	A176	1.50k	ol gray	70	30
456	A177	2k	red brn	30	8
457	A178	3k	rose brn	50	10
458	A176	5k	dp bl	*3.00*	*2.00*
459	A179	8k	gray	1.00	35
		Nos. 455-459 (5)		*5.50*	*2.83*

Issued to commemorate the 30th anniversary of the founding of the Czechoslovak Communist Party.

Antonin Dvorák
A180

Design: 1.50k, 3k, Friedrich Smetana.

1951, May 30

460	A180	1k	redsh brn	20	15
461	A180	1.50k	ol gray	*1.00*	*40*
462	A180	2k	dk redsh brn	*1.25*	*90*
463	A180	3k	rose brn	20	15

International Music Festival, Prague.

Portrait Type of 1950.

1951, June 21

Portrait: Bohumir Smeral (facing right).

464	A157	1.50k	dk gray	*55*	*45*
465	A157	3k	rose brn	40	15

Issued to commemorate the 10th anniversary of the death of Bohumir Smeral, political leader.

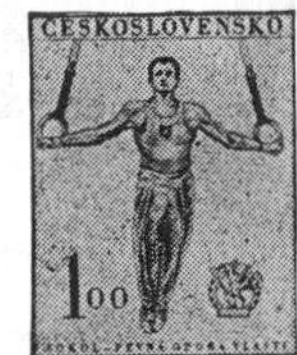

Gymnast on Rings
A181

Designs: 1.50k, Discus Thrower. 3k, Soccer. 5k, Skier.

1951, June 21

466	A181	1k	dk grn	80	45
467	A181	1.50k	dk brn	80	45
468	A181	3k	brn car	1.40	45
469	A181	5k	dp bl	*3.00*	*2.00*

Issued to honor the 9th Congress of the Czechoslovak Sokol Federation.

Scene from "Fall of Berlin"
A182

Scene from "The Great Citizen"
A183

1951, July 14

470	A182	80h	rose brn	35	25
471	A183	1.50k	dk gray	45	35
472	A182	4k	gray bl	*1.75*	*1.10*

Issued on the occasion of the International Film Festival, Karlovy Vary, July 14–29, 1951.

Alois Jirásek
A184

"Fables and Fate"
A185

Design: 4k, Scene from "Reign of Tabor."

1951, Aug. 23 Engr. ***Perf. 12½***

473	A184	1.50k	gray	25	15
474	A184	5k	dk bl	*2.50*	*1.75*

Photo. ***Perf. 14***

475	A185	3k	dk red	35	20
476	A185	4k	dk brn	50	25

Issued to commemorate the centenary of the birth of Alois Jirásek, author.

Portrait Type of 1950.

Design: Josef Hybes.

1951, July 21 **Engraved**

477	A157	1.50k	chocolate	20	10
478	A157	2k	rose brn	*90*	*50*

Issued to commemorate the centenary of the birth of Josef Hybes (1850–1921), cofounder of Czech Communist Party.

"Ostrava Region"
A186

Mining Iron Ore
A187

1951, Sept. 9

479	A186	1.50k	dk brn	12	8
480	A187	3k	rose brn	15	10
481	A186	5k	dp bl	*1.50*	*75*

Miner's Day, Sept. 9, 1951.

Soldiers on Parade
A188

Designs: 1k, Gunner and field gun. 1.50k, Klement Gottwald. 3k, Tankman and tank. 5k, Aviators.

Photo. (80h, 5k), Engr.

Perf. 14 (80h, 5k), 12½

1951, Oct. 6

Inscribed: "Den CS Armady 1951."

482	A188	80h	ol brn	20	15
483	A188	1k	dk ol grn	35	30
484	A188	1.50k	sepia	60	30
485	A188	3k	claret	75	30
486	A188	5k	blue	*1.50*	*1.10*
		Nos. 482-486 (5)		*3.40*	*2.15*

Issued to publicize Army Day, Oct. 6, 1951.

Joseph Stalin and Klement Gottwald
A189

Lenin, Stalin and Soldiers
A190

1951, Nov. 3 Engraved ***Perf. 12½***

487	A189	1.50k	sepia	15	10
488	A190	3k	red brn	20	8
489	A189	4k	dp bl	*1.25*	*65*

Issued to publicize the month of Czechoslovak-Soviet friendship, 1951.

Peter Jilemnicky
A191

Ladislav Zapotocky
A192

1951, Dec. 5 **Unwmkd.**

491	A191	1.50k	redsh brn	30	20
492	A191	2k	dl bl	*65*	*55*

Issued to commemorate the 50th anniversary of the birth of Peter Jilemnicky (1901–1949), writer.

1952, Jan. 12 ***Perf. 11½***

493	A192	1.50k	brn red	10	5
494	A192	4k	gray	*75*	*50*

Issued to commemorate the centenary of the birth of Ladislav Zapotocky, Bohemian socialist pioneer.

Jan Kollar
A193

Lenin and Lenin Hall
A194

1952, Jan. 30 ***Perf. 11½*** **Unwmkd.**

495	A193	3k	dk car	10	5
496	A193	5k	vio bl	*1.00*	*65*

Issued to commemorate the centenary of the death of Jan Kollar (1793–1852), poet.

1952, Jan. 30 ***Perf. 12½***

497	A194	1.50k	rose car	15	5
498	A194	5k	dp bl	*75*	*50*

Issued to commemorate the 40th anniversary of the Sixth All-Russian Party Conference.

Emil Holub and African
A195

Klement Gottwald Metallurgical Plant
A196

1952, Feb. 21 ***Perf. 11½***

499	A195	3k	red brn	50	35
500	A195	5k	gray	*1.75*	*1.50*

Issued to commemorate the 50th anniversary of the death of Emil Holub, explorer.

1952, Feb. 25 Photo. ***Perf. 14***

Designs: 2k, Foundry. 3k, Chemical plant.

501	A196	1.50k	sepia	15	10
502	A196	2k	red brn	*1.25*	*95*
503	A196	3k	scarlet	20	10

Student, Soldier and Worker
A197

Youths of Three Races
A198

1952, Mar. 21 ***Perf. 14*** **Unwmkd.**

504	A197	1.50k blue	12	10
505	A198	2k ol blk	25	15
506	A197	3k lake	1.00	80

International Youth Day, Mar. 25, 1952.

Similar to Type of 1951.

Portrait: Otakar Sevcik.

1952, Mar. 22 **Engr.** ***Perf. 12½***

507	A184	2k choc, *cr*	75	60
508	A184	3k rose brn, *cr*	25	15

Issued to commemorate the centenary of the birth of Otakar Sevcik, violinist.

Jan A. Komensky A199 — Industrial and Farm Women A200

1952, Mar. 28 **Cream Paper**

509	A199	1.50k dk brn	1.75	75
510	A199	11k dk bl	40	10

Issued to commemorate the 360th anniversary of the birth of Jan Amos Komensky (Comenius), teacher and philosopher.

1952, Mar. 8 **Cream Paper**

511	A200	1.50k dp bl	1.25	70

International Women's Day Mar. 8, 1952.

Woman and Children A201 — Antifascist A202

1952, Apr. 12 **Cream Paper**

512	A201	2k chocolate	90	65
513	A201	3k dp cl	20	10

Issued to publicize the International Conference for the Protection of Children, Vienna, April 12-16, 1952.

1952, Apr. 11 **Photo.** ***Perf. 14***

514	A202	1.50k red brn	15	8
515	A202	2k ultra	75	55

Issued to publicize the Day of International Solidarity of Fighters against Fascism, April 11, 1952.

Harvester A203

Design: 3k, Tractor and Seeders.

1952, Apr. 30

516	A203	1.50k dp bl	1.00	85
517	A203	2k brown	35	25
518	A203	3k brn red	35	25

Youths Carrying Flags A204

1952, May 1

519	A204	3k brn red	75	60
520	A204	4k dk red brn	90	75

Issued to publicize Labor Day, May 1, 1952.

Crowd Cheering Soviet Soldiers A205

1952, May 9

521	A205	1.50k dk red	75	50
522	A205	5k dp bl	1.50	1.25

Liberation of Czechoslovakia from German occupation, 7th anniversary.

Children A206 — J. V. Myslbek A207

Design: 3k, "Pioneer" teaching children.

1952, May 31 **Engr.** ***Perf. 12½***

Cream Paper.

523	A206	1.50k dk brn	10	5
524	A206	2k Prus grn	1.25	60
525	A206	3k rose brn	15	8

International Children's Day May 31, 1952.

1952, June 2

Design: 8k, Allegory, "Music."

526	A207	1.50k red brn	20	6
527	A207	2k dk brn	1.50	1.25
528	A207	8k gray grn	30	10

Issued to commemorate the 30th anniversary of the death of Joseph V. Myslbek (1848-1922), sculptor.

Beethoven A208 — House of Artists A209

1952, June 7 ***Perf. 11½*** **Unwmkd.**

529	A208	1.50k sepia	50	40
530	A209	3k red brn	50	40
531	A208	5k indigo	1.75	1.25

International Music Festival, Prague, 1952.

Lidice, Symbol of a New Life A210

1952, June 10 ***Perf. 12½***

532	A210	1.50k dk vio brn	20	8
533	A210	5k dk bl	85	65

Destruction of Lidice, 10th anniversary.

Jan Hus A211 — Bethlehem Chapel A212

1952, July 5

534	A211	1.50k brown	10	6
535	A212	3k red brn	15	8
536	A211	5k black	1.40	1.00

Issued to commemorate the 550th anniversary of the installation of Jan Hus as pastor of Bethlehem Chapel, Prague.

Doctor Examining Patient A213

Design: 2k, Doctor, Nurse, Mother and child.

1952, July 31

537	A213	1.50k dk brn	1.00	65
538	A213	2k bl vio	15	6
539	A213	3k rose brn	25	8

Czechoslovakia's Unified Health Service.

Relay Race—A214

Designs: 2k, Canoeing. 3k, Cycling. 4k, Hockey.

1952, Aug. 2 ***Perf. 11½***

540	A214	1.50k dk brn	80	45
541	A214	2k grnsh blk	2.00	1.00
542	A214	3k red brn	60	45
543	A214	4k dp bl	3.50	2.75

Issued to publicize Czechoslovakia's Unified Physical Education program.

F. L. Celakovski A215 — Mikulas Ales A216

1952, Aug. 5 ***Perf. 12½***

544	A215	1.50k dk brn	15	8
545	A215	2k dk grn	90	60

Issued to commemorate the centenary of the death of Frantisek L. Celakovski, poet and writer.

Perf. 11x11½

1952, Aug. 30 **Engraved** **Unwmkd.**

546	A216	1.50k dk gray grn	50	30
547	A216	6k red brn	2.75	2.00

Birth centenary of Mikulas Ales, painter.

17th Century Mining Towers A217 — Jan Zizka A218

Designs: 1.50k, Coal Excavator. 2k, Peter Bezruc mine. 3k, Automatic coaling crane.

1952, Sept. 14 ***Perf. 12½***

548	A217	1k sepia	1.25	75
549	A217	1.50k dk bl	10	6
550	A217	2k ol gray	20	10
551	A217	3k vio brn	25	8

Issued to publicize Miners' Day, Sept. 14, 1952. No. 550 also commemorates the 85th anniversary of the birth of Peter Bezruc (Vladimir Vasek), poet.

1952, Oct. 5 **Engraved** ***Perf. 11½***

Designs: 2k, Fraternization with Russians. 3k, Marching with flag.

Inscribed: ". . . . Armady 1952,"

552	A218	1.50k rose lake	15	6
553	A218	2k ol bis	20	5
554	A218	3k dk car rose	20	10
555	A218	4k gray	2.00	1.25

Issued to publicize Army Day, Oct. 5, 1952.

Souvenir Sheet.

Statues to Bulgarian Partisans and to Soviet Army—A219

1952, Oct. 18 ***Perf. 12½*** **Unwmkd.**

556	A219	Sheet of two	65.00	20.00
a.		2k dp car	25.00	7.50
b.		3k ultra	25.00	7.50

Issued to commemorate the National Philatelic Exhibition, Bratislava, Oct. 18–Nov. 2, 1952.

Danube River, Bratislava A220

1952, Oct. 18

557	A220	1.50k dk brn	25	10

National Philatelic Exhibition, Bratislava.

Conference with Lenin and Stalin A221 — Worker and Nurse Holding Dove and Olive Branch A222

1952, Nov. 7

558	A221	2k brn blk	85	70
559	A221	3k carmine	30	10

Issued to commemorate the 35th anniversary of the Russian Revolution and to publicize Czechoslovak-Soviet friendship.

1952, Nov. 15 **Photo.** ***Perf. 14***

560	A222	2k brown	85	60
561	A222	3k red	20	10

Issued to publicize the first State Congress of the Czechoslovak Red Cross.

Matej Louda, Hussite Leader, Painted by Mikulas Ales A223

Design: 3k, Dragon-killer Trutnov, painted by Ales.

1952, Nov. 18 Engraved *Perf. 11½*

562 A223 2k red brn 30 8
563 A223 3k grnsh gray 40 15

Issued to commemorate the centenary of the birth of Mikulas Ales, painter.

Gottwald Type of 1948–49.
Size: 19x24mm.

1952, June 2 *Perf. 12½* **Unwmkd.**

564 A135 1k dk grn 10 5

"Peace" Flags
A224

Dove by Picasso
A225

1952, Dec. 12 Photo. *Perf. 14*

565 A224 3k red brn 15 6
566 A224 4k dp bl 1.00 80

Issued to publicize the Congress of Nations for Peace, Vienna, Dec. 12–19, 1952.

1953, Jan. 17

Design: 4k, Czech Family.

567 A225 1.50k dk brn 10 5
568 A225 4k sl bl 70 40

2nd Czechoslovak Peace Congress.

Smetana Museum
A226

Design: 4k, Jirásek Museum.

1953, Feb. 10 Engraved *Perf. 11½*

569 A226 1.50k dk vio brn 10 6
570 A226 4k dk gray 1.00 75

Issued to commemorate the 75th anniversary of the birth of Prof. Zdenek Nejedly.

Martin Kukucin
A227

Jaroslav Vrchlicky
A228

Designs: 2k, Karel Jaromir Erben. 3k, Vaclav Matej Kramerius. 5k, Josef Dobrovsky.

1953, Feb. 28

571 A227 1k gray 10 5
572 A228 1.50k olive 8 5
573 A228 2k rose lake 8 5
574 A228 3k lt brn 25 15
575 A228 5k sl bl 1.50 1.50
Nos. 571-575 (5) 2.01 1.80

Issued to honor Czech writers and poets: 1k, 25th anniversary of death of Kukucin. 1.50k, birth centenary of Vrchlicky. 2k, centenary of completion of "Kytice" by Erben. 3k, birth bicentenary of Kramerius. 5k, birth bicentenary of Dobrovsky.

Militia
A229

Klement Gottwald
A230

Design: 8k, Portraits of Stalin and Gottwald and Peoples Assembly.

Perf. 13½x14

1953, Feb. 25 Photo. **Unwmkd.**

576 A230 1.50k dp bl 10 10
577 A230 3k red 20 15
578 A229 8k dk brn 1.50 1.00

Issued to commemorate the 5th anniversary of the defeat of the attempt to reinstate capitalism.

Book and Torch
A231

Design: 3k, Bedrich Vaclavek.

1953, Mar. 5 Engraved *Perf. 11½*

579 A231 1k sepia 80 60
580 A231 3k org brn 20 15

Issued to commemorate the 10th anniversary of the death of Bedrich Vaclavek (1897–1943), socialist writer.

Stalin Type of 1949.
Inscribed "21 XII 1879 - 5 III 1953."

1953, Mar. 12

581 A154 1.50k black 25 15

Death of Joseph Stalin, Mar. 5, 1953.

Mother and Child
A232

Girl Revolutionist
A233

1953, Mar. 8

582 A232 1.50k ultra 10 5
583 A233 2k brn red 50 40

International Women's Day.

Klement Gottwald
A234

1953, Mar. 19

584 A234 1.50k black 12 6
585 A234 3k black 12 6

Souvenir Sheet.
Imperf.

586 A234 5k black 2.75 2.00

No. 586 measures 68x97 mm., with marginal inscriptions and laurel branch.

Nos. 584-586 commemorate the death of President Klement Gottwald, March 14, 1953.

Josef Pecka, Ladislav Zapotocky and Josef Hybes—A236

1953, Apr. 7 *Perf. 11½* **Unwmkd.**

587 A236 2k lt vio brn 15 10

Issued to commemorate the 75th anniversary of the first congress of the Czech Social Democratic Party.

Cyclists
A237

1953, Apr. 29

588 A237 3k dp bl 60 30

Issued to commemorate the 6th International Peace Bicycle Race, Prague-Berlin-Warsaw.

Medal of "May 1, 1890"
A238

Designs: 1.50k, Lenin and Stalin. 3k, May Day Parade. 8k, Marx and Engels.

Engraved and Photogravure.

1953, Apr. 30 *Perf. 11½x11, 14*

Inscribed: "1 MAJ 1953"

589 A238 1k chocolate 1.50 1.35
590 A238 1.50k dk gray 10 6
591 A238 3k car lake 20 10
592 A238 8k dk gray grn 35 15

Issued to publicize Labor Day, May 1, 1953.

Sowing Grain
A239

Design: 7k, Reaper.

1953, May 8 Photo. *Perf. 14*

593 A239 1.50k brown 50 15
594 A239 7k dp grn 1.50 1.40

Issued to publicize the socialization of the village.

Dam
A240

Welder
A241

Design: 3k, Iron works.

1953, May 8 *Perf. 11½*

595 A240 1.50k gray 80 60
596 A241 2k bl gray 15 6
597 A240 3k red brn 15 5

Josef Slavik
A242

Leos Janacek
A243

1953, June 19

598 A242 75h dp gray bl 50 10
599 A243 1.60k dk brn 1.25 8

Issued on the occasion of the International Music Festival, Prague, 1953.

Gottwald Type of 1948–49.

1953 *Perf. 12½, 11½*

600 A135 15h yel grn 30 5
601 A135 20h dk vio brn 40 5
602 A135 1k purple 1.10 5
603 A135 3k brn car 15 5
604 A135 3k gray 1.30 5
Nos. 600-604 (5) 3.25 25

Nos. 600-604 vary slightly in size. Nos. 600 and 602 are perf. 12½; Nos. 601, 603-604 are perf. 11½.

Pres. Antonin Zapotocky
A244

1953, June 19 Photo. *Perf. 14*

605 A244 30h vio bl 45 5
606 A244 60h cerise 75 5

Julius Fucik
A245

Book and Carnation
A246

1953, Sept. 8 Engraved *Perf. 12½*

607 A245 40h dk vio brn 30 5
608 A246 60h pink 65 35

Issued to commemorate the 10th anniversary of the death of Julius Fucik, Communist leader executed by the Nazis.

Miner and Flag
A247

Design: 60h, Oil field and workers.

1953, Sept. 10 *Perf. 11½*

609 A247 30h gray 25 5
610 A247 60h brn vio 85 50

Issued to publicize Miner's Day, Sept. 10, 1953.

Volleyball Game
A248

Motorcyclist
A249

Design: 60h, Woman throwing javelin.

1953, Sept. 15

611	A248	30h brn red	*2.50*	*2.00*
612	A249	40h dk vio brn	4.00	1.25
613	A248	60h rose vio	4.00	1.25

Hussite Warrior A250 — Pres. Antonin Zapotocky A251

Designs: 60h, Soldier presenting arms. 1k, Red army soldiers.

Inscribed: "Den CS Armady 1953."

1953, Oct. 8

614	A250	30h brown	40	10
615	A250	60h rose lake	90	10
616	A250	1k brn red	*1.75*	*1.25*

Issued to publicize Army Day, Oct. 3, 1953.

1953 *Perf. 11½, 12½.* Unwmkd.

617	A251	30h vio bl	50	5
618	A251	60h car rose	60	5

No. 617 is perf. 11½ and measures 19x23 mm. No. 618 is perf. 12½ and measures 18½x23½.

See also No. 780.

Charles Bridge and Prague Castle A252 — Korean and Czech Girls A253

1953, Aug. 15 Engraved *Perf. 11½*

619	A252	5k gray	2.75	10

1953, Oct. 11 *Perf. 11x11½*

620	A253	30h dk brn	5.00	2.00

Issued to demonstrate Czechoslovakia's friendship with Korea.

Flags, Hradcany Castle and Kremlin A254

Designs: 60h, Lomonosov University, Moscow. 1.20k, Lenin Ship Canal.

1953, Nov. 7

621	A254	30h dk gray	*2.00*	*1.10*
622	A254	60h dk brn	2.25	1.25
623	A254	1.20k ultra	3.25	2.00

Issued to publicize the month of Czechoslovak-Soviet friendship.

Emmy Destinn, Opera Singer A255 — National Theater, Prague A256

Portrait: 2k, Eduard Vojan, actor.

1953, Nov. 18 *Perf. 14*

624	A255	30h bl blk	1.00	45
625	A256	60h brown	35	6
626	A255	2k sepia	*3.00*	*3.00*

Issued to commemorate the 70th anniversary of the founding of the National Theater.

Josef Manes A257 — Vaclav Hollar A258

1953, Nov. 28 *Perf. 11x11½*

627	A257	60h brn car	50	10
628	A257	1.20k dp bl	*1.50*	*85*

Issued to honor Josef Manes, painter.

1953, Dec. 5

Portrait: 1.20k, Head framed, facing right.

629	A258	30h brn blk	25	10
630	A258	1.20k dk brn	*1.25*	*75*

Issued to honor Vaclav Hollar, artist and etcher.

Leo N. Tolstoi A259

1953, Dec. 29 Unwmkd.

631	A259	60h dk grn	50	15
632	A259	1k chocolate	*1.50*	*1.00*

Issued to commemorate the 125th anniversary of the birth of Leo N. Tolstoi.

Locomotive A260

Design: 1k, Plane loading mail.

Engraved, Center Photogravure.

1953, Dec. 29 *Perf. 11½x11*

633	A260	60h brn org & gray vio	50	10
634	A260	1k org brn & brt bl	*2.00*	*1.25*

Lenin A261

Lenin Museum, Prague A262

1954, Jan. 21 Engraved *Perf. 11½*

635	A261	30h dk brn	75	35
636	A262	1.40k chocolate	*1.50*	*1.40*

Issued to commemorate the 30th anniversary of the death of Lenin.

Klement Gottwald A263

Design: 2.40k, Revolutionist with flag.

Perf. 11x11½, 14x13½.

1954, Feb. 18

637	A263	60h dk brn	50	5
638	A263	2.40k rose lake	*4.50*	*2.00*

Issued to commemorate the 25th anniversary of the fifth congress of the Communist Party in Czechoslovakia.

Gottwald Mausoleum, Prague A264

Gottwald and Stalin A265

Design: 1.20k, Lenin & Stalin mausoleum, Moscow.

1954, Mar. 5 *Perf. 11½, 14x13½*

639	A264	30h ol brn	35	10
640	A265	60h dp ultra	50	15
641	A264	1.20k rose brn	*2.00*	*1.35*

Issued to commemorate the first anniversary of the deaths of Joseph V. Stalin and Klement Gottwald.

Two Runners A266 — Group of Hikers A267

Design: 1k, Woman swimmer.

1954, Apr. 24 *Perf. 11½*

642	A266	30h dk brn	2.50	1.00
643	A267	80h dk grn	*5.50*	*5.00*
644	A266	1k dk vio bl	3.00	1.00

Nurse A268

Designs: 15h, Construction worker. 40h, Postwoman. 45h, Ironworker. 50h, Soldier. 75h, Lathe operator. 80h, Textile worker. 1k, Farm woman. 1.20k, Scientist and microscope. 1.60k, Miner. 2k, Physician and baby. 2.40k, Engineer. 3k, Chemist.

Perf. 12½x12, 11½x11.

1954

645	A268	15h dk grn	15
646	A268	20h lt vio	20
647	A268	40h dk brn	30
648	A268	45h dk gray bl	25
649	A268	50h dk gray grn	40
650	A268	75h dp bl	35
651	A268	80h vio brn	40
652	A268	1k green	60
653	A268	1.20k dk vio bl	45
654	A268	1.60k brn blk	1.00
655	A268	2k org brn	1.25
656	A268	2.40k vio bl	1.10
657	A268	3k carmine	1.50
		Nos. 645-657 (13)	7.95

Antonin Dvorák A269 — Prokop Divis A270

Portraits: 40h, Leos Janacek. 60h, Bedrich Smetana.

1954, May 22 *Perf. 11x11½*

658	A269	30h vio brn	1.75	25
659	A269	40h brick red	2.25	25
660	A269	60h dk bl	1.35	25

Issued to publicize the "Year of Czech Music," 1954.

1954, June 15

661	A270	30h gray	20	15
662	A270	75h vio brn	*1.10*	*75*

Issued to commemorate the 200th anniversary of the invention of a lightning conductor by Prokop Divis.

Slovak Insurrectionist A271 — Anton P. Chekhov A272

Design: 1.20k, Partisan woman.

1954, Aug. 28 *Perf. 11½*

663	A271	30h brn org	15	8
664	A271	1.20k dk bl	*1.25*	*90*

Issued to commemorate the 10th anniversary of the Slovak national uprising.

1954, Sept. 24

665	A272	30h dl gray grn	15	6
666	A272	45h dl gray brn	*1.25*	*95*

Issued to commemorate the 50th anniversary of the death of Anton P. Chekhov, writer.

Soviet Representative Giving Agricultural Instruction A273

Designs: 60h, Soviet industrial instruction. 2k, Dancers (cultural collaboration).

1954, Nov. 6 *Perf. 11½x11*

667	A273	30h yel brn	15	5
668	A273	60h dk bl	45	10
669	A273	2k vermilion	*1.60*	*1.50*

Issued to publicize the month of Czechoslovak-Soviet friendship.

Jan Neruda
A274

Portraits: 60h, Janko Jesensky. 1.60k, Jiri Wolker.

1954, Nov. 25 ***Perf. 11x11½***

670	A274	30h dk bl	1.50	15
671	A274	60h dl red	*2.25*	*75*
672	A274	1.60k sepia	1.25	30

Issued to honor Czechoslovak poets.

View of Telc
A275

Views: 60h, Levoca. 3k, Ceske Budejovice.

Engraved and Photogravure

1954, Dec. 10

673	A275	30h blk & bis	50	8
674	A275	60h brn & bis	50	8
675	A275	3k blk & bis	*2.75*	*2.25*

Pres. Antonin Zapotocky
A276

Attacking Soldiers
A278

1954, Dec. 18 Engraved ***Perf. 11½***

676	A276	30h blk brn	50	20
677	A276	60h dk bl	40	20

Souvenir Sheet
Imperf.

678	A276	2k dp cl	7.00	4.00

No. 678 measures 65 x 99½ mm., with arms and quotation in dark blue on sheet margins.
Nos. 676-678 commemorate the 70th birthday of President Antonin Zapotocky.
See also Nos. 829-831

1954, Oct. 3 ***Perf. 11½***

Design: 2k, Soldier holding child.

679	A278	60h dk grn	50	5
680	A278	2k dk brn	*1.60*	*1.40*

Issued to publicize Army Day, October 6, 1954.

Woman Holding Torch
A279

Comenius University Building
A280

Design: 45h, Ski jumper.

1955, Jan. 20 **Engraved**

681	A279	30h red	3.00	35

Engraved and Photogravure.

682	A279	45h blk & bl	3.00	25

Issued to publicize the First National Spartacist Games, 1955.

1955, Jan. 28 Engraved ***Perf. 11½***

Design: 75h, Jan A. Komensky medal.

683	A280	60h dp grn	40	10
684	A280	75h chocolate	*1.00*	*75*

Issued to commemorate the 35th anniversary of the founding of Comenius University, Bratislava.

Czechoslovak Automobile—A281

Designs: 60h, Textile worker. 75h, Lathe operator.

1955, Mar. 15 **Unwmkd.**

685	A281	45h dl grn	90	75
686	A281	60h dk vio bl	35	5
687	A281	75h sepia	75	10

Woman Decorating Soviet Soldier
A282

Stalin Memorial, Prague
A283

Designs: 35h, Tankman with flowers. 60h, Children greeting soldier.

1955, May 5 Engraved ***Perf. 11½***

688	A282	30h blue	20	5
689	A282	35h dk brn	*90*	*60*
690	A282	60h cerise	55	6

Photogravure.

691	A283	60h sepia	55	8

Issued to commemorate the 10th anniversary of Czechoslovakia's liberation.

Music and Spring
A284

Foundry Worker
A285

Design: 1k, Woman with lyre.

Engraved and Photogravure

1955, May 12

692	A284	30h blk & pale bl	40	8
693	A284	1k blk & pale rose	*1.50*	*1.25*

Issued on the occasion of the International Music Festival, Prague, 1955.

1955, May 12 **Engraved**

Design: 45h, Farm workers.

694	A285	30h violet	20	5
695	A285	45h green	*90*	*75*

Issued to publicize the third congress of the Trade Union Revolutionary Movement.

Woman Athlete
A286

Jakub Arbes
A287

Designs: 60h, Dancing couple. 1.60k, Athlete.

1955, June 21

696	A286	20h vio bl	*75*	*60*
697	A286	60h green	40	10
698	A286	1.60k red	1.00	40

Issued to publicize the first National Spartacist Games, Prague, June-July, 1955.

1955

Portraits: 30h, Jan Stursa. 40h, Elena Marothy-Soltesova. 60h, Josef Vaclav Sladek. 75h, Alexander Stepanovic Popov. 1.40k, Jan Holly. 1.60k, Pavel Josef Safarik.

699	A287	20h brown	35	5
700	A287	30h black	35	5
701	A287	40h gray grn	75	10
702	A287	60h black	35	5
703	A287	75h claret	*1.75*	*1.00*
704	A287	1.40k blk, *cr*	75	25
705	A287	1.60k dk bl	75	15
		Nos. 699-705 (7)	*5.05*	*1.65*

Issued to commemorate various anniversaries of prominent Slavs.

Girl and Boy of Two Races
A288

Costume of Ocova, Slovakia
A289

1955, July 20

706	A288	60h vio bl	50	5

Issued to commemorate the fifth World Festival of Youth in Warsaw, July 31–August 14, 1955.

1955, July 25

Regional Costumes: 75h, Detva man, Slovakia. 1.60k, Chodsko man, Bohemia. 2k, Hana woman, Moravia.

Frame and Outlines in Brown

707	A289	60h org & rose	*12.50*	*7.50*
708	A289	75h org & lil	*4.50*	*3.00*
709	A289	1.60k bl & org	*9.00*	*7.50*
710	A289	2k yel & rose	*12.50*	*9.00*

Carp
A290

Designs: 30h, Beetle. 35h, Gray Partridge. 1.40k, Butterfly. 1.50k, Hare.

1955, Aug. 8 **Engr. & Photo.**

711	A290	20h sep & lt bl	1.00	10
712	A290	30h sep & pink	80	10
713	A290	35h sep & buff	70	15
714	A290	1.40k sep & cr	*3.50*	*2.75*
715	A290	1.50k sep & lt grn	1.40	35
		Nos. 711-715 (5)	*7.40*	*3.45*

Tabor
A291

Designs: 45h, Prachatice. 60h, Jindrichuv Hradec.

1955, Aug. 26 **Engraved**

716	A291	30h vio brn	25	5
717	A291	45h rose car	*95*	*75*
718	A291	60h sage grn	25	5

Issued to publicize the architectural beauty of the towns of Southern Bohemia.

Souvenir Sheet.

Various Views of Prague—A292

Perf. 14x13½

1955, Sept. 10 **Engraved**

719	A292	Sheet of five	40.00	40.00
	a.	30h gray blk	6.50	6.50
	b.	45h gray blk	6.50	6.50
	c.	60h rose lake	6.50	6.50
	d.	75h rose lake	6.50	6.50
	e.	1.60k gray blk	6.50	6.50

Issued to commemorate the International Philatelic Exhibition, Prague, Sept. 10–25, 1955. Size: 145x110mm.

Exists imperf., price $55.

Motorcyclists
A293

Workers, Soldier and Pioneer
A294

1955, Aug. 28

720	A293	60h vio brn	3.75	50

Issued to commemorate the 30th International Motorcycle Races at Gottwaldov, Sept. 13-18, 1955.

1955, Oct. 6 ***Perf. 11½*** **Unwmkd.**

Design: 60h, Tanks and planes.

721	A294	30h vio brn	20	5
722	A294	60h slate	*1.50*	*1.45*

Army Day, Oct. 6.

Hans Christian Andersen
A295

Portraits: 40h, Friedrich von Schiller. 60h, Adam Mickiewicz. 75h, Walt Whitman.

1955, Oct. 27

723	A295	30h brn red	20	10
724	A295	40h dk bl	*1.25*	*1.00*
725	A295	60h dp cl	30	8
726	A295	75h grnsh blk	40	15

Issued in honor of these four poets and to mark the 100th anniversary of the publication of Walt Whitman's "Leaves of Grass".

Railroad Bridge
A296

Designs: 30h, Train crossing bridge. 60h, Train approaching tunnel. 1.60k, Miners' housing project.

Inscribed: "Stavba Socialismu."

1955, Dec. 15

No.	Type	Value	Color	Unused	Used
727	A296	20h	dl grn	15	15
728	A296	30h	vio brn	15	6
729	A296	60h	slate	30	5
730	A296	1.60k	car rose	80	10

Issued to publicize socialist public works.

Hydroelectric Plant
A297

Jewelry
A298

Designs: 10h, Miner with drill. 25h, Building construction. 30h, Harvester. 60h, Metallurgical plant.

Inscribed:

"Druhy Petilety Plan 1956–1960."

1956, Feb. 20 ***Perf. 11½x11***

No.	Type	Value	Color	Unused	Used
731	A297	5h	vio brn	15	5
732	A297	10h	gray blk	20	5
733	A297	25h	dk car rose	45	5
734	A297	30h	green	20	5
735	A297	60h	vio bl	25	5
			Nos. 731-735 (5)	1.25	25

Second Five Year Plan.

1956, Mar. 17 ***Perf. 11x11½***

Designs: 45h, Glassware. 60h, Ceramics. 75h, Textiles.

No.	Type	Value	Color	Unused	Used
736	A298	30h	gray grn	50	6
737	A298	45h	dk bl	*5.50*	*2.75*
738	A298	60h	claret	35	6
739	A298	75h	gray	45	8

Products of Czechoslovakian industries.

Karlovy Vary (Karlsbad)
A299

"We Serve our People"
A300

Various Spas: 45h, Marianske Lazne (Marienbad). 75h, Piestany. 1.20k, Tatry Vysne Ruzbachy (Tatra Mountains).

1956, Mar. 17

No.	Type	Value	Color	Unused	Used
740	A299	30h	ol grn	1.25	25
741	A299	45h	brown	1.25	30
742	A299	75h	claret	*8.00*	*5.00*
743	A299	1.20k	ultra	75	20

Issued to publicize Czechoslovakian spas.

1956, Apr. 9 Photo. ***Perf. 11x11½***

Designs: 60h, Russian War Memorial, Berlin. 1(k), Tank crewman with standard.

No.	Type	Value	Color	Unused	Used
744	A300	30h	ol brn	20	5
745	A300	60h	car rose	25	5
746	A300	1k	ultra	*5.25*	*4.50*

Issued to publicize the exhibition: "The Construction and Defense of our Country," Prague, April,'56.

Cyclists
A301

Girl Basketball Players
A302

Athletes and Olympic Rings
A303

Engraved and Photogravure.

1956, Apr. 25 ***Perf. 11½*** **Unwmkd.**

No.	Type	Value	Color	Unused	Used
747	A301	30h	grn & lt bl	2.50	30
748	A302	45h	dk bl & car	1.50	30
749	A303	75h	brn & lem	1.50	30

Issued to publicize the following: Ninth International Peace Cycling Race, Warsaw-Berlin-Prague, May 1-15, 1956 (No. 747). Fifth European Womens' Basketball Championship (No. 748). Summer Olympics, Melbourne, Nov. 22-Dec. 8, 1956 (No. 749).

Mozart
A304

Home Guard
A305

Designs: 45h, Josef Myslivecek. 60h, Jiri Benda. 1k, Bertramka House, Prague. 1.40k, Xaver Dusek (1731–1799) and wife Josepha. 1.60k, Nostic Theater, Prague.

1956, May 12 **Engraved**

Design in Gray Black.

No.	Type	Value	Color	Unused	Used
750	A304	30h	bister	75	35
751	A304	45h	gray grn	*15.00*	*10.00*
752	A304	60h	pale rose lil	75	8
753	A304	1k	salmon	50	15
754	A304	1.40k	lt bl	1.50	50
755	A304	1.60k	lemon	75	10
			Nos. 750-755 (6)	*19.25*	*11.18*

Issued to commemorate the 200th anniversary of the birth of Wolfgang Amadeus Mozart and to publicize the International Music Festival in Prague.

1956, May 25

No.	Type	Value	Color	Unused	Used
756	A305	60h	vio bl	40	5

Issued to commemorate the first meeting of the Home Guard, Prague, May 25-27, 1956.

Josef Kajetan Tyl
A306

River Patrol
A307

Portraits: 20h, Ludovit Stur. 30h, Frana Sramek. 1.40k, Karel Havlicek Borovsky.

1956, June 23

No.	Type	Value	Color	Unused	Used
757	A306	20h	dl pur	50	15
758	A306	30h	blue	50	10
759	A306	60h	black	30	6
760	A306	1.40k	claret	*3.00*	*2.00*

Issued to honor various Czechoslovakian writers. See also Nos. 781–784, 873–876.

1956, July 8 ***Perf. 11x11½***

Design: 60h, Guard and dog.

No.	Type	Value	Color	Unused	Used
761	A307	30h	ultra	95	40
762	A307	60h	green	20	5

Issued to honor men of Frontier Guard.

Type of 1956 and

Steeplechase—A308

1956, Sept. 8 ***Perf. 11½*** **Unwmkd.**

No.	Type	Value	Color	Unused	Used
763	A308	60h	ind & bis	2.00	50
764	A308	80h	brn vio & vio	1.25	20
765	A303	1.20k	sl & org	1.00	30

Issued to publicize: Steeplechase, Pardubice, 1956 (No. 763). Marathon race, Kosice, 1956 (No. 764). Olympic Games, Melbourne, Nov. 22–Dec. 8 (No. 765).

Woman Gathering Grapes
A309

Fishermen—A310

Designs: 35h, Women gathering hops. 95h, Logging.

1956, Sept. 20 **Engraved**

No.	Type	Value	Color	Unused	Used
766	A309	30h	brn lake	30	5
767	A309	35h	gray grn	50	20
768	A310	80h	dk bl	35	15
769	A310	95h	chocolate	*2.00*	*2.00*

Issued to publicize natural resources.

Locomotive, 1846
A311

Locomotive, 1855
A312

Locomotives: 40h, 1945. 45h, 1952. 60h, 1955. 1k, 1954.

1956, Nov. 9 ***Perf. 11½*** **Unwmkd.**

No.	Type	Value	Color	Unused	Used
770	A311	10h	brown	2.00	8
771	A312	30h	gray	1.00	8
772	A312	40h	green	3.00	20
773	A312	45h	brn car	*14.00*	*10.00*
774	A312	60h	indigo	1.00	5
775	A312	1k	ultra	1.50	20
			Nos. 770-775 (6)	*22.50*	*10.61*

Issued to commemorate the European Timetable Conference at Prague, Nov. 9–13.

Costume of Moravia
A313

Regional Costumes (women): 1.20k, Blata, Bohemia. 1.40k, Cicmany, Slovakia. 1.60k, Novohradsko, Slovakia.

1956, Dec. 15 ***Perf. 13½***

No.	Type	Value	Color	Unused	Used
776	A313	30h	brn, ultra & car	2.00	75
777	A313	1.20k	brn, car & ultra	1.50	45
778	A313	1.40k	brn, ocher & ver	*7.00*	*2.50*
779	A313	1.60k	brn, car & grn	2.00	60

See also Nos. 832-835.

Zapotocky Type of 1953.

1956, Oct. 7 ***Perf. 12½*** **Unwmkd.**

No.	Type	Value	Color	Unused	Used
780	A251	30h	blue	30	8

Portrait Type of 1956.

1957, Jan. 18 Engraved ***Perf. 11½***

Portraits: 15h, Ivan Olbracht. 20h, Karel Toman. 30h, F. X. Salda. 1.60k, Terezia Vansova.

Cream Paper.

No.	Type	Value	Color	Unused	Used
781	A306	15h	dk red brn	45	8
782	A306	20h	dk grn	15	8
783	A306	30h	dk brn	15	8
784	A306	1.60k	dk bl	75	12

Issued in honor of Czechoslovakian writers.

Kolin Cathedral
A315

Views: No. 786, Banska Stiavnica. No. 787, Uherske Hradiste. No. 788, Karlstein. No. 789, Charles Bridge, Prague. 1.25k, Moravska Trebova.

1957, Feb. 23

No.	Type	Value	Color	Unused	Used
785	A315	30h	dk bl gray	20	10
786	A315	30h	rose vio	20	10
787	A315	60h	dp rose	40	5
788	A315	60h	gray grn	40	5
789	A315	60h	brown	40	5
790	A315	1.25k	gray	*1.75*	*1.50*
			Nos. 785-790 (6)	*3.35*	*1.85*

Issued to commemorate anniversaries of various towns and landmarks.

Komensky Mausoleum, Naarden
A316

Jan A. Komensky (Comenius) A317 — Farm Woman A318

Old Prints: 40h, Komensky teaching. 1k, Sun, moon, stars and earth.

***Perf. 11½x11, 14* (A317)**

1957, Mar. 28 Engraved Unwmkd.

791	A316	30h pale brn	35	10
792	A316	40h dk grn	35	10
793	A317	60h chocolate	*1.75*	*80*
794	A316	1k car rose	60	15

Issued to commemorate the 300th anniversary of the publication of "Didactica Opera Omnia" by J. A. Komensky (Comenius). No. 793 issued in sheets of four.

1957, Mar. 22 *Perf. 11½*

795	A318	30h lt bl grn	35	10

Issued to publicize the 3rd Congress of Agricultural Cooperatives.

Cyclists—A319

Woman Archer—A320

Boxers
A321

Rescue Team—A322

Perf. 11½x11, 11x11½

1957, Apr. 30

796	A319	30h sep & ultra	35	8
797	A319	60h dl grn & bis	*2.50*	*1.75*
798	A320	60h gray & emer	35	10
799	A321	60h sep & org	35	10
800	A322	60h vio & choc	35	5
		Nos. 796-800 (5)	*3.90*	*2.08*

Issued to publicize: 10th International Peace Cycling Race, Prague-Berlin-Warsaw (Nos. 796–797). International Archery Championships (No. 798). European Boxing Championships, Prague (No. 799). Mountain Climbing Rescue Service (No. 800).

Jan V. Stamic
A323

Musicians: No. 802, Ferdinand Laub. No. 803, Frantisek Ondricek. No. 804, Josef B. Foerster. No. 805, Vitezslav Novak. No. 806, Josef Suk.

1957, May 12 *Perf. 11½*

801	A323	60h purple	25	6
802	A323	60h black	25	6
803	A323	60h sl bl	25	6
804	A323	60h brown	25	6
805	A323	60h dl red brn	35	6
806	A323	60h bl grn	25	6
		Nos. 801-806 (6)	1.60	36

Spring Music Festival, Prague.

Josef Bozek A324 — School of Engineering A325

Portraits: 60h, F. J. Gerstner. 1k, R. Skuhersky.

1957, May 25

807	A324	30h bluish blk	20	6
808	A324	60h gray brn	35	8
809	A324	1k rose lake	40	15
810	A325	1.40k bl vio	75	15

Issued to commemorate the 250th anniversary of the School of Engineering in Prague.

Pioneer and Philatelic Symbols
A326

Design: 60h, Girl and carrier pigeon.

Engraved and Photogravure.

1957, June 8 *Perf. 11½*

811	A326	30h ol grn & org	60	10

Engraved *Perf. 13½*

812	A326	60h brn & vio bl	*1.75*	*1.60*

Youth Philatelic Exhibition, Pardubice.

"Grief" A327 — Motorcyclists A328

Design: 60h, Rose, symbol of new life.

1957, June 10

813	A327	30h black	25	5
814	A327	60h blk & rose red	*75*	*35*

Destruction of Lidice, 15th anniversary.

1957, July 5 *Perf. 11½*

815	A328	60h dk gray & bl	75	8

32nd International Motorcycle Race.

Karel Klic A329 — Josef Ressel A330

1957, July 5

816	A329	30h gray blk	15	5
817	A330	60h vio bl	25	5

Issued to honor Karel Klic, inventor of photogravure, and Josef Ressel, inventor of the ship screw.

Chamois
A331

Gentian
A332

Designs: 30h, Brown bear. 60h, Edelweiss. 1.25k, Tatra Mountains.

1957, Aug. 28 Engr. *Perf. 11½*

Inscribed: "Tatransky Narodny Park."

818	A331	20h emer & brnsh gray	60	35
819	A331	30h lt bl & brn	30	5
820	A332	40h gldn brn & vio bl	45	5
821	A332	60h yel & grn	35	5
822	A332	1.25k ol grn & bis	*2.50*	*2.00*
		Nos. 818-822 (5)	*4.20*	*2.50*

Issued to publicize the Tatra Mountains National Park. No. 822 measures 48x28½ mm.

"Marycka Magdonova" A333 — Man Holding Banner of Trade Union Congress A334

Engraved and Photogravure

1957, Sept. 15 *Perf. 11½* Unwmkd.

823	A333	60h blk & dl red	35	5

Issued to commemorate the 90th birthday of Petr Bezruc, poet and author of "Marycka Magdonova."

1957, Sept. 28 Engraved

824	A334	75h rose red	40	10

Issued to publicize the fourth International Trade Union Congress, Leipzig, Oct. 4–15.

Television Transmitter and Antennas
A335

Design: 60h, Family watching television.

1957, Oct. 19 Engraved *Perf. 11½*

825	A335	40h dk bl & car	15	5
826	A335	60h redsh brn & emer	25	5

Issued to publicize the television industry.

Worker, Globe and Lenin
A336

Design: 60h, Worker, factory, hammer and sickle.

1957, Nov. 7 *Perf. 12x11½*

827	A336	30h claret	15	6
828	A336	60h gray bl	25	8

Russian Revolution, 40th anniversary.

Zapotocky Type of 1954 dated: 19 XII 1884 - 13 XI 1957

1957, Nov. 18 *Perf. 11½* Unwmkd.

829	A276	30h black	15	5
830	A276	60h black	30	5

Souvenir Sheet

Imperf.

831	A276	2k black	1.50	1.00

Issued to commemorate the death of Pres. Antonin Zapotocky.

No. 831 measures 69x99½mm. Olive branch below stamp; no marginal inscription.

Costume Type of 1956.

Regional Costumes: 45h, Pilsen woman, Bohemia. 75h, Slovacko man, Moravia. 1.25k, Hana woman, Moravia. 1.95k, Teshinsko woman, Silesia.

1957, Dec. 18 Engraved *Perf. 13½*

832	A313	45h brn, bl & dk red	3.25	1.25
833	A313	75h dk brn, red & grn	2.75	1.10

No.	Type	Description	Unused	Used
834	A313	1.25k dk brn, scar & ocher	4.00	1.00
835	A313	1.95k sep, bl & ver	*5.00*	*2.25*

Radio Telescope and Observatory A337

Meteorological Station in High Tatra A338

Design: 75h, Sputnik 2 over Earth.

1957, Dec. 20 ***Perf. 11½***

No.	Type	Description	Unused	Used
836	A337	30h vio brn & yel	2.75	1.25
837	A338	45h sep & lt bl	75	45
838	A337	75h cl & bl	3.50	1.50

International Geophysical Year, 1957–58. No. 838 also commemorates the launching of Sputnik 2, Nov. 3, 1957.

Girl Skater A339

Litomysl Castle A340

Designs: 40h, Canoeing. 60h, Volleyball. 80h, Parachutist. 1.60k, Soccer.

1958, Jan. 25 Engr. ***Perf. 11½x12***

No.	Type	Description	Unused	Used
839	A339	30h rose vio	65	20
840	A339	40h blue	30	5
841	A339	60h redsh brn	35	5
842	A339	80h vio bl	*2.25*	*85*
843	A339	1.60k brt grn	70	12
		Nos. 839-843 (5)	*4.25*	*1.27*

Issued to publicize various sports championship events in 1958.

1958, Feb. 10 ***Perf. 11½***

Design: 60h, Bethlehem Chapel.

No.	Type	Description	Unused	Used
844	A340	30h green	10	5
845	A340	60h redsh brn	20	5

Issued to commemorate the 80th anniversary of the birth of Zdenek Nejedly, restorer of Bethlehem Chapel.

Giant Excavator A341

Jewelry A342

Peace Dove and: 60h, Soldiers, flame and banner (horiz.). 1.60k, Harvester and rainbow (horiz.).

1958, Feb. 25

No.	Type	Description	Unused	Used
846	A341	30h gray vio & yel	25	5
847	A341	60h gray brn & car	35	8
848	A341	1.60k grn & dl yel	90	15

Issued to commemorate the 10th anniversary of the "Victorious February."

Engraved and Photogravure

1958 ***Perf. 11½*** **Unwmkd.**

Designs: 45h, Dolls. 60h, Textiles. 75h, Kaplan turbine. 1.20k, Glass.

No.	Type	Description	Unused	Used
849	A342	30h rose car & bl	15	5
850	A342	45h rose red & pale lil	20	5
851	A342	60h vio & aqua	25	5
852	A342	75h ultra & sal	*2.25*	*75*
853	A342	1.20k bl grn & pink	60	10
		Nos. 849-853 (5)	*3.45*	*1.00*

Issued for the Universal and International Exposition at Brussels.

King George of Podebrad

A343

Design: 60h, View of Prague, 1628.

1958, May 19 **Engraved**

No.	Type	Description	Unused	Used
854	A343	30h car rose	20	6
855	A343	60h vio bl	30	6

Issued to publicize the National Archives Exhibition, Prague, May 15–Aug. 15.

"Towards the Stars" A344

Women of Three Races A345

Boy, Girl and Globes

A346

1958, May 26

No.	Type	Description	Unused	Used
856	A344	30h car rose	85	30
857	A345	45h rose vio	50	15
858	A346	60h blue	25	5

Issued to publicize the following: The Society for Dissemination of Political and Cultural Knowledge (No. 856). The 4th Congress of the International Democratic Women's Federation (No. 857). The First World Trade Union Conference of Working Youths, held in Prague, July 14–20 (No. 858).

Grain, Hammer and Sickle

A347

Atomic Reactor—A348

Design: 45h, Map of Czechoslovakia, hammer and sickle.

1958, May 26

No.	Type	Description	Unused	Used
859	A347	30h dl red	10	5
860	A347	45h green	15	5
861	A348	60h dk bl	25	8

Issued to commemorate the 11th Congress of the Czech Communist Party and the 15th anniversary of the Russo-Czechoslovakian Treaty.

Karlovy Vary—A349

Various Spas: 40h, Podebrady. 60h, Marianske Lazne. 80h, Luhacovice. 1.20k, Strbske Pleso. 1.60k, Trencianske Teplice.

1958, June 25

No.	Type	Description	Unused	Used
862	A349	30h rose cl	10	5
863	A349	40h redsh brn	15	5
864	A349	60h gray grn	20	5
865	A349	80h sepia	25	5
866	A349	1.20k vio bl	50	8
867	A349	1.60k lt vio	*2.00*	*1.25*
		Nos. 862-867 (6)	*3.20*	*1.53*

Telephone Operator A350

Pres. Antonin Novotny A351

Design: 45h, Radio transmitter.

1958, June 20

No.	Type	Description	Unused	Used
868	A350	30h blk & brn org	25	5
869	A350	45h blk & lt grn	45	12

Issued to commemorate the Conference of Postal Ministers of Communist Countries, Prague, June 30–July 9.

1958–59 ***Perf. 12½, 11½***

No.	Type	Description	Unused	Used
870	A351	30h brt vio bl	10	5
870A	A351	30h lt vio ('59)	30	5
871	A351	60h car rose	35	5

Redrawn.

Perf. 11½

No.	Type	Description	Unused	Used
871A	A351	60h rose red ('59)	25	5

On No. 871 the top of the "6" turns down; on No. 871A it is open.

Czechoslovak Pavilion, Brussels

A352

1958, July 15 Photo. & Engraved

No.	Type	Description	Unused	Used
872	A352	1.95k lt bl & bis brn	1.25	18

Issued to mark Czechoslovakia Week at the Universal and International Exhibition at Brussels.

Portrait Type of 1956.

Portraits: 30h, Julius Fucik. 45h, G. K. Zechenter 60h, Karel Capek. 1.40k, Svatopluk Cech.

1958, Aug. 20 Engr. ***Perf. 11½***

No.	Type	Description	Unused	Used
873	A306	30h rose red	10	5
874	A306	45h violet	*1.50*	*50*
875	A306	60h dk bl gray	18	5
876	A306	1.40k gray	40	15

Death anniversaries of four famous Czechs.

The Artist and the Muse

A353

1958, Aug. 20 ***Perf. 14***

No.	Type	Description	Unused	Used
877	A353	1.60k black	3.25	1.25

Issued to commemorate the 85th birthday of Max Svabinsky, artist and engraver.

Children's Hospital, Brno—A354

Designs: 60h, New Town Hall, Brno. 1k, St. Thomas Church. 1.60k, View of Brno.

1958, Sept. 6 ***Perf. 11½*** **Unwmkd.**

Size: 40x23mm.

No.	Type	Description	Unused	Used
878	A354	30h violet	15	6
879	A354	60h rose red	35	8
880	A354	1k brown	65	15

Perf. 14

Size: 50x28mm.

No.	Type	Description	Unused	Used
881	A354	1.60k dk sl grn	*2.75*	*2.50*

Issued to commemorate the National Philatelic Exhibition, Brno, Sept. 9, 1958.

No. 881 sold for 3.10k, including entrance ticket to exhibition. Issued in sheets of four.

Lepiota Procera A355

Children on Beach A356

1958, Oct. 6 ***Perf. 14***

Mushrooms: 40h, Boletus edulis. 60h, Krombholzia rufescens. 1.40k, Amanita muscaria L. 1.60k, Armillariella mellea.

No.	Type	Description	Unused	Used
882	A355	30h dk brn, grn & buff	30	20
883	A355	40h vio brn & brn org	30	20
884	A355	60h blk, red & buff	45	20
885	A355	1.40k brn, scar & grn	60	40
886	A355	1.60k blk, red brn & ol	*4.00*	*1.75*
		Nos. 882-886 (5)	*5.65*	*2.75*

1958, Oct. 24 *Perf. 14* Unwmkd.

Designs: 45h, Mother, child and bird. 60h, Skier.

887	A356	30h bl, yel & red	20	5
888	A356	45h ultra & car	35	6
889	A356	60h brn, bl & yel	50	15

Issued to commemorate the opening of UNESCO (U.N. Educational, Scientific and Cultural Organization) Headquarters in Paris, Nov. 3.

Bozek's Steam Car of 1815
A357

Designs: 45h, "Präsident" car of 1897. 60h, "Skoda" sports car. 80h, "Tatra" sedan. 1k, "Autocar Skoda" bus. 1.25k, Trucks.

Engraved and Photogravure.

1958, Dec. 1 *Perf. 11½x11*

890	A357	30h vio blk & buff	50	10
891	A357	45h ol & lt ol grn	35	10
892	A357	60h ol gray & sal	50	10
893	A357	80h cl & bl grn	45	15
894	A357	1k brn & lt yel grn	45	20
895	A357	1.25k grn & buff	*3.00*	*80*
		Nos. 890-895 (6)	*5.25*	*1.45*

Issued to honor the automobile industry.

Stamp of 1918 and Allegory
A358

1958, Dec. 18 Engr. *Perf. 11x11½*

896	A358	60h dk bl gray	35	8

Issued to commemorate the 40th anniversary of the first Czechoslovakian postage stamp.

Ice Hockey—A359

Sports: 30h, Girl throwing javelin. 60h, Ice hockey. 1k, Hurdling. 1.60k, Rowing. 2k, High jump.

1959, Feb. 14 *Perf. 11½x11*

897	A359	20h dk brn & gray	35	8
898	A359	30h red brn & org brn	35	8
899	A359	60h dk bl & pale grn	25	8
900	A359	1k mar & cit	50	10
901	A359	1.60k dl vio & lt bl	75	10
902	A359	2k red brn & lt bl	*2.50*	*1.25*
		Nos. 897-902 (6)	*4.70*	*1.69*

Congress Emblem
A360

"Equality of All Races"
A361

Design: 60h, Industrial and agricultural workers and emblem.

1959, Feb. 27 *Perf. 11½*

903	A360	30h mar & lt bl	15	5
904	A360	60h dk bl & yel	20	5

Issued to commemorate the 4th Agricultural Co-operative Congress in Prague.

1959, Mar. 23

Designs: 1k, "Peace." 2k, Mother and Child: "Freedom for Colonial People."

905	A361	60h gray grn	30	8
906	A361	1k gray	35	10
907	A361	2k dk gray bl	*2.25*	*75*

Issued to commemorate the 10th anniversary of the signing of the Universal Declaration of Human Rights.

Girl Holding Doll
A362

Frederic Joliot Curie
A363

Engraved and Photogravure.

Designs: 40h, Pioneer studying map. 60h, Pioneer with radio. 80h, Girl pioneer planting tree.

1959, Mar. 28

908	A362	30h vio bl & yel	15	5
909	A362	40h ind & ultra	20	5
910	A362	60h blk & lil	20	5
911	A362	80h brn & lt grn	40	15

10th anniversary of the Pioneer organization.

1959, Apr. 17 Engraved

912	A363	60h sepia	90	20

Issued to honor Frederic Joliot Curie and the 10th anniversary of the World Peace Movement.

"Reaching for the Moon"
A364

Town Hall Pilsen
A365

1959, Apr. 17

913	A364	30h vio bl	1.00	25

Issued to publicize the Second Congress of the Czechoslovak Association for the Propagation of Political and Cultural knowledge.

1959, May 2

Designs: 60h, Part of steam condenser turbine. 1k, St. Bartholomew's Church, Pilsen. 1.60k, Part of lathe.

914	A365	30h lt brn	10	5
915	A365	60h vio & lt grn	20	5
916	A365	1k vio bl	65	15
917	A365	1.60k blk & yel	*2.00*	*1.00*

Issued to publicize the 2nd Pilsen Stamp Exhibition in connection with the centenary of the Skoda (Lenin) armament works.

Factory and Emblem
A366

Design: 60h, Dam.

Inscribed: "IV Vseodborovy sjezd, 1959."

1959, May 13

918	A366	30h rose & yel	12	5
919	A366	60h ol gray & bl	25	6

4th Trade Union Congress.

Zvolen Castle—A367

1959, June 13

920	A367	60h gray ol & yel	35	8

Regional Stamp Exhibition, Zvolen, 1959.

Frantisek Benda
A368

Aurel Stodola
A369

Portraits: 30h, Vaclav Kliment Klicpera. 60h, Karel V. Rais. 80h, Antonin Slavicek. 1k, Peter Bezruc.

1959, June 22 *Perf. 11½x11*

921	A368	15h vio bl	5	5
922	A368	30h org brn	10	5
923	A369	40h dl grn	15	5
924	A369	60h dl red brn	25	6
925	A369	80h dl vio	35	8
926	A368	1k dk brn	60	8
		Nos. 921-926 (6)	1.50	37

View of the Fair Grounds
A370

Designs: 60h, Fair emblem and world map. 1.60k, Pavilion "Z."

Inscribed: "Mezinarodni Veletrh Brne 6.-20.IX. 1959."

Engraved and Photogravure.

1959, July 20 *Perf. 11½* Unwmkd.

927	A370	30h lil & yel	20	5
928	A370	60h dl bl	45	5
929	A370	1.60k dk bl & bis	75	15

International Fair at Brno, Sept. 6–20.

Revolutionist and Flag—A371

Slovakian Fighter
A372

Design: 1.60k, Linden leaves, sun and factory.

Engraved.

1959, Aug. 29 *Perf. 11½* Unwmkd.

930	A371	30h blk & rose	25	5
931	A372	60h car rose	50	5
932	A371	1.60k dk bl & yel	1.00	8

Issued to commemorate the 15th anniversary of the national Slovakian revolution and the 40th anniversary of the Slovakian Soviet Republic.

Alpine Marmots—A373

Animals: 40h, Bison. 60h, Lynx (vert.). 1k, Wolf. 1.60k, Red deer.

Engraved and Photogravure.

1959, Sept. 25

933	A373	30h blk & gray	30	5
934	A373	40h dk brn & bluish grn	45	8
935	A373	60h brn red & yel	35	5
936	A373	1k ol brn & bl	*2.50*	*95*
937	A373	1.60k red brn & pink	75	15
		Nos. 933-937 (5)	*4.35*	*1.28*

Issued to commemorate the 10th anniversary of the establishment of the Tatra National Park.

Lunik 2 Hitting Moon and Russian Flag—A374

1959, Sept. 23 *Perf. 11½*

938	A374	60h dk red & lt ultra	1.00	20

Issued to commemorate the landing of the Soviet rocket on the moon, Sept. 13, 1959.

Stamp Printing Works, Peking
A375

1959, Oct. 1

939	A375	30h pale grn & red	18	6

Issued to commemorate 10 years of Czechoslovakian - Chinese friendship.

Haydn

A376

Great Spotted Woodpecker

A377

Design: 3k, Charles Darwin.

1959, Oct. 16 Engr. *Perf. 11½*

940	A376	60h vio blk	35	5
941	A376	3k dk red brn	*1.50*	*85*

150th anniversary of death of Franz Joseph Haydn, Austrian composer, and 150th anniversary of birth of Charles Darwin, English naturalist.

1959, Nov. 16 *Perf. 14*

Birds: 30h, Blue tits. 40h, Nuthatch. 60th, Golden oriole. 80h, Goldfinch. 1k, Bullfinch. 1.20k, European kingfisher.

942	A377	20h multi	30	20
943	A377	30h multi	20	20
944	A377	40h multi	*3.25*	*1.50*
945	A377	60h multi	40	15
946	A377	80h multi	50	25
947	A377	1k multi	50	20
948	A377	1.20k multi	85	40
		Nos. 942-948 (7)	*6.00*	*2.90*

Nikola Tesla—A378

Designs: 30h, Alexander S. Popov. 35h, Edouard Branly. 60h, Guglielmo Marconi. 1k, Heinrich Hertz. 2k, Edwin Howard Armstrong and research tower, Alpine, N. J.

Engraved and Photogravure.

1959, Dec. 7 *Perf. 11½*

949	A378	25h blk & pink	*80*	*20*
950	A378	30h blk & org	20	5
951	A378	35h blk & lt vio	25	5
952	A378	60h blk & bl	30	5
953	A378	1k blk & lt grn	40	6
954	A378	2k blk & bis	*2.25*	*60*
		Nos. 949-954 (6)	*4.20*	*1.01*

Issued to honor inventors in the fields of telegraphy and radio.

Gymnast

A379

Designs: 60h, Skier. 1.60k, Handball players.

Engraved and Photogravure.

1960, Jan. 20 *Perf. 11½*

955	A379	30h sal pink & brn	40	15
956	A379	60h lt bl & blk	50	15
957	A379	1.60k bis & brn	1.10	20

2nd Winter Spartacist Games.

1960, June 15 Unwmkd.

Designs: 30h, Two girls in "Red Ball" drill. 60h, Gymnast with stick. 1k, Three girls with hoops.

958	A379	30h lt grn & rose cl	25	5
959	A379	60h pink & blk	50	10
960	A379	1k ocher & vio bl	75	15

Issued to commemorate the 2nd Summer Spartacist Games, Prague, June 23–July 3.

River Dredge Boat

A380

Ships: 60h, River tug. 1k, Tourist steamer. 1.20k, Cargo ship "Lidice."

1960, Feb. 22 *Perf. 11½*

961	A380	30h sl grn & sal	50	8
962	A380	60h mar & pale bl	40	8
963	A380	1k dk vio & yel	75	15
964	A380	1.20k lil & pale grn	*1.25*	*1.00*

Ice Hockey Players—A381

Design: 1.80k, Figure skaters.

1960, Feb. 27

965	A381	60h sep & lt bl	60	25
966	A381	1.80k blk & lt grn	*4.50*	*3.25*

Issued to commemorate the 8th Olympic Winter Games, Squaw Valley, Calif., Feb. 18-29, 1960.

1960, June 15 Unwmkd.

Designs: 1k, Running. 1.80k, Women's gymnastics. 2k, Rowing.

967	A381	1k blk & org	65	25
968	A381	1.80k blk & sal pink	1.25	40
969	A381	2k blk & bl	*3.00*	*1.50*

Issued to commemorate the 17th Olympic Games, Rome, Aug. 25–Sept. 11.

Trencin Castle

A382

Wmk. 341

Castles: 10h, Bezdez. 20h, Kost. 30h, Pernstein. 40h, Kremnica. 50h, Krivoklát castle. 60h, Karlstein. 1k, Smolenice. 1.60k, Kokorin.

1960–63 Engraved *Perf. 11½*

970	A382	5h gray vio	8	5
971	A382	10h black	8	5
972	A382	20h brn org	15	5
973	A382	30h green	20	5
974	A382	40h brown	20	5
974A	A382	50h blk ('63)	25	5
975	A382	60h rose red	35	5
976	A382	1k lilac	50	5
977	A382	1.60k dk bl	1.00	5
		Nos. 970-977 (9)	2.86	45

Wmkd. Striped Ovals (341)

1961, Oct.

977A	A382	30h green	2.00	70

Lenin

A383

Soldier Holding Child

A384

1960, Apr. 22 Unwmkd.

978	A383	60h gray ol	50	15

90th anniversary of the birth of Lenin.

1960, May 5

Designs: No. 980, Child eating pie. No. 981, Soldier helping concentration camp victim. No. 982, Welder and factory (horiz.). No. 983, Tractor driver and farm (horiz.).

Engraved and Photogravure

979	A384	30h mar & lt bl	20	5
980	A384	30h dl red	20	5
981	A384	30h grn & dl bl	20	5
982	A384	60h dk bl & buff	35	5
983	A384	60h redsh brn & yel grn	40	5
		Nos. 979-983 (5)	1.35	25

15th anniversary of liberation.

Steelworker—A385

Design: 60h, Farm woman and child.

1960, May 24

984	A385	30h mar & gray	12	5
985	A385	60h grn & pale bl	25	5

Issued to publicize the 1960 parliamentary elections.

Red Cross Nurse Holding Dove—A386

Fire Fighters

A387

1960, May 26 Unwmkd.

986	A386	30h brn car & bl	20	5
987	A387	60h dk bl & pink	35	5

Issued to commemorate the 3rd Congress of the Czechoslovakian Red Cross (No. 986), and the 2nd Fire Fighters' Congress (No. 987).

Hand of Philatelist with Tongs and Two Stamps

A388

Design: 1k, Globe and 1937 Bratislava stamp (shown in miniature on 60h).

Engraved and Photogravure

1960, July 11 *Perf. 11½*

988	A388	60h blk & dl yel	35	5
989	A388	1k blk & bl	65	8

Issued to publicize the National Stamp Exhibition, Bratislava, Sept. 24–Oct. 9.

See Nos. C49–C50.

Stalin Mine, Ostrava-Hermanovice

A390

Viktorin Cornelius, Lawyer

A391

Designs: 20h, Power station, Hodonin. 30h, Gottwald iron works, Kuncice. 40h, Harvester. 60h, Oil refinery.

1960, July 25

992	A390	10h blk & pale grn	10	5
993	A390	20h mar & lt bl	15	5
994	A390	30h ind & pink	15	5
995	A390	40h grn & pale lil	25	5
996	A390	60h dk bl & yel	35	5
		Nos. 992-996 (5)	1.00	25

Issued to publicize the new five-year plan.

1960, Aug. 23 Engraved

Portraits: 20h, Karel Matej Capek-Chod, writer. 30h, Hana Kvapilova, actress. 40h, Oskar Nedbal, composer. 60h, Otakar Ostrcil, composer.

997	A391	10h black	15	5
998	A391	20h red brn	20	5
999	A391	30h rose red	25	5
1000	A391	40h dl grn	35	5
1001	A391	60h gray vio	45	8
		Nos. 997-1001 (5)	1.40	28

See also Nos. 1037–41.

Skoda Sports Plane Flying Upside Down

A392

1960, Aug. 28 Engr. & Photo.

1002	A392	60h vio bl & bl	75	10

Issued to commemorate the first aerobatic world championships, Bratislava.

Constitution and "Czechoslovakia"

A393

1960, Sept. 18

1003	A393	30h vio bl & pink	15	5

Issued to commemorate the proclamation of the new socialist constitution.

Workers Reading Newspaper
A394

Man Holding Newspaper
A395

1960, Sept. 18

1004	A394	30h sl & ver	12	6
1005	A395	60h blk & rose	24	6

Issued for the Day of the Czechoslovak Press, Sept. 21, 1960, and to commemorate the 40th anniversary of the Rudé Právo paper.

Globes and Laurel—A396

1960, Sept. 18 **Engraved**

1006	A396	30h dk bl & bis	15	5

Issued to commemorate the 15th anniversary of the World Federation of Trade Unions.

Black-crowned Night Heron
A397

Doronicum Clusii (Thistle)
A398

Birds: 30h, Great crested grebe. 40h, Lapwing. 60h, Gray heron. 1k, Graylag goose (horiz.). 1.60k, Mallard (horiz.).

Engraved and Photogravure

1960, Oct. 24 ***Perf. 11½*** **Unwmkd.**

Designs in Black

1007	A397	25h pale vio bl	20	5
1008	A397	30h pale cit	40	6
1009	A397	40h pale bl	25	6
1010	A397	60h pink	40	10
1011	A397	1k pale yel	50	20
1012	A397	1.60k lt vio	*3.25*	*1.10*
		Nos. 1007-1012 (6)	*5.00*	*1.57*

1960, Nov. 21 **Engraved** ***Perf. 14***

Flowers: 30h, Cyclamen. 40h, Primrose. 60h, Hen-and-chickens. 1k, Gentian. 2k, Pasqueflower.

1013	A398	20h blk, yel & grn	9	5
1014	A398	30h blk, car rose & grn	15	5
1015	A398	40h blk, yel & grn	20	5
1016	A398	60h blk, pink & grn	25	5
1017	A398	1k blk, bl, vio & grn	45	20
1018	A398	2k blk, lil, yel & grn	*3.00*	*1.25*
		Nos. 1013-1018 (6)	*4.14*	*1.65*

Alfons Mucha
A399

1960, Dec. 18 **Engr.** ***Perf. 11½x12***

1019	A399	60h dk bl gray	30	5

Issued for the Day of the Czechoslovak Postage Stamp and to commemorate the centenary of the birth of Alfons Mucha, designer of the first Czechoslovakian stamp (Type A1).

Rolling-mill Control Bridge
A400

Athletes with Flags
A401

Designs: 30h, Turbo generator. 60h, Ditch-digging machine.

1961, Jan. 20 ***Perf. 11½*** **Unwmkd.**

1020	A400	20h blue	20	5
1021	A400	30h rose	25	5
1022	A400	60h brt grn	40	5

Third Five-Year Plan.

Perf. 11x11½, 11½x11

1961, Feb. 20 **Engr. & Photo.**

Designs: No. 1024, Motorcycle race (horiz.). 40h, Sculling (horiz.). 60h, Ice skater. 1k, Rugby. 1.20k, Soccer. 1.60k, Long-distance runners.

1023	A401	30h rose red & bl	15	5
1024	A401	30h dk bl & car	15	5
1025	A401	40h dk gray & car	40	5
1026	A401	60h lil & bl	35	5
1027	A401	1k ultra & yel	45	10
1028	A401	1.20k grn & buff	65	20
1029	A401	1.60k sep & sal	*2.00*	*1.00*
		Nos. 1023-1029 (7)	*4.15*	*1.50*

Various sports events.

Exhibition Emblem
A402

Rocket Launching
A403

1961, Mar. 6 **Engraved** ***Perf. 11½***

1030	A402	2k dk bl & red	2.50	8

Issued to publicize the "Praga 1962" International Stamp Exhibition, Prague, Sept. 1962.

1961, Mar. 6 **Engr. & Photo.**

Designs: 30h, Sputnik III (horiz.). 40h, As 20h, but inscribed "Start Kosmicke Rakety k Venusi—12.II.1961". 60h, Sputnik I (horiz.). 1.60k, Interplanetary station (horiz.). 2k, Similar to type A404, without commemorative inscription.

1031	A403	20h vio & pink	40	5
1032	A403	30h dk grn & buff	15	5
1033	A403	40h dk red & yel grn	20	5
1034	A403	60h vio & buff	40	5
1035	A403	1.60k dk bl & pale grn	95	20
1036	A403	2k mar & pale bl	*2.50*	*1.35*
		Nos. 1031-1036 (6)	*4.60*	*1.75*

Issued to publicize Soviet space research.

Portrait Type of 1960

Portraits: No. 1037, Jindrich Mosna. No. 1038, Pavol Orszagh Hviezdoslav. No. 1039, Alois Mrstik. No. 1040, Joza Uprka. No. 1041, Josef Hora.

1961, March 27 ***Perf. 11½***

1037	A391	60h green	30	5
1038	A391	60h dk bl	30	5
a.		"ORSZACH" instead of "ORSZAGH"	75	30
1039	A391	60h dl cl	30	5
1040	A391	60h gray	30	5
1041	A391	60h sepia	30	5
		Nos. 1037-1041 (5)	1.50	25

Man Flying into Space
A404

1961, Apr. 13 **Engraved and Photo.**

1042	A404	60h car & pale bl	50	5
1043	A404	3k ultra & yel	*2.50*	*80*

Issued to commemorate the first man in space, Yuri A. Gagarin, Apr. 12, 1961. See also No. 1036.

Flute Player
A405

Blast Furnace and Mine, Kladno
A406

Designs: No. 1045, Dancer. 60h, Lyre player.

1961, Apr. 24 **Engraved**

1044	A405	30h brn blk	35	5
1045	A405	30h brn red	35	5
1046	A405	60h vio bl	35	8

Issued to commemorate the 150th anniversary of the Prague Conservatory of Music.

1961, Apr. 24

1047	A406	3k dl red	1.50	5

Marching Workers
A407

Woman with Hammer and Sickle
A408

Klement Gottwald Museum
A409

Designs: No. 1050, Lenin Museum. No. 1051, Crowd with flags. No. 1053, Man saluting Red Star.

1961, May 10

1048	A407	30h dl vio	10	5
1049	A409	30h dk bl	10	5
1050	A409	30h redsh brn	10	5
1051	A407	60h vermilion	30	8
1052	A408	60h dk grn	30	8
1053	A408	60h carmine	30	8
		Nos. 1048-1053 (6)	1.20	39

Czech Communist Party, 40th anniversary.

Puppet
A410

Designs: Various Puppets.

Engraved and Photogravure

1961, June 20 ***Perf. 11½*** **Unwmkd.**

1054	A410	30h ver & yel	15	5
1055	A410	40h sep & bluish grn	15	5
1056	A410	60h vio bl & sal	25	5
1057	A410	1k grn & lt bl	40	6
1058	A410	1.60k mar & pale vio	*1.75*	*45*
		Nos. 1054-1058 (5)	*2.70*	*66*

Woman, Map of Africa and Flag of Czechoslovakia
A411

1961, June 26

1059	A411	60h red & bl	35	8

Issued to publicize the friendship between the people of Africa and Czechoslovakia.

Map of Europe and Fair Emblem
A412

Designs (Fair emblem and): 60h Horizontal boring machine (vert.). 1k, Scientists' meeting and nuclear physics emblem.

Engraved and Photogravure

1961, Aug. 14 *Perf. 11½*

1060	A412	30h dk bl & pale grn	15	6
1061	A412	60h grn & pink	25	5
1062	A412	1k vio brn & lt bl	50	8

Issued to publicize the International Trade Fair, Brno, Sept. 10–24.

Sugar Beet, Cup of Coffee and Bags of Sugar
A413

Charles Bridge, St. Nicholas Church and Hradcany
A414

Designs: 30h, Clover. 40h, Wheat. 60h, Hops. 1.40k, Corn. 2k, Potatoes.

1961, Sept. 18 *Perf. 11½* **Unwmkd.**

1063	A413	20h sl & lil	8	5
1064	A413	30h pale cl & bis	10	5
1065	A413	40h brn & org	15	5
1066	A413	60h sl grn & bis	20	5
1067	A413	1.40k brn & fawn	45	6
1068	A413	2k dl vio & bl	*2.50*	*75*
		Nos. 1063-1068 (6)	*3.48*	*1.01*

1961, Sept. 25

1069	A414	60h vio bl & car	1.25	10

Issued to commemorate the 26th session of the Governor's Council of the Red Cross Societies League, Prague.

Orlik Dam and Kaplan Turbine
A415

Designs: 30h, View of Prague, flags and stamps. 40h, Hluboká Castle, river and fish. 60h, Karlovy Vary and cup. 1k, Pilsen and beer bottle. 1.20k, North Bohemia landscape and vase. 1.60k, Tatra mountains, boots, ice pick and rope. 2k, Ironworks, Ostrava Kuncice and pulley. 3k, Brno and ball bearing. 4k, Bratislava and grapes. 5k, Prague and flags.

Engraved and Photogravure

1961 *Perf. 11½* **Unwmkd.**

Size: 41x23mm.

1070	A415	20h gray & bl	*50*	*45*
1071	A415	30h vio bl & red	35	25
1072	A415	40h dk bl & lt grn	*65*	*50*
1073	A415	60h dk bl & yel	*45*	*40*
1074	A415	1k mar & grn	1.00	75
1075	A415	1.20k grn & pink	*1.10*	*75*
1076	A415	1.60k brn & vio bl	1.50	75
1077	A415	2k blk & ocher	2.25	1.75
1078	A415	3k ultra & yel	*2.25*	*2.00*
1079	A415	4k pur & sal	*3.50*	*3.25*

Engraved
Perf. 13½
Size: 50x29mm.

1080	A415	5k multi	*30.00*	*25.00*
		Nos. 1070-1080 (11)	*43.55*	*35.85*

Issued to publicize the "PRAGA 1962 World Exhibition of Postage Stamps," Aug. 18–Sept. 2, 1962. No. 1080 was printed in sheet of four with marginal inscription.

Globe
A416

Engraved and Photogravure

1961, Nov. 27 *Perf. 11½*

1081	A416	60h red & ultra	50	10

Issued to publicize the Fifth World Congress of Trade Unions, Moscow, Dec. 4–16.

Orange Tip Butterfly
A417

Bicyclists
A418

Designs (butterflies): 20h, Zerynthia hypsipyle Sch. 30h, Apollo. 40h, Swallowtail. 60h, Peacock. 80h, Mourning cloak (Camberwell beauty). 1k, Underwing (moth). 1.60k, Red admiral. 2k, Brimstone (sulphur).

1961, Nov. 27 **Engraved**

Brown Frame and Inscriptions

1082	A417	15h bl, org & yel	10	6
1083	A417	20h bl, yel & red	10	10
1084	A417	30h bl, car & grn	15	10
1085	A417	40h bl, ocher & car	30	10
1086	A417	60h bl, red brn & yel	40	12
1087	A417	80h bl, yel, brn & grn	60	25
1088	A417	1k pale brn, pink & bl	70	35
1089	A417	1.60k multi	90	55
1090	A417	2k bl, yel & red	*5.00*	*2.25*
		Nos. 1082-1090 (9)	*8.25*	*3.88*

Printed in sheets of ten.

Engraved and Photogravure

1962, Feb. 5 *Perf. 11½* **Unwmkd.**

Sports: 40h, Woman gymnast. 60h, Figure skaters. 1k, Woman bowler. 1.20k, Goalkeeper, soccer. 1.60k, Discus thrower.

1091	A418	30h blk & vio bl	10	5
1092	A418	40h blk & yel	15	5
1093	A418	60h sl & grnsh bl	20	5
1094	A418	1k blk & pink	50	8
1095	A428	1.20k blk & grn	60	15
1096	A418	1.60k blk & dl grn	*2.00*	*1.00*
		Nos. 1091-1096 (6)	*3.55*	*1.38*

Various 1962 sports events.
No. 1095 does not have the commemorative inscription.

Karel Kovarovic
A419

Frantisek Zaviska and Karel Petr
A420

Designs: 20h, Frantisek Skroup. 30h, Bozena Nemcova. 60h, View of Prague and staff of Aesculapius. 1.60k, Ladislav Celakovsky. 1.80k, Miloslav Valouch and Juraj Hronec.

1962, Feb. 26 **Engraved**

1097	A419	10h red brn	5	5
1098	A419	20h vio bl	8	5
1099	A419	30h brown	12	5
1100	A420	40h claret	15	10
1101	A419	60h black	25	6
1102	A419	1.60k sl grn	60	6
1103	A420	1.80k dk bl	65	15
		Nos. 1097-1103 (7)	1.90	52

Various cultural personalities and events.

Miner and Flag—A421

1962, Mar. 19 **Engr. & Photo.**

1104	A421	60h ind & rose	35	8

Issued to commemorate the 30th anniversary of the miners' strike at Most.

"Man Conquering Space"
A422

Soviet Spaceship Vostok 2—A423

Designs: 40h, Launching of Soviet space rocket. 80h, Multi-stage automatic rocket. 1k, Automatic station on moon. 1.60k, Television satellite.

1962, Mar. 26 **Engr. & Photo.**

1105	A422	30h dk red & lt bl	30	5
1106	A422	40h dk bl & sal	30	5
1107	A423	60h dk bl & pink	35	
1108	A423	80h rose vio & lt grn	50	1
1109	A422	1k ind & cit	50	1
1110	A423	1.60k grn & buff	*3.00*	*1.2*
		Nos. 1105-1110 (6)	*4.95*	*1.6*

Issued to publicize space research.

Polar Bear
A424

Zoo Animals: 30h, Chimpanzee. 60h, Camel. 1k, African and Indian elephants (horiz.). 1.40k, Leopard (horiz.). 1.60k, Przewalski horse (horiz.).

1962, Apr. 24 *Perf. 11½* **Unwmkd.**

Design and Inscriptions in Black

1111	A424	20h grnsh bl	8	5
1112	A424	30h violet	10	5
1113	A424	60h orange	25	8
1114	A424	1k green	45	10
1115	A424	1.40k car rose	70	25
1116	A424	1.60k lt brn	*2.75*	*1.25*
		Nos. 1111-1116 (6)	*4.33*	*1.78*

Child and Grieving Mother
A425

Klary's Fountain, Teplice
A426

Design: 60h, Flowers growing from ruins of Ležáky.

1962, June 9 **Engr. and Photo.**

1118	A425	30h blk & red	20	5
1119	A425	60h blk & dl bl	50	5

Issued to commemorate the 20th anniversary of the destruction of Lidice and Ležáky by the Nazis.

1962, June 9

1120	A426	60h dl grn & yel	50	8

Issued to commemorate the 1,200th anniversary of the discovery of the medicinal springs of Teplice.

Malaria Eradication Emblem, Cross and Dove
A427

Soccer Goalkeeper
A428

Design: 3k, Dove and malaria eradication emblem.

1962, June 18 **Engr. & Photo.**

1121	A427	60h blk & crim	30	8
1122	A427	3k dk bl & yel	*2.50*	*80*

Issued for the World Health Organization drive to eradicate malaria.

1962, June 20 ***Perf. 11½*** **Unwmkd.**

1123	A428	1.60k grn & yel	1.25	18

Issued to commemorate Czechoslovakia's participation in the World Cup Soccer Championship, Chile, May 30–June 17. See No. 1095.

Soldier in Swimming Relay Race
A429

"Agriculture"
A430

1962, July 20

Designs: 40h, Soldier hurdling. 60h, Soccer player. 1k, Soldier with rifle in relay race.

1124	A429	30h grn & lt ultra	10	5
1125	A429	40h dk pur & yel	12	5
1126	A429	60h brn & grn	25	5
1127	A429	1k dk bl & sal pink	60	15

Issued to publicize the 2nd Summer Spartacist Games of Friendly Armies, Prague, September, 1962.

1962 **Engraved** ***Perf. 13½***

Designs: 60h, Astronaut in capsule. 80h, Boy with flute (horiz.). 1k, Workers of three races (horiz.). 1.40k, Children dancing around tree. 1.60k, Flying bird (horiz.). 5k, View of Prague (horiz.).

1128	A430	30h multi	1.75	1.25
1129	A430	60h multi	90	90
a.		Miniature sheet of 8	*15.00*	*15.00*
1130	A430	80h multi	2.00	1.50
1131	A430	1k multi	3.50	2.75
1132	A430	1.40k multi	4.25	3.75
1133	A430	1.60k multi	*7.00*	*4.00*
		Nos. 1128-1133 (6)	*19.40*	*14.15*

Souvenir Sheet

1134	A430	5k multi	*17.50*	*17.50*
a.		Imperf.	*70.00*	*70.00*

Issued to commemorate the "PRAGA 1962 World Exhibition of Postage Stamps," Aug. 18–Sept. 2, 1962. No. 1133 also commemorates FIP Day, Sept. 1 (Federation Internationale de Philatelie.) Printed in sheets of 10.

No. 1129a contains four stamps each of Nos. 1128–29 and two labels arranged in two rows of two se-tenant pairs of Nos. 1128–29 with a label between. Size: 170x107mm. Sold for 5k, only with ticket.

No. 1134 contains one large stamp (51x 30mm). Black marginal inscription. Size of sheet: 95x74mm. Sold only with ticket.

Children in Day Nursery and Factory
A431

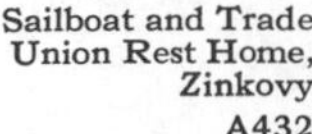

Sailboat and Trade Union Rest Home, Zinkovy
A432

Engraved and Photogravure

1962, Oct. 29 ***Perf. 11½*** **Unwmkd.**

1135	A431	30h blk & lt bl	12	5
1136	A432	60h brn & yel	25	5

Cruiser "Aurora"
A433

1962, Nov. 7

1137	A433	30h blk & gray bl	12	5
1138	A433	60h blk & pink	22	5

Issued to commemorate the 45th anniversary of the Russian October revolution.

Cosmonaut and Worker
A434

Lenin
A435

1962, Nov. 7

1139	A434	30h dk red & bl	12	5
1140	A435	60h blk & dp rose	22	5

40th anniversary of the U.S.S.R.

Symbolic Crane—A436

Designs: 40h, Agricultural products (vert.). 60h, Factories.

1962, Dec. 4

1141	A436	30h dk red & yel	10	5
1142	A436	40h gray bl & yel	20	5
1143	A436	60h blk & dp rose	45	15

Issued to commemorate the 12th Congress of the Communist Party of Czechoslovakia.

Ground Beetle
A437

Table Tennis
A438

Beetles: 30h, Cardinal beetle. 60h, Stag beetle (vert.). 1k, Great water beetle. 1.60k, Alpine longicorn (vert.). 2k, Ground beetle (vert.).

1962, Dec. 15 **Engraved** ***Perf. 14***

1144	A437	20h multi	15	5
1145	A437	30h multi	15	5
1146	A437	60h multi	25	8
1147	A437	1k multi	40	20
1148	A437	1.60k multi	1.50	50
1149	A437	2k multi	*4.25*	*1.75*
		Nos. 1144-1149 (6)	*6.70*	*2.63*

Engraved and Photogravure

1963, Jan. ***Perf. 11½***

Sports: 60h, Bicyclist. 80h, Skier. 1k, Motorcyclist. 1.20k, Weight lifter. 1.60k, Hurdler.

1150	A438	30h blk & dp grn	20	5
1151	A438	60h blk & org	25	5
1152	A438	80h blk & ultra	35	10
1153	A438	1k blk & vio	45	25
1154	A438	1.20k blk & pale brn	75	45
1155	A438	1.60k blk & car	1.25	45
		Nos. 1150-1155 (6)	3.25	1.35

Various 1963 sports events.

Industrial Plant, Laurel and Star
A439

Symbol of Child Welfare Home
A440

Industrial Plant and Symbol of Growth
A441

1963, Feb. 25 ***Perf. 11½*** **Unwmkd.**

1156	A439	30h car & lt bl	10	5
1157	A440	60h blk & car	25	5
1158	A441	60h blk & red	25	5

Issued to commemorate the 15th anniversary of the "Victorious February" and to publicize the 5th Trade Union Congress.

Artists' Guild Emblem
A442

Juraj Jánosik
A443

Eduard Urx
A444

National Theater, Prague
A445

Designs: No. 1163, Woman reading to children. No. 1164, Juraj Pálkovic. 1.60k, Max Svabinsky.

Engr. & Photo.; Engr. (A444)

1963, Mar. 25 ***Perf. 11½*** **Unwmkd.**

1159	A442	20h blk & Prus bl	5	5
1160	A443	30h car & lt bl	10	5
1161	A444	30h carmine	10	5
1162	A445	60h dl red brn & lt bl	20	5
1163	A444	60h green	20	5
1164	A444	60h black	35	5
1165	A444	1.60k brown	75	10
		Nos. 1159-1165 (7)	1.75	40

Various cultural personalities and events.

Boy and Girl with Flag
A446

Television Transmitter
A447

Engraved and Photogravure

1963, Apr. 18 ***Perf. 11½***

1166	A446	30h sl & rose red	25	6

The 4th Congress of Czechoslovak Youth.

1963, Apr. 25

Design: 40h, Television camera, mast and set (horiz.).

1167	A447	40h buff & sl	15	5
1168	A447	60h dk red & lt bl	35	5

Czechoslovak television, 10th anniversary.

Rocket to the Sun
A448

Designs: 50h, Rockets and Sputniks leaving Earth. 60h, Spacecraft to and from Moon. 1k, 3k, Interplanetary station and Mars 1. 1.60k, Atomic rocket and Jupiter. 2k, Rocket returning from Saturn.

1963, Apr. 25

1169	A448	30h red brn & buff	15	5
1170	A448	50h sl & bluish grn	20	10
1171	A448	60h dk grn & yel	30	5
1172	A448	1k dk gray & sal	50	15
1173	A448	1.60k gray brn & lt grn	80	25
1174	A448	2k dk pur & yel	*2.75*	*1.00*
		Nos. 1169-1174 (6)	*4.70*	*1.60*

Souvenir Sheet

Imperf.

1175	A448	3k Prus grn & org red	*4.50*	*4.50*

No. 1175 issued to commemorate the first Space Research Exhibition, Prague, Apr., 1963. Prussian green and red orange marginal inscription and design. Size: 85x70 mm.

Studio and Radio
A449

Design: 1k, Globe inscribed "Peace" and aerial mast (vert.).

Engraved and Photogravure

1963, May 18 ***Perf. 11½*** **Unwmkd.**

1176	A449	30h choc & pale grn	15	5
1177	A449	1k bluish grn & lil	35	5

40th anniversary of Czechoslovak radio.

Tupolev Tu-104B Turbojet
A450

Design: 1.80k, Ilyushin Il-18 Moskva.

1963, May 25

1178	A450	80h	vio & lt bl	35	6
1179	A450	1.80k	dk bl & lt grn	1.00	6

40th anniversary of Czechoslovak airlines.

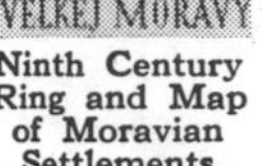

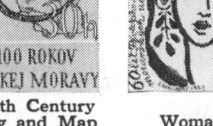

Ninth Century Ring and Map of Moravian Settlements
A451

Woman Singing
A452

Design: 1.60k, Falconer, 9th century silver disk.

1963, May 25

1180	A451	30h	lt grn & blk	15	5
1181	A451	1.60k	dl yel & blk	60	5

1100th anniversary of Moravian empire.

1963, May 25 **Engraved**

1182	A452	30h	brt red	45	5

Issued to commemorate the 60th anniversary of the founding of the Moravian Teachers' Singing Club.

Kromeriz Castle and Barley
A453

Centenary Emblem, Nurse and Playing Child
A454

Engraved and Photogravure

1963, June 20 *Perf. 11½* Unwmkd.

1183	A453	30h	sl grn & yel	45	6

Issued to publicize the National Agricultural Exhibition and to commemorate the 700th anniversary of Kromeriz.

1963, June 20

1184	A454	30h	dk gray & car	45	5

Centenary of the International Red Cross.

Bee, Honeycomb and Emblem
A455

Liberec Fair Emblem
A456

1963, June 20

1185	A455	1k	brn & yel	55	5

Issued to publicize the 19th International Beekeepers Congress, Apimondia, 1963.

1963, July 13

1186	A456	30h	blk & dp rose	45	5

Liberec Consumer Goods Fair.

Town Hall, Brno
A457

Cave, Moravian Karst
A458

1963, July 29

Design: 60h, Town Hall tower, Brno.

1187	A457	30h	lt bl & mar	10	5
1188	A457	60h	pink & dk bl	30	5

International Trade Fair, Brno.

1963, July 29

Designs: No. 1190, Trout, Hornad Valley. 60h, Great Hawk Gorge. 80h, Macocha mountains.

1189	A458	30h	brn & lt bl	35	5
1190	A458	30h	dk bl & dl grn	40	5
1191	A458	60h	grn & bl	35	5
1192	A458	80h	sep & pink	35	10

Blast Furnace
A459

Engraved and Photogravure

1963, Aug. 15 *Perf. 11½* Unwmkd.

1193	A459	60h	blk & bluish grn	35	5

Issued to publicize the 30th International Congress of Iron Founders, Prague.

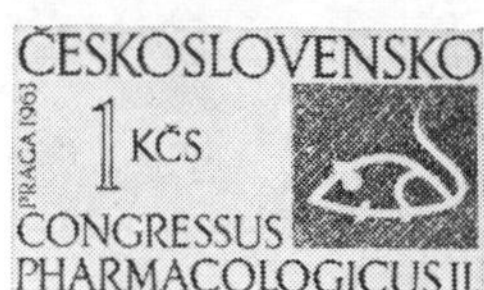

White Mouse—A460

1963, Aug. 15

1194	A460	1k	blk & car	45	5

Issued to publicize the second International Pharmacological Congress, Prague.

Farm Machinery for Underfed Nations
A461

Wooden Toys
A462

1963, Aug. 15 **Engraved**

1195	A461	1.60k	black	75	8

Issued for the "Freedom from Hunger" campaign of the U.N. Food and Agriculture Organization.

1963, Sept. 2 Engraved *Perf. 13½*

Folk Art (Inscribed "UNESCO"): 80h, Cock and flowers. 1k, Flowers in vase. 1.20k, Janosik, Slovak hero. 1.60k, Stag. 2k, Postilion.

1196	A462	60h	red & vio bl	20	10
1197	A462	80h	multi	30	15
1198	A462	1k	multi	40	20
1199	A462	1.20k	multi	50	20
1200	A462	1.60k	multi	60	30
1201	A462	2k	multi	*4.00*	*1.25*
			Nos. 1196-1201 (6)	*6.00*	*2.20*

Sheets of 10.

Canoeing
A463

Tree and Star
A464

Sports: 40h, Volleyball. 60h, Wrestling. 80h, Basketball. 1k, Boxing. 1.60k, Gymnastics.

Engraved and Photogravure

1963, Oct. 26 ***Perf. 11½***

1202	A463	30h	ind & grn	10	5
1203	A463	40h	red brn & lt bl	15	5
1204	A463	60h	brn red & yel	20	8
1205	A463	80h	dk pur & dp org	35	15
1206	A463	1k	ultra & dp rose	40	20
1207	A463	1.60k	vio bl & ultra	*3.00*	*1.25*
			Nos. 1202-1207 (6)	*4.20*	*1.78*

1964 Olympic Games, Tokyo.

1963, Dec. 11 *Perf. 11½* Unwmkd.

Design: 60h, Star, hammer and sickle.

1208	A464	30h	bis brn & lt bl	10	5
1209	A464	60h	car & gray	20	5

Issued to commemorate the 20th anniversary of the Russo-Czechoslovakian Treaty.

Atom Diagrams Surrounding Head
A465

Chamois
A466

1963, Dec. 12 **Engraved**

1210	A465	60h	dk pur	45	8

Issued to publicize the 3rd Congress of the Association for the Propagation of Scientific Knowledge.

1963, Dec. 14 ***Perf. 14***

Animals: 40h, Alpine ibex. 60h, Mouflon. 1.20k, Roe deer. 1.60k, Fallow deer. 2k, Red deer.

1211	A466	30h	multi	60	15
1212	A466	40h	multi	70	25
1213	A466	60h	brn, yel & grn	90	30
1214	A466	1.20k	multi	95	30
1215	A466	1.60k	multi	1.50	60
1216	A466	2k	multi	*5.00*	*2.75*
			Nos. 1211-1216 (6)	*9.65*	*4.35*

Figure Skating
A467

Ice Hockey
A468

Designs: 80h, Skiing (horiz.). 1k, Field ball player.

Engraved and Photogravure

1964, Jan. 20 *Perf. 11½* Unwmkd.

1217	A467	30h	vio bl & yel	20	5
1218	A467	80h	dk bl & org	50	8
1219	A467	1k	brn & lil	55	20

Issued to commemorate the International University Games (30h and 80h) and the World Field Ball Championships (1k).

1964, Jan. 20

Designs: 1.80k, Toboggan. 2k, Ski jump.

1220	A468	1k	pur & pale grn	75	45
1221	A468	1.80k	sl grn & bl gray	1.15	1.00
1222	A468	2k	dk bl & pale grn	*4.00*	*3.50*

Issued to commemorate the 9th Winter Olympic Games, Innsbruck, Jan. 29–Feb. 9, 1964.

Magura Rest Home, High Tatra
A469

Design: 80h, Slovak National Insurrection Rest Home, Low Tatra.

1964, Feb. 19 *Perf. 11½* Unwmkd.

1223	A469	60h	grn & yel	25	5
1224	A469	80h	vio bl & pink	30	5

Skiers and Ski Lift
A470

Designs: 60h, Automobile camp, Telč. 1k, Fishing, Spis Castle. 1.80k, Lake and boats, Český Krumlov.

1964, Feb. 19 **Engr. & Photo.**

1225	A470	30h	dk vio brn & bl	15	5
1226	A470	60h	sl & car	25	5
1227	A470	1k	brn & ol	50	8
1228	A470	1.80k	sl grn & org	75	15

Moses, Day and Night by Michelangelo
A471

Designs: 60h, "A Midsummer Night's Dream," by Shakespeare. 1k, Man, telescope and heaven (vert.). 1.60k, King George of Podebrad (1420–71).

1964, March 20

1229	A471	40h blk & yel grn	20	5
1230	A471	60h sl & car	20	5
1231	A471	1k blk & lt bl	35	8
1232	A471	1.60k blk & yel	75	15

Issued to commemorate the following: 400th anniversary of the death of Michelangelo (40h); 400th anniversary of the birth of Shakespeare (60h); 400th anniversary of the birth of Galileo (1k); 500th anniversary of the pacifist efforts of King George of Podebrad (1.60k).

Yuri A. Gagarin—A472

Astronauts: 60h, German Titov. 80h, John H. Glenn, Jr. 1k, Scott M. Carpenter (vert.). 1.20k, Pavel R. Popovich and Andrian G. Nikolayev. 1.40k, Walter M. Schirra (vert.). 1.60k, Gordon L. Cooper (vert.). 2k, Valentina Tereshkova and Valeri Bykovski (vert.).

Engraved and Photogravure

1964, Apr. 27 *Perf. 11½* Unwmkd.

Yellow Paper

1233	A472	30h blk & vio bl	60	10
1234	A472	60h dk grn & dk car	30	10
1235	A472	80h dk car & vio	35	10
1236	A472	1k ultra & rose vio	45	15
1237	A472	1.20k ver & ol gray	1.00	25
1238	A472	1.40k blk & dl grn	1.20	40
1239	A472	1.60k pale pur & Prus grn	*4.00*	*1.75*
1240	A472	2k dk bl & red	1.75	80
		Nos. 1233-1240 (8)	*9.65*	*3.65*

World's first 10 astronauts.

Creeping Bellflower A473

Film 'Flower' and Karlovy Vary Colonnade A474

Flowers: 80h, Musk thistle. 1k, Chicory. 1.20k, Yellow iris. 1.60k, Gentian. 2k, Corn poppy.

1964, June 15 Engraved *Perf. 14*

1241	A473	60h dk grn, lil & org	1.50	30
1242	A473	80h blk, grn & red lil	1.50	30
1243	A473	1k vio bl, grn & pink	1.50	40
1244	A473	1.20k blk, yel & grn	1.50	40
1245	A473	1.60k vio & grn	1.50	40
1246	A473	2k vio, red & grn	*9.00*	*2.75*
		Nos. 1241-1246 (6)	*16.50*	*4.55*

Engraved and Photogravure

1964, June 20 *Perf. 13½* Unwmkd.

1247	A474	60h blk, bl & car	1.25	15

Issued to commemorate the 14th International Film Festival at Karlovy Vary, July 4–19.

Silesian Coat of Arms A475

Young Miner of 1764 A476

1964, June 20 *Perf. 11½*

1248	A475	30h blk & yel	35	8

Issued to commemorate the 150th anniversary of the Silesian Museum, Opava.

1964, June 20

1249	A476	60h sep & lt grn	35	5

Issued to commemorate the bicentenary of the Mining School at Banska Stiavnica.

Skoda Fire Engine A477

1964, June 20

1250	A477	60h car rose & lt bl	35	5

Issued to commemorate the centenary of voluntary fire brigades in Bohemia.

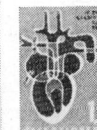

Gulls, Hradcany Castle, Red Cross A478

Human Heart A479

1964, July 10

1251	A478	60h car & bluish gray	35	5

Issued to commemorate the 4th Czechoslovak Red Cross Congress at Prague.

1964, July 10

1252	A479	1.60k ultra & car	80	8

Issued to commemorate the 4th European Cardiological Congress at Prague.

Partisans, Girl and Factories A480

Battle Scene, 1944 A481

Design: 60h, Partisans and flame.

Engraved and Photogravure

1964, Aug. 17 *Perf. 11½* Unwmkd.

1253	A480	30h brn & red	10	5
1254	A480	60h dk bl & red	30	5
1255	A481	60h blk & red	30	5

Issued to commemorate the 20th anniversary of the Slovak National Uprising; No. 1255 commemorates the 20th anniversary of the Battles of Dukla Pass.

Hradcany at Prague A482

Discus Thrower and Pole Vaulter A483

Design: 5k, Charles Bridge and Hradcany.

1964, Aug. 30 *Perf. 11½x12*

1256	A482	60h blk & red	75	10

Souvenir Sheet

Engraved *Imperf.*

1257	A482	5k dp cl	2.75	2.50

Millenium of the Hradcany, Prague. No. 1257 measures 76x98mm.; stamp size: 30x50mm.

Engraved and Photogravure

1964, Sept. 2 *Perf. 13½*

Designs: 60h, Bicycling (horiz.). 1k, Soccer. 1.20k, Rowing. 1.60k, Swimming (horiz.). 2.80k, Weight lifting (horiz.).

1258	A483	60h multi	30	12
1259	A483	80h multi	40	12
1260	A483	1k multi	50	18
1261	A483	1.20k multi	60	25
1262	A483	1.60k multi	1.00	50
1263	A483	2.80k multi	*5.50*	*3.00*
		Nos. 1258-1263 (6)	*8.30*	*4.17*

Issued to commemorate the 18th Olympic Games, Tokyo, Oct. 10–25. Sheets of 10.

Miniature Sheet

Space Ship Voskhod I, Astronauts and Globe—A484

Engraved and Photogravure

1964, Nov. 12 *Perf. 11½* Unwmkd.

1264	A484	3k dk bl & dl lil, *buff*	6.50	4.50

Issued to commemorate the Russian three-manned space flight of Vladimir M. Komarov, Boris B. Yegorov and Konstantin Feoktistov, Oct. 12–13. No. 1264 contains one stamp. Size of stamp: 49x30 mm.; size of sheet: 92x66mm.

Steam Engine and Atomic Power Plant A485

Diesel Engine "CKD Praha" A486

1964, Nov. 16 Engraved

1265	A485	30h dl red brn	15	5

Engraved and Photogravure

1266	A486	60h grn & sal	25	5

Issued to publicize traditions and development of engineering; No. 1265 commemorates the 150th anniversary of the First Brno Engineering Works, No. 1266 honors the engineering concern CKD Praha.

European Redstart A487

Birds: 60h, Green woodpecker. 80h, Hawfinch. 1k, Black woodpecker. 1.20k, European robin. 1.60k, European roller.

1964, Nov. 16 Litho. *Perf. 10½*

1267	A487	30h multi	15	5
1268	A487	60h blk & multi	30	5
1269	A487	80h multi	35	10
1270	A487	1k multi	45	20
1271	A487	1.20k lt vio bl & blk	50	25
1272	A487	1.60k yel & blk	1.00	75
		Nos. 1267-1272 (6)	2.75	1.40

Dancer A488

"In the Sun" Pre-school Children A489

Designs: 60h, "Over the Obstacles," teenagers. 1k, "Movement and Beauty," woman flag twirler. 1.60k, Runners at start.

Engraved and Photogravure

1965 *Perf. 11½* Unwmkd.

1273	A488	30h red & lt bl	15	5

Perf. 11½x12

1274	A489	30h vio bl & car	10	5
1275	A489	60h brn & ultra	20	5
1276	A489	1k blk & yel	40	6
1277	A489	1.60k mar & gray	75	30
		Nos. 1273-1277 (5)	1.60	51

Issued to publicize the Third National Spartacist Games. Issue dates: No. 1273, Jan. 3. Nos. 1274–1277, May 24.

Mountain Rescue Service A490

Arms and View, Beroun A491

1965, Jan. 15 *Perf. 11½* Unwmkd.

Designs: No. 1279, Woman gymnast. No. 1280, Bicyclists. No. 1281, Women hurdlers.

1278	A490	60h vio & bl	35	6

1279	A490	60h mar & ocher	35	6
1280	A490	60h blk & car	35	6
1281	A490	60h grn & yel	35	6

Issued to publicize: Mountain Rescue Service (No. 1278); First World Championship in Artistic Gymnastics, Prague, December 1965 (No. 1279); World Championship in Indoor Bicycling, Prague, Oct., 1965 (No. 1280); "Universiada 1965," Brno (No. 1281).

1965, Feb. 15 **Engr. and Photo.**

Designs: No. 1283, Town Square, Domazlice. No. 1284, Old and new buildings, Frydek-Mystek. No. 1285, Arms and view, Lipnik. No. 1286, Fortified wall, City Hall and Arms, Policka. No. 1287, View and hops, Zatek. No. 1288, Small fortress and rose, Terezin.

1282	A491	30h vio bl & lt bl	25	5
1283	A491	30h dl pur & yel	25	5
1284	A491	30h sl & gray	25	5
1285	A491	30h grn & bis	25	5
1286	A491	30h brn & tan	25	5
1287	A491	30h dk bl & cit	25	5
1288	A491	30h blk & rose	25	5
		Nos. 1282-1288 (7)	1.75	35

Nos. 1282–87 commemorate the 700th anniversary of the founding of various Bohemian towns; No. 1288 commemorates the 20th anniversary of the liberation of the Theresienstadt (Terezin) concentration camp.

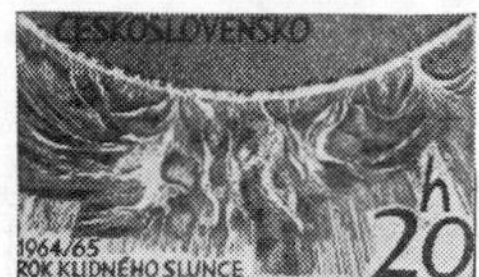

Sun's Corona—A492

Space Research: 30h, Sun. 60h, Exploration of the Moon. 1k, Twin space craft (vert.). 1.40k, Space station. 1.60k, Exploration of Mars (vert.). 2k, USSR and USA Meteorological collaboration.

Perf. 12x11½, 11½x12

1965, Mar. 15 **Engr. & Photo.**

1289	A492	20h rose & red lil	10	5
1290	A492	30h rose red & yel	12	5
1291	A492	60h bluish blk & yel	22	5
1292	A492	1k pur & pale bl	35	10
1293	A492	1.40k blk & sal	50	15
1294	A492	1.60k blk & pink	65	35
1295	A492	2k bluish blk & lt bl	*1.75*	*1.25*
		Nos. 1289-1295 (7)	*3.69*	*2.00*

Issued to publicize space research; Nos. 1289–1290 also commemorate the International Quiet Sun Year, 1964–65.

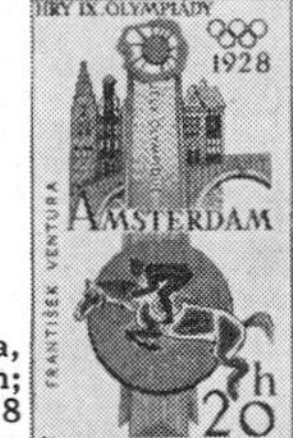

Frantisek Ventura, Equestrian; Amsterdam, 1928
A493

Czechoslovakian Olympic Victories: 30h, Discus, Paris, 1900. 60h, Running, Helsinki, 1952. 1k, Weight lifting, Los Angeles, 1932. 1.40k, Gymnastics, Berlin, 1936. 1.60k, Double sculling, Rome, 1960. 2k, Women's gymnastics, Tokyo, 1964.

1965, Apr. 16 ***Perf. 11½x12***

1296	A493	20h choc & gold	10	5
1297	A493	30h ind & emer	15	5
1298	A493	60h ultra & gold	25	10
1299	A493	1k red brn & gold	45	25
1300	A493	1.40k dk sl grn & gold	90	50
1301	A493	1.60k blk & gold	1.00	55
1302	A493	2k mar & gold	1.50	75
		Nos. 1296-1302 (7)	4.35	2.25

Astronauts Virgil Grissom and John Young—A494

Designs: No. 1304, Alexei Leonov floating in space. No. 1305, Launching pad at Cape Kennedy, U.S.A. No. 1306, Leonov leaving space ship.

1965, Apr. 17 ***Perf. 11x11½***

1303	A494	60h sl bl & lil rose	25	18
1304	A494	60h vio blk & bl	25	18
1305	A494	3k sl bl & lil rose	1.75	1.25
1306	A494	3k vio blk & bl	1.75	1.25

Issued to honor American and Soviet astronauts. Printed in sheets of 25; one sheet contains 20 No. 1303 and 5 No. 1305, the other sheet contains 20 No. 1304 and 5 No. 1306.

Russian Soldier, View of Prague and Guerrilla Fighters—A495

Designs: No. 1308, Blast furnace, workers and tank. 60h, Worker and factory. 1k, Worker and new constructions. 1.60k, Woman farmer, new farm buildings and machinery.

1965, May 5 **Engraved** ***Perf. 13½***

1307	A495	30h dk red, blk & ol	12	5
1308	A495	30h multi	12	5
1309	A495	60h vio bl, red & blk	25	5
1310	A495	1k dp org, blk & brn	40	10
1311	A495	1.60k yel, red & blk	75	20
		Nos. 1307-1311 (5)	1.64	45

Issued to commemorate the 20th anniversary of liberation from the Nazis.

Slovakian Kopov Dog—A496

Dogs: 40h, German shepherd. 60h, Czech hunting dog with pheasant. 1k, Poodle. 1.60k, Czech terrier. 2k, Afghan hound.

1965, June 10 ***Perf. 12x11½***

1312	A496	30h blk & red org	15	5
1313	A496	40h blk & yel	20	5
1314	A496	60h blk & ver	25	8
1315	A496	1k blk & dk car rose	50	10
1316	A496	1.60k blk & org	1.00	20
1317	A496	2k blk & org	2.00	95
		Nos. 1312-1317 (6)	4.10	1.43

Issued to publicize the World Dog Show at Brno and the International Dog Breeders Congress, Prague.

U.N. Headquarters Building, N.Y.
A497

Designs: 60h, U.N. Emblem and inscription. 1.60k, ICY emblem.

1965, June 24 ***Perf. 12x11½***

1318	A497	60h dk red brn & yel	25	6
1319	A497	1k ultra & lt bl	40	10
1320	A497	1.60k gold & dk red	75	35

Issued to commemorate the 20th anniversary of the United Nations and for the International Cooperation Year, 1965.

Trade Union Emblem
A498

1965, June 24 **Engraved**

1321	A498	60h dk red & ultra	35	5

Issued to commemorate the 20th anniversary of the International Trade Union Federation.

Women and Globe
A499

1965, June 24 ***Perf. 11½x12***

1322	A499	60h vio bl	35	5

Issued to commemorate the 20th anniversary of the International Women's Federation.

Children's House (Burgraves' Palace), Hradcany
A500

Matthias Tower
A501

1965, June 25 ***Perf. 11½***

1323	A500	30h sl grn	20	5
1324	A501	60h dk brn	40	5

Issued to publicize the Hradcany, Prague.

Marx and Lenin
A502

1965, July 1 **Engraved and Photo.**

1325	A502	60h car rose & gold	30	5

Issued to commemorate the 6th conference of Postal Ministers of Communist Countries, Peking, June 21–July 15.

Joseph Navratil
A503

Jan Hus
A504

Gregor Johann Mendel
A505

Costume Jewelry
A506

Bohuslav Martinu
A507

ITU Emblem and Communication Symbols
A509

Seated Woman and University of Bratislava
A508

Macromolecular Symposium Emblem
A510

Design: No. 1327, Ludwig Stur (diff. frame).

Engraved and Photogravure

1965 ***Perf. 11½*** **Unwmkd.**

1326	A503	30h blk & fawn	20	5
1327	A503	30h blk & dl grn	20	5
1328	A504	60h blk & crim	40	5
1329	A505	60h vio bl & red	40	5
1330	A506	60h pur & gold	40	5
1331	A507	60h blk & org	40	5
1332	A508	60h brn, *yel*	40	5
1333	A509	1k org & bl	60	8
1334	A510	1k blk & dp org	60	8
		Nos. 1326-1334 (9)	3.60	51

No. 1326 commemorates the centenary of the death of Josef Navratil (1798–1865), painter; No. 1327, the sesquicentennial of the birth of Ludwig Stur (1815–56), Slovak author and historian; No. 1328 commemorates the 550th anniversary of the death of Jan Hus, religious reformer; No. 1329, the centenary of publication of Mendel's laws of inheritance; No. 1330 publicizes the "Jablonec 1965" costume jewelry exhibition; No. 1331, the 75th anniversary of the birth of Bohuslav Martinu (1890–1959), composer; No. 1332, the 500th anniversary of the founding of the University of Bratislava as Academia Istropolitana; No. 1333, the centenary of the International Telecommunication Union; No. 1334, the International Symposium on Macromolecular Chemistry, Prague, Sept. 1–8.

"Young Woman at her Toilette," by Titian
A512

Help for Flood Victims
A513

Rescue of Flood Victims
A514

Miniature Sheet

1965, Aug. 12

1336	A512	5k multi	3.75	3.75

Issued to publicize the Hradcany Art Gallery. No. 1336 contains one stamp; size of sheet: 75x97mm.

1965, Sept. 6 Engraved

1337	A513	30h vio bl	15	7

Engraved and Photogravure

1338	A514	2k dk ol grn & ol	90	65

Help for Danube flood victims in Slovakia.

Dotterel
A515

Mountain Birds: 60h, Wall creeper (vert.). 1.20k, Lesser redpoll. 1.40k, Golden eagle (vert.). 1.60k, Ring ouzel. 2k, Eurasian nutcracker (vert.).

1965, Sept. 20 Litho. ***Perf. 11***

1339	A515	30h multi	15	5
1340	A515	60h multi	25	5
1341	A515	1.20k multi	60	10
1342	A515	1.40k multi	70	20
1343	A515	1.60k multi	80	25
1344	A515	2k multi	1.25	1.00
		Nos. 1339-1344 (6)	3.75	1.65

Levoca
A516

Coltsfoot
A517

Views of Towns: 10h, Jindrichuv Hradec. 20h, Nitra. 30h, Kosice. 40h, Hradec Králové. 50h, Telc. 60h, Ostrava. 1k, Olomouc. 1.20k, Ceske Budejovice. 1.60k, Cheb. 2k, Brno. 3k, Bratislava. 5k, Prague.

Engraved and Photogravure

1965–66 ***Perf. 11½x12***

Size: 23x19mm.

1345	A516	5h blk & yel	5	5
1346	A516	10h ultra & ol bis	6	5
1347	A516	20h blk & lt bl	12	5
1348	A516	30h vio bl & lt grn	20	5
1348A	A516	40h dk brn & lt bl ('66)	25	5
1348B	A516	50h blk & ocher ('66)	30	5
1348C	A516	60h red & gray ('66)	40	5
1348D	A516	1k pur & pale grn ('66)	60	5

Perf. 11½x11

Size: 30x23mm.

1349	A516	1.20k sl & lt bl	65	8
1350	A516	1.60k ind & yel	75	5
1351	A516	2k sl grn & pale yel	1.25	10
1352	A516	3k brn & yel	1.75	12
1353	A516	5k blk & pink	3.00	15
		Nos. 1345-1353 (13)	9.38	90

1965, Dec. 3 Engraved ***Perf. 14***

Medicinal Plants: 60h, Meadow saffron. 80h, Corn poppy. 1k, Foxglove. 1.20k, Arnica. 1.60k, Cornflower. 2k, Dog rose.

1354	A517	30h multi	15	8
1355	A517	60h multi	25	12
1356	A517	80h multi	30	15
1357	A517	1k multi	55	20
1358	A517	1.20k multi	75	25
1359	A517	1.60k multi	1.25	40
1360	A517	2k multi	*5.00*	*2.25*
		Nos. 1354-1360 (7)	*8.25*	*3.45*

Strip of "Stamps"—A518

Engraved and Photogravure

1965, Dec. 18 ***Perf. 11½***

1361	A518	1k dk red & gold	3.00	2.50

Issued for Stamp Day, 1965.

Romain Rolland
A519

Symbolic Musical Instruments and Names of Composers
A520

Portraits: No. 1362, Stanislav Sucharda. No. 1363, Ignac Josef Pesina. No. 1365, Donatello.

1966, Feb. 14 Engraved ***Perf. 11½***

1362	A519	30h dp grn	10	5
1363	A519	30h vio bl	10	5
1364	A519	60h rose lake	25	5
1365	A519	60h brown	25	5

Issued to commemorate the following: No. 1362, centenary of birth of Stanislav Sucharda (1866–1916), sculptor; No. 1363, bicentenary of birth of Ignac Josef Pesina (1766–1808), veterinarian. No. 1364, centenary of birth of Romain Rolland (1866–1944), French writer; No. 1365, 500th anniversary of death of Donatello (1386–1466), Italian sculptor.

1966, Feb. 15 Engr. and Photo.

1366	A520	30h blk & gold	55	20

Issued to commemorate the 70th anniversary of the Czech Philharmonic Orchestra.

Figure Skating Pair—A521

Designs: No. 1368, Man skater. No. 1369, Volleyball player, spiking (vert.). 1k, Volleyball player, saving (vert.). 1.60k, Woman skater. 2k, Figure skating pair.

1966, Feb. 17

1367	A521	30h dk car rose	15	5
1368	A521	60h green	30	5
1369	A521	60h car & buff	30	5
1370	A521	1k vio & lt bl	45	5
1371	A521	1.60k brn & yel	60	9
1372	A521	2k bl & grnsh bl	*2.50*	*80*
		Nos. 1367-1372 (6)	*4.30*	*1.09*

Nos. 1367–68 and 1371–72 commemorate the European Figure Skating Championships, Bratislava; Nos. 1369–70 commemorate the World Volleyball Championships.

Souvenir Sheet

Girl Dancing—A522

1966, Mar. 21 Engraved ***Imperf.***

1373	A522	3k sl bl, red & bl	2.25	2.25

Issued to commemorate the centenary of the opera "The Bartered Bride" by Bedrich Smetana. Opening chorus "Why shouldn't we be happy. ." in margin. Size: 85x105mm.

"Ajax" 1841
A523

Locomotives: 30h, "Karlstejn" 1865. 60h, Steam engine, 1946. 1k, Steam engine with tender, 1946. 1.60k, Electric locomotive, 1964. 2k, Diesel locomotive, 1964.

1966, March 21 ***Perf. 11½x11***

Buff Paper

1374	A523	20h sepia	10	5
1375	A523	30h dl vio	12	5
1376	A523	60h dl pur	30	5
1377	A523	1k dk bl	40	7
1378	A523	1.60k dk bl grn	70	30
1379	A523	2k dk red	*4.00*	*1.25*
		Nos. 1374-1379 (6)	*5.62*	*1.77*

European Perch
A524

Fish: 30h, Brown trout (vert.). 1k, Carp. 1.20k, Northern pike. 1.40k, Grayling. 1.60k, Eel.

Perf. 13x13½, 13½x13

1966, Apr. 22 Litho. **Unwmkd.**

1380	A524	30h multi	15	5
1381	A524	60h multi	25	5
1382	A524	1k multi	40	5
1383	A524	1.20k multi	50	15
1384	A524	1.40k multi	60	25
1385	A524	1.60k multi	*3.75*	*1.50*
		Nos. 1380-1385 (6)	*5.65*	*2.05*

Issued to publicize the International Fishing Championships, Svit, Sept. 3–5.

WHO Headquarters, Geneva
A525

Engraved and Photogravure

1966, Apr. 25 ***Perf. 12x11½***

1386	A525	1k dk bl & lt bl	45	10

Issued to commemorate the inauguration of the World Health Organization Headquarters, Geneva.

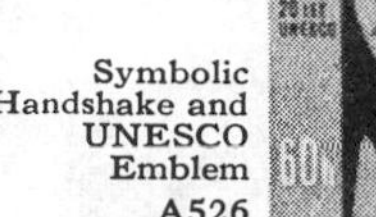

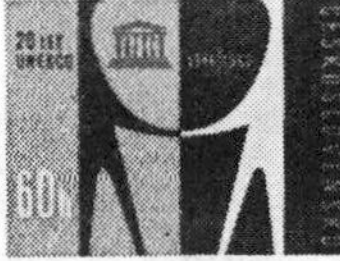

Symbolic Handshake and UNESCO Emblem
A526

1966, Apr. 25 ***Perf. 11½***

1387	A526	60h bis & ol gray	25	5

Issued to commemorate the 20th anniversary of UNESCO (U.N. Educational, Scientific and Cultural Organization).

Prague Castle Issue

Belvedere Palace and St. Vitus' Cathedral
A527

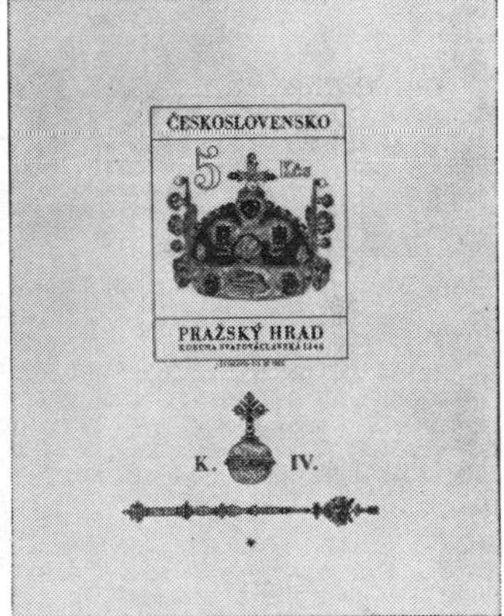

Crown of St. Wenceslas, 1346
A528

Design: 60h, Madonna, altarpiece from St. George's Church.

1966, May 9 Engraved ***Perf. 11½***

1388	A527	30h dk bl	25	5

Engraved and Photogravure

1389	A527	60h blk & yel bis	55	10

Souvenir Sheet

Engraved

1390	A528	5k multi	3.50	3.50

See also Nos. 1537–1539.

Tiger Swallowtail
A529

Butterflies and Moths: 60h, Clouded sulphur. 80h, European purple emperor. 1k, Apollo. 1.20k, Burnet moth. 2k, Tiger moth.

1966, May 23 Engraved *Perf. 14*

1391	A529	30h multi		10	8
1392	A529	60h multi		25	10
1393	A529	80h multi		35	12
1394	A529	1k multi		40	15
1395	A529	1.20k multi		60	20
1396	A529	2k multi		*3.75*	*1.50*
	Nos. 1391-1396 (6)			*5.45*	*2.15*

Sheets of ten.

Flags of Russia and Czechoslovakia
A530

Designs: 60h, Rays surrounding hammer and sickle "sun." 1.60k, Girl's head and stars.

Engraved and Photogravure

1966, May 31 *Perf. 11½*

1397	A530	30h dk bl & crim	12	5
1398	A530	60h dk bl & red	25	5
1399	A530	1.60k red & dk bl	70	15

Issued to commemorate the 13th Congress of the Communist Party of Czechoslovakia.

Dakota Chief
A531

Designs: 20h, Indians, canoe and tepee (horiz.). 30h, Tomahawk. 40h, Haida totem poles. 60h, Kachina, good spirit of the Hopis. 1k, Indian on horseback hunting buffalo (horiz.). 1.20k, Calumet, Dakota peace pipe.

1966, June 20 Engr. & Photo.

Size: 23x40mm.

1400	A531	20h vio bl & dp org	10	5
1401	A531	30h blk & dl org	10	5
1402	A531	40h blk & lt bl	10	8
1403	A531	60h grn & yel	30	10
1404	A531	1k pur & emer	40	20
1405	A531	1.20k vio bl & rose lil	60	40

Engraved

Perf. 14

Size: 23x37mm.

1406	A531	1.40k multi	*2.75*	*1.25*
	Nos. 1400-1406 (7)		*4.35*	*2.13*

Issued to commemorate the centenary of the Náprstek Ethnographic Museum, Prague, and in connection with "The Indians of North America" exhibition.

Model of Molecule
A532

Engraved and Photogravure

1966, July 4 *Perf. 11½* Unwmkd.

1407	A532	60h blk & lt bl	30	5

Issued to commemorate the centenary of the Czechoslovak Chemical Society.

"Guernica" by Pablo Picasso
A533

1966, July 5

Size: 75x30mm.

1408	A533	60h blk & pale bl	2.00	2.00

30th anniversary of International Brigade in Spanish Civil War.

Sheets of 15 stamps and 5 labels inscribed "Picasso-Guernica 1937."

Pantheon, Bratislava
A534

Designs: No. 1410, Devin Castle and Ludwig Stur. No. 1411, View of Nachod. No. 1412, State Science Library, Olomouc.

1966, July 25 Engraved

1409	A534	30h dl pur	10	5
1410	A534	60h dk bl	25	5
1411	A534	60h green	25	5
1412	A534	60h sepia	25	5

No. 1409 publicizes the Russian War Memorial, Bratislava; No. 1410, the 9th century Devin Castle as symbol of Slovak nationalism; No. 1411 commemorates the 700th anniversary of the founding of Nachod; No. 1412, the 400th anniversary of the State Science Library, Olomouc.

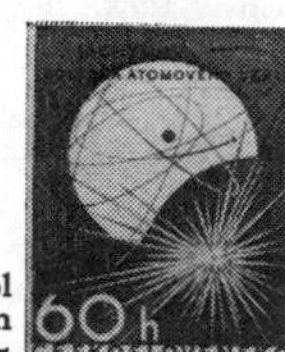

Atom Symbol and Sun
A535

Engraved and Photogravure

1966, Aug. 29 *Perf. 11½*

1413	A535	60h blk & red	30	5

Issued to publicize Jachýmov (Joachimsthal), where pitchblende was first discovered, "cradle of the atomic age."

Brno Fair Emblem
A536

Olympia Coin and Olympic Rings
A537

1966, Aug. 29

1414	A536	60h blk & red	30	5

8th International Trade Fair, Brno.

1966, Aug. 29

Design: 1k, Olympic flame, Czechoslovak flag and Olympic rings.

1415	A537	60h blk & gold	30	5
1416	A537	1k dk bl & red	55	30

Issued to commemorate the 70th anniversary of the Olympic Committee.

Missile Carrier, Tank and Jet Plane
A538

1966, Aug. 31

1417	A538	60h blk & ap grn	35	5

Issued to commemorate the maneuvers of the armies of the Warsaw Pact countries.

Mercury
A539

Designs: 30h, Moravian silver thaler, 1620, reverse and obverse (vert.). 1.60k, Old and new buildings of Brno State Theater. 5k, International Trade Fair Administration Tower and postmark (vert.).

1966, Sept. 10

1418	A539	30h dk red & blk	30	5
1419	A539	60h org & blk	30	5
1420	A539	1.60k blk & brt grn	75	35

Souvenir Sheet

1421	A539	5k multi	3.25	3.25

Issued to publicize the Brno Philatelic Exhibition, Sept. 11–25. No. 1421 contains one stamp (size: 30x40mm.). Marginal black inscription and exhibition emblem. Size: 73½x100mm.

First Meeting in Orbit—A540

Designs: 30h, Photograph of far side of Moon and Russian satellite. 60h, Photograph of Mars and Mariner 4. 80h, Soft landing on Moon. 1k, Satellite, laser beam and binary code. 1.20k, Telstar over Earth and receiving station.

Engraved and Photogravure

1966, Sept. 26 *Perf. 11½*

1422	A540	20h vio & lt grn	10	5
1423	A540	30h blk & sal pink	15	5
1424	A540	60h sl & lil	25	5
1425	A540	80h dk pur & lt bl	40	20
1426	A540	1k blk & vio	50	25
1427	A540	1.20k red & bl	*2.00*	*75*
	Nos. 1422-1427 (6)		*3.40*	*1.35*

Issued to publicize American and Russian achievements in space research.

Badger
A541

Game Animals: 40h, Red deer (vert.). 60h, Lynx. 80h, Hare. 1k, Red fox. 1.20k, Brown bear (vert.). 2k, Wild boar.

1966, Nov. 28 Litho. *Perf. 13½*

1428	A541	30h multi	12	5
1429	A541	40h multi	18	5
1430	A541	60h multi	25	5
1431	A541	80h multi (*europaens*)	35	12
a.		80h multi (*europaeus*)	2.00	2.00
1432	A541	1k multi	50	20
1433	A541	1.20k multi	60	25
1434	A541	2k multi	*4.00*	*2.00*
	Nos. 1428-1434 (7)		*6.00*	*2.72*

The sheet of 50 of the 80h contains 40 with misspelling "europaens" and 10 with "europaeus."

"Spring" by Vaclav Hollar, 1607–77
A542

Paintings: No. 1436, Portrait of Mrs. F. Wussin, by Jan Kupecký (1667–1740). No. 1437, Snow Owl by Karel Purkyne (1834–1868). No. 1438, Tulips by Vaclav Spála (1885–1964). No. 1439, Recruit by Ludovít Fulla (1902–).

1966, Dec. 8 Engraved *Perf. 14*

1435	A542	1k black	3.50	3.50
1436	A542	1k multi	3.50	3.50
1437	A542	1k multi	3.50	3.50
1438	A542	1k multi	3.50	3.50
1439	A542	1k multi	*15.00*	*12.00*
	Nos. 1435-1439 (5)		*29.00*	*26.00*

Printed in sheets of 4 stamps and 2 labels. The labels in sheet of No. 1435 are inscribed "Vaclav Hollar 1607–1677" in fancy frame. Other labels are blank.

See also No. 1484.

Symbolic Bird—A543

Engraved and Photogravure

1966, Dec. 17 *Perf. 11½*

1440	A543	1k dp bl & yel	95	95

Issued for Stamp Day.

Youth
A544

1967, Jan. 16 *Perf. 11½*

1441	A544	30h ver & lt bl	15	5

Issued to publicize the 5th Congress of the Czechoslovak Youth Organization.

Symbolic Flower and Machinery
A545

1967, Jan. 16 Engr. & Photo.

1442	A545	30h car & yel	15	5

6th Trade Union Congress, Prague.

Parents with Dead Child
A545a

1967, Jan. 16 *Perf. 11½*

1442A	A545a	60h blk & sal	30	6

Issued to publicize "Peace and Freedom in Viet Nam."

View of Jihlava and Tourist Year Emblem—A546

Views and Tourist Year Emblem: 40h, Spielberg Castle and churches, Brno. 1.20k, Danube, castle and churches, Bratislava. 1.60k, Vlatava River bridges, Hradany and churches, Prague.

1967, Feb. 13 Engraved *Perf. 11½*

Size: 40x23mm.

1443	A546	30h brn vio	12	5
1444	A546	40h maroon	18	5

Size: 75x30mm.

1445	A546	1.20k vio bl	65	20
1446	A546	1.60k black	*1.75*	*75*

International Tourist Year, 1967.

Black-tailed Godwit A547

Birds: 40h, Shoveler (horiz.). 60h, Purple heron. 80h, Penduline tit. 1k, Avocet. 1.40k, Black stork. 1.60k, Tufted duck (horiz.).

1967, Feb. 20 Litho. *Perf. 13½*

1447	A547	30h multi	10	5
1448	A547	40h multi	12	5
1449	A547	60h multi	20	5
1450	A547	80h multi	30	10
1451	A547	1k multi	40	12
1452	A547	1.40k multi	70	35
1453	A547	1.60k multi	*3.00*	*1.50*
		Nos. 1447-1453 (7)	*4.82*	*2.22*

Solar Research and Satellite A548

Space Research: 40h, Space craft, rocket and construction of station. 60h, Man on moon and orientation system. 1k, Exploration of solar system and rocket. 1.20k, Lunar satellites and moon photograph. 1.60k, Planned lunar architecture and moon landing.

Engraved and Photogravure

1967, March 24 *Perf. 11½*

1454	A548	30h yel & dk red	12	5
1455	A548	40h vio bl & blk	15	5
1456	A548	60h lil & grn	25	5
1457	A548	1k brt pink & sl	45	15
1458	A548	1.20k lt vio & blk	65	25
1459	A548	1.60k brn lake & blk	*2.00*	*90*
		Nos. 1454-1459 (6)	*3.62*	*1.45*

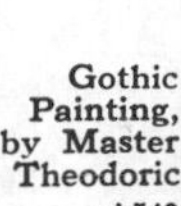

Gothic Painting, by Master Theodoric A549

Designs: 40h, "Burning of Master Hus," from Litomerice Hymnal. 60h, Modern glass sculpture. 80h, "The Shepherdess and the Chimney Sweep," Andersen fairy tale, painting by J. Trnka. 1k, Section of pressure vessel from atomic power station. 1.20k, Three ceramic figurines, by P. Rada. 3k, Montreal skyline and EXPO '67 emblem.

1967, Apr. 10 Engraved *Perf. 14*

Size: 37x23mm.

1460	A549	30h multi	15	5
1461	A549	40h multi	20	10
1462	A549	60h multi	30	15
1463	A549	80h multi	45	20
1464	A549	1k multi	50	30
1465	A549	1.20k multi	*1.50*	*80*
		Nos. 1460-1465 (6)	*3.10*	*1.60*

Souvenir Sheet

Perf. 11½

Size: 40x30mm.

1466	A549	3k multi	2.25	2.25

Issued to commemorate EXPO '67, International Exhibition, Montreal, Apr. 28–Oct. 27, 1967. No. 1466 contains one stamp with drawing of the Czechoslovakian pavilion in the margin. Size of sheet: 96x74mm.

Canoe Race A550

Women Playing Basketball A551

Designs: No. 1468, Wheels, dove and emblems of Warsaw, Berlin, Prague. 1.60k, Canoe slalom.

Perf. 12x11½, 11½x12

1967, Apr. 17 Engr. and Photo.

1467	A550	60h blk & brt bl	20	8
1468	A550	60h blk & sal	20	8
1469	A551	60h blk & grnsh bl	20	8
1470	A551	1.60k blk & brt vio	*1.75*	*70*

Issued to commemorate the following: No. 1467, 5th International Wild-Water Canoeing Championships; No. 1468, 20th Warsaw-Berlin-Prague Bicycle Race: No. 1469, Women's Basketball Championships; No. 1470, 10th International Water Slalom Championships.

"Golden Street" A552

Designs: 60h, Interior of Hall of King Wenceslas. 5k, St. Matthew, from illuminated manuscript, 11th century.

1967, May 9 *Perf. 11½x11*

1471	A552	30h rose cl	20	5
1472	A552	60h bluish blk	45	15

Souvenir Sheet

Perf. 11½

1473	A552	5k multi	4.00	4.00

Issued to publicize the Castle of Prague. No. 1473 contains one stamp with Latin marginal inscription in gold. Size: 75x95 mm.

Stylized Lyre with Flowers A553

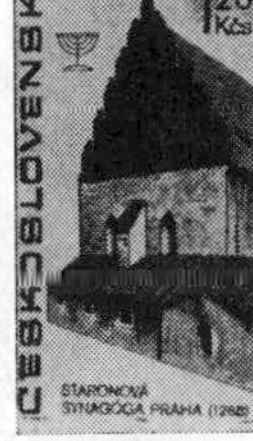

Old-New Synagogue, Prague A554

Engraved and Photogravure

1967, May 10 *Perf. 11½*

1474	A553	60h dl pur & brt grn	35	8

Prague Music Festival.

1967, May 22 *Perf. 11½*

Designs: 30h, Detail from Torah curtain, 1593. 60h, Prague Printer's emblem, 1530. 1k, Mikulov jug, 1804. 1.40k, Memorial for Concentration Camp Victims 1939–45, Pincas Synagogue (menorah and tablet). 1.60k, Tombstone of David Gans, 1613.

1475	A554	30h dl red & lt bl	45	10
1476	A554	60h blk & lt grn	60	10
1477	A554	1k dk bl & rose lil	90	25
1478	A554	1.20k dk brn & mar	1.25	45
1479	A554	1.40k blk & yel	1.50	60
1480	A554	1.60k grn & yel	*4.75*	*2.00*
		Nos. 1475-1480 (6)	*9.45*	*3.50*

Issued to show Jewish relics. The items shown on the 30h, 60h and 1k are from the State Jewish Museum, Prague.

"Lidice" A555

Prague Architecture A556

1967, June 9 *Perf. 11½* Unwmkd.

1481	A555	30h blk & brt rose	20	5

Issued to commemorate the 25th anniversary of the destruction of Lidice by the Nazis.

1967, June 10 Engr. & Photo.

1482	A556	1k blk & gold	45	30

Issued to publicize the 9th Congress of the International Union of Architects, Prague.

Petr Bezruc A557

1967, June 21

1483	A557	60h dl rose & blk	25	5

Issued to commemorate the centenary of the birth of Petr Bezruc, poet and writer.

Painting Type of 1966

Design: 2k, Henri Rousseau (1844–1910), self-portrait.

1967, June 22 Engr. *Perf. 11½*

1484	A542	2k multi	2.00	1.40

Issued to publicize Praga 68, World Stamp Exhibition, Prague, June 22–July 7, 1968. Printed in sheets of 4 stamps (2x2), separated by horizontal gutter with commemorative inscription and picture of National Gallery, site of Praga 68.

View of Skalitz A558

Designs: No. 1486, Mining tower and church steeple, Pribram. No. 1487, Hands holding book and view of Presov.

1967, Aug. 21 Engr. *Perf. 11½*

1485	A558	30h vio bl	10	5
1486	A558	30h sl grn	10	5
1487	A558	30h claret	10	5

Issued to commemorate anniversaries of the towns of Skalitz, Pribram and Presov.

Colonnade and Spring, Karlovy Vary and Communications Emblem A559

1967, Aug. 21 Engr. and Photo.

1488	A559	30h vio bl & gold	35	15

Issued to commemorate the 5th Sports and Cultural Festival of the Employees of the Ministry of Communications, Karlovy Vary.

Ondrejov Conservatory and Galaxy A560

1967, Aug. 22 Engraved

1489	A560	60h vio bl, rose lil & sil	95	25

Issued to commemorate the 13th International Congress of the Astronomic Union.

Orchid A561

Flowers from the Botanical Gardens: 30h, Cobaea scandens. 40h, Lycaste deppei. 60h, Glottiphyllum davisii. 1k, Anthurium. 1.20k, Rhodocactus. 1.40k, Moth orchid.

1967, Aug. 30 Litho. *Perf. 12½*

1490	A561	20h multi	8	5
1491	A561	30h pink & multi	12	5
1492	A561	40h multi	25	5
1493	A561	60h lt bl & multi	25	5
1494	A561	1k multi	55	15
1495	A561	1.20k lt yel & multi	95	18
1496	A561	1.40k multi	*2.75*	*90*
		Nos. 1490-1496 (7)	*4.95*	*1.43*

Red Squirrel
A562

Animals from the Tatra National Park: 60h, Wild cat. 1k, Ermine. 1.20k, Dormouse. 1.40k, Hedgehog. 1.60k, Pine marten.

Engraved and Photogravure

1967, Sept. 25 ***Perf. 11½***

1497	A562	30h	blk, yel & org	15	5
1498	A562	60h	blk & buff	30	6
1499	A562	1k	blk & lt bl	50	15
1500	A562	1.20k	brn, pale grn & yel	55	18
1501	A562	1.40k	blk, pink & yel	70	20
1502	A562	1.60k	blk, org & yel	*3.75*	*1.50*
			Nos. 1497-1502 (6)	*5.95*	*2.14*

Rockets and Weapons
A563

1967, Oct. 6 **Engraved** ***Perf. 11½***

1503	A563	30h	sl grn	30	5

Day of the Czechoslovak People's Army.

Cruiser "Aurora" Firing at Winter Palace—A564

Designs: 60h, Hammer and sickle emblems and Red Star (vert.). 1k, Hands reaching for hammer and sickle (vert.).

Engraved and Photogravure

1967, Nov. 7

1504	A564	30h	blk & dk car	10	5
1505	A564	60h	blk & dk car	20	5
1506	A564	1k	blk & dk car	50	10

Issued to commemorate the 50th anniversary of the Russian October Revolution.

The Conjurer, by Frantisek Tichy
A565

Paintings: 80h, Don Quixote, by Cyprian Majernik. 1k, Promenade in the Park, by Norbert Grund. 1.20k, Self-portrait, by Peter J. Brandl. 1.60k, Saints from Jan of Jeren Epitaph, by Czech Master of 1395.

1967, Nov. 13 **Engr.** ***Perf. 11½***

1507	A565	60h	multi	45	40
1508	A565	80h	multi	60	50
1509	A565	1k	multi	80	75
1510	A565	1.20k	multi	95	80
1511	A565	1.60k	multi	*4.75*	*4.25*
			Nos. 1507-1511 (5)	*7.55*	*6.70*

Sheets of 4. See Nos. 1589-1593, 1658-1662, 1711-1715, 1779-1783, 1847-1851, 1908-1913, 2043-2047, 2090-2093, 2147-2151, 2335-2339, 2534-2538, 2586-2590, 2634-2638.

Pres. Antonin Novotny
A566

1967, Dec. 9 **Engraved** ***Perf. 11½***

1512	A566	2k	bl gray	75	5
1513	A566	3k	brown	1.10	8

Czechoslovakia Nos. 65, 71 and 81 of 1920—A567

1967, Dec. 18

1514	A567	1k	mar & sil	1.25	1.10

Issued for Stamp Day.

Symbolic Flag and Dates
A568

1968, Jan. 15 **Engr.** ***Perf. 11½***

1515	A568	30h	red, dk bl & ultra	45	15

50th anniversary of Czechoslovakia.

Figure Skating and Olympic Rings
A569

Designs (Olympic Rings and): 1k, Ski course. 1.60k, Toboggan chute. 2k, Ice hockey.

1968, Jan. 29 **Engr. and Photo.**

1516	A569	60h	blk, yel & ocher	30	10
1517	A569	1k	ol grn, lt bl & lem	40	20
1518	A569	1.60k	blk, lil & bl grn	70	25
1519	A569	2k	blk, ap grn & lt bl	*2.50*	*75*

Issued to publicize the 10th Winter Olympic Games, Grenoble, France, Feb. 6–18.

Factories and Rising Sun
A570

Design: 60h, Workers and banner.

Engraved and Photogravure

1968, Feb. 25 ***Perf. 11½x12***

1520	A570	30h	car & dk bl	10	5
1521	A570	60h	car & dk bl	25	5

20th anniversary of February Revolution.

Map of Battle of Sokolow
A571

Human Rights Flame
A572

Engraved and Photogravure

1968, Mar. 8 ***Perf. 11½***

1522	A571	30h	blk, brt bl & car	35	5

Engraved

1523	A572	1k	rose car	55	25

No. 1522 commemorates the 25th anniversary of the Battle of Sokolow, Mar. 8, 1943, against the German Army; No. 1523 commemorates the International Human Rights Year.

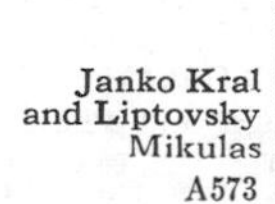

Janko Kral and Liptovsky Mikulas
A573

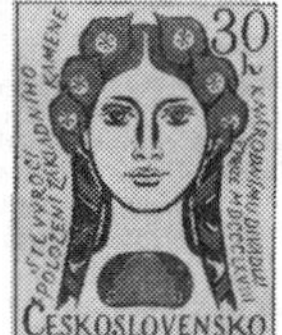

Karl Marx
A574

Girl's Head
A575

Arms and Allegory
A576

Head
A577

1968, Mar. 25 **Engraved**

1524	A573	30h	green	20	5
1525	A574	30h	claret	20	5

Engraved and Photogravure

1526	A575	30h	dk red & gold	20	5
1527	A576	30h	dk bl & dp org	20	5
1528	A577	1k	multi	1.10	35
			Nos. 1524-1528 (5)	1.90	55

Issued to commemorate the following: The writer Janko Kral and the Slovak town Liptovsky Mikulas (No. 1524); 150th anniversary of the birth of Karl Marx (No. 1525); centenary of the cornerstone laying of the Prague National Theater (No. 1526); 150th anniversary of the Prague National Museum (No. 1527); 20th anniversary of the World Health Organization (1k).

Symbolic Radio Waves
A578

Design: No. 1530, Symbolic television screens.

Engraved and Photogravure

1968, Apr. 29 ***Perf. 11½***

1529	A578	30h	blk, car & vio bl	15	6
1530	A578	30h	blk, car & vio bl	15	6

Issued to commemorate the 45th anniversary of Czechoslovak broadcasting (No. 1529), and the 15th anniversary of television (No. 1530).

Olympic Rings, Mexican Sculpture and Gymnast
A579

Olympic Rings and: 40h, Runner and "The Sanctification of Quetzalcoatl." 60h, Volleyball and Mexican ornaments. 1k, Czechoslovak and Mexican Olympic emblems and carved altar. 1.60k, Soccer and ornaments. 2k, View of Hradcany, weather vane and key.

1968, Apr. 30

1531	A579	30h	blk, bl & car	10	5
1532	A579	40h	multi	20	5
1533	A579	60h	multi	30	5
1534	A579	1k	multi	45	15
1535	A579	1.60k	multi	65	20
1536	A579	2k	blk & multi	*2.50*	*95*
			Nos. 1531-1536 (6)	*4.20*	*1.45*

Issued to publicize the 19th Olympic Games, Mexico City, Oct. 12–27.

Prague Castle Types of 1966

Designs: 30h, Tombstone of Bretislav I. 60h, Romanesque door knocker, St. Wenceslas Chapel. 5k, Head of St. Peter, mosaic from Golden Gate of St. Vitus Cathedral.

Photogravure and Engraved

1968, May 9 ***Perf. 11½***

1537	A527	30h	multi	20	5
1538	A527	60h	blk, red & cit	35	5

Souvenir Sheet

Engraved

1539	A528	5k	multi	4.50	4.50

No. 1539 contains one stamp, black ornament in margin. Size: 75x94mm.

Pres. Ludvik Svoboda
A580

1968–70 Engraved *Perf. 11½*

1540	A580	30h ultra	10	5
1540A	A580	50h grn ('70)	25	5
1541	A580	60h maroon	20	5
1541A	A580	1k rose car ('70)	55	10

Shades exist of No. 1541A.

"Business," Sculpture by Otto Gutfreund
A581

Cabaret Performer, by František Kupka
A582

Photo. & Engr.; Engr. (2k)

1968, June 5

Designs (The New Prague): 40h, Broadcasting Corporation Building. 60h, New Parliament. 1.40k, Tapestry by Jan Bauch "Prague 1787." 3k, Presidential standard.

1542	A581	30h blk & multi	9	5
1543	A581	40h blk & multi	15	5
1544	A581	60h dk brn & multi	30	7
1545	A581	1.40k dk brn & multi	65	18
1546	A582	2k ind & multi	*2.25*	*2.25*
1547	A581	3k blk & multi	1.25	95
		Nos. 1542-1547 (6)	*4.69*	*3.55*

1968, June 21 *Perf. 11½*

Designs (The Old Prague): 30h, St. George's Basilica. 60h, Renaissance fountain. 1k, Villa America-Dvorak Museum, 18th Century building. 1.60k, Emblem from the House of Three Violins, 18th century. 2k, Josefina, by Josef Manes. 3k, Emblem of Prague, 1475.

1548	A581	30h grn, gray & yel	9	5
1549	A581	60h dk vio, ap grn & gold	25	6
1550	A581	1k blk, lt bl & pink	50	15
1551	A581	1.60k sl grn & multi	65	20
1552	A582	2k brn & multi	*1.75*	*1.50*
1553	A581	3k blk, yel, bl & pink	1.35	75
		Nos. 1548-1553 (6)	*4.59*	*2.71*

Nos. 1542–1553 issued to publicize the Praga 68 Philatelic Exhibition. Nos. 1542–1545, 1547–1551 and 1553 issued in sheets of 15 stamps and 15 labels with Praga 68 emblem and inscription. Nos. 1546 and 1552 issued in sheets of 4 (2x2) with one horizontal label between top and bottom rows showing Praga 68 emblem.

Souvenir Sheet

View of Prague and Emblems
A583

Engraved and Photogravure

1968, June 22 *Imperf.*

1554	A583	10k multi	8.50	7.50

Issued for Praga 68 and to commemorate the 50th anniversary of Czechoslovak postage stamps. Type of 1918 issue and commemorative inscription in margin. Size: 75½x110mm. Sold only together with a 5k admission ticket to the Praga 68 philatelic Exhibition.

Madonna with the Rose Garlands, by Dürer
A584

1968, July 6 *Perf. 11½*

1555	A584	5k multi	4.50	3.50

Issued to commemorate FIP Day, July 6 (Féderation Internationale de Philatelie). Issued in sheets of 4 (2x2) with one horizontal label between, showing Praga 68 emblem.

Stage-coach on Rails
A585

Design: 1k, Steam and electric locomotives.

1968, Aug. 6 Engr. & Photo.

1556	A585	60h multi	55	20
1557	A585	1k multi	75	20

No. 1556 commemorates the 140th anniversary of the horse-drawn railroad České-Budějovice to Linz; No. 1557 commemorates the centenary of the České-Budějovice to Plzeň railroad.

Fanciful "S"
A586

1968, Aug. 7 *Perf. 11½*

1558	A586	30h vio bl & car	25	5

Issued to commemorate the 6th International Slavonic Congress in Prague.

Ardspach Rocks and Ammonite
A587

Designs: 60h, Basalt formation and frog skeleton fossil. 80h, Rocks, basalt veins and polished agate. 1k, Pelecypoda (fossil shell) and Belanske Tatra mountains. 1.60k, Trilobite and Barrande rock formation.

1968, Aug. 8

1559	A587	30h blk & cit	12	5
1560	A587	60h blk & rose cl	30	10
1561	A587	80h blk, lt vio & pink	35	15
1562	A587	1k blk & lt bl	45	20
1563	A587	1.60k blk & bis	*2.50*	*1.00*
		Nos. 1559-1563 (5)	*3.72*	*1.50*

Issued to publicize the 23rd International Geological Congress, Prague, Aug. 8–Sept. 3.

Raising Slovak Flag
A588

Design: 60h, Slovak partisans, and mountain.

1968, Sept. 9 Engraved *Perf. 11½*

1564	A588	30h ultra	10	5
1565	A588	60h red	20	5

No. 1564 honors the Slovak National Council, No. 1565 commemorates the 120th anniversary of the Slovak national uprising.

Flowerpot, by Jiri Schlessinger (age 10)
A589

Drawings by Children in Terezin Concentration Camp: 30h, Jew and Guard, by Jiri Beutler (age 10). 60h, Butterflies, by Kitty Brunnerova (age 11).

Engraved and Photogravure

1968, Sept. 30 *Perf. 11½*

1566	A589	30h blk, buff & rose lil	15	5
1567	A589	60h blk & multi	25	10

Perf. 12x11½

Size: 41x23mm.

1568	A589	1k blk & multi	50	25

30th anniversary of Munich Pact.

Arms of Banská Bystrica
A590

Arms of Prague
A591

Arms of Regional Capitals: No. 1570, Bratislava. No. 1571, Brno. No. 1572, České Budějovice. No. 1573, Hradec Králové. No. 1574, Košice. No. 1575, Ostrava (horse). No. 1576, Plzeň. No. 1577, Ustí nad Labem.

1968, Oct. 21 *Perf. 11½*

1569	A590	60h blk, red & sil	25	10
1570	A590	60h blk, red, sil & ultra	25	10
1571	A590	60h blk, red & sil	25	10
1572	A590	60h blk, red, sil & gold	25	10
1573	A590	60h blk, red, sil & gold	25	10
1574	A590	60h blk, bl, red & gold	25	10
1575	A590	60h blk, bl, yel & red	25	10
1576	A590	60h blk, emer, red & gold	25	10
1577	A590	60h blk, red, sil & gold	25	10

Perf. 11½x12

1578	A591	1k multi	75	45
		Nos. 1569-1578 (10)	3.00	1.35

No. 1578 issued in sheets of 10. See also Nos. 1652–1657, 1742–1747, 1886–1888, 2000–2001.

Flag and Linden Leaves
A592

Bohemian Lion Breaking Chains (Type SP1 of 1919)

A593

Design: 60h, Map of Czechoslovakia, linden leaves, Hradcany in Prague and Castle in Bratislava.

1968, Oct. 28 ***Perf. 12x11½***

1579	A592	30h dp bl & mag	20	5
1580	A592	60h blk, gold, red & ultra	25	8

Souvenir Sheet

Engraved ***Perf. 11½x12***

1581	A593	5k red	3.00	3.00

Issued to commemorate the 50th anniversary of the founding of Czechoslovakia. No. 1581 has violet blue marginal inscription and red ornament. Size: 75x100mm.

Ernest Hemingway (1899–1961) — A594

Cinderlad — A595

Caricatures: 30h, Karel Capek (1890–1938), writer. 40h, George Bernard Shaw (1856–1950), writer. 60h, Maxim Gorki (1868–1930), writer. 1k, Pablo Picasso (1881–1973), painter. 1.20k, Taikan Yokoyama (1868–1958), painter. 1.40k, Charlie Chaplin (1889–1977), actor.

Engraved and Photogravure

1968, Nov. 18 ***Perf. 11½x12***

1582	A594	20h blk, org & red	6	5
1583	A594	30h blk & multi	15	5
1584	A594	40h blk, lil & car	15	5
1585	A594	60h blk, sky bl & grn	18	8
1586	A594	1k blk, brn & yel	45	12
1587	A594	1.20k blk, dp car & vio	50	18
1588	A594	1.40k blk, brn & dp org	*2.50*	*85*
		Nos. 1582-1588 (7)	*3.99*	*1.38*

Issued to honor cultural personalities of the 20th century and UNESCO (United Nations Educational, Scientific and Cultural Organization). See Nos. 1628–1633.

Painting Type of 1967

Czechoslovakian Art: 60h, Cleopatra II, by Jan Zrzavy (1890–). 80h, Black Lake (man and horse), by Jan Preisler (1872–1918). 1.20k, Giovanni Francisci as a Volunteer, by Peter Michal Bohun (1822–1879). 1.60k, Princess Hyacinth, by Alfons Mucha (1860–1939). 3k, Madonna and Child, woodcarving, 1518, by Master Paul of Levoca.

1968, Nov. 29 Engraved ***Perf. 11½***

1589	A565	60h multi	35	30
1590	A565	80h multi	55	50
1591	A565	1.20k multi	90	80
1592	A565	1.60k multi	1.25	1.10
1593	A565	3k multi	*5.25*	*4.75*
		Nos. 1589-1593 (5)	*8.30*	*7.45*

Sheets of 4.

1968, Dec. 18 **Engr. and Photo.**

Slovak Fairy Tales: 60h, The Proud Lady. 80h, The Ruling Knight. 1k, Good Day, Little Bench. 1.20k, The Spellbound Castle. 1.80k, The Miraculous Hunter. The designs are from illustrations by Ludovit Fulla for "Slovak Stories."

1594	A595	30h multi	10	5
1595	A595	60h multi	25	7
1596	A595	80h multi	30	10
1597	A595	1k multi	35	13
1598	A595	1.20k multi	60	15
1599	A595	1.80k multi	*2.50*	*1.00*
		Nos. 1594-1599 (6)	*4.10*	*1.50*

ČESKOSLOVENSKO 1918 50 1968 1 KČS
DEN ČESKOSLOVENSKÉ POŠTOVNÍ ZNÁMKY

Czechoslovakia Nos. 2 and 3

A596

1968, Dec. 18

1600	A596	1k vio bl & gold	1.25	1.00

Issued to commemorate the 50th anniversary of Czechoslovakian postage stamps.

Crescent, Cross and Lion and Sun Emblems — A597

ILO Emblem — A598

Design: 60h, 12 crosses in circles forming large cross.

Engraved and Photogravure

1969, Jan. 31 ***Perf. 11½***

1601	A597	60h blk, red & gold	25	5
1602	A597	1k blk, ultra & red	45	15

No. 1601 commemorates the 50th anniversary of the Czechoslovak Red Cross; No. 1602 commemorates the 50th anniversary of the League of Red Cross Societies.

1969, Jan. 31

1603	A598	1k blk & gray	35	15

Issued to commemorate the 50th anniversary of the International Labor Organization.

Cheb Pistol

A599

Historical Firearms: 40h, Italian pistol with Dutch decorations, c. 1600. 60h, Wheellock rifle from Matej Kubik workshop c. 1720. 1k, Flintlock pistol, Devieuxe workshop, Liege, c. 1760. 1.40k, Dueling pistols, from Lebeda workshop, Prague, c. 1835. 1.60k, Derringer pistols, U.S.A., c. 1865.

1969, Feb. 18

1604	A599	30h blk & multi	9	5
1605	A599	40h blk & multi	15	5
1606	A599	60h blk & multi	20	6
1607	A599	1k blk & multi	45	10
1608	A599	1.40k blk & multi	70	25
1609	A599	1.60k blk & multi	*2.00*	*85*
		Nos. 1604-1609 (6)	*3.59*	*1.36*

Bratislava Castle, Muse and Book

A600

Designs: No. 1611, Science symbols and emblem (Brno University). No. 1612, Harp, laurel and musicians' names. No. 1613, Theatrical scene. No. 1614, Arms of Slovakia, banner and blossoms. No. 1615, School, outstretched hands and woman with linden leaves.

1969, Mar. 24 Engr. ***Perf. 11½***

1610	A600	60h vio bl	25	8

Engraved and Photogravure

1611	A600	60h blk, gold & sl	25	8
1612	A600	60h gold, bl, blk & red	25	8
1613	A600	60h blk & rose red	25	8
1614	A600	60h rose red, sil & bl	25	8
1615	A600	60h blk & gold	25	8
		Nos. 1610-1615 (6)	1.50	48

Nos. 1610–1614 issued to commemorate the 50th anniversary of: Komensky University in Bratislava (#1610); Brno University (#1611); Brno Conservatory of Music (#1612); Slovak National Theater (#1613); Slovak Soviet Republic (#1614); No. 1615 commemorates the centenary of the Zniev Gymnasium (academic high school).

Baldachin-top Car and Four-seat Coupé of 1900–1905—A601

Designs: 1.60k, Laurin & Klement Voiturette, 1907, and L & K touring car with American top, 1907. 1.80k, First Prague bus, 1907, and sectionalized Skoda bus, 1967.

1969, Mar. 25

1616	A601	30h blk, lil & lt grn	15	5
1617	A601	1.60k blk, org brn & lt bl	65	20
1618	A601	1.80k multi	*2.00*	*1.25*

Peace, by Ladislav Guderna

A602

Engraved and Photogravure

1969, Apr. 21 ***Perf. 11***

1619	A602	1.60k multi	90	55

Issued to commemorate the 20th anniversary of the Peace Movement. Issued in sheets of 15 stamps and 5 tabs.

Horse and Rider, by Vaclav Hollar

A603

Old Engravings of Horses: 30h, Prancing Stallion, by Hendrik Goltzius (horiz.). 80h, Groom Leading Horse, by Matthäus Merian (horiz.). 1.80k, Horse and Soldier, by Albrecht Dürer. 2.40k, Groom and Horse, by Johann E. Ridinger.

1969, Apr. 24 ***Perf. 11x11½, 11½x11***

Yellowish Paper

1620	A603	30h dk brn	10	5
1621	A603	80h vio brn	30	10
1622	A603	1.60k slate	65	20
1623	A603	1.80k sepia	80	30
1624	A603	2.40k multi	*2.50*	*95*
		Nos. 1620-1624 (5)	*4.35*	*1.60*

M. R. Stefánik as Astronomy Professor and French General

A604

1969, May 4 Engraved ***Perf. 11½***

1625	A604	60h rose cl	35	10

Issued to commemorate the 50th anniversary of the death of Gen. Milan R. Stefánik.

St. Wenceslas Pressing Wine, Mural by the Master of Litomerice

A605

Design: No. 1627, Coronation banner of the Estates, 1723, with St. Wenceslas and coats of arms of Bohemia and Czech Crown lands.

1969, May 9 Engraved ***Perf. 11½***

1626	A605	3k multi	2.50	2.00
1627	A605	3k multi	2.50	2.00

Issued to publicize the art treasures of the Castle of Prague. See Nos. 1689–1690.

Caricature Type of 1968

Caricatures: 30h, Pavol Orszagh Hviezdoslav (1849–1921), Slovak writer. 40h, Gilbert K. Chesterton (1874–1936), English writer. 60h, Vladimir Mayakovski (1893–1930), Russian poet. 1k, Henri Matisse (1869–1954), French painter. 1.80k, Ales Hrdlicka (1869–1943), Czech-born American anthropologist. 2k, Franz Kafka (1883–1924), Austrian writer.

Engraved and Photogravure

1969, June 17 ***Perf. 11½x12***

1628	A594	30h blk, red & bl	10	5

1629	A594	40h blk, bl & lt vio	15	8
1630	A594	60h blk, rose & yel	20	10
1631	A594	1k blk & multi	45	15
1632	A594	1.80k blk, ultra & ocher	75	25
1633	A594	2k blk, yel & brt grn	*2.00*	*60*
		Nos. 1628-1633 (6)	*3.65*	*1.23*

Issued to honor cultural personalities of the 20th century and UNESCO.

"Music," by Alfons Mucha
A606

Paintings by Mucha: 60h, "Painting." 1k, "Dance." 2.40k, "Ruby" and "Amethyst."

1969, July 14 ***Perf. 11½x11***

Size: 30x49mm.

1634	A606	30h blk & multi	10	5
1635	A606	60h blk & multi	20	10
1636	A606	1k blk & multi	35	15

Size: 39x51mm.

1637	A606	2.40k blk & multi	*2.50*	*1.75*

Issued to commemorate the 30th anniversary of the death of Alfons Mucha (1860–1930), painter and stamp designer (Type A1).

Pres. Svoboda and Partisans
A607

Design: No. 1639, Slovak fighters and mourners.

Engraved and Photogravure

1969, Aug. 29 ***Perf. 11***

1638	A607	30h ol grn & red, *yel*	12	5
1639	A607	30h vio bl & red, *yel*	12	5

Issued to commemorate the 25th anniversary of the Slovak uprising and of the Battle of Dukla.

Tatra Mountain Stream and Gentians
A608

Designs: 60h, Various views in Tatra Mountains. No. 1644, Mountain pass and gentians. No. 1645, Houses, Krivan Mountain and autumn crocuses.

1969, Sept. 8 **Engraved** ***Perf. 11***

Size: 71x33mm.

1640	A608	60h gray	35	10
1641	A608	60h dk bl	35	10
1642	A608	60h dl gray vio	35	10

Perf. 11½

Size: 40x23mm.

1643	A608	1.60k multi	75	25
1644	A608	1.60k multi	*1.50*	*60*
1645	A608	1.60k multi	75	25
		Nos. 1640-1645(6)	*4.05*	*1.40*

Issued to commemorate the 20th anniversary of the creation of the Tatra Mountains National Park. Nos. 1640–1642 are printed in sheets of 15 (3x5) with 5 labels showing mountain plants. Nos. 1643–1645 issued in sheets of 10.

Bronze Belt Ornaments
A609

Archaeological Treasures from Bohemia and Moravia: 30h, Gilt ornament with 6 masks. 1k, Jeweled earrings. 1.80k, Front and back of lead cross with Greek inscription. 2k, Gilt strap ornament with human figure.

Engraved and Photogravure

1969, Sept. 30 ***Perf. 11½x11***

1646	A609	20h gold & multi	10	5
1647	A609	30h gold & multi	10	5
1648	A609	1k red & multi	40	16
1649	A609	1.80k dl org & multi	80	30
1650	A609	2k gold & multi	*1.50*	*50*
		Nos. 1646-1650 (5)	*2.90*	*1.06*

"Mail Circling the World"
A610

1969, Oct. 1 **Engraved** ***Perf. 12***

1651	A610	3.20k multi	1.50	75

Issued to commemorate the 16th Universal Postal Union Congress, Tokyo, Oct. 1–Nov. 14. Issued in sheets of 4.

Coat of Arms Type of 1968

Engraved and Photogravure

1969, Oct. 25 ***Perf. 11½***

Multicolored

1652	A590	50h *Bardejov*	25	8
1653	A590	50h *Hranice*	25	8
1654	A590	50h *Kezmarok*	25	8
1655	A590	50h *Krnov*	25	8
1656	A590	50h *Litomerice*	25	8
1657	A590	50h *Manetin*	25	8
		Nos. 1652-1657 (6)	1.50	48

Painting Type of 1968

Designs: 60h, Requiem, 1944, by Frantisek Muzika. 1k, Resurrection, 1380, by the Master of the Trebon Altar. 1.60k, Crucifixion, 1950, by Vincent Hloznik. 1.80k, Girl with Doll, 1863, by Julius Bencur. 2.20k, St. Jerome, 1357–67, by Master Theodorik.

Engraved and Photogravure

1969, Nov. 25 ***Perf. 11½***

1658	A565	60h multi	30	25
1659	A565	1k multi	50	45
1660	A565	1.60k multi	75	65
1661	A565	1.80k multi	1.10	1.00
1662	A565	2.20k multi	*3.50*	*3.25*
		Nos. 1658-1662 (5)	*6.15*	*5.60*

Sheets of 4.

Symbolic Sheet of Stamps—A611

1969, Dec. 18 ***Perf. 11½x12***

1663	A611	1k dk brn, ultra & gold	65	50

Issued for Stamp Day 1969.

Ski Jump—A612

Designs: 60h, Long distance skier. 1k, Ski jump and slope. 1.60k, Woman skier.

Engraved and Photogravure

1970, Jan. 6 ***Perf. 11½***

1664	A612	50h multi	15	5
1665	A612	60h multi	18	5
1666	A612	1k multi	40	15
1667	A612	1.60k multi	*1.25*	*45*

Issued to publicize the International Ski Championships "Tatra 1970."

Ludwig van Beethoven (1770–1827)
A613

Portraits: No. 1669, Friedrich Engels (1820–1895), German socialist. No. 1670, Maximilian Hell (1720–1792), Slovakian Jesuit and astronomer. No. 1671, Lenin (1870–1924), Russian Communist leader. No. 1672, Josef Manes (1820–1871), Czech painter. No. 1673, John Amos Comenius (1592–1670), theologian and educator.

1970, Feb. 17 **Engr.** ***Perf. 11x11½***

1668	A613	40h black	15	8
1669	A613	40h dl red	15	8
1670	A613	40h yel brn	15	8
1671	A613	40h dl red	15	8
1672	A613	40h brown	15	8
1673	A613	40h black	15	8
		Nos. 1668-1673 (6)	90	48

Issued to commemorate the anniversaries of the birth of Beethoven, Engels, Hell, Lenin and Manes, the 300th anniversary of the death of Comenius, and to honor UNESCO.

Bells
A614

Designs: 80h, Machine tools and lathe. 1k, Folklore masks. 1.60k, Angel and Three Wise Men, 17th century icon from Koniec. 2k, View of Orlik Castle, 1787, by F. K. Wolf. 3k, "Passing through Koshu down to Mishima" from Hokusai's 36 Views of Fuji.

Engraved and Photogravure

1970, Mar. 13 ***Perf. 11½x11***

Size: 40x23mm.

1674	A614	50h multi	20	5
1675	A614	80h multi	30	8
1676	A614	1k multi	40	8

Size: 50x40mm.

Perf. 11½

1677	A614	1.60k multi	75	40
1678	A614	2k multi	1.00	50
1679	A614	3k multi	*2.50*	*2.00*
		Nos. 1674-1679 (6)	*5.15*	*3.11*

Issued to publicize EXPO '70 International Exhibition, Osaka, Japan, March 15–Sept. 13, 1970. Nos. 1674–1676 issued in sheets of 50, Nos. 1677–1679 in sheets of 4.

Kosice Townhall, Laurel and Czechoslovak Arms
A615

1970, Apr. 5 ***Perf. 11***

1680	A615	60h sl, ver & gold	50	8

Issued to commemorate the 25th anniversary of the government's Kosice Program.

"The Remarkable Horse" by Josef Lada
A616

Lenin
A617

Paintings by Josef Lada: 60h, Autumn, 1955 (horiz.). 1.80k, "The Water Sprite." 2.40k, Children in Winter, 1943 (horiz.).

1970, Apr. 21 ***Perf. 11½***

1681	A616	60h blk & multi	25	10
1682	A616	1k blk & multi	40	15
1683	A616	1.80k blk & multi	75	25
1684	A616	2.40k blk & multi	*1.75*	*1.00*

1970, Apr. 22 **Engr. & Photo.**

Design: 60h, Lenin without cap, facing left.

1685	A617	30h dk red & gold	12	5
1686	A617	60h blk & gold	30	6

Issued to commemorate the centenary of the birth of Lenin (1870–1924), Russian communist leader.

Fighters on the Barricades
A618

Design: No. 1688, Lilac, Russian tank and castle.

Engraved and Photogravure

1970, May 5 ***Perf. 11x11½***

1687	A618	30h dl pur, gold & bl	25	6
1688	A618	30h dl grn, gold & red	25	6

No. 1687 commemorates the 25th anniversary of the Prague uprising and No. 1688 the 25th anniversary of the liberation of Czechoslovakia from the Germans.

Prague Castle Art Type of 1969

Designs: No. 1689, Bust of St. Vitus, 1486. No. 1690, Hermes and Athena, by Bartholomy Springer (1546–1611), mural from White Tower.

1970, May 7 Engr. *Perf. 11½*

1689	A605	3k mar & multi	2.50	2.00
1690	A605	3k lt bl & multi	2.50	2.00

Issued to publicize art treasures of the Castle of Prague.

Compass Rose, U.N. Headquarters and Famous Buildings of the World
A619

Engraved and Photogravure

1970, June 26 *Perf. 11*

1691	A619	1k blk & multi	45	30

Issued to commemorate the 25th anniversary of the United Nations. Issued in sheets of 15 (3x5) and 5 labels showing U.N. emblem.

Cannon from 30 Years' War and Baron Munchhausen
A620

Historical Cannons: 60h, Cannon from Hussite war and St. Barbara. 1.20k, Cannon from Prussian-Austrian war, and legendary cannoneer Javurek. 1.80k, Early 20th century cannon and spaceship "La Colombiad" (Jules Verne). 2.40k, World War I cannon and "Good Soldier Schweik."

1970, Aug. 31 *Perf. 11½*

1692	A620	30h blk & multi	10	5
1693	A620	60h blk & multi	20	5
1694	A620	1.20k blk & multi	45	10
1695	A620	1.80k blk & multi	80	25
1696	A620	2.40k blk & multi	*2.25*	*1.00*
		Nos. 1692-1696 (5)	*3.80*	*1.45*

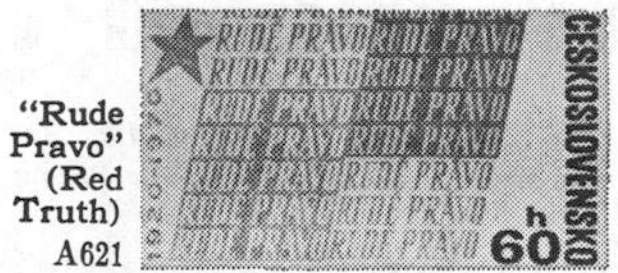

"Rude Pravo" (Red Truth)
A621

1970, Sept. 21 *Perf. 11½x11*

1697	A621	60h car gold & blk	25	5

Issued to commemorate the 50th anniversary of the Rude Pravo newspaper.

"Great Sun" House Sign and Old Town Tower Bridge, Prague
A622

Designs: 60h, "Blue Lion" and Town Hall Tower, Brno. 1k, Gothic corner stone and Town Hall Tower, Bratislava. 1.40k, Coat of Arms and Gothic Tower, Bratislava, and medallion. 1.60k, Moravian Eagle and Gothic Town Hall Tower, Brno. 1.80k, "Black Sun" and "Green Frog" house signs and New Town Hall, Prague.

Engr. & Photo.

1970, Sept. 23 *Perf. 11x11½*

1698	A622	40h blk & multi	12	6
1699	A622	60h blk & multi	18	10
1700	A622	1k blk & multi	35	16
1701	A622	1.40k blk & multi	*2.25*	*75*
1702	A622	1.60k blk & multi	60	24
1703	A622	1.80k blk & multi	75	28
		Nos. 1698-1703 (6)	*4.25*	*1.59*

Germany–Uruguay Semifinal Soccer Match—A623

Designs: 20h, Sundisk Games' emblem and flags of participating nations. 60h, England-Czechoslovakia match and coats of arms. 1k, Romania-Czechoslovakia match and coats of arms. 1.20k, Brazil-Italy, final match and emblems. 1.80k, Brazil-Czechoslovakia match and emblems.

1970, Oct. 29 *Perf. 11½*

1704	A623	20h blk & multi	6	5
1705	A623	40h blk & multi	12	5
1706	A623	60h blk & multi	20	5
1707	A623	1k blk & multi	40	6
1708	A623	1.20k blk & multi	45	15
1709	A623	1.80k blk & multi	*2.25*	*60*
		Nos. 1704-1709 (6)	*3.48*	*96*

Issued to commemorate the 9th World Soccer Championships for the Jules Rimet Cup, Mexico City, May 30–June 21.

Congress Emblem
A624

1970, Nov. 9 Engr. & Photo.

1710	A624	30h blk, gold, ultra & red	30	5

Congress of the Czechoslovak Socialist Youth Federation.

Painting Type of 1967

Paintings: 1k, Seated Mother, by Mikulas Galanda. 1.20k, Bridesmaid, by Karel Svolinsky. 1.40k, Walk by Night, 1944, by Frantisek Hudecek. 1.80k, Banska Bystrica Market, by Dominik Skutecky. 2.40k, Adoration of the Kings, from the Vysehrad Codex, 1085.

1970, Nov. 27 Engr. *Perf. 11½*

1711	A565	1k multi	40	35
1712	A565	1.20k multi	55	50
1713	A565	1.40k multi	75	65
1714	A565	1.80k multi	1.00	80
1715	A565	2.40k multi	*2.50*	*2.25*
		Nos. 1711-1715 (5)	*5.20*	*4.55*

Sheets of 4.

Radar
A625

Designs: 40h, Interkosmos 3, geophysical satellite. 60h, Molniya meteorological satellite. 1k, Astronaut and Vostok satellite. No. 1720, Interkosmos 4, solar research satellite. No. 1720A, Space satellite (Sputnik) over city. 1.60k, Two-stage rocket on launching pad.

Engraved and Photogravure

1970–71 *Perf. 11*

1716	A625	20h blk & multi	15	5
1717	A625	40h blk & multi	15	5
1718	A625	60h blk & multi	20	5
1719	A625	1k blk & multi	45	15
1720	A625	1.20k blk & multi	50	15
1720A	A625	1.20k blk & multi ('71)	60	15
1721	A625	1.60k blk & multi	*1.25*	*50*
		Nos. 1716-1721 (7)	*3.30*	*1.10*

Issued to publicize "Interkosmos," the collaboration of communist countries in various phases of space research. Issue dates: No. 1720A, Nov. 15, 1971; others, Nov. 30, 1970.

Face of Christ on Veronica's Veil
A626

Slovak Ikons, 16th–18th Centuries: 60h, Adam and Eve in the Garden (vert.). 2k, St. George and the Dragon. 2.80k, St. Michael (vert.).

1970, Dec. 17 Engraved *Perf. 11½*

Cream Paper

1722	A626	60h multi	30	30
1723	A626	1k multi	50	50
1724	A626	2k multi	95	95
1725	A626	2.80k multi	*2.50*	*2.25*

Sheets of 4.

Carrier Pigeon Type of 1920
A627

Engr. & Photo.

1970, Dec. 18 *Perf. 11x11½*

1726	A627	1k red, blk & yel grn	50	50

Stamp Day.

Song of the Barricades, 1938, by Karel Stika
A628

Designs (Czech and Slovak Graphic Art): 50h, Fruit Grower's Barge, 1941, by Cyril Bouda. 60h, Moon (woman) Searching for Lilies of the Valley, 1913, by Jan Zrzavy. 1k, At the Edge of Town (working man and woman), 1931, by Koloman Sokol. 1.60k, Summer, 1641, by Vaclav Hollar. 2k, Gamekeeper and Shepherd of Orava Castle, 1847, by Peter M. Bohun.

Engraved (40h, 60h, 1k); Engraved and Photogravure (others)

1971, Jan. 28 *Perf. 11½*

1727	A628	40h brown	15	6
1728	A628	50h blk & multi	18	8
1729	A628	60h slate	18	10
1730	A628	1k black	40	16
1731	A628	1.60k blk & buff	65	24
1732	A628	2k blk & multi	*1.75*	*50*
		Nos. 1727-1732 (6)	*3.31*	*1.14*

Saris Church A629 — Bell Tower, Hronsek—A630

Designs: 1k, Roofs and folk art, Horácko. 2.40k, House, Jicinsko. 3k, House and folk art, Cechy-Melnicko. 3.60k, Chrudimsko Church. 5k, Watch Tower, Cesky-Nachod. 5.40k, Baroque house, Posumavi. 6k, Cottage, Orava. 9k, Cottage, Turnovsko. 10k, Old houses, Liptov. 14k, House and wayside bell stand. 20k, Houses, Slovensko-Cicmany.

Perf. 11½x11, 11x11½

1971–72 Engr. and Photo.

1733	A630	1k blk & multi	40	5
1734	A629	1.60k blk, dk grn & vio	65	6
1735	A630	2k blk & multi	80	5
1736	A629	2.40k blk & multi	95	6
1736A	A630	3k blk & multi ('72)	1.20	8
1737	A629	3.60k blk & multi	1.50	6
1737A	A630	5k blk & multi ('72)	1.75	12
1738	A629	5.40k blk & multi	1.75	6
1739	A630	6k blk & multi	2.10	9
1740	A630	9k blk & multi	3.00	30
1740A	A629	10k blk & multi ('72)	3.75	30
1741	A629	14k blk & multi	5.00	25
1741A	A629	20k blk & multi ('72)	7.50	90
		Nos. 1733-1741A (13)	30.35	2.38

Nos. 1736A, 1738, 1740 are horizontal.

Coat of Arms Type of 1968

1971, Feb. 26 *Perf. 11½*

Multicolored

1742	A590	60h *Zilina*	25	8
1743	A590	60h *Levoca*	25	8
1744	A590	60h *Ceska Trebova*	25	8
1745	A590	60h *Uhersky Brod*	25	8
1746	A590	60h *Trutnov*	25	8
1747	A590	60h *Karlovy Vary*	25	8
		Nos. 1742-1747 (6)	1.50	48

"Fight of the Communards and Rise of the International"—A631

Design: No. 1749, World fight against racial discrimination, and "UNESCO."

1971, March 18 *Perf. 11*

1748	A631	1k multi	50	25
1749	A631	1k multi	50	25

No. 1748 commemorates the centenary of the Paris Commune. No. 1749 publicizes the Year against Racial Discrimination. Issued in sheets of 15 stamps and 5 labels.

Edelweiss, Mountaineering Map and Equipment
A632

Engraved and Photogravure

1971, Apr. 27 ***Perf. 11½x11***

1750	A632	30h multi	25	5

50th anniversary of Slovak Alpine Club.

Singer
A633

1971, Apr. 27 ***Perf. 11½***

1751	A633	30h multi	20	5

50th anniversary of Slovak Teachers' Choir.

Abbess' Crosier, 16th Century
A634

Design: No. 1753, Allegory of Music, 16th century mural.

1971, May 9

1752	A634	3k gold & multi	1.75	1.60
1753	A634	3k blk, dk brn & buff	1.75	1.60

See Nos. 1817-1818, 1884-1885, 1937-1938, 2040-2041, 2081-2082, 2114-2115, 2176-2177, 2238-2239, 2329-2330, 2420-2421.

Lenin
A635

Designs: 40h, Hammer and sickle allegory. 60h, Raised fists. 1k, Star, hammer and sickle.

1971, May 14 ***Perf. 11***

1754	A635	30h blk, red & gold	15	5
1755	A635	40h blk, ultra, red & gold	20	5
1756	A635	60h blk, ultra, red & gold	30	5
1757	A635	1k blk, ultra, red & gold	55	10

50th anniversary of the Czechoslovak Communist Party.

Star, Hammer-Sickle Emblems
A636

Design: 60h, Hammer-sickle emblem, fist and people (vert.).

Perf. 11½x11, 11x11½

1971, May 24 **Engr. & Photo.**

1758	A636	30h blk, red, gold & yel	15	5
1759	A636	60h blk, red, gold & bl	30	8

14th Congress of Communist Party of Czechoslovakia.

Ring-necked Pheasant
A637

Designs: 60h, Rainbow trout. 80h, Mouflon. 1k, Chamois. 2k, Stag. 2.60k, Wild boar.

1971, Aug. 17 ***Perf. 11½x11***

1760	A637	20h org & multi	6	5
1761	A637	60h lt bl & multi	18	6
1762	A637	80h yel & multi	24	6
1763	A637	1k lt grn & multi	30	10
1764	A637	2k lil & multi	75	30
1765	A637	2.60k bis & multi	*3.00*	*1.00*
		Nos. 1760-1765 (6)	*4.53*	*1.57*

World Hunting Exhibition, Budapest, Aug. 27-30.

Diesel Locomotive
A638

Gymnasts and Banners
A639

1971, Sept. 2 ***Perf. 11x11½***

1766	A638	30h lt bl, blk & red	12	5

Centenary of CKD, Prague Machine Foundry.

1971, Sept. 2 ***Perf. 11½x11***

1767	A639	30h red brn, gold & ultra	12	5

50th anniversary of Workers' Physical Exercise Federation.

Road Intersections and Bridge
A640

1971, Sept. 2 **Engr. & Photo.**

1768	A640	1k blk, gold, red & bl	45	20

14th World Highways and Bridges Congress. Sheets of 25 stamps and 25 labels printed se-tenant with continuous design.

Chinese Fairytale, by Eva Bednarova
A641

Designs: 1k, Tiger and other animals, by Mirko Hanak. 1.60k, The Miraculous Bamboo Shoot, by Yasuo Segawa (horiz.).

Perf. 11½x11, 11x11½

1971, Sept. 10

1769	A641	60h multi	30	10
1770	A641	1k multi	60	20
1771	A641	1.60k multi	1.40	60

Bratislava BIB 71 biennial exhibition of illustrations for children's books.

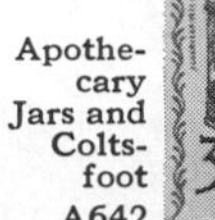

Apothecary Jars and Colts-foot
A642

Designs: 60h, Jars and dog rose. 1k, Scales and adonis vernalis. 1.20k, Mortars and valerian. 1.80k, Retorts and chicory. 2.40k, Mill, mortar and henbane.

1971, Sept. 20 ***Perf. 11½x11***

Yellow Paper

1772	A642	30h multi	9	5
1773	A642	60h multi	18	8
1774	A642	1k multi	35	12
1775	A642	1.20k multi	50	16
1776	A642	1.80k multi	85	30
1777	A642	2.40k multi	*1.75*	50
		Nos. 1772-1777 (6)	*3.72*	1.21

International Pharmaceutical Congress.

Painting Type of 1967

Paintings: 1k, "Waiting" (woman's head), 1967, by Imro Weiner-Král. 1.20k, Resurrection, by Master of Vyssi Brod, 14th century. 1.40k, Woman with Pitcher, by Milos Bazovsky. 1.80k, Veruna Cudova (in folk costume), by Josef Mánes. 2.40k, Detail from "Feast of the Rose Garlands," by Albrecht Dürer.

1971, Nov. 27 ***Perf. 11½***

1779	A565	1k multi	40	35
1780	A565	1.20k multi	60	45
1781	A565	1.40k multi	85	55
1782	A565	1.80k multi	1.10	85
1783	A565	2.40k multi	*2.25*	*2.00*
		Nos. 1779-1783 (5)	*5.20*	*4.20*

Sheets of 4.

Workers Revolt in Krompachy, by Julius Nemcik—A643

1971, Nov. 28 ***Perf. 11x11½***

1784	A643	60h multi	35	10

History of the Czechoslovak Communist Party.

Wooden Dolls and Birds
A644

Folk Art and UNICEF Emblem: 80h, Jug handles, carved. 1k, Horseback rider. 1.60k, Shepherd carrying lamb. 2k, Easter eggs and rattle. 3k, "Zbojnik," folk hero.

1971, Dec. 11 ***Perf. 11½***

1785	A644	60h multi	25	5
1786	A644	80h multi	35	8
1787	A644	1k multi	50	12
1788	A644	1.60k multi	75	20
1789	A644	2k multi	1.50	55
1790	A644	3k multi	2.75	80
		Nos. 1785-1790 (6)	6.10	1.80

25th anniversary of the United Nations International Children's Fund (UNICEF).

Runners, Parthenon, Czechoslovak Olympic Emblem
A645

Designs: 40h, Women's high jump, Olympic emblem and plan for Prague Stadium. 1.60k, Cross-country skiers, Sapporo '72 emblem and ski jump in High Tatras. 2.60k, Discus thrower, Discobolus and St. Vitus Cathedral.

1971, Dec. 16 **Engr. & Photo.**

1791	A645	30h multi	12	6
1792	A645	40h multi	15	9
1793	A645	1.60k multi	60	45
1794	A645	2.60k multi	1.50	60

75th anniversary of Czechoslovak Olympic Committee (30h, 2.60k); 20th Summer Olympic Games, Munich, Aug. 26–Sept. 10, 1972 (40h); 11th Winter Olympic Games, Sapporo, Japan, Feb. 3-13, 1972 (1.60k).

Post Horns and Lion—A646

1971, Dec. 17 ***Perf. 11x11½***

1795	A646	1k blk, gold, car & bl	55	30

Stamp Day.

Figure Skating
A647

"Lezáky"
A648

Designs (Olympic Emblems and): 50h, Ski jump. 1k, Ice hockey. 1.60k, Sledding, women's.

1972, Jan. 13 ***Perf. 11½***

1796	A647	40h pur, org & red	15	8
1797	A647	50h dk bl, org & red	20	8
1798	A647	1k mag, org & red	40	18
1799	A647	1.60k bl grn, org & red	*1.50*	*50*

11th Winter Olympic Games, Sapporo, Japan, Feb. 3-13.

1972, Feb. 16 **Engr. & Photo.**

Designs: No. 1801, Boy's head behind barbed wire (horiz.). No. 1802, Hand rising from ruins. No. 1803, Soldier and banner (horiz.).

1800	A648	30h blk, dl org & red	18	5
1801	A648	30h blk & brn org	18	5
1802	A648	60h blk, yel & red	25	5
1803	A648	60h sl grn & multi	25	5

30th anniversary of: destruction of Lezáky (No. 1800) and Lidice (1802); Terezin concentration camp (No. 1801); Czechoslovak Army unit in Russia (No. 1803).

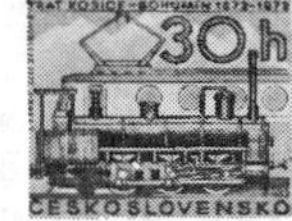

Book Year Emblem
A649

Steam and Diesel Locomotives
A650

1972, Mar. 17 ***Perf. 11½x11***

1804	A649	1k blk & org brn	40	10

International Book Year 1972.

1972, Mar. 17 *Perf. 11½x11*

1805	A650	30h multi	30	5

Centenary of the Kosice-Bohumin railroad.

"Pasture," by Vojtech Sedlacek
A651

Designs: 50h, Dressage, by Frantisek Tichy. 60th, Otakara Kubina, by Vaclav Fiala. 1k, The Three Kings, by Ernest Zmetak. 1.60k, Woman Dressing, by Ludovit Fulla.

Photogravure and Engraved

1972, Mar. 27 *Perf. 11½x11*

1806	A651	40h multi	13	5
1807	A651	50h multi	17	6
1808	A651	60h multi	30	8
1809	A651	1k multi	50	20
1810	A651	1.60k multi	1.40	1.25
		Nos. 1806-1810 (5)	2.50	1.64

Czech and Slovak graphic art. 1.60k issued in sheets of 4. See also Nos. 1859–1862, 1921–1924.

Ice Hockey
A652

Design: 1k, Two players.

1972, Apr. 7 *Perf. 11*

1811	A652	60h blk & multi	20	7
1812	A652	1k blk & multi	40	20

World and European Ice Hockey Championships, Prague.

Bicycling, Olympic Rings and Emblem
A653

1972, Apr. 7 **Multicolored**

1813	A653	50h *shown*	20	6
1814	A653	1.60k *Diving*	60	15
1815	A653	1.80k *Canoeing*	75	20
1816	A653	2k *Gymnast*	1.50	75

20th Olympic Games, Munich, Aug. 26–Sept. 11.

Prague Castle Art Type of 1971

Designs: No. 1817, Adam and Eve, column capital, St. Vitus Cathedral. No. 1818, Czech coat of arms (lion), c. 1500.

1972, May 9 *Perf. 11½*

1817	A634	3k blk & multi	3.00	2.50
1818	A634	3k blk, red, sil & gold	1.75	1.50

Art treasures of Castle of Prague. Sheets of 4.

Andrej Sladkovic (1820–1872), Poet
A654

Portraits: No. 1820, Janko Kral (1822–1876), poet. No. 1821, Ludmilla Podjavorinska (1872–1951), writer. No. 1822, Antonin Hudecek (1872–1941), painter. No. 1823, Frantisek Bilek (1872–1941), sculptor. No. 1824, Jan Preisler (1872–1918), painter.

Engraved and Photogravure

1972, June 14 *Perf. 11*

1819	A654	40h pur, ol & bl	20	8
1820	A654	40h dk grn, bl & yel	20	8
1821	A654	40h blk & multi	20	8
1822	A654	40h brn, grn & bl	20	8
1823	A654	40h choc, grn & org	20	8
1824	A654	40h grn, sl & dp org	20	8
		Nos. 1819-1824 (6)	1.20	48

Men with Banners
A655

1972, June 14 *Perf. 11x11½*

1825	A655	30h dk vio bl, red & yel	12	5

8th Trade Union Congress, Prague.

Art Forms of Wire
A656

Ornamental Wirework: 60h, Plane and rosette. 80h, Four-headed dragon and ornament. 1k, Locomotive and loops. 2.60k, Tray and owl.

1972, Aug. 28 *Perf. 11½x11*

1826	A656	20h sal & multi	7	5
1827	A656	60h multi	25	8
1828	A656	80h pink & multi	35	10
1829	A656	1k multi	50	18
1830	A656	2.60k rose & multi	1.75	60
		Nos. 1826-1830 (5)	2.92	1.01

"Jiskra"
A657

Engraved and Photogravure

1972, Sept. 27 *Perf. 11½x11*

Size: 40x22mm.

Multicolored Design on Blue Paper

1831	A657	50h *shown*	17	5
1832	A657	60h *"Mir"*	20	5
1833	A657	80h *"Republika"*	26	6

Size: 48x29mm.

Perf. 11x11½

1834	A657	1k *"Kosice"*	33	10
1835	A657	1.60k *"Dukla"*	53	16
1836	A657	2k *"Kladno"*	2.00	85
		Nos. 1831-1836 (6)	3.49	1.27

Czechoslovak sea-going vessels.

Hussar, 18th Century Tile
A658

1972, Oct. 24 *Perf. 11½x11*

Multicolored

1837	A658	30h *shown*	12	6
1838	A658	60h *Janissary*	25	8
1839	A658	80h *St. Martin*	30	12
1840	A658	1.60k *St. George*	75	18
1841	A658	1.80k *Nobleman's guard*	95	20
1842	A658	2.20k *Slovakian horseman*	2.00	1.00
		Nos. 1837-1842 (6)	4.37	1.64

Horsemen from 18th–19th century tiles or enamel paintings on glass.

Worker, Flag Hoisted on Bayonet
A659

Star, Hammer and Sickle
A660

1972, Nov. 7 *Perf. 11x11½*

1843	A659	30h gold & multi	12	6
1844	A660	60h rose car & gold	24	8

55th anniversary of the Russian October Revolution (30h); 50th anniversary of the Soviet Union (60h).

Nos. 1811–1812 Overprinted in Violet Blue or Black

CSSR

MAJSTROM

SVETA

1972 *Perf. 11*

1845	A652	60h multi (VBl)	8.00	8.00
1846	A652	1k multi (Bk)	8.00	8.00

Czechoslovakia's victorious ice hockey team. The overprint on the 60h is in Czech and reads ČSSR/MISTREM/SVĚTA; the overprint on the 1k (shown) is in Slovak.

Painting Type of 1967

Designs: 1k, "Nosegay" (nudes and flowers), by Max Svabinsky. 1.20k, Struggle of St. Ladislas with Kuman nomad, anonymous, 14th century. 1.40k, Lady with Fur Hat, by Vaclav Hollar. 1.80k, Midsummer Night's Dream, 1962, by Josef Liesler. 2.40k, Pablo Picasso, self-portrait.

1972, Nov. 27 **Photo. & Engr.**

1847	A565	1k multi	50	40
1848	A565	1.20k multi	60	55
1849	A565	1.40k blk & cr	1.25	1.00
1850	A565	1.80k multi	1.25	1.00
1851	A565	2.40k multi	3.00	2.75
		Nos. 1847-1851 (5)	6.60	5.70

Sheets of 4.

Goldfinch
A661

Songbirds: 60h, Warbler feeding young cuckoo. 80h, Cuckoo. 1k, Black-billed magpie. 1.60k, Bullfinch. 3k, Song thrush.

1972, Dec. 15

Size: 30x48½mm.

1852	A661	60h yel & multi	24	10
1853	A661	80h multi	32	14
1854	A661	1k lt bl & multi	40	16

Engraved

Size: 30x23mm.

1855	A661	1.60k multi	75	12
1856	A661	2k multi	95	30
1857	A661	3k multi	2.75	1.00
		Nos. 1852-1857 (6)	5.41	1.82

Post Horn and Allegory—A662

1972, Dec. 18 **Photo. & Engr.**

1858	A662	1k blk, red lil & gold	55	50

Stamp Day.

Art Type of 1972

1973, Jan. 25 *Perf. 11½x11*

Designs: 30h, Flowers in Window, by Jaroslav Grus. 60h, Quest for Happiness, by Josef Balaz. 1.60k, Balloon, by Kamil Lhotak. 1.80k, Woman with Viola, by Richard Wiesner.

1859	A651	30h multi	12	5
1860	A651	60h multi	24	10
1861	A651	1.60k multi	64	18
1862	A651	1.80k multi	1.50	70

Czech and Slovak graphic art.

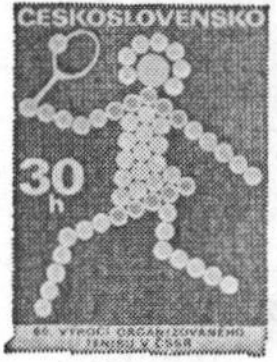

Tennis Player
A663

Figure Skater
A664

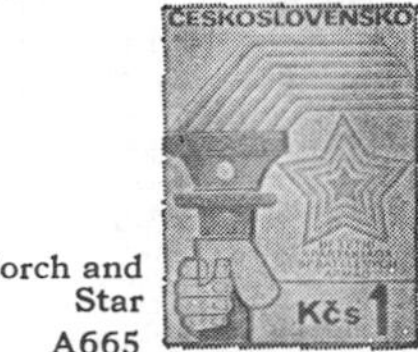

Torch and Star
A665

1973, Feb. 22 *Perf. 11*

1863	A663	30h vio & multi	12	5
1864	A664	60h blk & multi	24	10
1865	A665	1k multi	40	18

80th anniversary of the tennis organization in Czechoslovakia (30h); World figure skating championships, Bratislava (60h); 3rd summer army Spartakiad of socialist countries (1k).

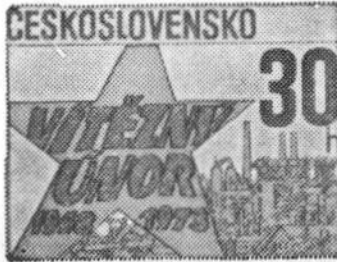

Star and Factories
A666

Workers' Militia, Emblem and Flag
A667

1973, Feb. 23 Photo. & Engr.

1866	A666	30h multi	12	5
1867	A667	60h multi	24	10

25th anniversary of the Communist revolution in Czechoslovakia and of the Militia.

Capt. Jan Nalepka, Major Antonin Sochor and Laurel—A668

Designs (Torch and): 40h, Evzen Rosicky, Mirko Nespor and ivy leaves. 60h, Vlado Clementis, Karol Smidke and linden leaves. 80h, Jan Osoha, Josef Molak and oak leaves. 1k, Marie Kuderikova, Jozka Jaburkova and rose. 1.60k, Vaclav Sinkule, Eduard Urx and palm leaf.

1973, Mar. 20 ***Perf. 11½x11***

Yellow Paper

1868	A668	30h blk, ver & gold	12	5
1869	A668	40h blk, ver & grn	16	7
1870	A668	60h blk, ver & gold	24	10
1871	A668	80h blk, ver & gold	32	14
1872	A668	1k blk, ver & grn	45	18
1873	A668	1.60k blk, ver & sil	*1.00*	*28*
		Nos. 1868-1873 (6)	*2.29*	*82*

Fighters against and victims of Fascism and Nazism during German Occupation.

Virgil I. Grissom, Edward H. White, Roger B. Chaffee—A669

Designs: 20h, Soviet planetary station "Vebera." 30h, "Intercosmos" station. 40h, Lunokhod on moon. 3.60k, Vladimir M. Komarov, Georgi T. Dobrovolsky, Vladislav N. Volkov, Victor I. Patsayev. 5k, Yuri A. Gagarin.

Photogravure and Engraved

1973, Apr. 12 ***Perf. 11½x11***

Size: 40x22mm.

1874	A669	20h multi	8	5
1875	A669	30h multi	12	5
1876	A669	40h multi	16	7

Engraved ***Perf. 11½***

Size: 49x30mm.

1877	A669	3k multi	1.35	75
1878	A669	3.60k multi	2.25	1.50
1879	A669	5k multi	*4.00*	*3.50*
		Nos. 1874-1879 (6)	*7.96*	*5.92*

In memory of American and Russian astronauts.

Radio
A670

Telephone and Map of Czechoslovakia
A671

Television
A672

1973, May 1 ***Perf. 11½x11***

1880	A670	30h blk & multi	12	5
1881	A671	30h lt bl, pink & blk	12	5
1882	A672	30h dp bl & multi	12	5

Czechoslovak anniversaries: 50 years of broadcasting (No. 1880); 20 years of telephone service to all communities (No. 1881); 20 years of television (No. 1882).

Coat of Arms and Linden Branch
A673

1973, May 9 ***Perf. 11x11½***

1883	A673	60h red & multi	24	10

25th anniversary of the Constitution of May 9.

Prague Castle Art Type of 1971

Designs: No. 1884, Royal Legate, 14th century. No. 1885, Seal of King Charles IV, 1351.

1973, May 9 ***Perf. 11½***

1884	A634	3k bl & multi	1.50	1.25
1885	A634	3k gold, grn & dk brn	2.00	1.75

Art treasures of Castle of Prague. Sheets of 4.

Coat of Arms Type of 1968

1973, June 20

Multicolored

1886	A590	60h *Mikulov*	24	15
1887	A590	60h *Zlutice*	24	15
1888	A590	60h *Smolenice*	24	15

Coats of arms of Czechoslovakian cities.

Heraldic Colors of Olomouc and Moravia
A674

Anthurium
A675

1973, Aug. 23 Photo. & Engr.

1889	A674	30h multi	15	8

400th anniversary of University of Olomouc.

1973, Aug. 23 ***Perf. 11½***

Sizes: 60h, 1k, 2k, 30x50mm.; 1.60k, 1.80k, 3.60k, 23x39mm.

Multicolored

1890	A675	60h *Tulips*	30	25
1891	A675	1k *Rose*	40	35
1892	A675	1.60k *shown*	70	35
1893	A675	1.80k *Iris*	90	75
1894	A675	2k *Chrysanthemum*	*2.50*	*2.25*
1895	A675	3.60k *Cymbidium*	1.60	1.35
		Nos. 1890-1895 (6)	*6.40*	*5.30*

Flower Show, Olomouc, Aug. 18–Sept. 2. 60h, 1k, 2k issued in sheets of 4, others in sheets of 10.

Irish Setter
A676

Designs: Hunting dogs.

1973, Sept. 5

Multicolored

1896	A676	20h *shown*	7	5
1897	A676	30h *Czech terrier*	12	5
1898	A676	40h *Bavarian hunting dog*	20	7
1899	A676	60h *German pointer*	35	12
1900	A676	1k *Cocker spaniel*	50	20
1901	A676	1.60k *Dachshund*	*1.50*	*35*
		Nos. 1896-1901 (6)	*2.74*	*84*

50th anniversary of the Czechoslovak United Hunting Organization.

St. John, the Baptist, by Svabinsky
A677

Works by Max Svabinsky: 60h, "August Noon" (woman). 80h, "Marriage of True Minds" (artist and muse). 1k, "Paradise Sonata I" (Adam dreaming of Eve). 2.60k, Last Judgment, stained glass window, St. Vitus Cathedral.

1973, Sept. 17 Litho. & Engr.

1902	A677	20h blk & pale grn	12	5
1903	A677	60h blk & buff	24	12

Engraved

1904	A677	80h black	45	30
1905	A677	1k sl grn	60	50
1906	A677	2.60k multi	*2.25*	*2.00*
		Nos. 1902-1906 (5)	*3.66*	*2.97*

Centenary of the birth of Max Svabinsky (1873–1962), artist and stamp designer. 20h and 60h issued in sheets of 25; 80h and 1k se-tenant in sheets of 4 checkerwise; 2.60k in sheets of 4.

Trade Union Emblem
A678

1973, Oct. 15 Photo. & Engr.

1907	A678	1k red, bl & yel	45	18

8th Congress of the World Federation of Trade Unions, Varna, Bulgaria.

Painting Type of 1967

Designs: 1k, Boy from Martinique, by Antonin Pelc. 1.20k, "Fortitude" (mountaineer), by Martin Benka. 1.80k, Rembrandt, self-portrait. 2k, Pierrot, by Bohumil Kubista. 2.40k, Ilona Kubinyiova, by Peter M. Bohun. 3.60k, Virgin and Child (Veveri Madonna), c. 1350.

Photogravure and Engraved

1973, Nov. 27 ***Perf. 11½***

1908	A565	1k multi, vio bl inscriptions	*1.75*	*1.60*
a.		1k multi, blk inscriptions	*6.00*	5.50
1909	A565	1.20k multi	*2.00*	*1.75*
1910	A565	1.80k multi	75	65
1911	A565	2k multi	80	70
1912	A565	2.40k multi	96	85
1913	A565	3.60k multi	1.45	1.30
		Nos. 1908-1913 (6)	*7.71*	*6.86*

Sheets of 4. Nos. 1910–1913 printed se-tenant with gold and black inscription on gutter.

Central background bluish gray on No. 1908, light bluish green on No. 1908a.

Postilion—A679

1973, Dec. 18

1914	A679	1k gold & multi	45	30

Stamp Day 1974 and 55th anniversary of Czechoslovak postage stamps. Printed with 2 labels showing telephone and telegraph.

"CSSR"
A680

Friedrich Smetana
A681

Pablo Neruda, Chilean Flag
A682

Comecon Building, Moscow
A683

1974, Jan. 1

1915	A680	30h red, gold & ultra	12	5

5th anniversary of Federal Government in the Czechoslovak Socialist Republic.

1974, Jan. 4 ***Perf. 11x11½***

Design: No. 1917, Josef Suk.

1916	A681	60h blk, bl & yel	24	12
1917	A681	60h grn & multi	24	12
1918	A682	60h bl, blk & red	24	12

Sesquicentennial of the birth of Friedrich Smetana (1824–1884), composer; centenary of the birth of Josef Suk (1874–1935), composer, and in memory of Pablo Neruda (Neftali Ricardo Reyes, 1904–1973), Chilean poet.

1974, Jan. 23

1919	A683	1k gold, red & vio bl	40	16

25th anniversary of the Council of Mutual Economic Assistance (COMECON).

Symbols of Postal Service—A684

1974, Feb. 20 *Perf. 11½*

1920	A684	3.60k multi	1.85	60

BRNO '74 National Stamp Exhibition, Brno, June 8–23.

Art Type of 1972

Designs: 60h, Tulips 1973, by Josef Broz. 1k, Structures 1961 (poppy and building), by Orest Dubay. 1.60k, Bird and flowers (Golden Sun-Glowing Day), by Adolf Zabransky. 1.80k, Artificial flowers, by Frantisek Gross.

1974, Feb. 21 *Perf. 11½x11*

1921	A651	60h multi	24	10
1922	A651	1k multi	50	20
1923	A651	1.60k multi	75	24
1924	A651	1.80k multi	1.25	40

Czech and Slovak graphic art.

Oskar Benes and Vaclav Prochazka A685

Portraits: 40h, Milos Uher and Anton Sedlacek. 60h, Jan Hajecek and Marie Sedlackova. 80h, Jan Sverma and Albin Grznar. 1k, Jaroslav Neliba and Alois Hovorka. 1.60k, Ladislav Exnar and Ludovit Kukorelli.

Photogravure and Engraved

1974, Mar. 21 *Perf. 11½x11*

1925	A685	30h ind & multi	12	5
1926	A685	40h ind & multi	16	6
1927	A685	60h ind & multi	24	8
1928	A685	80h ind & multi	32	12
1929	A685	1k ind & multi	40	14
1930	A685	1.60k ind & multi	1.00	35
		Nos. 1925-1930(6)	2.24	80

Partisan commanders and fighters.

"Water, the Source of Energy" A686

Symbolic Designs: 1k, Importance of water for agriculture. 1.20k, Study of the oceans. 1.60k, "Hydrological Decade." 2k, Struggle for unpolluted water.

1974, Apr. 25 Engr. *Perf. 11½*

1931	A686	60h multi	24	20
1932	A686	1k multi	40	30
1933	A686	1.20k multi	60	45
1934	A686	1.60k multi	90	75
1935	A686	2k multi	1.25	1.00
		Nos. 1931-1935 (5)	3.39	2.70

Hydrological Decade (UNESCO), 1965–1974. Sheets of 4.

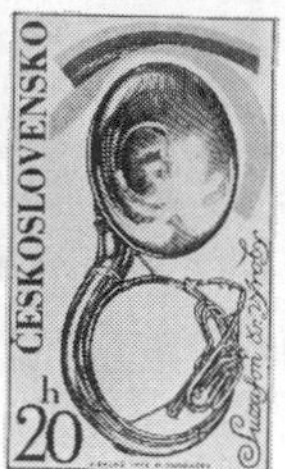

Allegory Holding "Molniya," and Ground Station A687

Sousaphone A688

1974, Apr. 30 Photo. & Engr.

1936	A687	30h vio bl & multi	20	10

"Intersputnik," first satellite communications ground station in Czechoslovakia.

Prague Castle Art Type of 1971

Designs: No. 1937, Golden Cock, 17th century locket. No. 1938, Glass monstrance, 1840.

1974, May 9 Engr. *Perf. 11½*

1937	A634	3k gold & multi	1.75	1.60
1938	A634	3k blk & multi	1.75	1.60

Art treasures of Castle of Prague. Sheets of 4.

Photogravure and Engraved

1974, May 12 *Perf. 11x11½*

Multicolored

1939	A688	20h *shown*	10	5
1940	A688	30h *Bagpipe*	12	8
1941	A688	40h *Violin, by Martin Benka*	18	12
1942	A688	1k *Pyramid piano*	40	18
1943	A688	1.60k *Tenor quinton, 1754*	1.25	30
		Nos. 1939-1943 (5)	2.05	73

Prague and Bratislava Music Festivals. The 1.60k also commemorates 25th anniversary of Slovak Philharmonic Orchestra.

Child A689

Photogravure and Engraved

1974, June 1 *Perf. 11½*

1944	A689	60h multi	30	12

Children's Day. Design is from illustration for children's book by Adolf Zabransky.

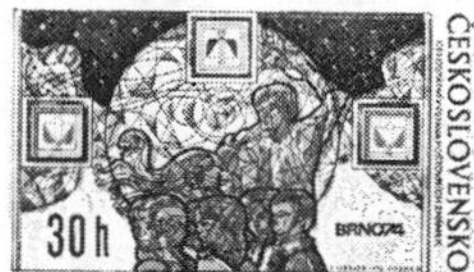

Globe, People and Exhibition Emblems A690

Design: 6k, Rays and emblems symbolizing "Oneness and Mutuality."

1974, June 1

1945	A690	30h multi	12	6
1946	A690	6k multi	2.75	1.20

BRNO 74 National Stamp Exhibition, Brno, June 8–23. Sheets of 16 stamps and 14 labels.

Resistance Fighter A691

Actress Holding Tragedy and Comedy Masks A692

Photogravure and Engraved

1974, Aug. 29 *Perf. 11½*

1947	A691	30h multi	12	6

Slovak National Uprising, 30th anniversary.

1974, Aug. 29

1948	A692	30h red, sil & blk	12	6

Bratislava Academy of Music and Drama, 25th anniversary.

Slovak Girl with Flower A693

1974, Aug. 29

1949	A693	30h multi	12	6

SLUK, Slovak folksong and dance ensemble, 25th anniversary.

Hero and Leander A694

Design: 2.40k, Hero watching Leander swim the Hellespont. No. 1952, Leander reaching shore. No. 1953, Hero mourning over Leander's body. No. 1954, Hermione, Leander's sister. No. 1955, Mourning Cupid. Designs are from 17th century English tapestries in Bratislava Council Palace.

1974–76 Photo. & Engr.

1950	A694	2k multi	2.50	1.50
1951	A694	2.40k multi	2.50	1.50
1952	A694	3k multi	2.50	1.75
1953	A694	3k multi	1.75	1.60
1954	A694	3.60k multi	2.50	1.75
1955	A694	3.60k multi	1.75	1.50
		Nos. 1950-1955 (6)	13.50	9.60

Issue dates: Nos. 1950–1951, Sept. 25, 1974. Nos. 1952, 1954, Aug. 29, 1975. Nos. 1953, 1955, May 9, 1976.

Soldier Standing Guard, Target, 1840 A695

Painted Folk-art Targets: 60h, Landscape with Pierrot and flags, 1828. 1k, Diana crowning champion marksman, 1832. 1.60k, Still life with guitar, 1839. 2.40k, Salvo and stag in flight, 1834. 3k, Turk and giraffe, 1831.

1974, Sept. 26 *Perf. 11½*

Size: 30x50mm.

1956	A695	30h blk & multi	12	6
1957	A695	60h blk & multi	24	12
1958	A695	1k blk & multi	40	25

Engraved *Perf. 12*

Size: 40x50mm.

1959	A695	1.60k grn & multi	80	60
1960	A695	2.40k sep & multi	1.25	1.00
1961	A695	3k multi	2.10	1.65
		Nos. 1956-1961 (6)	4.91	3.68

UPU Emblem and Postilion—A696

Designs (UPU Emblem and): 40h, Mail coach. 60h, Railroad mail coach, 1851. 80h, Early mail truck. 1k, Czechoslovak Airlines mail plane. 1.60k, Radar.

Photogravure and Engraved

1974, Oct. 9 *Perf. 11½*

1962	A696	30h multi	12	6
1963	A696	40h multi	16	8
1964	A696	60h multi	24	12
1965	A696	80h multi	35	16
1966	A696	1k multi	45	20
1967	A696	1.60k multi	1.00	32
		Nos. 1962-1967 (6)	2.32	94

Centenary of Universal Postal Union.

Post Horn, Old Town Bridge Tower A697

Sealed Letter A698

Stylized Bird A699

Postal Code Symbol A699a

Designs: 40h, Postilion. No. 1971, Carrier pigeon. No. 1979, Map of Czechoslovakia with postal code numbers.

Photogravure and Engraved

1974, Oct. 31 *Perf. 11½x11*

1968	A697	20h multi	8	5
1969	A698	30h brn, bl & red	12	5
1970	A697	40h multi	16	5
1971	A698	60h bl, yel & red	24	5

Coil Stamps

1975–76 Photogravure *Perf. 14*

1976	A699	30h brt bl	18	12
1977	A699	60h carmine	30	18
1978	A699a	30h emer, p. 11½ ('76)	12	5
1979	A699a	60h scar, p. 11½ ('76)	25	10

Nos. 1976–1979 have black control number on back of every fifth stamp.

Ludvik Kuba, Self-portrait, 1941
A700

Paintings: 1.20k, Violinist Frantisek Ondricek, by Vaclav Brozik. 1.60k, Vase with Flowers, by Otakar Kubin. 1.80k, Woman with Pitcher, by Janko Alexy. 2.40k, Bacchanalia, c. 1635, by Karel Skreta.

1974, Nov. 27 Engraved *Perf. 11½*

1980 A700 1k multi 40 40
1981 A700 1.20k multi 60 48
1982 A700 1.60k multi 80 70
1983 A700 1.80k multi 1.00 90
1984 A700 2.40k multi 1.35 1.20
Nos. 1980-1984 (5) 4.15 3.68

Czech and Slovak art. Sheets of 4.
See Nos. 2209-2211.

Post Horn—A701

Photogravure and Engraved

1974, Dec. 18 *Perf. 11x11½*

1985 A701 1k multi 50 30

Stamp Day.

Still-life with Hare, by Hollar
A702

Designs: 1k, The Lion and the Mouse, by Vaclav Hollar. 1.60k, Deer Hunt, by Philip Galle. 1.80k, Grand Hunt, by Jacques Callot.

Lithographed and Engraved

1975, Feb. 26 *Perf. 11½x11*

1988 A702 60h blk & buff 24 6
1989 A702 1k blk & buff 40 12
1990 A702 1.60k blk & yel 75 30
1991 A702 1.80k blk & buff 1.00 60

Hunting scenes from old engravings.

Guns Pointing at Family
A703

Young Woman and Globe
A704

Designs: 1k, Women and building on fire. 1.20k, People and roses. All designs include names of destroyed villages.

Photogravure and Engraved

1975, Feb. 26 *Perf. 11*

1992 A703 60h multi 30 6
1993 A703 1k multi 50 15
1994 A703 1.20k multi 48 18

Destruction of 14 villages by the Nazis, 30th anniversary.

1975, Mar. 7 *Perf. 11½x11*

1995 A704 30h red & multi 15 5

International Women's Year 1975.

Little Queens, Moravian Folk Custom
A705

Folk Customs: 1k, Straw masks (animal heads and blackened faces), Slovak. 1.40k, The Tale of Maid Dorothea (executioner, girl, king and devil). 2k, Drowning of Morena, symbol of death and winter.

1975, Mar. 26 Engr. *Perf. 11½*

1996 A705 60h blk & multi 60 25
1997 A705 1k blk & multi 50 45
1998 A705 1.40k blk & multi 60 55
1999 A705 2k blk & multi 1.00 90

Sheets of four.

Coat of Arms Type of 1968

Photogravure & Engraved

1975, Apr. 17 *Perf. 11½*

Multicolored

2000 A590 60h *Nymburk* 24 8
2001 A590 60h *Znojmo* 24 8

Coats of arms of Czechoslovakian cities.

Czech May Uprising—A706

Liberation by Soviet Army—A707

Czechoslovak-Russian Friendship—A708

1975, May 9 Photo. & Engr.

2002 A706 1k multi 40 15

Engraved

2003 A707 1k multi 40 15

Photogravure and Engraved

2004 A708 1k multi 40 15

30th anniversary of the May uprising of the Czech people and of liberation by the Soviet Army; 5th anniversary of the Czechoslovak-Soviet Treaty of Friendship, Cooperation and Mutual Aid.

Adolescents' Exercises—A709

Designs: 60h, Children's exercises. 1k, Men's and women's exercises.

Photogravure and Engraved

1975, June 15 *Perf. 12x11½*

2005 A709 30h lil & multi 15 5
2006 A709 60h multi 26 10
2007 A709 1k vio & multi 44 18

Spartakiad 1975, Prague, June 26–29. Nos. 2005–2007 each issued in sheets of 30 stamps and 40 labels, showing different Spartakiad emblems.

Datrioides Microlepis and Sea Horse—A710

Tropical Fish (Aquarium): 1k, Beta splendens regan and pterophyllum scalare. 1.20k, Carassius auratus. 1.60k, Amphiprion percula and chaetodon sp. 2k, Pomacanthodes semicirculatus, pomocanthus maculosus and paracanthorus hepatus.

1975, June 27 *Perf. 11½*

2008 A710 60h multi 26 8
2009 A710 1k multi 50 10
2010 A710 1.20k multi 65 25
2011 A710 1.60k multi 95 45
2012 A710 2k multi 1.75 50
Nos. 2008-2012 (5) 4.11 1.38

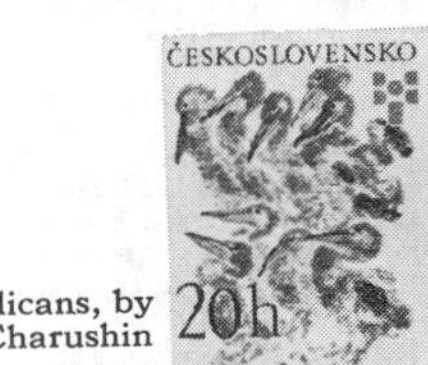

Pelicans, by Nikita Charushin
A711

Book Illustrations: 30h, The Dreamer, by Lieselotte Schwarz. 40h, Hero on horseback, by Val Muntenau. 60h, Peacock, by Klaus Ensikat. 80h, Man on horseback, by Robert Dubravec.

1975, Sept. 5

2013 A711 20h multi 10 6
2014 A711 30h multi 12 8
2015 A711 40h multi 15 10
2016 A711 60h multi 26 12
2017 A711 80h multi 40 20
Nos. 2013-2017 (5) 1.03 56

Bratislava BIB 75 biennial exhibition of illustrations for children's books.

Nos. 2013–2017 issued in sheets of 25 stamps and 15 labels with designs and inscriptions in various languages.

Strakonice, 1951
A712

Designs: Motorcycles.

Photogravure and Engraved

1975, Sept. 29 *Perf. 11½*

Multicolored

2018 A712 20h *shown* 8 5
2019 A712 40h *Jawa 250, 1945* 15 5
2020 A712 60h *Jawa 175, 1935* 24 10
2021 A712 1k *ITAR, 1921* 44 25
2022 A712 1.20k *ORION, 1903* 65 30
2023 A712 1.80k *Laurin & Klement, 1898* 1.25 35
Nos. 2018-2023 (6) 2.81 1.10

Study of Short-wave Solar Radiation
A713

Soyuz-Apollo Link-up in Space
A714

Designs: 60h, Study of aurora borealis and Oréol satellite. 1k, Study of ionosphere and cosmic radiation. 2k, Copernicus, radio map of the sun and satellite.

1975, Sept. 30

2024 A713 30h multi 12 5
2025 A713 60h yel, rose red & vio 24 8
2026 A713 1k bl, yel & vio 44 25
2027 A713 2k red, vio & yel 1.00 50

Engraved

2028 A714 5k vio & multi 3.00 2.50
Nos. 2024-2028 (5) 4.80 3.38

International cooperation in space research. No. 2028 issued in sheets of 4.

The design of No. 2026 appears to be inverted.

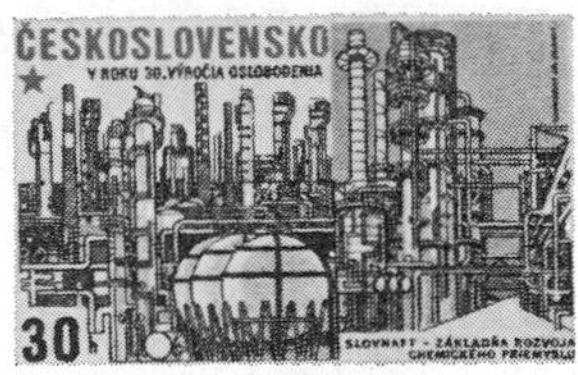

Slovnaft, Petrochemical Plant—A715

Designs: 60h, Atomic power station. 1k, Construction of Prague subway. 1.20k, Construction of Friendship pipeline. 1.40k, Combine harvesters. 1.60k, Apartment house construction.

1975, Oct. 28 Photo. & Engr.

2029 A715 30h multi 12 5
2030 A715 60h multi 24 8
2031 A715 1k multi 44 12
2032 A715 1.20k multi 65 15
2033 A715 1.40k multi 70 30
2034 A715 1.60k multi 90 35
Nos. 2029-2034 (6) 3.05 1.05

Socialist construction, 30th anniversary. Nos. 2029–2034 printed se-tenant with labels.

Pres. Gustav Husak
A716

1975, Oct. 28 Engraved

2035 A716 30h ultra 12 5
2036 A716 60h rose red 24 15

Prague Castle Art Type of 1971

Designs: 3k, Gold earring, 9th century. 3.60k, Arms of Premysl Dynasty and Bohemia from lid of leather case containing Bohemian crown, 14th century.

1975, Oct. 29

2040	A634	3k blk, grn, pur & gold	1.60	1.40
2041	A634	3.60k red & multi	1.75	1.50

Art treasures of Castle of Prague. Sheets of 4.

Miniature Sheet

Ludvik Svoboda, Road Map, Buzuluk to Prague, Carnations—A717

1975, Nov. 25

2042	A717	10k multi	15.00	15.00

Pres. Ludvik Svoboda, 80th birthday. Size of No. 2042: 75x95mm. (stamp size: 40x55mm.).

Exists imperf., price $60.

Art Type of 1967

Paintings: 1k, "May 1975" (Woman and doves for 30th anniversary of peace), by Zdenek Sklenar. 1.40k, Woman in national costume, by Eugen Nevan. 1.80k, "Liberation of Prague," by Alena Cermakova (horiz.). 2.40k, "Fire 1938" (woman raising fist), by Josef Capek. 3.40k, Old Prague, 1828, by Vincenc Morstadt.

1975, Nov. 27 **Engr.** ***Perf. 11½***

2043	A565	1k blk, buff & brn	44	40
2044	A565	1.40k multi	70	60
2045	A565	1.80k multi	1.00	80
2046	A565	2.40k multi	1.25	1.00
2047	A565	3.40k multi	2.40	1.70
		Nos. 2043-2047 (5)	5.79	4.50

Sheets of 4.

Carrier Pigeon—A718

Photogravure and Engraved

1975, Dec. 18 ***Perf. 11½***

2048	A718	1k red & multi	50	20

Stamp Day 1975.

Frantisek Halas
A719

Wilhelm Pieck
A720

Frantisek Lexa
A721

Jindrich Jindrich
A722

Ivan Krasko
A723

Photogravure and Engraved

1976, Feb. 25 ***Perf. 11½***

2049	A719	60h multi	24	10
2050	A720	60h multi	24	10
2051	A721	60h multi	24	10
2052	A722	60h multi	24	10
2053	A723	60h multi	24	10
		Nos. 2049-2053 (5)	1.20	50

Anniversaries: Frantisek Halas (1901–1949), poet (No. 2049); Wilhelm Pieck (1876–1960), president of German Democratic Republic (No. 2050); Frantisek Lexa (1876–1960), professor of Egyptology (No. 2051); Jindrich Jindrich (1876–1967), composer and writer (No. 2052); Ivan Krasko (1876–1958), Slovak poet (No. 2053). No. 2051 printed in sheets of 10, others in sheets of 50.

Ski Jump, Olympic Emblem
A724

Designs (Winter Olympic Games Emblem and): 1.40k, Figure skating, women's. 1.60k, Ice hockey.

Photogravure and Engraved

1976, Mar. 22 ***Perf. 12x11½***

2054	A724	1k gold & multi	44	15
2055	A724	1.40k gold & multi	60	25
2056	A724	1.60k gold & multi	70	30

12th Winter Olympic Games, Innsbruck, Austria, Feb. 4–15.

Javelin and Olympic Rings—A725

Designs (Olympic Rings and): 3k, Relay race. 3.60k, Shot put.

1976, Mar. 22 ***Perf. 11½***

2057	A725	2k multi	90	35
2058	A725	3k multi	1.30	50
2059	A725	3.60k multi	1.60	60

21st Olympic Games, Montreal, Canada, July 17–Aug. 1.

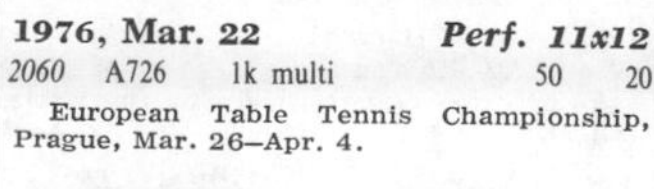

Table Tennis
A726

1976, Mar. 22 ***Perf. 11x12***

2060	A726	1k multi	50	20

European Table Tennis Championship, Prague, Mar. 26–Apr. 4.

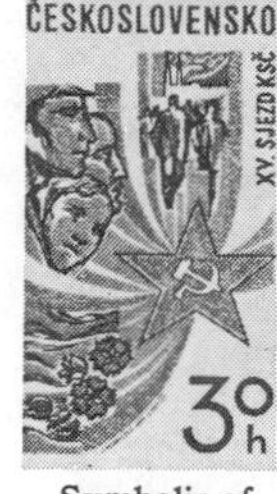

Symbolic of Communist Party
A727

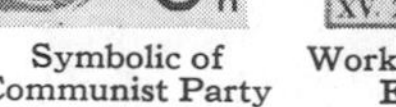

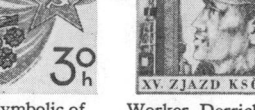

Worker, Derrick, Emblem
A728

1976, Apr. 12 ***Perf. 11x12***

2061	A727	30h gold & multi	12	5
2062	A728	60h gold & multi	24	8

15th Congress of the Communist Party of Czechoslovakia.

Radio Prague Orchestra
A729

Dancer, Violin, Tragic Mask
A730

Actors
A731

Folk Dancers
A732

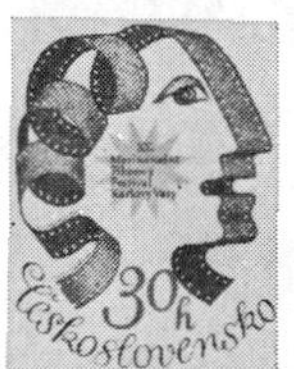

Film Festival—A733

1976, Apr. 26 ***Perf. 11½***

2063	A729	20h gold & multi	8	5
2064	A730	20h pink & multi	8	5
2065	A731	20h lt bl & multi	8	5
2066	A732	30h blk & multi	12	5
2067	A733	30h vio bl, rose & grn	12	5
		Nos. 2063-2067 (5)	48	25

Commemorating: Czechoslovak Radio Symphony Orchestra, Prague, 50th anniversary (No. 2063); Academy of Music and Dramatic Art, Prague, 50th anniversary (No. 2064); Nova Scena Theater Company, Bratislava, 30th anniversary (No. 2065); International Folk Song and Dance Festival, Straznice, 30th anniversary (No. 2066); 20th International Film Festival, Karlovy Vary (No. 2067).

Hammer and Sickle
A734 A735

Design: 6k, Hammer and sickle (horiz.).

1976, May 14

2068	A734	30h gold, red & dk bl	20	5
2069	A735	60h gold, red & dp car	45	15

Souvenir Sheet

2070	A735	6k red & multi	2.60	2.60

Czechoslovak Communist Party, 55th anniversary. No. 2070 contains one stamp (50x30mm.); violet blue marginal inscription and gold emblem. Size: 99x90mm.

Ships in Storm, by Frans Huys (1522–1562)
A736

Old Engravings of Ships: 60h, by Václav Hollar (1607–1677). 1k, by Regnier Nooms Zeeman (1623–1668). 2k, by Francois Chereau (1680–1729).

Photogravure and Engraved

1976, July 21 ***Perf. 11x11½***

2071	A736	40h buff & blk	16	6
2072	A736	60h gray, buff & blk	24	8
2073	A736	1k lt grn, buff & blk	44	15
2074	A736	2k lt bl, buff & blk	88	35

"UNESCO"
A737

1976, July 30 ***Perf. 11½***

2075	A737	2k gray & multi	88	50

30th anniversary of UNESCO. Sheets of 10.

Souvenir Sheet

Hands Holding Infant, Globe and Dove
A738

1976, July 30

2076	A738	6k, sheet of 2, multi	10.00	10.00

European Security and Cooperation Conference, Helsinki, Finland, 2nd anniversary. No. 2076 contains 2 stamps, marginal inscription and ornamental designs in blue and black. Size: 115x165mm.

Merino Ram
A739

Couple Smoking, WHO Emblem and Skull
A740

Designs: 40h, Bern-Hana milk cow. 1.60k, Kladruby stallion Generalissimus XXVII.

Photogravure and Engraved

1976, Aug. 28 ***Perf. 11½x12***

2077	A739	30h multi	12	5
2078	A739	40h multi	18	5
2079	A739	1.60k multi	70	25

Bountiful Earth Exhibition, Ceske Budejovice, Aug. 28–Sept. 12.

1976, Sept. 7 ***Perf. 12x11½***

2080	A740	2k multi	88	50

Fight against smoking, World Health Organization drive against drug addiction. Printed in sheets of 10 (2x5) with WHO emblems and inscription in margin.

Prague Castle Art Type of 1971

Designs: 3k, View of Prague Castle, by F. Hoogenberghe, 1572. 3.60k, Faun and Satyr, sculptured panel, 16th century.

1976, Oct. 22 **Engr.** ***Perf. 11½***

2081	A634	3k multi	1.30	1.15
2082	A634	3.60k multi	1.55	1.40

Art treasures of Castle of Prague.

Guernica 1937, by Imro Weiner-Kral
A741

1976, Oct. 22

2083	A741	5k multi	2.25	90

40th anniversary of the International Brigade in Spain.

Zebras
A472

Designs: 20h, Elephants (vert.). 30h, Cheetah. 40h, Giraffes (vert.). 60h, Rhinoceros. 3k, Bongos (vert.).

Photogravure and Engraved

Perf. 11½x11, 11x11½

1976, Nov. 3

2084	A742	10h multi	6	5
2085	A742	20h multi	8	5
2086	A742	30h multi	12	5
2087	A742	40h multi	16	5
2088	A742	60h multi	24	8
2089	A742	3k multi	1.50	45
		Nos. 2084-2089 (6)	2.16	73

African animals in Dvur Kralove Zoo.

Art Type of 1967

Paintings of Flowers: 1k, by Peter Matejka. 1.40k, by Cyril Bouda. 2k, by Jan Breughel. 3.60k, J. Rudolf Bys.

1976, Nov. 27 **Engr.** ***Perf. 11½***

2090	A565	1k multi	60	55
2091	A565	1.40k multi	85	80
2092	A565	2k multi	1.35	1.10
2093	A565	3.60k multi	2.00	1.85

Sheets of 4. Emblem and name of Praga 1978 on horizontal gutter.

Postrider, 17th Century, and Satellites—A743

1976, Dec. 18 **Photo. & Engr.**

2094	A743	1k multi	44	20

Stamp Day 1976.

Ice Hockey
A744

Arms of Vranov
A745

Designs: 1k, Biathlon. 1.60k, Ski jump. 2k, Downhill skiing.

Photogravure and Engraved

1977, Feb. 11 ***Perf. 11½***

2095	A744	60h multi	24	8
2096	A744	1k multi	44	12
2097	A744	1.60k multi	80	25
2098	A744	2k multi	88	35

6th Winter Spartakiad of Socialist Countries' Armies.

1977, Feb. 20

Designs: Coats of Arms of Czechoslovak towns.

Multicolored

2099	A745	60h *shown*	24	10
2100	A745	60h *Kralupy & Vltavou*	24	10
2101	A745	60h *Jicin*	24	10
2102	A745	60h *Valasske Mezirici*	24	10

See Nos. 2297-2300.

Window, Michna Palace
A746

Prague Renaissance Windows: 30h, Michna Palace. 40h, Thun Palace. 60h, Archbishop's Palace, Hradcany. 5k, St. Nicholas Church.

1977, Mar. 10

2103	A746	20h multi	8	5
2104	A746	30h multi	12	5
2105	A746	40h multi	16	5
2106	A746	60h multi	24	8
2107	A746	5k multi	2.20	1.00
		Nos. 2103-2107 (5)	2.80	1.23

PRAGA 1978 International Philatelic Exhibition, Prague, Sept. 8–17, 1978.

Children, Auxiliary Police
A747

Photogravure and Engraved

1977, Apr. 21 ***Perf. 11½***

2108	A747	60h multi	24	8

Auxiliary Police, 25th anniversary.

Warsaw, Polish Flag, Bicyclists
A748

Congress Emblem
A749

Designs: 60h, Berlin, DDR flag, bicyclists. 1k, Prague, Czechoslovakian flag, victorious bicyclist. 1.40k, Bicyclists on highways, modern views of Berlin, Prague and Warsaw.

1977, May 7

2109	A748	30h multi	12	5
2110	A748	60h multi	30	15
2111	A748	1k multi	50	25
2112	A748	1.40k multi	60	30

30th International Bicycle Peace Race Warsaw-Prague-Berlin.

Photogravure and Engraved

1977, May 25 ***Perf. 11½***

2113	A749	30h car, red & gold	12	5

9th Trade Union Congress, Prague 1977.

Prague Castle Art Type of 1971

Designs: 3k, Onyx footed bowl, 1350. 3.60k, Bronze horse, 1619.

1977, June 7 **Engraved**

2114	A634	3k multi	1.75	1.20
2115	A634	3.60k multi	1.75	1.50

Art treasures of Castle of Prague. Sheets of 4.

French Postrider, 19th Century, PRAGA '78 Emblem
A750

Postal Uniforms: 1k, Austrian, 1838. 2k, Austrian, late 18th century. 3.60k, Germany, early 18th century.

1977, June 8 **Photo. & Engr.**

2116	A750	60h multi	24	8
2117	A750	1k multi	44	15
2118	A750	2k multi	88	30
2119	A750	3.60k multi	1.50	65

PRAGA 1978 International Philatelic Exhibition, Prague, Sept. 8–17, 1978.

Nos. 2116–2119 issued in sheets of 50 and sheets of 4 with 4 labels and horizontal gutter.

Coffeepots, Porcelain Mark
A751

Mlada Boleslav Costume
A752

Czechoslovak Porcelain and Porcelain Marks: 30h, Urn. 40h, Vase. 60h, Cup and saucer, jugs. 1k, Candlestick and plate. 3k, Cup and saucer, coffeepot.

1977, June 15

2120	A751	20h multi	8	5
2121	A751	30h multi	12	5
2122	A751	40h multi	16	6
2123	A751	60h multi	24	8
2124	A751	1k multi	44	18
2125	A751	3k multi	1.50	45
		Nos. 2120-2125 (6)	2.54	87

1977, Aug. 31 **Engraved** ***Perf. 11½***

PRAGA Emblem and Folk Costumes from: 1.60k, Vazek. 3.60k, Zavadka. 5k, Belkovice.

2126	A752	1k multi	44	40
2127	A752	1.60k multi	68	60
2128	A752	3.60k multi	1.55	1.40
2129	A752	5k multi	2.20	2.00

Issued in sheets of 10 and in sheets of 8 plus 2 labels showing PRAGA '78 emblem.

Old Woman, Devil and Spinner, by Viera Bombova
A753

Book Illustrations: 60h, Bear and tiger, by Genadij Pavlisin. 1k, Coach drawn by 4 horses (Hans Christian Andersen), by Ulf Lovgren. 2k, Bear and flamingos (Lewis Carroll), by Nicole Claveloux. 3k, King with keys, and toys, by Jiri Trnka.

1977, Sept. 9 **Photo. & Engr.**

2130	A753	40h multi	16	6
2131	A753	60h multi	24	8
2132	A753	1k multi	44	15
2133	A753	2k multi	88	30
2134	A753	3k multi	1.30	45
		Nos. 2130-2134 (5)	3.02	1.04

Prize-winning designs, 6th biennial exhibition of illustrations for children's books, Bratislava.

Globe, Violin, Doves, View of Prague
A754

Photogravure and Engraved

1977, Sept. 28 ***Perf. 11½***

2135	A754	60h multi	24	8

Congress of International Music Council of UNESCO, Prague and Bratislava.

Souvenir Sheets

"For a Europe of Peace"
A755

Designs: 1.60k, "For a Europe of Cooperation." 2.40k, "For a Europe of Social Progress."

1977, Oct. 3 **Multicolored**

2136	A755	60h, Sheet of 2	55	50
2137	A755	1.60k, Sheet of 2	1.50	1.35
2138	A755	2.40k, Sheet of 2	2.25	2.00

2nd European Security and Cooperation Conference, Belgrade. Nos. 2136–2138 each contain 2 stamps and 2 blue on buff inscriptions and ornaments. Size: 130x80mm.

S. P. Koroljov, Sputnik I Emblem

A756

Sailors, Cruiser Aurora

A757

Designs: 30h, Yuri A. Gagarin and Vostok I. 40h, Alexei Leonov. 1k, Neil A. Armstrong and footprint on moon. 1.60k, Construction of orbital space station.

1977, Oct. 4

2139	A756	20h multi	8	5
2140	A756	30h multi	12	5
2141	A756	40h multi	16	6
2142	A756	1k multi	44	15
2143	A756	1.60k multi	75	25
		Nos. 2139-2143 (5)	1.55	56

Space research, 20th anniversary of first earth satellite.

1977, Nov. 7

2144	A757	30h multi	12	5

60th anniversary of Russian October Revolution.

"Russia" Arms of USSR, Kremlin

A758

"Science"

A759

1977, Nov. 7

2145	A758	30h multi	12	5

55th anniversary of the Union of Soviet Socialist Republics (USSR).

1977, Nov. 17

2146	A759	3k multi	1.35	55

Czechoslovak Academy of Science, 25th anniversary.

Art Type of 1967

Paintings: 2k, "Fear" (woman), by Jan Murdoch. 2.40k, Jan Francisci, portrait by Peter M. Bohun. 2.60k, Vaclav Hollar, self-portrait, 1647. 3k, Young Woman, 1528, by Lucas Cranach. 5k, Cleopatra, by Rubens.

1977, Nov. 27 **Engr.** ***Perf. 11½***

2147	A565	2k multi	88	80
2148	A565	2.40k multi	1.00	90
2149	A565	2.60k multi	1.15	1.00
2150	A565	3k multi	1.30	1.15
2151	A565	5k multi	2.50	2.10
		Nos. 2147-2151 (5)	6.83	5.95

Sheets of 4.

View of Bratislava, by Georg Hoefnagel—A760

Design: 3.60k, Arms of Bratislava, 1436.

1977, Dec. 6

2152	A760	3k multi	1.30	1.15
2153	A760	3.60k multi	1.55	1.40

Sheets of 4. See Nos. 2174-2175, 2270-2271, 2331-2332, 2364-2365, 2422-2423, 2478-2479, 2514-2515, 2570-2571, 2618-2619.

Stamp Pattern and Post Horn—A761

1977, Dec. 18 **Photo. & Engr.**

2154	A761	1k multi	45	15

Stamp Day.

Zdenek Nejedly

A762

Karl Marx

A763

Photogravure and Engraved

1978, Feb. 10 ***Perf. 11½***

2155	A762	30h multi	12	5
2156	A763	40h multi	16	6

Zdenek Nejedly (1878–1962), musicologist and historian; Karl Marx (1818–1883), political philosopher.

Civilians Greeting Guardsmen

A764

Intellectual, Farm Woman and Steel Worker, Flag—A765

1978, Feb. 25

2157	A764	1k gold & multi	45	15
2158	A765	1k gold & multi	45	15

30th anniversary of "Victorious February" (No. 2157), and National Front (No. 2158). See Note after 2190.

Yuri A. Gagarin and Vostok I

A766

10k Coin, 1964, and 25k Coin, 1965

A767

Design: 30h, 3.60k, like No. 2140.

Engr.; Overprint Photogravure (Blue and carmine on 30h, green and lilac rose on 3.60k)

1978, Mar. 2 ***Perf. 11½x12***

2159	A766	30h dk red	85	65
2160	A766	3.60k vio bl	8.50	6.50

Capt. V. Remek, first Czechoslovakian cosmonaut on Russian spaceship Soyuz 28, Mar. 2–9.

1978, Mar. 14 **Photo. & Engr.**

Designs: 40h, Medal for Culture, 1972. 1.40k, Charles University medal, 1948. 3k, Ferdinand I medal, 1568. 5k, Gold florin, 1335.

2161	A767	20h sil & multi	8	5
2162	A767	40h sil & multi	16	6
2163	A767	1.40k gold & multi	70	15
2164	A767	3k gold & multi	1.35	55
2165	A767	5k gold & multi	2.20	1.00
		Nos. 2161-2165 (5)	4.49	1.81

650th anniversary of Kremnica Mint.

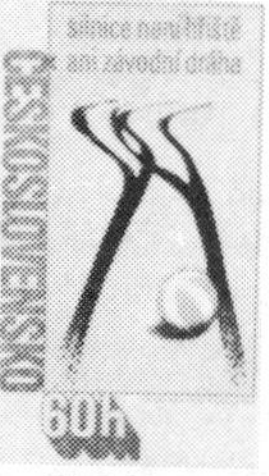

Tire Tracks and Ball

A768

Congress Emblem

A769

1978, Mar. 15

2166	A768	60h multi	24	8

Road safety.

Photogravure and Engraved

1978, Apr. 16 ***Perf. 11½***

2167	A769	1k multi	45	15

9th World Trade Union Congress, Prague 1978.

Shot Put and Praha '78 Emblem

A770

Designs: 1k, Pole vault. 3.60k, Women runners.

1978, Apr. 26

2168	A770	40h multi	16	6
2169	A770	1k multi	45	15
2170	A770	3.60k multi	1.55	38

5th European Athletic Championships, Prague 1978.

Ice Hockey—A771

Designs: 30h, Hockey. 2k, Ice hockey play.

1978, Apr. 26

2171	A771	30h multi	12	[illegible]
2172	A771	60h multi	25	[illegible]
2173	A771	2k multi	90	[illegible]

5th European Ice Hockey Championships and 70th anniversary of Bandy hockey.

Bratislava Type of 1977

Designs: 3k, Bratislava, 1955, by Orest Dubay. 3.60k, Fishpound Square, Bratislava, 1955, by Imro Weiner-Kral.

1978, May 9 **Engr.** ***Perf. 11½***

2174	A760	3k multi	1.30	1.15
2175	A760	3.60k multi	1.55	1.40

Sheets of 4.

Prague Castle Art Type of 1971

Designs: 3k, King Ottokar II, detail from tomb. 3.60k, Charles IV, detail from votiv panel by Jan Ocka.

1978, May 9

2176	A634	3k multi	1.30	1.15
2177	A634	3.60k multi	1.75	1.40

Art treasures of Castle of Prague. Sheets of 4.

Ministry of Post, Prague

A772

Photogravure and Engraved

1978, May 29 ***Perf. 12x11½***

2178	A772	60h multi	25	8

14th session of permanent COMECOM Commission (Ministers of Post and Telecommunications of Socialist Countries).

Palacky Bridge

A773

Prague Bridges and PRAGA '78 Emblem: 40h, Railroad bridge. 1k, Bridge of May 1. 2k, Manes Bridge. 3k, Svatopluk Cech Bridge. 5.40k, Charles Bridge.

1978, May 30

2179	A773	20h blk & multi	8	5
2180	A773	40h blk & multi	16	6
2181	A773	1k blk & multi	45	15
2182	A773	2k blk & multi	90	35
2183	A773	3k blk & multi	1.30	35
2184	A773	5.40k blk & multi	2.35	1.05
		Nos. 2179-2184 (6)	5.24	2.01

PRAGA 1978 International Philatelic Exhibition, Prague, Sept. 8–17.

St. Peter and Apostles, Clock Tower, and Emblem

A774

Town Hall Clock, Prague, by Josef Manes, and PRAGA '78 Emblem: 1k, Astronomical clock. 2k, Prague's coat of arms. 3k, Grape harvest (September). 3.60k, Libra. 10k, Arms surrounded by zodiac signs and scenes symbolic of 12 months (horiz.). 2k, 3k, 3.60k show details from design of 10k.

1978, June 20 *Perf. 11½x11*

2185	A774	40h multi	16	6
2186	A774	1k multi	45	15
2187	A774	2k multi	90	30
2188	A774	3k multi	1.70	45
2189	A774	3.60k multi	1.55	70
		Nos. 2185-2189 (5)	4.76	1.66

Souvenir Sheet

Perf. 12x12

2190	A774	10k multi	9.50	9.50

PRAGA'78 Intl. Philatelic Exhibition, Prague, Sept. 8-17. No. 1290 contains one stamp (50x40mm.): margin shows black clock tower, red inscription. Size: 90x125mm. Sheet exists imperf.

A non-valid souvenir sheet contains 4 imperf. copies of No. 2157. Blue marginal inscriptions, red PRAGA emblems. Sold only with PRAGA ticket.

Folk Dancers
A775

Photogravure and Engraved

1978, July 7 *Perf. 11½x12*

2191	A775	30h multi	12	5

25th Folklore Festival, Vychodna.

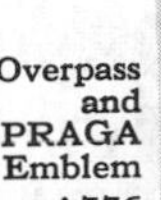

Overpass and PRAGA Emblem
A776

Designs (PRAGA Emblem and): 1k, 2k, Modern office buildings (diff.). 6k, Old and new Prague. 20k, Charles Bridge and Old Town, by Vincent Morstadt, 1828.

1978 *Perf. 12x11½*

2192	A776	60h blk & multi	25	8
2193	A776	1k blk & multi	45	15
2194	A776	2k blk & multi	90	30
2195	A776	6k blk & multi	2.60	75

Souvenir Sheet

Engraved

2196	A776	20k multi	9.50	9.00

PRAGA 1978 International Philatelic Exhibition, Prague, Sept. 8–17. No. 2196 also commemorates 60th anniversary of Czechoslovak postage stamps. Size of No. 2196: 95x76mm. (stamp 61x45mm.).

Issue dates: Nos. 2192–2195, Sept. 8; No. 2196, Sept. 10.

Souvenir Sheet

Apollo's Companion, by Titian
A777

Design: No. 2197b, King Midas. Stamps show details from "Apollo Flaying Marsya" by Titian.

1978, Sept. 12 *Perf. 11½*

2197		Sheet of 2	9.50	9.00
a.	A777	10k multi	4.50	4.00
b.	A777	10k multi	4.50	4.00

Titian (1488–1576), Venetian painter. Margin of No. 2197 shows painting from which stamp designs were taken, black inscription and red PRAGA emblem. Size: 109x165mm. No. 2197 with dark blue marginal inscription "FIP" was sold only with entrance ticket to PRAGA Philatelic Exhibition.

Exhibition Hall
A778

Photogravure and Engraved

1978, Sept. 13 *Perf. 11½x11*

2198	A778	30h multi	12	5

22nd International Engineering Fair, Brno.

Postal Newspaper Service
A779

TV Screen, Headquarters and Logo
A780

Newspaper, Microphone
A781

Photogravure and Engraved

1978, Sept. 21 *Perf. 11½*

2199	A779	30h multi	12	5
2200	A780	30h multi	12	5
2201	A781	30h multi	12	5

25th anniversaries: Postal News Service (No. 2199); Day of the Press (No. 2200); Broadcasting and Television Day (No. 2201).

Sulky Race
A782

Pardubice Steeplechase: 10h, Falling horses and jockeys at fence. 30h, Race. 40h, Horses passing post. 1.60k, Hurdling. 4.40k, Winner.

1978, Oct. 6 *Perf. 12x11½*

2202	A782	10h multi	5	5
2203	A782	20h multi	8	5
2204	A782	30h multi	12	5
2205	A782	40h multi	16	6
2206	A782	1.60k multi	70	30
2207	A782	4.40k multi	2.00	55
		Nos. 2202-2207 (6)	3.11	1.06

Woman Holding Arms of Czechoslovakia
A783

Photogravure and Engraved

1978, Oct. 28 *Perf. 11½*

2208	A783	60h multi	25	10

60th anniversary of independence.

Art Type of 1974

Paintings: 2.40k, Flowers, by Jakub Bohdan (1660–1724). 3k, The Dream of Salas, by Ludovit Fulla (1902–) (horiz.). 3.60k, Apostle with Censer, Master of the Spissko Capitals (c. 1480–1490).

1978, Nov. 27 **Engraved**

2209	A700	2.40k multi	1.05	90
2210	A700	3k multi	1.30	1.15
2211	A700	3.60k multi	1.60	1.40

Slovak National Gallery, 30th anniversary.

Musicians, by Jan Könyves
A784

Slovak Ceramics: 30h, Janosik on Horseback, by Jozef Franko. 40h, Woman in Folk Costume by Michal Polasko. 1k, Three Girls Singing, by Ignac Bizmayer. 1.60k, Janosik Dancing, by Ferdis Kostka.

Photogravure and Engraved

1978, Dec. 5 *Perf. 11½x12*

2212	A784	20h multi	8	5
2213	A784	30h multi	12	5
2214	A784	40k multi	16	6
2215	A784	1k multi	45	12
2216	A784	1.60k multi	70	18
		Nos. 2212-2216 (5)	1.51	46

Alfons Mucha and his Design for 1918 Issue—A785

1978, Dec. 18 *Perf. 11½*

2217	A785	1k multi	45	12

60th Stamp Day.

COMECON Building, Moscow
A786

Photogravure and Engraved

1979, Jan. 1 *Perf. 11½*

2218	A786	1k multi	45	10

Council for Mutual Economic Aid (COMECON), 30th anniversary.

Woman's Head and Grain
A787

Woman, Workers, Child, Doves
A788

1979, Jan. 1

2219	A787	30h multi	12	5
2220	A788	60h multi	25	8

Czechoslovakian Federation, 10th anniversary (30h); United Agricultural Production Association, 30th anniversary (60h).

Soyuz 28, Rockets and Capsule
A789

Designs: 60h, Astronauts Aleksei Gubarev and Vladimir Remek on launching pad (vert.). 1.60k, Soviet astronauts J. Romanenko and G. Grecko, Salyut 6 and recovery ship. 2k, Salyut-Soyuz orbital complex, post office in space and Czechoslovakia No. 2153. 4k, Soyuz 28, crew after landing and trajectory map (vert.). 10k, Gubarev and Remek, Intercosmos emblem, arms of Czechoslovakia and USSR.

1979, Mar. 2

2221	A789	30h multi	12	5
2222	A789	60h multi	25	8
2223	A789	1.60k multi	70	18
2224	A789	2k multi	90	30
2225	A789	4k multi	1.80	50
		Nos. 2221-2225 (5)	3.77	1.11

Souvenir Sheet

2226	A789	10k multi	5.00	4.75

First anniversary of joint Czechoslovak-Soviet space flight. Size of No. 2226: 76x93mm. (stamp 39x55mm.). No. 2226 exists imperf.

Alpine Bellflowers
A790

Stylized Satellite, Dial, Tape
A791

Mountain Flowers: 20h, Crocus. 30h, Pinks. 40h, Alpine hawkweed. 3k, Larkspur.

Photogravure and Engraved

1979, Mar. 23 *Perf. 11½*

2227	A790	10h multi	5	5
2228	A790	20h multi	8	5
2229	A790	30h multi	12	5
2230	A790	40h multi	16	6
2231	A790	3k multi	1.25	50
		Nos. 2227-2231 (5)	1.66	71

Mountain Rescue Service, 25th anniversary.

1979, Apr. 2

2232	A791	10h multi	12	5

Telecommunications research, 30th anniversary.

Artist and Model, Dove, Bratislava Castle—A792

Cog Wheels, Transformer and Student—A793

Musical Instruments, Bratislava Castle—A794

Pioneer Scarf, IYC Emblem—A795

Red Star, Man, Child and Doves A796

1979, Apr. 2

2233	A792	20h multi	12	5
2234	A793	20h multi	12	5
2235	A794	30h multi	12	5
2236	A795	30h multi	12	5
2237	A796	60h multi	25	10
		Nos. 2233-2237 (5)	73	30

Fine Arts Academy, Bratislava, 30th anniversary; Slovak Technical University, 40th anniversary; Radio Symphony Orchestra, Bratislava, 30th anniversary; Young Pioneers, 30th anniversary and International Year of the Child; Peace Movement, 30th anniversary.

Prague Castle Art Type of 1971

Designs: 3k, Burial crown of King Ottokar II. 3.60k, Portrait of Mrs. Reitmayer, by Karel Purkyne.

Photogravure and Engraved

1979, May 9 ***Perf. 11½***

2238	A634	3k multi	1.75	1.25
2239	A634	3.60k multi	1.75	1.35

Arms of Vlachovo Brezi, 1538 A797

Animals in Heraldry: 60h, Jesenik, 1509 (bear and eagle). 1.20k, Vysoke Myto, 1471 (St. George slaying dragon). 1.80k, Martin, 1854 (St. Martin giving coat to beggar). 2k, Zebrak, 1674 (mythological beast).

1979, May 25 ***Perf. 11½x12***

2240	A797	30h multi	12	5
2241	A797	60h multi	25	10
2242	A797	1.20k multi	50	20
2243	A797	1.80k multi	75	30
2244	A797	2k multi	85	30
		Nos. 2240-2244 (5)	2.47	95

Forest, Thriving and Destroyed A798

Designs: 1.80k, Water. 3.60k, City. 4k, Cattle. All designs show good and bad environment, separated by exclamation point; Man and Biosphere emblem.

1979, June 22 **Engr.** ***Perf. 11½***

2245	A798	60h multi	25	12
2246	A798	1.80k multi	75	25
2247	A798	3.60k multi	1.50	70
2248	A798	4k multi	1.70	70

Man and Biosphere Program of UNESCO.

Blast Furnace A799

Photogravure and Engraved

1979, Aug. 29 ***Perf. 11x11½***

2249	A799	30h multi	12	5

Slovak National Uprising, 35th anniversary.

Frog and Goat—A800

Book Illustrations (IYC Emblem and): 40h, Knight on horseback. 60h, Maidens. 1k, Boy with sled following rooster. 3k, King riding flying beast.

1979, Aug. 30 ***Perf. 11½x11***

2250	A800	20h multi	8	5
2251	A800	40h multi	16	6
2252	A800	60h multi	25	10
2253	A800	1k multi	45	18
2254	A800	3k multi	1.25	50
		Nos. 2250-2254 (5)	2.19	89

Prize-winning designs, 7th biennial exhibition of illustrations for children's books, Bratislava; International Year of the Child. Printed with labels showing story characters.

"Bone Shaker" Bicycles, 1870—A801

1979, Sept. 14 ***Perf. 12x11½***

Bicycles from: 20h, 1978. 40h, 1910. 60h, 1886. 3.60k, 1820.

2255	A801	20h multi	8	5
2256	A801	40h multi	16	6
2257	A801	60h multi	25	10
2258	A801	2k multi	90	30
2259	A801	3.60k multi	1.50	60
		Nos. 2255-2259 (5)	2.89	1.11

Bracket Clock, 18th Century—A802

Designs: 18th century clocks.

Photogravure and Engraved

1979, Oct. 1 ***Perf. 11½***

2260	A802	40h multi	16	6
2261	A802	60h multi	25	10
2262	A802	80h multi	32	12
2263	A802	1k multi	45	18
2264	A802	2k multi	90	30
		Nos. 2260-2264 (5)	2.08	76

Art Type of 1967

Paintings: 1.60k, Sunday by the River, by Alois Moravec. 2k, Self-portrait, by Gustav Mally. 3k, Self-portrait, by Ilia Yefimovic Repin. 3.60k, Horseback Rider, by Jan Bauch. 5k, Dancing Peasants, by Albrecht Dürer.

1979, Nov. 27 **Engraved** ***Perf. 12***

2265	A565	1.60k multi	72	50
2266	A565	2k multi	90	60
2267	A565	3k multi	1.35	70
2268	A565	3.60k multi	1.60	90
2269	A565	5k multi	2.25	1.50
		Nos. 2265-2269 (5)	6.82	4.20

Bratislava Type of 1977

Designs: 3k, Bratislava Castle on the Danube, by L. Janscha, 1787. 3.60k, Bratislava Castle, stone engraving by Wolf, 1815.

1979, Dec. 5

2270	A760	3k multi	1.35	60
2271	A760	3.60k multi	1.65	75

Stamp Day—A803

Engraved and Photogravure

1979, Dec. 18 ***Perf. 11½×12***

2272	A803	1k multi	45	15

Numeral—A804

1979-80 **Photo.** ***Perf. 11½×12***

2273	A804	50h red ('79)	22	8
2274	A804	1k brn ('79)	45	15
2275	A804	2k grn ('80)	90	30
2276	A804	3k lake ('80)	1.35	50

Runners and Dove—A805

1980, Jan. 29 Engr. & Photo. ***Perf. 12x11½***

2289	A805	50h multi	22	8

50th International Peace Marathon, Kosice, Oct. 4.

Downhill Skiing—A806

1980, Jan. 29 ***Perf. 11½x12***

2290	A806	1k *shown*	45	15
2291	A806	2k *Speed skating*	90	40
2292	A806	3k *Four-man bobsled*	1.35	50

13th Winter Olympic Games, Lake Placid, N.Y., Feb. 12-24.

Basketball—A807

1980, Jan. 29 ***Perf. 11½***

2293	A807	40h *shown*	18	6
2294	A807	1k *Swimming*	45	15
2295	A807	2k *Hurdles*	90	30
2296	A807	3.60k *Fencing*	1.60	55

22nd Olympic Games, Moscow, July 19-Aug. 3.

Arms Type of 1977

1980, Feb. 20 **Photo. & Engr.** ***Perf. 11½***

2297	A745	50h *Bystrice Nad Pernstejnem*	22	8
2298	A745	50h *Kunstat*	22	8
2299	A745	50h *Rozmital Pod Tremsinem*	22	8
2300	A745	50h *Zlata Idka*	22	8

Theatrical Mask A808

Slovak National Theater, Actors A809

1980, Mar. 1

2301	A808	50h multi	22	8
2302	A809	1k multi	45	15

50th Jiraskuv Hronov Theatrical Ensemble Review; Slovak National Theater, Bratislava, 60th anniversary.

Mouse in Space, Satellite
A810

Police Corps Banner, Emblem
A811

Intercosmos: 1k, Weather map, satellite. 1.60k, Intersputnik television transmission. 4k, Camera, satellite. 5k, Czech satellite station, 1978 (horiz.). 10k, Intercosmos emblem (horiz.).

1980, Apr. 12 ***Perf. 11½x12, 12x11½***

2303	A810	50h multi	22	8
2304	A810	1k multi	45	15
2305	A810	1.60k multi	80	30
2306	A810	4k multi	1.80	60
2307	A810	5k multi	2.25	75
		Nos. 2303-2307 (5)	5.52	1.88

Souvenir Sheet

2308	A810	10k multi	4.75	4.50

Intercosmos cooperative space program. No. 2308 has multicolored margin showing emblems, flags of participating countries. Size: 75½x94mm.

1980, Apr. 17 ***Perf. 11½***

2309	A811	50h multi	22	8

National Police Corps, 35th anniversary.

Lenin's 110th Birth Anniversary—A812

Design: No. 2311, Engel's 160th birth anniversary.

1980, Apr. 22

2310	A812	1k tan & brn	45	15
2311	A812	1k lt grn & brn	45	15

Old and Modern Prague, Czech Flag, Bouquet—A813

Boy Writing "Peace"—A814

Pact Members' Flags, Dove—A815

Czech and Soviet Arms, Prague and Moscow Views—A816

1980, May 6 ***Perf. 12x11½***

2312	A813	50h multi	22	8
2313	A814	1k multi	45	15
2314	A815	1k multi	45	15
2315	A816	1k multi	45	15

Liberation by Soviet army, 35th anniv.; Soviet victory in WWII, 35th anniv.; Signing of Warsaw Pact (Bulgaria, Czechoslovakia, German Democratic Rep., Hungary, Poland, Romania, USSR), 25th anniv.; Czechoslovak-Soviet Treaty of Friendship, Cooperation and Mutual Aid, 10th anniv.

Souvenir Sheet

United Nations, 35th Anniversary—A817

1980, June 3 **Engraved** ***Perf. 12***

2316	A817	4k sheet of 2	3.75	3.00

No. 2316 contains 2 stamps, marginal inscription and symbols of peace and destruction. Size: 111x165½mm.

Athletes Parading Banners in Strahov Stadium, Prague, Spartakiad Emblem—A818

1980, June 3 Photo. & Engr. ***Perf. 12x11½***

2317	A818	50h *shown*	22	8
2318	A818	1k *Gymnast*, vert.	45	15

Spartakiad 1980, Prague, June 26-29.

Aechmea Fasciata—A819

1980, Aug. 13 **Photo. & Engr.** ***Perf. 12***

2319	A819	50h *Gerbera Jamesonii*	22	8
2320	A819	1k *Aechmea fasciata*	45	30
2321	A819	2k *Strelitzia reginae*	90	50
2322	A819	4k *Paphiopedilum*	1.80	1.00

Olomouc and Bratislava Flower Shows.

Chad Girl, Embroidery—A820

Designs: Folktale character embroideries.

Photogravure & Engraved

1980, Sept. 24 ***Perf. 11½x12***

2323	A820	50h *shown*	22	8
2324	A820	1k *Punch and dog*	45	15
2325	A820	2k *Dandy and Posy*	90	30
2326	A820	4k *Lion and moon*	1.80	60
2327	A820	5k *Wallachian dance*	2.25	75
		Nos. 2323-2327 (5)	5.62	1.88

National Census—A821

Photogravure & Engraved

1980, Sept. 24 ***Perf. 12x11½***

2328	A821	1k multi	45	15

Prague Castle Type of 1971

Designs: 3k, Old Palace gateway. 4k, Armorial lion, 16th century.

1980, Oct. 28 ***Perf. 12***

2329	A634	3k multi	1.75	75
2330	A634	4k multi	1.80	1.10

Bratislava Type of 1977

Designs: 3k, View across the Danube, by J. Eder, 1810. 4k, The Old Royal Bridge, by J.A. Lantz, 1820.

1980, Oct. 28

2331	A760	3k multi	1.35	60
2332	A760	4k multi	1.80	90

10th Anniversay of Socialist Youth Federation—A822

1980, Nov. 9 ***Perf. 12x11½***

2333	A822	50h multi	22	8

No. 2137 Overprinted in Red: 3. / MEZINARODNI VELETRH ZNAMEK / ESSEN '80

1980, Nov. 18

2334	A755	1.60k multi	*15.00*	*15.00*

Czechoslovak Day / ESSEN '80, 3rd International Stamp Exhibition, No. 2334 has overprinted red marginal inscription.

Art Type of 1967

Designs: 1k, Pavel Jozef Safarik, by Jozef B. Klemens. 2k, Peasant Revolt mosaic, Anna Podzemma. 3k, St. Lucia, 14th century statue. 4k, Waste Heaps, by Jan Zrzavy (horiz.). 5k, Labor, sculpture by Jan Stursa.

1980, Nov. 27 **Engraved** ***Perf. 12***

2335	A565	1k multi	50	30
2336	A565	2k multi	1.00	60
2337	A565	3k multi	1.50	90
2338	A565	4k multi	2.00	1.25
2339	A565	5k multi	2.50	1.50
		Nos. 2335-2339 (5)	7.50	4.55

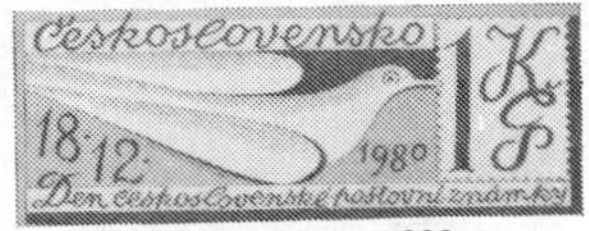

Stamp Day—A823

Photogravure & Engraved

1980, Dec. 18 ***Perf. 11½x12***

2340	A823	1k multi	45	15

7th Five-year Plan, 1981-1985—A824

1981, Jan. 1 **Photo. & Engr.** ***Perf. 11½***

2341	A824	50h multi	22	8

International Year of the Disabled—A825

1981, Feb. 24

2342	A825	1k multi	45	15

Landau, 1800—A826

1981, Feb. 25 ***Perf. 12x11½***

2343	A826	50h shown	22	8
2344	A826	1k Mail coach, 1830	45	15
2345	A826	3.60k Mail sled, 1840	1.65	55
2346	A826	5k 4-horse mail coach, 1860	2.25	75
2347	A826	7k Open carriage, 1840	3.15	1.05
a.		Sheet of 4	14.00	12.00
		Nos. 2343-2347 (5)	7.72	2.58

WIPA '81 Intl. Philatelic Exhibition, Vienna, Austria, May 22-31. No. 2347a has multicolored margin showing exhibition emblems. Size: 150x106mm. Issued May 10.

Wolfgang Amadeus Mozart—A827

Famous Men: No. 2348, Joesph Hlavka (1831-1908). No. 2349, Juraj Hronec (1881-1959). No. 2350, Jan Sverma (1901-1944). No. 2351, Mikulas Schneider-Trnavsky (1881-1958). No. 2352, B. Bolzano (1781-1848). No. 2353, Dimitri Shostakovich (1906-1975), composer. No. 2354, George Bernard Shaw (1856-1950), playwright.

1981, Mar. 10 Photo. & Engr. *Perf. 11½*

2348	A827	50h multi	22	8
2349	A827	50h multi	22	8
2350	A827	50h multi	22	8
2351	A827	50h multi	22	8
2352	A827	1k multi	45	15
2353	A827	1k multi	45	15
2354	A827	1k multi	45	15
2355	A827	1k multi	45	15
		Nos. 2348-2355 (8)	2.68	92

Souvenir Sheet

Yuri Gagarin—A828

1981, Apr. 5 *Perf. 12*

2356		Sheet of 2	5.50	3.50
a.	A828	6k multi	2.70	1.75

20th anniversary of first manned space flight. Margin shows satellites orbiting earth, intercosmos emblem and flags. Size: 108½x166mm.

Workers and Banner—A829

1981, Apr. 6 *Perf. 12x11½*

2357	A829	50h shown	22	8
2358	A829	1k Hands holding banner	45	15
2359	A829	4k Worker holding banner, vert.	1.80	60

Czechoslovakian Communist Party, 60th anniversary.

Congress Emblem, View of Prague—A830

1981, Apr. 6

2360	A830	50h shown	22	8
2361	A830	1k Bratislava	45	15

16th Communist Party Congress.

Agriculture Museum, 90th Anniv. A831

Natl. Assembly Elections A832

1981, May 14 *Perf. 11½x12*

2362	A831	1k multi	45	15

1981, June 1

2363	A832	50h multi	22	8

Bratislava Type of 1977

Designs: 3k, Bratislava Castle, by G.B. Probst, 1760. 4k, Grassalkovic Palace, by C. Bschor, 1815.

1981, June 10 *Perf. 12*

2364	A760	3k multi	1.35	60
2365	A760	4k multi	1.80	90

Uran and Red October Hotels—A833

Successes of Socialist Achievements Exhibition: 1k, Brno-Bratislava Highway, Jihlava. 2k, Nuclear power station, Jaslovske Bohunice.

1981, June 10 *Perf. 12x11½*

2366	A833	80h multi	36	12
2367	A833	1k multi	45	15
2368	A833	2k multi	90	30

Border Defense Units, 30th Anniv. A834

Civil Defense, 30th Anniv. A835

Army Cooperation, 30th Anniv.—A836

Rysy Youth Mountain Climbing Contest—A837

1981, July 11 Photo. & Engr. *Perf. 11½*

2369	A834	40h multi	18	6
2370	A835	50h multi	22	8
2371	A836	1k multi	45	15
2372	A837	3.60k multi	1.65	55

30th Natl. Festival of Amateur Puppet Ensembles—A838

1981, July 2 Photo. & Engr. *Perf. 11½*

2373	A838	2k Punch and Devil	90	30

Souvenir Sheet

Guernica, by Pablo Picasso—A839

1981, July 2 Engr. *Perf. 11½x12*

2374	A839	10k multi	4.75	3.75

Picasso's birth centenary; 45th anniv. of Intl. Brigades in Spain. No. 2374 has multicolored margin showing Picasso drawings. Size: 90x76mm.

Cat Holding Flower, by Etienne Delessert—A840

8th Biennial Exhibition of Children's Book Illustrations (Designs by): 50h, Albin Brunovsky (vert.). 1k, Adolf Born. 2k, Vive Tolli. 10k, Suekichi Akaba.

1981, Sept. 5 Photo. & Engr. *Perf. 11½*

2375	A840	50h multi	22	8
2376	A840	1k multi	45	20
2377	A840	2k multi	90	35
2378	A840	4k multi	1.80	75
2379	A840	10k multi	4.50	1.60
		Nos. 2375-2379 (5)	7.87	2.98

Prague Zoo, 50th Anniv.—A841

1981, Sept. 28 Photo. & Engr. *Perf. 11½x12*

2380	A841	50h Gorillas	22	8
2381	A841	1k Lions	45	20
2382	A841	7k Przewalski's horses	3.15	1.25

Anti-smoking Campaign—A842

1981, Oct. 27 Photo. & Engr. *Perf. 12*

2383	A842	4k multi	1.80	90

No. 2383 se-tenant with label.

Prague Castle Type of 1971

Designs: 3k, Carved dragon, Palais Lobkovitz, 16th cent. 4k, St. Vitus Cathedral, by J. Sember and G. Dobler, 19th cent.

1981, Oct. 28

2384	A634	3k multi	1.80	90
2385	A634	4k multi	1.80	1.25

Art Type of 1967

Designs: 1k, View of Prague, by Vaclav Hollar (1607-1677). 2k, Czechoslovak Academy medallion, engraved by Otakar Spaniel (1881-1955). 3k, Jihoceska Vysivka, by Zdenek Sklenar (b. 1910). 4k, Still Life, by A.M. Gerasimov (1881-1963). 5k, Standing Woman, by Pablo Picasso (1881-1973).

1981, Nov. 27 Engr. *Perf. 12*

2386	A565	1k multi	45	25
2387	A565	2k multi	90	50
2388	A565	3k multi	1.35	80
2389	A565	4k multi	1.80	1.25
2390	A565	5k multi	2.50	1.75
a.		Souvenir sheet of 4	10.50	9.50
		Nos. 2386-2390 (5)	7.00	4.55

Stamp Day—A843

1981, Dec. 18 Photo. & Engr. *Perf. 11½x12*

2391	A843	1k Engraver Edward Karel	45	15

Russian Workers' Party, Prague Congress, 70th Anniv.—A844

1982, Jan. 18 Photo. & Engr. *Perf. 12*

2392	A844	2k Lenin	90	40
a.		Sheet of 4	3.75	1.75

1982 World Cup Soccer—A845

Designs: Various soccer players.

1982, Jan. 29 *Perf. 12x11½*

2393	A845	1k multi	45	18
2394	A845	3.60k multi	1.65	60
2395	A845	4k multi	1.80	70

10th World Trade Union Congress, Havana A846

Arms of Hrob A847

1982, Feb. 10 *Perf. 11½*

2396	A846	1k multi	45	18

1982, Feb. 10 *Perf. 12x11½*

Arms of various cities.

2397	A847	50h shown	22	8
2398	A847	50h Nove Mesto Nad Metuji	22	8
	A847	50h Trencin	22	8
2400	A847	50h Mlada Boleslav	22	8

See Nos. 2499-2502, 2542-2544, 2595-2597.

50th Anniv. of the Great Strike at Most—A848

1982, Mar. 23 Photo. & Engr. *Perf. 11½*

2401	A848	1k multi	45	18

60th Intl. Railway Union Congress—A849

1982, Mar. 23 Photo. & Engr. *Perf. 12x11½*

2402	A849	6k Steam locomotive, 1922, electric, 1982	2.75	1.25

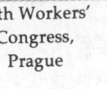

10th Workers' Congress, Prague — A850

George Dimitrov (1882-1947) First Bulgarian Prime Minister — A851

1982, Apr. 15

2403	A850	1k multi	45	15

1982, May 1

2404	A851	50h multi	22	8

The Muse Euterpe Playing a Flute, by Crispin de Passe (1565-1637) — A852

10th Lidice Intl. Children's Drawing Contest — A853

Engravings: 50h, The Lute Player, by Jacob de Gheyn (1565-1629). 1k, Woman Flautist, by Adriaen Collaert (1560-1618). 2k, Musicians in a Hostel, by Rembrandt (1606-1669). 3k, Hurdy-gurdy Player, by Jacques Callot (1594-1635).

1982, May 18 *Perf. 11½x12*

2405	A852	40h multi	18	15
2406	A852	50h multi	22	20
2407	A852	1k multi	45	40
2408	A852	2k multi	90	80
2409	A852	3k multi	1.35	1.00
		Nos. 2405-2409 (5)	3.10	2.55

1982, May 18

2410	A853	2k multi	90	80

Issued in sheets of 6.

40th Anniv. of Destruction of Lidice and Lezaky—A854

1982, June 4 *Perf. 11½*

2411	A854	1k Girl, rose	45	20
2412	A854	1k Hands, barbed wire	45	20

U.N. Disarmament Conference—A855

1982, June 4 *Perf. 12*

2413		Sheet of 2	5.50	4.75
a.		A855 6k Woman holding doves	2.75	2.25

Souvenir Sheet

2nd UN Conference on Peaceful Uses of Outer Space, Vienna, Aug. 9-21—A856

1982, Aug. 9 **Photo. & Engr.** *Perf. 12*

2414	A856	5k Sheet of 2	4.50	4.25

No. 2414 contains 2 stamps, marginal inscription, space themes. Size: 165x108mm.

Krivoklat Castle—A857

1982, Aug. 31 *Perf. 12x11½*

2415	A857	50h shown	22	8
2416	A857	1k Statues (Krivoklat)	45	15
2417	A857	2k Nitra Castle	90	30
2418	A857	3k Pottery, lock (Nitra)	1.35	45
a.		Souvenir Sheet of 4	3.00	2.75

No. 2418a contains Nos. 2415-2418. Size: 106x126mm.

50th Anniv. of Zizkov Hill Natl. Monument—A858

1982, Sept. 16

2419	A858	1k multi	45	18

Prague Castle Type of 1971

Designs: 3k, St. George and the Dragon, 1373. 4k, Tomb of King Vratislav I, 10th cent.

1982, Sept. 28 *Perf. 12*

2420	A634	3k multi	1.35	60
2421	A634	4k multi	1.80	85

Bratislava Type of 1977

Designs: 3k, Paddle steamer, Parnik, 1818. 4k, View from Bridge, 19th cent.

1982, Sept. 29

2422	A760	3k multi	1.35	60
2423	A760	4k multi	1.80	85

European Danube Commission—A859

1982, Sept. 29 *Perf. 11½x12*

2424	A859	3k Steamer, Bratislava Bridge	1.35	60
a.		Souvenir sheet of 4	6.50	6.00
2425	A859	3.60k Ferry, Budapest	1.65	75
a.		Souvenir sheet of 4	6.75	6.00

Nos. 2424a-2425a have multicolored margins showing flags and river map. Size: 129x127mm.

16th Communist Party Congress—A860

1982, Oct. 28 *Perf. 12x11½*

2426	A860	20h Agriculture	10	5
2427	A860	1k Industry	45	18
2428	A860	3k Engineering	1.35	60

30th Anniv. of Academy of Sciences—A861

1982, Oct. 29 *Perf. 11½*

2429	A861	6k Emblem	2.75	1.25

65th Anniv. of October Revolution—A862

Design: 1k, 60th anniv. of USSR.

1982, Nov. 7 *Perf. 12x11½*

2430	A862	50h multi	22	12
2431	A862	1k multi	45	18

Jaroslav Hasek, Writer, Sculpture by Josef Malejovsky—A863

Sculptures: 2k, Jan Zrzavy, freedom fighter, by Jan Simota. 4.40k, Leos Janacek, composer, by Milos Axman. 6k, Martin Kukucin, freedom fighter, by Jan Kulich. 7k, Peaceful Work, by Rudolf Pribis.

Photo. & Engr.

1982, Nov. 26 *Perf. 11½x12*

2432	A863	1k multi	45	15
2433	A863	2k multi	90	30
2434	A863	4.40k multi	2.00	68
2435	A863	6k multi	2.75	90
2436	A863	7k multi	3.25	1.05
		Nos. 2432-2436 (5)	9.35	3.08

Art Type of 1967

Paintings: 1k, Revolution in Spain, by Josef Sima (1891-1971). 2k, Woman Dressing, by Rudolf Kremlicka (1886-1932). 3k, The Girl Bride, by Dezider Milly (1906-1971). 4k, Performers, by Jan Zelibsky (b. 1907). 5k, The Complaint of the Birds, by Emil Filla (1882-1953).

1982, Nov. 27 *Perf. 12*

2437	A565	1k multi	45	15
2438	A565	2k multi	90	30
2439	A565	3k multi	1.35	45
2440	A565	4k multi	1.80	60
2441	A565	5k multi	2.25	75
		Nos. 2437-2441 (5)	6.75	2.25

Stamp Day—A864

1982, Dec. 8 **Photo. & Engr.** *Perf. 11½*

2442	A864	1k Engraver Jaroslav Goldschmied (1890-1977)	45	15

Pres. Gustav Husak, 70th Birthday — A865

1983, Jan. 10 **Engr.** *Perf. 12x11½*

2443	A865	50h dk bl	22	8

Jaroslav Hasek (1882-1923), Writer — A866

Designs: 1k, Julius Fucik (1903-1943), anti-fascist martyr. 2k, Martin Luther (1483-1546). 5k, Johannes Brahms (1833-1897), composer.

1983, Feb. 24 **Photo. & Engr.**

2444	A866	50h multi	22	8
2445	A866	1k multi	45	15
2446	A866	2k multi	90	30
a.		Souvenir sheet of 4	*15.00*	*5.00*
2447	A866	5k multi	2.25	75

Nordposta '83 Intl. Stamp Exhibition, Hamburg. Margin shows UNESCO emblem, Prague and Hamburg arms. Size: 110x80mm.

Workers Marching—A867

Family—A868

1983, Feb. 25 *Perf. 11½*

2448	A867	50h multi	22	8
2449	A868	1k multi	45	15

35th anniv. of "Victorious February" (50h), and Natl. Front (1k).

World Communications Year A869

7th World Ski-jumping Championships A870

Photo. & Engr.

1983, Mar. 16 *Perf. 11½, 12x11½ (2k)*

2450	A869	40h multi	18	5
2451	A869	1k multi	45	15
2452	A869	2k multi	90	30
2453	A869	3.60k multi	1.65	55

Various wave patterns. 2k, 40x23mm; 3.60k, 49x19mm.

1983, Mar. 16 *Perf. 11½*

2454	A870	1k multi	45	15

Souvenir Sheet

5th Anniv. of Czechoslovak-USSR Intercosmos Cooperative Space Program—A871

1983, Apr. 12 *Perf. 12*

2455	A871	10k Sheet of 2	9.00	3.00

Size: 109x166mm.

Protected Species—A872

1983, Apr. 28 *Perf. 12x11½*

2456	A872	50h Butterfly, violets	22	8
2457	A872	1k Water lilies, frog	45	15
2458	A872	2k Pine cones, crossbill	90	30
2459	A872	3.60k Herons	1.65	55
2460	A872	5k Gentians, lynx	4.50	1.50
2461	A872	7k Stag	5.40	1.80
		Nos. 2456-2461 (6)	13.12	4.38

30th Anniv. of Czechoslovak-Soviet Defense Treaty—A873

Soviet Marshals.

1983, May 5 Photo. & Engr. *Perf. 11½*

2462	A873	50h Ivan S. Konev	22	8
2463	A873	1k Andrei I. Sheremenko	45	15
2464	A873	2k Rodion J. Malinovsky	90	30

World Peace and Life Congress, Prague—A874

1983, July 13 *Perf. 12*

2465	A874	2k multi	90	30
a.		Souvenir sheet of 4	3.75	

No. 2465a has blue control number. Size: 108x83mm.

Emperor Rudolf II by Adrian De Vries (1560-1626)—A875

Art treasures of the Prague Castle: 5k, Kinetic relief, Timepiece, Rudolf Svoboda.

1983, Aug. 25 Photo. & Engr. *Perf. 11½*

2466	A875	4k multi	1.80	60
2467	A875	5k multi	2.25	75

See Nos. 2518-2519, 2610-2611.

9th Biennial of Illustrations for Children and Youth—A876

Illustrators: 50h, Oleg K. Zotov, USSR. 1k, Zbigniew Rychlicki, Poland. 4k, Lisbeth Zwerger, Austria. 7k, Antonio Dominques, Angola.

1983, Sept. 9 Photo. & Engr. *Perf. 11½*

2468	A876	50h multi	22	8
2469	A876	1k multi	45	15
2470	A876	4k multi	1.80	60
2471	A876	7k multi	3.15	1.05
a.		Souvenir sheet of 4	5.65	1.90

No. 2471a contains Nos. 2468-2471. Margin shows illustrations by Susan Jeffers, USA and Roald Als, Denmark. Size: 115x134mm.

World Communications Year—A877

Emblems and aircraft.

1983, Sept. 30 Photo. & Engr. *Perf. 11½*

2472	A877	50h red & blk	22	8
2473	A877	1k red & blk	45	15
2474	A877	4k red & blk	1.80	60

60th Anniv. of the Czechoslovak Airlines.

16th Party Congress Achievements—A878

1983, Oct. 20 Photo. & Engr. *Perf. 12x11½*

2475	A878	50h Civil engineering construction	22	8
2476	A878	1k Chemical industry	45	15
2477	A878	3k Health services	1.35	45

Bratislava Type of 1977

Designs: 3k, Two sculptures, Viktor Tilgner (1844-96). 4k, Mirbachov Palace, 1939, by Julius Schubert (1888-1947).

1983, Oct. 28 *Perf. 12*

2478	A760	3k multi	1.35	45
2479	A760	4k multi	1.80	60

Natl. Theater, Prague, Centenary—A879

1983, Nov. 8 Engr. *Perf. 11½*

2480	A879	50h Natl. Theater building	22	8
2481	A879	2k State Theater, Natl. Theater	90	30

Messenger of Mourning, by Mikolas Ales—A880

Designs: 2k, Genius, theater curtain by Vojtech Hynais (1854-1925). 3k, Music, Lyric drawings by Frantisek Zenisek (1849-1916). 4k, Symbolic figure of Prague, by Vaclav Brozik (1851-1901). 5k Hradcany Castle, by Julius Marak (1832-1899).

1983, Nov. 18 Engr.

2482	A880	1k multi	45	15
2483	A880	2k multi	90	30
2484	A880	3k multi	1.35	45
2485	A880	4k multi	1.80	60
2486	A880	5k multi	2.25	75
		Nos. 2482-2486 (5)	6.75	2.25

Warrior with Sword and Shield, Engraving, 17th Cent.—A881

Engravings of Costumes: 50h, Bodyguard of Rudolf II, by Jacob de Gheyn (1565-1629). 1k, Lady with Lace Collar, by Jacques Callot (1592-1635). 4k, Lady, by Vaclav Hollar (1607-77). 5k, Man, by Antoine Watteau (1684-1721).

1983, Dec. 2 Photo. & Engr. *Perf. 11½x12*

2487	A881	40h multi	18	6
2488	A881	50h multi	22	8
2489	A881	1k multi	45	15
2490	A881	4k multi	1.80	60
2491	A881	5k multi	2.25	75
		Nos. 2487-2491 (5)	4.90	1.64

Stamp Day—A882

1983, Dec. 18

2492	A882	1k Karl Seizinger (1889-1978), #114	45	1

Czechoslovak Federation, 15th Anniv.—A883

1984, Jan. 1 *Perf. 11½*

2493	A883	50h Bratislava, Prague Castles	22	8

35th Anniv. of COMECON—A884

1984, Jan. 23

2494	A884	1k Headquarters, Moscow	45	15

1984 Winter Olympics—A885

1984, Feb. 7 *Perf. 12x11½*

2495	A885	2k Cross-country skiing	90	30
2496	A885	3k Hockey	1.35	45
a.		Souvenir sheet of 4	5.50	5.50
2497	A885	5k Biathlon	2.25	75

No. 2496a contains 4 No. 2496. Size: 110x100mm.

Intl. Olympic Committee, 90th Anniv.—A886

1984, Feb. 7 Photo. & Engr. *Perf. 11½x12*

2498	A886	7k Rings, runners, torch	3.15	1.05

City Arms Type of 1982

1984, Mar. 1 *Perf. 12x11½*

2499	A847	50h Kutna Hora	22	8
2500	A847	50h Turnov	22	8
2501	A847	1k Martin	45	15
2502	A847	1k Milevsko	45	15

Intercosmos Space Program A887

Resistance Heroes A888

Various satellites. Nos. 2503-2507 se-tenant with labels showing flags.

1984, Apr. 12 Photo. & Engr. ***Perf. 11½x12***

2503	A887	50h multi	22	8
2504	A887	1k multi	45	15
2505	A887	2k multi	90	30
2506	A887	4k multi	1.80	60
2507	A887	5k multi	2.25	75
		Nos. 2503-2507 (5)	5.62	1.88

1984, May 9 ***Perf. 11x11½***

Designs: 50h, Vendelin Opatrny (1908-44). 1k, Ladislav Novomesky (1904-44). 2k, Rudolf Jasiok (1919-44). 4k, Jan Nalepka (1912-43).

2508	A888	50h multi	22	8
2509	A888	1k multi	45	15
2510	A888	2k multi	90	30
2511	A888	4k multi	1.80	60

Music Year—A889

1984, May 11 ***Perf. 11½***

2512	A889	50h Instruments	22	8
2513	A889	1k Organ pipes, vert.	45	15

Bratislava Type of 1977

Designs: 3k, Vintners' Guild arms, 19th cent. 4k, View of Bratislava (painting commemorating shooting competition, 1827).

1984, June 1 Photo. & Engr. ***Perf. 12***

2514	A760	3k multi	95	32
2515	A760	4k multi	1.25	42

Issued in sheetlets of 4.

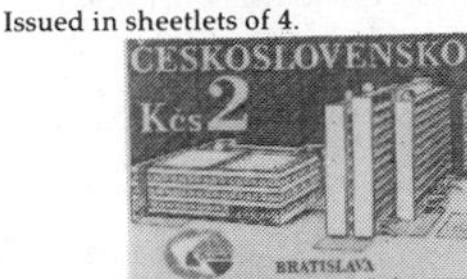

Central Telecommunications Building, Bratislava—A890

1984, June 1 ***Perf. 11½***

2516	A890	2k multi	62	20

1984 UPU Congress—A891

1984, June 12 ***Perf. 12***

2517	A891	5k UPU emblem, dove, globe	1.60	52

Issued in sheetlets of 4 with and without Philatelic Salon text.

Prague Castle Type of 1983

Designs: 3k, Crowing rooster, St. Vitus Cathedral, 19th cent. 4k, King David from the Roundnice, Book of Psalms illuminated manuscript, Bohemia, 15th cent.

1984, Aug. 9 Photo. & Engr. ***Perf. 12***

2518	A875	3k multi	90	30
2519	A875	4k multi	1.25	42

Jack of Spades, 16th Cent. Playing Card—A893

1984, Aug. 28 ***Perf. 11½x12***

2520	A893	50h shown	15	5
2521	A893	1k Queen of spades, 17th cent.	30	10
2522	A893	2k 9 of hearts, 18th cent.	60	20
2523	A893	3k Jack of clubs, 18th cent.	90	30
2524	A893	5k King of hearts, 19th cent.	1.50	50
		Nos. 2520-2524 (5)	3.45	1.15

Slovak Natl. Uprising, 40th Anniv.—A894

1984, Aug. 29 Photo. & Engr. ***Perf. 12x11½***

2525	A894	50h Family, factories, flowers	15	5

Battle of Dukla Pass (Carpathians), 40th Anniv.—A895

1984, Sept. 8 ***Perf. 11½x12***

2526	A895	2k Soldiers, flag	60	20

1984 Summer Olympics—A896

1984, Sept. 9 ***Perf. 12x11½***

2527	A896	1k Pole vault	30	10
2528	A896	2k Bicycling	60	20
2529	A896	3k Rowing	90	30
2530	A896	5k Weight lifting	1.50	50
a.		Souvenir sheet of 4	3.50	1.25

No. 2530a contains Nos. 2527-2530; margin shows Olympic rings. Size: 108x96mm.

16th Party Congress Goals and Projects—A897

1984, Oct. 28 Photo. & Engr. ***Perf. 12x11½***

2531	A897	1k Communications	30	10
2532	A897	2k Transportation	60	20
2533	A897	3k Transgas pipeline	90	30
a.		Souvenir sheet of 3	2.75	1.00

No. 2533a contains 3 Nos. 2533; multicolored margin shows map of Trans-European pipeline, flags. Size: 158x106mm.

Art Type of 1967

Paintings: 1k, The Milevsky River, by Karel Stehlik (b. 1912). 2k, Under the Trees, by Viktor Barvitius (1834-1902). 3k, Landscape with Flowers, by Zolo Palugyay (1898-1935). 4k, King in Palace, Visehrad Codex miniature, 1085. 5k, King in his Castle, Visehrad Codex, 1085. Nos. 2534-2537 horiz.; issued in sheets of 4.

1984, Nov. 16 ***Perf. 11½***

2534	A565	1k multi	30	10
2535	A565	2k multi	60	20
2536	A565	3k multi	90	30
2537	A565	4k multi	1.20	40
2538	A565	5k multi	1.50	50
		Nos. 2534-2538 (5).	4.50	1.50

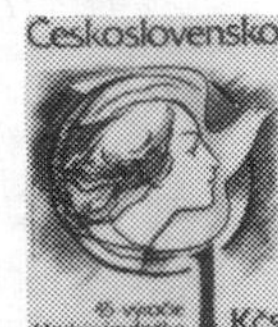

Students' Intl., 45th Anniv.—A898

1984, Nov. 17

2539	A898	1k Head, dove	30	10

Birth Centenary, Antonin Zapotocky—A899

1984, Dec. 18 Photo. & Engr. ***Perf. 11½***

2540	A899	50h multi	15	8

Stamp Day—A900

1984, Dec. 18 Photo. & Engr. ***Perf. 11½x12***

2541	A900	1k Engraver Bohumil Heinz (1894-1940)	30	10

City Arms Type of 1982

1985, Feb. 5 Photo. & Engr. ***Perf. 12x11½***

2542	A847	50h Kamyk nad Vltavou	15	8
2543	A847	50h Havirov	15	8
2544	A847	50h Trnava	15	8

University of Applied Arts, Prague, Centenary—A901

1985, Feb. 6 Photo. & Engr. ***Perf. 11½x12***

2545	A901	3k Art and Pleasure, sculpture	90	45

Trnava University, 350th Anniv.—A902

1985, Feb. 6 Photo. & Engr. ***Perf. 11½x12***

2546	A902	2k Town of Trnava	60	30

Military Museum Exposition—A903

1985, Feb. 7 ***Perf. 11½x12, 12x11½*** **Photo. & Engr.**

2547	A903	50h Armor, crossbow, vert.	15	8
2548	A903	1k Medals, vert.	30	15
2549	A903	2k Biplane, spacecraft	60	30

Vladimir I. Lenin (1870-1924), 1st Chairman of Russia—A904

1985, Mar. 15 Engr. ***Perf. 12***

2550	A904	2k multi	60	30

No. 2549 printed in sheets of 6.

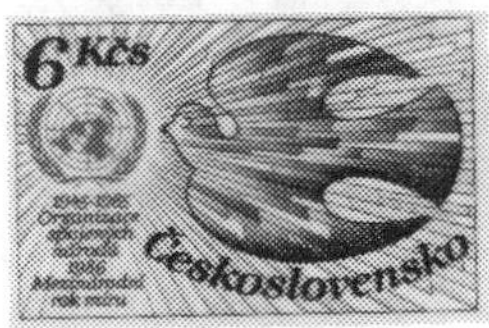

UN 40th Anniv., Peace Year 1986—A905

1985, Mar. 15

2551	A905	6k UN, Peace Year emblems	1.75	90

Kosice Govt. Plan, Apr. 5, 1945—A906

1985, Apr. 5 Photo. & Engr. ***Perf. 11½***

2552	A906	4k Natl. arms, twig, crowd	1.20	60

Natl. Security Forces, 40th Anniv.—A907

1985, Apr. 5

2553 A907 50h Natl. arms, flag, soldiers 15 8

Halley's Comet, INTERCOSMOS Project Vega—A908

Design: Emblem, space platform, interstellar map, intercept data.

1985, Apr. 12 *Perf. 12x11½*

2554 A908 5k multi 1.50 75
a. Souvenir sheet of 2 3.00 1.50

Project Vega, a joint effort of the USSR, France, German Democratic Republic, Austria, Poland, Bulgaria and CSSR, was for the geophysical study of Halley's Comet, airborne Dec. 1984-Mar. 1986. No. 2554a has multicolored margin picturing orbit and intercept data. Size: 106x98mm.

European Ice Hockey Championships, Prague, Apr. 17 - May 3—A909

1985, Apr. 13

2555 A909 1k Hockey players, emblem 30 15

Ovpt. "CSSR / WINNERS" in Violet-Blue.

1985, May 31 *Perf. 12x11½*

2556 A909 1k multi 30 15

Natl. Chess Org., 80th Anniv.—A910

1985, Apr. 13 *Perf. 11½*

2557 A910 6k Emblem, game board, chessmen 1.75 90

Anniversaries—A911

1985, May 5 *Perf. 11½x12*

2558 A911 1k May Uprising, 1945 30 15
2559 A911 1k Soviet Army in CSSR, 1945 30 15
2560 A911 1k Warsaw Treaty, 1950 30 15
2561 A911 1k Czech-Soviet Treaty, 1970 30 15

Spartakiad '85, Strahov Stadium, Prague, June 27—A912

Designs: 50h, Gymnasts warming up with rackets and balls. 1k, Rhythmic gymnastics floor exercise, Prague Castle.

1985, June 3 *Perf. 11½, 11½x12*

2562 A912 50h multi 15 8

Size: 53x22mm.

2563 A912 1k multi 30 15

WW II Anti-Fascist Political Art—A913

Drawings and caricatures: 50h, Fire, and From the Concentration Camp, by Joseph Capek (1887-1945). 2k, The Conference on Disarmament in Geneva, 1927 and The Prophecy of Three Parrots, 1933, by Frantisek Bidlo (1895-1945). 4k, The Unknown Warrior to Order, 1936, and The Almost Peaceful Dove, 1937, by Antonin Pelc (1895-1967).

1985, June 4 *Perf. 12x11½*

2564 A913 50h multi 15 8
2565 A913 2k multi 60 30
2566 A913 4k multi 1.20 60

Helsinki Conference on European Security and Cooperation, 10th Anniv.—A914

1985, July 1 Photo. & Engr. *Perf. 12x11½*

2567 A914 7k multi 2.00 1.00
a. Souvenir sheet of 4 8.00 8.00

No. 2567a has multicolored inscribed margin picturing doves, mother and child embracing, Finlandia Hall and map of Europe. Size: 107x136mm.

12th World Youth Festival, Moscow—A915

1985, July 2

2568 A915 1k Kremlin, youths 28 14

Federation of World Trade Unions, 40th Anniv.—A916

1985, Sept. 3 *Perf. 11½*

2569 A916 50h multi 14 8

Bratislava Type of 1977

Designs: 3k, Castle and river, lace embroidery by Elena Holeczyova (1906-1983). 4k, Pottery cups and mugs, 1600-1500 B.C.

1985, Sept. 4 Engr. *Perf. 12*

2570 A760 3k multi 85 42
2571 A760 4k multi 1.15 58

Issued in sheets of 4.

10th Biennial of Illustrations—A918

Children's book illustrations: 1k, Rocking Horse, by Kveta Pacovska, USSR. 2k, Fairies, by Gennadij Spirin, USSR. 3k, Butterfly and Girl, by Kaarina Kaila, Finland. 4k, Boy and Animals, by Erick Ingraham, USA.

1985, Sept. 5 Photo. & Engr. *Perf. 11½*

2572 A918 1k multi 28 14
2573 A918 2k multi 58 30
2574 A918 3k multi 85 42
2575 A918 4k multi 1.15 58
a. Souvenir Sheet of 4, #2572-2575

No. 2575a has black and red decorative margin inscribed in six languages and picturing the BIB '85 emblem and Playing Cards, by Dusan Kallay, Czech. Size: 95x129mm.

5-Year Development Plan—A919

1985, Oct. 28 *Perf. 12x11½*

2576 A919 50h Construction machinery 14 8
2577 A919 1k Prague subway, map 28 14
2578 A919 2k Modern textile spinning 58 30

16th Communist Party Congress goals.

Prague Castle—A920

Engr., Photo. & Engr. (3k)

1985, Oct. 28 *Perf. 12*

2579 A920 2k Presidential Palace Gate, 1768 58 30
2580 A920 3k St. Vitus Cathedral 85 42

Nos. 2579-2580 each issued in sheets of 6.

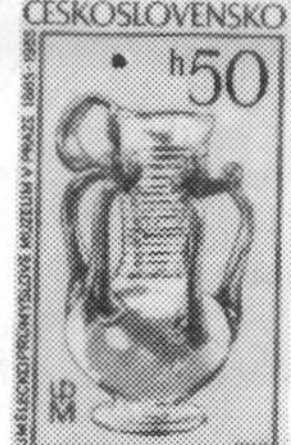

Arts and Crafts Museum, Prague, Cent.—A921

Glassware: 50h, Pitcher, Near East, 4th cent. 1k, Venetian pitcher, 16th cent. 2k, Bohemian goblet, c. 1720. 4k, Harrachov Bohemian vase, 18th cent. 6k, Jablonec Bohemian vase, c. 1900.

1985, Nov. 23 Photo. & Engr. *Perf. 11½x12*

2581 A921 50h multi 14 8
2582 A921 1k multi 28 14
2583 A921 2k multi 58 30
2584 A921 4k multi 1.15 58
2585 A921 6k multi 1.75 85
Nos. 2581-2585 (5) 3.90 1.95

Art Type of 1967

Designs: 1k, Young Woman in a Blue Gown, by Jozef Ginovsky (1800-1857). 2k, Lenin on the Charles Bridge, Prague, 1952, by Martin Sladky (b. 1920). 3k, Avenue of Poplars, 1935, by Vaclav Rabas (1885-1954). 4k, The Martyrdom of St. Dorothea, 1516, by Hans Baldung Grien (c. 1484-1545). 5k, Portrait of Jasper Schade van Westrum, 1645, by Frans Hals (c. 1581-1666).

1985, Nov. 27 Engr. *Perf. 12*

2586 A565 1k multi 28 14
2587 A565 2k multi 58 30
2588 A565 3k multi 85 42
2589 A565 4k multi 1.15 58
2590 A565 5k multi 1.40 70
Nos. 2586-2590 (5) 4.26 2.14

Nos. 2586-2590 each issued in sheets of 4.

Bohdan Roule (1921-1960), Engraver—A922

1985, Dec. 18 Photo & Engr. *Perf. 11½x12*

2591 A922 1k multi 28 14

Stamp Day 1985.

Intl. Peace Year—A923

1986, Jan. 2

2592 A923 1k multi 28 14

Philharmonic Orchestra, 90th Anniv. A924

EXPO '86, Vancouver A925

1986, Jan. 2 *Perf. 11½*
2593 A924 1k Victory Statue, Prague 28 14

1986, Jan. 23 *Perf. 11½*

Design: Z 50 LS monoplane, Cenyerth Prague-Kladno locomotive, Sahara Desert rock drawing, 5th-6th cent. B.C.

2594 A925 4k multi 1.15 58

City Arms Type of 1982

1986, Feb. 10 *Perf. 12x11½*
2595 A847 50h Myjava 14 8
2596 A847 50h Vodnany 14 8
2597 A847 50h Zamberk 14 8

17th Natl. Communist Party Congress, Prague, Mar. 24—A926

1986, Mar. 20 Photo. & Engr. *Perf. 11½*
2598 A926 50h shown 16 8
2599 A926 1k Industry 32 16

Natl. Communist Party, 65th Anniv.—A927

1986, Mar. 20 *Perf. 12x11½*
2600 A927 50h Star, man, woman 16 8
2601 A927 1k Hammer, sickle, laborers 32 16

Natl. Front Election Program—A928

1986, Mar. 28
2602 A928 50h multi 16 8

Karlovy Vary Intl. Film Festival, 25th Anniv.—A929

1986, Apr. 3 *Perf. 11½*
2603 A929 1k multi 32 16

Spring of Prague Music Festival A930

Prague-Moscow Air Service, 50th Anniv. A931

1986, Apr. 8 Photo. & Engr. *Perf. 11½*
2604 A930 1k multi 32 16

1986, Apr. 25
2605 A931 50h multi 16 8

Intl. Olympic Committee, 90th Anniv.—A932

1986, May 12 *Perf. 11½x12*
2606 A932 2k multi 65 32

1986 World Cup Soccer Championships, Mexico—A933

1986, May 15 *Perf. 12x11½*
2607 A933 4k multi 1.30 65

Women's World Volleyball Championships, Prague—A934

1986, May 19
2608 A934 1k multi 32 16

Souvenir Sheet

Intl. Philatelic Federation, FIP, 60th Anniv.—A935

Design: Portrait of Joseph Paar (1654-1725), postmaster, PRAGA '88 emblem, posthorn, covers and hand canceler from the Postal Museum, Prague.

1986, June 3 Engr. *Perf. 12*
2609 A935 20k multi 6.50 3.25

No. 2609 has multicolored inscribed margin picturing exhibition emblem and 19th century coach. Size: 110x82mm.

Prague Castle Type of 1983

Designs: 2k, Jewelled funerary pendant, 9th cent. 3k, Allegory of Blossoms, sculpture by Jaroslav Horejc (1886-1983), St. Vitus Cathedral.

1986, June 6 Engr. *Perf. 12*
2610 A875 2k multi 65 32
2611 A875 3k multi 1.00 50

UN Child Survival Campaign—A937

Toys.

1986, Sept. 1 Photo. & Engr. *Perf. 11½*
2612 A937 10h Rooster 5 5
2613 A937 20h Horse and rider 6 5
2614 A937 1k Doll 32 16
2615 A937 2k Doll, diff. 65 32
2616 A937 3k Tin omnibus, c. 1910 1.00 50
Nos. 2612-2616 (5) 2.08 1.08

UNICEF, 40th anniv.

Registration, Cent.—A938

1986, Sept. 2 *Perf. 11½x12*
2617 A938 4k Label, mail coach 1.30 65

Bratislava Type of 1977

1986, Sept. 11 Engr. *Perf. 12*
2618 A760 3k Sigismund Gate 95 48
2619 A760 4k St. Margaret, bas-relief 1.30 65

Sheets of four.

Owls—A939

1986, Sept. 18 Photo. & Engr. *Perf. 11½*
2620 A939 50h Bubo bubo 16 8
2621 A939 2k Asio otus 65 32
2622 A939 3k Strix aluco 95 48
2623 A939 4k Tyto alba 1.30 65
2624 A939 5k Asio flammeus 1.60 80
Nos. 2620-2624 (5) 4.66 2.33

Intl. Brigades in Spain—A940

Theater curtain: Woman Savaged by Horses, 1936, by Vladimir Sychra (1903-1963), Natl Gallery, Prague.

1986, Oct. 1 **Engr.** ***Perf. 12***

2625	A940	5k multi	1.60	80

No. 2625 issued in sheets of 2; inscribed margin pictures detail of curtain in black and white. Size: 165x108mm.

Locomotives and Streetcars—A941

1986, Oct. 6 **Photo. & Engr.** ***Perf. 12x11½***

2626	A941	50h KT-8	16	8
2627	A941	1k E458.1	32	16
2628	A941	3k T466.2	95	48
2629	A941	5k M152.0	1.60	80

Art Type of 1967

Designs: 1k, The Czech Lion, May 1918, by Vratislav H. Brunner (1886-1928). 2k, Boy with Mandolin, 1945, by Jozef Sturdik (b. 1920). 3k, Metra Building, 1984, by Frantisek Gross (1909-1985). 4k, Portrait of Maria Maximiliana at Sternberk, 1665, by Karel Skreta (1610-1674). 5k, Adam and Eve, 1538, by Lucas Cranach (1472-1553).

1986, Nov. 3 **Engr.** ***Perf. 12***

2634	A565	1k multi	32	16
2635	A565	2k multi	65	32
2636	A565	3k multi	95	48
2637	A565	4k multi	1.30	65
2638	A565	5k multi	1.60	80
		Nos. 2634-2638 (5)	4.82	2.41

Sheets of 4.

SEMI-POSTAL STAMPS.

Nos. B1–B123 were sold, in sets only, at 1½ times face value at the Philatelists' Window of the Prague P.O. for charity benefit. They were available for ordinary postage.

The overprints of Nos. B1–B123 have been well forged.

Austrian Stamps of 1916-18 Overprinted in Black or Blue

POŠTA
ČESKOSLOVENSKÁ
1919

a

1919 *Perf. 12½.*

B1	A37	3h	brt vio	20	20
B2	A37	5h	lt grn	20	20
B3	A37	6h	dp org (Bl)	60	60
B4	A37	6h	dp org (Bk)	*1,500.*	*1,500.*
B5	A37	10h	magenta	80	80
B6	A37	12h	lt bl	80	80
B7	A42	15h	dl red	20	20
B8	A42	20h	dk grn	20	20
a.		20h	grn	160.00	100.00
B9	A42	25h	blue	30	30
B10	A42	30h	dl vio	30	30
B11	A39	40h	ol grn	30	30
B12	A39	50h	dk grn	30	30
B13	A39	60h	dp bl	40	40
B14	A39	80h	org brn	30	30
B15	A39	90h	red vio	70	70
B16	A39	1k	car, *yel* (Bl)	50	50
B17	A39	1k	car, *yel* (Bk)	175.00	150.00
B18	A40	2k	lt bl	3.25	3.25
B18A	A40	2k	dk bl	*3,250.*	*2,500.*
B19	A40	3k	car rose	80.00	40.00
B19A	A40	3k	claret	1,200.	1,100.
B20	A40	4k	yel grn	20.00	12.00
B20A	A40	4k	dp grn	52.50	35.00
B21	A40	10k	violet	375.00	250.00
B21A	A40	10k	dp vio	525.00	325.00

The used price of No. B18A is for copies which have only a Czechoslovakian cancellation. Some of the copies of Austria No. 160 which were officially overprinted with type "a" and sold by the post office, had previously been used and lightly canceled with Austrian cancellations. These canceled-before-overprinting copies, which were postally valid, sell for about one-fourth as much.

Granite Paper.

B22	A40	2k	lt bl	2.50	2.50
B23	A40	3k	car rose	10.00	9.00
B24	A40	4k	yel grn		
B25	A40	10k	dp vio		

Excellent counterfeits of Nos. B1–B25 exist.

Austrian Newspaper Stamps Overprinted

b

Imperf.

On Stamp of 1908.

B26	N8	10h	carmine	2,000.	2,000.

On Stamps of 1916.

B27	N9	2h	brown	10	10
B28	N9	4h	green	40	40
B29	N9	6h	dp bl	25	25
B30	N9	10h	orange	5.00	5.00
B31	N9	30h	claret	2.00	2.00
			Nos. B27-B31 (5)	7.75	7.75

Austrian Special Handling Stamps Overprinted in Blue or Black.

Stamps of 1916 Overprinted

POŠTA
ČESKOSLOVENSKÁ
1919

c

Perf. 12½.

B32	SH1	2h	cl, *yel* (Bl)	40.00	35.00
B33	SH1	5h	dp grn, *yel*	*1,400.*	*1,000.*

Stamps of 1917 Overprinted

POŠTA
ČESKOSLOVENSKÁ
1919

d

B34	SH2	2h	cl, *yel* (Bl)	20	20
a.			Vert. pair, imperf. btwn.	*250.00*	
B35	SH2	2h	cl, *yel* (Bk)	85.00	50.00
B36	SH2	5h	grn, *yel* (Bk)	20	20

Austrian Air Post Stamps, Nos. C1–C3, Overprinted Type "c" Diagonally.

B37	A40	1.50k	on 2k lil	250.00	185.00
B38	A40	2.50k	on 3k ocher	250.00	185.00
B39	A40	4k	gray	1,000.	800.00

1919

Austrian Postage Due Stamps of 1908–13 Overprinted Type "b".

B40	D3	2h	carmine	*4,500.*	*4,000.*
B41	D3	4h	carmine	40.00	27.50
B42	D3	6h	carmine	20.00	15.00
B43	D3	14h	carmine	125.00	55.00
B44	D3	25h	carmine	80.00	40.00
B45	D3	30h	carmine	600.00	500.00
B46	D3	50h	carmine	1,200.	1,100.

Austria Nos. J49–J56 Overprinted Type "b".

B47	D4	5h	rose red	15	15
B48	D4	10h	rose red	20	20
B49	D4	15h	rose red	20	20
B50	D4	20h	rose red	3.00	3.00
B51	D4	25h	rose red	2.00	2.00
B52	D4	30h	rose red	60	60
B53	D4	40h	rose red	2.00	2.00
B54	D4	50h	rose red	425.00	375.00

Austria Nos. J57–J59 Overprinted Type "a".

B55	D5	1k	ultra	20.00	16.50
B56	D5	5k	ultra	80.00	50.00
B57	D5	10k	ultra	400.00	375.00

Austria Nos. J47–J48, J60–J63 Overprinted Type "c" Diagonally.

B58	A22	1h	gray	40.00	25.00
B59	A23	15h	on 2h vio	200.00	165.00
B60	A38	10h	on 24h bl	140.00	120.00
B61	A38	15h	on 36h vio	1.00	1.00
B62	A38	20h	on 54h org	140.00	120.00
B63	A38	50h	on 42h choc	1.00	1.00

Hungarian Stamps Overprinted Type "b".

Wmkd. Double Cross. (137)

1919 *Perf. 15.*

On Stamps of 1913-16.

B64	A4	1f	slate	1,650.	1,500.
B65	A4	2f	yellow	4.00	4.00
B66	A4	3f	orange	100.00	50.00
B67	A4	6f	ol grn	8.00	8.00
B68	A4	50f	lake, *bl*	2.00	1.50
B69	A4	60f	grn, *sal*	100.00	40.00
B70	A4	70f	red brn, *grn*	1,850.	1,250.

On Stamps of 1916.

B71	A8	10f	rose	375.00	275.00
B72	A8	15f	violet	200.00	150.00

On Stamps of 1916-18.

B73	A9	2f	brn org	15	15
B74	A9	3f	red lil	20	20
B75	A9	5f	green	10	10
B76	A9	6f	grnsh bl	80	80
B77	A9	10f	rose red	1.75	2.50
B78	A9	15f	violet	30	25
B79	A9	20f	gray brn	12.50	10.00
B80	A9	25f	dl bl	1.00	75
B81	A9	35f	brown	12.50	8.50
B82	A9	40f	ol grn	3.25	2.75

Overprinted Type "d".

B83	A10	50f	red vio & lil	1.25	1.25
B84	A10	75f	brt bl & pale bl	1.00	1.00
B85	A10	80f	yel grn & pale grn	2.00	2.00
B86	A10	1k	red brn & cl	2.50	2.50
B87	A10	2k	ol brn & bis	10.00	10.00
B88	A10	3k	dk vio & ind	67.50	50.00
B89	A10	5k	dk brn & lt brn	225.00	135.00
B90	A10	10k	vio brn & vio	1,200.	1,100.

Overprinted Type "b".

On Stamps of 1918.

B91	A11	10f	scarlet	25	25
B92	A11	20f	dk brn	35	35
B93	A11	25f	dp bl	2.50	2.50
B94	A12	40f	ol grn	2.75	2.75
B95	A12	50f	lilac	125.00	45.00

On Stamps of 1919.

B96	A13	10f	red	10.00	10.00
B97	A13	20f	dk brn	*4,000.*	*4,000.*

Same Overprint On Hungarian Newspaper Stamp of 1914.

Imperf.

B98	N5	(2f)	orange	15	15

Same Overprint On Hungarian Special Delivery Stamp.

Perf. 15.

B99	SD1	2f	gray grn & red	15	15

Same Overprint On Hungarian Semi-Postal Stamps.

B100	SP3	10f	+2f rose red	60	85
B101	SP4	15f	+2f vio	1.00	1.25
B102	SP5	40f	+2f brn car	8.00	5.00
			Nos. B98-B102 (5)	9.90	7.40

Hungarian Postage Due Stamps of 1903–18 Overprinted Type "b".

Wmkd. Crown in Circle. (135)

1919 *Perf. 11½, 12.*

B103	D1	50f	grn & blk	*750.00*	*750.00*

Wmkd. Crown. (136, 136a)

Perf. 11½x12, 15

B104	D1	1f	grn & blk	*700.00*	*700.00*
B105	D1	2f	grn & blk	*400.00*	*400.00*
B106	D1	12f	grn & blk	*3,000.*	*3,000.*
B107	D1	50f	grn & blk	225.00	225.00

Wmkd. Double Cross. (137)

Perf. 15.

On Stamps of 1914.

B110	D1	1f	grn & blk	600.00	575.00
B111	D1	2f	grn & blk	325.00	325.00
B112	D1	5f	grn & blk	750.00	750.00
B113	D1	12f	grn & blk	*2,500.*	*2,500.*
B114	D1	50f	grn & blk	225.00	225.00

On Stamps of 1915-18.

B115	D1	1f	grn & red	250.00	200.00
B116	D1	2f	grn & red	1.00	1.00
B117	D1	5f	grn & red	25.00	16.50
B118	D1	6f	grn & red	2.00	2.00
B119	D1	10f	grn & red	80	80
a.			Pair, one without overprint		
B120	D1	12f	grn & red	2.75	2.75
B121	D1	15f	grn & red	12.50	10.00
B122	D1	20f	grn & red	1.50	1.50
B123	D1	30f	grn & red	80.00	60.00
			Nos. B115-B123 (9)	375.55	294.55

Bohemian Lion Breaking its Chains
SP1

Mother and Child
SP2

1919 **Typographed.** **Unwmkd.**

Perf. 11½, 13½ and Compound.

Pinkish Paper.

B124	SP1	15(h)	gray grn	8	10
B125	SP1	25(h)	dk brn	8	10
a.		25(h)	lt brn	5.00	
B126	SP1	50(h)	dk bl	8	10

Photogravure.

Yellowish Paper.

B127	SP2	75(h)	slate	8	10
B128	SP2	100(h)	brn vio	8	10
B129	SP2	120(h)	vio, *yel*	8	10
			Nos. B124-B129 (6)	48	60

Nos. B124–B129 honor the Czecho-Slovak Legion. Nos. B124–B126 commemorate the first anniversary of Czechoslovak independence. Nos. B127–B129 were sold for the benefit of Legionnaires' orphans. Imperforates exist.

See No. 1581.

Regular Issues of Czechoslovakia Surcharged in Red:

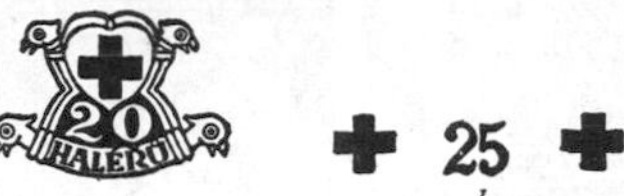

a b

1920 *Perf. 13½.*

B130	A1 (a)	40(h)	+20(h) bis	2.00	1.60
B131	A2 (a)	60(h)	+20h grn	2.00	1.60
B132	A4 (b)	125(h)	+25(h) gray bl	4.00	4.00

President Masaryk
SP3

Wmkd. Linden Leaves. (107)

1923 **Engraved** ***Perf. 13½x14½***

B133	SP3	50(h)	gray grn	1.25	75
B134	SP3	100(h)	carmine	2.50	1.25
B135	SP3	200(h)	blue	10.00	6.75
B136	SP3	300(h)	dk brn	11.00	6.75

Issued in commemoration of the fifth anniversary of the Republic.

The monogram "CSP" (Ceskoslovenska Posta) is printed on top of the gum in brown on the back of each stamp. These stamps were sold at double their face values, the excess being given to the Red Cross and other charitable organizations.

International Olympic Congress Issue.

1925

Semi-Postal Stamps of 1923 Overprinted in Blue or Red

CONGRES OLYMP. INTERNAT.
PRAHA1925

B137	SP3	50(h)	gray grn (Bl)	10.00	8.00
B138	SP3	100(h)	car (Bl)	17.50	13.00
B139	SP3	200(h)	bl (R)	110.00	90.00

These stamps were sold at double their face values, the excess being divided between a fund for post office clerks and the Olympic Games Committee.

Sokol Issue.

1926

Semi-Postal Stamps of 1923 Overprinted in Blue or Red

VIII. SLET VŠESOKOLSKÝ PRAHA 1926

B140	SP3	50 (h) gray grn (Bl)	8.00	6.75
B141	SP3	100 (h) car (Bl)	8.00	7.25
B142	SP3	200 (h) bl (R)	37.50	30.00
a.		Double overprint		
B143	SP3	300 (h) dk brn (R)	65.00	52.50

These stamps were sold at double their face values, the excess being given to the Congress of Sokols, June, 1926.

Midwife Presenting Newborn Child to its Father; after a Painting by Josef Manes
SP4 SP5

Engraved.

1936 *Perf. 12½* **Unwmkd.**

B144	SP4	50h +50h grn	60	60
B145	SP5	1k +50h cl	1.00	1.00
B146	SP4	2k +50h bl	2.50	2.50

"Lullaby" by Stanislav Sucharda
SP6 SP7

1937 *Perf. 12½.*

B147	SP6	50h +50h dl grn	50	50
B148	SP6	1k +50h rose lake	1.00	1.00
B149	SP7	2k +1k dl bl	2.00	2.00

President Masaryk and Little Girl in Native Costume
SP8

1938 *Perf. 12½*

B150	SP8	50h +50h dp grn	60	60
B151	SP8	1k +50h rose lake	70	70

Souvenir Sheet.
Imperf.

B152	SP8	2k +3k blk	4.50	4.50

No. B152 measures 72x90mm. with marginal inscriptions of "TGM" and Masaryk's signature.

Issued to commemorate the 88th anniversary of the birth of President Masaryk (1850–1937).

Souvenir Sheet.

Symbol of the Republic
SP9

1938 *Perf. 12½*

B153	SP9	2k (+8k) dk bl, sheet	4.50	4.50

Issued in sheets measuring 79x90mm. The surtax was devoted to national relief for refugees.

"Republic" and Congress Emblem
SP10

St. George Slaying the Dragon
SP11

1945 Engraved

B154	SP10	1.50(k) +1.50(k) car rose	20	10
B155	SP10	2.50(k) +2.50(k) bl	30	20

Issued to commemorate the Students' World Congress at Prague, Nov. 17, 1945.

1946

B156	SP11	2.40k +2.60k car rose	25	15
B157	SP11	4k +6k bl	60	30

Souvenir Sheet.
Imperf.

B158	SP11	4k +6k bl	1.50	1.50

No. B158 measures 70x90mm., with marginal inscriptions: "Pravda Vitezi Kveten 1945 1946." Nos. B156–B158 commemorate the 1st anniversary of Czechoslovakia's liberation. The surtax aided World War II orphans.

Souvenir Sheet.

SP13

1946, Aug. 3 *Imperf.*

B159	SP13	2.40k rose brn	1.00	1.00

Issued for the Brno National Stamp Exhibition, August, 1946.

The sheet measures 70x89mm. It was sold for 10k.

"You Went Away"
SP14

"You Remained Ours"
SP15

"You Came Back"
SP16

1946, Oct. 28 Photo. *Perf. 14*

B160	SP14	1.60k +1.40k red brn	30	30
B161	SP15	2.40k +2.60k scar	45	45
B162	SP16	4k +4k dp bl	75	75

The surtax was for repatriated Slovaks.

Barefoot Boy
SP17

Woman and Child
SP18

Designs: 2k+1k, Mother and child. 3k+1k, Little girl.

Engraved.

1948, Dec. 18 *Perf. 12½* **Unwmkd.**

B163	SP17	1.50(k) +1(k) rose lil	25	10
B164	SP17	2(k) +1(k) dp bl	25	10
B165	SP17	3(k) +1(k) rose car	35	30

The surtax was for child welfare.

Labels alternate with stamps in sheets of Nos. B163–B165.

Inscribed: "Detem 1949."

1949, Dec. 18 *Perf. 12½*

Design: 3k+1k, Man lifting child.

B166	SP18	1.50k +50h gray	3.50	1.75
B167	SP18	3k +1k cl	4.50	2.25

The surtax was for child welfare.

Dove Carrying Olive Branch
SP19 SP20

1949, Dec. 18

B168	SP19	1.50k +50h cl	4.00	1.75
B169	SP20	3k +1k rose red	4.00	1.75

The surtax was for the Red Cross.

AIR POST STAMPS.

Stamps of 1918-19 Surcharged in Red, Blue or Green:

14 Kč

1920 *Imperf.* **Unwmkd.**

C1	A1	14k on 200(h) ultra (R)	17.50	17.50
a.		Inverted surcharge	75.00	
C2	A2	24k on 500(h) red brn (Bl)	45.00	45.00
a.		Inverted surcharge	110.00	
C3	A2	28k on 1000 (h) vio (G)	45.00	45.00
a.		Inverted surcharge	115.00	
b.		Double surch.	125.00	

Perf. 14, 14x13½

C4	A1	14k on 200 (h) ultra (R)	35.00	35.00
a.		Perf. 14 x 13½	80.00	75.00
C5	A2	24k on 500 (h) red brn (Bl)	80.00	80.00
a.		Perf. 14 x 13½	110.00	110.00
C6	A2	28k on 1000(h) vio (G)	60.00	47.50
a.		Inverted surcharge	110.00	110.00
b.		Perf. 14	600.00	500.00

Excellent counterfeits of the overprint are known.

Stamps of 1920 Surcharged in Black or Violet:

1922, June 15

C7	A8	50(h) on 100(h) dl grn (Bk)	4.00	3.00
a.		Inverted surcharge	50.00	
b.		Double surcharge	45.00	
C8	A8	100(h) on 200(h) vio (Bk)	5.00	4.00
a.		Inverted surcharge	50.00	
C9	A8	250(h) on 400(h) brn (V)	11.00	10.00
a.		Inverted surcharge	50.00	

Fokker Monoplane
AP3

Smolik S 19
AP4

Smolik S 19—AP5

ČESKOSLOVENSKO

Fokker over Prague—AP6

Engraved.

1930, Dec. 16 *Perf. 13½*

C10	AP3	50(h) dp grn	25	25
a.		Perf. 12	3.00	3.00
C11	AP3	1k dp red	40	30
a.		Perf. 12	30.00	30.00
b.		Perf. 12 x 13½	4.50	4.50
C12	AP4	2k dk grn	90	85
a.		Perf. 12	22.50	22.50
b.		Perf. 13½ x 12	15.00	15.00
C13	AP4	3k red vio	2.00	1.50
C14	AP5	4k indigo	1.50	1.25
a.		Perf. 12	10.00	10.00
C15	AP5	5k red brn	2.25	1.75
a.		Perf. 12	750.00	
C16	AP6	10k vio bl	5.50	5.25
a.		10k ultra	10.00	10.00
C17	AP6	20k gray vio	6.75	5.00
a.		Perf. 12	6.75	5.00
b.		Perf. 13½x12	600.00	
		Nos. C10-C17 (8)	19.55	16.15

Two types exist of the 50h, 1k and 2k, and three types of the 3k, differing chiefly in the size of the printed area. A "no hill at left" variety of the 3k exists.

Imperforate copies of Nos. C10 to C17 are proofs.

Type of 1930 with hyphen in Cesko - Slovensko.

1939, Apr. 22 *Perf. 13½*

C18	AP3	30h rose lil	10	7

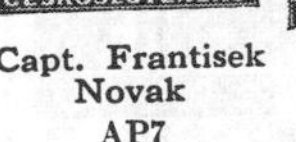

Capt. Frantisek Novak
AP7

Plane over Bratislava Castle
AP8

Plane over Charles Bridge Prague
AP9

1946–47 *Perf. 12½*

C19	AP7	1.50k rose red	25	10
C20	AP7	5.50k dk gray bl	60	20
C21	AP7	9k sep ('47)	1.50	20
C22	AP8	10k dl grn	1.25	50
C23	AP7	16k violet	1.75	60
C24	AP8	20k lt bl	2.00	80
C25	AP9	24k dk bl, *cr*	1.50	2.00
C26	AP9	24k rose lake	2.75	1.25
C27	AP9	50k dk gray bl	5.00	2.50
		Nos. C19-C27 (9)	16.60	8.15

No. C25 was issued June 12, 1946, for use on the first Prague-New York flight.

Nos. C19 to C24, C26 and C27 Surcharged with New Value and Bars in Various Colors.

1949, Sept. 1 *Perf. 12½*

C28	AP7	1k on 1.50k rose red (Bl)	12	10
C29	AP7	3k on 5.50k dk gray bl (C)	18	12
C30	AP7	6k on 9k sep (Br)	30	20
C31	AP7	7.50k on 16k vio (C)	60	20
C32	AP8	8k on 10k dl grn (G)	75	35
C33	AP8	12.50k on 20k lt bl (Bl)	1.00	35
C34	AP9	15k on 24k rose lake (Bl)	2.00	50
C35	AP9	30k on 50k dk gray bl (Bl)	2.50	75
		Nos. C28-C35 (8)	7.45	2.57

Karlovy Vary (Karlsbad)
AP10

Designs: 10k, Plestany. 15k, Marienbad. 20k, Silac.

1951, Apr. 2 **Engraved** *Perf. 13½*

C36	AP10	6k sage grn	3.00	60
C37	AP10	10k dp plum	4.00	85
C38	AP10	15k dp ultra	6.00	60
C39	AP10	20k sepia	*10.00*	*3.50*

View of Cesky Krumlov
AP11

Views: 1.55k, Olomouc. 2.35k, Banska Bystrica. 2.75k, Bratislava. 10k, Prague.

Perf. 11½

1955, Feb. 20 (10k) and Mar. 28

Cream Paper

C40	AP11	80h ol grn	1.75	8
C41	AP11	1.55k vio brn	1.75	15
C42	AP11	2.35k vio bl	2.75	25
C43	AP11	2.75k rose brn	4.00	1.00
C44	AP11	10k indigo	5.50	1.75
		Nos. C40-C44 (5)	15.75	3.23

Airline: Moscow-Prague-Paris
AP12

Design: 2.35k, Airline: Prague - Cairo - Beirut-Damascus.

Engraved and Photogravure.

1957, Oct. 15 *Perf. 11½* **Unwmkd.**

C45	AP12	75h ultra & rose	75	15
C46	AP12	2.35k ultra & org yel	1.50	30

Planes at First Czech Aviation School, Pardubice
AP13

Design: 1.80k, Jan Kasper and flight of first Czech plane, 1909.

1959, Oct. 15

C47	AP13	1k gray & yel	40	10
C48	AP13	1.80k blk & pale bl	1.20	18

Issued to commemorate the 50th anniversary of Jan Kasper's first flight Aug. 25, 1909, at Pardubice.

Mail Coach, Plane and Arms of Bratislava
AP14

Design: 2.80k, Helicopter over Bratislava.

Engraved and Photogravure

1960, Sept. 24 *Perf. 11½* **Unwmkd.**

C49	AP14	1.60k dk bl & gray	*2.75*	*1.50*
C50	AP14	2.80k grn & buff	*4.50*	*2.50*

Issued to publicize the National Stamp Exhibition, Bratislava, Sept. 24–Oct. 9.

Prague Hails Gagarin
AP15

Design: 1.80k, Gagarin, rocket and dove.

1961, June 22

C51	AP15	60h gray & car	25	5
C52	AP15	1.80k gray & bl	1.10	25

No. C51 commemorates Maj. Gagarin's visit to Prague, Apr. 28–29; No. C52 commemorates the first man in space, Yuri A. Gagarin, Apr. 12, 1961.

Dove and Nest of Eggs
AP16

Designs ("PRAGA" emblem and): 1.40k, Dove. 2.80k, Symbolic flower with five petals. 4.20k, Five leaves.

1962, May 14 **Engraved** *Perf. 14*

C53	AP16	80h multi	75	60
C54	AP16	1.40k blk, dk red & bl	2.00	1.50
C55	AP16	2.80k multi	3.25	2.75
C56	AP16	4.20k multi	4.75	3.50

Issued to publicize the "PRAGA 1962" World Exhibition of Postage Stamps, Aug. 18–Sept. 2, 1962.

Vostok 5 and Lt. Col. Valeri Bykovski—AP17

Design: 2.80k, Vostok VI and Lt. Valentina Tereshkova.

1963, June 26

C57	AP17	80h sl bl & pink	60	15
C58	AP17	2.80k dl red brn & lt bl	1.25	35

Issued to commemorate the space flights of Valeri Bykovski, June 14–19, and Valentina Tereshkova, first woman astronaut, June 16–19, 1963.

PRAGA 1962 Emblem, View of Prague and Plane
AP18

Designs: 60h, Istanbul '63 (Hagia Sophia). 1k, Philatec Paris 1964 (Ile de la Cité.) 1.40k, WIPA 1965 (Belvedere Palace, Vienna). 1.60k, SIPEX 1966 (Capitol, Washington). 2k, Amphilex '67 (harbor and old town, Amsterdam). 5k, PRAGA 1968 (View of Prague).

Engraved and Photogravure

1967, Oct. 30 *Perf. 11½*

Size: 30x50mm.

C59	AP18	30h choc, yel & rose	10	5
C60	AP18	60h dk grn, yel & lil	25	15
C61	AP18	1k blk, brick red & lt bl	40	20
C62	AP18	1.40k vio, yel & dp org	55	28
C63	AP18	1.60k ind, tan & lil	65	45
C64	AP18	2k dk grn, org & red	90	60

Size: 40x50mm.

C65	AP18	5k multi	*4.00*	*3.75*
		Nos. C59-C65 (7)	*6.85*	*5.48*

Issued to publicize the PRAGA 1968 World Stamp Exhibition, Prague, June 22–July 7, 1968. No. C59–C64 issued in sheets of 15 stamps and 15 bilingual labels. No. C65 issued in sheets of 4 stamps and one center label with commemorative inscription and airplane design.

Glider L-13
AP19

Airplanes: 60h, Sports plane L-40. 80h, Aero taxi L-200. 1k, Crop-spraying plane Z-37. 1.60k, Aerobatics trainer Z-526. 2k, Jet trainer L-29.

1967, Dec. 11 **Engr. and Photo.**

C66	AP19	30h multi	10	5
C67	AP19	60h multi	22	10
C68	AP19	80h multi	35	10
C69	AP19	1k multi	40	15
C70	AP19	1.60k multi	60	20
C71	AP19	2k multi	*2.00*	*80*
		Nos. C66-C71 (6)	*3.67*	*1.40*

Charles Bridge, Prague, and Balloon
AP20

Astronaut, Moon and Manhattan
AP21

Designs: 1k, Belvedere, fountain and early plane. 2k, Hradcany, Prague, and airship.

1968, Feb. 5 *Perf. 11½* **Unwmkd.**

C72	AP20	60h multi	30	15
C73	AP20	1k multi	45	20
C74	AP20	2k multi	75	35

Issued to publicize the PRAGA 1968 World Stamp Exhibition, Prague, June 22–July 7, 1968.

1969, July 21 **Engr. and Photo.**

Design: 3k, Lunar landing module and J. F. Kennedy Airport, New York.

C75	AP21	60h blk, vio, yel & sil	35	10
C76	AP21	3k blk, bl, ocher & sil	1.65	75

Issued to commemorate man's first landing on the moon, July 20, 1969, U. S. astronauts Neil A. Armstrong and Col. Edwin E. Aldrin, Jr., with Lieut. Col. Michael Collins piloting Apollo 11.

Nos. C75–C76 printed with label inscribed with names of astronauts and European date of moon landing.

TU-104A over Bitov Castle
AP22

Designs: 60h, IL-62 over Bezdez Castle. 1.40k, TU-134A over Orava Castle. 1.90k, IL-18 over Veveri Castle. 2.40k, IL-14 over Pernstejn Castle. 3.60k, TU-154 over Trencin Castle.

1973, Oct. 24 Engr. *Perf. 11½*

C77	AP22	30h multi	12	5
C78	AP22	60h multi	24	8
C79	AP22	1.40k multi	55	15
C80	AP22	1.90k multi	75	22
C81	AP22	2.40k multi	*5.00*	*1.00*
C82	AP22	3.60k multi	1.00	45
		Nos. C77-C82 (6)	*7.66*	*1.95*

50 years of Czechoslovakian aviation.

Old Water Tower and Manes Hall—AP23

Designs (Praga 1978 Emblem, Plane Silhouette and): 1.60k, Congress Hall. 2k, Powder Tower (vert.). 2.40k, Charles Bridge and Old Bridge Tower. 4k, Old Town Hall on Old Town Square (vert.). 6k, Prague Castle and St. Vitus Cathedral (vert.).

Engraved and Photogravure

1976, June 23 *Perf. 11½*

C83	AP23	60h ind & multi	25	8
C84	AP23	1.60k ind & multi	65	18
C85	AP23	2k ind & multi	90	20
C86	AP23	2.40k ind & multi	1.00	35
C87	AP23	4k ind & multi	1.75	45
C88	AP23	6k ind & multi	6.00	1.25
		Nos. C83-C88 (6)	10.55	2.51

PRAGA 1978 International Philatelic Exhibition, Prague, Sept. 8–17, 1978.

Zeppelin, 1909 and 1928 AP24

Designs (PRAGA '78 Emblem and): 1k, Ader, 1890, L'Eole and Dunn, 1914. 1.60k, Jeffries-Blanchard balloon, 1785. 2k, Otto Lilienthal's glider, 1896. 4.40k, Jan Kaspar's plane, Pardubice, 1911.

Photogravure and Engraved

1977, Sept. 15 *Perf. 11½*

C89	AP24	60h multi	20	8
C90	AP24	1k multi	40	10
C91	AP24	1.60k multi	65	20
C92	AP24	2k multi	90	30
C93	AP24	4.40k multi	3.50	1.00
		Nos. C89-C93 (5)	5.65	1.68

History of aviation.

SPECIAL DELIVERY STAMPS.

Doves
SD1

Typographed.

1919-20 *Imperf.* Unwmkd.

E1	SD1	2(h) red vio, *yel*	10	10
E2	SD1	5(h) yel grn, *yel*	10	10
E3	SD1	10(h) red brn, *yel* ('20)	80	65

1921 White Paper.

E1a	SD1	2(h) red vio	6.00	
E2a	SD1	5(h) yel grn	5.00	
E3a	SD1	10(h) red brn	100.00	

It is doubted that Nos. E1a-E3a were regularly issued.

PERSONAL DELIVERY STAMPS.

PD1

Design: No. EX2, "D" in each corner.

Photogravure

1937 *Perf. 13½* Unwmkd.

EX1	PD1	50h blue	30	40
EX2	PD1	50h carmine	30	40

PD3

1946 *Perf. 13½*

EX3	PD3	2k dp bl	45	30

POSTAGE DUE STAMPS.

D1

D2

Typographed.

1918-20 *Imperf.* Unwmkd.

J1	D1	5(h) dp bis	5	5
J2	D1	10(h) dp bis	8	5
J3	D1	15(h) dp bis	8	5
J4	D1	20(h) dp bis	8	5
J5	D1	25(h) dp bis	30	8
J6	D1	30(h) dp bis	8	5
J7	D1	40(h) dp bis	60	25
J8	D1	50(h) dp bis	65	25
J9	D1	100(h) blk brn	65	10
J10	D1	250(h) orange	12.50	1.50
J11	D1	400(h) scarlet	12.50	1.50
J12	D1	500(h) gray grn	3.75	30
J13	D1	1000(h) purple	5.00	10
J14	D1	2000(h) dk bl	25.00	60
		Nos. J1-J14 (14)	61.32	4.93

1922 Blue Surcharge

J15	D2	20(h) on 3(h) red vio	50	25
J16	D2	50(h) on 75(h) sl	1.75	15
J17	D2	60(h) on 80(h) ol grn	60	12
J18	D2	100(h) on 80(h) ol grn	60	10
J19	D2	200(h) on 400(h) pur	1.35	15
		Nos. J15-J19 (5)	4.80	77

1923-26 Violet Surcharge.

J20	D2	10(h) on 3(h) red vio	10	10
J21	D2	20(h) on 3(h) red vio	10	8
J22	D2	30(h) on 3(h) red vio	15	8
J23	D2	40(h) on 3(h) red vio	30	8
J24	D2	50(h) on 75(h) sl	1.50	8
J25	D2	60(h) on 50(h) dk vio ('26)	2.75	1.40
J26	D2	60(h) on 50(h) dk bl ('26)	2.75	1.25
J27	D2	60(h) on 75(h) sl	1.50	8
J28	D2	100(h) on 80(h) ol grn	50.00	75
J29	D2	100(h) on 120(h) gray blk	1.75	10
J30	D2	100(h) on 400(h) pur ('26)	1.00	15
J31	D2	100(h) on 1000(h) dp vio ('26)	2.25	15
		Nos. J20-J31 (12)	64.15	4.30

Nos. J15, J19, J20, J22, J23 and J30 were surcharged on stamps of type A1; others of the groups J15 to J31 were surcharged on stamps of type A2.

Postage Due Stamp of 1918-20 Surcharged in Violet **50**

1924

J32	D1	50(h) on 400(h) scar	1.75	15
J33	D1	60(h) on 400(h) scar	4.50	1.00
J34	D1	100(h) on 400(h) scar	3.50	25

Postage Due Stamps of 1918-20 Surcharged with New Values in Violet as in 1924.

1925

J35	D1	10(h) on 5(h) bis	8	8
J36	D1	20(h) on 5(h) bis	8	8
J37	D1	30(h) on 15(h) bis	40	40
J38	D1	40(h) on 15(h) bis	50	8
J39	D1	50(h) on 250(h) org	1.75	25
J40	D1	60(h) on 250(h) org	2.25	65
J41	D1	100(h) on 250(h) org	5.00	45
		Nos. J35-J41 (7)	10.06	1.99

Stamps of 1918-19 Surcharged with New Values in Violet as in 1922.

1926 *Perf. 14, 11½*

J42	D2	30(h) on 15(h) red	1.00	60
J43	D2	40(h) on 15(h) red	75	25

D3

D4

Violet Surcharge.

1926 *Perf. 14*

J44	D3	30(h) on 100(h) dk grn	20	15
J45	D3	40(h) on 200(h) vio	25	10
J46	D3	40(h) on 300(h) ver	95	25
a.		Perf. 14x13½		35.00
J47	D3	50(h) on 500(h) dp grn	70	8
a.		Perf. 14x13½	3.50	
J48	D3	60(h) on 400(h) brn	1.50	15
J49	D3	100(h) on 600(h) dp vio	3.50	15
a.		Perf. 14x13½	35.00	1.50
		Nos. J44-J49 (6)	7.10	88

1927 Violet Surcharge.

J50	D4	100(h) dk brn	90	10
a.		Perf. 13½	*275.00*	18.50

Surcharged with New Value in Violet.

1927

J51	D4	40(h) on 185(h) org	25	5
J52	D4	50(h) on 20(h) car	30	12
a.		50(h) on 50(h) car (error)		8,000.
J53	D4	50(h) on 150(h) rose	40	10
a.		Perf. 13½	12.00	2.50
J54	D4	60(h) on 25(h) brn	60	25
J55	D4	60(h) on 185(h) org	70	15
J56	D4	100(h) on 25(h) brn	80	25
		Nos. J50-J56 (7)	3.95	1.02

No. J52a is known only used.

No. J12 Surcharged in Violet **200**

1927 *Imperf.*

J57	D1	200(h) on 500(h) gray grn	5.50	3.75

D5

D6

1928 *Perf. 14x13½.*

J58	D5	5h dk red	5	5
J59	D5	10h dk red	5	5
J60	D5	20h dk red	8	5
J61	D5	30h dk red	8	5
J62	D5	40h dk red	8	5
J63	D5	50h dk red	8	5
J64	D5	60h dk red	8	5
J65	D5	1k ultra	25	10
J66	D5	2k ultra	75	10
J67	D5	5k ultra	1.25	10
J68	D5	10k ultra	2.50	15
J69	D5	20k ultra	5.00	15
		Nos. J58-J69 (12)	10.25	95

1946-48 Photogravure *Perf. 14*

J70	D6	10h dk bl	5	5
J71	D6	20h dk bl	6	5
J72	D6	50h dk bl	10	5
J73	D6	1k car rose	25	5
J74	D6	1.20k car rose	50	5
J75	D6	1.50k car rose ('48)	60	5
J76	D6	1.60k car rose	70	5
J77	D6	2k car rose ('48)	75	5
J78	D6	2.40k car rose	1.25	5
J79	D6	3k car rose	1.75	5
J80	D6	5k car rose	3.25	5
J81	D6	6k car rose ('48)	3.50	5
		Nos. J70-J81 (12)	12.76	60

D7

D8

1954-55 Engraved *Perf. 12½, 11½*

J82	D7	5h gray grn ('55)	5	5
J83	D7	10h gray grn ('55)	6	5
J84	D7	30h gray grn	20	5
J85	D7	50h gray grn ('55)	25	5
J86	D7	60h gray grn ('55)	28	5
J87	D7	95h gray grn	60	5
J88	D8	1k violet	60	5
J89	D8	1.20k vio ('55)	60	5
J90	D8	1.50k violet	1.25	5
J91	D8	1.60k vio ('55)	80	5
J92	D8	2k violet	1.50	5
J93	D8	3k violet	2.00	5
J94	D8	5k vio ('55)	2.50	25
		Nos. J82-J94 (13)	10.69	85

Perf. 11½ stamps are from a 1963 printing which lacks the 95h, 1.60k, and 2k.

Stylized Flower
D9

Designs: Various stylized flowers.

Engraved and Photogravure

1971-72 *Perf. 11½*

J95	D9	10h vio bl & pink ('72)	8	5
J96	D9	20h vio & lt bl ('72)	10	5
J97	D9	30h emer & lil rose ('72)	10	5
J98	D9	60h pur & emer ('72)	20	5
J99	D9	80h org & vio bl ('72)	27	5

J100	D9	1k dk red & emer ('72)	50	5
J101	D9	1.20k grn & org ('72)	40	5
J102	D9	2k bl & red ('72)	80	5
J103	D9	3k blk & yel ('72)	95	10
J104	D9	4k brn & ultra ('72)	1.60	10
J105	D9	5.40k red & lil	2.00	25
J106	D9	6k brick red & org ('72)	2.75	35
		Nos. J95-J106 (12)	9.75	1.20

OFFICIAL STAMPS.

Coat of Arms
O1

Lithographed.

1945 ***Perf. 10½x10.*** **Unwmkd.**

O1	O1	50h dp sl grn	10	5
O2	O1	1k dp bl vio	15	5
O3	O1	1.20k plum	30	20
O4	O1	1.50k crim rose	15	5
O5	O1	2.50k brt ultra	30	20
O6	O1	5k dk vio brn	40	30
O7	O1	8k rose pink	60	50
		Nos. O1-O7 (7)	2.00	1.35

Redrawn.

1947 Photogravure. ***Perf. 14.***

O8	O1	60h red	5	5
O9	O1	80h dk ol grn	5	5
O10	O1	1k dk lil gray	5	5
O11	O1	1.20k dp plum	8	5
O12	O1	2.40k dk car rose	12	6
O13	O1	4k brt ultra	25	20
O14	O1	5k dk vio brn	30	25
O15	O1	7.40k purple	50	40
		Nos. O8-O15 (8)	1.40	1.11

There are many minor changes in design, size of numerals, etc., of the redrawn stamps.

NEWSPAPER STAMPS.

Windhover
N1

Typographed.

1918-20 ***Imperf.*** **Unwmkd.**

P1	N1	2(h) gray grn	5	5
P2	N1	5(h) grn ('20)	5	5
a.		5(h) dk grn	50	15
P3	N1	6(h) red	75	40
P4	N1	10(h) dl vio	5	5
P5	N1	20(h) blue	10	5
P6	N1	30(h) gray brn	25	15
P7	N1	50(h) org ('20)	50	25
P8	N1	100(h) red brn ('20)	75	40
		Nos. P1-P8 (8)	2.50	1.40

Nos. P1 to P8 exist privately perforated.

Stamps of 1918-20 Surcharged in Violet

5
* *

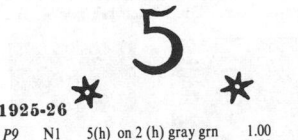

1925-26

P9	N1	5(h) on 2 (h) gray grn	1.00	50
P10	N1	5(h) on 6 (h) red ('26)	75	50

Special Delivery Stamps of 1918-20 Overprinted in Violet

NOVINY

1926

P11	SD1	5(h) ap grn, *yel*	35	30
a.		5(h) dl grn, *yel*	75	50
P12	SD1	10(h) red brn, *yel*	25	20

With Additional Surcharge of New Value.

P13	SD1	5(h) on 2(h) red vio, *yel*	25	18

Newspaper Stamps of 1918-20 Overprinted in Violet

O.T.

1934

P14	N1	10(h) dl vio	5	5
P15	N1	20(h) blue	5	5
P16	N1	30(h) gray brn	25	25

Overprinted for use by commercial firms only.

Carrier Pigeon
N2

1937 ***Imperf.***

P17	N2	2h bis brn	5	5
P18	N2	5h dl bl	5	5
P19	N2	7h red org	5	5
P20	N2	9h emerald	5	5
P21	N2	10h hn brn	5	5
P22	N2	12h ultra	5	5
P23	N2	20h dk grn	6	5
P24	N2	50h dk brn	6	5
P25	N2	1k ol gray	15	10
		Nos. P17-P25 (9)	57	50

Bratislava Philatelic Exhibition Issue.

Souvenir Sheet.

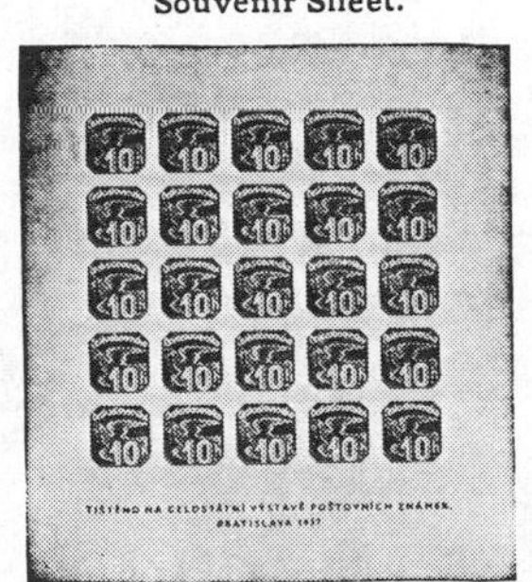

N3

1937 ***Imperf.***

P26	N3	10h hn brn, sheet of 25	3.50	3.50

Issued in sheets measuring 150x165mm.

Newspaper Delivery Boy
N4

Typographed.

1945 ***Imperf.*** **Unwmkd.**

P27	N4	5h dl bl	5	5
P28	N4	10h red	5	5
P29	N4	15h emerald	5	5
P30	N4	20h dk sl grn	5	5
P31	N4	25h brt red vio	5	5
P32	N4	30h ocher	5	5
P33	N4	40h red org	5	5
P34	N4	50h brn red	8	5
P35	N4	1k sl gray	15	8
P36	N4	5k dp vio bl	25	15
		Nos. P27-P36 (10)	83	63

Czechoslovak Legion Post

The Czechoslovak Legion in Siberia issued these stamps for use on its mail and that of local residents. Forgeries exist.

Urn and Cathedral at Irkutsk
A1

Armored Railroad Car
A2

Sentinel
A3

Lion of Bohemia
A4

1919 Lithographed. ***Perf. 11½.***

1	A1	25(k) carmine	13.50
a.		Imperf.	14.00
2	A2	50(k) yel grn	13.50
a.		Imperf.	14.00
3	A3	1 (r) red brn	30.00
a.		Imperf.	32.50

Originals of Nos. 1-3 and 1a-3a have yellowish gum. Ungummed remainders, which were given a white gum, exist imperforate and perforated 11½ and 14. Price per set, $3.

Embossed.

Perce en Arc in Blue.

4	A4	(25k) bl & rose	2.50

Two types: (I) Six points on star-like mace head at right of goblet; large saber handle; measures 19¼ x 24¾ mm. (II) Five points on mace head; small saber handle; measures 20 x 25mm.

1920 No. 4 Overprinted **1920**

5	A4	(25k) bl & rose	10.00

Both types of No. 4 received overprint.

No. 5 Surcharged with New Values in Green **2**

6	A4	2(k) bl & rose	35.00
7	A4	3(k) bl & rose	35.00
8	A4	5(k) bl & rose	35.00
9	A4	10(k) bl & rose	35.00
10	A4	15(k) bl & rose	35.00
11	A4	25(k) bl & rose	35.00
12	A4	35(k) bl & rose	35.00
13	A4	50(k) bl & rose	35.00
14	A4	1r bl & rose	35.00
		Nos. 6-14 (9)	315.00

BOHEMIA AND MORAVIA

(bō·hē'mĭ·ȧ & mō·rā'vĭ·ȧ)

German Protectorate.

Stamps of Czechoslovakia, 1928-39, Overprinted in Black

BÖHMEN u. MÄHREN

ČECHY a MORAVA

Perf. 10, 12½, 12x12½.

1939, July 15 **Unwmkd.**

No.	Type	Denom.	Color	Unused	Used
1	A29	5h	dk ultra	12	*30*
2	A29	10h	brown	10	*30*
3	A29	20h	red	10	*30*
4	A29	25h	green	12	*30*
5	A29	30h	red vio	10	*30*
6	A61a	40h	dk bl	3.75	*7.00*
7	A85	50h	dp grn	10	*30*
8	A63	60h	dl vio	3.75	*7.00*
9	A60	1k	rose lake (212)	1.10	*2.50*
10	A60	1k	rose lake (256)	42	*1.25*
11	A64	1.20k	rose lil	4.50	*9.00*
12	A65	1.50k	carmine	3.75	*7.00*
13	A79	1.60k	ol grn	3.75	*7.00*
a.			"Mähnen"	27.50	*40.00*
14	A66	2k	dk bl grn	1.75	*2.50*
15	A67	2.50k	dk bl	4.50	*6.50*
16	A68	3k	brown	4.50	*7.00*
17	A70	4k	dk vio	5.00	*7.50*
18	A71	5k	green	5.00	*8.50*
19	A72	10k	blue	6.75	*14.00*
			Nos. 1-19 (19)	49.16	*88.55*

The size of the overprint varies with the size of the stamps, Nos. 1 to 10 measure 17½x15½mm., Nos. 11 to 16 measure 19x18mm., Nos. 17 and 19 measure 28x17½ and No. 18 measures 23½x23mm.

Linden Leaves and Closed Buds

A1

1939-41 **Photogravure** ***Perf. 14***

No.	Type	Denom.	Color	Unused	Used
20	A1	5h	dk bl	5	5
21	A1	10h	blk brn	5	5
22	A1	20h	crimson	5	5
23	A1	25h	dk bl grn	6	12
24	A1	30h	dp plum	5	8
24A	A1	30h	gldn brn ('41)	5	5
25	A1	40h	org ('40)	5	8
26	A1	50h	sl grn ('40)	8	12
			Nos. 20-26 (8)	44	60

See also Nos. 49–51.

Castle at Zvikov

A2

Karlstein Castle

A3

St. Barbara's Church, Kutna Hora

A4

Cathedral at Prague

A5

Brno Cathedral

A6

Town Square, Olomouc

A7

1939 **Engraved.** ***Perf. 12½.***

No.	Type	Denom.	Color	Unused	Used
27	A2	40h	dk bl	5	8
28	A3	50h	dk bl grn	5	5
29	A4	60h	dl vio	5	5
30	A5	1k	dp rose	5	5
31	A6	1.20k	rose lil	25	*50*
32	A6	1.50k	rose car	5	5
33	A7	2k	dk bl grn	6	6
34	A7	2.50k	dk bl	5	8
			Nos. 27-34 (8)	61	*92*

No. 31 measures 23½x29½mm., while No. 42 measures 18½x23mm.

Zlin—A8

Iron Works at Moravská Ostrava

A9

Prague

A10

1939–40

No.	Type	Denom.	Color	Unused	Used
35	A8	3k	dl rose vio	15	15
36	A9	4k	sl ('40)	6	8
37	A10	5k	green	35	*40*
38	A10	10k	lt ultra	25	*75*
39	A10	20k	yel brn	75	*1.65*
			Nos. 35-39 (5)	1.56	*3.03*

Types of 1939 and

Neuhaus

A11

Lainsitz Bridge near Bechyne

A14

Pernstein Castle

A12

Samson Fountain Budweis

A15

Pardubice Castle

A13

Kromeriz

A16

Wallenstein Palace, Prague

A17

1940 **Engraved.** ***Perf. 12½***

No.	Type	Denom.	Color	Unused	Used
40	A11	50h	dk bl grn	5	8
41	A12	80h	dp bl	12	*40*
42	A6	1.20k	vio brn	25	25
43	A13	2k	gray grn	10	8
44	A14	5k	dk bl grn	10	10
45	A15	6k	brn vio	10	*25*
46	A16	8k	sl grn	10	*30*
47	A17	10k	blue	28	30
48	A10	20k	sepia	65	*1.50*
			Nos. 40-48 (9)	1.75	*3.26*

No. 42 measures 18½x23mm.; No. 31, 23½x29½mm.

Types of 1939–40.

1941

No.	Type	Denom.	Color	Unused	Used
49	A1	60h	violet	5	8
50	A1	80h	red org	6	8
51	A1	1k	brown	6	8
52	A5	1.20k	rose red	5	12
53	A4	1.50k	lil rose	8	12
53A	A13	2k	lt bl	5	12
53B	A6	2.50k	ultra	5	8
53C	A12	3k	olive	10	12
			Nos. 49-53C (8)	50	80

Nos. 49–51 show buds open. Nos. 52 and 53B measure 18¾x23½mm. and have no inscriptions below design.

Antonin Dvorák

A18

1941, Aug. 25 **Engr.** ***Perf. 12½***

No.	Type	Denom.	Color	Unused	Used
54	A18	60h	dl lil	12	*28*
55	A18	1.20k	sepia	25	40

Birth centenary of Antonin Dvorák (1841–1904), composer.

Labels alternate with stamps in sheets of Nos. 54–55.

Farming Scene

A19

Factories

A20

1941, Sept. 7 **Photo.** ***Perf. 13½***

No.	Type	Denom.	Color	Unused	Used
56	A19	30h	dk red brn	5	12
57	A19	60h	dk grn	5	12
58	A20	1.20k	dk plum	10	*30*
59	A20	2.50k	sapphire	12	*40*

Issued to publicize the Prague Fair.

Nos. 52 and 53B Overprinted in Blue or Red

1942, Mar. 15 ***Perf. 12½***

No.	Type	Denom.	Color	Unused	Used
60	A5	1.20k	rose red (Bl)	25	*60*
61	A6	2.50k	ultra (R)	42	*60*

Issued to commemorate the third anniversary of the Protectorate of Bohemia and Moravia.

Adolf Hitler

A21

17th Century Messenger

A22

1942 **Photogravure.** ***Perf. 14.***

Size: 17½x21½mm.

No.	Type	Denom.	Color	Unused	Used
62	A21	10(h)	gray blk	5	5
63	A21	30(h)	bis brn	5	5
64	A21	40(h)	sl bl	5	5
65	A21	50(h)	sl grn	5	5
66	A21	60(h)	purple	5	5
67	A21	80(h)	org ver	5	5

Engraved.

Perf. 12½

Size: 18x21mm.

No.	Type	Denom.	Color	Unused	Used
68	A21	1k	dl brn	5	5
69	A21	1.20(k)	carmine	5	5
70	A21	1.50(k)	claret	5	5
71	A21	1.60(k)	Prus grn	8	*20*
72	A21	2k	lt bl	5	5
73	A21	2.40(k)	fawn	8	*25*

Size: 18½x24mm.

No.	Type	Denom.	Color	Unused	Used
74	A21	2.50(k)	ultra	5	5
75	A21	3k	ol grn	6	5
76	A21	4k	brt red vio	6	5
77	A21	5k	myr grn	5	5
78	A21	6k	cl brn	5	10
79	A21	8k	indigo	5	10

Size: 23½x29¾mm.

No.	Type	Denom.	Color	Unused	Used
80	A21	10k	dk gray grn	8	10
81	A21	20k	gray vio	18	*30*
82	A21	30k	red	42	*1.00*
83	A21	50k	dp bl	90	*2.00*
			Nos. 62-83 (22)	2.56	*4.75*

1943, Jan. 10 **Photo.** ***Perf. 13½***

No.	Type	Denom.	Color	Unused	Used
84	A22	60(h)	dk rose vio	5	8

Stamp Day.

Scene from "Die Meistersinger"—A23

Richard Wagner

A24

Scene from "Siegfried"

A25

1943, May 22

No.	Type	Denom.	Color	Unused	Used
85	A23	60(h)	violet	5	8
86	A24	1.20(k)	car rose	6	8
87	A25	2.50(k)	dp ultra	6	*20*

130th anniversary of the birth of Richard Wagner (1813–1883).

St. Vitus' Cathedral, Prague
A26

Adolf Hitler
A27

1944, Nov. 21 Engr. Perf. 12½

88	A26	1.50(k) dl rose brn	5	12
89	A26	2.50(k) dl lil bl	8	*25*

1944

90	A27	4.20(k) green	12	*35*

SEMI-POSTAL STAMPS.

Nurse and Wounded Soldier
SP1

Red Cross Nurse and Patient
SP2

Perf. 13½

1940, June 29 Photo. Unwmkd.

B1	SP1	60h +40h ind	50	*80*
B2	SP1	1.20k +80h dp plum	60	*1.00*

Surtax for German Red Cross.
Labels alternate with stamps in sheets of Nos. B1–B2.

1941, Apr. 20

B3	SP2	60h +40h ind	25	*50*
B4	SP2	1.20k +80h dp plum	25	*60*

Surtax for German Red Cross.
Labels alternate with stamps in sheets of Nos. B3–B4.

Old Theater, Prague
SP3

Wolfgang Amadeus Mozart
SP4

1941, Oct. 26

B5	SP3	30h +30h brn	5	10
B6	SP3	60h +60h Prus grn	5	10
B7	SP4	1.20k +1.20k scar	12	*40*
B8	SP4	2.50k +2.50k dk bl	25	*55*

150th anniversary of Mozart's death.
Labels alternate with stamps in sheets of Nos. B5–B8. The labels with Nos. B5–B6 show two bars of Mozart's opera "Don Giovanni." Those with Nos. B7–B8 show Mozart's piano.

Adolf Hitler
SP5

Nurse and Soldier
SP6

1942, Apr. 20 Engr. Perf. 12½

B9	SP5	30(h) +20(h) dl brn vio	8	12
B10	SP5	60(h) +40(h) dl grn	8	12
B11	SP5	1.20(k) +80(h) dp cl	8	12
B12	SP5	2.50(k) +1.50(k) dl bl	12	*22*

Issued to commemorate Hitler's 53rd birthday.

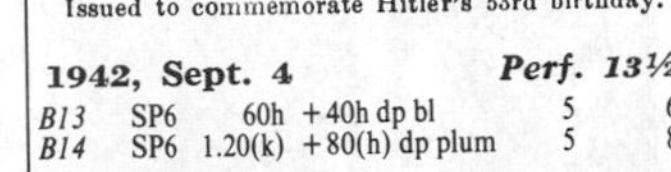

1942, Sept. 4 Perf. 13½

B13	SP6	60h +40h dp bl	5	6
B14	SP6	1.20(k) +80(h) dp plum	5	8

The surtax aided the German Red Cross.

Emperor Charles IV
SP7

Peter Parler
SP8

John the Blind, King of Bohemia
SP9

Adolf Hitler
SP10

1943, Jan. 29

B15	SP7	60(h) +40(h) vio	6	8
B16	SP8	1.20(k) +80(h) car	5	10
B17	SP9	2.50(k) +1.50(k) vio bl	8	14

The surtax was for the benefit of the German wartime winter relief.

1943, Apr. 20 Engr. Perf. 12½

B18	SP10	60(h) +1.40(k) dl vio	5	*12*
B19	SP10	1.20(k) +3.80(k) car	8	*25*

Issued to commemorate Hitler's 54th birthday.

Deathmask of Reinhard Heydrich
SP11

Eagle and Red Cross
SP12

1943, May 28 Photo. Perf. 13½

B20	SP11	60(h) +4.40(h) blk	22	*45*

No. B20 exists in a miniature sheet containing a single copy. It was given to officials attending Heydrich's funeral.

1943, Sept. 16 Perf. 13

B21	SP12	1.20(k) +8.80(k) blk & car	7	12

The surtax aided the German Red Cross.

Native Costumes
SP13

Nazi Emblem and Arms of Bohemia, Moravia
SP14

1944, Mar. 15 Perf. 13½

B22	SP13	1.20(k) +3.80(k) rose lake	5	10
B23	SP14	4.20(k) +10.80(k) gldn brn	5	10
B24	SP13	10k +20k saph	10	*30*

Fifth anniversary of protectorate.

Adolf Hitler
SP15

Friedrich Smetana
SP16

1944, Apr. 20

B25	SP15	60(h) +1.40(k) ol blk	5	8
B26	SP15	1.20(k) +3.80(k) sl grn	8	12

1944, May 12 Engr. Perf. 12½

B27	SP16	60(h) +1.40(k) dk gray grn	5	6
B28	SP16	1.20(k) +3.80(k) brn car	8	12

Issued to commemorate the 60th anniversary of the death of Friedrich Smetana (1824-84), Czech composer and pianist.

PERSONAL DELIVERY STAMPS.

PD1

Photogravure.

1939–40 Perf. 13½ Unwmkd.

EX1	PD1	50h ind & bl ('40)	60	*1.25*
EX2	PD1	50h car & rose	75	*1.50*

POSTAGE DUE STAMPS.

D1

Typographed.

1939–40 Perf. 14 Unwmkd.

J1	D1	5h dk car	6	8
J2	D1	10h dk car	6	8
J3	D1	20h dk car	6	8
J4	D1	30h dk car	6	8
J5	D1	40h dk car	8	10
J6	D1	50h dk car	8	10
J7	D1	60h dk car	8	10
J8	D1	80h dk car	8	10
J9	D1	1k brt ultra	12	*30*
J10	D1	1.20k brt ultra ('40)	18	*35*
J11	D1	2k brt ultra	55	*1.00*
J12	D1	5k brt ultra	60	*1.10*
J13	D1	10k brt ultra	90	*1.75*
J14	D1	20k brt ultra	2.50	*4.50*
		Nos. J1-J14 (14)	5.41	*9.72*

OFFICIAL STAMPS.

Numeral
O1

Eagle
O2

Typographed.

1941, Jan. 1 Perf. 14 Unwmkd.

O1	O1	30h ocher	12	5
O2	O1	40h indigo	12	5
O3	O1	50h emerald	12	5
O4	O1	60h sl grn	12	5
O5	O1	80h org red	55	20
O6	O1	1k red brn	20	5
O7	O1	1.20k carmine	20	5
O8	O1	1.50k dp plum	38	12
O9	O1	2k brt bl	38	8
O10	O1	3k olive	38	8
O11	O1	4k red vio	60	50
O12	O1	5k org yel	1.50	1.00
		Nos. O1-O12 (12)	4.67	2.28

1943, Feb. 15

O13	O2	30(h) bister	5	5
O14	O2	40(h) indigo	5	5
O15	O2	50(h) yel grn	5	5
O16	O2	60(h) dp vio	5	5
O17	O2	80(h) org red	5	5
O18	O2	1k chocolate	5	5
O19	O2	1.20(k) carmine	5	5
O20	O2	1.50(k) brn red	5	12
O21	O2	2k lt bl	6	12
O22	O2	3k olive	6	12
O23	O2	4k red vio	8	12
O24	O2	5k dk grn	12	*30*
		Nos. O13-O24 (12)	72	*1.13*

NEWSPAPER STAMPS.

Carrier Pigeon
N1 N2

Typographed.

1939 Imperf. Unwmkd.

P1	N1	2h ocher	5	8
P2	N1	5h ultra	5	8
P3	N1	7h red org	5	8
P4	N1	9h emerald	5	8
P5	N1	10h hn brn	5	12
P6	N1	12h dk ultra	5	8
P7	N1	20h dk grn	6	*25*
P8	N1	50h red brn	8	*35*
P9	N1	1k grnsh gray	12	*35*
		Nos. P1-P9 (9)	56	*1.47*

1940

No. P5 Overprinted in Black **GD-OT**

P10	N1	10h hn brn	12	*30*

Overprinted for use by commercial firms.

1943, Feb. 15

P11	N2	2(h) ocher	5	5
P12	N2	5(h) lt bl	5	5
P13	N2	7(h) red org	5	5
P14	N2	9(h) emerald	5	5
P15	N2	10(h) hn brn	5	5
P16	N2	12(h) dk ultra	5	5
P17	N2	20(h) dk grn	5	8
P18	N2	50(h) red brn	5	8
P19	N2	1k sl grn	5	*25*
		Nos. P11-P19 (9)	45	*71*

Helpful notes abound in the "Information for Collectors" section at the front of this volume.

CARPATHO-UKRAINE

(kär·pä'thô-ū'krān)

A former province of Czechoslovakia known as Ruthenia, which in 1938 became an autonomous Czechoslovak state as a result of the Munich Agreement. On Mar. 16, 1939, it was incorporated in the Kingdom of Hungary.

100 Haleru = 1 Koruna

View of Jasina
A1

Perf. 12½

1939, Mar. 15 Engr. Unwmkd.

1	A1	3k ultra	12.00	*35.00*

Issued in commemoration of the inauguration of the Carpatho-Ukraine Diet, March 2, 1939.

SLOVAKIA

(slô·vä'kĭ·ȧ)

LOCATION—Central Europe.
GOVT.—Nominally independent republic.
AREA—14,848 sq. mi.
POP.—2,450,000.
CAPITAL—Bratislava.

Formerly a province of Czechoslovakia, Slovakia declared its independence in March, 1939. A treaty was immediately concluded with Germany guaranteeing Slovakian independence but providing for German "protection" for 25 years.

In 1945 the republic ended and Slovakia again became a part of Czechoslovakia.

100 Halierov = 1 Koruna

Czechoslovakia No. 226 Surcharged in Orange Red

Otvorenie slovenského snemu 18. I. 1939

300 h

1939, Jan. 18 *Perf. 12½* Unwmkd.

1	A72	300h on 10k bl	90	*5.00*

Issued to commemorate the opening of the Slovakian Parliament.

Stamps of Czechoslovakia, 1928-39, Overprinted in Red or Blue

Slovenský štát 1939

1939 *Perf. 10, 12½, 12x12½*

2	A29	5h dk ultra (R)	75	1.25
3	A29	10h brn (R)	12	18
4	A29	20h red (Bl)	8	10
5	A29	25h grn (R)	1.50	2.50
6	A29	30h red vio (Bl)	10	18
7	A61a	40h dk bl (R)	12	25
8	A73	50h dp grn (R)	8	8
9	A63	50h dp grn (R)	8	8
10	A63	60h dl vio (R)	10	18
11	A63	60h dk bl (R)	8.50	12.50
12	A60	1k rose lake (Bl) (On No. 212)	8	8

Overprinted Diagonally.

13	A64	1.20k rose lil (Bl)	30	45
14	A65	1.50k car (Bl)	30	45
15	A79	1.60k ol grn (Bl)	2.25	3.75
16	A66	2k dk bl grn (R)	2.25	3.75
17	A67	2.50k dk bl (R)	45	75
18	A68	3k brn (R)	60	90
19	A69	3.50k dk vio (R)	24.00	37.50

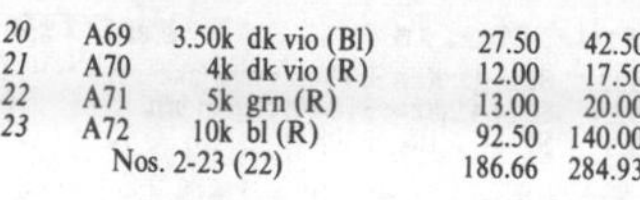

20	A69	3.50k dk vio (Bl)	27.50	42.50
21	A70	4k dk vio (R)	12.00	17.50
22	A71	5k grn (R)	13.00	20.00
23	A72	10k bl (R)	92.50	140.00
		Nos. 2-23 (22)	186.66	284.93

Excellent counterfeit overprints exist.

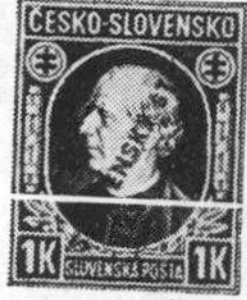

Andrej Hlinka
A1 A2

Overprinted in Red or Blue.
Photogravure.

1939, Apr. *Perf. 12½* Unwmkd.

24	A1	50h dk grn (R)	1.75	1.00
a.		Perf. 10½	1.75	1.50
b.		Perf. 10½x12½	4.00	4.50
25	A1	1k dk car rose (Bl)	1.50	1.00
a.		Perf. 10½	70.00	110.00
b.		Perf. 10½x12½	7.50	10.00

1939 *Perf. 12½* Unwmkd.

26	A2	5h brt ultra	45	75
27	A2	10h ol grn	75	1.10
a.		Perf. 10½x12½	24.00	8.00
b.		Perf. 10½	24.00	20.00
28	A2	20h org red	75	1.10
a.		Imperf.	60	1.00
29	A2	30h dp vio	75	1.10
a.		Imperf.	90	1.50
b.		Perf. 10½x12½	6.00	9.00
c.		Perf. 10½	9.00	10.00
30	A2	50h dk grn	75	1.10
31	A2	1k dk car rose	90	1.10
32	A2	2.50k brt bl	90	50
33	A2	3k blk brn	2.50	50
		Nos. 26-33 (8)	7.75	7.25

On Nos. 32 and 33 a pearl frame surrounds the medallion. See Nos. 55–57, 69.

General Stefánik and Memorial Tomb
A3

Rev. Josef Murgas and Radio Towers
A4

1939, May *Perf. 12½*

Size: 25x20mm.

34	A3	40h dk bl	90
35	A3	60h sl grn	90
36	A3	1k gray vio	90

Size: 30x23¾ mm.

37	A3	2k bl vio & sep	90

Prepared to commemorate the 20th anniversary of the death of Gen. Milan Stefánik, but not issued.

1939 Unwmkd.

38	A4	60h purple	30	45
39	A4	1.20k sl blk	60	30

Issued in commemoration of the 10th anniversary of the death of Rev. Josef Murgas. See No. 65.

Girl Weaving
A5

Woodcutter
A6

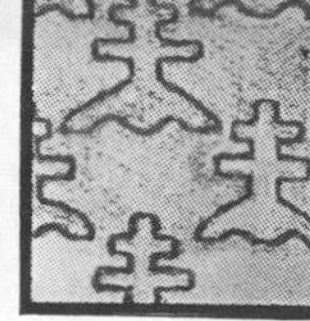

Girl at Spring
A7

Wmk. 263

Wmkd.
Double-Barred Cross Multiple.
(263)

1939–44 *Perf. 12½*

40	A5	2k dk bl grn	5.50	50
41	A6	4k cop brn	1.25	1.00
42	A7	5k org red	1.00	50
a.		Perf. 10 ('44)	75	50

Dr. Josef Tiso
A8

Presidential Residence
A9

1939–44 *Perf. 12½* Wmk. 263

43	A8	50h sl grn	45	50
43A	A8	70h dk red brn ('42)	30	25
b.		Perf. 10½ ('44)	60	25

See also No. 88.

1940, Mar. 14

44	A9	10k dp bl	90	1.00

Tatra Mountains
A10

Krivan Peak
A11

Edelweiss in the Tatra Mountains
A12

Chamois
A13

Church at Javorina
A14

1940–43 *Perf. 12½* Wmk. 263

Size: 17x21mm.

45	A10	5h dk ol grn	12	8
46	A11	10h dp brn	10	8
47	A12	20h bl blk	8	8
48	A13	25h ol brn	45	25
49	A14	30h chnt brn	20	20
a.		Perf. 10½ ('43)	35	25
		Nos. 45-49 (5)	95	69

See Nos. 84–87, 103–107.

Hlinka Type of 1939

1940–42 *Perf. 12½* Wmk. 263

55	A2	1k dk car rose	75	90
56	A2	2.50k brt bl ('42)	90	1.00
a.		Perf. 10½	60	1.00
57	A2	3k blk brn ('41)	1.25	1.00
a.		Perf. 10½	90	1.00

On Nos. 56 and 57 a pearl frame surrounds the medallion.

Stiavnica
A15

Lietava
A16

Spissky Hrad
A17

Bojnice
A18

1941 *Perf. 12½*

58	A15	1.20(k) rose lake	20	30
59	A16	1.50(k) rose pink	20	30
60	A17	1.60(k) ryl bl	30	12
61	A18	2k dk gray grn	20	8

Slovakian Castles.

S. M. Daxner and Stefan Moyses
A19

Andrej Hlinka
A20

1941, May 26 Photo. Wmk. 263

62	A19	50h ol grn	1.75	2.50
63	A19	1k sl bl	7.50	10.00
64	A19	2k black	7.50	10.00

Issued in commemoration of the 80th anniversary of the Memorandum of the Slovak Nation.

Murgas Type of 1939

1941 Wmk. 263

65	A4	60h purple	20	30

1942

69	A20	1.30k dk pur	45	12

Post Horn and Miniature Stamp
A21

Philatelist
A22

Philatelist—A23

1942, May 23

70	A21	30h dk grn	1.00	1.50
71	A22	70h dk car rose	1.00	1.50
72	A23	80h purple	1.00	1.50
73	A21	1.30k dk brn	1.00	1.50

Issued to commemorate the National Philatelic Exhibition at Bratislava.

On No. 70 the miniature stamp bears the coat-of-arms of Bratislava; on No. 73 it shows the National arms of Slovakia.

St. Stephen's Cathedral, Vienna
A24

1942, Oct. 12 *Perf. 14*

74	A24	70h bl grn	90	1.50
75	A24	1.30k ol grn	90	1.50
76	A24	2k sapphire	1.75	4.00

Issued to commemorate the European Postal Congress held in Vienna.

Slovakian Educational Society
A25

1942, Dec. 14

77	A25	70h black	12	20
78	A25	1k rose red	30	38
79	A25	1.30k sapphire	12	30
80	A25	2k chnt brn	30	38
81	A25	3k dk grn	45	50
82	A25	4k dl pur	45	60
		Nos. 77-82 (6)	1.74	2.36

Slovakian Educational Society, 150th anniversary.

Andrej Hlinka
A26

1943 **Wmk. 263**

83	A26	1.30k brt ultra	12	12

See also Nos. 93-94A.

Types of 1939–40

1943 *Perf. 12½.* **Unwmkd.**

84	A11	10h dp brn	18	12
85	A12	20h bl blk	45	25
86	A13	25h ol brn	45	25
87	A14	30h chnt brn	30	20
88	A8	70h dk red brn	55	50
		Nos. 84-88 (5)	1.93	1.32

Presov Church A27 — Locomotive A28

Railway Tunnel A29 — Viaduct A30

1943, Sept. 5 *Perf. 14*

89	A27	70h dk rose vio	45	50
90	A28	80h sapphire	45	50
91	A29	1.30k black	45	50
92	A30	2k dk vio brn	60	80

Issued to commemorate the inauguration of the new railroad line between Presov and Strazske.

Hlinka Type of 1943 and

Ludwig Stur A31 — Martin Razus A32

1944 **Unwmkd.**

93	A31	80h sl grn	18	12
94	A32	1k brn red	24	12
94A	A26	1.30k brt ultra	60	50

Prince Pribina
A33

Designs: 70h, Prince Mojmir. 80h, Prince Ratislav. 1.30k, King Svatopluk. 2k, Prince Kocel. 3k, Prince Mojmir II. 5k, Prince Svatopluk II. 10k, Prince Braslav.

1944, Mar. 14

95	A33	50h dk grn	8	10
96	A33	70h lil rose	8	10
97	A33	80h red brn	8	10
98	A33	1.30k brt ultra	12	12
99	A33	2k Prus bl	12	30
100	A33	3k dk brn	30	45
101	A33	5k violet	60	1.00
102	A33	10k black	1.65	3.00
		Nos. 95-102 (8)	3.03	5.17

Scenic Types of 1940
Size: 18x23mm.

1944, Apr. 1 *Perf. 14*

103	A11	10h brt car	18	35
104	A12	20h brt bl	18	35
105	A13	25h brn red	18	35
106	A14	30h red vio	18	35
107	A10	50h dp grn	18	35
		Nos. 103-107 (5)	90	1.75

Issued to honor the 5th anniversary of Slovakia's independence.

Symbolic of National Protection A41 — President Josef Tiso A42

1944, Oct. 6 **Wmk. 263**

108	A41	2k green	45	50
109	A41	3.80k red vio	45	75

1945 **Unwmkd.**

110	A42	1k orange	90	1.00
111	A42	1.50k brown	24	25
112	A42	2k green	30	25
113	A42	4k rose red	90	1.00
114	A42	5k sapphire	90	1.00

Wmk. 263

115	A42	10k red vio	60	50
		Nos. 110-115 (6)	3.84	4.00

To commemorate the sixth anniversary of the Republic of Slovakia's declaration of independence, March 14, 1939.

SEMI-POSTAL STAMPS.

Josef Tiso
SP1

Perf. 12½

1939, Nov. 6 **Photo.** **Wmk. 263**

B1	SP1	2.50k +2.50k ryl bl	3.00	4.50

The surtax was used for Child Welfare.

Medical Corpsman and Wounded Soldier
SP2

1941, Nov. 10

B2	SP2	50h +50h dl grn	45	75
B3	SP2	1k +1k rose lake	60	1.00
B4	SP2	2k +1k brt bl	2.00	2.50

Mother and Child SP3 — Soldier and Hlinka Youth SP4

1941, Dec. 10

B5	SP3	50h +50h dl grn	90	1.25
B6	SP3	1k +1k brn	90	1.25
B7	SP3	2k +1k vio	90	1.25

The surtax was for the benefit of child welfare.

1942, Mar. 14

B8	SP4	70h +1k brn org	45	60
B9	SP4	1.30k +1k brt bl	60	75
B10	SP4	2k +1k rose red	1.50	1.75

The surtax aided the Hlinka Youth Society "Hlinkova Mladez."

National Costumes
SP5 SP6 SP7

1943 *Perf. 14.*

B11	SP5	50h +50h dk sl grn	30	35
B12	SP6	70h +1k dp car	30	35
B13	SP7	80h +2k dk bl	30	35

The surtax was for the benefit of children, the Red Cross and winter relief of the Slovakian popular party.

Infantrymen
SP8

Aviator—SP9

Tank and Gun Crew
SP10

1943, July 28

B14	SP8	70h +2k rose brn	60	1.00
B15	SP9	1.30k +2k saph	60	1.00
B16	SP10	2k +2k ol grn	75	1.25

The surtax was for soldiers' welfare.

"The Slovak Language Is Our Life"— L. Stur SP11 — Slovakian National Museum SP12

Slovakian Foundation SP13 — Slovakian Peasant SP14

1943, Oct. 16

B17	SP11	30h +1k brn red	45	50
B18	SP12	70h +1k sl grn	60	50
B19	SP13	80h +2k sl bl	45	50
B20	SP14	1.30k +2k dl brn	45	50

The surtax was for the benefit of Slovakian cultural institutions.

Soccer Player SP15 — Skier SP16

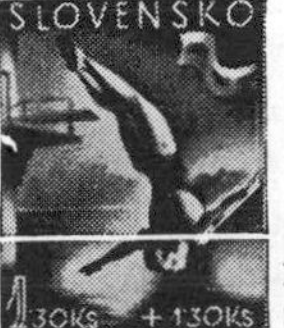

Diver
SP17

Relay Race
SP18

1944, Apr. 30 **Unwmkd.**

B21	SP15	70h +70h sl grn	60	1.25
B22	SP16	1k +1k vio	75	1.50
B23	SP17	1.30k +1.30k Prus bl	75	1.50
B24	SP18	2k +2k chnt brn	90	2.00

Symbolic of National Protection
SP19

Children
SP20

1944, Oct. 6 **Wmk. 263**

B25	SP19	70h +4h saph	1.00	2.25
B26	SP19	1.30k +4k red brn	1.00	2.25

The surtax was for the benefit of social institutions.

1944, Dec. 18

B27	SP20	2k +4k lt bl	3.50	6.00
a.		Sheet of 8 + Label	45.00	75.00

The surtax was to aid social work for Slovak youth.

AIR POST STAMPS.

Planes over Tatra Mountains
AP1 AP2

Perf. 12½

1939, Nov. 20 **Photo.** **Unwmkd.**

C1	AP1	30h violet	30	50
C2	AP1	50h dk grn	30	50
C3	AP1	1k vermilion	35	50
C4	AP2	2k grnsh blk	55	60
C5	AP2	3k dk brn	1.00	1.25
C6	AP2	4k sl bl	1.75	2.75
		Nos. C1-C6 (6)	4.25	6.10

See also No. C10.

Plane in Flight
AP3

Perf. 12½

1940, Nov. 30 **Wmk. 263**

C7	AP3	5k dk vio brn	1.25	2.00
C8	AP3	10k gray blk	1.50	2.50
C9	AP3	20k myr grn	1.75	3.00

Type of 1939.

1944, Sept. 15 **Wmk. 263**

C10	AP1	1k vermilion	35	50

PERSONAL DELIVERY STAMPS

PD1
Photogravure.

1940 *Imperf.* **Wmk. 263**

EX1	PD1	50h ind & bl	90	2.50
EX2	PD1	50h car & rose	90	2.50

POSTAGE DUE STAMPS.

D1

Letter, Post Horn
D2

Photogravure.

1939 *Perf. 12½* **Unwmkd.**

J1	D1	5h brt bl	30	75
J2	D1	10h brt bl	30	75
J3	D1	20h brt bl	30	75
J4	D1	30h brt bl	1.25	1.25
J5	D1	40h brt bl	60	1.00
J6	D1	50h brt bl	1.50	1.10
J7	D1	60h brt bl	1.25	1.10
J8	D1	1k dk car	13.00	11.00
J9	D1	2k dk car	13.00	3.50
J10	D1	5k dk car	4.50	3.50
J11	D1	10k dk car	35.00	10.00
J12	D1	20k dk car	15.00	12.50
		Nos. J1-J12 (12)	86.00	47.20

1940-41 **Wmk. 263**

J13	D1	5h brt bl ('41)	60	75
J14	D1	10h brt bl ('41)	30	38
J15	D1	20h brt bl ('41)	45	38
J16	D1	30h brt bl ('41)	6.00	6.00
J17	D1	40h brt bl ('41)	60	75
J18	D1	50h brt bl ('41)	75	1.25
J19	D1	60h brt bl	90	1.25
J20	D1	1k dk car ('41)	90	1.50
J21	D1	2k dk car ('41)	9.00	10.00
J22	D1	5k dk car ('41)	2.50	3.50
J23	D1	10k dk car ('41)	3.00	4.25
		Nos. J13-J23 (11)	25.00	30.01

1942 *Perf. 14.* **Unwmkd.**

J24	D2	10h dp brn	5	12
J25	D2	20h dp brn	5	30
J26	D2	40h dp brn	12	30
J27	D2	50h dp brn	90	30
J28	D2	60h dp brn	18	30
J29	D2	80h dp brn	24	30
J30	D2	1k rose red	30	30
J31	D2	1.10k rose red	60	80
J32	D2	1.30k rose red	35	30
J33	D2	1.60k rose red	45	30
J34	D2	2k rose red	60	30
J35	D2	2.60k rose red	1.25	1.50
J36	D2	3.50k rose red	7.50	10.00
J37	D2	5k rose red	2.75	3.50
J38	D2	10k rose red	3.00	4.25
		Nos. J24-J38 (15)	18.34	22.87

NEWSPAPER STAMPS.

Newspaper Stamps of Czechoslovakia, 1937, Overprinted in Red or Blue

1939
SLOVENSKÝ ŠTÁT

1939, Apr. *Imperf.* **Unwmkd.**

P1	N2	2h bis brn (Bl)	35	50
P2	N2	5h dl bl (R)	35	50
P3	N2	7h red org (Bl)	35	50
P4	N2	9h emer (R)	35	50
P5	N2	10h hn brn (Bl)	35	50
P6	N2	12h ultra (R)	35	50
P7	N2	20h dk grn (R)	75	1.10
P8	N2	50h dk brn (Bl)	2.50	3.50
P9	N2	1k grnsh gray (R)	8.50	12.50
		Nos. P1-P9 (9)	13.85	20.10

Excellent counterfeits exist of Nos. P1 to P9.

Arms of Slovakia
N1

10h
SLOVENSKO

Type Block "N" (for "Noviny"—Newspaper)
N2

1939 **Typographed.**

P10	N1	2h ocher	12	20
P11	N1	5h ultra	30	45
P12	N1	7h red org	24	30
P13	N1	9h emerald	24	30
P14	N1	10h hn brn	1.40	1.25
P15	N1	12h dk ultra	24	35
P16	N1	20h dk grn	1.25	1.25
P17	N1	50h red brn	1.50	1.50
P18	N1	1k grnsh gray	1.25	1.25
		Nos. P10-P18 (9)	6.54	6.85

1940-41 **Wmk. 263**

P20	N1	5h ultra	10	12
P23	N1	10h hn brn	10	20
P24	N1	15h brt pur ('41)	20	20
P25	N1	20h dk grn	45	50
P26	N1	25h lt bl ('41)	35	50
P27	N1	40h red org ('41)	45	50
P28	N1	50h chocolate	75	75
P29	N1	1k grnsh gray ('41)	75	75
P30	N1	2k emer ('41)	1.50	1.75
		Nos. P20-P30 (9)	4.65	5.27

1943 **Photogravure.** **Unwmkd.**

P31	N2	10h green	12	25
P32	N2	15h dk brn	12	25
P33	N2	20h ultra	18	25
P34	N2	50h rose red	22	38
P35	N2	1k sl grn	45	60
P36	N2	2k int bl	75	1.25
		Nos. P31-P36 (6)	1.84	2.98

DAHOMEY

(dä·hō′mā)

LOCATION—West coast of Africa.
GOVT.—Republic.
AREA—43,483 sq. mi.
POP.—3,030,000 (est. 1974).
CAPITAL—Porto-Novo.

Formerly a native kingdom including Benin, Dahomey was annexed by France in 1894. It became part of the colonial administrative unit of French West Africa in 1895. Stamps of French West Africa superseded those of Dahomey in 1945. The Republic of Dahomey was proclaimed Dec. 4, 1958.

The republic changed its name to the People's Republic of Benin on Nov. 30, 1975. See Benin for stamps issued after that date.

100 Centimes = 1 Franc

Navigation and Commerce
A1

Perf. 14x13½.

1899–1905 **Typo.** **Unwmkd.**

Name of Colony in Blue or Carmine.

1	A1	1c *lil bl* (01)	65	65
2	A1	2c brn, *buff* ('04)	85	85
3	A1	4c cl, *lav*('04)	1.50	1.50
4	A1	5c yel grn ('04)	2.50	2.50
5	A1	10c red ('01)	2.50	1.65
6	A1	15c gray ('01)	1.90	95
7	A1	20c red, *grn*('04)	9.50	9.50
8	A1	25c *rose* ('99)	9.50	7.00
9	A1	25c bl ('01)	9.50	7.75
10	A1	30c brn *bis*('04)	10.00	9.50
11	A1	40c red *straw* ('04)	12.00	9.50
12	A1	50c brn, *az* (name in red) ('01)	12.00	8.75
12A	A1	50c brn, *az* (name in bl) ('05)	21.00	15.00
13	A1	75c dp vio, *org* ('04)	60.00	45.00
14	A1	1fr brnz grn, *straw* ('04)	30.00	24.00
15	A1	2fr vio, *rose* ('04)	82.50	65.00
16	A1	5fr red lil, *lav* ('04)	110.00	95.00
		Nos. 1-16 (17)	375.90	304.10

Gen. Louis Faidherbe
A2

Oil Palm
A3

Dr. Noel Eugène Ballay
A4

1906–07 *Perf. 13½x14.*

Name of Colony in Red or Blue.

17	A2	1c slate	70	70
18	A2	2c chocolate	70	70
19	A2	4c choc, *gray bl*	1.50	1.25
20	A2	5c green	5.75	1.25
21	A2	10c car (B)	11.00	1.40
22	A3	20c *azure*	8.75	6.00
23	A3	25c bl, *pnksh*	11.00	6.50
24	A3	30c choc, *pnksh*	10.50	6.50
25	A3	35c *yellow*	65.00	7.75
26	A3	45c choc, *grnsh* ('07)	11.00	8.75
27	A3	50c dp vio	12.00	8.75
28	A3	75c bl, *org*	13.00	10.50
29	A4	1fr blk, *az*	15.00	10.50
30	A4	2fr bl, *pink*	90.00	82.50
31	A4	5fr car, *straw*(B)	75.00	65.00
		Nos. 17-31 (15)	330.90	218.05

Stamps of 1901–05 Surcharged in Black or Carmine

05 **10**

a *b*

1912 *Perf. 14x13½.*

32	(a)	5c on 2c brn, *buff*	52	52
33	(a)	5c on 4c cl, *lav*(C)	90	90
a.		Double surcharge	160.00	
34	(a)	5c on 15c gray (C)	90	90
35	(a)	5c on 20c red, *grn*	90	90
36	(a)	5c on 25c bl (C)	90	90
a.		Inverted surcharge	135.00	
37	(b)	5c on 30c brn, *bis* (C)	90	90
38	(b)	10c on 40c red, *straw*	90	90
a.		Inverted surcharge	210.00	
39	(b)	10c on 50c brn, *az*, name in bl (C)	1.00	1.00
40	(b)	10c on 50c brn, *az*, name in red (C)	875.00	950.00
41	(b)	10c on 75c vio, *org*	4.25	4.25
		Nos. 32-39, 41 (9)	11.17	11.17

Two spacings between the surcharged numerals are found on Nos. 32 to 41.

Man Climbing Oil Palm
A5

1913–39 ***Perf. 13½x14.***

42	A5	1c vio & blk	5	5
43	A5	2c choc & rose	5	5
44	A5	4c blk & brn	5	5
45	A5	5c yel grn & bl grn	15	15
46	A5	5c vio brn & vio ('22)	18	18
47	A5	10c org red & rose	60	42
48	A5	10c yel grn & bl grn ('22)	25	25
49	A5	10c red & ol ('25)	6	6
50	A5	15c brn org & dk vio ('17)	18	18
51	A5	20c gray & choc	18	15
52	A5	20c bluish grn & grn ('26)	5	5
53	A5	20c mag & blk ('27)	6	6
54	A5	25c ultra & dp bl	1.00	52
55	A5	25c vio brn & org ('22)	48	48
56	A5	30c choc & vio	1.40	1.10
57	A5	30c red org & rose ('22)	1.40	1.40
58	A5	30c yel & vio ('25)	6	6
59	A5	30c dl grn & grn ('27)	15	15
60	A5	35c brn & blk	60	52
61	A5	35c bl grn & grn ('38)	15	15
62	A5	40c blk & red org	25	18
63	A5	45c gray & ultra	25	25
64	A5	50c choc & brn	2.75	2.25
65	A5	50c ultra & bl ('22)	70	70
66	A5	50c brn red & bl ('26)	6	6
67	A5	55c gray grn & choc ('38)	15	15
68	A5	60c vio, *pnksh* ('25)	6	6
69	A5	65c yel brn & ol grn ('26)	52	52
70	A5	75c bl & vio	48	40
71	A5	80c hn brn & ultra ('38)	15	15
72	A5	85c dk bl & ver ('26)	80	80
73	A5	90c rose & brn red ('30)	48	42
74	A5	90c yel bis & red org ('39)	48	35
75	A5	1fr bl grn & blk	90	52
76	A5	1fr dk bl & ultra ('26)	90	90
77	A5	1fr yel brn & lt red ('28)	95	60
78	A5	1fr dk red & red org ('38)	60	40
79	A5	1.10fr vio & bis ('28)	1.50	1.50
80	A5	1.25fr dp bl & dk brn ('33)	14.00	5.25
81	A5	1.50fr dk bl & lt bl ('30)	60	42
82	A5	1.75fr dk brn & dp buff ('33)	2.25	1.25
83	A5	1.75fr ind & ultra ('38)	52	35
84	A5	2fr yel org & choc	90	70
85	A5	3fr red vio ('30)	1.50	1.10
86	A5	5fr vio & dp bl	1.50	1.25
		Nos. 42-86 (45)	40.35	26.56

The 1c gray and yellow green and 5c dull red and black are Togo Nos. 193a, 196a.

Common Design Types

pictured in section at front of book.

Type of 1913 Surcharged

60 60

1922–25

87	A5	60c on 75c vio, *pnksh*	42	42
a.		Double surcharge	130.00	130.00
88	A5	65c on 15c brn org & dk vio ('25)	1.00	1.00
89	A5	85c on 15c brn org & dk vio ('25)	1.00	1.00

Stamps and Type of 1913–39 Surcharged with New Value and Bars.

1924–27

90	A5	25c on 2fr org & choc	42	42
91	A5	90c on 75c cer & brn red ('27)	1.25	1.25
92	A5	1.25fr on 1fr dk bl & ultra (R) ('26)	42	42
93	A5	1.50fr on 1fr dk bl & grnsh bl ('27)	1.40	1.40
94	A5	3fr on 5fr olvn & dp org ('27)	7.00	7.00
95	A5	10fr on 5fr bl vio & red brn ('27)	6.00	6.00
96	A5	20fr on 5fr ver & dl grn ('27)	6.00	6.00
		Nos. 90-96 (7)	22.49	22.49

Colonial Exposition Issue.
Common Design Types

1931 Engraved. ***Perf. 12½.***

Name of Country in Black.

97	CD70	40c dp grn	3.50	3.50
98	CD71	50c violet	3.50	3.50
99	CD72	90c red org	3.50	3.50
100	CD73	1.50fr dl bl	3.50	3.50

Paris International Exposition Issue.
Common Design Types

1937 Engraved. ***Perf. 13.***

101	CD74	20c dp vio	70	70
102	CD75	30c dk grn	90	90
103	CD76	40c car rose	90	90
104	CD77	50c dk brn	70	70
105	CD78	90c red	70	70
106	CD79	1.50fr ultra	90	90
		Nos. 101-106 (6)	4.80	4.80

Souvenir Sheet.
Imperf.

107	CD77	3fr dp bl & blk	4.00	4.00

Size of No. 107: 118x99mm.

Caillié Issue.
Common Design Type

1939, Apr. 5 Engr. ***Perf. 12½x12***

108	CD81	90c org brn & org	95	95
109	CD81	2fr brt vio	1.00	1.00
110	CD81	2.25fr ultra & dk bl	1.10	1.10

New York World's Fair Issue.
Common Design Type

1939 Engraved.

111	CD82	1.25fr car lake	60	60
112	CD82	2.25fr ultra	60	60

Man Poling a Canoe
A7

Pile House
A8

Sailboat on Lake Nokoué
A9

Dahomey Warrior
A10

1941 ***Perf. 13.***

113	A7	2c scarlet	6	6
114	A7	3c dp bl	6	6
115	A7	5c brn vio	30	30
116	A7	10c green	18	18
117	A7	15c black	5	5
118	A8	20c vio brn	5	5
119	A8	30c dk vio	18	18
120	A8	40c scarlet	48	48
121	A8	50c sl grn	48	48
122	A8	60c black	18	18
123	A8	70c brt red vio	18	18
124	A9	80c brn blk	40	40
125	A9	1fr violet	52	52
126	A9	1.30fr brn vio	60	60
127	A9	1.40fr green	75	75
128	A9	1.50fr brt rose	75	75
129	A9	2fr brn org	95	95
130	A10	2.50fr dk bl	75	75
131	A10	3fr scarlet	80	80
132	A10	5fr sl grn	65	65
133	A10	10fr vio brn	1.25	1.25
134	A10	20fr black	1.75	1.75
		Nos. 113-134 (22)	11.37	11.37

Stamps of type A8 without "RF" were issued in 1944 by the Vichy Government, but were not placed on sale in the colony.

Pile House and Marshal Pétain
A11

1941 ***Perf. 12½x12.***

135	A11	1fr green	48
136	A11	2.50fr blue	48

Republic

Village Ganvié—A12

Engraved

1960, Mar. 1 ***Perf. 12*** **Unwmkd.**

137	A12	25fr dk bl, brn & red	40	10

Imperforates

Most Dahomey stamps from 1960 onward exist imperforate in issued and trial colors, and also in small presentation sheets in issued colors.

C.C.T.A. Issue
Common Design Type

1960, May 16

138	CD106	5fr rose lil & ultra	40	35

Issued to commemorate the 10th anniversary of the Commission for Technical Co-operation in Africa South of the Sahara (C.C.T.A.).

Emblem of the Entente
A13

Prime Minister Hubert Maga
A14

Council of the Entente Issue

1960, May 29 Photo. ***Perf. 13x13½***

139	A13	25fr multi	60	50

Issued to commemorate the first anniversary of the Council of the Entente (Dahomey, Ivory Coast, Niger and Upper Volta).

1960, Aug. Engraved ***Perf. 13***

140	A14	85fr dp cl & blk	1.20	35

Issued on the occasion of Dahomey's proclamation of independence, Aug. 1, 1960.

Weaver
A15

Doves, U.N. Building and Emblem
A16

Designs: 2fr, 10fr, Wood sculptor. 3fr, 15fr, Fisherman and net (horiz.). 4fr, 20fr, Potter (horiz.).

1961, Feb. 17 Engraved ***Perf. 13***

141	A15	1fr rose, org & red lil	6	5
142	A15	2fr bis brn & choc	5	5
143	A15	3fr grn & org	8	6
144	A15	4fr ol bis & cl	12	10
145	A15	6fr rose, lt vio & ver	12	10
146	A15	10fr bl & grn	25	12
147	A15	15fr red lil & vio	27	18
148	A15	20fr bluish vio & Prus bl	40	25
		Nos. 141-148 (8)	1.35	91

No. 140 Surcharged with New Value, Bars and: "Président de la République"

1961, Aug. 1

149	A14	100fr on 85fr dp cl & blk	1.60	1.50

First anniversary of Independence.

1961, Sept. 20 ***Perf. 13*** **Unwmkd.**

150	A16	5fr multi	30	20
151	A16	60fr multi	90	80

Issued to commemorate the first anniversary of Dahomey's admission to the United Nations. See No. C16 and souvenir sheet No. C16a.

No. 137 Overprinted:
"JEUX SPORTIFS D'ABIDJAN
24 AU 31 DECEMBRE 1961"

1961, Dec. 24

152	A12	25fr dk bl, brn & red	50	40

Abidjan Games, Dec. 24–31.

Interior of Burned-out Fort Ouidah and Wrecked Car—A17

1962, July 31 Photo. *Perf. 12½*

153	A17	30fr multi	45	20
154	A17	60fr multi	90	50

Issued to commemorate the first anniversary of the evacuation of Fort Ouidah by the Portuguese, and its occupation by Dahomey.

African and Malgache Union Issue

Common Design Type

1962, Sept. 8 *Perf. 12½x12*

155	CD110	30fr red lil, bluish grn, red & gold	70	30

Issued to commemorate the first anniversary of the African and Malgache Union.

Red Cross Nurses and Map
A18

Engraved

1962, Oct. 5 *Perf. 13* Unwmkd.

156	A18	5fr bl, choc & red	10	5
157	A18	20fr bl, dk grn & red	30	25
158	A18	25fr bl, brn & red	40	30
159	A18	30fr bl, blk & red	50	30

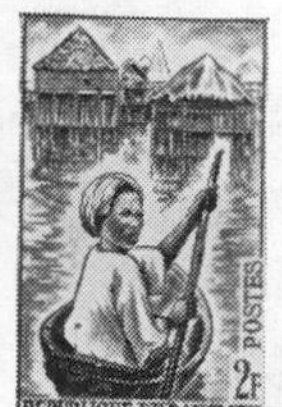

Ganvié Woman in Canoe
A19

Peuhl Herdsman and Cattle
A20

Designs: 3fr, 65fr, Bariba chief of Nikki. 15fr, 50fr, Ouidah witch doctor, rock python. 20fr, 30fr, Nessoukoué women carrying vases on heads, Abomey. 25fr, 40fr, Dahomey girl. 60fr, Peuhl herdsman and cattle. 85fr, Ganvié woman in canoe.

1963, Feb. 18 *Perf. 13* Unwmkd.

160	A19	2fr grnsh bl & vio	5	5
161	A19	3fr bl & blk	6	5
162	A20	5fr brn, blk & grn	10	6
163	A19	15fr brn, bl grn & red brn	25	15
164	A19	20fr grn, blk & car	30	20
165	A20	25fr dk brn, bl & bl grn	35	15
166	A19	30fr brn org, choc & mag	45	20
167	A20	40fr choc, grn & brt bl	60	30
168	A19	50fr blk, grn, brn & red brn	75	35
169	A20	60fr choc, org red & ol	85	40
170	A19	65fr org brn & choc	90	50
171	A19	85fr brt bl & choc	1.25	75
		Nos. 160-171 (12)	5.91	3.16

Boxers
A21

Designs: 1fr, 20fr, Soccer goalkeeper (horiz.). 2fr, 5fr, Runners.

1963, Apr. 11 Engraved

172	A21	50c grn & bl	5	5
173	A21	1fr ol, blk & brn	5	5
174	A21	2fr ol, bl & brn	6	6
175	A21	5fr brn, crim & blk	10	8
176	A21	15fr dk vio & brn	25	20
177	A21	20fr multi	40	30
		Nos. 172-177 (6)	91	74

Friendship Games, Dakar, Apr. 11–21.

President's Palace, Cotonou
A22

1963, Aug. 1 Photo. *Perf. 12½x12*

178	A22	25fr multi	40	25

Third anniversary of independence.

Gen. Toussaint L'Ouverture
A23

U.N. Emblem, Flame and "15"
A24

1963, Nov. 18 *Perf. 12x13* Unwmkd.

179	A23	25fr multi	40	25
180	A23	30fr multi	45	30
181	A23	100fr ultra, brn & red	1.50	1.00

Issued to honor Pierre Dominique Toussaint L'Ouverture (1743–1803), Haitian general, statesman and descendant of the kings of Allada (Dahomey).

1963, Dec. 10 *Perf. 12*

182	A24	4fr multi	8	8
183	A24	6fr multi	10	8
184	A24	25fr multi	40	30

Issued to commemorate the 15th anniversary of the Universal Declaration of Human Rights.

Somba Dance
A25

Regional Dances: 3fr, Nago dance, Pobe-Ketou (horiz.). 10fr, Dance of the baton. 15fr, Nago dance, Ouidah (horiz.). 25fr, Dance of the Sakpatassi. 30fr, Dance of the Nessouhouessi (horiz.).

1964, Aug. 8 Engraved *Perf. 13*

185	A25	2fr red, emer & blk	5	5
186	A25	3fr dl red, bl & grn	6	5
187	A25	10fr pur, blk & red	15	10
188	A25	15fr mag, blk & grn	25	15
189	A25	25fr Prus bl, brn & org	40	25
190	A25	30fr dk red, choc & org	45	35
		Nos. 185-190 (6)	1.36	95

Runner
A26

Design: 85fr, Bicyclist.

1964, Oct. 20 Photo. *Perf. 11*

191	A26	60fr lt brn & grn	75	55
192	A26	85fr vio bl & red lil	1.25	90

18th Olympic Games, Tokyo, Oct. 10–25.

Cooperation Issue

Common Design Type

1964, Nov. 7 Engraved *Perf. 13*

193	CD119	25fr org, vio & dk brn	40	25

UNICEF Emblem, Mother and Child
A27

IQSY Emblem and Apollo Satellite
A28

Design: 25fr, Mother holding child in her arms.

1964, Dec. 11 *Perf. 13* Unwmkd.

194	A27	20fr yel grn, dk red & blk	30	25
195	A27	25fr bl, dk red & blk	40	25

Issued for the 18th anniversary of the United Nations International Children's Emergency Fund (UNICEF).

1964, Dec. 22 Photo. *Perf. 13x12½*

Design: 100fr, IQSY emblem and Nimbus weather satellite.

196	A28	25fr grn & lt yel	50	20
197	A28	100fr dp plum & yel	1.50	90

International Quiet Sun Year, 1964–65.

Abomey Tapestry
A29

Designs (Abomey tapestries): 25fr, Warrior and fight scenes. 50fr, Birds and warriors (horiz.). 85fr, Animals, ship and plants (horiz.).

1965, Apr. 12 Photo. *Perf. 12½*

198	A29	20fr multi	30	20
199	A29	25fr multi	40	30
200	A29	50fr multi	75	50
201	A29	85fr multi	1.25	90
a.		Min. sheet of 4	2.75	2.75

Issued to publicize the local rug weaving industry. No. 201a contains one each of Nos. 198–201. Size: 194x100mm.

Baudot Telegraph Distributor and Ader Telephone
A30

1965, May 17 Engraved *Perf. 13*

202	A30	100fr lil, org & blk	1.50	60

Issued to commemorate the centenary of the International Telecommunication Union.

Cotonou Harbor—A31

Design: 100fr, Cotonou Harbor, denomination at left.

1965, Aug. 1 Photo. *Perf. 12½*

203	A31	25fr multi	45	25
204	A31	100fr multi	1.65	1.00

Issued to commemorate the opening of Cotonou Harbor. Nos. 203–204 printed se-tenant show a panoramic view of the harbor.

Cybium Tritor
A32

Fish: 25fr, Dentex filosus. 30fr, Atlantic sailfish. 50fr, Blackish tripletail.

1965, Sept. 20 Engraved *Perf. 13*

205	A32	10fr blk & brt bl	15	12
206	A32	25fr brt bl, org & blk	40	30
207	A32	30fr vio bl & grnsh bl	45	30
208	A32	50fr blk, gray bl & org	75	50

Independence Monument
A33

1965, Oct. 28 Photo. *Perf. 12x12½*

209	A33	25fr gray, blk & red	40	20
210	A33	30fr lt ultra, blk & red	45	25

October 28 Revolution, 2nd anniversary.

No. 165 Surcharged 1 F

1965, Nov. Engraved *Perf. 13*

211	A20	1fr on 25fr dk brn, bl & bl grn	8	6

Porto Novo Cathedral
A34

Designs: 50fr, Ouidah Pro-Cathedral (vert.). 70fr, Cotonou Cathedral.

1966, March 21 Engraved *Perf. 13*

212	A34	30fr Prus bl, vio brn & grn	45	30
213	A34	50fr vio brn, Prus bl & brn	75	45
214	A34	70fr grn, Prus bl & vio brn	1.10	65

Jewelry
A35

Designs: 30fr, Architecture. 50fr, Musician. 70fr, Crucifixion, sculpture.

1966, Apr. 4 Engr. *Perf. 13*

215	A35	15fr dl red brn & blk	25	15
216	A35	30fr dk brn, ultra & brn red	45	25
217	A35	50fr brt bl & dk brn	75	40
218	A35	70fr red brn & blk	1.10	65

Issued to commemorate the International Negro Arts Festival, Dakar, Senegal, Apr. 1–24.

Nos. 203–204 Surcharged

ACCORD DE COOPERATION
FRANCE - DAHOMEY
5e Anniversaire - 24 Avril 1966
15 F

1966, Apr. 24 Photo. *Perf. 12½*

219	A31	15fr on 25fr multi	25	15
220	A31	15fr on 100fr multi	25	15

Issued to commemorate the fifth anniversary of the Cooperation Agreement between France and Dahomey.

WHO Headquarters from the East
A36

1966, May 3 *Perf. 12½x13*

Size: 35x22½mm.

221	A36	30fr multi	45	30

Issued to commemorate the inauguration of the World Health Organization Headquarters, Geneva. See No. C32.

Boy Scout Signaling
A37

Designs: 10fr, Patrol standard with pennant (vert.). 30fr, Campfire and map of Dahomey (vert.). 50fr, Scouts building foot bridge.

1966, Oct. 17 Engraved *Perf. 13*

222	A37	5fr dk brn, ocher & red	10	5
223	A37	10fr blk, grn & rose cl	15	6
224	A37	30fr org, red brn & pur	40	25
225	A37	50fr vio bl, grn & dk brn	70	40
a.		Minature sheet of 4	1.65	1.65

No. 225a contains one each of Nos. 222–225. Size: 168x94mm.

Clappertonia Ficifolia
A38

Lions Emblem, Dancing Children and Bird
A39

Flowers: 3fr, Hewittia sublobata. 5fr, Butterfly pea. 10fr, Water lily. 15fr, Commelina forskalaei. 30fr, Eremomastax speciosa.

1967, Feb. 20 Photo. *Perf. 12x12½*

226	A38	1fr multi	8	5
227	A38	3fr multi	12	5
228	A38	5fr multi	15	8
229	A38	10fr multi	25	10
230	A38	15fr multi	30	18
231	A38	30fr multi	60	30
		Nos. 226-231 (6)	1.50	76

Nos. 170–171 Surcharged with New Value and Heavy Bar

1967, Mar. 1 Engraved *Perf. 13*

232	A19	30fr on 65fr org brn & choc	45	35
a.		Double surch.	22.50	
233	A19	30fr on 85fr brt bl & choc	45	35
a.		Double surch.	35.00	
b.		Invtd. surch.	35.00	

1967, March 20

234	A39	100fr dl vio, dp bl & grn	1.60	50

50th anniversary of Lions International.

EXPO '67 "Man in the City" Pavilion
A40

Design: 70fr, "The New Africa" exhibit.

1967, June 12 Engraved *Perf. 13*

235	A40	30fr grn & choc	45	20
236	A40	70fr grn & brn red	1.00	65

Issued to commemorate EXPO '67, International Exhibition, Montreal, Apr. 28–Oct. 27, 1967. See No. C57 and miniature sheet No. C57a.

Europafrica Issue, 1967

Trade (Blood) Circulation, Map of Europe and Africa
A41

1967, July 20 Photo. *Perf. 12x12½*

237	A41	30fr multi	40	20
238	A41	45fr multi	65	25

Scouts Climbing Mountain, Jamboree Emblem
A42

Design: 70fr, Jamboree emblem and Scouts launching canoe.

1967, Aug. 7 Engraved *Perf. 13*

239	A42	30fr brt bl, red brn & sl	45	20
240	A42	70fr brt bl, sl grn & dk brn	1.00	65

Issued to commemorate the 12th Boy Scout World Jamboree, Farragut State Park, Idaho, Aug. 1–9. For souvenir sheet see No. C59a.

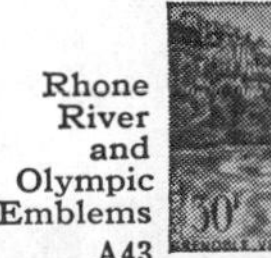

Rhone River and Olympic Emblems
A43

Designs (Olympic Emblems and): 45fr, View of Grenoble (vert.). 100fr, Rhone Bridge, Grenoble, and Pierre de Coubertin.

1967, Sept. 2 Engraved *Perf. 13*

241	A43	30fr bis, dp bl & grn	50	20
242	A43	45fr ultra, grn & brn	85	25
243	A43	100fr choc, grn & brt bl	1.65	90
a.		Miniature sheet of 3	3.25	3.25

Issued to publicize the 10th Winter Olympic Games, Grenoble, Feb. 6–18, 1968. No. 243a contains one each of Nos. 241–243. Size: 129x100mm.

Monetary Union Issue
Common Design Type

1967, Nov. 4 Engraved *Perf. 13*

244	CD125 30fr grn, dk car & dk brn	45	25

Issued to commemorate the 5th anniversary of the West African Monetary Union.

Cape Buffalo
A45

Animals from the Pendjari Reservation: 30fr, Lion. 45fr, Buffon's kob. 70fr, African slender-snouted crocodile. 100fr, Hippopotamus.

1968, Mar. 18 Photo. *Perf. 12½x13*

245	A45	15fr multi	25	15
246	A45	30fr pur & multi	45	20
247	A45	45fr bl & multi	70	30
248	A45	70fr multi	1.00	45
249	A45	100fr multi	1.50	80
		Nos. 245-249 (5)	3.90	1.90

WHO Emblem
A46

1968, Apr. 22 Engraved *Perf. 13*

250	A46	30fr dk bl, red brn & brt bl	45	20
251	A46	70fr multi	1.00	55

Issued to commemorate the 20th anniversary of the World Health Organization.

Leopard
A47

Animals: 5fr, Warthog. 60fr, Spotted hyena. 75fr, Anubius baboon. 90fr, Hartebeest.

1969, Feb. 10 Photo. *Perf. 12½x12*

252	A47	5fr dk brn & multi	8	5
253	A47	30fr dp ultra & multi	45	20
254	A47	60fr dk grn & multi	90	40
255	A47	75fr dk bl & multi	1.10	55
256	A47	90fr dk grn & multi	1.35	70
		Nos. 252-256 (5)	3.88	1.90

Heads, Symbols of Agriculture and Science, and Globe
A48

1969, Mar. 10 Engraved *Perf. 13*

257	A48	30fr org & multi	45	20
258	A48	70fr mar & multi	1.00	50

Issued to commemorate the 50th anniversary of the International Labor Organization.

Arms of Dahomey
A49

1969, June 30 Litho. *Perf. 13½x13*

259	A49	5fr yel & multi	8	6
260	A49	30fr org red & multi	40	25

See also No. C101.

Development Bank Issue

Cornucopia and Bank Emblem
A50

1969, Sept. 10 Photo. *Perf. 13*

261 A50 30fr blk, grn & ocher 50 25

Issued to commemorate the 5th anniversary of the African Development Bank.

Europafrica Issue

Ambary (Kenaf) Industry, Cotonou
A51

Design: 45fr, Cotton industry, Parakou.

1969, Sept. 22 Litho. *Perf. 14*

262 A51 30fr multi 40 25
263 A51 45fr multi 60 30

See Nos. C105–C105a.

Sakpata Dance and Tourist Year Emblem
A52

Dances and Tourist Year Emblem: 30fr, Guelede dance. 45fr, Sato dance.

1969, Dec. 15 Litho. *Perf. 14*

264 A52 10fr multi 20 10
265 A52 30fr multi 45 20
266 A52 45fr multi 65 35

See No. C108.

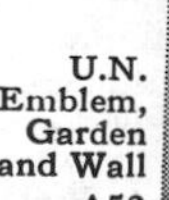

U.N. Emblem, Garden and Wall
A53

1970, Apr. 6 Engraved *Perf. 13*

267 A53 30fr ultra, red org & sl 45 20
268 A53 40fr ultra, brn & sl grn 60 30

25th anniversary of the United Nations.

ASECNA Issue
Common Design Type

1970, June 1 Engraved *Perf. 13*

269 CD132 40fr red & pur 60 35

Mt. Fuji, EXPO '70 Emblem, Monorail Train
A54

1970, June 15 Litho. *Perf. 13½x14*

270 A54 5fr grn, red & vio bl 12 8

Issued to publicize EXPO '70 International Exhibition, Osaka, Japan, Mar. 15–Sept. 13, 1970. See Nos. C124–C125.

Alkemy, King of Ardres
A55

Designs: 40fr, Sailing ships "La Justice" and "La Concorde," Ardres, 1670. 50fr, Matheo Lopes, ambassador of the King of Ardres and his coat of arms. 200fr, Louis XIV and fleur-de-lis.

1970, July 6 Engraved *Perf. 13*

271 A55 40fr brt grn, ultra & brn 65 22
272 A55 50fr dk car, choc & emer 75 27
273 A55 70fr gray, lem & choc 1.00 40
274 A55 200fr Prus bl, dk car & choc 2.75 1.20

Issued to commemorate the 300th anniversary of the mission from the King of Ardres to the King of France, and of the audience with Louis XIV on Dec. 19, 1670.

Star of the Order of Independence
A56

Bariba Warrior
A57

1970, Aug. 1 Photo. *Perf. 12*

275 A56 30fr multi 35 20
276 A56 40fr multi 50 25

The 10th anniversary of independence.

1970, Aug. 24 *Perf. 12½x13*

Designs: 2fr, 50fr, Two horsemen. 10fr, 70fr, Horseman facing left.

277 A57 1fr yel & multi 6 5
278 A57 2fr gray grn & multi 8 6
279 A57 10fr bl & multi 15 10
280 A57 40fr yel grn & multi 55 30
281 A57 50fr gold & multi 65 30
282 A57 70fr lil rose & multi 1.00 50
Nos. 277-282 (6) 2.49 1.31

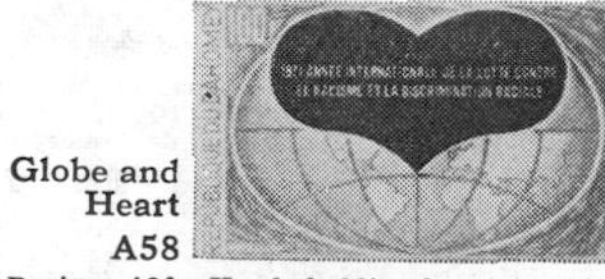

Globe and Heart
A58

Design: 40fr, Hands holding heart (vert.).

1971, June 7 Engraved *Perf. 13*

283 A58 40fr red, grn & dk brn 50 30
284 A58 100fr grn, red & bl 1.10 60

International year against racial discrimination.

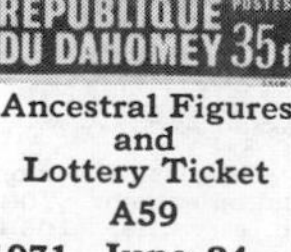

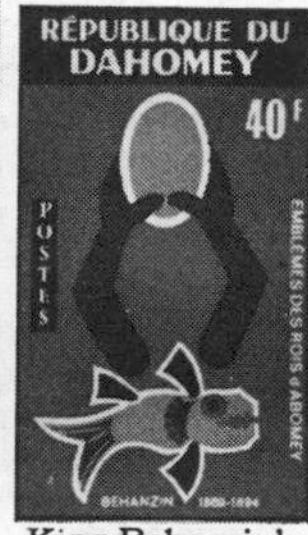

Ancestral Figures and Lottery Ticket
A59

King Behanzin's Emblem (1889–1894)
A60

1971, June 24 Litho. *Perf. 14*

285 A59 35fr multi 40 20
286 A59 40fr multi 50 25

4th anniversary of the National Lottery.

Photo.; Litho. (25fr, 135fr)

1971–72 *Perf. 12½*

Emblems of the Kings of Abomey: 25fr, Agoliagbo (1894–1900). 35fr, Ganyehoussou (1620–1645), bird and cup (horiz.). 100fr, Guezo (1818–1858), bull, tree and birds. 135fr, Ouegbadja (1645–1685) (horiz.). 140fr, Glèle (1858–1889), lion and sword (horiz.)

287 A60 25fr multi ('72) 30 15
288 A60 35fr grn & multi 45 20
289 A60 40fr grn & multi 50 25
290 A60 100fr red & multi 1.25 45
291 A60 135fr multi ('72) 1.40 70
292 A60 140fr brn & multi 1.75 85
Nos. 287-292 (6) 5.65 2.60

Issue dates: 25fr, 135fr, July 17, 1972. Others, Aug. 3, 1971.

Kabuki Actor, Long-distance Skiing
A61

Brahms and "Soir d'été"
A62

1972, Feb. Engraved *Perf. 13*

293 A61 35fr dk car, brn & bl grn 50 25

11th Winter Olympic Games, Sapporo, Japan, Feb. 3–13. See No. C153.

No. 268 Surcharged

1972

294 A53 35fr on 40fr multi 45 25

1972, June 29 Engraved *Perf. 13*

Design: 65fr, Brahms, woman at piano and music (horiz.).

295 A62 30fr red brn, blk & lil 40 25
296 A62 65fr red brn, blk & lil 80 50

75th anniversary of the death of Johannes Brahms (1833–1897), German composer.

The Hare and The Tortoise, by La Fontaine—A63

Fables: 35fr, The Fox and The Stork (vert.). 40fr, The Cat, The Weasel and Rabbit.

1972, Aug. 28 Engr. *Perf. 13*

297 A63 10fr multi 15 10
298 A63 35fr dk red & multi 45 25
299 A63 40fr ultra & multi 50 30

Jean de La Fontaine (1621–1695), French fabulist.

West African Monetary Union Issue
Common Design Type

1972, Nov. 2 Engraved *Perf. 13*

300 CD136 40fr choc, ocher & gray 40 25

10th anniversary of West African Monetary Union.

Dr. Hansen, Microscope, Bacilli
A65

Design: 85 fr, Portrait of Dr. Hansen.

1973, May 14 Engr. *Perf. 13*

301 A65 35fr ultra, vio brn & brn 30 20
302 A65 85fr yel grn, bis & ver 75 50

Centenary of the discovery by Dr. Armauer G. Hansen of the Hansen bacillus, the cause of leprosy.

Arms of Dahomey
A66

1973, June 25 Photo. *Perf. 13*

303 A66 5fr ultra & multi 8 5
304 A66 35fr ocher & multi 30 15
305 A66 40fr red org & multi 35 17

INTERPOL Emblem and Spiderweb
A67

Design: 50fr, INTERPOL emblem and communications symbols (vert.).

1973, July Engraved

306 A67 35fr ver, grn & brn 35 20
307 A67 50fr grn, brn & red 50 30

50th anniversary of International Criminal Police Organization (INTERPOL).

Education in Hygiene and Nutrition
A68

Design: 100fr, Prenatal examination and care, WHO emblem.

1973, Aug. 2 Photo. *Perf. 12½x13*

308 A68 35fr multi 35 15
309 A68 100fr multi 85 50

World Health Organization, 25th anniversary.

No. 248 Surcharged with New Value, 2 Bars, and Overprinted in Red: "SECHERESSE SOLIDARITE AFRICAINE"

1973, Aug. 16

310 A45 100fr on 70fr multi 1.20 65

African solidarity in drought emergency.

African Postal Union Issue
Common Design Type

1973, Sept. 12 Engraved *Perf. 13*

311 CD137 100fr red, pur & blk 1.00 55

Epinephelus Aeneus—A69

Fish: 15fr, Drepane africana. 35fr, Pragus ehrenbergi.

1973, Sept. 18

312	A69	5fr sl bl & ind	12	7
313	A69	15fr blk & brt bl	12	10
314	A69	35fr emer, ocher & sep	30	15

Chameleon A70

Design: 40fr, Emblem over map of Dahomey (vert.).

1973, Nov. 30 Photo. *Perf. 13*

315	A70	35fr ol & multi	35	20
316	A70	40fr multi	40	30

1st anniversary of the Oct. 26 revolution.

The Chameleon in the Tree—A71

Designs: 5fr, The elephant, the hen and the dog (vert.). 10fr, The sparrowhawk and the dog (vert.). 25fr, The chameleon in the tree. 40fr, The eagle, the viper and the hen.

1974, Feb. 14 Photo. *Perf. 13*

317	A71	5fr emer & multi	8	5
318	A71	10fr sl bl & multi	10	7
319	A71	25fr sl bl & multi	20	15
320	A71	40fr lt bl & multi	35	17

Folktales of Dahomey.

German Shepherd—A72

1974, Apr. 25 Photo. *Perf. 13*

Multicolored

321	A72	40fr *shown*	35	20
322	A72	50fr *Boxer*	40	25
323	A72	100fr *Saluki*	85	60

Council Issue

Map and Flags of Members A73

1974, May 29 Photo. *Perf. 13x12½*

324	A73	40fr bl & multi	35	20

15th anniversary of the Council of Accord.

Locomotive 232, 1911—A74

Designs: Locomotives.

1974, Sept. 2 Photo. *Perf. 13x12½*

Multicolored

325	A74	35fr *shown*	30	20
326	A74	40fr *Freight, 1877*	35	20
327	A74	100fr *Crampton, 1849*	85	60
328	A74	200fr *Stephenson, 1846*	1.65	1.25

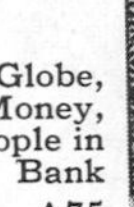

Globe, Money, People in Bank A75

1974, Oct. 31 Engraved *Perf. 13*

329	A75	35fr multi	35	20

World Savings Day.

Dompago Dance, Hissi Tribe A76

Flags of Dahomey and Nigeria over Africa A77

Folk Dances: 25fr, Fetish Dance, Vaudou-Tchinan. 40fr, Bamboo Dance, Agbehoun. 100fr, Somba Dance, Sandoua (horiz.).

1975, Aug. 4 Litho. *Perf. 12*

330	A76	10fr yel & multi	12	6
331	A76	25fr dk grn & multi	20	12
332	A76	40fr red & multi	32	22
333	A76	100fr multi	85	50

1975, Aug. 11 Photo. *Perf. 12½x13*

Design: 100fr, Arrows connecting maps of Dahomey and Nigeria (horiz.).

334	A77	65fr multi	55	35
335	A77	100fr grn & multi	85	55

Year of intensified cooperation between Dahomey and Nigeria.

Map, Pylons, Emblem—A78

Benin Electric Community Emblem and Pylon A79

1975, Aug. 18

336	A78	40fr multi	35	25
337	A79	150fr multi	1.25	85

Benin Electric Community and Ghana-Togo-Dahomey cooperation.

Map of Dahomey, Rising Sun A80

Albert Schweitzer, Nurse, Patient A81

1975, Aug. 25 Photo. *Perf. 12½x13*

338	A80	35fr multi	28	15

Cooperation Year for the creation of a new Dahoman society.

1975, Sept. 22 Engr. *Perf. 13*

339	A81	200fr ol, grn & red brn	1.65	1.10

Birth centenary of Albert Schweitzer (1875–1965), medical missionary and musician.

Woman Speaking on Telephone, IWY Emblem A82

Design: 150fr, International Women's Year emblem and linked rings.

1975, Oct. 20 Engr. *Perf. 12½x13*

340	A82	50fr Prus bl & lil	40	25
341	A82	150fr emer, brn & org	1.25	65

International Women's Year 1975. Later issues are listed under Benin.

SEMI-POSTAL STAMPS.

Regular Issue of 1913 Surcharged in Red

1915 *Perf. 14x13½.* **Unwmkd.**

B1 A5 10c +5c org red & rose 75 60

Curie Issue
Common Design Type

1938 *Perf. 13*

B2 CD80 1.75fr +50c brt ultra 7.00 7.00

French Revolution Issue
Common Design Type

Name and Value Typo. in Black.

1939 Photogravure.

B3 CD83 45(c) +25(c) grn 5.25 5.25
B4 CD83 70(c) +30(c) brn 5.75 5.75
B5 CD83 90(c) +35(c) red org 5.75 5.75
B6 CD83 1.25fr +1fr rose pink 5.75 5.75
B7 CD83 2.25fr +2fr bl 5.75 5.75
Nos. B3-B7 (5) 28.25 28.25

Postage Stamps of 1913-38 Surcharged in Black

SECOURS + 1 fr. NATIONAL

1941 *Perf. 13½x14.*

B8 A5 50c +1fr brn red & bl 1.00 1.00
B9 A5 80c +2fr hn brn & ultra 3.25 3.25
B10 A5 1.50fr +2fr dk bl & lt bl 4.25 4.25
B11 A5 2fr +3fr yel org & choc 4.25 4.25

Common Design Type and

Radio Operator
SP1

Senegalese Artillerymen
SP2

1941 Photogravure. *Perf. 13½.*

B12 SP1 1fr +1fr red 1.00
B13 CD86 1.50fr +3fr cl 1.00
B14 SP2 2.50fr +1fr bl 1.00

The surtax was for the defense of the colonies.

Stamps of type A11 surcharged "OEUVRES COLONIALES" and new values were issued in 1944 by the Vichy Government, but were not placed on sale in the colony.

Republic

Anti-Malaria Issue
Common Design Type

1962, Apr. 7 Engr. *Perf. 12½x12*

B15 CD108 25fr +5fr org brn 65 65

Issued for the World Health Organization drive to eradicate malaria.

Freedom from Hunger Issue
Common Design Type

1963, Mar. 21 *Perf. 13* **Unwmkd.**

B16 CD112 25fr +5fr ol, brn red & brn 65 65

AIR POST STAMPS.

Common Design Type
Engraved.

1940 *Perf. 12½* **Unwmkd.**

C1 CD85 1.90fr ultra 22 22
C2 CD85 2.90fr dk red 30 30
C3 CD85 4.50fr dk gray grn 48 48
C4 CD85 4.90fr yel bis 65 65
C5 CD85 6.90fr dp org 95 95
Nos. C1-C5 (5) 2.60 2.60

Common Design Types

1942

C6 CD88 50c car & bl 18
C7 CD88 1fr brn & blk 22
C8 CD88 2fr dk grn & red brn 30
C9 CD88 3fr dk bl & scar 60
C10 CD88 5fr vio & brn red 60

Frame Engr., Center Typo.

C11 CD89 10fr ultra, ind & org 75
C12 CD89 20fr rose car, mag & gray blk 75
C13 CD89 50fr yel grn, dl grn & dp bl 1.75 2.50
Nos. C6-C13 (8) 5.15

There is doubt whether Nos. C6-C12 were officially placed in use.

Republic

Somba House—AP4

Design: 500fr, Royal Court of Abomey.

Engraved

1960, Apr. 1 *Perf. 13* **Unwmkd.**

C14 AP4 100fr ind, ocher & vio brn 1.50 45
C15 AP4 500fr bis brn, brn red & dk grn 7.00 1.25

Type of Regular Issue, 1961.

1961, Sept. 20

C16 A16 200fr multi 2.75 2.00
a. Souvenir sheet of three 4.25 4.25

Issued to commemorate the first anniversary of Dahomey's admission to the United Nations. No. C16a contains one each of Nos. 150-151 and C16. Bistre marginal inscription. Size: 129x85mm.

Air Afrique Issue
Common Design Type

1962, Feb. 17 *Perf. 13*

C17 CD107 25fr ultra, blk & org brn 50 25

Issued to commemorate the founding of Air Afrique (African Airlines).

Palace of the African and Malgache Union, Cotonou
AP5

1963, July 27 Photo. *Perf. 13x12*

C18 AP5 250fr dk & lt bl, ocher & grn 3.50 2.00

Issued to commemorate the assembly of chiefs of state of the African and Malgache Union held at Cotonou in July.

African Postal Union Issue
Common Design Type

1963, Sept. 8 *Perf. 12½* **Unwmkd.**

C19 CD114 25fr brt bl, ocher & red 45 30

See note after Cameroun No. C47.

Boeing 707—AP6

Designs (Boeing 707): 200fr, On the ground. 300fr, Over Cotonou airport. 500fr, In the air.

1963, Oct. 25 Engraved *Perf. 13*

C20 AP6 100fr dk pur, grn & bis 1.25 40
C21 AP6 200fr vio, brn org & grn 2.50 1.25
C22 AP6 300fr bl, red brn & brt grn 3.50 1.75
C23 AP6 500fr brn org, dk brn & yel grn 6.00 2.50

Priests Carrying Funerary Boat, Isis Temple, Philae
AP7

1964, March 9 *Perf. 13* **Unwmkd.**

C24 AP7 25fr vio bl & brn 70 50

Issued to publicize the UNESCO world campaign to save historic monuments in Nubia.

Weather Map and Symbols
AP8

1965, Mar. 23 Photo. *Perf. 12½*

C25 AP8 50fr multi 80 50

Fifth World Meteorological Day.

ICY Emblem and Men of Various Races—AP9

1965, June 26 Engraved *Perf. 13*

C26 AP9 25fr dl pur, mar & grn 40 20
C27 AP9 85fr dp bl, mar & sl grn 1.25 80

International Cooperation Year, 1965.

Winston Churchill
AP10

1965, June 15 Photo. *Perf. 12½*

C28 AP10 100fr multi 1.65 1.25

Issued in memory of Sir Winston Churchill (1874-1965), statesman and World War II leader.

Abraham Lincoln—AP11

1965, July 15 *Perf. 13*

C29 AP11 100fr multi 1.65 1.25

Centenary of death of Abraham Lincoln.

John F. Kennedy and Arms of Dahomey
AP12

1965, Nov. 22 Photo. *Perf. 12½*

C30 AP12 100fr dp grn & blk 1.65 1.25

Issued in memory of President John F. Kennedy (1917-63).

Dr. Albert Schweitzer and Patients
AP13

1966, Jan. 17 Photo. *Perf. 12½*

C31 AP13 100fr multi 1.65 1.25

Issued in memory of Dr. Albert Schweitzer (1875-1965), medical missionary, theologian and musician.

WHO Type of Regular Issue

Design: 100fr, WHO Headquarters from the West.

1966, May 3 *Perf. 13* **Unwmkd.**

Size: 47x28mm.

C32 A36 100fr ultra, yel & blk 1.65 1.00

Issued to commemorate the inauguration of the World Health Organization Headquarters, Geneva.

Pygmy Goose
AP14

Broad-billed Rollers
AP15

Birds: 100fr, Firey-breasted bush-shrike. 250fr, Emerald cuckoos. 500fr, Emerald starling.

1966-67 *Perf. 12½*

C33	AP14	50fr multi	1.00	40
C34	AP14	100fr multi	1.75	65
C35	AP15	200fr multi ('67)	3.25	1.35
C36	AP15	250fr multi ('67)	4.00	1.85
C37	AP14	500fr multi	7.00	3.50
		Nos. C33-C37 (5)	17.00	7.75

Issue dates: 50fr, 100fr, 500fr, June 13, 1966. Others, Jan. 20, 1967.

Industrial Symbols
AP16

1966, July 21 Photo. *Perf. 12x13*

C38	AP16	100fr multi	1.50	90

3rd anniversary of agreement between European Economic Community and the African and Malagache Union.

Pope Paul VI and St. Peter's, Rome—AP17

Pope Paul VI and U.N. General Assembly
AP18

Design: 70fr, Pope Paul VI and view of New York City.

1966, Aug. 22 Engraved *Perf. 13*

C39	AP17	50fr brt grn, rose car & org brn	85	40
C40	AAP17	70fr dk bl, sl grn & lake	1.25	60
C41	AP18	100fr dk grn, brn vio & sl bl	1.85	1.00
a.		Min. sheet of 3	4.00	4.00

Issued to commemorate Pope Paul's appeal for peace before the U.N. General Assembly, Oct. 4, 1965. No. C41a contains one each of Nos. C39-C41. Size: 178x100mm.

Air Afrique Issue, 1966
Common Design Type

1966, Aug. 31 Photo. *Perf. 12½*

C42	CD123	30fr dk vio, blk & gray	50	25

Issued to commemorate the introduction of DC-8F planes by Air Afrique.

"Science"—AP20

Designs: 45fr, "Art" (carved female statue, vert.). 100fr, "Education" (book and letters).

1966, Nov. 4 Engraved *Perf. 13*

C43	AP20	30fr mag, ultra & vio brn	40	25
C44	AP20	45fr mar & grn	70	40
C45	AP20	100fr blk, mar & brt bl	1.50	90
a.		Min. sheet of 3	3.50	3.50

Issued to commemorate the 20th anniversary of UNESCO (United Nations Educational, Scientific and Cultural Organization). No. C45a contains one each of Nos. C43-C45 Size: 169x100mm.

Madonna by Alessio Baldovinetti
AP21

Designs: 50fr, Nativity after 15th century Beaune tapestry. 100fr, Adoration of the Shepherds, by José Ribera.

1966, Dec. 25 Photo. *Perf. 12½x12*

C46	AP21	50fr multi	2.25	1.35
C47	AP21	100fr multi	4.00	2.75
C48	AP21	200fr multi	6.75	5.00

Christmas 1966.
See Nos. C95-C96, C109-C115.

1967, Apr. 10 *Perf. 12½x12*

Paintings by Ingres: No. C49, Self-portrait, 1804. No. C50, Oedipus and the Sphinx.

C49	AP21	100fr multi	2.00	1.50
C50	AP21	100fr multi	2.00	1.50

Issued to commemorate the centenary of the death of Jean Auguste Dominique Ingres (1780-1867), French painter.

Three-master Suzanne—AP22

Windjammers: 45fr, Three-master Esmeralda (vert.). 80fr, Schooner Marie Alice (vert.). 100fr, Four-master Antonin.

1967, May 8 *Perf. 13*

C51	AP22	30fr multi	50	25
C52	AP22	45fr multi	70	45
C53	AP22	80fr multi	1.20	60
C54	AP22	100fr multi	1.50	85

Nos. C29-C30 Surcharged

29 MAI 1967
50e Anniversaire
de la naissance
de
John F. Kennedy

125F

1967, May 29 Photo. *Perf. 13, 12½*

C55	AP11	125fr on 100fr multi	2.00	1.00
a.		Surch. invtd.	22.50	
C56	AP12	125fr on 100fr dp grn & blk	2.00	1.00
a.		Surch. invtd.	25.00	

Issued to commemorate the 50th anniversary of the birth of President John F. Kennedy.

EXPO '67 "Man In Space" Pavilion
AP23

1967, June 12 Engraved *Perf. 13*

C57	AP23	100fr dl red & Prus bl	1.50	85
a.		Min. sheet of 3	3.25	3.25

Issued to commemorate EXPO '67, International Exhibition, Montreal, Apr. 28-Oct. 27, 1967. No. C57a contains one each of Nos. 235-236 and C57. Size: 149x100mm.

Europafrica Issue, 1967

Konrad Adenauer, by Oscar Kokoschká
AP24

1967, July 19 Photo. *Perf. 12½x12*

C58	AP24	70fr multi	1.25	90
a.		Souv. sheet of 4	5.00	5.00

Issued in memory of Konrad Adenauer (1876-1967), chancellor of West Germany (1949-1963). No. C58a contains 4 No. C58. Dark gray marginal inscription. Size: 140x158mm.

Jamboree Emblem, Ropes and World Map
AP25

1967, Aug. 7 Engr. *Perf. 13*

C59	AP25	100fr lil, sl grn & dp bl	1.50	90
a.		Souv. sheet of 3	3.75	3.50

Issued to commemorate the 12th Boy Scout World Jamboree, Farragut State Park, Idaho, Aug. 1-9. No. C59a contains one each of Nos. 239-240 and C59. Bright blue marginal inscription. Size: 149x100mm.

No. C48 Surcharged in Red

150F

RICCIONE
12-29
Août
1967

1967, Aug. 12 Photo. *Perf. 12½x12*

C60	AP21	150fr on 200fr multi	2.50	2.00
a.		"150F" omitted	125.00	125.00

Issued to publicize the Riccione, Italy, Stamp Exhibition.

African Postal Union Issue, 1967
Common Design Type

1967, Sept. 9 Engraved *Perf. 13*

C61	CD124	100fr red, brt lil & emer	1.50	1.00

Charles de Gaulle
AP26

1967, Nov. 21 Photo. *Perf. 12½x13*

C62	AP26	100fr multi	2.50	2.00
a.		Souv. sheet of 4	10.00	10.00

Issued to honor Pres. Charles de Gaulle of France on the occasion of Pres. Christophe Soglo's state visit to Paris, Nov. 1967. No. C62a contains 4 No. C62. Black marginal inscription. Size: 140x161 mm.

Madonna, by Matthias Grunewald
AP27

Paintings: 50fr, Holy Family by the Master of St. Sebastian (horiz.). 100fr, Adoration of the Magi by Ulrich Apt the Elder. 200fr, Annunciation, by Matthias Grunewald.

1967, Dec. 11 Photo. ***Perf. 12½***

C63 AP27 30fr multi 35 25
C64 AP27 50fr multi 70 40
C65 AP27 100fr multi 1.50 90
C66 AP27 200fr multi 3.00 1.40

Christmas 1967.

Venus de Milo and Mariner 5
AP28

Gutenberg Monument, Strasbourg Cathedral
AP29

Design: No. C68, Venus de Milo and Venus 4 Rocket.

1968, Feb. 17 Photo. ***Perf. 13***

C67 AP28 70fr grnsh bl & multi 1.25 60
C68 AP28 70fr dp bl & multi 1.25 60
a. Souv. sheet of 2 2.50 2.50

Issued to commemorate the explorations of the planet Venus, Oct. 18–19, 1967. No. C68a contains one each of Nos. C67–C68. Black marginal inscription. Size: 106x96mm.

1968, May 20 Litho. ***Perf. 14x13½***

Design: 100fr, Gutenberg Monument, Mainz, and Gutenberg press.

C69 AP29 45fr grn & org 70 35
C70 AP29 100fr dk & lt bl 1.35 65
a. Souv. sheet of 2 2.25 2.25

Issued to commemorate the 500th anniversary of the death of Johann Gutenberg, inventor of printing from movable type. No. C70a contains one each of Nos. C69–C70. Marginal inscription in green and dark blue. Size: 130x100mm.

Martin Luther King, Jr.
AP30

Designs: 30fr, "We must meet hate with creative love" in French, English and German. 100fr, Full-face portrait.

Perf. 12½, 13½x13

1968, June 17 Photogravure

Size: 26x46mm.

C71 AP30 30fr red brn, yel & blk 40 20

Size: 26x37mm.

C72 AP30 55fr multi 70 40
C73 AP30 100fr multi 1.25 65
a. Min. sheet of 3 2.75 2.75

Issued in memory of the Rev. Dr. Martin Luther King, Jr. (1929–1968), American civil rights leader. No. C73a contains one each of Nos. C71–C73. Size: 150x114mm.

Robert Schuman—AP31

Designs: 45fr, Alcide de Gasperi. 70fr, Konrad Adenauer.

1968, July 20 Photo. ***Perf. 13***

C74 AP31 30fr dp yel, blk & grn 40 20
C75 AP31 45fr org, dk brn & ol 60 30
C76 AP31 70fr multi 1.00 45

Issued to commemorate the 5th anniversary of the economic agreement between the European Economic Community and the African and Malgache Union.

Battle of Montebello, by Henri Philippoteaux
AP32

Paintings: 45fr, 2nd Zouave Regiment at Magenta, by Riballier. 70fr, Battle of Magenta, by Louis Eugène Charpentier. 100fr, Battle of Solferino, by Charpentier.

1968, Aug. 12 ***Perf. 12½x12***

C77 AP32 30fr multi 45 20
C78 AP32 45fr multi 70 30
C79 AP32 70fr multi 1.00 50
C80 AP32 100fr multi 1.50 75

Issued for the Red Cross.

Mail Truck in Village—AP33

Designs: 45fr, Mail truck stopping at rural post office. 55fr, Mail truck at river bank. 70fr, Mail truck and train.

1968, Oct. 7 Photo. ***Perf. 13x12½***

C81 AP33 30fr multi 30 20
C82 AP33 45fr multi 60 30
C83 AP33 55fr multi 70 40
C84 AP33 70fr multi 85 50

Aztec Stadium, Mexico City
AP34

Designs (Olympic Rings and); 45fr, Ball player, Mayan sculpture (vert.). 70fr, Wrestler, sculpture from Uxpanapan (vert.). 150fr, Olympic Stadium, Mexico City.

1968, Nov. 20 Engraved ***Perf. 13***

C85 AP34 30fr dp cl & sl grn 45 20
C86 AP34 45fr ultra & dk rose brn 60 25
C87 AP34 70fr sl grn & dk brn 90 40
C88 AP34 150fr dk car & dk brn 2.10 1.00
a. Min. sheet of 4 4.50 4.50

Issued to commemorate the 19th Olympic Games, Mexico City, Oct. 12–27.

No. C88a contains one each of Nos. C85–C88. It is folded down the vertical gutter separating Nos. C85–C86 se-tenant at left and Nos. C87–C88 se-tenant at right. Size: 235x102mm.

The Annunciation, by Foujita
AP35

Paintings by Foujita: 30fr, Nativity (horiz.). 100fr, The Virgin and Child. 200fr, The Baptism of Christ.

Perf. 12x12½, 12½x12

1968, Nov. 25 Photogravure

C89 AP35 30fr multi 50 20
C90 AP35 70fr multi 90 45
C91 AP35 100fr multi 1.50 65
C92 AP35 200fr multi 3.00 1.35

Christmas 1968.

PHILEXAFRIQUE Issue

Painting: 100fr, Diderot, by Louis Michel Vanloo.

1968, Dec. 16 ***Perf. 12½x12***

C93 AP35 100fr multi 1.50 1.00

Issued to publicize PHILEXAFRIQUE, Philatelic Exhibition in Abidjan, Feb. 14–23. Printed with alternating bluish violet label.

2nd PHILEXAFRIQUE Issue
Common Design Type

Design: 50fr, Dahomey No. 119 and aerial view of Cotonou.

1969, Feb. 14 Engraved ***Perf. 13***

C94 CD128 50fr bl, brn & pur 75 60

Issued to commemorate the opening of PHILEXAFRIQUE, Feb. 14.

Type of Painting (Christmas) Issue, 1966

Paintings: No. C95, Virgin of the Rocks, by Leonardo da Vinci. No. C96, Virgin with the Scales, by Cesare da Sesto.

1969, Mar. 17 Photo. ***Perf. 12½x12***

C95 AP21 100fr vio & multi 1.35 65
C96 AP21 100fr grn & multi 1.35 65

Issued to commemorate the 450th anniversary of the death of Leonardo da Vinci (1452–1519).

General Bonaparte, by Jacques Louis David
AP36

Paintings: 60fr, Napoleon I in 1809, by Robert J. Lefevre. 75fr, Napoleon on the Battlefield of Eylau, by Antoine Jean Gros (horiz.). 200fr, Gen. Bonaparte at Arcole, by Gros.

1969, Apr. 14 Photo. ***Perf. 12½x12***

C97 AP36 30fr multi 1.20 85
C98 AP36 60fr multi 1.75 1.25
C99 AP36 75fr multi 2.50 1.65
C100 AP36 200fr multi 5.50 3.25

Bicentenary of the birth of Napoleon I.

Arms Type of Regular Issue, 1969

1969, June 30 Litho. ***Perf. 13½x13***

C101 A49 50fr multi 60 30

Apollo 8 Trip Around the Moon
AP37

Embossed on Gold Foil

1969, July ***Die-cut Perf. 10½***

C102 AP37 1000fr gold 15.00 15.00

Issued to commemorate the U.S. Apollo 8 mission, which put the first men into orbit around the moon, Dec. 21–27, 1968.

ALUNISSAGE
APOLLO XI
JUILLET 1969

Nos. C67–C68 Surcharged

125F

1969, Aug. 1 Photo. ***Perf. 13***

C103 AP28 125fr on 70fr grnsh bl & multi 2.00 1.00
C104 AP28 125fr on 70fr dp bl & multi 2.00 1.00

Issued to commemorate man's first landing on the moon, July 20, 1969; U. S. astronauts Neil A. Armstrong and Col. Edwin E. Aldrin, Jr., with Lieut. Col. Michael Collins piloting Apollo 11.

Europafrica Issue
Type of Regular Issue, 1969

Design: 100fr, Oil palm industry, Cotonou.

1969, Sept. 22 Litho. ***Perf. 14***

C105 A51 100fr multi 1.25 65
a. Souv. sheet of 3 2.25 2.25

No. C105a contains one each of Nos. 262–263 and C105. Black marginal inscription. Size: 107½x148mm.

Dahomey Rotary Emblem
AP38

1969, Sept. 25 ***Perf. 14x13½***

C106 AP38 50fr multi 75 40

No. C33 Surcharged

1969, Nov. 15 Photo. *Perf. 12½*

C107 AP14 10fr on 50fr multi 12 6

Dance Type of Regular Issue

Design: 70fr, Teke dance and Tourist Year emblem.

1969, Dec. 15 Litho. *Perf. 14*

C108 A52 70fr multi 90 40

Painting Type of 1966

Paintings: 30fr, Annunciation, by Vrancke van der Stockt. 45fr, Nativity, Swabian School (horiz.). 110fr, Madonna and Child, by the Master of the Gold Brocade. 200fr, Adoration of the Kings, Antwerp School.

Perf. 12½x12, 12x12½

1969, Dec. 20

C109 AP21 30fr multi 50 35
C110 AP21 45fr red & multi 75 50
C111 AP21 110fr multi 2.00 1.20
C112 AP21 200fr multi 3.50 2.25

Christmas 1969.

1969, Dec. 27 *Perf. 12½x12*

Paintings: No. C113, The Artist's Studio (detail), by Gustave Courbet. No. C114, Self-portrait with Gold Chain, by Rembrandt. 150fr, Hendrickje Stoffels, by Rembrandt.

C113 AP21 100fr red & multi 1.25 75
C114 AP21 100fr grn & multi 1.25 75
C115 AP21 150fr multi 2.00 1.00

Franklin D. Roosevelt AP39

Astronauts, Rocket and U.S. Flag AP40

1970, Feb. Photo. *Perf. 12½*

C116 AP39 100fr ultra, yel grn & blk 1.25 50

Issued to commemorate the 25th anniversary of the death of Pres. Franklin Delano Roosevelt (1882–1945).

1970, Mar. 9 Photo. *Perf. 12½*

Designs: 50fr, Astronauts riding rocket through space. 70fr, Astronauts in landing module approaching moon. 110fr, Astronauts planting U.S. flag on moon.

C117 AP40 30fr multi 40 25

Souvenir Sheet

C118 AP40 Sheet of 4 3.50 3.50
a. 50fr vio bl & multi 60 60
b. 70fr vio bl & multi 85 85
c. 110fr vio bl & multi 1.25 1.25

See note after No. C104. No. C118 contains one each of Nos. C117, C118a, C118b and C118c; violet blue marginal inscription in French, German and English. Size: 120x157mm.

Walt Whitman and Dahoman Huts AP41

1970, Apr. 30 Engraved *Perf. 13*

C119 AP41 100fr Prus bl, brn & emer 1.25 50

Issued to honor Walt Whitman (1818–1892), American poet.

No. C117 Surcharged in Silver with New Value, Heavy Bar and:

"APOLLO XIII / SOLIDARITE / SPATIALE / INTERNATIONALE"

1970, May 15 Photo. *Perf. 12½*

C120 AP40 40fr on 30fr multi 65 65

The flight of Apollo 13.

Soccer Players and Globe—AP42

Designs: 50fr, Goalkeeper catching ball. 200fr, Players kicking ball.

1970, May 19

C121 AP42 40fr multi 60 35
C122 AP42 50fr multi 70 40
C123 AP42 200fr multi 3.00 1.40

Issued to publicize the 9th World Soccer Championships for the Jules Rimet Cup, Mexico City, May 30–June 21, 1970.

EXPO '70 Type of Regular Issue

Designs (EXPO '70 Emblems and): 70fr, Dahomey pavilion. 120fr, Mt. Fuji, temple and torii.

1970, June 15 Litho. *Perf. 13½x14*

C124 A54 70fr yel, red & dk vio 85 40
C125 A54 120fr yel, red & grn 1.50 75

Issued to publicize EXPO '70 International Exhibition Osaka, Japan, Mar. 15–Sept. 13, 1970.

No. C123 Surcharged with New Value and Overprinted:

"Bresil-Italie / 4–1"

1970, July 13 Photo. *Perf. 12½*

C126 AP42 100fr on 200fr multi 1.50 65

Issued to commemorate Brazil's victory in the 9th World Soccer Championships, Mexico City.

Mercury, Map of Africa and Europe AP43

Ludwig van Beethoven AP44

Europafrica Issue, 1970

1970, July 20 Photo. *Perf. 12x13*

C127 AP43 40fr multi 50 30
C128 AP43 70fr multi 85 40

1970, Sept. 21 Litho. *Perf. 14x13½*

C129 AP44 90fr brt bl & vio blk 1.25 50
C130 AP44 110fr yel grn & dk brn 1.35 70

Issued to commemorate the bicentenary of the birth of Ludwig van Beethoven (1770–1827), composer.

Symbols of Learning AP45

1970, Nov. 6 Photo. *Perf. 12½*

C131 AP45 100fr multi 1.25 50

Issued to commemorate the laying of the foundation stone for the University at Calavi.

Annunciation, Rhenish School, c.1340 AP46

Paintings of Rhenish School, circa 1340: 70fr, Nativity. 110fr, Adoration of the Kings. 200fr, Presentation at the Temple.

1970, Nov. 9 *Perf. 12½x12*

C132 AP46 40fr gold & multi 50 25
C133 AP46 70fr gold & multi 90 35
C134 AP46 110fr gold & multi 1.35 60
C135 AP46 200fr gold & multi 2.75 1.10

Christmas 1970.

Charles de Gaulle, Arc de Triomphe and Flag AP47

Design: 500fr, de Gaulle as old man and Notre Dame Cathedral, Paris.

1971, March 15 Photo. *Perf. 12½*

C136 AP47 40fr multi 60 30
C137 AP47 500fr multi 6.00 3.00

In memory of Gen. Charles de Gaulle (1890–1970), President of France.

L' Indifférent, by Watteau AP48

Painting: No. C139, Woman playing stringed instrument, by Watteau.

1971, May 3 Photo. *Perf. 13*

C138 AP48 100fr red brn & multi 1.20 80
C139 AP48 100fr red brn & multi 1.20 80

250th death anniversary of Jean Antoine Watteau (1684–1721), French painter.

1971, May 29 Photo. *Perf. 13*

Dürer Paintings: 100fr, Self-portrait, 1498. 200fr, Self-portrait, 1500.

C140 AP48 100fr bl grn & multi 1.20 80
C141 AP48 200fr dk grn & multi 2.75 1.60

500th anniversary of the birth of Albrecht Dürer (1471–1528), German painter and engraver. See Nos. C151–C152, C174–C175.

Johannes Kepler and Diagram AP49

Designs: 200fr, Kepler, trajectories, satellite and rocket.

1971, July 12 Engraved *Perf. 13*

C142 AP49 40fr brt rose lil, blk & vio bl 50 25
C143 AP49 200fr red, blk & dk bl 2.75 1.20

400th anniversary of the birth of Johannes Kepler (1571–1630), German astronomer.

Europafrica Issue

Jet Plane, Maps of Europe and Africa—AP50

Designs: 100fr, Ocean liner, maps of Europe and Africa.

1971, July 19 Photo. *Perf. 12½x12*

C144 AP50 50fr blk, lt bl & org 60 30
C145 AP50 100fr multi 1.20 60

African Postal Union Issue, 1971
Common Design Type

Design: 100fr, Dahomey coat of arms and UAMPT building, Brazzaville, Congo.

1971, Nov. 13 *Perf. 13x13½*

C146 CD135 100fr bl & multi 1.20 60

Flight into Egypt, by Van Dyke AP51

Paintings: 40fr, Adoration of the Shepherds, by the Master of the Hausbuch, c. 1500 (vert.). 70fr, Adoration of the Kings, by Holbein the Elder (vert.). 200fr, The Birth of Christ, by Dürer.

1971, Nov. 22 *Perf. 13*

C147 AP51 40fr gold & multi 50 25
C148 AP51 70fr gold & multi 90 45

C149	AP51	100fr gold & multi	1.20	50
C150	AP51	200fr gold & multi	2.40	1.20

Christmas 1971.

Painting Type of 1971 Inscribed: "25e ANNIVERSAIRE DE L'UNICEF"

Paintings: 40fr, Prince Balthazar, by Velasquez. 100fr, Infanta Margarita Maria, by Velázquez.

1971, Dec. 11

C151	AP48	40fr gold & multi	50	30
C152	AP48	100fr gold & multi	1.20	50

25th anniversary of the United Nations International Children's Fund (UNICEF).

Olympic Games Type of Regular Issue

Design: 150fr, Sapporo '72 emblem, ski jump and stork flying.

1972, Feb. Engraved *Perf. 13*

C153	A61	150fr brn, dp rose lil & bl	2.00	1.00

11th Winter Olympic Games, Sapporo, Japan, Feb. 3–13.

Boy Scout and Scout Flag
AP52

Designs: 40fr, Scout playing marimba. 100fr, Scouts doing farm work.

1972, Mar. 19 Photo. *Perf. 13*

Size: 26x35mm.

C154	AP52	35fr multi	30	20
C155	AP52	40fr multi	50	25

Size: 26x46mm.

C156	AP52	100fr yel & multi	1.20	60
a.		Souvenir sheet of 3	2.25	2.25

World Boy Scout Seminar, Cotonou, March 1972. No. C156a contains Nos. C154–C156 with perf. 12½. Red marginal inscription and black control number. Size: 150x115mm.

Workers Training Institute and Friedrich Naumann—AP53

Design: 250fr, Workers Training Institute and Pres. Theodor Heuss of Germany.

1972, Mar. 29 Photo. *Perf. 13x12*

C157	AP53	100fr brt rose, blk & vio	1.10	55
C158	AP53	250fr bl, blk & vio	3.00	1.25

Laying of foundation stone for National Workers Training Institute.

Mosaic Floor, St. Mark's, Venice—AP54

12th Century Mosaics from St. Mark's Basilica: 40fr, Roosters carrying fox on a pole. 65fr, Noah sending out dove.

1972, Apr. 10 *Perf. 13*

C159	AP54	35fr gold & multi	50	30
C160	AP54	40fr gold & multi	60	40
C161	AP54	65fr gold & multi	90	60

UNESCO campaign to save Venice.

Neapolitan and Dahoman Dancers
AP55

1972, May 3 *Perf. 13½x13*

C162	AP55	100fr multi	1.20	70

12th Philatelic Exhibition, Naples.

Running, German Eagle, Olympic Rings
AP56

Designs (Olympic Rings and): 85fr, High jump and Glyptothek, Munich. 150fr, Shot put and Propylaeum, Munich.

1972, June 12 Engraved *Perf. 13*

C163	AP56	20fr ultra, grn & brn	25	15
C164	AP56	85fr brn, grn & ultra	90	40
C165	AP56	150fr grn, brn & ultra	1.75	90
a.		Miniature sheet of 3	3.50	3.50

20th Olympic Games, Munich, Aug. 26–Sept. 10. No. C165a contains one each of Nos. C163–C165. Size: 130x99mm.

Louis Blériot and his Plane—AP57

1972, June 26

C166	AP57	100fr vio, cl & brt bl	1.20	65

Birth centenary of Louis Blériot (1872–1936), French aviation pioneer.

Adam, by Lucas Cranach
AP58

Design: 200fr, Eve, by Lucas Cranach.

1972, Oct. 24 Photogravure

C167	AP58	150fr multi	2.00	1.00
C168	AP58	200fr multi	2.50	1.10

500th anniversary of the birth of Lucas Cranach (1472–1553), German painter.

Pauline Borghese, by Canova
AP59

1972, Nov. 8

C169	AP59	250fr multi	3.00	1.50

Sesquicentennial of the death of Antonio Canova (1757–1822), Italian sculptor.

Nos. C163–C165 Overprinted:

a. 5.00m.–10.00m. / VIREN / 2 MEDAILLES D'OR
b. HAUTEUR DAMES / MEYFARTH / MEDAILLE D'OR
c. POIDS / KOMAR / MEDAILLE D'OR

1972, Nov. 13 Engraved *Perf. 13*

C170	AP56 (a)	20fr multi	30	20
C171	AP56 (b)	85fr multi	1.00	50
C172	AP56 (c)	150fr multi	2.00	1.10
a.		Miniature sheet of 3	3.75	3.75

Gold medal winners in 20th Olympic Games: Lasse Viren, Finland, 5,000m. and 10,000m. races (20fr); Ulrike Meyfarth, Germany, women's high jump (85fr); Wladyslaw Komar, Poland, shot put (150fr).

Louis Pasteur
AP60

1972, Nov. 30

C173	AP60	100fr brt grn, lil & brn	1.20	65

Sesquicentennial of the birth of Louis Pasteur (1822–1895), chemist and bacteriologist.

Painting Type of 1971

Paintings by Georges de La Tour: 35fr, Vielle player. 150fr, The Newborn (horiz.).

1972, Dec. 11 Photogravure

C174	AP48	35fr multi	42	20
C175	AP48	150fr multi	2.00	1.10

320th death anniversary of Georges de La Tour (1593–1652), French painter.

Annunciation, School of Agnolo Gaddi
AP61

Paintings: 125fr, Nativity, by Simone dei Crocifissi. 140fr, Adoration of the Shepherds, by Giovanni di Pietro. 250fr, Adoration of the Kings, by Giotto.

1972, Dec. 15

C176	AP61	35fr gold & multi	40	20
C177	AP61	125fr gold & multi	1.20	60
C178	AP61	140fr gold & multi	1.60	80
C179	AP61	250fr gold & multi	2.60	1.50

Christmas 1972. See Nos. C195–C198, C218, C223, C225–C226.

Statue of St. Teresa, Basilica of Lisieux—AP62

Design: 100fr, St. Teresa, roses, and globe (vert.).

1973, May 14 Photo. *Perf. 13*

C180	AP62	40fr blk, gold & lt ultra	40	25
C181	AP62	100fr gold & multi	1.00	55

Centenary of the birth of St. Teresa of Lisieux (Therese Martin, 1873–97), Carmelite nun.

Scouts, African Scout Emblem—AP63

Designs (African Scout Emblem and): 20fr, Lord Baden-Powell (vert.). 40fr, Scouts building bridge.

1973, July 2 Engraved *Perf. 13*

C182	AP63	15fr bl, grn & choc	15	10
C183	AP63	20fr ol & Prus bl	20	15
C184	AP63	40fr grn, Prus bl & brn	40	20
a.		Souvenir sheet of 3	85	85

24th Boy Scout World Conference, Nairobi, Kenya, July 16–21. No. C184a contains 3 stamps similar to Nos. C182–C184 in changed colors (15fr in ultramarine, slate green and chocolate; 20fr in chocolate, ultramarine and indigo; 40fr in slate green, indigo and chocolate). Ultramarine marginal inscription and border. Size: 180x100 mm.

Copernicus, Venera and Mariner Satellites—AP64

Design: 125fr, Copernicus, sun, earth and moon (vert.).

1973, Aug. 20 Engr. *Perf. 13*

C185	AP64	65fr blk, dk brn & org	80	45
C186	AP64	125fr bl, sl grn & pur	1.25	65

500th anniversary of the birth of Nicolaus Copernicus (1473–1543), Polish astronomer.

Head and City Hall, Brussels
AP64a

1973, Sept. 17 Engraved *Perf. 13*

C187	AP64a	100fr blk, Prus bl & dk grn	90	60

African Weeks, Brussels, Sept. 15–30, 1973.

WMO Emblem, World Weather Map—AP65

1973, Sept. 25

C188	AP65	100fr ol grn & lt brn	1.00	60

Centenary of international meteorological cooperation.

Europafrica Issue

"EUROPAFRIQUE"—AP66

Design: 40fr, similar to 35fr.

1973, Oct. 1 Engraved *Perf. 13*

C189	AP66	35fr multi	35	20
C190	AP66	40fr bl, sep & ultra	40	30

John F. Kennedy AP67

1973, Oct. 18

C191	AP67	200fr bl grn, vio & sl grn	2.00	1.20
a.		Souvenir sheet	2.50	2.50

10th anniversary of the death of President John F. Kennedy (1917–1963). No. C191a contains one stamp in changed colors (bright blue, magenta & brown). Magenta marginal inscription and border. Size: 140x109mm.

Soccer—AP68

Designs: 40fr, Two soccer players. 100fr, Three soccer players.

1973, Nov. 19 Engr. *Perf. 13*

C192	AP68	35fr multi	30	20
C193	AP68	40fr multi	40	25
C194	AP68	100fr multi	90	65

World Soccer Cup, Munich 1974.

Painting Type of 1972

Designs: 35fr, Annunciation, by Dirk Bouts. 100fr, Nativity, by Giotto. 150fr, Adoration of the Kings, by Botticelli. 200fr, Adoration of the Shepherds, by Jacopo Bassano (horiz.).

1973, Dec. 20 Photo. *Perf. 13*

C195	AP61	35fr gold & multi	35	25
C196	AP61	100fr gold & multi	1.00	60
C197	AP61	150fr gold & multi	1.50	1.00
C198	AP61	200fr gold & multi	2.00	1.30

Christmas 1973.

No. C188 Surcharged in Violet with New Value and: "OPERATION SKYLAB / 1973–1974"

1974, Feb. 4 Engraved *Perf. 13*

C199	AP65	200fr on 100fr multi	1.75	1.25

Skylab U.S. space missions, 1973–74.

Skiers, Snowflake, Olympic Rings AP69

1974, Feb. 25 Engraved *Perf. 13*

C200	AP69	100fr vio bl, brn & brt bl	90	65

50th anniversary of first Winter Olympic Games, Chamonix, France.

REPUBLIQUE DU DAHOMEY 125F POSTE AERIENNE 1974 MARIE CURIE 1867-1934

Marie Curie AP70

Designs: 50fr, Lenin. 150fr, Churchill.

1974, June 7 Engr. *Perf. 13*

C201	AP70	50fr dk red & brt lil	45	30
C202	AP70	125fr ol & dl red	1.10	75
C203	AP70	150fr brt lil & Prus bl	1.35	90

50th anniversary of the death of Lenin (50fr); 40th anniversary of the death of Marie Sklodowska Curie (125fr); centenary of the birth of Winston Churchill (150fr).

Bishop, Persian, 18th Century AP71

Frederic Chopin AP72

Design: 200fr, Queen, Siamese chess piece, 19th century.

1974, June 14 Photo. *Perf. 12½x13*

C204	AP71	50fr org & multi	50	35
C205	AP71	200fr brt grn & multi	1.75	1.25

21st Chess Olympiad, Nice, June 6–30, 1974.

1974, June 24 Engr. *Perf. 13*

Design: No. C207, Ludwig van Beethoven.

C206	AP72	150fr blk & cop red	1.25	90
C207	AP72	150fr blk & cop red	1.25	90

Famous musicians, Frederic Chopin (1810–1849) and Ludwig van Beethoven (1770–1827).

Astronaut on Moon, and Earth AP73

1974, July 10 Engraved *Perf. 13*

C208	AP73	150fr multi	1.25	1.00

5th anniversary of the first moon walk.

Nos. C182–C183 Surcharged and Overprinted in Black or Red: "XIe JAMBOREE PANARABE DE BATROUN-LIBAN"

1974, July 19

C209	AP63	100fr on 15fr multi	75	45
C210	AP63	140fr on 20fr multi (R)	1.20	75

11th Pan-Arab Jamboree, Batrun, Lebanon, Aug. 1974. Overprint includes 2 bars over old denomination; 2-line overprint on No. C209, 3 lines on No. C210.

Nos. C193–C194 Overprinted and Surcharged with New Value and Two Bars: "R F A 2 / HOLLANDE 1"

1974, July 26 Engraved *Perf. 13*

C211	AP68	100fr on 40fr	80	35
C212	AP68	150fr on 100fr	1.20	55

World Cup Soccer Championship, 1974, victory of German Federal Republic.

Earth and UPU Emblem—AP74

Designs (UPU Emblem and): 65fr, Concorde in flight. 125fr, French railroad car, c. 1860. 200fr, African drummer and Renault mail truck, pre-1939.

1974, Aug. 5 Engraved *Perf. 13*

C213	AP74	35fr rose cl & vio	30	10
C214	AP74	65fr Prus grn & cl	60	20
C215	AP74	125fr multi	1.10	42
C216	AP74	200fr multi	1.75	70

Centenary of Universal Postal Union.

Painting Type of 1972 and

Lion of Belfort by Frederic A. Bartholdi—AP75

Painting: 250fr, Girl with Falcon, by Philippe de Champaigne.

1974, Aug. 20 Engraved *Perf. 13*

C217	AP75	100fr rose brn	1.00	35
C218	AP61	250fr multi	2.50	1.00

Rhamphorhynchus—AP76

Prehistoric Animals: 150fr, Stegosaurus. 200fr, Tyrannosaurus.

1974, Sept. 23 Photogravure

C219	AP76	35fr multi	30	12
C220	AP76	150fr multi	1.20	55
C221	AP76	200fr multi	1.50	70

Europafrica Issue

Globe, Cogwheel, Emblem—AP77

1974, Dec. 20 Typo. *Perf. 13*

C222	AP77	250fr red & multi	2.50	1.00

Printed tête bêche in sheets of 10.

Christmas Type of 1972 and

Nativity, by Martin Schongauer AP78

Paintings: 35fr, Annunciation, by Schongauer. 100fr, Virgin in Rose Arbor, by Schongauer. 250fr, Virgin and Child, with St. John the Baptist, by Botticelli.

1974, Dec. 23 Photo. *Perf. 13*

C223	AP61	35fr gold & multi	30	15
C224	AP78	40fr gold & multi	40	25
C225	AP61	100fr gold & multi	1.00	35
C226	AP61	250fr gold & multi	2.50	1.00

Apollo and Soyuz Spacecraft AP79

Designs: 200fr, American and Russian flags, rocket take-off. 500fr, Apollo-Soyuz link-up.

1975, July 16 Litho. *Perf. 12½*

C227	AP79	35fr multi	30	15
C228	AP79	200fr vio bl, red & bl	1.60	70
C229	AP79	500fr vio bl, ind & red	4.00	2.25

Apollo Soyuz space test project (Russo-American cooperation); launching July 15; link-up, July 17.

Nos. C227–C228 Surcharged in Silver or Black:
"RENCONTRE / APOLLO-SOYOUZ / 17 Juil. 1975"

1975, July 17 Litho. *Perf. 12½*

C230	AP79	100fr on 35fr (S)	80	35
C231	AP79	300fr on 200fr	2.40	1.00

Apollo-Soyuz link-up in space, July 17, 1975.

ARPHILA Emblem, "Stamps" and Head of Ceres—AP80

1975, Aug. 22 Engr. *Perf. 13*

C232	AP80	100fr blk, bl & lil	90	35

ARPHILA 75, International Philatelic Exhibition, Paris, June 6–16.

Holy Family, by Michelangelo AP81 — Infantry and Stars AP82

Europafrica Issue

1975, Sept. 29 Litho. *Perf. 12*

C233	AP81	300fr gold & multi	2.75	1.00

1975, Nov. 18 Engr. *Perf. 13*

Designs (Stars and): 135fr, Drummers and fifer. 300fr, Artillery with cannon. 500fr, Cavalry.

C234	AP82	75fr grn car & pur	60	25
C235	AP82	135fr bl, mag & sep	1.10	45
C236	AP82	300fr vio bl, ver & choc	2.40	1.00
C237	AP82	500fr ver, dk grn & brn	4.00	1.75

American bicentennial.

Diving and Olympic Rings AP83

Design: 250fr, Soccer and Olympic rings.

1975, Nov. 24

C238	AP83	40fr vio, grnsh bl & ol brn	35	15
C239	AP83	250fr red, emer & brn	2.00	90

Pre-Olympic Year 1975.

AIR POST SEMI-POSTAL STAMPS.

V1

V2

V3

V4

Stamps of the preceding designs were issued in 1942 by the Vichy Government, but were not placed in use in the colony.

AIR POST PARCEL POST STAMPS

Nos. C20–C23, C14 Surcharged in Black or Red

■ 300F

COLIS POSTAUX

1967–69 Engraved *Perf. 13*

CQ1	AP6	200fr on 200fr multi	4.00	3.00
CQ2	AP6	300fr on 100fr multi	4.75	4.00
CQ3	AP6	500fr on 300fr multi	9.00	6.25
CQ4	AP6	1000fr on 500fr multi	18.00	15.00
CQ5	AP4	5000fr on 100fr multi (R) ('69)	80.00	80.00
		Nos. CQ1-CQ5 (5)	115.75	108.25

On No. CQ5, "Colis Postaux" is at top, bar at right.

POSTAGE DUE STAMPS.

Dahomey Natives D1 — Numeral of Value D2

Typographed.

1906 *Perf. 14x13½.* Unwmkd.

J1	D1	5c grn, *grnsh*	1.75	1.75
J2	D1	10c red brn	3.00	3.00
J3	D1	15c dk bl	5.75	5.75
J4	D1	20c *yellow*	4.00	4.00
J5	D1	30c red, *straw*	4.75	4.75
J6	D1	50c violet	17.00	17.00
J7	D1	60c *buff*	10.50	10.50
J8	D1	1fr *pinkish*	27.50	27.50
		Nos. J1-J8 (8)	74.25	74.25

1914

J9	D2	5c green	6	6
J10	D2	10c rose	15	15
J11	D2	15c gray	40	40
J12	D2	20c brown	60	60
J13	D2	30c blue	60	60
J14	D2	50c black	95	95
J15	D2	60c orange	1.40	1.40
J16	D2	1fr violet	1.40	1.40
		Nos. J9-J16 (8)	5.56	5.56

1927

Type of 1914 Issue Surcharged **2F.**

J17	D2	2fr on 1fr lil rose	3.50	3.50
J18	D2	3fr on 1fr org brn	3.00	3.00

Carved Mask D3

1941 Engraved *Perf. 14x13*

J19	D3	5c black	6	6
J20	D3	10c lil rose	6	6
J21	D3	15c dk bl	6	6
J22	D3	20c brt yel grn	18	18
J23	D3	30c orange	30	30
J24	D3	50c vio brn	60	60
J25	D3	60c sl grn	80	80
J26	D3	1fr rose red	1.00	1.00
J27	D3	2fr yellow	1.00	1.00
J28	D3	3fr dk pur	1.40	1.40
		Nos. J19-J28 (10)	5.46	5.46

Stamps of type D3 with value numerals replacing "RF" at upper left corner were issued in 1943-44 by the Vichy Government, but were not placed on sale in the colony.

Republic

Panther and Man—D4

Perf. 14x13½

1963, July 22 Typo. Unwmkd.

J29	D4	1fr grn & rose cl	5	5
J30	D4	2fr brn & emer	15	15
J31	D4	5fr org & vio bl	25	25
J32	D4	10fr mag & blk	60	60
J33	D4	20fr vio bl & org	95	95
		Nos. J29-J33 (5)	2.00	2.00

Mail Boat—D5

Designs: No. J35, Heliograph. No. J36, Morse receiver. No. J37, Mailman on bicycle. No. J38, Early telephone. No. J39, Autorail. No. J40, Mail truck. No. J41, Radio tower. No. J42, DC-8F jet plane. No. J43, Early Bird communications satellite.

1967, Oct. 24 Engraved *Perf. 11*

J34	D5	1fr brn, dl pur & bl	8	8
J35	D5	1fr dl pur, brn & bl	8	8
J36	D5	3fr dk brn, dk grn & org	12	12
J37	D5	3fr dk grn, dk brn & org	12	12
J38	D5	5fr ol bis, lil & bl	30	30
J39	D5	5fr lil, ol bis & bl	30	30
J40	D5	10fr brn org, vio & grn	50	50
J41	D5	10fr vio, brn org & grn	50	50
J42	D5	30fr Prus bl, mar & vio	80	80
J43	D5	30fr vio, Prus bl & mar	80	80
		Nos. J34-J43 (10)	3.60	3.60

The two designs of each value in Nos. J34–J43 were printed tête bêche, se-tenant at the base.

PARCEL POST STAMPS

COLIS POSTAUX

Nos. 141–146 and 148 Surcharged

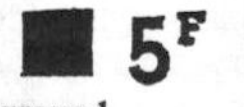

Engraved

1967, Jan. *Perf. 13* Unwmkd.

Q1	A15	5fr on 1fr multi	15	15
Q2	A15	10fr on 2fr multi	30	30
Q3	A15	20fr on 6fr multi	40	40
Q4	A15	25fr on 3fr multi	55	55
Q5	A15	30fr on 4fr multi	65	65
Q6	A15	50fr on 10fr multi	1.00	1.00
	a.	"20" instead of "50"	80.00	
Q7	A15	100fr on 20fr multi	2.00	2.00
		Nos. Q1-Q7 (7)	5.05	5.05

The surcharge is arranged to fit the shape of the stamp.

No. Q6a occurred once on the sheet of the 50fr on 10fr.

DALMATIA

(dăl·mā'shĭ·*ȧ*; -sh*ȧ*)

LOCATION—A promontory in the northwestern part of the Balkan Peninsula, together with several small islands in the Adriatic Sea.

GOVT.—Part of the former Austro-Hungarian crownland of the same name.

AREA—113 sq. mi.

POP.—18,719 (1921).

CAPITAL—Zara.

Stamps were issued during Italian occupation. This territory was subsequently annexed by Italy.

100 Centesimi = 1 Corona = 1 Lira

Issued under Italian Occupation.

Italy No. 87 Surcharged — una corona

Wmkd. Crown. (140)

1919, May 1 — *Perf. 14*

1	A46	1cor on 1 l brn & grn	60	*2.50*

Italian Stamps of 1906-08 Surcharged — 5 centesimi di corona — *a*

1921–22

2	A48	5c on 5c grn	30	*75*
3	A48	10c on 10c cl	30	*75*
4	A49	25c on 25c bl ('22)	50	*1.25*
5	A49	50c on 50c vio ('22)	75	*2.00*

Italian Stamps of 1901-10 Surcharged — 1 corona — *b*

6	A46	1cor on 1 l brn & grn ('22)	1.00	*2.50*
7	A46	5cor on 5 l bl & rose ('22)	4.50	*14.00*
8	A51	10cor on 10 l gray grn & red ('22)	7.00	*20.00*
		Nos. 1-8 (8)	14.95	*43.75*

Surcharges similar to these but differing in style or arrangement of type were used in Austria under Italian occupation.

SPECIAL DELIVERY STAMPS.

Italian Special Delivery Stamp No. E1 Surcharged — 25 centesimi di corona

Wmkd. Crowns. (140)

1921 — *Perf. 14*

E1	SD1	25c on 25c rose red	40	*1.50*
a.		Double surcharge	40.00	

Italian Special Delivery Stamp Surcharged — LIRE 1,20 DI CORONA

1922

E2	SD2	1.20 l on 1.20 l bl & rose	30.00	

No. E2 was not placed in use.

POSTAGE DUE STAMPS.

Italian Postage Due Stamps Surcharged types "a" or "b"

Wmkd. Crown. (140)

1922 — *Perf. 14.*

J1	D3 (a)	50c on 50c buff & mag	1.00	*2.50*
J2	D3 (b)	1cor on 1 l bl & red	1.25	*4.00*
J3	D3 (b)	2cor on 2 l bl & red	4.75	*14.00*
J4	D3 (b)	5cor on 5 l bl & red	7.00	*20.00*

DANISH WEST INDIES

LOCATION—A group of islands in the West Indies, lying east of Puerto Rico.

GOVT.—A former Danish colony.

AREA—132 sq. mi.

POP.—27,086 (1911).

CAPITAL—Charlotte Amalie.

The United States bought these islands in 1917 and they became the U. S. Virgin Islands, using U. S. stamps and currency.

100 Cents = 1 Dollar
100 Bits = 1 Franc (1905)

Coat of Arms
A1

Wmk. 111

Yellowish Paper.
Yellow Wavy-line Burelage, UL to LR
Wmkd. Small Crown (111)

1856 — **Typographed** — *Imperf.*

1	A1	3c dk car, brn gum	200.00	200.00
a.		3c dk car, yel gum	250.00	250.00
b.		3c dk car, white gum	2,000.	

White Paper
Yellow Wavy-line Burelage, UR to LL

1866

2	A1	3c rose	75.00	70.00

1872 — *Perf. 12½*

3	A1	3c rose	150.00	170.00

1873 — **Without Burelage.**

4	A1	4c dl bl	275.00	350.00
a.		Imperf., (pair)	950.00	1,200.
b.		Horiz. pair, imperf. vert.	750.00	900.00

No. 2 reprints, unwatermarked: 1930, carmine, price $120. 1942, rose carmine, back-printed across each row ("Nytryk 1942 G.A. Hagemann Danmark og Dansk Vestindiens Frimaerker Bind 2"), price $60. 1981, carmine, back-printed across two stamps ("Reprint by Dansk Post og Telegrafmuseum 1978"), price, pair, $7.

No. 4 reprints, unwatermarked, imperf.: 1930, ultramarine, price $120. 1942, blue, back-printed like 1942 reprint of No. 2, price $60.

Numeral of Value
A2

NORMAL FRAME — INVERTED FRAME

The arabesques in the corners have a main stem and a branch. When the frame is in normal position, in the upper left corner the branch leaves the main stem half way between two little leaflets. In the lower right corner the branch starts at the foot of the second leaflet. When the frame is inverted the corner designs are, of course, transposed.

Wmk. 112

White Wove Paper, Varying from Thin to Thick.
Perf. 14x13½

1874-79 — **Wmkd. Crown. (112)**

5	A2	1c grn & brn red	25.00	22.50
a.		1c grn & rose lil	37.50	30.00
b.		1c grn & red vio	37.50	30.00
c.		1c grn & vio	80.00	80.00
e.		Inverted frame	25.00	22.50
6	A2	3c bl & car	27.50	17.00
d.		Imperf., pair	600.00	
e.		Inverted frame	27.50	16.00
7	A2	4c brn & dl bl	20.00	20.00
b.		4c brn & ultra	225.00	160.00
c.		Diagonal half used as 2c on cover		225.00
d.		Inverted frame	750.00	550.00
8	A2	5c grn & gray ('76)	32.50	20.00
b.		Inverted frame	32.50	20.00
9	A2	7c lil & org	30.00	70.00
a.		7c lil & yel	70.00	80.00
b.		Inverted frame	60.00	90.00
10	A2	10c bl & brn ('76)	32.50	20.00
b.		Period between "t" & "s" of "cents"	45.00	32.50
c.		Inverted frame	30.00	20.00
11	A2	12c red lil & yel grn ('77)	35.00	42.50
a.		12c lil & dp grn	80.00	65.00
12	A2	14c lil & grn	700.00	825.00
a.		Inverted frame	1,800.	2,250.
13	A2	50c vio ('79)	120.00	140.00
a.		50c gray vio	150.00	170.00

Nos. 9 and 13 Surcharged in Black

I CENT — *a*

10 CENTS 1895 — *b*

1887–95

14	A2 (a)	1c on 7c lil & org	75.00	100.00
a.		1c on 7c lil & yel	120.00	140.00
b.		Double surcharge	250.00	300.00
c.		Inverted frame	110.00	120.00
15	A2 (b)	10c on 50c vio ('95)	30.00	40.00

Type of 1873

1896–1901 — *Perf. 13*

16	A2	1c grn & red vio ('98)	13.00	13.00
a.		Normal frame	300.00	300.00

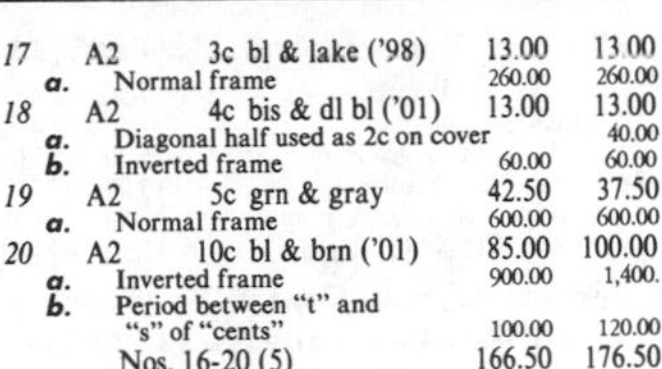

17	A2	3c bl & lake ('98)	13.00	13.00
a.		Normal frame	260.00	260.00
18	A2	4c bis & dl bl ('01)	13.00	13.00
a.		Diagonal half used as 2c on cover		40.00
b.		Inverted frame	60.00	60.00
19	A2	5c grn & gray	42.50	37.50
a.		Normal frame	600.00	600.00
20	A2	10c bl & brn ('01)	85.00	100.00
a.		Inverted frame	900.00	1,400.
b.		Period between "t" and "s" of "cents"	100.00	120.00
		Nos. 16-20 (5)	166.50	176.50

Arms
A5

1900

21	A5	1c lt grn	2.50	2.50
22	A5	5c lt bl	15.00	15.00

See also Nos. 29–30.

Nos. 6, 17, 20 Surcharged:

2 CENTS 1902 — *c*

8 Cents 1902 — *d*

Surcharge "c" in Black

1902 — *Perf. 14x13½*

23	A2	2c on 3c bl & car	500.00	550.00
a.		"2" in date with straight tail	525.00	575.00
b.		Normal frame	1,250.	

Perf. 13

24	A2	2c on 3c bl & lake	10.00	12.00
a.		"2" in date with straight tail	11.00	13.00
b.		Dated "1901"	400.00	450.00
c.		Normal frame	225.00	275.00
d.		Dark grn surch.	1,400.	
e.		As "d" & "a"	1,500.	
f.		As "d" & "c"		
25	A2	8c on 10c bl & brn	25.00	35.00
a.		"2" with straight tail	27.50	37.50
b.		On No. 20b	35.00	45.00
c.		Inverted frame	325.00	350.00

Surcharge "d" in Black

27	A2	2c on 3c bl & lake	12.50	17.50
a.		Normal frame	275.00	300.00
28	A2	8c on 10c bl & brn	11.00	11.00
a.		On No. 20b	18.00	18.00
b.		Inverted frame	275.00	275.00

Wmk. 113

1903 — **Wmkd. Crown (113)**

29	A5	2c carmine	13.00	13.00
30	A5	8c brown	27.50	32.50

King Christian IX
A8

St. Thomas Harbor
A9

1905		Typographed	*Perf. 13*	
31	A8	5b green	7.50	4.00
32	A8	10b red	7.50	4.00
33	A8	20b grn & bl	15.00	15.00
34	A8	25b ultra	15.00	15.00
35	A8	40b red & gray	12.50	12.50
36	A8	50b yel & gray	12.50	15.00

Frame Typo., Center Engraved
Wmkd. Two Crowns. (113)
Perf. 12

37	A9	1fr grn & bl	20.00	30.00
38	A9	2fr org red & brn	42.50	60.00
39	A9	5fr yel & brn	110.00	250.00
		Nos. 31-39 (9)	242.50	405.50

Nos. 18, 22, 30 Surcharged in Black

5
BIT
1905

Wmkd. Crown. (112)

1905			*Perf. 13*	
40	A2	5b on 4c bis & dl bl	22.50	45.00
a.		Inverted frame	42.50	60.00
41	A5	5b on 5c lt bl	14.00	27.50

Wmkd. Crown. (113)

42	A5	5b on 8c brn	14.00	27.50

King Frederik VIII
A10

Frame Typo., Center Engraved

1907		*Perf. 13*	Wmk. 113	
43	A10	5b green	2.50	1.30
44	A10	10b red	2.50	1.30
45	A10	15b vio & brn	5.00	5.00
46	A10	20b grn & bl	37.50	20.00
47	A10	25b bl & dk bl	3.25	2.00
48	A10	30b cl & sl	62.50	37.50
49	A10	40b ver & gray	6.50	8.00
50	A10	50b yel & brn	7.00	10.00
		Nos. 43-50 (8)	126.75	85.10

King Christian X
A11

Wmk. 114

Wmkd. Multiple Crosses. (114)

1915			*Perf. 14x14½*	
51	A11	5b yel grn	3.00	*6.00*
52	A11	10b red	3.00	*52.50*
53	A11	15b lil & red brn	3.00	*52.50*
54	A11	20b grn & bl	3.00	*52.50*
55	A11	25b bl & dk bl	3.00	*12.00*
56	A11	30b cl & blk	3.00	*52.50*
57	A11	40b org & blk	3.00	*52.50*
58	A11	50b yel & brn	3.00	*52.50*
		Nos. 51-58 (8)	24.00	*333.00*

Forged and favor cancellations exist.

POSTAGE DUE STAMPS.

Royal Cipher, "Christian 9 Rex"
D1

Lithographed

1902		*Perf. 11½*	Unwmkd.	
J1	D1	1c dk bl	8.00	14.00
J2	D1	4c dk bl	12.50	17.50
J3	D1	6c dk bl	32.50	52.50
J4	D1	10c dk bl	25.00	35.00

There are five types of each value. On the 4c they may be distinguished by differences in the figures "4"; on the other values the differences are minute.

Counterfeits of Nos. J1–J4 exist.

D2

1905–13			*Perf. 13*	
J5	D2	5b red & gray	6.50	8.00
J6	D2	20b red & gray	14.00	20.00
J7	D2	30b red & gray	8.50	13.00
J8	D2	50b red & gray	12.50	18.00
a.		Perf. 14x14½ ('13)	20.00	80.00
b.		Perf. 11½	275.00	

All values of this issue are known imperforate, but were not regularly issued.
Counterfeits of Nos. J5–J8 exist.

Used prices of Nos. J1-J8 are for canceled copies. Uncanceled examples without gum have probably been used. Price 60% of unused.

DANZIG

(dăn[t]'sĭg; dăn'zĭg)

LOCATION—In northern Europe bordering on the Baltic Sea.
GOVT.—Former free city and state.
AREA—754 sq. mi.
POP.—407,000 (approx. 1939).
CAPITAL—Danzig.

Established as a "Free City and State" under the protection of the League of Nations in 1920, Danzig was seized by Germany in 1939. It became a Polish province in 1945.

100 Pfennig = 1 Gulden (1923)
100 Pfennig = 1 Mark

Used Prices of 1920–23
are for favor-canceled stamps unless otherwise noted. Postally used copies bring higher prices.

German Stamps of 1906-20 Overprinted in Black

Danzig

Wmkd. Lozenges. (125)

1920			*Perf. 14, 14½, 15x14½*	
1	A16	5pf green	30	25
2	A16	10pf car rose	30	25
3	A22	15pf vio brn	30	25
4	A16	20pf bl vio	30	25
5	A16	30pf org & blk, *buff*	40	30
6	A16	40pf car rose	35	25
7	A16	50pf pur & blk, *buff*	40	30
8	A17	1m red	90	75
9	A17	1.25m green	90	75
10	A17	1.50m yel brn	1.10	1.25
11	A21	2m blue	1.75	1.75
a.		Double ovpt.	*1,000.*	
12	A21	2.50m lil rose	2.25	3.50
13	A19	3m blk vio	8.00	14.00
14	A16	4m blk & rose	6.00	8.50
15	A20	5m sl & car	2.50	3.00
a.		Center inverted	*6,000.*	
b.		Invtd. ovpt.		*10,000.*
		Nos. 1-15 (15)	25.75	35.35

The 5pf brown, 10pf orange and 40pf lake and black with this overprint were not regularly issued. Price for trio, $450.

"Germania"
A1

German Stamps of 1906-20
Surcharged in Violet, Red, Green or Brown.

1920				
19	A1	5pf on 30pf org & blk, *buff* (V)	18	20
20	A1	10pf on 20pf bl vio (R)	18	15
a.		Double surch.	175.00	250.00
21	A1	25pf on 30pf org & blk, *buff* (G)	18	20
a.		Inverted surcharge	175.00	250.00
22	A1	60pf on 30pf org & blk, *buff* (Br)	70	85
a.		Double surch.	175.00	250.00
23	A1	80pf on 30pf org & blk, *buff* (V)	70	85

A2

A3

A4

A5

A6

A7

Surcharged in Black, Red, Blue or Green

Gray Burelage with Points Up.

25	A2	1m on 30pf org & blk, *buff* (Bk)	75	2.00
a.		Pair, one without surcharge		
26	A3	1¼m on 3pf brn (R)	75	2.00
27	A4	2m on 35pf red brn (Bl)	90	2.00
d.		Surch. omitted	90.00	150.00
28	A5	3m on 7½pf org (G)	90	2.00
29	A6	5m on 2pf gray (R)	90	2.00
30	A7	10m on 7½pf org (Bk)	3.00	10.50

Gray Burelage with Points Down.

26a	A3	1¼m on 3pf brn	30.00	45.00
27a	A4	2m on 35pf red brn	350.00	375.00
28a	A5	3m on 7½pf org	13.00	15.00
29a	A6	5m on 2pf gray	10.00	30.00
30a	A7	10m on 7½pf org	6.00	11.00

Violet Burelage with Points Up.

25b	A2	1m on 30pf org & blk, *buff*	35.00	50.00
26b	A3	1 ¼m on 3pf brn	4.00	7.50
27b	A4	2m on 35pf red brn	15.00	25.00
28b	A5	3m on 7½pf org	1.50	2.50
29b	A6	5m on 2pf gray	1.40	2.25
30b	A7	10m on 7½pf org	1.40	2.25

Violet Burelage with Points Down.

25c	A2	1m on 30pf org & blk, *buff*	1.10	3.50
26c	A3	1¼m on 3pf brn	4.00	15.00
27c	A4	2m on 35pf red brn	15.00	55.00
28c	A5	3m on 7½pf org	40.00	110.00
29c	A6	5m on 2pf gray	4.50	12.00
30c	A7	10m on 7½pf org	15.00	35.00

Excellent counterfeits of the surcharges are known.

German Stamps of 1906-20 Overprinted in Blue

1920				
31	A22	2pf gray	130.00	250.00
32	A22	2½pf gray	200.00	400.00
33	A16	3pf brown	11.00	22.50
a.		Dbl. overprint	100.00	100.00
34	A16	5pf green	35	40
a.		Dbl. overprint	50.00	
35	A22	7½pf orange	40.00	75.00
36	A16	10pf carmine	4.00	7.50
37	A22	15pf dk vio	55	75
b.		Dbl. overprint	50.00	
38	A16	20pf bl vio	55	75

Overprinted in Carmine or Blue.

39	A16	25pf org & blk, *yel*	55	75
40	A16	30pf org & blk, *buff*	62.50	110.00
42	A16	40pf lake & blk	2.00	4.00
a.		Inverted overprint		
b.		Double ovpt.		
43	A16	50pf pur & blk, *buff*	210.00	400.00
44	A16	60pf mag (Bl)	2,250.	*4,000.*
45	A16	75pf grn & blk	55	75
46	A16	80pf lake & blk, *rose*	5.50	5.00
47	A17	1m carmine	1,000.	*1,600.*
a.		Dbl. ovpt.	*5,000.*	

Overprinted in Carmine

48	A21	2m gray bl	1,150.	*1,800.*

Counterfeit overprints of Nos. 31 to 48 exist.

Nos. 44, 47 and 48 were issued in small quantities and usually affixed directly to the mail by the postal clerk.

Hanseatic Trading Ship
A8 A9

Wmk. 108

Serrate Roulette 13½.

Wmkd. Honeycomb. (108)

1921, Jan. 31 Typographed

49	A8	5(pf) brn & vio	40	38
50	A8	10(pf) org & dk vio	40	38
51	A8	25(pf) grn & car rose	75	1.00
52	A8	40(pf) car rose	4.00	5.00
53	A8	80(pf) ultra	50	75
54	A9	1m car rose & blk	2.00	2.50
55	A9	2m dk bl & dk grn	6.25	7.50
56	A9	3m blk & grnsh bl	2.00	3.00
57	A9	5m ind & rose red	2.00	3.00
58	A9	10m dk grn & brn org	3.75	7.50
		Nos. 49-58 (10)	22.05	31.01

Issued in commemoration of the Constitution.

Nos. 49 and 50 with center in red instead of violet and Nos. 49, 50 and 54 with center inverted are probably proofs. All values of this issue exist imperforate but are not known to have been regularly issued in that condition.

1921, Mar. 11 *Perf. 14*

59	A8	25(pf) grn & car rose	90	1.25
60	A8	40(pf) car rose	90	1.50
61	A8	80(pf) ultra	5.50	13.00

No. 45 Surcharged in Black

A10

1921, May 6 **Wmk. 125**

62	A10	60pf on 75pf grn & blk	60	1.25
a.		Double surcharge	90.00	90.00

Arms A11

Coat of Arms A12

Wmkd. Honeycomb. (108)

(Vertical or Horizontal.)

1921-22 *Perf. 14*

63	A11	5(pf) orange	35	30
64	A11	10(pf) dk brn	25	20
65	A11	15(pf) green	25	20
66	A11	20(pf) slate	25	20
67	A11	25(pf) dk grn	25	25
68	A11	30(pf) bl & car	35	35
a.		Center inverted	37.50	
69	A11	40pf grn & car	25	20
a.		Center inverted	37.50	
70	A11	50pf dk grn & car	25	20
71	A11	60pf carmine	40	45
72	A11	80pf blk & car	45	75

Paper With Faint Gray Network.

73	A11	1m org & car	25	50
a.		Center inverted	37.50	
74	A11	1.20m bl vio	1.75	1.50
75	A11	2m gray & car	4.00	5.00
76	A11	3m vio & car	12.00	16.00

Serrate Roulette 13½

77	A12	5m grn, red & blk	1.90	3.00
78	A12	9m rose, red & org ('22)	3.75	9.00
79	A12	10m ultra, red & blk	1.90	3.00
80	A12	20m red & blk	1.90	3.00
		Nos. 63-80 (18)	30.50	44.10

In this and succeeding issues the mark values usually have the face of the paper covered with a gray network. This network is often very faint and occasionally is omitted.

Nos. 64, 66, 69-76 exist imperf. Price, each $20-$40.

See Nos. 81-93, 99-105.

Type of 1921 and

Coat of Arms

A13 A13a

1922 *Perf. 14* **Wmk. 108**

81	A11	75(pf) dp vio	20	25
82	A11	80(pf) green	20	25
83	A11	1.25m vio & car	20	25
84	A11	1.50m sl gray	22	35
85	A11	2m car rose	22	25
86	A11	2.40m dk brn & car	1.10	2.25
87	A11	3m car lake	22	35
88	A11	4m dk bl	1.10	1.75
89	A11	5m dp grn	12	30
90	A11	6m car lake	12	38
a.		6m car rose, wmk. 109 horiz. (error)	2,500.	
91	A11	8m lt bl	35	1.00
92	A11	10m orange	12	35
93	A11	20m org brn	12	35
94	A13	50m gold & car	1.75	4.00
a.		50m gold & red	11.00	17.50
95	A13a	100m metallic grn & red	4.00	6.50
		Nos. 81-95 (15)	10.04	18.58

No. 95 has buff instead of gray network.

Nos. 81-83, 85-86, 88 exist imperf. Price, each $15.

Nos. 94-95 exist imperf. Price, each $50

Nos. 87, 88 and 91 Surcharged in Black or Carmine

l

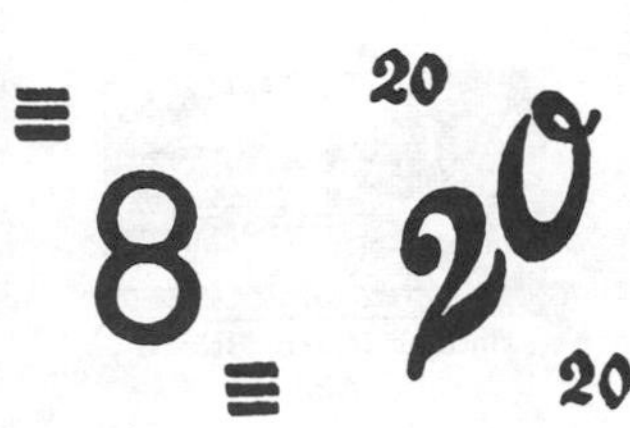

m n

1922

96	A11 (l)	6m on 3m car lake	25	45
a.		Dbl. surch.		
97	A11 (m)	8m on 4m dk bl	25	75
a.		Dbl. surch.	85.00	85.00
98	A11 (n)	20m on 8m lt bl (C)	30	60

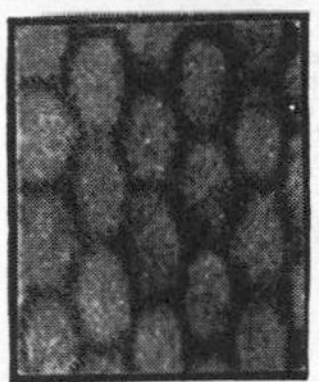

Wmk. 109

Wmkd. Webbing. (109)

(Vertical or Horizontal.)

1922-23 *Perf. 14*

99	A11	4m dk bl	18	38
100	A11	5m dk grn	18	38
102	A11	10m orange	18	38
103	A11	20m org brn	18	38

Paper Without Network.

104	A11	40m pale bl	18	30
105	A11	80m red	18	30
		Nos. 99-105 (6)	1.08	2.12

Nos. 104-105 exist imperf. Price, each $15.

Coat of Arms

A15 A15a

Coat of Arms

A16

1923 *Perf. 14*

Paper With Gray Network.

106	A15	50m pale bl & red	18	38
107	A15a	100m dk grn & red	18	38
108	A15a	150m vio & red	18	38
109	A16	250m vio & red	22	50
110	A16	500m gray blk & red	22	50
111	A16	1000m brn & red	22	50
112	A16	5000m sil & red	1.50	*6.50*

Paper Without Network.

113	A15	50m pale bl	18	30
114	A15a	100m dp grn	18	30
115	A15	200m orange	18	30
		Nos. 106-115 (10)	3.24	*10.04*

Nos. 109-112 exist imperf. Price, each $22.50.

Nos. 113-115 exist imperf. Price, each $17.50.

A17

1923 *Perf. 14*

Paper With Gray Network.

117	A17	250m vio & red	18	35
118	A17	300m bl grn & red	12	40
119	A17	500m gray & red	18	35
120	A17	1000m brn & red	18	35
121	A17	3000m vio & red	18	35
123	A16	10,000m org & red	45	75
124	A16	20,000m pale bl & red	60	1.25
125	A16	50,000m grn & red	45	1.00
		Nos. 117-125 (8)	2.34	4.80

Nos. 117-125 exist imperf. Price, each $17.50.

Surcharged in Red

100 000

1923, Aug. 14

126	A16	100,000m on 20,000m pale bl & red	1.50	*6.00*

1923 *Perf. 14*

Paper Without Network.

127	A17	1000m brown	18	40
129	A17	5000m rose	18	40
131	A17	20,000m pale bl	18	40
132	A17	50,000m green	18	40

Paper With Gray Network.

133	A17	100,000m dp bl	18	40
134	A17	250,000m violet	18	40
135	A17	500,000m slate	18	40
		Nos. 127-135 (7)	1.26	2.80

Nos. 126-135 exist imperf.

Abbreviations.

th=(tausend) thousand

mil=million

Stamps of Preceding Issues Surcharged

100 Tausend

1923 *Perf. 14*

Paper Without Network.

137	A15	40th m on 200m org	90	*2.50*
a.		Double surcharge	87.50	
138	A15	100th m on 200m org	90	*2.50*
139	A15	250th m on 200m org	8.50	*15.00*
140	A15a	400th m on 100m dp grn	50	75
141	A17	500th m on 50,000m grn	50	75
142	A17	1 mil m on 10,000m org	4.00	*9.00*

The surcharges on Nos. 140 to 142 differ in details from those on Nos. 137 to 139.

Type of 1923 Surcharged

10 Millionen

Paper With Gray Network.

143	A16	10 mil m on 1,000,000m org	60	50
		Nos. 137-143 (7)	15.90	*31.00*

Nos. 142-143 exist imperf. Price, each $17.50.

Type of 1923 Surcharged

1 Million

Perf. 14.

Paper Without Network.

144	A17	1 mil m on 10,000m rose	30	50
145	A17	2 mil m on 10,000m rose	30	50
146	A17	3 mil m on 10,000m rose	30	50
147	A17	5 mil m on 10,000m rose	30	50
b.		Dbl. surch.	87.50	
148	A17	10 mil m on 10,000m gray lil	50	75
149	A17	20 mil m on 10,000m gray lil	50	75
150	A17	25 mil m on 10,000m gray lil	40	75
151	A17	40 mil m on 10,000m gray lil	40	75
a.		Double surcharge	75.00	
152	A17	50 mil m on 10,000m gray lil	40	75

Type of 1923 Surcharged in Red

300 Millionen

No.	Type	Description	Unused	Used
153	A17	100 mil m on 10,000m gray lil	40	75
154	A17	300 mil m on 10,000m gray lil	40	75
155	A17	500 mil m on 10,000m gray lil	40	75
		Nos. 144-155 (12)	4.60	8.00

Nos. 144–147 exist imperf. Price, each $15.

Nos. 153–155 exist imperf. Price, each $20.

Types of 1923 Surcharged

10 Pfennige

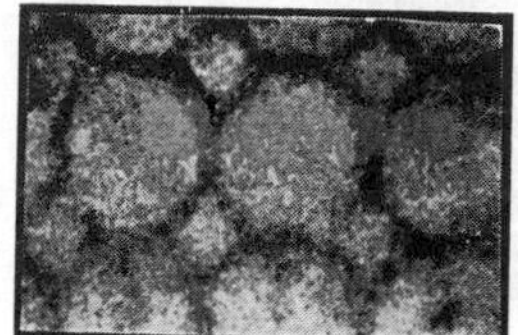

Wmk. 110

Wmkd. Octagons. (110)

1923 ***Perf. 14***

No.	Type	Description	Unused	Used
156	A15	5pf on 50m rose	90	60
157	A15	10pf on 50m rose	90	60
158	A15a	20pf on 100m rose	90	75
159	A15	25pf on 50m rose	8.00	14.00
160	A15	30pf on 50m rose	4.75	3.00
161	A15a	40pf on 100m rose	3.50	3.50
162	A15a	50pf on 100m rose	5.00	4.00
163	A15a	75pf on 100m rose	14.00	22.50

Type of 1923 Surcharged

2 Gulden

No.	Type	Description	Unused	Used
164	A16	1g on 1 mil m rose	8.00	9.00
165	A16	2g on 1 mil m rose	21.00	22.50
166	A16	3g on 1 mil m rose	50.00	85.00
167	A16	5g on 1 mil m rose	50.00	90.00
		Nos. 156-167 (12)	166.95	255.45

Coat of Arms
A19

Wmkd. Webbing. (109)

1924–37 ***Perf. 14***

No.	Type	Description	Unused	Used
168	A19	3(pf) brn, *yelsh* ('36)	1.50	1.10
a.		3(pf) dp brn, *white* ('27)	2.75	1.50
170	A19	5(pf) org, *yelsh* ('36)	4.50	40
a.		White paper	6.50	45
b.		Bklt. pane of 10		
c.		Tête bêche pair	750.00	
d.		Syncopated perf., #170 ('37)	16.00	14.00
e.		Syncopated perf., #170a ('32)	27.50	14.00
171	A19	7(pf) yel grn ('33)	2.00	2.50
172	A19	8(pf) yel grn ('37)	2.75	6.00

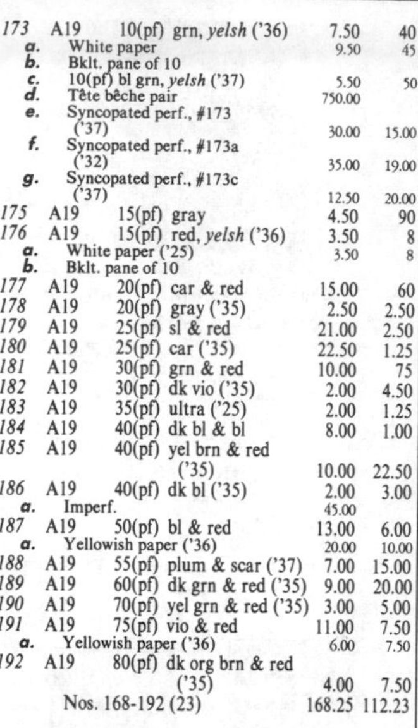

No.	Type	Description	Unused	Used
173	A19	10(pf) grn, *yelsh* ('36)	7.50	40
a.		White paper	9.50	45
b.		Bklt. pane of 10		
c.		10(pf) bl grn, *yelsh* ('37)	5.50	50
d.		Tête bêche pair	750.00	
e.		Syncopated perf., #173 ('37)	30.00	15.00
f.		Syncopated perf., #173a ('32)	35.00	19.00
g.		Syncopated perf., #173c ('37)	12.50	20.00
175	A19	15(pf) gray	4.50	90
176	A19	15(pf) red, *yelsh* ('36)	3.50	8
a.		White paper ('25)	3.50	8
b.		Bklt. pane of 10		
177	A19	20(pf) car & red	15.00	60
178	A19	20(pf) gray ('35)	2.50	2.50
179	A19	25(pf) sl & red	21.00	2.50
180	A19	25(pf) car ('35)	22.50	1.25
181	A19	30(pf) grn & red	10.00	75
182	A19	30(pf) dk vio ('35)	2.00	4.50
183	A19	35(pf) ultra ('25)	2.00	1.25
184	A19	40(pf) dk bl & bl	8.00	1.00
185	A19	40(pf) yel brn & red ('35)	10.00	22.50
186	A19	40(pf) dk bl ('35)	2.00	3.00
a.		Imperf.	45.00	
187	A19	50(pf) bl & red	13.00	6.00
a.		Yellowish paper ('36)	20.00	10.00
188	A19	55(pf) plum & scar ('37)	7.00	15.00
189	A19	60(pf) dk grn & red ('35)	9.00	20.00
190	A19	70(pf) yel grn & red ('35)	3.00	5.00
191	A19	75(pf) vio & red	11.00	7.50
a.		Yellowish paper ('36)	6.00	7.50
192	A19	80(pf) dk org brn & red ('35)	4.00	7.50
		Nos. 168-192 (23)	168.25	112.23

The 5pf and 10pf with syncopated perforations (Netherlands type C) are coils.
See also Nos. 225–232.

Oliva Castle and Cathedral
A20

St. Mary's Church
A23

Council Chamber on the Langenmarkt
A24

Wmk. 125

Designs: 2g, Mottlau River and Krantor. 3g, View of Zoppot.

Wmkd. Lozenges. (125)

1924–32 **Engraved.** ***Perf. 14.***

No.	Type	Description	Unused	Used
193	A20	1g yel grn & blk	40.00	50.00
		Parcel post cancel		25.00
194	A20	1g org & gray blk ('25)	25.00	2.50
a.		1g red org & blk ('32)	25.00	10.00
		Parcel post cancel		2.00
195	A20	2g red vio & blk	82.50	125.00
		Parcel post cancel		72.50
196	A20	2g rose & blk ('25)	3.50	5.00
		Parcel post cancel		3.50
197	A20	3g dk bl & blk	5.00	7.50
		Parcel post cancel		3.75
198	A23	5g brn red & blk	7.50	10.00
		Parcel post cancel		3.75
199	A24	10g dk brn & blk	50.00	90.00
		Parcel post cancel		45.00
		Nos. 193-199 (7)	213.50	290.00

See also No. 233.

Stamps of 1924-25 Overprinted in Black, Violet or Red

1920
15. November
1930

Wmkd. Webbing. (109)

1930, Nov. 15 **Typographed**

No.	Type	Description	Unused	Used
200	A19	5(pf) orange	3.50	3.50
201	A19	10(pf) yel grn (V)	5.50	5.00
202	A19	15(pf) red	8.00	11.00
203	A19	20(pf) car & red	4.00	6.00
204	A19	25(pf) sl & red	7.00	11.00
205	A19	30(pf) grn & red	15.00	27.50
206	A19	35(pf) ultra (R)	65.00	90.00
207	A19	40(pf) dk bl & bl (R)	17.50	32.50
208	A19	50(pf) dp bl & red	65.00	87.50
209	A19	75(pf) vio & red	65.00	87.50

Wmkd. Lozenges. (125)

Engraved.

No.	Type	Description	Unused	Used
210	A20	1g org & blk (R)	65.00	87.50
		Nos. 200-210 (11)	320.50	449.00

10th anniversary of the Free State. Counterfeits exist.

Nos. 171 and 183 Surcharged in Red Blue or Green:

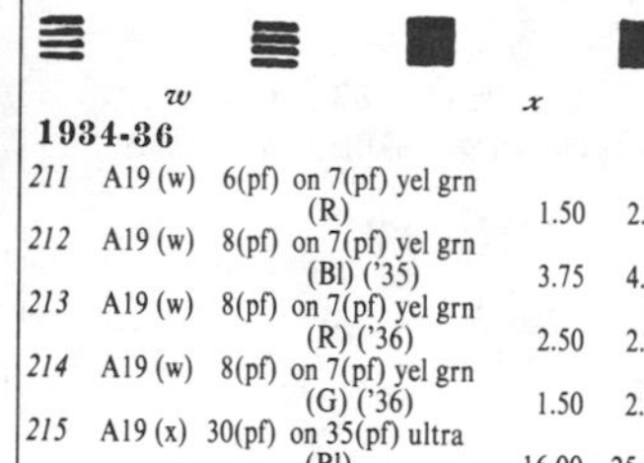

w *x*

1934-36

No.	Type	Description	Unused	Used
211	A19 (w)	6(pf) on 7(pf) yel grn (R)	1.50	2.25
212	A19 (w)	8(pf) on 7(pf) yel grn (Bl) ('35)	3.75	4.25
213	A19 (w)	8(pf) on 7(pf) yel grn (R) ('36)	2.50	2.75
214	A19 (w)	8(pf) on 7(pf) yel grn (G) ('36)	1.50	2.50
215	A19 (x)	30(pf) on 35(pf) ultra (Bl)	16.00	25.00
		Nos. 211-215 (5)	25.25	36.75

Bathing Beach, Brösen
A25

View of Brösen Beach
A26

War Memorial at Brösen
A27

Skyline of Danzig
A28

Wmkd. Webbing. (109)

1936, June 23 **Typo.** ***Perf. 14***

No.	Type	Description	Unused	Used
216	A25	10pf dp grn	75	1.50
217	A26	25pf rose red	1.25	3.00
218	A27	40pf brt bl	2.00	5.00

Village of Brösen, 125th anniversary. Exist imperf. Price of set, $110.

1937, Mar. 27

No.	Type	Description	Unused	Used
219	A28	10(pf) dk bl	90	2.00
220	A28	15(pf) vio brn	1.25	2.75

Air Defense League.

Danzig Philatelic Exhibition Issue.

Souvenir Sheet.

St. Mary's Church
A29

1937, June 6 ***Perf. 14*** **Wmk. 109**

No.	Type	Description	Unused	Used
221	A29	50pf dk grn	1.75	5.00

Issued for the Danzig Philatelic Exhibition, June 6–8, 1937. Sheet measures 149x104mm.

Arthur Schopenhauer
A30 A31

Design: 40(pf), Full-face portrait, white hair.

Perf. 14

1938, Feb. 22 **Photo.** **Unwmkd.**

No.	Type	Description	Unused	Used
222	A30	15(pf) dl bl	1.50	3.50
223	A31	25(pf) sepia	4.00	8.50
224	A31	40(pf) org ver	2.00	5.50

Issued in commemoration of the 150th anniversary of the birth of Schopenhauer.

Wmk. 237

Type of 1924-35.
Wmkd. Swastikas. (237)

1938–39 Typographed *Perf. 14*

225	A19	3(pf) brown	1.00	*7.00*
226	A19	5(pf) orange	1.00	1.75
a.		Booklet pane of 10		
b.		Syncopated perf.	2.00	*7.50*
227	A19	8(pf) yel grn	6.50	*17.00*
228	A19	10(pf) bl grn	1.00	1.25
a.		Booklet pane of 10		
b.		Syncopated perf.	3.00	*9.50*
229	A19	15(pf) scarlet	3.00	*8.00*
a.		Booklet pane of 10		
230	A19	25(pf) carmine	3.00	*8.00*
231	A19	40(pf) dk bl	3.00	*10.00*
232	A19	50(pf) brt bl & red ('39)	3.75	*11.00*

Engraved.

233	A20	1g red org & blk	7.00	*14.00*
		Nos. 225-233 (9)	29.25	78.00

No. 233 measures 32½x21¼mm; No. 194, 31x21mm.

Nos. 226b and 228b are coils with Netherlands type C perforation.

Knights in Tournament, 1500
A33

French Leaving Danzig, 1814
A35

Designs: 10(pf), Signing of Danzig-Sweden neutrality treaty, 1630. 25(pf), Battle of Weichselmünde, 1577.

Photogravure.

1939, Jan. 7 *Perf. 14* Unwmkd.

234	A33	5(pf) dk grn	1.00	*3.00*
235	A33	10(pf) cop brn	1.25	*3.50*
236	A35	15(pf) sl blk	1.50	*4.00*
237	A35	25(pf) brn vio	1.75	*5.00*

Stamp Day.

Scientists Issue.

Gregor Mendel
A37

Designs: 15(pf), Dr. Robert Koch. 25(pf), Wilhelm Roentgen.

1939, Apr. 29 Photo. *Perf. 13x14*

238	A37	10(pf) cop brn	50	1.25
239	A37	15(pf) indigo	75	1.50
240	A37	25(pf) dk ol grn	1.00	2.50

Issued in honor of the achievements of Mendel, Koch and Roentgen.

Issued under German Administration

Stamps of Danzig, 1925-39, Surcharged in Black:

Rpf 4 Deutsches Reich Rpf 4
a

Rpf 4 Deutsches Reich Rpf 4
b

1 Reichsmark

Deutsches Reich
c

Wmkd. Webbing. (109)

1939 *Perf. 14.*

241	A19(b)	4rpf on 35(pf) ultra	1.25	2.25
242	A19(b)	12rpf on 7(pf) yel grn	1.40	2.50
243	A19(a)	20rpf gray	4.00	7.50

Wmkd. Swastikas. (237)

244	A19(a)	3rpf brown	1.25	2.25
245	A19(a)	5rpf orange	1.25	2.25
246	A19(a)	8rpf yel grn	2.00	3.75
247	A19(a)	10rpf bl grn	2.50	4.25
248	A19(a)	15rpf scarlet	6.25	6.00
249	A19(a)	25rpf carmine	6.25	6.00
250	A19(a)	30rpf dk vio	2.25	4.00
251	A19(a)	40rpf dk bl	3.50	6.00
252	A19(a)	50rpf brt bl & red	4.50	8.00
253	A20(c)	1rm on 1g red org & blk	17.50	35.00

Wmkd. Lozenges. (125)

254	A20(c)	2rm on 2g rose & blk	25.00	42.50
		Nos. 241-254 (14)	78.90	132.25

Nos. 241 to 254 were valid throughout Germany.

SEMI-POSTAL STAMPS.

St. George and Dragon
SP1

Wmkd. Honeycomb. (108)

Size: 19x22 mm.

1921, Oct. 16 Typo. *Perf. 14*

B1	SP1	30pf +30pf grn & org	90	75
B2	SP1	60pf +60pf rose & org	2.00	2.00

Size: 25x30 mm.

Serrate Roulette 13½.

B3	SP1	1.20m +1.20m dk bl & org	3.50	3.50

Aged Pensioner
SP2

Wmkd. Webbing. (109)

Paper With Gray Network.

1923, Mar. *Perf. 14*

B4	SP2	50m +20m lake	28	50
B5	SP2	100m +30m red vio	28	50

Philatelic Exhibition Issue.

Neptune Fountain
SP3

Various Frames.

1929, July 7 Engr. Unwmkd.

B6	SP3	10(pf) yel grn & gray	3.75	4.00
B7	SP3	15(pf) car & gray	3.75	4.00
B8	SP3	25(pf) ultra & gray	12.50	10.00
a.		25(pf) vio bl & blk	60.00	120.00

These stamps were sold exclusively at the Danzig Philatelic Exhibition, June 7th to 14th, 1929. They were sold at double their face values, the excess being for the aid of the exhibition.

Regular Issue of 1924-25 Surcharged in Black

5
W. H. W.

1934, Jan. 15 Wmk. 109

B9	A19	5(pf) +5(pf) org	15.00	25.00
B10	A19	10(pf) +5(pf) yel grn	40.00	55.00
B11	A19	15(pf) +5(pf) car	25.00	35.00

Surtax for winter welfare. Counterfeits exist.

Stock Tower
SP4

George Hall
SP6

City Gate, 16th Century
SP5

1935, Dec. 16 Typo. *Perf. 14*

B12	SP4	5(pf) +5pf org	80	2.00
B13	SP5	10(pf) +5pf grn	1.25	3.00
B14	SP6	15(pf) +10pf scar	2.25	5.00

Surtax for winter welfare.

Milk Can Tower
SP7

Frauentor
SP8

Krantor
SP9

Langgarter Gate
SP10

High Gate
SP11

1936, Nov. 25

B15	SP7	10pf +5pf dk bl	2.00	3.00
a.		Imperf.	75.00	
B16	SP8	15pf +5pf dl grn	2.00	4.00
B17	SP9	25pf +10pf red brn	2.50	4.50
B18	SP10	40pf +20pf brn & red brn	4.00	6.00
B19	SP11	50pf +20pf bl & dk bl	6.00	10.00
		Nos. B15-B19 (5)	16.50	27.50

Surtax for winter welfare.

SP12 SP13

1937, Oct. 30

B20	SP12	25(pf) +25(pf) dk car	3.50	7.00
B21	SP13	40(pf) +40(pf) bl & red	3.50	7.00
a.		Souvenir sheet of two	27.50	55.00

Founding of Danzig community at Magdeburg.

No. B21a contains one each of Nos. B20–B21 with marginal inscriptions including "1937." Size: 146x105mm.

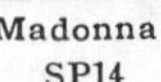

Madonna
SP14

Mercury
SP15

Weather Vane, Town Hall
SP16

Neptune Fountain
SP17

St. George and Dragon
SP18

1937, Dec. 13

B23	SP14	5pf +5pf brt vio	3.25	5.50
B24	SP15	10pf +10pf dk brn	3.25	6.25
B25	SP16	15pf +5pf bl & yel brn	4.00	8.25
B26	SP17	25pf +10pf bl grn & grn	4.50	9.00
B27	SP18	40pf +25pf brt car & bl	7.50	15.00
		Nos. B23-B27 (5)	22.50	44.00

Surtax for winter welfare. Designs are from frieze of the Artushof.

"Peter von Danzig" Yacht Race
SP19

Ships: 10+5pf, Dredger Fu Shing. 15+10pf, S. S. Columbus. 25+10pf, S. S. City of Danzig. 40+15pf, Peter von Danzig, 1472.

1938, Nov. 28 Photo. Unwmkd.

B28	SP19	5(pf) +5(pf) dk bl grn	1.50	3.00
B29	SP19	10(pf) +5(pf) gldn brn	2.00	4.00
B30	SP19	15(pf) +10(pf) ol grn	2.25	4.50
B31	SP19	25(pf) +10(pf) ind	3.00	6.00
B32	SP19	40(pf) +15(pf) vio brn	3.75	7.50
		Nos. B28-B32 (5)	12.50	25.00

Surtax for winter welfare.

AIR POST STAMPS.

AP1

AP2

No. 6 Surcharged in Blue or Carmine.

Wmkd. Lozenges. (125)

1920, Sept. 29 ***Perf. 14***

C1	AP1	40(pf) on 40pf car rose	1.75	3.75
a.		Double surcharge	300.00	300.00
C2	AP1	60(pf) on 40pf car rose (C)	1.75	3.75
a.		Double surcharge	300.00	300.00
C3	A2	1m on 40pf car rose	1.75	3.75

Plane faces left on No. C2.

Plane over Danzig
AP3 AP4

Wmkd. Honeycomb. (108)

1921-22 Typographed. ***Perf. 14.***

C4	AP3	40(pf) bl grn	40	75
C5	AP3	60(pf) dk vio	40	75
C6	AP3	1m carmine	40	75
C7	AP3	2m org brn	40	75

Serrate Roulette 13½.

Size: 34½x23mm.

C8	AP4	5m vio bl	1.25	2.25
C9	AP4	10m dp grn ('22)	2.75	4.75
		Nos. C4-C9 (6)	5.60	10.00

Nos. C4–C9 exist imperf. Price, each $45.

Wmkd. Webbing. (109)

1923 ***Perf. 14.***

C10	AP3	40(pf) bl grn	45	*2.25*
C11	AP3	60(pf) dk vio	45	*2.25*
a.		Double impression	75.00	
C12	AP3	1m carmine	45	*2.75*
C13	AP3	2m org brn	45	*2.75*
C14	AP3	25m pale bl	45	70

Serrate Roulette 13½.

Size: 34½x23mm.

C15	AP4	5m vio bl	45	1.00
C16	AP4	10m dp grn	45	1.00

Paper With Gray Network.

C17	AP4	20m org brn	45	1.00

Size: 40x23mm.

C18	AP4	50m orange	45	80
C19	AP4	100m red	45	80
C20	AP4	250m dk brn	45	80
C21	AP4	500m car rose	45	80
		Nos. C10-C21 (12)	5.40	*16.90*

Nos. C14, C18–C21 exist imperf. Price, each $35.

Post Horn and Airplanes
AP5

1923, Oct. 18 ***Perf. 14***

Paper Without Network.

C22	AP5	250,000m scarlet	42	1.75
C23	AP5	500,000m scarlet	42	1.75

Exist imperf. Price, each $37.50.

Surcharged **2 Millionen**

C24	AP5	2mil m on 100,000m scar	42	1.75
C25	AP5	5mil m on 50,000m scar	42	1.75
b.		Cliché of 10,000m in sheet of 50,000m	30.00	60.00

Exist imperf. Price, each $45.
Nos. C24 and C25 were not regularly issued without surcharge, although copies have been passed through the post. Price, uncanceled, each $7.50.

Plane over Danzig
AP6 AP7

1924

C26	AP6	10(pf) vermilion	25.00	4.50
C27	AP6	20(pf) car rose	2.25	2.00
C28	AP6	40(pf) ol brn	5.00	3.00
C29	AP6	1g dp grn	5.00	3.00
C30	AP7	2½g vio brn	37.50	50.00
		Nos. C26-C30 (5)	74.75	62.50

Exist imperf. Price #C30, $150, others, each $62.50.

Regular Issue of 1924 Surcharged in Various Colors

10 ▬▬▬ 10
Luftpost-Ausstellung
1932

1932 Wmkd. Lozenges. (125)

C31	A20	10(pf) on 1g yel grn & blk (G)	15.00	20.00
C32	A20	15(pf) on 2g red vio & blk (V)	15.00	20.00
C33	A20	20(pf) on 3g dk bl & blk (Bl)	15.00	20.00
C34	A23	25(pf) on 5g brn red & blk (R)	15.00	20.00
C35	A24	30(pf) on 10g dk brn & blk (Br)	15.00	20.00
		Nos. C31-C35 (5)	75.00	100.00

Issued in connection with the International Air Post Exhibition of 1932. The surcharges were variously arranged to suit the shapes and designs of the stamps. The stamps were sold at double their surcharged values, the excess being donated to the exhibition funds.

Airplane
AP8 AP9

1935 Wmkd. Webbing. (109)

C36	AP8	10pf scarlet	2.50	1.10
C37	AP8	15pf yellow	3.00	2.00
C38	AP8	25pf dk grn	2.50	2.00
C39	AP8	50pf gray bl	10.00	12.50
C40	AP9	1g magenta	7.00	*18.00*
		Nos. C36-C40 (5)	25.00	*35.60*

See also Nos. C42–C45.

Souvenir Sheet

St. Mary's Church—AP10

1937, June 6 ***Perf. 14***

C41	AP10	50pf dk bl	1.50	4.25

Issued for the Danzig Philatelic Exhibition, June 6–8, 1937. Size: 149x104mm.

Type of 1935.

1938-39 Wmkd. Swastikas. (237)

C42	AP8	10pf scarlet	1.75	*8.00*
C43	AP8	15pf yel ('39)	1.75	*8.75*
C44	AP8	25pf dk grn	1.75	*8.75*
C45	AP8	50pf gray bl ('39)	6.00	*20.00*

POSTAGE DUE STAMPS.

Danzig Coat of Arms
D1 D2

Wmkd. Honeycomb. (108)

1921-22 Typographed. ***Perf. 14***

Paper Without Network.

J1	D1	10(pf) dp vio	40	45
J2	D1	20(pf) dp vio	40	45
J3	D1	40(pf) dp vio	40	45
J4	D1	60(pf) dp vio	40	45
J5	D1	75(pf) dp vio ('22)	40	45
J6	D1	80(pf) dp vio	40	45
J7	D1	120(pf) dp vio	40	45
J8	D1	200(pf) dp vio ('22)	1.40	1.40
J9	D1	240(pf) dp vio	40	1.40
J10	D1	300(pf) dp vio ('22)	1.40	1.40
J11	D1	400(pf) dp vio	1.40	1.40
J12	D1	500(pf) dp vio	1.40	1.40
J13	D1	800(pf) dp vio ('22)	1.40	1.40
J14	D1	20m dp vio ('22)	1.40	1.40
		Nos. J1-J14 (14)	11.60	12.95

Nos. J1–J14 exist imperf. Price, each $15.

1923 Wmkd. Webbing. (109)

J15	D1	100(pf) dp vio	60	65
J16	D1	200(pf) dp vio	3.50	3.75
J17	D1	300(pf) dp vio	60	60
J18	D1	400(pf) dp vio	60	60
J19	D1	500(pf) dp vio	60	60
J20	D1	800(pf) dp vio	1.00	1.00
J21	D1	10m dp vio	60	70
J22	D1	20m dp vio	60	70
J23	D1	50m dp vio	60	70

Paper With Gray Network.

J24	D1	100m dp vio	60	70
J25	D1	500m dp vio	60	70
		Nos. J15-J25 (11)	9.90	10.70

Nos. J22–J25 exist imperf. Price, each $12.50.

Nos. J22–J23 and type of 1923 Surcharged **10000 ≡**

1923, Oct. 1

Paper Without Network.

J26	D1	5000(m) on 50m	35	60
J27	D1	10,000(m) on 20m	35	60
J28	D1	50,000(m) on 500m	35	60
J29	D1	100,000(m) on 20m	1.40	1.50

On No. J26 the numerals of the surcharge are all of the larger size.
A 1000(m) on 100m deep violet was prepared but not issued. Price, $110.
Nos. J26–J28 exist imperf. Price, each $25.

1923-28 Wmkd. Octagons. (110)

J30	D2	5(pf) bl & blk	1.00	1.00
J31	D2	10(pf) bl & blk	75	75
J32	D2	15(pf) bl & blk	1.50	1.50
J33	D2	20(pf) bl & blk	1.75	2.50
J34	D2	30(pf) bl & blk	11.00	2.50
J35	D2	40(pf) bl & blk	3.00	4.00
J36	D2	50(pf) bl & blk	3.00	3.00
J37	D2	60(pf) bl & blk	20.00	27.50
J38	D2	100(pf) bl & blk	20.00	11.00
J39	D2	3g bl & car	11.00	*60.00*
a.		"Guldeu" instead of "Gulden"	250.00	*500.00*
		Nos. J30-J39 (10)	73.00	*113.75*

Used prices of Nos. J30–J39 are for postally used copies.

Postage Due Stamps of 1923 Issue Surcharged in Red

1932, Dec. 20

J40	D2	5(pf) on 40(pf) bl & blk	3.00	11.00
J41	D2	10(pf) on 60(pf) bl & blk	55.00	12.50
J42	D2	20(pf) on 100(pf) bl & blk	3.25	9.00

Type of 1923.

Wmkd. Swastikas. (237)

1938-39 *Perf. 14.*

J43	D2	10(pf) bl & blk ('39)	1.50	20.00
J44	D2	30(pf) bl & blk	2.25	22.50
J45	D2	40(pf) bl & blk ('39)	7.00	47.50
J46	D2	60(pf) bl & blk ('39)	8.75	47.50
J47	D2	100(pf) bl & blk	10.50	47.50
		Nos. J43-J47 (5)	30.00	185.00

OFFICIAL STAMPS.

Regular Issues of 1921–22 Overprinted

D M

a

Wmkd. Honeycomb. (108)

1921-22 *Perf. 14x14½.*

O1	A11	5(pf) orange	40	45
O2	A11	10(pf) dk brn	30	35
a.		Invtd. ovpt.	75.00	
O3	A11	15(pf) green	30	35
O4	A11	20(pf) slate	30	35
O5	A11	25(pf) dk grn	30	35
O6	A11	30(pf) bl & car	75	85
O7	A11	40(pf) grn & car	35	40
O8	A11	50(pf) dk grn & car	35	40
O9	A11	60(pf) carmine	35	40
O10	A11	75(pf) dp vio ('22)	15	45
O11	A11	80(pf) blk & car	2.00	2.00
O12	A11	80(pf) grn ('22)	15	45

Paper With Faint Gray Network

O14	A11	1m org & car	30	40
O15	A11	1.20m bl vio	2.00	2.00
O16	A11	1.25m vio & car ('22)	15	45
O17	A11	1.50m sl gray ('22)	18	30
O18	A11	2m gray & car	22.50	21.00
a.		Invtd. ovpt.		
O19	A11	2m car rose ('22)	15	45
O20	A11	2.40m dk brn & car ('22)	1.25	3.25
O21	A11	3m vio & car	15.00	19.00
O22	A11	3m car lake ('22)	18	30
O23	A11	4m dk bl ('22)	1.25	3.25
O24	A11	5m dp grn ('22)	18	30
O25	A11	6m car lake ('22)	18	38
O26	A11	10m org ('22)	18	38
O27	A11	20m org brn ('22)	18	30
		Nos. O1-O27 (26)	49.38	58.56

Double overprints exist on Nos. O1–O2, O5–O7, O10 and O12. Price, each $17.50.

Same Overprint on No. 96

O28	A11	6m on 3m car lake	25	90
a.		Inverted overprint	40.00	

No. 77 Overprinted

1922 *Serrate Roulette 13½*

O29	A12	5m grn, red & blk	4.00	8.50

Nos. 99–103, 106–107 Overprinted Type "a"

Wmkd. Webbing. (109)

1923 *Perf. 14*

O30	A11	4m dk bl	20	40
O31	A11	5m dk grn	30	55
O32	A11	10m orange	20	40
O33	A11	20m org brn	20	40
O34	A15	50m pale bl & red	20	38
O35	A15a	100m dk grn & red	20	38

Nos. 113–115, 118–120 Overprinted Type "a"

O36	A15	50m pale bl	22	38
a.		Inverted overprint	30.00	
O37	A15a	100m dk grn	22	38
O38	A15	200m orange	22	38
a.		Inverted overprint	30.00	

Paper With Gray Network.

O39	A17	300m bl grn & red	20	35
O40	A17	500m gray & red	22	38
O41	A17	1000m brn & red	22	38
		Nos. O30-O41 (12)	2.60	4.76

Regular Issue of 1924-25 Overprinted

Dienst-marke

1924-25 *Perf. 14x14½*

O42	A19	5(pf) orange	2.50	1.75
O43	A19	10(pf) yel grn	2.50	1.75
O44	A19	15(pf) gray	2.50	1.75
O45	A19	15(pf) red ('25)	25.00	11.00
O46	A19	20(pf) car & red	3.00	1.75
O47	A19	25(pf) sl & red	25.00	27.50
O48	A19	30(pf) grn & red	4.00	3.00
O49	A19	35(pf) ultra ('25)	55.00	65.00
O50	A19	40(pf) dk bl & dl bl	8.00	9.00
O51	A19	50(pf) dp bl & red	25.00	30.00
O52	A19	75(pf) vio & red	50.00	100.00
		Nos. O42-O52 (11)	202.50	252.50

Double overprints exist on Nos. O42–O44, O47, O50–O52. Price, each $65.

DENMARK

(děn′märk)

LOCATION — northern part of a peninsula which separates the North and Baltic Seas, and includes the surrounding islands.
GOVT.—Kingdom.
AREA—16,631 sq. mi.
POP.—5,112,130 (1984).
CAPITAL—Copenhagen.

96 Skilling = 1 Rigsbank Daler

100 Ore = 1 Krone (1875)

> **Prices of early Denmark stamps vary according to condition. Quotations for Nos. 1–15 are for fine copies. Very fine to superb specimens sell at much higher prices, and inferior or poor copies sell at reduced prices, depending on the condition of the individual specimen.**

Numeral and Inscription of Value

A1

Royal Emblems

A2

Wmk. 111

Wmkd. Small Crown. (111)

1851 **Typographed.** *Imperf.*

With Yellow Brown Burelage.

1	A1	2rs blue	4,000.	1,300.
a.		First printing	7,500.	3,000.
2	A2	4rs brown	800.00	55.00
a.		First printing	1,000.	100.00
b.		4rs yel brn	1,000.	85.00

The first printing of Nos. 1 and 2 had the burelage printed from a copper plate, giving a clear impression with the lines in slight relief. The subsequent impressions had the burelage typographed, with the lines fainter and not rising above the surface of the paper.

Nos. 1–2 were reprinted in 1885 and 1901 on heavy yellowish paper, unwatermarked and imperforate, with a brown burelage. No. 1 was also reprinted without burelage, on both yellowish and white paper. Price for least costly reprint of No. 1, $40.

No. 2 was reprinted in 1951 in 10 shades with "Colour Specimen 1951" printed on the back. It was also reprinted in 1961 in 2 shades without burelage and with "Farve Nytryk 1961" printed on the back. Price for least costly reprint of No. 2, $8.50.

Dotting in Spandrels

A3

Wavy Lines in Spandrels

A4

1854-57

3	A3	2s bl ('55)	125.00	70.00
4	A3	4s brown	325.00	13.00
a.		4s yel brn	325.00	13.00
5	A3	8s grn ('57)	600.00	100.00
a.		8s yel grn	600.00	100.00
6	A3	16s gray lil ('57)	900.00	275.00

1858-62

7	A4	4s brown	80.00	8.00
a.		4s yel brn	80.00	8.00
b.		Wmk. 112 ('62)	80.00	10.00
8	A4	8s green	650.00	125.00

Nos. 2 to 8 inclusive are known with unofficial perforation 12 or 13, and Nos. 4, 5, 7 and 8 with unofficial roulette 9½.

Nos. 3, 6–8 were reprinted in 1885 on heavy yellowish paper, unwatermarked, imperforate and without burelage. Nos. 4–5 were reprinted in 1924 on white paper, unwatermarked, imperforate, gummed and without burelage. Price for No. 3, $9; Nos. 4–5, each $85; No. 6, $15; Nos. 7–8, each $7.50.

Wmk. 112

Wmkd. Crown. (112)

1863 *Rouletted 11*

9	A4	4s brown	125.00	22.50
a.		4s dp brn	125.00	22.50
10	A3	16s violet	2,000.	1,200.

Royal Emblems

A5

1864-68 *Perf. 13.*

11	A5	2s bl ('65)	125.00	60.00
a.		Imperf., (pair)	300.00	300.00
b.		Perf. 12½	475.00	425.00
12	A5	3s red vio ('65)	140.00	90.00
a.		Imperf., (pair)	400.00	
b.		Perf. 12½	500.00	400.00
13	A5	4s red	70.00	8.00
a.		Imperf., (pair)	180.00	300.00
14	A5	8s bis ('68)	550.00	125.00
a.		Imperf., (pair)	1,100.	
b.		Perf. 12½	625.00	350.00
15	A5	16s ol grn	625.00	170.00
a.		Imperf., (pair)	1,400.	
b.		Perf. 12½	1,250.	1,250.

Nos. 11–15 were reprinted in 1886 on heavy yellowish paper, unwatermarked, imperforate and without gum. The reprints of all values except the 4s were printed in two vertical rows of six, inverted with respect to each other, so that horizontal pairs are always tête bêche. Price $8 each.

Nos. 13 and 15 were reprinted in 1942 with printing on the back across each horizontal row: "Nytryk 1942. G. A. Hagemann: Danmarks og Vestindiens Frimaerker, Bind 2." Price, $50 each.

A6

NORMAL FRAME

INVERTED FRAME

The arabesques in the corners have a main stem and a branch. When the frame is in normal position, in the upper left corner the branch leaves the main stem half way between two little leaflets. In the lower right corner the branch starts at the foot of the second leaflet. When the frame is inverted the corner designs are, of course, transposed.

1870–71 ***Perf. 14x13½*** **Wmk. 112**

Paper Varying from Thin to Thick.

16	A6	2s gray & ultra ('71)	90.00	35.00
a.		2s gray & bl	90.00	32.50
b.		Imperf., (pair)	200.00	
c.		Inverted frame	1,250.	850.00
17	A6	3s gray & brt lil ('71)	200.00	110.00
a.		Imperf., (pair)	550.00	
b.		Inverted frame	2,500.	1,750.
18	A6	4s gray & car	110.00	15.00
a.		Imperf., (pair)	275.00	
b.		Inverted frame	1,100.	170.00
19	A6	8s gray & brn ('71)	300.00	100.00
a.		Imperf., (pair)	600.00	
b.		Inverted frame	2,000.	1,100.
20	A6	16s gray & grn ('71)	450.00	225.00
a.		Imperf., (pair)	900.00	
b.		Inverted frame	1,700.	1,400.

Perf. 12½.

21	A6	2s gray & bl ('71)	2,500.	3,250.
22	A6	4s gray & car	275.00	130.00
24	A6	48s brn & lil	900.00	350.00
a.		Imperf., (pair)	1,200.	
b.		Inverted frame	3,500.	2,500.

Nos. 16–20, 24 were reprinted in 1886 on thin white paper, unwatermarked, imperforate and without gum. These were printed in sheets of 10 in which 1 stamp has the normal frame (price $22.50 each and 9 the inverted (price $9 each; No. 24, $12).

1875–79 *Perf. 14x13½.*

25	A6	3ø gray bl & gray	16.00	11.00
a.		First "A" of "DANMARK" missing	70.00	100.00
b.		Imperf.		
c.		Inverted frame	16.00	11.00

26 A6 4ö sl & bl 14.00 30
a. 4ö gray & bl 14.00 30
b. 4ö sl & ultra 85.00 13.00
c. 4ö gray & ultra 85.00 13.00
d. Imperf., (pair) 225.00
e. Inverted frame 17.00 25
27 A6 5ö rose & bl ('79) 45.00 75.00
a. Ball of lower curve of large "5" missing 225.00 325.00
b. Inverted frame 1,500. 2,000.
28 A6 8ö sl & car 18.00 30
a. 8ö gray & car 50.00 3.00
b. Imperf., (pair) 275.00
c. Inverted frame 22.50 30
29 A6 12ö sl & dl lake 13.00 4.00
a. 12ö gray & brt lil 60.00 15.00
b. 12ö gray & dl mag 13.00 4.00
c. Inverted frame 16.00 4.00
30 A6 16ö sl & brn 70.00 4.50
a. 16ö lt gray & brn 80.00 13.00
b. Inverted frame 35.00 4.00
31 A6 20ö rose & gray 85.00 25.00
a. 20ö car & gray 85.00 25.00
b. Inverted frame 85.00 25.00
32 A6 25ö gray & grn 80.00 30.00
a. Inverted frame 110.00 60.00
33 A6 50ö brn & vio 85.00 25.00
a. 50ö brn & bl vio 550.00 125.00
b. Inverted frame 100.00 27.50
34 A6 100ö gray & org ('77) 125.00 42.50
a. Imperf., (pair) 450.00
b. Inverted frame 175.00 70.00

The stamps of this issue on thin semi-transparent paper are far scarcer than those on thicker paper.

See also Nos. 41-42, 44, 46-47, 50-52.

Arms
A7

Two types of numerals in corners:

1882

Small Corner Numerals.

35 A7 5ö green 250.00 125.00
37 A7 20ö blue 225.00 40.00

1884-85

Larger Corner Numerals.

38 A7 5ö green 14.00 2.00
a. Imperf.
39 A7 10ö car ('85) 15.00 1.25
a. Small numerals in corners 625.00 625.00
b. Imperf., pair 250.00
c. Pair, Nos. 39,39a 700.00 800.00
40 A7 20ö blue 25.00 1.25
a. Pair, Nos. 37, 40 500.00 800.00
b. Imperf., pair 2,500.

Stamps with large corner numerals have white line around crown and lower oval touches frame.

The plate of the 10 ore, No. 39, was damaged and three clichés in the bottom row were replaced by clichés for post cards, which had small numerals in the corners, making the variety No. 39a.

Two clichés with small numerals were inserted in the plate of No. 40.

Wmkd. Crown. (112)

1895-1901 *Perf. 13.*

41 A6 3ö bl & gray 12.00 5.00
b. Inverted frame 14.00 5.50
42 A6 4ö sl & bl ('96) 6.00 25
a. Inverted frame 6.00 25
43 A7 5ö green 10.00 1.10
44 A6 8ö sl & car 6.00 20
a. Inverted frame 6.00 20
45 A7 10ö rose car 10.00 1.00
46 A6 12ö sl & dl lake 7.00 4.00
a. Inverted frame 16.00 4.00
47 A6 16ö sl & brn 25.00 5.00
a. Inverted frame 30.00 5.00
48 A7 20ö blue 12.50 2.00
49 A7 24ö brn ('01) 14.00 3.50
50 A6 25ö gray & grn ('98) 75.00 15.00
a. Inverted frame 65.00 25.00

51 A6 50ö brn & vio ('97) 75.00 25.00
a. Inverted frame 90.00 40.00
52 A6 100ö sl & org 80.00 35.00
a. Inverted frame 90.00 42.50

1902-04 Wmkd. Crown. (113)

41c A6 3ö bl & gray 3.75 3.50
d. Invtd. frame 75.00 50.00
42b A6 4ö sl & bl 25.00 7.50
c. Invtd. frame 150.00 90.00
43a A7 5ö green 2.75 25
44d A6 8ö sl & car 600.00 375.00
45a A7 10ö rose car 2.75 25
48a A7 20ö blue 12.00 2.75
50b A6 25ö gray & grn 14.00 6.00
c. Invtd. frame 140.00 55.00
51b A6 50ö brn & vio 45.00 18.00
c. Invtd. frame 275.00 160.00
52b A6 100ö sl & org 32.50 18.00
c. Invtd. frame 300.00 175.00

Wmk. 113

1902 Wmkd. Crown. (113)

53 A7 1ö orange 1.00 50
a. Imperf., pair 275.00
54 A7 15ö lilac 15.00 90
a. Imperf., pair

Nos. 44d, 44, 49 Surcharged:

4 ØRE
a

15 15 ØRE
b

1904-12 Wmkd. Crown. (113)

55 A6(a) 4ö on 8ö sl & car 3.00 3.00
a. Wmk. 112 ('12) 30.00 60.00
b. As "a", inverted frame

Wmkd. Crown. (112)

56 A7(b) 15ö on 24ö brn 5.00 5.00
a. Short "15" at right 45.00 65.00

DANMARK 4 ØRE ØRE POSTFRIMÆRKE

Numeral of Value
A10

King Christian IX
A11

King Frederik VIII
A12

Wmkd. Crown. (113)

1905-17 Typographed. *Perf. 13.*

57 A10 1ö org ('06) 1.75 50
58 A10 2ö carmine 2.00 20
a. Perf. 14x14½ ('17) 5.00 4.00
59 A10 3ö gray 5.00 45
60 A10 4ö dl bl 5.00 20
a. Perf. 14x14½ ('17) 13.00 8.00
61 A10 5ö dp grn ('12) 6.00 20
62 A10 10ö dp rose ('12) 6.50 20
63 A10 15ö lilac 22.50 60
64 A10 20ö dk bl ('12) 40.00 1.00
Nos. 57-64 (8) 88.75 3.35

The three wavy lines in design A10 are symbolical of the three waters which separate the principal Danish islands.

See also Nos. 85-96.

1904-05 Engraved.

65 A11 10ö scarlet 5.50 20
66 A11 20ö blue 20.00 1.00
67 A11 25ö brn ('05) 20.00 3.00
68 A11 50ö dl vio ('05) 60.00 60.00

69 A11 100ö ocher ('05) 35.00 45.00
Nos. 65-69 (5) 140.50 109.20

1905-06 Re-engraved.

70 A11 5ö green 6.00 20
71 A11 10ö scar ('06) 16.00 25

The re-engraved stamps are much clearer than the originals, and the decoration on the king's left breast has been removed.

1907-12

72 A12 5ö green 1.75 12
a. Imperf.
73 A12 10ö red 2.75 8
a. Imperf.
74 A12 20ö indigo 8.00 40
a. 20ö brt bl ('11) 12.00 1.25
75 A12 25ö ol brn 15.00 75
76 A12 35ö dp org ('12) 11.00 4.50
77 A12 50ö claret 45.00 6.00
78 A12 100ö bis brn 100.00 3.50
Nos. 72-78 (7) 183.50 15.35

Nos. 47, 31 and 09 Surcharged:

35 ØRE
c

35 ØRE FRIMÆRKE
d

Dark Blue Surcharge.

1912 Wmkd. Crown. (112) *Perf. 13.*

79 A6(c) 35ö on 16ö sl & brn 18.00 55.00
a. Inverted frame 275.00 500.00

Perf. 14x13½.

80 A6(c) 35ö on 20ö rose & gray 15.00 45.00
a. Inverted frame 85.00 175.00

Black Surcharge.

81 O1(d) 35ö on 32ö grn 30.00 70.00

General Post Office, Copenhagen
A15

Wmkd. Two Crowns. (113)

1912 Engraved *Perf. 13*

82 A15 5k dk red 475.00 125.00
See No. 135.

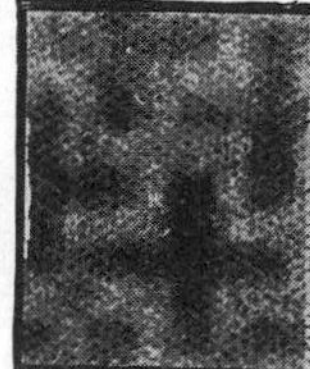

Wmk. 114

Wmkd. Multiple Crosses. (114)

1913-30 Typo. *Perf. 14x14½*

85 A10 1ö dp org ('14) 70 30
a. Booklet pane of 4, (2 No. 85, 2 No. 91 + 2 labels) 25.00
86 A10 2ö car ('13) 1.00 15
a. Imperf., (pair) 250.00 400.00
b. Booklet pane, 4+2 labels 32.50
87 A10 3ö gray ('13) 2.00 20
88 A10 4ö bl ('13) 6.00 20
a. Half used as 2ö on cover 1,300.
89 A10 5ö dk brn ('21) 1.00 10
a. Imperf., pair 350.00
b. Booklet pane, 4+2 labels 17.00

Unused Prices through 1960 are for hinged copies in fine condition.

90 A10 5ö lt grn ('30) 1.50 12
a. Booklet pane, 4+2 labels 17.00
b. Booklet pane of 50
91 A10 7ö ap grn ('26) 2.00 18
a. Booklet pane, 4+2 labels 20.00
92 A10 7ö dk vio ('30) 8.00 2.50
93 A10 8ö gray ('21) 5.00 75
94 A10 10ö grn ('21) 1.00 8
a. Imperf., (pair) 350.00
b. Booklet pane, 4+2 labels 45.00
95 A10 10ö bis brn ('30) 1.75 12
a. Booklet pane, 4+2 labels 18.00
b. Booklet pane of 50
96 A10 12ö vio ('26) 14.00 2.00
Nos. 85-96 (12) 43.95 6.70

No. 88a was used with No. 97 in Faroe Islands Jan. 3-23, 1919.

King Christian X
A16 A17

1913-28 Typo. *Perf. 14x14½*

97 A16 5ö green 1.50 6
a. Booklet pane of 4 20.00
98 A16 7ö org ('18) 2.50 50
99 A16 8ö dk gray ('20) 4.50 2.00
100 A16 10ö red 1.75 6
a. Imperf., (pair) 350.00
b. Booklet pane of 4 20.00
101 A16 12ö gray grn ('18) 11.00 9.00
102 A16 15ö violet 2.25 6
103 A16 20ö dp bl 7.50 30
104 A16 20ö brn ('21) 1.00 6
105 A16 20ö red ('26) 2.50 20
106 A16 25ö dk brn 9.00 40
107 A16 25ö brn & blk ('20) 50.00 3.50
108 A16 25ö red ('22) 3.50 50
109 A16 25ö yel grn ('25) 3.00 30
110 A16 27ö ver & blk ('18) 45.00 60.00
111 A16 30ö grn & blk ('18) 11.00 1.50
112 A16 30ö org ('21) 3.00 70
113 A16 30ö dk bl ('25) 3.00 60
114 A16 35ö orange 12.00 3.00
115 A16 35ö yel & blk ('19) 10.00 2.25
116 A16 40ö vio & blk ('18) 10.00 1.75
117 A16 40ö gray bl & blk ('20) 25.00 6.00
118 A16 40ö dk bl ('22) 5.00 1.50
119 A16 40ö org ('25) 3.00 55
120 A16 50ö claret 30.00 2.75
121 A16 50ö cl & blk ('19) 65.00 1.50
122 A16 50ö lt gray ('22) 6.00 20
a. 50ö dk gray ('21) 40.00 2.00
123 A16 60ö brn & bl ('19) 35.00 2.75
a. 60ö brn & ultra ('19) 140.00 14.00
124 A16 60ö grn bl ('21) 9.00 1.00
125 A16 70ö brn & grn ('20) 20.00 2.00
126 A16 80ö bl grn ('15) 60.00 20.00
127 A16 90ö brn & red ('20) 20.00 2.00
128 A16 1k brn & bl ('22) 45.00 1.65
129 A16 2k gray & cl ('25) 75.00 15.00
130 A16 5k vio & brn ('27) 12.00 7.00
131 A16 10k ver & yel grn ('28) 375.00 40.00
Nos. 97-131 (35) 979.00 190.64

No. 97 surcharged "2 ORE" is Faroe Islands No. 1.

Nos. 87 and 98, 89 and 94, 89 and 104, 90 and 95, 97 and 103, 100 and 102 exist se-tenant in coils for use in vending machines.

1913-20 Engraved

132 A17 1k yel brn 95.00 1.00
133 A17 2k gray 100.00 4.50
134 A17 5k pur ('20) 22.50 10.00

G.P.O. Type of 1912

Engraved

1915 ***Perf. 14x14½*** **Wmk. 114**

No.	Type	Description	Unused	Used
135	A15	5k dk red ('15)	525.00	125.00

Nos. 46 and 010 Surcharged in Black

DANMARK
80
ØRE
POSTFRIM.
e

Typographed

Perf. 13

1915 **Wmkd. Crown. (112)**

No.	Type	Description	Unused	Used
136	A6 (c)	80ö on 12ö sl & dl lake	45.00	125.00
a.		Invtd. frame	550.00	900.00
137	O1 (e)	80ö on 8ö car	50.00	140.00
a.		"POSTERIM"	85.00	175.00

POSTFRIM.

Newspaper Stamps Surcharged

ØRE 27 ØRE

DANMARK

On Issue of 1907.

1918 ***Perf. 13*** **Wmkd. Crown. (113)**

No.	Type	Description	Unused	Used
138	N1	27ö on 1ö ol	140.00	250.00
139	N1	27ö on 5ö bl	140.00	250.00
140	N1	27ö on 7ö car	140.00	250.00
141	N1	27ö on 10ö dp lil	140.00	250.00
142	N1	27ö on 68ö yel brn	8.00	25.00
143	N1	27ö on 5k rose & yel grn	9.00	15.00
144	N1	27ö on 10k bis & bl	8.00	22.50
		Nos. 138-144 (7)	585.00	1,062.50

On Issue of 1914–15.

Wmkd. Multiple Crosses. (114)

Perf. 14x14½.

No.	Type	Description	Unused	Used
145	N1	27ö on 1ö ol gray	4.50	11.00
146	N1	27ö on 5ö bl	9.00	22.50
147	N1	27ö on 7ö rose	4.00	8.00
148	N1	27ö on 8ö grn	5.00	14.00
149	N1	27ö on 10ö dp lil	4.00	9.00
150	N1	27ö on 20ö grn	4.00	11.00
151	N1	27ö on 29ö org yel	4.00	9.00
152	N1	27ö on 38ö org	45.00	85.00
153	N1	27ö on 41ö yel brn	10.00	*40.00*
154	N1	27ö on 1k bl grn & mar	4.00	7.00
		Nos. 145-154 (10)	93.50	*216.50*

Kronborg Castle
A20

Sonderborg Castle
A21

Roskilde Cathedral
A22

Perf. 14½x14, 14x14½

1920, Oct. 5 **Typographed**

No.	Type	Description	Unused	Used
156	A20	10ö red	5.50	50
157	A21	20ö slate	5.00	50
158	A22	40ö dk brn	20.00	6.00

This issue was to commemorate the reunion of Northern Schleswig with Denmark.

1921

No.	Type	Description	Unused	Used
159	A20	10ö green	8.00	50
160	A22	40ö dk bl	40.00	7.50

Stamps of 1918 Surcharged in Blue 8 8

1921-22

No.	Type	Description	Unused	Used
161	A16	8ö on 7ö org ('22)	3.50	2.75
162	A16	8ö on 12ö gray grn	3.50	5.00

No. 87 Surcharged 8

1921

No.	Type	Description	Unused	Used
163	A10	8ö on 3ö gray	2.75	2.75

King Christian X
A23

King Christian IV
A24

A25

A26

1924, Dec. 1 ***Perf. 14x14½.***

No.	Type	Description	Unused	Used
164	A23	10ö green	5.50	1.75
165	A24	10ö green	5.50	1.75
166	A25	10ö green	5.50	1.75
167	A26	10ö green	5.50	1.75
168	A23	15ö violet	5.50	1.75
169	A24	15ö violet	5.50	1.75
170	A25	15ö violet	5.50	1.75
171	A26	15ö violet	5.50	1.75
172	A23	20ö dk brn	5.50	1.75
173	A24	20ö dk brn	5.50	1.75
174	A25	20ö dk brn	5.50	1.75
175	A26	20ö dk brn	5.50	1.75
		3 Blocks of 4, #164-175	95.00	110.00
		Nos. 164-175 (12)	66.00	21.00

Issued to commemorate the 300th anniversary of the Danish postal service.

The sheets of each value are composed of stamps of types A23, A24, A25 and A26, arranged in groups of four as illustrated.

Stamps of 1921-22 Surcharged:

20 20
k

20 20
l

1926

No.	Type	Description	Unused	Used
176	A16 (k)	20ö on 30ö org	6.00	10.00
177	A16 (l)	20ö on 40ö dk bl	9.00	14.00

A27

A28

1926, Mar. 11 ***Perf. 14x14½.***

No.	Type	Description	Unused	Used
178	A27	10ö dl grn	1.50	15
179	A28	20ö dk red	2.00	15
180	A28	30ö dk bl	9.00	90

Issued in commemoration of the 75th anniversary of the introduction of postage stamps in Denmark.

Stamps of 1913-26 Surcharged in Blue or Black

7
m

7 7
n

1926-27 ***Perf. 14x14½.***

No.	Type	Description	Unused	Used
181	A10 (m)	7ö on 8ö gray (Bl)	1.75	4.00
182	A16 (n)	7ö on 27ö ver & blk	6.50	15.00
183	A16 (n)	7ö on 20ö red ('27)	90	80
184	A16 (n)	12ö on 15ö vio	4.00	6.50

Surcharged on Official Stamps of 1914-23.

No.	Type	Description	Unused	Used
185	O1 (e)	7ö on 1ö org	4.50	9.00
186	O1 (e)	7ö on 3ö gray	11.00	25.00
187	O1 (e)	7ö on 4ö bl	4.50	14.00
188	O1 (e)	7ö on 5ö grn	80.00	125.00
189	O1 (e)	7ö on 10ö grn	4.50	11.00
190	O1 (e)	7ö on 15ö vio	5.50	11.00
191	O1 (e)	7ö on 20ö ind	22.50	42.50
a.		Double surcharge	*650.00*	*650.00*
		Nos. 181-191 (11)	145.65	263.80

Caravel
A30

King Christian X
A31

1927 **Typographed.** ***Perf. 14x14½.***

No.	Type	Description	Unused	Used
192	A30	15ö red	4.00	6
193	A30	20ö gray	6.50	40
194	A30	25ö lt bl	70	10
195	A30	30ö ocher	70	10
196	A30	35ö red brn	15.00	40
197	A30	40ö yel grn	15.00	15
		Nos. 192-197 (6)	41.90	1.21

See also Nos. 232–238J.

1930, Sept. 26

No.	Type	Description	Unused	Used
210	A31	5ö ap grn	2.50	10
a.		Booklet pane, 4 + 2 labels	32.50	
211	A31	7ö violet	9.00	3.00
212	A31	8ö dk gray	42.50	10.00
213	A31	10ö yel brn	6.50	30
a.		Booklet pane, 4 + 2 labels	45.00	
214	A31	15ö red	15.00	15
215	A31	20ö lt gray	37.50	3.00
216	A31	25ö lt bl	14.00	40
217	A31	30ö yel buff	15.00	2.00
218	A31	35ö red brn	15.00	4.00
219	A31	40ö dp grn	15.00	1.25
		Nos. 210-219 (10)	172.00	24.20

60th birthday of King Christian X.

Wavy Lines and Numeral of Value
A32

Type of 1905–12 Issue.

Engraved, Redrawn

1933–40 ***Perf. 13*** **Unwmkd.**

No.	Type	Description	Unused	Used
220	A32	1ö gray blk	5	5
221	A32	2ö scarlet	10	5
222	A32	4ö blue	50	15
223	A32	5ö yel grn	1.75	15
a.		5ö gray grn	30.00	30.00
b.		Tête bêche pair	15.00	15.00
c.		Booklet pane of 4	12.00	
d.		Booklet pane of 4, (1 No. 223a & 3 No. B6)	35.00	
224	A32	5ö rose lake ('38)	5	5
a.		Booklet pane of 4	50	
b.		Booklet pane of 10	1.00	
224C	A32	6ö org ('40)	40	6
225	A32	7ö violet	3.00	25
226	A32	7ö yel grn ('38)	2.00	30
226A	A32	7ö lt brn ('40)	40	15
227	A32	8ö gray	80	15
227A	A32	8ö yel grn ('40)	45	10
228	A32	10ö yel org	17.50	20
a.		Tête bêche pair	60.00	32.50
b.		Booklet pane of 4	87.50	
229	A32	10ö lt brn ('37)	15.00	10
a.		Booklet pane of 4	75.00	
b.		Booklet pane of 4, (1 No. 229 & 3 No. B7)	35.00	
230	A32	10ö vio ('38)	80	5
a.		Booklet pane of 4	4.00	
b.		Bklt. pane of 4, (2 No. 230 & 2 No. B10)	6.00	
		Nos. 220-230 (14)	42.80	1.81

The stamps of 1905–12 were typographed. They had a solid background with groups of small hearts below the heraldic lions in the upper corners and below "DA" and "RK" of "DANMARK." The numerals of value were enclosed in single-lined ovals.

The 1933–40 stamps are line-engraved and have a background of crossed lines. The hearts have been removed and the numerals of value are now in double-lined ovals. Two types exist of some values.

The 1ö, No. 220, was issued on fluorescent paper in 1969.

No. 230 with wide margins is from booklet pane No. 230b.

Of the tête bêche pairs, those with gutters are twice as plentiful. Prices are for the less costly.

Surcharges of 20, 50 and 60öre on Nos. 220, 224 and 224C are listed as Faroe Islands Nos. 2–3, 5–6.

See Nos. 318, 333, 382, 416, 437-437A, 493-498, 629, 631, 688-695.

Certain Tête Bêche

pairs of 1938–55 issues which reached the market in 1971, and were not regularly issued, are not listed. This group comprises 24 different major-number vertical pairs of types A32, A47, A61 and SP3 (13 with gutters, 11 without), and pairs of some minor numbers and shades. They were removed from booklet pane sheets.

Type of 1927 Issue.

1933–34 **Engraved.** ***Perf. 13***

Type I.

Type I—Two columns of squares between sail and left frame line.

No.	Type	Description	Unused	Used
232	A30	20ö gray	17.00	20
233	A30	25ö blue	85.00	8.00
234	A30	25ö brn ('34)	55.00	15
235	A30	30ö org yel	2.50	1.50
236	A30	30ö bl ('34)	2.50	15
237	A30	35ö violet	1.25	20
238	A30	40ö yel grn	6.00	18
		Nos. 232-238 (7)	169.25	10.38

Type II.

Type II—One column of squares between sail and left frame line.

1933–40

No.	Type	Description	Unused	Used
238A	A30	15ö dp red	6.00	6
k.		Booklet pane of 4	30.00	
l.		Booklet pane of 4, (1 No. 238A, 3 No. B8)	45.00	
238B	A30	15ö yel grn ('40)	14.00	20
238C	A30	20ö gray blk ('39)	8.00	20
238D	A30	20ö red ('40)	1.50	5
238E	A30	25ö dp brn ('39)	1.50	20
238F	A30	30ö bl ('39)	6.00	45
238G	A30	30ö org ('40)	1.25	10
238H	A30	35ö vio ('40)	1.75	55
238I	A30	40ö yel grn ('39)	17.00	30
238J	A30	40ö bl ('40)	2.00	12
		Nos. 238A-238J (10)	59.00	2.23

Nos. 232–238J, engraved, have cross-hatched background. Nos. 192–197, typographed, have solid background.

No. 238A surcharged 20ore is listed as Faroe Islands No. 4.

King Christian X
A33

1934–41 ***Perf. 13***

No.	Type	Description	Unused	Used
239	A33	50ö gray	2.50	15
240	A33	60ö bl grn	6.00	20
240A	A33	75ö dk bl ('41)	1.00	20
241	A33	1k lt brn	6.50	10
242	A33	2k dl red	14.00	75
243	A33	5k violet	22.50	3.25
		Nos. 239-243 (6)	52.50	4.65

Nos. 233, 235 Surcharged in Black 4

1934, June 9

No.	Type	Description	Unused	Used
244	A30	4ö on 25ö bl	75	35
245	A30	10ö on 30ö org yel	5.00	2.25

"The Ugly Duckling" A34 — Hans Christian Andersen A35 — "The Little Mermaid" A36

1935, Oct. 4 *Perf. 13*

246	A34	5ŏ lt grn	6.00	12
a.		Tête bêche pair	20.00	12.00
b.		Bklt. pane of 4	27.50	
247	A35	7ŏ dl vio	5.00	1.00
248	A36	10ŏ orange	9.00	15
a.		Tête bêche pair	30.00	20.00
b.		Bklt. pane of 4	50.00	
249	A35	15ŏ red	22.50	10
a.		Tête bêche pair	60.00	30.00
b.		Bklt. pane of 4	125.00	
250	A35	20ŏ gray	20.00	80
251	A35	30ŏ dl bl	6.00	40
		Nos. 246-251 (6)	68.50	2.57

Issued to commemorate the centenary of the publication of the earliest installment of Hans Christian Andersen's "Fairy Tales."

Note on tête bêche pair prices after No. 230 applies to Nos. 246a, 248a and 249a.

Nikolai Church A37 — Hans Tausen A38

Ribe Cathedral A39

1936 *Perf. 13*

252	A37	5ŏ green	3.00	20
a.		Bklt. pane of 4	30.00	
253	A37	7ŏ violet	3.00	1.00
254	A38	10ŏ lt brn	4.00	15
a.		Bklt. pane of 4	32.50	
255	A38	15ŏ dl rose	6.00	10
256	A39	30ŏ blue	25.00	55
		Nos. 252-256 (5)	41.00	2.00

Issued in commemoration of the 400th anniversary of the Church Reformation in Denmark.

No. 229 Overprinted in Blue

K.P.K.
17.-26. SEPT.
19 37

1937, Sept. 17

257	A32	10ŏ lt brn	3.00	3.00

Issued in commemoration of the Jubilee Exhibition held by the Copenhagen Philatelic Club on the occasion of their 50th anniversary. The stamps were on sale at the Exhibition only, each holder of a ticket of admission (1kr.) being entitled to purchase 20 stamps at face value, and each holder of a season ticket (5kr.) being entitled to purchase 100 stamps.

Yacht and Summer Palace, Marselisborg A40 — King Christian X in Streets of Copenhagen A41

Equestrian Statue of King Frederik V and Amalienborg Palace A42

1937, May 15 *Perf. 13*

258	A40	5ŏ green	3.00	35
a.		Bklt. pane of 4	17.50	
259	A41	10ŏ brown	3.00	18
a.		Bklt. pane of 4	17.50	
260	A42	15ŏ scarlet	3.00	18
a.		Bklt. pane of 4	20.00	
261	A41	30ŏ blue	25.00	2.00

Issued in commemoration of the 25th anniversary of the accession to the throne of King Christian X.

Emancipation Column, Copenhagen A43

1938, June 20 *Perf. 13*

262	A43	15ŏ scarlet	1.25	20

Issued to commemorate the 150th anniversary of the abolition of serfdom in Denmark.

No. 223 Overprinted in Red on Alternate Stamps

D.F.U.
FRIM-UDST.
19 38

1938, Sept. 2

263	A32	5ŏ yel grn (pair)	6.00	6.50

10th Danish Philatelic Exhibition.

Bertel Thorvaldsen A44 — Statue of Jason A45

1938, Nov. 17 **Engr.** *Perf. 13*

264	A44	5ŏ rose lake	1.00	15
265	A45	10ŏ purple	1.00	12
266	A44	30ŏ dk bl	3.50	55

The return to Denmark in 1838 of Bertel Thorvaldsen, Danish sculptor.

Stamps of 1933-39 Surcharged with New Values in Black:

6 (*a*) **15** (*b*) **20** (*c*)

1940

267	A32 (a)	6ŏ on 7ŏ yel grn	35	35
268	A32 (a)	6ŏ on 8ŏ gray	30	20
269	A30 (b)	15ŏ on 40ŏ yel grn (On No. 238)	2.00	4.50
270	A30 (b)	15ŏ on 40ŏ yel grn (On No. 238I)	2.00	1.00
271	A30 (c)	20ŏ on 15ŏ dp red	2.25	15
272	A30 (b)	40ŏ on 30ŏ bl (On No. 238F)	2.00	35
		Nos. 267-272 (6)	8.90	6.55

Bering's Ship A46

1941, Nov. 27 **Engr.** *Perf. 13*

277	A46	10ŏ dk vio	60	20
278	A46	20ŏ red brn	1.25	40
279	A46	40ŏ dk bl	80	50

Issued in commemoration of the 200th anniversary of the death of Vitus Bering, explorer.

King Christian X A47

1942-46 *Perf. 13* **Unwmkd.**

280	A47	10ŏ violet	25	5
281	A47	15ŏ yel grn	60	6
282	A47	20ŏ red	60	5
283	A47	25ŏ brn ('43)	1.00	6
284	A47	30ŏ org ('43)	75	10
285	A47	35ŏ brt red vio ('44)	75	20
286	A47	40ŏ bl ('43)	75	10
286A	A47	45ŏ ol brn ('46)	1.00	20
286B	A47	50ŏ gray ('45)	1.50	10
287	A47	60ŏ bluish grn ('44)	1.25	10
287A	A47	75ŏ dk bl ('46)	1.00	20
		Nos. 280-287A (11)	9.45	1.22

Round Tower A48 — Condor Plane A49

1942, Nov. 27

288	A48	10ŏ violet	25	20

Issued to commemorate the 300th anniversary of the Round Tower, Copenhagen.

1943, Oct. 29

289	A49	20ŏ red	30	20

Issued to commemorate the 25th anniversary of the Danish Aviation Company (Det Danske Luftfartsselskab).

Ejby Church A50

Designs: 15ŏ, Oesterlars Church. 20ŏ, Hvidbjerg Church.

1944 **Engraved.** *Perf. 13*

290	A50	10ŏ violet	30	20
291	A50	15ŏ yel grn	40	60
292	A50	20ŏ red	30	20

Ole Roemer A53 — King Christian X A54

1944, Sept. 25

293	A53	20ŏ hn brn	30	20

Issued to commemorate the 300th anniversary of the birth of Ole Roemer, astronomer.

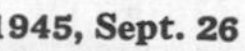

1945, Sept. 26

294	A54	10ŏ lilac	20	10
295	A54	20ŏ red	40	10
296	A54	40ŏ dp bl	90	25

75th birthday of King Christian X.

Small State Seal A55 — Tycho Brahe A56

1946-47 *Perf. 13* **Unwmkd.**

297	A55	1k brown	1.00	5
298	A55	2k red ('47)	80	5
299	A55	5k dl bl	1.50	6

Nos. 297-299 issued on ordinary and fluorescent paper.

See Nos. 395-400, 441A-444D, 499-506, 644-650. 716-720A.

1946, Dec. 14 **Engraved**

300	A56	20(ŏ) dk red	30	10

Issued to commemorate the 400th anniversary of the birth of Tycho Brahe, astronomer.

First Danish Locomotive A57 — Modern Steam Locomotive A58

Diesel Locomotive A59

1947, June 27

301	A57	15(ŏ) stl bl	50	40
302	A58	20(ŏ) red	50	20
303	A59	40(ŏ) dp bl	1.75	1.00

Issued to commemorate the centenary of the inauguration of the Danish State Railways.

Jacob C. Jacobsen A60 — King Frederik IX A61

1947, Nov. 10 *Perf. 13*

304	A60	20(ŏ) dk red	45	20

Issued to commemorate the 60th anniversary of the death of Jacob Christian Jacobsen, founder of the Glyptothek Art Museum, Copenhagen.

1948-50 *Perf. 13* **Unwmkd.**

Three types among 15ŏ, 20ŏ, 30ŏ:

I. Background of horizontal lines. No outline at left for cheek and ear. King's uniform textured in strong lines.

II. Background of vertical and horizontal lines. Contour of cheek and ear at left. Uniform same.

III. Background and facial contour lines as in II. Uniform lines double and thinner.

306	A61	15(ŏ) grn (II)	3.00	6
a.		Type III ('49)	2.00	6

307 A61 20(ö) dk red (I) 1.25 6
a. Type III ('49) 1.25 6
308 A61 25(ö) lt brn 1.75 10
309 A61 30(ö) org (II) 18.00 15
a. Type III ('50) 20.00 15
310 A61 40(ö) dl bl ('49) 5.00 60
311 A61 45(ö) ol ('50) 2.00 10
312 A61 50(ö) gray ('49) 2.00 10
313 A61 60(ö) grnsh bl ('50) 3.00 10
314 A61 75(ö) lil rose ('50) 1.50 10
Nos. 306-314 (9) 37.50 1.37

See also Nos. 319-326, 334-341, 354.

Legislative Assembly, 1849 A62

Symbol of U.P.U. A63

1949, June 5

315 A62 20(ö) red brn 50 15

Issued to commemorate the centenary of the adoption of the Danish constitution.

1949, Oct. 9

316 A63 40ö dl bl 1.25 85

Issued to commemorate the 75th anniversary of the formation of the Universal Postal Union.

Kalundborg Radio Station and Masts A64

1950, Apr. 1 Engr. *Perf. 13*

317 A64 20ö brn red 60 25

Issued to commemorate the 25th anniversary of radio broadcasting in Denmark.

Types of 1933-50.

1950–51 *Perf. 13* **Unwmkd.**

318 A32 10ö green 5 5
a. Booklet pane of #12 (4 #318, 4 #493, 4 #494) ('85) 3.25
b. Booklet pane of 10 (2 #318, 2 #688, 6 #494) ('84) 1.75
319 A61 15(ö) lilac 90 5
b. 15(ö) gray lil 4.00 5
320 A61 20(ö) lt brn 50 5
321 A61 25(ö) dk red 4.50 5
322 A61 35(ö) gray grn ('51) 1.20 15
323 A61 40(ö) gray 1.20 6
324 A61 50(ö) dk bl 4.00 20
325 A61 55(ö) brn ('51) 22.50 2.50
326 A61 70(ö) dp grn 3.75 10
Nos. 318-326 (9) 38.60 3.21

Warship of 1701 A65

Hans Christian Oersted A66

1951, Feb. 26 Engr. *Perf. 13*

327 A65 25(ö) dk red 80 25
328 A65 50(ö) dp bl 4.50 1.25

Issued to commemorate the 250th anniversary of the foundation of the Naval Officers' College.

1951, Mar. 9 **Unwmkd.**

329 A66 50(ö) blue 2.25 75

Issued to commemorate the centenary of the death of Hans Christian Oersted, physicist.

Post Chaise ("Ball Post") A67

Marine Rescue A68

1951, Apr. 1 *Perf. 13*

330 A67 15(ö) purple 1.50 25
331 A67 25(ö) hn brn 1.50 25

Issued to commemorate the centenary of Denmark's first postage stamp.

1952, Mar. 26

332 A68 25(ö) red brn 80 30

Issued to commemorate the centenary of the foundation of the Danish Lifesaving Service.

Types of 1933-50.

1952–53 *Perf. 13*

333 A32 12(ö) lt yel grn 50 5
334 A61 25(ö) lt bl 1.60 25
335 A61 30(ö) brn red 1.00 5
336 A61 50(ö) aqua ('53) 80 6
337 A61 60(ö) dp bl ('53) 1.00 6
338 A61 65(ö) gray ('53) 1.00 10
339 A61 80(ö) org ('53) 1.00 6
340 A61 90(ö) ol ('53) 4.00 6
341 A61 95(ö) red org ('53) 1.75 35
Nos. 333-341 (9) 12.65 1.04

Jelling Runic Stone A69

Designs: 15(ö), Vikings' camp, Trelleborg. 20(ö), Church of Kalundborg. 30(ö), Nyborg castle. 60(ö), Goose tower, Vordinborg.

1953–56 *Perf. 13*

342 A69 10(ö) dp grn 15 5
343 A69 15(ö) lt rose vio 15 5
344 A69 20(ö) brown 20 8
345 A69 30(ö) red ('54) 25 8
346 A69 60(ö) dp bl ('54) 60 20

Designs: 10(ö), Manor house, Spottrup. 15(ö), Hammershus castle ruins. 20(ö), Copenhagen stock exchange. 30(ö), Statue of Frederik V, Amalienborg. 60(ö), Soldier statue at Fredericia.

347 A69 10(ö) grn ('54) 15 5
348 A69 15(ö) lil ('55) 15 5
349 A69 20(ö) brn ('55) 20 8
350 A69 30(ö) red ('55) 25 8
351 A69 60(ö) dp bl ('56) 1.10 20
Nos. 342-351 (10) 3.20 92

Nos. 342-351 were issued to commemorate the 1000th anniversary of the Kingdom of Denmark. Each stamp represents a different century.

Telegraph Equipment of 1854 A70

King Frederik V A71

1954, Feb. 2 *Perf. 13*

352 A70 30(ö) red brn 80 15

Issued to commemorate the centenary of the telegraph in Denmark.

1954, Mar. 31

353 A71 30(ö) dk red 1.00 15

Issued to commemorate the 200th anniversary of the founding of the Royal Academy of Fine Arts.

Type of 1948-50

1955, Apr. 27

354 A61 25(ö) lilac 40 5

Nos. 224C and 226A Surcharged with New Value in Black. Nos. 307 and 321 Surcharged with New Value and 4 Bars.

1955–56

355 A32 5ö on 6ö org 20 20
356 A32 5ö on 7ö lt brn 20 20
357 A61 30(ö) on 20(ö) dk red (I) 40 10
a. Type III 70 15
b. Double surch. 550.00 550.00
358 A61 30(ö) on 25(ö) dk red ('56) 90 6
a. Double surch.

Sören Kierkegaard—A72

Ellehammer's Plane—A73

1955, Nov. 11 **Unwmkd.**

359 A72 30(ö) dk red 60 15

Issued to commemorate the 100th anniversary of the death of Sören Kierkegaard, philosopher and theologian.

1956, Sept. 12 **Engraved**

360 A73 30ö dl red 90 15

Issued to commemorate the 50th anniversary of the first flight made by Jacob Christian Hansen Ellehammer in a heavier-than-air craft.

Northern Countries Issue.

Whooper Swans A74

1956, Oct. 30 *Perf. 13*

361 A74 30ö rose red 5.00 35
362 A74 60ö ultra 3.00 1.00

Issued to emphasize the close bonds among the northern countries: Denmark, Finland, Iceland, Norway and Sweden.

Prince's Palace A75

Harvester A76

Design: 60ö, Sun God's Chariot.

1957, May 15 **Unwmkd.**

363 A75 30ö dl red 1.75 25
364 A75 60ö dk bl 1.75 60

Issued to commemorate the 150th anniversary of the National Museum.

1958, Sept. 4 Engr. *Perf. 13*

365 A76 30ö fawn 40 15

Centenary of the Royal Veterinary and Agricultural College.

King Frederik IX A77

Ballet Dancer A78

1959, Mar. 11

366 A77 30ö rose red 1.00 15
367 A77 35ö rose lil 60 60
368 A77 60ö ultra 60 35

King Frederik's 60th birthday.

1959, May 16

369 A78 35ö rose lil 40 20

Issued to publicize the Danish Ballet and Music Festival, May 17–31. See also Nos. 401, 422.

No. 319 Surcharged

1960, Apr. 7

370 A61 30ö on 15ö pur 40 20

Issued to publicize World Refugee Year, July 1, 1959–June 30, 1960.

Seeder and Farm A79

Designs: 30ö, Harvester combine. 60ö, Plow.

1960, Apr. 28 Engr. *Perf. 13*

371 A79 12ö green 20 20
372 A79 30ö dl red 40 20
373 A79 60ö dk bl 85 35

King Frederik IX and Queen Ingrid A80

1960, May 24 **Unwmkd.**

374 A80 30ö dl red 80 20
375 A80 60ö blue 80 30

Issued to commemorate the 25th anniversary of the marriage of King Frederik IX and Queen Ingrid.

Bascule Light A81

Niels R. Finsen A82

1960, June 8 **Engraved**

376 A81 30ö dl red 45 15

Issued to commemorate the 400th anniversary of the Lighthouse Service.

1960, Aug. 1 *Perf. 13*

377 A82 30ö dk red 45 15

Issued to commemorate the centenary of the birth of Dr. Niels R. Finsen, physician and scientist.

Nursing Mother A83

DC-8 Airliner A84

1960, Aug. 16 **Unwmkd.**

378 A83 60ø ultra 1.00 35

Issued to commemorate the 10th meeting of the regional committee for Europe of the World Health Organization, Copenhagen, Aug. 16–20.

Europa Issue, 1960

Common Design Type

1960, Sept. 19 ***Perf. 13***

Size: 28x21mm.

379 CD3 60ø ultra 1.25 35

SAS Issue

1961, Feb. 24

380 A84 60ø ultra 1.00 35

Issued to commemorate the 10th anniversary of the Scandinavian Airlines System, SAS.

Landscape A85 — Frederik IX A86

1961, Apr. 21 ***Perf. 13***

381 A85 30ø cop brn 35 8

Issued to commemorate the 50th anniversary of Denmark's Society of Nature Lovers.

Fluorescent Paper

as well as ordinary paper, was used in printing many definitive and commemorative stamps, starting in 1962. These include No. 220; the 15, 20, 25, 30, 35 (Nos. 386 and 387), 50 and 60ø, 1.20k, 1.50k and 25k definitives of following set, and Nos. 297–299, 318, 318a–b, 333, 380, 401–427, 429–435, 438–439, 493, 543, 548, B30.

Only fluorescent paper was used for Nos. 436–437, 437A and 440 onward; in semi-postals from B31 onward.

1961-63 **Engraved** ***Perf. 13***

382	A32	15ø grn ('63)	30	5
383	A86	20ø brown	80	5
384	A86	25ø brn ('63)	40	5
385	A86	30ø rose red	1.00	5
386	A86	35ø ol grn	1.00	50
387	A86	35ø rose red ('63)	40	5
388	A86	40ø gray	1.50	5
389	A86	50ø aqua	1.00	6
390	A86	60ø ultra	1.25	10
391	A86	70ø green	2.25	20
392	A86	80ø red org	2.50	10
393	A86	90ø ol bis	6.50	20
394	A86	95ø cl ('63)	1.25	60
		Nos. 382-394 (13)	20.15	2.06

See also Nos. 417–419, 438–441.

State Seal Type of 1946–47

1962–65

395	A55	1.10k lil ('65)	5.00	1.00
396	A55	1.20k gray	4.00	8
397	A55	1.25k orange	4.00	12
398	A55	1.30k grn ('65)	5.00	50
399	A55	1.50k red lil	2.00	6
400	A55	25k yel grn	7.50	25
		Nos. 395-400 (6)	27.50	2.01

Dancer Type of 1959

Inscribed "15-31 MAJ"

1962, Apr. 26

401 A78 60ø ultra 60 25

Issued to publicize the Danish Ballet and Music Festival, May 15–31. No. 369 is dated "17-31 MAJ."

Old Mill A87

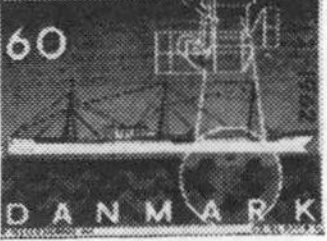

M.S. Selandia A88

1962, May 10 ***Perf. 13*** **Unwmkd.**

402 A87 10ø red brn 15 10

Issued to commemorate the centenary of the abolition of mill monopolies.

1962, June 14 **Engraved**

403 A88 60ø dk bl 3.00 2.50

Issued to commemorate the 50th anniversary of M.S. Selandia, the first Diesel ship.

Violin Scroll, Leaves, Lights and Balloon—A89

1962, Aug. 31

404 A89 35ø rose vio 30 10

Issued to commemorate the 150th anniversary of the birth of Georg Carstensen, founder of Tivoli amusement park, Copenhagen.

Cliffs on Möen Island A90 — Germinating Wheat A91

1962, Nov. 22

405 A90 20ø pale brn 15 5

Issued to publicize preservation of natural treasures and landmarks.

1963, Mar. 21 **Engraved**

406 A91 35ø fawn 40 12

Issued for the "Freedom from Hunger" campaign of the U.N. Food and Agriculture Organization.

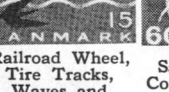

Railroad Wheel, Tire Tracks, Waves and Swallow A92 — Sailing Vessel, Coach, Postilions and Globe A93

1963, May 14 ***Perf. 13*** **Unwmkd.**

407 A92 15ø green 30 15

Issued to commemorate the inauguration of the "Bird Flight Line" railroad link between Denmark and Germany.

1963, May 27

408 A93 60ø dk bl 80 30

Issued to commemorate the centenary of the first International Postal Conference, Paris, 1863.

Niels Bohr and Atom Diagram A94 — Early Public School Drawn on Slate A95

1963, Nov. 21 **Engraved**

409	A94	35ø red brn	45	10
410	A94	60ø dk bl	90	20

Issued to commemorate the 50th anniversary of Prof. Niels Bohr's (1885–1962) atom theory.

1964, June 19 ***Perf. 13*** **Unwmkd.**

411 A95 35ø red brn 30 10

Issued to commemorate the 150th anniversary of the royal decrees for the public school system.

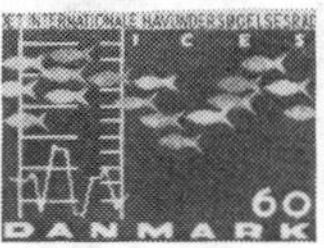

Fish and Chart A96

Danish Watermarks and Perforations A97

1964, Sept. 7 **Engraved**

412 A96 60ø vio bl 60 30

Issued to commemorate the Conference of the International Council for the Exploration of the Sea, Copenhagen.

1964, Oct. 10 ***Perf. 13***

413 A97 35ø pink 40 12

Issued for the 25th anniversary of Stamp Day and to publicize the Odense Stamp Exhibition, Oct. 10–11.

Landscape A98

Calculator, Ledger and Inkwell A99

1964, Nov. 12 **Engraved**

414 A98 25ø brown 25 10

Issued to publicize preservation of natural treasures and landmarks.

1965, Mar. 8 **Unwmkd.**

415 A99 15ø lt ol grn 20 15

Issued to commemorate the centenary of the first Business School in Denmark.

Types of 1933 and 1961

1965, May 15 **Engraved** ***Perf. 13***

416	A32	25ø ap grn	35	5
417	A86	40ø brown	35	5
418	A86	50ø rose red	45	5
419	A86	80ø ultra	1.25	10

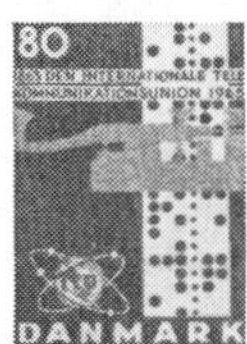

ITU Emblem, Telegraph Key and Teletype Paper A100 — Carl Nielsen A101

1965, May 17

420 A100 80ø dk bl 60 15

Issued to commemorate the centenary of the International Telecommunication Union.

1965, June 9 **Engraved**

421 A101 50ø brn red 30 10

Issued to commemorate the centenary of the birth of Carl Nielsen (1865–1931), composer.

Dancer Type of 1959

Inscribed "15-31 MAJ"

1965, Sept. 23

422 A78 50ø rose red 40 15

Issued to publicize the Danish Ballet and Music Festival, May 15–31.

Bogo Windmill A102 — Mylius Dalgas Surveying Wasteland A103

1965, Nov. 10 **Engraved** ***Perf. 13***

423 A102 40ø brown 40 1

Issued to publicize the preservation of natural treasures and landmarks.

1966, Feb. 24

424 A103 25ø ol grn 30 1

Issued to commemorate the centenary of the Danish Heath Society (reclamation of wastelands), founded by Enrico Mylius Dalgas.

Christen Kold A104

1966, March 29 ***Perf. 13***

425 A104 50ø dl red 40 10

Issued to commemorate the 150th anniversary of the birth of Christen Kold (1816–70), educator.

Poorhouse, Copenhagen A105

Holte Allée, Bregentved A106

Dolmen (Grave) in Jutland A107

1966 **Unwmkd.**

426	A105	50ø dl red	40	10
427	A106	80ø dk bl	1.00	20
428	A107	1.50k dk sl grn	1.50	25

Nos. 426–428 issued to publicize preservation of national treasures and ancient monuments. Issue dates: 50ø, May 12; 80ø, June 16; 1.50k, Nov. 24.

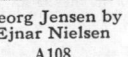

Georg Jensen by Ejnar Nielsen A108

Music Bar and Instruments A109

1966, Aug. 31 **Engr.** ***Perf. 13***

429 A108 80ø dk bl 1.00 20

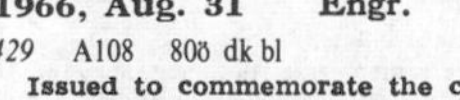

Issued to commemorate the centenary of the birth of Georg Jensen, silversmith.

1967, Jan. 9

430	A109	50ö dk red	40	12

Issued to commemorate the centenary of the Royal Danish Academy of Music.

Cogwheels, and Broken Customs Duty Ribbon
A110

1967, Mar. 2

431	A110	80ö dk bl	1.10	25

Issued to publicize the European Free Trade Association. Industrial tariffs were abolished Dec. 31, 1966, among EFTA members: Austria, Denmark, Finland, Great Britain, Norway, Portugal, Sweden and Switzerland.

Windmill and Medieval Fortress
A111

Designs: 40ö, Ship's rigging and baroque house front. 50ö, Old Town Hall. 80ö, New building construction.

1967 Engraved *Perf. 13*

432	A111	25ö green	60	20
433	A111	40ö sepia	50	20
434	A111	50ö red brn	50	20
435	A111	80ö dk bl	1.50	35

The 800th anniversary of Copenhagen.
Issue dates: Nos. 432-433, Apr. 6; Nos. 434-435, May 11.

Princess Margrethe and Prince Henri
A112

1967, June 10

436	A112	50ö red	60	10

Issued to commemorate the marriage of Crown Princess Margrethe and Prince Henri de Monpezat.

Types of 1933-1961

1967-71 Engraved *Perf. 13*

437	A32	30ö dk grn	35	5
437A	A32	40ö org ('71)	35	8
438	A86	50ö brown	1.25	6
439	A86	60ö rose red	1.25	5
440	A86	80ö green	1.00	5
441	A86	90ö ultra	1.40	10
441A	A55	1.20k Prus grn ('71)	3.00	30
442	A55	2.20k orange	5.50	10
443	A55	2.80k gray	4.50	20
444	A55	2.90k rose vio	5.50	20
444A	A55	3k dk sl grn ('69)	1.10	10
444B	A55	3.10k plum ('70)	7.50	20
444C	A55	4k gray ('69)	1.50	10
444D	A55	4.10k ol ('70)	7.50	20
		Nos. 437-444D (14)	41.70	1.79

Issue dates: Nos. 437-441, June 30, 1967; Nos. 442-443, July 8, 1967; No. 444, Apr. 29, 1968; Nos. 444A, 444C, Aug. 28, 1969; Nos. 444B, 444D, Aug. 27, 1970; Nos. 437A, 441A, June 24, 1971.

Hans Christian Sonne
A113

Cross-anchor and Porpoise
A114

1967, Sept. 21

445	A113	60ö red	40	10

Issued to commemorate the 150th anniversary of the birth of Hans Christian Sonne, pioneer of the cooperative movement in Denmark.

1967, Nov. 9 Engraved *Perf. 13*

446	A114	90ö dk bl	80	40

Issued to commemorate the centenary of the Danish Seamen's Church in Foreign Ports.

Esbjerg Harbor
A115

Koldinghus
A116

1968, Apr. 24

447	A115	30ö dk yel grn	30	15

Centenary of Esbjerg Harbor.

1968, June 13

448	A116	60ö cop red	40	12

700th anniversary of Koldinghus Castle.

Shipbuilding Industry
A117

Sower
A118

Designs: 50ö, Chemical industry. 60ö, Electric power. 90ö, Engineering.

1968, Oct. 24 Engraved *Perf. 13*

449	A117	30ö green	35	20
450	A117	50ö brown	35	10
451	A117	60ö red brn	40	10
452	A117	90ö dk bl	60	40

Issued to publicize Danish industries.

1969, Jan. 29

453	A118	30ö gray grn	30	12

Issued to commemorate the 200th anniversary of the Royal Agricultural Society of Denmark.

Five Ancient Ships
A119

Frederik IX
A120

Nordic Cooperation Issue

1969, Feb. 28 Engraved *Perf. 13*

454	A119	60ö brn red	1.75	25
455	A119	90ö blue	2.50	1.00

Issued to commemorate the 50th anniversary of the Nordic Society and to commemorate the centenary of postal cooperation among the northern countries: Denmark, Finland, Iceland, Norway and Sweden. The design is taken from a coin found at the site of Birka, an ancient Swedish town.

1969, Mar. 11

456	A120	50ö sepia	35	10
457	A120	60ö dl red	35	10

70th birthday of King Frederik IX.

Europa Issue, 1969
Common Design Type

1969, Apr. 28
Size: 28x20mm.

458	CD12	90ö chlky bl	1.25	60

Kronborg Castle
A121

Danish Flag
A122

1969, May 22 Engraved *Perf. 13*

459	A121	50ö brown	35	10

Issued to commemorate the 50th anniversary of the association of Danes living abroad.

1969, June 12

460	A122	60ö bluish blk, red & gray	50	10

Issued to commemorate the 750th anniversary of the fall of the Dannebrog (Danish flag) from heaven.

Martin Andersen Nexø
A123

Niels Stensen
A124

1969, Aug. 28

461	A123	80ö dp grn	60	15

Issued to commemorate the centenary of the birth of Martin Andersen Nexø (1869-1954), novelist.

1969, Sept. 25

462	A124	1k dp brn	65	15

Issued to commemorate the 300th anniversary of the publication of Niels Stensen's geological work "On Solid Bodies."

Abstract Design
A125

Symbolic Design
A126

1969, Nov. 10 Engraved *Perf. 13*

463	A125	60ö rose, red & ultra	40	10

1969, Nov. 20

464	A126	30ö ol grn	40	10

Issued to commemorate the centenary of the birth of Valdemar Poulsen (1869-1942), electrical engineer and inventor.

Post Office Bank
A127

School Safety Patrol
A128

1970, Jan. 15 Engraved *Perf. 13*

465	A127	60ö dk red & org	40	10

Issued to commemorate the 50th anniversary of post office banking service.

1970, Feb. 19

466	A128	50ö brown	40	10

Issued to publicize road safety.

Candle in Window
A129

Deer
A130

1970, May 4 Engraved *Perf. 13*

467	A129	50ö sl, dl bl & yel	40	10

Issued to commemorate the 25th anniversary of liberation from the Germans.

1970, May 28

468	A130	60ö yel grn, red & brn	40	10

Tercentenary of Jaegersborg Deer Park.

Elephant Figurehead, 1741
A131

"The Homecoming" by Povl Christensen
A132

1970, June 15 *Perf. 11½*

469	A131	30ö multi	40	35

Royal Naval Museum, tercentenary.

1970, June 15 *Perf. 13*

470	A132	60ö org, dl vio & ol grn	40	10

Issued to commemorate the 50th anniversary of the union of North Schleswig and Denmark.

Electromagnet
A133

1970, Aug. 13 Engraved

471	A133	80ö gray grn	65	12

Issued to commemorate the 150th anniversary of Hans Christian Oersted's discovery of electromagnetism.

Bronze Age Ship
A134

Ships: 50ö, Viking shipbuilding, from Bayeux tapestry. 60ö, Thuroe schooner with topgallant. 90ö, Tanker.

1970, Sept. 24

472	A134	30ö ocher & brn	40	35
473	A134	50ö brn red & rose brn	40	20
474	A134	60ö gray ol & red brn	70	20
475	A134	90ö bl grn & ultra	1.25	1.00

U.N. Emblem
A135

1970, Oct. 22 Engraved *Perf. 13*

476	A135	90ö bl, grn & red	1.00	70

25th anniversary of the United Nations.

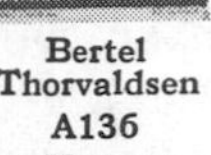

Bertel Thorvaldsen
A136

Mathilde Fibiger
A137

1970, Nov. 19

477	A136	2k sl bl	1.25	25

Issued to commemorate the bicentenary of the birth of Bertel Thorvaldsen (1768–1844), sculptor.

1971, Feb. 25

478	A137	80ö ol grn	60	12

Danish Women's Association centenary.

Refugees
A138

Hans Egede
A139

1971, March 26 Engr. *Perf. 13*

479	A138	50ö brown	40	15
480	A138	60ö brn red	60	10

Joint northern campaign for the benefit of refugees.

1971, May 27

481	A139	1k brown	70	15

250th anniversary of arrival of Hans Egede in Greenland and beginning of its colonization.

Swimming
A140

Designs: 50ö, Gymnastics. 60ö, Soccer. 90ö, Sailing.

1971, Oct. 14

482	A140	30ö bl & grn	40	35
483	A140	50ö dk red & brn	40	15
484	A140	60ö gray, yel & dk bl	60	15
485	A140	90ö ultra, pale grn & vio	1.00	60

Georg Brandes
A141

1971, Nov. 11 Engr. *Perf. 13*

486	A141	90ö dk bl	70	25

Centenary of first lectures given by Georg Brandes (1842–1927), writer and literary critic.

Sugar Production
A142

1972, Jan. 27

487	A142	80ö sl grn	60	15

Centenary of Danish sugar production.

King Frederik IX
A143

1972, Mar. 11 Engr. *Perf. 13*

488	A143	60ö red brn	45	10

In memory of King Frederik IX (1899–1972).

Abstract Design
A144

1972, Mar. 11

489	A144	1.20k brt rose lil, bl gray & brn	1.00	75

Centenary of the Danish Meteorological Institute.

Nikolai F. S. Grundtvig
A145

Locomotive, 1847, Ferry, Travelers
A146

1972, May 4 Engraved *Perf. 13*

490	A145	1k sepia	60	30

Centenary of the death of Nikolai Frederik Severin Grundtvig (1783–1872), theologian and poet.

1972, June 26

491	A146	70ö rose red	60	20

125th anniversary of Danish State Railways.

Rebild Hills
A147

"Tinker Turned Politician"
A148

1972, June 26

492	A147	1k bl, sl grn & mar	60	25

Types of 1933–46

1972–78 Engraved *Perf. 13*

493	A32	20ö sl bl ('74)	8	5
494	A32	50ö sep ('74)	18	5
495	A32	60ö ap grn ('76)	2.75	10
496	A32	60ö gray ('78)	1.00	50
497	A32	70ö red	1.50	5
498	A32	70ö ap grn ('77)	25	8
499	A55	2.50k orange	2.50	15
500	A55	2.80k ol ('75)	1.25	30
501	A55	3.50k lilac	3.00	10
502	A55	4.50k olive	7.00	10
503	A55	6k vio blk ('76)	1.75	20
504	A55	7k red lil ('78)	2.00	15
505	A55	9k brn ol ('77)	2.75	15
506	A55	10k lem ('76)	3.00	15
		Nos. 493-506 (14)	29.01	2.13

1972, Sept. 14

507	A148	70ö dk red	50	10

250th anniversary of the comedies of Ludvig Holberg (1684–1754) on the Danish stage.

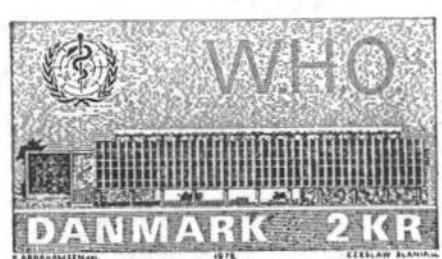

WHO Building, Copenhagen
A149

1972, Sept. 14

508	A149	2k bl, blk & lt red brn	1.25	50

Opening of World Health Organization Building, Copenhagen.

Bridge Across Little Belt
A150

Aeroskobing House c. 1740
A151

Designs (Diagrams): 60ö, Hanstholm Harbor. 70ö, Lim Fjord Tunnel. 90ö, Knudshoved Harbor.

1972, Oct. 19 Engraved *Perf. 13*

509	A150	40ö dk grn	35	30
510	A150	60ö dk brn	60	10
511	A150	70ö dk red	60	10
512	A150	90ö dk bl grn	75	35

Highway engineering.

1972, Nov. 23

Danish Architecture: 60ö, East Bornholm farmhouse, 17th century (horiz.). 70ö, House, Christianshavn, c. 1710. 1.20k, Hvide Sande farmhouse, c. 1810 (horiz.).

Size: 20x28mm., 27x20mm.

513	A151	40ö red, brn & blk	60	40
514	A151	60ö blk, vio bl & grn	60	40

Size: 18x37mm., 36x20mm.

515	A151	70ö red, dk red & blk	70	18
516	A151	1.20k dk brn, red & grn	1.00	90

Johannes V. Jensen
A152

Guard Rails and Cogwheels
A153

1973, Feb. 22 Engraved *Perf. 13*

517	A152	90ö green	50	15

Centenary of the birth of Johannes Vilhelm Jensen (1873–1950), lyric poet and novelist.

1973, Mar. 22

518	A153	50ö sepia	40	15

Centenary of first Danish Factory Act for labor protection.

P. C. Abildgaard
A154

Rhododendron
A155

1973, Mar. 22

519	A154	1k dl bl	60	60

Bicentenary of Royal Veterinary College, Christianshaven, founded by Prof. P. C. Abildgaard.

1973, Apr. 26

Design: 70ö, Dronningen of Denmark rose.

520	A155	60ö brn, grn & vio	70	20
521	A155	70ö dk red, rose & grn	70	20

Centenary of the founding of the Horticultural Society of Denmark.

Nordic Cooperation Issue 1973

Nordic House, Reykjavik
A156

1973, June 26 Engr. *Perf. 13*

522	A156	70ö multi	75	30
523	A156	1k multi	3.00	50

A century of postal cooperation among Denmark, Finland, Iceland, Norway and Sweden, and in connection with the Nordic Postal Conference, Reykjavik.

Sextant, Stella Nova and Cassiopeia
A157

St. Mark, from 11th Century Book of Dalby
A158

1973, Oct. 18 Engraved *Perf. 13*

524	A157	2k dk bl	1.00	30

400th anniversary of the publication of "De Nova Stella," by Tycho Brahe.

1973, Oct. 18 Photo. *Perf. 14x14½*

525	A158	120ö buff & multi	1.25	80

300th anniversary of Royal Library.

Devil and Gossips, Fanefjord Church, 1480
A159

Frescoes: No. 527, Queen Esther and King Ahasuerus, Tirsted Church, c.1400. No. 528, Miraculous Harvest, Jetsmark Church, c.1474. No. 529, Jesus carrying cross, and wearing crown of thorns, Biersted Church, c.1400. No. 530, Creation of Eve, Fanefjord Church, c.1480.

1973, Nov. 28 Engr. *Perf. 13*

Cream Paper

526	A159	70ö dk red, yel & grn	1.50	50
527	A159	70ö dk red, yel & grn	1.50	50
528	A159	70ö dk red, yel & grn	1.50	50

529	A159	70ö dk red, yel & grn	1.50	50
530	A159	70ö dk red, yel & grn	1.50	50
a.		Booklet pane of 10	45.00	
		Nos. 526-530 (5)	7.50	2.50

Nos. 526–530 printed se-tenant in sheets of 50 (5x10). No. 530a contains 2 each of Nos. 526–530.

Blood Donors A160 — Queen Margrethe A161

1974, Jan. 24

531	A160	90ö pur & red	60	20

"Blood Saves Lives."

1974-81 Engraved *Perf. 13*

532	A161	60ö brown	60	25
533	A161	60ö orange	60	5
534	A161	70ö red	60	5
535	A161	70ö dk brn	60	5
536	A161	80ö green	60	15
537	A161	80ö dp brn ('76)	60	25
538	A161	90ö red lil	60	5
539	A161	90ö dl red	60	5
540	A161	90ö sl grn ('76)	60	25
541	A161	100ö dp ultra	80	10
542	A161	100ö gray ('75)	80	25
543	A161	100ö red ('76)	60	5
544	A161	100ö brn ('77)	60	25
a.		Bklt. pane of 5 (#544, #494, 2 #493, #318)	2.25	
545	A161	110ö org ('78)	60	25
546	A161	120ö slate	80	6
547	A161	120ö red ('77)	60	6
548	A161	130ö ultra ('75)	2.50	1.00
549	A161	150ö vio bl ('78)	1.00	70
550	A161	180ö sl grn ('77)	80	50
551	A161	200ö bl ('81)	1.25	50
		Nos. 532-551 (20)	15.75	4.87

See Nos. 630, 632-643.

Pantomime Theater A162

1974, May 16

552	A162	100ö indigo	70	20

Centenary of the Pantomime Theater, Tivoli.

Hverringe A163

Views: 60ö, Norre Lyndelse, Carl Nielsen's childhood home. 70ö, Odense, Hans Chr. Andersen's childhood home. 90ö, Hesselagergaard (vert.). 120ö, Hindsholm.

1974, June 20 Engr. *Perf. 13*

553	A163	50ö brn & multi	70	30
554	A163	60ö sl grn & multi	60	35
555	A163	70ö red brn & multi	60	35
556	A163	90ö dk grn & mar	80	15
557	A163	120ö red org & dk grn	1.10	50
		Nos. 553-557 (5)	3.80	1.65

Emblem, Runner with Map A164 — Iris A165

Design: 80ö, Compass.

1974, Aug. 22 Engr. *Perf. 13*

558	A164	70ö dk bl & brn	60	40
559	A164	80ö brn & vio bl	60	40

World Orienteering Championships 1974.

1974, Sept. 19

Design: 120ö, Purple orchid.

560	A165	90ö brn, vio bl & sl grn	60	20
561	A165	120ö ind, lil & sl grn	90	40

Copenhagen Botanical Garden centenary.

Mailman, 1624, and Postilion, 1780 A166

Carrier Pigeon A167

Design: 90ö, Balloon and sailing ships.

1974, Oct. 9 Engraved *Perf. 13*

562	A166	70ö lem & dk brn	60	40
563	A166	90ö dl grn & sep	75	20
564	A167	120ö dk bl	1.00	35

350th anniversary of Danish Post Office (70ö, 90ö) and centenary of Universal Postal Union (120ö).

Souvenir Sheet

Ferslew's Essays, 1849 and 1852—A168

Engr. & Photo.

1975, Feb. 27 *Perf. 13*

565	A168	Sheet of 4, multi	7.00	7.50
a.		70ö *Coat of arms*	1.60	1.70
b.		80ö *King Frederik VII*	1.60	1.70
c.		90ö *King Frederik VII*	1.60	1.70
d.		100ö *Mercury*	1.60	1.70

HAFNIA 76 International Stamp Exhibition, Copenhagen, Aug. 20–29, 1976. Size of No. 565: 68x93mm. Sold for 5k.

See No. 585.

Early Radio Equipment A169 — Flora Danica Plate A170

1975, Mar. 20 Engr. *Perf. 13*

566	A169	90ö dl red	75	18

Danish broadcasting, 50th anniversary.

1975, May 22

Danish China: 90ö, Flora Danica tureen. 130ö, Vase and tea caddy, blue fluted china.

567	A170	50ö sl grn	50	18
568	A170	90ö brn red	1.00	15
569	A170	130ö vio bl	1.50	1.25

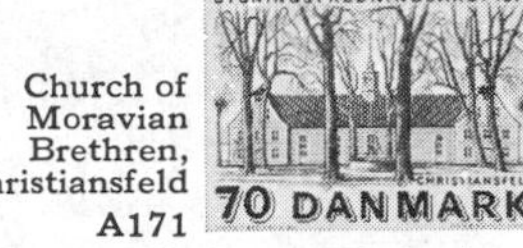

Church of Moravian Brethren, Christiansfeld A171

Designs: 120ö, Kongsgaard farmhouse, Lejre. 150ö, Anna Queenstraede, Helsingor (vert.).

1975, June 19

570	A171	70ö sepia	50	40
571	A171	120ö ol grn	1.50	50
572	A171	150ö vio blk	80	20

European Architectural Heritage Year 1975.

Hans Christian Andersen A172 — Watchman's Square, Abenra A173

Designs: 70ö, Numbskull Jack, drawing by Vilh. Pedersen. 130ö, The Marshking's Daughter, drawing by L. Frohlich.

1975, Aug. 28 Engr. *Perf. 13*

573	A172	70ö brn & blk	1.00	1.00
574	A172	90ö brn red & dk brn	1.75	20
575	A172	130ö bl blk & sep	2.25	2.25

Hans Christian Andersen (1805–1875), writer, death centenary.

1975, Sept. 25

Designs: 90ö, Haderslev Cathedral (vert.). 100ö, Mögeltönder Polder. 120ö, Mouth of Vidaaen at Höjer Floodgates.

576	A173	70ö multi	60	40
577	A173	90ö multi	70	20
578	A173	100ö multi	70	20
579	A173	120ö multi	1.00	50

European Kingfisher A174

Designs: 70ö, Hedgehog. 90ö, Cats. 130ö, Avocets. 200ö, Otter.

1975, Oct. 23 Engr. *Perf. 13*

580	A174	50ö vio blk	70	35
581	A174	70ö black	70	35
582	A174	90ö brown	70	20
583	A174	130ö bluish blk	1.25	1.10
584	A174	200ö brn blk	1.10	25
		Nos. 580-584 (5)	4.45	2.25

Protected animals, and for the centenary of the Danish Society for the Prevention of Cruelty to Animals (90ö).

Souvenir Sheet

HAFNIA Type of 1974

1975, Nov. 20 Engr. & Photo.

585	A168	Sheet of 4, multi	3.50	4.00
a.		50ö buff & brn No. 2	80	90
b.		70ö buff, brn & bl, No. 1	80	90
c.		90ö buff, bl & brn, No. 11	80	90
d.		130ö ol, brn & buff, No. 19	80	90

HAFNIA 76 International Stamp Exhibition, Copenhagen, Aug. 20–29, 1976. Size of No. 585: 68x93mm. Sold for 5k.

Copenhagen, Center A175

View from Round Tower A176

Copenhagen, Views: 100ö, Central Station, interior. 130ö, Harbor.

1976, Mar. 25 Engr. *Perf. 12½*

586	A175	60ö multi	80	30
587	A176	80ö multi	80	25
588	A176	100ö multi	50	10
589	A175	130ö multi	2.25	2.25

Postilion, by Otto Bache A177 — Emil Chr. Hansen, Physiologist, in Laboratory A178

1976, June 17 Engr. *Perf. 12½*

590	A177	130ö multi	2.00	1.50

Souvenir Sheet

591	A177	130ö multi	8.00	10.00

HAFNIA 76 International Stamp Exhibition, Copenhagen, Aug. 20–29. No. 591 contains one stamp similar to No. 590 with design continuous into sheet margin. Sheet shows painting "A String of Horses Outside an Inn" of which No. 590 shows a detail. Black marginal inscription and HAFNIA emblem. Size: 103x81mm. Sheet sold for 15k including exhibition ticket.

1976, Sept. 23 Engr. *Perf. 13*

592	A178	100ö org red	50	10

Carlsberg Foundation (art and science), centenary.

Glass Blower Molding Glass A179 — Five Water Lilies A180

Danish Glass Production: 80ö, Finished glass removed from pipe. 130ö, Glass cut off from foot. 150ö, Glass blown up in mold.

1976, Nov. 18 Engr. *Perf. 13*

593	A179	60ö slate	30	30
594	A179	80ö dk brn	40	30
595	A179	130ö dk bl	1.10	1.10
596	A179	150ö red brn	80	20

Photogravure and Engraved

1977, Feb. 2 *Perf. 12½*

597	A180	100ö brt grn & multi	60	35
598	A180	130ö ultra & multi	2.00	2.00

Nordic countries cooperation for protection of the environment and 25th Session of Nordic Council, Helsinki, Feb. 19.

Road Accident
A181

1977, Mar. 24 Engr. *Perf. 12½*

599	A181 100ö brn red		40	10

Road Safety Traffic Act, May 1, 1977.

Europa Issue 1977

Allinge
A182

Design: 1.30k, View, Ringsted.

1977, May 2 Engr. *Perf. 12½*

600	A182	1k dl red	70	25
601	A182	1.30k dk bl	3.50	3.00

Kongeåen
A183

Landscapes, Southern Jutland: 90ö, Skallingen. 150ö, Tørskind. 200ö, Jelling.

1977, June 30 Engr. *Perf. 12½*

602	A183	60ö multi	1.25	1.25
603	A183	90ö multi	60	40
604	A183	150ö multi	80	50
605	A183	200ö multi	90	30

See Nos. 616-619, 655-658.

Hammers and Horseshoes
A184

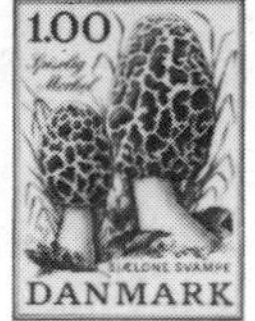

Globe Flower
A185

Designs: 1k, Chisel, square and plane. 1.30k, Trowel, ceiling brush and folding ruler.

1977, Sept. 22 Engr. *Perf. 12½*

606	A184	80ö dk brn	50	40
607	A184	1k red	60	15
608	A184	1.30k vio bl	1.10	50

Danish crafts.

1977, Nov. 17 Engr. *Perf. 12½*

Design: 1.50k, Cnidium dubium.

609	A185	1k multi	60	20
610	A185	1.50k multi	1.25	85

Endangered flora.

Handball
A186

1978, Jan. 19 *Perf. 12½*

611	A186	1.20k red	42	16

Men's World Handball Championships.

Christian IV, Frederiksborg Castle
A187

Frederiksborg Museum
A188

1978, Mar. 16

612	A187	1.20k brn red	60	16
613	A188	1.80k black	1.00	45

Frederiksborg Museum, centenary.

Europa Issue

Jens Bang's House, Aalborg
A189

Frederiksborg Castle, Ground Plan and Elevation
A190

1978, May 11 Engr. *Perf. 12½*

614	A189	1.20k red	42	16
615	A190	1.50k dk bl & vio bl	1.25	1.00

Landscape Type of 1977

Landscapes, Central Jutland: 70ö, Kongenshus Memorial Park. 120ö, Post Office, Old Town in Aarhus. 150ö, Lignite fields, Soby. 180ö, Church wall, Stadil Church.

1978, June 15 Engr. *Perf. 12½*

616	A183	70ö multi	35	30
617	A183	120ö multi	60	25
618	A183	150ö multi	75	75
619	A183	180ö multi	85	60

Boats in Harbor
A191

Edible Morel
A192

Designs: 1k, Eel traps. 1.80k, Boats in berth. 2.50k, Drying nets.

1978, Sept. 7 Engr. *Perf. 12½*

620	A191	70ö ol gray	60	40
621	A191	1k redsh brn	60	25
622	A191	1.80k slate	60	40
623	A191	2.50k sepia	1.25	60

Danish fishing industry.

1978, Nov. 16 Engr. *Perf. 12½*

Design: 1.20k, Satan's mushroom.

624	A192	1k sepia	60	30
625	A192	1.20k dl red	80	30

Telephones
A193

1979, Jan. 25 Engr. *Perf. 12½*

626	A193	1.20k dl red	50	20

Centenary of Danish telephone.

University Seal
A194

Pentagram: University Faculties
A195

1979, Apr. 5 Engr. *Perf. 12½*

627	A194	1.30k vermilion	60	20
628	A195	1.60k dk vio bl	80	70

University of Copenhagen, 500th anniversary.

Types of 1933–1974

1979-82 Engr. *Perf. 13*

629	A32	80o green	32	10
630	A161	90o slate	1.50	1.25
631	A32	100o dp grn ('81)	40	15
632	A161	110o brown	45	5
a.		Bklt. pane of 5 (#493-494, #632, 2 #318) ('79)	1.00	
a.		Booklet pane of 10 (2 each #629, 438, 632, 4 #633) ('79)	7.00	
633	A161	130o red	52	6
634	A161	130o brn ('81)	80	35
a.		Bklt. pane of 10, 2 each #494, 629, 632, 4 #633 ('79)	4.00	
635	A161	140o red org ('80)	1.25	1.00
636	A161	150o red org ('81)	90	65
637	A161	160o ultra	1.00	80
638	A161	160o red ('81)	75	15
a.		Bklt. pane of 14 (2 each #318, 634, 638, 8 #494)	8.00	
639	A161	180o ultra ('80)	1.00	90
640	A161	210o gray ('80)	1.25	1.10
641	A161	230o ol grn ('81)	1.25	25
642	A161	250o bl grn ('81)	1.25	50
643	A55	2.80k dl grn	1.00	20
644	A55	3.30k brn red ('81)	1.00	30
645	A55	3.50k grnsh bl ('82)	1.10	60
646	A55	4.30k brn red ('80)	1.75	1.10
647	A55	4.70k rose lil ('81)	1.75	1.25
648	A55	8k orange	2.50	20
649	A55	12k red brn ('81)	3.75	65
650	A55	14k dk red brn ('82)	4.25	65
		Nos. 629-650 (22)	29.74	12.26

Europa Issue 1979

Mail Cart, 1785
A196

Design: 1.60k, Morse key and amplifier.

1979, May 10 *Perf. 12½*

651	A196	1.30k red	45	20
652	A196	1.60k dk bl	1.00	1.00

Gripping Beast Pendant
A197

Viking Art: 2k, Key with gripping beast design.

1979, June 14 Engr. *Perf. 13*

653	A197	1.10k sepia	40	20
654	A197	2k grnsh gray	60	20

Landscape Type of 1977

Landscapes, Northern Jutland: 80ö, Mols Bjerge. 90ö, Orslev Kloster. 200ö, Trans. 280ö, Bovbjerg.

1979, Sept. 6 Engr. *Perf. 12½*

655	A183	80ö multi	40	40
656	A183	90ö multi	90	80
657	A183	200ö multi	70	20
658	A183	280ö multi	1.00	75

Adam Oehlenschläger—A198

1979, Oct, 4 Engraved *Perf. 13*

659	A198	1.30k dk car	45	20

Adam Oehlenschläger (1799-1850), poet and dramatist.

Score, Violin, Dancing Couple
A199

Ballerina
A200

1979, Nov. 8 Engraved *Perf. 13×12½*

660	A199	1.10k brown	35	25
661	A200	1.60k ultra	65	40

Jacob Gade (b. 1879), composer; August Bournoville (1805-1879), ballet master.

Royal Mail Guards' Office, Copenhagen, 1779—A201

1980, Feb. 14 Engraved *Perf. 13*

662	A201	1.30k brn red	45	20

National Postal Service, 200th anniversary.

Symbols of Occupation, Health and Education—A202

1980, May 5 Engraved *Perf. 13*

663	A202	1.60k dk bl	80	65

World Conference of the U.N. Decade for Women, Copenhagen, July 14-30.

Europa Issue 1980

Karen Blixen (1885-1962), writer—A203

Design: 1.60k, August Krogh (1874-1949), physiologist.

1980, May 5

664	A203	1.30k red	45	20
665	A203	1.60k blue	80	80

Landscape Type of 1977

Landscapes, Northern Jutland: 80o, Viking ship burial grounds, Lindholm Hoje. 110o, Lighthouse, Skagen (vert.). 200o, Boreglum Monastery. 280o, Fishing boats, Vorupor Beach.

1980, June 19 **Engraved** *Perf. 13*

666 A183 80ŏ multi 40 40
667 A183 110ŏ multi 40 40
668 A183 200ŏ multi 60 20
669 A183 280ŏ multi 1.00 80

Nordic Cooperation Issue

Silver Tankard, by Borchardt Rollufse, 1641—A204

1980, Sept. 9 **Engr.** *Perf. 13*

670 A204 1.30k *shown* 45 20
671 A204 1.80k *Bishop's bowl, Copenhagen faience, 18th century* 1.00 1.00

Frisian Sceat Facsimile, Obverse and Reverse, 9th Century—A205

Coins: 1.40k Silver coin of Valdemar the Great and Absalom, 1157-1182, 1.80k, Gold 12-mark coin of Christian VII, 1781.

1980, Oct. 9 **Engraved** *Perf. 13*

672 A205 1.30k red & redsh brn 45 20
673 A205 1.40k ol gray & sl grn 80 70
674 A205 1.80k dk bl & sl bl 80 70

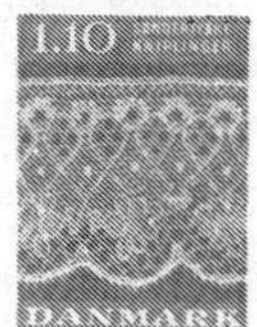

Tonder Lace Pattern, North Schleswig—A206

Designs: Tonder lace patterns.

1980, Nov. 13 **Engraved** *Perf. 13*

675 A206 1.10k brown 45 35
676 A206 1.30k brn red 52 20
677 A206 2k ol gray 80 30

Nyboder Development, Copenhagen, 350th Anniversary—A207

Design: 1.30k, View of Nyboder (diff.).

1981, Mar. 19

678 A207 1.30k dp org & ocher 60 50
679 A207 1.60k dp org & ocher 60 20

Tilting at a Barrel on Shrovetide A208

Design: 2k, Midsummer's Eve bonfire.

1981, May 4 **Engr.** *Perf. 13*

680 A208 1.60k brn red 60 25
681 A208 2k dk bl 80 45

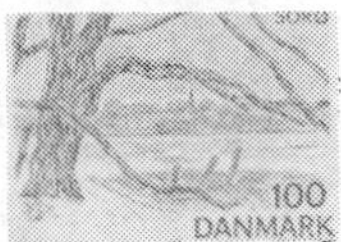

Soro Lake and Academy, Zealand—A209

Designs: Views of Zealand.

1981, June 18 **Engr.** *Perf. 13*

682 A209 100o shown 40 15
683 A209 150o Poet N.F.S. Grundtvig's home, Udby 60 35
684 A209 160o Kaj Munk's home, Opager 65 25
685 A209 200o Gronsund 65 40
686 A209 230o Bornholm Isld. 80 50
Nos. 682-686 (5) 3.10 1.65

European Urban Renaissance Year A210

1981, Sept. 10 **Engr.** *Perf. 12½x13*

687 A210 1.60k dl red 50 25

Type of 1933

1981-85 **Engr.** *Perf. 13*

688 A32 30o orange 12 5
689 A32 40o purple 16 6
690 A32 80o ol bis ('85) 18 8
691 A32 100o bl ('83) 45 10
b. Booklet pane of 8 (2 #494, 4 #691, 2 #706) ('83) 6.00
692 A32 150o dk grn ('82) 60 25
693 A32 200o grn ('83) 70 40
694 A32 230o brt yel grn ('84) 45 22
695 A32 250o brt yel grn ('85) 55 22

Ellehammer's 18-horsepower Biplane, 1906—A211

1981, Oct. 8 **Engr.** *Perf. 13*

696 A211 1k shown 40 40
697 A211 1.30k R-1 Fokker CV reconnaissance plane, 1926 70 60
698 A211 1.60k Bellanca J-300, 1931 50 25
699 A211 2.30k DC-7C, 1957 80 50

Queen Margrethe II, 10th Anniv. of Accession A212

1982-85 **Engr.** *Perf. 13*

700 A212 1.60k dl red 75 10
701 A212 1.60k dk ol grn 80 70
702 A212 1.80k sepia 1.00 40
703 A212 2k dl red 1.00 10
b. Bklt. pane of 10 (4 #494, 2 each #493, 702, 703) 10.00
704 A212 2.20k ol grn ('83) 55 40
705 A212 2.30k violet 1.00 10
706 A212 2.50k org red ('83) 1.00 30
707 A212 2.70k dk bl 1.10 35
708 A212 2.70k cop red ('84) 52 25
c. Booklet pane of 8 (3 #688, 2 #494, 3 #708) ('84) 5.00
709 A212 2.80k cop red ('85) 50 25
b. Booklet pane of 8 (3 #493, 2 #494, 3 #709) ('85) 4.00
710 A212 3k vio ('83) 1.25 35
711 A212 3.30k bluish blk ('84) 72 28
712 A212 3.50k bl ('83) 1.25 20
713 A212 3.50k dk vio ('85) 62 30
714 A212 3.70k dp bl ('84) 85 32
715 A212 3.80k dk bl ('85) 65 32

Arms Types of 1946

Engr. *Perf. 13*

716 A55 4.30k dk ol grn ('85) 95 38
717 A55 5.50k dk bl grn ('85) 1.25 50
718 A55 16k cop red ('85) 3.50 1.40
719 A55 17k cop red ('85) 3.75 1.50
720 A55 18k brn vio ('85) 3.00 1.50
720A A55 50k dk red ('85) 8.75 4.25

World Figure Skating Championships—A213

1982, Feb. 25

721 A213 2k dk bl 60 25

Customs Service Centenary—A214

1982, Feb. 25 **Engr.** *Perf. 12½*

722 A214 1.60k Revenue schooner Argus 60 18

Europa Issue, 1982—A215

1982, May 3 **Engr.** *Perf. 12½*

723 A215 2k Abolition of adscription, 1788 60 15
724 A215 2.70k Women's voting right, 1915 1.00 65

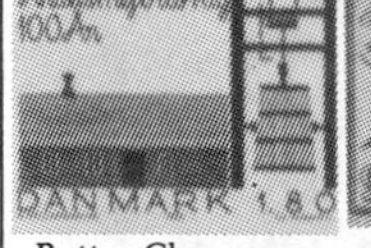

Butter Churn, Barn, Hjedding A216

Records Office, 400th Anniv. A217

1982, June 10 **Engr.** *Perf. 13*

725 A216 1.80k brown 60 30

Cooperative dairy farming centenary.

1982, June 10

726 A217 2.70k green 1.00 25

Steen Steensen Blicher (1782-1848), Poet, by J.V. Gertner—A218

1982, Aug. 26 **Engr.** *Perf. 13*

Robert Storm Petersen (1882-1949), Cartoonist A219

Printing in Denmark, 500th Anniv. A220

Characters: 1.50k, Three little men and the number man. 2k, Peter and Ping the penguin (horiz.).

1982, Sept. 23 **Engr.** *Perf. 12½*

728 A219 1.50k dk bl & red 60 40
729 A219 2k red & ol grn 65 30

1982, Sept. 23

730 A220 1.80k Press, text, ink balls 60 30

500th Anniv. of University Library—A221

1982, Nov. 4

731 A221 2.70k Library seal 1.00 40

World Communications Year—A222

1983, Jan. 27 **Engr.** *Perf. 13*

732 A222 2k multi 65 30

Amusement Park, 400th Anniv. A223

Badminton Championship A224

1983, Feb. 24

733 A223 2k multi 65 30

1983, Feb. 24

734 A224 2.70k multi 1.00 35

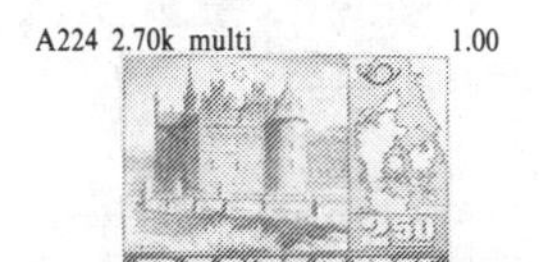

Nordic Cooperation Issue—A225

1983, Mar. 24

735 A225 2.50k Egeskov Castle 75 30
736 A225 3.50k Troll Church, North

50th Anniv. of Steel Plate Printed Stamps—A226

1983, Mar. 24 **Engr.** ***Perf. 13***
737 A226 2.50k car rose 75 30

Europa 1983 A227

Weights and Measures Ordinance, 300th Anniv. A228

1983, May 5 **Engr.** ***Perf. 13***
738 A227 2.50k Kildekovshallen Recreation Center, Copenhagen 75 30
739 A227 3.50k Salling Sound Bridge 1.25 80

1983, June 16
740 A228 2.50k red 75 30

300th Anniv. of Christian V Danish Law—A229

1983, Sept. 8 **Engr.**
741 A229 5k Codex titlepage 1.65 60

Life Saving and Salvage Services—A230

1983, Oct. 6 **Engr.** ***Perf. 13***
742 A230 1k Car crash, police 40 20
743 A230 2.50k Fire, ambulance service 80 30
744 A230 3.50k Sea rescue 1.25 80

Elderly in Society—A231

1983, Oct. 6
745 A231 2k Stages of life 65 40
746 A231 2.50k Train passengers 80 20

N.F.S. Grundtvig (1783-1872), Poet—A232

Street Scene, by C.W. Eckersberg (1783-1853)—A233

1983, Nov. 3 **Engr.**
747 A232 2.50k brn red 80 30
748 A233 2.50k brn red 80 30

Plant a Tree Campaign—A234

1984 Billiards World Championships, Copenhagen, May 10-13—A235

1984, Jan. 26 **Litho. & Engr.**
749 A234 2.70k Shovel, sapling 85 22

Engr.
750 A235 3.70k Game 1.25 40

Hydrographic Dept. Bicentenary—A236

Pilotage Service, 300th Anniv.—A237

1984, Mar. 22 **Engr.** ***Perf. 13***
751 A236 2.30k Compass 75 50
752 A237 2.70k Boat 90 40

2nd European Parliament Elections—A238

Scouts Around Campfire, Emblems—A239

1984, Apr. 12 **Litho. & Engr.** ***Perf. 13***
753 A238 2.70k org & dk bl 90 22
754 A239 2.70k multi 90 22

Europa (1959-84)—A240

1984, May 3 **Engr.** ***Perf. 12½***
755 A240 2.70k red 90 22
756 A240 3.70k blue 1.25 80

Prince Henrik, 50th Birthday A241

D Day, 40th Anniv. A242

1984, June 6 **Engr.**
757 A241 2.70k brn red 90 22
758 A242 2.70k War Memorial, Copenhagen 90 22

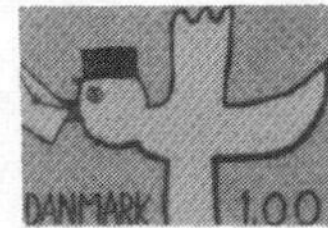

17th Cent. Inn—A243

1984, June 6
759 A243 3k multi 1.00 40

Fishing and Shipping—A244

1984, Sept. 6 **Engr.**
760 A244 2.30k Research (Herring) 80 60
761 A244 2.70k Sea transport 90 22
762 A244 3.30k Deep-sea fishing 1.10 50
763 A244 3.70k Deep-sea, diff. 1.25 60

Post Bird—A245

1984, Oct. 5 **Litho. & Engr.**
764 A245 1k multi 40 15

Holberg Meets with an Officer, by Wilhelm Marstrand (1810-73)—A246

1984, Oct. 5
765 A246 2.70k multi 90 22

Ludvig Holberg (1684-1754), writer.

Jewish Community in Copenhagen, 300th Anniv.—A247

1984, Oct. 5
766 A247 3.70k Woman blessing Sabbath candles 1.25 60

Carnival in Rome, by Christoffer W. Eckersberg (1783-1853)—A248

Paintings: 10k, Ymer and Odhumble (Nordic mythology figures), by Nicolai A. Abildgaard (1743-1809) (vert.).

Perf. 12½x13, 13x12½

1984, Nov. 22 **Litho. & Engr.**
767 A248 5k multi 1.65 1.40
768 A248 10k multi 3.25 2.50

German and French Reform Church, 300th Anniv.—A249

1985, Jan. 24 **Engr.** ***Perf. 13***
769 A249 2.80k magenta 90 20

Bonn-Copenhagen Declarations, 30th Anniv.—A250

1985, Feb. 21 **Litho.** ***Perf. 14***
770 A250 2.80k Map, flags 90 20

Intl. Youth Year—A251

1985, Mar. 14 *Perf. 13*
771 A251 3.80k multi 1.20 70

Souvenir Sheet

Early Postal Ordinances—A252

1985, Mar. 14 **Litho. & Engr.**

772 Sheet of 4 4.75 5.00
- ***a.*** A252 1k Christian IV's Ordinance on Postmen, 1624 1.10 1.25
- ***b.*** A252 2.50k Plague Mandate, 1711 1.10 1.25
- ***c.*** A252 2.80k Ordinance on Prohibition of Mail by Means other than the Post, 1775 1.10 1.25
- ***d.*** A252 3.80k Act on Postal Articles, 1831 1.10 1.25

HAFNIA '87 philatelic exhibition. Size: 93x68mm. Sold for 15k.

Europa 1985—A253

1985, May 2
773 A253 2.80k Musical staff 90 40
774 A253 3.80k Musical staff, diff. 1.25 70

Arrival of Queen Ingrid in Denmark, 50th Anniv.—A254

1985, May 21
775 A254 2.80k Queen Mother, chrysanthemums 90 20

See Greenland No. 163.

Opening of the Faro Bridges—A255

1985, May 21 **Litho.** *Perf. 13*
776 A255 2.80k Faro-Falster Bridge 90 20

St. Cnut's Land Grant to Lund Cathedral, 900th Anniv.—A256

Seal of King Cnut and: 2.80k, Lund Cathedral. 3k, City of Helsingdorg, Sweden.

1985, May 21 **Engr.**
777 A256 2.80k multi 90 20
778 A256 3k multi 95 60

See Sweden Nos. 1538-1539.

U.N. Decade for Women
A257

Sports
A258

1985, June 27 **Litho. & Engr.**
779 A257 3.80k Cyclist 1.25 60

1985, June 27
780 A258 2.80k Women's floor exercise 90 30
781 A258 3.80k Canoe & kayak 1.25 60
782 A258 6k Cycling 1.75 1.00

Kronborg Castle, Elsinore, 400th Anniv.—A259

1985, Sept. 5 **Litho. & Engr.**
783 A259 2.80k multi 90 22

U.N. 40th Anniv.—A260

1985, Sept. 5
784 A260 3.80k Dove, emblem 1.25 60

Niels Bohr (1885-1962), Physicist—A261

Perf. 13x12½

1985, Oct. 3 **Litho. & Engr.**
785 A261 2.80k With wife Margrethe 90 60

Winner of 1922 Nobel Prize in Physics for theory of atomic structure.

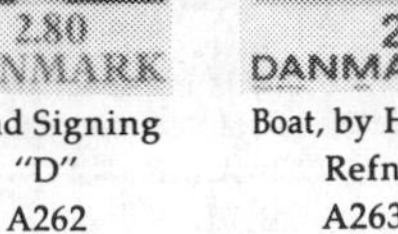

Hand Signing "D"
A262

Boat, by Helge Refn
A263

1985, Nov. 7 **Engr.** *Perf. 13*
786 A262 2.80k multi 90 50

Danish Assoc. for the Deaf, 50th anniv.

1985, Nov. 7 **Litho.**
787 A263 2.80k multi 90 50

Abstract Iron Sculpture by Robert Jacobsen—A264

Perf. 13x12½

1985, Nov. 7 **Litho. & Engr.**
788 A264 3.80k multi 1.25 80

Abstract Painting by Bjorn Wiinblad—A265

1986, Jan. 23 **Litho.** *Perf. 13x12½*
789 A265 2.80k multi 62 25

Amnesty Intl., 25th Anniv.—A266

1986, Jan. 23 **Litho. & Engr.** *Perf. 13*
790 A266 2.80k multi 62 30

Miniature Sheet

HAFNIA '87—A267

1986, Feb. 20

791 Sheet of 4 3.50 3.50
- ***a.*** A267 100o Holstein carriage, c.1840 85 85
- ***b.*** A267 250o Iceboat, c. 1880 85 85
- ***c.*** A267 280o 1st mail van, 1908 85 85
- ***d.*** A267 380o Airmail service, 1919 85 85

Size: 71x94mm. Sold for 15k.

Changing of the Guard—A268

1986, Mar. 20 *Perf. 13*
792 A268 2.80k multi 70 35

Royal Danish Life Guards barracks and Rosenborg Drilling Ground, bicent.

Arms Type of 1946

1986, Jan. 9 **Engr.** *Perf. 13*
807 A55 6.50k dp grn 1.50 75
811 A55 20k dp ultra 4.50 2.25

1987, Jan. 3 **Engr.** *Perf. 13*
812 A55 22k hn brn ('87) 6.00 3.00

Soro Academy, 400th Anniv.—A269

1986, Apr. 28 **Litho. & Engr.**
816 A269 2.80k multi 70 35

Intl. Peace Year—A270

1986, Apr. 28
817 A270 3.80k multi 95 48

Crown Prince Frederik, 18th Birthday—A271

1986, May 26 **Litho.**
818 A271 2.80k multi 70 35

Nordic Cooperation Issue 1986—A272

Sister towns.

1986, May 27 **Engr.**
819 A272 2.80k Aalborg Harbor 70 35
820 A272 3.80k Thisted Church and Town Hall 95 48

Hoje Tastrup Train Station Opening, May 31—A273

1986, May 27 **Litho.**
821 A273 2.80k multi 70 35

Mailbox, Telegraph Lines, Telephone
A274

Natl. Bird Candidates
A275

1986, June 19 **Litho.** ***Perf. 13***
822 A274 2.80k multi 68 35

19th European Intl. PTT Congress, Copenhagen, Aug. 12-16.

1986, June 19 **Litho. & Engr.**

Finalists: No. 823a, Corvus corax. No. 823b, Sturnus vulgaris. No. 823c, Cygnus olor (winner). No. 823d, Vanellus vanellus. No. 823e, Alauda arvensis.

823 Strip of 5 3.40 1.70
a.-e. A275 2.80k, any single 68 35

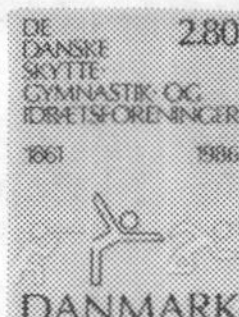

Danish Rifle, Gymnastics and Sports Club, 125th Anniv.—A276

1986, June 19
824 A276 2.80k multi 68 35

Souvenir Sheet

HAFNIA '87—A277

1986, Sept. 4
825 Sheet of 4 3.75 3.75
a. A277 100o Mailcoach, c. 1841 90 90
b. A277 250o Postmaster, c. 1840 90 90
c. A277 280o Postman, c. 1851 90 90
d. A277 380o Rural postman, c. 1893 90 90

Sold for 15k.

Europa 1986—A278

1986, Sept. 4 **Engr.**
826 A278 2.80k Street sweeper 72 35
827 A278 3.80k Garbage truck 98 50

Cupid—A279

1986, Oct. 9 **Litho.**
828 A279 3.80k multi 1.00 50

Premiere of The Whims of Cupid and the Ballet Master, by Vincenzo Galeotti, bicent.

Refugee—A280

1986, Oct. 9 **Litho. & Engr.**
829 A280 2.80k multi 75 38

Danish Refugee Council Relief Campaign.

Protestant Reformation in Denmark, 450th Anniv.—A281

Design: Sermon, altarpiece detail, 1561, Thorslunde Church, Copenhagen.

1986, Oct. 9 **Litho.** ***Perf. 13***
830 A281 6.50k multi 1.75 88

Organization for Economic Cooperation and Development, 25th Anniv.—A282

1986, Nov. 6 **Litho. & Engr.**
831 A282 3.80k multi 1.00 50

Abstract by Lin Utzon
A283

Danish Consumer Council, 40th Anniv.
A284

1987, Jan. 22 **Litho.** ***Perf. 13***
832 A283 2.80k multi 82 40

Art appreciation.

1987, Feb. 26 **Engr.** ***Perf.***
833 A284 2.80k 82 40

Religious Art (Details) from Ribe Cathedral—A285

1987, Apr. 9 **Litho.** ***Perf.***
834 A285 3k Fresco 90 45
835 A285 3.80k Stained-glass window 1.15 58
836 A285 6.50k Mosaic 1.90 95

Ribe Cathedral redecoration, 1982-1987, by Carl-Henning Pedersen.

SEMI-POSTAL STAMPS.

Nos. 159, 157 Surcharged in Red

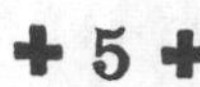

Wmkd. Multiple Crosses. (114)

1921, June 17 *Perf. 14½x14*

B1	A20	10ö +5ö grn	25.00	35.00
B2	A21	20ö +10ö sl	30.00	45.00

Crown and Staff of Aesculapius
SP1

Dybbol Mill
SP2

1929, Aug. 1 **Engraved**

B3	SP1	10ö yel grn	5.50	5.50
a.		Bklt. pane of 2	25.00	
B4	SP1	15ö brick red	7.00	7.00
a.		Bklt. pane of 2	30.00	
B5	SP1	25ö dp bl	30.00	30.00
a.		Bklt. pane of 2	125.00	

These stamps were sold at a premium of 5 öre each for benefit of the Danish Cancer Committee.

1937, Jan. 20 *Perf. 13* **Unwmkd.**

B6	SP2	5(ö) +5(ö) grn	1.50	1.50
B7	SP2	10(ö) +5(ö) lt brn	5.00	5.00
B8	SP2	15(ö) +5(ö) car	5.00	5.00

The surtax was for a fund in memory of H. P. Hanssen, statesman.
Nos. 223a and B6, Nos. 229 and B7, Nos. 238A and B8 are found se-tenant in booklets. For booklet panes, see Nos. 223d, 229b and 238e.

Queen Alexandrine
SP3

Princesses Ingrid and Margrethe
SP4

1939–41 *Perf. 13*

B9	SP3	5ö +3ö rose lake & red ('40)	40	40
a.		Booklet pane of 4	2.00	2.00
B10	SP3	10ö +5ö dk vio & red	50	35
B11	SP3	15ö +5ö scar & red	1.00	1.00

The surtax was for the Danish Red Cross.
Nos. 230 and B10 have been issued se-tenant in booklets. See No. 230b. In this pane No. 230 measures 23½x31mm. from perf. to perf.

1941-43

B12	SP4	10(ö) +5(ö) dk vio	40	40
a.		Bklt. pane of 10	25.00	
B13	SP4	20(ö) +5(ö) red ('43)	40	40

The surtax was for the Children's Charity Fund.

No. 288 Surcharged in Red

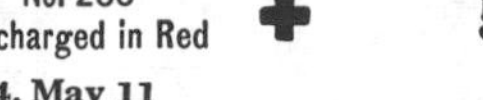

1944, May 11

B14	A48	10ö +5ö vio	30	30
a.		Bklt. pane of 10	35.00	

The surtax was for the Danish Red Cross.

Symbols of Freedom
SP5

Explosions at Rail Junction
SP6

Danish Flag
SP7

Princess Anne-Marie
SP8

1947, May 4 **Engr.** *Perf. 13*

B15	SP5	15(ö) +5(ö) grn	50	50
B16	SP6	20(ö) +5(ö) dk red	50	50
B17	SP7	40(ö) +5(ö) dp bl	1.25	1.25

Issued in memory of the Danish struggle for liberty and the liberation of Denmark. The surtax was for the Liberty Fund.

1950, Oct. 19 **Unwmkd.**

B18	SP8	25ö +5ö rose brn	1.00	1.00

The surtax was for the National Children's Welfare Association.

S. S. Jutlandia
SP9

1951, Sept. 13 *Perf. 13*

B19	SP9	25(ö) +5(ö) red	1.25	1.25

The surtax was for the Red Cross.

No. 335 Surcharged in Black **NL + 10**

1953, Feb. 13

B20	A61	30(ö) +10(ö) brn red	2.25	2.25

The surtax was for flood relief in the Netherlands.

Stone Memorial
SP10

1953, Mar. 26 *Perf. 13*

B21	SP10	30(ö) +5(ö) dk red	2.25	2.25

The surtax was for cultural work of the Danish Border Union.

Nos. B15 and B16 Surcharged with New Value and Ornamental Screen in Black

1955, Feb. 17

B22	SP5	20(ö) +5 (ö) on No. B15	1.75	1.75
B23	SP6	30(ö) +5(ö) on No. B16	1.75	1.75

The surtax was for the Liberty Fund.

No. 341 Surcharged **30 + 5 Ungarns-hjælpen**

1957, Mar. 25

B24	A61	30ö +5ö on 95ö red org	85	85

The surtax went to the Danish Red Cross for aid to Hungary.

No. 335 Surcharged: "Gronlandsfonden + 10"

1959, Feb. 23

B25	A61	30ö +10ö brn red	1.50	1.50

The surtax was for the Greenland Fund.

Globe Encircled by Red Cross Flags
SP11

Queen Ingrid
SP12

1959, June 24 **Engr.** *Perf. 13*

B26	SP11	30ö +5ö rose red	85	65
B27	SP11	60ö +5ö lt ultra & car	1.50	1.25

Issued to commemorate the centenary of the International Red Cross idea. The surtax was for the Red Cross. Crosses photogravure on No. B27.

1960, Oct. 25 **Unwmkd.**

B28	SP12	30ö +10ö dk red	1.50	1.30

Issued to commemorate Queen Ingrid's 25th anniversary as a Girl Scout. The surtax was for the Scouts' fund for needy and sick children.

African Mother and Child
SP13

Healthy and Crippled Hands
SP14

1962, May 24

B29	SP13	30ö +10ö dk red	1.50	1.50

Issued to aid underdeveloped countries.

1963, June 24 *Perf. 13*

B30	SP14	35ö +10ö dk red	1.75	1.75

The surtax was for the benefit of the Cripples' Foundation.

Old Bridge at Danish-German Border
SP15

1964, May 28 **Engraved**

B31	SP15	35ö +10ö hn brn	1.00	1.00

The surtax was for the Danish Border Union.

Princesses Margrethe, Benedikte and Anne-Marie
SP16

Happy Child
SP17

1964, Aug. 24

B32	SP16	35ö +10ö dl red	1.25	1.25
B33	SP16	60ö +10ö dk bl & red	1.75	1.75

The surtax was for the Red Cross.

1965, Oct. 21 **Engr.** *Perf. 13*

B34	SP17	50ö +10ö brick red	85	85

The surtax was for the National Children's Welfare Association.

"Red Cross" in 32 Languages and Red Cross, Red Lion and Sun, and Red Crescent Emblems
SP18

1966, Jan. 20 **Engraved** *Perf. 13*

B35	SP18	50ö +10ö red	75	75

Engraved and Photogravure

B36	SP18	80ö +10ö dk bl & red	1.50	1.50

The surtax was for the Red Cross.

"Refugees 66"
SP19

Symbolic Rose
SP20

1966, Oct. 24 **Engraved** *Perf. 13*

B37	SP19	40ö +10ö sep	1.25	1.25
B38	SP19	50ö +10ö rose red	1.25	1.25
B39	SP19	80ö +10ö bl	1.75	1.75

The surtax was for aid to refugees.

1967, Oct. 12

B40	SP20	60ö +10ö brn red	75	75

The surcharge was for the Salvation Army.

Two Greenland Boys in Round Tower
SP21

1968, Sept. 12 **Engraved** *Perf. 13*

B41	SP21	60ö +10ö dk red	1.10	1.10

The surtax was for child welfare work in Greenland.

Princess Margrethe and Prince Henrik with Prince Frederik
SP22

1969, Dec. 11

B42 SP22 50ø +10ø brn & red 1.00 1.00
B43 SP22 60ø +10ø brn red & red 1.00 1.00

The surtax was for the Danish Red Cross.

Child Seeking Help
SP23

1970, Mar. 13

B44 SP23 60ø +10ø brn red 85 85

Surtax for "Save the Children Fund."

Child
SP24

1971, Apr. 29 Engraved *Perf. 13*

B45 SP24 60ø +10ø cop red 85 85

Surtax was for the National Children's Welfare Association.

Marsh Marigold
SP25

1972, Aug. 17

B46 SP25 70ø +10ø grn & yel 85 85

Centenary of the Society and Home for the Disabled.

Heimaey Town and Volcano
SP26

1973, Oct. 17 Engraved *Perf. 13*

B47 SP26 70ø +20ø vio bl & red 85 85

The surtax was for the victims of the eruption of Heimaey Volcano, Jan. 23, 1973.

Queen Margrethe, IWY Emblem
SP27

1975, Mar. 20 Engr. *Perf. 13*

B48 SP27 90ø +20ø red & buff 1.50 1.50

International Women's Year 1975. Surtax was for a foundation to benefit women primarily in Greenland and Faroe Islands.

Skuldelev I
SP28

Ships: 90ø+20ø, Thingvalla, emigrant steamer. 100ø+20ø, Liner Frederick VIII, c. 1930. 130ø+20ø, Three-master Danmark.

1976, Jan. 22 Engr. *Perf. 13*

B49 SP28 70 +20ø ol brn 1.25 1.25
B50 SP28 90 +20ø brick red 1.25 1.25
B51 SP28 100 +20ø ol grn 1.50 1.50
B52 SP28 130 +20ø vio bl 1.50 1.50

Bicentenary of American Declaration of Independence.

People and Red Cross
SP29

Invalid in Wheelchair
SP30

1976, Feb. 26 Engr. *Perf. 13*

B53 SP29 100ø +20ø red & blk 60 60
B54 SP29 130ø +20ø bl, red & blk 85 85

Centenary of Danish Red Cross.

1976, May 6 Engr. *Perf. 13*

B55 SP30 100ø +20ø ver & blk 60 60

The surtax was for the Foundation to Aid the Disabled.

Mother and Child
SP31

Anti-Cancer Campaign
SP32

1977, Mar. 24 Engr. *Perf. 12½*

B56 SP31 1k +20ø multi 60 60

Danish Society for the Mentally Handicapped, 25th anniversary. Surtax was for the Society.

1978, Oct. 12 Engr. *Perf. 13*

B57 SP32 120ø +20ø red 60 60

Danish Anti-Cancer Campaign, 50th anniversary. Surtax was for campaign.

Child and IYC Emblem
SP33

1979, Jan. 25 Engr. *Perf. 12½*

B58 SP33 1.20k +20ø red & brn 85 85

International Year of the Child.

Foundation for the Disabled, 25th Anniversary—SP34

1980, Apr. 10 Engraved *Perf. 13*

B59 SP34 130ø +20ø brn red 60 60

Children Playing Ball—SP35

1981, Feb. 5 Engraved *Perf. 12½x13*

B60 SP35 1.60k +20ø brn red 85 85

Surtax was for child welfare.

Intl. Year of the Disabled—SP36

1981, Sept. 10 Engr. *Perf. 12½x13*

B61 SP36 2k +20ø dk bl 85 85

Stem and Broken Line—SP37

1982, May 3 Engr. *Perf. 13*

B62 SP37 2k +40ø dl red 1.00 1.00

Surtax was for Danish Multiple Sclerosis Society.

Nurse with Patient—SP38

1983, Jan. 27 Engr.

B63 SP38 2k +40ø multi 1.00 1.00

1984 Olympic Games—SP39

1984, Feb. 23 Litho. & Engr. *Perf. 13*

B64 SP39 2.70k +40ø multi 1.00 1.00

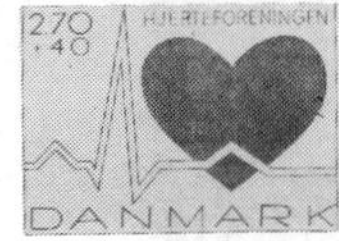

Electrocardiogram Reading, Heart—SP40

1984, Sept. 6 Engr. *Perf. 12½*

B65 SP40 2.70k +40ø red 1.00 1.00

Surtax was for Heart Foundation.

Liberation from German Occupation, 40th Anniv.—SP41

1985, May 2 Litho. *Perf. 13*

B66 SP41 2.80k +50ø multi 1.25 1.25

Surtax for benefit of World War II veterans.

Natl. Society for the Welfare of the Mentally Ill, 25th Anniv.—SP42

Design: Tapestry detail, by Caroline Ebbeson (1852-1936), former patient, St. Hans Hospital, [illegible]

1985, Oct. 3 Litho. & Engr.

B67 SP42 2.80k +40ø multi 1.25 1.00

Surtax benefited the mentally ill.

Danish Arthritis Assoc., 50th Anniv.—SP43

1986, Mar. 20 Litho. *Perf. 13*

B68 SP43 2.80k + 50ø multi 80 40

Surtax for the Arthritis Assoc.

Poul Reichhart (1913-1985), as Papageno in The Magic Flute—SP44

1986, Feb. 6 Litho. *Perf. 13*

B69 SP44 2.80k + 50ø multi 85 42

Surtax for the physically handicapped.

AIR POST STAMPS.

Airplane and Plowman
AP1

Towers of Copenhagen
AP2

Wmkd. Multiple Crosses. (114)

1925-29 Typo. ***Perf. 12x12½***

C1	AP1	10ö yel grn	20.00	30.00
C2	AP1	15ö vio ('26)	45.00	50.00
C3	AP1	25ö scarlet	40.00	45.00
C4	AP1	50ö lt gray ('29)	100.00	140.00
C5	AP1	1k choc ('29)	90.00	100.00
		Nos. C1-C5 (5)	295.00	365.00

Perf. 13

1934, June 9 **Engr.** **Unwmkd.**

C6	AP2	10ö orange	1.50	1.50
C7	AP2	15ö red	5.00	6.00
C8	AP2	20ö Prus bl	6.00	6.00
C9	AP2	50ö ol blk	5.00	6.00
C10	AP2	1k brown	16.00	17.00
		Nos. C6-C10 (5)	33.50	36.50

LATE FEE STAMPS

Numeral
LF1

Coat of Arms
LF2

Wmkd. Multiple Crosses. (114)

1923 **Typographed** ***Perf. 14x14½***

I1	LF1	10ö green	9.00	1.75
a.		Double ovpt.		

No. I1 was, at first, not a postage stamp but represented a tax for the services of the post office clerks in filling out postal forms and writing addresses. In 1923 it was put into use as a Late Fee stamp.

1926-31

I2	LF2	10ö green	3.00	1.75
I3	LF2	10ö brn ('31)	2.75	60

Engraved

1934 ***Perf. 13*** **Unwmkd.**

I4	LF2	5ö green	40	15
I5	LF2	10ö orange	40	20

POSTAGE DUE STAMPS.

Regular Issues of 1913-20

Overprinted **PORTO**

Wmkd. Multiple Crosses. (114)

1921, May 1 ***Perf. 14x14½***

J1	A10	1ö dp org	2.00	1.50
J2	A16	5ö green	3.00	1.75
J3	A16	7ö orange	3.00	1.50
J4	A16	10ö red	18.00	9.00
J5	A16	20ö dp bl	10.00	4.50
J6	A16	25ö brn & blk	15.00	2.50
J7	A16	50ö cl & blk	7.00	2.00
		Nos. J1-J7 (7)	58.00	22.75

Same Overprint in Dark Blue
On Military Stamp of 1917

1921, Nov. 23

J8	A16	10ö red	7.00	4.50
a.		"S" inverted	140.00	170.00

Numeral of Value
D1

Typographed (Solid Panel).

1921-30 ***Perf. 14x14½.***

No.	Type	Denomination / Color	Unused	Used
J9	D1	1ő org ('22)	60	60
J10	D1	4ő bl ('25)	1.75	1.75
J11	D1	5ő brn ('22)	1.50	1.00
J12	D1	5ő lt grn ('30)	1.00	80
J13	D1	7ő ap grn ('27)	16.00	16.00
J14	D1	7ő dk vio ('30)	24.00	24.00
J15	D1	10ő yel grn ('22)	1.25	60
J16	D1	10ő lt brn ('30)	1.10	50
J17	D1	20ő grnsh bl ('21)	1.50	75
a.		Double impression	1,600.	
J18	D1	20ő gray ('30)	2.00	1.25
J19	D1	25ő scar ('23)	2.50	1.10
J20	D1	25ő vio ('26)	2.50	1.40
J21	D1	25ő lt bl ('30)	5.00	3.50
J22	D1	1k dk bl ('21)	45.00	7.00
J23	D1	1k brn & dk bl ('25)	15.00	4.25
J24	D1	5k pur ('25)	25.00	8.00
		Nos. J9-J24 (16)	145.70	72.50

Engraved (Lined Panel).

1934-55 ***Perf. 13*** **Unwmkd.**

No.	Type	Denomination / Color	Unused	Used
J25	D1	1ő slate	18	10
J26	D1	2ő carmine	18	10
J27	D1	5ő yel grn	18	6
J28	D1	6ő dk ol ('41)	60	12
J29	D1	8ő mag ('50)	2.00	2.25
J30	D1	10ő orange	18	6
J31	D1	12ő dp ultra ('55)	45	40
J32	D1	15ő vio ('37)	60	10
J33	D1	20ő gray	45	10
J34	D1	25ő blue	60	18
J35	D1	30ő grn ('53)	60	18
J36	D1	40ő cl ('49)	75	18
J37	D1	1k brown	1.00	18
		Nos. J25-J37 (13)	7.77	4.01

No. 96 Surcharged in Black

PORTO

15

1934 ***Perf. 14x14½*** **Wmk. 114**

No.	Type	Denomination / Color	Unused	Used
J38	A10	15ő on 12ő vio	3.00	1.25

MILITARY STAMPS.

Nos. 97 and 100 Overprinted in Blue **S F**

Wmkd. Multiple Crosses. (114)

1917 ***Perf. 14x14½.***

No.	Type	Denomination / Color	Unused	Used
M1	A16	5ő green	22.50	32.50
a.		'S' inverted	250.00	375.00
M2	A16	10ő red	17.50	27.50
a.		'S' inverted	200.00	275.00

The letters "S F" are the initials of "Soldater Frimaerke" (Soldier's Stamp).

OFFICIAL STAMPS.

Small State Seal
O1

Wmkd. Crown. (112)

1871 **Typographed** ***Perf. 14x13½***

No.	Type	Denomination / Color	Unused	Used
O1	O1	2s blue	125.00	90.00
a.		2s ultra	125.00	90.00
b.		Imperf., pair	500.00	
O2	O1	4s carmine	70.00	16.00
a.		Imperf.,pair	500.00	
O3	O1	16s green	325.00	250.00
a.		Imperf., pair	650.00	

Perf. 12½.

No.	Type	Denomination / Color	Unused	Used
O4	O1	4s carmine	4,000.	400.00
O5	O1	16s green	350.00	350.00

Nos. O1, O2 and O3 were reprinted in 1886 upon white wove paper, unwatermarked and imperforate. Price $10 each.

1875 ***Perf. 14x13½.***

No.	Type	Denomination / Color	Unused	Used
O6	O1	3ő violet	3.50	12.00
O7	O1	4ő grnsh bl	5.50	3.00
O8	O1	8ő carmine	5.50	1.65
a.		Imperf., pair		
O9	O1	32ő green	40.00	35.00

1899-02 ***Perf. 13.***

No.	Type	Denomination / Color	Unused	Used
O9A	O1	3ő red lil ('02)	4.00	4.00
c.		Imperf., pair	375.00	
O9B	O1	4ő blue	2.00	1.75
O10	O1	8ő carmine	20.00	13.00

1902-06 **Wmkd. Crown. (113)**

No.	Type	Denomination / Color	Unused	Used
O11	O1	1ő orange	2.50	2.50
O12	O1	3ő red lil ('06)	1.00	1.00
O13	O1	4ő bl ('03)	1.75	1.50
O14	O1	5ő green	1.50	35
O15	O1	10ő carmine	1.50	1.40
		Nos. O11-O15 (5)	8.25	6.75

Wmkd. Multiple Crosses. (114)

1914-23 ***Perf. 14x14½.***

No.	Type	Denomination / Color	Unused	Used
O16	O1	1ő orange	1.75	1.50
O17	O1	3ő gray ('18)	4.50	4.50
O18	O1	4ő bl ('16)	32.50	37.50
O19	O1	5ő grn ('15)	1.00	35
O20	O1	5ő choc ('23)	4.50	*18.00*
O21	O1	10ő red ('17)	4.00	1.25
O22	O1	10ő grn ('21)	1.50	2.00
O23	O1	15ő vio ('19)	32.50	37.50
O24	O1	20ő ind ('20)	11.00	7.00
		Nos. O16-O24 (9)	93.25	*109.60*

The use of Official stamps was discontinued April 1, 1924.

NEWSPAPER STAMPS.

Numeral of Value
N1

Wmkd. Crown. (113)

1907 **Typographed** ***Perf. 13***

No.	Type	Denomination / Color	Unused	Used
P1	N1	1ő olive	5.00	2.00
P2	N1	5ő blue	20.00	12.00
P3	N1	7ő carmine	6.00	70
P4	N1	10ő dp lil	12.00	3.00
P5	N1	20ő green	11.00	1.00
P6	N1	38ő orange	16.00	1.00
P7	N1	68ő yel brn	35.00	22.50
P8	N1	1k bl grn & cl	12.00	1.50
P9	N1	5k rose & yel grn	90.00	22.50
P10	N1	10k bis & bl	100.00	22.50
		Nos. P1-P10 (10)	307.00	88.70

Wmkd. Multiple Crosses. (114)

1914-15 ***Perf. 14x14½.***

No.	Type	Denomination / Color	Unused	Used
P11	N1	1ő ol gray	5.00	60
P12	N1	5ő blue	14.00	7.00
P13	N1	7ő rose	11.00	60
P14	N1	8ő grn ('15)	12.00	60
P15	N1	10ő dp lil	12.00	60
P16	N1	20ő green	140.00	1.75
a.		Imperf., pair	*550.00*	
P17	N1	29ő org yel ('15)	18.00	1.40
P18	N1	38ő orange	3,250.	160.00
P19	N1	41ő yel brn ('15)	18.00	1.25
P20	N1	1k bl grn & mar	30.00	65
		Nos. P11-P17, P19-P20 (9)	260.00	14.45

PARCEL POST STAMPS.

These stamps were for use on postal packets sent by the Esbjerg-Fanö Ferry Service.

Regular Issues of 1913–30 Overprinted

POSTFÆRGE

Wmkd. Multiple Crosses. (114)

1919-41 ***Perf. 14x14½.***

No.	Type	Denomination / Color	Unused	Used
Q1	A10	10ő grn ('22)	16.00	11.00
Q2	A10	10ő bis brn ('30)	14.00	6.00
Q3	A16	10ő red	60.00	70.00
a.		"POSFFAERGE"	225.00	450.00
Q4	A16	15ő violet	22.50	27.50
a.		"POSFFAERGE'	225.00	*450.00*
Q5	A16	30ő org ('22)	16.00	16.00
Q6	A16	30ő dk bl ('26)	4.00	4.00
Q7	A16	50ő cl & blk ('20)	250.00	275.00
Q8	A16	50ő lt gray ('22)	22.50	10.00
a.		50ő dk gray ('22)	150.00	175.00
Q9	A16	1k brn & bl ('24)	60.00	18.00
Q9A	A16	5k vio & brn ('41)	4.00	3.50
Q10	A16	10k ver & grn ('30)	90.00	90.00

Engraved.

No.	Type	Denomination / Color	Unused	Used
Q11	A17	1k yel brn	150.00	150.00
a.		"POSFFAERGE"	1,700.	2,750.
		Nos. Q1-Q11 (12)	559.00	531.00

1927-30

No.	Type	Denomination / Color	Unused	Used
Q12	A30	15ő red ('27)	22.50	14.00
Q13	A30	30ő ocher ('27)	22.50	15.00
Q14	A30	40ő yel grn ('30)	20.00	8.50

Overprinted on Regular Issues of 1933-40.

1936-42 ***Perf. 13*** **Unwmkd.**

No.	Type	Denomination / Color	Unused	Used
Q15	A32	5ő rose lake ('42)	25	20
Q16	A32	10ő yel org	35.00	27.50
Q17	A32	10ő lt brn ('38)	2.00	2.00
Q18	A32	10ő pur ('39)	35	35
Q19	A30	15ő dp red	1.25	1.50
Q20	A30	30ő bl, I	7.00	6.00
Q21	A30	30ő bl, II ('40)	10.00	12.50
Q22	A30	30ő org, II ('42)	1.00	90
Q23	A30	40ő yel grn, I	7.00	6.00
Q24	A30	40ő yel grn, II ('40)	10.00	11.00
Q25	A30	40ő bl, II ('42)	1.25	1.25
Q26	A33	50ő gray	2.25	2.25
Q27	A33	1k lt brn	1.75	1.50
		Nos. Q15-Q27 (13)	79.10	72.95

Overprinted on Nos. 284, 286 and 286B

1945

No.	Type	Denomination / Color	Unused	Used
Q28	A47	30ő orange	2.00	1.75
Q29	A47	40ő blue	1.75	1.75
Q30	A47	50ő gray	2.25	1.75

Overprinted on Nos. 318, 309, 310, 312 and 297.

1949-53

No.	Type	Denomination / Color	Unused	Used
Q31	A32	10ő grn ('53)	35	35
Q32	A61	30ő orange	2.50	2.00
Q33	A61	40ő dl bl	2.50	2.00
Q34	A61	50ő gray ('50)	15.00	3.50
Q35	A55	1k brn ('50)	2.00	1.75
		Nos. Q31-Q35 (5)	22.35	9.60

Overprinted on Nos. 335, 323, 336, 326 and 397.

1955-65

No.	Type	Denomination / Color	Unused	Used
Q36	A61	30ő brn red	1.20	1.10
Q37	A61	40ő gray	1.00	1.00
Q38	A61	50ő aqua	1.25	1.25
Q39	A61	70ő dp grn	1.25	1.25
Q40	A55	1.25k org ('65)	7.00	8.00
		Nos. Q36-Q40 (5)	11.70	12.60

Overprinted on Nos. 417 and 419.

1967 **Engraved** ***Perf. 13***

No.	Type	Denomination / Color	Unused	Used
Q41	A86	40ő brown	1.00	1.00
Q42	A86	80ő ultra	1.00	1.00

Nos. 224, 438, 441, 297–299 Overprinted

POSTFÆRGE

1967-74 **Engraved** ***Perf. 13***

No.	Type	Denomination / Color	Unused	Used
Q43	A32	5ő rose lake	30	30
Q44	A86	50ő brn ('74)	70	70
Q45	A86	90ő ultra ('70)	1.40	1.40
Q46	A55	1k brown	1.75	1.50
Q47	A55	2k red ('72)	2.25	2.25
Q48	A55	5k dl bl ('72)	5.00	4.50
		Nos. Q43-Q48 (6)	11.40	10.65

Nos. Q44–Q45, Q47–Q48 are on fluorescent paper.

Overprinted on No. 544

1975, Feb. 27

No.	Type	Denomination / Color	Unused	Used
Q49	A161	100ő dp ultra	1.25	1.25

DIEGO-SUAREZ

(dyä'gō swä'räs)

LOCATION—A town at the northern end of Madagascar.

GOVT.—Former French colony.

POP.—12,237.

From 1885 to 1896 Diégo-Suarez, (Antsirane), a French naval base, was a separate colony and issued its own stamps. These were succeeded by stamps of Madagascar.

100 Centimes = 1 Franc

Stamps of French Colonies Handstamp Surcharged in Violet

1890 ***Perf. 14x13½.*** **Unwmkd.**

No.	Type	Description	Unused	Used
1	A9	15c on 1c *bl*	225.00	70.00
2	A9	15c on 5c grn, *grnsh*	575.00	70.00
3	A9	15c on 10c *lav*	250.00	70.00
4	A9	15c on 20c red, *grn*	575.00	70.00
5	A9	15c on 25c *rose*	95.00	35.00

This surcharge is found inverted, double, etc. Counterfeits exist.

Ship Flying French Flag
A2

Symbolical of Union of France and Madagascar
A3 A4

France
A5

1890 **Lithographed.** ***Imperf.***

No.	Type	Description	Unused	Used
6	A2	1c black	950.00	250.00
7	A3	5c black	925.00	190.00
8	A4	15c black	225.00	87.50
9	A5	25c black	250.00	100.00

A6

1891

No.	Type	Description	Unused	Used
10	A6	5c black	225.00	87.50

Excellent counterfeits exist of Nos. 6 to 10.

Stamps of French Colonies Surcharged in Red or Black:

a

b

1892 ***Perf. 14x13½***

No.	Type	Description	Unused	Used
11	A9 (a)	5c on 10c *lav* (R)	175.00	77.50
a.		Inverted surcharge	350.00	275.00
12	A9 (b)	5c on 20c red, *grn*	160.00	57.50
a.		Inverted surcharge	350.00	275.00

Stamps of French Colonies Overprinted in Black or Red

c

1892

No.	Type	Description	Unused	Used
13	A9	1c bl (R)	21.00	11.00
a.		Inverted overprint	160.00	130.00
14	A9	2c brn, *buff*	21.00	11.00
a.		Inverted overprint	160.00	130.00
15	A9	4c cl, *lav*	37.50	25.00
16	A9	5c grn, *grnsh*	82.50	60.00
a.		Inverted overprint	160.00	130.00
17	A9	10c *lavender*	25.00	19.00
a.		Inverted overprint	160.00	130.00
18	A9	15c *blue*	21.00	14.00
19	A9	20c red, *grn*	25.00	17.00
20	A9	25c *rose*	19.00	11.00
a.		Inverted overprint	160.00	130.00
21	A9	30c brn, *bis* (R)	1,000.	700.00
a.		Inverted overprint		1,300.
22	A9	35c *yellow*	1,000.	700.00
a.		Inverted overprint		1,300.
23	A9	75c car, *rose*	52.50	32.50
24	A9	1fr brnz grn, *straw* (R)	52.50	32.50
a.		Double overprint	190.00	160.00

Navigation and Commerce
A10 A11

1892 **Typographed.**

Name of Colony in Blue or Carmine.

No.	Type	Description	Unused	Used
25	A10	1c *blue*	1.65	1.65
26	A10	2c brn, *buff*	1.75	1.65
27	A10	4c cl, *lav*	1.50	1.50
28	A10	5c grn, *grnsh*	4.00	2.50
29	A10	10c *lavender*	5.50	3.00
30	A10	15c bl, quadrille paper	6.50	5.25
31	A10	20c red, *grn*	12.00	9.50
32	A10	25c *rose*	10.50	7.75
33	A10	30c brn, *bis*	13.00	9.50
34	A10	40c red, *straw*	16.00	11.00
35	A10	50c car, *rose*	32.50	17.50
36	A10	75c vio, *org*	32.50	20.00
37	A10	1fr brnz grn, *straw*	50.00	30.00
		Nos. 25-37 (13)	187.40	120.80

1894

No.	Type	Description	Unused	Used
38	A11	1c *blue*	90	1.00
39	A11	2c brn, *buff*	1.75	1.50
40	A11	4c cl, *lav*	1.75	1.50
41	A11	5c grn, *grnsh*	3.50	2.75
42	A11	10c *lavender*	5.25	3.50
43	A11	15c bl, quadrille paper	5.25	3.50
44	A11	20c red, *grn*	11.00	7.75
45	A11	25c *rose*	6.00	3.50
46	A11	30c brn, *bis*	7.00	4.25
47	A11	40c red, *straw*	7.75	4.25
48	A11	50c car, *rose*	11.00	8.75
49	A11	75c vio, *org*	7.75	4.25
50	A11	1fr brnz grn, *straw*	17.50	14.00
		Nos. 38-50 (13)	86.40	60.50

Bisected stamps of type A11 are mentioned in note after Madagascar No. 62.

POSTAGE DUE STAMPS.

D1

D2

Lithographed.

1891 ***Imperf.*** **Unwmkd.**

No.	Type	Description	Unused	Used
J1	D1	5c violet	130.00	52.50
J2	D2	50c black	130.00	52.50

Excellent counterfeits exist of Nos. J1 and J2.

Postage Due Stamps of French Colonies Overprinted Type "c" in Black

1892

No.	Type	Description	Unused	Used
J3	D1	1c black	95.00	47.50
J4	D1	2c black	95.00	47.50
a.		Inverted overprint	350.00	250.00
J5	D1	3c black	95.00	52.50
J6	D1	4c black	95.00	52.50
J7	D1	5c black	95.00	52.50
J8	D1	10c black	26.00	22.50
a.		Inverted overprint	350.00	250.00
J9	D1	15c black	26.00	22.50
a.		Double overprint	525.00	425.00
J10	D1	20c black	160.00	100.00
J11	D1	30c black	82.50	52.50
a.		Inverted overprint	350.00	250.00
J12	D1	60c black	1,100.	700.00
J13	D1	1fr brown	1,750.	1,100.

DJIBOUTI

(jĕ'bōō'tē')

LOCATION — East Africa.
GOVT.—Republic.
AREA—8,880 sq. mi.
POP.—340,000 (est. 1983).
CAPITAL—Djibouti.

The French territory of Afars and Issas became the Republic of Djibouti June 27, 1977. For 1894-1902 issues with "Djibouti" or "DJ." see Somali Coast.

Afars and Issas Issues of 1972–1977 Overprinted and Surcharged with Bars and "REPUBLIQUE DE DJIBOUTI" in Black, Dark Green, Blue or Brown

Printing and Perforations as Before

1977

Multicolored

No.	Type	Description	Unused	Used
439	A63	1fr on 4fr (#358;B)	5	5
440	A81	2fr on 5fr (#433;B)	5	5
441	A75	5fr on 20fr (#421;B)	15	15
442	A70	8fr (#380;B)	22	22
443	A71	20fr (#387;DG)	45	45
444	A81	30fr (#434;B)	60	60
445	A71	40fr (#388;DG)	75	75
446	A71	45fr (#389;Bl)	90	90
447	A78	45fr (#428;B)	90	90
448	A72	50fr (#394;B)	1.10	1.10
449	A71	60fr (#391;Br)	1.25	1.25
450	A79	70fr (#430;B)	1.50	1.50
451	A81	70fr (#435;B)	1.50	1.50
452	A74	100fr (#418;B)	2.00	2.00
453	A72	150fr (#399;B)	3.00	3.00
454	A76	200fr (#422;B)	4.00	4.00
455	A80	200fr (#432;B)	4.00	4.00
456	A74	300fr (#419;B)	6.75	6.75
		Nos. 439-456, C106-8 (21)	41.92	41.17

Map and Flag of Djibouti
A83

Water Pipe
A84

Design: 65fr, Map and flag of Djibouti, map of Africa (horiz.).

1977, June 27 **Litho.** ***Perf. 12½***

No.	Type	Description	Unused	Used
457	A83	45fr multi	1.00	60
458	A83	65fr multi	1.50	75

Independence, June 27.

1977, July 4

Designs: 10fr, Headrest (horiz.). 25fr, Pitcher.

No.	Type	Description	Unused	Used
459	A84	10fr multi	22	15
460	A84	20fr multi	45	18
461	A84	25fr multi	60	28

Ostrich
A85

Design: 100fr, Weaver.

1977, Aug. 11 **Litho.** ***Perf. 12½***

No.	Type	Description	Unused	Used
462	A85	90fr multi	1.75	1.25
463	A85	100fr multi	2.25	1.50

Snail
A86

Designs: 15fr, Fiddler crab. 50fr, Klipspringers. 70fr, Green turtle. 80fr, Priacanthus hamrur (fish). 150fr, Dolphinfish.

1977 **Litho.** ***Perf. 12½***

No.	Type	Description	Unused	Used
464	A86	15fr multi	22	18
465	A86	45fr multi	45	38
466	A86	50fr multi	90	55
467	A86	70fr multi	85	50
468	A86	80fr multi	1.00	60
469	A86	150fr multi	3.00	1.75
		Nos. 464-469 (6)	6.42	3.96

Issue dates: 45fr, 70fr, 80fr, Sept. 14. Others, Dec. 5.

Pres. Hassan Gouled Aptidon and Djibouti Flag
A87

1978, Feb. 12 **Litho.** ***Perf. 13***

No.	Type	Description	Unused	Used
470	A87	65fr multi	1.10	60

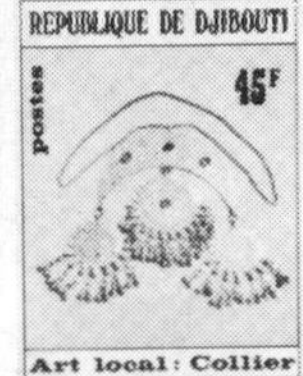

Charaxes Hansali A88 — Necklace A89

Butterflies: 20fr, Colias electo. 25fr, Acraea chilo. 150fr, Junonia hierta.

1978, Mar. 13 Litho. *Perf. 12½x13*

471	A88	5fr multi	5	5
472	A88	20fr multi	22	11
473	A88	25fr multi	45	28
474	A88	150fr multi	2.00	85

1978, May 29 Litho. *Perf. 12½x13*

Design: 55fr, Necklace (different).

475	A89	45fr pink & multi	60	35
476	A89	55fr bl & multi	70	40

Bougainvillea A90

Flowers: 35fr, Hibiscus schizopetalus. 250fr, Caesalpinia pulcherrima.

1978, July 10 Photo. *Perf. 12½x13*

477	A90	15fr multi	22	12
478	A90	35fr multi	50	28
479	A90	250fr multi	3.00	1.25

Charonia Nodifera—A91

Sea Shell: 80fr, Charonia variegata.

1978, Oct. 9 Litho. *Perf. 13*

480	A91	10fr multi	15	6
481	A91	80fr multi	1.10	45

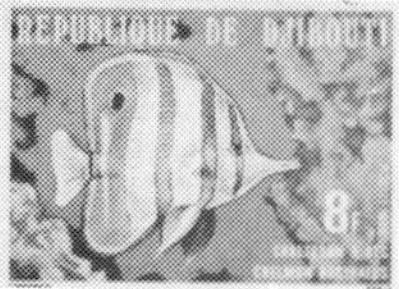

Chaetodon A92

Fish: 30fr, Yellow surgeonfish. 40fr, Harlequinfish.

1978, Nov. 20 Litho. *Perf. 13x12½*

482	A92	8fr multi	12	6
483	A92	30fr multi	35	15
484	A92	40fr multi	45	22

Alsthom BB 1201 at Dock—A93

Locomotives: 55fr, Steam locomotive 231. 60fr, Steam locomotive 130 and map of route. 75fr, Diesel.

1979, Jan. 29 Litho. *Perf. 13*

485	A93	40fr multi	60	22
486	A93	55fr multi	75	30
487	A93	60fr multi	90	30
488	A93	75fr multi	1.25	38

Djibouti-Addis Ababa railroad.

Children and IYC Emblem—A94

Design: 200fr, Mother and child, IYC emblem.

1979, Feb. 26 Litho. *Perf. 13*

489	A94	20fr multi	30	15
490	A94	200fr multi	2.75	1.75

International Year of the Child.

Plane over Ardoukoba Volcano—A95

Design: 30fr, Helicopter over Ardoukoba Volcano (vert.).

1979, Mar. 19

491	A95	30fr multi	45	38
492	A95	90fr multi	1.35	75

Rowland Hill, Postal Clerks, No. C109—A96

Designs: 100fr, Somali Coast No. 22, Djibouti No. 457, letters, Rowland Hill. 150fr, Letters hoisted onto ship, smoke signals, Rowland Hill.

1979, Apr. 17 Litho. *Perf. 13x12½*

493	A96	25fr multi	38	15
494	A96	100fr multi	1.40	60
495	A96	150fr multi	2.00	1.00

Sir Rowland Hill (1795–1879), originator of penny postage.

View of Djibouti, Bird and Local Woman—A97

Design: 80fr, Map and flag of Djibouti, UPU emblem, Concorde, train and mail runner.

1979, June 8 Litho. *Perf. 13x12½*

496	A97	55fr multi	1.25	90
497	A97	80fr multi	1.75	1.25

Philexafrique II, Libreville, Gabon, June 8–17. Nos. 496, 497 each printed in sheets of 10 with 5 labels showing exhibition emblem.

Solanacea A98

Flowers: 2fr, Opuntia (vert.). 15fr, Trichodesma. 45fr, Acacia etbaica. 50fr, Thunbergia alata (vert.).

Perf. 13x13½, 13½x13

1979, June 18

498	A98	2fr multi	5	5
499	A98	8fr multi	12	8
500	A98	15fr multi	18	8
501	A98	45fr multi	45	18
502	A98	50fr multi	60	18
		Nos. 498-502 (5)	1.40	57

Running—A99

Olympic Emblem and: 70fr, Basketball 200fr, Soccer (horiz.).

Perf. 12½×13, 13×12½

1979, Oct. 22 Litho.

503	A99	70fr multi	85	38
504	A99	120fr multi	1.75	75
505	A99	200fr multi	2.75	1.10

Pre-Olympic Year.

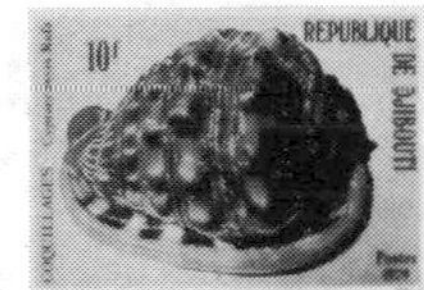

Cypraecassis Rufa—A100

Shells: 40fr, Lambis chiragra arthritica. 300fr, Harpa connaidalis.

1979, Dec. 22 Litho. *Perf. 13*

506	A100	10fr multi	12	8
507	A100	40fr multi	50	22
508	A100	300fr multi	3.75	1.60

Rotary International, 75th Anniversary—A101

1980, Feb. 19 Litho. *Perf. 13x12½*

509	A101	90fr multi	1.35	65

See "Special Notices" at the front of this volume for data on the listing methods of this Catalogue, abbreviations, condition, prices and examination.

Lions Club of Djibouti—A102

1980, Feb. 19

510	A102	100fr multi	1.65	75

Colotis Danae—A103

1980, Mar. 17 *Perf. 13x13½*

511	A103	5fr *shown*	8	5
512	A103	55fr *Danaus chrysippus*	70	30

Chess Players, Knight—A104

Chess Federation Creation: 75fr, Chess Game, Florence, 1493.

1980, June 9 Litho. *Perf. 13*

513	A104	20fr multi	38	12
514	A104	75fr multi	1.10	40

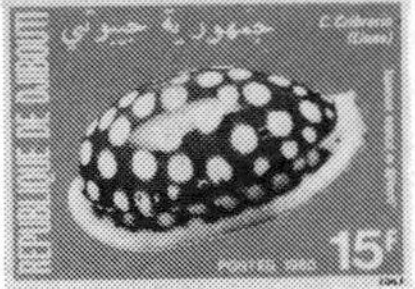

Cribraria—A105

1980, Aug. 12 Litho. *Perf. 13*

515	A105	15fr *shown*	18	8
516	A105	85fr *Nautilius pompilius*	1.00	45

Alexander Fleming, Discoverer of Penicillin—A106

Design: 130fr, Jules Verne, French science fiction writer; earth, moon and spacecraft.

1980, Sept. 1

517	A106	20fr multi	30	12
518	A106	130fr multi	1.75	70

Capt. Cook and Endeavor—A107

Capt James Cook Death Bicentenary: 90fr, Ships and Maps of voyages.

1980, Nov. 20 **Litho.** ***Perf. 13***

519	A107	55fr multi	60	30
520	A107	90fr multi	1.10	55

Souvenir sheets of 1 exist, perf. 12½x12.

Angel Fish—A108

1981, Apr. 13 **Litho.** ***Perf. 12½***

521	A108	25fr shown	30	12
522	A108	55fr Moorish idol	60	28
523	A108	70fr Scad	75	45

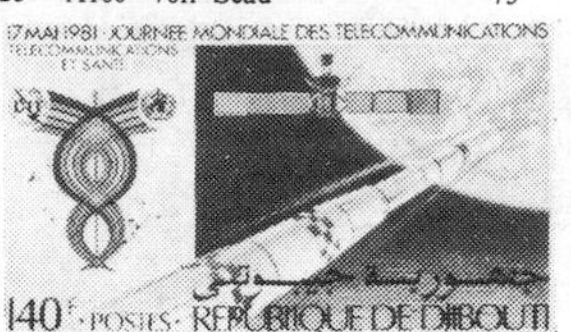

13th World Telecommunications Day—A109

1981, May 17 **Litho.** ***Perf. 13***

524	A109	140fr multi	1.75	75

Type 231 Steam Locomotive, Germany, 1958 and Amtrak, US, 1980—A110

Locomotives: 55fr, Stephenson and his Rocket, Djibouti Railways 230 engine. 65fr, Type TGV, France, Type 962, Japan.

1981, June 9 **Litho.** ***Perf. 13***

525	A110	40fr multi	45	28
526	A110	55fr multi	60	30
527	A110	65fr multi	75	35

Radio Amateurs Club—A111

1981, June 25

528	A111	250fr multi	3.00	1.50

Prince Charles and Lady Diana—A112

1981, June 29

529	A112	180fr shown	2.25	1.25
530	A112	200fr Couple, diff.	2.50	1.50

Royal Wedding.

Lord Nelson and Victory—A113

1981, July 6 **Litho.** ***Perf. 13x12½***

531	A113	100fr multi	1.25	75
532	A113	175fr multi	2.00	1.25

Lord Horatio Nelson (1758-1805).

Scout Tending Campfire—A114

1981, July 16 **Litho.** ***Perf. 13***

533	A114	60fr shown	75	45
534	A114	105fr Scout giving sign	1.25	60

28th World Scouting Conference, Dakar, Aug. (60fr); 4th Pan-African Scouting Conference, Abidjan, Aug. (105fr).

Pawn and Queen, Swedish Bone Chess Pieces, 13th Cent.—A115

1981, Oct. 15 **Litho.** ***Perf. 13***

535	A115	50fr shown	60	38
536	A115	130fr Pawn, knight, Chinese, 19th cent., vert.	1.75	1.00

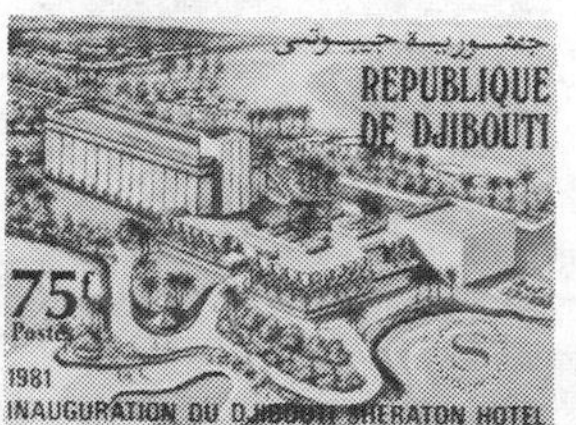

Sheraton Hotel Opening—A116

1981, Nov. 15 **Litho.** ***Perf. 13x12½***

537	A116	75fr multi	90	55

Acacia Mellifera—A117

1981, Dec. 21 ***Perf. 13***

538	A117	10fr Clitoria ternatea, vert.	12	8
539	A117	30fr shown	38	18
540	A117	35fr Punica granatum	40	28
541	A117	45fr Malvaceous plant, vert.	50	30

Nos. 535-536 Overprinted with Winners' Names.

1981, Dec. **Litho.** ***Perf. 13***

542	A115	50fr multi	60	45
543	A115	130fr multi	1.75	1.10

World Chess Championship.

TB Bacillus Centenary—A117a

1982 **Litho.** ***Perf. 13***

544	A117a	305fr Koch, slide, microscope	2.25	1.50

1982 World Chess Championship A117b

14th World Telecommunications Day A118

1982, Apr. 8 **Litho.** ***Perf. 13***

545	A117b	125fr Ivory bishop	1.50	1.00
546	A117b	175fr Queen, pawn, 19th cent.	2.25	1.25

1982, May 17

547	A118	150fr multi	1.75	1.25

Bus and Jeep—A119

1982, July 27 **Litho.** ***Perf. 13***

548	A119	20fr shown	22	15
549	A119	25fr Dhow, ferry	30	22
550	A119	55fr Train, jet	65	45

Shells from the Red Sea—A120

1982, Nov. 20 **Litho.** ***Perf. 12½***

551	A120	10fr Cypraea erythraeensis	12	8
552	A120	15fr Conus sumatrensis	18	12
553	A120	25fr Cypraea pulchra	30	18
554	A120	30fr Conus inscriptus	38	22
555	A120	70fr Casmaria ponderosa	85	55
556	A120	150fr Cypraea exusta	1.75	1.25
		Nos. 551-556 (6)	3.58	2.40

See Nos. 563-567.

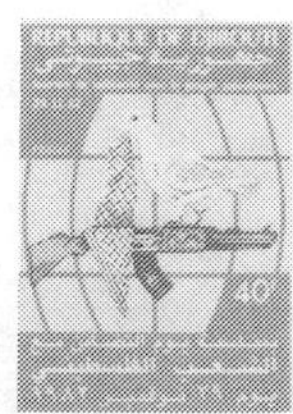

Intl. Palestinian Solidarity Day—A121

1982, Nov. 29 **Litho.** ***Perf. 13***

557	A121	40fr multi	60	40

Local Flowers—A122

Various flowers. 5fr, 55fr vert.

1983, Apr. 14 **Litho.** ***Perf. 13***

558	A122	5fr multi	8	6
559	A122	50fr multi	80	60
560	A122	55fr multi	90	65

World Communications Year—A123

1983, June 20 **Litho.** ***Perf. 13***

561	A123	500fr multi	8.00	6.00

Conference of Donors, Nov. 21-23—A124

1983, Nov. 21 **Litho.** ***Perf. 13x12½***

562	A124	75fr multi	1.10	80

Shell Type of 1982

1983, Dec. 20 Litho. *Perf. 12½*

563	A120	15fr	Marginella obtusa	22	16
564	A120	30fr	Conus jickelli	42	32
565	A120	55fr	Cypraea macandrewi	78	58
566	A120	80fr	Conus cuvieri	1.10	90
567	A120	100fr	Turbo petholatus	1.40	1.10
			Nos. 563-567 (5)	3.92	3.06

Local Butterflies—A125

1984, Jan. 24 Litho. *Perf. 13½x13*

568	A125	5fr	Colotis chrysonome	8	6
569	A125	20fr	Colias erate	28	22
570	A125	30fr	Junonia orithyia	42	32
571	A125	75fr	Acraea doubledayi	1.10	80
572	A125	110fr	Byblia ilithya	1.50	1.10
			Nos. 568-572 (5)	3.38	2.50

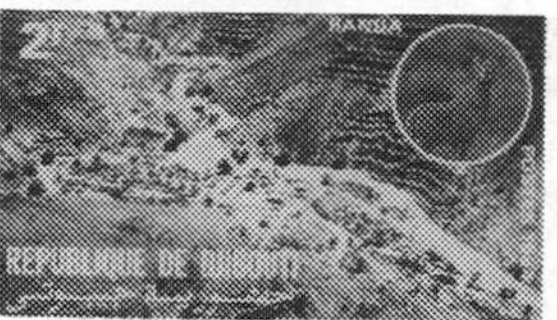

Landscapes and Animals—A126

1984, Apr. 29 Litho. *Perf. 13*

573	A126	2fr	Randa Klipspringer	5	5
574	A126	8fr	Ali Sabieh, gazelles	12	10
575	A126	10fr	Lake Assal, oryz	14	10
576	A126	15fr	Tadjoura, gazelle	22	16
577	A126	40fr	Alaila Dada, jackal, vert.	55	42
578	A126	45fr	Lake Abbe, warthog	65	50
579	A126	55fr	Obock, seagull	80	60
580	A126	125fr	Presidential Palace, bird	1.75	1.25
			Nos. 573-580 (8)	4.28	3.18

Fire Prevention—A127

1984, Sept. 9 Litho. *Perf. 13*

581	A127	25fr	Fire truck	35	28
582	A127	95fr	Hook & ladder	1.40	1.00
583	A127	100fr	Fire plane	1.40	1.10

International Olympic Committee Membership A128

1984, July 22 Litho. *Perf. 13*

584	A128	45fr	Runners	65	50

Motor Carriage, 1886—A128a

1984, Nov. 11 Litho. *Perf. 12½*

585	A128a	35fr	shown	50	38
586	A128a	65fr	Cabriolet, 1896	90	68
587	A128a	90fr	Phoenix, 1900	1.30	1.00

Gottlieb Daimler (1834-1900), pioneer automobile manufacturer.

Marie and Pierre Curie A129

1984, Dec. 3 Litho. *Perf. 12½*

588	A129	150fr	Pierre Curie	2.00	1.65
589	A129	150fr	Marie Curie	2.00	1.65

Audubon Bicentenary—A130

1985, Jan. 27 Litho. *Perf. 13*

590	A130	5fr	Merops albicollis	8	6
591	A130	15fr	Pterocles exustus	22	16
592	A130	20fr	Trachyphonus margaritatus somalicus	28	22
593	A130	25fr	Coracias garrulus	35	28

Intl. Youth Year—A131

1985, Mar. 26 Litho. *Perf. 13*

594	A131	10fr	multi	14	12
595	A131	30fr	multi	42	32
596	A131	40fr	multi	55	42

German Railways, 150th Anniv.—A132

Designs: 55fr, Engine No. 29, Addis Ababa - Djibouti Railways. 75fr, Adler, museum facsimile of the first German locomotive.

1985, April 22 Litho. *Perf. 13*

597	A132	55fr	multi	80	60
598	A132	75fr	multi	1.10	80

Scouting—A133

1985, May 23

599	A133	35fr	Planting saplings	50	38
600	A133	65fr	Hygiene, family health care	90	70

Victor Hugo (1802-1885), Novelist—A134

Authors: 100fr, Arthur Rimbaud (1854-1891), poet.

1985, June 24 Litho.

601	A134	80fr	brt bl & sl	1.10	85
602	A134	100fr	multi	1.40	1.10

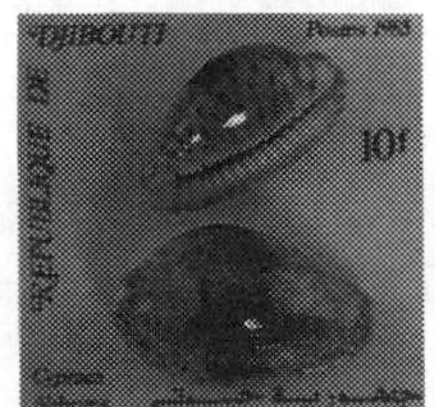

Sea Shells—A135

1985, July 15 Litho. *Perf. 12½*

603	A135	10fr	Cypraea nebrites	14	12
604	A135	15fr	Cypraea turdus	22	16
605	A135	30fr	Conus acuminatus	42	32
606	A135	40fr	Cypraea camelopardalis	55	42
607	A135	55fr	Conus terebra	78	60
			Nos. 603-607 (5)	2.11	1.62

1st World Cup Marathon '85, Hiroshima—A136

1985, Sept. 2 *Perf. 12½x13*

608	A136	75fr	Winners	1.05	80
609	A136	100fr	Approaching finish	1.40	1.05

Halley's Comet—A137

Designs: 85fr, Bayeux Tapestry, Comet and Halley. 90fr, Vega 1, Giotto space probes, map of planets, comet trajectory.

1986, Jan. 27 Litho. *Perf. 13*

610	A137	85fr	multi	1.20	90
611	A137	90fr	multi	1.25	95

ISERST Solar Energy Installation—A138

Designs: 50fr, Runners on beach. 150fr, Windmill, headquarters, power control station.

1986, Mar. 20

612	A138	50fr	multi	70	52
613	A138	150fr	multi	2.10	1.60

Ships from Columbus's Fleet, 1492—A139

1986, Apr. 14

614	A139	60fr	Santa Maria	85	65
615	A139	90fr	Nina, Pinta	1.25	95

Fish, Red Sea—A140

1986, June 16 **Litho.** ***Perf. 13½x13***

616 A140 20fr Elagatis bipinnulatus 28 22
617 A140 25fr Valamugil seheli 35 28
618 A140 55fr Lutjanus rivulatus 78 58

Public Buildings—A141

1986, July 21 **Litho.** ***Perf. 13***

619 A141 105fr People's Palace 1.50 1.15
620 A141 115fr Ministry of the Interior, Posts and Telecommunications 1.65 1.25

Sea-Me-We Building, Keyboard—A142

1986, Sept. 8 **Litho.** ***Perf. 13***

621 A142 100fr multi 1.40 1.05

Souvenir Sheet
Perf. 12½

622 A142 250fr multi 3.50 2.65

Southeast Asia, Middle East, Western Europe Submarine Cable System inauguration. No. 622 has multicolored margin picturing map and ship Vercors. Size: 125x95mm.

No. 537 Surcharged "5e ANNIVERSAIRE."

1986, Nov. 15 ***Perf. 13x12½***

623 A116 55fr on 75fr multi 78 60

Pasteur Institute, Cent.—A143

1987, Feb. 19 **Litho.** ***Perf. 13***

624 A143 220fr multi 3.25 2.50

Natl. Vaccination Campaign.

AIR POST STAMPS

Afars and Issas Nos. C104–C105, C103 Overprinted with Bars and "REPUBLIQUE DE DJIBOUTI" in Brown or Black

1977 Engraved *Perf. 13*
C106 AP37 55fr multi (Br) 1.50 1.50
C107 AP37 75fr multi 1.75 1.75

Litho. *Perf. 12*
C108 AP36 500fr multi 9.50 8.75

Map of Djibouti, Dove, UN Emblem—AP38

1977, Oct. 19 Photo. *Perf. 13*
C109 AP38 300fr multi 5.25 3.75

Djibouti's admission to the United Nations.

Marcel Brochet MB 101, 1955—AP39

Designs: 85fr, Tiger Moth, 1960. 200fr, Rallye-Commodore, 1973.

1978, Feb. 27 Litho. *Perf. 13*
C110 AP39 60fr multi 90 50
C111 AP39 85fr multi 1.25 75
C112 AP39 200fr multi 3.00 1.50

Djibouti Aero Club.

Old Man, by Rubens AP40

Design: 500fr, Hippopotamus Hunt, by Rubens (horiz.).

1978, Apr. 24 Photo. *Perf. 13*
C113 AP40 50fr multi 75 45
C114 AP40 500fr multi 7.50 4.50

Peter Paul Rubens (1577–1640), 400th birth anniversary.

Player Holding Soccer Cup AP41

Design: 300fr, Soccer player, map of South America with Argentina, Cup and emblem.

1978, June 20 Litho. *Perf. 13*
C115 AP41 100fr multi 1.50 60
C116 AP41 300fr multi 4.50 1.65

11th World Cup Soccer Championship, Argentina, June 1–25.

Nos. C115–C116 Overprinted:
a. ARGENTINE / CHAMPION 1978
b. ARGENTINE / HOLLANDE / 3–1

1978, Aug. 20 Litho. *Perf. 13*
C117 AP41(a)100fr multi 1.25 55
C118 AP41(b)300fr multi 3.75 1.75

Argentina's victory in 1978 Soccer Championship.

Tahitian Women, by Gauguin—AP42

Young Hare, by Dürer AP43

Perf. 13x12½, 12½x13
1978, Sept. 25 Lithographed
C119 AP42 100fr multi 1.50 60
C120 AP43 250fr multi 3.75 2.50

Paul Gauguin (1848–1903) and Albrecht Dürer (1471–1528), painters.

Philexafrique II—Essen Issue
Common Design Types

Designs: No. C121, Lynx and Djibouti No. 456. No. C122, Jay and Brunswick No. 3.

1978, Dec. 13 Litho. *Perf. 13x12½*
C121 CD138 90fr multi 1.75 1.50
C122 CD139 90fr multi 1.75 1.50

Nos. C121–C122 printed se-tenant.

UPU Emblem, Map of Djibouti, Dove AP44

1978, Dec. 18 Engr. *Perf. 13*
C123 AP44 200fr multi 3.00 1.75

Centenary of Congress of Paris.

Common Design Types
pictured in section at front of book.

Junkers JU-52 and Dewoitine D-338—AP45

Powered Flight, 75th Anniversary: 250fr, Potez P63-11, 1941 and Supermarine Spitfire HF-VII, 1942. 500fr, Concorde, 1969 and Sikorsky S-40 "American Clipper," 1931.

1979, May 21 Litho. *Perf. 13x12½*
C124 AP45 140fr multi 1.75 75
C125 AP45 250fr multi 3.25 1.50
C126 AP45 500fr multi 7.50 2.75

The Laundress, by Honore Daumier AP46

1979, July 10 Litho. *Perf. 12½x13*
C127 AP46 500fr multi 6.75 3.75

Olympic Emblem, Skis, Sleds—AP47

1980, Jan. 21 Litho. *Perf. 13*
C128 AP47 150fr multi 2.25 90

13th Winter Olympic Games, Lake Placid, N.Y., Feb. 12-24.

Cathedral of the Archangel, Basketball, Moscow '80 Emblem—AP48

1980, Apr. 10 Litho. *Perf. 13*
C129 AP48 60fr *shown* 75 30
C130 AP48 120fr *Lomonossov Univ., Moscow, Soccer* 1.50 60
C131 AP48 250fr *Cathedral of the Annunciation, Running* 3.00 1.40

22nd Summer Olympic Games, Moscow, July 18-Aug. 3.

Air Djibouti, 1st Anniversary—AP49

1980, Mar. 29 Litho. *Perf. 13x12½*
C132 AP49 400fr multi 4.75 1.75

No. C128 Surcharged in Black and Blue or Purple:

80fr. A.M. MOSER-PROEL / AUTRICHE / DESCENTE DAMES / MEDAILLE D'OR

200fr. HEIDEN / USA / 5 MEDAILLES D'OR / PATINAGE DE VITESSE

1980, Apr. 5 Litho. *Perf. 13*
C133 AP47 80fr on 150fr multi 1.00 60
C134 AP47 200fr on 150fr multi (P) 2.50 1.75

Apollo 11 Moon Landing, 10th Anniversary—AP50

Space Conquests: 300fr, Apollo-Soyuz space project, 5th anniversary.

1980, May 8
C135 AP50 200fr multi 2.75 90
C136 AP50 300fr multi 3.75 1.40

Satellite Earth Station Inauguration—AP51

1980, July 3 Litho. *Perf. 13*
C137 AP51 500fr multi 6.00 2.75

Graf Zeppelin—AP52

1980, Oct. 2 Litho. *Perf. 13*
C138 AP52 100fr *shown* 1.25 60
C139 AP52 150fr *Ferdinand von Zeppelin, blimp* 1.75 90

Zeppelin flight, 80th anniversary.

Voyager Passing Saturn—AP53

1980, Dec. 21 Litho. *Perf. 13*

C140	AP53	250fr multi	3.00	1.50

Soccer Players—AP54

World Cup Soccer Preliminary Games: 200fr, Players (diff.).

1981, Jan. 14

C141	AP54	80fr multi	1.00	45
C142	AP54	200fr multi	2.50	1.10

European—African Economic Convention—AP55

1981, Feb. 10 Litho. *Perf. 13*

C143	AP55	100fr multi	1.25	60

5th Anniversary of Viking I Take-off to Mars—AP56

20th Anniversary of Various Space Flights: 75fr, Vostok I, Yuri Gagarin (vert.). 150fr, Freedom 7, Alan B. Shepard (vert.).

1981, Mar. 9 Litho. *Perf. 13*

C144	AP56	75fr multi	90	45
C145	AP56	120fr multi	1.50	65
C146	AP56	150fr multi	1.75	90

Football Players, by Picasso (1881-1973)—AP57

Design: 400fr Man Wearing a Turban, by Rembrandt (1606-1669) (vert.).

1981, Aug. 3 Litho. *Perf. 13x12½, 12½x13*

C147	AP57	300fr multi	3.75	1.75
C148	AP57	400fr multi	4.75	2.75

Columbia Space Shuttle—AP58

1981, Sept. 24 Litho. *Perf. 13*

C149	AP58	90fr Shuttle, diff., vert.	1.10	60
C150	AP58	120fr shown	1.50	90

Nos. C149-C150 Overprinted in Brown with Astronauts' Names and Dates.

1981, Nov. 12 Litho. *Perf. 13*

C151	AP58	90fr multi	1.10	75
C152	AP58	120fr multi	1.50	1.10

1982 World Cup Soccer—AP59

Designs: Various soccer players.

1982, Jan. 20

C153	AP59	110fr multi	1.25	75
C154	AP59	220fr multi	2.50	1.50

Space Anniversaries—AP60

Designs: 40fr, Luna 9 moon landing, 15th (vert.). 60fr, John Glenn's flight, 20th (vert.). 180fr, Viking I Mars landing, 5th.

1982, Feb. 15

C155	AP60	40fr multi	45	30
C156	AP60	60fr multi	75	45
C157	AP60	180fr multi	2.10	1.25

21st Birthday of Princess Diana of Wales—AP61

1982, Apr. 29 Litho. *Perf. 12½x13*

C158	AP61	120fr Portrait	1.50	1.10
C159	AP61	180fr Portrait, diff.	2.25	1.40

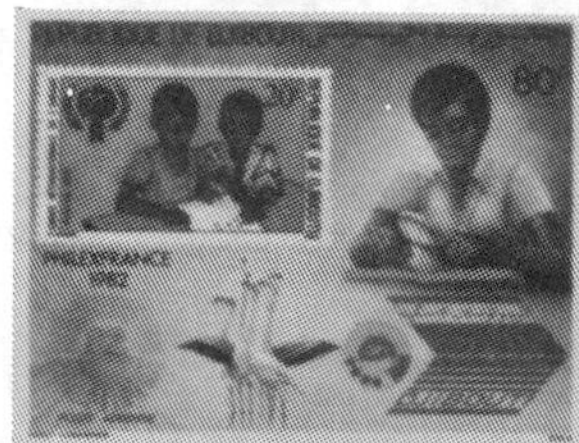

No. 489, Boy Examining Collection—AP62

1982, May 10 *Perf. 13x12½*

C160	AP62	80fr shown	1.00	75
C161	AP62	140fr No. 495	1.75	1.25

PHILEXFRANCE '82 Stamp Exhibition, Paris, June 11-21. Nos. C160-C161 se-tenant with label showing show emblem, dates.

1350th Anniv. of Mohamed's Death at Medina—AP63

1982, June 8 Litho. *Perf. 13*

C162	AP63	500fr Medina Mosque	6.00	3.50

Scouting Year—AP64

1982, June 28

C163	AP64	95fr Baden-Powell	1.25	75
C164	AP64	200fr Camp, scouts	2.50	1.50

2nd UN Conference on Peaceful Uses of Outer Space, Vienna, Aug. 9-21—AP65

1982, Aug. 19

C165	AP65	350fr multi	4.25	2.25

Nos. C153-C154 Overprinted with Winner's Name and Scores.

1982, July 21 Litho. *Perf. 13*

C166	AP59	110fr multi	1.25	90
C167	AP59	220fr multi	2.50	1.75

Italy's victory in 1982 World Cup.

Nos. C158-C159 Overprinted in Blue or Red with Date, Name, and Title.

1982, Aug. 9 *Perf. 12½x13*

C168	AP61	120fr multi	1.50	1.10
C169	AP61	180fr multi (R)	2.25	1.50

Birth of Prince William of Wales, June 21.

Franklin D. Roosevelt (1882-1945)—AP66

1982, Oct. 7 Litho. *Perf. 13*

C170	AP66	115fr shown	1.25	75
C171	AP66	250fr George Washington	3.00	1.50

Manned Flight Bicentenary AP67

Pre-olympic Year AP68

1983, Jan. 20 Litho.

C172	AP67	35fr Montgolfiere, 1783	48	32
C173	AP67	45fr Giffard, Paris Exposition, 1878	68	42
C174	AP67	120fr Double Eagle II, 1978	1.75	1.25

1983, Feb. 15

C175	AP68	75fr Volleyball	1.15	75
C176	AP68	125fr Wind surfing	1.85	1.25

50th Anniv. of Air France—AP69

1983, Mar. 20 Litho. *Perf. 13*

C177	AP69	25fr	Bloch 220	38	25
C178	AP69	100fr	DC-4	1.50	1.00
C179	AP69	175fr	Boeing 747	2.60	1.75

Martin Luther King, Jr. (1929-1968), Civil Rights Leader—AP70

Design: 250fr, Alfred Nobel (1833-1896)

1983, May 18 Litho. *Perf. 13*

C180	AP70	180fr	multi	2.90	2.00
C181	AP70	250fr	multi	4.00	3.00

Service Clubs—AP71

Designs: 90fr, Rotary Club International, Sailing Show, Toronto, June 5-9. 150fr, Lions Club International, Honolulu Meeting, June 22-24, Djibouti lighthouse.

1983, July 18 Litho. *Perf. 13*

C182	AP71	90fr	multi	1.35	90
C183	AP71	150fr	multi	2.25	1.50

Printed se-tenant with label showing emblems.

Vintage Motor Cars—AP72

1983, July 18 Litho. *Perf. 13x12½*

C184	AP72	60fr	Renault, 1904	90	60
C185	AP72	80fr	Mercedes, 1910	1.20	80
C186	AP72	110fr	Lorraine- Dietrich, 1912	1.65	1.10

Vostok VI—AP74

1983, Oct. 20 Litho. *Perf. 12*

C188	AP74	120fr	shown	1.80	1.20
C189	AP74	200fr	Explorer I	3.00	2.00

1984 Winter Olympics—AP75

1984, Feb. 14 Litho. *Perf. 13*

C190	AP75	70fr	Speed skating	1.00	75
C191	AP75	130fr	Figure skating	1.75	1.40

Souvenir Sheet

Ship—AP76

1984, Feb. 14 Litho. *Perf. 12½*

C192	AP76	250fr	multi	3.50	2.75

Sea-Me-We (South-east Asia-Middle East-Western Europe) submarine cable construction agreement. Multicolored margin shows map of cable. Size: 127x97mm.

Motorized Hang Gliders—AP77

Various hang gliders.

1984, Mar. 12 *Perf. 13x12½*

C193	AP77	65fr	multi	90	70
C194	AP77	85fr	multi	1.25	90
C195	AP77	100fr	multi	1.40	1.10

Nos. C190-C191 Overprinted with Winners' Names and Country

1984, Mar. 28 *Perf. 13*

C196	AP75	70fr	multi	1.00	75
C197	AP75	130fr	multi	1.90	1.40

Portrait of Marguerite Matisse, 1910, by Henri Matisse—AP78

Design: 200fr, Portrait of Mario Varvogli, by Amedeo Modigliani.

1984, Apr. 15 Litho. *Perf. 12½x13*

C198	AP78	150fr	multi	2.25	1.50
C199	AP78	200fr	multi	2.75	2.25

1984 Summer Olympics—AP79

1984, May 24 *Perf. 13*

C200	AP79	50fr	Running	70	52
C201	AP79	60fr	High jump	85	65
C202	AP79	80fr	Swimming	1.10	90

Battle Scene—AP80

1984, June 16 Litho. *Perf. 13x12½*

C203	AP80	300fr	multi	4.25	3.25

125th anniv. of Battle of Solferino and 120th anniv. of Red Cross.

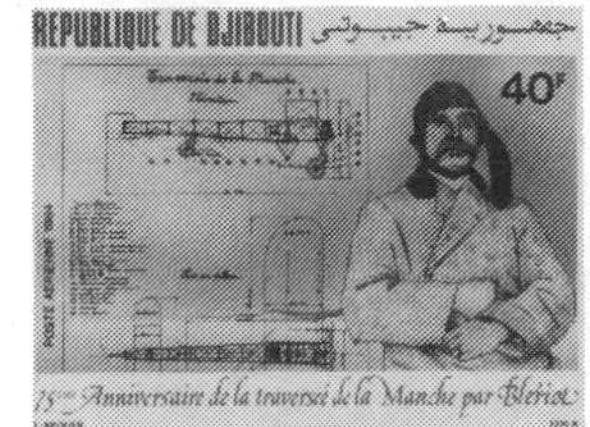

Bleriot's Flight over English Channel, 75th Anniv.—AP81

1984, July 8

C204	AP81	40fr	14-Bis plans	60	45
C205	AP81	75fr	Britten-Norman Islander	1.10	80
C206	AP81	90fr	Air Djibouti jet	1.25	1.00

375th Anniv., Galileo's telescope—AP82

1984, Oct. 7 Litho. *Perf. 13*

C207	AP82	120fr	Telescopes, spacecraft	1.75	1.25
C208	AP82	180fr	Galileo, telescopes	2.50	1.90

1984 Soccer Events—AP83

1984, Oct. 20 Litho. *Perf. 13*

C209	AP83	80fr	Euro Cup	1.10	90
C210	AP83	80fr	Los Angeles Olympics	1.10	90

Issued se-tenant, separated by pictorial label.

Service Clubs—AP84

1985, Feb. 23 Litho. *Perf. 13*

C211	AP84	50fr	Lions, World Leprosy Day	70	52
C212	AP84	60fr	Rotary, chess board, pieces	85	65

Telecommunications Technology—AP85

Designs: No. C213, Technician, researchist, operator. No. C214, Offshore oil rig, transmission tower, government building.

1985, July 2 *Perf. 13x12½*

C213	AP85	80fr	multi	1.15	80
C214	AP85	80fr	multi	1.15	80

PHILEXAFRICA '85, Lome. Nos. C213-C214 printed se-tenant with center label picturing map of Africa or UAPT emblem.

Telecommunications Development—AP86

1985, Oct. 2 *Perf. 13*

C215	AP86	50fr	Intl. transmission center	70	52
C216	AP86	90fr	Ariane rocket, vert.	1.30	1.00
C217	AP86	120fr	ARABSAT satellite	1.70	1.30

Youths Windsurfing, Playing Tennis—AP87

Design: No. C219, Tadjoura Highway construction.

1985, Nov. 13 ***Perf. 13x12½***

C218	AP87	100fr multi	1.40	1.05
C219	AP87	100fr multi	1.40	1.05

PHILEXAFRICA '85, Lome, Togo, Nov. 16-24. Nos. C218-C219 printed se-tenant with center label picturing map of Africa or UAPT emblem.

1986 World Cup Soccer Championships, Mexico—AP88

1986, Feb. 24 **Litho.** ***Perf. 13***

C220	AP88	75fr shown	1.05	78
C221	AP88	100fr Players, stadium	1.40	1.05

Statue of Liberty, Cent.—AP89

1986, May 21

C222	AP89	250fr multi	3.50	2.75

Nos. C220-C221 Ovptd. with Winners.

1986, Sept. 15 **Litho.** ***Perf. 13***

C223	AP88	75fr "FRANCE-BELGIQUE/4-2"	1.05	80
C224	AP88	100fr "3-2 ARGENTINE - RFA"	1.40	1.05

1986 World Chess Championships, May 1-19—AP89

Malayan animal chess pieces.

1986, Oct. 13 **Litho.** ***Perf. 13***

C225	AP89	80fr Knight, bishops	1.15	88
C226	AP89	120fr Rook, king, pawn	1.70	1.30

Yuri Gagarin, Sputnik Spacecraft—AP90

1986, Nov. 27 **Litho.** ***Perf. 13***

C227	AP90	150fr shown	2.15	1.65
C228	AP90	200fr Space rendezvous, 1966	2.85	2.15

First man in space, 25th anniv.; Gemini 8-Agena link-up, 20th anniv.

Historic Flights—AP91

1987, Jan. 22 **Litho.** ***Perf. 13***

C229	AP91	55fr Amiot 370	80	60
C230	AP91	80fr Spirit of St. Louis	1.15	85
C231	AP91	120fr Voyager	1.75	1.30

First flight from Istria to Djibouti, 1942; Lindbergh's Transatlantic flight, 1927; nonstop world circumnavigation without refueling.

DOMINICAN REPUBLIC

(dô·mĭn'ĭ·kăn rē·pŭb'lĭk)

LOCATION — Comprises about two-thirds of the island of Hispaniola in the West Indies.
GOVT.—Republic.
AREA—18,700 sq. mi.
POP.—5,982,000 (est. 1983).
CAPITAL—Santo Domingo.

8 Reales = 1 Peso
100 Centavos = 1 Peso (1880)
100 Centimos = 1 Franco (1883)
100 Centavos = 1 Peso (1885)

Prices of early Dominican Republic stamps vary according to condition. Quotations for Nos. 1–31 are for fine copies. Very fine to superb specimens sell at much higher prices, and inferior or poor copies sell at reduced prices, depending on the condition of the individual specimen.

Coat of Arms
A1 A2

Typographed

1865 *Imperf.* **Unwmkd.**

Wove Paper.

1	A1	½r *rose*	375.00	375.00
2	A1	1r *dp grn*	850.00	850.00

Twelve varieties of each.

Laid Paper.

3	A2	½r *pale grn*	550.00	500.00
4	A2	1r *straw*	1,300.	1,200.

Twelve varieties of the ½r, ten varieties of the 1r.

A3 A4

1866 **Laid Paper** **Unwmkd.**

5	A3	½r *straw*	200.00	150.00
6	A3	1r *pale grn*	900.00	900.00
7	A4	1r *pale grn*	175.00	150.00

Nos. 5–8 have 21 varieties (sheets of 21).

Wmk. 115

Wmkd. Diamonds. (115)

8	A3	1r *pale grn*	2,500.	2,500.

1866–67 **Wove Paper.** **Unwmkd.**

9	A3	½r *rose* ('67)	55.00	55.00
10	A3	1r *pale grn*	100.00	90.00
a.		Inscription double, top and bottom	*400.00*	*400.00*
11	A3	1r *bl* ('67)	45.00	35.00
a.		1r *lt bl* ('67)	45.00	35.00
b.		No space between "Un" and "real"	300.00	250.00
c.		Without inscription at top & bottom	450.00	200.00
d.		Inscription invtd., top & bottom		

1867-71 **Pelure Paper.**

13	A3	½r *rose*	135.00	100.00
15	A3	½r *lav* ('68)	275.00	275.00
a.		Without inscription at top and bottom		700.00
b.		Double inscriptions, one inverted		*550.00*
16	A3	½r *grnsh gray* ('68)	275.00	275.00
18	A3	½r *ol* ('69)	2,750.	2,750.
23	A3	1r *lavender*	250.00	225.00
24	A4	1r *rose* ('68)	250.00	225.00
25	A4	1r *mag* ('69)	1,400.	1,400.
26	A4	1r *sal* ('71)	250.00	225.00

1870-73 **Ordinary Paper.**

27	A3	½r *magenta*	1,000.	1,000.
28	A3	½r bl, *rose* (blk inscription) ('71)	65.00	55.00
a.		Blue inscription	650.00	650.00
b.		Without inscription at top and bottom		
29	A3	½r *yel* ('73)	40.00	27.50
a.		Without inscription at top and bottom	500.00	500.00
30	A4	1r *vio* ('73)	40.00	27.50
a.		Without inscription at top and bottom	600.00	600.00
31	A4	1r *dk grn*	80.00	65.00

Nos. 9–31 have 21 varieties (sheets of 21). Nos. 29 and 30 are known pin-perforated, unofficially.

Bisects are known of several of the early 1r stamps.

Coat of Arms
A5 A6

1879 ***Perf. 12½x13***

32	A5	½r violet	3.50	2.00
a.		Imperf., pair	12.00	12.00
b.		Horiz. pair, imperf. vert.	22.50	
33	A5	½r vio, *bluish*	3.50	2.00
a.		Imperf., pair	12.00	10.00
34	A5	1r carmine	3.50	2.00
a.		Imperf., pair	13.00	10.00
b.		Perf. 13	10.00	9.00
c.		Perf. 13x12½	10.00	9.00
35	A5	1r car, *sal*	3.50	2.00
a.		Imperf., pair	11.00	11.00

In 1891 15 stamps of 1879–83 were surcharged "U P U," new values and crossed diagonal lines.

Rouletted in Color

1880 **Typographed**

36	A6	1c green	1.50	1.00
b.		Laid paper	60.00	60.00
37	A6	2c red	1.00	75
a.		Pelure paper	45.00	45.00
b.		Laid paper	45.00	45.00
38	A6	5c blue	1.50	75
39	A6	10c rose	3.75	1.00
40	A6	20c brown	2.25	1.00
41	A6	25c violet	2.75	1.25
42	A6	50c orange	3.00	1.75
43	A6	75c ultra	6.00	3.00
a.		Laid paper	45.00	45.00
44	A6	1p gold	8.00	5.00
a.		Laid paper	65.00	65.00
b.		Double impression	55.00	55.00
		Nos. 36-44 (9)	29.75	15.50

1881 **Network Covering Stamp.**

45	A6	1c green	1.00	60
46	A6	2c red	1.00	60
47	A6	5c blue	1.50	60
48	A6	10c rose	1.75	75
49	A6	20c brown	1.75	90
50	A6	25c violet	2.25	1.00
51	A6	50c orange	2.50	1.25
52	A6	75c ultra	8.00	4.50
53	A6	1p gold	10.00	7.50
		Nos. 45-53 (9)	29.75	17.70

Preceding Issues Surcharged with Value in New Currency:

5 céntimos. (a)
5 céntimos (b)
5 céntimos. (c)
1 franco. (d)
1 Franco. (e)
1 franco (f)
1 franco, 25 céntimos. (g)
5 francos. (h)
5 francos (i)

1883 **Without Network.**

54	(a)	5c on 1c grn	2.50	1.50
b.		Inverted surcharge	27.50	27.50
c.		Surcharged "25 céntimos"	65.00	65.00
d.		Surcharged "10 céntimos"	35.00	35.00
55	(b)	5c on 1c grn	27.50	11.00
b.		Double surch.	125.00	
c.		Inverted surcharge	75.00	75.00
56	(c)	5c on 1c grn	20.00	10.00
b.		Surcharged "10 céntimos"	45.00	45.00
c.		Surcharged "25 céntimos"	50.00	50.00
57	(a)	10c on 2c red	6.50	4.00
a.		Inverted surcharge	37.50	37.50
d.		Surcharged "5 céntimos"	70.00	70.00
e.		Surcharged "25 céntimos"	100.00	100.00
58	(c)	10c on 2c red	6.00	4.00
a.		"Céntimso"		
b.		Inverted surcharge	50.00	50.00
c.		Surcharged "25 céntimos"	80.00	80.00
d.		"10" omitted	80.00	
59	(a)	25c on 5c bl	7.50	4.50
a.		Surcharged "5 céntimos"	70.00	
b.		Surcharged "10 céntimos"	70.00	70.00
c.		Surcharged "50 céntimos"	100.00	100.00
d.		Inverted surcharge	55.00	55.00
60	(c)	25c on 5c bl	7.50	3.50
a.		Inverted surcharge	60.00	50.00
b.		Surcharged "10 céntimos"	60.00	50.00
e.		"25" omitted	100.00	
f.		Surcharged on back		100.00
61	(a)	50c on 10c rose	27.50	15.00
a.		Inverted surcharge	65.00	60.00
62	(c)	50c on 10c rose	40.00	22.50
a.		Inverted surcharge	70.00	70.00
63	(d)	1fr on 20c brn	20.00	13.00
64	(e)	1fr on 20c brn	22.50	13.00
a.		Comma after "Franco,"	35.00	35.00
65	(f)	1fr on 20c brn	30.00	20.00
a.		Inverted surcharge		100.00
66	(g)	1fr25c on 25c vio	27.50	20.00
a.		Inverted surcharge	85.00	85.00
67	(g)	2fr50c on 50c org	17.50	13.00
a.		Inverted surcharge	45.00	35.00
68	(g)	3fr75c on 75c ultra	32.50	27.50
b.		Inverted surcharge	70.00	70.00
c.		Laid paper	85.00	85.00
70	(i)	5fr on 1p gold	675.00	600.00
a.		"s" of "francos" inverted	900.00	900.00

With Network.

71	(a)	5c on 1c grn	4.00	3.00
b.		Inverted surcharge	30.00	30.00
c.		Double surch.	27.50	27.50
d.		Surcharged "25 céntimos"	55.00	55.00
e.		"5" omitted	100.00	100.00
72	(b)	5c on 1c grn	27.50	12.00
b.		Inverted surcharge	65.00	65.00
73	(c)	5c on 1c grn	32.50	13.00
b.		Surcharged "10 céntimos"	55.00	50.00
c.		Surcharged "25 céntimos"	80.00	
74	(a)	10c on 2c red	5.00	3.00
a.		Surcharged "5 céntimos"	70.00	60.00
b.		Surcharged "25 céntimos"	90.00	90.00
c.		"10" omitted	75.00	
75	(c)	10c on 2c red	4.00	2.00
a.		Inverted surcharge	37.50	22.50
76	(a)	25c on 5c bl	9.00	4.00
a.		Surcharged "10 céntimos"	100.00	
b.		Surcharged "5 céntimos"	80.00	
c.		Surcharged "50 céntimos"	90.00	
77	(c)	25c on 5c bl	80.00	40.00
a.		Inverted surcharge		
b.		Surcharged on back		
78	(a)	50c on 10c rose	32.50	10.00
a.		Inverted surcharge	40.00	25.00
b.		Surcharged "25 céntimos"	75.00	
79	(c)	50c on 10c rose	35.00	12.50
a.		Inverted surcharge	70.00	
80	(d)	1fr on 20c brn	15.00	12.00
81	(e)	1fr on 20c brn	17.50	14.00
a.		Comma after "Franco,"	45.00	45.00
b.		Inverted surcharge	100.00	
82	(f)	1fr on 20c brn	30.00	22.50
83	(g)	1fr25c on 25c vio	55.00	32.50
a.		Inverted surcharge	85.00	
84	(g)	2fr50c on 50c org	25.00	16.50
a.		Inverted surcharge	45.00	35.00
85	(g)	3fr75c on 75c ultra	55.00	50.00
86	(h)	5fr on 1p gold	225.00	225.00
a.		Inverted surcharge		
87	(i)	5fr on 1p gold	250.00	250.00

Many minor varieties exist in Nos. 54– 87: accent on "i" of "centimos"; "5" with straight top; "1" with straight serif.

Coat of Arms
A7 A7a

1885–91 **Engraved** ***Perf. 12***

88	A7	1c green	1.00	60
89	A7	2c vermilion	1.00	60
90	A7	5c blue	1.50	60
91	A7a	10c orange	2.50	75
92	A7a	20c dk brn	2.50	1.00
93	A7a	50c vio ('91)	8.50	6.50
94	A7	1p car ('91)	24.00	14.00
95	A7	2p red brn ('91)	30.00	16.00
		Nos. 88-95 (8)	71.00	40.05

Nos. 93, 94 and 95 were issued without gum.

Imperf. varieties are proofs.

Coat of Arms
A8

1895–97 ***Perf. 12½x14***

96	A8	1c green	1.50	60
a.		Perf. 14 ('97)	1.75	70
97	A8	2c org red	1.50	60
a.		Perf. 14 ('97)	8.00	1.00
98	A8	5c blue	1.50	60
a.		Perf. 14 ('97)	1.75	1.00
99	A8	10c orange	3.00	1.75
a.		Perf. 14 ('97)	3.50	2.00

Nos. 96 to 99 are known imperforate but were not issued in this condition.

Columbus Mausoleum Issue.

Voyage of Diego Méndez from Jamaica—A9

Enriquillo's Revolt
A10

Sarcophagus of Columbus
A11

"Española" Guarding Remains of Columbus
A12

Toscanelli Replying to Columbus
A13

Bartolomé de las Casas Defending Indians
A14

Columbus at Salamanca
A15

Columbus' Mausoleum
A16

1899, Feb. 27 **Litho.** ***Perf. 11½***

100	A9	1c brn vio	6.00	5.00
a.		Imperf., pair	20.00	
102	A10	2c rose red	2.00	1.00
a.		Imperf., pair	7.00	
103	A11	5c blue	2.25	1.00
a.		Imperf., pair	8.00	
104	A12	10c orange	5.00	1.75
a.		Tête bêche pair	60.00	60.00
b.		Imperf. pair	12.50	
105	A13	20c brown	8.50	5.50
a.		Imperf. pair	20.00	
106	A14	50c yel grn	9.00	6.50
a.		Tête bêche pair	80.00	80.00
b.		Imperf. pair	25.00	
c.		as "a," imperf.	175.00	
107	A15	1p *gray bl*	22.50	17.50
a.		Imperf. pair	60.00	
108	A16	2p bis brn	45.00	45.00
a.		Imperf. pair	100.00	

1900, Jan.

109	A11	¼c black	1.00	1.00
a.		Imperf. pair	3.00	3.50
110	A15	½c black	1.00	1.00
b.		Imperf. pair	3.00	3.50
110A	A9	1c gray grn	1.00	75
c.		Imperf. pair	5.00	
		Nos. 100-110A (11)	103.25	86.00

Nos. 100–110A were issued to raise funds for a Columbus mausoleum.

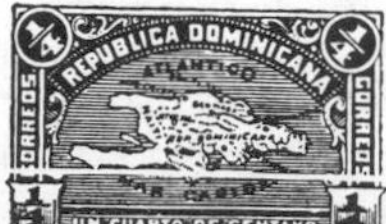

Map of Hispaniola
A17

Coat of Arms
A18

1900, Oct. 21 ***Perf. 14*** **Unwmkd.**

111	A17	¼c dk bl	90	60
112	A17	½c rose	90	60
113	A17	1c ol grn	90	60
114	A17	2c dp grn	90	60
115	A17	5c red brn	90	60
a.		Vertical pair, imperf. between	25.00	

Perf. 12.

116	A17	10c orange	90	60
117	A17	20c lilac	4.00	3.00
a.		20c rose (error)	8.00	8.00
118	A17	50c black	3.50	3.00
119	A17	1p brown	4.00	3.00
		Nos. 111-119 (9)	16.90	12.60

Several varieties in design are known in this issue. They were deliberately made. Counterfeits of Nos. 111–119 abound.

1901–06 **Typographed** ***Perf. 14***

120	A18	½c car & vio	90	50
121	A18	½c blk & org ('05)	1.75	1.00
122	A18	½c grn & blk ('06)	1.00	35
123	A18	1c ol grn & vio	90	25
124	A18	1c blk & ultra ('05)	2.00	1.00
125	A18	1c car & blk ('06)	90	40
126	A18	2c dp grn & vio	85	25
127	A18	2c blk & vio ('05)	2.00	75
128	A18	2c org brn & blk ('06)	90	20
129	A18	5c org brn & vio	90	30
130	A18	5c blk & cl ('05)	2.50	1.25
131	A18	5c bl & blk ('06)	1.00	40
132	A18	10c org & vio	1.50	50
133	A18	10c blk & grn ('05)	5.00	2.50
134	A18	10c red vio & blk ('06)	1.25	50
135	A18	20c brn vio & vio	2.75	1.00
136	A18	20c blk & ol ('05)	16.00	9.00
137	A18	20c ol grn & blk ('06)	8.00	3.50
138	A18	50c gray blk & vio	10.00	6.00
139	A18	50c blk & red brn ('05)	50.00	30.00
140	A18	50c brn & blk ('06)	9.00	8.00
141	A18	1p brn & vio	22.50	13.50
142	A18	1p blk & gray ('05)	250.00	250.00
143	A18	1p vio & blk ('06)	25.00	15.00
		Nos. 120-143 (24)	416.60	346.15

Issue dates: Nov. 15, 1901, May 11, 1905, Aug. 17, 1906.
See also Nos. 172–176.

Francisco Sánchez
A19

Juan Pablo Duarte
A20

Ramón Mella
A21

Ft. Santo Domingo
A22

1902, Feb. 25 **Engraved** ***Perf. 12***

144	A19	1c dk grn & blk	35	35
a.		Center inverted	4.50	
145	A20	2c scar & blk	35	35
a.		Center inverted	4.50	
146	A20	5c bl & blk	35	35
a.		Center inverted	4.50	
147	A19	10c org & blk	35	35
148	A21	12c pur & blk	35	35
a.		Center inverted	4.50	
149	A21	20c rose & blk	50	50
a.		Center inverted	4.50	
150	A22	50c brn & blk	75	75
a.		Center inverted	4.50	
		Nos. 144-150 (7)	3.00	3.00

400th anniversary of Santo Domingo. Imperforate varieties of Nos. 144 to 150 were never sold to the public.

Nos. 138, 141 Surcharged in Black

2
dos cts

1904, Aug.

151	A18	2c on 50c blk & vio	10.00	7.50
a.		Inverted surcharge	20.00	20.00
152	A18	2c on 1p brn & vio	15.00	10.00
a.		Inverted surcharge	20.00	20.00
b.		"2" omitted	70.00	70.00
c.		As "b," inverted	100.00	100.00
153	A18	5c on 50c blk & vio	4.50	3.00
a.		Inverted surcharge	6.00	5.00
154	A18	5c on 1p brn & vio	5.00	4.00
a.		Inverted surcharge	9.00	9.00
155	A18	10c on 50c blk & vio	10.00	8.00
a.		Inverted surcharge	20.00	20.00
156	A18	10c on 1p brn & vio	10.00	8.00
a.		Inverted surcharge	14.00	14.00
		Nos. 151-156 (6)	54.50	40.50

Official Stamps of 1902 Overprinted

16 de Agosto
1904

Red Overprint.

1904, Aug. 16

157	O1	5c dk bl & blk	6.00	3.25
a.		Inverted overprint	8.00	7.00

Black Overprint.

158	O1	2c scar & blk	15.00	5.00
a.		Inverted overprint	9.00	7.00
159	O1	5c dk bl & blk	800.00	800.00
160	O1	10c yel grn & blk	13.00	10.00
a.		Inverted overprint	16.00	16.00

16 de Agosto

Surcharged

1 1904 1

161	O1	1c on 20c yel & blk	5.00	4.00
a.		Inverted surcharge	7.50	6.50

Nos. J1–J2 Surcharged or Overprinted

REPUBLICA
DOMINICANA
1
CENTAVOS
CORREOS

Surcharged "CENTAVOS".

1904-05 Black Surcharge.

162	D1	1c on 2c ol gray	135.00	135.00
a.		"entavos"		
b.		"Dominican"	250.00	250.00
c.		"Centavo"	250.00	250.00

Carmine Surcharge or Overprint.

163	D1	1c on 2c ol gray	2.75	1.25
a.		Inverted surcharge	3.50	3.00
b.		"Domihicana"	17.50	17.50
c.		Same as "b," inverted	45.00	45.00
d.		"Dominican"	14.00	14.00
e.		"Centavos" omitted	35.00	35.00
g.		"entavos"	30.00	
163F	D1	1c on 4c ol gray	37.50	8.00
164	D1	2c ol gray	1.00	50
a.		"Domihicana"	12.50	12.50
b.		Inverted overprint	2.50	2.50
c.		Same as "a," inverted	25.00	25.00
d.		"Dominican"	7.00	7.00
e.		"Centavo" omitted	15.00	12.00
f.		"entavos"	12.50	12.50
g.		Same as "f," inverted	40.00	40.00
h.		Same as "d," inverted	40.00	40.00

Surcharged "CENTAVO".

165	D1	1c on 4c ol gray	1.00	75
a.		"Domihicana"	14.00	14.00
c.		Inverted surcharge	2.50	2.50
d.		"1" omitted	4.00	4.00
e.		Same as "a," invtd.	45.00	45.00
f.		Same as "d," invtd.	55.00	55.00
g.		Double surcharge	35.00	35.00

No. 92 Surcharged in Red

DOS
1905
CENTAVOS

1905, Apr. 4

166	A7a	2c on 20c dk brn	10.00	6.00
a.		Inverted surcharge	20.00	20.00
167	A7a	5c on 20c dk brn	5.00	2.00
a.		Inverted surcharge	22.50	22.50
b.		Double surcharge	35.00	35.00
168	A7a	10c on 20c dk brn	10.00	6.00

Nos. 166–168 exist with inverted "A" for "V" in "CENTAVOS" in surcharge.

Nos. J2, J4, J3 Surcharged:

REPUBLICA
DOMINICANA.
UN
centavo.

REPUBLICA
DOMINICANA.
DOS
centavos.

1906, Jan. 16 ***Perf. 14***

Red Surcharge.

169	D1	1c on 4c ol gray	1.00	60
a.		Inverted surcharge	15.00	15.00

1906, May 1

Black Surcharge.

170	D1	1c on 10c ol gray	1.25	60
a.		Inverted surcharge	15.00	15.00
b.		Double surcharge	20.00	20.00
c.		'OMINICANA'	27.50	27.50
171	D1	2c on 5c ol gray	1.25	60
a.		Inverted surcharge	15.00	15.00

The varieties small "C" or small "A" in "REPUBLICA" are found on Nos. 169, 170 and 171.

Arms Type of 1901–06.

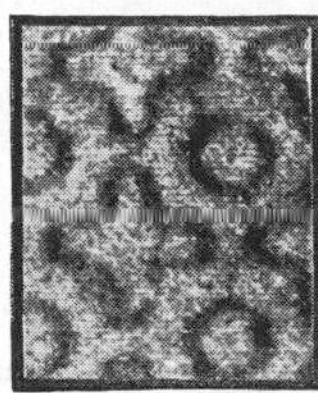

Wmk. 116

Wmkd. Crosses and Circles. (116)

1907-10

172	A18	½c grn & blk ('08)	80	25
173	A18	1c car & blk	80	20
174	A18	2c org brn & blk	80	20
175	A18	5c bl & blk	90	30
176	A18	10c red vio & blk ('10)	9.00	1.50
		Nos. 172-176 (5)	12.30	2.45

No. 06 Overprinted in Red

HABILITADO
1911

Perf. 13½x14, 13½x13

1911, July 11

177	O2	2c scar & blk	1.50	75
a.		'HABILITAOO'	12.50	8.50
b.		Inverted overprint	30.00	
c.		Double overprint	30.00	

Coat of Arms A23 Juan Pablo Duarte A24

1911-13 *Perf. 14.*

Center in Black

178	A23	½c org ('13)	35	20
179	A23	1c green	35	15
180	A23	2c carmine	35	15
181	A23	5c gray bl ('13)	75	20
182	A23	10c red vio	1.50	60
183	A23	20c ol grn	10.00	7.00
184	A23	50c yel brn ('12)	4.00	3.50
185	A23	1p vio ('12)	7.00	4.00
		Nos. 178-185 (8)	24.30	15.80

See Nos. 230–232.

1914, Apr. 13 *Perf. 13x14*

Background Red, White and Blue.

186	A24	½c org & blk	70	55
187	A24	1c grn & blk	70	55
188	A24	2c rose & blk	70	55
189	A24	5c sl & blk	85	60
190	A24	10c mag & blk	1.25	85
191	A24	20c ol grn & blk	3.00	3.00
192	A24	50c brn & blk	4.00	4.00
193	A24	1p dl lil & blk	6.50	6.50
		Nos. 186-193 (8)	17.70	16.60

To commemorate the centenary of the birth of Juan Pablo Duarte (1813–1876), patriot and revolutionary.

Official Stamps of 1909–12 Surcharged in Violet or Overprinted in Red:

Habilitado Habilitado

1915

MEDIO CENTAVO 1915

a b

1915, Feb. *Perf. 13½x13, 13½x14*

194	O2 (a)	½c on 20c org & blk	75	50
a.		Inverted surcharge	8.50	8.50
b.		Double surcharge	12.50	12.50
c.		'Habilitado' omitted	7.50	7.50
195	O2 (b)	1c bl grn & blk	1.00	35
a.		Inverted overprint	8.50	8.50
b.		Double overprint	10.00	
c.		Overprinted '1915' only	17.50	
196	O2 (b)	2c scar & blk	1.00	35
a.		Inverted overprint	7.50	7.50
b.		Double overprint	11.00	11.00
c.		Overprinted '1915' only	12.50	
d.		'1915' double		
197	O2 (b)	5c dk bl & blk	1.25	35
a.		Inverted overprint	10.00	10.00
b.		Double overprint	12.50	12.50
c.		Double overprint, one inverted	40.00	
d.		Overprinted '1915' only	12.00	
198	O2 (b)	10c yel grn & blk	3.50	2.75
a.		Inverted overprint	12.50	
199	O2 (b)	20c org & blk	12.00	9.00
a.		'Habilitado' omitted		
		Nos. 194-199 (6)	19.50	13.30

Nos. 194, 196–198 are known with both perforations. Nos. 195 and 199 are only perf. 13½x13.

The variety capital "I" for "1" in "Habilitado" occurs once in each sheet in all denominations.

A25

Type of 1911–13 Redrawn Overprinted "1915" in Red. Lithographed.

1915 *Perf. 11½* **Unwmkd.**

TWO CENTAVOS:

Type I. "DOS" in small letters.

Type II. "DOS" in larger letters with white dot at each end of the word.

200	A25	½c vio & blk	90	25
a.		Imperf., pair	8.00	
201	A25	1c yel brn & blk	90	12
a.		Imperf., pair	9.00	
b.		Vert. pair, imperf. horiz.	15.00	
c.		Horiz. pair, imperf. vert.	15.00	
202	A25	2c ol grn & blk (I)	4.00	35
a.		Imperf., pair	9.00	
203	A25	2c ol grn & blk (II)	7.00	25
a.		Center omitted	125.00	
b.		Frame omitted	125.00	
c.		Imperf., pair	9.00	
d.		Horiz. pair, imperf. vert.	15.00	
204	A25	5c mag & blk	4.00	35
a.		Pair, one without overprint	75.00	
b.		Imperf., pair	9.00	
205	A25	10c gray bl & blk	4.00	50
a.		Imperf., pair	11.00	
b.		Horiz. pair, imperf. vert.	50.00	
206	A25	20c rose red & blk	9.00	1.75
a.		Imperf., pair	17.50	
207	A25	50c grn & blk	11.00	5.00
a.		Imperf., pair	35.00	
208	A25	1p org & blk	22.50	10.00
a.		Imperf., pair	60.00	
		Nos. 200-208 (9)	63.30	18.57

Type of 1915 Overprinted "1916" in Red.

1916

209	A25	½c vio & blk	1.25	15
a.		Imperf., pair	30.00	
210	A25	1c grn & blk	2.25	15
a.		Imperf., pair	30.00	

Type of 1915 Overprinted "1917" in Red.

1917-19

213	A25	½c red lil & blk	2.25	40
a.		Horizontal pair, imperf. between	60.00	60.00
214	A25	1c yel grn & blk	2.00	10
215	A25	2c ol grn & blk	1.50	10
a.		Imperf., pair	45.00	
216	A25	5c mag & blk	15.00	1.00

Type of 1915 Overprinted "1919" in Red

1919

219	A25	2c ol grn & blk	10.00	15

Type of 1915 Overprinted "1920" in Red.

1920-27

220	A25	½c lil rose & blk	70	30
a.		Horizontal pair, imperf. between	35.00	35.00
b.		Inverted overprint		
c.		Double overprint		
d.		Double overprint, one inverted		
221	A25	1c yel grn & blk	90	12
a.		Overprint omitted	100.00	
222	A25	2c ol grn & blk	1.00	8
a.		Vertical pair, imperf. between	40.00	
223	A25	5c dp rose & blk	11.00	70
224	A25	10c bl & blk	7.00	30
225	A25	20c rose red & blk ('27)	9.00	75
226	A25	50c grn & blk ('27)	75.00	25.00
		Nos. 220-226 (7)	104.60	27.25

Type of 1915 Overprinted "1921" in Red.

1921

227	A25	1c yel grn & blk	3.00	40
a.		Horizontal pair, imperf. between	60.00	60.00
b.		Imperf., pair	60.00	60.00
228	A25	2c ol grn & blk	5.00	45

Redrawn Design of 1915 without Overprint

1922

230	A25	1c green	2.00	15
231	A25	2c car (II)	2.50	15
232	A25	5c blue	4.50	35

Exist imperf.

Arms of Dominican Republic

A26 A27

Second Redrawing.

TEN CENTAVOS:

Type I. Numerals 2 mm. high. "DIEZ" in thick letters with large white dot at each end.

Type II. Numerals 3 mm. high. "DIEZ" in thin letters with white dot with colored center at each end.

1924-27

233	A26	1c green	70	10
a.		Vertical pair, imperf. between	50.00	50.00
234	A26	2c red	85	10
235	A26	5c blue	1.00	12
236	A26	10c pale bl & blk (I) ('26)	15.00	2.00
236A	A26	10c pale bl & blk (II)	32.50	1.00
236B	A26	50c gray grn & blk ('26)	65.00	37.50
237	A26	1p org & blk ('27)	22.50	14.00
		Nos. 233-237 (7)	137.55	54.82

In the second redrawing the shield has a flat top and the design differs in many details from the stamps of 1911–13 and 1915–22.

1927

238	A27	½c lil rose & blk	40	10

Exhibition Pavilion
A28

1927 *Perf. 12.* **Unwmkd.**

239	A28	2c carmine	1.00	70
240	A28	5c ultra	1.75	70

Issued to commemorate the National and West Indian Exhibition at Santiago de los Caballeros.

Ruins of Columbus' Fortress
A29

1928

241	A29	½c lil rose	80	50
242	A29	1c dp grn	60	15
a.		Horizontal pair, imperf. between	30.00	
243	A29	2c red	70	15
244	A29	5c dk bl	1.75	40
245	A29	10c lt bl	2.00	40
246	A29	20c rose	3.50	60
247	A29	50c yel grn	15.00	9.00
248	A29	1p org yel	27.50	20.00
		Nos. 241-248 (8)	51.85	31.20

Reprints exist of 1c, 2c and 10c.

Issue dates: 1c, 2c, 10c, Oct. 1. Others, Dec.

Horacio Vasquez A30 Convent of San Ignacio de Loyola A31

1929, May-June

249	A30	½c dl rose	70	35
a.		Imperf., pair	17.50	
250	A30	1c gray grn	70	20
a.		Imperf., pair	17.50	
251	A30	2c red	80	20
a.		Imperf., pair	17.50	
252	A30	5c dk ultra	1.75	40
a.		Imperf., pair	20.00	

253 A30 10c pale bl 2.50 70
Nos. 249-253 (5) 6.45 1.85

Issued in commemoration of the signing of the "Frontier" treaty between the Dominican Republic and Haiti.

1930, May 1 ***Perf. 11½***

254 A31 ½c red brn 90 65
a. Imperf., pair 75.00 75.00
255 A31 1c dp grn 70 15
256 A31 2c vermilion 70 15
257 A31 5c dp bl 1.75 50
258 A31 10c lt bl 4.00 1.50
Nos. 254-258 (5) 8.05 2.95

Cathedral of Santo Domingo, First Church in America
A32

1931 ***Perf. 12.***

260 A32 1c dp grn 75 20
a. Imperf., pair 70.00
261 A32 2c scarlet 75 20
a. Imperf., pair 70.00
262 A32 3c violet 85 15
263 A32 7c dk bl 2.50 35
264 A32 8c bister 3.75 1.00
265 A32 10c lt bl 5.50 1.50
a. Imperf., pair 50.00

Issue dates: 3c-8c, Aug. 1. Others, July 11.

A33

Overprinted or Surcharged in Black.

1932, Dec. 20 ***Perf. 12***
Cross in Red

265B A33 1c yel grn 75 60
265C A33 3c on 2c vio 1.00 70
265D A33 5c blue 5.50 4.00
265E A33 7c on 10c turq bl 6.50 6.00

Proceeds of sale given to Red Cross. Valid Dec. 20, to Jan. 5, 1933.

Fernando Arturo de Merino As Archbishop
A34

As President
A35

Cathedral of Santo Domingo A36

Designs: ½, 5, 8c, Tomb of Merino.

1933, Feb. 27 **Engraved** ***Perf. 14***

266 A35 ½c lt vio 35 35
267 A34 1c yel grn 40 20
268 A35 2c lt red 1.00 90
269 A34 3c dp vio 50 20
270 A35 5c dk bl 70 35
271 A35 7c ultra 1.35 50
272 A35 8c dk grn 1.75 1.25
273 A34 10c org yel 1.50 40
274 A35 20c car rose 3.50 2.25
275 A36 50c lemon 14.00 8.50
276 A36 1p dk brn 35.00 22.50
Nos. 266-276 (11) 60.05 37.40

Issued in commemoration of the centenary of the birth of Fernando Arturo de Meriño (1833–1906)

Tower of Homage, Ozama Fortress
A37

1932 **Lithographed** ***Perf. 12***

278 A37 1c green 50 20
279 A37 3c violet 75 10

Issue dates: 1c, July 2; 3c, June 22.

"CORREOS" added at left.

1933, May 28

283 A37 1c dk grn 70 20

President Rafael L. Trujillo
A38 A39

1933, Aug. 16 **Engraved** ***Perf. 14***

286 A38 1c yel grn & blk 85 60
287 A39 3c dp vio & blk 1.00 30
288 A38 7c ultra & blk 3.00 1.25

Commemorating the 42nd anniversary of the birth of President Rafael Leonidas Trujillo Molina.

San Rafael Bridge
A40

1934 **Lithographed.** ***Perf. 12.***

289 A40 ½c dl vio 90 40
290 A40 1c dk grn 1.25 25
291 A40 3c violet 2.00 12

Opening of San Rafael Bridge.
Issue dates: ½c, Mar. 31; 1c, Feb. 17; 3c, Mar. 3.

Trujillo Bridge
A41

1934

292 A41 ½c red brn 90 35
293 A41 1c green 1.25 12
294 A41 3c purple 1.75 15

Issued in commemoration of the opening of the General Trujillo Bridge near Ciudad Trujillo.

Issue dates: 1c, Aug. 24. Others, Sept. 7.

Ramfis Bridge
A42

1935, Apr. 6

295 A42 1c green 65 12
296 A42 3c yel brn 70 12
297 A42 5c brn vio 2.25 1.50
298 A42 10c rose 4.50 2.00

Issued in commemoration of the opening of the Ramfis Bridge over the Higuamo River.

President Trujillo—A43

A44

A45

1935 ***Perf. 11***

299 A43 3c yel brn 45 25
300 A44 5c org red, bl, red & bis 55 15
301 A45 7c ultra, bl, red & brn 80 15
302 A44 10c red vio, bl, red & bis 1.25 15

Issue dates: 3c, Oct. 29; 5c, 10c, Nov. 25; 7c, Nov. 5.

Issued in commemoration of the ratification of a treaty setting the frontier between Dominican Republic and Haiti.

National Palace—A46

1935, Apr. 1 ***Perf. 11½***

303 A46 25c yel org 3.25 25

Issued for obligatory use on all mail addressed to the president and cabinet ministers.

Post Office, Santiago
A47

1936

304 A47 ½c brt vio 45 40
305 A47 1c green 45 12

Issue dates: ½c, Jan. 14; 1c, Jan. 4.

George Washington Ave., Ciudad Trujillo
A48

1936, Feb. 22

306 A48 ½c brn & vio brn 55 50
a. Imperf., pair 75.00
307 A48 2c car & brn 55 40
308 A48 3c yel org & red brn 90 25
309 A48 7c ultra, bl & brn 1.50 1.00
a. Imperf., pair 75.00

Issued in commemoration of the dedication of George Washington Avenue, Ciudad Trujillo.

José Nuñez de Cáceres
A49

Felix M. del Monte
A55

Proposed National Library
A56

Designs: 1c, Gen. Gregorio Luperon. 2c, Emiliano Tejera. 3c, President Trujillo. 5c, Jose Reyes. 7c, Gen. Antonio Duverge. 25c, Francisco J. Peynado. 30c, Salome Urena. 50c, Gen. Jose M. Cabral. 1p, Manuel de Jesus Galvan. 2p, Gaston F. Deligne.

Engraved.

1936 ***Perf. 13½, 14.*** **Unwmkd.**

310 A49 ½c dl vio 50 25
311 A49 1c dk grn 40 15
312 A49 2c carmine 40 20
313 A49 3c violet 45 10
314 A49 5c dp ultra 80 40
315 A49 7c sl bl 1.50 80
316 A55 10c orange 1.50 45
317 A56 20c ol grn 6.00 3.25
318 A55 25c gray vio 7.50 4.50
319 A55 30c scarlet 9.00 6.00
320 A55 50c blk brn 11.00 4.75
321 A55 1p black 35.00 35.00
322 A55 2p yel brn 90.00 80.00
Nos. 310-322 (13) 164.05 135.85

The funds derived from the sale of these stamps were returned to the National Treasury Fund for the erection of a building for the National Library and Archives.

Issue dates: 3c, 7c, Mar. 18; others, May 22.

President Trujillo and Obelisk
A62

1937, Jan. 11 **Litho.** ***Perf. 11½***

323 A62 1c green 30 10
324 A62 3c violet 60 15
325 A62 7c bl & turq bl 1.75 1.50

Issued in commemoration of the first anniversary of naming Ciudad Trujillo.

Discus Thrower and Flag
A63

1937, Aug. 14

Flag in Red and Blue.

326	A63	1c dk grn	5.00	1.25
327	A63	3c violet	6.00	75
328	A63	7c dk bl	10.00	5.00

Issued in commemoration of the First National Olympic Games, August 16, 1937.

Symbolical of Peace, Labor and Progress—A64

1937, Sept. 18 ***Perf. 12***

329	A64	3c purple	50	12

"8th Year of the Benefactor."

Monument to Father F. X. Billini
A65

1937, Dec. 29

330	A65	½c dp org	25	12
331	A65	5c purple	70	25

Issued in commemoration of the centenary of the birth of Father Francisco Xavier Billini (1837–1890).

Globe and Torch of Liberty
A66

1938, Feb. 22 ***Perf. 11½***

332	A66	1c green	60	10
333	A66	3c purple	85	10
334	A66	10c orange	1.75	30

Issued in commemoration of the 150th anniversary of the Constitution of the United States of America.

Pledge of Trinitarians, City Gate and National Flag
A67

1938, July 16 ***Perf. 12***

335	A67	1c grn, red & dk bl	60	30
336	A67	3c pur, red & bl	75	25
337	A67	10c org, red & bl	1.50	70

Issued in commemoration of the Trinitarians and patriots, Francisco Del Rosario Sanchez, Ramon Matias Mella and Juan Pablo Duarte, who helped free their country from foreign domination.

Seal of the University of Santo Domingo
A68

1938, Oct. 28

338	A68	½c orange	45	30
339	A68	1c dp grn & lt grn	50	15
340	A68	3c pur & pale vio	60	15
341	A68	7c dp bl & lt bl	1.25	65

Issued in commemoration of the fourth centenary of the founding of the University of Santo Domingo, on October 28, 1538.

Trylon and Perisphere, Flag and Proposed Columbus Lighthouse—A69

1939, Apr. 30 Litho. ***Perf. 12***

Flag in Blue and Red.

342	A69	½c red org & org	50	25
343	A69	1c grn & lt grn	55	20
344	A69	3c pur & pale vio	60	18
345	A69	10c org & yel	1.75	70
		Nos. 342-345, C33 (5)	5.65	2.18

New York World's Fair.

José Trujillo Valdez
A70

1939, Sept. Typographed

346	A70	½c blk & pale gray	45	25
347	A70	1c blk & yel grn	60	15
348	A70	3c blk & yel brn	70	15
349	A70	7c blk & dp ultra	1.75	1.25
350	A70	10c blk & brt red vio	2.50	65
		Nos. 346-350 (5)	6.00	2.45

Issued in commemoration of the fourth anniversary of the death of José Trujillo Valdez (1863–1935), father of President Trujillo Molina.

Map of the Americas and Flags of 21 American Republics
A71

Sir Rowland Hill
A72

1940, Apr. 14 Litho. ***Perf. 11½***

Flags in National Colors

351	A71	1c dp grn	40	15
352	A71	2c carmine	55	30
353	A71	3c red vio	80	10
354	A71	10c orange	1.60	30
355	A71	1p chestnut	25.00	20.00
		Nos. 351-355 (5)	28.35	20.85

Issued in commemoration of the 50th anniversary of the founding of the Pan American Union.

1940, May 6 ***Perf. 12***

356	A72	3c brt red vio & rose lil	5.00	60
357	A72	7c dk bl & lt bl	10.00	2.25

Centenary of first postage stamp.

Julia Molina Trujillo—A73

1940, May 26

358	A73	1c grn, lt grn & dk grn	45	12
359	A73	2c brt red, buff & dp rose	60	40
360	A73	3c org, dl org & brn org	75	12
361	A73	7c bl, pale bl & dk bl	1.75	65

Issued in commemoration of Mother's Day.

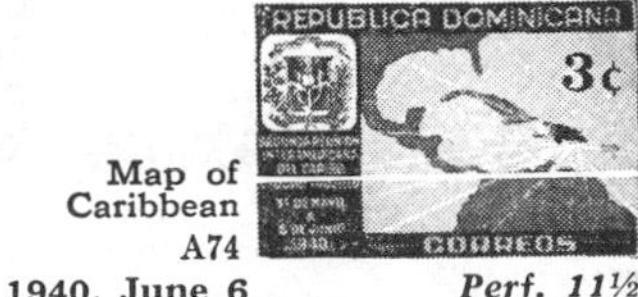

Map of Caribbean
A74

1940, June 6 ***Perf. 11½***

362	A74	3c brt car & pale rose	60	15
363	A74	7c dk bl & lt bl	1.25	25
364	A74	1p yel grn & pale grn	12.50	8.50

Issued in commemoration of the second Inter-American Caribbean Conference held at Ciudad Trujillo, May 31 to June 6.

Marion Military Hospital
A75

1940, Dec. 24

365	A75	½c chnt & fawn	40	30

Fortress, Ciudad Trujillo
A76

Statue of Columbus, Ciudad Trujillo
A77

1941

366	A76	1c dk grn & lt grn	20	8
367	A77	2c brt red & rose	25	12
368	A77	10c org brn & buff	85	15

Issue dates: 1c, Mar. 27; others, Apr. 7.

Sánchez, Duarte, Mella and Trujillo—A78

1941, May 16

369	A78	3c brt red lil & red vio	35	12
370	A78	4c brt red, crim & pale rose	50	20
371	A78	13c dk bl & lt bl	1.00	30
372	A78	15c org brn & buff	3.50	2.00
373	A78	17c lt bl, bl & pale bl	3.50	2.00
374	A78	1p org, yel brn & pale org	13.00	9.00
375	A78	2p lt gray & pale gray	27.50	12.00
		Nos. 369-375 (7)	49.35	25.62

Issued in commemoration of the Trujillo-Hull Treaty signed September 24, 1940 and effective April 1, 1941.

Bastion of February
A79

1941, Oct. 20

376	A79	5c brt bl & lt bl	80	30

School, Torch of Knowledge, Pres. Trujillo—A80

1941

377	A80	½c chnt & fawn	30	12
378	A80	1c dk grn & lt grn	40	15

Education campaign.
Issue dates: ½c, Dec. 12, 1c, Dec. 2.

Reserve Banl of Dominican Republic
A81

1942 **Unwmkd.**

379	A81	5c lt brn & buff	60	15
380	A81	17c dp bl & lt bl	1.50	60

Issued to commemorate the founding of the Reserve Bank, October 24, 1941.

Representation of Transportation
A82

1942, Aug. 15

No.	Type	Description	Unused	Used
381	A82	3c dk brn, grn yel & lt bl	70	10
382	A82	15c pur, grn, yel & lt bl	1.75	60

Issued in commemoration of the 8th anniversary of the Day of Posts and Telegraph.

Virgin of Altagracia
A83

1942, Aug. 15

No.	Type	Description	Unused	Used
383	A83	½c gray & pale gray	1.25	15
384	A83	1c dp grn & lt grn	2.50	10
385	A83	3c brt red lil & lil	16.00	10
386	A83	5c dk vio brn & vio brn	3.50	15
387	A83	10c rose pink & pink	11.00	40
388	A83	15c dp bl & lt bl	12.00	50
		Nos. 383-388 (6)	46.25	1.40

Issued to commemorate the 20th anniversary of the coronation of Our Lady of Altagracia.

Bananas A84 — Cows A85

1942-43

No.	Type	Description	Unused	Used
389	A84	3c dk brn & grn ('43)	70	15
390	A84	4c ver & blk ('43)	75	40
391	A85	5c dp bl & cop brn	65	15
392	A85	15c dk pur & bl grn	1.25	55

Issue date: 5c, 15c, Aug. 18.

Emblems of Dominican and Trujillista Parties
A86

1943, Jan. 15

No.	Type	Description	Unused	Used
393	A86	3c orange	55	10
394	A86	4c dk red	75	25
395	A86	13c brt red lil	1.60	30
396	A86	1p lt bl	7.50	2.75

Issued in commemoration of the re-election of President Rafael Trujillo Molina, May 16, 1942.

Model Market, Ciudad Trujillo
A87

1944

No.	Type	Description	Unused	Used
397	A87	2c dk brn & buff	25	15

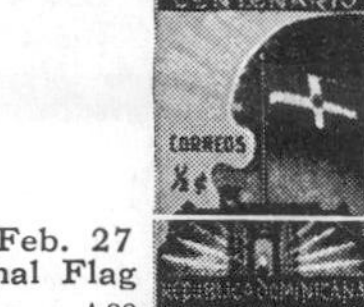

Bastion of Feb. 27 and National Flag
A88

1944, Feb. 27 **Unwmkd.**

Flag in Dark Blue and Carmine.

No.	Type	Description	Unused	Used
398	A88	½c ocher	12	10
399	A88	1c yel grn	12	8
400	A88	2c scarlet	20	12
401	A88	3c brt red vio	25	10
402	A88	5c yel org	30	15
403	A88	7c brt bl	40	35
404	A88	10c org brn	60	50
405	A88	20c ol grn	1.00	80
406	A88	50c lt bl	3.00	2.25
		Nos. 398-406, C46-C48 (12)	10.84	7.27

Souvenir Sheet.

Imperf.

No.	Type	Description	Unused	Used
407		Sheet of 12, multi	150.00	150.00
a.-l.		Single stamp	5.00	5.00

Centenary of Independence.

No. 407 contains one each of Nos. 398-406, C46-C48 with simulated perforations. Inscribed in brown: "Serie Conmemorativa del Centenario de la Republica 27 de Febrero." Size: 141x205mm.

Battlefield and Nurse with Child
A90

1944, Aug. 1

No.	Type	Description	Unused	Used
408	A90	1c dk bl grn, buff & car	25	10
a.		Vertical pair, imperf. between	20.00	
b.		Horiz. pair, imperf. vert.	20.00	
409	A90	2c dk brn, buff & car	50	15
410	A90	3c brt bl, buff & car	50	10
411	A90	10c rose car, buff & car	1.00	25

Issued to honor the 80th anniversary of the International Red Cross.

Municipal Building, San Cristóbal A91 — Emblem of Communications A92

Lithographed.

1945, Jan. 10 ***Perf. 12*** **Unwmkd.**

No.	Type	Description	Unused	Used
412	A91	½c bl & lt bl	10	10
413	A91	1c dk grn & grn	15	8
414	A91	2c red org & org	15	10
415	A91	3c dk brn & brn	20	12
416	A91	10c ultra & gray bl	70	20
		Nos. 412-416 (5)	1.30	60

Centenary of the constitution.

1945, Sept. 1

Center in Dark Blue and Carmine.

No.	Type	Description	Unused	Used
417	A92	3c orange	20	8
418	A92	20c yel grn	1.20	30
419	A92	50c lt bl	2.50	90
		Nos. 417-419, C53-C56 (7)	5.90	2.38

Palace of Justice, Ciudad Trujillo
A93

1946 ***Perf. 11½.***

No.	Type	Description	Unused	Used
420	A93	3c dk red brn & buff	30	10

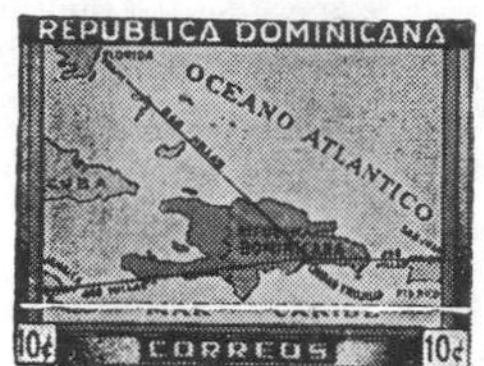

Map of Hispaniola
A94

1946, Aug. 4 ***Perf. 12***

No.	Type	Description	Unused	Used
421	A94	10c rose brn, yel, lil, bl, red & grn	60	25

Issued to commemorate the 450th anniversary of the founding of Santo Domingo. See also Nos. C62-C63.

Waterfall of Jimenoa—A95

1946-47

Center Multicolored

No.	Type	Description	Unused	Used
422	A95	1c yel grn ('47)	20	8
423	A95	2c car ('47)	20	10
424	A95	3c dp bl	25	8
425	A95	13c red vio ('47)	70	40
426	A95	20c choc ('47)	1.50	40
427	A95	50c org ('47)	2.75	1.50
		Nos. 422-427, C64-C67 (10)	5.40	5.11

Nos. 422-423, 425-427 issued Mar. 18.

Executive Palace
A96

1948, Feb. 27

No.	Type	Description	Unused	Used
428	A96	1c yel grn	12	8
429	A96	3c dp bl	18	8

See also Nos. C68-C69.

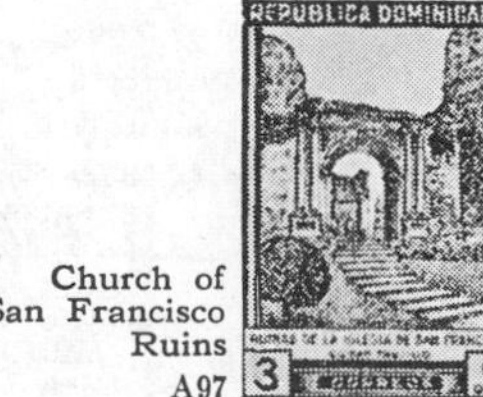

Church of San Francisco Ruins
A97

1949, Apr. 13 ***Perf. 11½***

No.	Type	Description	Unused	Used
430	A97	1c dk grn & pale grn	15	6
431	A97	3c dp bl & pale bl	20	8
		Nos. 430-431, C70-C73 (6)	2.55	1.46

Gen. Pedro Santana A98 — Pigeon and Globe A99

1949, Aug. 10

No.	Type	Description	Unused	Used
432	A98	3c dp bl & bl	25	10

Issued to commemorate the centenary of the Battle of Las Carreras. See No. C74.

1949, Sept. 15

Center and Inscriptions in Brown.

No.	Type	Description	Unused	Used
433	A99	1c grn & pale grn	18	12
434	A99	2c yel grn & yel	22	8
435	A99	5c bl & pale bl	30	10
436	A99	7c dk vio bl & pale bl	65	25

Issued to commemorate the 75th anniversary of the formation of the Universal Postal Union.

Hotel Jimani—A100

Hotels: 1c, 2c, Hamaca. 5c, Montana. 15c, San Cristobal. 20c, Maguana.

1950-52

No.	Type	Description	Unused	Used
437	A100	½c org brn & buff	10	8
438	A100	1c dp grn & grn ('51)	15	8
439	A100	2c red org & sal ('52)	15	8
440	A100	5c bl & lt bl	30	8
441	A100	15c dp org & yel	65	12
442	A100	20c lil & rose lil	1.25	20
443	A100	1p choc & yel	5.00	2.00
		Nos. 437-443, C75-C76 (9)	10.75	5.01

Issue dates: 1c, Dec. 1, 1951; 2c, Jan. 11, 1952. Others, Sept. 8, 1950.

The ½c, 15c and 20c exist imperf.

Ruins of Church and Hospital of San Nicolas de Bari
A101

School of Medicine A102 — Queen Isabella I A103

1950, Oct. 2

444 A101 2c dk grn & rose brn 30 10
445 A102 5c vio bl & org brn 40 12

13th Pan-American Health Conference. Exist imperf. See No. C77.

1951, Oct. 12

446 A103 5c dk bl & red brn 35 15

500th anniversary of the birth of Queen Isabella I of Spain. Exists imperf.

Dr. Salvador B. Gautier Hospital
A104

1952, Aug.

447 A104 1c dk grn 12 6
448 A104 2c red 18 6
449 A104 5c vio bl 35 10
Nos. 447-449, C78-C79 (5) 3.50 2.52

Columbus Lighthouse and Flags of 21 Republics
A105

1953, Jan. 6 Engraved *Perf. 13*

450 A105 2c dk grn 25 6
451 A105 5c dp bl 35 8
452 A105 10c dp car 60 30
Nos. 450-452, C80-C86 (10) 5.00 3.34

Miniature sheet containing Nos. 450-452 and C80-C86 is listed as No. C86a.

Treasury Building, Ciudad Trujillo
A106

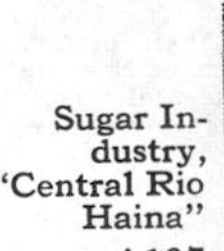

Sugar Industry, "Central Rio Haina"
A107

1953 Lithographed. *Perf. 11½.*

453 A106 ½c brown 8 6
454 A106 2c dk bl 10 8
455 A107 5c bl & vio brn 20 8
456 A106 15c orange 75 25

José Marti
A108

Monument to the Peace of Trujillo
A109

1954 *Perf. 12½.*

457 A108 10c dp bl & dk brn 45 18

Centenary of the birth of José Marti (1853-1895), Cuban patriot.

1954, May 25

458 A109 2c green 8 6
459 A109 7c blue 25 8
460 A109 20c orange 80 15

See also No. 493.

Rotary Emblem
A110

1955, Feb. 23 *Perf. 12*

461 A110 7c dp bl 70 25

50th anniversary, Rotary International. See No. C90.

Gen. Rafael L. Trujillo
A111

Designs: 4c, Trujillo in civilian clothes. 7c, Trujillo statue. 10c, Symbols of culture and prosperity.

1955, May 16 Engr. *Perf. 13½x13*

462 A111 2c red 10 6
463 A111 4c lt ol grn 15 8
464 A111 7c indigo 25 12
465 A111 10c brown 50 20
Nos. 462-465, C91-C93 (7) 3.15 1.58

25th anniversary of the Trujillo era.

General Rafael L. Trujillo
A112

Angelita Trujillo
A113

1955, Dec. 20 *Perf. 13* Unwmkd.

466 A112 7c dp cl 35 12
467 A112 10c dk bl 55 18

See also No. C94.

1955, Dec. 20 Litho. *Perf. 12½*

468 A113 10c bl & ultra 55 18

Nos. 466-468 were issued to publicize the International Fair of Peace and Brotherhood in Ciudad Trujillo, Dec. 1955.

Airport
A114

1956, Apr. 6 *Perf. 12½*

469 A114 1c brown 12 8
470 A114 2c red org 18 8

Issued to commemorate the third Caribbean conference of the International Civil Aviation Organization. See No. C95.

Cedar
A115

See also No. 493.

1956, Dec. 8 *Perf. 11½x12*

471 A115 5c car rose & grn 30 10
472 A115 6c red vio & grn 35 15

Issued to publicize the reforestation program. See No. C96.

Fair Emblem
A116

Fanny Blankers-Koen, Netherlands
A117

1957, Jan. 10 *Perf. 12½*

473 A116 7c bl, lt brn & ver 35 15

Issued to publicize the 2nd International Livestock Show, Ciudad Trujillo, Jan. 10-20, 1957. Exists imperf.

Engraved & Lithographed

1957, Jan. 24 *Perf. 11½*

Olympic Winners and Flags: 2c, Jesse Owens, United States. 3c, Kee Chung Sohn, Japan. 5c, Lord Burghley, England. 7c, Bob Mathias, United States.

Flags in National Colors.

474 A117 1c brn, lt bl, vio & mar 5 5
475 A117 2c dk brn, lt bl & vio 5 5
476 A117 3c red lil & red 5 5
477 A117 5c red org & vio 8 8
478 A117 7c grn & vio 10 10
Nos. 474-478, C97-C99 (8) 68 68

To commemorate the 16th Olympic Games, Melbourne, Nov. 22-Dec. 8, 1956. Exist imperf.

Miniature sheets of 5 exist, perf. and imperf., containing one each of Nos. 474-478. Sheets measure 169 x 86 mm. and have no marginal inscriptions. Price, 2 sheets, perf. and imperf., $6.

Lars Hall, Sweden, Pentathlon
A118

Olympic Winners and Flags: 2c, Betty Cuthbert, Australia, 100 & 200 meter dash. 3c, Egil Danielsen, Norway, javelin. 5c, Alain Mimoun, France, marathon. 7c, Norman Read, New Zealand, 50 km. walk.

Perf. 13½

1957, July 18 Photo. Unwmkd.

Flags in National Colors.

479 A118 1c brn & brt bl 5 5
480 A118 2c org ver & dk bl 5 5
481 A118 3c dk bl 5 5
482 A118 5c ol & dk bl 8 8
483 A118 7c rose brn & dk bl 10 10
Nos. 479-483, C100-C102 (8) 73 73

Issued in honor of the 1956 Olympic winners. Exist imperf.

Miniature sheets of 8 exist, perf. and imperf., containing one each of Nos. 479-483 and C100-C102. The center label in these sheets is printed in two forms: Olympic gold medal or Olympic flag. Sheets measure 140x140mm. Price, 4 sheets, perf. and imperf., medal and flag, $18.

A third set of similar miniature sheets (perf. and imperf.) with center label showing an incorrect version of the Dominican Republic flag (colors transposed) was printed. These sheets are said to have been briefly sold on the first day, then withdrawn as the misprint was discovered.

Price, 2 sheets, perf. & imperf., $150.

Gerald Ouellette, Canada, Small Bore Rifle, Prone—A119

Ron Delaney, Ireland, 1,500 Meter Run—A120

Olympic Winners and Flags: 3c, Tenley Albright, United States, figure skating. 5c, Joaquin Capilla, Mexico, platform diving. 7c, Ercole Baldini, Italy, individual road race (cycling).

Engraved and Lithographed

1957, Nov. 12 *Perf. 13½*

Flags in National Colors

484 A119 1c red brn 5 5
485 A120 2c gray brn 5 5
486 A119 3c violet 5 5
487 A120 5c red org 8 8
488 A119 7c Prus grn 10 10
Nos. 484-488, C103-C105 (8) 73 73

Issued in honor of the 1956 Olympic winners. Exist imperf.

Miniature sheets of 5 exist, perf. and imperf., containing one each of Nos. 484-488. Sheets have no marginal inscriptions. Price, 2 sheets, perf. and imperf., $5.50.

Mahogany Flower
A121

1957-58 Lithographed *Perf. 12½*

489 A121 2c grn & mar 12 8

Perf. 12

490 A121 4c lil & rose ('58) 18 12
491 A121 7c ultra & gray grn 35 12
492 A121 25c brn & org ('58) 85 35

Sizes: No. 489, 25x29¼mm.; Nos. 490-492, 24x28¾mm. In 1959, the 2c was reissued in size 24¼x28½mm. with slightly different tones of green and maroon.

Issue dates: 2c, Oct. 24; 7c, Nov. 6; 4c and 25c, Apr. 7, 1958.

Type of 1954, Redrawn

Perf. 12x11½

1957, June 12 **Unwmkd.**

493 A109 7c brt bl 55 20

On No. 493 the "$" is smaller, the shading of the sky and steps stronger and the letters in "Correos" shorter and bolder.

Cervantes, Globe and Book
A122

1958, Apr. 23 **Litho.** ***Perf. 12½***

494 A122 4c yel grn 15 6
495 A122 7c red lil 20 10
496 A122 10c lt ol brn 35 15

Fourth Book Fair, Apr. 23-28. Exist imperf.

Gen. Rafael L. Trujillo
A123

1958, Aug. 16 ***Perf. 12***

497 A123 2c red lil & yel 6 6
498 A123 4c grn & yel 15 8
499 A123 7c brn & yel 25 12
a. Souv. sheet of 3 90 75

Issued to commemorate the 25th anniversary of Gen. Trujillo's designation as "Benefactor of his country."

No. 499a measures 152x101mm and contains one each of Nos. 497-499, imperf. Brown marginal inscription.

S. S. Rhadames
A124

1958, Oct. 27 ***Perf. 12½***

500 A124 7c brt bl 40 18

Day of the Dominican Merchant Marine. Exists imperf.

Shozo Sasahara, Japan, Featherweight Wrestling
A125

Olympic Winners and Flags: 1c, Gillian Sheen, England, fencing (vert.). 2c, Milton Campbell, United States, decathlon (vert.). 5c, Madeleine Berthod, Switzerland, downhill skiing. 7c, Murray Rose, Australia, 400 & 1,500 meter freestyle.

1958, Oct. 30 **Photo.** ***Perf. 13½***

Flags in National Colors

501 A125 1c rose, ind & ultra 5 5
502 A125 2c brn & bl 5 5
503 A125 3c gray, vio, blk & buff 5 5
504 A125 5c rose, dk bl, brn & red 8 8
505 A125 7c lt brn, dk bl & red 10 10
Nos. 501-505, C106-C108 (8) 73 73

To honor 1956 Olympic winners. Exist imperf.

Miniature sheets of 5 exist, perf. and imperf. containing one each of Nos. 501-505. Size: 140x119½mm. Price, 2 sheets, perf. and imperf., $3.

Globe and Symbolic Fire
A126

1958, Nov. 3 **Litho.** ***Perf. 11½***

506 A126 7c bl & dp car 25 15

Issued to commemorate the opening of UNESCO (U. N. Educational, Scientific and Cultural Organization) Headquarters in Paris, Nov. 3.

Dominican Republic Pavilion, Brussels Fair
A127

1958, Dec. 9 ***Perf. 12½*** **Unwmkd.**

507 A127 7c bl grn 30 15

Issued for the Universal and International Exposition at Brussels. See Nos. C109-C110a.

Gen. Trujillo Placing Wreath on Altar of the Nation
A128

1959, July 10 ***Perf. 12***

508 A128 9c brn, grn, red & gold 30 15
a. Souv. sheet 60 60

Issued to commemorate the 29th anniversary of the Trujillo regime.

No. 508a contains one 9c, imperf. Size: 141x90mm.

Lt. Leonidas Rhadames Trujillo, Team Captain
A129

Jamaican Polo Team
A130

Design: 10c, Lt. Trujillo on polo pony.

1959, May 15

509 A129 2c violet 18 12
510 A130 7c yel brn 45 25
511 A130 10c green 50 35

Jamaica-Dominican Republic polo match at Ciudad Trujillo.

See also No. C111.

Symbolical of Census
A131

1959, Aug. 15 **Litho.** ***Perf. 12½***

Flag in Ultramarine and Red.

512 A131 1c bl & blk 12 10
513 A131 9c grn & blk 30 25
514 A131 13c org & blk 50 35

Issued to publicize the 1960 census.

Trujillo Stadium
A132

1959, Aug. 27

515 A132 9c grn & gray 50 30

Issued to publicize the 3rd Pan American Games Chicago, Aug. 27-Sept. 7.

Charles V
A133

1959, Oct. 12 ***Perf. 12*** **Unwmkd.**

516 A133 5c brt pink 20 10
517 A133 9c vio bl 30 15

Issued to commemorate the 400th anniversary of the death of Charles V (1500-1558), Holy Roman Emperor.

Rhadames Bridge
A134

Designs: 1c and No. 520, Different view of bridge.

1959-60 **Lithographed.** ***Perf. 12***

518 A134 1c grn & gray ('60) 12 10
519 A134 2c ultra & gray 20 12
520 A134 2c red & gray ('60) 20 10
521 A134 5c brn & dl red brn 30 18

Issue dates: No. 519, Oct. 22; 5c, Nov. 30; 1c and No. 520, Feb. 6, 1960.

Sosua Refugee Settlement and WRY Emblem—A135

1960, Apr. 7 ***Perf. 12½***

Center in Gray

522 A135 5c red brn & yel grn 15 10
523 A135 9c car & lt bl 30 15
524 A135 13c org & grn 40 25
Nos. 522-524, C113-C114 (5) 2.05 1.50

Issued to publicize World Refugee Year, July 1, 1959-June 30, 1960.

Sholam Takhti, Iran, Lightweight Wrestling—A136

Olympic Winners: 2c, Mauru Furukawa, Japan, 200 meter breast stroke. 3c, Mildred McDaniel, U.S.A., high jump. 5c, Terence Spinks, England, featherweight boxing. 7c, Carlo Pavesi, Italy, fencing.

Perf. 13½

1960, Sept. 14 **Photo.** **Unwmkd.**

Flags in National Colors

525 A136 1c red, yel grn & blk 5 5
526 A136 2c org, grnsh bl & brn 5 5
527 A136 3c hn brn & bl 5 5
528 A136 5c brn & ultra 8 8
529 A136 7c grn, bl & rose brn 10 10
Nos. 525-529, C115-C117 (8) 73 73

Issued to commemorate the 17th Olympic Games, Rome, Aug. 25-Sept. 11. Exist imperf.

Miniature sheets of 5 exist, perf. and imperf., containing one each of Nos. 525-529, and a Dominican Republic flag in national colors. Sheet size: 160x121mm.

Price, 2 sheets, perf. & imperf., $4.

Post Office, Ciudad Trujillo
A137

1960, Aug. 26 **Litho.** ***Perf. 11½x12***

530 A137 2c ultra & gray 18 10

Exists imperf.

Cattle—A138

1960, Aug. 30

531 A138 9c car & gray 35 18

Issued to publicize the Agricultural and Industrial Fair, San Juan de la Maguana.

Nos. 518, 490–491, 453, 427 Surcharged in Red, Black or Blue

HABILITADO PARA 2¢

1960–61 ***Perf. 12***

536 A134 2c on 1c grn & gray (R) 20 10
537 A121 9c on 4c lil & rose 70 15
a. Inverted surcharge 35.00
538 A121 9c on 7c ultra & gray grn (R) ('61) 70 20
539 A106 36c on ½c brn ('61) 2.25 1.25
a. Inverted surcharge 30.00
540 A95 1p on 50c multi (Bl) ('61) 5.00 3.00
Nos. 536-540 (5) 8.85 4.70

Issue dates: No. 536, Dec. 30, 1960; No. 537, Dec. 20, 1960. Others, Feb. 4, 1961.

Trujillo Memorial

A139

Coffee and Cacao

A140

1961 ***Perf. 11½*** **Unwmkd.**

548 A139 1c brown 12 5
549 A139 2c green 15 5
550 A139 4c rose lil 75 75
551 A139 5c lt bl 35 12
552 A139 9c red org 45 30
Nos. 548-552 (5) 1.82 1.27

Issued in memory of Gen. Rafael L. Trujillo (1891–1961).

1961, Dec. 30 **Litho.** ***Perf. 12½***

553 A140 1c bl grn 5 5
554 A140 2c org brn 8 5
555 A140 4c violet 15 8
556 A140 5c blue 15 8
557 A140 9c gray 35 8
Nos. 553-557, C118-C119 (7) 2.03 1.59

Exist imperf.

Dagger Pointing at Mosquito

A141

1962, Apr. 29 **Photo.** ***Perf. 12***

558 A141 10c brt pink & red lil 25 18
559 A141 20c pale brn & brn 50 45
560 A141 25c pale grn & yel grn 65 50
Nos. 558-560, B39-B40, C120-C121, CB24-CB25 (9) 4.60 4.13

Issued for the World Health Organization drive to eradicate malaria.

Broken Fetters and Laurel

A142

"Justice" and Map of Dominican Republic

A143

Farm, Factory and Flag

A144

Design: 20c, Flag, torch and inscription.

1962, May 30 **Litho.** ***Perf. 12½***

561 A142 1c grn, yel, ultra & red 15 10
562 A143 9c bis ultra & red 40 18
563 A142 20c lt bl, ultra & red 75 40
a. Souv. sheet of 3 1.00 1.00
564 A143 1p lil, ultra & red 4.00 2.50
Nos. 561-564, C122-C123 (6) 6.62 3.91

First anniversary of end of Trujillo era. Exist imperf.

No. 563a contains one each of Nos. 561–563, imperf. with ultramarine inscription on pink background. Size: 154x91mm.

1962, May 22

565 A144 1c ultra, red & grn 5 5
566 A144 2c ultra & red 10 5
567 A144 3c ultra, red & brn 12 6
568 A144 5c ultra, red & bl 20 8
569 A144 15c ultra, red & org 40 20
Nos. 565-569 (5) 87 44

Map and Laurel

A145

1962, June 14 **Lithographed**

570 A145 1c black 35 20

Issued to honor the martyrs of June 1959 revolution.

Western Hemisphere and Carrier Pigeon

A146

Archbishop Adolfo Alejandro Nouel

A147

1962, Oct. 23 ***Perf. 12½*** **Unwmkd.**

571 A146 2c rose red 12 6
572 A146 9c orange 35 18
573 A146 14c bl grn 22 10
Nos. 571-573, C124-C125 (5) 1.69 1.14

Issued to commemorate the 50th anniversary of the founding of the Postal Union of the Americas and Spain, UPAE.

1962, Dec. 18

574 A147 2c bl grn & dl bl 8 5
575 A147 9c org & red brn 35 18
576 A147 13c mar & vio brn 45 30
Nos. 574-576, C126-C127 (5) 2.13 1.53

Issued to commemorate the centenary of the birth of Archbishop Adolfo Alejandro Nouel, President of Dominican Republic in 1911.

Globe, Banner and Emblems

A148

1963, Apr. 15 ***Perf. 11½*** **Unwmkd.**

Banner in Dark Blue & Red

577 A148 2c green 10 5
578 A148 5c brt rose lil 25 10
579 A148 9c orange 40 18
Nos. 577-579, B41-B43 (6) 1.29 84

Issued for the "Freedom from Hunger" campaign of the U.N. Food and Agriculture Organization.

Juan Pablo Duarte

A149

Designs: 7c, Francisco Sanchez. 9c, Ramon Mella.

1963, July 7 **Litho.** ***Perf. 12x11½***

580 A149 2c ultra 6 5
581 A149 7c dl grn 18 18
582 A149 9c red lil 25 20

Issued to commemorate the 120th anniversary of separation from Haiti. See also No. C128.

Ulises F. Espaillat, Benigno F. de Rojas and Pedro F. Bono

A150

Designs: 4c, Generals Santiago Rodriguez, José Cabrera and Benito Moncion. 5c, Capotillo monument. 9c, Generals Gaspar Polanco, Gregorio Luperon and José A. Salcedo.

1963, Aug. 16 ***Perf. 11½*** **Unwmkd.**

583 A150 2c green 8 5
584 A150 4c red org 12 10
585 A150 5c brown 15 12
586 A150 9c brt bl 25 20
a. Souv. sheet of 4 75 75

Issued to commemorate the centenary of the Restoration. No. 586a contains 4 imperf. stamps similar to Nos. 583–586. Brown marginal inscription. Size: 229x106½mm.

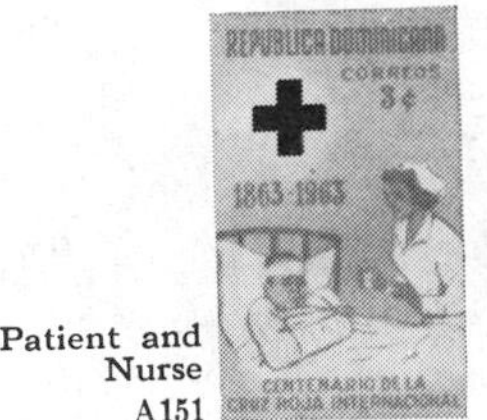

Patient and Nurse

A151

1963, Oct. 25 ***Perf. 12½*** **Unwmkd.**

587 A151 3c gray & car 12 12
588 A151 6c emer & red 25 15

Centenary of International Red Cross. Exist imperf. See No. C129.

Scales, Globe and UNESCO Emblem

A152

1963, Dec. 10 **Lithographed**

589 A152 6c pink & dp pink 18 12
590 A152 50c lt grn & grn 1.10 85

Universal Declaration of Human Rights, 15th anniversary. Exist imperf. See also Nos. C130–C131.

Ramses II Battling the Hittites (from Abu Simbel)—A153

Design: 6c, Two heads of Ramses II.

1964, March 8 ***Perf. 12½*** **Unwmkd.**

591 A153 3c pale pink & ver 10 8
592 A153 6c pale bl & ultra 20 15
593 A153 9c pale rose & red brn 30 20
Nos 591-593, C132-C133 (5) 1.35 1.03

Issued to publicize the UNESCO world campaign to save historic monuments in Nubia.

Maximo Gomez

A154

Palm Chat

A155

1964, Apr. 30 **Lithographed**

594 A154 2c lt bl & bl 6 6
595 A154 6c dl pink & dl cl 18 12

Issued to commemorate the bicentenary of the founding of the town of Bani.

1964, June 8 ***Perf. 12½*** **Unwmkd.**

Design: 6c, Hispaniolan parrot.

Size: 27x37½mm.

596 A155 3c ultra, brn & yel 18 15
597 A155 6c gray & multi 25 20

See also Nos. 602–604, C134.

Rocket Leaving Earth

A156

Designs: 1c, Launching of rocket (vert.). 3c, Space capsule orbiting earth. 6c, As 2c.

1964, July 28 **Lithographed**

598 A156 1c sky bl 10 8
599 A156 2c emerald 15 10
600 A156 3c blue 20 15
601 A156 6c sky bl 35 18
Nos. 598-601, C135-C136 (6) 1.70 1.16

Issued to commemorate the conquest of space.

Bird Type of 1964

Designs: 1c, Narrow-billed tody. 2c, Hispaniolan emerald hummingbird. 6c, Hispaniolan trogon.

1964, Nov. 7 ***Perf. 11½***

Size: 26x37mm.

Birds in Natural Colors

602	A155	1c brt pink	12	10
603	A155	2c dk brn	15	10
604	A155	6c blue	30	20

Universal Postal Union and United Nations Emblems
A157

1964, Dec. 5 **Litho.** ***Perf. 12½***

605	A157	1c red	7	5
606	A157	4c green	18	10
607	A157	5c orange	20	12

Issued to commemorate the 15th Universal Postal Union Congress, Vienna, Austria, May–June 1964. See also No. C138.

International Cooperation Year Emblem—A158

1965, Feb. 16 ***Perf. 12½*** **Unwmkd.**

608	A158	2c lt bl & ultra	6	5
609	A158	3c emer & dk grn	8	6
610	A158	6c sal pink & red	18	10

Issued to publicize the United Nations International Cooperation Year. See No. C139.

Virgin of Altagracia
A159

Flags of 21 American Nations
A160

Design: 2c, Hands holding lily.

1965, Mar. 18 ***Perf. 12½*** **Unwmkd.**

611	A159	2c grn, emer & dp rose	12	8
612	A159	6c multi	50	40

Issued to commemorate the Fourth Mariological Congress and the Eleventh International Marian Congress. No. 612 exists imperf. See No. C140.

1965, Apr. 14 **Litho.** ***Perf. 11½***

613	A160	2c brn, yel & multi	6	5
614	A160	6c red lil & multi	18	12

Organization of American States.

Stamp of 1865 (No. 1)
A161

1965, Dec. 28 **Litho.** ***Perf. 12½***

615	A161	1c pink, buff & blk	8	6
616	A161	2c bl, buff & blk	10	7
617	A161	6c emer, buff & blk	20	15
a.		Souv. sheet of 2	1.00	1.00
		Nos. 615-617, C142-C143 (5)	1.13	93

Issued to commemorate the centenary of the first Dominican postage stamps. No. 617a shows replicas of Nos. 1–2. Bright blue marginal inscription. Size: 100x65 mm. Sold for 50c.

WHO Headquarters, Geneva
A162

1966, May 21 **Litho.** ***Perf. 12½***

618	A162	6c blue	18	10
619	A162	10c red lil	30	18

Issued to commemorate the inauguration of World Health Organization Headquarters, Geneva.

Man Holding Map of Republic
A163

1966, May 23

620	A163	2c blk & brt grn	6	5
621	A163	6c blk & dp org	18	10

Issued to publicize the general elections, June 1, 1966.

Ascia Monuste
A164

National Altar
A165

1966 **Lithographed** ***Perf. 12½***

Various Butterflies in Natural Colors

Size: 31x21mm.

622	A164	1c bl & vio bl	10	10
623	A164	2c lt grn & brt grn	15	15
624	A164	3c lt gray & gray	20	20
625	A164	6c pink & mag	30	30
626	A164	8c buff & brn	50	50
		Nos. 622-626, C146-C148 (8)	4.75	3.80

Issue dates: 1c, Sept. 7; 3c, Sept. 11; others, Nov. 8.

1967, Jan. 18 **Litho.** ***Perf. 11½***

627	A165	1c brt bl	5	5
628	A165	2c car rose	5	5
629	A165	3c emerald	6	5
630	A165	4c gray	8	6
631	A165	5c org yel	10	8
632	A165	6c orange	12	10
		Nos. 627-632, C149-C151 (9)	1.36	1.09

Map of Republic and Emblem
A166

1967, Mar. 30 **Litho.** ***Perf. 12½***

633	A166	2c yel, bl & blk	7	5
634	A166	6c org, bl & blk	20	10
635	A166	10c emer, bl & blk	35	18

Development Year, 1967.

Rook and Knight
A167

1967, June 23 **Litho.** ***Perf. 12½***

636	A167	25c multi	1.00	60

Issued to commemorate the 5th Central American Chess Championships, Santo Domingo. See also Nos. C152–C152a.

Alliance for Progress
A168

Institute Emblem
A169

1967, Sept. 16 **Litho.** ***Perf. 12½***

637	A168	1c brt grn	5	5

Issued to commemorate the 6th anniversary of the Alliance for Progress. See Nos. C153–C154.

1967, Oct. 7

638	A169	3c brt grn	9	7
639	A169	6c sal pink	18	12

Issued to commemorate the 25th anniversary of the Inter-American Agriculture Institute. See also No. C155.

Globe and Satellite
A170

1968, June 15 **Typo.** ***Perf. 12***

640	A170	6c blk & multi	35	25

Issued to commemorate World Meteorological Day, Mar. 23. See Nos. C156–C157.

Boxers
A171

1968, June 29

641	A171	6c rose red & dp cl	25	20

Issued to commemorate the fight between Carlos Ortiz, Puerto Rico, and Teo Cruz, Dominican Republic, for the World Lightweight Boxing Championship. See Nos. C158–C159.

Lions Emblem
A172

1968, Aug. 9 **Litho.** ***Perf. 11½***

642	A172	6c brn & multi	20	12

Issued to commemorate the 50th anniversary (in 1967) of Lions International. See No. C160.

Wrestling and Olympic Emblem
A173

Designs (Olympic Emblem and): 6c, Running. 25c, Boxing.

1968, Nov. 12 **Litho.** ***Perf. 11½***

643	A173	1c sky bl & multi	15	8
644	A173	6c pale grn & multi	35	15
645	A173	25c pale lil & multi	1.25	60
		Nos. 643-645, C161-C162 (5)	3.20	2.18

Issued to commemorate the 19th Olympic Games, Mexico City, Oct. 12–27.

Map of Americas and House
A174

Stool in Human Form
A175

1969, Jan. 25 **Litho.** ***Perf. 12½***

646	A174	6c brt bl, lt bl & grn	25	12

Issued to publicize the 7th Inter-American Conference for Savings and Loans, Santo Domingo, Jan. 25–31. See No. C163.

1969, Jan. 31 **Litho.** ***Perf. 12½***

Taino Art: 2c, Wood carved mother figure (vert.). 3c, Face carved on 3-cornered stone. 4c, Stone hatchet (vert.). 5c, Clay pot.

647	A175	1c yel, org & blk	6	5
648	A175	2c lt grn, grn & blk	8	6
649	A175	3c cit, ol & brt grn	12	10
650	A175	4c lt lil, lil & brt grn	18	15
651	A175	5c yel, org & brn	20	18
		Nos. 647-651, C164-C166 (8)	1.69	1.34

Taino art flourished in the West Indies at the time of Columbus.

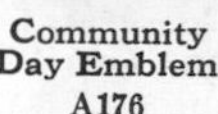

Community Day Emblem
A176

COTAL Emblem
A177

Headquarters Building and COTAL Emblem
A178

1969, Mar. 25 Litho. *Perf. 12½*

652	A176	6c dl grn & gold	20	10

Issued for Community Development Day, March 22.

1969, May 25 Litho. *Perf. 12½*

Design: 2c, Boy and COTAL emblem.

653	A177	1c lt & dk bl & red	5	5
654	A177	2c emer & dk grn	10	5
655	A178	6c ver & pink	18	10

Issued to publicize the 12th Congress of the Confederation of Latin American Tourist Organizations (COTAL), Santo Domingo, May 25–29.

See No. C167.

ILO Emblem A179 Sliding into Base A180

1969, June 27 Litho. *Perf. 12½*

656	A179	6c lt grnsh bl, grnsh bl & blk	40	10

Issued to commemorate the 50th anniversary of the International Labor Organization. See No. C168.

1969, Aug. 15 Litho. *Perf. 12½*

Designs: 1c, Catching a fly ball. 2c, View of Cibao Stadium (horiz.).

Size: 21x31mm. (1c, 3c); 43x30mm. (2c).

657	A180	1c grn & gray	15	8
658	A180	2c grn & lt grn	18	12
659	A180	3c pur & red brn	22	15
		Nos. 657-659, C169-C171 (6)	5.05	3.30

Issued to publicize the 17th World Amateur Baseball Championships, Santo Domingo.

Las Damas Dam
A181

Tavera Dam—A182

Designs: 2c, Las Damas hydroelectric station (vert.). 6c, Arroyo Hondo substation.

1969 Lithographed *Perf. 12*

660	A181	2c grn & multi	6	5
661	A181	3c dk bl & multi	9	5
662	A181	6c brt rose lil	18	10
663	A182	6c multi	18	10
		Nos. 660-663, C172-C173 (6)	1.16	65

Issued to publicize the national electrification plan.

Issue dates: Nos. 660–662, Sept. 15. No. 663, Oct. 15.

Juan Pablo Duarte
A183

Map of Republic, People, Census Emblem
A184

1970, Jan. 26 Litho. *Perf. 12*

664	A183	1c emer & dk grn	5	5
665	A183	2c sal pink & dp car	6	5
666	A183	3c brt pink & plum	9	5
667	A183	6c bl & vio bl	18	10
		Nos. 664-667, C174 (5)	68	43

Issued for Duarte Day in memory of Juan Pablo Duarte (1813–1876), liberator.

1970, Feb. 6 *Perf. 11*

Design: 6c, Census emblem and inscription.

668	A184	5c emer & blk	15	8
669	A184	6c ultra & bl	18	10

Census of 1970. See No. C175.

Abelardo Rodriguez Urdaneta
A185

"One of Many"
A186

1970, Feb. 20 Litho. *Perf. 12½*

670	A185	3c ultra	15	8
671	A186	6c grn & yel grn	25	12

Issued to honor Abelardo Rodriguez Urdaneta, sculptor. See No. C176.

Masonic Symbols
A187

1970, Mar. 2

672	A187	6c green	20	10

Issued to publicize the 8th Inter-American Masonic Conference, Santo Domingo, Mar. 1–7. See No. C177.

Communications Satellite—A188

1970, May 25 Litho. *Perf. 12½*

673	A188	20c ol & gray	75	45

Issued for World Telecommunications Day. See No. C178.

U.P.U. Headquarters, Bern
A189

1970, June 5 *Perf. 11*

674	A189	6c gray & brn	18	10

Issued to commemorate the inauguration of the new Universal Postal Union Headquarters in Bern. See No. C179.

Education Year Emblem
A190

Pedro Alejandrino Pina
A191

1970, June 26 Litho. *Perf. 12½*

675	A190	4c rose lil	12	6

Issued for International Education Year, 1970. See No. C180.

1970, Aug. 24 Litho. *Perf. 12½*

676	A191	6c lt red brn & blk	18	10

Issued to commemorate the 150th anniversary of the birth and the centenary of the death of Pedro Alejandrino Pina (1820–70), author.

Children Reading
A192

1970, Oct. 12 Litho. *Perf. 12½*

677	A192	5c dl grn	15	8

Issued to publicize the First World Exhibition of Books and Culture Festival, Santo Domingo, Oct. 11–Dec. 11. See Nos. C181–C182.

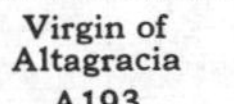

Virgin of Altagracia
A193

Manuel Rodriguez Objio
A194

1971, Jan. 20 Litho. *Perf. 12½*

678	A193	3c multi	20	10

Inauguration of the Basilica of Our Lady of Altagracia. See No. C184.

1971, June 18 Litho. *Perf. 11*

679	A194	6c lt bl	20	10

Centenary of the death of Manuel Rodriguez Objio (1838–1871), poet.

Boxing and Canoeing
A195

Design: 5c, Basketball.

1971, Sept. 10

680	A195	2c brn & org	12	8
681	A195	5c brn & lt grn	28	12

2nd National Games. See No. C186.

Goat and Fruit
A196

Designs: 2c, Cow and goose. 3c, Cacao and horse. 6c, Bananas, coffee and pig.

1971, Sept. 29 *Perf. 12½*

682	A196	1c brn & multi	5	5
683	A196	2c plum & multi	6	5
684	A196	3c grn & multi	9	8
685	A196	6c bl & multi	18	12
		Nos. 682-685, C187 (5)	1.03	80

6th National agriculture and livestock census.

José Nuñez de Cáceres—A197

Shepherds and Star—A198

1971, Dec. 1 *Perf. 11*

686	A197	6c lt bl, lil & dk bl	18	10

Sesquicentennial of first national independence. See No. C188.

1971, Dec. 10 *Perf. 12½*

687	A198	6c bl, brn & yel	25	12

Christmas 1971. See No. C189.

UNICEF Emblem, Child on Beach
A199

1971, Dec. 14 Litho. *Perf. 11*

688 A199 6c gray bl & multi 18 10

25th anniversary of the United Nations International Children's Fund (UNICEF). See No. C190.

Book Year Emblem A200 **Taino Mask A201**

1972, Jan. 25 *Perf. 12½*

689 A200 1c grn, ultra & red 5 5
690 A200 2c brn, ultra & red 6 5

International Book Year 1972. See No. C191.

1972, May 10 Litho. *Perf. 11*

Taino Art: 4c, Ladle and amulet. 6c, Human figure.

691 A201 2c pink & multi 12 5
692 A201 4c blk, bl & ocher 18 8
693 A201 6c gray & multi 30 15
Nos. 691-693, C194-C196 (6) 1.90 1.01

Taino art. See note after No. 651.

Globe A202

1972, May 17 *Perf. 12½*

694 A202 6c bl & multi 20 10

4th World Telecommunications Day. See No. C197.

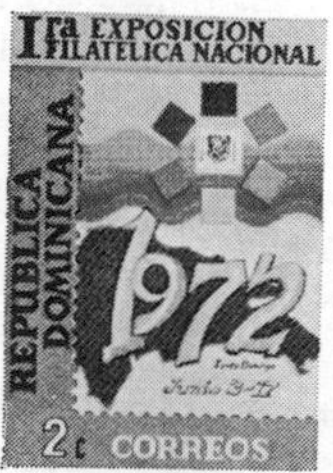

"1972," Stamps and Map of Dominican Republic A203

1972, June 3

695 A203 2c grn & multi 6 5

First National Philatelic Exhibition, Santo Domingo, June 3-17. See No. C198.

Basketball A204

1972, Aug. 25 Litho. *Perf. 12½*

696 A204 2c bl & multi 15 10

20th Olympic Games, Munich, Aug. 26-Sept. 11. See No. C199.

Club Emblem A205

1972, Sept. 29 Litho. *Perf. 10½*

697 A205 1c lt grn & multi 8 5

50th anniversary of the Club Activo 20-30 Internacional. See No. C200.

Emilio A. Morel A206

1972, Oct. 20 *Perf. 12½*

698 A206 6c brt pink & multi 18 10

Emilio A. Morel (1884-1958), poet and journalist. See No. C201.

Central Bank Building A207

Design: 5c, One peso note.

1972, Oct. 23

699 A207 1c blk & multi 5 5
700 A207 5c red, blk & grn 15 8

25th anniversary of Central Bank. See No. C202.

Holy Family A208

Mail Box and Student A210

Poinsettia A209

1972, Nov. 21

701 A208 2c rose lil, pur & gold 12 6
702 A209 6c red & multi 30 12

Christmas 1972. See No. C203.

1972, Dec. 15

703 A210 2c rose red 6 5
704 A210 6c blue 18 10
705 A210 10c emerald 30 15

Publicity for correspondence schools.

Tavera Dam A211

1973, Feb. 26 Litho. *Perf. 12½*

706 A211 10c multi 30 15

Inauguration of the Tavera Dam.

Various Sports—A212

1973, Mar. 30 *Perf. 13½x13*

707 A212 2c brn, yel & grn, block of 4 60 35
a. Upper left 15 8
b. Upper right 15 8
c. Lower left 15 8
d. Lower right 15 8
708 A212 25c dk grn & yel grn, block of 4 3.50 2.00
a. Upper left 75 40
b. Upper right 75 40
c. Lower left 75 40
d. Lower right 75 40
Nos. 707-708, C204-C205 (4 blocks of 4) 7.60 4.60

Publicity for the 12th Central American and Caribbean Games, Santo Domingo, Summer 1974.

Christ Carrying the Cross A213

Design: 6c, Belfry of Church of Our Lady of Carmen (vert.).

1973, Apr. 18 Litho. *Perf. 10½*

709 A213 2c multi 12 6
710 A213 6c multi 30 15

Holy Week, 1973. See No. C206.

WMO Emblem, Weather Satellite, "Weather" A214 **Mask, Cibao A215**

1973, Aug. 10 Litho. *Perf. 13½x13*

711 A214 6c mag & multi 18 12

Centenary of international meteorological cooperation. See No. C208.

1973, Oct. 12 Litho. *Perf. 10½*
Multicolored

712 A215 1c *Maguey drum* (horiz.) 5
713 A215 2c *Carved amber* (horiz.) 6
714 A215 4c *shown* 12
715 A215 6c *Pottery* 18
Nos. 712-715, C210-C211 (6) 92 6

Opening of Museum of Mankind in Santo Domingo.

Nativity A216

Design: 6c, Stained glass window (vert.).

Perf. 13½x13, 13x13½

1973, Nov. 26

716 A216 2c blk, bl & yel 10 6
717 A216 6c rose & multi 25 15

Christmas 1973. See No. C212.
No. 717 exists imperf.

Dominican Scout Emblem A217

Design: 5c, Scouts and flag.

1973, Dec. 7 Lithographed *Perf. 12*
Size: 35x35mm.

718 A217 1c ultra & multi 8 5

Size: 26x36mm.

719 A217 5c blk & multi 20 10

50th anniversary of Dominican Republic Boy Scouts. See No. C213.

Sports Palace, Basketball Players A218

Design: 6c, Bicyclist and race track.

1974, Feb. 25 Litho. *Perf. 13½*

720 A218 2c red brn & multi 10 6
721 A218 6c yel & multi 25 15

12th Central American and Caribbean Games, Santo Domingo, 1974. See Nos. C214-C215.

Bell Tower, Cathedral of Santo Domingo A219

Mater Dolorosa A220

1974, June 27 Litho. *Perf. 13½*

722 A219 2c multi 12 6
723 A220 6c multi 30 15

Holy Week 1974. See No. C216.

Francisco del Rosario Sanchez Bridge—A221

1974, July 12 *Perf. 12*

724	A221	6c multi	18	12

See No. C217.

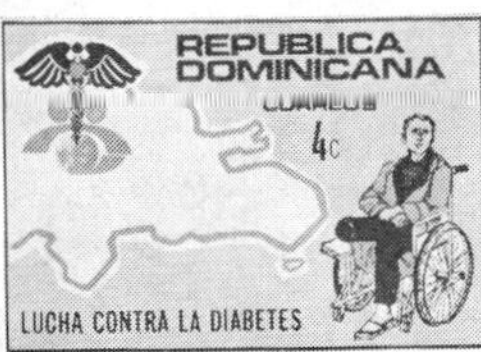

Map, Emblem and Patient A222

Design: 5c, Map of Dominican Republic, diabetics' emblem and pancreas.

1974, Aug. 22 Litho. *Perf. 13*

725	A222	4c bl & multi	12	8
726	A222	5c yel grn & multi	12	10

Fight against diabetes. See Nos. C218–C219.

Train and UPU Emblem A223

Design: 6c, Mail coach and UPU emblem.

1974, Oct. 9 Litho. *Perf. 13¼*

727	A223	2c bl & multi	10	5
728	A223	6c brn & multi	20	12

Centenary of Universal Postal Union. See Nos. C220–C221a.

Golfers A224

Design: 2c, Championship emblem and badge of Dominican Golf Association (horiz.).

Perf. 13x13½, 13½x13

1974, Oct. 24

729	A224	2c yel & blk	12	8
730	A224	6c bl & multi	30	18

World Amateur Golf Championships. See Nos. C222–C223.

Christmas Decorations A225

Virgin and Child A226

1974, Dec. 3 Litho. *Perf. 12*

731	A225	2c multi	10	6
732	A226	6c multi	25	15

Christmas 1974. See No. C224.

Tomatoes, FAO Emblem A227

1974, Dec. 5

Multicolored

733	A227	2c *shown*	8	5
734	A227	3c *Avocados*	12	6
735	A227	5c *Coconuts*	20	10

World Food Program, 10th anniversary. See No. C225.

Fernando A. Defillo A228

Tower, Our Lady of the Rosary Convent A229

1975, Feb. 14 Litho. *Perf. 13½x13*

736	A228	1c dl brn	5	5
737	A228	6c dl grn	18	12

Dr. Fernando A. Defillo (1874–1949), physician.

1975, Mar. 26 Litho. *Perf. 13½*

Design: 2c, Jesus saying "I am the Resurrection and the Life."

738	A229	2c brn & multi	15	5
739	A229	6c multi	25	12

Holy Week 1975. See No. C226.

Hands (Steel Beams) with Symbols of Agriculture, Industry A230

1975, May 19 Litho. *Perf. 10½x10*

740	A230	6c dl bl & multi	18	12

16th Assembly of the Governors of the International Development Bank, Santo Domingo, May 1975. See No. C228.

Satellite Tracking Station A231

1975, June 21 Litho. *Perf. 13½*

741	A231	5c multi	20	15

Opening of first earth satellite tracking station in Dominican Republic. See No. C229.

Apollo A232

Design: 4c, Soyuz.

1975, July 24

Size: 35x25mm.

742	A232	1c bl & multi	8	6
743	A232	4c vio bl & multi	20	15

Apollo Soyuz space test project (Russo-American cooperation), launching July 15; link-up, July 17. See No. C230.

Father Rafael C. Castellanos A233

1975, Aug. 6 Litho. *Perf. 12*

744	A233	6c brn & buff	18	12

Father Rafael C. Castellanos (1875–1934), first Apostolic Administrator in Dominican Republic, birth centenary.

Women and Men Around IWY Emblem A234

1975, Aug. 6 *Perf. 13*

745	A234	3c org & multi	12	6

International Women's Year 1975.

Guacanagarix A235

Basketball A236

Indian Chiefs: 2c, Guarionex. 3c, Caonabo. 4c, Bohechio. 5c, Cayacoa. 6c, Anacona (woman). 9c, Hatuey.

1975, Sept. 27 Litho. *Perf. 12*

746	A235	1c yel & multi	5	5
747	A235	2c sal & multi	6	5
748	A235	3c vio bl & multi	9	6
749	A235	4c grn & multi	12	8
750	A235	5c bl & multi	15	10
751	A235	6c vio & multi	18	12
752	A235	9c rose & multi	15	15
		Nos. 746-752, C231-C233 (10)	1.85	1.26

1975, Oct. 24 Litho. *Perf. 12*

Design: 6c, Baseball and Games' emblem.

753	A236	2c pink & multi	12	6
754	A236	6c org & multi	30	15

7th Pan-American Games, Mexico City, Oct. 13–26. See Nos. C234–C235.

Carolers A237

Design: 6c, Dominican nativity with farmers and shepherds.

1975, Dec. 12 Litho. *Perf. 13x13½*

755	A237	2c yel & multi	10	5
756	A237	6c bl & multi	20	12

Christmas 1975. See No. C236.

Abudefdul Marginatus—A238

1976, Jan. 23 Litho. *Perf. 13*

Multicolored

757	A238	10c *shown*	45	40
758	A238	10c *Doncella*	45	40
759	A238	10c *Carajuelo*	45	40
760	A238	10c *Reina de los Angeles*	45	40
761	A238	10c *Pargo Colorado*	45	40
		Nos. 757-761 (5)	2.25	2.00

Nos. 757–761 printed se-tenant.

Ascension, by J. Priego A239

"Separacion Dominicana" and Adm. Cambiaso A240

Design: 2c, Mary Magdalene, by Enrique Godoy.

1976, Apr. 14 Litho. *Perf. 13½*

762	A239	2c bl & multi	12	8
763	A239	6c yel & multi	30	10

Holy Week 1976. See No. C238.

1976, Apr. 15 *Perf. 13½x13*

764	A240	20c multi	20	20

Naval Battle off Tortuga, Apr. 15, 1844.

Maps of US and Dominican Republic A241

Design: 9c, Maps within cogwheels.

1976, May 29 Litho. *Perf. 13½*

765	A241	6c vio bl & multi	20	10
766	A241	9c vio bl & multi	10	5

American Bicentennial. See Nos. C239–C240.

Flags of Dominican Republic and Spain
A242

1976, May 31

767 A242 6c multi 55 10

Visit of King Juan Carlos I and Queen Sofia of Spain. See No. C241.

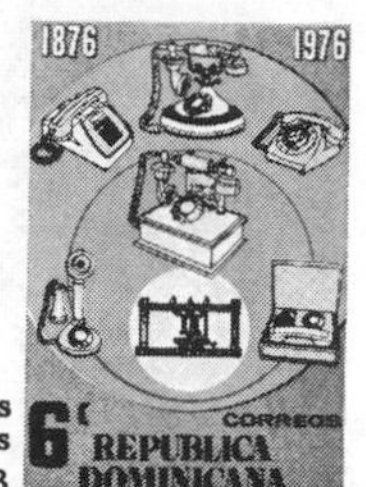

Various Telephones
A243

1976, July 15 ***Perf. 12x12½***

768 A243 6c multi 18 8

Centenary of first telephone call by Alexander Graham Bell, Mar. 10, 1876. See No. C242.

Vision of Duarte, by Luis Desangles
A244

Juan Pablo Duarte, by Rhadames Mejia
A245

1976, July 20 Litho. ***Perf. 13x13½***

769 A244 2c multi 10 5

Perf. 13½

770 A245 6c multi 25 8

Juan Pablo Duarte, liberation hero, death centenary. See Nos. C243–C244.

Fire Hydrant
A246

Design: 6c, Firemen's emblem.

1976, Sept. 13 Litho. ***Perf. 12***

771 A246 4c multi 12 6
772 A246 6c multi 18 8

Honoring firemen. Nos. 771–772 inscribed "Correos". See No. C245.

Radio and Atom Symbols
A247

1976, Oct. 8 Lithographed ***Perf. 13½***

773 A247 6c red & blk 20 8

Dominican Radio Club, 50th anniversary. See No. C246.

Spain, Central and South America, Galleon
A248

1976, Oct. 22 Litho. ***Perf. 13½***

774 A248 6c multi 20 8

Spanish heritage. See No. C247.

Boxing and Montreal Emblem
A249

Design: 3c, Weight lifting.

1976, Oct. 22 ***Perf. 12***

775 A249 2c bl & multi 12 5
776 A249 3c multi 12 5

21st Olympic Games, Montreal, Canada, July 17–Aug. 1. See Nos. C248–C249.

Virgin and Child
A250

Three Kings
A251

1976, Dec. 8 Litho. ***Perf. 13½***

777 A250 2c multi 15 5
778 A251 6c multi 30 12

Christmas 1976. See No. C250.

Cable Car and Beach Scenes
A252

1977, Jan. 7

779 A252 6c multi 25 12

Tourist publicity. See Nos. C251–C253.

Championship Emblem
A253

1977, Mar. 4 Litho. ***Perf. 13½***

780 A253 3c rose & multi 10 6
781 A253 5c yel & multi 15 10

10th Central American and Caribbean Children's and Young People's Swimming Championships, Santo Domingo. See Nos. C254–C255.

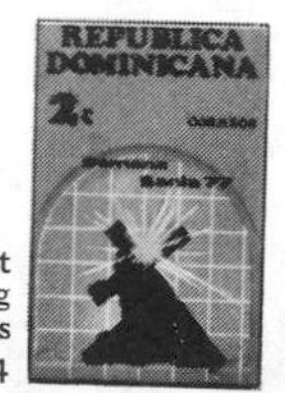

Christ Carrying Cross
A254

Design: 6c, Head with crown of thorns.

1977, Apr. 18 Litho. ***Perf. 13½x13***

782 A254 2c multi 15 5
783 A254 6c blk & rose 30 8

Holy Week 1977. See No. C256.

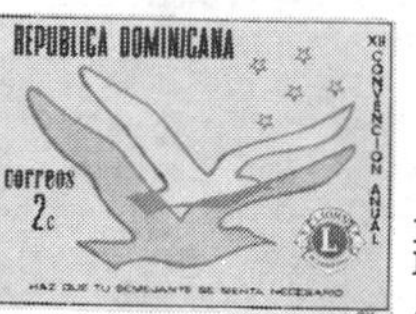

Doves, Lions Emblem
A255

1977, May 6 ***Perf. 13½x13***

784 A255 2c lt bl & multi 6 5
785 A255 6c sal & multi 18 8

12th annual Dominican Republic Lions Convention. See No. C257.

Battle Scene
A256

1977, June 15 Litho. ***Perf. 13x13½***

786 A256 20c multi 60 40

Dominican Navy.

Water Lily
A257

Designs: 4c, "Flor de Mayo" (orchid). 6c, Sebesten.

1977, Aug. 19 Litho. ***Perf. 12***

787 A257 2c multi 10 5
788 A257 4c multi 15 6
789 A257 6c multi 20 8

Nos. 787-789, C259-C260 (5) 1.01 64

National Botanical Garden.

Chart and Computers
A258

1977, Nov. 30 Litho. ***Perf. 13***

790 A258 6c multi 25 8

7th Interamerican Statistics Conference. See No. C261.

Solenodon Paradoxus
A259

Design: 20c, Iguana and Congress emblem.

1977, Dec. 29 Litho. ***Perf. 13***

791 A259 6c multi 25 8
792 A259 20c multi 70 40

8th Pan-American Veterinary and Zootechnical Congress. See Nos. C262–C263.

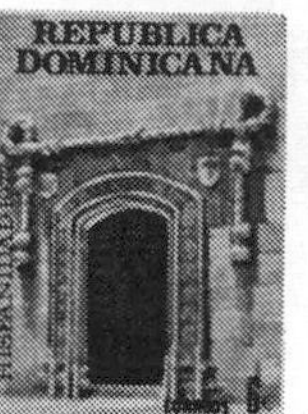

Main Gate, Casa del Cordon, 1503
A260

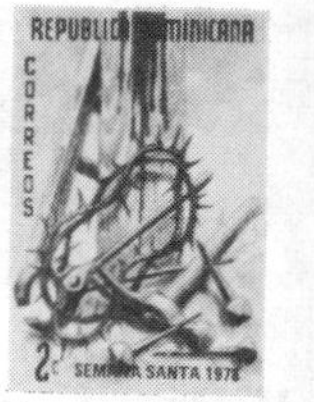

Crown of Thorns, Tools at the Cross
A261

1978, Jan. 19 ***Perf. 13x13½***

Size: 26x36mm.

793 A260 6c multi 18 8

Spanish heritage. See No. C264.

1978, Mar. 21 Litho. ***Perf. 12***

Design: 6c, Head of Jesus with crown of thorns.

Size: 22x33mm.

794 A261 2c multi 12 5
795 A261 6c slate 30 8

Holy Week 1978. See Nos. C265–C266.

Cardinal Octavio A. Beras Rojas
A262

Pres. Manuel de Troncoso
A263

1978, May 5 Litho. ***Perf. 13***

796 A262 6c multi 20 8

First Cardinal from Dominican Republic, consecrated May 24, 1976. See No. C268.

1978, June 12 Litho. ***Perf. 13½***

797 A263 2c blk, rose & brn 6 5
798 A263 6c blk, gray & brn 18 8

Manuel de Jesus Troncoso de la Concha (1878–1955), president of Dominican Republic 1940–1942.

Father Juan N. Zegri y Moreno
A264

1978, July 11 Litho. *Perf. 13x13½*

799 A264 6c multi 20 8

Congregation of the Merciful Sisters of Charity, centenary. See No. C273.

Boxing and Games' Emblem
A265

Design: 6c, Weight lifting.

1978, July 21 *Perf. 12*

800 A265 2c multi 12 5
801 A265 6c multi 25 8

13th Central American and Caribbean Games, Medellin, Colombia. See Nos. C274-C275.

Sun over Landscape
A266

Ships of Columbus, Map of Dominican Republic
A267

Design: 6c, Sun over beach and boat.

1978, Sept. 12 Litho. *Perf. 12*

802 A266 2c multi 6 5
803 A266 6c multi 18 8

Tourist publicity. See Nos. C280-C281.

1978, Oct. 12 Litho. *Perf. 13½*

804 A267 2c multi 10 6

Spanish heritage. See No. C282.

Dove, Lamp, Poinsettia
A268

Design: 6c, Dominican family and star (vert.).

1978, Dec. 5 Litho. *Perf. 12*

805 A268 2c multi 15 6
806 A268 6c multi 30 10

Christmas 1978. See No. C284.

Starving Child, ICY Emblem
A269

1979, Feb. 26 Litho. *Perf. 12*

807 A269 2c org & blk 10 5

International Year of the Child. See Nos. C287-C289.

Crucifixion
A270

Design: 3c, Jesus carrying cross (horiz.).

1979, Apr. 9 Litho. *Perf. 13½*

808 A270 2c multi 12 8
809 A270 3c multi 20 8

Holy Week. See No. C290.

Stigmaphyllon Periplocifolium
A271

1979, May 17 Litho. *Perf. 12*

810 A271 50c multi 50 35

"Dr. Rafael M. Moscoso" National Botanical Garden. See Nos. C293-C295.

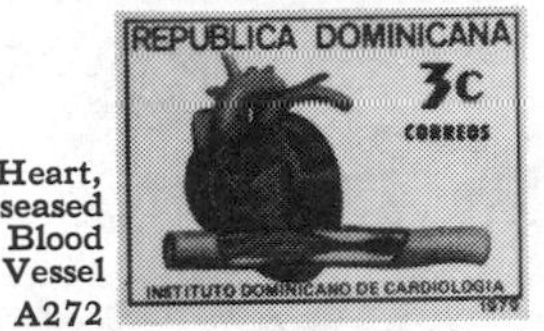

Heart, Diseased Blood Vessel
A272

Design: 1p, Cardiology Institute and heart.

1979, June 2 Litho. *Perf. 13½*

811 A272 3c multi 12 5
812 A272 1p multi 1.00 60

Dominican Cardiology Institute. See No. C296.

Baseball, Games' Emblem
A273

Design: 3c, Bicycling and Games' emblem (vert.).

1979, June 20

813 A273 2c multi 10 5
814 A273 3c multi 18 5

8th Pan American Games, Puerto Rico, June 30-July 15. See No. C297.

Soccer
A274

Thomas A. Edison
A275

Design: 25c, Swimming (horiz.).

1979, Aug. 9 Litho. *Perf. 12*

815 A274 2c multi 10 5
816 A274 25c multi 25 20

Third National Games. See No. C298.

1979, Aug. 27 *Perf. 13½*

817 A275 25c multi 75 50

Centenary of invention of electric light. See No. C300.

Hand Holding Electric Plug
A276

Design: 6c, Filling automobile gas tank.

1979, Aug. 30

818 A276 2c multi 5 5
819 A276 6c multi 18 12

Energy conservation.

Parrot—A277

Birds: 6c, Temnotrogon roseigaster.

1979, Sept. 12 Litho. *Perf. 12*

820 A277 2c multi 10 5
821 A277 6c multi 25 12
Nos. 820-821, C301-C303 (5) 1.50 1.17

Lions Emblem, Map of Dominican Republic—A278

1979, Nov. 13 Litho. *Perf. 12*

822 A278 20c multi 65 35

Lions International Club of Dominican Republic, 10th anniversary. See No. C304.

Holy Family—A279

1979, Dec. 18 Litho. *Perf. 12*

823 A279 2c multi 12 5

Christmas 1979. See No. C305.

See "Special Notices" at the front of this volume for data on the listing methods of this Catalogue, abbreviations, condition, prices and examination.

Jesus Carrying Cross—A280

1980, Mar. 27 Litho. *Perf. 12*

824 A280 3c multi 18 5

Holy Week. See Nos. C306-C307.

Cacao Harvest (Agriculture Year)—A281

1980, May 15 Litho. *Perf. 13½*

825 A281 1c *shown* 5 5
826 A281 2c *Coffee* 6 5
827 A281 3c *Plantain* 10 5
828 A281 4c *Sugar cane* 12 8
829 A281 5c *Corn* 15 10
Nos. 825-829 (5) 48 33

Cotuf Gold Mine, Pueblo Viejo, Flag of Dominican Republic—A282

1980, July 8 Litho. *Perf. 13½*

830 A282 6c multi 20 15

Nationalization of gold mining. See Nos. C310-C311.

Blind Man's Buff—A283

1980, July 21 *Perf. 12*

831 A283 3c *shown* 10 5
832 A283 4c *Marbles* 12 8
833 A283 5c *Drawing in sand* 5 5
834 A283 6c *Hopscotch* 18 12

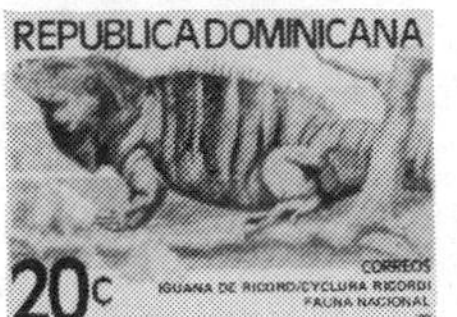

Iguana—A284

1980, Aug. 30 Litho. *Perf. 12*

835 A284 20c multi 70 50
Nos. 835, C314-C317 (5) 2.50 2.20

Dance, by Jaime Colson—A285

1980, Sept. 23 **Litho.** ***Perf. 13x13½, 13½x13***

836	A285	3c *shown*	10	8
837	A285	50c *Woman, by Gilberto Hernandez Ortega,* vert.	60	40

See Nos. C318-C319.

Three Kings—A286

1980, Dec. 5 **Litho.** ***Perf. 13½***

838	A286	3c *shown*	12	8
839	A286	6c *Carolers*	20	15

Christmas 1980. See No. C327.

Salcedo Province Centenary—A287

1981, Jan. 14 **Litho.** ***Perf. 13½***

840	A287	6c multi	20	15

See No. C328.

Juan Pablo Duarte—A288

1981, Feb. 6 **Litho.** ***Perf. 12***

841	A288	2c sep & dp bis	5	5

Juan Pablo Duarte, liberation hero, 105th anniversary of death.

Gymnast

A289

Mother Mazzarello
A290

1981, Mar. 31 **Litho.** ***Perf. 13½***

842	A289	1c shown	5	5
843	A289	2c Running	8	5
844	A289	3c Pole vault	12	6
845	A289	6c Boxing	20	12
		Nos. 842-845, C331 (5)	55	38

5th National Games. See No. C331.

1981, Apr. 14 ***Perf. 12***

846	A290	6c multi	18	12

Mother Maria Mazzarello (1837-1881), founder of Daughters of Mary.

Pedro Henriquez Urena, Historian (1884-1946)
A291

1981, May 18 **Litho.** ***Perf. 13½***

847	A291	6c gray vio & lt gray	18	12

Forest Conservation
A292

1981, June 30 **Litho.** ***Perf. 12***

848	A292	2c shown	6	5
849	A292	6c River, forest	18	12

Family in House, Census Emblem—A293

1981, Aug. 14 **Litho.** ***Perf. 12***

850	A293	3c shown	15	8
851	A293	6c Farmer	25	15

1981 natl. population and housing census.

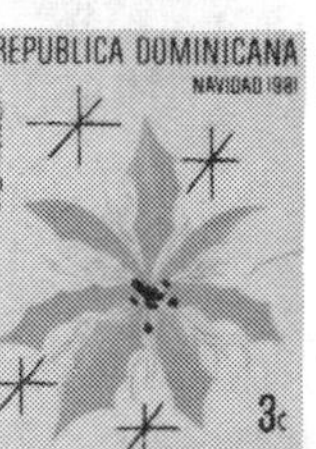

Christmas 1981—A294

1981, Dec. 23 **Litho.** ***Perf. 13½***

852	A294	2c Bells	5	5
853	A294	3c Poinsettia	10	6

See No. C353

Juan Pablo Duarte—A295

1982, Jan. 29 **Litho.** ***Perf. 13½***

854	A295	2c bl & pale bl	8	5

National Elections—A296

Designs: Voters casting votes. 3c, 6c vert.

1982, Mar. 30 **Litho.** ***Perf. 13½***

855	A296	2c multi	6	6
856	A296	3c multi	8	5
857	A296	6c multi	12	8

Energy Conservation

A297

Emilio Prud'Homme (1856-1932), Composer
A298

Designs: Various forms of energy.

1982, May 10 **Litho.** ***Perf. 12***

858	A297	1c multi	5	5
859	A297	2c multi	5	5
860	A297	3c multi	8	5
861	A297	4c multi	10	5
862	A297	5c multi	5	5
863	A297	6c multi	15	8
		Nos. 858-863 (6)	48	33

1982, Aug. 2 ***Perf. 12x12½***

864	A298	6c multi	12	5

Pres. Antonio Guzman Fernandez (1911-1982)—A299

1982, Aug. 4 ***Perf. 13x13½***

865	A299	6c multi	15	8

14th Central American and Caribbean Games—A300

1982, Aug. 13 ***Perf. 12***

866	A300	3c Baseball	5	5

See Nos. C368-C370. Exist imperf.

San Pedro de Macoris Province Centenary—A301

1982, Aug. 26 ***Perf. 13***

867	A301	1c Wagon	8	8
868	A301	2c Stained-glass window	8	8
869	A301	5c Views	12	12

Size of 1c, 5c, 42x29mm. See No. C375.

St. Teresa of Jesus of Avila (1515-1582)—A302

1982, Nov. 17 **Litho.** ***Perf. 13½***

870	A302	6c multi	12	10

Christmas 1982

A303

Environmental Protection
A304

Various Christmas balls.

1982, Dec. 8

871	A303	6c multi	15	8

See No. C380.

1982, Dec. 15 ***Perf. 12***

872	A304	2c Bird	5	5
873	A304	3c Water	6	5
874	A304	6c Forest	12	8
875	A304	20c Fish	20	20

Natl. Literacy Campaign—A305

1983, Mar. 9 **Litho.** ***Perf. 13½***

No.	Type	Description	Unused	Used
876	A305	2c Vowels on blackboard	8	5
877	A305	3c Writing, reading	6	5
878	A305	6c Children, pencil	18	8

Mao City Centenary—306

1983, Apr. 4 ***Perf. 12***

No.	Type	Description	Unused	Used
879	A306	1c multi	8	6
880	A306	5c multi	15	8

Antonio del Monte y Tejada (1780-1861)—A307

Famous Men: 3c, Manuel Ubaldo Gomez (1857-1941). 5c, Emiliano Tejera (1841-1923). 6c, Bernardo Pichardo (1877-1924). 7c, Americo Lugo (1870-1952). 10c, José Gabriel Garcia (1834-1910). 7c, 10c airmail.

1983, Apr. 25 **Litho.** ***Perf. 12***

No.	Type	Description	Unused	Used
881	A307	2c multi	6	5
882	A307	3c multi	6	5
883	A307	5c multi	5	5
884	A307	6c multi	5	5
885	A307	7c multi	10	10
886	A307	10c multi	20	15
		Nos. 881-886 (6)	52	45

National Anthem, 100th Anniv.—A308

Design: Emilia Prud Homme, Poet, and Jose Reyes, composer.

1983, Sept. 13 **Litho.** ***Perf. 13½***

No.	Type	Description	Unused	Used
887	A308	6c cop red & blk	10	8

Free Masons, 125th Anniv. — A309

Church of Our Lady of Regla, 300th Anniv. — A310

1983, Oct. 24 **Litho.** ***Perf. 12***

No.	Type	Description	Unused	Used
888	A309	4c Emblem	6	5

1983, Nov. 5 ***Perf. 13½***

No.	Type	Description	Unused	Used
889	A310	3c Church	5	5
890	A310	6c Statue	10	6

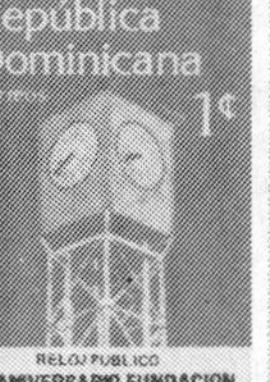

450th Anniv. of Monte Cristi Province A311

6th Natl. Games A312

1983, Nov. 25 ***Perf. 12***

No.	Type	Description	Unused	Used
891	A311	1c Tower	8	6
892	A311	2c Arms	8	6
893	A311	5c Cuban independence site, horiz.	8	6
894	A311	7c Workers, horiz.	10	8

1983, Dec. 9

No.	Type	Description	Unused	Used
895	A312	6c Bicycling, boxing, baseball	6	5
896	A312	10c Gymnast, weight lifting, swimming	10	6

10c airmail.

Restoration of the Republic, 120th Anniv.—A313

1983, Dec. 30 **Litho.** ***Perf. 13½***

No.	Type	Description	Unused	Used
897	A313	1c Capotillo Heroes Monument	5	5

140th Anniv. of Independence—A314

Designs: 6c, Matia Ramon Mella (Patriot), flag. 25c, Mella's Blunderbuss rifle, Gate of Deliverance (independence declaration site).

1984, Feb. 24 **Litho.** ***Perf. 13½***

No.	Type	Description	Unused	Used
898	A314	6c multi	6	5
899	A314	25c multi	25	15

Heriberto Pieter (1884-1972), Physician, First Negro Graduate—A315

1984, Mar. 16

No.	Type	Description	Unused	Used
900	A315	3c multi	5	5

Battle of Barranquita, 67th Anniv.—A316

1983, Dec. 30 ***Perf. 12***

No.	Type	Description	Unused	Used
901	A316	5c multi	5	5

Battle of Santiago, 140th Anniv.—A317

1984, Mar. 29 ***Perf. 13½***

No.	Type	Description	Unused	Used
902	A317	7c multi	8	5

Coast Guard Ship DC-1, 1934—A318

1984, Apr. 13 **Litho.**

No.	Type	Description	Unused	Used
903	A318	10c multi	10	6

Navy Day and 140th anniv. of Battle of Tortuguero.

Birth Centenary of Pedro Henriquez Urena—A319

1984, June 29 **Litho.** ***Perf. 12***

No.	Type	Description	Unused	Used
904	A319	7c Salome Urena	8	6
905	A319	10c Text	10	8
906	A319	22c Urena	22	18

Monument to Heroes of June 1959—A320

1984, June 20 ***Perf. 13½***

No.	Type	Description	Unused	Used
907	A320	6c sil & bl	6	5

Gesta de Constanza Maimon and Estero Hondo 25th anniv.

1984 Summer Olympics—A321

1984, Aug. 2

No.	Type	Description	Unused	Used
908	A321	1p Hurdles	1.00	80
909	A321	1p Weightlifting	1.00	80
910	A321	1p Boxing	1.00	80
911	A321	1p Baseball	1.00	80

Nos. 908-911 se-tenant.

Protection of Fauna—A322

1984, Oct. 3 **Litho.** ***Perf. 12***

No.	Type	Description	Unused	Used
912	A322	10c Owl	10	10
913	A322	15c Flamingo	15	15
914	A322	25c Wild Pig	25	25
915	A322	35c Solenodon	35	35

500th Anniv. of Discovery of America—A323

1984, Oct. 10 **Litho.** ***Perf. 13½x13***

No.	Type	Description	Unused	Used
916	A323	10c Landing on Hispaniola	10	10
917	A323	35c Distruction of Ft. Navidad	35	35
918	A323	65c First Mass in America	65	65
919	A323	1p Battle of Santo Cerro	1.00	1.00

Visit of Pope John Paul II—A324

1984, Oct. 11 Litho. *Perf. 13x13½*

920 Block of 4 3.00 3.00
a. A324 75c Shown 75 75
b. A324 75c Pope, map of Caribbean 75 75
c. A324 75c Pope, globe 75 75
d. A324 75c Bishop's crozier 75 75

150th Anniv. of Birth of Maximo Gomez—A325

1984, Dec. 6 Litho. *Perf. 13½*

921 A325 10c Gomez on horseback 10 10
922 A325 20c Maximo Gomez 20 20

Christmas 1984—A326

1984, Dec. 14 Litho. *Perf. 13½x13, 13x13½*

923 A326 5c multi 5 5
924 A326 10c multi, vert. 10 10

Sacrifice of the Child, by Eligio Pichardo—A327

Paintings and sculpture: 10c, The Pumpkin Sellers, by Gaspar Mario Cruz; 25c, The Market, by Celeste Woss y Gil; 50c, Horses in the Rain, by Dario Suro.

1984, Dec. 19 Litho. *Perf. 13½*

925 A327 5c multi 5 5
926 A327 10c multi, vert. 8 5
927 A327 25c multi 18 10
928 A327 50c multi 36 18

Day of Our Lady of Altagracia—A328

1985, Jan. 21

929 A328 5c Old church at Higuey, 1572 5 5
930 A328 10c Our Lady of Altagracia 1514, vert. 8 5
931 A328 25c Basilica of the Protector, Higuey, 1971, vert. 18 10

Independence, 141st Anniv.—A329

Painting: The Fathers of Our Country (Duarte, Sanchez and Mella).

1985, Mar. 8 *Perf. 12½*

932 A329 5c multi 5 5
933 A329 10c multi 8 5
934 A329 25c multi 18 10

Battle of Azua, 141st Anniv.—A330

1985, Apr. 8 Litho. *Perf. 13½*

935 A330 10c Gen. Antonio Duverge, Statue 8 5

Battle of Tortuguero, 141st Anniv.—A331

1985, Apr. 15 Litho.

936 A331 25c Santo Domingo Lighthouse, 1853 18 10

American Airforces Cooperation System, 25th Anniv.—A332

1985, Apr. 15 Litho. *Perf. 12*

937 A332 35c multi 70 48

Espaillat Province Cent. A333

1985, May 24 Litho. *Perf. 13½*

938 A333 10c Don Carlos M. Rojas, 1st gov. 8 5

MOCA '85, 7th Natl. Games—A334

1985, July 5 Litho. *Perf. 12*

939 A334 5c Table tennis 10 6
940 A334 10c Walking race 20 14

Intl. Youth Year—A335

1985, July 29 *Perf. 13½*

941 A335 5c Youth 10 6
942 A335 25c The Haitises 50 35
943 A335 35c Mt. Duarte summit 70 48
944 A335 2p Mt. Duarte 4.00 2.75

Interamerican Development Bank, 25th Anniv.—A336

Designs: 10c, Haina Harbor. 25c, Map of development sites. 1p, Tavera-Bao-Lopez Hydroelectric Complex.

1985, Aug. 23

945 A336 10c multi 20 14
946 A336 25c multi 50 35
947 A336 1p multi 2.00 1.35

Intl. Decade for Women A337

15th Central American and Caribbean Games, Santiago A338

Design: Evangelina Rodriguez (1879-1947), first Dominican woman doctor.

1985, Sept. 26

948 A337 10c multi 20 14

1985, Oct. 9 *Perf. 12*

949 A338 5c multi 10 6
950 A338 25c multi 50 35

4th Christopher Columbus Regatta, Casa de Espana—A339

Designs: 50c, Founding of Santo Domingo, 1496. 65c, Chapel of Our Lady of the Rosary, 1496, Santo Domingo. 1p, Columbus, American Indian and old Spanish coat of arms.

1985, Oct. 10 *Perf. 13½*

951 A339 35c multi 70 48
952 A339 50c multi 1.00 68
953 A339 65c multi 1.30 88
954 A339 1p multi 2.00 1.35

Discovery of America, 500th anniv. (in 1992).

Cacique Enriquillo A340

Archbishop Fernando Arturo de Merino A341

Designs: 5c, Enriquillo in the Bahuroco Mountains, mural detail. 10c, Shown.

1985, Oct. 31

955 A340 5c multi 10 6
956 A340 10c multi 20 14

Enriquillo (d. 1536), leader of revolution against Spain. Size of No. 955:

1985, Dec. 3 *Perf. 12*

957 A341 25c multi 50 35

Cent. of holy orders granted to Merino (1833-1906), president of the republic 1880-82.

Mirabal Sisters, Political Martyrs 1960—A342

985, Dec. 18 *Perf. 13½*

58	A342	10c multi	20	15

Christmas—A343

1985, Dec. 18

959	A343	10c multi	20	14
960	A343	25c multi	50	35

Day of Independence, Feb. 27—A344

Design: Mausoleum of founding fathers Duarte, Sanchez and Mella.

1986, Feb. 26 **Litho.** *Perf. 13½*

961	A344	5c multi	10	6
962	A344	10c multi	20	14

Holy Week—A345

Colonial churches.

1986, Apr. 10

963	A345	5c San Miguel	10	6
964	A345	5c San Andres	10	6
965	A345	10c Santa Barbara	20	14
966	A345	10c San Lazaro	20	14
967	A345	10c San Carlos	20	14
		Nos. 963-967 (5)	80	54

Navy Day—A346

Design: Juan Bautista Cambiaso, Juan Bautista Maggiolo and Juan Alejandro Acosta, 1884 independence battle heroes.

1986, Apr. 15

968	A346	10c multi	20	14

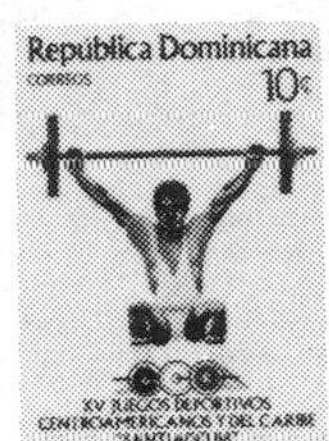

Natl. Elections A347

Natl. Postal Institute Inauguration A348

1986, Apr. 29

969	A347	5c Voters, map	10	6
970	A347	10c Ballot box	20	14

1986, June 10

971	A348	10c gold, bl & red	20	14
972	A348	25c sil, bl & red	50	35
973	A348	50c blk, bl & red	1.00	68

Central America and Caribbean Games, Santiago—A349

1986, July 17 **Litho.** *Perf. 13½*

974	A349	10c Weight lifting	20	14
975	A349	25c Gymnastics	50	35
976	A349	35c Diving	70	48
977	A349	50c Equestrian	1.00	68

Historians—A350

Designs: 5c, Ercilia Pepin (b. 1886), vert. 10c, Ramon Emilio Jimenez (b. 1886) and Victor Garrido (1886-1972).

1986, Aug. 1 **Litho.** *Perf. 13½*

978	A350	5c sil & dl brn	10	6
979	A350	10c sil & dl brn	20	14

A351

A352

Discovery of America, 500th Anniv. (in 1992)—A353

Designs: 25c, Yachts racing, 5th Admiral Columbus Regatta, Casa de Espana. 50c, Columbus founding La Isabela City. 65c, Exploration of the hidalgos. 1p, Columbus returning to the Court of Ferdinand and Isabella. 1.50p, Emblems.

1986, Oct. 10 **Litho.** *Perf. 13½*

980	A351	25c multi	50	35
981	A352	50c multi	1.00	68
982	A352	65c multi	1.30	88
983	A352	1p multi	2.00	1.35

Textured Paper
Size: 86x58mm.
Imperf.

984	A353	1.50p multi	3.00	2.00
		Nos. 980-984 (5)	7.80	5.26

1986 World Cup Soccer Championships, Mexico A354

Medicinal Plants A355

Various soccer plays.

1986, Oct. 21 *Perf. 13½*

985	A354	50c multi	1.00	68
986	A354	75c multi	1.50	1.00

1986, Dec. 15

987	A355	5c Zea mays	10	6
988	A355	10c Bixa orellana	20	14
989	A355	25c Momordica charantia	50	35
990	A355	50c Annona muricata	1.00	68

Second Caribbean Pharmacopeia Seminar.

Christmas—A356

1986, Dec. 19

991	A356	5c Urban scene	10	6
992	A356	25c Rural scene	50	35

Maximo Gomez y Baez (1836-1905), Revolutionary, Statesman—A357

1986, Dec. 31 **Litho.** *Perf. 13½*

993	A357	10c shown	20	15
994	A357	25c Portrait, c. 1900	50	35

SEMI-POSTAL STAMPS

Nos. 474-478 Surcharged in Red

Engraved and Lithographed.

1957, Feb. 8 *Perf. 11½* **Unwmkd.**

Flags in National Colors

B1	A117	1c +2c brn, lt bl, vio & mar	10	10
B2	A117	2c +2c dk brn, lt bl & vio	10	10
B3	A117	3c +2c red lil & red	15	15
B4	A117	5c +2c red org & vio	25	25
B5	A117	7c +2c grn & vio	35	35
		Nos. B1-B5, CB1-CB3 (8)	2.50	2.50

The surtax was to aid Hungarian refugees. A similar 25c surcharge was applied to the miniature sheets described in the footnote following No. 478. Price, 2 sheets, perf. and imperf., $17.50.

Nos. 479-483 Surcharged in Red Orange

1957, Sept. 9 Photo. *Perf. 13½*

Flags in National Colors

B6	A118	1c +2c brn & brt bl	25	25
B7	A118	2c +2c org ver & dk bl	35	35
B8	A118	3c +2c dk bl	40	40
B9	A118	5c +2c ol & dk bl	55	55
B10	A118	7c +2c rose brn & dk bl	65	65
		Nos. B6-B10, CB4-CB6 (8)	4.70	4.65

Issued to commemorate the centenary of the birth of Lord Baden Powell and the 50th anniversary of the Scout Movement. The surtax was for the Dominican Republic Boy Scouts.

A similar 5c surcharge was applied to the miniature sheets described in the footnote following No. 483. Price 4 sheets, perf. and imperf., medal and flag, $40.

Types of Olympic Regular Issue, 1957, Surcharged in Carmine

REFUGIADOS REFUGIADOS

a *b*

1958, May 26 **Engr. & Litho.**

Flags in National Colors

Pink Paper

B11	A119(a)	1c +2c red brn	25	25
B12	A119(b)	1c +2c red brn	25	25
B13	A120(a)	2c +2c gray brn	30	30
B14	A120(b)	2c +2c gray brn	30	30
B15	A119(a)	3c +2c vio	30	30
B16	A119(b)	3c +2c vio	30	30
B17	A120(a)	5c +2c red org	40	40
B18	A120(b)	5c +2c red org	40	40
B19	A119(a)	7c +2c Prus grn	50	50
B20	A119(b)	7c +2c Prus grn	50	50
		Nos. B11-B20, CB7-CB12 (16)	6.50	6.50

The surtax was for the United Nations Relief and Works Agency for Palestine Refugees.

A similar 5c surcharge, plus marginal United Nations emblem and "UNRWA," was applied to the miniature sheets described in the footnote following No. 488. Price, 4 sheets, perf. and imperf., $30.

Nos. 501-505 Surcharged

Perf. 13½

1959, Apr. 13 Photo. **Unwmkd.**

Flags in National Colors

B21	A125	1c +2c rose, ind & ultra	35	35
B22	A125	2c +2c brn & bl	45	45
B23	A125	3c +2c gray, vio, blk & buff	50	50
B24	A125	5c +2c rose, dk bl, brn & red	60	60
B25	A125	7c +2c lt brn, dk bl & red	65	65
		Nos. B21-B25, CB13-CB15 (8)	5.80	5.80

International Geophysical Year, 1957–58.

A similar 5c surcharge was applied to the miniature sheets described in the footnote following No. 505. Price, 2 sheets, perf. and imperf., $22.50.

Type of 1957 Surcharged in Red

Engraved and Lithographed

1959, Sept. 10 *Imperf.* **Unwmkd.**

Flags in National Colors

B26	A117	1c +2c brn, lt bl, vio & mar	30	30
B27	A117	2c +2c dk brn, lt bl & vio	30	30
B28	A117	3c +2c red lil & red	35	35
B29	A117	5c +2c red org & vio	40	40
B30	A117	7c +2c grn & vio	50	50
		Nos. B26-B30, CB16-CB18 (8)	3.90	3.90

3rd Pan American Games, Chicago, Aug. 27–Sept. 7, 1959.

World Refugee Year Issue

Nos. 522–524 Surcharged in Red

+5 ¢

1960, Apr. 7 Litho. *Perf. 12½*

Center in Gray

B31	A135	5c +5c red brn & yel grn	25	25
B32	A135	9c +5c car & lt bl	30	30
B33	A135	13c +5c org & grn	60	60
		Nos. B31-B33, CB19-CB20 (5)	2.50	2.50

Issued to publicize World Refugee Year, July 1, 1959–June 30, 1960. The surtax was for aid to refugees.

Souvenir sheets exist perf. and imperf., containing one each of Nos. B31–B33 and CB19–CB20. Size: 152x99mm. Black marginal inscription. Price, 2 sheets, perf. and imperf., $10.

Nos. 525–529 Surcharged: "XV ANIVERSARIO DE LA UNESCO +2c"

1962, Jan. 8 Photo. *Perf. 13½*

Flags in National Colors

B34	A136	1c +2c red, yel grn & blk	8	8
B35	A136	2c +2c org, grnsh bl & brn	10	10
B36	A136	3c +2c hn brn & bl	12	12
B37	A136	5c +2c brn & ultra	18	18
B38	A136	7c +2c grn, bl & rose brn	20	20
		Nos. B34-B38, CB21-CB23 (8)	2.08	2.08

Issued to commemorate the 15th anniversary (in 1961) of UNESCO (U.N. Educational, Scientific and Cultural Organization).

A similar 5c surcharge was applied to the miniature sheets described in the footnote following No. 529. Price, 2 sheets, perf. and imperf., $7.50.

Anti-Malaria Type of Regular Issue, 1962

1962, Apr. 29 Litho. *Perf. 12*

B39	A141	10c +2c brt pink & red lil	30	25
B40	A141	20c +2c pale brn & brn	50	40

Issued for the World Health Organization drive to eradicate malaria.

Type of Regular Issue, 1963

1963, Apr. 15 *Perf. 11½* **Unwmkd.**

Banner in Dark Blue & Red

B41	A148	2c +1c grn	6	6
B42	A148	5c +2c brt rose lil	18	15
B43	A148	9c +2c org	30	30

Issued for the "Freedom from Hunger" campaign of the U.N. Food and Agriculture organization. A souvenir sheet contains three imperf. stamps similar to Nos. B41–B43. Dark blue marginal inscription. Size: 172x102mm. Price, $1.25.

Nos. 591–593 Surcharged

1964, March 8 *Perf. 12½*

B44	A153	3c +2c pale pink & ver	20	20
B45	A153	6c +2c pale bl & ultra	25	25
B46	A153	9c +2c pale rose & red brn	40	40
		Nos. B44-B46, CB26-CB27 (5)	1.15	1.15

Issued to publicize the UNESCO world campaign to save historic monuments in Nubia.

Nos. 622–626 Surcharged

PRO DAMNIFICADOS CICLON INES

1966, Dec. 9 Litho. *Perf. 12½*

Size: 31x21mm.

B47	A164	1c +2c multi	10	10
B48	A164	2c +2c multi	5	5
B49	A164	3c +2c multi	5	5
B50	A164	6c +4c multi	10	10
B51	A164	8c +4c multi	15	15
		Nos. B47-B51, CB28-CB30 (8)	2.05	2.05

The surtax was for victims of hurricane Inez.

AIR POST STAMPS

Map of Hispaniola—AP1

Perf. 11½

1928, May 31 Litho. **Unwmkd.**

C1	AP1	10c dp ultra	7.50	4.00

1930

C2	AP1	10c ocher	5.00	4.00
a.		Vertical pair imperf. between	1,000.	
C3	AP1	15c scarlet	10.00	5.50
C4	AP1	20c dl grn	4.50	85
C5	AP1	30c violet	10.00	6.50

Nos. C2 to C5 have only "CENTAVOS" in lower panel. Dates of issue: 10c, 20c, Jan. 24; 15c, 30c, Feb. 14.

1930

C6	AP1	10c lt bl	2.50	1.00
C7	AP1	15c bl grn	5.00	1.50
C8	AP1	20c yel brn	5.50	7
a.		Imperf. vertically (pair)	600.00	600.
C9	AP1	30c chocolate	9.00	2.5

Dates of issue: 10c, 15c, 20c, Sept.; 30c, Oct.

Batwing Sundial Erected in 1753

AP2

1931-33 *Perf. 12*

C10	AP2	10c carmine	5.50	8
C11	AP2	10c lt bl ('32)	2.25	75
C12	AP2	10c dk grn ('33)	9.00	3.50
C13	AP2	15c rose lil	4.00	75
C14	AP2	20c dk bl	9.00	2.75
a.		Numerals reading up at left and down at right	10.00	4.00
b.		Imperf., pair	400.00	
C15	AP2	30c green	3.50	50
C16	AP2	50c red brn	9.00	1.00
C17	AP2	1p dp org	15.00	3.50
		Nos. C10-C17 (8)	57.25	13.60

Issue dates: Aug. 16, 1931; July 2, 1932; May 28, 1933.

Airplane and Ozama Fortress

AP3

1933, Nov. 20

C18	AP3	10c dk bl	5.50	85

Airplane and Trujillo Bridge

AP4

1934, Sept. 20

C19	AP4	10c dk bl	4.50	85

Symbolic of Flight

AP5

1935, Apr. 29

C20	AP5	10c lt bl & dk bl	2.25	65

AP6

1936, Feb. 11 *Perf. 11½*

C21	AP6	10c dk bl & turq bl	3.75	65

Allegory of Flight
AP7

1936, Oct. 17

C22	AP7	10c dk bl, bl & turq bl	3.25	50

Macorís Airport
AP8

1937, Oct. 22

C23	AP8	10c green	1.50	20

Fleet of Columbus
AP9

Air Fleet
AP10

Proposed Columbus Lighthouse
AP11

1937, Nov. 9 ***Perf. 12***

C24	AP9	10c rose red	2.50	1.50
C25	AP10	15c purple	2.00	1.00
C26	AP11	20c dk bl & lt bl	2.00	1.25
C27	AP10	25c red vio	3.00	1.50
C28	AP11	30c yel grn	2.75	1.25
C29	AP10	50c brown	5.50	1.75
C30	AP11	75c dk ol grn	15.00	15.00
C31	AP9	1p orange	9.00	3.00
		Nos. C24-C31 (8)	41.75	26.25

Issued in commemoration of the goodwill flight to all American countries by the planes "Colon", "Pinta", "Niña" and "Santa Maria".

Pan American Clipper
AP12

1938, July 30

C32	AP12	10c green	1.50	20

Trylon and Perisphere, Plane and Proposed Columbus Lighthouse—AP13

1939, Apr. 30

C33	AP13	10c grn & lt grn	1.75	85

New York World's Fair.

Airplane
AP14

1939, Oct. 18

C34	AP14	10c grn & dp grn	2.25	30
a.		Pair, imperf. between	*750.00*	

Proposed Columbus Lighthouse, Plane and Caravels—AP15

Christopher Columbus and Proposed Lighthouse
AP16

Proposed Lighthouse
AP17

Christopher Columbus
AP18

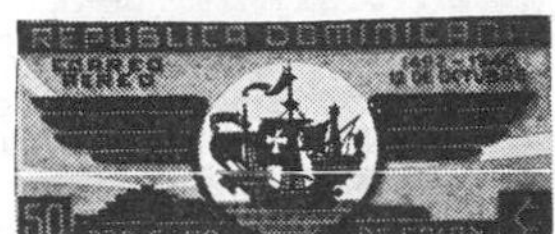

Caravel—AP19

1940, Oct. 12

C35	AP15	10c saph & lt bl	75	75
C36	AP16	15c org brn & brn	1.15	1.00
C37	AP17	20c rose red & red	1.15	1.00
C38	AP18	25c brt red lil & red vio	1.15	50
C39	AP19	50c grn & lt grn	2.25	2.00
		Nos. C35-C39 (5)	6.45	5.25

Discovery of America by Columbus and proposed Columbus memorial lighthouse in Dominican Republic.

Posts and Telegraph Building, San Cristobal
AP20

1941, Feb. 21

C40	AP20	10c brt red lil & pale lil rose	65	25

Globe, Wing and Letter
AP21

1942, Feb. 13

C41	AP21	10c dk vio brn	80	8
C42	AP21	75c dp org	5.00	3.00

Plane
AP22

1943, Sept. 1

C43	AP22	10c brt red lil	60	12
C44	AP22	20c dp bl & bl	70	18
C45	AP22	25c yel ol	8.00	4.00

Plane, Flag, Coat of Arms and Torch of Liberty
AP23

1944, Feb. 27 ***Perf. 11½***

Flag in Gray, Dark Blue, Carmine

C46	AP23	10c multi	60	12
C47	AP23	20c multi	75	20
C48	AP23	1p multi	3.50	2.50

Centenary of Independence. See No. 407 for souvenir sheet listing.

Communications Building, Ciudad Trujillo
AP24

1944, Nov. 12 **Litho.** ***Perf. 12***

C49	AP24	9c yel grn & bl	30	15
C50	AP24	13c dl brn & rose car	35	10
C51	AP24	25c org & dl red	60	15
b.		Vert. pair, imperf. between	75.00	
C52	AP24	30c blk & ultra	1.25	1.10

Twenty booklets of 100 (25 panes of 4) of the 25c were issued. Single panes are unknown to experts.

Emblem of Communications
AP25

1945, Sept. 1

Center in Dark Blue and Carmine.

C53	AP25	7c dp yel grn	30	35
C54	AP25	12c red org	35	25
C55	AP25	13c dp bl	45	20
C56	AP25	25c org brn	90	30

AP26

Flags and National Anthem
AP27

Lithographed.

1946, Feb. 27 ***Perf. 12*** **Unwmkd.**

Center in Dark Blue, Deep Carmine and Black.

C57	AP26	10c carmine	70	60
C58	AP26	15c blue	1.75	1.25
C59	AP26	20c chocolate	2.00	1.25
C60	AP26	35c orange	2.00	1.00
C61	AP27	1p grn, yel grn & cit	20.00	16.00
		Nos. C57-C61 (5)	26.45	20.10

Nos. C57–C61 exist imperf.

Map of Hispaniola
AP28

1946, Aug. 4

C62	AP28	10c multi	50	20
C63	AP28	13c multi	85	20

See note after No. 421.

Waterfall of Jimenoa
AP29

1947, Mar. 18 **Lithographed**

Center Multicolored.

C64	AP29	18c lt bl	60	60
C65	AP29	23c carmine	60	60
C66	AP29	50c red vio	60	60
C67	AP29	75c chocolate	75	75

Executive Palace
AP30

1948, Feb. 27

C68	AP30	37c org brn	1.25	1.00
C69	AP30	1p org yel	3.50	2.50

Church of San Francisco Ruins
AP31

Las Carreras Monument
AP32

1949 ***Perf. 11½*** **Unwmkd.**

C70	AP31	7c ol grn & pale ol grn	20	15
C71	AP31	10c org brn & buff	25	12
C72	AP31	15c brt rose & pale pink	75	35
C73	AP31	20c grn & pale grn	1.00	70

Issue dates: 10c, Apr. 4; others, Apr. 13.

1949, Aug. 10

C74	AP32	10c red & pink	35	8

Issued to commemorate the centenary of the Battle of Las Carreras.

Hotel Montana
AP33

Design: 37c, Hotel San Cristobal.

1950, Sept. 8

C75	AP33	12c dk bl & bl	40	12
C76	AP33	37c car & pink	2.75	2.25

Map, Plane and Caduceus
AP34

1950, Oct. 2

C77	AP34	12c org brn & yel	60	15

The 13th Pan-American Health Conference. Exists imperf.

Dr. Salvador B. Gautier Hospital
AP35

1952, Aug.

C78	AP35	23c dp bl	85	80
C79	AP35	29c carmine	2.00	1.50

Columbus Lighthouse and Plane
AP36

Ano Mariano Initials in Monogram
AP37

1953, Jan. 6 **Engraved** ***Perf. 13***

C80	AP36	12c ocher	35	25
C81	AP36	14c dk bl	15	15
C82	AP36	20c blk brn	75	60
C83	AP36	23c dp plum	30	20
C84	AP36	25c dk bl	85	70
C85	AP36	29c dp grn	40	40
C86	AP36	1p red brn	1.00	60
a.		Miniature sheet of 10	5.00	5.00
		Nos. C80-C86 (7)	3.80	2.90

No. C86a is lithographed and contains one each of Nos. 450–452 and C80–C86, in slightly different shades. Sheet measures 190x130mm. and is imperf. with simulated perforations printed in dark blue. No marginal inscriptions.

A miniature sheet similar to No. C86a, but measuring 200x163mm. and in folder, exists. Price $65.

1954, Aug. 5 **Litho.** ***Perf. 11½***

C87	AP37	8c claret	25	15
C88	AP37	11c blue	10	5
C89	AP37	33c brn org	1.00	65

Marian Year. Nos. C87–C89 exist imperf.

Rotary Type of Regular Issue, 1955.

1955, Feb. 23 ***Perf. 12***

C90	A110	11c rose red	45	20

Rotary International, 50th anniversary.

Flags
AP39

Portraits of General Hector B. Trujillo: 25c, In civilian clothes. 33c, In uniform.

Engraved.

1955, May 16 ***Perf. 13½x13***

C91	AP39	11c bl, yel & car	45	12
C92	AP39	25c rose vio	70	40
C93	AP39	33c org brn	1.00	60

The center of No. C91 is lithographed. Issued to commemorate the 25th anniversary of the inauguration of the Trujillo era.

Fair Type of Regular Issue, 1955

1955, Dec. 20 ***Perf. 13*** **Unwmkd.**

C94	A112	11c vermilion	40	12

Issued to publicize the International Fair of Peace and Brotherhood in Ciudad Trujillo, Dec. 1955.

ICAO Type of Regular Issue, 1956.

1956, Apr. 6 **Litho.** ***Perf. 12½***

C95	A114	11c ultra	35	12

Issued to commemorate the third Caribbean conference of the International Civil Aviation Organization.

Tree Type of Regular Issue, 1956.

Design: 13c, Mahogany tree.

1956, Dec. 8 **Litho.** ***Perf. 11½x12***

C96	A115	13c org & grn	45	18

Issued to publicize the reforestation program.

Type of Regular Issue, 1957.

Olympic Winners and Flags: 11c, Paavo Nurmi, Finland. 16c, Ugo Frigerio, Italy. 17c, Mildred Didrikson ("Didrickson" on stamp), United States.

Engraved and Lithographed.

1957, Jan. 24 ***Perf. 11½*** **Unwmkd.**

Flags in National Colors

C97	A117	11c ultra & red org	10	10
C98	A117	16c car & lt grn	15	15
C99	A117	17c blk, vio & red	15	15

Issued to commemorate the 16th Olympic Games, Melbourne, Nov. 22–Dec. 8, 1956. Exist imperf.

Souvenir sheets of 3 exist, perf. and imperf., containing one each of Nos. C97–C99. Sheets measure 169x86mm., with Olympic flag and motto on left margin.

Price, 2 sheets, perf. & imperf., $7.

Type of Regular Issue, 1957.

Olympic Winners and Flags: 11c, Robert Morrow, United States, 100 & 200 meter dash. 16c, Chris Brasher, England, steeplechase. 17c, A. Ferreira Da Silva, Brazil, hop, step and jump.

1957, July 18 **Photo.** ***Perf. 13½***

Flags in National Colors

C100	A118	11c yel grn & dk bl	10	10
C101	A118	16c lil & dk bl	15	15
C102	A118	17c brn & bl grn	15	15

1956 Olympic winners. Exist imperf.

See note on miniature sheets following No. 483.

Types of Regular Issue, 1957.

Olympic Winners and Flags: 11c, Hans Winkler, Germany, individual jumping. 16c, Alfred Oerter, United States, discus throw. 17c, Shirley Strickland, Australia, 800 meter hurdles.

Engraved and Lithographed.

Flags in National Colors

1957, Nov. 12 ***Perf. 13½*** **Unwmkd.**

C103	A119	11c ultra	10	10
C104	A120	16c rose car	15	15
C105	A119	17c claret	15	15

1956 Olympic winners. Exist imperf.

Miniature sheets of 3 exist, perf. and imperf., containing one each of Nos. C103–C105. Sheets have no marginal inscriptions. Price, 2 sheets, perf. and imperf., $5.50.

Type of Regular Issue, 1958.

Olympic Winners and Flags: 11c, Charles Jenkins, 400 & 800 meter run, and Thomas Courtney, 1,600 meter relay, United States. 16c, Field hockey team, India. 17c, Yachting team, Sweden.

Photogravure.

1958, Oct. 30 ***Perf. 13½*** **Unwmkd.**

Flags in National Colors

C106	A125	11c bl, ol & brn	10	10
C107	A125	16c lt grn, org & dk bl	15	15
C108	A125	17c ver, bl & yel	15	15

1956 Olympic winners. Exist imperf.

Miniature sheets of 3 exist, perf. and imperf., containing one each of Nos. C106–C108. Size: 140x78½mm. Price, 2 sheets, perf. and imperf., $3.

Fair Type of Regular Issue, 1958.

1958, Dec. 9 **Litho.** ***Perf. 12½***

C109	A127	9c gray	30	2
C110	A127	25c lt vio	75	4
a.		Souvenir sheet of 3, imperf.	2.25	1.7

No. C110a contains one each of Nos. C109 - C110 and 507 and measures 137x72½mm. Black marginal inscription.

Issued for the Universal and International Exposition at Brussels.

Polo Type of Regular Issue, 1959

Design: 11c, Dominican polo team.

1959, May 15 ***Perf. 12***

C111	A130	11c orange	45	4

Jamaica-Dominican Republic polo match at Ciudad Trujillo.

"San Cristobal" Plane
AP42

Lithographed.

1960, Feb. 25 ***Perf. 11½*** **Unwmkd.**

C112	AP42	13c org, bl, grn & gray	45	25

Dominican Civil Aviation.

Children and WRY Emblem
AP43

1960, Apr. 7 ***Perf. 12½***

C113	AP43	10c plum, gray & grn	55	45
C114	AP43	13c gray & grn	65	55

Issued to publicize World Refugee Year, July 1, 1959–June 30, 1960.

Olympic Type of Regular Issue.

Olympic Winners: 11c, Pat McCormick, U.S.A., diving. 16c, Mithat Bayrack, Turkey, welterweight wrestling. 17c, Ursula Happe, Germany, 200 meter breast stroke.

Photogravure

1960, Sept. 14 ***Perf. 13½***

Flags in National Colors

C115	A136	11c bl, gray & brn	10	10
C116	A136	16c red, brn & ol	15	15
C117	A136	17c blk, bl & ocher	15	15

Issued to commemorate the 17th Olympic Games, Rome, Aug. 25–Sept. 11. Exist imperf.

Miniature sheets of 3 exist, perf. and imperf., containing one each of Nos. C115–C117, with no marginal inscription. Size: 160x76mm. Price, 2 sheets, perf. and imperf., $3.75.

Coffee-Cacao Type of Regular Issue, 1961

1961, Dec. 30 **Litho.** ***Perf. 12½***

C118	A140	13c org ver	40	40
C119	A140	33c brt yel	85	85

Exist imperf.

Anti-Malaria Type of Regular Issue, 1962

1962, Apr. 29 ***Perf. 12*** **Unwmkd.**

C120	A141	13c pink & red	35	30

C121 A141 33c org & dp org 75 75

Issued for the World Health Organization drive to eradicate malaria.

Type of Regular Issue, 1962.

Designs: 13c, Broken fetters and laurel. 50c, Flag, torch and inscription.

1962, May 30 ***Perf. 12½***

C122 A142 13c brn, yel, ol, ultra & red 40 30
C123 A142 50c rose lil, ultra & red 1.50 1.00

First anniversary, end of Trujillo era. No. C122 exists imperf.

UPAE Type of Regular Issue, 1962

1962, Oct. 23 ***Perf. 12½***

C124 A146 13c brt bl 50 30
C125 A146 22c dl red brn 50 50

Issued to commemorate the 50th anniversary of the founding of the Postal Union of the Americas and Spain, UPAE. Exist imperf.

Nouel Type of Regular Issue, 1962

Design: Frame altered with rosary and cross surrounding portrait.

1962, Dec. 18

C126 A147 13c bl & pale bl 50 30
C127 A147 25c vio & pale vio 75 70
a. Souv. sheet 50 50

Birth centenary of Archbishop Adolfo Alejandro Nouel, president of Republic in 1911. Exist imperf.

No. C127a contains one each of Nos. C126–C127 imperf. Pale violet margin with blue inscription. Size: 153x93mm.

Sanchez, Duarte, Mella
AP44

1963, July 7 Litho. ***Perf. 11½x12***

C128 AP44 15c orange 40 30

Issued to commemorate the 120th anniversary of separation from Haiti.

World Map
AP45

1963, Oct. 25 ***Perf. 12½*** **Unwmkd.**

C129 AP45 10c gray & car 40 35

Centenary of International Red Cross. Exists imperf.

Human Rights Type of Regular Issue, 1963

1963, Dec. 10 **Lithographed**

C130 A152 7c fawn & red brn 30 25
C131 A152 10c lt bl & bl 35 25

15th anniversary, Universal Declaration of Human Rights. Exist imperf.

Ramses II Battling the Hittites (from Abu Simbel)
AP46

1964, March 8 ***Perf. 12½***

C132 AP46 10c brt vio 35 25
C133 AP46 13c yellow 40 35

UNESCO world campaign to save historic monuments in Nubia. Exist imperf.

Striated Woodpecker—AP47

1964, June 8 **Lithographed**

C134 AP47 10c multi 40 30

Type of Space Issue, 1964

Designs: 7c, Rocket leaving earth. 10c, Space capsule orbiting earth.

1964, July 28 ***Perf. 12½*** **Unwmkd.**

C135 A156 7c brt grn 40 25
C136 A156 10c vio bl 50 40
a. Souv. sheet 5.00 5.00

Issued to commemorate the conquest of space.

No. C136a contains 7c and 10c stamps similar to Nos. C135–C136 with gray border, violet blue inscription and simulated perforation. Size: 149x82mm.

Pres. John F. Kennedy
AP48

1964, Nov. 22 ***Perf. 11½***

C137 AP48 10c buff & dk brn 60 40

Issued in memory of President John F. Kennedy (1917–63). Sheets of 10 (5x2) with brown marginal inscription and date and sheets of 50.

U.P.U. Type of Regular Issue

1964, Dec. 5 Litho. ***Perf. 12½***

C138 A157 7c blue 20 22

Issued to commemorate the 15th Universal Postal Union Congress, Vienna, Austria, May–June, 1964.

ICY Type of Regular Issue, 1965

1965, Feb. 16 ***Perf. 12½*** **Unwmkd.**

C139 A158 10c lil & vio 35 30

Issued to publicize the United Nations International Cooperation Year.

Basilica of Our Lady of Altagracia
AP49

1965, Mar. 18 ***Perf. 12½*** **Unwmkd.**

C140 AP49 10c multi 50 35

Issued to commemorate the Fourth Mariological Congress and the Eleventh International Marian Congress.

Abraham Lincoln
AP50

1965, Apr. 15 Litho. ***Perf. 12½***

C141 AP50 17c brt bl 50 40

Issued to commemorate the centenary of the death of Abraham Lincoln.

Stamp Centenary Type of Regular Issue, 1965

Design: Stamp of 1865, (No. 2).

1965, Dec. 28 Litho. ***Perf. 12½***

C142 A161 7c vio, lt grn & blk 35 30
C143 A161 10c yel, lt grn & blk 40 35

Issued to commemorate the centenary of the first Dominican postage stamps.

ITU Emblem, Old and New Communication Equipment
AP51

1966, Apr. 6 Litho. ***Perf. 12½***

C144 AP51 28c pink & car 1.00 80
C145 AP51 45c brt grn & grn 1.50 1.50

Issued to commemorate the centenary (in 1965) of the International Telecommunication Union.

Butterfly Type of Regular Issue

1966, Nov. 8 Litho. ***Perf. 12½***

Various Butterflies in Natural Colors
Size: 35x24mm.

C146 A164 10c lt vio & vio 50 30
C147 A164 50c org & dp org 2.00 1.25
C148 A164 75c pink & rose red 1.00 1.00

Altar Type of Regular Issue

1967, Jan. 18 Litho. ***Perf. 11½***

C149 A165 7c lt ol grn 20 15
C150 A165 10c lilac 25 20
C151 A165 20c yel brn 45 35

Chess Type of Regular Issue

Design: 10c, Pawn and Bishop.

1967, June 23 Litho. ***Perf. 12½***

C152 A167 10c ol, lt ol & blk 60 35
a. Souv. sheet 1.25 1.25

Issued to commemorate the 5th Central American Chess Championships, Santo Domingo. No. C152a contains 2 imperf. stamps similar to Nos. 636 and C152. Gray chessboard design in margin with map of Dominican Republic and black inscription. Size: 117x76mm.

Alliance for Progress Type of Regular Issue

1967, Sept. 16 Litho. ***Perf. 12½***

C153 A168 8c gray 30 30
C154 A168 10c blue 28 18

Alliance for Progress, 6th anniversary.

Cornucopia and Emblem
AP52

Latin American Flags
AP53

1967, Oct. 7

C155 AP52 12c multi 35 25

Issued to commemorate the 25th anniversary of the Inter-American Agriculture Institute.

Satellite Type of Regular Issue

1968, June 15 Typo. ***Perf. 12***

C156 A170 10c dp bl & multi 40 30
C157 A170 15c pur & multi 60 45

World Meteorological Day, Mar. 23.

Boxing Type of Regular Issue

Designs: Two views of boxing match.

1968, June 29

C158 A171 7c org yel & grn 25 25
C159 A171 10c gray & bl 35 20

See note after No. 641.

Lions Type of Regular Issue

1968, Aug. 9 Litho. ***Perf. 11½***

C160 A172 10c ultra & multi 35 25

Issued to commemorate the 50th anniversary (in 1967) of Lions International.

Olympic Type of Regular Issue

Designs (Olympic Emblem and): 10c, Weight lifting. 33c, Pistol shooting.

1968, Nov. 12 Litho. ***Perf. 11½***

C161 A173 10c buff & multi 35 35
C162 A173 33c pink & multi 1.10 1.00

Issued to commemorate the 19th Olympic Games, Mexico City, Oct. 12–27.

1969, Jan. 25 Litho. ***Perf. 12½***

C163 AP53 10c pink & multi 30 18

Issued to publicize the 7th Inter-American Savings and Loan Conference, Santo Domingo, Jan. 25–31.

Taino Art Type of Regular Issue

Taino Art: 7c, Various spatulas with human heads (vert.). 10c, Female torso forming drinking vessel. 20c, Vase with human head (vert.).

1969, Jan. 31 Litho. ***Perf. 12½***

C164 A175 7c lt bl, bl & lem 20 15
C165 A175 10c pink, ver & brn 35 25
C166 A175 20c yel, org & brn 50 40

COTAL Type of Regular Issue

Design: 10c, Airport of the Americas and COTAL emblem.

1969, May 25 Litho. ***Perf. 12½***

C167 A178 10c brn & pale fawn 30 20

See note after No. 655.

ILO Type of Regular Issue

1969, June 27 Litho. ***Perf. 12½***

C168 A179 10c rose, red & blk 30 18

Issued to commemorate the 50th anniversary of the International Labor Organization.

Baseball Type of Regular Issue

Designs: 7c, Bleachers, Tetelo Vargas Stadium (horiz.). 10c, Batter, catcher and umpire. 1p, Quisqueya Stadium (horiz.).

1969, Aug. 15 Litho. ***Perf. 12½***

Size: 43x30mm. (7c, 1p);
21x31mm. (10c).

C169 A180 7c mag & org 40 30
C170 A180 10c mar & rose red 60 40
C171 A180 1p vio bl & brn 3.50 2.25

Issued to publicize the 17th World Amateur Baseball Championships.

Electrification Types of Regular Issue

Design: No. C172, Rio Haina steam plant. No. C173, Valdesa Dam.

1969 Lithographed ***Perf. 12***

C172 A181 10c org ver 30 15
C173 A182 10c multi 35 20

Issued to publicize the national electrification plan.

Issue dates: No C172, Sept. 15; No. C173, Oct. 15.

Duarte Type of Regular Issue

1970, Jan. 26 Litho. ***Perf. 12***

C174 A183 10c brn & dk brn 30 18

Issued for Duarte Day in memory of Juan Pablo Duarte (1813–1876), liberator.

Census Type of Regular Issue

Design: 10c, Buildings and census emblem.

1970, Feb. 6 ***Perf. 11***

C175 A184 10c lt bl & multi 35 25

Issued to publicize the 1970 census.

Sculpture Type of Regular Issue

Design: 10c, The Prisoner, by Abelardo Rodriguez Urdaneta (vert.).

1970, Feb. 20 Litho. ***Perf. 12½***

C176 A186 10c bluish gray 40 25

Issued to honor Abelardo Rodriguez Urdaneta, sculptor.

Masonic Type of Regular Issue

1970, Mar. 2

C177 A187 10c brown 25 18

The 8th Inter-American Masonic Conference, Santo Domingo, Mar. 1–7.

Satellite Type of Regular Issue

1970, May 25 Litho. ***Perf. 12½***

C178 A188 7c bl & gray 30 20

World Telecommunications Day.

U.P.U. Type of Regular Issue

1970, June 5 ***Perf. 11***

C179 A189 10c yel & brn 25 18

Inauguration of new Universal Postal Union headquarters, Bern.

Education Year Type of Regular Issue

1970, June 26 Litho. ***Perf. 12½***

C180 A190 15c brt pink 35 25

International Education Year, 1970.

Dancers

AP54

Album, Globe and Emblem

AP55

Design: 10c, U.N. emblem and wheel.

1970, Oct. 12 Litho. ***Perf. 12½***

C181 AP54 7c bl & multi 30 15
C182 AP54 10c pink & multi 30 18

Issued to publicize the First World Exhibition of Books and Culture Festival, Santo Domingo, Oct. 11–Dec. 11.

1970, Oct. 26 Litho. ***Perf. 11***

C183 AP55 10c multi 40 25

Issued to publicize EXFILCA 70, 2nd Interamerican Philatelic Exhibition, Caracas, Venezuela, Nov. 27–Dec. 6.

Basilica of Our Lady of Altagracia

AP56

1971, Jan. 20 Litho. ***Perf. 12½***

C184 AP56 17c multi 65 35

Inauguration of the Basilica of Our Lady of Altagracia.

Map of Dominican Republic, CARE Package

AP57

1971, May 28 Litho. ***Perf. 12½***

C185 AP57 10c bl & grn 25 18

25th anniversary of CARE, a U.S.-Canadian Cooperative for American Relief Everywhere.

Sports Type of Regular Issue

Design: 7c, Volleyball.

1971, Sept. 10 ***Perf. 11***

C186 A195 7c lil & gray 30 15

2nd National Games.

Animal Type of Regular Issue

Design: 25c, Cock and grain.

1971, Sept. 29 ***Perf. 12½***

C187 A196 25c blk & multi 65 50

6th National agriculture and livestock census.

Independence Type of Regular Issue

Design: 10c, Dominican-Colombian flag of 1821.

1971, Dec. 1 ***Perf. 11***

C188 A197 10c vio bl, yel & red 35 18

Sesquicentennial of first national independence.

Christmas Type of Regular Issue

Design: 10c, Bell, 1493.

1971, Dec. 10 ***Perf. 12½***

C189 A198 10c red, grn & yel 30 18

Christmas 1971.

UNICEF Type of Regular Issue

Design: 15c, UNICEF emblem and child on beach.

1971, Dec. 14 ***Perf. 11***

C190 A199 15c multi 50 40

25th anniversary of the United Nations International Children's Fund (UNICEF).

Book Year Type of Regular Issue

1972, Jan. 25 Litho. ***Perf. 12½***

C191 A200 12c lil, dk bl & red 25 20

International Book Year 1972.

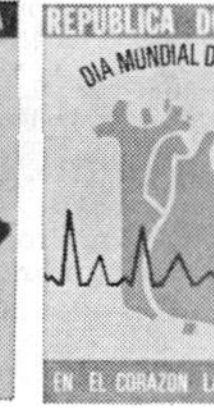

Magnifying Glass over Peru on Map of Americas

AP58

REPUBLICA DOMINICANA
DIA MUNDIAL DE LA SALUD
CORREO AEREO
7c
EN EL CORAZON LATE LA SALUD

"Your Heart is your Health"

AP59

1972, Mar. 7 Litho. ***Perf. 12***

C192 AP58 10c bl & multi 50 30

EXFILIMA '71, 3rd Inter-American Philatelic Exposition, Lima, Peru, Nov. 6–14, 1971.

1972, Apr. 27 Litho. ***Perf. 11***

C193 AP59 7c red & multi 20 12

World Health Day.

Taino Art Type of 1972

Taino Art: 8c, Ritual vessel showing human figures. 10c, Trumpet (shell). 25c, Carved vomiting spoons. All horiz.

1972, May 10 Litho. ***Perf. 11***

C194 A201 8c multi 15 15
C195 A201 10c lt bl & multi 40 18
C196 A201 25c multi 75 40

Telecommunications Type of Regular Issue

1972, May 17 ***Perf. 12½***

C197 A202 21c yel & multi 30 30

4th World Telecommunications Day.

Exhibition Type of Regular Issue

1972, June 3

C198 A203 33c org & multi 1.00 50

First National Philatelic Exhibition, Santo Domingo, June 3–17.

Olympic Type of Regular Issue.

Design: 33c, Running.

1972, Aug. 25 Litho. ***Perf. 12½***

C199 A204 33c yel & multi 1.00 60

20th Olympic Games, Munich, Aug. 26–Sept. 11.

Club Type of Regular Issue

1972, Sept. 29 Litho. ***Perf. 10½***

C200 A205 20c bl & multi 55 30

50th anniversary of the Club Activo 20–30 Internacional.

Morel Type of Regular Issue

1972, Oct. 20 Litho. ***Perf. 12½***

C201 A206 10c multi 25 15

Emilio A. Morel (1884–1958), poet and journalist.

Bank Type of Regular Issue

Design: 25c, Silver coin, 1947, and entrance to the Mint.

1972, Oct. 23

C202 A207 25c ocher & multi 75 35

25th anniversary of the Central Bank.

"La Navidad" Fortress, 1492

AP60

1972, Nov. 21 Litho. ***Perf. 12½***

C203 AP60 10c multi 30 12

Christmas 1972.

Sports Type of Regular Issue

Designs: Various sports.

1973, Mar. 30 Litho. ***Perf. 13½x13***

C204	A212	8c blk & lt bl, block of 4	1.50	1.50
a.		Upper left	35	35
b.		Upper right	35	35
c.		Lower left	35	35
d.		Lower right	35	35
C205	A212	10c dk bl & lil rose, block of 4	2.00	1.75
a.		Upper left	45	40
b.		Upper right	45	30
c.		Lower left	45	40
d.		Lower right	45	40

Publicity for the 12th Central American and Caribbean Games, Santo Domingo, Summer 1974.

Easter Type 1973

Design: 10c, Belfry of Church of Our Lady of Help.

1973, Apr. 18 Litho. ***Perf. 10½***

C206 A213 10c multi 40 15

Holy Week 1973.

North and South America on Globe

AP61

1973, May 29 Litho. ***Perf. 12***

C207 AP61 7c multi 25

Pan-American Health Organization, 70th anniversary (in 1972).

WMO Type of Regular Issue

1973, Aug. 10 Litho. ***Perf. 13½x13***

C208 A214 7c grn & multi 25 1

Centenary of international meteorological cooperation.

INTERPOL Emblem Police Scientist

AP62

1973, Sept. 28 Litho. ***Perf. 10½***

C209 AP62 10c vio bl, bl & emer 30 20

50th anniversary of International Criminal Police Organization.

Handicraft Type of Regular Issue

1973, Oct. 12

Multicolored

C210 A215 7c *Sailing ship, mosaic* 21 15
C211 A215 10c *Maracas rattlesif (horiz.)* 30 20

Opening of Museum of Mankind in Santo Domingo.

Christmas Type of Regular Issue

Design: 10c, Angels adoring Christ Child.

1973, Nov. 26 Litho. ***Perf. 13½x13***

C212 A216 10c multi 35 20

Christmas 1973.

Scout Type of Regular Issue

Design: 21c, Scouts cooking and Lord Baden-Powell.

1973, Dec. 7 Litho. ***Perf. 12***

C213 A217 21c red & multi 25 25

50th anniversary of Dominican Republic Boy Scouts.

Sport Type of Regular Issue

Designs: 10c, Olympic swimming pool and diver. 25c, Olympic Stadium, soccer and discus.

1974, Feb. 25 Litho. ***Perf. 13½***

C214 A218 10c bl & multi 10 10
C215 A218 25c multi 25 25

12th Central American and Caribbean Games, Santo Domingo, 1974.

The Last Supper

AP63

1974, June 27 Litho. ***Perf. 13½***

C216 AP63 10c multi 40 20

Holy Week 1974.

Bridge Type of 1974

Design: 10c, Higuamo Bridge.

1974, July 12 ***Perf. 12***

C217 A221 10c multi 35 20

Diabetes Type of 1974

Designs (Map of Dominican Republic, Diabetics' Emblem and): 7c, Kidney. 33c, Eye and heart.

1974, Aug. 22 Litho. ***Perf. 13***

C218 A222 7c yel & multi 25 20
C219 A222 33c lt bl & multi 1.50 85

Fight against diabetes.

UPU Type of 1974

Designs (UPU Emblem and): 7c, Ships. 33c, Jet.

1974, Oct. 9 Litho. *Perf. 13½*

C220 A223 7c grn & multi 25 20
C221 A223 33c red & multi 40 40
a. Souvenir sheet of 4 75 75

Centenary of Universal Postal Union. No. C221a contains one each of Nos. 727-728 and C220-C221 forming continuous design. Red marginal inscription. Size: 120x91mm.

Golfers and Championship Emblem AP64

Design: 20c, Golfer and Golf Association emblem.

1974, Oct. 24 Litho. *Perf. 13x13½*

C222 AP64 10c grn & multi 40 30
C223 AP64 20c grn & multi 70 60

World Amateur Golf Championships.

Hand Holding Dove AP65

1974, Dec. 3 Litho. *Perf. 12*

C224 AP65 10c multi 40 20

Christmas 1974.

FAO Type of 1974

Design: 10c, Bee, beehive and barrel of honey.

1974, Dec. 5

C225 A227 10c multi 40 25

World Food Program, 10th anniversary.

Chrismon, Lamb, Candle and Palm AP66

Spain No. 1, España 75 Emblem AP67

1975, Mar. 26 Litho. *Perf. 13½*

C226 AP66 10c gold & multi 40 20

Holy Week 1975.

1975, Apr. 10

C227 AP67 12c red, yel & blk 15 15

España 75, International Philatelic Exhibition, Madrid, Apr. 4-13.

Development Bank Type of 1975

1975, May 19 Litho. *Perf. 10½x10*

C228 A230 10c rose car & multi 35 30

16th Assembly of the Governors of the International Development Bank, Santo Domingo, May 1975.

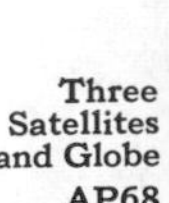

Three Satellites and Globe AP68

1975, June 21 Litho. *Perf. 13½*

C229 AP68 15c multi 55 40

Opening of first earth satellite tracking station in Dominican Republic.

Apollo Type of 1975

Design: 2p, Apollo-Soyuz link-up over earth.

1975, July 24 *Perf. 13*

Size: 42x28mm.

C230 A232 2p multi 2.00 2.00

Apollo Soyuz space test project (Russo-American cooperation), launching July 15; link-up, July 17.

Indian Chief Type of 1975

Designs: 7c, Mayobanex. 8c, Cotubanama and Juan de Esquivel. 10c, Enriquillo and Mencia.

1975, Sept. 27 Litho. *Perf. 12*

C231 A235 7c lt grn & multi 30 20
C232 A235 8c org & multi 40 30
C233 A235 10c gray & multi 45 30

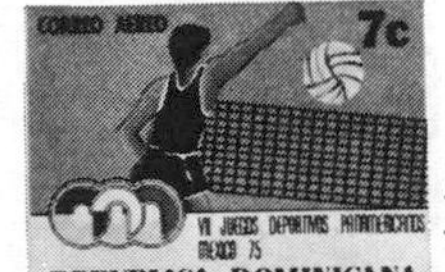

Volleyball AP69

Design: 10c, Weight lifting and Games' emblem.

1975, Oct. 24 Litho. *Perf. 12*

C234 AP69 7c bl & multi 30 20
C235 AP69 10c multi 40 30

7th Pan-American Games, Mexico City, Oct. 13-26.

Christmas Type of 1975

Design: 10c, Dove and peace message.

1975, Dec. 12 Litho. *Perf. 13x13½*

C236 A237 10c yel & multi 40 20

Christmas 1975.

Valdesia Dam—AP70

1976, Jan. 26 Litho. *Perf. 13*

C237 AP70 10c multi 30 20

Holy Week Type 1976

Design: 10c, Crucifixion, by Eliezer Castillo.

1976, Apr. 14 Litho. *Perf. 13½*

C238 A239 10c multi 40 30

Holy Week 1976.

Bicentennial Type of 1976 and

George Washington, Independence Hall AP71

Design: 10c, Hands holding maps of US and Dominican Republic.

1976, May 29 Litho. *Perf. 13½*

C239 A241 10c vio bl, grn & blk 40 25
C240 AP71 75c blk & org 75 60

American Bicentennial; No. C240 also for Interphil 76 International Philatelic Exhibition, Philadelphia, Pa., May 29-June 6.

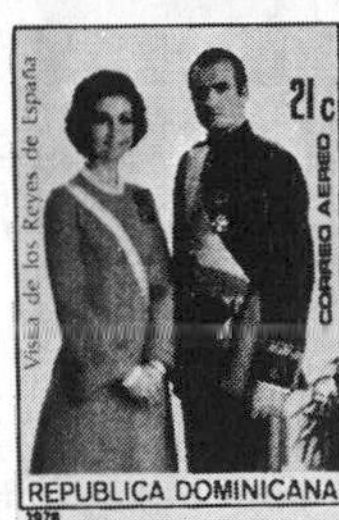

King Juan Carlos I and Queen Sofia AP72

1976, May 31

C241 AP72 21c multi 75 50

Visit of King Juan Carlos I and Queen Sofia of Spain.

Telephone Type of 1976

Design: 10c, Alexander Graham Bell and telephones, 1876 and 1976.

1976, July 15

C242 A243 10c multi 30 25

Centenary of first telephone call by Alexander Graham Bell, Mar. 10, 1876.

Duarte Types of 1976

Designs: 10c, Scroll with Duarte letter and Dominican flag. 33c, Duarte leaving for Exile, by E. Godoy.

1976, July 20 Litho. *Perf. 13½*

C243 A245 10c bl & multi 35 20

Perf. 13x13½

C244 A244 33c brn & multi 1.25 75

Juan Pablo Duarte, liberation hero, death centenary.

Fire Engine AP73

1976, Sept. 13 Litho. *Perf. 12*

C245 AP73 10c multi 30 20

Honoring firemen.

Radio Club Type of 1976

1976, Oct. 8 Lithographed *Perf. 13½*

C246 A247 10c bl & blk 40 25

Dominican Radio Club, 50th anniversary.

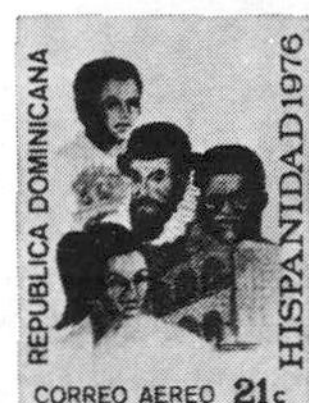

Various People AP74

1976, Oct. 15 Litho. *Perf. 13½*

C247 AP74 21c multi 30 30

Spanish heritage.

Olympic Games Type of 1976

Design (Montreal Olympic Games Emblem and): 10c, Running. 25c, Basketball.

1976, Oct. 22 *Perf. 12*

C248 A249 10c ocher & multi 30 20
C249 A249 25c grn & multi 45 30

21st Olympic Games, Montreal, Canada, July 17-Aug. 1.

Christmas Type of 1976

Design: 10c, Angel with bells.

1976, Dec. 8 Litho. *Perf. 13½*

C250 A251 10c multi 40 30

Tourist Activities AP75

Designs: 12c, Angling and hotel. 25c, Horseback riding and waterfall (vert.).

1977, Jan. 7

Size: 36x36mm.

C251 AP75 10c multi 30 20

Size: 34x25½, 25½x34mm.

C252 AP75 12c multi 15 15
C253 AP75 25c multi 80 60

Tourist publicity.

Championship Type of 1977

1977, Mar. 4 Litho. *Perf. 13½*

C254 A253 10c yel grn & multi 35 20
C255 A253 25c lt brn & multi 45 25

10th Central American and Caribbean Children's and Young People's Swimming Championships, Santo Domingo.

Holy Week Type 1977

Design: 10c, Belfry and open book.

1977, Apr. 18 Litho. *Perf. 13½x13*

C256 A254 10c multi 40 20

Holy Week 1977.

Lions Type of 1977

1977, May 6 *Perf. 13½x13*

C257 A255 7c lt grn & multi 25 15

12th annual Dominican Republic Lions Convention.

Caravel under Sail AP76

1977, July 16 Litho. *Perf. 13*

C258 AP76 10c multi 30 20

Miss Universe Contest, held in Dominican Republic.

Melon Cactus AP77

Design: 33c, Coccothrinax (tree).

1977, Aug. 19 Litho. *Perf. 12*

C259 AP77 7c multi 21 15
C260 AP77 33c multi 35 30

National Botanical Garden.

Chart and Factories
AP78

1977, Nov. 30 Litho. *Perf. 13x13½*

C261 AP78 28c multi 30 25
7th Interamerican Statistics Conference.

Animal Type of 1977

Designs (Congress Emblem and): 10c, "Dorado," red Roman stud bull. 25c, Flamingo (vert.).

1977, Dec. 29 Litho. *Perf. 13*

C262 A259 10c multi 35 20
C263 A259 25c multi 75 50
8th Pan-American Veterinary and Zootechnical Congress.

Spanish Heritage Type of 1978

Design: 21c, Window, Casa del Tostado, 16th century.

1978, Jan. 19 *Perf. 13x13½*
Size: 28x41mm.

C264 A260 21c multi 70 60

Holy Week Type, 1978

Designs: 7c, Facade, Santo Domingo Cathedral. 10c, Facade of Dominican Convent.

1978, Mar. 21 Litho. *Perf. 12*
Size: 27x36mm.

C265 A261 7c multi 30 25
C266 A261 10c multi 40 30
Holy Week 1978.

Schooner Duarte
AP79

1978, Apr. 15 Litho. *Perf. 13½*

C267 AP79 7c multi 25 14
Dominican naval forces training ship.

Cardinal Type of 1978

1978, May 5 Litho. *Perf. 13*

C268 A262 10c multi 30 25
Octavio A. Beras Rojas, first Cardinal from Dominican Republic.

Antenna
AP80

1978, May 17 Litho. *Perf. 13½*

C269 AP80 25c sil & multi 75 50
10th World Telecommunications Day.

No. C1 and Map
AP81

1978, June 6

C270 AP81 10c multi 40 20
50th anniversary of first Dominican Republic airmail stamp.

Globe, Soccer Ball, Emblem
AP82

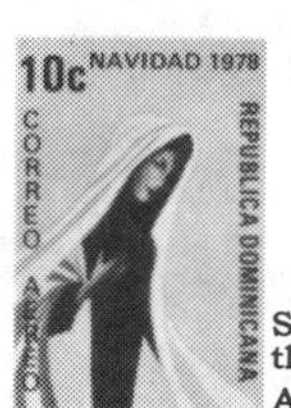

Crown, Cross and Rosary Emblem
AP83

Design: 33c, Soccer field, Argentina '78 emblem and globe.

1978, June 29

C271 AP82 12c multi 45 40
C272 AP82 33c multi 40 40
11th World Cup Soccer Championship, Argentina, June 1–25.

1978, July 11 *Perf. 13x13½*

C273 AP83 21c multi 25 25
Congregation of the Merciful Sisters of Charity, centenary.

Sports Type of 1978

Designs (Games' Emblem and): 7c, Baseball (vert.). 10c, Soccer (vert.).

1978, July 21 Litho. *Perf. 13½*

C274 A265 7c multi 25 14
C275 A265 10c multi 35 25
13th Central American and Caribbean Games, Medellin, Colombia.

Wright Brothers and Glider, 1902
AP84

Designs: 7c, Diagrams of Flyer I and jet (vert.). 13c, Diagram of air flow over wing. 45c, Flyer I over world map.

1978, Aug. 8 *Perf. 12*

C276 AP84 7c multi 30 25
C277 AP84 10c multi 45 25
C278 AP84 13c multi 70 45
C279 AP84 45c multi 45 45
75th anniversary of first powered flight.

Tourist Type of 1978

Designs: 7c, Sun and musical instruments. 10c, Sun and plane over Santo Domingo.

1978, Sept. 12 Litho. *Perf. 12*

C280 A266 7c multi 22 14
C281 A266 10c multi 30 30
Tourist publicity.

People and Globe
AP85

1978, Oct. 12 Litho. *Perf. 13½*

C282 AP85 21c multi 25 25
Spanish heritage.

Dominican Republic and UN Flags
AP86

1978, Oct. 23 *Perf. 12*

C283 AP86 33c multi 35 35
33rd anniversary of the United Nations.

Statue of the Virgin
AP87

1978, Dec. 5 Litho. *Perf. 12*

C284 AP87 10c multi 40 30
Christmas 1978.

Pope John Paul II
AP88

1979, Jan. 25 Litho. *Perf. 13½*

C285 AP88 10c multi 4.00 75
Visit of Pope John Paul II to the Dominican Republic, Jan. 25–26.

Map of Beata Island
AP89

1979, Jan. 25 *Perf. 12*

C286 AP89 10c multi 30 20
First expedition of radio amateurs to Beata Island.

Year of the Child Type, 1979

Designs (ICY Emblem and): 7c, Children reading book. 10c, Symbolic head and protective hands. 33c, Hands and jars.

1979, Feb. 26

C287 A269 7c multi 25 20
C288 A269 10c multi 35 25
C289 A269 33c multi 35 35
International Year of the Child.

Pope John Paul II Giving Benediction
AP90

Adm. Juan Bautista Cambiaso
AP91

1979, Apr. 9 Litho. *Perf. 13½*

C290 AP90 10c multi 40 30
Holy Week.

1979, Apr. 14 *Perf. 12*

C291 AP91 10c multi 30 20
135th anniversary of the Battle of Tortuguero.

Map of Dominican Rep., Album, Magnifier
AP92

1979, Apr. 18

C292 AP92 33c multi 35 30
EXFILNA, 3rd National Philatelic Exhibition, Apr. 18–22.

Flower Type of 1979

Designs: 7c, Passionflower. 10c, Isidorea pungens. 13c, Calotropis procera.

1979, May 17 Litho. *Perf. 12*

C293 A271 7c multi 15 15
C294 A271 10c multi 40 25
C295 A271 13c multi 20 20
"Dr. Rafael M. Moscoso" National Botanical Garden.

Cardiology Type, 1979

Design: 10c, Figure of man showing blood circulation (vert.).

1979, June 2 Litho. *Perf. 13½*

C296 A272 10c multi 30 20
Dominican Cardiology Institute.

Sports Type of 1979

Design: 7c, Runner and Games' emblem (vert.).

1979, June 20

C297 A273 7c multi 25 20
8th Pan American Games, Puerto Rico, June 30–July 15.

Soccer Type of 1979

Design: 10c, Tennis (vert.).

1979, Aug. 9 Litho. *Perf. 12*

C298 A273 10c multi 40 30
Third National Games.

Rowland Hill, Dominican Republic No. 1
AP93

1979, Aug. 21 *Perf. 13½*

C299 AP93 2p multi 2.00 1.50
Sir Rowland Hill (1795–1879), originator of penny postage.

Electric Light Type of 1979

Design: 10c, "100" and light bulb (horiz).

1979, Aug. 27 *Perf. 13½*

C300 A275 10c multi 40 30
Centenary of invention of electric light.

Bird Type of 1979

Birds: 7c, Phaenicophilus palmarum. 10c, Calyptophilus frugivorus tertius. 45c, Icterus dominicensis.

1979, Sept. 12 Litho. *Perf. 12*

C301 A277 7c multi 30 25
C302 A277 10c multi 40 35
C303 A277 45c multi 45 40

Lion Type of 1979

Design:10c, Melvin Jones, organization founder.

979, Nov. 13 **Litho.** ***Perf. 12***

C304	A278	10c multi	40	15

Lions International Club of Dominican Republic, 0th anniversary.

Christmas Type of 1979

Christmas 1979: 10c, Three Kings riding camels.

1979, Dec. 18 **Litho.** ***Perf. 12***

C305	A279	10c multi	40	30

Holy Week Type of 1980

Holy Week: 7c, Crucifixion. 10c, Resurrection.

980, Mar. 27 **Litho.** ***Perf. 12***

C306	A280	7c multi	25	25
C307	A280	10c multi	35	30

Navy Day—AP94

1980, Apr. 15 **Litho.** ***Perf. 13½***

C308	AP94	21c multi	25	20

Dominican Philatelic Society, 25th Anniversary—AP95

1980, Apr. 18

C309	AP95	10c multi	30	20

Gold Type of 1980

1980, July 8 **Litho.** ***Perf. 13½***

C310	A282	10c *Drag line mining*	40	25
C311	A282	33c *Mine*	70	35

Nationalization of gold mining.

Tourism Secretariat Emblem—AP96

1980, Aug. 26 **Litho.** ***Perf. 13½***

C312	AP96	10c *shown*	45	35
C313	AP96	33c *Conference emblem*	1.50	85

World Tourism Conference, Manila, Sept. 27.

Iguana Type of 1980

1980, Aug. 30 ***Perf. 12***

C314	A284	7c *American crocodile*	30	30
C315	A284	10c *Cuban rat*	40	40
C316	A284	25c *Manatee*	50	45
C317	A284	45c *Turtle*	60	55

Painting Type of 1980

1980, Sept. 23 **Litho.** ***Perf. 13½x13***

C318	A285	10c *Abstract, by Paul Guidicelli*, vert.	45	35
C319	A285	17c *Farmer, by Yoryi Morel*, vert.	70	60

Visit of Radio Amateurs to Catalina Island—AP97

1980, Oct. 3

C320	AP97	7c multi	25	25

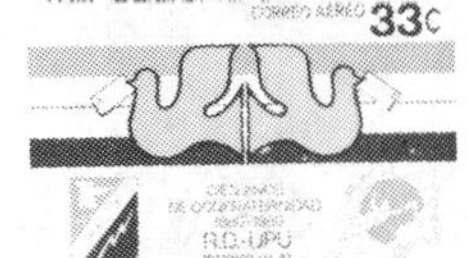

Rotary International, 75th Anniversary—AP98

1980, Oct. 23 **Litho.** ***Perf. 12***

C321	AP98	10c *Globe, emblem*, vert.	40	30
C322	AP98	33c *shown*	60	50

Carrier Pigeons, UPU Emblem—AP99

1980, Oct. 31 ***Perf. 13½***

C323	AP99	33c *shown*	35	35
C324	AP99	45c *Pigeons*, diff.	45	45
C325	AP99	50c *Pigeon, stamp*	50	50

Souvenir Sheet
Imperf.

C326	AP99	1.10p *UPU emblem*	1.25	1.25

Universal Postal Union membership centenary. No. C326 contains one stamp (48½x31mm); brown marginal inscription. Size: 102½x70mm.

Christmas Type of 1980

1980, Dec. 5 **Litho.** ***Perf. 13½***

C327	A286	10c *Holy Family*	40	30

Christmas 1980.

Salcedo Type of 1981

Design: Map and arms of Salcedo.

1981, Jan. 14 **Litho.** ***Perf. 13½***

C328	A287	10c multi	40	30

Industrial Symbols, Seminar Emblem—AP100

1981, Feb. 18 **Litho.** **Perf 13½**

C329	AP100	10c shown	40	30
C330	AP100	33c Seminar emblem	40	35

CODIA Chemical Engineering Seminar.

National Games Type of 1981

1981, Mar. 31 **Litho.** ***Perf. 13½***

C331	A289	10c Baseball	10	10

Admiral Juan Alejandro Acosta—AP101

1981, Apr. 15

C332	AP101	10c multi	30	25

Battle of Tortuguero anniversary.

13th World Telecommunications Day—AP102

1981, May 16 **Litho.** ***Perf. 12***

C333	AP102	10c multi	35	20

Heinrich von Stephan AP103

Worker in Wheelchair AP104

1981, July 15 **Litho.** ***Perf. 13½***

C334	AP103	33c tan & lt red brn	35	35

Birth sesquicentennial of Universal Postal Union founder.

1981, July 24

C335	AP104	7c Stylized people	15	10
C336	AP104	33c shown	35	35

Intl. Year of the Disabled.

EXPURIDOM '81 Intl. Stamp Show, Santo Domingo, July 31—Aug. 2 AP105

1981, July 31

C337	AP105	7c multi	25	25

Bullet Holes in Target, Competition Emblem—AP106

1981, Aug. 12

C338	AP106	10c shown	30	25
C339	AP106	15c Riflemen	45	40
C340	AP106	25c Pistol shooting	75	65

2nd World Sharpshooting Championship.

Exports—AP107

1981, Oct. 16 **Litho.** ***Perf. 12***

C341	AP107	7c Jewelry	30	25
C342	AP107	10c Handicrafts	40	35
C343	AP107	11c Fruit	15	15
C344	AP107	17c Vegetables	70	50

World Food Day—AP108

1981, Oct. 16 **Litho.** ***Perf. 13½***

C345	AP108	10c Fruits	40	30
C346	AP108	50c Vegetables	50	50

5th Natl. Games—AP109

1981, Dec. 5 **Litho.** ***Perf. 13½***

C347	AP109	10c Javelin, vert.	40	35
C348	AP109	50c Cycling	1.75	1.50

Orchids—AP110

1981, Dec. 14

C349	AP110	7c Encyclia cochleata	25	20
C350	AP110	10c Broughtonia domingensis	35	30
C351	AP110	25c Encyclia truncata	25	25
C352	AP110	75c Elleanthus capitatus	75	60

Christmas Type of 1981

1981, Dec. 23

C353	A294	10c Dove, sun	40	30

Battle of Tortuguero Anniv.—AP111

1982, Apr. 15 **Litho.** *Perf. 13½*

C354 AP111 10c Naval Academy, cadets 20 20

1982 World Cup Soccer AP112

American Air Forces Cooperation System AP113

Designs: Various soccer players.

1982, Apr. 19

C355 AP112 10c multi 35 25
C356 AP112 21c multi 25 20
C357 AP112 33c multi 35 30

1982, Apr. 12 *Perf. 12*

C358 AP113 10c multi 20 12

Scouting Year—AP114

1982, Apr. 30 **Litho.** *Perf. 13½*

C359 AP114 10c Baden-Powell, vert. 20 15
C360 AP114 15c Globe 30 25
C361 AP114 25c Baden-Powell, scout, vert. 50 30

Dancers AP115

Espamer '82 Emblem AP116

1982, June 1 **Litho.** *Perf. 13½*

C362 AP115 7c Emblem 12 12
C363 AP115 10c Cathedral, Casa del Tostado, Santo Domingo 15 12
C364 AP115 33c shown 75 50

Tourist Org. of the Americas, 25th Congress (COTAL '82), Santo Domingo.

1982, July 5

Espamer '82 Intl. Stamp Exhibition, San Juan, Oct. 12-17: Symbolic stamps. 7c, 13c horiz.

C365 AP116 7c multi 20 10
C366 AP116 13c multi 18 18
C367 AP116 50c multi 50 45

Sports Type of 1982

1982, Aug. 13 *Perf. 12*

C368 A300 10c Basketball 20 12
C369 A300 13c Boxing 15 15
C370 A300 25c Gymnast 25 25

Exist imperf.

Harbor, by Alejandro Bonilla—AP117

Paintings: 10c, Portrait of a Woman, by Leopoldo Navarro. 45c, Amelia Francasci, by Luis Desangles. 2p, Portrait, by Abelardo Rodriguez Urdaneta. 10c, 45c, 2p vert.

1982, Aug. 20 *Perf. 13*

C371 AP117 7c multi 20 15
C372 AP117 10c multi 25 20
C373 AP117 45c multi 45 30
C374 AP117 2p multi 2.00 1.75

Exist imperf.

San Pedro de Macoris Type of 1982

1982, Aug. 26

Size: 42x29mm.

C375 A301 7c Lake 25 20

35th Anniv. of Central Bank—AP118

1982, Oct. 22 **Litho.** *Perf. 13½x13*

C376 AP118 10c multi 20 15

490th Anniv. of Discovery of America—AP119

1982, Oct. 7 **Litho.** *Perf. 13½*

C377 AP119 7c Map 15 15
C378 AP119 10c Santa Maria, vert. 20 20
C379 AP119 21c Columbus, vert. 25 25

Christmas Type of 1982

1982, Dec. 8

C380 A303 10c multi 15 12

French Alliance Centenary—AP120

1983, Mar. 31 **Litho.** *Perf. 13½*

C381 AP120 33c multi 35 30

Battle of Tortuguero Anniv.—AP121

1983, Apr. 15 **Litho.** *Perf. 13½*

C382 AP121 15c Frigate Mella-451 30 20

World Communications Year—AP122

1983, May 6 **Litho.** *Perf. 13½*

C383 AP122 10c dk bl & bl 20 14

Simon Bolivar (1783-1830)—AP123

1983, July 5 **Litho.** *Perf. 13½*

C384 AP123 9c multi 10 10

9th Pan American Games, Caracas, Aug. 13-28—AP124

1983, Aug. 22 **Litho.** *Perf. 12*

C385 AP124 7c Gymnast, basketball 10 10
C386 AP124 10c Highjump, boxing 20 14
C387 AP124 15c Baseball, weight lifting, bicycling 18 18

491st Anniv. of Discovery of America—AP125

1983, Oct. 11 **Litho.** *Perf. 13½*

C388 AP125 10c Columbus' ships, map 22 1
C389 AP125 21c Santa Maria (trophy) 35 1
C390 AP125 33c Yacht Sotavento, vert. 40 2

Size: 103x103mm. ***Imperf.***

C391 AP125 50c Ship models

10th Anniv. of Latin American Civil Aviation Commission—AP126

1983, Dec. 7

C392 AP126 10c dk bl 10 6

Funeral Procession, by Juan Bautista Gomez—AP127

Designs: 15c, Meeting of Maximo Gomez and Jose Marti in Guayubin, by Enrique Garcia Godoy. 21c, St. Francis, by Angel Perdomo (vert.). 33c, Portrait of a Girl, by Adriana Billini (vert.).

1983, Dec. 26 *Perf. 13½*

C393 AP127 10c multi 10 6
C394 AP127 15c multi 15 8
C395 AP127 21c multi 22 15
C396 AP127 33c multi 32 20

Christmas 1983—AP128

1983, Dec. 13 **Litho.** *Perf. 13½*

C397 AP128 10c Bells, ornaments 12 8

AIR POST SEMI-POSTAL STAMPS

Nos. C97-C99 Surcharged in Red

Engraved and Lithographed.

1957, Feb. 8 *Perf. 11½* **Unwmkd.**

Flags in National Colors

CB1	A117	11c +2c ultra & red org	40	40
CB2	A117	16c +2c car & lt grn	55	55
CB3	A117	17c +2c blk, vio & red	60	60

The surtax was to aid Hungarian refugees. A similar 25c surcharge was applied to the souvenir sheets described in the footnote following No. C99. Price, 2 sheets, perf. and imperf., $17.50.

Nos. C100-C102 Surcharged in Red Orange

1957, Sept. 9 Photo. *Perf. 13½*

Flags in National Colors

CB4	A118	11c +2c yel grn & dk bl	70	65
CB5	A118	16c +2c lil & dk bl	85	85
CB6	A118	17c +2c brn & bl grn	95	95

See note after No. B10.

A similar 5c surcharge was applied to the miniature sheets described in the footnote following No. 483. Price, 4 sheets, Perf. & imperf., medal and flag, $40.

Types of Olympic Air Post Stamps, 1957, Surcharged in Carmine

+2¢ +2¢

REFUGIADOS REFUGIADOS

a b

Engraved and Lithographed

1958, May 26 *Perf. 13½*

Flags in National Colors

Pink Paper

CB7	A119(a)	11c +2c ultra	40	40
CB8	A119(b)	11c +2c ultra	40	40
CB9	A120(a)	16c +2c rose car	50	50
CB10	A120(b)	16c +2c rose car	50	50
CB11	A119(a)	17c +2c cl	60	60
CB12	A119(b)	17c +2c cl	60	60
		Nos. CB7-CB12 (6)	3.00	3.00

The surtax was for the United Nations Relief and Works Agency for Palestine Refugees.

A similar 5c surcharge, plus marginal United Nations emblem and "UNRWA," was applied to the miniature sheets described in the footnote following No. C105. Price, 4 sheets, perf. and imperf., $30.

Nos. C106-C108 Surcharged

Photogravure.

1959, Apr. 13 *Perf. 13½* **Unwmkd.**

Flags in National Colors

CB13	A125	11c +2c bl, ol & brn	75	75
CB14	A125	16c +2c lt grn, org & dk bl	1.00	1.00
CB15	A125	17c +2c ver bl & yel	1.50	1.50

Issued for the International Geophysical Year.

A similar 5c surcharge was applied to the miniature sheets described in the footnote following No. C108. Price, 2 sheets, perf. and imperf., $25.

Type of Regular Issue 1957 Surcharged in Red

Engraved and Lithographed

1959, Sept. 10 *Imperf.*

Flags in National Colors

CB16	A117	11c +2c ultra & red org	60	60
CB17	A117	16c +2c car & lt grn	70	70
CB18	A117	17c +2c blk, vio & red	75	75

Issued for the 3rd Pan American Games, Chicago, Aug. 27-Sept. 7, 1959.

World Refugee Year Issue.

Nos. C113-C114 Surcharged in Red

1960, Apr. 7 Litho. *Perf. 12½*

CB19	AP43	10c +5c plum, gray & grn	15	15
CB20	AP43	13c +5c gray & grn	20	20

For souvenir sheets see note after No. B33.

Nos. C115-C117 Surcharged: "XV ANIVERSARIO DE LA UNESCO +2c"

Photogravure

1962, Jan. 8 *Perf. 13½* **Unwmkd.**

Flags in National Colors

CB21	A136	11c +2c bl, gray & brn	35	35
CB22	A136	16c +2c red, brn & ol	50	50
CB23	A136	17c +2c blk, bl & ocher	55	55

See note after No. B38.

A similar 5c surcharge was applied to the miniature sheets described in the footnote following No. C117. Price, 2 sheets, perf. and imperf., $7.50.

Anti-Malaria Type of Regular Issue, 1962.

1962, Apr. 29 Litho. *Perf. 12*

CB24	A141	13c +2c pink & red	15	15
CB25	A141	33c +2c org & dp org	35	35

Issued for the World Health Organization drive to eradicate malaria. Souvenir sheets exist, perf. and imperf. containing one each of Nos. B39-B40, CB24-CB25 and a 25c+2c pale green and yellow green. Dark brown marginal inscription. Size: 169x102mm.

Nos. C132-C133 Surcharged

1964, March 8

CB26	AP46	10c +2c brt vio	15	15
CB27	AP46	13c +2c yel	15	15

Issued to publicize the UNESCO world campaign to save historic monuments in Nubia.

Nos. C146-C148 Surcharged Like Semi-Postal Issue B47-B51

1966, Dec. 9 Litho. *Perf. 12½*

Size: 35x24mm.

CB28	A164	10c +5c multi	15	15
CB29	A164	50c +10c multi	60	60
CB30	A164	75c +10c multi	85	85

Surtax for victims of hurricane Inez.

AIR POST OFFICIAL STAMPS.

OAP1

Typographed.

Blue Overprint.

1930, Dec. 3 *Perf. 12* **Unwmkd.**

CO1	OAP1	10c lt bl	17.50	15.00
a.		Pair, one without overprint	1,500.	
CO2	OAP1	20c orange	17.50	15.00

SPECIAL DELIVERY STAMPS.

Biplane

SD1

Lithographed.

1920, Apr. *Perf. 11½.* **Unwmkd.**

E1	SD1	10c dp ultra	9.00	2.00
a.		Imperf., pair		

Special Delivery Messenger

SD2

1925

E2	SD2	10c dk bl	22.50	6.00

SD3

1927

E3	SD3	10c red brn	9.00	2.00
a.		"E EXPRESO" at top	90.00	90.00

Type of 1927.

Redrawn.

1941

E4	SD3	10c yel grn	3.50	1.50
E5	SD3	10c dk bl grn	2.25	85

The redrawn design differs slightly from SD3.

Issue dates: E4, Mar. 27; E5, Aug. 7.

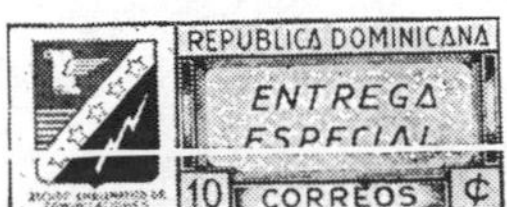

Emblem of Communications

SD4

1945, Sept. 1 *Perf. 12*

E6	SD4	10c rose car, car & dk bl	75	30

1950 Lithographed. **Unwmkd.**

E7	SD5	10c multi	75	30

Exists imperf.

Modern Communications System

SD6

1956, Aug. 18 *Perf. 11½*

E8	SD6	25c green	1.50	50

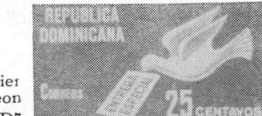

Carrier Pigeon

SD7

1967 Lithographed *Perf. 11½*

E9	SD7	25c lt bl	90	40

Carrier Pigeon, Globe

SD8

1978, Aug. 2 Litho. *Perf. 13½*

E10	SD8	25c multi	75	50

Messenger and Plane—SD9

1979, Nov. 30 *Perf. 13½*

E11	SD9	25c multi	25	25

INSURED LETTER STAMPS.

PRIMA
VALORES DECLARADOS
SERVICIO INTERIOR
8
CENTAVOS

Merino Issue of 1933 Surcharged in Red or Black

1935, Feb. 1 *Perf. 14.* Unwmkd.

G1	A35	8c on 7c ultra	80	25
a.		Invtd. surcharge	25.00	
G2	A34	15c on 10c org yel	70	20
a.		Invtd. surcharge	25.00	
G3	A35	30c on 8c dk grn	2.75	1.25
G4	A35	45c on 20c car rose (Bk)	4.00	1.75
G5	A36	70c on 50c lem	8.50	1.50
		Nos. G1-G5 (5)	16.75	4.95

PRIMA
VALORES DECLARADOS
SERVICIO INTERIOR
8
CENTAVOS

Merino Issue of 1933 Surcharged in Red

1940

G6	A35	8c on ½c lt vio	3.50	3.00
G7	A35	8c on 7c ultra	3.50	3.00

Coat of Arms
IL1

1940–45 Lithographed. *Perf. 11½*

Arms in Black

G8	IL1	8c brn red	1.00	10
a.		8c dk red, no shading on inner frame	1.75	12
G9	IL1	15c dp org ('45)	1.50	20
G10	IL1	30c dk grn ('41)	2.50	20
a.		30c yel grn	2.50	20
G11	IL1	45c ultra ('44)	2.50	50
G12	IL1	70c ol brn ('44)	3.00	45
		Nos. G8-G12 (5)	10.50	1.45

Redrawn Type of 1940-45.

1952–53 Arms in Black.

G13	IL1	8c car lake ('53)	1.25	60
G14	IL1	15c red org ('53)	2.50	1.00
G15	IL1	70c dp brn car	7.00	2.00

Larger and bolder numerals on 8c and 15c. Smaller and bolder "70." There are many other minor differences in the design.

1954 Type of 1940-45

Arms in Black, 15x16mm.

G16	IL1	10c carmine	1.00	25

Coat of Arms
IL2

Lithographed.

1955–69 *Perf. 11½* Unwmkd.

Arms in Black, 13½x11½mm.

G17	IL2	10c car rose	50	12
G18	IL2	15c red org ('56)	2.75	1.75
G19	IL2	20c red org ('58)	1.00	50
a.		20c org ('69)	1.25	45
b.		20c org, retouched ('69)	3.25	1.75
G20	IL2	30c dk grn ('55)	2.00	45
G21	IL2	40c dk grn ('58)	2.50	1.25
a.		40c lt yel grn ('62)	2.00	75
G22	IL2	45c ultra ('56)	4.50	2.00
G23	IL2	70c dp brn car ('56)	4.50	2.50
		Nos. G17-G23 (7)	17.75	8.57

On No. G19b the horizontal shading lines of shield are omitted.

Type of 1940–45
Second Redrawing

1963 *Perf. 12½*

Arms in Black, 17x16mm.

G24	IL1	10c red org	1.50	40
G25	IL1	20c orange	1.75	75

Third Redrawing

1966 Lithographed *Perf. 12½*

Arms in Black, 14x14mm.

G26	IL1	10c violet	60	30
G27	IL1	40c orange	2.25	1.50

Type of 1955–62

1968 Lithographed *Perf. 11½*

Arms in Black, 13½x11½mm.

G28	IL2	20c red	1.75	1.25
G29	IL2	60c yellow	1.00	1.00

1973–76 Lithographed *Perf. 12½*

Arms in Black, 11x11mm.

G30	IL2	10c car rose ('76)	50	30
G31	IL2	20c yellow	1.75	1.50
G32	IL2	20c org ('76)	1.50	70
G33	IL2	40c yel grn	2.75	1.75
a.		40c grn ('76)	3.00	1.75
G34	IL2	70c blue	1.00	1.00

1973 *Perf. 11½*

Arms in Black, 13½x11½mm.

G35	IL2	10c dk vio	1.50	40

1978, Aug. 9 *Perf. 10½*

Arms in Black, 11x11mm.

G36	IL2	10c rose mag	60	25
G37	IL2	40c brt grn	1.75	1.00

IL3

1982-83 Litho. *Perf. 10½*

Arms in Black.

G38	IL3	10c dp mag	20	5
G39	IL3	20c dp org	40	28
G40	IL3	40c bluish grn	80	54

IL4

1986 Litho. *Perf. 10½*

Arms in Black.

G41	IL4	20c brt rose lil	40	28
G42	IL4	60c orange	1.20	80
G43	IL4	1p lt bl	2.00	1.35
G44	IL4	1.25p pink	2.50	1.65
G45	IL4	1.50p vermilion	3.00	2.00
G46	IL4	3p lt grn	6.00	4.00
G47	IL4	3.50p ol bis	7.00	4.65
G48	IL4	4p yellow	8.00	5.35
G49	IL4	4.50p lt bl grn	9.00	6.00
G50	IL4	5p brn ol	10.00	6.75
G51	IL4	6p gray	12.00	8.00
G52	IL4	6.50p lt ultra	13.00	8.65
		Nos. G41-G52 (12)	74.10	49.48

POSTAGE DUE STAMPS.

Numeral of Value
D1

Typographed.

1901 *Perf. 14.* Unwmkd.

J1	D1	2 (c) ol gray	1.00	20
J2	D1	4 (c) ol gray	1.25	25
J3	D1	5 (c) ol gray	2.00	40
J4	D1	10 (c) ol gray	3.00	1.00

Wmkd. Crosses and Circles. (116)

1909

J5	D1	2 (c) ol gray	1.00	30
J6	D1	4 (c) ol gray	1.00	40
J7	D1	6 (c) ol gray	2.50	1.00
J8	D1	10 (c) ol gray	5.00	2.50

1913

J9	D1	2 (c) ol grn	60	20
J10	D1	4 (c) ol grn	70	25
J11	D1	6 (c) ol grn	85	30
J12	D1	10 (c) ol grn	1.25	50

Lithographed.

1922 *Perf. 11½.* Unwmkd.

J13	D1	1 (c) ol grn	60	60

Numeral of Value
D2 D3

1942

J14	D2	1c dk red & pale pink	20	10
J15	D2	2c dk bl & pale bl	20	15
J16	D2	4c dk grn & pale grn	20	20
J17	D2	6c brn & buff	30	25
J18	D2	8c yel org & pale yel	30	30
J19	D2	10c mag & pale pink	40	40
		Nos. J14-J19 (6)	1.60	1.40

1959

Size: 20½x25mm.

J20	D2	2c dk bl	2.00	1.50

1960–66 Lithographed *Perf. 11½*

Size: 21x25½mm.

J21	D3	1c dk car rose	1.75	1.75
J22	D3	2c dk bl ('66)	1.75	1.75
J23	D3	4c green	4.00	4.00

OFFICIAL STAMPS.

Bastion of February 27
O1

Lithographed

1902, Feb. 25 *Perf. 12* Unwmkd.

O1	O1	2c scar & blk	60	20
O2	O1	5c dk bl & blk	80	25
O3	O1	10c yel grn & blk	90	50
O4	O1	20c yel & blk	1.25	60
a.		Imperf., pair	12.50	

Bastion of February 27
O2

Columbus Lighthouse
O3

Wmkd. Crosses and Circles. (116)

Typographed

1909–12 *Perf. 13½x13, 13½x14*

O5	O2	1c bl grn & blk	20	20
O6	O2	2c scar & blk	25	25
O7	O2	5c dk bl & blk	60	30
O8	O2	10c yel grn & blk ('12)	1.25	75
O9	O2	20c org & blk ('12)	2.00	1.25
		Nos. O5-O9 (5)	4.30	2.75

The 2c and 5c are found in both perforations; 1c and 20c only perf. 13½x13; 10c only perf. 13½x14.

1928 *Perf. 12.* Unwmkd.

O10	O3	1c green	10	8
O11	O3	2c red	15	15
O12	O3	5c ultra	25	25
O13	O3	10c lt bl	35	35
O14	O3	20c orange	50	50
		Nos. O10-O14 (5)	1.35	1.33

Proposed Columbus Lighthouse
O4

1937 Lithographed. *Perf. 11½.*

O15	O4	3c dk pur	60	20
O16	O4	7c ind & bl	70	40
O17	O4	10c org yel	90	60

Proposed Columbus Lighthouse
O5

1939–41

O18	O5	1c dp grn & lt grn	10	6
O19	O5	2c crim & pale pink	12	8
O20	O5	3c pur & lt vio	15	8
O21	O5	5c dk bl & lt bl ('40)	35	18
O21A	O5	5c lt bl ('41)	1.00	30
O22	O5	7c brt bl & lt bl ('41)	40	15
O23	O5	10c yel org & pale org ('41)	60	25
O24	O5	20c brn org & buff ('41)	1.50	40
O25	O5	50c brt red lil & pale lil ('41)	3.00	1.25
		Nos. O18-O25 (9)	7.22	2.75

Type of 1939.
1950 Redrawn.

O26	O5	50c dp car & rose	2.00	1.25

The numerals "50" measure 3mm., and are close to left and right frames; numerals measure 4mm. on No. O25. There are other minor differences.

Denominations in "Centavos Oro."

1950

O27	O5	5c lt bl	30	15
O28	O5	10c yel & pale yel	60	25
O29	O5	20c dl org brn & buff	90	60

Letters of top inscription are 1½mm. high.

Type of 1939-41.
Second Redrawing.
Denominations in "Centavos Oro."

1956 *Perf. 11½* Unwmkd.

O30	O5	7c bl & lt bl	25	15
O31	O5	20c yel brn & buff	60	40
O32	O5	50c red lil & brt pink	1.50	1.00

The letters of top inscription are 2mm. high, the trees at base of monument have been redrawn, etc. On No. O32 the numerals are similar to No. O26.

POSTAL TAX STAMPS.

Santo Domingo after Hurricane
PT1

Hurricane's Effect on Capital
PT2

Lithographed.

1930, Dec. *Perf. 12.* Unwmkd.

RA1	PT1	1c grn & rose	25	15
a.		Tête Bêche pair	2.50	2.50
RA2	PT1	2c red rose	30	25
a.		Tête Bêche pair	2.50	2.00
RA3	PT2	5c ultra & rose	50	25
a.		Tête Bêche pair	3.00	3.00
RA4	PT2	10c yel & rose	60	50
a.		Tête Bêche pair	3.00	3.00

Imperf.

RA5	PT1	1c grn & rose	60	40
a.		Tête Bêche pair	2.50	2.50
RA6	PT1	2c red & rose	70	45
a.		Tête Bêche pair	2.50	2.50
RA7	PT2	5c ultra & rose	90	70
a.		Tête Bêche pair	3.00	3.00
RA8	PT2	10c yel & rose	1.25	1.00
a.		Tête Bêche pair	3.00	3.00
		Nos. RA1-RA8 (8)	5.10	3.70

Dr. Martos Sanatorium
PT3

Nurse and Child
PT4

1944, Apr. 1 Litho. *Perf. 11½*

RA9	PT3	1c dp bl, sl bl & red	35	15

1947, Apr. 1 Unwmkd.

RA10	PT4	1c dp bl, pale bl & car	35	15

Sanatorium of the Holy Help
PT5

1949, Apr. 1

RA11	PT5	1c dp bl, pale bl & car	30	15

Youth Holding Banner
PT6

"Suffer Little Children to Come Unto Me"
PT7

1950, Apr. 1 *Perf. 11½*

RA12	PT6	1c dp bl, pale bl & car	30	15

1950, Dec. 1 *Perf. 12, 12½*

Size: 22½ x 32mm.

RA13	PT7	1c lt bl & pale bl	75	15

Vertical line centering side borders merges into dots toward the bottom. See also Nos. RA13A, RA17, RA19, RA26, RA32, RA35.

The tax was for child welfare.

1951, Dec. 1 Redrawn

RA13A	PT7	1c lt bl & pale bl	2.25	25

In the redrawn stamp, the standing child, a blonde in No. RA13, is changed to a brunette; more foliage has been added above child's head and to branches showing in upper right corner. Vertical dashes in side borders.

Tuberculosis Sanatorium, Santiago—PT8

1952, Apr. 1 Litho. *Perf. 11½*

RA14	PT8	1c lt bl & car	30	15

Sword, Serpent and Crab
PT9

1953, Feb. 1 *Perf. 12.* Unwmkd.

RA15	PT9	1c carmine	40	15

The tax was for the Dominican League Against Cancer. See also Nos. RA18, RA21, RA43, RA46, RA51, RA56, RA61, RA67, RA72, RA76, RA82, RA88.

Tuberculosis Dispensary for Children—PT10

1953, Apr. 1 Litho. *Perf. 12½*

RA16 PT10 1c dp bl, pale bl & red 30 15

Jesus Type of 1950
Second Redrawing

1953, Dec. 1 *Perf. 11½*

Size: 22x31mm.

RA17 PT7 1c blue 60 15

Solid shading in sky reduced to a few scattered dots. Girl's left arm indicated. Rough white dots in side borders.

Cancer Type of 1952

1954, Oct. 1 Redrawn *Perf. 12½*

RA18 PT9 1c rose car 35 12
a. 1c red org ('58) 50 15
b. 1c car ('70) 75 25

Upper right serif of numeral "1" eliminated; diagonal line added through "C" and period removed; sword extended, placing top on a line with top of "1." Dots of background screen arranged diagonally. Many other differences.

The tax was for the Dominican League Against Cancer. No. RA18a exists imperf.

On No. RA18b background screen eliminates white outline of crab.

Jesus Type of 1950

1954, Dec. 1 Third Redrawing

Size: 23x32¾mm.

RA19 PT7 1c brt bl 40 15
a. 1c pale bl ('59) 20 10

Center completely screened. Tiny white horizontal rectangles in side borders.

Lorraine Cross as Bell Clapper PT11

1955, Apr. 1 Litho. *Perf. 11½x12*

RA20 PT11 1c blk, yel & red 25 12

Cancer Type of 1952.
Second Redrawing.

1956, Oct. 1 *Perf. 12½*

RA21 PT9 1c carmine 50 20
a. 1c red org ('64) 1.50 75

Similar to No. RA18, but dots of background screen arranged in vertical and horizontal rows. Outlines of central device, lettering and frame clearly delineated. "C" of "¢" smaller. Upper claw in solid color.

TB Dispensary Type of 1953

1954, Apr. 1 Redrawn

RA22 PT10 1c bl & red 35 15
a. Red (cross) omitted 80.00

No. RA22 has third color omitted; clouds added; bolder letters and numerals.

Angelita Trujillo PT12 — Lorraine Cross PT13

1955, Dec. 1 *Perf. 12½* Unwmkd.

RA23 PT12 1c violet 25 15

The tax was for child welfare.

1956, Apr. 1 Litho. *Perf. 11½*

RA24 PT13 1c blk, grn, lem & red 25 12

The tax was for the Anti-Tuberculosis League. Inscribed: B.C.G. (Bacillus Calmette-Guerin).

Children PT14 — Lorraine Cross PT15

1957, Apr. 1

RA25 PT14 1c red, blk, yel, grn & bl 25 12

Jesus Type of 1950
Fourth Redrawing.

1956, Dec. 1 *Perf. 12* Unwmkd.

Size: 21¾x31¼mm.

RA26 PT7 1c blue 30 12

Thin white lines around numeral boxes. Girl's bouquet touches Jesus' sleeve. Tiny white squares or rectangles in side borders. Foliage at either side of "Era de Trujillo" panel.

1958, Apr. 1 Litho. *Perf. 12½*

RA27 PT15 1c brn car & red 20 12

Type of 1958 Inscribed "1959"

1959, Apr. 1

RA28 PT15 1c brn car & red 20 12

Lorraine Cross PT16 — Lorraine Cross PT17

1960, Apr. 1 Litho. *Perf. 12*

RA29 PT16 1c bl, pale yel & red 30 20

The tax was for the Anti-Tuberculosis League.

1961, Apr. 1 *Perf. 11½* Unwmkd.

RA30 PT17 1c bl & red 15 12

The tax was for the Anti-Tuberculosis League.

Maria de los Angeles M. de Trujillo and Housing Project PT18

1961, Aug. 1 Lithographed *Perf. 12*

RA31 PT18 1c car rose 30 12

The tax was for aid to the needy. Nos. RA31—RA33 exist imperf.

Jesus Type of 1950
Fifth Redrawing

1961, Dec. 1 *Perf. 12½* Unwmkd.

RA32 PT7 1c blue 25 15

No. RA32 is similar to No. RA19, but "Era de Trujillo" has been replaced by a solid color panel.

Type of 1961 Dated "1962."

1962, Apr. 1 *Perf. 12½*

RA33 PT17 1c bl & red 15 12

The tax was for the Anti-Tuberculosis League.

Man's Chest and Lorraine Cross PT19 — Hibiscus PT20

1963, Apr. 1 *Perf. 12x11½*

RA34 PT19 1c ultra & red 25 12

Jesus Type of 1950
Sixth Redrawing

1963, Dec. 1 *Perf. 11½*

Size: 21¾x32mm.

RA35 PT7 1c blue 20 12
a. 1c dp bl ('64) 20 12

No. RA35 is similar to No. RA26, but "Era de Trujillo" panel has been omitted.

1966, Apr. 1 Litho. *Perf. 11½*

RA36 PT20 1c emer & car 20 12

The tax was for the Anti-Tuberculosis League.

Domingoa Nodosa PT21 — Civil Defense Emblem PT22

1967, Apr. 1 Litho. *Perf. 12½*

RA37 PT21 1c lil & red 20 12

The tax was for the Anti-Tuberculosis League.

1967, July 1 Litho. *Rouletted 13*

RA38 PT22 1c multi 30 18

The tax was for the Civil Defense Organization.

Boy, School and Yule Bells PT23 — Hand Holding Invalid PT24

1967, Dec. 1 Litho. *Perf. 12½*

RA39 PT23 1c rose red & pink 35 12

1968 *Perf. 11*

RA40 PT23 1c vermilion 45 18

No. RA40 has screened background; No. RA39, smooth background.

The tax was for child welfare.

See Nos. RA49A, RA52, RA57, RA62, RA68, RA73, RA77, RA81.

1968, Mar. 19 Litho. *Perf. 12½*

RA41 PT24 1c grn & yel 15 8
a. 1c ol grn & dp yel, perf. 11½x12 ('69) 15 8

The tax was for the rehabilitation of the handicapped. See Nos. RA47, RA50, RA54.

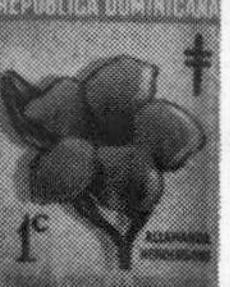

Dogbane PT25 — Schoolyard and Torch PT26

1968, Apr. 25 Litho. *Perf. 12½*

RA42 PT25 1c emer, yel & red 8 5

The tax was for the Anti-Tuberculosis League. See Nos. RA45, RA49.

Redrawn Cancer Type of 1955

1968, Oct. 1 Litho. *Perf. 12*

RA43 PT9 1c emerald 15 8

The tax was for the Dominican League against Cancer.

1969, Feb. 1 Litho. *Perf. 12½*

RA44 PT26 1c lt bl 8 5

Issued for Education Year 1969.

Flower Type of 1968

Design: No. RA45, Violets.

1969, Apr. 25 Litho. *Perf. 12½*

RA45 PT25 1c emer, lil & red 15 8

The tax was for the Anti-Tuberculosis League.

Redrawn Cancer Type of 1955

1969, Oct. 1 Litho. *Perf. 11*

RA46 PT9 1c brt rose lil 20 5

The tax was for the Dominican League against Cancer.

Invalid Type of 1968

1970, Mar. 2 *Perf. 12½*

RA47 PT24 1c blue 18 12

The tax was for the rehabilitation of the handicapped.

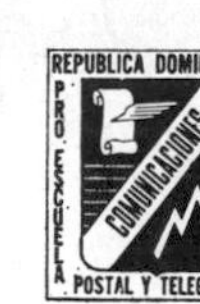

Book, Sun and Education Year Emblem PT27 — Communications Emblem PT28

1970, Feb. 6 *Perf. 11*

RA48 PT27 1c brt pink 8 5

International Education Year.

Flower Type of 1968

Design: 1c, Eleanthus capitatus; cross in upper left corner, denomination in lower right.

1970, Apr. 30 *Perf. 11*

RA49 PT25 1c emer, red & yel 15 8

Tax for Anti-Tuberculosis League.

Boy Type of 1967

1970, Dec. 1 *Perf. 12½*

RA49A PT23 1c orange 35 20

1971, Jan. 2 Litho. *Perf. 11*

Size: 17½x20½mm.

RA49B PT28 1c vio bl & red (white frame) 30 10

Tax was for Postal and Telegraph Communications School.

See Nos. RA53, RA58, RA63, RA69, RA78.

Invalid Type of 1968

1971, Mar. 1 **Litho.** ***Perf. 11***

RA50 PT24 1c brt rose lil 15 8

Tax was for rehabilitation of the handicapped.

Cancer Type of 1952 Third Redrawing

1971, Oct. 1 ***Perf. 11½***

RA51 PT9 1c dp yel grn 25 10

Background of No. RA51 appears white and design stands out. No. RA43 has greenish background and design appears faint. Numeral "1" on No. RA51 is 3½mm. high, on No. RA43 it is 3mm.

Boy Type of 1967

1971, Dec. 1 **Litho.** ***Perf. 11***

RA52 PT23 1c green 35 10

Communications Type of 1971

1972, Jan. 3 **Litho.** ***Perf. 12½***

Size: 19x22mm.

RA53 PT28 1c dk bl & red (bl frame) 20 8

Tax was for the Postal and Telegraph Communications School.

Invalid Type of 1968

1972, Mar. 1 **Litho.** ***Perf. 11½***

RA54 PT24 1c brown 15 10

Orchid PT29

1972, Apr. 2 ***Perf. 11***

RA55 PT29 1c lt grn, red & yel 25 10

Tax was for the Anti-Tuberculosis League.

Redrawn Cancer Type of 1954–58

1972, Oct. 2 ***Perf. 12½***

RA56 PT9 1c orange 18 10

Tax was for Dominican League against Cancer.

Boy Type of 1967

1972, Dec. 1 ***Perf. 12***

RA57 PT23 1c violet 25 10

Tax was for child welfare.

Communications Type of 1971

1973, Jan. 2 ***Perf. 10½***

Size: 19x22mm.

RA58 PT28 1c dk bl & red (red frame) 10 8

Tax was for Postal and Telegraph Communications School.

Invalid PT30

Hibiscus PT31

1973, Mar. 1 **Litho.** ***Perf. 12½***

Size: 21x25mm.

RA59 PT30 1c olive 15 8

Tax was for the Dominican Rehabilitation Association. See Nos. RA66, RA70, RA74, RA79, RA86.

1973, Apr. 17 **Litho.** ***Perf. 10½***

RA60 PT31 1c multi 20 10

Tax was for Anti-Tuberculosis League. Exists imperf.

Cancer Type of 1952 Redrawn and "1973" Added

1973, Oct. 1 ***Perf. 13½***

RA61 PT9 1c ol grn 15 8

Tax was for Dominican League Against Cancer.

Boy Type of 1967

1973, Dec. 1 **Litho.** ***Perf. 13x13½***

RA62 PT23 1c blue 25 15

Communications Type of 1971

1973, Nov. 3 ***Perf. 10½***

Size: 19x22mm.

RA63 PT28 1c bl & red (lt grn frame) 10 6

Tax was for Postal and Telegraph Communications School. Exists imperf.

Invalid Type of 1972

1974, Mar. 1 **Litho.** ***Perf. 10½***

Size: 22x27½mm.

RA66 PT30 1c lt ultra 25 15

See note after No. RA59.

Cancer Type of 1952 Redrawn and "1974" Added

1974, Oct. 1 ***Perf. 12***

RA67 PT9 1c orange 15 8

Tax was for Dominican League Against Cancer.

Boy Type of 1967

1974, Dec. 2 **Litho.** ***Perf. 11½***

RA68 PT23 1c dk brn & buff 15 8

Communications Type of 1971

1974, Nov. 13 ***Perf. 10½***

RA69 PT28 1c bl & red (yel frame) 15 8

Invalid Type of 1972 Dated "1975"

1975, Mar. 1 ***Perf. 13½x13***

Size: 21x32mm.

RA70 PT30 1c ol brn 15 8

Tax was for the Dominican Rehabilitation Association.

Catteeyopsis Rosea PT32

Oncidium Colochilum PT33

1975, Apr. 1 ***Perf. 12***

RA71 PT32 1c bl & multi 15 8

Tax was for Anti-Tuberculosis League.

Cancer Type of 1952 Redrawn and "1975" Added

1975, Oct. 1 **Litho.** ***Perf. 12***

RA72 PT9 1c vio bl 15 8

Tax was for Dominican League Against Cancer. Exists imperf.

Boy Type of 1967

1975, Dec. 1 **Litho.** ***Perf. 12***

RA73 PT23 1c red org 15 8

Tax was for child welfare.

Invalid Type of 1973 Dated "1976"

1976, Mar. 1 **Litho.** ***Perf. 12***

Size: 21x31mm.

RA74 PT30 1c ultra 15 8

Tax was for Dominican Rehabilitation Association.

1976, Apr. 6 ***Perf. 13x13½***

RA75 PT33 1c grn & multi 15 8

Tax was for Anti-Tuberculosis League. See No. RA80, RA84.

Cancer Type of 1952 Redrawn and "1976" Added

1976, Oct. 1 **Litho.** ***Perf. 13½***

RA76 PT9 1c green 15 8

Tax was for Dominican League Against Cancer.

Boy Type of 1967

1976, Dec. 1 **Litho.** ***Perf. 13½***

RA77 PT23 1c purple 15 8

Tax was for child welfare.

Communications Type of 1971

1977, Jan. 7 **Litho.** ***Perf. 10½***

Size: 19x22mm.

RA78 PT28 1c bl & red (lil frame) 15 8

Tax was for Postal and Telegraph Communications School.

Invalid Type of 1973 Dated "1977"

1977, Mar. 11 ***Perf. 12***

Size: 21x31mm.

RA79 PT30 1c ultra 15 8

Tax was for Dominican Rehabilitation Association.

Orchid Type of 1976 Dated "1977"

Orchid: Oncidium variegatum.

1977, Apr. 22 **Litho.** ***Perf. 13½***

RA80 PT33 1c multi 15 8

Tax was for Anti-Tuberculosis League.

Boy Type of 1967

1977, Dec. 27 **Litho.** ***Perf. 12***

RA81 PT23 1c emerald 15 8

Tax was for child welfare.

Cancer Type of 1952 Redrawn and "1977" Added

1978, Oct. 2 **Litho.** ***Perf. 13½***

RA82 PT9 1c lil rose 15 8

Tax was for Dominican League Against Cancer.

Mother, Child and Holly PT34

University Seal PT35

1978, Dec. 1 **Litho.** ***Perf. 13½***

RA83 PT34 1c green 15 8

Tax was for child welfare.

See No. RA89.

Orchid Type of 1973 Dated "1978"

Flower: Yellow alder.

1979, Apr. **Litho.** ***Perf. 13½***

RA84 PT33 1c lt bl & multi 15 8

Tax was for Anti-Tuberculosis League.

1979, Feb. 10 **Litho.** ***Perf. 13½***

RA85 PT35 2c ultra & gray 15 5

450th anniversary of University of Santo Domingo.

Invalid Type of 1973 Dated "1978"

1979, Mar. 1 **Litho.** ***Perf. 12***

RA86 PT30 1c emerald 8 5

Tax was for Dominican Rehabilitation Association.

Invalid —PT36

Turnera Ulmifolia (Marilope)—PT37

1980, Mar. 28 **Litho.** ***Perf. 13½***

RA87 PT36 1c ol & cit 8 5

Cancer Type of 1952 Redrawn and "1980" Added

1980, Oct. 1

RA88 PT9 1c vio & dk pur 8 5

Mother and Child Type of 1978

1980, Dec. 1 **Litho.** ***Perf. 13½***

RA89 PT34 1c brt bl 8 5

1981, Apr. 27 **Litho.** ***Perf. 12***

RA90 PT37 1c multi 8 5

Tax was for Anti-Tuberculosis League.

Communications Type of 1971

1981 **Litho.** ***Perf. 10½***

RA91 PT28 1c bl & red (lt bl frame) 8 5

Mother and Child Type of 1978

1982, Dec. 1 **Litho.** ***Perf. 12x12½***

RA92 PT34 1c lt bluish grn 8 5

Inscribed 1981.

Cancer Type of 1952 Redrawn and "1981" Added.

1982, Oct. 1 **Litho.** ***Perf. 13½***

RA93 PT9 1c bl & dp bl 8 5

PT38

Disabled—PT39

1983, Apr. 29 **Litho.** ***Perf. 12***

RA94 PT38 1c multi 8 5

Tax was for Red Cross.

1984, Mar. 1 **Litho.** ***Perf. 13½***

RA95 PT39 1c sky bl 8 5

Cancer Type of 1952 Redrawn and "1983" Added.

1983, Oct. 1 **Litho.** ***Perf. 13½***

RA96 PT9 1c lt bluish grn & dk grn 8 5

Mother and Child Type of 1978

1983, Dec. 1 **Litho.** ***Perf. 12***

RA97 PT34 1c lt grn 8 5

Inscribed 1983.

POSTAL TAX AIR POST STAMPS.

HABILITADO PARA
CORREO AEREO

Postal Tax Stamps Surcharged in Red or Gold

+5

1930, Dec. 3 ***Perf. 12*** **Unwmkd.**

RAC1 PT2	5c +5c blk & rose (R)	25.00	25.00
a.	Tête bêche pair	175.00	
b.	"Habilitado Para" missing	75.00	
RAC2 PT2	10c +10c blk & rose (R)	25.00	25.00
a.	Tête bêche pair	175.00	
b.	"Habilitado Para" missing	75.00	
c.	Gold surch.	225.00	225.00
d.	As "c," tête bêche pair	750.00	
e.	As "c," "Habilitado Para" missing	400.00	

Nos. RAC1–RAC2 were on sale only on Dec. 3, 1930.

RAC4 PT2	5c +5c ultra & rose (R)	10.00	10.00
a.	Tête bêche pair	75.00	
b.	Inverted surcharge	70.00	
c.	Tête bêche pair, inverted surcharge	1,000.	
d.	Pair, one without surcharge	300.00	
e.	"Habilitado Para" missing	25.00	
RAC5 PT2	10c +10c yel & rose (G)	7.50	7.50
a.	Tête bêche pair	70.00	
b.	"Habilitado Para" missing	30.00	

Imperf.

RAC6 PT2	5c +5c ultra & rose (R)	10.00	10.00
a.	Tête bêche pair	85.00	
b.	"Habilitado Para" missing	30.00	
RAC7 PT2	10c +10c yel & rose (G)	10.00	10.00
a.	Tête bêche pair	85.00	
b.	"Habilitado Para" missing	30.00	

It was obligatory to use Nos. RA1 to RA8 and RAC1 and RAC7 on all postal matter, in amounts equal to the ordinary postage.

This surtax was for the aid of sufferers from the hurricane of Sept. 3rd, 1930.

No. 261 Overprinted in Green

CORREO AEREO INTERNO

1933, Oct. 11

RAC8 A32	2c scarlet	60	45
a.	Double overprint	15.00	
b.	Pair, one without ovpt.	500.00	

By official decree a copy of this stamp, in addition to the regular postage, had to be used on every letter, etc., sent by the internal air post service.

DUTCH INDIES

(See Netherlands Indies.)

DUTCH NEW GUINEA

(See Netherlands New Guinea.)

EASTERN RUMELIA

(ēs'tērn rōō·mē'lĭ·ȧ ; -mēl'yȧ)

(South Bulgaria)

LOCATION—In southern Bulgaria

GOVT.—A former autonomous unit of the Turkish Empire.

CAPITAL—Philippopolis (Plovdiv).

In 1885 the province of Eastern Rumelia revolted against Turkish rule and united with Bulgaria, adopting the new name of South Bulgaria. This union was assured by the Treaty of Bucharest in 1886, following the war between Serbia and Bulgaria.

40 Paras = 1 Piastre

Counterfeits of all overprints are plentiful.

A1

A2

A3

Stamps of Turkey, 1876-84, Overprinted in Blue.

1880		*Perf. 13½*	Unwmkd.	
1	A1	½pi on 20pa yel grn	35.00	35.00
2	A1	2pi on 2pi yel brn		
3	A2	10pa blk & rose	40.00	
4	A2	20pa vio & grn	37.50	37.50
5	A2	1pi blk & bl		
6	A2	2pi blk & buff	75.00	75.00
7	A2	5pi red & bl	250.00	250.00
8	A3	10pa blk & red lil	25.00	

Nos. 2, 3, 5 and 8 were not placed in use.
Inverted and double overprints of all values exist.

Same, with Extra Overprint "R. O."

9	A3	10pa blk & red lil	40.00	40.00

Crescent and Turkish Inscriptions of Value
A4

1881		Typographed	*Perf. 13½*	
10	A4	5pa blk & ol	2.00	60
11	A4	10pa blk & grn	7.00	60
12	A4	20pa blk & rose	30	60
13	A4	1pi blk & bl	3.00	2.50
14	A4	5pi rose & bl	25.00	35.00

Tête bêche pairs, imperforates and all perf. 11½ copies of Nos. 10 to 14 were not placed in use, and were found only in the remainder stock. This is true also of a 10pa cliché in the 20pa plate, and of a cliché of Turkey No. 63 in the 1pi plate.

1884			*Perf. 11½, 13½*	
15	A4	5pa lil & pale lil	20	20
16	A4	10pa grn & pale grn	10	20
17	A4	20pa car & pale rose	20	
18	A4	1pi bl & pale bl	20	
19	A4	5pi brn & pale brn	150.00	

No. 17–19 were not placed in use.
Nos. 15 to 19 imperf. are from the remainder stock.

South Bulgaria.

Counterfeits of all overprints are plentiful.

Nos. 10 to 14 Overprinted in Two Types:

a

b

Type a: Four toes on each foot.
Type b: Three toes on each foot.

1885		*Perf. 13½.*	Unwmkd.	
		Blue Overprint.		
20	A4	5pa blk & ol	100.00	100.00
21	A4	10pa blk & grn	350.00	350.00
22	A4	20pa blk & rose	100.00	100.00
23	A4	1pi blk & bl	20.00	22.50
24	A4	5pi rose & bl	300.00	325.00
		Black Overprint.		
25	A4	1pi blk & bl	16.50	20.00
26	A4	5pi rose & bl	400.00	400.00

Same Overprint on Nos. 15 to 17.
Perf. 11½, 13½

		Blue Overprint.		
27	A4	5pa lil & pale lil, perf. 11½	9.00	14.00
a.		Perf. 13½	22.50	27.50
28	A4	10pa grn & pale grn	9.00	14.00
29	A4	20pa car & pale rose	80.00	90.00
		Black Overprint.		
30	A4	5pa lil & pale lil	16.00	20.00
31	A4	10pa grn & pale grn	16.00	20.00
32	A4	20pa car & pale rose	14.00	20.00

Nos. 10 to 14 Handstamped in Black in Two Types:

a

b

Type a: First letter at top circular.
Type b: First letter at top oval.

1885			*Perf. 13½*	
33	A4	5pa blk & ol	300.00	
34	A4	10pa blk & grn	300.00	
35	A4	20pa blk & rose	55.00	65.00
36	A4	1pi blk & bl	40.00	45.00
a.		On Turkey No. 63 (error)		
37	A4	5pi rose & bl	500.00	600.00

Same Handstamp in Black on Nos. 15 to 17.
Perf. 11½, 13½.

38	A4	5pa lil & pale lil, perf. 13½	11.00	11.00
a.		Perf. 11½	100.00	125.00
39	A4	10pa grn & pale grn	10.00	11.00
40	A4	20pa car & pale rose	10.00	15.00

Nos. 20 to 40 exist with inverted and double handstamps. Overprints in unlisted colors are proofs.
The stamps of South Bulgaria were superseded in 1886 by those of Bulgaria.

EASTERN SILESIA

(ēs'tērn sĭ·lē'shĭ·ȧ ; -shȧ)

LOCATION—In central Europe.

GOVT.—Former Austrian crown-land.

AREA—1,987 sq. mi.

POP.—680,422 (estimated 1920).

CAPITAL—Troppau.

After World War I, this territory was occupied by Czechoslovakia and eventually was divided between Poland and Czechoslovakia, the dividing line running through Teschen.

100 Heller = 1 Krone
100 Fennigi = 1 Marka

Plebiscite Issues.

Stamps of Czechoslovakia 1918-20, Overprinted in Black, Blue, Violet or Red — **SO 1920**

1920		*Imperf.*	Unwmkd.	
1	A2	1(h) dk brn	35	35
2	A1	3(h) red vio	12	12
3	A2	5(h) bl grn	40.00	30.00
4	A2	15(h) red	20.00	10.00
5	A1	20(h) bl grn	15	15
6	A2	25(h) dl vio	1.25	1.25
7	A1	30(h) bis (R)	25	25
8	A1	40(h) red org	25	25
9	A2	50(h) dl vio	50	50
10	A2	50(h) dk bl	1.75	1.75
11	A2	60(h) org (Bl)	75	75
12	A2	75(h) sl (R)	50	50
13	A2	80(h) ol grn (R)	50	50
14	A1	100(h) brown	70	70
15	A2	120(h) gray blk (R)	1.75	1.75
16	A1	200(h) ultra (R)	1.75	1.75
17	A2	300(h) grn (R)	2.50	2.50
18	A1	400(h) pur (R)	2.00	2.00
20	A2	500(h) red brn (Bl)	6.00	4.75
a.		Black overprint	12.00	10.00
21	A2	1000(h) vio (Bl)	16.00	10.00
a.		Black ovpt.	200.00	125.00
		Nos. 1-21 (20)	97.07	69.82

		Perf. 11½, 14		
22	A2	1(h) dk brn	5	5
23	A2	5(h) bl grn	25	25
24	A2	10(h) yel grn	15	15
a.		Imperf.	400.00	400.00
25	A2	15(h) red	15	15
26	A2	20(h) rose	35	35
a.		Imperf.	500.00	500.00
27	A2	25(h) dl vio	35	35
28	A2	30(h) red vio (Bl)	35	35
29	A2	60(h) org (Bl)	50	50
30	A1	200(h) ultra (R)	3.75	3.75
		Nos. 22-30 (9)	5.90	5.90

The letters "S. O." are the initials of "Silésie Orientale".
Forged cancellations are found on Nos. 1-30.

Overprinted — **19 SO 20**

31	A4	500(h) sl, *grysh* (C)	120.00	
32	A4	1000(h) blk brn, *brnsh* (V)	120.00	

Excellent counterfeits of this overprint exist.

Stamps of Poland, 1919, Overprinted — **S. O. 1920.**

1920			*Perf. 11½*	
41	A10	5f green	6	8
42	A10	10f red brn	6	8
43	A10	15f lt red	6	8
44	A11	25f ol grn	6	8
45	A11	50f bl grn	6	8

Overprinted **S. O. 1920.**

46	A17	1k dp grn	6	8
47	A17	1.50k brown	6	8
48	A17	2k dk bl	6	8
49	A18	2.50k dl vio	10	15
50	A19	5k sl bl	12	20
		Nos. 41-50 (10)	70	99

SPECIAL DELIVERY STAMPS.

Czechoslovakia Special Delivery Stamps Overprinted — **S O 19 20**

1920		*Imperf.*	Unwmkd.	
		Blue Overprint.		
E1	SD1	2(h) red vio, *yel*	8	8
a.		Black overprint	1.00	80
E2	SD1	5(h) yel grn, *yel*	8	10
a.		Black overprint	6.00	5.00

POSTAGE DUE STAMPS.

Czechoslovakia Postage Due Stamps Overprinted In Blue or Red — **SO 1920**

1920		*Imperf.*	Unwmkd.	
J1	D1	5(h) dp bis (Bl)	12	12
a.		Black ovpt.	55.00	45.00
J2	D1	10(h) dp bis	20	12
J3	D1	15(h) dp bis	20	12
J4	D1	20(h) dp bis	40	20
J5	D1	25(h) dp bis	40	25
J6	D1	30(h) dp bis	40	25
J7	D1	40(h) dp bis	60	50
J8	D1	50(h) dp bis	60	50
J9	D1	100(h) blk brn (R)	1.25	85
J10	D1	500(h) gray grn (R)	5.00	3.75
J11	D1	1000(h) pur (R)	9.50	8.50
		Nos. J1-J11 (11)	18.67	15.16

Forged cancellations exist.

NEWSPAPER STAMPS.

Czechoslovakia Newspaper Stamps Overprinted in Black — **SO 1920**

1920		*Imperf.*	Unwmkd.	
P1	N1	2(h) gray grn	40	40
P2	N1	6(h) red	10	10
P3	N1	10(h) dl vio	30	30
P4	N1	20(h) blue	40	40
P5	N1	30(h) gray brn	40	40
		Nos. P1-P5 (5)	1.60	1.60

ECUADOR

(ĕk'wȧ·dôr)

LOCATION — On the northwest coast of South America, bordering on the Pacific Ocean.
GOVT.—Republic.
AREA—116,270 sq. mi.
POP.—8,420,000 (est. 1984).
CAPITAL—Quito.

The Republic of Ecuador was so constituted on May 11, 1830, after the Civil War which separated the original members of the Republic of Colombia, founded by Simon Bolivar by uniting the Presidency of Quito with the Viceroyalty of New Grenada and the Captaincy of Venezuela. The Presidency of Quito became the Republic of Ecuador.

8 Reales = 1 Peso
100 Centavos = 1 Sucre (1881)

Coat of Arms
A1 A2

Typographed.
Quadrille Paper.

1865-72	**Imperf.**	**Unwmkd.**		
1	A1	1r yel ('72)	37.50	35.00
		Wove Paper		
2	A1	½r ultra	16.00	12.00
a.		½r gray bl ('67)	16.00	12.00
b.		Batonne paper ('70)	32.50	20.00
c.		Blue paper ('72)	165.00	110.00
3	A1	1r buff	25.00	15.00
a.		1r org buff	30.00	17.50
4	A1	1r yellow	17.50	12.50
a.		1r ol yel ('66)	25.00	15.00
b.		Laid paper	160.00	110.00
c.		Diagonal half used as ½r on cover		300.00
d.		Batonne paper	32.50	25.00
5	A1	1r green	250.00	55.00
a.		Diagonal half used as ½r on cover		300.00
6	A2	4r red ('66)	275.00	135.00
a.		4r red brn ('66)	275.00	135.00
b.		Arms in circle	275.00	135.00
c.		Printed on both sides	700.00	
d.		Half used as 2r on cover		1,500.

Letter paper embossed with arms of Ecuador was used in printing a number of sheets of Nos. 2, 4–6.

Papermakers' watermarks are known on No. 2 ("Bath" and crown) and No. 4 ("Rolland Freres").

On the 4r the oval holding the coat of arms is usually 13½–14mm. wide, but on about one-fifth of the stamps in the sheet it is 15–15½mm. wide, almost a circle.

The 2r, 8r and 12r, type A1, are bogus.

Proofs of the ½r, type A1, are known in black and green.

An essay of type A2 shows the condor's head facing right.

1871-72		**Blue-surface Paper**		
7	A1	½r ultra	30.00	19.00
8	A1	1r yellow	165.00	60.00

Unofficial reprints of types A1-A2 differ in color, have a different sheet makeup and lack gum. Type A1 reprints usually have a double frameline at left. All stamps on blue paper with horiz. blue lines are reprints.

Coat of Arms
A3 A4

Lithographed

1872		**White Paper**	***Perf. 11***	
9	A3	½r blue	17.50	4.00
10	A4	1r yellow	20.00	6.00
11	A3	1p rose	4.00	*12.00*

The 1r surcharged 4c is fraudulent.

Coat of Arms
A5 A6

A7 A8

A9 A10

1881, Nov. 1		**Engraved**	***Perf. 12***	
12	A5	1c yel brn	10	10
13	A6	2c lake	15	15
14	A7	5c blue	3.00	50
15	A8	10c orange	15	15
16	A9	20c gray vio	20	20
17	A10	50c bl grn	1.00	*3.00*
		Nos. 12-17 (6)	4.60	*4.10*

The 1c surcharged 3c, and 20c surcharged 5c are fraudulent.

No. 17 Surcharged in Black

DIEZ

CENTAVOS

1883, April				
18	A10	10c on 50c bl grn	25.00	20.00
a.		Double surcharge		

A12 A13

A14 A15

1887				
19	A12	1c bl grn	30	15
20	A13	2c vermilion	50	15
21	A14	5c blue	1.50	30
22	A15	80c ol grn	3.00	*7.50*

President Juan Flores
A16

1892				
23	A16	1c orange	15	10
24	A16	2c dk brn	15	10
25	A16	5c vermilion	15	10
26	A16	10c green	15	10
27	A16	20c red brn	15	10
28	A16	50c maroon	15	*40*
29	A16	1s blue	25	*1.00*
30	A16	5s purple	75	*1.50*
		Nos. 23-30 (8)	1.90	*3.40*

The issues of 1892, 1894, 1895 and 1896 were printed by the Hamilton Bank Note Co., New York, to the order of N. F. Seebeck, who held a contract for stamps with the government of Ecuador.

No. 30 in green is said to be an essay or color trial.

Nos. 29 and 30 Surcharged in Black

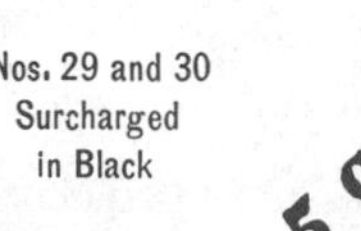

1893

Surcharge Measures 25½x2½ mm.

31	A16	5c on 1s bl	2.50	2.00
32	A16	5c on 5s pur	7.00	5.00
a.		Double surcharge		

Surcharge Measures 24x2¼ mm.

33	A16	5c on 1s bl	1.75	1.50
a.		Double surcharge, one inverted		
34	A16	5c on 5s pur	7.50	6.00
a.		Double surcharge, one inverted		

Nos. 28–30 Surcharged in Black

35	A16	5c on 50c mar	75	65
a.		Inverted surch.	2.50	
36	A16	5c on 1s bl	1.25	1.00
37	A16	5c on 5s pur	6.00	5.00

President Juan Flores
A19

President Vicente Rocafuerte
A20

38	A19	5c on 5s lake	1.00	75

It is stated that No. 38 was used exclusively as a postage stamp and not for telegrams.

1894		**Dated 1894.**	***Perf. 12.***	
		Various Frames		
39	A20	1c blue	30	30
40	A20	2c yel brn	30	30
41	A20	5c green	30	30
b.		Perf. 14	4.00	1.50
42	A20	10c vermilion	50	40
43	A20	20c black	75	50
44	A20	50c orange	4.00	1.50
45	A20	1s carmine	6.00	3.00
46	A20	5s dk bl	8.00	6.00
		Nos. 39-46 (8)	20.15	12.30

1895		**Same, Dated "1895".**		
47	A20	1c blue	60	5
48	A20	2c yel brn	60	5
49	A20	5c green	50	3
50	A20	10c vermilion	50	3
51	A20	20c black	75	6
52	A20	50c orange	2.50	1.2
53	A20	1s carmine	12.50	5.0
54	A20	5s dk bl	6.00	2.5
		Nos. 47-54 (8)	23.95	11.0

Reprints of the 2c, 10c, 50c, 1s and 5s of the 1894–95 issues are generally on thick paper. Original issues are on thin to medium thick paper. To distinguish reprints from originals, a comparison of paper thickness, paper color, gum, printing clarity and direction of paper weave is necessary. Price 10 cents each.

Coat of Arms
A21 A22

A23 A24

A25 A26

A27 A28

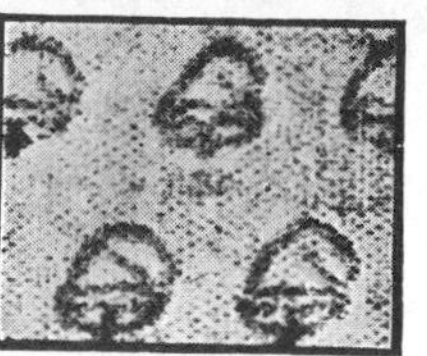

Wmk. 117

1896		**Wmkd. Liberty Cap. (117)**		
55	A21	1c dk grn	50	45
56	A22	2c red	50	20
57	A23	5c blue	50	20
58	A24	10c bis brn	40	*50*
59	A25	20c orange	70	*1.00*
60	A26	50c dk bl	1.25	*2.00*
61	A27	1s yel brn	2.50	*2.50*
62	A28	5s violet	5.00	*4.00*
		Nos. 55-62 (8)	11.35	*10.85*

Unwmkd.

62A	A21	1c dk grn	60	20
62B	A22	2c red	60	20
62C	A23	5c blue	60	20
62D	A24	10c bis brn	50	*1.00*
62E	A25	20c orange	3.75	*4.00*
62F	A26	50c dk bl	50	*2.00*
62G	A27	1s yel brn	3.50	*6.00*
62H	A28	5s violet	3.75	*4.00*
		Nos. 62A-62H (8)	13.80	*17.60*

Reprints of Nos. 55-62H are on very thick paper, with paper weave direction vertical. Price 10 cents each.

Vicente Roca, Diego Noboa and José Olmedo
A28a

General Juan Francisco Elizalde
A28b

Lithographed

1896, Oct. 9 *Perf. 11½* Unwmkd.

63	A28a	1c rose	50	50
64	A28b	2c blue	50	50
65	A28a	5c green	60	60
66	A28b	10c ocher	60	60
67	A28a	20c red	75	*1.25*
68	A28b	50c violet	1.00	*2.00*
69	A28a	1s orange	2.00	*2.50*
		Nos. 63-69 (7)	5.95	*7.95*

Issued in commemoration of the success of the Liberal Party in 1845 and 1895.

Coat of Arms
A29 A30

Black Surcharge.

1896, Nov. *Perf. 12*

70	A29	1c on 1c ver, '1893-1894'	60	40
a.		Inverted surcharge	1.75	1.50
b.		Double surcharge	6.00	5.00
71	A29	2c on 2c bl, "1893-1894"	1.50	1.25
a.		Invtd. surcharge	3.00	2.50
72	A29	5c on 10c org, "1887-1888"	60	40
a.		Inverted surcharge	1.50	1.25
b.		Double surcharge	3.50	3.00
c.		Surcharged "2cts"	75	60
d.		"1893-1894"	4.00	3.50
73	A29	10c on 4c brn, '1887-1888'	1.00	75
a.		Inverted surcharge	1.50	1.25
b.		Double surcharge	3.00	2.50
c.		Double surcharge, one inverted		
d.		Surcharged "1 cto"	2.25	2.00
e.		"1891-1892"	12.50	10.00

Similar surcharges of type A29 include: Dated "1887–1888"—1c on 1c blue green, 1c on 2c red, 1c on 4c brown, 1c on 10c yellow; 2c on 2c red, 2c on 10c yellow; 10c on 1c green. Dated "1891–1892"—1c on 1c blue green, 1c on 4c brown. Dated "1893–1894"—2c on 10c yellow; 10c on 1c vermilion, 10c on 10s black.

Wmkd. Liberty Cap. (117)

Surcharge in Black or Red

1896, Oct.

74	A30	5c on 20c org	30.00	30.00
76	A30	10c on 50c dk bl (R)	30.00	30.00
a.		Double surcharge		

The surcharge is diagonal, horizontal, or vertical.

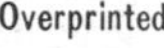

On Issue of 1894.

1897 Unwmkd.

77	A20	1c blue	1.50	1.00
78	A20	2c yel brn	1.25	65
79	A20	5c green	60	40
80	A20	10c vermilion	1.75	1.25
81	A20	20c black	2.00	1.50
82	A20	50c orange	4.50	1.25
83	A20	1s carmine	13.00	3.00
84	A20	5s dk bl	55.00	40.00
		Nos. 77-84 (8)	79.60	49.05

On Issue of 1895.

85	A20	1c blue	4.00	3.50
86	A20	2c yel brn	1.50	1.25
87	A20	5c green	1.25	75
88	A20	10c vermilion	4.50	4.00
89	A20	20c black	1.25	1.25
90	A20	50c orange	22.50	9.00
91	A20	1s carmine	10.00	5.00
92	A20	5s dk bl	10.00	8.00
		Nos. 85-92 (8)	55.00	32.75

Overprinted 1897 1898

On Issue of 1894.

93	A20	1c blue	1.00	60
94	A20	2c yel brn	75	50
95	A20	5c green	40	20
96	A20	10c vermilion	2.25	1.25
97	A20	20c black	2.50	1.25
98	A20	50c orange	4.50	1.75
99	A20	1s carmine	8.00	4.50
100	A20	5s dk bl	55.00	45.00
		Nos. 93-100 (8)	74.40	55.05

On Issue of 1895.

101	A20	1c blue	2.25	80
102	A20	2c yel brn	1.00	80
103	A20	5c green	1.25	70
104	A20	10c vermilion	4.00	2.50
105	A20	20c black	3.50	80
106	A20	50c orange	1.30	85
107	A20	1s carmine	6.00	4.00
108	A20	5s dk bl	7.00	5.00
		Nos. 101-108 (8)	26.30	15.45

Overprints on Nos. 77–108 are to be found reading upward from left to right and downward from left to right, as well as inverted.

Overprinted 1897 Y 1898

1897 On Issue of 1894.

109	A20	10c vermilion	*60.00*	*55.00*

On Issue of 1895.

110	A20	2c yel brn	*50.00*	*45.00*
111	A20	1s carmine	*60.00*	*55.00*
112	A20	5s dk bl	*60.00*	*45.00*

Nos. 56, 59 Overprinted

1897, June Wmk. 117

113	A22	2c red	50.00	40.00
114	A25	20c orange	60.00	45.00

Many forged overprints on Nos. 77–114 exist, made on original stamps and reprints.

Same Overprint on Stamps or Types of 1896.

1897 *Perf. 11½.* Unwmkd.

115	A28a	1c rose	1.75	1.50
116	A28b	2c blue	1.50	1.25
117	A28b	10c ocher	1.50	1.25
118	A28a	1s yellow	4.50	4.00

No. 63 Overprinted

1897

119	A28a	1c rose	90	75

Nos. 63–66 Overprinted in Black

1897

122	A28a	1c rose	3.50	3.00
a.		Inverted overprint	4.50	4.00
123	A28b	2c blue	3.50	3.00
a.		Inverted overprint	4.50	4.00
124	A28a	5c green	3.50	3.00
a.		Inverted overprint	4.50	4.00
125	A28b	10c ocher	3.50	3.00
a.		Double overprint	8.00	7.00
b.		Inverted overprint	4.00	4.00

The 20c, 50c and 1s with this overprint in black and all values of the issue overprinted in blue are reprints.

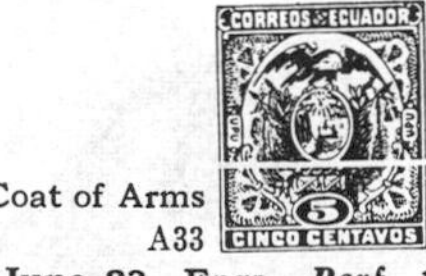

Coat of Arms
A33

1897, June 23 Engr. *Perf. 14–16*

127	A33	1c dk yel grn	15	15
128	A33	2c org red	20	15
129	A33	5c lake	20	20
130	A33	10c dk brn	20	25
131	A33	20c yellow	40	*60*
132	A33	50c dl bl	40	*1.00*
133	A33	1s gray	50	*1.25*
134	A33	5s dk lil	75	*1.75*
		Nos. 127-134 (8)	2.80	*5.35*

A34

A35

1899, May

135	A34	1c on 2c org red	2.25	75
136	A35	5c on 10c brn	1.75	50
a.		Double surcharge		

Luis Vargas Torres
A36

Abdón Calderón
A37

Juan Montalvo
A38

José Mejia
A39

Santa Cruz y Espejo
A40

Pedro Carbo
A41

José Joaquín Olmedo
A42

Pedro Moncayo
A43

1899 *Perf. 12½–16*

137	A36	1c gray bl & blk	25	12
a.		Imperf. vertically		
138	A37	2c brn lil & blk	25	10
139	A38	5c lake & blk	35	12
140	A39	10c vio & blk	35	10
141	A40	20c grn & blk	35	12
142	A41	50c lil rose & blk	1.25	60
143	A42	1s ocher & blk	6.00	2.00
144	A43	5s lil & blk	10.00	5.00
		Nos. 137-144 (8)	18.80	8.16

1901

145	A36	1c scar & blk	15	10
146	A37	2c grn & blk	20	10
147	A38	5c gray lil & blk	20	10
148	A39	10c dp bl & blk	20	15
149	A40	20c gray & blk	25	15
150	A41	50c lt bl & blk	1.25	75
151	A42	1s brn & blk	5.00	2.50
152	A43	5s gray blk & blk	7.50	5.00
		Nos. 145-152 (8)	14.75	8.85

In July, 1902, following the theft of a quantity of stamps during a fire at Guayaquil, the Government authorized the governors of the provinces to handstamp their stocks. Many varieties of these handstamps exist.

Other control marks were used in 1907.

A44

Surcharged on Revenue Stamp Dated 1901-1902.

1903-06 *Perf. 14, 15.*

153	A44	1c on 5c gray lil ('06)	30	25
154	A44	1c on 20c gray ('06)	4.50	3.00
155	A44	1c on 25c yel	60	25
a.		Double surcharge		
156	A44	1c on 1s bl ('06)	37.50	25.00
157	A44	3c on 5c gray lil ('06)	4.50	2.50
158	A44	3c on 20c gray ('06)	11.00	7.50
159	A44	3c on 25c yel ('06)	11.00	7.50
159A	A44	3c on 1s bl ('06)	1.25	1.00
		Nos. 153-159A (8)	70.65	47.00

Counterfeits are plentiful. See Nos. 191–197.

Capt. Abdón Calderón
A45 A46

1904, July 31 *Perf. 12*

160	A45	1c red & blk	45	35
161	A45	2c bl & blk	45	35
162	A46	5c yel & blk	1.75	1.20
163	A45	10c red & blk	3.50	1.20
164	A45	20c bl & blk	9.00	3.00
165	A46	50c yel & blk	75.00	50.00
		Nos. 160-165 (6)	90.15	56.10

Issued in commemoration of the centenary of the birth of Abdón Calderón, 1804–1904.

President Vicente Roca
A47

President Diego Noboa
A48

President Francisco Robles
A49

President José M. Urvina
A50

President García Moreno
A51

President Jerónimo Carrión
A52

President Javier Espinoza
A53

President Antonio Borrero
A54

1907, July *Perf. 14, 15*

166	A47	1c red & blk	25	15
167	A48	2c pale bl & blk	35	20
168	A49	3c org & blk	50	20
169	A50	5c lil rose & blk	60	15
170	A51	10c dp bl & blk	2.00	25
171	A52	20c yel grn & blk	2.50	30
172	A53	50c vio & blk	6.00	75
173	A54	1s grn & blk	8.50	2.00
		Nos. 166-173 (8)	20.70	4.00

The stamps of the 1907 issue frequently have control marks similar to those found on the 1899 and 1901 issues. These marks were applied to distinguish the stamps issued in the various provinces and to serve as a check on local officials.

Locomotive
A55

García Moreno
A56

Gen. Eloy Alfaro
A57

Abelardo Moncayo
A58

Archer Harman
A59

James Sivewright
A60

Mt. Chimborazo
A61

1908, June 25

174	A55	1c red brn	90	90
175	A56	2c bl & blk	1.50	1.20
176	A57	5c cl & blk	3.00	2.50
177	A58	10c ocher & blk	1.75	1.50
178	A59	20c grn & blk	1.75	1.75
179	A60	50c gray & blk	1.75	1.75
180	A61	1s black	3.75	3.75
		Nos. 174-180 (7)	14.40	13.35

Issued in commemoration of the opening of the Guayaquil-Quito Railway.

José Mejía Vallejo
A62

Francisco J. E. Santa Cruz y Espejo
A63

Francisco Ascásubi
A64

Juan Salinas
A65

Juan Pio de Montúfar
A66

Carlos de Montúfar
A67

Juan de Dios Morales
A68

Manuel R. de Quiroga
A69

Principal Exposition Building
A70

1909, Aug. 10 *Perf. 12.*

181	A62	1c green	35	60
182	A63	2c blue	35	60
183	A64	3c orange	35	75
184	A65	5c claret	35	75
185	A66	10c yel brn	40	75
186	A67	20c gray	40	1.10
187	A68	50c vermilion	40	1.10
188	A69	1s ol grn	40	1.50
189	A70	5s violet	1.20	3.00
		Nos. 181-189 (9)	4.20	10.15

National Exposition of 1909.

Surcharged CINCO CENTAVOS

1909

190	A68	5c on 50c ver	85	75

Revenue Stamps Surcharged as in 1903.

1910 *Perf. 14, 15*

Stamps Dated 1905-1906.

191	A44	1c on 5c grn	1.50	1.00
192	A44	5c on 20c bl	5.00	1.25
193	A44	5c on 25c vio	8.00	2.25

Stamps Dated 1907-1908.

194	A44	1c on 5c grn	30	15
195	A44	5c on 20c bl	9.00	6.00
196	A44	5c on 25c vio	30	25

Stamp Dated 1909—1910

197	A44	5c on 20c bl	*45.00*	*37.50*

President Roca
A71

President Noboa
A72

President Robles
A73

President Urvina
A74

President Moreno
A75

President Borrero
A76

1911-28 *Perf. 12.*

198	A71	1c scar & blk	15	8
199	A71	1c org ('16)	15	8
200	A71	1c lt bl ('25)	15	8
201	A72	2c bl & blk	35	8
202	A72	2c grn ('16)	15	8
203	A72	2c dk vio ('25)	15	8
204	A73	3c org & blk ('13)	1.25	35
205	A73	3c blk ('15)	15	8
206	A74	5c scar & blk	60	8
207	A74	5c vio ('15)	25	8
208	A74	5c rose ('25)	25	8
209	A74	5c dk brn ('28)	30	8
210	A75	10c dp bl & blk	1.00	8
211	A75	10c dp bl ('15)	1.00	20
212	A75	10c yel grn ('25)	25	8
213	A75	10c blk ('28)	75	10
214	A76	1s grn & blk	5.00	1.50
215	A76	1s org & blk ('27)	3.00	30
		Nos. 198-215 (18)	14.90	3.49

A77

1912 *Perf. 14, 15*

216	A77	1c on 1s grn	60	60
217	A77	2c on 2s car	90	90
218	A77	2c on 5s dl bl	90	90
219	A77	2c on 10s yel	2.00	1.50
	a.	Inverted surcharge	4.00	3.50

No. 216 exists with narrow "V" and small "U" in "UN" and Nos. 217, 218 and 219 with "D" with serifs or small "O" in "DOS".

Enrique Váldez
A78

Jerónimo Carrión
A79

Javier Espinoza
A80

1915-17 *Perf. 12*

220	A78	4c red & blk	20	8
221	A79	20c grn & blk ('17)	2.00	25
222	A80	50c dp vio & blk	3.50	50

Olmedo
A86

Monument to "Fathers of the Country"
A95

Laurel Wreath and Star
A104

Designs: 2c, Rafael Ximena. 3c, Roca. 4c, Luis F. Viviero. 5c, Luis Febres Cordero. 6c, Francisco Lavayen. 7c, Jorge Antonio de Elizalde. 8c, Baltazar Garcia. 9c, Jose de Antepara. 15c, Luis Urdaneta. 20c, Jose M. Villamil. 30c, Miguel Letamendi. 40c, Gregorio Escobedo. 50c, Gen. Antonio Jose de Sucre. 60c, Juan Illingworth. 70c, Roca. 80c, Rocafuerte. 1s, Simon Bolivar.

1920

223	A86	1c	yel grn	30	10
224	A86	2c	carmine	25	15
225	A86	3c	yel brn	25	15
226	A86	4c	myr grn	40	20
227	A86	5c	pale bl	40	10
228	A86	6c	red org	75	40
229	A86	7c	brown	1.75	75
230	A86	8c	ap grn	1.00	50
231	A86	9c	lake	3.50	1.50
232	A95	10c	lt bl	1.50	20
233	A86	15c	dk gray	1.75	50
234	A86	20c	dk vio	1.75	25
235	A86	30c	brt vio	3.50	1.25
236	A86	40c	dk brn	4.50	2.00
237	A86	50c	dk grn	4.00	50
238	A86	60c	dk bl	6.00	2.25
239	A86	70c	gray	10.00	5.00
240	A86	80c	org yel	9.00	5.00
241	A104	90c	green	10.00	5.00
242	A86	1s	pale bl	15.00	8.00
			Nos. 223-242 (20)	75.60	33.80

Nos. 223 to 242 were issued in commemoration of the centenary of the independence of Guayaquil.

Postal Tax Stamp of 1924 Overprinted

POSTAL

1925

259	PT6	20c	bis brn	1.50	50

Stamps of 1915-25 Overprinted in Black or Red (Upright or Inverted)

QUITO
1926
ESMERALDAS

1926

260	A71	1c	lt bl	3.50	3.00
261	A72	2c	dk vio	3.50	3.00
262	A73	3c	blk (R)	3.50	3.00
263	A86	4c	myr grn	3.50	3.00
264	A74	5c	rose	3.50	3.00
265	A75	10c	yel grn	3.50	3.00
			Nos. 260-265 (6)	21.00	18.00

Quito-Esmeraldas railway opening.

Postal Tax Stamps of 1920-24 Overprinted

POSTAL

1927

266	PT6	1c	ol grn	15	8
a.			"POSTAI"	2.00	1.25
b.			Double overprint	2.00	1.25
c.			Inverted overprint	2.00	1.25
267	PT6	2c	dp grn	15	8
a.			"POSTAI"	2.00	1.25
b.			Double overprint	2.00	1.25
268	PT6	20c	bis brn	1.00	15
a.			"POSTAI"	12.50	7.50

Quito Post Office
A109

1927, June

269	A109	5c	orange	20	10
270	A109	10c	dk grn	25	15
271	A109	20c	violet	30	25

Opening of new Quito P.O.

Postal Tax Stamp of 1924 Overprinted **POSTAL** in Dark Blue.

1928

273	PT6	20c	bis brn	30	10
a.			Double overprint, one inverted	2.00	1.00

A110

Nos. 235, 239-240 Overprinted in Red Brown and Surcharged in Dark Blue.

1928, July 8

274	A110	10c	on 30c vio	3.00	3.00
a.			Surch. invtd.		
275	A110	50c	on 70c gray	4.00	4.00
276	A110	1s	on 80c org yel	5.00	5.00
a.			Surch. invtd.		

Quito-Cayambe railway opening.

Stamps of 1920 Surcharged

ASAMBLEA
NCNAL. 1928
5 CTVOS.

1928, Oct. 9

277	A86	1c	on 1c yel grn	12.00	10.00
278	A86	1c	on 2c car	20	15
279	A86	2c	on 3c yel brn	1.25	1.00
a.			Double surcharge, one reading up	6.00	6.00
280	A86	2c	on 4c myr grn	90	75
281	A86	2c	on 5c lt bl	50	35
a.			Double surcharge	6.00	6.00
282	A86	2c	on 7c brn	16.00	12.50
283	A86	5c	on 6c red org	25	20
a.			"5 ctvos." omitted	20.00	20.00
284	A86	10c	on 7c brn	75	60
285	A86	20c	on 8c ap grn	25	20
a.			Double surcharge		
286	A95	40c	on 10c bl	3.50	3.00
287	A86	40c	on 15c dk gray	60	50
288	A86	50c	on 20c dk vio	11.00	9.00
289	A86	1s	on 40c dk brn	2.25	2.00
290	A86	5s	on 50c dk grn	3.00	2.25
291	A86	10s	on 60c dk bl	13.00	9.00

With Additional Surcharge in Red

0,10

292	A86	10c	on 2c on 7c brn	20	20
a.			Red surcharge double	6.00	6.00
			Nos. 277-292 (16)	65.65	51.70

National Assembly of 1928.
Counterfeit overprints exist of Nos. 277-291.

A111

A112

Surcharged in Various Colors

1928, Oct. 31 ***Perf. 14***

293	A111	5c	on 20c gray lil (Bk)	1.25	1.00
294	A111	10c	on 20c gray lil (R)	1.25	1.00
295	A111	20c	on 1s grn (O)	1.25	1.00
296	A111	50c	on 1s grn (Bl)	1.50	75
297	A111	1s	on 1s grn (V)	2.00	1.00
298	A111	5s	on 2s red (G)	6.00	5.00
299	A111	10s	on 2s red (Br)	7.50	7.50
a.			Black surcharge	8.00	8.00
			Nos. 293-299 (7)	20.75	17.25

Quito-Otavalo railway opening.

Postal Tax Stamp of 1924 Overprinted in Red **POSTAL**

1929 ***Perf. 12.***

302	PT6	2c	dp grn	10	10

There are two types of overprint on No. 302 differing slightly.

1929 Red Overprint.

303	A112	1c	dk bl	10	10
a.			Overprint reading down	10	10

See also Nos. 586-587.

Plowing
A113

Cultivating Cacao
A114

Cacao Pod
A115

Growing Tobacco
A116

Exportation of Fruits
A117

Landscape—A118

Loading Sugar Cane
A119

Scene in Quito
A120

Scene in Quito
A121

Olmedo
A122

Sucre
A123

Bolívar
A124

Monument to Simón Bolívar
A125

1930, Aug. 1 *Perf. 12½*

No.	Type	Description	Unused	Used
304	A113	1c yel & car	20	10
305	A114	2c yel & grn	20	10
306	A115	5c dp grn & vio brn	25	15
307	A116	6c yel & red	30	25
308	A117	10c org & ol grn	35	15
309	A118	16c red & yel grn	50	40
310	A119	20c ultra & yel	50	18
311	A120	40c org & sep	60	18
312	A121	50c org & sep	75	18
313	A122	1s dp grn & blk	2.50	25
314	A123	2s dk bl & blk	5.00	50
315	A124	5s dk vio & blk	9.00	75
316	A125	10s car rose & blk	25.00	6.00
		Nos. 304-316 (13)	45.15	9.19

Centenary of founding of republic.

A126

A127

1933 **Red Overprint.** *Perf. 15.*

No.	Type	Description	Unused	Used
317	A126	10c ol brn	25	15

Blue Overprint.

No.	Type	Description	Unused	Used
318	A127	10c ol brn	25	10
a.		Inverted overprint	5.00	5.00

Nos. 307, 309 Surcharged in Black

1933 *Perf. 12½*

No.	Type	Description	Unused	Used
319	A116	5c on 6c yel & red	30	15
320	A118	10c on 16c red & yel grn	40	15
a.		Inverted ovpt.	4.00	4.00

Landscape
A128

Mt. Chimborazo
A129

1934-45 *Perf. 12.*

No.	Type	Description	Unused	Used
321	A128	5c violet	15	8
322	A128	5c blue	15	8
323	A128	5c dk brn	15	8
323A	A128	5c sl blk ('45)	15	8
324	A128	10c rose	15	8
325	A128	10c dk grn	15	8
326	A128	10c brown	15	8
327	A128	10c orange	15	8
328	A128	10c ol grn	15	8
329	A128	10c gray blk ('35)	20	8
329A	A128	10c red lil ('44)	15	8

Perf. 14.

No.	Type	Description	Unused	Used
330	A129	1s car rose	1.50	60
		Nos. 321-330 (12)	3.20	1.48

Stamps of 1930 Surcharged or Overprinted in various colors similar to:

INAUGURACION MONUMENTO A BOLIVAR

QUITO, 24 DE JULIO DE 1935

1935 *Perf. 12½.*

No.	Type	Description	Unused	Used
331	A116	5c on 6c yel & red (Bl)	30	15
332	A116	10c on 6c yel & red (G)	35	15
333	A119	20c ultra & yel (R)	40	20
334	A120	40c org & sep (G)	50	30
335	A121	50c org & sep (G)	70	50
336	A124	1s on 5s dk vio & blk (Gold)	2.00	90
337	A124	2s on 5s dk vio & blk (Gold)	3.00	1.35
338	A125	5s on 10s car rose & blk (Bl)	5.00	3.25
		Nos. 331-338, C35-C38 (12)	32.25	26.80

Unveiling of a monument to Bolivar at Quito, July 24, 1935.

The five-stamp Sociedad Colombista Panamericana series of 1935 and five air-mail stamps of a similar design are not recognized by this Catalogue as having been issued primarily for postal purposes.

Telegraph Stamp Overprinted Diagonally in Red

POSTAL

1935 *Perf. 14½*

No.	Type	Description	Unused	Used
339	A126	10c ol brn	12	8

Map of Galápagos Islands
A130

Galapagos Land Iguana
A131

Galápagos Tortoise
A132

Charles R. Darwin
A133

Columbus
A134

Island Scene
A135

1936 *Perf. 14.*

No.	Type	Description	Unused	Used
340	A130	2c black	25	10
341	A131	5c ol grn	35	15
342	A132	10c brown	60	15
343	A133	20c dk vio	60	20
344	A134	1s dk car	1.25	50
345	A135	2s dk bl	2.25	1.00
		Nos. 340-345 (6)	5.30	2.10

Issued to commemorate the centenary of the visit of Charles Darwin to the Galápagos Islands, September 17, 1835.

Tobacco Stamp Overprinted in Black

POSTAL

1936 *Rouletted 7.*

No.	Type	Description	Unused	Used
346	PT7	1c rose red	12	8
a.		Horiz. pair, imperf. vertical		
b.		Double surcharge		

No. 346 is similar to type PT7 but does not include "CASA CORREOS".

Louis Godin, Charles M. de la Condamine and Pierre Bouguer
A136

Portraits: 5c, 20c, Antonio Ulloa, La Condamine and Jorge Juan.

1936 **Engraved.** *Perf. 12½*

No.	Type	Description	Unused	Used
347	A136	2c dp bl	8	8
348	A136	5c dk grn	10	8
349	A136	10c dp org	12	8
350	A136	20c violet	30	15
351	A136	50c dk red	60	35
		Nos. 347-351, C39-C42 (9)	2.80	1.41

Bicentenary of Geodesical Mission to Quito.

Independence Monument
A137

1936 *Perf. 13½x14.*

No.	Type	Description	Unused	Used
352	A137	2c green	1.75	30
353	A137	5c dk vio	1.75	30
354	A137	10c car rose	1.75	35
355	A137	20c black	1.75	50
356	A137	50c blue	3.00	1.50
357	A137	1s dk red	3.50	1.75
		Nos. 352-357, C43-C50 (14)	45.30	36.20

Issued to commemorate the first International Philatelic Exhibition at Quito.

Coat of Arms
A138

Overprint in Black or Red

1937 *Perf. 12½*

No.	Type	Description	Unused	Used
359	A138	5c ol grn	25	10
360	A138	10c dk bl (R)	25	10

Andean Landscape
A139

Atahualpa, the Last Inca
A140

Hat Weavers
A141

Coast Landscape
A142

Gold Washing
A143

1937, Aug. 19 *Perf. 11½*

No.	Type	Description	Unused	Used
361	A139	2c green	15	8
362	A140	5c dp rose	20	8
363	A141	10c blue	25	5
364	A142	20c dp rose	60	25
365	A143	1s ol grn	85	35
		Nos. 361-365 (5)	2.05	81

"Liberty" Carrying Flag of Ecuador
A144

Engraved and Lithographed

1938, Feb. 22 *Perf. 12*

Center Multicolored

No.	Type	Description	Unused	Used
366	A144	2c blue	20	10
367	A144	5c violet	25	10
368	A144	10c black	30	10
369	A144	20c brown	40	15
370	A144	50c black	60	15
371	A144	1s ol blk	1.00	25
372	A144	2s dk brn	2.00	40
		Nos. 366-372, C57-C63 (14)	10.40	1.85

U.S. Constitution, 150th anniversary.

Winged Figure Holding Globe
A145

Cactus and Winged Wheel
A146

"Communications"
A147

"Construction"
A148

Engraved.

1938, Oct. 30 *Perf. 13, 13x13½*

373	A145	10c brt ultra	10	5
374	A146	50c dp red vio	20	10
375	A147	1s cop red	40	10
376	A148	2s dk grn	60	10

Progress of Ecuador Exhibition.

Parade of Athletes A149

Runner A150

Basketball A151

Wrestlers A152

Diver A153

1939, Mar. *Perf. 12*

377	A149	5c car rose	2.50	50
378	A150	10c dp bl	3.00	60
379	A151	50c gray ol	3.50	75
380	A152	1s dl vio	6.50	75
381	A153	2s dl ol grn	9.00	1.00
		Nos. 377-381, C65-C69 (10)	46.25	5.75

First Bolivarian Games (1938), La Paz.

Dolores Mission A154

Trylon and Perisphere A155

1939, June 16 *Perf. 12½x13*

382	A154	2c bl grn	5	5
383	A154	5c rose red	10	5
384	A154	10c ultra	10	5
385	A154	50c yel brn	30	20
386	A154	1s black	50	20
387	A154	2s purple	1.00	20
		Nos. 382-387, C73-C79 (13)	3.30	1.40

Golden Gate International Exposition.

1939, June 30

388	A155	2c lt ol grn	10	5
389	A155	5c red org	10	5
390	A155	10c ultra	15	10
391	A155	50c sl gray	50	20
392	A155	1s rose car	75	25
393	A155	2s blk brn	1.25	30
		Nos. 388-393, C80-C86 (13)	4.55	1.75

New York World's Fair.

Flags of the 21 American Republics A156

Francisco J. E. Santa Cruz y Espejo A157

1940 *Perf. 12.*

394	A156	5c dp rose & blk	10	8
395	A156	10c dk bl & blk	15	8
396	A156	50c Prus grn & blk	40	12
397	A156	1s dp vio & blk	60	25
		Nos. 394-397, C87-C90 (8)	3.60	1.63

Pan American Union, 50th anniversary.

1941, Dec. 15

398	A157	30c blue	25	10
399	A157	1s red org	60	20

Issued to commemorate the Exposition of Journalism held under the auspices of the National Newspaper Men's Union. See Nos. C91-C92.

Francisco de Orellana A158

Gonzalo Pizarro A159

View of Guayaquil—A160

View of Quito—A161

1942, Jan. 30

400	A158	10c sepia	15	10
401	A159	40c dp rose	30	10
402	A160	1s violet	50	20
403	A161	2s dk bl	90	40
		Nos. 400-403, C93-C96 (8)	5.25	1.90

Issued to commemorate the 400th anniversary of the discovery and exploration of the Amazon River by Francisco de Orellana.

Remigio Crespo Toral A162

Alfredo Baquerizo Moreno A163

1942 *Perf. 13½*

404	A162	10c green	10	6
405	A162	50c brown	25	10

See also No. C97.

1942

406	A163	10c green	10	6

Mt. Chimborazo A164

1942–47 *Perf. 12*

407	A164	30c red brn	20	8
407A	A164	30c lt bl ('43)	20	8
407B	A164	30c red org ('44)	20	8
407C	A164	30c grn ('47)	20	8

View of Guayaquil A165

1942–44

408	A165	20c red	15	10
408A	A165	20c dp bl ('44)	15	10

Gen. Eloy Alfaro A166

Devil's Nose A167

Designs: 30c, Military College. 1s, Montecristi, Alfaro's birthplace.

1942

409	A166	10c dk rose & blk	20	8
410	A167	20c ol blk & red brn	20	10
411	A167	30c ol gray & grn	30	12
412	A167	1s sl & sal	60	25
		Nos. 409-412, C98-C101 (8)	5.30	2.80

Issued to commemorate the centenary of the birth of President Alfaro (1842–1903).

Nos. 370–372
Overprinted in Red Brown

BIENVENIDO — WALLACE

Abril 15 — 1943

1943, Apr. 15 *Perf. 11½*

413	A144	50c multi	50	50
414	A144	1s multi	1.00	1.00
415	A144	2s multi	1.50	1.50
		Nos. 413-415, C102-C104 (6)	7.75	5.25

Visit of Vice-President Henry A. Wallace of the United States.

"30 Centavos"
A170

Black Surcharge.

1943 *Perf. 12½*

416	A170	30c on 50c red brn	20	10
	a.	Without bars	20	10

Map Showing United States and Ecuador
A171

1943, Oct. 9 *Perf. 12*

417	A171	10c dl vio	25	20
418	A171	20c red brn	25	20
419	A171	30c orange	35	25
420	A171	50c ol grn	40	25
421	A171	1s dp vio	50	40
422	A171	10s ol bis	5.00	3.00
		Nos. 417-422, C114-C118 (11)	16.10	11.90

Issued to commemorate the good will tour of President Arroyo del Rio in 1942.

1944, Feb. 7

423	A171	10c yel grn	15	10
424	A171	20c rose pink	20	15
425	A171	30c dk gray brn	25	20
426	A171	50c dp red lil	40	30
427	A171	1s ol gray	50	40
428	A171	10s red org	5.00	3.00
		Nos.423-428, C119-C123 (11)	11.50	7.85

No. 385
Surcharged in Black

30
Centavos

1944 *Perf. 12½x13* **Unwmkd.**

429	A154	30c on 50c yel brn	20	10

Archbishop Federico González Suárez A172

Government Palace, Quito A173

1944 *Perf. 12*

430	A172	10c dp bl	15	8
431	A172	20c green	20	8
432	A172	30c dk vio brn	25	6
433	A172	1s dl vio	50	20
		Nos. 430-433, C124-C127 (8)	5.05	2.77

Birth centenary of Archbishop Federico Gonzalez Suarez.

Air Post Stamps
Nos. C76 and C83
Surcharged in Black

POSTAL
30
Centavos

1944 *Perf. 12½x13*

434	AP15	30c on 50c rose vio	20	10
435	AP16	30c on 50c sl grn	20	10

Nos. 382 and 388
Surcharged in Black

CINCO
Centavos

1944–45

436	A154	5c on 2c bl grn	15	12
	a.	Double surcharge		
437	A155	5c on 2c lt ol grn ('45)	15	12

1944 Engraved Perf. 11

438	A173	10c dk grn	15	10
439	A173	30c blue	15	10

Symbol of the Red Cross
A174

1945, Apr. 25 Perf. 12

Cross in Rose.

440	A174	30c bis brn	60	25
441	A174	1s red brn	75	30
442	A174	5s turq grn	1.50	1.00
443	A174	10s scarlet	4.00	2.50
		Nos. 440-443, C131-C134 (8)	16.33	10.55

International Red Cross, 80th anniversary.

Nos. 370 to 372
Overprinted in Dark Blue and Gold

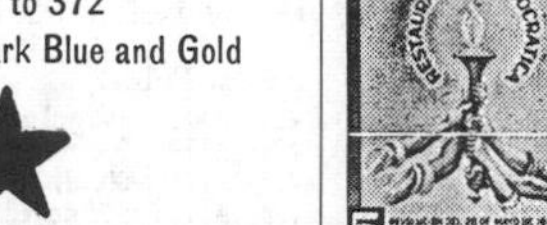

LOOR A CHILE
OCTUBRE 2 1945

1945, Oct. 2 Perf. 11½

Center Multicolored.

444	A144	50c black	25	20
a.		Double overprint		
445	A144	1s ol blk	40	30
446	A144	2s dk brn	90	75
		Nos. 444-446, C139-C141 (6)	3.45	3.15

Visit of Pres. Juan Antonio Rios of Chile.

General Antonio José de Sucre
A175

1945, Nov. 14 Engraved Perf. 12

447	A175	10c olive	5	5
448	A175	20c red brn	10	8
449	A175	40c ol gray	12	10
450	A175	1s dk grn	25	20
451	A175	2s sepia	60	35
		Nos. 447-451, C142-C146 (10)	4.67	3.45

150th anniversary of birth of Gen. Antonio José de Sucre.

No. 438 Surcharged in Blue

VEINTE
CENTAVOS

1945 Perf. 11

452	A173	20c on 10c dk grn	15	10
a.		Fancy bar omitted		

Map of Pan-American Highway and Arms of Loja
A176

1946, Apr. 22 Engraved Perf. 12

453	A176	20c red brn	10	6
454	A176	30c brt grn	15	10
455	A176	1s brt ultra	20	20
456	A176	5s dp red lil	1.00	75
457	A176	10s scarlet	2.00	1.50
		Nos. 453-457, C147-C151 (10)	7.60	4.91

Torch of Democracy
A177

Popular Suffrage
A178

Flag of Ecuador
A179

Pres. José M. Velasco Ibarra
A180

1946, Aug. 9 Perf. 12½ Unwmkd.

458	A177	5c dk bl	5	5
459	A178	10c Prus grn	10	5
460	A179	20c carmine	25	10
461	A180	30c chocolate	40	15
		Nos. 458-461, C152-C155 (8)	2.35	1.20

Issued to commemorate the 2nd anniversary of the Revolution of May 28, 1944.

"30 Ctvs."
A181
Black Surcharge.

1946

462	A181	30c on 50c red brn	10	10

Nos. CO13–CO14
With Additional Overprint in Black

POSTAL

1946 Perf. 11½

463	AP7	10c chestnut	10	10
464	AP7	20c ol blk	10	10

Instructor and Student
A182

1946, Sept. 16 Perf. 12½

465	A182	10c dp bl	15	10
466	A182	20c chocolate	15	10
467	A182	30c dk grn	20	15
468	A182	50c bluish blk	40	20
469	A182	1s dk red	60	20
470	A182	10s dk vio	4.00	1.00
		Nos. 465-470, C156-C160 (11)	11.15	3.95

Campaign for adult education.

Mariana de Jesus Paredes y Flores
A183

Urn
A184

1946, Nov. 28

471	A183	10c blk brn	20	10
472	A183	20c green	20	10
473	A183	30c purple	25	15
474	A184	1s rose brn	50	35
		Nos. 471-474, C161-C164 (8)	4.20	2.90

Issued to commemorate the 300th anniversary of the death of the Blessed Mariana de Jesus Paredes y Flores.

Pres. Vicente Rocafuerte
A185

Jesuits' Church Quito
A186

F.J.E. de Santa Cruz y Espejo
A187

1947, Nov. 27 Perf. 12

475	A185	5c redsh brn	10	5
476	A185	10c sepia	10	5
477	A185	15c gray blk	12	5
478	A186	20c redsh brn	20	5
479	A186	30c red vio	20	8
480	A186	40c brt ultra	25	15
481	A187	45c dk sl grn	30	15
482	A187	50c ol blk	40	20
483	A187	80c org red	50	15
		Nos. 475-483, C165-C171 (16)	3.62	1.63

Type of 1946,
Overprinted "POSTAL" in Black but
Without Additional Surcharge.

1948 Engraved.

484	A181	10c orange	60	10

Andrés Bello
A188

Flagship of Columbus
A189

1948, Apr. 21 Perf. 13

485	A188	20c lt bl	20	10
486	A188	30c rose car	25	10
487	A188	40c bl grn	30	15
488	A188	1s blk brn	60	20
		Nos. 485-488, C172-C174 (7)	2.85	3.95

83rd anniversary of the death of Andrés Bello (1781–1865), educator.

No. 480
Overprinted
in Black

CONFERENCIA
ECONOMICA
GRANCOLOMBIANA
MAYO 24 DE 1.948

1948, May 24 Perf. 12

489	A186	40c brt ultra	25	20

See also No. C175.

1948 Perf. 14

490	A189	10c dk bl grn	15	6
491	A189	20c brown	25	8
492	A189	30c dk pur	30	8
493	A189	50c dp cl	40	10
494	A189	1s ultra	50	15
495	A189	5s carmine	1.75	35
		Nos. 490-495, C176-C180 (11)	7.95	2.32

Issued to publicize the proposed Columbus Memorial Lighthouse near Ciudad Trujillo. Dominican Republic.

No. 483
Overprinted
in Blue

Feria Nacional
1948
de hoy y del
ECUADOR
MAÑANA

1948 Perf. 12

"MANANA" Reading Down.

496	A187	80c org red	40	35

Issued to publicize the National Fair of Today and Tomorrrow, 1948. See No. C181.

Telegrafo I in Flight
A190

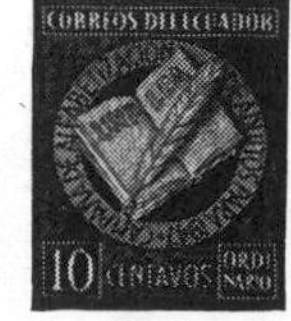

Book and Pen
A191

1948 Engraved. Perf. 12½

497	A190	30c red org	20	8
498	A190	40c rose lil	20	8
499	A190	60c vio bl	20	10
500	A190	1s brn red	25	10
501	A190	3s brown	90	25
502	A190	5s gray blk	1.00	40
		Nos. 497-502, C182-C187 (12)	5.55	3.21

25th anniversary (in 1945) of the first postal flight in Ecuador.

1948, Oct. 12 ***Perf. 14*** **Unwmkd.**

503	A191	10c dp cl	10	6
504	A191	20c brown	15	8
505	A191	30c dk grn	20	10
506	A191	50c red	25	12
507	A191	1s purple	35	15
508	A191	1s dl bl	3.00	50
		Nos. 503-508, C188-C192 (11)	6.70	2.46

Campaign for adult education.

Franklin D. Roosevelt and Two of "Four Freedoms"
A192 A193

1948, Oct. 24 ***Perf. 12½***

509	A192	10c rose brn & gray	20	15
510	A192	20c brn ol & bl	25	15
511	A193	30c ol bis & car rose	30	20
512	A193	40c red vio & sep	40	20
513	A193	1s org brn & car	50	40
		Nos. 509-513, C193-C197 (10)	4.05	1.85

Issued in tribute to Franklin D. Roosevelt (1882–1945).

Maldonado and Map
A194

Riobamba Aqueduct
A195

Maldonado on Bank of Riobamba
A196

Pedro V. Maldonado
A197

1948, Nov. 17 **Engraved** **Unwmkd.**

514	A194	5c gray blk & ver	20	8
515	A195	10c car & gray blk	25	8
516	A196	30c bis brn & ultra	35	12
517	A195	40c sage grn & vio	40	12
518	A194	50c grn & car	50	15
519	A197	1s brn & sl bl	60	20
		Nos. 514-519, C198-C201 (10)	3.60	1.35

Bicentenary of the death of Pedro Vicente Maldonado, geographer.

A198

Miguel de Cervantes Saavedra
A199

1949, May 2 ***Perf. 12½x12***

520	A198	30c dk car rose & dp ultra	20	12
521	A199	60c bis & brn vio	40	20
522	A198	1s grn & rose car	50	25
523	A199	2s gray blk & red brn	1.25	40
524	A198	5s choc & aqua	2.25	75
		Nos. 520-524, C202-C206 (10)	10.35	4.12

Issued to commemorate the 400th anniversary of the birth of Miguel de Cervantes Saavedra, novelist, playwright and poet.

No. 480 Surcharged in Carmine

II CONGRESO
Junio 1949
0.10
Eucarístico Ncl.

1949, June 15 ***Perf. 12***

525	A186	10c on 40c brt ultra	25	10
526	A186	20c on 40c brt ultra	35	15
a.		Double surcharge		
527	A186	30c on 40c brt ultra	40	20
		Nos. 525-527, C207-C209 (6)	1.60	1.05

Issued to commemorate the Second National Eucharistic Congress, Quito, June, 1949.

No. 526 exists se-tenant with No. 527

Monument on Equator
A200

Arms of Ecuador
R1

1949, June **Engr.** ***Perf. 12½x12***

528	A200	10c dp plum	30	12

No. 542 Surcharged in Black and Carmine

0.30
75 ANIVERSARIO
U.
P.
U.

1949 ***Perf. 12x12½***

529	A203	10c on 50c grn	15	10
530	A203	20c on 50c grn	20	10
531	A203	30c on 50c grn	30	10
		Nos.529-531, C210-C213 (7)	4.30	1.75

Universal Postal Union, 75th anniversary.

Consular Service Stamps Surcharged in Black

POSTAL
20 ctvs.

1949 ***Perf. 12***

532	R1	20c on 25c red brn	10	5
533	R1	30c on 50c gray	10	5

Nos. RA10A and RA55 Overprinted in Black

POSTAL
a

1950 ***Perf. 12.*** **Unwmkd.**

534	PT18	5c green	10	5
535	PT21	5c blue	10	5

Overprint 15 mm. on No. 534.

Nos. 528 and 517 to 519 Overprinted or Surcharged

ALFABETIZACION

in Black or Carmine.

1950, Feb. 10 ***Perf. 12½x12***

536	A200	10c dp plum	10	10

Perf. 12½

537	A195	20c on 40c sage grn & vio	10	10
538	A195	30c on 40c sage grn & vio	15	15
539	A194	50c grn & car	20	15
540	A197	1s brn & sl bl (C)	25	15

No. C220 Overprinted Type "a" in Carmine.

Perf. 11

Overprint 15 mm. long.

541	AP28	10s violet	2.00	75
		Nos. 536-541, C216-C220 (11)	6.20	3.00

Nos. 536 to 541 were issued to publicize adult education.

San Pablo Lake
A203

Perf. 12x12½

1950, May **Engraved** **Unwmkd.**

542	A203	50c green	20	15

Consular Service Stamp Surcharged "CORREOS" and New Value Vertically in Black.

1950 ***Perf. 12***

544	R1	30c on 50c gray	15	5

Coat of Arms
R2

Consular Service Stamps Overprinted or Surcharged in Black.

POSTAL
20 Ctvs. 20
b

POSTAL
c

CORREOS
d

50
ctvs.
POSTAL
e

1951 ***Perf. 12.*** **Unwmkd.**

545	R1 (b)	5c on 10c car rose	10	5
546	R1 (c)	10c car rose	10	5
547	R1 (d)	10c car rose	10	5
548	R1 (b)	20c on 25c red brn	10	5
549	R1 (b)	30c on 50c gray	15	5
550	R2 (b)	40c on 25c bl	15	10
551	R2 (e)	50c on 25c bl	20	10
		Nos. 545-551 (7)	90	45

Surcharge on No. 545 expressed: "5 ctvs." Small (lower case) "c" in "ctvs." on No. 550.

Consular Service Stamps Surcharged in Black

CAMPAÑA
Alfabetización
20 Ctvs. 20

1951

552	R2	20c on 25c bl	20	10
553	R2	30c on 25c bl	20	10

Adult education. See Nos. C225–C226.

Consular Service Stamp Surcharged Type "e" in Black.

1951

554	R2	"$0,30" on 50c car rose	20	10

Reliquary of St. Mariana and Vatican
A204

Perf. 12½x12

1952, Feb. **Engraved** **Unwmkd.**

555	A204	10c emer & red brn	10	5
556	A204	20c dp bl & pur	15	10
557	A204	30c car & bl grn	25	10
		Nos. 555-557, C227-C230 (7)	2.30	95

Issued to publicize the canonization of Mariana de Jesus Paredes y Flores.

Presidents Galo Plaza and Harry Truman
A205

Design: 2s, Pres. Plaza addressing U. S. Congress.

1952, Mar. 26 ***Perf. 12***

558	A205	1s rose car & gray blk	30	20
559	A205	2s dl bl & sep	60	25

Issued to commemorate the 1951 visit of Pres. Galo Plaza y Lasso to the United States. See Nos. C231–C232.

R3

Fiscal Stamps Surcharged or Overprinted Type "c" Horizontally in Carmine or Black. Engraved.

1952 ***Perf. 12.*** **Unwmkd.**

560	R3	20c on 30c dp bl (C)	10	5
561	R3	30c dp bl	10	5

Diagonal Overprint.

562	A138	50c purple	10	5

Pres. José M. Urvina, Slave and "Liberty"

A206

Lithographed.

1952 ***Hyphen-hole Perf. 7x6½***

563	A206	20c red & grn	15	5
564	A206	30c red & vio bl	20	5
565	A206	50c bl & car	35	10
		Nos. 563-565, C236-C239 (7)	4.70	1.35

Centenary of abolition of slavery in Ecuador. Counterfeits exist.

Consular Service Stamps Surcharged in Black

POSTAL
10
Centavos
f

1952-53 ***Perf. 12.*** **Unwmkd.**

566	R1	10c on 20s bl ('53)	10	5
567	R1	20c on 10s gray ('53)	10	5
568	R1	20c on 20s bl	10	5
569	R1	30c on 10s gray ('53)	10	5
570	R1	30c on 20s bl	15	5
		Nos. 566-570 (5)	55	25

Similar surcharges of 60c and 90c on the 20s blue are said to be bogus.

Teacher and Students

A207

New Citizens Voting

A208

Designs: 10c, Instructor with student. 30c, Teaching the alphabet.

1953, Apr. 13 **Engraved**

571	A207	5c lt bl	15	5
572	A207	10c dk car rose	20	5
573	A208	20c brt brn org	30	5
574	A208	30c dp red lil	40	10
		Nos. 571-574, C240-C241 (6)	2.40	45

1952 adult education campaign.

A209 **Cuicocha Lagoon** A210

Black Surcharge.

1953

575	A209	40c on 50c pur	40	20

1953 **Engraved.** ***Perf. 13x12½.***

Designs: 10c, Equatorial Line monument. 20c, Quininde countryside. 30c, Tomebamba river. 40c, La Chilintosa rock. 50c, Iliniza Mountains.

Frames in Black.

576	A210	5c brt bl	5	5
577	A210	10c brt grn	5	5
578	A210	20c purple	8	6
579	A210	30c brown	8	6
580	A210	40c orange	10	10
581	A210	50c dp car	30	10
		Nos. 576-581 (6)	66	42

Carlos Maria Cardinal de la Torre and Arches

A211

1954, Jan. **Photo.** ***Perf. 8½***

582	A211	30c blk & ver	15	5
583	A211	50c blk & rose lil	20	8
		Nos. 582-583, C253-C255 (5)	1.35	58

Issued to commemorate the first anniversary of the elevation of Archbishop de la Torre to Cardinal.

Queen Isabella I

A212

1954, Apr. 22

584	A212	30c blk & gray	20	8
585	A212	50c blk brn & yel	20	10
		Nos. 584-585, C256-C260 (7)	1.65	1.18

Issued to commemorate the 500th anniversary of the birth of Queen Isabella I (1451–1504) of Spain.

Type of 1929; "POSTAL" Overprint Larger, No Letterspacing.

1954–55 ***Perf. 12*** **Unwmkd.**

586	A112	5c ol grn ('55)	15	5
587	A112	10c orange	20	5

The normal overprint on Nos. 586–587 reads up. It also exists reading down.

Indian Messenger A213 — **Products of Ecuador** A214

1954, Aug. 2 **Litho.** ***Perf. 11***

588	A213	30c dk brn	15	10

Issued to publicize the Day of the Postal Employee. See also No. C263.

1954, Sept. 24 **Photogravure**

589	A214	10c orange	8	5
590	A214	20c vermilion	10	5
591	A214	30c rose pink	15	5
592	A214	40c dk gray grn	20	8
593	A214	50c yel brn	30	10
		Nos. 589-593 (5)	83	33

José Abel Castillo A215 — **Babahoyo River Los Rios** A216

Perf. 11½x11

1955, Oct. 19 **Engraved** **Unwmkd.**

594	A215	30c ol bis	10	10
595	A215	5c dk gray	15	10
		Nos. 594-595, C282-C286 (7)	2.60	1.35

Issued to commemorate the 30th anniversary of the first flight of the "Telegrafo I" and to honor José Abel Castillo, aviation pioneer.

1955–56 **Photogravure** ***Perf. 13***

Designs: 5c, Palms, Esmeraldas. 10c, Fishermen, Manabi. 30c, Guayaquil, Guayas. 50c, Pital River, El Oro. 70c, Cactus, Galapagos Isls. 80c, Orchids, Napo-Pastaza. 1s, Aguacate Mission, Zamora-Chinchipe. 2s, Jibaro Indian, Morona-Santiago.

596	A216	5c yel grn ('56)	5	5
597	A216	10c bl ('56)	10	5
598	A216	20c brown	10	5
599	A216	30c dk gray	10	5
600	A216	50c bl grn	15	5
601	A216	70c ol ('56)	20	5
602	A216	80c dp vio ('56)	40	10
603	A216	1s org ('56)	30	10
604	A216	2s rose red ('56)	60	20
		Nos. 596-604 (9)	2.00	70

See also Nos. 620–630, 670, C288–C297, C310–C311.

Brother Juan Adam Schwarz, S. J.

A217

1956, Aug. 27 **Engraved** ***Perf. 13½***

605	A217	5c yel grn	5	5
606	A217	10c org red	5	5
607	A217	20c lt vio	5	5
608	A217	30c dk grn	5	5
609	A217	40c blue	10	5
610	A217	50c dp ultra	15	5
611	A217	70c orange	20	5
		Nos. 605-611, C302-C305 (11)	2.60	1.35

Issued to commemorate the bicentennial of printing in Ecuador and in honor of Brother Juan Adam Schwarz, S.J.

Andres Hurtado de Mendoza

A218

Gil Ramirez Davalos

A219

Designs: 20c, Brother Vincent Solano.

1957, Apr. 7 ***Perf. 12*** **Unwmkd.**

612	A218	5c dk bl, *pink*	10	5
613	A219	10c grn, *grnsh*	10	5
614	A218	20c choc, *buff*	15	5
a.		Souvenir sheet of 4	50	50
		Nos. 612-614, C312-C314 (6)	80	45

Issued to commemorate the fourth centenary of the founding of Cuenca.

No. 614a contains two 5c gray and two 20c brown red stamps in designs similar to Nos. 612 and 614. It was printed on white ungummed paper, is imperf. and is inscribed "II Exposicion Filatelica Nacional, Cuenca, 11 al 20 de Abril de 1957." Size: 140x120mm.

Francisco Marcos, Gen. Pedro Alcantara Herran and Santos Michelena

A220

1957, Sept. 5 **Engr.** ***Perf. 14½x14***

615	A220	40c yellow	15	5
616	A220	50c ultra	15	5
617	A220	2s dk red	50	20

7th Postal Congress of the Americas and Spain (in 1955).

Souvenir Sheets

Various Railroad Scenes

A221

Lithographed.

1957 ***Perf. 10½x11***

618	A221	Sheet of five 20c	80	80
619	A221	Sheet of five 30c	60	50

Issued to commemorate the opening of the Quito-Ibarra-San Lorenzo railroad.

Nos. 618–619 measure 118x110mm. with ultramarine inscriptions and contain 2 orange yellow, 1 ultramarine and 2 carmine stamps, each in a different design.

Scenic Type of 1955–56.

Designs as before, except: 40c, Cactus, Galapagos Islands. No. 629, San Pablo, Imbabura.

1957-58 **Photogravure.** ***Perf. 13***

620	A216	5c	lt bl	10	5
621	A216	10c	brown	10	5
622	A216	20c	crim rose	10	5
623	A216	20c	yel grn	10	5
624	A216	30c	rose red	15	5
625	A216	40c	chlky bl	40	5
626	A216	50c	lt vio	15	5
627	A216	90c	brt ultra	40	5
628	A216	1s	dk brn	20	10
629	A216	1s	gray blk ('58)	20	10
630	A216	2s	brown	50	20
			Nos. 620-630 (11)	2.40	80

Blue and Yellow Macaw
A222

Birds: 20c, Red-breasted toucan. 30c, Condor. 40c, Black-tailed and sword-tailed hummingbirds.

Perf. 13½x13

1958, Jan. 7 **Litho.** **Unwmkd.**

Birds in Natural Colors.

634	A222	10c	red brn	15	5
635	A222	20c	dk gray	15	8
636	A222	30c	brt yel grn	40	10
637	A222	40c	red org	40	10

Carlos Sanz de Santamaria
A223

Richard M. Nixon and Flags
A224

Design: No. 640, Dr. Ramon Villeda Morales and flags. 2.20s, José Carlos de Macedo Soares and horizontal flags.

1958 ***Perf. 12***

Flags in Red, Blue, Yellow & Green.

638	A223	1.80s dl vio	50	15
639	A224	2s dk grn	50	20
640	A224	2s dk brn	50	20
641	A223	2.20s blk brn	50	20

No. 638 commemorates the visit of Colombia's Foreign Minister Dr. Carlos Sanz de Santamaria to Ecuador.

No. 639 commemorates the visit of U. S. Vice President Richard M. Nixon to Ecuador, May 9-10.

No. 640 commemorates the visit of President Ramon Villeda Morales of Honduras.

No. 641 commemorates the visit of Brazil's Foreign Minister José Carlos de Macedo Soares to Ecuador. See Nos. C419–C421.

Locomotive of 1908
A225

Garcia Moreno, Jose Caamano, L. Plaza and Eloi Alfaro
A226

Design: 50c, Diesel locomotive.

Perf. 13½x14, 14

1958, Aug. 9 **Photo.** **Unwmkd.**

642	A225	30c brn blk	10	5
643	A225	50c dk car	15	8
644	A226	5s dk brn	75	50

Issued to commemorate the 50th anniversary of the Guayaquil-Quito railroad.

Cardinal
A227

Birds: 30c, Andean cock-of-the-rock. 50c, Glossy cowbird. 60c, Red-fronted Amazon.

1958 **Lithographed.** ***Perf. 13½x13***

Birds in Natural Colors.

645	A227	20c	bluish grn, blk & red	10	5
646	A227	30c	buff, blk & brt bl	10	5
647	A227	50c	org, blk & grn	15	10
648	A227	60c	pale rose, blk & bluish grn	20	10

UNESCO Building and Eiffel Tower, Paris
A228

1958, Nov. 3 **Engraved** ***Perf. 12½***

649	A228	80c brown	25	15

Issued to commemorate the opening of UNESCO (U. N. Educational, Scientific and Cultural Organization) Headquarters in Paris, Nov. 3.

Globe and Satellites
A229

Virgin of Quito
A230

1958, Dec. 20 **Photo.** ***Perf. 14x13½***

650	A229	1.80s dk bl	1.25	50

Issued to commemorate the International Geophysical Year, 1957–58.

1959, Sept. 8 ***Perf. 13*** **Unwmkd.**

651	A230	5c ol grn	5	5
652	A230	10c yel brn	5	5
653	A230	20c purple	5	5
654	A230	30c ultra	10	5
655	A230	80c dk car rose	15	8
		Nos. 651-655 (5)	40	28

See also No. C290.

Uprooted Oak Emblem
A231

1960, Apr. 7 **Litho.** ***Perf. 14x13***

656	A231	80c rose car & grn	20	10

Issued to publicize World Refugee Year, July 1, 1959–June 30, 1960.

Great Anteater and Arms
A232

Animals: 40c, Tapir and map. 80c, Spectacled bear and arms. 1s, Puma and map.

1960, May 14 **Photo.** ***Perf. 13***

657	A232	20c	org, grn & blk	10	10
658	A232	40c	yel grn, bl grn & brn	15	10
659	A232	80c	bl, blk & red brn	25	15
660	A232	1s	Prus bl, plum & ocher	50	25

Issued to commemorate the 4th centenary of the founding of the city of Baeza.

See also Nos. 676–679.

Hotel Quito
A233

Designs: No. 662, Dormitory, Catholic University. No. 663, Dormitory, Central University. No. 664, Airport, Quito. No. 665, Overpass on Highway to Quito. No. 666, Security Bank. No. 667, Ministry of Foreign Affairs. No. 668, Government Palace. No. 669, Legislative Palace.

Perf. 11x11½

1960, Aug. 8 **Engraved** **Unwmkd.**

661	A233	1s	dk pur & redsh brn	15	10
662	A233	1s	dk bl & brn	15	10
663	A233	1s	blk & red	15	10
664	A233	1s	dk bl & ultra	15	10
665	A233	1s	dk pur & dk car rose	15	10
666	A233	1s	blk & ol bis	15	10
667	A233	1s	dk pur & turq	15	10
668	A233	1s	dk bl & grn	15	10
669	A233	1s	blk & vio	15	10
			Nos. 661-669 (9)	1.35	90

11th Inter-American Conference, Quito.

Souvenir Sheet

Type of Regular Issue, 1955–56.

Design: Orchids, Napo-Pastaza.

1960 **Photogravure** ***Perf. 13***

Yellow Paper.

670	A216	Sheet of two	30	30
a.		80c dp vio	10	10
b.		90c dp grn	10	10

Issued to commemorate the 25th anniversary of Asociacion Filatelica Ecuatoriana. Marginal inscription in silver. Size: 85x55mm. Exists with silver inscription omitted.

"Freedom of Expression"
A234

Manabi Bridge
A235

Designs: 10c, "Freedom to vote." 20c, "Freedom to work." 30c, Coins, "Monetary stability."

1960, Aug. 29 **Litho.** ***Perf. 13***

671	A234	5c	dk bl	5	5
672	A234	10c	lt vio	5	5
673	A234	20c	orange	10	5
674	A234	30c	bluish grn	10	5
675	A235	40c	brn & bluish grn	15	5
			Nos. 671-675 (5)	45	25

Issued to publicize the achievements of President Camilo Ponce Enriquez. See Nos. C370–C374.

Animal Type of 1960.

Animals: 10c, Collared peccary. 20c, Kinkajou. 80c, Jaguars. 1s, Mountain coati.

Photogravure

1961, July 13 ***Perf. 13*** **Unwmkd.**

676	A232	10c	grn, rose red & blk	5	5
677	A232	20c	vio, grnsh bl & brn	10	5
678	A232	80c	red org, dl yel & blk	20	10
679	A232	1s	brn, brt grn & org	25	15

Issued to commemorate the 400th anniversary of the founding of the city of Tena.

Graphium Pausianus
A236

Butterflies: 30c, Papilio torquatus leptalea. 50c, Graphium molops molops. 80c, Battus lycidas.

1961, July 13 **Litho.** ***Perf. 13½***

680	A236	20c	pink & multi	10	5
681	A236	30c	lt ultra & multi	10	5
682	A236	50c	org & multi	15	10
683	A236	80c	bl grn & multi	20	10

See also Nos. 711–713.

Galapagos Islands Nos. L1-L3 Overprinted in Black or Red

1961

Estación de Biología Marítima de Galápagos

XXXXXXXXXXX

1961, Oct. 31 **Photo.** ***Perf. 12***

684	A1	20c dk brn	20	10
685	A2	50c violet	20	10
686	A1	1s dk ol grn (R)	40	20
		Nos. 684-686, C389-C391 (6)	2.15	95

Establishment of maritime biological stations on Galapagos Islands by UNESCO. Overprint arranged differently on 20c, 1s. See Nos. C389-C391.

Daniel Enrique Proano School
A237

Designs: 60c, Loja-Zamora highway (vert.). 80c, Aguirre Abad College, Guayaquil. 1s, Army quarters, Quito.

Perf. 11x11½, 11½x11

1962, Jan. 10 Engr. Unwmkd.

687	A237	50c dl bl & blk	10	5
688	A237	60c ol grn & blk	10	5
689	A237	80c org red & blk	20	10
690	A237	1s rose lake & blk	25	10

Pres. Arosemena, Flags of Ecuador, U.S.
A238

Protection for The Family
A239

Designs (Arosemena and): 10c, Flags of Ecuador. 20c, Flags of Ecuador and Panama.

1963, July 1 Litho. *Perf. 14*

691	A238	10c buff & multi	5	5
692	A238	20c multi	10	5
693	A238	60c multi	15	5
		Nos. 691-693, C409-C411 (6)	1.50	75

Issued to commemorate Pres. Carlos J. Arosemena's friendship trip, July 1962.

1963, July 9 *Perf. 14* Unwmkd.

694	A239	10c ultra, red, gray & blk	10	5

Issued to commemorate the 25th anniversary of Social Insurance. See No. C413.

No. 655 Overprinted or Surcharged in Black or Blue

1961 DIA DEL EMPLEADO POSTAL 10

1963 Photogravure *Perf. 13*

695	A230	10c on 80c dk car rose	5	5
696	A230	20c on 80c dk car rose	10	5
697	A230	50c on 80c dk car rose	10	10
698	A230	60c on 80c dk car rose (Bl)	15	10
699	A230	80c dk car rose	25	10
		Nos. 695-699 (5)	65	40

Nos. 661-669 Surcharged **0,10** XXXXX

1964, Apr. 20 Engr. *Perf. 11x11½*

700	A233	10c on 1s dk pur & redsh brn	5	5
701	A233	10c on 1s dk pur & turq	5	5
702	A233	20c on 1s dk bl & brn	5	5
703	A233	20c on 1s dk bl & grn	5	5
704	A233	30c on 1s dk pur & dk car rose	10	5
705	A233	40c on 1s blk & ol bis	10	5
706	A233	60c on 1s blk & red	15	10
707	A233	80c on 1s dk bl & ultra	20	10
708	A233	80c on 1s blk & vio	20	10
		Nos. 700-708 (9)	95	60

No. 656 Overprinted in Black or Light Ultramarine **1961**

1964 Lithographed *Perf. 14x13*

709	A231	80c rose car & grn	2.00	60

Butterfly Type of 1961

Butterflies: Same as on Nos. 680, 682-683.

1964, June Litho. *Perf. 13½*

711	A236	20c brt grn & multi	5	5
712	A236	50c sal pink & multi	10	5
713	A236	80c lt red brn & multi	15	10

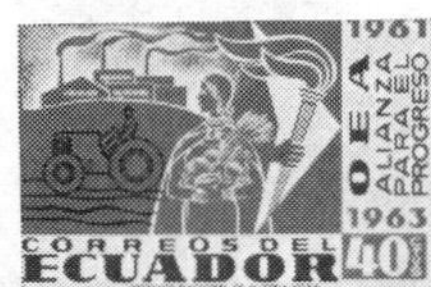

Alliance for Progress Emblem, Agriculture and Industry
A240

Designs: 50c, Emblem, gear wheels, mountain and seashore. 80c, Emblem, banana worker, fish, factory and ship.

1964, Aug. 26 *Perf. 12* Unwmkd.

715	A240	40c bis brn & vio	10	5
716	A240	50c red org & blk	15	5
717	A240	80c bl & dk brn	20	10

Issued to publicize the Alliance for Progress which aims to stimulate economic growth and raise living standards in Latin America.

No. 650 Overprinted in Red **FARO DE COLON**

1964 Photogravure *Perf. 14x13½*

718	A229	1.80s dk bl	2.00	1.00

No. 656 Overprinted

(Reduced Size)
Overprint covers four stamps

1964, July Litho. *Perf. 14x13*

719	A231	80c rose car & grn (block of 4)	2.50	1.00

Organization of American States.

World Map and Banana Tree
A241

1964, Oct. 26 *Perf. 12½x12*

720	A241	50c dk brn, gray & gray ol	5	5
721	A241	80c blk, org & gray ol	10	5

Issued to publicize the Banana Conference, Oct.-Nov. 1964. See Nos. C427-C428a.

King Philip II of Spain and Map of Upper Amazon River
A242

Designs (Map and): 20c, Juan de Salinas de Loyola. 30c, Hernando de Santillan.

1964, Dec. 6 Litho. *Perf. 13½*

722	A242	10c rose, blk & buff	5	5
723	A242	20c bl grn, blk & buff	10	5
724	A242	30c bl, blk & buff	10	5

Issued to commemorate the 4th centenary of the establishment of the Royal High Court in Quito.

Pole Vaulting
A243

1964, Dec. 16 *Perf. 14x13½*

725	A243	80c vio bl, yel grn & brn	15	10

Issued to commemorate the 18th Olympic Games, Tokyo, Oct. 10-25. See also Nos. C432-C434.

Peter Fleming and Two-toed Sloth
A244

Designs: 20c, James Elliot and armadillo. 30c, T. Edward McCully, Jr., and squirrel. 40c, Roger Youderian and deer. 60c, Nathaniel (Nate) Saint and plane over Napo River.

1965 *Perf. 13½* Unwmkd.

726	A244	20c emer & multi	5	5
727	A244	30c yel & multi	5	5
728	A244	40c lil & multi	5	5
729	A244	60c multi	10	10
730	A244	80c multi	15	10
		Nos. 726-730 (5)	40	35

Issued in memory of five American Protestant missionaries, killed by the Auca Indians, Jan. 8, 1956. Issue dates: 80c, May 11; others, July 8.

Juan B. Vázquez and Benigno Malo College
A245

1965, June 6 Litho. *Perf. 14*

731	A245	20c blk, yel & vio bl	5	5
732	A245	60c blk, red, yel & vio bl	10	5
733	A245	80c blk, emer, yel & vio bl	10	10

Issued to commemorate the centenary (in 1964) of the founding of Benigno Malo National College.

National Anthem, Juan Leon Mera and Antonio Neumane
A246

1965, Aug. 10 Litho. *Perf. 13½*

734	A246	50c pink & blk	5	5
735	A246	80c lt grn & blk	10	10
736	A246	5s bis & blk	50	40
737	A246	10s lt ultra & blk	90	75

Issued to commemorate the centenary of the national anthem. The name of the poet Juan Leon Mera is misspelled on the stamps.

Torch and Athletes (Shot Put, Discus, Javelin and Hammer Throw)
A247

Torch and Athletes: 50c, 1s, Runners. 60c, 1.50s, Soccer.

1965, Nov. 20 *Perf. 12x12½*

738	A247	40c org, gold, & blk	5	5
739	A247	50c org ver, gold & blk	5	5
740	A247	60c bl, gold & blk	10	5
741	A247	80c brt yel grn, gold & blk	10	10
742	A247	1s lt vio, gold & blk	15	10
743	A247	1.50s brt pink, gold & blk	20	15
		Nos. 738-743, C435-C440 (12)	2.40	1.70

Issued to publicize the 5th Bolivarian Games, held at Guayaquil and Quito.

Stamps of 1865
A248

1965, Dec. 30 Litho. *Perf. 13½*

Stamps of 1865 in Yellow, Ultramarine & Green

744	A248	80c rose red	15	10
745	A248	1.30s rose lil	20	10
746	A248	2s chocolate	30	15
747	A248	4s black	50	25
a.		Souv. sheet of 4	1.50	1.50

Issued to commemorate the centenary of Ecuadorian postage stamps. No. 747a contains four imperf. stamps similar to Nos. 744-747. Dark blue marginal inscription and black control number. Size: 140x125 mm.

Pavonine Quetzal
A249

Bust of Peñaherrera, Central University, Quito
A250

Birds: 50c, Blue-crowned motmot. 60c, Paradise tanager. 80c, Wire-tailed manakin.

1966, June 17 Litho. *Perf. 13½*

Birds in Natural Colors

748	A249	40c dl rose & blk	5	5
749	A249	50c sal & blk	5	5
750	A249	60c lt ocher & blk	10	10
751	A249	80c lt bl & blk	10	10
		Nos. 748-751, C441-C448 (12)	2.15	1.60

Various Surcharges on Issues of 1956-66

1967-68

752	AP72	30c on 1.10s multi (C337)	5	5
753	AP66	40c on 1.70s yel brn (C292)	5	5
754	A247	40c on 3.50s lt vio, gold & blk (C438)	5	5
755	A246	50c on 5s bis & blk (736) ('68)	10	5
756	A247	80c on 1.50s brt pink, gold & blk (743)	15	5
757	A249	80c on 2.50s lt yel grn & multi (C445)	15	5
758	A249	1s on 4s gray & multi (C447)	15	5
759	AP66	1.30s on 1.90s ol (C293)	20	15
760	A246	2s on 10s lt ultra & blk (737) ('68)	30	15
		Nos. 752-760, C449-C450 (11)	1.30	55

The surcharge on Nos. 754-755, 757 and 759-760 includes "Resello." The obliteration of old denomination and arrangement of surcharges differ on each stamp.

Perf. 12x12½, 12½x12

1967, Dec. 29 Lithographed

Designs: 50c, Law books. 80c, Open book and laurel (horiz.).

761	A250	50c brt grn & blk	5	5
762	A250	60c rose & blk	5	5
763	A250	80c rose lil & blk	10	5
		Nos. 761-763, C451-C452 (5)	50	35

Issued to commemorate the centenary (in 1964) of the birth of Dr. Victor Manuel Peñaherrera (1864-1932), author of the civil and criminal codes of Ecuador.

Otto Arosemena Gomez
A251

Lions Emblem
A252

1968, May 9 Litho. *Perf. 13½x14*

Design: 1s, Page from the Constitution.

764	A251	80c lil & multi	5	5
765	A251	1s multi	10	5

First anniversary of the administration of Pres. Otto Arosemena Gomez. See Nos. C453-C454.

1968, May 24 Litho. *Perf. 13½x14*

766	A252	80c multi	10	10
767	A252	1.30s multi	15	10
768	A252	2s pink & multi	20	15
a.		Souv. sheet of 1	3.00	3.00

Issued to commemorate the 50th anniversary (in 1967) of Lions International.

No. 768a contains one 5s stamp (size: 39x49mm.). Violet blue marginal inscriptions and red control numbers. Size: 71x104mm. Exists imperf.

Nos. C331 and C326 Surcharged in Violet and Dark Blue

RESELLO

$ 0,40

a

$ 0,50

RESELLO

b

1969, Jan. 10 *Perf. 11½, 14x13½*

769	AP79 (a)	40c on 1.30s grn & brn red (V)	5	5
770	AP76 (b)	50c on 1.30s dk grn & lt brn (DBl)	5	5

Type of 1958 Surcharged and Overprinted in Plum and Black

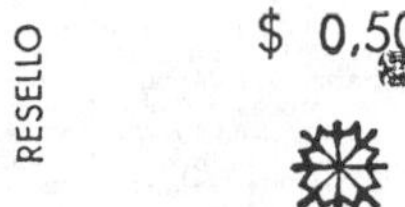

Design: Ignacio Luis Arcaya, Foreign Minister of Venezuela.

1969, Mar. Litho. *Perf. 12*

Flags in Red, Blue and Yellow.

771	A223	50c on 2s sep	5	5
772	A223	80c on 2s sep	10	5
773	A223	1s on 2s sep	10	10
774	A223	2s sepia	20	15
		Nos. 771-774, C455-C457 (7)	75	65

Nos. 771-774 were not issued without overprint. The obliteration of old denomination on No. 772 is a small square around a star. Overprint is plum, except for the black small coat of arms on right flag.

Map of Ecuador and Oriental Region
A253

Surcharge Typographed in Dark Blue, Red Brown, Black or Lilac

1969 Lithographed *Perf. 14*

775	A253	20c on 30c multi (DBl)	5	5
776	A253	40c on 30c multi (RBr)	5	5
777	A253	50c on 30c multi (DBl)	5	5
778	A253	60c on 30c multi (DBl)	5	5
779	A253	80c on 30c multi (Bk)	10	10
780	A253	1s on 30c multi (L)	10	10
781	A253	1.30s on 30c multi (Bk)	15	10
782	A253	1.50s on 30c multi (Bk)	20	15
783	A253	2s on 30c multi (DBl)	25	20
784	A253	3s on 30c multi (DBl)	35	25
785	A253	4s on 30c multi (Bk)	25	15
786	A253	5s on 30c multi (Bk)	30	20
		Nos. 775-786 (12)	1.90	1.45

Not issued without surcharge.

M. L. King, John and Robert Kennedy
A254

Thecla Coronata
A255

1969-70 Typographed *Perf. 12½*

787	A254	4s blk, bl, grn & buff	40	15

Perf. 13½

788	A254	4s blk, lt bl & grn ('70)	40	15

In memory of John F. Kennedy, Robert F. Kennedy and Martin Luther King, Jr.

1970 Lithographed *Perf. 12½*

Butterflies: 20c, Papilio zabreus. 30c, Heliconius chestertoni. 40c, Papilio pausanias. 50c, Pereute leucodrosime. 60c, Metamorpha dido. 80c, Morpho cypris. 1s, Catagramma astarte.

789	A255	10c buff & multi	5	5
790	A255	20c lt grn & multi	5	5
791	A255	30c pink & multi	5	5
792	A255	40c lt bl & multi	5	5
793	A255	50c gold & multi	5	5
794	A255	60c sal & multi	10	5
795	A255	80c sil & multi	10	5
796	A255	1s lt grn & multi	10	5
		Nos. 789-796, C461-C462 (10)	75	60

Same, White Background

1970 *Perf. 13½*

797	A255	10c multi	5	5
798	A255	20c multi	5	5
799	A255	30c multi	5	5
800	A255	40c multi	5	5
801	A255	50c multi	5	5
802	A255	60c multi	5	5
803	A255	80c multi	10	5
804	A255	1s multi	10	5
		Nos. 797-804, C463-C464 (10)	70	50

Surcharged Revenue Stamps
A256 A257

1970, June 16 Litho. *Perf. 14*

Red Surcharge

805	A256	1s on 1s lt bl	10	5
806	A256	1.30s on 1s lt bl	15	5
807	A256	1.50s on 1s lt bl	20	10
808	A256	2s on 1s lt bl	20	10
809	A256	5s on 1s lt bl	50	20
810	A256	10s on 1s lt bl	1.00	40
		Nos. 805-810 (6)	2.15	90

1970 Typographed *Perf. 12*

Black Surcharge

811	A257	60c on 1s vio	10	5
812	A257	80c on 1s vio	10	5
813	A257	1s on 1s vio	10	5
814	A257	1.10s on 1s vio	10	5
815	A257	1.30s on 1s vio	10	5
816	A257	1.50s on 1s vio	15	5
817	A257	2s on 1s vio	20	5
818	A257	2.20s on 1s vio	30	5
819	A257	3s on 1s vio	40	10
		Nos. 811-819 (9)	1.55	50

1970

820	A257	1.10s on 2s grn	10	10
821	A257	1.30s on 2s grn	15	10
822	A257	1.50s on 2s grn	15	10
823	A257	2s on 2s grn	20	10
824	A257	3.40s on 2s grn	35	10
825	A257	5s on 2s grn	50	15
826	A257	10s on 2s grn	90	20
827	A257	20s on 2s grn	1.50	40
828	A257	50s on 2s grn	4.00	1.00
		Nos. 820-828 (9)	7.85	2.25

1970

829	A257	3s on 5s bl	30	5
830	A257	5s on 5s bl	50	10
831	A257	10s on 40s org	75	20

Arms of Zamora Chinchipe
A258

Flags of Ecuador and Chile
A259

Design: 1s, Arms and flag of Esmeraldas.

1971 Lithographed *Perf. 10½*

832	A258	50c pale yel & multi	5	5
833	A258	1s sal & multi	10	5
		Nos. 832-833, C465-C469 (7)	1.65	1.25

1971, Sept. *Perf. 12½*

840	A259	1.30s blk & multi	10	10

Visit of Pres. Salvador Allende of Chile, Aug. 24. See Nos. C481-C482.

Ismael Pérez Pazmiño
A260

1971, Sept. 16 *Perf. 12x11½*

841	A260	1s grn & multi	10	5

50th anniversary of "El Universo," newspaper founded by Ismael Pérez Pazmiño. See Nos. C485-C486.

CARE Package
A261

Flags of Ecuador and Argentina
A262

1971-72 *Perf. 12½*

842	A261	30c lil ('72)	5	5
843	A261	40c emer ('72)	5	5
844	A261	50c blue	5	5
845	A261	60c carmine	5	5
846	A261	80c lt brn ('72)	10	5
		Nos. 842-846 (5)	30	25

25th anniversary of CARE, a U.S.-Canadian Cooperative for American Relief Everywhere.

1972 *Perf. 11½*

847	A262	1s blk & multi	10	5

Visit of Lt. Gen. Alejandro Agustin Lanusse, president of Argentina, Jan. 25. See Nos. C491-C492.

Jesus Giving Keys to St. Peter, by Miguel de Santiago
A263

Ecuadorian Paintings: 1.10s, Virgin of Mercy, Quito School. 2s, Virgin Mary, by Manuel Samaniego.

1972, Apr. 24 Litho. *Perf. 14x13½*

848	A263	50c blk & multi	5	5
849	A263	1.10s blk & multi	10	10
850	A263	2s blk & multi	20	15
a.		Souv. sheet of 3	40	40
		Nos. 848-850, C494-C495 (5)	1.30	95

No. 850a contains 3 imperf. stamps similar to Nos. 848–850. Blue marginal inscription. Size: 129x110mm.

1972, May 4

Ecuadorian Statues: 50c, Our Lady of Sorrow, by Caspicara. 1.10s, Nativity. Quito School (horiz.). 2s, Virgin of Quito, anonymous.

851	A263	50c blk & multi	5	5
852	A263	1.10s blk & multi	10	10
853	A263	2s blk & multi	20	10
a.		Souv. sheet of 3	40	40
		Nos. 851-853, C496-C497 (5)	1.35	95

Letters of "Ecuador" 3mm. high on Nos. 851–853, 7mm. high on Nos. 848–850. No. 853a contains 3 imperf. stamps similar to Nos. 851–853. Blue marginal inscription. Size. 129x110mm.

Gen. Juan Ignacio Pareja
A264

Designs: 40c, Juan José Flores. 50c, Leon de Febres Cordero. 60c, Ignacio Torres. 70c, Francisco de Paula Santander. 1s, José M. Cordova.

1972, May 24 *Perf. 12½*

854	A264	30c bl & multi	5	5
855	A264	40c bl & multi	5	5
856	A264	50c bl & multi	5	5
857	A264	60c bl & multi	5	5
858	A264	70c bl & multi	10	5
859	A264	1s bl & multi	10	5
		Nos. 854-859, C498-C503 (12)	3.70	2.60

Sesquicentennial of the Battle of Pichincha and the liberation of Quito.

Woman Wearing Poncho
A265

Designs: 3s, Striped poncho. 5s, Embroidered poncho. 10s, Metal vase.

1972, July Photo. *Perf. 13*

860	A265	2s multi	20	10
861	A265	3s multi	25	20
862	A265	5s multi	50	15
863	A265	10s dp bl & multi	1.00	40
a.		Souvenir sheet of 4	2.00	2.00
		Nos. 860-863, C504-C507 (8)	2.80	1.90

Handicraft of Ecuador. No. 863a contains 4 imperf. stamps similar to Nos. 860–863. Gray green marginal inscription and ornament. Black control number. Size 104x164mm.

Sucre Statue, Santo Domingo
A266

Radar Station
A267

Wmk. 367

Wmkd. Liberty Cap, Emblem and Inscription (367)

1972, Dec. 6 Litho. *Perf. 11½*

Designs: 1.80s, San Agustin Convent. 2.30s, Plaza de la Independencia. 2.50s, Bolivar statue, La Alameda. 4.75s, Chapel door.

864	A266	1.20s yel & multi	15	10
865	A266	1.80s yel & multi	15	10
866	A266	2.30s yel & multi	20	15
867	A266	2.50s yel & multi	30	20
868	A266	4.75s yel & multi	50	25
		Nos. 864-868, C518-C524 (12)	4.51	2.80

Sesquicentennial of the Battle of Pichincha.

1973, Apr. 5 Litho. *Perf. 11½*

869	A267	1s multi	20	10

Inauguration of earth telecommunications station, Oct. 19, 1972.

Blue-footed Boobies
A268

1973 Lithographed *Perf. 11½x12*

Multicolored

870	A268	30c *shown*	5	5
871	A268	40c *Blue-faced booby*	5	5
872	A268	50c *Oyster-catcher*	5	5
873	A268	60c *California sea lions*	10	10
874	A268	70c *Galapagos giant tortoise*	15	10
875	A268	1s *California sea lion*	20	10
		Nos. 870-875, C527-C528 (8)	1.00	65

Elevation of Galapagos Islands to a province of Ecuador.
Issue dates: 50c, Oct. 3; others Aug. 16.

Black-chinned Mountain Tanager
A269

Birds of Ecuador: 2s, Moriche oriole. 3s, Toucan barbet (vert.). 5s, Masked crimson tanager (vert.). 10s, Blue-necked tanager (vert.).

Perf. 11x11½, 11½x11

1973, Dec. 6 Litho. Unwmkd.

876	A269	1s brick red & multi	15	10
877	A269	2s lt bl & multi	25	10
878	A269	3s lt grn & multi	25	10
879	A269	5s pale lil & multi	60	25
880	A269	10s pale yel grn & multi	1.25	60
		Nos. 876-880 (5)	2.50	1.15

Two souvenir sheets exist: one contains 2 imperf. stamps similar to Nos. 876–877 with yellow margin and black inscription; the other 3 stamps similar to Nos. 878–880; gray margin and black inscription including "Aereo." Both sheets dated "1972." Size: 143x84mm.

Marco T. Varea, Botanist
A270

Portraits: 60c, Pio Jaramillo Alvarado, writer. 70c, Prof. Luciano Andrade M. No. 883, Marco T. Varea, botanist. No. 884, Dr. Juan Modesto Carbo Noboa, medical researcher. No. 885, Alfredo J. Valenzuela. No. 886, Capt. Edmundo Chiriboga G. 1.20s, Francisco Campos R., scientist. 1.80s, Luis Vernaza Lazarte, philanthropist.

1974 *Perf. 12x11½* Unwmkd.

881	A270	60c crim rose	5	5
882	A270	70c lilac	5	5
883	A270	1s ultra	10	5
884	A270	1s orange	10	5
885	A270	1s emerald	10	5
886	A270	1s brown	10	5
887	A270	1.20s ap grn	15	10
889	A270	1.80s lt bl	25	15
		Nos. 881-889 (8)	90	55

Arcade
A271

Designs: 30c, Monastery, entrance. 40c, Church. 50c, View of Church through gate (vert.). 60c, Chapel (vert.). 70c, Church and cemetery (vert.).

Perf. 11½x12, 12x11½

1975, Feb. 4 Lithographed

896	A271	20c yel & multi	5	5
897	A271	30c yel & multi	5	5
898	A271	40c yel & multi	5	5
899	A271	50c yel & multi	5	5
900	A271	60c yel & multi	10	5
901	A271	70c yel & multi	10	5
		Nos. 896-901 (6)	40	30

Colonial Monastery, Tilipulo, Cotopaxi Province.

Angel Polibio Chaves, Founder of Bolivar Province
A272

Portrait: No. 903, Emilio Estrada Ycaza (1916–1961), archeologist.

1975 Litho. *Perf. 12x11½*

902	A272	80c vio bl & lt bl	10	10
903	A272	80c ver & pink	10	10

Issue dates: No. 902, Feb. 21; No. 903, Mar. 25.

R. Rodriguez Palacios and A. Duran Quintero
A273

"Woman of Action"
A274

1975, Apr. 1 Litho. *Perf. 12x11½*

910	A273	1s multi	10	10

Meeting of the Ministers for Public Works of Ecuador and Colombia, July 27, 1973.
See Nos. C547–C548.

1975, June

Design: No. 912, 1s, "Woman of Peace."

911	A274	1s yel & multi	10	10
912	A274	1s bl & multi	10	10

International Women's Year 1975.

Planes, Soldier and Ship
A275

1975, July 9 *Perf. 11½x12*

913	A275	2s multi	20	15

Three years of National Revolutionary Government.

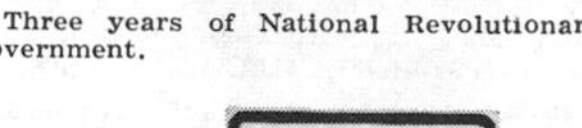

Hurdling
A276

Designs: Modern sports drawn Inca style.

1975, Sept. 11 Litho. *Perf. 11½*

914	A276	20c *shown*	5	5
915	A276	20c *Chess*	5	5
916	A276	30c *Basketball*	5	5
917	A276	30c *Boxing*	5	5
918	A276	40c *Bicycling*	5	5
919	A276	40c *Steeplechase*	5	5
920	A276	50c *Soccer*	5	5
921	A276	50c *Fencing*	5	5
922	A276	60c *Golf*	5	5
923	A276	60c *Vaulting*	5	5
924	A276	70c *Judo (standing)*	10	5
925	A276	70c *Wrestling*	10	5
926	A276	80c *Swimming*	10	5
927	A276	80c *Weight lifting*	10	5

928 A276 1s *Table Tennis* 10 5
929 A276 1s *Paddle ball* 10 5
Nos. 914-929, C554-C558 (21) 2.50 1.20

3rd Ecuadorian Games.

Genciana
A277

Designs: Ecuadorian plants.

Perf. 12x11½, 11½x12

1975, Nov. 18 Lithographed

Multicolored

930 A277 20c *Orchid* (vert.) 5 5
931 A277 30c *shown* 5 5
932 A277 40c *Bromeliaceae cactacceae (vert.)* 5 5
933 A277 50c *Orchid* 5 5
934 A277 60c *Orchid* 5 5
935 A277 80c *Flowering cactus* 10 5
936 A277 1s *Orchid* 10 5
Nos. 930-936, C559-C563 (12) 1.70 1.05

Venus, Chorrera Culture
A278

Female Mask, Tolita Culture
A279

Designs: 30c, Venus, Valdivia Culture. 40c, Seated man, Chorrera Culture. 50c, Man with poncho, Panzaleo Culture (late). 60c, Mythical head, Cashaloma Culture. 80c, Musician, Tolita Culture. No. 943, Chief Priest, Manteña Culture. No. 945, Ornament, Tolita Culture. No. 946, Angry mask, Tolita Culture.

1976, Feb. 12 Litho. *Perf. 11½*

937 A278 20c multi 5 5
938 A278 30c multi 5 5
939 A278 40c multi 5 5
940 A278 50c multi 5 5
941 A278 60c multi 5 5
942 A278 80c multi 10 5
943 A278 1s multi 10 5
944 A279 1s multi 10 5
945 A279 1s multi 10 5
946 A279 1s multi 10 5
Nos. 937-946, C568-C572 (15) 1.90 1.10

Archaeological artifacts.

Strawberries
A280

Carlos Amable Ortiz (1859–1937)
A281

1976, Mar. 30

947 A280 1s bl & multi 10 5

25th Flower and Fruit Festival, Ambato. See Nos. C573–C574.

1976, Mar. 15 Litho. *Perf. 11½*

Portraits: No. 949, Sixto Maria Duran (1875–1947). No. 950, Segundo Cueva Celi (1901–1969). No. 951, Cristobal Ojeda Davila (1910–1952). No. 952, Luis Alberto Valencia (1918–1970).

948 A281 1s ver & multi 10 5
949 A281 1s org & multi 10 5
950 A281 1s lt grn & multi 10 5
951 A281 1s bl & multi 10 5
952 A281 1s lt brn & multi 10 5
Nos. 948-952 (5) 50 25

Ecuadorian composers and musicians.

Institute Emblem
A282

1977, Aug. 15 Litho. *Perf. 11½x12*

953 A282 2s multi 20 10

11th General Assembly of Pan-American Institute of Geography and History, Quito, Aug. 15–30. See Nos. C597–C597a.

Hands Holding Rotary Emblem
A283

José Peralta
A284

1977, Aug. 31 Litho. *Perf. 12*

954 A283 1s multi 10 5
955 A283 2s multi 20 10

Souvenir Sheets

Imperf.

956 A283 5s multi 50 30
957 A283 10s multi 1.00 60

Rotary Club of Guayaquil, 50th anniversary. Nos. 956–957 have black control numbers. Size: 90x115mm.

1977 Litho. *Perf. 11½*

Design: 2.40s, Peralta statue.

958 A284 1.80s multi 15 10
959 A284 2.40s multi 20 10

José Peralta (1855–1937), writer, 40th death anniversary. See No. C609.

Blue-faced Booby
A285

Galapagos Birds: 1.80s, Red-footed booby. 2.40s, Blue-footed boobies. 3.40s, Gull. 4.40s, Galapagos hawk. 5.40s, Map of Galapagos Islands and boobies (vert.).

Perf. 11½x12, 12x11½

1977, Nov. 29 Lithographed

960 A285 1.20s multi 10 5
961 A285 1.80s multi 15 10
962 A285 2.40s multi 20 10
963 A285 3.40s multi 25 15
964 A285 4.40s multi 35 20
965 A285 5.40s multi 50 20
Nos. 960-965 (6) 1.55 80

Dr. Corral Moscoso Hospital, Cuenca
A286

1978, Apr. 12 Litho. *Perf. 11½x12*

966 A286 3s multi 25 15

Inauguration (in 1977) of Dr. Vicente Corral Moscoso Regional Hospital, Cuenca. See Nos. C613–C614.

Surveyor Plane over Ecuador
A287

Latin-American Lions Emblem
A288

1978, Apr. 12 Litho. *Perf. 11½*

967 A287 6s multi 50 30

Military Geographical Institute, 50th anniversary. See Nos. C619–C620.

1978

968 A288 3s multi 25 15
969 A288 4.20s multi 40 20

7th meeting of Latin American Lions, Jan. 25–29. See Nos. C621–C623.

70th Anniversary Emblem
A289

1978, Sept. Litho. *Perf. 11½*

970 A289 4.20s gray & multi 40 20

70th anniversary of Filanbanco (Philanthropic Bank). See No. C626.

Goalmouth and Net—A290

Designs: 1.80s, "Gauchito" and Games emblem (vert.). 4.40s, "Gauchito" (vert.).

1978, Nov. 1 Litho. *Perf. 12*

971 A290 1.20s multi 10 5
972 A290 1.80s multi 15 10
973 A290 4.40s multi 35 20
Nos. 971-973, C627-C629 (6) 2.20 1.20

11th World Cup Soccer Championship, Argentina, June 1–25.

Symbols for Male and Female
A291

1979, Feb. 15 Litho. *Perf. 12x11½*

974 A291 3.40s multi 30 15

Inter-American Women's Commission, 50th anniversary.

Emblem
A292

1979, June 21 Litho. *Perf. 11½x12*

975 A292 4.40s multi 40 20
976 A292 5.40s multi 50 20

Ecuadorian Mortgage Bank, 16th anniversary.

Street Scene, Quito
A293

Unwmkd.

1979, Aug. 3 Litho. *Perf. 12x11½*

977 A293 3.40s multi 30 15

National heritage: Quito and Galapagos Islands. See Nos. C651–C653.

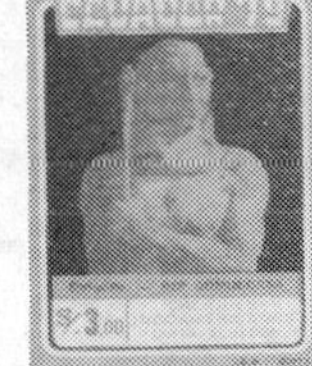
Jose Joaquin de Olmedo (1780-1847), Physician
A294

Chief Enriquillo, Dominican Republic
A295

1980, Apr. 29 Litho. *Perf. 12x11½*

978 A294 3s multi 25 10
979 A294 5s multi 40 20

First President of Free State of Guayaquil, 1820. See No. C662.

1980, May 12

Indo-American Tribal Chiefs: 3.40s, Guaycaypuro, Venezuela. No. 982, Abayuba, Uruguay. No. 983, Atlacatl, Salvador.

980 A295 3s multi 25 10
981 A295 3.40s multi 35 15
982 A295 5s multi 50 25
983 A295 5s multi 50 25
Nos. 980-983, C663-C678 (20) 18.90 9.40

King Juan Carlos and Queen Sofia, Visit to Ecuador—A296

1980, May 18 *Perf. 11½x12*

984 A296 3.40s multi 30 15

See No. C679.

Cofan Indian, Napo Province—A297

1980, June 10 Litho. *Perf. 12x11½*

985 A297 3s *shown* 25 10
986 A297 3.40s *Zuleta woman, Imbabura* 30 15
987 A297 5s *Chota woman Imbabura* 50 25
Nos. 985-987, C681-C684 (7) 4.45 2.35

Basilica, Our Lady of Mercy Church, Quito—A298

1980, July 7 Litho. *Perf. 11½*

988 A298 3.40s *shown* 30 15
989 A298 3.40s *Balcony*, vert. 30 15
Nos. 988-989, C685-C691 (9) 9.40 4.69

Souvenir Sheet

990 A298 5s multi 50 25

Virgin of Mercy, patron saint of Ecuadorian armed forces. No. 990 contains designs of Nos. C686, C690, 989; black control number. Size: 91x116mm.

Olympic Torch and Rings—A299

1980, July 19 *Perf. 12x11½*

991 A299 5s multi 40 20
992 A299 7.60s multi 60 30

Souvenir Sheet
Imperf.

993 A299 30s multi 2.50 1.25

22nd Summer Olympic Games, Moscow, July 19-Aug. 3. See Nos. C695-C696.

No. 993 contains vignettes in designs of Nos. 991 and C695, black control number. Size: 116x90mm.

Coronation of Virgin of Cisne, 50th Anniversary—A300

1980 Litho. *Perf. 11½*

994 A300 1.20s *shown* 10 5
995 A300 3.40s *Different statue* 30 15

J.J. Olmeda, Father de Velasco, Flags of Ecuador and Riobamba, Constitution—A301

1980, Sept. 20 Litho. *Perf. 11½*

996 A301 3.40s multi 30 15
997 A301 5s multi 50 20

Souvenir Sheet
Imperf.

998 A301 30s multi 3.00 1.25

Constitutional Assembly of Riobamba sesquicentennial. No. 998 contains vignettes in designs of Nos. 996-997, black control number. Size: 116x90mm. See Nos. C700-C702.

First Lady Mrs. Aguilera—A302

Wmk. 367
1980, Oct. 9 Litho. *Perf. 12x11½*

999 A302 1.20s multi 10 5
1000 A302 3.40s multi 30 15

Democratic government, 1st anniversary. See Nos. C703-C705.

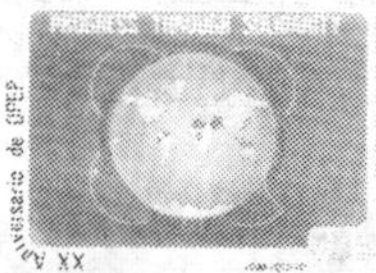

OPEC Emblem—A303

1980, Nov. 8 *Perf. 11½x12*

1001 A303 3.40s multi 30 15

20th anniversary of OPEC. See No. C706.

Decorative Hedges, Capitol Gardens, Carchi—A304

1980, Nov. 21 *Perf. 13*

1002 A304 3s multi 25 10

Carchi province centennial. See Nos. C707-C708.

Cattleya Maxima—A305

Designs: Orchids.

1980, Nov. 22 *Perf. 11½x12*

1003 A305 1.20s *shown* 10 5
1004 A305 3s *Comparattia speciosa* 25 10
1005 A305 3.40s *Cattleya iricolor* 30 15
Nos. 1003-1005, C709-C712 (7) 5.75 3.60

Souvenir Sheet
Imperf.

1006 A305 20s multi 2.00 1.00

No. 1006 contains vignettes in desings of Nos. 1003-1005; black control number. Size: 115x90mm.

Pope John Paul II and Children—A306

1980, Dec. 27 *Perf. 12*

1007 A306 3.40s multi 30 15

Christmas 1980/visit of Pope John Paul II. See Nos. C715-C716.

Carlos and Jorge Ortega, Editors of El Comercio—A307

El Comercio Newspaper, 75th Anniversary: 3.40s, Editors Cesar and Carlos Jacome.

1981, Jan. 6

1008 A307 2s multi 15 10
1009 A307 3.40s multi 25 15

Soldier on Map of Ecuador—A308

National Defense (Map of Ecuador and): No. 1011, Pres. Roldos.

1981, Mar. 10 Litho. *Perf. 13*

1010 A308 3.40s multi 25 15
1011 A308 3.40s multi 25 15

Theodore E. Gildred and Ecuador I
A309

1981, Mar. 31 Litho. *Perf. 13*

1012 A309 2s lt bl & blk 15 10

Ecuador-U.S. flight, 50th anniv.

Octavio Cordero Palacios (1870-1930), Humanist—A310

1981, Apr. 10

1013 A310 2s multi 15 10

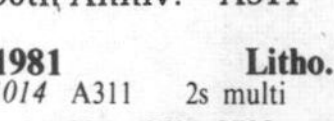

Radio Station HCJB
50th Anniv.—A311

1981 Litho. *Perf. 13*

1014 A311 2s multi 15 10

See Nos. C721-C722.

Virgin of Dolorosa—A312

1981, Apr.30 Litho. *Perf. 12*

1015 A312 2s shown 15 10
1016 A312 2s San Gabriel College Church 15 10

Miracle of the painting of the Virgin of Dolorosa at San Gabriel College, 75th anniv.

Dr. Rafael Mendoza Aviles Bridge Inauguration—A313

1981, July 25 *Perf. 13*

1017 A313 2s multi 15 10

REPUBLICA DEL ECUADOR
DIA MUNDIAL DE LA ALIMENTACION s/ 5.00

World Food Day—A314

1981, Dec. 31 Litho. *Perf. 13½x13*

1018 A314 5s multi 50 20

See No. *C732*

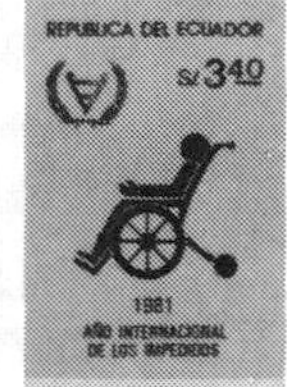

Transnave Shipping Co. 10th Anniv.
A315

Intl. Year of the Disabled
A316

1982, Jan. 21 Litho. *Perf. 13*

1019 A315 3.50s Freighter Isla Salango 35 15

1982, Feb. 25

1020 A316 3.40s Man in wheelchair 30 15

See Nos. *C733 C734*

Arch

A317

Juan Montalvo Birth Sesquicentennial

A318

1982, May **Litho.** ***Perf. 13***

1021	A317	2s shown	15	10
1022	A317	3s Houses	25	10

Souvenir Sheet

1023		Sheet of 4 18th cent. map of Quito	2.50	1.00
a.-d.		A317 6s multi	60	25

QUITEX '82, 4th Natl. Stamp Exhibition, Quito, Apr. 16-22. No. 1023 contains 4 stamps (48x31mm., perf. 12½); black control number, inscription. Size: 109x89mm.

1982

1024	A318	2s Portrait	15	10
1025	A318	3s Mausoleum	20	10

See No. *C735*

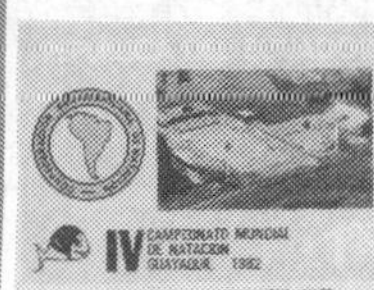

American Air Forces Cooperation System A319

4th World Swimming Champ., Guayaquil A320

1982

1026	A319	5s Emblem	40	20

1982, July 30

1027	A320	1.80s Stadium	15	10
1028	A320	3.40s Water polo	25	15

See Nos. C732-C733.

Juan L. Mera (1832-?), Writer, by Victor Mideros—A321

1982, Dec. **Litho.** ***Perf. 13***

1029	A321	5.40s shown	40	20
1030	A321	6s Statue	45	20

St. Teresa of Jesus of Avila (1515-1582)—A322

1983, Mar. 28 **Litho.** ***Perf. 13***

1031	A322	2s multi	15	10

Sea Lions A323

Flamingoes A324

1983, June 17 **Litho.** ***Perf. 13***

1032	A323	3s multi	15	5
1033	A324	5s multi	20	10

Sesquicentennial of Ecuadorian rule over Galapagos Islds (3s); Charles Darwin (1809-1882).

Pres. Vicente Rocafuerte Birth Bicentenary A325

Simon Bolivar A326

Wmk. 367

1983, Aug. 26 **Litho.** ***Perf. 13x13½***

1034	A325	5s Statue	20	10
1035	A325	20s Portrait	75	35
1036	A326	20s Portrait	75	35

Vicente Rocafuerte Bejarano, president, 1833-39 (Nos. 1034-1035).

Paute Hydroelectric Plant Opening—A327

1983, Sept. 3

1037	A327	5s River	15	10
1038	A327	10s Dam	30	20

Souvenir Sheet

Imperf.

1039	A327	20s Dam, river	60	40

No. 1039 has black control number, airmail. Size: 110x90mm.

World Communications Year—A328

Wmk. 367

1983, Nov. 10 **Litho.** ***Perf. 13***

1040	A328	2s multi	10	5

Centenary of Bolivar and El Oro Provinces (1984)—A329

Wmk. 367

1983, Sept. **Litho.** ***Perf. 13***

1041	A329	3s multi	6	5

450 AÑOS DE LA MUERTE DE ATAHUALPA

Atahualpa (1497-1529), Last Incan Rulers—A330

1984, Mar. **Litho.** ***Perf. 13***

1042	A330	15s Engraving	30	15

Christmas 1983—A331

Creche figures.

1984, July 7 **Litho.** ***Perf. 13½x13, 13x13½***

1043	A331	5s Jesus and lawyers	10	5
1044	A331	5s Three kings	10	5
1045	A331	5s Holy Family	10	5
1046	A331	6s Priest, vert.	12	6

REPUBLICA DEL ECUADOR

Foreign Policy of Pres. Hurtado—A332

State visits.

1984, July 10 ***Perf. 13½x13***

1047	A332	8s Brazil	16	8
1048	A332	9s People's Rep. of China	18	10
1049	A332	24s U.N.	48	24
1050	A332	28s U.S.	56	28
1051	A332	29s Venezuela	58	30
1052	A332	37s Latin-American Economic Conference, Quito	75	38
		Nos. 1047-1052 (6)	2.71	1.38

Miguel Diaz Cueva (1884-1942), Lawyer—A333

1984, Aug. 8 **Litho.** ***Perf. 13½x13***

1053	A333	10s Cueva, arms	35	18

1984 Winter Olympics A334

Manned Flight Bicentenary A335

1984, Aug. 15 ***Perf. 13x13½, 12x11½ (6s)***

1054	A334	2s Emblem	8	5
1055	A334	4s Ice skating	14	8
1056	A334	6s Skating, diff.	22	12
1057	A334	10s Skiing	35	18

1984, Aug. 15 ***Perf. 13x13½***

1058	A335	3s Montgolfier	10	5
1059	A335	6s Charlier's balloon, Paris, 1789	22	12

Souvenir Sheet

1060	A335	20s Graf Zeppelin, Montgolfier	75	50

No. 1060 is airmail and contains one stamp (50x37mm., imperf.); multicolored margin shows balloons, plane; red control number. Size: 110x90mm.

SAN MATEO '83, Esmeraldas—A336

1984 **Litho.** ***Perf. 13***

1061	A336	8s La Marimba folk dance	35	18

Size: 89x110mm.

Imperf.

1061A	A336	15s La Marimba, diff.	40	20

No. 1061A airmail, has bronze control number. Size: 90x110mm.

Jose Maria de Jesus Yerovi (b. 1824), 4th Archbishop of Quito—A337

1984

1062	A337	5s multi	18	10

Canonization of Brother Miguel—A338

1984 **Litho.** ***Perf. 13***

1063	A338	9s Academy of Languages	30	18
1064	A338	24s Vatican City, vert.	70	42
1065	A338	28s Home of Brother Miguel	80	50

No. 1065, airmail, has black control number, Size: 110x90mm.

State Visit of Pope John Paul II
A339

Beatification of Mercedes de Jesus Molina
A340

1985, Jan. 23 **Litho.** ***Perf. 13x13½***

1066	A339	1.60s	Papal arms	5	5
1067	A339	5s	Blessing crowd	12	6
1068	A339	9s	World map, itinerary	24	12
1069	A339	28s	Pope waving	70	35
1070	A339	29s	Portrait	75	38
			Nos. 1066-1070 (5)	1.86	96

Size: 90x109mm.
Imperf.

1071	A339	30s	Pope holding crosier	2.00	1.00

No. 1071 has black control number.

1985, Jan. 23

Paintings, sculpture.

1072	A340	1.60s	Portrait	5	5
1073	A340	5s	Czestochowa Madonna	12	6
1074	A340	9s	Alborada Madonna	15	8

Size: 90x110mm.
Imperf.

1075	A340	20s	Mercedes de Jesus, children	2.00	1.00

Visit of Pope John Paul II, birth bimillennium of the Virgin Mary. No. 1075 has red control number.

Samuel Valarezo Delgado, Naturalist, Politician—A341

1985, Feb.

1076	A341	2s	Bird	5	5
1077	A341	3s	Swordfish, tuna	5	5
1078	A341	6s	Portrait	15	8

ESPANA '84, Madrid—A342

1985, Apr. 25 ***Perf. 13½x13***

1079	A342	6s	Emblem	12	6
1080	A342	10s	Spanish royal family	28	14

Size: 110x90mm.
Imperf.

1081	A342	15s	Retiro Park, exhibition site	1.00	50

No. 1081 has black control number.

Dr. Pio Jaramillo Alvarado (1884-1968), Historian, Author—A343

1985, May 17

1082	A343	6s	multi	12	6

Ingenio Valdez Sugar Refinery—A344

Designs: 50s, Sugar cane, emblem. 100s, Rafael Valdez Cervantes, founder.

1985, June **Litho.** ***Perf. 13***

1082A	A344	50s	multi	1.00	50
1082B	A344	100s	multi	2.00	1.00

Imperf.

Size: 110x90mm.

1083	A344	30s	multi	60	30

No. 1083 has red control number.

Chamber of Commerce, 10th Anniv.—A345

Design: 50s, Natl. and American Statues of Liberty.

1985, Aug. 15 ***Perf. 13½x13***

1084	A345	24s	multi	50	25
1085	A345	28s	multi	60	30

Size: 110x90mm.
Imperf.

1086	A345	50s	multi	1.10	55

No. 1086 has black control number.

Natl. Philatelic Assoc., AFE, 50th Anniv.—A346

1985, Aug. 25 ***Perf. 12***

1087	A346	25s	AFE emblem	52	25
1088	A346	30s	No. 357, horiz.	65	32

Guayaquil Fire Dept., 150th Anniv.—A347

1985, Oct. 10 ***Perf. 13½x13***

1089	A347	6s	Steam fire pump, 1882	12	6
1090	A347	10s	Fire Wagon, 1899	20	10
1091	A347	20s	Anniv. emblem, natl. flag	38	20

Natl. Infant Survival Campaign
A348

1st Natl. Philatelic Congress, Quito, Nov. 25-28
A349

1985, Oct. ***Perf. 13x13½***

1092	A348	10s	Boy, girl, tree	20	10

1985, Nov. ***Perf. 13x13½, 13½x13***

20th century illustrations, natl. cultural collection: 5s, Supreme Court, Quito, by J. M. Roura. 10s, Riobamba Cathedral, by O. Munaz. 15s, House of 100 Windows, by J. M. Roura, horiz. 20s, Rural cottage near Cuenca, by J. M. Roura. No. 1097a, Stampless cover, 1779, Riobamba. No. 1097b, Hand press, 1864, Quito. No. 1097c, Postrider, 1880, Cuenca. No. 1097d, Monoplane, 1st airmail flight, 1919, Guayaquil.

1093	A349	5s	multi	10	5
1094	A349	10s	multi	18	9
1095	A349	15s	multi	28	14
1096	A349	20s	multi	38	16

Souvenir Sheet

1097			Sheet of 4	1.00	50
a.-d.	A349	5s,	any single	25	14

AFE, 50th anniv. No. 1097 contains 4 stamps (size: 53x42mm, perf. 13x12½ on 2 sides); black control number. Size: 109x90mm.

10th Bolivarian Games, Cuenca—A350

1985, Nov. ***Perf. 13½x13***

1098	A350	10s	Boxing	18	10
1099	A350	25s	Women's gymnastics	48	24
1100	A350	30s	Discus	55	28

BAE Calderon, Navy Cent.—A351

Military anniversaries: No. 1102, Fighter plane, Air Force 65th anniv. No. 1103, Army and paratroops emblems, Special Forces 30th anniv.

1985, Dec. ***Perf. 13x13½***

1101	A351	10s	multi	18	10
1102	A351	10s	multi	18	10
1103	A351	10s	multi	18	10

UN, 40th Anniv.—A352

1985, Oct. **Litho.** ***Perf. 13***

1104	A352	10s	UN flag	18	9
1105	A352	20s	Natl. flag	38	16

Size: 110x90mm.
Imperf.

1106	A352	50s	UN Building	1.00	50

No. 1106 bears black control number.

Christmas
A353

Indigenous Flowers
A354

1985, Nov.

1107	A353	5s	Child riding donkey	10	5
1108	A353	10s	Baked goods	18	10
1109	A353	15s	Riding donkey, diff.	28	14

Size: 90x110mm.
Imperf.

1110	A353	30s	like 5s	60	30

No. 1110 bears green control number.

1986, Feb. 6

1111	A354	24s	Embotrium grandiforum	45	22
1112	A354	28s	Topobea sp.	50	25
1113	A354	29s	Befaria resinosa mutis	52	25

Size: 110x90mm.
Imperf.

1114	A354	15s	multi	28	14

No. 1114 contains designs of Nos. 1111, 1113, 1112; black control number.

Discovery of the Galapagos Isls., 450th Anniv.—A355

Map of the Islands—A356

1986, Feb. 13

1115	A355	10s Land iguana	18	10
1116	A355	20s Sea lion	35	18
1117	A355	30s Frigate birds	52	25
1118	A355	40s Penguins	70	35
1119	A355	50s Sea turtle	85	42
1120	A355	100s Charles Darwin	1.75	88
1121	A355	200s Bishop Tomas de Berlenga, discoverer	3.50	1.75

Nos. 1115-1121 (7)

Perf. 12½

1122	Sheet of 4	3.50	1.75
a.-d.	A356 50s, Map of the islands	85	42

No. 1122 contains 4 stamps (size: 53x42mm, perf. 12½ on 2 sides); red control number. Size: 110x90mm.

Inter—American Development Bank, 25th Anniv.—A357

Designs: 5s, Antonio Ortiz Mena, president 1971- . 10s, Felipe Herrera, president 1960-1971. 50s, Emblem.

1986, Mar. 6

1123	A357	5s multi	8	5
1124	A357	10s multi	18	8
1125	A357	50s multi	80	40

Guayaquil Tennis Club, 75th Anniv.—A358

1986, Mar. 7

1126	A358	10s Emblem	14	8
1127	A358	10s Francisco Segura Cano, vert.	14	8
1128	A358	10s Andres Gomez Santos, vert.	14	8

1986 World Cup Soccer Championships, Mexico—A359

1986, May 5

1129	A359	5s shot	8	5
1130	A359	10s Block	14	8

An imperf. stamp exists picturing flags, player and emblem. Black control number.

Meeting of Presidents Cordero and Betancourt of Colombia, Feb. 1985—A360

1986 Litho. *Perf. 13½x13*

1131	A360	20s Presidents	28	15
1132	A360	20s Embracing	28	15

Exports—A361

Designs: 35s, 1137c, Shrimp. 40s, No. 1137b, Tuna. 45s, No. 1137a, Sardines. No. 1137d, MICIP emblem.

1986, Apr. 12

1133	A361	35s ultra & ver	50	25
1134	A361	40s red & yel grn	55	28
1135	A361	45s car & dk yel	62	30

Perf. 12½ on 2 Sides

1137	Sheet of 4	60	32
a.-d.	A361 10s, any single	14	8

No. 1137 contains 4 stamps (Size: 53x42mm); black control number. Size: 110x90mm.

A362

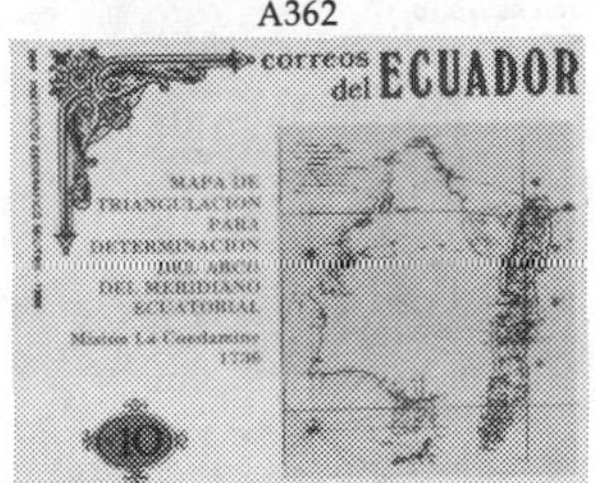

La Condamine's First Geodesic Mission, 250th Anniv.—A363

Designs: No. 1141a, Triangulation map for determining equatorial meridian, 1736. No. 1141b, Partial map of the Maranon and Amazon Rivers, by Samuel Fritz, 1743-1744. No. 1141c, Base of measurement, Yaruqui plains. No. 1141d, Caraburo and Dyambaru Pyramids near Quito. Nos. 1141c-1141d printed se-tenant in a continuous design.

1986, July 10 Litho. *Perf. 13½x13*

1138	A362	10s La Condamine	14	8
1139	A362	15s Maldonado	22	12
1140	A362	20s Middle of the World, Quito	28	15

Souvenir Sheet

Perf. 12½ on 2 Sides

1141	Sheet of 4	60	32
a.-d.	A363 10s, any single	14	8

No. 1141 has black control number. Size: 110x90mm.

Chambers of Commerce—A364

1986 Litho. *Perf. 13½x13*

1142	A364	10s Pichincha	18	10
1143	A364	10s Cuenca	18	10
1144	A364	10s Guayaquil	18	10

Civil Service and Communications Ministry, 57th Anniv.—A365

Organization emblems.

1986, Dec. Litho. *Perf. 13x13½*

1145	A365	5s State railway	10	5
1146	A365	10s Post office	20	10
1147	A365	15s Communications	30	15
1148	A365	20s Ministry of Public Works	40	20

SEMI-POSTAL STAMPS.

Nos. 423-428
Surcharged in Carmine or Blue:

Hospital

Méndez + $ 0,50

1944, May 9 **Perf. 12** Unwmkd.

B1	A171	10c +10c yel grn (C)	50	35
B2	A171	20c +20c rose pink	50	40
B3	A171	30c +20c dk gray brn	50	50
B4	A171	50c +20c dp red lil	1.00	75
B5	A171	1s +50c ol gray (C)	1.50	1.25
B6	A171	10s +2s red org	6.00	3.50
		Nos. B1-B6 (6)	10.00	6.75

The surtax aided Mendez Hospital.

AIR POST STAMPS.

In 1928–30, the internal airmail service of Ecuador was handled by the Sociedad Colombo-Alemana de Transportes Aereos ("SCADTA") under government sanction. During this period SCADTA issued stamps which were the only legal franking for airmail service except that handled under contract with Pan American-Grace Airways. SCADTA issues are Nos. C1–C6, C16–C25.

Colombia Air Post Stamps of 1923 Surcharged in Carmine

PROVISIONAL

50 50

"Provisional" at 45° Angle.

Perf. 14x14½

1928, Aug. 28 Wmk. 116

C1	AP6	50c on 10c grn	150.00	100.00
C2	AP6	75c on 15c car	300.00	200.00
C3	AP6	1s on 20c gray	100.00	60.00
C4	AP6	1½s on 30c bl	75.00	50.00
C5	AP6	3s on 60c brn	125.00	75.00
		Nos. C1-C5 (5)	750.00	485.00

"Provisional" at 41° Angle.

1929, Mar. 20

C1a	AP6	50c on 10c grn	165.00	150.00
C2a	AP6	75c on 15c car	200.00	175.00
C3a	AP6	1s on 20c gray	165.00	175.00

Same with "Cts." Between Surcharged Numerals

C6	AP6	50c on 10c grn	*1,250.*	*1,000.*

A 75c on 15c carmine with "Cts." between the surcharged numerals exists. There is no evidence that it was regularly issued or used.

Plane over River Guayas
AP1

Engraved.

1929, May 5 **Perf. 12** Unwmkd.

C8	AP1	2c black	20	10
C9	AP1	5c car rose	20	10
C10	AP1	10c dp brn	25	6
C11	AP1	20c dk vio	40	8
C12	AP1	50c dp grn	1.25	35
C13	AP1	1s dk bl	3.50	1.75
C14	AP1	5s org yel	10.00	5.00
C15	AP1	10s org red	50.00	40.00
		Nos. C8-C15 (8)	65.80	47.44

Issued to commemorate the establishing of commercial air service in Ecuador. The stamps were available for all forms of postal service and were largely used for franking ordinary letters.

Nos. C13–C15 show numerals in color on white background. Counterfeits of No. C15 exist.

See Nos. C26–C31.

Quito Cathedral
AP2

Mount Chimborazo
AP3

Lithographed.

1929, Apr. 1 **Perf. 14** Wmk. 127

C16	AP2	50c red brn	2.50	2.50
C17	AP2	75c green	2.50	2.50
C18	AP2	1s rose	3.50	2.50
C19	AP2	1½s gray bl	3.50	3.00
C20	AP2	2s violet	12.50	10.00
C21	AP2	3s brown	12.50	10.00
C22	AP3	5s lt bl	40.00	30.00
C23	AP3	10s lt red	85.00	65.00
C24	AP3	15s violet	150.00	125.00
C25	AP3	25s ol grn	200.00	150.00
		Nos. C16-C25 (10)	512.00	400.50

Plane Type of 1929

Engraved.

1930-44 **Perf. 12.** Unwmkd.

C26	AP1	1s car lake	3.50	50
C27	AP1	1s grn ('44)	60	12
C28	AP1	5s ol grn	5.00	4.00
C29	AP1	5s pur ('44)	1.25	12
C30	AP1	10s black	15.00	5.00
C31	AP1	10s brt ultra ('44)	2.25	12
		Nos. C26-C31 (6)	27.60	9.86

Nos. C26–C31 show numerals in color on white background.

Overprinted in Various Colors.

AP4

1930, June 4

C32	AP4	1s car lake (Bk)	30.00	30.00
a.		Double overprint (R Br+Bk)	100.00	
C33	AP4	5s ol grn (Bl)	30.00	30.00
C34	AP4	10s blk (R Br)	30.00	30.00

Issued to commemorate the flight of Capt. Benjamin Mendez from Bogota to Quito, bearing a crown of flowers for the tomb of Grand Marshal Sucre.

Air Post Official Stamps of 1929–30
Overprinted in Various Colors

INAUGURACION MONUMENTO A BOLIVAR QUITO, 24 DE JULIO DE 1935

or Surcharged Similarly in Upper & Lower Case

1935, July 24

C35	AP1	50c dp grn (Bl)	5.00	5.00
C36	AP1	50c ol brn (R)	5.00	5.00
C37	AP1	1s on 5s ol grn (Bk)	5.00	5.00
a.		Double surcharge	100.00	
C38	AP1	2s on 10s blk (R)	5.00	5.00

Issued to commemorate the unveiling of a monument to Bolivar at Quito, July 24th, 1935.

Geodesical Mission Issue

Nos. 349–351 Overprinted in Blue or Black

AÉREO

1936, July 3 **Perf. 12½**

C39	A136	10c dp org (Bl)	25	10
C40	A136	20c vio (Bk)	25	10
C41	A136	50c dk red (Bl)	40	12

Charles M. de la Condamine and Pedro Maldonado
AP5

C42	AP5	70c black	70	35

Bicentenary of Geodesical Mission visit to Quito.

Philatelic Exhibition Issue

Type of Regular Issue Overprinted "AEREA"

1936, Oct. 20 **Perf. 13½x14**

C43	A137	2c rose	5.00	5.00
C44	A137	5c brn org	5.00	5.00
C45	A137	10c brown	5.00	5.00
C46	A137	20c ultra	5.00	5.00
C47	A137	50c red vio	5.00	5.00
C48	A137	1s green	5.00	5.00
		Nos. C43-C48 (6)	30.00	30.00

Condor and Plane—AP6

Perf. 13½

C49	AP6	70c org brn	90	65
C50	AP6	1s dl vio	90	85

Nos. C43–C50 were issued to commemorate the first International Philatelic Exhibition at Quito.

Condor over "El Altar"
AP7

1937–46 **Perf. 11½, 12**

C51	AP7	10c chestnut	10	5
C52	AP7	20c ol blk	20	6
C53	AP7	40c rose car ('46)	20	6
C54	AP7	70c blk brn	25	15
C55	AP7	1s gray blk	35	25
C56	AP7	2s dk vio	75	35
		Nos. C51-C56 (6)	1.85	92

Issue dates: 40c, Oct. 7, 1946; others, Aug. 19, 1937.

Portrait of Washington, American Eagle and Flags
AP8

Engraved and Lithographed.

1938, Feb. 9 **Perf. 12**

Center Multicolored.

C57	AP8	2c brown	20	10
C58	AP8	5c black	20	10
C59	AP8	10c brown	25	10
C60	AP8	20c dk bl	50	10
C61	AP8	50c violet	75	20
C62	AP8	1s black	1.25	25
C63	AP8	2s violet	2.50	75
		Nos. C57-C63 (7)	5.65	1.60

Issued in commemoration of the 150th anniversary of the Constitution of the United States of America.

In 1947, Nos. C61 to C63 were overprinted in dark blue: "Primero la Patria!" and plane. These revolutionary propaganda stamps were later renounced by decree.

No. RA35 Surcharged in Red

AEREO
SEDTA

0,65

1938, Nov. 16 **Perf. 13½**

C64	PT12	65c on 3c ultra	15	10

A national airmail concession was given to the Sociedad Ecuatoriano de Transportes Aereos (SEDTA)) in July, 1938. No. RA35 was surcharged for SEDTA postal requirements. SEDTA operated through 1940.

Army Horseman
AP9

Woman Runner
AP10

Tennis
AP11

Boxing
AP12

Olympic Fire
AP13

1939, Mar. Engraved **Perf. 12**

C65	AP9	5c lt grn	75	15
C66	AP10	10c salmon	1.00	25
C67	AP11	50c redsh brn	5.00	25
C68	AP12	1s blk brn	6.00	50
C69	AP13	2s rose car	9.00	1.00
		Nos. C65-C69 (5)	21.75	2.15

First Bolivarian Games (1938), La Paz.

Plane over Chimborazo
AP14

1939, May 1 **Perf. 13x12½**

C70	AP14	1s yel brn	25	15
C71	AP14	2s rose vio	50	15
C72	AP14	5s black	1.25	15

Golden Gate Bridge and Mountain Peak
AP15

Empire State Building and Mountain Peak
AP16

1939 ***Perf. 12½x13***

C73	AP15	2c black	5	5
C74	AP15	5c rose red	5	5
C75	AP15	10c indigo	5	5
C76	AP15	50c rose vio	10	10
C77	AP15	1s chocolate	15	10
C78	AP15	2s yel brn	25	10
C79	AP15	5s emerald	60	20
		Nos. C73-C79 (7)	1.25	65

Golden Gate International Exposition.

1939

C80	AP16	2c brn org	5	5
C81	AP16	5c dk car	5	5
C82	AP16	10c indigo	5	5
C83	AP16	50c sl grn	10	10
C84	AP16	1s dp org	20	10
C85	AP16	2s dk red vio	40	25
C86	AP16	5s dk gray	75	20
		Nos. C80-C86 (7)	1.60	80

New York World's Fair.

Map of the Americas and Airplane
AP17

Francisco J. E. Santa Cruz y Espejo
AP18

1940, July 9

C87	AP17	10c red org & bl	20	10
C88	AP17	70c sep & bl	25	10
C89	AP17	1s cop brn & bl	40	15
C90	AP17	10s blk & bl	1.50	75

Pan American Union, 50th anniversary.

1941, Dec. 15

C91	AP18	3s rose car	1.25	20
C92	AP18	10s yel org	2.50	30

See note after No. 399.

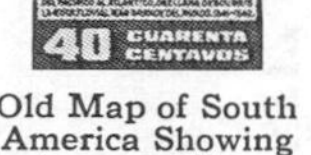

Old Map of South America Showing Amazon River
AP19

Panoramic View of Amazon River
AP20

Designs: 70c, Gonzalo de Pineda. 5s, Painting of the expedition.

1942, Jan. 30

C93	AP19	40c blk & buff	40	15
C94	AP19	70c olive	75	10
C95	AP20	2s dk grn	75	25
C96	AP19	5s rose	1.50	60

See note after No. 403.

Remigio Crespo Toral
AP21

1942, Sept. 1 ***Perf. 13½***

C97	AP21	10c dl vio	25	10

Gen. Eloy Alfaro
AP22

Devil's Nose
AP23

Designs: 3s, Military College. 5s, Montecristi, Alfaro's birthplace.

1943, Feb. 16 ***Perf. 12***

C98	AP22	70c dk rose & blk	50	20
C99	AP23	1s ol blk & red brn	75	40
C100	AP23	3s ol gray & grn	1.00	75
C101	AP23	5s sl & sal	1.75	90

Issued to commemorate the centenary of the birth of President Alfaro (1842-1903).

Nos. C61-C63 Overprinted in Red Brown
BIENVENIDO — WALLACE
Abril 15 — 1943

1943, Apr. 15 ***Perf. 11½***

Center Multicolored.

C102	AP8	50c violet	1.25	50
C103	AP8	1s black	1.50	75
C104	AP8	2s violet	2.00	1.00

Issued to commemorate the visit of Vice-President Henry A. Wallace of the United States.

Nos. 374-376 Overprinted "AEREO LOOR A BOLIVIA JUNIO 11—1943" (like Nos. C111-C113).

1943, June 11 ***Perf. 13***

C105	A146	50c dp red vio	20	20
C106	A147	1s cop red	40	30
C107	A148	2s dk grn	60	35

Issued to commemorate the visit of President Enrique Penaranda of Bolivia.
Vertical overprints on Nos. C105-C106.

Nos. 374-376 Overprinted "AEREO LOOR A PARAGUAY JULIO 5—1943" (like Nos. C111-C113).

1943, July 5

C108	A146	50c dp red vio	20	20
a.		Double ovpt.	40.00	
C109	A147	1s cop red	40	30
C110	A148	2s dk grn	60	35

Issued to commemorate the visit of President Higinio Morinigo of Paraguay.
Vertical overprints on Nos. C108-C109.

Nos. 374-376 Overprinted in Black
AEREO
LOOR A VENEZUELA
JULIO 23 — 1943

1943, July 23

C111	A146	50c dp red vio	20	20
C112	A147	1s cop red	40	30
C113	A148	2s dk grn	60	35

Issued to commemorate the visit of President Isaias Medina Angarita of Venezuela.
Vertical overprint on Nos. C111-C112.
See also Nos. C105-C110.

President Arroyo del Rio Addressing U.S. Congress
AP26

1943, Oct. 9 ***Perf. 12***

C114	AP26	50c dk brn	50	40
C115	AP26	70c brt rose	60	60
C116	AP26	3s dk bl	75	60
C117	AP26	5s dk grn	1.50	1.00
C118	AP26	10s ol blk	6.00	5.00
		Nos. C114-C118 (5)	9.35	7.60

Issued to commemorate the good will tour of President Arroyo del Rio in 1942.

1944, Feb. 7

C119	AP26	50c dp red lil	50	40
C120	AP26	70c red brn	75	40
C121	AP26	3s turq grn	75	40
C122	AP26	5s brt ultra	1.25	1.00
C123	AP26	10s scarlet	1.75	1.50
		Nos. C119-C123 (5)	5.00	3.70

Church of San Francisco, Quito
AP27

1944, Feb. 13

C124	AP27	70c turq grn	60	40
C125	AP27	1s olive	60	40
C126	AP27	3s red org	1.00	60
C127	AP27	5s car rose	1.25	75

See note after No. 433.

Government Palace, Quito
AP28

1944 **Engraved** ***Perf. 11***

C128	AP28	3s orange	50	10
C129	AP28	5s dk brn	75	10
C130	AP28	10s dk red	1.50	20

See also No. C221.

Symbol of the Red Cross
AP29

1945, Apr. 25 ***Perf. 12*** **Unwmkd.**

Cross in Rose.

C131	AP29	2s dp bl	75	75
C132	AP29	3s green	1.25	75
C133	AP29	5s dk vio	2.00	1.25
C134	AP29	10s car rose	5.00	3.75

Issued to commemorate the 80th anniversary of the founding of the International Red Cross.

No. RA55 Surcharged in Black
AEREO
40
Ctvs.

1945, June 8

C135	PT21	40c on 5c bl	20	10
a.		Double surcharge	10.00	

Counterfeits exist.

Nos. C128 to C130 Overprinted in Green
V
SETIEMBRE 5
1945

1945, Sept. 6 ***Perf. 11***

C136	AP28	3s orange	60	60
a.		Inverted ovpt.	30.00	
b.		Double ovpt.	30.00	
C137	AP28	5s dk brn	75	75
C138	AP28	10s dk red	2.50	2.50

Nos. C61-C63 Overprinted in Dark Blue and Gold

LOOR A CHILE
OCTUBRE 2 1945

1945, Oct. 2 ***Perf. 12***

Center Multicolored.

C139	AP8	50c violet	60	60
C140	AP8	1s black	65	65
C141	AP8	2s violet	65	65

Visit of Pres. Juan Antonio Rios of Chile.

Monument to Liberty
AP30

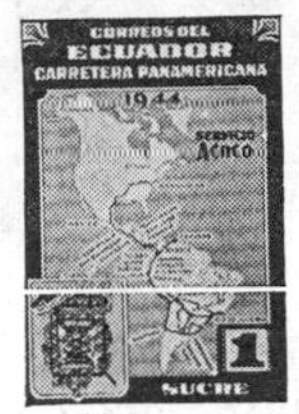

Map of Pan-American Highway and Arms of Cuenca
AP31

1945, Nov. 14 **Engraved.**

C142	AP30	30c blue	20	10
C143	AP30	40c rose car	25	10
C144	AP30	1s dl vio	60	25
C145	AP30	3s gray blk	1.00	75
C146	AP30	5s pur brn	1.50	1.00
		Nos. C142-C146 (5)	3.55	2.20

Issued to commemorate the 150th anniversary of the birth of General Antonio José de Sucre.

1946, Apr. 22 **Unwmkd.**

C147	AP31	1s car rose	40	30
C148	AP31	2s violet	50	40
C149	AP31	3s turq grn	75	50
C150	AP31	5s red org	1.00	60
C151	AP31	10s dk bl	1.50	50
		Nos. C147-C151 (5)	4.15	2.30

Revolution Types of Regular Issue

1946, Aug. 9 ***Perf. 12½***

C152	A177	40c dp cl	10	10
C153	A178	1s sepia	15	10
C154	A179	2s indigo	40	20
C155	A180	3s ol grn	60	40

Issued to commemorate the 2nd anniversary of the Revolution of May 28, 1944.

National Union of Periodicals, Initials and Quill Pen
AP36

1946, Sept. 16

C156	AP36	50c dl pur	40	25
C157	AP36	70c dk grn	50	30
C158	AP36	3s red	75	40
C159	AP36	5s indigo	1.00	50
C160	AP36	10s chocolate	3.00	75
		Nos. C156-C160 (5)	5.65	2.20

Issued to publicize a campaign for adult education.

The Blessed Mariana Teaching Children
AP37

"Lily of Quito"
AP38

1946, Nov. 28 **Unwmkd.**

C161	AP37	40c chocolate	30	10
C162	AP37	60c dp bl	40	35
C163	AP38	3s org yel	85	75
C164	AP38	5s green	1.50	1.00

Issued to commemorate the 300th anniversary of the death of the Blessed Mariana de Jesus Paredes y Flores.

Juan de Velasco
AP39

Riobamba Irrigation Canal
AP40

1947, Nov. 27 ***Perf. 12***

C165	AP39	60c dk grn	10	5
C166	AP39	70c purple	15	5
C167	AP39	1s blk brn	15	5
C168	AP39	1.10s car rose	15	10
C169	AP40	1.30s dp bl	20	15
C170	AP40	1.90s ol bis	35	20
C171	AP40	2s ol grn	35	10
		Nos. C165-C171 (7)	1.45	70

Andrés Bello
AP41

Christopher Columbus
AP42

1948, Apr. 21 ***Perf. 13***

C172	AP41	60c magenta	20	10
C173	AP41	1.30s dk bl grn	40	20
C174	AP41	1.90s dk rose car	30	20

No. C166 Overprinted in Black

CONFERENCIA
ECONOMICA
GRANCOLOMBIANA
MAYO 24 DE 1.948

1948, May 24 ***Perf. 12***

C175	AP39	70c purple	50	30

1948, May 26 ***Perf. 14***

C176	AP42	50c ol grn	15	15
C177	AP42	70c rose car	20	20
C178	AP42	3c ultra	50	40
C179	AP42	5s brown	1.00	35
C180	AP42	10s dp vio	1.75	40
		Nos. C176-C180 (5)	3.60	1.50

See note after No. 495.

No. C169 Overprinted in Carmine

Feria Nacional
1948
ECUADOR de hoy y del MAÑANA

1948, Aug. 26 ***Perf. 12*** **Unwmkd.**

C181	AP40	1.30s dp bl	50	35

Issued to publicize the National Fair of Today and Tomorrow, 1948.

Elia Liut and Telegrafo I
AP43

Teacher and Pupils
AP44

1948, Sept. 10 ***Perf. 12½***

C182	AP43	60c rose red	30	25
C183	AP43	1s green	30	25
C184	AP43	1.30s dp cl	30	30
C185	AP43	1.90s dp vio	35	30
C186	AP43	2s dk brn	50	40
C187	AP43	5s blue	1.00	60
		Nos. C182-C187 (6)	2.75	2.10

Issued to commemorate the 25th anniversary (in 1945) of the first postal flight in Ecuador.

1948, Oct. 12 ***Perf. 14***

C188	AP44	50c violet	25	20
C189	AP44	70c dp bl	25	20
C190	AP44	3s dk grn	40	30
C191	AP44	5s red	50	25
C192	AP44	10s brown	1.25	50
		Nos. C188-C192 (5)	2.65	1.45

Campaign for adult education.

Franklin D. Roosevelt and Two of "Four Freedoms"
AP45 AP46

1948, Oct. 24 ***Perf. 12½***

C193	AP45	60c emer & org brn	15	15
C194	AP45	1s car rose & sl	15	15
C195	AP46	1.50s grn & red brn	25	20
C196	AP46	2s red & blk	60	25
C197	AP46	5s ultra & blk	1.00	25
		Nos. C193-C197 (5)	2.15	1.00

Issued in tribute to Franklin D. Roosevelt, 1882-1945.

Maldonado Types of Regular Issue

1948, Nov. 17

C198	A196	60c dp org & rose car	25	10
C199	A197	90c red & gray blk	25	10
C200	A196	1.30s pur & dp org	40	20
C201	A197	2s dp bl & dl grn	40	20

See note after No. 519.

Juan Montalvo and Cervantes
AP47

Don Quixote
AP48

1949, May 2 **Engr.** ***Perf. 12½x12***

C202	AP47	1.30s ol brn & ultra	2.00	1.50
C203	AP48	1.90s grn & rose car	50	30
C204	AP47	3s vio & org brn	50	30
C205	AP48	5s red & gray blk	1.25	15
C206	AP47	10s red lil & aqua	2.00	15
		Nos. C202-C206 (5)	6.25	2.40

Issued to commemorate the 400th anniversary of the birth of Miguel de Cervantes Saavedra, novelist, playwright and poet, and the 60th anniversary of the death of Juan Montalvo (1832-1889), Ecuadorean writer.

No. C168 Surcharged in Blue

II CONGRESO
Junio 1949
Eucarístico Ncl.
50 —— 50

1949, June 15 ***Perf. 12***

C207	AP39	50c on 1.10s car rose	15	15
C208	AP39	60c on 1.10s car rose	20	20
C209	AP39	90c on 1.10s car rose	25	25

Issued to commemorate the Second Eucharistic Congress, Quito, June 1949.

No. C128 Surcharged in Black

75 Aniversario
* U. P. U. *
60 centavos 60

1949, Oct. 11 ***Perf. 11***

C210	AP28	60c on 3s org	50	40
a.		Double surcharge	20.00	
C211	AP28	90c on 3s org	40	25
C212	AP28	1s on 3s org	50	35
C213	AP28	2s on 3s org	1.25	50

"SUCRE(S)" in capitals on Nos. C212-C213.
Issued to commemorate the 75th anniversary of the formation of the Universal Postal Union.

AP49

Black Surcharge.

1950 ***Perf. 12*** **Unwmkd.**

C214	AP49	60c on 50c gray	15	5
a.		Double surcharge	20.00	

No. C170 Surcharged with New Value in Black.

C215	AP40	90c on 1.90s ol bis	40	15

Nos. C168, C128-C129 and Type of 1944 Surcharged or Overprinted
ALFABETIZACION
in Black or Carmine.

1950, Feb. 10 ***Perf. 12***

C216	AP39	50c on 1.10s car rose	20	15
C217	AP39	70c on 1.10s car rose	25	20

Perf. 11

C218	AP28	3s orange	50	40
C219	AP28	5s dk brn (C)	90	50
C220	AP28	10s vio (C)	1.50	35
		Nos. C216-C220 (5)	3.35	1.60

Issued to publicize adult education.

Govt. Palace Type of 1944

1950, May 15 **Engr.** ***Perf. 11***

C221	AP28	10s violet	1.00	10

No. C169 Surcharged with New Value in Black.

1950 ***Perf. 12***

C222	AP40	90c on 1.30s dp bl	20	10

See No. C235.

Nos. C128-C129 Overprinted in Black

20.000 Cruce
Línea Ecuatorial
PANAGRA
26-Julio-1951

1951, July 28 ***Perf. 11*** **Unwmkd.**

C223	AP28	3s orange	60	60
C224	AP28	5s dk brn	1.00	75

Issued to commemorate the 20,000th crossing of the equator by Pan American-Grace Airways planes.

Nos. C202-C203 Surcharged in Black

CAMPANA

Alfabetización
60 Ctvs. 60
a

CAMPAÑA
ALFABETIZACION
1,00 Sucre 1,00
b

1951 ***Perf. 12½x12*** **Unwmkd.**

C225	AP47 (a)	60c on 1.30s ol brn & ultra	25	10

C226	AP48 (b)	1s on 1.90s grn & rose car	25	10
a.		Inverted surcharge	17.50	

Issued to publicize adult education.

St. Mariana de Jesus
AP50

1952, Feb. 15 **Engraved.**

C227	AP50	60c plum & aqua	40	20
C228	AP50	90c dk grn & lt ultra	40	15
C229	AP50	1s car & dk grn	50	20
C230	AP50	2s ind & rose lil	50	15

Issued to publicize the canonization of Mariana de Jesus Paredes y Flores.

Presidents
Galo Plaza and Harry Truman
AP51

Design: 5s, Pres. Plaza addressing U. S. Congress.

1952, Mar. 26 ***Perf. 12***

C231	AP51	3s lil & bl grn	50	40
C232	AP51	5s red brn & ol gray	1.00	75
a.		Souvenir sheet	3.00	3.00

No. C232a measures 126 x 61 mm., and contains one each of Nos. C231 and C232, with marginal inscriptions in lilac and red brown.

Issued to commemorate the 1951 visit of Pres. Galo Plaza y Lasso to the United States.

Consular Service Stamps Surcharged "AEREO" and New Value in Black.

1952 ***Perf. 12*** **Unwmkd.**

C233	R2	60c on 1s grn	10	5
C234	R2	1s on 1s grn	15	5

Type R2 illustrated above No. 545.

No. C169 Surcharged with New Value in Carmine.

C235	AP40	90c on 1.30s dp bl	10	5

See No. C222.

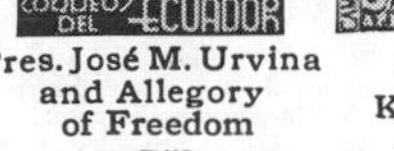

Pres. José M. Urvina and Allegory of Freedom
AP52

Torch of Knowledge
AP53

Hyphen-hole Perf. 7x6½

1952, Nov. 18 **Lithographed.**

C236	AP52	60c rose red & bl	1.00	30
C237	AP52	90c lil & red	1.00	40
C238	AP52	1s org & grn	1.00	20
C239	AP52	2s red brn & bl	1.00	25

Centenary of abolition of slavery in Ecuador. Counterfeits exist.

Engraved.

Design: 2s, Aged couple studying alphabet.

1953, Apr. 13 ***Perf. 12*** **Unwmkd.**

C240	AP53	1s dk bl	50	10
C241	AP53	2s red org	75	10

1952 adult education campaign.

Globe Showing Part of Western Hemisphere
AP54

1953, June 5 ***Perf. 12½x12***

C242	AP54	60c org yel	30	30
C243	AP54	90c dk bl	35	30
C244	AP54	3s carmine	75	50

Issued to publicize the crossing of the equator by the Pan-American highway.

Consular Service Stamps Surcharged in Black

AEREO
1
SUCRE
a

1 SUCRE
AEREO
b

1953-54 ***Perf. 12.***

C245	R1 (a)	60c on 2s brn	20	10
C246	R2 (a)	60c on 5s sep ('54)	20	10
C247	R2 (a)	70c on 5s sep ('54)	25	15
C248	R2 (a)	90c on 50c car rose ('54)	35	10
C249	R1 (b)	1s on 2s brn	35	15
C250	R1 (a)	1s on 2s brn ('54)	35	10
C251	R1 (a)	2s on 2s brn ('54)	40	20
C252	R1 (a)	3s on 5s vio ('54)	75	20
		Nos. C245-C252 (8)	2.85	1.10

The surcharge reads upward on Nos. C250–C252.

Carlos Maria Cardinal de la Torre
AP55

Queen Isabella I
AP56

1954, Jan. 13 **Photo.** ***Perf. 8½.***

Center in Black.

C253	AP55	60c rose lil	20	10
C254	AP55	90c green	25	10
C255	AP55	3s orange	35	25

Issued to commemorate the first anniversary of the elevation of Archbishop de la Torre to Cardinal.

1954, April 22

C256	AP56	60c dk grn & grn	10	10
C257	AP56	90c lil rose	15	15
C258	AP56	1s blk & pale lil	15	15
C259	AP56	2s blk brn & pale bl	25	20
C260	AP56	5s blk brn & buff	60	40
		Nos. C256-C260 (5)	1.25	1.00

See note after No. 585.

Post Office, Guayaquil—AP57

Engraved.

1954, May 19 ***Perf. 12½x12.***

Black Surcharge

C261	AP57	80c on 20c red	20	15
C262	AP57	1s on 20c red	25	15

Issued to commemorate the 25th anniversary of Pan American-Grace Airways' operation in Ecuador.

Plane, Gateway and Wheel
AP58

Lithographed

1954, Aug. 2 ***Perf. 11*** **Unwmkd.**

C263	AP58	80c blue	15	10

Issued to publicize the Day of the Postal Employee.

San Pablo Lagoon
AP59

1954, Sept. 24 **Photogravure**

C264	AP59	60c orange	10	5
C265	AP59	70c rose pink	10	5
C266	AP59	90c dp grn	15	5
C267	AP59	1s dk gray grn	20	5
C268	AP59	2s blue	30	10
C269	AP59	3s yel brn	40	15
		Nos. C264-C269 (6)	1.25	45

Glorification of Abdon Calderon Garaicoa
AP60

Capt. Calderon
AP61

1954, Oct. 1

C270	AP60	80c rose pink	25	15
C271	AP61	90c blue	25	15

Issued to commemorate the 150th anniversary of the birth of Capt. Abdon Calderon Garaicoa.

El Cebollar College
AP62

Brother Miguel Instructing Boys
AP63

Designs: 90c, Francisco Febres Cordero (Brother Miguel). 2.50s, Tomb of Brother Miguel. 3s, Monument to Brother Miguel.

1954, Dec. 8 ***Perf. 11*** **Unwmkd.**

C272	AP62	70c dk grn	10	10
C273	AP63	80c dk brn	15	10
C274	AP63	90c dk gray bl	15	10
C275	AP63	2.50s indigo	25	20
C276	AP62	3s lil rose	50	35
		Nos. C272-C276 (5)	1.15	85

Issued to commemorate the centenary of the birth of Francisco Febres Cordero (Brother Miguel).

No. C221 Surcharged in Various Colors

E. M. P. 1955

$ 1,00

1955, May 25

C277	AP28	1s on 10s vio (Bk)	25	10
C278	AP28	1.70s on 10s vio (C)	40	15
C279	AP28	4.20s on 10s vio (Br)	75	50

Denomination in larger type on No. C279.

Issued to publicize the National Exhibition of Daily Periodicals.

"La Rotonda," Guayaquil, and Rotary Emblem
AP64

Design: 90c, Eugenio Espejo hospital, Quito, and Rotary emblem.

1955, July 9 **Engraved** ***Perf. 12½***

C280	AP64	80c dk brn	40	30
C281	AP64	90c dk grn	40	35

Issued to commemorate the 50th anniversary of the founding of Rotary International.

José Abel Castillo
AP65

Design:
2s, 5s, José Abel Castillo and Map of Ecuador.

1955, Oct. 19 ***Perf. 11x11½***

C282	AP65	60c chocolate	40	15
C283	AP65	90c lt ol grn	40	15
C284	AP65	1s lilac	40	15
C285	AP65	2s vermilion	40	20
C286	AP65	5s ultra	75	50
		Nos. C282-C286 (5)	2.35	1.15

See note after No. 595.

No. C29 Surcharged in Black.

1
X SUCRE X

1955, Oct. 24 ***Perf. 12***

C287	AP1	1s on 5s pur	25	20

A similar surcharge on No. C29, set in two lines with letters 5mm. high and no X's or black-out line of squares, was privately applied.

San Pablo, Imbabura
AP66

Designs: 50s, Rumichaca Caves. 1.30s, Virgin of Quito. 1.50s, Cotopaxi Volcano. 1.70s, Tungurahua Volcano, Tungurahua. 1.90s, Guanacos. 2.40s, Mat market. 2.50s, Ruins at Incapirca. 4.20s, El Carmen, Cuenca, Azuay. 4.80s, Santo Domingo Church.

1956, Jan. 2 **Photo.** ***Perf. 13***

C288	AP66	50c sl bl	30	10
C289	AP66	1s ultra	30	10
C290	AP66	1.30s crimson	35	15
C291	AP66	1.50s dp grn	25	10
C292	AP66	1.70s yel brn	20	10
C293	AP66	1.90s olive	30	25
C294	AP66	2.40s red org	35	25
C295	AP66	2.50s violet	35	25
C296	AP66	4.20s black	40	30
C297	AP66	4.80s yel org	60	50
		Nos. C288-C297 (10)	3.40	2.10

See also Nos. C310-C311.

Honorato Vazquez
AP67

Title Page of First Book
AP68

1956, May 28 **Engraved**

Various Portraits.

C298	AP67	1s yel grn	20	15
C299	AP67	1.50s red	25	20
C300	AP67	1.70s brt bl	20	20
C301	AP67	1.90s sl bl	25	20

Birth centenary (in 1955) of Honorato Vazquez, statesman.

1956, Aug. 27 ***Perf. 13½*** **Unwmkd.**

C302	AP68	1s black	15	10
C303	AP68	1.70s sl bl	20	15
C304	AP68	2s blk brn	30	20
C305	AP68	3s redsh brn	35	30

Bicentenary of printing in Ecuador.

Hands Reaching for U.N. Emblem
AP69

1956, Oct. 24 ***Perf. 14***

C307	AP69	1.70s red org	50	20

Issued to commemorate the tenth anniversary of the United Nations (in 1955).
See also No. C319.

Coat of Arms and Basketball Player
AP70

Designs: 1.70s, Map of South America with flags and girl basketball players.

Photogravure.

1956, Dec. 28 ***Perf. 14½x14***

C308	AP70	1s red lil	25	10
C309	AP70	1.70s dp grn	40	20

Issued to commemorate the 6th South American Women's Basketball Championship, August 1956.

Scenic Type of 1956.

1957, Jan. 2 ***Perf. 13***

C310	AP66	50c bl grn	25	10
C311	AP66	1s orange	30	15

Type of Regular Issue, 1957

Designs: 50c, Map of Cuenca, 16th century. 80c, Cathedral of Cuenca. 1s, Modern City Hall.

Photogravure.

1957, Apr. 7 ***Perf. 12*** **Unwmkd.**

C312	A219	50c brn, *cr*	10	5
a.		Souvenir sheet of 4	75	75
C313	A219	80c red, *bluish*	15	15
C314	A219	1s pur, *yel*	20	10
a.		Souvenir sheet of 3	1.25	1.25

Issued to commemorate the fourth centenary of the founding of Cuenca.

No. C312a contains four imperf. 50c stamps similar to No. 613, but inscribed "AEREO" and printed in green. The sheet measures 140x120mm. and is printed on white ungummed paper. It is inscribed "IV Reunion de Consulta de la Comision del Instituto Panamericano de Geografia e Historia, Cuenca 4 al 12 de Abril de 1957."

No. C314a contains three imperf. stamps in designs similar to Nos. C312–C314, but with colors changed to orange (50c), brown (80c), violet (1s). The sheet measures 140x120mm. and is printed on white ungummed paper. It is inscribed "III Congreso de Ingenieros y Arquitectos del Ecuador, Cuenca, 6 al 9 de Abril de 1957."

Gabriela Mistral
AP71

Arms of Espejo, Carchi
AP72

Lithographed.

1957, Sept. 18 ***Perf. 14*** **Unwmkd.**

C315	AP71	2s lt bl, blk & red	30	20

Issued to honor Gabriela Mistral (1889–1957), Chilean poet and educator.
See also Nos. C406–C407.

Province of Carchi.

1957, Nov. 16 ***Perf. 14½x13½***

Arms of Cantons: 2s, Montufar. 4.20s, Tulcan.

Coat of Arms Multicolored.

C316	AP72	1s carmine	20	10
C317	AP72	2s black	25	15
C318	AP72	4.20s ultra	60	40

See also Nos. C334–C337, C355–C364, C392–C395.

Redrawn U.N. Type of 1956.

1957, Dec. 10 **Engraved.** ***Perf. 14***

C319	AP69	2s grnsh bl	50	35

Issued to honor the United Nations. Dates, as on No. C307, are omitted; inscribed: "Homenaje a las Naciones Unidas."

Mater Dolorosa, San Gabriel College
AP73

Rafael Maria Arizaga
AP74

Design: Nos. C321 & 1s, Door of San Gabriel College, Quito.

1958, Apr. 27 **Engraved.** ***Perf. 14***

C320	AP73	30c rose cl, *dp rose*	20	10
C321	AP73	30c rose cl, *dp rose*	20	10
C322	AP73	1s dk bl, *lt bl*	20	10
C323	AP73	1.70s dk bl, *lt bl*	25	20

Issued to commemorate the 50th anniversary of the miracle of San Gabriel College, Quito.
Issued in 2 sheets of 50. One sheet contains alternate copies of Nos. C320-C321, the other Nos. C322-C323.

1958, July 21 **Lithographed**

C324	AP74	1s multi	15	10

Issued to commemorate the centenary of the birth of Rafael Maria Arizaga (1858–1933), writer.
See also Nos. C343, C350, C412.

Daule River Bridge
AP75

Engraved.

1958, July 25 ***Perf. 13½x14***

C325	AP75	1.30s green	25	15

Issued to commemorate the opening of the River Daule bridge in Guayas province.
See also Nos. C367–C369.

Basketball Player
AP76

Symbolical of the Eucharist
AP77

Photogravure

1953, Sept. 1 ***Perf. 14x13½***

C326	AP76	1.30s dk grn & lt brn	50	40

South American basketball championships.

1958, Sept. 25 **Litho.** **Unwmkd.**

Design: 60c, Cathedral of Guayaquil.

C327	AP77	10c vio & buff	10	10
C328	AP77	60c org & vio brn	10	10
C329	AP77	1s brn & lt bl	20	10

Souvenir Sheet

Symbolical of the Eucharist
AP78

Perf. 13½x14

C330	AP78	Sheet of four	75	75
a.		40c dk bl (any position)	15	15

Nos. C327-C330 issued to commemorate the 3rd National Eucharistic Congress.
No. C330 measures 115 x 88½mm.

Stamps of 1865 and 1920
AP79

Designs: 2s, Stamps of 1920 and 1948. 4.20s, Municipal museum and library.

Photogravure.

1958, Oct. 8 ***Perf. 11½*** **Unwmkd.**

Granite Paper

C331	AP79	1.30s grn & brn red	25	20
C332	AP79	2s bl & vio	50	30
C333	AP79	4.20s dk brn	90	60

Issued to publicize the National Philatelic Exposition (EXFIGUA), Guayaquil, Oct. 4-14.

Coat of Arms Type of 1957.

Province of Imbabura.

Arms of Cantons: 50c, Cotacachi. 60c, Antonio Ante. 80c, Otalvo. 1.10s, Ibarra.

Lithographed.

1958, Nov. 9 ***Perf. 14½x13½***

Coats of Arms Multicolored.

C334	AP72	50c blk & red	10	10
C335	AP72	60c blk, bl & red	10	10
C336	AP72	80c blk & yel	15	10
C337	AP72	1.10s blk & red	20	10

Charles V
AP80

Paul Rivet
AP81

Engraved & Photogravure

Perf. 14x13½

1958, Dec. 12 **Unwmkd.**

C338	AP80	2s brn red & dk brn	30	15
C339	AP80	4.20s dk gray & red brn	60	50

Issued to commemorate the 400th anniversary of the death of Charles V, Holy Roman Emperor.

1958, Dec. 29 **Photo.** ***Perf. 11½***

Granite Paper.

C340	AP81	1s brown	15	10

Issued in honor of Paul Rivet (1876–1958), French anthropologist.

1959, May 6

Portrait: 2s, Alexander von Humboldt.

C341 AP81 2s slate 20 10

Issued to commemorate the centenary of the death of Alexander von Humboldt, German naturalist and geographer.

Front Page of "El Telegrafo"
AP82

1959, Feb. Litho. *Perf. 13½*

C342 AP82 1.30s bl grn & blk 20 15

Issued to commemorate the 75th anniversary of Ecuador's oldest newspaper.

Portrait Type of 1958

Portrait: José Luis Tamayo.

1959, June 26 *Perf. 14* Unwmkd.

Portrait Multicolored.

C343 AP74 1.30s lt grn, bl & sal 20 15

Issued to commemorate the centenary of the birth of José Luis Tamayo (1858–1947), lawyer.

El Sagrario and House of Manuela Canizares
AP83

Condor
AP84

Designs: 80c, Hall at San Agustin. 1s, First words of the constitutional act. 2s, Entrance to Cuartel Real. 4.20s, Allegory of Liberty.

Photogravure.

1959, Aug. 28 *Perf. 14* Unwmkd.

C344 AP83 20c ultra & lt brn 10 5
C345 AP83 80c brt bl & dp org 10 5
C346 AP83 1s dk red & dk ol 15 10
C347 AP84 1.30s brt bl & org 25 10
C348 AP84 2s ultra & org brn 25 15
C349 AP84 4.20s scar & brt bl 60 40
Nos. C344-C349 (6) 1.45 85

Sesquicentennial of the revolution.

Portrait Type of 1958

Portrait: 1s, Alfredo Baquerizo Moreno.

1959, Sept. 26 Litho. *Perf. 14*

C350 AP74 1s gray, red & sal 15 10

Issued to commemorate the centenary of the birth of Alfredo Baquerizo Moreno (1859–1951), statesman.

Pope Pius XII
AP85

1959, Oct. 9 *Perf. 14½* Unwmkd.

C351 AP85 1.30s multi 30 25

Issued in memory of Pope Pius XII.

Flags of Argentina, Bolivia, Brazil, Guatemala, Haiti, Mexico and Peru
AP86

Flags of: 80c, Chile, Costa Rica, Cuba, Dominican Republic, Panama, Paraguay, United States. 1.30s, Colombia, Ecuador, Honduras, Nicaragua, Salvador, Uruguay, Venezuela.

1959, Oct. 12 *Perf. 13½.*

C352 AP86 50c multi 15 10
C353 AP86 80c yel, red & bl 20 15
C354 AP86 1.30s multi 25 20

Organization of American States.

Coat of Arms Type of 1957
Province of Pichincha.

Arms of Cantons: 10c, Rumiñahui. 40c, Pedro Moncayo. 1s, Mejia. 1.30s, Cayambe. 4.20s, Quito.

Lithographed.

1959–60 *Perf. 14½x13½* Unwmkd.

Coat of Arms Multicolored.

C355 AP72 10c blk & dk red ('60) 5 5
C356 AP72 40c blk & yel 10 5
C357 AP72 1s blk & brn ('60) 10 10
C358 AP72 1.30s blk & grn ('60) 20 10
C359 AP72 4.20s blk & org 40 30
Nos. C355-C359 (5) 85 60

Province of Cotopaxi.

Arms of Cantons: 40c, Pangua. 60c, Pujili. 70c, Saquisili. 1s, Salcedo. 1.30s, Latacunga.

1960

Coat of Arms Multicolored

C360 AP72 40c blk & car 5 5
C361 AP72 60c blk & bl 10 5
C362 AP72 70c blk & turq 20 10
C363 AP72 1s blk & red org 20 10
C364 AP72 1.30s blk & org 25 15
Nos. C360-C364 (5) 80 45

Flags of American Nations
AP87

1960, Feb. 23 *Perf. 13x12½*

C365 AP87 1.30s multi 15 10
C366 AP87 2s multi 25 20

Issued to commemorate the 11th Inter-American Conference, Feb. 1960.

Bridge Type of 1958.

Bridges: No. C367, Juntas. No. C368, Saracay. 2s, Railroad bridge, Ambato.

1960 Lithographed *Perf. 13½*

C367 AP75 1.30s chocolate 15 10

Photo. *Perf. 12½*

C368 AP75 1.30s emerald 15 10
C369 AP75 2s brown 25 15

Building of three new bridges.

Bahia-Chone Road
AP88

Pres. Camilo Ponce Enriquez
AP89

Designs: 4.20s, Public Works Building, Cuenca. 5s, El Coca airport. 10s, New Harbor, Guayaquil.

1960, Aug. Litho. *Perf. 14*

C370 AP88 1.30s blk & dl yel 20 10
C371 AP88 4.20s rose car & lt grn 40 40
C372 AP88 5s dk brn & yel 60 50
C373 AP88 10s dk bl & bl 1.25 1.00

Perf. 11x11½

C374 AP89 2s org brn & blk 2.00 40
Nos. C370-C374 (5) 4.45 2.40

Nos. C370–C374 issued to publicize the achievements of Pres. Camilo Ponce Enriquez (1956–1960).

Issue dates: Nos. C370–C373, Aug. 24. No. C374, Aug. 31.

Red Cross Building, Quito and Henri Dunant—AP90

1960, Oct. 5 *Perf. 13x14* Unwmkd.

C375 AP90 2s rose vio & car 40 20

Centenary (in 1959) of Red Cross idea.

El Belen Church, Quito
AP91

1961, Jan. 14 *Perf. 12½*

C376 AP91 3s multi 50 25

Issued to commemorate Ecuador's participation in the 1960 Barcelona Philatelic Congress.

Map of Ecuador and Amazon River System
AP92

1961, Feb. 27 Litho. *Perf. 10½*

C377 AP92 80c sal, cl & grn 20 15
C378 AP92 1.30s gray, sl & grn 25 20
C379 AP92 2s beige, red & grn 30 25

Issued to commemorate Amazon Week, and the 132nd anniversary of the Battle of Tarqui against Peru.

Juan Montalvo, Juan Leon Mera, Juan Benigno Vela
AP93

Hugo Ortiz G.
AP94

1961, Apr. 13 *Perf. 13* Unwmkd.

C380 AP93 1.30s sal & blk 30 10

Centenary of Tungurahua province.

1961, May 25 *Perf. 14x14½*

Design: No. C382, Ortiz monument.

C381 AP94 1.30s grnsh bl, blk & yel 20 10
C382 AP94 1.30s grnsh bl, pur, ol & brn 20 10

Issued in memory of Lieutenant Hugo Ortiz G., killed in battle Aug. 2, 1941.

Condor and Airplane Stamp of 1936
AP95

Designs: 1.30s, Map of South America and stamp of 1865. 2s, Bolivar monument stamp of 1930.

Perf. 10½

1961, May 25 Litho. Unwmkd.

Size: 41x28mm.

C383 AP95 80c org & vio 25 15

Size: 41x34mm.

C384 AP95 1.30s bl, yel, ol & car 40 20

Size: 40½x37mm.

C385 AP95 2s car rose & blk 50 30

Issued to publicize the Third National Philatelic Exhibition, Quito, May 25–June 3, 1961.

Arms of Los Rios and Egret
AP96

1961, May 27 ***Perf. 14½x13½***
Coat of Arms Multicolored

C386 AP96 2s bl & blk 40 25

Centenary (in 1960) of Los Rios province.

Gabriel Garcia Moreno
AP97

Remigio Crespo Toral
AP98

1961, Sept. 24 ***Perf. 12*** **Unwmkd.**

C387 AP97 1s bl, brn & buff 20 10

Issued to commemorate the centenary of the restoration of national integrity.

1961, Nov. 3 ***Perf. 14*** **Unwmkd.**

C388 AP98 50c multi 10 10

Issued to commemorate the centenary of the birth of Remigio Crespo Toral, poet laureate of Ecuador.

Galapagos Islands Nos. LC1–LC3 Overprinted in Black or Red: "Estacion de Biologia Maritima de Galapagos" and "UNESCO 1961" (Similarly to Nos. 684–686).

1961, Oct. 31 **Photo.** ***Perf. 12***

C389 A1 1s dp bl 30 20
 a. "de Galapagos" on top line 1.25 1.25
C390 A1 1.80s rose vio 40 25
 a. UNESCO emblem omitted 75 75
C391 A1 4.20s blk (R) 65 50

Issued to commemorate the establishment of maritime biological stations on Galapagos Islands by UNESCO.

Coat of Arms Type of 1957.
Province of Tungurahua.

Arms of Cantons: 50c, Pillaro. 1s, Pelileo. 1.30s, Baños. 2s, Ambato.

Perf. 14½x13½

1962, Mar. 30 **Litho.** **Unwmkd.**
Coats of Arms Multicolored

C392 AP72 50c black 10 5
C393 AP72 1s black 15 10
C394 AP72 1.30s black 20 10
C395 AP72 2s black 30 20

Pres. Arosemena and Prince Philip, Arms of Ecuador and Great Britain and Equator Monument
AP99

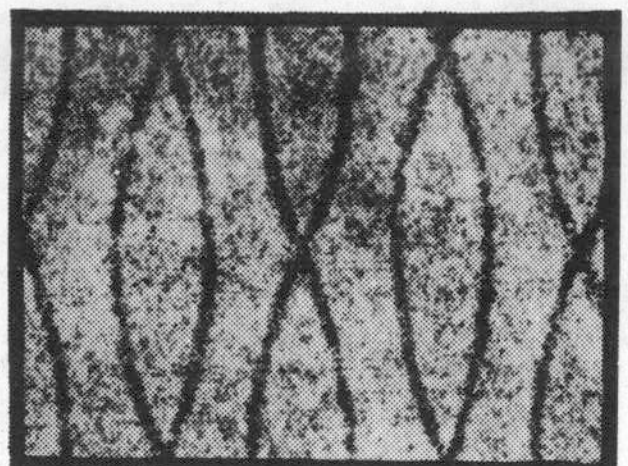

Wmk. 340

Wmkd. Alternating Interlaced Wavy Lines. (340)

1962, Feb. 17 ***Perf. 14x13½***

C396 AP99 1.30s bl, sep, red & yel 20 15
C397 AP99 2s multi 25 20

Issued to commemorate the visit of Prince Philip, Duke of Edinburgh, to Ecuador, Feb. 17–20, 1962.

Mountain Farming
AP100

Lithographed

1963, Mar. 21 ***Perf. 12½*** **Unwmkd.**

C398 AP100 30c emer, yel & blk 10 10
C399 AP100 3s dl red, grn & org 40 25
C400 AP100 4.20s bl, blk & yel 60 40

Issued for the "Freedom from Hunger" campaign of the U.N. Food and Agriculture Organization.

Mosquito and Malaria Eradication Emblem
AP101

1963, Apr. 17 ***Perf. 12½*** **Unwmkd.**

C401 AP101 50c dl yel, car rose & blk 10 10
C402 AP101 80c brt grn, car rose & blk 10 10
C403 AP101 2s brt pink, dp cl & blk 25 25

Issued for the World Health Organization drive to eradicate malaria.

Stagecoach and Jet Plane
AP102

1963, May 7 **Lithographed**

C404 AP102 2s org & car rose 40 20
C405 AP102 4.20s cl & ultra 60 40

Issued to commemorate the centenary of the first International Postal Conference, Paris, 1863.

Type of 1957 Inscribed "Islas Galapagos," Surcharged with New Value and Overprinted "Ecuador" in Black or Red.

1963, June 19 ***Perf. 14*** **Unwmkd.**

C406 AP71 5s on 2s gray, dk bl & red 40 30
C407 AP71 10s on 2s gray, dk bl & red (R) 1.00 75

The basic 2s exists without surcharge and overprint. No. C407 exists with "ECUADOR" omitted, and with both "ECUADOR" and "10 SUCRES" double.

No. C375 Overprinted: "1863–1963/Centenario/de la Fundación/de la Cruz Roja/Internacional"

Photogravure

1963, June 21 ***Perf. 13x14***

C408 AP90 2s rose vio & car 30 20

Issued to commemorate the centenary of the founding of the International Red Cross.

Type of Regular Issue, 1963.

Designs (Arosemena and): 70c, Flags of Ecuador. 2s, Flags of Ecuador and Panama. 4s, Flags of Ecuador and U.S.

1963, July 1 **Lithographed** ***Perf. 14***

C409 A238 70c pale bl & multi 15 10
C410 A238 2s pink & multi 30 15
C411 A238 4s lt bl & multi 75 35

Issued to commemorate Pres. Arosemena's friendship trip, July 1962.

Portrait Type of 1958

Portrait: 2s, Dr. Mariano Cueva.

Lithographed

1963, July 4 ***Perf. 14*** **Unwmkd.**

C412 AP74 2s lt grn & multi 25 15

Issued to commemorate the 150th anniversary of the birth of Dr. Mariano Cueva (1812–1882).

Social Insurance Symbol
AP103

Mother and Child
AP104

1963, July 9 **Lithographed**

C413 AP103 10s brn, bl, gray & ocher 75 60

25th anniversary of Social Insurance.

1963, July 28 ***Perf. 12½***

C414 AP104 1.30s org, dk bl & blk 25 15
C415 AP104 5s gray, red & brn 50 35

Issued to publicize the 7th Pan-American and South American Pediatrics Congresses, Quito.

Simon Bolivar Airport, Guayaquil
AP105

1963, July 25 ***Perf. 14***

C416 AP105 60c gray 10 5
C417 AP105 70c dl grn 15 10
C418 AP105 5s brn vio 50 35

Issued to commemorate the opening of Simon Bolivar Airport, Guayaquil, July 15, 1962.

Nos. 638, 640–641 Overprinted "AEREO"

1964 ***Perf. 12***
Flags in National Colors

C419 A223 1.80s dl vio 50 35
C420 A224 2s dk brn 50 35
C421 A223 2.20s blk brn 50 35

On 1.80s and 2.20s, "AEREO" is vertical, reading down.

No. 650 Overprinted in Gold: "FARO DE COLON / AEREO"

1964 **Photo.** ***Perf. 14x13½***

C422 A229 1.80s dk bl 2.50 1.50

Nos. C352–C354 Overprinted **1961**

1964 **Lithographed** ***Perf. 13½***

C423 AP86 50c bl & multi 60 30
C424 AP86 80c yel & multi 60 30
C425 AP86 1.30s pale grn & multi 60 30

No. C307 Overprinted: "DECLARACION / DERECHOS HUMANOS / 1964 / XV-ANIV"

Engraved

1964, Sept. 29 ***Perf. 14*** **Unwmkd.**

C426 AP69 1.70s red org 40 20

Issued to commemorate the 15th anniversary (in 1963) of the Universal Declaration of Human Rights.

Banana Type of Regular Issue

1964, Oct. 26 **Litho.** ***Perf. 12½x12***

C427 A241 4.20s blk, bis & gray ol 40 30
C428 A241 10s blk, scar & gray ol 75 60
 a. Souv. sheet of 4 1.50 1.50

Issued to publicize the Banana Conference, Oct.–Nov. 1964. No. C428a contains four imperf. stamps similar to Nos. 720–721 and C427–C428. Pale blue margin with black inscription and red control number. Size: 120x95mm.

John F. Kennedy, Flag-draped Coffin and John Jr.
AP106

1964, Nov. 22 **Litho.** ***Perf. 14***

C429 AP106 4.20s multi 75 60
C430 AP106 5s multi 1.00 75
C431 AP106 10s multi 1.50 1.00
 a. Souv. sheet of 3 6.00 6.00

Issued in memory of President John F. Kennedy (1917–63).

No. C431a contains stamps similar to Nos. C429–C431, imperf. Pale lilac margin with brown and white inscriptions. Red control number. Size: 114x130mm.

Olympic Type of Regular Issue

Designs: 1.30s, Gymnast (vert.). 1.80s, Hurdler. 2s, Basketball.

Perf. 13½x14, 14x13½

1964, Dec. 16 **Unwmkd.**

C432 A243 1.30s vio bl, ver & brn 25 15
C433 A243 1.80s vio bl & multi 25 20

C434	A243	2s red & multi	35	25
a.		Souv. sheet of 4	3.00	3.00

18th Olympic Games, Tokyo, Oct. 10–25.

No. C434a contains stamps similar to Nos. 725 and C432–C434, imperf. Pale olive margin with black and white inscriptions and red control number. Size: 139x107mm.

Sports Type of Regular Issue, 1965

Torch and Athletes: 2s, 3s, Diver, gymnast, wrestlers and weight lifter. 2.50s, 4s, Bicyclists. 3.50s, 5s, Jumpers.

1965, Nov. 20 Litho. *Perf. 12x12½*

C435	A247	2s bl, gold & blk	20	15
C436	A247	2.50s org, gold & blk	25	20
C437	A247	3s brt pink, gold & blk	25	20
C438	A247	3.50s lt vio, gold & bl	30	25
C439	A247	4s brt yel grn, gold & blk	35	30
C440	A247	5s red org, gold & blk	40	35
a.		Souv. sheet of 12	4.00	4.00
		Nos. C435-C440 (6)	1.75	1.45

Issued to commemorate the 5th Bolivarian Games, held at Guayaquil and Quito. No. C440a contains 12 imperf. stamps similar to Nos. 738–743 and C435–C440. Black and red inscriptions. Size: 215x129mm.

Bird Type of Regular Issue

Birds: 1s, Yellow grosbeak. 1.30s, Black-headed parrot. 1.50s, Scarlet tanager. 2s, Sapphire quail-dove. 2.50s, Violet-tailed sylph. 3s, Lemon-throated barbet. 4s, Yellow-tailed oriole. 10s, Collared puffbird.

1966, June 17 Litho. *Perf. 13½*

Birds in Natural Colors

C441	A249	1s lt red brn & blk	10	5
C442	A249	1.30s pink & blk	10	5
C443	A249	1.50s pale grn & blk	10	10
C444	A249	2s sal & blk	15	10
C445	A249	2.50s lt yel grn & blk	20	15
C446	A249	3s sal & blk	25	20
C447	A249	4s gray & blk	30	25
C448	A249	10s beige & blk	75	60
		Nos. C441-C448 (8)	1.95	1.50

Nos. C436 and C443 Surcharged

1967

C449	A247	80c on 2.50s org, gold & blk	10	5
C450	A249	80c on 1.50s multi	10	5

Old denomination on No. C449 is obliterated with heavy bar; the surcharge on No. C450 includes "Resello" and an ornament over old denomination.

Peñaherrera Monument, Quito
AP107

Design: 2s, Peñaherrera statue.

1967, Dec. 29 Litho. *Perf. 12x12½*

C451	AP107	1.30s blk & org	15	10
C452	AP107	2s blk & lt ultra	15	10

See note after No. 763.

Arosemena Type of Regular Issue, 1968

Designs: 1.30s, Inauguration of Pres. Arosemena. 2s, Pres. Arosemena speaking in Punta del Este.

1968, May 9 Litho. *Perf. 13½x14*

C453	A251	1.30s multi	10	10
C454	A251	2s multi	15	15

First anniversary of administration of Pres. Otto Arosemena Gomez.

No. C448 Surcharged In Plum, Dark Blue or Green

RESELLO

$ 0,80

1969, Jan. 9 Litho. *Perf. 13½*

Bird in Natural Colors

C455	A249	80c on 10s beige (P)	5	5
C456	A249	1s on 10s beige (DBl)	10	10
C457	A249	2s on 10s beige (G)	15	15

"Operation Friendship"
AP108

1969–70 Typo. *Perf. 13½*

C458	AP108	2s yel, blk, red & lt bl	15	15
a.		Perf. 12½	15	15
C459	AP108	2s bl, blk, car & yel ('70)	15	15

Friendship campaign. Medallion background on Nos. C458 and C458a is blue; on No. C459, yellow.

No. 639 Surcharged in Gold "S/. 5 AEREO" and Bar

1969, Nov. 25 Litho. *Perf. 12*

C460	A224	5s on 2s multi	1.25	75

Butterfly Type of Regular Issue

Butterflies: 1.30s, Morpho peleides. 1.50s, Anartia amathea.

1970 Lithographed *Perf. 12½*

C461	A255	1.30s multi	10	10
C462	A255	1.50s pink & multi	10	10

Same, White Background

1970 *Perf. 13½*

C463	A255	1.30s multi	10	10
C464	A255	1.50s multi	10	10

Arms Type of Regular Issue

Provincial Arms and Flags: 1.30s, El Oro. 2s, Loja. 3s, Manabi. 5s, Pichincha. 10s, Guayas.

1971 Lithographed *Perf. 10½*

C465	A258	1.30s pink & multi	10	10
C466	A258	2s multi	15	10
C467	A258	3s multi	20	15
C468	A258	5s multi	40	30
C469	A258	10s multi	75	60
		Nos. C465-C469 (5)	1.60	1.25

Presentation of the Virgin
AP109

Pres. Allende and Chilean Flag
AP110

Art of Quito: 1.50s, Blessed Anne at Prayer. 2s, St. Theresa de Jesus. 2.50s, Altar of Carmen (horiz.). 3s, Descent from the Cross. 4s, Christ of St. Mariana de Jesus. 5s, Shrine of St. Anthony. 10s, Cross of San Diego.

1971 *Perf. 11½*

Inscriptions in Black

C473	AP109	1.30s multi	15	10
C474	AP109	1.50s multi	20	10
C475	AP109	2s multi	25	10
C476	AP109	2.50s multi	30	15
C477	AP109	3s multi	40	20
C478	AP109	4s multi	60	25
C479	AP109	5s multi	60	30
C480	AP109	10s multi	1.20	60
		Nos. C473-C480 (8)	3.70	1.80

Design: 2.10s, Pres. José M. Velasco Ibarra of Ecuador, Pres. Salvador Allende of Chile and national flags.

1971, Aug. 24 *Perf. 12½*

C481	AP110	2s multi	15	10
C482	AP110	2.10s multi	15	10

Visit of Pres. Salvador Allende of Chile, Aug. 24.

Globe and Emblem
AP111

1971

C483	AP111	5s black	60	35
C484	AP111	5.50s dl pur & blk	60	40

Opening of Postal Museum, Aug. 24, 1971.

Pazmiño Type of Regular Issue

1971, Sept. 16 *Perf. 12x11½*

C485	A260	1.50s grn & multi	10	10
C486	A260	2.50s grn & multi	20	15

50th anniversary of "El Universo," newspaper founded by Ismael Pérez Pazmiño.

Map of Americas
AP112

Designs: 10s, Converging roads and map. 20s, Map of Americas and Equator. 50s, Mountain road and monument on Equator.

1971 *Perf. 11½*

C487	AP112	5s org & multi	60	35
C488	AP112	10s org & blk	1.00	75
C489	AP112	20s blk, bl & brt rose	1.50	1.25
C490	AP112	50s bl, blk & gray	2.50	2.25

11th Pan-American Road Congress.

Issue dates: 5s, 10s, 50s, Nov. 15; 20s, Nov. 22.

Arms of Ecuador and Argentina
AP113

Design: 5s, Presidents José M. Velasco Ibarra and Alejandro Agustin Lanusse.

1972

C491	AP113	3s blk & multi	25	20
C492	AP113	5s blk & multi	40	30

Visit of Lt. Gen. Alejandro Agustin Lanusse, president of Argentina, Jan. 25.

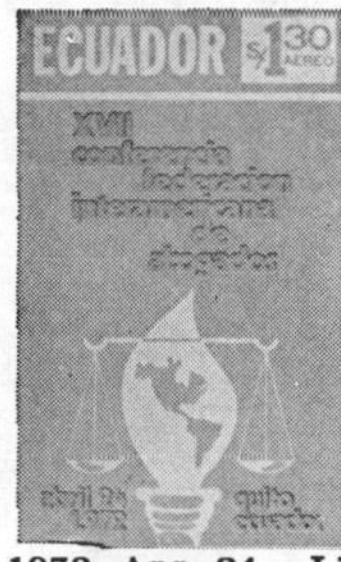

Flame, Scales, Map of Americas
AP114

1972, Apr. 24 Litho. *Perf. 12½*

C493	AP114	1.30s bl & red	10	10

17th Conference of the Interamerican Federation of Lawyers, Quito, Apr. 24.

Religious Paintings Type of Regular Issue

Ecuadorian Paintings: 3s, Virgin of the Flowers, by Miguel de Santiago. 10s, Virgin of the Rosary, by Quito School.

1972, Apr. 24 *Perf. 14x13½*

C494	A263	3s blk & multi	20	15
C495	A263	10s blk & multi	75	50
a.		Souv. sheet of 2	1.00	1.00

No. C495a contains one each of Nos. C494–C495. Blue marginal inscription. Size: 98x110½mm.

1972, May 4

Ecuadorian Statues: 3s, St. Dominic, Quito School. 10s, St. Rosa of Lima, by Bernardo de Legarda.

C496	A263	3s blk & multi	25	20
C497	A263	10s blk & multi	75	50
a.		Souv. sheet of 2	1.00	1.00

No. C497a contains one each of Nos. C496–C497. Blue marginal inscription. Size: 98x110½mm. Letters of "Ecuador" 3mm. high on Nos. C496–C497, 7mm. high on Nos. C494–C495.

Portrait Type of Regular Issue

Designs (Generals, from Paintings): 1.30s, José Maria Saenz. 3s, Tomás Wright. 4s, Antonio Farfan. 5s, Antonio José de Sucre. 10s, Simon Bolivar. 20s, Arms of Ecuador.

1972, May 24

C498	A264	1.30s bl & multi	10	10
C499	A264	3s bl & multi	25	20
C500	A264	4s bl & multi	30	20
C501	A264	5s bl & multi	40	30
C502	A264	10s bl & multi	75	50
C503	A264	20s bl & multi	1.50	1.00
		Nos. C498-C503 (6)	3.30	2.30

Sesquicentennial of the Battle of Pichincha and the liberation of Quito.

Artisan Type of Regular Issue

Designs: 2s, Woman wearing flowered poncho. 3s, Striped poncho. 5s, Poncho with roses. 10s, Gold sunburst sculpture.

1972, July Photo. *Perf. 13*

C504	A265	2s multi	15	10
C505	A265	3s multi	20	15
C506	A265	5s multi	40	30
C507	A265	10s org red & multi	75	50
a.		Souvenir sheet of 4	1.75	1.75

Handicraft of Ecuador. No. C507a contains one each of Nos. C504–C507. Pale claret marginal inscription and ornament. Black control number. Size 104x164mm.

Epidendrum Orchid
AP115

1972 Photogravure *Perf. 12½*

Multicolored; Flowers in Natural Colors

C508	AP115	4s *shown*	40	25
C509	AP115	6s *Canna*	50	30
C510	AP115	10s *Jimson weed*	1.00	60
a.		Souv. sheet of 3	2.25	2.25

No. C510a contains one each of Nos. C508–C510. Blue marginal inscription and ornaments. Black control number. Size: 166x106mm. Exists imperf.

Oil Drilling Towers
AP116

Coat of Arms
AP117

1972, Oct. 17 Litho. *Perf. 11½*

C511	AP116	1.30s bl & multi	15	10

Ecuadorian oil industry.

1972, Nov. 18 Litho. *Perf. 11½*

Arms Multicolored

C512	AP117	2s black	20	15
C513	AP117	3s black	30	20
C514	AP117	4s black	40	25
C515	AP117	4.50s black	40	25
C516	AP117	6.30s black	75	40
C517	AP117	6.90s black	75	40
		Nos. C512-C517 (6)	2.80	1.65

Pichincha Type of Regular Issue

Designs: 2.40s, Corridor, San Agustin. 4.50s, La Merced Convent. 5.50s, Column base. 6.30s, Chapter Hall, San Agustin. 6.90s, Interior, San Agustin. 7.40s, Crucifixion, Cantuña Chapel. 7.90s, Decorated ceiling, San Agustin.

1972, Dec. 6 Wmk. 367

C518	A266	2.40s yel & multi	20	15
C519	A266	4.50s yel & multi	35	25
C520	A266	5.50s yel & multi	40	30
C521	A266	6.30s yel & multi	50	40
C522	A266	6.90s yel & multi	50	40
C523	A266	7.40s yel & multi	60	50
C524	A266	7.90s yel & multi	65	50
		Nos. C518-C524 (7)	3.20	2.50

Sesquicentennial of the Battle of Pichincha.

UN Emblem
AP118

OAS Emblem
AP119

1973, Mar. 23 Litho. Unwmkd.

Perf. 11½

C525	AP118	1.30s lt bl & blk	20	10

25th anniversary of the Economic Committee for Latin America (CEPAL).

Wmk. 367

1973, Apr. 14 Litho. *Perf. 11½*

C526	AP119	1.50s multi	20	10
a.		Unwatermarked		

Day of the Americas and "Philately for Peace."

Bird Type of Regular Issue

1973 *Perf. 11½x11* Unwmkd.

C527	A268	1.30s *Blue-footed booby*	20	10
C528	A268	3s *Brown pelican*	20	10

Elevation of Galapagos Islands to a province of Ecuador.

Presidents Lara and Caldera
AP120

1973, June 15 Wmk. 367

C529	AP120	3s multi	40	20

Visit of Pres. Rafael Caldera of Venezuela, Feb. 5–7.

Silver Coin, 1934
AP121

Globe, OPEC Emblem, Oil Derrick
AP122

Ecuadorian Coins: 10s, Silver coin, obverse. 50s, Gold coin, 1928.

Perf. 14

1973, Dec. 14 Photo. Unwmkd.

C530	AP121	5s multi	40	20
C531	AP121	10s multi	75	40
C532	AP121	50s multi	3.75	2.00
a.		Souvenir sheet of 3	5.00	5.00

No. C532a contains one each of Nos. C530–C532; light blue margin with gold and black inscription, coat of arms and control numbers. Dated "1972." Size: 115x 88mm. Exists imperf.

A gold marginal overprint was applied in 1974 to No. C532a (perf. and imperf.): "X Campeonato Mundial de Football / Munich—1974".

A carmine overprint was applied in 1974 to No. C532a (perf. and imperf.): "Seminario de Telecommunicaciones Rurales, / Septiembre—1974 / Quito—Ecuador" and ITU emblem.

1974, June 15 Litho. *Perf. 11½*

C533	AP122	2s multi	20	10

Meeting of Organization of Oil Exporting Countries, Quito, June 15–24.

Ecuadorian Flag, UPU Emblem
AP123

1974, July 15 Litho. *Perf. 11½*

C534	AP123	1.30s multi	15	10

Centenary of Universal Postal Union.

Teodoro Wolf
AP124

Capt. Edmundo Chiriboga
AP125

1974 Lithographed *Perf. 12x11½*

C535	AP124	1.30s blk & ultra	10	5
C536	AP125	1.50s gray	10	5

Teodoro Wolf, geographer; Edmundo Chiriboga, national hero. Issue dates, No. C535, Nov. 29; No. C536, Dec. 4.

Congress Emblem
AP126

1974, Dec. 8 Litho. *Perf. 11½x12*

C537	AP126	5s bl & multi	40	20

8th Inter-American Postmasters' Congress, Quito.

Map of Americas and Coat of Arms
AP127

Manuel J. Calle, Journalist
AP128

1975, Feb. 1 *Perf. 12x11½*

C538	AP127	3s bl & multi	25	15

EXFIGUA Stamp Exhibition and 5th General Assembly of Federacion Inter-Americana de Filatelia, Guayaquil, Nov. 1973.

1975 *Perf. 12x11½*

Portraits: No. C540, Leopoldo Benites V., president of U.N. General Assembly, 1973–74; No. C541, Adofo H. Simmonds G. (1892–1969), journalists; No. C542, Juan de Dios Martinez Mera, President of Ecuador, birth centenary.

C539	AP128	5s lil rose	40	20
C540	AP128	5s gray	40	20
C541	AP128	5s violet	40	20
C542	AP128	5s blk & rose red	40	20

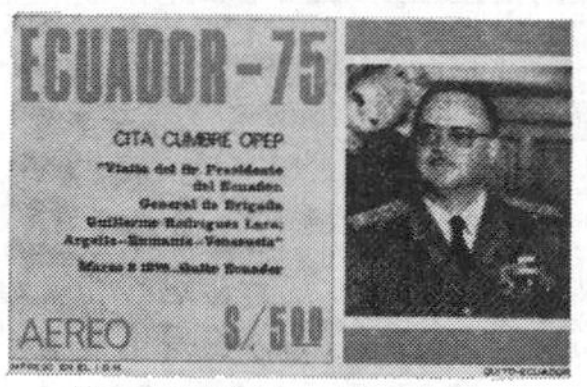

Pres. Guillermo Rodriguez Lara—AP129

1975 *Perf. 12* Unwmkd.

C546	AP129	5s ver & blk	50	20

State visit of Pres. Guillermo Rodriguez Lara to Algeria, Romania and Venezuela.

Meeting Type of 1975

Designs: 1.50s, Rafael Rodriguez Palacio and Argelino Duran Quintero meeting at border in Ruichacha. 2s, Signing border agreement.

1975, Apr. 1 Litho. *Perf. 12x11½*

C547	A273	1.50s multi	10	10
C548	A273	2s multi	20	10

Meeting of the Ministers for Public Works of Ecuador and Colombia, July 27, 1973.

Sacred Heart (Painting)
AP130

Quito Cathedral
AP131

Design: 2s, Monstrance.

1975, Apr. 28 Litho. *Perf. 12x11½*

C549	AP130	1.30s yel & multi	15	5
C550	AP130	2s bl & multi	20	10
C551	AP131	3s multi	30	10

3rd Bolivarian Eucharistic Congress, Quito, June 9–16, 1974.

J. Delgado Panchana with Trophy
AP132

J. Delgado Panchana Swimming
AP133

Perf. 12x11½, 11½x12

1975, June 12 Unwmkd.

C552	AP132	1.30s bl & multi	20	5
C553	AP133	3s blk & multi	30	10

Jorge Delgado Panchana. South American swimming champion, 1971 and 1974.

Sports Type of 1975

1975, Sept. 11 Litho. *Perf. 11½*

C554	A276	1.30s *Tennis*	10	5
C555	A276	2s *Target shooting*	20	10
C556	A276	2.80s *Volleyball*	25	10
C557	A276	3s *Raft with sails*	25	10
C558	A276	5s *Mask*	40	15
		Nos. C554-C558 (5)	1.20	50

3rd Ecuadorian Games.

Flower Type of 1975

1975, Nov. 18 Litho. *Perf. 11½x12*

C559	A277	1.30s *Pitcairnia pungens*	10	5
C560	A277	2s *Scarlet sage*	20	10
C561	A277	3s *Amaryllis*	25	15
C562	A277	4s *Opuntia quitense*	30	20
C563	A277	5s *Amaryllis*	40	20
		Nos. C559-C563 (5)	1.25	70

Tail Assemblies and Emblem
AP134

Planes over Map of Ecuador
AP135

1975, Dec. 17 Litho. *Perf. 11½*

C564	AP134	1.30s bl & multi	15	5
C565	AP135	3s multi	25	10

TAME, Military Transport Airline, 13th anniversary.

Benalcázar Statue
AP136

1976, Feb. 6 Litho. *Perf. 11½*

C566	AP136	2s multi	20	10
C567	AP136	3s multi	30	10

Sebastián de Benalcázar (1495–1550), Spanish conquistador, founder of Quito.

Archaeology Type of 1975

Designs: 1.30s, Seated man, Carchi Culture. 2s, Funerary urn, Tuncahuan Culture. 3s, Priest, Bahia de Caraquez Culture. 4s, Snail's shell, Cuasmal Culture. 5s, Bowl supported by figurines, Guangala Culture.

1976, Feb. 12 Litho. *Perf. 11½*

C568	A278	1.30s multi	10	5
C569	A278	2s multi	15	10
C570	A278	3s multi	20	10
C571	A278	4s multi	30	15
C572	A278	5s multi	40	20
		Nos. C568-C572 (5)	1.15	60

Archaeological artifacts.

Fruit Type of 1976

Designs: 2s, Apples. 5s, Rose.

1976, Mar. 30

C573	A280	2s bl & multi	15	10
C574	A280	5s bl & multi	40	20

25th Flower and Fruit Festival, Ambato.

Lufthansa Jet
AP137

1976, June 25 Litho. *Perf. 12*

C575	AP137	10s bl & multi	90	50

Lufthansa, 50th anniversary.

An imperf. 20s miniature sheet exists, similar to No. C575 enlarged, with overprinted black bar covering line below "Lufthansa." Size: 90x115mm.

Projected Post Office, Quito
AP138

Fruit Peddler
AP139

1976, Aug. 10 Litho. *Perf. 12*

C576	AP138	5s blk & multi	40	20

Design for new General Post Office, Quito.

1976, July 25

Designs: No. C578, Longshoreman. No. C579, Cerros del Carmen and Santa Ana, hills of Guayaquil (horiz.). No. C580, Sebastián de Belalcázar. No. C581, Francisco de Orellana. No. C582, Chief Guayas and his wife Quila.

C577	AP139	1.30s red & multi	10	5
C578	AP139	1.30s red & multi	10	5
C579	AP139	1.30s red & multi	10	5
C580	AP139	2s red & multi	15	10
C581	AP139	2s red & multi	15	10
C582	AP139	2s red & multi	15	10
		Nos. C577-C582 (6)	75	45

Founding of Quayaquil, 441st anniversary.

Emblem and Laurel
AP140

1976, Aug. 9

C583	AP140	1.30s yel & multi	10	5

Bolivarian Society of Ecuador, 50th anniversary.

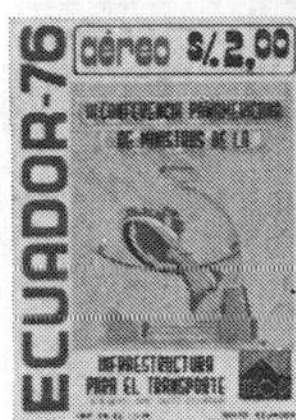

Western Hemisphere and Equator Monument
AP141

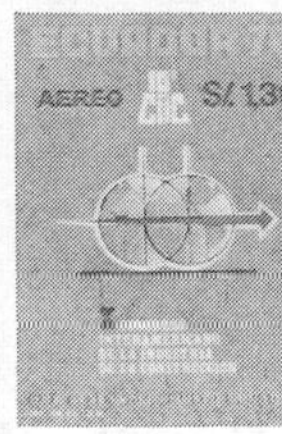

Congress Emblem
AP142

1976, Sept. 6

C584	AP141	2s multi	15	10

Souvenir Sheet

Imperf.

C585	AP141	5s multi	2.50	2.50

3rd Conference of Pan-American Transport Ministers, Quito, Sept. 6–11. No. C585 contains design similar to No. C584 with black denomination and red control number in margin. Size: 95x114mm.

1976, Sept. 27 Litho. *Perf. 11½*

C586	AP142	1.30s bl & multi	10	5
C587	AP142	3s bl & multi	20	10

Souvenir Sheet

Imperf.

C588	AP142	10s bl & multi	1.00	1.00

10th Inter-American Congress of the Construction Industry, Quito, Sept. 27–30. No. C588 has black control number. Size: 89x115mm.

George Washington
AP143

Design: 5s, Naval battle, Sept. 23, 1779, in which the Bonhomme Richard, commanded by John Paul Jones, defeated and captured the Serapis, British man-of-war, off Yorkshire coast (horiz.).

1976, Oct. 18 Litho. *Perf. 12*

C589	AP143	3s blk & multi	50	15
C590	AP143	5s red brn & yel	70	25

American Bicentennial.

Dr. Hideyo Noguchi
AP144

Luis Cordero
AP145

1976 Litho. *Perf. 11½*

C591	AP144	3s yel & multi	25	10

Dr. Hideyo Noguchi (1876–1928), bacteriologist (at Rockefeller Institute), birth centenary. A 10s imperf. miniature sheet in same design exists with red control number and without "Aereo." Size: 95x114 mm.

1976, Dec. Litho. *Perf. 11½*

C592	AP145	2s multi	15	10

Luis Cordero (1833–1912), president of Ecuador.

Mariuxi Febres Cordero
AP146

1976, Dec. *Perf. 11½*

C593	AP146	3s multi	25	10

Mariuxi Febres Cordero, South American swimming champion.

Flags and Monument
AP147

1976, Nov. 9 *Perf. 12*

C594	AP147	3s multi	25	10

Miniature Sheet

Imperf.

C595	AP147	5s multi	50	50

2nd Meeting of the Agriculture Ministers of the Andean Countries, Quito, Nov. 8–10. No. C595 has red control number. Size: 95x115mm.

See "Special Notices" at the front of this volume for data on the listing methods of this Catalogue, abbreviations, condition, prices and examination.

Sister Catalina
AP148

Congress Hall, Quito
AP149

1977, June 17 Litho. *Perf. 12x11½*

C596	AP148	1.30s blk & pale ol	10	5

Sister Catalina de Jesus Herrera (1717–1795), writer.

1977, Aug. 15 Litho. *Perf. 12x11½*

C597	AP149	5s multi	40	20
a.		10s souvenir sheet	1.00	1.00

11th General Assembly of Pan-American Institute of Geography and History, Quito, Aug. 15–30. No. C597a contains the designs of types A282 and AP149 without denominations and with simulated perforations; black and blue inscriptions, black control number. Size: 90x115mm.

Pres. Alfonso López Michelsen, Flag of Colombia—AP150

Designs: 5s, Pres. López M. of Colombia, Pres. Alfredo Povedo B. of Ecuador and aide. 7s, as 5s (vert.). 9s, 10s, Presidents with aides.

1977 *Perf. 12*

C598	AP150	2.60s multi	30	10
C599	AP150	5s multi	60	20
C600	AP150	7s multi	60	30
C601	AP150	9s multi	90	45

Imperf.

C602	AP150	10s multi	1.00	1.00

Meeting of the Presidents of Ecuador and Colombia and Declaration of Putumayo, Feb. 25, 1977. Nos. C598–C602 are overprinted in multiple fluorescent, colorless rows: INSTITUTO GEOGRAFICO MILITAR GOBIERNO DEL ECUADOR. No. C602 has black control number. Size: 115x91mm.

Ceramic Figure, Tolita Culture
AP151

Designs: 9s, Divine Shepherdess, sculpture by Bernardo de Legarda. 11s, The Fruit Seller, sculpture by Legarda. 20s, Sun God, pre-Columbian gold mask.

1977, Aug. 24 *Perf. 12*

C603	AP151	7s gold & multi	60	30
C604	AP151	9s gold & multi	80	40
C605	AP151	11s gold & multi	1.00	50

Souvenir Sheet
Gold Embossed ***Imperf.***

C606 AP151 20s vio, bl, blk & gold 2.00 2.00

Central Bank of Ecuador, 50th anniversary. No. C606 has black control number. Size: 89x115mm. Nos. C603–C605 overprinted like Nos. C598–C602.

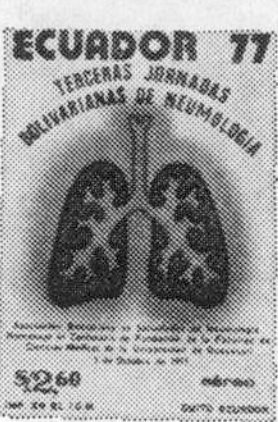

Lungs **AP152**

Brother Miguel, St. Peter's, Rome **AP153**

1977, Oct. 5 Litho. ***Perf. 12x11½***

C607 AP152 2.60s multi 20 10

3rd Congress of the Bolivarian Pneumonic Society and centenary of the founding of the medical faculty of the University of Guayaquil.

1977

C608 AP153 2.60s multi 20 10

Beatification of Brother Miguel.

Peralta Type of 1977

Design: 2.60s, Titles of works by Peralta and his bookmark.

1977 ***Perf. 11½***

C609 A284 2.60s multi 20 10

José Peralta (1855–1937), writer, 40th death anniversary.

Broadcast Tower **AP154**

Remigio Romero y Cordero **AP155**

1977, Dec. 2 Litho. ***Perf. 12x11½***

C610 AP154 5s multi 40 20

9th World Telecommunications Day.

1978, Mar. 2 Litho. ***Perf. 12½x11½***

C611 AP155 3s multi 20 10
C612 AP155 10.60s multi 80 40

Imperf.

C612A AP155 10s multi 80 40

Remigio Romero y Cordero (1895–1967), poet.

No. C612A contains a vignette similar to Nos. C611–C612, poem and black control number. Size: 90x114mm.

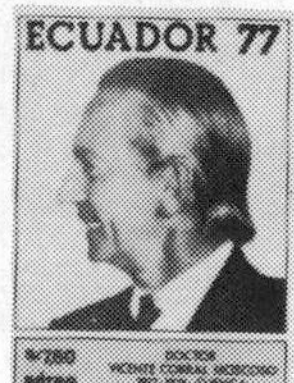

Dr. Vicente Corral Moscoso **AP156**

Faces **AP157**

Design: 5s, Hospital emblem with Caduceus.

1978, Apr. 12 Litho. ***Imperf.***

C613 AP156 5s multi 40 20

Perf. 12x11½

C614 APP156 7.60s multi 60 30

Inauguration (in 1977) of Dr. Vicente Corral Moscoso Regional Hospital, Cuenca.

No. C613 has black control number. Size: 89x114mm.

1978, Mar. 17

Designs: 9s, Emblems and flags of Ecuador. 10s, 11s, Hands reaching for light.

C615 AP157 7s multi 60 30
C616 AP157 9s multi 80 40
C617 AP157 11s multi 90 45

Imperf.

C618 AP157 10s multi 80 40

Ecuadorian Social Security Institute, 50th anniversary.

No. C618 has black control number. Size: 89x114mm.

Geographical Institute Type of 1978

Design: 7.60s, Plane over map of Ecuador with mountains.

1978, Apr. 12 Litho. ***Perf. 11½***

C619 A287 7.60s multi 60 30

Imperf.

C620 A287 10s multi 90 45

Military Geographical Institute, 50th anniversary. No. C620 contains 2 vignettes with simulated perforations in designs of Nos. 967 and C619, Institute emblem, black control number. Size: 115x89mm.

Lions Type of 1978

1978 ***Perf. 11½***

C621 A288 5s multi 40 20
C622 A288 6.20s multi 50 25

Imperf.

C623 A288 10s multi 80 40

7th meeting of Latin American Lions, Jan. 25–29. No. C623 contains a vignette similar to Nos. C621–C622, inscriptions and black control number. Size: 115x90mm.

San Martin **AP158**

1978, Apr. 13 Litho. ***Perf. 12***

C624 AP158 10.60s multi 90 45

Imperf.

C625 AP158 10s multi 80 40

Gen. José de San Martin (1778–1850), soldier and statesman. No. C625 contains a vignette similar to No. C624, inscriptions and black control number. Size: 115x90mm.

Bank Type of 1978

Design: 5s, Bank emblem.

1978, Sept. Litho. ***Perf. 11½***

C626 A289 5s gray & multi 40 20

70th anniversary of Filanbanco (Philanthropic Bank).

Soccer Type of 1978

Designs: 2.60s, "Gauchito" and Games' emblem. 5s, "Gauchito." 7s, Soccer ball. 9s, Games' emblem (vert.). 10s, Games' emblem.

1978, Nov. 1 ***Perf. 12***

C627 A290 2.60s multi 20 15
C628 A290 7s multi 60 30
C629 A290 9s multi 80 40

Imperf.

C630 A290 5s blk & bl 40 20
C631 A290 10s blk & bl 80 40

11th World Cup Soccer Championship, Argentina, June 1–25. Nos. C630–C631 have black control numbers. Size: 115x90mm.

Bernardo O'Higgins **AP159**

Old Men of Vilcabamba **AP160**

1978, Nov. 11 Litho. ***Perf. 12x11½***

C632 AP159 10.60s multi 90 45

Imperf.

C633 AP159 10s multi 80 40

Gen. Bernardo O'Higgins (1778–1842), Chilean soldier and statesman. No. C633 contains a vignette similar to No. C632, inscriptions and black control number. Size: 115x90mm.

1978, Nov. 11 ***Perf. 12x11½***

C634 AP160 5s multi 40 20

Vilcabamba, valley of longevity.

Hubert H. Humphrey **AP161**

Virgin and Child **AP162**

1978, Nov. 27 Litho. ***Perf. 12x11½***

C635 AP161 5s multi 40 20

Hubert H. Humphrey (1911–1978), Vice President of the U.S.

1978

Children's Drawings: 4.60s, Holy Family. 6.20s, Candle and children.

C636 AP162 2.20s multi 20 10
C637 AP162 4.60s multi 40 20
C638 AP162 6.20s multi 60 25

Christmas 1978.

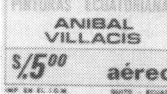

Village, by Anibal Villacis **AP163**

Ecuadorian Painters: No. C640, Mountain Village, by Gilberto Almeida. No. C641, Bay, by Roura Oxandaberro. No. C642, Abstract, by Luis Molinari. No. C643, Statue, by Oswaldo Viteri. No. C644, Tools, by Enrique Tabara.

1978, Dec. 9 ***Perf. 12***

C639 AP163 5s multi 40 20
C640 AP163 5s multi 40 20
C641 AP163 5s multi 40 20
C642 AP163 5s multi 40 20
C643 AP163 5s multi 40 20
C644 AP163 5s multi 40 20
Nos. C639-C644 (6) 2.40 1.20

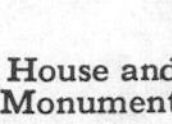

House and Monument **AP164**

Design: 3.40s, Monument (vert.).

1979, Feb. 27 Litho. ***Perf. 12***

C645 AP164 2.40s multi 20 10
C646 AP164 3.40s multi 25 10

Imperf.

C647 AP164 10s multi 90

Sesquicentennial of Battle of Portete and Tarqui. No. C647 contains vignettes similar to Nos. C645–C646; inscriptions and black control number. Size: 115x90mm.

Fish and Ship **AP165**

Flags of Ecuador and U.S. **AP166**

Designs: 7s, Map of Ecuador and Galapagos showing territorial waters (horiz.). 9s, Map of South America with west-coast territorial waters.

Perf. 12x11½, 11½x12

1979, July 23 Litho. Wmk. 367

C648 AP165 5s multi 40 20
C649 AP165 7s multi 60 30
C650 AP165 9s multi 80 40

Declaration of 200-mile territorial limit, 25th anniversary.

1979, Aug. 3 ***Perf. 12x11½***

Designs: 10.60s, Bells in Quito clock tower (horiz.). 13.60s, Aerial view of Galapagos coast.

C651 A293 10.60s multi 90 45
C652 A293 13.60s multi 1.00 50

Souvenir Sheet
Imperf. **Unwmkd.**

C653 A293 10s multi 90 45

National heritage: Quito and Galapagos Islands. No. C653 contains vignettes similar to Nos. 977, C651–C652; black control number, black and blue inscriptions. Size: 115x90mm.

1979, Aug. ***Perf. 11½x12*** **Wmk. 367**

C654 AP166 7.60s multi 60 30
C655 AP166 10.60s multi 90 45

Souvenir Sheet
Imperf. **Unwmkd.**

C656 AP166 10s multi 90 45

5th anniversary of Ecuador–U.S. Chamber of Commerce. No. C656 contains vignettes similar to Nos. C654–C655; black control number and marginal inscription. Size: 115x90mm.

Smiling Girl, IYC Emblem **AP167**

1979, Sept. 7 Litho. ***Perf. 12x11½***

C657 AP167 10s multi 90 45

International Year of the Child.

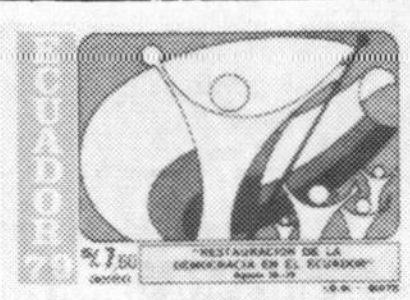

Citizens and Flag of Ecuador—AP168

Design: 10.60s, Pres. Jaime Roldas Aguilera, flag of Ecuador (vert.).

Unwmkd.

1979, Sept. 27 **Litho.** ***Perf. 11½***

C658 AP168 7.60s multi 75 40

Wmk. 367

C659 AP168 10.60s multi 90 45

Restoration of democracy to Ecuador.

Ecuador Coat of Arms, Olympic Rings and Eagle—AP169

1979, Nov. 23 **Litho.** ***Perf. 12×11½***

C660 AP169 28s multi 1.50 75

5th National Games, Cuenca.

CIESPAL Building, Quito—AP170

1979, Dec. 26 ***Perf. 11½×12½***

C661 AP170 10.60s multi 90 45

Opening of Ecuadorian Institute of Engineers building.

Olmedo Type of 1980

1980, Apr. 29 **Litho.** ***Perf. 12x11½***

C662 A294 10s multi 90 45

Tribal Chief Type of 1980

1980, May 12

Indo-American Tribal Chiefs: No. C663, Cuauhtemoc, Mexico. No. C664, Lempira, Honduras No. C665, Nicaragua. No. C666, Lambaré, Paraguay. No. C667, Urraca, Panama. No. C668, Anacaona, Haiti No. C669, Caupolican, Chile. No. C670, Tacun-Uman, Guatemala. No. C671, Calarca, Colombia. No. C672. Garabito, Costa Rica. No. C673, Hatuey, Cuba. No. C674, Cmarao, Brazil. No. C675, Tehuelche, Argentina. No.C676, Tupaj Katri, Bolivia. 17.80s, Sequoya, U.S. 22.80s, Ruminahui, Ecuador.

C663 A295 7.60s multi 70 35
C664 A295 7.60s multi 70 35
C665 A295 7.60s multi 70 35
C666 A295 10s multi 90 45
C667 A295 10s multi 90 45
C668 A295 10.60s multi 90 45
C669 A295 10.60s multi 90 45
C670 A295 10.60s multi 90 45
C671 A295 12.80s multi 1.20 60
C672 A295 12.80s multi 1.20 60
C673 A295 12.80s multi 1.20 60
C674 A295 13.60s multi 1.20 60
C675 A295 13.60s multi 1.20 60
C676 A295 13.60s multi 1.20 60
C677 A295 17.80s multi 1.50 75
C678 A295 22.80s multi 2.00 1.00
Nos. C663-C678 (16) 17.30 8.65

Royal Visit Type of 1980

1980, May 18 ***Perf. 11½x12***

C679 A296 10.60s multi 90 45

Pichincha Provincial Development Council Building AP171

1980, June 1 ***Perf. 12x11½***

C680 AP171 10.60s multi 90 45

Progress in Pichincha Province.

Indian Type of 1980

1980, June 10 **Litho.** ***Perf. 12x11½***

C681 A297 7.60s *Salasaca boy, Tungurahua* 70 35
C682 A297 10s *Amula woman, Chimborazo* 90 45
C683 A297 10.60s *Canar woman, Canar* 90 45
C684 A297 13.60s *Colorado Indian, Pichincha* 1.20 60

Virgin of Mercy Type of 1980

1980, July 7 **Litho.** ***Perf. 11½***

C685 A298 7.60s *Cupola, cloisters* 70 35
C686 A298 7.60s *Gold screen* 70 35
C687 A298 7.60s *Quito from basilica tower* 70 35
C688 A298 10.60s *Retable* 90 45
C689 A298 10.60s *Pulpit* 90 45
C690 A298 13.60s *Cupola* 1.20 60
C691 A298 13.60s *Statue of Virgin* 1.20 60
Nos. C685-C691 (7) 6.30 3.15

Virgin of Mercy, patron saint of Ecuadorian armed forces.

U.P.U. Monument AP172

Marshal Sucre, by Marco Sales AP173

Design: 17.80s, Mail box, 1880.

1980, July 7 ***Perf. 12***

C692 AP172 10.60s multi 90 45
C693 AP172 17.80s multi 1.50 75

Souvenir Sheet

C694 AP172 25s multi 2.50 1.25

Universal Postal Union membership centenary. No. C694 contains designs of C692 and C693 (horiz.), perf. 11½. Black control number. Size: 116x91mm.

Olympic Type of 1980.

Design: 10.60s, 13.60s, Moscow '80 emblem, Olympic rings.

1980, July 19 ***Perf. 12x11½***

C695 A299 10.60s multi 90 45
C696 A299 13.60s multi 1.20 60

Souvenir Sheet ***Imperf.***

C697 A299 30s multi 2.50 1.25

22nd Summer Olympic Games, Moscow, July 19-Aug. 3.

No. C697 contains vignettes in designs of Nos. 991 and C695, black control number. Size: 116x90mm.

1980

C698 AP173 10.60s multi 90 45

Marshal Antonio Jose de Sucre, death sesquicentennial.

Rotary International, 75th Anniversary—AP174

1980, Aug. 4 ***Perf. 11½***

C699 AP174 10s multi 90 45

Riobamba Type of 1980

Design: 7.60s, 10.60s, Monstrance, Riobamba Cathedral (vert.).

1980, Sept. 20 **Litho.** ***Perf. 11½***

C700 A301 7.60s multi 70 35
C701 A301 10.60s multi 90 45

Souvenir Sheet
Imperf.

C702 A301 30s multi 2.50 1.25

Constitutional Assembly of Riobamba sesquicentennial. No. C702 contains vignettes in designs of Nos. 996-997, black control number. Size: 116x90mm.

Democracy Type of 1980

Designs: 7.60s, 10.60s, Pres. Aguilera and voter.

Wmk. 367

1980, Oct. 9 **Litho.** ***Perf. 12x11½***

C703 A302 7.60s multi 70 35
C704 A302 10.60s multi 90 45

Souvenir Sheet
Imperf.

C705 A302 15s multi 1.30 65

No. C705 contains vignettes in designs of Nos. 999 and C703; control number.

OPEC Type of 1980

20th Anniversary of OPEC: 7.60s, Men holding OPEC emblem (vert.).

1980, Nov. 8 ***Perf. 11½x12***

C706 A303 7.60s multi 70 35

Carchi Province Type of 1980

Designs: 10.60s, Governor's Palace (vert.). 17.80s, Victory Museum, Central Square (vert.).

1980, Nov. 21 ***Perf. 13***

C707 A304 10.60s multi 90 45
C708 A304 17.80s multi 1.50 75

Orchid Type of 1980

1980, Nov. 22 ***Perf. 12x11½, 11½x12***

C709 A305 7.60s *Anguloa uniflora* 70 35
C710 A305 10.60s *Scuticaria salesiana* 90 45
C711 A305 50s *Helcia sanguinolenta*, vert. 1.50 1.00
C712 A305 100s *Anguloa virginalis* 2.00 1.50

Souvenir Sheets
Imperf.

C713 A305 20s multi 1.75 85
C714 A305 20s multi 1.75 85

Nos. C713-C714 contain vignettes in designs of Nos. C709-C710 and C711-C712 respectively; blue control numbers: 115 x 90 mm.

Christmas Type of 1980

Designs: 7.60s, Pope blessing crowd (vert.). 10.60s, Portrait (vert.).

1980, Dec. 27 ***Perf. 12***

C715 A306 7.60s multi 70 35
C716 A306 10.60s multi 90 45

Isidro Cueva AP175

Simon Bolivar, by Marco Salas AP176

1980, Nov. 20 ***Perf. 13***

C717 AP175 18.20s multi 1.75 85

Dr. Isidro Ayora Cueva, former president, birth centenary.

1980, Dec. 17 ***Perf. 11½***

C718 AP176 13.60s multi 1.20 60

Simon Bolivar death sesquicentennial.

Turtle, Galapagos Islands—AP177

Design: 100s, Oldest Ecuadorian mail box, 1793 (vert.).

1981, Feb. 12 **Litho.** ***Perf. 13***

C719 AP177 50s multi 2.00 1.00
C720 AP177 100s multi 3.00 2.00

HCJB Type of 1981

1981 **Litho.** ***Perf. 13***

C721 A311 7.60s Emblem, horiz. 70 35
C722 A311 10.60s Emblem, diff. 90 45

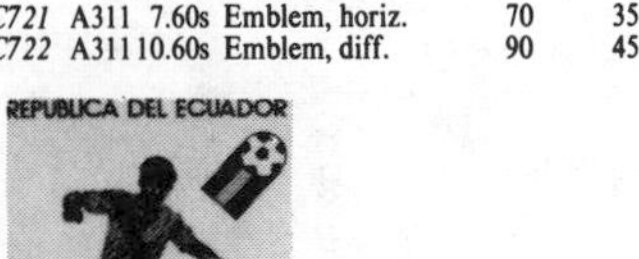

Soccer Players AP178

1981, July 8

C723 AP178 7.60s Emblem 70 35
C724 AP178 10.60s shown 90 45
C725 AP178 13.60s World Cup 1.20 60

Souvenir Sheets

C726 AP178 20s multi 1.75 85
C727 AP178 20s multi 1.75 85

1982 World Cup Soccer Championship. Nos. C726-C727 contain vignettes in designs of Nos. C723 and C724 respectively; black control numbers. Size: 115x90mm.

Picasso Type of 1981

1981, Oct. 26 **Litho.** ***Perf. 13***

C728 A313a 7.60s Still-life 65 32
C729 A313a 10.60s First Communion, vert. 90 45
C730 A313a 13.60s Las Meninas, vert. 1.15 58

Size: 110x90mm.
Imperf.

C731 A313a 20s multi 1.75 90

No. C731 contains designs of Nos. C730, C729; black control number.

World Food Day Type of 1981

1981, Dec. 31 **Litho.** ***Perf. 13x13½***

C732	A314	10s Farming, vert.	90	45

IYD Type of 1982

1982, Feb. 25 **Litho.** ***Perf. 13***

C733	A316	7.60s Emblem	70	35
C734	A316	10.60s Man with crutch	90	45

Montalvo Type of 1982

1982 **Litho.** ***Perf. 13***

C735	A318	5s Home, horiz.	40	20

Swimming Type of 1982

1982, July 30

C736	A320	10.20s Emblem, vert.	90	45
C737	A320	14.20s Diving, vert.	1.20	60

Pres. Jaime Roldos, (1940-81), Mrs. Martha Roldos, Independence Monument, Quito—AP179

1983, May 25 **Litho.** ***Perf. 12***

C738	AP179	13.60s multi	65	30

Souvenir Sheet
Imperf.

C739	AP179	20s multi	1.00	50

AIR POST SEMI-POSTAL STAMPS.

Nos. C119-C123 Surcharged in Blue or Red:

Hospital

Méndez + $ 0,50

1944, May 9 ***Perf. 12*** **Unwmkd.**

CB1	AP26	50c +50c dp red lil	5.00	5.00
CB2	AP26	70c +30c red brn	5.00	5.00
CB3	AP26	3s +50c turq grn (R)	5.00	5.00
CB4	AP26	5s +1s brt ultra (R)	5.00	5.00
CB5	AP26	10s +2s scar	5.00	5.00
		Nos. CB1-CB5 (5)	25.00	25.00

The surtax aided Mendez Hospital.

AIR POST REGISTRATION STAMPS.

Issued by Sociedad Colombo-Alemana de Transportes Aereos (SCADTA)

Nos. C3 and C3a Overprinted "R" in Carmine.

1928-29 ***Perf. 14x14½*** **Wmk. 116**

CF1	AP6	1s on 20c gray (#C3)	200.00	175.00
a.		1s on 20c gray (C3a) ('29)	225.00	200.00

No. C18 Overprinted "R" in Black.

1929, Apr. 1 ***Perf. 14*** **Wmk. 127**

CF2	AP2	1s rose	90.00	75.00

AIR POST OFFICIAL STAMPS.

in Red or Black **OFICIAL**

1929, May ***Perf. 12*** **Unwmkd.**

CO1	AP1	2c blk (R)	60	60
CO2	AP1	5c car rose	60	60
CO3	AP1	10c dp brn	60	60
CO4	AP1	20c dk vio	60	60
CO5	AP1	50c dp grn	2.00	1.50
CO6	AP1	1s dk bl	2.00	1.75
a.		Invtd. ovpt.	425.00	
CO7	AP1	5s org yel	7.50	7.50
CO8	AP1	10s org red	100.00	75.00
		Nos. CO1-CO8 (8)	113.90	88.15

Establishment of commercial air service in Ecuador.
Counterfeits of No. CO8 exist.

1930, Jan. 9

CO9	AP1	50c ol brn	1.50	1.35
CO10	AP1	1s car lake	2.50	2.00
CO11	AP1	5s ol grn	5.00	5.00
CO12	AP1	10s black	10.00	10.00

Air Post Stamps of 1937 Overprinted in Black **OFICIAL**

1937, Aug. 19 ***Perf. 11½***

CO13	AP7	10c chestnut	25	20
CO14	AP7	20c ol blk	35	20
CO15	AP7	70c blk brn	35	20
CO16	AP7	1s gray blk	50	20
CO17	AP7	2s dk vio	60	40
		Nos. CO13-CO17 (5)	2.05	1.20

No. C79 Overprinted in Black **OFICIAL**

1940, Aug. 1 ***Perf. 12½x13***

CO18	AP15	5s emerald	1.25	90

Nos. C352-C354 Overprinted: "1961 oficial"

1964 ***Perf. 13½***

CO19	AP86	50c bl & multi	1.00	1.00
CO20	A86	80c yel & multi	1.00	1.0
CO21	A86	1.30s pale grn & multi	1.00	1.0

SPECIAL DELIVERY STAMPS.

SD1

1928 ***Perf. 12.*** **Unwmkd.**

E1	SD1	2c on 2c bl	4.50	6.00
E2	SD1	5c on 2c bl	4.00	6.00
E3	SD1	10c on 2c bl	4.50	4.00
a.		10 CTVOS inverted	14.00	17.50
E4	SD1	20c on 2c bl	6.00	6.00
E5	SD1	50c on 2c bl	6.00	6.00
		Nos. E1-E5 (5)	25.00	28.00

No. RA49A Surcharged in Red **EXPRESO 20 Ctvs.**

1945

E6	PT18	20c on 5c grn	25	10

LATE FEE STAMP.

No. RA49A Surcharged in Black **U. H. 10 Ctvs.**

1945 ***Perf. 12.*** **Unwmkd.**

I1	PT18	10c on 5c grn	15	12

POSTAGE DUE STAMPS.

Numeral D1

Coat of Arms D2

Wmkd. Liberty Cap. (117)

1896 **Engraved** ***Perf. 12***

J1	D1	1c bl grn	1.25	2.00
J2	D1	2c bl grn	40	1.00
J3	D1	5c bl grn	1.25	1.25
J4	D1	10c bl grn	85	1.50
J5	D1	20c bl grn	35	2.00
J6	D1	50c bl grn	30	2.50
J7	D1	100c bl grn	60	5.00
		Nos. J1-J7 (5)	5.00	15.25

Reprints are on very thick paper with distinct watermark and vertical paper-weave direction. Price 5c each.

Unwmkd.

J8	D1	1c bl grn	1.75	4.00
J9	D1	2c bl grn	1.75	4.00
J10	D1	5c bl grn	1.75	4.00
J11	D1	10c bl grn	1.75	4.00
J12	D1	20c bl grn	2.25	5.00
J13	D1	50c bl grn	3.00	7.00
J14	D1	100c bl grn	4.00	10.00
		Nos. J8-J14 (7)	16.25	38.00

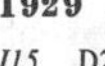

1929

J15	D2	5c dp bl	15	8
J16	D2	10c org yel	20	12
J17	D2	20c red	30	25

Numeral D3

Lithographed

1958, Nov. *Perf. 13½* **Unwmkd.**

J18 D3 10c brt lil 5 5
J19 D3 50c emerald 10 6
J20 D3 1s maroon 20 15
J21 D3 2s red 30 25

OFFICIAL STAMPS.

Regular Issues of 1881 and 1887 Handstamped in Black

OFICIAL

1886 *Perf. 12* **Unwmkd.**

O1 A5 1c yel brn 50 50
O2 A6 2c lake 75 75
O3 A7 5c blue 1.25 1.25
O4 A8 10c orange 1.00 1.00
O5 A9 20c gray vio 1.00 1.00
O6 A10 50c bl grn 4.00 3.50
Nos. O1-O6 (6) 8.50 8.00

1887

O7 A12 1c green 75 75
O8 A13 2c vermilion 75 75
O9 A14 5c blue 1.00 1.00
O10 A15 80c ol grn 4.00 3.00

Nos. O1 to O10 are known with red handstamp but these are believed to be speculative.

The overprint on the 1886–87 issues is handstamped and is found in various positions.

Flores O1

Arms O1a

1892 Carmine Overprint.

O11 O1 1c ultra 12 25
O12 O1 2c ultra 12 25
O13 O1 5c ultra 12 25
O14 O1 10c ultra 12 20
O15 O1 20c ultra 12 10
O16 O1 50c ultra 12 50
O17 O1 1s ultra 40 50
Nos. O11-O17 (7) 1.12 2.05

1894

O18 O1a 1c sl grn (R) 10.00
O19 O1a 2c lake (Bk) 10.00

Nos. O18 and O19 were not placed in use.

Rocafuerte O2

Dated 1894.

1894 Carmine Overprint

O20 O2 1c gray blk 25 50
O21 O2 2c gray blk 25 25
O22 O2 5c gray blk 25 25
O23 O2 10c gray blk 10 20
O24 O2 20c gray blk 30 25
O25 O2 50c gray blk 1.50 1.50
O26 O2 1s gray blk 2.00 2.00
Nos. O20-O26 (7) 4.65 4.95

Dated 1895

1895 Carmine Overprint.

O27 O2 1c gray blk 2.25 2.25
O28 O2 2c gray blk 3.00 3.00
O29 O2 5c gray blk 50 50
O30 O2 10c gray blk 3.00 3.00
O31 O2 20c gray blk 5.00 5.00
O32 O2 50c gray blk 12.50 12.50
O33 O2 1s gray blk 1.50 1.50
Nos. O27-O33 (7) 27.75 27.75

Reprints of 1894–95 issues are on very thick paper with paper weave found both horizontal and vertical for all denominations. Generally they are blacker than originals.

Overprinted FRANQUEO OFICIAL in Carmine.

1896 **Wmkd. Liberty Cap. (117)**

O34 A21 1c ol bis 35 35
O35 A22 2c ol bis 35 35
O36 A23 5c ol bis 35 35
O37 A24 10c ol bis 35 35
O38 A25 20c ol bis 35 35
O39 A26 50c ol bis 35 35
O40 A27 1s ol bis 1.00 75
O41 A28 5s ol bis 1.75 1.65
Nos. O34-O41 (8) 4.85 4.50

Reprints of Nos. O34-O41 are on thick paper with vertical paper weave direction.

Unwmkd.

O42 A21 1c ol bis 1.00 1.00
O43 A22 2c ol bis 1.00 1.00
O44 A23 5c ol bis 1.00 70
O45 A24 10c ol bis 75 60
O46 A25 20c ol bis 1.00 1.00
O47 A26 50c ol bis 1.00 1.50
O48 A27 1s ol bis 2.00 1.25
O49 A28 5s ol bis 3.00 2.25
Nos. O42-O49 (8) 10.75 9.30

Reprints of Nos. O42-O49 all have overprint in black. Price 10¢ each.

Issue of 1894 Overprinted 1897 1898

1897–98

O50 O2 1c gray blk *5.00* *5.00*
O51 O2 2c gray blk *6.00* *6.00*
O52 O2 5c gray blk *50.00* *50.00*
O53 O2 10c gray blk *6.00* *6.00*
O54 O2 20c gray blk *2.75* *1.75*
O55 O2 50c gray blk *10.00* *10.00*
O56 O2 1s gray blk *15.00* *15.00*
Nos. O50-O56 (7) *94.75* *93.75*

Issue of 1894 Overprinted 1897 1898

O57 O2 1c gray blk *1.50* *1.50*
O58 O2 2c gray blk *3.50* *1.25*
O59 O2 5c gray blk *6.00* *6.00*
O60 O2 10c gray blk *50.00* *50.00*
O61 O2 20c gray blk *1.50* *1.50*
O62 O2 50c gray blk *6.00* *5.00*
O63 O2 1s gray blk *65.00* *65.00*
Nos. O57-O63 (7) *133.50* *130.25*

Issue of 1894 Overprinted 1897 y 1898

O64 O2 1c gray blk *12.00* *12.00*
O65 O2 2c gray blk *12.00* *12.00*
O66 O2 5c gray blk *12.00* *12.00*
O67 O2 10c gray blk *12.00* *12.00*
O68 O2 20c gray blk *12.00* *12.00*
O69 O2 50c gray blk *12.00* *12.00*
O70 O2 1s gray blk *12.00* *12.00*
Nos. O64-O70 (7) *84.00* *84.00*

Issue of 1895 Overprinted in Black 1897 1898

O71 O2 1c gray blk *3.00* *3.00*
O72 O2 2c gray blk *2.00* *2.00*
O73 O2 5c gray blk *3.00* *3.00*
O74 O2 10c gray blk *3.00* *3.00*
O75 O2 20c gray blk *5.00* *5.00*
O76 O2 50c gray blk *22.50*
O77 O2 1s gray blk *45.00* *45.00*
Nos. O71-O77 (7) *83.50*

Issue of 1895 Overprinted 1897 1898

O78 O2 1c gray blk *1.25* *1.25*
O79 O2 2c gray blk *90* *90*
O80 O2 5c gray blk *2.50* *2.50*
O81 O2 10c gray blk *90* *90*
O82 O2 20c gray blk *1.00* *60*
O83 O2 50c gray blk *2.00* *75*
O84 O2 1s gray blk *7.50* *7.50*
Nos. O78-O84 (7) *16.05* *14.40*

Issue of 1895 Overprinted 1897 y 1898

O85 O2 1c gray blk *45.00* *45.00*
O86 O2 2c gray blk *1.50* *1.50*
O87 O2 5c gray blk *1.10* *85*
O88 O2 10c gray blk *40.00* *40.00*
O89 O2 20c gray blk *65.00* *65.00*
O90 O2 50c gray blk *16.00* *16.00*
O91 O2 1s gray blk *82.50* *82.50*
Nos. O85-O91 (7) *251.10* *250.85*

Many forged overprints of Nos. O50–O91 exist, made on the original stamps and reprints.

O3

Black Surcharge.

1898–99 *Perf. 15, 16*

O92 O3 5c on 50c lil 30 30
a. Inverted surcharge 1.50 1.50
O93 O3 10c on 20s org 85 85
a. Double surcharge 2.25 2.25
O94 O3 10c on 50c lil *80.00* *80.00*
O95 O3 20c on 50c lil 2.50 2.50
O96 O3 20c on 50s grn 2.25 2.25
Nos. O92-O96 (5) *85.90* *85.90*

Green Surcharge.

O97 O3 5c on 50c lil 1.25 1.25
a. Double surcharge 2.00
b. Double surcharge, blk and grn 6.50
c. Same as 'b', blk surcharge inverted 2.00

1899 Red Surcharge.

O98 O3 5c on 50c lil 1.25 1.25
a. Double surcharge 2.00
b. Double surcharge, blk and red 2.50
O99 O3 20c on 50s grn 2.50 2.50
a. Inverted surcharge 5.00
b. Double surcharge, red and blk 8.00

Similar Surcharge. Value in Words in Two Lines. Black Surcharge.

O100 O3 1c on 5c bl *30.00*

Red Surcharge

O101 O3 2c on 5c bl *65.00*
O102 O3 4c on 20c bl *55.00*

Types of Regular Issue of 1899 Overprinted in Black OFICIAL

1899 *Perf. 14, 15*

O103 A37 2c org & blk 40 1.00
O104 A39 10c org & blk 40 1.00
O105 A40 20c org & blk 30 1.50
O106 A41 50c org & blk 30 2.00

OFICIAL

The above overprint was applied to remainders of the postage stamps of 1904 with the idea of increasing their salability. They were never regularly in use as official stamps.

Regular Issue of 1911-13 Overprinted in Black OFICIAL

1913 *Perf. 12.*

O107 A71 1c scar & blk 75 75
O108 A72 2c bl & blk 75 75
O109 A73 3c org & blk 40 35
O110 A74 5c scar & blk 1.00 75
O111 A75 10c bl & blk 1.00 30
Nos. O107-O111 (5) 3.90 2.90

Regular Issue of 1911-13 Overprinted OFICIAL

Overprint 22x3½ mm.

1916–17

O112 A72 2c bl & blk 7.50 7.50
O113 A74 5c scar & blk 7.50 7.50
O114 A75 10c bl & blk 4.50 4.50

Overprint 25x4 mm.

O115 A71 1c scar & blk 75 75
O116 A72 2c bl & blk 1.00 1.00
a. Invtd. ovpt. 1.50 1.50
O117 A73 3c org & blk 60 60
O118 A74 5c scar & blk 1.00 1.00
O119 A75 10c bl & blk 1.00 50
Nos. O115-O119 (5) 4.35 3.85

Same Overprint On Regular Issue of 1915-17.

O120 A71 1c orange 30 30
O121 A72 2c green 30 30
O122 A73 3c black 50 40
O123 A78 4c red & blk 50 50
a. Invtd. ovpt. 1.00
O124 A74 5c violet 30 25
O125 A75 10c blue 55 55
O126 A79 20c grn & blk 3.50 3.50
Nos. O120-O126 (7) 5.95 5.80

Regular Issues of 1911-17 Overprinted in Black or Red OFICIAL

O127 A71 1c orange 20 15
O128 A72 2c green 20 20
O129 A73 3c blk (Bk) 15 10
O130 A73 3c blk (R) 20 20
a. Inverted overprint
O131 A78 4c red & blk 20 10
O132 A74 5c violet 35 20
O133 A75 10c bl & blk 1.00 50
O134 A75 10c blue 20 20
O135 A79 20c grn & blk 1.00 40
Nos. O127-O135 (9) 3.50 2.05

Regular Issue of 1920 Overprinted OFICIAL

1920

O136 A86 1c green 50 40
a. Inverted overprint 6.00 6.00
O137 A86 2c carmine 40 30
O138 A86 3c yel brn 50 40
O139 A86 4c dk grn 75 60
a. Inverted overprint 6.00 10.00
O140 A86 5c blue 75 60
O141 A86 6c orange 50 40
O142 A86 7c brown 75 60
O143 A86 8c yel grn 1.00 75

O144 A86 9c red 1.25 1.00
O145 A95 10c blue 75 60
O146 A86 15c gray 4.00 3.00
O147 A86 20c dp vio 5.00 3.50
O148 A86 30c violet 6.00 4.00
O149 A86 40c dk brn 8.00 4.00
O150 A86 50c dk grn 5.00 4.00
O151 A86 60c dk bl 6.00 5.00
O152 A86 70c gray 6.00 5.00
O153 A86 80c yellow 7.50 6.00
O154 A104 90c green 8.00 7.00
O155 A86 1s blue 15.00 12.00
Nos. O136-O155 (20) 77.65 59.15

Nos. O136 to O155 were issued in commemoration of the centenary of the independence of Guayaquil.

Stamps of 1911 Overprinted

OFICIAL

1922

O156 A71 1c scar & blk 2.00 75
O157 A72 2c bl & blk 1.00 75

Revenue Stamps of 1919-1920 Overprinted like Nos. O156 and O157

1924

O158 PT3 1c dk bl 40 30
O159 PT3 2c green 2.00 1.25

Regular Issues of 1911-17 Overprinted

OFICIAL

1924

O160 A71 1c orange 1.50 1.50
a. Inverted overprint 2.50

Overprinted in Black or Red

OFICIAL

O161 A72 2c green 25 25
O162 A73 3c blk (R) 30 30
O163 A78 4c red & blk 60 60
O164 A74 5c violet 75 40
O165 A75 10c dp bl 60 50
O166 A76 1s grn & blk 2.00 2.00
Nos. O160-O166 (7) 6.00 5.55

No. O106 with Additional Overprint

Acuerdo No 4.228

1924 *Perf. 14, 15*

O167 A41 50c org & blk 1.25 1.25

Nos. O160 to O167 inclusive exist with inverted overprint.

No. 199 Overprinted

OFICIAL

1924 *Perf. 12*

O168 A71 1c orange 1.00 1.00

Regular Issues of 1911-25 Overprinted

OFICIAL

1925

O169 A71 1c scar & blk 1.50 70
a. Invtd. ovpt. 1.50

O170 A71 1c orange 20 15
a. Invtd. ovpt. 1.00
O171 A72 2c green 15 15
a. Invtd. ovpt. 1.00
O172 A73 3c blk (Bk) 25 25
O173 A73 3c blk (R) 30 30
O174 A78 4c red & blk 15 15
O175 A74 5c violet 25 25
O176 A74 5c rose 25 25
O177 A75 10c dp bl 15 15
Nos. O169-O177 (9) 3.20 2.35

Regular Issues of 1916-25 Overprinted Vertically Up or Down

OFICIAL

1927, Oct.

O178 A71 1c orange 40 30
O179 A86 2c carmine 40 30
O180 A86 3c yel brn 40 30
O181 A86 4c myr grn 40 30
O182 A86 5c pale bl 40 30
O183 A75 10c yel grn 40 30
Nos. O178-O183 (6) 2.40 1.80

Regular Issues of 1920-27 Overprinted

OFICIAL

1928

O184 A71 1c lt bl 15 12
O185 A86 2c carmine 15 12
O186 A86 3c yel brn 15 15
a. Invtd. ovpt. 1.00
O187 A86 4c myr grn 15 15
O188 A86 5c lt bl 15 15
O189 A75 10c yel grn 15 15
O190 A109 20c violet 2.00 50
a. Ovpt. reading up 50 50
Nos. O184-O190 (7) 2.90 1.34

The overprint is placed vertically reading down on No. O190.

Regular Issue of 1936 Overprinted in Black

OFICIAL

1936 *Perf. 14.*

O191 A131 5c ol grn 8 6
O192 A132 10c brown 10 12
O193 A133 20c dk vio 12 10
O194 A134 1s dk car 30 25
O195 A135 2s dk bl 50 40
Nos. O191-O195 (5) 1.10 93

Regular Postage Stamps of 1937 Overprinted in Black

OFICIAL

1937 *Perf. 11½*

O196 A139 2c green 5 5
O197 A140 5c dp rose 10 10
O198 A141 10c blue 10 10
O199 A142 20c dp rose 10 10
O200 A143 1s ol grn 25 20
Nos. O196-O200 (5) 60 55

Tobacco Stamp, Overprinted in Black

CORRESPONDENCIA OFICIAL

1946 *Rouletted.* **Unwmkd.**

O201 PT7 1c rose red 6 6

Communications Building, Quito
O4

Lithographed.

1947 *Perf. 11* **Unwmkd.**

O202 O4 30c brown 15 15
O203 O4 30c grnsh bl 15 10
a. Imperf., pair
O204 O4 30c purple 15 10

Nos. O202 to O204 overprinted "Primero la Patria!" and plane in dark blue are said to be essays.

No. 719 with Additional Diagonal Overprint:

oficial

1964 *Perf. 14x13*

O205 A231 80c rose car & grn (block of 4) 3.00 3.00

The "OEA" overprint covers four stamps, the "oficial" overprint is applied to every stamp.

A set of 20 imperforate items in the above Roosevelt design, some overprinted with the initials of various government ministries, was released in 1949. Later that year a set of eight miniature sheets, bearing the same design plus a marginal inscription, "Presidencia (or Vicepresidencia) de la Republica," and a frame-line were released. In the editors' opinion, information justifying the listing of these issues has not been received.

POSTAL TAX STAMPS.

Roca
PT1

1920 *Perf. 12.* **Unwmkd.**

RA1 PT1 1c orange 35 15

PT2 PT3

RA2 PT2 1c red & bl 25 15
a. "de" inverted 2.00 2.00
b. Double overprint 2.00 60
c. Inverted overprint 2.00 60
RA3 PT3 1c dp bl 30 10
a. Inverted ovpt. 1.25 1.00
b. Double ovpt. 1.25 1.00

PT4 PT5

Red or Black Surcharge or Overprint.

Stamp Dated 1911-1912.

RA4 PT4 20c dp bl 27.50 12.00

Stamp Dated 1913-1914.

RA5 PT4 20c dp bl (R) 1.50 50

Stamp Dated 1917-1918.

RA6 PT4 20c ol grn (R) 2.00 75
a. Dated 1919-20 9.00
RA7 PT5 1c on 2c grn 30 12

Stamp Dated 1911-1912.

RA8 PT5 1c on 5c grn 25 10
a. Double surcharge

Stamp Dated 1913-1914.

RA9 PT5 1c on 5c grn 2.50 50
a. Double surcharge 3.00 2.00

On Nos. RA7, RA8 and RA9 the surcharge is found reading upward or downward.

Post Office
PT6

1920-24 **Engraved.**

RA10 PT6 1c ol grn 15 10
RA11 PT6 2c dp grn 20 10
RA12 PT6 20c bis brn ('24) 75 20
RA13 PT6 2s violet 3.00 3.00
RA14 PT6 5s blue 5.00 5.00
Nos. RA10-RA14 (5) 9.10 8.40

Revenue Stamps of 1917-18 Surcharged Vertically in Red reading up or down

Casa de Correos
VEINTE CTS.
1921—1922

1921-22

RA15 PT5 20c on 1c dk bl 20.00 3.00
RA16 PT5 20c on 2c grn 20.00 3.00

No. RA12 Surcharged in Green

DOS
CENTAVOS
—2—

1924

RA17 PT6 2c on 20c bis brn 20 10
a. Invtd. surch. 2.00 2.00
b. Dbl. surch. 3.00 3.00

PT7

1924 *Rouletted 7*

RA18 PT7 1c rose red 25 15
a. Inverted overprint 1.50

Similar Design, Eagle at left

Perf. 12

RA19 PT7 2c blue 30 12
a. Inverted overprint 1.50 1.00

PT8

Inscribed "Timbre Fiscal".

1924

RA20 PT8 1c yellow 1.00 75
RA21 PT8 2c dk bl 40 20

Inscribed "Region Oriental".

RA22 PT8 1c yellow 35 15
RA23 PT8 2c dk bl 35 30

Overprint on No. RA22 reads down or up.

Revenue Stamp Overprinted in Blue

CASA
de
Correos y
Telegrafos
de
Guayaquil

1934

RA24 2c green 15 10
a. Blue overprint inverted 2.00 1.50
b. Blue overprint double, one inverted 2.50 1.50

Postage Stamp of 1930 Overprinted in Red

Perf. 12½.

RA25 A119 20c ultra & yel 25 20

Telegraph Stamp Overprinted in Red, like No. RA24, and Surcharged diagonally in Black

1934 *Perf. 14*

RA26 2c on 10c ol brn 20 15
a. Double surcharge 2.00

Overprint Blue, Surcharge Red.

RA27 2c on 10c ol brn 25 15

PT9

PT10

1934–36 *Perf. 12.*

RA28 PT9 2c green 15 10
a. Both overprints in red ('36) 15 10

Postal Tax stamp of 1920–24, overprinted in red "POSTAL" has been again overprinted "CASA de Correos y Teleg. de Guayaquil" in black.

Symbols of Post and Telegraph Service
PT11

Wmk. 233

Photogravure.

Wmkd.

"Harrison & Sons, London" in Script Letters. (233)

1934 *Perf. 14½x14.*

RA29 PT10 2c yel grn 15 10

Issued to pay a postal tax of 2c for the rebuilding of the General Post Office at Guayaquil.

1935

RA30 PT11 20c claret 15 10

Issued to pay a postal tax of 20c for the rebuilding of the General Post Office at Guayaquil.

No. RA29 Surcharged in Red and Overprinted in Black

3 ctvs,
Seguro Social del Campesino Quito, 16 de Otbre.-1935

1935

RA31 PT10 3c on 2c yel grn 15 10
a. Double surcharge

Issued for the Social and Rural Workers' Insurance Fund.

Tobacco Stamp Surcharged in Black

Seguro Social 3
del Campesino ctvs

1936 *Rouletted 7.* **Unwmkd.**

RA32 PT7 3c on 1c rose red 15 10
a. Lines of words reversed 18 12
b. Imperf. vertically (pair)

Issued for the Social and Rural Workers' Insurance Fund.

No. 310 Overprinted in Black

Casa de Correos y Telégrafos de Guayaquil

1936 *Perf. 12½*

RA33 A119 20c ultra & yel 15 8
a. Double overprint

Tobacco Stamp Surcharged in Black

SEGURO SOCIAL 3
DEL CAMPESINO ctvs.

1936 *Rouletted 7*

RA34 PT7 3c on 1c rose red 15 10

Issued for the Social and Rural Workers' Insurance Fund.

PT12

PT13

Worker

1936 **Engraved** *Perf. 13½*

RA35 PT12 3c ultra 10 5

Issued for the Social and Rural Workers' Insurance Fund.

Surcharged in Black.

1936

RA36 PT13 5c on 3c ultra 15 12

This combines the 2c for the rebuilding of the post office with the 3c for the Social and Rural Workers' Insurance Fund.

National Defense Issue.

Tobacco Stamp, Surcharged in Black.

TIMBRE PATRIOTICO
DIEZ CENTAVOS

1936 *Rouletted 7.*

RA37 PT7 10c on 1c rose 20 12
a. Double surch.

Symbolical of Defense
PT14

1937–42 *Perf. 13½*

RA38 PT14 10c dp bl 20 10

A 1s violet and 2s green exist in type PT14.

PT15

Overprinted or Surcharged in Black.

1937–42 **Engr. & Typo.** *Perf. 13½*

RA39 PT15 5c lt brn & red 50 20
d. Invert. ovpt. 5.00

Perf. 12, 11½.

RA39A PT15 20c on 5c rose pink & red ('42) 35.00
RA39B PT15 20c on 1s yel brn & red ('42) 35.00
RA39C PT15 20c on 2s grn & red ('42) 35.00

A 50c dark blue and red exists in type PT15.

5 5

No. RA38 Surcharged in Red

POSTAL ADICIONAL

1937 **Engraved** *Perf. 12½*

RA40 PT14 5c on 10c dp bl 25 12

Map of Ecuador
PT16

1938 *Perf. 14x13½.*

RA41 PT16 5c car rose 18 10

Issued for the Social and Rural Workers' Insurance Fund.

No. C42 Surcharged in Red

20 20
CASA DE CORREOS
Y TELEGRAFOS
DE GUAYAQUIL
20 20

1938 *Perf. 12½.*

RA42 AP5 20c on 70c blk 30 10

No. 307 Surcharged in Red

CAMPAÑA CONTRA EL CANCER
5 5

1938

RA43 A116 5c on 6c yel & red 15 6

This stamp was obligatory on all mail from Nov. 23rd to 30th, 1938. The tax was for the International Union for the Control of Cancer.

Tobacco Stamp, Surcharged in Black

POSTAL ADICIONAL
CINCO CENTAVOS

1939 *Rouletted.*

RA44 PT7 5c on 1c rose 12 10
a. Double surcharge
b. Triple surcharge

Tobacco Stamp, Surcharged in Blue

CASAS DE CORREOS
Y TELEGRAFOS
CINCO CENTAVOS

1940

RA45 PT7 5c on 1c rose red 15 10
a. Double surcharge 1.00 1.00

No. 370 Surcharged in Carmine

CASA DE
CORREOS y TELEGRAFOS
DE GUAYAQUIL
20 20

1940 *Perf. 11½.*

RA46 A144 20c on 50c blk & multi 15 12
a. Double surcharge, one inverted

Tobacco Stamp, Surcharged in Black

TIMBRE PATRIOTICO
VEINTE CENTAVOS

1940 *Rouletted*

RA47 PT7 20c on 1c rose red 15 7

Farmer Plowing
PT17

Communication Symbols
PT18

1940 *Perf. 13x13½.*

RA48 PT17 5c car rose 25 10

1940-43 *Perf. 12.*

RA49 PT18 5c cop brn 15 10
RA49A PT18 5c grn ('43) 15 10

Pursuit Planes
PT19

1941 *Perf. 11½x13*

RA50 PT19 20c ultra 25 6

The tax was used for national defense.

Warrior Shielding Women
PT20

1942–46 **Engraved** *Perf. 12*

RA51 PT20 20c dk bl 25 10
RA51A PT20 40c blk brn ('46) 25 10

The tax was used for national defense.

A 20c carmine, 20c brown and 30c gray exist lithographed in type PT20.

No. 370 Surcharged in Carmine

CASA DE
CORREOS y TELEGRAFOS
DE GUAYAQUIL
VEINTE CENTAVOS

1942 *Perf. 11½*

RA52 A144 20c on 50c blk & multi 25 15
a. Double surch. 2.50

No. RA35 Surcharged in Red

ADICIONAL CINCO CENTAVOS

1943 *Perf. 13½.*

RA53 PT12	5c on 3c ultra	10	5

No. RA53 with Additional Surcharge in Black

5 Centavos CASA DE CORREOS DE GQUIL. y

1943

RA54 PT12	5c on 5c on 3c ultra	10	5

Peons PT21

1943 *Perf. 12*

RA55 PT21	5c blue	20	10

The tax was for farm workers.

Revenue Stamp (as No. RA64) Overprinted in Black

TIMBRE PATRIOTICO

1943 *Perf. 12½*

RA56	20c red org	60.00	1.00

Revenue Stamp (as No. RA64) Surcharged in Black

TIMBRE PATRIOTICO VEINTE CENTAVOS

1943 *Perf. 12*

RA57	20c on 10c org	55	10
a.	Double surch.		

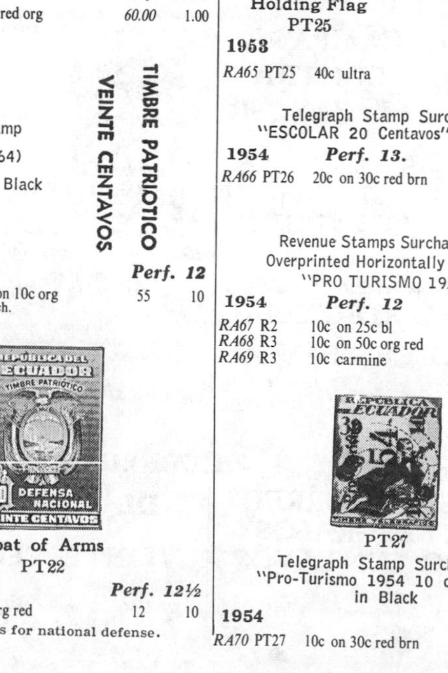

Coat of Arms PT22

1943 *Perf. 12½*

RA58 PT22	20c org red	12	10

The tax was for national defense.

No. RA58 Surcharged in Black

30 Centavos

1944

RA59 PT22	30c on 20c org red	15	10
a.	Double surcharge		

Consular Service Stamps Surcharged in Black

TIMBRE ESCOLAR 20 ctvs. 20

1951 *Perf. 12.* **Unwmkd.**

RA60 R1	20c on 1s red	15	8
RA61 R1	20c on 2s brn	15	8
RA62 R1	20c on 5s vio	15	8

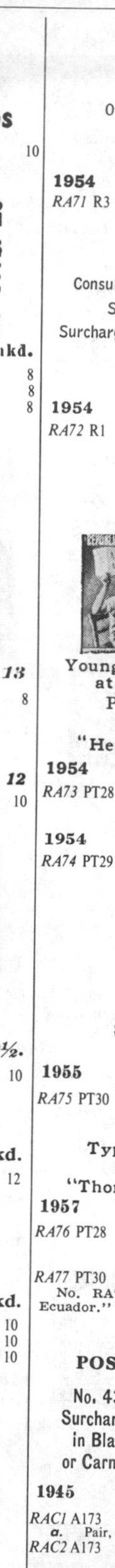

Teacher and Pupils in Schoolyard PT23

PT24

1952 **Engraved.** *Perf. 13*

RA63 PT23	20c bl grn	15	8

Revenue Stamp Overprinted "PATRIOTICO / SANITARIO"

1952 *Perf. 12*

RA64 PT24	40(c) ol grn	20	10

Woman Holding Flag PT25

PT26

1953 *Perf. 12½.*

RA65 PT25	40c ultra	30	10

Telegraph Stamp Surcharged "ESCOLAR 20 Centavos" in Black

1954 *Perf. 13.* **Unwmkd.**

RA66 PT26	20c on 30c red brn	30	12

Revenue Stamps Surcharged or Overprinted Horizontally in Black "PRO TURISMO 1954"

1954 *Perf. 12* **Unwmkd.**

RA67 R2	10c on 25c bl	25	10
RA68 R3	10c on 50c org red	25	10
RA69 R3	10c carmine	25	10

PT27

Telegraph Stamp Surcharged "Pro-Turismo 1954 10 ctvs. 10" in Black

1954 *Perf. 13*

RA70 PT27	10c on 30c red brn	35	12

Revenue Stamp Overprinted in Black

ESCOLAR

1954 *Perf. 12*

RA71 R3	20c ol blk	35	12

Consular Service Stamp Surcharged in Black

0,20 ESCOLAR Veinte centavos 0,20

1954

RA72 R1	20c on 10s gray	35	12

Young Student at Desk PT28

Globe, Ship and Plane PT29

Imprint: "Heraclio Fournier.—Vitoria"

1954 **Photo.** *Perf. 11*

RA73 PT28	20c rose pink	35	12

See also No. RA76.

1954 **Engraved** *Perf. 12*

RA74 PT29	10c dp mag	35	12

Soldier Kissing Flag PT30

1955 **Photogravure.** *Perf. 11*

RA75 PT30	40c blue	35	12

See also No. RA77.

Types of 1954-55 Redrawn. Imprint: "Thomas de la Rue & Co. Ltd."

1957 *Perf. 13* **Unwmkd.**

RA76 PT28	20c rose pink	15	8

Perf. 14x14½

RA77 PT30	40c blue	40	20

No. RA77 is inscribed "Republica del Ecuador."

AIR POST POSTAL TAX STAMPS.

No. 438 Surcharged in Black or Carmine

FOMENTO-AERO-COMUNICACIONES 20 Ctvs.

1945 *Perf. 11.* **Unwmkd.**

RAC1 A173	20c on 10c dk grn	35	15
a.	Pair, one without surch.	45.00	
RAC2 A173	20c on 10c dk grn (C)	35	15

Obligatory on letters and parcel post carried on planes in the domestic service.

Liberty, Mercury and Planes PTAP1

1946 **Engraved.** *Perf. 12.*

RAC3 PTAP1	20c org brn	25	15

Galapagos Islands
(Columbus Archipelago)

Issued for use in the Galapagos Islands, a province of Ecuador, but were commonly used throughout the country.

Sea Lions A1

Map A2

Design: 1s, Marine iguana.

Photogravure.

1957, July 15 *Perf. 12* **Unwmkd.**

L1	A1	20c dk brn	30	15
L2	A2	50c violet	20	15
L3	A1	1s dl ol grn	1.00	40

Issued to commemorate the 125th anniversary of Ecuador's possession of the Galapagos Islands, and to publicize the islands.

AIR POST STAMPS

Type of Regular Issue, 1957.

Designs: 1s, Santa Cruz Island. 1.80s, Map of Galapagos archipelago. 4.20s, Galapagos giant tortoise.

Photogravure.

1957, July 19 *Perf. 12* **Unwmkd.**

LC1	A1	1s dp bl	25	15
LC2	A1	1.80s rose vio	50	25
LC3	A1	4.20s black	1.50	60

Issued to commemorate the 125th anniversary of Ecuador's possession of the Galapagos Islands and to publicize the islands.

Redrawn Type of Ecuador, 1956

1959, Jan. 3 **Engraved.** *Perf. 14*

LC4 AP69	2s lt ol grn	75	50

Issued to honor the United Nations.

See note after No. C407.

EGYPT

(ē′jĭpt)

LOCATION — Northern Africa, bordering on the Mediterranean and the Red Sea.
GOVT.—Republic.
AREA—386,900 sq. mi.
POP.—46,000,000 (est. 1984).
CAPITAL—Cairo.

Modern Egypt was a part of Turkey until 1914 when a British protectorate was declared over the country and the Khedive was deposed in favor of Hussein Kamil under the title of sultan. In 1922 the protectorate ended and the reigning sultan was declared king of the new monarchy. Egypt became a republic on June 18, 1953. Egypt merged with Syria in 1958 to form the United Arab Republic. Syria left this union in 1961. In 1971 Egypt took the name of Arab Republic of Egypt.

40 Paras = 1 Piastre
1000 Milliemes = 100 Piastres = 1 Pound (1888)
1000 Milliemes = 1 Pound

Turkish Suzerainty

Turkish Inscriptions
A1

A2 A3

A4 A5

A6 A7

Wmk. 118

Surcharged in Black

Wmkd. Pyramid and Star. (118)

Perf. 12½

1866, Jan. 1 Lithographed

1	A1	5pa sl grn	35.00	25.00
a.		Imperf. pair	275.00	
b.		Pair, imperf. btwn.	350.00	
c.		Perf. 12½x13	50.00	50.00
d.		Perf. 13	350.00	450.00
2	A2	10pa brown	45.00	30.00
a.		Imperf. pair	250.00	
b.		Pair, imperf. btwn.	250.00	
c.		Perf. 13	250.00	
d.		Perf. 12½x15	325.00	350.00
3	A3	20pa blue	70.00	35.00
a.		Imperf. pair	350.00	
b.		Pair, imperf. btwn.	500.00	
c.		Perf. 12½x13	125.00	125.00
d.		Perf. 13	600.00	350.00
4	A4	2pi yellow	90.00	45.00
a.		Imperf.	125.00	75.00
b.		Imperf. vert or horiz. pair	350.00	350.00
c.		Perf. 12½x15	150.00	
d.		Diagonal half used as 1 pi on cover		1,500.
e.		Perf. 12½x13, 13x12½	120.00	50.00
5	A5	5pi rose	250.00	200.00
a.		Imperf.	300.00	300.00
b.		Imperf. vert. or horiz. pair	*1,000.*	
d.		Inscription of 10 pi, imperf.	500.00	
e.		Perf. 12½x13, 13x12½	300.00	300.00
f.		As "d" perf. 12½x15	600.00	600.00
6	A6	10pi sl bl	275.00	250.00
a.		Imperf.	275.00	275.00
b.		Pair, imperf. btwn.	*2,000.*	
c.		Perf. 12½x13, 13x12½	500.00	500.00
d.		Perf. 13	*2,000.*	

Unwmkd.

Typographed

7	A7	1pi rose lil	50.00	5.00
a.		Imperf.	100.00	
b.		Pair, imperf. vert.	350.00	
c.		Perf. 12½x13, 13x12½	100.00	35.00
d.		Perf. 13	350.00	200.00

Single imperforates of types A1–A10 are sometimes simulated by trimming wide-margined copies of perforated stamps.

Proofs of Nos. 1–7 are on smooth white paper, unwatermarked and imperforate. Proofs of No. 7 are on thinner paper than No. 7a.

Sphinx and Pyramid
A8

Wmk. 119

Wmkd. Crescent and Star. (119)

1867 Litho. *Perf. 15x12½*

8	A8	5pa orange	13.00	10.00
a.		Imperf.	50.00	50.00
b.		Imperf. vert. or horiz. pair	200.00	
9	A8	10pa lilac	37.50	10.00
a.		10pa vio	35.00	10.00
b.		Half used as 5pa on newspaper piece		600.00
11	A8	20pa bl grn	37.50	15.00
a.		20pa yel grn	40.00	15.00
13	A8	1pi rose red	6.00	1.25
a.		Imperf.	60.00	
b.		Pair, imperf. btwn.	200.00	
c.		Half used as 20pa on cover		700.00
d.		Rouletted	50.00	
14	A8	2pi blue	75.00	12.00
a.		Imperf.	150.00	
b.		Imperf. vert., pair	500.00	
c.		Diagonal half used as 1pi on cover		
d.		Perf. 12½	300.00	
15	A8	5pi brown	350.00	150.00

There are four types of each value, so placed that any block of four contains all four types.

A9 A10

Typographed by the Government at Boulac

Clear Impressions. Thick Opaque Paper.

Perf. 12½x13½, Clean-cut.

1872 Wmk. 119

19	A9	5pa brown	9.00	4.50
20	A9	10pa lilac	8.00	3.00
21	A9	20pa blue	25.00	3.50
22	A9	1pi rose red	25.00	60
h.		Half used as 20pa on cover		300.00
23	A9	2pi dl yel	50.00	5.00
24	A9	2½pi dl vio	45.00	5.00
25	A9	5pi green	200.00	30.00
j.		Tête bêche pair		

Perf. 13½, Clean-cut.

19a	A9	5pa brown	20.00	12.00
20a	A9	10pa dl lil	8.00	3.00
21a	A9	20pa blue	45.00	15.00
22a	A9	1pi rose red	50.00	2.75
23a	A9	2pi dl yel	20.00	3.50
24a	A9	2½pi dl vio	800.00	250.00
25a	A9	5pi green	300.00	75.00

Lithographed

21m	A9	20pa bl, perf. 12½x13½	120.00	40.00
21n	A9	20pa bl, perf. 13½	200.00	75.00
21p	A9	20pa bl, imperf.	200.00	
22m	A9	1pi rose red, perf. 12½x13½	250.00	3.00
22n	A9	1pi rose red, perf. 13½		5.00

Typographed

Blurred Impressions. Thinner Paper.

Wmkd. Crescent and Star. (119)

1874-75 *Perf. 12½, Rough.*

26	A10	5pa brn ('75)	6.00	2.50
e.		Imperforate		40.00
f.		Imperforate horiz., pair	150.00	150.00
g.		Tête bêche pair	50.00	50.00
20b	A9	10pa gray lil	6.00	3.00
g.		Tête bêche pair	200.00	200.00
21b	A9	20pa gray bl	40.00	3.00
k.		Half used as 10pa on cover		400.00
22b	A9	1pi vermilion	4.00	85
f.		Imperforate	8.00	7.00
g.		Tête bêche pair	75.00	75.00
23b	A9	2pi yellow	30.00	4.00
j.		Tête bêche pair	500.00	500.00
24b	A9	2½pi dp vio	5.00	2.50
e.		Imperforate	22.50	22.50
f.		Tête bêche pair	400.00	400.00
25b	A9	5pi yel grn	35.00	10.00
e.		Imperforate	25.00	

No. 26f normally occurs tête-bêche.

Perf. 13½x12½, Rough.

26c	A10	5pa brown	4.00	2.50
j.		Tête bêche pair	35.00	35.00
20c	A9	10pa gray lil	6.00	2.50
j.		Tête bêche pair	200.00	200.00
21c	A9	20pa gray bl	4.00	2.75
h.		Pair, imperf. between	250.00	
22c	A9	1pi vermilion	11.00	1.00
j.		Tête bêche pair	300.00	300.00
23c	A9	2pi yellow	5.00	4.00
g.		Tête bêche pair	400.00	400.00
k.		Half used as 1pi on cover		*850.00*

Perf. 12½x13½, Rough.

23d	A9	2pi yel ('75)	16.50	5.00
h.		Tête bêche pair		
24d	A9	2½pi dp vio ('75)	15.00	9.00
j.		Tête bêche pair	700.00	700.00
25d	A9	5pi yel grn ('75)	250.00	150.00

Stamp of 1872-75 Surcharged in Black

Perf. 12½, 12½x13½, Rough

1879, Jan. 1

27	A9	5pa on 2½pi dl vio	6.00	6.00
a.		Imperf.	35.00	35.00
b.		Tête bêche pair	*3,000.*	
c.		Inverted surcharge	60.00	60.00
d.		Perf. 12½x13½	6.00	6.50
e.		As "d," tête bêche pair		
f.		As "c," perf. 12½x13½	110.00	110.00
28	A9	10pa on 2½pi dl vio	6.00	6.00
a.		Imperf.		
b.		Tête bêche pair	1,500.	
c.		Inverted surcharge	70.00	70.00
d.		Perf. 12½x13½	10.00	10.00
e.		As "c," perf. 12½x13½	90.00	90.00

A11 A12

A13 A14

A15 A16

1879-93 Typo. *Perf. 14x13½*

29	A11	5pa brown	30	15
30	A12	10pa violet	27.50	3.00
31	A12	10pa lil rose ('81)	45.00	4.00
32	A12	10pa gray ('82)	10.00	75
33	A12	10pa grn ('84)	30	12
34	A13	20pa ultra	60.00	1.25
35	A13	20pa rose ('84)	8.00	40
36	A14	1pi rose	15.00	25
37	A14	1pi ultra ('84)	1.75	10
38	A15	2pi org yel	15.00	35
39	A15	2pi org brn	10.00	35
40	A16	5pi green	80.00	5.50
41	A16	5pi gray ('84)	12.50	40
		Nos. 29-41 (13)	285.35	16.62

Imperf. examples of Nos. 29–31, 35–38 and 40 are proofs.

A17

1884, Feb. 1

42	A17	20pa on 5pi grn	10.00	1.00
a.		Inverted surcharge	45.00	35.00

A18 A19

A20

1888

43	A18	1m brown	25	5
44	A19	2m green	50	6
45	A20	5m car rose	1.00	5

Imperf. examples of Nos. 43–45 are proofs.

A21 A22

1889-93

46	A21	3m mar ('92)	2.50	80
47	A21	3m org ('93)	1.25	15
48	A22	10pi purple	21.00	50

Nos. 37, 39, 41, 43 to 45, 47 and 48 exist on both ordinary and chalky paper.

A23

1906 Chalk-surfaced Paper.

49	A23	4m brn red	1.50	60

Boats on Nile A24 — Cleopatra A25

Ras-el-Tin Palace A26 — Giza Pyramids A27

Sphinx A28 — Colossi of Thebes A29

Pylon of Karnak and Temple of Khonsu A30 — Citadel at Cairo A31

Rock Temple of Abu Simbel A32 — Aswan Dam A33

Perf. 13½x14

1914, Jan. 8 Wmk. 119

Chalk-surfaced Paper

50	A24	1m ol brn	12	8
51	A25	2m dp grn	30	12
52	A26	3m orange	50	15
53	A27	4m red	1.00	50
54	A28	5m lake	60	5
a.		Bklt. pane of 6		
55	A29	10m dk bl	1.25	8

Perf. 14

56	A30	20m ol grn	3.00	15
57	A31	50m red vio	5.00	50
58	A32	100m black	10.00	50
59	A33	200m plum	25.00	85
		Nos. 50-59 (10)	46.77	2.98

All values of this issue exist imperforate on both watermarked and unwatermarked paper but are not known to have been issued in that condition.

See also Nos. 61-72.

British Protectorate

No. 52 Surcharged

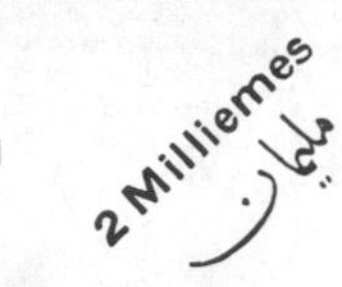

1915, Oct. 15

60	A26	2m on 3m org	60	50
a.		Inverted surcharge	150.00	150.00

Scenic Types of 1914 and

Statue of Ramses II

A34 — A35

Wmk. 120

Wmkd. Triple Crescent and Star. (120)

1921-22 *Perf. 13½x14*

Chalk-surfaced Paper

61	A24	1m ol brn	15	7
62	A25	2m dp grn	1.50	1.00
63	A25	2m red ('22)	40	20
64	A26	3m orange	1.25	35
65	A27	4m grn ('22)	1.50	1.25
66	A28	5m lake	50	6
67	A28	5m pink	1.00	6
68	A29	10m dp bl	2.00	10
69	A29	10m lake ('22)	1.50	25
70	A34	15m ind ('22)	1.25	15
71	A35	15m ind ('22)	12.50	1.00

Perf. 14

72	A30	20m ol grn	3.50	15
73	A31	50m maroon	7.00	30
74	A32	100m black	25.00	3.00
		Nos. 61-74 (14)	59.05	7.94

Independent Kingdom

Stamps of 1921-22 Overprinted

1922, Oct. 10

78	A24	1m ol brn	30	15
a.		Inverted overprint	60.00	60.00
b.		Double overprint	75.00	75.00
79	A25	2m red	50	10
a.		Double overprint	60.00	60.00
80	A26	3m orange	1.00	50
81	A27	4m green	75	50
a.		Double ovpt.	100.00	
b.		Inverted ovpt.		
82	A28	5m pink	60	5
83	A29	10m lake	1.00	6
84	A34	15m indigo	2.50	10
85	A35	15m indigo	1.25	25

Perf. 14

86	A30	20m ol grn	2.25	20
a.		Inverted overprint	200.00	200.00
b.		Double overprint	125.00	125.00
87	A31	50m maroon	3.00	20
a.		Inverted overprint	425.00	400.00
b.		Double overprint		
88	A32	100m black	10.00	60
a.		Inverted overprint	225.00	225.00
b.		Double overprint	225.00	225.00
		Nos. 78-88 (11)	23.15	2.71

Same Overprint on Nos. 58-59

Wmkd. Crescent and Star (119)

90	A32	100m black	75.00	40.00
91	A33	200m plum	10.00	60
a.		Inverted overprint		375.00

Nos. 78-91 were issued to commemorate the proclamation of the Egyptian monarchy. The overprint signifies "The Egyptian Kingdom, March 15, 1922". It exists in four types, one lithographed and three typographed on Nos 78-87, but lithographed only on Nos. 88-91.

King Fuad

A36 — A37

Wmkd. Triple Crescent and Star. (120)

Size 18x22½ mm.

1923-24 Photo. *Perf. 13½*

92	A36	1m orange	25	6
93	A36	2m black	40	6
94	A36	3m brown	75	18
a.		Imperf., pair	225.00	
95	A36	4m yel grn	75	15
96	A36	5m org brn	40	5
a.		Imperf., pair	30.00	
97	A36	10m rose	60	5
98	A36	15m ultra	75	5
a.		Imperf., pair	225.00	

Perf. 14

Size 22x28 mm.

99	A36	20m dk grn	1.50	10
100	A36	50m myr grn	5.00	10
101	A36	100m red vio	8.00	25
102	A36	200m vio ('24)	15.00	1.00
a.		Imperf., pair	375.00	
103	A37	£1 ultra & dk vio ('24)	100.00	10.00
a.		Imperf., pair	900.00	
		Nos. 92-103 (12)	133.40	12.05

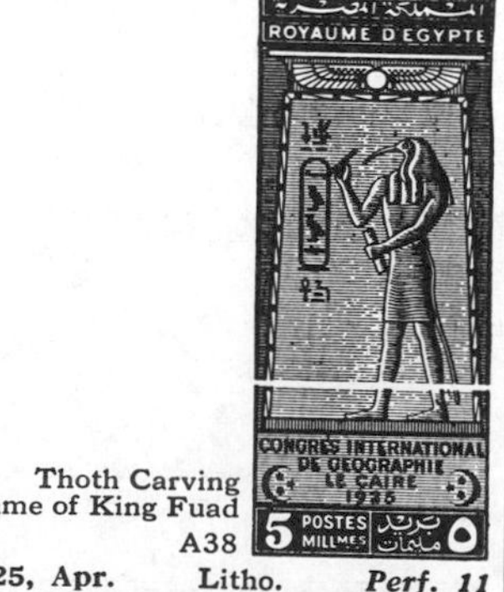

Thoth Carving Name of King Fuad

A38

1925, Apr. Litho. *Perf. 11*

105	A38	5m brown	4.00	4.00
106	A38	10m rose	5.50	5.50
107	A38	15m ultra	8.00	8.00

International Geographical Congress, Cairo.

Nos. 106-107 exist with both white and yellowish gum.

Oxen Plowing

A39

Wmk. 195

Wmkd. Multiple Crown and Arabic F. (195)

1926 *Perf. 13x13½*

108	A39	5m lt brn	1.00	70
109	A39	10m brt rose	1.00	70
110	A39	15m dp bl	1.00	70
111	A39	50m Prus grn	5.00	4.00
112	A39	100m brn vio	11.00	7.00
113	A39	200m brt vio	15.00	12.00
		Nos. 108-113 (6)	34.00	25.10

Issued to commemorate the 12th Agricultural and Industrial Exhibition at Gezira. "F" in watermark stands for Fuad.

King Fuad

A40

Perf. 14x14½

1926, Apr. 2 Photo. Wmk. 120

114	A40	50pi brn vio & red vio	70.00	10.00

58th birthday of King Fuad.

Nos. 111-113 Surcharged **5 MILLIEMES**

Perf. 13x13½

1926, Aug. 24 Wmk. 195

115	A39	5m on 50m Prus grn	1.50	1.25
116	A39	10m on 100m brn vio	1.50	1.25
117	A39	15m on 200m brt vio	1.50	1.25
a.		Dbl. surcharge	200.00	

Ship of Hatshepsut—A41

1926, Dec. 9 Litho. *Perf. 13x13½*

118	A41	5m brn & blk	2.00	1.00
119	A41	10m dp red & blk	2.50	1.25
120	A41	15m dp bl & blk	2.50	1.25

International Navigation Congress, Cairo.

Nos. 118-120, 114 Overprinted

PORT FOUAD
a

PORT FOUAD
b

1926, Dec. 21

121	A41 (a)	5m brn & blk	100.00	75.00
122	A41 (a)	10m dp red & blk	100.00	75.00
123	A41 (a)	15m dp bl & blk	100.00	75.00

***Perf. 14x14½* Wmk. 120**

124	A40 (b)	50pi brn vio & red vio	1,300.	1,100.

Inauguration of Port Fuad opposite Port Said.

Nos. 121-123 have a block over "Le Caire" at lower left.

Forgeries of Nos. 121-124 exist.

Branch of Cotton
A42

Perf. 13x13½

1927, Jan. 25 Wmk. 195

125	A42	5m dk brn & sl grn	1.00	1.00
126	A42	10m dp red & sl grn	2.50	1.50
127	A42	15m dp bl & sl grn	2.50	1.50

International Cotton Congress, Cairo.

King Fuad
A43 A44

A45

A46

Photogravure.

1927-37 *Perf. 13x13½* Wmk. 195

128	A43	1m orange	10	5
129	A43	2m black	15	5
130	A43	3m ol brn	15	8
131	A43	3m dp grn ('30)	25	6
132	A43	4m yel grn	45	15
133	A43	4m brn ('30)	50	20
134	A43	4m dp grn ('34)	75	18
135	A43	5m dk red brn ('29)	25	5
b.		5m chnt	30	5
136	A43	10m dk red ('29)	60	5
a.		10m org red	90	6
137	A43	10m pur ('34)	1.30	8
138	A43	13m car rose ('32)	50	12
139	A43	15m ultra	1.00	5
140	A43	15m dk vio ('34)	2.00	5
141	A43	20m ultra ('34)	3.50	8

Early printings of Nos. 128, 129, 130, 132, 135, 136 and 139 were from plates with screen of vertical dots in the vignette; later printings show screen of diagonal dots.

Perf. 13½x14

142	A44	20m ol grn	1.00	5
143	A44	20m ultra ('32)	2.25	6
144	A44	40m ol brn ('32)	1.25	6
145	A44	50m Prus grn	1.00	5
a.		50m grnsh bl	1.50	5
146	A44	100m brn vio	4.00	6
a.		100m ol	4.00	8
147	A44	200m dp vio	5.00	25

Printings of Nos. 142, 145 and 146, made in 1929 and later, were from new plates with stronger mpressions and darker colors.

Lithographed; Center Photogravure.

Perf. 13x13½

148	A45	500m choc & Prus bl ('32)	40.00	6.00
a.		Entirely photogravure	50.00	8.00
149	A46	£1 dk grn & org brn ('37)	50.00	5.00
a.		Entirely photogravure	50.00	5.00
		Nos. 128-149 (22)	116.00	12.78

Statue of Amenhotep, Son of Hapu
A47

1927, Dec. 29 Photo. *Perf. 13½x13*

150	A47	5m org brn	50	40
151	A47	10m cop red	1.00	55
152	A47	15m dp bl	2.00	65

Statistical Congress, Cairo.

Imhotep
A48

Mohammed Ali Pashe
A49

1928, Dec. 15

153	A48	5m org brn	75	35
154	A49	10m cop red	75	35

Issued to commemorate the International Congress of Medicine at Cairo and the centenary of the Faculty of Medicine at Cairo.

Prince Farouk
A50

1929, Feb. 11 Lithographed

155	A50	5m choc & gray	1.00	1.00
156	A50	10m dl red & gray	2.00	1.00
157	A50	15m ultra & gray	2.00	1.00
158	A50	20m Prus bl & gray	2.00	1.00

Ninth birthday of Prince Farouk.

1929

155a	A50	5m choc & blk	110.00	110.00
156a	A50	10m dl red & brn	110.00	110.00
157a	A50	15m ultra & brn	110.00	110.00
158a	A50	20m Prus bl & brn	110.00	110.00

Nos. 155a to 158a are trial color proofs. They were sent to the Universal Postal Union, but were never placed on sale to the public, although some are known used.

Tomb Fresco at El-Bersheh
A51

1931, Feb. 15 *Perf. 13x13½*

163	A51	5m brown	70	60
164	A51	10m cop red	1.50	60
165	A51	15m dk bl	2.00	75

Issued to commemorate the 14th Agricultural and Industrial Exhibition, Cairo.

Nos. 114 and 103 Surcharged with Bars and

MILLS 50 ٥٠ مليما
a

MILLS 100 ١٠٠ مليم
b

1932 *Perf. 14x14½* Wmk. 120

166	A40	50m on 50pi brn vio & red vio	5.00	1.25

Perf. 14

167	A37	100m on £1 ultra & dk vio	135.00	100.00

Locomotive of 1852
A52

Designs (Locomotives): 13m, Of 1859. 15m, Of 1862. 20m, Of 1932.

Perf. 13x13½

1933, Jan. 19 Litho. Wmk. 195

168	A52	5m brn & blk	2.50	1.50
169	A52	13m dl red & blk	10.00	7.50
170	A52	15m pur & blk	10.00	7.50
171	A52	2m dp bl & blk	10.00	7.50

International Railroad Congress, Heliopolis.

Commercial Passenger Airplane
A56

Dornier Do-X—A57

Graf Zeppelin
A58

1933, Dec. 20 Photogravure

172	A56	5m brown	3.25	1.50
173	A56	10m brt vio	10.00	6.00
174	A57	13m brn car	12.00	6.00
175	A57	15m violet	12.00	6.00
176	A58	20m blue	18.00	12.50
		Nos. 172-176 (5)	55.25	32.00

International Aviation Congress, Cairo.

Khedive Ismail Pasha
A59 A60

1934, Feb. 1 *Perf. 13½*

177	A59	1m dp org	15	15
178	A59	2m black	20	15
179	A59	3m brown	20	20
180	A59	4m bl grn	30	30
181	A59	5m red brn	30	15
182	A59	10m violet	60	25
183	A59	13m cop red	90	60
184	A59	15m dl vio	70	25
185	A59	20m ultra	1.00	40
186	A59	50m Prus bl	3.00	40
187	A59	100m ol grn	6.50	60
188	A59	200m dp vio	20.00	3.00

Perf. 13½x13

189	A60	50pi brown	100.00	42.50
190	A60	£1 Prus bl	175.00	65.00
		Nos. 177-190 (14)	308.85	113.95

10th Congress of Universal Postal Union, Cairo.

King Fuad
A61

1936-37 *Perf. 13½*

191	A61	1m dl org	12	5
192	A61	2m black	25	5
193	A61	4m dk grn	30	10
194	A61	5m chestnut	25	5
195	A61	10m pur ('37)	1.00	10
196	A61	15m brn vio	1.50	8
197	A61	20m sapphire	2.00	10
		Nos. 191-197 (7)	5.42	53

Entrance to Agricultural Building
A62

Agricultural Building
A63

Design: 15m, 20m, Industrial Building.

1936, Feb. 15 *Perf. 13½x13*

198	A62	5m brown	55	50

Perf. 13x13½

199	A63	10m violet	80	75
200	A63	13m cop red	1.75	1.25
201	A63	15m dk vio	1.00	75
202	A63	20m blue	2.00	2.00
		Nos. 198-202 (5)	6.10	5.25

Issued to commemorate the 15th Agricultural and Industrial Exhibition, Cairo.

Signing of Treaty—A65

1936, Dec. 22 *Perf. 11*

203	A65	5m brown	50	40
204	A65	15m dk vio	75	50
205	A65	20m sapphire	1.50	70

Signing of Anglo-Egyptian Treaty, Aug. 26, 1936.

King Farouk
A66

Medal for Montreux Conference
A67

1937–44 *Perf. 13x13½* **Wmk. 195**

206	A66	1m brn org	5	5
207	A66	2m vermilion	5	5
208	A66	3m brown	5	5
209	A66	4m green	10	5
210	A66	5m red brn	10	5
211	A66	6m lt yel grn ('40)	20	5
212	A66	10m purple	20	5
213	A66	13m rose car	20	12
214	A66	15m dk vio brn	25	5
215	A66	20m blue	30	5
216	A66	20m lil gray ('44)	35	6
		Nos. 206-216 (11)	1.85	63

1937, Oct. 15 *Perf. 13½x13*

217	A67	5m red brn	50	30
218	A67	15m dk vio	85	50
219	A67	20m sapphire	1.00	60

Issued in commemoration of the International Treaty signed at Montreux, Switzerland, under which foreign privileges in Egypt were to end in 1949.

Eye of Ré
A68

1937, Dec. 8 *Perf. 13x13½*

220	A68	5m brown	60	55
221	A68	15m dk vio	1.00	60
222	A68	20m sapphire	1.40	60

15th Ophthalmological Congress, Cairo, December, 1937.

King Farouk, Queen Farida—A69

1938, Jan. 20 *Perf. 11*

223	A69	5m red brn	10.00	2.50

Royal wedding of King Farouk and Farida Zulficar.

Inscribed: "11 Fevrier 1938"

1938, Feb. 11

224	A69	£1 grn & sep	125.00	100.00

King Farouk's 18th birthday.

Cotton Picker
A70

1938, Jan. 26 *Perf. 13½x13*

225	A70	5m red brn	65	60
226	A70	15m dk vio	2.00	1.25
227	A70	20m sapphire	1.50	1.00

Issued to commemorate the 18th International Cotton Congress at Cairo.

Pyramids of Giza and Colossus of Thebes—A71

1938, Feb. 1 *Perf. 13x13½*

228	A71	5m red brn	80	75
229	A71	15m dk vio	1.50	1.00
230	A71	20m sapphire	2.00	1.00

International Telecommunication Conference, Cairo.

Branch of Hydnocarpus—A72

1938, Mar. 21 *Perf. 13x13½*

231	A72	5m red brn	85	50
232	A72	15m dk vio	1.50	70
233	A72	20m sapphire	1.50	70

International Leprosy Congress, Cairo.

King Farouk and Pyramids
A73

A74 King Farouk A75

Backgrounds: 40m, Hussan Mosque. 50m, Cairo Citadel. 100m, Aswan Dam. 200m, Cairo University.

1939–46 **Photo.** *Perf. 14x13½*

234	A73	30m gray	35	5
a.		30m sl gray	30	5
234B	A73	30m ol grn ('46)	35	5
235	A73	40m dk brn	50	5
236	A73	50m Prus grn	55	5
237	A73	100m brn vio	80	5
238	A73	200m dk vio	2.50	8

Perf. 13½x13

239	A74	50pi grn & sep	5.00	50
240	A75	£1 dp bl & dk brn	10.00	70
		Nos. 234-240 (8)	20.05	1.53

For £1 with A77 portrait, see No. 269D. See Nos. 267–269D.

King Fuad
A76

King Farouk
A77

1944, Apr. 28 *Perf. 13½x13*

241	A76	10m dk vio	25	20

Issued to commemorate the eighth anniversary of the death of King Fuad.

1944–50 *Perf. 13x13½* **Wmk. 195**

242	A77	1m yel brn ('45)	6	5
243	A77	2m red org ('45)	6	5
244	A77	3m sep ('46)	25	15
245	A77	4m dp grn ('45)	25	20
246	A77	5m red brn ('46)	10	5
247	A77	10m dp vio	18	5
247A	A77	13m rose red ('50)	1.50	75
248	A77	15m dk vio ('45)	20	5
249	A77	17m ol grn	25	8
250	A77	20m dk gray ('45)	30	6
251	A77	22m dp bl ('45)	40	10
		Nos. 242-251 (11)	3.55	1.59

King Farouk
A78

Khedive Ismail Pasha
A79

1945, Feb. 10 *Perf. 13½x13*

252	A78	10m dp vio	25	20

25th birthday of King Farouk.

1945, Mar. 2 **Photogravure**

253	A79	10m dk ol	25	20

50th anniversary of death of Khedive Ismail Pasha.

Flags of Arab Nations
A80

1945, July 29

254	A80	10m violet	12	12
255	A80	22m dp yel grn	30	30

League of Arab Nations Conference, Cairo, Mar. 22, 1945.

Flags of Egypt and Saudi Arabia
A81

Perf. 13x13½

1946, Jan. 10 **Wmk. 195**

256	A81	10m dp yel grn	15	15

Visit of King Ibn Saud, Jan., 1946.

Citadel, Cairo
A82

1946, Aug. 9

257	A82	10m yel brn & dp yel grn	25	25

Withdrawal of British troops from Cairo Citadel, Aug. 9, 1946.

King Farouk and Inchas Palace, Cairo
A83

Portraits: 2m, Prince Abdullah, Yemen. 3m, Pres. Bechara el-Khoury, Lebanon. 4m, King Abdul Aziz ibn Saud, Saudi Arabia. 5m, King Faisal II, Iraq. 10m, Amir Abdullah ibn Hussein, Jordan. 15m, Pres. Shukri el Kouatly, Syria.

1946, Nov. 9

258	A83	1m dp yel grn	8	8
259	A83	2m sepia	8	8
260	A83	3m dp bl	10	10
261	A83	4m brn org	12	12
262	A83	5m brn red	15	15
263	A83	10m dk gray	18	18
264	A83	15m dp vio	20	20
		No. 258-264 (7)	91	91

Issued to commemorate the Arab League Congress at Cairo, May 28, 1946.

Parliament Building, Cairo
A84

1947, Apr. 7 **Photogravure**

265	A84	10m green	18	18

Issued to commemorate the 36th conference of the Interparliamentary Union, April, 1947.

Raising Egyptian Flag over Kasr-el-Nil Barracks
A85

King Farouk
A85a

1947, May 6 *Perf. 13½x13*

266 A85 10m dp plum & yel grn 15 15

Issued to commemorate the withdrawal of British troops from the Nile Delta.

Farouk Types 1939 Redrawn

1947–51 *Perf. 14x13½* **Wmk. 195**

267	A73	30m ol grn	30	5
268	A73	40m dk brn	40	5
269	A73	50m Prus grn ('48)	55	5
269A	A73	100m dk brn vio ('49)	1.65	8
269B	A73	200m dk vio ('49)	5.00	20

Perf. 13½13

269C	A85a	50pi grn & sep ('51)	12.00	3.75
269D	A75	£1 dp bl & dk brn ('50)	30.00	2.00
		Nos. 267-269D (7)	49.90	6.18

The king faces slightly to the left and clouds have been added in the sky on Nos. 267–269B. Backgrounds as in 1939–46 issue. Portrait on £1 as on type A77.

Field and Branch of Cotton
A86

Map and Infantry Column
A87

Perf. 13½x13

1948, Apr. 1 **Wmk. 195**

270 A86 10m ol grn 30 25

Issued to commemorate the International Cotton Congress held at Cairo in April, 1948.

1948, June 15 *Perf. 11½x11*

271 A87 10m green 35 35

Arrival of Egyptian troops at Gaza, May 15, 1948.

Ibrahim Pasha
A88

1948, Nov. 10 *Perf. 13x13½*

272 A88 10m brn red & dp grn 25 25

Issued to commemorate the centenary of the death of Ibrahim Pasha (1789–1848).

Statue, "The Nile"
A89

Protection of Industry and Agriculture
A90

Perf. 13x13½

1949, Mar. 1 **Photo.** **Wmk. 195**

273	A89	1m dk grn	10	10
274	A89	10m purple	20	20
275	A89	17m crimson	25	25
276	A89	22m dp bl	30	30

Perf. 11½x11

277	A90	30m dk brn	40	40
		Nos. 273-277 (5)	1.25	1.25

Souvenir Sheets.
Photogravure and Lithographed.
Imperf.

278	A89	Sheet of 4	1.25	1.25
a.		1m red brn	25	25
b.		10m dk brn	25	25
c.		17m brn org	25	25
d.		22m dk Prus grn	25	25
279	A90	Sheet of 2	1.75	1.75
a.		10m vio gray	75	75
b.		30m red org	75	75

Nos. 273–279 were issued to publicize the 16th Agricultural and Industrial Exposition, Cairo.

No. 278 has frame and marginal inscriptions in dark green. Size: 127x104½ mm.

No. 279 has frame and marginal inscriptions in dark violet. Size: 108x123 mm.

Mohammed Ali and Map
A93

Globe
A94

Perf. 11½x11

1949, Aug. 2 **Photo.** **Wmk. 195**

280 A93 10m org brn & grn 25 25

Centenary of death of Mohammed Ali.

1949, Oct. 9 *Perf. 13½x13*

281	A94	10m rose brn	35	30
282	A94	22m violet	60	50
283	A94	30m dl bl	80	70

75th anniversary of the formation of the Universal Postal Union.

Scales of Justice
A95

1949, Oct. 14 *Perf. 13x13½*

284 A95 10m dp ol grn 20 20

Issued to commemorate the end of the Mixed Judiciary System, Oct. 14, 1949.

Desert Scene
A96

1950, Dec. 27

285 A96 10m vio & red brn 25 25

Issued to commemorate the opening of the Fuad I Institute of the Desert.

Fuad I University
A97

1950, Dec. 27

286 A97 22m dp grn & cl 35 35

Issued to commemorate the 25th anniversary of the founding of Fuad I University.

Globe and Khedive Ismail Pasha
A98

1950, Dec. 27

287 A98 30m cl & dp grn 40 40

75th anniversary of Royal Geographic Society of Egypt.

Picking Cotton
A99

1951, Feb. 24

290 A99 10m ol grn 25 20

International Cotton Congress, 1951.

King Farouk and Queen Narriman
A100

1951, May 6 **Photo.** *Perf. 11x11½*

291	A100	10m grn & red brn	1.00	1.00
a.		Souvenir sheet	1.50	1.50

Issued to commemorate the marriage of King Farouk and Narriman Sadek, May 6, 1951.

No. 291a was issued in sheets measuring 129x112 mm., with ornamental border and inscriptions in gray and black.

Stadium Entrance
A101

Arms of Alexandria and Olympic Emblem
A102

King Farouk
A103

1951, Oct. 5 *Perf. 13x13½, 13½x13*

292	A101	10m brown	50	50
293	A102	22m dp grn	90	90
294	A103	30m bl & dp grn	1.00	1.00
a.		Souvenir sheet	5.00	5.00

Issued to publicize the first Mediterranean Games, Alexandria, Oct. 5–20, 1951.

No. 294a measures 189x117mm., and contains one each of Nos. 292–294 with ornamental frame and background in buff.

Winged Figure and Map
A105

Designs: 22m, King Farouk and Map. 30m, King Farouk and Flag.

Dated "16 Oct. 1951."

1952, Feb. 11 *Perf. 13½x13*

296	A105	10m dp grn	50	50
297	A105	22m plum & dp grn	90	90
298	A105	30m grn & brn	1.00	1.00
a.		Souvenir sheet	5.00	5.00

Issued to commemorate the abrogation of the Anglo-Egyptian treaty.

No. 298a measures 134 x 113mm., and contains one each of Nos. 296 to 298, with ornamental border and Arabic inscriptions in gray.

Stamps of 1937-51 Overprinted in Various Colors

ملك مصر والسودان
١٦ اكتوبرسنة ١٩٥١

Perf. 13x13½

1952, Jan. 17 **Wmk. 195**

299	A77	1m yel brn	10	8
300	A77	2m red org (Bl)	10	8
301	A66	3m brn (Bl)	12	10
302	A77	4m dp grn (RV)	12	8
303	A66	6m lt yel grn (RV)	60	15
304	A77	10m dp vio (C)	20	5
305	A77	13m rose red (Bl)	75	15
306	A77	15m dk vio (C)	60	22
307	A77	17m ol grn (C)	90	15
308	A77	20m dk gray (RV)	1.00	15
309	A77	22m dp bl (C)	1.50	80

No. 244, the 3m sepia, exists with this overprint but was not regularly issued or used.

Same Overprint, 24½mm. Wide on Nos. 267 to 269B.
Perf. 14x13½

310	A73	30m ol grn	55	8
a.		Dark bl overprint	35	6

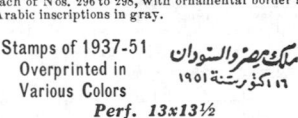

No.	Type	Description	Unused	Used
311	A73	40m dk brn (G)	50	18
312	A73	50m Prus grn (C)	65	10
313	A73	100m dk brn vio (C)	1.00	25
314	A73	200m dk vio (C)	2.50	30

Same Overprint, 19mm. Wide, on Nos. 269C–269D.

Perf. 13½x13.

No.	Type	Description	Unused	Used
315	A85a	50pi grn & sep (C)	12.00	3.50
316	A75	£1 dp bl & dk brn (Bl)	25.00	3.75
		Nos. 299-316 (18)	48.19	10.17

The overprint translates: King of Egypt and the Sudan, Oct. 16, 1951.

Egyptian Flag
A106

Perf. 13½x13

1952, May 6 Photo. Wmk. 195

No.	Type	Description	Unused	Used
317	A106	10m org yel, dp bl & dp grn	25	25
a.		Souvenir sheet	1.25	1.25

Issued to commemorate the birth of Crown Prince Ahmed Fuad, January 16, 1952.

No. 317a measures 115½ x 137½mm., with ornamental border and Arabic inscriptions in deep blue, salmon and green.

"Dawn of New Era"
A107

Symbolical of Egypt Freed
A108

Designs: 10m, "Egypt" with raised sword. 22m, Citizens marching with flag.

Perf. 13x13½, 13½x13

1952, Nov. 23

Dated: "23 Juillet 1952."

No.	Type	Description	Unused	Used
318	A107	4m dp grn & org	10	10
319	A107	10m dp grn & cop brn	15	15
320	A108	17m brn org & dp grn	25	25
321	A108	22m choc & dp grn	35	35

Change of government, July 23, 1952.

Republic

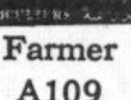

Farmer
A109

Soldier
A110

Mosque of Sultan Hassan
A111

Queen Nefertiti
A112

1953–56 ***Perf. 13x13½***

No.	Type	Description	Unused	Used
322	A109	1m red brn	5	5
323	A109	2m dk lil	6	5
324	A109	3m brt bl	6	5
325	A109	4m dk grn	6	5
326	A110	10m dk brn (*"Defence"*)	12	6
327	A110	10m dk brn (*"Defense"*)	8	5
328	A110	15m gray	15	5
329	A110	17m dk grnsh bl	18	6
330	A110	20m purple	18	6

Perf. 13½.

No.	Type	Description	Unused	Used
331	A111	30m dl grn	20	5
332	A111	32m brt bl	25	10
333	A111	35m vio ('55)	50	5
334	A111	37m gldn brn ('56)	1.75	15
335	A111	40m red brn	30	5
336	A111	50m vio brn	45	5
337	A112	100m hn brn	1.00	10
338	A112	200m dk grnsh bl	2.50	20
339	A112	500m purple	5.00	90
340	A112	£1 dk grn, blk & red	12.00	1.00
		Nos. 332-340 (19)	24.89	3.13

Nos. 327–330 are inscribed "Defense." See No. 490.

Nos. 206, 208 and 211 Overprinted in Black with Three Bars to Obliterate Portrait.

1953 ***Perf. 13x13½***

No.	Type	Description	Unused	Used
342	A66	1m brn org	5.00	5.00
343	A66	3m brown	1.00	1.00
344	A66	6m lt yel grn	25	25

Same Overprint on Stamps of 1939–51

Perf. 13x13½, 13½x13.

No.	Type	Description	Unused	Used
345	A77	1m yel brn	6	6
346	A77	2m red org	6	6
347	A77	3m sepia	6	6
348	A77	4m dp grn	8	6
349	A77	10m dp vio	12	10
350	A77	13m rose red	18	15
351	A77	15m dk vio	18	10
352	A77	17m ol grn	20	15
353	A77	20m dk gray	25	12
354	A77	22m dp bl	30	25
355	A73	30m ol grn (#267)	35	18
356	A73	50m Prus grn (#269)	50	20
357	A73	100m dk brn vio (#269A)	75	25
358	A73	200m dk vio (#269B)	2.50	35
359	A85a	50pi grn & sep	6.00	2.00
360	A75	£1 dp bl & dk brn (#269D)	15.00	5.00
		Nos. 345-360 (16)	26.59	9.09

Same Overprint on Nos. 299-309, 311 and 314.

No.	Type	Description	Unused	Used
360A	A77	1m yel brn	2.00	2.00
360B	A77	2m red org	25	20
360C	A66	3m brown	2.00	2.00
360D	A77	4m dp grn	2.00	2.00
360E	A66	6m lt yel grn	2.50	2.50
361	A77	10m dp vio	1.00	1.00
362	A77	13m rose red	50	30
362A	A77	15m dk vio	7.00	7.00
362B	A77	17m ol grn	7.00	7.00
362C	A77	20m dk gray	7.00	7.00
362D	A77	22m dp bl	25.00	25.00

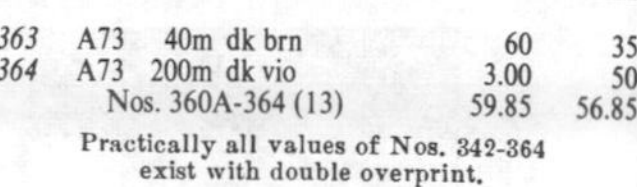

No.	Type	Description	Unused	Used
363	A73	40m dk brn	60	35
364	A73	200m dk vio	3.00	50
		Nos. 360A-364 (13)	59.85	56.85

Practically all values of Nos. 342-364 exist with double overprint.

Symbols of Electronic Progress
A113

1953, Nov. 23 Photo. ***Perf. 13x13½***

No.	Type	Description	Unused	Used
365	A113	10m brt bl	30	25

Electronics Exposition, Cairo, Nov. 23.

Crowd Acclaiming the Republic
A114

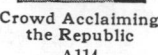

Farmer
A115

Design: 30m, Crowd, flag and eagle.

Perf. 13½x13

1954, June 18 Wmk. 195

No.	Type	Description	Unused	Used
366	A114	10m brown	15	15
367	A114	30m dp bl	35	35

Issued to commemorate the first anniversary of the proclamation of the republic.

1954-55 ***Perf. 13x13½.***

No.	Type	Description	Unused	Used
368	A115	1m red brn	5	5
369	A115	2m dk lil	5	5
370	A115	3m brt bl	6	5
371	A115	4m dk grn ('55)	6	6
372	A115	5m dp car ('55)	12	8
		Nos. 368-372 (5)	34	29

Egyptian Flag and Map
A116

Globe
A117

Design: 35m, Bugler, soldier and map.

1954, Nov. 4 ***Perf. 13½x13***

No.	Type	Description	Unused	Used
373	A116	10m rose vio & grn	15	15
374	A116	35m ver, blk & bl grn	50	50

Issued to commemorate the agreement of Oct. 19, 1954, with Great Britain for the evacuation of the Suez Canal zone by British troops.

Arab Postal Union Issue.

1955, Jan. 1

No.	Type	Description	Unused	Used
375	A117	5m yel brn	10	10
376	A117	10m green	20	20
377	A117	37m violet	60	60

Issued to commemorate the founding of the Arab Postal Union, July 1, 1954.

Paul P. Harris and Rotary Emblem
A118

Design: 35m, Globe, wings and Rotary emblem.

Perf. 13½x13

1955, Feb. 23 Wmk. 195

No.	Type	Description	Unused	Used
378	A118	10m claret	30	15
379	A118	35m blue	60	40

Issued to commemorate the 50th anniversary of the founding of Rotary International.

Nos. 375-377 Overprinted مؤتمر البريد العربي القاهرة-١٩٥٥/٣/١٥

1955, Nov. 1

No.	Type	Description	Unused	Used
381	A117	5m yel brn	10	10
382	A117	10m green	20	20
383	A117	37m violet	55	55

Issued to commemorate the Arab Postal Union Congress held at Cairo, March 15, 1955.

Map of Africa and Asia, Olive Branch and Rings
A119

Globe, Torch, Dove and Olive Branch
A120

Perf. 13x13½, 13½x13

1956, July 29

No.	Type	Description	Unused	Used
384	A119	10m chnt & grn	20	15
385	A120	35m org yel & dl pur	45	40

Afro-Asian Festival, Cairo, July, 1956.

Map of Suez Canal and Ship
A121

Queen Nefertiti
A122

Perf. 11½x11

1956, Sept. 26 **Wmk. 195**

386 A121 10m bl & buff 50 25

Nationalization of the Suez Canal, July 26, 1956. See also No. 393.

1956, Oct. 15 ***Perf. 13½x13***

387 A122 10m dk grn 1.50 45

Issued to publicize the International Museum Week (UNESCO), Oct. 8-14.

Egyptians Defending Port Said
A123

1956, Dec. 20 Litho. ***Perf. 11x11½***

388 A123 10m brn vio 30 20

Issued in honor of the defenders of Port Said.

No. 388 Overprinted in Carmine Rose — الجلاء ٢٣/١٢/٥٦ EVACUATION 22-12-56

1957, Jan. 14

389 A123 10m brn vio 50 20

Issued to commemorate the evacuation of Port Said by British and French troops, Dec. 22, 1956.

Old and New Trains
A124

1957, Jan. 30 Photo. ***Perf. 13x13½***

390 A124 10m red vio & gray 25 15

Issued to commemorate the 100th anniversary of the Egyptian Railway System (in 1956).

Mother and Children
A125

1957, Mar. 21

391 A125 10m crimson 25 15

Mother's Day, 1957.

Battle Scene
A126

Perf. 13x13½

1957, Mar. 28 **Wmk. 195**

392 A126 10m brt bl 25 15

Issued to commemorate the 150th anniversary of the victory over the British at Rosetta.

Type of 1956;
New Inscriptions in English

1957, Apr. 15 ***Perf. 11½x11***

393 A121 100m bl & yel grn 1.00 65

Issued to commemorate the reopening of the Suez Canal.

No. 393 is inscribed: "Nationalisation of Suez Canal Co. Guarantees Freedom of Navigation" and "Reopening 1957".

Map of Gaza Strip
A127

Perf. 13½x13

1957, May 4 Photo. **Wmk. 195**

394 A127 10m Prus bl 25 18

"Gaza Part of Arab Nation."

Al Azhar University
A128

1957, Apr. 27 ***Perf. 13x13½***

New Arabic Date in Red.

395 A128 10m brt vio 25 15
396 A128 15m vio brn 30 20
397 A128 20m dk gray 40 25

Millenary of Al Azhar University, Cairo.

Shepheard's Hotel, Cairo
A129

Gate, Palace and Eagle
A130

Perf. 13½x13

1957, July 20 **Wmk. 195**

398 A129 10m brt vio 25 12

Reopening of Shepheard's Hotel, Cairo.

Wmk. 315

Wmkd. Multiple Eagle (315)

1957, July 22 ***Perf. 11½x11***

399 A130 10m yel & brn 25 12

First meeting of New National Assembly.

Amasis I in Battle of Avaris, 1580 B. C.—A131

Designs: No. 401, Sultan Saladin, Hitteen, 1187 A. D. No. 402, Louis IX of France in chains, Mansourah, 1250 (vertical). No. 403, Map of Middle East, Ein Galout, 1260. No. 404, Port Said, 1956.

Inscribed:
"Egypt Tomb of Aggressors 1957"
Perf. 13x13½, 13½x13

1957, July 26

400 A131 10m car rose 30 10
401 A131 10m dk ol grn 30 10
402 A131 10m brn vio 30 10
403 A131 10m grnsh bl 30 10
404 A131 10m yel brn 30 10
Nos. 400-404 (5) 1.50 50

No. 400 exists with Wmk. 195.

Ahmed Arabi Speaking to the Khedive—A132

Perf. 13x13½

1957, Sept. 16 **Wmk. 315**

405 A132 10m dp vio 25 12

75th anniversary of Arabi Revolution.

Hafez Ibrahim
A133

Portrait: No. 407, Ahmed Shawky.

1957, Oct. 14 ***Perf. 13½x13***

406 A133 10m dl red brn 15 12
407 A133 10m ol grn 15 12

Nos. 406–407 are printed se-tenant in sheets of 50. Issued to commemorate the 25th anniversary of the deaths of Hafez Ibrahim and Ahmed Shawky, poets.

MiG and Ilyushin Planes—A134

Design: No. 409, Viscount plane.

1957, Dec. 19 ***Perf. 13x13½***

408 A134 10m ultra 25 15
409 A134 10m green 25 15

Issued to commemorate the 25th anniversaries of the Egyptian Air Force and of Misrair, the Egyptian airline. Nos. 408–409 printed se-tenant.

Pyramids, Dove and Globe—A135

1957, Dec. 26 Photo. **Wmk. 315**

410 A135 5m brn org 12 8
411 A135 10m green 18 12
412 A135 15m brt vio 25 20

Issued to publicize the Afro-Asian Peoples Conference, Cairo, Dec. 26–Jan. 2.

Farmer's Wife
A136

Ramses II
A137

1957-58 ***Perf. 13½*** **Wmk. 315**

413 A136 1m bl grn ('58) 5 5
414 A137 10m violet 12 8

"Industry"
A138

Wmk. 318

Wmkd. Multiple Eagle and "Misr" (318)

1958

415 A136 1m lt bl grn 5 5
416 A138 5m brown 6 5
417 A137 10m violet 12 5

See also Nos. 438–444, 474–488.

Cyclists
A139

Mustafa Kamel
A140

Perf. 13½x13

1958, Jan. 12 **Wmk. 315**

418 A139 10m lt red brn 25 15

Issued to publicize the fifth International Bicycle Race, Egypt, Jan. 12–26.

1958, Feb. 10 Photo. **Wmk. 318**

419 A140 10m bl gray 25 15

Issued to commemorate the 50th anniversary of the death of Mustafa Kamel, orator and politician.

United Arab Republic

Linked Maps of Egypt and Syria
A141

Cotton
A142

Perf. 11½x11

1958, Mar. 22 **Wmk. 318**

436 A141 10m yel & grn 15 12

Birth of United Arab Republic. See No. C90.

1958, Apr. 5 ***Perf. 13½x13***

437 A142 10m Prus bl 15 12

Issued for the International Fair for Egyptian Cotton, April, 1958.

Types of 1957–58 Inscribed "U.A.R. EGYPT" and

Princess Nofret
A143

Designs: 1m, Farmer's wife. 2m, Ibn-Tulun's Mosque. 4m, 14th century glass lamp (design lacks "1963" of A217). 5m. "Industry" (factories and cogwheel). 10m, Ramses II. 35m, "Commerce" (eagle, ship and cargo).

1958 ***Perf. 13½x14***

438	A136	1m crimson	5	5
439	A138	2m blue	5	5
440	A143	3m dk red brn	5	5
441	A217	4m green	5	5
442	A138	5m brown	6	5
443	A137	10m violet	12	5
444	A138	35m lt ultra	80	5
		Nos. 438-444 (7)	1.18	35

See Nos. 474–488, 532–535.

Qasim Amin
A144

Doves, Broken Chain and Globe
A145

1958, Apr. 23 ***Perf. 13½x13***

445 A144 10m dp bl 18 12

50th anniversary of the death of Qasim Amin, author of "Emancipation of Women."

1958, June 18

446 A145 10m violet 15 10

Issued on the fifth anniversary of the republic to publicize the struggle of peoples and individuals for freedom.

Cement Industry
A146

Industries: No. 448, Textile. No. 449, Iron & steel. No. 450, Petroleum (Oil). No. 451, Electricity and fertilizers.

Perf. 13½x13

1958, July 23 **Photo.** **Wmk. 318**

447	A146	10m red brn	15	10
448	A146	10m bl grn	15	10
449	A146	10m brt red	15	10
450	A146	10m ol grn	15	10
451	A146	10m dk bl	15	10
		Nos. 447-451 (5)	75	50

Nos. 447–451 are printed in one sheet of 25 in vertical rows of five.

Souvenir Sheet

U. A. R. Flag—A147

1958, July 23 ***Imperf.***

452 A147 50m grn, dp car & blk 10.00 10.00

No. 452 measures 80½x75½mm. with black marginal inscription. Nos. 447–452 issued on the 6th anniversary of the Revolution of July 23, 1952.

Sayed Darwich
A148

Hand Holding Torch, Broken Chain and Flag
A149

1958, Sept. 15 ***Perf. 13½x13***

453 A148 10m vio brn 12 10

Issued to commemorate the 35th anniversary of the death of Sayed Darwich, Arab composer.

1958, Oct. 14 **Photo.** **Wmk. 318**

454 A149 10m car rose 12 10

Establishment of the Republic of Iraq.

Maps and Cogwheels
A150

1958, Dec. 8 ***Perf. 13x13½***

455 A150 10m blue 18 10

Issued to publicize the Economic Conference of Afro-Asian Countries, Cairo, Dec. 8.

Overprinted in Red in English and Arabic in 3 Lines: "Industrial and Agricultural Production Fair."

1958, Dec. 9

456 A150 10m lt red brn 18 10

Issued to publicize the Industrial and Agricultural Production Fair, Cairo, Dec. 9.

Dr. Mahmoud Azmy and U.N. Emblem—A151

1958, Dec. 10

457	A151	10m dl vio	20	15
458	A151	35m green	55	45

Tenth anniversary of the signing of the Universal Declaration of Human Rights.

University Building, Sphinx, "Education" and God Thoth
A152

1958, Dec. 21 **Photo.** **Wmk. 318**

459 A152 10m grnsh blk 12 10

50th anniversary of Cairo University.

الجمهورية العربية المتحدة
٥٥

No. 337 Surcharged

UAR
55

1959, Jan. 20 ***Perf. 13½*** **Wmk. 195**

460 A112 55m on 100m hn brn 45 30

Emblem
A153

1959, Feb. 2 ***Perf. 13x13½***

461 A153 10m lt ol grn 12 10

Afro-Asian Youth Conference, Cairo, Feb. 2.

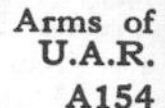

Arms of U.A.R.
A154

Perf. 13½x13

1959, Feb. 22 **Photo.** **Wmk. 318**

462 A154 10m grn, blk & red 12 10

First anniversary, United Arab Republic.

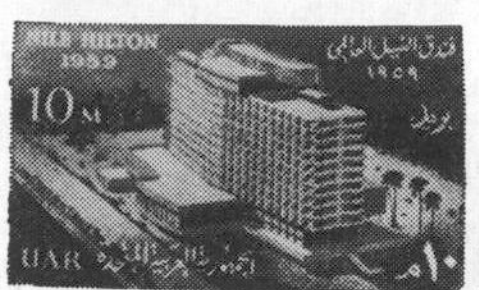

Nile Hilton Hotel
A155

1959, Feb. 22 ***Perf. 13x13½***

463 A155 10m dk gray 12 10

Opening of the Nile Hilton Hotel, Cairo.

Globe, Radio and Telegraph—A156

1959, Mar. 1

464 A156 10m violet 12 10

Arab Union of Telecommunications.

United Arab States Issue

Flags of U. A. R. and Yemen
A157

1959, Mar. 8

465 A157 10m sl grn, car & blk 12 10

First anniversary of United Arab States.

Oil Derrick and Pipe Line
A158

Perf. 13½x13

1959, Apr. 16 **Litho.** **Wmk. 318**

466 A158 10m lt bl & dk bl 12 8

First Arab Petroleum Congress, Cairo.

Railroad
A159

Designs: No. 468, Bus on highway. No. 469, River barge. No. 470, Ocean liner. No. 471, Telecommunications on map. No. 472, Stamp printing building, Heliopolis.

1959, July 23 **Photo.** ***Perf. 13x13½***

Frame in Gray.

467	A159	10m maroon	7	7
468	A159	10m green	7	7
469	A159	10m violet	7	7
470	A159	10m dk bl	8	8
471	A159	10m dl pur	8	8

472	A159	10m scarlet	8	8
		Nos. 467-472 (6)	45	45

An imperf. souvenir sheet, issued with this set, commemorates the seventh anniversary of the Egyptian revolution of 1952. The sheet carries a single 50m green and red stamp, 57x32mm., picturing a ship, train, plane and motorcycle mail carrier. Marginal Arabic inscriptions in black; size: 80x74mm. The government printed 140,000 of this sheet and sold it only if the buyer also bought five sets of Nos. 467-472.

Globe, Swallows and Map A160

1959, Aug. 8 ***Perf. 13½x13***

473	A160	10m maroon	10	8

Issued to commemorate the convention of the Association of Arab Emigrants in the United States.

Types of 1953–58 without "Egypt" and

St. Simon's Gate, Bosra, Syria A161

Wmk. 328

Designs: 1m, Farmer's wife. 2m, Ibn-Tulun's Mosque. 3m, Princess Nofret. 4m, 14th century glass lamp (design lacks "1963" of A217). 5m, "Industry" (factories and cogwheel). 10m, Ramses II. 15m, Omayyad Mosque, Damascus. 20m, Lotus vase, Tutankhamen treasure. 35m, Eagle, ship and cargo. 40m, Scribe statue. 45m, Saladin's citadel, Aleppo. 55m, Eagle, cotton and wheat. 60m, Dam and factory. 100m, Eagle, hand, cotton and grain. 200m, Palmyra ruins, Syria. 500m, Queen Nefertiti, inscribed "UAR" (no ovpt.).

Wmkd. U A R. (328)

Photogravure.

1959-60 ***Perf. 13½x14, 14x13½.***

474	A136	1m vermilion	5	5
475	A138	2m dp bl ('60)	5	5
476	A143	3m maroon	5	5
477	A217	4m grn ('60)	5	5
478	A138	5m blk ('60)	5	5
479	A137	10m dk ol grn	10	5
480	A138	15m dp cl	15	5
481	A138	20m crim ('60)	20	5
482	A161	30m brn vio	30	6
483	A138	35m lt vio bl ('60)	40	6
484	A143	40m sepia	60	8
485	A161	45m lil gray ('60)	1.00	8
486	A138	55m brt bl grn	1.00	8
487	A138	60m dp pur ('60)	60	8
488	A138	100m org & sl grn ('60)	2.00	10
489	A161	200m lt bl & mar	3.50	10
490	A112	500m dk gray & red ('60)	6.00	30
		Nos. 474-490 (17)	16.10	1.34

Shield and Cogwheel A162

Perf. 13½x13

1959, Oct. 20 **Photo.** **Wmk. 328**

491	A162	10m brt car rose	12	8

Issued for Army Day, 1959.

Cairo Museum—A163

1959, Nov. 18 ***Perf. 13x13½***

492	A163	10m ol gray	12	8

Centenary of Cairo museum.

Abu Simbel Temple of Ramses II A164

1959, Dec. 22 ***Perf. 11x11½***

493	A164	10m lt red brn, *pnksh*	25	20

Issued as propaganda to save historic monuments in Nubia threatened by the construction of Aswan High Dam.

Postrider, 12th century A165

1960, Jan. 2 ***Perf. 13x13½***

494	A165	10m dk bl	12	8

Issued for Post Day, Jan. 2.

Hydroelectric Power Station, Aswan Dam—A166

1960, Jan. 9

495	A166	10m vio blk	15	8

Issued to commemorate the inauguration of the Aswan Dam hydroelectric power station, Jan. 9.

Arabic and English Description of Aswan High Dam—A167

Architect's Drawing of Aswan High Dam—A168

1960, Jan. 9 ***Perf. 11x11½***

496	A167	10m claret	15	8
497	A168	35m claret	45	25

Issued to commemorate the start of work on the Aswan High Dam. Nos. 496–497 printed se-tenant vertically in sheet.

Symbols of Agriculture and Industry A169

Arms and Flag A170

1960, Jan. 16 ***Perf. 13½x13***

498	A169	10m gray grn & sl grn	12	8

Industrial and Agricultural Fair, Cairo.

1960, Feb. 22 **Photo.** **Wmk. 328**

499	A170	10m grn, blk & red	12	8

Issued to commemorate the 2nd anniversary of the proclamation of the United Arab Republic.

No. 340 Overprinted "UAR" in English and Arabic in Red

1960 ***Perf. 13½*** **Wmk. 195**

500	A112	£1 dk grn, blk & red	10.00	1.00
a.		Double ovpt.	*50.00*	

"Art" A171

Perf. 13½x13

1960, Mar. 1 **Wmk. 328**

501	A171	10m brown	12	8

Issued to publicize the 3rd Biennial Exhibition of Fine Arts in Alexandria.

Arab League Center, Cairo—A172

1960, Mar. 22 **Photo.** ***Perf. 13x13½***

502	A172	10m dl grn & blk	12	8

Opening of Arab League Center and Arab Postal Museum, Cairo.

Refugees Pointing to Map of Palestine—A173

1960, Apr. 7

503	A173	10m org ver	10	8
504	A173	35m Prus bl	35	30

Issued to publicize World Refugee Year, July 1, 1959–June 30, 1960.

Weight Lifter A174

Stadium, Cairo—A175

Sports: No. 506, Basketball. No. 507, Soccer. No. 508, Fencing. No. 509, Rowing. 30m, Steeplechase (horiz.). 35m, Swimming (horiz.)

Perf. 13½x13

1960, July 23 **Photo.** **Wmk. 328**

505	A174	5m gray	5	5
506	A174	5m brown	5	5
507	A174	5m dp cl	10	5
508	A174	10m brt car	15	5
509	A174	10m gray grn	15	5
510	A174	30m purple	35	15
511	A174	35m dk bl	45	20
		Nos. 505-511 (7)	1.30	60

Souvenir Sheet

Imperf.

512	A175	100m car & brn	1.25	75

Nos. 505–511 issued to commemorate the 17th Olympic Games, Rome, Aug. 25–Sept. 11.

Nos. 505–509 are printed in one sheet of 25 in vertical rows of five.

No. 512 measures 80x75mm. with black marginal inscription.

Dove and U.N. Emblem A176

Design: 35m, Lights surrounding U.N. emblem (horiz.).

Perf. 13½x13

1960, Oct. 24 Wmk. 328

513 A176 10m purple 10 8
514 A176 35m brt rose 30 25

15th anniversary of United Nations.

Abu Simbel Temple of Queen Nefertari—A177

Perf. 11x11½

1960, Nov. 14 Photo. Wmk. 328

515 A177 10m ocher, *buff* 30 20

Issued as propaganda to save historic monuments in Nubia and in connection with the UNESCO meeting, Paris, Nov. 14.

Model Post Office A178

1961, Jan. 2 *Perf. 13x13½*

516 A178 10m brt car rose 12 8

Issued for Post Day, Jan. 2.

Eagle, Fasces and Victory Wreath A179

Wheat and Globe Surrounded by Flags A180

1961, Feb. 22 *Perf. 13½x13*

517 A179 10m dl vio 12 8

3rd anniversary of United Arab Republic.

1961, March 21 Wmk. 328

518 A180 10m vermilion 12 8

Issued to publicize the International Agricultural Exhibition, Cairo, March 21–April 20.

Patrice Lumumba and Map A181

Reading Braille and WHO Emblem A182

1961, March 30 *Perf. 13½x13*

519 A181 10m black 12 8

Issued for Africa Day, Apr. 15 and to commemorate the 3rd Conference of Independent African States, Cairo, March 25–31.

1961, Apr. 6 Photogravure

520 A182 10m red brn 12 8

World Health Organization Day. See No. B21.

Tower of Cairo A183

Arab Woman and Son, Palestine Map A184

1961, Apr. 11 *Perf. 13½x13*

521 A183 10m grnsh bl 12 8

Issued to commemorate the opening of the 600-foot Tower of Cairo, on island of Gizireh. See also No. C95.

1961, May 15 Wmk. 328

522 A184 10m brt grn 20 8

Issued for Palestine Day.

Symbols of Industry and Electricity A185

Chart and Workers—A186

Designs: No. 524, New buildings and family. No. 525, Ship, train, bus and radio. No. 526, Dam, cotton and field. No. 527, Hand holding candle and family.

Photogravure

1961, July 23 *Perf. 13x13½*

523 A185 10m dp car 8 5
524 A185 10m brt bl 8 5
525 A185 10m dk vio brn 8 5
526 A185 35m dk grn 28 5
527 A185 35m brt pur 28 6
Nos. 523-527 (5) 80 26

Souvenir Sheet

Imperf.

528 A186 100m red brn 1.25 1.25

Nos. 523–528 issued to commemorate the ninth anniversary of the revolution. No. 528 has pale brown border with black inscription. Size: 82x75mm.

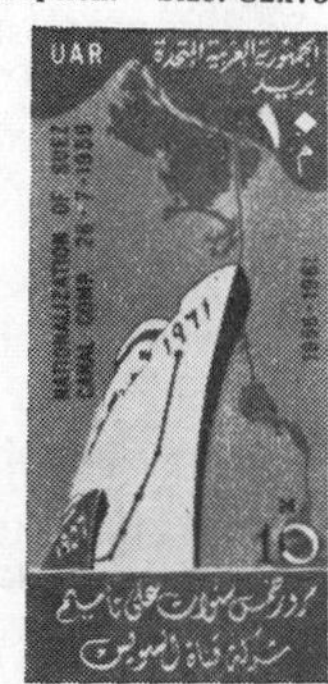

Map of Suez Canal and Ships A187

Perf. 11½x11

1961, July 26 Unwmkd.

529 A187 10m olive 12 8

Fifth anniversary of the nationalization of the Suez Canal Company.

Various Enterprises of Misr Bank A188

Perf. 13x13½

1961, Aug. 22 Wmk. 328

530 A188 10m red brn, *pnksh* 12 8

The 41st anniversary of Misr Bank.

Flag, Ship's Wheel and Battleship A189

1961, Aug. 29 Photo. *Perf. 13½x13*

531 A189 10m dp bl 12 8

Issued for Navy Day.

Eagle of Saladin over Cairo A190

U.N. Emblem, Book, Cogwheel and Corn A191

Type A143 of 1958 Redrawn and Type A190

1961, Aug. 31 *Perf. 11½* Unwmkd.

Designs: 1m, Farmer's wife. 4m, 14th century glass lamp. 35m, "Commerce."

532 A143 1m blue 5 5
533 A143 4m olive 5 5
534 A190 10m purple 10 5
535 A143 35m sl bl 30 6

Smaller of two Arabic inscriptions in new positions: 1m, at right above Egyptian numeral; 4m, upward to spot beside waist of lamp; 35m, upper left corner below "UAR." On 4m, "UAR" is 2mm. deep instead of 1mm. "Egypt" omitted as in 1959–60.

Perf. 13½x13

1961, Oct. 24 Photo. Wmk. 328

Design: 35m, Globe and cogwheel (horiz.).

536 A191 10m blk & ocher 10 8
537 A191 35m bl grn & brn 30 25

Issued to honor the United Nations' Technical Assistance Program and to commemorate the 16th anniversary of the United Nations.

Trajan's Kiosk, Philae—A192

1961, Nov. 4 *Perf. 11½* Unwmkd.

Size: 60x27mm.

538 A192 10m dp vio bl 35 20

Issued to commemorate the 15th anniversary of UNESCO, and to publicize UNESCO's help in safeguarding the monuments of Nubia.

Palette, Brushes and Map of Mediterranean A193

Atom and Educational Symbols A194

1961, Dec. 14 *Perf. 13½* Wmk. 328

539 A193 10m dk red brn 12 8

Issued to publicize the 4th Biennial Exhibition of Fine Arts in Alexandria.

1961, Dec. 18

540 A194 10m dl pur 12 8

Issued to publicize Education Day.

Arms of U.A.R. A195

1961, Dec. 23 *Perf. 11½* Unwmkd.

541 A195 10m brt pink, brt grn & blk 20 8

Issued to commemorate Victory Day.

Sphinx at Giza A196

1961, Dec. 27 *Perf. 11x11½*

542 A196 10m black 12 8

Issued to publicize the "Sound and Light" Project, the installation of floodlights and sound equipment at the site of the Pyramids and Sphinx.

Post Office Printing Plant, Nasser City—A197

1962, Jan. 2 Photo. ***Perf. 11½x11***

543 A197 10m dk brn 12 8

Issued for Post Day, Jan. 2.

Map of Africa, King Mohammed V of Morocco and Flags
A198

1962, Jan. 4 ***Perf. 11x11½***

544 A198 10m indigo 12 8

Issued to commemorate the first anniversary of the African Charter, Casablanca.

Girl Scout Saluting and Emblem
A199

Perf. 13x13½

1962, Feb. 22 **Wmk. 328**

545 A199 10m brt bl 25 15

Egyptian Girl Scouts' 25th anniversary.

Arab Refugees, Flag and Map
A200

Mother and Child
A201

1962, March 7 ***Perf. 13½x13***

546 A200 10m dk sl grn 12 8

Issued to commemorate the 5th anniversary of the liberation of the Gaza Strip.

1962, March 21 **Photogravure**

547 A201 10m dk vio brn 12 8

Issued for Arab Mother's Day, March 21.

Map of Africa and Post Horn
A202

1962, Apr. 23 **Wmk. 328**

548 A202 10m crim & ocher 12 8
549 A202 50m dp bl & ocher 40 30

Establishment of African Postal Union.

Cadets on Parade and Academy Emblem—A203

1962, June 18 ***Perf. 13x13½***

550 A203 10m green 12 8

Issued to commemorate the 150th anniversary of the Egyptian Military Academy.

Malaria Eradication Emblem
A204

Theodor Bilharz
A205

1962, June 20 ***Perf. 13½x13***

551 A204 10m dk brn & red 12 8
552 A204 35m dk grn & bl 30 28

Issued for the World Health Organization drive to eradicate malaria.

1962, June 24 ***Perf. 11x11½***

553 A205 10m brn org 12 8

Issued to commemorate the centenary of the death of Dr. Theodor Bilharz (1825–1862), German physician who first described bilharziasis, an endemic disease in Egypt.

Patrice Lumumba and Map of Africa
A206

Hand on Charter
A207

Wmk. 342

Watermarked Coat of Arms, Multiple (342)

1962, July 1 **Photogravure**

554 A206 10m rose & red 25 10

Issued in memory of Patrice Lumumba (1925–61), Premier of Congo.

1962, July 10 ***Perf. 11x11½***

555 A207 10m brt bl & dk brn 12 8

Proclamation of the National Charter.

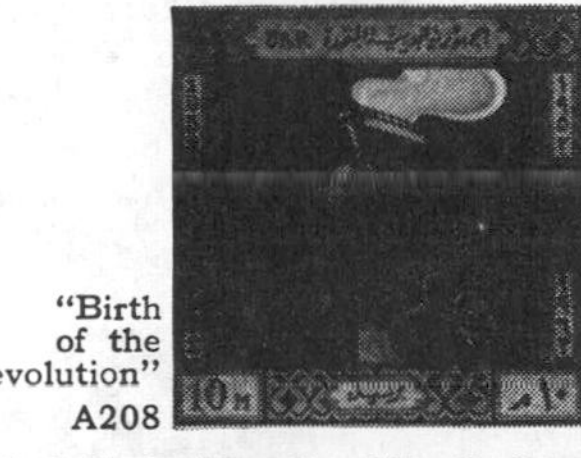

"Birth of the Revolution"
A208

Symbolic Designs: No. 557, Proclamation (Scroll and book). No. 558, Agricultural Reform (Farm and crescent). No. 559, Bandung Conference (Dove, globe and olive branch). No. 560, Birth of UAR (Eagle and flag). No. 561, Industrialization (cogwheel, factory, ship and bus). No. 562, Aswan High Dam. No. 563, Social Revolution (Modern buildings and emblem). 100m, Arms of UAR, emblems of Afro-Asian and African countries and United Nations emblem.

1962, July 23 ***Perf. 11½***

556 A208 10m brn, dk red brn & pink 15 8
557 A208 10m dk bl & sep 15 8
558 A208 10m sep & brt bl 15 8
559 A208 10m ol & dk ultra 15 8
560 A208 10m grn, blk & red 15 8
561 A208 10m brn org & ind 15 8
562 A208 10m brn org & vio blk 15 8
563 A208 10m org & blk 15 8
Nos. 556-563 (8) 1.20 64

Souvenir Sheets

Perf. 11½, Imperf.

564 A208 100m grn, pink, red & blk 1.25 1.00

Issued to commemorate the tenth anniversary of the revolution. No 564 contains one stamp; green marginal inscription. Size: 71x79mm.

Mahmoud Moukhtar, Museum and Sculpture—A209

1962, July 24 ***Perf. 11½x11***

565 A209 10m lt vio bl & ol 12 8

Issued to commemorate the opening of the Moukhtar Museum, Island of Gezireh. The sculpture is "La Vestale de Secrets" by Moukhtar.

Flag of Algeria and Map of Africa Showing Algeria
A210

1962, Aug. 15 ***Perf. 11x11½***

566 A210 10m multi 12 8

Algeria's independence, July 1, 1962.

Rocket, Arms of U.A.R. and Atom Symbol
A211

1962, Sept. 1 Photo. **Wmk. 342**

567 A211 10m brt grn, red & blk 12 8

Launching of U.A.R. rockets.

Rifle and Target—A212

Map of Africa, Table Tennis Paddle, Net and Ball—A213

1962, Sept. 18 ***Perf. 11½***

568 A212 5m grn, blk & red 5 5
569 A213 5m grn, blk & red 6 5
570 A212 10m bis, bl & dk grn 12 10
571 A213 10m bis, bl & dk grn 12 10
572 A212 35m dp ultra, red & blk 40 30
573 A213 35m dp ultra, red & blk 40 30
Nos. 568-573 (6) 1.15 90

Issued to commemorate the 38th World Shooting Championships and the First African Table Tennis Tournament. Types A212 and A213 are printed se-tenant at the base in sheets of 70.

Dag Hammarskjold and U.N. Emblem—A214

Perf. 11½x11

1962, Oct. 24 Photo. **Wmk. 342**

Portrait in Slate Blue

574 A214 5m dp lil 5 5
575 A214 10m olive 15 8
576 A214 35m dp ultra 30 30

Issued to honor Dag Hammarskjold, Secretary General of the United Nations, 1953–61, and to commemorate the 17th anniversary of the United Nations.

Queen Nefertari Crowned by Isis and Hathor
A215

1962, Oct. 31 ***Perf. 11½***

577	A215	10m bl & ocher	25	15

Issued to publicize the UNESCO campaign to safeguard the monuments of Nubia.

Jet Trainer, Hawker Hart Biplane and College Emblem
A216

1962. Nov. 2 ***Perf. 11½x11***

578	A216	10m bl, dk bl & crim	12	8

25th anniversary of Air Force College.

14th Century Glass Lamp and "1963"
A217

Yemen Flag and Hand with Torch
A218

1963, Feb. 20 ***Perf. 11x11½***

579	A217	4m dk brn, grn & car	6	5

Issued for use on greeting cards. See also nos. 441, 477.

1963, Mar. 14 Photo. Wmk. 342

580	A218	10m ol & brt car	12	8

Establishment of Yemen Arab Republic.

Tennis Player, Pyramids and Globe
A219

Perf. 11½x11

1963, Mar. 20 **Unwmkd.**

581	A219	10m gray, blk & brn	12	8

Issued to commemorate the International Lawn Tennis Championships, Cairo.

Cow, U.N. and F.A.O. Emblems
A220

Designs: 10m, Corn, wheat and emblems (vert.). 35m, Wheat, corn and emblems.

Perf. 11½x11, 11x11½

1963, Mar. 21 **Wmk. 342**

582	A220	5m vio & dp org	10	5
583	A220	10m ultra & yel	15	10
584	A220	35m bl, yel & blk	35	30

Issued for the "Freedom from Hunger" campaign of the U.N. Food and Agriculture Organization.

Centenary Emblem
A221

Design: 35m, Globe and emblem.

Perf. 11x11½

1963, May 8 **Unwmkd.**

585	A221	10m lt bl, red & mar	10	8
586	A221	35m lt bl & red	30	25

Centenary of the Red Cross.

Arab Socialist Union Emblem
A222

Design: 50m, Tools, torch and symbol of National Charter.

Photogravure

1963, July 23 ***Perf. 11½*** **Wmk. 342**

587	A222	10m sl & rose pink	10	8

Souvenir Sheets

Perf. 11½, Imperf.

588	A222	50m vio bl & org yel	1.00	1.00

Issued to commemorate the 11th anniversary of the revolution and to publicize the Arab Socialist Union. No. 588 contains one stamp, violet blue marginal inscription. Size: 69x80mm.

Television Station, Cairo, and Screen
A223

1963, Aug. 1 ***Perf. 11½x11***

589	A223	10m dk bl & yel	12	8

Issued to publicize the 2nd International Television Festival, Alexandria, Sept. 1–10.

Queen Nefertari
A224

Swimmer and Map of Suez Canal
A225

Designs: 10m, Great Hypostyle Hall, Abu Simbel. 35m, Ramses in moonlight.

Photogravure

1963, Oct. 1 ***Perf. 11*** **Wmk. 342**

Size: 25x42mm. (5m, 35m); 28x61mm. (10m)

590	A224	5m brt vio bl & yel	5	5
591	A224	10m gray, blk & red org	10	8
592	A224	35m org yel & blk	30	28

Issued to publicize the UNESCO world campaign to save historic monuments in Nubia.

1963, Oct. 15

593	A225	10m bl & sal rose	10	8

Issued to commemorate the International Suez Canal Swimming Championship.

Ministry of Agriculture—A226

Perf. 11½x11

1963, Nov. 20 **Wmk. 342**

594	A226	10m multi	10	8

Issued to commemorate the 50th anniversary of the Ministry of Agriculture.

Modern Building and Map of Africa and Asia—A227

1963, Dec. 7

595	A227	10m multi	10	8

Afro-Asian Housing Congress, Dec. 7–12.

Scales, Globe, UN Emblem—A228

1963, Dec. 10

596	A228	5m dk grn & yel	8	5
597	A228	10m bl, gray & blk	15	8
598	A228	35m rose red, pink & red	40	28

Issued to commemorate the 15th anniversary of the Universal Declaration of Human Rights.

Sculpture, Arms of Alexandria and Palette with Flags
A229

1963, Dec. 12 ***Perf. 11x11½***

599	A229	10m pale bl, dk bl & brn	10	8

Issued to publicize the 5th Biennial Exhibition of Fine Arts in Alexandria.

Lion and Nile Hilton Hotel
A230

Vase, 13th Century
A231

Pharaoh Userkaf (5th Dynasty)
A232

Designs: 1m, Vase, 14th century. 2m, Ivory headrest. 3m, Pharaonic calcite boat. 4m, Minaret and gate. 5m, Nile and Aswan High Dam. 10m, Eagle of Saladin over pyramids. 15m, Window, Ibn Tulun's mosque. No 608, Mitwalli Gate, Cairo. 35m, Nefertari. 40m, Tower Hotel. 55m, Sultan Hassan's Mosque. 60m, Courtyard, Al Azhar University. 200m, Head of Ramses II. 500m, Funerary mask of Tutankhamen.

Photogravure

1964–67 ***Perf. 11*** **Unwmkd.**

Size: Nos. 608, 612, 19x24mm.; others, 24x29mm.

600	A231	1m cit & ultra	5	5
601	A230	2m mag & bis	10	5
602	A230	3m sal, org & bl	10	5
603	A235	4m ocher, blk & ultra	25	10
604	A230	5m brn & brt bl	10	10
a.		5m brn & dk bl	10	10
605	A231	10m grn, dk brn & lt brn	10	10
606	A230	15m ultra & yel	10	8
607	A230	20m brn org & blk	15	8
608	A231	20m lt ol grn ('67)	25	8
609	A231	30m yel & brn	35	10
610	A231	35m sal, ocher & ultra	30	10
611	A231	40m ultra & yel	35	10
612	A231	55m brt red lil ('67)	50	20
613	A231	60m grnsh bl & yel brn	45	20

Wmk. 342

614	A232	100m dk vio brn & sl	1.50	25
615	A232	200m bluish blk & yel brn	3.50	50
616	A232	500m ultra & dp org	6.00	1.00
		Nos. 600-616 (17)	14.15	3.14

Nos. 603 and N107 lack the vertically arranged dates which appear at lower right on No. 619.

HSN Commission Emblem
A233

Perf. 11x11½

1964, Jan. 10 Wmk. 342

617 A233 10m dl bl, dk bl & yel 10 5

Issued to commemorate the first conference of the Commission of Health, Sanitation and Nutrition.

Arab League Emblem—A234

1964, Jan. 13 *Perf. 11*

618 A234 10m brt grn & blk 20 10

Issued to commemorate the first meeting of the Heads of State of the Arab League, Cairo, January.

Minaret at Night
A235

1964 *Perf. 11* Unwmkd.

619 A235 4m emer, blk & red 8 5

Issued for use on greeting cards. See also No. 603.

Old and New Dwellings and Map of Nubia—A236

Perf. 11½x11

1964, Feb. 27 Photo. Wmk. 342

620 A236 10m dl vio & yel 10 8

Resettlement of Nubian population.

Map of Africa and Asia and Train
A237

1964, March 21

621 A237 10m dl bl, dk bl & yel 8 8

Asian Railway Conference, Cairo, Mar. 21.

Ikhnaton and Nefertiti with Children
A238

1964, Mar. 21 *Perf. 11x11½*

622 A238 10m dk brn & ultra 8 8

Issued for Arab Mother's Day, March 21.

Arab Postal Union Emblem
A239

World Health Organization Emblem
A240

1964, Apr. 1 Photo. Wmk. 342

623 A239 10m org brn & bl, *sal* 8 8

Issued to commemorate the 10th anniversary of the Permanent Office of the Arab Postal Union.

1964, Apr. 7

624 A240 10m dk bl & red 8 8

World Health Day (Anti-Tuberculosis).

Statue of Liberty, World's Fair Pavilion and Pyramids
A241

1964, Apr. 22 *Perf. 11½x11*

625 A241 10m brt grn & ol, *grysh* 15 15

New York World's Fair, 1964–65.

Nile and Aswan High Dam
A242

1964, May 15 *Perf. 11½* Unwmkd.

626 A242 10m blk & bl 8 8

The diversion of the Nile.

"Land Reclamation"—A243

Design: No. 628, "Electricity," Aswan High Dam hydroelectric station.

1964, July 23 *Perf. 11½*

627 A243 10m yel & emer 8 8
628 A243 10m grn & blk 8 8

Issued to publicize land reclamation and hydroelectric power due to the Aswan High Dam.

An imperf. souvenir sheet, issued July 23, contains two 50m black and blue stamps showing Aswan High Dam before and after diversion of the Nile. Black portrait of President Nasser and blue inscription in margin. Size of stamps: 42x26 mm.; size of sheet: 104x81mm. Price $2.25.

Map of Africa and 34 Flags
A244

1964, July 17 Photogravure

629 A244 10m brn, brt bl & blk 8 8

Issued to commemorate the Assembly of Heads of State and Government of the Organization for African Unity at Cairo in July.

Jamboree Emblem—A245

Design: No. 631, Emblem of Air Scouts.

1964, Aug. 28 *Perf. 11½* Unwmkd.

630 A245 10m red, grn & blk 12 8
631 A245 10m grn & red 12 8

The 6th Pan Arab Jamboree, Alexandria.

Flag of Algeria—A246

1964, Sept. 5 *Perf. 11½x11*

Flags in Original Colors

632 A246 10m grn (*Algeria*) 25 12
633 A246 10m grn (*Iraq*) 25 12
634 A246 10m grn (*Jordan*) 25 12
635 A246 10m grn (*Kuwait*) 25 12
636 A246 10m grn (*Lebanon*) 25 12
637 A246 10m grn (*Libya*) 25 12
638 A246 10m grn (*Morocco*) 25 12
639 A246 10m grn (*Saudi Arabia*) 25 12
640 A246 10m bl (*Sudan*) 25 12
641 A246 10m grn (*Syria*) 25 12
642 A246 10m grn (*Tunisia*) 25 12
643 A246 10m grn (*U.A.R.*) 25 12
644 A246 10m grn (*Yemen*) 25 12
Nos. 632-644 (13) 3.25 1.56

Issued to commemorate the second meeting of the Heads of State of the Arab League, Alexandria, Sept. 1964.

World Map, Dove, Olive Branches and Pyramids—A247

1964, Oct. 5 *Perf. 11½*

645 A247 10m sl bl & yel 8 8

Issued to commemorate the Conference of Heads of State of Non-Aligned Countries, Cairo, Oct. 1964.

Pharaonic Athletes—A248

Designs from ancient decorations: 10m, Four athletes (vert.). 35m, Wrestlers (vert.). 50m, Pharaoh in chariot hunting.

Perf. 11½x11, 11x11½

1964, Oct. 10 Photo. Unwmkd.

Sizes: 39x22mm., 22x39mm.

646 A248 5m lt grn & org 5 5
647 A248 10m sl bl & lt brn 8 8
648 A248 35m dl vio & lt brn 38 35

Size: 58x24mm.

649 A248 50m ultra & brn org 40 40

18th Olympic Games Tokyo, Oct. 10–25.

Emblem, Map of Africa and Asia
A249

Map of Africa, Communication Symbols
A250

1964, Oct. 10 *Perf. 11x11½*

650 A249 10m vio & yel 8 8

First Afro-Asian Medical Congress.

1964, Oct. 24

651 A250 10m grn & blk 8 8

Issued to commemorate the Pan-African and Malagasy Posts and Telecommunications Congress, Cairo, Oct. 24–Nov. 6.

Horus and Façade of Nefertari Temple, Abu Simbel—A251

Ramses II
A252

Designs: 35m, A god holding rope of life, Abu Simbel. 50m, Isis of Kalabsha (horiz.).

1964, Oct. 24 ***Perf. 11½, 11x11½***

652 A251 5m grnsh bl & yel brn 15 15
653 A252 10m sep & brt yel 30 15
654 A251 35m brn org & ind 75 50

Souvenir Sheet
Imperf.

655 A252 50m ol & vio blk 1.00 1.00

Issued to publicize the "Save the Monuments of Nubia" campaign. No. 655 contains one horizontal stamp; violet black and olive marginal inscription. Size: 106x63mm.

Emblems of Cooperation, Rural Handicraft and Women's Work
A253

Perf. 11½x11

1964, Dec. 8 **Photo.** **Unwmkd.**

656 A253 10m yel & dk bl 8 8

Issued to commemorate the 25th anniversary of the Ministry of Social Affairs.

United Nations and UNESCO Emblems, Pyramids
A254

Minaret, Mardani Mosque
A255

1964, Dec. 24 ***Perf. 11x11½***

657 A254 10m ultra & yel 8 8

Issued for UNESCO Day.

1965, Jan. 20 **Photo.** ***Perf. 11***

658 A255 4m bl & dk brn 5 5

Issued for use on greeting cards.

Police Emblem over City
A256

Oil Derrick and Emblem
A257

Perf. 11x11½

1965, Jan. 25 **Wmk. 342**

659 A256 10m blk & yel 8 8

Issued for Police Day.

1965, Mar. 16 **Photogravure**

660 A257 10m dk brn & yel 8 8

Issued to publicize the 5th Arab Petroleum Congress and the 2nd Arab Petroleum Exhibition.

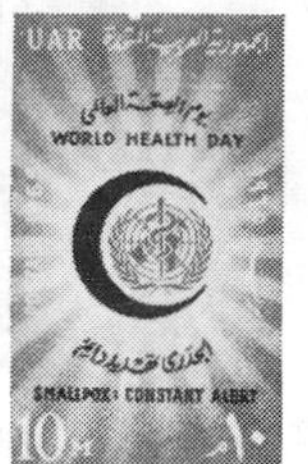

Flags and Emblem of the Arab League
A258

Red Crescent and WHO Emblem
A259

Design: 20m, Arab League emblem (horiz.).

1965, Mar. 22 **Wmk. 342**

661 A258 10m grn, red & blk 15 15
662 A258 20m ultra & brn 16 15

20th anniversary of the Arab League.

1965, Apr. 7 **Photogravure**

663 A259 10m bl & crim 8 8

Issued to commemorate World Health Day (Smallpox: Constant Alert).

Dagger in Map of Palestine
A260

1965, Apr. 9 ***Perf. 11x11½***

664 A260 10m blk & red 50 25

Deir Yassin massacre, Apr. 9, 1948.

ITU Emblem, Old and New Communication Equipment
A261

1965, May 17 ***Perf. 11½x11***

665 A261 5m vio blk & yel 5 5
666 A261 10m red & yel 8 5
667 A261 35m dk bl, ultra & yel 28 25

Issued to commemorate the centenary of the International Telecommunication Union.

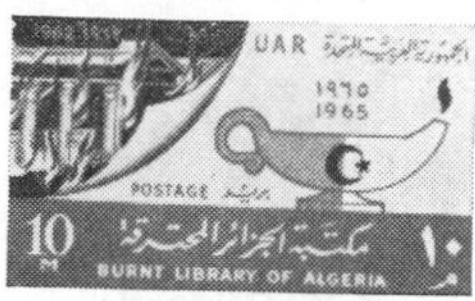

Library Aflame and Lamp
A262

1965, June 7 **Photo.** **Wmk. 342**

668 A262 10m blk, grn & red 8 5

Issued to commemorate the burning of the Library of Algiers, June 7, 1962.

Sheik Mohammed Abdo
A263

1965, July 11 ***Perf. 11x11½***

669 A263 10m Prus bl & bis brn 6 5

Issued to commemorate the 60th anniversary of the death of Mohammed Abdo (1850–1905), Mufti of Egypt.

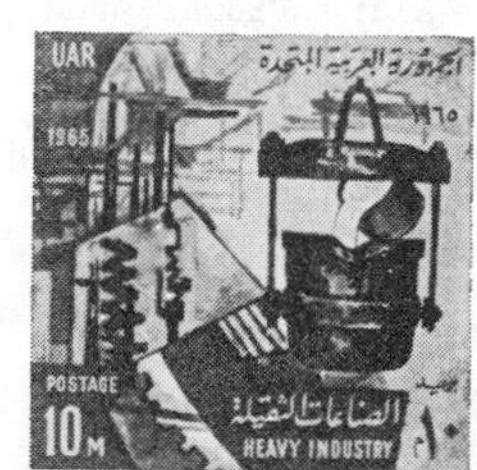

Pouring Ladle (Heavy Industry)
A264

President Gamal Abdel Nasser and Emblems of Arab League, African Unity Organization, Afro-Asian Countries and United Nations
A265

1965, July 23 ***Perf. 11½***

Designs: No. 670, Search for off-shore oil. No. 672, Housing, construction in Nassar City (diamond shaped).

670 A264 10m ind & lt bl 15 10
671 A264 10m brn & yel 15 10
672 A264 10m yel brn & blk 15 10
673 A265 100m lt grn & blk 2.50 1.75

13th anniversary of the revolution.

The 100m was printed in sheets of six, consisting of two singles and two vertical pairs. Margins and gutters contain multiple UAR coat of arms in light green. Size: 240x330mm.

4th Pan Arab Games Emblem
A266

Map and Emblems of Previous Games
A267

Designs: No. 675, Swimmers Zeitun and Abd el Gelil and arms of Alexandria. 35m, Race horse "Saadoon."

Perf. 11½x11; 11½ (#676)

1965, Sept. 2 **Photo.** **Wmk. 342**

674 A266 5m bl & red 5 5
675 A266 10m dp bl & dk brn 15 10
676 A267 10m org brn & dp bl 15 10
677 A266 35m grn & brn 28 25

Issued to publicize the 4th Pan Arab Games, Cairo, Sept. 2–11. No. 675 commemorates the long-distance swimming competition at Alexandria, a part of the Games.

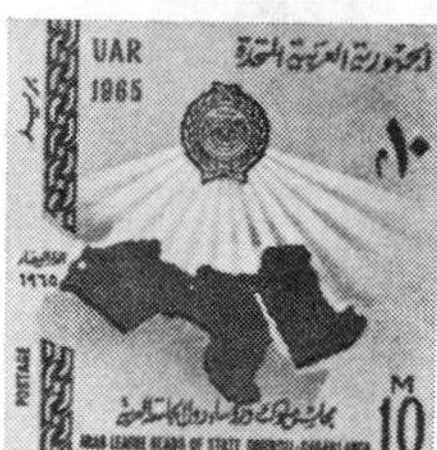

Map of Arab Countries, Emblem of Arab League and Broken Chain—A268

1965, Sept. 13 **Photo.** ***Perf. 11½***

678 A268 10m brn & yel 6 5

Issued to commemorate the Third Arab Summit Conference, Casablanca, Sept. 13.

Land Forces Emblem and Sun
A269

Perf. 11x11½

1965, Oct. 20 Wmk. 342

679 A269 10m bis brn & blk 6 5

Issued for Land Forces Day.

Map of Africa, Torch and Olive Branches—A270

1965, Oct. 21 ***Perf. 11½***

680 A270 10m dl pur & car rose 6 5

Issued to commemorate the Assembly of Heads of State of the Organization for African Unity.

Ramses II, Abu Simbel, and ICY Emblem
A271

Pillars, Philae, and U.N. Emblem
A272

Designs: 35m, Two Ramses II statues, Abu Simbel and UNESCO emblem. 50m, Cartouche of Ramses II and ICY emblem (horiz.).

Photogravure

1965, Oct. 24 ***Perf. 11½*** **Wmk. 342**

681	A271	5m yel & sl grn	10	10
682	A272	10m bl & blk	35	15
683	A271	35m dk vio & yel	75	25

Souvenir Sheet

Imperf.

684 A272 50m brt ultra & dk brn 1.25 1.00

Issued to publicize the international cooperation in saving the Nubian monuments. No. 684 also commemorates the 20th anniversary of the United Nations. No. 684 contains one stamp (42x25m.) and has marginal inscription in bright ultramarine and dark brown. Size: 105x63mm.

Al-Maqrizi, Buildings and Books
A273

Perf. 11½x11

1965, Nov. 20 Photo. Wmk. 342

685 A273 10m ol & dk sl grn 6 5

Issued to commemorate the 600th anniversary of the birth of Ahmed Al-Maqrizi (1365-1443), historian.

Flag of U.A.R., Arms of Alexandria and Art Symbols—A274

1965, Dec. 16 ***Perf. 11x11½***

686 A274 10m multi 6 5

Issued to publicize the 6th Biennial Exhibition of Fine Arts in Alexandria, Dec. 16, 1965–March 31, 1966.

Parchment Letter, Carrier Pigeon and Postrider—A275

1966, Jan. 2 ***Perf. 11½*** **Wmk. 342**

687 A275 10m multi 10 10

Post Day, Jan. 2. See Nos. CB1–CB2.

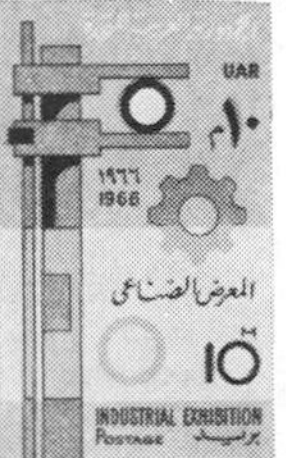

Lamp and Arch
A276

Exhibition Poster
A277

1966, Jan. 10 ***Perf. 11*** **Unwmkd.**

688 A276 4m vio & dp org 5 5

Issued for use on greeting cards.

Perf. 11x11½

1966, Jan. 27 Wmk. 342

689 A277 10m lt bl & blk 6 5

Industrial Exhibition, Jan. 29–Feb.

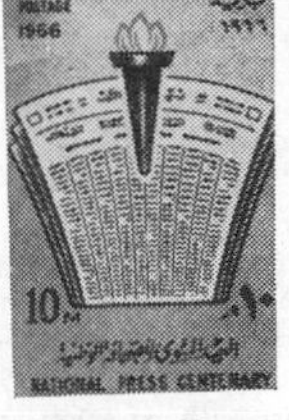

Arab League Emblem
A278

Printed Page and Torch
A279

1966, March 22 Photo. Wmk. 342

690 A278 10m brt yel & pur 6 5

Arab Publicity Week, March 22–28.

1966, March 25 ***Perf. 11x11½***

691 A279 10m dp org & sl bl 6 5

Centenary of the national press.

Traffic Signal at Night
A280

Hands Holding Torch, Flags of U.A.R. and Iraq
A281

1966, May 4 Photo. Wmk. 342

692 A280 10m grn & red 6 5

Issued for Traffic Day.

1966. May 26 ***Perf. 11x11½***

693 A281 10m dp cl, rose red & brt grn 6 5

Friendship between U.A.R. and Iraq.

Workers and U.N. Emblem
A282

Perf. 11½x11

1966, June 1 Photo. Wmk. 342

694	A282	5m bl grn & blk	5	5
695	A282	10m brt rose lil & grn	10	5
696	A282	35m org & blk	35	25

Issued to commemorate the 50th session of the International Labor Organization.

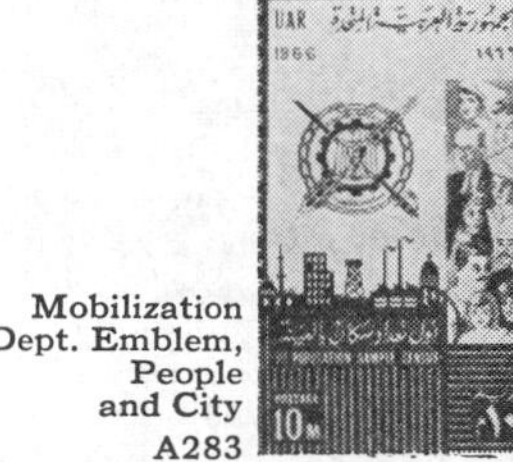

Mobilization Dept. Emblem, People and City
A283

1966, June 30 ***Perf. 11x11½***

697 A283 10m dl pur & brn 10 5

Population sample, May 31–June 16.

"Salah el Din," Crane and Cogwheel
A284

Present-day Basket Dance and Pharaonic Dance—A285

Designs: No. 699, Transfer of first stones of Abu Simbel. No. 700, Development of Sinai (map of Red Sea area and Sinai Peninsula). No. 701, El Maadi Hospital and nurse with patient.

Perf. 11½

1966, July 23 Photo. Wmk. 342

698	A284	10m org & multi	12	10
699	A284	10m brt grn & multi	12	10
700	A284	10m yel & multi	12	10
701	A284	10m lt bl & multi	12	10

Souvenir Sheet

Imperf.

702 A285 100m multi 1.25 1.00

Issued to commemorate the 14th anniversary of the revolution. No. 702 contains one stamp. Size: 115x67mm.

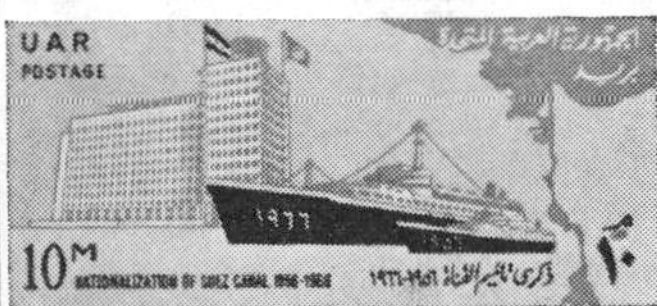

Suez Canal Headquarters, Ships and Map of Canal—A286

1966, July 26 ***Perf. 11½***

703 A286 10m bl & crim 20 10

Issued to commemorate the 10th anniversary of the nationalization of the Suez Canal.

Cotton, Farmers with Plow and Tractor
A287

Designs: 10m, Rice. 35m, Onions.

Perf. 11½x11

1966, Sept. 9 Photo. Wmk. 342

704	A287	5m pur & lt bl	5	5
705	A287	10m emer & yel brn	10	10
706	A287	35m bl & org	28	25

Issued for Farmer's Day.

WHO Headquarters, Geneva
A288

Designs: 10m, U.N. refugee emblem. 35m, UNICEF emblem.

Perf. 11½x11

1966. Oct. 24 Wmk. 342

707	A288	5m ol & brt pur	5	5
708	A288	10m org & brt pur	10	10
709	A288	35m lt bl & brt pur	28	25

21st anniversary of the United Nations.

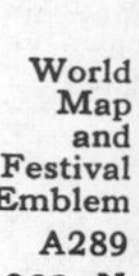

World Map and Festival Emblem
A289

1966, Nov. 8 Photogravure

710	A289	10m brt pur & yel	6	5

Issued to publicize the 5th International Television Festival, Nov. 1-10.

Arms of UAR, Rocket and Pylon
A290

1966, Dec. 23 *Perf. 11½* Wmk. 342

711	A290	10m brt grn & car rose	10	10

Issued for Victory Day.

Jackal
A291

Design: 35m, Alabaster head from Tutankhamen treasure.

1967, Jan. 2 Photogravure

712	A291	10m sl, yel & brn	75	20
713	A291	35m bl, dk vio & ocher	1.40	45

Issued for Post Day, Jan. 2.

Carnations
A292

Workers Planting Tree
A293

1967, Jan. 10 *Perf. 11* Unwmkd.

714	A292	4m cit & pur	5	5

Issued for use on greeting cards.

Perf. 11x11½

1967, Mar. 15 Wmk. 342

715	A293	10m brt grn & blk vio	10	5

Issued to publicize the Tree Festival.

Gamal el-Dine el-Afaghani and Arab League Emblem
A294

1967, Mar. 22 Photo. Wmk. 342

716	A294	10m dp grn & dk brn	10	5

Arab Publicity Week, March 22-28.

Census Emblem, Man, Woman and Factory—A295

1967, Apr. 23 *Perf. 11½x11*

717	A295	10m blk & dp org	10	5

First industrial census.

Brickmaking Fresco, Tomb of Rekhmire, Thebes, 1504-1450 B.C.—A296

1967, May 1 Photo. Wmk. 342

718	A296	10m ol & org	10	5

Issued for Labor Day, 1967.

Ramses II and Queen Nefertari
A297

Design: 35m, Shooting geese, frieze from tomb of Atet at Meidum, c. 2724 B. C.

Perf. 11½x11

1967, June 7 Photo. Wmk. 342

719	A297	10m multi	50	20
720	A297	35m dk grn & org	75	45
		Nos. 719-720, C113-C115 (5)	4.25	1.85

Issued for International Tourist Year, 1967.

President Nasser, Crowd and Map of Palestine
A298

1967, June 22 *Perf. 11½*

721	A298	10m dp org, yel & ol	45	30

Issued to publicize Arab solidarity for "the defense of Palestine."

Souvenir Sheet

National Products—A299

1967, July 23 *Imperf.* Wmk. 342

722	A299	100m multi	1.00	90

Issued to commemorate the 15th anniversary of the revolution. No. 722 contains one stamp with yellow, green and brown margin. Size: 111½x66mm.

Salama Higazi
A300

Perf. 11x11½

1967, Oct. 14 Photo. Wmk. 342

723	A300	20m brn & dk bl	12	8

Issued to commemorate the 50th anniversary of the death of Salama Higazi, pioneer of Egyptian lyric stage.

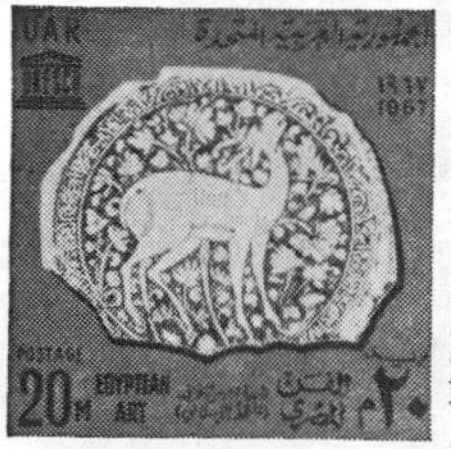

Stag on Ceramic Disk
A301

Design: 55m, Apse showing Christ in Glory, Madonna and Saints, Coptic Museum, and UNESCO Emblem.

1967, Oct. 24 *Perf. 11½*

724	A301	20m dl rose & dk bl	15	10
725	A301	55m dk sl grn & yel	50	30

Issued to commemorate the 22nd anniversary of the United Nations. See No. C117.

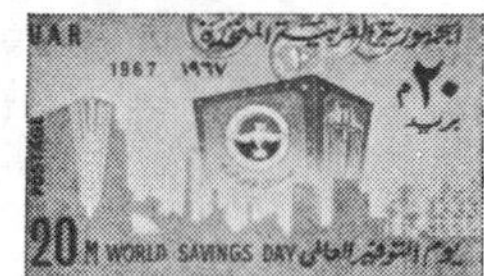

Savings Bank and Postal Authority Emblems—A302

1967, Oct. 31 *Perf. 11½x11*

726	A302	20m sal pink & dk bl	12	8

International Savings Day.

Rose
A303

Photogravure

1967, Dec. 15 *Perf. 11* Unwmkd.

727	A303	5m grn & rose lil	5	5

Issued for use on greeting cards.

Pharaonic Dress
A304

Aswan High Dam and Power Lines
A305

Designs: Various pharaonic dresses from temple decorations.

Perf 11x11¼

1968, Jan. 2 Wmk. 342

728	A304	20m brn, grn & buff	50	15
729	A304	55m lt grn, yel & sep	1.10	35
730	A304	80m dk brn, bl & brt rose	1.50	75

Issued for Post Day, Jan. 2.

1968, Jan. 9

731	A305	20m yel, bl & dk brn	10	8

Issued to commemorate the first electricity generated by the Aswan Hydroelectric Station.

Alabaster Vessel, Tutankhamen Treasure
A306

Girl, Moon and Paint Brushes
A308

Capital of Coptic Limestone Pillar
A307

Perf. 11x11½, 11½

1968, Jan. 20 Photo. Wmk. 342

732	A306	20m dk ultra, yel & brn	15	10
733	A307	80m lt grn, dk pur & ol grn	40	35

2nd International Festival of Museums.

1968, Feb. 15 ***Perf. 11x11½***

734	A308	20m brt bl & blk	10	8

Issued to publicize the 7th Biennial Exhibition of Fine Arts, Alexandria, Feb. 15.

Cattle and Veterinarian
A309

Perf. 11½x11

1968, May 4 Photo. **Wmk. 342**

735	A309	20m brn, yel & grn	10	8

8th Arab Veterinary Congress, Cairo.

Human Rights Flame
A310

Perf. 11x11½

1968, July 1 Photo. **Wmk. 342**

736	A310	20m cit, crim & grn	15	8
737	A310	60m sky bl, crim & grn	40	30

International Human Rights Year, 1968.

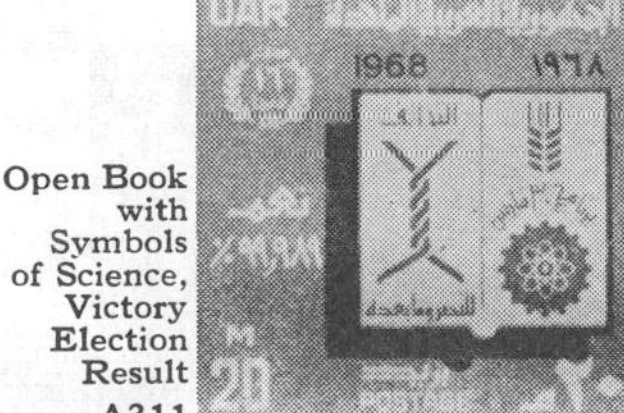

Open Book with Symbols of Science, Victory Election Result
A311

Workers, Cogwheel with Coat of Arms and Open Book
A312

1968, July 23 ***Perf. 11½***

738	A311	20m rose red & sl grn	12	8

Souvenir Sheet
Imperf.

739	A312	10m lt grn, org & pur	1.00	1.00

16th anniversary of the revolution.
No. 739 has orange marginal inscription and the ornaments. Size: 116x68mm.

Imhotep and WHO Emblem—A313

Design: No. 741, Avicenna and WHO emblem.

Perf. 11½x11

1968, Sept. 1 Photo. **Wmk. 342**

740	A313	20m bl, yel & brn	30	10
741	A313	20m yel, bl & brn	30	10

Issued to commemorate the 20th anniversary of the World Health Organization. Nos. 740–741 printed in checkerboard sheets of 50 (5x10).

Table Tennis
A314

Perf. 11x11½

1968, Sept. 20 Photo. **Wmk. 342**

742	A314	20m lt grn & dk brn	12	8

First Mediterranean Table Tennis Tournament, Alexandria, Sept. 20–27.

Factories and Fair Emblem
A315

1968, Oct. 20 ***Perf. 11½*** **Wmk. 342**

743	A315	20m bl gray, red & sl bl	12	8

Cairo International Industrial Fair.

Temples of Philae—A316

Refugees, Map of Palestine, Refugee Year Emblem
A317

Design: 55m, Temple at Philae and UNESCO emblem.

1968, Oct. 24 **Photogravure**

744	A316	20m multi	12	8
745	A317	30m multi	1.00	20
746	A317	55m lt bl, yel & blk	50	26

Issued for United Nations Day, Oct. 24.

Egyptian Boy Scout Emblem
A318

1968, Nov. 1

747	A318	10m dl org & vio bl	25	10

50th anniversary of Egyptian Boy Scouts.

Pharaonic Sports
A319

Design: 30m, Pharaonic sports (different).

1968, Nov. 1

748	A319	20m pale ol, pale sal & blk	12	8
749	A319	30m pale bl, buff & pur	18	15

Issued to commemorate the 19th Olympic Games, Mexico City, Oct. 12–27.

Aly Moubarak
A320

Lotus
A321

1968, Nov. 9 ***Perf. 11½***

750	A320	20m grn, brn & bis	25	8

Issued to honor Aly Moubarak (1823–1893), founder of the modern educational system in Egypt.

1968, Dec. 11 Photo. **Wmk. 342**

751	A321	5m brt bl, grn & yel	30	15

Issued for use on greeting cards.

Son of Ramses III
A322

Hefni Nassef
A323

Pharaonic Dress: No. 753, Ramses III. No. 754, Girl carrying basket on her head. 55m, Queen of the New Empire in transparent dress.

1969, Jan. 2 Photo. ***Perf. 11½***

752	A322	5m bl & multi	50	25
753	A322	20m bl & multi	75	50
754	A322	20m bl & multi	1.00	75
755	A322	55m bl & multi	70	35

Issued for Post Day, Jan. 2.

Perf. 11x11½

1969, Mar. 2 Photo. **Wmk. 342**

Portrait: No. 757, Mohammed Farid.

756	A323	20m pur & brn	30	10
757	A323	20m emer & brn	30	10

Issued to commemorate the 50th anniversaries of the death of Hefni Nassef (1860–1919) writer and government worker, and of Mohammed Farid (1867–1919), lawyer and Speaker of the Nationalist Party. Nos. 756–757 printed se-tenant in sheets of 50 (10x5).

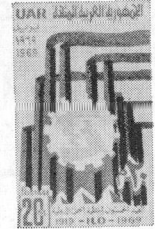

Teacher and Children
A324

ILO Emblem and Factory Chimneys
A325

1969, Mar. 2 ***Perf. 11x11½***

758	A324	20m multi	25	8

Arab Teacher's Day.

1969, Apr. 11 Photo. **Wmk. 342**

759	A325	20m brn, ultra & car	25	8

Issued to commemorate the 50th anniversary of the International Labor Organization.

Flag of Algeria, Africa Day and Tourist Year Emblems—A326

Wmk. 342

1969, May 25 Litho. ***Perf. 11½x11***

760	A326	10m grn (*Algeria*)	30	20
761	A326	10m grn (*Botswana*)	50	30
762	A326	10m grn (*Burundi*)	50	30
763	A326	10m grn (*Cameroun*)	50	30
764	A326	10m bl (*Cent. Afr. Rep.*)	50	30
765	A326	10m bl (*Chad*)	50	30
766	A326	10m grn (*Congo, ex-Belgian*)	50	30
767	A326	10m grn (*Congo, ex-French*)	50	30
768	A326	10m grn (*Dahomey*)	50	30
769	A326	10m bl (*Equatorial Guinea*)	50	30
770	A326	10m bl (*Ethiopia*)	50	30
771	A326	10m bl (*Gabon*)	50	30
772	A326	10m grn (*Gambia*)	50	30
773	A326	10m grn (*Ghana*)	50	30
774	A326	10m grn (*Guinea*)	50	30
775	A326	10m grn (*Ivory Coast*)	50	30
776	A326	10m grn (*Kenya*)	50	30
777	A326	10m grn (*Lesotho*)	50	30
778	A326	10m bl (*Liberia*)	50	30
779	A326	10m grn (*Libya*)	50	30
780	A326	10m grn (*Malagasy*)	50	30
781	A326	10m grn (*Malawi*)	50	30
782	A326	10m grn (*Mali*)	50	30
783	A326	10m grn (*Mauritania*)	50	30
784	A326	10m bl (*Mauritius*)	50	30
785	A326	10m grn (*Morocco*)	50	30
786	A326	10m grn (*Niger*)	50	30
787	A326	10m grn (*Nigeria*)	50	30
788	A326	10m grn (*Rwanda*)	50	30
789	A326	10m grn (*Senegal*)	50	30
790	A326	10m grn (*Sierra Leone*)	50	30
791	A326	10m grn (*Somalia*)	50	30
792	A326	10m bl (*Sudan*)	50	30
793	A326	10m vio (*Swaziland*)	50	30
794	A326	10m bl (*Tanzania*)	50	30
795	A326	10m grn (*Togo*)	50	30
796	A326	10m grn (*Tunisia*)	50	30
797	A326	10m blk (*Uganda*)	50	30
798	A326	10m grn (*U.A.R.*)	50	30
799	A326	10m grn (*Upper Volta*)	50	30
800	A326	10m bl (*Zambia*)	50	30
		Nos. 760-800 (41)	20.30	12.20

El Fetouh Gate, Cairo
A327

Sculptures from the Egyptian Museum, Cairo—A328

Millenary of Cairo—A329

Designs: No. 802, Al Azhar University. No. 803, The Citadel. No. 805, Sculptures, Coptic Museum. No. 806, Glass plate and vase, Fatimid dynasty, Islamic Museum. No. 807a, Islamic coin. No. 807b, Fatimist era jewelry. No. 807c, Copper vase. No. 807d, Coins and plaque.

Perf. 11½x11

1969, July 23 Photo. Wmk. 342

801 A327 10m dk brn & multi 25 5
802 A327 10m grn & multi 25 5
803 A327 10m bl & multi 25 5

Perf. 11½

804 A328 20m yel grn & multi 60 10
805 A328 20m dp ultra & multi 60 10
806 A328 20m brn & multi 60 10
Nos. 801-806 (6) 2.55 45

Souvenir Sheet

807 A329 Souv. sheet of 4 5.00 5.00
a. 20m dk bl & multi 18 12
b. 20m lil & multi 18 12
c. 20m yel & multi 18 12
d. 20m dk grn & multi 18 12

Issued to commemorate the millenium of the founding of Cairo. No. 807 has pale lilac margin and dark blue inscription. Size: 128x70mm.

African Development Bank Emblem
A330

Perf. 11x11½

1969, Sept. 10 Photo. Wmk. 342

808 A330 20m emer, yel & vio 25 8

Issued to publicize the 5th anniversary of the African Development Bank.

Pharaonic Boat and UN Emblem
A331

Temple of Philae Inundated and UNESCO Emblem
A332

Design: 5m, King and Queen from Abu Simbel Temple and UNESCO Emblem (size: 21x38mm.).

Perf. 11x11½, 11½x11

1969, Oct. 24 Photo. Wmk. 342

809 A332 5m brn & multi 8 5
810 A331 20m yel & ultra 30 10

Perf. 11½

811 A332 55m yel & multi 50 25

Issued for United Nations Day.

Ships of 1869 and 1967 and Maps of Africa and Suez Canal—A333

1969, Nov. 15 ***Perf. 11½x11***

812 A333 20m lt bl & multi 25 8

Centenary of the Suez Canal.

Cairo Opera House and Performance of Aida—A334

1969, Nov. 15

813 A334 20m multi 25 8

Centenary of the Cairo Opera House.

Crowd with Egyptian and Revolutionary Flags—A335

1969, Nov. 15 ***Perf. 11½x11***

814 A335 20m brt grn, dl lil & red 25 8

Revolution of 1919.

Ancient Arithmetic and Computer Cards—A336

Perf. 11½x11

1969, Dec. 17 Photo. Wmk. 342

815 A336 20m multi 25 8

Issued to publicize the International Congress for Scientific Accounting, Cairo, Dec. 17–19.

Poinsettia
A337

Sakkara Step Pyramid
A338

El Fetouh Gate, Cairo
A339

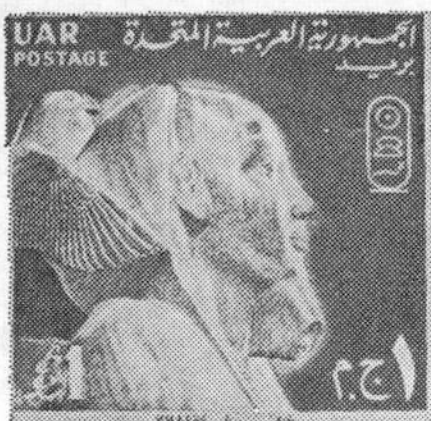

Fountain, Sultan Hassan Mosque, Cairo
A340

King Khafre (Ruled c. 2850 B.C.)
A341

1969, Dec. 24 ***Perf. 11*** **Unwmkd.**

816 A337 5m yel, grn & car 5 5

Issued for use on greeting cards.

Photo.; Engr. (20m, 55m)

Unwmkd.; Wmk. 342 (20m, £1)

1969–70 ***Perf. 11***

Designs: 5m, Al Azhar Mosque. 10m, Luxor Temple. 50m, Qaitbay Fort, Alexandria.

817 A338 1m multi ('70) 10 5
818 A338 5m multi ('70) 15 5
819 A338 10m multi ('70) 25 5
820 A339 20m dk brn 50 8
821 A338 50m multi ('70) 75 20
822 A340 55m sl grn 1.00 22

Perf. 11½

Photo. and Engr.

823 A341 £1 org & sl grn ('70) 8.50 4.00
Nos. 817-823 (7) 11.25 4.65

See Nos. 889–891, 893–897, 899, 901–902, 904.

Veiled Women, by Mahmoud Said
A342

Perf. 11x11½

1970, Jan. 2 Photo. Wmk. 342

Size: 45x89mm.

824 A342 100m bl & multi 1.75 45

Post Day, Jan. 2. Sheet of 8 with two panes of 4.

Parliament, Scales, Globe and Laurel—A343

1970, Feb. 2 ***Perf. 11½x11***

825 A343 20m bl, vio bl & ocher 25 8

Issued to publicize the International Conference of Parliamentarians on the Middle East Crisis, Cairo, Feb. 2–5.

Map of Arab League Countries, Flag and Emblem—A344

Perf. 11½x11

1970, Mar. 22 Photo. Wmk. 342

826 A344 30m brn org, grn & dk pur 25 12

Issued to commemorate the 25th anniversary of the Arab League. See No. B42.

Mena House and Sheraton Hotel
A345

1970, Mar. 23

827 A345 20m ol, org & bl 25 8

Issued to commemorate the centenary of Mena House and the inauguration of the Cairo Sheraton Hotel.

Manufacture of Medicine—A346

1970, Apr. 20

828	A346	20m brn, yel & bl	25	8

Issued to commemorate the 30th anniversary of the production of medicines in Egypt.

Mermaid
A347

1970, Apr. 20 *Perf. 11x11½*

829	A347	20m org, blk & ultra	25	8

Issued to publicize the 8th Biennial Exhibition of Fine Arts, Alexandria, March 12.

Misr Bank and Talaat Harb
A348

ITU Emblem
A349

1970, May 7 Photo. **Wmk. 342**

830	A348	20m multi	25	8

50th anniversary of Misr Bank.

1970, May 17 *Perf. 11x11½*

831	A349	20m dk brn, yel & dl bl	25	8

World Telecommunications Day.

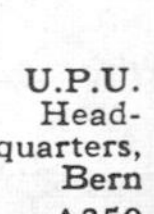

U.P.U. Headquarters, Bern
A350

1970, May 20 *Perf. 11½x11*

832	A350	20m multi	25	8

Issued to commemorate the inauguration of the new Universal Postal Union Headquarters in Bern. See No. C128.

Basketball Player and Map of Africa
A351

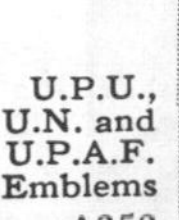

U.P.U., U.N. and U.P.A.F. Emblems
A352

Designs: No. 834, Soccer player, map of Africa and cup (horiz.).

Perf. 11x11½, 11½x11

1970, May 25 Photo. **Wmk. 342**

833	A351	20m lt bl, yel & brn	30	8
834	A351	20m yel & multi	30	8
835	A352	20m ocher, grn & blk	30	8

Issued for Africa Day. No. 833 also commemorates the 5th African basketball championship for men; No. 834 the annual African Soccer championship and No. 835 publicizes the African Postal Union seminar.

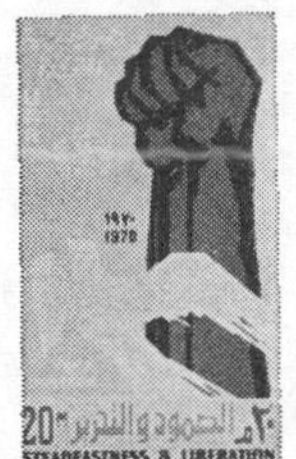

Fist and Freed Bird
A353

1970, July 23 Photo. *Perf. 11*

836	A353	20m lt grn, org & blk	25	8

Souvenir Sheet
Imperf.

837	A353	100m lt bl, dp org & blk	1.00	45

Issued to commemorate the 18th anniversary of the revolution. No. 837 contains one stamp; U.N. emblem, Scales of Justice and orange commemorative inscription in margin. Size: 110x70mm.

Al Aqsa Mosque on Fire—A354

1970, Aug. 21 *Perf. 11* **Wmk. 342**

838	A354	20m multi	30	8
839	A354	60m brt bl & multi	60	24

First anniversary of the burning of Al Aqsa Mosque, Jerusalem.

Standardization Emblems
A355

1970, Oct. 14 *Perf. 11* **Wmk. 342**

840	A355	20m yel, ultra & grn	25	8

Issued to commemorate World Standards Day and the 25th anniversary of the International Standardization Organization, ISO.

U.N. Emblem, Scales and Dove
A356

Temple at Philae
A357

Child, Education Year and U.N. Emblems
A358

Designs: 10m, U.N. emblem. No. 845, Second Temple at Philae (denomination at left).

Perf. 11 (5m), 11½ (others)

1970, Oct. 24 Photo. **Wmk. 342**

841	A356	5m lt bl, rose lil & sl	10	10
842	A357	10m yel, brn & lt bl	15	10
843	A358	20m sl & multi	25	15
844	A357	55m brn, bl & ocher	45	25
845	A357	55m brn, bl & ocher	45	25
		Strip of 3 (#842,844-845)	1.05	60
		Nos. 841-845, B43 (6)	2.90	1.60

Issued to commemorate the 25th anniversary of the United Nations. No. 843 also commemorates International Education Year; Nos. 842, 844–845 commemorate the work of UNESCO in saving the Temples of Philae; Nos. 842, 844–845 printed se-tenant in sheets of 35 (15 No. 842 and 10 each Nos. 844–845). Nos. 844–845 show continuous picture of the Temples at Philae.

Gamal Abdel Nasser
A359

1970, Nov. 6 *Perf. 11* **Wmk. 342**

846	A359	5m sky bl & blk	10	5
847	A359	20m gray grn & blk	25	8

Issued in memory of Gamal Abdel Nasser (1918–1970), President of Egypt. See Nos. C129–C130.

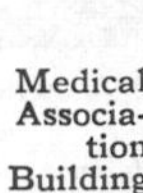

Medical Association Building
A360

Designs: No. 849, Old and new National Library. No. 850, Egyptian Credo (Nasser quotation). No. 851, Engineering Society, old and new buildings. No. 852, Government Printing Offices, old and new buildings.

1970, Dec. 20 Photo. *Perf. 11*

848	A360	20m yel, grn & brn	30	8
849	A360	20m grn & multi	30	8
850	A360	20m lt bl & brn	30	8
851	A360	20m bl, yel & brn	30	8
852	A360	20m bl, yel & brn	30	8
		Nos. 848-852 (5)	1.50	40

Nos. 848–852 printed se-tenant in sheets of 50 (5x10) commemorate: 50th anniversary of Egyptian Medical Association (No. 848); centenary of National Library (No. 849); Egyptian Engineering Association (No. 851) sesquicentennial of Government Printing Offices (No. 852).

Map and Flags of UAR, Libya, Sudan
A361

1970, Dec. 27 *Perf. 11½*

853	A361	20m lt grn, car & blk	25	8

Signing of the Charter of Tripoli affirming the unity of UAR, Libya and the Sudan, Dec. 27, 1970.

Qalawun Minaret
A362

Designs (Minarets): 10m, As Saleh. 20m, Isna. 55m, Al Hakim.

1971, Jan. 2 *Perf. 11* **Wmk. 342**

854	A362	5m grn & multi	45	15
855	A362	10m grn & multi	1.25	20
856	A362	20m grn & multi	2.50	25
857	A362	55m grn & multi	4.25	60
		Strip of 4 (#854-857) + label	10.00	1.50

Post Day, 1971. Nos. 854–857 printed se-tenant in sheets of 40 stamps and 10 blue and yellow labels.
See Nos. 905–908, 932–935.

Gamal Abdel Nasser
A363

Photogravure and Engraved

1971 *Perf. 11½* **Wmk. 342**

858	A363	200m brn vio & dk bl	2.50	1.00
859	A363	500m bl & blk	6.00	2.75

Souvenir Sheet
Design: Portrait facing right.
Imperf.

860	A363	Sheet of 2	6.00	3.75
a.		100m lt grn & blk	3.00	1.00
b.		200m bl & blk	2.25	1.75

No. 860 commemorates inauguration of the Aswan High Dam, which is shown in margin. Green and blue marginal inscription. Size: 134x79mm.
Issue dates: No. 860, Jan. 15; Nos. 858–859, Feb. 1.
See No. 903.

Cotton and Globe
A364

1971, Mar. 6 Photo. *Perf. 11½x11*

861 A364 20m lt grn, bl & brn 25 10

Egyptian cotton.

Arab Countries, and Arab Postal Union Emblem
A365

1971, Mar. 6 Wmk. 342

862 A365 20m lt bl, org & sl grn 25 10

9th Arab Postal Congress, Cairo, March 6–25. See No. C131.

Cairo Fair Emblem
A366

1971, Mar. 6 *Perf. 11x11½*

863 A366 20m plum, blk & org 25 10

Cairo International Fair, March 2–23.

Nesy Ra, Apers Papyrus and WHO Emblem—A367
Perf. 11½x11

1971, Apr. 30 Photo. Wmk. 342

864 A367 20m yel bis & pur 25 10

World Health Organization Day.

Gamal Abdel Nasser
A368

1971, May 1 *Perf. 11*

865 A368 20m pur & bl gray 15 8

866 A368 55m bl & pur 45 20

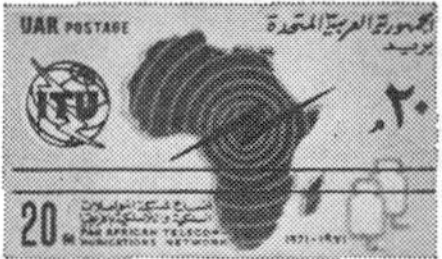

Map of Africa, Telecommunications Symbols
A369

1971, May 17 *Perf. 11½x11*

867 A369 20m bl & multi 25 10

Pan-African telecommunications system.

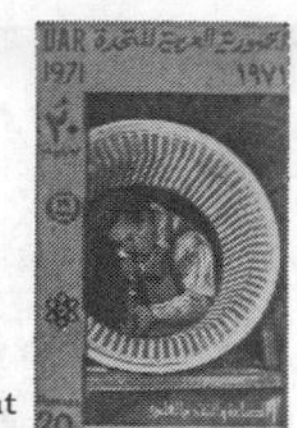

Wheelwright
A370

Hand Holding Wheat and Laurel
A371

Candle Lighting Africa—A372
Perf. 11x11½

1971, July 23 Photo. Wmk. 342

868 A370 20m yel & multi 25 8

869 A371 20m tan, grn & ocher 25 8

Souvenir Sheet
Imperf.

870 A372 100m bl & multi 1.00 60

19th anniversary of the July Revolution. No. 870 contains one stamp with simulated perforations in gold and with blue marginal inscription. Portrait of Pres. Nasser in margin. Size: 115x70mm.

Arab Postal Union Emblem
A373

1971, Aug. 3 *Perf. 11½*

871 A373 20m blk, yel & grn 25 8

25th anniversary of the Conference of Sofar, Lebanon, establishing the Arab Postal Union. See No. C135.

Arab Republic of Egypt

Three Links
A374

Perf. 11½x11

1971, Sept. 28 Photo. Wmk. 342

872 A374 20m gray, org brn & blk 25 10

Confederation of Arab Republics (Egypt, Syria and Libya). See No. C136.

Gamal Abdel Nasser
A375

Blood Donation
A376

1971, Sept. 28 *Perf. 11x11½*

873 A375 5m sl grn & vio brn 8 8

874 A375 20m vio brn & ultra 20 10

875 A375 30m ultra & brn 30 15

876 A375 55m brn & emer 50 25

First anniversary of the death of President Gamal Abdel Nasser.

1971, Oct. 24

877 A376 20m grn & car 25 8

"Blood Saves Lives."

Princess Nursing Child, UNICEF Emblem
A377

Submerged Pillar, Philae, UNESCO Emblem
A379

Equality Year Emblem
A378

Perf. 11x11½, 11½x11

1971, Oct. 24 Photo. Wmk. 342

878 A377 5m buff, blk & org brn 5 5

879 A378 20m red brn, grn, yel & blk 25 8

880 A379 55m blk, lt bl, yel & brn 50 20

United Nations Day. No. 878 honors U.N. International Children's Fund; No. 879 for International Year Against Racial Discrimination; No. 880 honors U.N. Educational, Scientific and Cultural Organization. See No. C137.

Postal Traffic Center, Alexandria
A380

1971, Oct. 31 *Perf. 11½x11*

881 A380 20m bl & bis 25 8

Opening of Postal Traffic Center in Alexandria.

Sunflower
A381

Abdalla El Nadim
A382

1971, Nov. 13 *Perf. 11*

882 A381 5m lt bl & multi 10 5

For use on greeting cards.

1971, Nov. 14 *Perf. 11x11½*

883 A382 20m grn & brn 25 10

Abdalla El Nadim (1845–1896), journalist, publisher, connected with Orabi Revolution.

Section of Earth's Crust, Map of Africa on Globe
A383

1971, Nov. 27 *Perf. 11½x11*

884 A383 20m ultra, yel & brn 25 10

75th anniversary of Egyptian Geological Survey and International Conference, Nov. 27–Dec. 1.

Postal Union Emblem, Letter and Dove
A384

Design: 55m, African Postal Union emblem and letter.

1971, Dec. 2

885 A384 5m multi 5 5

886 A384 20m ol, blk & org 25 8

887 A384 55m red, blk & bl 50 20

10th anniversary of African Postal Union. See No. C138.

Money and Safe Deposit Box
A385

1971, Dec. 23 *Perf. 11½*

888 A385 20m rose, brn & grn 25 8

70th anniversary of Postal Savings Bank.

Types of 1969–70, 1971 Inscribed "A. R. Egypt" and

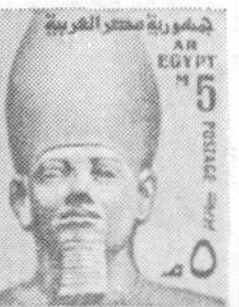

Ramses II
A385a

Designs as before and: No. 894, King Citi I. No. 897, Queen Nefertari. No. 900, Sphinx and Middle Pyramid. 100m, Cairo Mosque. 200m, Head of Pharaoh Userkaf.

Unwmkd., Wmk. 342 (#892A, 901-904)

1972-76 Photo. *Perf. 11*

No.	Type	Description	Unused	Used
889	A338	1m multi	5	5
890	A338	1m dk brn ('73)	5	5
891	A338	5m multi	5	5
892	A385a	5m ol ('73)	5	5
892A	A385a	5m bis ('76)	5	5
893	A338	10m multi	7	5
894	A338	10m lt brn ('73)	5	5
895	A339	20m olive	40	20
896	A339	20m pur ('73)	10	5
897	A338	50m multi	33	22
898	A385a	50m dl bl ('73)	25	15
899	A340	55m red lil	36	24
900	A340	55m grn ('74)	75	40
901	A339	100m lt bl, dp org & blk	50	35

Perf. 11½

Photogravure and Engraved

No.	Type	Description	Unused	Used
902	A341	200m yel grn & brn	1.25	70
903	A363	500m bl & choc	5.00	3.00
904	A341	£1 org & sl grn	8.00	5.00
		Nos. 889-904 (17)	17.31	10.66

Minaret Type of 1971

Designs: 5m, West Minaret, Nasser Mosque. 20m, East Minaret, Nasser Mosque. 30m, Minaret, Al Gawli Mosque. 55m, Minaret, Ibn Tulun Mosque.

Photogravure

1972, Jan. 2 *Perf. 11* Wmk. 342

No.	Type	Description	Unused	Used
905	A362	5m dk grn & multi	45	15
906	A362	20m dk grn & multi	1.40	20
907	A362	30m dk grn & multi	3.00	30
908	A362	55m dk grn & multi	4.25	60
		Strip of 4 (#905-908) + label	11.00	1.75

Post Day, 1972. Nos. 905–908 printed se-tenant in sheets of 40 stamps and 10 blue and yellow labels.

Police Emblem and Activities
A386

1972, Jan. 25 *Perf. 11½*

No.	Type	Description	Unused	Used
909	A386	20m dl bl, brn & yel	25	9

Police Day 1972.

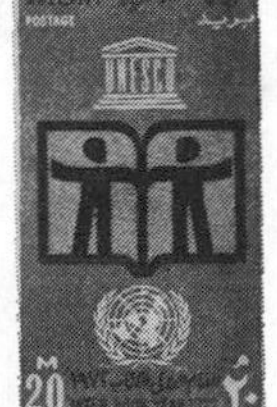

UNESCO, U.N. and Book Year Emblems
A387

1972, Jan. 25 *Perf. 11x11½*

No.	Type	Description	Unused	Used
910	A387	20m lt yel grn, vio bl & yel	25	9

International Book Year 1972.

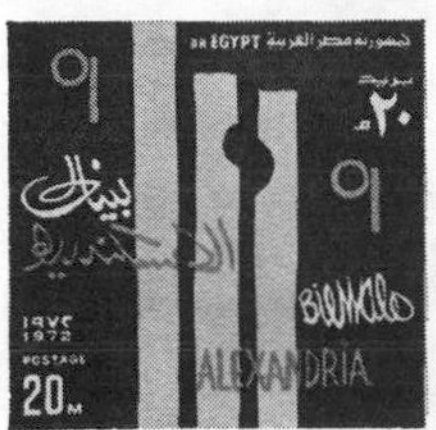

Alexandria Biennale
A388

1972, Feb. 15 *Perf. 11½* Wmk. 342

No.	Type	Description	Unused	Used
911	A388	20m blk, brt rose & yel	14	9

9th Biennial Exhibition of Fine Arts, Alexandria, March, 1972.

Fair Emblem
A389

Abdel Moniem Riad
390

1972, March 5 *Perf. 11x11½*

No.	Type	Description	Unused	Used
912	A389	20m bl, org & yel grn	25	9

International Cairo Fair.

1972, Mar. 21 Photo. Wmk. 342

No.	Type	Description	Unused	Used
913	A390	20m bl & brn	25	9

In memory of Brig. Gen. Abdel Moniem Riad (1919–1969), military hero.

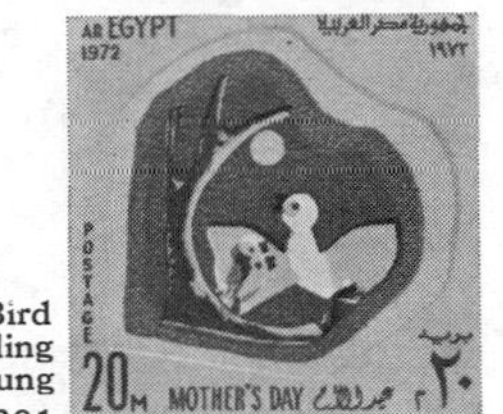

Bird Feeding Young
A391

1972, Mar. 21 *Perf. 11½*

No.	Type	Description	Unused	Used
914	A391	20m yel & multi	25	9

Mother's Day.

Tutankhamen
A392

Design: 55m, Back of chair with king's name and symbols of eternity.

1972, May 22 Unwmkd.

No.	Type	Description	Unused	Used
915	A392	20m gray, blk & ocher	75	25
916	A392	55m pur & yel	1.50	45

50th anniversary of the discovery of the tomb of Tutankhamen by Howard Carter and Lord Carnarvon. See Nos. C142–C144.

Queen Nefertiti
A393

Perf. 11½

1972, May 22 Photo. Wmk. 342

No.	Type	Description	Unused	Used
917	A393	20m red, blk & gold	10	7

50th anniversary of the Society of the Friends of Art.

Map of Africa
A394

1972, May 25 *Perf. 11x11½*

No.	Type	Description	Unused	Used
918	A394	20m pur, bl & brn	25	7

Africa Day.

Atom Symbol, "Faith and Science"
A395

Design: No. 920, Egyptian coat of arms.

1972, July 23 *Perf. 11½*

No.	Type	Description	Unused	Used
919	A395	20m bl, cl & blk	15	7
920	A395	20m ol grn, gold & blk	15	7

20th anniversary of the revolution.

Boxing, Olympic and Motion Emblems—A396

Designs (Olympic and Motion Emblems and): 10m, Wrestling. 20m, Basketball.

1972, Aug. 17 *Perf. 11½x11*

No.	Type	Description	Unused	Used
921	A396	5m bl & multi	5	5
922	A396	10m yel & multi	5	5
923	A396	20m ver & multi	10	7
		Nos. 921-923, C149-C152 (7)	1.05	66

20th Olympic Games, Munich, Aug. 26–Sept. 11.

Flag of Confederation of Arab Republics—A397

1972, Sept. 1 *Perf. 11½* Wmk. 342

No.	Type	Description	Unused	Used
924	A397	20m car, bis & blk	25	15

First anniversary of Confederation of Arab Republics.

Red Crescent, TB and UN Emblems
A398

Heart and WHO Emblem
A399

Refugees, UNRWA Emblem, Map of Palestine—A400

Design: 55m, Inundated Temple of Philae, UNESCO emblem.

1972, Oct. 24 Photo. *Perf. 11x11½*

No.	Type	Description	Unused	Used
925	A398	10m brn org, red & bl	25	10

Perf. 11½

No.	Type	Description	Unused	Used
926	A399	20m grn, yel & blk	50	15

Perf. 11

No.	Type	Description	Unused	Used
927	A400	30m lt bl, pur & lt brn	75	25

Perf. 11½

No.	Type	Description	Unused	Used
928	A399	55m brn, gold & bluish gray	1.40	55

United Nations Day. No. 925 commemorates the 14th Regional Tuberculosis Conference, Cairo, 1972; No. 926 is for World Health Month; No. 927 publicizes aid to refugees and No. 928 the U.N. campaign to save the Temples at Philae.

Morning Glory
A401

1972, Oct. 24 *Perf. 11*

No.	Type	Description	Unused	Used
929	A401	10m yel, lil & grn	5	5

For use on greeting cards.

"Seeing Eye"
A402

1972, Nov. 30 *Perf. 11½*

No.	Type	Description	Unused	Used
930	A402	20m multi	15	7

Social Work Day.

Sculling Race, View of Luxor—A403

1972, Dec. 17 *Perf. 11* Wmk. 342

No.	Type	Description	Unused	Used
931	A403	20m bl & brn	10	7

Third Nile International Rowing Festival, Dec. 1972.

Minaret Type of 1971

Minarets: 10m, Al Maridani, 1338. 20m, Bashtak, 1337. 30m, Qusun, 1330. 55m, Al Gashankir, 1306.

1973, Jan. 2

Frame in Brt. Yel. Green

932	A362	10m multi	90	20
933	A362	20m multi	1.40	30
934	A362	30m multi	3.00	50
935	A362	55m multi	4.25	1.25
		Strip of 4 (#932-935) + Label	10.00	4.00

Post Day, 1973. Nos. 932-935 printed se-tenant in sheets of 40 stamps and 10 yellow and green labels.

Cairo Fair Emblem
A404

Perf. 11½x11

1973, Mar. 21 Photo. Wmk. 342

936 A404 20m gray & multi 10 7

International Cairo Fair.

Family
A405

1973, Mar. 21 *Perf. 11x11½*

937 A405 20m multi 10 7

Family planning.

Sania Girls' School and Hoda Sharawi
A406

Perf. 11½x11

1973, July 15 Photo. Wmk. 342

938 A406 20m ultra, grn & brn 10 7

Centenary of education for girls and 50th anniversary of the Egyptian Women's Union, founded by Hoda Sharawi.

Rifaa el Tahtawi
A407

1973, July 15 *Perf. 11x11½*

939 A407 20m brt grn, ol & brn 10 7

Centenary of the death of Rifaa el Tahtawi, champion of democracy and principal of language school.

Omar Makram
A408

Abdel Rahman al Gabarti, Historian
A409

"Reconstruction and Battle"—A410

Design: No. 941, Mohamed Korayem, martyr.

1973, July 23

940	A408	20m yel grn, bl & brn	10	7
941	A408	20m lt grn, bl & brn	10	7
942	A409	20m ocher & brn	10	7

Souvenir Sheet

Imperf.

943 A410 110m gold, bl & blk 1.00 1.00

21st anniversary of the revolution establishing the republic. No. 943 contains one stamp and has gold marginal inscription. Size: 97x102mm.

Grain, Cow, FAO Emblem
A411

Perf. 11½x11

1973, Oct. 24 Wmk. 342

944 A411 10m brn, dk bl & yel grn 5 5

10th anniversary of the World Food Organization.

Inundated Temples at Philae
A412

1973, Oct. 24 *Perf. 11½*

945 A412 55m bl, pur & org 40 18

UNESCO campaign to save the temples at Philae.

Bank Building
A413

1973, Oct. 24

946 A413 20m brn org, grn & blk 10 8

75th anniversary of the National Bank of Egypt.

Rose
A414

1973, Oct. 24 *Perf. 11*

947 A414 10m bl & multi 5 5

For use on greeting cards.

Human Rights Flame
A415

Taha Hussein
A416

Perf. 11x11½

1973, Dec. 8 Photo. Wmk. 342

948 A415 20m yel grn, dk bl & car 10 8

25th anniversary of the Universal Declaration of Human Rights.

1973, Dec. 10

949 A416 20m dk bl, brn & emer 10 8

In memory of Dr. Taha Hussein (1893-1973), "Father of Education" in Egypt, writer, philosopher.

Pres. Sadat, Flag and Battle of Oct. 6—A417

1973, Dec. 23 *Perf. 11x11½*

950 A417 20m yel, blk & red 2.50 1.00

Crossing of Suez Canal by Egyptian forces, Oct. 6, 1973.

WPY Emblem and Chart
A418

Cairo Fair Emblem
A419

1974, Mar. 21 *Perf. 11* **Wmk. 342**

951 A418 55m org, grn & dk bl 30 18

World Population Year.

1974, Mar. 21 Photogravure

952 A419 20m bl & multi 15 8

Cairo International Fair.

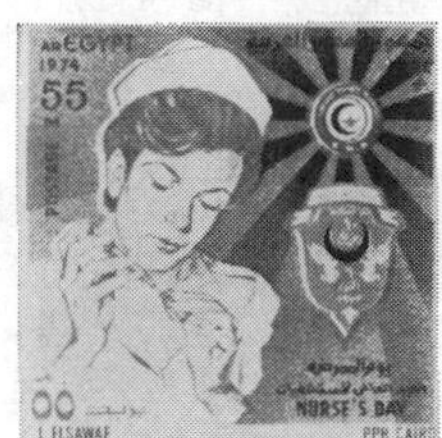

Nurse and Medal of Angels of Ramadan 10
A420

1974, May 15 *Perf. 11½*

953 A420 55m multi 28 18

Nurses' and World Hospital Day.

Workers, Relief Carving from Queen Tee's Tomb, Sakhara—A421

1974, May 15 *Perf. 11*

954 A421 20m yel, bl & brn 25 10

Workers' Day.

Pres. Sadat, Troops Crossing Suez Canal
A422

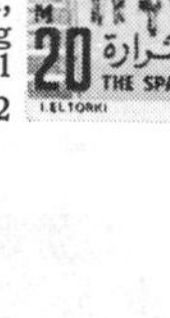

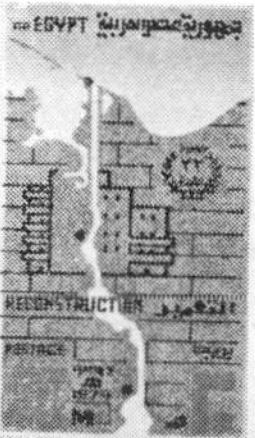

"Reconstruction," Map of Suez Canal and New Building
A423

Sheet of Aluminum
A424

Design: 110m, Pres. Sadat's "October Working Paper," symbols of science and development.

1974, July 23 Photo. *Perf. 11x11½*

955	A422	20m multi	45	15
956	A423	20m bl, gold & blk	45	15

Perf. 11½

957	A424	20m plum & sil	45	15

Souvenir Sheet

Imperf.

958	A424	110m grn & multi	1.00	75

22nd anniversary of the revolution establishing the republic and for the end of the October War. No. 958 contains one stamp (52x59mm.). Gold and green marginal inscription. Size: 72½x108mm.

Pres. Sadat and Flag—A425

Perf. 11x11½

1974, Oct. 6 Wmk. 342

959	A425	20m yel, blk & red	1.50	75

First anniversary of Battle of Oct. 6.

Palette and Brushes
A426

1974, Oct. 6 *Perf. 11½*

960	A426	30m pur, yel & blk	15	12

6th Exhibition of Plastic Art.

Teachers and Pupils
A427

1974, Oct. 6 *Perf. 11x11½*

961	A427	20m multi	10	8

Teachers' Day.

Souvenir Sheet

UPU Monument, Bern—A428

1974, Oct. 6 *Imperf.*

962	A428	110m gold & multi	1.75	1.00

Centenary of Universal Postal Union. No. 962 contains one stamp, yellow green marginal inscription. Size: 75x100mm.

Emblems, Cogwheel and Calipers—A429

Refugee Camp under Attack and UN Refugee Organization Emblem
A430

Child and UNICEF Emblem
A431

Temple of Philae
A432

1974, Oct. 24 *Perf. 11½, 11x11½*

963	A429	10m blk, bl & yel	25	15
964	A430	20m dp org, bl & blk	50	25
965	A431	30m grn, bl & brn	60	30
966	A432	55m blk, bl & yel	90	45

United Nations Day. World Standards Day (10m); Palestinian refugee repatriation (20m); Family Planning (30m); Campaign to save Temple of Philae (55m).

Calla Lily
A433

1974, Nov. 7 *Perf. 11*

967	A433	10m ultra & multi	5	5

For use on greeting cards.

10m-coins, Smoke-stacks and Grain
A434

1974, Nov. 7 *Perf. 11½x11*

968	A434	20m yel grn, dk bl & sil	10	8

International Savings Day.

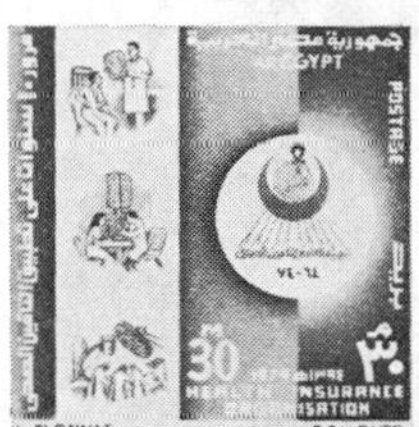

Organization Emblem and Medical Services
A435

1974, Nov. 7 *Perf. 11½*

969	A435	30m vio, red & gold	15	12

Health Insurance Organization, 10th anniversary.

Mustafa Lutfy El Manfalouty
A436

Abbas Mahmoud El Akkad
A437

Perf. 11x11½

1974, Dec. 8 Photo. Wmk. 342

970	A436	20m bl blk & brn	15	8
971	A437	20m brn & bl blk	15	8

Arab writers; Mustafa Lutfy El Manfalouty (1876–1924) and Abbas Mahmoud El Akkad (1889–1964). Nos. 970–971 printed se-tenant in sheets of 50.

Goddess Maat Facing God Thoth—A438

Fish-shaped Vase—A439

Pharaonic Golden Vase
A440

Sign of Life, Mirror
A441

Perf. 11½

1975, Jan. 2 Photo. Wmk. 342

972	A438	20m sil & multi	25	15
973	A439	30m multi	30	25
974	A440	55m multi	40	30
975	A441	110m bl & multi	1.00	65

Post Day 1975. Egyptian art works from 12th–5th centuries B.C.

Om Kolthoum
A442

Perf. 11½

1975, Mar. 3 Photo. Unwmkd.

976	A442	20m brown	20	12

In memory of Om Kolthoum, singer.

Crescent, Globe, Al Aqsa and Kaaba
A443

Cairo Fair Emblem
A444

1975, Mar. 25

977	A443	20m multi	25	10

Mohammed's Birthday.

Perf. 11x11½

1975, Mar. 25 Wmk. 342

978	A444	20m multi	10	8

International Cairo Fair.

Kasr El Ainy Hospital WHO Emblem A445

Perf. 11½x11

1975, May 7 Photo. Wmk. 342

979	A445	20m dk brn & bl	10	8

World Health Organization Day.

Children Reading Book A446

Children and Line Graph A447

1975, May 7 *Perf. 11x11½*

980	A446	20m multi	10	8
981	A447	20m multi	10	8

Science Day.

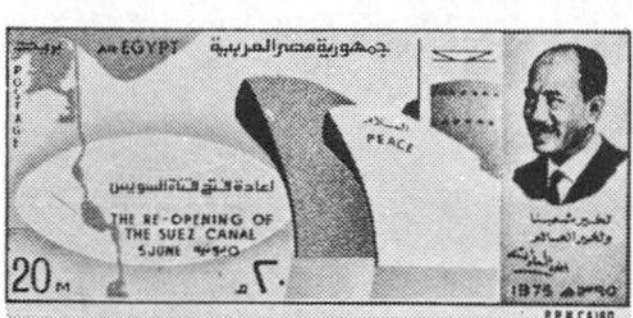

Suez Canal, Globe, Ships, Pres. Sadat—A448

1975, June 5 *Perf. 11½*

982	A448	20m bl, brn & blk	70	30

Reopening of the Suez Canal, June 5. See Nos. C166–C167.

Belmabgoknis Flowers A449

1975, July 30 Photo. Wmk. 342

983	A449	10m grn & bl	5	5

For use on greeting cards.

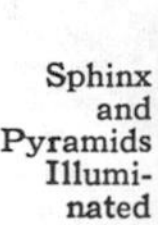

Sphinx and Pyramids Illuminated A450

Rural Electrification A451

Map of Egypt with Tourist Sites—A452

1975, July 23

984	A450	20m blk, org & grn	15	8
985	A451	20m dk bl & brn	15	8

Perf. 11

986	A452	110m multi	1.75	1.50

23rd anniversary of the revolution establishing the republic. No. 986 printed in sheets of 6 (2x3). Size: 71x80mm.

Volleyball A453

1975, Aug. 2 Photo. *Perf. 11x11½*

Orange & Green

987	A453	20m *shown*	20	10
988	A453	20m *Running*	20	10
989	A453	20m *Torch and flag bearers*	20	10
990	A453	20m *Basketball*	20	10
991	A453	20m *Soccer*	1.50	10
		Nos. 987-991 (5)	2.30	50

6th Arab School Tournament. Nos. 987–991 printed se-tenant in sheets of 50.

Egyptian Flag and Tanks A454

Perf. 11½

1975 Photo. Unwmkd.

992	A454	20m multi	1.00	25

Two-line Arabic Inscription in Bottom Panel, "M" over "20"

992A	A454	20m multi	1.00	25

No. 992 commemorates 2nd anniversary of Battle of Oct. 6, "The Spark;" No. 992A, the International Symposium on War of October 1973, Cairo University, Oct. 27–31. Issue dates: No. 992, Oct. 6. No. 992A, Oct. 24.

Arrows Pointing to Fluke, and Emblems A455

Submerged Wall and Sculpture, UNESCO Emblem A456

Perf. 11x11½

1975, Oct. 24 Wmk. 342

993	A455	20m multi	15	10
994	A456	55m multi	85	30

United Nations Day. 20m publicizes International Conference on Schistosomiasis (Bilharziasis); 55m commemorates UNESCO help in saving temples at Philae. See Nos. C169–C170.

Pharaonic Gate, University Emblem A457

Al Biruni A458

1975, Nov. 15 Photo. Wmk. 342

995	A457	20m multi	25	15

Ain Shams University, 25th anniversary.

1975, Dec. 23 Photo. *Perf. 11x11½*

Designs: No. 997, Al Farabi and lute. No. 998, Al Kanady, book and compass.

996	A458	20m bl, brn & grn	12	8
997	A458	20m bl, brn & grn	12	8
998	A458	20m bl, brn & grn	12	8

Arab philosophers.

Ibex (Prow) A459

Designs (from Tutankhamen's Tomb): 30m, Lioness. 55m, Cow's head (Goddess Hawthor). 110m, Hippopotamus' head (God Horus).

1976, Jan. 2 *Perf. 11½* Unwmkd.

999	A459	20m multi	35	15

Wmk. 342

1000	A459	30m brn, gold & ultra	65	30
1001	A459	55m multi	85	35
1002	A459	110m multi	1.25	75

Post Day 1976.

Lake, Aswan Dam, Industry and Agriculture—A460

Perf. 11½x11

1976, Jan. 27 Photo. Wmk. 342

1003	A460	20m multi	10	8

Filling of lake formed by Aswan High Dam.

Fair Emblem A461

Commemorative Medal A462

1976, Mar. 15 *Perf. 11x11½*

1004	A461	20m org & pur	10	8

9th International Cairo Fair, Mar. 8–27.

1976, Mar. 15 Wmk. 342

1005	A462	20m ol, yel & blk	10	8

11th Biennial Exhibition of Fine Arts, Alexandria.

Hands Shielding Invalid A463

1976, Apr. 7 Photo. *Perf. 11½*

1006	A463	20m dk grn, lt grn & yel	10	8

Founding of Faithfulness and Hope Society.

Eye and WHO Emblem A464

1976, Apr. 7

1007	A464	20m dk brn, yel & grn	10	8

World Health Day: "Foresight prevents blindness."

Pres. Sadat, Legal Department Emblem A465

Perf. 11½x11

1976, May 15 Photo. Wmk. 342

1008	A465	20m ol & multi	25	15

Centenary of State Legal Department.

Scales of Justice
A466

1976, May 15 ***Perf. 11x11½***

1009 A466 20m car, blk & grn 10 8

5th anniversary of Rectification Movement.

Al-Ahram Front Page, First Issue
A467

Perf. 11½x11

1976, June 25 Photo. Wmk. 342

1010 A467 20m bis & multi 10 8

Centenary of Al-Ahram newspaper.

World Map, Pres. Sadat and Emblems—A468

1976, July 23 ***Perf. 11x11½***

1011 A468 20m bl, blk & yel 50 35

Souvenir Sheet

Imperf.

1012 A468 110m bl, blk & yel 2.00 1.00

24th anniversary of the revolution. No. 1012 shows design of No. 1011 enlarged to fill entire area. Size: 85x76mm.

Scarborough Lily
A469

1976, Sept. 10 Photo. ***Perf. 11***

1013 A469 10m multi 5 5

For use on greeting cards.

Reconstruction of Sinai by Irrigation—A470

Abu Redice Oil Wells and Refinery
A471

Unknown Soldier, Memorial Pyramid for October War—A472

1976, Oct. 6 ***Perf. 11x11½***

1014 A470 20m multi 25 15
1015 A471 20m multi 25 15
1016 A472 110m grn, bl & blk 2.00 1.00

October War (crossing of Suez Canal), 3rd anniversary. Size of No. 1016: 65x77 mm.

Papyrus with Children's Animal Story—A473

Al Aqsa Mosque, Palestinian Refugees
A474

Designs: 55m, Isis, from Philae Temple, UNESCO emblem (vert.). 110m, UNESCO emblem and "30".

Perf. 11½, 11½x11

1976, Oct. 24 Photo. Wmk. 342

1017 A473 20m dk bl, bis & brn 25 10
1018 A474 30m brn, grn & blk 45 25
1019 A473 55m dk bl & bis 75 35
1020 A474 110m lt grn, vio bl & red 1.50 60

30th anniversary of UNESCO.

Census Chart
A475

1976, Nov. 22 Photo. ***Perf. 11½x11***

1021 A475 20m multi 15 8

10th General Population and Housing Census.

Nile and Commemorative Medal—A476

Ikhnaton
A477

1976, Nov. 22 ***Perf. 11x11½***

1022 A476 20m grn & brn 15 8

Geographical Society of Egypt, centenary (in 1975).

1977, Jan. 2 Photo. ***Perf. 11x11½***

Designs: 30m, Ikhnaton's daughter. 55m, Nefertiti, Ikhnaton's wife. 110m, Ikhnaton, front view.

1023 A477 20m multi 35 15
1024 A477 30m multi 30 20
1025 A477 55m multi 75 30
1026 A477 110m multi 1.50 75

Post Day 1977.

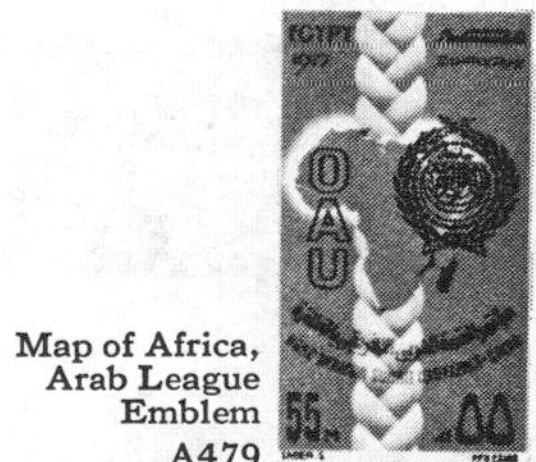

Policeman, Emblem and Emergency Car—A478

Wmk. 342

1977, Feb. 25 Photo. ***Perf. 11½x11***

1027 A478 20m multi 20 8

Police Day.

Map of Africa, Arab League Emblem
A479

1977, Mar. 7 ***Perf. 11x11½***

1028 A479 55m multi 40 20

First Afro-Arab Summit Conference, Cairo.

Fair Emblem, Pharaonic Ship—A480

1977, Mar. 7 ***Perf. 11½x11***

1029 A480 20m grn, blk & red 20 8

10th International Cairo Fair.

King Faisal
A481

1977, Mar. 22 Photo. ***Perf. 11x11½***

1030 A481 20m ind & brn 50 25

King Faisal Ben Abdel-Aziz Al Saud of Saudi Arabia (1906–1975).

Healthy and Crippled Children
A482

1977, Apr. 12 Wmk. 342

1031 A482 20m multi 10 8

National campaign to fight poliomyelitis.

APU Emblem, Members' Flags
A483

1977, Apr. 12 ***Perf. 11½***

1032 A483 20m bl & multi 15 10
1033 A483 30m gray & multi 20 15

25th anniversary of Arab Postal Union (APU).

Children's Village
A484

Perf. 11½x11

1977, May 7 Photo. Wmk. 342

1034 A484 20m multi 10 8
1035 A484 55m multi 30 18

Inauguration of Children's Village, Cairo.

Loom, Spindle and Factory
A485

1977, May 7

1036 A485 20m multi 10 8

Egyptian Spinning and Weaving Company, El Mehalla el Kobra, 50th anniversary.

Satellite, Globe, ITU Emblem
A486

1977, May 17 ***Perf. 11x11½***

1037 A486 110m dk bl & multi 1.00 75

World Telecommunications Day.

Flag and "25" A487

Egyptian Flag and Eagle—A488

Wmk. 342

1977, July 23 Photo. *Perf. 11½x11*

1038	A487	20m sil, car & blk	20	8

Perf. 11x11½

1039	A488	110m multi	1.25	75

25th anniversary of July 23rd Revolution. No. 1039 printed in sheets of six. Size: 75x83mm.

Saad Zaghloul A489

Archbishop Capucci, Map of Palestine A490

Perf. 11x11½

1977, Aug. 23 Photo. Wmk. 342

1040	A489	20m dk grn & dk brn	20	8

Saad Zaghloul, leader of 1919 Revolution, 50th death anniversary.

1977, Sept. 1

1041	A490	45m emer & bl	45	18

Palestinian Archbishop Hilarion Capucci, jailed by Israel in 1974.

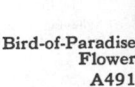

Bird-of-Paradise Flower A491

1977, Sept. 3

1042	A491	10m multi	10	5

For use on greeting cards.

Proclamation Greening the Land A492

Wmk. 342

1977, Sept. 25 Photo. *Perf. 11x11½*

1043	A492	20m multi	20	8

Agrarian Reform Law, 25th anniversary.

Soldier, Tanks, Medal of Oct. 6 A493

Anwar El Sadat—A494

1977, Oct. 6 *Perf. 11½x11*

1044	A493	20m multi	50	25

Unwmkd. *Perf. 11*

1045	A494	140m dk brn, gold & red	5.00	2.75

Crossing of Suez Canal, 4th anniversary. No. 1045 printed in sheets of 16.

Refugees Looking at Al Aqsa Mosque A495

Goddess Taueret and Spirit of Flight (Horus) A496

Mural Relief, Temple of Philae A497

Wmk. 342

1977, Oct. 24 Photo. *Perf. 11*

1046	A495	45m grn, red & blk	25	20
1047	A496	55m dp bl & yel	30	25
1048	A497	140m ol bis & dk brn	70	50

United Nations Day.

Electric Trains, First Egyptian Locomotive A498

1977, Oct. 22

1049	A498	20m multi	12	8

125th anniversary of Egyptian railroads.

Film and Eye A499

1977, Nov. 16 *Perf. 11½x11*

1050	A499	20m gray, blk & gold	12	8

50th anniversary of Egyptian cinema.

Natural Gas Well and Refinery A500

1977, Nov. 17 Photogravure

1051	A500	20m multi	25	15

National Oil Festival, celebrating the acquisition of Sinai oil wells.

Pres. Sadat and Dome of the Rock—A501

Wmk. 342

1977, Dec. 31 Photo. *Perf. 11½x11*

1052	A501	20m grn, brn & blk	25	15
1053	A501	140m grn, blk & brn	1.15	75

Pres. Sadat's peace mission to Israel.

Ramses II A502

Design: 45m, Queen Nefertari, bas-relief.

1978, Jan. 2 *Perf. 11½*

1054	A502	20m grn, blk & gold	10	8
1055	A502	45m org, blk & ol	25	16

Post Day 1978.

Water Wheels, Fayum A503

Flying Duck, from Floor in Ikhnaton's Palace—A504

Designs: 5m, Birdhouse. 10m, Statue of Horus. 20m, Al Rifa'i Mosque, Cairo. 50m, Monastery, Wadi al-Natrun. 55m, Ruins of Edfu Temple. 70m, Bridge of Oct. 6. 85m, Medum pyramid. 100m, Facade, El Morsi Mosque, Alexandria. 200m, Column, Alexandria, and Sphinx. 500m, Arabian stallion.

Wmk. 342

1978-82 *Perf. 11½*

1056	A503	1m sl bl	5	5
1057	A503	5m bis brn	5	5
1058	A503	10m brt grn	5	5
1059	A503	20m dk brn	10	8
1059A	A503	30m sepia	15	15
1060	A503	50m brt bl	25	15
1061	A503	55m olive	28	18
1062	A503	70m ol ('79)	35	20
1062A	A503	80m like #1062 ('82)	40	40
1063	A503	85m dp pur	42	30
1064	A503	100m brown	50	40
1065	A503	200m bl & ind	1.00	80
1066	A504	500m multi	2.50	1.25
1067	A504	£1 multi	5.00	2.50
		Nos. 1056-1067 (14)	11.10	6.56

Issue dates: 500m, £1, Feb. 27. Others, July 23, 70m, Aug. 22, 1979.

Fair Emblem and Wheat A505

1978, Mar. 15 *Perf. 11½*

1072	A505	20m multi	10	8

11th Cairo International Fair, Mar. 11-25.

Emblem, Kasr El Ainy School A506

1978, Mar. 18 *Perf. 11½x11*

1073	A506	20m lt bl, blk & gold	10	8

Kasr El Ainy School of Medicine, 150th anniversary.

Soldiers and Emblem A507

Youssef El Sebai A508

1978, Mar. 30 *Perf. 11x11½*

1074 A507 20m multi 10 8
1075 A508 20m bis brn 10 8

Nos. 1069–1070 printed se-tenant.
Youssef El Sebai, newspaper editor, assassinated on Cyprus and in memory of the commandos killed in raid on Cyprus.

Biennale Medal, Statue for Entrance to Port Said
A509

1978, Apr. 1 *Perf. 11½*

1076 A509 20m bl, grn & blk 10 8

12th Biennial Exhibition of Fine Arts, Alexandria.

Child with Smallpox, UN Emblem
A510

1978, Apr. 7 Photo. *Perf. 11½*

1077 A510 20m multi 10 8

Eradication of smallpox.

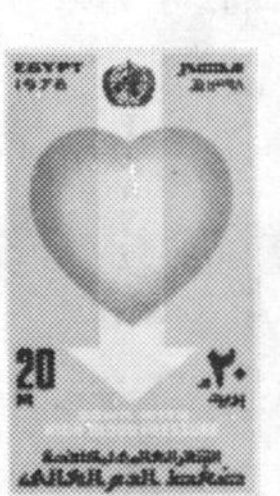

Heart and Arrow, UN Emblem
A511

Anwar El Sadat
A512

1978, Apr. 7 **Wmk. 342**

1078 A511 20m multi 10 8

Fight against hypertension.

1978, May 15 Photo. *Perf. 11½x11*

1079 A512 20m grn, brn & gold 25 15

7th anniversary of Rectification Movement.

Social Security Emblem—A513

1978, May 16 *Perf. 11*

1080 A513 20m lt grn & dk brn 10 8

General Organization of Insurance and Pensions (Social Security), 25th anniversary.

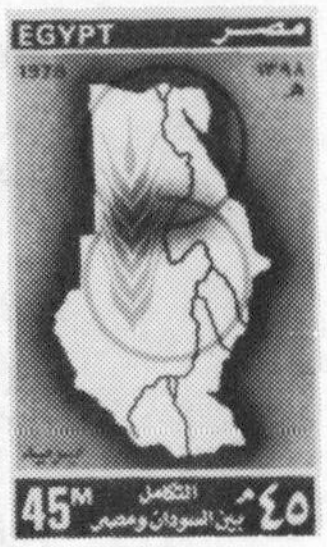

New Cities on Map of Egypt
A514

Map of Egypt and Sudan, Wheat
A515

Wmk. 342

1978, July 23 Photo. *Perf. 11½*

1081 A514 20m multi 35 8
1082 A515 45m multi 60 16

26th anniversary of July 23rd revolution.

Symbols of Egyptian Ministries
A516

1978, Aug. 28 Photo. *Perf. 11½x11*

1083 A516 20m multi 10 8

Centenary of Egyptian Ministerial System.

Pres. Nasser and "Spirit of Egypt" Showing Way—A517

1978, Oct. 6 Photo. *Perf. 11x11½*

1084 A517 20m multi 25 15

Crossing of Suez Canal, 5th anniversary.

Human Rights Emblem
A518

Dove and Human Rights Emblem
A520

Kobet al Sakra Mosque, Refugee Camp
A519

Design: 55m, Temple at Biga and UNESCO emblem (horiz.).

Perf. 11, 11½ (45m)

1978, Oct. 24 Photo. **Wmk. 342**

1085 A518 20m multi 10 8
1086 A519 45m multi 75 50
1087 A518 55m multi 28 18
1088 A520 140m multi 70 48

United Nations Day.

Pilgrims, Mt. Arafat and Holy Kaaba—A521

1978, Nov. 7 Photo. *Perf. 11*

1089 A521 45m multi 25 16

Pilgrimage to Mecca.

Tahtib Horse Dance
A522

1978, Nov. 7

1090 A522 10m multi 5 5
1091 A522 20m multi 10 8

U.N. Emblem, Globe and Grain
A523

1978, Nov. 11 Photo *Perf. 11½*

1092 A523 20m grn, dk bl & yel 10 8

Technical Cooperation Among Developing Countries Conference, Buenos Aires, Argentina, Sept. 1978.

Pipes, Map and Emblem of Sumed Pipeline—A524

1978, Nov. 11

1093 A524 20m brn, bl & yel 10 8

Inauguration of Sumed pipeline from Suez to Alexandria, 1st anniversary.

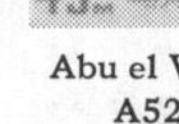

Mastheads
A525

Abu el Walid
A526

1978, Dec. 24 *Perf. 11x11½*

1094 A525 20m brn & blk 10 8

150th anniversary of the newspaper El Wakea el Masriya.

1978, Dec. 24

1095 A526 45m brt grn & ind 22 18

800th death anniversary of Abu el Walid ibn Rashid.

Helwan Observatory and Sky—A527

1978, Dec. 30 **Wmk. 342**

1096 A527 20m multi 10 8

Helwan Observatory, 75th anniversary.

Second Daughter of Ramses II
A528

Ramses Statues, Abu Simbel, and Cartouches
A529

1979, Jan. 2 Photo. *Perf. 11*

1097 A528 20m brn & yel 10 8

Perf. 11½x11

1098 A529 140m multi 70 48

Post Day 1978.

Book, Reader and Globe
A530

Wmk. 342

1979, Feb. 1 Photo. *Perf. 11½x11*

1099	A530	20m yel grn & brn	10	10

Cairo 11th International Book Fair.

Wheat, Globe, Fair Emblem—A531

Perf. 11x11½

1979, Mar. 17 Photo. Unwmkd.

1100	A531	20m bl, org & blk	10	10

12th Cairo International Fair, March–Apr.

Skull, Poppy, Agency Emblem—A532

1979, Mar. 20 *Perf. 11*

1101	A532	70m multi	40	35

Anti-Narcotics General Administration, 50th anniversary.

Isis Holding Horus
A533

1979, Mar. 21

1102	A533	140m multi	80	70

Mother's Day.

World Map and Book—A534

Perf. 11x11½

1979, Mar. 22 Wmk. 342

1103	A534	45m yel, bl & brn	25	20

Cultural achievements of the Arabs.

Pres. Sadat's Signature, Peace Doves
A535

Wmk. 342

1979, Mar. 31 Photo. *Perf. 11½*

1104	A535	70m brt grn & red	35	35
1105	A535	140m yel grn & red	70	70

Signing of Peace Treaty between Egypt and Israel, Mar. 26.

1979, May 26 Photo. *Perf. 11½*

1106	A535	20m yel & dk brn	10	10

Return of Al Arish to Egypt.

Honey-comb with Food Symbols
A536

1979, May 15

1107	A536	20m multi	12	10

8th anniversary of movement to establish food security.

Coins, 1959, 1979
A537

Photogravure

Perf. 11½x11

1979, June 1 Wmk. 342

1108	A537	20m yel & gray	12	10

25th anniversary of the Egyptian Mint.

Egypt No. 1104 under Magnifying Glass—A538

1979, June 1 *Perf. 11*

1109	A538	20m grn, blk & brn	25	10

Philatelic Society of Egypt, 50th anniversary.

See "Special Notices" at the front of this volume for data on the listing methods of this Catalogue, abbreviations, condition, prices and examination.

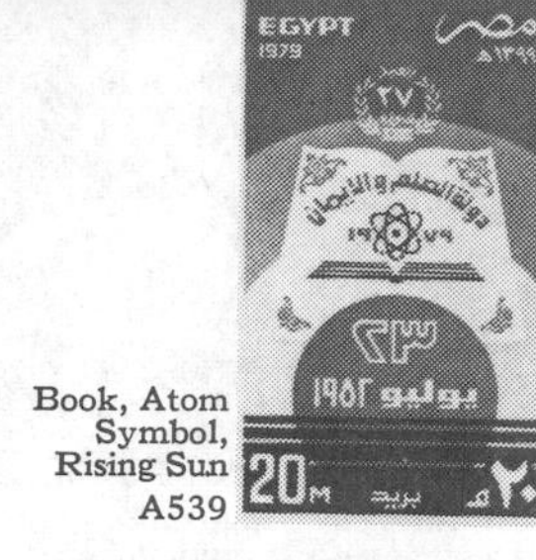

Book, Atom Symbol, Rising Sun
A539

"23 July," "Revolution" and "Peace"—A540

Perf. 11½x11

1979, July 23 Wmk. 342

1110	A539	20m multi	10	10

Miniature Sheet

Imperf.

1111	A540	140m multi	85	85

27th anniversary of July 23rd revolution. Size of No. 1111: 50x62mm.

Musicians
A541

1979, Aug. 22 *Perf. 11½*

1112	A541	10m multi	8	6

For use on greeting cards.

Dove over Map of Suez Canal
A542

Wmk. 342

1979, Oct. 6 Photo. *Perf. 11½*

1113	A542	20m bl & brn	15	12

Crossing of Suez Canal, 6th anniversary.

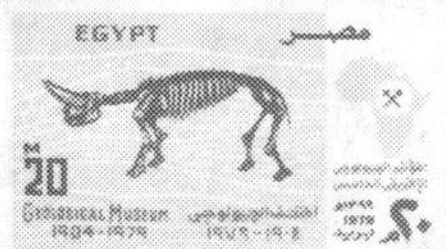

Dinosaur Skeleton, Map of Africa
A543

Wmk. 342

1979, Oct. 9 Photo. *Perf. 11½×11*

1114	A543	20m multi	12	10

Egyptian Geological Museum, 75th anniversary.

T Square on Drawing Board—A544

1979, Oct. 11 *Perf. 11*

1115	A544	20m multi	12	10

Engineers Day.

Human Rights Emblem Over Globe
A545

Boy Balancing IYC Emblem
A546

Unwmkd.

1979, Oct. 24 Photo. *Perf. 11½*

1116	A545	45m multi	30	25
1117	A546	140m multi	90	70

United Nations Day and International Year of the Child.

International Savings Day—A547

1979, Oct. 31

1118	A547	70m multi	45	35

Shooting Championship Emblem
A548

1979, Nov. 16

1119	A548	20m multi	15	10

20th International Military Shooting Championship, Cairo.

International Palestinian Solidarity Day
A549

1979, Nov. 29 ***Perf. 11×11½***

1120 A549 140m multi 85 70

Dove Holding Grain, Rotary Emblem, Globe—A550

1979, Dec. 3 **Photo.** ***Perf. 11½***

1121 A550 45m multi 30 25

Rotary International, 75th anniversary; Cairo Rotary Club, 50th anniversary.

Arms Factories, 25th Anniversary
A551

Wmk. 342

1979, Dec. 23 **Photo.** ***Perf. 11½×11***

1122 A551 20m lt ol grn & brn 10 10

Aly El Garem
(1881-1949)
A552

Pharaonic
Capital
A553

Poets: No. 1124, Mahmoud Samy El Baroudy (1839-1904).

1979, Dec. 25 ***Perf. 11×11½***

1123 A552 20m dk brn & yel brn 10 10
1124 A552 20m brn & dk brn 10 10

Nos. 1123-1124 printed se-tenant.

1980, Jan. 2 **Unwmkd.** ***Perf. 11½***

Post Day: Various Pharaonic capitals. Printed se-tenant.

1125 A553 20m multi 25 10
1126 A553 45m multi 40 20
1127 A553 70m multi 65 35
1128 A553 140m multi 1.00 70

Golden Goddess of Writing, Fair Emblem
A554

Exhibition Catalogue and Medal
A555

1980, Feb. 2 **Photo.** ***Perf. 11½***

1129 A554 20m multi 25 15

12th Cairo International Book Fair, Jan. 24-Feb. 4.

1980, Feb. 2

1130 A555 20m multi 10 10

13th Biennial Exhibition of Fine Arts, Alexandria.

13th Cairo International Fair—A556

1980, Mar. 8 **Photo.** ***Perf. 11x11½***

1131 A556 20m multi 10 10

Kiosk of Trajan—A557

1980, Mar. 10 ***Perf. 11½***

1132 Strip of 4 plus label 2.75 2.75
a. A557 70m, single stamp 45 45

UNESCO campaign to save Nubian monuments, 20th anniversary. Shown on stamps are Temples of Philae, Kalabsha, Korasy.

Physicians' Day—A558

1980, Mar. 18 ***Perf. 11x11½***

1133 A558 20m multi 10 10

Rectification Movement, 9th Anniversary—A559

Wmk. 342

1980, May 15 **Photo.** ***Perf. 11½x11***

1134 A559 20m multi 25 15

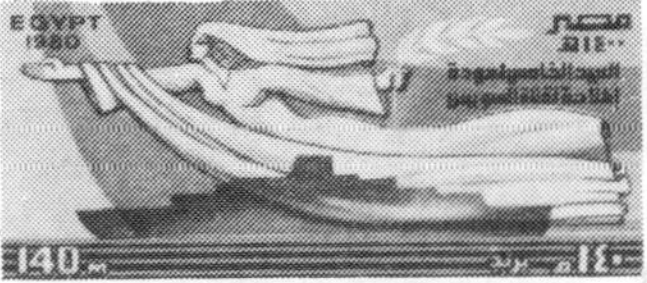

Re-opening of Suez Canal, 5th Anniversary—A560

1980, June 5 ***Perf. 11½***

1135 A560 140m multi 70 70

Prevention of Cruelty to Animals Week—A561

1980, June 5

1136 A561 20m lt yel grn & gray 10 10

Industry Day—A562

Wmk. 342

1980, July 12 **Photo.** ***Perf. 11½x11***

1137 A562 20m multi 10 10

Leaf with Text—A563

Family Protection Emblem—A564

1980, July 23 ***Perf. 11½***

1138 A563 20m multi 10 10

Souvenir Sheet
Imperf.

1139 A564 140m multi 75 75

July 23rd Revolution, 28th anniversary; Social Security Year. Size of No. 1139: 51x67mm.

Erksous Seller and Nakrazan Player—A565

Photo.

1980, Aug. 8 ***Perf. 11½*** **Unwmkd.**

1140 A565 10m multi 5 5

For use on greeting cards.

7th Anniversary of Suez Canal Crossing—A566

1980, Oct. 6 **Litho.**

1141 A566 20m multi 10 10

Islamic and Coptic Columns—A567

International Telecommunications Union Emblem—A568

Wmk. 342

1980, Oct. 24 **Photo.** ***Perf. 11½***

1142	A567	70m multi	35	35
1143	A568	140m multi	70	70

United Nations Day. Campaign to save Egyptian monuments (70m), International Telecommunications Day (140m).

Hegira (Pilgrimage Year)—A569

1980, Nov. 9 **Litho.** ***Perf. 11x11½***

1144	A569	45m multi	22	22

Opening of Suez Canal Third Branch—A570

Wmk. 342

1980, Dec. 16 **Photo.** ***Perf. 11½x11***

1145	A570	70m multi	35	35

Mustafa Sadek El-Rafai (1880-1927), Writer—A571

Famous Men: No. 1147, Ali Mustafa Mousharafa (1898-1950), mathematician, No. 1148, Ali Ibrahim (1880-1947), surgeon Nos. 1146-1148 se-tenant.

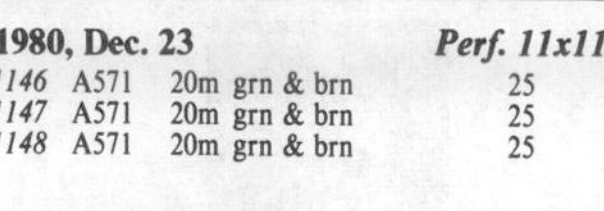

1980, Dec. 23 ***Perf. 11x11½***

1146	A571	20m grn & brn	25	15
1147	A571	20m grn & brn	25	15
1148	A571	20m grn & brn	25	15

Ladybug Scarab Emblem A572

Heinrich von Stephan, UPU A573

Unwmkd.

1981, Jan. 2 **Photo.** ***Perf. 11½***

1149	A572	70m *shown*	35	35
1150	A572	70m *Scarab, reverse*	35	35

Post Day.

1981, Jan. 7 **Wmk. 342** ***Perf. 11x11½***

1151	A573	140m grnsh bl & dk brn	70	70

Heinrich von Stephan (1831-1897), founder of Universal Postal Union, birth sesquicentennial.

13th Cairo International Book Fair—A574

1981, Feb. 1 ***Perf. 11½x11***

1152	A574	20m multi	10	10

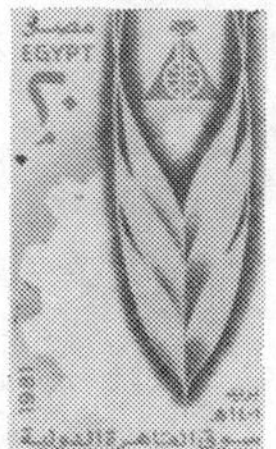

14th Cairo International Fair, Mar. 14-28—A575

Wmk. 342

1981, Mar. 14 **Photo.** ***Perf. 11x11½***

1153	A575	20m multi	10	10

Rural Electrification Authority, 10th Anniversary—A576

1981, Mar. 18

1154	A576	20m multi	10	10

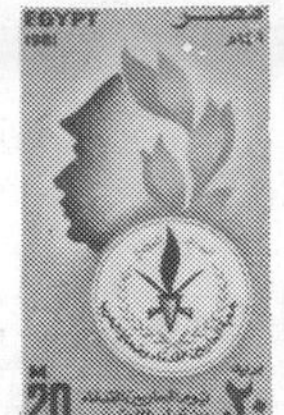

Veterans' Day—A577

1981, Mar. 26

1155	A577	20m multi	10	10

International Dentistry Conference, Cairo—A578

Wmk. 342

1981, Apr. 14 **Photo.** ***Perf. 11x11½***

1156	A578	20m red & ol	10	10

Trade Union Emblem A579

Nurses' Day A580

Wmk. 342

1981, May 1 **Photo.** ***Perf. 11x11½***

1157	A579	20m brt bl & dk brn	10	10

International Confederation of Arab Trade Unions, 25th anniv.

1981, May 12

1158	A580	20m multi	10	10

Irrigation Equipment (Electrification Movement) A581

1981, May 15 ***Perf. 11½***

1159	A581	20m multi	10	10

Air Force Day—A582

Wmk. 342

1981, June 30 **Photo.** ***Perf. 11x11½***

1160	A582	20m multi	10	10

Flag Surrounding Map of Suez Canal—A583

Wmk. 342

1981, July 23 **Photo.** ***Perf. 11½***

1161	A583	10m multi	5	5
1162	A583	20m Emblems	10	10

July 23rd Revolution, 29th anniv.; Social Defense Year.

1981 Feasts—A584

Wmk. 342

1981, July 29 **Photo.** ***Perf. 11***

1163	A584	10m multi	5	5

Kemal Ataturk—A585

1981, Aug. 10 ***Perf. 11x11½***

1164	A585	140m dk grn & brn	70	70

Arabi Pasha, Leader of Egyptian Force A586

Athlete, Pyramids, Sphinx A587

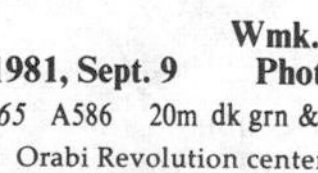

Wmk. 342

1981, Sept. 9 **Photo.** ***Perf. 11x11½***

1165	A586	20m dk grn & brn	10	10

Orabi Revolution centenary.

1981, Sept. 14

1166	A587	45m multi	22	22

World Muscular Athletics Championships, Cairo.

Ministry of Industry and Mineral Resources, 25th Anniv.—A588

Wmk. 342

1981, Sept. 26 **Photo.** ***Perf. 11x11½***

1167 A588 45m multi 22 22

20th Intl. Occupational Health Congress, Cairo—A589

1981, Sept. 28 ***Perf. 11½x11***

1168 A589 20m multi 10 10

8th Anniv. of Suez Canal Crossing—A590

1981, Oct. 6

1169 A590 20m multi 10 10

World Food Day—A591

13th World Telecommunications Day A592

Intl. Year of the Disabled A593

Fight Against Apartheid—A594

Wmk. 342

1981, Oct. 24 Photo. ***Perf. 11½x11, 11x11½***

1170 A591 10m multi 5 5

1171 A592 20m multi 10 10

1172 A593 45m multi 22 22

1173 A594 230m multi 1.15 1.15

United Nations Day.

Pres. Anwar El-Sadat (1917-1981)—A595

1981, Nov. 14 **Unwmkd.** ***Perf. 11x11½***

1174 A595 30m multi 45 35

1175 A595 230m multi 1.75 1.50

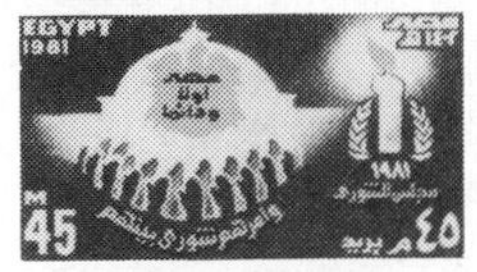

Establishment of Shura Family Council—A596

Wmk. 342

1981, Dec. 12 **Photo.** ***Perf. 11½x11***

1176 A596 45m pur & yel 22 22

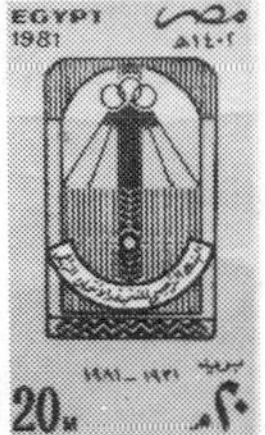

Agricultural Credit and Development Bank, 50th Anniv.—A597

1981, Dec. 15 ***Perf. 11x11½***

1177 A597 20m multi 10 10

Famous Men Type of 1980

Designs: 30m, Ali el-Ghayati (1885-1956), journalist. 60m, Omar Ebn sl-Fared (1181-1234), Sufi poet. Nos. 1178-1179 se-tenant.

Wmk. 342

1981, Dec. 21 **Photo.** ***Perf. 11x11½***

1178 A571 30m grn & brn 15 15

1179 A571 60m grn & brn 30 30

20th Anniv. of African Postal Union—A598

1981, Dec. 21 ***Perf. 11½x11***

1180 A598 60m multi 30 30

14th Cairo Intl. Book Fair A599

Arab Trade Union of Egypt, 25th Anniv. A600

1982, Jan. 28

1181 A599 3p brn & yel 15 15

1982, Jan. 30

1182 A600 3p multi 15 15

Khartoum Branch of Cairo University, 25th Anniv.—A601

1982, Mar. 4 **Wmk. 342** ***Perf. 11½x11***

1183 A601 6p bl & grn 30 30

15th Cairo Intl. Fair—A602

1982, Mar. 13 ***Perf. 11x11½***

1184 A602 3p multi 15 15

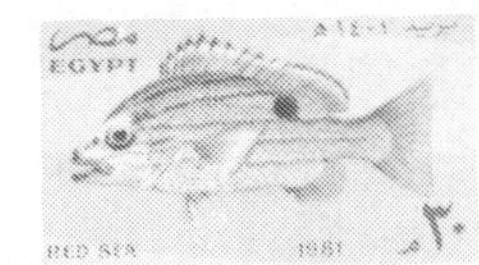

50th Anniv. of Al-Ghardaka Marine Biological Station—A603

Fish of the Red Sea. Nos. 1185-1188 se-tenant in continuous design.

1982, Apr. 24 **Litho.** ***Perf. 11½x11***

1185 A603 10m Blue-banded sea perch 5 5

1186 A603 30m Lined butterfly fish 15 15

1187 A603 60m Batfish 30 30

1188 A603 230m Blue-spotted boxfish 1.15 1.15

Liberation of the Sinai—A604

1982, Apr. 25 **Photo.** ***Perf. 11x11½***

1189 A604 3p multi 15 15

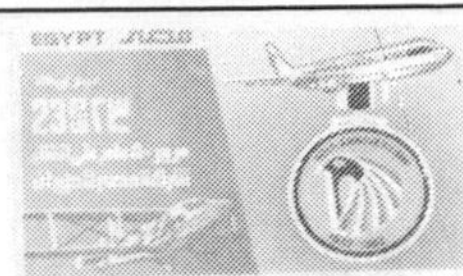

50th Anniv. of Egypt Air—A605

1982, May 7 **Photo.** ***Perf. 11½x11***

1190 A605 23p multi 1.15 1.15

Minaret—A606

Souvenir Sheet

Al Azhar Mosque—A607

Wmk. 342

1982, June 28 **Photo.** ***Perf. 11x11½***

1191 Strip of 4 plus label 1.25 1.25

a. A606 6p, any single multi 30 30

Unwmkd. ***Imperf.***

1192 A607 23p multi 1.25 1.25

Al Azhar Mosque millennium. Size of No. 1192: 61x60mm.

Dove—A608

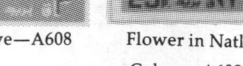

Flower in Natl. Colors—A609

Wmk. 342

1982, July 23 **Photo.** ***Perf. 11x11½***

1193 A608 3p multi 15 15

Souvenir Sheet

Imperf.

1194 A609 23p multi 1.25 1.25

30th anniv. of July 23rd Revolution. Size of No. 1194: 55x74mm.

World Tourism Day—A610

Wmk. 342
1982, Sept. 27 Photo. *Perf. 11½x11*
1195 A610 23p Sphinx, pyramid of Cheops, St. Catherine's Tower 1.25 1.25

10th Anniv. of Suez Canal Crossing—A611

1982, Oct. 6
1196 A611 3p Memorial, map 15 15

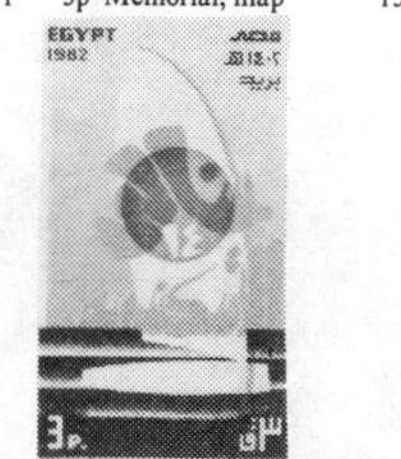

Biennale of Alexandria Art Exhibition—A612

1982, Oct. 17 *Perf. 11x11½*
1197 A612 3p multi 15 15

10th Anniv. of UN Conference on Human Environment—A613

2nd UN Conference on Peaceful Uses of Outer Space, Vienna, Aug. 9-21—A614

Scouting Year—A615

TB Bacillus Centenary—A616

1982, Oct. 24 *Perf. 11½x11, 11½ (A615)*
1198 A613 3p multi 15 15
1199 A614 6p multi 30 30
1200 A615 6p multi 30 30
1201 A616 8p multi 40 40

United Nations Day.

50th Anniv. of Air Force—A617

1982, Nov. 2 *Perf. 11½x11*
1202 A617 3p Jet, plane 15 15

Ahmed Chawki (1868-1932) and Hafez Ibrahim (1871-1932), Poets—A618

Wmk. 342
1982, Nov. 25 Photo. *Perf. 11½x11*
1203 A618 6p multi 30 30

Natl. Research Center, 25th Anniv.—A619

1982, Dec. 12 Photo. *Perf. 11x11½*
1204 A619 3p red & bl 15 15

50th Anniv. of Arab Language Society—A620

1982, Dec. 25 *Perf. 11½x11*
1205 A620 6p multi 30 30

Year of the Aged A621 | Post Day A622

1982, Dec. 25 *Perf. 11x11½*
1206 A621 23p multi 1.15 1.15

1983, Jan. 2 *Perf. 11½*
1207 A622 3p multi 15 15

15th Cairo Intl. Book Fair—A623

Wmk. 342
1983, Jan. 25 Photo. *Perf. 11x11½*
1208 A623 3p bl & red 15 15

Police Day—A624

1983, Jan. 25 *Perf. 11½x11*
1209 A624 3p multi 15 15

16th Cairo Intl. Fair A625 | 5th UN African Map Conference, Cairo A626

Wmk. 342
1983, Mar. 2 Photo. *Perf. 11x11½*
1210 A625 3p multi 15 15

1983, Mar. 2
1211 A626 3p lt grn & bl 15 15

African Ministers of Transport, Communications and Planning, 3rd Conference—A627

1983, Mar. 8 *Perf. 11½x11*
1212 A627 23p grn & bl 1.15 1.15

Victory in African Soccer Cup—A628

1983, Mar. 20 *Perf. 11x11½*
1213 A628 3p Heading 15 15
1214 A628 3p Kick 15 15

World Health Day and Natl. Blood Donation Campaign—A629

Wmk. 342
1983, Apr. 2 Photo. *Perf. 11x11½*
1215 A629 3p ol & red 15 15

Org. of African Trade Union Unity—A630

Wmk. 342
1983, Apr. 21 Photo. *Perf. 11½x11*
1216 A630 3p multi 15 15

First Anniv. of Sinai Liberation—A631

1983, Apr. 25 *Perf. 11x11½*
1217 A631 3p multi 15 15

75th Anniv. of Entomology Society—A632

1983, May 23
1218 A632 3p Emblem (Holy Scarab) 15 15

Flowers—A633

1983, June 11 Photo. *Perf. 11½x11*
1219 A633 20m grn & org red 10 6

5th African Handball Championship, Cairo—A634

Wmk. 342

1983, July 22 **Photo.** ***Perf. 11½x11***
1220 A634 6p brn & dk grn 30 30

31st Anniv. of Revolution—A635

Simon Bolivar (1783-1830)—A636

1983, July 23 ***Perf. 11½***
1221 A635 3p multi 15 15

1983, Aug. ***Perf. 11x11½***
1222 A636 23p brn & dl grn 1.15 1.15

Centenary of Arrival of Natl. Hero Orabi in Ceylon—A637

Wmk. 342

1983, Aug. 25 **Photo.** ***Perf. 11½x11***
1223 A637 3p Map, Orabi, El-Zahra School 15 15

Islamic Vase, Museum Building—A638

1983, Sept. 14 **Photo.** ***Perf. 11½x11***
1224 A638 3p yel brn & dk brn 15 15

Reopening of Islamic Museum.

10th Anniv., Sinai Crossing A639

2nd Pharaonic Race A640

1983, Oct. 6 ***Perf. 11½***
1225 A639 3p multi 15 15

1983, Oct. 17 ***Perf. 11½***
1226 A640 23p multi 1.15 1.15

United Nations Day—A641

1983, Oct. 24 **Photo.** ***Perf. 11***
1227 A641 3p IMO, ships 15 15
1228 A641 6p ITU, UPU 30 30
1229 A641 6p FAO, UN, grain 30 30
1230 A641 23p UN, ocean 1.15 1.15

4th World Karate Championship, Cairo—A642

1983, Nov. **Photo.** ***Perf. 13***
1231 A642 3p multi 15 15

Intl. Palestinian Cooperation Day—A643

1983, Nov. 29 **Photo.** ***Perf. 13x13½***
1232 A643 6p Dome of the Rock 30 30

75th Anniv. of Faculty of Fine Arts, Cairo—A644

1983, Nov. 30 ***Perf. 13***
1233 A644 3p multi 15 15

75th Anniv. of Cairo University—A645

1983, Nov. 30 ***Perf. 11x11½***
1234 A645 3p multi 15 15

Intl. Egyptian Society of Mother and Child Care—A646

1983, Nov. 30 ***Perf. 11½x11***
1235 A646 3p multi 15 15

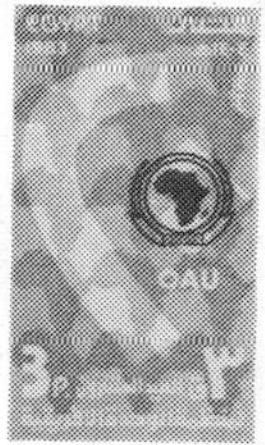

Org. of African Unity, 20th Anniv. A647

World Heritage Convention, 10th Anniv. A648

Wmk. 342

1983, Dec. 20 **Photo.** ***Perf. 11x11½***
1236 A647 3p multi 15 15

1983, Dec. 24
1237 Strip of 3 45 45
a. A648 3p Wood carving, Islamic 15 15
b. A648 3p Coptic tapestry 15 15
c. A648 3p Ramses II, Thebes 15 15

Post Day—A649

Restored Forts: 6p, Quatbay. 23p, Mosque, Salah El-Din.

1984, Jan. 2 ***Perf. 13***
1238 A649 6p multi 30 30
1239 A649 23p multi 1.15 1.15

Misr Insurance Co., 50 Anniv.—A650

1984, Jan. 14 ***Perf. 11½x11***
1240 A650 3p multi 15 15

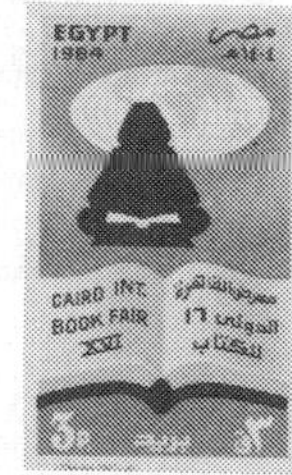

16th Cairo Intl. Book Fair—A651

Wmk. 342

1984, Jan. 26 **Photo.** ***Perf. 13½x13***
1241 A651 3p multi 15 15

17th Cairo Intl. Fair—A652

Wmk. 342

1984, Mar. 10 **Photo.** ***Perf. 11½x11***
1242 A652 3p multi 15 15

25th Anniv. of Assiout University—A653

1984, Mar. 10 ***Perf. 11x11½***
1243 A653 3p multi 15 15

75th Anniv. of Cooperative Unions—A654

1984, Mar. 17
1244 A654 3p multi 15 15

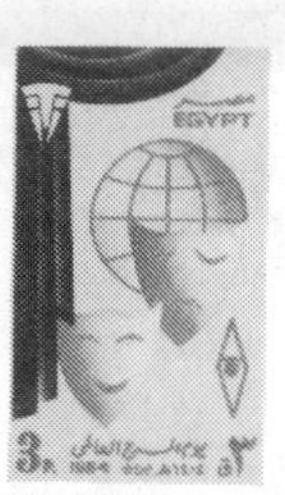

World Theater Day
A655

Mahmoud Mokhtar (1891-1934), Sculptor
A656

Perf. 11x11½, 11½x11

1984, Mar. 27 **Photo.** **Wmk.**

1245 A655 3p Masks 15 15
1246 A656 3p Pride of the Nile 15 15

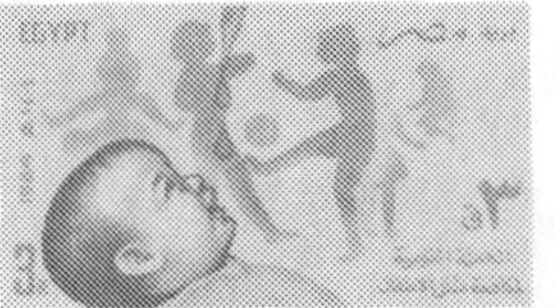

World Health Day and Fight Against Polio—A657

Wmk. 342

1984, Apr. 7 **Photo.** *Perf. 11½x11*

1247 A657 3p Polio vaccine 15 15

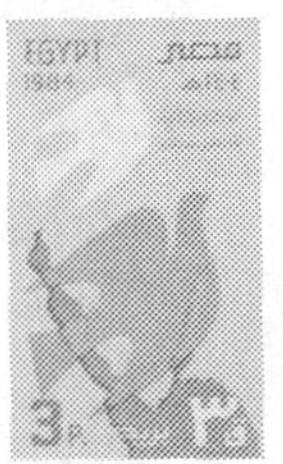

2nd Anniv. of Sinai Liberation—A658

1984, Apr. 25

1248 A658 3p Doves, map 15 15

Africa Day—A659

Wmk. 342

1984, May 25 **Photo.** *Perf. 12½x13½*

1249 A659 3p Map, UN emblem 15 15

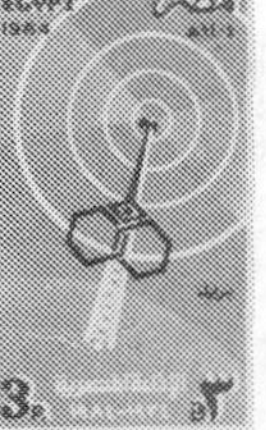

Satellite, Waves
A660

Flower
A661

1984, May 31 *Perf. 11x11½*

1250 A660 3p multi 15 15

Radio broadcasting in Egypt, 50th anniv.

1984, June 1

1251 A661 2p red & grn 10 10

Intl. Cairo Arab Arts Biennale—A662

1984, June 1 *Perf. 13½x12½*

1252 A662 3p multi 15 15

July Revolution, 32nd Anniv.—A663

Wmk. 342

1984, July 23 **Photo.** *Perf. 11*

1253 A663 3p Atomic energy, agriculture 15 15

1984 Summer Olympics—A664

Designs: a. Boxing. b. Basketball. c. Volleyball. d. Soccer.

1984, July 28

1254 Strip of 4 + label 60 60
a.-d. A664 3p, any single 15 15

Imperf.

1255 A664 30p Like #1254 1.50 1.50

Size of No. 1255: 130x80mm.

2nd Genl. Conference of Egyptians Abroad, Aug. 11-15, Cairo—A665

Wmk. 342

1984, Aug. 13 **Photo.** *Perf. 11*

1256 A665 3p bl & multi 15 15
1257 A665 23p grn & multi 1.15 1.15

Youth Hostels, 30th Anniv.
A666

Egypt Tour Co., 50th Anniv.
A667

Wmk. 342

1984, Sept. 22 **Photo.** *Perf. 11x11½*

1258 A666 3p Youths, emblem 15 15

1984, Sept. 27

1259 A667 3p Emblem, sphinx 15 15

Sinai Crossing, 11th Anniv.
A668

Egypt-Sudan Unity
A669

1984, Oct. 6

1260 A668 3p Map, eagle 15 15

1984, Oct. 12

1261 A669 3p Map of Nile, arms 15 15

UN Day—A670

Wmk. 342

1984, Oct. 24 **Photo.** *Perf. 13½x12½*

1262 A670 3p UNICEF Emblem, child 15 15

UN campaign for infant survival.

Tanks, Emblem—A671

1984, Nov. 10

1263 A671 3p multi 15 15

Military Equipment Exhibition, Cairo, Nov. 10-14.

Tolon Mosque, Egypt—A672

1984, Dec. 23 **Photo.** *Perf. 11½x11*

1264 A672 3p multi 15 15

Ahmed Ebn Tolon (A.D. 835-884), Gov. of Egypt, founder of Kataea City.

Kamel el-Kilany (1897-1959), Author—A673

1984, Dec. 23 *Perf. 11x11½*

1265 A673 3p multi 15 15

Globe and Congress Emblem—A674

Wmk. 342

1984, Dec. 26 **Photo.** *Perf. 11x11½*

1266 A674 3p lt bl, ver & blk 15 15

29th Intl. Congress on the History of Medicine, Dec. 27, 1984-Jan. 1, 1985, Cairo.

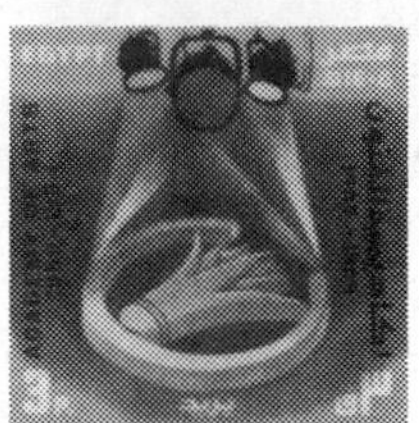

Academy of the Arts, 25th Anniv.—A675

1984, Dec. 31 *Perf. 13*

1267 A675 3p Emblem in spotlights 15 15

Pharaoh Receiving Message, Natl. Postal Museum, Cairo—A676

1985, Jan. 2 *Perf. 11½x11*

1268 A676 3p brn, lt bl & ver 15 15

Postal Museum, 50th anniv.

Intl. Union of Architects, 15th Conference, Jan. 14-Feb. 15—A677

1985, Jan. 20

1269 A677 3p multi 15 15

Seated Pharaonic Scribe A678

Wheat, Cogwheels, Fair Emblem A679

1985, Jan. 22 ***Perf. 11x11½***

1270 A678 3p brt org & dk bl grn 15 15

17th Intl. Book Fair, Jan. 22-Feb. 3, Cairo.

1985, Mar. 9 ***Perf. 13½x13***

1271 A679 3p multi 15 15

18th Intl. Fair, Mar. 9-22, Cairo.

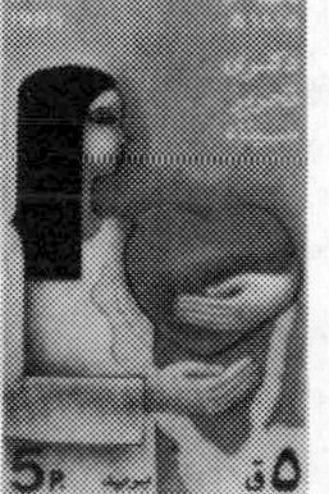

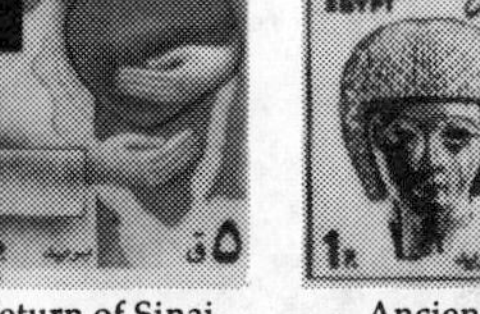

Return of Sinai to Egypt, 3rd Anniv. A680

Ancient Artifacts A681

1985, Apr. 25 **Wmk. 342** **Litho.**

1272 A680 5p multi 25 25

Wmk. 342

1985 **Photo.** ***Perf. 11½***

Designs: 1p, God Mout, limestone sculpture, 360-340 B.C. 2p, Five wading birds, bas-relief. 3p, 5p, Seated statue, Ramses II, Temple of Luxor. 8p, 15p, Slave bearing votive fruit offering, mural. 11p, Sculpted head of woman. 35p, Temple of Karnak carved capitals.

1273	A681	1p brn ol	5	5
1274	A681	2p brt grnsh bl	10	10
1275	A681	3p yel brn	15	15
1276	A681	5p dk vio	25	25
1277	A681	8p pale ol grn, sep & brn	40	40
1279	A681	11p dk vio	55	55
1282	A681	15p pale yel, sep & brn	75	75
1283	A681	20p yel grn ('86)	1.00	1.00
1285	A681	35p sep & pale yel	1.75	1.75
		Nos. 1273-1285 (9)	5.00	5.00

Issue dates: 1p, 2p, 3p, 5p, 8p, 11p, 15p, May 1. 35p, July 7.

Helwan University School of Music, 50th Anniv.—A682

1985, May 15

1287 A682 5p multi 25 25

El-Moulid Bride, Folk Doll—A683

1985

1288 A683 2p org & multi 10 10

1289 A683 5p red & multi 25 25

Festivals 1985. Issue dates: 2p, June 11. 5p, Aug. 10.

1985 Africa Cup Soccer Championships—A684

Designs and winning teams: Nos. 1287a, 1287b, Cairo Sports Stadium. No. 1287c, El-Mokawiloon Club, white uniform, 1983. No. 1287d, Natl. Club, red uniform, 1984. No. 1287e, El-Zamalek Club, orange uniform, 1984.

1985, June 17 ***Perf. 13½x13***

1290 Strip of 5 1.25 1.25

a.-e. A684 5p, Any single 25 25

Cairo Sports Stadium, 25th anniv. Nos. 1287a-1287b se-tenant in a continuous design.

Egyptian Television, 25th Anniv.—A685

1985, July 23 ***Perf. 11½x11***

1291 A685 5p bl, brn & yel 25 25

Egyptian Revolution, 33rd anniv.

Suez Canal Reopening, 10th Anniv.—A686

Wmk. 342

1985, July 23 **Litho.** ***Perf. 13x13½***

1292 A686 5p multi 25 25

Egyptian Revolution, 33rd anniv.

Ahmed Hamdi Memorial Underwater Tunnel—A687

1985, July 23 ***Perf. 13½x13***

1293 A687 5p bl, vio & org 25 25

Egyptian Revolution, 33rd anniv.

Souvenir Sheet

Aswan High Dam, 25th Anniv.—A688

Wmk. 342

1985, July 23 **Photo.** ***Imperf.***

1294 A688 30p multi 1.50 1.50

No. 1294 has multicolored margin. Size: 97x79m.

Heart, Map, Olive Laurel, Conference Emblem—A689

1985, Aug. 10 **Litho.** ***Perf. 13½x13***

1295 A689 15p multi 75 75

Egyptian Emigrants, 3rd general conference, Aug. 10-14, Cairo.

Natl. Tourism Ministry, 50th Anniv.—A691

1985, Sept. 10 ***Perf. 13x13½***

1296 A690 5p multi 25 25

Sinai Crossing, 12th Anniv.—A690

1985, Oct. 6

1297 A691 5p multi 25 25

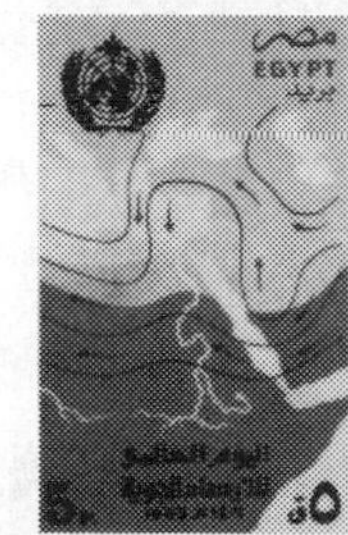

Air Scouts Assoc., 30th Anniv.—A692

1985, Oct. 15 **Photo.** ***Perf. 11½***

1298 A692 5p Emblem 25 25

UN Day, Meteorology Day—A693

1985, Oct. 24

1299 A693 5p UN emblem, weather map 25 25

UN, 40th Anniv. A694

Intl. Youth Year A695

1985, Oct. 24

1300 A694 15p multi 75 75

1985, Oct. 24

1301 A695 5p multi 25 25

Intl. Communications Development Program
A696

2nd Intl. Dentistry Conference
A697

1985, Oct. 24
1302 A696 15p bl & int bl 75 75

1985, Oct. 29 ***Perf. 11x11½***

Emblem, hieroglyphics of Hassi Raa, 1st known dentist.
1303 A697 5p beige & pale bl vio 25 25

Emblem, Squash Player—A698

1985, Nov. **Photo.** ***Perf. 11½***
1304 A698 5p dl org yel, grn & sep 25 25

1985 World Squash Championships, Nov. 18-Dec. 4.

4th Intl. Conference on the Biography and Sunna of Mohammed
A699

1st Conference on the Development of Vocational Training
A700

1985, Nov. 2 **Litho.** ***Perf. 13½x13***
1305 A699 5p multi 25 25

1985, Dec. 1 **Photo.** ***Perf. 11x11½***
1306 A700 5p multi 25 25

Natl. Olympic Committee, 75th Anniv.
A701

18th Intl. Book Fair, Cairo
A702

1985, Dec. 28 **Photo.** ***Perf. 13x13½***
1307 A701 5p multi 25 25

1986, Jan. 21 ***Perf. 11x11½***
1308 A702 5p Pharaonic scribe 25 25

CODATU III—A703

1986, Jan. 26 ***Perf. 11½***
1309 A703 5p lt ol grn, ver & grnsh bl 25 25

3rd Intl. Conference on Urban Transportation in Developing Countries, Cairo.

Central Bank, 25th Anniv.—A704

1986, Jan. 30 ***Perf. 13x13½***
1310 A704 5p multi 25 25

Cairo Postal Traffic Center Inauguration—A705

1986, Jan. 30 ***Perf. 11½x11***
1311 A705 5p bl & dk brn 25 25

Pharaonic Mural, Btah Hotteb's Tomb at Saqqara—A706

1986, Feb. 27 **Photo.** ***Perf. 11½x11***
1312 A706 5p yel, gldn brn & brn 25 25

Faculty of Commerce, Cairo University, 75th anniv.

Cairo Intl. Fair, Mar. 8-21—A707

1986, Mar. 8 **Litho.** ***Perf. 13½x13***
1313 A707 5p multi 25 25

Queen Nefertiti, Sinai—A708

Wmk. 342
1986, Mar. 25 **Litho.** ***Perf. 13x13½***
1314 A708 5p multi 25 25

Return of the Sinai to Egypt, 4th anniv.

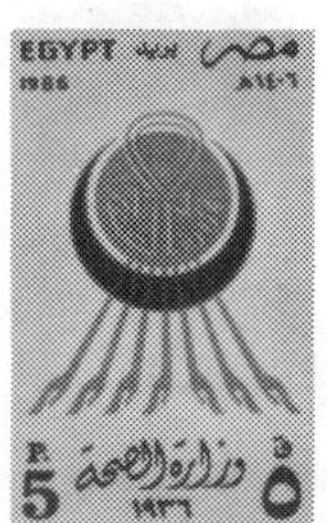

Ministry of Health, 50th Anniv.—A709

1986, Apr. 10 ***Perf. 13½x13***
1315 A709 5p multi 25 25

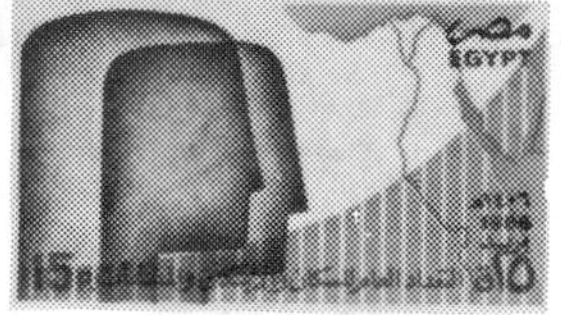

1986 Census—A710

1986, May 26 **Photo.** ***Perf. 11½***
1316 A710 15p brn, grnsh bl & yel bis 75 75

Egypt, Winner of African Soccer Cup
A711

Festivals, Roses
A712

1986, May 31 ***Perf. 13½x13***
1317 A711 5p English inscription below cup 25 25
1318 A711 5p Arabic 25 25

Nos. 1317-1318 printed se-tenant.

1986, June 2 ***Perf. 11½***
1319 A712 5p multi 25 25

World Environment Day—A713

1986, June 5 ***Perf. 13½x13***
1320 A713 15p Emblem, smokestacks 75 75

July 23rd Revolution, 34th Anniv.—A714

1986, July 23 **Litho.** ***Perf. 13***
1321 A714 5p gray grn, scar & yel bis 25 25

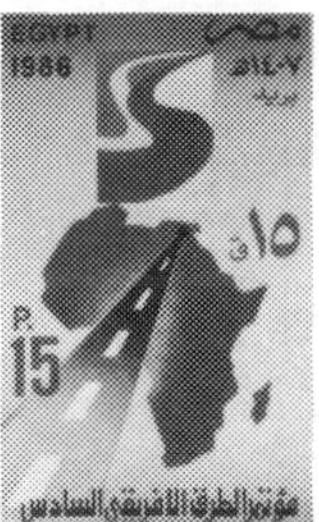

6th African Roads Conference, Cairo, Sept. 22-26—A715

1986, Sept. 21 **Litho.** ***Perf. 13½x13***
Wmk. 342
1322 A715 15p multi 75 75

Suez Canal Crossing, 13th Anniv.—A716

1986, Oct. 6 **Litho.** ***Perf. 13***
1323 A716 5p multi 25 25

Engineers' Syndicate, 40th Anniv.—A717

1986, Oct. 11 **Photo.** ***Perf. 11½***
1324 A717 5p lt bl, brn & pale grn 25 25

Workers' Cultural Education Assoc., 25th Anniv.
A718

Intl. Peace Year
A719

1986, Oct. 11 ***Perf. 11x11½***
1325 A718 5p org & rose vio 25 25

1986, Oct. 24
1326 A719 5p bl, grn & pale sal 25 25

First Oil Well in Egypt, Cent.—A720

1986, Nov. 7 **Photo.** ***Perf. 11½***
1327 A720 5p dl grn, blk & pale yel 25 25

UN Child Survival Campaign—A721

1986, Nov. 20 **Litho.** ***Perf. 13***
1328 A721 5p multi 25 25

Ahmed Amin, Philosopher
A722

National Theater, 50th Anniv.
A723

1986, Dec. 20 ***Perf. 11½***
1329 A722 5p pale grn, pale yel & brn 25 25

1986, Dec. 20 ***Perf. 13½x13***
1330 A723 5p multi 25 25

Post Day—A724

Design: Step Pyramid, Saqqara, King Zoser (2780-2760 B.C.)

Wmk. 342
1987, Jan. 2 **Litho.** ***Perf. 13x13½***
1331 A724 5p multi 25 25

19th Intl. Book Fair, Cairo—A725

1987, Jan. 25 **Litho.** ***Perf. 13***
1332 A725 5p multi 25 25

SEMI-POSTAL STAMPS.

Princess Ferial
SP1

Wmkd. Multiple Crown and Arabic F. (195)

1940, May 17 Photo. *Perf. 13½x14*

B1	SP1	5m +5m cop brn	50	45

No. B1 Overprinted in Green **1943** ١٩٤٣

1943, Nov. 17

B2	SP1	5m +5m cop brn	5.00	4.00
a.		Arabic date "1493"	175.00	175.00

The surtax on Nos. B1 and B2 was for the children's fund.

First Postage Stamp of Egypt
SP2

Khedive Ismail Pasha
SP3

Designs: 17m+17m, King Fuad. 22m+22m, King Farouk.

Perf. 13x13½

1946, Feb. 28 Wmk. 195

B3	SP2	1m +1m gray	10	10
B4	SP3	10m +10m vio	15	15
B5	SP3	17m +17m brn	25	25
B6	SP3	22m +22m yel grn	30	30
a.		Souvenir sheet, perf. 8½	40.00	35.00
b.		As "a," imperf.	40.00	35.00

Issued to commemorate the 80th anniversary of Egypt's first postage stamp.

Nos. B6a and B6b measure 129x171mm, and contain one each of Nos. B3 to B6, with inscriptions in top and bottom margins.

Goddess Hathor, King Men-kau-Re (Mycerinus) and Jackal-headed Goddess
SP7

Ramesseum, Thebes—SP8

Queen Nefertiti
SP9

Funerary Mask of King Tutankhamen
SP10

Perf. 13½x13

1947, Mar. 9 Wmk. 195

B9	SP7	5m +5m sl	25	25
B10	SP8	15m +15m dp bl	50	40
B11	SP9	30m +30m hn brn	70	70
B12	SP10	50m +50m brn	1.00	1.00

Issued to commemorate the International Exposition of Contemporary Art, Cairo.

Boy Scout Emblem
SP11

Scout Emblems: 20m+10m, Sea Scouts. 35m+15m, Air Explorers.

Photogravure.

1956, July 25 *Perf. 13½x13*

B13	SP11	10m +10m grn	35	30
B14	SP11	20m +10m ultra	50	45
B15	SP11	35m +15m bl	70	65

Issued to commemorate the 2nd Arab Scout Jamboree, Alexandria-Aboukir, 1956.

Souvenir sheets, perf. and imperf., contain one each of Nos. B13-B15. Size: 118×158mm. Price $400 each.

Ambulance
SP12

1957, May 13 *Perf. 13x13½*

B16	SP12	10m +5m rose red	20	18

Issued to commemorate the 50th anniversary of the Public Aid Society.

United Arab Republic

Eye and Map of Africa, Europe and Asia
SP13

Postal Emblem
SP14

Perf. 13½x13

1958, Mar. 1 Photo. Wmk. 318

B17	SP13	10m +5m org	60	60

Issued to commemorate the First Afro-Asian Congress of Ophthalmology, Cairo.

The surtax was for centers to aid the blind.

1959, Jan. 2

B18	SP14	10m +5m bl grn, red & blk	20	12

Issued for Post Day, Jan. 2. The surtax went to the social fund for postal employees.

Children and U. N. Emblem
SP15

Arab League Building, Cairo, and Emblem
SP16

1959, Oct. 24 Wmk. 328

B19	SP15	10m +5m brn lake	20	12
B20	SP15	35m +10m dk bl	40	35

Issued for International Children's Day and to honor UNICEF.

Braille Type of Regular Issue, 1961.

1961, Apr. 6 *Perf. 13½x13*

B21	A182	35m +15m yel & brn	50	50

World Health Organization Day.

1962, Mar. 22 Photo. Wmk. 328

B22	SP16	10m +5m gray	25	25

Arab Publicity Week, Mar. 22–28.

Postal Emblem
SP17

Stamp of 1866—SP18

1963, Jan. 2 *Perf. 11½* Wmk. 342

B23	SP17	20m +10m brt grn, red & blk	60	60
B24	SP18	40m +20m blk & brn org	90	90
B25	SP18	40m +20m brn org & blk	90	90

Issued for Post Day, Jan. 2 and to publicize the 1966 exhibition of the Federation International de Philatelie. Nos. B24–B25 printed se-tenant.

Arms of U.A.R. and Pyramids
SP19

1964, Jan. 2 *Perf. 11* Wmk. 342

B26	SP19	10m +5m org yel & grn	1.00	75
B27	SP19	80m +40m grnsh bl & blk	2.00	1.50
B28	SP19	115m +55m org brn & blk	2.50	2.00

Issued for Post Day. Jan. 2.

Type of 1963 and

Postal Emblem—SP20

Designs: No. B30, Emblem of Postal Secondary School. 80m+40m, Postal emblem, gearwheel and laurel wreath.

Photogravure

1965, Jan. 2 *Perf. 11½* Unwmkd.

B29	SP20	10m +5m lt grn & car	12	12
B30	SP20	10m +5m ultra, car & blk	12	12
B31	SP18	80m +40m rose, brt grn & blk	95	95

Issued for Post Day, Jan. 2. No. B31 also publicizes the Stamp Centenary Exhibition.

Souvenir Sheet

Stamps of Egypt, 1866—SP21

1966, Jan. 2 *Imperf.* Wmk. 342

B32	SP21	140m +60m blk, sl bl & rose	2.50	2.50

Issued for Post Day, 1966, and to commemorate the centenary of the first Egyptian postage stamps. Size: 105x62mm.

Pharaonic "Mediator"
SP22

Design: 115m+40, Pharaonic guard.

1967, Jan. 2 *Perf. 11½* Wmk. 342

B33	SP22	80m +20m multi	1.50	1.25
B34	SP22	115m +40m multi	2.75	1.75

Issued for Post Day, Jan. 2.

Grand Canal, Doges' Palace, Venice, and Santa Maria del Fiore, Florence—SP23

Design: 115m+30m, Piazetta and Campanile, Venice, and Palazzo Vecchio, Florence.

Perf. 11½x11

1967, Dec. 9 Photo. Wmk. 342

B35	SP23	80m +20m grn, yel & brn	65	65
B36	SP23	115m +30m ol, yel & sl bl	1.00	1.00

The surtax was to help save the cultural monuments of Venice and Florence, damaged in the 1966 floods.

Boy and Girl SP24

Emblem and Flags of Arab League SP25

Design: No. B38, Five children and arch.

Perf. 11

1968, Dec. 11 Photo. Wmk. 342

B37	SP24	20m +10m car, bl & lt brn	25	20
B38	SP24	20m +10m vio bl, sep & lt grn	25	20

Issued for Children's Day and to commemorate the 22nd anniversary of UNICEF (United Nations Children's Fund).

1969, Mar. 22 *Perf. 11x11½*

B39	SP25	20m +10m multi	35	18

Arab Publicity Week, March 22–28.

Refugee Family SP26

Perf. 11½

1969, Oct. 24 Photo. Wmk. 342

B40	SP26	30m +10m multi	75	50

Issued for United Nations Day.

Men of Three Races, Human Rights Emblem SP27

1970, Mar. 21 *Perf. 11½x11*

B41	SP27	20m +10m multi	25	18

Issued to publicize the International Day for the Elimination of Racial Discrimination.

Arab League Type of Regular Issue

1970, Mar. 22 Wmk. 342

B42	A344	20m +10m bl, grn & brn	75	50

25th anniversary of Arab League.

Map of Palestine and Refugees SP28

Perf. 11½x11

1970, Oct. 24 Photo. Wmk. 342

B43	SP28	20m +10m multi	1.50	75

Issued to commemorate the 25th anniversary of the United Nations and to draw attention to the plight of the Palestinian refugees.

Arab Republic of Egypt

Blind Girl, WHO and Society Emblems SP29

1973, Oct. 24 Photo. *Perf. 11x11½*

B44	SP29	20m +10m bl & gold	25	15

25th anniversary of the World Health Organization and for the Light and Hope Society, which educates and helps blind girls.

Map of Africa, OAU Emblem SP30

Social Work Day Emblem SP31

Perf. 11x11½

1973, Dec. 8 Photo. Wmk. 342

B45	SP30	55m +20m multi	1.50	1.50

10th anniversary of the Organization for African Unity.

1973, Dec. 8

B46	SP31	20m +10m multi	25	15

Social Work Day.

Jehane al Sadat Consoling Wounded Man—SP32

1974, Mar. 21 *Perf. 11* Wmk. 342

B47	SP32	20m +10m multi	50	25

Faithfulness and Hope Society.

AIR POST STAMPS.

Mail Plane in Flight AP1

Wmkd. Multiple Crown and Arabic F. (195)

Photogravure.

1926, Mar. 10 *Perf. 13x13½.*

C1	AP1	27m dp vio	14.00	8.00

1929, July 17

C2	AP1	27m org brn	5.00	3.00

Zeppelin Issue.

No. C2 Surcharged in Blue or Violet

GRAF ZEPPELIN
AVRIL 1931
50

1931, Apr. 6

C3	AP1	50m on 27m org brn (Bl)	37.50	32.50
a.		"1951" instead of "1931"	70.00	70.00
C4	AP1	100m on 27m org brn (V)	37.50	32.50

Airplane over Giza Pyramids AP2

1933–38 Lithographed *Perf. 13x13½*

C5	AP2	1m org & blk	10	8
C6	AP2	2m gray & blk	1.00	55
C7	AP2	2m org red & blk ('38)	80	75
C8	AP2	3m ol brn & blk	20	20
C9	AP2	4m grn & blk	50	45
C10	AP2	5m dp brn & blk	35	10
C11	AP2	6m dk grn & blk	70	65
C12	AP2	7m dk bl & blk	45	45
C13	AP2	8m vio & blk	25	15
C14	AP2	9m dp red & blk	80	80
C15	AP2	10m vio & brn	50	15
C16	AP2	20m dk grn & brn	35	10
C17	AP2	30m dl bl & brn	50	20
C18	AP2	40m dp red & brn	10.00	20
C19	AP2	50m org & brn	7.25	20
C20	AP2	60m gray & brn	2.75	20
C21	AP2	70m dk bl & bl grn	1.50	20
C22	AP2	80m ol brn & bl grn	1.50	20
C23	AP2	90m org & bl grn	2.50	20
C24	AP2	100m vio & bl grn	3.00	25
C25	AP2	200m dp red & bl grn	6.00	50
		Nos. C5-C25 (21)	41.00	6.58

Type of 1933.

1941–43 Photogravure

C34	AP2	5m cop brn ('43)	15	12
C35	AP2	10m violet	40	20
C36	AP2	25m dk vio brn ('43)	40	20
C37	AP2	30m green	50	20

No. C37 Overprinted in Black

مؤتمر الملاحة الجوية الدولى للشرق الأوسط

Le Caire 1946 - ١٩٤٦ القاهرة

1946, Oct. 1

C38	AP2	30m green	40	20
a.		Double overprint	125.00	125.00
b.		Inverted overprint	200.00	200.00

Issued to commemorate the Middle East International Air Navigation Congress, Cairo, October 1946.

King Farouk, Delta Dam and DC-3 Plane—AP3

Perf. 13x13½

1947, Feb. 19 Photo. Wmk. 195

C39	AP3	2m red org	10	5
C40	AP3	3m dk brn	10	10
C41	AP3	5m red brn	10	10
C42	AP3	7m dp yel org	12	12
C43	AP3	8m green	15	10
C44	AP3	10m violet	15	8
C45	AP3	20m brt bl	25	15
C46	AP3	30m brn vio	35	18
C47	AP3	40m car rose	50	20
C48	AP3	50m Prus grn	60	25
C49	AP3	100m ol grn	1.50	45
C50	AP3	200m dk gray	2.50	1.25
		Nos. C39-C50 (12)	6.42	3.03

Nos. C49 and C50 Surcharged in Black

Mills 13 ١٣ مليم

S. A. I. D. E.

23-8-1948 ١٩٤٨

1948, Aug. 23

C51	AP3	13m on 100m ol grn	45	45
C52	AP3	22m on 200m dk gray	55	55
a.		Date omitted		

Issued to commemorate the inaugural flights of "Services Aeriens Internationaux d'Egypte" from Cairo to Athens and Rome, August 23, 1948.

Nos. C39 to C50 Overprinted in Various Colors

ملك مصر والسودان
١٦ اكتوبر سنة ١٩٥١

Overprint 27mm. Wide.

1952, Jan. *Perf. 13x13½* Wmk. 195

C53	AP3	2m red org (Bl)	8	8
C54	AP3	3m dk brn (RV)	10	10
C55	AP3	5m red brn	12	10
C56	AP3	7m dp yel org (Bl)	25	25
C57	AP3	8m grn (RV)	18	18
C58	AP3	10m vio (G)	25	25
C59	AP3	20m brt bl (RV)	1.25	1.00
C60	AP3	30m brn vio (G)	50	40
C61	AP3	40m car rose	2.50	80
C62	AP3	50m Prus grn (RV)	1.50	1.00
C63	AP3	100m ol grn	3.00	1.85
C64	AP3	200m dk gray (RV)	4.25	3.25
		Nos. C53-C64 (12)	13.98	9.26

See note after No. 316.

Delta Dam and Douglas DC-3 AP4

1953 Photogravure.

C65	AP4	5m red brn	15	8
C66	AP4	15m ol grn	45	15

Nos. C39-C49 Overprinted in Black with Three Bars to Obliterate Portrait.

1953

C67	AP3	2m red org	20	20
C68	AP3	3m dk brn	40	40
C69	AP3	5m red brn	10	10
C70	AP3	7m dp yel org	50	15
C71	AP3	8m green	20	20
C72	AP3	10m violet	10.00	8.00
C73	AP3	20m brt bl	25	20
C74	AP3	30m brn vio	40	35
C75	AP3	40m car rose	45	45
C76	AP3	50m Prus grn	60	55
C77	AP3	100m ol grn	1.00	1.00
C77A	AP3	200m gray	20.00	15.00
		Nos. C67-C77A (12)	34.10	26.60

Nos. C53-C64 Overprinted in Black with Three Bars to Obliterate Portrait.

1953

C78	AP3	2m red org	8	8
C79	AP3	3m dk brn	12	12
C80	AP3	5m red brn	8	8
C81	AP3	7m dp yel org	4.50	4.50
C82	AP3	8m green	18	18
C83	AP3	10m violet	25	25
C84	AP3	20m brt bl	20.00	20.00
C85	AP3	30m brn vio	35	35
C86	AP3	40m car rose	20.00	20.00
C87	AP3	50m Prus grn	50	45
C88	AP3	100m ol grn	75	75
C89	AP3	200m dk gray	7.50	2.75
		Nos. C78-C89 (12)	54.31	49.51

Practically all values of Nos. C67-C89 exist with double overprint.

United Arab Republic

Type of Regular Issue

Perf. 11½x11

1958, March 22 Photo. Wmk. 318

C90	A141	15m ultra & red brn	30	20

Birth of United Arab Republic.

Pyramids at Giza AP5

Al Azhar University AP6

Designs: 15m, Colossi of Memnon, Thebes. 90m, St. Catherine Monastery, Mt. Sinai.

1959-60 *Perf. 13x13½* Wmk. 328

C91	AP5	5m brt red	5	5
C92	AP5	15m dk dl vio	15	15
C93	AP6	60m dk grn	50	50
C94	AP5	90m brn car ('60)	1.00	40

Nos. C91-C93 exist imperf. See also Nos. C101, C105.

Type of Regular Issue, Redrawn (Tower of Cairo)

1961, May 1 *Perf. 13½x13*

C95	A183	50m brt bl	40	35

Top inscription has been replaced by two airplanes.

Weather Vane, Anemometer and U.N. World Meteorological Organization Emblem—AP7

Perf. 11½x11

1962, Mar. 23 Photo. Unwmkd.

C96	AP7	60m yel & dp bl	50	50

2nd World Meteorological Day, Mar. 23.

Patrice Lumumba and Map of Africa AP8

Perf. 13½x13

1962, July 1 Wmk. 328

C97	AP8	35m multi	30	30

Issued in memory of Patrice Lumumba (1925-61), Premier of Congo.

Maritime Station, Alexandria AP9

Designs: 30m, International Airport, Cairo. 40m, Railroad Station, Luxor.

1963, Mar. 18 *Perf. 13x13½*

C98	AP9	20m dk brn	16	12
C99	AP9	30m car rose	25	20
C100	AP9	40m black	35	30

Type of 1959-60 and

Temple of Queen Nefertari, Abu Simbel—AP10

Arch and Tower of Cairo AP11

Designs: 80m, Al Azhar University seen through arch. 140m, Ramses II, Abu Simbel.

Perf. 11½x11, 11x11½

1963, Oct. 24 Photo. Wmk. 342

C101	AP6	80m vio blk & brt bl	3.00	50
C102	AP10	115m brn & yel	95	70
C103	AP10	140m pale vio, blk & org red	1.15	90

Unwmkd.

C104	AP11	50m yel brn & brt bl ('64)	50	40
C105	AP6	80m vio bl & lt bl ('65)	2.50	50

Weather Vane, Anemometer and WMO Emblem—AP12

Perf. 11½x11

1965, Mar. 23 Wmk. 342

C106	AP12	80m dk bl & rose lil	65	50

Fifth World Meteorological Day.

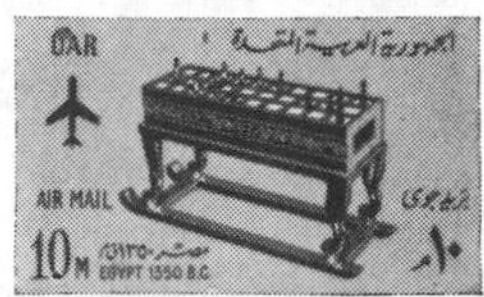

Game Board from Tomb of Tutankhamen—AP13

1965, July 1 Photo. Unwmkd.

C107	AP13	10m yel & dk bl	50	25

Temples at Abu Simbel—AP14

1966, Apr. 28 *Perf. 11½* Wmk. 342

C108	AP14	20m multi	12	10
C109	AP14	80m multi	60	35

Issued to commemorate the transfer of the temples of Abu Simbel to a hilltop, 1963-66.

Scout Camp and Jamboree Emblem—AP15

1966, Aug. 10 *Perf. 11½x11*

C110	AP15	20m ol & rose	25	10

Issued to commemorate the 7th Pan-Arab Boy Scout Jamboree, Good Daim, Libya, Aug. 12.

St. Catherine Monastery, Mt. Sinai AP16

1966, Nov. 30 Photo. Wmk. 342

C111	AP16	80m multi	60	35

Issued to commemorate the 1400th anniversary of St. Catherine Monastery, Sinai.

Cairo Airport AP17

1967, Apr. 26 *Perf. 11½x11*

C112	AP17	20m sky bl, sl grn & lt brn	12	10

Hotel El Alamein and Map of Nile Delta AP18

Designs: 80m, The Virgin's Tree, Virgin Mary and Child. 115m, Fishing in the Red Sea.

1967, June 7 *Perf. 11½* Wmk. 342

C113	AP18	20m dl pur, sl grn & dl org	25	10
C114	AP18	80m bl & multi	1.00	35
C115	AP18	115m brn, org & bl	1.75	75

Issued for International Tourist Year, 1967.

Oil Derricks, Map of Egypt—AP19

1967, July 23 Photogravure

C116	AP19	50m org & bluish blk	45	26

15th anniversary of the revolution.

Type of Regular Issue, 1967

Design: 80m, Back of Tutankhamen's throne and UNESCO emblem.

1967, Oct. 24 *Perf. 11½* Wmk. 342

C117	A301	80m bl & yel	50	35

22nd anniversary of the United Nations.

Koran—AP20

1968, Mar. 25 *Perf. 11½* Wmk. 342

C118	AP20	30m lil, bl & yel	75	50
C119	AP20	80m lil, bl & yel	1.50	1.00

Issued to commemorate the 1400th anniversary of the Koran. Nos. C118-C119 are printed in miniature sheets of 4 containing 2 each of Nos. C118-C119, decorative border and gutters. Size: 240x158 mm.

St. Mark and St. Mark's Cathedral—AP21

1968, June 25 *Perf. 11½* Wmk. 342

C120	AP21	80m brt grn, dk brn & dp car	60	35

Issued to commemorate the 1900th anniversary of the martyrdom of St. Mark and to commemorate the consecration of St. Mark's Cathedral, Cairo.

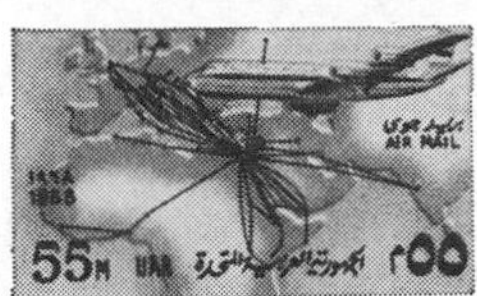

Map of United Arab Airlines and Boeing 707—AP22

Design: No. C122, Ilyushin 18 and routes of United Arab Airlines.

1968-69 Photo. *Perf. 11½x11*

C121	AP22	55m bl, ocher & car	35	25
C122	AP22	55m bl, yel & vio blk ('69)	35	25

Issued to commemorate the first flights of a Boeing 707 (No. C121) and an Ilyushin 18 (No. C122) for United Arab Airlines.

Mahatma Gandhi, Arms of India and UAR AP23

Imam El Boukhary AP24

1969, Sept. 10 *Perf. 11x11½*

C123	AP23	80m lt bl, ocher & brn	65	35

Issued to commemorate the centenary of the birth of Mohandas K. Gandhi (1869-1948), leader in India's fight for independence.

1969, Dec. 27 Photo. Wmk. 342

C124	AP24	30m lt ol & dk brn	20	15

Issued to commemorate the 1100th anniversary of the death of the Imam El Boukhary (824-870), philosopher and writer.

Azzahir Beybars Mosque AP25

1969, Dec. 27 Engr. *Perf. 11½x11*

C125	AP25	30m red lil	18	15

700th anniversary of the founding of the Azzahir Beybars Mosque, Cairo.

Lenin AP26

Perf. 11x11½

1970, Apr. 22 Photo. Wmk. 342

C126	AP26	80m lt grn & brn	50	35

Issued to commemorate the centenary of the birth of Lenin (1870-1924).

Phantom Fighters and Destroyed Factory—AP27

1970, May 1 *Perf. 11½x11*

C127	AP27	80m yel, grn & dk vio brn	75	35

Issued to commemorate the destruction of the Abu-Zaabal factory by Israeli planes.

U.P.U. Type of Regular Issue

1970, May 20 Photo. Wmk. 342

C128	A350	80m multi	50	35

Issued to commemorate the inauguration of the new Universal Postal Union Headquarters in Bern.

Nasser and Burial Mosque AP28

1970, Nov. 6 *Perf. 11* Wmk. 342

C129	AP28	30m ol & blk	35	15
C130	AP28	80m brn & blk	75	35

Issued in memory of Gamal Abdel Nasser (1918-1970), President of Egypt.

Postal Congress Type of Regular Issue

Perf. 11½x11

1971, Mar. 6 Photo. Wmk. 342

C131	A365	30m lt ol, org & sl grn	25	15

9th Arab Postal Congress, Cairo, March 6-25.

Nasser, El Rifaei and Sultan Hussein Mosques—AP29

Designs: 85m, Nasser and Ramses Square, Cairo. 110m, Nasser, Sphinx and pyramids.

Perf. 11½x11

1971, July 1 Photo. Wmk. 342

C132	AP29	30m multi	50	15
C133	AP29	85m multi	1.25	35
C134	AP29	110m multi	1.75	50

APU Type of Regular Issue

1971, Aug. 3 *Perf. 11½* Wmk. 342

C135	A373	30m brn, yel & bl	18	15

25th anniversary of the Conference of Sofar, Lebanon, establishing the Arab Postal Union.

Arab Republic of Egypt

Confederation Type of Regular Issue

Perf. 11½x11

1971, Sept. 28 Photo. Wmk. 342

C136	A374	30m gray, sl grn & dk pur	18	12

Confederation of Arab Republics (Egypt, Syria and Libya).

Al Aqsa Mosque and Woman AP30

Perf. 11½

1971, Oct. 24 Photo. Wmk. 342

C137	AP30	30m bl, yel, brn & grn	75	50

25th anniversary of the United Nations (in 1970) and for the return of Palestinian refugees.

Postal Union Type of Regular Issue

Design: 30m, African Postal Union emblem and letter.

1971, Dec. 2 *Perf. 11½x11*

C138	A384	30m grn, blk & bl	18	12

10th anniversary of African Postal Union.

Aida, Triumphal March AP31

1971, Dec. 23 *Perf. 11½* Wmk. 342

C139	AP31	110m dk brn, yel & sl grn	80	40

Centenary of the first performance of the opera Aida, by Giuseppe Verdi.

Globe, Glider, Rocket Club Emblem AP32

St. Catherine's Monastery on Fire AP33

1972, Feb. 11 *Perf. 11x11½*

C140	AP32	30m bl, ocher & yel	18	12

International Aerospace Education Conference, Cairo, Jan. 11-13.

Perf. 11½x11

1972, Feb. 15 Unwmkd.

C141	AP33	110m dp car, org & blk	70	40

The burning of St. Catherine's Monastery in Sinai Desert, Nov. 30, 1971.

Tutankhamen in Garden AP34

Tutankhamen, from 2nd Sarcophagus—AP35

Design: No. C143, Ankhesenamun.

1972, May 22 Photo. *Perf. 11½*

C142	AP34	110m brn org, bl & grn	2.50	75
C143	AP34	110m brn org, bl & grn	2.50	75

Souvenir Sheet

Imperf.

C144	AP35	200m gold & multi	5.00	5.00

50th anniversary of the discovery of the tomb of Tutankhamen. Nos. C142-C143 printed se-tenant in sheets of 50. The continuous design is from a painted ivory plaque on lid of a coffer.

No. C144 has blue inscription and gold scarab ornaments in margin. Size: 97x102 mm.

Souvenir Sheet

Flag of Confederation of Arab Republics—AP36

1972, July 23 Photo. *Imperf.*

C145	AP36	110m gold, dp car & blk	1.75	1.50

20th anniversary of the revolution. No. C145 has gold commemorative inscription and black portraits of Presidents Nasser and Anwar El Sadat in margin. Size: 107x69 mm.

Temples at Abu Simbel
AP37

Designs: 30m, Al Azhar Mosque and St. George's Church. 110m, Pyramids at Giza.

1972 ***Perf. 11½x11*** **Wmk. 342**

C146	AP37	30m bl brn & buff	15	10
C147	AP37	85m bl, brn & ocher	45	30
C148	AP37	110m multi	60	32

Issue dates: Nos. C146, C148, Nov. 22; No. C147, Aug. 1.

Olympic Type of Regular Issue

Designs (Olympic and Motion Emblems and): No. C149, Handball. No. C150, Weight lifting. 50m, Swimming. 55m, Gymnastics. All vertical.

1972, Aug. 17 ***Perf. 11x11½***

C149	A396	30m multi	15	10
C150	A396	30m yel & multi	15	10
C151	A396	50m bl & multi	25	16
C152	A396	55m multi	28	16

Champollion, Rosetta Stone, Hieroglyphics—AP38

1972, Oct. 16

C153	AP38	110m gold, grn & blk	1.25	50

Sesquicentennial of the deciphering of Egyptian hieroglyphics by Jean-François Champollion.

World Map, Telephone, Radar, ITU Emblem—AP39

1973, Mar. 21 **Photo.** ***Perf. 11***

C154	AP39	30m lt bl, dk bl & blk	15	10

5th World Telecommunications Day.

Karnak Temple, Luxor
AP40

Hand Dripping Blood and Falling Plane
AP41

1973, Mar. 21

C155	AP40	110m dp ultra, blk & rose	1.00	70

Sound and light at Karnak.

1973, May 1 ***Perf. 11x11½***

C156	AP41	110m multi	1.50	75

Israeli attack on Libyan civilian plane, Feb. 1973.

WMO Emblem, Weather Vane
AP42

1973, Oct. 24 ***Perf. 11x11½***

C157	AP42	110m bl, gold & pur	1.00	50

Centenary of international meteorological cooperation.

Refugees, Map of Palestine
AP43

1973, Oct. 24 ***Perf. 11½***

C158	AP43	30m dk brn, yel & bl	1.00	35

Plight of Palestinian refugees.

INTERPOL Emblem
AP44

Postal and UPU Emblems
AP45

Perf. 11x11½

1973, Dec. 8 **Photo.** **Wmk. 342**

C159	AP44	110m blk & multi	75	35

50th anniversary of the International Criminal Police Organization.

1974, Jan. 2 ***Perf. 11*** **Unwmkd.**

Designs (UPU Emblems and): 30m, Arab Postal Union emblem. 55m, African Postal Union emblem. 110m, Universal Postal Union emblem.

Size: 26x46½mm.

C160	AP45	20m gray, red & blk	10	8
C161	AP45	30m sal, blk & pur	15	10
C162	AP45	55m emer, blk & brt mag	70	25

Size: 37x37½mm. ***Perf. 11½***

C163	AP45	110m lt bl, blk & gold	1.00	50

Post Day 1974.

Solar Bark of Khufu (Cheops)
AP46

Photogravure

1974, Mar. 21 ***Perf. 11½*** **Wmk. 342**

C164	AP46	110m bl, gold & brn	1.00	50

Solar Bark Museum.

Hotel Meridien
AP47

1974, Oct. 6 ***Perf. 11½x11***

C165	AP47	110m multi	1.00	50

Opening of Hotel Meridien, Cairo.

Suez Canal Type of 1975

1975, June 5 ***Perf. 11½***

C166	A448	30m bl, yel grn & ind	60	25
C167	A448	110m ind & bl	1.50	50

Reopening of the Suez Canal, June 5.

Irrigation Commission Emblem
AP48

1975, July 20

C168	AP48	110m org & dk grn	1.00	50

9th International Congress on Irrigation and Drainage, Moscow, and 25th anniversary of the International Commission on Irrigation and Drainage.

Refugees and UNWRA Emblem—AP49

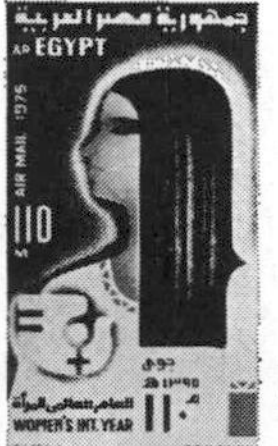

Woman and IWY Emblem
AP50

Perf. 11x11½

1975, Oct. 24 **Photo.** **Wmk. 342**

C169	AP49	30m multi	75	50

Unwmkd.

C170	AP50	110m ol, org & blk	1.10	65

United Nations Day. 30m publicizes U.N. help for refugees; 110m is for International Women's Year 1975.

Step Pyramid, Sakhara, and Entrance Gate
AP51

Designs: 45m, Plane over Giza Pyramids. 140m, Plane over boats on Nile.

Perf. 11½x11

1977, Nov. 15 **Photo.** **Wmk. 342**

C171	AP51	45m yel & brn	22	16
C171A	AP51	60m olive	30	30
C172	AP51	115m bl & brn	60	30
C173	AP51	140m bl & pur	70	48

Flyer and U.N. ICAO Emblem
AP52

Wmk. 342

1978, Dec. 30 **Photo.** ***Perf. 11x11½***

C174	AP52	140m bl, blk & brn	70	55

75th anniversary of 1st powered flight.

Seeing Eye Medallion—AP53

Wmk. 342

1981, Oct. 1 **Photo.** ***Perf. 11½x11***

C175	AP53	230m multi	1.15	60

Hilton Ramses Hotel Opening—AP54

Wmk. 342

1982, Mar. 15 **Photo.** ***Perf. 11x11½***

C176	AP54	18½p multi	10	5

Temple of Horus, Edfu—AP55

Designs: 15p, like 6p. 18½p, 25p, Statue of Akhnaton, Thebes, hieroglyphics, vert. 23p, 30p, Gizeh pyramids.

1985 **Photo.** ***Perf. 11½x11, 11x11½***

C177	AP55	6p lt bl & dk bl grn	30	30
C178	AP55	15p grnsh bl & brn	75	75
C179	AP55	18½p grn, sep & dp yel	90	90
C180	AP55	23p grnsh bl, sep & yel bis	1.15	1.15
C181	AP55	25p lt bl, sep & yel bis	1.25	1.25
C182	AP55	30p grnsh bl, sep & org yel	1.50	1.50
		Nos. C177-C182 (6)	5.85	5.85

Issue dates: 6p, 18½p, 23p, Mar. 1. 15p, 25p, 30p, May 1.

Post Day—AP56

Narmer Board, oldest known hieroglyphic inscriptions: No. C183a, Tablet obverse. No. C183b, Reverse.

1986, Jan. 2 Photo. *Perf. 13½x13*

C183		Pair	1.50	1.50
a.-b.	AP56	15p any single	75	75

Map, Jet, AFRAA Emblem—AP57

1986, Apr. 7 Photo. *Perf. 11½*

C184	AP57	15p bl, yel & blk	38	38

African Airlines Assoc., 18th General Assembly, Cairo, Apr. 7-10.

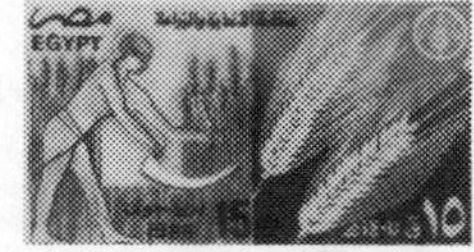

World Food Day—AP58

UNESCO, 40th Anniv.—AP59

1986, Oct. 24 Litho. *Perf. 13½x13, 13x13½*

C185	AP58	15p multi	75	75
C186	AP59	15p multi	75	75

UN Day.

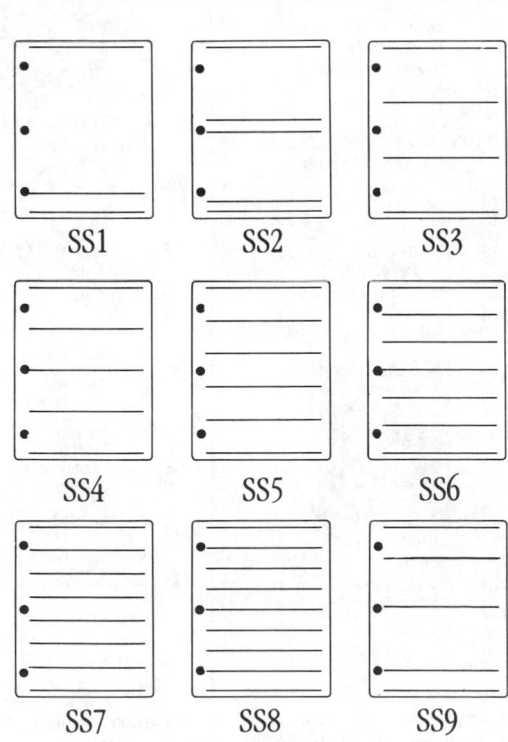

AIR POST SEMI-POSTAL STAMPS

United Arab Republic

Pharaonic Mail Carriers and Papyrus Plants
SPAP1

Design: 115m+55m, Jet plane, world map and stamp of Egypt, 1926 (No. C1).

Photogravure

1966, Jan. 2 Perf. 11½ Wmk. 342

CB1 SPAP1 80m +40m yel, grn, brn, lil & bl 90 70
CB2 SPAP1 115m +55m bl, yel & lil 1.10 85

Issued for Post Day, Jan. 2. Nos. CB1–CB2 printed se-tenant in sheets of 28.

SPECIAL DELIVERY STAMPS.

Motor-cycle Postman
SD1

Wmkd.
Multiple Crown and Arabic F. (195)

1926, Nov. 28 Photo. Perf. 13x13½

E1 SD1 20m dk grn 6.50 2.00

1929, Sept.

E2 SD1 20m brn red & blk 75 40

Inscribed "Postes Expres."

1943–44 Lithographed

E3 SD1 26m brn red & gray blk 1.00 90
E4 SD1 40m dl brn & pale gray ('44) 75 30

No. E4 Overprinted in Black
ملك مصر والسودان
١٦ اكتوبر سنة ١٩٥١

Overprint 27mm. Wide.

1952, Jan.

E5 SD1 40m dl brn & pale gray 60 45

See note after No. 316.

POSTAGE DUE STAMPS.

D1 D2

Wmkd. Crescent and Star. (119)

1884, Jan. 1 Litho. Perf. 10½

J1 D1 10pa red 10.00 2.00
a. Imperf. vert., pair 125.00
J2 D1 20pa red 18.00 4.00
J3 D1 1pi red 32.50 7.50
J4 D1 2pi red 50.00 4.00
J5 D1 5pi red 12.50 10.00

1886, Aug. 1 Unwmkd.

J6 D1 10pa red 3.00 1.00
a. Imperf. vert., pair 75.00 60.00
J7 D1 20pa red 75.00 10.00
J8 D1 1pi red 2.50 1.00
J9 D1 2pi red 2.50 50

1888, Jan. 1 Perf. 11½

J10 D2 2m green 1.50 75
a. Horiz. pair, imperf. between 75.00
J11 D2 5m rose red 2.50 75
J12 D2 1pi blue 25.00 8.50
J13 D2 2pi yellow 20.00 3.50
J14 D2 5pi gray 75.00 50.00
a. Period after 'PIASTRES' 100.00 75.00
Nos. J10-J14 (5) 124.00 63.50

Excellent counterfeits of J1 to J14 are plentiful. There are four types of each of Nos. J1 to J14, so placed that any block of four contains all four types.

D3 D4

Typographed.

1889 Perf. 14x13½ Wmk. 119

J15 D3 2m green 90 10
a. Half used as 1m on cover 5.00
J16 D3 4m maroon 60 8
J17 D3 1pi ultra 1.50 8
J18 D3 2pi orange 1.75 25

Nos. J15–J18 exist on both ordinary and chalky paper. Imperf. examples of Nos. J15–J17 are proofs.

Black Surcharge.

1898

J19 D4 3m on 2pi org 30 25
a. Inverted surch. 30.00 30.00
b. Double surcharge 100.00 100.00
c. Pair, one without surcharge 175.00

There are two types of this surcharge. In one type, the spacing between the last two Arabic characters at the right is 2mm. In the other type, this spacing is 3mm., and there is an added sign on top of the second character from the right.

D5 D6

Wmkd.
Triple Crescent and Star. (120)

1921 Perf. 14x13½

J20 D5 2m green 40 35
J21 D5 4m vermilion 1.50 75
J22 D6 10m dp bl 1.50 1.00

1921-22

J23 D5 2m vermilion 35 15
J24 D5 4m green 35 15
J25 D6 10m lake ('22) 50 10

Nos. J18, J23–J25 Overprinted

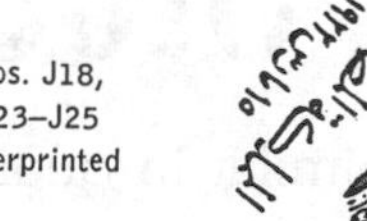

1922, Oct. 10 Wmk. 119

J26 D3 2pi orange 4.00 1.00
a. Ovpt. right side up 8.00 5.00

Wmk. 120

J27 D5 2m vermilion 50 25
J28 D5 4m green 75 50
J29 D6 10m lake 1.25 60

Overprint on Nos. J26–J29 is inverted.

Arabic Numeral
D7

Wmkd.
Multiple Crown and Arabic F. (195)

1927–56 Lithographed Perf. 13x13½

Size: 18x22½ mm.

J30 D7 2m slate 50 15
J31 D7 2m org ('38) 25 15
J32 D7 4m green 40 15
J33 D7 4m ol brn ('32) 1.50 20
J34 D7 5m brown 1.00 30
J35 D7 6m gray grn ('41) 50 20
J36 D7 8m brn vio 50 25
J37 D7 10m brick red ('29) 65 25
a. 10m dp red 75 35
J38 D7 12m rose lake ('41) 90 25
J38A D7 20m dk red ('56) 1.50 75

Perf. 13½x14

Size: 22x28 mm.

J39 D7 30m purple 3.50 1.50
Nos. J30-J39 (11) 11.20 4.15

Postage Due Stamps and Type of 1927 Overprinted in Various Colors
ملك مصر والسودان
١٦ اكتوبر سنة ١٩٥١

1952, Jan. 16 Perf. 13x13½

J40 D7 2m org (Bl) 15 15
J41 D7 4m green 30 30
J42 D7 6m gray grn (RV) 45 35
J43 D7 8m brn vio (Bl) 40 35
J44 D7 10m dl rose (Bl) 1.00 35
a. 10m brn red (Bk) 65 40
J45 D7 12m rose lake (Bl) 50 30

Perf. 14

J46 D7 30m pur (C) 1.50 55
Nos. J40-J46 (7) 4.30 2.35

See note after No. 316.

United Arab Republic

1960 Perf. 13x13½ Wmk. 318

Size: 18x22½ mm.

J47 D7 2m orange 45 15
J48 D7 4m lt grn 55 20
J49 D7 6m green 75 25
J50 D7 8m brn vio 55 35
J51 D7 12m rose brn 1.00 50
J52 D7 20m dl rose brn 1.50 50

Perf. 14

Size: 22x28 mm.

J53 D7 30m violet 5.00 1.00
Nos. J47-J53 (7) 9.80 2.95

1962 Perf. 13x13½ Wmk. 328

Size: 18x22½mm.

J54 D7 2m salmon 35 25
J55 D7 4m lt grn 70 35
J56 D7 10m red brn 1.00 50
J57 D7 12m rose brn 1.75 75
J58 D7 20m dl rose brn 2.50 1.50

Perf. 14

Size: 22x28mm.

J59 D7 30m lt vio 3.25 2.25
Nos. J54-J59 (6) 9.55 5.60

D8

Photogravure

1965 Perf. 11 Unwmkd.

J60 D8 2m org & vio blk 15 10
J61 D8 8m lt bl & dk bl 20 15
J62 D8 10m yel & emer 25 15
J63 D8 20m lt bl & vio blk 30 15
J64 D8 40m org & emer 60 20
Nos. J60-J64 (5) 1.50 75

A little time given to study of the arrangement of the Scott Catalogue can make it easier to use effectively.

MILITARY STAMPS

From November 1, 1932 to February 29, 1936 members of the British Forces in Egypt were permitted to send letters to Great Britain at reduced rates. Special seals were used in place of Egyptian stamps. These seals were replaced by special stamps March 1, 1936.

Fuad Type of 1927.
Inscribed "Army Post".
Wmkd.
Multiple Crown and Arabic F. (195)

1936, Mar. 1 Photo. Perf. 13½x14

M1 A44 3m green 50 15
M2 A44 10m carmine 1.50 30

King Farouk
M1

1939, Dec. 16 Perf. 13x13½

M3 M1 3m green 50 3.00
M4 M1 10m car rose 1.50 20

United Arab Republic

Arms of UAR and Military Emblems
M2

Perf. 11x11½

1971, Apr. 15 Photo. Wmk. 342

M5 M2 10m purple 12 12

OFFICIAL STAMPS.

O1

Wmkd. Crescent and Star. (119)

1893, Jan. 1 Typo. Perf. 14x13½

O1 O1 org brn 30 15

No. O1 exists on ordinary and chalky paper.
Imperf. examples of No. O1 are proofs.

Regular Issues of 1884-93 Overprinted
O.H.H.S.
اميري

1907

O2 A18 1m brown 15 6
O3 A19 2m green 20 6
a. Double ovpt.
O4 A21 3m orange 20 6
O5 A20 5m car rose 35 5
O6 A14 1pi ultra 60 6
O7 A16 5pi gray 3.50 20
Nos. O2-O7 (6) 5.00 49

Imperf. examples of Nos. O2–O3, O5–O7 are proofs.

Overprinted
O.H.H.S.

1913

O8 A20 5m car rose 30 15
a. Inverted overprint 100.00 50.00
b. No period after "S" 6.50 3.50

Regular Issues Overprinted
O.H.H.S.
اميرى

1914–15 On Issues of 1888–1906

O9 A19 2m green 30 20
a. Inverted ovpt. 20.00 20.00
b. Dbl. ovpt. 250.00 250.00
c. No period after "S" 6.00 6.00

O10 A23 4m brn red 50 20
a. Inverted ovpt. 140.00 110.00

On Issue of 1914.

O11 A24 1m ol brn 20 12
a. No period after "S" 2.50 2.50
O12 A26 3m orange 25 15
a. No period after "S" 5.00 5.00
O13 A28 5m lake 50 8
a. No period after "S" 4.00 4.00
b. Two periods after "S" 4.00 4.00
Nos. O9-O13 (5) 1.75 75

Regular Issues Overprinted O.H.H.S. أميرى

On Issues of 1888–1906

1915, Oct.

O14 A19 2m green 45 12
a. Inverted overprint 10.00 10.00
b. Double overprint 15.00
O15 A23 4m brn red 75 15

On Issue of 1914.

O16 A28 5m lake 35 18
a. Pair, one without ovpt. 200.00

On Issue of 1921-22.

1922 Wmk. 120

O17 A24 1m ol brn 5.00 1.50
a. Two periods after "S" 300.00
O18 A25 2m red 5.00 1.50
O19 A26 3m orange 100.00 85.00
O20 A28 5m pink 5.00 1.50
a. Double ovpt. 100.00

Regular Issues of 1921–22 Overprinted O.H.E.M.S. الحكومة الملكيةالمصرية

1922

O21 A24 1m ol brn 35 25
a. Two periods after "S" 35.00
O22 A25 2m red 40 30
O23 A26 3m orange 1.75 80
O24 A27 4m green 2.50 1.50
a. Two periods after "H" none after "S" 100.00 100.00
O25 A28 5m pink 60 25
a. Two periods after "H" none after "S" 50.00 50.00
O26 A29 10m dp bl 1.75 1.00
O27 A34 15m indigo 2.00 1.25
O28 A35 15m indigo 125.00 75.00
a. Two periods after "H" none after "S" 300.00 300.00
O29 A31 50m maroon 10.00 3.75
Nos. O21-O29 (9) 144.35 84.10

1923

O30 A29 10m lake 3.00 1.25
a. Two periods after "H" none after "S" 75.00 75.00

Regular Issue of 1923 Overprinted in Black or Red أمرى

1924 Perf. 13½x14

O31 A36 1m orange 60 20
O32 A36 2m gray (R) 75 45
O33 A36 3m brown 2.00 70
O34 A36 4m yel grn 2.50 1.00
O35 A36 5m org brn 75 30
O36 A36 10m rose 2.25 45
O37 A36 15m ultra 2.50 75

Perf. 14

O38 A36 50m myr grn 6.00 1.75
Nos. O31-O38 (8) 17.35 5.60

O2 O3

Wmkd. Multiple Crown and Arabic F. (195)

1926–35 Litho. Perf. 13x13½

Size 18½x22mm.

O39 O2 1m lt org 6 6
O40 O2 2m black 6 6
O41 O2 3m ol brn 8 8
O42 O2 4m lt grn 10 8
O43 O2 5m brown 15 6
O44 O2 10m dl red 50 8
O45 O2 10m brt vio ('34) 25 8
O46 O2 15m dp bl 75 10
O47 O2 15m brn vio ('34) 30 8
O48 O2 20m dp bl ('35) 40 10

Perf. 13½

Size 22½x27½ mm.

O49 O2 20m ol grn 2.00 20
O50 O2 50m myr grn 1.50 15
Nos. O39-O50 (12) 6.15 1.13

1938, Dec. Size 22½x19mm.

O51 O3 1m orange 5 5
O52 O3 2m red 6 6
O53 O3 3m ol brn 8 8
O54 O3 4m yel grn 10 8
O55 O3 5m brown 10 6
O56 O3 10m brt vio 12 8
O57 O3 15m rose vio 18 10
O58 O3 20m blue 25 12

Perf. 14x13½.

Size 26½x22 mm.

O59 O3 50m myr grn 50 15
Nos. O51-O59 (9) 1.44 78

Nos. O51 to O59 Overprinted in Various Colors ملك مصر والسودان ١٦ اكتوبر سنة ١٩٥١

Overprint 19mm. Wide.

1952, Jan. Perf. 13x13½

O60 O3 1m org (Br) 5 5
O61 O3 2m red 5 5
O62 O3 3m ol brn (Bl) 8 8
O63 O3 4m yel grn (Bl) 10 10
O64 O3 5m brn (Bl) 10 10
O65 O3 10m brt vio (Bl) 15 10
O66 O3 15m rose vio (Bl) 20 15
O67 O3 20m blue 30 30

Overprint 24½mm. Wide.

Perf. 14x13½.

O68 O3 50m myr grn (RV) 75 60
Nos. O60-O68 (9) 1.78 1.53

See note after No. 316.

United Arab Republic

Numeral O4 Arms of U.A.R. O5

Perf. 13x13½

1959 Lithographed Wmk. 318

O69 O4 10m brn vio 50 8
O70 O4 35m chlky bl 1.00 12

1962-63 Wmk. 328

O71 O4 1m org ('63) 5 5
O72 O4 4m yel grn ('63) 5 5
O73 O4 5m brown 5 5
O74 O4 10m dk brn 5 5
O75 O4 35m dk bl 35 35
O76 O4 50m green 50 50
O77 O4 100m vio ('63) 1.00 50
O78 O4 200m rose red ('63) 2.00 1.00
O79 O4 500m gray ('63) 5.00 3.00
Nos. O71-O79 (9) 9.05 5.55

Photogravure

1966–68 Perf. 11½x11 Unwmkd.

O80 O5 1m ultra 5 5
O81 O5 4m brown 5 5
O82 O5 5m olive 5 5
O83 O5 10m brn blk 10 10
O84 O5 20m magenta 15 15
O85 O5 35m dk pur 30 30
O86 O5 50m orange 35 35
O87 O5 55m dk pur 40 40

Wmk. 342

O88 O5 100m brt grn & brick red 70 50
O89 O5 200m bl & brick red 1.25 1.00
O90 O5 500m ol & brick red 3.50 2.50
Nos. O80-O90 (11) 6.90 5.45

1969 Wmk. 342

O91 O5 10m magenta 8 8

Arab Republic of Egypt

Arms of Egypt O6

Perf. 11

1972, June 30 Photo. Wmk. 342

O92 O6 1m blk & vio bl 5 5
a. 1m blk & lt bl ('75) 5 5
O93 O6 10m blk & car 8 8
a. 10m blk & rose red ('76) 8 8
O94 O6 20m blk & ol 15 15
O95 O6 50m blk & org 30 30
O96 O6 55m blk & pur 35 35
Nos. O92-O96 (5) 93 93

1973

O97 O6 20m lil & sep 15 15
a. 20m pur & lt brn ('76) 15 15
O98 O6 70m blk & grn ('79) 50 50

1982 Photo. Unwmkd. Perf. 11

O99 O6 30m pur & brn 15 15
O100 O6 60m blk & org 30 30
O101 O6 80m blk & grn 40 40

Issue dates: 30m, Feb. 12; 60m, Feb. 24; 80m, Feb. 18.

Arms of Egypt—O7

1985, May 1 Photo. Perf. 11½

O102 O7 1p vermilion 5 5
O103 O7 3p sepia 15 15
O104 O7 5p org yel 25 25
O105 O7 8p green 40 40
O106 O7 15p dl vio 75 75
Nos. O102-O106 (5) 1.60 1.60

OCCUPATION STAMPS

For Use in Palestine.

فلسطين

Nos. 208, 211 and 213 Overprinted in Green or Black

PALESTINE
a

Perf. 13x13½

1948, May 15 Wmk. 195

N1 A66 3m brown 15 15
N2 A66 6m lt yel grn (Bk) 20 20
N3 A66 13m rose car 25 25

Same Overprint in Red, Green or Black on Stamps of Egypt, 1939–46.

Perf. 13x13½, 13½x13

N4 A77 1m yel brn (G) 15 15
N5 A77 2m red org (G) 15 15
N6 A77 4m dp grn 15 15
N7 A77 5m red brn (Bk) 15 15
N8 A77 10m dp vio 20 20
N9 A77 15m dk vio 20 20
N10 A77 17m ol grn 25 25
N11 A77 20m dk gray 25 25
N12 A77 22m dp bl 35 35
N13 A74 50pi grn & sep 6.00 5.00
N14 A75 £1 dp bl & dk brn 12.00 10.00

The two lines of the overprint are more widely separated on Nos. N13 and N14.

Nos. 267–269, 237 and 238 Overprinted in Red

فلسطين

PALESTINE
b

Perf. 14x13½.

N15 A73 30m ol grn 75 75
N16 A73 40m dk brn 75 75
N17 A73 50m Prus grn 1.00 1.00
N18 A73 100m brn vio 1.50 1.50
N19 A73 200m dk vio 5.00 5.00
Nos. N1-N19 (19) 29.45 26.45

Overprint arranged to fit size of stamps.

Nos. N1-N19 Overprinted in Black with Three Bars to Obliterate Portrait

Perf. 13x13½, 13½x13, 14x13½

1953 Wmk. 195

N20 A77 1m yel brn 8 8
N21 A77 2m red org 8 8
N22 A66 3m brown 12 12
N23 A77 4m dp grn 12 12
N24 A77 5m red brn 12 12
N25 A66 6m lt yel grn 20 20
N26 A77 10m dp vio 25 25
N27 A66 13m rose car 30 30
N28 A77 15m dk vio 30 30
N29 A77 17m ol grn 35 35
N30 A77 20m dk gray 35 35
N31 A77 22m dp bl 50 50
N32 A73 30m ol grn 60 60
N33 A73 40m dk brn 90 90
N34 A73 50m Prus grn 1.25 1.25
N35 A73 100m brn vio 3.00 3.00
N36 A73 200m dk vio 6.00 6.00
N37 A74 50pi grn & sep 17.50 17.50
N38 A75 £1 dp bl & dk brn 30.00 30.00
Nos. N20-N38 (19) 62.02 62.02

Regular Issue of 1953–55 Overprinted Type "a" in Blue or Red

1954-55 Perf. 13x13½

N39 A115 1m red brn 5 5
N40 A115 2m dk lil 5 5
N41 A115 3m brt bl (R) 8 8
N42 A115 4m dk grn (R) 10 10
N43 A115 5m dp car 10 10
N44 A110 10m dk brn 15 15
N45 A110 15m gray (R) 15 15

N46 A110 17m dk grnsh bl (R) 20 20
N47 A110 20m pur (R) ('54) 20 20

فلسطين

Nos. 331–333 and
335–340 Overprinted
in Blue or Red

PALESTINE
c

1955-56 ***Perf. 13½.***

N48 A111 30m dl grn (R) 30 30
N49 A111 32m brt bl (R) 35 35
N50 A111 35m vio (R) 40 40
N51 A111 40m red brn 60 60
N52 A111 50m vio brn 65 65
N53 A112 100m hn brn 1.50 1.50
N54 A112 200m dk grnsh bl (R) 3.00 3.00
N55 A112 500m pur (R) 12.50 12.50
N56 A112 £1 dk grn, blk & red (R) ('56) 20.00 20.00
Nos. N39-N56 (18) 40.38 40.38

Type of 1957
Overprinted in Red

فلسطين
PALESTINE
d

1957 ***Perf. 13½x13*** **Wmk. 195**

N57 A127 10m bl grn 1.25 1.25

Nos. 414-417
Overprinted Type "d" in Red.

1957-58 ***Perf. 13½*** **Wmk. 315**

N58 A137 10m violet 20 20

Wmk. 318

N59 A136 1m lt bl grn ('58) 8 8
N60 A138 5m brn ('58) 10 10
N61 A137 10m vio ('58) 15 15

United Arab Republic

Nos. 438–444 Overprinted Type "d"
in Red or Green

Photogravure.

1958 ***Perf. 13½x14*** **Wmk. 318**

N62 A136 1m crimson 5 5
N63 A138 2m blue 5 5
N64 A143 3m dk red brn (G) 5 5
N65 A217 4m green 6 6
N66 A138 5m brown 10 10
N67 A137 10m violet 10 10
N68 A138 35m lt ultra 40 40
Nos. N62-N68 (7) 81 81

Same Overprint in Red on
Freedom Struggle
Type of 1958

1958 ***Perf. 13½x13***

N69 A145 10m dk brn 1.00 1.00

Same Overprint in Green
on Declaration of Human
Rights Type of 1958.

1958 ***Perf. 13x13½***

N70 A151 10m rose vio 1.00 1.00
N71 A151 35m red brn 1.50 1.50

No. 460 Overprinted Type "d"
in Green

1959 ***Perf. 13½*** **Wmk. 195**

N72 A112 55m on 100m hn brn 75 75

"PALESTINE" Added in English and
Arabic to Stamps of Egypt

World Refugee Year Type

1960 ***Perf. 13x13½*** **Wmk. 328**

N73 A173 10m org brn 10 10
N74 A173 35m dk bl gray 35 35

Type of Regular Issue 1959–60

1960 ***Perf. 13½x14***

N75 A136 1m brn org 5 5
N76 A217 4m ol gray 5 5
N77 A138 5m dk dl pur 10 10
N78 A137 10m dk ol grn 15 15

Palestine Day Type

1961, May 15 ***Perf. 13½x13***

N79 A184 10m purple 15 15

WHO Day Type

1961 ***Perf. 13½x13*** **Wmk. 328**

N80 A182 10m blue 20 20

U.N.T.A.P. Type

1961, Oct. 24

N81 A191 10m dk bl & org 10 10
N82 A191 35m ver & blk 30 30

Education Day Type

1961, Dec. 18 **Photo.** ***Perf. 13½***

N83 A194 10m red brn 10 10

Victory Day Type

1961, Dec. 23 ***Perf. 11½*** **Unwmkd.**

N84 A195 10m brn org & brn 15 15

Gaza Strip Type

Perf. 13½x13

1962, March 7 **Wmk. 328**

N85 A200 10m red brn 10 10

Arab Publicity Week Type

1962, March 22 ***Perf. 13½x13***

N86 SP16 10m dk pur 10 10

Anti-Malaria Type

1962, June 20 **Photogravure**

N87 A204 10m brn & dk car rose 15 15
N88 A204 35m blk & yel 40 40

Hammarskjold Type

Perf. 11½x11

1962, Oct. 24 **Wmk. 342**

Portrait in Slate Blue

N89 A214 5m brt rose 10 10
N90 A214 10m brown 20 20
N91 A214 35m blue 40 40

Lamp Type of Regular Issue

Perf. 11x11½

1963, Feb. 20 **Unwmkd.**

N92 A217 4m dk brn, org & ultra 10 10

"Freedom from Hunger" Type

Perf. 11½x11, 11x11½

1963, Mar. 21 **Wmk. 342**

N93 A220 5m lt grn & dp org 5 5
N94 A220 10m ol & yel 10 10
N95 A220 35m dl pur, yel & blk 35 35

Red Cross Centenary Type

Designs: 10m, Centenary emblem, bottom panel added. 35m, Globe and emblem, top and bottom panels added.

Perf. 11x11½

1963, May 8 **Unwmkd.**

N96 A221 10m dk bl & crim 10 10
N97 A221 35m crim & dk bl 35 35

"Save Abu Simbel" Type, 1963

1963, Oct. 15 ***Perf. 11*** **Wmk. 342**

N98 A224 5m blk & yel 5 5
N99 A224 10m gray, blk & yel 10 10
N100 A224 35m org yel & vio 35 35

Human Rights Type, 1963

1963, Dec. 10 **Photo.** ***Perf. 11½x11***

N101 A228 5m dk brn & yel 5 5
N102 A228 10m dp cl, gray & blk 10 10
N103 A228 35m lt grn, pale grn & blk 35 35

Types of Regular Issue, 1964

1964 ***Perf. 11*** **Unwmkd.**

N104 A231 1m cit & lt vio 10 10
N105 A230 2m org & sl 10 10
N106 A230 3m bl & ocher 10 10
N107 A235 4m ol gray, ol, brn & rose 10 10
N108 A230 5m rose & brt bl 15 15
a. 5m rose & dk bl 1.50 1.50
N109 A231 10m ol, rose & brn 20 20
N110 A230 15m lil & yel 35 35
N111 A230 20m brn blk & ol 20 20
N112 A231 30m dp org & ind 35 35
N113 A231 35m buff, ocher & emer 50 50
N114 A231 40m ultra & emer 50 50
N115 A231 60m grnsh bl & brn org 1.00 1.00

Wmk. 342

N116 A232 100m bluish blk & yel brn 1.00 1.00
Nos. N104-N116 (13) 4.65 4.65

Arab League Council Type, 1964

1964, Jan. 13 **Photogravure**

N117 A234 10m ol & blk 5 5

Minaret Type, 1964

1964 ***Perf. 11*** **Unwmkd.**

N118 A235 4m ol, red brn & red 5 5

Arab Postal Union Type, 1964

1964, Apr. 1 ***Perf. 11*** **Wmk. 342**

N119 A239 10m emer & ultra, *lt grn* 10 10

WHO Type, 1964

1964, Apr. 7

N120 A240 10m vio blk & red 10 10

Minaret Type, 1965

1965, Jan. 20 ***Perf. 11*** **Unwmkd.**

N121 A255 4m grn & dk brn 6 6

Arab League Type, 1965

1965, Mar. 22 ***Perf. 11*** **Wmk. 342**

N122 A258 10m grn, red & blk 10 10
N123 A258 20m grn & brn 20 20

World Health Day Type, 1965

1965, Apr. 7 ***Perf. 11*** **Wmk. 342**

N124 A259 10m brt grn & crim 10 10

Massacre Type, 1965

1965, Apr. 9 **Photogravure**

N125 A260 10m sl bl & red 15 15

ITU Type, 1965

1965, May 17 ***Perf. 11*** **Wmk. 342**

N126 A261 5m sl grn, sl bl & yel 5 5
N127 A261 10m car, rose red & gray 10 10
N128 A261 35m vio bl, ultra & yel 30 30

United Nations Type, 1966

Designs: 5m, WHO Headquarters Building, Geneva. 10m, U.N. Refugee emblem. 35m, UNICEF emblem.

1966, Oct. 24 ***Perf. 11*** **Wmk. 342**

N129 A288 5m rose & brt pur 5 5
N130 A288 10m yel brn & brt pur 6 6
N131 A288 35m brt grn & brt pur 30 30

Victory Day Type, 1966

Photogravure

1966, Dec. 23 ***Perf. 11½*** **Wmk. 342**

N132 A290 10m ol & car rose 6 6

Arab Publicity Week Type, 1967

Perf. 11x11½

1967, Mar. 22 **Photo.** **Wmk. 342**

N133 A294 10m vio bl & brn 6 6

Labor Day Type, 1967

Perf. 11½x11

1967, May 1 **Photo.** **Wmk. 342**

N134 A296 10m ol & sep 6 6

OCCUPATION AIR POST STAMPS.

Nos. C39–C50 Overprinted
Type "b" in Black, Carmine or Red.

Perf. 13x13½

1948, May 15 **Wmk. 195**

NC1 AP3 2m red org (Bk) 15 15
NC2 AP3 3m dk brn (C) 15 15
NC3 AP3 5m red brn (Bk) 15 15
NC4 AP3 7m dp yel org (Bk) 15 15
NC5 AP3 8m grn (C) 15 15
NC6 AP3 10m violet 20 20
NC7 AP3 20m brt bl 35 35
NC8 AP3 30m brn vio (Bk) 50 50
NC9 AP3 40m car rose (Bk) 65 65
NC10 AP3 50m Prus grn 90 90
NC11 AP3 100m ol grn 1.50 1.50
NC12 AP3 200m dk gray 5.00 5.00
Nos. NC1-NC12 (12) 9.85 9.85

Nos. NC1-NC12 Overprinted in Black
with Three Bars to Obliterate Portrait

1953

NC13 AP3 2m red org 90 90
NC14 AP3 3m dk brn 15 15
NC15 AP3 5m red brn 3.50 3.50
NC16 AP3 7m dp yel org 50 50
NC17 AP3 8m green 75 75
NC18 AP3 10m violet 25 25
NC19 AP3 20m brt bl 60 60
NC20 AP3 30m brn vio 50 50
NC21 AP3 40m car rose 75 75
NC22 AP3 50m Prus grn 4.00 4.00
NC23 AP3 100m ol grn 20.00 20.00
NC24 AP3 200m dk gray 7.50 7.50
Nos. NC13-NC24 (12) 39.40 39.40

Nos. NC1-NC3, NC6, NC10, NC11
with Additional
Overprint in
Various Colors

ملك مصر والسودان
١٦ اكتوبر سنة ١٩٥١

Overprinted in Black with Three Bars
to Obliterate Portrait

NC25 AP3 2m red org (Bk+Bl) 15 15
NC26 AP3 3m dk brn (Bk+RV) 2.50 2.50
NC27 AP3 5m red brn (Bk) 15 10
NC28 AP3 10m vio (R+G) 5.00 5.00
NC29 AP3 50m Prus grn (R+RV) 2.50 2.50
NC30 AP3 100m ol grn (R+Bk) 12.50 12.50
Nos. NC25-NC30 (6) 22.80 22.75

Nos. C65-C66 Overprinted Type "b"
in Black or Red

1955 ***Perf. 13x13½*** **Wmk. 195**

NC31 AP4 5m red brn 90 90
NC32 AP4 15m ol grn (R) 1.25 1.25

United Arab Republic

"PALESTINE" Added in Arabic and
English to Air Post Stamps.

Type of 1963

Perf. 11½x11

1963, Oct. 24 **Photo.** **Wmk. 342**

NC33 AP6 80m blk & brt bl 1.25 75
NC34 AP10 115m blk & yel 1.75 1.00
NC35 AP10 140m bl, ultra & org red 2.25 1.25

Cairo Tower Type, 1964

Perf. 11x11½

1964, Nov. 2 **Unwmkd.**

NC36 AP11 50m dl vio & lt bl 50 50

World Meteorological Day Type

1965, Mar. 23 ***Perf. 11*** **Wmk. 342**

NC37 AP12 80m dk bl & org 1.00 1.00

Type of Regular Issue, 1965
(Game Board)

1965, July 1 **Photo.** ***Perf. 11***

NC38	AP13	10m brn org & brt grn	25	25

OCCUPATION SPECIAL DELIVERY STAMP.

No. E4 Overprinted Type "b" in Carmine.

1948 ***Perf. 13x13½.*** **Wmk. 195**

NE1	SD1	40m dl brn & pale gray	1.00	1.00

OCCUPATION POSTAGE DUE STAMPS.

Postage Due Stamps of Egypt, 1927-41, Overprinted Type "a" in Black or Rose.

1948 ***Perf. 13x13½.*** **Wmk. 195**

NJ1	D7	2m orange	10	10
NJ2	D7	4m grn (R)	10	10
NJ3	D7	6m gray grn	15	15
NJ4	D7	8m brn vio	20	20
NJ5	D7	10m brick red	20	20
NJ6	D7	12m rose lake	30	30

Overprinted Type "b" in Red.
Perf. 14.
Size: 22x28mm.

NJ7	D7	30m purple	75	75
		Nos. NJ1-NJ7 (7)	1.80	1.80

ELOBEY, ANNOBON AND CORISCO

(ȧ-lō'bȧ, än'ȯ-bōn' & kȯ-ris'kō)

LOCATION — A group of islands near the Guinea Coast of western Africa.

GOVT. — Spanish colonial possessions administered as part of the Continental Guinea District. A second district under the same governor-general included Fernando Po.

AREA—13¾ sq. mi.

POP.—2,950 (estimated 1910).

CAPITAL—Santa Isabel.

100 Centimos = 1 Peseta

King Alfonso XIII
A1

Typographed.
Control Numbers on Back

1903 ***Perf. 14*** **Unwmkd.**

1	A1	¼c carmine	55	25
2	A1	½c dk vio	55	25
3	A1	1c black	55	25
4	A1	2c red	55	25
5	A1	3c dk grn	55	25
6	A1	4c dk bl grn	55	25
7	A1	5c violet	55	25
8	A1	10c rose lake	1.10	75
9	A1	15c org buff	3.25	75
10	A1	25c dk bl	5.50	2.25
11	A1	50c red brn	7.75	3.50
12	A1	75c blk brn	7.75	4.50
13	A1	1p org red	11.50	6.50
14	A1	2p chocolate	30.00	17.50
15	A1	3p dp ol grn	45.00	22.50
16	A1	4p claret	100.00	32.50
17	A1	5p bl grn	115.00	32.50
18	A1	10p dl bl	225.00	47.50
		Nos. 1-18 (18)	555.70	172.50

Same as A1, Dated "1905".

1905 **Control Numbers on Back**

19	A1	1c carmine	1.00	30
20	A1	2c dp vio	4.50	30
21	A1	3c black	1.00	30
22	A1	4c dl red	1.00	30
23	A1	5c dp grn	1.00	30
24	A1	10c bl grn	3.50	45
25	A1	15c violet	4.50	2.00
26	A1	25c rose lake	4.50	2.00
27	A1	50c org buff	8.00	2.75
28	A1	75c dk bl	8.00	2.75
29	A1	1p red brn	16.00	6.50
30	A1	2p blk brn	17.50	9.00
31	A1	3p org red	17.50	9.00
32	A1	4p dk brn	120.00	37.50
33	A1	5p brnz grn	120.00	37.50
34	A1	10p claret	325.00	110.00
		Nos. 19-34 (16)	653.00	220.95

Nos. 19–22 Surcharged in Black or Red

1906
10 CÉNTS.

1906

35	A1	10c on 1c rose (Bk)	11.00	6.75
a.		Inverted surcharge	11.00	6.75
b.		Value omitted	32.50	17.50
c.		Frame omitted	17.00	8.00
d.		Double surcharge	11.00	6.75
e.		Surcharged "15 cents"	35.00	17.50
f.		Surcharged "25 cents"	50.00	25.00
g.		Surcharged "50 cents"	50.00	25.00
h.		"1906" omitted	17.50	8.00
36	A1	15c on 2c dp vio (R)	11.00	6.75
a.		Frame omitted	12.00	6.50
b.		Surcharged "25 cents"	17.00	10.00
c.		Inverted surcharge	11.00	6.75
d.		Double surcharge	11.00	6.75
36E	A1	15c on 2c dp vio (Bk)	17.00	10.00
37	A1	25c on 3c blk (R)	11.00	6.75
a.		Inverted surcharge	11.00	6.75
b.		Double surcharge	11.00	6.75
c.		Surcharged "15 cents"	17.00	10.00
d.		Surcharged "50 cents"	25.00	12.00
37E	A1	25c on 3c blk (Bk)	17.00	10.00
f.		Inverted surcharge	17.00	10.00
g.		Surcharged "15 cents"	17.00	11.50
h.		Surcharged "10 cents"	25.00	11.00
38	A1	50c on 4c red (Bk)	11.00	6.75
a.		Inverted surcharge	11.00	6.75
b.		Value omitted	40.00	20.00
c.		Frame omitted	17.50	8.50
e.		Double surcharge	11.00	6.75
f.		"1906" omitted	17.50	8.50
g.		Surcharged "10 cents"	35.00	17.50
h.		Surcharged "25 cents"	35.00	17.50
		Nos. 35-38 (6)	78.00	47.00

Eight other surcharges were prepared but not issued: 10c on 50c, 75c, 1p, 2p and 3p; 15c on 50c and 5p; 50c on 5c.

King Alfonso XIII
A2

1907 **Control Numbers on Back**

39	A2	1c dk vio	50	40
40	A2	2c black	50	40
41	A2	3c red org	50	40
42	A2	4c dk grn	50	40
43	A2	5c bl grn	50	40
44	A2	10c violet	5.50	2.25
45	A2	15c carmine	2.00	75
46	A2	25c orange	2.00	75
47	A2	50c blue	2.00	75
48	A2	75c brown	6.00	1.25
49	A2	1p blk brn	10.00	2.25
50	A2	2p org red	14.00	3.75
51	A2	3p dk brn	13.00	3.75
52	A2	4p brnz grn	14.00	3.25
53	A2	5p claret	20.00	3.75
54	A2	10p rose	47.50	11.00
		Nos. 39-54 (16)	138.50	35.50

Stamps of 1907 Surcharged

HABILITADO
PARA
05CTMS

1908-09 **Black Surcharge.**

55	A2	5c on 3c red org ('09)	3.25	1.50
56	A2	5c on 4c dk grn ('09)	3.25	1.50
57	A2	5c on 10c vio	6.75	6.00
58	A2	25c on 10c vio	32.50	17.00

1910 **Red Surcharge.**

59	A2	5c on 1c dk vio	3.25	1.50
60	A2	5c on 2c blk	3.25	1.50

Nos. 55–60 exist with surcharge inverted (price each $10 unused, $7.50 used); with double surcharge, one black, one red (price $15 each); with "PARA" omitted (price each $15 unused, $7.50 used).

The same 5c surcharge was also applied to Nos. 45–54, but these were not issued. Price $10 each.

In 1909, stamps of Spanish Guinea replaced those of Elobey, Annobon and Corisco.

1909
CORREOS
10 cen de peseta

Revenue stamps surcharged as above were unauthorized although some were postally used.

EPIRUS

(ė-pī'rŭs)

LOCATION—Southeastern Europe comprising parts of Greece and Albania.

This territory formerly belonged to Turkey but is now divided between Greece and Albania. The northern part of the Greek section, now a part of Albania, set up a provisional government during 1912–13 and issued postage stamps but it collapsed in 1916, following Greek occupation. The name "Epirus" is taken from the Greek word meaning "Mainland."

100 Lepta = 1 Drachma

Chimarra Issue.

Double-headed Eagle, Skull and Crossbones
A1

Handstamped. Without Gum.

1914 (Feb.) ***Imperf.*** **Unwmkd.**

Control Mark in Blue.

1	A1	1 l blk & bl		
2	A1	5 l bl & red		
3	A1	10 l red & blk		
4	A1	25 l bl & red		
		Nos. 1-4 (4)	*400.00*	*360.00*

All values exist without control mark. This mark is a solid blue oval, about 12x8 mm., containing the colorless Greek letters "SP," the first two letters of Spiromilios, the Chimarra commander.

All four exist with value inverted and the 1, 5 and 10 l with value double.

Some students question the official character of this issue. Counterfeits are plentiful.

Provisional Government Issues

Infantryman with Rifle
A2 **A3**

Serrate Roulette 13½

1914 (March) **Lithographed**

5	A2	1 l orange	75	75
6	A2	5 l green	50	50
7	A3	10 l carmine	50	50
8	A3	25 l dp bl	50	50
9	A2	50 l brown	2.00	2.00
10	A2	1d violet	3.00	3.00
11	A2	2d blue	17.50	15.00
12	A2	5d gray grn	18.00	17.50
		Nos. 5-12 (8)	42.75	39.75

Turkish stamps surcharged "Epirus Autonomous" and new values in Greek were on sale for a few days in Argyrokastron (Gjinokaster).

Flag of Epirus
A5

1914 (Aug.)

15	A5	1 l brn & bl	65	65
16	A5	5 l grn & bl	65	65
17	A5	10 l rose red & bl	90	90
18	A5	25 l dk bl & bl	1.25	1.25
19	A5	50 l vio & bl	1.25	1.25
20	A5	1d car & bl	6.00	6.00
21	A5	2d org & bl	1.25	1.25
22	A5	5d dk grn & bl	6.00	6.00
		Nos. 15-22 (8)	17.95	17.95

Koritsa Issue.

A7

1914

26	A7	25 l dk bl & bl	5.00	6.00
27	A7	50 l vio & bl	7.50	9.00

Chimarra Issue.

1911-23 Issues of Greece Overprinted

ΕΛΛΗΝΙΚΗ
1914
ΧΕΙΜΑΡΡΑ

1914 (Aug.)

34	A24	1 l green	6.00	5.00
35	A25	2 l carmine	5.25	6.00
36	A24	3 l vermilion	7.00	8.00
37	A26	5 l green	12.00	10.00
38	A24	10 l carmine	13.00	8.50
39	A25	20 l slate	21.00	19.00
40	A25	25 l blue	27.50	25.00
41	A26	50 l vio brn	35.00	32.50
		Nos. 34-41 (8)	126.75	114.00

The 2 l and 3 l are engraved stamps of the 1911–21 issue, the others are lithographed stamps of the 1912–23 issue.

Overprint reads: "Greek Chimarra 1914".

Stamps of this issue are with or without a black monogram (S.S., for S. Spiromilios) in manuscript. Counterfeits are plentiful.

Foreign postal stationery (stamped envelopes, postal cards and air letter sheets) lies beyond the scope of this Catalogue which is limited to adhesive postage stamps.

Stamps of the following designs were not regularly issued for postal purposes in the opinion of the editors.

Three varieties, 1914

Six varieties, 1914

Seven varieties, 1914.

Fifteen varieties, 1914.

Four varieties, 1920.

OCCUPATION STAMPS.

Issued under Greek Occupation.

Greek Occupation Stamps of 1913 Overprinted Horizontally

B. ΗΠΕΙΡΟΣ

Serrate Roulette 13½.

1914-15 Black Overprint. **Unwmkd.**

N1	O1	1 l brown	2.00	2.00
N2	O2	2 l red	2.00	2.00
b.		2 l rose	3.00	3.00
N4	O2	3 l orange	2.00	2.00
N5	O1	5 l green	4.00	3.00
N6	O1	10 l rose red	5.00	3.25
N7	O1	20 l violet	7.50	7.50
N8	O2	25 l pale bl	7.50	7.50
N9	O1	30 l gray grn	27.50	25.00
N10	O2	40 l indigo	27.50	25.00
N11	O1	50 l dk bl	27.50	25.00
N12	O2	1d vio brn	85.00	80.00
		Nos. N1-N12 (11)	197.50	182.25

The overprint exists double on 4 denominations (1 l, 2 l red, 3 l and 1d); inverted on 7 (1 l, 2 l red, 3 l, 5 l, 10 l, 20 l and 1d). Prices twice or triple normal copies.

Red Overprint.

N1a	1 l brown	5.00
N2a	2 l red	5.00
N4a	3 l orange	5.00
N5a	5 l green	5.00

Nos. N1a–N5a were not issued. Exist canceled.

Regular Issues of Greece, 1911–23, Overprinted

B. ΗΠΕΙΡΟΣ

On Issue of 1911-21

1916 **Engraved.**

N17	A24	3 l vermilion	2.25	2.25
N18	A26	30 l car rose	40.00	40.00
N19	A27	1d ultra	75.00	75.00
N20	A27	2d vermilion	75.00	75.00
N21	A27	3d car rose	75.00	75.00
N22	A27	5d ultra	275.00	275.00
a.		Double overprint	275.00	275.00
		Nos. N17-N22 (6)	542.25	542.25

On Issue of 1912-23.

1916 Lithographed

N23	A24	1 l green	2.50	2.50
N24	A25	2 l carmine	2.50	2.50
N25	A24	3 l vermilion	2.50	2.50
N26	A26	5 l green	2.50	2.50
N27	A24	10 l carmine	5.00	5.00
N28	A25	20 l slate	7.50	7.50
N29	A25	25 l blue	10.00	10.00
N30	A26	30 l rose	17.50	17.50
N31	A25	40 l indigo	17.50	17.50
N32	A26	50 l vio brn	17.50	17.50
		Nos. N23-N32 (10)	85.00	85.00

In each sheet there are two varieties in the overprint: the "I" in "Epirus" omitted and an inverted "L" in place of the first letter of the word.

Counterfeits exist of Nos. N1–N32.

Postage stamps issued in 1940–41, during Greek occupation, are listed under Greece.

EQUATORIAL GUINEA

LOCATION—Gulf of Guinea, West Africa.
GOVT.—Republic.
AREA—10,832 sq. mi.
POP.—310,000 (est. 1974).
CAPITAL—Malabo.

The Spanish provinces Fernando Po and Rio Muni united and became independent as the Republic of Equatorial Guinea, Oct. 12, 1968.

100 Centimos = 1 Peseta

Clasped Hands and Laurel
A1

Pres. Francisco Macias Nguema
A2

Photogravure

1968, Oct. 12 *Perf. 13* **Unwmkd.**

1	A1	1p dp bl, gold & sep	8	8
2	A1	1.50p dk grn, gold & brn	8	8
3	A1	6p cop red, gold & brn	20	10

Issued to commemorate the attainment of independence, Oct. 12, 1968.

1970, Jan. 27 *Perf. 13x12½*

4	A2	50c dl org, brn & crim	8	8
5	A2	1p pink, grn & lil	8	8
6	A2	1.50p pale ol, brn & bl grn	8	8
7	A2	2p buff, grn & ol	10	8
8	A2	2.50p pale grn, dk grn & dk bl	10	10
9	A2	10p bis, Prus bl & vio brn	1.00	15
10	A2	25p gray, blk & brn	1.75	25
		Nos. 4-10 (7)	3.19	82

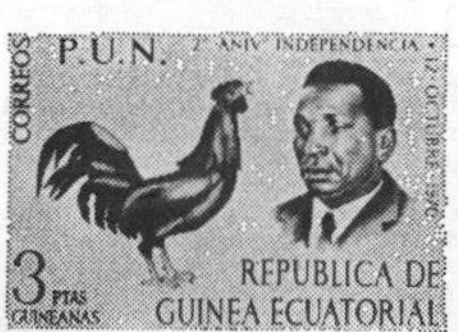

Pres. Macias Nguema and Cock
A3

1971, Apr. **Photogravure** *Perf. 13*

11	A3	3p lt bl & multi	10	10
12	A3	5p buff & multi	20	10
13	A3	10p pale lil & multi	40	10
14	A3	25p pale grn & multi	60	30

2nd anniversary of independence, Oct. 12, 1970.

Torch, Bow and Arrows—A4

1972 Photogravure *Perf. 11½*

15	A4	50p ocher & multi	1.75	65

"3rd Triumphal Year."

SPECIAL DELIVERY STAMPS

Archer with Crossbow—SD1

1971, Oct. 12 Photo. *Perf. 12½x13*

E1	SD1	4p bl & multi	15	10
E2	SD1	8p rose & multi	25	10

3rd anniversary of independence.

ERITREA

(ĕr'ē-trā'ä)

LOCATION—In northeast Africa, bordering on the Red Sea.
GOVT.—Former Italian Colony.
AREA—15,754 sq. mi. (1936).
POP.—600,573 (1931).
CAPITAL—Asmara.

Eritrea was incorporated as a State of Italian East Africa in 1936.

100 Centesimi = 1 Lira

Stamps of Italy Overprinted

Colonia Eritrea
a

b

Wmk. 140

Wmkd. Crown (140)

1892 *Perf. 14.*

Overprinted Type "a" in Black.

1	A6	1c brnz grn	1.50	90
a.		Invtd. overprint	185.00	130.00
b.		Double ovpt.	400.00	
2	A7	2c org brn	55	45
a.		Invtd. overprint	300.00	185.00
b.		Double ovpt.	400.00	
3	A33	5c green	19.00	1.65
a.		Invtd. overprint	2,750.	1,250.

Overprinted Type "b" in Black.

4	A17	10c claret	7.50	1.25
5	A17	20c orange	47.50	1.25
6	A17	25c blue	150.00	6.75
7	A25	40c brown	3.00	3.25
8	A26	45c sl grn	3.25	4.75
9	A27	60c violet	3.25	5.50
10	A28	1 l brn & yel	5.50	7.50
11	A38	5 l bl & rose	120.00	62.50

1895-99

Overprinted type "a" in Black.

12	A39	1c brn ('99)	3.00	4.50
13	A40	2c org brn ('99)	45	75
14	A41	5c green	45	60
a.		Inverted ovpt.	300.00	850.00

Overprinted type "b" in Black.

15	A34	10c cl ('98)	55	75
16	A35	20c orange	75	80
17	A36	25c blue	95	1.25
18	A37	45c ol grn	3.00	6.25

Overprinted type "a" in Black.

1903-28

19	A42	1c brown	15	45
a.		Inverted ovpt.	26.00	45.00
20	A43	2c org brn	15	38
21	A44	5c bl grn	12.00	45
22	A45	10c claret	16.00	45
23	A45	20c orange	38	45
24	A45	25c blue	82.50	4.50
a.		Double ovpt.	110.00	110.00
25	A45	40c brown	67.50	6.75
26	A45	45c ol grn	75	3.25
27	A45	50c violet	37.50	4.25
28	A46	75c dk red & rose ('28)	9.00	4.50
29	A46	1 l brn & grn	75	38
30	A46	1.25 l bl & ultra ('28)	7.50	3.00
31	A46	2 l dk grn & org ('25)	10.50	26.00
32	A46	2.50 l dk grn & org ('28)	26.00	16.00
33	A46	5 l bl & rose	9.00	5.50
		Nos. 19-33 (15)	279.68	76.31

Surcharged in Black

Colonia Eritrea
C. 15

1905

34	A45	15c on 20c org	7.50	1.25

Overprinted type "a" in Black

1908-28

35	A48	5c green	30	22
36	A48	10c cl ('09)	30	22
37	A48	15c sl ('20)	2.50	1.50
38	A49	20c grn ('25)	2.25	3.75
39	A49	20c lil brn ('28)	2.25	3.25
40	A49	25c bl ('09)	90	65
41	A49	30c gray ('25)	2.25	3.75
42	A49	40c brn ('16)	11.00	19.00
43	A49	50c vio ('16)	75	75
44	A49	60c brn car ('18)	5.50	6.75
45	A49	60c brn org ('28)	22.50	62.50
46	A51	10 l gray grn & red ('16)	92.50	250.00
		Nos. 35-46 (12)	143.00	352.34

See also No. 53.

Government Building at Massaua
A1 A2

Engraved.

1910-29 *Perf. 13½* **Unwmkd.**

47	A1	15c slate	42.50	4.00
a.		Perf. 11 ('29)	26.00	16.00
48	A2	25c dk bl	1.10	1.50
a.		Perf. 12		

Farmer Plowing

A3 A4

1914-28

No.	Type	Description	Unused	Used
49	A3	5c green	38	38
a.		Perf. 11 ('28)	100.00	20.00
50	A4	10c carmine	1.10	1.50
a.		Perf. 11 ('28)	19.00	16.00
b.		Perf. 13½x14	15.00	30.00

No. 47 Surcharged in Red or Black

Cent. 5

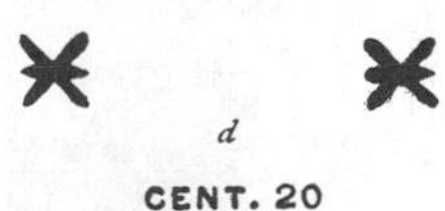

d

CENT. 20

e

1916

No.	Type	Description	Unused	Used
51	A1(d)	5c on 15c sl (R)	2.25	6.75
52	A1(e)	20c on 15c sl	75	75
a.		"CEN" for "CENT"	11.00	22.50
b.		"CENT" omitted	45.00	90.00
c.		"ENT"	15.00	30.00

Italy No. 113 Overprinted in Black ERITREA *f*

1921 *Perf. 14.* **Wmk. 140**

No.	Type	Description	Unused	Used
53	A50	20c brn org	1.25	4.50

Victory Issue.

Italian Victory Stamps of 1921 Overprinted type "f" 13mm. long.

1922

No.	Type	Description	Unused	Used
54	A64	5c ol grn	55	2.25
55	A64	10c red	55	2.25
56	A64	15c sl grn	75	3.75
57	A64	25c ultra	75	3.00

Somalia Nos. 10–16 Overprinted ERITREA *g* In Black and Bars over Original Values,

1922 **Wmkd. Crowns. (140)**

No.	Type	Description	Unused	Used
58	A1	2c on 1b brn	2.50	5.50
59	A1	5c on 2b bl grn	2.50	3.75
60	A2	10c on 1a cl	2.50	75
61	A2	15c on 2a brn org	2.50	90
62	A2	25c on 2½a bl	2.50	90
63	A2	50c on 5a yel	3.25	2.25
a.		"ERITREA" double		375.00
64	A2	1 l on 10a LI	4.00	5.75
a.		"ERITREA" double	225.00	300.00
		Nos. 58-64 (7)	19.75	19.80

See Nos. 81–87.

Propagation of the Faith Issue.

Italy Nos. 143–146 Overprinted ERITREA

1923

No.	Type	Description	Unused	Used
65	A68	20c ol grn & brn org	1.65	8.25
66	A68	30c cl & brn org	1.65	8.25
67	A68	50c vio & brn org	1.25	6.75
68	A68	1 l bl & brn org	1.25	6.75

Fascisti Issue.

Italy Nos. 159–164 Overprinted in Red or Black

ERITREA *j*

1923 *Perf. 14* **Unwmkd.**

No.	Type	Description	Unused	Used
69	A69	10c dk grn (R)	1.50	6.75
70	A69	30c dk vio (R)	1.50	6.75
71	A69	50c brn car	1.50	6.75

Wmkd. Crowns. (140)

No.	Type	Description	Unused	Used
72	A70	1 l blue	1.50	6.75
73	A70	2 l brown	1.50	6.75
74	A71	5 l blk & bl (R)	1.50	11.50
		Nos. 69-74 (6)	9.00	45.25

Manzoni Issue.

Italy Nos. 165-170 Overprinted ERITREA in Red.

1924 *Perf. 14.*

No.	Type	Description	Unused	Used
75	A72	10c brn red & blk	75	7.50
76	A72	15c bl grn & blk	75	7.50
77	A72	30c blk & sl	75	7.50
78	A72	50c org brn & blk	75	7.50
79	A72	1 l bl & blk	12.00	82.50
80	A72	5 l vio & blk	275.00	1,200.
		Nos. 75-79 (5)	15.00	112.50

On Nos. 79 and 80 the overprint is placed vertically at the left side.

Somalia Nos. 10–16 Overprinted type "g" in Blue or Red.

1924

Bars over Original Values.

No.	Type	Description	Unused	Used
81	A1	2c on 1b brn	6.00	15.00
82	A1	5c on 2b bl grn (R)	3.75	9.00
83	A2	10c on 1a rose red	2.25	4.50
84	A2	15c on 2a brn org	2.25	4.50
a.		Pair, one without "ERITREA"	550.00	
85	A2	25c on 2½a bl (R)	2.25	4.50
a.		Double surch.	225.00	
86	A2	50c on 5a yel	3.75	8.25
87	A2	1 l on 10a lil (R)	4.00	10.50
		Nos. 81-87 (7)	24.25	56.25

Stamps of Italy, 1901–08 Overprinted type "j" in Black.

1924

No.	Type	Description	Unused	Used
88	A42	1c brown	1.50	3.75
a.		Inverted ovpt.	110.00	
89	A43	2c org brn	1.10	3.75
90	A48	5c green	1.90	3.75

Victor Emmanuel Issue.

Italy Nos. 175–177 Overprinted ERITREA *k*

1925–26 *Perf. 11* **Unwmkd.**

No.	Type	Description	Unused	Used
91	A78	60c brn car	25	2.25
a.		Perf. 13½	1.90	11.00
92	A78	1 l dk bl	30	2.25
a.		Perf. 13½	6,750.	1,400.

Perf. 13½

No.	Type	Description	Unused	Used
93	A78	1.25 l dk bl ('26)	75	10.00
a.		Perf. 11	1.25	10.00

Saint Francis of Assisi Issue.

Italian Stamps of 1926 Overprinted

ERITREA

1926 *Perf. 14* **Wmk. 140**

No.	Type	Description	Unused	Used
94	A79	20c gray grn	90	4.50
95	A80	40c dk vio	90	4.50
96	A81	60c red vio	90	4.50

Overprinted in Red **Eritrea**

Perf. 11 **Unwmkd.**

No.	Type	Description	Unused	Used
97	A82	1.25 l dk bl	90	4.50

Perf. 14

No.	Type	Description	Unused	Used
98	A83	5 l +2.50 l ol grn	2.25	8.00
		Nos. 94-98 (5)	5.85	26.00

Italian Stamps of 1926 Overprinted type "f" in Black.

1926 *Perf. 14.* **Wmk. 140**

No.	Type	Description	Unused	Used
99	A46	75c dk red & rose	11.00	5.25
a.		Double ovpt.	125.00	
100	A46	1.25 l bl & ultra	7.50	2.25
101	A46	2.50 l dk grn & org	26.00	15.00

Volta Issue.

Type of Italy, 1927, Overprinted **Eritrea** *o*

1927

No.	Type	Description	Unused	Used
102	A84	20c purple	3.00	11.00
103	A84	50c dp org	3.75	7.50
a.		Double overprint	19.00	
104	A84	1.25 l brt bl	4.50	11.00

Italian Stamps of 1925-28 Overprinted type "a" in Black.

1928-29

No.	Type	Description	Unused	Used
105	A86	7½c lt brn ('29)	5.50	19.00
106	A86	50c brt vio	11.00	15.00

Italian Stamps of 1927-28 Overprinted type "f."

1928-29

No.	Type	Description	Unused	Used
107	A86	50c brt vio	13.00	22.50

Perf. 11. **Unwmkd.**

No.	Type	Description	Unused	Used
107A	A85	1.75 l dp brn	9.00	7.50

Italy No. 192 Overprinted type "o."

1928 *Perf. 14* **Wmk. 140**

No.	Type	Description	Unused	Used
108	A85	50c brn & sl	3.75	1.50

Monte Cassino Issue.

Types of 1929 Issue of Italy Overprinted in Red or Blue ERITREA

1929 *Perf. 14.*

No.	Type	Description	Unused	Used
109	A96	20c dk grn (R)	1.65	7.50
110	A96	25c red org (Bl)	1.65	7.50
111	A98	50c +10c crim (Bl)	1.65	11.00
112	A98	75c +15c ol brn (R)	1.65	11.00
113	A96	1.25 l +25c dl vio (R)	3.25	11.00
114	A98	5 l +1 l saph (R)	3.25	11.00

Overprinted in Red **Eritrea**

Unwmkd.

No.	Type	Description	Unused	Used
115	A100	10 l +2 l gray brn	3.25	15.00
		Nos. 109-115 (7)	16.35	74.00

Royal Wedding Issue.

Type of Italian Stamps of 1930 Overprinted ERITREA

1930 **Wmk. 140**

No.	Type	Description	Unused	Used
116	A101	20c yel grn	75	3.00
117	A101	50c +10c dp org	55	3.75
118	A101	1.25 l +25c rose red	55	4.50

Lancer A5

Scene in Massaua A6

Designs: 2c, 35c, Lancer. 5c, 10c, Postman. 15c, Lineman. 25c, Askari (infantryman). 2 l, Railroad viaduct. 5 l, Asmara Deghe Selam. 10 l, Camels.

Lithographed

1930 *Perf. 14* **Wmk. 140**

No.	Type	Description	Unused	Used
119	A5	2c brt bl & blk	55	1.50
120	A5	5c dk vio & blk	75	65
121	A5	10c yel brn & blk	75	38
122	A5	15c dk grn & blk	75	55
123	A5	25c gray grn & blk	75	38
124	A5	35c red brn & blk	2.25	4.50
125	A6	1 l dk bl & blk	90	22
126	A6	2 l choc & blk	1.75	4.50
127	A6	5 l ol grn & blk	3.00	7.50
128	A6	10 l dl bl & blk	3.25	10.00
		Nos. 119-128 (10)	14.70	30.18

Ferrucci Issue.

Types of Italian Stamps of 1930 Overprinted type "f" in Red or Blue.

1930

No.	Type	Description	Unused	Used
129	A102	20c vio (R)	55	2.25
130	A103	25c dk grn (R)	55	2.25
131	A103	50c blk (R)	55	2.25
132	A103	1.25 l dp bl (R)	55	2.25
133	A104	5 l +2 l dp car (Bl)	2.25	4.50
		Nos. 129-133 (5)	4.45	13.50

Virgil Issue.

Types of Italian Stamps of 1930 Overprinted in Red or Blue

ERITREA

1930 **Photogravure.**

No.	Type	Description	Unused	Used
134	A106	15c vio blk	38	2.25
135	A106	20c org brn	38	2.25
136	A106	25c dk grn	38	1.90
137	A106	30c lt brn	38	2.25
138	A106	50c dl vio	38	1.90
139	A106	75c rose red	38	2.25
140	A106	1.25 l gray bl	38	2.25

Engraved.

Unwmkd.

No.	Type	Description	Unused	Used
141	A106	5 l +1.50 l dk vio	2.00	9.00
142	A106	10 l +2.50 l ol brn	2.00	9.00
		Nos. 134-142 (9)	6.66	33.05

Saint Anthony of Padua Issue.

Types of Italian Stamps of 1931 Overprinted type "f" in Blue, Red or Black

1931 **Photogravure.** **Wmk. 140**

No.	Type	Description	Unused	Used
143	A116	20c brn (Bl)	75	3.25
144	A116	25c grn (R)	75	3.25
145	A118	30c gray brn (Bl)	75	3.25
146	A118	50c dl vio (Bl)	75	2.25
147	A120	1.25 l sl bl (R)	75	3.25

Engraved.

Unwmkd.

No.	Type	Description	Unused	Used
148	A121	75c blk (R)	75	3.25
149	A122	5 l +2.50 l dk brn (Bk)	2.25	11.00
		Nos. 143-149 (7)	6.75	29.50

King Victor Emmanuel III A13

1931 Photo. Wmkd. Crown. (140)

No.	Type	Description	Unused	Used
150	A13	7½c ol brn	38	75
151	A13	20c sl bl & car	30	12
152	A13	30c ol grn & brn vio	38	12
153	A13	40c bl & yel grn	30	12
154	A13	50c bis brn & ol	15	12
155	A13	75c car rose	75	18
156	A13	1.25 l vio & ind	90	12
157	A13	2.50 l dl grn	1.25	90
		Nos. 150-157 (8)	4.41	2.43

Camel A14

Temple Ruins A18

Designs: 2c, 10, Camel. 5c, 15c, Shark fishery. 25c, Baobab tree. 35c, Pastoral scene. 2 l, African elephant. 5 l, Eritrean man. 10 l, Eritrean woman.

1934 Photo. Wmkd. Crowns. (140)

No.	Type	Description	Unused	Used
158	A14	2c dp bl	45	90
159	A14	5c black	55	55
160	A14	10c brown	75	38
161	A14	15c org brn	90	80
162	A14	25c gray grn	55	25
163	A14	35c purple	1.65	3.25
164	A18	1 l dk bl gray	25	12
165	A14	2 l ol blk	4.50	1.10
166	A18	5 l car rose	2.50	1.50
167	A18	10 l red org	3.25	2.00
		Nos. 158-167 (10)	15.35	10.85

Abruzzi Issue.

Types of 1934 Issue Overprinted in Black or Red ONORANZE AL DUCA DEGLI ABRUZZI

1934

No.	Type	Description	Unused	Used
168	A14	10c dl bl (R)	3.00	11.00
169	A14	15c blue	3.00	11.00
170	A14	35c grn (R)	1.90	11.00
171	A18	1 l cop red	1.90	11.00
172	A14	2 l rose red	4.50	11.00
173	A18	5 l pur (R)	2.25	11.00
174	A18	10 l ol grn (R)	2.25	11.00
		Nos. 168-174 (7)	18.80	77.00

Grant's Gazelle A22

1934 Photogravure

No.	Type	Description	Unused	Used
175	A22	5c ol grn & brn	1.65	6.25
176	A22	10c yel brn & blk	1.65	6.25
177	A22	20c scar & ind	1.65	6.25
178	A22	50c dk vio & brn	1.65	6.25
179	A22	60c org brn & ind	1.65	6.25
180	A22	1.25 l dk bl & grn	1.65	6.25
		Nos. 175-180 (6)	9.90	37.50

Second Colonial Arts Exhibition, Naples. See also Nos. C1–C6.

SEMI-POSTAL STAMPS.

Many issues of Italy and Italian Colonies include one or more semipostal denominations. To avoid splitting sets, these issues are generally listed as regular postage, airmail, etc., unless all values carry a surtax.

Italy Nos. B1–B3 Overprinted type "f."

1915-16 Perf. 14. Wmk. 140

No.	Type	Description	Unused	Used
B1	SP1	10c +5c rose	1.50	3.25
a.		"EPITREA"	9.00	13.00
b.		Inverted ovpt.	130.00	185.00
B2	SP2	15c +5c sl	3.75	9.00
B3	SP2	20c +5c org	2.25	4.75
a.		"EPITREA"	13.00	21.00
b.		Inverted overprint	75.00	110.00
c.		Pair, one without ovpt.		925.00

No. B2 Surcharged 20

1916

No.	Type	Description	Unused	Used
B4	SP2	20c on 15c+5c sl	3.75	9.00
a.		"EPITREA"	22.50	32.50
b.		Pair, one without overprint	200.00	

Counterfeits exist of the minor varieties of Nos. B1, B3–B4.

Holy Year Issue.

Italy Nos. B20–B25 Overprinted in Black or Red ERITREA

1925 Perf. 12

No.	Type	Description	Unused	Used
B5	SP4	20c +10c dk grn & brn	1.00	4.50
B6	SP4	30c +15c dk brn & brn	1.00	4.50
a.		Double overprint		
B7	SP4	50c +25c vio & brn	1.00	4.50
B8	SP4	60c +30c dp rose & brn	1.00	4.50
a.		Inverted overprint		
B9	SP8	1 l +50c dp bl & vio (R)	1.00	4.50
B10	SP8	5 l +2.50 l org brn & vio (R)	1.00	4.50
		Nos. B5-B10 (6)	6.00	27.00

Colonial Institute Issue.

"Peace" Substituting Spade for Sword SP1

1926 Typographed Perf. 14

No.	Type	Description	Unused	Used
B11	SP1	5c +5c brn	25	2.50
B12	SP1	10c +5c ol grn	25	2.50
B13	SP1	20c +5c bl grn	25	2.50
B14	SP1	40c +5c brn red	25	2.50
B15	SP1	60c +5c org	25	2.50
B16	SP1	1 l +5c bl	25	2.50
		Nos. B11-B16 (6)	1.50	15.00

The surtax of 5c on each stamp was for the Italian Colonial Institute.

Types of Italian Semi-Postal Stamps of 1926 Overprinted type "k."

1927 Perf. 11½ Unwmkd.

No.	Type	Description	Unused	Used
B17	SP10	40c +20c dk brn & blk	1.00	5.25
B18	SP10	60c +30c brn red & ol brn	1.00	5.25
B19	SP10	1.25 l +60c dp bl & blk	1.00	5.25
B20	SP10	5 l +2.50 l dk grn & blk	1.50	6.75

The surtax on these stamps was for the charitable work of the Voluntary Militia for Italian National Defense.

Fascism and Victory SP2

Typographed.

1928 Perf. 14. Wmk. 140

No.	Type	Description	Unused	Used
B21	SP2	20c +5c bl grn	75	3.75
B22	SP2	30c +5c red	75	3.75
B23	SP2	50c +10c pur	75	3.75
B24	SP2	1.25 l +20c dk bl	75	3.75

The surtax was for the Society Africana d'Italia, whose 46th anniversary was commemorated by the issue.

Types of Italian Semi-Postal Stamps of 1928 Overprinted type "f."

1929 Perf. 11. Unwmkd.

No.	Type	Description	Unused	Used
B25	SP10	30c +10c red & blk	1.25	5.50
B26	SP10	50c +20c vio & blk	1.25	5.50
B27	SP10	1.25 l +50c brn & bl	1.50	7.50
B28	SP10	5 l +2 l ol grn & blk	1.50	7.50

The surtax was for the charitable work of the Voluntary Militia for Italian National Defense.

Types of Italian Semi-Postal Stamps of 1929 Overprinted type "f" in Black or Red.

1930 Perf. 14.

No.	Type	Description	Unused	Used
B29	SP10	30c +10c dk grn & bl grn (Bk)	4.00	15.00
B30	SP10	50c +10c dk grn & vio (R)	4.00	15.00
B31	SP10	1.25 l +30c ol brn & red brn (R)	4.00	15.00
B32	SP10	5 l +1.50 l ind & grn (R)	12.00	47.50

The surtax was for the charitable work of the Voluntary Militia for Italian National Defense.

Agriculture SP3

1930 Photogravure Wmk. 140

No.	Type	Description	Unused	Used
B33	SP3	50c +20c ol brn	1.10	6.00
B34	SP3	1.25 l +20c dp bl	1.10	6.00
B35	SP3	1.75 l +20c grn	1.10	6.00
B36	SP3	2.55 l +50c pur	1.65	6.00
B37	SP3	5 l +1 l dp car	1.65	6.00
		Nos. B33-37 (5)	6.60	30.00

Italian Colonial Agricultural Institute, 25th anniversary. The surtax aided that institution.

AIR POST STAMPS

Desert Scene—AP1

Design: 80c, 1 l, 2 l, Plane and globe.

Wmkd. Crowns. (140)

1934 Photogravure. Perf. 14.

No.	Type	Description	Unused	Used
C1	AP1	25c sl bl & org red	1.65	6.25
C2	AP1	50c grn & ind	1.65	6.25
C3	AP1	75c brn & org red	1.65	6.25
C4	AP1	80c org brn & ol grn	1.65	6.25
C5	AP1	1 l scar & ol grn	1.65	6.25
C6	AP1	2 l dk bl & brn	1.65	6.25
		Nos. C1-C6 (6)	9.90	37.50

Second Colonial Arts Exhibition, Naples.

Plowing AP3

Plane and Cacti AP6

Designs: 25c, 1.50 l, Plowing. 50c, 2 l, Plane over mountain pass. 60c, 5 l, Plane and trees. 75c, 10 l, Plane and cacti. 1 l, 3 l, Bridge.

1936 Photogravure.

No.	Type	Description	Unused	Used
C7	AP3	25c dp grn	75	1.50
C8	AP3	50c dk brn	45	30
C9	AP3	60c brn org	1.10	3.75
C10	AP6	75c org brn	90	75
C11	AP3	1 l dp bl	22	12
C12	AP3	1.50 l purple	65	40
C13	AP3	2 l gray bl	90	75
C14	AP3	3 l cop red	7.50	6.75
C15	AP3	5 l green	3.75	1.25
C16	AP6	10 l rose red	10.00	2.25
		Nos. C7-C16 (10)	26.22	17.82

AIR POST SEMI-POSTAL STAMPS.

King Victor Emmanuel III SPAP1

Photogravure.

1934 Perf. 14 Wmk. 140

No.	Type	Description	Unused	Used
CB1	SPAP1	25c +10c gray grn	1.90	1.90
CB2	SPAP1	50c +10c brn	1.90	1.90
CB3	SPAP1	75c +15c rose red	1.90	1.90
CB4	SPAP1	80c +15c blk brn	1.90	1.90
CB5	SPAP1	1 l +20c red brn	1.90	1.90
CB6	SPAP1	2 l +20c brt bl	1.90	1.90
CB7	SPAP1	3 l +25c pur	17.50	17.50
CB8	SPAP1	5 l +25c org	17.50	17.50
CB9	SPAP1	10 l +30c dp vio	17.50	17.50
CB10	SPAP1	25 l +2 l dp grn	17.50	17.50
		Nos. CB1-CB10 (10)	81.40	81.40

Issued in commemoration of the 65th birthday of King Victor Emmanuel III and the nonstop flight from Rome to Mogadiscio. Used prices are for stamps canceled to order.

AIR POST SEMI-POSTAL OFFICIAL STAMP.

Type of Air Post Semi-Postal Stamps, 1934, Overprinted Crown and "SERVIZIO DI STATO" in Black.

1934 Perf. 14. Wmk. 140

No.	Type	Description	Unused	Used
CBO1	SPAP1	25 l +2 l cop red	1,400.	

SPECIAL DELIVERY STAMPS.

Special Delivery Stamps of Italy, Overprinted type "a."

1907 Perf. 14 Wmk. 140

No.	Type	Description	Unused	Used
E1	SD1	25c rose red	5.50	5.50
a.		Double ovpt.		

1909

No.	Type	Description	Unused	Used
E2	SD2	30c bl & rose	30.00	62.50

1920

No.	Type	Description	Unused	Used
E3	SD1	50c dl red	1.90	5.50

"Italia"
SD1

1924 Engraved. Unwmkd.

No.	Type	Description	Unused	Used
E4	SD1	60c dk red & brn	3.25	7.50
a.		Perf. 13½	9.00	19.00
E5	SD1	2 l dk bl & red	4.00	11.00

Nos. E4 and E5 Surcharged in Dark Blue or Red:

70 ٧٠

v

2,50 ٢,٥٠

w

1926

No.	Type	Description	Unused	Used
E6	SD1 (v)	70c on 60c dk red & brn (Bl)	3.25	7.50
E7	SD1 (w)	2.50 l on 2 l dk bl & red (R)	4.00	11.00

Type of 1924 Surcharged in Blue or Black:

LIRE
1,25

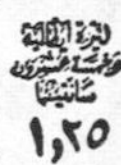

١,٢٥

1927–35 Perf. 11

No.	Type	Description	Unused	Used
E8	SD1	1.25 l on 60c dk red & brn (Bl)	3.00	75
a.		Perf. 14 (Bl) ('35)	60.00	5.50
b.		Perf. 11 (Bk) ('35)	3,000.	165.00
c.		Perf. 14 (Bk) ('35)	165.00	9.00

AUTHORIZED DELIVERY STAMP.

Authorized Delivery Stamp of Italy, No. EY2, Overprinted Type "f" in Black.

1939–41 Perf. 14 Wmk. 140

No.	Type	Description	Unused	Used
EY1	AD2	10c dk brn ('41)	25	
a.		10c redsh brn	17.00	21.00

On No. EY1a, which was used in Eritrea, the overprint hits the figures "10." On No. EY1, which was sold in Rome, the overprint falls above the 10's.

POSTAGE DUE STAMPS.

Postage Due Stamps of Italy Overprinted type "a" at Top

1903 Perf. 14 Wmk. 140

No.	Type	Description	Unused	Used
J1	D3	5c buff & mag	6.75	9.00
a.		Double overprint	75.00	
J2	D3	10c buff & mag	4.50	7.50
J3	D3	20c buff & mag	4.50	7.50
J4	D3	30c buff & mag	6.75	9.00
J5	D3	40c buff & mag	16.00	22.50
J6	D3	50c buff & mag	19.00	26.00
J7	D3	60c buff & mag	6.75	13.00
J8	D3	1 l bl & mag	4.50	2.25
J9	D3	2 l bl & mag	19.00	26.00
J10	D3	5 l bl & mag	62.50	100.00
J11	D3	10 l bl & mag	600.00	62.50

Same with Overprint at Bottom

1920–22

No.	Type	Description	Unused	Used
J1b	D3	5c buff & mag	38	1.90
c.		Numeral and ovpt. inverted	75.00	
J2a	D3	10c buff & mag	75	2.25
J3a	D3	20c buff & mag	82.50	92.50
J4a	D3	30c buff & mag	6.75	11.00
J5a	D3	40c buff & mag	4.50	11.00
J6a	D3	50c buff & mag	4.50	11.00
J7a	D3	60c buff & mag	6.75	15.00
J8a	D3	1 l bl & mag	10.50	11.00
J9a	D3	2 l bl & mag	550.00	400.00
J10a	D3	5 l bl & mag	75.00	130.00
J11a	D3	10 l bl & mag	3.75	19.00

1903 Wmk. 140

No.	Type	Description	Unused	Used
J12	D4	50 l yellow	130.00	82.50
J13	D4	100 l blue	75.00	22.50

1927

No.	Type	Description	Unused	Used
J14	D3	60c buff & brn	18.00	45.00

Postage Due Stamps of Italy, 1934, Overprinted type "j" in Black.

1934

No.	Type	Description	Unused	Used
J15	D6	5c brown	30	1.10
J16	D6	10c blue	30	1.10
J17	D6	20c rose red	1.25	1.50
a.		Inverted ovpt.	62.50	
J18	D6	25c green	1.25	1.50
J19	D6	30c red org	1.25	2.50
J20	D6	40c blk brn	1.25	3.25
J21	D6	50c violet	1.25	55
J22	D6	60c black	2.00	4.50
J23	D7	1 l red org	2.00	75
J24	D7	2 l green	16.00	22.50
J25	D7	5 l violet	21.00	26.00
J26	D7	10 l blue	21.00	26.00
J27	D7	20 l car rose	24.00	35.00
		Nos. J15-J27 (13)	92.85	126.25

PARCEL POST STAMPS.

These stamps were used by affixing them to the way bill so that one half remained on it following the parcel, the other half staying on the receipt given the sender. Most used halves are right halves. Complete stamps were obtainable canceled, probably to order. Both unused and used prices are for complete stamps.

Parcel Post Stamps of Italy, 1914-17, Overprinted type "j" in Black on Each Half.

1916 Perf. 13½. Wmk. 140

No.	Type	Description	Unused	Used
Q1	PP2	5c brown	32.50	60.00
Q2	PP2	10c dp bl	1,500.	2,250.
Q3	PP2	25c red	45.00	90.00
Q4	PP2	50c orange	16.00	30.00
Q5	PP2	1 l violet	16.00	30.00
Q6	PP2	2 l green	13.00	30.00
Q7	PP2	3 l bister	90.00	150.00
Q8	PP2	4 l slate	90.00	150.00

Halves Used

Q1, Q7-Q8	2.00
Q2	30.00
Q3	1.00
Q4	25
Q5-Q6	30

Overprinted type "f" on Each Half.

1917-24

No.	Type	Description	Unused	Used
Q9	PP2	5c brown	1.10	3.00
Q10	PP2	10c dp bl	1.10	3.00
Q11	PP2	20c black	1.10	3.00
Q12	PP2	25c red	1.10	3.00
Q13	PP2	50c orange	1.10	3.00
Q14	PP2	1 l violet	1.10	3.00
Q15	PP2	2 l green	1.10	3.00
Q16	PP2	3 l bister	1.50	3.75
Q17	PP2	4 l slate	2.25	4.50
Q18	PP2	10 l rose lil ('24)	26.00	45.00
Q19	PP2	12 l red brn ('24)	55.00	100.00
Q20	PP2	15 l ol grn ('24)	55.00	100.00
Q21	PP2	20 l brn vio ('24)	55.00	100.00
		Nos. Q9-Q21 (13)	202.45	374.25

Halves Used

Q9-Q16	10
Q17	12
Q18	40
Q19	75
Q20	1.25
Q21	2.00

Parcel Post Stamps of Italy, 1927-39, Overprinted type "f" on Each Half.

1927–37

No.	Type	Description	Unused	Used
Q21A	PP3	10c dp bl ('37)	2,500.	150.00
Q22	PP3	25c red ('37)	200.00	7.50
Q23	PP3	30c ultra ('29)	18	1.50
Q24	PP3	50c org ('36)	200.00	7.50
Q25	PP3	60c red ('29)	18	1.50
Q26	PP3	1 l brn vio ('36)	110.00	3.75
a.		1 l lil	150.00	3.75
Q27	PP3	2 l grn ('36)	30.00	6.00
Q28	PP3	3 l bister	45	3.75
Q29	PP3	4 l gray	55	6.00
Q30	PP3	10 l rose lil ('36)	130.00	190.00
Q31	PP3	20 l lil brn ('36)	150.00	225.00
		Nos. Q22-Q31 (10)	821.36	452.50

Halves Used

Q21A	8.00
Q22-Q25, Q27-Q28	20
Q26, Q26a, Q27	30
Q30	75
Q31	1.50

ESTONIA

(ĕs·tō'nĭ·ȧ)

LOCATION—In Northern Europe, bordering on the Baltic Sea and the Gulf of Finland.

GOVT.—Former independent republic.

AREA—18,353 sq. mi.

POP.—1,126,413 (1940).

CAPITAL—Tallinn.

Formerly a part of Russia, Estonia declared its independence in 1918. In 1940 it was incorporated in the Union of Soviet Socialist Republics.

100 Kopecks = 1 Ruble
100 Penni = 1 Mark (1919)
100 Sents = 1 Kroon (1928)

A1

A2

Lithographed.

1918–19 Imperf. Unwmkd.

No.	Type	Description	Unused	Used
1	A1	5k pale red	75	75
2	A1	15k brt bl	75	75
3	A2	35p brn ('19)	1.50	1.50
a.		Printed on both sides	100.00	
b.		olive	20.00	20.00
4	A2	70p ol grn ('19)	2.00	2.00

Nos. 1–4 exist privately perforated.

Russian Stamps of 1909-17 Handstamped in Violet or Black

Eesti Post

1919 Perf. 14, 14½x15, 13½.

No.	Type	Description	Unused	Used
8	A14	1k orange	2,500.	2,500.
9	A14	2k green	35.00	35.00
10	A14	3k red	40.00	40.00
11	A14	5k claret	30.00	30.00
12	A15	10k dk bl (Bk)	45.00	45.00
13	A15	10k dk bl	110.00	110.00
14	A14	10k on 7k lt bl (Bk)	400.00	400.00
15	A11	15k red brn & bl	40.00	40.00
16	A11	25k grn & vio	45.00	45.00
17	A11	35k red brn & grn	1,200.	1,200.
18	A8	50k vio & grn	100.00	100.00
19	A9	1r pale brn, brn & org	150.00	150.00
20	A13	10r scar, yel & gray	3,000.	3,000.

Imperf.

No.	Type	Description	Unused	Used
21	A14	1k orange	40.00	40.00
22	A14	2k green	400.00	400.00
23	A14	3k red	75.00	75.00
24	A9	1r pale brn, brn & red org	300.00	300.00
25	A12	3½r mar & grn	400.00	400.00
26	A13	5r dk bl, grn & pale bl	500.00	500.00

This overprint has been extensively counterfeited.

No. 20 is always creased.

Gulls
A3

1919, May 13 Imperf.

No.	Type	Description	Unused	Used
27	A3	5p yellow	2.00	1.50

A4

A5

A6

A7

Viking Ship
A8

1919–20 Perf. 11½

No.	Type	Description	Unused	Used
28	A4	10p green	50	50

Imperf.

No.	Type	Description	Unused	Used
29	A4	5p orange	20	20
30	A4	10p green	20	20
31	A5	15p rose	20	20
32	A6	35p blue	40	40
33	A7	70p dl vio ('20)	40	40
34	A8	1m bl & blk brn	1.00	50
a.		Gray granite paper ('20)	60	35
35	A8	5m yel & blk	2.50	1.00
a.		Gray granite paper ('20)	1.50	50
b.		Inverted center (white paper)	400.00	400.00
36	A8	15m yel grn & vio ('20)	4.50	1.00
37	A8	25m ultra & blk brn ('20)	6.75	3.00
		Nos. 28-37 (10)	16.65	7.40

See also Nos. 76–77.

Skyline of Tallinn
A9

1920–24 Imperf. Pelure Paper

No.	Type	Description	Unused	Used
39	A9	25p green	40	20
40	A9	25p yel ('24)	65	50
41	A9	35p rose	40	15
42	A9	50p grn ('21)	40	15
43	A9	1m vermilion	75	15
44	A9	2m blue	1.00	15
45	A9	2m ultra	75	15
46	A9	2.50m blue	60	30
		Nos. 39-46 (8)	4.95	1.75

Nos. 39 to 46 with sewing machine perforation are unofficial.

Stamps of 1919-20 Surcharged

1 Mk.
a

2 Mk.
b

1920 Imperf.

No.	Type	Description	Unused	Used
55	A5	1m on 15p rose	35	35

56	A9	1m on 35p rose	35	35
57	A7	2m on 70p dl vio	35	35

Weaver A10 — Blacksmith A11

1922–23 Typographed. *Imperf.*

58	A10	½m org ('23)	2.50	3.25
59	A10	1m brn ('23)	2.50	3.00
60	A10	2m yel grn	3.00	3.00
61	A10	2½m claret	3.00	3.00
62	A11	5m rose	5.00	3.00
63	A11	9m red ('23)	8.00	6.00
64	A11	10m dp bl	5.50	3.50
		Nos. 58-64 (7)	29.50	24.75

1922-25 *Perf. 14.*

65	A10	½m org ('23)	1.00	15
66	A10	1m brn ('23)	1.50	15
67	A10	2m yel grn	2.50	15
68	A10	2½m claret	2.50	15
69	A10	3m bl grn ('24)	2.50	15
70	A11	5m rose	4.00	15
71	A11	9m red ('23)	2.50	1.25
72	A11	10m dp bl	4.50	15
73	A11	12m red ('25)	4.00	1.75
74	A11	15m plum ('25)	3.50	50
75	A11	20m ultra ('25)	12.00	30
		Nos. 65-75 (11)	40.50	4.85

See also No. 89.

Viking Ship Type of 1920.

1922, June 8 *Perf. 14x13½*

76	A8	15m yel grn & vio	5.00	60
77	A8	25m ultra & blk brn	7.50	2.00

Map of Estonia
A13

1923–24

Paper with Lilac Network.

78	A13	100m ol grn & bl	20.00	2.00

Paper with Buff Network.

79	A13	300m brn & bl ('24)	45.00	8.00

National Theater, Tallinn
A14

1924, Dec. 9 *Perf. 14x13½.*

Paper with Blue Network.

81	A14	30m vio & blk	8.50	3.00

Paper with Rose Network.

82	A14	70m car rose & blk	12.50	3.50

Vanemuine Theater, Tartu
A15

1927, Oct. 25

Paper with Lilac Network.

83	A15	40m dp bl & ol brn	7.50	1.25

Stamps of 1922–25 Surcharged in New Currency in Red or Black

1918 24/II 1928
S. S.

1928 *Perf. 14.*

84	A10	2s yel grn	1.00	20
85	A11	5s rose red	1.00	15
86	A11	10s dp bl	1.25	15
a.		Imperf., pair	500.00	500.00
87	A11	15s plum	3.50	50
88	A11	20s ultra	3.00	60
		Nos. 84-88 (5)	9.75	1.60

10th anniversary of independence.

3rd Philatelic Exhibition Issue
Blacksmith Type of 1922–23.

1928, July 6

89	A11	10m gray	5.00	5.50
a.		Imperf., pair		

Sold only at Tallinn Philatelic Exhibition.

Arms
A16

Paper with Network as in Parenthesis.

1928-40 *Perf. 14, 14½x14*

90	A16	1s dk gray (bl)	60	15
a.		Thick gray-toned laid paper ('40)	7.50	9.00
91	A16	2s yel grn (org)	75	10
92	A16	4s grn (brn) ('29)	1.00	15
93	A16	5s red (grn)	75	10
a.		5 feet on lowest lion	20.00	25.00
94	A16	8s vio (buff) ('29)	3.25	15
95	A16	10s lt bl (lil)	2.00	10
96	A16	12s crim (grn)	3.00	20
97	A16	15s yel (bl)	3.00	20
98	A16	15s car (gray) ('35)	10.00	90
99	A16	20s sl bl (red)	4.50	20
100	A16	25s red vio (grn) ('29)	11.00	30
101	A16	25s bl (brn) ('35)	10.00	75
102	A16	40s red org (bl) ('29)	7.50	50
103	A16	60s gray (brn) ('29)	8.00	60
104	A16	80s brn (bl) ('29)	15.00	2.00
		Nos.90-104 (15)	80.35	6.40

Types of 1924 Issues Surcharged:

KROON 1 KROON
a

2 KROONI 2
b

3 KROONI 3
c

1930, Sept. 1 *Perf. 14x13½.*

Paper with Green Network.

105	A14	1k on 70m car & blk	8.50	5.00

Paper with Rose Network.

106	A13	2k on 300m brn & bl	15.00	8.00

Paper with Blue Network.

107	A13	3k on 300m brn & bl	35.00	20.00

University Observatory
A17

University of Tartu
A18

Paper with Network as in Parenthesis.

1932, June 1 *Perf. 14.*

108	A17	5s red (yel)	6.50	60
109	A18	10s lt bl (lil)	2.00	20
110	A17	12s car (bl)	9.50	1.75
111	A18	20s dk bl (grn)	8.00	35

University of Tartu tercentenary.

Narva Falls
A19

Ancient Bard Playing Harp
A20

1933, Apr. 1 Photo. *Perf. 14x13½.*

112	A19	1k gray blk	7.50	85

See also No. 149.

Paper with Network as in Parenthesis.

1933, May 29 Typo. *Perf. 14*

113	A20	2s grn (org)	3.00	40
114	A20	5s red (grn)	4.00	40
115	A20	10s bl (lil)	5.00	25

Tenth National Singing Festival.

Woman Harvester
A21

President Konstantin Päts
A22

1935, Mar. 1 Engr. *Perf. 13½.*

116	A21	3k blk brn	90	1.50

1936-40 Typographed. *Perf. 14.*

117	A22	1s chocolate	60	15
118	A22	2s yel grn	60	15
119	A22	3s dp org ('40)	7.00	5.00
120	A22	4s rose vio	1.40	25
121	A22	5s lt bl grn	1.40	20
122	A22	6s rose lake	1.25	25
123	A22	6s dp grn ('40)	27.50	22.50
124	A22	10s grnsh bl	1.50	20
125	A22	15s crim rose ('37)	2.50	30
126	A22	15s dp bl ('40)	7.50	50
127	A22	18s dp car ('39)	20.00	9.00
128	A22	20s brt vio	2.50	20
129	A22	25s dk bl ('38)	8.25	30
130	A22	30s bis ('38)	8.50	30
131	A22	30s ultra ('39)	15.00	2.50
132	A22	50s org brn	7.50	1.00
133	A22	60s brt pink	12.00	1.75
		Nos. 117-133(17)	125.00	44.55

St. Brigitta Convent Entrance
A23

Ruins of Convent, Pirita River
A24

Front View of Convent
A25

Seal of Convent
A26

Paper with Network as in Parenthesis.

1936, June 10 *Perf. 13½.*

134	A23	5s grn (buff)	65	20
135	A24	10s bl (lil)	90	20
136	A25	15s red (org)	1.40	1.90
137	A26	25s ultra (brn)	1.75	2.75

St. Brigitta Convent, 500th anniversary.

Harbor at Tallinn
A27

1938, Apr. 11 Engraved *Perf. 14*

138	A27	2k blue	1.00	2.00

Friedrich R. Faehlmann
A28

Friedrich R. Kreutzwald
A29

1938 Typographed. *Perf. 13½.*

139	A28	5s dk grn	1.00	1.00
140	A29	10s dp brn	1.00	1.00
141	A29	15s dk car	1.25	1.75
142	A28	25s ultra	2.25	2.75
a.		Sheet of four	13.00	22.50

Society of Estonian Scholars centenary.

No. 142a contains one each of Nos. 139–142, with inscription in top margin. Size: 89x138mm.

Hospital at Pärnu
A30

Seashore Hotel
A31

1939, June 20 Typographed

144	A30	5s dk grn	1.40	75
145	A31	10s dp red vio	1.00	75
146	A30	18s dk car	2.75	2.75
147	A31	30s dp bl	3.25	3.25
a.		Sheet of four	20.00	40.00

Centenary of health resort and baths at Pärnu.

No. 147a contains one each of Nos. 144–147, with inscription at left. Size: 137x90mm.

Narva Falls Type of 1933.

1940, Apr. 15 Engraved

149	A19	1k sl grn	1.00	2.50

The sky consists of heavy horizontal lines and the background consists of horizontal and vertical lines.

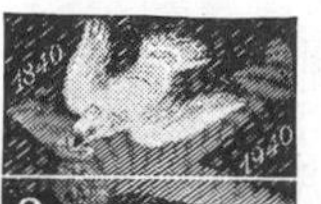

Carrier Pigeon and Plane
A32

1940, July 30 **Typographed**

150	A32	3s red org	20	15
151	A32	10s purple	20	15
152	A32	15s rose brn	25	15
153	A32	30s dk bl	2.00	1.25

Centenary of the first postage stamp.

SEMI-POSTAL STAMPS.

Assisting Wounded Soldier
SP1

Offering Aid to Wounded Hero
SP2

Lithographed

1920, June ***Imperf.*** **Unwmkd.**

B1	SP1 35p +10p red & ol grn		40	65
B2	SP2 70p +15p dp bl & brn		40	65

Surcharged **2 Mk**

1920

B3	SP1 1m on 35p+10p red & ol grn	60	60
B4	SP2 2m on 70p+15p dp bl & brn	60	60

Nurse and Wounded Soldier
SP3

1921, Aug. 1 ***Imperf.***

B5	SP3 2½ (3½)m org, brn & car	1.00	1.40
B6	SP3 5 (7)m ultra, brn & car	1.00	1.40

1922, Apr. 26 ***Perf. 13½x14***

B7	SP3 2½ (3½)m org, brn & car	1.50	2.00
a.	Vert. pair, imperf. horiz.	15.00	20.00
B8	SP3 5 (7)m ultra, brn & car	1.50	2.00
a.	Vert. pair, imperf. horiz.	15.00	20.00

Nos. B5–B8 Overprinted **Aita hädalist.**

1923 ***Imperf.***

B9	SP3 2½ (3½)m	25.00	35.00
B10	SP3 5 (7)m	30.00	40.00

Perf. 13½x14.

B11	SP3 2½ (3½)m	35.00	45.00
a.	Vert. pair, imperf. horiz.	125.00	175.00
B12	SP3 5 (7)m	40.00	50.00
a.	Vert. pair, imperf. horiz.	125.00	175.00

Excellent forgeries are plentiful.

Nos. B7 and B8 Surcharged **5 5** / **6 6**

1926, June 15

B13	SP3 5 (6)m on 2½(3½)m	2.50	4.00
a.	Vert. pair, imperf. horiz.	15.00	20.00
B14	SP3 10 (12)m on 5(7)m	2.50	4.00
a.	Vert. pair, imperf. horiz.	15.00	20.00

Nos. B5–B14 had the franking value of the lower figure. They were sold for the higher figure, the excess going to the Red Cross Society.

Kuressaare Castle
SP4

Tartu Cathedral
SP5

Tallinn Castle—SP6

Narva Fortress
SP7

View of Tallinn
SP8

Wmk. 207

Reduced illustration. Watermark covers a large part of sheet.

Laid Paper.

Wmkd. Arms of Finland in the Sheet. (207)

1927, Nov. 19 Typo. ***Perf. 14½x14***

B15	SP4 5m +5m bl grn & ol, *grysh*	60	1.00
B16	SP5 10m +10m dp bl & brn, *cr*	60	1.00
B17	SP6 12m +12m rose red & ol grn, *bluish*	60	1.50

Perf. 14x13½

B18	SP7 20m +20m bl & choc, *gray*	1.00	2.00
B19	SP8 40m +40m org brn & sl, *buff*	1.00	2.00
	Nos. B15-B19 (5)	3.80	7.50

The money derived from the surtax was donated to the Committee for the commemoration of War for Liberation.

Red Cross Issue.

Symbolical of Succor to Injured
SP9

Symbolical of "Light of Hope"
SP10

1931, Aug. 1 ***Perf. 13½*** **Unwmkd.**

B20	SP9 2s +3s grn & car	8.00	10.00
B21	SP10 5s +3s red & car	8.00	10.00
B22	SP10 10s +3s lt bl & car	8.00	10.00
B23	SP9 20s +3s dk bl & car	13.00	15.00

Nurse and Child
SP11

Lorraine Cross and Flower
SP13

Taagepera Sanatorium
SP12

Paper with Network as in Parenthesis.

1933, Oct. 1 ***Perf. 14, 14½.***

B24	SP11 5s +3s ver (grn)	8.50	8.50
B25	SP12 10s +3s lt bl & red (vio)	8.50	8.50
B26	SP13 12s +3s rose & red (grn)	9.50	9.50
B27	SP12 20s +3s dk bl & red (org)	15.00	15.00

The surtax was for a fund to combat tuberculosis.

Arms of Narva
SP14

Arms of Pärnu
SP15

Arms of Tartu
SP16

Arms of Tallinn
SP17

Paper with Network as in Parenthesis.

1936, Feb. 1 ***Perf. 13½***

B28	SP14 10s +10s grn & ultra (gray)	6.25	7.50
B29	SP15 15s +15s car & bl (gray)	6.25	7.50
B30	SP16 25s +25s gray bl & red (brn)	8.50	10.00
B31	SP17 50s +50s blk & dl org (ol)	20.00	27.50

Arms of Paide
SP18

Arms of Rakvere
SP19

Arms of Valga
SP20

Arms of Viljandi
SP21

Paper with Network as in Parenthesis.

1937, Jan. 2

B32	SP18 10s +10s grn (gray)	5.50	7.50
B33	SP19 15s +15s red brn (gray)	5.50	7.50
B34	SP20 25s +25s dk bl (lil)	8.00	10.00
B35	SP21 50s +50s dk vio (gray)	15.00	20.00

Arms of Baltiski
SP22

Arms of Vöru
SP23

Arms of Haapsalu
SP24

Arms of Kuressaare
SP25

Designs are the armorial bearings of various cities.

1938, Jan. 21

Paper with Gray Network.

B36	SP22 10s +10s dk brn	5.00	6.50
B37	SP23 15s +15s car & grn	6.00	7.00
B38	SP24 25s +25s dk bl & car	8.00	10.00
B39	SP25 50s +50s blk & org yel	12.00	17.50
a.	Sheet of four	35.00	50.00

Annual charity ball, Tallinn, Jan. 2, 1938. No. B39a contains one each of Nos. B36-B39. Size: 106x150mm.

Arms of Viljandi
SP27

Arms of Pärnu
SP28

Arms of Tartu
SP29

Arms of Harju
SP30

Designs are the armorial bearings of various districts.

1939, Jan. 10

Paper with Gray Network.

B41	SP27	10s +10s dk bl grn	5.00	6.00
B42	SP28	15s +15s car	6.00	7.00
B43	SP29	25s +25s dk bl	8.00	9.50
B44	SP30	50s +50s brn lake	12.50	20.00
a.		Sheet of four	37.50	50.00

No. B44a measures 90x138mm., and contains one each of Nos. B41 to B44, with marginal inscriptions.

Arms of Võru
SP32

Arms of Järva
SP33

Arms of Lääne
SP34

Arms of Saare
SP35

Paper with Gray Network.

1940, Jan. 2 Typo. *Perf. 13½*

Designs are the armorial bearings of various districts.

B46	SP32	10s +10s dp grn & ultra	4.50	6.00
B47	SP33	15s +15s dk car & ultra	4.50	6.00
B48	SP34	25s +25s dk bl & scar	5.50	10.00
B49	SP35	50s +50s ocher & ultra	7.50	16.00

AIR POST STAMPS.

Airplane
AP1

Typographed.

1920, Mar. 13 *Imperf.* Unwmkd.

C1	AP1	5m yel, blk & lt grn	2.25	3.00

No. C1 Overprinted "1923" in Red.

1923, Oct. 1

C2	AP1	5m multi	7.00	10.00

No. C1 Surcharged in Red

1923, Oct. 1

C3	AP1	15m on 5m multi	10.00	12.00

Pairs of No. C1 Surcharged in Black or Red

45 Marka

1923

1923, Oct.

C4	AP1	10m on 5m+5m (B)	10.00	*14.00*
C5	AP1	20m on 5m+5m (R)	22.50	30.00
C6	AP1	45m on 5m+5m (R)	75.00	90.00

Rough Perf. 11½.

C7	AP1	10m on 5m+5m (B)	*250.00*	*300.00*
C8	AP1	20m on 5m+5m (R)	*150.00*	*200.00*

The pairs comprising Nos. C7 and C8 are imperforate between. Forged surcharges and perforations abound.

Monoplane in Flight—AP2

Designs: Various views of planes in flight.

1924, Feb. 12 *Imperf.*

C9	AP2	5m yel & blk	2.50	3.50
C10	AP2	10m bl & blk	2.50	3.50
C11	AP2	15m red & blk	2.50	3.50
C12	AP2	20m grn & blk	2.50	3.50
C13	AP2	45m vio & blk	2.50	3.50
		Nos. C9-C13 (5)	12.50	17.50

The paper is covered with a faint network in pale shades of the frame colors. There are four varieties of the frames and five of the pictures.

1925, July 15 *Perf. 13½.*

C14	AP2	5m yel & blk	2.00	3.00
C15	AP2	10m bl & blk	2.00	3.00
C16	AP2	15m red & blk	2.00	3.00
C17	AP2	20m grn & blk	2.00	3.00
C18	AP2	45m vio & blk	2.00	3.00
		Nos. C14-C18 (5)	10.00	15.00

Counterfeits of Nos. C1 to C18 are plentiful.

OCCUPATION STAMPS.

Issued under German Occupation.

For Use in Tartu (Dorpat)

Russian Stamps of 1909-12 Surcharged

20 Pfg.

1918 *Perf. 14x14½* Unwmkd.

N1	A15	20pf on 10k dk bl	35.00	*60.00*
N2	A8	40pf on 20k bl & car	35.00	*60.00*

Forged overprints exist.

Estonian Arms and Swastika
OS1

Perf. 11½

1941, Aug. Typo. Unwmkd.

N3	OS1	15k brown	15.00	15.00
N4	OS1	20k green	11.00	11.00
N5	OS1	30k dk bl	11.00	11.00

Exist imperf. Price, set, $60.

Nos. N3-N5 were issued on both ordinary paper with colorless gum and thick chalky paper with yellow gum. Same prices.

SEMI-POSTAL STAMPS

Castle Tower, Tallinn—OSP1

Designs: 20k+20k, Stone Bridge, Tartu (horiz.). 30k+30k, Narva Castle (horiz.). 50k+50k, Tallinn view (horiz.). 60k+60k, Tartu University. 100k+100k, Narva Castle, close view.

Paper with Gray Network

Perf. 11½

1941, Sept. 29 Photo. Unwmkd.

NB1	OSP1	15k +15k dk brn	45	*5.00*
NB2	OSP1	20k +20k red lil	45	*5.00*
NB3	OSP1	30k +30k dk bl	45	*5.00*
NB4	OSP1	50k +50k bluish grn	45	*5.00*
NB5	OSP1	60k +60k car	65	*5.00*
NB6	OSP1	100k +100k gray	1.40	*6.00*
		Nos. NB1-NB6 (6)	3.85	*31.00*

Nos. NB1-NB6 exist imperf. Price, set unused $14, used $30.

A miniature sheet containing one each of Nos. NB1-NB6, imperf., exists in various colors. It was not postally valid.

ETHIOPIA

(ē'thĭ-ō'pĭ-ȧ)

(Abyssinia)

LOCATION — Northeastern Africa.
GOVT.—Provisional military.
AREA—471,800 sq. mi.
POP.—40,000,000 (est. 1984).
CAPITAL—Addis Ababa.

16 Guerche = 1 Menelik Dollar
or 1 Maria Theresa Dollar
100 Centimes = 1 Franc (1905)
40 Paras = 1 Piastre (1908)
16 Mehalek = 1 Thaler or Talari (1928)
100 Centimes = 1 Thaler (1936)
100 Cents = 1 Ethiopian Dollar (1946)
100 Cents = 1 Birr (1978)

Excellent forgeries of Nos. 1-86 exist.

Menelik II
A1

Lion of Judah
A2

Typographed

1894 *Perf. 14x13½* Unwmkd.

1	A1	¼g green	2.00	2.00
2	A1	½g red	1.50	1.50
3	A1	1g blue	1.50	1.50
4	A1	2g dk brn	1.50	1.50
5	A2	4g lil brn	1.50	1.50
6	A2	8g violet	1.50	1.50
7	A2	16g black	1.75	1.75
		Nos. 1-7 (7)	11.25	11.25

For 4g, 8g and 16g stamps of type A1, see Nos. J3a, J4a, and J7a.

Nos. 1-7 Handstamped in Violet, Blue or Black

Ethiopie

1901

8	A1	¼g green	8.00	8.00
9	A1	½g red	8.00	8.00
10	A1	1g blue	8.00	8.00
11	A1	2g dk brn	8.00	8.00
12	A2	4g lil brn	11.00	11.00
13	A2	8g violet	14.00	14.00
14	A2	16g black	15.00	15.00
		Nos. 8-14 (7)	72.00	72.00

Two types of overprint on Nos. 8-14: 9½mm. and 8½mm. wide.

Handstamped in Violet, Blue or Black

ቦስጣ።

1902

15	A1	¼g green	5.00	5.00
16	A1	½g red	6.00	5.00
17	A1	1g blue	7.50	7.50
18	A1	2g dk brn	7.50	7.50
19	A2	4g lil brn	12.50	12.50
20	A2	8g violet	17.50	17.50
21	A2	16g black	30.00	30.00
		Nos. 15-21 (7)	86.00	85.00

The handstamp reads "Bosta" (Post).

Handstamped in Violet, Blue or Black

መልክት።

1903

22	A1	¼g green	5.00	5.00
a.		On stamp No. 15		
23	A1	½g red	5.00	5.00
24	A1	1g blue	7.50	7.50
a.		On stamp No. 17		
25	A1	2g dk brn	10.00	10.00
26	A2	4g lil brn	10.00	10.00
27	A2	8g violet	22.50	22.50
28	A2	16g black	30.00	30.00
		Nos. 22-28 (7)	90.00	90.00

The handstamp reads "Malekt." (Message).

Handstamped in Violet or Blue

ምልክት

1904

36	A1	¼g green	10.00	10.00
37	A1	½g red	10.00	10.00
38	A1	1g blue	12.00	12.00
39	A1	2g dk brn	15.00	15.00
40	A2	4g lil brn	20.00	20.00
41	A2	8g violet	32.50	32.50
42	A2	16g black	47.50	47.50
		Nos. 36-42 (7)	147.00	147.00

The handstamp reads "Malekt." (Message).

Preceding Issues Surcharged with New Values in French Currency in Blue, Violet, Rose or Black:

05 *a* 1.60 *b*

1905

On Nos. 1 to 7.

43	A1 (a)	5c on ¼g grn	6.00	6.00
44	A1 (a)	10c on ½g red	6.00	6.00
45	A1 (a)	20c on 1g bl	6.00	6.00
46	A1 (a)	40c on 2g dk brn	8.00	8.00
47	A2 (a)	80c on 4g lil brn	13.00	13.00
48	A2 (b)	1.60fr on 8g vio	12.50	17.50
49	A2 (b)	3.20fr on 16g blk	25.00	25.00
		Nos. 43-49 (7)	76.50	81.50

On No. 8.

50	A1 (a)	5c on ¼g grn	75.00	75.00

On Nos. 15 to 20.

51	A1 (a)	5c on ¼g grn	15.00	15.00
51B	A1 (a)	10c on ½g red	*275.00*	*275.00*
51C	A1 (a)	20c on 1g bl	*20.00*	
51D	A1 (a)	40c on 2g dk brn	*67.50*	

51E	A2 (a)	80c on 4g lil brn	*110.00*	
51F	A2 (b)	1.60fr on 8g vio	*140.00*	

On Nos. 22, 24 & 26.

52	A1 (a)	5c on ¼g grn	32.50	32.50
52B	A1 (a)	20c on 1g bl	*52.50*	
52D	A2 (a)	80c on 4g lil brn	*140.00*	

On No. 36.

53	A1 (a)	5c on ¼g grn	35.00	35.00

The status of Nos. 51C–51F, 52B–52D is questioned.

5

5%m centimes.

c *d*

On No. 2.

54	A1 (c)	5c on half of ½g red	3.50	3.50

On Nos. 15 & 21.

54B	A1(c)	5c on ¼g grn	50.00	50.00
55	A2(d)	5c on 16g blk	90.00	90.00

On No. 28.

56	A2(d)	5c on 16g blk	90.00	90.00

The overprints and surcharges on Nos. 8 to 56 inclusive were handstamped, the work being very roughly done. Apparently any color of ink that was at hand was used. It is not at all improbable that other varieties may exist.

As is usual with handstamped overprints and surcharges there are many inverted and double.

Surcharged with New Values in Various Colors and ምኒልክ in Violet.

1906, Jan. 1

57	A1	5c on ¼g grn	6.00	6.00
58	A1	10c on ½g red	8.00	8.00
59	A1	20c on 1g bl	8.00	8.00
60	A1	40c on 2g dk brn	8.00	8.00
61	A2	80c on 4g lil brn	10.00	10.00
62	A2	1.60fr on 8g vio	14.00	14.00
63	A2	3.20fr on 16g blk	37.50	37.50
		Nos. 57-63 (7)	91.50	91.50

Two types of the 4-character overprint ("Menelik"): 15x3½mm. and 16½x4½ mm.

Surcharged with New Values and ምኒልክ። in Violet.

1906, July 1

64	A1	5c on ¼g grn	6.00	6.00
a.		Surcharged "20"	40.00	40.00
65	A1	10c on ½g red	7.00	7.00
66	A1	20c on 1g bl	10.00	10.00
67	A1	40c on 2g dk brn	10.00	10.00
68	A2	80c on 4g lil brn	14.00	14.00
69	A2	1.60fr on 8g vio	14.00	14.00
70	A2	3.20fr on 16g blk	35.00	35.00
		Nos. 64-70 (7)	96.00	96.00

The control overprint reads "Menelik."

Surcharged in Violet:

☆1/2☆ ✳ 1.✳

e *f*

1907, July 1

71	A1(e)	¼ on ¼g grn	6.00	6.00
72	A1(e)	½ on ½g red	6.00	6.00
73	A1(f)	1 on 1g bl	7.50	7.50
74	A1(f)	2 on 2g dk brn	9.00	9.00
a.		Surcharged "40"	45.00	
75	A2(f)	4 on 4g lil brn	9.00	9.00
a.		Surcharged "80"	42.50	
76	A2(f)	8 on 8g vio	18.00	18.00
77	A2(f)	16 on 16g blk	25.00	25.00
		Nos. 71-77 (7)	80.50	80.50

Nos. 71–72 are also found with stars farther away from figures.

The control overprint reads "Dagmawi" ("Second"), meaning Emperor Menelik II.

Nos. 2, 23 Surcharged in Blue

1 PIASTRE

1908, Mar. 25

78	A1	1pi on ½g red (#2)	6.00	6.00
79	A1	1pi on ½g red (#23)	*250.00*	*250.00*

The surcharges on Nos. 57 to 79 are handstamped and are found double, inverted, etc.

Surcharged in Black

1/4 piastre

1908, Nov. 1

80	A1	¼p on ¼g grn	1.25	1.25
81	A1	½p on ½g red	1.25	1.25
82	A1	1p on 1g bl	2.00	2.00
83	A1	2p on 2g dk brn	3.00	3.00
84	A2	4p on 4g lil brn	4.75	4.75
85	A2	8p on 8g vio	10.00	10.00
86	A2	16p on 16g blk	16.00	16.00
		Nos. 80-86 (7)	38.25	38.25

Surcharges on Nos. 80–85 are found double, inverted, etc.

King Solomon's Throne
A3

Menelik in Native Costume
A4

Menelik in Royal Dress
A5

1909, Mar. 27 ***Perf. 11½***

87	A3	¼g bl grn	60	50
88	A3	½g rose	60	50
89	A3	1g grn & org	3.25	1.25
90	A4	2g blue	2.50	1.50
91	A4	4g grn & car	3.75	3.00
92	A5	8g ver & dp grn	6.25	4.50
93	A5	16g ver & car	9.00	7.50
		Nos. 87-93 (7)	25.95	18.75

Nos. 1–7 Handstamped and Surcharged in ms.

AFF EXCEP
FAUTE TIMB

1911, Oct. 1 ***Perf. 14x13½***

94	A1	¼g on ¼g grn	90.00	40.00
95	A1	½g on ½g red	90.00	40.00
96	A1	1g on 1g bl	90.00	40.00
97	A1	2g on 2g dk brn	90.00	40.00
98	A2	4g on 4g lil brn	90.00	40.00
99	A2	8g on 8g vio	90.00	40.00
100	A2	16g on 16g blk	90.00	40.00
		Nos. 94-100 (7)	630.00	280.00

Nos. 94–100 are provisionals used at Dire-Dawa for 5 days. The overprint is abbreviated from "Affranchissement Exceptionnel Faute Timbres" (Special Franking Lacking Stamps). Nos. 94–100 exist without ms. surcharge. Forgeries exist.

Stamps of 1909 Handstamped in Violet or Black:

11-2-1917

g

11-2-1917

h

1917, Mar. 30 ***Perf. 11½***

101	A3(g)	¼g bl grn (V)	3.00	3.00
102	A3(g)	½g rose (V)	3.00	3.00
104	A4(h)	2g bl (Bk)	4.00	4.00
105	A4(h)	4g grn & car (Bk)	7.00	7.00
106	A5(h)	8g ver & dp grn (Bk)	12.00	12.00
107	A5(h)	16g ver & car (Bk)	25.00	25.00
		Nos. 101-107 (6)	54.00	54.00

Coronation of Empress Zauditu.

Nos. 101–107 exist with overprint inverted and Nos. 101–106 with it double.

Stamps of 1909 Overprinted in Blue, Black or Red:

11/2/1917 11/2/1917

i *j*

1917, Apr. 5

108	A3(i)	¼g Bl grn (bl)	25	25
109	A3(i)	½g rose (Bl)	25	25
110	A3(i)	1g grn & org (Bl)	1.75	1.75
111	A4(i)	2g bl (R)	67.50	75.00
112	A4(j)	2g bl (Bk)	30	25
113	A4(j)	4g grn & car (Bl)	75	75
a.		Black ovpt.	10.00	10.00
114	A5(j)	8g ver & dp grn (Bl)	60	60
115	A5(j)	16g ver & car (Bl)	1.00	1.00
		Nos. 108-115 (8)	72.40	79.85

Coronation of Empress Zauditu.

Nos. 108–115 all exist with double overprint and inverted overprint. Nos. 108, 112, 113, 114 and 115 exist with double overprint, one inverted, and various combinations.

Preceding Issue with Additional Surcharge

1/4 1/2 1 2

k *l* *m* *n*

1917, May 28

116	A5(k)	¼g on 8g ver & dp grn	2.50	2.50
117	A5(l)	½g on 8g ver & dp grn	2.50	2.50
118	A5(m)	1g on 16g ver & car	6.50	6.50
119	A5(n)	2g on 16g ver & car	6.50	6.50

Nos. 116 to 119 all exist with the numerals double and inverted and No. 116 with the Amharic surcharge double.

Sommering's Gazelle
A6

Ras Tafari
A9

Cathedral of St. George—A12

Empress Waizeri Zauditu
A18

Designs: ⅛g, Giraffes. ½g, Leopard. 2g, Ras Tafari. 4g, Regent Tafari. 8g, White rhinoceros. 12g, Somali ostriches. 1t, African elephant. 2t, Water buffalo. 3t, Lions. 5t, 10t, Empress Zauditu.

1919, June 16 **Typo.** ***Perf. 11½.***

120	A6	⅛g vio & brn	10	6
121	A6	¼g bl grn & db	10	6
122	A6	½g scar & ol grn	10	6
123	A9	1g rose lil & gray grn	8	5
124	A9	2g dp ultra & fawn	8	6
125	A9	4g turq bl & org	10	10
126	A12	6g lt bl & org	10	10
127	A12	8g ol grn & blk brn	25	12
128	A12	12g red vio & gray	40	20
129	A12	1t rose & gray blk	70	30
130	A12	2t blk & brn	1.75	1.10
131	A12	3t grn & dp org	2.00	1.40
132	A18	4t brn & lil rose	2.25	2.00
133	A18	5t car & gray	3.00	3.00
134	A18	10t gray grn & bis	6.00	4.00
		Nos. 120-134 (15)	17.01	12.61

Reprints differ slightly in color from originals. Reprints exist imperf. and some values with inverted centers. Price for set, unused or canceled, $1.50.

No. 132 Surcharged in Blue

፬ ግርሽ ።
4guerches

1919, Oct.

135	A18	4g on 4t brn & lil rose	90	90

The Amharic surcharge indicates the new value and, therefore, varies on Nos. 135 to 154. There are numerous defective letters and figures, several types of the "2" of "½," the errors "guerhce," "gnerche," etc.

Stamps of 1919 Surcharged

አንድ ፡
ግርሽ ።
1 guerche

1921-22

136	A6	½g on ⅛g vio & brn ('22)	50	50
137	A6	1g on ¼g grn & db	50	50
138	A9	2g on 1g lil brn & gray grn ('22)	75	75
139	A18	2g on 4t brn & lil rose ('22)	27.30	27.50
140	A6	2½g on ½g scar & ol grn	75	75
141	A9	4g on 2g ultra & fawn ('22)	75	75
		Nos. 136-141 (6)	30.55	30.75

Stamps and Type of 1919 Surcharged

፩ ግርሽ ፡
1 guerche

1925-28

142	A12	½g on 1t rose & gray blk ('26)	75	75
a.		Without colon ('28)	10.00	10.00
143	A18	½g on 5t car & gray ('26)	40	40
144	A12	1g on 6g bl & org	40	40
145	A12	1g on 12g lil & gray	80.00	80.00
146	A12	1g on 3t grn & org ('26)	17.50	17.50
147	A18	1g on 10t gray grn & bis ('26)	50	50
		Nos. 142-147 (6)	99.55	99.55

On No. 142 the surcharge is at the left side of the stamp, reading upward. On No. 142a it is at the right, reading downward. The two surcharges are from different, though similar, settings. On No. 146 the surcharge is at the right, reading upward. See note following No. 154.

There are also many irregularly produced settings in imitation of Nos. 136-154 which differ slightly from the originals.

Type of 1919 Surcharged

፩ ግርሽ ፡

= 1 guerche =

1926

147A	A12	1g on 12g lil & gray	55.00	55.00
b.		Vertical bars at lower right corner	65.00	

Stamps of 1919 Surcharged

አንድ ፡ ግርሽ ፡

1 guerche

1926

148	A12	½g on 8g ol grn & blk brn	1.00	1.00
149	A12	1g on 6g bl & org	22.50	22.50
150	A12	1g on 12g lil & gray	65.00	65.00

Stamps of 1919 Surcharged

የግርሽ ፡ አላድ ፡

1/2 guerche

1927

151	A12	½g on 8g ol grn & blk brn	75	75
152	A12	1g on 6g bl & org	35.00	35.00
153	A12	1g on 12g lil & gray	1.00	1.00
154	A12	1g on 3t grn & org	80.00	80.00

Many varieties of surcharge, such as double, inverted, lines transposed or omitted, and inverted "2" in "½," exist on Nos. 136-154.

Ras Tafari
A22

Empress Zauditu
A23

1928, Sept. 5 Typo. *Perf. 13½x14*

155	A22	⅛m org & lt bl	50	40
156	A23	¼m ind & red org	30	30
157	A22	½m gray grn & blk	50	40
158	A23	1m dk car & blk	30	25
159	A22	2m dk bl & blk	30	25
160	A23	4m yel & ol	30	25
161	A22	8m vio & ol	80	60
162	A23	1t org brn & vio	1.00	80
163	A22	2t grn & bis	1.40	1.40
164	A23	3t choc & grn	2.00	1.50
		Nos. 155-164 (10)	7.40	6.15

Preceding Issue Overprinted in Black, Violet or Red

፲፱፻፳፩

ፖ፡ ቴ፡ ቴ፡
የተመረቀበት:
ቀን: መታሰቢያ:

1928, Sept. 1

165	A22	⅛m org & lt bl (Bk)	1.00	1.00
166	A23	¼m ind & red org (V)	1.00	1.00
167	A22	½m gray grn & blk (V)	1.00	1.00
168	A23	1m dk car & blk (V)	1.00	1.00
169	A22	2m dk bl & blk (R)	1.00	1.00
170	A23	4m yel & ol (Bk)	1.00	1.00
171	A22	8m vio & ol (R)	1.00	1.00
172	A23	1t org brn & vio (Bk)	1.00	1.00
173	A22	2t grn & bis (V)	1.50	1.50
174	A23	3t choc & grn (R)	2.00	2.00
		Nos. 165-174 (10)	11.50	11.50

Opening of General Post Office, Addis Ababa.

Stamps of 1928 Issue Handstamped in Violet, Red or Black

ንጉሥ ፡ ተፈሪ
NEGOUS TEFERI

1928, Oct. 7

175	A22	⅛m org & lt bl (V)	1.00	1.00
176	A22	½m gray grn & blk (R)	1.00	1.00
177	A22	2m dk bl & blk (R)	1.00	1.00
178	A22	8m vio & ol (Bk)	1.00	1.00
179	A22	2t grn & bis (V)	1.00	1.00
		Nos. 175-179 (5)	5.00	5.00

Crowning of Regent Tafari Makonen as Negus on Oct. 7, 1928.

Nos. 175-177 exist with overprint vertical.

Stamps of 1928 Overprinted in Red or Green

ቀዳማዊ
ኃይለ ሥላሴ
መጋቢት ጽ፭ ቀን
፲፱፻፳፪

HAYLE SELASSIE Ier
3 Avril 1930

1930, Apr. 3

180	A22	⅛m org & lt bl (R)	20	15
181	A23	¼m ind & red org (G)	25	20
182	A22	½m gray grn & blk (R)	20	15
183	A23	1m dk car & blk (G)	25	20
184	A22	2m dk bl & blk (R)	25	20
185	A23	4m yel & ol (R)	40	30
186	A22	8m vio & ol (R)	75	75
187	A23	1t org brn & vio (R)	1.75	1.75
188	A22	2t grn & bis (R)	2.25	2.25
189	A23	3t choc & grn (R)	3.00	3.00
		Nos. 180-189 (10)	9.30	8.95

Issued in commemoration of the proclamation of the Negus Tafari as King of Kings of Abyssinia under the name "Haile Selassie I."

A similar overprint, set in four vertical lines, was printed on all denominations of the 1928 issue. It was not considered satisfactory and was rejected. The trial impressions were not placed on sale to the public, but some copies reached private hands and have been passed through the post.

Stamps of 1928 Overprinted in Red or Olive Brown

ቀዳማዊ ፡
ኃይለ ፡ ሥላሴ ፡
መጋቢት፡ጽ፭፡ቀን፡
፲፱፻፳፪

HAILE SELASSIE 1er
3 Avril 1930

1930, Apr. 3

190	A22	⅛m org & lt bl	25	20
191	A23	¼m ind & red org (OB)	25	25
192	A22	½m gray grn & blk	25	20
193	A23	1m dk car & blk (OB)	25	25
194	A22	2m dk bl & blk	25	25
195	A23	4m yel & ol	50	50
196	A22	8m vio & ol	75	75
197	A23	1t org brn & vio	1.75	1.75
198	A22	2t grn & bis	2.25	2.25
199	A23	3t choc & grn	3.00	3.00
		Nos. 190-199 (10)	9.50	9.40

Issued in commemoration of the proclamation of the Negus Tafari as Emperor Haile Selassie I.

All stamps of this series exist with "H" of "HAILE" omitted.

Stamps of 1928 Handstamped in Violet or Red

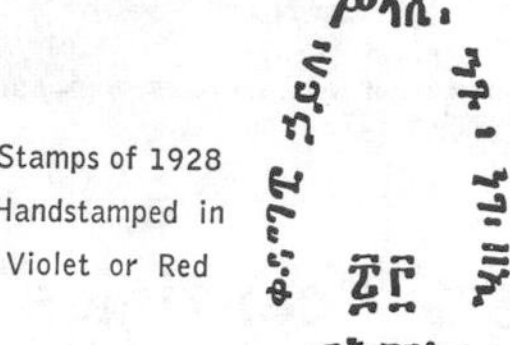

1930, Nov. 2

200	A22	⅛m org & lt bl (V)	30	25
201	A23	¼m ind & red org (V)	30	25
202	A22	½M gray grn & blk (R)	30	25
203	A23	1m dk car & blk (V)	30	25
204	A22	2m dk bl & blk (R)	30	25
205	A23	4m yel & ol (V)	30	25
206	A22	8m vio & ol (V or R)	75	75
207	A23	1t org brn & vio (V)	1.00	1.00
208	A22	2t grn & bis (V or R)	1.50	1.50
209	A23	3t choc & grn (V or R)	2.25	2.25
		Nos. 200-209 (10)	7.30	7.00

Issued in commemoration of the coronation of the Emperor Haile Selassie I, November 2nd, 1930.

Haile Selassie Coronation Monument, Symbols of Empire
A24

1930, Nov. Engraved *Perf. 12½*

210	A24	1g orange	20	20
211	A24	2g ultra	20	20
212	A24	4g violet	20	20
213	A24	8g dl grn	35	30
214	A24	1t brown	50	50
215	A24	3t green	75	75
216	A24	5t red brn	75	75
		Nos. 210-216 (7)	2.95	2.90

Coronation of Emperor Haile Selassie I.

Reprints of Nos. 210 to 216 exist. Paper is thinner and gum whiter than the originals. Price 7c each.

Stamps of 1928 Surcharged in Green, Red or Blue

1/8 Mehalek

Type I — Type II

1931, Mar. 20 *Perf. 13½x14.*

217	A23	⅛m on 1m dk car & blk (G)	30	30
218	A22	⅛m on 2m dk bl & blk (R)	30	30

219	A23	⅛m on 4m yel & ol (G)	30	30
220	A23	¼m on 1m dk car & blk (Bl)	30	30
221	A22	¼m on 2m dk bl & blk (R)	75	75
222	A23	¼m on 4m yel & ol (G)	75	75
225	A23	½m on 1m dk car & blk (Bl)	75	75
226	A22	½m on 2m dk bl & blk (R)	75	75
227	A23	½m on 4m yel & ol (G) (II)	75	75
a.		½m on 4m yel & ol (I)	7.50	7.50
228	A23	½m on 3t choc & grn (R)	6.00	6.00
230	A22	1m on 2m dk bl & blk (R)	1.00	1.00
		Nos. 217-230 (11)	11.95	11.95

The ½m on 1/8m orange and light blue and ½m on ¼m indigo and red orange were clandestinely printed and never sold at the post office.

No. 230 with double surcharge in red and blue is a color trial.

Ras Makonnen
A25

Empress Menen
A27

View of Hawash River and Railroad Bridge—A26

Designs: 2g, 8g, Haile Selassie I (profile). 4g, 1t, Statue of Menelik II. 3t, Empress Menen (full face). 5t, Haile Selassie I (full face).

Perf. 12½, 12x12½, 12½x12.

1931, June 27 **Engraved**

232	A25	⅛g red	15	15
233	A26	¼g ol grn	15	15
234	A25	½g dk vio	20	15
235	A27	1g red org	20	20
236	A27	2g ultra	25	25
237	A25	4g violet	35	35
238	A27	8g bl grn	1.10	1.10
239	A25	1t chocolate	2.00	2.00
240	A27	3t yel grn	3.25	3.25
241	A27	5t red brn	6.00	5.00
		Nos. 232-241 (10)	13.65	12.60

Reprints of Nos. 232 to 241 are on thinner and whiter paper than the originals. Price 5c each.

Stamps of 1931 Surcharged in Blue or Carmine similar to cut

2 c

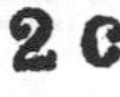

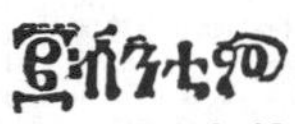

1936 ***Perf. 12x12½, 12½x12.***

242	A25	1c on ⅛g red	1.10	75
243	A26	2c on ¼g ol grn (C)	1.10	75
244	A25	3c on ½g dk vio	1.10	85
245	A27	5c on 1g red org	2.00	1.25
246	A27	10c on 2g ultra (C)	2.50	1.50
		Nos. 242-246 (5)	7.80	5.10

Haile Selassie I
A32 A33

Lithographed

1942, Mar. 23 ***Perf. 14x13½***

247	A32	4c lt bl grn, ind & blk	30	25
248	A32	10c rose, ind & blk	1.00	50
249	A32	20c dp ultra, ind & blk	2.00	90

1942-43 **Unwmkd.**

250	A33	4c lt bl grn & ind	20	15
251	A33	8c yel org & ind	25	15
252	A33	10c rose & ind	40	20
253	A33	12c dl vio & ind	45	25
254	A33	20c dp ultra & ind	65	40
255	A33	25c dl grn & ind ('43)	1.10	60
256	A33	50c dl brn & ind ('43)	1.50	1.00
257	A33	60c lil & ind ('43)	2.50	1.25
		Nos. 250-257 (8)	7.05	4.00

OBELISK
3 Nov. 1943

Nos. 250–254 Surcharged in Black or Brown

3

1943, Nov. 3

258	A33	5c on 4c lt bl grn & ind	30.00	30.00
259	A33	10c on 8c yel org & ind	30.00	30.00
260	A33	15c on 10c rose & ind	30.00	30.00
261	A33	20c on 12c dl vio & ind (Br)	30.00	30.00
262	A33	30c on 20c dp ultra & ind (Br)	30.00	30.00
		Nos. 258-262 (5)	150.00	150.00

Restoration of the Obelisk in Myazzia Place, Addis Ababa, and the 14th anniversary of the coronation of Emperor Haile Selassie I.

On No. 262, "3" is surcharged on "2" of "20" to make "30."

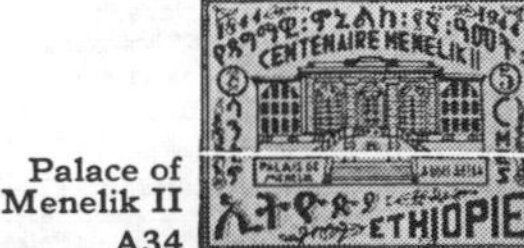

Palace of Menelik II
A34

Menelik II
A35

Statue
A36

Designs: 50c, Mausoleum. 65c, Menelik II (with scepter).

1944, Dec. 31 **Litho.** ***Perf. 10½***

263	A34	5c green	1.50	75
264	A35	10c red lil	2.00	1.00
265	A36	20c dp bl	3.50	2.00
266	A34	50c dl pur	4.00	2.00
267	A35	65c bis brn	7.50	3.00
		Nos. 263-267 (5)	18.50	8.75

Issued to commemorate the centenary of the birth of Emperor Menelik II, August 18, 1844.

Unissued Semi-Postal Stamps Overprinted in Carmine:

Nurse and Baby
A39

Various Designs Inscribed "Croix Rouge".

1945, Aug. 7 **Photo.** ***Perf. 11½***

268	A39	5c brt grn	40	40
269	A39	10c brt red	40	40
270	A39	25c brt bl	40	40
271	A39	50c dk yel brn	2.25	1.75
272	A39	1t brt vio	3.50	2.50
		Nos. 268-272 (5)	6.95	5.45

Nos. 268 to 272 without overprint were ordered printed in Switzerland before Ethiopia fell to the invading Italians, so were not delivered to Addis Ababa. After that country's liberation, the set was overprinted "V" and issued for ordinary postage. These stamps exist without overprint, but were not so issued. Price $1.25.

See Nos. B36–B40.

Lion of Judah
A44

Menelik II
A45

Mail Transport, Old and New
A46

Designs: 50c, Old Post Office, Addis Ababa. 70c, Menelik II and Haile Selassie I.

1947, Apr. 18 **Engraved** ***Perf. 13***

273	A44	10c yel org	1.75	60
274	A45	20c dp bl	2.25	75
275	A46	30c org brn	3.50	1.25
276	A46	50c dk sl grn	8.00	2.50
277	A46	70c red vio	15.00	5.00
		Nos. 273-277 (5)	30.50	10.10

Issued to commemorate the 50th anniversary of Ethiopia's postal system.

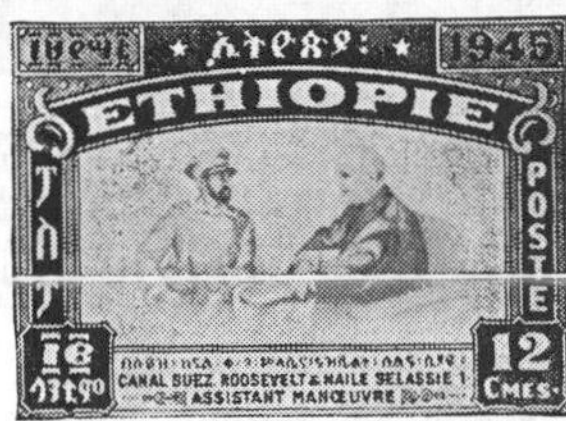

Haile Selassie and Franklin D. Roosevelt—A49

Design: 65c, Roosevelt and U. S. Flags.

Engraved and Photogravure.

1947, May 23 ***Perf. 12½*** **Unwmkd.**

278	A49	12c car lake & bl grn	35	20
279	A49	25c dk bl & rose	75	40
280	A49	65c blk, red & dp bl	1.50	1.00
		Nos. 278-280, C21-C22 (5)	18.00	14.00

Negus Sahle Selassie—A50

Negus Sahle Selassie
A52

Design: 30c, View of Ankober.

1947, May 1 **Engraved** ***Perf. 13***

281	A50	20c dp bl	1.50	75
282	A50	30c dk pur	2.50	1.00
283	A52	$1 dp grn	6.00	3.00

150th anniversary of Selassie dynasty.

No. 255 Surcharged in Orange

12 centimes

1947, July 14 ***Perf. 14x13½***

284	A33	12c on 25c dl grn & ind	40.00	40.00

Amba Alaguie—A53

Wmk. 282

Designs: 2c, Trinity Church. 4c, Debra Sina. 5c, Mecan, near Achanguie. 8c, Lake Tana. 12c, 15c, Parliament Building, Addis Ababa. 20c, Aiba, near Mai Cheo. 30c, Bahr Bridge over Blue Nile. 60c, 70c, Canoe on Lake Tana. $1, Omo Falls. $3, Mt. Alamata. $5, Ras Dashan Mountains.

Wmkd.
Ethiopian Star and Amharic Characters, Multiple. (282)

1947–53 Engraved *Perf. 13x13½*

285	A53	1c rose vio	10	5
286	A53	2c bl vio	15	8
287	A53	4c green	25	12
288	A53	5c dk grn	25	12
289	A53	8c dp org	40	20
290	A53	12c red	50	20
290A	A53	15c dk ol brn ('53)	45	20
291	A53	20c blue	75	30
292	A53	30c org brn	1.25	40
292A	A53	60c red ('51)	1.50	70
293	A53	70c rose lil	2.00	50
294	A53	$1 dk car rose	3.50	50
295	A53	$3 brt bl	9.00	2.00
296	A53	$5 olive	15.00	4.00
		Nos. 285-296 (14)	35.10	9.37

Issue dates: 15c, May 25, 1953; 60c, Feb. 10, 1951; others, Aug. 23, 1947.

Empress Waizero Menen and Emperor Haile Selassie I
A54

1949, May 5 *Perf. 13* Wmk. 282

297	A54	20c blue	1.00	50
298	A54	30c yel org	1.00	65
299	A54	50c purple	2.50	1.25
300	A54	80c green	3.00	1.50
301	A54	$1 red	5.50	2.50
		Nos. 297-301 (5)	13.00	6.40

Central ornaments differ on each denomination.

Issued to commemorate the eighth anniversary of Ethiopia's liberation from Italian occupation.

Dejach Balcha Hospital—A55

Abuna Petros
A56

Designs: 20c, Haile Selassie raising flag. 30c, Lion of Judah statue. 50c, Empress Waizero Menen, Haile Selassie and building.

Perf. 13x13½, 13½x13.
1950, Nov. 2 Engr. Wmk. 282

302	A55	5c purple	60	30
303	A56	10c dp plum	1.50	60
304	A56	20c dp car	2.00	75
305	A56	30c green	3.50	1.50
306	A55	50c dp bl	6.00	3.00
		Nos. 302-306 (5)	13.60	6.15

Issued to commemorate the 20th anniversary of the coronation of Emperor Haile Selassie and Empress Menen.

Abbaye Bridge
A57

1951, Jan. 1 *Perf. 14* Unwmkd.

308	A57	5c dk grn & dk brn	3.50	30
309	A57	10c dp org & blk	5.00	35
310	A57	15c dp bl & org brn	7.00	50
311	A57	30c ol & lil rose	12.50	65
312	A57	60c brn & dp bl	17.50	1.50
313	A57	80c pur & grn	22.50	2.25
		Nos. 308-313 (6)	68.00	5.55

Issued to commemorate the opening of the Abbaye Bridge over the Blue Nile.

Tomb of Ras Makonnen
A58

1951, Mar. 2

Center in Black.

314	A58	5c dk grn	1.75	25
315	A58	10c dp ultra	1.75	35
316	A58	15c blue	2.50	35
317	A58	30c claret	6.00	1.35
318	A58	80c rose car	8.00	2.00
319	A58	$1 org brn	10.00	2.00
		Nos. 314-319 (6)	30.00	6.30

55th anniversary of the Battle of Adwa.

Emperor Haile Selassie I
A59

1952, July 23 *Perf. 13½*

320	A59	5c dk grn	35	20
321	A59	10c red org	60	25
322	A59	15c black	85	35
323	A59	25c ultra	1.25	35
324	A59	30c violet	1.50	60
325	A59	50c rose red	2.25	85
326	A59	65c chocolate	3.75	1.50
		Nos. 320-326 (7)	10.55	4.10

60th birthday of Haile Selassie I.

Open Road to Sea
A60

Designs: 25c, 50c, Road and broken chain. 65c, Map. 80c, Allegory: Reunion. $1, Haile Selassie raising flag. $2, Ethiopian flag and seascape. $3, Haile Selassie addressing League of Nations.

Engraved.
1952, Sept. 11 *Perf. 13* Wmk. 282

327	A60	15c brn car	75	30
328	A60	25c red brn	1.00	50
329	A60	30c yel brn	1.75	75
330	A60	50c purple	2.25	90
331	A60	65c gray	3.00	1.10
332	A60	80c bl grn	3.50	75
333	A60	$1 rose car	7.00	1.75
334	A60	$2 dp bl	13.00	3.00
335	A60	$3 magenta	27.50	5.00
		Nos. 327-335 (9)	59.75	14.05

Issued to celebrate Ethiopia's federation with Eritrea, effected Sept. 11, 1952.

Haile Selassie and New Ethiopian Port
A61

Design: 15c, 30c, Haile Selassie on deck of ship.

1953, Oct. 4

337	A61	10c red & dk brn	1.25	75
338	A61	15c bl & dk grn	1.50	75
339	A61	25c org & dk brn	2.50	1.25
340	A61	30c red brn & dk grn	4.50	1.50
341	A61	50c pur & dk brn	8.50	3.25
		Nos. 337-341 (5)	18.25	7.50

Issued to commemorate the first anniversary of the federation of Ethiopia and Eritrea.

Princess Tsahai at a Sickbed
A62

Perf. 13x13½
1955, July 8 Engr. Wmk. 282
Cross Typographed in Red

342	A62	15c choc & ultra	1.00	50
343	A62	20c grn & org	1.50	60
344	A62	30c ultra & grn	2.50	75

Issued to commemorate the 20th anniversary of the founding of the Ethiopian Red Cross.

Promulgating the Constitution
A63

Bishops' Consecration by Archbishop
A64

Designs: 25c, Kagnew Battalion. 35c, Reunion with the Motherland. 50c, "Progress." 65c, Empress Waizero Menen and Emperor Haile Selassie I.

Engraved.
1955, Nov. 3 *Perf. 12½* Unwmkd.

345	A63	5c grn & choc	50	25
346	A64	20c car & grn	1.10	35
347	A64	25c mag & gray	1.50	50
348	A63	35c brn & red org	2.00	65
349	A64	50c dk brn & ultra	3.00	1.00
350	A64	65c vio & car	4.25	1.50
		Nos. 345-350 (6)	12.35	4.25

Issued to commemorate the silver jubilee of the coronation of Emperor Haile Selassie I and Empress Waizero Menen.

Emperor Haile Selassie and Fair Emblem
A65

1955, Nov. 5 Wmk. 282

351	A65	5c grn & ol grn	60	15
352	A65	10c car & dp ultra	90	25
353	A65	15c vio blk & grn	1.25	35
354	A65	50c mag & red brn	1.75	90

Silver Jubilee Fair, Addis Ababa.

Nos. 291 and 292A Overprinted

የዓለም ስደተኞች ዓመት
World Refugee Year
1959-1960

1960, Apr. 7 *Perf. 13x13½*

355	A53	20c blue	35	25
356	A53	60c red	75	50

Issued to publicize World Refugee Year, July 1, 1959–June 30, 1960.

Map of Africa, "Liberty" and Haile Selassie
A66

Emperor Haile Selassie
A67

Perf. 13½
1960, June 14 Engr. Unwmkd.

357	A66	20c org & grn	60	60
358	A66	80c org & vio	1.50	60
359	A66	$1 org & mar	1.75	80

Issued to commemorate the 2nd Conference of Independent African States at Tunis. Issued in sheets of 10.

1960, Nov. 2 *Perf. 14* Wmk. 282

360	A67	10c brn & bl	40	20
361	A67	25c vio & emer	80	25
362	A67	50c dk bl & org yel	1.50	1.00
363	A67	65c sl grn & sal pink	2.00	1.00
364	A67	$1 ind & rose vio	3.00	1.50
		Nos. 360-364 (5)	7.70	3.95

Issued to commemorate the 30th anniversary of the coronation of Emperor Haile Selassie I.

Africa Hall, U.N. Economic Commission for Africa
A68

1961, Apr. 15 *Perf. 14* Wmk. 282

365	A68	80c ultra	1.00	50

Issued for Africa Freedom Day, Apr. 15. Issued in sheets of 10.

Map of Ethiopia, Olive Branch and Emperor Haile Selassie I
A69

1961, May 5 *Perf. 13x13½*

366	A69	20c green	20	15
367	A69	30c vio bl	30	20
368	A69	$1 brown	1.25	60

Issued to commemorate the 20th anniversary of Ethiopia's liberation from Italian occupation.

African Wild Ass
A70

Designs: 15c, Eland. 25c, Elephant. 35c, Giraffe. 50c, Beisa. $1, Lion.

1961, June 16 *Perf. 14* Wmk. 282

369	A70	5c blk & emer	15	5
370	A70	15c red brn & grn	20	5
371	A70	25c sep & emer	30	15
372	A70	35c lt red brn & grn	40	20
373	A70	50c brn red & emer	50	35
374	A70	$1 red brn & grn	1.50	85
		Nos. 369-374 (6)	3.05	1.65

Issued in sheets of 10.

Emperor Haile Selassie I and Empress Waizero Menen
A71

1961, July 27 *Perf. 11* Unwmkd.

375	A71	10c green	50	25
376	A71	50c vio bl	1.00	50
377	A71	$1 car rose	1.75	1.00

Issued to commemorate the golden wedding anniversary of the Emperor and Empress.

Warlike Horsemanship (Guks)
A72

Designs: 15c, Hockey. 20c, Bicycling. 30c, Soccer. 50c, Marathon runner, Olympic winner, 1960.

Photogravure and Engraved

1962, Jan. 14 *Perf. 12x11½*

378	A72	10c yel grn & car	15	5
379	A72	15c pink & dk brn	20	6
380	A72	20c red & blk	25	10
381	A72	30c ultra & dl pur	35	15
382	A72	50c yel & grn	75	25
		Nos. 378-382 (5)	1.70	61

Issued to commemorate the Third Africa Football (soccer) Cup, Addis Ababa, Jan. 14–22.

Malaria Eradication Emblem, World Map and Mosquito
A73

Engraved

1962, Apr. 7 *Perf. 13½* Wmk. 282

383	A73	15c black	20	10
384	A73	30c purple	40	25
385	A73	60c red brn	1.00	60

Issued for the World Health Organization drive to eradicate malaria.

Abyssinian Ground Hornbill
A74

Birds: 15c, Abyssinian roller. 30c, Bataleur (vert.). 50c, Double-toothed barbet (vert.). $1, Didric cuckoo.

Photogravure

1962, May 5 *Perf. 11½* Unwmkd.

Granite Paper

386	A74	5c multi	20	10
387	A74	15c emer, brn & ultra	40	15
388	A74	30c lt brn, blk & red	75	25
389	A74	50c multi	1.50	60
390	A74	$1 multi	3.00	1.25
		Nos. 386-390 (5)	5.85	2.35

See also Nos. C77–C81, C97–C101, C107–C111.

Assab Hospital
A75

Designs: 15c, School at Assab. 20c, Church at Massawa. 50c, Mosque at Massawa. 60c, Assab port.

Engraved

1962, Sept. 11 *Perf. 13½* Wmk. 282

391	A75	3c purple	15	5
392	A75	15c dk bl	20	10
393	A75	20c green	25	10
394	A75	50c brown	50	25
395	A75	60c car rose	75	35
		Nos. 391-395 (5)	1.85	85

Issued to commemorate the tenth anniversary of the Federation of Ethiopia and Eritrea.

King Bazen, Madonna and Stars over Bethlehem—A76

Designs: 15c, Ezana, obelisks and temple. 20c, Kaleb and sailing fleet. 50c, Lalibela, rock-church and frescoes (vert.). 60c, Yekuno Amlak and priests preaching in village. 75c, Zara Yacob and procession around tree. $1, Lebna Dengel and tournament.

Photogravure

1962, Nov. 2 *Perf. 14½* Unwmkd.

396	A76	10c multi	15	10
397	A76	15c multi	25	10
398	A76	20c multi	30	10
399	A76	50c multi	50	20
400	A76	60c multi	55	30
401	A76	75c multi	90	50
402	A76	$1 multi	1.25	75
		Nos. 396-402 (7)	3.90	2.05

Issued on the 32nd anniversary of the coronation of Emperor Haile Selassie I and to commemorate ancient kings and saints.

Map of Ethiopian Telephone Network
A77

Wheat Emblem
A78

Designs: 50c, Radio mast and waves. 60c, Telegraph pole and rising sun.

Perf. 13½x14

1963, Jan. 1 Engraved Wmk. 282

403	A77	10c dk red	40	10
404	A77	50c ultra	1.00	40
405	A77	60c brown	1.25	50

Issued to commemorate the 10th anniversary of the Imperial Board of Telecommunications.

1963, Mar. 21 *Perf. 13½* Unwmkd.

406	A78	5c dp rose	10	5
407	A78	10c rose car	15	10
408	A78	15c vio bl	20	10
409	A78	30c emerald	30	20

Issued for the "Freedom from Hunger" campaign of the U.N. Food and Agriculture Organization.

Abuna Salama
A79

Queen of Sheba
A80

Spiritual Leaders: 15c, Abuna Aregawi. 30c, Abuna Tekle Haimanot. 40c. Yared. 60c, Zara Yacob.

1964, Jan. 3 *Perf. 13½* Unwmkd.

410	A79	10c blue	25	10
411	A79	15c dk grn	35	15
412	A79	30c brn red	60	35
413	A79	40c dk bl	1.00	60
414	A79	60c brown	1.50	1.10
		Nos. 410-414 (5)	3.70	2.30

1964, March 2 Photo. *Perf. 11½*

Ethiopian Queens: 15c, Helen. 50c, Seble Wongel. 60c, Mentiwab. 80c, Taitu, consort of Menelik II.

Granite Paper

415	A80	10c multi	50	15
416	A80	15c multi	60	20
417	A80	50c multi	1.25	55
418	A80	60c multi	2.00	85
419	A80	80c multi	2.50	1.25
		Nos. 415-419 (5)	6.85	3.00

Priest Teaching Alphabet to Children
A81

Eleanor Roosevelt
A82

Designs: 10c, Classroom. 15c, Woman learning to read (vert.). 40c, Students in chemistry laboratory (vert.). 60c, Graduation procession (vert.).

1964, June 1 *Perf. 11½* Unwmkd.

Granite Paper

420	A81	5c brown	15	7
421	A81	10c emerald	15	10
422	A81	15c rose vio	20	14
423	A81	40c vio bl	60	25
424	A81	60c dk pur	1.00	50
		Nos. 420-424 (5)	2.10	1.06

Issued to publicize education.

1964, Oct. 11 Photogravure

Granite Paper

Portrait in Slate Blue

425	A82	10c yel bis	15	8
426	A82	60c org brn	80	50
427	A82	80c grn & gold	1.00	70

Issued to honor Eleanor Roosevelt (1884–1962).

King Serse Dengel and View of Gondar, 1563
A83

Ethiopian Leaders: 10c, King Fasiladas and Gondar in 1632. 20c, King Yassu the Great and Gondar in 1682. 25c, Emperor Theodore II and map of Ethiopia. 60c, Emperor John IV and Battle of Gura, 1876. 80c, Emperor Menelik II and Battle of Adwa, 1896.

1964, Dec. 12 Photo. *Perf. 14½x14*

428	A83	5c multi	10	5
429	A83	10c multi	15	6
430	A83	20c multi	30	15
431	A83	25c multi	50	20
432	A83	60c multi	1.00	55
433	A83	80c multi	1.25	75
		Nos. 428-433(6)	3.30	1.76

Ethiopian Rose
A84

Flowers: 10c, Kosso tree. 25c, St.-John's-wort. 35c, Parrot's-beak. 60c, Maskal daisy.

1965, Mar. 30 *Perf. 12x13½*

434	A84	5c multi	10	5
435	A84	10c multi	15	5
436	A84	25c multi	50	15
437	A84	35c multi	90	30
438	A84	60c grn, yel & org	1.25	50
		Nos. 434-438 (5)	2.90	1.05

ITU Emblem, Old and New Communication Symbols
A85

Perf. 13½x14½

1965, May 17 Litho. Unwmkd.

439	A85	5c bl, ind & yel	15	6
440	A85	10c bl, ind & org	25	10
441	A85	60c bl, ind & lil rose	90	50

Issued to commemorate the centenary of the International Telecommunication Union.

Laboratory
A86

Designs: 5c, Textile spinning mill. 10c, Sugar factory. 20c, Mountain road. 25c, Autobus. 30c, Diesel locomotive and bridge. 35c, Railroad station, Addis Ababa.

1965, July 19 Photo. *Perf. 11½*

Granite Paper

Portrait in Black

442	A86	3c sepia	8	5
443	A86	5c dl pur & buff	10	5
444	A86	10c blk & gray	12	5
445	A86	20c grn & pale yel	25	10
446	A86	25c dk brn & yel	35	15
447	A86	30c mar & gray	55	25
448	A86	35c dk bl & gray	65	35
		Nos. 442-448 (7)	2.10	1.00

ICY Emblem
A87

1965, Oct. 24 *Perf. 11½* Unwmkd.

Granite Paper

449	A87	10c bl & red brn	20	10
450	A87	50c dp bl & red brn	75	40
451	A87	80c vio bl & red brn	1.00	60

International Cooperation Year, 1965.

National Bank Emblem
A88

Designs: 10c, Commercial Bank emblem. 60c, National and Commercial Bank buildings.

1965, Nov. 2 Photo. *Perf. 13*

452	A88	10c dp car, blk & ind	35	10
453	A88	30c ultra, blk & ind	65	30
454	A88	60c blk, yel & ind	95	50

Issued to publicize the National and Commercial Banks of Ethiopia.

"Light and Peace" Press Building
A89

1966, Apr. 5 Engraved *Perf. 13*

455	A89	5c pink & blk	8	5
456	A89	15c lt yel grn & blk	35	12
457	A89	30c org yel & blk	60	30

Issued to commemorate the opening of the "Light and Peace" Printing Press building.

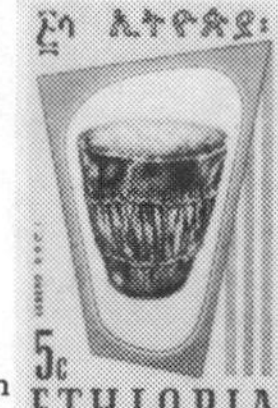

Kebero Drum
A90

Musical Instruments: 10c, Begena harp. 35c, Mesenko guitar. 50c, Krar lyre. 60c, Washent flutes.

1966, Sept. 9 Photo. *Perf. 13½*

458	A90	5c brt grn & blk	10	5
459	A90	10c dl bl & blk	15	8
460	A90	35c org & blk	55	25
461	A90	50c yel & blk	80	35
462	A90	60c rose car & blk	1.00	60
		Nos. 458-462 (5)	2.60	1.33

Emperor Haile Selassie—A91

1966, Nov. 1 *Perf. 12* Unwmkd.

463	A91	10c blk, gold & grn	15	5
464	A91	15c blk, gold & dp car	30	10
465	A91	40c blk & gold	90	60

Issued to commemorate 50 years of leadership of Emperor Haile Selassie.

UNESCO Emblem and Map of Africa
A92

Lithographed

1966, Nov. 30 *Perf. 13½* Wmk. 282

466	A92	15c bl car & blk	35	10
467	A92	60c ol, brn & dk bl	90	45

Issued to commemorate the 20th anniversary of UNESCO (United Nations Educational, Scientific and Cultural Organization).

WHO Headquarters, Geneva
A93

1966, Nov. 30

468	A93	5c ol, ultra & brn	20	5
469	A93	40c brn, pur & emer	65	35

Issued to commemorate the opening of World Health Organization Headquarters, Geneva.

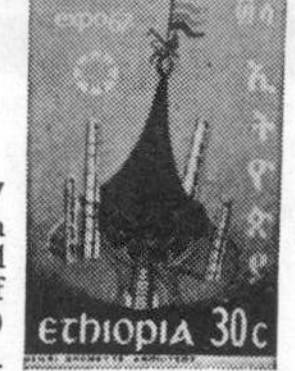

Expo '67 Ethiopian Pavilion and Columns of Axum (Replica)
A94

Perf. 12x13½

1967, May 2 Photo. Unwmkd.

470	A94	30c brt bl & multi	60	25
471	A94	45c multi	75	35
472	A94	80c gray & multi	1.50	60

Issued to commemorate EXPO '67, International Exhibition, Montreal, Apr. 28–Oct. 27, 1967.

Diesel Train and Map—A95

1967, June 7 Photo. *Perf. 12*

473	A95	15c multi	35	15
474	A95	30c multi	75	30
475	A95	50c multi	1.25	35

Issued to commemorate the 50th anniversary of the Djibouti-Addis Ababa railroad.

Papilionidae Aethiops
A96

Various Butterflies.

Perf. 13½x13

1967, June 30 Photo. Unwmkd.

476	A96	5c buff & multi	10	5
477	A96	10c lil & multi	25	6
478	A96	20c multi	50	15
479	A96	35c bl & multi	1.00	35
480	A96	40c multi	1.25	40
		Nos. 476-480 (5)	3.10	1.01

Emperor Haile Selassie and Lion of Judah
A97

1967, July 21 *Perf. 11½*

Granite Paper

481	A97	10c dk brn, emer & gold	25	12
482	A97	15c dk brn, yel & gold	40	15
483	A97	$1 dk brn, red & gold	1.75	75

Souvenir Sheet

484	A97	$1 dk brn, pur & gold	4.00	3.75

Issued to commemorate the 75th birthday of Emperor Haile Selassie. No. 484 contains one stamp; brown marginal inscription. Size 120x75mm.

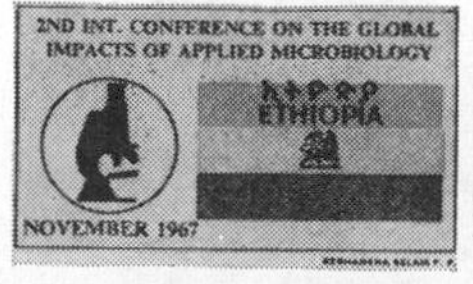

Microscope and Ethiopian Flag
A98

1967, Nov. 6 Litho. *Perf. 13*

Flag in Grn., Yel., Red & Blk.

485	A98	5c blue	15	5
486	A98	30c ocher	50	25
487	A98	$1 violet	1.75	80

Issued to commemorate the 2nd International Conference on the Global Impact of Applied Microbiology, Addis Ababa, Nov. 6–12.

Wall Painting from Debre Berhan Selassie Church, Gondar, 17th Century—A99

Designs (ITY Emblem and): 25c, Votive throne from Atsbe Dera, 4th Century B.C. (vert.). 35c, Prehistoric cave painting, Harar Province. 50c, Prehistoric stone tools, Melke Kontoure (vert.).

1967, Nov. 20 Photo. *Perf. 14½*

488	A99	15c multi	50	20
489	A99	25c yel grn, buff & blk	70	30
490	A99	35c grn, brn & blk	80	50
491	A99	50c yel & blk	1.00	75

International Tourist Year, 1967.

Processional Bronze Cross, Biet-Maryam Church
A100

Emperor Theodore
A101

Crosses of Lalibela: 10c, Processional copper cross. 15c, Copper cross, Biet-Maryam church. 20c, Lalibela-style cross. 50c, Chiseled copper cross, Madhani Alem church.

1967, Dec. 7 Photo. *Perf. 14½*

Crosses in Silver

492	A100	5c yel & blk	8	5
493	A100	10c red org & blk	15	6
494	A100	15c vio & blk	25	10
495	A100	20c brt rose & blk	30	15
496	A100	50c org yel & blk	1.10	50
		Nos. 492-496 (5)	1.88	86

Perf. 14x13½

1968, Apr. 18 Litho. Unwmkd.

Designs: 20c, Emperor Theodore and lions (horiz.). 50c, Imperial crown.

497	A101	10c lt vio, ocher & brn	15	6
498	A101	20c lil, brn & dk vio	35	15
499	A101	50c dk grn, org & rose cl	1.00	40

Issued to commemorate the centenary of the death of the Emperor Theodore (1818? –1868).

Human Rights Flame
A102

1968, May 31 *Perf. 14½* Unwmkd.

No.	Type	Description	Unused	Used
500	A102	15c pink, red & blk	30	30
501	A102	$1 lt bl, brt bl & blk	1.50	1.50

International Human Rights Year, 1968.

Shah Riza Pahlavi, Emperor and Flags—A103

1968, June 3 Litho. *Perf. 13½*

No.	Type	Description	Unused	Used
502	A103	5c multi	12	12
503	A103	15c multi	25	25
504	A103	30c multi	85	85

Issued to commemorate the visit of Shah Mohammed Riza Pahlavi of Iran.

Emperor Haile Selassie Appealing to League of Nations, 1935

A104

Designs: 35c, African Unity Building and map of Africa. $1, World map, symbolizing international relations.

1968, July 22 Photo. *Perf. 14x13½*

No.	Type	Description	Unused	Used
505	A104	15c bl, red, blk & gold	25	25
506	A104	35c blk, emer, red & gold	55	55
507	A104	$1 dk bl, lil, blk & gold	1.75	1.75

Ethiopia's struggle for peace.

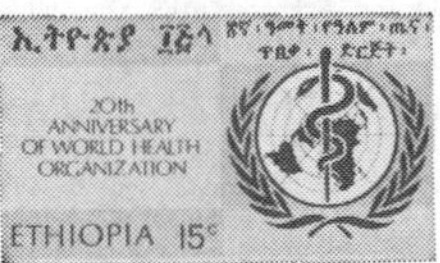

WHO Emblem

A105

Perf. 14x13½

1968, Aug. 30 Litho. Unwmkd.

No.	Type	Description	Unused	Used
508	A105	15c brt grn & blk	25	25
509	A105	60c red lil & blk	90	90

Issued to commemorate the 20th anniversary of the World Health Organization.

Running

A106

Designs: 15c, Soccer. 20c, Boxing. 40c, Basketball. 50c, Bicycling.

1968, Oct. 12 *Perf. 11½*

No.	Type	Description	Unused	Used
510	A106	10c lt grn & multi	15	15
511	A106	15c brt vio & multi	25	25
512	A106	20c bl & multi	30	30
513	A106	40c multi	60	60
514	A106	50c beige & multi	90	90
		Nos. 510-514 (5)	2.20	2.20

Issued to commemorate the 19th Olympic Games, Mexico City, Oct. 12–27.

Arrussi Woman

A107

Regional Costumes: 15c, Man from Gemu Gefa. 20c, Gojam man. 30c, Kefa man. 35c, Harer woman. 50c, Ilubabor grass coat. 60c, Woman from Eritrea.

Perf. 13½x13

1968, Dec. 10 Photo. Unwmkd.

No.	Type	Description	Unused	Used
515	A107	5c sil & multi	7	7
516	A107	15c sil & multi	15	15
517	A107	20c sil & multi	20	20
518	A107	30c sil & multi	30	30
519	A107	35c sil & multi	35	35
520	A107	50c sil & multi	60	60
521	A107	60c sil & multi	85	85
		Nos. 515-521 (7)	2.52	2.52

See Nos. 575–581.

Message Stick and Amharic Postal Emblem—A108

1969, Mar. 10 Litho. *Perf. 14*

No.	Type	Description	Unused	Used
522	A108	10c emer, blk & brn	20	20
523	A108	15c yel, blk & brn	30	30
524	A108	35c multi	75	75

Issued to commemorate the 75th anniversary of Ethiopian postal service.

ILO Emblem

A109

1969, Apr. 11 Litho. *Perf. 14½*

No.	Type	Description	Unused	Used
525	A109	15c org & blk	30	30
526	A109	60c emer & blk	1.25	1.25

Issued to commemorate the 50th anniversary of the International Labor Organization.

Dove, Red Cross, Crescent, Lion and Sun Emblems—A110

1969, May 8 *Perf. 13* Wmk. 282

No.	Type	Description	Unused	Used
527	A110	5c lt ultra, blk & red	8	8
528	A110	15c lt ultra, grn & red	30	30
529	A110	30c lt ultra, vio bl & red	60	60

Issued to commemorate the 50th anniversary of the League of Red Cross Societies.

Endybis Silver Coin, 3rd Century

A111

Ancient Ethiopian Coins: 10c, Gold coin of Ezana, 4th century. 15c, Gold coin of Kaleb, 6th century. 30c, Bronze coin of Armah, 7th century. 40c, Bronze coin of Wazena, 7th century. 50c, Silver coin of Gersem, 8th century.

1969, June 19 Photo. *Perf. 14½*

No.	Type	Description	Unused	Used
530	A111	5c ultra, blk & sil	10	10
531	A111	10c brt red, blk & gold	18	18
532	A111	15c brn, blk & gold	30	30
533	A111	30c dp car, blk & brnz	60	60
534	A111	40c dk grn, blk & brnz	70	70
535	A111	50c dp vio, blk & sil	90	90
		Nos. 530-535 (6)	2.78	2.78

Zebras and Tourist Year Emblem

A112

Designs: 10c, Camping. 15c, Fishing. 20c, Water skiing. 25c, Mountaineering (vert.).

Perf. 13x13½, 13½x13

1969, Aug. 29 Litho. Unwmkd.

No.	Type	Description	Unused	Used
536	A112	5c multi	10	10
537	A112	10c multi	15	15
538	A112	15c multi	25	25
539	A112	20c multi	40	40
540	A112	25c multi	50	50
		Nos. 536-540 (5)	1.40	1.40

International Year of African Tourism.

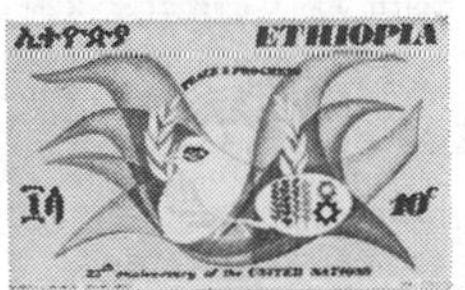

Stylized Bird and U.N. Emblem

A113

Designs: 30c, Stylized flowers, U.N. and peace emblems (vert.). 60c, Stylized bird, U.N. emblem and plane.

1969, Oct. 24 *Perf. 11½* Unwmkd.

No.	Type	Description	Unused	Used
541	A113	10c lt bl & multi	15	15
542	A113	30c lt bl & multi	45	45
543	A113	60c lt bl & multi	1.00	1.00

25th anniversary of the United Nations.

See "Special Notices" at the front of this volume for data on the listing methods of this Catalogue, abbreviations, condition, prices and examination.

Ancient Cross and Holy Family

A114

Designs: Various ancient crosses.

Photogravure

1969, Dec. 10 *Perf. 14½x13½*

No.	Type	Description	Unused	Used
544	A114	5c blk, yel & dk bl	10	10
545	A114	10c blk & yel	15	15
546	A114	25c blk, yel & grn	50	50
547	A114	60c blk & ocher	1.25	1.25

Ancient Figurines—A115

Ancient Ethiopian Pottery: 20c, Vases, Yeha period, 4th–3rd centuries B.C. 25c, Vases and jugs, Axum, 4th–6th centuries A.D. 35c, Bird-shaped jug and jugs, Matara, 4th–6th centuries A.D. 60c, Decorated pottery, Adulis, 6th–7th centuries A.D.

1970, Feb. 6 Photo. *Perf. 14½*

No.	Type	Description	Unused	Used
548	A115	10c blk & multi	15	15
549	A115	20c blk & multi	30	30
550	A115	25c blk & multi	35	35
551	A115	35c blk & multi	60	60
552	A115	60c blk & multi	1.10	1.10
		Nos. 548-552 (5)	2.50	2.50

Medhane Alem Church—A116

Rock Churches of Lalibela, 12th–13th Centuries: 10c, Bieta Emmanuel. 15c, The four Rock Churches of Lalibela. 20c, Bieta Mariam. 50c, Bieta Giorgis.

1970, Apr. 15 *Perf. 13* Unwmkd.

No.	Type	Description	Unused	Used
553	A116	5c brn & multi	8	8
554	A116	10c brn & multi	15	15
555	A116	15c brn & multi	30	30
556	A116	20c brn & multi	50	50
557	A116	50c brn & multi	1.15	1.15
		Nos. 553-557 (5)	2.18	2.18

Sailfish Tang

A117

Tropical Fish: 10c, Undulate triggerfish. 15c, Orange butterflyfish. 25c, Butterflyfish. 50c, Imperial Angelfish.

1970, June 19 Photo. *Perf. 12½*

No.	Type	Description	Unused	Used
558	A117	5c multi	10	10

559	A117	10c multi	15	15
560	A117	15c multi	25	25
561	A117	25c multi	60	60
562	A117	50c multi	1.25	1.25
		Nos. 558-562 (5)	2.35	2.35

Education Year Emblem
A118

1970, Aug. 14 *Perf. 13½* Unwmkd.

563	A118	10c multi	15	15
564	A118	20c gold, ultra & emer	35	35
565	A118	50c gold, emer & org	85	85

Issued for International Education Year.

Map of Africa
A119

Designs: 30c, Flag of Organization of African Unity. 40c, OAU Headquarters, Addis Ababa.

1970, Sept. 21 Photo. *Perf. 13½*

566	A119	20c multi	27	27
567	A119	30c multi	40	40
568	A119	40c grn & multi	75	75

Organization of African Unity.

Emperor Haile Selassie
A120

1970, Oct. 30 *Perf. 14½* Unwmkd.

569	A120	15c Prus bl & multi	18	18
570	A120	50c multi	65	65
571	A120	60c multi	1.25	1.25

Issued to commemorate the 40th anniversary of the coronation of Emperor Haile Selassie I.

Posts, Telecommunications and G.P.O. Buildings—A121

1970, Dec. 30 Litho. *Perf. 13½*

572	A121	10c ver & multi	18	18
573	A121	50c brn & multi	1.00	1.00
574	A121	80c multi	1.25	1.25

Opening of new Posts, Telecommunications and General Post Office buildings.

Costume Type of 1968

Regional Costumes: 5c, Warrior from Begemedir and Semain. 10c, Woman from Bale. 15c, Warrior from Wolega. 20c, Woman from Showa. 25c, Man from Sidamo. 40c, Woman from Tigre. 50c, Man from Wello.

1971, Feb. 17 Photo. *Perf. 11½*

Granite Paper

575	A107	5c gold & multi	8	8
576	A107	10c gold & multi	15	15
577	A107	15c gold & multi	25	25
578	A107	20c gold & multi	30	30
579	A107	25c gold & multi	40	40
580	A107	40c gold & multi	50	50
581	A107	50c gold & multi	1.00	1.00
		Nos. 575-581 (7)	2.68	2.68

Plane's Tail with Emblem
A122

Designs: 10c, Ethiopian scenes. 20c, Nose of Boeing 707. 60c, Pilots in cockpit, and engine. 80c, Globe with routes shown.

1971, Apr. 8 *Perf. 14½x14*

582	A122	5c multi	8	8
583	A122	10c multi	15	15
584	A122	20c multi	30	30
585	A122	60c multi	1.00	1.00
586	A122	80c multi	1.35	1.35
		Nos. 582-586 (5)	2.88	2.88

Ethiopian Airlines, 25th anniversary.

Fountain of Life, 15th Century Gospel Book
A123

Ethiopian Paintings: 10c, King David, 15th century manuscript. 25c, St. George, 17th century painting on canvas. 50c, King Lalibela, 18th century painting on wood. 60c, Yared singing before King Kaleb, mural in Axum Cathedral.

1971, June 15 Photo. *Perf. 11½*

Granite Paper

587	A123	5c tan & multi	8	8
588	A123	10c pale sal & multi	15	15
589	A123	25c lem & multi	30	30
590	A123	50c yel & multi	80	80
591	A123	60c gray & multi	1.25	1.25
		Nos.587-591 (5)	2.58	2.58

Black and White Heads, Globes
A124

Designs: 60c, Black and white hand holding globe. 80c, Four races, globes.

1971, Aug. 31 Unwmkd.

592	A124	10c org, red brn & blk	20	20
593	A124	60c grn, bl & blk	75	75
594	A124	80c bl, org, yel & blk	1.25	1.25

International Year Against Racial Discrimination.

Emperor Menelik II and Reading of Treaty of Ucciali
A125

Contemporary Paintings: 30c, Menelik II on horseback gathering the tribes. 50c, Ethiopians and Italians in Battle of Adwa. 60c, Menelik II at head of his army.

1971, Oct. 20 Litho. *Perf. 13½*

595	A125	10c multi	20	20
596	A125	30c multi	50	50
597	A125	50c multi	75	75
598	A125	60c multi	1.25	1.25

75th anniversary of victory of Adwa over the Italians, March 1, 1896.

Haile Selassie Broadcasting and Map of Ethiopia
A126

Designs: 5c, Two telephones, 1897, Menelik II and Ras Makonnen. 30c, Ethiopians around television set. 40c, Telephone microwave circuits. 60c, Map of Africa on globe and telephone dial.

1971, Nov. 2

599	A126	5c brn & multi	6	6
600	A126	10c yel & multi	12	12
601	A126	30c vio bl & multi	40	40
602	A126	40c blk & multi	55	55
603	A126	60c vio bl & multi	1.10	1.10
		Nos. 599-603 (5)	2.23	2.23

75th anniversary of telecommunications in Ethiopia.

UNICEF Emblem, Mother and Child
A127

Designs (UNICEF Emblem and): 10c, Children drinking milk. 15c, Man holding sick child. 30c, Kindergarten class. 50c, Father and son.

1971, Dec. 15 Unwmkd.

604	A127	5c yel & multi	8	8
605	A127	10c pale brn & multi	15	15
606	A127	15c rose & multi	22	22
607	A127	30c vio & multi	45	45
608	A127	50c grn & multi	75	75
		Nos. 604-608 (5)	1.65	1.65

25th anniversary of the United Nations International Children's Fund (UNICEF).

Nos. 445-448 Overprinted

U.N. SECURITY COUNCIL
FIRST MEETING
IN AFRICA 1972

1972, Jan. 28 Photo. *Perf. 11*

Portrait in Black

609	A86	20c grn & pale yel	30	30
610	A86	25c dk brn & yel	45	45
611	A86	30c mar & gray	65	65
612	A86	35c dk bl & gray	80	80

First meeting of U.N. Security Council in Africa.

River Boat on Lake Haik—A128

1972, Feb. 7 Litho. *Perf. 11½*

Granite Paper; Multicolored

613	A128	10c *shown*	15	15
614	A128	20c *Boats on Lake Abaya*	30	30
615	A128	30c *on Lake Tana*	60	60
616	A128	60c *on Baro River*	1.25	1.25

Proclamation of Cyrus the Great
A129

1972, Mar. 28 Photo. *Perf. 14x14½*

617	A129	10c red & multi	15	15
618	A129	60c emer & multi	90	90
619	A129	80c gray & multi	1.25	1.25

2500th anniversary of the founding of the Persian empire by Cyrus the Great.

Houses, Sidamo Province
A130

Ethiopian Architecture: 10c, Tigre Province. 20c, Eritrea Province. 40c, Addis Ababa. 80c, Shoa Province.

1972, Apr. 11 Litho. *Perf. 13½*

620	A130	5c blk & multi	8	8
621	A130	10c blk, gray & brn	15	15
622	A130	20c blk & multi	30	30
623	A130	40c blk, bl grn & brn	60	60
624	A130	80c blk, brn & red brn	1.35	1.35
		Nos. 620-624 (5)	2.48	2.48

Hands Holding Map of Ethiopia
A131

Designs: 10c, Hands shielding Ethiopians. 25c, Map of Africa, hands reaching for African Unity emblem. 50c, Brown and white hands clasped, U.N. emblem. 60c, Hands protecting dove. Each denomination shows different portrait of the Emperor.

Perf. 14½x14

1972, July 21 Litho. Unwmkd.

625	A131	5c scar & multi	7	7
626	A131	10c ultra & multi	13	13
627	A131	25c vio bl & multi	33	33
628	A131	50c lt bl & multi	65	65

629	A131	60c brn & multi	80	80
		Nos. 625-629 (5)	1.98	1.98

80th birthday of Emperor Haile Selassie.

Running, Flags of Mexico, Japan, Italy
A132

1972, Aug. 25 ***Perf. 13½x13***

Multicolored

630	A132	10c *shown*	13	13
631	A132	30c *Soccer*	40	40
632	A132	50c *Bicycling*	80	80
633	A132	60c *Boxing*	1.10	1.10

20th Olympic Games, Munich, Germany, Aug. 26–Sept. 11.

Open Bible, Cross and Orbit
A133

Designs: 50c, First and 1972 headquarters of the British and Foreign Bible Society (vert.). 80c, First Amharic Bible.

1972, Sept. 25 Photo. ***Perf. 13½***

634	A133	20c dp red & multi	27	27
635	A133	50c dp red & multi	65	65
636	A133	80c dp red & multi	1.25	1.25

United Bible Societies World Assembly, Addis Ababa, Sept. 1972.

Security Council Meeting
A134

Designs: 60c, Building where Security Council met. 80c, Map of Africa with flags of participating members.

1972, Nov. 1 Litho. ***Perf. 13½***

637	A134	10c lt bl & vio bl	13	13
638	A134	60c multi	75	75
639	A134	80c multi	1.50	1.50

First United Nations Security Council meeting, Addis Ababa, Jan. 28–Feb. 4, 1972.

Fish in Polluted Sea
A135

Designs: 30c, Fisherman, beacon, family. 80c, Polluted seashore.

1973, Feb. 23 Photo. ***Perf. 13½***

640	A135	20c gold & multi	30	30
641	A135	30c gold & multi	45	45
642	A135	80c gold & multi	1.25	1.25

World message from the sea, Ethiopian anti-pollution campaign.

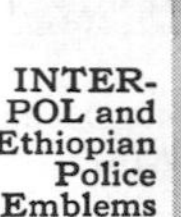

INTERPOL and Ethiopian Police Emblems
A136

Designs: 50c, INTERPOL emblem and General Secretariat, Paris. 60c, INTERPOL emblem.

1973, Mar. 20 Photo. ***Perf. 13½***

643	A136	40c dl org & blk	65	65
644	A136	50c bl, blk & yel	85	85
645	A136	60c dk car & blk	1.00	1.00

50th anniversary of International Criminal Police Organization (INTERPOL).

Virgin of Emperor Zara Yaqob
A137

Ethiopian Art: 15c, Crucifixion, Zara Yaqob period. 30c, Virgin and Child, from Entoto Mariam Church. 40c, Christ, contemporary mosaic. 80c, The Evangelists, contemporary bas-relief.

1973, May 15 Photo. ***Perf. 11½***

Granite Paper

646	A137	5c brn & multi	7	7
647	A137	15c dp bl & multi	20	20
648	A137	30c gray grn & multi	55	55
649	A137	40c multi	60	60
650	A137	80c sl & multi	1.50	1.50
		Nos. 646-650 (5)	2.92	2.92

Free African States in 1963 and 1973
A138

Designs (Map of Africa and): 10c, Flags of OAU members. 20c, Symbols of progress. 40c, Dove and people. 80c, Emblems of various UN agencies.

1973 May 25 ***Perf. 14½x14***

651	A138	5c red & multi	8	8
652	A138	10c ol gray & multi	17	17
653	A138	20c grn & multi	33	33
654	A138	40c sep & multi	65	65
655	A138	80c lt bl & multi	1.75	1.75
		Nos. 651-655 (5)	2.98	2.98

Organization for African Unity, 10th anniversary.

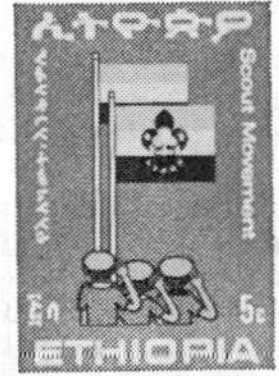

Scouts Saluting Ethiopian and Scout Flags
A139

Designs: 15c, Road and road sign. 30c, Girl Scout reading to old man. 40c, Scout and disabled people. 60c, Ethiopian Boy Scout.

1973, July 10 Photo. ***Perf. 11½***

Granite Paper

656	A139	5c bl & multi	7	7
657	A139	15c lt grn & multi	20	20
658	A139	30c yel & multi	42	42
659	A139	40c crim & multi	60	60
660	A139	60c vio & multi	1.10	1.10
		Nos. 656-660 (5)	2.39	2.39

24th Boy Scout World Conference, Nairobi, Kenya, July 16–21.

WMO Emblem
A140

Designs: 50c, WMO emblem and anemometer. 60c, Weather satellite over earth, and WMO emblem.

1973, Sept. 4 Photo. ***Perf. 13½***

661	A140	40c blk, bl & dl bl	55	55
662	A140	50c dl bl & blk	65	65
663	A140	60c dl bl & multi	1.00	1.00

Centenary of international meteorological cooperation.

Prince Makonnen, Duke of Harer
A141

Human Rights Flame
A142

Designs: 5c, Old wall of Harer. 20c, Operating room. 40c, Boy Scouts learning first aid, and hospital. 80c, Prince Makonnen and hospital.

1973, Nov. 1 ***Perf. 14½*** **Unwmkd.**

664	A141	5c gray & multi	5	5
665	A141	10c red brn & multi	10	10
666	A141	20c grn & multi	30	30
667	A141	40c brn red & multi	65	65
668	A141	80c ultra & multi	1.35	1.35
		Nos. 664-668 (5)	2.45	2.45

Opening of Prince Makonnen Memorial Hospital.

Perf. 11½

1973, Nov. 16 Photo. **Unwmkd.**

Granite Paper

669	A142	40c yel, gold & dk grn	60	60
670	A142	50c lt grn, gold & dk grn	75	75
671	A142	60c org, gold & dk grn	1.00	1.00

25th anniversary of the Universal Declaration of Human Rights.

Emperor Haile Selassie
A143

1973, Nov. 5 Photo. ***Perf. 11½***

672	A143	5c yel & multi	5	5
673	A143	10c brt bl & multi	12	5
674	A143	15c grn & multi	18	7
675	A143	20c dl yel & multi	25	10
676	A143	25c multi	30	13
677	A143	30c multi	35	15
678	A143	35c multi	42	17
679	A143	40c ultra & multi	48	20
680	A143	45c multi	55	22
681	A143	50c org & multi	60	25
682	A143	55c mag & multi	75	50
683	A143	60c multi	90	65
684	A143	70c red org & multi	1.00	70
685	A143	90c brt vio & multi	1.20	85
686	A143	$1 multi	1.60	1.10
687	A143	$2 org & multi	3.00	2.00
688	A143	$3 multi	4.50	3.00
689	A143	$5 multi	7.50	5.00
		Nos. 672-689 (18)	23.75	15.19

Wicker Furniture
A144

Designs: Various wicker baskets, wall hangings, dinnerware.

1974, Jan. 31 Photo. ***Perf. 11½***

Granite Paper

690	A144	5c vio bl & multi	5	5
691	A144	10c vio bl & multi	10	10
692	A144	30c vio bl & multi	30	30
693	A144	50c vio bl & multi	60	60
694	A144	60c vio bl & multi	75	75
		Nos. 690-694 (5)	1.80	1.80

Cow, Calf, Syringe
A145

Designs: 15c, Inoculation of cattle. 20c, Bullock and syringe. 50c, Laboratory technician, cow's head, syringe. 60c, Map of Ethiopia, cattle, syringe.

1974, Feb. 20 Litho. ***Perf. 13½x13***

695	A145	5c sep & multi	5	5
696	A145	15c ultra & multi	15	15
697	A145	20c ultra & multi	20	20
698	A145	50c org & multi	75	75
699	A145	60c gold & multi	1.00	1.00
		Nos. 695-699 (5)	2.15	2.15

Campaign against cattle plague.

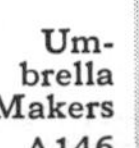

Umbrella Makers
A146

Designs: 30c, Weaving. 50c, Child care. 60c, Foundation headquarters.

1974, Apr. 17 Photo. ***Perf. 14½***

700	A146	10c lt lil & multi	10	10
701	A146	30c multi	30	30
702	A146	50c multi	60	60
703	A146	60c bl & multi	75	75

20th anniversary of Haile Selassie I Foundation.

Ceremonial Robe
A147

Designs: Ceremonial robes.

1974, June 26 Lithographed ***Perf. 13***

704	A147	15c multi	15	15
705	A147	25c ocher & multi	25	25
706	A147	35c grn & multi	50	50
707	A147	40c lt brn & multi	60	60
708	A147	60c gray & multi	85	85
		Nos. 704-708 (5)	2.35	2.35

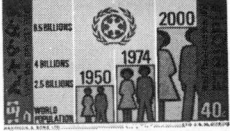

World Population Statistics
A148

Designs: 50c, "Larger families—lower living standard." 60c, Rising population graph.

1974, Aug. 19 Photo. *Perf. 14½*

709 A148 40c yel & multi 50 50
710 A148 50c vio & multi 60 60
711 A148 60c grn & multi 75 75

World Population Year 1974.

UPU Emblem, Letter Carrier's Staff
A149

Celebration Around "Damara" Pillar
A150

Designs (UPU Emblem and): 50c, Letters and flags. 60c, Globe. 70c, Headquarters, Bern.

1974, Oct. 9 Photo. *Perf. 11½*

Granite Paper

712 A149 15c yel & multi 15 15
713 A149 50c multi 60 60
714 A149 60c ultra & multi 75 75
715 A149 70c multi 85 85

Centenary of Universal Postal Union.

1974, Dec. 17 Photo. *Perf. 14x14½*

Designs: 5c, Site of Gishen Mariam Monastery. 20c, Cross and festivities. 80c, Torch (Chibos) Parade.

716 A150 5c yel & multi 5 5
717 A150 10c yel & multi 10 10
718 A150 20c yel & multi 25 25
719 A150 80c yel & multi 1.00 1.00

Meskel Festival, Sept. 26–27, commemorating the finding in the 4th century of the True Cross, of which a fragment is kept at Gishen Mariam Monastery in Wollo Province.

Precis Clelia
A151

Adoration of the Kings
A152

Butterflies: 25c, Charaxes achaemenes. 45c, Papilio dardanus. 50c, Charaxes druceanus. 60c, Papilio demodocus.

1975, Feb. 18 Photo. *Perf. 12x12½*

720 A151 10c sil & multi 10 10
721 A151 25c gold & multi 25 25
722 A151 45c pur & multi 65 65
723 A151 50c grn & multi 85 85
724 A151 60c brt bl & multi 1.00 1.00
Nos. 720-724 (5) 2.85 2.85

1975, Apr. 23 Photo. *Perf. 11½*

Designs: 10c, Baptism of Jesus. 15c, Jesus teaching in the Temple. 30c, Jesus giving sight to the blind. 40c, Crucifixion. 80c, Resurrection.

Granite Paper

725 A152 5c brn & multi 5 5
726 A152 10c blk & multi 10 10
727 A152 15c dk brn & multi 15 15
728 A152 30c dk brn & multi 30 30
729 A152 40c blk & multi 60 60
730 A152 80c sl & multi 1.10 1.10
Nos. 725-730 (6) 2.30 2.30

Murals from Ethiopian churches.

Warthog
A153

Designs: Wild animals.

1975, May 27 Photo. *Perf. 11½*

Multicolored; Granite Paper

731 A153 5c *shown* 5 5
732 A153 10c *Aardvark* 10 10
733 A153 20c *Semien wolf* 20 20
734 A153 40c *Gelada baboon* 50 50
735 A153 80c *Civet* 1.10 1.10
Nos. 731-735 (5) 1.95 1.95

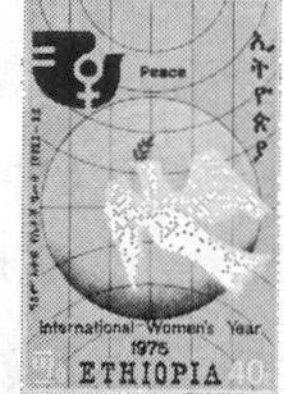

"Peace," Dove, Globe, IWY Emblem
A154

Designs (IWY Emblem and): 50c, Symbols of development. 90c, Equality between men and women.

1975, June 30 Litho. *Perf. 14x14½*

736 A154 40c bl & blk 50 50
737 A154 50c sal & multi 60 60
738 A154 90c multi 1.25 1.25

International Women's Year 1975.

Postal Museum
A155

Designs: Various interior views of Postal Museum.

1975, Aug. 19 Photo. *Perf. 13x12½*

739 A155 10c ocher & multi 10 10
740 A155 30c pink & multi 30 30
741 A155 60c multi 75 75
742 A155 70c lt grn & multi 85 85

Ethiopian National Postal Museum, opening.

Map of Ethiopia and Sun
A156

1975, Sept. 11 Photo. *Perf. 11½*

Granite Paper

743 A156 5c lil & multi 5 5
744 A156 10c ultra & multi 10 10
745 A156 25c brn & multi 25 25
746 A156 50c yel & multi 60 60
747 A156 90c brt grn & multi 1.10 1.10
Nos. 743-747 (5) 2.10 2.10

1st anniversary of Ethiopia Tikdem (Socialism).

U.N. Emblem
A157

1975, Oct. 24 Photo. *Perf. 11½*

748 A157 40c lil & multi 50 50
749 A157 50c multi 60 60
750 A157 90c bl & multi 1.10 1.10

United Nations, 30th anniversary.

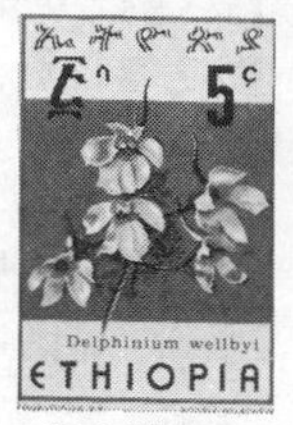

Ilubabor Hair Style
A158

Delphinium Wellbyi
A159

Regional Hair Styles: 15c, Arusi. 20c, Eritrea. 30c, Bale. 35c, Kefa. 50c, Begemdir. 60c, Shewa.

1975, Dec. 15 Photo. *Perf. 11½*

751 A158 5c multi 5 5
752 A158 15c multi 15 15
753 A158 20c multi 25 25
754 A158 30c multi 35 35
755 A158 35c multi 50 50
756 A158 50c multi 60 60
757 A158 60c multi 75 75
Nos. 751-757 (7) 2.65 2.65

See Nos. 832–838.

1976, Jan. 15 Photo. *Perf. 11½*

Flowers: 10c, Plectocephalus varians. 20c, Brachystelma asmarensis (horiz.). 40c, Ceropegia inflata. 80c, Erythrina brucei.

758 A159 5c multi 5 5
759 A159 10c multi 10 10
760 A159 20c multi 25 25
761 A159 40c multi 50 50
762 A159 80c multi 1.00 1.00
Nos. 758-762 (5) 1.90 1.90

Goalkeeper, Map of Africa, Games' Emblem
A160

Designs: Various scenes from soccer, map of Africa and ball.

1976, Feb. 27 Photo. *Perf. 14½*

763 A160 5c org & multi 5 5
764 A160 10c yel & multi 10 10
765 A160 25c lil & multi 30 30
766 A160 50c grn & multi 60 60
767 A160 90c brt grn & multi 1.10 1.10
Nos. 763-767 (5) 2.15 2.15

10th African Cup of Nations, Addis Ababa and Dire Dawa, Feb. 29–Mar. 14.

Telephones, 1876 and 1976
A161

Ethiopian Jewelry
A162

Designs: 60c, Alexander Graham Bell. 90c, Transmission tower.

1976, Mar. 10 Litho. *Perf. 12x13½*

768 A161 30c lt ocher & multi 35 35
769 A161 60c emer & multi 75 75
770 A161 90c ver, blk & buff 1.10 1.10

Centenary of first telephone call by Alexander Graham Bell, Mar. 10, 1876.

Granite Paper

1976, May 14 Photo. *Perf. 11½*

Designs: Women wearing various kinds of Ethiopian jewelry.

771 A162 5c bl & multi 5 5
772 A162 10c plum & multi 10 10
773 A162 20c gray & multi 30 30
774 A162 40c grn & multi 60 60
775 A162 80c org & multi 1.10 1.10
Nos. 771-775 (5) 2.15 2.15

Boxing
A163

Hands Holding Map of Ethiopia
A164

Designs (Montreal Olympic Emblem and): 80c, Runner and maple leaf. 90c, Bicycling.

1976, July 15 Litho. *Perf. 12½x12*

776 A163 10c multi 10 10
777 A163 80c brt red, blk & grn 1.00 1.00
778 A163 90c brt red & multi 1.10 1.10

21st Olympic Games, Montreal, Canada, July 17–Aug. 1.

1976, Aug. 5 Photo. *Perf. 14½*

779 A164 5c rose & multi 5 5
780 A164 10c ol & multi 10 10
781 A164 25c org & multi 25 25
782 A164 50c multi 60 60
783 A164 90c dk bl & multi 1.10 1.10
Nos. 779-783 (5) 2.10 2.10

Development through cooperation.

Revolution Emblem: Eye and Map
A165

1976, Sept. 9 Photo. *Perf. 13½*

784 A165 5c multi 5 5
785 A165 10c multi 10 10
786 A165 25c multi 25 25
787 A165 50c yel & multi 60 60
788 A165 90c grn & multi 1.10 1.10
Nos. 784-788 (5) 2.10 2.10

2nd anniversary of the revolution (Tikdem).

Sunburst Around Crest
A166

Plane Over Man with Donkey
A167

1976, Sept. 13 Photo. *Perf. 11½*

789 A166 5c grn gold & blk 5 5
790 A166 10c org, gold & blk 10 5
791 A166 15c grnsh bl, gold & blk 15 8
792 A166 20c lil, gold & blk 20 10
793 A166 25c brt grn, gold & blk 25 12
794 A166 30c car, gold & blk 30 15
795 A166 35c yel, gold & blk 35 18

796 A166 40c ol, gold & blk 40 20
797 A166 45c brt grn, gold & blk 45 22
798 A166 50c car rose, gold & blk 50 25
799 A166 55c ultra, gold & blk 55 28
800 A166 60c fawn, gold & blk 60 30
801 A166 70c rose, gold & blk 70 35
802 A166 90c bl, gold & blk 90 45
803 A166 $1 dl grn, gold & blk 1.00 50
804 A166 $2 gray, gold & blk 2.00 1.00
805 A166 $3 brn vio, gold & blk 3.00 1.50
806 A166 $5 sl bl, gold & blk 5.00 2.50
Nos. 789-806 (18) 16.50 8.28

1976, Oct. 28 Litho. *Perf. 12x12½*

Designs: 10c, Globe showing routes. 25c, Crew and passengers forming star. 50c, Propeller and jet engine. 90c, Airplanes surrounding map of Ethiopia.

807 A167 5c dl bl & multi 5 5
808 A167 10c lil & multi 10 10
809 A167 25c multi 25 25
810 A167 50c org & multi 50 50
811 A167 90c ol & multi 90 90
Nos. 807-811 (5) 1.80 1.80

Ethiopian Airlines, 30th anniversary.

Tortoises
A168

Hand Holding Makeshift Hammer
A169

Reptiles: 20c, Chameleon. 30c, Python. 40c, Monitor lizard. 80c, Nile crocodiles.

1976, Dec. 15 Photo. *Perf. 14½*

812 A168 10c multi 10 10
813 A168 20c multi 20 20
814 A168 30c multi 30 30
815 A168 40c multi 40 40
816 A168 80c multi 80 80
Nos. 812-816 (5) 1.80 1.80

1977, Jan. 20 Litho. *Perf. 12½*

Designs: 5c, Hands holding bowl and plane dropping food. 45c, Infant with empty bowl, and bank note. 60c, Map of affected area, footprints and tire tracks. 80c, Film strip, camera and Ethiopian sitting between eggshells.

817 A169 5c multi 5 5
818 A169 10c multi 10 10
819 A169 45c multi 45 45
820 A169 60c multi 60 60
821 A169 80c multi 80 80
Nos. 817-821 (5) 2.00 2.00

Ethiopian Relief and Rehabilitation Commission for drought and disaster areas.

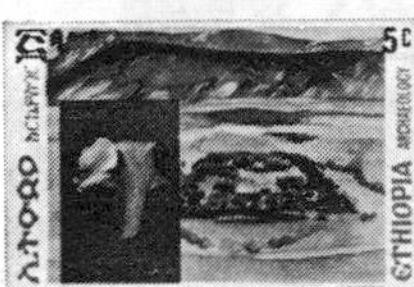

Elephant and Ruins, Axum, 7th Century
A170

Designs: 10c, Ibex and temple, 5th century, B.C., Yeha. 25c, Megalithic dolmen and pottery, Sourre Kabanawa. 50c, Awash Valley, stone axe, Acheulean period. 80c, Omo Valley, hominid jawbone.

1977, Mar. 15 Photo. *Perf. 13½*

822 A170 5c gold & multi 5 5
823 A170 10c gold & multi 10 10
824 A170 25c gold & multi 25 25
825 A170 50c gold & multi 50 50
826 A170 80c gold & multi 80 80
Nos. 822-826 (5) 1.70 1.70

Archaeological sites and finds in Ethiopia.

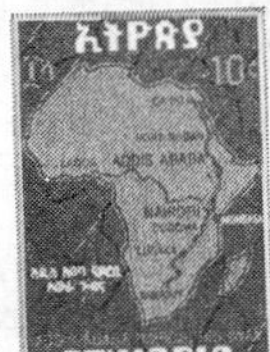

Map of Africa with Trans-East Highway
A171

1977, Mar. 30 *Perf. 14*

827 A171 10c gold & multi 10 10
828 A171 20c gold & multi 20 20
829 A171 40c gold & multi 40 40
830 A171 50c gold & multi 50 50
831 A171 60c gold & multi 60 60
Nos. 827-831 (5) 1.80 1.80

Addis Ababa to Nairobi Highway and projected highways to Cairo, Egypt, and Gaborone, Botswana.

Hairstyle Type of 1975

Regional Hairstyles: 5c, Wollega. 10c, Gojjam. 15c, Tigre. 20c, Harrar. 25c, Gemu Gofa. 40c, Sidamo. 50c, Wollo.

1977, Apr. 28 Photo. *Perf. 11½*

832 A158 5c multi 5 5
833 A158 10c multi 10 10
834 A158 15c multi 15 15
835 A158 20c multi 20 20
836 A158 25c multi 25 25
837 A158 40c multi 45 45
838 A158 50c multi 60 60
Nos. 832-838 (7) 1.80 1.80

Addis Ababa
A172

Towns of Ethiopia: 10c, Asmara. 25c, Harer. 50c, Jima. 90c, Dese.

1977, June 20 Photo. *Perf. 14½*

839 A172 5c sil & multi 5 5
840 A172 10c sil & multi 10 10
841 A172 25c sil & multi 25 25
842 A172 50c sil & multi 50 50
843 A172 90c sil & multi 90 90
Nos. 839-843 (5) 1.80 1.80

Terebratula Abyssinica
A173

Fractured Imperial Crown
A174

Fossil Shells: 10c, Terebratula subalata. 25c, Cucullaea lefeburiaua. 50c, Ostrea plicatissima. 90c, Trigonia cousobrina.

1977, Aug. 15 Photo. *Perf. 14x13½*

844 A173 5c multi 5 5
845 A173 10c multi 10 10
846 A173 25c multi 25 25
847 A173 50c multi 50 50
848 A173 90c multi 90 90
Nos. 844-848 (5) 1.80 1.80

1977, Sept. 9 Litho. *Perf. 15*

Designs: 10c, Symbol of the Revolution (spade, axe, torch). 25c, Warriors, hammer and sickle, map of Ethiopia. 60c, Soldier, farmer and map. 80c, Map and emblem of revolutionary government.

849 A174 5c multi 5 5
850 A174 10c multi 10 10
851 A174 25c multi 25 25
852 A174 60c multi 60 60
853 A174 80c multi 80 80
Nos. 849-853 (5) 1.80 1.80

Third anniversary of the revolution.

Cicindela Petitii
A175

Lenin, Globe, Map of Ethiopia and Emblem
A176

Insects: 10c, Heliocopris dillonii. 25c, Poekilocerus vignaudii. 50c, Pepsis heros. 90c, Pepsis dedjaz.

1977, Sept. 30 Photo. *Perf. 14x13½*

854 A175 5c multi 5 5
855 A175 10c multi 10 10
856 A175 25c multi 25 25
857 A175 50c multi 50 50
858 A175 90c multi 90 90
Nos. 854-858 (5) 1.80 1.80

1977, Nov. 15 Litho. *Perf. 12*

859 A176 5c org & multi 5 5
860 A176 10c multi 10 10
861 A176 25c sal & multi 25 25
862 A176 50c lt bl & multi 50 50
863 A176 90c yel & multi 90 90
Nos. 859-863 (5) 1.80 1.80

60th anniversary of Russian October Revolution.

Chondrostoma Dilloni
A177

Salt-water Fish: 10c, Ostracion cubicus. 25c, Serranus summana. 50c, Serranus luti. 90c, Tetraodon maculatus.

1978, Jan. 20 Litho. *Perf. 15½*

864 A177 5c multi 5 5
865 A177 10c multi 10 10
866 A177 25c multi 25 25
867 A177 50c multi 50 50
868 A177 90c multi 90 90
Nos. 864-868 (5) 1.80 1.80

Cattle
A178

Domestic Animals: 10c, Mules. 25c, Goats. 50c, Dromedaries. 90c, Horses.

1978, Mar. 27 Litho. *Perf. 13½x14*

869 A178 5c yel & multi 5 5
870 A178 10c multi 10 10
871 A178 25c grn & multi 25 25
872 A178 50c ver & multi 50 50
873 A178 90c ultra & multi 90 90
Nos. 869-873 (5) 1.80 1.80

Foreign postal stationery (stamped envelopes, postal cards and air letter sheets) lies beyond the scope of this Catalogue which is limited to adhesive postage stamps.

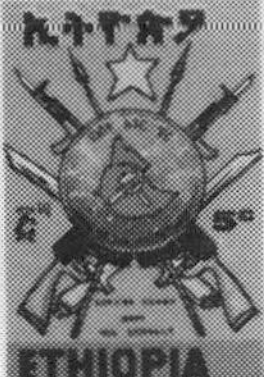

Weapons and Shield, Map of Ethiopia
A179

Bronze Ibex, 5th Century B.C.
A180

Designs: (Map of Ethiopia and): 10c, Civilian fighters. 25c, Map of Africa. 60c, Soldiers. 80c, Red Cross nurse and wounded man.

1978, May Litho. *Perf. 15½*

874 A179 5c multi 5 5
875 A179 10c multi 10 10
876 A179 25c multi 25 25
877 A179 60c multi 60 60
878 A179 80c multi 80 80
Nos. 874-878 (5) 1.80 1.80

"Call of the Motherland."

1978, June 21 Litho. *Perf. 15½*

Ancient Bronzes: 10c, Lion, Yeha, 5th century B.C. (horiz.). 25c, Lamp with ibex attacked by dog, Matara, 1st century B.C. 50c, Goat, Axum, 3rd century A.D. (horiz.). 90c, Ax, chisel and sickle, Yeha, 5th–4th centuries B.C.

879 A180 5c multi 5 5
880 A180 10c multi 10 10
881 A180 25c multi 25 25
882 A180 50c multi 50 50
883 A180 90c multi 90 90
Nos. 879-883 (5) 1.80 1.80

Globe and Argentina '78 Emblem
A181

Designs (Argentina '78 Emblem and): 20c, Soccer player kicking ball. 30c, Two players embracing, net and ball. 55c, World map and ball. 70c, Soccer field (vert.).

Perf. 14x13½, 13½x14
1978, July 19 Lithographed

884 A181 5c multi 5 5
885 A181 20c multi 20 20
886 A181 30c multi 30 30
887 A181 55c multi 55 55
888 A181 70c multi 70 70
Nos. 884-888 (5) 1.80 1.80

11th World Cup Soccer Championship, Argentina, June 1–25.

Map of Africa, Oppressed African
A182

Designs (Map of Africa and): 10c, Policeman pointing gun. 25c, Sniper with gun. 60c, African caught in net. 80c, Head of free man.

1978, Aug. 25 *Perf. 12½x13½*

889 A182 5c multi 5 5
890 A182 10c multi 10 10
891 A182 25c multi 25 25
892 A182 60c multi 60 60
893 A182 80c multi 80 80
Nos. 889-893 (5) 1.80 1.80

Namibia Day.

Soldiers, Guerrilla and Jets
A183

Design: 1b, People looking toward sun, crushing snake, flags.

1978, Sept. 8 **Photo.** ***Perf. 14***

894	A183	80c multi	80	80
895	A183	1b multi	1.00	1.00

4th anniversary of revolution.

Hand and Globe with Tools
A184

Designs: 15c, Symbols of energy, communications, education, medicine, agriculture and industry. 25c, Cogwheels and world map. 60c, Globe and hands passing wrench. 70c, Flying geese and turtle over globe.

1978, Nov. 10 **Litho.** ***Perf. 12x12½***

896	A184	10c multi	10	10
897	A184	15c multi	15	15
898	A184	25c multi	25	25
899	A184	60c multi	60	60
900	A184	70c multi	70	70
		Nos. 896-900 (5)	1.80	1.80

Technical Cooperation Among Developing Countries Conference, Buenos Aires, Argentina, Sept. 1978.

Human Rights Emblem
A185

1978, Dec. 7 **Photo.** ***Perf. 12½x13½***

901	A185	5c multi	5	5
902	A185	15c multi	15	15
903	A185	25c multi	25	25
904	A185	35c multi	35	35
905	A185	1b multi	1.00	1.00
		Nos. 901-905 (5)	1.80	1.80

Declaration of Human Rights, 30th anniversary.

Broken Chain, Anti-Apartheid Emblem
A186

Stele from Osole
A187

1978, Dec. 28 **Litho.** ***Perf. 12½x12***

906	A186	5c multi	5	5
907	A186	20c multi	20	20
908	A186	30c multi	30	30
909	A186	55c multi	55	55
910	A186	70c multi	70	70
		Nos. 906-910 (5)	1.80	1.80

Anti-Apartheid Year.

1979, Jan. 25 ***Perf. 14***

Ancient Carved Stones, Soddo Region: 10c, Anthropomorphous stele, Gorashino. 25c, Leaning stone, Wado. 60c, Round stones, Ambeut. 80c, Bas-relief, Tiya.

911	A187	5c multi	5	5
912	A187	10c multi	10	10
913	A187	25c multi	25	25
914	A187	60c multi	60	60
915	A187	80c multi	80	80
		Nos. 911-915 (5)	1.80	1.80

Cotton and Shemma Valley
A188

Shemma Industry: 10c, Women spinning cotton yarn. 20c, Man reeling cotton. 65c, Weaver. 80c, Cotton garments.

1979, Mar. 15 **Litho.** ***Perf. 15½***

916	A188	5c multi	5	5
917	A188	10c multi	10	10
918	A188	20c multi	20	20
919	A188	65c multi	65	65
920	A188	80c multi	80	80
		Nos. 916-920 (5)	1.80	1.80

"Grar" Tree
A189

Designs: Ethiopian trees.

1979, Apr. 26 **Photo.** ***Perf. 13½x14***

921	A189	5c multi	5	5
922	A189	10c multi	10	10
923	A189	25c multi	25	25
924	A189	50c multi	50	50
925	A189	90c multi	90	90
		Nos. 921-925 (5)	1.80	1.80

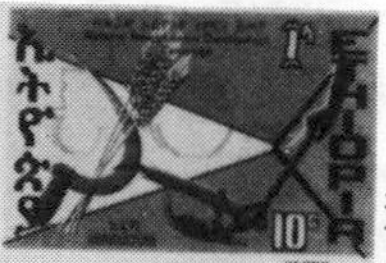

Agricultural Development
A190

Revolutionary Development Campaign: 15c, Industry. 25c, Transportation and communication. 60c, Education and health. 70c, Commerce.

1979, July 3 **Litho.** ***Perf. 12x12½***

926	A190	10c multi	10	10
927	A190	15c multi	15	15
928	A190	25c multi	25	25
929	A190	60c multi	60	60
930	A190	70c multi	70	70
		Nos. 926-930 (5)	1.80	1.80

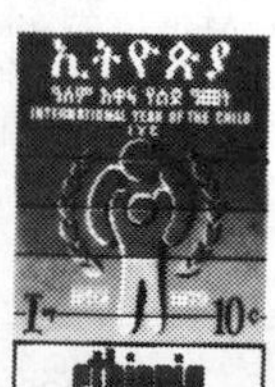

IYC Emblem
A191

Designs: 15c, Adults leading children. 25c, Adult helping child. 60c, IYC emblem surrounded by children. 70c, Adult and children embracing.

Perf. 12x12½

1979, Aug. 16 **Lithographed**

931	A191	10c multi	10	10
932	A191	15c multi	15	15
933	A191	25c multi	25	25
934	A191	60c multi	60	60
935	A191	70c multi	70	70
		Nos. 931-935 (5)	1.80	1.80

International Year of the Child.

Guerrilla Fighters—A192

Designs: 15c, Soldiers. 25c, Map of Africa within cogwheel and star. 60c, Students with book and torch. 70c, Family, hammer and sickle emblem.

1979, Sept. 11 **Photo.** ***Perf. 14***

936	A192	10c multi	10	10
937	A192	15c multi	15	15
938	A192	25c multi	25	25
939	A192	60c multi	60	60
940	A192	70c multi	70	70
		Nos. 936-940 (5)	1.80	1.80

Fifth anniversary of revolution.

Telephone Receiver
A193

Telecom Emblem and: 5c, Symbolic waves. 35c, Satellite beaming to earth. 45c, Dish antenna. 65c, Television cameraman.

1979, Sept. **Photo.** ***Perf. 11½***

941	A193	5c multi	5	5
942	A193	30c multi	30	30
943	A193	35c multi	35	35
944	A193	45c multi	45	45
945	A193	65c multi	65	65
		Nos. 941-945 (5)	1.80	1.80

3rd World Telecommunications Exhibition, Geneva, Sept. 20–26.

Incense Container—A194

1979, Nov. 15 **Litho.** ***Perf. 15***

946	A194	5c *shown*	5	5
947	A194	10c *Vase*	10	10
948	A194	25c *Earthenware cover*	25	25
949	A194	60c *Milk container*	60	60
950	A194	80c *Storage container*	80	80
		Nos. 946-950 (5)	1.80	1.80

Wooden Grain Bowl
A195

Lappet-faced Vulture
A196

1980, Jan. **Litho.** ***Perf. 13½x13***

Multicolored

951	A195	5c *shown*	5	5
952	A195	30c *Chair, stool*	30	30
953	A195	35c *Mortar, pestle*	35	35
954	A195	45c *Buckets*	45	45
955	A195	65c *Storage jars*	65	65
		Nos. 951-955 (5)	1.80	1.80

1980, Feb. 12 ***Perf. 13½x14***

Birds of Prey: 15c, Long-crested hawk eagle. 25c, Secretary bird. 60c, Abyssinian long-eared owl. 70c, Lanner falcon.

956	A196	10c multi	10	10
957	A196	15c multi	15	15
958	A196	25c multi	25	25
959	A196	60c multi	60	60
960	A196	70c multi	70	70
		Nos. 956-960 (5)	1.80	1.80

Fight Against Cigarette Smoking
A197

1980, Apr. 7 **Photo.** ***Perf.13x13½***

961	A197	20c *shown*	20	20
962	A197	60c *Cigarette*	60	60
963	A197	1b *Respiratory system*	1.00	1.00

"110" and Lenin House Museum
A198

Lenin, 110th "Birthday" (Paintings): 15c, In hiding. 20c, As a young man. 40c, Returning to Russia. 1b, Speaking on the Goelro Plan.

1980, Apr. 22 **Litho.** ***Perf. 12×12½***

964	A198	5c multi	5	5
965	A198	15c multi	15	15
966	A198	20c multi	20	20
967	A198	40c multi	40	40
968	A198	1b multi	1.00	1.00
		Nos. 964-968 (5)	1.80	1.80

Grévy's Zebras—A199

1980, June 10 **Litho.** ***Perf. 12½x12***

969	A199	10c *shown*	10	10
970	A199	15c *Gazelles*	15	15
971	A199	25c *Wild hunting dogs*	25	25
972	A199	60c *Swayne's hartebeests*	60	60
973	A199	70c *Cheetahs*	70	70
		Nos. 969-973 (5)	1.80	1.80

Runner, Moscow '80 Emblem—A200

1980, July 19 **Photo.** *Perf. 11½×12*

974	A200	30c *shown*	30	30
975	A200	70c *Gymnast*	70	70
976	A200	80c *Boxing*	80	80

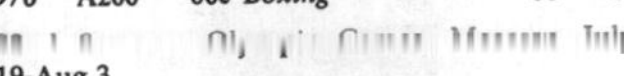

[illegible] Olympic Games, Moscow, July 19-Aug.3.

Taking off Blindfold—A201

1980, Sept. 11 **Photo.** *Perf. 14x13½*

977	A201	30c *shown*	30	30
978	A201	40c *Revolutionary*	40	40
979	A201	50c *Woman breaking chain*	50	50
980	A201	70c *Russian and Ethiopian flags*	70	70

6th anniversary of revolution.

Bamboo Food Basket—A202

1980, Oct. 23 **Litho.** *Perf. 14*

981	A202	5c *shown*	5	5
982	A202	15c *Hand basket*	15	15
983	A202	25c *Stool*	25	25
984	A202	35c *Fruit basket*	35	35
985	A202	1b *Lamp shade*	1.00	1.00
		Nos. 981-985 (5)	1.80	1.80

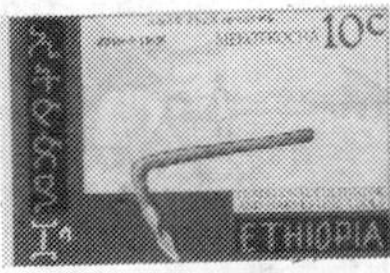

Mekotkocha (Used in Weeding)—A203

Traditional Harvesting Tools: 15c, Layda (grain separater). 40c, Mensh (fork). 45c, Medekdekia (soil turner). 70c, Plow and yoke.

1980, Dec. 18 **Litho.** *Perf. 12½x12*

986	A203	10c multi	10	10
987	A203	15c multi	15	15
988	A203	40c multi	40	40
989	A203	45c multi	45	45
990	A203	70c multi	70	70
		Nos. 986-990 (5)	1.80	1.80

Baro River Bridge Opening—A204

1981, Feb. 28 **Photo.** *Perf. 13½ x 13*

991	A204	15c *Canoes and ferry*	15	15
992	A204	65c *Bridge construction*	65	65
993	A204	1b *shown*	1.00	1.00

Simion National Park—A205

World Heritage Year: 5c, Wawel Castle, Poland. 15c, Quito Cathedral, Ecuador. 20c, Old Slave Quarters, Goree Island, Senegal. 30c, Mesa Verde Indian Village, US. 1b, L'Anse aux Meadows excavation, Canada.

1981, Mar. 10 **Photo.** *Perf. 11x11½, 11½x11*

994	A205	5c multi	5	5
995	A205	15c multi	15	15
996	A205	20c multi	20	20
997	A205	30c multi	30	30
998	A205	80c multi	80	80
999	A205	1b multi	1.00	1.00

1981, June 16 **Photo.**

Designs: 10c, Biet Medhami Alem Church, Ethiopia. 15c, Nahenni National Park, Canada. 20c, Yellowstone River Lower Falls, U.S. 30c, Aachen Cathedral, Germany. 80c, Kicker Rock, San Cristobal Island, Ecuador. 1b, The Lizak corridor, Holy Cross Chapel, Cracow, Poland (vert.).

1000	A205	10c multi	10	10
1001	A205	15c multi	15	15
1002	A205	20c multi	20	20
1003	A205	30c multi	30	30
1004	A205	80c multi	80	80
1005	A205	1b multi	1.00	1.00
		Nos. 994-1005 (12)	5.05	5.05

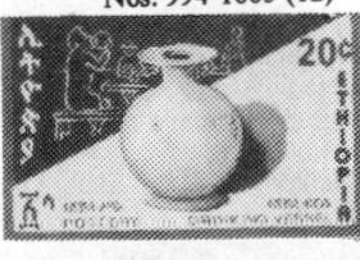

Ancient Drinking Vessel A206

1981, May 5 **Litho.** *Perf. 12½x12*

1006	A206	20c shown	20	20
1007	A206	25c Spice container	25	25
1008	A206	35c Jug	35	35
1009	A206	40c Cooking pot holder	40	40
1010	A206	60c Animal figurine	60	60
		Nos. 1006-1010 (5)	1.80	1.80

Intl. Year of the Disabled A207

7th Anniv. of Revolution A208

1981, July 16 **Photo.** *Perf. 11½x12*

1011	A207	5c Prostheses	5	5
1012	A207	15c Boys writing	15	15
1013	A207	20c Activities	20	20
1014	A207	40c Knitting	40	40
1015	A207	1b Weaving	1.00	1.00
		Nos. 1011-1015 (5)	1.80	1.80

1981, Sept. 10 *Perf. 14*

1016	A208	20c Children's Center	20	20
1017	A208	60c Heroes' Center	60	60
1018	A208	1b Serto Ader (state newspaper)	1.00	1.00

World Food Day—A209

1981, Oct. 15 **Litho.** *Perf. 13½x12½*

1019	A209	5c Wheat airlift	5	5
1020	A209	15c Plowing	15	15
1021	A209	20c Malnutrition	20	20
1022	A209	40c Agriculture education	40	40
1023	A209	1b Cattle, corn	1.00	1.00
		Nos. 1019-1023 (5)	1.80	1.80

Ancient Bronze Type of 1978

1981, Dec. 15 **Litho.** *Perf. 14x13½*

1024	A180	15c Pitcher	15	15
1025	A180	45c Tsenatsil (musical instrument)	45	45
1026	A180	50c Pitcher, diff.	50	50
1027	A180	70c Pot	70	70

Horn Artifacts—A210

1982, Feb. 18 **Photo.** *Perf. 12x12½*

1028	A210	10c Tobacco containers	10	10
1029	A210	15c Cup	15	15
1030	A210	40c Container, diff.	40	40
1031	A210	45c Goblet	45	45
1032	A210	70c Spoons	70	70
		Nos. 1028-1032 (5)	1.80	1.80

Coffee Cultivation—A211

1982, Apr. 20 **Photo.** *Perf 13½*

1033	A211	5c Plants	5	5
1034	A211	15c Bushes	15	15
1035	A211	25c Mature bushes	25	25
1036	A211	35c Picking beans	35	35
1037	A211	1b Drinking coffee	1.00	1.00
		Nos. 1033-1037 (5)	1.80	1.80

1982 World Cup—A212

1982, June 10 **Litho.** *Perf. 13½x12½*

1038	A212	5c multi	5	5
1039	A212	15c multi	15	15
1040	A212	20c multi	20	20
1041	A212	40c multi	40	40
1042	A212	1b multi	1.00	1.00
		Nos. 1038-1042 (5)	1.80	1.80

TB Bacillus Centenary A213

8th Anniv. of Revolution A214

1982, July 12 **Litho.** *Perf. 13½x12½*

1043	A213	15c Cow	15	15
1044	A213	20c Magnifying glass	20	20
1045	A213	30c Koch, microscope	30	30
1046	A213	35c Koch	35	35
1047	A213	80c Man coughing	80	80
		Nos. 1043-1047 (5)	1.80	1.80

1982, Sept. 10 *Perf. 12½x13½*

Designs: Symbols of justice.

1048	A214	80c multi	80	80
1049	A214	1b multi	1.00	1.00

World Standards Day—A215

1982, Oct. 14 **Litho.** *Perf. 13½x12½*

1050	A215	5c Hand, foot, square	5	5
1051	A215	15c Scales	15	15
1052	A215	20c Rulers	20	20
1053	A215	40c Weights	40	40
1054	A215	1b Emblem	1.00	1.00
		Nos. 1050-1054 (5)	1.80	1.80

10th Anniv. of UN Conference on Human Environment—A216

1982, Dec. 13 **Litho.** *Perf. 12*

1055	A216	5c Wildlife conservation	5	5
1056	A216	15c Environmental health and settlement	15	15
1057	A216	20c Forest protection	20	20
1058	A216	40c Natl. literacy campaign	40	40
1059	A216	1b Soil and water conservation	1.00	1.00
		Nos. 1055-1059 (5)	1.80	1.80

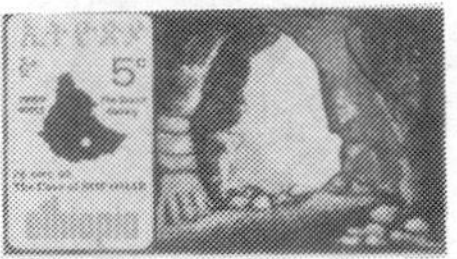

Cave of Sof Omar—A217

Various views.

1983, Feb. 10 **Photo.** *Perf. 13½*

1060	A217	5c multi	5	5
1061	A217	10c multi	10	10
1062	A217	15c multi	15	15
1063	A217	70c multi	70	70
1064	A217	80c multi	80	80
		Nos. 1060-1064 (5)	1.80	1.80

25th Anniv. of Economic Commission for Africa—A218

1983, Apr. 29 **Photo.** ***Perf. 14***

1065	A218	80c multi	80	80
1066	A218	1b multi	1.00	1.00

25th Anniv. of Intl. Maritime Org.—A219

1983, June 3 **Photo.** ***Perf. 12½x11½***

1067	A219	85c Emblem	85	85
1068	A219	1b Lighthouse, ship	1.00	1.00

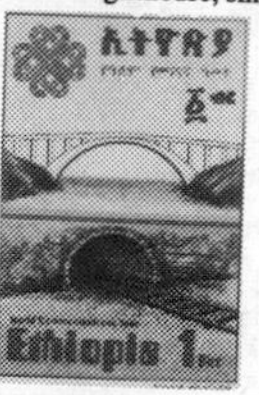

World Communications Year—A220

1983, July 22 **Litho.**

1069	A220	25c UPU emblem	25	25
1070	A220	55c Dish antenna, emblems	55	55
1071	A220	1b Bridge, tunnel	1.00	1.00

9th Anniv. of Revolution—A221

1983, Sept. 10 **Litho.** ***Perf. 14½***

1072	A221	25c Dove	25	25
1073	A221	55c Star	55	55
1074	A221	1b Emblems	1.00	1.00

Musical Instruments—A222

1983, Oct. 17 **Litho.** ***Perf. 12½x13½***

1075	A222	5c Hura	5	5
1076	A222	15c Dinke	15	15
1077	A222	20c Meleket	20	20
1078	A222	40c Embilta	40	40
1079	A222	1b Tom	1.00	1.00
		Nos. 1075-1079 (5)	1.80	1.80

Charaxes Galawadiwosi—A223

1983, Dec. 13 **Photo.** ***Perf. 14***

1080	A223	10c shown	10	10
1081	A223	15c Epiphora elianae	15	15
1082	A223	55c Batuana rougeoti	55	55
1083	A223	1b Achaea saboeareginae	1.00	1.00

Intl. Anti—Apartheid Year (1983)—A224

1984, Feb. 10 **Litho.** ***Perf. 13½x12½***

1084	A224	5c multi	5	5
1085	A224	15c multi	15	15
1086	A224	20c multi	20	20
1087	A224	40c multi	40	40
1088	A224	1b multi	1.00	1.00
		Nos. 1084-1088 (5)	1.80	1.80

Local Flowers—A225

1984, Apr. 13 **Litho.** ***Perf. 13½***

1089	A225	5c Protea gaguedi	5	5
1090	A225	25c Sedum epidendrum	25	25
1091	A225	50c Echinops amplexicaulis	50	50
1092	A225	1b Canarina eminii	1.00	1.00

Traditional Houses—A226

1984, Aug. 3 **Photo.**

1093	A226	15c Konso	15	15
1094	A226	65c Dorze	65	65
1095	A226	$1 Harer	1.00	1.00

10th Anniv. of the Revolution—A227

1984, Sept. 10 **Photo.** ***Perf. 11½***

1096	A227	5c September 12, 1974	5	5
1097	A227	10c March 4, 1975	10	10
1098	A227	15c April 20, 1976	15	15
1099	A227	20c February 11, 1977	20	20
1100	A227	25c March 1978	25	25
1101	A227	40c July 8, 1980	40	40
1102	A227	45c December 17, 1980	45	45
1103	A227	50c September 15, 1980	50	50
1104	A227	70c September 18, 1981	70	70
1105	A227	1b June 6, 1983	1.00	1.00
		Nos. 1096-1105	3.80	3.80

Traditional Sports—A228

1984, Dec. 7 **Photo.** ***Perf. 14***

1106	A228	5c Gugs	5	5
1107	A228	25c Tigil	25	25
1108	A228	50c Genna	50	50
1109	A228	1b Gebeta	1.00	1.00

Birds—A229

1985, Jan. 4 **Photo.** ***Perf. 14½***

1110	A229	5c Francolinus harwoodi	5	5
1111	A229	15c Rallus rougetti	15	15
1112	A229	80c Merops pusillus	80	80
1113	A229	85c Malimbus rubriceps	85	85

Indigenous Fauna—A230

1985, Feb. 4 **Litho.** ***Perf. 12½x12***

1114	A230	20c Hippopotamus amphibius	20	20
1115	A230	25c Litocranius walleri	25	25
1116	A230	40c Sylivicapra grimmia	40	40
1117	A230	1b Rhynchotragus guentheri	1.00	1.00

Freshwater Fish—A321

1985, Apr. 3 ***Perf. 13½***

1118	A231	10c Barbus degeni	10	10
1119	A231	20c Labeo cylindricus	20	20
1120	A231	55c Protopterus annectens	55	55
1121	A231	1b Alestes dentex	1.00	1.00

Medicinal Plants—A232

1985, May 23 ***Perf. 11½x12½***

1122	A232	10c Securidaca longependunculata	10	10
1123	A232	20c Plumbago zeylanicum	20	20
1124	A232	55c Brucea antidysenteric	55	55
1125	A232	1b Dorstenia barminiana	1.00	1.00

Ethiopian Red Cross Soc., 50th Anniv.—A233

1985, Aug. 6 **Litho.** ***Perf. 13½x13***

1126	A233	35c multi	35	35
1127	A233	55c multi	55	55
1128	A233	1b multi	1.00	1.00

Ethiopian Revolution, 11th Anniv.—A234

Designs: 10c, Kombolcha Mills, Wollo Region. 80c, Muger Cement Factory, Mokoda, Shoa. 1b, Relocating famine and drought victims.

1985, Sept. 10 **Litho.** ***Perf. 13½***

1129	A234	10c multi	10	10
1130	A234	80c multi	80	80
1131	A234	1b multi	1.00	1.00

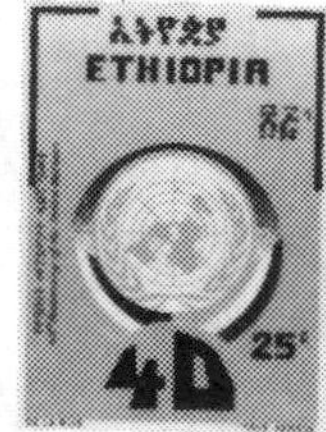

U.N. 40th Anniv.—A235

1985, Nov. 22 **Litho.** ***Perf. 13½x14***

1132	A235	25c multi	25	25
1133	A235	55c multi	55	55
1134	A235	1b multi	1.00	1.00

Anti-Polio Campaign—A236

1986, Jan. 10 **Litho.** ***Perf. 11½x12½***

1135	A236	5c Boy, prosthesis	5	5
1136	A236	10c Boy on crutches	10	10
1137	A236	20c Nurse, boy	20	20
1138	A236	55c Man, sewing machine	55	55
1139	A236	1b Nurse, mother, child	1.00	1.00
		Nos. 1135-1139 (5)	1.90	1.90

Indigenous Trees—A237

1986, Feb. 10 *Perf. 13½x14½*

1140	A237	10c Millettia ferruginea	10	10
1141	A237	30c Syzyigum guineense	30	30
1142	A237	50c Cordia africana	50	50
1143	A237	1b Hagenia abyssinica	1.00	1.00

Spices—A238

1986, Mar. 10 *Perf. 13½*

1144	A238	10c Zingiber officinale rosc	10	10
1145	A238	15c Ocimum bacilicum	15	15
1146	A238	55c Sinapsis alba	55	55
1147	A238	1b Cuminum cyminum	1.00	1.00

Current Coins, Obverse and Reverse—A239

1986, May 9 **Litho.** *Perf. 13½x14*

1148	A239	5c 1-cent	5	5
1149	A239	10c 25-cent	10	10
1150	A239	35c 5-cent	35	35
1151	A239	50c 50-cent	50	50
1152	A239	1b 10-cent	1.00	1.00
		Nos. 1148-1152 (5)	2.00	2.00

Discovery of 3.5 Million Year-old Hominid Skeleton, Dinkinesh—A240

1986, July 4 *Perf. 13½*

1153	A240	2b multi	2.00	2.00

Ethiopian Revolution, 12th Anniv.—A241

Designs: 20c, Military service. 30c, Tiglachin monument. 55c, Delachin Exhibition emblem. 85c, Food processing plant, Merti.

1986, Sept. 10 **Litho.** *Perf. 14*

1154	A241	20c multi	20	20
1155	A241	30c multi	30	30
1156	A241	55c multi	52	52
1157	A241	85c multi	82	82

Ethiopian Airlines, 40th Anniv. A242

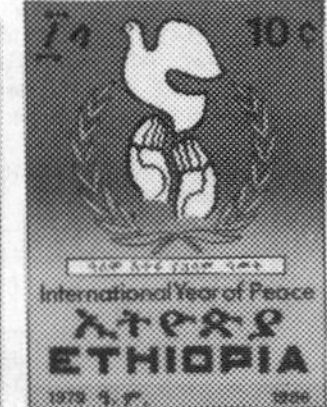

Intl. Peace Year A243

1986, Oct. 14

1158	A242	10c DC-7	10	10
1159	A242	20c DC-3	20	20
1160	A242	30c Personnel, jet tail	30	30
1161	A242	40c Engine	38	38
1162	A242	1b DC-7, map	95	95
		Nos. 1158-1162 (5)	1.93	1.93

1986, Nov. 13 *Perf. 13½*

1163	A243	10c multi	10	10
1164	A243	80c multi	78	78
1165	A243	1b multi	95	95

UN Child Survival Campaign—A244

1986, Dec. 11 *Perf. 12½*

1166	A244	10c Breast feeding	10	10
1167	A244	35c Immunization	35	35
1168	A244	50c Hygiene	48	48
1169	A244	1b Growth monitoring	95	95

Umbrellas—A245

1987, Feb. 10 *Perf.*

1170	A245	35c Axum	35	35
1171	A245	55c Negele-Borena	52	52
1172	A245	1b Jimma	95	95

SEMI-POSTAL STAMPS.

Types of 1931, Overprinted in Red at Upper Left +

Perf. 12x12½, 12½x12.

1936, Feb. 25 **Unwmkd.**

B1	A27	1g lt grn	35	30
B2	A27	2g rose	35	30
B3	A25	4g blue	35	30
B4	A27	8g brown	50	50
B5	A25	1t purple	50	50
		Nos. B1-B5 (5)	2.05	1.90

Nos. B1–B5 were sold at twice face value, the surtax going to the Red Cross.

Nos. 289, 290 and 292 to 294 Surcharged in Blue

EXPOSITION 1949 +8c

Perf. 13x13½

1949, June 13 **Wmk. 282**

B6	A53	8c +8c dp org	1.25	1.25
B7	A53	12c +5c red	1.25	1.25
B8	A53	30c +15c org brn	2.50	2.50
B9	A53	70c +70c rose lil	16.50	16.50
B10	A53	$1 +80c dk car rose	20.00	20.00
		Nos. B6-B10 (5)	41.50	41.50

Type A39 Surcharged in Carmine

+ 10 ct.

Photogravure.

1950, May 8 ***Perf. 11½*** **Unwmkd.**

Various Designs

Inscribed "Croix Rouge"

B11	A39	5c +10c brt grn	1.00	1.00
B12	A39	10c +10c brt red	1.50	1.50
B13	A39	25c +10c brt bl	2.50	2.50
B14	A39	50c +10c dk yel brn	7.00	7.00
B15	A39	1t +10c brt vio	11.00	11.00
		Nos. B11-B15 (5)	23.00	23.00

The surtax was for the Red Cross.

Nos. B6-B10 Overprinted in Black

1951

Perf. 13x13½

1951, Nov. 17 **Wmk. 282**

B16	A53	8c +8c dp org	75	75
B17	A53	12c +5c red	75	75
B18	A53	30c +15c org brn	1.10	1.10
B19	A53	70c +70c rose lil	10.00	10.00
B20	A53	$1 +80c dk car rose	15.00	15.00
		Nos. B16-B20 (5)	27.60	27.60

Tree, Staff and Snake
SP1

Engraved

1951, Nov. 25 ***Perf. 13*** **Wmk. 282**

Lower Panel in Red.

B21	SP1	5c +2c dp bl grn	30	15
B22	SP1	10c +3c org	50	25
B23	SP1	15c +3c dp bl	60	40
B24	SP1	30c +5c red	1.35	1.00
B25	SP1	50c +7c red brn	3.00	2.00
B26	SP1	$1 +10c pur	5.25	3.00
		Nos. B21-B26 (6)	11.00	6.80

The surtax was for anti-tuberculosis work.

1958, Dec. 1

Lower Panel in Red

B27	SP1	20c +3c dl pur	40	30
B28	SP1	25c +4c emer	50	35
B29	SP1	35c +5c rose vio	75	40
B30	SP1	60c +7c vio bl	1.50	80
B31	SP1	65c +7c vio	3.00	1.75
B32	SP1	80c +9c car rose	5.00	3.00
		Nos. B27-B32 (6)	11.15	6.60

The surtax was for anti-tuberculosis work.
Nos. B27-B32 were the only stamps on sale from Dec. 1-25, 1958.

Type of Regular Issue, 1955, Surcharged

RED CROSS CENTENARY 1859 1959 +2c

Engraved; Cross Typographed in Red

1959, May 30 **Wmk. 282**

B33	A62	15c +2c ol bis & rose red	60	60
B34	A62	20c +3c vio & emer	75	75
B35	A62	30c +5c rose car & grnsh bl	1.25	1.25

Issued to commemorate the centenary of the International Red Cross idea. The surtax was for the Red Cross.

Type A39 Surcharged

Silver Jubilee 1960
+ 5 ct.

Perf. 11½

1960, May 7 **Photo.** **Unwmkd.**

B36	A39	5c +1c brt grn	35	25
B37	A39	10c +2c brt red	50	30
B38	A39	25c +3c brt bl	1.10	75
B39	A39	50c +4c dk yel brn	1.75	1.50
B40	A39	1t +5c brt vio	3.00	2.75
		Nos. B36-B40 (5)	6.70	5.55

25th anniversary of Ethiopian Red Cross.

Crippled Boy on Crutches
SP2

Engraved

1963, July 23 ***Perf. 13½*** **Wmk. 282**

B41	SP2	10c +2c ultra	25	25
B42	SP2	15c +3c red	35	30
B43	SP2	50c +5c brt grn	1.10	1.00
B44	SP2	60c +5c red lil	1.75	1.25

The surtax was to aid the disabled.

AIR POST STAMPS.

Regular Issue of 1928 Handstamped in Violet, Red, Black or Green

Perf. 13½x14

1929, Aug. 17 **Unwmkd.**

C1	A22	⅛m org & lt bl	75	90
C2	A23	¼m ind & red org	75	90
C3	A22	½m gray grn & blk	75	90
C4	A23	1m dk car & blk	75	90
C5	A22	2m dk bl & blk	90	1.10
C6	A23	4m yel & ol	90	1.10
C7	A22	8m vio & ol	90	1.10
C8	A23	1t org brn & vio	1.10	1.10
C9	A22	2t grn & bis	1.50	1.75
C10	A23	3t choc & grn	1.50	1.75
		Nos. C1-C10 (10)	9.80	11.50

The overprint signifies "16 August 1929—Airplane of the Ethiopian Government." The stamps commemorate the arrival at Addis Ababa of the first air mail carried by an airplane of the Ethiopian Government. There are three types of the overprint: (I) 19½mm. high; "colon" at right of bottom word. (II) 20mm. high; same "colon." (III) 19½-mm. high; no "colon." Many errors exist.

Symbols of Empire, Airplane and Map
AP1

931, June 17 **Engr.** ***Perf. 12½***

C11	AP1	1g org red	20	30
C12	AP1	2g ultra	25	35
C13	AP1	4g violet	30	50
C14	AP1	8g bl grn	70	1.00
C15	AP1	1t ol brn	1.75	1.25
C16	AP1	2t carmine	3.00	4.50
C17	AP1	3t yel grn	4.50	6.00
		Nos. C11-C17 (7)	10.70	13.90

Nos. C11 to C17 exist imperforate.

Reprints of C11 to C17 exist. Paper is thinner and gum whiter than the originals. Reprints usually sell at about one-tenth of above prices.

Nos. 250, 255 and 257 Surcharged in Black

a: 20 - 4 - 39

b: AERIENNE / REPRISE POSTE / ETHIOPIENNE / 29/12/46 / Eth. Doll. 0,50

Perf. 14x13½

1947, Mar. 20 **Unwmkd.**

C18	A33 (a)	12c on 4c lt bl grn & ind	30.00	30.00
C19	A33 (b)	50c on 25c dl grn & ind	30.00	30.00
a.		"26-12-46"	125.00	
C20	A33 (b)	$2 on 60c lil & ind	50.00	50.00
a.		"26-12-46"	125.00	

Resumption of airmail service, Dec. 29, 1946.

Franklin D. Roosevelt
AP2

Design: $2, Haile Selassie.

Engraved and Photogravure.

1947, May 23 ***Perf. 12½***

C21	AP2	$1 dk pur & sep	4.00	3.50
C22	AP2	$2 car & dp bl	6.00	5.00

Farmer Plowing
AP3

Designs: 10c, 25c, Zoquala, extinct volcano. 30c, 35c, Tesissat Falls, Abai River. 65c, 70c, Amba Alaguie. $1, Sacala, source of Nile. $3, Gorgora and Dembia, Lake Tana. $5, Magdala, former capital. $10, Ras Dashan, mountain peak.

Engraved

1947–55 ***Perf. 13x13½*** **Wmk. 282**

C23	AP3	8c pur brn	20	10
C24	AP3	10c brt grn	20	10
C25	AP3	25c dl pur ('52)	35	20
C26	AP3	30c org yel	50	15
C27	AP3	35c bl ('55)	50	25
C28	AP3	65c pur ('51)	60	40
C29	AP3	70c red	90	40
C30	AP3	$1 dp bl	1.00	50
C31	AP3	$3 rose lil	4.00	2.50
C32	AP3	$5 red brn	7.50	3.50
C33	AP3	$10 rose vio	15.00	9.00
		Nos. C23-C33 (11)	30.75	17.10

U. P. U. Monument, Bern—AP4

1950, Apr. 3 ***Perf. 12½*** **Unwmkd.**

C34	AP4	5c grn & red	20	15
C35	AP4	15c dk sl grn & car	25	25
C36	AP4	25c org yel & grn	30	25
C37	AP4	50c car & ultra	75	60

Issued to commemorate the 75th anniversary of the formation of the Universal Postal Union.

Convair Plane over Mountains
AP5

Engraved and Lithographed

1955, Dec. 30 ***Perf. 12½*** **Unwmkd.**

Center Multicolored

C38	AP5	10c gray grn	40	20
C39	AP5	15c carmine	50	25
C40	AP5	20c violet	75	40

10th anniversary of Ethiopian Airlines.

Promulgating the Constitution
AP6

Perf. 14x13½

1956, July 16 **Engr.** **Wmk. 282**

C41	AP6	10c redsh brn & ultra	30	20

C42	AP6	15c dk car rose & ol grn	40	25
C43	AP6	20c bl & org red	60	40
C44	AP6	25c pur & grn	75	50
C45	AP6	30c dk grn & red brn	1.00	75
		Nos. C41-C45 (5)	3.05	2.10

25th anniversary of the constitution.

Aksum
AP7

Ancient Capitals: 10c, Lalibela. 15c, Gondar. 20c, Mekele. 25c, Ankober.

1957, Feb. 7 ***Perf. 14***

Centers in Green.

C46	AP7	5c red brn	50	25
C47	AP7	10c rose car	50	25
C48	AP7	15c red org	60	30
C49	AP7	20c ultra	85	45
C50	AP7	25c claret	1.25	65
		Nos. C46-C50 (5)	3.70	1.90

Amharic "A"
AP8

Designs: Various Amharic characters and views of Addis Ababa. The characters, arranged by values, spell Addis Ababa.

1957, Feb. 14 **Engraved**

Amharic Letters in Scarlet.

C51	AP8	5c ultra, *sal pink*	15	10
C52	AP8	10c ol grn, *pink*	25	15
C53	AP8	15c dl pur, *yel*	35	15
C54	AP8	20c grn, *buff*	50	25
C55	AP8	25c plum, *pale bl*	75	30
C56	AP8	30c red, *pale grn*	90	35
		Nos. C51-C56 (6)	2.90	1.30

70th anniversary of Addis Ababa.

Map, Rock Church at Lalibela and Obelisk—AP9

1958, April 15 ***Perf. 13½*** **Wmk. 282**

C57	AP9	10c green	20	10
C58	AP9	20c rose red	30	20
C59	AP9	30c brt bl	50	25

Issued to commemorate the conference of Independent African States, Accra, April 15–22.

Map of Africa and U. N. Emblem
AP10

1958, Dec. 29 ***Perf. 13***

C60	AP10	5c emerald	15	5
C61	AP10	20c car rose	25	20
C62	AP10	25c ultra	30	25
C63	AP10	50c pale pur	60	40

Issued to commemorate the first session of the United Nations Economic Conference for Africa, opened in Addis Ababa Dec. 29.

Nos. C23–29 Overprinted

የአየር ፖስት ፴ኛ ዓመት
30th Airmail Ann.
1929 - 1959

Perf. 13x13½

1959, Aug. 16 **Engraved** **Wmk. 282**

C64	AP3	8c pur brn	30	25
C65	AP3	10c brt grn	40	30
C66	AP3	25c dl pur	60	35
C67	AP3	30c org yel	65	50
C68	AP3	35c blue	85	55
C69	AP3	65c purple	1.25	85
C70	AP3	70c red	1.60	1.10
		Nos. C64-C70 (7)	5.65	3.90

30th anniversary of Ethiopian airmail service.

Ethiopian Soldier and Map of Congo
AP11

Globe with Map of Africa
AP12

Photogravure

1962, July 23 ***Perf. 11½*** **Unwmkd.**

Granite Paper

C71	AP11	15c org, bl, brn & grn	20	10
C72	AP11	50c pur, bl, brn & grn	40	30
C73	AP11	60c red, bl, brn & grn	70	35

Issued to commemorate the second anniversary of the Ethiopian contingent of the United Nations forces in the Congo and in honor of the 70th birthday of Emperor Haile Selassie.

1963, May 22 **Granite Paper**

C74	AP12	10c mag & blk	20	10
C75	AP12	40c emer & BK	40	25
C76	AP12	60c bl & blk	70	35

Issued to commemorate the conference of African heads of state for African Unity, Addis Ababa.

Bird Type of Regular Issue, 1962

Birds: 10c, Black-headed forest oriole. 15c, Broad-tailed paradise whydah (vert.). 20c, Lammergeier (vert.). 50c, White-checked touraco. 80c, Purple indigo bird.

1963, Sept. 12 ***Perf. 11½***

Granite Paper

C77	A74	10c multi	20	12
C78	A74	15c multi	25	18
C79	A74	20c bl, blk & ocher	45	25
C80	A74	50c lem & multi	75	45
C81	A74	80c ultra, blk & brn	1.50	75
		Nos. C77-C81 (5)	3.15	1.75

Swimming
AP13

Sport: 10c, Basketball (vert.). 15c, Javelin. 80c, Soccer game in stadium.

Perf. 14x13½

1964, Sept. 15 **Litho.** **Unwmkd.**

C82	AP13	5c multi	10	15
C83	AP13	10c multi	15	15
C84	AP13	15c multi	30	30
C85	AP13	80c multi	1.25	60

18th Olympic Games, Tokyo, Oct. 10–25.

Queen Elizabeth II and Emperor Haile Selassie
AP14

1965, Feb. 1 **Photo.** ***Perf. 11½***

Granite Paper

C86	AP14	5c multi	12	5
C87	AP14	35c multi	50	30
C88	AP14	60c multi	85	50

Issued to commemorate the visit of Queen Elizabeth II of Great Britain, Feb. 1–8.

Koka Dam and Power Plant
AP15

Designs: 15c, Sugar cane field. 50c, Blue Nile bridge. 60c, Gondar castles. 80c, Coffee tree. $1, Cattle at water hole. $3, Camels at well. $5, Ethiopian Air Lines jet plane.

1965, July 19 ***Perf. 11½*** **Unwmkd.**

Granite Paper

Portrait in Black

C89	AP15	15c vio brn & buff	20	15
C90	AP15	40c vio bl & lt bl	50	30
C91	AP15	50c grn & lt bl	60	35
C92	AP15	60c cl & yel	75	45
C93	AP15	80c grn, yel & red	90	50
C94	AP15	$1 brn & lt bl	1.10	60
C95	AP15	$3 cl & pink	3.50	1.65
C96	AP15	$5 ultra & lt bl	7.50	3.00
		Nos. C89-C96 (8)	15.05	7.00

Bird Type of Regular Issue, 1962

Birds: 10c, White-collared kingfisher. 15c, Blue-breasted bee-eater. 25c, African paradise flycatcher. 40c, Village weaver. 60c, White-collared pigeon.

1966, Feb. 15 **Photo.** ***Perf. 11½***

Granite Paper

C97	A74	10c dl yel & multi	20	15
C98	A74	15c lt bl & multi	30	15
C99	A74	25c gray & multi	65	35
C100	A74	40c pink & multi	1.25	50
C101	A74	60c multi	1.50	75
		Nos. C97-C101 (5)	3.90	1.90

Black Rhinoceros—AP16

Animals: 10c, Leopard. 20c, Black-and-white colobus (monkey). 30c, Mountain nyala. 60c, Nubian ibex.

1966, June 20 **Litho.** ***Perf. 13***

C102	AP16	5c dp grn, blk & gray	15	7
C103	AP16	10c grn, blk & ocher	20	10
C104	AP16	20c cit, blk & grn	40	15
C105	AP16	30c yel grn, blk & ocher	60	18
C106	AP16	60c yel grn, blk & dk brn	1.25	30
		Nos. C102-C106 (5)	2.60	80

Bird Type of Regular Issue, 1962

Birds: 10c, Blue-winged goose (vert.). 15c, Yellow-billed duck. 20c, Wattled ibis. 25c, Striped swallow. 40c, Black-winged lovebird (vert.).

1967, Sept. 29 **Photo.** ***Perf. 11½***

Granite Paper

C107	A74	10c lt ultra & multi	20	15
C108	A74	15c grn & multi	25	15
C109	A74	20c yel & multi	30	15
C110	A74	25c sal & multi	50	15
C111	A74	40c pink & multi	1.00	40
		Nos. C107-C111 (5)	2.25	1.00

SPECIAL DELIVERY STAMPS.

Motorcycle Messenger
SD1

Addis Ababa Post Office
SD2

Engraved.

1947, Apr. 24 ***Perf. 13*** **Unwmkd.**

E1	SD1	30c org brn	60	50
E2	SD2	50c blue	2.00	1.50

1954–62 **Wmk. 282**

E3	SD1	30c org brn ('62)	1.00	75
E4	SD2	50c blue	90	50

POSTAGE DUE STAMPS.

Menelik II
D1

Perf. 14x13½

1896, June 10 **Unwmkd.**

Black Overprint.

J1	D1	¼g green	1.00	
J2	D1	½g red	1.00	
J3	D1	4g lil brn	75	
a.		Without overprint	75	
J4	D1	8g violet	75	
a.		Without overprint	75	

Red Overprint.

J5	D1	1g blue	1.00	
J6	D1	2g dk brn	1.00	
J7	D1	16g black	75	
a.		Without overprint	75	
		Nos. J1-J7 (7)	6.25	

Regular Issue of 1894
Handstamped in Various Colors:

1905, Jan. 1

J8	A1 (a)	¼g green	14.00	14.00
J9	A1 (a)	½g red	14.00	14.00

J10	A1 (a)	1g blue	14.00	14.00
J11	A1 (a)	2g dk brn	14.00	14.00
J12	A2 (a)	4g lil brn	14.00	14.00
J13	A2 (a)	8g violet	20.00	20.00
J14	A2 (a)	16g black	40.00	40.00
J15	A1 (b)	¼g green	14.00	14.00
J16	A1 (b)	½g red	14.00	14.00
J17	A1 (b)	1g blue	14.00	14.00
J18	A1 (b)	2g dk brn	14.00	14.00
J19	A2 (b)	4g lil brn	14.00	14.00
J20	A2 (b)	8g violet	20.00	20.00
J21	A2 (b)	16g black	40.00	40.00
		Nos. J8-J21 (14)	260.00	260.00

Excellent forgeries of Nos. J8–J42 exist.

Regular Issue of 1894 Handstamped in Blue or Violet

TAXE
A
PERCEVOIR
T

1906, July 1

J22	A1	¼g green	9.00	9.00
J23	A1	½g red	9.00	9.00
J24	A1	1g blue	9.00	9.00
J25	A1	2g dk brn	9.00	9.00
J26	A2	4g lil brn	9.00	9.00
J27	A2	8g violet	14.00	14.00
J28	A2	16g black	20.00	20.00
		Nos. J22-J28 (7)	79.00	79.00

Nos. J22, J24, J25 and J26 exist with inverted overprint, also No. J22 with double overprint.

With Additional Surcharge of Value Handstamped as on Regular Issue of 1907.

1907, July 1

J29	A1(e)	¼ on ¼g grn	15.00	15.00
J30	A1(e)	½ on ½g red	15.00	15.00
J31	A1(f)	1 on 1g bl	15.00	15.00
J32	A1(f)	2 on 2g dk brn	15.00	15.00
J33	A2(f)	4 on 4g lil brn	15.00	15.00
J34	A2(f)	8 on 8g vio	15.00	15.00
J35	A2(f)	16 on 16g blk	25.00	25.00
		Nos. J29-J35 (7)	115.00	115.00

Nos. J30, J31, J32 and J33 exist with inverted surcharge.

Regular Issue of 1894 Handstamped in Black

1908, Dec. 1

J36	A1	¼g green	1.00	75
J37	A1	½g red	1.00	75
J38	A1	1g blue	1.00	75
J39	A1	2g dk brn	1.25	1.00
J40	A2	4g lil brn	1.75	1.50
J41	A2	8g violet	4.00	4.00
J42	A2	16g black	12.00	12.00
		Nos. J36-J42 (7)	22.00	20.75

Nos. J36 to J42 exist with inverted overprint and Nos. J36, J37, J38 and J40 with double overprint.

Same Handstamp on Regular Issue of 1909.

1912, Dec. 1 *Perf. 11½*

J43	A3	¼g bl grn	1.00	75
J44	A3	½g rose	1.50	1.00
J45	A3	1g grn & org	3.50	2.50
J46	A4	2g blue	4.00	3.50
J47	A4	4g grn & car	6.00	4.00
J48	A5	8g ver & dp grn	8.00	6.50
J49	A5	16g ver & car	20.00	15.00
		Nos. J43-J49 (7)	44.00	33.25

Nos. J43 to J49, all exist with inverted overprint.

Same Handstamp on Regular Issue of 1919 in Blue Black

1925-27 *Perf. 11½*

J50	A6	⅛g vio & brn	*22.50*	*22.50*
J51	A6	¼g bl grn & db	*22.50*	*22.50*
J52	A6	½g scar & ol grn	*25.00*	*25.00*
J53	A9	1g rose lil & gray grn	3.00	3.00
J54	A9	2g dp ultra & fawn	*25.00*	*25.00*

Same Handstamp on Nos. 110 and 112.

1930 (?)

J55	A3(i)	1g grn & org	*25.00*	*25.00*
J56	A4(j)	2g blue	*25.00*	*25.00*

D2

Lithographed.

1951, Apr. 2 *Perf. 11½* **Unwmkd.**

J57	D2	1c emerald	25	10
J58	D2	5c rose red	35	15
J59	D2	10c violet	50	20
J60	D2	20c ocher	75	55
J61	D2	50c brt ultra	1.50	1.10
J62	D2	$1 rose lil	3.00	1.75
		Nos. J57-J62 (6)	6.35	3.85

OCCUPATION STAMPS.

Issued under Italian Occupation.

100 Centesimi = 1 Lira

Victor Emmanuel III

OS1

Emperor Victor Emmanuel

OS2

Wmk. 140

1936 Wmkd. Crowns. (140) *Perf. 14*

N1	OS1	10c org brn	40	40
N2	OS1	20c purple	75	75
N3	OS2	25c dk grn	50	50
N4	OS2	30c dk brn	50	50
N5	OS2	50c rose car	50	50
N6	OS1	75c dp org	75	75
N7	OS1	1.25l dp bl	1.50	1.50
		Nos. N1-N7 (7)	4.90	4.90

For later issues see Italian East Africa.

The first price column gives the catalogue value of an unused stamp, the second that of a used stamp.

FAR EASTERN REPUBLIC

(fär ēs′tẽrn rē·pŭb′lĭk)

LOCATION—In Siberia east of Lake Baikal.

GOVT.—Republic.

AREA—900,745 sq. mi.

POP.—1,560,000 (approx. 1920)

CAPITAL—Chita.

A short-lived independent government was established here in 1920.

100 Kopecks = 1 Ruble

Vladivostok Issue.

Russian Stamps Surcharged or Overprinted:

ДВР

a

К.7 К. К.10 К.

b c

On Stamps of 1909–17.

Perf. 14, 14½x15, 13½.

1920 **Unwmkd.**

2	A14(a)	2k green	13.00	20.00
3	A14(a)	3k red	11.00	14.00
4	A11(b)	3k on 35k red brn & grn	14.00	20.00
5	A15(a)	4k carmine	11.00	14.00
6	A11(b)	4k on 70k brn & org	9.00	9.00
8	A11(b)	7k on 15k red brn & bl	4.00	5.50
a.		Inverted surcharge	50.00	
b.		Pair, one overprinted "DBP" only		
9	A15(a)	10k dk bl	80.00	110.00
a.		Overprint on back	150.00	
10	A12(c)	10k on 3½r mar & lt grn	30.00	35.00
11	A11(a)	14k bl & rose	30.00	35.00
12	A11(a)	15k red brn & bl	14.00	16.00
13	A8(a)	20k bl & car	85.00	110.00
14	A11(b)	20k on 14k bl & rose	9.00	10.00
a.		Surch. on back	60.00	
15	A11(a)	25k grn & vio	17.50	22.50
16	A11(a)	35k red brn & grn	50.00	60.00
17	A8(a)	50k brn vio & grn	16.50	22.50
18	A9(a)	1r pale brn, dk brn & org	400.00	500.00

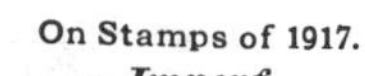

On Stamps of 1917.

Imperf.

21	A14(a)	1k orange	12.50	14.00
22	A14(a)	2k gray grn	5.50	5.50
23	A14(a)	3k red	16.00	20.00
25	A11(b)	7k on 15k red brn & dp bl	5.50	5.50
a.		Pair, one without surcharge		
b.		Pair, one overprinted "DBP" only		
26	A12(c)	10k on 3½r mar & lt grn	16.00	20.00
27	A9(a)	1r pale brn, brn & red org	20.00	22.50

On Stamps of Siberia 1919.

Perf. 14, 14½x15.

30	A14(a)	35k on 2k grn	6.00	7.50
a.		"DBP" on back	40.00	80.00

Imperf.

31	A14(a)	35k on 2k grn	14.00	15.00
32	A14(a)	70k on 1k org	7.50	9.00

Counterfeit surcharges and overprints abound.

Postal Savings Stamps Surcharged for Postal Use.

A1

Wmk. 171

Wmkd. Diamonds. (171)

Perf. 14½x15.

35	A1(b)	1k on 5k grn, *buff*	15.00	20.00
36	A1(b)	2k on 10k brn, *buff*	20.00	25.00

The letters on these stamps resembling "DBP," are the Russian initials of "Dalni Vostochini Respoublika" (Far Eastern Republic).

Chita Issue.

A2

A2a

Typographed.

1921 *Imperf.* **Unwmkd.**

38	A2	2k gray grn	1.50	1.75
39	A2a	4k rose	1.50	1.75
40	A2	5k claret	2.00	3.00
41	A2a	10k blue	3.00	3.50

Blagoveshchensk Issue.

A3

1921 Lithographed *Imperf.*

42	A3	2r red	4.00	5.00
43	A3	3r dk grn	4.00	5.00
44	A3	5r dk bl	4.00	5.00
a.		Tête bêche pair	40.00	50.00
45	A3	15r dk brn	4.00	5.00
46	A3	30r dk vio	4.00	5.00
a.		Tête bêche pair	40.00	50.00
		Nos. 42-46 (5)	20.00	25.00

Remainders of Nos. 42–46 were canceled in colored crayon or by typographed bars. These sell for half of foregoing prices.

Chita Issue.

A4

A5

1922 Lithographed. *Imperf.*

49	A4	1k orange	90	1.50
50	A4	3k dl red	50	90
51	A5	4k dp rose & buff	50	90
52	A4	5k org brn	1.25	90
53	A4	7k lt bl	1.25	2.50
a.		Perf. 11½	1.25	2.50
b.		Rouletted 9	2.25	4.00
c.		Perf. 11½x rouletted	4.00	6.00
54	A5	10k dk bl & red	60	1.25
55	A4	15k dl rose	90	1.50
56	A5	20k bl & red	90	1.50
57	A5	30k grn & red org	1.00	2.00
58	A5	50k blk & red org	1.75	3.00
		Nos. 49-58 (10)	9.55	15.95

The 4k exists with "4" omitted.

Vladivostok Issue.

Stamps of 1921 Overprinted in Red

1917
7-XI
1922

1922 *Imperf.*

62	A2	2k gray grn	12.50	17.50
a.		Inverted overprint	42.50	
63	A2a	4k rose	12.50	17.50
a.		Inverted overprint	75.00	
b.		Double overprint	60.00	
64	A2	5k claret	15.00	22.50
a.		Inverted overprint	75.00	
b.		Double overprint	60.00	
65	A2a	10k blue	15.00	22.50
a.		Inverted overprint	150.00	

Issued to commemorate the fifth anniversary of the Russian revolution of November, 1917.

Once in the setting the figures "22" of 1922 have the bottom stroke curved instead of straight. Price $15 apiece.

Vladivostok Issue.

Russian Stamps of 1922-23 Surcharged in Black or Red

Д. 1 В.
коп. коп.
ЗОЛОТОМ

1923 *Imperf.*

66	A50	1k on 100r red	60	1.50
a.		Invtd. surch.	55.00	
67	A50	2k on 70r vio	60	1.50
68	A49	5k on 10r bl (R)	60	1.50
69	A50	10k on 50r brn	1.00	2.50
a.		Invtd. surch.	37.50	

Perf. 14½x15.

70	A50	1k on 100r red	1.00	2.50
		Nos. 66-70 (5)	3.80	9.50

OCCUPATION STAMPS.

Issued under Occupation of General Semenov. Chita Issue.

Russian Stamps of 1909-12 Surcharged:

р. 1 р.
a

2р.50к.
b

Р. 5 Р.
c

1920 *Perf. 14, 14x15½* Unwmkd.

N1	A15 (a)	1r on 4k car	30.00	40.00
N2	A8 (b)	2r50k on 20k bl & car	30.00	40.00
N3	A14 (c)	5r on 5k cl	17.50	27.50
a.		Double surch.	35.00	
N4	A11 (a)	10r on 70k brn & org	30.00	40.00

FAROE ISLANDS
(The Faroes)

LOCATION — North Atlantic Ocean.
GOVT.—Self-governing part of Kingdom of Denmark.
AREA—540 sq. mi.
POP.—52,347 (1984).
CAPITAL—Thorshavn.

100 Ore = 1 Krone

Denmark No. 97 Handstamp Surcharged

2
ØRE

1919, Jan. Typo. *Perf. 14x14½*

1	A16	2ø on 5ø grn	1,200.	600.00

Counterfeits of surcharge exist.

Denmark No. 88a, the bisect, was used with Denmark No. 97 in Faroe Islands Jan. 3–23, 1919.

Denmark Nos. 220, 224, 238A, 224C Surcharged in Blue or Black

50 ≡ 50
b

20 |||| 20
c

20
d

1940–41 Engraved *Perf. 13*

2	A32 (b)	20(ø) on 1ø gray blk (Bl) ('41)	70.00	100.00
3	A32 (c)	20(ø) on 5ø rose lake (Bl) ('41)	52.50	35.00
4	A30 (d)	20(ø) on 15ø dp red (Bk)	70.00	20.00
5	A32 (b)	50(ø) on 5ø rose lake (Bk)	325.00	90.00
6	A32 (b)	60(ø) on 6ø org (Bk)	140.00	225.00
		Nos. 2-6 (5)	657.50	470.00

Nos. 2–6 were issued during British administration.

Map of Islands, 1673
A1

Map of North Atlantic, 1573
A2

West Coast, Sandoy
A3

Vidoy and Svinoy, by Eyvindur Mohr
A4

Designs: 50ø, 90ø, like 5ø. 60ø, 80ø, 120ø, like 10ø. 200ø, like 70ø. 250ø, 300ø, View of Streymoy and Vagar. 450ø, Houses, Nes, by Ruth Smith. 500ø, View of Hvitanes and Skalafjordur, by S. Joensen-Mikines.

Perf. 13

1975, Jan. 30 Engr. Unwmkd.

7	A1	5ø sepia	5	5
8	A2	10ø emer & dk bl	5	5
9	A1	50ø grysh grn	18	18
10	A2	60ø brn & dk bl	2.00	2.00
11	A3	70ø vio bl & sl grn	2.00	2.00
12	A2	80ø ocher & dk bl	1.00	1.00
13	A1	90ø red brn	2.00	2.00
14	A2	120ø brt bl & dk bl	1.00	70
15	A3	200ø vio bl & sl grn	1.00	1.00
16	A3	250ø multi	90	90
17	A3	300ø multi	10.00	3.00

Photo. *Perf. 12½x13*

18	A4	350ø multi	1.25	1.25
19	A4	450ø multi	1.50	1.50
20	A4	500ø multi	1.50	1.50
		Nos. 7-20 (14)	24.43	17.13

Faroe Boat
A5

Faroe Flag
A6

Faroe Mailman
A7

Engr.; Litho. (A6)

1976, Apr. 1 *Perf. 12½x13, 12 (A6)*

21	A5	125ø cop red	4.00	2.00
22	A6	160ø multi	60	60
23	A7	800ø olive	1.75	1.50

Faroe Islands independent Postal service, Apr. 1, 1976.

Motor Fishing Boat
A8

Faroese Fishing Vessels and Map of Islands: 125ø, Inland fishing cutter. 160ø, Modern seine fishing vessel. 600ø, Deep-sea fishing trawler.

1977, Apr. 28 Photo. *Perf. 14½x14*

24	A8	100ø grn & blk	11.00	8.00
25	A8	125ø car & blk	3.00	3.00
26	A8	160ø bl & blk	1.00	1.00
27	A8	600ø brn & blk	1.50	1.25

Common Snipe
A9

Birds: 180ø, Oystercatcher. 250ø, Whimbrel.

Photogravure & Engraved

1977, Sept. 29 *Perf. 14½x14*

28	A9	70ø multi	30	30
29	A9	180ø multi	60	60
30	A9	250ø multi	90	90

See "Special Notices" at the front of this volume for data on the listing methods of this Catalogue, abbreviations, condition, prices and examination.

North Coast, Puffins
A10

Mykines Village
A11

Mykines Island: 140ø, Tilled fields and coast. 150ø, Aerial view. 180ø, Map.

Perf. 13x13½, 13½x13

1978, Jan. 26 Photogravure

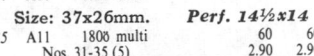

Size: 21x28mm., 28x21mm

31	A10	100ø multi	35	35
32	A11	130ø multi	45	45
33	A11	140ø multi	90	90
34	A10	150ø multi	60	60

Size: 37x26mm. *Perf. 14½x14*

35	A11	180ø multi	60	60
		Nos. 31-35 (5)	2.90	2.90

Gannets
A12

Old Library
A13

Sea Birds: 180ø, Puffins. 400ø, Guillemots.

Lithographed and Engraved

1978, Apr. 13 *Perf. 12x12½*

36	A12	140ø multi	1.25	1.25
37	A12	180ø multi	1.65	1.65
38	A12	400ø multi	1.25	1.25

1978, Dec. 7 *Perf. 13*

Design: 180ø, New Library.

39	A13	140ø gray grn & lt grn	1.25	1.25
40	A13	180ø brn & buff	1.25	85

Completion of New Library Building.

Girl Guide, Tent and Fire
A14

1978, Dec. 7 Photo. *Perf. 13½*

41	A14	140ø multi	1.65	1.65

Faroese Girl Guides, 50th anniversary.

Ram
A15

Lithographed and Engraved

1979, Mar. 19 *Perf. 12*

42	A15	25k multi	7.50	6.00

Europa Issue 1979

Denmark No. 88a
A16

Design: 180ö, Faroe Islands No. 1.

Lithographed and Engraved

1979, May 7 *Perf. 12½*

43	A16	140o yel & bl	1.25	1.25
44	A16	180o rose, grn & blk	1.25	1.25

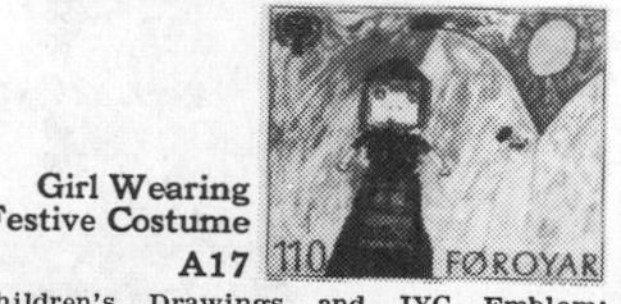

Girl Wearing Festive Costume
A17

Children's Drawings and IYC Emblem: 150ö, Fisherman. 200ö, Two friends.

Lithographed and Engraved

1979, Oct. 1 *Perf. 12*

45	A17	110ö multi	35	35
46	A17	150ö multi	50	50
47	A17	200ö multi	65	65

International Year of the Child.

Sea Plantain—A18

1980, Mar. 17 **Photo.** *Perf. 12x11½*

48	A18	90ö *shown*	30	30
49	A18	110ö *Glacier buttercup*	35	35
50	A18	150ö *Purple saxifrage*	50	50
51	A18	200ö *Starry saxifrage*	70	70
52	A18	400ö *Lady's mantle*	1.25	1.25
		Nos. 48-52 (5)	3.10	3.10

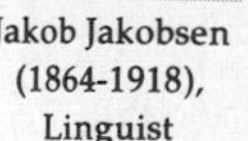

Jakob Jakobsen (1864-1918), Linguist
A19

Coat of Arms, Virgin and Child, Gothic Pew Gable
A20

Europa Issue 1980

Design: 200ö, Vensel Ulrich Hammershaimb (1819-1909), theologian, linguist and folklorist.

1980, Oct. 6 **Engr.** *Perf. 11½*

53	A19	150ö dl grn	60	60
54	A19	200ö dl red brn	80	80

1980, Oct. 6 **Photo. & Engr.** *Perf. 13½*

Kirkjubour Pew Gables, 15th Century: 140ö, Norwegian coat of arms, John the Baptist. 150ö, Christ's head, St. Peter. 200ö, Hand in halo, Apostle Paul.

55	A20	110ö multi	35	35
56	A20	140ö multi	55	55
57	A20	150ö multi	55	55
58	A20	200ö multi	70	70

See Nos. 102-105.

Fishing Boats, Old Torshavn—A21

Designs: Sketches of Old Torshavn by Ingalzur Reyni.

1981, Mar. 2 **Engraved**

59	A21	110ö dk grn	35	35
60	A21	140ö black	60	60
61	A21	150ö dk brn	60	60
62	A21	200o dk bl	80	80

Europa Issue 1981

The Ring Dance—A22

Design: 200o. The garter dance.

1981, June 1 **Engr.** *Perf. 13x14*

63	A22	150o pale rose & grn	70	70
64	A22	200o pale yel grn & dk brn	80	80

Rune Stones, 800-1000 AD—A23

Historic Writings: 1k, Folksong, 1846. 3k, Sheep Letter excerpt, 1298. 6k, Seal and text, 1533. 10k, Titlepage from Faeroae et Faeroa, by Lucas Jacobson Debes, library.

1981, Oct. 19 **Photo. & Engr.** *Perf. 11½*

65	A23	10o multi	10	10
69	A23	1k multi	34	34
72	A23	3k multi	90	90
75	A23	6k multi	1.75	1.75
78	A23	10k multi	3.25	3.25
		Nos. 65-80 (5)	6.34	6.34

Europa 1982—A24

1982, Mar. 15 **Engr.** *Perf. 13½*

81	A24	1.50k Viking North Atlantic routes	70	70
82	A24	2k Viking house foundation	80	80

View of Gjogv, by Ingalvur av Reyni—A25

1982, June 7 **Litho.** *Perf. 12½x13*

83	A25	180o shown	65	65
84	A25	220o Hvalvik	3.25	1.25
85	A25	250o Kvivik	90	90

Ballad of Harra Paetur and Elinborg—A26

Designs: Scenes from the medieval ballad of chivalry.

1982, Sept. 27 **Litho.**

86	A26	220o multi	85	85
87	A26	250o multi	85	85
88	A26	350o multi	1.25	1.25
89	A26	450o multi	1.65	1.65

Cargo Ships—A27

1983, Feb. 21 **Litho.** *Perf. 14x14½*

90	A27	220o Arcturus, 1856	85	85
91	A27	250o Laura, 1882	85	85
92	A27	700o Thyra, 1866	2.25	2.25

Chessmen, by Pol i Buo (1791-1857)—A28

1983, May 2 **Engr.** *Perf. 13 Vert.*

93	A28	250o King	1.25	1.25
94	A28	250o Queen	1.25	1.25
a.		Bklt. pane of 6 (3 each #93-94)	7.50	

Nos. 93-94 issued only in booklets.

Europa 1983—A29

Nobel Prizewinners in Medicine: 250o, Niels R. Finsen (1860-1903), ultraviolet radiation pioneer. 400o, Alexander Fleming (1881-1955), discoverer of penicillin.

1983, June 6 **Engr.** *Perf. 12x11½*

95	A29	250o dk bl	75	75
96	A29	400o red brn	1.40	1.40

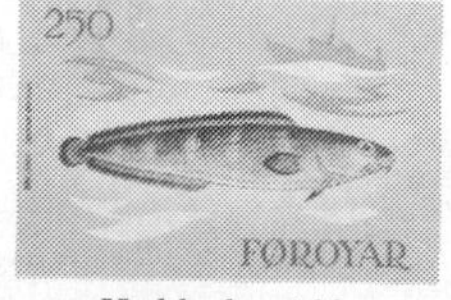

Haddock—A30

1983, Sept. 19 **Litho.** *Perf. 12½x13*

97	A30	250o Tusk	80	80
98	A30	280o shown	1.00	1.00
99	A30	500o Halibut	1.50	1.50
100	A30	900o Catfish	2.75	2.75

Souvenir Sheet

Traditional Costumes—A31

Various national costumes.

1983, Nov. 4 **Litho.** *Perf. 12*

101		Sheet of 3	7.00	7.50
a.	A31	250o multi	2.25	2.50
b.	A31	250o multi	2.25	2.50
c.	A31	250o multi	2.25	2.50

Nordic House Cultural Center opening. Margin shows Scandinavian flags. Size: 120x67mm.

Pew Gables Type of 1980

Designs: 250o, John, shield with three crowns. 300o, St. Jacob, shield with crossed keys. 350o, Thomas, shield with crossbeam. 400o, Judas Taddeus, Toulouse cross halo.

1984, Jan. 30 **Photo. & Engr.** *Perf. 14x13½*

102	A20	250o lil, pur & dk brn	75	75
103	A20	300o red brn, dk buff & dk brn	90	90
104	A20	350o blk, lt gray & dk brn	1.05	1.05
105	A20	400o ol grn, pale yel & dk brn	1.20	1.20

Europa (1959-84)—A33

1984, Apr. 2 **Engr.** ***Perf. 13½***

106	A33	250o red	75	75
107	A33	500o dk bl	2.00	2.00

Sverri Patursson (1871-1960), Writer—A34

Poets: 2.50k, Joannes Patursson (1866-1946). 3k, J. H. O. Djurhuus (1881-1948). 4.50k, H.A. Djurhuus (1883-1951).

1984, May 28 **Engr.** ***Perf. 13½***

108	A34	2k ol grn	60	60
109	A34	2.50k red	75	75
110	A34	3k dk bl	90	90
111	A34	4.50k violet	1.35	1.35

Faroese Smack (Fishing Boat)—A35

Perf. 12½x13, 13x12½

1984, Sept. 10 **Engr.**

112	A35	280o shown	90	90
113	A35	300o Fishermen, vert.	90	90
114	A35	12k Helmsman, vert.	3.60	3.60

Fairytale Illustrations by Elinborg Lutzen—A36

1984, Oct. 29 **Litho.** ***Perf. 13 Vert.***

115	A36	140o Beauty of the Veils	1.10	1.10
116	A36	280o Veils, diff.	1.10	1.10
117	A36	280o Girl Shy Prince	1.10	1.10
118	A36	280o The Glass Sword	1.10	1.10
119	A36	280o Little Elin	1.10	1.10
120	A36	280o The Boy and the Ox	1.10	1.10
a.		Bklt. pane of 6 (#115-120)	6.75	
		Nos. 115-120 (6)	6.60	6.60

View of Torshavn and the Forts, by Edward Dayes—A37

Dayes' Landscapes, 1789: 280o, Skaeling. 550o, View Towards the North Seen from the Hills Near Torshavn in Stremoy, Faroes. 800o, The Moving Stones in Eysturoy, Faroes. Nos. 121-124 se-tenant.

1985, Feb. 4 **Litho. & Engr.** ***Perf. 13***

121	A37	250o multi	75	75
122	A37	280o multi	1.75	1.75
123	A37	550o multi	1.65	1.65
124	A37	800o multi	2.50	2.50

Europa 1985—A38

Children taking music lessons.

1985, Apr. 1 **Litho.** ***Perf. 13½x14½***

125	A38	280o multi	90	90
126	A38	550o multi	1.65	1.65

Paintings, Faroese Museum of Art—A39

Designs: 550o, Winter's Day in Nolsoy, 1959, by Steffan Danielsen (1922-1976). 450o, Self-Portrait, 1952, by Ruth Smith (1913-1958). 280o, The Garden, Hoyvik, 1973, by Thomas Arge (1942-1978).

1985, June 3 **Litho. & Engr.** ***Perf. 12½***

127	A39	280o multi	90	90
128	A39	450o multi, vert.	1.40	1.40
129	A39	550o multi	1.65	1.65

Lighthouses—A40

1985, Sept. 23 **Litho.** ***Perf. 13½x14***

130	A40	270o Nolsoy, 1893	85	85
131	A40	320o Thorshavn, 1909	95	95
132	A40	350o Mykines, 1909	1.10	1.10
133	A40	470o Map of locations	1.40	1.40

Passenger Aviation in the Faroes, 22nd Anniv.—A41

1985, Oct. 28 **Photo.** ***Perf. 13½ Horiz.***

134	A41	300o Douglas DC-3	90	90
135	A41	300o Fokker Friendship	90	90
136	A41	300o Boeing 737	90	90
137	A41	300o Interisland LM-IKB	90	90
138	A41	300o Helicopter Snipan	90	90
a.		Bklt. pane of 5, #134-138	4.50	4.50

Nos. 134-138 printed in booklets only.

Skrimsla, Ancient Folk Ballad—A42

1986, Feb. 3 **Litho.** ***Perf. 12½x13***

139	A42	300o Peasant in woods	90	90
140	A42	420o Meets Giant	1.25	1.25
141	A42	550o Giant loses game	1.65	1.65
142	A42	650o Giant grants Peasant's wish	2.00	2.00

Europa 1986 — A43

Amnesty Intl., 25th Anniv. — A44

1986, Apr. 7 **Litho.** ***Perf. 13½***

143	A43	300o shown	90	90
144	A43	550o Sea pollution	1.65	1.65

1986, June 2 ***Perf. 14x13½***

Winning design competition artwork.

145	A44	300o Olivur vid Neyst	90	90
146	A44	470o Eli Smith	1.40	1.40
147	A44	550o Ranna Kunoy	1.65	1.65

Nos. 145-146 horiz.

Souvenir Sheet

HAFNIA '87, Copenhagen—A45

Design: East Bay of Torshavn, watercolor, 1782, by Christian Rosenmeyer (1728-1802).

1986, Aug. 29 **Litho.** ***Perf. 13x13½***

148		Sheet of 3	6.00	6.00
a.		A45 3k multi	2.00	2.00
b.		A45 4.70k multi	2.00	2.00
c.		A45 6.50k multi	2.00	2.00

No. 148 has multicolored inscribed margin continuing the painting. Sold for 20k. Size:

Old Stone Bridges—A46

Designs: 2.70k, Glyvrar on Eysturoy. 3k, Leypanagjogv on Vagar, vert. 13k, Skaelinger on Streymoy.

Perf. 13½x14½, 14½x13½

1986, Oct. 13 **Engr.**

149	A46	2.70k	dp brn vio	80	80
150	A46	3k	bluish blk	90	90
151	A46	13k	gray grn	4.00	4.00

Farmhouses—A47

Traditional architecture: 300o, Depil on Borooy, 1814. 420o, Depil, diff. 470o, Frammi vio Gjonna on Streymoy, c. 1814. 650o, Frammi, diff.

1987, Feb. 9 **Engr.** ***Perf. 13x14½***

152	A47	300o	pale bl & bl	72	72
153	A47	420o	buff & brn	1.00	1.00
154	A47	470o	pale grn & dp grn	1.15	1.15
155	A47	650o	pale gray & blk	1.55	1.55

Europa 1987—A48

Nordic House: 300o, Exterior. 550o, Interior.

1987, Apr. 6 ***Perf. 13x14***

156	A48	300o	dk bl	90	90
157	A48	550o	dk brn	1.65	1.65

FERNANDO PO

(fĕr·năn'dō pō')

LOCATION—An island in the Gulf of Guinea off west Africa.

GOVT.—Province of Spain.

AREA—800 sq. mi.

POP.—62,612 (1960).

CAPITAL—Santa Isabel.

Together with the islands of Elobey, Annobon and Corisco, Fernando Po came under the administration of Spanish Guinea. Postage stamps of Spanish Guinea were used until 1960.

The provinces of Fernando Po and Rio Muni united Oct. 12, 1968, to form the Republic of Equatorial Guinea.

100 Centimos=1 Escudo=2.50 Pesetas
100 Centimos = 1 Peseta
1000 Milesimas = 100 Centavos = 1 Peso (1882)

Queen Isabella II A1 — King Alfonso XII A2

Typographed.

1868 *Perf. 14* **Unwmkd.**

1	A1	20c brown	400.00	125.00

Forgeries exist.

1879 **Centimos de Peseta.**

2	A2	5c green	35.00	6.75
3	A2	10c rose	35.00	6.75
4	A2	50c blue	55.00	6.75

1882-89 **Centavos de Peso.**

5	A2	1c green	10.00	2.75
6	A2	2c rose	15.00	4.75
7	A2	5c gray bl	32.50	6.25
8	A2	10c dk brn ('89)	55.00	5.00

Nos. 5-7 Handstamp Surcharged in Blue, Black or Violet

a

1884-95

9	A2	50c on 1c grn ('95)	70.00	14.00
11	A2	50c on 2c rose	22.50	4.50
12	A2	50c on 5c bl ('87)	80.00	17.50

Inverted and double surcharges exist.

King Alfonso XIII A4

1894-97 *Perf. 14*

13	A4	⅛c sl ('96)	20.00	3.00
14	A4	2c rose ('96)	15.00	2.00
15	A4	5c bl grn ('97)	15.00	2.00
16	A4	6c dk vio ('96)	12.00	2.75
17	A4	10c brn vio ('94)	125.00	27.50
18	A4	10c lake ('95)	32.50	5.75
19	A4	10c org brn ('96)	10.00	2.00
20	A4	12½c dk brn ('96)	11.00	2.75
21	A4	20c sl bl ('96)	11.00	2.75
22	A4	25c cl ('96)	20.00	2.75
		Nos. 13-22 (10)	271.50	53.25

Stamps of 1894-97 Handstamped in Blue, Black or Red

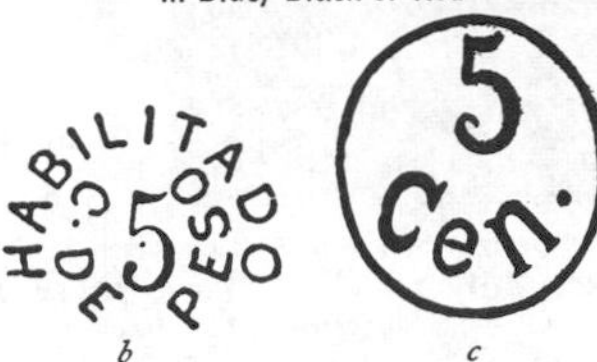

b — c

Type "b" Surcharge

1896-98

23	A4	5c on 2c rose (Bl)	27.50	4.75
24	A4	5c on 10c brn vio (Bl)	85.00	12.00
25	A4	5c on 12½c brn (Bl)	21.00	4.25
a.		Black surcharge	21.00	4.25

Type "c" Surcharge

26	A4	5c on ⅛c sl (Bk)	18.00	5.00
27	A4	5c on 2c rose (Bl)	18.00	5.00
a.		Black surcharge	18.00	5.00
28	A4	5c on 5c grn (R)	90.00	15.00
29	A4	5c on 6c dk vio (R)	12.50	9.00
a.		Violet surcharge	14.00	11.50
30	A4	5c on 10c org brn (Bk)	90.00	18.00
31	A4	5c on 12½c brn (R)	37.50	7.25
32	A4	5c on 20c sl bl (R)	22.50	5.00
33	A4	5c on 25c cl (Bk)	22.50	7.25
a.		Blue surcharge	22.50	7.25

Type "a" Surcharge

1898-99

34	A4	50c on 2c rose (Bl)	47.50	7.00
35	A4	50c on 10c brn vio (Bl)	110.00	20.00
36	A4	50c on 10c lake (Bl)	120.00	20.00
37	A4	50c on 10c org brn (Bl)	110.00	20.00
38	A4	50c on 12½c brn (Bk)	95.00	15.00

The "a" surcharge also exists on 1/8c, 5c and 25c.

Arms

A5 — A6

Revenue Stamps Handstamped in Blue

1897-98 *Imperf.*

39	A5	5c on 10c rose	40.00	20.00
40	A6	10c rose	40.00	20.00

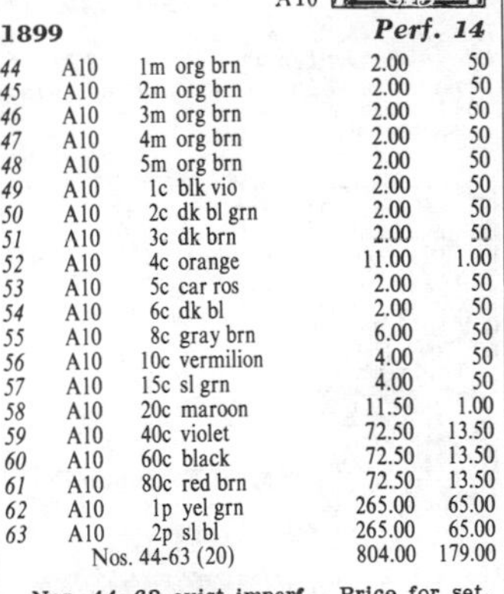

A7

Arms—A8

A9

A9a

Revenue Stamps Handstamped in Black or Red

1899 *Imperf.*

41	A7	15c on 10c grn	50.00	27.50
a.		Blue surcharge, vertical	50.00	27.50
42	A8	10c on 25c grn	135.00	90.00
43	A9	15c on 25c grn	200.00	135.00
43A	A9a	15c on 25c grn (R)	*4,000.*	*2,250.*
b.		Black surcharge	*4,000.*	*2,250.*

Surcharge on No. 41 is either horizontal, inverted or vertical.

On No. 42 "CORREOS" is overprinted in red.

King Alfonso XIII A10

1899 *Perf. 14*

44	A10	1m org brn	2.00	50
45	A10	2m org brn	2.00	50
46	A10	3m org brn	2.00	50
47	A10	4m org brn	2.00	50
48	A10	5m org brn	2.00	50
49	A10	1c blk vio	2.00	50
50	A10	2c dk bl grn	2.00	50
51	A10	3c dk brn	2.00	50
52	A10	4c orange	11.00	1.00
53	A10	5c car ros	2.00	50
54	A10	6c dk bl	2.00	50
55	A10	8c gray brn	6.00	50
56	A10	10c vermilion	4.00	50
57	A10	15c sl grn	4.00	50
58	A10	20c maroon	11.50	1.00
59	A10	40c violet	72.50	13.50
60	A10	60c black	72.50	13.50
61	A10	80c red brn	72.50	13.50
62	A10	1p yel grn	265.00	65.00
63	A10	2p sl bl	265.00	65.00
		Nos. 44-63 (20)	804.00	179.00

Nos. 44-63 exist imperf. Price for set, $1,400.

1900 Surcharged type "a",

64	A10	50c on 20c mar	17.00	3.75
a.		Blue surcharge	30.00	6.50

Surcharged type "b".

64B	A10	5c on 20c mar	175.00	9.00

Surcharged type "c".

65	A10	5c on 20c mar	12.00	3.75

Dated "1900"

1900

66	A10	1m black	3.00	50
67	A10	2m black	3.00	50
68	A10	3m black	3.00	50
69	A10	4m black	3.00	50
70	A10	5m black	3.00	50
71	A10	1c green	3.00	50
72	A10	2c violet	3.00	50
73	A10	3c rose	3.00	50
74	A10	4c blk brn	3.00	50
75	A10	5c blue	3.00	50
76	A10	6c orange	3.00	1.50
77	A10	8c brnz grn	3.00	1.50
78	A10	10c claret	3.00	50
79	A10	15c dk vio	3.00	50
80	A10	20c ol brn	3.00	50
81	A10	40c brown	6.75	1.50
82	A10	60c green	16.00	1.50
83	A10	80c dk bl	16.00	2.75
84	A10	1p red brn	85.00	17.50
85	A10	2p orange	135.00	37.50
		Nos. 66-85 (20)	303.75	70.25

Nos. 66-85 exist imperf.

A11 — A12

Revenue Stamps Overprinted or Surcharged with Handstamp in Red or Black

1900 *Imperf.*

86	A11	10c bl (R)	50.00	16.00
87	A12	5c on 10c bl	125.00	57.50

Nos. 52 and 80 Surcharged type "a" in Violet or Black.

1900

88	A10	50c on 4c org (V)	20.00	5.75
a.		Green surcharge	32.50	16.00
88B	A10	50c on 20c ol brn	15.00	5.50

A13

A14

1901 *Perf. 14*

89	A13	1c black	2.00	50
90	A13	2c org brn	2.00	50
91	A13	3c dk vio	2.00	50
92	A13	4c lt vio	2.00	50
93	A13	5c org red	1.25	50
94	A13	10c vio brn	1.25	50
95	A13	25c dp bl	1.25	50
96	A13	50c claret	2.00	50
97	A13	75c dk brn	1.50	50
98	A13	1p bl grn	42.50	3.50
99	A13	2p red brn	27.50	5.50
100	A13	3p ol grn	27.50	7.25
101	A13	4p dl red	27.50	7.25
102	A13	5p dk grn	32.50	7.25
103	A13	10p buff	70.00	17.50
		Nos. 89-103 (15)	242.75	52.75

Dated "1902"

1902 **Control Numbers on Back.**

104	A13	5c dk grn	2.00	30
105	A13	10c slate	2.00	30
106	A13	25c claret	5.00	75
107	A13	50c vio brn	12.00	2.25
108	A13	75c lt vio	12.00	2.25
109	A13	1p car rose	15.00	3.50
110	A13	2p ol grn	30.00	8.00
111	A13	5p org red	45.00	18.00
		Nos. 104-111 (8)	123.00	35.35

Nos. 104-111 exist imperf. Price for set, $425.

1903 *Perf. 14*

Control Numbers on Back

112	A14	¼c dk vio	30	20
113	A14	½c black	30	20

114	A14	1c scarlet	30	20
115	A14	2c dk grn	30	20
116	A14	3c bl grn	30	20
117	A14	4c violet	30	20
118	A14	5c rose lake	40	20
119	A14	10c org buff	50	25
120	A14	15c bl grn	2.00	75
121	A14	25c red brn	2.25	1.00
122	A14	50c blk brn	3.75	1.75
123	A14	75c carmine	13.00	3.00
124	A14	1p dk brn	19.00	4.50
125	A14	2p dk ol grn	25.00	6.25
126	A14	3p claret	25.00	6.25
127	A14	4p dk bl	32.50	10.00
128	A14	5p dp dl bl	45.00	12.00
129	A14	10p dl red	100.00	18.00
		Nos. 112-129 (18)	270.20	65.15

Dated "1905"

1905 Control Numbers on Back.

136	A14	1c dp vio	30	25
137	A14	2c black	30	25
138	A14	3c vermilion	30	25
139	A14	4c dp grn	30	25
140	A14	5c bl grn	40	25
141	A14	10c violet	1.25	40
142	A14	15c car lake	1.25	40
143	A14	25c org buff	9.00	1.10
144	A14	50c green	6.75	1.65
145	A14	75c red brn	8.00	5.25
146	A14	1p dp gray brn	9.00	5.25
147	A14	2p carmine	17.00	7.50
148	A14	3p dp brn	26.00	8.75
149	A14	4p brnz grn	30.00	10.00
150	A14	5p claret	47.50	16.00
151	A14	10p dp bl	75.00	22.50
		Nos. 136-151 (16)	232.35	80.05

King Alfonso XIII
A15

1907 Control Numbers on Back.

152	A15	1c bl blk	20	25
153	A15	2c car rose	20	6
154	A15	3c dp vio	20	6
155	A15	4c black	20	6
156	A15	5c org buff	25	20
157	A15	10c maroon	1.20	35
158	A15	15c brnz grn	40	20
159	A15	25c dk brn	17.50	6.50
160	A15	50c bl grn	25	15
161	A15	75c vermilion	30	15
162	A15	1p dl bl	1.75	35
163	A15	2p brown	6.75	2.50
164	A15	3p lake	6.75	2.50
165	A15	4p violet	6.75	2.50
166	A15	5p blk brn	6.75	2.50
167	A15	10p org brn	6.75	2.50
		Nos. 152-167 (16)	56.20	20.83

No. 157 Handstamp Surcharged in Black or Blue

HABILITADO
PARA
05CTMS

1908

168	A15	5c on 10c mar (Bk)	4.00	2.50
169	A15	5c on 10c mar (Bl)	14.00	6.75

The surcharge on Nos. 168–169 exists inverted, double and otherwise.

Seville-Barcelona Issue of Spain, 1929, Overprinted FERNANDO POO in Blue or Red

1929 ***Perf. 11.***

170	A52	5c rose lake	15	15
171	A53	10c grn (R)	15	15
a.		Perf. 14	60	50
172	A50	15c Prus bl (R)	15	15
173	A51	20c pur (R)	15	15
174	A50	25c brt rose	15	15
175	A52	30c blk brn	15	15
176	A53	40c dk bl (R)	30	30
177	A51	50c dp org	50	45
178	A52	1p bl blk (R)	1.50	1.00
179	A53	4p dp rose	7.50	6.00
180	A53	10p brown	9.50	7.50
		Nos. 170-180 (11)	20.20	16.15

Virgin Mary
A16

Photogravure

1960 ***Perf. 13x12½*** **Unwmkd.**

181	A16	25c dl gray vio	6	6
182	A16	50c brn ol	6	6
183	A16	75c vio brn	6	6
184	A16	1p org ver	12	6
185	A16	1.50p lt bl grn	12	6
186	A16	2p red lil	12	6
187	A16	3p dk bl	3.50	1.10
188	A16	5p lt red brn	30	12
189	A16	10p lt ol grn	55	20
		Nos. 181-189 (9)	4.89	1.78

Tricorn and Windmill from "The Three-Cornered Hat" by Falla
A17

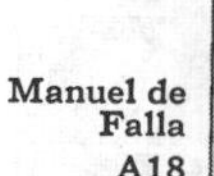

Manuel de Falla
A18

1960 ***Perf. 13x12½, 12½x13***

190	A17	35c sl grn	10	5
191	A18	80c Prus grn	10	6

Issued to honor Manuel de Falla (1876–1946), Spanish composer.

See Nos. B1–B2.

Map of Fernando Po
A19

General Franco
A20

Designs: 70c, Santa Isabel Cathedral.

Perf. 13x12½, 12½x13

1961, Oct. 1 **Photo.** **Unwmkd.**

192	A19	25c gray vio	10	5
193	A20	50c ol brn	10	6
194	A19	70c brt grn	10	6
195	A20	1p red org	10	6

Issued to commemorate the 25th anniversary of the nomination of Gen. Francisco Franco as Chief of State.

Ocean Liner
A21

Design: 50c, S.S. San Francisco.

1962, July 10 ***Perf. 12½x13***

196	A21	25c dl vio	10	5
197	A21	50c gray ol	10	5
198	A21	1p org brn	10	6

Mailman
A22

Mail Transport Symbols
A23

Perf. 13x12½, 12½x13

1962, Nov. 23 **Unwmkd.**

199	A22	15c dk grn	10	5
200	A23	35c lil rose	10	5
201	A22	1p brown	10	6

Issued for Stamp Day.

Fetish
A24

1963, Jan. 29 ***Perf. 13x12½***

202	A24	50c ol gray	10	5
203	A24	1p dp mag	10	6

Issued to help the victims of the Seville flood.

Nuns
A25

Design: 50c, Nun and child (vert.).

Perf. 12½x13, 13x12½

1963, July 6 **Photo.** **Unwmkd.**

204	A25	25c brt lil	10	5
205	A25	50c dl grn	10	5
206	A25	1p red org	10	6

Issued for child welfare.

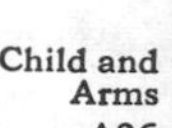

Child and Arms
A26

1963, July 12 ***Perf. 12½x13***

207	A26	50c brn ol	6	6
208	A26	1p car rose	6	6

Issued for Barcelona flood relief.

Governor Chacon
A27

Orange Blossoms
A28

Men in Dugout Canoe
A29

1964, Mar. 6 ***Perf. 12½x13, 13x12½***

209	A27	25c vio blk	10	5
210	A28	50c dk ol	10	5
211	A27	1p brn red	10	6

Issued for Stamp Day 1963.

1964, June 1 **Photo.** ***Perf. 13x12½***

Design: 50c, Pineapple.

212	A29	25c purple	10	6
213	A28	50c dl ol	10	6
214	A29	1p dp cl	10	5

Issued for child welfare.

Ring-necked Francolin
A30

1964, July 1

Designs: 15c, 70c, 3p, Ring-necked francolin. 25c, 1p, 5p, Two mallards. 50c, 1.50p, 10p, Head of great blue touraco.

215	A30	15c chestnut	6	5
216	A30	25c dl vio	6	5
217	A30	50c dk ol grn	6	5
218	A30	70c green	6	5
219	A30	1p brn org	12	5
220	A30	1.50p grnsh bl	15	6
221	A30	3p vio bl	75	15
222	A30	5p dl pur	2.00	25
223	A30	10p brt grn	2.75	1.00
		Nos. 215-223 (9)	6.01	1.71

The Three Kings
A31

Designs: 50c, 1.50p, Caspar (vert.).

Perf. 13x12½, 12½x13

1964, Nov. 23 **Unwmkd.**

224	A31	50c green	5	5
225	A31	1p org ver	5	5
226	A31	1.50p dp grn	18	6
227	A31	3p ultra	2.00	1.10

Issued for Stamp Day, 1964.

Boy
A32

Woman Fruit Picker
A33

Design: 1.50p, Girl learning to write, and church.

1964, Mar. 1 Photo. *Perf. 13x12½*

228	A32	50c indigo	5	5
229	A33	1p dk red	6	6
230	A33	1.50p grnsh bl	15	6

Issued to commemorate 25 years of peace.

Plectrocnemia Cruciata
A34

Design: 1p, Metopodontus savagei (horiz.).

Perf. 13x12½, 12½x13

1965, June 1 Photo. Unwmkd.

231	A34	50c sl grn	5	5
232	A34	1p rose red	6	6
233	A34	1.50p Prus bl	15	6

Issued for child welfare.

Pole Vault
A35

Arms of Fernando Po
A36

Perf. 12½x13, 13x12½

1965, Nov. 23 Photo. Unwmkd.

234	A35	50c yel grn	5	5
235	A36	1p brt org brn	6	6
236	A35	1.50p brt bl	15	6

Issued for Stamp Day, 1965.

Children Reading
A37

Design: 1.50p, St. Elizabeth of Hungary (vert.).

Perf. 12½x13, 13x12½

1966, June 1 Photo. Unwmkd.

237	A37	50c dk grn	5	5
238	A37	1p brn red	6	6
239	A37	1.50p dk bl	15	6

Issued for child welfare.

White-nosed Monkey
A38

Designs: 40c, 4p, Head of moustached monkey (vert.).

1966, Nov. 23 Photo. *Perf. 13*

240	A38	10c dk bl & yel	5	5
241	A38	40c lt brn, bl & blk	5	5
242	A38	1.50p ol bis, brn org & blk	10	6
243	A38	4p sl grn, brn org & blk	20	15

Issued for Stamp Day, 1966.

Flowers
A39

Designs: 40c, 4p, Six flowers.

1967, June 1 Photo. *Perf. 13*

244	A39	10c brt car & pale grn	5	5
245	A39	40c red brn & org	5	5
246	A39	1.50p red lil & lt red brn	10	6
247	A39	4p dk bl & lt grn	20	15

Issued for child welfare.

Linsang
A40

Designs: 1.50p, Needle-clawed galago (vert.). 3.50p, Fraser's scaly-tailed flying squirrel.

1967, Nov. 23 Photo. *Perf. 13*

248	A40	1p blk & bis	15	6
249	A40	1.50p brn & ol	15	10
250	A40	3.50p rose lake & dl grn	25	20

Issued for Stamp Day 1967.

Stamp of 1868, No. 1, and Arms of San Carlos—A41

Designs: 1.50p, Fernando Po No. 1 and arms of Santa Isabel. 2.50p, Fernando Po No. 1 and arms of Fernando Po.

1968, Feb. 4 Photo. *Perf. 13*

251	A41	1p brt plum & brn org	15	10
252	A41	1.50p dp bl & brn org	15	10
253	A41	2.50p brn & brn org	20	15

Centenary of the first postage stamp.

Zodiac Issue

Libra
A42

Signs of the Zodiac: 1.50p, Leo. 2.50p, Aquarius.

1968, Apr. 25 Photo. *Perf. 13*

254	A42	1p brt mag, *lt yel*	15	10
255	A42	1.50p brn, *pink*	15	10
256	A42	2.50p dk vio, *yel*	20	15

Issued for child welfare.

SEMI-POSTAL STAMPS

Types of Regular Issue, 1960

Designs: 10c+5c, Manuel de Falla. 15c+5c, Dancers from "Love, the Magician."

Perf. 12½x13, 13x12½

1960 Photogravure Unwmkd.

B1	A18	10c +5c mar	10	5
B2	A17	15c +5c dk brn & bis	10	5

The surtax was for child welfare.

Whale
SP1

Design: 20c+5c, 50c+20c, Harpooning whale.

1961 *Perf. 12½x13*

B3	SP1	10c +5c rose brn	6	5
B4	SP1	20c +5c dk sl grn	6	5
B5	SP1	30c +10c ol brn	6	5
B6	SP1	50c +20c dk brn	20	6

Issued for Stamp Day, 1960.

Hand Blessing Woman
SP2

Design: 25c+10c, Boy making sign of the cross, and crucifix.

1961, June 21 *Perf. 13x12½*

B7	SP2	10c +5c rose brn	10	5
B8	SP2	25c +10c gray vio	10	5
B9	SP2	80c +20c dk grn	10	5

The surtax was for child welfare.

Ethiopian Tortoise
SP3

Design: 25c+10c, 1p+10c, Native carriers, palms and shore.

1961, Nov. 23 *Perf. 12½x13*

B10	SP3	10c +5c rose red	10	5
B11	SP3	25c +10c dk pur	10	5
B12	SP3	30c +10c vio brn	10	5
B13	SP3	1p +10c red org	10	6

Issued for Stamp Day 1961.

FEZZAN

(See Libya, Occupation Stamps).

FINLAND

(fĭn'lănd)

(Suomi)

LOCATION — Northern Europe bordering on the Gulfs of Bothenia and Finland.
GOVT.—Republic.
AREA—130,119 sq. mi.
POP.—4,869,858 (1984).
CAPITAL—Helsinki.

Finland was a Grand Duchy of the Russian Empire from 1809 until December 1917, when it declared its independence.

100 Kopecks = 1 Ruble
100 Pennia = 1 Markka (1866)

Issues under Russian Empire.

Prices of early Finland stamps vary according to condition. Quotations for Nos. 1–3B are for fine copies. Used prices are for pen-canceled copies. Very fine to superb specimens sell at much higher prices, and inferior or poor copies sell at reduced prices, depending on the condition of the individual specimen.

Coat of Arms
A1

Typographed.

1856 *Imperf.* Unwmkd.

Small Pearls in Post Horns.

Wove Paper.

1	A1	5k blue	*8,000.*	1,400.
		Pen and town cancellation		*2,000.*
		Town cancellation		*3,000.*
a.		Tête bêche pair		*30,000.*
		As "a," pen and town cancellation		*37,500.*
2	A1	10k rose	8,000.	325.00
		Pen and town cancellation		725.00
		Town cancellation		975.00
a.		Tête bêche pair		*20,000.*
		As "a," pen and town cancellation		*27,500.*

1858

Wide Vertically Laid Paper

2C	A1	10k rose	1,200.
		Pen and town cancellation	1,800.
		Town cancellation	2,250.
d.		Tête bêche pair	

The wide vertically laid paper has 13–14 distinct lines per 2 cm. The 10k rose also exists on a narrow laid paper with lines sometimes indistinct. Price, 60 per cent of that for a wide laid paper example.

A 5k blue with small pearls exists on narrow vertically laid paper.

Stamps on diagonally laid paper are envelope cut squares.

Large Pearls in Post Horns.

Wove Paper.

3	A1	5k blue	*7,000.*	1,200.
		Pen and town cancellation		1,600.
		Town cancellation		2,500.
a.		Tête bêche pair		*30,000.*
		As "a," pen and town cancellation		*37,500.*

1859

Wide Vertically Laid Paper

3B	A1	5k blue		*11,000.*
		Pen and town cancellation		*14,000.*

Reprints of Nos. 2 and 3, made in 1862, are on brownish paper, on vertically laid paper, and in tête bêche pairs on normal and vertically laid paper. Reprints of 1871, 1881 and 1893 are on yellowish or white paper. Price for least costly of each, $70.

In 1956, Nos. 2 and 3 were reprinted for the Centenary with post horn watermark and gum. Price, $65 each.

Coat of Arms
A2

Serpentine Roulette 7½, 8

1860

Nos. 4–13, with serpentine roulette, are seldom in perfect condition. Usually some of the "teeth" are missing. In average condition, one or two teeth are gone. Prices are for average specimens. Copies with all teeth intact sell for many times more.

Four types of indentation are noted:

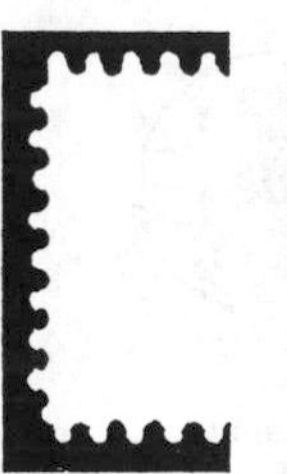

I. Depth 1–1¼mm.

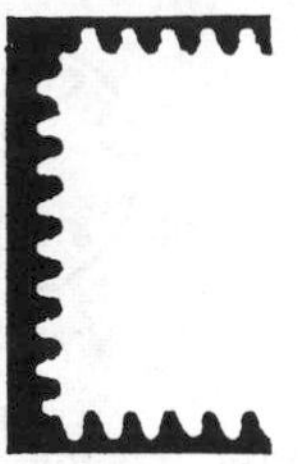

II. Depth 1½–1¾mm.

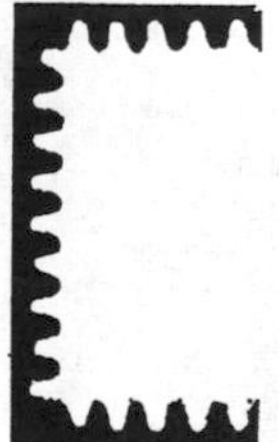

III. Depth 2–2¼mm.

IV. Shovel-shaped teeth. Depth 1¼–1½mm.

Wove Paper.

4	A2	5k bl, *bluish*, roulette I	450.00	100.00
a.		Roulette II	600.00	110.00
b.		Imperf. vert.		
5	A2	10k rose, *pale rose*, roulette I	325.00	35.00
a.		Roulette II	700.00	45.00

A3

A4

1866–74 ***Serpentine Roulette***

6	A3	5p pur brn, *lil*, roulette I ('73)	180.00	50.00
a.		Roulette II		1,400.
b.		5p red brn, *lil*, roulette III ('71)	180.00	50.00
7	A3	8p *grn*, roulette III ('67)	175.00	75.00
a.		Ribbed paper, roulette III ('72)	750.00	175.00
b.		Roulette II ('74)	180.00	75.00
c.		As "b,"ribbed paper ('74)	250.00	85.00
d.		Roulette I ('73)	275.00	90.00
e.		As "d," ribbed paper	750.00	175.00
f.		Serp. roulette 10½ ('67)		*8,000.*
8	A3	10p *yel*, roulette III ('70)	260.00	75.00
a.		10p *buff*, roulette II	450.00	100.00
b.		10p *buff*, roulette I ('73)	325.00	100.00
9	A3	20p bl, *bl*, roulette III	250.00	22.50
a.		Roulette II	250.00	22.50
b.		Roulette I ('73)	350.00	32.50
c.		Roulette IV ('74)	*1,100.*	*500.00*
d.		Imperf. horiz.		*300.00*
e.		Printed on both sides (40p bl on back)		*6,500.*
10	A3	40p rose, *lil rose*, roulette III	250.00	27.50
a.		Ribbed paper, roulette III ('73)	325.00	40.00
b.		Roulette II	250.00	27.50
c.		As "b," ribbed paper ('73)	325.00	40.00
d.		Roulette I	525.00	42.50
e.		As "d," ribbed paper	375.00	42.50
f.		Roulette IV		*1,200.*
g.		As "f," ribbed paper		*1,500.*
h.		Serp. roulette 10½		*4,500.*
11	A4	1m yel brn, roulette III ('67)	1,000.	400.00
a.		Roulette II	1,800.	700.00
b.		Final "A" of "MARKKA" covered by color spot	1,400.	500.00

Nos. 7f and 10h are also known in compound serpentine roulette 10½ and 7½.

Nos. 4 to 11 were reprinted in 1893 on thick wove paper. Colors differ from originals. Roulette type IV. Price for Nos. 4-10, each $30. Price for No. 11, $42.50.

Thin or Thick Laid Paper.

12	A3	5p red brn, *lil*, roulette III	180.00	50.00
a.		Roulette II	180.00	50.00
b.		Roulette I	180.00	60.00
d.		5p *buff*, roul. III (error)		*7,000.*
e.		Tête bêche pair		*10,000.*
13	A3	10p *buff*, roulette III	275.00	80.00
a.		10p *yel*, roulette II	325.00	80.00
b.		10p *yel*, roulette I	1,000.	125.00
c.		10p red brn, *lil*, roul. III (error)	*6,000.*	*3,500.*

A5

A6

1875 ***Perf. 14x13½***

16	A5	32p lake	2,000.	700.00

1875–81 ***Perf. 11***

17	A5	2p gray	60.00	60.00
18	A5	5p orange	175.00	15.00
a.		5p yel	175.00	15.00
19	A5	8p bl grn	250.00	80.00
a.		8p yel grn	250.00	80.00
20	A5	10p brn ('81)	475.00	75.00
21	A5	20p ultra	175.00	4.00
a.		20p bl	175.00	4.00
b.		20p Prus bl	200.00	20.00
c.		Tête bêche pair	3,000.	2,500.
22	A5	25p car ('79)	200.00	18.00
a.		25p rose	200.00	27.50
23	A5	32p carmine	375.00	45.00
a.		32p rose	375.00	50.00
24	A5	1m vio ('77)	600.00	175.00

A souvenir card was issued in 1974 for NORDIA 1975 reproducing a block of four of the unissued "1 MARKKAA" design.

Nos. 19 and 23 were reprinted in 1893, perf. 12½. Price $17.50 each.

1881–83 ***Perf. 12½***

25	A5	2p gray	20.00	20.00
a.		Imperf., pair	150.00	
26	A5	5p orange	55.00	7.50
a.		Tête bêche pair	3,500.	3,000.
b.		Imperf. vert., pair	150.00	150.00
c.		Imperf. horiz., pair		175.00
27	A5	10p brown	130.00	20.00
28	A5	20p ultra	65.00	2.25
a.		20p bl	65.00	2.25
b.		Tête bêche pair	1,800.	2,250.
c.		Imperf., pair	100.00	
29	A5	25p rose	65.00	11.00
a.		25p car	65.00	11.00
b.		Tête bêche pair	4,000.	4,500.
30	A5	1m vio ('82)	425.00	65.00

Nos. 27–29 were reprinted in 1893 in deeper shades, perf. 12½. Price $35 each.

1881 ***Perf. 11x12½***

26d	A5	5p orange	375.00	80.00
27a	A5	10p brown	1,200.	300.00
28d	A5	20p ultra	550.00	50.00
28e	A5	20p blue	550.00	50.00
29c	A5	25p rose	525.00	140.00
29d	A5	25p carmine	525.00	140.00
30a	A5	1m violet		1,500.

1881 ***Perf. 12½x11***

26e	A5	5p orange	375.00	80.00
27b	A5	10p brown	1,200.	300.00
28f	A5	20p ultra	550.00	50.00
28g	A5	20p blue	550.00	50.00
29e	A5	25p rose	525.00	140.00
29f	A5	25p carmine	525.00	140.00

1885 ***Perf. 12½.***

31	A5	5p emerald	25.00	50
a.		5p yel grn	25.00	50
b.		Tête bêche pair	5,500.	4,500.
32	A5	10p carmine	35.00	3.50
a.		10p rose	35.00	3.50
33	A5	20p orange	35.00	50
a.		20p yel	40.00	3.25
b.		Tête bêche pair	3,250.	2,750.
34	A5	25p ultra	65.00	2.50
a.		25p bl	65.00	2.50
35	A5	1m gray & rose	37.50	18.00
36	A5	5m grn & rose	600.00	4.25
37	A5	10m brn & rose	925.00	800.00

1889–92 ***Perf. 12½***

38	A6	2p sl ('90)	1.00	1.00
39	A6	5p grn ('90)	35.00	35
40	A6	10p car ('90)	60.00	65
a.		10p rose ('90)	60.00	65
41	A6	20p org ('92)	55.00	30
a.		20p yel ('90)	60.00	1.50
42	A6	25p ultra ('91)	60.00	65
a.		25p bl	60.00	70
43	A6	1m sl & rose ('92)	8.00	5.50
a.		1m brnsh gray & rose ('90)	40.00	5.50
44	A6	5m grn & rose ('90)	55.00	65.00
45	A6	10m brn & rose ('90)	85.00	110.00

The 2p slate, perf. 14x13, is believed to be an essay.

See also Nos. 60–63.

Imperial Arms of Russia

A7 A8 A9

A10

A11

Wmk. 168

Laid Paper.

Wmkd.

Wavy Lines and Letters. (168)

1891–92 ***Perf. 14½x15***

46	A7	1k org yel	8.50	11.00
47	A7	2k green	8.50	11.00
48	A7	3k carmine	15.00	18.00
49	A8	4k rose	16.00	18.00
50	A7	7k dk bl	9.00	3.00
51	A8	10k dk bl	22.50	18.00
52	A9	14k bl & rose	30.00	25.00
53	A8	20k bl & car	22.50	20.00
54	A9	35k vio & grn	35.00	50.00
55	A8	50k vio & grn	50.00	40.00

Perf. 13½.

56	A10	1r brn & org	130.00	100.00
57	A11	3½r blk & gray	525.00	550.00
a.		3½r blk & yel (*error*)	*6,500.*	*5,500.*
58	A11	7r blk & yel	350.00	300.00
		Nos. 46-58 (13)	1,222.	1,164.

Forgeries of Nos. 57, 57a, 58 exist.

Type of 1889–90.

Wove Paper.

1895–96 ***Perf. 14x13*** **Unwmkd.**

60	A6	5p green	75	25
61	A6	10p rose	1.00	25
a.		Imperf.	125.00	125.00
62	A6	20p orange	1.00	25
a.		Imperf.	110.00	125.00
63	A6	25p ultra	2.00	50
a.		25p bl	2.00	50
b.		Imperf.	125.00	125.00

A12

A13

A14

A15

1901 Lithographed ***Perf. 14½x15***

Chalky Paper.

64	A12	2p yellow	5.00	4.00
65	A12	5p green	15.00	70
66	A13	10p carmine	25.00	1.25
67	A12	20p dk bl	50.00	55
68	A14	1m vio & grn	225.00	7.50

Perf. 13½.

69	A15	10m blk & gray	350.00	300.00
		Nos. 64-69 (6)	670.00	314.00

Imperf. sheets of 10p and 20p, stolen during production, were privately perforated 11½ to defraud the P.O. Uncanceled imperfs. of Nos. 65–68 are believed to be proofs.

Types of 1901 Redrawn.

No. 64.

No. 70.

2p. On No. 64, the "2" below "II" is shifted slightly leftward. On No. 70, the "2" is centered below "II."

No. 65.

No. 71.

5p. On No. 65, the frame lines are very close. On No. 71, a clear white space separates them.

Nos. 66, 67.

Nos. 72, 73.

10p, 20p. On Nos. 66–67, the horizontal central background lines are faint and broken. On Nos. 72–73, they are clear and solid, though still thin.

20p. On No. 67, "H" close to "2" with period midway. On No. 73 they are slightly separated with period close to "H".

No. 68.

Nos. 74, 74a.

1m. On No. 68, the "1" following "MARKKA" lacks serif at base. On Nos. 74–74a, this "1" has serif.

No. 69.

No. 75.

10m. On No. 69, the serifs of "M" and "A" in top and bottom panels do not touch. On No. 75, the serifs join.

1901–14 Typo. ***Perf. 14, 14½x15***

Ordinary Paper.

70	A12	2p orange	90	90
a.		Imperf.	250.00	*275.00*
71	A12	5p green	2.25	20
b.		Imperf.	100.00	140.00
72	A13	10p carmine	70	25
a.		Imperf.	100.00	110.00
b.		Background inverted	22.50	2.50
73	A12	20p dk bl	60	25
a.		Imperf.	100.00	110.00
74	A14	1m lil & grn, perf. 14 ('14)	1.30	50
a.		1m vio & bl grn, perf. 14½x15 ('02)	11.00	50
b.		Imperf.	125.00	150.00
		Nos. 70-74 (5)	5.75	2.10

Perf. 13½.

75	A15	10m blk & db ('03)	160.00	62.50

A16

A17

A18

1911–16 ***Perf. 14, 14½x15***

77	A16	2p orange	25	25
78	A16	5p green	40	25
a.		Imperf.	100.00	100.00
b.		Perf. 14½x15	250.00	40.00
79	A17	10p rose	30	25
a.		Imperf.	60.00	70.00
b.		Perf. 14½x15	1.65	1.10
80	A16	20p dp bl	30	25
a.		Imperf.	60.00	60.00
81	A18	40p vio & bl	20	20
a.		Perf. 14½x15	1,800.	1,800.
		Nos. 77-81 (5)	1.45	1.20

There are three minor types of No. 79.

Perf. 14½

82	A15	10m blk & grnsh gray ('16)	200.00	225.00
a.		Horiz. pair, imperf. vert.	1,250.	

Republic.

Helsinki Issue.

Arms of the Republic
A19

Two types of the 40p.
Type I—Thin figures of value.
Type II—Thick figures of value.

Perf. 14, 14½x15

1917-29 **Unwmkd.**

83	A19	5p green	15	8
84	A19	5p gray ('19)	15	8
85	A19	10p rose	25	8
a.		Imperf., pair	250.00	325.00
86	A19	10p grn ('19)	1.75	10
a.		Perf. 14½x15		1,400.
87	A19	10p lt bl ('21)	15	8
88	A19	20p buff	25	10
89	A19	20p rose ('20)	50	10
90	A19	20p brn ('24)	50	35
91	A19	25p blue	30	10
92	A19	25p lt brn ('19)	18	10
93	A19	30p grn ('23)	40	25
94	A19	40p vio (I)	25	8
a.		Perf. 14½x15	180.00	15.00
95	A19	40p bl grn (II) ('29)	25	50
a.		Type I ('24)	10.00	4.50
96	A19	50p org brn	25	8
97	A19	50p dp bl ('19)	4.00	12
a.		Perf. 14½x15		500.00
98	A19	50p grn ('21)	30	20
99	A19	60p red vio ('21)	50	8
a.		Imperf., pair	100.00	135.00
100	A19	75p yel ('21)	25	30
101	A19	1m dl rose & blk	14.00	10
102	A19	1m red org ('25)	40	*12.00*
103	A19	1½m bl grn & red vio ('29)	20	20
104	A19	2m grn & blk ('21)	3.00	60
105	A19	2m dk bl & ind ('22)	1.00	12
106	A19	3m bl & blk ('21)	110.00	30
107	A19	5m red vio & blk	25.00	15
108	A19	10m brn & gray blk, perf. 14	85	85
a.		10m lt brn & blk, perf. 14½x15 ('29)	7.00	*400.00*
110	A19	25m dl red & yel ('21)	1.00	*20.00*
		Nos. 83-108, 110 (27)	165.83	*37.10*

Copies of a 2½p gray of this type exist. They are proofs from the original die which were distributed through the Universal Postal Union. No plate was made for this denomination.

See also Nos. 127–140, 143–152.

Vasa Issue

A20

1918 Lithographed. ***Perf. 11½.***

111	A20	5p green	40	60
112	A20	10p red	35	55
113	A20	30p slate	1.00	2.00
114	A20	40p brn vio	30	60
115	A20	50p org brn	50	1.40
116	A20	70p gray brn	2.25	13.00
117	A20	1m red & gray	50	1.00
118	A20	5m red vio & gray	100.00	140.00
		Nos. 111-118 (8)	105.30	159.15

Nos. 111–118 exist imperforate but were not regularly issued in that condition.

Sheet margin copies, perf. on 3 sides, imperf. on margin side, were sold by post office.

Stamps and Type of 1917–29 Surcharged **50** 50 50

1919 ***Perf. 14***

119	A19	10p on 5p grn	40	40
120	A19	20p on 10p rose	40	40
121	A19	50p on 25p bl	90	40
122	A19	75p on 20p org	40	40

Stamps and Type of 1917–29 Surcharged:

30 P (a) **1½ M** (b)

1921

123	A19 (a)	30p on 10p grn	80	40
124	A19 (a)	60p on 40p red vio	4.00	60
125	A19 (a)	90p on 20p rose	25	25
126	A19 (a)	1½m on 50p bl	1.75	20
a.		Thin "2" in "½"	8.00	4.50
b.		Imperf., pair	200.00	400.00

Wmk. 121

Arms Type of 1917–29.

Wmkd. Multiple Swastika. (121)

1925–29 ***Perf. 14, 14½x15***

127	A19	10p ultra ('27)	60	1.00
128	A19	20p brown	60	80
129	A19	25p brn org ('29)	1.00	*37.50*
130	A19	30p yel grn	25	25
131	A19	40p bl grn (I)	3.00	25
a.		Type II	3.00	25
132	A19	50p gray grn ('27)	50	25
133	A19	60p red vio	25	25
134	A19	1m dp org	5.00	25
135	A19	1½m bl grn & red vio	8.50	25
136	A19	2m dk bl & ind	40	50
137	A19	3m chlky bl & blk	1.25	25
138	A19	5m red vio & blk	35	25
139	A19	10m lt brn & blk ('27)	5.00	11.00
140	A19	25m dp org & yel ('27)	30.00	*275.00*
		Nos. 127-140 (14)	56.70	

A21

Wmk. 208

Wmkd. Post Horn. (208)

1927. Dec. 6 Typo. ***Perf. 14***

141	A21	1½m dp vio	25	50
142	A21	2m dp bl	40	1.50

Issued in commemoration of the tenth anniversary of Finnish independence.

Arms Type of 1917–29.

Perf. 14½x15

1927–29 **Wmk. 208**

143	A19	20p lt brn ('29)	1.75	*7.00*
144	A19	40p bl grn (II) ('28)	25	25
145	A19	50p gray grn ('28)	25	25
146	A19	1m dp org	25	25
a.		Imperf., pair	160.00	200.00
b.		Perf. 14	1.50	25
147	A19	1½m bl grn & red vio ('28)	3.25	15
a.		Perf. 14	675.00	15.00
148	A19	2m dk bl & ind ('28)	50	50
149	A19	3m chlky bl & blk	50	50
a.		Perf. 14	2.75	2.75
150	A19	5m red vio & blk ('28)	50	50
151	A19	10m lt brn & blk	1.50	*37.50*
152	A19	25m brn org & yel	1.75	*140.00*
		Nos. 143-152 (10)	10.50	

Philatelic Exhibition Issue.

A22

Overprint in Black

1928, Nov. 10 Litho. Wmk. 208

153	A22	1m dp org	11.00	18.00
154	A22	1½m bl grn & red vio	11.00	18.00

Nos. 153 and 154 were sold exclusively at the Helsinki Philatelic Exhibition, Nov. 10–18, 1928, and were valid only during that period.

S. S. "Bore" Leaving Turku
A23

Turku Cathedral
A24

Turku Castle
A25

Typographed

1929, May 22 ***Perf. 14*** **Wmk. 208**

155	A23	1m ol grn	1.75	4.00
156	A24	1½m chocolate	3.00	3.50
157	A25	2m dk gray	1.00	4.00

Issued to commemorate the 700th anniversary of the founding of the city of Turku (Abo).

A26

1930–46 ***Perf. 14*** **Unwmkd.**

158	A26	5p chocolate	10	10
159	A26	10p dl vio	10	10
160	A26	20p yel grn	40	50
161	A26	25p yel brn	15	10
162	A26	40p bl grn	3.50	25
163	A26	50p yellow	60	50
164	A26	50p bl grn ('32)	15	6
b.		Imperf., pair	160.00	175.00
165	A26	60p dk gray	50	60
165A	A26	75p dp org ('42)	15	10
166	A26	1m red org	60	8
a.		Booklet pane of 4	2.75	
166B	A26	1m yel grn ('42)	25	10
167	A26	1.20m crimson	50	75
168	A26	1.25m yel ('32)	30	10
169	A26	1½m red vio	3.50	10
170	A26	1½m car ('32)	20	10
170A	A26	1½m sl ('40)	20	8
170B	A26	1.75m org yel ('40)	75	15
171	A26	2m indigo	40	15
172	A26	2m dp vio ('32)	10.00	10
173	A26	2m car ('36)	25	8
173B	A26	2m yel org ('42)	40	10
173C	A26	2m bl grn ('45)	25	10
174	A26	2½m brt bl ('32)	3.00	15
174A	A26	2½m car ('42)	20	8
174B	A26	2.75m rose vio ('40)	20	10
175	A26	3m ol blk	40.00	15
175B	A26	3m car ('45)	30	10
175C	A26	3m yel ('45)	50	60
176	A26	3½m brt bl ('36)	8.00	15
176A	A26	3½m ol ('42)	20	8
176B	A26	4m ol ('45)	50	8
176C	A26	4½m saph ('42)	20	20
176D	A26	5m saph ('45)	50	10
176E	A26	5m pur ('45)	50	15
j.		Imperf., pair	160.00	175.00
176F	A26	5m yel ('46)	1.00	10
k.		Imperf., pair	140.00	160.00
176G	A26	6m car ('45)	50	15
m.		Imperf., pair	160.00	175.00
176H	A26	8m pur ('46)	20	10
176I	A26	10m saph ('45)	1.00	10
		Nos. 158-176I (38)	80.05	6.69

See also Nos. 257–262, 270–274, 291–296, 302–304.

Stamps of types A26–A29 overprinted "ITA KARJALA" are listed under Karelia, Nos. N1–N15.

Castle in Savonlinna
A27

Lake Saima
A28

Woodchopper
A29

1930 **Engraved**

177	A27	5m blue	30	6
178	A28	10m gray lil	120.00	4.75
179	A29	25m blk brn	1.25	25

See also Nos. 205 and 305.

Elias Lönnrot
A30

Seal of Finnish Literary Society
A31

1931, Jan. 1 **Typographed**

180	A30	1m ol brn	4.00	4.00
181	A31	1½m dl bl	15.00	4.00

Centenary of Finnish Literary Society.

A32

1931, Feb. 28

182	A32	1½m red	3.50	5.00
183	A32	2m blue	3.50	6.00

75th anniversary of first use of postage stamps in Finland.

Nos. 162-163 Surcharged

50 PEN.
=

1931, Dec.

195	A26	50p on 40p bl grn	1.50	30
196	A26	1.25m on 50p yel	4.00	70

President P. E. Svinhufvud
A33

Alexis Kivi
A34

1931, Dec. 15

197	A33	2m gray bl & blk	2.25	2.50

Issued to commemorate the 70th birthday of President Pehr Eyvind Svinhufvud.

Lake Saima Type of 1930.

1932–43 **Re-engraved**

205	A28	10m red vio ('43)	75	10
a.		10m dk vio	25.00	70

On Nos. 205 and 205a the lines of the islands, the clouds and the foilage are much deeper and stronger than on No. 178.

1934, Oct. 10 **Typographed**

206	A34	2m red vio	2.75	3.50

Issued in commemoration of the centenary of the birth of Alexis Kivi, Finnish poet (1834–1872).

Bards Reciting the "Kalevala"
A35

Goddess Louhi, As Eagle Seizing Magic Mill
A36

Kullervo
A37

1935, Feb. 28 **Engraved**

207	A35	1¼m brn lake	1.50	1.50
208	A36	2m black	4.50	1.25
209	A37	2½m blue	4.50	2.50

Issued to commemorate the centenary of the publication of the "Kalevala" (Finnish National Epic).

No. 170 Surcharged in Black

2
MARKKAA
=

1937, Feb.

212	A26	2m on 1½m car	5.50	65

Field Marshal Gustaf Mannerheim
A38

Swede-Finn Co-operation in Colonization
A39

1937, June 4 **Photo.** ***Perf. 14***

213	A38	2m ultra	85	1.25

Issued in commemoration of the 70th birthday of Field Marshal Baron Carl Gustaf Mannerheim, June 4th, 1937.

1938, June 1

214	A39	3½m dk brn	1.80	3.00

Tercentenary of the colonization of Delaware by Swedes and Finns.

Early Post Office
A40

Designs: 1¼m, Mail delivery in 1700. 2m, Modern mail plane. 3½m, Helsinki post office.

1938, Sept. 6 **Photo.** ***Perf. 14***

215	A40	50p green	45	90
216	A40	1¼m dk bl	1.75	3.50
217	A40	2m scarlet	2.00	1.00
218	A40	3½m sl blk	7.00	9.00

Issued in commemoration of the 300th anniversary of the Finnish Postal System.

Post Office, Helsinki
A44

1939–42 **Photogravure**

219	A44	4m brn blk	25	15
		Engraved		
219A	A44	7m blk brn ('42)	75	15
219B	A44	9m rose lake ('42)	75	15

See also No. 248.

University of Helsinki
A45

1940, May 1 **Photogravure**

220	A45	2m dp bl & bl	80	1.00

Issued in commemoration of the 300th anniversary of the founding of the University of Helsinki.

Nos. 168 and 173 Surcharged in Black

mk
1:75
=

1940, June 16 **Typographed**

221	A26	1.75m on 1.25m yel	1.10	1.40
222	A26	2.75m on 2m car	3.25	40

President Kallio Reviewing Military Band
A46

1941, May 24 **Engraved**

223	A46	2.75m black	80	1.00

Issued in memory of President Kyösti Kallio (1873–1940).

Castle at Viborg
A47

1941, Aug. 30 **Typographed**

224	A47	1.75m yel org	50	1.00
225	A47	2.75m rose vio	50	1.00
226	A47	3.50m blue	1.00	2.00

Field Marshal Mannerheim
A48

Wmk. 273

Wmkd. Roses. (273)

1941, Dec. 31 **Engraved** ***Perf. 14***

227	A48	50p dl grn	80	1.25
228	A48	1.75m dp brn	80	1.25
229	A48	2m dk red	80	1.25
230	A48	2.75m dl vio brn	80	1.25
231	A48	3.50m dp bl	80	1.25
232	A48	5m sl bl	80	1.25
		Nos. 227-232 (6)	4.80	7.50

President Risto Ryti
A49

233	A49	50p dl grn	80	1.25
234	A49	1.75m dp brn	80	1.25
235	A49	2m dk red	80	1.25
236	A49	2.75m dl vio brn	80	1.25
237	A49	3.50m dp bl	80	1.25
238	A49	5m sl bl	80	1.25
		Nos. 233-238 (6)	4.80	7.50

Types A48–A49 overprinted "ITA KARJALA" are listed under Karelia, Nos. N16–N27.

Häme Bridge, Tampere
A50

South Harbor, Helsinki
A51

1942 **Unwmkd.**

239	A50	50m dl brn vio	2.00	12
240	A51	100m indigo	2.50	20

See also No. 350.

Altar and Open Bible
A52

17th Century Printer
A53

1942, Oct. 10

241	A52	2.75m dk brn	50	1.00
242	A53	3.50m vio bl	1.00	1.75

Issued to commemorate the 300th anniversary of the printing of the first Bible in Finnish, 1642.

No. 174B Surcharged in Black

3½mk

1943, Feb. 1

243	A26	3.50m on 2.75m rose vio	20	20

Minna Canth
A54

1944, Mar. 20

244	A54	3.50m dk ol grn	60	1.00

Issued to commemorate the centenary of the birth of Minna Canth (1844–96), author and playwright.

President P. E. Svinhufvud
A55

K. J. Stahlberg
A56

1944, Aug. 1

245	A55	3.50m black	60	1.00

Death of President Svinhufvud (1861–1944).

1945, May 16 **Engraved** ***Perf. 14***

246	A56	3.50m brn vio	30	80

80th birthday of Dr. K. J. Stahlberg.

Castle in Savonlinna
A57

Jean Sibelius
A58

1945, Sept. 4

247	A57	15m lil rose	1.25	15
248	A44	20m sepia	1.50	8

For a 35m of type A57, see No. 280.

1945, Dec. 8

249	A58	5m dk sl grn	25	50

80th birthday of Jean Sibelius (1865–1957), composer.

No. 176E Surcharged with New Value and Bars in Black.

1946, Mar. 16

250	A26	8(m) on 5m pur	20	20

Victorious Athletes
A59

Lighthouse at Uto
A60

1946, June 1 **Engraved** ***Perf. 13½***

251	A59	8m brn vio	50	80

Issued to commemorate the 3rd Sports Festival, Helsinki, June 27–30, 1946.

1946, Sept. 19

252	A60	8m dp vio	50	80

Issued to commemorate the 250th anniversary of the Finnish Department of Pilots and Lighthouses.

Post Bus
A61

1946–47 ***Perf. 14*** **Unwmkd.**

253	A61	16m gray blk	50	90
253A	A61	30m gray blk ('47)	1.75	20

Old Town Hall, Porvoo
A62

Cathedral, Porvoo
A63

1946, Dec. 3

254	A62	5m gray blk	30	45
255	A63	8m dp cl	50	65

Issued to commemorate the 600th anniversary of the founding of the city of Porvoo (Borga).

Waterfront, Tammisaari
A64

1946, Dec. 14

256	A64	8m grnsh blk	50	65

Issued to commemorate the 400th anniversary of the founding of the town of Tammisaari (Ekenas).

Lion Type of 1930.

1947 **Typographed** ***Perf. 14***

257	A26	2½m dk grn	40	10
258	A26	3m sl gray	20	8
259	A26	6m dp org	1.00	12
260	A26	7m carmine	40	10
261	A26	10m purple	2.50	8
262	A26	12m dp bl	1.25	8
		Nos. 257-262 (6)	5.75	56

Pres. Juho K. Paasikivi
A65

Postal Savings Emblem
A66

1947, Mar. 15 **Engraved**

263	A65	10m gray blk	50	65

1947, Apr. 1

264	A66	10m brn vio	50	65

Issued to commemorate the 60th anniversary of the foundation of the Finnish Postal Savings Bank.

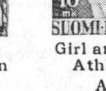

Ilmarinen, the Plowman
A67

Girl and Boy Athletes
A68

1947, June 2

265	A67	10m gray blk	50	65

Issued to mark the second year of peace following World War II.

1947, June 2

266	A68	10m brt bl	50	65

Issued to commemorate the Finnish Athletic Festival, Helsingfors, June 29–July 3, 1947.

Wheat and Savings Bank Association Emblem
A69

Sower
A70

1947, Aug. 21

267	A69	10m red brn	50	65

Issued to commemorate the 125th anniversary of the Finnish Savings Bank Association.

1947, Nov. 1

268	A70	10m gray blk	50	65

Issued to commemorate the 50th anniversary of Finnish Agricultural Societies.

Koli Mountain and Lake Pielisjärvi
A71

Statue of Michael Agricola
A72

1947, Nov. 1

269	A71	10m indigo	50	65

Issued to commemorate the 60th anniversary of the Finnish Touring Association.

Lion Type of 1930.

1948 **Typographed.** ***Perf. 14***

270	A26	3m dk grn	2.00	15
271	A26	6m yel grn	60	50
272	A26	9m carmine	45	8
273	A26	15m dk bl	4.00	8
274	A26	24m brn lake	1.25	30
		Nos. 270-274 (5)	8.30	1.11

No. 261 Surcharged with New Value and Bars in Black.

1948, Feb. 9

275	A26	12(m) on 10m pur	1.00	18

1948, Oct. 2 **Engraved** ***Perf. 14***

Design: 12m, Agricola translating New Testament.

276	A72	7m rose vio	1.25	1.75
277	A72	12m gray bl	1.25	1.75

Issued to commemorate the 400th anniversary of publication of the Finnish translation of the New Testament, by Michael Agricola.

Sveaborg Fortress
A73

Post Rider
A74

1948, Oct. 15

278	A73	12m dp grn	1.75	1.75

Issued to commemorate the 200th anniversary of the construction of Sveaborg Fortress on the Gulf of Finland.

1948, Oct. 27

279	A74	12m green	22.50	32.50

Issued to commemorate the Helsinki Philatelic Exhibition. Sold only at exhibition, for 62m of which 50m was entrance fee.

1949 **Castle Type of 1945.**

280	A57	35m violet	5.50	15

Sawmill and Cellulose Plant
A75

Pine Tree and Globe
A76

Woman with Torch
A77

1949, June 15

281 A75 9m brown 3.00 3.00
282 A76 15m dl grn 3.00 3.00

Issued to publicize the Third World Forestry Congress, Helsinki, July 10–20, 1949.

1949, July 16 Engraved *Perf. 14*

283 A77 5m dl grn 5.00 *12.00*
284 A77 15m red (*Worker*) 5.00 *12.00*

Issued to commemorate the 50th anniversary of the Finnish labor movement.

Harbor of Lappeenranta (Willmanstrand)
A78

Raahe (Brahestad)
A79

1949

285 A78 5m dk bl grn 1.00 90
286 A79 9m brn car 1.25 1.25
287 A78 15m brt bl (*Kristiinan-kaupunki*) 2.00 2.00

Issued to commemorate the 300th anniversary of the founding of Willmanstrand, Brahestad and Kristinestad (Kristiinankaupunki).

Issue dates: 5m, Aug. 6; 9m, Aug. 13; 15m, July 30.

Technical High School Badge
A80

Hannes Gebhard
A81

1949, Sept. 13

288 A80 15m ultra 1.00 1.00

Issued to commemorate the centenary of the founding of the technical school.

1949, Oct. 2

289 A81 15m dl grn 1.00 1.00

Issued to commemorate the 50th anniversary of the establishment of Finnish cooperatives.

Finnish Lake Country
A82

1949, Oct. 8

290 A82 15m blue 2.00 1.50

Issued to commemorate the 75th anniversary of the formation of the Universal Postal Union.

Lion Type of 1930

1950 Typographed *Perf. 14.*

291 A26 8m brt grn 65 1.00
292 A26 9m red org 1.00 50
293 A26 10m vio brn 4.50 10
294 A26 12m scarlet 65 15
295 A26 15m plum 12.00 10
296 A26 20m dp bl 4.50 10
Nos. 291-296 (6) 23.30 1.95

Forsell's Map of Old Helsinki
A83

J. A. Ehrenstrom and C. L. Engel
A84

City Hall
A85

1950, June 11 Engraved

297 A83 5m emerald 90 90
298 A84 9m brown 1.50 1.50
299 A85 15m dp bl 1.00 1.00

Issued to commemorate the 400th anniversary of the founding of Helsinki.

J. K. Paasikivi
A86

View of Kajaani
A87

1950, Nov. 27

300 A86 20m dp ultra 90 65

80th birthday of Pres. J. K. Paasikivi.

1951, July 7 *Perf. 14* Unwmkd.

301 A87 20m red brn 1.00 90

Tercentenary of Kajaani.

Lion and Chopper Types of 1930

1952 Typographed

302 A26 10m emerald 2.25 15
303 A26 15m red 3.25 12
304 A26 25m blue 4.00 10

Engraved

305 A29 40m blk brn 3.00 12

Arms of Pietarsaari
A88

Rooftops of Vaasa
A89

1952, June 19 *Perf. 14* Unwmkd.

306 A88 25m blue 1.25 1.00

Issued to commemorate the 300th anniversary of the founding of Pietarsaari (Jacobstad).

1952, Aug. 3

307 A89 25m brown 1.25 1.00

Centenary of the burning of Vaasa.

Chess Symbols
A90

1952, Aug. 10

308 A90 25m gray 3.00 3.00

Issued to publicize the 10th Chess Olympics, Helsinki, Aug. 10–31, 1952.

Torch Bearers
A91

1953, Jan. 27

309 A91 25m blue 1.50 1.00

Issued to commemorate the centenary of the temperance movement in Finland.

Air View of Hamina (Fredrikshamn)
A92

Ivar Wilskman
A93

1953, June 20

310 A92 25m dk gray grn 1.00 90

Tercentenary of Hamina.

1954, Feb. 26

311 A93 25m blue 1.00 65

Issued to commemorate the centenary of the birth of Prof. Ivar Wilskman, "father of gymnastics in Finland."

Arms of Finland
A94

"In the Outer Archipelago"
A95

1954–59 *Perf. 11½*

312 A94 1m red brn ('55) 60 8
313 A94 2m grn ('55) 60 8
314 A94 3m dp org 60 8
314A A94 4m gray ('58) 50 8
315 A94 5m vio bl 1.00 8
316 A94 10m bl grn 1.50 5
a. Bklt. pane of 5 (vert. strip) 30.00
317 A94 15m rose red 4.50 5
318 A94 15m yel org ('57) 10.00 8
319 A94 20m rose lil 12.00 10
320 A94 20m rose red ('56) 4.00 5
321 A94 25m dp bl 5.00 5
322 A94 25m rose lil ('59) 18.00 8
323 A94 30m lt ultra ('56) 4.00 5
Nos. 312-323 (13) 62.30 91

See Nos. 398, 400–405A, 457–459, 461A–462, 464–464B.

1954, July 21 *Perf. 14*

324 A95 25m black 1.00 75

Issued to commemorate the centenary of the birth of Albert Edelfelt, painter.

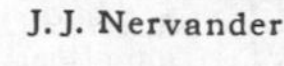

J. J. Nervander
A96

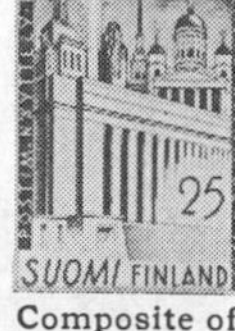

Composite of Finnish Public Buildings
A97

1955, Feb. 23

325 A96 25m blue 1.50 1.00

Issued to commemorate the 150th anniversary of the birth of J. J. Nervander, astronomer and poet.

1955, Mar. 20 Engraved *Perf. 14*

326 A97 25m gray 22.50 25.00

Sold for 125m, which included the price of admission to the National Postage Stamp Exhibition, Helsinki, March 30 to April 3, 1955.

Bishop Henrik with Foot on Lalli, his Murderer
A98

Conference Hall, Helsinki
A99

Design: 25m, Arrival of Bishop Henrik and monks.

1955, May 19

327 A98 15m rose brn 1.50 1.00
328 A98 25m green 1.50 1.00

Issued to commemorate the 800th anniversary of the adoption of Christianity in Finland.

1955, Aug. 25

329 A99 25m bluish grn 2.00 1.50

Issued to commemorate the 44th conference of the Interparliamentarian Union, Helsinki, Aug. 25-31, 1955.

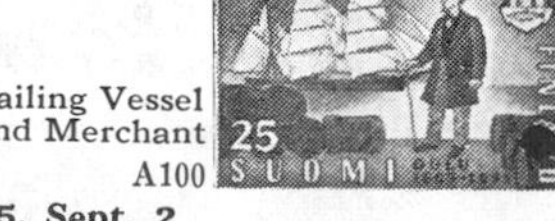

Sailing Vessel and Merchant
A100

1955, Sept. 2

330 A100 25m sepia 2.00 1.50

350th anniversary of founding of Oulu.

Town Hall, Lahti
A101

Radio Sender and Map of Finland
A102

1955, Nov. 1 *Perf. 14x13½*

331 A101 25m vio bl 1.75 1.25

50th anniversary of founding of Lahti.

1955, Dec. 10 *Perf. 14*

Designs: 15m, Otto Nyberg. 25m, Telegraph wires and pines under snow.

Inscribed:
Lennatin 1855-1955 Telegrafen.

332 A102 10m green 1.75 1.65
333 A102 15m dl vio 1.75 80
334 A102 25m lt ultra 1.75 80

Issued to commemorate the centenary of the telegraph in Finland.

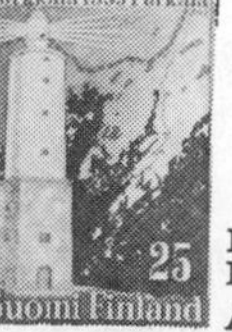

Lighthouse and Porkkala Peninsula
A103

1956, Jan. 26 *Perf. 14* **Unwmkd.**

335 A103 25m grnsh bl 1.25 80

Issued to commemorate the return of the Porkkala Region to Finland by Russia, Jan. 1956.

Church at Lammi
A104

Designs: 40m, House of Parliament. 60m, Fortress of Olavinlinna (Olofsborg).

1956–57 *Perf. 11½*

336	A104	30m gray ol	1.00	15
337	A104	40m dl pur	4.00	20
338	A104	50m gray ol ('57)	7.00	20
338A	A104	60m pale pur ('57)	16.00	20

See Nos. 406–408A.

Johan V. Snellman
A105

Gymnast and Athletes
A106

1956, May 12 Engraved *Perf. 14*

339 A105 25m dk vio brn 1.25 80

Issued to commemorate the 150th anniversary of the birth of Johan V. Snellman (1806–1881), statesman.

1956, June 28

340 A106 30m vio bl 1.50 1.00

Issued to commemorate the Finnish Gymnastic and Sports Games, Helsinki, June 28–July 1, 1956.

A107

Rouletted

1956, July 7 Typo. **Wmk. 208**

341 A107 30m dp ultra 5.00 7.00
a. Tête bêche pair 10.00 15.00
b. Pane of 10 55.00 80.00

Issued to publicize the FINLANDIA Philatelic Exhibition, Helsinki, July 7–15, 1956.

Printed in sheets containing four 2x5 panes, with white margins around each group. The stamps in each double row are printed tete-beche, making the position of the watermark differ in the vertical row of each pane of ten.

Sold for 155m, price including entrance ticket to exhibition.

Town Hall at Vasa
A108

Engraved.

1956, Oct. 2 *Perf. 14* **Unwmkd.**

342 A108 30m brt bl 1.25 80

350th anniversary of Vasa.

Northern Countries Issue.

Whooper Swans
A108a

1956, Oct. 30 *Perf. 12½*

343	A108a	20m rose red	5.00	2.50
344	A108a	30m ultra	16.00	2.25

See footnote after Denmark No. 362.

University Clinic, Helsinki
A109

Scout Sign, Emblem and Globe
A110

1956, Dec. 17 *Perf. 11½*

345 A109 30m dl grn 1.50 80

Issued to commemorate the bicentenary of public health service in Finland.

1957, Feb. 22 *Perf. 14*

346 A110 30m ultra 2.50 1.50

50th anniversary of Boy Scouts.

Arms Holding Hammers and Laurel
A111

"Lex" from Seal of Parliament
A112

Design: 20m, Factories and cogwheel.

1957 Engraved *Perf. 13½*

347	A111	20m dk bl	1.25	75
348	A111	30m carmine	1.25	1.00

50th anniv.: Central Fed. of Finnish Employers (20m, issued 9/27); Finnish Trade Union Movement (30m, issued 4/15).

1957, May 23 *Perf. 14*

349 A112 30m ol gray 1.25 1.00

Issued to commemorate the 50th anniversary of the Finnish parliament.

Harbor Type of 1942.

1957 *Perf. 14* **Unwmkd.**

350 A51 100m grnsh bl 9.00 20

Ida Aalberg
A114

Arms of Finland
A115

1957, Dec. 4 *Perf. 14*

351 A114 30m vio gray & mar 1.25 80

Issued to commemorate the centenary of the birth of Ida Aalberg, Finnish actress.

1957, Dec. 6 *Perf. 11½*

352 A115 30m blue 1.25 80

Issued to commemorate the 40th anniversary of Finland's independence.

Jean Sibelius
A116

Ski Jump
A117

1957, Dec. 8 *Perf. 14*

353 A116 30m black 1.25 80

Issued in memory of Jean Sibelius (1865–1957), composer.

1958, Feb. 1 Engraved *Perf. 11½*

Design: 30m, Skier (vertical).

354	A117	20m sl grn	1.25	1.25
355	A117	30m blue	1.50	75

Issued to publicize the Nordic championships of the International Ski Federation, Lahti.

"March of the Bjorneborgienses," by Edelfelt
A118

South Harbor, Helsinki
A119

1958, Mar. 8

356 A118 30m vio gray 2.00 1.00

Issued to commemorate the 400th anniversary of the founding of Pori (Bjorneborg).

1958, June 2 *Perf. 11½* **Unwmkd.**

357 A119 100m bluish grn 25.00 15

See No. 410.

Seal of Jyväsky lä Lyceum
A120

1958, Oct. 1 *Perf. 11½*

358 A120 30m rose car 2.00 1.25

Issued to commemorate the centenary of the founding of the first Finnish secondary school.

Chrismon and Globe
A121

Diet at Porvoo, 1809
A122

1959, Jan. 19

359 A121 30m dl vio 1.40 60

Issued to commemorate the centenary of the Finnish Missionary Society.

1959, Mar. 22 *Perf. 11½*

360 A122 30m dk bl gray 1.40 60

Issued to commemorate the 150th anniversary of the inauguration of the Diet at Porvoo.

Saw Cutting Log
A123

Pyhakoski Power Station
A124

Design: 30m, Forest.

1959, May 13 **Engraved**

361	A123	10m redsh brn	80	60
362	A123	30m green	1.00	1.00

No. 361 commemorates the centenary of the establishment of the first steam sawmill in Finland; No. 362, the centenary of the Department of Forestry.

1959, May 24

363 A124 75m gray 6.00 25

See No. 409.

Oil Lamp
A125

Woman Gymnast
A126

1959, Dec. 19

364 A125 30m blue 1.00 65

Issued to commemorate the centenary of the liberation of the country trade.

1959, Nov. 14 **Unwmkd.**

365 A126 30m rose lil 1.00 65

Issued to honor Finnish women's gymnastics and the centenary of the birth of Elin Oihonna Kallio, pioneer of Finnish women's physical education.

Arms of Six New Towns
A127

1960, Jan. 2 *Perf. 14*

366 A127 30m lt vio 1.00 65

Issued to commemorate the founding of new towns in Finland: Hyvinkaa, Kouvola, Riihimaki, Rovaniemi, Salo and Seinajoki.

Type of 1860 Issue
A128

Typographed

1960, Mar. 25 *Rouletted 4½*

367 A128 30m bl & gray 11.00 12.50

Issued to commemorate the centenary of Finland's serpentine roulette stamps, and in connection with HELSINKI 1960, 40th anniversary exhibition of the Federation of Philatelic Societies of Finland, March 25–31. Sold only at the exhibition for 150m including entrance ticket.

Mother and Child, Waiting Crowd and Uprooted Oak Emblem
A129

1960, Apr. 7 Engraved *Perf. 11½*

368	A129	30m rose cl	90	60
369	A129	40m dk bl	90	60

Issued to publicize World Refugee Year, July 1, 1959–June 30, 1960.

Johan Gadolin A130 **Hj. Nortamo A131**

1960, June 4 *Perf. 11½*

370	A130	30m dk brn	1.25	85

Issued to commemorate the bicentennary of the birth of Johan Gadolin, chemist.

1960, June 13 Unwmkd.

371	A131	30m gray grn	1.25	60

Issued to commemorate the centenary of the birth of Hj. Nortamo (Hjalmar Nordberg), writer.

Symbolic Tree and Cuckoo A132

1960, June 18

372	A132	30m vermilion	1.25	60

Karelian National Festival, Helsinki, June 18–19.

Geodetic Instrument A133 **Urho Kekkonen A134**

Design: 30m, Aurora borealis and globe.

1960, July 26 *Perf. 13½* Unwmkd.

373	A133	10m bl & pale brn	80	60
374	A133	30m ver & rose car	1.50	75

Issued to publicize the 12th General Assembly of the International Union of Geodesy and Geophysics, Helsinki.

1960, Sept. 3 Engraved *Perf. 11½*

375	A134	30m vio bl	1.25	60

Issued to honor President Urho Kekkonen on his 60th birthday.

Europa Issue, 1960
Common Design Type

1960, Sept. 19 *Perf. 13½*
Size: 30½x21mm.

376	CD3	30m dk bl & Prus bl	75	60
377	CD3	40m dk brn & plum	1.00	75

A 30m gray similar to No. 376 was printed with simulated perforations in a non-valid souvenir sheet privately released in London for STAMPEX 1961.

Uno Cygnaeus A135 **"Pommern" and Arms of Mariehamn A136**

1960, Oct. 13 *Perf. 11½*

378	A135	30m dl vio	1.25	60

Issued to commemorate the 150th anniversary of the birth of Pastor Uno Cygnaeus, founder of elementary schools.

1961, Feb. 21 *Perf. 11½*

379	A136	30m grnsh bl	4.25	1.75

Centenary of the founding of Mariehamn.

Lake and Rowboat
A137

Turku Castle
A138

1961 Engraved Unwmkd.

380	A137	5m green	50	20
381	A138	125m sl grn	30.00	60

See also Nos. 399, 411.

Postal Savings Bank Emblem A139 **Symbol of Standardization A140**

1961, May 24

382	A139	30m Prus grn	1.25	60

Issued to commemorate the 75th anniversary of Finland's Postal Savings Bank.

Lithographed

1961, June 5 *Perf. 14x13½*

383	A140	30m dk sl grn & org	1.25	60

Issued to commemorate the meeting of the International Organization for Standardization, ISO, Helsinki, June 5.

Juhani Aho A141

Engraved

1961, Sept. 11 *Perf. 11½* Unwmkd.

384	A141	30m red brn	1.25	60

Issued to commemorate the centenary of the birth of Juhani Aho (1861–1921), writer.

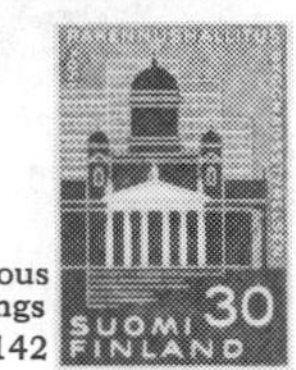

Various Buildings A142

1961, Oct. 16 *Perf. 11½*

385	A142	30m slate	1.25	60

Issued to commemorate 150 years of the Central Board of Buildings.

Arvid Jarnefelt A143

1961, Nov. 16

386	A143	30m dp cl	1.25	60

Issued to commemorate the centenary of the birth of Arvid Jarnefelt, writer.

Bank of Finland A144 **First Finnish Locomotive A145**

1961, Dec. 12 Engraved *Perf. 11½*

387	A144	30m brn vio	1.25	60

150th anniversary of Bank of Finland.

1962, Jan. 31 *Perf. 11½* Unwmkd.

Designs: 30m, Steam locomotive and timber car. 40m, Diesel locomotive and passenger train.

388	A145	10m gray grn	1.25	60
389	A145	30m vio bl	1.50	60
390	A145	40m dl red brn	4.00	80

Centenary of the Finnish State Railways.

Mora Stone A146

1962, Feb. 15

391	A146	30m gray brn	1.25	60

Issued to commemorate 600 years of political rights of the Finnish people.

Senate Place, Helsinki
A147

1962, Apr. 8 *Perf. 11½* Unwmkd.

392	A147	30m vio brn	1.25	60

Issued to commemorate the sesquicentennial of the proclamation of Helsinki as capital of Finland.

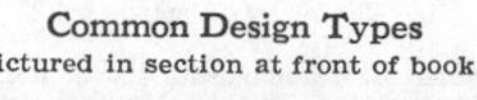

Common Design Types pictured in section at front of book.

Customs Emblem A148 **Staff of Mercury A149**

1962, Apr. 11

393	A148	30m red	1.25	60

Issued to commemorate the sesquicentennial of the Finnish Board of Customs.

1962, May 21 Engraved

394	A149	30m bluish grn	1.25	60

Issued to commemorate the centenary of the first commercial bank in Finland.

Santeri Alkio A150 **Finnish Labor Emblem and Conveyor Belt A151**

1962, June 17 *Perf. 11½* Unwmkd.

395	A150	30m brn car	1.25	60

Issued to commemorate the centenary of the birth of Santeri Alkio, writer and pioneer of the young people's societies in Finland.

1962, Oct. 19

396	A151	30m chocolate	1.25	60

National production progress.

Survey Plane and Compass A152

1962, Nov. 14

397	A152	30m yel grn	1.25	60

Issued to commemorate the 150th anniversary of the Finnish Land Survey Board.

Types of 1954–61 and

Log Floating A153

Parainen Bridge A154

Farm on Lake Shore A155

Ristikallio in Kuusamo—A156

Designs: 40p, House of Parliament. 50p, Church at Lammi. 60p, 65p, Fortress of Olavinlinna. 2.50m, Aerial view of Punkaharju.

1963–67 Engraved *Perf. 11½*

398	A94	5p vio bl	40	6
a.		Booklet pane of 2 (vert. pair)	27.50	
b.		Bklt. pane of 2 (horiz. pair)	35.00	
399	A137	5p green	30	8
400	A94	10p bl grn	50	6
a.		Booklet pane of 2 (vert pair)	27.50	
401	A94	15p yel org	1.40	6
402	A94	20p rose red	90	6
a.		Booklet pane of 1	27.50	
b.		Bklt. pane of 3 (2 No. 400, 1 No. 402 + label; horiz. strip)	50.00	
c.		Bklt. pane of 5 (2 No. 398, 2 No. 400, 1 No. 402; horiz. strip)	6.00	
403	A94	25p rose lil	60	6
404	A94	30p lt ultra	7.00	6
404A	A94	30p bl gray ('65)	75	6
405	A94	35p blue	1.50	6
405A	A94	40p ultra ('67)	2.00	6
406	A104	40p dl pur	2.00	10
407	A104	50p gray ol	2.00	10
408	A104	60p pale pur	5.00	10
408A	A104	65p pale pur ('67)	1.50	10
409	A124	75p gray	2.00	10
410	A119	1m bluish grn	55	5
411	A138	1.25m sl grn	2.25	10
412	A153	1.50m dk grnsh gray	1.10	8
413	A154	1.75m blue	1.75	10
414	A155	2m grn ('64)	2.25	20
414A	A155	2.50m ultra & yel ('67)	3.00	25
415	A156	5m dk sl grn ('64)	7.00	60
		Nos. 398-415 (22)	45.75	2.50

Pennia denominations expressed: "0,05", "0,10", etc.

Four stamps of type A94 (5p, 10p, 20p, 25p) come in two types: I. Four vertical lines in "O" of SUOMI. II. Three lines in "O."

See also Nos. 457–464B.

Mother and Child A157

1963, Mar. 21 *Perf. 11½* Unwmkd.

416	A157	40p red brn	1.00	60

Issued for the "Freedom from Hunger" campaign of the U.N. Food and Agriculture Organization.

"Christ Today" A158

Design: 10p, Crown of thorns and medieval cross of consecration.

1963, July 30 Engraved *Perf. 11½*

417	A158	10p maroon	60	60
418	A158	30p dk grn	1.00	60

Issued to commemorate the 4th assembly of the Lutheran World Federation, Helsinki, July 30–Aug. 8.

Europa Issue, 1963

Common Design Type

1963, Sept. 16

Size: 30x20mm.

419	CD6	40p red lil	1.50	60

Assembly Building, Helsinki A159

1963, Sept. 18

420	A159	30p vio bl	1.25	60

Issued to commemorate the centenary of the Representative Assembly of Finland.

Convair Metropolitan A160

M. A. Castrén A161

Design: 40p, Caravelle jetliner.

1963, Nov. 1

421	A160	35p sl grn	1.25	60
422	A160	40p brt ultra	1.25	60

40th anniversary of Finnish air traffic.

1963, Dec. 2 Unwmkd.

423	A161	35p vio bl	1.25	60

Issued to commemorate the 150th anniversary of the birth of Matthias Alexander Castrén (1813–52), ethnologist and philologist.

Stone Elk's Head, 2000 B.C. A162

Emil Nestor Setälä A163

1964, Feb. 5 Litho. *Perf. 11½*

424	A162	35p ocher & sl grn	1.25	60

Issued to commemorate the centenary of the Finnish Artists' Association. The soapstone sculpture was found at Huittinen.

1964, Feb. 27 Engraved

425	A163	35p dk red brn	1.25	60

Issued to commemorate the centenary of the birth of Emil Nestor Setälä (1864–1946), philologist, minister of education and foreign affairs and chancellor of Abo University.

Staff of Aesculapius A164

1964, June 13 *Perf. 11½* Unwmkd.

426	A164	40p sl grn	1.25	60

Issued to commemorate the 18th General Assembly of the World Medical Association, Helsinki, June 13–19, 1964.

Ice Hockey A165

1965, Jan. 4 Engraved

427	A165	35p dk bl	1.25	60

Issued to publicize the World Ice Hockey Championships, Finland, March 3–14, 1965.

Design from Centenary Medal A166

1965, Feb. 6 *Perf. 11½* Unwmkd.

428	A166	35p ol gray	1.25	60

Issued to commemorate the centenary of communal self-government in Finland.

K. J. Stahlberg and "Lex" by W. Runeberg A167

1965, Mar. 22 Engraved

429	A167	35p brown	1.25	60

Issued to commemorate the centenary of the birth of Kaarlo Juho Stahlberg (1865–1952), first President of Finland.

International Cooperation Year Emblem A168

1965, Apr. 2 Lithographed *Perf. 14*

430	A168	40p bis, dl red, blk & grn	1.25	60

U.N. International Cooperation Year.

"Fratricide" by Gallen-Kallela A169

Sibelius, Piano and Score A170

Design: 35p, Girl's Head by Aksell Gallen-Kallela.

1965, Aug. 26 *Perf. 13½x14*

431	A169	25p multi	1.50	65
432	A169	35p multi	1.50	65

Issued to commemorate the centenary of the birth of the painter Aksell Gallen-Kallela.

1965, May 15 Engraved *Perf. 11½*

Design: 35p, Musical score and bird.

433	A170	25p violet	1.25	55
434	A170	35p dl grn	1.25	55

Issued to commemorate the centenary of the birth of Jean Sibelius (1865–1957), composer.

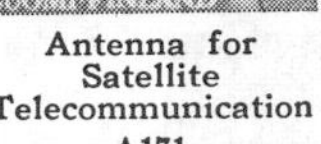

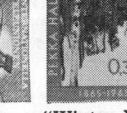

Antenna for Satellite Telecommunication A171

"Winter Day" by Pekka Halonen A172

1965, May 17

435	A171	35p blue	1.25	60

Issued to commemorate the centenary of the International Telecommunication Union.

Perf. 14x13½

1965, Sept. 23 Litho. Unwmkd.

436	A172	35p gold & multi	1.25	60

Issued to commemorate the centenary of the birth of the painter Pekka Halonen.

Europa Issue, 1965

Common Design Type

Engraved and Lithographed

1965, Sept. 27 *Perf. 13½x14*

437	CD8	40p bis, red brn, dk bl & grn	1.25	60

"Growth" A173

Old Post Office A174

1966, May 11 Litho. *Perf. 14*

438	A173	35p vio bl & bl	1.00	45

Issued to commemorate the centenary of the promulgation of the Elementary School Decree.

1966, June 11 Litho. *Perf. 14*

439	A174	35p ocher, yel, dk bl & blk	11.00	12.50

Issued to commemorate the centenary of the first postage stamps in Finnish currency, and in connection with the NORDIA Stamp Exhibition, Helsinki, June 11–15. The stamp was sold only to buyers of a 1.25m exhibition entrance ticket.

UNESCO Emblem and World Map A175

Finnish Police Emblem A176

Lithographed and Engraved

1966, Oct. 9 *Perf. 14*

440	A175	40p grn, yel, blk & brn org	1.25	45

Issued to commemorate the 20th anniversary of UNESCO (United Nations Educational, Scientific and Cultural Organization).

1966, Oct. 15

441	A176	35p dp ultra, blk & sil	1.25	45

Issued to honor the Finnish police.

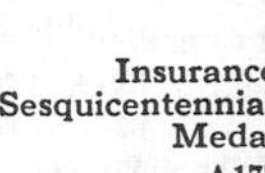

Insurance Sesquicentennial Medal A177

Engraved and Photogravure

1966, Oct. 28 *Perf. 14*

442	A177	35p mar, ol & blk	1.25	45

Issued to commemorate the 150th anniversary of the Finnish insurance system.

UNICEF Emblem A178

1966, Nov. 14

443 A178 15p lt ultra, pur & grn 75 40

Issued to publicize the activities of UNICEF (United Nations Children's Emergency Fund).

"FINEFTA," Finnish Flag and Circle
A179

1967, Feb. 15 Engraved *Perf. 14*

444 A179 40p ultra 1.25 40

Issued to publicize the European Free Trade Association, EFTA. See note after Denmark No. 431.

Windmill and Arms of Uusikaupunki
A180

Mannerheim Monument by Aimo Tukiainen
A181

Lithographed and Engraved

1967, Apr. 19 *Perf. 14*

445 A180 40p multi 1.25 40

Issued to commemorate the 350th anniversary of Uusikaupunki (Nystad).

1967, June 4 *Perf. 14*

446 A181 40p vio & multi 1.25 40

Issued to commemorate the centenary of the birth of Field Marshal Carl Gustav Emil Mannerheim.

Double Mortise Corner
A182

Watermark of Thomasböle Paper Mill
A183

Lithographed and Photogravure

1967, June 16

447 A182 40p multi 1.25 40

Issued to honor Finnish settlers in Sweden.

Lithographed and Engraved

1967, Sept. 6 *Perf. 14*

448 A183 40p ol & blk 1.25 40

Issued to commemorate the 300th anniversary of the Finnish paper industry.

Martin Luther, by Lucas Cranach
A184

Photogravure and Engraved

1967, Nov. 4 *Perf. 14*

449 A184 40p bis & brn 1.25 40

450th anniversary of the Reformation.

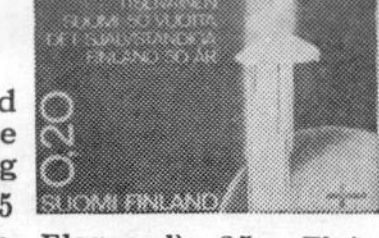

"Wood and Water" Globe and Flag
A185

Designs (Globe, Flag and): 25p, Flying swan. 40p, Ear of wheat.

1967, Dec. 5 *Perf. 11½*

450	A185	20p grn & bl	1.25	40
451	A185	25p ultra & bl	1.25	40
452	A185	40p mag & bl	1.25	40

Issued to commemorate the 50th anniversary of Finland's independence.

Zachris Topelius and Blue Bird
A186

1968, Jan. 14 Litho. *Perf. 14*

453 A186 25p bl & multi 1.25 40

Issued to commemorate the 150th anniversary of the birth of Zachris Topelius (1818–1898), writer and educator.

Skiers and Ski Lift
A187

1968, Feb. 19 Photo. *Perf. 14*

454 A187 25p multi 1.25 40

Issued to publicize Winter Tourism in Finland.

Paper Making, by Hannes Autere
A188

Wmk. 363

Wmkd. Tree Stump (363)

1968, Mar. 12 Lithographed

455 A188 45p dk red, brn & org 1.25 40

Issued to publicize the Finnish paper industry and to commemorate the 150th anniversary of the oldest Finnish paper mill, Tervakoski, whose own watermark was used for this stamp.

World Health Organization Emblem
A189

Lithographed and Photogravure

1968, Apr. 6 *Perf. 14* Unwmkd.

456 A189 40p red org, dk bl & gold 1.25 40

To honor World Health Organization.

Lion Type of 1954–58 and

Market Place and Mermaid Fountain, Helsinki
A190

Keuru Wooden Church, 1758
A191

Häme Bridge, Tampere—A192

Finnish Arms from Grave of King Gustav Vasa, 1581
A194

Designs: 25p, Post bus. 30p, Aquarium-Planetarium, Tampere. No. 463, P.O., Tampere. No. 465, National Museum, Helsinki (vert.). No. 467A, like 70p. 1.30m, Helsinki railroad station.

Engr. (type A94); Litho. (#465 & type A190); Engr. & Litho. (others).

Perf. 11½; 12½ (type A190); 14 (#465, 470A); 13½ (#470).

1968–78

457	A94	1p lt red brn	50	10
458	A94	2p gray grn	50	10
459	A94	4p gray	50	10
460	A192	25p multi ('71)	50	10
461	A191	30p multi ('71)	1.25	15
461A	A94	35p dl org ('74)	50	6
b.		Bklt. pane of 4 (#398, #461A, #400, #464A) + label	4.00	
462	A94	40p org ('73)	75	10
a.		Bklt. pane of 3 (2 #404A, #462) + 2 labels	10.00	
463	A192	40p multi ('73)	1.25	10
464	A94	50p lt ultra ('70)	1.25	5
c.		Bklt. pane of 5 (#401, #403, #464, 2 #398) + 5 labels	12.00	
464A	A94	50p rose lake ('74)	1.00	5
d.		Bklt. pane of 4 (#400, 2 #402, #464A) + label	3.00	
464B	A94	60p bl ('73)	75	5
465	A191	60p multi ('73)	60	10
466	A190	70p multi ('73)	1.00	10
467	A191	80p multi ('70)	3.00	10
467A	A190	80p multi ('76)	60	10
468	A192	90p multi	2.50	10
469	A191	1.30m multi ('71)	1.25	12
470	A194	10m multi ('74)	4.00	60
470A	A194	20m multi ('78)	8.00	1.50
		Nos. 457-470A (19)	29.70	3.68

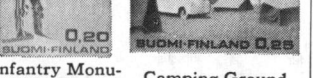

Infantry Monument, Vaasa
A195

Camping Ground
A196

Designs: 25p, War Memorial (cross), Hietaniemi Cemetery. 40p, Soldier, 1968.

1968, June 4 Photo. *Perf. 14*

471	A195	20p lt vio & multi	1.50	45
472	A195	25p lt bl & multi	1.50	45
473	A195	40p org & multi	1.50	45

To honor Finnish national defense.

1968, June 10 Lithographed

474 A196 25p multi 1.25 40

Issued to publicize Finland for summer vacations.

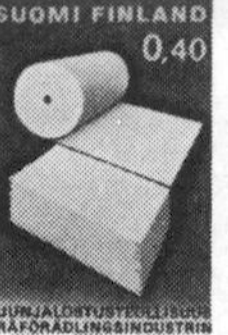

Paper, Pulp and Pine
A197

Mustola Lock, Saima Canal
A198

Lithographed and Embossed

1968, July 2 *Perf. 14* Unwmkd.

475 A197 40p multi 1.25 40

Finnish wood industry.

1968, Aug. 5 Litho. *Perf. 14*

476 A198 40p multi 1.25 40

Opening of the Saima Canal.

Oskar Merikanto and Pipe Organ
A199

1968, Aug. 5 Unwmkd.

477 A199 40p vio, sil & lt brn 1.25 40

Issued to commemorate the centenary of the birth of Oskar Merikanto, composer.

Ships in Harbor and Emblem of Central Chamber of Commerce
A200

Welder
A201

1968, Sept. 13 Litho. *Perf. 14*

478 A200 40p lt bl, brt bl & blk 1.25 40

Issued to publicize economic development and to commemorate the 50th anniversary of the Central Chamber of Commerce of Finland.

1968, Oct. 11 Lithographed *Perf. 14*

479 A201 40p bl & multi 1.25 40

Finnish metal industry.

Lyre, Students' Emblem
A202

Five Ancient Ships
A203

Lithographed and Engraved

1968, Nov. 24 *Perf. 14*

480 A202 40p ultra, vio bl & gold 1.25 40

Issued to publicize the work of the student unions in Finnish social life.

Nordic Cooperation Issue

1968, Feb. 28 Engraved *Perf. 11½*

481 A203 40p lt ultra 3.00 45

See footnote after Denmark No. 455.

Town Hall and Arms of Kemi
A203a

1969, Mar. 5 **Photo.** ***Perf. 14***

482 A203a 40p multi 1.25 40

Centenary of the town of Kemi.

Europa Issue, 1969
Common Design Type

1969, Apr. 28 **Photo.** ***Perf. 14***
Size: 30x20mm.

483 CD12 40p dl rose, vio bl & dk bl 3.00 70

I.L.O. Emblem
A204

Armas Järnefelt
A205

Lithographed and Engraved

1969, June 2 ***Perf. 11½***

484 A204 40p dp rose & vio bl 1.25 40

Issued to commemorate the 50th anniversary of the International Labor Organization.

1969, Aug. 14 **Photo.** ***Perf. 14***

485 A205 40p multi 1.25 40

Centenary of the birth of Armas Järnefelt (1869–1958), composer and conductor. Portrait on stamp by Vilho Sjöström.

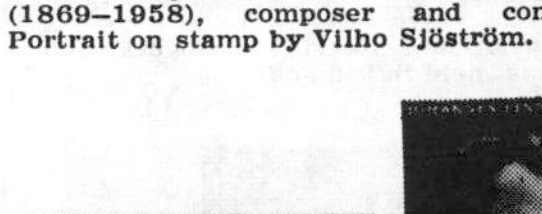

Emblems and Flag
A206

Johannes Linnankoski
A207

1969, Sept. 19 **Photo.** ***Perf. 14***

486 A206 40p lt bl, blk, grn & lil 1.25 40

Issued to publicize the importance of National and International Fairs in Finnish economy.

1969, Oct. 18 **Lithographed**

487 A207 40p dk brn red & multi 1.25 40

Issued to commemorate the centenary of the birth of Johannes Linnankoski (1869–1913), writer.

Educational Symbols
A208

Lithographed and Engraved

1969, Nov. 24 ***Perf. 11½***

488 A208 40p gray, vio & grn 1.25 40

Centenary of the Central School Board.

DC-8-62 CF Plane and Helsinki Airport
A209

1969, Dec. 22 **Photo.** ***Perf. 14***

489 A209 25p sky bl & multi 1.25 40

Golden Eagle
A210

1970, Feb. 10 **Litho.** ***Perf. 14***

490 A210 30p multi 4.00 1.00

Year of Nature Conservation, 1970.

Swatches in Shape of Factories
A211

1970, Mar. 9 **Litho.** ***Perf. 14***

491 A211 50p multi 1.25 40

Finnish textile industry.

Molecule Diagram and Factories
A212

UNESCO Emblem and Lenin
A213

Atom Diagram and Laurel
A214

U.N. Emblem and Globe
A215

1970, Mar. 26 **Photo.** ***Perf. 14***

492 A212 50p multi 1.25 40

Finnish chemical industry.

1970 **Litho. and Engraved**

493 A213 30p gold & multi 1.25 40
494 A214 30p red & multi 1.25 40

Photogravure and Gold Embossed

495 A215 50p bl, vio bl & gold 1.25 40

Issued to commemorate the 25th anniversary of the United Nations. No. 493 also publicizes the UNESCO-sponsored Lenin Symposium, Tampere, Apr. 6–10. No. 494 also publicizes the Nuclear Data Conference of the Atomic Energy Commission, Otaniemi (Helsinki), June 15–19.

Issue dates: No. 493, Apr. 6; No. 494, June 15; No. 495, Oct. 24.

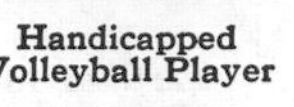

Handicapped Volleyball Player
A216

Meeting of Auroraseura Society
A217

1970, June 27 **Litho.** ***Perf. 14***

496 A216 50p org, red & blk 1.50 40

Issued to publicize the position of handicapped civilians and war veterans in society and their potential contributions to it.

1970, Aug. 15 **Photo.** ***Perf. 14***

497 A217 50p multi 1.25 40

Issued to commemorate the 200th anniversary of the Auroraseura Society, dedicated to the study of Finnish history, geography, economy and language. The design of the stamp is after a painting by Eero Jarnefelt.

Uusikaarlepyy Arms, Church and 17th Century Building—A218

Urho Kekkonen, Medal by Aimo Tukiainen
A219

Design: No. 499, Arms of Kokkola, harbor, Sports Palace and 17th century building.

1970 ***Perf. 14***

498 A218 50p multi 1.25 40
499 A218 50p multi 1.25 40

Issued to commemorate the 350th anniversaries of the towns of Uusikaarlepyy and Kokkola. Issue dates: No. 498, Aug. 21; No. 499, Sept. 17.

1970, Sept. 3 **Litho. & Engr.**

500 A219 50p ultra, sil & blk 1.25 40

70th birthday of Pres. Urho Kekkonen.

Globe, Maps of U.S., Finland, U.S.S.R.—A220

Pres. Paasikivi by Essi Renavall
A221

Lithographed and Gold Embossed

1970, Nov. 2

501 A220 50p blk, bl, pink & gold 1.25 40

Issued to publicize the Strategic Arms Limitation Talks (SALT) between the U.S. and U.S.S.R., Helsinki, Nov. 2–Dec. 18.

1970, Nov. 27 **Photo.** ***Perf. 14***

502 A221 50p gold, brt bl & sl 1.75 40

Centenary of the birth of Juho Kusti Paasikivi (1870–1956), President of Finland.

Cogwheels
A222

1971, Jan. 28 **Litho.** ***Perf. 14***

503 A222 50p multi 1.25 40

Finnish industry.

Europa Issue, 1971
Common Design Type

1971, May 3 **Litho.** ***Perf. 14***
Size: 30x20mm.

504 CD14 50p dp rose, yel & blk 2.75 60

Tornio Church
A223

Front Page, January 15, 1771
A224

1971, May 12 **Litho.** ***Perf. 14***

505 A223 50p multi 1.25 40

350th anniversary of the town of Tornio.

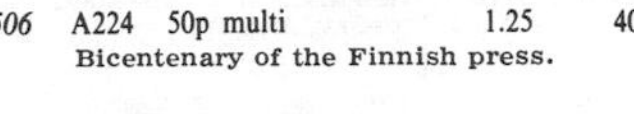

1971, June 1 **Litho.** ***Perf. 14***

506 A224 50p multi 1.25 40

Bicentenary of the Finnish press.

Athletes in Helsinki Stadium
A225

Design: 50p, Running and javelin in Helsinki Stadium.

1971, July 5 Lithographed ***Perf. 14***

507 A225 30p multi 1.25 60
508 A225 50p multi 2.75 60

European Athletic Championships.

Sailboats
A226

1971, July 14

509 A226 50p multi 1.50 60

International Lightning Class Championships, Helsinki, July 14–Aug. 1.

Silver Tea Pot, Guild's Emblem, Tools
A227

1971, Aug. 6

510 A227 50p lil & multi 1.25 40

600th anniversary of Finnish goldsmiths' art.

"Plastic Buttons and Houses"
A228

Photogravure and Embossed

1971, Oct. 20 *Perf. 14*

511 A228 50p multi 1.25 40

Finnish plastics industry.

Europa Issue 1972

Common Design Type

1972, May 2 Litho. *Perf. 14*

Size: 20x30mm.

512 CD15 30p dk red & multi 2.00 60
513 CD15 50p lt brn & multi 3.00 60

Finnish National Theater
A229

1972, May 22 Litho. *Perf. 14*

514 A229 50p lt vio & multi 1.25 40

Centenary of the Finnish National Theater, founded by Kaarlo and Emilie Bergbom.

Globe, U.S. and U.S.S.R. Flags
A230

1972, June 2

515 A230 50p multi 1.75 50

Strategic Arms Limitation Talks (SALT), final meeting, Helsinki, Mar. 28–May 26; treaty signed, Moscow, May 26.

Map and Arms of Aland
A231

Training Ship Suomen Joutsen
A232

1972, June 9

516 A231 50p multi 5.50 1.25

50th anniversary of first Provincial Meeting of Aland.

1972, June 19

517 A232 50p org & multi 1.50 50

Tall Ships' Race 1972, Helsinki, Aug. 20.

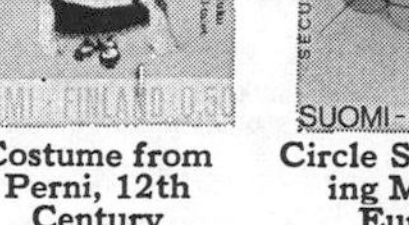

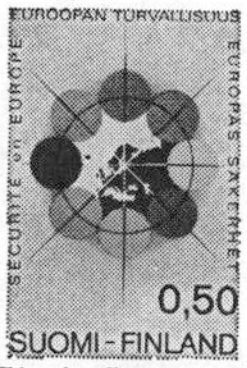

Costume from Perni, 12th Century
A233

Circle Surrounding Map of Europe
A234

1972, Nov. 19 Litho. *Perf. 13*

Multicolored

518 A233 50p *shown* 1.75 40
519 A233 50p *Couple, Tenhola, 18th cent.* 1.75 40
520 A233 50p *Girl, Nastola, 19th century* 1.75 40
521 A233 50p *Man, Voyni, 19th century* 1.75 40
522 A233 50p *Lapps, Inari, 19th century* 1.75 40
a. Booklet pane of 10 20.00
Nos. 518-522 (5) 8.75 2.00

Regional costumes. Nos. 518–522 printed se-tenant.

No. 522a contains 2 each of Nos. 518–522.

See Nos. 533–537.

1972, Dec. 11 *Perf. 14x13½*

523 A234 50p multi 4.00 75

Preparatory Conference on European Security and Cooperation.

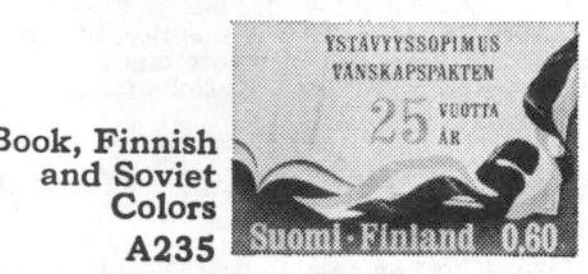

Book, Finnish and Soviet Colors
A235

Litho.; Gold Embossed

1973, Apr. 6 *Perf. 14*

524 A235 60p gold & multi 1.50 40

25th anniversary of the Soviet-Finnish Treaty of Friendship.

Pres. Kyösti Kallio
A236

1973, Apr. 10 Litho. *Perf. 13*

525 A236 60p multi 1.50 40

Centenary of the birth of Kyösti Kallio (1873–1940), president of Finland.

Europa Issue 1973

Common Design Type

1973, Apr. 30 Photo. *Perf. 14*

Size: 31x21mm.

526 CD16 60p bl, brt bl & emer 1.25 50

Nordic Cooperation Issue

Nordic House, Reykjavik
A236a

1973, June 26 Engr. *Perf. 12½*

527 A236a 60p multi 1.50 50
528 A236a 70p multi 1.50 50

A century of postal cooperation among Denmark, Finland, Iceland, Norway and Sweden, and in connection with the Nordic Postal Conference, Reykjavik.

Map of Europe, "EUROPA" as a Maze
A237

Litho., Embossed

1973, July 3 *Perf. 13*

529 A237 70p multi 1.25 40

Conference for European Security and Cooperation, Helsinki, July 1973.

Paddling
A238

Radiosonde, WMO Emblem
A239

1973, July 18 Litho. *Perf. 14*

530 A238 60p multi 1.25 40

Canoeing World Championships, Tampere, July 26–29.

1973, Aug. 6 Litho. *Perf. 14*

531 A239 60p multi 1.25 40

Centenary of international meteorological cooperation.

Eliel Saarinen and Design for Parliament, Helsinki
A240

1973, Aug. 20 *Perf. 12½x13*

532 A240 60p multi 1.25 40

Centenary of the birth of Eliel Saarinen (1873–1950), architect.

Costume Type of 1972

1973, Oct. 10 Litho. *Perf. 13*

Multicolored

533 A233 60p *Woman, Kaukola* 3.75 40
534 A233 60p *Woman, Jaaski* 3.75 40
535 A233 60p *Married couple, Koivisto* 3.75 40
536 A233 60p *Mother and son, Sakyla* 3.75 40
537 A233 60p *Girl, Hainavesi* 3.75 40
Nos. 533-537 (5) 18.75 2.00

Regional costumes. Nos. 533–537 printed se-tenant.

DC10–30 Jet
A241

1973, Nov. 1 Litho. *Perf. 14*

538 A241 60p multi 1.25 40

50th anniversary of regular air service, Finnair.

Santa Claus in Reindeer Sleigh
A242

1973, Nov. 15 Litho. *Perf. 14*

539 A242 30p multi 1.00 25

Christmas 1973.

"The Barber of Seville"
A243

1973, Nov. 21

540 A243 60p multi 1.25 40

Centenary of opera in Finland.

Production of Porcelain Jug
A244

Nurmi, by Waino Aaltonen
A245

1973, Nov. 23

541 A244 60p bl & multi 1.25 40

Finnish porcelain.

1973, Dec. 11

542 A245 60p multi 1.25 40

Paavo Nurmi (1897–1973), runner, Olympic winner, 1920–1924–1928.

Arms, Map and Harbor of Hanko
A246

1974, Jan. 10 Litho. *Perf. 14*

543 A246 60p bl & multi 1.25 40

Centenary of the town of Hanko.

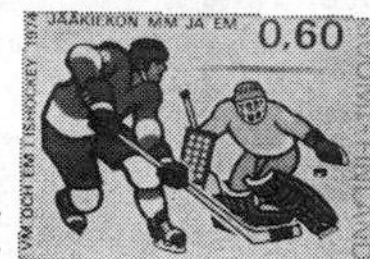

Ice Hockey
A247

1974, Mar. 5 Lithographed *Perf. 14*

544 A247 60p multi 1.25 40

European and World Ice Hockey Championships, held in Finland.

Seagulls (7 Baltic States)
A248

1974, Mar. 18 *Perf. 12½*

545 A248 60p multi 1.25 40

Protection of marine environment of the Baltic Sea.

Goddess of Freedom, by Waino Aaltonen
A249

Ilmari Kianto and Old Pine
A250

Europa Issue, 1974

1974, Apr. 29 Litho. *Perf. 13x12½*

546 A249 70p multi 1.25 40

1974, May 7 *Perf. 13*

547 A250 60p multi 1.25 40

Ilmari Kianto (1874–1970), writer.

Society Emblem, Symbol
A251

Lithographed and Embossed

1974, June 12 *Perf. 13½x14*

548 A251 60p gold & multi 1.25 40

Centenary of Adult Education.

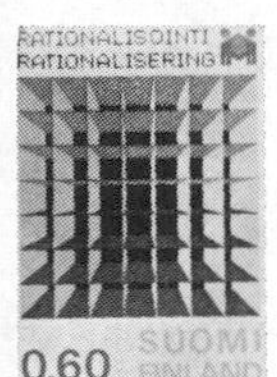

Grid
A252

UPU Emblem
A253

1974, June 14 Litho. *Perf. 14x13½*

549 A252 60p multi 1.25 40

Rationalization Year in Finland, dedicated to economic and business improvements.

1974, Oct. 10 Litho. *Perf. 13½x14*

550 A253 60p multi 1.25 40
551 A253 70p multi 1.25 40

Centenary of Universal Postal Union.

Elves Distributing Gifts
A254

Concrete Bridge and Granite Bridge, Aunessilta
A255

1974, Nov. 16 Litho. *Perf. 14x13½*

552 A254 35p multi 1.00 40

Christmas 1974.

Lithographed and Engraved

1974, Dec. 17 *Perf. 14*

553 A255 60p multi 1.25 40

Royal Finnish Directorate of Roads and Waterways, 175th anniversary.

Coat of Arms, 1581
A256

Chimneyless Log Sauna
A256a

Cheese Frames
A257

Carved Wooden Distaffs
A258

Kirvu Weather Vane
A258a

Design: 1.50m, Wood-carved high drinking bowl, 1542.

Perf. 11½; 14 (2m)

1975–79 **Engraved**

No.	Type	Value	Unused	Used
555	A256	10p red lil ('78)	6	5
a.		Bklt. pane of 4 (#555, 2 #556, #559) + label	1.25	
b.		Bklt. pane of 5 (2 #555, #557, #563, #564)	2.25	
c.		As #555a, no label	60	
556	A256	20p ol ('77)	12	5
557	A256	30p car ('77)	18	5
558	A256	40p orange	22	5
559	A256	50p grn ('76)	28	5
560	A256	60p blue	35	5
561	A256	70p sepia	40	5
562	A256	80p dl red & bl grn ('76)	45	5
563	A256	90p vio ('77)	50	5
564	A256	1.10m yel ('79)	55	8
565	A256	1.20m dk bl ('79)	60	10
566	A258	1.50m multi ('76)	70	10
567	A256a	2m multi, litho. ('77)	90	25

Lithographed and Engraved

No.	Type	Value	Unused	Used
568	A257	2.50m multi ('76)	1.10	25
569	A258	4.50m multi ('76)	2.00	25
570	A258a	5m multi ('77)	2.25	25
		Nos. 555-570 (16)	10.66	1.73

Finland No. 16
A259

Girl Combing Hair, by Magnus Enckell
A260

Lithographed and Typographed

1975, Apr. 26 *Perf. 13*

571 A259 70p multi 4.50 5.00

Nordia 75 Philatelic Exhibition, Helsinki, Apr. 26–May 1. Sold only at exhibition for 3m including entrance ticket.

Europa Issue 1975

Design: 90p, Washerwoman, by Tyko Sallinen (1879–1955).

1975, Apr. 28 Litho. *Perf. 13x12½*

572 A260 70p gray & multi 1.25 40
573 A260 90p tan & multi 1.25 40

Balance of Justice, Sword of Legality
A261

Rescue Boat and Sinking Ship
A262

1975, May 7 *Perf. 14*

574 A261 70p vio bl & multi 1.00 40

Sesquicentennial of State Economy Comptroller's Office.

1975, June 2 Litho. *Perf. 14*

575 A262 70p multi 1.25 40

12th International Salvage Conference, Finland, stressing importance of coordinating sea, air and communications resources in salvage operations.

Safe and Unsafe Levels of Drugs
A263

1975, July 21 Litho. *Perf. 14*

576 A263 70p multi 1.00 40

Importance of pharmacological studies and for the 6th International Pharmacology Congress, Helsinki.

Olavinlinna Castle
A264

1975, July 29 *Perf. 13*

577 A264 70p multi 1.00 40

500th anniversary of Olavinlinna Castle.

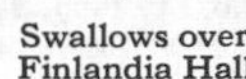

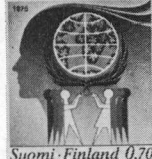

Swallows over Finlandia Hall
A265

"Men and Women Working for Peace"
A266

1975, July 30

578 A265 90p multi 1.25 40

European Security and Cooperation Conference, Helsinki, July 30–Aug. 1. (The swallows of the design represent freedom, mobility and continuity.) See No. 709

1975, Oct. 24 Litho. *Perf. 13x12½*

579 A266 70p multi 1.00 40

International Women's Year 1975.

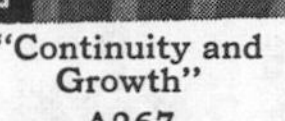

"Continuity and Growth"
A267

Boys as Three Kings and Herod
A268

1975, Oct. 29 *Perf. 13*

580 A267 70p brn & multi 1.00 40

Industrial Art and for the centenary of the Finnish Society of Industrial Art.

1975, Nov. 8 *Perf. 14*

581 A268 40p bl & multi 1.00 25

Christmas 1975.

Top Border of State Debenture
A269

Lithographed and Engraved

1976, Jan. 9 *Perf. 11½*

582 A269 80p multi 1.00 40

Centenary of State Treasury.

Glider over Lake Region
A270

1976, Jan. 13 Litho. *Perf. 14*

583 A270 80p multi 1.50 40

15th World Glider Championships, Rayskala, June 13–27.

Heikki Klemetti
A271

1976, Feb. 14 Litho. *Perf. 13*

584 A271 80p grn & multi 1.00 40

Prof. Heikki Klemetti (1876–1953), musician and writer, birth centenary.

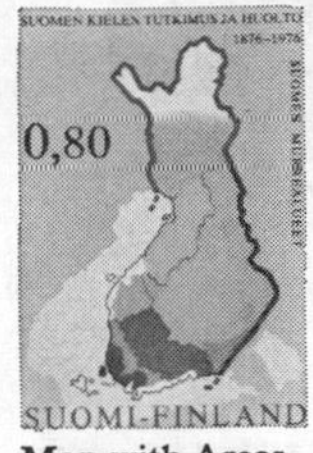

Map with Areas of Different Dialects
A272

Aino Ackté, by Albert Edelfelt
A273

1976, Mar. 10 Litho. *Perf. 13*

585 A272 80p multi 1.00 40

Finnish Language Society, centenary.

1976, Apr. 23

586 A273 70p yel & multi 1.00 40

Aino Ackté (1876–1944), opera singer, birth centenary.

Europa Issue 1976

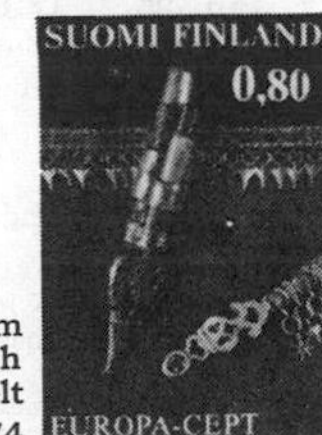

Knife from Voyri, Sheath and Belt
A274

1976, May 3 Litho. *Perf. 13*

587 A274 80p vio bl & multi 3.00 50

Radio and Television
A275

1976, Sept. 9 Litho. *Perf. 13*

588 A275 80p multi 1.00 40

Radio broadcasting in Finland, 50th anniversary.

Christmas Morning Ride to Church
A276

1976, Oct. 23 Litho. *Perf. 14*

589 A276 50p multi 1.00 30

Christmas 1976.

Turku Chapter Seal (Virgin and Child)
A277

1976, Nov. 1 Litho. *Perf. 12½*

590 A277 80p buff, brn & red 1.00 40

700th anniversary of the Cathedral Chapter of Turku.

Alvar Aalto, Finlandia Hall, Helsinki
A278

1976, Nov. 4

591 A278 80p multi 1.00 40

Hugo Alvar Henrik Aalto (1898–1976), architect.

Ice Dancers
A280

Five Water Lilies
A281

1977, Jan. 25 Litho. *Perf. 13*

592 A280 90p multi 1.00 40

European Figure Skating Championships, Finland, Jan. 25–29.

Photogravure and Engraved

1977, Feb. 2 *Perf. 12½*

593 A281 90p brt grn & multi 1.50 55
594 A281 1m ultra & multi 1.50 55

Nordic countries cooperation for protection of the environment and 25th Session of Nordic Council, Helsinki, Feb. 19.

Icebreaker Rescuing Merchantman
A282

1977, Mar. 2 Litho. *Perf. 13*

595 A282 90p multi 1.00 40

Winter navigation between Finland and Sweden, centenary.

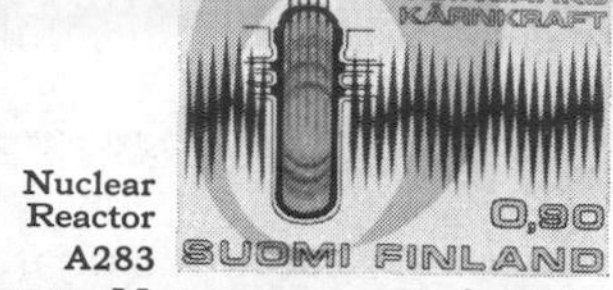

Nuclear Reactor
A283

1977, Mar. 3 *Perf. 12½x13*

596 A283 90p multi 1.00 40

Opening of nuclear power station on Hästholmen Island.

Europa Issue 1977

Autumn Landscape, Northern Finland
A284

1977, May 2 Litho. *Perf. 12½x13*

597 A284 90p multi 1.25 40

Tree, Birds and Nest
A285

Orthodox Church, Valamo Cloister
A286

1977, May 4 *Perf. 13x12½*

598 A285 90p multi 1.00 40

75th anniversary of cooperative banks.

1977, May 31 Litho. *Perf. 14*

599 A286 90p multi 1.00 40

Consecration festival of new Orthodox Church at Valamo Cloister, Heinävesi; 800th anniversary of introduction of orthodoxy in Karelia and of founding of Valamo Cloister.

Paavo Ruotsalainen
A287

1977, July 8 Litho. *Perf. 13*

600 A287 90p multi 1.00 40

Paavo Ruotsalainen (1777–1852), lay leader of Pietists in Finland.

People Fleeing Fire and Water
A288

Volleyball
A289

1977, Sept. 14 Litho. *Perf. 14*

601 A288 90p multi 1.00 40

Civil defense for security.

1977, Sept. 15

602 A289 90p multi 1.00 40

European Women's Volleyball Championships, Finland, Sept. 29–Oct. 2.

Children Bringing Water for Sauna
A290

1977, Oct. 25

603 A290 50p multi 1.00 25

Christmas 1977.

Finnish Flag
A291

Wall Telephone, 1880, New Telephone
A292

1977, Dec. 5 Litho. *Perf. 14*

Size: 31x21mm.

604 A291 80p multi 1.00 40

Size: 37x25mm. ***Perf. 13***

605 A291 1m multi 1.40 40

60th anniversary of Finland's declaration of independence.

1977, Dec. 9 *Perf. 14*

606 A292 1m multi 1.00 40

Centenary of first telephone in Finland.

Harbor, Sunila Factory, Kotka Arms
A293

1978, Jan. 2 Litho. *Perf. 14*

607 A293 1m multi 1.00 40

Centenary of founding of Kotka.

Europa Issue 1978

Paimio Sanitarium by Alvar Aalto
A294

Design: 1.20m, Hvittrask studio house, 1902 (horiz.).

1978, May 2 Litho. *Perf. 13*

608 A294 1m multi 3.00 75
609 A294 1.20m multi 6.00 5.50

Rural Bus Service
A295

1978, June 8 Litho. *Perf. 14*

610 A295 1m multi 1.00 40

Eino Leino and Eagle
A296

1978, July 6 Litho. *Perf. 13*

611 A296 1m multi 1.00 40

Eino Leino (1878–1926), poet.

Function Theory and Rhythmical Lines
A297

1978, Aug. 15 Litho. *Perf. 14*

612 A297 1m multi 1.00 40

ICM 78, International Congress of Mathematicians, Helsinki, Aug. 15–23.

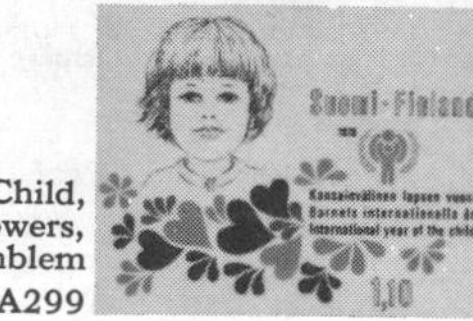

Child Feeding Birds
A298

1978, Oct. 23 Litho. *Perf. 14*

613 A298 50p multi 1.00 25

Christmas 1978.

Child, Flowers, IYC Emblem
A299

1979, Jan. 2 Litho. *Perf. 13*

614 A299 1.10m multi 3.50 50

International Year of the Child.

Runner
A300

1979, Feb. 7 Litho. *Perf. 14*

615 A300 1.10m multi 1.40 40

8th Orienteering World Championships, Finland, Sept. 1–4.

Old School, Hamina, Academy Flag
A301

1979, Mar. 20 Litho. *Perf. 14*

616 A301 1.10m multi 1.00 40

200th anniversary of Finnish Military Academy.

Turku Cathedral and Castle, Prinkkala House, Brahe Statue
A302

1979, Mar. 31

617 A302 1.10m multi 1.00 40

Streetcar, Helsinki
A303

1979, May 2 Litho. *Perf. 14*

618 A303 1.10m multi 1.00 40

Non-polluting urban transportation.

View of Tampere, 1779
A304

View of Tampere, 1979—A305

1979, May 2

619 A304 90p multi 1.00 40

1979, Oct. 1 Litho. *Perf. 13*

620 A305 1.10m multi 1.00 40

Bicentenary of founding of Tampere.

Europa Issue 1979

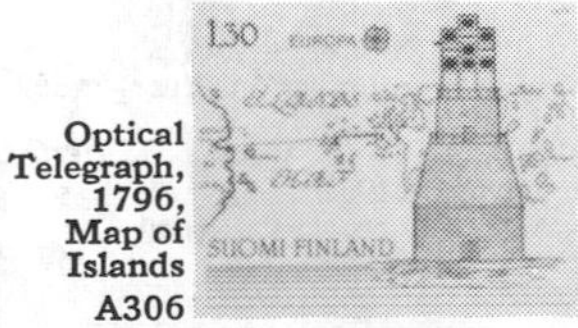

Optical Telegraph, 1796, Map of Islands
A306

Design: 1.10m, Letter of Queen Christina to Per Brahe, 1638, establishing postal service (vert.).

1979, May 2 *Perf. 13*

621 A306 1.10m multi 1.00 40
622 A306 1.30m multi 1.65 1.00

Shops and Merchants' Signs—A307

1979, Sept. 26 *Perf. 14*

623 A307 1.10m multi 1.00 40

Business and industry regulation centenary.

See "Special Notices" at the front of this volume for data on the listing methods of this Catalogue, abbreviations, condition, prices and examination.

Old and New Cars, Street Crossing
A308

1979, Oct. 1

624 A308 1.10m multi 1.00 40

Road safety.

Elves Feeding Horse—A309

1979, Oct. 24

625 A309 60p multi 80 25

Christmas 1979.

Korppi House, Lapinjarvi—A310

Farm houses, First Row: Syrjala House, Tammela, 2 stamps in continuous design; Murtovaara House, Valtimo; Antila House, Lapua. Second row: Lofts, Pohjanmaa; Courtyard gate, Kanajarvi House, Kalvola; Main door, Havuselka House, Kauhajoki; Maki-Rasinpera House and dinner bell tower; Gable and eaves, Rasula Kuortane granary.

1979, Oct. 27 Litho. *Perf. 13*

626 A310 Bklt. pane of 10 9.00
a-j. 1.10m, single stamp 90 50

See Nos. 672, 737.

Type of 1975

Kauhaneva Swamp
A315

Hame Castle, Hameenlinna
A316

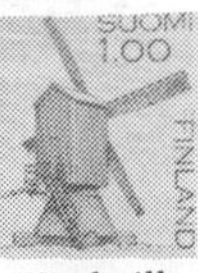

Windmill, Harrstrom
A318

Multiharju Forest, Seitseminen Natl. Park—A319

Shuttle, Raanu Designs—A322

Kaspaikka Towel Design
A323

Bridal Rug, Teisko, 1815
A324

Iron-forged Door, Hollola Church
A325

Iron Fish Spear c.1100—A326

Litho. & Engr., Litho., Engr.

Perf. 11½, 14

1979-85

627 A315 70p multi ('81) 40 18
628 A316 90p brn red ('82) 45 25
629 A256 1m red brn ('81) 50 20
630 A318 1m bl & red brn ('83) 50 20
631 A256 1.30m dk grn ('83) 60 20
632 A256 1.40m pur ('84) 65 20
633 A256 1.50m grnsh bl ('85) 70 20
634 A319 1.60m multi 75 30
635 A315 1.80m Eastern Gulf natl. park ('83) 80 30
636 A322 3m multi 1.40 25
637 A323 6m multi ('80) 2.75 40
638 A324 7m multi ('82) 3.25 50
639 A325 8m multi ('83) 3.50 60
640 A326 9m blk & dk bl ('84) 4.00 60
Nos. 627-640 (14) 20.25 4.38

Coil Stamp

Perf. 11½ Vert.

641 A316 90p brn red ('82) 45 30

Perf. 12½ Horiz.

642 A318 1m bl & red brn ('83) 50 32

Maria Jotuni (1880-1943), Writer
A327

1980, Apr. 9 **Litho.**

643 A327 1.10m multi 80 30

Europa Issue 1980

Frans Eemil Sillanpaa (1888-1964), Writer—A328

Design: 1.30m, Artturi Ilmari Virtanen (1895-1973), chemist (vert.).

1980, Apr. 28 *Perf. 13*

644 A328 1.10m multi 1.25 40
645 A328 1.30m multi 1.25 50

Pres. Urho Kekkonen, 80th Birthday—A329

1980, Sept. 3 **Litho.** *Perf. 13*

646 A329 1.10m multi 80 35

Nordic Cooperation Issue

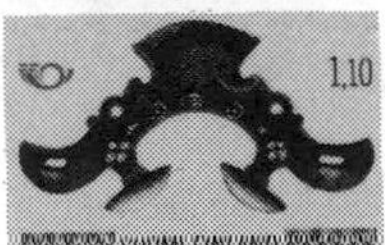

Back-piece Harness, 19th century—A330

1980, Sept. 9 *Perf. 14*

647 A330 1.10m *shown* 1.00 40
648 A330 1.30m *Collar harness, vert.* 1.00 50

Biathlon—A331

1980, Oct. 17 **Litho.** *Perf. 14*

649 A331 1.10m multi 80 35

World Biathlon Championship, Lahti, Feb. 10-15, 1981.

Pull the Roller, Weighing out the Salt—A332

Christmas 1980 (Traditional Games): 1.10m, Putting out the shoemaker's eye.

1980, Oct. 27

650 A332 60p multi 35 16
651 A332 1.10m multi 1.00 25

Boxing Match A333

Glass Blowing A334

1981, Feb. 28 **Litho.** ***Perf. 14***

652 A333 1.10m multi 60 30

European Boxing Championships, Tampere, May 2-10.

1981, Mar. 12

653 A334 1.10m multi 60 30

Glass industry, 300th anniversary.

Mail Boat Furst Menschikoff, 1836—A335

1981, May 6 **Litho. & Engr.** ***Perf. 13***

654 A335 1.10m brn & tan 4.00 4.50

Nordia '81 Stamp Exhibition, Helsinki, May 6-10. Sold only at exhibition for 3m including entrance ticket.

Europa Issue 1981

Rowing to Church—A336

1981, May 18 **Litho.** ***Perf. 13***

655 A336 1.10m shown 1.00 38
656 A336 1.50m Midsummer's Eve dance 1.00 52

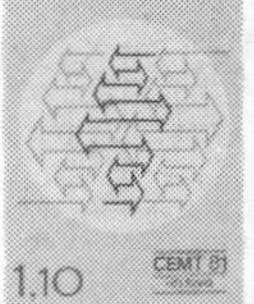

Traffic Conference Emblem A337

Boy and Girl Riding Pegasus A338

1981, May 26 **Litho.** ***Perf. 14***

657 A337 1.10m multi 60 30

European Conference of Ministers of Transport, May 25-28.

1981, June 11

658 A338 1m multi 55 30

Youth associations centenary.

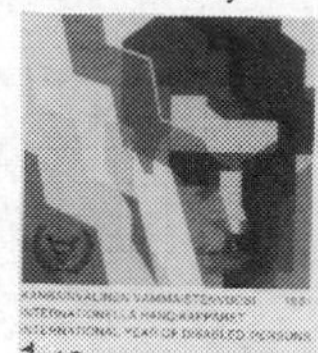

Intl. Year of the Disabled—A339

1981, Sept. 2 **Litho.** ***Perf. 13***

659 A339 1.10m multi 60 30

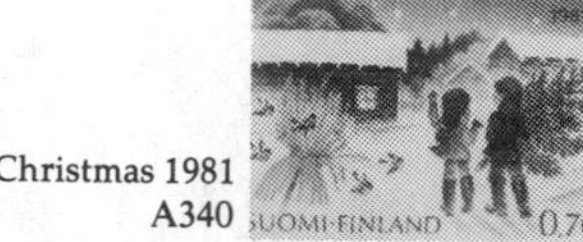

Christmas 1981 A340

1981, Oct. 27 **Litho.** ***Perf. 14***

660 A340 70p Children, Christmas tree 40 22
661 A340 1.10m Decorating tree, vert. 60 40

"Om Konsten att Ratt Behaga" First Issue (Periodicals Bicentenary)—A341

1982, Jan. 15

662 A341 1.20m multi 65 30

Kuopio Bicentenary A343

Score, String Instrument Neck A344

1982, Mar. 4 **Litho.** ***Perf. 14***

664 A343 1.20m multi 65 30

1982, Mar. 11 ***Perf. 13***

665 A344 1.20m multi 65 30

Centenaries of Sibelius Academy of Music and Helsinki Orchestra.

Electric Power Plant Centenary—A345

1982, Mar. 15 ***Perf. 14***

666 A345 1.20m multi 65 30

Gardening—A346

1982, Apr. 16 **Litho.** ***Perf. 14***

667 A346 1.10m multi 65 30

Europa Issue 1982—A347

Designs: 1.20m, Publication of Abckiria (first Finnish book), 1543. (Sculpture of Mikael Agricola, printer, by Oskari Jauhiainen, 1951). 1.50m, Turku Academy, first Finnish university (Turku Academy Inaugural Procession, 1640, after Albert Edelfelt).

1982, Apr. 29 **Litho.** ***Perf. 13x12½***

668 A347 1.20m multi 65 35

Size: 47x31mm. ***Perf. 12½***

669 A347 1.50m multi 70 60

Intl. Monetary Fund and World Bank Emblems—A348

1982, May 12 ***Perf. 14***

670 A348 1.60m multi 72 30

IMF interim Committee and IMF-WB Joint Development Committee Meeting, Helsinki, May 12-14.

75th Anniv. of Unicameral Parliament—A349

1982, May 25

671 A349 2.40m Future, by Waino Aaltonen, Parliament 1.10 50

House Type of 1979

Manor Houses, First Row: a, Kuitia, Parainen, 1490. b, Louhisaari, Askainen, 1655. c, Frugard, Joroinen, 1780. d, Jokioinen, 1798. e, Moisio, Elimaki, 1820. Second Row: f, Sjundby, Siuntio, 1560. g, Fagervik, Inkoo, 1773. h, Mustio, Karjaa, 1792. i, Fiskars, Pohja, 1818. j, Kotkaniemi, Vihti, 1836.

1982, June 14 **Litho.** ***Perf. 13x13½***

672 A310 Bklt. pane of 10 6.00
a-j. 1.20m, single stamp 60 40

Christmas 1982—A350

1982, Oct. 25

673 A350 90p Feeding forest animals 60 30
674 A350 1.20m Children eating porridge 60 30

Nordic Cooperation—A351

1983, Mar. 24 **Litho.** ***Perf. 14***

675 A351 1.20m Panning for gold 60 30
676 A351 1.30m Kitkajoki River rapids 65 30

World Communications Year—A352

1983, Apr. 9 **Litho.** ***Perf. 13***

677 A352 1.30m Postal services 65 30
678 A352 1.70m Sound waves, optical cables 85 50

Europa 1983—A353

1983, May 2 **Litho.** ***Perf. 12½x13***

679 A353 1.30m Flash smelting method 65 30
680 A353 1.70m Temppeliaukio Church 85 50

Pres. Lauri Kristian Relander (1883-1942) A354

Running A355

1983, May 31 Litho. *Perf. 14*
681 A354 1.30m multi 65 30

1983, June 6
682 A355 1.20m Javelin, horiz. 60 40
683 A355 1.30m shown 65 30

First World Athletic Championships, Helsinki, Aug. 7-14.

Toivo Kuula (1883-1918), Composer—A356

1983, July 7 *Perf. 14*
684 A356 1.30m multi 65 30

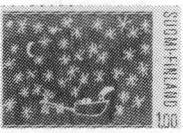

Christmas 1983—A357

Childrens drawings: 1m, Santa, reindeer, sled and gifts by Eija Myllyviita. 1.30m, Two candles by Camilla Lindberg.

Engr., Litho.

1983, Nov. 4 *Perf. 12, 14*
685 A357 1m dk bl 50 30
686 A357 1.30m multi, vert. 65 30

President Mauno Henrik Koivisto, 60th Birthday—A358

1983, Nov. 25 Litho. *Perf. 14*
687 A358 1.30m brt bl & blk 65 30

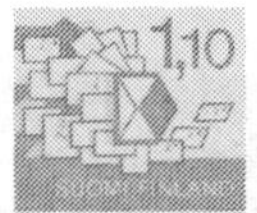

Inauguration of Nordic Postal Rates—A360

1984, Mar. 1 Engr. *Perf. 12*
689 A360 1.10m Letters (2nd class rate) 50 20

Photo. & Engr.
690 A360 1.40m Automated sorting (1st class rate), vert. 65 20

Museum Pieces A361

Work and Skill A362

Designs: No. 691, Pottery, 3200 B.C.; Silver chalice, 1416; Crossbow, 16th cent. No. 692, Kaplan hydraulic turbine.

1984, Apr. 30 Litho. *Perf. 13½*
691 A361 1.40m multi 65 32
692 A362 1.40m multi 65 32

Europa (1959-84)—A363

1984, May 7 *Perf. 12½x13*
693 A363 1.40m multi 65 32
694 A363 2m multi 90 50

Dentistry—A364

1984, Aug. 27 Litho. *Perf. 14*
695 A364 1.40m Dentist, teeth 65 32

Astronomy—A365

1984, Sept. 12
696 A365 1.10m Observatory, planets, sun 50 25

Aleksis Kivi (1934-72), Writer—A366

1984, Oct. 10 Litho. *Perf. 14*
697 A366 1.40m Song of my Heart 65 32

Christmas 1984—A367

1984, Nov. 30 Litho. & Engr. *Perf. 12*
698 A367 1.10m Father Christmas, brownie 50 25

Common Law of 1734—A368

1984, Dec. 6 *Perf. 14*
699 A368 2m Statute Book 90 40

25th Anniv. of EFTA—A369

1985, Feb. 2 Litho.
700 A369 1.20m multi 55 25

100th Anniv. of Society of Swedish Literature in Finland—A370

1985, Feb. 5 Litho.
701 A370 1.50m Johan Ludvig Runeberg 70 30

100th Anniv. of Order of St. Sergei and St. Herman—A371

1985, Feb. 18 Litho. *Perf. 11½x12*
702 A371 1.50m Icon 70 30

150th Anniv. of Kalevala—A372

Perf. 13x12½

1985, Feb. 28 Litho. & Engr.
703 A372 1.50m Pedri Semeikka 70 30
704 A372 2.10m Larin Paraske 95 45

NORDIA 1985—A373

1985, May 15 Litho. & Engr. *Perf. 13*
705 A373 1.50m Mermaid and sea lions 4.50 5.00

NORDIA 1985 philatelic exhibition, May 15-19. Sold for 10m, which included admission ticket.

Finnish Banknote Centenary—A374

Designs: Finnish banknotes of 1886, 1909, 1922, 1945 and 1955.

1985, May 18 Photo. & Engr. *Perf. 11½*
706 Booklet pane of 8 6.00 6.00
a.-h. A374 1.50m Any single 70 30

Europa 1985—A375

Designs: 1.50m, Children playing the recorder. 2.10m, Excerpt "Ramus Virens Olivarum" from the "Piae Cantiones," 1582.

1985, June 17 Litho. *Perf. 13*
707 A375 1.50m multi 70 30
708 A375 2.10m multi 95 45

Security Conference Type of 1975

1985, June 19 Litho.
709 A265 2.10m multi 95 45

European Security and Cooperation Conference, 10th Anniv.

Provincial Administration Established by Count Per Brahe, 350th Anniv.—A376

1985, Sept. 5 Litho. *Perf. 14*
710 A376 1.50m Provincial arms, Count's seal 70 30

Arms Type of 1975

1986, Jan. 2 **Engr.** ***Perf. 11½***

715	A256 1.60m ver ('86)		75	20
716	A256 1.70m ('87)		75	20

Tulip Damask Table Cloth, 18th Century—A377

1985, Sept. 13 **Litho.** ***Perf. 14***

723	A377	12m multi	5.50	1.25

Miniature Sheet

Postal Map, 1698—A378

Designs: No. 728a, Postman on foot. No. 728c, Sailing vessel, diff. No. 728d, Postrider, vert.

1985, Oct. 16 **Litho. & Engr.** ***Perf. 14***

728	Sheet of 4	4.00	4.00
a.-d.	A378 1.50m, Any single	1.00	1.00

FINLANDIA '88, 350th anniv. of Finnish Postal Service, founded in 1638 by Gov.-Gen. Per Brahe. Sheet sold for 8m. Size: 135x90mm.

Intl. Youth Year A379

Christmas 1985 A380

1985, Nov. 1 **Litho.** ***Perf. 13***

729	A379 1.50m multi		70	30

1985, Nov. 29 ***Perf. 14***

730	A380 1.20m	Bird, tulips	55	30
731	A380 1.20m	Cross of St. Thomas, hyacinths	55	30

Natl. Geological Society, Cent.—A390

1986, Feb. 8 **Litho.** ***Perf. 14***

732	A390 1.30m	Orbicular granite	60	30
733	A390 1.60m	Rapaviki	75	50
734	A390 2.10m	Veined gneiss	95	50

Europa 1986—A391

1986, Apr. 10 ***Perf. 12½x13***

735	A391 1.60m	Saimaa ringed seal	75	50
736	A391 2.20m	Environmental conservation	1.00	50

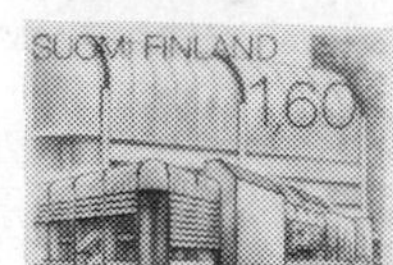

Conference Palace, Baghdad, 1982—A392

Natl. Construction Year. No. 737b, Lahti Theater, 1983. No. 737c, Kuusamo Municipal Offices, 1978. No. 737d, Hamina Court Building, 1983. No. 737e, Finnish Embassy, New Delhi, 1986. No. 737f, Western Sakyla Daycare Center, 1980.

1986, Apr. 19 ***Perf. 14***

737	Bklt. pane of 6	4.50	
a.-f.	A392 1.60m, any single	75	30

Nordic Cooperation Issue 1986—A393

Sister towns.

1986, May 27 **Litho.** ***Perf. 14***

738	A393 1.60m	Joensuu	75	40
739	A393 2.20m	Jyvaskyla	1.00	50

Souvenir Sheet

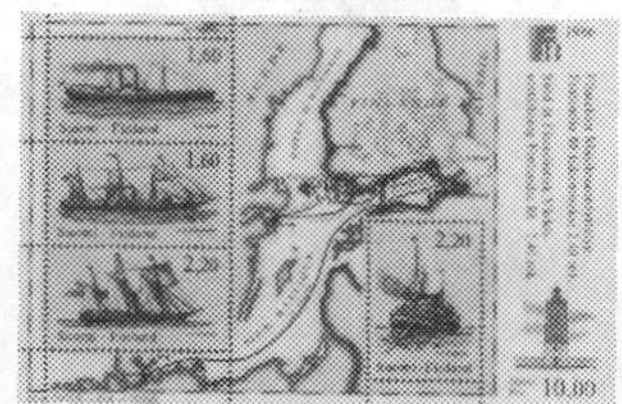

FINLANDIA '88—A394

Postal ships: No. 740a, Iron paddle steamer Aura, Stockholm-St. Petersburg, 1858. No. 740b, Screw vessel Alexander, Helsinki-Tallinn-Lubeck, 1859. No. 740c, Steamship Nicolai, Helsinki-Tallinn-St. Petersburg, 1858. No. 740d, 1st Ice steamship Express II, Helsinki-Stockholm, 1877-98, vert.

1986, Aug. 29 **Litho. & Engr.** ***Perf. 13***

740	Sheet of 4	4.50	5.00
a.-b.	A394 1.60m, any single	1.10	1.25
c.-d.	A394 2.20m, any single	1.10	1.25

No. 740 has multicolored margin picturing map of Sweden, Aland Isls., Germany, Finland and Russia, showing postal ship routes. Sold for 10k. Size: 135x90mm.

Pierre-Louis Moreau de Maupertuis (1698-1759)—A395

1986, Sept. 5 **Litho.** ***Perf. 12½x13***

741	A395 1.60m multi		75	30

Lapland Expedition, 250th anniv., proved Earth's poles are flattened.

See France No. 2016.

Urho Kaleva Kekkonen (1900-1986), President A396

Intl. Peace Year A397

1986, Sept. 30 **Engr.** ***Perf. 14***

742	A396	5m black	2.25	2.25

1986, Oct. 13 **Litho.** ***Perf. 13***

743	A397 1.60m multi		75	30

A398

Christmas—A399

1986, Oct. 31 **Photo. & Engr.** ***Perf. 12***

744	A398 1.30m	shown	60	30
745	A398 1.30m	Denomination at right	60	30
746	A399 1.60m	Elves	75	40

Nos. 744-745 printed se-tenant in a continuous design.

Postal Savings Bank, Cent.—A400

1987, Jan. 2 **Litho.** ***Perf. 14***

747	A400	1.70m multi	75	38

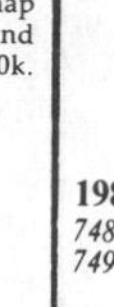

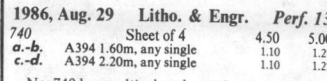

Natl. Tourism, Cent.—A401

1987, Feb. 4 **Litho.** ***Perf. 14***

748	A401	1.70m Winter	75	38
749	A401	2.30m Summer	1.05	52

Metric System in Finland, Cent.—A402

1987, Feb. 4 ***Perf. 14***

750	A402	1.40m multi	65	32

SEMI-POSTAL STAMPS

Arms
SP1 1M+50 P

Typographed.

1922, May 15 ***Perf. 14*** **Unwmkd.**

No.	Type	Denomination	Color	Unused	Used
B1	SP1	1m+50p	gray & red	1.00	*9.00*
a.		Perf. 13x13½		7.00	

Red Cross Standard SP2 — Symbolic SP3 — Ship of Mercy SP4

1930, Feb. 6

No.	Type	Denomination	Color	Unused	Used
B2	SP2	1m +10p	red org & red	2.00	*10.00*
B3	SP3	1½m +15p	grysh grn & red	1.25	*10.00*
B4	SP4	2m +20p	dk bl & red	3.50	*35.00*

The surtax on this and subsequent similar issues was for the benefit of the Red Cross Society of Finland.

Church in Hattula SP5 — SP8

Designs: 1½m+15p, Castle of Hameenlinna. 2m+20p, Fortress of Viipuri.

1931, Jan. 1 **Engraved**

Cross in Red.

No.	Type	Denomination	Color	Unused	Used
B5	SP5	1m +10p	gray grn	2.00	*8.00*
B6	SP5	1½m +15p	lil brn	11.00	11.00
B7	SP5	2m +20p	dl bl	1.85	*15.00*

Typographed.

1931, Oct. 15 ***Rouletted 4, 5***

No.	Type	Denomination	Color	Unused	Used
B8	SP8	1m +4m	blk	32.50	*60.00*

The surtax was to assist the Postal Museum of Finland in purchasing the Richard Granberg collection of entire envelopes.

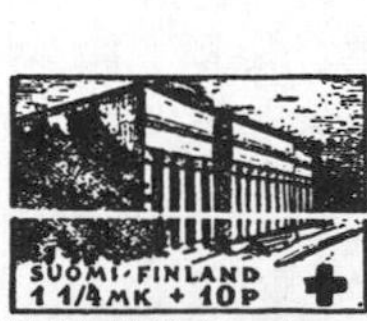

Helsinki University Library SP9 — Nikolai Church at Helsinki SP10

Design: 2½m+25p, Parliament Building, Helsinki.

1932, Jan. 1 ***Perf. 14***

No.	Type	Denomination	Color	Unused	Used
B9	SP9	1¼m +10p	ol bis & red	2.00	*12.50*
B10	SP10	2m +20p	dp vio & red	1.00	*6.00*
B11	SP9	2½m +25p	lt bl & red	1.50	*20.00*

Bishop Magnus Tawast SP12 — Michael Agricola SP13

Design: 2½m+25p, Isacus Rothovius.

1933, Jan. 20 **Engraved**

No.	Type	Denomination	Color	Unused	Used
B12	SP12	1¼m +10p	blk brn & red	2.50	4.50
B13	SP13	2m +20p	brn vio & red	75	1.50
B14	SP13	2½m +25p	ind & red	1.00	2.00

Evert Horn SP15

Designs: 2m+20p, Torsten Stalhandske. 2½m+25p, Jakob (Lazy Jake) de la Gardie.

1934, Jan. **Cross in Red.**

No.	Type	Denomination	Color	Unused	Used
B15	SP15	1¼m +10p	brn	1.00	2.00
B16	SP15	2m +20p	gray lil	1.80	3.50
B17	SP15	2½m +25p	gray	1.00	2.50

Mathias Calonius SP18 — Robert Henrik Rehbinder SP21

Designs: 2m+20p, Henrik C. Porthan. 2½m+25p, Anders Chydenius.

1935, Jan. 1 **Cross in Red.**

No.	Type	Denomination	Color	Unused	Used
B18	SP18	1¼m +15p	brn	1.00	2.00
B19	SP18	2m +20p	gray lil	1.50	3.00
B20	SP18	2½m +25p	gray bl	75	2.50

1936, Jan. 1

Designs: 2m+20p, Count Gustaf Mauritz Armfelt. 2½m+25p, Count Arvid Bernard Horn.

Cross in Red.

No.	Type	Denomination	Color	Unused	Used
B21	SP21	1¼m +15p	dk brn	75	2.00
B22	SP21	2m +20p	vio brn	4.00	5.50
B23	SP21	2½m +25p	bl	75	3.00

The "Uusimaa" SP24 — The "Turunmaa" SP25

Design: 3½m+35p, The "Hameenmaa."

1937, Jan. 1 **Cross in Red.**

No.	Type	Denomination	Color	Unused	Used
B24	SP24	1¼m +15p	brn	1.00	2.50
B25	SP25	2m +20p	brn lake	18.50	6.00
B26	SP24	3½m +35p	ind	1.00	3.00

Aukuste Makipeska SP27 — Skiing SP31

Designs: 1¼m+15p, Robert Isidor Orn. 2m+20p, Edward Bergenheim. 3½m+35p, Johan Mauritz Nordenstam.

1938, Jan. 5 **Engraved**

Cross in Red

No.	Type	Denomination	Color	Unused	Used
B27	SP27	50p +5p	dk grn	70	1.00
B28	SP27	1¼m +15p	dk brn	1.00	2.00
B29	SP27	2m +20p	rose lake	9.00	7.00
B30	SP27	3½m +35p	dk bl	90	3.50

1938, Jan. 18

Designs: 2+1m, Ski jumper. 3.50+1.50m, Skier.

No.	Type	Denomination	Color	Unused	Used
B31	SP31	1.25m +75p	sl grn	6.00	11.00
B32	SP31	2m +1m	dk car	6.00	11.00
B33	SP31	3.50m +1.50m	dk bl	6.00	11.00

Issued to commemorate the ski championships held at Lahti.

Soldier—SP34

1938, May 16

No.	Type	Denomination	Color	Unused	Used
B34	SP34	2m +½m	bl	2.00	4.00

Issued to commemorate the victory of the White Army over the Red Guards. The surtax was for the benefit of the members of the Union of the Finnish Front.

Battlefield at Solferino SP35

1939, Jan. 2 **Cross in Scarlet.**

No.	Type	Denomination	Color	Unused	Used
B35	SP35	50p +5p	dk grn	1.00	1.50
B36	SP35	1¼m +15p	dk brn	1.00	2.50
B37	SP35	2m +20p	lake	18.50	10.00
B38	SP35	3½m +35p	dk bl	80	3.50

Issued in commemoration of the 75th anniversary of the founding of the International Red Cross Society.

Soldiers with Crossbows SP36 — Arms of Finland SP40

Designs: 1¼m+15p, Cavalryman. 2m+20p, Soldier of Charles XII of Sweden. 3½m+35p, Officer and soldier of War with Russia, 1808–1809.

1940, Jan. 3 **Cross in Red.**

No.	Type	Denomination	Color	Unused	Used
B39	SP36	50p +5p	dk grn	70	1.50
B40	SP36	1¼m +15p	dk brn	1.50	2.50
B41	SP36	2m +20p	lake	2.00	2.50
B42	SP36	3½m +35p	dp ultra	2.00	3.50

The surtax aided the Finnish Red Cross.

1940, Feb. 15 **Lithographed**

No.	Type	Denomination	Color	Unused	Used
B43	SP40	2m +2m	ind	60	1.10

The surtax was given to a fund for the preservation of neutrality.

Mason SP41 — Soldier's Emblem SP45

Designs: 1.75m+15p, Farmer plowing. 2.75m+25p, Mother and child. 3.50m+35p, Finnish flag.

1941, Jan. 2 **Engraved**

Cross in Red.

No.	Type	Denomination	Color	Unused	Used
B44	SP41	50p +5p	grn	50	1.10
B45	SP41	1.75m +15p	brn	1.25	2.00
B46	SP41	2.75m +25p	brn car	6.50	10.00
B47	SP41	3.50m +35p	dp ultra	1.25	3.00

See also Nos. B65–B68.

1941, May 24 **Unwmkd.**

No.	Type	Denomination	Color	Unused	Used
B48	SP45	2.75m +25p	brt ultra	1.00	1.25

The surtax was for the aid of the soldiers who fought in the Russo-Finnish War.

Aaland Arms SP46 — Lapland Arms SP51

Designs: Coats of Arms—1.75m+15p, Nyland. 2.75m+25p, Finland's first arms. 3.50m+35p, Karelia. 4.75m+45p, Satakunta.

1942, Jan. 2 ***Perf. 14***

Cross in Red.

No.	Type	Denomination	Color	Unused	Used
B49	SP46	50p +5p	grn	1.00	1.50
B50	SP46	1.75m +15p	brn	1.25	2.25
B51	SP46	2.75m +25p	dk red	1.25	2.25
B52	SP46	3.50m +35p	dp ultra	1.25	2.25
B53	SP46	4.75m +45p	dk sl grn	1.00	2.25
		Nos. B49-B53 (5)		5.75	10.50

The surtax aided the Finnish Red Cross.

1943, Jan. 6 **Inscribed "1943."**

Designs: Coats of Arms—2m+20p, Hame. 3.50m+35p, Eastern Bothnia. 4.50m+45p, Savo.

Cross in Red.

No.	Type	Denomination	Color	Unused	Used
B54	SP51	50p +5p	grn	50	1.25
B55	SP51	2m +20p	brn	1.00	2.00
B56	SP51	3.50m +35p	dk red	1.00	2.00
B57	SP51	4.50m +45p	brt ultra	1.50	5.00

The surtax aided the Finnish Red Cross.

Soldier's Helmet and Sword SP55 — Mother and Children SP56

1943, Feb. 1 ***Perf. 13***

No.	Type	Denomination	Color	Unused	Used
B58	SP55	2m +50p	dk brn	75	1.00
B59	SP56	3.50m +1m	brn red	75	1.00

The surtax was for national welfare.

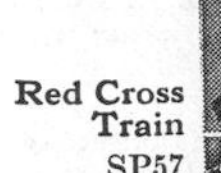

Red Cross Train
SP57

Designs: 2m+50p, Ambulance. 3.50m+75p, Red Cross Hospital, Helsinki. 4.50m+1m, Hospital plane.

Inscribed "1944"

1944, Jan. 2 *Perf. 14*

Cross in Red.

B60	SP57	50p	+25p grn	50	50
B61	SP57	2m	+50p sep	70	1.00
B62	SP57	3.50m	+75p ver	70	1.00
B63	SP57	4.50m	+1m brt ultra	1.25	2.00

The surtax aided the Finnish Red Cross.

Symbols of Peace SP61 | Wrestling SP62

1944, Dec. 1

B64	SP61	3.50m	+1.50m dk red brn	65	1.00

The surtax was for national welfare.

Types of 1941 Inscribed "1945."
Photogravure and Engraved.

1945, May 2 Cross in Red.

B65	SP41	1m	+25p grn	20	50
B66	SP41	2m	+50p brn	40	80
B67	SP41	3.50m	+75p brn car	40	80
B68	SP41	4.50m	+1m dp ultra	80	1.50

The surtax was for the Finnish Red Cross.

1945, Apr. 16 Engraved *Perf. 13½*

Designs: 2+1m, Gymnast. 3.50+1.75m, Runner. 4.50+2.25m, Skier. 7+3.50m, Javelin thrower.

B69	SP62	1m	+50p bluish grn	30	1.00
B70	SP62	2m	+1m dp red	30	1.00
B71	SP62	3.50m	+1.75m dl vio	30	1.00
B72	SP62	4.50m	+2.25m ultra	60	1.25
B73	SP62	7m	+3.50m dl brn	90	2.00
			Nos.B69-B73 (5)	2.40	6.25

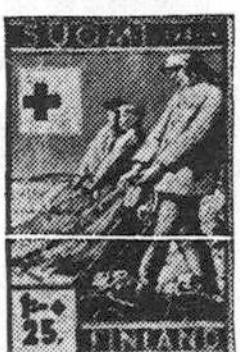

Fishing SP67 | Nurse and Children SP71

Designs: 3+75p, Churning. 5+1.25m, Reaping. 10+2.50m, Logging.

Engraved; Cross Typo. in Red

1946, Jan. 7

B74	SP67	1m	+25p dl grn	60	75
B75	SP67	3m	+75p lil brn	45	50
B76	SP67	5m	+1.25m rose red	60	75
a.			Red cross omitted	*500.00*	
B77	SP67	10m	+2.50m ultra	75	1.00

The surtax was for the Finnish Red Cross.

1946, Sept. 2 Engraved

Design: 8+2m, Doctor examining infant.

B78	SP71	5m	+1m grn	60	80
B79	SP71	8m	+2m brn vio	60	80

The surtax was for the prevention of tuberculosis.

Nos. B78 and B79 Surcharged with New Values in Black.

1947, Apr. 1

B80	SP71	6m	+1m on 5m +1m grn	60	1.00
B81	SP71	10m	+2m on 8m+2m brn vio	60	1.00

The surtax was for the prevention of tuberculosis.

Medical Examination of Infants
SP73 SP74

Designs: 10+2.50m, Infant held by the feet. 12+3m, Mme. Alli Paasikivi and a child. 20+5m, Infant standing.

1947, Sept. 15 Engraved

B82	SP73	2.50m	+1m grn	60	1.00
B83	SP74	6m	+1.50m dk red	80	1.00
B84	SP74	10m	+2.50m red brn	1.00	1.00
B85	SP73	12m	+3m dp bl	1.25	1.25
B86	SP74	20m	+5m dk red vio	1.50	1.50
			Nos. B82-B86 (5)	5.15	5.75

The surtax was for the prevention of tuberculosis.

Zachris Topelius
SP78

Designs: 7+2m, Fredrik Pacius. 12+3m, Johan L. Runeberg. 20+5m, Fredrik Cygnaeus.

Engraved; Cross Typo. in Red

1948, May 10 *Perf. 14* Unwmkd.

B87	SP78	3m	+1m grn	80	1.00
B88	SP78	7m	+2m rose red	1.00	1.10
B89	SP78	12m	+3m brt bl	1.10	1.25
B90	SP78	20m	+5m dk vio	1.25	1.50

The surtax was for the Finnish Red Cross.

Nos. B83, B84 and B86 Surcharged with New Values and Bars in Black.

1948, Sept. 13 Engr. *Perf. 13½*

B91	SP74	7m	+2m on 6m+1.50m dk red	1.75	2.50
B92	SP74	15m	+3m on 10m+2.50m red brn	1.75	2.50
B93	SP74	24m	+6m on 20m+5m dk red vio	2.00	2.50

The surtax was for the prevention of tuberculosis.

Tying Birch Boughs SP79 | Wood Anemone SP83

Designs: 9+3m, Bathers in Sauna house. 15+5m, Rural bath house. 30+10m, Cold plunge in lake.

Engraved; Cross Typo. in Red

1949, May 5 *Perf. 13½x14*

B94	SP79	5m	+2m dl grn	60	85
B95	SP79	9m	+3m dk car	1.00	1.25
B96	SP79	15m	+5m dp bl	1.00	1.25
B97	SP79	30m	+10m dk vio brn	1.75	3.00

The surtax was for the Finnish Red Cross.

1949, June 2 Engraved

Designs: 9+3m, Wild rose. 15+5m, Coltsfoot.

Inscribed: "1949"

B98	SP83	5m	+2m grn	80	1.25
B99	SP83	9m	+3m car	1.00	1.25
B100	SP83	15m	+5m ol bis	1.25	1.75

The surtax was for the prevention of tuberculosis.

Similar to Type of 1949.

Designs: 5+2m, Water lily. 9+3m, Pasqueflower. 15+5m, Bell flower cluster.

1950, Apr. 1 Inscribed: "1950."

B101	SP83	5m	+2m emer	2.00	2.00
B102	SP83	9m	+3m rose car	1.75	1.75
B103	SP83	15m	+5m bl	1.75	1.75

The surtax was for the prevention of tuberculosis.

Hospital Entrance, Helsinki SP84 | Blood Donor's Medal SP86

Design: 12+3m, Giving blood.

Engraved; Cross Typo. in Red

1951, Mar. 17 *Perf. 14* Unwmkd.

B104	SP84	7m	+2m choc	1.75	1.75
B105	SP84	12m	+3m bl vio	1.75	1.75
B106	SP86	20m	+5m car	3.25	3.25

The surtax was for the Finnish Red Cross.

Capercaillie
SP87

Designs: 12m+3m, European cranes. 20m+5m, Caspian terns.

1951, Oct. 26 Engraved

B107	SP87	7m	+2m dk grn	2.75	2.75
B108	SP87	12m	+3m rose brn	2.75	2.75
B109	SP87	20m	+5m bl	2.75	2.75

The surtax was for the prevention of tuberculosis.

Diver SP88 | Soccer Players SP89

Designs: 20m+3m, Stadum, Helsinki. 25m+4m, Runners.

1951–52

Inscribed: "XV Olympia 1952."

B110	SP88	12m	+2m rose car	1.25	1.50
B111	SP89	15m	+2m grn ('52)	1.25	1.50
B112	SP88	20m	+3m dp bl	1.25	1.50
B113	SP89	25m	+4m brn ('52)	1.25	1.50

Issued to publicize the XV Olympic Games, Helsinki, 1952. The surtax was to help finance the games.

Margin blocks of four of each denomination were cut from regular or perf.-through-margin sheets and pasted by the selvage, overlapping, in a printed folder to create a kind of souvenir booklet. Price $35.

Field Marshal Mannerheim SP90 | Great Titmouse SP91

Engraved; Cross Typo. in Red

1952, Mar. 4

B114	SP90	10m	+2m gray	2.25	2.25
B115	SP90	15m	+3m rose vio	2.25	2.25
B116	SP90	25m	+5m bl	2.25	2.25

The surtax was for the Red Cross.

1952, Dec. 4 Engraved

Designs: 15m+3m, Spotted flycatchers and nest. 25m+5m, Swift.

B117	SP91	10m	+2m grn	2.50	2.50
B118	SP91	15m	+3m plum	2.50	2.50
B119	SP91	25m	+5m dp bl	2.50	2.50

The surtax was for the prevention of tuberculosis.

European Red Squirrel SP92 | Children Receiving Parcel from Welfare Worker SP93

Designs: 15m+3m, Brown bear. 25m+5m, European elk.

Engraved.

1953, Nov. 16 *Perf. 14* Unwmkd.

B120	SP92	10m	+2m red brn	2.50	2.50
B121	SP92	15m	+3m vio	2.50	2.50
B122	SP92	25m	+5m dk grn	2.50	2.50

The surtax was for the prevention of tuberculosis.

Engraved; Cross Typographed in Red

1954, Mar. 8 *Perf. 11½*

Designs: 15m+3m, Aged woman knitting. 25m+5m, Blind basket-maker and dog.

B123	SP93	10m	+2m dk ol grn	1.75	1.75
B124	SP93	15m	+3m dk bl	1.75	1.75
B125	SP93	25m	+5m dk brn	1.75	1.75

The surtax was for the Finnish Red Cross.

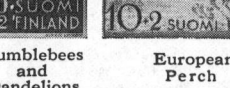

Bumblebees and Dandelions SP94 | European Perch SP95

Designs: 15m+3m, Butterfly. 25m+5m, Dragonfly.

Engraved; Cross Typographed in Red

1954, Dec. 7 ***Perf. 14***

B126 SP94 10m +2m brn 1.75 1.75
B127 SP94 15m +3m car 1.75 1.75
B128 SP94 25m +5m bl 1.75 1.75

The surtax was for the prevention of tuberculosis.

Engraved; Cross Typographed in Red

1955, Sept. 26 ***Perf. 14***

Designs: 15m+3m, Northern pike. 25m+5m, Atlantic salmon.

B129 SP95 10(m) +2(m) dl grn 1.75 1.75
B130 SP95 15(m) +3(m) vio brn 1.75 1.75
B131 SP95 25(m) +5(m) dk bl 1.75 1.75

The surtax was for the Anti-Tuberculosis Society.

Gen. von Dobeln in Battle of Juthas, 1808
SP96

Waxwing
SP97

Illustrations by Albert Edelfelter from J. L. Runeberg's "Tales of Ensign Stal": 15(m)+3(m), Col. J. Z. Duncker holding flag. 25(m)+5(m), Son of fallen Soldier.

Engraved; Cross Typographed in Red.

1955, Nov. 24

B132 SP96 10(m) +2(m) dp ultra 1.75 1.75
B133 SP96 15(m) +3(m) dk red brn 1.75 1.75
B134 SP96 25(m) +5(m) grn 1.75 1.75

The surtax was for the Red Cross.

Engraved; Cross Typographed in Red.

Birds: 20m+3m, Eagle owl. 30m+5m, Mute swan.

1956, Sept. 25 ***Perf. 11½***

B135 SP97 10m +2m dl red brn 1.65 1.65
B136 SP97 20m +3m bl grn 1.75 1.75
B137 SP97 30m +5m bl 1.75 1.75

The surtax was for the Anti-Tuberculosis Society.

Pekka Aulin
SP98

Wolverine (Glutton)
SP99

Portraits: 10m+2m, Leonard von Pfaler. 20m+3m, Gustaf Johansson. 30m+5m, Viktor Magnus von Born.

Engraved; Cross Typographed in Red.

1956, Nov. 26 **Unwmkd.**

B138 SP98 5m +1m grysh grn 1.25 1.25
B139 SP98 10m +2m brn 1.50 1.50
B140 SP98 20m +3m mag 1.75 1.75
B141 SP98 30m +5m lt ultra 1.75 1.75

The surtax was for the Red Cross.

Engraved; Cross Typographed in Red

1957, Sept. 5 ***Perf. 11½***

Designs: 20m+3m, Lynx. 30m+5m, Reindeer.

B142 SP99 10m +2m dl pur 1.50 1.50
B143 SP99 20m +3m sep 1.75 1.75
B144 SP99 30m +5m dk bl 1.75 1.75

The surtax was for the Anti-Tuberculosis Society. See also Nos. B160–B165.

Red Cross Flag
SP100

Raspberry
SP101

1957, Nov. 25 **Engraved** ***Perf. 14***

Cross in Red.

B145 SP100 10m +2m ol grn 2.25 2.25
B146 SP100 20m +3m mar 2.25 2.25
B147 SP100 30m +5m dl bl 2.25 2.25

Issued to commemorate the 80th anniversary of the Finnish Red Cross.

Type of 1952.

Flowers: 10m+2m, Lily of the valley. 20m+3m, Red clover. 30m+5m, Hepatica.

Engraved; Cross Typographed in Red

1958, May 5 ***Perf. 14*** **Unwmkd.**

B148 SP91 10m +2m grn 1.50 1.50
B149 SP91 20m +3m lil rose 1.75 1.75
B150 SP91 30m +5m ultra 1.75 1.75

The surtax was for the Anti-Tuberculosis Society.

Engraved; Cross Typographed in Red.

1958, Nov. 20 ***Perf. 11½***

Designs: 20m+3m, Cowberry. 30m+5m, Blueberry.

B151 SP101 10m +2m org 1.25 1.25
B152 SP101 20m +3m red 1.75 1.75
B153 SP101 30m +5m dk bl 1.75 1.75

The surtax was for the Red Cross.

Daisy
SP102

Reindeer
SP103

Designs: 20m+5m, Primrose. 30m+5m, Cornflower.

Engraved; Cross Typographed in Red.

1959, Sept. 7 **Unwmkd.**

B154 SP102 10m +2m grn 3.25 1.75
B155 SP102 20m +3m lt brn 4.00 2.25
B156 SP102 30m +5m bl 4.00 2.25

The surtax was for the Anti-Tuberculosis Society.

Engraved; Cross Typographed in Red

1960, Nov. 24 ***Perf. 11½***

Designs: 20m+3m, Lapp and lasso. 30m+5m, Mountains.

B157 SP103 10m +2m dk gray 1.50 1.50
B158 SP103 20m +3m gray vio 2.25 2.25
B159 SP103 30m +5m rose vio 2.25 2.25

The surtax was for the Red Cross.

Animal Type of 1957.

Designs: 10m+2m, Muskrat. 20m+3m, Otter. 30m+5m, Seal.

Engr.; Cross at right, Typo. in Red

1961, Sept. 4

B160 SP99 10m +2m brn car 1.50 1.50
B161 SP99 20m +3m sl bl 2.25 2.25
B162 SP99 30m +5m bl grn 2.25 2.25

The surtax was for the Anti-Tuberculosis Society.

Animal Type of 1957.

Designs: 10m+2m, Hare. 20m+3m, Pine marten. 30m+5m, Ermine.

Engraved; Cross Typographed in Red

1962, Oct. 1

B163 SP99 10m +2m gray 1.50 1.50
B164 SP99 20m +3m dl red brn 2.00 2.00
B165 SP99 30m +5m vio bl 2.00 2.00

The surtax was for the Anti-Tuberculosis Society.

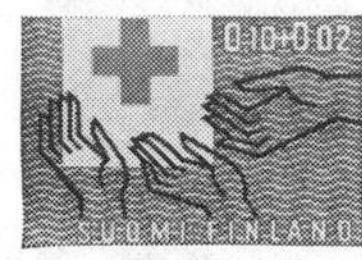

Cross and Outstretched Hands
SP104

Engraved; Cross Typographed in Red

1963, May 8 ***Perf. 11½*** **Unwmkd.**

B166 SP104 10p +2p red brn 1.25 1.25
B167 SP104 20p +3p vio 1.50 1.50
B168 SP104 30p +5p grn 1.50 1.50

The surtax was for the Red Cross.

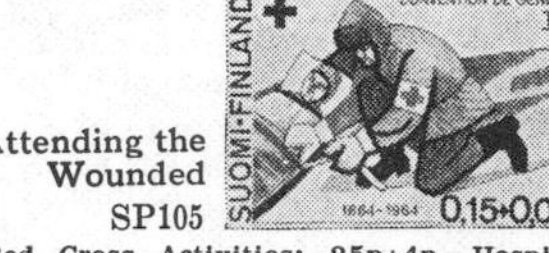

Attending the Wounded
SP105

Red Cross Activities: 25p+4p, Hospital ship. 35p+5p, Prisoner-of-war health examination. 40p+7p, Gift parcel distribution.

Engraved; Cross Typographed in Red

1964, May 26 ***Perf. 11½***

B169 SP105 15p +3p vio bl 1.10 1.10
B170 SP105 25p +4p grn 1.50 1.25
B171 SP105 35p +5p vio brn 1.50 1.25
B172 SP105 40p +7p dk ol grn 1.50 1.25

The surtax was for the Red Cross.

Finnish Spitz
SP106

Artificial Respiration
SP107

Designs: 25p+4p, Karelian bear dog. 35p+5p, Finnish hunting dog.

Engraved; Cross Typographed in Red

1965, May 10 ***Perf. 11½***

B173 AP106 15p +3p org brn 1.50 1.50
B174 AP106 25p +4p blk 1.75 1.75
B175 AP106 35p +5p gray brn 1.75 1.75

Surtax for Anti-Tuberculosis Society.

1966, May 7 Lithographed ***Perf. 14***

First Aid: 25p+4p, Skin diver rescuing occupants of submerged car. 35p+5p, Helicopter rescue in winter.

B176 SP107 15p +3p multi 1.50 1.50
B177 SP107 25p +4p multi 1.50 1.50
B178 SP107 35p +5p multi 1.50 1.50

The surtax was for the Red Cross.

Birch
SP108

Horse-drawn Ambulance
SP109

Trees: 25p+4p, Pine. 40p+7p, Spruce.

1967, May 12 **Litho.** ***Perf. 14***

B179 SP108 20p +3p multi 1.25 1.25
B180 SP108 25p +4p multi 1.25 1.25
B181 SP108 40p +7p multi 1.25 1.25

Surtax for Anti-Tuberculosis Society. See Nos. B185–B187.

1967, Nov. 24 **Litho.** ***Perf. 14***

Designs: 25p+4p, Ambulance, 1967. 40p+7p, Red Cross.

Cross in Red

B182 SP109 20p +3p dl yel, grn & blk 1.25 1.25
B183 SP109 25p +4p vio & blk 1.25 1.25
B184 SP109 40p +7p dk grn, blk & dk bl 1.25 1.25

The surtax was for the Red Cross.

Tree Type of 1967

Trees: 20p+3p, Juniper. 25+4p, Aspen. 40p+7p, Chokecherry.

1969, May 12 **Litho.** ***Perf. 14***

B185 SP108 20p +3p multi 1.25 1.25
B186 SP108 25p +4p multi 1.25 1.25
B187 SP108 40p +7p multi 1.25 1.25

Surtax for Anti-Tuberculosis Society.

"On the Lapp's Magic Rock"
SP110

Designs: 30p+6p, Juhani blowing horn on Impivaara Rock (vert.). 50+10p, The Pale Maiden. The designs are from illustrations by Askeli Gallen-Kallelas for "The Seven Brothers" by Aleksis Kivi.

1970, May 8 **Litho.** ***Perf. 14***

B188 SP110 25p +5p multi 1.00 1.00
B189 SP110 30p +6p multi 1.00 1.00
B190 SP110 50p +10p multi 1.00 1.00

The surtax was for the Red Cross.

Cutting and Loading Timber
SP111

Designs: 30p+6p, Floating logs downstream. 50p+10p, Sorting logs at saw-mill.

1971, Apr. 25 **Litho.** ***Perf. 14***

B191 SP111 25p +5p multi 1.00 1.00
B192 SP111 30p +6p multi 1.00 1.00
B193 SP111 50p +10p multi 1.00 1.00

Surtax for Anti-Tuberculosis Society.

Blood Donor and Nurse
SP112

Designs: 30p+6p, Blood research (microscope, slides; vert.). 50p+10p, Blood transfusion.

1972, Oct. 23

B194 AP112 25p +5p multi 1.00 1.00
B195 AP112 30p +6p multi 1.00 1.00
B196 AP112 50p +10p multi 1.00 1.00

Surtax was for the Red Cross.

Girl with Lamb, by Hugo Simberg
SP113

Paintings: 40p+10p, Summer Evening, by Vilho Sjöström. 60p+15p, Woman at Mountain Fountain, by Juho Rissanen.

1973, Sept. 12 Litho. *Perf. 13x12½*

B197	SP113	30p	+5p multi	1.00	1.00
B198	SP113	40p	+10p multi	1.50	1.50
B199	SP113	60p	+15p multi	1.50	1.50

Surtax for the Finnish Anti-Tuberculosis Assoc. Birth centenaries of featured artists.

Morel
SP114

Mushrooms: 50p+10p, Chanterelle. 60p+15p, Boletus edulis.

1974, Sept. 24 Litho. *Perf. 12½x13*

B200	SP114	35p	+5p multi	1.50	1.25
B201	SP114	50p	+10p multi	1.50	1.25
B202	SP114	60p	+15p multi	1.50	1.25

Finnish Red Cross.

Echo, by Ellen Thesleff (1869–1954)
SP115

Paintings: 60p+15p, Hilda Wiik, by Maria Wiik (1853–1928). 70p+20p, At Home (old woman in chair), by Helene Schjerfbeck (1862–1946).

1975, Sept. 30 Litho. *Perf. 13x12½*

B203	SP115	40p	+10p multi	1.00	1.00
B204	SP115	60p	+15p multi	1.25	1.25
B205	SP115	70p	+20p multi	1.25	1.25

Finnish Red Cross. In honor of International Women's Year paintings by women artists were chosen.

Disabled Veterans' Emblem
SP116

Lithographed and Photogravure

1976, Jan. 15 *Perf. 14*

B206	SP116	70p	+30p multi	2.00	1.40

The surtax was for hospitals for disabled war veterans.

Wedding Procession
SP117

Designs: 70p+15p, Wedding dance (vert.). 80p+20p, Bride, groom, matron and pastor at wedding dinner.

1976, Sept. 15 Litho. *Perf. 13*

B207	SP117	50p	+10p multi	75	75
B208	SP117	70p	+15p multi	1.00	1.00
B209	SP117	80p	+20p multi	1.10	1.10

Surtax for Anti-Tuberculosis Society.

Disaster Relief
SP118

Designs: 80p+15p, Community work. 90p+20p, Blood transfusion service.

1977, Jan. 19 Litho. *Perf. 14*

B210	SP118	50p	+10p multi	75	75
B211	SP118	80p	+15p multi	1.10	1.10
B212	SP118	90p	+20p multi	1.10	1.10

Finnish Red Cross centenary.

Long-distance Skiing
SP119

Design: 1m+50p, Ski jump.

1977, Oct. 5 Litho. *Perf. 13*

B213	SP119	80p	+40p multi	3.25	3.25
B214	SP119	1m	+50p multi	2.25	2.25

Surtax was for World Ski Championships, Lahti, Feb. 17–26, 1978.

Saffron Milkcap
SP120

Edible Mushrooms: 80p+15p, Parasol mushrooms (vert.). 1m+20p, Gypsy mushrooms.

1978, Sept. 13 Litho. *Perf. 13*

B215	SP120	50p	+10p multi	75	75
B216	SP120	80p	+15p multi	1.10	1.10
B217	SP120	1m	+20p multi	1.10	1.10

Surtax was for Red Cross.

See Nos. B221-B223.

Pehr Kalm, 1716-1779—SP121

Finnish Scientists: 90p + 15p, Title page of Pehr Adrian Gadd's (1727-1797) book (vert.). 1.10m +20p, Petter Forsskal (1732-1763).

Perf. 12½×13, 13×12½

1979, Sept. 26 Litho.

B218	SP121	60p	+10p multi	70	70
B219	SP121	90p	+15p multi	1.10	1.10
B220	SP121	1.10m	+20p multi	1.10	1.10

Surtax was for the Finnish Anti-Tuberculosis Assocation.

Mushroom Type of 1978

Edible Mushrooms: 60p+10p, Woolly milkcap. 90p+15p, Orange-cap boletus (vert.). 1.10m+20p, Russula paludosa.

1980, Apr. 19 Litho. *Perf. 13*

B221	SP120	60p	+10p multi	60	60
B222	SP120	90p	+15p multi	90	90
B223	SP120	1.10m	+20p multi	90	90

Surtax was for Red Cross.

Fuchsia—SP122

1981, Aug. 24 Litho. *Perf. 13*

B224	SP122	70p	+10p shown	45	45
B225	SP122	1m	+15p African violet	60	60
B226	SP122	1.10m	+20p Geranium	75	75

Surtax was for Red Cross.

Garden Dormouse—SP123

1982, Aug. 16 Litho. *Perf. 13*

B227	SP123	90p	+10p shown	50	50
B228	SP123	1.10m	+15p Flying squirrels	65	65
B229	SP123	1.20m	+20p European minks	70	70

Surtax was for Red Cross. No. B228 vert.

Forest and Wetland Plants—SP124

Designs: 1m+20p, Chickweed wintergreen. 1.20m+25p, Marsh violet. 1.30m+30p, Marsh marigold. Surtax was for Finnish Anti-Tuberculosis Assoc.

1983, July 7 Litho. *Perf. 13*

B230	SP124	1m	+20p multi	60	60
B231	SP124	1.20m	+25p multi	80	80
B232	SP124	1.30m	+30p multi	80	80

Globe Puzzle—SP125

Design: 2m+40p, Symbolic world communication. Surtax was for Red Cross.

1984, May 28 Litho. *Perf. 13*

B233	SP125	1.40m	+35p multi	80	80
B234	SP125	2m	+40p multi	1.10	1.10

Butterflies—SP126

1986, May 22 Litho. *Perf. 13*

B235	SP126	1.60m	+40p Anthocharis cardamines	1.00	1.00
B236	SP126	2.10m	+45p Nymphalis antiopa	1.40	1.40
B237	SP126	5m	+50p Parnassius apollo	2.50	2.50

Surtax for Red Cross.

AIR POST STAMPS.

No. 178 Overprinted in Red **ZEPPELIN 1930**

1930, Sept. 24 ***Perf. 14*** **Unwmkd.**

C1	A28	10m gray lil	160.00	250.00
a.		1830 for 1930	2,750.	4,250.

Issued Sept. 24, 1930; overprinted expressly for use on mail carried in "Graf Zeppelin" on her return flight from Finland to Germany on Sept. 24, 1930, after which trip the stamps ceased to be valid for postage. Forgeries of Nos. C1 and C1a are almost always on No. 205, rather than No. 178.

Douglas DC-2
AP1

1944 **Engraved**

C2	AP1	3.50m dk brn	70	*1.10*

Issued to commemorate the 20th anniversary of Air Transport Service, 1923-43.

Douglas DC-6 Over Winter Landscape
AP2

1950, Feb. 13

C3	AP2	300m blue	20.00	10.00

Available also for ordinary postage.

Type of 1950 Redrawn

1958, Jan. 20 ***Perf. 11½***

C4	AP2	300 (m) bl	27.50	1.10

On No. C4 "mk" is omitted.

Convair 440 over Lakes
AP3

1958, Oct. 31 ***Perf. 11½*** **Unwmkd.**

C5	AP3	34m blue	1.30	55

No. C5 Surcharged with New Value and Bars

1959, Apr. 5

C6	AP3	45m on 34m bl	3.00	3.00

1959, Nov. 2

C7	AP3	45m blue	3.00	75

1963, Feb. 15

C8	AP3	45p blue	2.00	20

DC-6 Type, Comma After "3"

1963, Oct. 10

C9	AP2	3m bl, Type II ('73)	2.50	35
a.		Type I		

Convair Type of 1958

1970, July 15

C10	AP3	57p ultra	2.00	80

MILITARY STAMPS.

M1

Typographed.

1941, Nov. 1 ***Imperf.*** **Unwmkd.**

M1	M1	(4m) *dk org*	40	*80*

No. M1 has simulated roulette printed in black.

Type of 1930-46 Overprinted in Black **KENTTÄ-POSTI FÄLTPOST**

1943, Oct. 16 ***Perf. 14***

M2	A26	2m dp org	40	*60*
M3	A26	3½m grnsh bl	40	*60*

Post Horn and Sword
M2

1943 **Size: 29½x19½mm.**

M4	M2	(2m) green	30	*60*
M5	M2	(3m) rose vio	30	*60*

1944 **Size: 20x16mm.**

M6	M2	(2m) green	25	30
M7	M2	(3m) rose vio	25	30

Post Horns and Arms of Finland
M3

1963, Sept. 26 **Litho.** ***Perf. 14***

M8	M3	vio bl	*225.00*	*200.00*

Used during maneuvers Sept. 30–Oct. 5, 1963. Valid from Sept. 26.

No. M8 with overprint "19 83" was issued in that year.

PARCEL POST STAMPS

PP1

Wmkd. Rose & Triangles Multiple
Rouletted 6 on 2 or 3 Sides

1949–50 **Typographed**

Q1	PP1	1m brt grn & blk	2.00	4.50
Q2	PP1	5m red & blk	16.00	14.00
Q3	PP1	20m org & blk	30.00	22.50
Q4	PP1	50m bl & blk ('50)	11.00	11.00
Q5	PP1	100m brn & blk ('50)	12.50	11.00
		Nos. Q1-Q5 (5)	71.50	63.00

Mail Bus
PP2

Engraved

1952–58 ***Perf. 14*** **Unwmkd.**

Q6	PP2	5m car rose	4.00	4.00
Q7	PP2	20m orange	10.00	7.00
Q8	PP2	50m bl ('54)	25.00	10.00
Q9	PP2	100m brn ('58)	30.00	15.00

Mail Bus
PP3

1963 ***Perf. 12***

Q10	PP3	5p red & blk	3.00	3.00
Q11	PP3	20p org & blk	2.75	1.50
Q12	PP3	50p bl & blk	5.00	2.00
Q13	PP3	1m brn & blk	1.25	1.25

Nos. Q1–Q13 were issued only in booklets: panes of 6 for Nos. Q1–Q5, 10 for Nos. Q6–Q9 and 5 for Nos. Q10–Q13.

Used prices are for regular postal or mail-bus cancels. Pen strokes, cutting or other cancels sell for half as much.

1981 SISU Bus—PP4

Perf. 12 Horiz.

1981, Dec. 7 **Photo. & Engr.**

Q14	PP4	50p dk bl & blk	50	*3.00*
Q15	PP4	1m dk brn & blk	75	*3.00*
Q16	PP4	5m grn & blk	3.00	*5.00*
Q17	PP4	10m red & blk	6.00	*10.00*

Parcel post stamps invalid after Jan. 9, 1985.

ALAND ISLANDS

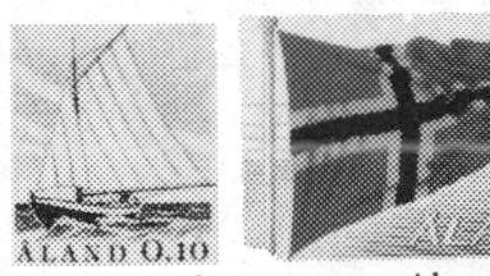

Gaff-rigged Sloop A1 — Aland Flag A2

Midsummer Pole A3 — Landscapes A4

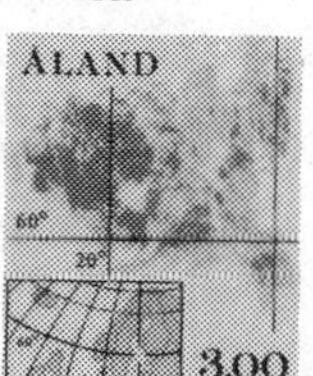

Map of Scandinavia A5

Seal of St. Olaf and Aland Province, 1326— A6

Artifacts—A7

Sea Birds—A8

Designs: 5m, Outer Aland Archipelago. 8m, Farm and windmill.

Designs: 1.60m, Burial site, clay hands. 2.20m, Bronze Staff of Finby, apostolic decoration. 20m, Ancient court site, contemporary monument, horiz.

1984-86		**Engr.**		***Perf. 12***
1	A1	10p mag ('85)	5	5
2	A1	20p brn ol	8	8
4	A1	50p brt grn	18	18
6	A1	1.10m dp bl	38	38
7	A1	1.20m blk ('85)	42	42
8	A1	1.30m ('86)	45	45
		Litho.		***Perf. 14***
10	A2	1.40m multi	48	48
11	A3	1.50m multi	52	52
		Litho.		***Perf. 13***
12	A7	1.60m multi ('86)	62	62
13	A8	1.70m Somateria mollissima	70	70
14	A4	2m Grove, vert.	70	70
15	A7	2.20m multi ('86)	85	85
15A	A8	2.30m Aythya fuligula	95	95
16	A5	3m multi	1.00	1.00
18	A4	5m Outer Aland Archipelago	1.75	1.75
20	A4	8m Farm, windmill	2.75	2.75
		Litho. & Engr.		
21	A6	10m multi	3.50	3.50
		Litho.		
21A	A8	12m Melantha fusca	5.00	5.00
22	A7	20m multi ('86)	7.75	7.75

Issue dates: Nos. 1, 7, 11, Jan. 2, 1985. Nos. 2, 4, 6, 10, 16, 21, Mar. 1, 1984. No. 8, Jan. 2, 1986. Nos. 14, 18, 20, Sept. 16, 1985.

1.60m, 2.20m, 20m, Apr. 4.

Bark Pommern and Car Ferries, Mariehamn West Harbor A10

1984, Mar. 1		**Litho**		***Perf. 14***
23	A10	2m multi	3.00	3.00

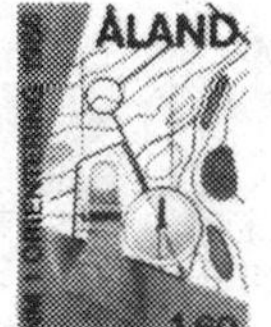

1986 Nordic Orienteering Championships, Aug. 30-31—A11

1986, Jan. 2		**Litho.**		***Perf. 14***
24	A11	1.60m multi	58	58

Onningeby Artists' Colony, Cent.—A12

Design: Pallette, pen and ink drawing of Onningeby landscape, 1891, by Victor Westerholm (1860-1919), founder.

1986, Sept. 1		**Litho.**		***Perf.***
25	A12	3.70m multi	1.50	1.50

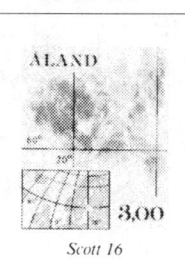

FIUME

(fyōō'mȧ)

LOCATION—A city and surrounding territory on the Adriatic Sea.

GOVT.—Formerly a part of Italy.

AREA—8 sq. mi.

POP.—44,956 (estimated 1924).

Formerly a port of Hungary, Fiume was claimed by Jugoslavia and Italy following World War I. During the discussion, the poet, Gabriele d'Annunzio, organized his legionnaires and seized Fiume, together with the islands of Arbe, Carnaro and Veglia, in the name of Italy. Jugoslavia recognized Italy's claim and the city was annexed in January, 1924.

100 Filler = 1 Korona
100 Centesimi = 1 Corona (1919)
100 Centesimi = 1 Lira

Hungarian Stamps of 1916-18 Overprinted **FIUME**

Wmkd. Double Cross. (137)

1918, Dec. 2 *Perf. 15*

On Stamps of 1916.

White Numerals.

1	A8	10f rose	25.00	7.50
2	A8	15f violet	12.00	5.00

Nos. 1–2 overprints are handstamped.

On Stamps of 1916–18.

Colored Numerals.

3	A9	2f brn org	30	20
4	A9	3f red vio	30	20
5	A9	5f green	30	20
6	A9	6f grnsh bl	30	20
7	A9	10f rose red	22.50	7.50
8	A9	15f violet	30	20
9	A9	20f gray brn	30	20
10	A9	25f dp bl	50	40
11	A9	35f brown	60	60
12	A9	40f ol grn	9.00	2.00

White Numerals

13	A10	50f red vio & lil	50	40
14	A10	75f brt bl & pale bl	1.75	60
15	A10	80f grn & pale grn	1.25	40
16	A10	1k red brn & cl	8.50	1.75
17	A10	2k ol brn & bis	60	40
18	A10	3k dk vio & ind	5.50	1.75
19	A10	5k dk brn & lt brn	8.50	3.50
20	A10	10k vio brn & vio	60.00	35.00

Inverted or double overprints exist on most of Nos. 4–15.

On Stamps of 1918.

21	A11	10f scarlet	50	25
22	A11	20f dk brn	50	25
23	A12	40f ol grn	4.00	1.50

The overprint on Nos. 3–23 was applied both by press and handstamp. Prices are for the less costly. Prices of Nos. 7, 12, 20 and 23 are for handstamps.

Forgeries of Nos. 1–23 abound.

A1

A2

Postage Due Stamps of Hungary, 1915-20 Overprinted and Surcharged in Black.

1919, Jan.

24	A1	45f on 6f grn & red	1.75	75
25	A1	45f on 20f grn & red	1.75	75

Hungarian Savings Bank Stamp Surcharged in Black.

1919, Jan. 29

26	A2	15f on 10f dk vio	1.75	75

"Italy"

A3

Italian Flag on Clock-Tower in Fiume

A4

"Revolution"

A5

Sailor Raising Italian Flag at Fiume (1918)

A6

Lithographed.

1919 *Perf. 11½* **Unwmkd.**

27	A3	2c dl bl	15	15
28	A3	3c gray brn	15	15
29	A3	5c yel grn	15	15
30	A4	10c rose	15	15
31	A4	15c violet	15	15
32	A4	20c green	15	15
33	A5	25c dk bl	15	15
34	A6	30c dp vio	15	15
35	A5	40c brown	20	20
36	A5	45c orange	15	15
37	A6	50c yel grn	15	15
38	A6	60c claret	15	15
39	A6	1cor brn org	20	20
40	A6	2cor brt bl	25	25
41	A6	3cor org red	25	25
42	A6	5cor dp brn	25	25
43	A6	10cor ol grn	1.00	1.00
		Nos. 27-43 (17)	3.80	3.80

The earlier printings of January and February are on thin grayish paper and in sheets of 70. A March printing is on semi-transparent white paper, also in sheets of 70. An April printing is on white paper of medium thickness and in sheets of 100. Part-perforate examples of most of this series are known.

A7

A8

A9

A10

1919, July 28 *Perf. 11½*

46	A7	5c yel grn	15	15
47	A8	10c rose	15	15
48	A9	30c violet	20	15
49	A10	40c yel brn	85	85
50	A10	45c orange	20	20
51	A9	50c yel grn	22	22
52	A9	60c claret	22	22
a.		Perf. 13x12½	30.00	30.00
53	A9	10cor ol grn	1.00	1.00
a.		Perf. 13x12½	30.00	30.00
b.		Perf. 10½	30.00	30.00
		Nos. 46-53 (8)	2.99	2.94

Five other denominations—25c, 1cor, 2cor, 3cor and 5cor—were not officially issued. Some copies of the 25c are known canceled.

Stamps of 1919 Handstamp Surcharged **FRANCO 5**

1919–20

58	A4	5c on 20c grn ('20)	15	20
59	A10	5c on 25c bl	15	20
60	A5	10c on 45c org	15	20
61	A9	15c on 30c vio ('20)	15	20
62	A10	15c on 45c org	15	20
63	A9	15c on 60c cl ('20)	15	30
64	A6	25c on 50c yel grn ('20)	1.00	1.10
65	A9	25c on 50c yel grn ('20)	25	30
66	A6	55c on 1cor brn org	1.00	1.10
67	A6	55c on 2cor brt bl	1.00	1.10
68	A6	55c on 3cor org red	1.00	1.10
69	A6	55c on 5cor dp brn	1.00	1.10
70	A9	55c on 10cor ol grn	1.35	1.25
		Nos. 58-70 (13)	7.50	8.35

Semi-Postal Stamps of 1919 Surcharged:

Valore globale Cent. 5 — *a*

Valore globale Cent. 45 — *b*

1919–20

73	SP6(a)	5c on 5c grn	15	15
74	SP6(a)	10c on 10c rose	15	15
75	SP6(a)	15c on 15c gray	15	15
76	SP6(a)	20c on 20c org	20	20
77	SP9(a)	25c on 25c bl ('20)	25	25
78	SP7(b)	45c on 45c ol grn	25	25
79	SP7(b)	60c on 60c rose	25	25
80	SP7(b)	80c on 80c vio	30	30
81	SP7(b)	1cor on 1cor sl	30	30
82	SP8(a)	2cor on 2cor red brn	40	40
83	SP8(a)	3cor on 3cor blk brn	85	85
84	SP8(a)	5cor on 5cor yel brn	1.00	1.00
85	SP8(a)	10cor on 10cor dk vio ('20)	50	50
		Nos. 73-85 (13)	4.75	4.75

Double or inverted surcharges, or imperf. varieties, exist on most of Nos. 73–85.

There were three settings of the surcharges on Nos. 73–85 except No. 77 which is known only with one setting.

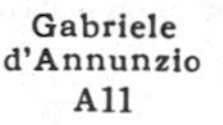

Gabriele d'Annunzio

A11

Severing the Gordian Knot

A12

Pale Buff Background.

1920, Sept. 12 Typo. *Perf. 11½*

86	A11	5c green	20	20
87	A11	10c carmine	20	20
88	A11	15c dk gray	30	30
89	A11	20c orange	30	30
90	A11	25c dk bl	50	50
91	A11	30c red brn	50	50
92	A11	45c ol gray	75	75
93	A11	50c lilac	75	75
94	A11	55c bister	75	75
95	A11	1 l black	1.20	1.20
96	A11	2 l red vio	2.50	2.50
97	A11	3 l dk grn	2.50	2.50
98	A11	5 l brown	2.50	2.50
99	A11	10 l gray vio	3.00	3.00
		Nos. 86-99 (14)	15.95	15.95

Counterfeits of Nos. 86 to 99 are plentiful.

1920, Sept. 12

Designs: 10c, Ancient emblem of Fiume. 20c Head of "Fiume." 25c, Hands holding daggers.

100	A12	5c green	7.50	7.50
101	A12	10c dp rose	1.50	1.50
102	A12	20c brn org	2.00	1.50
103	A12	25c dk bl	15.00	11.00

These stamps were issued to mark the anniversary of the occupation of Fiume by d'Annunzio. They were available for franking the correspondence of the legionnaires on the day of issue only, Sept. 12, 1920

Counterfeits of Nos. 100 to 103 are plentiful.

Commemorative Stamps of 1920 Overprinted in Black or Red and New Values **Reggenza Italiana del Carnaro**

1920, Nov. 20

104	A12	1c on 5c grn	20	20
105	A12	2c on 25c bl (R)	20	20
106	A12	5c green	20	20
107	A12	10c rose	30	30
108	A12	15c on 10c rose	30	30
109	A12	15c on 20c brn org	30	30
110	A12	15c on 25c bl (R)	40	40
111	A12	20c brn org	40	40
112	A12	25c bl (R)	40	40
113	A12	25c bl (Bk)	40.00	32.50
114	A12	25c on 10c rose	1.35	1.35
115	A12	50c on 20c brn org	50	50
116	A12	55c on 5c grn	50	50
117	A12	1 l on 10c rose	2.00	2.00
118	A12	1 l on 25c bl (R)	150.00	90.00
119	A12	2 l on 5c grn	4.00	4.00
120	A12	5 l on 10c rose	25.00	13.00
121	A12	10 l on 20c brn org	90.00	32.50
		Nos. 104-121 (18)	316.05	179.05

The Fiume Legionnaires of d'Annunzio occupied the islands of Arbe and Veglia in the Gulf of Carnaro from Nov. 13, 1920, until Jan. 5, 1921.

Varieties of overprint or surcharge exist for most of Nos. 104–121.

Same Overprint with **ARBE** at top

1920, Nov. 18

122	A12	5c green	1.25	1.00
123	A12	10c rose	1.50	1.25
124	A12	20c brn org	2.00	1.50
125	A12	25c dp bl	8.00	5.00
126	A12	50c on 20c brn org	2.75	1.75
127	A12	55c on 5c grn	2.75	1.75
		Nos.122-127 (6)	18.25	12.25

The overprint on Nos. 122–125 comes in two widths: 11mm. and 14mm. Prices are for the 11mm. width.

Same Overprint with **VEGLIA** at top.

1920, Nov. 18

128	A12	5c green	1.25	1.00
129	A12	10c rose	1.50	1.25
130	A12	20c brn org	2.00	1.50
131	A12	25c dp bl	8.00	5.00
132	A12	50c on 20c brn org	2.75	1.75
133	A12	55c on 5c grn	2.75	1.75
		Nos. 128-133 (6)	18.25	12.25

The overprint on Nos. 128–131 comes in two widths: 17mm. and 19mm. Prices are for the 17mm. width.

Nos. 122–133 exist with double and inverted overprints.

Counterfeits of these overprints exist.

Stamps of 1920 Overprinted **Governo Provvisorio**

1921, Feb. 2

Pale Buff Background.

134	A11	5c green	20	20
135	A11	10c carmine	20	20
136	A11	15c dk gray	30	30
137	A11	20c orange	30	30
138	A11	25c dk bl	40	40
139	A11	30c red brn	40	40
140	A11	45c ol gray	50	50
141	A11	50c lilac	50	50
142	A11	55c bister	50	50
143	A11	1 l black	20.00	22.50

144	A11	2 l red vio	1.00	75
145	A11	3 l dk grn	1.50	1.50
146	A11	5 l brown	2.00	75
147	A11	10 l gray vio	2.25	2.00

With Additional Surcharge LIRE UNA

148	A11	1 l on 30c red brn	50	30
		Nos. 134-148 (15)	30.55	31.10

Most of Nos. 134–143, 148 and E10–E11 exist with inverted or double overprint. **See Nos. E10–E11.**

First Constituent Assembly.

24 - IV - 1921

Semi-Postal Stamps of 1919 Overprinted

1921, Apr. 24

149	SP6	5c bl grn	40	25
150	SP6	10c rose	30	25
151	SP6	15c gray	30	25
152	SP6	20c orange	30	25
153	SP7	45c ol grn	50	35
154	SP7	60c car rose	60	50
155	SP7	80c brt vio	75	60

With Additional Overprint "L".

156	SP7	1 l on 1cor dk sl	1.00	85
157	SP8	2 l on 2cor red brn	3.00	50
158	SP8	3 l on 3cor blk brn	5.00	6.00
159	SP8	5 l on 5cor yel brn	9.00	50
160	SP8	10 l on 10cor dk vio	9.00	10.00
		Nos. 149-160 (12)	30.15	20.30

The overprint exists inverted on several denominations.

Second Constituent Assembly.

"Constitution" Issue of 1921 With Additional Overprint "1922".

1922

161	SP6	5c bl grn	1.50	40
162	SP6	10c rose	15	20
163	SP6	15c gray	3.00	60
164	SP6	20c orange	15	20
165	SP7	45c ol grn	20	25
166	SP7	60c car rose	20	25
167	SP7	80c brt vio	20	25
168	SP7	1 l on 1cor dk sl	20	25
169	SP8	2 l on 2cor red brn	20	35
170	SP8	3 l on 3cor blk brn	25	50
171	SP8	5 l on 5cor yel brn	30	75
		Nos. 161-171 (11)	6.35	4.00

Nos. 161–171 have the overprint in heavier type than Nos. 149–160 and "IV" in Roman instead of sans-serif numerals.
The overprint exists inverted or double on almost all values.

Venetian Ship
A16

Roman Arch
A17

St. Vitus
A18

Rostral Column
A19

1923, Mar. 23 *Perf. 11½*

Pale Buff Background.

172	A16	5c bl grn	20	20
173	A16	10c violet	20	20
174	A16	15c brown	20	20
175	A17	20c org red	20	20
176	A17	25c dk gray	20	20
177	A17	30c dk grn	20	20
178	A18	50c dl bl	20	20
179	A18	60c rose	30	30
180	A18	1 l dk bl	30	30
181	A19	2 l vio brn	1.50	1.00
182	A19	3 l ol bis	8.00	6.00
183	A19	5 l yel brn	3.50	3.00
		Nos. 172-183 (12)	15.00	12.00

Stamps of 1923 Overprinted REGNO D'ITALIA

1924, Feb. 22

Pale Buff Background.

184	A16	5c bl grn	15	30
185	A16	10c violet	15	30
186	A16	15c brown	15	30
187	A17	20c org red	15	30
188	A17	25c dk gray	15	30
189	A17	30c dk grn	15	30
190	A18	50c dl bl	15	30
191	A18	60c red	15	30
192	A18	1 l dk bl	15	30
193	A19	2 l vio brn	50	1.00
194	A19	3 l olive	1.75	3.50
195	A19	5 l yel brn	1.75	3.50
		Nos. 184-195 (12)	5.35	10.70

The overprint exists inverted on almost all values.

Stamps of 1923 Overprinted

22 Febb. 1924

1924, Mar. 1

Pale Buff Background.

196	A16	5c bl grn	15	30
197	A16	10c violet	15	30
198	A16	15c brown	15	30
199	A17	20c org red	15	30
200	A17	25c dk gray	15	30
201	A17	30c dk grn	15	30
202	A18	50c dl bl	15	30
203	A18	60c red	15	30
204	A18	1 l dk bl	15	30
205	A19	2 l vio brn	75	1.50
206	A19	3 l olive	75	1.50
207	A19	5 l yel brn	75	1.50
		Nos. 196-207 (12)	3.60	7.20

Postage stamps of Fiume were superseded by stamps of Italy.

SEMI-POSTAL STAMPS.

Semi-Postal Stamps of Hungary, 1916-17. Overprinted FIUME

Wmkd. Double Cross. (137)

1918, Dec. 2 *Perf. 15*

B1	SP3	10f +2f rose	85	30
a.		Inverted overprint	25.00	7.50
B2	SP4	15f +2f dl vio	90	30
a.		Inverted overprint	25.00	6.00
B3	SP5	40f +2f brn car	1.25	90
a.		Inverted overprint	25.00	6.00

Examples of Nos. B1–B3 with overprint hand-stamped sell for higher prices.

Statue of Romulus and Remus Being Suckled by Wolf
SP6

Venetian Galley
SP7

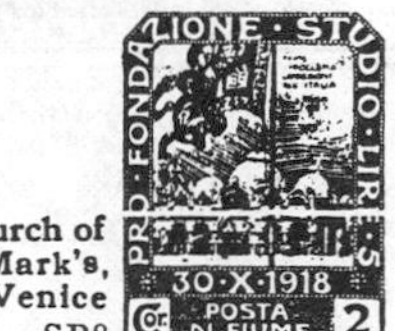

Church of St. Mark's, Venice
SP8

Typographed.

1919, May 18 *Perf. 11½* **Unwmkd.**

B4	SP6	5c +5 l bl grn	1.35	1.40
B5	SP6	10c +5 l rose	1.35	1.40
B6	SP6	15c +5 l dk gray	1.35	1.40
B7	SP6	20c +5 l org	1.35	1.40
B8	SP7	45c +5 l ol grn	1.35	1.40
B9	SP7	60c +5 l car rose	1.35	1.40
B10	SP7	80c +5 l brt vio	1.35	1.40
B11	SP7	1cor +5 l dk sl	1.35	1.40
B12	SP8	2cor +5 l red brn	1.35	1.40
B13	SP8	3cor +5 l blk brn	1.35	1.40
B14	SP8	5cor +5 l yel brn	1.35	1.40
B15	SP8	10cor +5 l dk vio	1.35	1.40
		Nos. B4-B15 (12)	16.20	16.80

Nos. B4 to B15 were issued in commemoration of the 200th day of peace. The surtax aided Fiume students in Italy. "Posta di Fiume" is printed on the back of Nos. B4–B16.

Dr. Antonio Grossich
SP9

1919, Sept. 20

B16	SP9	25c +2 l bl	15	15

The surtax benefited the Dr. Grossich Foundation.

SPECIAL DELIVERY STAMPS

Special Delivery Stamp of Hungary, 1916, Overprinted FIUME

1918, Dec. 2 *Perf. 15* **Wmk. 137**

E1	SD1	2f gray grn & red	40	25

No. E1 with overprint handstamped sells for more.

SD3

Typographed.

1920, Sept. 12 *Perf. 11½* **Unwmkd.**

E2	SD3	30c sl bl	1.00	1.00
E3	SD3	50c rose	1.00	1.00

Nos. 102 and 100 Surcharged

Reggenza Italiana del Carnaro 50 50 ESPRESSO

1920, Nov.

E4	A12	30c on 20c brn org	30.00	20.00
E5	A12	50c on 5c grn	10.00	5.00

Same Surcharge with **ARBE** at top.

E6	A12	30c on 20c brn org	35.00	17.50
E7	A12	50c on 5c grn	10.00	11.50

Overprint on Nos. E6–E7 is 11mm. wide.

Same Surcharge with **VEGLIA** at top.

E8	A12	30c on 20c brn org	35.00	17.50
E9	A12	50c on 5c grn	10.00	11.50

Overprint on Nos. E8–E9 is 17mm. wide.

Nos. E2 and E3 Overprinted

Governo Provvisorio

1921, Feb. 2

E10	SD3	30c sl bl	1.00	1.00
E11	SD3	50c rose	1.00	1.00

Fiume in 16th Century
SD4

1923, Mar. 23 *Perf. 11, 11½.*

E12	SD4	60c rose & buff	50	50
E13	SD4	2 l dk bl & buff	50	50

Stamps of 1923 Overprinted

1924, Feb. 22

E14	SD4	60c car & buff	50	1.00
E15	SD4	2 l dk bl & buff	50	1.00

1924, Mar. 1 Overprinted

22 Febbraio 1924

E16	SD4	60c car & buff	50	1.00
E17	SD4	2 l dk bl & buff	50	1.10

POSTAGE DUE STAMPS.

Postage Due Stamps of Hungary, 1915–1916, Overprinted FIUME

1918, Dec. *Perf. 15* **Wmk. 137**

J1	D1	6f grn & blk	70.00	22.50
J2	D1	12f grn & blk	55.00	22.50
J3	D1	50f grn & blk	30.00	11.50
J4	D1	1f grn & red	9.00	5.50
J5	D1	2f grn & red	30	20
J6	D1	5f grn & red	4.00	1.50
J7	D1	6f grn & red	30	20
J8	D1	10f grn & red	5.00	2.00
J9	D1	12f grn & red	30	20
J10	D1	15f grn & red	7.50	5.00

J11 D1 20f grn & red 30 20
J12 D1 30f grn & red 6.00 4.00

The overprint on Nos. J1–J12 was applied both by press and handstamp. Prices are for the less costly. Inverted and double overprints exist. Excellent forgeries exist.

Eagle
D2

Typographed

1919, July 28 *Perf. 11½* **Unwmkd.**

J13 D2 2c brown 15 15
J14 D2 5c brown 15 15

Semi-Postal Stamps of 1919 with Overprint "Valore Globale" Surcharged:

Segnatasse

L. 0.02

a

1921, Mar. 21

J15 SP6 2c on 15c gray 25 30
J16 SP6 4c on 10c rose 15 20
J17 SP9 5c on 25c bl 15 20
J18 SP6 6c on 20c org 15 20
J19 SP6 10c on 20c org 40 50

Surcharged:

Segnatasse

L. 0.20

b

J20 SP7 20c on 45c ol grn 30 40
J21 SP7 30c on 1cor dk sl 30 45
J22 SP7 40c on 80c vio 20 30
J23 SP7 50c on 60c car 25 40
J24 SP7 60c on 45c ol grn 30 40
J25 SP7 80c on 45c ol grn 30 45

Surcharged type "a."

J26 SP8 1 l on 2cor red brn 50 75
Nos. J15-J26 (12) 3.25 4.55

See note below No. 85 regarding settings of "Valore Globale" overprint.

NEWSPAPER STAMPS.

Newspaper Stamp of Hungary, 1914, Overprinted FIUME

1918, Dec. 2 *Imperf.* **Wmk. 137**

P1 N5 (2f) orange 45 30

No. P1 with overprint handstamped sells for more.

Eagle
N1

1919 *Perf. 11½* **Unwmkd.**

P2 N1 2c dp buff 45 75

Re-engraved

P3 N1 2c dp buff 75 1.40

In the re-engraved stamp the top of the "2" is rounder and broader, the feet of the eagle show clearly and the diamond at bottom has six lines instead of five.

Steamer
N2

1920, Sept. 12

P4 N2 1c gray grn 22 38
No. P4 exists imperf.

See note on FIUME-KUPA Zone, Italian Occupation, after Jugoslavia No. NJ22.

FRANCE

(frâns)

LOCATION — Western Europe.
GOVT.—Republic.
AREA—210,033 sq. mi.
POP.—54,539,000 (est. 1984).
CAPITAL—Paris.

100 Centimes = 1 Franc

Prices of early French stamps vary according to condition. Quotations for Nos. 1–48 are for fine copies. Very fine to superb specimens sell at much higher prices, and inferior or poor copies sell at reduced prices, depending on the condition of the individual specimen.

Ceres
A1

FORTY CENTIMES.

4 Type I. 4 Type II.

Typographed

1849–50 *Imperf.* **Unwmkd.**

1 A1 10c bis, *yelsh* ('50) 1,400. 350.00
a. 10c dk bis, *yelsh* 1,650. 400.00
b. 10c grnsh bis 2,750. 550.00
c. Tête bêche pr. 57,500. 12,000.
2 A1 15c yel grn, *grnsh* ('50) 12,000. 1,250.
a. 15c grn, *grnsh* 13,500. 1,350.
b. Tête bêche pair 135,000.
3 A1 20c blk, *yelsh* 300.00 52.50
a. 20c blk 500.00 60.00
b. 20c blk, *buff* 1,650. 375.00
c. Tête bêche pair 6,000. 6,000.
4 A1 20c dk bl 1,500.
a. 20c bl, *bluish* 1,650.
b. 20c bl, *yelsh* 2,000.
c. Tête bêche pair 30,000.
6 A1 25c lt bl, *bluish* 3,750. 37.50
a. 25c bl, *bluish* ('50) 4,500. 60.00
b. 25c bl, *yelsh* 3,750. 52.50
c. Tête bêche pr. 100,000. 9,000.
7 A1 40c org, *yelsh* (I)('50) 2,250. 525.00
a. 40c org ver, *yelsh* (I) 2,750. 675.00
b. 40c org, *yelsh* (II) 15,000. 3,750.
c. Pair, types I and II 22,500. 8,000.
8 A1 1fr dl org red 30,000. 13,500.
a. 1fr ver, *yelsh* 55,000. 20,000.
b. Tête bêche pair 225,000. 165,000.
c. 1fr pale ver ("Vervelle") 18,000.
9 A1 1fr dk car, *yelsh* 6,750. 1,000.
a. Tête bêche pair 100,000. 21,000.
b. 1fr brn car 9,000. 1,350.
c. 1fr lt car 7,000. 1,000.

No. 4, which lacks gum, was not issued due to a rate change to 25c after the stamps were prepared.

An ungummed sheet of No. 8c was found in 1895 among the effects of Anatole A. Hulot, the printer. It was sold to Ernest Vervelle, a Parisian dealer, by whose name the stamps are known.

Nos. 1, 4, 6, 7 and 13 are of similar designs and colors to French Colonies Nos. 9, 11, 12, 14, and 8. There are numerous shades of each. They can seldom be correctly allocated except by the cancellations.

See Nos. 329–329e, 612–613, 624.

1862 **Re-issue.**

1d A1 10c bister 300.00
2d A1 15c yel grn 400.00
3d A1 20c blk, *yelsh* 260.00
4d A1 20c blue 260.00
6d A1 25c blue 260.00
7d A1 40c org (I) 350.00
7e A1 40c org (II) 10,000.
9d A1 1fr pale lake 450.00

The re-issues are in lighter colors and on whiter paper than the originals. An official imitation of the essay, 25c on 20c blue, was made at the same time as the re-issues.

President Louis Napoleon
A2

Emperor Napoleon III
A3

1852

10 A2 10c pale bis, *yelsh* 22,500. 600.00
a. 10c dk bis, *yelsh* 25,000. 675.00
11 A2 25c bl, *bluish* 2,500. 52.50

1862 **Re-issue.**

10b A2 10c bister 375.00
11a A2 25c blue 275.00

The re-issues are in lighter colors and on whiter paper than the originals.

1853–60 *Imperf.*

Die I. The curl above the forehead directly below "R" of "EMPIRE" is made up of two lines very close together, often appearing to form a single thick line. There is no shading across the neck.

Die II. The curl is made of two distinct, more widely separated lines. There are lines of shading across the upper neck.

12 A3 1c ol grn, *pale bl* (II) ('60) 140.00 80.00
a. 1c brnz grn, *pale bluish* 165.00 90.00
13 A3 5c grn, *grnsh* (I) ('54) 600.00 80.00
14 A3 10c bis, *yelsh* (I) 375.00 8.25
a. 10c yel, *yelsh* (I) 1,800. 82.50
b. 10c bis brn, *yelsh* (I) 525.00 25.00
c. 10c bis, *yelsh* (II) ('60) 525.00 30.00
15 A3 20c bl, *bluish* (I) ('54) 165.00 1.00
a. 20c dk bl, *bluish* (I) 250.00 1.65
b. 20c mlky bl (I) 275.00 15.00
c. 20c bl, *lil* (I) 3,500. 90.00
d. 20c bl, *bluish* (II) ('60) 375.00 5.25
e. As "d," tête bêche pair 100,000.
16 A3 20c bl, *grnsh* (I) 4,000. 180.00
a. 20c bl, *grnsh* (II) 4,000. 225.00
17 A3 25c bl, *bluish* (I) 2,000. 275.00

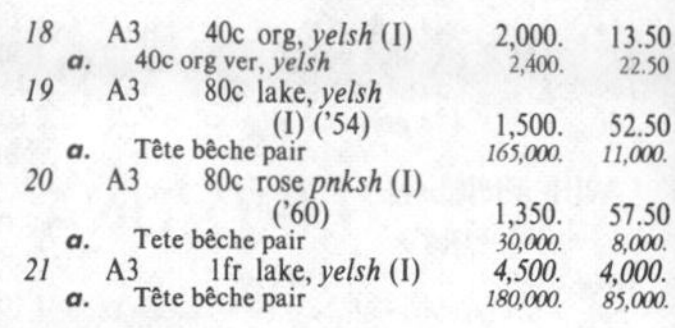

18 A3 40c org, *yelsh* (I) 2,000. 13.50
a. 40c org ver, *yelsh* 2,400. 22.50
19 A3 80c lake, *yelsh* (I) ('54) 1,500. 52.50
a. Tête bêche pair 165,000. 11,000.
20 A3 80c rose *pnksh* (I) ('60) 1,350. 57.50
a. Tete bêche pair 30,000. 8,000.
21 A3 1fr lake, *yelsh* (I) 4,500. 4,000.
a. Tête bêche pair 180,000. 85,000.

Most values of the 1853–60 issue are known unofficially rouletted, pin-perf., perf. 7 and percé en scie.

1862 **Re-issue.**

17c A3 25c bl (I) 250.00
20c A3 80c rose (I) 1,350.
21c A3 1fr lake (I) 1,100.
d. Tête bêche pair 13,500.

The re-issues are in lighter colors and on whiter paper than the originals.

1862-71 *Perf. 14x13½*

22 A3 1c ol grn, *pale bl* (II) 100.00 40.00
a. 1c brnz grn, *pale bl* (II) 100.00 42.50
23 A3 5c yel grn, *grnsh*(I) 150.00 9.00
a. dp grn, *grnsh* (I) 185.00 12.50
24 A3 5c grn, *pale bl* ('71) (I) 900.00 75.00
25 A3 10c bis, *yelsh* (II) 900.00 4.00
a. 10c yel brn, *yelsh* (II) 1,000. 5.00
26 A3 20c bl, *bluish* (II) 185.00 75
a. Tête bêche pair (II) 3,250. 1,000.
27 A3 40c org, *yelsh* (I) 1,000. 6.50
28 A3 80c rose, *pnksh* (I) 850.00 37.50
a. 80c brt rose, *pnksh* (I) 1,000. 60.00
b. Tête bêche pair (I) 11,000. 4,250.

Napoleon III
A4 A5

Napoleon III
A6

1863–70 *Perf. 14x13½*

29 A4 1c brnz grn, *pale bl* ('70) 21.00 12.50
a. 1c ol grn, *pale bl* 24.00 15.00
b. Imperf. 1,000.
30 A4 2c red brn, *yelsh* 57.50 25.00
a. Imperf. 185.00
31 A4 4c gray 135.00 52.50
a. Tête bêche pair 10,000. 7,500.
b. Imperf. 150.00
32 A5 10c bis, *yelsh* ('67) 225.00 5.00
a. Imperf. 150.00
33 A5 20c bl, *bluish* ('67) 165.00 1.25
a. Imperf. 275.00
34 A5 30c brn, *yelsh* ('67) 575.00 18.00
a. 30c dk brn, *yelsh* 825.00 37.50
c. Imperf. 150.00
35 A5 40c org, *yelsh* ('68) 650.00 11.00
a. 40c pale org, *yelsh* 675.00 13.00
b. Imperf. 200.00

36	A5	80c rose, *pnksh* ('68)	600.00	20.00
a.		80c car, *yelsh*	775.00	32.50
b.		Imperf.	450.00	
37	A6	5fr gray lil *lav* ('69)	*5,500.*	850.00
a.		"5" and "F" omitted		*45,000.*
b.		Imperf.	*7,500.*	

No. 33 exists in two types, differing in the size of the dots at either side of POSTES.

On No. 37, the "5" and "F" vary in height from 3¾mm. to 4½mm. All known copies of No. 37a are more or less damaged.

The imperforate varieties of Nos. 29–36 constitute the "Rothschild Issue," said to have been authorized exclusively for the banker to use on his correspondence. Used copies exist.

No. 29 was reprinted in 1887 by authority of Granet, Minister of Posts. The reprints show a yellowish shade under the ultraviolet lamp. Price $850.

Ceres

A7 A8

A9 Type I

A10 Type II

A11 Type III

Bordeaux Issue.
Lithographed.

On the lithographed stamps, except for type I of the 20c, the shading on the cheek and neck is in lines or dashes, not in dots. On the typographed stamps the shading is in dots.

The 2c, 10c and 20c (types II and III) occur in two or more types. The most easily distinguishable are:

2c—Type A. To the left of and within the top of the left "2" are lines of shading composed of dots.

2c—Type B. These lines of dots are replaced by solid lines.

10c—Type A. The inner frame lines are of the same thickness as all other frame lines.

10c—Type B. The inner frame lines are much thicker than the others.

Three Types of the 20c.

A9—Type I. The inscriptions in the upper and lower labels are small and there is quite a space between the upper label and the circle containing the head. There is also very little shading under the eye and in the neck.

A10—Type II. The inscriptions in the labels are similar to those of the first type, the shading under the eye and in the neck is heavier and the upper label and circle almost touch.

A11—Type III. The inscriptions in the labels are much larger than those of the two preceding types, and are similar to those of the other values of the same type in the set.

1870–71 ***Imperf.***

38	A7	1c ol grn, *pale bl*	85.00	90.00
a.		1c brnz grn, *pale bl*	120.00	125.00
39	A7	2c red brn, *yelsh* (B)	225.00	250.00
a.		2c brick red, *yelsh* (B)	1,000.	850.00
b.		2c mar, *yelsh* (B)	1,350.	900.00
c.		2c choc, *yelsh* (A)	900.00	875.00
40	A7	4c gray	250.00	250.00
41	A8	5c grn, *grnsh*	250.00	165.00
a.		5c yel grn, *grnsh*	275.00	185.00
b.		5c emer, *grnsh*	2,500.	1,000.
42	A8	10c bis, *yelsh* (A)	700.00	82.50
a.		10c bis, *yelsh* (B)	825.00	95.00
43	A9	20c bl, *bluish*(I)	*10,000.*	675.00
a.		20c dk bl, *bluish*(I)	*11,000.*	850.00
44	A10	20c bl, *bluish* (II)	850.00	57.50
a.		20c dk bl, *bluish* (II)	1,150.	100.00
b.		20c ultra, *bluish* (II)	*16,500.*	*3,000.*
45	A11	20c bl, *bluish* (III) ('71)	850.00	18.00
a.		20c ultra, *bluish* (III)	2,250.	675.00
46	A8	30c brn, *yelsh*	375.00	275.00
a.		30c blk brn, *yelsh*	1,500.	825.00
47	A8	40c org, *yelsh*	400.00	125.00
a.		40c yel org, *yelsh*	400.00	125.00
b.		40c red org, *yelsh*	600.00	180.00
c.		40c scar, *yelsh*	*5,250.*	*1,900.*
48	A8	80c rose, *pnksh*	575.00	275.00
a.		80c dl rose, *pnksh*	625.00	275.00

All values of the 1870 issue are known rouletted, pin-perf. and perf. 14, unofficially.

A12

Blue Surcharge

1871 Typographed. ***Perf. 14x13½.***

49	A12	10(c) on 10c bis	1,500.	

No. 49 was never placed in use. Counterfeits exist.

Ceres

A13 A14

Two types of the 40c as in the 1849–50 issue.

1870–73 Typo. ***Perf. 14x13½***

50	A7	1c ol grn, *pale bl*	30.00	12.00
a.		1c brnz grn, *pale bl* ('72)	37.50	12.50
51	A7	2c red brn, *yelsh* ('72)	67.50	12.00
52	A7	4c gray ('72)	300.00	37.50
53	A7	5c yel grn, *pale bl*('72)	120.00	7.50
a.		5c grn	125.00	9.00
54	A13	10c bis, *yelsh*	400.00	50.00
a.		Tête bêche pair	*4,000.*	2,000.
55	A13	10c bis, *rose*('73)	300.00	8.75
a.		Tête bêche pair	3,000.	1,500.
56	A13	15c bis, *yelsh* ('71)	300.00	3.75
a.		Tête bêche pair	*27,500.*	*7,000.*
57	A13	20c dl bl, *bluish*	225.00	6.00
a.		20c brt bl, *bluish*	240.00	9.00
b.		Tête bêche pair	2,750.	1,350.
58	A13	25c bl, *bluish* ('71)	95.00	90
a.		25c dk bl, *bluish*	100.00	1.00
b.		Tête bêche pair	*5,000.*	*2,500.*
59	A13	40c org, *yelsh* (I)	450.00	4.50
a.		40c org yel, *yelsh* (I)	575.00	6.00
b.		40c org, *yelsh* (II)	2,250.	150.00
c.		40c org yel, *yelsh* (II)	2,250.	150.00
d.		Pair, types I and II	*4,000.*	500.00

No. 58 exists in three main plate varieties, differing in one or another of the flower-like corner ornaments.

Nos. 54, 57 and 58 were reprinted imperf. in 1887. See note after No. 37.

1872-75 Larger Numerals.

60	A14	10c bis, *rose* ('75)	250.00	8.75
a.		Cliché of 15c in plate of 10c	*3,250.*	*3,750.*
b.		As "a," se-tenant with #60	*4,500.*	*4,750.*
61	A14	15c bis ('73)	250.00	4.50
62	A14	30c brn, *yelsh*	475.00	6.00
63	A14	80c rose, *pnksh*	550.00	12.50

Peace and Commerce ("Type Sage")

A15

Type I. The "N" of "INV" is under the "B" of "REPUBLIQUE".

Type II. The "N" of "INV" is under the "U" of "REPUBLIQUE".

1876-78 Type I.

64	A15	1c grn, *grnsh*	115.00	52.50
a.		Imperf.	165.00	
65	A15	2c grn, *grnsh*	1,150.	275.00
a.		Imperf.	1,100.	
66	A15	4c grn, *grnsh*	100.00	45.00
a.		Imperf.	165.00	
67	A15	5c grn, *grnsh*	600.00	45.00
a.		Imperf.	525.00	
68	A15	10c grn, *grnsh*	750.00	22.50
a.		Imperf.	600.00	
69	A15	15c gray lil, *grysh*	675.00	18.00
a.		Imperf.	600.00	
70	A15	20c red brn, *straw*	500.00	16.00
a.		Imperf.	400.00	
71	A15	20c bl, *bluish*	*13,500.*	
72	A15	25c ultra, *bluish*	*5,250.*	52.50
73	A15	30c brn, *yelsh*	300.00	8.25
a.		Imperf.	275.00	
74	A15	40c red, *straw* ('78)	375.00	30.00
a.		Imperf.	275.00	
75	A15	75c car, *rose*	750.00	11.00
a.		Imperf.	600.00	
76	A15	1fr brnz grn, *straw*	525.00	10.00
a.		Imperf.	450.00	

No. 71 was never put into use.

The reprints of No. 71 are of the second type. They are imperforate or with forged perforation.

1876-77 Type II.

77	A15	2c grn, *grnsh*	82.50	19.00
78	A15	5c grn, *grnsh*	18.50	30
a.		Imperf.	185.00	
79	A15	10c grn, *grnsh*	1,000.	250.00
80	A15	15c gray lil, *grysh*	450.00	1.25
81	A15	25c ultra, *bluish*	350.00	30
a.		25c bl, *bluish*	375.00	50
b.		Pair, types I & II	*32,500.*	*10,000.*
c.		Imperf.	350.00	
82	A15	30c yel brn, *yelsh*	32.50	65
a.		30c brn, *yelsh*	37.50	75
b.		Imperf.	525.00	
83	A15	75c car, *rose* ('77)	1,800.	85.00
84	A15	1fr brnz grn, *straw* ('77)	65.00	5.25
a.		Imperf.	525.00	

1877-80

86	A15	1c *lil bl*	2.25	60
a.		1c *gray bl*	2.50	65
b.		Imperf.	67.50	
87	A15	1c *Prus bl* ('80)	*9,000.*	*4,000.*
88	A15	2c brn, *straw*	3.25	75
a.		2c brn, *yel*	4.50	1.50
b.		Imperf.	67.50	
89	A15	3c yel, *straw* ('78)	190.00	4.50
a.		Imperf.	120.00	
90	A15	4c cl, *lav*	3.25	1.65
a.		4c vio brn, *lav*	5.25	3.00
b.		Imperf.	67.50	
91	A15	10c *lavender*	30.00	85
a.		10c *rose lil*	32.50	1.25
b.		10c *lil*	32.50	1.25
c.		Imperf.	75.00	
92	A15	15c bl ('78)	18.00	30
a.		Imperf.	95.00	
b.		15c bl, *bluish*	325.00	3.75
93	A15	25c *red* ('78)	775.00	22.50
a.		Imperf.	700.00	
94	A15	35c *yel* ('78)	400.00	32.50
a.		35c *yel org*	450.00	37.50
b.		Imperf.	400.00	
95	A15	40c red, *straw* ('80)	52.50	1.25
a.		Imperf.	250.00	
96	A15	5fr vio, *lav*	500.00	85.00
a.		5fr red lil, *lav*	525.00	90.00
b.		Imperf.	800.00	

1879-90

97	A15	3c gray, *grysh*('80)	2.25	1.00
a.		Imperf.	67.50	
98	A15	20c red, *yel grn*	30.00	2.25
a.		20c red, *dp grn* ('84)	40.00	4.50
b.		Imperf.	82.50	
99	A15	25c yel, *straw*	275.00	4.00
a.		Imperf.	285.00	
100	A15	25c *pale rose* ('86)	32.50	45
a.		Imperf.	120.00	
101	A15	50c [illegible] ('90)	[illegible]	1.00
a.		50c car, *rose*	125.00	1.00
102	A15	75c dp vio, *org* ('90)	185.00	30.00
a.		75c dp vio, *yel*	190.00	37.50

1892 Quadrille Paper

103	A15	15c blue	11.00	28
a.		Imperf.	135.00	

1898–1900 Ordinary Paper

104	A15	5c yel grn	12.00	28
a.		Imperf.	90.00	

Type I.

105	A15	5c yel grn	9.00	65
a.		Imperf.	325.00	
106	A15	10c *lavender*	15.00	2.00
a.		Imperf.	180.00	
107	A15	50c car, *rose*	125.00	30.00
108	A15	2fr brn, *az* ('00)	110.00	37.50
b.		Imperf.	*2,100.*	

See also No. 226.

Reprints of A15, type II, were made in 1887 and left imperf. See note after No. 37. Price for set of 27, $2,750.

Liberty, Equality and Fraternity

A16

"The Rights of Man"

A17

Liberty and Peace

A18

1900–29 ***Perf. 14x13½***

109	A16	1c gray	70	15
a.		Imperf.	37.50	
110	A16	2c vio brn	80	10
a.		Imperf.	55.00	
111	A16	3c orange	90	15
a.		3c red	20.00	5.00
b.		Imperf.	40.00	
112	A16	4c yel brn	3.50	75
a.		Imperf.	180.00	
113	A16	5c green	3.00	8
a.		Imperf.	75.00	
b.		Bklt. pane of 10	35.00	
114	A16	7½c lil ('26)	75	32
115	A16	10c lil ('29)	6.00	15
116	A17	10c carmine	26.00	75
a.		Numerals printed separately	30.00	10.00
b.		Imperf., #116 or 116a	300.00	*200.00*
117	A17	15c orange	9.00	30
a.		Imperf.	225.00	*165.00*
118	A17	20c brn vio	75.00	8.25
119	A17	25c blue	135.00	1.25
a.		Numerals printed separately	135.00	7.00
b.		Imperf. #119 or 119a	650.00	*400.00*
120	A17	30c violet	95.00	5.50
121	A18	40c red & pale bl	20.00	50
a.		Imperf.	225.00	150.00
122	A18	45c grn & bl ('06)	27.50	1.25
a.		Imperf.	225.00	165.00

123	A18	50c	bis brn & lav	135.00	1.40
a.	Imperf.			350.00	275.00
124	A18	60c	vio & ultra ('20)	1.40	45
a.	Imperf.			525.00	375.00
125	A18	1fr	cl & ol grn	40.00	30
a.	Imperf.			210.00	165.00
126	A18	2fr	gray vio & yel	950.00	80.00
a.	Imperf.			*2,500.*	*1,500.*
127	A18	2fr	org & pale bl ('20)	60.00	32
a.	Imperf.			600.00	450.00
128	A18	3fr	vio & bl ('25)	30.00	7.50
129	A18	3fr	brt vio & rose ('27)	75.00	1.65
a.	Imperf.			450.00	
130	A18	5fr	dk bl & buff	125.00	4.00
a.	Imperf.			1,100.	600.00
131	A18	10fr	grn & red ('26)	150.00	16.00
132	A18	20fr	mag & grn ('26)	225.00	37.50
			Nos. 109-132 (24)	2,194.55	168.62

In the 10c and 25c values, the first printings show the numerals to have been impressed by a second operation, whereas, in later printings, the numerals were inserted in the plates. Two operations were used for all 20c and 30c, and one operation for the 15c.

No. 114 was issued precanceled only. Prices for precanceled stamps in first column are for those which have not been through the post and have original gum. Prices in the second column are for postally used, gumless stamps.

See also No. P7.

Flat Plate & Rotary Press

The following stamps were printed by both flat plate and rotary press: Nos. 109-113, 144-146, 163, 166, 168, 170, 177-178, 185, 192 and P7.

"Rights of Man"—A19

Sower A20

1902

133	A19	10c	rose red	30.00	45
a.	Imperf., without gum			225.00	
134	A19	15c	pale red	11.00	30
a.	Imperf., without gum			400.00	
135	A19	20c	brn vio	110.00	15.00
a.	Imperf., without gum			450.00	
136	A19	25c	blue	125.00	1.65
137	A19	30c	lilac	300.00	12.50
a.	Imperf., without gum			750.00	
			Nos. 133-137 (5)	576.00	29.90

1903-38

138	A20	10c	rose	11.00	22
a.	Imperf.			120.00	75.00
139	A20	15c	sl grn	3.75	5
a.	Imperf.			110.00	70.00
b.	Booklet pane of 10			50.00	
140	A20	20c	vio brn	90.00	1.35
a.	Imperf.			200.00	110.00
141	A20	25c	dl bl	100.00	1.25
a.	Imperf.			225.00	110.00
142	A20	30c	violet	225.00	6.00
a.	Imperf.			600.00	300.00
143	A20	45c	lt vio ('26)	7.00	65
144	A20	50c	dl bl ('21)	32.50	60
a.	Imperf.			110.00	
145	A20	50c	gray grn ('26)	8.00	30
a.	Imperf.			135.00	
146	A20	50c	ver ('26)	45	5
a.	Booklet pane of 10			9.00	
b.	Imperf.			90.00	
147	A20	50c	grnsh bl ('38)	1.50	15
a.	Imperf.			60.00	
148	A20	60c	lt vio ('24)	8.00	80
149	A20	65c	rose ('24)	3.25	60
a.	Imperf.			185.00	
150	A20	65c	gray grn ('27)	9.00	90
151	A20	75c	rose lil ('26)	5.75	30
a.	Imperf.			475.00	
152	A20	80c	ver ('26)	40.00	7.25
153	A20	85c	ver ('24)	16.00	60
154	A20	1fr	dl bl ('26)	8.25	22
			Nos. 138-154 (17)	569.45	21.29

See also Nos. 941, 942A.

Sower, Ground under Feet

A21

Sower, no Ground under Feet

A22

1906

With Ground Under Feet of Figure

155	A21	10c	red	4.00	65
a.	Imperf., pair, without gum			225.00	

1906-37

TEN AND THIRTY-FIVE CENTIMES.

Type I. Numerals and letters of the inscriptions thin.

Type II. Numerals and letters thicker.

No Ground Under the Feet.

156	A22	1c	ol bis ('33)	15	15
157	A22	2c	dk grn ('33)	22	10
158	A22	3c	ver ('33)	15	10
159	A22	5c	green	2.75	5
a.	Imperf., pair			27.50	
b.	Bklt. pane of 10			42.50	
160	A22	5c	org ('21)	2.25	15
a.	Bklt. pane of 10			40.00	
161	A22	5c	cer ('34)	22	15
162	A22	10c	red (II)	2.75	5
a.	Imperf., pair			27.50	
b.	10c red (I) ('06)			11.00	30
c.	Booklet pane of 10 (I)			140.00	
d.	Booklet pane of 10 (II)			85.00	
e.	Booklet pane of 6 (II)			275.00	
163	A22	10c	grn (II) ('21)	75	10
a.	10c grn (I) ('27)			35.00	30.00
b.	Booklet pane of 10 (II)			17.50	
c.	Booklet pane of 10 (I)			475.00	
164	A22	10c	ultra ('32)	1.40	22
165	A22	15c	red brn ('26)	32	5
a.	Booklet pane of 10			27.50	
166	A22	20c	brown	4.50	30
a.	Imperf., pair			45.00	
167	A22	20c	red vio ('26)	32	10
a.	Bklt. pane of 10			7.50	
168	A22	25c	blue	2.75	10
a.	Bklt. pane of 10			35.00	
b.	Imperf., pair			45.00	
169	A22	25c	brn ('27)	22	10
170	A22	30c	orange	18.00	90
a.	Imperf., pair			140.00	
171	A22	30c	red ('21)	12.00	1.65
172	A22	30c	cer ('25)	1.40	30
a.	Booklet pane of 10			14.00	
173	A22	30c	lt bl ('25)	3.75	22
a.	Bklt. pane of 10			40.00	
174	A22	30c	cop red ('37)	45	10
a.	Booklet pane of 10			9.00	
175	A22	35c	vio (II) ('26)	15.00	50
a.	Imperf., pair			140.00	
b.	35c vio (I) ('06)			225.00	5.25
176	A22	35c	grn ('37)	85	20
177	A22	40c	ol ('25)	1.50	30
b.	Bklt. pane of 10			37.50	
178	A22	40c	ver ('26)	2.50	22
a.	Bklt. pane of 10			30.00	
179	A22	40c	vio ('27)	3.00	22
180	A22	40c	lt ultra ('28)	2.25	15
181	A22	1.05fr	ver ('25)	10.00	2.75
182	A22	1.10fr	cer ('27)	15.00	1.50
183	A22	1.40fr	cer ('26)	22.50	16.00
184	A22	2fr	Prus grn ('31)	18.00	45
			Nos. 156-184 (29)	144.95	27.18

The 10c and 35c, type I, were slightly retouched by adding thin white outlines to the sack of grain, the underside of the right arm and the back of the skirt. It is difficult to distinguish the retouches except on clearly-printed copies. The white outlines were made stronger on the stamps of type II.

Stamps of types A16, A18, A20 and A22 were printed in 1916-20 on paper of poor quality, usually grayish and containing bits of fiber. This is called G. C. (Grande Consommation) paper.

Nos. 160, 162b, 163, 175b and 176 also exist imperf.

See also Nos. 241-241b, P8.

Louis Pasteur

A23

1923-26

185	A23	10c	green	80	22
a.	Booklet pane of 10			11.00	
186	A23	15c	grn ('24)	2.25	22
187	A23	20c	grn ('26)	3.50	45
188	A23	30c	red	50	32
189	A23	30c	grn ('26)	90	22
190	A23	45c	red ('24)	2.25	1.00
191	A23	50c	blue	5.25	15
192	A23	75c	bl ('24)	4.50	30
a.	Imperf., pair			275.00	
193	A23	90c	red ('26)	13.50	3.00
194	A23	1fr	bl ('25)	26.00	15
195	A23	1.25fr	bl ('26)	24.00	6.00
196	A23	1.50fr	bl ('26)	6.50	15
			Nos. 185-196 (12)	89.95	12.18

Nos. 185, 188 and 191 were issued to commemorate the centenary of the birth of Pasteur.

No. 125 Overprinted in Blue

CONGRES PHILATELIQUE
DE
BORDEAUX
1923

1923, June 15

197	A18	1fr	cl & ol grn	475.00	475.00

Allegory of Olympic Games at Paris

A24

The Trophy

A25

Milo of Crotona

A26

Victorious Athlete

A27

Perf. 14x13½, 13½x14

1924, Apr. 1

198	A24	10c	gray grn & yel grn	1.90	50
199	A25	25c	rose & dk rose	2.75	28
200	A26	30c	brn red & blk	10.00	8.00
201	A27	50c	ultra & dk bl	22.50	4.00

8th Olympic Games, Paris. Exist imperf.

Pierre de Ronsard

A28

1924, Oct. 6 *Perf. 14x13½*

219	A28	75c	bl, *bluish*	1.75	1.00

Issued to commemorate the 400th anniversary of the birth of Pierre de Ronsard, poet (1524-1585).

"Light and Liberty" Allegory—A29

Majolica Vase

A30

Potter Decorating Vase—A31

Terrace of Château—A32

1924-25 *Perf. 14x13½, 13½x14.*

220	A29	10c	dk grn & yel ('25)	75	45
221	A30	15c	ind & grn ('25)	75	45
a.	Imperf.			225.00	
222	A31	25c	vio brn & garnet	90	22
223	A32	25c	gray bl & vio ('25)	1.40	50
a.	Imperf.			400.00	
224	A31	75c	ind & ultra	3.75	1.40
225	A29	75c	dk bl & lt bl ('25)	15.00	6.00
a.	Imperf.			300.00	
			Nos. 220-225 (6)	22.55	9.02

Issued to commemorate the International Exhibition of Decorative Modern Arts at Paris, 1925.

Philatelic Exhibition Issue.
Souvenir Sheet.

A32a

1925, May 2 *Perf. 14x13½*

No.	Type	Description	Unused	Used
226	A32a	5fr car (A15, type II) sheet of four	1,000.	1,000.
a.		Imperf. sheet	4,750.	
b.		Single stamp, perf.	120.00	110.00
c.		Single stamp, imperf.	900.00	

Issued in sheets measuring 140x220 mm.
These were not on sale at post offices but solely at the International Philatelic Exhibition, Paris, May, 1925.

Stamps of 1907–26 Surcharged **=25c**

1926-27

No.	Type	Description	Unused	Used
227	A22	25c on 30c lt bl	38	22
228	A22	25c on 35c vio	38	30
a.		Double surcharge	300.00	
229	A20	50c on 60c lt vio ('27)	1.50	60
230	A20	50c on 65c rose ('27)	1.25	30
231	A23	50c on 75c bl	3.25	30
232	A20	50c on 80c ver ('27)	1.50	60
233	A20	50c on 85c ver ('27)	2.50	30
234	A22	50c on 1.05fr ver ('27)	2.00	45
235	A23	50c on 1.25fr bl	2.00	30
236	A20	55c on 60c lt vio	135.00	52.50
238	A22	90c on 1.05fr ver	4.00	2.75
240	A22	1.10fr on 1.40fr cer	1.40	45
		Nos. 227-240 (12)	155.16	59.07

No. 236 is known only precanceled. See second note after No. 132.
Nos. 229, 230, 234, 238 and 240 have three bars instead of two. The 55c surcharge has thinner, larger numerals and a rounded "c." Width, including bars, is 17mm., instead of 13mm.

Strasbourg Exhibition Issue.
Souvenir Sheet.

A32b

1927, June 4

No.	Type	Description	Unused	Used
241	A32b	Sheet of two	950.00	950.00
a.		5fr lt ultra (A22)	190.00	190.00
b.		10fr car rose (A22)	190.00	190.00

Issued in sheets measuring 111x140mm. Sold at the Strasbourg Philatelic Exhibition as souvenirs.

Marcelin Berthelot—A33

1927, Sept. 7

No.	Type	Description	Unused	Used
242	A33	90c dl rose	1.75	32

Issued to commemorate the centenary of the birth of Marcelin Berthelot (1827–1907), chemist and statesman.

Lafayette, Washington, S. S. Paris and Airplane "Spirit of St. Louis"

A34

1927, Sept. 15

No.	Type	Description	Unused	Used
243	A34	90c dl red	1.00	65
a.		Value omitted	1,250.	
244	A34	1.50fr dp bl	3.00	90
a.		Value omitted	1,100.	

Visit of American Legionnaires to France, September, 1927. Exist imperf.

Joan of Arc

A35

1929, Mar.

No.	Type	Description	Unused	Used
245	A35	50c dl bl	1.50	18
a.		Booklet pane of 10	16.00	
b.		Imperf.	135.00	

Issued in commemoration of the 500th anniversary of the relief of Orleans by the French forces led by Joan of Arc.

Le Havre Exhibition Issue.

A36

Blue Overprint.

1929, May 18

No.	Type	Description	Unused	Used
246	A36	2fr org & pale bl	575.00	575.00

No. 246 was sold exclusively at the International Philatelic Exhibition, Le Havre, May, 1929. Sold for 7fr, which included a 5fr admission ticket.
Excellent counterfeits of No. 246 exist.

Reims Cathedral

A37

Dies I, II & III. Die IV

Die I Die II Die III

3fr—Die I. The window of the first turret on the left is made of two lines. The horizontal line of the frame surrounding 3F is not continuous.
3fr—Die II. Same as Die I but the line under 3F is continuous.
3fr—Die III. Same as Die II but there is a deeply cut line separating 3 and F.
3fr—Die IV. The window of the first turret on the left is made of three lines.

Mont-Saint-Michel

A38

Die I. Die II.

5fr—Die I. The line at the top of the spire is broken.
5fr—Die II. The line is unbroken.

Port of La Rochelle

A39

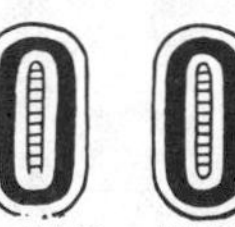

Dies I & II. Die III.

10fr—Die I. The top of the "E" of "POSTES" has a serif. The oval of shading inside the "0" of "10 fr" and the outer oval are broken at their bases.
10fr—Die II. The same top has no serif. Interior and exterior of "0" broken as in Die I.
10fr—Die III. Top of "E" has no serif. Interior and exterior of "0" complete.

Pont du Gard, Nimes

A40

Dies I & II.

Die III.

20fr—Die I. Shading of the first complete arch in the left middle tier is made of horizontal lines. Size 36 x 20¾ mm. Perf. 13½.
20fr—Die II. Same, size 35½ x 21 mm. Perf. 11.
20fr—Die III. Shading of same arch is made of three diagonal lines. Thin paper. Perf. 13.

Engraved.

1929-33 *Perf. 11, 13, 13½*

No.	Type	Description	Unused	Used
247	A37	3fr dk gray ('30) (I)	95.00	2.50
247A	A37	3fr dk gray ('30) (II)	150.00	4.00
247B	A37	3fr dk gray ('30) (III)	475.00	20.00
248	A37	3fr bluish sl ('31) (IV)	95.00	2.50
249	A38	5fr brn ('30) (I)	27.50	1.90
250	A38	5fr brn ('31) (II)	24.00	38
251	A39	10fr lt ultra (I)	135.00	13.00
251A	A39	10fr ultra (II)	150.00	22.50
252	A39	10fr dk ultra ('31) (III)	110.00	6.75
253	A40	20fr red brn (I)	375.00	37.50
254	A40	20fr brt red brn ('33) (II)	1,100.	250.00
254A	A40	20fr org brn ('31) (III)	325.00	32.50

View of Algiers

A41

1929, Jan. 1 **Typographed**

No.	Type	Description	Unused	Used
255	A41	50c bl & rose red	2.75	32

Issued in commemoration of the centenary of the first French settlement in Algeria.

Nos. 146 and 196 Overprinted **CONGRÈS DU B. I. T. 1930**

1930, Apr. 23 *Perf. 14x13½*

No.	Type	Description	Unused	Used
256	A20	50c vermilion	2.75	1.50
257	A23	1.50fr blue	18.00	13.00

International Labor Bureau, 48th Congress, Paris.

Colonial Exposition Issue.

Fachi Woman

A42

French Colonials

A43

1930-31 **Typo.** *Perf. 14x13½*

No.	Type	Description	Unused	Used
258	A42	15c gray blk	65	22
259	A42	40c dk brn	1.75	22
260	A42	50c dk red	60	5
a.		Booklet pane of 10	12.00	
261	A42	1.50fr dp bl	12.50	30

Photogravure.
Perf. 13½.

No.	Type	Description	Unused	Used
262	A43	1.50fr dp bl ('31)	52.50	1.10
		Nos. 258-262 (5)	68.00	1.89

Arc de Triomphe

A44

Peace with Olive Branch

A45

1931 **Engraved** *Perf. 13*

No.	Type	Description	Unused	Used
263	A44	2fr red brn	32.50	45

1932-39 **Typo.** *Perf. 14x13½*

No.	Type	Description	Unused	Used
264	A45	30c dp grn	1.00	38
265	A45	40c brt vio	38	6
266	A45	45c yel brn	2.75	60
267	A45	50c rose red	15	5
a.		Imperf., pair	110.00	
b.		Booklet pane of 10	7.50	
268	A45	55c dl vio ('37)	1.00	28
269	A45	60c ocher ('37)	30	28
270	A45	65c vio brn	50	22
271	A45	65c brt ultra ('37)	45	10
a.		Booklet pane of 10	10.00	
272	A45	75c ol grn	22	15
273	A45	80c org ('38)	18	18
274	A45	90c dk red	40.00	1.75
275	A45	90c brt grn ('38)	10	6

276	A45	90c ultra ('38)	1.00	5
a.		Booklet pane of 10	14.00	
277	A45	1fr orange	3.00	15
278	A45	1fr rose pink ('38)	3.00	15
279	A45	1.25fr brn ol	87.50	2.75
280	A45	1.25fr rose car ('39)	2.75	1.00
281	A45	1.40fr brt red vio ('39)	8.50	4.00
282	A45	1.50fr dp bl	30	22
283	A45	1.75fr magenta	6.25	22
		Nos. 264-283 (20)	159.33	12.65

The 50c is found in 4 types, differing in the lines below belt and size of "c."

Le Puy-en-Velay—A46

1933 Engraved *Perf. 13*

290	A46	90c rose	3.75	45

Aristide Briand A47

Paul Doumer A48

Victor Hugo A49

1933, Dec. 11 Typo. *Perf. 14x13½*

291	A47	30c bl grn	21.00	8.25
292	A48	75c red vio	24.00	75
293	A49	1.25fr claret	6.00	75

Dove and Olive Branch A50

Joseph Marie Jacquard A51

1934, Feb. 20

294	A50	1.50fr ultra	70.00	15.00

1934, Mar. 14 Engr. *Perf. 14x13*

295	A51	40c blue	3.00	75

Issued to commemorate the centenary of the death of Joseph Marie Jacquard (1752–1834), inventor of an improved loom for figured weaving.

Jacques Cartier A52

1934, July 18 *Perf. 13*

296	A52	75c rose lil	22.50	1.50
297	A52	1.50fr blue	52.50	2.75

Issued to commemorate the 400th anniversary of Carter's discovery of Canada.

No. 279 Surcharged

50c

1934, Nov. *Perf. 14x13½*

298	A45	50c on 1.25fr brn ol	5.75	28

Breton River Scene A53

1935, Feb. Engraved *Perf. 13*

299	A53	2fr bl grn	45.00	50

S. S. Normandie—A54

1935, April

300	A54	1.50fr dk bl	18.00	1.10
a.		1.50fr bl ('36)	75.00	15.00
b.		1.50fr bl grn ('36)	4,000.	

Issued in commemoration of the maiden voyage of the transatlantic steamship, the "Normandie".

Benjamin Delessert A55

1935, May 20

301	A55	75c bl grn	25.00	75

Issued in commemoration of the opening of the International Savings Bank Congress, May 20, 1935.

View of St. Trophime at Arles A56

Victor Hugo A57

1935, May 3

302	A56	3.50fr dk brn	37.50	2.50

1935, May 30 *Perf. 14x13*

303	A57	1.25fr magenta	6.00	1.25

Victor Hugo (1802–1885), 50th anniversary of death.

Cardinal Richelieu A58

Jacques Callot A59

1935, June 12 *Perf. 13*

304	A58	1.50fr dp rose	25.00	1.25

Issued in commemoration of the tercentenary of the founding of the French Academy by Cardinal Richelieu.

1935, Nov. *Perf. 14x13*

305	A59	75c red	15.00	38

Issued in commemoration of the 300th anniversary of the death of Jacques Callot, engraver.

André Marie Ampère A60

1936, Feb. 27 *Perf. 13*

306	A60	75c brown	25.00	90

Issued to commemorate the centenary of the death of André Marie Ampère (1775–1836), scientist. (Portrait by Louis Boilly.)

Windmill at Fontvielle, Immortalized by Daudet—A61

1936, Apr. 27

307	A61	2fr ultra	2.25	22

Issued in commemoration of the 70th anniversary of the publication, in 1866, of Alphonse Daudet's "Lettres de mon Moulin".

Pilâtre de Rozier and his Balloon A62

1936, June 4

308	A62	75c Prus bl	25.00	2.25

Issued in commemoration of the 150th anniversary of the death of Jean Joseph Pilâtre de Rozier, balloonist.

Rouget de Lisle A63

"La Marseillaise" A64

1936, June 27

309	A63	20c Prus grn	3.25	75
310	A64	40c dk brn	6.75	2.25

Centenary of the death of Claude Joseph Rouget de Lisle, composer of "La Marseillaise."

Canadian War Memorial at Vimy Ridge—A65

1936, July 26

311	A65	75c hn brn	9.75	1.50
312	A65	1.50fr dl bl	17.50	7.00

Issued to commemorate the unveiling of the Canadian War Memorial at Vimy Ridge, July 26, 1936.

Jean Léon Jaurès A66

Jean Jaurès A67

1936, July 30

313	A66	40c red brn	3.25	60
314	A67	1.50fr ultra	13.00	2.25

Issued in commemoration of the assassination of Jean Léon Jaurès (1859–1914), socialist and politician.

Herald A68

Allegory of Exposition A69

1936, Sept. 15 Typo. *Perf. 14x13½*

315	A68	20c brt vio	45	30
316	A68	30c Prus grn	2.75	95
317	A68	40c ultra	1.25	30
318	A68	50c red org	90	15
319	A69	90c carmine	15.00	7.00
320	A69	1.50fr ultra	30.00	2.00
		Nos. 315-320 (6)	50.35	10.70

Publicity for the 1937 Paris Exposition.

"Peace" A70

1936, Oct. 1 Engr. *Perf. 13*

321	A70	1.50fr blue	18.00	2.25

Skiing A71

1937, Jan. 18

322	A71	1.50fr dk bl	11.00	1.50

Issued in commemoration of the International Ski Meet at Chamonix—Mont Blanc.

Pierre Corneille, Portrait by Charles Le Brun A72

1937, Feb. 15

323	A72	75c brn car	2.50	90

Issued to commemorate the 300th anniversary of the publication of "Le Cid."

Paris Exposition Issue.

Exposition Allegory—A73

1937, Mar. 15

324	A73	1.50fr turq bl	1.75	70

Jean Mermoz A74

Memorial to Mermoz A75

1937, Apr. 27

325	A74	30c dk sl grn	90	45
326	A75	3fr dk vio	8.25	3.25
a.		3fr vio	9.00	3.75

Issued in honor of aviator Jean Mermoz (1901–36).

Electric Train A76

Streamlined Locomotive A77

1937, May 31

327	A76	30c dk grn	1.90	1.10
328	A77	1.50fr dk ultra	11.00	7.00

13th International Railroad Congress.

International Philatelic Exhibition Issue.
Souvenir Sheet

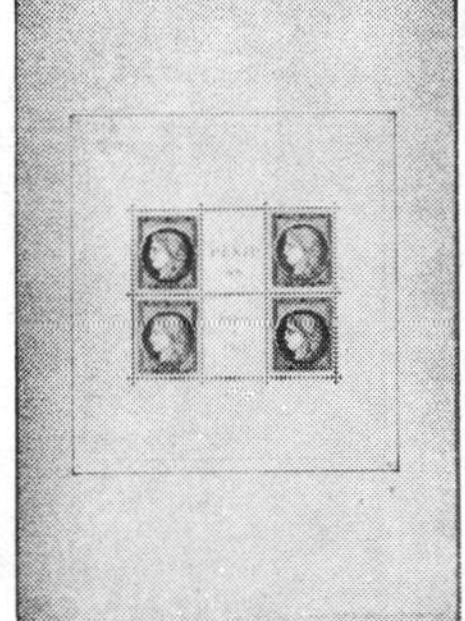

A77a
Ceres Type of 1849–50.

1937, June 18 Typo. ***Perf. 14x13½***

329	A77a	Sheet of four (A1)	250.00	250.00
a.		5c ultra & dk brn	45.00	45.00
b.		15c red & rose red	45.00	45.00
c.		30c ultra & rose red	45.00	45.00
d.		50c red & dk brn	45.00	45.00
e.		Imperf. sheet of four	1,500.	

Issued in sheets measuring 150x220mm. The sheets were sold only at the exhibition in Paris, a ticket of admission being required for each sheet purchased.

René Descartes, by Frans Hals A78

1937, June Engraved ***Perf. 13***

Inscribed: "Discours sur la Méthode."

330	A78	90c cop red	1.50	90

Inscribed "Discours de la Méthode"

331	A78	90c cop red	4.75	90

Issued in commemoration of the third centenary of the publication of "Discours de la Méthode" by René Descartes.

France Congratulating U.S.A.
A79

1937, Sept. 17

332	A79	1.75fr ultra	2.25	1.40

Issued to commemorate the 150th anniversary of the Constitution of the United States of America.

No. 277 Surcharged in Red

80c

1937, Oct. ***Perf. 14x13½***

333	A45	80c on 1fr org	45	30
a.		Inverted surch.	600.00	

Mountain Road at Iseran
A80

1937, Oct. 4 Engraved ***Perf. 13***

334	A80	90c dk grn	90	18

Issued in commemoration of the opening of the mountain road at Iseran, Savoy.

Ceres
A81

1938–40 Typo. ***Perf. 14x13½***

335	A81	1.75fr dk ultra	1.40	22
336	A81	2fr car rose ('39)	30	15
337	A81	2.25fr ultra ('39)	12.00	38
338	A81	2.50fr grn ('39)	3.00	22
339	A81	2.50fr vio bl ('40)	1.10	45
340	A81	3fr rose lil ('39)	1.10	22
		Nos. 335-340 (6)	18.90	1.64

Léon Gambetta A82

1938, Apr. 2 Engraved ***Perf. 13***

341	A82	55c dk vio	50	38

Issued in commemoration of the centenary of the birth of Léon Gambetta (1838-1882), lawyer and statesman.

Arc de Triomphe of Orange
A82a

Miners
A83

Keep and Gate of Vincennes
A86

Palace of the Popes, Avignon
A84

Medieval Walls of Carcassonne
A85

Port of St. Malo—A87

1938

342	A82a	2fr brn blk	1.25	90
343	A83	2.15fr vio brn	3.00	45
344	A84	3fr car brn	14.00	3.25
345	A85	5fr dp ultra	70	38
346	A86	10fr brn, *bl*	2.25	1.50
347	A87	20fr dk bl grn	55.00	17.50
		Nos. 342-347 (6)	76.20	23.98

Clément Ader
A88

1938, June 16

348	A88	50fr ultra (thin paper)	110.00	75.00
a.		50fr dk ultra (thick paper)	125.00	90.00

Issued in honor of Clément Ader, air pioneer.

Soccer Players
A89

1938, June 1

349	A89	1.75fr dk ultra	13.00	8.25

World Cup Soccer Championship.

Costume of Champagne Region
A90

Jean de La Fontaine
A91

1938, June 13

350	A90	1.75fr dk ultra	5.25	3.25

Issued in commemoration of the tercentenary of the birth of Dom Pierre Pérignon, discoverer of the champagne process.

1938, July 8

351	A91	55c dk bl grn	75	50

Issued to honor Jean de La Fontaine (1621-1695) the fabulist.

Seal of Friendship and Peace, Victoria Tower and Arc de Triomphe—A92

1938, July 19

352	A92	1.75fr ultra	1.10	95

Issued in honor of the visit of King George VI and Queen Elizabeth of Great Britain to France.

Mercury
A93

Paul Cézanne, Self-portrait
A95

1938–42 Typo. ***Perf. 14x13½***

353	A93	1c dk brn ('39)	5	5
354	A93	2c sl grn ('39)	5	5
355	A93	5c rose	5	5
356	A93	10c ultra	5	5
357	A93	15c red org	5	5
358	A93	15c org brn ('39)	1.00	30
359	A93	20c red vio	5	5
360	A93	25c bl grn	15	5
361	A93	30c rose red ('39)	5	5
362	A93	40c dk vio ('39)	5	5
363	A93	45c lt grn ('39)	80	30
364	A93	50c dp bl ('39)	3.75	15
365	A93	50c dk grn ('41)	75	15
366	A93	50c grnsh bl ('42)	15	10
367	A93	60c red org ('39)	22	10

368	A93	70c mag ('39)	25	8
369	A93	75c dk org brn ('39)	7.50	1.65
		Nos. 353-369 (17)	14.97	3.28

No. 366 exists imperforate. See also Nos. 455-458.

1939, Mar. 15 Engr. *Perf. 13*

370	A95	2.25fr Prus bl	5.50	2.50

Issued in commemoration of the centenary of the birth of Paul Cézanne (1839-1906), painter.

Georges Clemenceau and Battleship Clemenceau—A96

1939, Apr. 18

371	A96	90c ultra	50	42

Issued to commemorate the laying of the keel of the warship "Clemenceau" January 17, 1939.

Statue of Liberty, French Pavilion, Trylon and Perisphere—A97

1939-40

372	A97	2.25fr ultra	7.50	3.75
373	A97	2.50fr ultra ('40)	4.75	3.25

New York World's Fair.

Joseph Nicéphore Niepce and Louis Jacques Mandé Daguerre A98

1939. Apr. 24

374	A98	2.25fr dk bl	6.75	4.25

Centenary of photography.

Iris A99

Pumping Station at Marly A100

1939-44 Typo. *Perf. 14x13½*

375	A99	80c red brn ('40)	30	22
376	A99	80c yel grn ('44)	6	5
377	A99	1fr green	75	5
378	A99	1fr crim ('40)	22	5
a.		Bklt. pane of 10	7.50	
379	A99	1fr grnsh bl ('44)	6	6
380	A99	1.20fr vio ('44)	6	5
381	A99	1.30fr ultra ('40)	22	22
382	A99	1.50fr red org ('41)	30	30
383	A99	1.50fr hn brn ('44)	6	6
384	A99	2fr vio brn ('44)	15	15
385	A99	2.40fr car rose ('44)	15	15
386	A99	3fr org ('44)	22	8
387	A99	4fr ultra ('44)	30	22
		Nos. 375-387 (13)	2.85	1.66

1939 Engraved. *Perf. 13.*

388	A100	2.25fr brt ultra	9.00	3.00

Issued in commemoration of France's participation in the International Water Exposition at Liège.

St. Gregory of Tours A101

1939, June 10

389	A101	90c red	75	60

Issued to commemorate the 14th centenary of the birth of St. Gregory of Tours, historian and bishop.

"The Oath of the Tennis Court" by Jacques David—A102

1939, June 20

390	A102	90c dp sl grn	1.65	90

150th anniversary of French Revolution.

Cathedral of Strasbourg A103

1939, June 23

391	A103	70c brn car	1.10	75

Issued to commemorate the 500th anniversary of the completion of Strasbourg Cathedral.

Porte Chaussée, Verdun—A104

1939, June 23

392	A104	90c blk brn	1.25	1.00

Issued to commemorate the 23rd anniversary of the Battle of Verdun.

View of Pau A105

1939, Aug. 25

393	A105	90c brt rose, *gray bl*	1.50	50

Maid of Languedoc A106

Bridge at Lyons A107

1939

394	A106	70c blk, *bl*	50	45
395	A107	90c dl brn vio	75	45

Imperforates

Nearly all French stamps issued from 1940 onward exist imperforate. Officially 20 sheets, ranging from 25 to 100 subjects, were left imperforate.

Georges Guynemer A108

1940, Nov. 7

396	A108	50fr ultra	13.00	9.00

Issued in honor of Georges Guynemer (1894-1917), World War I ace.

Stamps of 1938-39 Surcharged in Carmine **1F**

1940-41 *Perf. 14x13½.*

397	A81	1fr on 1.75fr dk ultra	18	18
398	A81	1fr on 2.25fr ultra ('41)	18	18
399	A81	1fr on 2.50fr grn ('41)	55	55

Stamps of 1932-39 Surcharged in Carmine, Red or Black **= 1F**

Perf. 13, 14x13½.

400	A22	30c on 35c grn (C) ('41)	10	10
401	A45	50c on 55c dl vio (C) ('41)	15	15
a.		Invtd. surch.	375.00	
402	A45	50c on 65c brt ultra (C) ('41)	10	10
403	A45	50c on 75c ol grn (C) ('41)	22	22
404	A93	50c on 75c dk org brn (C) ('41)	22	22
405	A45	50c on 80c org (C) ('41)	22	22
406	A45	50c on 90c ultra (C) ('41)	15	15
a.		Invtd. surch.	225.00	
b.		"05" instead of "50"	3,750.	
407	A45	1fr on 1.25fr rose car (Bk) ('41)	22	22
408	A45	1fr on 1.40fr brt red vio (R) ('41)	22	22
a.		Dble. surch.	600.00	
409	A45	1fr on 1.50fr dk bl (C) ('41)	55	55
410	A83	1fr on 2.15fr vio brn (C)	22	22
411	A85	2.50fr on 5fr dp ultra (C) ('41)	25	25
a.		Dble. surch.	180.00	82.50
412	A86	5fr on 10fr brn, *bl* (C) ('41)	1.75	1.75
413	A87	10fr on 20fr dk bl grn (C) ('41)	1.25	1.25
414	A88	20fr on 50fr dk ultra (#348a) (C) ('41)	42.50	42.50
a.		20fr on 50fr ultra, thin paper (#348)	52.50	45.00
		Nos. 400-414 (15)	48.12	48.12

Marshal Pétain A109

Frédéric Mistral A110

1941 *Perf. 13.*

415	A109	40c red brn	50	38
416	A109	80c turq bl	75	50
417	A109	1fr red	22	22
418	A109	2.50fr dp ultra	1.50	90

1941, Feb. 20 *Perf. 14x13*

419	A110	1fr brn lake	15	15

Issued in honor of Frédéric Mistral, poet and Nobel prize winner for literature in 1904.

Beaune Hospital A111

View of Angers A112

Ramparts of St. Louis, Aiguesmortes A113

1941

420	A111	5fr brn blk	30	22
421	A112	10fr dk vio	45	30
422	A113	20fr brn blk	60	50

1942

Inscribed "Postes Francaises". Imprint: "FELTESSE" at right.

423	A111	15fr brn lake	50	30

Marshal Pétain A114 A115

Marshal Pétain A116 A117

Marshal Pétain A118

1941–42 Typo. *Perf. 14x13½*

No.	Type	Value	Color	Unused	Used
427	A114	20c	lil ('42)	5	5
428	A114	30c	rose red	5	5
429	A114	40c	ultra	10	6
431	A115	50c	dp grn	5	5
432	A115	60c	vio ('42)	8	8
433	A115	70c	saph ('42)	8	8
434	A115	70c	org ('42)	8	6
435	A115	80c	brown	10	10
436	A115	80c	emer ('42)	8	8
437	A115	1fr	rose red	6	6
438	A115	1.20fr	red brn ('42)	5	5
439	A116	1.50fr	rose	15	10
440	A116	1.50fr	dl red brn ('42)	5	5
a.			Booklet pane of 10	3.50	
441	A116	2fr	bl grn ('42)	5	5
443	A116	2.40fr	rose red ('42)	15	15
444	A116	2.50fr	ultra	90	45
445	A116	3fr	orange	8	6
446	A115	4fr	ultra ('42)	15	15
447	A115	4.50fr	dk grn ('42)	90	25
			Nos. 427-447 (19)	3.21	1.98

Nos. 431 to 438 measure 16½ x 20½ mm.

No. 440 was forged by the French Underground ("Defense de la France") and used to frank clandestine journals, etc., from February to June, 1944. The forgeries were ungummed, both perforated 11½ and imperforate, with a back handstamp covering six stamps and including the words: "Atelier des Faux."

1942 Engraved. *Perf. 14x13.*

No.	Type	Value	Color	Unused	Used
448	A115	4fr	brt ultra	25	20
449	A115	4.50fr	dk grn	25	10
450	A117	5fr	Prus grn	15	15

Perf. 13

No.	Type	Value	Color	Unused	Used
451	A118	50fr	black	4.00	3.00

Nos. 448 and 449 measure 18x21½mm.

Jules Massenet A119

Stendhal (Marie Henri Beyle) A120

1942, June 22 *Perf. 14x13*

No.	Type	Value	Color	Unused	Used
452	A119	4fr	Prus grn	22	18

Issued to commemorate the centenary of the birth of Jules Massenet (1842–1912), composer.

1942, Sept. 14 *Perf. 13*

No.	Type	Value	Color	Unused	Used
453	A120	4fr	blk brn & org red	32	32

Issued to commemorate the centenary of the death of Stendhal (1783–1842), writer.

André Blondel A121

Town-Hall Belfry, Arras A122

1942, Sept. 14

No.	Type	Value	Color	Unused	Used
454	A121	4fr	dl bl	32	32

Issued in honor of André Eugène Blondel (1863–1938), physicist.

Mercury Type of 1938–42 Inscribed "Postes Françaises".

1942 *Perf. 14x13½*

No.	Type	Value	Color	Unused	Used
455	A93	10c	ultra	6	6
456	A93	30c	rose red	6	6

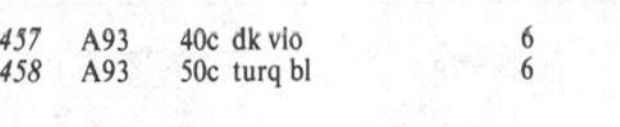

No.	Type	Value	Color	Unused	Used
457	A93	40c	dk vio	6	6
458	A93	50c	turq bl	6	6

1942, Dec. 8 Engraved *Perf. 13*

No.	Type	Value	Color	Unused	Used
459	A122	10fr	green	22	22

Coats of Arms.

Lyon A123

Brittany A124

Provence A125

Ile de France A126

1943 Typographed. *Perf. 14x13½*

No.	Type	Value	Color	Unused	Used
460	A123	5fr	vio bl, org, red org & blk	32	22
461	A124	10fr	ocher & blk	40	30
462	A125	15fr	vio bl, org, red & blk	2.00	1.40
463	A126	20fr	vio bl, org, & dl brn	1.40	90

Antoine Lavoisier A127

1943, July 5 Engr. *Perf. 14x13*

No.	Type	Value	Color	Unused	Used
464	A127	4fr	ultra	15	15

Issued to commemorate the 200th anniversary of the birth of Lavoisier (1743-94), French scientist.

Lake Lerie and Meije Dauphiné Alps—A128

1943, July 5 *Perf. 13*

No.	Type	Value	Color	Unused	Used
465	A128	20fr	dl gray grn	60	60

Nicolas Rolin, Guigone de Salins and Hospital of Beaune—A129

1943, July 21

No.	Type	Value	Color	Unused	Used
466	A129	4fr	blue	30	30

Issued to commemorate the 500th anniversary of the founding of the Hospital of Beaune.

Coats of Arms.

Flanders A130

Languedoc A131

Orléans A132

Normandy A133

1944, Mar. 27 Typo. *Perf. 14x13½*

No.	Type	Value	Color	Unused	Used
467	A130	5fr	ver, org & blk	15	15
468	A131	10fr	brn, blk, dl red & yel	22	22
469	A132	15fr	brn, brt ultra & org	80	60
470	A133	20fr	ultra, dl red org & blk	1.00	75

Edouard Branly A134

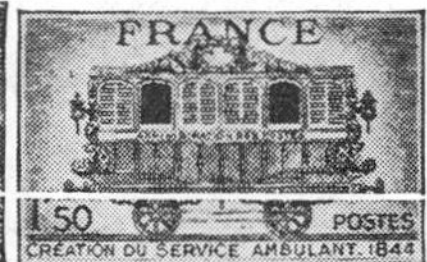

Early Postal Car A135

1944, Feb. 21 Engraved *Perf. 14x13*

No.	Type	Value	Color	Unused	Used
471	A134	4fr	ultra	18	15

Issued to commemorate the centenary of the birth of Edouard Branly, electrical inventor.

1944, June 10 *Perf. 13*

No.	Type	Value	Color	Unused	Used
472	A135	1.50fr	dk bl grn	40	30

Issued to commemorate the centenary of France's traveling postal service.

Chateau de Chenonceaux A136

Claude Chappe A137

1944, June 10

No.	Type	Value	Color	Unused	Used
473	A136	15fr	lil brn	50	50
a.		15fr	blk brn	7.50	1.75
b.		15fr	blk	47.50	

1944, Aug. 14 *Perf. 14x13*

No.	Type	Value	Color	Unused	Used
474	A137	4fr	dk ultra	15	15

Issued to commemorate the 150th anniversary of the invention of an optical telegraph by Claude Chappe (1763–1805).

Gallic Cock A138

Marianne A139

1944 Lithograped *Perf. 12*

No.	Type	Value	Color	Unused	Used
477	A138	10c	yel grn	10	10
478	A138	30c	dk rose vio	22	22
479	A138	40c	blue	10	10
480	A138	50c	dk red	6	6
481	A139	60c	ol brn	10	10
482	A139	70c	rose lil	12	12
483	A139	80c	yel grn	65	65
484	A139	1fr	violet	8	8
485	A139	1.20fr	dp car	10	10
486	A139	1.50fr	dp bl	8	8
487	A138	2fr	indigo	10	10
488	A139	2.40fr	red org	1.25	1.25
489	A139	3fr	dp bl grn	22	22
490	A139	4fr	grnsh bl	22	22
491	A139	4.50fr	black	18	18
492	A139	5fr	vio bl	4.25	4.25
493	A138	10fr	violet	4.75	4.75
494	A138	15fr	ol brn	4.75	4.75
495	A138	20fr	dk sl grn	4.75	4.75
			Nos. 477-495 (19)	22.08	22.08

Nos. 477–495 were issued first in Corsica after the Allied landing, and released in Paris Nov. 15, 1944.

Chateau de Chenonceaux—A140

1944, Oct. 30 Engraved *Perf. 13*

No.	Type	Value	Color	Unused	Used
496	A140	25fr	black	55	55

Thomas Robert Bugeaud A141

1944, Nov. 20

No.	Type	Value	Color	Unused	Used
497	A141	4fr	myr grn	18	18

Issued to commemorate the 100th anniversary of the Battle of Isly, August 14th, 1844.

Church of St. Denis A142

1944, Nov. 20

No.	Type	Value	Color	Unused	Used
498	A142	2.40fr	brn car	15	15

Issued to commemorate the 800th anniversary of the Church of St. Denis.

Type of 1938-42, Overprinted in Black RF Inscribed "Postes Francaises"

1944 *Perf. 14x13½.*

No.	Type	Value	Color	Unused	Used
499	A93	10c	ultra	5	5
500	A93	30c	rose red	15	15
501	A93	40c	dk vio	15	15
502	A93	50c	grnsh bl	15	15

The overprint "RF" in various forms, with or without Lorraine Cross, was also applied to stamps of the French State at Lyon and fourteen other cities.

French Forces of the Interior and Symbol of Liberation A143

1945, Jan.

No.	Type	Value	Color	Unused	Used
503	A143	4fr	dk ultra	35	30

Issued to commemorate the Liberation.

Stamps of the above design, and of one incorporating "FRANCE" in the top panel, were printed by photogravure in England during World War II upon order of the Free French Government. They were not issued. There are three values in each design; 25c green, 1fr red, 2.50fr blue. Price: set, above design, $135; set inscribed "FRANCE," $525.

Marianne
A144

Perf. 11½x12½.

1944–45		Engraved	Unwmkd.	
505	A144	10c ultra	5	5
506	A144	30c bister	5	5
507	A144	40c indigo	5	5
508	A144	50c red org	5	5
509	A144	60c chlky bl	5	5
510	A144	70c sepia	5	5
511	A144	80c dp grn	5	5
512	A144	1fr lilac	5	5
513	A144	1.20fr dk ol grn	5	5
514	A144	1.50fr rose ('44)	5	5
515	A144	2fr dk brn	6	5
516	A144	2.40fr red	6	6
517	A144	3fr brt ol grn	6	5
518	A144	4fr brt ultra	5	5
519	A144	4.50fr sl gray	15	15
520	A144	5fr brt org	22	22
521	A144	10fr yel grn	32	30
522	A144	15fr lake	32	30
523	A144	20fr brn org	1.50	95
523A	A144	50fr dp pur	4.00	2.50
		Nos. 505-523A (20)	7.24	5.13

The 2.40fr exists imperf. in a miniature sheet of 4 which was not issued.

Coat of Arms A145 · Ceres A146 · Marianne A147

1945–47		Typo.	Perf. 14x13½.	
524	A145	10c brn blk	5	5
525	A145	30c dk bl grn	10	10
526	A145	40c lil rose	10	10
527	A145	50c vio bl	5	5
528	A146	60c brt ultra	10	10
530	A146	80c brt grn	5	5
531	A146	90c dl grn ('46)	75	35
532	A146	1fr rose red	10	6
533	A146	1.20fr brn blk	18	15
534	A146	1.50fr rose lil	10	6
535	A147	1.50fr rose pink	15	15
536	A147	2fr myr grn	10	6
536A	A146	2fr lt bl grn ('46)	18	10
537	A147	2.40fr scarlet	38	30
538	A146	2.50fr brn ('46)	18	15
539	A147	3fr sepia	10	6
540	A147	3fr dp rose ('46)	15	6
541	A147	4fr ultra	15	15
541A	A147	4fr vio ('46)	15	12
541B	A147	4.50fr ultra ('47)	10	5
542	A147	5fr lt grn	15	5
542A	A147	5fr rose pink ('47)	6	5
543	A147	6fr brt ultra	38	30
544	A147	6fr crim rose ('46)	25	8
545	A147	10fr red org	38	15
546	A147	10fr ultra ('46)	1.25	42
547	A147	15fr brt red vio	2.50	85
		Nos. 524-547 (27)	8.19	4.17

No. 531 is known only precanceled. See second note after No. 132.

Due to a reduction of the domestic postage rate, No. 542A was sold for 4.50fr.

See also Nos. 576 to 580, 594 to 602, 614, 615, 650 to 654.

Engraved.

1945–46			Perf. 14x13	
548	A147	4fr dk bl	18	15
549	A147	10fr dp bl ('46)	48	22
550	A147	15fr brt red vio ('46)	6.00	1.50
551	A147	20fr bl grn ('46)	95	22
552	A147	25fr red ('46)	4.75	1.00
		Nos. 548-552 (5)	12.36	3.09

Marianne
A148

1945		Engraved	Perf. 13	
553	A148	20fr dk grn	1.50	60
554	A148	25fr violet	1.90	95
555	A148	50fr red brn	2.00	90
556	A148	100fr brt rose car	12.00	4.50

CFA

French stamps inscribed or surcharged "CFA" and new value are listed under Réunion in Vol. IV.

Arms of Metz A149 · Arms of Strasbourg A150

1945, Mar. 3			Perf. 14x13	
557	A149	2.40fr dl bl	18	18
558	A150	4fr blk brn	18	18

Liberation of Metz and Strasbourg.

Costumes of Alsace and Lorraine and Cathedrals of Strasbourg and Metz—A151

1945, May 16			Perf. 13	
559	A151	4fr hn brn	18	18

Liberation of Alsace and Lorraine.

World Map Showing French Possessions—A152

1945, Sept. 17				
560	A152	2fr Prus bl	18	18

No. B193 Surcharged with New Value in Black.

1946			Perf. 14x13½	
561	SP147	3fr on 2fr + 1fr red org	15	15

Coats of Arms.

Corsica A153 · Alsace A154

Lorraine A155 · County of Nice A156

Typographed.

1946		Perf. 14x13½.	Unwmkd.	
562	A153	10c dp ultra & blk	5	5
563	A154	30c blk, red org & yel	6	5
564	A155	50c brn, yel & red	6	5
565	A156	60c red, ultra & blk	6	6

Reaching for "Peace" A157 · Holding the Dove of Peace A158

1946, July 29		Engraved	Perf. 13	
566	A157	3fr Prus grn	18	18
567	A158	10fr dk bl	18	18

Peace Conference of Paris, 1946.

Vézelay
A159

Luxembourg Palace
A160

Rocamadour
A161

Pointe du Raz, Finistère
A162

1946		Perf. 13.	Unwmkd.	
568	A159	5fr rose vio	22	22
569	A160	10fr dk bl	22	15
570	A161	15fr dk vio brn	90	22
571	A162	20fr sl gray	30	15

See also Nos. 591–592.

Globe and Wreath
A163

1946, Nov.				
572	A163	10fr dk bl	25	25

Issued to honor the general conference of the United Nations Educational, Scientific and Cultural Organization, Paris, 1946.

Cannes
A164

Stanislas Square, Nancy
A165

1946–48		Engraved	Perf. 13	
573	A164	6fr rose red	45	30
574	A165	25fr blk brn	90	15
575	A165	25fr dk bl ('48)	4.50	80

Ceres & Marianne Types of 1945.
Typographed.

1947		Perf. 14x13½	Unwmkd.	
576	A146	1.30fr dl bl	30	30
577	A147	3fr green	90	15
578	A147	3.50fr brn red	60	25
579	A147	5fr blue	22	10
580	A147	6fr carmine	50	40
		Nos. 576-580 (5)	2.52	1.20

Colonnade of the Louvre
A166

La Conciergerie, Paris Prison
A167

La Cité, Oldest Section of Paris
A168

Place de la Concorde
A169

1947, May 7		Engraved	Perf. 13	
581	A166	3.50fr chocolate	38	38
582	A167	4.50fr dk sl gray	38	38
583	A168	6fr red	70	70
584	A169	10fr brt ultra	70	70

Issued to commemorate the 12th Congress of the Universal Postal Union, Paris, May 7 to July 7, 1947.

Auguste Pavie A170 | Francois Fénelon A171

1947, May 30

585	A170	4.50fr sepia	22	22

Issued to commemorate the centenary of the birth of Auguste Pavie, French pioneer in Laos.

1947, July 12

586	A171	4.50fr chocolate	22	22

Issued to honor Francois de Salignac de la Mothe-Fénelon, prelate and writer.

Fleur-de-Lis and Double Carrick Bend A172

1947, Aug. 2 **Unwmkd.**

587	A172	5fr brown	22	22

Issued to commemorate the 6th World Boy Scout Jamboree held at Moisson, August 9th to 18th, 1947.

Captured Patriot A173 | View of Conques A174

1947, Nov. 10 **Engraved** ***Perf. 13***

588	A173	5fr sepia	60	60

No. 576 Surcharged in Carmine.

1947, Nov. **Typo.** ***Perf. 14x13½***

589	A146	1fr on 1.30fr dl bl	15	15

1947, Dec. 18 **Engraved** ***Perf. 13***

590	A174	15fr hn brn	55	30

Types of 1946-47.

1948 **Re-engraved.**

591	A160	12fr rose car	45	30
592	A160	15fr brt red	30	30
593	A174	18fr dk bl	75	30

"FRANCE" substituted for inscriptions "RF" and "REPUBLIQUE FRANCAISE."

Marianne Type of 1945.

1948-49 **Typo.** ***Perf. 14x13½***

594	A147	2.50fr brown	2.50	1.50
595	A147	3fr lil rose	22	10
596	A147	4fr lt bl grn	30	10
597	A147	4fr brn org	1.50	45
598	A147	5fr lt bl grn	60	5
599	A147	8fr blue	32	15
600	A147	10fr brt vio	20	5
601	A147	12fr ultra ('49)	1.50	15
602	A147	15fr crim rose ('49)	50	5
a.		Bklt. pane of 10	80.00	
		Nos. 594-602 (9)	7.64	2.60

No. 594 known only precanceled. See second note after No. 132.

François René de Chateaubriand A175

1948, July 3 **Engraved** ***Perf. 13***

603	A175	18fr dk bl	30	30

Issued to commemorate the centenary of the death of Vicomte de Chateaubriand (1768–1848).

Philippe François M. de Hautecloque (Gen. Jacques Leclerc)—A176

1948, July 3

604	A176	6fr gray blk	38	32

See also Nos. 692-692A.

Chaillot Palace A177

A178

1948, Sept. 21

605	A177	12fr car rose	38	38
606	A178	18fr indigo	45	45

Issued to commemorate the meeting of the United Nations General Assembly, Paris, 1948.

Genissiat Dam A179 | Paul Langevin A180

1948, Sept. 21

607	A179	12fr car rose	48	45

1948, Nov. 17 ***Perf. 14x13***

Design: 8fr, Jean Perrin.

608	A180	5fr dk brn car	18	18
609	A180	8fr dk grnsh bl	18	18

Issued to commemorate the placing of the ashes of physicists Paul Langevin (1872–1946) and Jean Perrin (1870–1942) in the Pantheon.

No. 544 Surcharged with New Value and Bars in Black.

1949, Jan. ***Perf. 14x13½***

610	A147	5fr on 6fr crim rose	15	15

Arctic Scene A181

1949, May 2 ***Perf. 13***

611	A181	15fr indigo	38	38

Issued to publicize French polar explorations.

Types of 1849 and 1945.

1949, May 9 **Engraved** ***Imperf.***

612	A1	15fr red	4.75	4.75
a.		Strip of 4 (1 each Nos. 612 to 615) + label	21.00	21.00
613	A1	25fr dp bl	4.75	4.75

Perf. 14x13

614	A147	15fr red	4.75	4.75
615	A147	25fr dp bl	4.75	4.75

Printed in sheets containing a horizontal row of ten each of Nos. 612 to 615, the imperforate and perforated stamps separated by a row of labels.

Nos. 612 to 615 were issued to commemorate the centenary of the first French postage stamps.

Arms of Burgundy A182

Designs (Arms): 50c, Guyenne (Aquitania). 1fr, Savoy. 2fr, Auvergne. 4fr, Anjou.

1949, May 11 **Typo.** ***Perf. 14x13½***

616	A182	10c bl, red & yel	6	6
617	A182	50c bl, red & yel	10	10
618	A182	1fr brn & red	15	15
619	A182	2fr grn, yel & red	22	15
620	A182	4fr bl, red & yel	42	38
		Nos. 616-620 (5)	95	84

See also Nos. 659–663, 694–699, 733–739, 782–785.

Collegiate Church of St. Barnard and Dauphiné Arms—A183

1949, May 14 **Engraved** ***Perf. 13***

621	A183	12fr red brn	32	30

Issued to commemorate the 600th anniversary of France's acquisition of the Dauphiné region.

U.S. and French Flags, Plane and Steamship—A184

1949, May 14

622	A184	25fr bl & car	55	48

Issued to publicize Franco-American friendship.

Cloister of St. Wandrille Abbey A185

1949, May 18

623	A185	25fr dp ultra	30	15

See also No. 649.

Type of 1849 Inscribed "1849–1949" in Lower Margin.

1949, June 1

624	A1	10fr brn org	60.00	52.50
a.		Sheet of 10	600.00	600.00

Issued to commemorate the centenary of the first French postage stamp.

No. 624 has wide margins, measuring 40 x 52 mm., from perforation to perforation. Sold for 110 francs which included cost of admission to the Centenary International Exhibition, Paris, June 1949.

Claude Chappe A186 | Jean Racine A187

Designs: 15fr, François Arago and André M. Ampère. 25fr, Emile Baudot. 50fr, Gen. Gustave A. Ferrié.

Inscribed. "C.I.T.T. PARIS 1949".

1949, June 13 ***Perf. 13*** **Unwmkd.**

625	A186	10fr vermilion	65	60
626	A186	15fr sepia	1.25	90
627	A186	25fr dp cl	3.25	3.00
628	A186	50fr dp bl	5.25	3.00

Issued to publicize the International Telegraph and Telephone Conference, Paris, May–July 1949.

1949

629	A187	12fr sepia	38	38

Issued to commemorate the 250th anniversary of the death of Jean Racine, dramatist.

Abbey of St. Bertrand de Comminges A188

Meuse Valley, Ardennes A189

Mt. Gerbier de Jonc, Vivarais A190

1949 **Engraved.**

630	A188	20fr dk red	30	15
631	A189	40fr Prus grn	10.50	22
632	A190	50fr sepia	2.00	15

A191

1949, Oct. 18

633	A191	15fr dp car	30	30

Issued to commemorate the 50th anniversary of the Assembly of Presidents of Chambers of Commerce of the French Union.

U.P.U. Allegory A192

1949, Nov. 7

634	A192	5fr dk grn	32	30
635	A192	15fr dp car	40	30
636	A192	dp bl	1.25	1.00

Issued to commemorate the 75th anniversary of the formation of the Universal Postal Union.

Raymond Poincaré
A193

François Rabelais
A195

Charles Péguy and Cathedral at Chartres—A194

1950, May 27 ***Perf. 13*** **Unwmkd.**

637	A193	15fr indigo	32	30

1950, June

638	A194	12fr dk brn	32	32
639	A195	12fr red brn	40	40

Chateau of Chateaudun
A196

1950, Nov. 25

640	A196	8fr choc & bis brn	32	32

Madame Récamier
A197

Marie de Sévigné
A198

1950

641	A197	12fr dk grn	38	38
642	A198	15fr ultra	30	30

Palace of Fontainbleau
A199

1951, Jan. 20

643	A199	12fr dk brn	38	38

Jules Ferry
A200

Jean-Baptiste de la Salle
A202

Hands Holding Shuttle
A201

1951, Mar. 17

644	A200	15fr brt red	50	45

1951, Apr. 9

645	A201	25fr dp ultra	1.00	90

Issued to publicize the International Textile Exposition at Lille, April–May, 1951.

1951, Apr. 28

646	A202	15fr chocolate	38	38

Issued to commemorate the 300th anniversary of the birth of Jean-Baptiste de la Salle, educator and saint.

Map and Anchor
A203

1951, May 12

647	A203	15fr dp ultra	50	45

Issued to commemorate the 50th anniversary of the creation of the French colonial troops.

Vincent d'Indy
A204

1951, May 15

648	A204	25fr dp grn	2.25	1.65

Issued to commemorate the centenary of the birth of Vincent d'Indy, composer.

Abbey Type of 1949.

1951

649	A185	30fr brt bl	5.50	4.50

Marianne Type of 1945–47.

1951 Typographed. ***Perf. 14x13½***

650	A147	5fr dl vio	50	5
651	A147	6fr green	5.50	45
652	A147	12fr red org	1.10	15
653	A147	15fr ultra	22	6
a.		Booklet pane of 10	22.50	
654	A147	18fr cerise	15.00	1.00
		Nos. 650-654 (5)	22.32	1.71

Professors Nocard, Bouley and Chauveau; Gate at Lyons School—A205

1951, June 8 Engraved ***Perf. 13***

655	A205	12fr red vio	60	50

Issued to honor Veterinary Medicine.

Gen. Picqué, Cols. Roussin and Villemin; Val de Grace Dome
A206

1951, June 17 **Unwmkd.**

656	A206	15fr red brn	65	50

Issued to honor Military Medicine.

St. Nicholas, by Jean Didier
A207

1951, June 23

657	A207	15fr ind, dp cl & org	65	50

Chateau Bontemps, Arbois
A208

1951, June 23

658	A208	30fr indigo	75	22

Arms Type of 1949

Arms of: 10c, Artois. 50c, Limousin. 1fr, Béarn. 2fr, Touraine. 3fr, Franche-Comté.

1951, June Typo. ***Perf. 14x13½***

659	A182	10c red, vio bl & yel	6	5
660	A182	50c grn, red & blk	15	15
661	A182	1fr bl, red & yel	22	15
662	A182	2fr vio bl, red & yel	65	22
663	A182	3fr red, vio bl & yel	80	30
		Nos. 659-663 (5)	1.88	87

Seal of Paris
A209

Maurice Noguès and Globe
A210

Engraved

1951, July 7 ***Perf. 13*** **Unwmkd.**

664	A209	15fr dp bl, dk brn & red	45	38

Issued to commemorate the 2,000th anniversary of the founding of Paris.

1951, Oct. 13

665	A210	12fr ind & bl	75	50

Issued to honor Maurice Nogues, aviation pioneer.

Charles Baudelaire
A211

Poets: 12fr, Paul Verlaine. 15fr, Arthur Rimbaud.

1951, Oct. 27

666	A211	8fr purple	40	40
667	A211	12fr gray	55	55
668	A211	15fr dp grn	65	65

Georges Clemenceau
A212

1951, Nov. 11

669	A212	15fr blk brn	30	30

Issued to commemorate the centenary of the birth of Georges Clemenceau.

Chateau du Clos, Vougeot
A213

1951, Nov. 17

670	A213	30fr blk brn & brn	4.00	1.65

Chaillot Palace and Eiffel Tower
A214

1951, Nov. 6

671	A214	18fr red	90	80
672	A214	30fr dp ultra	1.40	1.00

Issued to publicize the opening of the Geneva Assembly of the United Nations, Paris, Nov. 6, 1951.

Observatory, Pic du Midi
A215

Abbaye aux Hommes, Caen
A216

1951, Dec. 22

673	A215	40fr violet	5.50	22
674	A216	50fr blk brn	4.00	22

Marshal Jean de Lattre de Tassigny—A217

1952, May 8 ***Perf. 13*** **Unwmkd.**

675	A217	15fr vio brn	90	45

Issued to honor Marshal Jean de Lattre de Tassigny, 1890–1952.

See also No. 717.

Gate of France, Vaucouleurs
A218

1952, May 11

676 A218 12fr brn blk 1.65 1.00

Flags and Monument at Narvik, Norway
A219

1952, May 28

677 A219 30fr vio bl 3.00 2.00

Issued to commemorate the 12th anniversary of the Battle of Narvik, May 27, 1940.

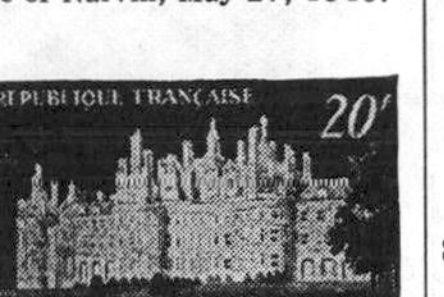

Chateau de Chambord
A220

1952, May 30

678 A220 20fr dk pur 50 22

Assembly Hall, Strasbourg
A221

1952, May 31

679 A221 30fr dk grn 11.00 7.50

Issued to honor the Council of Europe.

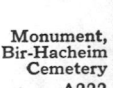

Monument, Bir-Hacheim Cemetery
A222

1952, June 14

680 A222 30fr rose lake 3.75 2.25

Issued to commemorate the 10th anniversary of the defense of Bir-Hacheim.

Abbey of the Holy Cross, Poitiers
A223

1952, June 21

681 A223 15fr brt red 40 38

Issued to commemorate the 14th centenary of the foundation of the Abbey of the Holy Cross at Poitiers.

Leonardo da Vinci, Amboise Chateau and La Signoria, Florence—A224

1952, July 9

682 A224 30fr dp ultra 8.50 5.50

Issued to commemorate the 500th anniversary of the birth of Leonardo da Vinci.

Garabit Viaduct
A225

1952, July 5

683 A225 15fr dk bl 80 60

Sword and Military Medals, 1852-1952
A226

Dr. René Laënnec
A227

1952, July 5

684 A226 15fr choc, grn & yel 48 40

Issued to commemorate the centenary of the creation of the Military Medal.

1952, Nov. 7

685 A227 12fr dk grn 50 45

Versailles Gate, Painted by Utrillo
A228

1952, Dec. 20

686 A228 18fr vio brn 2.00 1.50

Publicity for the restoration of Versailles Palace. See also No. 728.

Mannequin
A229

1953, Apr. 24 ***Perf. 13*** **Unwmkd.**

687 A229 30fr bl blk & rose vio 90 45

Issued to publicize the dressmaking industry of France.

Gargantua of François Rabelais
A230

Célimène from The Misanthrope
A231

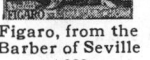

Figaro, from the Barber of Seville
A232

Hernani of Victor Hugo
A233

1953

688 A230 6fr dp plum & car 30 30
689 A231 8fr ind & ultra 22 18
690 A232 12fr vio brn & dk grn 22 15
691 A233 18fr vio brn & blk brn 65 45

Type of 1948
Inscribed "Général Leclerc Maréchal de France"

1953–54

692 A176 8fr red brn 65 50
692A A176 12fr dk grn & gray grn ('54) 2.25 1.50

Issued to honor the memory of General Jacques Leclerc.

Map and Cyclists, 1903–1953
A234

1953, July 26

693 A234 12fr red brn, ultra & blk 1.75 1.25

Issued to commemorate the 50th anniversary of the inauguration of the Bicycle Tour of France.

Arms Type of 1949.

Coats of Arms: 50c, Picardy. 70c, Gascony. 80c, Berri. 1fr, Poitou. 2fr, Champagne. 3fr, Dauphiné.

1953 Typographed. ***Perf. 14x13½***

694 A182 50c bl, yel & red 30 30
695 A182 70c red, bl & yel 28 28
696 A182 80c bl, red & yel 28 28
697 A182 1fr blk, red & yel 30 22
698 A182 2fr brn, bl & yel 30 22
699 A182 3fr red, bl & yel 60 30
Nos. 694-699 (6) 2.06 1.60

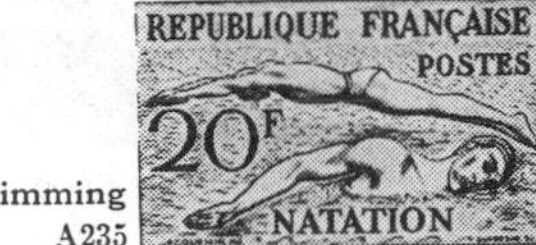

Swimming
A235

Sports: 25fr, Track. 30fr, Fencing. 40fr, Canoe racing. 50fr, Rowing. 75fr, Equestrian.

1953, Nov. 28 Engr. ***Perf. 13***

700 A235 20fr car & dk brn 3.00 22
701 A235 25fr dk grn & dk brn 11.00 50
702 A235 30fr ultra & dk brn 3.00 30
703 A235 40fr choc & ind 10.50 30
704 A235 50fr bl grn & dk brn 6.00 22
705 A235 75fr org & cl 40.00 15.00
Nos. 700-705 (6) 73.50 16.54

No. 654 Surcharged with New Value and Bars in Black.

1954 ***Perf. 14x13½***

706 A147 15fr on 18fr cer 75 18

Farm Woman
A236

Gallic Cock
A237

1954 Typographed

707 A236 4fr blue 38 15
708 A236 8fr brn red 6.00 1.00
709 A237 12fr cerise 4.00 45
710 A237 24fr bl grn 17.50 4.75

Nos. 707–710 are known only precanceled. See also Nos. 833–834, 840–844, 910–913, 939 and 952–955. See second note after No. 132.

Tapestry and Gobelin Workshop
A238

Entrance to Exhibition Park
A239

Designs: 30fr, Book manufacture. 40fr, Porcelain and glassware. 50fr, Jewelry and metalsmith's work. 75fr, Flowers and perfumes.

1954, May 6 Engr. ***Perf. 13***

711 A238 25fr red brn car & blk brn 8.50 30
712 A238 30fr dk grn & lil gray 1.65 10
713 A238 40fr dk brn, vio brn & org brn 2.50 10
714 A238 50fr brt ultra, dl grn & org brn 1.75 6
715 A238 75fr dp car & mag 10.00 45
Nos. 711-715 (5) 24.40 1.01

1954, May 22

716 A239 15fr bl & dk car 48 45

Issued to commemorate the 50th anniversary of the founding of the Fair of Paris.

De Lattre Type of 1952

1954, June 5

717 A217 12fr vio bl & ind 2.25 1.50

Allied Landings
A240

1954, June 5

718 A240 15fr scar & ultra 1.00 65

The 10th anniversary of the liberation.

View of Lourdes
A241

Street Corner, Quimper
A242

Views: 8fr, Seine valley, Les Andelys. 10fr, Beach at Royan. 18fr, Cheverny Chateau. 20fr, Beach, Gulf of Ajaccio.

1954

No.	Type	Description	Unused	Used
719	A241	6fr ultra, ind & dk grn	32	30
720	A241	8fr brt bl & dk grn	32	15
721	A241	10fr aqua & org brn	32	12
722	A242	12fr rose vio & dk vio	32	6
723	A241	18fr bl, dk grn & ind	2.50	60
724	A241	20fr blk brn, bl grn & red brn	2.00	15
		Nos. 719-724 (6)	5.78	1.38

See also No. 873.

Abbey Ruins, Jumièges
A243

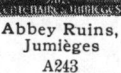

St. Philibert Abbey, Tournus
A244

1954, June 13

No.	Type	Description	Unused	Used
725	A243	12fr vio bl, ind & dk grn	1.65	1.25

13th centenary of Abbey of Jumièges.

1954, June 18

No.	Type	Description	Unused	Used
726	A244	30fr ind & bl	8.50	5.50

Issued to publicize the first conference of the International Center of Romance Studies.

View of Stenay
A245

1954, June 26

No.	Type	Description	Unused	Used
727	A245	15fr dk brn & org brn	1.00	75

Issued to commemorate the 300th anniversary of the acquisition of Stenay by France.

Versailles Type of 1952

1954, July 10

No.	Type	Description	Unused	Used
728	A228	18fr dp bl, ind & vio brn	7.75	4.75

Villandry Chateau
A246

1954, July 17

No.	Type	Description	Unused	Used
729	A246	18fr dk bl & dk bl grn	5.50	4.00

Napoleon Awarding Legion of Honor Decoration—A247

1954, Aug. 14

No.	Type	Description	Unused	Used
730	A247	12fr scarlet	1.65	1.00

Issued to commemorate the 150th anniversary of the first Legion of Honor awards at Camp de Boulogne.

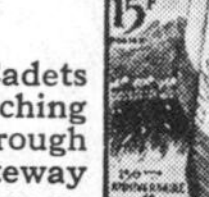

Cadets Marching Through Gateway
A248

1954, Aug. 1

No.	Type	Description	Unused	Used
731	A248	15fr vio gray, dk bl & car	1.65	1.00

Issued to commemorate the 150th anniversary of the founding of the Military School of Saint-Cyr.

Allegory
A249

Duke de Saint-Simon
A250

1954, Oct. 4

No.	Type	Description	Unused	Used
732	A249	30fr ind & choc	9.00	6.00

Issued to publicize the fact that the metric system was first introduced in France.

Arms Type of 1949

Arms: 50c, Maine. 70c, Navarre. 80c, Nivernais. 1fr, Bourbonnais. 2fr, Angoumois. 3fr, Aunis. 5fr, Saintonge.

1954 Typographed. *Perf. 14x13½*

No.	Type	Description	Unused	Used
733	A182	50c multi	15	15
734	A182	70c grn, red & yel	30	30
735	A182	80c bl, red & yel	30	30
736	A182	1fr red, bl & yel	18	15
737	A182	2fr blk, red & yel	6	5
738	A182	3fr brn, red & yel	5	5
739	A182	5fr bl & yel	6	5
		Nos. 733-739 (7)	1.10	1.05

1955, Feb. 5 Engr. *Perf. 13*

No.	Type	Description	Unused	Used
740	A250	12fr dk brn & vio brn	80	60

Issued to commemorate the 200th anniversary of the death of Louis de Rouvroy, Duke de Saint-Simon (1675–1755).

Allegory and Rotary Emblem
A251

Marianne
A252

1955, Feb. 23

No.	Type	Description	Unused	Used
741	A251	30fr vio bl, bl & org	1.75	1.25

Issued to commemorate the 50th anniversary of the founding of Rotary International.

1955–59 Typo. *Perf. 14x13½*

No.	Type	Description	Unused	Used
751	A252	6fr fawn	4.00	2.25
752	A252	12fr green	3.25	1.50
a.		Bklt. pane of 10 + 2 labels	37.50	
753	A252	15fr carmine	30	5
a.		Bklt. pane of 10	8.50	
754	A252	18fr grn ('58)	30	15
755	A252	20fr ultra ('57)	45	5
756	A252	25fr rose red ('59)	1.00	5
a.		Bklt. pane of 8	10.00	
b.		Bklt. pane of 10	11.00	
		Nos. 751-756 (6)	9.30	4.05

No. 751 was issued in coils of 1,000.
No. 752 was issued in panes of 10 stamps and two labels with marginal instructions for folding to form a booklet.
Nos. 754–755 are found in two types, distinguished by the numerals. On the 18fr there is no serif at base of "1" on the earlier type.

Philippe Lebon, Inventor of Illuminating Gas—A253

Inventors: 10fr, Barthélemy Thimonnier, sewing machine. 12fr, Nicolas Appert, canned foods. 18fr, Dr. E. H. St. Claire Deville, aluminum. 25fr, Pierre Martin, steel making. 30fr, Bernigaud de Chardonnet, rayon.

1955, Mar. 5 Engraved

No.	Type	Description	Unused	Used
757	A253	5fr dk vio bl & bl	1.00	65
758	A253	10fr dk brn & org brn	1.00	75
759	A253	12fr dk grn	1.40	80
760	A253	18fr dk vio bl & ind	3.25	3.00
761	A253	25fr dk brnsh pur & vio	3.25	2.50
762	A253	30fr rose car & scar	3.25	2.50
		Nos. 757-762 (6)	13.15	10.20

St. Stephen Bridge, Limoges
A254

1955, Mar. 26 *Perf. 13* Unwmkd.

No.	Type	Description	Unused	Used
763	A254	12fr yel brn & dk vio brn	1.75	1.25

Gloved Model in Place de la Concorde
A255

1955, Mar. 26

No.	Type	Description	Unused	Used
764	A255	25fr blk brn, vio bl & blk	1.00	22

Issued to publicize French glove manufacturing.

Jean Pierre Claris de Florian
A256

1955, Apr. 2

No.	Type	Description	Unused	Used
765	A256	12fr bl grn	80	50

200th anniversary of the birth of Jean Pierre Claris de Florian, fabulist.

Eiffel Tower and Television Antennas
A257

1955, Apr. 16

No.	Type	Description	Unused	Used
766	A257	15fr ind & ultra	75	45

Issued to publicize French advancement in television.

Wire Fence and Guard Tower
A258

1955, Apr. 23

No.	Type	Description	Unused	Used
767	A258	12fr dk gray bl & brn blk	75	60

Issued to commemorate the 10th anniversary of the liberation of concentration camps.

Electric Train
A259

1955, May 11

No.	Type	Description	Unused	Used
768	A259	12fr blk brn & sl bl	1.90	1.10

Issued to publicize the electrification of the Valenciennes-Thionville railroad line.

Jacquemart of Moulins
A260

1955, May 28

No.	Type	Description	Unused	Used
769	A260	12fr blk brn	1.40	90

Jules Verne and Nautilus
A261

1955, June 3

No.	Type	Description	Unused	Used
770	A261	30fr indigo	8.25	6.25

Issued to commemorate the 50th anniversary of the death of Jules Verne.

Auguste and Louis Lumière and Motion Picture Projector
A262

1955, June 12

No.	Type	Description	Unused	Used
771	A262	30fr rose brn	5.50	4.75

Issued to commemorate the 60th anniversary of the invention of motion pictures.

Jacques Coeur and His Mansion at Bourges
A263

1955, June 18

772	A263	12fr	violet	2.50	1.75

Issued to commemorate the 5th centenary of the death of Jacques Coeur (1395?–1456), French merchant.

Corvette "La Capricieuse"
A264

1955, July 9

773	A264	30fr	aqua & dk bl	6.75	5.25

Issued to commemorate the centenary of the voyage of La Capricieuse to Canada.

Bordeaux
A265

Designs: 8fr, Marseilles. 10fr, Nice. 12fr, Valentre bridge, Cahors. 18fr, Uzerche. 25fr, Fortifications, Brouage.

1955, Oct. 15

774	A265	6fr	car lake	28	22
775	A265	8fr	indigo	40	15
776	A265	10fr	dp ultra	32	6
777	A265	12fr	vio & brn	32	6
778	A265	18fr	bluish grn & ind	70	15
779	A265	25fr	org brn & red brn	80	18
			Nos. 774-779 (6)	2.82	82

See Nos. 838–839.

Mount Pelée, Martinique
A266

1955, Nov. 1

780	A266	20fr	dk & lt pur	2.50	15

Gérard de Nerval
A267

1955, Nov. 11

781	A267	12fr	lake & sep	50	32

Issued to commemorate the centenary of the death of Gérard de Nerval (Labrunie), author.

Arms Type of 1949.

Arms of: 50c, County of Foix. 70c, Marche. 80c, Roussillon. 1fr, Comtat Venaissin.

Perf. 14x13½

1955, Nov. 19 Typo. Unwmkd.

782	A182	50c	multi	6	6
783	A182	70c	red, bl & yel	15	15
784	A182	80c	brn, yel & red	15	15
785	A182	1fr	bl, red & yel	6	5

Concentration Camp Victim and Monument
A268

Belfry at Douai
A269

1956, Jan. 14 Engr. *Perf. 13*

786	A268	15fr	brn blk & red brn	50	50

No. 786 shows the national memorial for Nazi deportation victims erected at the Natzwiller Struthof concentration camp in Alsace.

1956, Feb. 11

787	A269	15fr	ultra & ind	38	38

Col. Emil Driant
A270

1956, Feb. 21

788	A270	15fr	dk bl	32	32

Issued to commemorate the 40th anniversary of the death of Col. Emil Driant during the battle of Verdun.

Trench Fighting
A271

1956, Mar. 3

789	A271	30fr	ind & dk ol	2.25	1.40

40th anniversary of Battle of Verdun.

Jean Henri Fabre, Entomology
A272

Scientists: 15fr, Charles Tellier, Refrigeration. 18fr, Camille Flammarion, Popular Astronomy. 30fr, Paul Sabatier, Catalytic Chemistry.

1956, Apr. 7

790	A272	12fr	vio brn & org brn	65	45
791	A272	15fr	vio bl & int blk	1.00	65
792	A272	18fr	brt ultra	2.75	1.50
793	A272	30fr	Prus grn & dk grn	3.75	2.50

Grand Trianon, Versailles
A273

1956, Apr. 14

794	A273	12fr	vio brn & gray grn	1.75	1.25

Symbols of Latin American and French Culture
A274

1956, Apr. 21

795	A274	30fr	brn & red brn	2.50	1.65

Issued in recognition of the friendship between France and Latin America.

"The Smile of Reims" and Botticelli's "Spring"
A275

1956, May 5

796	A275	12fr	blk & grn	90	60

Issued to emphasize the cultural and artistic kinship of Reims and Florence.

Leprosarium and Maltese Cross
A276

1956, May 12

797	A276	12fr	sep, red brn & red	50	45

Issued in honor of the Knights of Malta.

St. Yves de Treguier
A277

1956, May 19

798	A277	15fr	bluish gray & blk	38	32

Issued in honor of St. Yves, patron saint of lawyers.

Marshal Franchet d'Esperey
A278

Miners Monument
A279

1956, May 26

799	A278	30fr	dp cl	3.00	1.65

Issued to commemorate the centenary of the birth of Marshal Louis Franchet d'Esperey.

1956, June 2

800	A279	12fr	vio brn	50	45

Issued to commemorate the 100th anniversary of the town Montceau-les-Mines.

Basketball
A280

"Rebuilding Europe"
A281

Sports: 40fr, Pelota (Jai alai). 50fr, Rugby. 75fr, Mountain climbing.

1956, July 7

801	A280	30fr	gray vio & blk	1.10	18
802	A280	40fr	brn & vio brn	3.25	28
803	A280	50fr	rose vio & vio	2.25	15
804	A280	75fr	ind, grn & bl	6.75	1.65

Europa Issue.

Perf. 13½x14

1956, Sept. 15 Typo. Unwmkd.

805	A281	15fr	rose & rose lake	1.50	30

Engraved.

Perf. 13

806	A281	30fr	lt bl & vio bl	7.50	1.25

Issued to symbolize the cooperation among the six countries comprising the Coal and Steel Community.

No. 805 measures 21x35½mm., No. 806 measures 22x35½mm.

Dam at Donzère-Mondragon
A282

Cable Railway to Pic du Midi
A283

Rhine Port of Strasbourg
A284

1956, Oct. 6 Engraved *Perf. 13*

807	A282	12fr	gray vio & vio brn	1.75	1.00
808	A283	18fr	indigo	2.75	1.50
809	A284	30fr	ind & dk bl	8.25	3.00

French technical achievements.

Antoine-Augustin Parmentier
A285

1956, Oct. 27

810	A285	12fr brn red & brn	48	45

Issued in honor of A. A. Parmentier, nutrition chemist, who popularized the potato in France.

Petrarch—A286

Portraits: 12fr, J. B. Lully. 15fr, J. J. Rousseau. 18fr, Benjamin Franklin. 20fr, Frederic Chopin. 30fr, Vincent van Gogh.

1956, Nov. 10

811	A286	8fr green	75	60
812	A286	12fr claret	75	60
813	A286	15fr dk red	1.10	75
814	A286	18fr ultra	3.00	2.25
815	A286	20fr brt vio	3.75	1.75
816	A286	30fr brt grnsh bl	4.75	3.25
		Nos. 811-816 (6)	14.10	9.20

Issued in honor of famous men who lived in France.

Pierre de Coubertin and Olympic Stadium—A287

1956, Nov. 24

817	A287	30fr dk bl gray & pur	1.75	1.25

Issued in honor of Baron Pierre de Coubertin, founder of the modern Olympic Games.

Homing Pigeon
A288

1957, Jan. 12

818	A288	15fr dp ultra, ind & red brn	38	32

Victor Schoelcher
A289

1957, Feb. 16 **Engraved**

819	A289	18fr lil rose	50	38

Issued in honor of Victor Schoelcher, who freed the slaves in the French Colonies.

Sèvres Porcelain
A290

1957, Mar. 23 ***Perf. 13*** **Unwmkd.**

820	A290	30fr ultra & vio bl	75	60

Issued to commemorate the the bicentenary of the porcelain works at Sèvres (in 1956).

Gaston Planté and Storage Battery
A291

Designs: 12fr, Antoine Béclère and X-ray apparatus. 18fr, Octave Terrillon, autoclave, microscope and surgical instruments. 30fr, Etienne Oemichen and early helicopter.

1957, Apr. 13

821	A291	8fr gray blk & dp cl	45	45
822	A291	12fr dk bl, blk & emer	50	50
823	A291	18fr rose red & mag	1.65	1.65
824	A291	30fr grn & sl grn	2.50	2.50

Uzès Chateau
A292

1957, Apr. 27

825	A292	12fr sl bl & bis brn	38	38

Jean Moulin **Le Quesnoy**
A293 **A294**

Portraits: 10fr, Honoré d'Estienne d'Orves. 12fr, Robert Keller. 18fr, Pierre Brossolette. 20fr, Jean-Baptiste Lebas.

1957, May 18

826	A293	8fr vio brn	65	50
827	A293	10fr blk & vio bl	60	50
828	A293	12fr brn & sl grn	65	45
829	A293	18fr pur & blk	1.90	1.25
830	A293	20fr Prus bl & dk bl	1.10	60
		Nos. 826-830 (5)	4.90	3.30

Issued in honor of the heroes of the French Underground of World War II.

See also Nos. 879–882, 915–919, 959–963, 990–993.

1957, June 1

831	A294	8fr dk sl grn	18	18

See also No. 837.

Symbols of Justice
A295

1957, June 1

832	A295	12fr sep & ultra	30	30

Issued to commemorate the 150th anniversary of the French Cour des Comptes.

Farm Woman Type of 1954.

1957-59 ***Perf. 14x13½***

833	A236	6fr orange	10	10
833A	A236	10fr brt grn ('59)	75	6
834	A236	12fr red lil	18	15

Nos. 833-834 issued without precancellation.

Symbols of Public Works
A296

1957, June 20 **Engr.** ***Perf. 13***

835	A296	30fr sl grn, brn & ocher	1.25	75

Brest
A297

1957, July 6

836	A297	12fr gray grn & brn ol	65	48

Scenic Types of 1955, 1957.

Designs: 15fr, Le Quesnoy. 35fr, Bordeaux. 70fr, Valentre bridge, Cahors.

1957, July 19 **Unwmkd.**

837	A294	15fr dk bl grn & sep	18	5
838	A265	35fr dk bl grn & sl grn	1.90	45
839	A265	70fr blk & dl grn	8.25	1.50

Gallic Cock Type of 1954.

1957 **Typo.** ***Perf. 14x13½***

840	A237	5fr ol bis	38	30
841	A237	10fr brt bl	90	38
842	A237	15fr plum	2.25	60
843	A237	30fr brt red	5.25	1.25
844	A237	45fr green	35.00	18.00
		Nos. 840-844 (5)	43.78	20.53

Nos. 840–844 are known only precanceled. See second note after No. 132.

Leo Lagrange and Stadium
A298

1957, Aug. 31 **Engr.** ***Perf. 13***

845	A298	18fr lil gray & blk	45	32

Issued to commemorate the International University Games, Paris, Aug. 31-Sept. 8.

"United Europe" **Auguste Comte**
A299 **A300**

1957, Sept. 16

846	A299	20fr red brn & grn	50	30
847	A299	35fr dk brn & bl	1.50	60

Issued to publicize a united Europe for peace and prosperity.

1957, Sept. 14

848	A300	35fr brn red & sep	60	60

Issued to commemorate the centenary of the death of Auguste Comte, mathematician and philosopher.

Roman Amphitheater, Lyon
A301

1957, Oct. 5 ***Perf. 13***

849	A301	20fr brn org & brn vio	48	38

Issued to commemorate the 2,000th anniversary of the founding of Lyon.

Sens River, Guadeloupe
A302

Beynac-Cazenac, Dordogne **Nicolaus Copernicus**
A303 **A304**

Designs: 10fr, Elysee Palace. 25fr, Chateau de Valencay, Indre. 35fr, Rouen Cathedral. 50fr, Roman Ruins, Saint-Remy. 65fr, Evian-les-Bains.

1957, Oct. 19

850	A302	8fr grn & lt brn	15	15
851	A302	10fr dk ol bis & vio brn	15	12
852	A303	18fr ind & dk brn	28	15
853	A302	25fr bl gray & vio brn	38	15
854	A303	35fr car rose & lake	38	6
855	A302	50fr ol grn & ol bis	55	6
856	A302	65fr dk bl & ind	90	18
		Nos. 850-856 (7)	2.79	87

See also Nos. 907–909.

1957, Nov. 9 **Engraved** ***Perf. 13***

Portraits: 10fr, Michelangelo. 12fr, Miguel de Cervantes. 15fr, Rembrandt. 18fr, Isaac Newton. 25fr, Mozart. 35fr, Johann Wolfgang von Goethe.

857	A304	8fr dk brn	90	60
858	A304	10fr dk grn	95	60
859	A304	12fr dk pur	1.00	60
860	A304	15fr brn & org brn	1.25	45
861	A304	18fr dp bl	1.75	1.25
862	A304	25fr lil & cl	1.75	65
863	A304	35fr blue	2.00	1.65
		Nos. 857-863 (7)	9.60	5.80

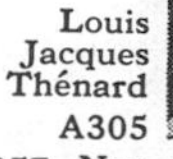

Louis Jacques Thénard
A305

1957, Nov. 30 **Unwmkd.**

864	A305	15fr ol bis & grnsh blk	45	45

Issued to commemorate the centenary of the death of L. J. Thenard, chemist, and the founding of the Charitable Society of the Friends of Science.

Dr. Philippe Pinel
A306

Joseph Louis Lagrange
A307

Doctors' Portraits: 12fr, Fernand Widal. 15fr, Charles Nicolle. 35fr, René Leriche.

1958, Jan. 25

865	A306	8fr brn ol	1.00	75
866	A306	12fr brt vio bl	1.00	75
867	A306	15fr dp bl	1.65	90
868	A306	35fr black	2.25	1.40

Issued in honor of famous French physicians.

1958, Feb. 15 *Perf. 13*

Portraits: 12fr, Urbain Jean Joseph Leverrier. 15fr, Jean Bernard Leon Foucault. 35fr, Claude Louis Berthollet.

869	A307	8fr bl grn & vio bl	1.10	75
870	A307	12fr sep & gray	1.25	95
871	A307	15fr sl grn & grn	2.50	1.25
872	A307	35fr mar & cop red	2.75	1.50

Issued to honor French scientists.

Lourdes Type of 1954.

1958

873	A241	20fr grnsh bl & ol	38	22

Le Havre
A308

Maubeuge
A309

Designs: 18fr, Saint-Die. 25fr, Sete.

1958, Mar. 29 Engr. *Perf. 13*

874	A308	12fr ol grn & car rose	75	60
875	A309	15fr brt pur & brn	80	60
876	A309	18fr ultra & ind	1.25	1.00
877	A308	25fr dk bl, bl grn & brn	1.65	1.00

Reconstruction of war-damaged cities.

French Pavilion, Brussels
A310

1958, Apr. 12

878	A310	35fr brn, dk grn & bl	38	32

Issued for the Universal and International Exposition at Brussels.

Heroes Type of 1957.

Portraits: 8fr, Jean Cavaillès. 12fr, Fred Scamaroni. 15fr, Simone Michel-Levy. 20fr, Jacques Bingen.

1958, Apr. 19

879	A293	8fr vio & blk	55	45
880	A293	12fr ultra & grn	55	45
881	A293	15fr brn & gray	1.65	1.25
882	A293	20fr ol & ultra	1.40	95

Issued in honor of the heroes of the French Underground in World War II.

Bowling
A311

Sports: 15fr, Naval joust. 18fr, Archery (vert.). 25fr, Breton wrestling (vert.).

1958, Apr. 26

883	A311	12fr rose & brn	1.00	50
884	A311	15fr bl, ol gray & grn	1.25	75
885	A311	18fr grn & brn	2.25	1.25
886	A311	25fr brn & ind	3.00	1.65

Senlis Cathedral
A312

1958. May 17

887	A312	15fr ultra & ind	40	40

Bayeux Tapestry Horsemen
A313

1958, June 21

888	A313	15fr bl & car	45	38

Europa Issue, 1958

Common Design Type

Size: 22x36mm.

1958, Sept. 13 **Engraved** *Perf. 13*

889	CD1	20fr rose red	45	22
890	CD1	35fr ultra	75	45

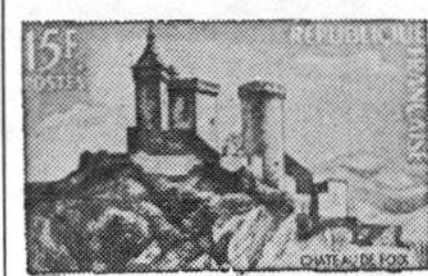

Foix Chateau
A314

1958, Oct. 11

891	A314	15fr ultra, grn & ol brn	22	22

Common Design Types pictured in section at front of book.

City Halls, Paris and Rome
A315

1958, Oct. 11

892	A315	35fr gray, grnsh bl & rose red	50	45

Issued to publicize the cultural ties between Rome and Paris and the need for European unity.

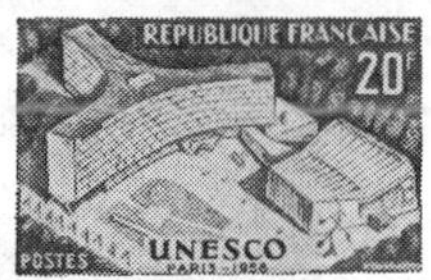

UNESCO Building, Paris
A316

Design: 35fr, Different view of building.

1958, Nov. 1 *Perf. 13*

893	A316	20fr grnsh bl & ol bis	18	18
894	A316	35fr dk sl grn & red org	28	28

Issued to commemorate the opening of UNESCO (U.N. Educational, Scientific and Cultural Organization) Headquarters in Paris, Nov. 3.

Soldier's Grave in Wheat Field
A317

Arms of Marseilles
A318

1958, Nov. 11

895	A317	15fr dk grn & ultra	22	22

Issued to commemorate the 40th anniversary of the World War I armistice.

1958–59 Typo. *Perf. 14x13½*

Arms (Cities): 70c, Lyon. 80c, Toulouse. 1fr, Bordeaux. 2fr, Nice. 3fr, Nantes. 5fr, Lille. 15fr, Algiers.

896	A318	50c dk bl & ultra	5	5
897	A318	70c multi	5	5
898	A318	80c red, bl & yel	5	5
899	A318	1fr dk bl, yel & red	6	5
900	A318	2fr dk bl, red & grn	6	5
901	A318	3fr multi	10	10
902	A318	5fr dk brn & red	10	5
903	A318	15fr multi ('59)	18	15
		Nos. 896-903 (8)	65	55

See also Nos. 938, 940, 973, 1040–1042, 1091–1095, 1142–1144.

Arc de Triomphe and Flowers
A319

1959, Jan. 17 **Engraved** *Perf. 13*

904	A319	15fr brn, bl, grn, cl & red	30	25

Paris Flower Festival.

Symbols of Learning and Medal
A320

1959, Jan. 24 *Perf. 13*

905	A320	20fr lake, blk & vio	25	25

Issued to commemorate the sesquicentennial of the Palm Leaf Medal of the French Academy.

Charles de Foucauld
A321

1959, Jan. 31

906	A321	50fr dp brn, bl & mar	65	55

Issued to honor Father Charles de Foucauld, explorer and missionary of the Sahara.

Type of 1957

Designs: 30fr, Elysee Palace. 85fr, Evian-les Bains. 100fr, Sens River, Guadeloupe.

1959, Feb. 10

907	A302	30fr dk sl grn	90	15
908	A302	85fr dp cl	2.50	18
909	A302	100fr dp vio	13.00	30

Gallic Cock Type of 1954.

1959 Typographed. *Perf. 14x13½*

910	A237	8fr violet	60	22
911	A237	20fr yel grn	2.50	65
912	A237	40fr hn brn	5.50	3.25
913	A237	55fr emerald	24.00	14.00

Nos. 910–913 were issued with precancellation. See second note after No. 132.

Miners' Tools and School
A322

1959, Apr. 11 Engr. *Perf. 13*

914	A322	20fr red, blk & bl	18	18

Issued to commemorate the 175th anniversary of the National Mining School.

Heroes Type of 1957.

Portraits: No. 915, The five martyrs of the Buffon school. No. 916, Yvonne Le Roux. No. 917, Médéric-Védy. No. 918, Louis Martin-Bret. 30fr, Gaston Moutardier.

1959, Apr. 25 Engr. *Perf. 13*

915	A293	15fr blk & vio	38	30
916	A293	15fr mag & rose vio	45	40
917	A293	20fr grn & grnsh bl	48	40
918	A293	20fr org brn & brn	80	55
919	A293	30fr mag & vio	90	55
		Nos. 915-919 (5)	3.01	2.20

Dam at Foum el Gherza
A323

Marcoule Atomic Center
A324

Designs: 30fr, Oil field at Hassi Messaoud, Sahara. 50fr, C. N. I. T. Building (Centre National des Industries et des Techniques).

1959, May 23

920	A323	15fr ol & grnsh bl	38	30
921	A324	20fr brt car & red brn	50	38
922	A324	30fr dk bl, brn & grn	75	38
923	A323	50fr ol grn & sl bl	1.40	60

Issued to publicize French technical achievements.

Marceline Desbordes-Valmore
A325

1959, June 20

924	A325	30fr bl, brn & grn	32	32

Issued to commemorate the centenary of the death of Marceline Desbordes-Valmore, poet.

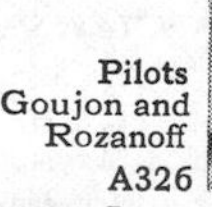

Pilots Goujon and Rozanoff
A326

1959, June 13

925	A326	20fr lt bl & org brn	32	32

Issued in honor of Charles Goujon and Col. Constantin Rozanoff, test pilots.

Tancarville Bridge
A327

1959, Aug. 1 Engr. *Perf. 13*

926	A327	30fr dk bl, brn & ol	32	25

Marianne and Ship of State
A328

Jean Jaures
A329

1959, July Typo. *Perf. 14x13½*

927	A328	25fr blk & red	40	6

See also No. 942.

1959, Sept. 12 Engr. *Perf. 13*

928	A329	50fr chocolate	50	40

Issued to commemorate the centenary of the birth of Jean Jaures, socialist leader.

Europa Issue, 1959
Common Design Type
1959, Sept. 19
Size: 22x36mm

929	CD2	25fr brt grn	45	30
930	CD2	50fr brt vio	90	45

Blood Donors
A330

1959, Oct. 17 Engraved

931	A330	20fr mag & gray	30	25

French-Spanish Handshake
A331

1959, Oct. 24 *Perf. 13*

932	A331	50fr bl, rose car & org	60	45

Issued to commemorate the 300th anniversary of the signing of the Treaty of the Pyrenees.

Polio Victim Holding Crutches
A332

Henri Bergson
A333

1959, Oct. 31

933	A332	20fr dk bl	22	15

Vaccination against poliomyelitis.

1959, Nov. 7

934	A333	50fr lt red brn	48	40

Issued to commemorate the centenary of the birth of Henri Bergson, philosopher.

Avesnes-sur-Helpe
A334

Design: 30fr, Perpignan.

1959, Nov. 14

935	A334	20fr sep & bl	30	25
936	A334	30fr brn, dp cl & bl	38	30

New NATO Headquarters, Paris
A335

1959, Dec. 12

937	A335	50fr grn, brn & ultra	95	65

Issued to commemorate the 10th anniversary of the North Atlantic Treaty Organization.

Types of 1958–59 and

Farm Woman
A336

Sower
A337

Designs: 5c, Arms of Lille. 15c, Arms of Algiers. 25c, Marianne and Ship of State.

Typographed.

1960–61 *Perf. 14x13½* Unwmkd.

938	A318	5c dk brn & red	10.00	22
939	A336	10c brt grn	38	5
940	A318	15c red, ultra, yel & grn	75	18
941	A337	20c grnsh bl & car rose	25	10
942	A328	25c ver & ultra	3.00	15
b.		Bklt. pane of 8	27.50	
c.		Bklt. pane of 10	32.50	
942A	A337	30c gray & ultra ('61)	2.50	45
		Nos. 938-942A (6)	16.88	1.15

Earlier stamps of Farm Woman type (A336), but with no decimals in denominations, are listed as Nos. 707–708, 833–834 (A236). Nos. 938–942A are in the New Franc currency (100 old francs equal 1 New Franc).

Laon Cathedral
A338

Kerrata Gorge
A339

Designs: 30c, Fougères Chateau. 50c, Mosque, Tlemcen. 65c, Sioule Valley. 85c, Chaumont Viaduct. 1fr, Cilaos Church, Reunion.

1960, Jan. 16 Engr. *Perf. 13*

943	A338	15c bl & ind	22	22
944	A338	30c bl, sep & grn	2.25	15
945	A339	45c brt vio & ol gray	75	12
946	A339	50c sl grn & lt cl	75	5
947	A338	65c sl grn, bl & blk brn	90	18
948	A338	85c bl, sep & grn	2.25	18
949	A339	1fr vio bl, bl & grn	1.50	12
		Nos. 943-949 (7)	8.62	1.02

Pierre de Nolhac
A340

1960, Feb. 13

950	A340	20c blk & gray	75	50

Issued to commemorate the centenary of the birth of Pierre de Nolhac, curator of Versailles and historian.

Museum of Art and Industry, Saint-Etienne
A341

1960. Feb. 20

951	A341	30c brn, car & sl	75	50

Gallic Cock Type of 1954.

1960 Typographed. *Perf. 14x13½*

952	A237	8c violet	1.10	6
953	A237	20c yel grn	3.75	45
954	A237	40c hn brn	9.25	2.50
955	A237	55c emerald	35.00	16.00

Nos. 952–955 were issued only precanceled. See second note after No. 132.

View of Cannes
A342

1960, Mar. 5 Engr. *Perf. 13*

956	A342	50c red brn & lt grn	95	75

Issued to commemorate the meeting of European municipal administrators, Cannes, March, 1960.

Woman of Savoy and Alps
A343

Woman of Nice and Shore
A344

1960 *Perf. 13* Unwmkd.

957	A343	30c sl grn	55	55
958	A344	50c brn, yel & rose	60	45

Issued to commemorate the centenary of the annexation of Nice and Savoy.

Heroes Type of 1957.

Portraits: No. 959, Edmund Debeaumarché. No. 960, Pierre Massé. No. 961, Maurice Ripoche. No. 962, Leonce Vieljeux. 50c, Abbé René Bonpain.

1960, Mar. 26

959	A293	20c bis & blk	2.50	1.65
960	A293	20c pink & rose cl	2.50	1.65
961	A293	30c vio & brt vio	2.50	1.65
962	A293	30c sl bl & brt bl	2.75	2.50
963	A293	50c sl grn & red brn	3.50	3.00
		Nos. 959-963 (5)	13.75	10.45

Issued in honor of the heroes of the French Underground of World War II.

"Education" and Children
A345

1960, May 21 Engraved *Perf. 13*

964	A345	20c rose lil, pur & blk	32	30

Issued to commemorate the 150th anniversary of the first secondary school in Strasbourg.

Blois Chateau
A346

View of La Bourboule
A347

1960, May

965	A346	30c dk bl, sep & grn	75	45
966	A347	50c ol brn, car & grn	90	60

Lorraine Cross
A348

Marianne
A349

1960, June 18

967	A348	20c red brn, dk brn & yel grn	45	30

Issued to commemorate the 20th anniversary of the French Resistance Movement in World War II.

Typographed

1960, June 18 *Perf. 14x13½*

968	A349	25c lake & gray	18	5
a.		Bklt. pane of 8	6.00	
b.		Bklt. pane of 10	4.50	

Jean Bouin and Stadium
A350

1960, July 9 Engraved *Perf. 13*

969	A350	20c bl, mag & ol gray	32	30

Issued to commemorate the 17th Olympic Games, Rome, Aug. 25–Sept. 11.

Europa Issue, 1960.
Common Design Type

1960, Sept. 17 *Perf. 13*

Size: 36x22mm.

970	CD3	25c grn & bluish grn	18	18
971	CD3	50c mar & red lil	40	30

Lisieux Basilica
A351

1960, Sept. 24 *Perf. 13*

972	A351	15c bl, gray & blk	30	30

Arms Type of 1958–59.
Design: Arms of Oran.

Typographed

1960, Oct. 15 *Perf. 14x13½*

973	A318	5c red, bl, yel & emer	25	5

Madame de Staël by François Gerard
A352

1960, Oct. 22 Engraved *Perf. 13*

974	A352	30c dl cl & brn	32	30

Issued to honor Madame de Staël (1766–1817), writer.

Gen. J. B. E. Estienne
A353

1960, Nov. 5

975	A353	15c lt lil & blk	22	22

Issued to commemorate the centenary of the birth of Gen. Jean Baptiste Eugene Estienne.

Marc Sangnier and Youth Hostel at Bierville
A354

1960, Nov. 5

976	A354	20c bl, blk & lil	22	18

Issued to honor Marc Sangnier, founder of the French League for Youth Hostels.

Badge of Order of Liberation
A355

1960, Nov. 14 Engraved *Perf. 13*

977	A355	20c blk & brt grn	38	30

Order of Liberation, 20th anniversary.

Lapwings
A356

Birds: 30c, Puffin. 45c, European teal. 50c, European bee-eaters.

1960, Nov. 12

978	A356	20c multi	38	30
979	A356	30c multi	38	38
980	A356	45c multi	1.25	75
981	A356	50c multi	80	38

Issued to publicize wildlife protection.

André Honnorat
A357

1960, Nov. 19

982	A357	30c bl, blk & grn	38	30

Issued to honor André Honnorat, statesman, fighter against tuberculosis and founder of the University City of Paris, an international students' community.

St. Barbara and Medieval View of School
A358

1960, Dec. 3 Engraved

983	A358	30c red, bl & ol brn	40	40

Issued to commemorate the 500th anniversary of St. Barbara School, Paris.

"Mediterranean" by Aristide Maillol
A359

Marianne by Cocteau
A360

1961, Feb. 18 *Perf. 13* **Unwmkd.**

984	A359	20c car & ind	30	25

Issued to commemorate the centenary of the birth of Aristide Maillol, sculptor.

1961, Feb. 23

985	A360	20c bl & car	25	5

A second type has an extra inverted-V-shaped mark (a blue flag top) at right of hair tip. Price unused $2.50, used 50 cents.

Paris Airport, Orly
A361

1961, Feb. 25

986	A361	50c blk, dk bl, & bluish grn	55	45

Issued to commemorate the inauguration of new facilities at Orly airport.

George Méliès and Motion Picture Screen
A362

1961, March 11

987	A362	50c pur, ind & ol bis	90	50

Issued to commemorate the centenary of the birth of George Méliès, motion picture pioneer.

Jean Baptiste Henri Lacordaire
A363

1961, Mar. 25 *Perf. 13*

988	A363	30c lt brn & blk	30	30

Issued to commemorate the centenary of the death of the Dominican monk Lacordaire, orator and liberal Catholic leader.

A364

1961, Mar. 25

989	A364	30c grn, red brn & red	30	30

Introduction of tobacco use into France, fourth centenary. By error stamp portrays Jan Nicquet instead of Jean Nicot.

Heroes Type of 1957.

Portraits: No. 990, Jacques Renouvin. No. 991, Lionel Dubray. No. 992, Paul Gateaud. No. 993, Mère Elisabeth.

1961, Apr. 22

990	A293	20c bl & lil	90	60
991	A293	20c gray grn & bl	90	65
992	A293	30c brn org & blk	1.25	80
993	A293	30c vio & blk	1.50	90

Bagnoles-de-l'Orne
A365

1961, May 6

994	A365	20c ol, ocher, bl & grn	30	25

Dove, Olive Branch and Federation Emblem
A366

1961, May 6

995	A366	50c brt bl, grn & mar	40	38

World Federation of Ex-Service Men.

Deauville in 19th Century
A367

1961, May 13 Engraved

996	A367	50c rose cl	1.75	1.25

Centenary of Deauville.

La Champmeslé
A368

Mont-Dore, Snowflake and Cable Car
A369

French actors: No. 998, Talma. No. 999, Rachel. No. 1000, Gérard Philipe. No. 1001, Raimu.

1961, June 10 *Perf. 13* Unwmkd.

Dark Carmine Frame

997	A368	20c choc & yel grn	45	30
998	A368	30c brn & crim	50	38
999	A368	30c yel grn & sl grn	50	38
1000	A368	50c ol & choc	90	60
1001	A368	50c bl grn & red brn	90	45
		Nos. 997-1001 (5)	3.25	2.11

Issued to honor great French actors and in connection with the Fifth World Congress of the International Federation of Actors.

1961, July 1

1002	A369	20c org & rose lil	32	25

Pierre Fauchard

A370

St. Theobald's Church, Thann

A371

1961, July 1

1003	A370	50c dk grn & blk	60	45

Issued to commemorate the bicentenary of the death of Pierre Fauchard, first surgeon dentist.

1961, July 1

1004	A371	20c sl grn, vio & brn	75	45

800th anniversary of Thann.

Europa Issue, 1961

Common Design Type

1961, Sept. 16 *Perf. 13*

Size: 35x22mm.

1005	CD4	25c vermilion	18	15
1006	CD4	50c ultra	38	30

Saint-Paul, Maritime Alps

A372

Designs: 30c, Beach and sailboats, Arcachon. 45c, Sully-sur-Loire Chateau. 50c, View of Cognac. 65c, Rance Valley and Dinan. 85c, City hall and Rodin's Burghers, Calais. 1fr, Roman gates of Lodi, Medea, Algeria.

1961, Oct. 9 Engraved *Perf. 13*

1007	A372	15c bl & pur	15	15
1008	A372	30c ultra, sl grn & lt brn	25	15
1009	A372	45c vio bl, red brn & grn	32	5
1010	A372	50c grn, Prus bl & sl	48	12
1011	A372	65c red brn, sl grn & bl	48	10
1012	A372	85c sl grn, sl & red brn	75	16
1013	A372	1fr dk bl, sl & bis	2.75	15
		Nos. 1007-1013 (7)	5.18	88

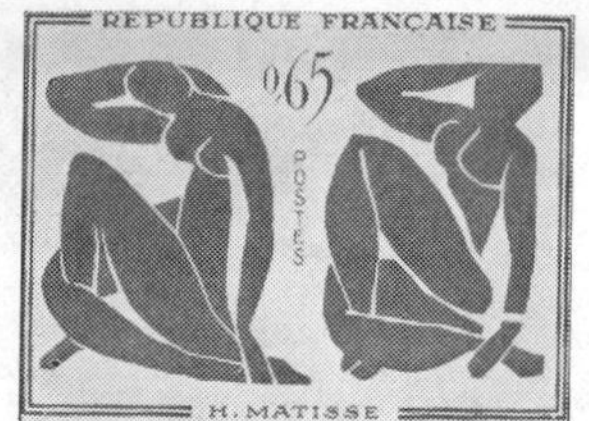

Blue Nudes, by Matisse—A373

Paintings: 50c, "The Messenger," by Braque. 85c, "The Cardplayers," by Cézanne. 1fr, "The 14th July," by Roger de La Fresnaye.

1961, Nov. 10 *Perf. 13x12*

1014	A373	50c dk brn, bl, blk & gray	3.75	2.25
1015	A373	65c grn, vio, & ultra	4.50	3.00
1016	A373	85c blk, brn, red & ol	3.25	2.25
1017	A373	1fr multi	5.50	3.75

Liner France

A374

1962, Jan. 11 Engraved *Perf. 13*

1018	A374	30c dk bl, blk & car	75	48

New French liner France.

Skier Going Downhill

A375

Maurice Bourdet

A376

Design: 50c, Slalom.

1962, Jan. 27 *Perf. 13*

1019	A375	30c ultra & dk vio bl	30	30
1020	A375	50c dk grn, bl & lil	50	38

Issued to publicize the World Ski Championships, Chamonix, Feb. 1962.

1962, Feb. 17

1021	A376	30c slate	30	30

Issued to commemorate the 60th anniversary of the birth of Maurice Bourdet, radio commentator and resistance hero.

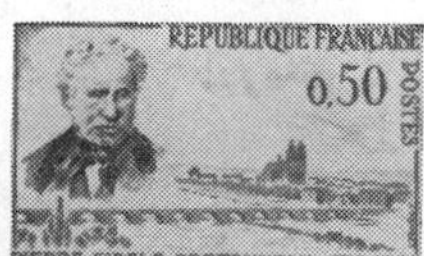

Pierre-Fidele Bretonneau

A377

1962, Feb. 17

1022	A377	50c brt lil & bl	45	32

Issued to commemorate the centenary of the death of Pierre-Fidele Bretonneau, physician.

Chateau and Bridge, Laval, Mayenne

A378

Gallic Cock

A379

1962, Feb. 24

1023	A378	20c bis brn & sl grn	30	25

1962–65 *Perf. 13*

1024	A379	25c ultra, car & brn	30	10
a.		Bklt. pane of 4 (horiz. strip)	3.25	
1024B	A379	30c gray grn, red & brn ('65)	1.40	5
c.		Bklt. pane of 5	8.00	
d.		Bklt. pane of 10	16.00	

No. 1024 was also issued on experimental luminescent paper in 1963.

Ramparts of Vannes

A380

Dunkirk

A381

Paris Beach, Le Touquet

A381a

1962 Engraved *Perf. 13*

1025	A380	30c dk bl	65	60
1026	A381	95c grn, bis & red lil	1.50	22
1027	A381a	1fr grn, red brn & bl	60	5

No. 1026 commemorates the 300th anniversary of Dunkirk.

Stage Setting and Globe

A382

1962, Mar. 24 Unwmkd.

1028	A382	50c sl grn, ocher & mag	50	45

International Day of the Theater, Mar. 27.

Memorial to Fighting France, Mont Valerien

A383

Resistance Heroes' Monument, Vercors

A384

Design: 50c, Ile de Sein monument.

1962, Apr. 7

1029	A383	20c ol & sl grn	75	38
1030	A384	30c bluish blk	60	45
1031	A384	50c bl & ind	1.00	60

Issued to publicize memorials for the French Underground in World War II.

Malaria Eradication Emblem and Swamp

A385

Nurses with Child and Hospital

A386

1962, Apr. 14 Engraved

1032	A385	50c dk bl & dk red	45	38

Issued for the World Health Organization drive to eradicate malaria.

1962, May 5 *Perf. 13* Unwmkd.

1033	A386	30c bl grn, gray & red brn	22	22

National Hospital Week, May 5–12.

Glider—A387

Design: 20c, Planes showing development of aviation.

1962, May 12

1034	A387	15c org red & brn	45	45
1035	A387	20c lil rose & rose cl	50	50

Issued to publicize sports aviation.

School Emblem
A388

1962, May 19 **Engraved**

1036 A388 50c mar, ocher & dk vio 50 50

Issued to commemorate the centenary of the Watchmaker's School at Besançon.

Louis XIV and Workers Showing Modern Gobelin—A389

1962, May 26 ***Perf. 13*** **Unwmkd.**

1037 A389 50c ol, sl grn & car 50 45

Issued to commemorate the 300th anniversary of the Gobelin tapestry works, Paris.

Blaise Pascal—A390

1962, May 26

1038 A390 50c sl grn & dp org 60 50

Issued to commemorate 300th anniversary of the death of Blaise Pascal (1623–1662), mathematician, scientist and philosopher.

Palace of Justice, Rennes
A391

1962, June 12

1039 A391 30c blk, grysh bl & grn 1.50 90

Arms Type of 1958–59

Arms: 5c, Amiens. 10c, Troyes. 15c, Nevers.

1962–63 **Typo.** ***Perf. 14x13½***

1040 A318 5c ver, ultra & yel 7 6
1041 A318 10c red, ultra & yel ('63) 5 5
1042 A318 15c ver, ultra & yel 10 5

Phosphor Tagging

In 1970 France began to experiment with luminescence. Phosphor bands have been added to Nos. 1041, 1143, 1231, 1231C, 1292A-1294B, 1494-1498, 1560-1579B, etc.

Rose
A392

Design: 30c, Old-fashioned rose.

1962, Sept. 8 **Engraved** ***Perf. 13***

1043 A392 20c ol, grn & brt car 45 30
1044 A392 30c dk sl grn, ol & car 60 45

Europa Issue, 1962

Common Design Type

1962, Sept. 15

Size: 36x22mm.

1045 CD5 25c violet 18 15
1046 CD5 50c hn brn 38 30

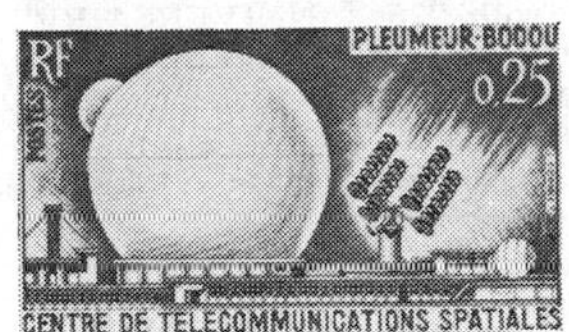

Space Communications Center, Pleumeur-Bodou, France—A394

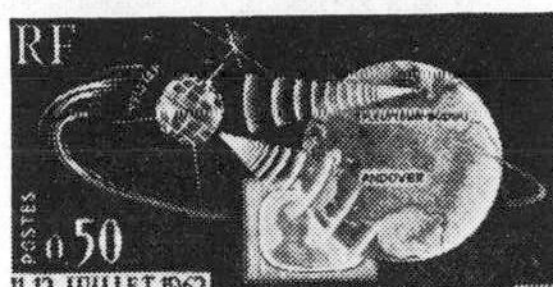

Telstar, Earth and Television Set
A395

1962, Sept. 29 **Engraved** ***Perf. 13***

1047 A394 25c gray, yel & grn 22 15
1048 A395 50c dk bl, grn & ultra 40 38

Issued to commemorate the first television connection of the United States and Europe through the Telstar satellite, July 11–12.

"Bonjour Monsieur Courbet" by Gustave Courbet—A396

Paintings: 65c, "Madame Manet on Blue Sofa," by Edouard Manet. 1fr, "Guards officer on horseback," by Theodore Géricault (vert.).

1962, Nov. 9 ***Perf. 13x12, 12x13***

1049 A396 50c multi 4.75 2.50
1050 A396 65c multi 3.25 2.25
1051 A396 1fr multi 6.75 4.00

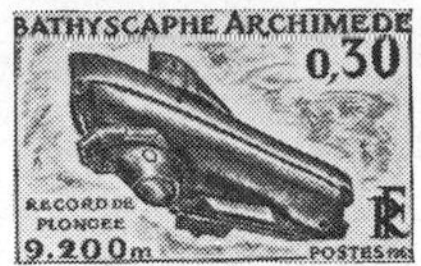

Bathyscaph "Archimede"
A397

1963, Jan. 26 ***Perf. 13*** **Unwmkd.**

1052 A397 30c dk bl & blk 32 30

French deep-sea explorations.

Flowers and Nantes Chateau
A398

1963, Feb. 11

1053 A398 30c vio bl, car & sl grn 32 30

Nantes flower festival.

St. Peter, Window at St. Foy de Conches—A399

Design: 50c, Jacob Wrestling with the Angel, by Delacroix.

1963, Mar. 2 ***Perf. 12x13***

1054 A399 50c multi 4.50 3.00
1055 A399 1fr multi 6.75 4.75

See also Nos. 1076–1077.

Hungry Woman and Wheat Emblem
A400

1963, Mar. 21 **Engraved** ***Perf. 13***

1056 A400 50c sl grn & brn 40 32

Issued for the "Freedom from Hunger" campaign of the U.N. Food and Agriculture Organization.

Cemetery and Memorial, Glières
A401

Design: 50c, Memorial, Ile de la Cité, Paris.

1963, Mar. 23 ***Perf. 13*** **Unwmkd.**

1057 A401 30c dk brn & ol 40 40
1058 A401 50c indigo 48 48

Issued to commemorate the heroes of the resistance against the Nazis.

Beethoven, Birthplace at Bonn and Rhine
A402

Designs: No. 1060, Emile Verhaeren, memorial at Roisin and residence. No. 1061, Giuseppe Mazzini, Marcus Aurelius statue and Via Appia, Rome. No. 1062, Emile Mayrisch, Colpach Chateau and blast furnace, Esch. No. 1063, Hugo de Groot, Palace of Peace, The Hague and St. Agatha Church, Delft.

1963, Apr. 27 ***Perf. 13*** **Unwmkd.**

1059 A402 20c ocher, sl & brt grn 38 38
1060 A402 20c pur, blk & mar 38 38
1061 A402 20c mar, sl & ol 38 38
1062 A402 20c mar, dk brn & ocher 38 38
1063 A402 30c dk brn, vio & ocher 38 38
Nos. 1059-1063 (5) 1.90 1.90

Issued to honor famous men of the European Common Market countries.

Hotel des Postes and Stagecoach, 1863
A403

1963, May 4

1064 A403 50c grysh blk 45 38

Issued to commemorate the first International Postal Conference, Paris, 1863.

Lycée Louis-le-Grand, Belvédère, Panthéon and St. Étienne du Mont Church
A404

1963, May 18

1065 A404 30c sl grn 32 30

Issued to commemorate the 400th anniversary of the Jesuit Clermont secondary school, named after Louis XIV.

St. Peter's Church and Ramparts, Caen
A405

1963, June 1 ***Perf. 13*** **Unwmkd.**

1066 A405 30c gray bl & brn 32 32

Radio Telescope, Nançay—A406

1963, June 8 **Engraved**

1067	A406	50c dk bl & dk brn	40	38

Amboise Chateau
A407

Saint-Flour
A408

Designs: 50c, Côte d'Azur Varoise. 85c, Vittel. 95c, Moissac.

1963, June 15

1068	A407	30c sl, grn & bis	30	15
1069	A407	50c dk grn, dk bl & hn brn	45	5
1070	A408	60c ultra, dk grn & hn brn	50	32
1071	A407	85c dk grn, yel grn & brn	1.40	18
1072	A408	95c dk brn & blk	90	30
		Nos. 1068-1072 (5)	3.55	1.00

Water Skiing Slalom
A409

1963, Aug. 31 ***Perf. 13*** **Unwmkd.**

1073	A409	30c sl grn, blk & car	32	30

Issued to commemorate the World Water Skiing Championships, Vichy.

Europa Issue, 1963
Common Design Type

1963, Sept. 14

Size: 36x22mm.

1074	CD6	25c red brn	25	15
1075	CD6	50c green	40	30

Type of 1963

Designs: 85c, "The Married Couple of the Eiffel Tower" by Marc Chagall. 95c, "The Fur Merchants," window, Chartres Cathedral.

1963, Nov. 9 Engraved ***Perf. 12x13***

1076	A399	85c multi	1.90	1.40
1077	A399	95c multi	1.00	75

Philatec Issue
Common Design Type

1963, Dec. 14 ***Perf. 13*** **Unwmkd.**

1078	CD118	25c dk gray, sl grn & dk car	22	15

Radio and Television Center, Paris
A411

1963, Dec. 15 **Engraved**

1079	A411	20c org brn, sl & ol	18	15

Fire Brigade Insignia, Symbols of Fire, Water and Civilian Defense
A412

1964, Feb. 8 **Engraved** ***Perf. 13***

1082	A412	30c bl, org & red	38	30

Issued to honor the fire brigades and civilian defense corps.

Handicapped Laboratory Technician
A413

1964, Feb. 22 ***Perf. 13*** **Unwmkd.**

1083	A413	30c grn, red brn & brn	30	25

Rehabilitation of the handicapped.

John II the Good (1319–64) by Girard d'Orleans
A414

1964, Apr. 25 ***Perf. 12x13***

1084	A414	1fr multi	2.75	1.90

The lack of a price for a listed item does not necessarily indicate rarity.

Stamp of 1900
A415

Mechanized Mail Handling
A416

Designs: No. 1086, Stamp of 1900, Type A17. No. 1088, Telecommunications.

1964, May 9 ***Perf. 13***

1085	A415	25c bis & dk car	30	30
1086	A415	25c bis & bl	30	30
1087	A416	30c blk, bl & org brn	30	30
1088	A416	30c blk, car rose & bluish grn	30	30
a.		Strip of 4 (1 each Nos. 1085-1088 + label)	1.25	1.25

Printed in sheets of 20 stamps, containing five No. 1088a. The label shows the Philatec emblem in green.

Type of Semi-Postal Issue, 1959 with "25e ANNIVERSAIRE" added

1964, May 9

1089	SP208	25c multi	30	18

25th anniversary, night airmail service.

Madonna and Child from Rose Window of Notre Dame
A417

1964, May 23 ***Perf. 12x13***

1090	A417	60c multi	60	60

Issued to commemorate the 800th anniversary of Notre Dame Cathedral, Paris.

Arms Type of 1958–59

Arms: 1c, Niort. 2c, Guéret. 12c, Agen. 18c, Saint-Denis, Réunion. 30c, Paris.

1964–65 **Typo.** ***Perf. 14x13½***

1091	A318	1c vio bl & yel	6	6
1092	A318	2c emer, vio bl & yel	6	6
1093	A318	12c blk, red & yel	10	5
1094	A318	18c multi	22	22
1095	A318	30c vio, bl & red ('65)	45	5
a.		Bklt. pane of 10	8.50	
		Nos. 1091-1095 (5)	89	44

Gallic Coin
A418

Perf. 13½x14

1964–66 **Typographed** **Unwmkd.**

1096	A418	10c emer & bis	1.40	15
1097	A418	15c org & bis ('66)	45	15
1098	A418	25c lil & brn	75	32
1099	A418	50c brt bl & brn	1.50	65

Nos. 1096–1099 are known only precanceled. See second note after No. 132. See Nos. 1240–1242, 1315–1318, 1421–1424.

Postrider, Rocket and Radar Equipment—A419

1964, June 5 **Engraved** ***Perf. 13***

1100	A419	1fr brn, dk red & dk bl	30.00	26.00

Sold for 4fr, including 3fr admission to PHILATEC. Issued in sheets of 8 stamps and 8 labels (2x8 subjects with labels in horizontal rows 1, 4, 5, 8; stamps in rows 2, 3, 6, 7). Commemorative inscriptions on side margins.

Caesar's Tower, Provins
A420

Chapel of Notre Dame du Haut, Ronchamp—A421

1964–65

1101	A421	40c sl grn, dk brn & brn ('65)	30	10
1102	A420	70c sl, grn & car	45	6
1103	A421	1.25fr brt bl, sl grn & ol	90	38

The 40c was issued in vertical coils in 1971. Every 10th coil stamp has a red control number printed twice on the back.

Georges Mandel
A422

Judo
A423

1964, July 4 ***Perf. 13*** **Unwmkd.**

1104	A422	30c vio brn	22	22

Issued to commemorate the 20th anniversary of the death of Georges Mandel (1885–1944), Cabinet minister, executed by the Nazis.

1964, July 4

1105	A423	50c dk bl & vio brn	38	30

Issued to publicize the 18th Olympic Games, Tokyo, Oct. 10–25, 1964.

Champlevé Enamel from Limoges, 12th Century—A424

Design: No. 1107, The Lady (Claude Le Viste ?) with the Unicorn, 15th century tapestry.

1964 *Perf. 12x13*

1106	A424	1fr multi	2.00	1.25
1107	A424	1fr multi	75	60

No. 1106 shows part of an enamel sepulchral plate portraying Geoffrey IV, Count of Anjou and Le Maine (1113–1151), who was called Geoffrey Plantagenet.

Issue dates: No. 1106, July 4. No. 1107, Oct. 31.

Paris Taxis Carrying Soldiers to Front, 1914
A425

1964, Sept. 5 *Perf. 13* **Unwmkd.**

1108	A425	30c blk, bl & red	30	30

50th anniversary of Battle of the Marne.

Europa Issue, 1964
Common Design Type

1964, Sept. 12 **Engraved**

Size: 22x36mm.

1109	CD7	25c dk car, dp ocher & grn	18	15
1110	CD7	50c vio, yel grn & dk car	32	30

Cooperation Issue
Common Design Type

1964, Nov. 6 *Perf. 13* **Unwmkd.**

1111	CD119	25c red brn, dk brn & dk bl	22	22

Joux Chateau
A427

1965, Feb. 6 **Engraved**

1112	A427	1.30fr redsh brn, brn red & dk brn	1.00	20

"The English Girl from the Star" by Toulouse-Lautrec—A428

St. Paul on the Damascus Road, Window, Cathedral of Sens
A429

Leaving for the Hunt
A430

Apocalypse Tapestry, 14th Century
A431

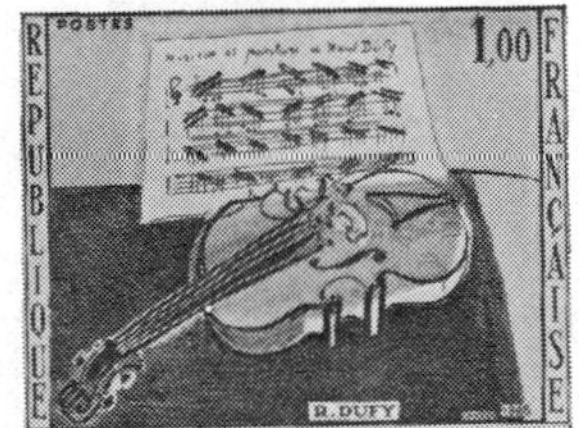

"The Red Violin" by Raoul Dufy
A432

Designs: No. 1115, "August" miniature of Book of Hours of Jean de France, Duc de Berry ("Les Très Riches Heures du Duc de Berry"), painted by Flemish brothers, Pol, Hermant and Jannequin Limbourg, 1411–16. No. 1116, Scene from oldest existing set of French tapestries, showing the Winepress of the Wrath of God (Revelations 14: 19–20).

1965 *Perf. 12x13, 13x12*

1113	A428	1fr multi	50	50
1114	A429	1fr multi	45	45
1115	A430	1fr multi	45	45
1116	A431	1fr multi	45	45
1117	A432	1fr blk, pink & car	45	45
		Nos. 1113-1117 (5)	2.30	2.30

No. 1114 issued to commemorate the 800th anniversary of the Cathedral of Sens.

Dates of issue: No. 1113, Mar. 12. No. 1114, June 5. No. 1115, Sept. 25. No. 1116, Oct. 30. No. 1117, Nov. 6.

Paris Parade of Returning Deportees, 1945
A433

1965, Apr. 1 *Perf. 13* **Unwmkd.**

1118	A433	40c Prus grn	48	38

Issued to commemorate the 20th anniversary of the return of people deported during World War II.

House of Youth and Culture, Troyes
A434

1965, Apr. 10 **Engraved**

1119	A434	25c ind, brn & dk grn	32	25

Issued to publicize the 20th anniversary of the establishment of recreational cultural centers for young people.

Woman Carrying Flowers
A435

Flags of France, USA, USSR and Great Britain Crushing Swastika
A436

1965, Apr. 24 *Perf. 13* **Unwmkd.**

1120	A435	60c dk grn, dp org & ver	40	38

Issued to publicize the tourist Campaign of Welcome and Amiability.

1965, May 8

1121	A436	40c blk, car & ultra	38	30

Issued to commemorate the 20th anniversary of victory in World War II.

Telegraph Key, Syncom Satellite and Pleumeur-Bodou Station
A437

1965, May 17

1122	A437	60c dk bl, brn & blk	40	38

Issued to commemorate the centenary of the International Telecommunication Union.

Croix de Guerre
A438

1965, May 22 **Engraved**

1123	A438	40c red, brn & brt grn	48	38

Issued to commemorate the 50th anniversary of the Croix de Guerre medal.

Cathedral of Bourges
A439

Moustiers-Sainte-Marie
A440

Views: 30c, Road and tunnel, Mont Blanc. 60c, Aix-les-Bains, sailboat. 75c, Tarn Gorge, Lozère mountains. 95c, Vendée River, man poling boat, and windmill. 1fr, Prehistoric stone monuments, Carnac.

1965, June–July

1124	A439	30c bl, vio bl & brn vio	25	22
1125	A439	40c gray bl & redsh brn	30	25
1126	A440	50c grn, bl gray & bis	32	10
1127	A439	60c bl & red brn	40	15
1128	A439	75c brn, bl & grn	95	48
1129	A440	95c brn, grn & bl	2.00	22
1130	A440	1fr gray grn & brn	80	6
		Nos. 1124-1130 (7)	5.02	1.48

No. 1124 was issued July 17 to commemorate the opening of the Mont Blanc Tunnel. No. 1125 (Bourges Cathedral) was issued in connection with the French Philatelic Societies Federation Congress, held at Bourges.

Europa Issue, 1965
Common Design Type

1965, Sept. 25 *Perf. 13*

Size: 36x22mm.

1131	CD8	30c red	22	15
1132	CD8	60c gray	38	38

Planting Seedling
A441

Etienne Régnault, "Le Taureau" and Coast of Reunion
A442

1965, Oct. 2

1133	A441	25c sl grn, yel grn & red brn	22	22

National reforestation campaign.

1965. Oct. 2

1134	A442	30c ind & dk car	22	18

Tercentenary of settlement of Reunion.

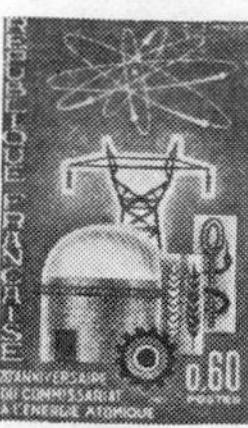

Atomic Reactor and Diagram, Symbols of Industry, Agriculture and Medicine

A443

1965, Oct. 9

1135 A443 60c brt bl & blk 75 60

Issued to commemorate the 20th anniversary of the Atomic Energy Commission.

Air Academy and Emblem

A444

1965, Nov. 6 ***Perf. 13***

1136 A444 25c dk bl & grn 25 22

Issued to commemorate the 50th anniversary of the Air Academy, Salon-de-Provence.

French Satellite A-1 Issue

Common Design Type

Design: 60c, A-1 satellite.

1965, Nov. 30 **Engraved** ***Perf. 13***

1137 CD121 30c Prus bl, brt bl & blk 22 22
1138 CD121 60c blk, Prus bl & brt bl 32 30
a. Strip of 2 + label 60 60

Issued to commemorate the launching of France's first satellite, Nov. 26, 1965. No. 1138a contains one each of Nos. 1137–1138 and bright blue label with commemorative inscription. Each sheet contains 16 triptychs (2x8).

Arms of Auch

A446

Arms (Cities): 20c, Saint-Lô. 25c, Mont-de-Marsan.

Typo.; Photo. (20c)

1966 ***Perf. 14x13; 14 (20c)***

1142 A446 5c bl & red 5 5
1143 A446 20c vio bl, sil, gold & red 18 5
1144 A446 25c red brn & ultra 38 15

The 5c and 20c were issued in sheets and in vertical coils. In the coils, every 10th stamp has a red control number on the back.

French Satellite D-1 Issue

Common Design Type

1966, Feb. 18 **Engraved** ***Perf. 13***

1148 CD122 60c bl blk, grn & cl 32 30

Launching of the D-1 satellite at Hammaguir, Algeria, Feb. 17, 1966.

Horses from Bronze Vessel of Vix

A448

"The Newborn" by Georges de La Tour

A449

The Baptism of Judas (4th Century Bishop of Jerusalem)

A450

"The Moon and the Bull" Tapestry by Jean Lurçat

A451

"Crispin and Scapin" by Honoré Daumier

A452

1966 ***Perf. 13x12, 12x13***

1149 A448 1fr multi 45 45
1150 A449 1fr multi 45 45
1151 A450 1fr multi 50 50
1152 A451 1fr multi 50 50
1153 A452 1fr multi 50 50
Nos. 1149-1153 (5) 2.40 2.40

The design of No. 1149 is a detail from a 6th century B.C. vessel, found in 1953 in a grave near Vix, Cote d'Or.

The design of No. 1151 is from a stained glass window in the 13th century Sainte-Chapelle, Paris.

Issue dates: No. 1149, Mar. 26. No. 1150, June 25. No. 1151, Oct. 22. No. 1152, Nov. 19. No. 1153, Dec. 10.

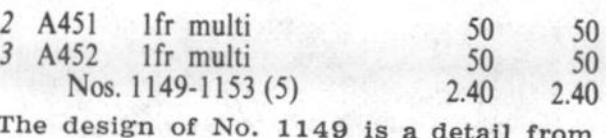

Chessboard, Knight, Emblems for King and Queen

A453

St. Michael Slaying the Dragon

A455

Rhone Bridge, Pont-Saint-Esprit

A454

1966, Apr. 2 **Engraved** ***Perf. 13***

1154 A453 60c sep, gray & dk vio bl 60 50

Issued to publicize the Chess Festival.

1966, Apr. 23 ***Perf. 13*** **Unwmkd.**

1155 A454 25c blk & dl bl 22 18

1966, Apr. 30 **Litho. and Engr.**

1156 A455 25c multi 22 18

Millenium of Mont-Saint-Michel.

Stanislas Leszczynski, Lunéville Chateau

A456

1966, May 6 **Engraved**

1157 A456 25c sl, grn & brn 22 18

Issued to commemorate the 200th anniversary of the reunion of Lorraine and Bar (Barrois) with France.

St. Andrew's and Sèvre River, Niort

A457

1966, May 28 **Engraved** ***Perf. 13***

1158 A457 40c brt bl, ind & grn 30 25

Bernard Le Bovier de Fontenelle and 1666 Meeting Room

A458

1966, June 4

1159 A458 60c dk car rose & brn 40 38

300th anniversary, Académie des Sciences.

William the Conqueror, Castle and Norman Ships—A459

1966, June 4

1160 A459 60c brn red & dp bl 45 45

900th anniversary of Battle of Hastings.

Tracks, Globe and Eiffel Tower

A460

1966, June 11

1161 A460 60c dk brn, car & dl bl 80 50

19th International Railroad Congress.

Oléron Bridge

A461

1966, June 20

1162 A461 25c Prus bl, brn & bl 22 18

Issued to commemorate the opening of Oléron Bridge, connecting Oléron Island in the Bay of Biscay with the French mainland.

Europa Issue, 1966

Common Design Type

1966, Sept. 24 **Engraved** ***Perf. 13***

Size: 22x36mm.

1163 CD9 30c Prus bl 18 15
1164 CD9 60c red 40 38

Vercingetorix at Gergovie, 52 B.C.

A462

Bishop Remi Baptizing King Clovis, 496 A.D.
A463

Design: 60c, Charlemagne attending school (page holding book for crowned king).

1966, Nov. 5 ***Perf. 13***

1165 A462 40c choc, grn & gray bl 25 25
1166 A463 40c dk red brn & blk 25 25
1167 A463 60c pur, rose car & brn 38 30

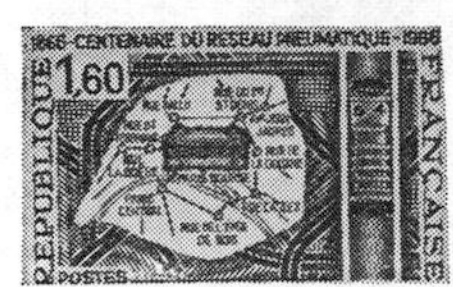

Map of Pneumatic Post and Tube
A464

1966, Nov. 11

1168 A464 1.60fr mar & ind 90 50

Centenary of Paris pneumatic post system.

Val Chateau
A465

1966, Nov. 19 **Engraved** ***Perf. 13***

1169 A465 2.30fr dk bl, sl grn & brn 2.25 18

Rance Power Station
A466

1966, Dec. 3

1170 A466 60c dk bl, sl grn & brn 45 30

Issued to publicize the tidal power station in the estuary of the Rance River on the English Channel.

European Broadcasting Union Emblem
A467

1967, Mar. 4 **Engraved** ***Perf. 13***

1171 A467 40c dk bl & rose brn 30 30

Issued to publicize the 3rd International Congress of the European Broadcasting Union, Paris, March 8–22.

"Father Juniet's Gig" by Henri Rousseau—A468

Francois I by Jean Clouet
A469

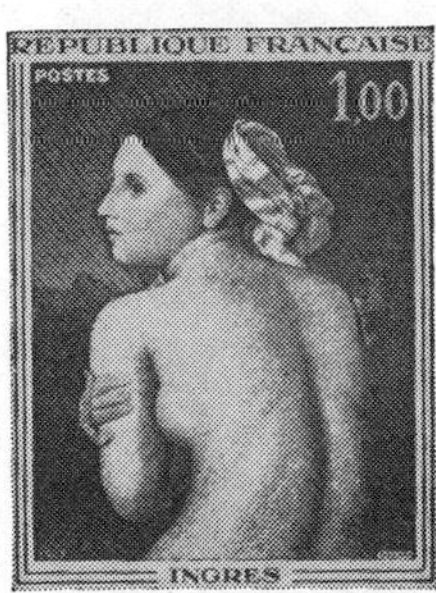

The Bather, by Jean-Dominique Ingres
A470

St. Eloi, the Goldsmith, at Work
A471

1967 **Engr.** ***Perf. 13x12, 12x13***

1172 A468 1fr multi 50 50
1173 A469 1fr multi 50 50
1174 A470 1fr multi 48 45
1175 A471 1fr multi 48 45

The design of No. 1175 is from a 16th century stained glass window in the Church of Sainte Madeleine, Troyes.

Issue dates: No. 1172, Apr. 15. No. 1173, July 1. No. 1174, Sept. 9. No. 1175, Oct. 7.

Snow Crystal and Olympic Rings
A472

1967, Apr. 22 Photogravure ***Perf. 13***

1176 A472 60c brt & lt bl & red 45 30

Issued to publicize the 10th Winter Olympic Games, Grenoble, Feb. 6–18, 1968.

French Pavilion, EXPO '67
A473

1967, Apr. 22 **Engraved**

1177 A473 60c dl bl & bl grn 40 30

Issued to commemorate the International Exhibition EXPO '67, Montreal, Apr. 28–Oct. 27, 1967.

Europa Issue, 1967
Common Design Type

1967, Apr. 29
Size: 22x36mm.

1178 CD10 30c bl & gray 18 15
1179 CD10 60c brn & lt bl 32 30

Great Bridge, Bordeaux—A474

1967, May 8

1180 A474 25c ol, blk & brn 30 22

Nungesser, Coli and "L'Oiseau Blanc"
A475

1967, May 8

1181 A475 40c sl, dk & lt brn 45 30

Issued to commemorate the 40th anniversary of the attempted transatlantic flight of Charles Nungesser and François Coil, French aviators.

Goüin House, Tours
A476

1967, May 13 **Engraved** ***Perf. 13***

1182 A476 40c vio bl, red brn & red 32 30

Issued to publicize the Congress of the Federation of French Philatelic Societies in Tours.

Ramon and Alfort Veterinary School
A477

1967, May 27

1183 A477 25c brn, dp bl & yel grn 18 15

Issued to commemorate the 200th anniversary of the Alfort Veterinary School and to honor Professor Gaston Ramon (1886–1963).

Robert Esnault-Pelterie, Diamant Rocket and A-1 Satellite—A478

1967, May 27

1184 A478 60c sl & vio bl 45 38

Issued to honor Robert Esnault-Pelterie (1881–1957), aviation and space expert.

City Hall, Saint-Quentin
A479

Saint-Germain-en-Laye
A480

Views: 60c, Clock Tower, Vire. 75c, Beach, La Baule, Brittany. 95c, Harbor, Boulogne-sur-Mer. 1fr, Rodez Cathedral. 1.50fr, Morlaix; old houses, grotesque carving, viaduct.

1967

1185 A479 50c bl, sl bl & brn 38 8
1186 A479 60c dp bl, sl bl & dk red brn 45 30
1187 A480 70c rose car, red brn & bl 45 6
1188 A480 75c multi 65 48
1189 A480 95c sky bl, lil & sl grn 75 45
1190 A479 1fr ind & bl gray 60 10
1191 A479 1.50fr brt bl, brt grn & red brn 1.25 32
Nos. 1185-1191 (7) 4.53 1.79

Issue Dates: 1fr, 1.50fr, June 10; 70c, June 17; 50c, 60c, 95c, July 8; 75c, July 24.

Orchids

A481

Cross of Lorraine, Soldiers and Sailors

A483

Scales of Justice, City and Harbor

A482

1967, July 29 **Engr.** ***Perf. 13***

1192	A481	40c dp car, brt pink & pur	45	30

Orleans flower festival.

1967, Sept. 4

1193	A482	60c dk plum, dl bl & ocher	38	30

Issued to publicize the 9th International Accountancy Congress, Paris, Sept. 6–12.

1967, Oct. 7 **Engraved** ***Perf. 13***

1194	A483	25c brn, dp ultra & bl	22	18

Issued to commemorate the 25th anniversary of the Battle of Bir Hacheim.

Marie Curie, Bowl Glowing with Radium

A484

1967, Oct. 23 **Engr.** ***Perf. 13***

1195	A484	60c dk bl & ultra	45	32

Issued to commemorate the centenary of the birth of Marie Curie (1867–1934), scientist who discovered radium and polonium, Nobel prize winner for physics and chemistry.

Lions Emblem

A485

Marianne (by Cheffer)

A486

1967, Oct. 28

1196	A485	40c dk car & vio bl	38	28

50th anniversary of Lions International.

1967, Nov. 4 **Engraved**

1197	A486	25c dk bl	60	30
1198	A486	30c brt lil	65	5
a.		Bklt. pane of 5	5.00	
b.		Bklt. pane of 10	11.00	

Coils (vertical) of Nos. 1197 and 1231 show a red number on the back of every 10th stamp.

See Nos. 1230–1231C.

King Philip II (Philip Augustus) at Battle of Bouvines

A487

Designs: No. 1200, Election of Hugh Capet as King (horiz.). 60c, King Louis IX (St. Louis) holding audience for the poor.

1967, Nov. 13 **Engraved** ***Perf. 13***

1199	A487	40c gray & blk	32	30
1200	A487	40c stl bl & ultra	32	30
1201	A487	60c grn & dk red brn	45	30

Commemorative Medal

A488

1968, Jan. 6 **Engraved** ***Perf. 13***

1202	A488	40c dk sl grn & bis	30	30

Issued to commemorate the 50th anniversary of postal checking service.

Various Road Signs

A489

1968, Feb. 24

1203	A489	25c lil, red & dk bl grn	22	18

Issued to publicize road safety.

Prehistoric Paintings, Lascaux Cave—A490

"Arearea" (Merriment) by Paul Gauguin—A491

The Dance, by Emile Antoine Bourdelle

A492

Portrait of the Model, by Auguste Renoir

A493

1968 **Engr.** ***Perf. 13x12, 12x13***

1204	A490	1fr multi	50	45
1205	A491	1fr multi	60	50
1206	A492	1fr car & gray ol	60	50
1207	A493	1fr multi	60	50

Issue dates: No. 1204, Apr. 13. No. 1205, Sept. 21. No. 1206, Oct. 26. No. 1207, Nov. 9.

Audio-visual Institute, Royan

A494

1968, Apr. 13 ***Perf. 13***

1208	A494	40c sl grn, brn & Prus bl	30	30

Issued to publicize the 5th Conference for World Cooperation with the theme of teaching living languages by audio-visual means.

Europa Issue, 1968

Common Design Type

1968, Apr. 27

Size: 36x22mm

1209	CD11	30c brt red lil & ocher	22	15
1210	CD11	60c brn & lake	38	30

Alain René Le Sage

A495

1968, May 4

1211	A495	40c bl & rose vio	30	22

Issued to commemorate the 300th anniversary of the birth of Alain René Le Sage (1668–1747), novelist and playwright.

Chateau de Langeais

A496

1968, May 4

1212	A496	60c sl bl, grn & red brn	45	38

Pierre Larousse

A497

1968, May 11 **Engraved** ***Perf. 13***

1213	A497	40c rose vio & brn	30	22

Issued to honor Pierre Larousse (1817–1875), grammarian, lexicographer and encyclopedist.

Gnarled Trunk and Fir Tree

A498

1968, May 18 **Engraved** ***Perf. 13***

1214	A498	25c grnsh bl, brn & grn	22	22

Issued to commemorate the twinning of Rambouillet Forest in France and the Black Forest in Germany.

Map of Papal Enclave, Valréas, and John XXII Receiving Homage—A499

1968, May 25

1215	A499	60c brn, bis brn & pur	40	38

Issued to commemorate the 650th anniversary of the papal enclave at Valréas.

Louis XIV, Arms of France and Flanders

A500

1968, June 29

1216	A500	40c rose car, gray & lem	30	22

Issued to commemorate the 300th anniversary of the Treaty of Aachen which reunited Flanders with France.

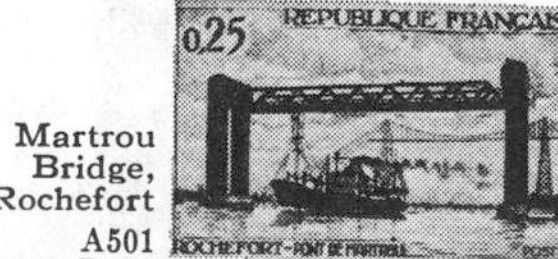

Martrou Bridge, Rochefort

A501

1968, July 20

1217	A501	25c sky bl, blk & dk red brn	18	18

Letord Lorraine Bimotor Plane over Map of France—A502

1968, Aug. 17 Engraved *Perf. 13*

1218 A502 25c brt bl, ind & red 55 30

Issued to commemorate the 50th anniversary of the first regularly scheduled air mail route in France from Paris to St. Nazaire.

Tower de Constance, Aigues-Mortes A503

1968, Aug. 31

1219 A503 25c red brn, sky bl & ol bis 30 22

Bicentenary of the release of Huguenot prisoners from the Tower de Constance, Aigues-Mortes.

Cathedral and Pont Vieux, Beziers A504

1968, Sept. 7 Engraved *Perf. 13*

1220 A504 40c ind, bis & grn 25 15

"Victory" over White Tower of Salonika A505

1968, Sept. 28

1221 A505 40c red lil & plum 32 30

Issued to commemorate the 50th anniversary of the armistice on the eastern front in World War I, Sept. 29, 1918.

Louis XV, Arms of France and Corsica A506

1968, Oct. 5 *Perf. 13*

1222 A506 25c ultra, grn & blk 22 15

Issued to commemorate the 200th anniversary of the return of Corsica to France.

Relay Race A507

1968, Oct. 12

1223 A507 40c ultra, brt grn & ol brn 38 30

Issued to commemorate the 19th Olympic Games, Mexico City, Oct. 12–27.

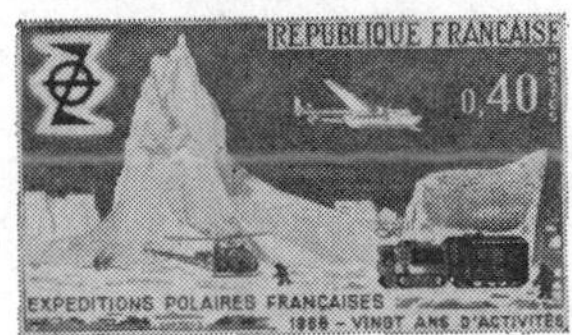

Polar Camp with Helicopter, Plane and Snocat Tractor—A508

1968, Oct. 19

1224 A508 40c Prus bl, lt grnsh bl & brn red 38 30

20 years of French Polar expeditions.

Leon Bailby, Paris Opera Staircase and Hospital Beds A509

"Victory" over Arc de Triomphe and Eternal Flame A510

1968, Oct. 26

1225 A509 40c ocher & mar 30 25

Issued to publicize the 50th anniversary of the "Little White Beds" children's hospital fund.

1968, Nov. 9 Engraved *Perf. 13*

1226 A510 25c dk car rose & dp bl 22 18

Issued to commemorate the 50th anniversary of the armistice which ended World War I.

Death of Bertrand Du Guesclin at Chateauneuf-de-Randon, 1380 A511

1968, Nov. 16

Designs: No. 1228, King Philip IV (the Fair) and first States-General assembly, 1302 (horiz.). 60c, Joan of Arc leaving Vaucouleurs, 1429.

1227 A511 40c cop red, grn & gray 30 30
1228 A511 40c grn, ultra & brn 30 30
1229 A511 60c vio bl, sl bl & bis 38 30

See also No. 1260.

Marianne Type of 1967

1969–70 Engraved *Perf. 13*

1230 A486 30c green 25 15
a. Bklt. pane of 10 4.00
1231 A486 40c dp car 40 5
a. Bklt. pane of 5 (horiz. strip) 3.50
b. Bklt. pane of 10 5.75
d. With label ('70) 60 38

Typographed *Perf. 14x13*

1231C A486 30c bl grn 22 5

No. 1231d was issued in sheets of 50 with alternating labels showing coat of arms of Perigueux, arranged checkerwise, to commemorate the inauguration of the Perigueux stamp printing plant.

The 40c coil is noted after No. 1198.

Church of Brou, Bourg-en-Bresse A512

Views: 80c, Vouglans Dam, Jura. 85c, Chateau de Chantilly. 1.15fr, Sailboats in La Trinité-sur-Mer harbor.

1969 Engraved *Perf. 13*

1232 A512 45c ol, bl & red brn 32 22
1233 A512 80c ol bis, brn red & dk brn 60 10
1234 A512 85c sl grn, dl bl & gray 70 65
1235 A512 1.15fr brt bl, gray grn & brn 75 45

"February" Bas-relief from Amiens Cathedral A513

Philip the Good, by Roger van der Weyden A514

Sts. Savin and Cyprian before Ladicius, Mural, St. Savin, Vienne—A515

The Circus, by Georges Seurat A515a

1969 *Perf. 12x13*

1236 A513 1fr dk grn & brn 60 50
1237 A514 1fr multi 60 50
1238 A515 1fr multi 60 50
1239 A515a 1fr multi 60 50

Issue dates: No. 1236, Feb. 22; No. 1237, May 3; No. 1238, June 28; No. 1239, Nov. 8.

Gallic Coin Type of 1964–66

1969 Typographed *Perf. 13½x14*

1240 A418 22c brt grn & vio 1.00 22
1241 A418 35c red & ultra 2.00 55
1242 A418 70c ultra & red brn 7.75 3.00

Nos. 1240–1242 are known only precanceled. See note after No. 132.

Hautefort Chateau A516

1969, Apr. 5 Engraved *Perf. 13*

1243 A516 70c bl, sl & bis 50 45

Irises A517

1969, Apr. 12 Photogravure

1244 A517 45c multi 38 38

Issued to publicize the 3rd International Flower Show, Paris, Apr. 23–Oct. 5.

Europa Issue, 1969

Common Design Type

1969, Apr. 26 Engraved *Perf. 13*

Size: 36x22mm.

1245 CD12 40c car rose 25 15
1246 CD12 70c Prus bl 40 38

Albert Thomas and Thomas Memorial, Geneva A518

1969, May 10 Engraved *Perf. 13*

1247 A518 70c brn, ol bis & ind 50 45

Issued to commemorate the 50th anniversary of the International Labor Organization and to honor Albert Thomas (1878–1932), director of the ILO 1920–1932.

Garigliano Battle Scene, 1944
A519

1969, May 10

1248	A519	45c blk & vio	38	30

Issued to commemorate the 25th anniversary of the Battle of the Garigliano against the Germans.

Chateau du Marché, Chalons-sur-Marne
A520

Parachutists over Normandy Beach
A521

1969, May 24

1249	A520	45c bis, dl bl & grn	45	32

Federation of French Philatelic Societies, 42nd congress.

1969, May 31

1250	A521	45c dk bl & vio bl	60	45

Issued to commemorate the 25th anniversary of the landing of Special Air Service and Free French commandos in Normandy, June 6, 1944.

Monument of the French Resistance, Mt. Mouchet
A522

1969, June 7

1251	A522	45c dk grn, sl & ind	60	45

Issued to commemorate the 25th anniversary of the battle of Mt. Mouchet between French resistance fighters and the Germans, June 2 and 10, 1944.

French Troops Landing in Provence
A523

1969, Aug. 23 Engraved *Perf. 13*

1252	A523	45c sl & blk brn	60	45

Issued to commemorate the 25th anniversary of the landing of French and American forces in Provence, Aug. 15, 1944.

Russian and French Aviators
A524

1969, Oct. 18 Engraved *Perf. 13*

1253	A524	45c sl, dp bl & car	60	45

Issued to honor the French aviators of the Normandy-Neman Squadron who fought on the Russian Front, 1942–45.

Kayak on Isère River
A525

1969, Aug. 2 Engraved *Perf. 13*

1254	A525	70c org brn, ol & dk bl	55	45

Issued to commemorate the International Canoe and Kayak Championships, Bourg-Saint-Maurice, Savoy, July 31–Aug. 6.

Napoleon as Young Officer and his Birthplace, Ajaccio—A526

1969, Aug. 16

1255	A526	70c brt grnsh bl, ol & rose vio	55	45

Issued to commemorate the 200th anniversary of the birth of Napoleon Bonaparte (1769–1821).

Drops of Water and Diamond
A527

Mediterranean Mouflon
A528

1969, Sept. 27

1256	A527	70c blk, dp bl & brt grn	60	45

European Water Charter.

1969, Oct. 11

1257	A528	45c ol, blk & org brn	45	45

Issued to publicize wildlife protection.

Central School of Arts and Crafts
A529

1969, Oct. 18

1258	A529	70c dk grn, yel grn & org	45	38

Issued to commemorate the inauguration of the Central School of Arts and Crafts at Chatenay-Malabry.

Nuclear Submarine "Le Redoutable"
A530

1969, Oct. 25

1259	A530	70c dp bl, grn & sl grn	50	45

Type of 1968 and

Henri IV and Edict of Nantes
A531

Designs: No. 1260, Pierre Terrail de Bayard wounded at Battle of Brescia (after a painting in Versailles). No. 1262, Louis XI, Charles the Bold and map of France.

1969, Nov. 8 Engraved *Perf. 13*

1260	A511	80c brn, bis & blk	50	38
1261	A531	80c blk & vio bl	60	38
1262	A531	80c ol, dp grn & dk red brn	50	38

"Firecrest" and Alain Gerbault
A532

1970, Jan. 10 Engraved *Perf. 13*

1263	A532	70c ind, brt bl & gray	60	45

Issued to commemorate the 40th anniversary of the completion of Alain Gerbault's trip around the world aboard the "Firecrest," 1923–29.

Gendarmery Emblem, Mountain Climber, Helicopter, Motorcyclists and Motorboat—A533

1970, Jan. 31

1264	A533	45c sl grn, dk bl & brn	50	38

Issued to honor the National Gendarmery, founded 1791.

Field Ball Player
A534

1970, Feb. 21 Engraved *Perf. 13*

1265	A534	80c sl grn	60	32

Issued to publicize the 7th International Field Ball Games, Feb. 26–March 8.

Alphonse Juin and Church of the Invalides—A535

1970, Feb. 28

1266	A535	45c gray bl & dk brn	38	30

Issued to honor Marshal Alphonse Pierre Juin (1888–1967), military leader.

Aerotrain
A536

1970, Mar. 7

1267	A536	80c pur & gray	60	32

Issued to publicize the introduction of the aerotrain, which reaches a speed of 320 miles per hour.

Pierre Joseph Pelletier, Joseph Bienaimé Caventou, Quinine Formula and Cell—A537

1970, Mar. 21 Engraved *Perf. 13*

1268	A537	50c sl grn, sky bl & dp car	45	30

Discovery of quinine, 150th anniversary.

Pink Flamingos
A538

Diamant B Rocket and Radar
A539

1970, Mar. 21

1269	A538	45c ol, gray & pink	40	30

European Nature Conservation Year, 1970.

1970, Mar. 28

1270	A539	45c brt grn	45	30

Issued to publicize the space center in Guyana and the launching of the Diamant B rocket, Mar. 10, 1970.

Europa Issue, 1970

Common Design Type

1970, May 2 Engraved *Perf. 13*

Size: 36x22mm.

1271	CD13	40c dp car	25	15
1272	CD13	80c sky bl	48	38

Annunciation, by Primitive Painter of Savoy, 1480
A540

The Triumph of Flora, by Jean Baptiste Carpeaux—A541

Diana Returning from the Hunt, by François Boucher—A542

Dancer with Bouquet, by Edgar Degas
A543

1970 *Perf. 12x13, 13x12*

1273	A540	1fr multi	65	50
1274	A541	1fr red brn	65	50
1275	A542	1fr multi	65	60
1276	A543	1fr multi	65	60

Issue dates: No. 1273, May 9. No. 1274, July 4. No. 1275, Oct. 10. No. 1276, Nov. 14.

Arms of Lens, Miner's Lamp and Pit Head
A544

1970, May 16 Engraved *Perf 13*

1277	A544	40c scarlet	30	22

Issued to publicize the 43rd National Congress of the Federation of French Philatelic Societies, Lens, May 14–21.

Diamond Rock, Martinique
A545

Haute Provence Observatory and Spiral Nebula
A546

Designs: 95c, Chancelade Abbey, Dordogne. 1fr, Gosier Islet, Guadeloupe.

1970, June 20 Engraved *Perf. 13*

1278	A545	50c sl grn, brt bl & plum	32	15
1279	A545	95c lt ol, car & brn	1.10	60
1280	A545	1fr sl grn, brt bl & dk car rose	60	6
1281	A546	1.30fr dk bl, vio bl & dk grn	1.75	90

Hand Reaching for Freedom
A547

Handicapped Javelin Thrower
A548

1970, June 27

1282	A547	45c vio bl, bl & bis	50	30

Liberation of concentration camps, 25th anniversary.

1970, June 27

1283	A548	45c rose car, ultra & emer	50	38

Issued to publicize the International Games of the Handicapped, St. Etienne, June 1970.

Pole Vault
A549

1970, Sept. 11 Engraved *Perf. 13*

1284	A549	45c car, bl & ind	50	38

Issued to publicize the First European Junior Athletic Championships, Colombes, Sept. 11–13.

Royal Salt Works, Arc-et-Senans
A550

1970, Sept. 26

1285	A550	80c bl, brn & dk grn	65	45

Issued to publicize the restoration of the 18th century Royal Salt Works buildings, by Claude Nicolas Ledoux (1736–1806) at Arc-et-Senans, for use as a center for studies of all aspects of future human life.

Armand Jean du Plessis, Duc de Richelieu—A551

Designs: No. 1287, Battle of Fontenoy, 1745. No. 1288, Louis XIV and Versailles.

1970, Oct. 17 Engraved *Perf. 13*

1286	A551	45c blk, sl & car rose	38	30
1287	A551	45c org, brn & ind	38	30
1288	A551	45c sl grn, lem & org brn	38	30

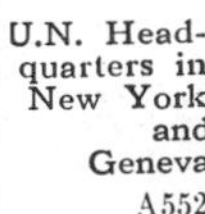

U.N. Headquarters in New York and Geneva
A552

1970, Oct. 24 Engr. *Perf. 13*

1289	A552	80c ol, dp ultra & dk pur	50	45

25th anniversary of the United Nations.

View of Bordeaux and France No. 43—A553

1970, Nov. 7

1290	A553	80c vio bl & gray bl	50	45

Centenary of the Bordeaux issue.

Col. Denfert-Rochereau and Lion of Belfort, by Frederic A. Bartholdi—A554

1970, Nov. 14

1291	A554	45c dk bl, ol & red brn	40	30

Centenary of the siege of Belfort during Franco-Prussian War.

Marianne (by Bequet)
A555

1971–74 Typographed *Perf. 14x13*

1292	A555	45c sky bl	45	10
1292A	A555	60c grn ('74)	1.40	5

Engraved *Perf. 13*

1293	A555	50c rose car	50	5
a.		Bklt. pane of 5 (horiz. strip)	3.75	
b.		Bklt. pane of 10	6.00	
1294	A555	60c grn ('74)	6.25	15
a.		Booklet pane of 10	62.50	
1294B	A555	80c car rose ('74)	75	5
c.		Booklet pane of 5	6.00	
d.		Booklet pane of 10	12.00	

Nos. 1294 and 1294B issued also in vertical coils with control number on back of every 10th stamp.

No. 1293 issued only in booklets and in vertical coils with red control number on back of every 10th stamp.

See Nos. 1494–1498.

St. Matthew, Sculpture from Strasbourg Cathedral
A556

Winnower, by François Millet
A557

The Dreamer, by Georges Rouault
A558

1971 Engraved *Perf. 12x13*

1295	A556	1fr dk red brn	65	60
1296	A557	1fr multi	65	50
1297	A558	1fr multi	65	50

Issue dates: No. 1295, Jan. 23; No. 1296, Apr. 3; No. 1297, June 5.

Figure Skating Pair—A560

1971, Feb. 20 Engraved *Perf. 13*

1299	A560	80c vio bl, sl & aqua	60	38

World Figure Skating Championships, Lyons, Feb. 23–28.

Underwater Exploration
A561

1971, March 6

1300	A561	80c bl blk & bl grn	60	38

International Exhibition of Ocean Exploration, Bordeaux, March 9–14.

Cape Horn Clipper "Antoinette" and Solidor Castle, Saint-Malo
A562

1971, Apr. 10 Engraved *Perf. 13*

1301	A562	80c bl, pur & sl	50	45

Pyrenean Chamois
A563

1971, Apr. 24 Engraved *Perf. 13*

1302	A563	65c bl, dk brn & brn ol	50	30

National Park of Western Pyrenees.

Europa Issue, 1971

Common Design Type and

Santa Maria della Salute, Venice
A564

1971, May 8 Engraved *Perf. 13*

1303	A564	50c bl gray & ol bis	38	15

Size: 36x22mm.

1304	CD14	80c rose lil	50	45

Cardinal, Nobleman and Lawyer—A565

Storming of the Bastille—A566

Design: No. 1306, Battle of Valmy.

1971

1305	A565	45c bl, rose red & pur	40	30
1306	A565	45c bl, ol bis & brn red	40	38
1307	A566	65c dk brn, gray bl & mag	60	45

No. 1305 commemorates the opening of the Estates General, May 5, 1789; No. 1306, Battle of Valmy (Sept. 20, 1792) between French and Prussian armies; 65c, Storming of the Bastille, Paris, July 14, 1789.

Issue dates: No. 1305, May 8; No. 1306, Sept. 18; 65c, July 10.

Grenoble
A568

1971, May 29 Engraved *Perf. 13*

1308	A568	50c ocher, lil & rose red	30	15

44th National Congress of the Federation of French Philatelic Societies, Grenoble, May 30–31.

"Rural Family Aid" Shedding Light on Village
A569

1971, June 5

1309	A569	40c vio, bl & grn	30	22

Aid for rural families.

Chateau and Fort de Sedan
A570

Pont d'Arc, Ardèche Gorge
A571

Views: 60c, Sainte Chapelle, Riom. 65c, Fountain and tower, Dole. 90c, Tower and street, Riquewihr.

1971 Engraved *Perf. 13*

1310	A571	60c blk, grn & bl	32	18
1311	A571	65c lil, ocher & blk	45	18
1312	A571	90c grn, vio brn & red brn	55	15
1313	A570	1.10fr sl grn, Prus bl & brn	75	30
1314	A571	1.40fr sl grn, bl & dk brn	90	22
		Nos. 1310-1314 (5)	2.97	1.03

Issue dates: 60c, June 19; 65c, 90c, July 3; 1.10fr, 1.40fr, June 12.

Gallic Coin Type of 1964–66

1971, July 1 Typo. *Perf. 13½x14*

1315	A418	26c lil & brn	75	22
1316	A418	30c lt brn & brn	1.25	30
1317	A418	45c dl grn & brn	2.50	45
1318	A418	90c red & brn	3.00	75

Nos. 1315–1318 are known only precanceled. See second paragraph after No. 132.

Bourbon Palace
A572

1971, Aug. 28 Engraved *Perf. 13*

1319	A572	90c vio bl	60	38

59th Conference of the Interparliamentary Union.

Embroidery and Tool Making
A573

1971, Oct. 16

1320	A573	90c brn red, brt lil & cl	75	45

40th anniversary of the first assembly of presidents of artisans' guilds.

Reunion Chameleon
A574

1971, Nov. 6 Photo. *Perf. 13*

1321	A574	60c brn, yel, grn & blk	1.50	48

Nature protection.

De Gaulle Issue

Common Design Type and

De Gaulle in Brazzaville, 1944
A576

Designs: No. 1324, De Gaulle entering Paris, 1944. No. 1325, Pres. de Gaulle, 1970.

1971, Nov. 9 Engraved

1322	CD134	50c black	75	45
1323	A576	50c ultra	75	45
1324	A576	50c rose red	75	45
1325	CD134	50c black	75	45
a.		Strip of 4 + label	3.00	2.75

First anniversary of the death of Charles de Gaulle (1890–1970). Nos. 1322–1325 printed se-tenant in sheets of 20 containing 5 strips of 4 plus label with Cross of Lorraine and inscription.

Antoine Portal and first Session of Academy—A577

1971, Nov. 13

1326	A577	45c dk pur & mag	38	30

Sesquicentennial of the founding of the National Academy of Medicine; Baron Antoine Portal was first president.

L'Etude, by Jean Honoré Fragonard
A578

Women in Garden, by Claude Monet
A579

St. Peter Presenting Pierre de Bourbon, by Maitre de Moulins
A580

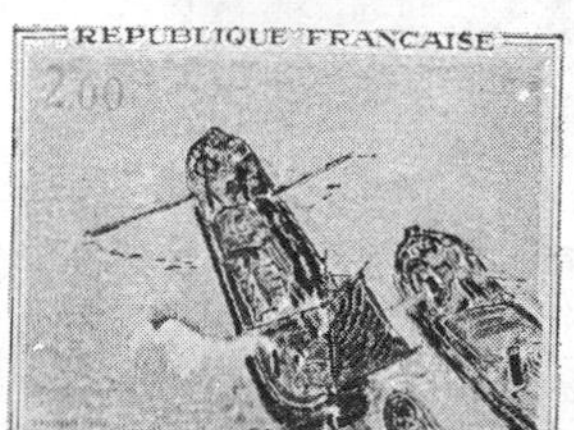

Boats, by André Derain—A581

1972 Engr. ***Perf. 12x13, 13x12***

1327	A578	1fr blk & multi	65	50
1328	A579	1fr sl grn & multi	95	50
1329	A580	2fr dk brn & multi	2.50	1.25
1330	A581	2fr yel & multi	3.75	1.40

Issue dates: No. 1327, Jan. 22; No. 1328, June 17; No. 1329, Oct. 14; No. 1330, Dec. 16.

Map of South Indian Ocean, Penguin and Ships
A582

1972, Jan. 29 ***Perf. 13***

1331	A582	90c blk, bl & ocher	90	60

Bicentenary of discovery of the Crozet and Kerguelen Islands.

Slalom and Olympic Emblems
A583

1972, Feb. 7

1332	A583	90c dk ol & dp car	75	45

11th Winter Olympic Games, Sapporo, Japan, Feb. 3–13.

Hearts, U.N. Emblem, Caduceus and Pacemaker—A584

1972, Apr. 8 Engr. ***Perf. 13***

1333	A584	45c dk car, org & gray	45	30

"Your heart is your health," world health month.

Red Deer, Sologne Plateau
A585

Charlieu Abbey
A585a

Bazoches-du-Morvand Chateau
A586

Saint-Just Cathedral, Narbonne
A587

1972 ***Perf. 13***

1334	A585	1fr ocher & red brn	75	15
1335	A585a	1.20fr sl & dl brn	65	18
1336	A586	2fr sl grn, blk & red brn	1.25	15
1337	A587	3.50fr bl, gray ol & car rose	1.90	32

Issue dates: 1fr, Sept. 10; 1.20fr, Apr. 29; 2fr, Sept. 9; 3.50fr, Apr. 8.

Eagle Owl
A588

Design: 60c, Salmon (horiz.).

1972

1338	A588	60c grn, ind & brt bl	2.25	90
1339	A588	65c sl, ol brn & sep	1.40	48

Nature protection. Issue dates: 60c, May 27; 65c, Apr. 15.

Europa Issue 1972

Common Design Type and

Aix-la-Chapelle Cathedral
A589

1972, Apr. 22 Engr. ***Perf. 13***

1340	A589	50c yel, vio brn & dk ol	32	15

Photogravure
Size: 22x36mm.

1341	CD15	90c red org & multi	60	45

Bouquet Made of Hearts and Blood Donors' Emblem
A590

Newfoundlander "Côte d'Emeraude"
A591

1972, May 5 Engraved

1342	A590	40c red	38	30

20th anniversary of the Blood Donors Association of Post and Telecommunications Employees.

1972, May 6

1343	A591	90c org, vio bl & sl grn	65	50

Cathedral, Saint-Brieuc
A592

1972, May 20

1344	A592	50c lil rose	38	22

45th Congress of the Federation of French Philatelic Societies, Saint-Brieuc, May 21–22.

Hand Holding Symbol of Postal Code
A593

1972, June 3 Typo. ***Perf. 14x13***

1345	A593	30c grn, blk & car	22	10
1346	A593	50c car, blk & yel	38	6

Introduction of postal code system.

Old and New Communications
A594

1972, July 1 Engraved ***Perf. 13***

1347	A594	45c sl & vio bl	32	30

21st International Congress of P.T.T. (Post, Telegraph and Telephone) Employees, Paris, July 1–7.

Hurdler and Olympic Rings
A595

1972, July 8

1348	A595	1fr dp ol	75	32

20th Olympic Games, Munich, Aug. 26–Sept. 11.

Hikers and Mt. Aigoual
A596

Bicyclist
A597

1972, July 15 Photo. ***Perf. 13***

1349	A596	40c brt rose & multi	2.00	90

International Year of Tourism and 25th anniversary of the National Hikers Association.

1972, July 22 Engraved

1350	A597	1fr gray, brn & lil	2.00	90

World Bicycling Championships, Marseille, July 29–Aug. 2.

"Incroyables and Merveilleuse," 1794
A598

Designs: 60c, Bonaparte at the Arcole Bridge. 65c, Egyptian expedition (soldiers and scientists finding antiquities; pyramids in background).

1972 Engraved ***Perf. 13***

1351	A598	45c ol, dk grn & car rose	45	30
1352	A598	60c red, blk & ind	50	38
1353	A598	65c ocher, ultra & choc	50	45

French history. Issue dates: 45c, Oct. 7; 60c, 65c, Nov. 11.

Champollion, Rosetta Stone with Key Inscription—A599

1972, Oct. 14

1354	A599	90c vio bl, brn red & blk	75	50

Sesquicentennial of the deciphering of hieroglyphs by Jean-François Champollion.

St. Teresa, Portal of Notre Dame of Alençon
A600

1973, Jan. 6 Engraved ***Perf. 13***

1355	A600	1fr Prus bl & ind	90	45

Centenary of the birth of St. Teresa of Lisieux, the Little Flower (Thérèse Martin, 1873–1897), Carmelite nun.

Anthurium (Martinique)
A601

1973, Jan. 20 Photogravure

1356	A601	50c gray & multi	38	30

Colors of France and Germany Interlaced—A602

1973, Jan. 22

Size: 48x27mm.

1357	A602	50c multi	38	30

10th anniversary of the Franco-German Cooperation Treaty. See Germany No. 1101.

Polish Immigrants—A603

1973, Feb. 3 Engraved *Perf. 13*

1358	A603	40c sl grn, dp car & brn	30	30

50th anniversary of Polish immigration into France, 1921–1923.

Last Supper, St. Austremoine Church, Issoire
A604

Kneeling Woman, by Charles Le Brun
A605

Angel, Wood, Moutier-D'Ahun
A606

Lady Playing Archlute, by Antoine Watteau
A607

1973 Engraved *Perf. 12x13*

1359	A604	2fr brn & multi	2.25	1.25
1360	A605	2fr dk red & yel	2.25	1.25
1361	A606	2fr ol brn & vio brn	2.25	1.25
1362	A607	2fr blk & multi	1.75	1.10

Issue dates: No. 1359, Feb. 10; No. 1360, Apr. 28; No. 1361, May 26; No. 1362, Sept. 22.

Tuileries Palace, Telephone Relays
A608

Oil Tanker, Francis I Lock
A609

Airbus A300-B
A610

1973

1363	A608	45c ultra, sl grn & bis	45	22
1364	A609	90c plum, blk & bl	75	25
1365	A610	3fr dk grn, bl & blk	2.50	1.25

French technical achievements.
Issue dates: 45c, May 15; 90c, Oct. 27; 3fr, Apr. 7.

Europa Issue 1973

Common Design Type and

City Hall, Brussels, CEPT Emblem
A611

1973, Apr. 14 Engr. *Perf. 13*

1366	A611	50c brt pink & choc	45	15

Photogravure
Size: 36x22mm.

1367	CD16	90c sl grn & multi	1.00	45

Masonic Lodge Emblem
A612

1973, May 12 Engr. *Perf. 13*

1368	A612	90c mag & vio bl	75	45

Bicentenary of the Free Masons of France.

Guadeloupe Raccoon
A613

White Storks
A614

1973

1369	A613	40c lil, sep & ol	45	30
1370	A614	60c blk, aqua & org red	60	38

Nature protection.
Issue dates: 40c, June 23; 60c, May 12.

Tourist Issue

Doubs Waterfall
A615

Clos-Lucé, Amboise
A617

Palace of Dukes of Burgundy, Dijon
A616

Design: 90c, Gien Chateau.

1973 Engraved *Perf. 13*

1371	A615	60c multi	30	18
1372	A616	65c red & pur	45	18
1373	A616	90c Prus bl, ind & brn	50	18
1374	A617	1fr ocher, bl & sl grn	50	15

Issue dates: 60c, Sept. 8; 65c, May 19; 90c, Aug. 18; 1fr, June 23.

Academy Emblem
A618

1973, May 26

1375	A618	1fr lil, sl grn & red	60	38

50th anniversary of the Academy of Overseas Sciences.

Racing Car and Clocks
A619

1973, June 2

1376	A619	60c dk brn & bl	75	60

50th anniversary of the 24-hour automobile race at Le Mans.

Five-master France II—A620

1973, June 9

1377	A620	90c ultra, Prus bl & ind	60	38

Tower and Square, Toulouse
A621

1973, June 9

1378	A621	50c pur & red brn	38	22

46th Congress of the Federation of French Philatelic Societies, Toulouse, June 9–12.

Dr. Armauer G. Hansen
A622

Ducretet and his Transmission Diagram
A623

1973, Sept. 29 Engraved *Perf. 13*

1379	A622	45c grn, dk ol & ocher	40	30

Centenary of the discovery of the Hansen bacillus, the cause of leprosy.

1973, Oct. 6

1380	A623	1fr yel grn & mag	60	30

75th anniversary of the first transmission of radio signals from the Eiffel Tower to the Pantheon by Eugene Ducretet (1844–1915).

Molière as Sganarelle
A624

1973, Oct. 20

1381	A624	1fr dk red & ol brn	60	32

Tercentenary of the death of Molière (Jean-Baptiste Poquelin; 1622–1673), playwright and actor.

Pierre Bourgoin and Philippe Kieffer
A625

1973, Oct. 27

1382 A625 1fr red, rose cl & vio bl 75 38

Pierre Bourgoin (1907–70), and Philippe Kieffer (1899–1963), heroes of the Free French forces in World War II.

Napoleon, Jean Portalis and Palace of Justice, Paris—A626

Exhibition Halls—A627

The Coronation of Napoleon, by Jean Louis David
A628

1973 Engraved *Perf. 13*

1383 A626 45c bl, choc & gray 30 30
1384 A627 60c ol, sl grn & brn 45 30
1385 A628 1fr sl grn, ol & cl 65 32

History of France. No. 1383 commemorates the preparation of the Code Napoleon; No. 1384, Napoleon's encouragement of industry and No. 1385 his coronation. Issue dates: 45c, Nov. 3; 60c, Nov. 24; 1fr, Nov. 12.

Eternal Flame, Arc de Triomphe
A629

Weather Vane
A630

1973, Nov. 10

1386 A629 40c pur, vio bl & red 32 30

50th anniversary of the Eternal Flame at the Arc de Triomphe, Paris.

1973, Dec. 1

1387 A630 65c ultra, blk & grn 40 30

50th anniversary of the Department of Agriculture.

Human Rights Flame and Man
A631

Postal Museum
A632

1973, Dec. 8 Engraved *Perf. 13*

1388 A631 45c car, org & blk 30 22

25th anniversary of the Universal Declaration of Human Rights.

1973, Dec. 19

1389 A632 50c mar & bis 30 15

Opening of new post and philately museum, Paris.

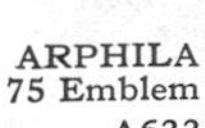
ARPHILA 75 Emblem
A633

1974, Jan. 19 Engraved *Perf. 13*

1390 A633 50c brn, bl & brt lil 38 18

ARPHILA 75 Philatelic Exhibition, Paris, June 1975.

Concorde over Charles de Gaulle Airport
A634

Turbotrain T.G.V. 001
A635

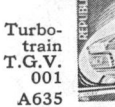

Phenix Nuclear Power Station
A636

1974 Engraved *Perf. 13*

1391 A634 60c pur & ol gray 60 38
1392 A635 60c multi 1.50 60
1393 A636 65c multi 45 30

French technical achievements.
Issue dates: No. 1391, Mar. 18; No. 1392, Aug. 31; 65c, Sept. 21.

Cardinal Richelieu, by Philippe de Champaigne—A637

Painting by Joan Miró—A638

Canal du Loing, by Alfred Sisley
A639

"In Honor of Nicolas Fouquet," Tapestry by Georges Mathieu
A640

Engr.; Photo. (#1395, 1397)

1974 *Perf. 12x13, 13x12*

1394 A637 2fr multi 1.75 1.10
1395 A638 2fr multi 1.75 1.10
1396 A639 2fr multi 2.00 1.10
1397 A640 2fr multi 2.00 1.10

Nos. 1394–1397 are printed in sheets of 25 with alternating labels publicizing "ARPHILA 75," Paris, June 6–16, 1975.
Issue dates: No. 1394, Mar. 23; No. 1395, Sept. 14; No. 1396, Nov. 9; No. 1397, Nov. 16.

French Alps and Gentian
A641

1974, Mar. 30 Engr. *Perf. 13*

1398 A641 65c vio bl & gray 48 38

Centenary of the French Alpine Club.

Europa Issue 1974

"Age of Bronze," by Auguste Rodin
A642

"Air," by Aristide Maillol
A643

1974, Apr. 20 *Perf. 13*

1399 A642 50c brt rose lil & blk 45 22
1400 A643 90c ol & brn 90 38

Sea Rescue—A644

1974, Apr. 27

1401 A644 90c multi 50 38

Reorganized sea rescue organization.

Council Building, View of Strasbourg and Emblem—A645

1974, May 4 Engr. *Perf. 13*

1402 A645 45c ind, bis & bl 32 22

25th anniversary of the Council of Europe.

Tourist Issue

View of Salers
A646

Basilica of St. Nicolas de Porte
A647

Seashell over Corsica
A648

Design: 1.10fr, View of Lot Valley.

1974 Engraved *Perf. 13*

1403	A646	65c yel grn & choc	38	30
1404	A646	1.10fr choc & sl grn	65	38
1405	A647	2fr gray & lil	1.25	25
1406	A648	3fr multi	1.50	45

Issue dates: 65c, June 22; 1.10fr, Sept. 7; 2fr, Oct. 12; 3fr, May 11.

Bison
A649

Giant Armadillo of Guyana
A650

1974

1407	A649	40c bis, choc & bl	40	22
1408	A650	65c sl, ol & grn	40	30

Nature protection.
Issue dates: No. 1407, May 25; No. 1408, Oct. 19.

Americans Landing in Normandy and Arms of Normandy—A651

General Marie-Pierre Koenig
A652

Order of the French Resistance
A653

1974

1409	A651	45c grn, rose & ind	50	30
1410	A652	1fr multi	75	30
1411	A653	1fr multi	60	30

30th anniversary of the liberation of France from the Nazis. Design of No. 1410 includes diagram of battle of Bir-Hakeim and Free French and Bir-Hakeim memorials.
Issue dates, 45c, June 8; No. 1410, May 25. No. 1411, Nov. 23. See No. B478.

Pfister House, 16th Century, Colmar
A654

1974, June 1

1412	A654	50c multi	30	15

47th Congress of the Federation of French Philatelic Societies, Colmar, May 30–June 4.

Chess
A655

1974, June 8

1413	A655	1fr dk brn & multi	80	50

21st Chess Olympiad, Nice, June 6–30.

Facade with Statue of Louis XIV, and 1675 Medal
A656

1974, June 15

1414	A656	40c ind, bl & brn	30	22

300th anniversary of the founding of the Hotel des Invalides (Home for poor and sick officers and soldiers).

Peacocks Holding Letter, and Globe—A657

1974, Oct. 5 Engraved *Perf. 13*

1415	A657	1.20fr ultra, dp grn & dk car	65	48

Centenary of Universal Postal Union.

Copernicus and Heliocentric System—A658

1974, Oct. 12

1416	A658	1.20fr multi	60	45

500th anniversary of the birth of Nicolaus Copernicus (1473–1543), Polish astronomer.

Tourist Issue

Palace of Justice, Rouen
A659

Saint-Pol-de-Leon
A660

Chateau de Rochechouart
A661

1975 Engraved *Perf. 13*

1417	A659	85c multi	50	18
1418	A660	1.20fr bl, bis & choc	60	22
1419	A661	1.40fr brn, ind & grn	75	22

Issue dates: 85c, Jan. 25; 1.20fr, Jan. 18; 1.40fr, Jan. 11.

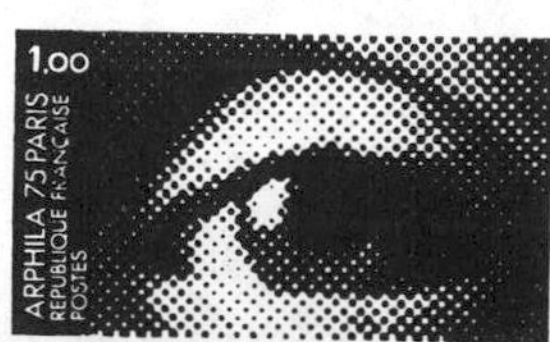

Snowy Egret
A662

Gallic Coin
A663

1975, Feb. 15 Engraved *Perf. 13*

1420	A662	70c brt bl & bis	48	38

Nature protection.

1975, Feb. 16 Typo. *Perf. 13½x14*

1421	A663	42c org & mag	1.65	38
1422	A663	48c lt bl & red brn	2.00	38
1423	A663	70c brt pink & red	3.25	75
1424	A663	1.35fr lt grn & brn	4.00	1.10

Nos. 1421–1424 are known only precanceled. See second note after No. 132. See Nos. 1460–1463, 1487–1490.

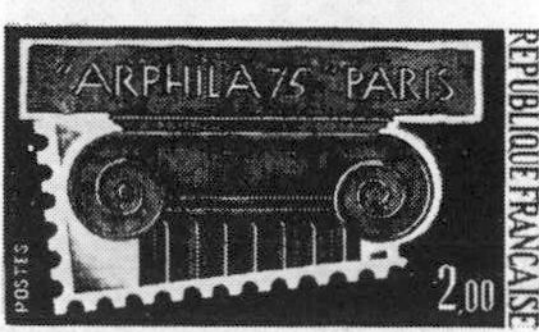

The Eye—A664

Ionic Capital—A665

Graphic Art—A666

Ceres—A667

1975 Engraved *Perf. 13*

1425	A664	1fr red, pur & org	65	30
1426	A665	2fr grn, sl grn & mag	1.00	45
1427	A666	3fr dk car & ol grn	1.50	65
1428	A667	4fr red, sl grn & bis	2.00	90

Souvenir Sheet

1429		Sheet of 4	12.00	12.00
a.	A664	2fr dp car & sl bl	1.75	1.75
b.	A665	3fr brt bl, sl bl & dp car	2.25	2.25
c.	A666	4fr sl bl, brt bl & plum	3.25	3.25
d.	A667	6fr brt bl, sl bl & plum	4.25	4.00

ARPHILA 75, International Philatelic Exhibition, Paris, June 6–16. No. 1429 has ornamental border and commemorative inscription. Size: 150x143mm. Issue dates: 1fr, Mar. 1; 2fr, Mar. 22; 3fr, Apr. 19; 4fr, May 17; souvenir sheet, Apr. 2.

Pres. Georges Pompidou
A668

Paul as Harlequin, by Picasso
A669

1975, Apr. 3 Engraved *Perf. 13*

1430	A668	80c blk & gray	45	15

Georges Pompidou (1911–74), President of France, 1969–74.

Europa Issue 1975

1975, Apr. 26 Photo. *Perf. 13*

Design: 1.20fr, Woman on Balcony, by Kees van Dongen (horiz.).

1431	A669	80c multi	60	22
1432	A669	1.20fr multi	90	38

Machines, Globe, Emblem
A670

1975, May 3 Engraved

1433	A670	1.20fr bl, blk & red	60	45

World Machine Tool Exhibition, Paris, June 17–26.

Senate Assembly Hall
A671

1975, May 24 Engraved *Perf. 13*

1434	A671	1.20fr ol & dk car	60	45

Centenary of the Senate of the Republic.

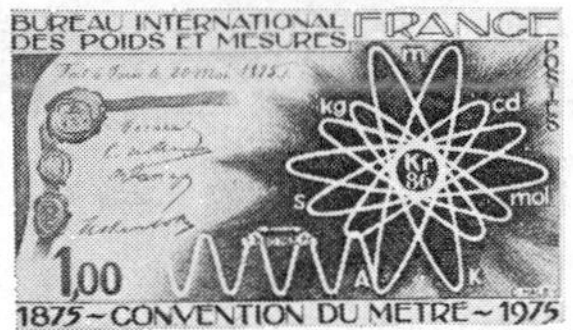
Meter Convention Document, Atom Diagram and Waves—A672

1975, May 31

1435	A672	1fr multi	50	32

Centenary of International Meter Convention, Paris, 1875.

Metro Regional Train
A673

"Gazelle" Helicopter
A674

1975

1436	A673	1fr ind & brt bl	1.25	38
1437	A674	1.30fr vio bl & grn	95	60

French technical achievements.
Issue dates: 1fr, June 21; 1.30fr, May 31.

Youth and Flasks, Symbols of Study and Growth
A675

1975, June 21

1438	A675	70c red pur & blk	38	30

Student Health Foundation.

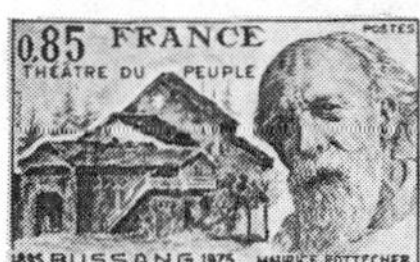
People's Theater, Bussang, and Maurice Pottecher—A676

1975, Aug. 9 Engraved *Perf. 13*

1439	A676	85c multi	45	30

80th anniversary of the People's Theater at Bussang, founded by Maurice Pottecher.

Regions of France

Central France
A677

Aquitaine
A678

Limousin
A679

Picardy
A680

Burgundy
A681

Loire
A682

Guyana
A683

Auvergne
A684

Poitou-Charentes
A685

Southern Pyrenees—A686

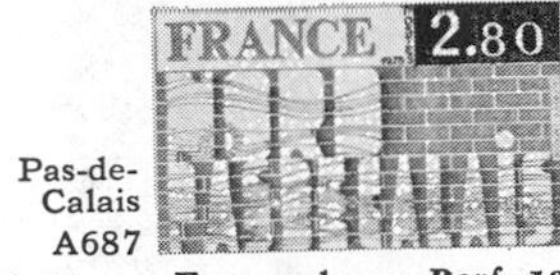
Pas-de-Calais
A687

1975–76 Engraved *Perf. 13*

1440	A677	25c bl & yel grn	30	22
1441	A678	60c multi	32	25
1442	A679	70c multi	65	25
1443	A680	85c bl, grn & org	95	30
1444	A681	1fr red, yel & mar	90	30
1445	A682	1.15fr bl, bis & grn	90	38
1446	A683	1.25fr multi	75	45
1447	A684	1.30fr dk bl & red	75	30
1448	A685	1.90fr sl, ol & Prus bl	1.25	30
1449	A686	2.20fr multi	1.40	75
1450	A687	2.80fr car, bl & blk	2.00	80
		Nos. 1440-1450 (11)	10.17	4.30

Issue dates—1975: 85c, Nov. 15; 1fr, Oct. 25; 1.15fr, Sept. 6; 1.30fr, Oct. 4; 1.90fr, Dec. 6; 2.80fr, Dec. 13. 1976: 25c, Jan. 31; 2.20fr, Jan. 10; 60c, May 22; 70c, May 29; 125fr, Oct. 16.

French Flag, F.-H. Manhes, Jean Verneau, Pierre Kaan
A690

1975, Sept. 27

1453	A690	1fr multi	50	38

Liberation of concentration camps, 30th anniversary. F.-H. Manhes (1889–1959), Jean Verneau (1890–1944) and Pierre Kaan (1903–1945) were French resistance leaders, imprisoned in concentration camps.

Monument, by Joseph Riviere
A691

1975, Oct. 11

1454	A691	70c multi	38	30

Land Mine Demolition Service, 30th anniversary. Monument was erected in Alsace to honor land mine victims.

Symbols of Suburban Living
A692

1975, Oct. 18

1455	A692	1.70fr brn, bl & grn	1.00	75

Creation of new towns.

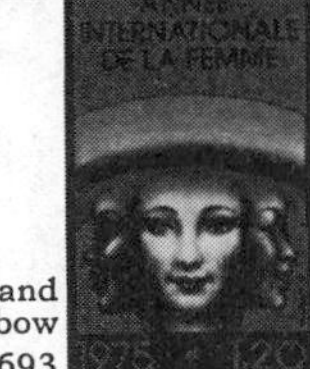
Women and Rainbow
A693

1975, Nov. 8 Photogravure

1456	A693	1.20fr sil & multi	65	45

International Women's Year 1975.

Saint-Nazaire Bridge
A694

1975, Nov. 8 Engraved

1457	A694	1.40fr bl, ind & grn	90	32

French and Russian Flags
A695

Frigate Melpomene
A696

1975, Nov. 22

1458	A695	1.20fr bl, red & ocher	65	45

Franco-Soviet diplomatic relations, 50th anniversary.

1975, Dec. 6

1459	A696	90c multi	50	30

Gallic Coin Type of 1975

1976, Jan. 1 Typo. *Perf. 13½x14*

1460	A663	50c lt grn & brn	1.65	45
1461	A663	60c lil & brn	2.50	45
1462	A663	90c org & brn	3.00	1.00
1463	A663	1.60fr vio & brn	5.50	3.00

Nos. 1460–1463 are known only precanceled. See second note after No. 132.

Lintel, St. Genis des Fontaines Church—A697

Venus of Brassempouy (Paleolithic)
A698

"The Joy of Life," by Robert Delaunay—A699

Ramses II, from Abu Simbel Temple, Egypt—A700

Still Life, by Maurice de Vlaminck—A701

1976 Engr. *Perf. 13*

1464	A697	2fr bl & sl bl	1.25	90
1465	A698	2fr dk brn & yel	1.25	90

Photo. *Perf. 12½x13*

1466	A699	2fr multi	1.25	90

Engr. *Perf. 13x12½*

1467	A700	2fr multi	1.10	75

Perf. 13

1468	A701	2fr multi	1.10	75
		Nos. 1464-1468 (5)	5.95	4.20

Issue dates: No. 1464, Jan. 24; No. 1465, Mar. 6; No. 1466, July 24; No. 1467, Sept. 4; No. 1468, Dec. 18.

Tourist Issue

Chateau Fort de Bonaguil
A702

Lodève Cathedral
A703

Biarritz
A704

Thiers
A705

Ussel
A706

Chateau de Malmaison
A707

1976 Engraved *Perf. 13*

1469	A702	1fr multi	45	15
1470	A703	1.10fr vio bl	55	30
1471	A704	1.40fr multi	60	22
1472	A705	1.70fr multi	75	18
1473	A706	2fr multi	1.25	22
1474	A707	3fr multi	1.40	32
		Nos. 1469-1474 (6)	5.00	1.39

Issue dates: 1fr, 2fr, July 10; 1.10fr, Nov. 13; 1.40fr, Sept. 25; 1.70fr, Oct. 9; 3fr, Apr. 10.

Destroyers, Association Emblem
A708

1976, Apr. 24

1475	A708	1fr vio bl, mag & lem	75	32

Naval Reserve Officers Association, 50th anniversary.

Gate, Rouen
A709

Young Person
A710

1976, Apr. 24

1476	A709	80c ol gray & sal	45	18

49th Congress of the Federation of French Philatelic Societies, Rouen, Apr. 23–May 2.

1976, Apr. 27

1477	A710	60c bl grn, ind & car	50	18

JUVAROUEN 76, International Youth Philatelic Exhibition, Rouen, Apr. 25–May 2.

Europa Issue 1976

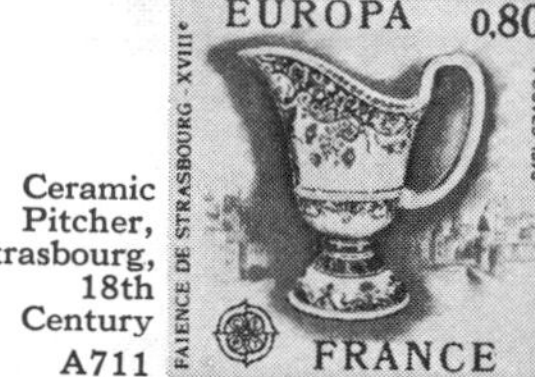

Ceramic Pitcher, Strasbourg, 18th Century
A711

Design: 1.20fr, Sevres porcelain plate and CEPT emblem.

1976, May 8 Photo. *Perf. 13*

1478	A711	80c multi	48	22
1479	A711	1.20fr multi	75	32

Count de Vergennes and Benjamin Franklin—A712

1976, May 15 Engr. *Perf. 13*

1480	A712	1.20fr multi	60	45

American Bicentennial.

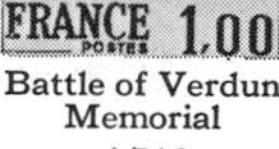

Battle of Verdun Memorial
A713

Communication
A714

1976, June 12 Engraved

1481	A713	1fr multi	60	32

Battle of Verdun, 60th anniversary.

1976, June 12 Photogravure

1482	A714	1.20fr multi	60	38

Troncais Forest
A715

Cross of Lorraine
A716

1976, June 19 Engraved

1483	A715	70c grn & multi	40	30

Protection of the environment.

1976, June 19

1484	A716	1fr multi	50	30

Association of Free French, 30th anniversary.

Symphonie Communications Satellite
A717

1976, June 26 Photogravure

1485	A717	1.40fr multi	80	38

French technical achievements.

Gallic Coin Type of 1975

1976, July 1 Typo. *Perf. 13½x14*

1487	A663	52c ver & dk brn	90	30
1488	A663	62c vio & dk brn	1.75	60
1489	A663	95c tan & dk brn	2.25	90
1490	A663	1.70fr dk bl & dk brn	4.00	2.25

Nos. 1487–1490 are known only precanceled. See second note after No. 132.

Paris Summer Festival
A719

1976, July 10 Engraved

1491	A719	1fr multi	75	32

Summer festival in Tuileries Gardens, Paris.

Emblem and Soldiers
A720

1976, July 8

1492	A720	1fr blk, dp bl & mag	50	30

Officers Reserve Corps, centenary.

Sailing
A721

1976, July 17

1493	A721	1.20fr bl, blk & vio	60	45

21st Olympic Games, Montreal, Canada, July 17–Aug. 1.

Marianne Type of 1971–74

1976 Typographed *Perf. 14x13*

1494	A555	80c green	50	5

Engraved *Perf. 13*

1495	A555	80c green	60	15
	a.	Booklet pane of 10	6.00	
1496	A555	1fr car rose	60	5
	a.	Booklet pane of 5	5.00	
	b.	Booklet pane of 10	9.00	

No. 1495 issued in booklets only. "POSTES" 6mm. long on Nos. 1292A and 1494; 4mm. on others.

Nos. 1494 and 1496 were issued untagged in 1977.

Coil Stamps

1976, Aug. 1 Engr. *Perf. 13 Horiz.*

1497	A555	80c green	60	38
1498	A555	1fr car rose	60	30

Red control number on back of every 10th stamp.

Woman's Head, by Jean Carzou—A722

1976, Sept. 18 Engr. *Perf. 13x12½*

1499	A722	2fr multi	1.10	65

Old and New Telephones—A723

1976, Sept. 25 Engr. *Perf. 13*

1500	A723	1fr multi	50	22

Centenary of first telephone call by Alexander Graham Bell, Mar. 10, 1876.

Festival Emblem and Trophy, Pyrenees, Hercules and Pyrène
A724

Police Emblem
A725

1976, Oct. 2

1501	A724	1.40fr multi	75	45

10th International Tourist Film Festival, Tarbes, Oct. 4–10.

1976, Oct. 9 Engr. *Perf. 13*

1502	A725	1.10fr ultra, red & ol	65	30

National Police, help and protection.

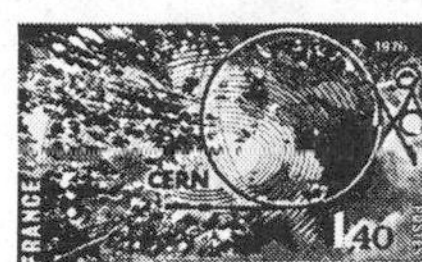

Atomic Particle Accelerator, Diagram—A726

1976, Oct. 22 Photogravure

1503	A726	1.40fr multi	90	38

European Center for Nuclear Research (CERN).

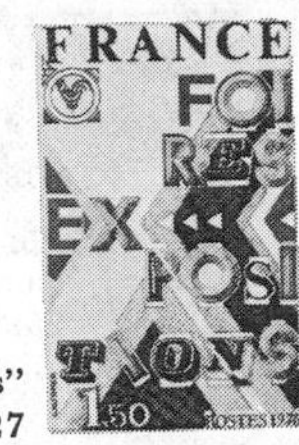

"Exhibitions"
A727

1976, Nov. 20 Engr. *Perf. 13*

1504	A727	1.50fr multi	75	45

Trade Fairs and Exhibitions.

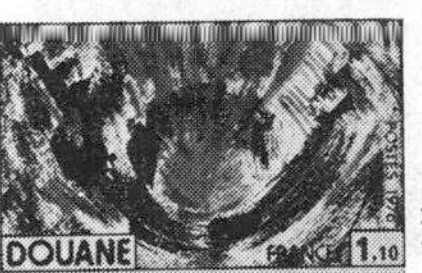

Abstract Design
A728

1976, Nov. 27 Photogravure

1505	A728	1.10fr multi	65	32

Customs Service.

Atlantic Museum, Port Louis—A729

1976, Dec. 4 Engraved

1506	A729	1.45fr grnsh bl & ol	75	45

Regions of France

Réunion
A730

Martinique
A731

Franche-Comté
A732

Brittany
A733

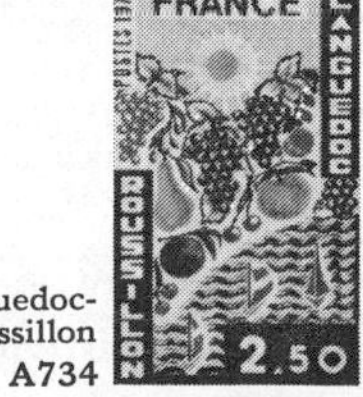

Languedoc-Roussillon
A734

Rhône-Alps
A735

Champagne-Ardennes
A736

Alsace
A737

Photo. (1.45fr, 1.50fr, 2.50fr); Engr.

1977 *Perf. 13*

1507	A730	1.45fr grn & lil rose	75	30
1508	A731	1.50fr multi	80	38
1509	A732	2.10fr multi	1.10	50
1510	A733	2.40fr multi	1.50	32
1511	A734	2.50fr multi	1.50	50
1512	A735	2.75fr Prus bl	1.75	48
1513	A736	3.20fr multi	1.90	80
1514	A737	3.90fr multi	2.50	90
		Nos. 1507-1514 (8)	11.80	4.18

Issue dates: 1.45fr, Feb. 5; 1.50fr, Jan. 29; 2.10fr, Jan. 8; 2.40fr, Feb. 19; 2.50fr, Jan. 15; 2.75fr, Jan. 22; 3.20fr, Apr. 16; 3.90fr, Feb. 26.

Pompidou Cultural Center—A738

1977, Feb. 5 Engr. *Perf. 13*

1515	A738	1fr multi	50	22

Inauguration of the Georges Pompidou National Center for Art and Culture, Paris.

Dunkirk Harbor
A739

1977, Feb. 12

1516	A739	50c multi	32	18

Expansion of Dunkirk harbor facilities.

Bridge at Mantes, by Corot—A740

Virgin and Child, by Rubens
A741

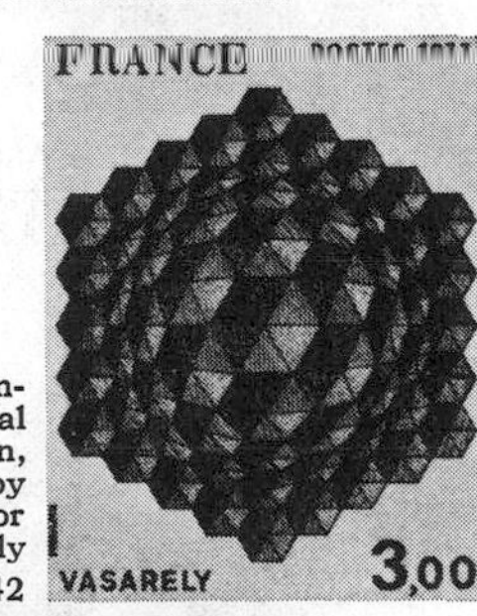

Tridimensional Design, by Victor Vasarely
A742

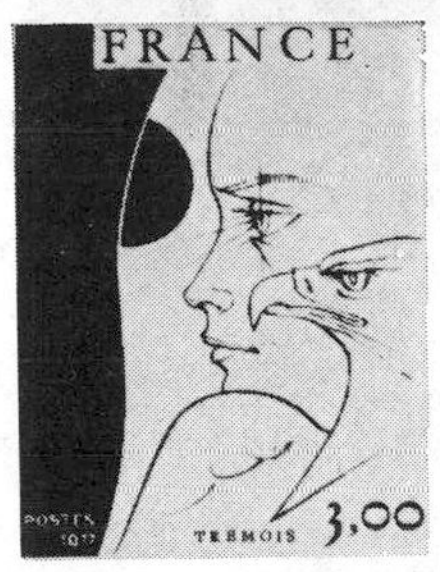

Head and Eagle, by Pierre-Yves Tremois
A743

1977 Engr. *Perf. 13x12½*

1517	A740	2fr multi	1.10	75
		Perf. 12x13		
1518	A741	2fr multi	1.10	75
		Perf. 12½x13		
1519	A742	3fr ultra & sl grn	1.50	75
		Photogravure		
1520	A743	3fr dk red & blk	1.90	90

Issue dates: No. 1517, Feb. 12; No. 1518, Nov. 5; No. 1519, Apr. 7; No. 1520, Sept. 17.

Hand Holding Torch and Sword
A744

Pisces
A745

1977, Mar. 5 Engr. *Perf. 13*

1521	A744	80c ultra & multi	55	22

"France remembers its dead."

1977–78 Engraved *Perf. 13*

Zodiac Signs: 58c, Cancer. 61c, Sagittarius. 68c, Taurus. 73c, Aries. 78c, Libra. 1.05fr, Scorpio. 1.15fr, Capricorn. 1.25fr, Leo. 1.85fr, Aquarius. 2fr, Virgo. 2.10fr, Gemini.

1522	A745	54c vio bl	90	45
1523	A745	58c emerald	1.40	50

1524 A745 61c brt bl 75 45
1525 A745 68c dp brn 1.10 60
1526 A745 73c rose car 2.00 95
1527 A745 78c vermilion 95 60
1528 A745 1.05fr brt lil 2.00 1.25
1529 A745 1.15fr orange 3.25 1.90
1530 A745 1.25fr lt ol grn 1.65 1.00
1531 A745 1.85fr sl grn 3.75 1.50
1532 A745 2fr bl grn 4.00 3.00
1533 A745 2.10fr lil rose 2.25 1.65
Nos. 1522-1533 (12) 24.00 13.85

Issue dates: 54c, 68c, 1.05fr, 1.85fr, Apr. 1, 1977. Others, 1978.

Nos. 1522–1533 are known only precanceled. See second note after No. 132.

Europa Issue

Village in Provence
A746

Design: 1.40fr, Brittany port.

1977, Apr. 23

1534 A746 1fr multi 50 15
1535 A746 1.40fr multi 75 30

Flowers and Gardening
A747

1977, Apr. 23 Engr. *Perf. 13*

1536 A747 1.70fr multi 90 45

National Horticulture Society, centenary.

Symbolic Flower
A748

1977, May 7

1537 A748 1.40fr multi 65 60

International Flower Show, Nantes, May 12–23.

Battle of Cambray
A749

1977, May 14

1538 A749 80c multi 50 30

300th anniversary of the capture of Cambray and the incorporation of Cambresis District into France.

Carmes Church, School, Map of France
A750

Modern Constructions
A751

1977, May 14

1539 A750 1.10fr multi 60 30

Catholic Institutes in France.

1977, May 21

1540 A751 1.10fr multi 55 38

European Federation of the Construction Industry.

Annecy Castle
A752

1977, May 28

1541 A752 1fr multi 55 22

Congress of the Federation of French Philatelic Societies, Annecy, May 28–30.

Tourist Issue

Abbey, Pont-à-Mousson
A753

Abbey Tower, Saint-Amand-les-Eaux
A754

Collegiate Church of Dorat
A755

Fontenay Abbey
A756

Bayeux Cathedral
A757

Chateau de Vitré
A758

1977 Engraved *Perf. 13*

1542 A753 1.25fr multi 60 22
1543 A754 1.40fr multi 65 22
1544 A755 1.45fr multi 65 25
1545 A756 1.50fr multi 75 30
1546 A757 1.90fr blk & yel 90 38
1547 A758 2.40fr blk & yel 1.10 30
Nos. 1542-1547 (6) 4.65 1.67

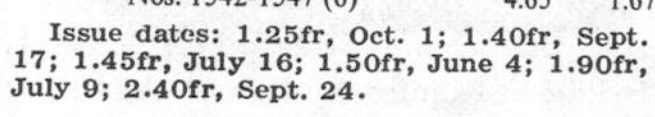

Issue dates: 1.25fr, Oct. 1; 1.40fr, Sept. 17; 1.45fr, July 16; 1.50fr, June 4; 1.90fr, July 9; 2.40fr, Sept. 24.

Polytechnic School and "X"
A759

1977, June 4 Engr. *Perf. 13*

1548 A759 1.70fr multi 80 32

Relocation at Palaiseau of Polytechnic School, founded 1794.

Soccer and Cup—A760

1977, June 11

1549 A760 80c multi 80 32

Soccer Cup of France, 60th anniversary.

De Gaulle Memorial
A761

Stylized Map of France
A762

Photogravure & Embossed

1977, June 18

1550 A761 1fr gold & multi 75 18

5th anniversary of dedication of De Gaulle memorial at Colombey-les-Deux-Eglises.

1977, June 18 Engr. *Perf. 13*

1551 A762 1.10fr ultra & red 65 30

French Junior Chamber of Commerce.

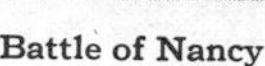

Battle of Nancy
A763

Arms of Burgundy
A764

1977, June 25

1552 A763 1.10fr bl & sl 1.25 60

Battle of Nancy between the Dukes of Burgundy and Lorraine, 500th anniversary.

1977, July 2

1553 A764 1.25fr ol brn & sl grn 75 32

Annexation of Burgundy by the French Crown, 500th anniversary.

Association Emblem
A765

1977, July 8

1554 A765 1.40fr ultra, ol & red 65 38

French-speaking Parliamentary Association.

Red Cicada
A766

1977, Sept. 10 Photo. *Perf. 13*

1555 A766 80c multi 50 25

Nature protection.

French Handicrafts
A767

1977, Oct. 1 Engraved *Perf. 13*

1556 A767 1.40fr multi 60 30

French craftsmen.

Industry and Agriculture
A768

1977, Oct. 22

1557 A768 80c brn & ol 45 30

Economic and Social Council, 30th anniversary.

Table Tennis
A769

1977, Dec. 17 Engr. *Perf. 13*

1558 A769 1.10fr multi 1.10 38

French Table Tennis Federation, 50th anniversary, and French team, gold medal winner, Birmingham.

Abstract, by Roger Excoffon—A770

1977, Dec. 17 *Perf. 13x12½*

1559 A770 3fr multi 1.75 75

Sabine, after David
A771

1977–78		Engraved	Perf. 13	
1560	A771	1c slate	10	5
1561	A771	2c brt vio	10	5
1562	A771	5c sl grn	10	5
1563	A771	10c red brn	10	5
1564	A771	15c Prus bl	15	15
1565	A771	20c brt grn	15	6
1566	A771	30c orange	15	6
1567	A771	50c red lil	22	15
1568	A771	80c green	1.50	25
a.		Bklt. pane of 10	16.00	
1569	A771	80c olive	38	5
1570	A771	1fr red	1.65	5
a.		Bklt. pane of 5	10.00	
b.		Bklt. pane of 10	19.00	
1571	A771	1fr green	75	5
a.		Bklt. pane of 10	8.00	
1572	A771	1.20fr red	75	5
a.		Bklt. pane of 5	6.00	
b.		Bklt. pane of 10	11.00	
1573	A771	1.40fr brt bl	2.50	25
1574	A771	1.70fr grnsh bl	90	30
1575	A771	2fr emerald	90	6
1576	A771	2.10fr lil rose	95	10
1577	A771	3fr dk brn	1.25	40
		Nos. 1560-1577 (18)	12.60	2.18

Coil Stamps

1978			Perf. 13 Horiz.	
1578	A771	80c brt grn	1.65	60
1579	A771	1fr brt grn	1.25	45
1579A	A771	1fr brt red	1.65	60
1579B	A771	1.20fr brt red	1.25	45

See Nos. 1658-1677.

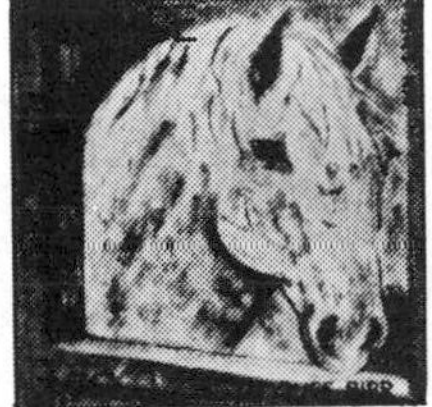

Percheron, by Jacques Birr
A772

Osprey
A773

1978		Photo.	Perf. 13	
1580	A772	1.70fr multi	1.25	60
		Engraved		
1581	A773	1.80fr multi	1.00	32

Nature protection.
Issue dates: 1.70fr, Jan. 7; 1.80fr, Oct. 14.

Examination

The Catalogue editors cannot undertake to appraise, identify or pass upon genuineness or condition of stamps.

Tournament, 1662, Etching
A774

Institut de France and Pont des Arts, Paris, by Bernard Buffet
A776

Horses, by Yves Brayer—A777

1978		Engr.	Perf. 12x13	
1582	A774	2fr black	2.00	90
		Perf. 13x12		
1584	A776	3fr multi	2.25	60
1585	A777	3fr multi	1.50	60

Issue dates: 2fr, Jan. 14; No. 1584, Feb. 4; No. 1585, Dec. 9.

Communications School and Tower
A778

1978, Jan. 19		Engr.	Perf. 13	
1586	A778	80c Prus bl	38	22

National Telecommunications School, centenary.

Swedish and French Flags, Map of Saint Barthelemy—A779

1978, Jan. 19				
1587	A779	1.10fr multi	60	25

Centenary of the reunion with France of Saint Barthelemy Island, West Indies.

Regions of France

Ile de France
A780

Tanker, Refinery, Flower, Upper Normandy
A781

Lower Normandy
A782

1978		Photo.	Perf. 13	
1588	A780	1fr red, bl & blk	60	30
		Engr.		
1589	A781	1.40fr multi	65	30
		Photogravure		
1590	A782	1.70fr multi	1.10	45

Issue dates. 1fr, Mar. 4; 1.40fr, Jan. 21; 1.70fr, Mar. 31.

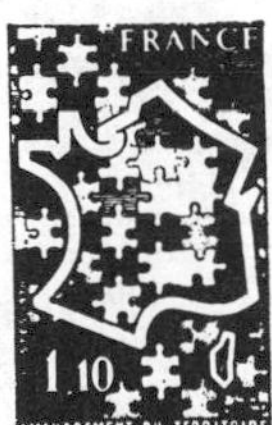

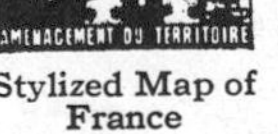

Stylized Map of France
A788

Young Stamp Collector
A789

1978, Feb. 11		Engr.	Perf. 13	
1596	A788	1.10fr vio & grn	60	25

Program of administrative changes, 15th anniversary.

1978, Feb. 25				
1597	A789	80c multi	40	22

JUVEXNIORT, Youth Philatelic Exhibition, Niort, Feb. 25—March 5.

Tourist Issue

Verdon Gorge
A790

Saint-Saturnin Church
A792

Pont Neuf, Paris
A791

Our Lady of Bec-Hellouin Abbey
A793

Chateau D'Esquelbecq
A794

Aubazine Abbey
A795

Fontevraud Abbey
A796

1978		Engraved	Perf. 13	
1598	A790	50c multi	25	15
1599	A791	80c multi	48	22
1600	A792	1fr black	50	15
1601	A793	1.10fr multi	65	22
1602	A794	1.10fr multi	50	32
1603	A795	1.25fr car & brn	65	30
1604	A796	1.70fr multi	95	32
		Nos. 1598-1604 (7)	3.98	1.68

Issue dates: 1.25fr, Feb. 18; 50c, Mar. 6; No. 1601, Mar. 26; 80c, May 27; 1fr, June 10; 1.70fr, June 3; No. 1602, June 17.

Fish and Under-water Flora
A797

1978, Apr. 15		Photo.	Perf. 13	
1605	A797	1.25fr multi	80	60

Port Cros National Park, 15th anniversary.

Flowers, Butterflies and Houses
A798

1978, Apr. 22		Engr.	Perf. 13	
1606	A798	1.70fr multi	3.00	45

50th anniversary of the beautification of France campaign.

Hands Shielding Source of Heat and Light—A799

1978, Apr. 22

1607	A799	1fr multi	80	18

Energy conservation.

World War I Memorial near Lens
A800

Fountain of the Innocents, Paris
A801

1978, May 6

1608	A800	2fr lem & mag	1.25	45

Colline Notre Dame de Lorette memorial of World War I.

Europa Issue 1978

Design: 1.40fr, Flower Park Fountain, Paris.

1978, May 6

1609	A801	1fr multi	50	15
1610	A801	1.40fr multi	65	30

Maurois Palace, Troyes
A802

1978, May 13

1611	A802	1fr multi	50	22

51st Congress of the Federation of French Philatelic Societies, Troyes, May 13–15.

Roland Garros Tennis Court and Player—A803

1978, May 27

1612	A803	1fr multi	1.40	38

Roland Garros Tennis Court, 50th anniversary.

Hand and Plant
A804

Printing Office Emblem—A805

1978, Sept. 9 **Engr.** ***Perf. 13***

1613	A804	1.30fr brn, red & grn	65	32

Encouragement of handicrafts.

1978, Sept. 23

1614	A805	1fr multi	50	22

National Printing Office, established 1538.

Fortress, Besançon, and Collegiate Church, Dole
A806

Valenciennes and Maubeuge
A807

1978

1615	A806	1.20fr multi	65	22
1616	A807	1.20fr multi	65	22

Reunion of Franche-Comté and Valenciennes and Maubeuge with France, 300th anniversary.

Issue dates: No. 1615, Sept. 23, No. 1616, Sept. 30.

Sower Type of 1906–1937 and Academy Emblem
A808

Gymnasts, Strasbourg Cathedral, Storks
A809

1978, Oct. 7

1617	A808	1fr multi	50	25

Academy of Philately, 50th anniversary.

1978, Oct. 21

1618	A809	1fr multi	65	25

19th World Gymnastics Championships, Strasbourg, Oct. 23–26.

Various Sports
A810

Polish Veterans' Monument
A811

1978, Oct. 21

1619	A810	1fr multi	1.10	45

Sports for all.

1978, Nov. 11

1620	A811	1.70fr multi	80	38

Polish veterans of World War II.

Railroad Car and Monument, Compiègne Forest, Rethondes—A812

1978, Nov. 11 **Engr.** ***Perf. 13***

1621	A812	1.20fr indigo	75	22

60th anniversary of World War I armistice.

Handicapped People
A813

1978, Nov. 18

1622	A813	1fr multi	50	22

Rehabilitation of the handicapped.

Human Rights Emblem
A814

1978, Dec. 9 **Engr.** ***Perf. 13***

1623	A814	1.70fr dk brn & bl	80	45

30th anniversary of Universal Declaration of Human Rights.

Child and IYC Emblem
A815

1979, Jan. 6 **Engr.** ***Perf. 13***

1624	A815	1.70fr multi	4.75	2.25

International Year of the Child.

"Music," 15th Century Miniature
A816

1979, Jan. 13 ***Perf. 13x12½***

1625	A816	2fr multi	1.40	75

Diana Taking a Bath, d'Ecouen Castle
A817

Church at Auvers-on-Oise, by Vincent Van Gogh—A818

Head of Marianne, by Salvador Dali
A819

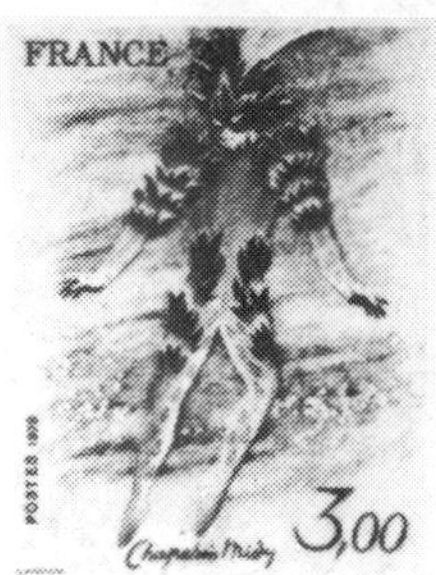

Fire Dancer from The Magic Flute, by Chaplain Midy—A820

1979 **Photo.** ***Perf. 12½×13***

1626	A817	2fr multi	95	60
1627	A818	2fr multi	2.00	60
1628	A819	3fr multi	1.40	60
1629	A820	3fr multi	1.40	75

Issue dates: No. 1626, Sept. 22; No. 1627, Oct. 27; No. 1628, Nov. 19; No. 1629, Nov. 26.

Orange Agaric
A821

Mushrooms: 83c, Death trumpet. 1.30fr, Olive wood pleurotus. 2.25fr, Cauliflower claveria.

1979, Jan. 15 Engr. *Perf. 13*

1630	A821	64c orange	50	38
1631	A821	83c brown	65	45
1632	A821	1.30fr yel bis	1.00	65
1633	A821	2.25fr brn pur	1.50	1.10

Nos. 1630–1633 are known only precanceled. See second note after No. 132.

Victor Segalen
A822

1979, Jan. 20

1634 A822 1.50fr multi 60 30

Victor Segalen (1878–1919), physician, explorer and writer.

Hibiscus and Palms
A823

1979, Feb. 3

1635 A823 35c multi 18 15

International Flower Festival, Martinique.

Buddha, Stupas, Temple of Borobudur
A824

1979, Feb. 24

1636 A824 1.80fr ol & sl grn 80 45

Save the Temple of Borobudur, Java, campaign.

Boy, by Poulbot
A825

1979, Mar. 24 Photogravure

1637 A825 1.30fr multi 55 22

Francisque Poulbot (1879–1946).

Tourist Issue

Chateau de Maisons, Laffitte
A826

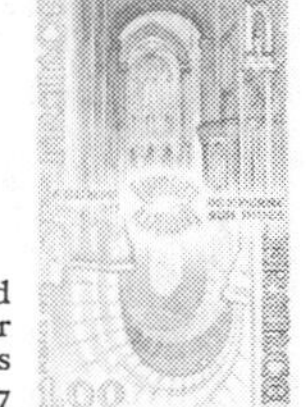

Bernay and St. Pierre sur Dives Abbeys
A827

View of Auray
A827a

Steenvorde Windmill
A828

Wall Painting, Niaux Cave
A829

Royal Palace, Perpignan
A830

1979 Engraved *Perf. 13*

1638	A826	45c multi	22	15
1639	A827	1fr multi	45	22
1640	A827a	1fr multi	45	22
1641	A828	1.20fr multi	60	18
1642	A829	1.50fr multi	65	30
1643	A830	1.70fr multi	75	30
		Nos. 1638-1643 (6)	3.12	1.37

Issue dates: 45c, Oct. 6; No. 1639, June 16; No. 1640, June 30; 1.20fr, May 12; 1.50fr, July 9; 1.70fr, Apr. 21.

Honey Bee
A831

1979, Mar. 31 Engr. *Perf. 13*

1644 A831 1fr multi 50 18

Nature protection.

St. Germain des Prés Abbey
A832

1979, Apr. 21

1645 A832 1.40fr multi 60 30

Europa Issue 1979

Simoun Mail Monoplanes, 1935, and Map of Mail Routes—A833

Design: 1.70fr, Floating spheres used on Seine during siege of Paris, 1870.

1979, Apr. 28

1646	A833	1.20fr multi	60	22
1647	A833	1.70fr multi	75	38

Ship and View of Nantes
A834

1979, May 5 Engr. *Perf. 13*

1648 A834 1.20fr multi 50 22

52nd National Congress of French Philatelic Societies, Nantes, May 5–7.

Royal Palace, 1789
A835

1979, May 19

1649 A835 1fr car rose & pur 45 30

European Elections
A836

1979, May 19 Photo. *Perf. 13*

1650 A836 1.20fr multi 60 18

European Parliament, first direct elections, June 10.

Joan of Arc Monument
A837

1979, May 24 Engraved

1651 A837 1.70fr brt lil rose 1.00 45

Joan of Arc, the Maid of Orleans (1412–1431).

Felix Guyon and Catheters
A840

1979, June 23

1652 A840 1.80fr sep & bl 75 30

Felix Guyon (1831–1920), urologist.

Lantern Tower, La Rochelle
A841

Telecom '79
A842

Towers: 88c, Chartres Cathedral. 1.40fr, Bourges Cathedral. 2.35fr, Amiens Cathedral.

1979, Aug. 13 Engr. *Perf. 13*

1653	A841	68c vio brn & blk	50	45
1654	A841	88c ultra & blk	65	45
1655	A841	1.40fr gray grn & blk	1.00	80
1656	A841	2.35fr dl brn & blk	1.50	95

Nos. 1653–1656 are known only precanceled. See second note after No. 132.

See Nos. 1684-1687.

1979, Sept. 22

1657 A842 1.10fr multi 45 18

3rd World Telecommunications Exhibition.

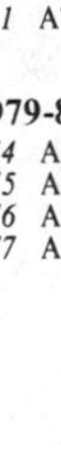

Sabine Type of 1977–78

1979-81 Engr. *Perf. 13*

1658	A771	40c brn ('81)	18	15
1659	A771	60c red brn ('81)	25	18
1660	A771	70c vio bl	30	15
1661	A771	90c brt lil ('81)	38	22
1662	A771	1fr gray ol	38	5
1663	A771	1.10fr green	95	5
1664	A771	1.20fr grn ('80)	60	5
1665	A771	1.30fr rose red	95	5
1666	A771	1.40fr rose red ('80)	65	5
1667	A771	1.60fr purple	1.25	15
1668	A771	1.80fr ocher	95	18
1669	A771	3.50fr lt ol grn ('81)	1.25	22
1670	A771	4fr brt car ('81)	1.40	30
1671	A771	5fr brt grnsh bl ('81)	1.75	15
		Nos. 1658-1671 (14)	11.24	1.95

Coil Stamps

1979-80 *Perf. 13 Horiz.*

1674	A771	1.10fr green	1.50	30
1675	A771	1.20fr grn ('80)	65	30
1676	A771	1.30fr rose red	1.50	30
1677	A771	1.40fr rose red ('80)	75	30

Lorraine Region—A845

1979, Nov. 10

1678 A845 2.30fr multi 95 32

Gears—A847

1979, Nov. 17 ***Perf. 13***

1680 A847 1.80fr multi 75 45

Central Technical School of Paris, 150th anniv.

Judo Throw—A848

1979, Nov. 24 **Engr.**

1681 A848 1.60fr multi 65 38

World Judo Championships, Paris, Dec.

Violins—A849

1979, Dec. 10

1682 A849 1.30fr multi 75 22

Eurovision—A850

1980, Jan. 12 **Engraved** ***Perf. 13×13½***

1683 A850 1.80fr multi 1.25 60

Tower Type of 1979

Designs: 76c, Chateau d'Angers. 99c, Chateau de Kerjean. 1.60fr, Chateau de Pierrefonds. 2.65fr, Chateau de Tarascon.

1980, Jan. 21 **Engraved**

1684	A841	76c	grnsh bl & blk	38	38
1685	A841	99c	sl grn & blk	50	45
1686	A841	1.60fr	red & blk	90	80
1687	A841	2.65fr	brn org & blk	1.50	95

Nos. 1684-1687 are known only precanceled. See second note after No. 132.

Self-portrait , by Albrecht Dürer, Philexfrance '82 Emblem—A851

Woman Holding Fan, by Ossip Zadkine—A852

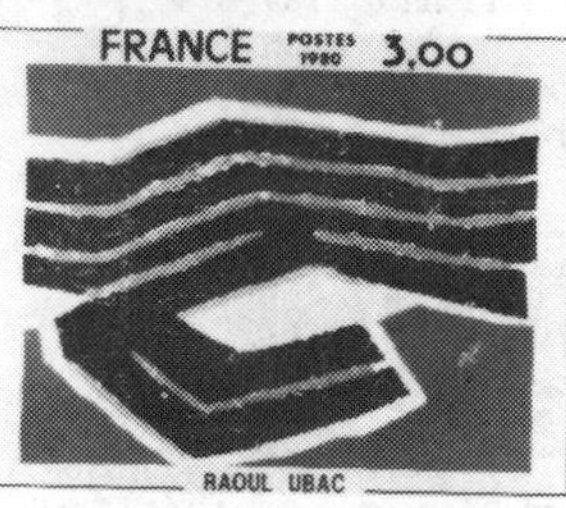

Abstract, by Raoul Ubak—A853

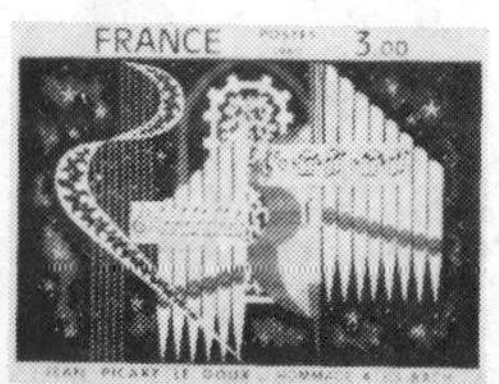

Hommage to J.S. Bach, by Jean Picart Le Doux—A854

Peasant, by Louis Le Nain—A855

Woman with Blue Eyes, by Modigliani—A856

Abstract, by Hans Hartung—A857

Perf. 12½x13, 13x12½

1980 **Engr., Engr. & Photo**

1688	A851	2fr	multi	75	60
1689	A852	3fr	multi	1.40	60
1690	A853	3fr	multi	1.40	60
1691	A854	3fr	multi	1.40	65
1692	A855	3fr	multi	1.40	50
1693	A856	4fr	multi	1.90	50
1694	A857	4fr	ultra & blk	1.75	50
		Nos. 1688-1694 (7)		10.00	3.95

Issue dates: #1688, June 7; #1689, Jan. 19; #1690, Feb. 2; #1691, Sept. 20; #1693, Oct. 26; #1692, Nov. 10; #1694, Dec. 20.

Giants of the North Festival—A858

1980, Feb. 16 ***Perf. 13***

1695 A858 1.60fr multi 65 45

French Cuisine—A859

1980, Feb. 23

1696 A859 90c red & lt brn 38 22

Woman Embroidering A860

Fight Against Cigarette Smoking A861

Photo. & Engr.

1980, Mar. 29 ***Perf. 13***

1697 A860 1.10fr multi 55 22

Photo. ***Perf. 13***

1980, Apr. 5

1698 A861 1.30fr multi 55 22

Europa Issue

Aristide Briand—A862

Design: 1.80fr, St. Benedict.

1980, Apr. 26 **Engraved** ***Perf. 13***

1699 A862 1.30fr multi 50 15

1700 A862 1.80fr red & red brn 80 25

Aristide Briand (1862-1932), prime minister, 1909-1911, 1921-1922; St. Benedict, patron saint of Europe.

Liancourt, College, Map of Northwestern France—A863

1980, May 19 **Engraved** ***Perf. 13***

1701 A863 2fr dk grn & pur 75 30

National College of Arts and Handicrafts (founded by Larochefoucauld Liancourt) bicentenary

Cranes, Town Hall Tower, Dunkirk
A864

1980, May 24

1702 A864 1.30fr multi 50 18

53rd National Congress of French Federation of Philatelic Societies, Dunkirk, May 24-26.

Tourist Issue

Cordes
A865

Montauban
A867

Chateau de Maintenon—A866

St. Peter's Abbey, Solesmes—A868

Puy Cathedral
A869

1980		**Engraved**	**Perf. 13**	
1703	A865	1.50fr multi	60	22
1704	A866	2fr multi	75	18
1705	A867	2.30fr multi	90	30
1706	A868	2.50fr multi	1.00	15
1707	A869	3.20fr multi	1.25	38
		Nos. 1703-1707 (5)	4.50	1.23

Issue dates: #1703, Apr. 5; #1704, June 7; #1705, May 7; #1706, Sept. 20; #1707, May 12.

Graellsia Isabellae—A870

1980, May 31 **Photo.**

1708 A870 1.10fr multi 75 30

See "Special Notices" at the front of this volume for data on the listing methods of this Catalogue, abbreviations, condition, prices and examination.

Association Emblem
A871

Marianne, French Architecture
A872

1980, June 10 **Photo.**

1709 A871 1.30fr red & bl 48 22

International Public Relations Association, 25th anniversary.

1980, June 21 **Engr.**

1710 A872 1.50fr bluish & gray blk 75 32

Heritage Year.

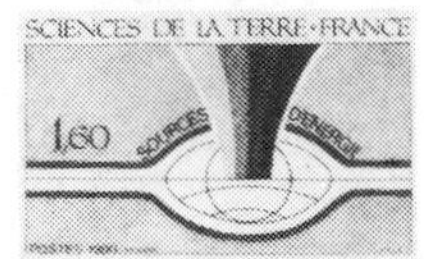

Earth Sciences—A873

1980, July 5

1711 A873 1.60fr dk brn & red 60 38

International Geological Congress.

Rochambeau's Landing—A874

1980, July 15

1712 A874 2.50fr multi 1.25 48

Rochambeau's landing at Newport, R.I. (American Revolution), bicentenary.

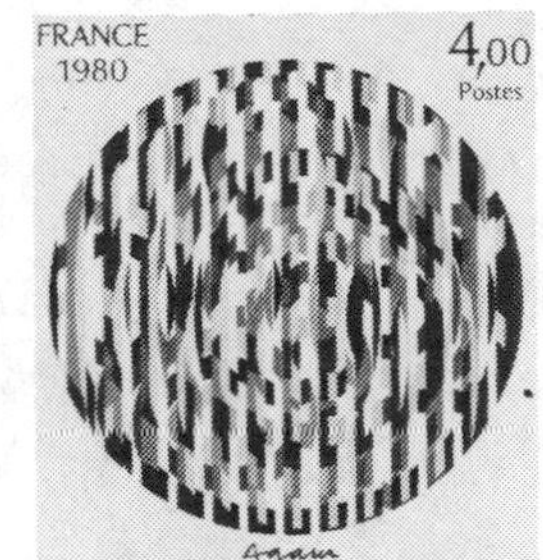

Message of Peace, by Yaacov Agam—A875

1980, Oct. 4 **Photo.** ***Perf. 11½x13***

1713 A875 4fr multi 2.50 90

French Golf Federation—A876

1980, Oct. 18 **Engraved**

1714 A876 1.40fr multi 65 22

Comedie Francaise, 300th Anniversary—A877

1980, Oct. 18

1715 A877 2fr multi 75 30

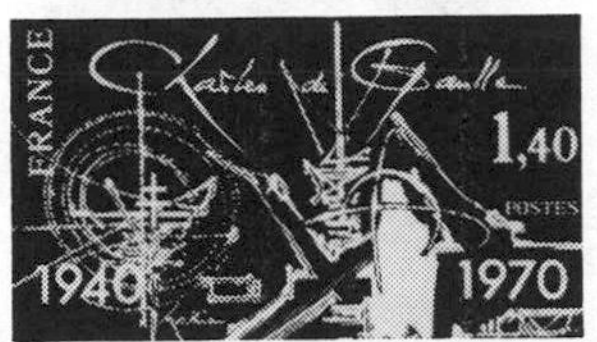

Charles de Gaulle—A878

1980, Nov. 10 **Photo.** ***Perf. 13***

1716 A878 1.40fr multi 80 15

40th anniversary of De Gaulle's appeal of June 18, and 10th anniversary of his death.

Guardsman—A879

1980, Nov. 24 **Engr.** ***Perf. 13***

1717 A879 1.70fr multi 65 45

Rambouillet Chateau—A880

1980, Dec. 6 **Engraved** ***Perf. 13***

1718 A880 2.20fr multi 90 22

Tower Type of 1979

Designs: 88c, Imperial Chapel, Ajaccio. 1.14fr, Astronomical Clock, Besancon. 1.84fr, Coucy Castle ruins. 3.05fr, Font-de-Gaume cave drawing, Les Eyzies de Tayac.

1981, Jan. 11		**Engraved**	***Perf. 13***	
1719	A841	88c dp mag & blk	45	30
1720	A841	1.14fr ultra & blk	60	38
1721	A841	1.84fr dk grn & blk	90	60
1722	A841	3.05fr brn red & blk	1.50	95

Nos. 1719-1722 are known only precanceled. See second note after No. 132.

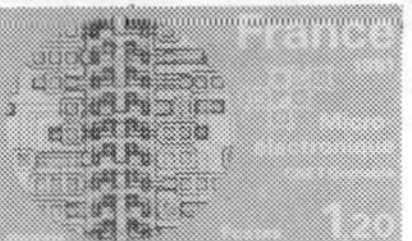

Microelectronics—A881

1981		**Photogravure**		
1723	A881	1.20fr shown	90	18
1724	A881	1.20fr Biology	50	25
1725	A881	1.40fr Energy	65	32
1726	A881	1.80fr Marine exploration	80	45
1727	A881	2fr Telemetry	1.00	25
		Nos. 1723-1727 (5)	3.85	1.45

Issue dates: No. 1723, Feb. 5; others, Mar. 28.

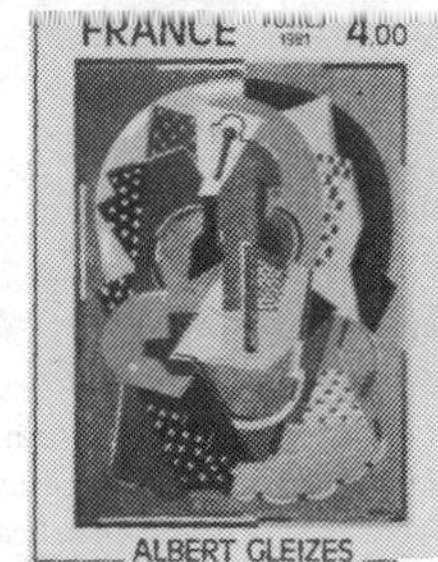

Abstract, by Albert Gleizes—A882

1981, Feb. 28 ***Perf. 12½x13***

1728 A882 4fr multi 1.65 65

The Footpath by Camille Pissaro—A883

1981, Apr. 18 **Engr.** ***Perf. 13x12½***

1729 A883 2fr multi 90 45

Child Watering Smiling Map of France—A884

1981, Mar. 14 **Engraved** ***Perf. 13***

1730 A884 1.40fr multi 50 18

Sully Chateau, Rosny-sur-Seine—A885

1981, Mar. 21

1731 A885 2.50fr multi 1.10 15

Tourist Issue

Roman Temple, Nimes—A886

1981, Apr. 11 ***Perf. 13***

1732 A886 1.70fr multi 65 30

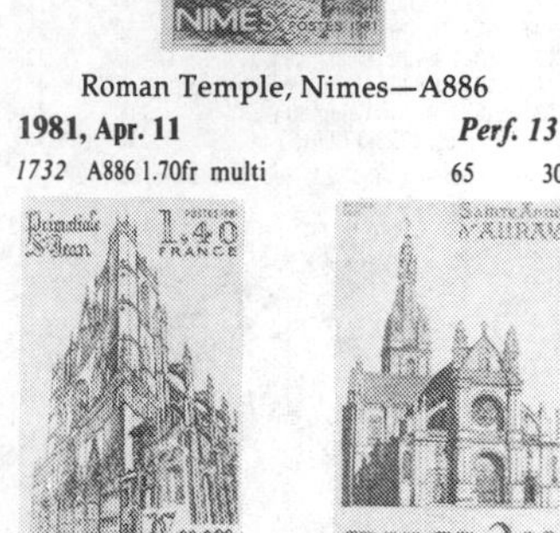

Church of St. Jean, Lyon A887

St. Anne d'Auray Basilica A888

1981 Engr. ***Perf. 13***

1733 A887 1.40fr dk red & dk brn 50 18
1734 A888 2.20fr bl & blk 90 30

Issue dates: 1.40fr, May 30; 2.20fr, July 4.

Vaucelles Abbey—A889

Notre Dame of Louviers—A890

1981

1735 A889 2fr red & blk 65 22
1736 A890 2.20fr red brn & dk brn 80 38

Issue dates: 2fr, Sept. 19; 2.20fr, Sept. 26.

Europa Issue 1981

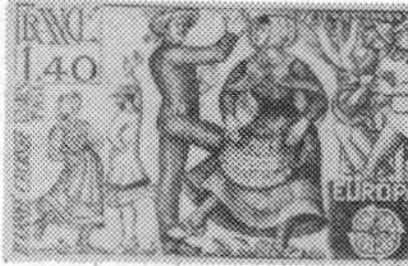

Bouree—A891

Folkdances: 2fr, Sardane.

1981, May 4 ***Perf. 13***

1737 A891 1.40fr multi 50 15
1738 A891 2fr multi 80 25

Bookbinding A892

Cadets A893

1981, Apr. 4 ***Perf. 13***

1739 A892 1.50fr ol & car rose 60 30

1981, May 16

1740 A893 2.50fr multi 95 22

Military College at St. Maixent centenary.

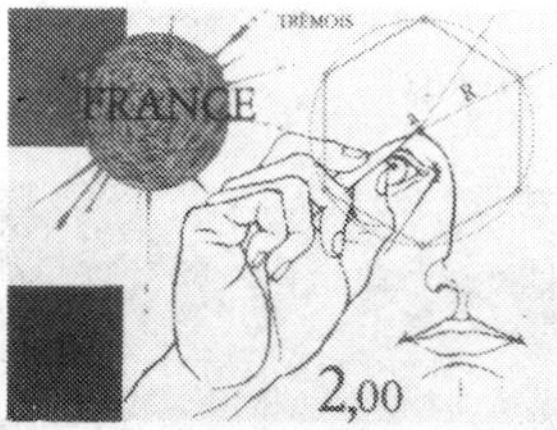

Man Drawing Geometric Diagram—A894

1981, May 23 **Photo.**

1741 A894 2fr shown 1.25 60
1742 A894 2fr Faces 1.25 60

PHILEXFRANCE '82 Stamp Exhibition, Paris, June 11-21, 1982. Nos. 1741-1742 se-tenant with label showing exhibition emblem.

Theophraste Renaudot and Emile de Girardin A895

Public Gardens, Vichy A896

1981, May 30 **Engr.**

1743 A895 2.20fr blk & red 85 45

350th anniversary of La Gazette (founded by Renaudot), and death centenary of founder of Le Journal (de Girardin).

1981, June 6

1744 A896 1.40fr multi 50 22

54th National Congress of French Federation of Philatelic Societies, Vichy.

Higher National College for Commercial Studies Centenary—A897

1981, June 20 ***Perf. 13***

1745 A897 1.40fr multi 55 22

Sea Shore Conservation—A898

1981, June 20

1746 A898 1.60fr multi 75 25

World Fencing Championship, Clermont-Ferrand, July 2-13—A899

1981, June 27

1747 A899 1.80fr multi 80 32

Sabine, after David—A900

1981, Sept. 1 **Engr.**

1755 A900 1.40fr green 50 6
1756 A900 1.60fr red 60 6
1757 A900 2.30fr blue 80 30

Coil Stamps

1981 Engr. ***Perf. 13 Horiz.***

1758 A900 1.40fr green 60 30
1759 A900 1.60fr red 65 22

Highway Safety ("Drink or Drive")—A901

1981, Sept. 5 ***Perf. 13***

1768 A901 1.60fr multi 60 15

45th Intl. PEN Club Congress A902

Jules Ferry, Statesman A903

1981, Sept ***Perf. 13***

1769 A902 2fr multi 90 32

1981, Sept. 28 ***Perf. 12½x13***

1770 A903 1.60fr multi 75 22

Free compulsory public school centenary.

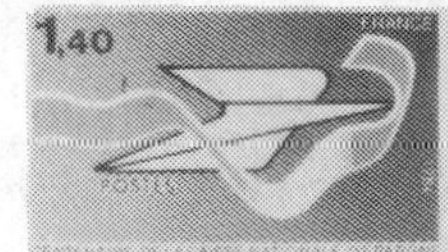

Natl. Savings Bank Centenary—A904

1981, Sept. 21 **Photo.** ***Perf. 13***

1771 A904 1.40fr multi 50 22
1772 A904 1.60fr multi 60 22

The Divers, by Edouard Pignon—A905

1981, Oct. 3 ***Perf. 13x12½***

1773 A905 4fr multi 1.65 45

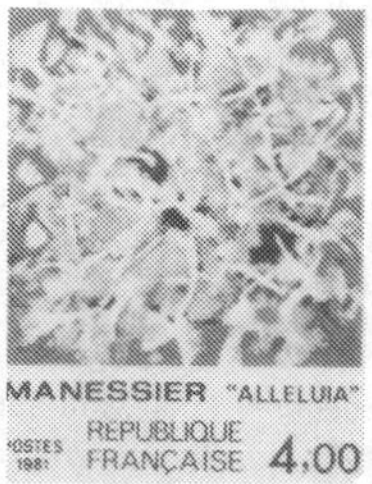

Alleluia, by Alfred Manessier—A906

1981, Dec. 19 **Photo.** ***Perf. 12x13***

1774 A906 4fr multi 1.65 45

Tourist Issue

Saint-Emilion—A907

Crest—A908

1981 Engr. ***Perf. 13x12½, 13 (2.90fr)***

1775 A907 2.60fr dk red & lt ol grn 95 18
1776 A908 2.90fr dk grn 1.00 10

Issue dates: #1775, Oct. 10; #1776, Nov. 28.

150th Anniv. of Naval Academy—A909

1981, Oct. 17 ***Perf. 13***

1777 A909 1.40fr multi 60 22

St. Hubert Kneeling Before the Stag, 15th Cent. Sculpture A910

1981, Oct. 24

1778	A910	1.60fr multi	60	18

Museum of hunting and nature.

V. Schoelcher, J. Jaures, J. Moulin and the Pantheon—A911

1981, Nov. 2

1779	A911	1.60fr bl & dl pur	60	22

Intl. Year of the Disabled—A912

1981, Nov. 7

1780	A912	1.60fr multi	60	15

Men Leading Cattle, 2nd Cent. Roman Mosaic—A913

1981, Nov. 14 ***Perf. 13x12***

1781	A913	2fr multi	90	45

Virgil's birth bimillennium.

Martyrs of Chateaubriant A914

1981, Dec. 12 **Engr.** ***Perf. 13***

1782	A914	1.40fr multi	60	18

Liberty, after Delacroix—A915

1982 **Engr.** ***Perf. 13***

1783	A915	5c dk grn	5	5
1784	A915	10c dl red	5	5
1785	A915	15c brt rose lil	5	5
1786	A915	20c brt grn	6	6
1787	A915	30c orange	8	5
1788	A915	40c brown	10	10
1789	A915	50c lilac	12	8
1790	A915	60c lt red brn	15	10
1791	A915	70c ultra	18	10
1792	A915	80c lt ol grn	20	10
1793	A915	90c brt lil	22	18
1794	A915	1fr ol grn	25	6
1795	A915	1.40fr green	65	10
1796	A915	1.60fr green	48	6
1797	A915	1.60fr red	75	6
1798	A915	1.80fr red	60	6
1799	A915	2fr brt yel grn	60	6
1800	A915	2.30fr blue	65	30
1801	A915	2.60fr blue	75	30
1802	A915	3fr chocolate	75	6
1803	A915	4fr brt car	1.00	15
1804	A915	5fr gray bl	1.25	15
		Nos. 1783-1804 (22)	8.99	2.28

Coil Stamps
Perf. 13 Horiz.

1805	A915	1.40fr green	1.00	38
1806	A915	1.60fr red	1.25	38
1807	A915	1.60fr green	50	22
1807A	A915	1.80fr red	65	18

See Nos. 1881-1896.

Tourist Issue

St. Pierre and Miquelon A916

Corsica A917

1982, Jan. 9 **Engr.** ***Perf. 12½***

1808	A916	1.60fr dk bl & blk	50	15
1809	A917	1.90fr bl & red	65	30

Renaissance Fountain, Aix-en Provence—A918

Collonges-la-Rouge—A919

Castle of Henry IV, Pau—A920

1982 ***Perf. 13***

1810	A918	2fr multi	65	15
1811	A919	3fr multi	90	22
1812	A920	3fr ultra & dk bl	90	15

Issue dates, Aix-en-Provence, June 21, Collonges-la-Rouge, July 5, Pau, May 15.

Lille A921

Chateau Ripaille, Haute-Savoie A921a

1982 ***Perf. 13x12½***

1813	A921	1.80fr dl red & ol	55	15
1813A	A921a	2.90fr multi	90	10

Issue dates: 1.80fr, Oct. 16; 2.90fr, Sept. 4.

Tower Type of 1979

Designs: 97c, Tanlay Castle, Yonne. 1.25fr, Salses Fort, Pyrenees-Orientales. 2.03fr, Montlhery Tower, Essonne. 3.36fr, Chateau d'If Bouches-du-Rhone.

1982, Jan. 11 **Engr.** ***Perf. 13***

1814	A841	97c ol grn & blk	50	32
1815	A841	1.25fr red & blk	60	40
1816	A841	2.03fr sep & blk	90	60
1817	A841	3.36fr ultra & blk	1.50	95

Nos. 1814-1817 are known only precanceled. See second note after No. 132.

800th Birth Anniv. of St. Francis of Assisi—A922

1982, Feb. 6 **Photo & Engr.**

1818	A922	2fr blk & bl	90	30

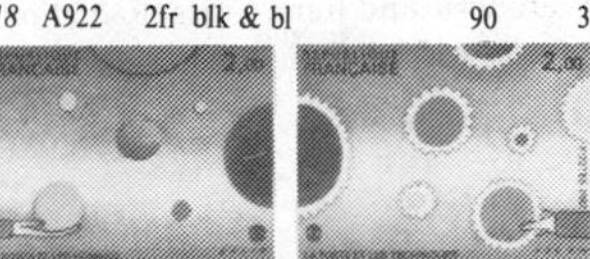

Posts and Mankind A923

Posts and Technology A924

1982, Feb. 13 **Photo.**

1819	A923	2fr multi	2.50	75
1820	A924	2fr multi	2.50	75

PHILEXFRANCE '82 Stamp Exhibition, Paris, June 11-21. Nos. 1819-1820 se-tenant with label showing emblem.

Souvenir Sheet

Marianne, by Jean Cocteau—A925

1982, June 11

1821		Sheet of 2	25.00	25.00
a.	A925	4fr red & bl	*11.00*	*11.00*
b.	A925	6fr bl & red	*12.00*	*12.00*

No. 1821 has gray marginal inscription, show emblem. Size: 100x71mm. Sold only with 20fr show admission ticket.

Scouting Year—A926

1982, Feb. 20 **Engr.**

1822	A926	2.30fr yel grn & blk	90	45

31st Natl. Census A927

Bale-Mulhouse Airport Opening A928

1982, Feb. 27 **Photo.**

1823	A927	1.60fr multi	50	22

1982, Mar. 15 **Engr.** ***Perf. 13***

1824	A928	1.90fr multi	80	38

Fight Against Racism A929

Blacksmith A930

1982, Mar. 20

1825	A929	2.30fr brn & red org	90	45

1982, Apr. 17

1826	A930	1.40fr multi	50	30

Europa 1982—A931

1982, Apr. 24

1827	A931	1.60fr Treaty of Rome, 1957	50	15
1828	A931	2.30fr Treaty of Verdun, 843	75	25

1982 World Cup—A932

1982, Apr. 28

1829 A932 1.80fr multi 75 18

Young Greek Soldier, Hellenic Sculpture, Agude—A933

1982, May 15 ***Perf. 12½x13***

1830 A933 4fr multi 1.40 50

Embarkation for Ostia, by Claude Gellee—A934

The Lacemaker, by Vermeer—A935

Turkish Chamber, by Balthus—A936

Perf. 13x12½, 12½x13

1982 **Photo.**

1831 A934 4fr multi 1.40 50
1832 A935 4fr multi 1.40 50
1833 A936 4fr multi 1.40 45

Issue dates: No. 1831, June 19; No. 1832, Sept. 4; No. 1833, Nov. 8.

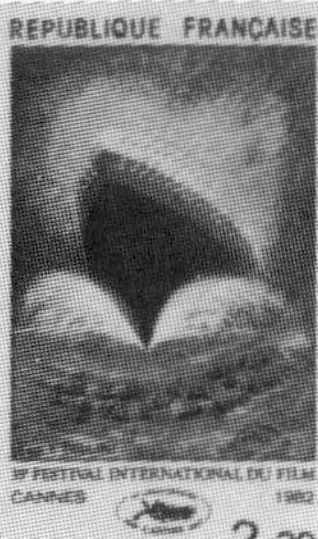

35th Intl. Film Festival, Cannes A937

Natl. Space Studies Center, 20th Anniv. A938

1982, May 15 **Photo.** ***Perf. 13***

1834 A937 2.30fr multi 75 45

1982, May 15 **Engr.**

1835 A938 2.60fr multi 1.00 45

Industrialized Countries' Summit Meeting, Versailles, June 4-6—A939

1982, June 4 **Photo**

1836 A939 2.60fr multi 95 45

Jules Valles (1832-1885), Writer—A940

1982, June 4 **Engr.** ***Perf. 13***

1837 A940 1.60fr ol grn & dk grn 90 18

Frederic and Irene Curie, Radiation Diagrams—A941

1982, June 26

1838 A941 1.80fr multi 65 22

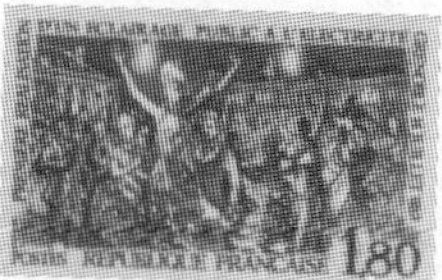

Electric Street Lighting Centenary—A942

1982, July 10

1839 A942 1.80fr dk bl & vio 75 22

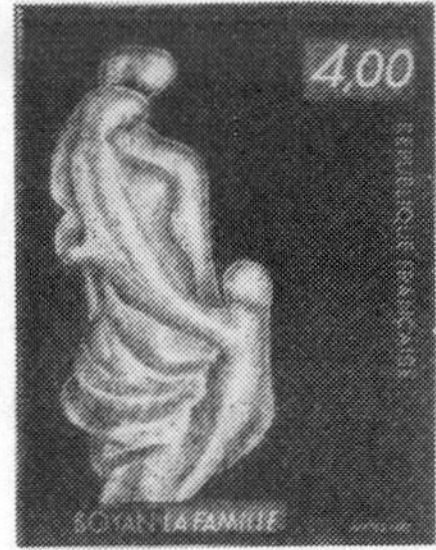

The Family, by Marc Boyan—A943

Photo. & Engr.

1982, Sept. 18 ***Perf. 12½x13***

1840 A943 4fr multi 1.40 45

Natl. Federation of Firemen Centenary A944

Marionettes A945

1982, Sept. 18 **Engr.** ***Perf. 13***

1841 A944 3.30fr red & sep 1.25 25

1982, Sept. 25

1842 A945 1.80fr multi 50 15

Rugby—A946

1982, Oct. 9

1843 A946 1.60fr multi 50 22

Higher Education—A947

1982, Oct. 16

1844 A947 1.80fr red & blk 60 18

TB Bacillus Centenary—A948

1982, Nov. 13

1845 A948 2.60fr red & blk 75 38

St. Teresa of Avila (1515-1582)—A949

1982, Nov. 20

1846 A949 2.10fr multi 60 30

Leon Blum (1872-1950), Politician—A950

1982, Dec. 18 **Engr.** ***Perf. 13***

1847 A950 1.80fr dk brn & brn 55 18

Cavelier de la Salle (1643-1687), Explorer—A951

1982, Dec. 18 ***Perf. 13x12½***

1848 A951 3.25fr multi 1.00 30

Spring—A952

1983, Jan. 17 **Engr.** ***Perf. 13***

1849 A952 1.05fr shown 45 25
1850 A952 1.35fr Summer 60 32
1851 A952 2.19fr Autumn 80 50
1852 A952 3.63fr Winter 1.50 90

Nos. 1849-1852 known only pre-canceled. See second note after No. 132.

Provence—Alpes-Cote d'Azur—A953

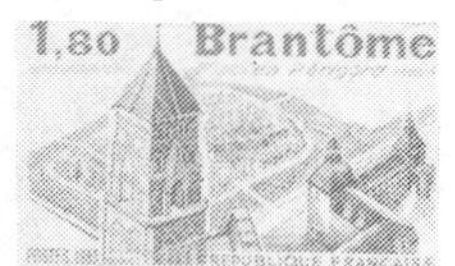

Brantome (Perigord)—A954

Perf. 13, 13x12½

1983 **Photo., Engr.**

1853 A953 1fr multi 38 10
1854 A954 1.80fr multi 60 8

Issue dates: 1fr, Jan. 8; 1.80fr, Feb. 5.

Concarneau—A955

Noirlac Abbey—A956

1983 **Engr.** ***Perf. 13, 13x12½***

1855	A955	3fr multi	95	22
1856	A956	3.60fr multi	1.10	30

Issue dates: No. 1855, June 11; No. 1856, July 2.

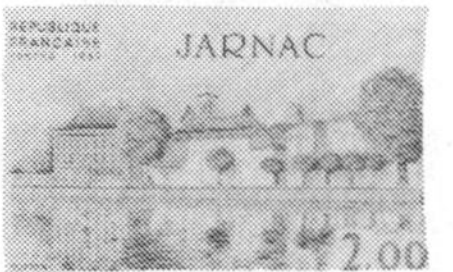

Jarnac—A957

Charleville-Mezieres—A958

1983 **Engr.** ***Perf. 13x12½***

1857	A957	2fr multi	55	10
1858	A958	3.10fr multi	95	75

Issue dates: No. 1857, Oct. 8; No. 1858, Sept. 17.

Martin Luther (1483-1546)—A959

1983, Feb. 12 **Engr.** ***Perf. 13***

1859	A959	3.30fr dk brn & tan	1.00	30

Alliance Francaise Centenary—A960

1983, Feb. 19

1860	A960	1.80fr multi	55	22

Danielle Casanova (d. 1942), Resistance Leader—A961

1983, Mar. 8

1861	A961	3fr blk & red brn	1.00	30

World Communications Year—A962

1983, Mar. 12 **Photo.**

1862	A962	2.60fr multi	75	30

Manned Flight Bicentenary—A963

1983, Mar. 19 **Photo.** ***Perf. 13***

1863	A963	2fr Hot air balloon	75	45
1864	A963	3fr Hydrogen balloon	1.00	60

Se-tenant with label.

Female Nude, by Raphael—A964

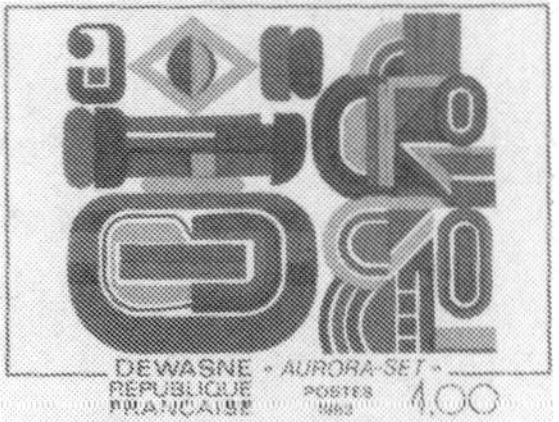

Aurora-Set, by Dewasne—A965

1983 **Engr., Photo.** ***Perf. 13***

1865	A964	4fr multi	1.40	60
1866	A965	4fr multi	1.40	60

Issue dates: No. 1866, Mar. 19; No. 1865, Apr. 9.

Illustration from Perrault's Folk Tales, by Gustave Dore—A966

1983, June 18 **Engr.** ***Perf. 13***

1867	A966	4fr red & blk	1.40	60

Homage to Jean Effel—A967

1983, Oct. 15

1868	A967	4fr multi	1.40	45

Le Lapin Agile, by Utrillo—A968

1983, Dec. 3 ***Perf. 13x12½***

1869	A968	4fr multi	1.25	60

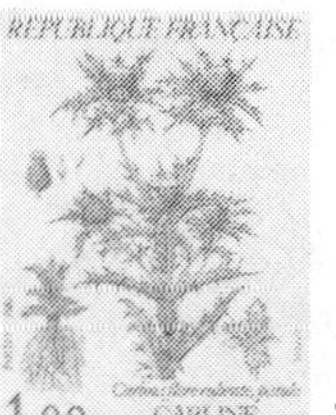

Thistle—A969

1983, Apr. 23 **Engr.** ***Perf. 12½x12***

1870	A969	1fr shown	32	15
1871	A969	2fr Martagon lily	90	15
1872	A969	3fr Aster	1.00	25
1873	A969	4fr Aconite	1.40	45

Europa 1983—A970

1983, Apr. 29 ***Perf. 13***

1874	A970	1.80fr Symbolic shutter	1.65	22
1875	A970	2.60fr Lens-to-screen diagram	2.00	38

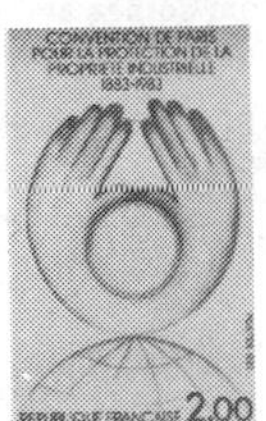

Centenary of Paris Convention for the Protection of Industrial Property—A971

1983, May 14 **Photo.** ***Perf. 13***

1876	A971	2fr multi	60	18

French Philatelic Societies Congress, Marseilles—A972

1983, May 21 **Engr.** ***Perf. 13***

1877	A972	1.80fr multi	75	18

Liberty Type of 1982

1983-86 **Engr.** ***Perf. 13***

1881	A915	1.70fr grn ('84)	50	8
1882	A915	1.80fr emer ('85)	48	8
1882B	A915	1.90fr emer grn ('86)	58	12
1883	A915	2fr red	60	6
1884	A915	2.10fr red ('84)	60	8
1885	A915	2.20fr red ('85)	60	10
a		Bklt. pane of 10 ('86)	5.25	
1887	A915	2.80fr blue	80	30
1888	A915	3fr bl ('84)	90	22
1889	A915	3.20fr saph ('85)	85	10
1890	A915	3.40fr dp bl ('86)	1.00	20
1891	A915	10fr purple	2.50	10
1892	A915	(1.90fr) emer grn ('86)	58	12
		Nos. 1881-1892 (12)	9.99	1.56

No. 1892 is inscribed "A."

Coil Stamps

Engr. ***Perf. 13 Horiz.***

1893	A915	1.70fr emer ('85)	40	8
1894	A915	1.80fr emer ('85)	42	8
1894A	A915	1.90fr emer grn ('86)	58	12
1895	A915	2fr red	65	22
1895A	A915	2.10fr crim ('84)	75	30
1896	A915	2.20fr red ('85)	52	10

50th Anniv. of Air France—A973

1983, June 18

1898	A973	3.45fr multi	1.10	50

Treaties of Versailles and Paris Bicentenary—A974

1983, Sept. 2 ***Perf. 13x12½***

1899	A974	2.80fr multi	90	45

Jewelry Making—A975

1983, Sept. 10 **Photo.** ***Perf. 13***

1900	A975 2.20fr multi		65	30

30th Anniv. of Customs Cooperation Council—A976

1983, Sept. 22 **Engr.** ***Perf. 13x12½***

1901	A976 2.30fr multi		70	30

Michaux's Bicycle—A977

1983, Oct. 1 **Engr.** ***Perf. 13***

1902	A977 1.60fr multi		60	22

Natl. Weather Forecasting—A978

1983, Oct. 22 **Engr.** ***Perf. 12½x13***

1903	A978 1.50fr multi		45	15

Berthie Albrecht (1893-1943)—A979

1983, Nov. 5

1904	A979 1.60fr dk brn & ol		50	15
1905	A979 1.60fr Rene Levy (1906-1943)		50	15

Resistance heroines.

Pierre Mendes France (1907-1982), Premier—A980

1983, Dec. 16

1906	A980	2fr dk gray & red	60	15

Trade Union Centenary—A981

1984, Mar. 22 ***Perf. 13***

1907	A981 3.60fr Union leader Waldeck-Rousseau		1.10	38

Homage to the Cinema, by Cesar—A982

1984, Feb. 4 **Engr.** ***Perf. 12½x13***

1908	A982	4fr multi	1.25	60

Four Corners of the Sky, by Jean Messagier—A983

1984, Mar. 31 **Photo.** ***Perf. 13x12½***

1909	A983	4fr multi	1.25	60

Dining Room Corner, at Cannet, by Pierre Bonnard—A984

1984, Apr. 14 Photo. & Engr. ***Perf. 12½x12***

1910	A984	4fr multi	1.25	60

Pythia, by Andre Masson—A985

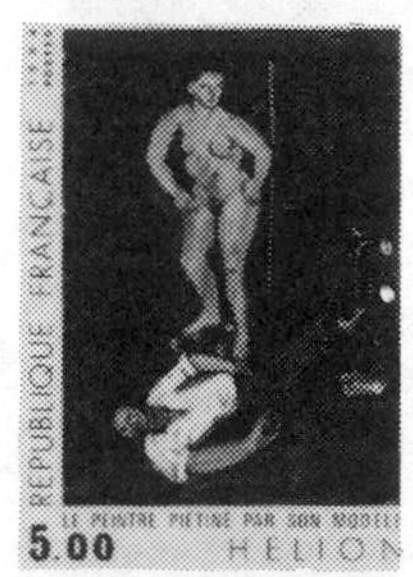

Painter at the Feet of His Model, by Helion—A986

1984 **Photo.** ***Perf. 12x13***

1911	A985	5fr multi	1.50	45
1912	A986	5fr multi	1.50	45

Issue dates: No. 1911, Oct. 13; No. 1912, Dec. 1.

Guadeloupe—A987

1984, Feb. 25 ***Perf. 13***

1913	A987 2.30fr Map, West Indian dancers		70	22

Vauban Citadel, Belle Ile-en-Mer—A988

Phare de Cordouan—A989

1984 **Engr.** ***Perf. 13***

1914	A988 2.50fr multi		75	22
1915	A989 3.50fr multi		1.00	22

Issue dates: No. 1914, May 26; No. 1915, June 23.

La Grande Chartreuse Monastery, 900th Anniv.—A990

Palais Ideal, Hauterives-Drome—A991

Montsegur Chateau—A992

1984 **Engr.** ***Perf. 13***

1916	A990 1.70fr multi		50	15
1917	A991 2.10fr multi		80	10
1917A	A992 3.70fr multi		1.10	18

Issue dates: 1.70fr, July 7; 2.10fr, June 30; 3.70fr, Sept. 15.

Flora Tristan (1803-44), Feminist—A992a

1984, Mar. 8

1918	A992a 2.80fr multi		80	30

Playing Card Suits—A993

1984, Apr. 11 **Engr.**

1919	A993 1.14fr Hearts		45	25
1920	A993 1.47fr Spades		50	32
1921	A993 2.38fr Diamonds		80	60
1922	A993 3.95fr Clubs		1.50	1.00

Nos. 1919-1922 known only precanceled. See second note after No. 132.

450th Anniv. of Cartier's Landing in Quebec—A994

1984, Apr. 20 **Photo. & Engr.**

1923	A994	2fr multi	75	15

See Canada No. 1011.

Philex '84, Dunkirk—A995

1984, Apr. 21 *Perf. 13x12½*

1924 A995 1.60fr multi 48 22

Europa (1959-84)—A996

1984, Apr. 28 **Engr.** *Perf. 13*

1925 A996 2fr red brn 60 15
1926 A996 2.80fr blue 90 38

2nd European Parliament Election—A997

1984, Mar. 24 **Photo.** *Perf. 13*

1927 A997 2fr multi 75 10

Foreign Legion—A998

1984, Apr. 30 **Engr.** *Perf. 13x12½*

1928 A998 3.10fr multi 95 38

40th Anniv. of Liberation—A999

1984, May 8 **Photo. & Engr.** *Perf. 12½x13*

1929 A999 2fr Resistance 60 30
1930 A999 3fr Landing 90 45

Se-tenant with label showing Order of Liberation emblem.

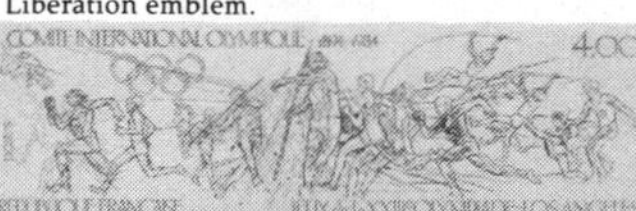

Olympic Events—A1000

1984, June 1 *Perf. 13*

1931 A1000 4fr multi 1.50 75

Intl. Olympic Committee, 90th anniv. and 1984 Summer Olympics.

Engraving—A1001

1984, June 8 **Engr.**

1932 A1001 2fr multi 60 15

Bordeaux—A1002

1984, June 9 *Perf. 13x12½*

1933 A1002 2fr red 60 15

French Philatelic Societies Congress, Bordeaux.

Natl. Telecommunications College, 40th Anniv.—A1003

1984, June 16 **Photo.** *Perf. 13*

1934 A1003 3fr Satellite, phone, keyboard 90 30

25th Intl. Geography Congress, Paris—A1004

1984, Aug. 25 **Engr.** *Perf. 13x12½*

1935 A1004 3fr Alps 1.00 30

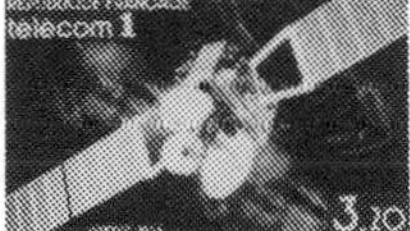

Telecom I Satellite—A1005

1984, Sept. 1 **Photo.** *Perf. 13*

1936 A1005 3.20fr multi 1.10 30

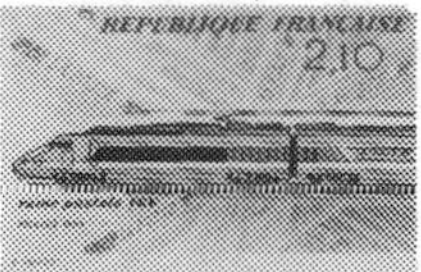

High-speed Train Mail Transport—A1006

1984, Sept. 8

1937 A1006 2.10fr Electric train, Paris-Lyon 75 22

Local Birds A1007

Marx Dormoy (1888-1941) A1008

1984, Sept. 22 **Photo. & Engr.** *Perf. 12½x12*

1938 A1007 1fr Gypaetus barbatus 30 22
1939 A1007 2fr Circaetus gallicus 75 22
1940 A1007 3fr Accipiter nisus 90 30
1941 A1007 5fr Peregrine falcon 1.50 45

1984, Sept. 22 **Engr.** *Perf. 13*

1942 A1008 2.40fr multi 75 18

100th Anniv. of the Automobile—A1009

1984, Oct. 6 **Engr.** *Perf. 12½x13*

1943 A1009 3fr Plans for automobile 95 18

Pres. Vincent Auriol (1884-1966)—A1010

1984, Nov. 3

1944 A1010 2.10fr multi 65 10

9th 5-Year Plan—A1011

1984, Dec. 8 **Photo.** *Perf. 13*

1945 A1011 2.10fr dk bl & scar 75 10

French Language Promotion—A1012

1985, Jan. 15 **Engr.** *Perf. 12½x13*

1946 A1012 3fr multi 90 18

Tourism Issue

View of Vienne—A1013

Cathedral at Montpelier—A1014

St. Michel de Cuxa (Codalet) Abbey—A1015

Talmont Church, Saintonge Romane—A1016

Solutre—A1017

1985 *Perf. 13x12½*

1947 A1013 1.70fr ol blk & dk grn 50 8
1948 A1014 2.10fr sep & org 65 10
1949 A1015 2.20fr multi 65 10
1950 A1016 3fr multi 75 12
1951 A1017 3.90fr multi 1.00 18
Nos. 1947-1951 (5) 3.55 58

Issue dates: 1.70fr, Jan. 19; 2.10fr, Mar. 30; 2.20fr, July 6; 3fr, June 15; 3.90fr, Sept. 28.

French TV, 50th Anniv.—A1018

1985, Jan. 26 **Photo.** *Perf. 13*

1952 A1018 2.50fr multi 75 10

Months of the Year—A1019

Designs: 1.22fr, January. 1.57fr, February. 2.55fr, March. 4.23fr, April.

1985, Feb. 11 **Engr.**

1953 A1019 1.22fr brt pur & blk 45 5
1954 A1019 1.57fr dp bl & sl bl 50 6
1955 A1019 2.55fr dk ol grn & dk brn 80 10
1956 A1019 4.23fr org brn & dk ol grn 1.50 18

Nos. 1953-1956 are known only precanceled. See second note after No. 132.

1986, Feb. 10 **Engr.** ***Perf. 13***

Designs: 1.28fr, May. 1.65fr, June. 2.67fr, July. 4.44fr, August.

1957 A1019 1.28fr sage grn & lil rose 35 8
1958 A1019 1.65fr Prus bl & brt yel grn 45 10
1959 A1019 2.67fr dk red & saph 75 15
1960 A1019 4.44fr dk ol bis & org 1.25 25

Nos. 1957-1960 are known only precanceled. See second note after No. 132.

1987, Feb. 16 **Engr.** ***Perf.***

Designs: 1.31fr, September. 1.69fr, October. 2.74fr, November. 4.56fr, December.

1961 A1019 1.31fr 45 10
1962 A1019 1.69fr 58 12
1963 A1019 2.74fr 92 18
1964 A1019 4.56fr 1.55 32

Nos. 1961-1964 are known only precanceled. See second note after No. 132.

St. Valentine, by Raymond Peynet—A1020

1985, Feb. 14 **Photo.** ***Perf. 13x12½***

1965 A1020 2.10fr multi 65 10

Pauline Kergomard (1838-1925)—A1021

1985, Mar. 8 **Engr.** ***Perf. 13x12½***

1966 A1021 1.70fr int bl & cop red 55 8

Art Issue

Stained Glass Window, Strasbourg Cathedral—A1022

Still-life with Candle, Nicolas de Stael—A1023

Perf. 12x13, 13x12

1985 **Engr.** **Photo. (#1968)**

1967 A1022 5fr multi 1.50 22
1968 A1023 5fr multi 1.50 22

Issue dates: No. 1967, Apr. 13; No. 1968, June 1.

Untitled Abstract by Jean Dubuffet—A1024

Octopus Overlaid on Manuscript, by Pierre Alechinsky—A1025

1985 **Photo.; Engr. (#1970)** ***Perf. 13x12½***

1969 A1024 5fr multi 1.40 24
1970 A1025 5fr multi 1.40 24

Issue dates: No. 1969, Sept. 14; No. 1970, Oct. 12.

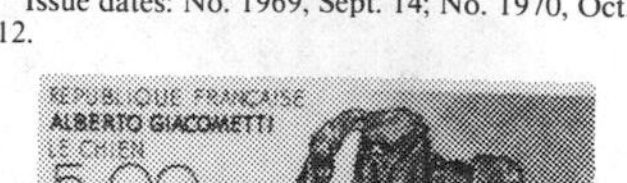

The Dog, Abstract by Alberto Giacometti (1901-1966)—A1026

1985, Dec. 7 **Engr.** ***Perf. 13x12½***

1971 A1026 5fr grnsh blk & lt lem 1.25 25

Housing in Givors—A1027

Contemporary architecture by Jean Renaude.

1985, Apr. 20 **Engr.** ***Perf. 13***

1972 A1027 2.40fr blk, yel org & ol grn 55 12

Landevennec Abbey, 1500th Anniv.—A1028

1985, Apr. 20 ***Perf. 13x12½***

1973 A1028 1.70fr grn & brn vio 40 8

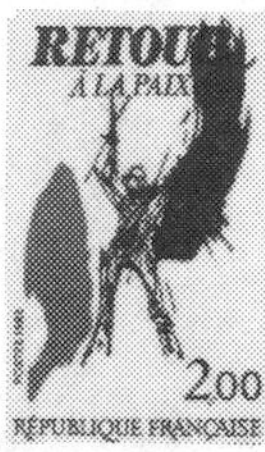

Europa 1985

A1029 Composers

Liberation of France from German Occupation Forces, 40th Anniv. A1030

1985, Apr. 27 ***Perf. 12½x13***

1974 A1029 2.10fr Adam de la Halle (1240-1285), composer 45 10
1975 A1029 3fr Darius Milhaud (1892-1974), composer 65 14

1985, May 8 ***Perf. 13x12½***

1976 A1030 2fr Return of peace 45 10
1977 A1030 3fr Return of liberty 65 14
a. Pair with label 1.10

Nos. 1976-1977 se-tenant with central label inscribed for 40th anniv. of the victory.

Natl. Philatelic Congress, Tours—A1031

1985, May 25 ***Perf. 12½x13***

1978 A1031 2.10fr Tours Cathedral 46 10

Rabies Vaccine Cent.—A1032

1985, June 1 ***Perf. 13x12½***

1979 A1032 1.50fr Pasteur inoculating patient 32 6

Mystere Falcon-900—A1033

1985, June 1 ***Perf. 13***

1980 A1033 10fr blue 2.15 45

Lake Geneva Life-Saving Society Cent.—A1034

1985, June 15

1981 A1034 2.50fr brt ultra & blk 55 12

United Nations, 40th Anniv.—A1035

1985, June 26 ***Perf. 13x12½***

1982 A1035 3fr multi 65 14

Huguenot Cross—A1036

1985, Aug. 31 **Engr.** ***Perf. 12½x13***

1983 A1036 2.50fr dp vio, dk red brn & dk red 60 12

King Louis XIV revoked the Edict of Nantes on Oct. 18, 1685, dispossessing French Protestants of religious and civil liberty.

Trees—A1037

Trees, leaves and fruit of the beech, elm, oak and pine varieties.

1985, Sept. 21 **Engr.** ***Perf. 12½***

1984 A1037 1fr shown 25 5
1985 A1037 2fr Ulmus montana 50 10
1986 A1037 3fr Quercus pedunculata 75 15
1987 A1037 5fr Picea abies 1.25 25

La France Mourning the Dead, Eternal Flame A1038

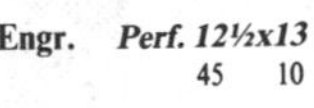

Charles Dullin, 1885-1949, Impressario, Theater A1039

1985, Nov. 2 **Engr.** ***Perf. 12½x13***

1988	A1038 1.80fr		45	10

Memorial Day.

1985, Nov. 9 **Engr.**

1989	A1039 3.20fr		80	16

National Information System—A1040

1985, Nov. 16 **Engr.** ***Perf. 13x12½***

1990	A1040 2.20fr		55	12

Thai Ambassadors at the Court of King Louis XIV, Painting—A1041

1986, Jan. 25 **Engr.** ***Perf. 13***

1991	A1041 3.20fr	rose lake & blk	85	18

Normalization of diplomatic relations with Thailand, 300th anniv.

Leisure, by Fernand Leger—A1042

1986, Feb. 1 **Photo.** ***Perf. 13***

1992	A1042 2.20fr	multi	60	12

1936 Popular Front, 50th anniv.

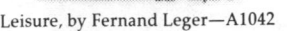

Venice Carnival, Paris—A1043

1986, Feb. 12 ***Perf. 12½x13***

1993	A1043 2.20fr	multi	60	12

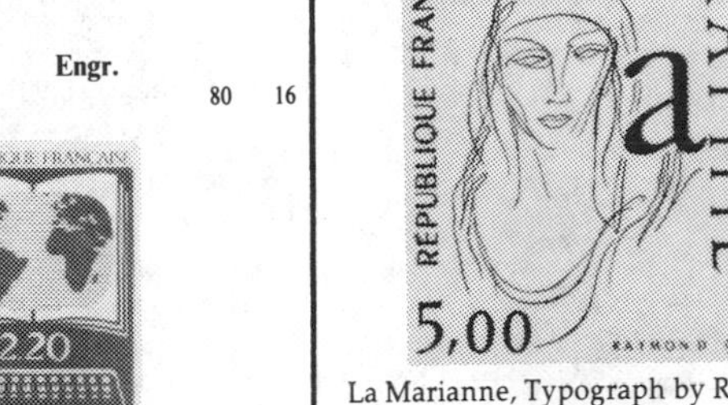

La Marianne, Typograph by Raymond Gid—A1044

1986, Mar.3 Photo. & Engr. ***Perf.12½x13½***

1994	A1044	5fr blk & dk red	1.50	30

Tourism Series

Filitosa, South Corsica—A1045

Loches Chateau—A1046

Norman Manor, St. Germain de Livet A1047

Notre-Dame-en-Vaux Monastery, Marne—A1048

Market Square, Bastide de Monpazier, Dordogne—A1049

1986 **Engr.** ***Perf. 13, 13x12½ (#1999)***

1995	A1045	1.80fr multi	52	10
1996	A1046	2fr int bl & blk	60	12
1997	A1047	2.20fr grnsh bl, brn & grn	65	14
1998	A1048	2.50fr HENNA brn & sep	75	15
1999	A1049	3.90fr blk & yel org	1.10	22

Issue dates: 2fr, June 14; 2.50fr, June 9. 1.80fr, 3.90fr, July 5.

Louise Michel (1830-1905), Anarchist—A1050

1986, Mar. 10 **Engr.**

2000	A1050 1.80fr	dk red & gray blk	38	8

City of Science and Industry, La Villette—A1051

1986, Mar. 17

2001	A1051 3.90fr	multi	85	18

Center for Modern Asia-Africa Studies—A1052

1986, Apr. 12 **Photo.** ***Perf. 13***

2002	A1052 3.20fr	Map	90	18

Art Series

Skibet,Abstract by Maurice Esteve—A1053

1986, Apr. 14 **Photo.** ***Perf. 12½x13***

2003	A1053	5fr multi	1.10	22

Virginia, Abstract by Alberto Magnelli—A1054

1986, June 25 **Photo.** ***Perf. 13x12½***

2004	A1054	5fr multi	1.40	28

Abstract, by Pierre Soulages—A1055

1986, Dec. 22 **Engr.** ***Perf. 13x12½***

2005	A1055	5fr brt vio, blk & brn gray	1.55	32

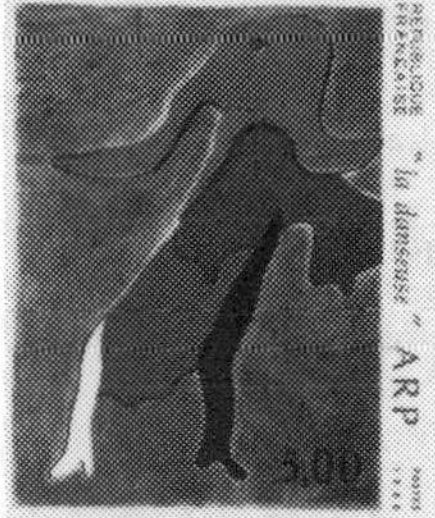

The Dancer, by Jean Arp—A1056

1986 , Nov. 10. **Photo.** ***Perf. 12½x13***

2006	A1056	5fr multi	1.50	30

Isabelle d'Este, by Leonardo da Vinci—A1057

1986, Nov. 10 **Engr.**

2007	A1057	5fr blk, red brn & grnsh yel	1 60	32

Victor Basch (1863-1944),IPY Emblem

1986, Apr. 28 **Engr.** ***Perf. 13***
2008 A1058 2.50fr blk & yel grn 55 12

International Peace Year.

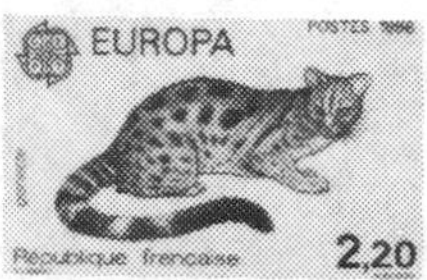

Europa 1986—A1059

1986, Apr. 28 ***Perf.***
2009 A1059 2.20fr Civet cat 48 10
2010 A1059 3.20fr Bat 68 14

St. Jean-Marie Vianney, Curé of Ars—A1060

1986, May 3 **Engr.** ***Perf. 13x12½***
2011 A1060 1.80fr sep, brn org & brn 52 10

Philatelic Societies Federation Congress, Nancy—A1061

1986, May 17 ***Perf. 13***
2012 A1061 2.20fr Exposition Center 62 12

Men's World Volleyball Championships A1062

Statue of Liberty, Cent. A1063

1986, May 24 **Engr.** ***Perf. 13***
2013 A1062 2.20fr dk vio, brn vio & scar 62 12

1986, July 4 ***Perf. 13***
2014 A1063 2.20fr scar & dk bl 62 12

See US No. 2224.

1st Ascent of Mt. Blanc, 1786—A1064

1986, Aug. 8 **Engr.** ***Perf. 13x12½***
2015 A1064 2fr J. Balmat, M.G. Paccard 60 12

Pierre-Louis Moreau de Maupertuis (1698-1759), La Condamine and Sextant—A1065

1986, Sept. 5
2016 A1065 3fr lt bl, int bl & brt ultra 88 18

Lapland Expedition, 250th anniv., proved Earth's poles are flattened.

See Finland No. 741.

Marcassite—A1066

1986, Sept. 13 ***Perf. 12½***
2017 A1066 2fr shown 60 12
2018 A1066 3fr Quartz 88 18
2019 A1066 4fr Calcite 1.20 24
2020 A1066 5fr Fluorite 1.50 30

Souvenir Sheet

Natl. Film Industry, 50th Anniv.—A1067

Personalities and film scenes: No. 2021a, Louis Feuillade, The Vampires. No. 2021b, Max Linder. No. 2021c, Sacha Guitry, Romance of the Trickster. No. 2021d, Jean Renoir, The Great Illusion. No. 2021e, Marcel Pagnol, The Baker's Woman. No. 2021f, Jean Epstein, The Three-Sided Mirror. No. 2021g, Rene Clair, Women of the Night. No. 2021h, Jean Gremillon, Talk of Love. No. 2021i, Jacques Becker, Helmet of Gold. No. 2021j, Francois Truffaut, The Young Savage.

1986, Sept. 20 **Photo.** ***Perf. 13x12½***
2021 Sheet of 10 6.50 6.50
a.-j. 2.20fr, any single 65 65

No. 2021 has a multicolored inscribed margin picturing film clips. Size:

Scene from Le Grand Meaulnes, by Henry Alain-Fournier (b. 1886), Novelist A1068

Professional Education, Cent. A1069

1986, Oct. 4 **Engr.** ***Perf. 12½x13***
2022 A1068 2.20fr blk & dk red 68 14

1986, Oct. 4
2023 A1069 1.90fr brt vio & dp lil rose 58 12

World Energy Conference, Cannes—A1070

1986, Oct. 5 **Photo.** ***Perf. 13***
2024 A1070 3.40fr multi 1.10 22

Mulhouse Technical Museum—A1071

1986, Dec. 1 **Engr.**
2025 A1071 2.20fr int bl, dk red & blk 70 14

Museum at Orsay, Opening—A1072

1986, Dec. 10 **Photo.**
2026 A1072 3.70fr BLSH blk & pck bl 1.15 24

Fulgence Bienvenue (1852-1934), and the Metro—A1073

1987, Jan. 17 **Engr.** ***Perf.***
2027 A1073 2.50fr vio. brn, brn & dk grn 80 16

Raoul Follereau (1903-1977), Care for Lepers—A1074

1987, Jan. 24 ***Perf.***
2028 A1074 1.90fr grn & grnsh blk 60 12

Cutlery Industry, Thiers—A1075

1987, Mar. 7 **Engr.** ***Perf.***
2029 A1075 1.90fr 65 14

Tourism Series

Redon, Ille et Vilaine—A1076

1987, Mar. 7 **Engr.** ***Perf.***
2030 A1076 2.20fr 75 20

Jean Jenneret Le Corbusier (1887-1965), Architect—A1081

1987, Apr. 11	**Photo.**	***Perf.***	
2035 A1081 3.70fr Abstract		1.25	32

Europa 1987—A1082

Modern architecture: 2.20fr, Metal factory at Boulogne-Billancourt, by architect Claude Vasconi. 3.40fr, Rue Mallet-Stevens housing, by Rob Mallet-Stevens.

1987, Apr. 25	**Engr.**	***Perf.***	
2036 A1082 2.20fr		75	20
2037 A1082 3.40fr		1.15	30

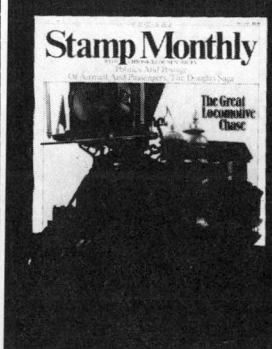

INDEX of Commemorative Issues

SEMI-POSTAL STAMPS.

SP1

SP2

Red Surcharge on No. B1

Typographed

1914 ***Perf. 14x13½*** **Unwmkd.**

No.	Type	Description	Unused	Used
B1	SP1	10c +5c red	6.75	5.50
B2	SP2	10c +5c red	42.50	3.75
a.		Bklt. pane of 10	625.00	

Issue dates: No. B1, Aug. 11; No. B2, Sept. 10.

Widow at Grave

SP3

War Orphans

SP4

Woman Plowing

SP5

"Trench of Bayonets"

SP6

Lion of Belfort

SP7

"La Marseillaise"

SP8

1917-19

No.	Type	Description	Unused	Used
B3	SP3	2c +3c vio brn	4.50	4.50
B4	SP4	5c +5c grn ('19)	14.00	6.75
B5	SP5	15c +10c gray grn	22.50	22.50
B6	SP5	25c +15c dp bl	95.00	55.00
B7	SP6	35c +25c sl & vio	150.00	120.00
B8	SP7	50c +50c pale brn & dk brn	250.00	190.00
B9	SP8	1fr +1fr cl & mar	450.00	350.00
B10	SP8	5fr +5fr dp bl & blk	1,800.	1,250.
		Nos. B3-B10 (8)	2,786.	1,998.75

Hospital Ship and Field Hospital

SP9

1918, Aug.

No.	Type	Description	Unused	Used
B11	SP9	15c +5c sl & red	180.00	67.50

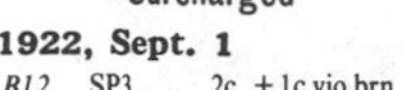

Semi-Postal Stamps of 1917-19 Surcharged

+5c

1922, Sept. 1

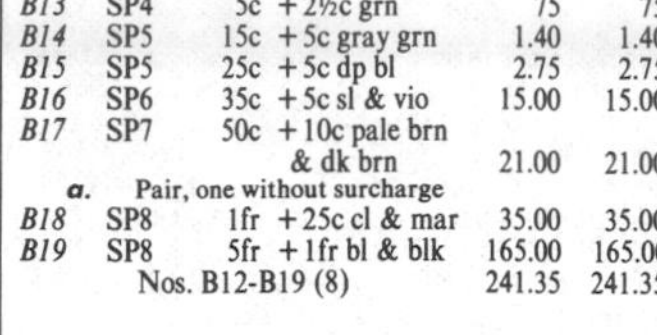

No.	Type	Description	Unused	Used
B12	SP3	2c +1c vio brn	45	45
B13	SP4	5c +2½c grn	75	75
B14	SP5	15c +5c gray grn	1.40	1.40
B15	SP5	25c +5c dp bl	2.75	2.75
B16	SP6	35c +5c sl & vio	15.00	15.00
B17	SP7	50c +10c pale brn & dk brn	21.00	21.00
a.		Pair, one without surcharge		
B18	SP8	1fr +25c cl & mar	35.00	35.00
B19	SP8	5fr +1fr bl & blk	165.00	165.00
		Nos. B12-B19 (8)	241.35	241.35

Style and arrangement of surcharge differs for each denomination.

Types of 1917-19.

1926-27

No.	Type	Description	Unused	Used
B20	SP3	2c +1c vio brn	1.10	1.10
B21	SP7	50c +10c ol brn & dk brn	30.00	12.50
B22	SP8	1fr +25c dp rose & red brn	67.50	40.00
B23	SP8	5fr +1fr sl bl & blk	125.00	100.00

Sinking Fund Issues.

Types of Regular Issues of 1903-07 Surcharged in Red or Blue

Caisse d'Amortissement +10c

1927, Sept. 26

No.	Type	Description	Unused	Used
B24	A22	40c +10c lt bl (R)	6.00	6.00
B25	A20	50c +25c grn (Bl)	9.00	9.00

Type of Regular Issue of 1923 Surcharged in Black

C A +50c

No.	Type	Description	Unused	Used
B26	A23	1.50fr +50c org	14.00	14.00

Industry and Agriculture

SP10

1928, May **Engraved** ***Perf. 13½***

No.	Type	Description	Unused	Used
B27	SP10	1.50fr +8.50fr dl bl	150.00	150.00
a.		bl grn	400.00	400.00

Types of 1903-23 Issues Surcharged as in 1927.

1928, Oct. 1 ***Perf. 14x13½***

No.	Type	Description	Unused	Used
B28	A22	40c +10c gray lil (R)	11.00	11.00
B29	A20	50c +25c org brn (Bl)	32.50	30.00
B30	A23	1.50fr +50c rose lil (Bk)	45.00	40.00

Types of 1903-23 Issues Surcharged as in 1927.

1929, Oct. 1

No.	Type	Description	Unused	Used
B31	A22	40c +10c grn	19.00	16.00
B32	A20	50c +25c lil rose	32.50	27.50
B33	A23	1.50fr +50c chnt	60.00	55.00

"The Smile of Reims"

SP11

1930, Mar. 15 **Engraved** ***Perf. 13***

No.	Type	Description	Unused	Used
B34	SP11	1.50fr +3.50fr red vio	90.00	90.00
a.		Bklt. pane of 4	400.00	400.00

Types of 1903-07 Issues Surcharged

Caisse d'Amortissement +10c

1930, Oct. 1 ***Perf. 14x13½***

No.	Type	Description	Unused	Used
B35	A22	40c +10c cer	22.50	19.00
B36	A20	50c +25c gray brn	45.00	32.50
B37	A22	1.50fr +50c vio	75.00	62.50

Allegory, French Provinces

SP12

1931, Mar. 1 ***Perf. 13***

No.	Type	Description	Unused	Used
B38	SP12	1.50fr +3.50fr grn	165.00	165.00

Types of 1903-07 Issues Surcharged

Caisse d'Amortissement +10c

1931, Oct. 1 ***Perf. 14x13½***

No.	Type	Description	Unused	Used
B39	A22	40c +10c ol grn	37.50	32.50
B40	A20	50c +25c gray vio	120.00	90.00
B41	A22	1.50fr +50c dp red	120.00	110.00

"France" Giving Aid to an Intellectual

SP13

Symbolic of Music

SP14

1935, Dec. 9 **Engraved** ***Perf. 13***

No.	Type	Description	Unused	Used
B42	SP13	50c +10c ultra	4.50	2.50
B43	SP14	50c +2fr dl red	70.00	47.50

The surtax was for the aid of distressed and exiled intellectuals.

Statue of Liberty

SP15

Children of the Unemployed

SP16

1936-37

No.	Type	Description	Unused	Used
B44	SP15	50c +25c dk bl ('37)	5.25	4.00
B45	SP15	75c +50c vio	12.50	7.50

The surtax was for the aid of political refugees.

1936, May

No.	Type	Description	Unused	Used
B46	SP16	50c +10c cop red	7.50	4.75

The surtax was for the aid of children of the unemployed.

Type of 1935 Semi-Postal Surcharged in Black

+20c

1936, Nov.

No.	Type	Description	Unused	Used
B47	SP14	20c on 50c+2fr dl red	4.50	3.75

Jacques Callot

SP17

Anatole France (Jacques Anatole Thibault)

SP18

Hector Berlioz

SP19

Victor Hugo

SP20

Auguste Rodin

SP21

Louis Pasteur

SP22

1936-37 **Engraved**

No.	Type	Description	Unused	Used
B48	SP17	20c +10c brn car	3.25	3.00
B49	SP18	30c +10c emer ('37)	3.75	2.25
B50	SP19	40c +10c emer	4.00	3.25
B51	SP20	50c +10c cop red	6.00	3.25
B52	SP21	90c +10c rose red ('37)	8.25	5.50
B53	SP22	1.50fr +50c dp ultra	32.50	20.00
		Nos. B48-B53 (6)	57.75	37.25

The surtax was used for relief of unemployed intellectuals.

1938

No.	Type	Description	Unused	Used
B54	SP18	30c +10c brn car	2.25	2.25
B55	SP17	35c +10c dl grn	3.75	3.00
B56	SP19	55c +10c dl vio	6.75	3.75
B57	SP20	65c +10c ultra	6.75	4.00
B58	SP21	1fr +10c car lake	6.75	4.00
B59	SP22	1.75fr +25c dp bl	19.00	10.50
		Nos. B54-B59 (6)	45.25	27.50

Tug of War
SP23

Foot Race
SP24

Hiking
SP25

1937, June 16

B60	SP23	20c +10c brn	3.00	2.25
B61	SP24	40c +10c red brn	3.00	2.25
B62	SP25	50c +10c blk brn	3.00	2.25

The surtax was for the Recreation Fund of the employees of the Post, Telephone and Telegraph.

Pierre Loti
(Louis Marie Julien Viaud)
SP26

1937, Aug.

B63	SP26	50c +20c rose car	4.50	3.25

The surtax was for the Pierre Loti Monument Fund.

"France" and Infant
SP27

1937–39

B64	SP27	65c +25c brn vio	3.25	2.50
B65	SP27	90c +30c pck bl ('39)	2.25	1.75

The surtax was used for public health work.

Winged Victory of Samothrace
SP28

Jean Baptiste Charcot
SP29

1937, Aug.

B66	SP28	30c bl grn	95.00	45.00
B67	SP28	55c red	95.00	45.00

On sale at the Louvre for 2.50 fr. The surtax of 1.65 fr. was for the benefit of the Louvre Museum.

1938-39

B68	SP29	65c +35c dk bl grn	1.75	1.75
B69	SP29	90c +35c brt red vio ('39)	10.50	9.00

The surtax was for the benefit of French seamen.

Palace of Versailles
SP30

1938, May 9

B70	SP30	1.75fr +75c dp bl	22.50	18.00

Issued in commemoration of the National Exposition of Painting and Sculpture at Versailles. The surtax was for the benefit of the Versailles Concert Society.

French Soldier
SP31

Monument
SP32

1938, May 16

B71	SP31	55c +70c brn vio	5.25	3.75
B72	SP31	65c +1.10fr pck bl	5.25	3.75

The surtax was for a fund to erect a monument to the glory of the French Infantrymen.

1938, May 25

B73	SP32	55c +45c ver	12.00	9.00

The surtax was for a fund to erect a monument in honor of the Army Medical Corps.

Reims Cathedral
SP33

"France" Welcoming Her Sons
SP34

1938, July 10

B74	SP33	65c +35c ultra	10.50	9.00

Issued to commemorate the completion of the reconstruction of Reims Cathedral, July 10, 1938.

1938, Aug. 8

B75	SP34	65c +60c rose car	6.75	5.25

The surtax was for the benefit of French volunteers repatriated from Spain.

Curie Issue
Common Design Type

1938, Sept. 1

B76	CD80	1.75fr +50c dp ultra	9.50	8.25

Victory Parade
Passing Arc de Triomphe
SP36

1938, Oct. 8

B77	SP36	65c +35c brn car	6.00	4.50

20th anniversary of the Armistice.

Student and Nurse—SP37

1938, Dec. 1

B78	SP37	65c +60c pck bl	7.50	5.25

The surtax was for Student Relief.

Blind Man and Radio
SP38

1938, Dec.

B79	SP38	90c +25c brn vio	8.25	6.25

The surtax was used to help provide radios for the blind.

Civilian Facing Firing Squad
SP39

Red Cross Nurse
SP40

1939, Feb. 1

B80	SP39	90c +35c blk brn	8.25	6.75

The surtax was used to erect a monument to civilian victims of World War I.

1939, Mar. 24

B81	SP40	90c +35c dk sl grn, turq bl & red	7.00	5.50

Issued in commemoration of the 75th anniversary of the founding of the International Red Cross Society.

Army Engineer—SP41

1939, Apr. 3

B82	SP41	70c +50c ver	7.00	5.50

Issued in honor of the Army Engineering Corps. The surtax was used to erect a monument to those members who died in World War I.

Ministry of Post, Telegraph and Telephone
SP42

1939, Apr. 8

B83	SP42	90c +35c turq bl	18.00	13.00

The surtax was used to aid orphans of employees of the postal system. Issued to commemorate the opening of the new building for the Ministry of Post, Telegraph and Telephones.

Mother and Child
SP43

Eiffel Tower
SP44

1939, Apr. 24

B84	SP43	90c +35c red	3.25	2.50

The surtax was used to aid children of the unemployed.

1939, May 5

B85	SP44	90c +50c red vio	9.00	6.75

Issued in commemoration of the 50th anniversary of the Eiffel Tower. The surtax was used for celebration festivities.

Puvis de Chavannes
SP45

Claude Debussy
SP46

Honoré de Balzac
SP47

Claude Bernard
SP48

1939–40

B86	SP45	40c	+10c ver	1.50	1.25
B87	SP46	70c	+10c brn vio	1.90	1.65
B87A	SP46	80c	+10c brn vio ('40)	3.00	3.00
B88	SP47	90c	+10c brt red vio	3.00	2.50
B88A	SP47	1fr	+10c brt red vio ('40)	3.00	3.00
B89	SP48	2.25fr	+25c brt ultra	9.25	5.00
B89A	SP48	2.50fr	+25c brt ultra ('40)	3.00	3.00
		Nos. B86-B89A (7)		24.65	19.40

The surtax was used to aid unemployed intellectuals.

Mothers and Children
SP49 SP50

1939, June 15

B90	SP49	70c	+80c bl, grn & vio	3.75	3.25
B91	SP50	90c	+60c dk brn, dl vio & brn	4.50	4.00

The surtax was used to aid France's repopulation campaign.

"The Letter" by Jean Honoré Fragonard
SP51

Statue of Widow and Children
SP52

1939, July 6

B92	SP51	40c	+60c brn, sep & pur	4.50	3.75

The surtax was used for the Postal Museum.

1939, July 20

B93	SP52	70c	+30c brn vio	9.00	6.75

The surtax was for the benefit of French seamen.

French Soldier
SP53

Colonial Trooper
SP54

1940, Feb. 15

B94	SP53	40c	+60c sep	1.75	1.25
B95	SP54	1fr	+50c turq bl	1.75	1.25

The surtax was used to assist the families of mobilized men.

World Map Showing French Possessions
SP55

1940, Apr. 15

B96	SP55	1fr	+25c scar	3.00	2.25

Marshal Joseph J .C. Joffre
SP56

Marshal Ferdinand Foch
SP57

Gen. Joseph S. Gallieni
SP58

Woman Plowing
SP59

1940, May 1

B97	SP56	80c	+45c choc	3.00	3.00
B98	SP57	1fr	+50c dk vio	3.25	3.25
B99	SP58	1.50fr	+50c brn red	3.25	3.25
B100	SP59	2.50fr	+50c ind & dl bl	4.00	4.00

The surtax was used for war charities.

Doctor, Nurse, Soldier and Family
SP60

Nurse and Wounded Soldier
SP61

1940, May 12

B101	SP60	80c	+1fr dk grn & red	6.25	4.50
B102	SP61	1fr	+2fr sep & red	6.25	4.50

The surtax was used for the Red Cross.

Nurse with Injured Children
SP62

1940, Nov. 12

B103	SP62	1fr	+2fr sep	1.10	90

The surtax was used for victims of the war.

Wheat Harvest
SP63

Sowing
SP64

Picking Grapes
SP65

Grazing Cattle
SP66

1940, Dec. 2

B104	SP63	80c	+2fr brn blk	1.90	1.65
B105	SP64	1fr	+2fr chnt	1.90	1.65
B106	SP65	1.50fr	+2fr brt vio	1.90	1.65
B107	SP66	2.50fr	+2fr dp grn	2.25	1.75

The surtax was for national relief.

Prisoners of War
SP67 SP68

1941, Jan. 1

B108	SP67	80c	+5fr dk grn	1.25	1.25
B109	SP68	1fr	+5fr rose brn	1.25	1.25

The surtax was for prisoners of war.

Science Fighting Cancer
SP69

1941, Feb. 20

B110	SP69	2.50fr	+50c sl blk & brn	1.40	1.40

The surtax was used for the control of cancer.

Type of 1941 Surcharged "+10c" in Blue.

1941, Mar. 4

B111	A109	1fr	+10c crim	18	18

Men Hauling Coal
SP70

"France" Aiding Needy Man
SP71

1941

B112	SP70	1fr	+2fr sep	1.10	90
B113	SP71	2.50fr	+7.50fr dk bl	4.00	2.00

The surtax was for Marshal Pétain's National Relief Fund.

Liner Pasteur
SP72

Red Surcharge

1941, July 17

B114	SP72	1fr	+1fr on 70c dk bl grn	18	18

World Map, Mercator Projection
SP73

1941

B115	SP73	1fr	+1fr multi	60	50

Fisherman
SP74

1941, Oct. 23

B116	SP74	1fr +9fr dk bl grn	1.00	1.00

Surtax for benefit of French seamen.

Arms of Various Cities.

Nancy
SP75

Lille
SP76

Rouen
SP77

Bordeaux
SP78

Toulouse
SP79

Clermont-Ferrand
SP80

Marseilles
SP81

Lyon
SP82

Rennes
SP83

Reims
SP84

Montpellier
SP85

Paris
SP86

1941 *Perf. 14x13.*

B117	SP75	20c +30c brn blk	2.75	2.75
B118	SP76	40c +60c org brn	3.00	3.00
B119	SP77	50c +70c grnsh bl	3.00	3.00
B120	SP78	70c +80c rose vio	3.00	3.00
B121	SP79	80c +1fr dp rose	3.00	3.00
B122	SP80	1fr +1fr blk	3.00	3.00
B123	SP81	1.50fr +2fr dk bl	3.00	3.00
B124	SP82	2fr +2fr dk vio	3.00	3.00
B125	SP83	2.50fr +3fr brt grn	3.00	3.00
B126	SP84	3fr +5fr org brn	3.00	3.00
B127	SP85	5fr +6fr brt ultra	3.00	3.00
B128	SP86	10fr +10fr dk red	3.25	3.25
		Nos. B117-B128 (12)	36.00	36.00

Count de La Pérouse
SP87

1942, Mar. 23 *Perf. 13*

B129	SP87	2.50fr +7.50fr ultra	1.00	1.00

Issued to commemorate the 200th anniversary of the birth of Jean Francois de Galaup de La Pérouse, (1741–1788), French navigator and explorer. The surtax was for National Relief.

Planes over Fields
SP88

1942, Apr. 4

B130	SP88	1.50fr +3.50fr lt vio	50	50

The surtax was for the benefit of French airmen and their families.

Alexis Chabrier
SP89

1942, May 18

B131	SP89	2fr +3fr sep	90	90

Emmanuel Chabrier (1841–1894), composer, birth centenary. The surtax was for works of charity among musicians.

Symbolical of French Colonial Empire
SP90

1942, May 18

B132	SP90	1.50fr +8.50fr blk	75	75

The surtax was for National Relief.

Jean de Vienne
SP91

1942, June 16

B133	SP91	1.50fr +8.50fr sep	90	90

Issued in commemoration of the 600th anniversary of the birth of Jean de Vienne, first admiral of France. The surtax was for the benefit of French seamen.

Type of Regular Issue, 1941 Surcharged in Carmine

+ 50

S N

1942, Sept. 10 *Perf. 14x13½*

B134	A116	1.50fr +50c brt ultra	15	15

The surtax was for national relief ("Secours National").

Arms of Various Cities.

Chambéry
SP92

La Rochelle
SP93

Poitiers
SP94

Orléans
SP95

Grenoble
SP96

Angers
SP97

Dijon
SP98

Limoges
SP99

Le Havre
SP100

Nantes
SP101

Nice
SP102

St. Etienne
SP103

Engraved.

1942, Oct. *Perf. 14x13* **Unwmkd.**

B135	SP92	50c +60c blk	3.00	3.00
B136	SP93	60c +70c grnsh bl	3.00	3.00
B137	SP94	80c +1fr rose	3.00	3.00
B138	SP95	1fr +1.30fr dk grn	3.25	3.25
B139	SP96	1.20fr +1.50fr rose vio	3.25	3.25
B140	SP97	1.50fr +1.80fr sl bl	3.25	3.25
B141	SP98	2fr +2.30fr dp rose	3.25	3.25
B142	SP99	2.40fr +2.80fr sl grn	3.25	3.25
B143	SP100	3fr +3.50fr dp vio	3.25	3.25
B144	SP101	4fr +5fr lt ultra	3.25	3.25
B145	SP102	4.50fr +6fr red	3.25	3.25
B146	SP103	5fr +7fr brt red vio	3.50	3.50
		Nos. B135-B146 (12)	38.50	38.50

The surtax was for national relief.

Tricolor Legion—SP104

1942, Oct. 12 *Perf. 13*

B147	SP104	1.20 +8.80fr dk bl	8.25	8.25
a.		Vert. strip of 3 (1 each Nos. B147, B148 + albino impression)	18.00	18.00
B148	SP104	1.20 +8.80fr crim	8.25	8.25

These stamps were printed in sheets of 20 stamps and 5 albino impressions arranged: 2 horizontal rows of 5 dark blue stamps, 1 row of 5 albino impressions, and 2 rows of 5 crimson stamps.

Marshal Henri Philippe Pétain
SP105 SP106

1943, Feb. 8

B149	SP105	1fr +10fr rose red	3.25	3.25
a.		Strip of 4 (1 each Nos. B149-B152 + label)	15.00	15.00
B150	SP105	1fr +10fr bl	3.25	3.25
B151	SP106	2fr +12fr rose red	3.25	3.25
B152	SP106	2fr +12fr bl	3.25	3.25

The surtax was for national relief. Printed in sheets of 20, the 10 blue stamps at left, the 10 rose red at right, separated by a vertical row of five white labels bearing a tri-colored battle-ax.

Marshal Pétain
SP107

"Work"
SP108

"Family"
SP109

"State"
SP110

Marshal Pétain
SP111

1943, June 7

B153	SP107	1.20fr	+1.40fr dl vio	12.50	12.50
a.	Strip of 5 (1 each Nos. B153 to B157)			67.50	67.50
B154	SP108	1.50fr	+2.50fr red	12.50	12.50
B155	SP109	2.40fr	+7fr brn	12.50	12.50
B156	SP110	4fr	+10fr dk vio	12.50	12.50
B157	SP111	5fr	+15fr red brn	12.50	12.50
	Nos. B153-B157 (5)			62.50	62.50

Issued to commemorate Pétain's 87th birthday.
The surtax was for national relief.
Printed in sheets of 25 (5x5). Each horizontal strip includes the five values, arranged by denomination.

Civilians Under Air Attack
SP112

Civilians Doing Farm Work
SP113

Prisoner's Family Doing Farm Work
SP114

1943, Aug. 23

B158	SP112	1.50fr	+3.50fr blk	55	55

Surtax was for bomb victims at Billancourt, Dunkirk, Lorient, Saint-Nazaire.

1943, Sept. 27

B159	SP113	1.50fr	+8.50fr sep	90	90
B160	SP114	2.40fr	+7.60fr dk grn	90	90

The surtax was for families of war prisoners.

Michel de Montaigne
SP115

Picardy Costume
SP121

Designs: 1.20fr+1.50fr, Francois Clouet. 1.50fr+3fr, Ambrose Paré. 2.40fr+4fr, Chevalier Pierre de Bayard. 4fr+6fr, Duke of Sully. 5fr+10fr, Henri IV.

1943, Oct. 2

B161	SP115	60c	+80c Prus grn	1.90	1.90
B162	SP115	1.20fr	+1.50fr blk	1.90	1.90
B163	SP115	1.50fr	+3fr dp ultra	1.90	1.90
B164	SP115	2.40fr	+4fr red	2.00	2.00
B165	SP115	4fr	+6fr dl brn red	2.50	2.50
B166	SP115	5fr	+10fr dl grn	2.50	2.50
	Nos. B161-B166 (6)			12.70	12.70

The surtax was for national relief. Issued to honor famous 16th century Frenchmen.

1943, Dec. 27

Designs: 18th Century Costumes: 1.20fr+2fr, Brittany. 1.50fr+4fr, Ile de France. 2.40+5fr, Burgundy. 4fr+6fr, Auvergne. 5fr+7fr, Provence.

B167	SP121	60c	+1.30fr sep	2.25	2.25
B168	SP121	1.20fr	+2fr lt vio	2.25	2.25
B169	SP121	1.50fr	+4fr turq bl	2.25	2.25
B170	SP121	2.40fr	+5fr rose car	2.25	2.25
B171	SP121	4fr	+6fr chlky bl	3.00	3.00
B172	SP121	5fr	+7fr red	3.00	3.00
	Nos. B167-B172 (6)			15.00	15.00

The surtax was for national relief.

Admiral Tourville
SP127

Charles Gounod
SP128

1944, Feb. 21

B173	SP127	4fr	+6fr dl red brn	55	55

Issued to commemorate the 300th anniversary of the birth of Admiral Anne-Hilarion de Cotentin Tourville (1642–1701).

1944, Mar. 27 ***Perf. 14x13***

B174	SP128	1.50fr	+3.50fr sep	30	30

Issued to commemorate the 50th anniversary of the death of Charles Gounod, composer (1818–1893).

Marshal Pétain
SP129

Farming
SP130

Industry
SP131

1944, Apr. 24 ***Perf. 13***

B175	SP129	1.50fr	+3.50fr sep	3.00	3.00
B176	SP130	2fr	+3fr dp ultra	60	60
B177	SP131	4fr	+6fr rose red	60	60

Marshal Henri Pétain's 88th birthday.

Modern Streamliner and 19th Century Train
SP132

Molière (Jean-Baptiste Poquelin)
SP133

1944, Aug. 14

B178	SP132	4fr	+6fr blk	1.65	1.65

Issued to commemorate the centenary of the Paris-Rouen, Paris-Orléans railroad.

1944, July 31

Designs: 80c+2.20fr, Jules Hardouin Mansart. 1.20fr+2.80fr, Blaise Pascal. 1.50fr+3.50fr, Louis II of Bourbon. 2fr+4fr, Jean-Baptiste Colbert. 4fr+6fr, Louis XIV.

B179	SP133	50c	+1.50fr rose car	1.25	1.25
B180	SP133	80c	+2.20fr dk grn	1.25	1.25
B181	SP133	1.20fr	+2.80fr blk	1.25	1.25
B182	SP133	1.50fr	+3.50fr brt ultra	1.25	1.25
B183	SP133	2fr	+4fr dl brn red	1.25	1.25
B184	SP133	4fr	+6fr red	1.25	1.25
	Nos. B179-B184 (6)			7.50	7.50

Noted 17th century Frenchmen.

French Cathedrals.

Angoulême
SP139

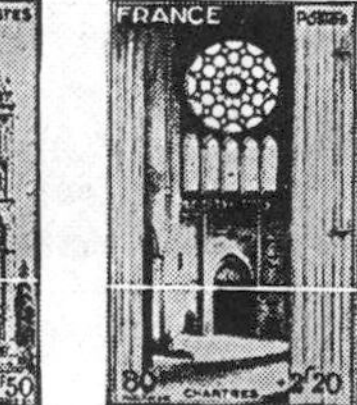

Chartres
SP140

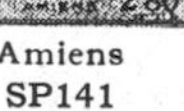

Amiens
SP141

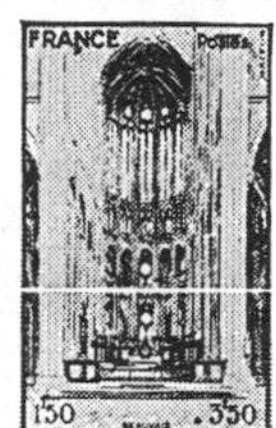

Beauvais
SP142

Albi
SP143

1944, Nov. 20

B185	SP139	50c	+1.50fr blk	30	30
B186	SP140	80c	+2.20fr rose vio	45	45
B187	SP141	1.20fr	+2.80fr brn car	65	65
B188	SP142	1.50fr	+3.50fr dp bl	65	65
B189	SP143	4fr	+6fr org red	65	65
	Nos. B185-B189 (5)			2.70	2.70

Coat of Arms of Renouard de Villayer
SP144

Sarah Bernhardt
SP145

1944, Dec. 9 **Engraved**

B190	SP144	1.50fr	+3.50fr dp brn	18	15

Stamp Day.

1945, May 16 ***Perf. 13*** **Unwmkd.**

B191	SP145	4fr	+1fr dk vio brn	30	30

Issued to commemorate the 100th anniversary of the birth of Sarah Bernhardt, actress.

War Victims
SP146

Tuberculosis Patient
SP147

1945, May 16

B192	SP146	4fr	+6fr dk vio brn	15	15

The surtax was for war victims of the P.T.T.

1945, May 16 Typo. ***Perf. 14x13½***

B193	SP147	2fr	+1fr red org	15	10

The surtax was for the aid of tuberculosis victims.

Boy and Girl
SP148

Burning of Oradour Church
SP149

1945, July 9 **Engraved** ***Perf. 13***

B194	SP148	4fr	+2fr Prus grn	18	18

The surtax was used for child welfare.

1945, Oct. 13

B195	SP149	4fr	+2fr sep	18	18

Destruction of Oradour, June, 1944.

Louis XI and Post Rider
SP150

1945, Oct. 13

B196	SP150	2fr	+3fr dp ultra	22	22

Stamp Day.

Ruins of Dunkirk
SP151

Ruins of Rouen—SP152

Ruins of Caen—SP153

Ruins of Saint-Malo
SP154

1945, Nov. 5

B197	SP151	1.50fr	+1.50fr red brn	25	25
B198	SP152	2fr	+2fr vio	25	25
B199	SP153	2.40fr	+2.60fr bl	25	25
B200	SP154	4fr	+4fr blk	25	25

The surtax was to aid the suffering residents of Dunkirk, Rouen, Caen and Saint Malo.

Alfred Fournier
SP155

Henri Becquerel
SP156

1946, Feb. 4 **Engraved** ***Perf. 13***

B201	SP155	2fr	+3fr red brn	18	18
B202	SP156	2fr	+3fr vio	18	18

Issued to raise funds for the fight against veneral disease (B201) and for the struggle against cancer (B202).

No. B202 commemorated the 50th anniversary of the discovery of radio-activity by Henri Becquerel.

See also No. B221.

Church of the Invalides,
Paris—SP157

1946, Mar. 11

B203	SP157	4fr	+6fr red brn	22	22

The surtax was to aid disabled war veterans.

French Warships
SP158

1946, Apr. 8

B204	SP158	2fr	+3fr gray blk	18	18

The surtax was for naval charities.

"The Letter"
by Jean Siméon
Chardin
SP159

Fouquet
de la Varane
SP160

1946, May 25

B205	SP159	2fr	+3fr brn red	38	38

The surtax was used for the Postal Museum.

1946, June 29

B206	SP160	3fr	+2fr sep	38	38

Stamp Day.

François Villon
SP161

Designs: 3fr+1fr, Jean Fouquet. 4fr+3fr, Philippe de Commynes. 5fr+4fr, Joan of Arc. 6fr+5fr, Jean de Gerson. 10fr+6fr, Charles VII.

1946, Oct. 28

B207	SP161	2fr	+1fr dk Prus grn	1.40	1.40
B208	SP161	3fr	+1fr dk bl vio	1.40	1.40
B209	SP161	4fr	+3fr hn brn	1.40	1.40
B210	SP161	5fr	+4fr ultra	1.40	1.40
B211	SP161	6fr	+5fr sep	1.40	1.40
B212	SP161	10fr	+6fr red	1.50	1.50
	Nos. B207-B212 (6)			8.50	8.50

Church of
St. Sernin,
Toulouse
SP167

Notre Dame
du Port,
Clermont-Ferrand
SP168

Cathedral of St. Front, Perigueux
SP169

Cathedral of St. Julien, Le Mans
SP170

Cathedral of
Notre Dame,
Paris
SP171

François Michel
le Tellier
de Louvois
SP172

1947 **Engraved**

B213	SP167	1fr	+1fr car rose	65	65
B214	SP168	3fr	+2fr dk bl vio	90	90
B215	SP169	4fr	+3fr hn brn	1.25	1.25
B216	SP170	6fr	+4fr dp bl	1.65	1.65
B217	SP171	10fr	+6fr dk gray grn	2.25	2.25
	Nos. B213-B217 (5)			6.70	6.70

1947, Mar. 15

B218	SP172	4.50fr	+5.50fr car rose	1.25	1.25

Stamp Day, March 15, 1947.

Submarine Pens, Shipyard
and Monument
SP173

1947, Aug. 2

B219	SP173	6fr	+4fr bluish blk	30	30

Issued to commemorate the British commando raid on the Nazi U-boat base at St. Nazaire, 1942.

Liberty
Highway Marker
SP174

Louis
Braille
SP175

1947, Sept. 5

B220	SP174	6fr	+4fr dk grn	45	45

The surtax was to help defray maintenance costs of the Liberty Highway.

Fournier Type of 1946

1947, Oct. 20

B221	SP155	2fr	+3fr ind	25	25

1948, Jan. 19

B222	SP175	6fr	+4fr pur	30	30

Etienne
Arago
SP176

Alphonse
de Lamartine
SP177

1948, Mar. 6

B223	SP176	6fr	+4fr blk brn	45	45

Stamp Day, March 6–7, 1948.

1948, Apr. 5 **Engraved** ***Perf. 13***

Designs: 3fr+2fr, Alexandre A. Ledru-Rollin. 4fr+3fr, Louis Blanc. 5fr+4fr, Albert (Alexandre Martin). 6fr+5fr, Pierre J. Proudhon. 10fr+6fr, Louis Auguste Blanqui. 15fr+7fr, Armand Barbés. 20fr+8fr, Dennis A. Affre.

B224	SP177	1fr	+1fr dk grn	1.40	1.40
B225	SP177	3fr	+2fr hn brn	1.50	1.50
B226	SP177	4fr	+3fr vio brn	1.50	1.50
B227	SP177	5fr	+4fr lt bl grn	1.90	1.90
B228	SP177	6fr	+5fr ind	1.90	1.90
B229	SP177	10fr	+6fr car rose	1.90	1.90
B230	SP177	15fr	+7fr sl blk	3.00	3.00
B231	SP177	20fr	+8fr pur	3.25	3.25
	Nos. B224-B231 (8)			16.35	16.35

Centenary of the Revolution of 1848.

Dr. Léon Charles Albert Calmette
SP178

1948, June 18

B232	SP178	6fr	+4fr dk grnsh bl	25	25

Issued to mark the first International Congress on the Calmette-Guerin bacillus vaccine.

Farmer
SP179

Designs: 5fr+3fr, Fisherman. 8fr+4fr, Miner. 10fr+6fr, Metal worker.

1949, Feb. 14

B233	SP179	3fr	+1fr cl	80	60
B234	SP179	5fr	+3fr dk bl	90	90
B235	SP179	8fr	+4fr ind	1.00	75
B236	SP179	10fr	+6fr dk red	1.40	1.10

Étienne François de Choiseul and Post Cart
SP180

Baron de la Brède et de Montesquieu
SP181

1949, Mar. 26

B237	SP180	15fr +5fr dk grn	1.25	1.25

Stamp Day, March 26–27, 1949.

1949, Nov. 14

Designs: 8fr+2fr, Voltaire. 10fr+3fr, Antoine Watteau. 12fr+4fr, Georges de Buffon. 15fr+5fr, Joseph F. Dupleix. 25fr+10fr, A. R. J. Turgot.

B238	SP181	5fr +1fr dk grn	4.50	4.50
B239	SP181	8fr +2fr ind	4.50	4.50
B240	SP181	10fr +3fr brn red	4.50	4.50
B241	SP181	12fr +4fr pur	4.50	4.50
B242	SP181	15fr +5fr rose car	6.00	6.00
B243	SP181	25fr +10fr ultra	6.00	6.00
		Nos. B238-B243 (6)	30.00	30.00

"Spring"
SP182

Designs: 8fr+2fr, Summer. 12fr+3fr, Autumn. 15fr+4fr, Winter.

1949, Dec. 19

B244	SP182	5fr +1fr grn	2.25	2.25
B245	SP182	8fr +2fr yel org	2.25	2.25
B246	SP182	12fr +3fr pur	3.00	3.00
B247	SP182	15fr +4fr dp bl	3.25	3.25

Postman
SP183

1950, Mar. 11

B248	SP183	12fr +3fr dp bl	3.75	3.00

Stamp Day, March 11–12, 1950.

André de Chénier
SP184

Alexandre Brongniart, Bust by Houdon
SP185

Portraits: 8fr+3fr, J. L. David. 10fr+4fr, Lazare Carnot. 12fr+5fr, G. J. Danton. 15fr+6fr, Maximilian Robespierre. 20fr+10fr, Louis Hoche.

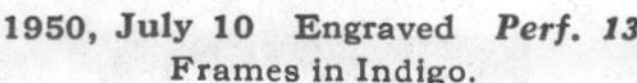

1950, July 10 Engraved *Perf. 13*

Frames in Indigo.

B249	SP184	5fr +2fr brn vio	9.50	9.50
B250	SP184	8fr +3fr blk brn	9.50	9.50
B251	SP184	10fr +4fr lake	9.50	9.50
B252	SP184	12fr +5fr red brn	10.50	10.50
B253	SP184	15fr +6fr dk grn	12.00	12.00
B254	SP184	20fr +10fr dk vio bl	12.00	12.00
		Nos. B249-B254 (6)	63.00	63.00

1950, Dec. 22

Design: 15fr–3fr, "L'Amour" by Etienne M. Falconet.

B255	SP185	8fr +2fr ind & car	3.00	3.00
B256	SP185	15fr +3fr red brn & car	3.00	3.00

The surtax was for the Red Cross.

Mail Car Interior
SP186

Alfred de Musset
SP187

1951, Mar. 10 *Perf. 13* Unwmkd.

B257	SP186	12fr +3fr lil gray	3.25	3.25

Stamp Day, March 10–11, 1951.

1951, June 2

Designs: 8fr+2fr, Eugène Delacroix. 10fr+3fr, J.-L. Gay-Lussac. 12fr+4fr, Robert Surcouf. 15fr+5fr, C. M. Talleyrand. 30fr+10fr, Napoleon I.

Frames in Dark Brown.

B258	SP187	5fr +1fr dk grn	8.25	8.25
B259	SP187	8fr +2fr vio brn	9.00	9.00
B260	SP187	10fr +3fr grnsh blk	9.25	9.25
B261	SP187	12fr +4fr dk vio brn	9.25	9.25
B262	SP187	15fr +5fr brn car	9.50	9.50
B263	SP187	30fr +10fr ind	14.00	14.00
		Nos. B258-B263 (6)	59.25	59.25

Child at Prayer by Le Maître de Moulins
SP188

18th Century Child by Quentin de la Tour
SP189

1951, Dec. 15

Cross in Red.

B264	SP188	12fr +3fr dk brn	3.75	3.75
B265	SP189	15fr +5fr dp ultra	3.75	3.75

The surtax was for the Red Cross.

Stagecoach of 1844
SP190

1952, Mar. 8 *Perf. 13*

B266	SP190	12fr +3fr dp grn	3.25	3.25

Stamp Day, March 8, 1952.

Gustave Flaubert
SP191

Portraits: 12fr+3fr, Edouard Manet. 15fr+4fr, Camille Saint-Saens. 18fr+5fr, Henri Poincaré. 20fr+6fr, Georges-Eugene Haussmann. 30fr+7fr, Adolphe Thiers.

1952, Oct. 18

Frames in Dark Brown.

B267	SP191	8fr +2fr ind	6.75	6.75
B268	SP191	12fr +3fr vio bl	6.75	6.75
B269	SP191	15fr +4fr dk grn	6.75	6.75
B270	SP191	18fr +5fr dk brn	6.75	6.75
B271	SP191	20fr +6fr car	9.00	9.00
B272	SP191	30fr +7fr pur	9.00	9.00
		Nos. B267-B272 (6)	45.00	45.00

Cupid from Diana Fountain Versailles
SP192

Design: 15fr+5fr, Similar detail, cupid facing left.

1952, Dec. 13

Cross in Red.

B273	SP192	12fr +3fr dk grn	5.25	5.25
B274	SP192	15fr +5fr ind	5.25	5.25
a.		Bklt. pane of 10	70.00	

The surtax was for the Red Cross.

Count d'Argenson
SP193

St. Bernard
SP194

1953, Mar. 14

B275	SP193	12fr +3fr dp bl	3.00	3.00

Issued to commemorate the Day of the Stamp. The surtax was for the Red Cross.

1953, July 9

Portraits: 12fr+3fr, Olivier de Serres. 15fr+4fr, Jean Philippe Rameau. 18fr+5fr, Gaspard Monge. 20fr+6fr, Jules Michelet. 30fr+7fr, Marshal Hubert Lyautey.

B276	SP194	8fr +2fr ultra	7.00	7.00
B277	SP194	12fr +3fr dk grn	7.00	7.00
B278	SP194	15fr +4fr brn car	9.50	9.50
B279	SP194	18fr +5fr dk bl	9.50	9.50
B280	SP194	20fr +6fr dk pur	9.50	9.50
B281	SP194	30fr +7fr brn	11.00	11.00
		Nos. B276-B281 (6)	53.50	53.50

The surtax was for the Red Cross.

Madame Vigée-Lebrun and her Daughter
SP195

Count Antoine de La Vallette
SP196

Design: 15fr+5fr, "The Return from Baptism," by Louis Le Nain.

1953, Dec. 12

Cross in Red

B282	SP195	12fr +3fr red brn	9.00	9.00
a.		Bklt. pane (4 #B282, 4 #B283 with gutter btwn.)	90.00	
B283	SP195	15fr +5fr ind	10.50	10.50

The surtax was for the Red Cross.

1954, Mar. 20 Engraved *Perf. 13*

B284	SP196	12fr +3fr dp grn & choc	4.75	4.50

Stamp Day, March 20, 1954.

Louis IX
SP197

"The Sick Child," by Eugene Carrière
SP198

Portraits: 15fr+5fr, Jacques Benigne Bossuet. 18fr+6fr, Sadi Carnot. 20fr+7fr, Antoine Bourdelle. 25fr+8fr, Dr. Emile Roux. 30fr+10fr, Paul Valéry.

1954, July 10

B285	SP197	12fr +4fr dp bl	20.00	20.00
B286	SP197	15fr +5fr pur	21.00	21.00
B287	SP197	18fr +6fr dk brn	21.00	21.00
B288	SP197	20fr +7fr crim	27.50	27.50
B289	SP197	25fr +8fr ind	27.50	27.50
B290	SP197	30fr +10fr dp cl	27.50	27.50
		Nos. B285-B290 (6)	144.50	144.50

See also Nos. B303–B308 and B312–B317.

1954, Dec. 18

Design: 15fr+5fr, "Young Girl with Doves," by Jean Baptiste Greuze.

Cross in Red

B291	SP198	12fr +3fr vio gray & ind	9.50	9.50
a.		Bklt. pane (4 #B291, 4 #B292 with gutter btwn.)	90.00	
B292	SP198	15fr +5fr dk brn & org brn	9.50	9.50

No. B291a was issued to commemorate the 90th anniversary of the Red Cross. The gutter between panes is inscribed in red.

The surtax was for the Red Cross.

Balloon Post, 1870
SP199

1955, Mar. 19 ***Perf. 13*** **Unwmkd.**

B293 SP199 12fr +3fr dk grnsh bl, vio brn & ol grn 6.75 5.25

Stamp Day, March 19–20, 1955.

King Philip II
SP200

Child with Cage by Pigalle
SP201

Portraits: 15fr+6fr, Francois de Malherbé. 18fr+7fr, Sebastien de Vauban. 25fr+8fr, Charles G. de Vergennes. 30fr+9fr, Pierre S. de Laplace. 50fr+15fr, Pierre Auguste Renoir.

1955, June 11

B294	SP200	12fr +5fr brt pur	16.00	16.00
B295	SP200	15fr +6fr dp bl	16.00	16.00
B296	SP200	18fr +7fr dp grn	18.00	18.00
B297	SP200	25fr +8fr gray	24.00	24.00
B298	SP200	30fr +9fr rose brn	25.00	25.00
B299	SP200	50fr +15fr bl grn	27.50	27.50
		Nos. B294-B299 (6)	126.50	126.50

See also Nos. B321–B326.

1955, Dec. 17

Design: 15fr+5fr, Child with Goose, by Boethus of Chalcedon.

Cross in Red.

B300	SP201	12fr +3fr cl	6.00	6.00
B301	SP201	15fr +5fr dk bl	6.00	6.00
a.		Booklet pane of 10	72.50	

The surtax was for the Red Cross.

Francois of Taxis
SP202

1956, Mar. 17 **Engraved** ***Perf. 13***

B302 SP202 12fr +3fr ultra, grn & dk brn 2.50 2.50

Stamp Day, March 17–18, 1956.

Portrait Type of 1954.

Portraits: No. 303, Guillaume Budé. No. B304, Jean Goujon. No. B305, Samuel de Champlain. No. B306, Jean Simeon Chardin. No. B307, Maurice Barrès. No. B308, Maurice Ravel.

1956, June 9 ***Perf. 13***

B303	SP197	12fr +3fr saph	6.75	6.75
B304	SP197	12fr +3fr lil gray	6.75	6.75
B305	SP197	12fr +3fr brt red	8.25	8.25
B306	SP197	15fr +5fr grn	8.25	8.25
B307	SP197	15fr +5fr vio brn	9.00	9.00
B308	SP197	15fr +5fr dp vio	9.50	9.50
		Nos. B303-B308 (6)	48.50	48.50

Peasant Boy by Le Nain
SP203

Design: 15fr+5fr, Gilles by Watteau.

1956, Dec. 8 **Unwmkd.**

Cross in Red

B309	SP203	12fr +3fr ol gray	3.75	3.75
a.		Bklt. pane (4 #B309, 4 #B310 with gutter btwn.)	35.00	
B310	SP203	15fr +5fr rose lake	3.75	3.75

The surtax was for the Red Cross.

Genoese Felucca, 1750
SP204

1957, Mar. 16 ***Perf. 13***

B311 SP204 12fr +3fr bluish gray & brn blk 2.00 1.65

Issued to commemorate the Day of the Stamp, March 16, 1957, and to honor the Maritime Postal Service.

Portrait Type of 1954

1957, June 15

Portraits: No. B312, Jean de Joinville. No. B313, Bernard Palissy. No. B314, Quentin de la Tour. No. B315, Hugues Félicité Robert de Lamennais. No. B316, George Sand. No. B317, Jules Guesde.

B312	SP197	12fr +3fr ol gray & ol grn	3.00	3.00
B313	SP197	12fr +3fr grnsh blk & grnsh bl	3.25	3.25
B314	SP197	15fr +5fr cl & brt red	3.75	3.75
B315	SP197	15fr +5fr ultra & ind	4.00	4.00
B316	SP197	18fr +7fr grnsh blk & dk grn	4.50	4.50
B317	SP197	18fr +7fr dk vio brn & red brn	5.25	5.25
		Nos. B312-B317 (6)	23.75	23.75

Blind Man and Beggar, Engraving by Jacques Callot
SP205

Design: 20fr+8fr, Women beggars.

1957, Dec. 7 **Engraved** ***Perf. 13***

B318	SP205	15fr +7fr ultra & red	3.25	3.25
a.		Bklt. pane (4 #B318, 4 #B319 with gutter btwn.)	32.50	
B319	SP205	20fr +8fr dk vio brn & red	3.25	3.25

The surtax was for the Red Cross.

Motorized Mail Distribution
SP206

1958, Mar. 15

B320 SP206 15fr +5fr ol gray, ol grn & red brn 1.75 1.50

Stamp Day, Mar. 15.

Portrait Type of 1955.

Portraits: No. B321, Joachim du Bellay. No. B322, Jean Bart. No. B323, Denis Diderot. No. B324, Gustave Courbet. 20fr+8fr, J. B. Carpeaux. 35fr+15fr, Toulouse-Lautrec.

1958, June 7 **Engraved** ***Perf. 13***

B321	SP200	12fr +4fr yel grn	2.25	2.25
B322	SP200	12fr +4fr dk bl	2.25	2.25
B323	SP200	15fr +5fr dl cl	2.50	2.50
B324	SP200	15fr +5fr ultra	2.50	2.50
B325	SP200	20fr +8fr brt red	3.00	3.00
B326	SP200	35fr +15fr grn	3.00	3.00
		Nos. B321-B326 (6)	15.50	15.50

St. Vincent de Paul
SP207

Portrait: 20fr+8fr, J. H. Dunant.

1958, Dec. 6 **Unwmkd.**

Cross in Carmine.

B327	SP207	15fr +7fr grysh grn	1.50	1.50
a.		Bklt. pane (4 #B327, 4 #B328 with gutter btwn.)	14.00	
B328	SP207	20fr +8fr vio	1.50	1.50

The surtax was for the Red Cross.

Plane Landing at Night
SP208

1959, Mar. 21

B329 SP208 20fr +5fr sl grn, blk & rose 60 60

Issued for the Day of the Stamp, March 21, and to publicize night air mail service. The surtax was for the Red Cross.

See also No. 1089.

Geoffroi de Villehardouin and Ships
SP209

Designs: No. B331, André Le Nôtre and formal garden. No. B332, Jean Le Rond d'Alembert, books and wheel. No. B333, David d'Angers, statue and building. No. B334, M. F. X. Bichat and torch. No. B335, Frédéric Auguste Bartholdi, Statue of Liberty and Lion of Belfort.

1959, June 13 **Engraved** ***Perf. 13***

B330	SP209	15fr +5fr vio bl	1.65	1.65
B331	SP209	15fr +5fr dk sl grn	1.65	1.65
B332	SP209	20fr +10fr ol bis	1.90	1.90
B333	SP209	20fr +10fr dk gray	1.90	1.90
B334	SP209	30fr +10fr dk car rose	2.50	2.50
B335	SP209	30fr +10fr org brn	2.50	2.50
		Nos. B330-B335 (6)	12.10	12.10

The surtax was for the Red Cross.

No. 927 Surcharged

FREJUS +5f

1959, Dec. **Typo.** ***Perf. 14x13½***

B336 A328 25fr +5fr blk & red 38 38

The surtax was for the flood victims at Frejus.

Charles Michel de l'Épée
SP210

Design: 25fr+10fr, Valentin Hauy.

1959, Dec. 5 **Engraved** ***Perf. 13***

Cross in Carmine

B337	SP210	20fr +10fr blk & cl	1.25	1.25
a.		Bklt. pane (4 #B337, 4 #B338 with gutter btwn.)	12.00	
B338	SP210	25fr +10fr dk bl & blk	1.25	1.25

The surtax was for the Red Cross.

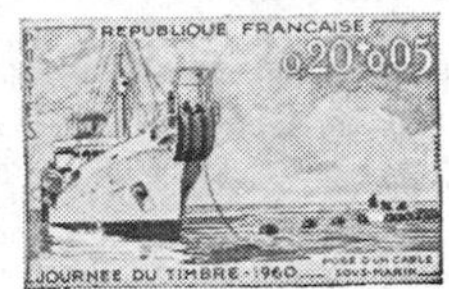

Ship Laying Underwater Cable
SP211

1960, Mar. 12

B339 SP211 20c +5c grnsh bl & dk bl 1.50 1.50

Issued for the Day of the Stamp. The surtax went to the Red Cross.

Refugee Girl Amid Ruins
SP212

1960, Apr. 7

B340 SP212 25c +10c grn, brn & ind 38 32

Issued to publicize World Refugee Year, July 1, 1959–June 30, 1960. The surtax was for aid to refugees.

Michel de L'Hospital
SP213

Designs: No. B342, Henri de la Tour D'Auvergne, Viscount of Turenne. No. B343, Nicolas Boileau (Despreaux). No. B344, Jean-Martin Charcot, M.D. No. B345, Georges Bizet. 50c+15c, Edgar Degás.

1960, June 11 **Engraved** ***Perf. 13***

B341	SP213	10c +5c pur & rose car	2.50	2.50
B342	SP213	20c +10c ol & vio brn	2.75	2.75
B343	SP213	20c +10c Prus grn & dp yel grn	3.25	3.25
B344	SP213	30c +10c rose car & rose red	3.25	3.25

B345 SP213 30c +10c dk bl & vio bl 4.00 4.00
B346 SP213 50c +15c sl bl & gray 4.50 4.50
Nos. B341-B346 (6) 20.25 20.25

The surtax was for the Red Cross. See also Nos. B350–B355.

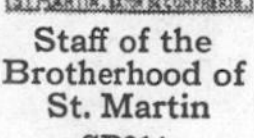

Staff of the Brotherhood of St. Martin
SP214

Letter Carrier, Paris 1760
SP215

Design: 25c+10c, St. Martin, 16th century wood sculpture.

1960, Dec. 3 *Perf. 13* Unwmkd.

B347 SP214 20c +10c rose cl & red 3.00 3.00
a. Bklt. pane (4 #B347, 4# B348 with gutter btwn.) 30.00
B348 SP214 25c +10c lt ultra & red 3.00 3.00

The surtax was for the Red Cross.

1961, March 18 *Perf. 13*

B349 SP215 20c +5c sl grn, brn & red 1.00 80

Stamp Day. Surtax for Red Cross.

Famous Men Type of 1960

Designs: 15+5c, Bertrand Du Guesclin. B351, Pierre Puget. B352, Charles Coulomb. 30+10c, Antoine Drouot. 45c+10c, Honoré Daumier. 50+15c, Guillaume Apollinaire.

1961, May 20 Engraved

B350 SP213 15c +5c red brn & blk 2.00 2.00
B351 SP213 20c +10c dk grn & lt bl 2.00 2.00
B352 SP213 20c +10c ver & rose car 2.00 2.00
B353 SP213 30c +10c blk & brn org 2.00 2.00
B354 SP213 45c +10c choc & dk grn 3.00 3.00
B355 SP213 50c +15c dk car rose & vio 3.00 3.00
Nos. B350-B355 (6) 14.00 14.00

"Love" by Rouault
SP216

Medieval Royal Messenger
SP217

Designs from "Miserere" by Georges Rouault: 25c+10c, "The Blind Consoles the Seeing."

1961, Dec. 2 *Perf. 13*

B356 SP216 20c +10c brn, blk & red 2.50 2.50
a. Bklt. pane (4 #B356, 4 #B357 with gutter btwn.) 22.50
B357 SP216 25c +10c brn, blk & red 2.50 2.50

The surtax was for the Red Cross.

1962, March 17

B358 SP217 20c +5c rose red, bl & sep 90 65

Stamp Day. Surtax for Red Cross.

Denis Papin, Scientist
SP218

Rosalie Fragonard by Fragonard
SP219

Portraits: No. B360, Edme Bouchardon, sculptor. No. B361, Joseph Lakanal, educator. 30c+10c, Gustave Charpentier, composer. 45c+15c, Edouard Estaunié, writer. 50c+20c, Hyacinthe Vincent, physician and bacteriologist.

1962, June 2 Engraved

B359 SP218 15c +5c bluish grn & dk gray 3.00 3.00
B360 SP218 20c +10c cl brn 3.00 3.00
B361 SP218 20c +10c gray & sl 3.00 3.00
B362 SP218 30c +10c brt bl & ind 3.75 3.75
B363 SP218 45c +15c org brn & choc 4.00 4.00
B364 SP218 50c +20c grnsh bl & blk 4.00 4.00
Nos. B359-B364 (6) 20.75 20.75

The surtax was for the Red Cross.

1962, Dec. 8

Design: 25c+10c, Child dressed as Pierrot.

Cross in Red

B365 SP219 20c +10c redsh brn 1.25 1.25
a. Bklt. pane (4 #B365, 4 #B366 with gutter btwn.) 11.00
B366 SP219 25c +10c dl grn 1.25 1.25

The surtax was for the Red Cross.

Jacques Amyot, Classical Scholar
SP220

Portraits: 30c+10c, Pierre de Marivaux, playwright. 50c+20c, Jacques Daviel, surgeon.

1963, Feb. 23 *Perf. 13* Unwmkd.

B367 SP220 20c +10c mar, gray & pur 1.50 1.50
B368 SP220 30c +10c Prus grn & mar 1.40 1.40
B369 SP220 50c +20c ultra, ocher & ol 1.50 1.50

The surtax was for the Red Cross.

Roman Chariot
SP221

1963, March 16 Engraved

B370 SP221 20c +5c brn org & vio brn 32 32

Stamp Day. Surtax for Red Cross.

Étienne Méhul, Composer
SP222

Designs: 30c+10c, Nicolas-Louis Vauquelin, chemist. 50c+20c, Alfred de Vigny, poet.

1963, May 25 *Perf. 13* Unwmkd.

B371 SP222 20c +10c dp bl, dk brn & dp org 1.75 1.75
B372 SP222 30c +10c mag, gray ol & blk 1.40 1.40
B373 SP222 50c +20c sl, blk & brn 2.25 2.25

The surtax was for the Red Cross.

"Child with Grapes" by David d'Angers and Centenary Emblem
SP223

Design: 25c+10c, "The Fifer," by Edouard Manet.

1963, Dec. 9 *Perf. 13* Unwmkd.

B374 SP223 20c +10c blk & red 65 65
a. Bklt. pane (4 #B374, 4 #B375 with gutter btwn.) 5.50
B375 SP223 25c +10c sl grn & red 65 65

Issued to commemorate the centenary of the International and the French Red Cross. The surtax was for the Red Cross.

Post Rider, 18th Century
SP224

1964, March 14 Engraved

B376 SP224 20c +5c Prus grn 30 25

Issued for Stamp Day.

Resistance Memorial by Watkin, Luxembourg Gardens
SP225

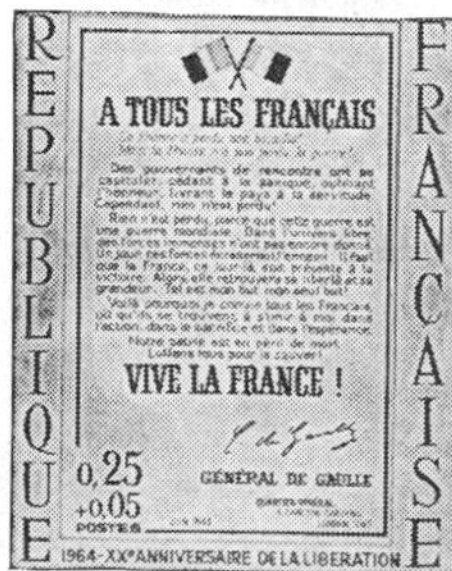

De Gaulle's 1940 Poster "A Tous les Francais"
SP226

Allied Troops Landing in Normandy and Provence—SP227

Designs: 20c+5c, "Deportation," concentration camp with watchtower and barbed wire. No. B380, Street fighting in Paris and Strasbourg.

1964 Engraved *Perf. 13*

B377 SP225 20c +5c sl blk 75 75

Perf. 12x13

B378 SP226 25c +5c dk red, bl, red & blk 1.00 1.00

Perf. 13

B379 SP227 30c +5c blk, bl & org brn 75 75
B380 SP227 30c +5c org brn, cl & blk 90 90
B381 SP225 50c +5c dk grn 1.00 1.00
Nos. B377-B381 (5) 4.40 4.40

Issued to commemorate the 20th anniversary of liberation from the Nazis.

Issue dates: Nos. B377, B381, Mar. 21; No. B378, June 18; No. B379, June 6; No. B380, Aug. 22.

President René Coty
SP229

Jean Nicolas Corvisart
SP230

Portraits: No. B383, John Calvin. No. B384, Pope Sylvester II (Gerbert).

1964 *Perf. 13* Unwmkd.

B382 SP229 30c +10c dp cl & blk 32 32
B383 SP229 30c +10c dk grn, blk & brn 32 32
B384 SP229 30c +10c sl & cl 32 32

The surtax was for the Red Cross.

Issue dates: No. B382, Apr. 25; No. B383, May 25; No. B384, June 1.

1964, Dec. 12 Engraved

Portrait; 25c+10c, Dominique Larrey.

Cross in Carmine

B385 SP230 20c +10c blk 38 30
a. Bklt. pane (4 #B385, 4 #B386 with gutter btwn.) 3.75
B386 SP230 25c +10c blk 38 30

Issued to honor Jean Nicolas Corvisart (1755–1821), physician of Napoleon I, and Dominique Larrey (1766–1842), Chief Surgeon of the Imperial Armies. The surtax was for the Red Cross.

Paul Dukas, Composer
SP231

Portraits: No. B387, Duke François de La Rochefoucauld, writer. No. B388, Nicolas Poussin, painter. No. B389, Duke Charles of Orléans, poet.

1965, Feb. Engraved *Perf. 13*

B387	SP231	30c +10c org brn & dk bl	48	48
B388	SP231	30c +10c car & dk red brn	48	48
B389	SP231	40c +10c dk red brn, dk red & Prus bl	60	60
B390	SP231	40c +10c dk brn & sl bl	60	60

The surtax was for the Red Cross.
Nos. B387 and B390 were issued Feb. 13; Nos. B388–B389 were issued Feb. 20.

Packet "La Guienne"
SP232

1965, Mar. 29 *Perf. 13* Unwmkd.

B391	SP232	25c +10c ultra, blk & sl grn	48	48

Issued for Stamp Day, 1965. "La Guienne" was used for transatlantic mail service. Surtax was for the Red Cross.

Infant with Spoon by Auguste Renoir
SP233

Design: 30c+10c, Coco Writing (Renoir's daughter Claude).

1965, Dec. 11 Engraved *Perf. 13*

Cross in Carmine

B392	SP233	25c +10c sl	25	25
a.		Bklt. pane (4 #B392, 4 #B393 with gutter btwn.)	3.00	
B393	SP233	30c +10c dl red brn	32	32

The surtax was for the Red Cross.

Francois Mansart and Carnavalet Palace, Paris—SP234

Designs: No. B395, St. Pierre Fourier and Basilica of St. Pierre Fourier, Mirecourt. No. B396, Marcel Proust and St. Hilaire Bridge, Illiers. No. B397, Gabriel Fauré, monument and score of "Penelope." No. B398, Elie Metchnikoff, microscope and Pasteur Institute. No. B399, Hippolyte Taine and birthplace.

1966 Engraved *Perf. 13*

B394	SP234	30c +10c dk red brn & grn	38	38
B395	SP234	30c +10c blk & gray grn	38	38
B396	SP234	30c +10c ind, sep & grn	38	38
B397	SP234	30c +10c bis brn & ind	38	38
B398	SP234	30c +10c blk & dl brn	38	38
B399	SP234	30c +10c grn & ol brn	38	38
		Nos. B394-B399 (6)	2.28	2.28

The surtax was for the Red Cross.
Issue dates: Nos. B394–B396, Feb. 12. Others, June 25.

Engraver Cutting Die and Tools
SP235

1966, March 19 Engraved *Perf. 13*

B400	SP235	25c +10c sl, dk brn & dp org	45	45

Stamp Day. Surtax for Red Cross.

Angel of Victory, Verdun Fortress, Marching Troops
SP236

First Aid on Battlefield, 1859
SP237

1966, May 28 *Perf. 13*

B401	SP236	30c +5c Prus bl, ultra & dk bl	32	32

Victory of Verdun, 50th anniversary.

1966, Dec. 10 Engraved *Perf. 13*

Design: 30c+10c, Nurse giving first aid to child, 1966.

Cross in Carmine

B402	SP237	25c +10c grn	38	38
a.		Bklt pane (4 #B402, 4 # B403 with gutter btwn.)	3.75	
B403	SP237	30c +10c sl	38	38

The surtax was for the Red Cross.

Emile Zola
SP238

Letter Carrier, 1865
SP239

Portraits: No. B405, Beaumarchais (pen name of Pierre Augustin Caron). No. B406, St. Francois de Sales (1567–1622). No. B407, Albert Camus (1913–1960).

1967 Engraved *Perf. 13*

B404	SP238	30c +10c sl bl & bl	38	38
B405	SP238	30c +10c rose brn & lil	38	38
B406	SP238	30c +10c dl vio & pur	38	38
B407	SP238	30c +10c brn & dl cl	38	38

The surtax was for the Red Cross.
Issue dates: Nos. B404–B405, Feb. 4. Others, June 24.

1967, Apr. 8

B408	SP239	25c +10c ind, grn & red	32	32

Issued for Stamp Day.

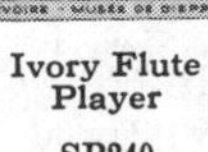

Ivory Flute Player
SP240

Ski Jump and Long Distance Skiing
SP241

Design: 30c+10c, Violin player, ivory carving.

1967, Dec. 16 Engraved *Perf. 13*

Cross in Carmine

B409	SP240	25c +10c dl vio & lt brn	38	38
a.		Bklt. pane (4 #B409, 4 #B410 with gutter btwn.)	3.75	
B410	SP240	30c +10c grn & lt brn	38	38

The surtax was for the Red Cross.

1968, Jan. 27

Designs: 40c+10c, Ice hockey. 60c+20c, Olympic flame and snowflakes. 75c+25c, Woman figure skater. 95c+35c, Slalom.

B411	SP241	30c +10c ver, gray & brn	25	25
B412	SP241	40c +10c lil, lem & brt mag	32	32
B413	SP241	60c +20c dk grn, org & brt vio	45	45
B414	SP241	75c +25c brt pink, yel grn & blk	60	60
B415	SP241	95c +35c bl, brt pink & red brn	75	75
		Nos. B411-B415 (5)	2.37	2.37

Issued for the 10th Winter Olympic Games, Grenoble, Feb. 6–18.

Rural Mailman, 1830
SP242

1968, Mar. 16 Engraved *Perf. 13*

B416	SP242	25c +10c bl gray, ultra & red	30	30

Issued for Stamp Day.

François Couperin, Composer, and Instruments
SP243

Portraits: No. B418, Gen. Louis Desaix de Veygoux (1768–1800) and scene showing his death at the Battle of Marengo, Italy. No. B419, Saint-Pol-Roux (pen name of Paul-Pierre Roux, 1861–1940), Christ on the Cross and ruins of Camaret-sur-Mer. No. B420, Paul Claudel (poet and diplomat, 1868–1955) and Joan of Arc at the stake.

1968 Engraved *Perf. 13*

B417	SP243	30c +10c pur & rose lil	30	30
B418	SP243	30c +10c dk grn & brn	30	30
B419	SP243	30c +10c cop red & ol bis	30	30
B420	SP243	30c +10c dk brn & lil	30	30

Issue dates: Nos. B417–B418, Mar, 23; Nos. B419–B420, July 6.

Spring, by Nicolas Mignard
SP244

Designs (Paintings by Nicolas Mignard): 30c+10c, Fall. No. B423, Summer. No. B424, Winter.

1968–69 Engraved *Perf. 13*

Cross in Carmine

B421	SP244	25c +10c pur & sl bl	32	32
a.		Bklt. pane (4 #B421, 4 #B422 with gutter btwn.)	3.00	
B422	SP244	30c +10c brn & rose car	32	32
B423	SP244	40c +15c dk brn & brn ('69)	40	40
a.		Bklt. pane (4 #B423, 4 #B424 with gutter btwn.)	3.75	
B424	SP244	40c +15c pur & Prus bl ('69)	40	40

The surtax was for the Red Cross.

Mailmen's Omnibus, 1881
SP245

1969, Mar. 15 Engraved *Perf. 13*

B425	SP245	30c +10c brn, grn & blk	30	30

Issued for Stamp Day.

Gen. Francois Marceau
SP246

Portraits: No. B427, Charles Augustin Sainte-Beuve (1804–1869), writer. No. B428, Albert Roussel (1869–1937), musician. No. B429, Marshal Jean Lannes (1769–1809). No. B430, Georges Cuvier (1769–1832), naturalist. No. B431, André Gide, (1869–1951), writer.

1969

B426	SP246	50c +10c brn red	60	60
B427	SP246	50c +10c sl bl	60	60
B428	SP246	50c +10c dp vio bl	60	60
B429	SP246	50c +10c choc	60	60
B430	SP246	50c +10c dp plum	60	60
B431	SP246	50c +10c bl grn	60	60
		Nos. B426-B431 (6)	3.60	3.60

The surtax was for the Red Cross.
Issue dates: Nos. B426–B428, Mar. 24. No. B429, May 10, Nos. B430–B431, May 17.

Gen. Jacques Leclerc, La Madeleine and Battle—SP247

1969, Aug. 23 Engraved *Perf. 13*

B432	SP247	45c +10c sl & ol	65	65

Issued to commemorate the 25th anniversary of the liberation of Paris, Aug. 25, 1944.

Same Inscribed
"Liberation de Strasbourg"

1969, Nov. 22 Engraved *Perf. 13*

B433	SP247	70c +10c brn, choc & ol	1.25	1.25

Issued to commemorate the 25th anniversary of the liberation of Strasbourg.

Philibert Delorme, Architect, and Chateau d'Anet—SP248

Designs: No. B435, Louis Le Vau (1612–1670), architect, and Vaux-le-Vicomte Chateau, Paris. No. B436, Prosper Merimée (1803–1870), writer, and Carmen. No. B437, Alexandre Dumas (1820–1870), writer, and Three Musketeers. No. B438, Edouard Branly (1844–1940), physicist, electric circuit and convent of the Carmes, Paris. No. B439, Maurice de Broglie (1875–1960), physicist, and X-ray spectrograph.

1970 Engraved *Perf. 13*

B434	SP248	40c	+10c sl grn	60	60
B435	SP248	40c	+10c dk car	60	60
B436	SP248	40c	+10c Prus bl	60	60
B437	SP248	40c	+10c vio bl	60	60
B438	SP248	40c	+10c dp brn	60	60
B439	SP248	40c	+10c dk gray	60	60
	Nos. B434-B439 (6)			3.60	3.60

The surtax was for the Red Cross.
Issue dates: No. B434–B436, Feb. 14; Nos. B437–B439, Apr. 11.

City Mailman, 1830
SP249

"Life and Death"
SP250

1970, Mar. 14

B440	SP249	40c	+10c blk, ultra & dk car rose	45	45

Issued for Stamp Day.

1970, Apr. 4

B441	SP250	40c	+10c brt bl, ol & car rose	40	40

Issued to publicize the fight against cancer in connection with Health Day, Apr. 7.

Marshal de Lattre de Tassigny
SP251

1970, May 8 Engraved *Perf. 13*

B442	SP251	40c	+10c sl & vio bl	60	45

Issued to commemorate the 25th anniversary of the entry into Berlin of French troops under Marshal Jean de Lattre de Tassigny, May 8, 1945.

Lord and Lady, Dissay Chapel Fresco
SP252

Design: No. B444, Angel holding whips, from fresco in Dissay Castle Chapel, Vienne, c. 1500.

1970, Dec. 12 Engraved *Perf. 13*

Cross in Carmine

B443	SP252	40c	+15c grn	80	75
a.			Bklt. pane (4 #B443, 4 #B444 with gutter btwn.)	8.50	
B444	SP252	40c	+15c cop red	80	75

The surtax was for the Red Cross.

Daniel-Francois Auber and "Fra Diavolo" Music
SP253

Designs: No. B446, Gen. Charles Diego Brosset (1898–1944), and Basilica of Fourvière. No. B447, Victor Grignard (1871–1935), chemist, and Nobel Prize medal. No. B448, Henri Farman (1874–1958) and plane. No. B449, Gen. Charles Georges Delestraint (1879–1945) and scroll. No. B450, Jean Eugène Robert-Houdin (1805–1871) and magician's act.

1971 Engraved *Perf. 13*

B445	SP253	50c	+10c brn vio & brn	1.25	1.00
B446	SP253	50c	+10c dk sl grn & ol gray	1.25	1.00
B447	SP253	50c	+10c brn red & ol	1.25	1.00
B448	SP253	50c	+10c vio bl & vio	1.25	1.00
B449	SP253	50c	+10c pur & cl	1.40	1.25
B450	SP253	50c	+10c sl grn & bl grn	1.40	1.25
	Nos. B445-B450 (6)			7.80	6.50

The surtax was for the Red Cross.
Issue dates: Nos. B445–B446, Mar. 6. No. B447, May 8. No. B448, May 29. Nos. B449–B450, Oct. 16.

Army Post Office, 1914–1918
SP254

1971, March 27 Engr. *Perf. 13*

B451	SP254	50c	+10c ol, brn & bl	50	45

Stamp Day, 1971.

Girl with Dog, by Greuze
SP255

Aristide Bergès (1833–1904)
SP256

Design: 50c+10c, "The Dead Bird," by Jean-Baptiste Greuze (1725–1805).

1971, Dec. 11

Cross in Carmine

B452	SP255	30c	+10c vio bl	75	75
a.			Bklt. pane (4 #B452, 4 #B453 with gutter btwn.)	7.50	
B453	SP255	50c	+10c dp car	75	75

The surtax was for the Red Cross.

1972 Engraved *Perf. 13*

Portraits: No. B455, Paul de Chomedey (1612–1676), founder of Montreal, and arms of Neuville-sur-Vanne. No. B456, Edouard Belin (1876–1963), inventor. No. B457, Louis Blériot (1872–1936), aviation pioneer. No. B458, Adm. François Joseph, Count de Grasse (1722–1788), hero of the American Revolution. No. B459, Théophile Gautier (1811–1872), writer.

B454	SP256	50c	+10c blk & grn	1.10	1.10
B455	SP256	50c	+10c blk & bl	1.10	1.10
B456	SP256	50c	+10c blk & lil rose	1.10	1.10
B457	SP256	50c	+10c red & blk	1.10	1.10
B458	SP256	50c	+10c org & blk	1.50	1.50
B459	SP256	50c	+10c blk & brn	1.50	1.50
	Nos. B454-B459 (6)			7.40	7.40

The surtax was for the Red Cross.
Issue dates: Nos. B454–B455, Feb. 19; No. B456, June 24; No. B457, July 1; Nos. B458–B459, Sept. 9.

Rural Mailman, 1894
SP257

Nicolas Desgenettes
SP258

1972, Mar. 18 Engr. *Perf. 13*

B460	SP257	50c	+10c bl, yel & ol gray	75	60

Stamp Day 1972.

1972, Dec. 16 Engraved *Perf. 13*

Designs: 30c+10c, René Nicolas Dufriche, Baron Desgenettes, M.D. (1762–1837). 50c+10c, François Joseph Broussais, M.D. (1772–1838).

B461	SP258	30c	+10c sl grn & red	95	80
a.			Bklt. pane (4 #B461, 4 #B462 with gutter btwn.)	9.25	
B462	SP258	50c	+10c red	95	80

The surtax was for the Red Cross.

Gaspard de Coligny
SP259

Portraits: No. B463, Gaspard de Coligny (1519–1572), admiral and Huguenot leader. No. B464, Ernest Renan (1823–1892), philologist and historian. No. B465, Alberto Santos Dumont (1873–1932), Brazilian aviator. No. B466, Gabrielle-Sidonie Colette (1873–1954), writer. No. B467, René Duguay-Trouin (1673–1736), naval commander. No. B468, Louis Pasteur (1822–1895), chemist, bacteriologist. No. B469, Tony Garnier (1869–1948), architect.

1973 Engraved *Perf. 13*

B463	SP259	50c	+10c multi	1.25	1.00
B464	SP259	50c	+10c multi	1.25	1.00
B465	SP259	50c	+10c multi	1.25	1.00
B466	SP259	50c	+10c multi	1.25	1.00
B467	SP259	50c	+10c multi	1.25	1.00
B468	SP259	50c	+10c multi	1.25	1.10
B469	SP259	50c	+10c multi	1.25	1.10
	Nos. B463-B469 (7)			8.75	7.20

Issue dates: No. B463, Feb. 17; No. B464, Apr. 28; No. B465, May 26; No. B466, June 2; No. B467, June 9; No. B468, Oct. 6; No. B469, Nov. 17.

Mail Coach, 1835
SP260

1973, Mar. 24 Engraved *Perf. 13*

B470	SP260	50c	+10c grnsh bl	50	45

Stamp Day, 1973.

Mary Magdalene
SP261

St. Louis-Marie de Montfort
SP262

Design: 50c+10c, Mourning woman. Designs are from 15th century Tomb of Tonnerre.

1973, Dec. 1

B471	SP261	30c	+10c sl grn & red	60	60
a.			Bklt. pane (4 # B471, 4 #B472 with gutter btwn.)	6.00	
B472	SP261	50c	+10c dk gray & red	75	75

Surtax was for the Red Cross.

1974, Feb. 23 Engraved *Perf. 13*

Portraits: No. B474, Francis Poulenc (1899–1963), composer. No. B475, Jules Barbey d'Aurevilly (1808–1889), writer. No. B476, Jean Giraudoux (1882–1944), writer.

B473	SP262	50c	+10c multi	1.65	1.65
B474	SP262	50c	+10c multi	1.10	1.10
B475	SP262	80c	+15c multi	1.25	1.25
B476	SP262	80c	+15c multi	1.25	1.25

Issue dates: No. B473, Mar. 9; No. B474, July 20; Nos. B475–B476, Nov. 16.

Automatically Sorted Letters
SP263

1974, Mar. 9 Engraved *Perf. 13*

B477	SP263	50c	+10c multi	38	32

Stamp Day 1974. Automatic letter sorting center, Orleans-la-Source, opened Jan. 30, 1973.

Order of Liberation and 5 Honored Cities—SP264

1974, June 15 Engraved *Perf. 13*

B478	SP264	1fr	+10c multi	75	60

30th anniversary of liberation from the Nazis.

"Summer" SP265 — "Winter" SP266

Designs: B481, "Spring" (girl on swing). B482, "Fall" (umbrella and rabbits).

1974, Nov. 30 — Engr. — *Perf. 13*

B479	SP265	60c +15c multi	65	60
a.		Bklt. pane (4 #B479, 4 # B480 with gutter btwn.)	6.00	
B480	SP266	80c +15c multi	80	75

1975, Nov. 29

B481	SP265	60c +15c multi	50	45
a.		Booklet pane (4#B481, 4#B482 with gutter btwn.)	6.00	
B482	SP266	80c +20c multi	80	75

Surtax was for the Red Cross.

Dr. Albert Schweitzer SP267 — Edmond Michelet SP268

André Siegfried and Map SP269

Portraits: No. B483, Albert Schweitzer (1875–1965), medical missionary, birth centenary. No. B484, Edmond Michelet (1899–1970), Resistance hero, statesman. No. B485, Robert Schuman (1886–1963), promoter of United Europe. No. B486, Eugene Thomas (1903–1969), minister of PTT. No. B487, André Siegfried (1875–1959), political science professor, writer, birth centenary.

1975 — Engraved — *Perf. 13*

B483	SP267	80c +20c multi	60	60
B484	SP268	80c +20c bl & ind	60	60
B485	SP268	80c +20c blk & ind	60	60
B486	SP268	80c +20c blk & sl	60	60
B487	SP269	80c +20c blk & bl	65	65
		Nos. B483-B487 (5)	3.05	3.05

Issue dates: No. B483, Jan. 11; No. B484, Feb. 22; No. B485, May 10; No. B486, June 28; No. B487, Nov. 15.

Second Republic Mailman's Badge SP270

1975, Mar. 8 — Photogravure

B488	SP270	80c +20c multi	50	48

Stamp Day.

"Sage" Type of 1876 SP271 — Marshal A. J. de Moncey SP272

1976, Mar. 13 — Engr. — *Perf. 13*

B489	SP271	80c +20c blk & lil	60	50

Stamp Day 1976.

1976 — Engraved — *Perf. 13*

Designs: No. B491, Max Jacob (1876–1944), Dadaist writer, by Picasso. No. B492, Jean Mounet-Sully (1841–1916), actor. No. B493, Gen. Pierre Daumesnil (1776–1832). No. B494, Eugène Fromentin (1820–1876), painter.

B490	SP272	80c +20c multi	65	65
B491	SP272	80c +20c red brn & ol	65	65
B492	SP272	80c +20c multi	65	65
B493	SP272	1fr +20c multi	75	75
B494	SP272	1fr +20c multi	75	75
		Nos. B490-B494 (5)	3.45	3.45

Issue dates: No. B490, May 22; No. B491, July 22. No. B492, Aug. 28; No. B493, Sept. 4; No. B494, Sept. 25.

Anna de Noailles SP273 — St. Barbara SP274

1976, Nov. 6 — Engr. — *Perf. 13*

B495	SP273	1fr +20c multi	75	75

Anna de Noailles (1876–1933), writer and poet.

1976, Nov. 20

Design: 1fr+25c, Cimmerian Sibyl. Sculptures from Brou Cathedral.

Cross in Carmine

B496	SP274	80c +20c vio	75	65
a.		Booklet pane (4 #B496, 4 #B497 with gutter between)	7.50	
B497	SP274	1fr +25c dk brn	90	80

Surtax was for the Red Cross.

Marckolsheim Relay Station Sign SP275

1977, Mar. 26 — Engr. — *Perf. 13*

B498	SP275	1fr +20c multi	60	60

Stamp Day.

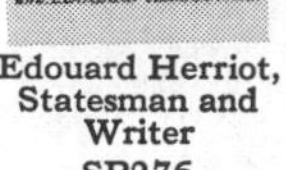

Edouard Herriot, Statesman and Writer SP276 — Christmas Figurine, Provence SP277

Designs: No. B500, Abbé Breuil (1877–1961), archaeologist. No. B501, Guillaume de Machault (1305–1377), poet and composer. No. B502, Charles Cros (1842–1888).

1977 — Engraved — *Perf. 13*

B499	SP276	1fr +20c multi	75	75
B500	SP276	1fr +20c multi	75	75
B501	SP276	1fr +20c multi	75	75
B502	SP276	1fr +20c multi	75	75

Issue dates: No. B499, Oct. 8; No. B500, Oct. 15; No. B501, Nov. 12; No. B502, Dec. 3.

1977, Nov. 26

Design: 1fr+25c, Christmas figurine (woman), Provence.

B503	SP277	80c +20c red & ind	65	65
a.		Booklet pane (4 #B503, 4 #B504 with gutter between)	6.50	
B504	SP277	1fr +25c red & sl grn	80	80

Surtax was for the Red Cross.

Marie Noël, Writer SP278 — Mail Collection, 1900 SP279

Designs: No. B506, Georges Bernanos (1888–1948), writer. No. B507, Leo Tolstoi (1828–1910), Russian writer. No. B508, Charles Marie Leconte de Lisle (1818–1894), poet. No. B509, Voltaire (1694–1778) and Jean Jacques Rousseau (1712–1778). No. B510, Claude Bernard (1813–1878), physiologist.

1978 — Engraved — *Perf. 13*

B505	SP278	1fr +20c multi	75	75
B506	SP278	1fr +20c multi	75	75
B507	SP278	1fr +20c multi	75	75
B508	SP278	1fr +20c multi	75	75
B509	SP278	1fr +20c multi	75	75
B510	SP278	1fr +20c multi	75	75
		Nos. B505-B510 (6)	4.50	4.50

Issue dates: No. B505, Feb. 11; No. B506, Feb. 18; No. B507, Apr. 15; No. B508, Mar. 26; No. B509, July 1; No. B510, Sept. 16.

1978, Apr. 8 — Engr. — *Perf. 13*

B511	SP279	1fr +20c multi	65	60

Stamp Day 1978.

The Hare and the Tortoise SP280

Design: 1.20fr+30c, The City Rat and the Country Rat.

1978, Dec. 2 — Engr. — *Perf. 13*

B512	SP280	1fr +25c multi	75	60
a.		Booklet pane (4 #B512, 4 #B513 with gutter between)	7.50	
B513	SP280	1.20fr +30c multi	90	75

Surtax was for the Red Cross.

Ladislas Marshal de Berchény (1689–1778) SP281

Design: No. B515, Leon Jouhaux (1879–1954), labor leader. No. B516, Peter Abelard (1079–1142), theologian and writer. No. B517, Georges Courteline (1860–1929), humorist. No. B518, Simone Weil (1909–1943), social philosopher. No. B519, André Malraux (1901–1976), novelist.

1979 — Engraved — *Perf. 13*

B514	SP281	1.20fr +30c multi	80	80
B515	SP281	1.20fr +30c multi	95	95
B516	SP281	1.20fr +30c multi	80	80
B517	SP281	1.20fr +30c multi	80	80
B518	SP281	1.30fr +30c multi	90	90
B519	SP281	1.30fr +30c multi	90	90
		Nos. B514-B519 (6)	5.15	5.15

Issue dates: Nos. B514, Jan. 13; B515, May 12; B516, June 9; B517, June 25; B518, Nov. 12; B519, Nov. 26.

General Post Office, from 1908 Post Card—SP282

1979, Mar. 10 — Engr. — *Perf. 13*

B520	SP282	1.20fr +30c multi	65	48

Stamp Day 1979.

Woman, Stained-Glass Window SP283

Stained-glass windows, Church of St. Joan of Arc, Rouen: 1.30fr + 30c, Simon the Magician.

1979, Dec. 1

B521	SP283	1.10fr +30c multi	65	60
a.		Bklt. pane (4# B521, 4# B522 with gutter between)	6.00	
B522	SP283	1.30fr +30c multi	80	65

Surtax was for the Red Cross.

Eugene Viollet le Duc (1814-1879), Architect—SP284

Jean-Marie de Le Mennais (1780-1860), Priest and Educator—SP285

Designs No. B524, Jean Monnet (1888-1979), economist and diplomat. No. B526, Frederic Mistral (1830-1914), poet. No. B527, Saint-John Perse (Alexis Leger, 1887-1975), poet and diplomat. No. B528, Pierre Paul de Riquet (1604-1680), canal builder.

1980 Engr. *Perf. 13*

B523	SP284	1.30fr +30c multi	75	65
B524	SP284	1.30fr +30c multi	80	80
B525	SP285	1.40fr +30c bl	80	75
B526	SP285	1.40fr +30c blk	80	75
B527	SP285	1.40fr +30c multi	80	75
B528	SP284	1.40fr +30c multi	80	75
		Nos. B523-B528 (6)	4.75	4.45

Issue dates: No. B523, Feb. 16; No. B524, Nos. B525-B526, Sept. 6; Nos. B527-B528, Oct. 11.

The Letter to Melie, by Avati, Stamp Day, 1980—SP286

1980, Mar. 8 Photo.

B529	SP286	1.30fr +30c multi	75	60

Filling the Granaries, Choir Stall Detail, Amiens Cathedral—SP287

Design: 1.40fr+30c, Grapes from the Promised Land.

1980, Dec. 6 Engraved *Perf. 13*

B530	SP287	1.20fr +30c red & dk red brn	60	50
B531	SP287	1.40fr +30c red & dk red brn	65	60
a.		Bklt. pane (4 #B530, 4 #B531 with gutter between)	5.25	

Sister Anne-Marie Javouhey (1779-1851), Founded Congregation of St. Joseph of Cluny—SP288

Designs: No. B532, Louis Armand (1905-1971), railway engineer. B533, Louis Jouvet (1887-1951), theater director. B534, Marc Boegner (1881-1970), peace worker. No. B536, Jacques Offenbach (1819-1880), composer. No. B537, Pierre Teilhard de Chardin (1881-1955), philosopher.

1981 Engr. *Perf. 13*

B532	SP288	1.20 +30c multi	60	60
B533	SP288	1.20 +30c multi	60	60
B534	SP288	1.40 +30c multi	95	65
B535	SP288	1.40 +30c multi	75	65
B536	SP288	1.40 +30c multi	75	65
B537	SP288	1.40 +30c multi	75	65
		Nos. B532-B537 (6)	4.40	3.80

Issue dates: #B532, May 23; #B533, June 13; #B534, Nov. 14; #B535, Feb. 7; #B536, Feb. 14; #B537, May 23.

The Love Letter, by Goya—SP289

1981, Mar. 7 *Perf. 13x12½*

B538	SP289	1.40 +30c multi	75	50

Stamp Day 1981.

Scourges of the Passion—SP290

Guillaume Postel (1510-1581), Theologian—SP291

Stained-glass Windows, Church of the Sacred Heart, Audincourt: 1.60fr+30c, "Peace."

1981, Dec. 5 Photo. *Perf. 13*

B539	SP290	1.40 +30c multi	60	55
B540	SP290	1.60 +30c multi	70	60
a.		Bklt. pane (4 #B539, 4 #B540 with gutter between)	6.00	

1982 Engr. *Perf. 13*

Designs: No. B542, Henri Mondor (1885-1962), physician. No. B543, Andre Chantemesse (1851-1919), Scientist. No. B544, Louis Pergand (1882-1915), writer. No. B545, Robert Debre (1882-1978), writer. No. B546, Gustave Eiffel (1832-1923), engineer.

B541	SP291	1.40 +30c multi	75	60
B542	SP291	1.40 +30c dk brn & dk bl	60	50
B543	SP291	1.60 +30c multi	70	65
B544	SP291	1.60 +40c multi	90	60
B545	SP291	1.60 +40c dk bl	75	60
B546	SP291	1.80 +40c sep	75	75
		Nos. B541-B546 (6)	4.45	3.70

Woman Reading, by Picasso—SP292

1982, Mar. 27 *Perf. 13x12½*

B547	SP292	1.60 +40c multi	90	45

Stamp Day.

Five Weeks in a Balloon, by Jules Verne—SP293

Design: 20,000 Leagues under the Sea.

1982, Nov 20 *Perf. 13*

B548	SP293	1.60 +30c multi	75	65
B549	SP293	1.80 +40c multi	75	65
a.		Bklt. pane (4 #B548, 4#B549 with gutter between)	6.50	

Surtax was for Red Cross.

Andre Messager (1853-1929)—SP294

Designs: No. B551, J.A. Gabriel (1698-1782), architect. No. B552, Hector Berlioz (1803-1869), composer. No. B553, Max Fouchet (1913-1980). No. B554, Rene Cassin (1887-1976). No. B555, Stendhal (Marie Henri Beyle, 1783-1842).

1983 Engr. *Perf. 12½x13*

B550	SP294	1.60 +30c multi	65	65
B551	SP294	1.60 +30c multi	65	65
B552	SP294	1.80 +40c dp lil & blk	75	75
B553	SP294	1.80 +40c multi	75	75
B554	SP294	2fr +40c multi	80	80
B555	SP294	2fr +40c multi	80	80
		Nos. B550-B555 (6)	4.40	4.40

Issue dates: No. B550, Jan. 15; No. B551, Apr. 16; No. B552, Jan. 22; No. B553, Apr. 29; No. B554, June 25; No. B555, Nov. 14.

Man Dictating a Letter, by Rembrandt—SP295

Photo. & Engr.

1983, Feb. 26 *Perf. 13x12½*

B556	SP295	1.80 +40c multi	80	45

Stamp Day.

Virgin with Child, Baillon, 14th Cent.—SP296

Design: No. B558, Virgin with Child, Genainville, 16th Cent.

1983, Nov. 26 Engraved *Perf. 13*

B557	SP296	1.60 +40c shown	60	50
B558	SP296	2fr +40c multi	75	60
a.		Bklt pane (4 #B557, 4 #B558 with gutter between)	6.50	

Emile Littre (1801-1881), Physician—SP297

Designs: No. B560, Jean Zay (1904-44). No. B561, Pierre Corneille (1606-1684). No. B562, Gaston Bachelard (1884-1962). No. B563, Jean Paulhan (1884-1968). No. B564, Evariste Galois (1811-1832).

1984 Engr. *Perf. 13*

B559	SP297	1.60fr +40c plum & blk	65	65
B560	SP297	1.60fr +40c dk grn & blk	65	65
B561	SP297	1.70fr +40c dp vio & blk	52	52
B562	SP297	2fr +40c gray & blk	56	56
B563	SP297	2.10fr +40c dk brn & blk	58	58
B564	SP297	2.10fr +40c ultra & blk	58	58

Diderot Holding a Letter, by L.M. Van Loo—SP298

1984, Mar. 17 Engr. *Perf. 12½x13*

B565	SP298	2fr +40c multi	90	60

The Rose Basket, by Caly—SP299

1984, Nov. 24 Photo. *Perf. 12½x13*

B566	SP299 2.10fr +50c pnksh (basket) & multi	60	60
a.	Sal (basket) & multi	60	60
b.	Bklt pane of #B566a + 2 labels	6.00	

Surtax was for the Red Cross.

Jules Romains (1885-1972)—SP300

Authors: No. B568, Jean-Paul Sartre (1905-1980). No. B569, Romain Rolland (1866-1944). No. B570, Roland Dorgeles (1885-1973). No. B571, Victor Hugo (1802-1885). No. B572, Francois Mauriac (1885-1970).

1985, Feb. 23 Engr. *Perf. 13*

B567	SP300 1.70fr +40c vio & dp vio	45	45
B568	SP300 1.70fr +40c dp vio & brn vio	45	45
B569	SP300 1.70fr +40c brn vio & dp vio	45	45
B570	SP300 2.10fr +50c brn vio & vio	58	58
B571	SP300 2.10fr +50c vio & brn vio	58	58
B572	SP300 2.10fr +50c dp vio & vio	58	58
a.	Bklt. pane of 6, #B567-B572		

Stamp Day—SP301

Design: Canceling apparatus invented by Eugene Daguin (1849-1888).

1985, Mar. 16 Engr. *Perf. 12½x13*

B573	SP301 2.10fr +50c brn blk & bluish gray	58	58

Issenheim Altarpiece Retable—SP302

1985, Nov. 23 Photo.

B574	SP302 2.20fr +.50fr multi	70	70
a.	Bklt. pane of 10	7.00	

Surtaxed for the Red Cross.

Francois Arago (1786-1853), Physician, Politician—SP303

Famous men: No. B576, Henri Moissan (1852-1907), chemist. No. B577, Henri Fabre (1882-1984), engineer. No. B578, Marc Seguin (1786-1875), engineer. No. B579, Paul Heroult (1863-1914), chemist.

1986, Feb. 22 Engr. *Perf. 13*

B575	SP303 1.80fr + 40c multi	60	12
B576	SP303 1.80fr + 40c multi	60	12
B577	SP303 1.80fr + 40c multi	60	12
B578	SP303 2.20fr + 50c multi	72	14
B579	SP303 2.20fr + 50c multi	72	14
a.	Bklt. pane of 5 + 3 labels	4.00	

Pierre Cot (1895-1977)—SP304

1986, Mar. 1 Engr. *Perf. 13x12½*

B580	SP304 2.20fr +50c brn blk	80	16

Mail Britzska—SP305

1986, Apr. 5 *Perf. 13*

B581	SP305 2.20fr +60c pale tan & dk vio brn	85	18

Engr. *Perf. 13*

B582	SP305 2.20fr + 60c buff & blk	85	18
a.	Bklt. pane of 6 + label	5.10	

No. B582 issued in booklets only.

Stained Glass Window (detail), by Vieira da Silva, St. Jacques of Reims Church, Marne—SP306

1986, Nov. 24 Photo. *Perf.*

B583	SP306 2.20fr + 60c multi	88	18
a.	Bklt. pane of 10	8.80	

Surtaxed to benefit the natl. Red Cross.

Physicians and Biologists—SP307

Designs: No. B584, Charles Richet (1850-1935). No. B585, Eugene Jamot (1879-1937). No. B586, Bernard Halpern (1904-1978). No. B587, Alexandre Yersin (1863-1943). No. B588, Jean Rostand (1894-1977). No. B589, Jacques Monod (1910-1976).

1987, Feb. 21 Engr. *Perf.*

B584	SP307 1.90fr + 50c	78	15
B585	SP307 1.90fr + 50c	78	15
B586	SP307 1.90fr + 50c	78	15
B587	SP307 2.20fr + 50c	88	18
B588	SP307 2.20fr + 50c	88	18
B589	SP307 2.20fr + 50c	88	18
a.	Bklt. pane of 6, #B584-B589	5.00	
	Nos. B584-B589 (6)	4.98	99

Stamp Day Type of 1986

Design: Berline carriage.

1987, Mar. 14 Engr. *Perf.*

B590	SP305 2.20fr + 60c	95	20

Booklet Stamp

B591	SP305 2.20fr + 60c	95	20
a.	Bklt. pane of 6 + 2 labels	5.75	

Stamp Day 1987. No. B591 issued in booklets only.

AIR POST STAMPS.

Nos. 127, 130 Overprinted in Dark Blue or Black

Poste Aérienne

Perf. 14x13½

1927, June 25 **Unwmkd.**

C1	A18	2fr org & bl (DB)	200.00	185.00
C2	A18	5fr dk bl & buff (Bk)	200.00	185.00

These stamps were on sale only at the International Aviation Exhibition at Marseilles, June, 1927. One set could be purchased by each holder of an admission ticket. Excellent counterfeits exist.

Nos. 242, 196 Surcharged **10 FR.**

1928, Aug. 23

C3	A33	10fr on 90c dl rose	1,650.	1,650.
a.		Inverted surcharge	*12,000.*	*12,000.*
b.		Space between "10" and bars 6½mm	*3,000.*	*3,000.*
C4	A23	10fr on 1.50fr bl	*8,250.*	*8,250.*
a.		Space between "10" and bars 6½mm	*10,000.*	*10,000.*

Nos. C3–C4 received their surcharge in New York by order of the French consul-general. They were for use in paying the 10fr fee for letters leaving the liner Ile de France on a catapulted hydroplane when the ship was one day off the coast of France on its eastward voyage.

The normal space between "10" and bars is 4½mm., but on 10 stamps in each pane of 50 the space is 6½mm. Counterfeits exist.

View of Marseille, Church of Notre Dame at Left
AP1

1930–31 **Engraved** ***Perf. 13***

C5	AP1	1.50fr dp car	24.00	2.00
C6	AP1	1.50fr dk bl ('31)	21.00	1.65
a.		1.50fr ultra	45.00	12.00
b.		With perf. initials (EIPA 30)	575.00	400.00

No. C6a was sold at the International Air Post Exhibition, Paris, Nov. 6–20, 1930, at face value plus 5 francs, the price of admission. Most of the stamps of the first printing were perforated "EIPA30".

Blériot's Monoplane—AP2

1934, Sept. 1 ***Perf. 13***

C7	AP2	2.25fr violet	21.00	6.00

Issued in commemoration of the first flight across the English Channel, by Louis Blériot.

Plane over Paris
AP3

1936

C8	AP3	85c dp grn	3.75	90
C9	AP3	1.50fr blue	11.00	3.75
C10	AP3	2.25fr violet	26.00	6.75
C11	AP3	2.50fr rose	37.50	7.50
C12	AP3	3fr ultra	22.50	65
C13	AP3	3.50fr org brn	75.00	19.00
C14	AP3	50fr emerald	1,000.	325.00
a.		50fr dp grn	1,350.	600.00
		Nos. C8-C14 (7)	1,175.75	363.55

Monoplane over Paris—AP4
Paper with Red Network Overprint

1936, July 10 ***Perf. 12½***

C15	AP4	50fr ultra	900.00	300.00

Airplane and Galleon
AP5

Airplane and Globe
AP6

1936, Aug. 17 ***Perf. 13***

C16	AP5	1.50fr dk ultra	19.00	2.25
C17	AP6	10fr Prus grn	375.00	110.00

Issued in commemoration of the 100th air mail flight across the South Atlantic Ocean.

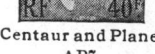

Centaur and Plane
AP7

Iris
AP8

Zeus Carrying Hebe
AP9

Chariot of the Sun
AP10

1946–47 **Engraved** **Unwmkd.**

C18	AP7	40fr dk grn	60	22
C19	AP8	50fr rose pink	60	22
C20	AP9	100fr dk bl ('47)	5.25	50
C21	AP10	200fr red	4.50	75

Ile de la Cité, Paris, and Gull
AP11

1947, May 7

C22	AP11	500fr dk Prus grn	47.50	37.50

Universal Postal Union 12th Congress, Paris, May 7–July 7, 1947.

View of Lille
AP12

Air View of Paris—AP13

Designs: 200fr, Bordeaux. 300fr, Lyon. 500fr, Marseille.

1949-50 ***Perf. 13.*** **Unwmkd.**

C23	AP12	100fr sepia	90	22
C24	AP12	200fr dk bl grn	9.50	75
C25	AP12	300fr purple	19.00	12.00
C26	AP12	500fr brt red	45.00	4.50
C27	AP13	1000fr sep & blk, *bl* ('50)	90.00	22.50
		Nos. C23-C27 (5)	164.40	39.97

Alexander III Bridge and Petit Palais, Paris—AP14

1949, June 13

C28	AP14	100fr brn car	9.50	6.75

Issued to publicize the International Telegraph and Telephone Conference, Paris, May–July 1949.

Jet Plane, Mystère IV
AP15

Planes: 200fr, Noratlas. 500fr, Miles Magister. 1000fr, Provence.

1954, Jan. 16

C29	AP15	100fr red brn & bl	1.50	15
C30	AP15	200fr blk brn & vio bl	5.25	22
C31	AP15	500fr car & org	80.00	12.00
C32	AP15	1000fr vio brn, bl grn & ind	90.00	16.00

Maryse Bastié and Plane
AP16

1955, June 4 ***Perf. 13*** **Unwmkd.**

C33	AP16	50fr dp plum & rose pink	8.25	5.25

Issued to honor Maryse Bastié, 1898-1952.

Caravelle—AP17

Designs: 300fr, Morane Saulnier 760 "Paris." 1000fr, Alouette helicopter.

1957-59 **Engraved.** ***Perf. 13***

C34	AP17	300fr sl grn, grnsh bl & sep ('59)	5.25	2.50
C35	AP17	500fr dp ultra & blk	45.00	2.25
C36	AP17	1000fr lil, ol blk & blk ('58)	70.00	26.00

Types of 1954-59.

Planes: 2fr, Noratlas. 3fr, MS760, Paris. 5fr, Caravelle. 10fr, Alouette helicopter.

1960, Jan. 11

C37	AP15	2fr vio bl & ultra	2.25	10
a.		2fr ultra	3.75	22
C38	AP17	3fr sl grn, grnsh bl & sep	1.90	5
C39	AP17	5fr dp ultra & blk	3.25	30
C40	AP17	10fr lil, ol blk & blk	18.00	1.50

Type of 1957–59.

Design: 2fr, Jet plane, Mystère 20.

1965, June 12 **Engraved** ***Perf. 13***

C41	AP17	2fr sl bl & ind	1.40	6

Concorde Issue
Common Design Type

1969, Mar. 2 **Engraved** ***Perf. 13***

C42	CD129	1fr ind & brt bl	1.90	38

Issued to commemorate the first flight of the prototype Concorde plane at Toulouse, March 1, 1969.

Jean Mermoz, Antoine de Saint-Exupéry and Concorde—AP19

1970, Sept. 19 **Engraved** ***Perf. 13***

C43	AP19	20fr bl & ind	6.25	45

Issued to honor Jean Mermoz (1901–1936) and the writer Antoine de Saint-Exupéry (1900–1944), aviators and air mail pioneers.

Balloon, Gare d'Austerlitz, Paris AP20

1971, Jan. 16 Engraved *Perf. 13*

C44 AP20 95c bl, vio bl, org & sl grn 1.25 90

Centenary of the balloon post from besieged Paris, 1870–71.

Didier Daurat, Raymond Vanier and Plane Landing at Night—AP21

1971, Apr. 17 Engraved *Perf. 13*

C45 AP21 5fr Prus bl, blk & lt grn 1.90 10

Honoring Didier Daurat (1891–1969) and Raymond Vanier (1895–1965), aviation pioneers.

Hélène Boucher, Maryse Hilsz and Caudron-Renault and Moth-Morane Planes—AP22

Design: 15fr, Henri Guillaumet, Paul Codos, Latécoère 521, Guillaumet's crashed plane in Andes, skyscrapers.

1972–73 Engraved *Perf. 13*

C46 AP22 10fr plum, red & sl 3.75 15
C47 AP22 15fr dp car, gray & brn ('73) 5.25 45

Hélène Boucher (1908–1934) and Maryse Hilsz (1901–1946), aviation pioneers.
Henri Guillaumet (1902–1940) and Paul Codos (1896–1960), aviation pioneers.
Issue dates: 10fr, June 10, 1972; 15fr, Feb. 24, 1973.

Concorde AP23

1976, Jan. 10 Engr. *Perf. 13*

C48 AP23 1.70fr brt bl, red & blk 1.00 50

First flight of supersonic jet Concorde from Paris to Rio de Janeiro, Jan. 21.

Planes over the Atlantic, New York-Paris—AP24

1977, June 4 Engr. *Perf. 13*

C49 AP24 1.90fr multi 1.00 60

First transatlantic flight by Charles A. Lindbergh from New York to Paris, 50th anniversary, and first attempted westbound flight by French aviators Charles Nungesser and Francois Coli.

Plane over Flight Route AP25

1978, Oct. 14 Engr. *Perf. 13*

C50 AP25 1.50fr multi 1.40 45

75th anniversary of first airmail route from Villacoublay to Pauillac, Gironde.

Rocket, Concorde, Exhibition Hall AP26

1979, June 9 Engr. *Perf. 13*

C51 AP26 1.70fr ultra, org & brn 1.10 50

33rd International Aerospace and Space Show, Le Bourget, June 11–15.

First Nonstop Transatlantic Flight, Paris-New York—AP27

1980, Aug. 30 Engr. *Perf. 13*

C52 AP27 2.50fr vio brn & ultra 80 32

34th Intl. Space and Aeronautics Exhibition, June 5-14—AP28

1981, June 6 Engr. *Perf. 13*

C53 AP28 2fr multi 2.00 45

Dieudonné Costes and Joseph Le Brix and their Breguet Bi-plane—AP29

1981, Sept. 12 Engr.

C54 AP29 10fr dk brn & red 3.75 22

First South Atlantic crossing, Oct. 14-15, 1927.

Seaplane Late-300—AP30

1982, Dec. 4 Engr.

C55 AP30 1.60fr multi 60 45

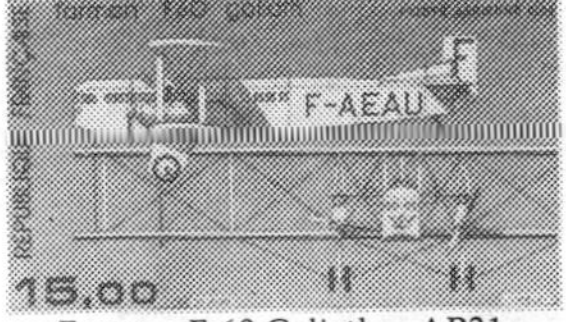

Farman F-60 Goliath—AP31

1984, Mar. 3 Engr. *Perf. 13x12½*

C56 AP31 15fr dk bl 3.75 45

CAMS-53 Seaplane—AP32

1985, Mar. 2 Engr. *Perf. 13*

C57 AP32 20fr dp org 5.25 60

Wibault 283 Monoplane—AP33

1986, Oct. 11 Engr.

C58 AP33 30fr brt vio 9.00 1.80

Dewoitine 338—AP34

1987, Apr. 11 Engr.

C59 AP34 50fr grn 17.00 3.00

AIR POST SEMI-POSTAL STAMPS.

Antoine de Saint-Exupéry SPAP1

Col. Jean Dagnaux SPAP2

Engraved

1948 *Perf. 13* Unwmkd.

CB1 SPAP1 50fr +30fr vio brn 1.75 1.75
CB2 SPAP2 100fr +70fr dk bl 2.75 2.75

Modern Plane and Ader's "Eole" SPAP3

1948, Feb.

CB3 SPAP3 40fr +10fr dk bl 1.10 1.10

Issued to commemorate the 50th anniversary of the flight of Clément Ader's plane, the Eole, in 1897.

POSTAGE DUE STAMPS.

D1

D2

Lithographed

1859–70 ***Imperf.*** **Unwmkd.**

J1	D1	10c black	*11,000.*	210.00
J2	D1	15c blk ('70)	125.00	225.00

In the lithographed stamps the central bar of the "E" of "CENTIMES" is very short, and the accent on "a" slants at an angle of 30°, for the 10c and 17° for the 15c, while on the typographed the central bar of the "E" is almost as wide as the top and bottom bars and the accent on the "a" slants at an angle of 47°.

No. J2 is known rouletted unofficially.

1859-78 Typographed.

J3	D1	10c black	21.00	16.50
J4	D1	15c blk ('63)	25.00	13.50
J5	D1	20c blk ('77)	*2,250.*	
J6	D1	25c blk ('71)	110.00	45.00
J7	D1	30c blk ('78)	185.00	120.00
J8	D1	40c bl ('71)	300.00	400.00
a.		40c ultra	*5,250.*	*6,000.*
b.		40c Prus bl	*2,500.*	
J9	D1	60c yel ('71)	500.00	*1,200.*
J10	D1	60c bl ('78)	60.00	100.00
a.		60c dk bl	550.00	650.00
J10B	D1	60c black	*2,250.*	

The 20c and 60c black were never put into use.

Nos. J3, J4, J6, J8 and J9 are known rouletted unofficially and Nos. J4, J6, J7 and J10 pin-perf. unofficially.

1882-92 ***Perf. 14 x 13½.***

J11	D2	1c black	75	75
J12	D2	2c black	13.50	14.00
J13	D2	3c black	13.50	15.00
J14	D2	4c black	25.00	18.00
J15	D2	5c black	52.50	15.00
J16	D2	10c black	50.00	1.50
J17	D2	15c black	26.50	6.00
J18	D2	20c black	150.00	82.50
J19	D2	30c black	100.00	1.50
J20	D2	40c black	60.00	30.00
J21	D2	50c blk ('92)	275.00	100.00
J22	D2	60c blk ('84)	275.00	30.00
J23	D2	1fr black	350.00	225.00
J24	D2	2fr blk ('84)	650.00	500.00
J25	D2	5fr blk ('84)	1,500.	1,000.

Excellent counterfeits exist of Nos. J23-J25.

1884

J26	D2	1fr brown	225.00	67.50
J27	D2	2fr brown	135.00	100.00
J28	D2	5fr brown	265.00	200.00

1893–1941

J29	D2	5c bl ('94)	45	22
J30	D2	10c brown	45	15
J31	D2	15c lt grn ('94)	18.00	1.35
J32	D2	20c ol grn ('06)	3.00	22
J33	D2	25c rose ('23)	3.75	2.65
J34	D2	30c red ('94)	45	15
J35	D2	30c org red ('94)	450.00	70.00
J36	D2	40c rose ('25)	6.75	2.65
J37	D2	45c grn ('24)	5.00	3.50
J38	D2	50c brn vio ('95)	45	15
a.		50c lil	45	15
J39	D2	60c bl grn ('25)	55	20
J40	D2	1fr rose, *straw* ('96)	450.00	375.00
J41	D2	1fr red brn, *straw* ('20)	3.75	15
J42	D2	1fr red brn ('35)	75	18
J43	D2	2fr red org ('10)	180.00	50.00
J44	D2	2fr brt vio ('26)	55	30
J45	D2	3fr mag ('26)	55	30
J45A	D2	5fr red org ('41)	1.50	1.50

D3

D4

1908–25

J46	D3	1c ol grn	90	45
J47	D3	10c violet	1.00	30
a.		Imperf., pair	180.00	
J48	D3	20c bis ('19)	18.00	50
J49	D3	30c bis ('09)	9.50	30
J50	D3	50c red ('09)	210.00	52.50
J51	D3	60c red ('25)	2.25	1.10
		Nos. J46-J51 (6)	241.65	55.15

"Recouvrements" stamps were used to recover charges due on undelivered or refused mail which was returned to the sender.

Nos. J49–J50 Surcharged **20c.**

1917

J52	D3	20c on 30c bis	9.00	2.40
J53	D3	40c on 50c red	9.00	2.10
a.		Double surch.	165.00	

In Jan. 1917 several values of the current issue of postage stamps were handstamped "T" in a triangle and used as postage due stamps.

Recouvrements Stamps of 1908-25 Surcharged **50**

1926

J54	D3	50c on 10c lil	3.50	1.50
J55	D3	60c on 1c ol grn	5.25	2.50
J56	D3	1fr on 60c red	13.50	6.00
J57	D3	2fr on 60c red	13.50	6.75

1927-31

J58	D4	1c ol grn ('28)	1.10	38
J59	D4	10c rose ('31)	16.50	38
J60	D4	30c bister	3.75	22
J61	D4	60c red	3.25	30
J62	D4	1fr violet	12.00	2.40
J63	D4	1fr Prus grn ('31)	13.50	45
J64	D4	2fr blue	40.00	25.00
J65	D4	2fr ol brn ('31)	125.00	18.00
		Nos. J58-J65 (8)	215.10	47.13

Nos. J62 to J65 have the numerals of value double-lined.

Nos. J64, J62 Surcharged in Red or Black **1F20**

1929

J66	D4	1.20fr on 2fr bl	30.00	4.50
J67	D4	5fr on 1fr vio (Bk)	37.50	6.00

No. J61 Surcharged **UN FRANC**

1931

J68	D4	1fr on 60c red	15.00	1.50

D5

D6

Sheaves of Wheat

Typographed.

1943-46 ***Perf. 14x13½.*** **Unwmkd.**

J69	D5	10c sepia	15	15
J70	D5	30c brt red vio	15	15
J71	D5	50c bl grn	15	15
J72	D5	1fr brt ultra	15	15
J73	D5	1.50fr rose red	30	30
J74	D5	2fr turq bl	35	30
J75	D5	3fr brn org	35	30
J76	D5	4fr dp vio ('45)	4.00	2.75
J77	D5	5fr brt pink	45	30
J78	D5	10fr red org ('45)	3.75	30
J79	D5	20fr ol bis ('46)	6.75	2.40
		Nos. J69-J79 (11)	16.55	7.25

Type of 1943.
Inscribed "Timbre Taxe."

1946-53

J80	D5	10c sep ('47)	1.35	1.00
J81	D5	30c brt red vio ('47)	1.00	90
J82	D5	50c bl grn ('47)	8.00	4.50
J83	D5	1fr brt ultra ('47)	22	22
J85	D5	2fr turq bl	22	22
J86	D5	3fr brn org	22	22
J87	D5	4fr dp vio	30	22
J88	D5	5fr brt pink ('47)	30	15
J89	D5	10fr red org ('47)	30	15
J90	D5	20fr ol bis ('47)	1.50	30
J91	D5	50fr dk grn ('50)	13.50	30
J92	D5	100fr dp grn ('53)	47.50	4.75
		Nos. J80-J92 (12)	74.41	12.93

1960 **Typographed.** ***Perf. 14x13½***

J93	D6	5c brt pink	1.65	30
J94	D6	10c red org	2.10	30
J95	D6	20c ol bis	3.75	30
J96	D6	50c dk grn	11.00	1.20
J97	D6	1fr dp grn	42.50	1.65
		Nos. J93-J97 (5)	61.00	3.75

Corn Poppy
D7

Flowers: 5c, Centaury. 10c, Gentian. 20c, Violets. 30c, Forget-me-not. 40c, Columbine. 50c, Clover. 1fr, Soldanel.

1964–71 **Typo.** ***Perf. 14x13½***

J98	D7	5c car rose, red & grn ('65)	5	5
J99	D7	10c car rose, brt bl & grn ('65)	10	5
J100	D7	15c brn, grn & red	15	15
J101	D7	20c dk grn, grn & vio ('71)	15	10
J102	D7	30c brn, ultra & grn	18	6
J103	D7	40c dk grn, scar & yel ('71)	27	15
J104	D7	50c vio bl, car & grn ('65)	27	6
J105	D7	1fr vio bl, lil & grn ('65)	45	12
		Nos. J98-J105 (8)	1.62	74

Ampedus Cinnabarinus—D8

1982–83 **Engr.** ***Perf. 13***

J106	D8	10c shown	5	5
J107	D8	20c Dorcadion fuliginator	6	5
J108	D8	30c Leptura cordigera	12	5
J109	D8	40c Paederus littoralis	12	6
J110	D8	50c Pyrochroa coccinea	15	5
J111	D8	1fr Scarites laevigatus	30	5
J112	D8	2fr Trichius gallicus	55	5
J113	D8	3fr Adalia alpina	90	6
J114	D8	4fr Apoderus coryli	1.20	5
J115	D8	5fr Trichodes alvearius	1.50	10
		Nos. J106-J115 (10)	4.95	57

MILITARY STAMPS

Regular Issue Overprinted in Black or Red **F. M.**

1901-39 ***Perf. 14x13½*** **Unwmkd.**

M1	A17	15c org ('01)	67.50	7.50
a.		Inverted overprint	200.00	82.50
b.		Imperf., pair	325.00	
M2	A19	15c pale red ('03)	70.00	5.25
M3	A20	15c sl grn ('04)	47.50	6.00
a.		No period after "M"	100.00	40.00
b.		Imperf., pair	210.00	
M4	A20	10c rose ('06)	30.00	8.25
a.		No period after "M"	85.00	40.00
b.		Imperf., pair	200.00	
M5	A22	10c red ('07)	60	30
a.		Inverted overprint	90.00	47.50
b.		Imperf., pair	175.00	
M6	A20	50c ver ('29)	4.50	90
a.		No period after "M"	40.00	15.00
b.		Period in front of F	40.00	15.00
M7	A45	50c rose red ('34)	2.25	30
a.		No period after "M"	20.00	12.50
b.		Invtd. ovpt.	95.00	45.00
M8	A45	65c brt ultra (R) ('38)	38	22
a.		No period after "M"	27.50	22.50
M9	A45	90c ultra (R) ('39)	45	38

"F. M." are initials of Franchise Militaire (Military Frank). See No. S1.

M1

Flag—M2

1946-47 **Typographed.**

M10	M1	dk grn	1.40	65
M11	M1	rose red ('47)	22	10

Nos. M10-M11 were valid also in the French colonies.

1964, July 20 ***Perf. 13x14***

M12	M2	multi	30	22

OFFICIAL STAMPS

For the Council of Europe.

For use only on mail posted in the post office in the Council of Europe Building, Strasbourg.

France No. 854 Overprinted: "CONSEIL DE L'EUROPE." Engraved.

1958, Jan. 14 ***Perf. 13*** **Unwmkd.**

1O1	A303	35fr car rose & lake	1.90	3.00

Council of Europe Flag O1

1958-59

Flag in Ultramarine.

1O2	O1	8fr red org & brn vio	22	22
1O3	O1	20fr yel & lt brn	45	38
1O4	O1	25fr lil rose & sl grn ('59)	1.10	50
1O5	O1	35fr red	80	80
1O6	O1	50fr lil rose ('59)	1.90	1.75
		Nos. 1O2-1O6 (5)	4.47	3.65

1963, Jan. 3

Flag in Ultramarine

1O7	O1	20c yel & lt brn	1.90	75
1O8	O1	25c lil rose & sl grn	3.00	1.65
1O9	O1	50c lil rose	3.00	2.50

1965-71

Flag in Ultramarine & Yellow

1O10	O1	25c ver, yel & sl grn	1.25	95
1O11	O1	30c ver & yel	1.25	95
1O12	O1	40c ver, yel & gray ('69)	1.90	95
1O13	O1	50c red, yel & grn ('71)	3.80	1.75
1O14	O1	60c ver, yel & vio	1.50	95
1O15	O1	70c ver, yel & dk brn ('69)	5.50	3.75
		Nos. 1O10-1O15 (6)	15.20	9.30

Issue dates: 25c, 30c, 60c, Jan. 16, 1965. 50c, Feb. 20, 1971. Others, Mar. 24, 1969.

Type of 1958 Inscribed "FRANCE"

1975-76 **Engraved** ***Perf. 13***

Flag in Ultramarine & Yellow

1O16	O1	60c org, yel & emer	1.65	1.00
1O17	O1	80c yel & mag	2.50	1.65
1O18	O1	1fr car, yel & gray ol ('76)	5.50	4.50
1O19	O1	1.20fr org, yel & bl	7.00	3.75

Issue dates: 1fr, Oct. 16, 1976. Others, Nov. 22, 1975.

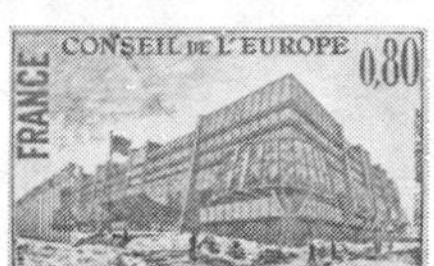

New Council Headquarters, Strasbourg O2

1977, Jan. 22 **Engr.** ***Perf. 13***

1O20	O2	80c car & multi	1.10	75
1O21	O2	1fr brn & multi	1.10	75
1O22	O2	1.40fr gray & multi	2.25	1.50

Human Rights Emblem in Upper Left Corner

1978, Oct. 14

1O23	O2	1.20fr red lil & multi	65	60
1O24	O2	1.70fr bl & multi	95	80

30th anniversary of the Universal Declaration of Human Rights.

Council Headquarters Type of 1977

1980, Nov. 24 **Engraved** ***Perf. 13***

1O25	O2	1.40fr olive	75	65
1O26	O2	2fr bl gray	90	80

New Council Headquarters, Strasbourg—O3

1981, Nov. 21 **Engr.**

1O27	O3	1.40fr multi	60	60
1O28	O3	1.60fr multi	60	60
1O29	O3	2.30fr multi	95	95

1982, Nov. 13 **Engr.**

1O30	O3	1.80fr multi	80	80
1O31	O3	2.60fr multi	95	95

1983, Nov. 21 **Engraved**

1O32	O3	2fr multi	90	90
1O33	O3	2.80fr multi	1.10	1.10

1984, Nov. 5 **Engr.** ***Perf. 13***

1O34	O3	1.70fr emerald	40	40
1O35	O3	2.10fr red	45	45
1O36	O3	3fr brt bl	65	65

Youth's Leg, Sneaker, Shattered Eggshell—O4

1985, Aug. 31 **Engr.** ***Perf. 13***

1O37	O4	1.80fr brt grn	42	8
1O38	O4	2.20fr vermilion	52	10
1O39	O4	3.20fr brt bl	75	15

New Council Headquarters, Strasbourg—O5

1986, Dec. 13 **Engr.** ***Perf.***

1O40	O5	1.90fr green	60	12
1O41	O5	2.20fr red	70	14
1O42	O5	3.40fr blue	1.05	22

For the United Nations Educational, Scientific and Cultural Organization

For use only on mail posted in the post office in the UNESCO Building, Paris.

Khmer Buddha and Hermes by Praxiteles
O1

Engraved

1961–65 ***Perf. 13*** **Unwmkd.**

201	O1	20c dk gray, ol bis & bl	45	38
202	O1	25c blk, lake & grn	60	45
203	O1	30c choc & bis brn ('65)	1.00	90
204	O1	50c blk, red & vio bl	2.50	1.90
205	O1	60c grnsh bl, red brn & rose lil ('65)	2.25	1.90
		Nos. 201-205 (5)	6.80	5.53

Book and Globe
O2

1966, Dec. 17

206	O2	25c gray	75	75
207	O2	30c dk red	95	95
208	O2	60c green	1.65	1.65

20th anniversary of UNESCO.

Human Rights Flame
O3

1969–71 **Engraved** ***Perf. 13***

209	O3	30c sl grn, red & dp brn	90	60
2010	O3	40c dk car rose, red & dp brn	1.40	90
2011	O3	50c ultra, car & brn ('71)	3.00	2.25
2012	O3	70c pur, red & sl	4.50	3.75

Universal Declaration of Human Rights.

Type of 1969 Inscribed "FRANCE"

1975, Nov. 15 **Engr.** ***Perf. 13***

2013	O3	60c grn, red & dk brn	1.65	1.00
2014	O3	80c ocher, red & red brn	2.50	1.65
2015	O3	1.20fr ind, red & brn	6.25	4.50

O4

1976–78 **Engr.** ***Perf. 13***

2016	O4	80c multi	1.10	90
2017	O4	1fr multi	1.10	90
2018	O4	1.20fr multi ('78)	65	60
2019	O4	1.40fr multi	3.00	1.75
2020	O4	1.70fr multi ('78)	95	80
		Nos. 2016-2020 (5)	6.80	4.95

Issue dates: 1.20fr, 1.70fr, Oct. 14, 1978. Others, Oct. 23, 1976.

Slave Quarters, Senegal—O5

Designs: 1.40fr, Mohenjo-Daro excavations, Pakistan. 2fr, Sans-Souci Palace, Haiti.

1980, Nov. 17 **Engr.** ***Perf. 13***

2021	O5	1.20fr multi	65	55
2022	O5	1.40fr multi	75	60
2023	O5	2fr multi	1.00	80

Fort St. Elmo, Malta—O6

Designs: 1.40fr, Building, Fez, Morocco (vert.). 1.60fr, Seated deity, Sukhotai, Thailand (vert.).

1981, Dec. 12

2024	O6	1.40fr multi	65	60
2025	O6	1.60fr multi	65	60
2026	O6	2.30fr multi	1.00	90

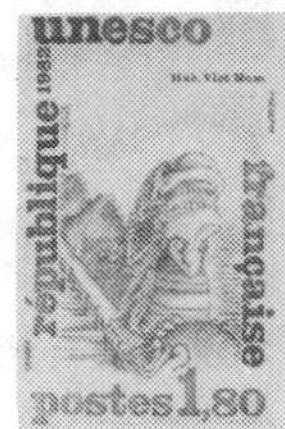

Hue, Vietnam—O7

1982, Oct. 23 **Engr.**

2027	O7	1.80fr shown	75	75
2028	O7	2.60fr St. Michael Church ruins, Brazil	90	90

Mosque, Chinguetti, Mauritania—O8

1983, Oct. 10 **Engraved**

2029	O8	2fr shown	80	80
2030	O8	2.80fr Enclosure wall, interior, Istanbul	95	95

1984, Oct. 22 **Engr.** ***Perf. 13x12½***

2031	O8	1.70fr Church, Lalibela, Ethiopia	40	40
2032	O8	2.10fr San'a, Yemen	45	45
2033	O8	3fr Church, Kotor, Jugoslavia	65	65

Architecture Type of 1983-84

Designs: 1.80fr, Roman Theater and female standing sculpture, Carthage, Tunisia. 2.20fr, Old Town Square and wrought iron latticework, Havana. 3.20fr, Temple of Anuradhapura and bas-relief of two women, Sri Lanka.

1985, Oct. 26 **Engr.** ***Perf. 12½x13***

2034	O8	1.80fr multi	42	8
2035	O8	2.20fr multi	52	10
2036	O8	3.20fr multi	75	15

UNESCO restoration projects, 1985-86.

Tikal Temple, Guatemala—O9

1986, Dec. 6 **Engr.** ***Perf. 13***

2037	O9	1.90fr shown	60	12
2038	O9	3.40fr Bagerhat Mosque, Bangladesh	1.05	22

NEWSPAPER STAMPS.

Coat of Arms
N1

Typographed.

1868 ***Imperf.*** **Unwmkd.**

P1	N1	2c lilac	250.00	60.00
P2	N1	2c (+2c) bl	525.00	250.00

Perf. 12½.

P3	N1	2c lilac	37.50	20.00
P4	N1	2c (+4c) rose	135.00	90.00
P5	N1	2c (+2c) bl	62.50	30.00
P6	N1	5c lilac	1,000.	650.00

Nos. P2, P4, and P5 were sold for face plus an added fiscal charge indicated in parenthesis. Nos. P1, P3 and P6 were used simply as fiscals.

The 2c rose and 5c lilac imperforate and the 5c rose and 5c blue, both imperforate and perforated, were never put into use.

Nos. P1–P6 were reprinted for the 1913 Ghent Exhibition and the 1937 Paris Exhibition (PEXIP).

No. 109 Surcharged in Red **½ centime**

1919 ***Perf. 14x13½***

P7	A16	½c on 1c gray	30	22
	a.	Inverted surcharge	1,000.	450.00

No. 156 Surcharged.

1933

P8	A22	½c on 1c ol bis	45	38

FRANCHISE STAMP.

No. 276 Overprinted "F".

1939 ***Perf. 14x13½*** **Unwmkd.**

S1	A45	90c ultra	2.25	2.25
	a.	Period after "F"	27.50	22.50

No. S1 was for the use of Spanish refugee soldiers in France. "F" stands for "Fugitives."

OCCUPATION STAMPS.

Issued under German Occupation.

(Alsace and Lorraine).

O1

Perf. 13½x14.

1870 **Typographed** **Unwmkd.**

Network with Points Up.

N1	O1	1c ol grn	52.50	100.00
N2	O1	2c red brn	100.00	125.00
	a.	2c dk brn	120.00	160.00
N3	O1	4c gray	92.50	60.00
N4	O1	5c yel grn	60.00	10.00
N5	O1	10c yel brn	30.00	3.50
	a.	10c bis brn	55.00	4.75
	b.	Network lem yel	72.50	8.00
N6	O1	20c ultra	65.00	10.00
N7	O1	25c brown	120.00	65.00
	a.	25c blk brn	160.00	95.00

There are three varieties of the 4c and two of the 10c, differing in the position of the figures of value, and several other setting varieties.

Network with Points Down.

No.	Type	Description	Unused	Used
N8	O1	1c ol grn	325.00	*750.00*
N9	O1	2c red brn	150.00	*675.00*
N10	O1	4c gray	160.00	120.00
N11	O1	5c yel grn	2,400.	325.00
N12	O1	10c bister	80.00	9.50
a.		Network lem yel	265.00	80.00
N13	O1	20c ultra	225.00	110.00
N14	O1	25c brown	475.00	240.00

Official imitations have the network with points downward. The "P" of "Postes" is 2½mm. from the border in the imitations and 3mm. in the originals. The word "Postes" measures 12¾ to 13mm. on the imitations, and from 11 to 12½mm. on the originals.

The imitations are perf. 13½x14½; originals, perf. 13½x14¼.

The stamps for Alsace and Lorraine were replaced by stamps of the German Empire on Jan. 1, 1872.

German Stamps of 1905–16 Surcharged:

3 Cent. (a) 1 F (b)

✱ 1F.25Cent. ✱ (c)

Wmkd. Lozenges. (125)

1916 *Perf. 14, 14½.*

No.	Type	Description	Unused	Used
N15	A16(a)	3c on 3pf brn	50	50
N16	A16(a)	5c on 5pf grn	50	75
N17	A22(a)	8c onn 7½pf org	60	1.00
N18	A16(a)	10c on 10pf car	50	50
N19	A22(a)	15c on 15pf yel brn	50	50
N20	A16(a)	25c on 20pf bl	75	75
a.		25c on 20pf ultra	1.25	2.50
N21	A16(a)	40c on 30pf org & blk, *buff*	1.00	2.00
N22	A16(a)	50c on 40pf lake & blk	1.00	2.00
N23	A16(a)	75c on 60pf mag	5.00	6.00
N24	A16(b)	1fr on 80pf lake & blk, *rose*	5.00	9.00
N25	A17	1fr25c on 1m car	22.50	25.00
a.		Double surcharge	100.00	
N26	A21	2fr50c on 2m gray bl	22.50	20.00
a.		Double surcharge	100.00	
		Nos. N15-N26 (12)	60.35	68.00

These stamps were also used in parts of Belgium occupied by the German forces.

Alsace.

Issued under German Occupation.

Stamps of Germany 1933-36 Overprinted in Black **Elsaß**

Wmkd. Swastikas. (237)

1940 *Perf. 14*

No.	Type	Description	Unused	Used
N27	A64	3(pf) ol bis	28	50
N28	A64	4(pf) dl bl	45	1.00
N29	A64	5(pf) brt grn	28	50
N30	A64	6(pf) dk grn	28	50
N31	A64	8(pf) vermilion	28	50
N32	A64	10(pf) chocolate	28	90
N33	A64	12(pf) dp car	30	60
N34	A64	15(pf) maroon	45	1.00
N35	A64	20(pf) brt bl	45	1.00
N36	A64	25(pf) ultra	60	1.35
N37	A64	30(pf) ol grn	1.15	1.60
N38	A64	40(pf) red vio	1.15	1.60
N39	A64	50(pf) dk grn & blk	1.65	2.50
N40	A64	60(pf) cl & blk	2.00	3.50
N41	A64	80(pf) dk bl & blk	2.25	5.00
N42	A64	100(pf) org & blk	3.25	3.00
		Nos. N27-N42 (16)	15.10	25.05

Lorraine.

Issued under German Occupation.

Stamps of Germany 1933-36

Overprinted in Black **Lothringen**

Wmkd. Swastikas. (237)

1940 *Perf. 14.*

No.	Type	Description	Unused	Used
N43	A64	3(pf) ol bis	50	*1.00*
N44	A64	4(pf) dl bl	50	*1.00*
N45	A64	5(pf) brt grn	50	*1.00*
N46	A64	6(pf) dk grn	50	50
N47	A64	8(pf) vermilion	50	*1.00*
N48	A64	10(pf) chocolate	50	75
N49	A64	12(pf) dp car	50	75
N50	A64	15(pf) maroon	50	*1.25*
a.		Inverted surcharge	125.00	
N51	A64	20(pf) brt bl	50	*1.40*
N52	A64	25(pf) ultra	65	*1.40*
N53	A64	30(pf) ol grn	70	*1.50*
N54	A64	40(pf) red vio	70	*1.50*
N55	A64	50(pf) dk grn & blk	1.00	*2.50*
N56	A64	60(pf) cl & blk	1.00	*3.00*
N57	A64	80(pf) dk bl & blk	1.25	*3.75*
N58	A64	100(pf) org & blk	1.50	*6.00*
		Nos. N43-N58 (16)	11.30	*28.30*

Besetztes Gebiet Nordfrankreich

These three words, in a rectangular frame covering two stamps, were handstamped in black on Nos. 267, 367 and 369 and used in the Dunkerque region in July-August, 1940. The German commander of Dunkerque authorized the overprint.

Issued jointly by the Allied Military Government of the United States and Great Britain, for civilian use.

Arc de Triomphe
OS2
Lithographed

1944 *Perf. 11* Unwmkd.

No.	Type	Description	Unused	Used
2N1	OS2	5c brt red vio	5	5
2N2	OS2	10c lt gray	5	5
2N3	OS2	25c brown	5	5
2N4	OS2	50c ol bis	5	5
2N5	OS2	1fr pck grn	10	10
2N6	OS2	1.50fr rose pink	15	15
2N7	OS2	2.50fr purple	15	15
2N8	OS2	4fr ultra	15	15
2N9	OS2	5fr black	15	15
2N10	OS2	10fr yel org	21.50	18.50
		Nos. 2N1-2N10 (10)	22.40	19.40

1945

Denominations in Black.

No.	Type	Description	Unused	Used
2N11	OS2	30c orange	6	6
2N12	OS2	40c pale gray	6	6
2N13	OS2	50c ol bis	6	6
2N14	OS2	60c violet	10	10
2N15	OS2	80c emerald	10	10
2N16	OS2	1.20fr brown	15	15
2N17	OS2	1.50fr vermilion	15	15
2N18	OS2	2fr yellow	15	15
2N19	OS2	2.40fr dk rose	15	15
2N20	OS2	3fr brt red vio	15	15
		Nos. 2N11-2N20 (10)	1.13	1.13

FRENCH OFFICES ABROAD

OFFICES IN CHINA

Prior to 1923 several of the world powers maintained their own post offices in China for the purpose of sending and receiving overseas mail. French offices were maintained in Canton, Hoi Hao (Hoihow), Kwangchowan (Kouang - tchéou - wan), Mongtseu (Mong-tseu), Packhoi (Pak-noi), Tong King (Tchongking), Yunnan Fou (Yunnanfu).

100 Centimes = 1 Franc
100 Cents = 1 Piastre

Peace and Commerce
A1

Stamps of France Overprinted in Red or Black.
Perf. 14x13½.

1894–1900 Unwmkd.

No.	Type	Description	Unused	Used
1	A1	5c grn, *grnsh* (R)	1.40	1.00
2	A1	5c yel grn, I (R) ('00)	1.75	90
a.		Type II	35.00	17.50
3	A1	10c *lav*, I (R)	3.50	90
a.		Type II	14.00	9.50
4	A1	15c bl (R)	4.75	1.50
5	A1	20c red, *grn*	3.75	1.75
6	A1	25c *rose* (R)	3.75	1.10
7	A1	30c brn, *bis*	3.75	2.25
8	A1	40c red, *straw*	4.75	2.75
9	A1	50c car, *rose*, I	13.00	8.75
a.		Red overprint	42.50	
b.		Type II (Bk)	10.50	5.50
10	A1	75c dp vio, *org*(R)	57.50	40.00
11	A1	1fr brnz grn, *straw*	7.75	3.00
a.		Double overprint	225.00	
12	A1	2fr brn, *az* ('00)	26.00	16.00
12A	A1	5fr red lil, *lav*	52.50	35.00
b.		Red overprint	265.00	

Surcharged in Black **Chine 25**

No.	Type	Description	Unused	Used
13	A1	25c on 1fr brnz, grn, *straw*	47.50	27.50

Surcharged in Red **Chine 2 Cents**

1901

No.	Type	Description	Unused	Used
14	A1	2c on 25c *rose*	775.00	190.00
15	A1	4c on 25c *rose*	650.00	190.00
16	A1	6c on 25c *rose*	750.00	325.00
17	A1	16c on 25c *rose*	210.00	150.00
a.		Black surcharge		*5,750.*

Stamps of Indo-China Surcharged in Black

1902–04

No.	Type	Description	Unused	Used
18	A3	1c *lil bl*	1.25	1.00
19	A3	2c brn, *buff*	2.00	1.90
20	A3	4c cl, *lav*	1.40	1.25
21	A3	5c yel grn	1.50	1.40
22	A3	10c red	2.00	1.90
23	A3	15c gray	3.50	3.25
24	A3	20c red, *grn*	4.00	3.50
25	A3	25c *rose*	5.75	5.25
26	A3	25c bl ('04)	4.75	4.25
27	A3	30c brn, *bis*	2.75	2.50
28	A3	40c red, *straw*	14.00	12.00
29	A3	50c car, *rose*	47.50	42.50
30	A3	50c brn, *az* ('04)	7.00	6.00
31	A3	75c vio, *org*	22.50	17.50
32	A3	1fr brnz grn, *straw*	26.00	25.00
33	A3	5fr red lil, *lav*	65.00	57.50
		Nos. 18-33 (16)	210.90	186.70

The Chinese characters surcharged on Nos. 18–33 are the Chinese equivalents of the French values and therefore differ on each denomination. Another printing of these stamps was made in 1904 which differs from the first one principally in the size and shape of the letters in "CHINE", particularly the "H" which is much thinner in the second printing. Prices are for the less expensive variety. Many varieties of surcharge exist.

Liberty, Equality and Fraternity
A3

"Rights of Man"
A4

A5

1902–03 Typographed.

No.	Type	Description	Unused	Used
34	A3	5c green	1.00	90
35	A4	10c rose red ('03)	1.00	90
36	A4	15c pale red	1.50	1.00
37	A4	20c brn vio ('03)	3.00	3.00
38	A4	25c bl ('03)	2.50	1.40
39	A4	30c lil ('03)	3.00	3.00
40	A5	40c red & pale bl	7.00	6.00
41	A5	50c bis brn & lav	9.50	8.50
42	A5	1fr cl & ol grn	13.00	7.50
43	A5	2fr gray vio & yel	37.50	27.50
44	A5	5fr dk bl & buff	52.50	40.00
		Nos. 34-44 (11)	131.50	99.70

Surcharged in Black **5**

1903

No.	Type	Description	Unused	Used
45	A4	5c on 15c pale red	9.50	5.25
a.		Invtd. surcharge	60.00	60.00

Stamps of Indo-China, 1904–06, Surcharged as Nos. 18 to 33 in Black.

1904–05

No.	Type	Description	Unused	Used
46	A4	1c ol grn	90	90
47	A4	2c vio brn, *buff*	90	90
47A	A4	4c cl, *bluish*	775.00	575.00
48	A4	5c dp grn	1.00	1.00
49	A4	10c carmine	1.00	1.00
50	A4	15c org brn, *bl*	1.00	1.00
51	A4	20c red, *grn*	7.25	7.00
52	A4	25c dp bl	3.50	2.00
53	A4	40c *bluish*	3.25	2.50
54	A4	1fr pale grn	275.00	210.00
55	A4	2fr brn, *org*	19.00	15.00
56	A4	10fr org brn, *grn*	110.00	95.00
		Nos. 46-56 (12)	1,197.80	911.30

Many varieties of the surcharge exist on Nos. 46–55.

Stamps of 1902-03 Surcharged in Black **2 CENTS 仙二**

1907

No.	Type	Description	Unused	Used
57	A3	2c on 5c grn	60	52
58	A4	4c on 10c rose red	60	52
a.		Pair, one without surcharge	*35.00*	
59	A4	6c on 15c pale red	1.25	90
60	A4	8c on 20c brn vio	2.75	2.25
a.		"8" inverted	35.00	35.00
61	A4	10c on 25c bl	42	42
62	A5	20c on 50c bis brn & lav	1.75	1.40
a.		Double surcharge		
b.		Triple surch.	225.00	225.00
63	A5	40c on 1fr cl & ol grn	12.50	7.75

64	A5	2pi on 5fr dk bl & buff	13.00	7.75
a.		Double surcharge	1,000.	1,000.
		Nos. 57-64 (8)	32.87	21.51

Stamps of 1902-03 Surcharged in Black — 2 CENTS 分二

1911-22

65	A3	2c on 5c grn	60	42
66	A4	4c on 10c rose red	80	42
67	A4	6c on 15c org	1.40	60
68	A4	8c on 20c brn vio	1.00	60
69	A4	10c on 25c bl ('21)	1.25	60
70	A4	20c on 50c bl ('22)	35.00	26.00
71	A5	40c on 1fr cl & ol grn	1.90	1.25

No. 44 Surcharged — 2 $ 圓二

73	A5	$2 on 5fr bl & buff ('22)	110.00	90.00
		Nos. 65-73 (8)	151.95	119.89

Types of 1902-03 Surcharged in Black — 2 CENTS 分二

1922

75	A3	1c on 5c org	1.90	1.00
76	A4	2c on 10c grn	3.25	2.75
77	A4	3c on 15c org	4.75	3.75
78	A4	4c on 20c red brn	6.50	4.50
79	A4	5c on 25c dk vio	3.50	1.75
80	A4	6c on 30c red	7.50	5.25
82	A4	10c on 50c bl	7.50	5.25
83	A5	20c on 1fr cl & ol grn	22.50	18.00
84	A5	40c on 2fr org & pale bl	22.50	18.00
85	A5	$1 on 5fr dk bl & buff	110.00	110.00
		Nos. 75-85 (10)	189.90	170.25

POSTAGE DUE STAMPS.

Postage Due Stamps of France Handstamped In Red or Black — Chine

Perf. 14x13½.

1901-07 **Unwmkd.**

J1	D2	5c lt bl (R)	2.75	1.75
J2	D2	10c choc (R)	4.75	3.50
J3	D2	15c lt grn (R)	4.75	3.50
J4	D2	20c ol grn (R) ('07)	5.50	4.25
J5	D2	30c carmine	8.25	7.50
J6	D2	50c lilac	8.75	7.50
		Nos. J1-J6 (6)	34.75	28.00

Stamps of 1894-1900 Handstamped in Carmine — A PERCEVOIR

1903

J7	A1	5c yel grn	2,100.	700.00
a.		pur handstamp	2,100.	700.00
b.		5c grn, *grnsh*	4,750.	
J8	A1	10c *lavender*	5,250.	4,250.
a.		pur handstamp	5,250.	4,250.
J9	A1	15c blue	2,100.	650.00
a.		pur handstamp	2,100.	700.00
J10	A1	30c brn, *bis*	1,200.	75.00
a.		pur handstamp	1,200.	75.00

Same Handstamp on Stamps of 1902-03 in Carmine

1903

J14	A3	5c green	1,200.	700.00
a.		pur handstamp	1,200.	700.00
J15	A4	10c rose red	575.00	110.00
a.		pur handstamp	575.00	110.00
J16	A4	15c pale red	600.00	110.00
a.		pur handstamp	600.00	110.00

Stamps of 1894-1900 Handstamped in Carmine — A PERCEVOIR

1903

J20	A1	5c yel grn	1,400.	240.00
a.		pur handstamp	1,400.	240.00
b.		5c grn, *grnsh*	4,750.	
J21	A1	10c *lavender*	6,500.	5,250.
a.		pur handstamp	6,500.	5,250.
J22	A1	15c blue	875.00	75.00
a.		pur handstamp	875.00	75.00
J23	A1	30c brn, *bis*	450.00	57.50
a.		pur handstamp	450.00	57.50

Same Handstamp on Stamps of 1902-03 in Carmine or Purple

1903

J27	A3	5c grn (C)	950.00	425.00
a.		pur handstamp	950.00	425.00
J28	A4	10c rose red (C)	260.00	37.50
a.		pur handstamp	260.00	37.50
J29	A4	15c pale red (C)	575.00	42.50
a.		pur handstamp	575.00	42.50
J30	A4	30c lil (P)	6,500.	5,250.

The handstamps on Nos. J7-J30 are found inverted, double, etc.

The cancellations on these stamps should have dates between Sept. 1, and Nov. 30, 1903, to be genuine.

Postage Due Stamps of France 1893-1910 Surcharged in Black — 2 CENTS 分二

1911

J33	D2	2c on 5c bl	90	70
a.		Double surch.	70.00	70.00
J34	D2	4c on 10c choc	90	70
a.		Double surch.	70.00	70.00
J35	D2	8c on 20c ol grn	1.00	1.00
a.		Double surch.	70.00	70.00
J36	D2	20c on 50c lil	1.25	1.00

1922

J37	D2	1c on 5c bl	52.50	47.50
J38	D2	2c on 10c brn	70.00	65.00
J39	D2	4c on 20c ol grn	70.00	65.00
J40	D2	10c on 50c brn vio	70.00	65.00

CANTON

Stamps of Indo-China, 1892-1900, Overprinted in Red — CANTON 州廣

1901 *Perf. 14x13½.* **Unwmkd.**

1	A3	1c *lil bl*	1.00	1.00
1A	A3	2c brn, *buff*	1.00	1.00
2	A3	4c cl, *lav*	1.90	1.90
2A	A3	5c grn, *grnsh*	500.00	500.00
3	A3	5c yel grn	1.65	1.65
4	A3	10c *lavender*	3.50	3.50
5	A3	15c bl, quadrille paper	2.50	2.50
6	A3	15c gray	3.50	3.50
a.		Dbl. overprint	20.00	
7	A3	20c red, *grn*	5.75	5.75
8	A3	25c *rose*	5.75	5.75
9	A3	30c brn, *bis*	12.50	12.50
10	A3	40c red, *straw*	15.00	15.00
11	A3	50c car, *rose*	17.50	17.50
12	A3	75c dp vio, *org*	27.50	27.50
13	A3	1fr brnz grn, *straw*	24.00	24.00
14	A3	5fr red lil, *lav*	175.00	175.00
		Nos. 1-14 (16)	798.05	798.05

The Chinese characters in the overprint on Nos. 1-14 read "Canton." On Nos. 15-64, they restate the denomination of the basic stamp.

Surcharged in Black — CANTON 仙六

1903-04

15	A3	1c *lil bl*	1.90	1.90
16	A3	2c brn, *buff*	2.00	1.90
17	A3	4c cl, *lav*	2.00	1.90
18	A3	5c yel grn	1.90	1.75
19	A3	10c rose red	1.90	1.75
20	A3	15c gray	2.50	1.90
21	A3	20c red, *grn*	10.00	9.50
22	A3	25c blue	4.25	3.25
23	A3	25c *rose* ('04)	4.25	3.25
24	A3	30c brn, *bis*	12.50	11.00
25	A3	40c red, *straw*	32.50	27.50
26	A3	50c car, *rose*	275.00	240.00
27	A3	50c brn, *az* ('04)	50.00	42.50
28	A3	75c dp vio, *org*	50.00	42.50
a.		"INDO-CHINE" inverted	22,500.	
29	A3	1fr brnz grn, *straw*	40.00	37.50
30	A3	5fr red lil, *lav*	52.50	42.50
		Nos. 15-30 (16)	543.20	470.60

Many varieties of the surcharge exist on Nos. 15-30.

Stamps of Indo-China, 1892-1906, Surcharged in Red or Black — CANTON 花銀八厘

A second printing of the 1906 surcharges of Canton, Hoi Hao, Kwangchowan, Mongtseu, Packhoi, Tong King and Yunnan Fou was made in 1908. The inks are grayish instead of full black and vermilion instead of carmine. Prices are for the cheaper variety which usually is the second printing.

The 4c and 50c of the 1892 issue of Indo-China are known with this surcharge and similarly surcharged for other cities in China. The surcharges on these two stamps are always inverted. It is stated that they were irregularly produced and never issued.

1906

31	A4	1c ol grn (R)	1.00	1.00
32	A4	2c vio brn, *buff*	1.00	1.00
33	A4	4c cl, *bluish* (R)	1.00	1.00
34	A4	5c dp grn (R)	1.25	1.25
35	A4	10c carmine	1.50	1.40
36	A4	15c org brn, *bl*	1.90	1.90
37	A4	20c red, *grn*	1.50	1.50
38	A4	25c dp bl	1.50	1.50
39	A4	30c pale brn	2.75	2.50
40	A4	35c *yel* (R)	1.50	1.40
41	A4	40c *bluish* (R)	3.25	3.00
42	A4	50c bis brn	3.75	3.25
43	A3	75c dp vio, *org* (R)	37.50	32.50
44	A4	1fr pale grn	8.25	7.75
45	A4	2fr brn, *org* (R)	27.50	26.00
46	A3	5fr red lil, *lav*	60.00	50.00
47	A4	10fr org brn, *grn*	50.00	50.00
		Nos. 31-47 (17)	205.15	186.95

The surcharge exists inverted on 1c, 25c and 1fr.

Stamps of Indo-China, 1907, Surcharged "CANTON", and Chinese Characters, in Red or Blue.

1908

48	A5	1c ol brn & blk	65	65
49	A5	2c brn & blk	65	65
50	A5	4c bl & blk	1.00	1.00
51	A5	5c grn & blk	1.00	1.00
52	A5	10c red & blk (Bl)	1.00	1.00
53	A5	15c vio & blk	1.50	1.50
54	A6	20c vio & blk	1.50	1.50
55	A6	25c bl & blk	1.50	1.50
56	A6	30c brn & blk	4.00	3.75
57	A6	35c ol grn & blk	4.00	3.75
58	A6	40c brn & blk	5.75	4.25
59	A6	50c car & blk (Bl)	6.00	5.75
60	A7	75c ver & blk (Bl)	6.00	5.75
61	A8	1fr car & blk (Bl)	8.75	7.75
62	A9	2fr grn & blk	26.00	24.00
63	A10	5fr bl & blk	35.00	27.50
64	A11	10fr pur & blk	60.00	52.50
		Nos. 48-64 (17)	164.30	143.80

Nos. 48-64 Surcharged with New Values in Cents or Piastres in Black, Red or Blue

1919

65	A5	⅖c on 1c	60	60
66	A5	⅘c on 2c	60	60
67	A5	1⅗c on 4c (R)	80	75
68	A5	2c on 5c	80	75
69	A5	4c on 10c (Bl)	80	70
a.		Chinese "2" instead of "4"	21.00	21.00
70	A5	6c on 15c	1.25	95
71	A6	8c on 20c	1.25	1.10
72	A6	10c on 25c	1.40	95
73	A6	12c on 30c	1.40	95
a.		Double surcharge	87.50	87.50
74	A6	14c on 35c	1.40	95
a.		Closed "4"	7.00	7.00
75	A6	16c on 40c	1.40	1.10
76	A6	20c on 50c (Bl)	1.40	1.10
77	A7	30c on 75c (Bl)	1.40	95
78	A8	40c on 1fr (Bl)	6.00	4.25
79	A9	80c on 2fr (R)	7.75	5.75
80	A10	2pi on 5fr (R)	8.75	7.75
81	A11	4pi on 10fr (R)	10.00	9.50
		Nos. 65-81 (17)	47.00	38.70

HOI HAO

Stamps of Indo-China Overprinted in Red — HOI HAO 州瓊

1901 *Perf. 14x13½.* **Unwmkd.**

1	A3	1c *lil bl*	2.25	2.25
2	A3	2c brn, *buff*	2.25	2.25
3	A3	4c cl, *lav*	2.25	2.25
4	A3	5c yel grn	2.25	2.25
5	A3	10c *lavender*	4.00	4.00
6	A3	15c blue	1,400.	700.00
7	A3	15c gray	1.75	1.75
8	A3	20c red, *grn*	12.00	12.00
9	A3	25c *rose*	6.50	4.00
10	A3	30c brn, *bis*	17.50	16.00
11	A3	40c red, *straw*	17.50	16.00
12	A3	50c car, *rose*	27.50	24.00
13	A3	75c dp vio, *org*	165.00	140.00
14	A3	1fr brnz grn, *straw*	650.00	575.00
15	A3	5fr red lil, *lav*	525.00	475.00
		Nos. 1-15 (15)	2,835.75	1,976.75

The Chinese characters in the overprint on Nos. 1-15 read "Hoi Hao." On Nos. 16-66, they restate the denomination of the basic stamp.

Surcharged in Black — HOI HAO 仙六

1903-04

16	A3	1c *lil bl*	70	70
17	A3	2c brn, *buff*	70	70
18	A3	4c cl, *lav*	1.65	1.65
19	A3	5c yel grn	1.65	1.65
20	A3	10c red	1.65	1.65
21	A3	15c gray	1.65	1.65
22	A3	20c red, *grn*	4.25	4.25
23	A3	25c blue	1.90	1.90
24	A3	25c *rose* ('04)	1.90	1.90
25	A3	30c brn, *bis*	2.00	2.00
26	A3	40c red, *straw*	24.00	24.00
27	A3	50c car, *rose*	24.00	24.00
28	A3	50c brn, *az* ('04)	80.00	80.00
29	A3	75c dp vio, *org*	32.50	32.50
a.		"INDO-CHINE" inverted	22,000.	
30	A3	1fr brnz grn, *straw*	35.00	35.00
31	A3	5fr red lil, *lav*	140.00	140.00
		Nos. 16-31 (16)	353.55	353.55

Many varieties of the surcharge exist on Nos. 1-31.

Stamps of Indo-China, 1892-1906, Surcharged in Red or Black — HOI HAO 花銀八厘

1906

32	A4	1c ol grn (R)	1.25	1.25
33	A4	2c vio brn, *buff*	1.25	1.25
34	A4	4c cl, *bluish* (R)	1.90	1.90
35	A4	5c dp grn (R)	2.25	2.25
36	A4	10c carmine	2.25	2.25
37	A4	15c org brn, *bl*	2.25	2.25
38	A4	20c red, *grn*	3.75	3.75
39	A4	25c dp bl	5.25	5.25
40	A4	30c pale brn	5.25	5.25
41	A4	35c *yel* (R)	8.75	8.75
42	A4	40c *bluish* (R)	9.25	9.25
43	A4	50c gray brn	9.50	9.50

44	A3	75c	dp vio, *org* (R)	24.00	24.00
45	A4	1fr	pale grn	24.00	24.00
46	A4	2fr	brn, *org* (R)	24.00	24.00
47	A3	5fr	red lil, *lav*	92.50	92.50
48	A4	10fr	org brn, *grn*	110.00	110.00
			Nos. 32-48 (17)	327.40	327.40

Stamps of Indo-China, 1907, Surcharged "HOI HAO" and Chinese Characters, in Red or Blue.

1908

49	A5	1c	ol brn & blk	65	65
50	A5	2c	brn & blk	65	65
51	A5	4c	bl & blk	95	95
52	A5	5c	grn & blk	1.25	1.25
53	A5	10c	red & blk (Bl)	1.75	1.75
54	A5	15c	vio & blk	3.00	3.00
55	A6	20c	vio & blk	3.75	3.75
56	A6	25c	bl & blk	3.75	3.75
57	A6	30c	brn & blk	3.75	3.75
58	A6	35c	ol grn & blk	3.75	3.75
59	A6	40c	brn & blk	3.50	3.50
61	A6	50c	car & blk (Bl)	4.50	4.50
62	A7	75c	ver & blk (Bl)	5.00	5.00
63	A8	1fr	car & blk (Bl)	11.00	11.00
64	A9	2fr	grn & blk	25.00	25.00
65	A10	5fr	bl & blk	47.50	47.50
66	A11	10fr	pur & blk	67.50	67.50
			Nos. 49-66 (17)	187.25	187.25

Issue of 1908 Surcharged with New Values in Cents or Piastres in Black, Red or Blue.

1919

67	A5	⅖c	on 1c ol brn & blk	65	65
68	A5	⅘c	on 2c yel brn & blk	65	65
69	A5	1⅗c	on 4c bl & blk (R)	90	90
70	A5	2c	on 5c grn & blk	65	65
71	A5	4c	on 10c red & blk (Bl)	90	90
a.			Chinese "2" instead of "4"	4.25	4.25
72	A5	6c	on 15c vio & blk	90	90
73	A6	8c	on 20c vio & blk	1.25	1.25
a.			"S" of "CENTS" omitted	65.00	65.00
74	A6	10c	on 25c bl & blk	3.25	3.25
75	A6	12c	on 30c brn & blk	1.00	1.00
76	A6	14c	on 35c ol grn & blk	1.00	1.00
a.			Closed "4"	9.50	9.50
77	A6	16c	on 40c yel brn & blk	1.00	1.00
79	A6	20c	on 50c car & blk (Bl)	1.25	1.25
80	A7	30c	on 75c ver & blk (Bl)	1.90	1.90
81	A8	40c	on 1fr car & blk (Bl)	5.00	5.00
82	A9	80c	on 2fr grn & blk (R)	14.00	14.00
83	A10	2pi	on 5fr bl & blk (R)	42.50	42.50
a.			Triple surcharge of new value	350.00	
84	A11	4pi	on 10fr pur & blk (R)	130.00	130.00
			Nos. 67-84 (17)	206.80	206.80

KWANGCHOWAN

A Chinese Territory leased to France, 1898 to 1945.

Stamps of Indo-China, 1892–1906, Surcharged in Red or Black

Kouang Tchéou-Wan

廣州灣

1906 ***Perf. 14x13½*** **Unwmkd.**

1	A4	1c	ol grn (R)	1.75	1.75
2	A4	2c	vio brn, *buff*	1.75	1.75
3	A4	4c	cl, *bluish* (R)	2.50	2.50
4	A4	5c	dp grn (R)	2.50	2.50
5	A4	10c	carmine	2.50	2.50
6	A4	15c	org brn, *bl*	6.00	6.00
7	A4	20c	red, *grn*	2.50	2.50
8	A4	25c	dp bl	2.50	2.50
9	A4	30c	pale brn	3.00	3.00
10	A4	35c	*yel* (R)	4.25	4.25
11	A4	40c	*bluish* (R)	3.00	3.00
12	A4	50c	bis brn	12.00	12.00
13	A3	75c	dp vio, *org* (R)	17.00	17.00
14	A4	1fr	pale grn	21.00	21.00
15	A4	2fr	brn, *org* (R)	21.00	21.00
16	A3	5fr	red lil, *lav*	130.00	130.00
17	A4	10fr	org brn, *grn*	175.00	175.00
			Nos. 1-17 (17)	408.25	408.25

Various varieties of the surcharge exist on Nos. 2–10.

Stamps of Indo-China, 1907, Surcharged "KOUANG-TCHEOU" and Value in Chinese in Red or Blue.

1908

18	A5	1c	ol brn & blk	52	52
19	A5	2c	brn & blk	52	52
20	A5	4c	bl & blk	52	52
21	A5	5c	grn & blk	52	52
22	A5	10c	red & blk (Bl)	52	52
23	A5	15c	vio & blk	1.25	1.25
24	A6	20c	vio & blk	2.50	2.50
25	A6	25c	bl & blk	3.00	3.00
26	A6	30c	brn & blk	5.50	5.50
27	A6	35c	ol grn & blk	7.00	7.00
28	A6	40c	brn & blk	7.00	7.00
30	A6	50c	car & blk (Bl)	7.50	7.50
31	A7	75c	ver & blk (Bl)	7.50	7.50
32	A8	1fr	car & blk (Bl)	8.75	8.75
33	A9	2fr	grn & blk	22.50	22.50
34	A10	5fr	bl & blk	47.50	47.50
35	A11	10fr	pur & blk	70.00	70.00
a.			Double surch.	575.00	575.00
b.			Triple surch.	575.00	575.00
			Nos. 18-35 (17)	192.60	192.60

The Chinese characters overprinted on Nos. 1 to 35 repeat the denomination of the basic stamp.

Issue of 1908 Surcharged with New Values in Cents or Piastres in Black, Red or Blue.

1919

36	A5	⅖c	on 1c ol grn & blk	42	42
37	A5	⅘c	on 2c yel brn & blk	42	42
38	A5	1⅗c	on 4c bl & blk (R)	60	60
39	A5	2c	on 5c grn & blk	60	60
a.			"2 CENTS" inverted	47.50	
40	A5	4c	on 10c red & blk (Bl)	1.65	1.00
41	A5	6c	on 15c vio & blk	60	42
42	A6	8c	on 20c vio & blk	2.50	2.25
43	A6	10c	on 25c bl & blk	6.50	6.00
44	A6	12c	on 30c brn & blk	1.25	1.00
45	A6	14c	on 35c ol grn & blk	1.50	1.25
a.			Closed "4"	21.00	17.50
46	A6	16c	on 40c yel brn & blk	1.00	85
48	A6	20c	on 50c car & blk (Bl)	1.00	85
49	A7	30c	on 75c ver & blk (Bl)	4.50	4.25
50	A8	40c	on 1fr car & blk (Bl)	5.25	5.00
a.			"40 CENTS" inverted		
51	A9	80c	on 2fr grn & blk (R)	6.00	5.25
52	A10	2pi	on 5fr bl & blk (R)	110.00	100.00
53	A11	4pi	on 10fr pur & blk (R)	14.00	13.00
			Nos. 36-53 (17)	157.79	143.16

Stamps of Indo-China, 1922-23, Overprinted in Black, Red or Blue KOUANG-TCHEOU

1923

54	A12	⅒c	blk & sal (Bl)	8	8
55	A12	⅕c	dp bl & blk (R)	8	8
a.			Black ovpt.	65.00	
56	A12	⅖c	ol brn & blk (R)	18	18
57	A12	⅘c	brt rose & blk	22	22
58	A12	1c	yel brn & blk (Bl)	22	22
59	A12	2c	gray grn & blk (R)	60	60
60	A12	3c	vio & blk (R)	60	60
61	A12	4c	org & blk	60	60
62	A12	5c	car & blk	60	60
63	A13	6c	dl red & blk	85	85
64	A13	7c	ol grn & blk	60	60
65	A13	8c	blk (R)	1.00	1.00
66	A13	9c	yel & blk	1.00	1.00
67	A13	10c	bl & blk	1.00	1.00
68	A13	11c	vio & blk	1.00	1.00
69	A13	12c	brn & blk	1.00	1.00
70	A13	15c	org & blk	1.40	1.40
71	A13	20c	bl & blk, *straw* (R)	1.00	1.00
72	A13	40c	ver & blk, *bluish* (Bl)	2.00	2.00
73	A13	1pi	bl grn & blk, *grnsh*	3.30	3.30
74	A13	2pi	vio brn & blk, *pnksh* (Bl)	8.50	8.50
			Nos. 54-74 (21)	28.03	28.03

Indo-China Stamps of 1927 Overprinted in Black or Red KOUANG-TCHÉOU

1927

75	A14	⅒c	lt ol grn (R)	6	6
76	A14	⅕c	yellow	18	18
77	A14	⅖c	lt bl (R)	22	22
78	A14	⅘c	dp brn	22	22
79	A14	1c	orange	42	42
80	A14	2c	bl grn (R)	60	60
81	A14	3c	ind (R)	60	60
82	A14	4c	lil rose	60	60
83	A14	5c	dp vio	60	60
84	A15	6c	dp red	60	60
85	A15	7c	lt brn	60	60
86	A15	8c	gray grn (R)	60	60
87	A15	9c	red vio	85	85
88	A15	10c	lt bl (R)	85	85
89	A15	11c	orange	85	85
90	A15	12c	myr grn (R)	85	85
91	A16	15c	dl rose & ol brn	1.25	1.25
92	A16	20c	vio & sl (R)	1.50	1.50
93	A17	25c	org brn & lil rose	1.50	1.50
94	A17	30c	dp bl & ol gray (R)	1.10	1.10
95	A18	40c	ver & lt bl	1.00	1.00
96	A18	50c	lt grn & sl (R)	1.10	1.10
97	A19	1pi	dk bl, blk & yel (R)	3.00	3.00
98	A19	2pi	red, dp bl & org (R)	3.00	3.00
a.			Double ovpt.	75.00	
			Nos. 75-98 (24)	22.15	22.15

Stamps of Indo-China, 1931-41, Overprinted in Black or Red KOUANG-TCHÉOU

1937–41 ***Perf. 13, 13½***

99	A20	⅒c	Prus bl	5	5
100	A20	⅕c	lake	6	6
101	A20	⅖c	org red	8	8
102	A20	½c	red brn	8	8
103	A20	⅘c	dk vio	18	18
104	A20	1c	blk brn	18	18
105	A20	2c	dk grn	18	18
a.			Inverted ovpt.	95.00	
106	A21	3c	dk grn	52	52
107	A21	3c	yel brn ('41)	8	8
108	A21	4c	dk bl (R)	60	60
109	A21	4c	dk grn ('41)	18	18
110	A21	4c	yel org ('41)	1.25	1.25
111	A21	5c	dp vio	60	60
112	A21	5c	dp grn ('41)	25	25
113	A21	6c	org red	42	42
114	A21	7c	blk (R) ('41)	42	42
115	A21	8c	rose lake ('41)	42	42
116	A21	9c	blk, *yel* (R) ('41)	42	42
d.			Black ovpt.	5.50	5.50
117	A22	10c	dk bl (R)	85	85
118	A22	10c	ultra, *pink* (R) ('41)	60	60
119	A22	15c	dk bl (R)	42	42
120	A22	18c	bl (R) ('41)	8	8
121	A22	20c	rose	42	42
122	A22	21c	ol grn	42	42
123	A22	22c	grn ('41)	25	25
124	A22	25c	dp vio	1.90	1.90
125	A22	25c	dk bl (R) ('41)	42	42
126	A22	30c	org brn	42	42
127	A23	50c	dk brn	70	70
128	A23	60c	dl vio	70	70
129	A23	70c	lt bl (R) ('41)	42	42
130	A23	1pi	yel grn	95	95
131	A23	2pi	red	1.10	1.10
			Nos. 99-131 (33)	15.62	15.62

Colonial Arts Exhibition Issue.

Common Design Type

Souvenir Sheet.

1937 **Engraved.** ***Imperf.***

132	CD79	30c	grn & sep	3.50	3.50

Sheet size: 118x99mm.

New York World's Fair Issue.

Common Design Type

1939 ***Perf. 12½x12*** **Unwmkd.**

133	CD82	13c	car lake	65	65
134	CD82	23c	ultra	65	65

Petain Issue.

Indo-China Nos. 209–209A Overprinted "KOUANG TCHEOU" in Blue or Red.

1941 **Engraved** ***Perf. 12½x12***

135	A27a	10c	car lake (B)	35	
136	A27a	25c	bl (R)	35	

Nos. 135–136 were issued by the Vichy government, and were not placed on sale in Kwangchowan. This is also true of 16 stamps of Indo-China types A20–A23 without "RF" and overprinted "KOUANG-TCHEOU."

SEMI-POSTAL STAMPS.

French Revolution Issue

Common Design Type

Photogravure.

1939 ***Perf. 13.*** **Unwmkd.**

Name and Value Typo. in Black.

B1	CD83	6c	+2c grn	4.25	4.25
B2	CD83	7c	+3c brn	4.25	4.25
B3	CD83	9c	+4c red org	4.25	4.25
B4	CD83	13c	+10c rose pink	4.25	4.25
B5	CD83	23c	+20c bl	4.25	4.25
			Nos. B1-B5 (5)	21.25	21.25

Indo-China Nos. B19A and B19C Overprinted "KOUANG-TCHEOU" in Blue or Red, and Common Design Type

1941 **Photogravure** ***Perf. 13½***

B6	SP1	10c	+10c red (B)	48	
B7	CD86	15c	+30c mar & car	48	
B8	SP2	25c	+10c bl (R)	65	

Nos. B6–B8 were issued by the Vichy government, and were not placed on sale in Kwangchowan.

Nos. 135–136 were surcharged "OEUVRES COLONIALES" and surtax (including change of denomination of the 25c to 5c). These were issued in 1944 by the Vichy government, and not placed on sale in Kwangchowan.

Common Design Types

pictured in section at front of book.

AIR POST SEMI-POSTAL STAMPS.

Stamps of Indo-China types V4, V5 and V6 overprinted "KOUANG-TCHEOU" and type of Cameroons V10 inscribed "KOUANG-TCHEOU" were issued in 1942 by the Vichy Government, but were not placed on sale in the territory.

MONGTSEU
(Mengtsz)

Stamps of Indo-China Surcharged in Black

MONGTZE 仙 六

1903-04 ***Perf. 14x13½.*** **Unwmkd.**

1	A3	1c *lil bl*	4.25	4.25
2	A3	2c brn, *buff*	2.50	2.50
3	A3	4c cl, *lav*	4.25	4.25
4	A3	5c yel grn	3.50	3.50
5	A3	10c red	4.75	4.75
6	A3	15c gray	5.75	5.75
7	A3	20c red, *grn*	6.00	6.00
7C	A3	25c *rose*	500.00	500.00
8	A3	25c blue	6.75	6.75
9	A3	30c brn, *bis*	5.75	5.75
10	A3	40c red, *straw*	42.50	42.50
11	A3	50c car, *rose*	240.00	240.00
12	A3	50c brn, *az* ('04)	70.00	70.00
13	A3	75c dp vio, *org*	70.00	70.00
a.		"INDO-CHINE" inverted	31,000.	
14	A3	1fr brnz grn, *straw*	70.00	70.00
15	A3	5fr red lil, *lav*	70.00	70.00
		Nos. 1-15 (16)	1,106.	1,106.

Many varieties of the surcharge exist on Nos. 1–15.

Stamps of Indo-China, 1892–1906, Surcharged in Red or Black

Mong-Tseu 花銀八厘

1906

16	A4	1c ol grn (R)	1.00	1.00
17	A4	2c vio brn, *buff*	1.00	1.00
18	A4	4c cl, *bluish*(R)	1.00	1.00
19	A4	5c dp grn (R)	1.00	1.00
20	A4	10c carmine	1.25	1.25
21	A4	15c org brn, *bl*	1.25	1.25
22	A4	20c red, *grn*	2.50	2.50
23	A4	25c dp bl	2.50	2.50
24	A4	30c pale brn	4.25	4.25
25	A4	35c *yel* (R)	3.00	3.00
26	A4	40c *bluish* (R)	3.75	3.75
27	A4	50c bis brn	11.00	11.00
28	A3	75c dp vio, *org* (R)	26.00	26.00
a.		"INDO-CHINE" inverted	31,000.	
29	A4	1fr pale grn	12.00	12.00
30	A4	2fr brn, *org* (R)	32.50	32.50
31	A3	5fr red lil, *lav*	67.50	67.50
32	A4	10fr org brn, *grn*	92.50	92.50
a.		Chinese characters inverted	1,400.	1,750.
		Nos. 16-32 (17)	264.00	264.00

Inverted varieties of the surcharge exist on Nos. 19, 22 and 32.

Stamps of Indo-China, 1907, Surcharged "MONGTSEU" and Value in Chinese in Red or Blue.

1908

33	A5	1c ol brn & blk	42	42
34	A5	2c brn & blk	42	42
35	A5	4c bl & blk	65	65
36	A5	5c grn & blk	75	75
37	A5	10c red & blk (Bl)	1.00	1.00
38	A5	15c vio & blk	1.00	1.00
39	A6	20c vio & blk	3.00	3.00
40	A6	25c bl & blk	4.00	4.00
41	A6	30c brn & blk	2.50	2.50
42	A6	35c ol grn & blk	2.50	2.50
43	A6	40c brn & blk	2.50	2.50
45	A6	50c car & blk (Bl)	2.50	2.50
46	A7	75c ver & blk (Bl)	6.50	6.50
47	A8	1fr car & blk (Bl)	7.50	7.50
48	A9	2fr grn & blk	9.50	9.50
49	A10	5fr bl & blk	67.50	67.50
50	A11	10fr pur & blk	80.00	80.00
		Nos. 33-50 (17)	192.24	192.24

The Chinese characters overprinted on Nos. 1 to 50 repeat the denomination of the basic stamp.

Issue of 1908 Surcharged with New Values in Cents or Piastres in Black, Red or Blue.

1919

51	A5	2/5c on 1c ol brn & blk	42	42
52	A5	4/5c on 2c yel brn & blk	42	42
53	A5	1 3/5c on 4c bl & blk (R)	1.00	1.00
54	A5	2c on 5c grn & blk	60	60
55	A5	4c on 10c red & blk (Bl)	1.25	1.25
56	A5	6c on 15c vio & blk	1.25	1.25
57	A6	8c on 20c vio & blk	2.25	2.25
58	A6	10c on 25c bl & blk	1.90	1.90
59	A6	12c on 30c brn & blk	1.90	1.90
60	A6	14c on 35c ol grn & blk	1.90	1.90
a.		Closed "4"	9.50	9.50
61	A6	16c on 40c yel brn & blk	2.50	2.50
63	A6	20c on 50c car & blk (Bl)	2.50	2.50
64	A7	30c on 75c ver & blk (Bl)	2.25	2.25
65	A8	40c on 1fr car & blk (Bl)	5.25	5.25
66	A9	80c on 2fr grn & blk (R)	3.25	3.25
a.		Triple surcharge, one inverted	275.00	275.00
67	A10	2pi on 5fr bl & blk (R)	87.50	87.50
a.		Triple surcharge, one inverted	275.00	275.00
b.		Double surch.	275.00	275.00
68	A11	4pi on 10fr pur & blk (R)	15.00	15.00
		Nos. 51-68 (17)	131.14	131.14

PAKHOI

Stamps of Indo-China Surcharged in Black

PACKHOI 仙 六

1903–04 ***Perf. 14x13½*** **Unwmkd.**

1	A3	1c *lil bl*	4.00	4.00
2	A3	2c brn, *buff*	3.00	3.00
3	A3	4c cl, *lav*	2.50	2.50
4	A3	5c yel grn	2.50	2.50
5	A3	10c red	2.00	2.00
6	A3	15c gray	2.00	2.00
7	A3	20c red, *grn*	4.00	4.00
8	A3	25c blue	4.00	4.00
9	A3	25c *rose*('04)	3.00	3.00
10	A3	30c brn, *bis*	4.00	4.00
11	A3	40c red, *straw*	32.50	32.50
12	A3	50c car, *rose*	250.00	250.00
13	A3	50c brn, *az* ('04)	40.00	40.00
14	A3	75c dp vio, *org*	40.00	40.00
a.		"INDO-CHINE" inverted	22,000.	
15	A3	1fr brnz grn, *straw*	45.00	45.00
16	A3	5fr red lil, *lav*	72.50	72.50
		Nos. 1-16 (16)	511.00	511.00

Many varieties of the surcharge exist on Nos. 1–16.

Stamps of Indo-China 1892–1906, Surcharged in Red or Black

PAK-HOI 花銀八厘

1906

17	A4	1c ol grn (R)	90	90
18	A4	2c vio brn, *buff*	90	90
19	A4	4c cl, *bluish* (R)	90	90
20	A4	5c dp grn (R)	90	90
21	A4	10c carmine	90	90
22	A4	15c org brn, *bl*	3.00	3.00
23	A4	20c red, *grn*	2.00	2.00
24	A4	25c dp bl	2.00	2.00
25	A4	30c pale brn	2.00	2.00
26	A4	35c *yel* (R)	2.00	2.00
27	A4	40c *bluish*(R)	2.00	2.00
28	A4	50c bis brn	4.00	4.00
29	A3	75c dp vio, *org* (R)	27.50	27.50
30	A4	1fr pale grn	17.00	17.00
31	A4	2fr brn, *org*(R)	26.00	26.00
32	A3	5fr red lil, *lav*	67.50	67.50
33	A4	10fr org brn, *grn*	82.50	82.50
		Nos. 17-33 (17)	242.00	242.00

Various varieties of the surcharge exist on Nos. 17–24.

Stamps of Indo-China, 1907, Surcharged "PAKHOI" and Value in Chinese in Red or Blue.

1908

34	A5	1c ol brn & blk	30	30
35	A5	2c brn & blk	42	42
36	A5	4c bl & blk	42	42
37	A5	5c grn & blk	70	70
38	A5	10c red & blk (Bl)	70	70
39	A5	15c vio & blk	90	90
40	A6	20c vio & blk	90	90
41	A6	25c bl & blk	1.00	1.00
42	A6	30c brn & blk	1.50	1.50
43	A6	35c ol grn & blk	1.50	1.50
44	A6	40c brn & blk	1.50	1.50
46	A6	50c car & blk (Bl)	1.50	1.50
47	A7	75c ver & blk (Bl)	3.25	3.25
48	A8	1fr car & blk (Bl)	4.00	4.00
49	A9	2fr grn & blk	10.00	10.00
50	A10	5fr bl & blk	57.50	57.50
51	A11	10fr pur & blk	87.50	87.50
		Nos. 34-51 (17)	173.59	173.59

The Chinese characters overprinted on Nos. 1 to 51 repeat the denomination of the basic stamps.

Issue of 1908 Surcharged with New Values in Cents or Piastres in Black, Red or Blue.

1919

52	A5	2/5c on 1c ol brn & blk	42	42
a.		"PAK-HOI" and Chinese double	125.00	125.00
53	A5	4/5c on 2c yel brn & blk	42	42
54	A5	1 3/5c on 4c bl & blk (R)	42	42
55	A5	2c on 5c grn & blk	60	60
56	A5	4c on 10c red & blk (Bl)	1.50	1.50
57	A5	6c on 15c vio & blk	60	60
58	A6	8c on 20c vio & blk	1.50	1.50
59	A6	10c on 25c bl & blk	1.90	1.90
60	A6	12c on 30c brn & blk	80	80
a.		"12 CENTS" double	100.00	100.00
61	A6	14c on 35c ol grn & blk	42	42
a.		Closed "4"	6.00	6.00
62	A6	16c on 40c yel brn & blk	1.25	1.25
64	A6	20c on 50c car & blk (Bl)	80	80
65	A7	30c on 75c ver & blk (Bl)	1.25	1.25
66	A8	40c on 1fr car & blk (Bl)	6.00	6.00
67	A9	80c on 2fr grn & blk (R)	2.50	2.50
68	A10	2pi on 5fr bl & blk (R)	6.50	6.50
69	A11	4pi on 10fr pur & blk (R)	13.00	13.00
		Nos. 52-69 (17)	39.88	39.88

TCHONGKING
(Chungking)

Stamps of Indo-China Surcharged in Black

TCHONGKING 仙 六

1903–04 ***Perf. 14x13½*** **Unwmkd.**

1	A3	1c *lil bl*	1.90	1.90
2	A3	2c brn, *buff*	1.90	1.90
3	A3	4c cl, *lav*	1.90	1.90
4	A3	5c yel grn	1.90	1.90
5	A3	10c red	1.90	1.90
6	A3	15c gray	1.90	1.90
7	A3	20c red, *grn*	1.90	1.90
8	A3	25c blue	27.50	27.50
9	A3	25c *rose* ('04)	4.00	4.00
10	A3	30c brn, *bis*	6.00	6.00
11	A3	40c red, *straw*	27.50	27.50
12	A3	50c car, *rose*	150.00	150.00
13	A3	50c brn, *az* ('04)	87.50	87.50
14	A3	75c vio, *org*	27.50	27.50
15	A3	1fr brnz grn, *straw*	32.50	32.50
16	A3	5fr red lil, *lav*	62.50	62.50
		Nos. 1-16 (16)	438.30	438.30

Many varieties of the surcharge exist on Nos. 1–14.

Stamps of Indo-China and French China, issued in 1902 with similar overprint, but without Chinese characters, were not officially authorized.

Stamps of Indo-China, 1892–1906, Surcharged in Red or Black

Tch'ong K'ing 花銀八厘

1906

17	A4	1c ol grn (R)	1.25	1.25
18	A4	2c vio brn, *buff*	1.25	1.25
19	A4	4c cl, *bluish* (R)	1.25	1.25
20	A4	5c dp grn (R)	1.25	1.25
21	A4	10c carmine	1.25	1.25
22	A4	15c org brn, *bl*	3.75	3.75
23	A4	20c red, *grn*	1.25	1.25
24	A4	25c dp bl	2.50	2.50
25	A4	30c pale brn	1.90	1.90
26	A4	35c *yellow*(R)	1.90	1.90
27	A4	40c *bluish* (R)	3.75	3.75
28	A4	50c bis brn	3.75	3.75
29	A3	75c dp vio, *org* (R)	24.00	24.00
30	A4	1fr pale grn	17.00	17.00
31	A4	2fr brn, *org*(R)	17.00	17.00
32	A3	5fr red lil, *lav*	75.00	75.00
33	A4	10fr org brn, *grn*	87.50	87.50
		Nos. 17-33 (17)	245.55	245.55

Variety "T" omitted in surcharge occurs once in each sheet of Nos. 17–33. Other surcharge varieties exist, such as inverted surcharge on 1c and 2c.

Stamps of Indo-China, 1907, Surcharged "TCHONGKING" and Value in Chinese in Red or Blue.

1908

34	A5	1c ol brn & blk	14	14
35	A5	2c brn & blk	30	30
36	A5	4c bl & blk	40	40
37	A5	5c grn & blk	70	70
38	A5	10c red & blk (Bl)	95	95
39	A5	15c vio & blk	1.10	1.10
40	A6	20c vio & blk	1.90	1.90
41	A6	25c bl & blk	1.90	1.90
42	A6	30c brn & blk	2.00	2.00
43	A6	35c ol grn & blk	3.50	3.50
44	A6	40c brn & blk	8.25	8.25
45	A6	50c car & blk (Bl)	5.75	5.75
46	A7	75c ver & blk (Bl)	5.75	5.75
47	A8	1fr car & blk (Bl)	7.50	7.50
48	A9	2fr grn & blk	60.00	60.00
49	A10	5fr bl & blk	21.00	21.00
50	A11	10fr pur & blk	175.00	175.00
		Nos. 34-50 (17)	296.14	296.14

The Chinese characters overprinted on Nos. 1 to 50 repeat the denomination of the basic stamp.

Issue of 1908 Surcharged with New Values in Cents or Piastres in Black, Red or Blue.

1919

51	A5	2/5c on 1c ol brn & blk	52	52
52	A5	4/5c on 2c yel brn & blk	60	60
53	A5	1 3/5c on 4c bl & blk (R)	80	80
54	A5	2c on 5c grn & blk	70	52
55	A5	4c on 10c red & blk (Bl)	52	52
56	A5	6c on 15c vio & blk	52	52
57	A6	8c on 20c vio & blk	52	52
58	A6	10c on 25c bl & blk	80	70
59	A6	12c on 30c brn & blk	1.00	70
60	A6	14c on 35c ol grn & blk	1.00	60
a.		Closed "4"	9.50	9.50
61	A6	16c on 40c yel brn & blk	1.25	1.00
a.		"16 CENTS" dbl.	65.00	65.00

62	A6	20c on 50c car & blk (Bl)	6.00	6.00
63	A7	30c on 75c ver & blk (Bl)	1.25	1.25
64	A8	40c on 1fr car & blk (Bl)	1.90	1.25
65	A9	80c on 2fr grn & blk (R)	3.25	2.75
66	A10	2pi on 5fr bl & blk (R)	4.50	3.75
67	A11	4pi on 10fr pur & blk (R)	6.75	4.75
		Nos. 51-67 (17)	31.88	26.75

YUNNAN FOU
(Formerly Yunnan Sen, later known as Kunming)

Stamps of Indo-China Surcharged in Black **YUNNANSEN 仙六**

1903-04 ***Perf. 14x13½.*** **Unwmkd.**

1	A3	1c *lil bl*	4.25	3.50
2	A3	2c brn, *buff*	3.50	3.50
3	A3	4c cl, *lav*	3.50	3.50
4	A3	5c yel grn	3.50	3.00
5	A3	10c red	3.50	3.00
6	A3	15c gray	4.25	3.50
7	A3	20c red, *grn*	5.00	3.75
8	A3	25c blue	3.50	3.75
9	A3	30c brn, *bis*	5.50	3.75
10	A3	40c red, *straw*	52.50	32.50
11	A3	50c car, *rose*	265.00	250.00
12	A3	50c brn, *az* ('04)	130.00	130.00
13	A3	75c dp vio, *org*	35.00	32.50
a.		"INDO-CHINE" inverted	22,000.	
14	A3	1fr brnz grn, *straw*	37.50	35.00
15	A3	5fr red lil, *lav*	77.50	75.00
		Nos. 1-15 (15)	634.00	586.25

The Chinese characters overprinted on Nos. 1 to 15 repeat the denomination of the basic stamp.

Many varieties of the surcharge exist on Nos. 1-15.

Stamps of Indo-China, 1892–1906, Surcharged in Red or Black **Yunnan-Fou 花銀八厘**

1906 ***Perf. 14x13½.*** **Unwmkd.**

17	A4	1c ol grn (R)	1.50	1.50
18	A4	2c vio brn, *buff*	1.75	1.75
19	A4	4c cl, *bluish* (R)	2.00	2.00
20	A4	5c dp grn (R)	2.00	2.00
21	A4	10c carmine	2.00	2.00
22	A4	15c org brn, *bl*	4.00	4.00
23	A4	20c red, *grn*	2.50	2.50
24	A4	25c dp bl	3.25	3.25
25	A4	30c pale brn	2.50	2.50
26	A4	35c *yel* (R)	4.25	4.25
27	A4	40c *bluish* (R)	3.25	3.25
28	A4	50c bis brn	4.25	4.25
29	A3	75c dp vio, *org* (R)	32.50	32.50
30	A4	1fr pale grn	15.00	15.00
31	A4	2fr brn, *org* (R)	15.00	15.00
32	A3	5fr red lil, *lav*	52.50	52.50
33	A4	10fr org brn, *grn*	62.50	62.50
		Nos. 17-33 (17)	210.75	210.75

Various varieties of the surcharge exist on Nos. 18, 20, 21 and 27.

Stamps of Indo-China, 1907, Surcharged "YUNNANFOU", and Value in Chinese in Red or Blue.

1908

34	A5	1c ol brn & blk	60	60
35	A5	2c brn & blk	60	60
36	A5	4c bl & blk	60	60
37	A5	5c grn & blk	90	90
38	A5	10c red & blk (Bl)	60	60
39	A5	15c vio & blk	2.75	2.25
40	A6	20c vio & blk	3.00	2.50
41	A6	25c bl & blk	3.00	2.50
42	A6	30c brn & blk	4.25	3.50
43	A6	35c ol grn & blk	4.25	3.50
44	A6	40c brn & blk	4.75	4.75
45	A6	50c car & blk (Bl)	4.75	4.75
46	A7	75c ver & blk (Bl)	5.50	4.75
47	A8	1fr car & blk (Bl)	8.75	6.75
48	A9	2fr grn & blk	16.00	14.00
a.		"YUNANNFOU"	1,600.	1,600.
49	A10	5fr bl & blk	37.50	30.00
a.		"YUNANNFOU"	1,600.	1,600.
50	A11	10fr pur & blk	67.50	67.50
a.		"YUNANNFOU"	1,600.	1,600.
		Nos. 34-50 (17)	165.30	150.05

The Chinese characters overprinted on Nos. 17 to 50 repeat the denomination of the basic stamp.

1919

Issue of 1908 Surcharged with New Values in Cents or Piastres in Black, Red or Blue.

51	A5	⅖c on 1c ol brn & blk	52	52
a.		New value double	65.00	
52	A5	⅘c on 2c yel brn & blk	80	70
53	A5	1⅗c on 4c bl & blk (R)	90	80
54	A5	2c on 5c grn & blk	80	70
a.		Triple surcharge	110.00	
55	A5	4c on 10c red & blk (Bl)	80	70
56	A5	6c on 15c vio & blk	80	70
57	A6	8c on 20c vio & blk	1.00	90
58	A6	10c on 25c bl & blk	1.40	1.25
59	A6	12c on 30c brn & blk	1.25	1.00
60	A6	14c on 35c ol grn & blk	2.25	2.00
a.		Closed "4"	60.00	60.00
61	A6	16c on 40c yel brn & blk	2.50	2.00
62	A6	20c on 50c car & blk (Bl)	1.40	1.40
63	A7	30c on 75c ver & blk (Bl)	2.50	2.50
64	A8	40c on 1fr car & blk (Bl)	3.25	3.00
65	A9	80c on 2fr grn & blk (R)	4.25	4.25
a.		Triple surch., one inverted	175.00	
66	A10	2pi on 5fr bl & blk (R)	27.50	27.50
67	A11	4pi on 10fr pur & blk (R)	9.50	8.75
		Nos. 51-67 (17)	61.42	58.67

OFFICES IN CRETE

Austria, France, Italy and Great Britain maintained their own post offices in Crete during the period when that country was an autonomous state.

100 CENTIMES=1 FRANC

Liberty, Equality and Fraternity
A1

"Rights of Man"
A2

Liberty and Peace (Symbolized by Olive Branch)
A3

Typographed.

1902-03 ***Perf. 14x13½.*** **Unwmkd.**

1	A1	1c gray	95	95
2	A1	2c vio brn	1.00	1.00
3	A1	3c red org	1.00	1.00
4	A1	4c yel brn	1.00	1.00
5	A1	5c green	90	60
6	A2	10c rose red	1.25	90
7	A2	15c pale red ('03)	1.25	95
8	A2	20c brn vio ('03)	1.75	1.40
9	A2	25c bl ('03)	2.25	1.75
10	A2	30c lil ('03)	3.25	3.00
11	A3	40c red & pale bl	6.00	4.75
12	A3	50c bis brn & lav	9.50	7.00
13	A3	1fr cl & ol grn	13.00	11.00
14	A3	2fr gray vio & yel	20.00	19.00
15	A3	5fr dk bl & buff	32.50	27.50
		Nos. 1-15 (15)	95.60	81.80

A4

A5

Black Surcharge.

1903

16	A4	1pi on 25c bl	22.50	19.00
17	A5	2pi on 50c bis brn & lav	47.50	32.50
18	A5	4pi on 1fr cl & ol grn	67.50	60.00
19	A5	8pi on 2fr gray vio & yel	75.00	75.00
20	A5	20pi on 5fr dk bl & buff	125.00	110.00
		Nos. 16-20 (5)	337.50	296.50

OFFICES IN EGYPT

French post offices formerly maintained in Alexandria and Port Said.

100 CENTIMES=1 FRANC

ALEXANDRIA

A1

French Stamps Overprinted in Red, Blue or Black.

Perf. 14x13½

1899–1900 **Unwmkd.**

1	A1	1c *lil bl* (R)	65	65
a.		Double overprint	67.50	
b.		Triple overprint	67.50	
2	A1	2c brn, *buff* (Bl)	95	95
3	A1	3c gray, *grysh* (Bl)	1.25	1.00
4	A1	4c cl, *lav*(Bl)	1.10	90
5	A1	5c yel grn, (I) (R)	2.00	1.25
a.		Type II (R)	95.00	67.50
6	A1	10c *lav*, (I) (R)	4.50	3.75
a.		Type II (R)	37.50	18.00
7	A1	15c bl (R)	3.75	2.50
8	A1	20c red, *grn*	7.50	3.75
a.		Double ovpt.		
9	A1	25c *rose* (R)	3.00	2.25
a.		Inverted overprint	47.50	
b.		Double overprint, one inverted	82.50	
10	A1	30c brn, *bis*	9.00	6.00
11	A1	40c red, *straw*	6.75	6.75
12	A1	50c car, *rose* (II)	13.00	9.50
a.		Type I	110.00	9.50
13	A1	1fr brnz grn, *straw*	13.00	11.00
14	A1	2fr brn, *az* ('00)	70.00	47.50
15	A1	5fr red lil, *lav*	90.00	77.50
		Nos. 1-15 (15)	226.45	175.25

A2

A3

A4

1902-03

16	A2	1c gray	38	15
17	A2	2c vio brn	38	22
18	A2	3c red org	38	18
19	A2	4c yel brn	52	30
20	A2	5c green	70	38
21	A3	10c rose red	85	38
22	A3	15c orange	70	45
a.		15c pale red ('03)	1.00	52
23	A3	20c brn vio ('03)	1.10	60
24	A3	25c bl ('03)	52	22
25	A3	30c vio ('03)	3.00	1.75
26	A4	40c red & pale bl	2.50	1.10
27	A4	50c bis brn & lav	3.75	1.40
28	A4	1fr cl & ol grn	5.00	1.90
29	A4	2fr gray vio & yel	9.50	6.75
30	A4	5fr dk bl & buff	12.50	10.50
		Nos. 16-30 (15)	41.78	26.28

The 2c, 5c, 10c, 20c and 25c exist imperf. Price, each $15.

See also Nos. 77-86.

Stamps of 1902-03 Surcharged Locally in Black **4 Mill.**

1921

31	A2	2m on 5c grn	3.00	2.25
32	A2	3m on 3c red org	3.25	2.25
a.		Larger numeral	47.50	40.00
33	A3	4m on 10c rose	2.50	2.25
34	A2	5m on 1c dk gray	3.75	3.00
35	A2	5m on 4c yel brn	3.75	3.00
36	A3	6m on 15c org	1.75	1.75
a.		Larger numeral	45.00	45.00
37	A3	8m on 20c brn vio	3.00	2.25
a.		Larger numeral	21.00	19.00
38	A3	10m on 25c bl	1.10	1.10
a.		Inverted surcharge	22.50	22.50
b.		Double surcharge	22.50	22.50
39	A3	12m on 30c vio	8.25	8.25
40	A2	15m on 2c vio brn	3.25	3.25

Surcharged **15 Mill.**

41	A4	15m on 40c red & pale bl	9.00	8.25
42	A4	15m on 50c bis brn & lav	3.75	3.75
43	A4	30m on 1fr cl & ol grn	110.00	100.00
44	A4	60m on 2fr gray vio & yel	150.00	150.00
a.		Larger numeral	400.00	400.00

No.	Type	Description	Unused	Used
45	A4	150m on 5fr dk bl & buff	225.00	225.00

Port Said Nos. 20 and 19 Surcharged like Nos. 32 and 40.

No.	Type	Description	Unused	Used
45A	A2	3m on 3c red org	67.50	67.50
46	A2	15m on 2c vio brn	67.50	67.50

Alexandria No. 28 Surcharged with Two New Values.

1921

No.	Type	Description	Unused	Used
46A	A4	30m on 15m on 1fr cl & ol grn	750.00	750.00

The surcharge "15 Mill." was made in error and is cancelled by a bar.

The surcharges were lithographed on Nos. 31, 33, 38, 39 and 42 and typographed on the other stamps of the 1921 issue. Nos. 34, 36 and 37 were surcharged by both methods.

Alexandria Stamps of 1902-03 Surcharged in Paris — **2 MILLIEMES**

1921-23

No.	Type	Description	Unused	Used
47	A2	1m on 1c gray	90	90
48	A2	2m on 5c grn	85	85
49	A3	4m on 10c rose	1.50	1.40
50	A3	4m on 10c grn ('23)	1.00	85
51	A2	5m on 3c red org ('23)	3.25	3.00
52	A3	6m on 15c org	90	80
53	A3	8m on 20c brn vio	70	52
54	A3	10m on 25c bl	70	48
55	A3	10m on 30c vio	2.00	1.65
56	A3	15m on 50c bl ('23)	1.25	85

Surcharged — **15 MILLIÈMES**

No.	Type	Description	Unused	Used
57	A4	15m on 50c bis brn & lav	2.00	1.65
58	A4	30m on 1fr cl & ol grn	1.25	1.10
59	A4	60m on 2fr gray vio & yel	1,300.	1,300.
60	A4	60m on 2fr org & pale bl ('23)	6.00	4.00
61	A4	150m on 5fr bl & buff	7.00	4.25
		Nos. 47-58, 60-61 (14)	29.30	22.30

Stamps and Types of 1902-03 Surcharged with New Values and Bars in Black.

1925

No.	Type	Description	Unused	Used
62	A2	1m on 1c gray	45	45
63	A2	2m on 5c org	38	38
64	A2	2m on 5c grn	85	85
65	A3	4m on 10c grn	60	45
66	A2	5m on 3c red org	45	45
67	A3	6m on 15c org	60	45
68	A3	8m on 20c brn vio	60	52
69	A3	10m on 25c bl	38	38
70	A3	15m on 50c bl	85	70
71	A4	30m on 1fr cl & ol grn	95	75
72	A4	60m on 2fr org & pale bl	1.90	1.65
73	A4	150m on 5fr dk bl & buff	2.50	2.00
		Nos. 62-73 (12)	10.51	9.03

Types of 1902-03 Issue.

1927-28

No.	Type	Description	Unused	Used
77	A2	3m org ('28)	75	70
81	A3	15m sl bl	75	70
82	A3	20m rose lil ('28)	2.25	1.65
84	A4	50m org & bl	5.50	4.50
85	A4	100m sl bl & buff	7.00	5.50
86	A4	250m gray grn & red	13.00	9.25
		Nos. 77-86 (6)	29.25	22.30

SEMI-POSTAL STAMPS.

Regular Issue of 1902–03 Surcharged in Carmine — ✚5c

1915 *Perf. 14x13½.* **Unwmkd.**

No.	Type	Description	Unused	Used
B1	A3	10c +5c rose	45	45

Sinking Fund Issue.

Type of 1902-03 Issue Surcharged in Blue or Black — **+5 Mm** Caisse d'Amortissement

1927-30

No.	Type	Description	Unused	Used
B2	A3	15m +5m dp org	1.50	1.50
B3	A3	15m +5m red vio ('28)	2.25	2.25
a.		15m +5m vio ('30)	5.25	5.25

1929 Type of 1902-03 Issue Surcharged as in 1927-28.

No.	Type	Description	Unused	Used
B4	A3	15m +5m fawn	3.75	3.75

POSTAGE DUE STAMPS.

Postage Due Stamps of France, 1893-1920, Surcharged in Paris in Black — **2 MILLIEMES**

1922 *Perf. 14x13½.* **Unwmkd.**

No.	Type	Description	Unused	Used
J1	D2	2m on 5c bl	1.25	1.25
J2	D2	4m on 10c brn	1.25	1.25
J3	D2	10m on 30c rose red	1.50	1.50
J4	D2	15m on 50c brn vio	1.65	1.65
J5	D2	30m on 1fr red brn, *straw*	2.75	2.75
		Nos. J1-J5 (5)	8.40	8.40

D3

1928 **Typographed.**

No.	Type	Description	Unused	Used
J6	D3	1m slate	90	90
J7	D3	2m lt bl	75	75
J8	D3	4m lil rose	1.00	1.00
J9	D3	5m gray grn	70	70
J10	D3	10m lt red	90	90
J11	D3	20m vio brn	75	75
J12	D3	30m green	2.50	2.50
J13	D3	40m lt vio	2.25	2.25
		Nos. J6-J13 (8)	9.75	9.75

Nos. J6 to J13 were also available for use in Port Said.

PORT SAID

A1

Stamps of France Overprinted in Red, Blue or Black. *Perf. 14x13½.*

1899-1900 **Unwmkd.**

No.	Type	Description	Unused	Used
1	A1	1c *lil bl* (R)	75	52
2	A1	2c brn, *buff* (bl)	90	70
3	A1	3c gray, *grysh* (Bl)	1.00	85
4	A1	4c cl, *lav* (Bl)	1.00	85
5	A1	5c yel grn (I) (R)	5.00	2.50
a.		Type II (R)	27.50	7.50
6	A1	10c *lav* (I) (R)	6.75	6.75
a.		Type II (R)	42.50	27.50
7	A1	15c bl (R)	6.75	4.25
8	A1	20c red, *grn*	7.50	4.25
9	A1	25c *rose*(R)	7.00	1.50
a.		Double overprint	110.00	
10	A1	30c brn, *bis*	7.50	4.25
a.		Inverted overprint	110.00	
11	A1	40c red, *straw*	8.25	4.50
12	A1	50c car, *rose*(II)	11.00	5.75
a.		Type I	200.00	57.50
b.		Dbl. ovpt. (II)	150.00	
13	A1	1fr brnz grn, *straw*	15.00	7.50
14	A1	2fr brn, *az* ('00)	52.50	35.00
15	A1	5fr red lil, *lav*	75.00	50.00
		Nos. 1-15 (15)	205.90	129.17

Regular Issue Surcharged in Red — PORT SAID VINGT CINQ

1899

No.	Type	Description	Unused	Used
16	A1	25c on 10c *lav*	82.50	19.00

With Additional Surcharge "25."

No.	Type	Description	Unused	Used
17	A1	25c on 10c *lav*	300.00	120.00

A2

A3

A4

1902-03 **Typographed.**

No.	Type	Description	Unused	Used
18	A2	1c gray	38	30
19	A2	2c vio brn	38	30
20	A2	3c red org	45	30
21	A2	4c yel brn	52	38
22	A2	5c bl grn	52	45
a.		5c yel grn	1.75	1.50
23	A3	10c rose red	90	52
24	A3	15c pale red ('03)	90	90
a.		15c org	1.00	90
25	A3	20c brn vio ('03)	90	60
26	A3	25c bl ('03)	1.00	75
27	A3	30c vio ('03)	2.50	1.90
28	A4	40c red & pale bl	2.50	1.90
29	A4	50c bis brn & lav	3.50	2.50
30	A4	1fr cl & ol grn	5.00	3.25
31	A4	2fr gray vio & yel	8.00	6.75
32	A4	5fr dk bl & buff	17.00	14.00
		Nos. 18-32 (15)	44.45	34.80

See Nos. 83–92.

Stamps of 1902-03 Surcharged Locally — **2 Milliemes**

1921

No.	Type	Description	Unused	Used
33	A2	2m on 5c grn	3.75	3.75
a.		Inverted surcharge	24.00	24.00
34	A3	4m on 10c rose	3.75	3.75
a.		Inverted surcharge	24.00	24.00
35	A2	5m on 1c gray	5.25	5.25
a.		Inverted surcharge	45.00	45.00
c.		Surcharged "2 Milliemes"	30.00	30.00
36	A2	5m on 2c vio brn	6.75	6.75
a.		Surcharged "2 Milliemes"	37.50	37.50
b.		Sames as "a," inverted	62.50	62.50
37	A2	5m on 3c red org	5.25	5.25
a.		Inverted surcharge	26.00	26.00
b.		On Alexandria #18	190.00	190.00
38	A2	5m on 4c yel brn	5.25	5.25
a.		Inverted surcharge	45.00	45.00
39	A2	10m on 2c vio brn	6.75	6.75
40	A2	10m on 4c yel brn	10.50	10.50
a.		Inverted surcharge	45.00	45.00
41	A3	10m on 25c bl	3.25	3.25
a.		Inverted surcharge	45.00	45.00
42	A3	12m on 30c vio	19.00	19.00
43	A2	15m on 4c yel brn	4.00	4.00
a.		Inverted surcharge	45.00	45.00
44	A3	15m on 15c pale red	30.00	30.00
a.		Inverted surcharge	60.00	60.00
45	A3	15m on 20c brn vio	30.00	30.00
a.		Inverted surcharge	60.00	60.00
46	A4	30m on 50c bis brn & lav	200.00	200.00
47	A4	60m on 50c bis brn & lav	225.00	225.00
48	A4	150m on 50c bis brn & lav	275.00	275.00

Nos. 46, 47 and 48 have a bar between the numerals and "Millièmes", which is in capital letters.

Same Surcharge on Stamps of French Offices in Turkey, 1902-03.

No.	Type	Description	Unused	Used
49	A2	2m on 2c vio brn	60.00	60.00
50	A2	5m on 1c gray	52.50	52.50
a.		"5" inverted	475.00	475.00

Stamps of 1902-03 Surcharged — **15 MILLIEMES**

No.	Type	Description	Unused	Used
51	A4	15m on 40c red & pale bl	27.50	27.50
a.		"MILLtEMES"	70.00	67.50
52	A4	15m on 50c bis brn & lav	37.50	37.50
a.		"MILLtEMES"	180.00	180.00
b.		Bar below 15	30.00	30.00
53	A4	30m on 1fr cl & ol grn	150.00	150.00
a.		"MILLtEMES"	450.00	425.00
54	A4	60m on 2fr gray vio & yel	52.50	52.50
a.		"MILLtEMES"	190.00	150.00
55	A4	150m on 5fr dk bl & buff	190.00	190.00
a.		"MILLtEMES"	525.00	450.00

Stamps of 1902-03 Surcharged in Paris — **2 MILLIEMES**

1921-23

No.	Type	Description	Unused	Used
56	A2	1m on 1c gray	52	52
57	A2	2m on 5c grn	52	52
58	A3	4m on 10c rose	1.00	1.00
59	A2	5m on 3c red org	4.50	4.50
60	A3	6m on 15c org	1.25	1.25
a.		6m on 15c pale red	6.00	6.00
61	A3	8m on 20c brn vio	1.00	1.00
62	A3	10m on 25c bl	1.75	1.75
63	A3	10m on 30c vio	3.75	3.75
64	A3	15m on 50c bl	3.00	3.00

Surcharged — **15 MILLIÈMES**

No.	Type	Description	Unused	Used
65	A4	15m on 50c bis brn & lav	3.00	3.00
66	A4	30m on 1fr cl & ol grn	3.50	3.50
67	A4	60m on 2fr gray vio & yel	75.00	75.00
68	A4	60m on 2fr org & pale bl	5.25	5.25
69	A4	150m on 5fr bl & buff	4.50	4.50
		Nos. 56-69 (14)	108.54	108.54

Stamps and Types of 1902–03 Surcharged with New Values and Bars

1925

No.	Type	Description	Unused	Used
70	A2	1m on 1c gray	38	38
71	A2	2m on 5c grn	45	45
72	A3	4m on 10c rose red	45	45
73	A2	5m on 3c red org	45	45
74	A3	6m on 15c org	70	70
75	A3	8m on 20c brn vio	45	45
76	A3	10m on 25c bl	75	75
77	A3	15m on 50c bl	75	75
78	A4	30m on 1fr cl & ol grn	95	95
79	A4	60m on 2fr org & pale bl	1.10	1.10
80	A4	150m on 5fr dk bl & buff	1.75	1.75
		Nos. 70-80 (11)	8.18	8.18

Types of 1902-03 Issue.

1927-28

No.	Type	Description	Unused	Used
83	A2	3m org ('28)	75	75
87	A3	15m sl bl	85	85
88	A3	20m rose lil ('28)	95	95
90	A4	50m org & bl	1.90	1.90
91	A4	100m sl bl & buff	2.50	2.50
92	A4	250m gray grn & red	4.50	4.50
		Nos. 83-92 (6)	11.45	11.45

SEMI-POSTAL STAMPS.

Regular Issue of 1902-03 Surcharged in Carmine — ✚ 5c

1915 *Perf. 14x13½.* **Unwmkd.**

B1 A3 10c +5c rose 85 85

Sinking Fund Issue.

Type of 1902-03 Issue Surcharged in Blue or Black — +5 Mm Caisse d'Amortissement

1927-30

B2 A3 15m +5m dp org (Bl) 1.40 1.40
B3 A3 15m +5m red vio ('28) 1.40 1.40
a. 15m+5m vio ('30) 2.50 2.50
B4 A3 15m +5m fawn ('29) 1.50 1.50

POSTAGE DUE STAMPS.

Postage Due Stamps of France, 1893–1906, Surcharged Locally in Black — 15 Millièmes

1921 *Perf. 14x13½.* **Unwmkd.**

J1 D2 12m on 10c brn 30.00 30.00
J2 D2 15m on 5c bl 32.50 32.50
J3 D2 30m on 20c ol grn 37.50 37.50
a. Invtd. surch. 375.00 375.00
J4 D2 30m on 50c red vio 2,250. 2,250.

Same Surcharged in Red or Blue — 4 MILLIEMES

1921

J5 D2 2m on 5c bl (R) 30.00 30.00
a. Blue surcharge 180.00 180.00
J6 D2 4m on 10c brn (Bl) 32.50 32.50
a. Surcharged "15 Milliemes" 450.00 450.00
J7 D2 10m on 30c red (Bl) 30.00 30.00
a. Inverted surcharge 75.00 75.00
J8 D2 15m on 50c brn vio (Bl) 40.00 40.00
a. Inverted surcharge 77.50 77.50

Nos. J5–J8 exist with second "M" in "Milliemes" inverted, also with final "S" omitted.

Alexandria Nos. J6–J13 were also available for use in Port Said.

French Offices In Morocco

See French Morocco.

FRENCH OFFICES IN TURKISH EMPIRE (Levant)

Various powers maintained post offices in the Turkish Empire before World War I by authority of treaties which ended with the signing of the Treaty of Lausanne in 1923. The foreign post offices were closed Oct. 27, 1923.

100 CENTIMES=1 FRANC
25 CENTIMES=40 PARAS=1 PIASTRE

A1

Stamps of France Surcharged in Black or Red. *Perf. 14x13½.*

1885–1901 **Unwmkd.**

1 A1 1pi on 25c yel, *straw* ('85) 325.00 7.50
a. Inverted surch. 1,400. 1,400.
2 A1 1pi on 25c *rose* (R) ('86) 1.10 52
a. Inverted surch. 165.00 150.00
3 A1 2pi on 50c car, *rose* (II) ('90) 9.00 1.25
a. Type I ('01) 190.00 22.50
4 A1 3pi on 75c car, *rose* ('85) 14.00 6.00
5 A1 4pi on 1fr brnz grn, *straw* ('85) 11.00 5.25
6 A1 8pi on 2fr brn, *az* ('00) 22.50 12.50
7 A1 20pi on 5fr red lil, *lav* ('90) 55.00 24.00

A2

A3

A4

A5

A6

Typographed.

1902–07 *Perf. 14x13½.*

21 A2 1c gray 30 22
22 A2 2c vio brn 45 30
23 A2 3c red org 45 30
24 A2 4c yel brn 90 52
a. Imperf., pair 47.50
25 A2 5c grn ('06) 45 22
26 A3 10c rose red 55 18
27 A3 15c pale red ('03) 1.00 70
28 A3 20c brn vio ('03) 1.00 70
29 A3 25c bl ('07) 30.00 25.00
a. Imperf., pair 275.00
30 A3 30c lil ('03) 2.50 1.40
31 A4 40c red & pale bl 2.50 1.40
32 A4 50c bis brn & lav ('07) 110.00 95.00
a. Imperf., pair 600.00
33 A4 1fr cl & ol grn ('07) 275.00 275.00
a. Imperf., pair 675.00

Black Surcharge.

34 A5 1pi on 25c bl ('03) 55 18
a. Second "I" omitted 12.00 10.00
b. Double surch. 37.50 27.50
35 A6 2pi on 50c bis brn & lav 1.25 45
36 A6 4pi on 1fr cl & ol grn 1.65 60
a. Imperf., pair 500.00
37 A6 8pi on 2fr gray vio & yel 10.50 5.50
38 A6 20pi on 5fr dk bl & buff 3.75 1.65
Nos. 21-38 (18) 442.80 409.32

Nos. 29, 32–33 were used during the early part of 1907 in the French Offices at Harrar and Diredawa, Ethiopia. Djibouti and Port Said stamps were also used.

No. 27 Surcharged in Green — 1 Piastre Beyrouth

1905

39 A3 1pi on 15c pale red 1,200. 190.00
a. "Piastte" 3,750. 675.00

Stamps of France 1900-21 Surcharged:

1 PIASTRE 30 PARAS (a) — 20 PARAS (b) — 15 PIASTRES (c)

1921-22

40 A22 (a) 30pa on 5c grn 45 30
41 A22 (a) 30pa on 5c org 45 30
42 A22 (b) 1pi 20pa on 10c red 45 30
43 A22 (b) 1pi 20pa on 10c grn 45 30
44 A22 (b) 3pi 20pa on 25c bl 45 30
45 A22 (b) 4pi 20pa on 30c org 45 30
a. "4" omitted 550.00
46 A20 (b) 7pi 20pa on 50c bl 45 30
47 A18 (c) 15pi on 1fr car & ol grn 75 52
48 A18 (c) 30pi on 2fr org & pale bl 6.50 4.00
49 A18 (c) 75pi on 5fr dk bl & buff 4.00 2.50
Nos. 40-49 (10) 14.40 9.12

Stamps of France, 1903-07, Handstamped — 3 PIASTRES 30 PARAS

1923

52 A22 1pi 20pa on 10c red 30.00 30.00
54 A20 3pi 30pa on 15c gray grn 12.00 12.00
55 A22 7pi 20pa on 35c vio 14.00 14.00
a. 1pi 20pa on 35c vio 475.00 475.00

CAVALLE (Cavalla)

A1

A2

Stamps of France Overprinted or Surcharged in Red, Blue or Black *Perf. 14x13½.*

1893–1900 **Unwmkd.**

1 A1 5c grn, *grnsh* (R) 9.50 7.75
2 A1 5c yel grn (I) ('00) (R) 11.00 7.75
3 A1 10c *lav* (II) (Bl) 12.50 9.00
a. 10c *lav* (I) 95.00 82.50
4 A1 15c bl (R) 16.00 11.00
5 A2 1pi on 25c *rose* (Bl) 17.00 12.00
6 A2 2pi on 50c car, *rose* (Bl) 47.50 35.00
7 A2 4pi on 1fr brnz grn, *straw* (R) 47.50 40.00
8 A2 8pi on 2fr brn, *az* ('00) (Bk) 67.50 60.00
Nos. 1-8 (8) 228.50 182.50

A3

A4

A5

A6

1902-03

9 A3 5c green 75 75
10 A4 10c rose red ('03) 90 90
11 A4 15c orange 1.00 1.00
a. 15c pale red ('03) 4.50 4.50

Surcharged in Black.

12 A5 1pi on 25c bl 1.65 1.50
13 A6 2pi on 50c bis brn & lav 4.00 3.25
14 A6 4pi on 1fr cl & ol grn 5.75 5.00
15 A6 8pi on 2fr gray vio & yel 8.25 7.75
Nos. 9-15 (7) 22.30 20.15

DEDEAGH (Dedeagatch)

A1

A2

Stamps of France Overprinted or Surcharged in Red, Blue or Black. *Perf. 14x13½.*

1893-1900 **Unwmkd.**

1 A1 5c grn, *grnsh* (II) (R) 7.50 6.75
2 A1 5c yel grn (I) ('00) (R) 7.50 6.75
3 A1 10c *lav* (II) (Bl) 12.00 10.50
a. Type I 24.00 12.50
4 A1 15c bl (R) 16.00 10.50
5 A2 1pi on 25c *rose* (Bl) 16.00 14.00
6 A2 2pi on 50c car, *rose* (Bl) 35.00 25.00
7 A2 4pi on 1fr brnz grn, *straw* (R) 40.00 30.00
8 A2 8pi on 2fr brn, *az* ('00) (Bk) 62.50 47.50
Nos. 1-8 (8) 196.50 151.00

A3

A4

A5 A6

1902–03

9 A3 5c green 60 60
10 A4 10c rose red ('03) 85 60
11 A4 15c orange 1.25 90

Black Surcharge.

No.	Type	Description	Unused	Used
15	A5	1pi on 25c bl ('03)	1.50	90
16	A6	2pi on 50c bis brn & lav	4.00	3.25
a.		Double surcharge	95.00	
17	A6	4pi on 1fr cl & ol grn	8.25	6.50
18	A6	8pi on 2fr gray vio & yel	13.00	12.00
		Nos. 9-18 (7)	29.45	24.75

PORT LAGOS

A1

A2

Stamps of France Overprinted or Surcharged in Red or Blue.

1893 *Perf. 14x13½* Unwmkd.

No.	Type	Description	Unused	Used
1	A1	5c grn, *grnsh* (R)	15.00	11.00
2	A1	10c *lav* (Bl)	30.00	22.50
3	A1	15c bl (R)	55.00	45.00
4	A2	1pi on 25c *rose*	40.00	37.50
5	A2	2pi on 50c car, *rose* (Bl)	120.00	72.50
6	A2	4pi on 1fr brnz grn, *straw* (R)	67.50	57.50

VATHY
(Samos)

A1

A2

Stamps of France Overprinted or Surcharged in Red, Blue or Black.

Perf. 14x13½

1894-1900 Unwmkd.

No.	Type	Description	Unused	Used
1	A1	5c grn, *grnsh* (R)	5.25	5.00
2	A1	5c yel grn (I) ('00) (R)	5.25	5.00
a.		Type II	52.50	50.00
3	A1	10c *lav* (I) (Bl)	8.25	6.75
a.		Type II	32.50	18.00
4	A1	15c bl (R)	8.25	8.25
5	A2	1pi on 25c *rose* (Bl)	9.50	7.50
6	A2	2pi on 50c car, *rose* (Bl)	18.00	18.00
7	A2	4pi on 1fr brnz grn, *straw* (R)	19.00	18.00
8	A2	8pi on 2fr brn, *az* ('00) (Bk)	55.00	45.00
9	A2	20pi on 5fr lil, *lav* ('00) (Bk)	72.50	67.50
		Nos. 1-9 (9)	201.00	181.00

OFFICES IN ZANZIBAR

Until 1906 France maintained post offices in the Sultanate of Zanzibar, but in that year Great Britain assumed direct control over this protectorate and the French withdrew their postal system.

16 ANNAS=1 RUPEE

A1

A2

Stamps of France Surcharged in Red, Blue or Black.

1894–96 *Perf. 14x13½* Unwmkd.

No.	Type	Description	Unused	Used
1	A1	½a on 5c grn, *grnsh* (R)	3.50	3.00
2	A1	1a on 10c *lav* (Bl)	7.00	5.25
3	A1	1½a on 15c bl ('96) (R)	11.00	10.50
a.		"ANNAS"	55.00	55.00
4	A1	2a on 20c red, *grn* ('96) (Bk)	7.00	5.25
5	A1	2½a on 25c *rose* (Bl)	5.75	3.75
a.		Double surcharge	100.00	
6	A1	3a on 30c brn, *bis* ('96) (Bk)	11.00	9.50
7	A1	4a on 40c red, *straw* ('96) (Bk)	11.00	9.50
8	A1	5a on 50c car, *rose* (Bl)	18.00	15.00
9	A1	7½a on 75c vio, *org* ('96) (R)	285.00	250.00
10	A1	10a on 1fr brnz grn, *straw* (R)	30.00	24.00
11	A1	50a on 5fr red lil, *lav* ('96) (Bk)	210.00	175.00

1894

No.	Type	Description	Unused	Used
12	A2	½a & 5c on 1c *lil bl* (R)	100.00	100.00
13	A2	1a & 10c on 3c gray, *grysh* (R)	95.00	95.00
14	A2	2½a & 25c on 4c cl, *lav* (Bk)	135.00	135.00
15	A2	5a & 50c on 20c red, *grn* (Bk)	135.00	135.00
16	A2	10a & 1fr on 40c red, *straw* (Bk)	275.00	275.00

There are two distinct types of the figures 5c, four of the 25c and three of each of the others of this series.

A3

Surcharged in Red, Blue or Black.

1896-1900

No.	Type	Description	Unused	Used
17	A3	½a on 5c grn, *grnsh* (R)	4.00	3.00
18	A3	½a on 5c yel grn (I) (R)	4.00	3.00
a.		Type II	4.00	3.25
19	A3	1a on 10c *lav* (II) (Bl)	4.50	3.25
a.		Type I	8.25	7.50
20	A3	1½a on 15c bl (R)	4.00	3.00
21	A3	2a on 20c red, *grn* (Bk)	4.00	3.75
a.		"ZANZIBAR" double	62.50	
b.		"ZANZIBAR" triple	70.00	
22	A3	2½a on 25c *rose* (Bl)	5.50	4.50
23	A3	3a on 30c brn, *bis* (Bk)	5.00	4.50
24	A3	4a on 40c red, *straw* (Bk)	5.00	4.50
25	A3	5a on 50c rose, *rose* (II) (Bl)	21.00	16.00
a.		Type I	60.00	47.50
26	A3	10a on 1fr brnz grn, *straw* (R)	11.00	8.25
27	A3	20a on 2fr brn, *az* (Bk)	15.00	9.50
a.		"ZANZIBAS"	400.00	400.00
28	A3	50a on 5fr lil, *lav* (Bk)	40.00	26.00
a.		"ZANZIBAS"	*1,800.*	
		Nos. 17-28 (12)	123.00	89.25

A4

A5

1897

No.	Type	Description	Unused	Used
29	A4	2½a & 25c on ½a on 5c grn, *grnsh*	700.00	100.00
30	A4	2½a & 25c on 1a on 10c *lav*	*2,750.*	625.00
31	A4	2½a & 25c on 1½a on 15c bl	*2,750.*	525.00
32	A5	5a & 50c on 3a on 30c brn, *bis*	*2,750.*	450.00
33	A5	5a & 50c on 4a on 40c red, *straw*	*2,750.*	550.00

PosteFrance 2½ Annas 25c ZANZIBAR — A6   PosteFrance 5 Annas 50c ZANZIBAR — A7

Printed on the Margins of Sheets of French Stamps.

1897

No.	Type	Description	Unused	Used
34	A6	2½a & 25c grn, *grnsh*	675.00	
35	A6	2½a & 25c *lav*	1,900.	
36	A6	2½a & 25c bl	*1,900.*	
37	A7	5a & 50c brn, *bis*	*1,500.*	
38	A7	5a & 50c red, *straw*	*1,900.*	

There are several varieties of figures in the above surcharges.

A8

A9

A10

Surcharged in Red or Black.

1902-03

No.	Type	Description	Unused	Used
39	A8	½a on 5c grn (R)	2.50	2.25
40	A9	1a on 10c rose red ('03)	3.75	3.00
41	A9	1½a on 15c pale red ('03)	6.75	6.00
42	A9	2a on 20c brn vio ('03)	9.00	7.50
43	A9	2½a on 25c bl ('03)	9.00	7.50
44	A9	3a on 30c lil ('03)	7.00	5.25
a.		5a on 30c (error)	190.00	190.00
45	A10	4a on 40c red & pale bl	12.00	10.50
46	A10	5a on 50c bis brn & lav	9.50	8.25
47	A10	10a on 1fr cl & ol grn	16.00	13.00
48	A10	20a on 2fr gray vio & yel	35.00	30.00
49	A10	50a on 5fr dk bl & buff	57.50	57.50
		Nos. 39-49 (11)	168.00	150.75

Nos. 23–24 Surcharged in Black:

25 ▬ 2½ (a)   50 ▬ 5 (b)   1 fr ▬ 10 (c)

1904

No.	Type	Description	Unused	Used
50	A3	25(c) & 2½(a) on 4a on 40c red, *straw*	600.00	
51	A3	50(c) & 5(a) on 3a on 30c brn, *bis*	750.00	
52	A3	50(c) & 5(a) on 4a on 40c red, *straw*	750.00	
53	A3	1fr & 10(a) on 3a on 30c brn, *bis*	1,250.	
54	A3	1fr & 10(a) on 4a on 40c red, *straw*	1,250.	

Stamps of 1902-03 Issue Surcharged in Red or Black:

2 25 (d)   25c 2½ (e)   50c cinq (f)   1 fr dix (g)

No.	Type	Description	Unused	Used
55	A8 (d)	25(c) & 2(a) on ½a on 5c grn (R)	*1,650.*	67.50
56	A9 (e)	25c & 2½(a) on 1a on 10c rose red	*3,250.*	77.50
a.		Inverted surcharge		750.00
57	A9 (e)	25c & 2½(a) on 3c on 30c lil		*2,000.*
a.		Inverted surcharge		*2,000.*
b.		Double surcharge, both inverted		*2,500.*
58	A9 (f)	50c & 5(a) on 3a on 30c lil		675.00
59	A9 (g)	1fr & 10(a) on 3a on 30c lil		900.00

Postage Due Stamps of 1897 Issue With Various Surcharges.

Overprinted "Timbre" in Red.

No.	Type	Description	Unused	Used
60	D1	½a on 5c bl		250.00

Overprinted "Affrancht" in Black.

No.	Type	Description	Unused	Used
61	D1	1a on 10c brn		250.00

With Red Bars Across "CHIFFRE" and "TAXE"

No.	Type	Description	Unused	Used
62	D1	1½a on 15c grn		550.00

The illustrations are not exact reproductions of the new surcharges but are merely intended to show their relative positions and general styles.

POSTAGE DUE STAMPS.

D1

Stamps of France Surcharged in Red, Blue or Black.

1897 *Perf. 14x13½.* Unwmkd.

No.	Type	Description	Unused	Used
J1	D1	½a on 5c bl (R)	9.50	6.00
J2	D1	1a on 10c brn (Bl)	9.50	6.00
a.		Inverted surcharge	75.00	75.00
J3	D1	1½a on 15c grn (R)	13.00	8.25
J4	D1	3a on 30c car (Bk)	15.00	12.50
J5	D1	5a on 50c lil (Bl)	15.00	12.00
a.		2½a on 50c lil (Bl)	575.00	550.00
		Nos. J1-J5 (5)	62.00	44.75

Methods and style of listing are detailed in "Special Notices" at the front of this volume.

FRENCH COLONIES

From 1859 to 1906 and in 1944 and 1945 special stamps were issued for use in all French Colonies which did not have stamps of their own.

100 CENTIMES=1 FRANC

Perforations: Nos. 1–45 are known variously perforated unofficially.

Gum: Many of Nos. 1-45 were issued without gum. Some were gummed locally.

Reprints: Nos. 1-7, 9-12, 24, 26-42, 44 and 45 were reprinted officially in 1887. These reprints are ungummed and the colors of both design and paper are deeper or brighter than the originals. Price for Nos. 1-6, $30 each.

> Prices of early French Colonies stamps vary according to condition. Quotations for Nos. 1–23 are for fine copies. Very fine to superb specimens sell at much higher prices, and inferior or poor copies sell at reduced prices, depending on the condition of the individual specimen.

Eagle and Crown
A1

Typographed.

1859–65 *Imperf.* **Unwmkd.**

1	A1	1c ol grn, *pale bl* ('62)	13.00	16.00
2	A1	5c yel grn, *grnsh* ('62)	15.00	12.00
3	A1	10c bis, *yel*	18.00	6.75
a.		Pair, one sideways	700.00	400.00
4	A1	20c bl, *bluish* ('65)	22.50	12.00
5	A1	40c org, *yelsh*	15.00	8.25
6	A1	80c car rose, *pnksh* ('65)	55.00	47.50

Napoleon III
A2 A3

Ceres A4 — Napoleon III A5

1871–72 *Imperf.*

7	A2	1c ol grn, *pale bl* ('72)	55.00	55.00
8	A3	5c yel grn, *grnsh* ('72)	700.00	450.00
9	A4	10c bis, *yelsh*	265.00	120.00
a.		Tête bêche pair	*24,000.*	*18,000.*
10	A4	15c bis, *yelsh* ('72)	210.00	10.00
11	A4	20c bl, *bluish*	450.00	120.00
a.		Tête bêche pair		*12,500.*
12	A4	25c bl, *bluish* ('72)	120.00	10.00
13	A5	30c brn, *yelsh*	100.00	37.50
14	A4	40c org, *yelsh* (I)	210.00	12.00
a.		Type II	*3,000.*	*600.00*
b.		Pair, types I & II	*6,250.*	*1,600.*
15	A5	80c rose, *pnksh*	750.00	95.00

For types I and II of 40c see illustrations over No. 1 of France.

Ceres
A6 A7

1872–77 *Imperf.*

16	A6	1c ol grn, *pale bl* ('73)	12.50	13.00
17	A6	2c red brn, *yelsh* ('76)	450.00	750.00
18	A6	4c gray ('76)	*9,000.*	600.00
19	A6	5c grn, *pale bl*	12.50	9.00
20	A7	10c bis, *rose* ('76)	165.00	12.00
21	A7	15c bis ('77)	475.00	95.00
22	A7	30c brn, *yelsh*	80.00	18.00
23	A7	80c rose, *pnksh* ('73)	375.00	135.00

No. 17 was used only in Cochin China, 1876-77. Excellent forgeries of Nos. 17 and 18 exist.

With reference to the stamps of France and French Colonies in the same designs and colors see the note after France No. 9.

Peace and Commerce
A8

Commerce
A9

1877–78 Type I. *Imperf.*

24	A8	1c grn, *grnsh*	25.00	30.00
25	A8	4c grn, *grnsh*	15.00	11.00
26	A8	30c brn, *yelsh* ('78)	32.50	32.50
27	A8	40c ver, *straw*	22.50	19.00
28	A8	75c car, *rose* ('78)	67.50	55.00
29	A8	1fr brnz grn, *straw*	30.00	16.00

Type II.

30	A8	2c grn, *grnsh*	11.00	9.50
31	A8	5c grn, *grnsh*	15.00	4.50
32	A8	10c grn, *grnsh*	80.00	9.50
33	A8	15c gray, *grysh*	225.00	67.50
34	A8	20c red brn, *straw*	47.50	6.00
35	A8	25c ultra *bluish*	32.50	8.00
a.		25c bl, *bluish* ('78)	*4,750.*	165.00
36	A8	35c vio blk, *org*('78)	40.00	25.00

1878–80 Type II.

38	A8	1c *lil bl*	16.00	16.00
39	A8	2c brn, *buff*	15.00	11.00
40	A8	4c cl, *lav*	20.00	20.00
41	A8	10c *lav* ('79)	90.00	18.00
42	A8	15c bl ('79)	25.00	11.00
43	A8	20c red, *grn* ('79)	75.00	11.00
44	A8	25c *red*('79)	475.00	300.00
45	A8	25c yel, *straw*('80)	525.00	25.00

No. 44 was used only in Mayotte, Nossi-Bé and New Caledonia. Forgeries exist.

The 3c yellow, 3c gray, 15c yellow, 20c blue, 25c rose and 5fr lilac were printed together with the reprints, and were never issued.

1881-86 *Perf. 14 x 13½.*

46	A9	1c *lil bl*	2.50	2.50
47	A9	2c brn, *buff*	3.00	3.00
48	A9	4c cl, *lav*	3.00	3.00
49	A9	5c grn, *grnsh*	3.00	1.90
50	A9	10c *lavender*	6.00	3.00
51	A9	15c blue	9.00	1.90
52	A9	20c red, *yel grn*	26.00	13.00
53	A9	25c yel, *straw*	7.50	2.75
54	A9	25c *rose* ('86)	7.50	1.90
55	A9	30c brn, *bis*	21.00	13.00
56	A9	35c vio blk, *yel org*	24.00	18.00
a.		35c vio blk, *yel*	37.50	19.00
57	A9	40c ver, *straw*	26.00	20.00
58	A9	75c car, *rose*	75.00	37.50
59	A9	1fr brnz grn, *straw*	45.00	25.00

Nos. 46–59 exist imperforate. They are proofs and were not used for postage, except the 10c.

For stamps of type A9 surcharged with numerals see: Cochin China, Diego Suarez, Gabon, Madagascar, Nossi Be, New Caledonia, Reunion, Senegal, Tahiti.

SEMI-POSTAL STAMPS.

Resistance Fighters
SP1

Lithographed.

1943 *Rouletted* **Unwmkd.**

B1	SP1	1.50fr +98.50fr ind & gray	25.00	27.50

The surtax was for the benefit of patriots and the French Committee of Liberation.

No. B1 was printed in sheets of 10 (5x2) with adjoining labels for each stamp. The label shows the Lorraine cross in indigo in a gray frame.

Colonies Offering Aid to France
SP2

1943 *Perf. 12*

B2	SP2	9fr +41fr red vio	1.10	1.25

The surtax was for the benefit of French Patriots.

Patriots and Map of France
SP3

1943

B3	SP3	50c +4.50fr yel grn	75	90
B4	SP3	1.50fr +8.50fr cer	75	90
B5	SP3	3fr +12fr grnsh bl	75	90
B6	SP3	5fr +15fr ol gray	75	90

The surtax was for the aid of combatants and patriots.

Refugee Family
SP4

1943

B7	SP4	10fr +40fr dl bl	3.25	3.75

The surtax was for refugee relief work.

Woman and Child with Wing
SP5

1944

B8	SP5	10fr +40fr grnsh blk	3.75	4.00

The surtax was for the general benefit of aviation.

Nos. B1–B8 were originally prepared for use in the French Colonies, but after the landing of Free French troops in Corsica they were used there and later also in Southern France. They became valid throughout France in November 1944.

POSTAGE DUE STAMPS.

D1

Typographed.

1884-85 *Imperf.* **Unwmkd.**

J1	D1	1c black	1.90	1.90
J2	D1	2c black	1.90	1.90
J3	D1	3c black	1.90	1.90
J4	D1	4c black	2.50	1.90
J5	D1	5c black	3.25	2.50
J6	D1	10c black	5.25	3.25
J7	D1	15c black	8.25	6.00
J8	D1	20c black	8.25	7.50
J9	D1	30c black	10.00	5.25
J10	D1	40c black	13.00	5.25
J11	D1	60c black	21.00	13.00
J12	D1	1fr brown	18.00	13.00
a.		1fr blk	190.00	
J13	D1	2fr brown	16.00	12.00
a.		2fr blk	190.00	
J14	D1	5fr brown	60.00	40.00
a.		5fr blk	250.00	

Nos. J12a, J13a and J14a were not regularly issued.

1894-1906

J15	D1	5c pale bl	50	50
J16	D1	10c gray brn	50	50
J17	D1	15c pale grn	50	50
J18	D1	20c ol grn ('06)	50	50
J19	D1	30c carmine	90	75
J20	D1	50c lilac	90	75
J21	D1	60c brn, *buff*	2.00	1.50
a.		60c dk vio, *buff*	2.50	1.50
J22	D1	1fr red, *buff*	3.00	2.50
a.		1fr rose, *buff*	15.00	13.00
		Nos. J15-J22 (8)	8.80	7.50

D2

1945 Lithographed *Perf. 12*

J23	D2	10c sl bl	5	5
J24	D2	15c yel grn	5	5
J25	D2	25c dp org	12	12
J26	D2	50c grnsh blk	38	38
J27	D2	60c cop brn	38	38
J28	D2	1fr dp red lil	18	18
J29	D2	2fr red	38	18
J30	D2	4fr sl gray	1.50	1.50
J31	D2	5fr brt ultra	1.50	1.50
J32	D2	10fr purple	9.00	6.75
J33	D2	20fr dl brn	1.75	1.75
J34	D2	50fr dp grn	3.25	3.25
		Nos. J23-J34 (12)	18.54	16.29

FRENCH CONGO

(frĕnch kŏng'gō)

LOCATION—Central Africa.

GOVT.—French possession.

French Congo was originally a separate colony, but was joined in 1888 to Gabon and placed under one commissioner-general with a lieutenant-governor presiding in Gabon and another in French Congo. In 1894 the military holdings in Ubangi were attached to French Congo, and in 1900 the Chad military protectorate was added. Postal service was not established in Ubangi or Chad, however, at that time. In 1906 Gabon and Middle Congo were separated and French Congo ceased to exist as such. Chad and Ubangi remained attached to Middle Congo as the joint dependency of "Ubangi—Chari—Chad," and Middle Congo stamps were used there.

Issues of the Republic of the Congo are listed under Congo Republic (ex-French).

100 Centimes = 1 Franc

Stamps of French Colonies Surcharged Horizontally in Red or Black

Congo français

5c.

1891 ***Perf. 14x13½.*** **Unwmkd.**

1	A9	5c on 1c *lil bl*(R)	*6,000.*	*4,000.*
2	A9	5c on 1c *lil bl*	125.00	65.00
a.	Double surcharge		500.00	250.00
3	A9	5c on 15c bl	250.00	100.00
a.	Double surcharge		500.00	250.00
5	A9	5c on 25c *rose*	87.50	26.00
a.	Inverted surcharge		225.00	67.50

1891–92

First "O" of "Congo" is a Capital, "Francais" with Capital "F".

6	A9	5c on 20c red, *grn*	1,000.	350.00
7	A9	5c on 25c *rose*	130.00	57.50
a.	Surch. vert.		190.00	57.50
8	A9	10c on 25c *rose*	140.00	37.50
a.	Inverted surcharge		265.00	87.50
b.	Surch. vert.		150.00	65.00
c.	First "o" of "Congo" small		100.00	27.50
d.	Double surcharge		300.00	95.00
9	A9	10c on 40c red, *straw*	2,000.	325.00
10	A9	15c on 25c *rose*	130.00	27.50
a.	Surch. vert.		190.00	57.50
b.	Inverted surcharge		110.00	40.00
c.	Double surch.		265.00	82.50

First "O" of Congo small. Surcharge Vertical, Reading Down or Up. No period.

11	A9	5c on 25c *rose*
12	A9	10c on 25c *rose*
13	A9	15c on 25c *rose*

Postage Due Stamps of French Colonies Surcharged in Red or Black Reading Down or Up

Congo français
Timbres poste
10 c

1892 ***Imperf.***

14	D1	5c on 5c blk (R)	110.00	95.00
15	D1	5c on 20c blk (R)	120.00	92.50
16	D1	5c on 30c blk (R)	160.00	110.00
17	D1	10c on 1fr brn	130.00	92.50
a.	Double surcharge			
b.	Surch. horiz.			*1,400.*

Excellent counterfeits of Nos. 1-17 exist.

Navigation and Commerce
A3

1892–1900 Typo. ***Perf. 14x13½***

Colony Name in Blue or Carmine

18	A3	1c *lil bl*	1.25	1.00
19	A3	2c brn, *buff*	1.50	1.25
a.	Name double		100.00	87.50
20	A3	4c cl, *lav*	1.65	1.40
a.	Name in blk and in bl		100.00	87.50
21	A3	5c grn, *grnsh*	3.50	3.00
22	A3	10c *lavender*	14.00	9.50
a.	Name double		425.00	350.00
23	A3	10c red ('00)	1.50	1.00
24	A3	15c bl, quadrille paper	35.00	9.00
25	A3	15c gray ('00)	4.75	3.50
26	A3	20c red, *grn*	15.00	9.50
27	A3	25c *rose*	14.00	9.50
28	A3	25c bl ('00)	5.75	4.75
29	A3	30c brn, *bis*	20.00	12.00
30	A3	40c red, *straw*	32.50	17.00
31	A3	50c car, *rose*	32.50	17.00
32	A3	50c brn, *az* ('00)	5.75	4.75
a.	Name double		475.00	475.00
33	A3	75c dp vio, *org*	24.00	17.00
34	A3	1fr brnz grn, *straw*	40.00	20.00
		Nos. 18-34 (17)	252.65	141.15

Leopard
A4

Bakalois Woman
A5

Coconut Grove
A6

Wmk. 122

Wmkd. Thistle Branch. (122)

1900 ***Perf. 11***

35	A4	1c brn vio & gray lil	42	42
a.	Background inverted		40.00	40.00
36	A4	2c brn & org	42	42
a.	2c dk red & red		100.00	
b.	Imperf., pair		42.50	42.50
37	A4	4c scar & gray bl	60	42
a.	4c dk red & red		600.00	
b.	Background inverted		47.50	47.50
38	A4	5c grn & gray grn	1.00	42
a.	Imperf., pair		87.50	87.50
39	A4	10c dk red & red	3.50	1.50
a.	Imperf., pair		87.50	87.50
40	A4	15c dl vio & ol grn	1.25	52
a.	Imperf. pair		50.00	50.00

Wmk. 123

Wmkd. Rose Branch. (123)

41	A5	20c yel grn & org	1.25	80
42	A5	25c bl & pale bl	1.75	95
43	A5	30c car rose & org	2.00	1.00
44	A5	40c org brn & brt grn	3.00	1.40
a.	Imperf., pair		60.00	60.00
b.	Center inverted		92.50	92.50
45	A5	50c gray vio & lil	3.50	2.75
46	A5	75c red vio & org	6.50	5.00
a.	Imperf., pair		60.00	60.00

Wmk. 124

Wmkd. Olive Branch. (124)

47	A6	1fr gray lil & ol	14.00	9.50
a.	Center inverted		200.00	200.00
b.	Imperf., pair		87.50	87.50
48	A6	2fr car & brn	24.00	14.00
a.	Imperf., pair		175.00	175.00
49	A6	5fr brn org & gray	62.50	42.50
a.	5fr ocher & gray		600.00	600.00
b.	Center inverted		290.00	290.00
c.	Wmk. 123		190.00	
d.	Imperf., pair		400.00	400.00
		Nos. 35-49 (15)	125.69	81.60

Nos. 26 and 29 Surcharged in Black

Valeur
15

1900 ***Perf. 14x13½*** **Unwmkd.**

50	A3	5c on 20c red, *grn*	*17,500.*	*5,750.*
a.	Dbl. surch.			*11,000.*
51	A3	15c on 30c brn, *bis*	*9,500.*	*2,400.*
a.	Dbl. surch.			*4,750.*

Nos. 43 and 48 Surcharged in Black:

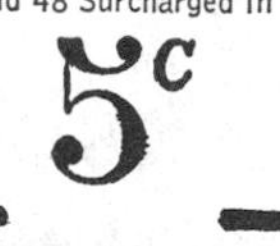

a

0,10

b

1903 ***Perf. 11*** **Wmk. 123**

52	A5	5c on 30c car rose & org	225.00	110.00
a.	Inverted surcharge		*1,750.*	

Wmk. 124

53	A6	10c on 2fr car & brn	325.00	110.00
a.	Inverted surcharge		*1,750.*	
b.	Double surcharge		*2,000.*	

Counterfeits of the preceding surcharges are known.

FRENCH EQUATORIAL AFRICA

(frĕnch ē'kwȧ·tō'rĭ·ǎl ăf'rĭ·kȧ)

LOCATION—North of Belgian Congo and south of Libya.

GOVT.—Former French Colony.

AREA—959,256 square miles.

POP.—4,491,785.

CAPITAL—Brazzaville.

In 1910 Gabon and Middle Congo, with its military dependencies, were politically united as French Equatorial Africa. The component colonies were granted administrative autonomy. In 1915 Ubangi-Chari-Chad was made an autonomous civilian colony and in 1920 Chad was made a civil colony. In 1934 the four colonies were administratively united as one colony, but this federation was not completed until 1936. Each colony had its own postal administration until 1936 when they were united. The postal issues of the former colonial subdivisions are listed under the names of those colonies.

In 1958, French Equatorial Africa was divided into four republics: Chad, Congo, Gabon and Central African Republic (formerly Ubangi-Chari).

100 Centimes = 1 Franc

Stamps of Gabon, 1932, Overprinted "Afrique Equatoriale Francaise" and Bars Similar to "a" and "b" in Black

Perf. 13x13½, 13½x13.

1936 **Unwmkd.**

1	A16	1c brn vio	6	6
2	A16	2c blk, *rose*	6	6
3	A16	4c green	42	30
4	A16	5c grnsh bl	40	30
5	A16	10c red, *yel*	40	35
6	A17	40c brn vio	1.00	80
7	A17	50c red brn	1.00	60
8	A17	1fr yel grn, *bl*	25.00	8.75
9	A18	1.50fr dl bl	1.75	90
10	A18	2fr brn red	11.00	5.25
		Nos. 1-10 (10)	41.09	17.37

Stamps of Middle Congo, 1933 Overprinted in Black:

AFRIQUE
ÉQUATORIALE
FRANÇAISE

a

AFRIQUE ÉQUATORIALE
FRANÇAISE

b

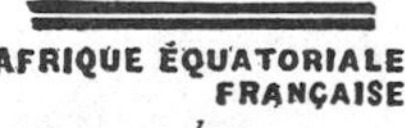

c

1936

11	A4 (b)	1c lt brn	6	6
12	A4 (b)	2c dl bl	6	6
13	A4 (b)	4c ol grn	35	22
14	A4 (b)	5c red vio	42	30
15	A4 (b)	10c slate	80	52
16	A4 (b)	15c dk vio	90	52
17	A4 (b)	20c red, *pink*	70	42
18	A4 (b)	25c orange	1.90	1.40

19	A5 (a)	40c org brn	2.00	1.50
20	A5 (c)	50c blk vio	1.75	1.25
21	A5 (c)	75c blk, *pink*	3.00	2.00
22	A5 (a)	90c carmine	1.75	1.40
23	A5 (c)	1.50fr dk bl	1.00	65
24	A6 (a)	5fr sl bl	42.50	22.50
25	A6 (a)	10fr black	22.50	16.00
26	A6 (a)	20fr dk brn	22.50	17.50
		Nos. 11-26 (16)	102.19	66.30

Paris International Exposition Issue.
Common Design Types

1937, Apr. 15 Engraved. *Perf. 13.*

27	CD74	20c dk vio	1.40	1.40
28	CD75	30c dk grn	1.40	1.40
29	CD76	40c car rose	1.50	1.50
30	CD77	50c dk brn & bl	1.25	1.25
31	CD78	90c red	1.50	1.50
32	CD79	1.50fr ultra	1.50	1.50
		Nos. 27-32 (6)	8.55	8.55

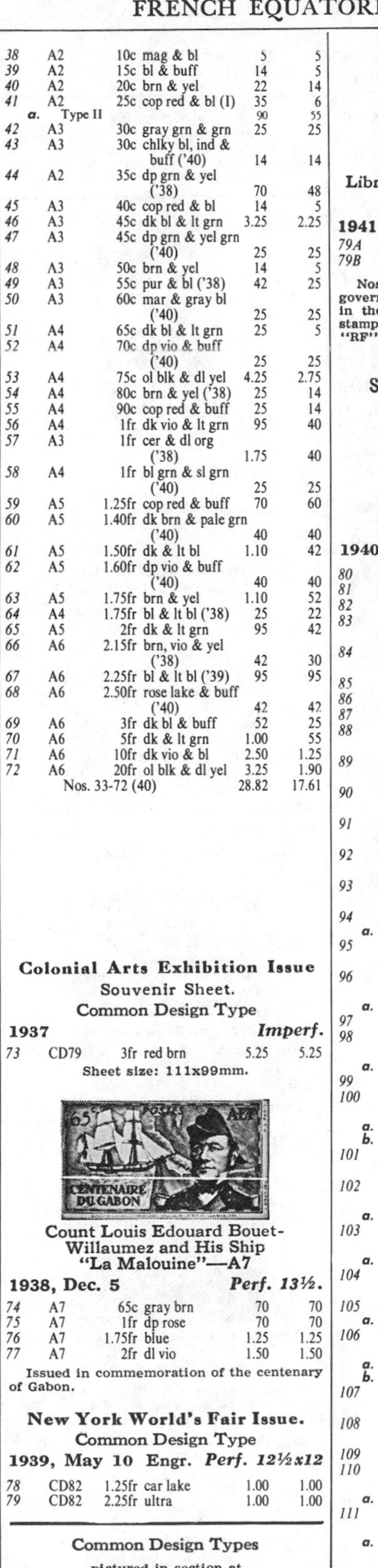

Logging on Loéme River
A1

People of Chad
A2

Pierre Savorgnan de Brazza
A3

Emile Gentil
A4

Paul Crampel
A5

Governor Victor Liotard
A6

Two types of 25c:
I. Wide numerals (4mm.).
II. Narrow numerals (3½mm.).

1937–40 Photo. *Perf. 13½x13*

33	A1	1c brn & yel	5	5
34	A1	2c vio & grn	6	6
35	A1	3c bl & yel ('40)	14	14
36	A1	4c mag & bl	6	6
37	A1	5c dk & lt grn	5	5
38	A2	10c mag & bl	5	5
39	A2	15c bl & buff	14	5
40	A2	20c brn & yel	22	14
41	A2	25c cop red & bl (I)	35	6
a.		Type II	90	55
42	A3	30c gray grn & grn	25	25
43	A3	30c chlky bl, ind & buff ('40)	14	14
44	A2	35c dp grn & yel ('38)	70	48
45	A3	40c cop red & bl	14	5
46	A3	45c dk bl & lt grn	3.25	2.25
47	A3	45c dp grn & yel grn ('40)	25	25
48	A3	50c brn & yel	14	5
49	A3	55c pur & bl ('38)	42	25
50	A3	60c mar & gray bl ('40)	25	25
51	A4	65c dk bl & lt grn	25	5
52	A4	70c dp vio & buff ('40)	25	25
53	A4	75c ol blk & dl yel	4.25	2.75
54	A4	80c brn & yel ('38)	25	14
55	A4	90c cop red & buff	25	14
56	A4	1fr dk vio & lt grn	95	40
57	A3	1fr cer & dl org ('38)	1.75	40
58	A4	1fr bl grn & sl grn ('40)	25	25
59	A5	1.25fr cop red & buff	70	60
60	A5	1.40fr dk brn & pale grn ('40)	40	40
61	A5	1.50fr dk & lt bl	1.10	42
62	A5	1.60fr dp vio & buff ('40)	40	40
63	A5	1.75fr brn & yel	1.10	52
64	A4	1.75fr bl & lt bl ('38)	25	22
65	A5	2fr dk & lt grn	95	42
66	A6	2.15fr brn, vio & yel ('38)	42	30
67	A6	2.25fr bl & lt bl ('39)	95	95
68	A6	2.50fr rose lake & buff ('40)	42	42
69	A6	3fr dk bl & buff	52	25
70	A6	5fr dk & lt grn	1.00	55
71	A6	10fr dk vio & bl	2.50	1.25
72	A6	20fr ol blk & dl yel	3.25	1.90
		Nos. 33-72 (40)	28.82	17.61

Colonial Arts Exhibition Issue
Souvenir Sheet.
Common Design Type

1937 ***Imperf.***

73	CD79	3fr red brn	5.25	5.25

Sheet size: 111x99mm.

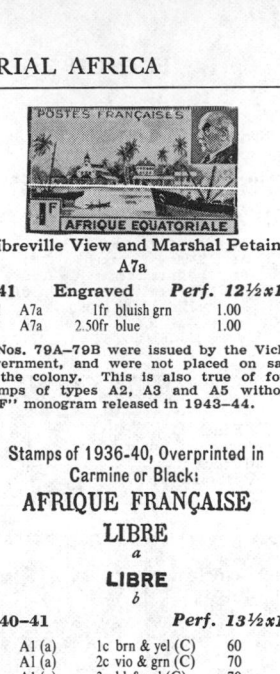

Count Louis Edouard Bouet-Willaumez and His Ship "La Malouine"—A7

1938, Dec. 5 ***Perf. 13½.***

74	A7	65c gray brn	70	70
75	A7	1fr dp rose	70	70
76	A7	1.75fr blue	1.25	1.25
77	A7	2fr dl vio	1.50	1.50

Issued in commemoration of the centenary of Gabon.

New York World's Fair Issue.
Common Design Type

1939, May 10 Engr. *Perf. 12½x12*

78	CD82	1.25fr car lake	1.00	1.00
79	CD82	2.25fr ultra	1.00	1.00

Common Design Types
pictured in section at front of book.

Libreville View and Marshal Petain
A7a

1941 Engraved *Perf. 12½x12*

79A	A7a	1fr bluish grn	1.00
79B	A7a	2.50fr blue	1.00

Nos. 79A–79B were issued by the Vichy government, and were not placed on sale in the colony. This is also true of four stamps of types A2, A3 and A5 without "RF" monogram released in 1943–44.

Stamps of 1936-40, Overprinted in Carmine or Black:

AFRIQUE FRANÇAISE
LIBRE
a

LIBRE
b

1940–41 ***Perf. 13½x13***

80	A1 (a)	1c brn & yel (C)	60	60
81	A1 (a)	2c vio & grn (C)	70	70
82	A1 (a)	3c bl & yel (C)	70	70
83	A4 (b)	4c ol grn (Bk) (No. 13)	7.25	7.00
84	A1 (a)	5c dk grn & lt grn (C)	80	80
85	A2 (a)	10c mag & bl (Bk)	95	95
86	A2 (a)	15c bl & buff (C)	95	95
87	A2 (a)	20c brn & yel (C)	1.25	1.25
88	A2 (a)	25c cop red & bl (Bk)	5.25	5.25
89	A3 (b)	30c gray grn & grn (C)	8.75	7.00
90	A3 (b)	30c gray grn & grn (Bk) ('41)	1.25	95
91	A3 (b)	30c chlky bl, ind & buff (C) ('41)	7.50	6.50
92	A3 (b)	30c chlky bl, ind & buff (Bk) ('41)	4.50	4.50
93	A2 (a)	35c dp grn & yel (C)	1.00	1.00
94	A3 (b)	40c cop red & bl (Bk)	42	42
a.		Double overprint	22.50	
95	A3 (b)	45c dp grn & yel grn (C)	80	52
96	A3 (b)	45c dp grn & yel grn (Bk) ('41)	42	42
a.		Double overprint	5.75	5.75
97	A3 (b)	50c brn & yel (C)	4.00	2.75
98	A3 (b)	50c brn & yel (Bk) ('41)	2.25	2.25
a.		Double overprint	40.00	
99	A3 (b)	55c pur & bl (C)	80	52
100	A3 (b)	55c pur & bl (Bk) ('41)	42	42
a.		Double overprint	7.00	7.00
b.		Double, one inverted	22.50	
101	A3 (b)	60c mar & gray bl (Bk)	42	40
102	A4 (b)	65c dk bl & lt grn (Bk)	42	40
a.		Double overprint	22.50	
103	A4 (b)	70c dp vio & buff (Bk)	42	40
a.		Double overprint	5.75	5.75
104	A4 (b)	75c ol blk & dl yel (Bk)	32.50	32.50
105	A4 (b)	80c brn & yel (Bk)	42	42
a.		Double overprint	22.50	
106	A4 (b)	90c cop red & buff (Bk)	70	70
a.		Double overprint	22.50	
b.		Double, one inverted	22.50	
107	A4 (b)	1fr bl grn & sl grn (Bk)	4.75	4.00
108	A4 (b)	1fr bl grn & sl grn (C) ('41)	4.00	3.00
109	A3 (b)	1fr cer & dl org (Bk)	95	90
110	A5 (b)	1.40fr dk brn & pale grn (Bk)	42	40
a.		Double overprint	4.75	4.75
111	A5 (b)	1.50fr dk bl & lt bl (Bk)	42	40
a.		Double overprint	7.00	7.00
112	A5 (b)	1.60fr dp vio & buff (Bk)	42	40
113	A5 (b)	1.75fr brn & yel (Bk)	90	60
114	A6 (b)	2.15fr brn, vio & yel (Bk)	70	60
a.		Double overprint	4.75	4.75
115	A6 (b)	2.25fr bl & lt bl (C)	80	65
a.		Double overprint	7.00	7.00
116	A6 (b)	2.25fr bl & lt bl (Bk) ('41)	1.25	1.10
a.		Double overprint	22.50	
117	A6 (b)	2.50fr rose lake & buff (Bk)	60	60
a.		Double overprint	22.50	
118	A6 (b)	3fr dk bl & buff (C)	80	65
119	A6 (b)	3fr dk bl & buff (Bk) ('41)	1.40	1.10
a.		Double overprint	6.25	6.25
120	A6 (b)	5fr dk grn & lt grn (C)	2.50	2.25
121	A6 (b)	5fr dk grn & lt grn (Bk) ('41)	95.00	47.50
122	A6 (b)	10fr dk vio & bl (C)	1.25	1.10
123	A6 (b)	10fr dk vio & bl (Bk) ('41)	65.00	47.50
a.		Double overprint		
124	A6 (b)	20fr ol blk & dl yel (C)	1.25	1.10
125	A6 (b)	20fr ol blk & dl yel (Bk) ('41)	7.25	7.25
		Nos. 80-125 (46)	275.10	201.37

Nos. 48, 51 Surcharged in Black or Carmine

LIBRE
75 c

1940

126	A3	75c on 50c brn & yel (Bk)	35	35
a.		Double surcharge		
127	A4	1fr on 65c dk bl & lt grn (C)	35	35
a.		Double surcharge	6.00	

Middle Congo No. 67
Overprinted in Carmine:

AFRIQUE FRANÇAISE LIBRE

Perf. 13½

128	A4	4c ol grn	35.00	32.50

Stamps of 1940
With Additional **24-10-40**
Overprint in Black

1940 ***Perf. 13½x13***

129	A4	80c brn & yel	11.00	9.50
a.		Overprint without "2"	25.00	
130	A4	1fr bl grn & sl grn	11.00	9.50
131	A3	1fr cer & dl org	11.00	9.50
132	A5	1.50fr dk bl & lt bl	11.00	9.50

These stamps were sold affixed to post cards and at a slight increase over face value to cover the cost of the cards.

Issued to commemorate the arrival of General de Gaulle in Brazzaville, capital of Free France, October 24, 1940.

Stamps of 1937-40
Overprinted in Black **Afrique Française Libre**

1941

133	A1	1c brn & yel	90	90
134	A1	2c vio & grn	90	90
135	A1	3c bl & yel	90	90
136	A1	5c dk & lt grn	90	90
137	A2	10c mag & bl	90	90
138	A2	15c bl & buff	90	90
139	A2	20c brn & yel	90	90
140	A2	25c cop red & bl	2.75	2.75
141	A2	35c dp grn & yel	2.25	2.25
a.		Double overprint	14.00	
		Nos. 133-141 (9)	11.30	11.30

There are two settings of the overprint on Nos. 133 to 141 and C10. The first has a space of 1mm. between lines of the overprint, the second has space of 2 mm.

Phoenix
A8

1941 Photogravure ***Perf. 14x14½***

142	A8	5c brown	5	5
143	A8	10c dk bl	5	5
144	A8	25c emerald	5	5
145	A8	30c dp org	6	6
146	A8	40c dk sl grn	25	22
147	A8	80c red brn	8	6
148	A8	1fr dp red lil	10	6
149	A8	1.50fr brt red	6	6
150	A8	2fr gray	18	18
151	A8	2.50fr brt ultra	42	40
152	A8	4fr dl vio	48	40
153	A8	5fr yel bis	48	40
154	A8	10fr dp brn	55	52
155	A8	20fr dp grn	90	52
		Nos. 142-155 (14)	3.71	3.03

Eboue Issue.
Common Design Type
Engraved.

1945 ***Perf. 13.*** **Unwmkd.**

156	CD91	2fr black	25	25
157	CD91	25fr Prus grn	1.25	1.25

Nos. 156 and 157 exist imperforate.

Nos. 142, 144 and 151
Surcharged with New Values and Bars
in Red, Carmine or Black.

1946 ***Perf. 14x14½***

158	A8	50c on 5c brn (R)	42	42
159	A8	60c on 5c brn (R)	42	42
160	A8	70c on 5c brn (R)	35	35
161	A8	1.20fr on 5c brn (C)	35	35
162	A8	2.40fr on 25c emer	65	65
163	A8	3fr on 25c emer	90	90
164	A8	4.50fr on 25c emer	90	90
165	A8	15fr on 2.50fr brt ultra (C)	90	90
		Nos. 158-165 (8)	4.89	4.89

Black Rhinoceros and Rock Python
A9

Jungle Scene
A10

Mountainous Shore Line
A11

Gabon Forest
A12

Niger Boatman
A13

Young Bacongo Woman
A14

Engraved.

1946 ***Perf. 12½*** **Unwmkd.**

166	A9	10c dp bl	5	5
167	A9	30c vio blk	5	5
168	A9	40c dp org	5	5
169	A10	50c vio bl	5	5
170	A10	60c dk car	35	25
171	A10	80c dk ol grn	40	25
172	A11	1fr dp org	40	25
173	A11	1.20fr dp cl	52	40
174	A11	1.50fr dk grn	80	65
175	A12	2fr dk vio brn	10	6
176	A12	3fr rose car	8	5
177	A12	3.60fr red brn	1.75	1.25
178	A12	4fr dp bl	25	18
179	A13	5fr dk brn	48	14
180	A13	6fr dp bl	40	18
181	A13	10fr black	48	18
182	A14	15fr brown	1.00	18
183	A14	20fr dp cl	1.00	18
184	A14	25fr black	1.50	25
		Nos. 166-184 (19)	9.71	4.65

Imperforates

Most French Equatorial Africa stamps from 1951 onward exist imperforate in issued and trial colors, and also in small presentation sheets in issued colors.

Pierre Savorgnan de Brazza
A15

1951, Nov. 5 ***Perf. 13***

185	A15	10fr ind & dk grn	90	25

Issued to commemorate the centenary of the birth of Pierre Savorgnan de Brazza, explorer.

Military Medal Issue.
Common Design Type
Engraved and Typographed.

1952, Dec. 1 ***Perf. 13***

186	CD101	15fr multi	4.25	3.50

Lt. Gov. Adolphe L. Cureau—A16

1954, Sept. 20 **Engraved**

187	A16	15fr ol grn & red brn	1.00	48

Savannah Monitor—A17

1955, May 2 **Unwmkd.**

188	A17	8fr dk grn & cl	1.25	60

Issued in connection with the International Exhibition for Wildlife Protection, Paris, May 1955.

FIDES Issue.

Boali Waterfall and Power Plant, Ubangi-Chari
A18

Designs: 10fr, Cotton, Chad. 15fr, Brazzaville Hospital, Middle Congo. 20fr, Libreville Harbor, Gabon.

1956, Apr. 25 ***Perf. 13x12½***

189	A18	5fr dk brn & cl	30	18
190	A18	10fr blk & bluish grn	40	25
191	A18	15fr ind & gray vio	48	14
192	A18	20fr dk red & red org	55	25

See note after Common Design Type CD103.

Coffee Issue.

Coffee
A19

1956, Oct. **Engraved** ***Perf. 13***

193	A19	10fr brn vio & vio bl	60	22

Leprosarium at Mayumba and Maltese Cross—A20

1957, Mar. 11

194	A20	15fr grn, bl grn & red	1.10	52

Issued in honor of the Knights of Malta.

Giant Eland
A21

Animals: 2fr, Lions. 3fr, Elephant. 4fr, Greater kudu. (3fr and 4fr vertical.)

1957, Nov. 4

195	A21	1fr grn & brn	22	18
196	A21	2fr Prus grn & ol grn	22	18
197	A21	3fr grn, gray & bl	25	22
198	A21	4fr mar & gray	25	25

WHO Building, Brazzaville
A22

1958, May 19 **Engraved.** ***Perf. 13***

199	A22	20fr dk grn & org brn	70	52

Issued to commemorate the 10th anniversary of the World Health Organization.

Flower Issue
Common Design Type

Design: 10fr, Euadania. 25fr, Spathodea.

1958, July 7 **Photo.** ***Perf. 12x12½***

200	CD104	10fr dk vio, yel & grn	42	35
201	CD104	25fr grn, yel & red	80	42

Human Rights Issue
Common Design Type

1958, Dec. 10 **Engraved.** ***Perf. 13***

202	CD105	20fr Prus grn & dk bl	1.25	95

SEMI-POSTAL STAMPS.

Common Design Type

1938, Oct. 24 **Engraved.**

B1	CD80	1.75fr +50c brt ultra	14.00	14.00

Stamps of 1937-38
Surcharged in Black or Red **+35c**

1938, Nov. 7 ***Perf. 13x13½***

B2	A4	65c +35c dk bl & lt grn (R)	1.50	1.25

B3	A4	1.75fr +50c bl & lt bl (Bk)	1.50	1.25

The surtax was for welfare.

French Revolution Issue
Common Design Type
Name and Value Typo. in Black.

1939, July 5 Photogravure.

B4	CD83	45(c) +25(c) grn	9.50	9.50
B5	CD83	70(c) +30(c) brn	9.50	9.50
B6	CD83	90(c) +35(c) red org	9.50	9.50
B7	CD83	1.25fr +1fr rose pink	9.50	9.50
B8	CD83	2.25fr +2fr bl	9.50	9.50
		Nos. B4-B8 (5)	47.50	47.50

Issued to commemorate the 150th anniversary of the French Revolution. The surtax was used for the defense of the colonies.

Common Design Type and

Native Artilleryman
SP1

Gabon Infantryman
SP2

1941 Photogravure *Perf. 13½*

B8A	SP1	1fr +1fr red	1.90
B8B	CD86	1.50fr +3fr mar	1.90
B8C	SP2	2.50fr +1fr bl	1.90

Nos. B8A-B8C were issued by the Vichy government and not placed on sale in the colony.

Nos. 79A-79B were surcharged "OEUVRES COLONIALES" and surtax (including change of denomination of the 2.50fr to 50c). These were issued in 1944 by the Vichy government and not placed on sale in the colony.

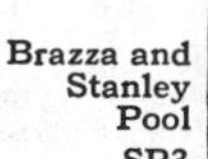

Brazza and Stanley Pool
SP3

1941 Photogravure. *Perf. 14½x14.*

B9	SP3	1fr +2fr dk brn & red	60	60

The surtax was for a monument to Pierre Savorgnan de Brazza.

Regular Stamps of 1937-39 Surcharged in Red

Afrique
Française
Combattante

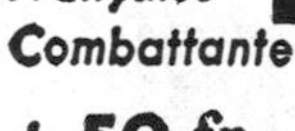

1943, June 28 *Perf. 13½x13*

B10	A6	2.25fr +50fr bl & lt bl	8.75	8.75
B11	A6	10fr +100fr dk vio & bl	26.00	26.00

Nos. 129 and 132 with additional Surcharge in Carmine

LIBÉRATION

+10 fr.

1944

B12	A4	80c +10fr brn & yel	14.00	14.00
B13	A5	1.50fr +15fr dk bl & lt bl	14.00	14.00

Same Surcharge printed Vertically on Stamps of 1941.

Perf. 14x14½.

B14	A8	5c +10fr brn	4.75	4.75
B15	A8	10c +10fr dk bl	4.75	4.75
B16	A8	25c +10fr emer	4.75	4.75
B17	A8	30c +10fr dp org	4.75	4.75
B18	A8	40c +10fr dk sl grn	4.75	4.75
B19	A8	1fr +10fr dp red lil	4.75	4.75
B20	A8	2fr +20fr gray	5.25	5.25
B21	A8	2.50fr +25fr brt ultra	5.25	5.25
		Nos. B12-B21 (10)	67.00	67.00

Nos. 129 and 132 with additional Surcharge in Carmine

RÉSISTANCE

+10 fr.

1944 *Perf. 13½x13*

B22	A4	80c +10fr brn & yel	13.00	13.00
B23	A5	1.50fr +15fr dk bl & lt bl	13.00	13.00

Same Surcharge printed Vertically on Stamps of 1941.

Perf. 14x14½

B24	A8	5c +10fr brn	4.75	4.75
B25	A8	10c +10fr dk bl	4.75	4.75
B26	A8	25c +10fr emer	4.75	4.75
B27	A8	30c +10fr dp org	4.75	4.75
B28	A8	40c +10fr dk sl grn	4.75	4.75
B29	A8	1fr +10fr dp red lil	4.75	4.75
B30	A8	2fr +20fr gray	4.75	4.75
B31	A8	2.50fr +25fr brt ultra	4.75	4.75
B32	A8	4fr +40fr dl vio	4.75	4.75
B33	A8	5fr +50fr yel bis	4.75	4.75
B34	A8	10fr +100fr dp brn	6.50	6.50
B35	A8	20fr +200fr dp grn	6.50	6.50
		Nos. B22-B35 (14)	86.50	86.50

Nos. B12 to B35 were issued to raise funds for the Committee to Aid the Fighting Men and Patriots of France.

Red Cross Issue
Common Design Type

1944 Photogravure. *Perf. 14½x14*

B38	CD90	5fr +20fr ryl bl	80	80

The surtax was for the French Red Cross and national relief.

Tropical Medicine Issue
Common Design Type

1950, May 15 Engraved. *Perf. 13*

B39	CD100	10fr +2fr dk bl grn & vio brn	4.00	4.00

The surtax was for charitable work.

AIR POST STAMPS.

Hydroplane over Pointe-Noire
AP1

Trimotor over Stanley Pool
AP2

Photogravure.

1937 *Perf. 13½* **Unwmkd.**

C1	AP1	1.50fr ol blk & yel	18	18
C2	AP1	2fr mag & bl	25	25
C3	AP1	2.50fr grn & buff	25	25
C4	AP1	3.75fr brn & lt grn	52	52
C5	AP2	4.50fr cop red & bl	52	52
C6	AP2	6.50fr bl & lt grn	90	90
C7	AP2	8.50fr red brn & yel	90	90
C8	AP2	10.75fr vio & lt grn	90	90
		Nos. C1-C8 (8)	4.42	4.42

V4

Stamps of types AP1 and AP2 without "R F" and stamp of the design shown above were issued in 1943 and 1944 by the Vichy Government, but were not placed on sale in the colony.

Nos. C1, C3-C7 Overprinted in Black

Afrique Française
Libre

1940-41

C9	AP1	1.50fr ('41)	175.00	175.00
a.		Double overprint		
C10	AP1	2.50fr	90	90
a.		Double overprint	50.00	
C11	AP1	3.75fr ('41)	175.00	175.00
C12	AP2	4.50fr	95	95
a.		Double overprint	50.00	50.00
C13	AP2	6.50fr	1.25	1.25
C14	AP2	8.50fr	90	90

No. C8 Surcharged in Carmine

Afrique Française
Libre
50 fr.

C15	AP2	50fr on 10.75fr	5.75	5.75

No. C3 Surcharged in Black

Afrique Française
Libre
10F

C16	AP1	10fr on 2.50fr ('41)	77.50	72.50
		Nos. C9-C16 (8)	437.25	432.25

Counterfeits of Nos. C9 and C11 exist. See note following No. 141.

Common Design Type

1941 Photogravure *Perf. 14½x14*

C17	CD87	1fr dk org	42	30
C18	CD87	1.50fr brt red	42	30
C19	CD87	5fr brn red	1.00	42
C20	CD87	10fr black	1.00	60
C21	CD87	25fr ultra	80	52
C22	CD87	50fr dk grn	52	52
C23	CD87	100fr plum	95	80
		Nos. C17-C23 (7)	5.11	3.46

Victory Issue
Common Design Type
Engraved.

1946, May 8 *Perf. 12½* **Unwmkd.**

C24	CD92	8fr lil rose	80	65

Chad to Rhine Issue
Common Design Types

1946, June 6

C25	CD93	5fr dk vio	60	60
C26	CD94	10fr sl grn	60	60
C27	CD95	15fr dp bl	1.00	1.00
C28	CD96	20fr red org	1.25	1.25
C29	CD97	25fr sepia	1.50	1.50
C30	CD98	50fr brn car	1.50	1.50
		Nos. C25-C30 (6)	6.45	6.45

Palms and Village—AP3

Village and Waterfront—AP4

Bearers in Jungle—AP5

1946 Engraved. *Perf. 13.*

C31	AP3	50fr red brn	1.75	60
C32	AP4	100fr grnsh blk	3.50	95
C33	AP5	200fr dp bl	6.00	1.50

UPU Issue
Common Design Type

1949, July 4

C34	CD99	25fr green	8.75	8.75

Brazza Holding Map—AP6

1951, Nov. 5

C35	AP6	15fr brn, ind & red	1.25	52

Issued to commemorate the centenary of the birth of Pierre Savorgnan de Brazza, explorer.

Archbishop Augouard and St. Anne Cathedral, Brazzaville
AP7

1952, Dec. 1

C36	AP7	15fr ol grn, dk brn & vio brn	4.00	2.00

Issued to commemorate the centenary of the birth of Archbishop Philippe-Prosper Augouard.

Anhingas—AP8

1953, Feb. 16

C37	AP8	500fr grnsh blk, blk & sl	32.50	4.75

Liberation Issue
Common Design Type

1954, June 6

C38	CD102	15fr vio & vio brn	4.00	4.00

Log Rafts—AP9

Designs: 100fr, Fishing boats and nets, Lake Chad. 200fr, Age of mechanization.

1955, Jan. 24 **Engraved**

C39	AP9	50fr ind, brn & dk grn	1.25	60
C40	AP9	100fr aqua, dk grn & blk brn	4.75	60
C41	AP9	200fr red & dp plum	6.50	1.75

Gov. Gen. Félix Eboué, View of Brazzaville and the Pantheon
AP10

1955, Apr. 30 ***Perf. 13*** **Unwmkd.**

C42	AP10	15fr sep, brn & sl bl	3.50	1.75

Gen. Louis Faidherbé and African Sharpshooter—AP11

1957, July 20

C43	AP11	15fr sep & org ver	2.25	1.40

Centenary of French African Troops.

AIR POST SEMI-POSTAL STAMPS.

French Revolution Issue
Common Design Type
Photogravure.

1939 ***Perf. 13.*** **Unwmkd.**

Name and Value Typo. in Orange.

CB1	CD83	4.50fr +4fr brn blk	21.00	21.00

V5

V6

V7

Stamps of the designs shown above and stamp of Cameroun type V10 inscribed "Afrique Equatoriale Frcaise" were issued in 1942 by the Vichy Government, but were not placed on sale in the colony.

No. C8 Surcharged in Red

Afrique
Française
Combattante

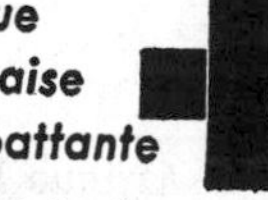

+200 fr.

1943, June 28 ***Perf. 13½***

CB2	AP2	10.75fr +200fr vio & lt grn	125.00	125.00

Counterfeits exist.

POSTAGE DUE STAMPS.

Numeral of Value on Equatorial Butterfly
D1 D2

Photogravure.

1937 ***Perf. 13*** **Unwmkd.**

J1	D1	5c redsh pur & lt bl	5	5
J2	D1	10c cop red & buff	6	6
J3	D1	20c dk grn & grn	6	6
J4	D1	25c red brn & buff	6	6
J5	D1	30c cop red & lt bl	14	14
J6	D1	45c mag & yel grn	40	40
J7	D1	50c dk ol grn & buff	35	35
J8	D1	60c redsh pur & yel	60	60
J9	D1	1fr brn & yel	70	70
J10	D1	2fr dk bl & buff	1.10	1.10
J11	D1	3fr red brn & lt grn	1.10	1.10
		Nos. J1-J11 (11)	4.62	4.62

1947 **Engraved.**

J12	D2	10c red	6	6
J13	D2	30c dp org	6	6
J14	D2	50c grnsh bl	6	6
J15	D2	1fr carmine	18	18
J16	D2	2fr emerald	18	18
J17	D2	3fr dp red lil	35	35
J18	D2	4fr dp ultra	40	40
J19	D2	5fr red brn	60	60
J20	D2	10fr pck bl	90	90
J21	D2	20fr sepia	1.00	1.00
		Nos. J12-J21 (10)	3.73	3.73

FRENCH GUIANA

(frĕnch gē-ä′nȧ)

LOCATION — On the northeast coast of South America bordering on the Atlantic Ocean.

GOVT.—Former French colony.

AREA—34,740 sq. mi.

POP.—28,537 (1946).

CAPITAL—Cayenne.

Formerly a colony, French Guiana became an overseas department of France in 1946.

100 Centimes = 1 Franc

Stamps of French Colonies Surcharged in Black

Déc. 1886.
GUY. FRANÇ.
0f 05
a

1886, Dec. ***Imperf.*** **Unwmkd.**

1	A8	5c on 2c grn, *grnsh*	425.00	425.00
b.		No "f" after "O"	600.00	600.00

Perf. 14x13½.

2	A9	5c on 2c brn, *buff*	425.00	400.00
b.		No "f" after "O"	350.00	325.00

Two types of No. 1: Surcharge 12mm. high, and surcharge 10½mm. high.

Avril 1887.
GUY FRANÇ
0f 20
b

Avril 1887.
GUY FRANÇ.
0f 25
c

Date Line Reads "ᴧVril 1887"

1887, Apr. ***Imperf.***

4	A8	20c on 35c *org*	35.00	30.00

Date Line Reads "Avril 1887"

5	A8	5c on 2c grn, *grnsh*	95.00	82.50
6	A8	20c on 35c *org*	240.00	190.00
7	A7	25c on 30c brn, *yelsh*	26.00	24.00

Variety "small 'f' omitted" occurs on Nos. 5–7.

French Colonies Nos. 22 and 26 Surcharged:

DÉC. 1887.
GUY. FRANÇ.
5c
d

8	A7	5c on 30c brn, *yelsh*	100.00	82.50
a.		Double surcharge	525.00	525.00
b.		Inverted surcharge	700.00	700.00
c.		Pair, one without surcharge	875.00	875.00
9	A8	5c on 30c brn, *yelsh*	1,000.	1,000.

French Colonies Nos. 22 and 28 Surcharged:

Février 1888
GUY. FRANÇ
5
e

Février 1888
GUY. FRANÇ
10
f

1888

10	A7	5c on 30c brn, *yelsh*	95.00	82.50
b.		Double surcharge	325.00	325.00
c.		Inverted surcharge	325.00	325.00
11	A8	10c on 75c car, *rose*	160.00	160.00

Stamps of French Colonies Overprinted in Black

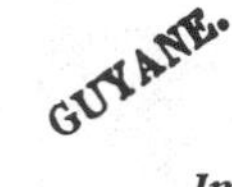

1892, Feb. 20 ***Imperf.***

12	A8	2c grn, *grnsh*	600.00	600.00
13	A7	30c brn, *yelsh*	100.00	100.00
14	A8	35c *orange*	*2,200.*	*1,750.*
15	A8	40c red, *straw*	82.50	75.00
16	A8	75c car, *rose*	87.50	75.00
a.		Inverted overprint	300.00	300.00
17	A8	1fr brnz grn, *straw*	100.00	100.00
a.		Inverted overprint	400.00	400.00

1892 ***Perf. 14x13½***

18	A9	1c *lil bl*	30.00	21.00
19	A9	2c brn, *buff*	26.00	21.00
20	A9	4c cl, *lav*	26.00	21.00
21	A9	5c grn, *grnsh*	26.00	21.00
a.		Inverted overprint	77.50	77.50
b.		Double overprint	77.50	
22	A9	10c *lavender*	42.50	26.00
a.		Inverted overprint	42.50	26.00
23	A9	15c blue	37.50	26.00
24	A9	20c red, *grn*	35.00	26.00
25	A9	25c *rose*	52.50	22.50
26	A9	30c brn, *bis*	27.50	22.50
27	A9	35c *orange*	150.00	150.00
28	A9	40c red, *straw*	92.50	82.50
a.		Inverted overprint	100.00	87.50
29	A9	75c car, *rose*	82.50	70.00
30	A9	1fr brnz grn, *straw*	160.00	150.00

French Colonies No. 51 Surcharged

1892, Dec.

31	A9	5c on 15c bl	21.00	17.50

Navigation and Commerce
A12

1892–1904 **Typographed**

Name of Colony in Blue or Carmine.

32	A12	1c *lil bl*	1.00	95
33	A12	2c brn, *buff*	70	75
34	A12	4c cl, *lav*	95	75
a.		"GUYANE" double	125.00	125.00
35	A12	5c grn, *grnsh*	6.50	5.25
36	A12	5c yel grn ('04)	80	42
37	A12	10c *lavender*	6.00	3.00
38	A12	10c red ('00)	2.25	80
39	A12	15c bl, quadrille paper	22.50	1.50

40	A12	15c gray, *lt gray* ('00)	77.50	57.50
41	A12	20c red, *grn*	14.00	7.25
42	A12	25c *rose*	12.00	2.25
43	A12	25c bl ('00)	10.00	9.25
44	A12	30c brn, *bis*	12.00	7.75
45	A12	40c red, *straw*	14.00	7.75
46	A12	50c car, *rose*	20.00	7.75
47	A12	50c brn, *az* ('00)	13.00	12.00
48	A12	75c dp vio, *org*	26.00	12.00
49	A12	1fr brn grn, *straw*	9.50	7.75
50	A12	2fr vio, *rose* ('02)	150.00	6.50
		Nos. 32-50 (19)	398.70	151.17

Great Anteater
A13

Washing Gold
A14

Palm Grove at Cayenne—A15

1905–28

51	A13	1c black	5	5
52	A13	2c blue	6	6
53	A13	4c red brn	6	6
54	A13	5c green	60	48
55	A13	5c org ('22)	5	5
56	A13	10c rose	18	14
57	A13	10c grn ('22)	14	14
58	A13	10c red, *bluish* ('25)	14	6
59	A13	15c violet	90	60
60	A14	20c red brn	18	14
61	A14	25c blue	1.10	42
62	A14	25c vio ('22)	52	18
63	A14	30c black	80	42
64	A14	30c rose ('22)	18	18
65	A14	30c red org ('25)	18	14
66	A14	30c dk grn, *grnsh* ('28)	65	65
67	A14	35c *yel* ('06)	18	14
68	A14	40c rose	18	14
69	A14	40c blk ('22)	30	18
70	A14	45c ol ('07)	52	18
71	A14	50c violet	1.75	1.25
72	A14	50c bl ('22)	18	18
73	A14	50c gray ('25)	52	22
74	A14	60c lil, *rose* ('25)	22	18
75	A14	65c myr grn ('26)	22	18
76	A14	75c green	70	42
77	A14	85c mag ('26)	42	18
78	A15	1fr rose	48	18
79	A15	1fr bl, *bluish* ('25)	52	18
80	A15	1fr bl, *yel grn* ('28)	1.65	1.65
81	A15	1.10fr lt red ('28)	85	85
82	A15	2fr blue	60	42
83	A15	2fr org red, *yel* ('26)	1.40	1.10
84	A15	5fr black	4.25	3.00
85	A15	10fr grn, *yel* ('24)	8.75	8.25
a.		Printed on both sides	30.00	30.00
86	A15	20fr brn lake ('24)	12.00	10.50
		Nos. 51-86 (36)	41.48	33.15

Issue of 1892 Surcharged in Black or Carmine

05 *j* 10 *k*

1912

87	A12	5c on 2c brn, *buff*	52	52
88	A12	5c on 4c cl, *lav* (C)	48	48
89	A12	5c on 20c red, *grn*	52	52
90	A12	5c on 25c *rose* (C)	2.25	2.25
91	A12	5c on 30c brn, *bis* (C)	80	80
92	A12	10c on 40c red, *straw*	48	48
93	A12	10c on 50c car, *rose*	1.50	1.50
a.		Double surcharge	325.00	
		Nos. 87-93 (7)	6.55	6.55

Two spacings between the surcharged numerals are found on Nos. 87 to 93.

No. 59 Surcharged in Various Colors **0,01** =

1922

94	A13	1c on 15c vio (Bk)	22	22
95	A13	2c on 15c vio (Bl)	22	22
a.		Inverted surch.	52.50	
96	A13	4c on 15c vio (G)	22	22
a.		Double surch.	52.50	
97	A13	5c on 15c vio (R)	22	22

Type of 1905–28 Surcharged in Blue

VINGT FRANCS — VINGT FRANCS

1923

98	A15	10fr on 1fr grn, *yel*	9.50	9.50
99	A15	20fr on 5fr lil, *rose*	9.50	9.50

Stamps and Types of 1905-28 Surcharged with New Value and Bars in Black or Red.

1924-27

100	A13	25c on 15c vio ('25)	22	22
101	A15	25c on 2fr bl ('24)	22	22
a.		Double surcharge	75.00	
b.		Triple surcharge	87.50	
102	A14	65c on 45c ol (R) ('25)	80	80
103	A14	85c on 45c ol (R) ('25)	80	80
104	A14	90c on 75c red ('27)	80	80
105	A15	1.05fr on 2fr lt yel brn ('27)	80	80
106	A15	1.25fr on 1fr ultra (R) ('26)	80	80
107	A15	1.50fr on 1fr lt bl ('27)	1.00	1.00
108	A15	3fr on 5fr vio ('27)	1.00	1.00
a.		No period after "F"	6.00	6.00
		Nos. 100-108 (9)	6.44	6.44

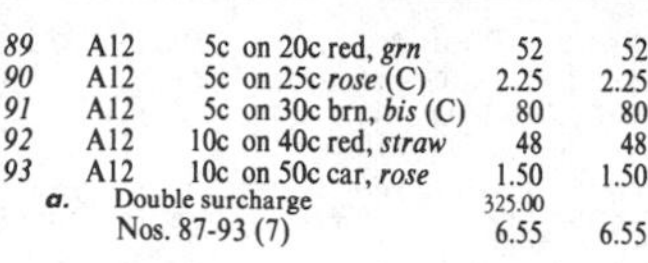

Carib Archer
A16

Shooting Rapids, Maroni River
A17

Government Building, Cayenne
A18

1929-40 ***Perf. 13½x14.***

109	A16	1c gray lil & grnsh bl	6	6
110	A16	2c dk red & bl grn	5	5
111	A16	3c gray lil & grnsh bl ('40)	5	5
112	A16	4c ol brn & red vio	18	18
113	A16	5c Prus bl & red org	6	6
114	A16	10c mag & brn	6	6
115	A16	15c yel brn & red org	6	6
116	A16	20c dk bl & ol grn	14	14
117	A16	25c dk red & dk brn	18	18

Perf. 14x13½.

118	A17	30c dl & lt grn	35	18
119	A17	30c grn & brn ('40)	5	5
120	A17	35c Prus grn & ol grn ('38)	48	48
121	A17	40c org brn & ol gray	14	14
122	A17	45c grn & dk brn	48	48
123	A17	45c ol grn & lt grn ('40)	18	18
124	A17	50c dk bl & ol gray	14	14
125	A17	55c vio bl & car ('38)	80	80
126	A17	60c sal & grn ('40)	18	18
127	A17	65c sal & grn	52	52
128	A17	70c ind & sl bl ('40)	65	65
129	A17	75c ind & sl bl	95	95
130	A17	80c blk & vio bl ('38)	40	35
131	A17	90c dk red & ver	52	52
132	A17	90c red vio & brn ('39)	65	65
133	A17	1fr lt vio & brn	52	52
134	A17	1fr car & lt red ('38)	1.50	1.25
135	A17	1fr blk & vio bl ('40)	18	18
136	A18	1.05fr ver & olvn	3.75	3.00
137	A18	1.10fr ol brn & red vio	3.75	3.00
138	A18	1.25fr blk brn & bl grn ('33)	52	52
139	A18	1.25fr rose & lt red ('39)	30	30
140	A18	1.40fr ol brn & red vio ('40)	65	65
141	A18	1.50fr dk bl & lt bl	6	6
142	A18	1.60fr ol brn & bl grn ('40)	30	30
143	A18	1.75fr brn red & blk brn ('33)	1.50	1.25
144	A18	1.75fr vio bl ('38)	52	52
145	A18	2fr dk grn & rose red	18	18
146	A18	2.25fr vio bl ('39)	65	65
147	A18	2.50fr cop red & brn ('40)	65	65
148	A18	3fr brn red & red vio	48	48
149	A18	5fr dl vio & yel grn	48	48
150	A18	10fr ol gray & dp ultra	85	85
151	A18	20fr ind & ver	1.25	1.10
		Nos. 109-151 (43)	25.42	23.05

Colonial Exposition Issue.
Common Design Types
Name of Country Printed in Black.

1931 Engraved. ***Perf. 12½.***

152	CD70	40c dp grn	2.50	2.50
153	CD71	50c violet	2.50	2.50
154	CD72	90c red org	2.75	2.75
155	CD73	1.50fr dl bl	2.75	2.75

Recapture of Cayenne by d'Estrées, 1676
A19

Products of French Guiana
A20

1935, Oct. 21 ***Perf. 13***

156	A19	40c gray brn	3.00	3.00
157	A19	50c dl red	7.00	4.25
158	A19	1.50fr ultra	3.00	3.00
159	A20	1.75fr lil rose	9.50	8.75
160	A20	5fr brown	7.00	6.00
161	A20	10fr bl grn	7.00	6.00
		Nos. 156-161 (6)	36.50	31.00

Issued to commemorate the tercentenary of the founding of French possessions in the West Indies.

Paris International Exposition Issue.
Common Design Types

1937, Apr. 15

162	CD74	20c dp vio	70	70
163	CD75	30c dk grn	70	70
164	CD76	40c car rose	70	70
165	CD77	50c dk brn	70	70
166	CD78	90c red	80	80
167	CD79	1.50fr ultra	80	80
		Nos. 162-167 (6)	4.40	4.40

Colonial Arts Exhibition Issue
Souvenir Sheet.
Common Design Type

1937 ***Imperf.***

168	CD75	3fr violet	3.50	3.50

Sheet size: 118x99mm.

New York World's Fair Issue
Common Design Type
Engraved.

1939, May 10 ***Perf. 12½x12***

169	CD82	1.25fr car lake	70	70
170	CD82	2.25fr ultra	70	70

View of Cayenne and Marshal Petain
A21a

1941 Engraved ***Perf. 12½x12***

170A	A21a	1fr dp lil	48	
170B	A21a	2.50fr blue	48	

Nos. 170A–170B were issued by the Vichy government and were not placed on sale in the colony. This is also true of three stamps of types A16–A18 without "RF" released in 1944.

Common Design Types
pictured in section at front of book.

Eboue Issue.
Common Design Type

1945 Engraved. *Perf. 13.*

171	CD91	2fr black	48	48
172	CD91	25fr Prus grn	75	75

This issue exists imperforate.

Arms of Cayenne
A22

1945 Lithographed *Perf. 12*

173	A22	10c dp gray vio	6	6
174	A22	30c brn org	6	6
175	A22	40c lt bl	6	6
176	A22	50c vio brn	6	6
177	A22	60c org yel	6	6
178	A22	70c pale brn	18	18
179	A22	80c lt grn	18	18
180	A22	1fr blue	14	14
181	A22	1.20fr brt vio	18	12
182	A22	1.50fr dp org	52	52
183	A22	2fr black	52	52
184	A22	2.40fr red	55	55
185	A22	3fr pink	55	55
186	A22	4fr dp ultra	55	55
187	A22	4.50fr dp yel grn	55	55
188	A22	5fr org brn	55	55
189	A22	10fr dk vio	55	55
190	A22	15fr rose car	75	75
191	A22	20fr ol grn	80	80
		Nos. 173-191 (19)	6.87	6.81

Hammock
A23

Guiana Girl
A26

Maroni River Bank
A24

Inini Scene
A25

Toucans
A27

Parrots—A28
Engraved

1947, June 2 *Perf. 13.* Unwmkd.

192	A23	10c dk bl grn	6	6
193	A23	30c brt red	6	6
194	A23	50c dk vio brn	6	6
195	A24	60c grnsh blk	6	6
196	A24	1fr red brn	18	18
197	A24	1.50fr blk brn	18	18
198	A25	2fr dp yel grn	35	18
199	A25	2.50fr dp ultra	35	30
200	A25	3fr red brn	48	42
201	A26	4fr blk brn	1.40	60
202	A26	5fr dp bl	85	60
203	A26	6fr red brn	90	60
204	A27	10fr dp ultra	3.50	2.50
205	A27	15fr blk brn	3.50	3.50
206	A27	20fr red brn	4.25	3.75
207	A28	25fr brt bl grn	5.75	4.25
208	A28	40fr blk brn	5.75	4.25
		Nos. 192-208 (17)	27.68	21.55

SEMI-POSTAL STAMPS.

Regular Issue of 1905–28 Surcharged in Red

+
5

1915 *Perf. 13½x14.* Unwmkd.

B1	A13	10c +5c rose	9.50	9.50
a.		Inverted surcharge	100.00	100.00
b.		Double surcharge	87.50	87.50

Regular Issue of 1905–28 Surcharged in Rose

+5c

B2	A13	10c +5c rose	52	52

Curie Issue
Common Design Type

1938 *Perf. 13.*

B3	CD80	1.75fr +50c brt ultra	7.00	7.00

French Revolution Issue
Common Design Type

1939 Photogravure

Name and Value in Black.

B4	CD83	45c +25c grn	6.00	6.00
B5	CD83	70c +30c brn	6.00	6.00
B6	CD83	90c +35c red org	6.00	6.00
B7	CD83	1.25fr +1fr rose pink	6.00	6.00
B8	CD83	2.25fr +2fr bl	6.00	6.00
		Nos. B4-B8 (5)	30.00	30.00

Common Design Type and

Colonial Infantryman
SP1

Colonial Policeman
SP2

1941 Photogravure *Perf. 13½*

B9	SP1	1fr +1fr red	70	
B10	CD86	1.50fr +3fr mar	95	
B11	SP2	2.50fr +1fr bl	70	

Nos. B9–B11 were issued by the Vichy government, and were not placed on sale in the colony.

Nos. 170A–170B were surcharged "OEUVRES COLONIALES" and surtax (including change of denomination of the 2.50fr to 50c). These were issued in 1944 by the Vichy government, and not placed on sale in the colony.

Red Cross Issue
Common Design Type

1944 *Perf. 14½x14.*

B12	CD90	5fr +20fr dk cop brn	65	65

The surtax was for the French Red Cross and national relief.

AIR POST STAMPS.

Cayenne—AP1
Photogravure.

1933, Nov. 20 *Perf. 13½* Unwmkd.

C1	AP1	50c org brn	22	22
C2	AP1	1fr yel grn	22	22
C3	AP1	1.50fr dk bl	22	22
C4	AP1	2fr orange	22	22
C5	AP1	3fr black	65	65
C6	AP1	5fr violet	30	30
C7	AP1	10fr ol grn	55	55
C8	AP1	20fr scarlet	65	65
		Nos. C1-C8 (8)	3.03	3.03

V4

V5

Stamp of type AP1 without "RF" and stamps of the designs shown above were issued in 1942 and 1944 by the Vichy Government, but were not placed on sale in the colony.

Common Design Type

1945 Photo. *Perf. 14½x14*

C9	CD87	50fr dk grn	90	90
C10	CD87	100fr plum	1.50	1.50

Victory Issue
Common Design Type

1946, May 8 Engraved. *Perf. 12½.*

C11	CD92	8fr black	1.00	1.00

Issued to commemorate the European victory of the Allied Nations in World War II.

Chad to Rhine Issue
Common Design Types

1946, June 6

C12	CD93	5fr dk sl bl	65	65
C13	CD94	10fr lil rose	75	75
C14	CD95	15fr dk vio brn	75	75
C15	CD96	20fr dk sl grn	85	85
C16	CD97	25fr vio brn	90	90
C17	CD98	50fr brt lil	1.25	1.25
		Nos. C12-C17 (6)	5.15	5.15

Eagles—AP2

Tapir
AP3

Toucans—AP4

1947, June 2 Engraved. *Perf. 13*

C18	AP2	50fr dp grn	10.50	10.50
C19	AP3	100fr red brn	10.50	10.50
C20	AP4	200fr dk gray bl	19.00	19.00

AIR POST SEMI-POSTAL STAMP
French Revolution Issue
Common Design Type
Photogravure

1939, July 5 *Perf. 13* Unwmkd.

Name & Value Typo. in Orange

CB1	CD83	5fr +4fr brn blk	12.00	12.00

V6

Stamps of the design shown above and stamp of Cameroun type V10 inscribed "Guyane Francaise" were issued in 1942 by the Vichy Government, but were not placed on sale in the colony.

POSTAGE DUE STAMPS.

Postage Due Stamps of France, 1893–1926, Overprinted

GUYANE FRANÇAISE

1925-27 *Perf. 14x13½.* Unwmkd.

J1	D2	5c lt bl	14	14
J2	D2	10c brown	22	22
J3	D2	20c ol grn	22	22
J4	D2	50c vio brn	55	42
J5	D2	3fr mag ('27)	6.25	5.25

Surcharged in Black

GUYANE FRANÇAISE 25 centimes à percevoir

No.	Type	Description	Unused	Used
J6	D2	15c on 20c ol grn	22	22
a.		Blue surcharge	30.00	
J7	D2	25c on 5c lt bl	52	35
J8	D2	30c on 20c ol grn	65	42
J9	D2	45c on 10c brn	40	30
J10	D2	60c on 5c lt bl	55	42
J11	D2	1fr on 20c ol grn	95	85
J12	D2	2fr on 50c vio brn	1.25	1.00
		Nos. J1-J12 (12)	11.92	9.81

Royal Palms

D3

Guiana Girl

D4

1929, Oct. 14 Typo. *Perf. 13½x14*

No.	Type	Description	Unused	Used
J13	D3	5c ind & Prus bl	14	14
J14	D3	10c bis brn & Prus grn	14	14
J15	D3	20c grn & rose red	14	14
J16	D3	30c ol brn & rose red	14	14
J17	D3	50c vio & ol brn	42	42
J18	D3	60c brn red & ol brn	65	65
J19	D4	1fr dp bl & org brn	95	95
J20	D4	2fr brn red & bluish grn	1.40	1.40
J21	D4	3fr vio & blk	2.50	2.50
		Nos. J13-J21 (9)	6.48	6.48

D5

1947, June 2 Engr. *Perf. 14x13*

No.	Type	Description	Unused	Used
J22	D5	10c dk car rose	5	5
J23	D5	30c dl grn	5	5
J24	D5	50c black	8	8
J25	D5	1fr brt ultra	22	22
J26	D5	2fr dk brn red	22	22
J27	D5	3fr dp vio	35	35
J28	D5	4fr red	60	60
J29	D5	5fr brn vio	75	75
J30	D5	10fr bl grn	1.25	1.25
J31	D5	20fr lil rose	1.75	1.75
		Nos. J22-J31 (10)	5.32	5.32

FRENCH GUINEA

(frĕnch gĭn'ī)

LOCATION—On the coast of West Africa, between Portuguese Guinea and Sierra Leone.

GOVT.—Former French colony.

AREA—89,436 sq. mi.

POP.—2,058,442 (est. 1941).

CAPITAL—Conakry.

French Guinea stamps were replaced by those of French West Africa around 1944–45. French Guinea became the Republic of Guinea Oct. 2, 1958. See "Guinea" for issues of the republic.

100 Centimes = 1 Franc.

Navigation and Commerce

A1

Fulah Shepherd

A2

Perf. 14x13½.

1892-1900 Typographed. Unwmkd.

Name of Colony in Blue or Carmine

No.	Type	Description	Unused	Used
1	A1	1c *lil bl*	90	90
2	A1	2c brn, *buff*	1.00	1.00
3	A1	4c cl, *lav*	1.25	1.25
4	A1	5c grn, *grnsh*	4.75	3.00
5	A1	10c *lavender*	4.25	3.00
6	A1	10c red ('00)	27.50	21.00
7	A1	15c bl, quadrille paper	4.75	3.00
8	A1	15c gray, *lt gray* ('00)	82.50	70.00
9	A1	20c red, *grn*	12.00	8.25
10	A1	25c *rose*	6.50	4.75
11	A1	25c bl ('00)	16.00	13.00
12	A1	30c brn, *bis*	24.00	16.00
13	A1	40c red, *straw*	24.00	16.00
a.		"GUINEE FRANCAISE" double	375.00	375.00
14	A1	50c car, *rose*	30.00	16.00
15	A1	50c brn, *az* ('00)	21.00	16.00
16	A1	75c dp vio, *org*	40.00	30.00
17	A1	1fr brnz grn, *straw*	30.00	20.00
		Nos. 1-17 (17)	330.40	243.15

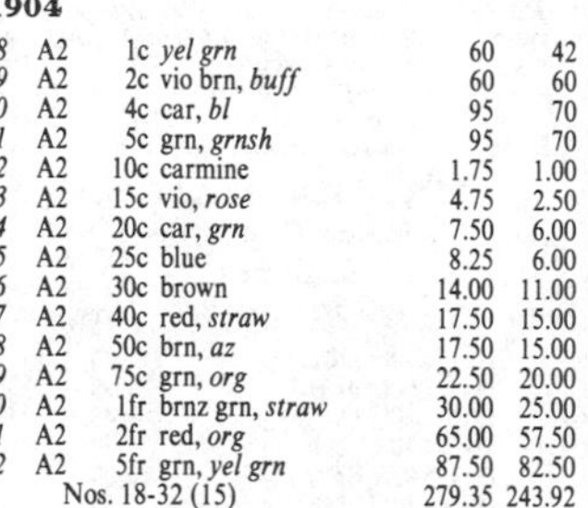

1904

No.	Type	Description	Unused	Used
18	A2	1c *yel grn*	60	42
19	A2	2c vio brn, *buff*	60	60
20	A2	4c car, *bl*	95	70
21	A2	5c grn, *grnsh*	95	70
22	A2	10c carmine	1.75	1.00
23	A2	15c vio, *rose*	4.75	2.50
24	A2	20c car, *grn*	7.50	6.00
25	A2	25c blue	8.25	6.00
26	A2	30c brown	14.00	11.00
27	A2	40c red, *straw*	17.50	15.00
28	A2	50c brn, *az*	17.50	15.00
29	A2	75c grn, *org*	22.50	20.00
30	A2	1fr brnz grn, *straw*	30.00	25.00
31	A2	2fr red, *org*	65.00	57.50
32	A2	5fr grn, *yel grn*	87.50	82.50
		Nos. 18-32 (15)	279.35	243.92

Gen. Louis Faidherbé

A3

Oil Palm

A4

Dr. Noel Eugène Ballay

A5

1906-07

Name of Colony in Red or Blue.

No.	Type	Description	Unused	Used
33	A3	1c gray	52	52
34	A3	2c brown	65	52
35	A3	4c brn, *bl*	85	70
36	A3	5c green	1.90	1.25
37	A3	10c car (B)	11.00	1.40
38	A4	20c *blue*	3.25	2.25
39	A4	25c bl, *pnksh*	4.25	3.50
40	A4	30c brn, *pnksh*	4.00	2.50
41	A4	35c *yellow*	1.75	1.25
42	A4	45c choc, *grnsh gray*	3.25	2.50
43	A4	50c dp vio	7.75	7.00
44	A4	75c bl, *org*	3.75	2.50
45	A5	1fr blk, *az*	14.00	13.00
46	A5	2fr bl, *pink*	30.00	27.50
47	A5	5fr car, *straw* (B)	42.50	42.50
		Nos. 33-47 (15)	129.42	108.89

Regular Issues Surcharged in Black or Carmine

05 *a*   10 *b*

1912

On Issue of 1892–1900

Surcharged Type *a*

No.	Type	Description	Unused	Used
48	A1	5c on 2c brn, *buff*	70	70
49	A1	5c on 4c cl, *lav* (C)	52	52
50	A1	5c on 15c bl (C)	52	52
51	A1	5c on 20c red, *grn*	2.50	2.50
52	A1	5c on 30c brn, *bis* (C)	2.75	2.75

Surcharged Type *b*

No.	Type	Description	Unused	Used
53	A1	10c on 40c red, *straw*	1.25	1.25
54	A1	10c on 75c dp vio, *org*	4.25	4.25
a.		Double surcharge, inverted	160.00	

On Issue of 1904.

Surcharged Type *a*

No.	Type	Description	Unused	Used
55	A2	5c on 2c vio brn, *buff*	60	60
a.		Pair, one without surcharge	425.00	
56	A2	5c on 4c car, *bl*	60	60
57	A2	5c on 15c vio, *rose*	60	60
58	A2	5c on 20c car, *grn*	60	60
59	A2	5c on 25c bl (C)	60	60
60	A2	5c on 30c brn (C)	85	85

Surcharged Type *b*

No.	Type	Description	Unused	Used
61	A2	10c on 40c red, *straw*	1.10	1.10
62	A2	10c on 50c brn, *az* (C)	2.75	2.75
		Nos. 48-62 (15)	20.19	20.19

Two spacings between the surcharged numerals are found on Nos. 48 to 62.

Ford at Kitim

A6

1913-33 *Perf. 13½x14*

No.	Type	Description	Unused	Used
63	A6	1c vio & bl	5	5
64	A6	2c brn & vio brn	5	5
65	A6	4c gray & blk	5	5
66	A6	5c yel grn & bl grn	18	18
67	A6	5c brn vio & grn ('22)	5	5
68	A6	10c red org & rose	18	18
69	A6	10c yel grn & bl grn ('22)	5	5
70	A6	10c vio & ver ('25)	6	5
71	A6	15c vio brn & rose ('16)	5	5
72	A6	15c gray grn & yel grn ('25)	5	5
73	A6	15c red brn & rose lil ('27)	15	5
74	A6	20c brn & vio	5	5
75	A6	20c grn & bl grn ('26)	60	40
76	A6	20c brn red & brn ('27)	15	6
77	A6	25c ultra & bl	80	70
78	A6	25c blk & vio ('22)	52	35
79	A6	30c vio brn & grn	45	42
80	A6	30c red org & rose ('22)	18	18
81	A6	30c rose red & grn ('25)	5	5
82	A6	30c dl grn & bl grn ('28)	95	80
83	A6	35c bl & rose	18	18
84	A6	40c grn & gray	65	52
85	A6	45c brn & red	85	65
86	A6	50c ultra & blk	4.00	2.50
87	A6	50c ultra & bl ('22)	48	22
88	A6	50c yel brn & ol ('25)	6	5
89	A6	60c vio, *pnksh* ('25)	15	15
90	A6	65c yel brn & sl bl ('26)	1.25	80
91	A6	75c red & ultra	1.00	90
92	A6	75c ind & dl bl ('25)	48	35
93	A6	75c mag & yel grn ('27)	95	70
94	A6	85c ol grn & red brn ('26)	55	42
95	A6	90c brn red & rose ('30)	3.50	3.25
96	A6	1fr vio & blk	90	52
97	A6	1.10fr vio & ol brn ('28)	4.25	4.00
98	A6	1.25fr vio & yel brn ('33)	1.00	70
99	A6	1.50fr dk bl & lt bl ('30)	3.00	1.75
100	A6	1.75fr ol brn & vio ('33)	1.25	1.00
101	A6	2fr org & vio brn	1.90	90
102	A6	3fr red vio ('30)	5.75	4.75
103	A6	5fr blk & vio	8.50	7.00
104	A6	5fr dl bl & blk ('22)	1.75	1.25
		Nos. 63-104 (42)	47.07	36.38

Nos. 66 and 68 exist on both ordinary and chalky paper, No. 71 on chalky paper only.

Type of 1913–33 Surcharged

60 = 60

1922

No.	Type	Description	Unused	Used
105	A6	60c on 75c vio, *pnksh*	42	42

Stamps and Type of 1913-33 Surcharged with New Value and Bars.

1924-27

106	A6	25c on 2fr org & brn (R)	8	8
107	A6	25c on 5fr dl bl & blk ('24)	6	6
108	A6	65c on 75c rose & ultra ('25)	90	90
109	A6	85c on 75c rose & ultra ('25)	90	90
110	A6	90c on 75c brn red & cer ('27)	1.25	1.25
111	A6	1.25fr on 1fr dk bl & ultra ('26)	42	42
112	A6	1.50fr on 1fr dp bl & lt bl ('27)	1.25	1.25
113	A6	3fr on 5fr mag & sl ('27)	2.75	2.75
114	A6	10fr on 5fr bl & bl grn, *bluish* ('27)	5.25	5.25
115	A6	20fr on 5fr rose lil & brn ol, *pnksh* ('27)	14.00	14.00
		Nos. 106-115 (10)	26.86	26.86

Colonial Exposition Issue.

Common Design Types

1931 Engraved. ***Perf. 12½.***

Name of Country in Black.

116	CD70	40c dp grn	2.75	2.50
117	CD71	50c violet	2.75	2.50
118	CD72	90c red org	2.75	2.50
119	CD73	1.50fr dl bl	2.25	1.90

Paris International Exposition Issue.

Common Design Types

1937 ***Perf. 13.***

120	CD74	20c dp vio	1.00	1.00
121	CD75	30c dk grn	1.00	1.00
122	CD76	40c car rose	1.25	1.25
123	CD77	50c dk brn	1.25	1.25
124	CD78	90c red	1.40	1.40
125	CD79	1.50fr ultra	1.40	1.40
		Nos. 120-125 (6)	7.30	7.30

Colonial Arts Exhibition Issue.

Souvenir Sheet.

Common Design Type

1937 ***Imperf.***

126	CD76	3fr Prus grn	3.50	3.50

Sheet size: 118x99mm.

Guinea Village—A7

Hausa Basket Workers—A8

Forest Waterfall—A9

Guinea Women
A10

1938–40 ***Perf. 13***

128	A7	2c vermilion	5	5
129	A7	3c ultra	5	5
130	A7	4c green	5	5
131	A7	5c rose car	5	5
132	A7	10c pck bl	5	5
133	A7	15c vio brn	5	5
134	A8	20c dk car	5	5
135	A8	25c pck bl	18	14
136	A8	30c ultra	14	14
137	A8	35c green	35	35
138	A8	40c blk brn ('40)	14	14
139	A8	45c dk grn ('40)	18	18
140	A8	50c red brn	15	15
141	A9	55c dk ultra	52	40
142	A9	60c dk ultra ('40)	65	65
143	A9	65c green	55	35
144	A9	70c grn ('40)	65	65
145	A9	80c rose vio	35	35
146	A9	90c rose vio ('39)	65	65
147	A9	1fr org red	1.50	1.10
148	A9	1fr brn blk ('40)	42	42
149	A9	1.25fr org red ('39)	85	85
150	A9	1.40fr brn ('40)	85	85
151	A9	1.50fr brown	1.50	1.10
152	A10	1.60fr org red ('40)	85	85
153	A10	1.75fr ultra	45	42
154	A10	2fr magenta	75	42
155	A10	2.25fr brt ultra ('39)	1.25	1.25
156	A10	2.50fr brn blk ('40)	85	85
157	A10	3fr pck bl	42	22
158	A10	5fr rose vio	52	42
159	A10	10fr sl grn	90	65
160	A10	20fr chocolate	1.50	1.25
		Nos. 128-160 (33)	17.47	15.15

Caillié Issue

Common Design Type

1939 Engraved ***Perf. 12½x12***

161	CD81	90c org brn & org	70	70
162	CD81	2fr brt vio	70	70
163	CD81	2.25fr ultra & dk bl	70	70

Issued to commemorate the centenary of the death of René Caillié, French explorer.

New York World's Fair Issue.

Common Design Type

1939

164	CD82	1.25fr car lake	70	70
165	CD82	2.25fr ultra	70	70

Ford at Kitim and Marshal Petain
A11

1941 ***Perf. 12x12½.***

166	A11	1fr green	42
167	A11	2.50fr dp bl	42

Nos. 166–167 were issued by the Vichy government. Seven stamps of types A7–A10 without "RF" are also Vichy issues (1943–44), but are believed not to have been placed on sale in the colony.

Stamps of French Guinea were followed by those of French West Africa.

Common Design Types pictured in section at front of book.

SEMI-POSTAL STAMPS.

Regular Issue of 1913 Surcharged in Red **✚ 5c**

1915 ***Perf. 13½x14.*** **Unwmkd.**

B1	A6	10c +5c org & rose	90	52

No. B1 exists on both ordinary and chalky paper.

Curie Issue

Common Design Type

1938 Engraved. ***Perf. 13.***

B2	CD80	1.75fr +50c brt ultra	6.50	6.50

French Revolution Issue

Common Design Type

1939 Photogravure.

Name and Value Typo. in Black.

B3	CD83	45(c) +25(c) grn	4.25	4.25
B4	CD83	70(c) +30(c) brn	4.25	4.25
B5	CD83	90(c) +35(c) red org	4.25	4.25
B6	CD83	1.25fr +1fr rose pink	4.25	4.25
B7	CD83	2.25fr +2fr bl	4.25	4.25
		Nos. B3-B7 (5)	21.25	21.25

Stamps of 1938, Surcharged in Black **SECOURS + 1 fr. NATIONAL**

1941 ***Perf. 13.*** **Unwmkd.**

B8	A8	50c +1fr red brn	90	90
B9	A9	80c +2fr rose vio	3.00	2.50
B10	A9	1.50fr +2fr brn	3.00	2.50
B11	A10	2fr +3fr mag	3.00	2.50

Common Design Type and

Senegalese Soldier
SP1

Colonial Infantryman
SP2

1941 ***Perf. 13*** **Unwmkd.**

B12	SP1	1fr +1fr red	70
B13	CD86	1.50fr +3fr mar	70
B14	SP2	2.50fr +1fr bl	70

Nos. B12–B14 were issued by the Vichy government, and were not placed on sale in the colony.

Nos. 166–167 were surcharged "OEUVRES COLONIALES" and surtax (including change of denomination of the 2.50fr to 50c). These were issued in 1944 by the Vichy government and not placed on sale in the colony.

AIR POST STAMPS.

Common Design Type

Engraved.

1940 ***Perf. 12½x12.*** **Unwmkd.**

C1	CD85	1.90fr ultra	30	30
C2	CD85	2.90fr dk red	35	35
C3	CD85	4.50fr dk gray grn	45	45
C4	CD85	4.90fr yel bis	60	60
C5	CD85	6.90fr dp org	90	90
		Nos. C1-C5 (5)	2.60	2.60

Common Design Types

1942 Engraved.

C6	CD88	50c car & bl	5
C7	CD88	1fr brn & blk	14
C8	CD88	2fr dk grn & red brn	14
C9	CD88	3fr dk bl & scar	35
C10	CD88	5fr vio & brn red	35

Frame Engraved, Center Typographed.

C11	CD89	10fr ultra, ind & vio	45	
C12	CD89	20fr rose car, mag & gray bl	45	
C13	CD89	50fr yel grn, dl grn & gray blk	80	1.90
		Nos. C6-C13 (8)	2.73	

There is doubt whether Nos. C6–C12 were officially placed in use.

AIR POST SEMI-POSTAL STAMPS.

Stamps of types of Dahomey V1, V2 and V3, and of Cameroun V10, inscribed "Guinée", "Guinée Frcaise" or "Guinée Francaise," were issued in 1942 by the Vichy Government, but were not placed on sale in the colony.

POSTAGE DUE STAMPS.

Fulah Woman
D1

Heads and Coast
D2

Typographed.

1905 ***Perf. 14x13½*** **Unwmkd.**

J1	D1	5c blue	90	1.00
J2	D1	10c brown	90	1.00
J3	D1	15c green	3.25	2.50
J4	D1	30c rose	3.50	2.00
J5	D1	50c black	7.25	6.25
J6	D1	60c dl org	9.50	7.00
J7	D1	1fr violet	27.50	25.00
		Nos. J1-J7 (7)	52.80	44.75

1906-08

J8	D2	5c grn, *grnsh* ('08)	14.00	10.50
J9	D2	10c vio brn ('08)	5.25	4.25
J10	D2	15c dk bl ('08)	3.50	4.25
J11	D2	20c *yellow*	3.50	3.00
J12	D2	30c red, *straw* ('08)	22.50	17.00
J13	D2	50c vio ('08)	17.50	17.00
J14	D2	60c blk, *buff* ('08)	17.00	14.00
J15	D2	1fr *pnksh* ('08)	10.50	9.25
		Nos. J8-J15 (8)	88.50	75.00

D3

D4

1914

J16	D3	5c green	6	6
J17	D3	10c rose	6	6
J18	D3	15c gray	30	30
J19	D3	20c brown	30	30
J20	D3	30c blue	30	30
J21	D3	50c black	60	60
J22	D3	60c orange	1.25	1.25
J23	D3	1fr violet	1.40	1.40
		Nos. J16-J23 (8)	4.27	4.27

Type of 1914 Issue Surcharged **2F.**

1927

J24	D3	2fr on 1fr lil rose	4.75	4.75
J25	D3	3fr on 1fr org brn	5.25	5.25

1938 Engraved.

J26	D4	5c dk vio	5	5
J27	D4	10c carmine	5	5
J28	D4	15c green	5	5
J29	D4	20c red brn	5	5
J30	D4	30c rose vio	30	30
J31	D4	50c chocolate	45	45
J32	D4	60c pck bl	75	75
J33	D4	1fr vermilion	75	75
J34	D4	2fr ultra	80	80
J35	D4	3fr black	1.10	1.10
		Nos. J26-J35 (10)	4.35	4.35

A 10c of type D4 without "RF" was issued in 1944 by the Vichy Government, but was not placed on sale in the colony.

FRENCH INDIA

(frĕnch ĭn′dĭ·ȧ)

LOCATION—East coast of India bordering on Bay of Bengal.

GOVT.—Former French Territory.

AREA—196 sq. mi.

POP.—323,295 (1941).

CAPITAL—Pondichéry.

French India was an administrative unit comprising the five settlements of Chandernagor, Karikal, Mahé, Pondichéry and Yanaon. These united with India in 1949 and 1954.

100 Centimes = 1 Franc

24 Caches = 1 Fanon (1923)

8 Fanons = 1 Rupie

Navigation and Commerce A1

A2

Perf. 14x13½.

1892-1907 Typographed. Unwmkd.

Colony Name in Blue or Carmine

No.	Type	Description	Unused	Used
1	A1	1c *lil bl*	90	70
2	A1	2c brn, *buff*	1.00	90
3	A1	4c cl, *lav*	1.10	1.00
4	A1	5c grn, *grnsh*	3.00	1.90
5	A1	10c *lavender*	5.25	1.90
6	A1	10c red ('00)	2.00	1.50
7	A1	15c bl, quadrille paper	5.25	3.50
8	A1	15c gray, *lt gray* ('00)	21.00	17.50
9	A1	20c red, *grn*	4.50	3.25
10	A1	25c *rose*	2.00	1.50
11	A1	25c bl ('00)	8.75	6.25
12	A1	30c brn, *bis*	40.00	35.00
13	A1	35c *yel* ('06)	8.75	6.00
14	A1	40c red, *straw*	3.75	3.00
15	A1	45c *gray grn* ('07)	3.25	2.25
16	A1	50c car, *rose*	3.75	3.00
17	A1	50c brn, *az* ('00)	7.75	5.75
18	A1	75c dp vio, *org*	5.75	5.75
19	A1	1fr brnz grn, *straw*	7.50	7.50
		Nos. 1-19 (19)	135.25	108.15

Nos. 10 and 16 Surcharged in Carmine or Black 0,05

1903

No.	Type	Description	Unused	Used
20	A1	5c on 25c *rose*	250.00	160.00
21	A1	10c on 25c *rose*	250.00	160.00
22	A1	15c on 25c *rose*	82.50	82.50
23	A1	40c on 50c car, *rose* (Bk)	425.00	375.00

Counterfeits of Nos. 20–23 abound.

1903

No.	Type	Description	Unused	Used
24	A2	5c gray bl & blk	16.00	16.00

Brahma A5

Kali Temple near Pondichéry A6

1914–22 *Perf. 13½x14, 14x13½*

No.	Type	Description	Unused	Used
25	A5	1c gray & blk	6	6
26	A5	2c brn vio & blk	6	6
27	A5	2c grn & brn vio ('22)	18	18
28	A5	3c brn & blk	15	15
29	A5	4c org & blk	18	18
30	A5	5c bl grn & blk	35	35
31	A5	5c vio brn & blk ('22)	18	18
32	A5	10c dp rose & blk	42	42
33	A5	10c grn & blk ('22)	30	30
34	A5	15c vio & blk	48	48
35	A5	20c org red & blk	75	75
36	A5	25c bl & blk	75	75
37	A5	25c ultra & fawn ('22)	42	42
38	A5	30c ultra & blk	85	85
39	A5	30c rose & blk ('22)	52	52
40	A6	35c choc & blk	85	85
41	A6	40c org red & blk	85	85
42	A6	45c bl grn & blk	85	85
43	A6	50c dp rose & blk	65	65
44	A6	50c ultra & bl ('22)	65	65
45	A6	75c bl & blk	1.50	1.50
46	A6	1fr yel & blk	1.50	1.50
47	A6	2fr vio & blk	3.25	3.25
48	A6	5fr ultra & blk	1.25	1.25
49	A6	5fr rose & blk ('22)	2.00	2.00
		Nos. 25-49 (25)	19.00	19.00

No. 34 Surcharged 0,01 ≡ in Various Colors.

1922

No.	Type	Description	Unused	Used
50	A5	1c on 15c (Bk)	42	42
51	A5	2c on 15c (Bl)	42	42
53	A5	5c on 15c (R)	42	42

Stamps and Types of 1914-22 Surcharged with New Values in Caches, Fanons and Rupies in Black, Red or Blue:

1 FANON

2 CACHES

12 CACHES

3 ROUPIES

1923-28

No.	Type	Description	Unused	Used
54	A5	1ca on 1c gray & blk (R)	6	6
55	A5	2ca on 5c vio brn & blk	18	18
a.		Horizontal pair, imperf. between		
56	A5	3ca on 3c brn & blk	30	30
57	A5	4ca on 4c org & blk	48	40
58	A5	6ca on 10c grn & blk	55	55
59	A6	6ca on 45c bl grn & blk (R)	42	42
60	A5	10ca on 20c dp red & bl grn ('28)	1.50	1.50
61	A5	12ca on 15c vio & blk	60	60
62	A5	15ca on 20c org & blk	85	85
63	A6	16ca on 35c lt bl & yel brn ('28)	1.50	1.50
64	A5	18ca on 30c rose & blk	85	85
65	A6	20ca on 45c grn & dl red ('28)	1.00	80
66	A5	1fa on 25c dp grn & rose red ('28)	1.90	1.90
67	A6	1fa3ca on 35c choc & blk (Bl)	85	85
68	A6	1fa6ca on 40c org & blk (R)	95	70
69	A6	1fa12ca on 50c ultra & bl (Bl)	85	85
70	A6	1fa12ca on 75c bl & blk (Bl)	85	85
a.		Double surch.	95.00	
71	A6	1fa16ca on 75c brn red & grn ('28)	2.00	1.50
72	A5	2fa9ca on 25c ultra & fawn (Bl)	1.00	85
73	A6	2fa12ca on 1fr vio & dk brn ('28)	1.75	1.75
74	A6	3fa3ca on 1fr yel & blk (R)	1.10	1.00
a.		Double surch.	95.00	
75	A6	6fa6ca on 2fr vio & blk (Bl)	3.50	3.00
76	A6	1r on 1fr grn & dp bl (R) ('26)	4.25	3.75
77	A6	2r on 5fr rose & blk (R)	4.25	3.75
a.		Double surch.	95.00	
78	A6	3r on 2fr gray & bl vio (R) ('26)	10.50	8.25
79	A6	5r on 5fr rose & blk, *grnsh* ('26)	14.00	11.00
		Nos. 54-79 (26)	56.04	48.01

Nos. 60, 63, 66 and 73 have the original value obliterated by bars.

A7

A8

1929

No.	Type	Description	Unused	Used
80	A7	1ca dk gray & blk	6	6
81	A7	2ca vio brn & blk	6	6
82	A7	3ca brn & blk	6	6
83	A7	4ca org & blk	6	6
84	A7	6ca gray grn & grn	22	22
85	A7	10ca brn, red & grn	22	22
86	A8	12ca grn & lt grn	42	35
87	A7	16ca brt bl & blk	60	52
88	A7	18ca brn red & ver	60	52
89	A7	20ca dk bl & grn, *bluish*	48	42
90	A8	1fa gray grn & rose red	42	35
91	A8	1fa6ca red org & blk	42	35
92	A8	1fa12ca dp bl & ultra	42	35
93	A8	1fa16ca rose red & grn	65	60
94	A8	2fa12ca brt vio & brn	75	60
95	A8	6fa6ca dl vio & blk	75	60
96	A8	1r gray grn & dp bl	52	42
97	A8	2r rose & blk	1.00	52
98	A8	3r lt gray & gray lil	1.50	1.10
99	A8	5r rose & blk, *grnsh*	2.25	1.90
		Nos. 80-99 (20)	11.46	9.28

Colonial Exposition Issue.

Common Design Types

1931 Engraved. *Perf. 12½.*

No.	Type	Description	Unused	Used
100	CD70	10ca dp grn	2.00	2.00
101	DC71	12ca violet	2.00	2.00
102	CD72	18ca red org	2.00	2.00
103	CD73	1fa12ca dl bl	2.00	2.00

Paris International Exposition Issue.

Common Design Types

1937 *Perf. 13.*

No.	Type	Description	Unused	Used
104	CD74	8ca dp vio	1.00	1.00
105	CD75	12ca dk grn	1.00	1.00
106	CD76	16ca car rose	1.00	1.00
107	CD77	20ca dk brn	1.00	1.00
108	CD78	1fa12ca red	1.00	1.00
109	CD79	2fa12ca ultra	1.00	1.00
		Nos. 104-109 (6)	6.00	6.00

Colonial Arts Exhibition Issue.

Souvenir Sheet.

Common Design Type

1937 *Imperf.*

No.	Type	Description	Unused	Used
110	CD79	5fa red vio	3.50	3.50

Sheet size: 118x99mm.

New York World's Fair Issue.

Common Design Type

1939 Engraved *Perf. 12½x12*

No.	Type	Description	Unused	Used
111	CD82	1fa12ca car lake	95	95
112	CD82	2fa12ca ultra	1.10	1.10

Temple near Pondichéry and Marshal Petain—A9

1941 Engraved *Perf. 12½x12*

No.	Type	Description	Unused	Used
112A	A9	1fa16ca car & red	42	
112B	A9	4fa4ca blue	42	

Nos. 112A–112B were issued by the Vichy government, and were not placed on sale in French India.

Stamps of 1923 Overprinted in Carmine or Blue:

FRANCE LIBRE

a *b*

Perf. 13½x14, 14x13½.

1941 Unwmkd.

No.	Type	Description	Unused	Used
113	A5 (a)	15ca on 20c org & blk (C)	52.50	52.50
114	A5 (a)	18ca on 30c rose & blk (C)	1.50	1.50
115	A6 (a)	1fa3ca on 35c choc & blk (C)	60.00	60.00
a.		Horiz. ovpt.	65.00	65.00
116	A5 (b)	2fa9ca on 25c ultra & fawn (Bl)	875.00	775.00
a.		Ovpt. "a" (Bl)	875.00	775.00
b.		Ovpt. "b" (C)	*1,400.*	

Common Design Types

pictured in section at front of book.

Stamps of 1929 Overprinted in Carmine or Blue.

No.	Type	Description	Unused	Used
117	A7 (a)	2ca vio brn & blk (C)	6.25	6.25
118	A7 (a)	3ca brn & blk (C)	1.50	1.50
119	A7 (a)	4ca org & blk (C)	3.75	3.25
120	A7 (a)	6ca gray grn & grn (C)	1.00	1.00
121	A7 (a)	10ca brn red & grn (Bl)	1.25	1.25
122	A8 (a)	12ca grn & lt grn (C)	1.25	1.25
123	A7 (a)	16ca brt bl & blk (C)	1.65	1.50
123A	A7 (a)	18ca brn red & ver (Bl)	575.00	525.00
124	A7 (a)	20ca dk bl & grn, *bluish* (C)	1.25	1.25
125	A8 (a)	1fa gray grn & rose red (Bl)	1.10	1.10
126	A8 (a)	1fa6ca red org & blk (C)	1.50	1.40
127	A8 (a)	1fa12ca dp bl & ultra (C)	3.00	2.50
128	A8 (a)	1fa16ca rose red & grn (C)	1.25	1.10
129	A8 (a)	2fa12ca brt vio & brn (C)	1.25	1.10
130	A8 (a)	6fa6ca dl vio & blk (C)	1.25	1.25
131	A8 (a)	1r gray grn & dp bl (C)	1.25	1.25
132	A8 (a)	2r rose & blk (C)	1.25	1.25
133	A8 (a)	3r lt gray & gray lil (C)	1.65	1.65
134	A8 (a)	5r rose & blk, *grnsh* (C)	6.25	4.75
		Nos. 113-115, 117-123, 124-134 (21)	151.65	148.60

Same Overprints on Paris Exposition Issue of 1937.

Perf. 13.

No.	Type	Description	Unused	Used
135	CD74 (b)	8ca dp vio (C)	4.25	4.25
135A	CD74 (b)	8ca dp vio (Bl)	175.00	175.00
135B	CD74 (a)	8ca dp vio (C)	110.00	110.00
135C	CD74 (a)	8ca dp vio (Bl)	165.00	165.00
136	CD75 (a)	12ca dk grn (C)	2.75	2.75
137	CD76 (a)	16ca car rose (Bl)	2.75	2.75
138	CD78 (a)	1fa12ca red (Bl)	2.75	2.75
139	CD79 (a)	2fa12ca ultra (C)	2.75	2.75
		Nos. 135-139 (8)	465.25	465.25

Inverted overprints exist.

Souvenir Sheet

No. 110 Overprinted "FRANCE LIBRE" Diagonally in Blue Violet

Two types of overprint:
- I. Overprint 37mm. With serifs.
- II. Overprint 24mm., as type "a" shown above No. 113. No serifs.

1941 ***Imperf.*** **Unwmkd.**

No.	Type	Description	Unused	Used
140	CD79	5fa red vio (I)	425.00	400.00
a.		Type II	600.00	600.00

Overprinted on New York World's Fair Issue, 1939.

Perf. 12½x12.

No.	Type	Description	Unused	Used
141	CD82 (a)	1fa12ca car lake (Bl)	2.00	2.00
142	CD82 (a)	2fa12ca ultra (C)	2.00	2.00

Lotus Flowers
A10

Photogravure

1942 ***Perf. 14x14½*** **Unwmkd.**

No.	Type	Description	Unused	Used
143	A10	2ca brown	18	18
144	A10	3ca dk bl	18	18
145	A10	4ca emerald	18	18
146	A10	6ca dk org	18	18
147	A10	12ca grnsh blk	18	18
148	A10	16ca rose vio	18	18
149	A10	20ca dk red brn	52	52
150	A10	1fa brt red	52	42
151	A10	1fa18ca sl blk	80	52
152	A10	6fa6ca brt ultra	90	75
153	A10	1r dl vio	80	75
154	A10	2r bister	90	90
155	A10	3r chocolate	1.25	1.00
156	A10	5r dk grn	1.75	1.25
		Nos. 143-156 (14)	8.52	7.19

Stamps of 1923–39 Overprinted in Blue or Carmine

FRANCE
LIBRE
c

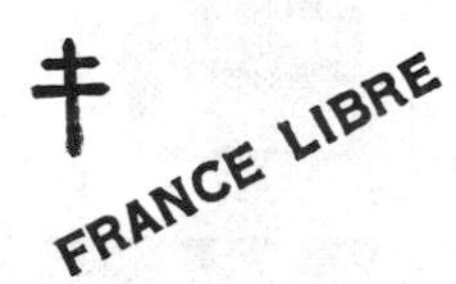

d

Perf. 13½x14, 14x13½.

1942–43

Overprinted on No. 64

No.	Type	Description	Unused	Used
156A	A5 (c)	18ca on 30c rose & blk (B)	210.00	160.00

Overprinted on Stamps of 1929

No.	Type	Description	Unused	Used
157	A7 (c)	2ca vio brn & blk (C)	65	65
a.		Black overprint	19.00	19.00
158	A7 (c)	3ca brn & blk (C)	75	75
159	A7 (c)	6ca gray grn & grn (Bl)	85	85
160	A8 (d)	12ca grn & lt grn (Bl)	1.65	1.65
161	A7 (c)	16ca brt bl & blk (C)	85	85
162	A7 (c)	18ca brn red & ver (Bl)	85	85
163	A7 (c)	20ca dk bl & grn, *bluish* (Bl) ('43)	3.00	2.50
164	A7 (c)	20ca dk bl & grn, *bluish* (C)	85	85
165	A8 (d)	1fa gray grn & rose red (Bl)	85	85
166	A8 (d)	1fa6ca red org & blk (C)	1.10	1.10
167	A8 (d)	1fa12ca dp bl & ultra (C)	1.00	1.00
168	A8 (d)	1fa16ca rose red & grn (Bl)	85	85
169	A8 (d)	2fa12ca brt vio & brn (Bl)	37.50	37.50
170	A8 (d)	2fa12ca brt vio & brn (C)	1.00	1.00
171	A8 (d)	6fa6ca dl vio & blk (C)	1.65	1.65
172	A8 (d)	1r gray grn & dp bl (C)	4.00	4.00
173	A8 (d)	2r rose & blk (C)	3.25	3.25
174	A8 (d)	3r lt gray & gray lil (C)	4.00	4.00
175	A8 (d)	3r lt gray & gray lil (Bl) ('43)	100.00	95.00
176	A8 (d)	5r rose & blk, *grnsh* (C)	4.25	4.25
		Nos. 156A-176 (21)	378.90	323.40

Same Overprints on Paris International Exposition Issue of 1937.

Perf. 13.

No.	Type	Description	Unused	Used
177	CD74 (c)	8ca dp vio (Bl)	4.75	4.25
178	CD75 (d)	12ca dk grn (Bl)	4.25	4.25
179	CD76 (d)	16ca car rose (Bl)	1,000.	875.00
180	CD78 (d)	1fa12ca red (Bl)	90	90
181	CD79 (d)	2fa12ca ultra (C)	2.25	2.25

Same Overprint on New York World's Fair Issue, 1939.

Perf. 12½x12.

No.	Type	Description	Unused	Used
182	CD82 (d)	1fa12ca car lake (Bl)	1.50	1.50
183	CD82 (d)	2fa12ca ultra (C)	2.50	2.50

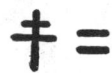

No. 87 Surcharged in Carmine

FRANCE
LIBRE

2 fa 9 ca

1942–43 ***Perf. 13½x14***

No.	Type	Description	Unused	Used
184	A7	1ca on 16ca	52.50	32.50
185	A7	4ca on 16ca ('43)	52.50	32.50
186	A7	10ca on 16ca	32.50	14.00
187	A7	15ca on 16ca	30.00	14.00
188	A7	1fa3ca on 16ca ('43)	52.50	27.50
189	A7	2fa9ca on 16ca ('43)	47.50	42.50
190	A7	3fa3ca on 16ca ('43)	37.50	15.00
		Nos. 184-190 (7)	305.00	178.00

Nos. 95–99 Surcharged in Carmine

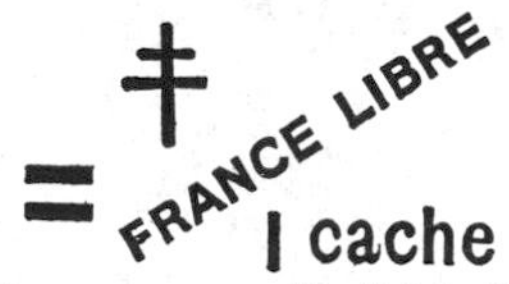

1943 ***Perf. 14x13½.***

No.	Type	Description	Unused	Used
191	A8	1ca on 6fa6ca dl vio & blk	7.50	6.00
192	A8	4ca on 6fa6ca dl vio & blk	8.75	7.75
193	A8	10ca on 6fa6ca dl vio & blk	1.75	1.25
194	A8	15ca on 6fa6ca dl vio & blk	3.50	1.50
195	A8	1fa3ca on 6fa6ca dl vio & blk	5.25	2.50
196	A8	2fa9ca on 6fa6ca dl vio & blk	4.25	3.50
197	A8	3fa3ca on 6fa6ca dl vio & blk	6.50	3.75
198	A8	1ca on 1r gray grn & dp bl	3.50	3.00
199	A8	2ca on 1r gray grn & dp bl	95	95
200	A8	4ca on 1r gray grn & dp bl	95	90
201	A8	6ca on 2r rose & blk	90	75
202	A8	10ca on 2r rose & blk	1.25	1.25
203	A8	12ca on 2r rose & blk	90	75
204	A8	15ca on 3r lt gray & gray lil	80	80
205	A8	16ca on 3r lt gray & gray lil	80	80
206	A8	1fa3ca on 3r lt gray & gray lil	90	90
207	A8	1fa6ca on 5r rose & blk, *grnsh*	1.25	1.25
208	A8	1fa12ca on 5r rose & blk, *grnsh*	1.25	1.00
209	A8	1fa16ca on 5r rose & blk, *grnsh*	1.25	1.00
		Nos. 191-209 (19)	52.20	39.60

In 1943, twenty-seven stamps were overprinted in red or dark blue, "FRANCE TOUJOURS" and a Lorraine Cross within a circle measuring 17½mm. in diameter. The stamps overprinted were 19 denominations of the regular 1929 postage series, plus Nos. 104 to 109 and Nos. 111 and 112. Of each stamp, 200 were overprinted.

No. 95 Surcharged in Carmine with New Value and Bars.

1943 ***Perf. 14x13½.*** **Unwmkd.**

No.	Type	Description	Unused	Used
209A	A8	1ca on 6fa6ca	19.00	12.00
209B	A8	4ca on 6fa6ca	19.00	12.00
209C	A8	10ca on 6fa6ca	6.00	4.25
209D	A8	15ca on 6fa6ca	6.00	4.25
209E	A8	1fa3ca on 6fa6ca	16.00	14.00
209F	A8	2fa9ca on 6fa6ca	16.00	14.00
209G	A8	3fa3ca on 6fa6ca	18.00	15.00
		Nos. 209A-209G (7)	100.00	75.50

Eboue Issue.

Common Design Type

1945 **Engraved.** ***Perf. 13.***

No.	Type	Description	Unused	Used
210	CD91	3fa8ca black	42	42
211	CD91	5r 1fa 16ca Prus grn	90	90

Nos. 210 and 211 exist imperforate.

Apsaras
A11

Brahman Ascetic
A12

Designs: 6ca, 8ca, 10ca, Dvarabalagar. 12ca, 15ca, 1fa, Vishnu. 1fa 6ca, 2fa, 2fa 2ca, Dvarabalagar (foot raised). 2fa 12ca, 3fa, 5fa, Temple Guardian. 7fa 12ca, 1r 2fa, 1r 4fa 12ca, Tigoupalagar.

1948 Photogravure ***Perf. 13x13½***

No.	Type	Description	Unused	Used
212	A11	1ca dk ol grn	5	5
213	A11	2ca org brn	6	6
214	A11	4ca vio, *cr*	6	6
215	A11	6ca yel org	60	30
216	A11	8ca gray blk	70	60
217	A11	10ca dl yel grn, *pale grn*	70	60
218	A11	12ca vio brn	30	22
219	A11	15ca Prus grn	30	22
220	A11	1fa vio, *pale rose*	85	42
221	A11	1fa6ca brn red	60	60
222	A11	2fa dk grn	60	42
223	A11	2fa 2ca bl, *cr*	1.00	70
224	A11	2fa12ca brown	1.00	90
225	A11	3fa dp org	1.50	95
226	A11	5fa red vio, *rose*	1.25	95
227	A11	7fa12ca dk brn	1.00	95
228	A11	1r2fa brn blk	3.50	3.00
229	A11	1r 4fa 12ca ol grn	3.75	3.50
		Nos. 212-229 (18)	17.82	14.50

1952

No.	Type	Description	Unused	Used
230	A12	18ca rose red	90	90
231	A12	1fa15ca vio bl	1.25	1.25
232	A12	4fa ol grn	1.75	1.75

Military Medal Issue.
Common Design Type

1952 Engr. and Typo. *Perf. 13*

233	CD101	1fa multi	2.50	2.50

SEMI-POSTAL STAMPS.

Regular Issue of 1914 Surcharged in Red ✚ 5c

1915 *Perf. 14x13½* Unwmkd.

B1	A5	10c +5c rose & blk	70	70
a.		Inverted surch.	52.50	52.50

There were two printings of this surcharge; in the first it was placed at the bottom of the stamp, in the second it was near the top.

Regular Issue of 1914 Surcharged in Red 5 ✚

1916

B2	A5	10c +5c rose & blk	9.50	9.50
a.		Inverted surch.	52.50	52.50
b.		Double surch.	47.50	47.50

Surcharged ✚ 5 C

B3	A5	10c +5c rose & blk	1.75	1.75

Surcharged ✚ 5 c

B4	A5	10c +5c rose & blk	90	90

Surcharged ✚ 5c

B5	A5	10c +5c rose & blk	90	90

Curie Issue
Common Design Type

1938 Engraved. *Perf. 13.*

B6	CD80	2fa12ca +20ca brt ultra	7.00	7.00

French Revolution Issue
Common Design Type

1939 Photogravure.
Name and Value Typo. in Black.

B7	CD83	18ca +10ca grn	4.25	4.25
B8	CD83	1fa6ca +12ca brn	4.25	4.25
B9	CD83	1fa12ca +16ca red org	4.25	4.25
B10	CD83	1fa16ca +1fa16ca rose pink	4.25	4.25
B11	CD83	2fa12ca +3fa bl	4.25	4.25
		Nos. B7-B11 (5)	21.25	21.25

Common Design Type and

Non-Commissioned Officer, Native Guard
SP1

Sepoy
SP2

1941 Photogravure *Perf. 13½*

B12	SP1	1fa16ca +1fa16ca red	75
B13	CD86	2fa12ca +5fa mar	75
B13A	SP2	4fa4ca +1fa16ca bl	75

Nos. B12–B13A were issued by the Vichy government, and were not placed on sale in French India.

Nos. 112A–112B were surcharged "OEUVRES COLONIALES" and surtax (including change of denomination of the 4fa 4ca to 20ca). These were issued in 1944 by the Vichy government and were not placed on sale in French India.

Red Cross Issue
Common Design Type

1944 Photogravure. *Perf. 14½x14.*

B14	CD90	3fa +1r 4fa dk ol brn	80	80

The surtax was for the French Red Cross and national relief.

Tropical Medicine Issue
Common Design Type

1950 Engraved. *Perf. 13.*

B15	CD100	1fa +10ca ind & dp bl	1.25	1.25

The surtax was for charitable work.

AIR POST STAMPS.

Common Design Type
Photogravure.

1942 *Perf. 14½x14.* Unwmkd.

C1	CD87	4fa dk org	48	48
C2	CD87	1r brt red	48	48
C3	CD87	2r brn red	85	85
C4	CD87	5r black	1.00	1.00
C5	CD87	8r ultra	1.50	1.50
C6	CD87	10r dk grn	1.75	1.75
		Nos. C1-C6 (6)	6.06	6.06

Victory Issue
Common Design Type

1946 Engraved. *Perf. 12½*

C7	CD92	4fa dk bl grn	70	70

Issued to commemorate the European Victory of the Allied Nations in World War II.

Chad to Rhine Issue
Common Design Types

1946, June 6

C8	CD93	2fa12ca ol bis	65	65
C9	CD94	5fa dk bl	65	65
C10	CD95	7fa12ca dk pur	85	85
C11	CD96	1r2fa green	85	85
C12	CD97	1r4fa12ca dk car	1.10	1.10
C13	CD98	3r1fa vio brn	1.10	1.10
		Nos. C8-C13 (6)	5.20	5.20

A 3r ultramarine and red, picturing the Temple of Chindambaram, was sold at Paris June 7 to July 8, 1948, but not placed on sale in the colony.

Bas-relief Figure of Goddess
AP1

Wing and Temple AP2 Bird over Palms AP3

Perf. 12x13, 13x12.

1949 Photogravure Unwmkd.

C14	AP1	1r yel & plum	3.50	2.00
C15	AP2	2r grn & dk grn	4.25	4.00
C16	AP3	5r lt bl & vio brn	14.00	10.00

UPU Issue
Common Design Type

1949 Engraved *Perf. 13*

C17	CD99	6fa lil rose	5.25	5.25

Issued to commemorate the 75th anniversary of the formation of the Universal Postal Union.

Liberation Issue
Common Design Type

1954, June 6

C18	CD102	1fa sep & vio brn	4.00	4.00

AIR POST SEMI-POSTAL STAMPS.

V4

Stamps of the above design and of Cameroun type V10 inscribed "Etabts Frcais dans l'Inde" were issued in 1942 by the Vichy Government, but were not placed on sale in French India.

POSTAGE DUE STAMPS.

Postage Due Stamps of France, 1893–1941.
Surcharged **6 CACHES**
like Regular Issue in Black, Blue or Red.

1923 *Perf. 14x13½.* Unwmkd.

J1	D2	6ca on 10c brn (Bl)	70	70
J2	D2	12ca on 25c rose (Bk)	70	70
J3	D2	15ca on 20c ol grn (R)	85	85
J4	D2	1fa6ca on 30c red (Bl)	85	85
J5	D2	1fa12a on 50c brn vio (Bl)	1.25	1.25
J6	D2	1fa15ca on 5c bl (Bk)	1.50	1.50
J7	D2	3fa3ca on 1fr red brn, *straw* (Bl)	2.00	2.00
		Nos. J1-J7 (7)	7.85	7.85

Types of Postage Due Stamps of French Colonies, 1884-85, Surcharged with New Values as in 1923 in Red or Black. Bars over Original Values.

1928

J8	D1	4ca on 20c gray lil	70	70
J9	D1	1fa on 30c org	1.00	1.00
J10	D1	1fa16ca on 5c bl blk (R)	1.25	1.25
J11	D1	3fa on 1 fr lt grn	1.75	1.75

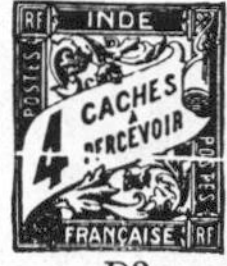

D3

D4

1929 Typographed

J12	D3	4ca dp red	42	42
J13	D3	6ca blue	52	52
J14	D3	12ca green	52	52
J15	D3	1fa brown	85	85
J16	D3	1fa12ca lil gray	85	85
J17	D3	1fa16ca buff	95	95
J18	D3	3fa lilac	1.50	1.50
		Nos. J12-J18 (7)	5.61	5.61

Photogravure.

1948 *Perf. 13x13½.* Unwmkd.

J19	D4	1ca dk vio	5	5
J20	D4	2ca dk brn	5	5
J21	D4	6ca bl grn	15	15
J22	D4	12ca dp org	35	35
J23	D4	1fa dk car rose	42	42
J24	D4	1fa12ca brown	60	60
J25	D4	2fa dk sl bl	80	80
J26	D4	2fa12ca hn brn	95	95
J27	D4	5fa dk ol grn	1.50	1.50
J28	D4	1r dk bl vio	2.25	2.25
		Nos. J19-J28 (10)	7.12	7.12

FRENCH MOROCCO

(frĕnch mô·rŏk'ō)

LOCATION—Northwest coast of Africa.
GOVT.—Former French Protectorate.
AREA—153,870 sq. mi.
POP.—8,340,000 (estimated 1954).
CAPITAL—Rabat.

French Morocco was a French Protectorate from 1912 until 1956 when it, along with the Spanish and Tangier zones of Morocco, became the independent country, Morocco.

Stamps inscribed "Tanger" were for use in the international zone of Tangier in northern Morocco.

100 Centimos = 1 Peseta
100 Centimes = 1 franc (1917)

French Offices in Morocco

A1

A2

Stamps of France Surcharged in Red or Black.
Perf. 14x13½.

1891–1900 Unwmkd.

1	A1	5c on 5c grn, *grnsh* (R)	6.00	2.25
a.		Imperf., pair	87.50	
2	A1	5c on 5c yel grn (I) (R) ('99)	24.00	21.00
a.		Type II	24.00	17.50
3	A1	10c on 10c *lav* (II) (R)	20.00	2.75
a.		Type I	26.00	12.00
b.		10c on 25c *rose*	775.00	
4	A1	20c on 20c red, *grn*	30.00	20.00
5	A1	25c on 25c *rose* (R)	20.00	1.00
a.		Double surcharge	140.00	
b.		Imperf., pair	95.00	
6	A1	50c on 50c car, *rose* (II)	72.50	25.00
a.		Type I	350.00	240.00

No.	Type	Description	Unused	Used
7	A1	1p on 1fr brnz grn, *straw*	77.50	55.00
8	A1	2p on 2fr brn, *az* (Bk) ('00)	225.00	190.00
		Nos. 1-8 (8)	475.00	317.00

No. 3b was never sent to Morocco.

France Nos. J15–J16
Overprinted in Carmine.

1893

No.	Type	Description	Unused	Used
9	A2	5c black	1,900.	875.00
10	A2	10c black	1,600.	575.00

Counterfeits exist.

A3

A4

A5

Surcharged in Red or Black.

1902–10

No.	Type	Description	Unused	Used
11	A3	1c on 1c gray (R)('08)	70	42
a.		Surcharge omitted		
12	A3	2c on 2c vio brn ('08)	90	65
13	A3	3c on 3c red org ('08)	1.00	65
14	A3	4c on 4c yel brn ('08)	7.00	4.25
15	A3	5c on 5c grn (R)	3.25	90
a.		Double surch.		140.00
16	A4	10c on 10c rose red ('03)	2.75	90
a.		Surcharge omitted		
17	A4	20c on 20c brn vio ('03)	17.50	11.00
18	A4	25c on 25c bl ('03)	17.50	1.40
19	A4	35c on 35c vio ('10)	27.50	16.00
20	A5	50c on 50c bis brn & lav ('03)	32.50	7.75
21	A5	1p on 1fr cl & ol grn ('03)	85.00	52.50
22	A5	2p on 2fr gray vio & yel ('03)	100.00	60.00
		Nos. 11-22 (12)	295.60	156.42

Nos. 11–14 exist spelled CFNTIMOS or GENTIMOS.

The 25c on 25c with surcharge omitted is listed as No. 81a.

Postage Due Stamps
Nos. J1–J2
Handstamped

1903

No.	Type	Description	Unused	Used
24	D2	5c on 5c lt bl	1,200.	875.00
25	D2	10c on 10c choc	2,400.	1,750.

Nos. 24 and 25 were used only on Oct. 10, 1903. Used copies were not canceled, the overprint serving as a cancelation.

Counterfeits exist.

Types of 1902–10 Issue
Surcharged in
Red or Blue

1
سنتيم

1911-17

No.	Type	Description	Unused	Used
26	A3	1c on 1c gray (R)	30	15
27	A3	2c on 2c vio brn	48	30
28	A3	3c on 3c org	52	30
29	A3	5c on 5c grn (R)	55	15
30	A4	10c on 10c rose	18	6
a.		Imperf. pair	180.00	
31	A4	15c on 15c org ('17)	1.40	1.25
32	A4	20c on 20c brn vio	3.00	2.00
33	A4	25c on 25c bl (R)	1.65	80
34	A4	35c on 35c vio (R)	6.00	2.00
35	A5	40c on 40c red & pale bl ('17)	5.00	4.00
36	A5	50c on 50c bis brn & lav (R)	20.00	10.00
37	A5	1p on 1fr cl & ol grn	13.00	5.00
		Nos. 26-37 (12)	52.08	26.01

Stamps of this design were issued by the Cherifien posts in 1912–13. The Administration Cherifienne des Postes, Telegraphes et Telephones was formed in 1911 under French guidance.

French Protectorate

A6

A7

A8

Issue of 1911-17
Overprinted "Protectorat Francais"

1914–21

No.	Type	Description	Unused	Used
38	A6	1c on 1c gray	30	30
39	A6	2c on 2c vio brn	30	22
40	A6	3c on 3c org	60	42
41	A6	5c on 5c grn	15	5
a.		New value omitted	190.00	190.00
42	A7	10c on 10c rose	15	5
a.		New value omitted	350.00	350.00
43	A7	15c on 15c org ('17)	18	5
a.		New value omitted	70.00	70.00
44	A7	20c on 20c brn vio	3.25	1.75
a.		"Protectorat Francais" double	225.00	225.00
45	A7	25c on 25c bl	75	5
a.		New value omitted	225.00	225.00
46	A7	25c on 25c vio ('21)	60	6
a.		"Protectorat Francais" omitted	42.50	42.50
b.		"Protectorat Francais" double	110.00	110.00
c.		"Protectorat Francais" double (R + Bk)	100.00	100.00
47	A7	30c on 30c vio ('21)	9.50	7.50
48	A7	35c on 35c vio	3.25	1.00
49	A8	40c on 40c red & pale bl	11.00	5.50
a.		New value omitted	225.00	225.00
50	A8	45c on 45c grn & bl ('21)	32.50	27.50
51	A8	50c on 50c bis brn & lav	52	18
a.		"Protectorat Francais" inverted	110.00	110.00
b.		"Protectorat Francais" double		
52	A8	1p on 1fr cl & ol grn	1.40	18
a.		"Protectorat Francais" inverted	250.00	250.00
b.		New value double	110.00	110.00
c.		New value double, one inverted	110.00	110.00
53	A8	2p on 2fr gray vio & yel	2.75	95
a.		New value omitted	125.00	125.00
b.		"Protectorat Francais" omitted	75.00	75.00
c.		New value double		
d.		New value double, one inverted		
54	A8	5p on 5fr dk bl & buff	10.50	3.00
		Nos. 38-54 (17)	77.70	48.76

Tower of Hassan, Rabat
A9

Mosque of the Andalusians, Fez
A10

City Gate, Chella
A11

Koutoubiah, Marrakesh
A12

Bab Mansour, Meknés
A13

Roman Ruins, Volubilis
A14

Engraved.

1917 *Perf. 13½x14, 14x13½*

No.	Type	Description	Unused	Used
55	A9	1c grnsh gray	18	18
56	A9	2c brn lil	35	30
57	A9	3c org brn	30	22
a.		Imperf., pair	42.50	42.50
58	A10	5c yel grn	22	6
59	A10	10c rose red	22	6
60	A10	15c dk gray	22	10
a.		Imperf., pair	35.00	35.00
61	A11	20c red brn	2.25	1.75
62	A11	25c dl bl	2.00	48
63	A11	30c gray vio	2.75	1.65
64	A12	35c orange	2.25	1.50
65	A12	40c ultra	95	48
66	A12	45c gray grn	13.00	6.50
67	A13	50c dk brn	4.25	2.00
a.		Imperf., pair	37.50	37.50
68	A13	1fr slate	5.25	2.50
a.		Imperf., pair	32.50	32.50
69	A14	2fr blk brn	165.00	82.50
70	A14	5fr dk gray grn	30.00	26.00
71	A14	10fr black	30.00	30.00
		Nos. 55-71 (17)	259.19	156.28

See note following No. 115.
See Nos. 93–105.

Types of the 1902-10 Issue Overprinted **TANGER**

1918-24 *Perf. 14x13½.*

No.	Type	Description	Unused	Used
72	A3	1c gray	15	15
73	A3	2c vio brn	18	18
74	A3	3c red org	30	30
75	A3	5c green	42	35
76	A3	5c org ('23)	85	80
77	A4	10c rose	42	42
78	A4	10c grn ('24)	42	35
79	A4	15c orange	95	70
80	A4	20c vio brn	1.50	1.25
81	A4	25c blue	1.75	1.00
a.		"TANGER" omitted	300.00	225.00
82	A4	30c red org ('24)	1.75	1.40
83	A4	35c violet	1.90	1.25
84	A5	40c red & pale bl	2.00	1.25
85	A5	50c bis brn & lav	17.50	10.00
86	A4	50c blue	11.00	7.00
87	A5	1fr cl & ol grn	7.50	3.25
88	A5	2fr org & pale bl ('24)	65.00	52.50
89	A5	5fr dk bl & buff ('24)	52.50	50.00
		Nos. 72-89 (18)	166.09	132.15

Types of 1917 and

Tower of Hassan, Rabat
A15

Bab Mansour, Meknès
A16

Roman Ruins, Volubilis
A17

1923–27 Photo. *Perf. 13½*

No.	Type	Description	Unused	Used
90	A15	1c ol grn	5	5
91	A15	2c brn vio	5	5
92	A15	3c yel brn	5	5
93	A10	5c orange	6	6
94	A10	10c yel grn	6	5
95	A10	15c dk gray	6	5
96	A11	20c red brn	6	5
97	A11	20c red vio ('27)	42	40
98	A11	25c ultra	6	6
99	A11	30c dp red	6	6
100	A11	30c turq bl ('27)	70	40
101	A12	35c violet	70	60
102	A12	40c org red	5	5
103	A12	45c dp grn	6	6
104	A16	50c dl turq	10	10
105	A12	50c dk ol grn ('27)	48	10
106	A16	60c lilac	35	22
107	A16	75c red vio ('27)	65	35
108	A16	1fr dp brn	48	30
109	A16	1.05fr red brn ('27)	1.00	75
110	A16	1.40fr dl rose ('27)	52	40
111	A16	1.50fr turq bl ('27)	75	10
112	A17	2fr ol brn	90	60
113	A17	3fr dp red ('27)	90	70
114	A17	5fr dk gray grn	2.50	1.65

No.	Type	Value	Color	Unused	Used
115	A17	10fr	black	7.50	4.75
		Nos. 90-115 (26)		18.57	12.01

Nos. 90–110, 112–115 exist imperf.

The stamps of 1917 were line engraved. Those of 1923–27 were printed by photogravure and have in the margin at lower right the imprint "Helio Vaugirard".

No. 102 Surcharged in Black

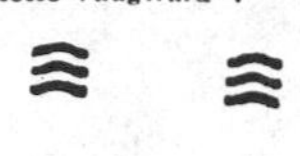

15c 15c

1930

No.	Type	Value	Color	Unused	Used
120	A12	15c	on 40c org red	1.00	1.00

Nos. 100, 106 and 110 Surcharged in Blue Similarly to No. 176.

1931

No.	Type	Value	Color	Unused	Used
121	A11	25c	on 30c turq bl	1.50	1.50
a.		Inverted surch.		65.00	47.50
122	A16	50c	on 60c lil	52	18
a.		Inverted surch.		75.00	70.00
123	A16	1fr	on 1.40fr rose	1.90	1.00
a.		Inverted surch.		75.00	70.00

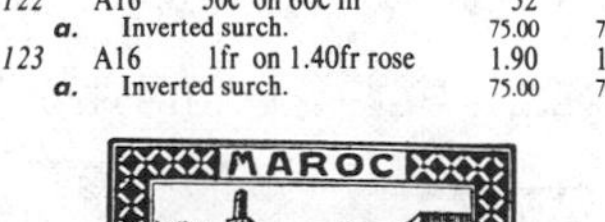

Old Treasure House and Tribunal, Tangier
A18

Roadstead at Agadir
A19

Post Office at Casablanca
A20

Moulay Idriss of the Zehroun
A21

Kasbah of the Oudayas, Rabat
A22

Court of the Medersa el Attarine at Fez
A23

Saadiens' Tombs at Marrakesh
A25

Kasbah of Si Madani el Glaoui at Ouarzazat—A24

1933–34 Engraved *Perf. 13*

No.	Type	Value	Color	Unused	Used
124	A18	1c	ol blk	6	5
125	A18	2c	red vio	6	6
126	A19	3c	dk brn	6	6
127	A19	5c	brn red	6	6
128	A20	10c	bl grn	15	6
129	A20	15c	black	6	6
130	A20	20c	red brn	18	10
131	A21	25c	dk bl	18	6
132	A21	30c	emerald	30	5
133	A21	40c	blk brn	30	10
134	A22	45c	brn vio	35	35
135	A22	50c	dk bl grn	30	5
a.		Booklet pane of 10			
136	A22	65c	brn red	6	6
a.		Booklet pane of 10			
137	A23	75c	red vio	30	6
138	A23	90c	org red	30	5
139	A23	1fr	dp brn	60	5
140	A23	1.25fr	blk ('34)	85	40
141	A24	1.50fr	ultra	35	5
142	A24	1.75fr	myr grn ('34)	30	5
143	A24	2fr	yel brn	2.50	5
144	A24	3fr	car rose	47.50	5.00
145	A25	5fr	red brn	5.00	75
146	A25	10fr	black	7.50	5.00
147	A25	20fr	bluish gray	8.00	5.00
		Nos. 124-147 (24)		75.32	17.58

No. 135 Surcharged in Red

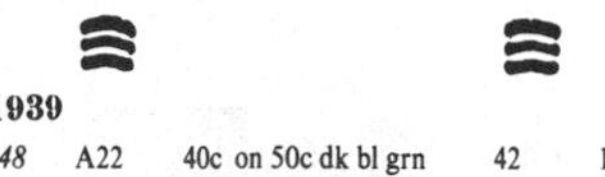

40c

1939

No.	Type	Value	Color	Unused	Used
148	A22	40c	on 50c dk bl grn	42	18

Mosque of Salé
A26

Sefrou
A27

Cedars
A28

Goatherd
A29

Ramparts of Salé
A30

Scimitar-horned Oryxes
A31

Fez
A33

Valley of Draa
A32

1939–42

No.	Type	Value	Color	Unused	Used
149	A26	1c	rose vio	5	5
150	A27	2c	emerald	5	5
151	A27	3c	ultra	5	5
152	A26	5c	dk bl grn	6	5
153	A27	10c	brt red vio	6	5
154	A28	15c	dk grn	6	5
155	A28	20c	blk brn	6	5
156	A29	30c	dp bl	6	5
157	A29	40c	chocolate	6	5
158	A29	45c	Prus grn	42	30
159	A30	50c	rose red	1.25	60
159A	A30	50c	Prus grn ('40)	18	6
160	A30	60c	turq bl	1.25	60
160A	A30	60c	choc ('40)	18	5
161	A31	70c	dk vio	6	5
162	A32	75c	grnsh blk	30	30
163	A32	80c	pck bl ('40)	10	5
163A	A32	80c	dk grn ('42)	10	5
164	A30	90c	ultra	10	5
165	A28	1fr	chocolate	10	5
165A	A32	1.20fr	rose vio ('42)	30	10
166	A32	1.25fr	hn brn	85	42
167	A32	1.40fr	rose vio	30	10
168	A30	1.50fr	cop red ('40)	6	6
168A	A30	1.50fr	rose ('42)	6	6
169	A33	2fr	Prus grn	6	6
170	A33	2.25fr	dk bl	25	25
170A	A26	2.40fr	red ('42)	10	5
171	A26	2.50fr	scarlet	85	42
171A	A26	2.50fr	dp bl ('40)	75	42
172	A33	3fr	blk brn	22	18
172A	A26	4fr	dp ultra ('42)	18	5
172B	A32	4.50fr	grnsh blk ('42)	42	18
173	A31	5fr	dk bl	42	18
174	A31	10fr	red	70	48
174A	A31	15fr	Prus grn ('42)	3.50	3.00
175	A31	20fr	dk vio brn	1.25	1.25
		Nos. 149-175 (37)		15.24	10.05

See also Nos. 197–219.

No. 136 Surcharged in Black

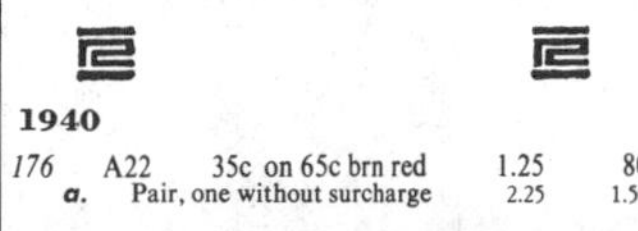

35c

1940

No.	Type	Value	Color	Unused	Used
176	A22	35c	on 65c brn red	1.25	80
a.		Pair, one without surcharge		2.25	1.50

The surcharge was applied on alternate rows in the sheet, making pairs, one stamp with a surcharge and one without. This was done to make a pair equal 1 franc, the new rate.

One Aim Alone —Victory
A34

Tower of Hassan, Rabat
A35

1943 Lithographed *Perf. 12.*

No.	Type	Value	Color	Unused	Used
177	A34	1.50fr	dp bl	18	5

1943

No.	Type	Value	Color	Unused	Used
178	A35	10c	rose lil	5	5
179	A35	30c	blue	5	5
180	A35	40c	lake	5	5
181	A35	50c	bl grn	5	5
182	A35	60c	dk vio brn	5	5
183	A35	70c	rose vio	5	5
184	A35	80c	gray grn	5	5
185	A35	1fr	car lake	5	5
186	A35	1.20fr	violet	5	5
187	A35	1.50fr	red	5	5
188	A35	2fr	lt bl grn	18	5
189	A35	2.40fr	car rose	6	5
190	A35	3fr	ol brn	10	5
191	A35	4fr	dk ultra	10	5
192	A35	4.50fr	sl blk	6	5
193	A35	5fr	dl bl	50	18
194	A35	10fr	org brn	30	6
195	A35	15fr	sl grn	1.00	22
196	A35	20fr	dp plum	1.40	35
		Nos. 178-196 (19)		4.20	1.56

Types of 1939-42.

Perf. 13½x14, 14x13½.

1945-47 Typographed. Unwmkd.

No.	Type	Value	Color	Unused	Used
197	A27	10c	red vio	6	6
199	A29	40c	chocolate	8	6
200	A30	50c	Prus grn	6	6
203	A28	1fr	choc ('46)	6	6
204	A32	1.20fr	vio brn ('46)	6	6
205	A27	1.30fr	bl ('47)	35	22
206	A30	1.50fr	dp red	28	25
207	A33	2fr	Prus grn	6	6
209	A33	3fr	blk brn	6	6
210	A29	3.50fr	dk red ('47)	50	42
212	A31	4.50fr	mag ('47)	25	6
214	A31	5fr	indigo	55	30
215	A32	6fr	chlky bl ('46)	25	6
216	A31	10fr	red	90	65
217	A31	15fr	Prus grn	1.00	55
218	A31	20fr	dk vio brn	1.50	1.00
219	A31	25fr	blk brn	2.00	1.50
		Nos. 197-219 (17)		8.02	5.43

The Terraces
A37

Mountain District
A39

Fortress
A38

Marrakesh
A40

Gardens of Fez—A41

Ouarzazat District A42

Engraved.

1947-48 ***Perf. 13*** **Unwmkd.**

No.	Type	Denomination	Unused	Used
221	A37	10c blk brn	5	5
222	A37	30c brt red	10	6
223	A37	50c brt grnsh bl	6	5
224	A37	60c brt red vio	6	5
225	A38	1fr black	6	5
226	A38	1.50fr blue	6	5
227	A39	2fr brt grn	22	18
228	A39	3fr brn red	6	6
229	A40	4fr dk bl vio	8	6
230	A41	5fr dk grn	42	22
231	A40	6fr crimson	8	5
232	A41	10fr dp bl ('47)	15	6
233	A42	15fr dk grn ('47)	90	65
234	A42	20fr hn brn ('47)	60	6
235	A42	25fr pur ('47)	1.50	65
		Nos. 221-235 (15)	4.40	2.30

1948-49

No.	Type	Denomination	Unused	Used
236	A37	30c purple	5	5
237	A38	2fr vio brn ('49)	6	5
238	A40	4fr green	8	5
239	A41	8fr org ('49)	35	12
240	A41	10fr blue	35	18
241	A42	10fr car rose	35	22
242	A38	12fr red	50	18
243	A42	18fr dp bl	95	75
		Nos. 236-243 (8)	2.69	1.60

No. 175 Surcharged with New Value and Wavy Lines in Carmine.

1948

No.	Type	Denomination	Unused	Used
244	A31	8fr on 20fr dk vio brn	60	42

Fortified Oasis—A43

Walled City—A44

1949

No.	Type	Denomination	Unused	Used
245	A43	5fr bl grn	15	5
246	A44	15fr red	90	5
247	A44	25fr ultra	95	10

See also No. 300.

Detail, Gate of Oudayas, Rabat A45

Nejjarine Fountain, Fez A46

Garden, Meknes A47

1949 ***Perf. 14x13***

No.	Type	Denomination	Unused	Used
248	A45	10c black	6	5
249	A45	50c rose brn	10	8
250	A45	1fr bl vio	6	6
251	A46	2fr dk car rose	6	6
252	A46	3fr dk bl	6	6
253	A46	5fr brt grn	18	5
254	A47	8fr dk bl grn	60	5
255	A47	10fr brt red	80	15
		Nos. 248-255 (8)	1.92	56

Postal Administration Building, Meknes A48

1949, Oct. ***Perf. 13***

No.	Type	Denomination	Unused	Used
256	A48	5fr dk grn	1.25	1.25
257	A48	15fr dp car	1.40	1.40
258	A48	25fr dp bl	1.75	1.75

Issued to commemorate the 75th anniversary of the formation of the Universal Postal Union.

Todra Valley A49

1950

No.	Type	Denomination	Unused	Used
259	A49	35fr red brn	1.00	18
260	A49	50fr indigo	1.00	8

See also No. 270.

Nos. 204 and 205 Surcharged in Black or Blue

1fr

1950 ***Perf. 14x13½, 13½x14***

No.	Type	Denomination	Unused	Used
261	A32	1fr on 1.20fr vio brn (Bk)	10	10
262	A27	1fr on 1.30fr bl (Bl)	10	10

The surcharge is transposed and spaced to fit the design on No. 262.

No. 231 Surcharged with New Value and Wavy Lines in Black.

1951 ***Perf. 13***

No.	Type	Denomination	Unused	Used
263	A40	5fr on 6fr crim	18	15

Statue of Gen. Jacques Leclerc A50

1951, Apr. 28 **Engraved**

No.	Type	Denomination	Unused	Used
264	A50	10fr bl grn	1.25	1.25
265	A50	15fr dp car	1.50	1.50
266	A50	25fr indigo	1.50	1.50

Issued to commemorate the unveiling of a monument to Gen. Leclerc at Casablanca, April 28, 1951. See No. C39.

Loustau Hospital, Oujda A51

Designs: 15fr, New Hospital, Meknes. 25fr, New Hospital, Rabat.

1951

No.	Type	Denomination	Unused	Used
267	A51	10fr ind & pur	1.00	1.00
268	A51	15fr Prus grn & red brn	1.00	1.00
269	A51	25fr dk brn & ind	1.50	1.50

Todra Valley Type of 1950.

1951

No.	Type	Denomination	Unused	Used
270	A49	30fr ultra	90	42

Pigeons at Fountain A52

Karaouine Mosque, Fez A53

Patio, Oudayas A54

Oudayas Point, Rabat A55

Patio of Old House A56

MAROC MAROC

Type I (No. 275) Type II (No. 276)

Perf. 14x13, 13.

1951-53 **Engraved.** **Unwmkd.**

No.	Type	Denomination	Unused	Used
271	A52	5fr mag ('52)	6	5
272	A53	6fr bl grn ('52)	22	22
273	A52	8fr brn ('52)	18	18
273A	A53	10fr rose red ('53)	22	5
274	A53	12fr dp ultra ('52)	42	6
275	A54	15fr red brn (I)	2.00	6
276	A54	15fr red brn (II)	48	5
277	A55	15fr pur ('52)	60	5
278	A55	18fr red ('52)	1.00	50
279	A56	20fr dp grnsh bl ('52)	70	48
		Nos. 271-279 (10)	5.88	1.70

See also Nos. 297-299.

8th-10th Century Capital A57

Casablanca Monument A58

Capitals: 20fr, XIIth Century. 25fr, XIIIth–XVIth Century. 50fr, XVIIth Century.

1952, Apr. 5 ***Perf. 13***

No.	Type	Denomination	Unused	Used
280	A57	15fr dp bl	2.25	2.25
281	A57	20fr red	2.25	2.25
282	A57	25fr purple	2.25	2.25
283	A57	50fr dp grn	2.50	2.50

1952, Sept. 22 **Engr. & Typo.**

No.	Type	Denomination	Unused	Used
284	A58	15fr multi	2.00	1.50

Issued to commemorate the centenary of the creation of the French Military Medal.

Daggers of South Morocco A59

Post Rider and Public Letter-writer A60

Designs: 20fr and 25fr, Antique brooches.

1953, Mar. 27 **Engraved.**

No.	Type	Denomination	Unused	Used
285	A59	15fr dk car rose	2.25	2.25
286	A59	20fr vio brn	2.25	2.25
287	A59	25fr dk bl	2.25	2.25

See No. C46.

1953, May 16

No.	Type	Denomination	Unused	Used
288	A60	15fr vio brn	1.25	1.25

Stamp Day, May 16, 1953.

Bine el Ouidane Dam A61

1953, Nov. 3 ***Perf. 13***

No.	Type	Denomination	Unused	Used
290	A61	15fr indigo	1.25	1.25

See also No. 295.

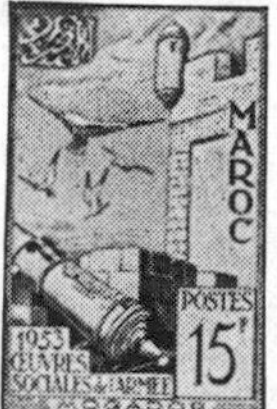

Mogador Fortress A62

Design: 30fr, Moorish knights.

1953, Dec. 4

No.	Type	Denomination	Unused	Used
291	A62	15fr green	1.25	1.25
292	A62	30fr red brn	1.25	1.25

Issued to aid Army Welfare Work.

Nos. 226 and 243 Surcharged with New Value and Wavy Lines in Black.

1954

293	A38	1fr on 1.50fr bl	10	10
294	A42	15fr on 18fr dp bl	52	52

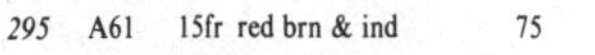

Dam Type of 1953.

1954, Mar. 8

295	A61	15fr red brn & ind	75	30

Station of Rural Automobile Post

A63

1954, Apr. 10

296	A63	15fr dk bl grn	70	70

Stamp Day, April 10, 1954.

Types of 1951–53

1954 Engraved. *Perf. 14x13*

297	A52	15fr dk bl grn	45	5

Typographed.

298	A52	5fr magenta	30	22
299	A55	15fr rose vio	60	35

Walled City Type of 1949

1954 Engraved. *Perf. 13*

300	A44	25fr purple	60	35

Marshal Lyautey at Rabat

A64

Lyautey, Builder of Cities

A65

Designs: 15fr, Marshal Lyautey at Khenifra. 50fr, Hubert Lyautey, Marshal of France.

1954, Nov. 17

301	A64	5fr indigo	2.25	2.25
302	A64	15fr dk grn	2.25	2.25
303	A65	30fr rose brn	2.75	2.75
304	A65	50fr dk red brn	2.75	2.75

Issued to commemorate the centenary of the birth of Marshal Hubert Lyautey.

Franco-Moslem Education

A66

Moslem Student at Blackboard

A67

Designs: 30fr, Moslem school at Camp Boulhaut. 50fr, Moulay Idriss College at Fez.

1955, Apr. 16 *Perf. 13* Unwmkd.

305	A66	5fr indigo	1.00	1.00
306	A67	15fr rose lake	1.25	1.25
307	A66	30fr chocolate	1.65	1.65
308	A67	50fr dk bl grn	1.75	1.75

Issued to publicize Franco-Moslem solidarity.

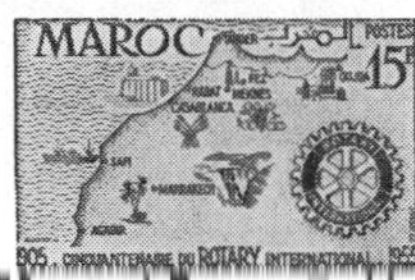

Map and Rotary Emblem

A68

1955, June 11

309	A68	15fr bl & org brn	1.25	1.00

Issued to commemorate the 50th anniversary of the founding of Rotary International.

Post Office, Mazagan

A69

1955, May 24

310	A69	15fr red	65	65

Stamp Day.

Bab el Chorfa, Fez

A70

Mahakma (Courthouse), Casablanca

A71

Fortress, Safi

A72

Designs: 50c, 1fr, 2fr, Mrissa Gate, Salé. 10fr, 12fr, 15fr, Minaret at Rabat. 30fr, Menara Garden, Marrakesh. 40fr, Tafraout Village. 50fr, Portuguese cistern, Mazagan. 75fr, Garden of Oudaya, Rabat.

1955 *Perf. 13½x13, 13x13½, 13*

311	A70	50c brn vio	6	5
312	A70	1fr blue	6	5
313	A70	2fr red lil	6	5
314	A70	3fr bluish blk	8	5
315	A70	5fr vermilion	75	30
316	A70	6fr green	18	18
317	A70	8fr org brn	65	40
318	A70	10fr vio brn	1.10	18
319	A70	12fr grnsh bl	30	5
320	A70	15fr magenta	95	5
321	A71	18fr dk grn	1.25	65
322	A71	20fr brn lake	52	5
323	A72	25fr brt ultra	1.65	18
324	A72	30fr green	1.65	42
325	A72	40fr org red	85	10
326	A72	50fr blk brn	5.00	30
327	A71	75fr grnsh bl	1.25	75
		Nos. 311-327 (17)	16.36	3.81

Succeeding issues, released under the Kingdom, are listed under Morocco in Vol. III.

SEMI-POSTAL STAMPS.

French Protectorate

No. 30 Surcharged in Red

+ 5c

1914 *Perf. 14x13½* Unwmkd.

B1	A4	10c +5c on 10c rose	22,500.	22,500.

No. B1 is known only with inverted surcharge.

Same Surcharge on No. 42 with "Protectorat Francais".

B2	A7	10c +5c on 10c rose	2.50	2.50
a.		Double surcharge	87.50	87.50
b.		Inverted surcharge	110.00	110.00
c.		"s" omitted	[illegible]	[illegible]

On Nos. B1 and B2 the cross is set up from pieces of metal (quads), the horizontal bar being made from two long pieces, the vertical bar from two short pieces. Each cross in the setting of twenty-five differs from the others.

No. 30 Handstamp Surcharged in Red

B3	A4	10c +5c on 10c rose	1,500.	1,100.

No. B3 was issued at Oujda. The surcharge ink is water-soluble.

No. 42 Surcharged in Vermilion or Carmine

B4	A7	10c +5c on 10c rose (V)	15.00	15.00
a.		Double surcharge	100.00	100.00
b.		Inverted surcharge	120.00	120.00
c.		Double surcharge, one inverted	120.00	120.00
B5	A7	10c +5c on 10c rose (C)	265.00	300.00

On Nos. B4 and B5 the horizontal bar of the cross is single and not as thick as on Nos. B1 and B2.

No. B5 was sold largely at Casablanca.

SP1

SP2

1915 Carmine Surcharge.

B6	SP1	5c +5c grn	1.75	1.40
a.		Inverted surcharge	160.00	160.00

No. B6 was not issued without the Red Cross surcharge.

B7	SP2	10c +5c rose	2.25	2.25

No. B7 was used in Tangier.

SP3

SP4

France No. B2 Overprinted in Black.

B8	SP3	10c +5c red	4.25	4.25

1917 Carmine Surcharge.

B9	SP4	10c +5c on 10c rose	1.90	1.90

On No. B9 the horizontal bar of the cross is made from a single, thick piece of metal.

Marshal Hubert Lyautey

SP5

1935, May 15 Photo. *Perf. 13x13½*

B10	SP5	50c +50c red	8.25	8.25
B11	SP5	1fr +1fr dk grn	8.25	8.25
B12	SP5	5fr +1fr blk brn	40.00	40.00

Stamps of 1933–34 Surcharged in Blue or Red

O.S.E.
+3 c

1938 *Perf. 13.*

B13	A18	2c +2c red vio (Bl)	4.25	4.25
B14	A19	3c +3c dk brn (Bl)	4.25	4.25
B15	A20	20c +20c red brn (Bl)	4.25	4.25
B16	A21	40c +40c blk brn (R)	4.25	4.25
B17	A22	65c +65c brn red (Bl)	4.25	4.25
B18	A23	1.25fr +1.25fr blk (R)	4.25	4.25
B19	A24	2fr +2fr yel brn (Bl)	4.25	4.25
B20	A25	3fr +3fr red brn (Bl)	4.25	4.25
		Nos. B13-B20 (8)	34.00	34.00

Stamps of 1939 Surcharged in Black

+2f
Enfants de France
au Maroc

1942

B21	A29	45c +2fr Prus grn	3.50	3.50
B22	A30	90c +4fr ultra	3.50	3.50
B23	A32	1.25fr +6fr hn brn	3.50	3.50
B24	A26	2.50fr +8fr scar	3.50	3.50

The arrangement of the surcharge differs slightly on each denomination.

No. 207 Surcharged in Black

AIDEZ
LES
TUBERCULEUX
+1f

1945 *Perf. 13½x14* Unwmkd.

B26	A33	2fr +1fr Prus grn	22	22

Mausoleum of Marshal Lyautey

SP7

Statue of Marshal Lyautey

SP8

1945 Lithographed *Perf. 11½*

B27	SP7	2fr +3fr dk bl	18	18

The surtax was for French works of solidarity.

No. B26 Surcharged in Red

3f

1946 *Perf. 13½x14*

B28	A33	3fr (+1fr) on 2fr+1fr Prus grn	10	6

Engraved.

1946, Dec. 16 ***Perf. 13½x14, 13***

B29	SP8	2fr +10fr blk	1.00	1.00
B30	SP8	3fr +15fr cop red	1.25	1.25
B31	SP8	10fr +20fr brt bl	1.90	1.90

The surtax was for works of solidarity.

JOURNÉE
DU
TIMBRE
1947

No. 212
Surcharged in
Rose Violet

+5F50

1947, Mar. 15 ***Perf. 13½x14***

B32	A31	4.50fr +5.50fr mag	1.00	1.00

Stamp Day, 1947.

Map and Symbols of Prosperity from Phosphates
SP9

1947 ***Perf. 13***

B33	SP9	4.50fr +5.50fr grn	65	65

Issued to commemorate the 25th anniversary of the exploitations of the Cherifien Office of Phosphates.

Power **SP10** — **Health** **SP11**

1948, Feb. 9

B34	SP10	6fr +9fr red brn	1.75	1.75
B35	SP11	10fr +20fr dp ultra	1.75	1.75

The surtax was for combined works of Franco-Moroccan solidarity.

Type of Regular Issue of 1923, Inscribed: "Journée du Timbre 1948."

1948, Mar. 6

B36	A16	6fr +4fr red brn	60	60

Stamp Day, Mar. 6, 1948.

Battleship off Moroccan Coast
SP12

1948, Aug.

B37	SP12	6fr +9fr pur	1.25	1.25

The surtax was for naval charities

Wheat Field near Meknès
SP13

Designs: 2fr+5fr, Olive grove, Taroudant. 3fr+7fr, Net and coastal view. 5fr+10fr, Aguedal Gardens, Marrakesh.

1949, Apr. 12 Engraved Unwmkd.

Inscribed: "SOLIDARITÉ 1948."

B38	SP13	1fr +2fr org	1.00	1.00
B39	SP13	2fr +5fr car	1.00	1.00
B40	SP13	3fr +7fr pck bl	1.00	1.00
B41	SP13	5fr +10fr dk brn vio	1.00	1.00
a.		Sheet of four	11.00	11.00
		Nos. B38-B41, CB31-CB34 (8)	5.60	5.60

No. B41a contains one each of Nos. B38–B41. Size: 120x96mm.

Gazelle Hunter, from 1899 Local Stamp—SP14

1949, May 1

B42	SP14	10fr +5fr choc & car rose	1.25	1.25

Stamp Day and 50th anniversary of Mazagan-Marrakesh local postage stamp.

Moroccan Soldiers and Flag **SP15** — **Rug Weaving** **SP16**

1949

B43	SP15	10fr +10fr brt red	1.00	1.00

The surtax was for Army Welfare Work.

1950, Apr. 11

Designs: 2fr+5fr, Pottery making. 3fr+7fr, Bookbinding. 5fr+10fr, Copper work.

Inscribed: "SOLIDARITE 1949."

B44	SP16	1fr +2fr dp car	1.75	1.75
B45	SP16	2fr +5fr dk grnsh bl	1.75	1.75
B46	SP16	3fr +7fr dk pur	1.75	1.75
B47	SP16	5fr +10fr red brn	1.75	1.75
a.		Sheet of four	11.00	11.00
		Nos. B44-B47, CB36-CB39 (8)	7.40	7.40

No. B47a contains one each of Nos. B44–B47. Size: 95½x120½mm.

Ruins of Sala Colonia at Chella
SP17

1950, Sept. 25 Engraved. ***Perf. 13***

B48	SP17	10fr +10fr dp mag	1.10	1.10
B49	SP17	15fr +15fr ind	1.10	1.10

The surtax was for Army Welfare Work.

AIR POST STAMPS.
French Protectorate

Biplane over Casablanca
AP1

Photogravure.

1922–27 ***Perf. 13½*** **Unwmkd.**

C1	AP1	5c dp org ('27)	18	18
a.		Imperf., pair	47.50	
C2	AP1	25c dp ultra	65	22
a.		Imperf., pair	57.50	
C3	AP1	50c grnsh bl	18	18
a.		Imperf., pair	47.50	
C4	AP1	75c dp bl	75.00	9.50
a.		Imperf., pair	525.00	
C5	AP1	75c dp grn	18	12
a.		Imperf., pair	62.50	
C6	AP1	80c vio brn ('27)	1.25	30
a.		Imperf., pair	50.00	
C7	AP1	1fr vermilion	18	12
a.		Imperf., pair	57.50	
C8	AP1	1.40fr brn lake ('27)	1.50	75
C9	AP1	1.90fr dp bl ('27)	1.90	1.25
C10	AP1	2fr blk vio	95	70
a.		2fr dp vio	1.25	90
b.		Imperf., pair	190.00	
C11	AP1	3fr gray blk ('27)	1.50	80
		Nos. C1-C11 (11)	83.47	14.12

The 25c, 50c, 75c deep green and 1fr each were printed in two or three types, differing in frameline thickness, or hyphen in "Helio-Vaugirard" imprint.

Nos. C8–C9 Surcharged in Blue or Black

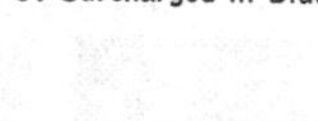

1fr

1931, Apr. 10

C12	AP1	1fr on 1.40fr (B)	1.25	1.25
a.		Inverted surcharge	250.00	250.00
C13	AP1	1.50fr om 1.90fr (Bk)	1.25	1.25

Rabat and Tower of Hassan
AP2

Casablanca—AP3

1933, Jan. **Engraved**

C14	AP2	50c dk bl	65	35
C15	AP2	80c org brn	42	30
C16	AP2	1.50fr brn red	52	22
C17	AP3	2.50fr car rose	3.50	42
C18	AP3	5fr violet	1.50	1.00
C19	AP3	10fr bl grn	75	75
		Nos. C14-C19 (6)	7.34	3.04

Storks and Minaret, Chella
AP4

Plane and Map of Morocco
AP5

1939–40 ***Perf. 13***

C20	AP4	80c Prus grn	5	5
C21	AP4	1fr dk red	5	5
C22	AP5	1.90fr ultra	5	6
C23	AP5	2fr red vio ('40)	6	5
C24	AP5	3fr chocolate	6	6
C25	AP4	5fr violet	75	52
C26	AP5	10fr turq bl	60	35
		Nos. C20-C26 (7)	1.62	1.14

Plane over Oasis
AP6

1944 **Lithographed** ***Perf. 11½***

C27	AP6	50c Prus grn	6	5
C28	AP6	2fr ultra	15	15
C29	AP6	5fr scarlet	15	15
C30	AP6	10fr violet	52	52
C31	AP6	50fr black	85	85
C32	AP6	100fr dp bl & red	2.50	2.50
		Nos. C27-C32 (6)	4.23	4.22

Plane—AP7

1945 **Engraved** ***Perf. 13***

C33	AP7	50fr sepia	60	60

Moulay Idriss
AP8

La Medina—AP9

1947–48

C34	AP8	9fr dk rose car	18	18
C35	AP8	40fr dk bl	70	30
C36	AP8	50fr dp cl ('47)	70	18
C37	AP9	100fr dp grnsh bl	1.90	70
C38	AP9	200fr hn brn	3.50	1.50
		Nos. C34-C38 (5)	6.98	2.86

Leclerc Type of Regular Issue

1951, Apr. 28

C39	A50	50fr purple	1.75	1.75

Issued to commemorate the unveiling of a monument to Gen. Leclerc at Casablanca, April 28, 1951.

Kasbah of the Oudayas, Rabat
AP11

1951, May 22

C40	AP11	300fr purple	17.50	10.50

Ben Smine Sanatorium
AP12

1951, June 4

C41	AP12	50fr pur & Prus grn	2.25	2.25

Fortifications, Chella
AP13

Plane Near Marrakesh
AP14

Fort, Anti-Atlas Mountains
AP15

View of Fez
AP16

1952, Apr. 19 ***Perf. 13*** **Unwmkd.**

C42	AP13	10fr bl grn	70	18
C43	AP14	40fr red	95	42
C44	AP15	100fr brown	2.50	42
C45	AP16	200fr purple	7.50	3.50

Antique Brooches
AP17

1953, Mar. 27

C46	AP17	50fr dk grn	2.25	2.25

"City" of the Agdal, Meknes
AP18

Designs: 20fr, Yakoub el Mansour, Rabat. 40fr, Ainchock, Casablanca. 50fr, El Aliya, Fedala.

1954, Mar. 8

C47	AP18	10fr ol brn	2.25	2.25
C48	AP18	20fr purple	2.25	2.25
C49	AP18	40fr red brn	2.25	2.25
C50	AP18	50fr dp grn	2.25	2.25

Franco-Moroccan solidarity.

Naval Vessel and Sailboat
AP19

Village in the Anti-Atlas
AP20

"Ksar es Souk," Rabat and Plane
AP21

1954, Oct. 18

C51	AP19	15fr dk bl grn	1.25	1.25
C52	AP19	30fr vio bl	1.50	1.50

1955, July 25 Engraved. ***Perf. 13***

Designs: 200fr, Estuary of Bou Regreg, Rabat and Plane.

C53	AP20	100fr brt vio	2.25	30
C54	AP20	200fr brt car	3.00	70
C55	AP21	500fr grnsh bl	9.50	4.00

AIR POST SEMI-POSTAL STAMPS.

French Protectorate

Moorish Tribesmen
SPAP1

Designs: 25c, Moor plowing with camel and burro. 50c, Caravan nearing Saffi. 75c, Walls, Marrakesh. 80c, Sheep grazing at Azrou. 1fr, Gate at Fez. 1.50fr, Aerial view of Tangier. 2fr, Aerial view of Casablanca. 3fr, Storks on old wall, Rabat. 5fr, Moorish fete.

Perf. 13½

1928, July 26 Photo. **Unwmkd.**

CB1	SPAP1	5c dp bl	3.50	3.50
CB2	SPAP1	25c brn org	3.50	3.50
CB3	SPAP1	50c red	3.50	3.50
CB4	SPAP1	75c org brn	3.50	3.50
CB5	SPAP1	80c ol grn	3.50	3.50
CB6	SPAP1	1fr orange	3.50	3.50
CB7	SPAP1	1.50fr Prus bl	3.50	3.50
CB8	SPAP1	2fr dp brn	3.50	3.50
CB9	SPAP1	3fr dp vio	3.50	3.50
CB10	SPAP1	5fr brn blk	3.50	3.50
		Nos. CB1-CB10 (10)	35.00	35.00

These stamps were sold in sets only and at double their face value. The money received for the surtax was divided among charitable and social organizations. The stamps were not sold at post offices but solely by subscription to the Moroccan Postal Administration.

Stamps of 1928

Overprinted **Tanger** in Red or Blue.

1929, Feb. 1

CB11	SPAP1	5c dp bl (R)	3.50	3.50
CB12	SPAP1	25c brn org (Bl)	3.50	3.50
CB13	SPAP1	50c red (Bl)	3.50	3.50
CB14	SPAP1	75c org brn (Bl)	3.50	3.50
CB15	SPAP1	80c ol grn (R)	3.50	3.50
CB16	SPAP1	1fr org (Bl)	3.50	3.50
CB17	SPAP1	1.50fr Prus bl (R)	3.50	3.50
CB18	SPAP1	2fr dp brn (R)	3.50	3.50
CB19	SPAP1	3fr dp vio (R)	3.50	3.50
CB20	SPAP1	5fr brn blk (R)	3.50	3.50
		Nos.CB11-CB20 (10)	35.00	35.00

These stamps were sold at double their face values and only in Tangier. The surtax benefited various charities.

Marshal Hubert Lyautey
SPAP10

1935, May 15 ***Perf. 13½***

CB21	SPAP10	1.50fr +1.50fr bl	19.00	17.50

Nos. C14, C19 Surcharged in Red **O.S.E. +50 c**

1938 ***Perf. 13***

CB22	AP2	50c +50c dk bl	4.75	4.75
CB23	AP3	10fr +10fr bl grn	4.75	4.75

Plane over Oasis
SPAP11

Statue of Marshal Lyautey
SPAP12

1944 Lithographed ***Perf. 11½***

CB23A	SPAP11	1.50fr +98.50fr red, dp bl & blk	1.25	1.25

The surtax was for charity among the liberated French.

No. C29 Surcharged in Black **+ 5F** 18 Juin 1940 ✠ 18 Juin 1946

1946, June 18 ***Perf. 11***

CB24	AP6	5fr +5fr scar	60	60

Issued to commemorate the 6th anniversary of the appeal made by Gen. Charles de Gaulle, June 18, 1940. The surtax was for the Free French Association of Morocco.

1946, Dec. Engraved. ***Perf. 13***

CB25	SPAP12	10fr +30fr dk grn	1.50	1.50

The surtax was for works of solidarity.

Replenishing Stocks of Food
SPAP13

Agriculture
SPAP14

1948, Feb. 9 **Unwmkd.**

CB26	SPAP13	9fr +16fr dp grn	1.25	1.25
CB27	SPAP14	20fr +35fr brn	1.25	1.25

The surtax was for combined works of Franco-Moroccan solidarity.

Tomb of Marshal Hubert Lyautey
SPAP15

1948, May 18 ***Perf. 13***

CB28	SPAP15	10fr +25fr dk grn	1.00	1.00

Lyautey Exposition, Paris, June, 1948.

P. T. T. Clubhouse
SPAP16

1948, June 7 **Engraved**

CB29	SPAP16	6fr +34fr dk grn	1.50	1.50
CB30	SPAP16	9fr +51fr red brn	1.65	1.65

The surtax was used for the Moroccan P. T. T. employees vacation colony at Ifrane.

View of Agadir
SPAP17

Plane over Globe
SPAP18

Designs: 6fr+9fr, Fez. 9fr+16fr, Atlas Mountains. 15fr+25fr, Valley of Draa.

1949, Apr. 12 ***Perf. 13***

Inscribed: "SOLIDARITÉ 1948."

CB31	SPAP17	5fr +5fr dk grn	1.25	1.25
CB32	SPAP17	6fr +9fr org red	1.25	1.25
CB33	SPAP17	9fr +16fr blk brn	1.25	1.25

CB34	SPAP17	15fr +25fr ind	1.25	1.25
a.		Sheet of four	11.00	11.00

No. CB34a contains one each of Nos. CB31–CB34. Size: 96x120mm.

1950, Mar. 11 — Engr. and Typo.

CB35	SPAP18	15fr +10fr bl grn & car	52	52

Issued to commemorate the "Day of the Stamp," March 11–12, 1950, and to mark the 25th anniversary of the first air post link between Casablanca and Dakar.

Scenes and Map: Northwest Corner
SPAP19

Designs (quarters of map): 6fr+9fr, Northeast. 9fr+16fr, Southwest. 15fr+25fr, Southeast.

1950, Apr. 11 — Engraved

Inscribed: "SOLIDARITÉ 1949."

CB36	SPAP19	5fr +5fr dp ultra	1.25	1.25
CB37	SPAP19	6fr +9fr Prus grn	1.25	1.25
CB38	SPAP19	9fr +16fr dk brn	1.25	1.25
CB39	SPAP19	15fr +25fr brn red	1.25	1.25
a.		Sheet of four	7.50	7.50

No. CB39a contains one each of Nos. CB36–CB39. Size: 120½x95½mm.

Arch of Triumph of Caracalla at Volubilis
SPAP20

1950, Sept. 25 — Unwmkd.

CB40	SPAP20	10fr +10fr sep	1.00	1.00
CB41	SPAP20	15fr +15fr bl grn	1.00	1.00

The surtax was for Army Welfare Work.

Casablanca Post Office and First Air Post Stamp—SPAP21

1952, Mar. 8 — *Perf. 13*

CB42	SPAP21	15fr +5fr red brn & dp grn	3.00	3.00

Issued to publicize the "Day of the Stamp," March 8, 1952, and to commemorate the 30th anniversary of French Morocco's first air post stamp.

POSTAGE DUE STAMPS.

French Offices in Morocco

Postage Due Stamps and Types of France Surcharged in Red or Black — 5 CENTIMOS

1896 — *Perf. 14x13½.* — Unwmkd.

On Stamps of 1891-93.

J1	D2	5c on 5c lt bl (R)	4.25	2.50
J2	D2	10c on 10c choc (R)	6.00	2.50
J3	D2	30c on 30c car	15.00	11.00
a.		Pair, one without surcharge		
J4	D2	50c on 50c lil	15.00	9.50
a.		"S" of "CENTIMOS" omitted		15.00
J5	D2	1p on 1fr lil brn	275.00	250.00

1909-10

On Stamps of 1908-10.

J6	D3	1c on 1c ol grn (R)	1.00	1.00
J7	D3	10c on 10c vio	22.50	19.00
J8	D3	30c on 30c bis	27.50	26.00
J9	D3	50c on 50c red	42.50	42.50

Postage Due Stamps of France Surcharged in Red or Blue — 5 (Arabic surcharge)

1911

On Stamps of 1893-96.

J10	D2	5c on 5c bl (R)	2.25	2.25
J11	D2	10c on 10c choc (R)	7.50	7.50
a.		Double surch.	87.50	87.50
J12	D2	50c on 50c lil (Bl)	9.50	9.50

On Stamps of 1908-10.

J13	D3	1c on 1c ol grn (R)	1.00	1.00
J14	D3	10c on 10c vio (R)	3.00	3.00
J15	D3	30c on 30c bis (R)	4.25	4.25
J16	D3	50c on 50c red (Bl)	8.25	8.25
		Nos. J10-J16 (7)	35.75	35.75

French Protectorate

D4

D5

1915–17

Type of 1911 Issue Overprinted "Protectorat Francais".

J17	D4	1c on 1c blk	18	18
a.		New value double	100.00	
J18	D4	5c on 5c bl	85	75
J19	D4	10c on 10c choc	1.25	1.00
J20	D4	20c on 20c ol grn	1.10	1.00
J21	D4	30c on 30c rose red	3.75	3.50
J22	D4	50c on 50c vio brn	6.25	3.00
		Nos. J17-J22 (6)	13.38	9.43

Nos. J13 to J16 With Additional Overprint "Protectorat Francais".

1915

J23	D3	1c on 1c ol grn	60	60
J24	D3	10c on 10c vio	1.25	1.00
J25	D3	30c on 30c bis	1.65	1.25
J26	D3	50c on 50c red	1.65	1.40

1917–26 — Typographed

J27	D5	1c black	5	5
J28	D5	5c dp bl	15	5
J29	D5	10c brown	18	10
J30	D5	20c ol grn	1.25	75
J31	D5	30c rose	18	6
J32	D5	50c lil brn	18	8
J33	D5	1fr red brn, *straw* ('26)	90	28
J34	D5	2fr vio ('26)	1.10	65
		Nos. J27-J34 (8)	3.99	2.02

Postage Due Stamps of France, 1882-1906 Overprinted TANGER

1918

J35	D2	1c black	30	30
J36	D2	5c blue	52	52
J37	D2	10c chocolate	85	85
J38	D2	15c green	2.50	2.50
J39	D2	20c ol grn	3.25	3.25
J40	D2	30c rose red	7.75	7.75
J41	D2	50c vio brn	12.50	12.50
		Nos. J35-J41 (7)	27.67	27.67

Postage Due Stamps of France, 1908-19 Overprinted TANGER

1918

J42	D3	1c ol grn	52	52
J43	D3	10c violet	90	90
J44	D3	20c bister	4.75	4.75
J45	D3	40c red	10.50	10.50

Nos. J31 and J29 Surcharged — 50c

1944 — *Perf. 14x13½* — Unwmkd.

J46	D5	50c on 30c rose	1.90	1.90
J47	D5	1fr on 10c brn	2.75	2.50
J48	D5	3fr on 10c brn	7.50	5.75

Type of 1917–1926

1945-52 — Typographed.

J49	D5	1fr brn lake ('47)	60	52
J50	D5	2fr rose lake ('47)	80	60
J51	D5	3fr ultra	30	18
J52	D5	4fr red org	30	22
J53	D5	5fr green	65	15
J54	D5	10fr yel brn	65	18
J55	D5	20fr car ('50)	1.00	75
J56	D5	30fr dl brn ('52)	1.75	1.25
		Nos. J49-J56 (8)	6.05	3.85

PARCEL POST STAMPS.

French Protectorate

PP1

1917 — *Perf. 13½x14* — Unwmkd.

Q1	PP1	5c green	48	22
Q2	PP1	10c carmine	52	30
Q3	PP1	20c lil brn	55	35
Q4	PP1	25c blue	95	48
Q5	PP1	40c dk brn	1.65	70
Q6	PP1	50c red org	1.75	60
Q7	PP1	75c pale sl	2.50	1.50
Q8	PP1	1f ultra	3.50	42
Q9	PP1	2f gray	5.25	60
Q10	PP1	5f violet	6.50	60
Q11	PP1	10f black	11.00	60
		Nos. Q1-Q11 (11)	34.65	6.37

FRENCH POLYNESIA

(French Oceania)

LOCATION — South Pacific Ocean.
GOVT.—French Overseas Territory.
AREA—1,522 sq. mi.
POP.—172,000 (est. 1984).
CAPITAL—Papeete.

In 1903 various French Establishments in the South Pacific were united to form a single colony. Most important of the island groups are the Society Islands, Marquesas Islands, the Tuamotu group and the Gambier, Austral, and Rapa Islands. Tahiti, largest of the Society group, ranks first in importance.

100 Centimes = 1 Franc

Navigation and Commerce
A1

Perf. 14x13½.

1892–1907 — Typographed — Unwmkd.

Name of Colony in Blue or Carmine.

1	A1	1c *lil bl*	80	70
2	A1	2c brn, *buff*	1.00	90
3	A1	4c cl, *lav*	1.75	1.40
4	A1	5c grn, *grnsh*	5.00	4.25
5	A1	5c yel grn ('06)	90	60
6	A1	10c *lavender*	12.50	6.00
7	A1	10c red ('00)	90	60
8	A1	15c bl, quadrille paper	10.50	5.25
9	A1	15c gray, *lt gray* ('00)	1.75	1.40
10	A1	20c red, *grn*	10.50	4.25
11	A1	25c *rose*	24.00	14.00
12	A1	25c bl ('00)	7.75	4.25
13	A1	30c brn, *bis*	8.75	6.50
14	A1	35c *yel* ('06)	3.50	1.90
15	A1	40c red, *straw*	77.50	47.50
16	A1	45c *gray grn* ('07)	2.50	1.75
17	A1	50c car, *rose*	5.50	3.50
18	A1	50c brn, *az* ('00)	140.00	110.00
19	A1	75c dp vio, *org*	7.00	4.25
20	A1	1fr brnz grn, *straw*	8.75	6.50
		Nos. 1-20 (20)	330.85	225.50

Tahitian Girl
A2

Kanakas
A3

Fautaua Valley
A4

1913-30

21	A2	1c vio & brn	14	14
22	A2	2c brn & blk	14	14
23	A2	4c org & bl	18	18
24	A2	5c grn & yel grn	18	18
25	A2	5c bl & blk ('22)	18	18
26	A2	10c rose & org	52	35
27	A2	10c bl grn & yel grn ('22)	30	30
28	A2	10c org red & brn red, *bluish* ('26)	60	60
29	A2	15c org & blk ('15)	18	18
a.		Imperf., pair	26.00	
30	A2	20c blk & vio	18	18
a.		Imperf., pair	35.00	
31	A2	20c grn & bl grn ('26)	25	25
32	A2	20c brn red & dk brn ('27)	60	60
33	A3	25c ultra & bl	40	18
34	A3	25c vio & rose ('22)	18	18
35	A3	30c gray & brn	1.50	1.25
a.		Imperf., pair	95.00	
36	A3	30c rose & red org ('22)	52	52
37	A3	30c blk & red org ('26)	18	18
38	A3	30c sl bl & bl grn ('27)	60	60
39	A3	35c grn & rose	40	18
40	A3	40c blk & grn	40	30
41	A3	45c org & red	40	35
42	A3	50c dk brn & blk	7.00	6.00
43	A3	50c ultra & bl ('22)	40	40
44	A3	50c gray & bl vio ('26)	40	40
45	A3	60c grn & blk ('26)	40	40
46	A3	65c ol brn & red vio ('27)	1.00	1.00
47	A3	75c vio brn & vio	95	65
48	A3	90c brn red & rose ('30)	8.25	8.25
49	A4	1fr rose & blk	1.10	80
50	A4	1.10fr vio & dk brn ('28)	90	90
51	A4	1.40fr bis brn & vio ('29)	2.25	2.25
52	A4	1.50fr ind & bl ('30)	8.25	8.25
53	A4	2fr dk brn & grn	2.25	1.25
54	A4	5fr vio & bl	5.75	4.75
		Nos. 21-54 (34)	46.93	42.32

No. 7 Overprinted

E F O
1915

1915

55	A1	10c red	1.75	1.75
a.		Inverted overprint	52.50	52.50

No. 29 Surcharged

10

1916

56	A2	10c on 15c org & blk	70	70

Nos. 22, 41 and 29 Surcharged

05
1921

1921

57	A2	5c on 2c brn & blk	17.50	17.50
58	A3	10c on 45c org & red	17.50	17.50
59	A2	25c on 15c org & blk	4.25	4.25

On No. 58 the new value and date are set wide apart and without bar.

Types of 1913-30 Issue Surcharged

60

1923-27

60	A3	60c on 75c bl & brn	18	18
61	A4	65c on 1fr dk bl & ol (R) ('25)	60	60
62	A4	85c on 1fr dk bl & ol (R) ('25)	65	65
63	A3	90c on 75c brn red & cer ('27)	65	65

No. 26 Surcharged

45 c.
1924

1924

64	A2	45c on 10c rose & org	1.00	1.00
a.		Inverted surch.	350.00	350.00

Stamps and Type of 1913–30 Surcharged with New Value and Bars

1924–27

65	A4	25c on 2fr dk brn & grn	52	52
66	A4	25c on 5fr vio & bl	60	60
67	A4	1.25fr on 1fr dk bl & ultra (R) ('26)	60	60
68	A4	1.50fr on 1fr dk bl & lt bl ('27)	1.00	1.00
69	A4	20fr on 5fr org & brt vio ('27)	14.00	11.00
		Nos. 65-69 (5)	16.72	13.72

Surcharged **TROIS FRANCS**

1926

70	A4	3fr on 5fr gray & bl (Bk)	1.00	70
71	A4	10fr on 5fr grn & blk (R)	2.75	2.25

Papetoai Bay, Moorea
A5

1929, Mar. 25

72	A5	3fr grn & dk brn	3.75	3.75
73	A5	5fr lt bl & dk brn	6.50	6.50
74	A5	10fr lt red & dk brn	21.00	21.00
75	A5	20fr lil & dk brn	25.00	25.00

Colonial Exposition Issue.

Common Design Types

1931, Apr. 13 Engr. ***Perf. 12½***

Name of Country Printed in Black.

76	CD70	40c dp grn	3.00	3.00
77	CD71	50c violet	3.00	3.00
78	CD72	90c red org	3.00	3.00
79	CD73	1.50fr dl bl	3.50	3.50

Spear Fishing
A12

Tahitian Girl
A13

Idols
A14

Photogravure.

1934–39 ***Perf. 13½, 13½x13***

80	A12	1c gray blk	6	6
81	A12	2c claret	8	8
82	A12	3c lt bl ('39)	8	8
83	A12	4c orange	22	22
84	A12	5c violet	42	42
85	A12	10c dk brn	8	8
86	A12	15c green	18	18
87	A12	20c red	6	6
88	A13	25c gray bl	18	18
89	A13	30c yel grn	60	60
90	A13	30c org brn ('39)	18	18
91	A14	35c dp grn ('38)	2.00	2.00
92	A13	40c red vio	18	18
93	A13	45c brn org	5.25	5.25
94	A13	45c dk grn ('39)	48	48
95	A13	50c violet	6	6
96	A13	55c bl ('38)	2.25	2.25
97	A13	60c blk ('39)	18	18
98	A13	65c brown	1.50	1.50
99	A13	70c brt pink ('39)	40	40
100	A13	75c ol grn	3.50	3.50
101	A13	80c vio brn ('38)	60	60
102	A13	90c rose red	40	40
103	A14	1fr red brn	18	18
104	A14	1.25fr brn vio	4.75	4.75
105	A14	1.25fr rose red ('39)	40	40
106	A14	1.40fr org yel ('39)	40	40
107	A14	1.50fr blue	40	40
108	A14	1.60fr dl vio ('39)	40	40
109	A14	1.75fr olive	3.25	3.25
110	A14	2fr red	40	40
111	A14	2.25fr dp bl ('39)	35	35
112	A14	2.50fr blk ('39)	48	48
113	A14	3fr brn org ('39)	48	48
114	A14	5fr red vio ('39)	48	48
115	A14	10fr dk grn ('39)	1.50	1.50
116	A14	20fr dk brn ('39)	2.00	2.00
		Nos. 80-116 (37)	34.41	34.41

Common Design Types
pictured in section at front of book.

Paris International Exposition Issue.

Common Design Types

1937 Engraved. ***Perf. 13.***

117	CD74	20c dp vio	1.25	1.25
118	CD75	30c dk grn	1.25	1.25
119	CD76	40c car rose	1.25	1.25
120	CD77	50c dk brn & bl	1.40	1.40
121	CD78	90c red	1.75	1.75
122	CD79	1.50fr ultra	1.90	1.90
		Nos. 117-122 (6)	8.80	8.80

Colonial Arts Exhibition Issue.

Souvenir Sheet.

Common Design Type

1937 ***Imperf.***

123	CD78	3fr emerald	4.25	4.25

Sheet size: 118x99mm.

New York World's Fair Issue.

Common Design Type

1939, May 10 Engr. ***Perf. 12½x12***

124	CD82	1.25fr car lake	1.00	1.00
125	CD82	2.25fr ultra	1.00	1.00

Fautaua Valley and Marshal Petain
A15

1941 Engraved ***Perf. 12½x12***

125A	A15	1fr bluish grn	40	
125B	A15	2.50fr dp bl	40	

Nos. 125A–125B were issued by the Vichy government, and were not placed on sale in the colony. This is also true of five stamps of types A12–A14 without "RF" released in 1942–44.

Stamps of 1929-39 Overprinted in Black or Red

FRANCE LIBRE

1941 ***Perf. 14x13½, 13½x13***

126	A14	1fr red brn (Bk)	2.50	2.50
127	A14	2.50fr blk (R)	3.50	3.50
128	A5	3fr grn & dk brn (R)	3.50	3.50
129	A14	3fr brn org (Bk)	3.50	3.50
130	A5	5fr lt bl & dk brn (R)	3.50	3.50
131	A14	5fr red vio (Bk)	3.50	3.50
132	A5	10fr lt red & dk brn (R)	8.75	8.75
133	A14	10fr dk grn (R)	35.00	35.00
134	A5	20fr lil & dk brn (R)	60.00	60.00
135	A14	20fr dk brn (R)	30.00	30.00
		Nos. 126-135 (10)	153.75	153.75

Ancient Double Canoe
A16

1942 Photo. ***Perf. 14½x14***

136	A16	5c dk brn	5	5
137	A16	10c dk gray bl	6	6
138	A16	25c emerald	6	6
139	A16	30c red org	6	6
140	A16	40c dk sl grn	6	6
141	A16	80c red brn	14	14
142	A16	1fr rose vio	14	14
143	A16	1.50fr brt red	25	22
144	A16	2fr gray blk	25	25
145	A16	2.50fr brt ultra	1.00	1.00
146	A16	4fr dl vio	42	40
147	A16	5fr bister	60	55
148	A16	10fr dp brn	60	55
149	A16	20fr dp grn	1.00	90
		Nos. 136-149 (14)	4.69	4.44

Eboue Issue.

Common Design Type

1945 Engraved ***Perf. 13***

150	CD91	2fr black	25	25
151	CD91	25fr Prus grn	1.00	1.00

Nos. 150 and 151 exist imperforate.

Nos. 136, 138 and 145 Surcharged with New Values and Bars in Carmine or Black.

1946 ***Perf. 14½x14.***

152	A16	50c on 5c (C)	18	18
153	A16	60c on 5c (C)	18	18
154	A16	70c on 5c (C)	22	22
155	A16	1.20fr on 5c (C)	22	22
156	A16	2.40fr on 25c (Bk)	70	70
157	A16	3fr on 25c (Bk)	42	42
158	A16	4.50fr on 25c (Bk)	1.00	1.00
159	A16	15fr on 2.50fr (C)	1.25	1.25
		Nos. 152-159 (8)	4.17	4.17

Coast of Mooréa
A17

Fisherman and Catch
A18

Tahitian Girl
A20

House at Faa
A19

Island of Borabora
A21

Island Women
A22

Engraved.

1948 ***Perf. 13*** **Unwmkd.**

160	A17	10c brown	6	6
161	A17	30c bl grn	6	6
162	A17	40c dp bl	6	6
163	A18	50c red brn	8	8
164	A18	60c dk brn ol	10	10
165	A18	80c brt bl	10	10
166	A19	1fr red brn	14	8
167	A19	1.20fr slate	25	18
168	A19	1.50fr dp ultra	35	25
169	A20	2fr sepia	60	48
170	A20	2.40fr red brn	85	85

No.	Type	Description	Unused	Used
171	A20	3fr purple	7.00	1.75
172	A20	4fr bl blk	70	70
173	A21	5fr sepia	85	70
174	A21	6fr stl bl	95	70
175	A21	10fr dk brn ol	1.50	60
176	A22	15fr vermilion	2.75	1.50
177	A22	20fr slate	3.00	1.50
178	A22	25fr sepia	3.50	1.90
		Nos. 160-178 (19)	22.90	11.65

Imperforates

Most French Polynesia stamps from 1948 onward exist imperforate in issued and trial colors, and also in small presentation sheets in issued colors.

Military Medal Issue.

Common Design Type

Engraved and Typographed.

1952, Dec. 1

No.	Type	Description	Unused	Used
179	CD101	3fr blk, grn, yel & pur	5.25	5.25

Girl of Borabora
A23

Girl Playing Guitar
A24

1955, Sept. 26 Engraved

No.	Type	Description	Unused	Used
180	A23	9fr dk brn, blk & red	10.50	8.75

FIDES Issue.

Common Design Type

Design: 3fr, Dry dock at Papeete.

1956, Oct. 22 Engr. *Perf. 13x12½*

No.	Type	Description	Unused	Used
181	CD103	3fr grnsh bl	1.25	1.00

1958, Nov. 3 *Perf. 13* Unwmkd.

Design : 4fr, 7fr, 9fr, Man with headdress. 10fr, 20fr, Girl with shells on beach.

No.	Type	Description	Unused	Used
182	A24	10c grn & redsh brn	38	38
183	A24	25c sl grn, cl & car	38	38
184	A24	1fr brt bl, brn & red org	52	52
185	A24	2fr brn, vio brn & vio	52	52
186	A24	4fr sl grn & org yel	70	70
187	A24	7fr red brn, grn & org	1.40	1.00
188	A24	9fr vio brn, grn & org	2.50	1.75
189	A24	10fr dk bl, brn & car	2.75	1.90
190	A24	20fr pur, rose red & brn	5.25	3.25
		Nos. 182-190 (9)	14.40	10.40

See Nos. 302-304.

Human Rights Issue

Common Design Type

1958, Dec. 10

No.	Type	Description	Unused	Used
191	CD105	7fr dk gray & dk bl	7.50	6.75

Flower Issue

Common Design Type

Design: 4fr, Breadfruit.

1959, Jan. Photo. *Perf. 12½x12*

No.	Type	Description	Unused	Used
192	CD104	4fr multi	3.75	3.00

Spear Fishing
A25

Tahitian Dancers
A26

1960, May 16 Engraved *Perf. 13*

No.	Type	Description	Unused	Used
193	A25	5fr grn, brn & lil	70	70
194	A26	17fr ultra, brt grn & red brn	3.50	2.25

Post Office, Papeete
A27

1960, Dec. 15 *Perf. 13* Unwmkd.

No.	Type	Description	Unused	Used
195	A27	16fr grn, bl & cl	4.00	3.00

Saraca Indica
A28

Design: 25fr, Hibiscus.

1962, July 12 Photo. *Perf. 13*

No.	Type	Description	Unused	Used
196	A28	15fr multi	9.00	7.50
197	A28	25fr multi	12.00	11.00

Map of Australia and South Pacific—A29

1962, July 18 *Perf. 13x12*

No.	Type	Description	Unused	Used
198	A29	20fr multi	7.50	6.00

Issued to commemorate the Fifth South Pacific Conference, Pago Pago, July 1962.

Spined Squirrelfish—A30

Fish: 10fr, One-spot butterflyfish. 30fr, Radiate lionfish. 40fr, Horned boxfish.

1962, Dec. 15 Engraved *Perf. 13*

No.	Type	Description	Unused	Used
199	A30	5fr blk, mag & bis	2.25	1.10
200	A30	10fr multi	3.00	1.90
201	A30	30fr multi	7.50	5.25
202	A30	40fr multi	11.00	8.25

South Pacific Games Issue

Soccer
A30a

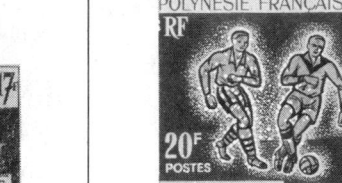

Design: 50fr, Throwing the javelin.

1963, Aug. 29 Photo. *Perf. 12½*

No.	Type	Description	Unused	Used
203	A30a	20fr brt ultra & brn	6.75	5.25
204	A30a	50fr brt car rose & ultra	10.50	7.50

Issued to publicize the South Pacific Games, Suva, Aug. 29–Sept. 7.

Red Cross Centenary Issue

Common Design Type

1963, Sept. 2 Engraved *Perf. 13*

No.	Type	Description	Unused	Used
205	CD113	15fr vio brn, gray & car	11.00	9.00

International Red Cross centenary.

Human Rights Issue

Common Design Type

1963, Dec. 10 *Perf. 13* Unwmkd.

No.	Type	Description	Unused	Used
206	CD117	7fr grn & vio bl	8.25	7.00

Philatec Issue

Common Design Type

1964, Apr. 9 *Perf. 13* Unwmkd.

No.	Type	Description	Unused	Used
207	CD118	25fr grn, dk sl grn & red	10.50	9.00

Tahitian Dancer
A31

1964, May 14 Engraved *Perf. 13*

No.	Type	Description	Unused	Used
208	A31	1fr multi	38	38
209	A31	3fr dp cl, blk & org	75	75

Soldiers, Truck and Battle Flag
A32

1964, July 10 Photo. *Perf. 12½*

No.	Type	Description	Unused	Used
210	A32	5fr multi	4.50	2.25

Issued to honor the Tahitian Volunteers of the Pacific Battalion. See No. C31.

Tuamotu Scene
A33

Views: 4fr, Borabora. 7fr, Papeete Harbor. 8fr, Paul Gauguin's tomb, Marquesas. 20fr, Mangareva, Gambier Islands.

1964, Dec. 1 Litho. *Perf. 12½x13*

No.	Type	Description	Unused	Used
211	A33	2fr multi	45	45
212	A33	4fr multi	85	45
213	A33	7fr multi	1.40	95
214	A33	8fr multi	1.75	95
215	A33	20fr multi	4.50	2.50
		Nos. 211-215, C32 (6)	14.20	8.35

Painting from a School Dining Room
A34

1965, Nov. 29 Engraved *Perf. 13*

No.	Type	Description	Unused	Used
216	A34	20fr dk brn, sl grn & dk car	12.00	9.00

Issued to publicize the School Canteen Program. See No. C38.

Outrigger Canoe on Lagoon
A35

Ships: 11fr, Large cruising yacht (vert.). 12fr, Motorboat for sport fishing. 14fr, Outrigger canoes with sails. 19fr, Schooner (vert.). 22fr, Modern coaster "Oiseau des Isles II."

1966, Aug. 30 Engraved *Perf. 13*

No.	Type	Description	Unused	Used
217	A35	10fr brt ultra, emer & mar	1.25	70
218	A35	11fr mar, dk bl & sl grn	1.50	1.25
219	A35	12fr emer, dk bl & red lil	2.25	1.50
220	A35	14fr brn, bl & sl grn	2.75	1.75
221	A35	19fr scar, sl grn & dp bl	3.75	1.75
222	A35	22fr multi	5.00	3.50
		Nos. 217-222 (6)	16.50	10.45

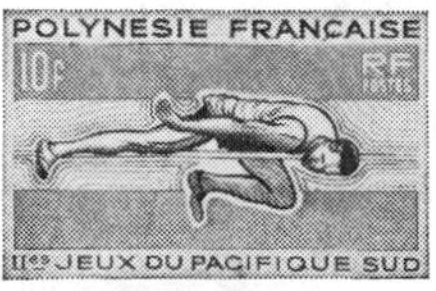

High Jump
A36

Designs: 20fr, Pole vault (vert.). 40fr, Women's basketball (vert.). 60fr, Hurdling.

1966, Dec. 15 Engraved *Perf. 13*

No.	Type	Description	Unused	Used
223	A36	10fr dk red, lem & blk	1.40	1.00
224	A36	20fr bl, emer & blk	3.25	1.50
225	A36	40fr emer, brt pink & blk	6.50	4.25
226	A36	60fr dl yel, bl & blk	11.00	7.50

Issued to commemorate the Second South Pacific Games, Nouméa, New Caledonia, Dec. 8–18.

Poi Pounder A37 — Javelin Throwing A38

1967, June 15 Engraved *Perf. 13*

227	A37	50fr org & blk	10.50	7.50

Issued to commemorate the 50th anniversary of the Society for Oceanic Studies.

1967, July 11

Designs: 5fr, Spring dance (horiz.). 15fr, Horse race (horiz.). 16fr, Fruit carriers' race. 21fr, Canoe race (horiz.).

228	A38	5fr multi	90	70
229	A38	13fr multi	1.75	1.10
230	A38	15fr multi	2.00	1.40
231	A38	16fr multi	3.50	2.25
232	A38	21fr multi	6.00	3.50
		Nos. 228-232 (5)	14.15	8.95

Issued to publicize the July Festival.

Earring A39

Art of the Marquesas Islands: 10fr, Carved mother-of-pearl. 15fr, Decorated canoe paddle. 23fr, Oil vessel. 25fr, Carved stilt stirrups. 30fr, Fan handles. 35fr, Tattooed man. 50fr, Tikis.

1967-68 Engraved *Perf. 13*

233	A39	10fr dp cl, dl red & ultra ('68)	1.40	70
234	A39	15fr blk & emer ('68)	2.00	95
235	A39	20fr ol gray, dk car & lt bl	2.50	1.65
236	A39	23fr dk brn, ocher & bl ('68)	3.75	2.75
237	A39	25fr dk brn, dk bl & lil	4.50	2.75
238	A39	30fr brn & red lil	6.00	3.00
239	A39	35fr ultra & dk brn ('68)	8.25	5.00
240	A39	50fr brn, sl grn & lt bl	9.00	5.50
		Nos. 233-240 (8)	37.40	22.30

Issue dates: 20fr, 25fr, 30fr, 50fr, Dec. 19, 1967; others Feb. 28, 1968.

WHO Anniversary Issue
Common Design Type

1968, May 4 Engraved *Perf. 13*

241	CD126	15fr bl grn, mar & dp vio	5.50	2.50
242	CD126	16fr org, lil & bl grn	6.50	3.25

Issued for the 20th anniversary of the World Health Organization.

Human Rights Year Issue
Common Design Type

1968, Aug. 10 Engraved *Perf. 13*

243	CD127	15fr bl, red & brn	5.50	3.75
244	CD127	16fr brn, brt pink & ultra	6.50	5.25

Tiare Apetahi A40

Flower: 17fr, Tiare Tahiti.

1969, Mar. 27 Photo. *Perf. 12½x13*

245	A40	9fr multi	1.90	90
246	A40	17fr multi	3.00	1.40

Runner A41

Designs: 9fr, Boxer (horiz.). 17fr, High jump. 22fr, Long jump.

1969, Aug. 13 Engraved *Perf. 13*

247	A41	9fr bl, vio & sep	1.50	75
248	A41	17fr red, sep & cl	2.25	1.50
249	A41	18fr bl, brn ol & cl	3.75	2.25
250	A41	22fr brt grn & choc	5.50	3.75

Issued to publicize the 3rd South Pacific Games, Port Moresby, Papua and New Guinea, Aug. 13-23.

ILO Issue
Common Design Type

1969, Nov. 24 Engraved *Perf. 13*

251	CD131	17fr org, emer & ol	5.50	3.25
252	CD131	18fr org, dk brn & vio bl	6.50	4.00

Territorial Assembly A42

Buildings: 14fr, Governor's Residence. 17fr, House of Tourism. 18fr, Maeva Hotel. 24fr, Taharaa Hotel.

1969, Dec. 22 Photo. *Perf. 12½x12*

253	A42	13fr blk & multi	1.40	90
254	A42	14fr blk & multi	2.00	1.40
255	A42	17fr blk & multi	3.00	2.25
256	A42	18fr blk & multi	4.50	2.25
257	A42	24fr blk & multi	7.00	4.50
		Nos. 253-257 (5)	17.90	11.30

Stone Figure with Globe A43

Designs: 40fr, Globe, plane, map of Polynesia and men holding "PATA" sign (horiz.). 60fr, Polynesian carrying globe.

1970, Apr. 7 Engraved *Perf. 13*

258	A43	20fr dp plum, gray & bl	3.00	2.25
259	A43	40fr emer, rose lil & ultra	6.50	4.50
260	A43	60fr red brn, bl & dk brn	12.00	8.25

Issued to publicize the 1970 Pacific Area Travel Association Congress (PATA).

U.P.U. Headquarters Issue
Common Design Type

1970, May 20 Engraved *Perf. 13*

261	CD133	18fr mar, pur & brn	5.00	3.75
262	CD133	20fr lil rose, ol & ind	6.50	4.50

Night Fishing—A44

1971, May 11 Photo. *Perf. 13*

263	A44	10fr multi	6.00	3.00

See Nos. C71-C73.

Flowers A45

Designs: Various flowers. 12fr is horiz.

Perf. 12½x13, 13x12½

1971, Aug. 27

264	A45	8fr multi	1.10	75
265	A45	12fr multi	2.25	1.10
266	A45	22fr multi	4.00	2.25

Day of a Thousand Flowers.

Water-skiing Slalom—A46

Designs: 20fr, Water-skiing, jump (vert.). 40fr, Figure water-skiing.

1971, Oct. 11 Engraved *Perf. 13*

267	A46	10fr grnsh bl, dk red & brn	2.25	1.50
268	A46	20fr car, emer & brn	5.25	3.00
269	A46	40fr brn, grn & lil	10.50	7.50

World water-skiing championships, Oct. 1971.

De Gaulle Issue
Common Design Type

Designs: 30fr, Gen. de Gaulle, 1940. 50fr, Pres. de Gaulle, 1970.

1971, Nov. 9 Engraved *Perf. 13*

270	CD134	30fr red lil & blk	6.00	4.50
271	CD134	50fr red lil & blk	9.00	6.75

First anniversary of the death of Charles de Gaulle (1890-1970), president of France.

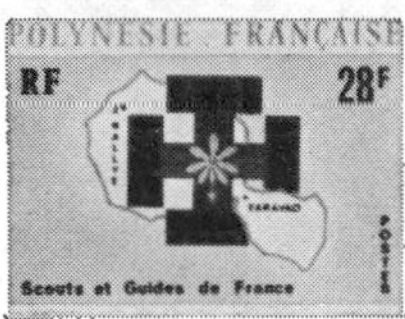

Map of Tahiti and Jerusalem Cross A47

1971, Dec. 18 Photo. *Perf. 13x12½*

272	A47	28fr lt bl & multi	8.25	6.00

2nd rally of French Boy Scouts and Guides, Taravao, French Polynesia.

"Alcoholism" A48 — Mother and Child A49

1972, Mar. 24 Photo. *Perf. 13*

273	A48	20fr brn & multi	4.50	2.50

Fight against alcoholism.

1973, Sept. 26 Photo. *Perf. 12½x13*

274	A49	28fr pale yel & multi	5.00	3.00

Day nursery.

Polynesian Golfer A50

Design: 24fr, Atimaono Golf Course.

1974, Feb. 27 Photogravure *Perf. 13*

275	A50	16fr multi	3.00	1.75
276	A50	24fr multi	3.75	2.75

Atimaono Golf Course.

Hand Throwing Life Preserver to Puppy—A51

1974, May 9 Photo. *Perf. 13*

277	A51	21fr brt bl & multi	6.00	3.00

Society for the Protection of Animals.

Around a Fire, on the Beach A52

Polynesian Views: 2fr, Lagoons and mountains. 6fr, Pebble divers. 10fr, Lonely Mountain and flowers (vert.). 15fr, Sailing ship at sunset. 20fr, Lagoon and mountain.

1974, May 22

278	A52	2fr multi	30	30
279	A52	5fr multi	60	52
280	A52	6fr multi	75	55
281	A52	10fr multi	90	65
282	A52	15fr multi	1.90	95
283	A52	20fr multi	3.00	1.50
		Nos. 278-283 (6)	7.45	4.47

Polynesian Woman and UPU Emblem
A53

Lion, Sun and Emblem
A54

1974, Oct. 9 Engraved *Perf. 13*

284	A53	65fr multi	8.25	5.25

Centenary of Universal Postal Union.

1975, June 17 Photogravure

285	A54	26fr multi	5.50	2.50

15th anniversary of Lions International in Tahiti.

Fish and Leaf—A55

1975, July 9 Litho. *Perf. 12*

286	A55	19fr dp ultra & grn	4.50	2.50

Polynesian Association for the Protection of Nature.

Pompidou Type of France 1975

1976, Feb. 16 Engr. *Perf. 13*

287	A668	49fr dk vio & blk	6.75	5.25

Georges Pompidou (1911–74), President of France (1965–74).

Alain Gerbault and Sailboat
A56

1976, May 25 Photo. *Perf. 13*

288	A56	90fr multi	9.00	7.50

50th anniversary of Alain Gerbault's arrival in Bora Bora.

Turtle
A57

Design: 42fr, Hand protecting bird.

1976, June 24 Litho. *Perf. 12½*

289	A57	18fr multi	4.00	1.90
290	A57	42fr multi	6.50	5.00

World Ecology Day.

A. G. Bell, Telephone, Radar and Satellite—A58

1976, Sept. 15 Engr. *Perf. 13*

291	A58	37fr multi	6.00	2.50

Centenary of first telephone call by Alexander Graham Bell, Mar. 10, 1876.

Marquesas Dugout Canoe—A59

Dugout Canoes from: 30fr, Raiatea. 75fr, Tahiti. 100fr, Tuamotu.

1976, Dec. 16 Litho. *Perf. 13x12½*

292	A59	25fr multi	1.50	1.10
293	A59	30fr multi	2.25	1.50
294	A59	75fr multi	5.25	2.75
295	A59	100fr multi	7.50	5.25

Sailing Ship—A60

Designs: Various sailing vessels.

1977, Dec. 22 Litho. *Perf. 13*

296	A60	20fr multi	1.50	1.10
297	A60	50fr multi	3.00	1.50
298	A60	85fr multi	4.50	2.75
299	A60	120fr multi	6.00	4.50

Hibiscus
A61

Girl with Shells on Beach
A62

Designs: 10fr, Vanda orchids. 16fr, Pua (fagraea berteriana). 22fr, Gardenia.

1978–79 Photo. *Perf. 12½x13*

300	A61	10fr multi	45	30
301	A61	13fr multi	1.10	70
302	A61	16fr multi	1.50	70
303	A61	22fr multi	75	52

Issue dates: Nos. 301–302, Aug. 23, 1978; Nos. 300, 303, Jan. 25, 1979.

1978, Nov. 3 Engr. *Perf. 13*

Designs (as type A24 with "1958 1978" added): 28fr, Man with headdress. 36fr, Girl playing guitar.

304	A62	20fr multi	1.25	52
305	A62	28fr multi	1.75	95
306	A62	36fr multi	2.50	1.50
a.		Souvenir sheet of 3	9.50	9.50

20th anniv. of stamps inscribed: Polynesie Francaise. No. 306a contains Nos. 304-306 in changed colors. Size: 130x100mm.

Tahiti—A63

Ships: 30fr, Monowai. 75fr, Tahitien. 100fr, Mariposa.

1978, Dec. 29 Litho. *Perf. 13x12½*

307	A63	15fr multi	1.10	90
308	A63	30fr multi	1.50	1.25
309	A63	75fr multi	3.75	2.00
310	A63	100fr multi	5.50	3.00

Porites Coral
A64

Design: 37fr, Montipora coral.

1979, Feb. 15 *Perf. 13x12½*

311	A64	32fr multi	1.50	75
312	A64	37fr multi	2.25	1.10

Raiatea
A65

Landscapes: 1fr, Moon over Bora Bora. 2fr, Mountain peaks, Ua Pou. 3fr, Sunset over Motu Tapu. 6fr, Palm and hut, Tuamotu.

1979, Mar. 8 *Perf. 13x13½*

313	A65	1fr multi	6	6
314	A65	2fr multi	6	6
315	A65	3fr multi	15	5
316	A65	4fr multi	22	6
317	A65	5fr multi	38	15
318	A65	6fr multi	45	38
		Nos. 313-318 (6)	1.32	76

Dance Costumes, Fetia
A66

Dance Costumes: 51fr, Teanuanua. 74fr, Temaeva.

1979, July 14 Litho. *Perf. 12½*

319	A66	45fr multi	1.50	90
320	A66	51fr multi	2.25	1.00
321	A66	74fr multi	3.00	1.75

Hill, Great Britain No. 53, Tahiti No. 28—A67

1979, Aug. 1 Engraved *Perf. 13*

322	A67	100fr multi	4.00	3.00

Sir Rowland Hill (1795–1879), originator of penny postage.

Hastula Strigilata
A68

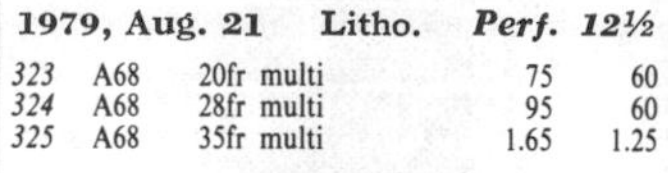

Shells: 28fr, Scabricola variegata. 35fr, Fusinus undatus.

1979, Aug. 21 Litho. *Perf. 12½*

323	A68	20fr multi	75	60
324	A68	28fr multi	95	60
325	A68	35fr multi	1.65	1.25

Statue Holding Rotary Emblem—A69

1979, Nov. 30 Litho. *Perf. 13*

326	A69	47fr multi	2.50	1.65

Rotary International, 75th anniversary; Papeete Rotary Club, 20th anniversary.

Myripristis Murdjan—A70

Fish: 8fr, Napoleon fish. 12fr, Emperor fish.

1980, Jan. 21 Litho. *Perf. 12½*

327	A70	7fr multi	45	18
328	A70	8fr multi	45	18
329	A70	12fr multi	75	45

No. 326 Overprinted and Surcharged in Gold:
"75eme / ANNIVERSAIRE / 1905-1980"

1980, Feb. 23 **Litho.** ***Perf. 13***

330	A69	77fr on 47fr multi	3.75	2.50

Rotary International, 75th anniversary.

CNEXO Fish Hatchery—A71

1980, Mar. 17 **Photo.** ***Perf. 13x13½***

331	A70	15fr *shown*	75	45
332	A70	22fr *Crayfish*	90	60

Papeete Post Office Building Opening—A72

1980, May 5 **Photo.** ***Perf. 13x12½***

333	A71	50fr multi	1.90	1.50

Tiki and Festival Emblem A73

1980, June 30 **Photo.** ***Perf. 13½***

334	A73	34fr *shown*	90	70
335	A73	39fr *Drum (pahu)*	1.40	1.00
336	A73	49fr *Ax (to'i)*	2.25	1.65
	a.	Souvenir sheet of 3	6.75	6.75

South Pacific Arts Festival, Port Moresby, Papua New Guinea. No. 336a contains Nos. 334-336; multicolored margin shows festival emblem. Size: 136x100mm.

Titmouse henparrot A74

Charles de Gaulle A75

Photogravure

1980, Oct. 20 ***Perf. 13x12½, 12½x13***

337	A74	25fr *White sea-swallow, horiz.*	85	52
338	A74	35fr *shown*	90	75
339	A74	45fr *Minor frigate bird, horiz.*	1.25	95

1980, Nov. 9 **Engr.** ***Perf. 12½x13***

340	A75	100fr multi	3.25	2.50

Naso Vlamingi (Karaua)—A76

1981, Feb. 5 **Litho.** ***Perf. 12½***

341	A76	13fr shown	45	38
342	A76	16fr Lutjanus vaigensis (toau)	60	38
343	A76	24fr Plectropomus leopardus (tonu)	90	45

Indoor Fish Breeding Tanks, Cnexo Hatchery—A77

1981, May 14 **Photo.** ***Perf. 13x13½***

344	A77	23fr shown	75	60
345	A77	41fr Mussels	1.10	90

Folk Dancers—A78

1981, July 10 **Litho.** ***Perf. 13x13½, 13½x13***

346	A78	26fr shown	70	45
347	A78	28fr Dancer	85	60
348	A78	44fr Dancers, vert.	1.50	90

Sterna Bergii—A79

1981, Sept. 24 **Litho.** ***Perf. 13***

349	A79	47fr shown	1.10	75
350	A79	53fr Ptilinopus purpuratus, vert.	1.40	90
351	A79	65fr Estrilda astrild, vert.	1.65	1.40

See Nos. 370-372

Huahine Island—A80

1981, Oct. 22 **Litho.** ***Perf. 12½***

352	A80	34fr shown	75	52
353	A80	134fr Maupiti	2.25	1.50
354	A80	136fr Bora-Bora	2.25	1.50

A81

1982, Feb. 4 **Photo.** ***Perf. 13x13½***

355	A81	30fr Parrotfish	60	52
356	A81	31fr Regal angel	60	52
357	A81	45fr Spotted bass	90	75

Pearl Industry—A82

1982, Apr. 22 **Photo.** ***Perf. 13x13½***

358	A82	7fr Pearl beds	14	6
359	A82	8fr Extracting pearls	18	14
360	A82	10fr Pearls	22	18

Tahiti "No. 1A," Emblem—A83

1982, May 12 **Engr.** ***Perf. 13***

361	A83	150fr multi	4.50	3.75
	a.	Souvenir sheet	8.25	8.25

PHILEXFRANCE Stamp Exhibition, Paris, June 11-21. No. 361a contains No. 361 in changed colors; blue marginal inscription. Size: 122x95mm.

King Holding Carved Scepter—A84

Designs: Coronation ceremony.

1982, July 14 **Photo.** ***Perf. 13½x13***

362	A84	12fr shown	30	18
363	A84	13fr King, priest	30	18
364	A84	17fr Procession	38	30

Championship Emblem—A85

1982, Aug. 13 ***Perf. 13***

365	A85	90fr multi	2.25	1.90

4th Hobie-Cat 16 World Catamaran Sailing Championship, Tahiti, Aug. 15-21.

First Colloquium on New Energy Sources—A86

1982, Sept. 29 **Litho.**

366	A86	46fr multi	1.10	90

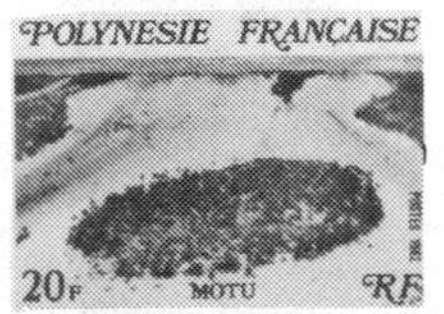

Motu, Tuamotu Islet—A87

1982, Oct. 12 **Litho.** ***Perf. 13***

367	A87	20fr shown	55	30
368	A87	33fr Tupai Atoll	65	45
369	A87	35fr Gambier Islds.	85	60

Bird Type of 1981

1982, Nov. 17 **Litho.** ***Perf. 13***

370	A79	37fr Sacred egret	75	45
371	A79	39fr Pluvialis dominica, vert.	85	60
372	A79	42fr Lonchura castaneothorax	95	60

Fish—A88

1983, Feb. 9 **Litho.** ***Perf. 13x13½***

373	A88	8fr Acanthurus lineatus	15	12
374	A88	10fr Caranx melampygus	22	12
375	A88	12fr Carcharhinus melanopterus	30	18

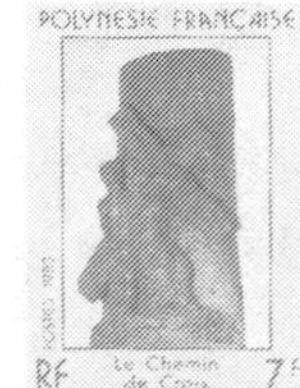

The Way of the Cross, Sculpture by Damien Haturau—A89

1983, Mar. 9 **Litho.** ***Perf. 13***

376	A89	7fr shown	15	6
377	A89	21fr Virgin and Child	42	18
378	A89	23fr Christ	48	30

Traditional Hats—A90

1983, May 24 Litho. *Perf. 13x12½*

379	A90	11fr	Acacia	22	18
380	A90	13fr	Niau	30	18
381	A90	25fr	Ofe	52	32
382	A90	35fr	Ofe, diff.	75	45

See Nos. 393-396

Chieftain in Traditional Costume, Sainte-Christine Isld.—A91

Traditional Costumes, Marquesas Islds.

1983, July 12 Photo. *Perf. 13*

383	A91	15fr	shown	30	22
384	A91	17fr	Man	38	30
385	A91	28fr	Woman	52	38

See Nos. 397-399

Polynesian Crowns—A92

Various flower garlands.

1983, Oct. 19 Litho. *Perf. 13*

386	A92	41fr	multi	90	75
387	A92	44fr	multi	1.00	75
388	A92	45fr	multi	1.00	75

See Nos. 400-402

Martin Luther (1483-1546), 500th Birth Anniv.—A93

1983, Nov. 19 Engr. *Perf. 13*

389	A93	90fr	blk, brn & lil gray	1.90	1.50

Tiki Carvings—A94

Various carvings.

1984, Feb. 8 Litho. *Perf. 12½x13*

390	A94	14fr	multi	30	22
391	A94	16fr	multi	38	25
392	A94	19fr	multi	45	25

Hat Type of 1983

1984, June 20 Litho. *Perf. 13x12½*

393	A90	20fr	Aeho ope	38	30
394	A90	24fr	Paeore	45	30
395	A90	26fr	Ofe fei	52	38
396	A90	33fr	Hua	70	45

Costume Type of 1983

1984, Aug. 21 Litho. *Perf. 13*

397	A91	34fr	Tahitian playing nose flute	70	45
398	A91	35fr	Priest, Oei-eitia	70	45
399	A91	39fr	Tahitian adult and child	75	52

Garland Type of 1983

1984, Oct. 24 Litho. *Perf. 13x12½*

400	A92	46fr	Moto'i Lei	85	52
401	A92	47fr	Pitate Lei	90	60
402	A92	53fr	Bougainvillea Lei	1.00	75

4th Pacific Arts Festival, Noumea, New Caledonia, Dec. 8-22—A95

1984, Nov. 20 Litho. *Perf. 13*

403	A95	150fr	Statue, headdress	2.50	2.00

See No. C213.

Paysage D'Anaa, by Jean Masson—A96

Paintings: 50fr, Sortie Du Culte, by Jacques Boulaire. 75fr, La Fete, by Robert Tatin. 85fr, Tahitiennes Sur La Plage, by Pierre Heyman.

1984, Dec. 12 Litho. *Perf. 12½x13, 13x12½*

404	A96	50fr	multi, vert.	85	60
405	A96	65fr	multi	1.00	60
406	A96	75fr	multi	1.25	90
407	A96	85fr	multi	1.50	1.10

Tiki Carvings A97 Polynesian Faces A98

1985, Jan. 23 Litho. *Perf. 13½*

408	A97	30fr	multi	52	38
409	A97	36fr	multi	60	45
410	A97	40fr	multi	70	52

1985, Feb. 20 Photo. *Perf. 12½x13*

411	A98	22fr	multi	38	30
412	A98	39fr	multi	70	45
413	A98	44fr	multi	75	60

Early Tahiti—A99

Perf. 13x12½, 12½x13
1985, Apr. 24 Litho.

414	A99	42fr	Entrance to Papeete	70	45
415	A99	45fr	Girls, vert.	75	52
416	A99	48fr	Papeete market	80	52

5th Intl. Congress on Coral Reefs, Tahiti—A100

1985, May 28 Litho. *Perf. 13½*

417	A100	140fr	Local reef formation	2.50	1.90

Printed se-tenant with label picturing congress emblem.

National Flag—A101

1985, June 28

418	A101	9fr	Flag, natl. arms	20	15

18th-19th Century Prints, Beslu Collection—A102

1985, July 17 *Perf. 13*

419	A102	38fr	Tahitian dancer	70	45
420	A102	55fr	Man and woman from Otahiti, 1806	90	70
421	A102	70fr	Traditional chief	1.25	90

Local Foods—A103

1985-6 Litho. *Perf. 13*

422	A103	25fr	Roasted pig	45	30
423	A103	35fr	Pit fire	60	45
423A	A103	80fr	Fish in coconut milk ('86)	1.40	90
423B	A103	110fr	Fafaru ('86)	1.90	1.40

Issue dates: 25fr, 35fr, Nov. 14. 80fr, 110fr, May 20.

Catholic Churches—A104

1985, Dec. 11 Litho. *Perf. 13*

424	A104	90fr	St. Anne's, Otepipi	1.50	1.10
425	A104	100fr	St. Michael's Cathedral, Rikitea	1.65	1.25
426	A104	120fr	Cathedral, exterior	2.00	1.50

Nos. 424-426 printed se-tenant with labels picturing local religious art.

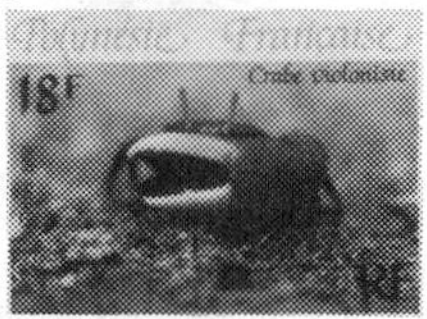

Crabs—A105

1986, Jan. 22 *Perf. 13½*

427	A105	18fr	Fiddler	30	22
428	A105	29fr	Hermit	48	35
429	A105	31fr	Coconut	52	38

Faces of Polynesia—A106

1986, Feb. 19 *Perf. 12½x13, 13x12½*

430	A106	43fr	Boy, fish	75	50
431	A106	49fr	Boy, coral	85	55
432	A106	51fr	Boy, turtle, vert.	90	58

Old Tahiti—A107

1986, Mar. 18 *Perf. 13x12½*

433	A107	52fr	Papeete	90	60
434	A107	56fr	Harpoon fishing	95	65
435	A107	57fr	Royal Palace, Papeete	95	68

Tiki Rock Carvings—A108

1986, Apr. 16

436	A108	58fr	Atuona, Hiva Oa	95	68
437	A108	59fr	Ua Huka Hill, Hane Valley	95	70

Landscapes Type of 1979 Redrawn.

1986, May *Perf. 13½*

439	A65	2fr	multi	5	5
440	A65	3fr	multi	5	5
442	A65	5fr	multi	8	6
443	A65	6fr	multi	10	8

Nos. 439-440, 442-443 printed in sharper detail, box containing island name is larger and margin inscribed "CARTOR" instead of "DELRIEU."

Traditional Crafts—A109

1986, July 17 Litho. *Perf. 13x12½, 12½x13*

444	A109	8fr	Quilting, vert.	15	12
445	A109	10fr	Baskets, hats	18	15
446	A109	12fr	Grass skirts	22	16

Building a Pirogue (Canoe)—A110

1986, Oct. 21 **Litho.** *Perf. 13½*

447	A110	46fr	Boat-builders	70	52
448	A110	50fr	Close-up	75	58

Medicinal Plants—A111

1986, Nov. 19 *Perf. 13*

449	A111	40fr	Phymatosorus	60	45
450	A111	41fr	Barringtonia asiatica	62	45
451	A111	60fr	Ocimum bacilicum	90	68

Polynesians—A112

1987, Jan. 21 **Litho.** *Perf. 13½*

452	A112	28fr	Old man	42	32
453	A112	30fr	Mother and child	45	35
454	A112	37fr	Old woman	55	42

Crustaceans—A113

1987, Feb. 18 *Perf. 12½x13*

455	A113	34fr	Carpilius maculatus	52	40
456	A113	35fr	Parribacus antarticus	55	42
457	A113	39fr	Justitia longimana	58	30

SEMI-POSTAL STAMPS.

Nos. 55 and 26 Surcharged in Red

1915 ***Perf. 14x13½*** **Unwmkd.**

B1	A1	10c +5c red	13.00	13.00
a.		"e" instead of "c"	24.00	24.00
b.		Inverted surcharge	65.00	55.00
B2	A2	10c +5c rose & org	4.25	4.25
a.		"e" instead of "c"	19.00	19.00
b.		"c" inverted	19.00	19.00
c.		Inverted surcharge	65.00	65.00

Surcharged in Carmine

B3	A2	10c +5c rose & org	1.25	1.25
a.		"e" instead of "c"	11.00	11.00
b.		Inverted surcharge	65.00	65.00

Surcharged in Carmine

1916

B4	A2	10c +5c rose & org	1.25	1.25

Curie Issue
Common Design Type

1938 **Engraved.** ***Perf. 13***

B5	CD80	1.75fr +50c brt ultra	8.75	8.75

French Revolution Issue
Common Design Type

1939 **Photogravure**

Name and Value Typo. in Black.

B6	CD83	45(c) +25(c) grn	7.75	7.75
B7	CD83	70(c) +30(c) brn	7.75	7.75
B8	CD83	90(c) +35(c) red org	7.75	7.75
B9	CD83	1.25fr +1fr rose pink	7.75	7.75
B10	CD83	2.25fr +2fr bl	7.75	7.75
		Nos. B6-B10 (5)	38.75	38.75

Common Design Type and

Marine Officer
SP1

"L'Astrolabe"
SP2

1941 **Photogravure** ***Perf. 13½***

B11	SP1	1fr +1fr red	1.00
B12	CD86	1.50fr +3fr mar	1.00
B12A	SP2	2.50fr +1fr bl	1.00

Nos. B11-B12A were issued by the Vichy government, and were not placed on sale in the colony.

Nos. 125A-125B were surcharged "OEUVRES COLONIALES" and surtax (including change of denomination of the 2.50fr to 50c). These were issued in 1944 by the Vichy government and not placed on sale in the colony.

Red Cross Issue
Common Design Type

1944 **Photogravure.** ***Perf. 14½x14.***

B13	CD90	5fr +20fr pck bl	60	60

The surtax was for the French Red Cross and national relief.

Tropical Medicine Issue
Common Design Type

1950 **Engraved.** ***Perf. 13.***

B14	CD100	10fr +2fr dk bl grn & dk grn	2.50	2.50

The surtax was for charitable work.

AIR POST STAMPS.

Seaplane in Flight
AP1

Photogravure.

1934, Nov. 5 ***Perf. 13½*** **Unwmkd.**

C1	AP1	5fr green	25	25

V4

Stamps of type AP1 without "RF" monogram and stamp of the above design were issued in 1944 by the Vichy Government, but were not placed on sale in the colony.

No. C1 Overprinted in Red

FRANCE LIBRE

1941

C2	AP1	5fr green	2.00	2.00

Common Design Type

1942 ***Perf. 14½x14.***

C3	CD87	1fr dk org	35	35
C4	CD87	1.50fr brt red	42	42
C5	CD87	5fr brn red	52	52
C6	CD87	10fr black	80	80
C7	CD87	25fr ultra	1.00	1.00
C8	CD87	50fr dk grn	1.00	1.00
C9	CD87	100fr plum	1.00	1.00
		Nos. C3-C9 (7)	5.09	5.09

Victory Issue
Common Design Type

1946, May 8 **Engr.** ***Perf. 12½***

C10	CD92	8fr dk grn	1.00	1.00

Issued to commemorate the European Victory of the Allied Nations in World War II.

Chad to Rhine Issue
Common Design Types

1946, June 6

C11	CD93	5fr red org	1.00	1.00
C12	CD94	10fr dk ol bis	1.00	1.00
C13	CD95	15fr dk yel grn	1.00	1.00
C14	CD96	20fr carmine	1.50	1.50
C15	CD97	25fr dk rose vio	1.50	1.50
C16	CD98	50fr black	2.50	2.50
		Nos. C11-C16 (6)	8.50	8.50

Shearwater and Moorea Landscape
AP2

Fishermen—AP3

Shearwater over Maupiti Shoreline
AP4

1948, Mar. 1 ***Perf. 13*** **Unwmkd.**

C17	AP2	50fr red brn	14.00	9.50
C18	AP3	100fr purple	10.50	7.75
C19	AP4	200fr bl grn	27.50	17.50

UPU Issue
Common Design Type

1949

C20	CD99	10fr dp bl	9.50	9.50

Gauguin's "Nafea faaipoipo"
AP5

1953, Sept. 24

C21	AP5	14fr dk brn, dk gray grn & red	70.00	70.00

Issued to commemorate the 50th anniversary of the death of Paul Gauguin.

Liberation Issue
Common Design Type

1954, June 6

C22	CD102	3fr dk grnsh bl & bl grn	2.50	2.50

Bahia Peak, Borabora—AP6

1955, Sept. 26 ***Perf. 13*** **Unwmkd.**

C23	AP6	13fr ind & bl	7.00	5.25

Mother-of-Pearl Artist
AP7

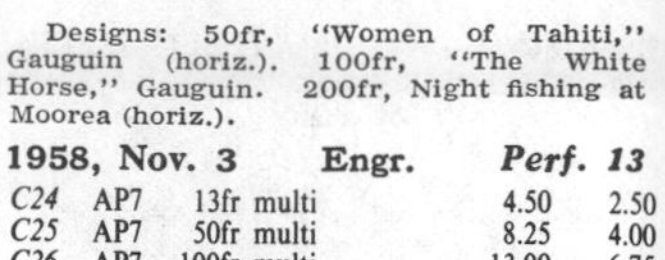

Designs: 50fr, "Women of Tahiti," Gauguin (horiz.). 100fr, "The White Horse," Gauguin. 200fr, Night fishing at Moorea (horiz.).

1958, Nov. 3 **Engr.** ***Perf. 13***

C24	AP7	13fr multi	4.50	2.50
C25	AP7	50fr multi	8.25	4.00
C26	AP7	100fr multi	13.00	6.75
C27	AP7	200fr lil & sl	32.50	20.00

Airport, Papeete—AP8

1960, Dec. 15

C28	AP8	13fr rose lil, vio, & yel grn	3.00	2.25

Telstar Issue
Common Design Type

1962, Dec. 5 ***Perf. 13***

C29	CD111	50fr red lil, mar & vio bl	11.00	7.50

Tahitian Dancer
AP10

1964, May 14 **Photo.** ***Perf. 13***

C30	AP10	15fr multi	3.00	1.75

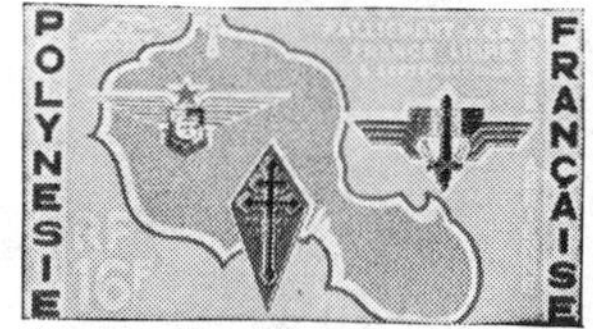

Map of Tahiti and Free French Emblems—AP11

1964, July 10 **Unwmkd.**

C31	AP11	16fr multi	9.50	5.25

Issued to commemorate the rallying of French Polynesia to the Free French cause.

Moorea Scene—AP12

1964, Dec. 1 **Litho.** ***Perf. 13***

C32	AP12	23fr multi	5.25	3.00

ITU Issue
Common Design Type

1965, May 17 **Engraved** ***Perf. 13***

C33	CD120	50fr vio, red brn & bl	82.50	45.00

Issued to commemorate the centenary of the International Telecommunication Union.

Paul Gauguin—AP13

Design: 25fr, Gauguin Museum (stylized). 40fr, Primitive statues at Gauguin Museum.

1965 Engraved *Perf. 13*

C34	AP13	25fr ol grn	6.00	3.75
C35	AP13	40fr bl grn	12.00	6.00
C36	AP13	75fr brt red brn	19.00	12.50

Opening of Gauguin Museum, Papeete.

Skin Diver with Spear Gun—AP14

1965, Sept. 1 Engraved *Perf. 13*

C37	AP14	50fr red brn, dl bl & dk grn	62.50	52.50

World Championships in Underwater Fishing, Tuamotu Archipelago, Sept. 1965.

Painting from a School Dining Room — AP15

Radio Tower, Globe and Palm — AP16

1965, Nov. 29

C38	AP15	80fr brn, bl, dl bl & red	18.00	13.00

School Canteen Program.

1965, Dec. 29 Engraved *Perf. 13*

C39	AP16	60fr org, grn & dk brn	16.00	12.50

50th anniversary of the first radio link between Tahiti and France.

French Satellite A-1 Issue

Common Design Type

Designs: 7fr, Diamant Rocket and launching installations. 10fr, A-1 satellite.

1966, Feb. 7

C40	CD121	7fr choc, dp grn & lil	4.75	4.75
C41	CD121	10fr lil, dp grn & dk brn	6.00	6.00
a.		Strip of 2 + label	11.00	11.00

Issued to commemorate the launching of France's first satellite, Nov. 26, 1965. No. C41a contains one each of Nos. C40-C41 and dark brown label with commemorative inscription. Each sheet contains 16 triptychs (2x8).

French Satellite D-1 Issue

Common Design Type

1966, May 10 Engraved *Perf. 13*

C42	CD122	20fr brn, brt grn & cl	6.50	4.50

Papeete Harbor—AP17

1966, June 30 Photo. *Perf. 13*

C43	AP17	50fr multi	13.00	10.50

"Vive Tahiti" by A. Benichou AP18

1966, Nov. 28 Photo. *Perf. 13*

C44	AP18	13fr multi	7.50	4.00

Explorer's Ship and Canoe—AP19

Designs: 60fr, Polynesian costume and ship. 80fr, Louis Antoine de Bougainville (vert.).

1968 Engraved *Perf. 13*

C45	AP19	40fr grn, bl & ocher	5.00	3.00
C46	AP19	60fr brt bl, org & blk	9.25	5.25
C47	AP19	80fr red lil, sal & lake	9.50	6.75
a.		Souv. sheet of 3	62.50	62.50

Issued to commemorate the 200th anniversary of the discovery of Tahiti by Louis Antoine de Bougainville. No. C47a contains one each of Nos. C45-C47. Ocher marginal inscription. Size: 174x99mm.

The Meal, by Paul Gauguin—AP20

1968, July 30 Photo. *Perf. 12x12½*

C48	AP20	200fr multi	32.50	26.00

See also Nos. C63-C67, C78-C82, C89-C93, C98.

Shot Put AP21

PATA 1970 Poster AP22

1968, Oct. 12 Engraved *Perf. 13*

C49	AP21	35fr dk car rose & brt grn	10.50	6.75

Issued to commemorate the 19th Olympic Games, Mexico City, Oct. 12-27.

Concorde Issue

Common Design Type

1969, Apr. 17

C50	CD129	40fr red brn & car rose	52.50	32.50

1969, July 9 Photo. *Perf. 12½x13*

C51	AP22	25fr bl & multi	7.50	5.25

Issued to publicize PATA 1970 (Pacific Area Travel Association Congress), Tahiti.

Underwater Fishing AP23

Design: 52fr, Hand holding fish made up of flags (vert.).

1969, Aug. 5 Photo. *Perf. 13*

C52	AP23	48fr blk, grnsh bl & red lil	9.50	6.00
C53	AP23	52fr bl, blk & red	15.00	12.00

Issued to publicize the World Underwater Fishing Championships.

Gen. Bonaparte as Commander of the Army in Italy, by Jean Sebastien Rouillard

AP24

1969, Oct. 15 Photo. *Perf. 12½x12*

C54	AP24	100fr car & multi	82.50	67.50

Bicentenary of the birth of Napoleon Bonaparte (1769-1821).

Eiffel Tower, Torii and EXPO Emblem AP25

Pearl Diver Descending, and Basket AP26

Design: 30fr, Mount Fuji, Tower of the Sun and EXPO emblem (horiz.).

1970, Sept. 15 Photo. *Perf. 13*

C55	AP25	30fr multi	6.00	4.50
C56	AP25	50fr multi	9.00	6.75

EXPO '70 International Exposition, Osaka, Japan, Mar. 15-Sept. 13.

1970, Sept. 30 Engraved *Perf. 13*

Designs: 5fr, Diver collecting oysters. 18fr, Implantation into oyster (horiz.). 27fr, Open oyster with pearl. 50fr, Woman with mother of pearl jewelry.

C57	AP26	2fr sl, grnsh bl & red brn	1.10	75
C58	AP26	5fr grnsh bl, ultra & org	1.90	1.10
C59	AP26	18fr sl, mag & org	3.25	2.25
C60	AP26	27fr brt pink, brn & dl lil	5.50	4.00
C61	AP26	50fr gray, red brn & org	10.50	6.75
		Nos. C57-C61(5)	22.25	14.85

Pearl industry of French Polynesia.

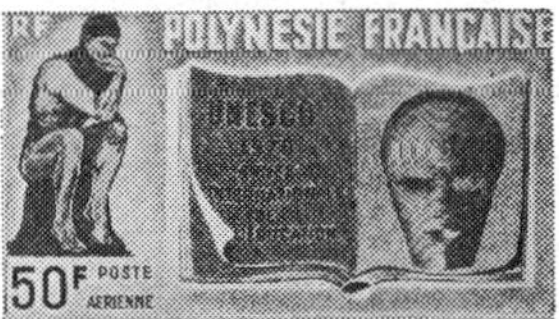

The Thinker, by Auguste Rodin and Education Year Emblem—AP27

1970, Oct. 15 Engraved *Perf. 13*

C62	AP27	50fr bl, ind & fawn	9.50	7.50

International Education Year.

Painting Type of 1968

Paintings by Artists Living in Polynesia: 20fr, Woman on the Beach, by Yves de Saint-Front. 40fr, Abstract, by Frank Fay. 60fr, Woman and Shells, by Jean Guillois. 80fr, Hut under Palms, by Jean Masson. 100fr, Polynesian Girl, by Jean-Charles Bouloc (vert.).

Perf. 12x12½, 12½x12

1970, Dec. 14 Photogravure

C63	AP20	20fr brn & multi	5.25	4.50
C64	AP20	40fr brn & multi	9.00	6.75
C65	AP20	60fr brn & multi	13.00	9.00
C66	AP20	80fr brn & multi	19.00	13.00
C67	AP20	100fr brn & multi	27.50	22.50
		Nos. C63-C67 (5)	73.75	55.75

South Pacific Games Emblem AP28

1971, Jan. 26 ***Perf. 12½***

C68	AP28	20fr ultra & multi	5.50	4.50

Publicity for 4th South Pacific Games, held in Papeete, Sept. 8-19, 1971.

Memorial Flame
AP29

1971, March 19 **Photo.** ***Perf. 12½***

C69	AP29	5fr multi	3.75	2.25

In memory of Charles de Gaulle.

Soldier and Badge—AP30

1971, Apr. 21

C70	AP30	25fr multi	7.50	6.00

30th anniversary of departure of Tahitian volunteers to serve in World War II.

Water Sports Type of Regular Issue

Designs: 15fr, Surfing (vert.). 16fr, Skin diving (vert.). 20fr, Water-skiing with kite.

1971, May 11 **Photo.** ***Perf. 13***

C71	A44	15fr multi	3.75	2.25
C72	A44	16fr multi	4.50	3.00
C73	A44	20fr multi	6.75	5.25

Sailing
AP31

Designs: 18fr, Golf. 27fr, Archery. 53fr, Tennis.

1971, Sept. 8 ***Perf. 12½***

C74	AP31	15fr multi	2.25	1.50
C75	AP31	18fr multi	3.00	2.25
C76	AP31	27fr multi	6.00	4.50
C77	AP31	53fr multi	9.50	6.75
a.		Souvenir sheet of 4	47.50	47.50

4th South Pacific Games, Papeete, Sept. 8-19. No. C77a contains one each of Nos. C74-C77. Black marginal inscription. Size: 136x169mm.

Painting Type of 1968

Paintings by Artists Living in Polynesia: 20fr, Hut and Palms, by Isabelle Wolf. 40fr, Palms on Shore, by André Dobrowolski. 60fr, Polynesian Woman, by Françoise Séli (vert.). 80fr, Holy Family, by Pierre Heymann (vert.). 100fr, Crowd, by Nicolai Michoutouchkine.

1971, Dec. 15 **Photo.** ***Perf. 13***

C78	AP20	20fr multi	4.50	3.75
C79	AP20	40fr multi	8.25	6.00
C80	AP20	60fr multi	13.00	9.00
C81	AP20	80fr multi	16.00	11.00
C82	AP20	100fr multi	27.50	22.50
		Nos. C78-C82 (5)	69.25	52.25

Papeete Harbor—AP32

1972, Jan. 13

C83	AP32	28fr vio & multi	7.50	6.00

Free port of Papeete, 10th anniversary.

Figure Skating and Dragon
AP33

1972, Jan. 25 **Engraved** ***Perf. 13***

C84	AP33	20fr ultra, lake & brt grn	7.00	5.00

11th Winter Olympic Games, Sapporo, Japan, Feb. 3-13.

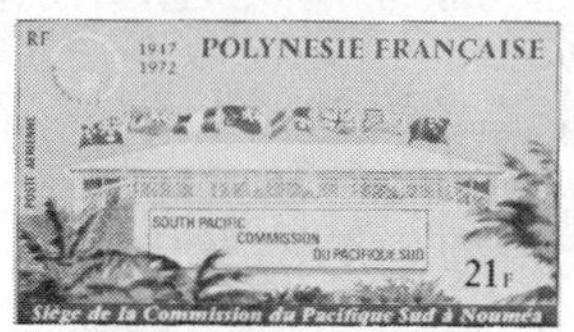

South Pacific Commission Headquarters, Noumea—AP34

1972, Feb. 5 **Photogravure** ***Perf. 13***

C85	AP34	21fr bl & multi	6.50	3.00

South Pacific Commission, 25th anniversary.

Festival Emblem
AP35

1972, May 9 **Engr.** ***Perf. 13***

C86	AP35	36fr org, bl & grn	6.75	5.25

South Pacific Festival of Arts, Fiji, May 6-20.

Kon Tiki and Route, Callao to Tahiti—AP36

1972, Aug. 18 **Photo.** ***Perf. 13***

C87	AP36	16fr dk & lt bl, blk & org	5.25	3.00

25th anniversary of the arrival of the raft Kon Tiki in Tahiti.

Charles de Gaulle and Memorial
AP37

1972, Dec. 9 **Engraved** ***Perf. 13***

C88	AP37	100fr slate	30.00	26.00

Gen. Charles de Gaulle (1890-1970), president of France.

Painting Type of 1968

Paintings by Artists Living in Polynesia; 20fr, Horses, by Georges Bovy. 40fr, Sailboats, by Ruy Juventin (vert.). 60fr, Harbor, by André Brooke. 80fr, Farmers, by Daniel Adam (vert.). 100fr, Dancers, by Aloysius Pilioko (vert.).

1972, Dec. 14 **Photogravure**

C89	AP20	20fr gold & multi	4.50	3.00
C90	AP20	40fr gold & multi	7.50	4.50
C91	AP20	60fr gold & multi	12.50	7.50
C92	AP20	80fr dk grn, buff & dk brn	19.00	10.50
C93	AP20	100fr gold & multi	24.00	19.00
		Nos. C89-C93 (5)	67.50	44.50

St. Teresa and Lisieux Basilica
AP38

1973, Jan. 23 **Engraved** ***Perf. 13***

C94	AP38	85fr multi	20.00	15.00

Centenary of the birth of St. Teresa of Lisieux (1873-1897), Carmelite nun.

Nicolaus Copernicus—AP39

1973, Mar. 7 **Engraved** ***Perf. 13***

C95	AP39	100fr brn, vio bl & red lil	20.00	15.00

500th anniversary of the birth of Nicolaus Copernicus (1473-1543), Polish astronomer.

Plane over Tahiti—AP40

1973, Apr. 3 **Photo.** ***Perf. 13***

C96	AP40	80fr ultra, gold & lt grn	18.00	13.00

Air France's World Tour via Tahiti.

DC-10 at Papeete Airport—AP41

1973, May 18 **Engraved** ***Perf. 13***

C97	AP41	20fr bl, ultra & sl grn	7.50	3.75

Start of DC-10 service.

Painting Type of 1968

Design: 200fr, "Ta Matete" (seated women), by Paul Gauguin.

1973, June 7 **Photo.** ***Perf. 13***

C98	AP20	200fr multi	22.50	19.00

70th anniversary of the death of Paul Gauguin (1848-1903), painter.

Pierre Loti and Characters from his Books—AP42

1973, July 4 **Engraved** ***Perf. 13***

C99	AP42	60fr multi	16.00	11.00

50th anniversary of the death of Pierre Loti (1850-1923), French naval officer and writer.

"Sun," by Jean Francois Favre
AP43

Paintings by Artists Living in Polynesia: 40fr, Woman with Flowers, by Eliane de Gennes. 60fr, Seascape, by Alain Sidet. 80fr, Crowded Bus, by Francois Ravello. 100fr, Stylized Boats, by Jackie Bourdin (horiz.).

1973, Dec. 13 **Photo.** ***Perf. 13***

C100	AP43	20fr gold & multi	3.00	2.25
C101	AP43	40fr gold & multi	6.75	3.75
C102	AP43	60fr gold & multi	9.00	6.75
C103	AP43	80fr gold & multi	15.00	12.00
C104	AP43	100fr gold & multi	22.50	16.00
		Nos. C100-C104 (5)	56.25	40.75

Bird, Fish, Flower and Water
AP44

1974, June 12 Photo. *Perf. 13*

C105	AP44	12fr bl & multi	5.50	2.50

Nature protection.

Catamaran under Sail
AP45

1974, July 22 Engraved *Perf. 13*

C106	AP45	100fr multi	16.00	12.00

2nd Catamaran World Championships.

Still-life, by Rosine Temarui-Masson
AP46

Paintings by Artists Living in Polynesia: 40fr, Palms and House on Beach, by Marcel Chardon. 60fr, Man, by Marie-Françoise Avril. 80fr, Polynesian Woman, by Henriette Robin. 100fr, Lagoon by Moonlight, by David Farsi (horiz.).

1974, Dec. 12 Photogravure *Perf. 13*

C107	AP46	20fr gold & multi	4.50	2.25
C108	AP46	40fr gold & multi	6.75	3.75
C109	AP46	60fr gold & multi	11.00	6.00
C110	AP46	80fr gold & multi	18.00	9.00
C111	AP46	100fr gold & multi	27.50	16.00
		Nos. C107-C111 (5)	67.75	37.00

See also Nos. C122–C126.

Polynesian Gods of Travel—AP47

Designs: 75fr, Tourville hydroplane, 1929. 100fr, Passengers leaving plane.

1975, Feb. 7 Engraved *Perf. 13*

C112	AP47	50fr sep, pur & brn	5.25	3.75
C113	AP47	75fr grn, bl & red	7.50	5.25
C114	AP47	100fr grn, sep & car	12.50	9.00

Fifty years of Tahitian aviation.

French Ceres Stamp and Woman
AP48

1975, May 29 Engr. *Perf. 13*

C115	AP48	32fr ver, brn & blk	3.50	3.75

ARPHILA 75 International Philatelic Exhibition, Paris, June 6–16.

Shot Put and Games' Emblem
AP50

Designs: 30fr, Volleyball. 40fr, Women's swimming.

1975, Aug. 1 Photo. *Perf. 13*

C117	AP50	25fr dk red & multi	3.00	2.25
C118	AP50	30fr emer & multi	3.75	2.25
C119	AP50	40fr vio bl & multi	5.25	3.75

5th South Pacific Games, Guam, Aug. 1–10.

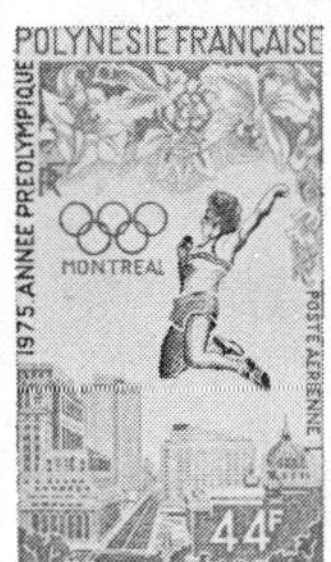

Flowers, Athlete, View of Montreal
AP51

1975, Oct. 15 Engr. *Perf. 13*

C120	AP51	44fr brt bl, ver & blk	6.00	3.75

Pre-Olympic Year 1975.

U.P.U. Emblem, Jet and Letters—AP52

1975, Nov. 5 Engr. *Perf. 13*

C121	AP52	100fr brn, bl & ol	12.50	9.00

World Universal Postal Union Day.

Paintings Type of 1974

Paintings by Artists Living in Polynesia: 20fr, Beach Scene, by R. Marcel Marius (horiz.). 40fr, Roofs with TV antennas, by M. Anglade (horiz.). 60fr, Street scene with bus, by J. Day (horiz.). 80fr, Tropical waters (fish), by J. Steimetz. 100fr, Women, by A. van der Heyde.

1975, Dec. 17 Litho. *Perf. 13*

C122	AP46	20fr gold & multi	2.25	1.50
C123	AP46	40fr gold & multi	3.00	1.90
C124	AP46	60fr gold & multi	5.25	3.25
C125	AP46	80fr gold & multi	9.00	6.00
C126	AP46	100fr gold & multi	12.00	7.50
		Nos. C122-C126 (5)	31.50	20.15

Concorde—AP53

1976, Jan. 21 Engr. *Perf. 13*

C127	AP53	100fr car, bl & ind	15.00	11.00

First commercial flight of supersonic jet Concorde from Paris to Rio de Janeiro, Jan. 21.

Adm. Rodney, Count de la Perouse, "Barfleur" and "Triomphant" in Battle—AP54

Design: 31fr, Count de Grasse and Lord Graves, "Ville de Paris" and "Le Teribie" in Chesapeake Bay Battle.

1976, Apr. 15 Engr. *Perf. 13*

C128	AP54	24fr grnsh bl, lt brn & blk	3.00	1.90
C129	AP54	31fr mag, red & lt brn	3.75	2.25

American Bicentennial.

King Pomaré I
AP55

Portraits: 21fr, King Pomaré II. 26fr, Queen Pomaré IV. 30fr, King Pomaré V.

1976, Apr. 28 Litho. *Perf. 12½*

C130	AP55	18fr ol & multi	1.10	60
C131	AP55	21fr multi	1.50	90
C132	AP55	26fr gray & multi	1.90	1.10
C133	AP55	30fr plum & multi	2.25	1.50

Pomaré Dynasty. See Nos. C141–C144.

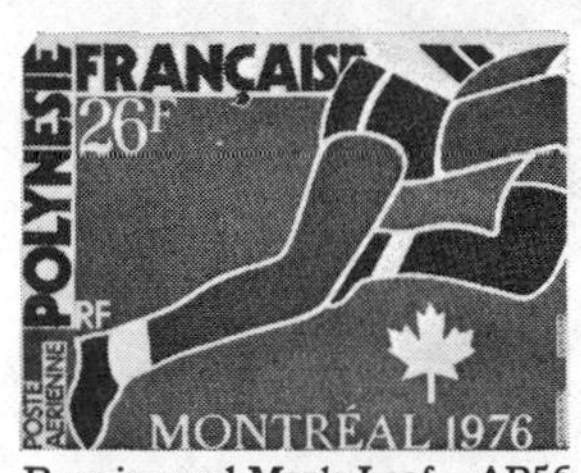

Running and Maple Leaf—AP56

Designs: 34fr, Long jump (vert.). 50fr, Olympic flame and flowers.

1976, July 19 Engr. *Perf. 13*

C134	AP56	26fr ultra & multi	2.50	1.90
C135	AP56	34fr ultra & multi	3.25	2.50
C136	AP56	50fr ultra & multi	6.00	4.50
a.		Miniature sheet of 3	26.00	26.00

21st Olympic Games, Montreal, Canada, July 17–Aug. 1. No. C136a contains one each of Nos. C134–C136. Size: 180x100 mm.

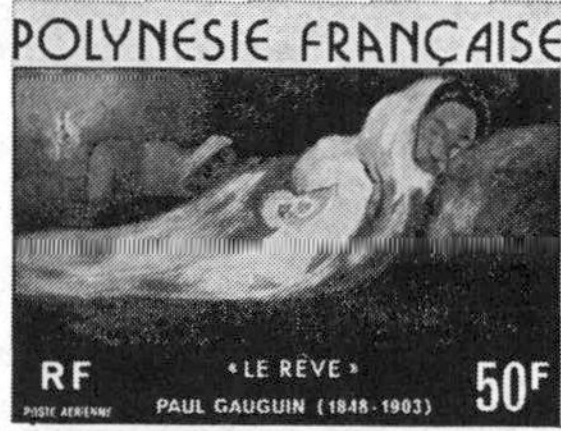

The Dream, by Paul Gauguin—AP57

1976, Oct. 17 Photo. *Perf. 13*

C137	AP57	50fr multi	6.50	4.50

Murex Steeriae
AP58

Pocillopora
AP59

Sea Shells: 27fr, Conus Gauguini. 35fr, Conus marchionatus.

1977, Mar. 14 Photo. *Perf. 12½x13*

C138	AP58	25fr vio bl & multi	1.50	85
C139	AP58	27fr ultra & multi	1.90	95
C140	AP58	35fr bl & multi	2.50	1.25

See Nos. C156–C158.

Royalty Type of 1976

Portraits: 19fr, King Maputeoa, Mangareva. 33fr, King Camatoa V, Raiatea. 39fr, Queen Vaekehu, Marquesas. 43fr, King Teurarii III, Rurutu.

1977, Apr. 19 Litho. *Perf. 12½*

C141	AP55	19fr dl red & multi	95	70
C142	AP55	33fr dk bl & multi	1.25	95
C143	AP55	39fr ultra & multi	1.50	1.10
C144	AP55	43fr grn & multi	1.90	1.40

Polynesian rulers.

Perf. 13x12½, 12½x13

1977, May 23 Photogravure

Design: 25fr, Acropora (horiz.).

C145	AP59	25fr multi	1.40	75
C146	AP59	33fr multi	2.00	1.10

3rd Symposium on Coral Reefs, Miami, Fla. See Nos. C162–C163.

De Gaulle Memorial
AP60

Tahitian Dancer
AP61

Photogravure and Embossed

1977, June 18 *Perf. 13*

C147 AP60 40fr gold & multi 3.25 2.50

5th anniversary of dedication of De Gaulle memorial at Colombey-les-Deux-Eglises.

1977, July 14 Litho. *Perf. 12½*

C148 AP61 27fr multi 1.90 95

Charles A. Lindbergh and Spirit of St. Louis—AP62

1977, Aug. 18 Litho. *Perf. 12½*

C149 AP62 28fr multi 3.00 2.25

Charles A. Lindbergh's solo transatlantic flight from New York to Paris, 50th anniversary.

Mahoe AP63 — Palms on Shore AP64

Design: 12fr, Frangipani.

1977, Sept. 15 Photo. *Perf. 12½x13*

C150 AP63 8fr multi 52 38
C151 AP63 12fr multi 75 52

1977, Nov. 8 Photo. *Perf. 12½x13*

C152 AP64 32fr multi 3.00 1.90

Ecology, protection of trees.

Rubens' Son Albert AP65

1977, Nov. 28 Engr. *Perf. 13*

C153 AP65 100fr grnsh blk & rose cl 7.50 6.00

Peter Paul Rubens (1577–1640), painter, 400th birth anniversary.

Capt. Cook and "Discovery"—AP66

Design: 39fr, Capt. Cook and "Resolution."

1978, Jan. 20 Engr. *Perf. 13*

C154 AP66 33fr multi 2.25 1.50
C155 AP66 39fr multi 3.00 1.90

Bicentenary of Capt. James Cook's arrival in Hawaii.

Shell Type of 1977

Sea Shells: 22fr, Erosaria obvelata. 24fr, Cypraea ventriculus. 31fr, Lambis robusta.

1978, Apr. 13 Photo. *Perf. 13½x13*

C156 AP58 22fr brt bl & multi 1.40 75
C157 AP58 24fr brt bl & multi 1.50 75
C158 AP58 31fr brt bl & multi 2.00 1.10

Tahitian Woman and Boy, by Gauguin AP67

1978, May 7 *Perf. 13*

C159 AP67 50fr multi 5.25 3.75

Paul Gauguin (1848–1903), 75th death anniversary.

Antenna and ITU Emblem AP68

1978, May 17 Litho. *Perf. 13*

C160 AP68 80fr gray & multi 5.25 3.75

10th World Telecommunications Day.

Soccer and Argentina '78 Emblem AP69

1978, June 1

C161 AP69 28fr multi 1.90 1.40

11th World Cup Soccer Championship, Argentina, June 1–25.

Coral Type of 1977

Designs: 26fr, Fungia (horiz.). 34fr, Millepora.

Perf. 13x12½, 12½x13

1978, July 13 **Photogravure**

C162 AP59 26fr multi 1.10 85
C163 AP59 34fr multi 1.50 95

Radar Antenna, Polynesian Woman AP70

1978, Sept. 5 Engr. *Perf. 13*

C164 AP70 50fr bl & blk 3.00 2.25

Papenoo earth station.

Bird and Rainbow over Island—AP71

1978, Oct. 5 **Photogravure**

C165 AP71 23fr multi 1.65 1.00

Nature protection.

Nos. C154-C155 Overprinted in Black or Violet Blue:
' "1779–1979" / BICENTENAIRE / DE LA / MORT DE'

1979, Feb. 14 Engr. *Perf. 13*

C166 AP66 33fr multi 2.00 1.10
C167 AP66 39fr multi (VBl) 2.50 1.90

Bicentenary of Capt. Cook's death. On No. C167 date is last line of overprint.

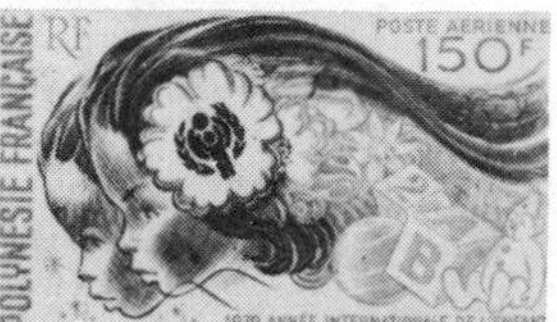

Children, Toys and IYC Emblem AP72

1979, May 3 Engr. *Perf. 13*

C168 AP72 150fr multi 7.50 6.00

International Year of the Child.

"Do you expect a letter?" by Paul Gauguin—AP73

1979, May 20 Photo. *Perf. 13*

C169 AP73 200fr multi 9.50 7.50

Shell and Carved Head—AP74

1979, June 30 Engr. *Perf. 13*

C170 AP74 44fr multi 2.25 1.90

Museum of Tahiti and the Islands.

See "Special Notices" at the front of this volume for data on the listing methods of this Catalogue, abbreviations, condition, prices and examination.

Conference Emblem over Island AP75

1979, Oct. 6 Photo. *Perf. 13*

C171 AP75 23fr multi 1.50 1.00

19th South Pacific Conference, Tahiti, Oct. 6–12.

Flying Boat "Bermuda"—AP76

Planes Used in Polynesia: 40fr, DC-4 over Papeete. 60fr, Britten-Norman "Islander." 80fr, Fairchild F-27A. 120fr, DC-8 over Tahiti.

1979, Dec. 19 Litho. *Perf. 13*

C172 AP76 24fr multi 90 60
C173 AP76 40fr multi 1.50 1.10
C174 AP76 60fr multi 2.50 1.65
C175 AP76 80fr multi 3.25 2.25
C176 AP76 120fr multi 5.25 3.25
Nos. C172-C176 (5) 13.40 8.85

See Nos. C180-C183.

Window on Tahiti, by Henri Matisse AP77

1980, Feb. 18 **Photo.**

C177 AP77 150fr multi 6.00 4.50

Marshi Metua No Tehamana, by Gauguin—AP78

1980, Aug. 18 Photo. *Perf. 13*

C178 AP78 500fr multi 16.00 12.50

Sydpex '80, Philatelic Exhibition, Sydney Town Hall—AP79

1980, Sept. 29 Photo. *Perf. 13*

C179 AP79 70fr multi 3.00 2.25

Aviation Type of 1979

1980, Dec. 15 Litho. *Perf. 13*

C180 AP76 15fr *Catalina* 45 45
C181 AP76 26fr *Twin Otter* 75 60
C182 AP76 30fr *CAMS 55* 1.00 75
C183 AP76 50fr *DC-6* 1.50 1.25

And The Gold of their Bodies, by Gauguin—AP80

1981, Mar. 15 Photo. *Perf. 13*

C184 AP80 100fr multi 3.25 2.25

20th Anniv. of Manned Space Flight—AP81

1981, June 13 Litho. *Perf. 12½*

C185 AP81 300fr multi 7.00 5.50

First Intl. Pirogue (6-man Canoe) Championship—AP82

1981, July 25 Litho. *Perf. 13x12½*

C186 AP82 200fr multi 5.50 4.50

Matavai Bay, by William Hodges—AP83

Paintings: 60fr, Poedea, by John Weber (vert.). 80fr, Omai, by Joshua Reynolds (vert.). 120fr, Point Venus, by George Tobin.

1981, Dec. 10 Photo. *Perf. 13*

C187 AP83 40fr multi 90 75
C188 AP83 60fr multi 1.40 1.10
C189 AP83 80fr multi 2.00 1.50
C190 AP83 120fr multi 2.75 2.25

See. Nos. C194-C197, C202-C205.

TB Bacillus Centenary—AP84

1982, Mar. 24 Engr. *Perf. 13*

C191 AP84 200fr multi 4.50 3.25

1982 World Cup—AP85

1982, May 18 Litho. *Perf. 13*

C192 AP85 250fr multi 6.75 5.25

French Overseas Possessions' Week, Sept. 18-25—AP86

1982, Sept. 17 Engr.

C193 AP86 110fr multi 2.50 1.90

Painting Type of 1981

Designs: 50fr, The Tahitian, by M. Radiguet (vert.). 70fr, Souvenir of Tahiti, by C. Giraud. 100fr, Beating Cloth Lengths, by Atlas JL the Younger. 160fr, Papeete Harbor, by C.F. Gordon Cumming.

1982, Dec. 15 Photo. *Perf. 13*

C194 AP83 50fr multi 1.10 75
C195 AP83 70fr multi 1.50 1.10
C196 AP83 100fr multi 2.25 1.90
C197 AP83 160fr multi 3.75 2.50

Wood Cutter, by Gauguin—AP87

1983, May 8 Photo. & Engr. *Perf. 12½x13*

C198 AP87 600fr multi 11.00 9.00

Voyage of Capt. Bligh—AP88

1983, June 9 Litho. *Perf. 13*

C199 AP88 200fr Map, fruit 4.00 3.00

BRASILIANA '83 Intl. Stamp Exhibition, Rio de Janeiro, July 29—Aug. 7—AP89

1983, July 29 Litho. *Perf. 13x12½*

C200 AP89 100fr multi 2.25 1.75
a. Souvenir sheet 2.75 2.75

Size of No. C200a: 132x93mm.

1983, Aug. 4 Litho. *Perf. 13x12½*

C201 AP89 110fr Bangkok '83 2.25 1.75
a. Souvenir sheet 3.00 3.00

Size of No. C201a:93x132mm.

Painting Type of 1981

20th Century Paintings: 40fr, View of Moorea, by William Alister MacDonald (1861-1956). 60fr, The Fruit Carrier, by Adrian Herman Gouwe (1875-1965, vert.). 80fr, Arrival of the Destroyer Escort, by Nicolas Mordvinoff (1911-1977, vert.). 100fr, Women on a Veranda, by Charles Alfred Le Moine (1872-1918).

1983, Dec. 22 Photo. *Perf. 13*

C202 AP83 40fr multi 75 60
C203 AP83 60fr multi 1.10 90
C204 AP83 80fr multi 1.50 1.10
C205 AP83 100fr multi 2.25 1.50

ESPANA '84—AP90

Design: Maori canoers.

1984, Apr. 27 Engr. *Perf. 13*

C206 AP90 80fr brn red & dk bl 1.75 1.40

Souvenir Sheet

C207 AP90 200fr dk bl & dk red 5.25 5.25

Margin of No. C207 continues design. Size: 144x101mm.

Woman with Mango, by Gauguin—AP91

1984, May 27 Photo. & Engr. *Perf. 12½x13*

C208 AP91 400fr multi 7.50 6.00

Ausipex '84—AP92

Details from Human Sacrifice of the Maori in Tahiti, 18th cent. engraving.

1984, Sept. 5 Litho. *Perf. 13x12½*

C209 AP92 120fr Worshippers 3.25 2.25
C210 AP92 120fr Preparation 3.25 2.25

Souvenir Sheet

C211 AP92 200fr Entire 9.00 9.00

Nos. C209-C210 se-tenant with label showing exhibition emblem. Size of No. C211: 128x94mm.

Painting by Gaugin (1848-1903)—AP93

Design: Where have we come from? What are we? Where are we going?

1985, Mar. 17 Litho. *Perf. 13½x13*

C212 AP93 550fr multi 9.00 7.50

No. C212 printed se-tenant with label showing self-portrait.

4th Pacific Arts Festival, Type of 1984

1985, July 3 Litho. *Perf. 13*

C213 A95 200fr Islander, tiki, artifacts 3.25 2.25

Intl. Youth Year—AP95

1985, Sept. 18 **Litho.**

C214	AP95	250fr Island youths, frigate bird	4.00	3.00

ITALIA '85—AP96

Design: Ship sailing into Papeete Harbor, 19th century print.

1985, Oct. 22 **Engr.**

C215	AP96	130fr multi	2.25	1.75

Souvenir Sheet

C216	AP96	240fr multi	4.00	2.00

No. C216 has multicolored margin continuing the design and picturing the exhibition emblem.

1st Intl. Marlin Fishing Contest, Feb. 27-Mar. 5—AP97

1986, Feb. 27 **Litho.** ***Perf. 12½***

C217	AP97	300fr multi	5.25	3.25

Arrival of a Boat, c. 1880—AP98

1986, June 24 **Engr.** ***Perf. 13***

C218	AP98	400fr int bl	6.75	4.50

STOCKHOLMIA '86—AP99

Design: Dr. Karl Solander and Anders Sparrmann, Swedish scientists who accompanied Capt. Cook, and map of Tahiti.

1986, Aug. 28 **Engr.** ***Perf. 13***

C219	AP99	150fr brt bl, dk bl & emer grn	2.50	2.25

Souvenir Sheet

C220	AP99	210fr brt ultra, Prus bl & emer grn	4.50	4.50

STOCKHOLMIA '86, Aug. 28-Sept. 7. No. 448 has bright ultramarine and emerald green margin picturing sea chart. Size: 143x106mm.

Protestant Churches—AP100

1986, Dec. 17 **Litho.** ***Perf. 13***

C221	AP100	80fr Tiva, 1955	1.20	90
C222	AP100	200fr Avera, 1880	3.00	2.25
C223	AP100	300fr Papetoai, 1822	4.50	3.40

AIR POST SEMI-POSTAL STAMP.

French Revolution Issue
Common Design Type
Photogravure.

1939, July 5 *Perf. 13* Unwmkd.
Name and Value Typo. in Orange.

CB1	CD83	5fr +4fr brn blk	14.00	14.00

V5

Stamps of the above design and of Cameroun type V10 inscribed "Etabts Frcais de l'Océanie" were issued in 1942 by the Vichy Government, but were not placed on sale in the colony.

POSTAGE DUE STAMPS.

Postage Due Stamps of French Colonies, 1894-1906, Overprinted

Établissements
Français

de l'Océanie

1926-27 *Perf. 14x13½* Unwmkd.

J1	D1	5c lt bl	25	25
J2	D1	10c brown	40	40
J3	D1	20c ol grn	60	60
J4	D1	30c dl red	60	60
J5	D1	40c rose	1.25	1.25
J6	D1	60c bl grn	90	90
J7	D1	1fr red brn, *straw*	1.10	1.10
J8	D1	3fr mag ('27)	5.25	5.25

With Additional Surcharge of New Value

J9	D1	2fr on 1fr org red	1.75	1.75
		Nos. J1-J9 (9)	12.10	12.10

Fautaua Falls, Tahiti
D2

Tahitian Youth
D3

1929 Typographed *Perf. 13½x14*

J10	D2	5c lt bl & dk brn	42	42
J11	D2	10c ver & grn	42	42
J12	D2	30c dk brn & dk red	90	90
J13	D2	50c yel grn & dk brn	42	42
J14	D2	60c dl vio & yel grn	2.00	2.00
J15	D3	1fr Prus bl & red vio	90	90
J16	D3	2fr brn red & dk brn	60	60
J17	D3	3fr bl vio & bl grn	90	90
		Nos. J10-J17 (8)	6.56	6.56

D4

Polynesian Club
D5

1948 Engraved. *Perf. 14x13.*

J18	D4	10c brt bl grn	6	6
J19	D4	30c blk brn	6	6
J20	D4	50c dk car rose	6	6
J21	D4	1fr ultra	25	25
J22	D4	2fr dk bl grn	52	52
J23	D4	3fr red	75	75
J24	D4	4fr violet	85	85
J25	D4	5fr lil rose	1.00	1.00
J26	D4	10fr slate	2.00	2.00
J27	D4	20fr red brn	2.75	2.75
		Nos. J18-J27 (10)	8.30	8.30

1958 *Perf. 14x13* Unwmkd.

J28	D5	1fr dk brn & grn	30	30
J29	D5	3fr bluish blk & hn brn	45	45
J30	D5	5fr brn & ultra	75	75

Tahitian Bowl—D6

1984, Mar. 16 Litho. *Perf. 13*

J31	D6	1fr Mother-of-pearl fish hook, vert.	5	5
J32	D6	3fr shown	6	5
J33	D6	5fr Marquesan fan	15	15
J34	D6	10fr Lamp stand, vert.	22	22

Unused Prices
Catalogue prices for unused stamps through 1960 are for hinged copies in fine condition.

See "Special Notices" at the front of this volume for data on the listing methods of this Catalogue, abbreviations, condition, prices and examination.

OFFICIAL STAMPS

Bread-fruit
O1

Polynesian Fruits: 2fr, 3fr, 5fr, like 1fr. 7fr, 8fr, 10fr, 15fr, "Vi Tahiti." 19fr, 20fr, 25fr, 35fr, Avocados. 50fr, 100fr, 200fr, Mangos.

1977, June 9 Litho. *Perf. 12½*

O1	O1	1fr ultra & multi	5	5
O2	O1	2fr ultra & multi	6	6
O3	O1	3fr ultra & multi	8	8
O4	O1	5fr ultra & multi	12	12
O5	O1	7fr red & multi	18	18
O6	O1	8fr red & multi	18	18
O7	O1	10fr red & multi	22	22
O8	O1	15fr red & multi	30	30
O9	O1	19fr blk & multi	45	45
O10	O1	20fr blk & multi	45	45
O11	O1	25fr blk & multi	52	52
O12	O1	35fr blk & multi	70	70
O13	O1	50fr blk & multi	90	90
O14	O1	100fr red & multi	2.75	2.75
O15	O1	200fr ultra & multi	6.25	6.25
		Nos. O1-O15 (15)	13.21	13.21

FRENCH SOUTHERN and ANTARCTIC TERRITORIES

AREA—9,000 sq. mi.
POP.—168 (1983).

Formerly dependencies of Madagascar, these areas, comprising the Kerguelen Archipelago; St. Paul, Amsterdam and Crozet Islands and Adelle Land in Antarctica achieved territorial status on August 6, 1955.

100 Centimes = 1 Franc

Madagascar No. 289 Overprinted in Red:

TERRES AUSTRALES ET
ANTARCTIQUES FRANÇAISES

Engraved.

1955, Oct. 28 *Perf. 13* Unwmkd.

1	A25	15f dk grn & dp ultra	21.00	26.00

Rockhopper Penguins, Crozet Archipelago—A1

New Amsterdam
A2

Design: 10fr, 15fr, Elephant seal.

1956, Apr. 25 Engr. *Perf. 13*

2	A1	50c dk bl, sep & yel	45	52
3	A1	1fr ultra, org & gray	45	52
4	A2	5fr bl & dp ultra	1.65	1.75
5	A2	8fr gray vio & dk brn	12.50	13.00
6	A2	10fr indigo	3.50	3.75
7	A2	15fr ind & brn vio	3.75	4.00
		Nos. 2-7 (6)	22.30	23.54

Polar Observation
A3

1957, Oct. 11

8	A3	5fr blk & vio	4.50	4.50
9	A3	10fr rose red	5.00	5.00
10	A3	15fr dk bl	5.00	5.00

International Geophysical Year, 1957–58.

Imperforates

Most stamps of this French possession exist imperforate in issued and trial colors, and also in small presentation sheets in issued colors.

Flower Issue
Common Design Type
Design: Pringlea (horiz.).

1959 Photogravure. *Perf. 12½x12*

11	CD104	10fr sal, grn & yel	4.50	5.25

Common Design Types
pictured in section at front of book.

Light-mantled Sooty Albatross
A4

Coat of Arms
A5

Designs: 40c, Skua (horiz.). 12fr, King shag.

1959, Sept. 14 Engraved. *Perf. 13*

12	A4	30c bl, grn & red brn	52	52
13	A4	40c blk, dl red brn & bl	52	52
14	A4	12fr lt bl & blk	9.50	9.50

Typographed
Perf. 13x14

15	A5	20fr ultra, lt bl & yel	19.00	19.00

Sheathbills
A6

Designs: 4fr, Sea leopard (horiz.). 25fr, Weddell seal at Kerguélen (horiz.). 85fr, King penguin.

1960, Dec. 15 Engraved *Perf. 13*

16	A6	2fr grnsh bl, gray & choc	1.25	1.25
17	A6	4fr bl, dk brn & dk grn	4.50	4.50
18	A6	25fr sl grn, bis brn & blk	40.00	30.00
19	A6	85fr grnsh bl, org & blk	24.00	24.00

Yves-Joseph de Kerguélen-Trémarec—A7

1960, Nov. 22

20	A7	25fr red org, dk bl & brn	22.50	22.50

Issued to honor Yves-Joseph de Kerguélen-Trémarec, discoverer of the Kerguélen Archipelago.

Charcot, Compass Rose and "Pourquoi-pas?"
A8

1961, Dec. 26 *Perf. 13* Unwmkd.

21	A8	25fr brn, grn & red	22.50	22.50

25th anniv. of the death of Commander Jean Charcot (1867-1936), Antarctic explorer.

Elephant Seals Fighting
A9

1963, Feb. 11 Engraved *Perf. 13*

22	A9	8fr dk bl, blk & cl	7.50	7.50

See No. C4.

Penguins and Camp on Crozet Island
A10

Design: 20fr, Research station and IQSY emblem.

1963, Dec. 16 *Perf. 13* Unwmkd.

23	A10	5fr blk, red brn & Prus bl	30.00	22.50
24	A10	20fr vio, sl & red brn	67.50	65.00

Issued to publicize the International Quiet Sun Year, 1964–65. See No. C6.

Great Blue Whale
A11

Black-browed Albatross
A12

Aurora Australis, Map of Antarctica and Rocket
A13

Designs: 10fr, Cape pigeons. 12fr, Phylica trees, Amsterdam Island. 15fr, Killer whale (orca).

1966–69 Engraved *Perf. 13*

25	A11	5fr brt bl & ind	7.50	7.50
26	A12	10fr sl, ind & ol brn ('69)	30.00	27.50
27	A11	12fr brt bl, sl grn & lem ('69)	15.00	12.00
27A	A11	15fr ol, dk bl & ind ('69)	7.50	7.50
28	A12	20fr sl, ol & org ('68)	425.00	350.00
		Nos. 25-28 (5)	485.00	404.50

Issue dates: 5fr, Dec. 12, 1966; 20fr, Jan. 31, 1968; 10fr, 12fr, Jan. 6, 1969; 15fr, Dec. 21, 1969.

1967, March 4 Engraved *Perf. 13*

29	A13	20fr mag, bl & blk	30.00	27.50

Issued to commemorate the launching of the first space rocket from Adelie Land, January, 1967.

Dumont d'Urville
A14

1968, Jan. 20

30	A14	30fr lt ultra, dk bl & dk brn	125.00	110.00

Jules Sébastien César Dumont D'Urville (1790–1842), French naval commander and South Seas explorer.

WHO Anniversary Issue
Common Design Type

1968, May 4 Engraved *Perf. 13*

31	CD126	30fr red, yel & bl	60.00	52.50

Issued for the 20th anniversary of the World Health Organization.

Human Rights Year Issue
Common Design Type

1968, Aug. 10 Engraved *Perf. 13*

32	CD127	30fr grnsh bl, red & brn	60.00	52.50

Polar Camp with Helicopter, Plane and Snocat Tractor
A15

1969, Mar. 17 Engraved *Perf. 13*

33	A15	25fr Prus bl, lt grnsh bl & brn red	19.00	15.00

20 years of French Polar expeditions.

ILO Issue
Common Design Type

1970, Jan. 1 Engraved *Perf. 13*

35	CD131	20fr org, dk bl & brn	16.00	12.50

U.P.U. Headquarters Issue
Common Design Type

1970, May 20 Engraved *Perf. 13*

36	CD133	50fr bl, plum & ol bis	32.50	27.50

Ice Fish—A16

Fish: Nos. 38–43, Antarctic cods, various species. 135fr, Zanchlorhynchus spinifer.

1971 Engraved *Perf. 13*

37	A16	5fr brt grn, ind & org	75	75
38	A16	10fr redsh brn & dp vio	90	90
39	A16	20fr dp cl, brt grn & org	1.40	1.40
40	A16	22fr pur, brn ol & mag	2.25	1.50
41	A16	25fr grn, ind & org	2.25	2.25
42	A16	30fr sep, gray & bl vio	3.75	3.75
43	A16	35fr sl grn, dk brn & ocher	3.00	2.25
44	A16	135fr Prus bl, dp org & ol grn	5.25	4.50
		Nos. 37-44 (8)	19.55	17.30

Issue dates: Nos. 37–39, 41–42, Jan. 1; Nos. 40, 43–44, Dec. 22.

Map of Antarctica
A17

TERRES AUSTRALES ET ANTARCTIQUES FRANÇAISES
MICROZETIA MIRABILIS
25F
POSTES

Microzetia Mirabilis
A18

1971, Dec. 22

45	A17	75fr red	32.50	32.50

Tenth anniversary of the Antarctic Treaty pledging peaceful uses of and scientific co-operation in Antarctica.

1972

Insects: 15fr, Christiansenia dreuxi. 22f, Phtirocoris antarcticus. 30fr, Antarctophytosus atriceps. 40fr, Paractora drenxi. 140fr, Pringleophaga Kerguelenensis.

46	A18	15fr cl, org & brn	3.00	2.25
47	A18	22fr vio bl, sl grn & yel	3.00	2.25
48	A18	25fr grn, rose lil & pur	3.00	2.50
49	A18	30fr bl & multi	3.75	3.00
50	A18	40fr dk brn, ocher & blk	3.00	2.50
51	A18	140fr bl, emer & brn	7.50	7.50
		Nos. 46-51 (6)	23.25	20.00

Issue dates: Nos. 48, 50–51, Jan. 3; Nos. 46–47, 49, Dec. 16.

De Gaulle Issue

Common Design Type

Designs: 50fr, Gen. de Gaulle, 1940. 100fr, Pres. de Gaulle, 1970.

1972, Feb. 1 Engraved *Perf. 13*

52	CD134	50fr brt grn & blk	12.50	10.50
53	CD134	100fr brt grn & blk	20.00	17.00

First anniversary of death of Charles de Gaulle (1890–1970), president of France.

Kerguelen Cabbage
A19

Designs: 61fr, Azorella selago (horiz.). 87fr, Acaena ascendens (horiz.).

1972–73

54	A19	45fr dl red, ultra & sl grn	4.00	3.75
55	A19	61fr multi ('73)	2.25	2.25
56	A19	87fr multi ('73)	3.00	3.00

Issue dates: 45fr, Dec. 18, 1972; others, Dec. 13, 1973.

Mailship Sapmer and Map of Amsterdam Island—A20

1974, Dec. 31 Engraved *Perf. 13*

57	A20	75fr bl, blk & dk brn	6.00	6.00

25th anniversary of postal service.

Antarctic Tern
A21

Designs: 50c, Antarctic petrel. 90c, Sea lioness. 1fr, Weddell seal. 1.20fr, Kerguelen cormorant (vert.). 1.40fr, Gentoo penguin (vert.).

1976, Jan. Engraved *Perf. 13*

58	A21	40c multi	2.25	1.50
59	A21	50c multi	3.00	2.25
60	A21	90c multi	4.50	3.75
61	A21	1fr multi	12.00	10.50
62	A21	1.20fr multi	12.00	12.00
63	A21	1.40fr multi	15.00	15.00
		Nos. 58-63 (6)	[illegible]	[illegible]

James Clark Ross
A22

James Cook
A23

Design: 30c, Climbing Mount Ross.

1976, Dec. 16 Engr. *Perf. 13*

64	A22	30c multi	3.75	3.00
65	A22	3fr multi	4.25	4.25

First climbing of Mount Ross, Kerguelen Island, by James Clark Ross, Jan. 5, 1875.

1976, Dec. 16

66	A23	70c multi	15.00	13.00

Bicentenary of Capt. Cook's voyage past Kerguelen Island. See No. C46.

Commerson's Dolphins
A24

Design: 1.10fr, Blue whale.

1977, Feb. 1 Engraved *Perf. 13*

67	A24	1.10fr bl & ind	3.00	2.25
68	A24	1.50fr multi	4.50	4.00

Macrocystis Algae—A25

Salmon Hatchery—A26

Magga Dan—A27

Designs: 70c, Durvillea algae. 90c, Albatross. 1fr, Underwater sampling and scientists (vert.). 1.40fr, Thala Dan and penguins.

1977, Dec. 20 Engr. *Perf. 13*

69	A25	40c ol brn & bis	45	38
70	A26	50c dk bl & pur	1.00	75
71	A25	70c blk, grn & brn	60	60
72	A26	90c grn, brt bl & brn	75	75
73	A27	1fr slate	90	90
74	A27	1.20fr multi	1.40	95
75	A27	1.40fr multi	1.65	1.25
		Nos. 69-75 (7)	6.75	5.58

See Nos. 77–79.

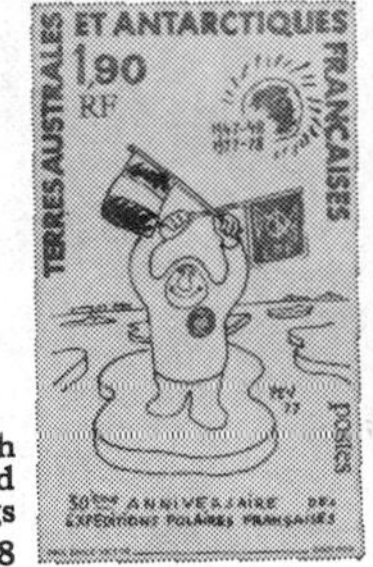

Explorer with French and Expedition Flags
A28

1977, Dec. 24

76	A28	1.90fr multi	3.75	3.00

French Polar expeditions, 1947–48, 30th anniversary.

Types of 1977

Designs: 40c, Forbin, destroyer. 50c Jeanne d'Arc, helicopter carrier. 1.40fr, Kerguelen cormorant.

1979, Jan. 1 Engr. *Perf. 13*

77	A27	40c blk & bl	1.25	1.25
78	A27	50c blk & bl	1.40	1.40
79	A26	1.40fr multi	1.40	1.25

R. Rallier du Baty
A29

1979, Jan. 1

80	A29	1.20fr cit & ind	1.25	1.25

French Navigators Monument, Hobart—A30

1979, Jan. 1

81	A30	1fr multi	85	85

French navigators and explorers.

Petrel—A31

1979 Engraved *Perf. 13*

82	A31	70c *Rockhopper penguins*, vert.	1.00	75
83	A31	1fr *shown*	1.00	75

Commandant Bourdais—A32

1979

84	A32	1.10fr *Doudart de Lagree*, vert.	70	70
85	A32	1.50fr *shown*	95	95

Admiral Antoine d'Entrecasteaux
A33

Sebastian de el Cano
A34

1979

86	A33	1.20fr multi	1.40	1.00

1979

Discovery of Amsterdam Island, 1522: 4fr, Victoria, horiz.

87	A34	1.40fr multi	1.00	75
88	A34	4fr multi	2.25	2.25

Adelie Penguins—A35

Adelie Penguin—A36

Sea Leopard—A37

1980, Dec. 15 **Engraved** ***Perf. 13***

89	A35	50c rose vio	1.50	1.50
90	A36	60c multi	1.10	95
91	A35	1.20fr multi	1.50	1.25
92	A37	1.30fr multi	95	85
93	A37	1.80fr multi	1.10	95
		Nos. 89-93 (5)	6.15	5.50

20th Anniv. of Antarctic Treaty—A38

1981, June 23 **Engr.** ***Perf. 13***

94	A38	1.80fr multi	6.75	6.75

Alouette II—A39

1981-82 **Engr.** ***Perf. 13***

95	A39	55c brn & multi	45	30
96	A39	65c bl & multi	45	30

Jean Loranchet—A40

1981

97	A40	1.40fr multi	75	60

Landing Ship Le Gros Ventre, Kerguelen—A41

1983, Jan. 3 **Engr.** ***Perf. 13***

98	A41	55c multi	45	45

Our Lady of the Winds Statue and Church, Kerguelen
A42

Martinde Vivies, Navigator

A43

1983, Jan. 3

99	A42	1.40fr multi	90	90
100	A43	1.60fr multi	90	75

Eaton's Ducks—A44

1983, Jan. 3

101	A44	1.50fr multi	60	60
102	A44	1.80fr multi	90	75

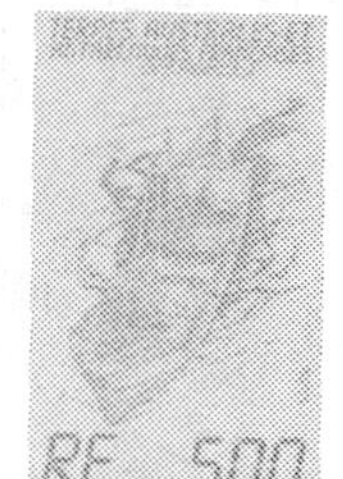

Trawler Austral—A45

1983, Jan. 3

103	A45	2.30fr multi	1.25	1.00

Freighter Lady Franklin—A46

1983, Aug. 4 **Engr.** ***Perf. 13***

104	A46	5fr multi	5.25	3.75

Glaciology—A47

Design: Scientists examining glacier, base.

1984, Jan. 1 **Engr.** ***Perf. 13***

105	A47	15c multi	38	38
106	A47	1.70fr multi	70	70

Crab-eating Seal—A48

Penguins—A49

1984, Jan. 1

107	A48	60c multi	45	45
108	A49	70c multi	45	45
109	A49	2fr multi	1.00	90
110	A48	5.90fr multi	1.75	1.75

Alfred Faure, Explorer—A50

1984, Jan. 1

111	A50	1.80fr multi	90	75

Biomass—A51

1985, Jan. 1 **Engr.** ***Perf. 13***

112	A51	1.80fr multi	60	60
113	A51	5.20fr multi	1.65	1.65

Emperor Penguins—A52

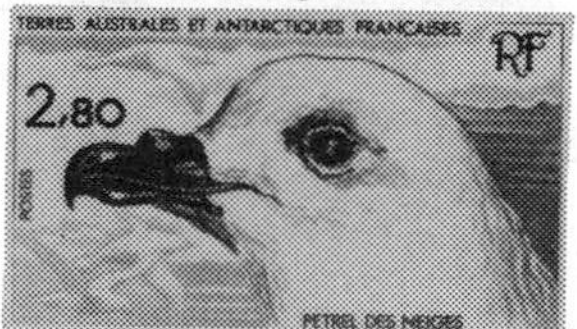

Snowy Petrel—A53

1985, Jan. 1 **Engr.** ***Perf. 13***

114	A52	1.70fr multi	75	60
115	A53	2.80fr multi	1.50	1.40

Port Martin

A54

Andre-Frank Liotard
A55

1985, Jan. 1 **Engr.** ***Perf. 13***

116	A54	2.20fr multi	90	75

1985, Jan. 1 **Engr.** ***Perf. 13***

117	A55	2fr multi	75	60

Antarctic Fulmar—A56

1986, Jan. 1 **Engr.** ***Perf. 13***

118	A56	1fr shown	30	30
119	A56	1.70fr Giant petrels	52	52

See No. C91.

Star Fish—A57

1986, Jan. 1

120	A57	1.90fr shown	60	60

Cotula Plumosa
A58

Shipping
A59

1986, Jan. 1

121	A58	2.30fr shown	75	75
122	A58	6.20fr Lycopodium saururus	1.90	1.90

1986, Jan. 1

123	A59	2.10fr Var research ship	90	90
124	A59	3fr Polarbjorn support ship	1.40	1.40

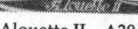

AIR POST STAMPS

Emperor Penguins and Map of Antarctica—AP1

Engraved

1956, April 25 ***Perf. 13*** **Unwmkd.**

C1	AP1	50fr lt ol grn & dk grn	40.00	32.50
C2	AP1	100fr dl bl & ind	37.50	32.50

Wandering Albatross—AP2

1959, Sept. 14

C3	AP2	200fr brn red, bl & blk	37.50	30.00

Adélie Penguins—AP3

1963, Feb. 11 ***Perf. 13*** **Unwmkd.**

C4	AP3	50fr blk, dk bl & dp cl	47.50	45.00

Telstar Issue

Common Design Type

1963, Feb. 11

C5	CD111	50fr dp bl, ol & grn	30.00	26.00

Radio Towers, Adelie Penguins and IQSY Emblem AP4

1963, Dec. 16 **Engraved**

C6	AP4	100fr bl, ver & blk	125.00	120.00

International Quiet Sun Year, 1964–65.

Discovery of Adelie Land—AP5

1965, Jan. 20 **Engraved** ***Perf. 13***

C7	AP5	50fr bl & ind	135.00	125.00

125th anniversary of the discovery of Adelie Land by Dumont d'Urville.

ITU Issue

Common Design Type

1965, May 17 ***Perf. 13*** **Unwmkd.**

C8	CD120	30fr Prus bl, sep & dk car rose	275.00	250.00

Issued to commemorate the centenary of the International Telecommunication Union.

French Satellite A-1 Issue

Common Design Type

Designs: 25fr, Diamant rocket and launching installations. 30fr, A-1 satellite.

1966, Mar. 2 **Engraved** ***Perf. 13***

C9	CD121	25fr dk grn, choc & sl	15.00	12.50
C10	CD121	30fr choc, sl & dk grn	15.00	12.50
a.		Strip of 2 + label	30.00	25.00

Issued to commemorate the launching of France's first satellite, Nov. 26, 1965. No. C10a contains one each of Nos. C9–C10 and label with dark green commemorative inscription. Each sheet contains 16 triptychs (2x8).

French Satellite D-1 Issue

Common Design Type

1966, Mar. 27

C11	CD122	50fr dk pur, lil & org	40.00	32.50

Issued to commemorate the launching of the D-1 satellite at Hammaguir, Algeria, Feb. 17, 1966.

Ionospheric Research Pylon, Adelie Land AP6

1966, Dec. 12

C12	AP6	25fr plum, bl & dk brn	21.00	18.00

Port aux Français, Emperor Penguin and Explorer—AP7

Design: 40fr, Aerial view of Saint Paul Island.

1968–69 **Engraved** ***Perf. 13***

C13	AP7	40fr brt bl & dk gray ('69)	40.00	37.50
C14	AP7	50fr lt ultra, dk grn & blk	140.00	135.00

Kerguelen Island and Rocket

AP8

Design: 30fr, Adelie Land.

1968, Apr. 22 **Engraved** ***Perf. 13***

C15	AP8	25fr sl grn, dk brn & Prus bl	18.00	15.00
C16	AP8	30fr dk brn, sl grn & Prus bl	18.00	15.00
a.		Strip of 2 + label	40.00	32.50

Issued to commemorate space explorations with Dragon rockets, 1967–68. No. C16a contains one each of Nos. C15–C16 and label with slate green and dark brown commemorative inscription.

Eiffel Tower, Antarctic Research Station, Ship from Paris Arms and Albatross AP9

1969, Jan. 13

C17	AP9	50fr brt bl	45.00	40.00

Issued to commemorate the 5th Consultative Meeting of the Antarctic Treaty Powers, Paris, Nov. 18, 1968.

Concorde Issue

Common Design Type

1969, Apr. 17

C18	CD129	85fr ind & bl	52.50	45.00

Map of Amsterdam Island AP10

Map of Kerguelen Island—AP11

Coat of Arms AP12

Designs: 50fr, Possession Island. 200fr, Point Geology Archipelago.

1969–71 **Engraved** ***Perf. 13***

C19	AP10	30fr brn ('70)	7.50	6.00
C20	AP11	50fr sl grn, bl & dk red ('70)	18.00	15.00
C21	AP11	100fr bl & blk	22.50	15.00
C22	AP10	200fr sl grn, brn & Prus bl ('71)	52.50	37.50
C23	AP12	500fr pck bl	13.00	13.00
		Nos. C19-C23 (5)	113.50	86.50

The 30fr commemorates the 20th anniversary of the Amsterdam Island Meteorological Station.

Issue dates: 30fr , Mar. 27, 1970; 50fr, Dec. 22, 1970; 100fr, 500fr, Dec. 21, 1969; 200fr, Jan. 1, 1971.

Port-aux-Français, 1970—AP13

Design: 40fr, Port-aux-Français, 1950.

1971, Mar. 9 **Engraved** ***Perf. 13***

C24	AP13	40fr bl, ocher & sl grn	9.00	7.50
C25	AP13	50fr bl, grn ol & sl grn	9.00	7.50
a.		Strip of 2 + label	19.00	16.00

20th anniversary of Port-aux-Français on Kerguelen Island. No. C25a contains one each of Nos. C24–C25 and label with blue and brown olive commemorative inscription.

Marquis de Castries Taking Possession of Crozet Island, 1772—AP14

Design: 250fr, Fleur-de-lis flag raising on Kerguelen Island.

1972 **Engraved** ***Perf. 13***

C26	AP14	100fr black	16.00	13.00
C27	AP14	250fr blk & dk brn	27.50	24.00

Bicentenary of the discovery of the Crozet and Kerguelen Islands. Issue dates: 100fr, Jan. 24; 250fr, Feb. 23.

M. S. Galliéni—AP15

1973, Jan. 25 **Engr.** ***Perf. 13***

C28	AP15	100fr blk & bl	18.00	15.00

Exploration voyages of the Galliéni.

"Le Mascarin," 1772—AP16

Sailing Ships: 145fr, "L'Astrolabe," 1840. 150fr, "Le Rolland," 1774. 185fr, "La Victoire," 1522.

1973, Dec. 13 Engraved *Perf. 13*

C29	AP16	120fr brn ol	3.75	3.00
C30	AP16	145fr brt ultra	3.75	3.25
C31	AP16	150fr slate	4.50	4.50
C32	AP16	185fr ocher	6.00	5.25

Ships used in exploring Antarctica.
See Nos. C37–C38.

Alfred Faure Base—AP17

Design: Nos. C33–C35 show panoramic view of Alfred Faure Base.

1974, Jan. 7 Engraved *Perf. 13*

C33	AP17	75fr Prus bl, ultra & brn	4.50	3.75
C34	AP17	110fr Prus bl, ultra & brn	6.75	4.50
C35	AP17	150fr Prus bl, ultra & brn	6.75	6.00
		Triptych (Nos. C33-C35)	19.00	16.00

10th anniversary of the Alfred Faure Antarctic Base. Nos. C33–C35 printed se-tenant.

Penguin, Map of Antarctica, Letters
AP18

1974, Oct. 9 Engraved *Perf. 13*

C36	AP18	150fr multi	6.75	6.00

Centenary of Universal Postal Union.

Ship Type of 1973

Designs: 100fr, "Le Français." 200fr, "Pourquoi-pas?"

1974, Dec. 16 Engraved *Perf. 13*

C37	AP16	100fr brt bl	3.75	2.50
C38	AP16	200fr dk car rose	5.25	4.00

Ships used in exploring Antarctica.

Rockets over Kerguelen Islands—AP19

Design: 90fr, Northern lights over map of northern coast of Russia.

1975, Jan. 26 Engraved *Perf. 13*

C39	AP19	45fr pur & multi	3.75	3.00
C40	AP19	90fr pur & multi	3.75	3.00
a.		Strip of 2 + label	8.25	6.75

Franco-Soviet magnetosphere research. No. C40a contains one each of Nos. C39–C40, and label with red inscription and indigo design. Sheets contain 5 No. C40a.

"La Curieuse"—AP20

Ships: 2.70fr, Commandant Charcot. 4fr, Marion-Dufresne.

1976, Jan. Engraved *Perf. 13*

C41	AP20	1.90fr multi	2.25	1.50
C42	AP20	2.70fr multi	3.75	3.00
C43	AP20	4fr red & multi	4.50	3.75

Dumont D'Urville Base, 1956—AP21

Design: 4fr, Dumont D'Urville Base, 1976, Adelie Land.

1976, Jan.

C44	AP21	1.20fr multi	3.00	2.25
C45	AP21	4fr multi	6.00	4.50
a.		Strip of 2 + label	10.00	8.25

20th anniversary of the Dumont D'Urville Antarctic Base. No. C45a contains one each of Nos. C44–C45 and label with map of Antarctica and penguins.

Capt. Cook's Ships Passing Kerguelen Island—AP22

1976, Dec. 31 Engr. *Perf. 13*

C46	AP22	3.50fr sl & bl	10.50	9.00

Bicentenary of Capt. Cook's voyage past Kerguelen Island.

Sea Lion and Cub
AP23

1977–79 Engr. *Perf. 13*

C47	AP23	4fr dk bl & grn ('79)	2.25	2.25
C48	AP23	10fr multi	10.50	9.50

Satellite Survey, Kerguelen—AP24

Designs: 70c, Geophysical laboratory. 1.90fr, Satellite and Kerguelen tracking station. 3fr, Satellites, Adelie Land.

1977–79 Engr. *Perf. 13*

C49	AP24	50c multi ('79)	75	75
C50	AP24	70c multi ('79)	75	70
C51	AP24	1.90fr multi ('79)	1.50	1.40
C52	AP24	2.70fr multi ('78)	2.25	2.25
C53	AP24	3fr multi	3.75	3.00
		Nos. C49-C53 (5)	9.00	8.10

Elephant Seals
AP25

1979, Jan. 1

C54	AP25	10fr blk & bl	5.25	5.25

Challenger—AP26

1979, Jan. 1

C55	AP26	2.70fr blk & bl	2.00	2.00

Antarctic expeditions to Crozet and Kerguelen Islands, 1972–1976.

La Recherche and L'Esperance—AP27

1979

C56	AP27	1.90fr dp bl	1.25	1.00

Arrival of d'Entrecasteaux and Kermadec at Amsterdam Island, Mar. 28, 1792.

Lion Rock—AP28

1979

C57	AP28	90c multi	75	75

Natural Arch, Kerguelen Island, 1840—AP29

1979

C58	AP29	2.70fr multi	1.40	1.25

Phylica Nitida, Amsterdam Island—AP30

1979

C59	AP30	10fr multi	4.50	4.50

Charles de Gaulle, 10th Anniversary of Death—AP31

1980, Nov. 9 Engraved *Perf. 13*

C60	AP31	5.40fr multi	11.00	11.00

HB-40 Castor Truck and Trailer—AP32

1980, Dec. 15

C61	AP32	2.40fr multi	1.00	1.00

Supply Ship Saint Marcouf—AP33

1980, Dec. 15

C62	AP33	3.50fr *shown*	1.50	1.40
C63	AP33	7.30fr *Icebreaker Norsel*	3.00	2.75

Glacial Landscape, Dumont D'Urville Sea—AP34

Chionis—AP35

Adele Dumont D'Urville (1798-1842)—AP36

Arcad III—AP37

25th Anniv. of Charcot Station—AP38

Antares—AP39

1981-82 **Engr.** ***Perf. 13, 12½x13 (2fr)***

C64	AP34	1.30fr multi	70	52
C65	AP35	1.50fr black	75	70
C66	AP36	2fr blk & lt brn	1.10	1.10
C67	AP37	3.85fr multi	1.50	1.50
C68	AP38	5fr multi	2.25	2.00
C69	AP39	8.40fr multi	3.00	3.00
		Nos. C64-C69 (6)	9.30	8.82

PHILEXFRANCE '82 Stamp Exhibition, Paris, June 11-21—AP40

1982, June 11 **Engr.** ***Perf. 13***

C70 AP40 8fr multi 6.00 6.00

French Overseas Possessions Week, Sept. 18-25—AP41

1982, Sept. 17 **Engr.** ***Perf. 13***

C71 AP41 5fr Commandant Charcot 2.25 2.25

Apotres Islands—AP42

1983, Jan. 3 **Engr.** ***Perf. 13***

C72 AP42 65c multi 45 30

Sputnik I—AP43

Orange Bay Base, Cape Horn, 1883—AP44

Intl. Polar Year Centenary and 24th Anniv. of Intl. Geophysical Year: 5.20fr, Scoresby Sound Base, Greenland, 1983. Nos. C73-C75 se-tenant.

1983, Jan. 3

C73	AP43	1.50fr multi	52	52
C74	AP44	3.30fr multi	1.40	1.40
C75	AP44	5.20fr multi	1.90	1.90

AP45

1983, Jan. 3

C76 AP45 4.55fr dk bl 3.00 2.50

Abstract, by G. Mathieu—AP46

1983, Jan. 3 **Photo.** ***Perf. 13x13½***

C77 AP46 25fr multi 9.50 9.50

Erebus otf Antarctic Ice Cap, 1842—AP47

Port of Joan of Arc, 1930—AP48

1984, Jan. 1 **Engr.** ***Perf. 13***

C78	AP47	2.60fr ultra & dk bl	1.00	90
C79	AP48	4.70fr multi	1.50	1.50

Aurora Polaris—AP49

1984, Jan. 1 **Photo.**

C80 AP49 3.50fr multi 2.25 1.50

Manned Flight Bicentenary (1983)—AP50

Various balloons and airships. Se-tenant with label showing anniv. emblem.

1984, Jan. 1 **Engr.**

C81	AP50	3.50fr multi	1.90	1.90
C82	AP50	7.80fr multi	3.00	3.00

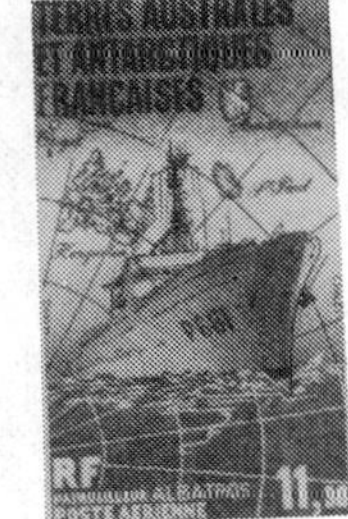
Patrol Boat Albatros—AP51

1984, July 2 **Engr.** ***Perf. 13***

C83 AP51 11.30fr multi 1.60 1.60

NORDPOSTA Exhibition—AP52

1984, Nov. 3 **Engr.** ***Perf. 13***

C84 AP52 9fr Scientific Vessel Gauss 3.00 3.00

Issued se-tenant with label.

Corsican Sheep AP53

Amsterdam Albatross AP54

1985, Jan. 1 **Engr.** ***Perf. 13***

C85	AP53	70c Mouflons	30	30
C86	AP54	3.90fr Diomedia amsterdamensis	1.50	1.25

La Novara, Frigate—AP55

1985, Jan. 1 **Engr.** ***Perf. 13***

C87 AP55 12.80fr La Novara at St. Paul 5.25 5.25

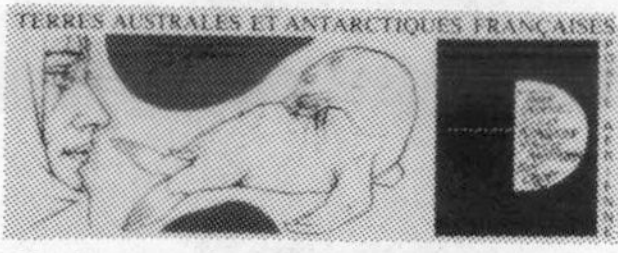

Explorer and Seal, by Tremois—AP56

1985, Jan. 1 **Photo.** ***Perf. 13x12½***

C88	AP56	30fr	Woman, seal, names of territories	10.00	10.00

Issued se-tenant with label containing artist's signature.

Sailing Ships, Ropes, Flora & Fauna—AP57

1985, Aug. 6 **Engr.** ***Perf. 13***

C89	AP57	2fr	blk, brt bl & ol grn	60	60
C90	AP57	12.80fr	blk, ol grn & brt bl	4.00	4.00

French Southern & Antarctic Territories, 30th anniv. Nos. C89-C90 printed se-tenant in continuous design with center label.

Bird Type of 1986

1986, Jan. 1 **Engr.** ***Perf. 13½x13***

C91	A56	4.60fr	Sea Gulls	1.50	1.50

Antarctic Atmospheric Research, 10th Anniv.—AP58

1986, Jan. 1

C92	AP58	14fr	blk, dk red & brt org	4.25	4.25

Jean Charcot (1867-1936), Explorer—AP59

1986, Jan. 1

C93	AP59	2.10fr	Ship Poquoi Pas	60	60
C94	AP59	14fr	Ship in storm	4.25	4.25

Nos. C93-C94 printed se-tenant with center label.

SPOT Satellite over the Antarctic—AP60

1986, May 26 **Engr.** ***Perf. 13***

C95	AP60	8fr	dp ultra, sep & dk ol grn	2.50	2.50

J.B. Charcot—AP61

1987, Jan. 1 **Engr.** ***Perf. 13x13½***

C96	AP61	14.60fr	dk bl, rose lake & rose brn	4.75	4.75

Marine Oil Drilling Program—AP62

1987, Jan. 1 ***Perf. 13½x13***

C97	AP62	16.80fr	lem, dk ultra & bluish blk	5.50	5.50

FRENCH SUDAN

(frĕnch sōō·dăn′; -dän′)

LOCATION—In northwest Africa, north of French Guinea and Ivory Coast.

GOVT.—Former French Colony.

AREA—590,966 sq. mi.

POP.—3,794,270 (1941).

CAPITAL—Bamako.

In 1899 French Sudan was abolished as a separate colony and was divided among Dahomey, French Guinea, Ivory Coast, Senegal and Senegambia and Niger. Issues for French Sudan were resumed in 1921.

From 1906 to 1921 a part of this territory was known as Upper Senegal and Niger. A part of Upper Volta was added in 1933. See Mali.

100 Centimes = 1 Franc

Navigation and Commerce
A1 A2

Stamps of French Colonies, Surcharged in Black.

1894 ***Perf. 14x13½*** **Unwmkd.**

1	A1	15c on 75c car, *rose*	*3,250.*	*1,900.*
2	A1	25c on 1fr brnz grn, *straw*	*4,000.*	*1,400.*

The imperforate stamp like No. 1 was made privately in Paris from a fragment of the lithographic stone which had been used in the Colony for surcharging No. 1.

Counterfeit surcharges exist.

1894-1900 **Typographed**

Name of colony in Blue or Carmine.

3	A2	1c *lil bl*	1.25	1.25
4	A2	2c brn, *buff*	1.40	1.40
5	A2	4c cl, *lav*	3.50	3.25
6	A2	5c grn, *grnsh*	4.25	4.00
7	A2	10c *lavender*	10.00	10.00
8	A2	10c red ('00)	2.50	2.50
9	A2	15c bl, quadrille paper	3.00	2.75
10	A2	15c gray, *lt gray* ('00)	4.25	4.25
11	A2	20c red, *grn*	16.00	15.00
12	A2	25c *rose*	16.00	15.00
13	A2	25c bl ('00)	4.00	4.00
14	A2	30c brn, *bis*	32.50	24.00
15	A2	40c red, *straw*	19.00	15.00
16	A2	50c car, *rose*	35.00	35.00
17	A2	50c brn, *az* ('00)	7.00	7.00
18	A2	75c dp vio, *org*	25.00	25.00
19	A2	1fr brnz grn, *straw*	6.00	6.00
		Nos. 3-19 (17)	190.65	175.40

Camel and Rider
A3

Stamps of Upper Senegal and Niger Overprinted in Black.

1921-30 ***Perf. 13½x14***

21	A3	1c brn vio & vio	6	6
22	A3	2c dk gray & dl vio	6	6

No.	Type	Description	Unused	Used
23	A3	4c blk & bl	6	6
24	A3	5c ol brn & dk brn	8	8
25	A3	10c yel grn & bl grn	8	8
26	A3	10c red vio & bl ('25)	8	8
27	A3	15c red brn & org	6	6
28	A3	15c yel grn & dp grn ('25)	8	8
29	A3	15c org brn & vio ('27)	95	95
30	A3	20c brn vio & blk	8	8
31	A3	25c blk & bl grn	35	35
a.		Booklet pane of 4		
32	A3	30c red org & rose	35	35
33	A3	30c bl grn & blk ('26)	18	18
34	A3	30c dl grn & bl grn ('28)	1.25	1.25
35	A3	35c rose & vio	8	8
36	A3	40c gray & rose	52	35
37	A3	45c bl & ol brn	35	30
38	A3	50c ultra & bl	48	40
39	A3	50c red org & bl ('26)	55	35
40	A3	60c vio, *pnksh* ('26)	35	22
41	A3	65c bis & pale bl ('28)	95	95
42	A3	75c org & ol brn	42	40
43	A3	90c brn red & pink ('30)	3.75	3.75
44	A3	1fr dk brn & dl vio	75	65
45	A3	1.10fr gray lil & red vio ('28)	1.75	1.75
46	A3	1.50fr dp bl & bl ('30)	3.75	3.75
47	A3	2fr grn & bl	1.50	1.25
48	A3	3fr red vio ('30)	6.50	6.50
a.		Double overprint	100.00	
49	A3	5fr vio & blk	4.00	3.25
		Nos. 21-49 (29)	29.42	27.67

1922

No.	Type	Description	Unused	Used
50	A3	60c on 75c vio, *pnksh*	35	35

Stamps and Type of 1921-30 Surcharged with New Values and Bars.

1925–27

No.	Type	Description	Unused	Used
51	A3	25c on 45c bl & ol brn ('25)	35	35
52	A3	65c on 75c org & ol brn ('25)	90	70
53	A3	85c on 2fr grn & bl ('25)	1.25	1.00
54	A3	85c on 5fr vio & blk ('25)	1.25	1.00
55	A3	90c on 75c brn red & sal pink ('27)	1.40	1.25
56	A3	1.25fr on 1fr dp bl & lt bl (R) ('26)	75	70
57	A3	1.50fr on 1fr dp bl & ultra ('27)	75	70
58	A3	3fr on 5fr dl red & brn org ('27)	2.50	1.75
59	A3	10fr on 5fr brn red & bl grn ('27)	12.00	10.00
60	A3	20fr on 5fr vio & ver ('27)	17.50	14.00
		Nos. 51-60 (10)	38.65	31.45

Sudanese Woman
A4

Entrance to the Residency at Djenné
A5

Sudanese Boatman
A6

1931–40 Typo. *Perf. 13x14.*

No.	Type	Description	Unused	Used
61	A4	1c dk red & blk	5	5
62	A4	2c dp bl & org	6	6
63	A4	3c dk red & blk ('40)	6	6
64	A4	4c gray lil & rose	6	6
65	A4	5c ind & grn	8	8
66	A4	10c ol grn & rose	6	6
67	A4	15c blk & brt vio	6	6
68	A4	20c hn brn & lt bl	8	8
69	A4	25c red vio & lt red	8	6
70	A5	30c grn & lt grn	30	8
71	A5	30c dk bl & red org ('40)	15	15
72	A5	35c ol grn & grn ('38)	8	6
73	A5	40c ol grn & pink	8	8
74	A5	45c dk bl & red org	42	35
75	A5	45c ol grn & grn ('40)	18	18
76	A5	50c red & blk	6	6
77	A5	55c ultra & car ('38)	30	30
78	A5	60c brt bl & brn ('40)	55	55
79	A5	65c brt vio & blk	10	8
80	A5	70c vio bl & car rose ('40)	18	18
81	A5	75c brt bl & ol brn	1.25	90
82	A5	80c car & brn ('38)	10	8
83	A5	90c dp red & red org	42	35
84	A5	90c brt vio & sl blk ('39)	30	30
85	A5	1fr ind & grn	4.75	80
86	A5	1fr rose red ('38)	2.50	55
87	A5	1fr car & brn ('40)	18	18
88	A6	1.25fr vio & dl vio ('33)	42	35
89	A6	1.25fr red ('39)	30	30
90	A6	1.40fr brt vio & blk ('40)	30	30
91	A6	1.50fr dk bl & ultra	22	10
92	A6	1.60fr brn & dp bl ('40)	30	30
93	A6	1.75fr dk brn & dp bl ('33)	30	30
94	A6	1.75fr vio bl ('38)	30	30
95	A6	2fr org brn & grn	42	8
96	A6	2.25fr vio bl & ultra ('39)	48	48
97	A6	2.50fr lt brn ('40)	60	60
98	A6	3fr Prus grn & brn	42	8
99	A6	5fr red & blk	1.00	55
100	A6	10fr dl bl & grn	1.40	90
101	A6	20fr red vio & brn	1.90	1.10
		Nos. 61-101 (41)	20.87	11.56

Colonial Exposition Issue.

Common Design Types

1931 Engraved *Perf. 12½*

Name of Country Printed in Black.

No.	Type	Description	Unused	Used
102	CD70	40c dp grn	1.50	1.50
103	CD71	50c violet	1.50	1.50
104	CD72	90c red org	1.50	1.50
105	CD73	1.50fr dl bl	1.50	1.50

Paris International Exposition Issue.

Common Design Types

1937 *Perf. 13.*

No.	Type	Description	Unused	Used
106	CD74	20c dp vio	85	85
107	CD75	30c dk grn	85	85
108	CD76	40c car rose	85	85
109	CD77	50c dk brn	85	85
110	CD78	90c red	85	85
111	CD79	1.50fr ultra	85	85
		Nos. 106-111 (6)	5.10	5.10

Colonial Arts Exhibition Issue.

Souvenir Sheet.

Common Design Type

1937 Engraved *Imperf.*

No.	Type	Description	Unused	Used
112	CD77	3fr mag & blk	3.50	3.50

Sheet size: 118x99mm.

Caillie Issue

Common Design Type

1939 *Perf. 12½x12.*

No.	Type	Description	Unused	Used
113	CD81	90c org brn & org	52	52
114	CD81	2fr brt vio	52	52
115	CD81	2.25fr ultra & dk bl	52	52

Centenary of the death of René Caillié (1799–1838), French explorer.

New York World's Fair Issue.

Common Design Type

1939, May 10

No.	Type	Description	Unused	Used
116	CD82	1.25fr car lake	65	65
117	CD82	2.25fr ultra	65	65

Entrance to the Residency at Djenné and Marshal Pétain
A7

1941 Engraved *Perf. 12x12½.*

No.	Type	Description	Unused	Used
118	A7	1fr green	35	35
119	A7	2.50fr blue	35	35

Stamps of types A4 and A5 without "RF" were issued in 1943 and 1944 by the Vichy Government, but were not placed on sale in the colony.

Stamps of French Sudan were superseded by those of French West Africa.

SEMI-POSTAL STAMPS.

Curie Issue

Common Design Type

Engraved.

1938 *Perf. 13* Unwmkd.

No.	Type	Description	Unused	Used
B1	CD80	1.75fr +50c brt ultra	7.75	7.75

French Revolution Issue

Common Design Type

1939 Photogravure.

Name and Value Typo. in Black.

No.	Type	Description	Unused	Used
B2	CD83	45(c) +25(c) grn	5.25	5.25
B3	CD83	70(c) +30(c) brn	5.25	5.25
B4	CD83	90(c) +35(c) red org	5.25	5.25
B5	CD83	1.25fr +1fr rose pink	5.25	5.25
B6	CD83	2.25fr +2fr bl	5.25	5.25
		Nos. B2-B6 (5)	26.25	26.25

Stamps of 1931–40, Surcharged in Black or Red

SECOURS
+ 1 fr.
NATIONAL

1941 *Perf. 13x14*

No.	Type	Description	Unused	Used
B7	A5	50c +1fr red & blk (R)	1.00	1.00
B8	A5	80c +2fr car & brn (Bk)	5.00	5.00
B9	A6	1.50fr +2fr dk bl & ultra (Bk)	5.00	5.00
B10	A6	2fr +3fr org brn & grn (Bk)	5.00	5.00

Common Design Type and

Native Officer
SP1

Aviation Officer
SP2

1941 Photogravure *Perf. 13½*

No.	Type	Description	Unused	Used
B11	SP1	1fr +1fr red	65	
B12	CD86	1.50fr +3fr cl	65	
B13	SP2	2.50fr +1fr bl	65	

The surtax was for the defense of the colonies.

Nos. B11–B13 were issued by the Vichy government and were not placed on sale in the colony.

Stamps of type A7, surcharged "OEUVRES COLONIALES" and new values, were issued in 1944 by the Vichy Government, but were not placed on sale in the colony.

AIR POST STAMPS.

Common Design Type

Engraved.

1940 *Perf. 12½x12.* Unwmkd.

No.	Type	Description	Unused	Used
C1	CD85	1.90fr ultra	22	22
C2	CD85	2.90fr dk red	30	30
C3	CD85	4.50fr dk gray grn	60	60
C4	CD85	4.90fr yel bis	60	60
C5	CD85	6.90fr dp org	65	65
		Nos. C1-C5 (5)	2.37	2.37

Common Design Types

1942

No.	Type	Description	Unused	Used
C6	CD88	50c car & bl	6	40
C7	CD88	1fr brn & blk	15	
C8	CD88	2fr dk grn & red brn	22	
C9	CD88	3fr dk bl & scar	35	
C10	CD88	5fr vio & brn red	35	

Frame Engraved, Center Typographed.

No.	Type	Description	Unused	Used
C11	CD89	10fr ultra, ind & gray blk	35	
C12	CD89	20fr rose car, mag & lt vio	42	
C13	CD89	50fr yel grn, dl grn & dl bl	1.00	1.50
		Nos. C6-C13 (8)	2.90	

There is doubt whether Nos. C7–C12 were officially placed in use.

AIR POST SEMI-POSTAL STAMPS.

Stamps of type of Dahomey V1, V2, V3 and V4 inscribed "Soudan Frcais", "Soudan" or "Soudan Francais" were issued in 1942 by the Vichy Government, but were not placed on sale in the colony.

POSTAGE DUE STAMPS.

D1

D2

Postage Due Stamps of Upper Senegal and Niger Overprinted in Black.

Typographed.

1921		*Perf. 14x13½*	Unwmkd.	
J1	D1	5c green	30	30
J2	D1	10c rose	42	42
J3	D1	15c gray	42	42
J4	D1	20c brown	60	60
J5	D1	30c blue	60	60
J6	D1	50c black	90	90
J7	D1	60c orange	1.25	1.25
J8	D1	1fr violet	1.50	1.50
		Nos. J1-J8 (8)	5.99	5.99

Type of 1921 Issue Surcharged **2F.**

1927				
J9	D1	2fr on 1fr lil rose	4.00	4.00
J10	D1	3fr on 1fr org brn	4.00	4.00

1931				
J11	D2	5c green	6	6
J12	D2	10c rose	6	6
J13	D2	15c gray	5	5
J14	D2	20c dk brn	6	6
J15	D2	30c dk bl	10	10
J16	D2	50c black	15	15
J17	D2	60c dp org	30	30
J18	D2	1fr violet	70	70
J19	D2	2fr lil rose	90	90
J20	D2	3fr red brn	90	90
		Nos. J11-J20 (10)	3.28	3.28

FRENCH WEST AFRICA

(frĕnch wĕst′ ăf′rĭ-kȧ)

LOCATION—Northwestern Africa.

GOVT.—Former French colonial administrative unit.

AREA—1,821,768 sq. mi.

POP.—18,777,163 (est.).

CAPITAL—Dakar.

French West Africa comprised the former colonies of Senegal, French Guinea, Ivory Coast, Dahomey, French Sudan, Mauritania, Niger and Upper Volta.

In 1958, these former colonies became republics, eventually issuing their own stamps. Until the republic issues appeared, stamps of French West Africa continued in use. The Senegal and Sudanese Republics issued stamps jointly as the Federation of Mali, starting in 1959.

Senegal No. 156 Surcharged in Red **50 fr.**

1943		*Perf. 12½x12.*	Unwmkd.	
1	A30	1.50fr on 65c dk vio	48	48
2	A30	5.50fr on 65c dk vio	55	55
3	A30	50fr on 65c dk vio	1.90	1.25

Mauritania No. 91 Surcharged in Red **5 fr.**

1944			*Perf. 13*	
4	A7	3.50fr on 65c dp grn	18	18
5	A7	4fr on 65c dp grn	40	22
6	A7	5fr on 65c dp grn	75	75
7	A7	10fr on 65c dp grn	80	52
		Nos. 1-7 (7)	5.06	3.95

Common Design Types pictured in section at front of book.

Senegal Nos. 143, 148 and 188 Surcharged with New Values in Black or Orange.

1944		*Perf. 12½x12*		
8	A29	1.50fr on 15c blk (O)	40	40
9	A29	4.50fr on 15c blk (O)	55	55
10	A29	5.50fr on 2c brn	1.10	1.10
11	A29	10fr on 15c blk (O)	1.50	1.25
12	CD81	20fr on 90c org brn & org	1.00	60
13	CD81	50fr on 90c org brn & org	2.50	2.25

Mauritania No. 109 Surcharged in Black.

14	CD81	15fr on 90c org brn & org	75	60
		Nos. 8-14 (7)	7.80	6.75

Eboue Issue.

Common Design Type

1945		Engraved	*Perf. 13*	
15	CD91	2fr black	52	52
16	CD91	25fr Prus grn	1.25	1.25

Nos. 15 and 16 exist imperforate.

Colonial Soldiers
A1

1945		Lithographed	*Perf. 12*	
17	A1	10c ind & buff	6	5
18	A1	30c ol & yel	6	5
19	A1	40c bl & buff	30	30
20	A1	50c red org & gray	6	6
21	A1	60c ol brn & bl	6	6
22	A1	70c mag & cit	35	35
23	A1	80c bl grn & pale lem	30	30
24	A1	1fr brn vio & cit	5	5
25	A1	1.20fr gray brn & cit	2.75	1.75
26	A1	1.50fr choc & pink	30	18
27	A1	2fr ocher & gray	52	30
28	A1	2.40fr red & gray	80	60
29	A1	3fr brn red & yelsh	18	5
30	A1	4fr ultra & pink	18	6
31	A1	4.50fr org brn & yelsh	18	15
32	A1	5fr dk pur & yelsh	18	6
33	A1	10fr ol grn & pink	95	15
34	A1	15fr org & yel	1.40	90
35	A1	20fr sl grn & grnsh	1.50	1.25
		Nos. 17-35 (19)	10.18	6.67

Rifle Dance, Mauritania
A2

Shelling Coconuts, Togo
A6

Bamako Dike, French Sudan
A3

Trading Canoe, Niger River
A4

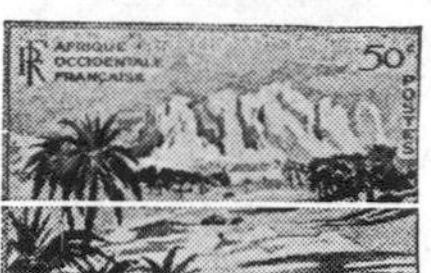

Oasis of Bilma, Niger
A5

Kouandé Weaving, Dahomey
A7

Donkey Caravan, Senegal
A8

Crocodile and Hippopotamus, Ivory Coast
A9

Bamako Fountain, French Sudan
A11

Gathering Coconuts, French Guinea
A10

Peul Woman of Djenné
A12

Bamako Market
A13

Dahomey Laborer
A14

Woman of Mauritania
A15

Fula Woman, French Guinea
A16

Djenné Mosque, French Sudan
A17

Monorail Train, Senegal
A18

Agni Woman, Ivory Coast
A19

Azwa Women at Niger River
A20

Engraved.

1947		*Perf. 12½*	Unwmkd.	
36	A2	10c blue	5	5
37	A3	30c red brn	5	5
38	A4	40c gray grn	5	5
39	A5	50c red brn	5	5
40	A6	60c gray blk	40	35
41	A7	80c brn vio	55	52
42	A8	1fr maroon	6	6
43	A9	1.20fr dk bl grn	80	52
44	A10	1.50fr ultra	1.00	70
45	A11	2fr red org	6	6
46	A12	3fr chocolate	40	18
47	A13	3.60fr brn red	1.10	80
48	A14	4fr dp bl	22	15
49	A15	5fr dk gray grn	22	15
50	A16	6fr dk bl	30	15
51	A17	10fr brn red	80	18
52	A18	15fr sepia	95	5
53	A19	20fr chocolate	80	18
54	A20	25fr grnsh blk	1.50	22
		Nos. 36-54 (19)	9.36	4.47

Types of 1947.

1948 Re-engraved.

55	A6	60c brn ol	52	35
56	A12	3fr chocolate	42	18

Nos. 40 and 46 are inscribed "TOGO" in lower margin. Inscription omitted on Nos. 55 and 56.

Imperforates

Most stamps of French West Africa from 1949 onward exist imperforate in issued and trial colors, and also in small presentation sheets in issued colors.

Military Medal Issue.
Common Design Type
Engraved and Typographed.

1952, Dec. 1 *Perf. 13*

57	CD101	15fr blk, grn, yel & blk brn	4.25	4.25

Treich Laplène and Map
A21

1952, Dec. 1 Engraved

58	A21	40fr brn lake	1.25	18

Issued to honor Marcel Treich Laplene, a leading contributor to the development of Ivory Coast.

Medical Laboratory
A22

1953, Nov. 18

59	A22	15fr brn, dk bl grn & blk brn	80	5

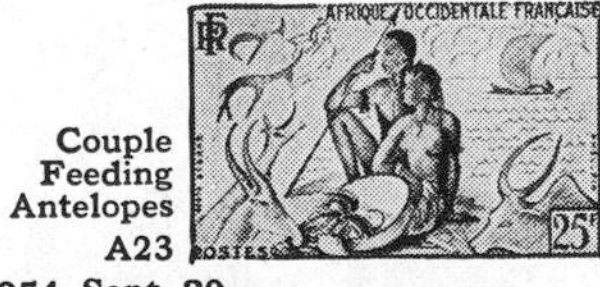

Couple Feeding Antelopes
A23

1954, Sept. 20

60	A23	25fr multi	1.00	18

Gov. Noel Eugène Ballay
A24

1954, Nov. 29

61	A24	8fr ind & brn	1.00	42

Chimpanzee
A25

Giant Pangolin
A26

1955, May 2 *Perf. 13* **Unwmkd.**

62	A25	5fr dk gray & dk brn	1.00	52
63	A26	8fr dk brn & bl grn	1.00	52

Issued in connection with the International Exhibition for Wildlife Protection, Paris, May 1955.

Map, Symbols of Industry, Rotary Emblem
A27

1955, July 4

64	A27	15fr dk bl	1.00	60

Issued to commemorate the 50th anniversary of the founding of Rotary International.

FIDES Issue

Mossi Railroad Upper Volta
A28

Designs: 1fr, Date grove, Mauritania. 2fr, Milo Bridge, French Guinea. 4fr, Cattle raising, Niger. 15fr, Farm machinery and landscape, Senegal. 17fr, Woman and Sansanding River, French Sudan. 20fr, Palm oil production, Dahomey. 30fr, Road construction, Ivory Coast.

1956 Engraved *Perf. 13x12½*

65	A28	1fr dk grn & dk bl grn	42	35
66	A28	2fr dk bl grn & bl	42	35
67	A28	3fr dk brn & red brn	80	60
68	A28	4fr dk car rose	80	60
69	A28	15fr ind & ultra	90	35
70	A28	17fr dk bl & ind	1.00	42
71	A28	20fr rose lake	1.00	42
72	A28	30fr dk pur & cl	1.10	80
		Nos. 65-72 (8)	6.44	3.89

See note after Cameroun No. 320.

Coffee Issue.

Coffee
A28a

1956, Oct. 22 *Perf. 13*

73	A28a	15fr dk bl grn	42	18

Mobile Leprosy Clinic and Maltese Cross
A29

1957, Mar. 11

74	A29	15fr dl red brn, pur & red	1.10	52

Issued in honor of the Knights of Malta.

Map of Africa
A30

1958, Feb. *Perf. 13* **Unwmkd.**

75	A30	20fr grnsh bl, blk & dl red brn	1.00	60

Issued to publicize the sixth International Congress for African Tourism at Dakar.

"Africa" and Communications Symbols
A31

1958, Mar. 15 Engraved

76	A31	15fr org, ultra & choc	1.00	52

Stamp Day. See No. 86.

Abidjan Bridge
A32

1958, Mar. 15

77	A32	20fr dk sl grn & grnsh bl	1.00	52

Bananas
A33

1958, May 19 *Perf. 13*

78	A33	20fr rose lil, dk grn & ol	70	25

Flower Issue
Common Design Type

Designs: 10fr, Gloriosa. 25fr, Adenopus. 30fr, Cyrtosperma. 40fr, Cistanche. 65fr, Crinum Moorei.

1958–59 Photogravure. *Perf. 12x12½*

79	CD104	10fr multi	52	22
80	CD104	25fr red, yel & grn ('59)	60	35
81	CD104	30fr multi	75	55
82	CD104	40fr blk brn, grn & yel ('59)	1.25	90
83	CD104	65fr multi	1.65	90
		Nos. 79-83 (5)	4.77	2.92

Moro Naba Sagha and Map
A34

1958, Nov. 1 Engraved *Perf. 13*

84	A34	20fr ol brn, car & vio	90	52

Issued to commemorate the 10th anniversary of the reestablishment of the Upper Volta territory.

Human Rights Issue
Common Design Type

1958, Dec. 10

85	CD105	20fr mar & dk bl	1.40	1.40

Type of 1958 Redrawn.

1959, Mar. 21 Engraved *Perf. 13*

86	A31	20fr red, grnsh bl & sl grn	1.75	1.25

Name of country omitted on No. 86; "RF" replaced by "CF," inscribed "Dakar-Abidjan."

Stamp Day.

SEMI-POSTAL STAMPS.

Red Cross Issue
Common Design Type
Photogravure.

1944 *Perf. 14½x14.* **Unwmkd.**

B1	CD90	5fr +20fr plum	4.25	4.25

The surtax was for the French Red Cross and national relief.

Type of France, 1945, Overprinted in Black **A O F**

1945 Engraved. *Perf. 13.*

B2	SP150	2fr +3fr org red	60	60

Tropical Medicine Issue
Common Design Type

1950, May 15 *Perf. 13*

B3	CD100	10fr +2fr red brn & sep	4.75	4.75

The surtax was for charitable work.

AIR POST STAMPS.

Common Design Type
Photogravure.

1945 *Perf. 14½x14* **Unwmkd.**

C1	CD87	5.50fr ultra	70	52
C2	CD87	50fr dk grn	2.25	52
C3	CD87	100fr plum	2.25	52

Victory Issue
Common Design Type

1946, May 8 Engr. *Perf. 12½*

C4	CD92	8fr violet	90	80

Chad to Rhine Issue
Common Design Types

1946, June 6

C5	CD93	5fr brn car	90	90
C6	CD94	10fr dp bl	90	90
C7	CD95	15fr brt vio	1.10	1.10
C8	CD96	20fr dk sl grn	1.40	1.40
C9	CD97	25fr ol brn	2.00	2.00
C10	CD98	50fr brown	2.75	2.75
		Nos. C5-C10 (6)	9.05	9.05

Antoine de Saint-Exupéry, Map and Natives
AP1

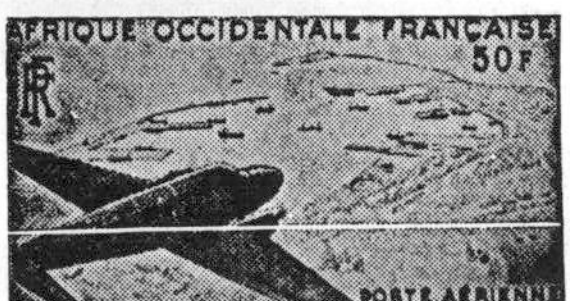

Plane over Dakar—AP2

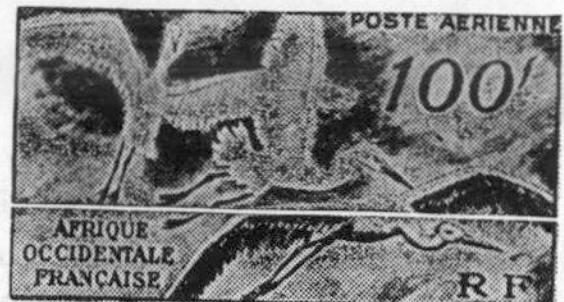

Great White Egrets in Flight—AP3

Natives and Phantom Plane—AP4

1947, Mar. 24 **Engraved**

C11	AP1	8fr red brn	42	35
C12	AP2	50fr rose vio	1.75	35
C13	AP3	100fr ultra	6.50	3.25
C14	AP4	200fr sl gray	9.50	2.25

UPU Issue
Common Design Type

1949, July 4 ***Perf. 13***

C15	CD99	25fr multi	6.50	6.50

Vridi Canal, Abidjan—AP5

1951, Nov. 5 ***Perf. 13*** **Unwmkd.**

C16	AP5	500fr red org, bl grn & dp ultra	20.00	4.25

Liberation Issue
Common Design Type

1954, June 6

C17	CD102	15fr ind & ultra	3.50	3.50

Logging—AP6

Designs: 100fr, Radiotelephone exchange. 200fr, Baobab trees.

1954, Sept. 20

C18	AP6	50fr ol grn & org brn	2.00	52
C19	AP6	100fr ind, dk brn & dk grn	3.00	75
C20	AP6	200fr bl grn, grnsh blk & brn lake	9.00	2.25

Gen. Louis Faidherbé and African Sharpshooter
AP7

1957, July 20 ***Perf. 13*** **Unwmkd.**

C21	AP7	15fr ind & bl	1.40	1.40

Centenary of French African troops.

Gorée Island and Woman—AP8

Designs: 20fr, Map with planes and ships. 25fr, Village and modern city. 40fr, Seat of Council of French West Africa. 50fr, Worker, ship and peanut plant. 100fr, Bay of N'Gor.

1958, March 15 **Engraved**

C22	AP8	15fr blk brn, grn & vio	80	55
C23	AP8	20fr blk brn, dk bl & red brn	80	55
C24	AP8	25fr blk vio, bis & grn	80	55
C25	AP8	40fr dk bl, brn & grn	80	55
C26	AP8	50fr vio, brn & grn	1.25	80
C27	AP8	100fr brn, bl & grn	4.00	1.25
a.		Souvenir sheet	10.00	10.00
		Nos. C22-C27 (6)	8.45	4.25

Issued to commemorate the centenary of Dakar.

No. C27a measures 185x125mm. and contains one each of Nos. C22–C27, with picture of old Dakar in center and inscribed: "Centenaire de Dakar."

Woman Playing Native Harp
AP9

1958, Dec. 1 ***Perf. 13*** **Unwmkd.**

C28	AP9	20fr red brn, blk & gray	1.00	70

Issued in connection with the inauguration of Nouakchot as capital of Mauritania.

POSTAGE DUE STAMPS.

D1

Engraved.

1947 ***Perf. 13*** **Unwmkd.**

J1	D1	10c red	6	6
J2	D1	30c dp org	6	6
J3	D1	50c grnsh blk	18	18
J4	D1	1fr carmine	18	18
J5	D1	2fr emerald	18	18
J6	D1	3fr red lil	22	22
J7	D1	4fr dp ultra	40	40
J8	D1	5fr red brn	1.00	1.00
J9	D1	10fr pck bl	1.50	1.50
J10	D1	20fr sepia	3.00	3.00
		Nos. J1-J10 (10)	6.78	6.78

OFFICIAL STAMPS

Mask
O1

Typographed.

1958 ***Perf. 14x13*** **Unwmkd.**

Various Masks.

O1	O1	1fr dk brn red	40	40
O2	O1	3fr brt grn	40	40
O3	O1	5fr crim rose	25	6
O4	O1	10fr lt ultra	35	6
O5	O1	20fr brt red	60	6
O6	O1	25fr purple	60	6
O7	O1	30fr green	90	70
O8	O1	45fr gray blk	1.00	90
O9	O1	50fr dk red	1.50	70
O10	O1	65fr brt ultra	2.25	90
O11	O1	100fr ol bis	4.00	70
O12	O1	200fr dp grn	7.75	2.50
		Nos. O1-O12 (12)	20.00	7.44

FUNCHAL

(fōō̆n·shäl')

LOCATION—A city and administrative district in the Madeira island group in the Atlantic Ocean northwest of Africa.

GOVT.—A part of the Republic of Portugal.

POP.—150,574 (1900).

Postage stamps of Funchal were superseded by those of Madeira. These, in turn, were displaced by the stamps of Portugal.

1000 Reis=1 Milreis

King Carlos
A1 A2

Perf. 11½, 12½, 13½

1892–93 **Typographed** **Unwmkd.**

1	A1	5r yellow	1.50	1.00
a.		Half used as 2½r on cover		25.00
b.		Perf. 11½	6.00	4.00
2	A1	10r red vio	1.50	1.10
3	A1	15r chocolate	2.75	1.50
4	A1	20r lavender	3.25	1.75
a.		Perf. 13½	6.50	4.50
5	A1	25r dk grn	2.50	1.25
6	A1	50r ultra	3.75	1.00
a.		Perf. 13½	7.50	2.00
7	A1	75r carmine	7.50	6.00
8	A1	80r yel grn	10.00	8.00
a.		Perf. 13½	13.00	11.00
9	A1	100r brn, *yel* ('93)	5.00	3.75
a.		Diagonal half used as 50r on cover		
10	A1	150r car, *rose* ('93)	32.50	22.50
11	A1	200r dk bl, *bl* ('93)	35.00	27.50
12	A1	300r dk bl, *sal* ('93)	40.00	30.00

The reprints of this issue have shiny white gum and clean-cut perforation 13½. The shades differ from those of the originals and the uncolored paper is thin. Price $4 each.

1897–1905 ***Perf. 12***

Name and Value in Black except Nos. 25 and 34.

13	A2	2½r gray	20	20
14	A2	5r orange	25	22
15	A2	10r lt grn	25	22
16	A2	15r brown	4.00	3.00
17	A2	15r gray grn ('99)	2.50	2.00
18	A2	20r gray vio	60	40
19	A2	25r sea grn	1.75	50
20	A2	25r car rose ('99)	75	25
a.		Booklet pane of 6		
21	A2	50r dk bl	3.00	1.10
a.		Perf. 12½	10.00	5.00
22	A2	50r ultra ('05)	60	40
23	A2	65r sl bl ('98)	60	40
24	A2	75r rose	90	70
25	A2	75r brn & red, *yel* ('05)	1.00	1.50
26	A2	80r violet	75	60
27	A2	100r dk bl, *bl*	75	60
a.		Diagonal half used as 50r on cover		
28	A2	115r org brn, *pink* ('98)	1.25	1.25
29	A2	130r gray brn, *buff* ('98)	1.25	1.25
30	A2	150r lt brn, *buff*	1.25	1.00
31	A2	180r sl, *pnksh* ('98)	1.25	1.25
32	A2	200r red vio, *pale lil*	2.25	2.25
33	A2	300r bl, *rose*	2.25	2.00
34	A2	500r blk & red, *bl*	2.25	1.75
a.		Perf. 12½	7.00	5.50
		Nos. 13-34 (22)	29.65	22.84

These stamps were received too late for inclusion in their proper places in the Catalogue. Later issues will be found listed in Scott's Chronicle of New Issues.

ALBANIA

War Martyrs Type of 1980

Portraits: 25q, Perlat Rexhepi (1919-1942) and Branko Kadia (1921-1942). 80q, Xheladin Beqiri (1908-1944) and Hajdar Dushi (1916-1944). 1.20 l, Koci Bako (1905-1941), Vasil Laci (1923-1941) and Mujo Ulqinaku (1898-1939). 1.35 l, Mine Peza (1875-1942) and Zoja Curo (1920-1944).

1981, May 5 Litho. *Perf. 12*

2012A	A410	25q sil & multi	25	12
2012B	A410	80q gold & multi	80	40
2012C	A410	1.20 l sil & multi	1.15	55
2012D	A410	1.35 l gold & multi	1.25	62

ALGERIA

AIR POST STAMP

Storks and Plane AP7

1979, Mar. 24 Photo. *Perf. 11½*

C19	AP7	10d multi	6.00	2.50

AUSTRIA

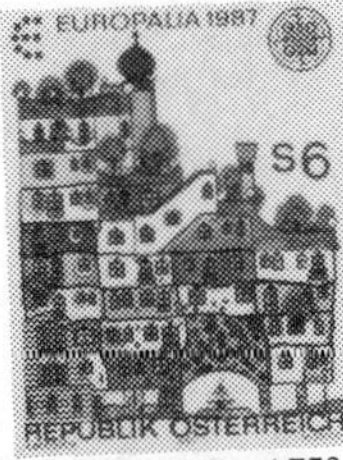

Europa 1987—A758

1987, Apr. 6 Photo. & Engr. *Perf.*

1389	A758	6s Hundertwasser House	95	55

POSTAGE DUE STAMPS

D17

1985 86 Photo. *Perf. 14*

Background Color

J260	D17	10g brt yel ('86)	5	5
J261	D17	20g pink ('86)	5	5
J262	D17	50g orange ('86)	8	6
J263	D17	1s lt bl ('86)	14	10
J264	D17	2s pale brn ('86)	28	20
J265	D17	3s vio ('86)	40	30
J266	D17	5s ocher	58	42

BHUTAN

Nos. 335-339 Ovptd. "75th ANNIVERSARY / GIRL GUIDES."

1986, July 23 Litho. *Perf. 14*

559	A46	3nu multi	50	35
560	A46	5nu multi	85	58
561	A46	15nu multi	2.50	1.75
562	A46	20nu multi	3.50	2.50

Souvenir Sheet

563	A46	25nu multi	4.25	3.00

A73

Statue of Liberty, Cent.—A74

Statue and ships: 50ch, Mircea, Romania. 1nu, Shalom, Israel. 2nu, Leonardo da Vinci, Italy. 3nu, Libertad, Argentina. 4nu, France, France. 5nu, SS United States, US. 15nu, Queen Elizabeth II, England. 20nu, Europa, West Germany. No. 582, Statue. No. 583, Statue, World Trade Center.

1986, Nov. 4

574	A73	50ch multi	10	8
575	A73	1nu multi	18	14
576	A73	2nu multi	35	28
577	A73	3nu multi	50	35
578	A73	4nu multi	68	52
579	A73	5nu multi	85	65
580	A73	15nu multi	2.50	1.90
581	A73	20nu multi	3.40	2.50
		Nos. 574-581 (8)	8.56	6.42

Souvenir Sheets

582	A74	25nu multi	4.25	3.00
583	A74	25nu multi, diff.	4.25	3.00

Nos. 582-583 have multicolored margins continuing the designs picturing Nippon Maru, Japan (#582), and flat-bottom boats, Netherlands (#583). Size: 114x83mm.

BRAZIL

POSTAL TAX STAMP

Fr. Pacheco Type of 1984

1986, Nov. 24 Litho. *Perf. 11½*

RA22	PT7	.10cz gray brn	5	5

Use of No. RA22 was required for one week. The tax was for the care and treatment of lepers.

CENTRAL AFRICA

1982 World Cup Soccer Championships, Spain—A152a

Various soccer plays.

1982, Sept. Litho. *Perf. 13½x13*

Overprinted in Silver or Gold.

545	A152a	60fr Italy, 1st, 2nd	25	12
546	A152a	150fr Poland, 3rd	62	30
547	A152a	300fr France, 4th	1.25	62

Souvenir Sheet

548	A152a	500fr Italy, 1st (G)	2.00	1.00

Not issued without overprint. No. 548 has multicolored margin inscribed with final score. Size: 104x81mm.

POSTAGE DUE STAMPS

Giant Anteater—D2

1985, Jan. 25 Litho. *Perf. 12½*

J13	D2	5fr multi	5	5
J14	D2	20fr multi	10	5
J15	D2	30fr multi	14	8

CHAD

1982 World Cup Soccer Championships, Spain—A108

1982 Litho. *Perf. 13½*

390	A108	30fr Hungary	12	6
391	A108	40fr Italy	16	8
392	A108	50fr Algeria	20	10
393	A108	60fr Argentina	25	12
		Nos. 390-393, C258-C259 (6)	2.30	1.14

CHINA

Plum Blossoms Type of 1979

1987, Jan. 5 Engr. *Perf. 13x12½*

2154b	Plain paper ('87)	1.00	80
2155a	Plain paper ('87)	2.50	2.00

Memorial Hall Type of 1981

1987, Jan. 16 *Perf. 12½x13½*

2237a	Photo.	5	5
2238a	Photo.	5	5

CONGO REPUBLIC

POSTAGE DUE STAMPS

Flowers and Fruit—D9

1986, June 5 Litho. *Perf. 13*

J52	D9	5fr Passiflora quadrangulares	5	5
J53	D9	10fr Cannaceae, vert.	6	5
J54	D9	15fr Ananas comosus, vert.	10	5

DOMINICAN REPUBLIC

POSTAL TAX STAMPS

Flower Type of 1981 Dated "1983" or "1984"

1983-85 Litho. *Perf. 12x12½*

RA98	PT37	1c 1983	5	5
RA99	PT37	1c 1984	5	5

Issue dates: No. RA98, Apr. 19, 1983. No. RA99, Apr. 1, 1985.

ECUADOR

Virgin of Mercy Type of 1980

1980, July 7 **Litho.**

Imperf.

990A A298 5s multi 50 25
990B A298 5s multi 50 25

Virgin of Mercy, patron saint of Ecuadorian armed forces. No. 990 contains designs of Nos. C686, C690, 989; No. 990A contains designs of Nos. 989, C687, C685, 988. No. 990B contains designs of Nos. C688, C691, C690. All have black control number. Sizes: 91x116mm, 116x91mm.

Pablo Picasso (1881-1973), Painter—A313a

1981, Oct. 26 **Litho.** ***Imperf.***

1017A A313a 20s multi 1.75 90

No. 1017A contains design of No. C728, additional portrait; black control number. See Nos. C728-C731.

EGYPT

SEMI-POSTAL STAMPS

Afghan Solidarity—SP33

Wmk. 342

1981, July 15 **Photo.** ***Perf. 11½***

B48 SP33 20m + 10m multi 15 15

Size: 30x25mm

1981 **Photo.** ***Perf. 11½***

B49 SP33 20m + 10m multi 15 15

Map of Sudan, Dunes, Dead Tree—SP34

1986, Mar. 25 **Photo.** ***Perf. 13x13½***

B50 SP34 15p + 5p multi 50 50

Fight against drought and desertification of the Sudan. Surtax for drought relief.

AIR POST STAMP

Step Pyramid Type of 1977

Wmk. 342

1984 **Photo.** ***Perf. 11½x11***

C173A AP51 185m bl, sep & gray brn 1.00 1.00

FRENCH SOUTHERN & ANTARCTIC TERRITORIES

Marine Life—A60

Flora—A61

Marret Base, Adelie Land—A62

Adm. Mouchez—A63

Reindeer—A64

Transport Ship Eure—A65

Macaroni Penguins—A66

1987, Jan. 1 **Engr.** ***Perf. 13½x13***

125 A60 50c dk bl & org 16 16

1987, Jan. 1

126 A61 1.80fr Poa cookii 58 58
127 A61 6.50fr Lichen, Neuropogon taylori 2.10 2.10

1987, Jan. 1

128 A62 2fr yel brn, dk ultra & lake 65 65

1987, Jan. 1

129 A63 2.20fr blk, brn & dk bl 72 72

1987, Jan. 1

130 A64 2.50fr black 80 80

1987, Jan. 1

131 A65 3.20fr dk ultra, Prus grn & dk grn 1.05 1.05

1987, Jan. 1 ***Perf. 13x12½***

132 A66 4.80fr multi 1.55 1.55

FOR THE RECORD

The items recorded here appeared on the stamp market in the 1960's and '70s, and have not been listed in the Scott Standard Catalogue. They are arranged chronologically and briefly described.

CONTENTS

AFGHANISTAN

Sets exist perf., imperf.

1963

GANEFO Games, Djakarta. *Sept. 3.* 2, 3, 4, 5, 10p, 9af; airmail, 300, 500p (8v). 2 souvenir sheets, 250, 300p.

Red Cross centenary. *Oct. 9.* 2, 3, 4, 5, 10p; airmail, 100, 200p, 4, 6af (9v). 2 souvenir sheets, 3, 4af.

Nubian Monuments Protection. *Nov. 16.* 100, 150, 200, 250, 500p; airmail, 5, 7.50, 10af (8v).

1964

Women's Day. *Jan. 5.* 2, 3, 4, 5, 10p (5v).

Afghan Boy and Girl Scouts. *Jan. 5.* 2, 3, 4, 5, 10p; airmail, 2af x 2, 2.50, 3, 4, 5, 12af (12v). 4 souvenir sheets, 5, 6x2, 10 af.

Children and Young People. *Jan. 22.* 2, 3, 4, 5, 10p; airmail, 200, 300p (7v).

Afghan Red Crescent Society. *Feb. 8.* 100, 200p, 2.50, 3.50af; airmail, 100p, 5, 7.50af (7v).

Teachers' Day. *Mar. 3.* 2, 3, 4, 5, 10p; airmail, 1.50, 2, 3, 3.50af (9v). 2 souvenir sheets, 4, 6af.

United Nations Day. *Mar. 9.* 2, 3, 4, 5, 10p; airmail, 100p, 2, 3af (8v). 2 souvenir sheets, 4, 5af, imperf.

Declaration of Human Rights, 15th anniversary. *Mar. 9.* Same values and sheets as United Nations Day set, each with 50p surcharge (8v).

UNICEF (United Nations Children's Fund). *Mar. 15.* 100, 150, 200, 250p; airmail, 5, 7.50, 10af (7v).

Fight Against Malaria. *Mar. 15.* 2, 3, 4, 5p; semi-postal, 4p+10p; airmail, 2, 5, 10af (8v). 2 souvenir sheets, 2af, perf.; 5af, imperf.

BHUTAN

1966

King Jigme Wangchuk, Coins, 40th anniversary of accession. *July 1.* Gold foil embossed. 10, 25, 50ch, 1, 1.30, 2, 3, 4, 5nu (9v).

Abominable Snowman (Yeti). *Oct. 12.* 1, 2, 3, 4, 5, 15, 30, 40, 50ch. *Nov. 15.* 1.25, 2.50, 3, 5, 6, 7nu (15v).

1967

Nos. 19–21, 38–39, 63–67 overprinted "Air Mail" in straight or curved lines. *Jan. 10.* (20v).

Flowers, *Feb. 9.* 3, 5, 7, 10, 50ch, 1, 2.50, 4, 5nu (9v).

Boy Scouts of Bhutan. *Mar. 28.* Perf., imperf. 5, 10, 15, 50ch, 1.25, 4nu (6v). Souvenir sheet of 2 (1.25, 4nu).

EXPO '67. *May 15.* Nos. 50–52 overprinted (3v). Souvenir sheet of 2 (1.50, 2.50nu) perf., imperf.

Churchill and Battle of Britain. *June 26.* Perf., imperf. 45ch, 2, 4nu (3v). Souvenir sheet of 2 (2, 4nu).

World Boy Scout Jamboree, Idaho. *Aug. 1.* Boy Scouts of Bhutan issue overprinted "World Jamboree/Idaho, U.S.A./Aug. 1–9/67." (6v and sheet).

Girl Scouts of Bhutan. *Sept. 18.* Perf., imperf. 5, 10, 15ch, 1.50, 2.50, 5nu (6v). Souvenir sheet of 2 (2.50, 5nu).

Astronauts. *Oct. 30.* Imperf., tridimensional. 3, 5, 7, 10, 15, 30, 50ch, 1.25nu; airmail, 2.50, 4, 5, 9nu (12v). 3 souvenir sheets of 4 (3, 5, 7, 10ch; 15, 30, 50ch, 1.25nu; 2.50, 4, 5, 9nu).

1968

Pheasants. *Jan. 20.* Perf., imperf. 1, 2, 4, 8, 15ch, 2, 4nu; *Apr. 23.* 5, 7, 9nu (10v).

10th Winter Olympics, Grenoble. Abominable Snowman issue of 1966 overprinted (2 types). *Feb. 16.* Perf., imperf. 40ch, 1.25, 3, 6nu (4v).

Mythological Creatures. *Mar. 14.* 2, 3, 4, 5, 15, 20, 30, 50ch, 1.25, 2nu; airmail, 1.50, 2.50, 4, 5, 10nu (15v).

Butterflies, *May 20.* Imperf., tridimensional. 15, 50ch, 1.25, 2nu; airmail, 3, 4, 5, 6nu (8v). 2 souvenir sheets of 4 (15, 50ch, 1.25, 2nu; 3, 4, 5, 6nu).

Paintings (relief printed). *July 8.* Imperf. 2, 4, 5, 10, 45, 80ch, 1.05, 1.40, 2, 3, 4, 5nu; *Aug. 28:* airmail, 1.50, 2.50, 6, 8nu (16v). (van Gogh, Millet, Monet, Corot). 4 souvenir sheets of 4 (2, 4, 5, 10ch; 45, 80ch, 1.05, 1.40nu; 2, 3, 4, 5nu; 1.50, 2.50, 6, 8nu).

19th Summer Olympics, Mexico City. *Oct. 1.* Perf., imperf. 5, 45, 60, 80ch, 1.05, 2, 3, 5nu (8v). Souvenir sheet of 2 (1.05, 5nu).

International Human Rights Year. *Nov. 12.* (Black and gold overprint on unissued gold foil coin set, 3 sizes) 15, 35ch, 9nu (3v).

Flood Relief. *Dec. 7.* Summer Olympics issue surcharged 5ch+5ch, 80ch+25ch, 2nu+50ch (3v).

Birds of Bhutan. *Dec. 7.* 2, 3, 4, 5, 15ch; *Dec. 28:* 20, 30, 50ch 1.25, 2nu; *Jan. 29, 1969:* Airmail, 1.50, 2.50, 4, 5, 10nu (15v).

1969

Fish. *Feb. 27.* Imperf., tridimensional. 15, 20, 30ch; airmail, 5, 6, 7nu (6v). Souvenir sheet of 4 (30ch, 5, 6, 7nu).

Insects. *Apr. 10.* Imperf., tridimensional. 10, 75ch, 1.25, 2nu; airmail, 3, 4, 5, 6nu (8v). 2 Souvenir sheets of 4 (10, 75ch, 1.25, 2nu; 3, 4, 5, 6nu).

Universal Postal Union, admission of Bhutan. *May 2.* Perf., imperf. 5, 10, 15, 45, 60ch, 1.05, 1.40, 4nu (8v).

History of Steel Making (printed on steel foil). Imperf. *June 2:* 2, 5, 15, 45, 75ch. 1.50, 1.75, 2nu; airmail, 3, 4, 5, 6nu (12v). *June 30.* 6 souvenir sheets of 2 (2, 45ch; 5, 15ch; 75ch, 2nu; 1.50, 1.7nu; 3, 6nu; 4, 5nu).

Birds, *Aug. 5.* Imperf., tridimensional. 15, 50ch, 1.25, 2nu; airmail, 3, 4, 5, 6nu (8v). *Aug. 28;* 2 souvenir sheets of 4 (15, 50ch, 1.25, 2nu; 3, 4, 5, 6nu).

Buddhist Prayer Banners (printed on silk). *Sept. 30.* Imperf. 15, 75ch, 2, 5, 6nu (5v). Souvenir sheet of 3 (75ch, 5, 6nu) perf., imperf.

Apollo 11 Moon Landing. *Nov. 3.* Imperf., tridimensional. 3, 5, 15, 20, 25, 45, 50ch, 1.75nu; airmail, 3, 4, 5, 6nu (12v). *Nov. 20.* 3 souvenir sheets of 4 (3, 5, 15, 20ch; 25, 45, 50ch, 1.75nu; 3, 4, 5, 6nu).

1970

Paintings, *Jan. 19.* Imperf., tridimensional. 5, 10,

15ch, 2.75nu; airmail, 3, 4, 5, 6nu (8v). (Clouet, van Eyck, David, Homer, Rubens, Gentileschi, Ghirlandaio, Raphael). 2 souvenir sheets of 4 (5, 10, 15ch, 2.75nu; 3, 4, 5, 6nu).

Flowers, paintings (relief printed). *May 6,* Imperf. 2, 3, 5, 10, 15, 75ch, 1, 1.40nu; *May 28.* Airmail, 80, 90ch, 1.10, 1.40, 1.60, 1.70, 3, 3.50nu (16v). (van Gogh, Redon, Kiyoteru Kuroda, Renoir, Monet, La Tour, Oudot). 4 souvenir sheets of 4 (2, 3, 5, 10ch; 15, 75ch, 1, 1.40nu; 80, 90ch, 1.10, 1.40nu; 1.60, 1.70, 3, 3.50nu).

Preceding Issues Surcharged, *June.*
Mythological Creatures issue of 1968. 5ch x 6; 20ch x 3.
No. 14 (Freedom from Hunger). 20ch.
Nos. 63–67 (Animals). 20ch x 5.
Abominable Snowman issue of 1966. 20ch x 6.
Flower issue of 1967. 20ch x 2.
Boy Scout issue of 1967. 20ch x 2.
Churchill. Battle of Britain issue of 1967. 20ch x 2.
Pheasant issue of 1968. 20ch x 3.
Birds issue of 1968. 20ch x 9.
UPU issue of 1969. 20ch x 3.

Animals, Imperf., tridimensional. *Sept. 17:* 5, 10, 20, 25, 30, 40, 65, 75, 85ch; *Oct. 15:* airmail. 2, 3, 4, 5nu (13v).

Space Conquest. Imperf., tridimensional. *Nov. 9:* 2, 5, 15, 25, 30, 50, 75ch, 1.50nu; *Nov. 30:* airmail, 2, 3, 6, 7nu (12v). 3 souvenir sheets of 4 (2, 5, 15, 25ch; 30, 50, 75ch, 1.50nu; 2, 3, 6, 7nu).

1971

History of Sculpture (plastic bas-relief sculptures from antiquity to Modigliani). *Mar.* Imperf. 10, 75ch, 1.25, 2nu; airmail, 3, 4, 5, 6nu (8v). 2 souvenir sheets of 4 (10, 75ch, 1.25, 2nu; 3, 4, 5, 6nu).

Apollo 15 and Lunokhod 1. *Mar. 20.* Imperf., tridimensional. 10ch, 1.70nu; airmail, 2.50, 4nu (4v). Souvenir sheet of 4 (10ch, 1.70, 2.50, 4nu).

Antique Cars. Imperf. *May 20:* 2, 5, 10, 15, 20, 30, 60ch; *June 10:* 75, 85ch, 1, 1.20, 1.55, 1.80, 2, 2.50nu; *July 5:* 4, 6, 7, 9, 10nu (20v).

Preceding Issues Surcharged. *July 1.*
Nos. 22–23, 55ch on 1.30nu, 90ch on 2nu.
Nos. 65–66, 55ch on 3nu, 90ch on 4nu.
Boy Scout issue of 1967, 90ch on 4nu.
Pheasant issue of 1968, 55ch on 5nu, 90ch on 9nu.
Mythology issue of 1968, 55ch on 4nu.
Olympic issue of 1968, 90ch on 1.05nu.
Birds issue of 1968, 90ch on 2nu.
UPU issue of 1969, 55ch on 60ch.
UPU issue of 1970, 90ch on 2.50nu.
Space issue of 1971 (Apollo 15), 90ch on 1.70nu.

1972

Paintings (relief printed). Imperf. *Jan. 29:* 15, 20, 90ch, 2.50nu; *Feb. 28:* airmail, 1.70, 4.60, 5.40, 6nu (8v). (Renoir, Manet, da Vinci, Millet, Rousseau, Gauguin, Degas, Guillaumin) 2 souvenir sheets of 4 (15, 20, 90ch, 2.50nu; 1.70, 4.60, 5.40, 6nu).

Famous Men (plastic bas-reliefs). *Apr. 22.* Imperf. 10, 15, 55ch; airmail; 2, 6, 8nu (6v). (Gandhi, J.F. Kennedy, Churchill, de Gaulle, Pope John XXIII, Eisenhower). Souvenir sheet of 4 (55ch, 2, 6, 8nu).

International Book Year. *May 15.* 2, 3, 5, 20ch (4v).

20th Summer Olympics, Munich. *June 6.* 10, 15, 20, 30, 45ch; airmail, 35ch. 1.35, 7nu (8v). Souvenir sheet of 3 (35ch, 1.35, 7nu) perf., imperf.

Apollo 16 (rockets and astronauts). *Sept. 1.* Imperf., tridimensional. 15, 20, 90ch, 2.50nu; airmail, 1.70, 4.60, 5.40, 6nu (8v). 2 souvenir sheets of (15, 20, 90ch, 2.50nu; 1.70, 4.60, 5.40, 6nu).

Dogs. *Oct. 5.* Perf., imperf. 5, 10, 15, 25, 55ch, 8nu, souvenir sheet of 2 (55ch, 8nu); *Jan. 1, 1973.* 2, 3, 15, 20, 30, 99ch, 2.50, 4nu, souvenir sheet of 3 (99ch, 2.50, 4nu); *Jan. 15.* Airmail souvenir sheet, 18nu. (14v).

1973

Roses (scented paper). *Jan. 30.* 15, 25, 30ch, 3nu; airmail, 6, 7nu (6v). Souvenir sheet of 2 (6, 7nu) perf., imperf.

Apollo 17 (astronauts on moon). *Feb. 23.* Imperf., tridimensional. 10, 15, 55ch, 2nu; airmail, 7, 9nu (6v). Souvenir sheet of 4 (10, 15, 55ch, 2nu); circular souvenir sheet of 2 (7, 9nu).

Folk Songs, on Record. *Apr. 15.* 10, 25ch, 1.25, 7, 8nu; airmail, 3, 9nu (7v).

King Jigme Dorji Wangchuk, memorial. *May 2.* Gold foil, 10, 25ch, 3nu; airmail, 6, 8nu (5v). Souvenir sheet of 2 (6, 8nu).

Mushrooms, *Sept. 25.* Imperf., tridimensional. 15, 25, 30ch, 3nu; airmail, 6, 7nu (6v). Souvenir sheet of 4 (15, 25, 30ch, 3nu) and of 2 (6, 7nu).

INDIPEX Philatelic Exhibition (Bhutanese mail service scenes). *Nov. 14.* 5, 10, 15, 25ch. 1.25, 3nu, airmail, 5, 6nu (8v). Souvenir sheet of 2 (5, 6nu).

1974

Reading and Writing, paintings. *Feb. 15.* 1, 2, 3, 5, 10, 15, 25, 50, 60, 80ch, 1, 1.25nu (12v). (Fragonard, Carpaccio, Liotard, Holbein, Terborch).

CAMBODIA (Khmer)

1972

20th Summer Olympics, Munich. *Nov. 2.* Gold foil, airmail, 900r x 4 (4v). 2 souvenir sheets of 2, 900r x 2.

Apollo 16. *Nov. 2.* Gold foil, airmail 900r x 2. (2v). Souvenir sheet of 2 (900r x 2) perf., imperf.

1973

World Cup Soccer Championships. Gold foil, airmail, 900r x 4 (4v).

1974

John F. Kennedy and Apollo 11 Astronauts on Moon. Gold foil, airmail, 1100r x 2 (2v). Souvenir sheet of 2 (1100r x 2).

Copernicus, 500th birth anniversary. Gold foil, airmail, 1200r. Souvenir sheet, 1200r.

UPU Centenary. Gold foil, airmail, 1200r x 2 (2v). Souvenir sheet, 1200r.

1975

World Cup Soccer Championships. *Feb.* 1, 5, 10, 25r; airmail, 50, 100, 150, 200, 250r (9v). 9 imperf. souvenir sheets; same with simulated perforations; 2 sheets, 200, 250r, perf. Gold foil, airmail, 1200r, same, souvenir sheet.

21st Summer Olympics, Montreal, 1976 (ancient and modern sports). 1, 5, 10, 25r; airmail, 50, 100, 150, 200, 250r (9v). 9 imperf. souvenir sheets; same with simulated perforations. 2 souvenir sheets, 200, 250r, perf. Gold foil, airmail, 1200r.

UPU Centenary. *April 12.* (Second issue) 15, 20, 70, 160, 180, 235r, airmail 500, 1000, 2000r (9v). 9 imperf. souvenir sheets; same with simulated perforations. 2 souvenir sheets, 1000, 2000r. Gold foil embossed, airmail, perf., imperf. 1000r x 2 (train & plane). Same, souvenir sheet, 1200r (Chinese junks).

CAMEROUN

1977

Winter Olympics, 1976, Innsbruck. *Aug. 10.* 40, 50fr; airmail, 140, 200, 350fr (5v). Airmail souvenir sheet, 500fr.

Apollo-Soyuz Project. *Aug. 10.* 40, 60fr; airmail, 100, 250, 350fr (5v). Airmail souvenir sheet, 500fr.

CHAD

1970

Apollo Program. *May.* 40fr; airmail, 15, 25fr (3v). Souvenir sheet, 50fr.

Napoleon. *June 12.* Perf., imperf. airmail, 10, 25, 32fr, se-tenant in sheets of 6 (3v). Souvenir sheet, 40fr. Gold foil, 10fr and souvenir sheet.

World Cup Soccer Championships, Mexico. *July 2.* Perf., imperf. 1, 4, 5fr x 2 (4v). Souvenir sheet; 15fr.

EXPO '70, Osaka, Japan (Japanese prints). *July.* Perf., imperf. 50c, 1, 2fr, se-tenant in sheets of 6 (3v).

19th Summer Olympics and 1970 Soccer Cup, Mexico. *July 1.* Airmail 5fr. Souvenir sheet, 15fr. Gold foil, 5 fr. Souvenir sheet, 5fr.

Christmas, paintings. *Aug. 19.* Perf., imperf. 3, 25fr; airmail, 32fr (3v). (Virgin and Child by Solario, Dürer, Fouquet).

Paintings, flowers and woman (Iba N'Diaye). *Aug. 28.* Airmail, 250 fr × 2.

20th Summer Olympics, Munich, 1972. *Sept.* 3, 8, 20fr; airmail, 10, 35fr (5v). Souvenir sheet, 40fr.

Apollo 11 and 12. *Sept.* Imperf. airmail gold foil, 25fr and souvenir sheet.

20th Summer Olympics, Munich, *Oct. 14.* Imperf. gold foil, 10fr and airmail souvenir sheet.

Napoleon II. *July 23.* 10fr, se-tenant with label. Souvenir sheet, 40fr. Embossed gold foil, 10fr perf., imperf. Same, 2 souvenir sheets. 10fr, perf., imperf.

French Royalty. *1970–71.* Perf., imperf. About 70 stamps and souvenir sheets showing paintings against gold background. Various denominations, both postage and airmail, printed se-tenant.

1971

11th Winter Olympics, Sapporo, 1972 (Kiyonaga paintings). *Feb. 16.* Perf., imperf. 50c, 1, 2fr (3v).

Flowers, paintings. *Apr. 28.* Perf., imperf. 1, 4, 5fr, printed se-tenant (3v). (Rubens, Van Os, Brueghel).

Space Exploration and John F. Kennedy. *Feb. 16.* Perf., imperf. 8, 10fr; airmail, 35fr (3v). Souvenir sheet, 40fr.

Olympic Games (sport and culture). *Apr. 28.* Perf., imperf. 15, 20fr; airmail, 25fr (3v). Airmail souvenir sheet, 50fr.

Peace and Sciences. *July 5.* Embossed gold foil. Perf. and imperf., 10fr and souvenir sheet, 10fr.

Christmas. *July 17.* Nos. 205–210 overprinted "Noel/ 1971" in gold (6v).

20th Summer Olympics, Munich. Soccer Cup issue of 1970 overprinted in gold. Airmail souvenir sheets: 15fr; 5fr × 2 and 2 labels.

11th Winter Olympics, Sapporo. *July 17.* EXPO '70 and Winter Olympic issues of 1971 overprinted in gold (6v).

1972–73

Soccer World Champions, Great Britain, 1966. Gold foil, 5fr and souvenir sheet, 5fr.

Summer Olympics, Munich. *June 24.* Nos. 181–204 overprinted (24v).

Wild Animals. *Nov.* Airmail, 20, 30, 100, 130, 150fr (5v). Souvenir sheet, 200fr.

20th Summer Olympics, Munich.

Olympic Flame and Athletes: *1973.* 20, 30, 50fr; airmail, 100, 130, 150fr (6v). Souvenir sheet, 200 fr.

Athletes and Abstract White Drawings of Athletes in Background: *1973.* 25, 40, 50, 75fr; airmail, 100, 150fr (6v). Souvenir sheet, 250fr.

Music, paintings. *Apr.* 30, 70, 100fr; airmail, 125, 150fr (5v). (Costa, Oudry, Saraceni, Metsu). Souvenir sheet, 300fr.

Easter. *Apr.* 60, 120fr; airmail, 40, 150, 250fr (5v). Souvenir sheet, 400fr.

Modern Trains. 10, 40, 50, 150, 200fr (5v). Souvenir sheet, 300fr.

Domestic Animals (sheep, dromedaries, cats, dogs, horses). 20, 30fr; airmail, 100, 130, 150fr (5v).

Horses, paintings. 20, 60, 100, 150fr (4v). (Gericault, Potter, Stubbs, Vernet). Souvenir sheet, 500fr.

Aircraft, Airmail, 5, 25, 70, 150, 200fr (5v). Souvenir sheet, 350fr.

Christmas, paintings. 30, 40, 55fr; airmail, 60, 250fr (5v). (Lotto, Tintoretto, Schongauer, Barocci, Lochner, Memling). Souvenir sheet, 400fr.

COMORO ISLANDS

Most sets exist perf., imperf.

1975

Apollo-Soyuz Space Issue. 10, 30, 50fr; airmail 100, 200, 400fr (6v). Souvenir sheet, 500fr. Embossed gold foil, airmail, 1500fr, same souvenir sheet, 1500fr.

1976

American Bicentennial. *Jan. 15.* 15, 25, 35, 40, 75fr; airmail 500fr (6v). Airmail souvenir sheet, 400fr. Embossed on gold foil, airmail, 1000fr, same, souvenir sheet, 1500fr.

12th Winter Olympics, Innsbruck. *Mar 30.* 5, 30, 35, 50fr; airmail, 200, 400fr (6v). Airmail souvenir sheet, 500fr. Embossed on gold foil, airmail, 1000fr, same airmail souvenir sheet, 1000fr.

21st Summer Olympics, Montreal. *Mar. 30.* 20, 25, 40, 75fr; airmail, 100, 500fr (6v). Airmail souvenir sheet, 400fr.

Telephone Centenary, *July 1.* 10, 25, 75fr; airmail, 100, 200, 500fr (6v). 2 airmail souvenir sheets, 400, 500fr.

American Bicentennial, Project Viking III. *Nov. 23.* 5, 10, 25, 35, 100fr; airmail, 500fr (6v). **Project Viking IV.** Embossed on gold foil, airmail, 1500fr (Pioneer and rocket). Same, airmail souvenir sheet, 1500fr (Mars landing vehicle).

United Nations Postal Administration, 25th anniversary. *Nov. 25.* 15, 30, 50, 75fr; airmail, 200, 400fr (6v). Airmail souvenir sheet, 500fr.

American Bicentennial, Civil War Battles. *Dec. 30.* 10, 30, 50fr; airmail, 100, 200, 400fr (6v). Airmail souvenir sheet, 500fr. Embossed on gold foil, airmail, 1500fr (Kennedy, moon landing). Same, airmail souvenir sheet, 1000fr (Abraham Lincoln).

Endangered Species. *Dec. 30.* 15, 20, 35, 40, 75fr; airmail, 400fr (6v). Airmail souvenir sheet, 500fr.

1977

Endangered Species. *Apr. 14.* 10, 30, 40, 50fr; airmail, 200, 400fr (6v). Airmail souvenir sheet, 500fr.

Airships and Railroads. *Apr. 14.* 20, 25, 50, 75fr; airmail, 200, 500fr (6v). Airmail souvenir sheet, 500fr.

Nobel Prize, 75th anniversary. *July 7.* 30, 40, 50, 100fr; airmail, 200, 400fr (6v). Airmail souvenir sheet, 500fr.

Peter Paul Rubens, 400th birth anniversary. *July 7.* 20, 25, 50, 75fr; airmail, 200, 500fr (6v). Airmail souvenir sheet, 500fr (self-portrait).

Silver Jubilee QEII. *July 7.* Embossed on gold foil, airmail, 500fr. Same, 2 airmail souvenir sheets, 500, 1000fr.

Fish, various local species. 30, 40, 50, 100fr; airmail, 200, 400fr (6v). Airmail souvenir sheet, 500fr.

Space Ships and Vehicles. 30, 50, 75, 100fr; airmail, 200, 400fr (6v). Airmail souvenir sheet, 500fr.

Concorde, "Paris-New-York-22 nov, 1977" overprinted in gold on UNPA 25th anniversary, 200fr airmail.

Fairy Tales. 15, 30, 35, 40, 50fr; airmail, 400fr (6v) (Hansel & Gretel, Alice in Wonderland, Pinocchio, Good Little Henri, Peter and the Wolf, 1001 Nights).

1978

Birds. *Feb. 6.* 15, 20, 35, 40, 75fr; airmail, 400fr (6v). Airmail souvenir sheet, 500fr.

World Cup Soccer, Argentina '78. *Feb. 6.* 30, 50, 75, 100fr; airmail, 200, 400fr (6v). Airmail souvenir sheet, 500fr. Embossed on gold foil, airmail, 1000fr. Same, airmail souvenir sheet, 1000fr.

Famous Composers. *Apr. 5.* 30, 40, 50, 100fr; airmail, 200, 400fr (6v). Airmail souvenir sheet, 500fr.

Albrecht Dürer, 450th death anniversary. *Apr. 5.* 20, 25, 50, 75fr; airmail, 200, 500fr (6v). Airmail souvenir sheet, 500fr.
Aug. 20, 30, 40fr; airmail, 100, 200, 400fr (6v). 3 airmail souvenir sheets, 500, 1000, 1500fr.

QE II Coronation, 25th anniversary. *May 25.* 10, 25, 40, 100fr; airmail, 200, 500fr (6v). Airmail souvenir sheet, 500fr. Embossed on gold foil, airmail, 500, 1000fr. Same, 2 souvenir sheets, 1000fr.

Butterflies. *May 8.* 15, 20, 30, 50, 75fr; airmail, 400fr (6v). Airmail souvenir sheet, 500fr.

World Telecommunications, 10th anniversary. *June.* 30, 50, 75, 100fr; airmail, 200, 400fr (6v).

History of Aviation. *June.* 30, 50, 75, 100fr; airmail, 200, 400fr (6v). Airmail souvenir sheet, 500fr.

Peter Paul Rubens, 400th anniversary. *June.* 10, 25, 35, 50, 75fr; airmail, 500fr (6v). 3 airmail souvenir sheets, 400, 1000, 1500fr.

Rowland Hill. *Aug.* 20, 30, 40, 75fr; airmail, 200, 400fr (6v). Airmail souvenir sheet, 500fr.

World Cup Soccer. *Sept.* Overprinted "Rep. Fed. Islamique / des Comores / 1 Argentine / 2 Hollande / 3 Bresil." 30, 50, 75, 100fr; airmail 200, 400fr (6v). Airmail souvenir sheet, 500fr.

Europe-Africa. *Sept.* 10, 25, 35, 50fr; airmail, 100, 500fr (6v). Airmail souvenir sheet, 500fr.

CONGO PEOPLE'S REPUBLIC

1970

Paintings. *Feb.* 3, 40fr; airmail, 25fr (3v). (Fragonard, Boucher).

Olympic Games. *Feb.* 2, 5, 15, 50fr (4v). Airmail souvenir sheet, 100fr.

Kennedys, King and Space. *Feb.* 1, 10, 20, 30fr (4v).

1971

13th World Boy Scout Jamboree, Japan. *July 14.* Gold foil, airmail, 1000fr and silver foil souvenir sheet of 4 (90fr × 4).

1977

History of Aviation, famous fliers. 60, 75, 100, 200, 300fr (5v). Souvenir sheet, 500fr.

Peter Paul Rubens, 400th birth anniversary. **Mao Tse-tung,** 1st anniversary of death. *Sept.* Embossed gold foil, 400, 600fr (2v).

Famous Persons. *Dec.* 200, 200, 250, 300fr (4v) (Baudouin, de Gaulle, QEII Silver Jubilee (2)). Airmail souvenir sheet, 500fr (QEII and Royal Family).

DAHOMEY

1974

World Cup Soccer Championships, Munich. *July 16.* Airmail, 35, 40, 100, 200, 300fr (5v). Souvenir sheet, 500fr. Embossed gold foil. 1000fr, same souvenir sheet.

UPU centenary. *Aug. 5.* Airmail, 50, 100, 125, 150, 200fr (5v). Souvenir sheet, 500fr. 6 souvenir sheets with simulated perforations. Airmail gold foil 1000fr, same souvenir sheet.

Conquest of Solar System's Planets. *Oct. 31.* Perf., imperf. Airmail 50, 100, 150, 200fr (4v). 4 souvenir sheets with simulated perforations. Souvenir sheet, 500fr.

World Soccer Champions, Germany. *Nov.* Perf., imperf. Airmail 100, 125, 150, 300fr (4v). 4 souvenir sheets with simulated perforations. Souvenir sheet, 500fr. Embossed gold foil, perf., imperf., 1000fr and 4 souvenir sheets.

ECUADOR

1966

International Telecommunication Union, centenary. *Jan. 27.* Perf., imperf. 10c × 2, 80c; airmail, 1.50, 3, 4s (6v). 2 souvenir sheets of 3 (10, 80c, 3s; 10c, 1.50, 4s).

Space Exploration. *Jan. 27.* 10c, 1s; airmail, 1.30, 2, 2.50, 3.50s (6v). Souvenir sheet of 3 (10c, 1.30, 3.50s) perf., imperf.

Dante and Galileo. 10, 80c; airmail, 2, 3s (4v). Souvenir sheet of 3 (10, 80c, 3s) perf., imperf.

Pope Paul VI. 10c; airmail, 1.30, 3.50s (3v). Souvenir sheet of 3 (10c, 1.30, 3.50s) perf., imperf.

Famous Men. *June 24.* 10c, 1s; airmail, 1.50, 2.50, 4s (5v). (Hammarskjold, Churchill, Schweitzer, J. F. Kennedy). Souvenir sheet of 3 (10c, 1.50, 4s).

Olympic Games. (Greek athletes, classic period). *June 27.* 10c × 2, 80c; airmail, 1.30, 3, 3.50s (6v). 2 souvenir sheets of 3 (10c, 1.30, 3.50s; 10, 80c, 3s) perf., imperf.

Winter Olympics, 1924–1968. 10c, 1s; airmail, 1.50, 2, 2.50, 4s (6v). Souvenir sheet of 3 (10c, 1.50, 4s) perf., imperf.

French-American Space Research. 10c; airmail, 1.50, 4s (3v). Souvenir sheet of 3 (10c, 1.50, 4s) perf., imperf.

Italian Space Research. 10c; airmail, 1.30, 3.50s (3v). Souvenir sheet of 3 (10c, 1.30, 3.50s) perf., imperf.

Moon Exploration. 10, 80c, 1s; airmail, 2, 2.50, 3s (6v). Souvenir sheet of 3 (10, 80c, 3s) perf., imperf.

1967

19th Summer Olympics, Mexico. *Mar. 13.* 10c, 1s; airmail, 1.30, 2, 2.50, 3.50s (6v). Souvenir sheet of 3 (10c, 1.30, 3.50s) perf., imperf. Diamond-shaped; 10c × 2, 80c; airmail, 1.50, 3, 4s (6v). 2 souvenir sheets of 3 (10c, 1.50, 4s; 10, 80c, 3s) perf., imperf.

National Eucharistic Congress, 4th. *May 10.* 10, 60, 80c, 1s; airmail, 1.50, 2s (6v). Souvenir sheet, 10s perf., imperf.

Madonnas, paintings. *May.* 10, 40, 50c; airmail, 1.30, 2.50, 3s (6v). (Reni, van Hemesen, Memling, Dürer, Raphael, Murillo).

Women, paintings. *Sept. 9.* 10c, 1s; airmail, 1.50, 2, 2.50, 4s (6v). (van der Weyden, Rubens, Dürer, Gainsborough, Manet, Raphael). Souvenir sheet of 3 (10c, 1.50, 4s) perf., imperf.

John F. Kennedy, 50th birth anniversary. *Sept. 11.* 10c × 2, 80c; airmail, 1.30, 3, 3.50s (6v). 2 souvenir sheets of 3 (10, 80c, 3s; 10c, 1.30, 3.50s) perf., imperf.

Christmas. *Dec. 29.* 10c × 2, 40, 50, 60c; airmail, 2.50s (6v).

1968

Christian Local Art. *Jan. 19.* 10, 80c, 1s; airmail, 1.30, 1.50, 2s (6v). Souvenir sheet of 3 (3, 3.50, 4s) perf., imperf.

Tourist Year (9th COTAL Congress). *Apr. 1.* 20, 30, 40, 50, 60, 80c, 1s; airmail, 1.30, 1.50, 2s (10v).

1969

Pope Paul VI, Latin American visit and **39th International Eucharistic Congress.** Bogota, 40, 60c, 1s; airmail, 1.30, 2s (5v). Souvenir sheets of 2 (1, 2s) and 3 (40, 60c, 1.30s); imperf.

Guayaquil University Centenary, religious paintings with university coat of arms ovptd. in silver. 40, 60c, 1s; airmail, 1.30, 2s (5v). (van der Weyden, Raphael, Veronese). Souvenir sheets of 3 (40, 60c, 2s) and 2 (1, 2s) imperf.

EQUATORIAL GUINEA

Most sets exist perf., imperf.
Most imperf. sets have surface colored paper

1972

Apollo 15. *Jan. 28.* 1, 3, 5, 8, 10p; airmail, 15, 25p (7v). 3 airmail semi-postal souvenir sheets 25p+200p, perf.; 50p+250p, imperf.; gold foil, 200p+25p, perf., 200p+50p, imperf.

11th Winter Olympics, Sapporo. *Feb. 3.* 1, 2, 3, 5, 8p; airmail, 15, 50p (7v). 2 airmail semi-postal souvenir sheets, 200p+25p, perf.; 250p+50p, imperf.; gold foil, 200p+25p, perf., 200p+50p, imperf., 2 each.

Christmas; paintings. *1971.* 1, 3, 5, 8, 10p; airmail, 15, 25p (7v). 2 airmail semi-postal souvenir sheets 25p+200p, perf.; 50p+200p, imperf. (Virgin and Child by da Vinci, Murillo, Raphael, Mabuse, van der Weyden, Dürer), gold foil, 200p+25p, perf., 250p+50p, imperf.

Easter. *Apr. 28.* 1, 3, 5, 8, 10p; airmail, 15, 25p (7v). 2 souvenir sheets (25, 200p), perf., semi-postal 250p+50p, imperf., gold foil airmail semi-postal 200p+25p, perf., 250+50p, imperf., 2 each with designs by Velazquez and El Greco.

20th Summer Olympics, Munich (sports; inscribed "Augsburgo"). *May 5.* 1, 2, 3, 5, 8p; airmail, 15, 50p (7v). 2 airmail semi-postal souvenir sheets 200p+25p, perf.; 250p+50p, imperf. Presentation folder with gold foil airmail semi-postal 200p+25p, perf., 200p+50p, imperf.

Gold Medal Winners, Sapporo. *May 25.* 1, 2, 3, 5, 8p; airmail, 15, 50p (7v). Airmail souvenir sheet, 250p+50p, imperf.; souvenir sheet of 2 (25, 200p) perf. Gold foil, 200p+25p, perf., 250p+50p, imperf., 6 each.

Black Gold Medal Winners, Munich. *June 26.* 1, 2, 3, 5, 8p; airmail, 15, 50p (7v). 2 airmail semi-postal souvenir sheets 200p+25p, perf.; 250p+50p, imperf. Gold foil, 200p+25p, perf., 250p+50p, imperf., 9 each.

Olympic Games, Regatta in Kiel & Oberschleissheim. *July 25.* 1, 2, 3, 5, 8p; airmail, 15, 50p (7v). 2 airmail semi-postal souvenir sheets 200p+25p, perf.; 250p+50p, imperf. Gold foil, 200p+25p, perf., 250p+50p, imperf., 2 each.

1972 Munich Olympics. *Aug. 10.* 1, 2, 3, 5, 8p; airmail, 15, 50p (7v). 2 airmail semi-postal souvenir sheets 200p+25p, perf.; 250p+50p, imperf. *Aug. 17.* 10 gold foil sheets, 200p+25p each, perf. Same, 10 imperf. sheets, 250p+50p each.

Olympic Equestrian Events. *Aug. 24.* 1, 2, 3, 5, 8p; airmail, 15, 50, 50p (7v). 2 airmail semi-postal souvenir sheets 200p+25p, perf.; 250p+50p, imperf. Gold foil souvenir sheets, 200p+25p, perf. Same, imperf. sheets, 250p+50p, 8 each. 2 stamps, 200p+25p, perf., 250p+50p, imperf. 3 sheets of 2, 200p+25p (2 perf., 1 imperf.)

Japanese Railroad centenary (locomotives). *Sept. 21.* 1, 3, 5, 8, 10p; airmail, 15, 25p (7v). 2 airmail semi-postal souvenir sheets 200p+25p, perf.; 250p+50p, imperf. 11 gold foil souvenir sheets of 1; (200p+25p, perf. (9), 200p+25p, imperf. (2). 2 sheets of 2, each 200p+25p. perf., imperf.

Gold Medal Winners, Munich Games. *Oct. 30.* 1, 2, 3, 5, 8p; airmail, 15, 50p (7v). 2 airmail semi-postal souvenir sheets 200p+25p, perf.; 250p+50p, imperf. 4 gold foil souvenir sheets, 200p+25p, perf., 250p+50p, imperf., 2 each.

Christmas and 500th birth anniversary of Lucas Cranach. (Madonnas and Christmas seals). *Nov. 22.* 1, 3, 5, 8, 10p; airmail, 15, 25p (7v). (Giotto, Schongauer, Fouquet, de Morales, Fini, David, Sassetta). 2 airmail semi-postal souvenir sheets, 200p+25p, perf., 250+50p, imperf. Gold foil souvenir sheets, 200p+25p (6), perf., 250p+50p (6) imperf. Souvenir sheets of 2, 200p+25p, perf., imperf. Ovptd. stamp 200p+25p.

American and Russian astronaut memorial. *Dec. 14.* 1, 3, 5, 8, 10p; airmail, 15, 25p (7v). 2 airmail semi-postal souvenir sheets 200p+25p, perf.; 250p+50p, imperf. Gold foil ovptd. "Apollo 16 and 17" 200p+25p, perf., 250p+50p, imperf., 2 each.

1973

Trans-Atlantic Yacht Race. *Jan. 22.* 1, 2, 3, 5, 8p; airmail, 15, 50p (7v). 2 airmail semi-postal souvenir sheets 200p+25p, perf.; 250p+50p, imperf.

Renoir paintings. *Feb. 22.* 1, 2, 3, 5, 8p; airmail, 15, 50p (7v). 2 airmail semi-postal souvenir sheets 25p+200p, perf.; 50p+250p, imperf. Golf foil, 200p+25p, perf., 250p+50p, imperf.

Conquest of Venus (spacecraft). *Mar. 22.* 1, 3, 5, 8, 10p; airmail, 15, 25p (7v). 2 airmail semi-postal souvenir sheets 200p+25p, perf.; 250p+50p, imperf.

Apollo Flights 11–17. *Mar. 22.* 18 gold foil airmail semi-postal souvenir sheets: 14 sheets of 1 (7 × 200p+25p, perf.; 7 × 250p+50p, imperf.); 4 sheets of 2, 200p+25p, perf., 250p+50p, imperf. 2 each.

National Workers Party. *April.* 1, 1.50, 2, 4, 5p (5v).

Independence, 4th anniversary. *April.* 1.50, 2, 3, 4, 5p (5v).

Easter, paintings. *Apr. 25.* 1, 3, 5, 8, 10p; airmail, 15, 25p (7v). (Verrocchio, Perugino, Tintoretto, Witz, Pontormo). 2 airmail semi-postal souvenir sheets 200p+25p, perf.; 250p+50p, imperf. Gold foil issue of 1972 ovptd. 4 sheets, 200p+25p, perf., 250p+50p, imperf. 2 each.

Copernicus. 500th birth anniversary (US and USSR space explorations). *May 15.* 4 gold foil airmail semi-postal souvenir sheets, 200p+25p, perf.; 250p+50p, imperf., 2 each.

Tour de France bicycle race. 59th. *May 22.* 1, 2, 3, 5, 8p; airmail, 15, 50p (7v). 2 airmail semi-postal souvenir sheets 200p+25p, perf.; 250p+50p, imperf.

Paintings. *June 29.* 1, 2, 3, 5, 8p; airmail, 15, 50p (7v). 2 airmail semi-postal souvenir sheets 200p+25p, perf.; 250p+50p, imperf.

World Cup Soccer Championships, Munich, 1974. *Aug. 30.* 5, 10, 15, 20, 25, 55, 60c; airmail, 5, 70p (9v). 2 airmail souvenir sheets, 130p, perf.; 200p, imperf.

Rubens paintings. *Sept. 23.* 1, 2, 3, 5, 8p; airmail, 15, 50p (7v). 2 souvenir sheets of 2 (200, 25p perf.; 250, 50p imperf.).

New Currency: Ekuele.

World Cup Soccer Championships, Munich, 1974. *Oct. 24.* 2 Gold foil souvenir sheets 130e × 2, perf.; 200e × 2, imperf. 2 souvenir sheets of 2, 130p, perf., 200p, imperf.

Christmas, paintings. *Oct. 30.* 1, 3, 5, 8, 10p; airmail, 15, 25p (7v). (Nativity by, van der Weyden, Bosco, de Carvajal, Mabuse, Lucas Jordon, P. Goecke, Maino, Fabriano, Lochner). 2 airmail semi-postal souvenir sheets 200p+25p, perf.; 250p+50p, imperf.

Apollo Program and J. F. Kennedy. *Nov. 10.* Gold foil airmail semi-postal 200p+25p, perf.; 250p+50p, imperf. and souvenir sheets (same).

World Cup Soccer (famous players). *Nov. 20.* 30, 35, 40, 45, 50, 65, 70c; airmail, 8, 60p (9v). 2 souvenir sheets, 130p, perf., 200p, imperf.

Princess Anne's Wedding. *Dec. 17.* Gold foil airmail souvenir sheets, 2 sheets of 1, 250e each; 1 sheet of 2, 250e × 2, perf., imperf.

Pablo Picasso Memorial (Blue Period paintings). *Dec. 20.* 30, 35, 40, 45, 50c; airmail, 8, 60e (7v). 2 souvenir sheets, 130e, perf.; 200e, imperf.

1974

Copernicus, 500th birth anniversary. *Feb. 8.* 5, 10, 15, 20c, 4e, airmail, 10, 70e (7v). 2 souvenir sheets 130e, perf.; 200e, imperf. *Apr. 10.* 8 gold foil souvenir sheets: 130e (3), perf.; 200e (3), imperf., 250e, perf., 300e, imperf. 4 souvenir sheets of 2, 250e, perf., 250e, imperf; 2 each.

World Cup Soccer Championships (final games) Munich. *Feb. 28.* 75, 80, 85, 90, 95c, 1, 1.25e; airmail, 10, 50e (9v). 2 souvenir sheets, 130e, perf.; 200e, imperf.

Easter, paintings. *Mar. 27.* 1, 3, 5, 8, 10p; airmail, 15, 25p (7v). (Fra Angelico, Castagno, Allori, Multscher, della Francesca, Pleydenwurff, Correggio). 2 airmail semi-postal souvenir sheets 200p+25p, perf.; 250p+50p, imperf.

Holy Year 1975 (famous churches). *Apr. 11.* 5, 10, 15, 20c, 3.50e; airmail, 10, 70e (7v). 2 souvenir sheets 130e, perf., 200e, imperf.

World Cup Soccer (contemporary players). *Apr. 30.* 1.50, 1.75, 2, 2.25, 2.50, 3, 3.50e; airmail, 10, 60e (9v). 2 souvenir sheets of 2, 65e × 2, perf.; 100e × 2, imperf.

UPU centenary (transportation from messenger to rocket). *May 30.* 60, 70, 80c, 1, 1.50e; airmail, 30, 50e (7v). 2 souvenir sheets, 225e, perf.; 150e × 2, imperf. *June 8.* 2 airmail deluxe souvenir sheets, 130e. 1 sheet of 2, 130e, perf.

Picasso Memorial (Pink Period paintings). *June 28.* 55, 60, 65, 70, 75c; airmail, 10, 50e (7v). 2 souvenir sheets 130e, perf.; 200e, imperf.

World Cup Soccer Championships. *July 8.* 6 gold foil airmail souvenir sheets: 4 sheets of 1, 130e (2), 250e (2); 2 sheets of 2, 130e × 2, 250e × 2.

Aleksander Solzhenitsyn. *July 25.* Gold foil airmail souvenir sheets, 250e perf., 300e imperf.

Opening of American West. *July 30.* 30, 35, 40, 45, 50c; airmail, 8, 60p (7v). 2 souvenir sheets 130p, perf.; 200p, imperf.

Flowers. *Aug. 20.* 5, 10, 15, 20, 25c, 1, 3, 5, 8, 10p; airmail, 5, 15, 25, 70p (14v). 4 souvenir sheets: 130p; 200p; 2 semi-postal, 200p+25p, 250p+50p.

Christmas. *Sept. 16.* 60, 70, 80c, 1, 1.50e; airmail, 30, 50e (7v). 2 souvenir sheets, 225e, perf.; 300e, imperf.

Barcelona soccer team, 75th anniversary. *Sept. 25.* 1, 3, 5, 8, 10e; airmail, 15, 60e (7v, miniature sheet of 7 plus label). 2 souvenir sheets 200e, perf.; 300e, imperf. 4 gold foil airmail souvenir sheets, 200e each, perf. and imperf.

UPU centenary and ESPANA 75. *Oct. 9.* 1.25, 1.50, 1.75, 2, 2.25e; airmail, 35, 60e (7v). 2 airmail souvenir sheets 225e, perf., 300e, imperf. *Oct. 14.* Gold foil sheets, 250e, 300e, 250e × 2 perf., imperf.

Nature protection, Australian animals: *Oct. 25.* 80, 85, 90, 95c. 1e; airmail, 15, 40e (7v). 2 souvenir sheets 130e, perf.; 200e, imperf. **African animals:** *Nov. 6.* 55, 60, 65, 70, 75c; airmail, 10, 70e (7v). 2 souvenir sheets 130e, perf.; 200e, imperf. **Australian and South American Birds:** *Nov. 26.* 1.25, 1.50, 1.75, 2, 2.25, 2.50, 2.75, 3, 3.50, 4p; airmail, 20, 25, 30, 35p (14v). 4 souvenir sheets 130p × 2, perf.; 200p × 2, imperf. **Endangered Species:** *Dec. 17.* 10, 15, 20, 25, 30, 35, 40, 45, 50, 55, 60c, 1, 2e; airmail, 10, 70e (15v se-tenant in sheet of 15).

Monkeys, various species. *Dec. 27.* Se-tenant in sheets of 16. 5, 10, 15, 20, 25, 30, 35, 40, 45, 50, 55, 60c, 1, 2e; airmail 10, 70e (16v).

Cats, various species. *Dec. 27.* Se-tenant in sheets of 16. 5, 10, 15, 20, 25, 30, 35, 40, 45, 50, 55, 60c, 1, 2e; airmail 10, 70e (16v).

Fish, various species. *Dec. 27.* Se-tenant in sheets of 16. 5, 10, 15, 20, 25, 30, 35, 40, 45, 50, 55, 60c, 1, 2e; airmail 10, 70e (16v).

Butterflies, various species. *Dec. 27.* Se-tenant in sheets of 16. 5, 10, 15, 20, 25, 30, 35, 40, 45, 50, 55, 60c, 1, 2e; airmail 10, 70e (16v).

1975

Picasso Memorial (Paintings from last period). *Jan. 27.* 5, 10, 15, 20, 25c; airmail, 5, 70e (7v). 2 souvenir sheets 130e, perf.; 200e, imperf.

ARPHILA 75 Philatelic Exhibition Paris. *Jan. 27.* 8 gold foil airmail souvenir sheets, 3 sheets of 1, 250e, 1 sheet of 2, 250e, perf.; 3 sheets of 1, 300e; 1 sheet of 2, 300e, imperf.

Easter and Holy Year 1975. *Feb. 15.* 60, 70, 80c, 1, 1.50e; airmail, 30, 50e (7v). 2 airmail souvenir sheets 225e, perf.; 300e, imperf.

12th Winter Olympics, Innsbruck, 1976. *Mar. 10.* 5, 10, 15, 20, 25, 30, 35, 40, 45c, 25, 70e (11v). 2 souvenir sheets 130e, perf.; 200e, imperf. 2 gold foil souvenir sheets, 1 sheet of 1, 250e, 1 sheet of 2, 250e × 2.

Don Quixote. *Apr. 4.* 30, 35, 40, 45, 50c; airmail, 25, 60e (7v). 2 souvenir sheets 130e, perf.; 200e, imperf.

American Bicentennial. *April 30.* (First Issue) 5, 20, 40, 75c, 2, 5, 8e; airmail 25, 30e (9v). Airmail souvenir sheets, 130e, perf., 200e, imperf.

April 30. (Second Issue) 10, 30, 50c, 1, 3, 6, 10e; airmail, 12, 40e (9v). 2 airmail souvenir sheets, 130e, perf., 200e, imperf.

July 4. (Presidents) 5, 10, 20, 30, 40, 50, 75c, 1, 2, 3, 5, 6, 8, 10e; airmail, 12, 25, 30, 40e (18v). 4 airmail souvenir sheets, 225e × 2, perf., 300e × 2, imperf. Embossed gold foil 6 souvenir sheets airmail 200e × 2, 200e (2) perf., 300e × 2, 300e (2) imperf.

Bull Fight. *May 26.* 80, 85, 90, 95c, 8e; airmail, 35, 40e (7v). 2 airmail souvenir sheets, 130e, perf., 200e, imperf.

Apollo-Soyuz Space Project. *June 20.* 1, 2, 3, 5, 5.50, 7, 7.50, 9, 15e; airmail, 20, 30e (11v). 2 airmail souvenir sheets, 225e, perf., 300e, imperf.

Apollo-Soyuz Space Project. *July 17.* Airmail souvenir sheet, 250e, perf.

Famous Painters, Nudes. *Aug. 10.* Se-tenant in sheets of 16. 5, 10, 15, 20, 25, 30, 35, 40, 45, 50, 55, 60c, 1, 2e; airmail 10, 70e (16v). (Egyptian, Greek, Roman, Indian art, Goes, Dürer, Liss, Beniort, Renoir, Gauguin, Stenlen, Picasso, Modigliani, Matisse, Padua). Airmail souvenir sheetlets embossed gold foil, 10 × 200p +25p, perf., 10 × 250p+50p, imperf.

Conquerors of the Seas. *Sept. 5.* 30, 35, 40, 45, 50, 55, 60, 65, 70, 75c; airmail 8, 10, 50, 60p (14v). 4 airmail souvenir sheets, 130p, perf., 200p, imperf., 2 each.

Christmas and Holy Year 1975. *Oct.* 60, 70, 80c, 1, 1.50e; airmail 30, 50e (7v) (Jordan, Barocci, Vereycke, Rubens, Mengs, Del Castillo, Cavedone). 2 airmail souvenir sheets, 225e, perf., 300e, imperf. Embossed gold foil, 4 souvenir sheets, 200e, perf., 300e, imperf. 2 gold foil miniature sheets of 2, 200e+200e, perf., 300e+300e, imperf.

President Macias, I.W.Y. *Dec. 25.* 1.50, 3, 3.50, 5, 7, 10e; airmail 100, 300e (8v). 2 airmail souvenir sheets (world events), 100 (U.S., Yorktown 2c), 300e, imperf.

1976

Uniforms, Cavalry. *Feb. 2.* 5, 10, 15, 20, 25c; airmail, 5, 70p (7v). 2 airmail souvenir sheets, 130p, perf., 200p, imperf.

12th Winter Olympics, Innsbruck '76. *Feb.* 50, 55, 60, 65, 70, 75, 80, 85, 90e; airmail 35, 60e (11v). 2 airmail souvenir sheets, 130e, perf., 200e, imperf.

21st Summer Olympics Montreal '76. Ancient to Modern Games. *Feb.* 50, 60, 70, 80, 90c; airmail 35, 60e (7v). 2 souvenir sheets airmail, 225e, perf., 300e, imperf.

21st Summer Olympics Montreal '76 *Mar. 5.* 50, 60, 70, 80, 90c; airmail 30, 60e (7v). 2 airmail souvenir sheets 225e, perf., 300e, imperf. 4 embossed gold foil airmail souvenir sheets, 250e, perf., 300e, imperf. 2 miniature sheets of 2, 250e×2, perf., 300e×2, imperf.

U.N. 30th Anniversary. *June.* Airmail souvenir sheet, 250e, perf.

El Greco, paintings. *Apr. 5.* 1, 3, 5, 8, 10e; airmail, 15, 25e (7v). 2 airmail semipostal souvenir sheets, 200+25e, perf., 250+50e, imperf.

21st Summer Olympics, Montreal, modern games. *May 7.* 50, 55, 60, 65, 70, 75, 80, 85, 90c; airmail, 35, 60e (11v). 2 airmail souvenir sheets, 225e, perf., 300e, imperf. 4 embossed on gold foil souvenir sheets, 250e, perf., 300e, imperf. (2 each). 2 miniature sheets of 2, 250e × 2, perf., 300e × 2, imperf.

Contemporary Automobiles, *June 10.* 1, 3, 5, 8, 10p; airmail, 15, 25p (7v). 2 airmail semipostal souvenir sheets, 200+25p, perf., 250+50p, imperf.

Nature Protection, European Animals. *July 1.* 5, 10, 15, 20, 25c; airmail, 5, 70p (7v). 2 airmail souvenir sheets, 130p, perf., 200p, imperf. **Asian Animals.** *Sept. 20.* 30, 35, 40, 45c, 8p; airmail 50c, 60p (7v). 2 airmail souvenir sheets, 130p, perf., 200p, imperf. **Asian Birds.** *Sept. 20.* 55, 60, 65, 70, 75c; airmail, 10, 50p (7v). 2 airmail souvenir sheets, 130p, perf., 200p, imperf. **European Birds.** *Sept. 20.* 5, 10, 15, 20, 25c; airmail, 5, 70p (7v). 2 airmail souvenir sheets, 130p, perf., 200p, imperf. **North American Birds.** *Sept. 20.* 80, 85, 90, 95c, 1p; airmail, 15, 40p (7v). 2 airmail souvenir sheets, 130p, perf., 200p, imperf.

Motorcycle Aces. *July 22.* 1e × 2, 2e × 2, 3e × 2, 4e × 2, 5e × 2, 10e × 2, 30e × 2, 40e × 2 (16v) in se-tenant blocks of 8 different values.

21st Summer Olympics, Montreal. *Aug.* 7, 10, 25e se-tenant strip of 3; airmail, 200e (4v). Airmail souvenir sheet, 300e, imperf.

Flowers. *Aug. 16.* **South America.** 30, 35, 40, 45, 50c;

airmail, 8, 60p (7v). 2 airmail souvenir sheets, 130p, perf., 200p, imperf. **Oceania.** 80, 85, 90, 95c, 1p; airmail, 15, 40p (7v). 2 airmail souvenir sheets, 130p, perf., 200p, imperf.

1977

Butterflies. *Jan.* 80, 85, 90, 95c, 8e; airmail, 35, 40e (7v). 2 airmail souvenir sheets, 130e, perf., 200e, imperf.

Madrid Real, 75th anniversary. *Jan.* 2, 4, 5, 8, 10, 15e; airmail, 20, 35, 150e (9v).

Ancient Carriages. *Feb.* 5, 10, 15, 20, 25, 30, 35, 40, 45, 50, 55, 60c, 1, 2e; airmail, 10, 70e (16v).

Chinese Art. *Feb.* 60, 70, 80c, 1, 1.50e; airmail, 30. 50e (7v). 2 airmail souvenir sheets, 130e, perf., 200e, imperf.

African Masks. *Mar.* 5, 10, 15, 20, 25c; airmail, 5, 70e (7v). 2 airmail souvenir sheets, 130e, perf., 200e, imperf.

North American Animals., 1.25, 1.50, 1.75, 2, 2.25e; airmail, 20, 50e (7v). 2 airmail souvenir sheets, 130e, perf., 200e, imperf.

World Championship Soccer, Argentina '78. *July 25.*

Famous Players. 2, 4, 5, 8, 10, 15e; airmail, 20, 35e (8v). 2 airmail souvenir sheets, 150e, perf., 250e, imperf.

Famous Teams. 2, 4, 5, 8, 10, 15e; airmail, 20, 35e (8v se-tenant). 2 gold foil embossed souvenir sheets, 500e (Amphilex '77, Cutty Sark, Concorde); airmail, 500e (World Cup).

Napoleon. *Aug. 20.*

Life and Battle Scenes. 5, 10, 15, 20, 25, 30, 35, 40, 45, 50, 55, 60c, 1, 2e; airmail, 10, 70e (se-tenant in sheet of 16).

Military Uniforms. 5, 10, 15, 20, 25, 30, 35, 40, 45, 50, 55, 60c, 1, 2e; airmail, 10, 70e (se-tenant in sheet of 16).

South American Animals, *Aug.* 2.50, 2.75, 3, 3.50, 4e; airmail, 25, 35e (7v). 2 airmail souvenir sheets, 130e, perf., 200e imperf.

U.S.S.R. Space Program, 20th anniversary. *Dec. 15.* 2, 4, 5, 8, 10, 15e; airmail, 20, 35e (8v). 2 airmail souvenir sheets, 150e, imperf., 250e, perf.

1978

Ancient Sailing Ships. *Jan. 6.* 5, 10, 15, 20, 25c; airmail, 5, 70e, also 5, 10, 20, 25, 70e (12v). 4 airmail souvenir sheets, 150, 225e, perf., 250, 300e, imperf. Gold foil embossed airmail souvenir sheets, 500e, perf., imperf.

Pre-Olympics '80. *Jan. 17.*

Winter Games, Lake Placid. 5, 10, 20, 25e; airmail, 70e (5v). 2 airmail souvenir sheets, 150e, perf., 250e, imperf. Gold foil embossed airmail souvenir sheet, 500e, perf., imperf.

Summer Games, Moscow. 2, 3, 5, 8, 10, 15e; airmail, 30, 50e (8v). 2 airmail souvenir sheets, 150e, perf., 250e, imperf. Gold foil embossed airmail souvenir sheet, 500e perf., imperf.

Summer Water Games, Talinn. 5, 10, 20, 25e; airmail, 70e (5v). 2 airmail souvenir sheets, 150e, perf., 250e, imperf. Gold foil embossed airmail souvenir sheet, 500e, perf., imperf.

QE II Coronation, 25th anniversary. *Apr. 25.* 2, 5, 8, 10, 12, 15e; airmail, 30, 50e (8v). 2 airmail souvenir sheets, 150e perf., 250e imperf.

English Knights of 1200–1350 A.D. *Apr. 25.* 5, 10, 15, 20, 25e; airmail, 15, 70e (7v). 2 airmail souvenir sheets, 130e perf., 250e imperf.

Old Locomotives. *Aug.* 1, 2, 3, 5, 10e; airmail, 25, 70e (7v). 2 airmail souvenir sheets, 150e perf., 250e imperf.

Prehistoric Animals. *Aug.* 30, 35, 40, 45, 50e; airmail, 25, 60e (7v). Airmail souvenir sheet, 130e.

Souvenir Sheets. *Aug.* Airmail: **Francisco Goya,** "Maja Vestida," 150e; **Peter Paul Rubens—UNICEF,** 250e; **Europa—CEPT—Eurphila, 78,** 250e; **30th International Stamp Fair, Riccione,** 150e; **1978 Events.** Sheet of 3, QE II Coronation, 150e; CEPT, 250e and World Cup Soccer, Argentina '78 and Spain '82, 150e; Christmas, Titian painting, "The Virgin," 150e.

INDEX AND IDENTIFIER

See also Addenda and For the Record.

NUMERICAL INDEX OF WATERMARK ILLUSTRATIONS (VOL. II)

Wmk.	Country	Page
a-g	Chile	532
84-90	Argentina	108-112
91	Austria	160
	Bosnia and Herzegovina	298
96	Belgium	215
97-101	Brazil	309-311
103	China	556
104-105	Cuba	767-768
106	Cuba	761
107	Czechoslovakia	788
108-110	Danzig	860-862
111-114	Danish West Indies	859, 860
	Denmark	865, 866
115-116	Dominican Republic	893, 895
116	Colombia	675
117	Ecuador	928
118-120	Egypt	963-964
121	Finland	1043
122-124	French Congo	1154
125	Albania	63
	Cameroun	456
	Caroline Islands	488
	Danzig	862
127	Colombia	675
140	Eritrea	1010
	Ethiopia	1034
145	Bulgaria	370
168	Bulgaria	367
	Finland	1042
171	Armenia	155
	Far Eastern Republic	1034
193	Brazil	311
194	Colombia	660
195	Egypt	964
205	Argentina	113
206	Brazil	311
207	Estonia	1015
208	Finland	1043
215	Chile	534
	Costa Rica	745
218	Brazil	311
220	Albania	35
221-222	Brazil	312
229	Colombia	660
	Costa Rica	744
	Cuba	771
232	Angola	99
233	Ecuador	961
236	Brazil	313
237	Danzig	551
245	Brazil	313
249	Brazil	314
255	Colombia	661
256	Brazil	315
261	China	561
263	Slovakia	844
264	Brazil	315
267-268	Brazil	317
270-271	Brazil	363
273	Finland	1044
275	Bulgaria	373
278	Croatia	765
281	Brazil	317
	China	569
282	Ethiopia	1020
287	Argentina	117
288	Argentina	114
315	Egypt	969
318	Egypt	969
321	Cuba	778
323	China	570
328	Egypt	971
331	Colombia	666
340	Ecuador	952
341	Czechoslovakia	804
342	Egypt	973
346	Colombia	668
363	Finland	1050
365	Argentina	126
367	Ecuador	940
368	China	582
370	China	582

Authorized SCOTT® Dealer Listing

Look for your nearby dealer in the listing below. If you can't find him, call us at 1-800-448-3611. We're adding names daily. And check your dealer's window for the Authorized Dealer Sign.

ALABAMA

Rash Enterprises
110 Victoria Drive
Enterprise, AL 36330

Hoover Stamps
3228 Lorna Road
Hoover, AL 35216

Ala Coin
912 Bob Wallace
Huntsville, AL 35801

ALASKA

Richard D. Sampson
P. O. Box 841
Barrow, AK 99723

ARKANSAS

The Coin & Stamp Shop
1 Donaghey Bldg.
Little Rock, AR 72201

Ye Old Hobby Shoppe
1400 W. Walnut Apt. 114
Rogers, AR 72756

ARIZONA

Bridgeport Stamp & Coin
HC72 Box 1289
Cottonwood, AZ 86326

BJ's Stamp Co.
6342 W. Bell Road
Glendale, AZ 85308

Mountain States Stamp & Coin
5740 W. Glendale Avenue
Glendale, AZ 85301

Southwest Collectibles
1344 W. University
Mesa, AZ 85201

A & F Coins & Stamps
3180 E. Indian School Rd.
Phoenix, AZ 85016

Maricopa Stamps
P. O. Box 60963-MS
Phoenix, AZ 85082

Amer. Philatelic Brokerage
7225 N. Oracle Road
Tucson, AZ 85704

Quail Trail Mail Stamp Co.
P. O. Box 50603
Tucson, AZ 85703-1603

Catalina Stamp Shop
4022 E. Grant
Tucson, AZ 85712

CALIFORNIA

Ed Denson Stamps
P. O. Box 158
Alderpoint, CA 95411

Brewart Coins & Stamps
403 W. Katella
Anaheim, CA 92802

OCPI-Steve's Stamp Store
1017-19 N. Euclid
Anaheim, CA 92801

SWCC
634 San Gabriel Ave.
Azusa, CA 91702

Shipwell Container Corp.
634 San Gabriel Avenue
Azusa, CA 91702

Harry Lewis Weiss
P. O. Box 3396
Beverly Hills, CA 90212

Berlyn Enterprises
B. G. Berg
Box 1807
Blue Jay, CA 92317

Coin & Stamp Mart
21510 Sherman Way
Canoga Park, CA 91303

B & B Stamp Shop
5825 Manzanita Avenue #3
Carmichael, CA 95608

Joseph I. Caldwell Stamps
6659 Arozona Lane
Carpenteria, CA 93013

Shnayer's Philatelic SVCS
1420 Mangrove Ave.
Chico, CA 95926

Postage Stamps & Supplies For Collectors
992 Helix Avenue
Chula Vista, CA 92011

RHO Enterprises
John Rhodes
2082 Waterbury
Chula Vista, CA 92010

Postmark Stamps
1460 Clovis Avenue
Clovis, CA 93612

Russell S. Bell
21 Tamac Vista
Corte Madera, CA 94925

CALIFORNIA

3-Cabins Stamp Co.
P. O. Box 689
Eureka, CA 95501

The Postmark-Stamps & Coins
11879 A Valley View
Garden Grove, CA 92645

Coin & Stamp Galleries Of Glendale
142 S. Brand Blvd.
Glendale, CA 91205

A&E Stamp & Coin
8853 Adams Avenue
Huntington Beach, CA 92646

Aliso Hills Stamp & Coin
25381 I Alicia Pkwy.
Laguna Hills, CA 92653

Laguna Hills Stamp Co.
25292 McIntyre Suite E
Laguna Hills, CA 92653

Stamps in the Attic
323 First St.
P. O. Box AE
Los Altos, CA 94023

M. Meghrig & Sons
5352 Wilshire Blvd.
Los Angeles, CA 90036

L&M Stamp Co.
2121A 10th St.
Los Osos, CA 93402

Ftacek Stamp Co.
1118 Virginia Street
Manteca, CA 95336

R.Schneider Co.
3096 Snell Place
Marina, CA 93944

Ron's Stamp
P. O. Box 2972
Merced, CA 95340

Pete Alexander
P. O. Box 2087
Napa, CA 94558

Quality Philatelic
P. O. Box 2871
Newport Beach, CA 92663

United Stamp Co.
P. O. Box 3001
No. Hollywood, CA 91609

CALIFORNIA

Calif. Coin & Stamp Co.
390 17th St.
Oakland, CA 94612

Stanley M. Piller & Assoc.
3351 Grand Avenue
Oakland, CA 94610

Yellowstone Stamps
388 South Tustin Avenue
Orange, CA 92666

Kett's Koin Kastle, Inc.
422 S. A. St.
Oxnard, CA 93030

Crown City Stamp & Coin Co.
16 N. Marengo Ave.
Suite 201
Pasadena, CA 91101

Alan Lipken Stamp
6 Petaluma Blvd. N.
Petaluma, CA 94952

Global Stamp Service
109 W. Center Street
Pomona, CA 91768

Stamps From Sylvia
P. O. Box 226
Redlands, CA 92373

Stamps R Us
6747 Tampa Avenue
Reseda, CA 91335

Tom & Jerry
P. O. Box 1166
Reseda, CA 91335

Giles A. Gibson
P. O. Drawer B
54 Willow Road
Rio Nido, CA 95471

C&H Stamps
2550 Alta Arden Expwy.
Sacramento, CA 95825

Duane D. Morford
P. O. Box 60769
Sacramento, CA 95860

Fred Coops & Co.
115 Central City Mall
San Bernadino, CA 92401

Robert E. Kohl
3745 Seventh Avenue #2
San Diego, CA 92103

Authorized SCOTT® Dealer Listing

Look for your nearby dealer in the listing below. If you can't find him, call us at 1-800-448-3611. We're adding names daily. And check your dealer's window for the Authorized Dealer Sign.

CALIFORNIA

United States Stamp Co. Inc.
368 Bush St.
San Francisco, CA 94104

Edward Weinberg Inc.
3404 Balboa Street
San Francisco, CA 94121

Michael R. Fried
Box 817
San Leandro, CA 94577

The Stamp Den
12 W. Figueroa Street
Santa Barbara, CA 93101

Stampcraft
933 Monroe P. O. Box 2425
Santa Clara, CA 95055

Santa Maria Coin & Stamp
2011-M S. Broadway
Santa Maria, CA 93454

Brosius Stamp & Coin
1510 2nd Street
Santa Monica, CA 90401

David Torre
P. O. Box 4298
Santa Rosa, CA 95402

Coins Stamps & More
P. O. Box 3455
Simi Valley, CA 93063

Americana Stamp & Coin
18385 Ventura Blvd.
Tarzana, CA 91356

Bullock's Dept. Store Stamp Dept.
21600 Hawthorn Blvd.
Torrance, CA 90503

South Bay Coins & Stamps
3535 Torrance Blvd.
Torrance, CA 90503

Bick International
P. O. Box 854
Van Nuys, CA 91408

Globe Stamp Store
Parker Haydon
1507 Cypress Street
Walnut Creek, CA 94596

Kenneth & Co. Limited
37 Carlos Court
Walnut Creek, CA 94596

CALIFORNIA

The Stamp Gallery
1515 Locust Street
Walnut Creek, CA 94596

Kabel Stamp Co.
P. O. Box 415
West Covina, CA 91793

Colony's
P. O. Box 1482
Whittier, CA 90609

Whittier Philatelic SVCS
6727 S. Washington Ave.
Whittier, Ca 90601

Woodland Hills Stamps & Coin Co.
20969 Ventura Blvd. 12A
Woodland Hills, CA 91364

Thomas F. Hut
18165 Cari Lane
Yorba Linda, CA 92686

COLORADO

Timm & Moses Stamp & Supplies Inc.
P. O. Box 31692
Aurora, CO 80041

Brighton S & C Center Ltd.
Kenneth M. Ott
119 Bridge Street
Brighton, CO 80601

Bauer Enterprises
5290 Silver Drive
P. O. Box 26196
Colorado Springs, CO 80918

Skyway Stamp Co.
P. O. Box 38266
Colo. Springs, CO 80937

Apollo Stamp Co.
The Stamp & Coin Dept.
The Denver
16th & California Sts.
Denver, CO 80202

Colorado Collectors Coin
1724 S. Broadway
Denver, CO 80210

Rocky Mountain Stamp
5940 E. Colfax Avenue
Denver, CO 80220

Evergreen Stamp Co.
4080 S. Skyline Drive
Evergreen, CO 80439

The Collector
141 Mountain Shadow Dr.
Glenwood Springs, CO 81801

COLORADO

Murray Paul Hayutin
2198 Green Oaks Drive
Greenwood Village, CO 80121

Aronohoe Coin & Stamp
1212 W. Littleton Blvd.
Littleton, CO 80120

CONNECTICUT

J. L. McGuire
P. O. Box 152
Colchester, CT 06415

Connecticut Yankee Stamps
P. O. Box 5008
Hamden, CT 06518

JMB Associates
130 Centerbrook Road
Hamden, CT 06518

W. C. Phillips & Co.
11 Asylum Street
Hartford, CT 06103

Su-Deb Coin & Stamp Co.
67 East Center Street
Manchester, CT 06040

Joseph A. Riley
5 Trading Cove Drive
Norwich, CT 06360

Marty's Stamp & Coin
161½ Boston Post Road
Orange, CT 06477

Pony Express Stamp & Coin
Heritage Village
Southbury, CT 06488

Dr. Robert Rabinowitz
37 Stanwick Place
Stamford, CT 06905

The Keeping Room
P. O. Box 257
Trumbull, CT 06611

Miller's Stamp Shop
41 New London Tpke.
Uncasville, CT 06382

Rouleau Stamp Co.
57 Echo Ridge Dr.
Vernon, CT 06066

The Perforation Gauge
P. O. Box 332
West Hartford, CT 06107

DELAWARE

Stamp Center
4115 Concord Pike
Wilmington, DE 19803

FLORIDA

Boca Raton Stamps
P. O. Box 7077
Boca Raton, FL 33431

Jerry Siegel
P. O. Box 290455
Davie, FL 33329

Philatelic Concepts
321 SE 3rd Terrace
Deerfield Beach, FL 33441

Rick Basini Stamps
1505 NE 26th Street
Ft. Lauderdale, FL 33305

Herbert A. Sawyer
4415 NW 33rd Court
Gainesville, FL 32606

Benjamin Liechtenstein
6089 Amber Tree Lane
Green Acres City, FL 33463

Heritage C & S Gallery
775 University Blvd. N.
Jacksonville, FL 32211

Jacksonville Stamp & Coin
39 University Blvd. N.
Jacksonville, FL 32211

A & R Stamp & Coin Inc.
1512 W. Vine St.
Kissimmee, FL 32741

Ruth & Millerd Stamp Co.
c/o Chini-Ka Pin
Route 4 Box 810
Lake City, FL 32055

Hauser Coin & Stamp
1233 Highway 98 S.
Lakeland, FL 33802

William Gerlah
P. O. Box 6637
Lake Worth, FL 33466

Dobson's Quality Stamps
P. O. Box 5362
Lake Worth, FL 33466

State Supply Co.
1849 7th Avenue North
Lake Worth, FL 33461

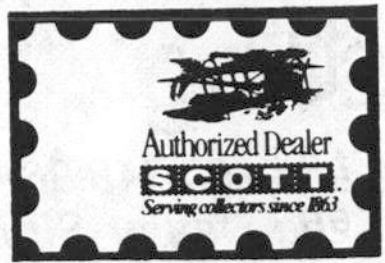

Authorized SCOTT® Dealer Listing

Look for your nearby dealer in the listing below. If you can't find him, call us at 1-800-448-3611. We're adding names daily. And check your dealer's window for the Authorized Dealer Sign.

IOWA

Iowa Stamps & Coins
Box 56
Ankeny, IA 50021

Richard F. Castner
Quad City Stamp Shop
538 14th Street
Bettendorf, IA 52722

Rivercity Stamps
1630 State Street
Suite 8
Bettendorf, IA 52722

Holman's
508 Water
Sioux City, IA 51103

Stamps N Stuff
2700 University Suite 204
West Des Moines, IA 50265

KANSAS

Plate Block Stamp Co.
Box 6417
Leawood, KS 66206

Ace Stamp Co.
9607 Metcalf
Overland Park, KS 66212

C & G Coins & Jewelry Inc.
Galen Glass
9814 W. Santa Fe
Overland Park, KS 66212

Suburban Stamp Gallery
5016 Linden Avenue
Roeland Park, KS 66205

Central Sales Inc.
P. O. Box 3178
Shawnee, KS 66203

Great Plains Stamps
1700 Medford
Topeka, KS 66604

KENTUCKY

Blue Grass Stamp Shop
166 Eastland Shopping Ctr.
Lexington, KY 40505

Glover's Bookery
862 S. Broadway
Lexington, KY 40504

C O & H E Stamps
1511 Bardstown Road
Louisville, KY 40205

Dupont Stamp Studio
1406 G Browns Lane
Louisville, KY 40207

KENTUCKY

Treasure Isld. Coin & Stamps
1433 Bardstown Road
Louisville, KY 40204

Col. R. K. Walker
6916 Southside Dr.
Louisville, KY 40214

LOUISIANA

The Little Stamp Co.
4500 Shores Drive
Metairie, LA 76006

J. M. Fussell
Box 24015
New Orleans, LA 70104

New Orleans Stamp & Coin Co.
P. O. Box 4097
New Orleans, LA 70178

Silen's Library Datr
2737 Bienville Avenue
New Orleans, LA 70119

The Stamp Place
333 St. Charles Avenue
New Orleans, LA 70130

Leonard Keim Stamps
P. O. Box 279
Robert, LA 70455

L & M Stamps
Mavalee Village
4438A Youree Drive
Shreveport, LA 71105

MAINE

Coins & Stamps
87 Spring Street
Brunswick, ME 04011

D&G Stamp & Coin
15 Water St.
Caribou, ME 04136

The Stamp Center
148 Summer Street
Kennebunk, ME 04043

CTC Stamps
426 Pleasant Street
Lewiston, ME 04240

MARYLAND

Annapolis Stamp & Coin Co.
208 W. Street
Annapolis, MD 21401

Maryland Stamps & Coins
7720 Wisconsin Ave.
Bethesda, MD 20014

MARYLAND

Commonwealth
Arthur F. Lafionatis
2908 Terrace Drive
Chevy Chase, MD 20815

Bob Beck Co.
1801 Taylor Avenue
Fort Washington, MD 20744

Buckinghamshire Stamp Co.
P. O. Box 3018
Gaithersburg, MD 20878

Rockville Stamp & Coin
1097 Rockville Pike
Rockville, MD 20852

Universal Stamps
1327-D Rockville Pike
Rockville, MD 20852

Frank and Laurese Katen
708 Cloverly Street
Silver Spring, MD 20904

Potomac Supply
P. O. Box 34113
W. Bethesda, MD 20817

MASSACHUSETTS

Collectors Shop Inc.
P. O. Box 131
Auburndale, MA 02166

H. F. Johnson
23 Hariet Avenue
Belmont, MA 02178

Waverly Exchange Inc.
503 Trapelo Road
Belmont, MA 02178

Olde Boston Co. Inc.
61 Bromfield Street
Boston, MA 02108

Robert Patkin
10 Oldefarms Road
Boxford, MA 01921

Westside Stamp & Coin Co.
432 West Street
Brockton, MA 02401

Danvers Coin & Stamp Shop
157 High Street
Danvers, MA 01923

D&D Stamp & Coin
163 New Boston Road
Fall River, MA 02720

Falmouth Stamp & Coin
Thomas A. Holland
Falmouth Mall
Falmouth, MA 02536

MASSACHUSETTS

Battle Green Stamp Co.
4-Muzzey Street
Lexington, MA 02173

Richard E. Murphy
52 Cedar Hill Road
Northbow, MA 01532

Tritown Stamp & Coin
55 Franklin St.
Quincy, MA 02169

Suburban Stamp
1071 St. James Avenue
Springfield, MA 01104

Bicentennial Stamps & Covers
10 Fenno Drive
Westminster, MA 01473

Economical Co.
6 King Philip Road
Worcester, MA 01606

J & N Fortier Inc.
484 Main Street
Worcester, MA 01608

Lincoln Stamp & Coin
50 Franklin St.
Worcester, MA 01608

Parnassus Book Service
Rte. 6A Box 33
Yarmouth Port, MA 02675

MICHIGAN

Robert Gesell
P. O. Box 8248
Ann Arbor, MI 48107

Mel Coon Stamps
3833 Twelve Mile
Berkley, MI 48072

Jones Coin & Stamp Co.
15332 W. Warren
Dearborn, MI 48126

RMJ Enterprises
Madelyn & Rich Slominski
7129 N. Beech Daly
Dearborn Hts., MI 48124

America's Stamp-West
25820 Middlebelt Road & 11 Mile Road
Farmington Hills, MI 48018

Steve Rubenfaer Stamps
30840 Northwestern Hwy. #100
Farmington Hills, MI 48018

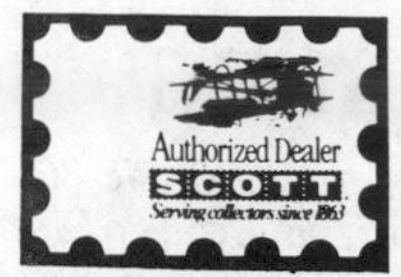

Authorized SCOTT® Dealer Listing

Look for your nearby dealer in the listing below. If you can't find him, call us at 1-800-448-3611. We're adding names daily. And check your dealer's window for the Authorized Dealer Sign.

MICHIGAN

Frankenmuth Stamp Store
126 South Main Street
Frankenmuth, MI 48734

Philatelic Appraisal Co.
9882 Sonora
Freeland, MI 48623

Richard H. Dick
31561 Bridge Street
Garden City, MI 48135

Bookery
150 E. Fulton
Grand Rapids, MI 49503

Kelly's Coin & Stamp
4324 W. Saginaw Hwy.
Lansing, MI 48917

House of Cards Gift & Stamp
40100 Hayes
Mt. Clemens, MI 48044

Prieh's Stamp & Coin
78 Macomb
Mt. Clemens, MI 48043

Jack White
263 S. Gratiot
Mt. Clemens, MI 48043

W E B's Stamps
W. E. Bentkowski
37829 Moravian Drive
Mt. Clemens, MI 48043

Clark Stamp Co.
5232 Airline Road
Muskegon, MI 49444

Michigan Stamp Dealer Supply Co.
10016 Wolfriver Drive
Plymouth, MI 48170

Plymouth Hobby & Teachers Corner
882 W. Ann Arbor Trail
Plymouth, MI 48170

Philatelics Intl. Inc.
3355 Sunnyview
Saginaw, MI 48604

Lakeshore Stamps
31500 St. Margaret
St. Clair Shores, MI 48082

W. Michigan Coin & Stamp Inc.
1878 28th Street SW
Wyoming, MI 49509

MINNESOTA

Bryce's
310 SW 1st Street
Austin, MN 55912

Stamp Professor
1500 E. 79th Street
Bloomington, MN 55420

Plaza Stamps & Coins Ltd.
3939 W. 50th Street
Edina, MN 55424

Bel-Aire Stamp & Coin
923 Marquette Avenue
Minneapolis, MN 55402

Minnesota Stamp & Coin Co.
720 2nd Ave. South
Minneapolis, MN 55402

Dick Rudolf
P. O. Box 19251
Minneapolis, MN 55419

Battle Creek Coins & Stamps
297 S McKnight Rd.
St. Paul, MN 55119

Bud Elvgren
P. O. Box 18120
St. Paul, MN 55118

Gopher Wholesale
P. O. Box 19653
St. Paul, MN 55119

Twin City Stamp & Coin
404 St. Peter Street
St. Paul, MN 55102

MISSOURI

Knolls Stamp Service
7220 Rightors Mill Rd.
Rockville, MO 20855

Rolla Rare Coin & Stamp
P. O. Box 902-700 Pine
Rolla, MO 65401

Gilmore Stamps & Coins
3004 E. Sunshine
Springfield, MO 65804

Arch City Supply
P. O. Box 10956
St. Louis, MO 63135

The Stamp Corner
8145 Delmar
St. Louis, MO 63130

MONTANA

Cottage Industries
1520 Beall
Bozeman, MT 59715

Cutler Stamps
608½ Central Avenue
Apt. 206
Great Falls, MT 59405

NEBRASKA

Hard-To-Find
Dianna Eveland
U.S. Hiway 92 Access
Box 152
Lemoyne, NE 69146

Chick Bartlett Stamp & Coin Gallery
766 NBC Center
Lincoln, NE 68508

Lin-Co
2641 N. 48th
Lincoln, NE 68504

Aksarben Stamp
10817 Prairiebrook Road
Rockbrook Village
Omaha, NE 68144

Natl. Stamp & Coin
210 S. 16th St.
Braiker/Brandeis Bldg.
Omaha, NE 68102

Tannutuva Stamp Co.
203 So. 72nd Street #3
Omaha, NE 68114

NEVADA

Shelly Stamp Co.
3661 Maryland Pkwy.
Las Vegas, NV 89109

NEW HAMPSHIRE

J&S Stamp Co.
12 Kimball Hill Rd.
Hudson, NH 03051

J&R Stamps
141 Paro Avenue
Keene, NH 03431

Sherran's Wholesale
Route 8, Box 363
Loudon, NH 03301

H. E. Harris & Co.
170 West Road
P. O. Box 7087
Portsmouth, NH 03801

Major Book Inc.
Newington Mall
Portsmouth, NH 03801

NEW HAMPSHIRE

David Ladner
1 Wakefield Street
Suite 212
Rochester, NH 03867

NEW JERSEY

Mr. P's Stamp & Hobby
6 Keswick Court
Belle Mead, NJ 08502

Lickem & Stickem
150 Grand St.
Carlstadt, NJ 07072

Gene Federman
Gene's Stamp & Coin
Cinnaminson Mall
Cinnaminson, NJ 08077

Romar-Lewis Corp.
Attn: Roger Lewis Broker
1539 Durie Ave.
Closter, NJ 07624

The Philatelists
P. O. Box 408
McAfee, NJ 07428

Penn Jersey Coin & Stamp Ex.
15 W. Park Avenue
Merchantville, NJ 08109

Aall Stamps
38 N. Main Street
Box 249
Milltown, NJ 08850

The Stamp Man
P. O. Box 2122
Neptune City, NJ 07754

Doriton House of Stamps
Route 1 Market
New Brunswick, NJ 07095

Lyceum Stamp Co.
18 Christy Lane
Ocean Township, NJ 07712

Frank Knina
474 Forest Avenue
Paramus, NJ 07652

Quality Stamps
P. O. Box 167
Plainfield, NJ 07161

Beachcomber Coin Supplies
Shore Mall
Pleasantville, NJ 08232

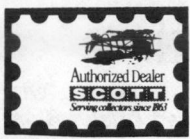

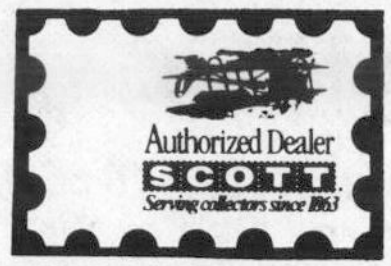

Authorized SCOTT® Dealer Listing

Look for your nearby dealer in the listing below. If you can't find him, call us at 1-800-448-3611. We're adding names daily. And check your dealer's window for the Authorized Dealer Sign.

UTAH

Highland Stamp Shop
4835 Highland Drive
Salt Lake City, UT 84117

Worldwide Coin Co.
933 Pennsylvania Place
Salt Lake City, UT 84102

VIRGINIA

Latherow & Co. Inc.
5054 Lee Highway
Arlington, VA 22207

Colonial Stamp Shoppe
P. O. Box 515
Colonial Heights, VA 23834

Red Dog Stamps
P. O. Box 885
Fairfax, VA 22030

Cee Jay Stamp Sales Inc.
100 N. Washington Street
Falls Church, VA 22046

Stamp Chest
115 Hillwood Avenue
Falls Church, VA 22046

John's Stamp Shop
Route 2 Box 52B
Grundy, VA 24614

Uhler's Stamp & Coin Mart
9029 Center Street
Manassas, VA 22110

Sam's Comics and Collectibles
13770 Warwick Blvd.
Newport News, VA 23602

R. J. Schultz Stamp
1919 Flintwood Drive
Richmond, VA 23233

Thalhimers Stamp & Coin
7th St. Platform
Richmond, VA 23261

A. H. Coins & Stamps
5302 Fairfield Shp. Cnt.
Virginia Beach, VA 23464

VIRGINIA

Beach Coins & Stamps
1621 Hilltop W. Shppg. Ctr.
Virginia Beach, VA 23451

DM Stamps
178 Highmeadow Place
Warrenton, VA 22186

WASHINGTON

Evergreen Stamp & Coin
Evergreen Village
Shopping Center
1645 140th NE
Bellevue, WA 98005

The Stamp Gallery
10335 Main Street
Bellevue, WA 98004

Washington Numismatic Gallery Inc.
1400 NE 20th
Bellevue, WA 98007

People's Stamp Serv.
4132 F. Street
Bremerton, WA 98312

Rainier Philatelic Inc.
15405 1st Avenue South
Burien, WA 98148

Odyssey Stamp & Coins #1
1615 Hewitt
Everett, WA 98201

Rel Stamp & Coin Co.
R. Trosper
1407 Hewitt Avenue
Everett, WA 98201

Pennies & Postage Inc.
Box 998
Mercer Island, WA 98040

Global Stamp
P. O. Box 7429
Olympia, WA 98507

Straits Stamp & Coin
112A S. Lincoln Street
Port Angeles, WA 98362

WASHINGTON

Wesley's Stamps
512 Rose Street
Port Angeles, WA 98362

A & M Stamps
P. O. Box 58157
Renton, WA 98058

Olo Enterprises
P. O. Box 207
Richland, WA 99352

Aurora Stamp Shop
18002 Aurora Avenue N.
Seattle, WA 98133

Halls Stamp & Gifts
West 1013 Sprague
Spokane, WA 99204

Ledo Supply Co.
North 3221 Park Road
Spokane, WA 99212

Tacoma Mall Coin & Stamp
320 Tacoma Mall
Tacoma, WA 98409

Almanac Postal Express
3409 Carol Avenue
Yakima, WA 98902

WASHINGTON, D.C.

John Arnosti
1426 HSA NW Suite 1027
Washington, DC 20005

WEST VIRGINIA

David Hill Ltd.
6424 U.S. Rte. 60 E.
Barboursville, WV 25504

RSA Stamps
Route 219, 250 South
Beverly, WV 26253

W. Va. Philatelic Classics
348 W. Main St.
Clarksburg, WV 26301

WEST VIRGINIA

Lubman & Rasmussen
224 Wilson Avenue
Morgantown, WV 26505

WISCONSIN

Cal's & Friends
4889 Pretty Lake Road
Dousman, WI 53118

Curtis E. Moore Co.
822 Green Bay Plaza
Green Bay, WI 54304

A-Mar
1033 Caledonia Street
La Crosse, WI 54603

Jim Luke's Stamp & Coin
P. O. Box 410
Manitowoc, WI 54220

Heritage Stamps
11400 W. Bluemound Road
Milwaukee, WI 53266

Northwestern Stamp Co., Inc.
152 W. Wisconsin Avenue
Milwaukee, WI 53203

America Coin & Stamp Co., Inc.
2724 16th Street
Racine, WI 53405

Wisconsin Valley Stamps
James R. Johnson
8503 Louis Street
Rothschild, WI 54474

Bob Korosec
Bob's Coins & Stamps
8307 W. Becher Street
West Allis, WI 53219

Rainbow Harvest Stamps
236 5th Avenue
Westbend, WI 53095

PUERTO RICO

Mr. Luis Pagan
Caribe Stamp & Coin Center
404 Munoz Rivera Avenue
Hato Rey, PR 00918

Authorized SCOTT® Dealer Listing

Look for your nearby dealer in the listing below. If you can't find him, call us at 1-800-448-3611. We're adding names daily. And check your dealer's window for the Authorized Dealer Sign.

The following wholesalers also handle Scott Products . . .

Anderson Import-Export Co.
P. O. Box 782
Florence, AL 35630

M. C. Clayton
910 San Mateo Avenue
San Bruno, CA 94066

Harold Cohn & Co. Inc.
3224 North Halsted Street
Chicago, IL 60657

Harry Edelman
111-37 Lefferts Blvd.
So. Ozone Park, NY 11420

Gold Coast Coin & Stamp
1007 NE 43rd Street
Ft. Lauderdale, FL 33334

Robert C. Gray
4219 Grove Street
Oakland, CA 94609

Grossman Stamp Co.
5 East 17th Street
New York, NY 10003

Hamps Coin & Stamp Co.
9440 Old Katy Road
Suite 121
Houston, TX 77055

Heart of America
1729 Stewart Street
Kansas City, KS 66104

Charles R. Heisler Inc.
500 Oak Grove Drive
Lancaster, PA 17601

Hopmeadow Trading Co.
P. O. Box 1269
Litchfield, CT 06759

Indy Stamp & Coin
10 North Sheffield
Indianapolis, IN 46222

Intercontinental Stamp
Ricardo Del Campo
4839 SW 75th Avenue
Miami, FL 33155

Jerry's Coin & Stamp Co.
Route 309
Line Lexington, PA 18932

Stephen Juskewycz
952 West 26th Street
Erie, PA 16508

Minkus Publishing Co.
41-45 West 25th Street
New York, NY 10010

Herman Most
7720 Wisconsin Avenue
Bethesda, MD 20014

Pollard Coin & Stamp
5220 East 23rd Street
Indianapolis, IN 46218

Harold Rice
993-995 Kenmore Avenue
Buffalo, NY 14217

Scott-Edelman Supply Co.
1111 East Truslow Avenue
Fullerton, CA 92631

Square Deal
18 Falkland Way
Portsmouth, NH 03801

Tonka Hobby Supply
297 S. McKnight Road
St. Paul, MN 55119

Trade Winds
159 West White Horse Pike
Berlin, NJ 08009

The Wholesale Co. Stamp & Coin Supplies
111 Nassau Street
New York, NY 10038

Williams Wholesale
114 Central Avenue
P. O. Box 6253
Albany, NY 12206

Serving collectors since 1863

Scott Publishing Co.
P. O. Box 828
Sidney, Ohio 45365

NUMBER CHANGES (VOL. 2)

No. in 1987 Cat.	No. in 1988 Cat.
ALBANIA	
27a, 29a	deleted
ALGERIA	
7a, 8a	deleted
18a, 20a	deleted
ARGENTINA	
1441	1442
1442	1441
BELGIAN CONGO	
61b	deleted
68a	deleted
144a, 146a, 148a, 149a, 151a	deleted
C1a, C2a	deleted
BELGIUM	
28a, 29a, 30a, 32a, 34a, 35a, 36b	deleted
37b	deleted
41a, 42b, 43a, 44a	deleted
45a, 46a, 47a, 48a	deleted
50a, 51a, 52b, 53a, 54a	deleted
56a, 57a	deleted
65a, 67a, 73a	deleted
85a, 86a, 87b, 88a, 90a	deleted
92a	deleted
103b	deleted
138a, 141a	deleted
270B	271
271-274	272-275
274A	276
274B-274C	278-279
274D	282
275-276	283-284
277-278	286-287
279-280	289-290
281-292	292-303
293-295	309-311
296-300	317-321
301-305	312-316
306-340	322-360
345-351	361-370
352	277
352A-353	280-281
354-383	371-400
385	401
388	402
389	405
390	407
391-392	409-410
393-396	413-416
397-399	418-420
400	285
401	288
402	291
403-406A	304-308
407-421	435-449
422-423	451-452
424	457
425-461	477-513
462	412
463	454
464	459
465-479	514-528
480	453
481-482	455-456
482A	458
483-487	460-466
488	468
489	450
490-499	529-538
500-501	403-404
502	408
502A	429
503	431
504-528	539-563
529-606	565-642
607-611	659-663
612	411
613	430
614	417
614A-614B	427-428
615	467
616-628	664-676
629-630	650-651
631-640	677-686
641-644	688-691
645	687
646-647	643-644
648-653	692-697
655-656	698-699
657	564
659-665	700-706
666-667	645-646
668-669	652-653
670-672	707-709
673-674	711-712
675	710
676-679	713-716
680	433
680A	472
680D	434
680G-681	473-474
681C-681D	475-476
682-690	717-725
691-692	654-655
693-710	726-743
711-712	647-648
713-714	744-745
714A-716	421-423
717-717A	746-747
717B	749
718-720A	751-754
720B-720C	756-757
721	759
722-723	761-762
724	764
724A	766
725	769
726	772
727	774
727A	778
728-738	789-799
738A-738C	469-471
739-750	800-811
751	649
752-754	656-658
755-792	812-849
793-798	857-862
799	850
800	852
801	863
802-803	782-783
804	785
805-816	864-875
865-872	876-883
873	851
874-875	853-854
876-877	884-885
878	406
882-884	424-426
890	748
891	750
893	755
894	758
895	760
896	763
897	765
898-899	767-768
900-901	770-771
902	773
903-905	775-777
906	779
910-911	780-781
923	432
924	784
925	787
929-930	855-856
980	786
981	788
B12a, B15a	deleted
B13a	B9a
P7a, P12a, P26a	deleted
BOSNIA & HERZEGOVINA	
126a, 126c, 126e, 126g	deleted
B1a	deleted
BRAZIL	
138a	deleted
152a, 155b, 157b	deleted
323	deleted
1928	1934
1930	1935
1932-1933	1936-1937
1935	1938
1987	1986
1990-1993	1988-1991
BULGARIA	
2871	2853E
2997	3000
CAMEROUN	
21a, 22a	deleted
133a, 135a	deleted
C335	C333
C333-C334	C334-C335
CAPE JUBY	
E1a	deleted
CHINA	
222a, 222b, 224a	deleted
297a, 297b, 299a, 299b	deleted
303a, 313a, 313b	deleted
1179a, 1179b, 1180a, 1180b, 1181a	deleted
1540a, 1541a, 1544a	deleted
PEOPLE'S REPUBLIC OF CHINA	
NORTH CHINA	
3LQ14a	3LQ19
3LQ19	3LQ14a
CILICIA	
65A	deleted
89	deleted
CONGO	
324a	deleted
COSTA RICA	
370-372 (Oct.)	371-373
CYRENAICA	
11a, 12a, 13a, 14a	deleted
B3a	deleted
CZECHOSLOVAKIA	
2392	2392a
2392a	2392
DANZIG	
36a, 37a	deleted
48a	47a
DENMARK	
633	deleted
634-645	633-644
645A	645
639a	638a
ECUADOR	
728-735	732-739
EGYPT	
67a	deleted
135a, 136b, 139a	deleted
194a	deleted
210a, 211a, 212a, 214a	deleted
245a, 247b, 251a	deleted
ESTONIA	
2a	deleted
93b, 95a	deleted
ETHIOPIA	
1448-1453	1148-1153
FINLAND	
161a, 164a, 166a, 168a, 173a	deleted
215a, 216a, 217a, 218a	deleted
FRANCE	
1949	1950
1950	1949
1994A	1995
1995 2fr	1996
1995 2.20fr	1997
1997	1998
1O39A	1O40
1O40	1O41
FRENCH GUINEA	
66a, 68a	deleted

Scott Catalogue Philatelic Marketplace

2

This "Yellow Pages" section of your Scott Catalogue contains advertisements to help you find what you need, when you need it . . . conveniently.

ACCESSORIES

APPROVALS

COLLECTIONS

1986 RUSSIA

Complete CTO 105 stamps + 9 S/S
Including 5 Deluxe Miniature Sheets $13.95

THE SMART COLLECTORS BUY BY THE YEAR,
THE PRACTICAL, ECONOMICAL WAY TO BUILD COLLECTIONS.

FREE LIST - 120 Countries

N.Y. Residents: Please add NY Sales Tax

WALLACE
Box 82, Port Washington, NY 11050

NEW ISSUES

SPECTACULAR NEW ISSUE SERVICE

Extensive Coverage of New Issues from the Entire World

Remember Our Specialty:
All Topicals and New Issues
Want Lists for Older Issues Serviced
Top Prices Paid for Collections and Accumulations

FREE ILLUSTRATED TOPICAL MONTHLY
NEW ISSUE LIST

COUNTY STAMP CENTER
P.O. Box 3373 ANNAPOLIS, MD 21403

PHILATELIC SERVICES

JAMES H. CRUM (APS, ASDA, ANS) (Est. 1929)
Thousands of Stamps plus Personal Helpful Advice
2720 E. Gage Ave., Huntington Park, CA 90255. 213-588-4467

PHILATELIC SOCIETIES

AMERICAN PHILATELIC SOCIETY
Service to 140,000 Stamp Collectors since 1886
Dept. TZ, P.O. Box 8000, State College, PA 16803

STAMP STORES

OMEGA STAMP & COIN CO.
Brooklyn's Largest Buys & Sells U.S. & Foreign Collections.
2076 East 17th St., Brooklyn, NY 11229. Ph. 718-339-9191

WHEN VISITING CENTRAL FLORIDA BE SURE TO STOP BY.

The Best Stamp/Postal History Inventory in Florida

Michael Rogers
WINTER PARK STAMP SHOP
340 Park Ave. North, Winter Park, FL 32789
Mon. through Sat. 10-6 (4 miles North of Orlando) **305-628-1120**

TOPICALS

TOPICALS • TOPICALS • TOPICALS • TOPICALS

CITY HALL STAMP CO., INC.
The TOPICAL Market SPECIALIST

- **Want lists filled on all topics.**
- **Always ready to buy topical collections.**
- **Absolute satisfaction guaranteed**

City Hall Stamp Co., Inc.

Wholesale-Retail
P.O. Box 52, East Station
Yonkers, N.Y. 10704
Phone 914-969-3554, 969-2023
Cable — Alkastamp, Yonkers, N.Y. • Telex #497 2032

TOPICALS • TOPICALS • TOPICALS • TOPICALS

PLAN NOW TO FEATURE YOUR ADVERTISING MESSAGE IN THE SCOTT 1989 CATALOGUES

Call or write us and we'll place your name on our prospect list to receive full information, as soon as it is available, on advertising rates and copy deadlines.

Scott Publishing Company
P.O. Box 828, Sidney, OH 45365 • Ph. 513-498-0802